CW00486835

THE BRITISH CIVIL AIRCRAFT REGISTERS 1919 - 1999

Compiled by Michael Austen

in collaboration with

Kevin Evans and Malcolm P. Fillmore

CONTENTS

Published by Air-Britain (Historians) Limited
Registered Office 12 Lonsdale Gardens, Tunbridge Wells, Kent
Sales Department 5 Bradley Road, Upper Norwood, London SE19 3NT
Membership Enquiries 36 Nursery Road, Taplow, Maidenhead, Berks SL6 0JZ

World-wide Web http://www.air-britain.com

A selection of the extraordinary variety of different types of flying machine which grace the British Register

Front Cover Photographs

Classic biplane	Moth Corporation DH.60M Moth G-AADR at Woburn (Rod W Simpson)
Trainer	Slingsby T.67M Firefly G-BWXE at Hucknall (Ian P Burnett)
Helicopter	Aerospatiale AS.355F1 Twin Squirrel G-OBIG at Ashton Court (Chris J Chatfield)
Airship	Colt AS.80 Mk.II Hot-Air Airship G-NDRW at Chateau d'Oex (Chris J Chatfield)
Turboprop	Short SC.7 Skyvan 3A G-BVXW at Oxford (Ian P Burnett)

Rear Cover Photographs

Hot-air balloon	Colt Santa Claus SS HAFB G-HOHO at Chateau d'Oex (Chris J Chatfield)
Commercial jet	Airbus A.340-313X G-VELD at Heathrow (Rod W Simpson)
Pioneer	Civilian CAC.1 Coupe G-ABNT at Woburn (Rod W Simpson)
Classic monoplane	Miles M.38 Messenger 2A G-AKIN at Sywell (Ian P Burnett)
Microlight	Cyclone Pegasus Quantum 15 G-MGTG at Popham (Rod W Simpson)
Exotic import	Yakovlev Yak-50 G-BVVO at Little Gransden (Ian P Burnett)
Business jet	BAe.125 Srs.800B G-BNEH at Hatfield (Chris J Chatfield)

ISBN 0 85130 281 5

THE BRITISH CIVIL AIRCRAFT REGISTERS 1919 - 1999

USER'S GUIDE

There are several purposes for this Monograph. The straightforward one is to list all aircraft that have been allocated or used a British or Irish civil registration, giving full details of their types and identities. This expands upon and sometimes corrects the official registers. However, we go well beyond that and include all other aircraft which have had "G-" marks allocated, including the various British Empire Territories in the early years.

Beyond that, we have tried to cater for the aviation specialist or historian, who wants to know more about particular aircraft - detailed information such as the known fate or the aircraft's first subsequent identity when it departed from the British or Irish civil registers.

A brief guide to what is in the main text is as follows:-

Registration

Set out in strict alphabetic order. A few aircraft, either real or static reproductions, have been painted in British or Irish civil marks for display or instructional purposes and in some case painted with incorrect marks in error. These are shown as "G-xxxx" or "EI-xxx". Sometimes, the same marks have been reissued or reallotted - particularly if the first holder or allottee did not use the marks. These are shown with the suffix (2) after the registration. Thankfully very few reissues or reallocations give reason for the suffix (3) or above.

Type

We adopt the full generally accepted or official type as set down by the manufacturer or designer. Where there is doubt, reference is usually made to the relevant issue of Janes All the Worlds Aircraft, or some similar leading authority. Indication is given if the manufacturer is a successor company or a licence builder - although not always if it is merely a sub-contractor. Additional explanatory notes include details of any unrepaired accidents and comments on the airframe's identity, including where the true position is at variance with the official position.

Constructors Number

This is the manufacturer's serial number, which may or not be quoted in the official register. Some aircraft may have more than one number - for example homebuilds can have the builder's own number, as well as the official sequential number allotted by the PFA and on occasion a plan or kit number. All are given where known. Some homebuilds and microlights were registered without any proper c/n - in this case the authorities generally used the owner's initials following by "01" etc. These numbers are replaced if the correct serial is subsequently identified. Many weightshift microlights are given separate c/n's for the trike unit and for the wing by the manufacturer. In many cases, the CAA only registers the wing c/n (although builders such as Hornet, Mainair and Medway issue a composite c/n comprising both units). Wherever known, both c/n's are shown - with the trike unit preceding the wing c/n.

Previous Identities

These are set out in reverse order, with the most recent identity first. Registrations shown in (brackets) were allotted but believed never officially used. The nationality of foreign military serials is indicated where it may not be apparent. Manufacturers test marks are given, where known, except in respect of where a standard generic mark has been used (such as for Pipers in the 60s).

Registration Date

This is the date of the original registration for those particular marks, even where subsequently removed and restored.

Fate or immediate subsequent identity (if known)

For current aircraft, this column will probably be without any comment. Included under this column are details of status (at latest reported date) if the C of A is not current or the aircraft is known to be under repair. Some aircraft are shown as TWFU (Temporary withdrawn from use) - this is where the CAA has not received an application from a new owner following a sale. A period of discretion is given by the CAA but if no response is received, the certificate is cancelled and the aircraft may not fly. This normally results in the forms being forthcoming by the new owner.

In the case of non-current aircraft, this column contains details of any known fate(s) or its first subsequent identity. Some Balloons have been cancelled by the CAA but were last known to be operating or based abroad, if details are known a comment indicating in what country it was last known to be operating is added.

EDITORIAL NOTE

The UK and Irish Registers include information available, including allocations, to the end of August 1999.

ABBREVIATIONS

Acft	- Aircraft	DBF	- Destroyed by fire	NTU	- Not taken up
AF	- Air Force	DBR	- Damaged beyond repair	PFA	- Popular Flying Association
Avn	- Aviation	DBER	- Damaged beyond economic repair	R	- Reservation
Canx	- Cancelled	HAFB	- (Hot-Air) Free Balloon	RAF	- Royal Air Force
CofA	- Certificate of Airworthiness	Intl	- International	WFU	- Withdrawn from use
c/n	- Constructors number	MOD	- Ministry of Defence	W/o	- Written off

INTRODUCTION AND EDITORIAL

We are pleased to present the first edition, by Air-Britain, of The British Civil Aircraft Registers 1919 - 1999 to celebrate eighty years since civil flying recommenced after World War One and the International Commision on Air Navigation decided that individual identification of civil registrations were necessary. Owing to the sheer weight of numbers of aircraft that have claim to a British or Irish registration, past and present, this A-B publication has taken longer than expected to prepare. The first four sections of this Monograph contain all the in-sequence British registrations as far as G-BZZZ, issued or yet to be issued, with further sections covering all known British out-of-sequence (including Microlight aircraft), UK Alphanumeric, Registrations used for Countries that formed parts of the former British Empire (Australia, Canada, India, New Zealand and South Africa) and further sections covering the Republic of Ireland Register of in-sequence and out-of-sequence registrations. Finally we have a section covering all known International Registration Prefixes allocated and/or used.

Future editions of the monograph will see a nominal increase in the number of pages as the in-sequence allocation of British registrations are currently near the mid portion of the G-BYxx registration block with only the mainly vacant G-BZxx registrations to be allotted. A greater expansion of the, currently, "out-of-sequence" registrations will be obvious as the G-Cxxx registrations presumably become "in sequence" registrations. Adding to this will be the continued growth of the Irish register. The Microlight register as an independent UK civil register reserved for Microlight class aircraft only, officially ceased to exist on September 15th 1998, after nearly seventeen and a half years, with all Microlights now being registered in the normal aircraft sequence. The registration blocks that were reserved for Microlight aircraft were in the G-MBAA, MGAA, MJAA, MMAA, MNAA, MTAA, MVAA, MWAA, MYAA and MZAA. All the G-Mxxx registered Microlight aircraft have been included in the main G-Mxxx out-of-sequence registration block in this monograph.

With the sheer volume of aircraft entries involved in producing this detailed coverage of the UK and Irish registers in a readable size print a decision was taken by the Monographs Committee to produce this title in hardback only form.

The British Glider Association (BGA) and Irish Glider Association registers have been excluded as they will to be covered in their own monograph currently under preparation for Air-Britain by the leading specialists in that area.

Special thanks to Kevin Evans for getting me started on the subject and to Malcolm P. Fillmore for proof-reading all the G-Axxx and the pre-G-A series of registered aircraft against his extensive records, without these gentlemen this monograph would still be only on the drawing board. Thanks are due to Alan Johnson for liaising with the CAA in London and to Paul Cunniffe and Colman Corcoran for similar in Ireland. Paul Crellin on his discoveries of aircraft that still remain but thought expired long since. The Australian (Colonial) Register information included in this monograph would not have anything like the extent of detailed coverage, as we are pleased to present, if it was not for the sterling efforts of John Hopton, Howard Rogers and Trevor Boughton of "Man and Aerial Machines". Also mention of thanks to David Hall, Donald Hannah, Graham Slack and Barry Towey for the supply of up-to-date relevant information. Finally I give credit to my other half, Wendy who managed to put up with the lengthy periods of an absent husband whilst this monograph was compiled.

SEPTEMBER 1999

MICHAEL AUSTEN
48 Greenman Road
NAVENBY
Lincoln
Lincs LN5 OJY

e-mail: michael@air-britain.demon.co.uk

The table below shows the approximate dates when each new registration sequence was initiated. Apart from being a guide to the date when any particular aircraft was registered, the table shows how the number of aircraft coming on to the Register has fluctuated with trade cycles, wars, surplus sales and other disasters.

Registration	Date	Registration	Date	Registration	Date	Registration	Date
G-EAAA	May 1919	G-ALAA	May 1948	G-BAAA	July 1972	G-BNAA	October 1986
G-EBAA	January 1922	G-AMAA	April 1950	G-BBAA	June 1973	G-BOAA	November 1987
G-AAAA	July 1928	G-ANAA	June 1953	G-BCAA	March 1974	G-BPAA	September 1988
G-ABAA	May 1930	G-AOAA	February 1955	G-BDAA	April 1975	G-BRAA	May 1989
G-ACAA	August 1932	G-APAA	March 1957	G-BEAA	June 1976	G-BSAA	February 1990
G-ADAA	November 1934	G-ARAA	April 1960	G-BFAA	August 1977	G-BTAA	November 1990
G-AEAA	January 1936	G-ASAA	May 1962	G-BGAA	October 1978	G-BUAA	January 1992
G-AFAA	July 1937	G-ATAA	January 1965	G-BHAA	August 1979	G-BVAA	June 1993
G-AGAA	October 1939	G-AVAA	October 1966	G-BIAA	July 1980	G-BWAA	February 1995
G-AHAA	January 1946	G-AWAA	December 1967	G-BJAA	June 1981	G-BXAA	October 1996
G-AIAA	August 1946	G-AXAA	February 1969	G-BKAA	March 1982	G-BYAA	July 1998
G-AJAA	January 1947	G-AYAA	March 1970	G-BLAA	October 1983	G-BZAA	-
G-AKAA	June 1947	G-AZAA	June 1971	G-BMAA	June 1985		

COMMENTS ON THE OUT-OF-SEQUENCE REGISTRATIONS IN THE BRITISH CIVIL AIRCRAFT REGISTER

Regular use of out-of-sequence registration allocations did not come about until 1974. Prior to then, very occasional lapses in strict order of allocation were allowed and then only if it could be shown that by the time the aircraft flew, it would be in-sequence. The Accountant G-ATEL was the first chink in this regime but it was possibly Concorde G-BSST in 1968 which opened the door, although it was some years before the CAA realised that they could exploit "cherished" marks and make money from their allocation. The in-sequence registrations have now progressed to the point of almost exhausting all remaining registrations in the G-Bxxx series with the vacant available marks in the G-Cxxx series presumably being the next block to be used up. It is at this point that this Monograph becomes ready for the millennium.

British Empire-based aircraft were initially registered in Great Britain, and used the British nationality letter G- followed by a four-letter group, the first of which indicated the Dominion concerned. Then, in the 1929 reorganisation, the nationality letter G- was used for Great Britain only, the Dominions being allotted new two-letter groups, while the Colonies, Protectorates and Mandates were lumped together under VP-, VQ- and VR-, the initial letter of the individual registration marking again denoting the Colony of origin.

The registrations from G-CAAA to G-CAXP were allocated to Canada in the 1920s, none are current. Also the registrations from G-CYAA to G-CYHZ and G-CYUA to G-CYZZ were allocated to Canadian military usage in 1929, again none are current.

Lighter-than-air Aircraft had individual registration marks beginning with the letter F, this gave rise to the registrations G-FAAA to G-FAAZ being used from 1919 until 1929, none are current.

Unmanned (Toy) balloons were allotted, by the CAA, the special sequences of G-FYAA to G-FZZZ with effect from 1.1.82. They have permitted the continuation in existance of all those registered in the normal sequence prior to then without re-registration. The number of registrations issued in this sequence has declined to the point that only one has been registered since 1992. These registrations have been included in the out-of-sequence with some of the allotted registrations used for non "mini-balloons".

The series from G-GAAA to G-GAAE was used by five gliders only in 1937 to allow them to participate in competitions at Wasserkuppe in Germany, none are current.

The registrations from G-IAAA to G-IAAZ were allocated to India in the 1920s, none are current.

One registration, G-KAA (which possibly should have been G-KAAA) was used in Kenya Colony.

The registration block from G-MBAA on is (with registrations in the G-MGAA, G-MJAA, G-MMAA, G-MNAA, G-MTAA, G-MVAA, G-MWAA, G-MYAA and G-MZAA series) reserved for Microlight or Minimum Aircraft and was started in 4/81. Several other Microlights are registered in the normal registration series. With effect from 15.9.98 the Microlight G-M... Register ceased to exist with all Microlights then being registered in the normal aircraft sequence. We have elected to keep this section seperate in this publication, but will in future editions include them in the G-M... part of the out-of-sequence registrations section of this monograph.

The registrations from G-NZAA to G-NZAZ and G-NZEA to G-NZEF were allocated to New Zealand in the 1920s, none are current.

The registrations from G-UAAA to G-UABD were allocated to the Union of South Africa in the 1920s, none are current.

The registration block from G-N94AA onwards was used for six British registered Concorde aircraft when British Airways entered into an agreement with US carriers Braniff Airlines for the latter to fly Concordes to Washington-Dallas as an extension of the former's London-Washington route, registration of the aircraft proved to be a problem. Under American law aircraft operated by a US carrier may not carry a foreign registration so the solution was to adopt a 'alphanumeric' registration system. Services were commenced on 12.1.79 by G-N94AE. The agreement was terminated by Braniff in 5.80. In theory aircraft went onto the American register at Washington and was 'restored' to the British register upon their return from Dallas.

We have tried to include any "reserved" registrations known to have been allotted. Prior to formal registration the CAA will allot a new registration pending completion of the paperwork and formal registration (which in the case of overseas built or registered aircraft requires evidence of de-registration or non-registration from that country). Some aircraft, for one reason or another, fail to take up these initially allotted British marks - they may elect and pay for an out-of-sequence allocation, they may fail to complete importation procedures or the owner changes his/her mind etc. Eventually the reserved marks are struck out and the registration cancelled as not allotted. We feel that it is important, in the context of aviation history, to record these "almosts" (and in fact many aircraft have actually worn their reserved marks).

SECTION 1 - TEMPORARY 'Ex SERVICE AIRCRAFT' SERIES UK REGISTER

British Civil Aviation came officially into existance on 1.5.19. As there were no international regulations controlling the registration of civil aircraft at the time, the Civil Aviation Department, formed on 12.2.19, specified its own system of temporary registration marks and the Air Ministry directed that all military aircraft sold for civil purposes and already bearing Service aerials would be allocated those serials as registration marks, although the Service ring (roundel) markings were to be obliterated. New aircraft and those built from spares, on the other hand, were allocated marks in a special Service sequence commencing at K-100.

Both systems were operated simultaneously by the Civil Aviation Department until a permanent system of international markings was formulated.

Regn	Type	c/n	Previous identity	Regn date	Fate or immediate subsequent identity (if known)
C6054	Airco DH.9	-		30. 4.19	Crashed on Portsdown Hill, N of Portsmouth at 5.30 am on 1.5.19 whilst performing the first civil flight to be made by a "civilian" registered aircraft. Allotted marks G-EAAA not used. Canx 1.9.19.
H9277	Airco DH.9	-		30. 4.19	Modified to a DH.9B and re-regd as K-109 in 4/19. Canx.
H9273	Airco DH.9	-		30. 4.19	Believed crashed in 5/19. Allotted G-EAAD but NTU. Canx 9.9.19.
D8350	Handley Page O/400	HP-16		30. 4.19	To G-EAAE 7/19. Canx.
F5414	Handley Page O/400 (Painted as G-5414)	HP-13		30. 4.19	To G-EAAF 7/19. Canx.
F5418	Handley Page O/400	HP-18		30. 4.19	To G-EAAG 7/19. Canx.
F5417	Handley Page O/400 (Painted as G-5417)	HP-14		2. 5.19	To G-EAAW 7/19. Canx.
E4222	Avro 504K	-		30. 4.19	To G-EAAK 7/19. Canx.
E4154	Avro 504K	-		30. 4.19	To G-EAAL 7/19. Canx.
E3289	Avro 504K	PL.6036		30. 4.19	To G-EAAM 7/19. Canx.
E4225	Avro 504K	-		30. 4.19	To G-EAAN 7/19. Canx.
C105	Vickers FB.27 Vimy	C105	B9952	1. 5.19	To G-EAAR 7/19. Canx.
C103	Vickers FB.14A	C103		1. 5.19	To G-EAAS 7/19. Project abandoned. Canx 7/19.
C102	Vickers FB.14A	C102		13. 5.19	To G-EAAT 7/19. Project abandoned. Canx 7/19.
C104	Vickers FB.19 Bullet	C104		13. 5.19	To G-EAAU 7/19. Project abandoned. Canx 7/19.
B4674	Maurice Farman S-11 Shorthorn	-		5. 5.19	To G-EAAZ 7/19. Canx.
D6205	Avro 504K	-		6. 5.19	To G-EAAX 7/19. Canx.
C724	Avro 504K	-		16. 5.19	To G-EAAY 7/19. Canx.
E3480	Avro 504K	-		6. 5.19	To G-EABA 7/19. Canx.
E4137	Avro 504K	-		6. 5.19	To G-EABE 7/19. Canx.
C748	Avro 504K	-		6. 5.19	To G-EABF 7/19. Canx.
C749	Avro 504K	-		6. 5.19	To G-EABG 7/19. Canx.
B8758	Avro 504K	P1/1848		6. 5.19	To G-EABH 7/19. Canx.
E4359	Avro 504K	359		19. 5.19	To G-EABJ 7/19. Canx.
D8287	Avro 504K	-		27. 5.19	To G-EABK 7/19. Canx.
E4324	Avro 504K	324		9. 5.19	To G-EABL 7/19. Canx.
E4360	Avro 504K	360		9. 5.19	To G-EABM 7/19. Canx.
D6229	Avro 504K	-		27. 5.19	To G-EABV 7/19. Canx.
C747	Avro 504K	-		20. 5.19	To G-EABW 7/19. Canx.
E4230	Avro 504K	-		10. 5.19	To G-EABX 7/19. Canx.
C723	Avro 504K	-		10. 5.19	To G-EABN 7/19. Canx.
D6202	Avro 504K	-		20. 5.19	To G-EABO 7/19. Canx.
F9802	Avro 504K	-		19. 5.19	To G-EABP 7/19. Canx.
D6201	Avro 504K	-		20. 5.19	To G-EABT 7/19. Canx.
B9629	Armstrong Whitworth FK.3	-		24. 5.19	To G-EABY 7/19. Canx.
B9518	Armstrong Whitworth FK.3	-		24. 5.19	To G-EABZ 7/19. Canx.
E6765	Avro 504K	-		29. 5.19	To G-EACA 7/19. Canx.
E1671	Avro 504K	-		9. 5.19	To G-EACB 7/19. Canx.
E4224	Avro 504K	-		15. 5.19	To G-EACD 7/19. Canx.
D9341	Avro 504K	-		29. 5.19	To G-EACS 7/19. Canx.
D9298	Avro 504K	-		20. 5.19	To G-EACL 7/19. Canx.
E4233	Avro 504K	-		29. 5.19	To G-EACV 7/19. Canx.
E1663	Avro 504K	-		29. 5.19	To G-EACW 7/19. Canx.
C7175	RAF B.E.2e	-		29. 5.19	To G-EACY 7/19. Canx.
E4221	Avro 504K	-		29. 5.19	To G-EADA 7/19. Canx.
E1665	Avro 504K	-		6. 6.19	To G-EADD 7/19. Canx.
B9981	Blackburn RT.1 Kangaroo	-	N1731	8. 6.19	DBR at Hendon in 29.6.19. Allotted G-EADE, but NTU. Canx 7/19.
B9982	Blackburn RT.1 Kangaroo	-	N1732	8. 6.19	Crashed at Hendon on 31.5.19 due to engine failure on take-off. Allotted G-EADF, but NTU. Canx 7/19.
B9985	Blackburn RT.1 Kangaroo	-	N1735	11. 6.19	To G-EADG 7/19. Canx.
E3502	Avro 504K	-		17. 6.19	To G-EADH 7/19. Canx.
E3292	Avro 504K	PL.6039		5. 6.19	To G-EADI 7/19. Canx.
H2581	Avro 504K Seaplane	-		5. 6.19	To G-EADJ 7/19. Canx.
H5282	Avro 504K Seaplane	-		. 6.19R	To G-EADK 7/19. Canx.
E4348	Avro 504K	348		5. 6.19	To G-EADL 7/19. Canx.
E4336	Avro 504K	336		5. 6.19	To G-EADM 7/19. Canx.
E3293	Avro 504K	PL.6040		5. 6.19	To G-EADN 7/19. Canx.
F8706	Avro 504K	-		5. 6.19	To G-EADO 7/19. Canx.
E3481	Avro 504K	-		5. 6.19	To G-EADP 7/19. Canx.
D7588	Avro 504K	-		5. 6.19	To G-EADQ 7/19. Canx.
N2986	Short 184	-		. 6.19R	To G-EAJT 8/19. Canx.

Regn	Type	c/n	Previous identity	Regn date	Fate or immediate subsequent identity (if known)
N2998	Short 184	-		. 6.19R	To G-EALC 8/19. Canx.
H1925	Avro 504K	-		. 6.19R	To G-EALD 8/19. Canx.
D6245	Avro 504K	-		6. 6.19	To G-EADR 7/19. Canx.
H2507	Avro 504K	-		6. 6.19	To G-EADS 7/19. Canx.
D9329	Avro 504K	-		6. 6.19	To G-EADU 7/19. Canx.
E4343	Avro 504K	343		6. 6.19	To G-EADW 7/19. Canx.
D6239	Avro 504K	-		6. 6.19	To G-EADX 7/19. Canx.
E3408	Avro 504K	-		6. 6.19	To G-EADY. Canx.
N2876	Fairey IIIA	F.246		6. 6.19	To G-EADZ 7/19. Canx.
D9304	Avro 504K	-		6. 6.19	To G-EAEA 7/19. Canx.
B8774	Avro 504K	-		6. 6.19	To G-EAEB 7/19. Canx.
E3501	Avro 504K	-		6. 6.19	To G-EAEC 7/19. Canx.
N1526	Supermarine Channel I	S.969		11. 6.19	To G-EAEM 7/19. Canx.
N1528	Supermarine Channel I	S.970		11. 6.19	To G-EAEL 7/19. Canx.
N1711	Supermarine Channel I	S.971		11. 6.19	To G-EAEK 7/19. Canx.
N1714	Supermarine Channel I	S.972		11. 6.19	To G-EAEJ 7/19. Canx.
N1715	Supermarine Channel I	S.973		11. 6.19	To G-EAEI 7/19. Canx.
N1716	Supermarine Channel I	S.974		11. 6.19	To G-EAEH 7/19. Canx.
N2451	Supermarine Channel I	S.975		11. 6.19	To G-EAEG 7/19. Canx.
N2452	Supermarine Channel I	S.976		11. 6.19	To G-EAEF 7/19. Canx.
N1710	Supermarine Channel I	S.977		11. 6.19	To G-EAEE 7/19. Canx.
N1529	Supermarine Channel I	S.978		11. 6.19	To G-EAED 7/19. Canx.
D9018	Avro 504K	-		11. 6.19	To G-EAEN 7/19. Canx.
E4362	Avro 504K	362		11. 6.19	To G-EAEO 7/19. Canx.
C4964	Bristol M.1c Monoplane	2782		13. 6.19	Allocated marks G-EAER in 7/19, but NTU. (See notes on G-EAER) Canx.
D5150	Armstrong Whitworth FK.8	-		15. 6.19	To G-EAET 7/19. Canx.
B9612	Armstrong Whitworth FK.3	-		18. 6.19	To G-EAEU 7/19. Canx.
H2560	Avro 504K	-		18. 6.19	To G-EAEY 7/19. Canx.
H2561	Avro 504K	-		18. 6.19	To G-EAEZ 7/19. Canx.
H2586	Avro 504K	-		18. 6.19	To G-EAEV 7/19. Canx.
E1660	Avro 504K	-		19. 6.19	To G-EAFC 7/19. Canx.
E4329	Avro 504K (Flown from Southport as D4329 in error)	-		19. 6.19	To G-EAFD 7/19. Canx.
D7648	Avro 504K	-		19. 6.19	To G-EAFE 7/19. Canx.
E3363	Avro 504K	PL.6110		25. 6.19	To G-EAFP 7/19. Canx.
E4180	Avro 504K	-		27. 6.19	To G-EAFQ 7/19. Canx.
D9340	Avro 504K	-		27. 6.19	To G-EAFS 7/19. Canx.
H2583	Avro 504K	-		30. 6.19	To G-EAFU 7/19. Canx.
H2584	Avro 504K	-		30. 6.19	To G-EAFV 7/19. Canx.
H2591	Avro 504K	-		1. 7.19	To G-EAFW 7/19. Canx.
H6543	Avro 504K	-		1. 7.19	To G-EAFX 7/19. Canx.
B2943	Airco DH.6	-		1. 7.19	To G-EAFT 7/19. Canx.
C7390	Airco DH.6	-		3. 7.19	To (G-EAFY)/G-EAJM 8/19. Canx.
C7320	Airco DH.6	-		3. 7.19	To G-EAFZ 7/19. Canx.
H5173	Avro 504K	-		4. 7.19	To G-EAGB 7/19. Canx.
H5172	Avro 504K	-		4. 7.19	To G-EAGC 7/19. Canx.
D5499	Avro 504K	-		4. 7.19	To G-EAGD 7/19. Canx.
C5224	Airco DH.6	-		4. 7.19	To G-EAGE 7/19. Canx.
C5220	Airco DH.6	-		4. 7.19	To G-EAGF 7/19. Canx.
C2101	Airco DH.6	-		4. 7.19	To G-EAGG 7/19. Canx.
C7101	RAF B.E.2e	-		4. 7.19	To G-EAGH 7/19. Canx.
E4234	Avro 504K	-		9. 7.19	To G-EAGI 7/19. Canx.
C746	Avro 504K	-		9. 7.19	To G-EAGJ 7/19. Canx.
D9343	Avro 504K	-		12. 7.19	To G-EAGO 7/19. Canx.
H2585	Avro 504K Seaplane	-		14. 7.19	To G-EAGU 7/19. Canx.
5570	Bristol Scout C	1060		10. 7.19	To G-EAGR 7/19. Canx.
D2617	Avro 504K	-		14. 7.19	To G-EAGT 7/19. Canx.
H6598	Avro 504K	-		14. 7.19	To G-EAGV 7/19. Canx.
H6599	Avro 504K	-		14. 7.19	To G-EAGW 7/19. Canx.
H9255	Airco DH.9	-		14. 7.19	To G-EAGX 7/19. Canx.
H9258	Airco DH.9	-		14. 7.19	To G-EAGY 7/19. Canx.
D8984	Avro 504K	GW.3254		14. 7.19	To G-EAGZ 7/19. Canx.
D3832	FE.2b	-		14. 7.19	To G-EAHC 7/19. Canx.
B2934	Airco DH.6	-		17. 7.19	To G-EAHD 7/19. Canx.
B2917	Airco DH.6	-		18. 7.19	To G-EAHE 7/19. Canx.
F2699	Airco DH.4A	-		18. 7.19	To G-EAHF 7/19. Canx.
F2694	Airco DH.4A	-		. 7.19R	To G-EAHG 7/19. Canx.
F3435	Airco DH.6	-		18. 7.19	To G-EAHH 7/19. Canx.
C6889	Airco DH.6	-		18. 7.19	To G-EAHI 7/19. Canx.
C9432	Airco DH.6	-		. 7.19R	To G-EAHJ 7/19. Canx.
E4340	Avro 504K	340		18. 7.19	To G-EAHK 7/19. Canx.
E4118	Avro 504K	-		18. 7.19	To G-EAHL 7/19. Canx.
E1707	Avro 504K	-		. 7.19R	To G-EAHM 7/19. Canx.
H1959	Avro 504K	-		7. 7.19	To G-EAHO 7/19. Canx.

The following aircraft were allotted reservations prior to 24.7.19

Regn	Type	c/n	Previous identity	Regn date	Fate or immediate subsequent identity (if known)
E1611	Avro 504K	-		. 7.19R	To G-EAHU 7/19. Canx.
H2297	Avro 504K	-		. 7.19R	To G-EAHV 9/19. Canx.
E1675	Avro 504K	-		. 7.19R	To G-EAIG 9/19. Canx.
E3364	Avro 504K	PL.6111		. 7.19R	To G-EAHW 8/19. Canx.
E3366	Avro 504K	PL.6113		. 7.19R	To G-EAHX 8/19. Canx.

Regn	Type	c/n	Previous identity	Regn date	Fate or immediate subsequent identity (if known)
H7513	Avro 504K	-		. 7.19R	To G-EAHY 8/19. Canx.
H2411	Avro 504K	-		. 7.19R	To G-EAHZ 8/19. Canx.
F8717	Avro 504K	-		. 7.19R	To G-EAIA 8/19. Canx.
D9303	Avro 504K	-		. 7.19R	To G-EAIB 8/19. Canx.
H4473	Armstrong Whitworth FK.8	-		. 7.19R	To G-EAIC 8/19. Canx.
H2595	Avro 504K	-		. 7.19R	To G-EAIH 7/19. Canx.
H2596	Avro 504K	-		. 7.19R	To G-EAII 7/19. Canx.
H2597	Avro 504K	-		. 7.19R	To G-EAIJ 7/19. Canx.
H2598	Avro 504K	-		. 7.19R	To G-EAJB 8/19. Canx.
N4634	Gosport Flying Boat (Felixstowe F.5)	G6/100		. 7.19R	To G-EAIK 8/19. Canx.
E3359	Avro 504K	PL.6106		. 7.19R	To G-EAIO 8/19. Canx.
E4143	Avro 504K	-		. 7.19R	To G-EAIP 8/19. Canx.

SECTION 2 - FIRST TEMPORARY 'K' SERIES UK REGISTER

Regn	Type	c/n	Previous identity	Regn date	Fate or immediate subsequent identity (if known)
K-100	Airco DH.6 (Non-standard rebuild)	-		30. 4.19	To G-EAAB. Canx in 7/19.
K-101	Sopwith Gnu	A.16		30. 4.19	Crashed and burnt on landing at Southport Sands, Lancs on 10.6.19. Allocated marks G-EAAH, but NTU. Canx in 7/19.
K-102	BAT FK.26	FK.26-29		30. 4.19	To G-EAAI. Canx in 7/19.
K-103	Fairey III	F.127	N9	1. 5.19	To G-EAAJ. Canx in 7/19.
K-104	Avro 536	ATC.2		30. 4.19	Crashed in Southwark Park, London 9.9.19 whilst still as K-104. Allocated marks G-EAAQ, but NTU. Canx in 9/20.
K-105	Avro 536	ATC.3		30. 4.19	Crashed at Sandhurst, Berks on 6.8.19 whilst still as K-105. Allocated marks G-EAAP, but NTU. Canx in 12/19.
K-106	Avro 504L	ATC.4		30. 4.19	To G-EAAO. Canx/Sold in 7/19.
K-107	Vickers Vimy Commercial	-		13. 5.19	To G-EAAV. Canx in 7/19.
K-108	Central Centaur IV	201		7. 5.19	To G-EABI. Canx in 7/19.
K-109	Airco DH.9B	-	H9277	30. 4.19	To G-EAAC. Canx in 7/19.
K-110	Bristol F.2c Badger X (Originally c/n 4257)	5658	F3497	30. 5.19	NTU - DBR when turned over on the ground at Filton on 22.5.19. Also allotted marks G-EABU but NTU. Canx in 7/19.
K-111	Grahame-White G.W.15	401		6. 5.19	NTU - No CofA issued. Also marks allocated G-EABB, but NTU. Canx in 7/19.
K-112	Grahame-White G.W.15	402		6. 5.19	NTU - No CofA issued. Also marks allocated G-EABC, but NTU. Canx in 7/19.
K-113	Grahame-White G.W.15	403		15. 5.19	NTU - No CofA issued. To G-EABD. Canx in 7/19.
K-114	Avro 504L (Converted to Seaplane in 6/19)	ATC.1		30. 6.19	To G-EACC. Canx in 7/19.
K-115	Caudron G.III	87/8271		29. 5.19	To G-EACF. Canx in 7/19.
K-116	Avro 536	ATC.9		20. 5.19	To G-EACG. Canx in 7/19.
K-117	London & Provincial Biplane	E.121		20. 5.19	Allocated marks G-EABQ, but NTU. Canx in 7/19.
K-118	London & Provincial Biplane	E.120		20. 5.19	Allocated marks G-EABR, but NTU. Canx in 7/19.
K-119	London & Provincial Biplane	D.147		20. 5.19	Allocated marks G-EABS, but NTU. Canx in 7/19.
K-120	Boulton & Paul P.6	P.6/1	X25	20. 5.19	Allocated marks G-EACJ, but NTU. Canx in 7/19.
K-121	Caudron G.III	3005		30. 5.19	To G-EACK. Canx in 7/19.
K-122	Sopwith Dove	2714		20. 5.19	To G-EACM. Canx in 7/19.
K-123	BAT FK.23 Bantam	FK.23-15	F1654	29. 5.19	To G-EACN. Canx in 7/19.
K-124	BAT FK.24 Baboon	FK.24-7	D9731	29. 5.19	To G-EACO. Canx in 7/19.
K-125	BAT FK.23 Bantam	FK.23-17	F1656	29. 5.19	To G-EACP. Canx in 7/19.
K-126	Westland Limousine I	WAC.1		27. 6.19	To G-EAFO. Canx in 7/19.
K-127	Caudron G.III	-		29. 5.19	To G-EACH. Canx in 7/19.
K-128	Caudron G.III	-		29. 5.19	To G-EACI. Canx in 7/19.
K-129	Boulton & Paul P.7 Bourges IA	P.7/1	F2903	20. 5.19	To G-EACE. Canx in 7/19.
K-130	Airco DH.16	DH.16/1		29. 5.19	To G-EACT. Canx in 7/19.
K-131	Avro 534 Baby	534/1		29. 5.19	To G-EACQ. Canx in 7/19.
K-132	Avro 538 Scout	530/1		25. 5.19	To G-EACR. Canx in 7/19.
K-133	Sopwith Dove	2769/1		24. 5.19	To G-EACU. Canx in 7/19.
K-134	Avro 504M	ATC.10		29. 5.19	To G-EACX. Canx in 7/19.
K-135	Sopwith Scooter (Originally F.1 Camel B9276)	2052		29. 5.19	To G-EACZ. Canx in 7/19.
K-136	Sopwith Gnu	2976/1		29. 5.19	To G-EADB. Canx in 7/19.
K-137	Avro 536	ATC.5		6. 6.19	To G-EADC. Canx in 7/19.
K-138	London & Provincial Biplane	E.122		11. 6.19	To G-EADT. Canx in 7/19.
K-139	Avro 536	ATC.11		6. 6.19	To G-EADV. Canx in 7/19.
K-140	Sopwith Gnu	2976/2		11. 6.19	To G-EAEP. Canx in 7/19.
K-141	Airco DH.4R	G7/67		16. 6.19	To G-EAEW. Canx in 7/19.
K-142	Airco DH.4	G7/63		16. 6.19	To G-EAEX. Canx in 7/19.
K-143	BAT FK.27	FK.27-33		17. 6.19	To G-EAFA. Canx in 7/19.
K-144	Avro 504L	E.1		18. 6.19	To G-EAFB. Canx in 7/19.
K-145	Avro 504L	ATC.12		19. 6.19	To G-EAFF. Canx in 7/19.
K-146	Avro 504L	ATC.13		19. 6.19	Crashed in fog off Alderney, Channel Islands on 5.10.19 while carrying newspapers to Guernsey. Allocated marks G-EAFG but NTU. Canx in 7/19.
K-147	Avro 504K	ATC.14		19. 6.19	To G-EAFH. Canx in 7/19.
K-148	Sopwith Dove	2769/2		19. 6.19	To G-EAFI. Canx in 7/19.
K-149	Sopwith RM.1 Snapper	PW.14		19. 6.19	To G-EAFJ. Canx in 7/19.

Regn	Type	c/n	Previous identity	Regn date	Fate or immediate subsequent identity (if known)
K-150	Grahame-White G.W.E.6 Bantam	GWE.6		20. 6.19	Crashed into the side of a hangar at Hendon on 6.7.19. Allocated marks G-EAFK, but NTU. Canx in 7/19.
K-151	Nieuport Nighthawk	LC.1/1		13. 6.19	To G-EAEQ. Canx in 7/19.
K-152	Martinsyde F.4A	E4/500		13. 6.19	To G-EAES. Canx in 7/19.
K-153	Grahame-White G.W.E.6 Bantam	GWE.6A		20. 6.19	To G-EAFL. Canx in 7/19.
K-154	BAT FK.23 Bantam	FK.23-16	F1655	24. 6.19	To G-EAFM. Canx in 7/19.
K-155	BAT FK.23 Bantam	FK.23-18	F1657	24. 6.19	Allocated marks G-EAFN, but NTU. Canx in 7/19.
K-156	Sopwith Gnu	3005/1		27. 6.19	To G-EAFR. Canx in 7/19.
K-157	Sopwith Dove	3004/1		3. 7.19	Allocated marks G-EAGA, NTU & to Australia. (See notes on G-EAGA) Canx in 7/19.
K-158	Austin Whippet	AU.1		14. 7.19	To G-EAGS. Canx in 7/19.
K-159	Alliance P.1	P.1		9. 7.19	To G-EAGK. Canx in 7/19.
K-160	Alliance P.2 Seabird	P.2		9. 7.19	To G-EAGL. Canx in 7/19.
K-161	Avro 536	ATC.6		10. 7.19	To G-EAGM, but crashed at Weston-super-Mare on 1.9.19 - prior to applying new marks. Canx.
K-162	Handley Page O/7 (Originally built as O/400, converted before registered)	HP.1	C9704	. 7.19	To G-EAGN. Canx in 7/19.
K-163	Sopwith Gnu	2976/3		12. 7.19	To G-EAGP. Canx in 7/19.
K-164	Sopwith Gnu	2976/4		14. 7.19	To G-EAGQ. Canx in 7/19.
K-165	Avro 536	ATC.7		14. 7.19	To G-EAHA. Canx in 7/19.
K-166	Avro 536	ATC.8		14. 7.19	To G-EAHB. Canx in 7/19.
K-167	BAT FK.26	FK.26-30		18. 7.19	To G-EAHN. Canx in 7/19.
K-168	Sopwith Dove	3004/2		22. 7.19	To G-EAHP. Canx in 7/19.
K-169	Sopwith Gnu	2976/5		22. 7.19	To G-EAHQ. Canx in 7/19.
K-170	Central Centaur IIA	101		22. 7.19	NTU - To G-EAHR. Canx in 7/19.
K-171	Central Centaur IV	202		23. 7.19	NTU - To G-EAHS. Canx in 7/19.
K-172	Airco DH.9R	GR/1		23. 7.19	NTU - To G-EAHT. Canx in 7/19.
K-173	Avro 536	B.1		31. 7.19	NTU - To G-EAID. Canx in 7/19.
K-174	Avro 536	B.2		24. 7.19	NTU - To G-EAIE. Canx in 7/19.
K-175	Avro 536	B.4		7. 8.19	NTU - To G-EAIF. Canx in 8/19.

Seen at Warrnambool, Victoria, Australia on 25.1.20 was Sopwith Dove K-157, c/n 3004/1, which was exported to Australia by the Larkin-Sopwith Aviation Co., and was certainly in use as K-157 by 11/12.1919. Then sold to Major George Aubrey Cadogan Cowper (who, with partners, operated as Aviation Ltd.) at Glenroy, Victoria. Its' history past this point is very vague, but this is possibly the Dove which Cowper gave to one F.J.Barnes circa 5.21, who died in 1925. What exactly happen to the Dove is not known, but an unregistered Dove, recorded as an "experimental machine", was crashed on a test-flight at Essendon, Victoria on 9.3.30, and it is suspected this may well have been K-157. It is believed that the remains brought to the UK circa 1987/88 and rebuilt as the replica (with regn G-BLOO) were from somewhere near Hamilton, and since then it has been (apparently) absolutely identified as the former K-157. Therefore the two entries for the marks G-EAGA, below, could be one and the same aircraft, and the previous identities for (2) could infact be; (G-BLOO)/(G-EAGA)/K-157. (John Hopton Collection)

SECTION 3 - FIRST PERMANENT UK REGISTER G-EAAA - G-EBZZ (See Section 5 for G-E registrations issued post-war)

The International Air Navigation Convention met in Paris during the first week in July 1919 and on the 22nd they published their Report. Using the British Government's Air Navigation Bill and Regulations as their model, the Convention made only a small number of alterations to reach agreement on international regulations. One of the Convention's main tasks was the allotment of nationality markings to twenty-six countries: that allotted to the British Empire was the letter G. Affecting all countries was the stipulation that the nationality mark was to be followed by a group of four letters, each group containing at least one vowel, and that for this purpose the letter Y would be considered a vowel in addition to A, E, I, O, U. This four letter group would be separated by a hyphen from the nationality marking. The agreement was signed in 10/19 and ratified in the U.K. by the 1920 Air Navigation Act.

In London, the report stopped the further registration of civil aircraft after 24.7.19, and this activity was not resumed until the 31st. During the interval, Committee discussions were in progress to formulate the manner of the four letter group. It was finally agreed that the first letter after G- would be E for powered flying machines and F for airships and balloons; gliders were not provided for at the time. The remaining three letters would be the aircraft's individual identity, and radio call sign, by the simple expedient of alphabetical progression, ie; AAA through to ZZZ. Commonwealth countries were allocated their own fixed first letter(s).

The first permanent United Kingdom Register of Civil Aircraft was inaugurated on 31.7.19 and the task of transferring aircraft from the temporary to the permanent register occupied the Civil Aviation Department until 7.8.19. Their eventual policy was to transfer all aircraft irrespective of their state of airworthiness. But, as will be seen, re-registration was not carried out in chronological order and the reasons why remain a matter for conjecture.

Regn	Type	c/n	Previous identity	Regn date	Fate or immediate subsequent identity (if known)
G-EAAA	Airco DH.9	-	C6054	22. 7.19	NTU - Crashed on Portsdown Hill, N of Portsmouth at 5.30 am on 1.5.19 whilst performing the first civil flight to be made by a "civilian" registered aircraft. (Was still regd as C6054) Canx 1.9.19.
G-EAAB	Airco DH.6	-	K-100	22. 7.19	Crashed at Croydon in 11/21. Canx 10.2.22.
G-EAAC	Airco DH.9J (Originally regd as DH.9B, modified to DH.9C in 1921, then to DH.9J in 7/26)	-	K-109 H9277	22. 7.19	CofA expired 28.1.33 & WFU. Scrapped in 1933. Canx in 12/33.
G-EAAD	Airco DH.9	-	H9273	22. 7.19	NTU - Believed crashed in 5/19 as H9273. CofA application canx on 29.5.19. Canx in 9/19.
G-EAAE	Handley Page 0/400	HP.16	D8320	22. 7.19	Canx as WFU in 8/20.
G-EAAF	Handley Page 0/7 (Originally regd as a 0/400, modified to 0/7 with new CofA issued on 14.8.19)	HP.13	F5414 "G-5414"	22. 7.19	CofA expired on 13.8.20. Canx as WFU 8/20.
G-EAAG	Handley Page 0/400	HP.18	F5418	22. 7.19	CofA expired 30.4.20 & WFU. Canx.
G-EAAH	Sopwith Gnu	A.16	K-101	22. 7.19	NTU - Crashed and burnt on landing at Southport Sands, Lancs on 10.6.19 whilst still marked as K-101. Canx in 7/19.
G-EAAI	BAT FK.26	FK.26-29	K-102	22. 7.19	CofA expired 28.7.20 & WFU. Stored at Willesden. To Holland for exhibition in 1937 - fate unknown. Canx.
G-EAAJ	Fairey III	F.127	K-103 N9	22. 7.19	To Norway as N-20 in 5/20. Canx in 5/20.
G-EAAK	Avro 504K	-	E4222	22. 7.19	WFU at Hounslow. CofA expired 8.5.20. Canx 10.11.21.
G-EAAL	Avro 548 (Originally regd as Avro 504K, modified in 11/25)	-	E4154	22. 7.19	Crashed near Stag Lane, Edgware on 3.6.28. Canx.
G-EAAM	Avro 504K	PL.6036	E3289	22. 7.19	WFU at Hounslow. CofA expired 8.5.20. Canx in 9/20.
G-EAAN	Avro 504K	-	E4225	22. 7.19	Crashed at Weston-super-Mare on 28.8.19. CofA expired 6.5.20. Canx in 5/20.
G-EAAO	Avro 536	ATC.4	K-106	22. 7.19	Canx/Sold in 7/19.
G-EAAP	Avro 536	ATC.3	K-105	22. 7.19	NTU - Crashed at Sandhurst, Berks 6.8.19 whilst still as K-105. Canx in 12/19.
G-EAAQ	Avro 536	ATC.2	K-104	22. 7.19	NTU - Crashed in Southwark Park, London 9.9.19 whilst still as K-104. Canx in 9/20.
G-EAAR	Vickers FB.27 Vimy	C105	C105 B9952	22. 7.19	NTU - No CofA issued. Canx in 5/20.
G-EAAS	Vickers FB.14A	C103	C103	22. 7.19	NTU - Project abandoned. Canx in 7/19.
G-EAAT	Vickers FB.14A	C102	C102	22. 7.19	NTU - Project abandoned. Canx in 7/19.
G-EAAU	Vickers FB.19 Bullet	C104	C104	22. 7.19	NTU - Project abandoned. Canx in 7/19.
G-EAAV	Vickers Vimy Commercial	-	K-107	22. 7.19	Crashed during take-off from Tabora, Tanganyika on 27.2.20. Canx in 4/20.
G-EAAW	Handley Page 0/400	HP.14	F5417 "G-5417"	22. 7.19	CofA expired 30.4.20 & WFU. Canx 10.1.23.
G-EAAX	Avro 504K	-	D6205	22. 7.19	CofA expired 11.5.21 & WFU. Canx.
G-EAAY	Avro 504K	-	C724	22. 7.19	CofA canx on 24.10.30 due to a prior accident. Canx in 12/32.
G-EAAZ	Farman S-11 Shorthorn	-	B4674	22. 7.19	No CofA issued. Canx in 1920.
G-EABA	Avro 504K	-	E3480	22. 7.19	WFU on 11.5.21. CofA expired 28.5.21. Canx.
G-EABB	Grahame-White G.W.15	401	(K-111)	22. 7.19	NTU - No CofA issued. Canx in 5/20.
G-EABC	Grahame-White G.W.15	402	(K-112)	22. 7.19	NTU - No CofA issued. Canx in 5/20.
G-EABD	Grahame-White G.W.15	403	(K-113)	22. 7.19	No CofA issued. Canx 10.1.23.
G-EABE	Avro 504K	-	E4137	22. 7.19	Crashed near Cambridge on 12.5.24. Canx.
G-EABF	Avro 504K	-	C748	22. 7.19	CofA expired 8.7.21 & WFU. Canx.
G-EABG	Avro 504K	-	C749	22. 7.19	CofA expired 31.5.21 & WFU. Canx 10.1.23.
G-EABH	Avro 504K	P1/1848	B8758	22. 7.19	CofA expired 1.8.21 & WFU. Canx.
G-EABI	Central Centaur IVA (Originally regd as a Mk.IV)	201	K-108	22. 7.19	No CofA issued. Scrapped at Shoreham in 4/30. Canx.
G-EABJ	Avro 504K	359	E4359	22. 7.19	CofA expired 18.5.20 & WFU. Canx in 5/20.
G-EABK	Avro 504K	-	D8287	22. 7.19	CofA expired 19.5.20 & WFU. Canx in 5/20.

Regn	Type	c/n	Previous identity	Regn date	Fate or immediate subsequent identity (if known)
G-EABL	Avro 504K	324	E4324	22. 7.19	CofA expired 18.5.20 & WFU. Canx in 5/20.
G-EABM	Avro 504K	360	E4360	22. 7.19	CofA expired 18.5.20 & WFU. Canx in 5/20.
G-EABN	Avro 504K	-	C723	22. 7.19	CofA expired 8.5.21 & WFU. Canx.
G-EABO	Avro 504K	-	D6202	27. 5.19	To Canada as G-CAAE on 16.7.20. Canx in 5/20.
G-EABP	Avro 504K	-	F9802	22. 7.19	CofA expired 19.5.21. To Belgian AF in 6/21. Canx 27.7.21.
G-EABQ	London & Provincial Biplane	E.121	K-117	22. 7.19	NTU - No CofA issued. Scrapped at Stag Lane in 8/19. Canx in 8/19.
G-EABR	London & Provincial Biplane	E.120	K-118	22. 7.19	NTU - No CofA issued. Scrapped at Stag Lane in 8/19. Canx in 8/19.
G-EABS	London & Provincial Biplane	D.147	K-119	22. 7.19	NTU - No CofA issued. Scrapped at Stag Lane in 8/19. Canx in 8/19.
G-EABT	Avro 504K	-	D6201	22. 7.19	No CofA issued & WFU. Canx in 8/19.
G-EABU	Bristol F.2c Badger X (Originally c/n 4257)	5658	K-110 F3497	22. 7.19	NTU - DBR when turned over on the ground at Filton on 22.5.19 prior to registration, not repaired. Canx in 5/20.
G-EABV	Avro 504K	-	D6229	22. 7.19	Crashed in 12/19. Canx in 12/19.
G-EABW	Avro 504K	-	C747	22. 7.19	CofA expired 18.7.22 & WFU. Canx 10.1.23.
G-EABX	Avro 504K	-	E4230	22. 7.19	CofA expired 21.5.22. Crashed at Rhos-on-Sea on 18.8.22. Canx in 8/23.
G-EABY	Armstrong Whitworth FK.3	-	B9629	22. 7.19	CofA expired 15.5.20 & WFU. Canx in 5/20.
G-EABZ	Armstrong Whitworth FK.3	-	B9518	22. 7.19	CofA expired 15.5.20 & WFU. Canx in 5/20.
G-EACA	Avro 504K	-	E6765	22. 7.19	CofA expired 12.6.20. Crashed at Earlham, Norwich on 28.9.21. Canx 1.10.21.
G-EACB	Avro 504K	-	E1671	22. 7.19	No CofA issued. Canx in 9/20.
G-EACC	Avro 536 Seaplane (Converted to Seaplane in 7/19)	ATC.1	K-114	22. 7.19	CofA expired 30.6.20 & WFU. Canx in 7/21.
G-EACD	Avro 504K	-	E4224	22. 7.19	Crashed in 12/19 (details?). Canx in 12/19.
G-EACE	Boulton & Paul P.7 IA	P.7/1	K-129 F2903	22. 7.19	No CofA issued. Scrapped in 5/20. Canx in 5/20.
G-EACF	Caudron G.III	87/8271	K-115	22. 7.19	No CofA issued. Canx in 1920.
G-EACG	Avro 536	ATC.9	K-116	22. 7.19	Crashed at Manston on 30.8.19. CofA canx on 19.11.19. Canx in 12/19.
G-EACH	Caudron G.III	-	K-127	22. 7.19	No CofA issued. Canx in 8/19.
G-EACI	Caudron G.III	-	K-128	22. 7.19	No CofA issued. Canx in 8/19.
G-EACJ	Boulton & Paul P.6	P.6/1	K-120 X25	22. 7.19	NTU. No CofA issued. Canx.
G-EACK	Caudron G.III	3005	K-121	22. 7.19	No CofA issued. Canx in 1920.
G-EACL	Avro 504K	-	D9298	22. 7.19	Overturned and crashed in a hayfield near Northampton on 5.8.19. Canx in 12/19.
G-EACM	Sopwith Dove	2714	K-122	22. 7.19	CofA expired 18.5.20 & WFU. To Canada as G-CAAY in 6/20. Canx in 5/20.
G-EACN	BAT FK.23 Bantam 1	FK.23-15	K-123 F1654	22. 7.19	NTU - No CofA issued. On display at Aviodome/Early Birds Foundation, Lelystad, Holland (On rebuild 1992)
G-EACO	BAT FK.24 Baboon	FK.24-7	K-124 D9731	22. 7.19	NTU - No CofA issued. Scrapped at Hendon in 1921. Canx.
G-EACP	BAT FK.23 Bantam (Clipped-wing racer)	FK.23-17	K-125 F1656	22. 7.19	NTU - No CofA issued. Last flown on 27.9.20. Scrapped at Hendon in 1921. Canx.
G-EACQ	Avro 534 Baby	534/1	K131	22. 7.19	To Australia in 6/21 - regd as G-AUCQ 12.7.21. Canx in 7/21 (Then to VH-UCQ in 10/30) On display at Queensland Cultural Centre, Brisbane, Australia in 2/96 marked as G-EACQ.
G-EACR	Avro 538 Scout	538/1	K-132	22. 7.19	No CofA issued. Scrapped. Canx in 9/20.
G-EACS	Avro 504K	-	D9341	22. 7.19	CofA expired 21.5.20 & WFU. Canx in 5/20.
G-EACT	Airco DH.16	DH.16/1	K-130	22. 7.19	Crashed in sea off Brighton on 18.3.20. CofA expired 26.5.20. Canx in 3/20.
G-EACU	Sopwith Dove	2769/1	K-133	22. 7.19	To Sweden as S-AFAA in 1/23. Canx 12.1.23.
G-EACV	Avro 504K	-	E4233	22. 7.19	Crashed in 4/20. Canx in 4/20.
G-EACW	Avro 504K	-	E1663	22. 7.19	Force landed in the sea at Southsea in 11/19. Canx in 11/19
G-EACX	Avro 504M	ATC.10	K-134	22. 7.19	CofA expired 23.5.20 & WFU. Canx.
G-EACY	RAF B.E.2e	-	C7175	22. 7.19	Crashed in 12/19. Canx in 12/19.
G-EACZ	Sopwith Scooter (Originally F.1 Camel B9276)	2052	K-135	22. 7.19	Sold as scrap in 1927. Canx.
G-EADA	Avro 504N (Originally regd as Avro 504K, modified in 1923)	-	E4221	22. 7.19	Canx in 1924.
G-EADB	Sopwith Gnu	2976/1	K-136	22. 7.19	Stalled on approach to a field at Horley, Surrey on 2.3.26. Canx.
G-EADC	Avro 536	ATC.5	K-137	22. 7.19	Scrapped at Hamble in 12/19. Canx.
G-EADD	Avro 504K	-	E1665	22. 7.19	WFU on 30.5.20. Canx.
G-EADE	Blackburn RT.1 Kangaroo	-	B9981 N1731	22. 7.19	NTU - Crashed at Hendon in 29.6.19 whilst still marked as B9981. Canx in 7/19.
G-EADF	Blackburn RT.1 Kangaroo	-	B9982 N1732	22. 7.19	NTU - No CofA issued. Crashed on take-off from Hendon on 31.5.19 whilst still marked as B9982. Canx in 7/19.
G-EADG	Blackburn RT.1 Kangaroo	-	B9985 N1735	22. 7.19	CofA expired 7.6.21 & WFU. Canx.
G-EADH	Avro 504K	-	E3502	22. 7.19	CofA expired 17.6.26 & WFU. Canx in 2/30.
G-EADI	Avro 504K (C/n also quoted as P1/8038)	PL.6039	E3292	22. 7.19	CofA expired 26.5.20 & WFU. Canx in 5/20.
G-EADJ	Avro 504K	-	H2581	22. 7.19	CofA expired 25.6.20 & WFU. Canx.
G-EADK	Avro 504K Seaplane	-	H2582	22. 7.19	CofA expired 17.7.21 & WFU. Canx.
G-EADL	Avro 504K	348	E4348	22. 7.19	DBR when aircraft broke its back in a difficult forced-landing at Kingswood, Bristol in 1/20, through engine failure. Canx.
G-EADM	Avro 504K	336	E4336	22. 7.19	CofA expired in 6/21. To Belgian AF in 6/21. Canx.
G-EADN	Avro 504K (C/n also quoted as P1/8039)	PL.6040	E3293	22. 7.19	Crashed at Llanelli on 12.9.19. CofA expired 30.6.20. Canx.

Regn	Type	c/n	Previous identity	Regn date	Fate or immediate subsequent identity (if known)
G-EADO	Avro 504K	-	F8706	22. 7.19	Crashed in 12/19. CofA canx on 7.12.19. Canx in 12/19.
G-EADP	Avro 504K	-	E3481	22. 7.19	Crashed at Morecambe Foreshore on 27.7.26. CofA expired 9.4.27. Canx in 11/31.
G-EADQ	Avro 504K	-	D7588	22. 7.19	CofA expired in 6/22. To Irish Air Corps as V-1 in 6/22. Canx 7.6.22.
G-EADR	Avro 504K	-	D6245	22. 7.19	Crashed at Werrington on 24.6.20. CofA expired in 7/20. Canx.
G-EADS	Avro 504K	-	H2507	22. 7.19	Crashed in 4/20. Canx.
G-EADT	London & Provincial Biplane	E.122	K-138	22. 7.19	No CofA issued. Canx in 10/20.
G-EADU	Avro 504K	-	D9329	22. 7.19	Crashed at High Wycombe on 19.11.23. CofA expired 8.10.24. Canx in 7/25.
G-EADV	Avro 536 (Experimental long-range 2-seater version)	ATC.11	K-139	22. 7.19	No CofA issued. Scrapped at Hamble in 12/19. Canx.
G-EADW	Avro 504K	343	E4343	22. 7.19	DBR by gales at Rhyl in 8/19. Canx 14.12.19.
G-EADX	Avro 504K	-	D6239	22. 7.19	CofA expired 25.5.20 & WFU. Canx in 5/20.
G-EADY	Avro 504K	-	E3408	22. 7.19	To South Africa in 1/21. Canx.
G-EADZ	Fairey IIIA	F.246	N2876	22. 7.19	NTU - No CofA issued. To G-EAMY in 9/19. Canx.
G-EAEA	Avro 504K	-	D9304	22. 7.19	To South Africa in 1/21. Canx.
G-EAEB	Avro 504K	P1/1864	B8774	22. 7.19	Crashed at Norwich on 25.9.21. Canx 3.10.21.
G-EAEC	Avro 504K	-	E3501	22. 7.19	To Australia in 6/21 - regd as G-AUDQ on 28.3.22. Canx.
G-EAED	Supermarine Channel I	978	N1529	22. 7.19	CofA expired 13.6.20 & WFU. Canx in 6/21.
G-EAEE	Supermarine Channel I	977	N1710	22. 7.19	Overturned and sank during a pleasure flight at Bournemouth on 15.8.19. Canx.
G-EAEF	Supermarine Channel I	976	N2452	22. 7.19	To Bermuda in 4/20. CofA expired 30.7.21. Canx.
G-EAEG	Supermarine Channel I	975	N2451	22. 7.19	To Bermuda in 4/20, then Trinidad in 3/21. CofA expired 16.5.21. Canx.
G-EAEH	Supermarine Channel I	974	N1716	22. 7.19	To Norway as N-9 in 6/20. Canx in 5/20.
G-EAEI	Supermarine Channel I	973	N1715	22. 7.19	To Norway as N-10 in 5/20. Canx in 5/20.
G-EAEJ	Supermarine Channel I	972	N1714	22. 7.19	To Bermuda in 4/20. CofA expired 8.8.20. Canx in 5/21.
G-EAEK	Supermarine Channel I	971	N1711	22. 7.19	Scrapped at Woolston in 2/21. Canx in 2/21.
G-EAEL	Supermarine Channel I	970	N1528	22. 7.19	NTU - Canx in 5/20. To Norway as N-11 in 7/20.
G-EAEM	Supermarine Channel I	969	N1526	22. 7.19	NTU - Canx in 5/20. To R.Norwegian Navy in 7/20.
G-EAEN	Avro 504K	-	D9018	22. 7.19	Crashed in 1/20. Canx in 1/20.
G-EAEO	Avro 504K	362	E4362	22. 7.19	CofA expired 14.6.20 & WFU. Canx.
G-EAEP	Sopwith Gnu	2976/2	K-140	22. 7.19	CofA expired 28.6.20 & WFU. Canx.
G-EAEQ	Nieuport Nighthawk	LC.1/1	K-151	22. 7.19	To India in 9/20. Canx.
G-EAER	Bristol M.1C	2782	C4964	22. 7.19	NTU - No CofA issued. Canx.
	Note: There is fairly conclusive evidence that this aircraft was sold to H.J.Butler at Minlaton, South Australia and arrived there sometime in late 1921 or early 1922. Upon Butler's death, the aircraft was stored until circa 1935 when acquired by Horrie Miller. From what can be worked out, the aircraft in the Memorial at Minlaton, South Australia was a hybrid made by combining components from both G-EAER and G-AUCH, to become VH-UQI on 15.10.31.				
G-EAES	Martinsyde F.4A	E4/500	K-152	22. 7.19	No CofA issued. Canx in 8/20.
G-EAET	Armstrong Whitworth FK.8	-	D5150	22. 7.19	No CofA issued. Canx in 8/19.
G-EAEU	Armstrong Whitworth FK.3	-	B9612	22. 7.19	Crashed in 12/19. Canx in 12/19.
G-EAEV	Avro 504K	-	H2586	22. 7.19	CofA expired 11.6.20 & WFU. Canx in 7/21.
G-EAEW	Airco DH.4R	G7/67	K-141	22. 7.19	No CofA issued. Scrapped in 1920. Canx in 6/20.
G-EAEX	Airco DH.4	G7/63	K-142	22. 7.19	No CofA issued. Scrapped in 1920. Canx in 4/20.
G-EAEY	Avro 504K	-	H2560	22. 7.19	Canx in 4/20.
G-EAEZ	Avro 504K	-	H2561	22. 7.19	Crashed near Tuxford on 18.10.19. Canx in 4/20.
G-EAFA	BAT FK.27	FK.27-33	K-143	22. 7.19	No CofA issued. Scrapped in 1921. Canx.
G-EAFB	Avro 504L	E.1	K-144	22. 7.19	CofA expired 24.6.21 & WFU. Canx.
G-EAFC	Avro 504K	-	E1660	22. 7.19	DBR by gales at Rhyl in 8/19. Canx.
G-EAFD	Avro 504K	-	E4329 "D4329"	22. 7.19	Canx in 3/21.
G-EAFE	Avro 504K	-	D7648	22. 7.19	Crashed on 8.9.21. Canx.
G-EAFF	Avro 504L	ATC.12	K-145	22. 7.19	To Belgian AF in 7/21. Canx.
G-EAFG	Avro 504L	ATC.13	K-146	22. 7.19	NTU - Crashed in fog off Alderney, Channel Islands on 5.10.19 while carrying newspapers to Guernsey, prior to re-registration. Canx.
G-EAFH	Avro 548 (Originally regd as Avro 504K, modified in 1920)	ATC.14	K-147	22. 7.19	Crashed at Southport on 31.5.35. Canx.
G-EAFI	Sopwith Dove	2769/2	K-148	22. 7.19	To Norway in 10/20. Canx.
G-EAFJ	Sopwith RM.1 Snapper	PW.14	K-149 F7031	22. 7.19	Restored to RAF as F7031 in 7/19. Canx.
G-EAFK	Grahame-White G.W.E.6 Bantam	GWE.6	K-150	22. 7.19	NTU - Crashed into the side of a hangar at Hendon on 5.7.19 whilst still marked as K-150. Canx.
G-EAFL	Grahame-White G.W.E.6 Bantam	GWE.6A	K-153	22. 7.19	Canx 10.1.23.
G-EAFM	BAT FK.23 Bantam	FK.23-16	K-154 F1655	22. 7.19	Crashed at Hendon on 23.3.20. Canx. (Also quoted as to USA as AS94111/P.167 in summer 1919 !)
G-EAFN	BAT FK.23 Bantam	FK.23-18	K-155 F1657	22. 7.19	Canx as registration lapsed in 6/20.
G-EAFO	Westland Limousine I	WAC.1	K-126	22. 7.19	W/o after being struck by RAF Fawn II J7220 on ground at Netheravon on 17.8.25. Canx 3.9.25.
G-EAFP	Avro 504K (C/n also quoted as P1/8109)	PL.6110	E3363	22. 7.19	To Australia in 12/21 - regd as G-AUFP on 17.12.23. Canx.
G-EAFQ	Avro 504K	-	E4180	22. 7.19	Crashed at Hildenborough, Kent on 26.11.21. Canx.
G-EAFR	Sopwith Gnu	3005/1	K-156	22. 7.19	NTU - To South Africa. Canx in 9/19.
G-EAFS	Avro 504K	-	D9340	22. 7.19	WFU on 3.7.20. Canx.
G-EAFT	Airco DH.6	-	B2943	22. 7.19	WFU on 22.9.20. Canx.
G-EAFU	Avro 504K	-	H2583	22. 7.19	NTU - To South Africa in 7/19. Canx.
G-EAFV	Avro 504K	-	H2584	22. 7.19	NTU - To South Africa in 7/19. Canx.
G-EAFW	Avro 504K	-	H2591	22. 7.19	NTU - To South Africa in 7/19. Canx.

Regn	Type	c/n	Previous identity	Regn date	Fate or immediate subsequent identity (if known)
G-EAFX	Avro 504K	-	H6543	22. 7.19	Badly damaged by gales at Rhyl in 8/19. Rebuilt as G-EASG. Canx.
G-EAFY	Airco DH.6	-	C7390	22. 7.19	NTU - To G-EAJM in 8/19. Canx.
G-EAFZ	Airco DH.6	-	C7320	22. 7.19	NTU - Used as spares for G-EAJM. Canx in 8/19.
G-EAGA(1)	Sopwith Dove	3004/1	K-157	22. 7.19	NTU - To Australia by 11/19, no marks issued. Canx in 9/19.
G-EAGA(2)	Sopwith Dove Replica	"3004/1"	(G-BLOO)	22.11.89	(On loan to The Shuttleworth Collection)
	Note: Sopwith Dove, c/n 3004/1, was exported to Australia by the Larkin-Sopwith Aviation Co., and was certainly in use as K-157 by 11/12.1919. Then sold to Major George Aubrey Cadogan Cowper (who, with partners, operated as Aviation Ltd.) at Glenroy, Victoria. Its' history past this point is very vague, but this is possibly the Dove which Cowper gave to one F.J.Barnes circa 5.21, who died in 1925. What exactly happen to the Dove is not known, but an unregistered Dove, recorded as an "experimental machine", was crashed on a test-flight at Essendon, Victoria on 9.3.30, and it is suspected this may well have been K-157. It is believed that the remains brought to the UK circa 1987/88 and rebuilt as the replica (with regn G-BLOO) were from somewhere near Hamilton, and since then it has been (apparently) absolutely identified as the former K-157. Therefore the two entries for the one marks could be one and the same aircraft, and the previous identities for (2) could infact be; (G-BLOO)/(G-EAGA)/K-157.				
G-EAGB	Avro 504K	-	H5173	22. 7.19	Crashed at Evesham on 10.9.23. Canx.
G-EAGC	Avro 504K	-	H5172	22. 7.19	Canx in 3/24.
G-EAGD	Avro 504K	-	D5499	22. 7.19	DBR in 1919; Rebuilt as G-EALE. Canx.
G-EAGE	Airco DH.6	-	C5224	22. 7.19	Canx as WFU 17.9.24.
G-EAGF	Airco DH.6	-	C5220	22. 7.19	CofA expired 21.8.21 & WFU. Canx.
G-EAGG	Airco DH.6	-	C2101	22. 7.19	NTU. Canx in 4/20.
G-EAGH	BE.2e	-	C7101	22. 7.19	Canx as WFU 27.9.20.
G-EAGI	Avro 504K	-	E4234	22. 7.19	Crashed near Twickenham on 19.3.20. Canx.
G-EAGJ	Avro 504K	-	C746	22. 7.19	Crashed at Twickenham in 12/19. Canx in 12/19.
G-EAGK	Alliance P.1	P.1	K-159	22. 7.19	Scrapped in 11/20. Canx in 11/20.
G-EAGL(1)	Alliance P.2 Seabird	P.2	K-160	22. 7.19	Canx in 11/20. (Possibly sold in Spain).
G-EAGL(2)	Cessna 421C Golden Eagle III	421C-0713	(N2656G)	8. 8.79	
G-EAGM	Avro 536	ATC.6	K-161	22. 7.19	NTU - Crashed at Weston-super-Mare on 1.9.19 still marked as K-161. Canx.
G-EAGN	Handley Page O/7	HP.1	K-162 C9704	22. 7.19	To China in 8/19. Canx 25.8.19.
G-EAGO	Avro 504K	-	D9343	22. 7.19	NTU - Crashed at Southport on 21.8.19, still as D9343. Canx.
G-EAGP	Sopwith Gnu	2976/3	K-163	22. 7.19	Crashed at Kings Lynn on 2.5.26. Canx.
G-EAGQ	Sopwith Gnu	2976/4	K-164	22. 7.19	WFU on 28.7.20. Canx.
G-EAGR	Bristol Type 1 Scout C	1060	5570	22. 7.19	Broken up in a scrap yard at South Cave, East Yorks., in 1933. Canx.
G-EAGS	Austin Whippet	AU.1	K-158	22. 7.19	CofA expired 19.11.21 & WFU. Canx.
G-EAGT	Avro 504K	-	D6217	22. 7.19	Canx in 3/21.
G-EAGU	Avro 504L Seaplane	-	H2585	22. 7.19	WFU on 15.8.20. Canx.
G-EAGV	Avro 504K	-	H6598	22. 7.19	Crashed at Scarborough on 3.8.20. Canx.
G-EAGW	Avro 504K	-	H6599	22. 7.19	Crashed at Scarborough in 7/20. Canx.
G-EAGX	Airco DH.9B	-	H9255	22. 7.19	Crashed in 8/20. Canx in 9/20.
G-EAGY	Airco DH.9B	-	H9258	22. 7.19	Sold abroad in 1/21. Canx in 1/21.
G-EAGZ	Avro 504K	GW.3254	D8984	22. 7.19	Canx in 6/20.
G-EAHA	Avro 536	ATC.7	K-165	22. 7.19	To Holland. Canx in 9/20.
G-EAHB	Avro 536	ATC.8	K-166	22. 7.19	Dismantled at Hamble in 12/19. Canx as WFU 14.7.20.
G-EAHC	FE.2b	-	D3832	22. 7.19	Crashed prior to 10.1.23. Canx as WFU 7.8.21.
G-EAHD	Airco DH.6	-	B2934	22. 7.19	Canx as WFU in 2/20.
G-EAHE	Airco DH.6	-	B2917	22. 7.19	Crashed on 25.2.20. Canx.
G-EAHF	Airco DH.4A	-	F2699	22. 7.19	Crashed at Caterham, Surrey on 11.12.19. Canx.
G-EAHG	Airco DH.4A	-	F2694	5. 8.19	Crashed into the English Channel on 30.10.19. Canx.
G-EAHH	Airco DH.6	-	F3435	22. 7.19	WFU on 10.8.20. Canx.
G-EAHI	Airco DH.6	-	C6889	22. 7.19	WFU on 30.7.22. Canx.
G-EAHJ	Airco DH.6	-	C9432	22. 7.19R	NTU. Canx in 7/19.
G-EAHK	Avro 504K	340	E4340	22. 7.19	WFU on 11.8.21. Canx.
G-EAHL	Avro 504K	-	E4118	22. 7.19	Crashed at Dunham Massey, Cheshire on 30.6.23. Canx 7.7.23.
G-EAHM	Avro 504K	-	E1707	2. 8.19	Crashed in 12/19. Canx in 12/19.
G-EAHN	BAT FK.26	FK.26-30	K-167	22. 7.19	Crashed in 7/20. Canx.
G-EAHO	Avro 504K	-	H1959	22. 7.19	Crashed at Aberystwyth on 28.8.19. Canx.
G-EAHP	Sopwith Dove	3004/2	K-168	22. 7.19	Sold abroad, probably to Australia. Canx in 9/19.
	Note: It is believed that this aircraft accompanied K-157/(G-EAGA) to Australia by 11/19; if this is the case, it would have been marked only as K-168.				
G-EAHQ	Sopwith Gnu	2976/5	K-169	22. 7.19	To Australia (by 2/20) - regd as G-AUBX on 28.6.21. Canx.
G-EAHR	Central Centaur IIA	101	(K-170)	22. 7.19	Crashed on take-off from Northolt in 7/19. Canx.
G-EAHS	Central Centaur IVA (Originally regd as a Mk.IV)	202	(K-171)	23. 7.19	To Belgium in 4.7.22. Canx.
G-EAHT	Airco DH.9R Racer	9R/1	(K-172)	23. 7.19	NTU - No CofA issued. Scrapped in 1922. Canx.
G-EAHU	Avro 504K	-	E1611	. 7.19	Crashed at Castle Bromwich on 10.6.22. Canx.
G-EAHV	Avro 504K	-	H2297	3. 9.19	WFU in 8/21. Canx 10.1.23.
G-EAHW	Avro 504K (C/n also quoted as P1/8110)	PL.6111	E3364	7. 8.19	Crashed at Southwark Park, London on 31.3.20. Canx.
G-EAHX	Avro 504K (C/n also quoted as P1/8112)	PL.6113	E3366	7. 8.19	WFU in 9/20. Canx in 8/21.
G-EAHY	Avro 504K	-	H7513	. 8.19	WFU in 8/28. Canx in 1/29.
G-EAHZ	Avro 504K	-	H2411	. 8.19	Crashed on 1.3.22. Canx 1.3.25.
G-EAIA	Avro 504K	-	F8717	. 8.19	WFU on 15.8.21. Canx in 3/24.
G-EAIB	Avro 504K	-	D9303	. 8.19	Canx in 6/21.
G-EAIC	Armstrong Whitworth FK.8	-	H4473	7. 8.19	Crashed in 6/20. Canx.
G-EAID	Avro 536	B.1	(K-173)	31. 7.19	Stored at Alexandra Park Aerodrome, Manchester in 8/21. Canx in 8/21

Regn	Type	c/n	Previous identity	Regn date	Fate or immediate subsequent identity (if known)
G-EAIE	Avro 536	B.2	(K-174)	24. 7.19	Stored at Alexandra Park Aerodrome, Manchester in 8/21. Canx in 8/21
G-EAIF	Avro 536	B.4	(K-175)	7. 8.19	Stored at Alexandra Park Aerodrome, Manchester in 8/21. Canx in 8/21
G-EAIG	Avro 504K	-	E1695	3. 9.19	NTU - Not converted. Canx in 10/19.
G-EAIH	Avro 504K	-	H2595	31. 7.19	To Belgian AF in 1921. Canx.
G-EAII	Avro 504K	-	H2596	31. 7.19	Crashed off Great Yarmouth on 1.8.20. Canx in 8/21.
G-EAIJ	Avro 504K	-	H2597	31. 7.19	WFU in 7/20. Canx in 8/21.
G-EAIK	Felixstowe F.5	G6/100	N4634	5. 8.19	Restored to RAF as N4634 in 8/20. Canx.
	(Register as 'Gosport Flying Boat' by the builders Gosport Aviation Co. Ltd)				
G-EAIL	Sopwith Gnu	2976/6		7. 8.19	To Australia in 4/20 - regd as G-AUBY on 28.6.21. Canx.
G-EAIM	Sopwith Gnu	3005/2		7. 8.19	To Australia in 11/19 - not regd (may have been w/o pre-registration). Canx.
G-EAIN	Sopwith Grasshopper	2698/1		. 8.19	WFU at Cramlington on 30.5.29. Canx.
G-EAIO	Avro 504K	PL.6106	E3359	6. 8.19	Canx in 8/20.
G-EAIP	Avro 504K	-	E4143	7. 8.19	Canx in 8/20.
G-EAIQ	Avro 504K	-	E4144	7. 8.19	Scrapped in 11/20. Canx.
G-EAIR	Avro 504K	-	E4164	7. 8.19	Crashed at Hayling Island on 11.8.23. Canx.
G-EAIS	Avro 504K	-	E4170	7. 8.19	Canx as sold abroad in 4/20.
G-EAIT	Blackburn RT.1 Kangaroo	-	B9978	1. 8.19	Fatal crash at Brough on 5.5.25. Canx.
	(Converted to dual trainer in 1924)		N1728		
G-EAIU	Blackburn RT.1 Kangaroo	-	B9973	1. 8.19	CofA expired 19.4.29 & WFU. Scrapped at Sherburn-in-Elmet in 1929. Canx.
	(Conv. to proto. dual trainer in 5/24)		N1723		
G-EAIV	Avro 504K	AAEC/1		7. 8.19	NTU - To Australia in 8/19 - regd as G-AUCB on 28.6.21. Canx.
G-EAIW	Avro 504K	AAEC/2		7. 8.19	NTU - To Australia in 8/19 - DBR in forced landing near Shepparton, Victoria on 20.4.21, with no regn issued. Canx.
G-EAIX	Avro 504K	AAEC/3		7. 8.19	NTU - To Australia in 8/19 - no regn issued. Shipped to New Zealand on 21.12.20 - crashed at Longlands, near hastings on 12.6.21, also without regn marks being issued. Canx.
G-EAIY	Avro 504K	AAEC/4		7. 8.19	NTU - To Australia in 8/19 - regd as G-AUBE on 28.6.21. Canx.
	Note: As far as can be ascertained, the above four aircraft were shipped directly from the factory to Mascot, New South Wales, Australia without having ever been erected in the UK. These were assembled by the A.A.& E.Co. and used as their "in house" demonstrators, fitted with the Clerget 9B of 130hp.				
G-EAIZ	Bristol 29 Tourer	5867		7. 8.19	WFU on 9.9.20. Canx.
G-EAJA	BE.2e	-	A1298	. 8.19	DBR by gales at Aylestone, Leics in 7/20. Canx in 7/20.
G-EAJB	Avro 548	-	H2598	. 8.19	Canx in 1/29.
	(Originally regd as Avro 504K, modified in 1927)				
G-EAJC	Airco DH.4A	-	F2702	7. 8.19	WFU on 18.8.20. Canx.
G-EAJD	Airco DH.4A	-	F2704	7. 8.19	WFU on 21.8.20. Canx.
G-EAJE	Avro 504K	-	H2549	1. 8.19	To Denmark as T-DOLM in 6/21. Canx 8.8.21.
G-EAJF	Avro 504K	-	H2556	1. 8.19	To Danish Army as AVRO.1 in 11/21. Canx 21.11.21.
G-EAJG	Avro 504K	-	H1956	7. 8.19	Crashed at Penshurst on 20.8.22. Canx.
G-EAJH	Avro 504L Seaplane	E.2		7. 8.19	Sank in sea off Hove, Sussex on 19.8.20. Canx.
G-EAJI	Sopwith Dove	3004/3		7. 8.19	To Australia in 9/20 - regd as G-AUDN on 28.6.21. Canx.
G-EAJJ	Sopwith Dove	3004/4		7. 8.19	To Australia in 3/20 - regd as G-AUJJ on 28.6.21. Canx.
G-EAJK	Avro 504K	-	D7619	. 8.19	Crashed in 8/21. Canx in 5/22.
G-EAJL	Westland Limousine II	WAC.2		6. 8.19	To Newfoundland, Canada in 8/22. Canx.
G-EAJM	Airco DH.6	-	(G-EAFY) C7390	7. 8.19	WFU on 6.8.20. Canx.
G-EAJN	BE.2e	-	A1404	. 8.19	WFU in 18.8.20. Scrapped. Canx in 10/21.
G-EAJO	Airco DH.10	-	E5488	7. 8.19	DBR in forced-landing in Pyrenees on 3.3.20. Canx in 4/20.
G-EAJP	Avro 504K	-	E1728	. 8.19	Sold Abroad. Canx in 1/21.
G-EAJQ	Avro 504K	-	H2587	. 8.19	Crashed at Honiton on 23.9.20. Canx.
G-EAJR	Avro 536	B.5		8. 8.19	Stored at Alexandra Park Aerodrome, Manchester in 8/21. Canx in 8/21
G-EAJS	Armstrong Whitworth FK.8	-	H4612	14. 8.19	To Sweden in 11/19. Canx.
G-EAJT	Short 184	-	N2986	28. 8.19	WFU on 30.7.29. Canx.
G-EAJU	Avro 504K	-	H2592	. 8.19	DBR at Brighton on 21.7.29. Canx.
G-EAJV	BE.2e	-	A1410	. 8.19	Crashed at Northallerton on 12.10.20. Canx 18.8.21.
G-EAJW	BAT FK.23 Bantam	FK.23-19	F1658	12. 8.19	To Holland as (H-NACQ) on 20.8.20. Canx.
G-EAJX	Avro 504L	ATC.16		12. 8.19	Canx in 10/20.
G-EAJY	Nieuport Nighthawk	LC.1/No.2		13. 8.19	Scrapped in 1921. Canx.
G-EAJZ	Avro 504K	-	H2594	14. 8.19	Crashed on 11.8.23. Canx.
G-EAKA	Avro 504L Seaplane	-	H2590	14. 8.19	WFU on 20.8.20. To Chile in 8/21. Canx.
G-EAKB	Avro 504K	-	H2588	14. 8.19	WFU on 21.8.20. Canx.
G-EAKC	De Bolotoff SDEB.14	14		14. 8.19	NTU. Canx.
G-EAKD	Avro 536	B.3		16. 8.19	Stored at Alexandra Park Aerodrome, Manchester in 8/21. Canx in 8/21
G-EAKE	Handley Page O/400	HP.22	J2252	14. 8.19	Crashed when engine failed on take-off from Srebro, near Stockholm, Sweden on 30.6.20. Canx.
G-EAKF	Handley Page O/400	HP.19	J2249	14. 8.19	CofA expired 1.10.20 & WFU. Canx.
G-EAKG	Handley Page O/400	HP.20	J2250	14. 8.19	CofA expired 29.8.20 & WFU. Canx.
G-EAKH	Sopwith Dove	3004/5		14. 8.19	To Australia in 3/20 - regd as G-AUKH on 28.6.21. Canx.
G-EAKI	Sopwith Schneider Seaplane	3067		. 8.19	Crashed at Hersham on 1.9.23. Canx.
G-EAKJ	Avro 536	B.6		18. 8.19	WFU on 16.5.26. Canx in 1/29.
G-EAKK	Avro 536	B.7		18. 8.19	WFU on 4.9.20. Stored at Alexandra Park Aerodrome, Manchester in 8/21. Canx.
G-EAKL	Avro 536	B.8		18. 8.19	Stored at Alexandra Park Aerodrome, Manchester in 8/21. Canx in 8/21. Rebuilt as G-EBOY in 1926 with c/n P.8.
G-EAKM	Avro 536	B.9		18. 8.19	Crashed at Taplow on 4.7.28. Canx.
G-EAKN	Avro 536	B.10		18. 8.19	Crashed at Dorton, near Brill on 12.8.24. Canx.

Regn	Type	c/n	Previous identity	Regn date	Fate or immediate subsequent identity (if known)
G-EAKO	Avro 536	B.11		18. 8.19	Stored at Alexandra Park Aerodrome, Manchester in 8/21. Canx in 8/21
G-EAKP	Avro 536	B.12		18. 8.19	WFU 14.7.26. Canx in 1/29.
G-EAKQ	Blackburn RT.1 Kangaroo	-	B9972 N1722	18. 8.19	To Peruvian Army Flying Service in 7/21. Canx in 7/21.
G-EAKR	Avro 504K	-	E4246	19. 8.19	Crashed at Laumes-Alesia, Cote D'or, France on 20.9.19. Canx.
G-EAKS	Sopwith Wallaby	3109		19. 8.19	Crashed at Bali on 17.4.20. Rebuilt in Australia - regd as G-AUDU on 30.8.22. Canx.
G-EAKT	Sopwith Dove	3004/6		19. 8.19	To Australia in 3/20: intended as G-AUDP but crashed prior to registration. Canx.
G-EAKU	Airco DH.6	K.151	(RAF)	. 8.19	WFU in 9/20. Canx in 1/21.
G-EAKV	Avro 504K	-	J803	20. 8.19	To Switzerland as CH-10 in 9/19. Canx 17.9.19.
G-EAKW	Avro 504K	-	H2593	20. 8.19	Crashed at Blackpill, near Swansea in 8/20. Canx in 9/20.
G-EAKX	Avro 504K	-	H2600	20. 8.19	Dismantled at Hooton Park in 9/34. Canx.
G-EAKY	Avro 504K	-	H2599	20. 8.19	WFU on 27.8.20. Canx.
G-EAKZ	Avro 504K	PL.6044	E3297	20. 8.19	WFU on 7.9.20. Canx.
G-EALA	Avro 504K	-	E1640	20. 8.19	Crashed 21.8.22.
G-EALB	Avro 504L Seaplane	-	H2589	20. 8.19	WFU on 15.6.20. Canx.
G-EALC	Short 184	-	N2998	28. 8.19	WFU on 6.3.20. Canx.
G-EALD	Avro 504K	-	H1925	. 8.19	Crashed at Kennington, Kent on 27.8.22. Canx.
G-EALE	Avro 504K	-	G-EAGD J5499	. 8.19	Crashed at Burton on 30.3.23. Canx as WFU 24.4.23.
G-EALF	Avro 548	-	J743	20. 8.19	W/o in 7/21. Canx.
	(Originally regd as Avro 504K, modified in 1920)				
G-EALG	Avro 539A Seaplane	539/1		21. 8.19	Canx in 1921. Rebuilt as Avro 539B Racer & re-regd G-EAXM.
	(Converted to landplane 7/20 with c/n 539A/1)				
G-EALH	Avro 504L	ATC.15		21. 8.19	WFU on 24.8.20. Canx.
G-EALI	Avro 504L	ATC.17		21. 8.19	WFU on 29.8.20. Canx.
G-EALJ	Airco DH.9	-	D2884	26. 8.19	Conversion abandoned. Canx in 10/20.
G-EALK	Armstrong Whitworth FK.3	-	B9603	25. 8.19	Scrapped in 1920. Canx as WFU 9.9.20.
G-EALL	Central Centaur IV	203		. 8.19	Scrapped at Shoreham in 4/30. Canx in 4/30.
G-EALM	Airco DH.16	4		26. 8.19	Crashed at Stanmore on 10.1.23. Canx.
G-EALN	Blackburn Sidecar	-		26. 8.19	Canx in 7/21.
G-EALO	Avro 504L	E.3		26. 8.19	Crashed in 2/21. Canx.
G-EALP	Supermarine Sea Lion I	-		26. 8.19	Crashed into the English Channel off Bournemouth Pier on 10.9.19. Canx.
G-EALQ	Fairey IIIA Seaplane	F.128	N10	28. 8.19	Canx in 12/22.
G-EALR	Grahame-White G.W.E.VII	GWE.7		28. 8.19	DBR in forced-landing at Hendon on 1.10.19. Wreck burned in 1920. Canx.
G-EALS	Airco DH.6	-	C7620	29. 8.19	NTU - Registration elapsed. Canx.
G-EALT	Airco DH.6	-	B3094	29. 8.19	WFU on 19.12.20. Canx.
G-EALU	Airco DH.16	P.1		29. 8.19	Broken up at Croydon in 8/22 for spares. Canx.
G-EALV	Caudron G.III	1005	A3032	29. 8.19	Canx in 9/20.
G-EALW	Armstrong Whitworth FK.8	-	F7484	3. 9.19	Fatal crash near Bedford on 16.8.20. Canx.
G-EALX	Handley Page O/400	HP.21	J2251	3. 9.19	Crashed in heavy landing in 4/20. Canx 27.10.20.
G-EALY	Handley Page O/400	HP.24	J2247	3. 9.19	CofA expired 9.10.20. Canx.
G-EALZ	Handley Page O/400	HP.23	J2243	3. 9.19	Canx as WFU 6.12.20.
G-EAMA	Handley Page O/400	HP.25	J2248	3. 9.19	Crashed at Golders Green, London on 14.12.20. Canx.
	(Was the first scheduled transport fatal accident)				
G-EAMB	Handley Page O/400	HP.26	D4623	3. 9.19	Canx in 10/20.
G-EAMC	Handley Page O/400	HP.27	D4624	3. 9.19	Crashed north of El Sherik, Sudan on 25.2.20. Canx in 10/20.
G-EAMD	Handley Page O/400	HP.28	D4633	3. 9.19	To Poland in 11/20. Canx.
G-EAME	Sopwith Gnu	3005/4		3. 9.19	Canx 8.9.21.
G-EAMF	Sopwith Gnu	3005/6		3. 9.19	Canx 8.9.21.
G-EAMG	Sopwith Gnu	3005/5		3. 9.19	Sold Abroad in 9/21. Canx 8.9.21.
G-EAMH	Sopwith Gnu	3005/3		3. 9.19	Canx 8.9.21.
G-EAMI	Avro 504K	PL.6146	E3399	5. 9.19	Crashed at Banbury on 16.4.21. Canx 7.12.21.
	(C/n also quoted as P1/8145)				
G-EAMJ	Blackburn RT.1 Kangaroo (Converted to dual trainer in 1924)	-	B9977 N1727	8. 9.19	CofA expired 2.2.29. Broken up at Sherburn-in-Elmet in 1929. Canx.
G-EAMK	Airco DH.6	-	C9448	. 9.19	To South Africa in 9/19. Crashed in 1921 still marked as G-EAMK. Canx 19.9.19.
G-EAML	Airco DH.6	-	C9449	. 9.19	To South Africa in 9/19. Preserved in South African Air Force Museum, Pretoria as G-EAML. Canx 19.9.19.
G-EAMM	BAT FK.23 Bantam	FK.23-20	F1659	8. 9.19	NTU - Broken up in 1920. Canx as registration lapsed in 9/20. Possibly not completed.
G-EAMN	Avro 504K	-	J747	10. 9.19	No CofA issued. Canx in 9/20.
G-EAMO	Avro 504K	-	J746	10. 9.19	CofA expired 22.9.20. To Chile 9/21. Canx 8.9.21.
G-EAMP	Avro 504K	-	J745	10. 9.19	CofA expired 6.10.20 & WFU. Canx.
G-EAMQ	Avro 504K	-	J748	10. 9.19	Crashed at Rhyl on 14.10.20. Canx.
G-EAMR	Martinsyde Type A Mk.I	E4/500		10. 9.19	Crashed into sea off St.Georges Bay, Crete on 17.12.19. Canx.
G-EAMS	Airco DH.6	-	B2689	11. 9.19	NTU - Conversion abandoned. Canx 9/20.
G-EAMT	Airco DH.6	-	A9613	11. 9.19	NTU - Conversion abandoned. Canx 9/20.
G-EAMU	Airco DH.4A	-	H5939	. 9.19	WFU on 11.3.24. Canx.
	(Originally regd as DH.4, modified in 1920)				
G-EAMV	Westland Limousine II	WAC.3		. 9.19	Sold Abroad. Canx 23.4.23.
G-EAMW	Grahame-White G.W.E.IX Ganymede	GWE.9	C3481	12. 9.19	Broken up and burned in 9/20. Canx.
G-EAMX	Airco DH.9	-	D5622	15. 9.19	To Newfoundland, Canada. Canx in 4/20.

Regn	Type	c/n	Previous identity	Regn date	Fate or immediate subsequent identity (if known)
G-EAMY	Fairey IIIC	F.246	G-EADZ	18. 9.19	Crashed near Gavle, Sweden on 22.7.20. Canx in 8/20.
	(Originally regd as a Mk.IIIA)		N2876		
G-EAMZ	Avro 504K	-	E3724	. 9.19	Crashed at Le Bourget, France on 9.6.25. Canx.
G-EANA	Central Centaur V	301		15. 9.19	NTU - Construction abandoned. Canx 1.9.22.
G-EANB	Avro 504L	ATC.18		16. 9.19	To Sweden as S-IAA/S-ABAA in 7/21. Canx.
G-EANC	Avro 504K	-	H2318	16. 9.19	Canx in 10/20.
G-EAND	Avro 504K	-	J749	18. 9.19	To Belgium as O-BADL in 6/21. Canx.
G-EANE	Avro 504K	-	J751	18. 9.19	CofA expired 22.10.20. To Chile 9/21. Canx 8.9.21.
G-EANF	Avro 504K	-	J752	18. 9.19	CofA expired 30.9.20. Canx in 10/20.
G-EANG	Avro 504K	-	J753	18. 9.19	To Belgium as O-BADM in 6/21. Canx.
G-EANH	Fokker D.VII	-		18. 9.19	Canx in 9/20.
G-EANI	BAT FK.26	FK.26-31		18. 9.19	DBR at Watford in 1942 & WFU. Canx.
G-EANJ	Airco DH.6	-	B2861	. 9.19	WFU on 18.4.22. Canx.
G-EANK	Airco DH.4	P.7	F2670	20. 9.19	Sold abroad in 4/20. Canx.
G-EANL	Airco DH.4	P.8	F2671	20. 9.19	Sold abroad in 4/20. Canx.
G-EANM	Martinsyde F.4	E4/500		23. 9.19	To Portuguese AF in 12/19. Canx.
G-EANN	Avro 504K	-	H2514	. 9.19	Crashed in France during 1920. Canx.
G-EANO	Avro 504K	-	J756	22. 9.19	CofA expired 8.10.20 & WFU. Canx.
G-EANP	Avro 504K	-	J754	22. 9.19	To Imperial Japanese Navy in 9/21. Canx 8.9.21.
G-EANQ	Avro 504K	-	J755	22. 9.19	Crashed in Solway Firth, Carlisle on 1.12.21. Canx.
G-EANR	Bristol 29 Tourer	5868		23. 9.19	Shipped to USA in 5/20, flown in Nicaragua. Canx.
G-EANS	Avro 504L	E.4		26. 9.19	Crashed in 9/20. Canx as WFU 29.9.20.
G-EANT	Avro 504K	PL.6105	E3358	26. 9.19	WFU on 20.2.23. Canx.
	(C/n also quoted as P1/8104)				
G-EANU	Airco DH.6	-	C5230	. 9.19	WFU on 6.5.24. Canx.
G-EANV	Handley Page O/7	HP.7		27. 9.19	Crashed near Beaufort West, South Africa on 19.2.20. Canx.
G-EANW	BE.2e	-	C7185	. 9.19	Destroyed in hangar collapse at Martlesham Heath in 2/29. Canx.
G-EANX	Avro 504K	-	J757	3.10.19	To Imperial Japanese Navy in 9/21. Canx 8.9.21.
G-EANY	Avro 504K	-	J758	3.10.19	To Imperial Japanese Navy in 9/21. Canx 7.9.21.
G-EANZ	Avro 504K	-	J759	3.10.19	To Imperial Japanese Navy in 9/21. Canx in 9.21.
G-EAOA	Avro 504K	-	J760	3.10.19	To Imperial Japanese Navy in 9/21. Canx 7.9.21.
G-EAOB	Avro 504K	-	J761	3.10.19	To Imperial Japanese Navy in 9/21. Canx 7.9.21.
G-EAOC	Avro 504K	-	J762	3.10.19	To Imperial Japanese Navy in 9/21. Canx 7.9.21.
G-EAOD	Avro 504K	-	J763	3.10.19	To Imperial Japanese Navy in 9/21. Canx 7.9.21.
G-EAOE	Avro 504K	-	E3505	.10.19	Crashed at Cleethorpes on 12.6.22. Canx.
G-EAOF	Airco DH.9A	-	E750	9.10.19	Returned to RAF as E750 in 6/20. Canx.
G-EAOG	Airco DH.9A	-	E752	9.10.19	Returned to RAF as E752 in 6/20. Canx.
G-EAOH	Airco DH.9A	-	E753	9.10.19	Returned to RAF as E753 in 4/20. Canx.
G-EAOI	Airco DH.9A	-	E754	9.10.19	Returned to RAF as E754 in 6/20. Canx.
G-EAOJ	Airco DH.9A	-	E756	9.10.19	Returned to RAF as E756 in 6/20. Canx.
G-EAOK	Airco DH.9A	-	E757	9.10.19	Returned to RAF as E757 in 6/20. Canx.
G-EAOL	Vickers FB.27A Vimy IV	-	F8625	16.10.19	To Spain in 1920. Canx.
G-EAOM	Avro 536	ATC.23		14.10.19	Canx as WFU 16.12.21.
G-EAON	Caudron G.III	3032	A3020	15.10.19	Canx at census 10.1.23.
G-EAOO	Caudron G.III	3030	A3030	15.10.19	Canx at census 10.1.23.
G-EAOP	Airco DH.9	-	H5579	20.10.19	W/o in 9/20. Canx.
G-EAOQ	Central Centaur IV	204		20.10.19	To Belgium in 10/21. Canx 11.10.21.
G-EAOR	Central Centaur IVB Seaplane	205		19.10.19	Crashed in 10/20. Canx in 10/20.
	(Originally regd as Mk.IVA, converted in 1920)				
G-EAOS	Central Centaur IVA	206		20.10.19	To Belgium in 10/21. Canx 7.10.21.
	(Originally regd as Mk.IV)				
G-EAOT	Airco DH.6	-	C7434	20.10.19	To Switzerland as CH-45 in 2/21. Canx 18.2.21.
G-EAOU	Vickers FB.27A Vimy IV	-	F8630	23.10.19	First aircraft to be flown by Australian's from England to Australia, taking-off on 12.11.19 and arriving on 10.12.19. Canx in 1920. Became A5-1 9/21 (see note). Partly rebuilt after fire in transit to exhibition hall at Smith Airport, Adelaide, Australia in 1958. On display in the museum at West Beach, Adelaide in 2/96, marked as G-EAOU.
	Note: The R.Australian AF serial A5-1 was a genuine allotment - the problem was it didn't actually belong th the RAAF at the time - it had been officially handed over to the Commonwealth Government and was stored at Point Cook; the gentlemen there simply included it in the 'stock-take' and allotted the serial number, in 9/21. They were quickly apprised of the real situation and shortly afterwards the aircraft was handed over to what was then known as thc Australian War Museum.				
"G-EAOU"	Vickers FB.27A Vimy IV Replica	01		----	Is NX71MY really - regd on 19.9.94.
G-EAOV	Vickers Viking I	1		21.10.19	Crashed north of Rouen, France on 18.12.19. Canx.
G-EAOW	Blackburn RT.1 Kangaroo	-	B9970 N1720	24.10.19	Abandoned after force landing at Suda Bay, Crete on 8.12.19. Canx.
G-EAOX	Alliance P.2 Seabird	P.2/2		23.10.19	Fatal crash at Surbiton, Surrey on 13.11.19. Canx.
G-EAOY	Norman-Thompson NT.4A	NA.4A/1	N2155	29.10.19	Canx in 10/22.
G-EAOZ	Airco DH.9B	P.32E	H5889	29.10.19	To Holland as H-NABF(2) in 8/21. Canx.
G-EAPA	Handley Page O/7	HP.11		3.11.19	To India as G-IAAC(1) in 5/20. Canx.
G-EAPB	Handley Page O/7	HP.12	J1934	3.11.19	To India in 6/20. Canx 1/21.
G-EAPC	Central Centaur IIA (Cabin model)	102		5.11.19	Fatal crash at Sharvel Lane, Hayes, Middlesex on 25.9.20. Canx.
G-EAPD	Boulton Paul P.9	P.9/1		6.11.19	To Australia in 11/20: did not attain regn. Canx in 11/20.
	Note: Possibly the aircraft acquired to one F.J.Barnes, from Hamilton in the Western District [about 100 miles southwest of Melbourne, Australia] circa 5/21 - his announced intention was to convert the P.9 (thought to be this one) into a monoplane, but what exactly was done with it, if anything, is as yet unknown.				
G-EAPE	Boulton Paul P.8	P.8/2		6.11.19	WFU in 1920. Canx.
G-EAPF	Austin Whippet	AU.2		.11.19	WFU at Shoreham in 1931. Canx.
G-EAPG	Airco DH.6	3100	C7430	8.11.19	Canx in 11/20.
G-EAPH	Airco DH.6	-	C7739	8.11.19	NTU - Conversion abandoned. Canx in 2/20.

Regn	Type	c/n	Previous identity	Regn date	Fate or immediate subsequent identity (if known)
G-EAPI	Martinsyde F.6	E4/500		10.11.19	To Canada as G-CYEQ in 10/20. Canx.
G-EAPJ	Handley Page W.8	W.8/1		11.11.19	Crashed near Poix, France on 10.7.23. Canx.
G-EAPK	BAT FK.26	FK.26-32		11.11.19	Canx 31.7.22.
G-EAPL	Airco DH.9B	P.33E	H5890	13.11.19	To Holland as H-NABE(2) in 4/21. Canx.
G-EAPM	Airco DH.16	P.2		13.11.19	WFU in 11/23. Canx.
G-EAPN	Martinsyde Type A Mk.I	E4/500/217		20.11.19	To Irish Air Corps. Canx.
G-EAPO	Airco DH.9B	P.34E		20.11.19	Canx in 9/20.
G-EAPP	Martinsyde F.4A	E4/500		21.11.19	WFU in 1920. Canx.
G-EAPQ	Avro 548	-	H2322	21.11.19	W/o on 19.10.22. Canx.
G-EAPR	Avro 552B	-	H2323	21.11.19	WFU in 1927. Rebuilt as Avro 586 & re-regd as G-EBTX in 1927. Canx.
	(Originally regd as Avro 545, then modified to 551, then 552, then 552A versions)				
G-EAPS	Avro 534A Water Baby	534/2		21.11.19	Crashed on 7.9.21. Canx.
G-EAPT	Airco DH.16	P.3		25.11.19	Dismantled on 6.7.23. Canx as WFU 7.7.23.
G-EAPU	Airco DH.9B	P.35E		25.11.19	Crashed in 11/20. Canx in 11/20.
G-EAPV	Fairey IIIC	F.302	N2255	1.12.19	To Sweden in 11/20. Canx.
G-EAPW	Airco DH.6	12486	C6503	2.12.19	NTU - No CofA issued. Canx.
G-EAPX	Alula (Martinsyde) Semiquaver	S.1		.12.19	Scrapped at Farnborough in 1921. Canx.
G-EAPY	Airco DH.14A	E.46	(J1940)	.12.19	Damaged in forced-landing at Hertford on 24.7.20. Repaired & restored to RAF as J1940 in 3/21. Canx in 3/21.
G-EAPZ	Short Shrimp Seaplane	S.540		.12.19	To Australia in 1/21 - regd as G-AUPZ on 19.6.22. Canx.
G-EAQA	Airco DH.9B	P.36E		10.12.19	Crashed in 1/21. Canx 1/21.
G-EAQB	Airco DH.6	-	C7815	11.12.19	WFU in 9/20. Canx.
G-EAQC	Airco DH.6	-	C7436	11.12.19	W/o in 11/21. Canx 6.11.21.
G-EAQD	Bristol 46A Babe III	5866		18.12.19	NTU. Canx in 12/20.
	(Originally regd as Type 30 Mk.I, converted to Type 46A Mk.III in 1920)				
G-EAQE	Central Centaur IVA	207		18.12.19	To Belgium as O-BOTH in 12/21. Canx 3.12.21.
G-EAQF	Central Centaur IVA	208		18.12.19	To Belgium as O-BOTI in 12/21. Canx 3.12.21.
G-EAQG	Airco DH.16	P.4		23.12.19	To Argentina as R-137 in 4/20. Canx.
G-EAQH	Martinsyde F.4A	FA.4		29.12.19	Canx in 12/20.
G-EAQI	Beardmore WB.IX	5404		30.12.19	NTU - Construction abandoned. Canx.
G-EAQJ	Beardmore WB.X	5442		30.12.19	Flew only once on 16.8.20. WFU in 1920. Canx.
G-EAQK	Caudron G.III	-		30.12.19	NTU. Canx 12/19.
G-EAQL	Airco DH.9B	P.38E		31.12.19	To Belgium in 7/21. Canx 27.7.21.
G-EAQM	Airco DH.9	-	F1278	31.12.19	NTU - Flew marked only as "P.D." To Australia in 1920 (arriving in 8/20). Canx 8.1.20. Stored until purchased by Australian War Museum in 1923. On display at Australian War Memorial Canberra, Australia.
	Note: This aircraft has absolutely no connection whatsoever with G-AUKI, whose exact pre-history is unknown at present - but it certainly isn't G-EAQM.				
G-EAQN	Airco DH.9B	P.37E		7. 1.20	Crashed at Le Bourget, France on 9.11.20. Canx in 12/20.
G-EAQO	Norman-Thompson NT.2B	-	N2290	9. 1.20	To Canada as G-CACG in 6/21. Canx.
G-EAQP	Airco DH.9B	P.39E		12. 1.20	Canx in 1/22.
G-EAQQ	Airco DH.6	-	C2136	. 1.20	To Peru in 1/21. Canx 1.10.24.
G-EAQR	BE.2c	-	9468	19. 1.20	Crashed on 24.8.21. Canx.
G-EAQS	Airco DH.16	P.5E		23. 1.20	WFU at Croydon in 12/20. Scrapped in 1922. Canx.
G-EAQT	Felixstowe-Short F.3	S.607	N4019	. 1.20	Shipped to Botany Bay, Australia in 1920 - did not attain registration. Canx.
	Note: This aircraft was sold to one Lebbeus Horbern and was erected - photographs published in the daily papers at the time show it being taxied on Botany Bay, but have been unable to find proof that it actually flew. But Mr.Hordern coundn't find a use for it, and in the end, donated the RR Eagle engines to the R.Australian AF, and local legend has it that the fuselage ended up as a "chook-coup" in the Sydney suburb of Manly. Around 1928, Charlie Pratt inspected it, with the view of an attempted trans-Tasman flight, but nothing came of it.				
G-EAQU	Avro 504K	-	E3021	4. 2.20	Canx in 2/21.
G-EAQV	Avro 504K	-	E9443	4. 2.20	Crashed at Friars Park, Kelso, Roxburgh on 25.5.20. Canx 24.2.21.
G-EAQW	London & Provincial Biplane	-		6. 2.20	Scrapped in 1920. Canx.
G-EAQX	Avro 547 Triplane	547/1		6. 2.20	To Australia in 11/20 - regd as G-AUCR on 28.6.21. Canx.
G-EAQY	Airco DH.6	-	'B3082' B2885	. 2.20	WFU on 23.5.24. Canx.
G-EAQZ	Handley Page O/7	HP.10		11. 2.20	Canx in 1/21.
G-EARA	Airco DH.6	-	C5527	11. 2.20	Crashed off Douglas, IoM on 25.5.20. Canx.
G-EARB	Airco DH.6	-	C5533	11. 2.20	WFU on 30.3.21. Canx.
G-EARC	Airco DH.6	-	C5547	11. 2.20	WFU on 3.8.24. Canx.
G-EARD	Airco DH.6	-	C7768	11. 2.20	Crashed off Ramsey, IoM on 3.8.20. Canx.
G-EARE	Westland Limousine II	WAC.4		11. 2.20	CofA expired 19.6.23 & WFU. Scrapped. Canx.
G-EARF	Westland Limousine II	WAC.5		11. 2.20	CofA expired 1.6.23 & WFU. Scrapped. Canx.
G-EARG	Westland Limousine II	WAC.6		11. 2.20	WFU on 27.9.23. To Canada. Canx.
G-EARH	Westland Limousine II	WAC.7		11. 2.20	NTU - Construction abandoned. Canx.
G-EARI	Airco DH.18	E.52		9. 3.20	Crashed at Wallington, Surrey on 16.8.20. Canx.
G-EARJ	Airco DH.6	-	B3061	. 3.20	WFU on 3.7.23. Canx.
G-EARK	Airco DH.6	-	B3065	. 3.20	WFU on 12.5.22. Canx.
G-EARL	Airco DH.6	-	B3003	. 3.20	WFU on 23.4.21. Canx.
G-EARM	Airco DH.6	-	B3068	. 3.20	WFU on 19.4.23. Canx.
G-EARN	Airco DH.23	E.58		9. 3.20	NTU - Construction abandoned. Canx.
G-EARO	Airco DH.18A	E.53		9. 3.20	Last flew on 10.11.27 & WFU. Canx.
G-EARP	Avro 504K	-		9. 3.20	WFU in 3/21. Canx in 4/21.
G-EARQ	Short Silver Streak	S.543		17. 3.20	To RAF as J6854 in 12/20. Canx 23.12.20.
G-EARR	Airco DH.6	-	B3067	. 3.20	WFU on 27.5.21. Canx.
G-EARS	Fairey IIIC Transatlantic	F.333	N9256	17. 3.20	To Canada as G-CYCF in 10/20. Canx.
G-EART	Bristol 47 Tourer	5876		17. 3.20	Canx as WFU in 2/21.
G-EARU	Airco DH.16	P.59		19. 3.20	Crashed at Swanley on 10.6.20. Stored at Croydon in 12/20. Scrapped in 1922. Canx.

Regn	Type	c/n	Previous identity	Regn date	Fate or immediate subsequent identity (if known)
G-EARV	Westland Limousine III	WAC.8		23. 3.20	To Canada in 1/21 - allocated marks G-CAET but NTU & scrapped at Luc a la Tortue, Quebec in 12/24. Canx.
G-EARW	BE.2e	-	C6953	23. 3.20	WFU on 9.4.21. Canx at census 10.1.23.
G-EARX	Beardmore WB.IIB	5441/1		24. 3.20	Crashed at Huntingdon on 12.12.20. Canx.
G-EARY	Beardmore WB.IIB	5441/2		24. 3.20	WFU in 1922. Canx 15.2.23.
G-EARZ	Avro 504K	-	H6551	31. 3.20	Crashed at Bournemouth on 7.8.20. Canx.
G-EASA	Avro 504K	-	F9809	31. 3.20	Crashed at Doncaster on 28.4.22. Canx.
G-EASB	Avro 504K	-	F9810	31. 3.20	Crashed near Ripley, Yorks on 15.12.26. Canx.
G-EASC	Vickers Viking II	2		26. 3.20	Crashed off Ostend, Belgium in 9/20. Canx.
G-EASD	Avro 504L Floatplane (130 hp Le Clerget)	E.5	SE-HAA S-AHAA/S-AAP/G-EASD/(RAF)	26. 3.20	(Stored 8/93, pending rebuild)
G-EASE	Avro 504L	E.6	(RAF)	26. 3.20	Sold Abroad. Canx 2.3.21.
G-EASF	Avro 504K	-	D5858	. 3.20	Dismantled at Hooton in 1937. Canx in 12/36.
G-EASG	Avro 504K	-	G-EAFX H6543	. 3.20	Crashed near Great Bookham on 2.9.26. Canx.
G-EASH	Bristol F.2b Fighter	5093	H1376	7. 4.20	WFU & Canx in 4/21.
G-EASI(1)	Vickers 66 Vimy Commercial	41		30. 4.20	WFU in 20.8.25. Scrapped in 1926. Canx.
G-EASI(2)	Short SD.3-30 Var.100	SH.3070	(G-BITW) G-14-3070	9. 6.81	Restored as G-BITW on 19.11.84. Canx.
G-EASJ	Boulton Paul P.9	P.9/2		. 4.20	To South Africa as G-UAAM in 1928. Canx.
G-EASK	Nieuport Goshawk	LS.3/No.1		13. 4.20	Crashed at Burnt Oak, Hendon on 12.7.21. Canx.
G-EASL	Handley Page O/11	HP.30	C9699	15. 4.20	WFU in 4/21. Canx.
G-EASM	Handley Page O/11	HP.31	C9731	15. 4.20	WFU in 4/21. Canx.
G-EASN	Handley Page O/11	HP.32	D4611	15. 4.20	WFU in 4/21. Canx.
G-EASO	Handley Page O/400	HP.33	F5444	15. 4.20	Broken up in 5/20. Canx.
G-EASP	Bristol 26 Pullman Triplane	5753	C4298	14. 4.20	Restored to RAF as C4298 in 5/20. Canx 13.5.20.
G-EASQ	Bristol 46A Babe III	5867		14. 4.20	Converted to low-wing monoplane Type 46B but not flown. WFU at Filton in 2/21. Canx in 2/21.
"G-EASQ"	Bristol 30/46 Babe Static Replica	-	BAPC.87	----	On display 5/99 at Bristol Aero Collection, Kemble. (Construction commenced in 70s by W.Sneesby)
G-EASR	Bristol M.1C (Type 20)	5885		14. 4.20	Canx as WFU 7.4.25.
G-EASS	Sopwith Antelope	3398		20. 4.20	To Australia (post-6/22) - regd as G-AUSS on 18.4.23. Canx.
G-EAST	Central Centaur VIII	400		26. 4.20	NTU - Not constructed. Canx.
G-EASU	Bristol F.2b Fighter	5356	H1639	29. 4.20	To Belgian AF. Canx 9/20.
G-EASV	Bristol F.2b Fighter	5355	H1638	29. 4.20	To Belgian AF. Canx 11/20.
G-EASW	Airco DH.16	P.6		29. 4.20	Stored at Croydon in 12/20. Broken up in 1922. Canx.
G-EASX	Handley Page O/10	HP.34	F308	30. 4.20	To India as G-IAAC(2) in 2/21. Canx.
G-EASY	Handley Page O/10	HP.35	D4614	30. 4.20	To India in 4/21. Canx.
G-EASZ	Handley Page O/11	HP.36	F310	30. 4.20	To India in 4/21. Canx.
G-EATA	Airco DH.9B	-	H9271	30. 4.20	Canx in 4/21.
G-EATB	Avro 504K	-	F8902	7. 5.20	WFU in 6/21. Canx 26.8.21.
G-EATC	Sopwith 5F.1 Dolphin	-	D5369	7. 5.20	Sold Abroad. Canx 10.1.23.
G-EATD	Martinsyde F.4	-	D4267	. 5.20	Canx 13.11.22.
G-EATE	SE.5A	-	F9022	. 5.20	Scrapped in 5/22. Canx.
G-EATF	Sopwith 7F.1 Snipe	365	J465	7. 5.20	No CofA issued. Sold Abroad in 3/22. Canx.
G-EATG	Handley Page O/10	HP.37	D4618	7. 5.20	WFU in 4/21. Canx.
G-EATH	Handley Page O/10	HP.38	D4631	7. 5.20	WFU in 9/23. Canx.
G-EATI	Airco DH.6	G5/100		18. 5.20	WFU on 13.7.22. Canx.
G-EATJ	Handley Page O/10	HP.39	F307	15. 5.20	WFU in 4/21. Canx.
G-EATK	Handley Page O/10	HP.40	J2262	15. 5.20	CofA expired 10.8.22 & WFU. Canx 22.11.22.
G-EATL	Handley Page O/10	HP.41	F312	18. 5.20	WFU on 30.12.21. Canx.
G-EATM	Handley Page O/10	HP.42	D4609	19. 5.20	Wrecked in gale after forced-landing at Berk-sur-Mer, France on 29.12.21. Canx.
G-EATN	Handley Page O/10	HP.43	J2261	26. 5.20	Crashed in fog at Senlis, France on 14.1.22. Canx 8.5.22.
G-EATO	Armstrong Whitworth FK.8	-	F7384	2. 6.20	WFU on 4.4.22. Scrapped in 1922. Canx.
G-EATP	Armstrong Whitworth FK.8	-	H4600	9. 6.20	Crashed in Norway during European tour in 1920. Canx in 10/20.
G-EATQ	Martinsyde F.6	61/3		8. 6.20	Sold Abroad in 1920. Canx.
G-EATR	Austin Kestrel	-		10. 6.20	WFU on 31.7.21. Sold for spares in 5/24. Canx.
G-EATS	Bristol 32B Bullet (Originally regd as Type 32, modified to Type 32A in 1920, converted to Type 32B in 1921)	5869		15. 6.20	Scrapped in 1924. Canx.
G-EATT	BE.2e	-	C6968	10. 6.20	WFU on 16.6.21. Dismantled. Canx.
G-EATU	Avro 504K	-	E3045	12. 6.20	Crashed near Shoreham on 5.9.27. Canx.
G-EATV	Avro 504K	-	D6387	12. 6.20	Crashed in 11/20. Canx.
G-EATW	BE.2e	-	C6964	24. 6.20	Crashed in 1/21. Canx.
G-EATX	Martinsyde F.4A	310		22. 6.20	Canx 4.8.22.
G-EATY	Martinsyde Type A Mk.II	218		22. 6.20	To Newfoundland, Canada in 10/21. Canx.
G-EATZ	Avro 504K	-	E3022	24. 6.20	To G-EAVC in 8/20. Canx.
G-EAUA	Short Shrimp Seaplane	S.541		28. 6.20	Scrapped in 1924. Canx.
G-EAUB	Short Shrimp Seaplane	S.542		28. 6.20	Scrapped in 1924. Canx.
G-EAUC	Airco DH.9B	-	H9282	28. 6.20	WFU on 5.7.21. Scrapped in 1922. Canx.
G-EAUD	Saunders Kittiwake	101		30. 6.20	Scrapped in 1921. Canx.
G-EAUE	Bristol 36 Seely Puma (Modified to Type 85 prior to sale in 12/23)	5870		3. 7.20	To RAF as J7004 in 10/23. Canx 22.12.23.
G-EAUF	Airco DH.18A	E.54		7. 7.20	Crashed at Argueil, France on 13.5.21. Canx.
G-EAUG	Avro 534B Baby	534B/1		9. 7.20	Crashed near Ipswich on 4.8.20. Canx.
G-EAUH	Airco DH.9B	-	H9196	13. 7.20	To Holland as H-NABP in 3/21. Canx 19.3.21.
G-EAUI	Airco DH.9B	-	H9197	13. 7.20	Sold Abroad in 6/23 (possibly to Spain). Canx 4.6.23.
G-EAUJ	Avro 547A Triplane	547A/1		9. 7.20	Sold as spares at Shoreham in 1928. Canx.
G-EAUK	Vickers Viking III Seaplane	3		. 7.20	To RAF as N147 in 2/21. Canx 2.2.21.
G-EAUL	Vickers FB.28 Vimy Commercial	40		10. 7.20	To China in 1921. Canx 11.8.21.
G-EAUM	Avro 543 Baby (Originally regd with c/n 543/1)	5062		12. 7.20	WFU on 8.11.34. Canx 12/34.

Regn	Type	c/n	Previous identity	Regn date	Fate or immediate subsequent identity (if known)
G-EAUN	Airco DH.9B	-	H9128	17. 7.20	To Spain as M-AGAG in 6/23. Canx.
G-EAUO	Airco DH.9B	-	H9187	17. 7.20	To Holland as H-NABO in 3/21. Canx 27.7.21.
G-EAUP	Airco DH.9B	-	H9176	17. 7.20	WFU on 6.9.21. Canx.
G-EAUQ	Airco DH.9B	-	H9125	17. 7.20	Crashed on 19.3.21. Canx.
G-EAUR	Martinsyde F.4	-	D4352	15. 7.20	Canx 10.1.23.
G-EAUS	Airco DH.6	-	C7763	. 7.20	WFU on 2.7.23. Sold as spares. Canx.
G-EAUT	Airco DH.6	-	C9436	. 7.20	WFU on 7.5.22. Canx.
G-EAUU	Sopwith 7F.1 Snipe	-	J459	24. 7.20	Crashed at Barnet on 28.7.20. Canx 12/20.
G-EAUV	Sopwith 7F.1 Snipe	-	J453	24. 7.20	Crashed at Kingsmead, Hertford on 28.7.20. Canx 12/20.
G-EAUW	Sopwith 7F.1 Snipe	-	J455	24. 7.20	NTU - No CofA issued. Canx 12/20.
G-EAUX	Martinsyde F.4	-	H7786	29. 7.20	WFU on 26.11.23. Canx.
G-EAUY	Vickers FB.28 Vimy Commercial	39	J6864	31. 7.20	NTU - To China in 1920. Canx in 2/21.
G-EAUZ	Austin Whippet	AU.3		30. 7.20	To Argentina as R-151 in 7/20. Canx.
G-EAVA	BE.2e	-	C7178	. 7.20	Crashed at Brooklands on 21.9.22. Canx.
G-EAVB	Sopwith 1½ Strutter	3541	N5504	7. 8.20	NTU. Canx.
G-EAVC	Avro 504K	-	G-EATZ E3022	17. 8.20	Not converted. Canx 1/21.
G-EAVD	Avro 504K	-	E6757	18. 8.20	Crashed in France in 8/20 whilst on delivery to Belgium. Canx 16.8.20.
G-EAVE	Supermarine Amphibian	1152		11. 8.20	Crashed at Great Bookham on 13.10.20. Canx.
G-EAVF	Sopwith Pup	3210 & 764		20. 8.20	NTU - Scrapped in 1921. Canx.
G-EAVG	Airco DH.6	-	(RAF)	16. 8.20	Force-landed on the Ribble mud flats and set on fire to attract rescuers from the shore (date?). Canx 3/21.
G-EAVH	Avro 548	548/4		23. 8.20	Crashed at Montevideo, Uruguay on 21.8.21. Canx.
G-EAVI	Avro 504K	-	E1644	23. 8.20	WFU on 12.8.24. Canx.
G-EAVJ	Handley Page W.8A	W.8A		6. 9.20	NTU. Canx 10.1.23.
G-EAVK	Airco DH.9B	P.60E		. 9.20	Sold Abroad. Canx 8.3.22.
G-EAVL	Airco DH.4A	-	H5905	13. 9.20	Crashed in 4/21. Canx.
G-EAVM	Airco DH.9	-	H9243	13. 9.20	To Denmark as T-DOKL in 9/22. Canx 18.9.22.
G-EAVN	Blackburn T.1 Swift I	BA.6368		22. 9.20	To RAF as N139 in 12/20. Canx 23.12.20.
G-EAVO	Bristol M.1C (Type 20)	5887		28. 9.20	To Spain as M-AFAA in 11/21. Canx.
G-EAVP	Bristol M.1D (Type 77)	5888		28. 9.20	Fatal crash at Fox Hills Estate, nr Chertsey, Surrey on 23.6.23. Canx.
G-EAVQ	Armstrong Whitworth FK.8	-	H4585	7.10.20	To Argentina? Canx 10.1.23.
G-EAVR	Airco DH.6	87/A1359	C7797	.10.20	WFU on 8.4.26. Canx.
G-EAVS	BE.2e	-	C7179	.10.20	Crashed on 10.5.22. Canx.
G-EAVT	Armstrong Whitworth FK.8	-	H4573	14.10.20	Sold Abroad. Canx 10.1.23.
G-EAVU	Bristol 47 Tourer (Dual control demonstrator)	5892		21.10.20	WFU on 25.10.21. Scrapped. Canx.
G-EAVV	Sopwith Pup	-	C440	4.11.20	NTU. Scrapped. Canx.
G-EAVW	Sopwith Pup	-	C312	27.10.20	Scrapped in 1921. Canx.
G-EAVX(1)	Sopwith Pup	-	B1807	2.11.20	DBR in nose-over at Henden on 21.7.21 & w/o. Canx.
G-EAVX(2)	Sopwith Pup (Claimed to be rebuild of original aircraft)	PFA/101-10523		16. 1.87	Status uncertain.
G-EAVY	Sopwith Pup	-	C438	4.11.20	NTU. Scrapped. Canx.
G-EAVZ	Sopwith Pup	-	C540	22.11.20	NTU. Scrapped. Canx.
G-EAWA	Bristol F.2b Fighter	-	H951	22.11.20	Canx as registration lapsed.
G-EAWB	Bristol 29 Tourer	6122		29.11.20	WFU on 31.12.21. Canx.
G-EAWC	Supermarine Channel II	1141		10. 1.21	To Trinidad in 4/21. Canx.
G-EAWD	Airco DH.6	'649'		12. 1.21	Crashed at Stanford Rivers, Essex on 27.8.23. Canx.
G-EAWE	Martinsyde F.4	-	H7780	14. 1.21	To Polish AF in 1/21. Canx.
G-EAWF	Westland Limousine III	WAC.9	(J6851)	20. 1.21	CofA expired 13.4.22. Canx 25.11.25.
G-EAWG	Alula DH.6 Parasol Monoplane	-		15. 2.21	Dismantled c 1921; Shipped to St.Cyr, near Paris, France. Canx.
G-EAWH	Airco DH.4A	-	F5764	17. 2.21	WFU in 1922. Canx 5.1.23.
G-EAWI	Avro 504K	-	E3672	25. 2.21	Crashed near Croydon in 9/21. Canx.
G-EAWJ	Avro 504K	-	D2035	25. 2.21	WFU in 2/22. Canx 28.2.22.
G-EAWK	Avro 504K	-	E3671	. 3.21	Crashed in Swansea Bay on 3.10.22. Canx.
G-EAWL	Avro 504K	-	E9341	. 3.21	WFU on 2.10.22. Dismantled in 4/23. Canx.
G-EAWM	Avro 504K	-	E9245	. 3.21	WFU on 2.10.22. Dismantled in 4/23. Canx.
G-EAWN	Sopwith 1F.1 Camel	-	H2700	11. 3.21	Dismantled at Stag Lane in 1922. Canx.
G-EAWO	DH.18A	DH.18A/4		23. 3.21	Destroyed in mid-air collision with Farman Goliath F-AEGP over Grandvilliers, Northern France on 7.4.22. Canx.
G-EAWP	Supermarine Channel II	1146		8. 4.21	To Fiji in 7/21. Canx.
G-EAWQ	Bristol 28 Coupe Tourer	6114		16. 4.21	To Spain as M-AAEA but crashed on delivery at San Sebastian on 23.4.21. Canx.
G-EAWR	Bristol 47 Tourer	6112		16. 4.21	To Spain as M-AEAA in 4/21. Canx.
G-EAWS	Boulton Paul P.9 Mk.II	P.9/6		21. 4.21	Crashed at Lympne on 30.3.29. Canx 15.5.29.
G-EAWT	Airco DH.6	4442	F3437	27. 4.21	WFU on 27.8.24. Canx.
G-EAWU	Airco DH.6	-	F3439	27. 4.21	WFU after a minor landing accident on Isle of Wight on 31.3.22. Canx.
G-EAWV	Airco DH.6	-	F3440	27. 4.21	Registration lapsed & WFU c 1925. Canx.
G-EAWW	DH.18B	E.56 & DH.18B/5	(J6899)	. 5.21	Ditched in sea off Felixstowe in Air Ministry flotation test on 2.5.24. Canx 29.12.24.
G-EAWX	DH.18B	E.57 & DH.18B/6	(J6900)	. 5.21	CofA expired 18.11.23 & WFU. Canx.
G-EAWY	Bristol 62 Ten-Seater	6124		. 5.21	WFU on 10.2.23. Canx.
G-EAWZ	Bristol F.2b Fighter	4999	H1282	23. 5.21	Crashed at Hamble on 25.5.21. Canx.
G-EAXA	Bristol 81 Puma Trainer (Originally regd as Type 29 Tourer)	6120		23. 5.21	Crashed on 10.5.24. Canx.
G-EAXB	Martinsyde F.4	-	D4279	1. 6.21	DBR in ground collision with SE.5A G-EAXU at Croydon on 17.4.22. Canx.
G-EAXC	Airco DH.9A	-	E8791	1. 6.21	Canx 13.11.22.
G-EAXD	Airco DH.4	-	F2686	3. 6.21	To Belgian AF in 6/21. Canx.

Regn	Type	c/n	Previous identity	Regn date	Fate or immediate subsequent identity (if known)
G-EAXE	Airco DH.4	-	F2697	3. 6.21	To Belgian AF in 6/21. Canx.
G-EAXF	Airco DH.4	-	H5934	3. 6.21	To Belgian AF in 6/21. Canx.
G-EAXG	Airco DH.9C (Originally regd as a DH.9)	DH.9C/16		14. 6.21	To Spain in 1/22. Canx 15.6.22.
G-EAXH	Airco DH.4	-	A7988	15. 6.21	To Belgian AF in 6/21. Canx.
G-EAXI	Airco DH.4	-	F2698	15. 6.21	To Belgian AF in 6/21. Canx.
G-EAXJ	Airco DH.4	-	F5794	15. 6.21	To Belgian AF in 6/21. Canx.
G-EAXK	Bristol 28 Coupe Tourer	6108		18. 6.21	To Australia in 11/21 - regd as G-AUDF on 28.11.21. Canx.
G-EAXL	Avro 534C Baby	534C/1		27. 6.21	Crashed into Southampton Water on 6.9.22. Canx.
G-EAXM	Avro 539B Napier-Racer	539B/1	G-EALG	27. 6.21	Destroyed in landing accident at Hamble on 15.7.21. Canx.
G-EAXN	Airco DH.4	-	F2678	27. 6.21	To Belgian AF in 7/21. Canx.
G-EAXO	Airco DH.4	-	F2680	27. 6.21	To Belgian AF in 7/21. Canx.
G-EAXP	Airco DH.4	-	F5774	27. 6.21	To Belgian AF in 7/21. Canx.
G-EAXQ	SE.5A	-	F5249	4. 7.21	WFU on 12.7.22. Canx 13.11.22.
G-EAXR	SE.5A	-	F5303	4. 7.21	Canx 17.7.22.
G-EAXS	SE.5A	-	F5285	4. 7.21	Canx 17.7.22.
G-EAXT	SE.5A	-	F5258	4. 7.21	Canx 13.11.22.
G-EAXU	SE.5A	-	F5333	4. 7.21	DBR in ground collision with Martinsyde F.4 G-EAXB at Croydon on 17.4.22. Canx in 5/22.
G-EAXV	SE.5A	-	F5253	4. 7.21	Scrapped in 1922. Canx 17.11.22.
G-EAXW	SE.5A	-	F5259	4. 7.21	Canx 13.11.22.
G-EAXX	SE.5A	-	F5257	4. 7.21	Canx 17.11.22.
G-EAXY	Avro 504K	-	D9058	4. 7.21	WFU on 2.8.23. Canx.
G-EAXZ	Gloster Mars I Bamel Floatplane (Modified to Gloster I in 1923)	1		7. 7.21	To RAF as J7234 in 10/23. Canx 4.10.23.
G-EAYA	BAT FK.23 Bantam	FK.23-22	F1661	7. 7.21	To Holland as H-NACH in 1923 but NTU, though to have been broken up in Holland. Canx.
G-EAYB	Avro 504K	-	H6608	. 7.21	Crashed at Croydon on 14.6.23. Canx.
G-EAYC	Avro 504K	-	H6609	. 7.21	Crashed on 22.5.22. Canx.
G-EAYD	Avro 548 (Originally regd as Avro 504K)	-	H7428	28. 7.21	Crashed on 13.10.21. Canx.
G-EAYE	Airco DH.4	-	F2675	30. 7.21	To Belgian AF in 8/21. Canx.
G-EAYF	Airco DH.4	-	F5779	30. 7.21	To Belgian AF in 8/21. Canx.
G-EAYG	Airco DH.4	-	H5902	30. 7.21	To Belgian AF in 8/21. Canx.
G-EAYH	Airco DH.4	-	F2684	30. 7.21	To Belgian AF in 8/21. Canx.
G-EAYI	Airco DH.4	-	F2693	25. 8.21	To Belgian AF in 9/21. Canx.
G-EAYJ	Airco DH.4	-	F2677	25. 8.21	To Belgian AF in 9/21. Canx.
G-EAYK	Martinsyde F.4	-		7. 9.21	WFU on 26.11.23. Canx.
G-EAYL	SE.5A	-	F5300	. 9.21	Canx 8.2.25.
G-EAYM	Avro 534D Baby (Originally regd with c/n 534D/1)	5049		17. 9.21	WFU at Calcutta, India in 1929. Canx.
G-EAYN	Gloster Grouse II (Originally regd as Mars III Sparrowhawk II with c/n MARS III, rebuilt as Grouse I with c/n 1 in 1923, converted to Grouse II in 1924)	2		19. 9.21	To Swedish Army as 62 in 12/25. Canx 9.12.25.
G-EAYO	DH.29 Doncaster	8	(J6850)	28. 9.21	Dismantled and wing to RAE for static tests in 2/24. Canx.
G-EAYP	Martinsyde F.4	-	D4275	4.10.21	WFU on 26.11.23. Canx.
G-EAYQ	Bristol F.2b Fighter	5106	H1389	4.10.21	Crashed in France in 10/21. Canx.
G-EAYR	Airco DH.4	-	F2689	4.10.21	To Belgian AF in 10/21. Canx.
G-EAYS	Airco DH.4	-	H5898	4.10.21	To Belgian AF in 10/21. Canx.
G-EAYT	Airco DH.9C	DH.9C/14		12.10.21	Landed in the sea off Venice Lido, Italy on 2.10.22. Canx.
G-EAYU	Airco DH.9C	DH.9C/15		12.10.21	To Hedjaz Government in 11/24. Canx 3.11.24.
G-EAYV	Airco DH.4	-	F5797	13.10.21	To Belgian AF in 11/21. Canx.
G-EAYW	Airco DH.9	-	H5619	13.10.21	To Belgian AF in 11/21. Canx.
G-EAYX	Airco DH.4	-	H5896	21.10.21	To Belgian AF in 11/21. Canx.
G-EAYY	Airco DH.9	-	H5833	31.10.21	To Switzerland as CH-82 in 12/21. Canx.
G-EAYZ	Airco DH.9	-	H5848	31.10.21	To Switzerland as CH-83 in 12/21. Canx.
G-EAZA	Airco DH.9	-	H5629	8.11.21	To Belgian AF in 11/21. Canx.
G-EAZB	Airco DH.9	-	H5705	8.11.21	To Belgian AF in 11/21. Canx.
G-EAZC	Airco DH.9	-	H5607	8.11.21	To Belgian AF in 11/21. Canx.
G-EAZD	Airco DH.9	-	H5856	8.11.21	To Belgian AF in 11/21. Canx.
G-EAZE	Airco DH.9	-	H5757	8.11.21	To Belgian AF in 11/21. Canx.
G-EAZF	Avro 504K	-	H7426	8.11.21	Crashed on test flight at Croydon. Canx 28.11.21. Was for Belgian AF.
G-EAZG	Avro 504K	-	H6605	8.11.21	To Belgian AF in 11/21. Canx.
G-EAZH	Airco DH.9	-	H5839	14.11.21	To Switzerland as CH-81 in 2/22. Canx.
G-EAZI	Airco DH.9	-	H5860	14.11.21	To Switzerland as CH-84 in 2/22. Canx.
G-EAZJ	Airco DH.9	-	H5666	19.11.21	To Belgian AF in 11/21. Canx.
G-EAZK	Avro 504K	-	H6611	19.11.21	To Belgian AF in 11/21. Canx.
G-EAZL	Avro 504K	-	H6601	19.11.21	To Belgian AF in 11/21. Crashed on test at Croydon. Canx.
G-EAZM	Airco DH.9	-	H5865	19.11.21	To Belgian AF in 11/21. Canx.
G-EAZN	Airco DH.9	-	H5707	22.11.21	To Belgian AF in 12/21. Canx.
G-EAZO	Airco DH.9	-	H5845	22.11.21	To Belgian AF in 12/21. Canx.
G-EAZP	Airco DH.9	-	H5868	22.11.21	To Belgian AF in 12/21. Canx.
G-EAZQ	Avro 504K	-	H2516	22.11.21	To Belgian AF in 12/21. Canx.
G-EAZR	Avro 504K	-	H2553	24.11.21	To Belgian AF in 12/21. Canx.
G-EAZS	Avro 504K	-	H2558	24.11.21	To Belgian AF in 12/21. Canx.
G-EAZT	SE.5A	-	E6013	30.11.21	DBR after standing on nose taxying at Bekesbourne in early 1923. Canx.
G-EAZU	Avro 504K	-	H2509	1.12.21	To Belgian AF in 12/21. Canx.
G-EAZV	Avro 504K	-	H2565	1.12.21	To Belgian AF in 12/21. Canx.
G-EAZW	Avro 504K	-	H2295	.12.21	Crashed at Brighouse, Yorks on 3.5.24. Canx.
G-EAZX	Avro 504K	-	E1860	.12.21	Crashed at Manchester on 2.8.24. Canx.
G-EAZY	Airco DH.9	-	H5706	5.12.21	To Belgian AF in 12/21. Canx.

Regn	Type	c/n	Previous identity	Regn date	Fate or immediate subsequent identity (if known)
G-EAZZ	Airco DH.9	-	H5668	5.12.21	To Belgian AF in 12/21. Canx.
G-EBAA	Airco DH.9	-	H5783	5.12.21	To Belgian AF in 12/21. Canx.
G-EBAB	Airco DH.9	-	H5851	5.12.21	To Belgian AF in 12/21. Canx.
G-EBAC	Airco DH.9A	17	E8788	5.12.21	Sold Abroad in 12/21. Canx 12.1.22.
G-EBAD	Airco DH.9	-	H5621	8.12.21	To Belgian AF in 12/21. Canx.
G-EBAE	Airco DH.9	-	H5736	8.12.21	To Belgian AF in 12/21. Canx.
G-EBAF	Avro 504K	-	H7467	8.12.21	To Belgian AF in 12/21. Canx.
G-EBAG	Avro 548	-	H2025	.12.21	WFU on 13.1.28. Canx 1/29.
G-EBAH	Supermarine Sea Lion II (Originally regd as Sea King II)	1154		16.12.21	To Royal Navy as N170 in 12/23. Canx.
G-EBAI	Airco DH.9	-	H5712	.12.21	To Belgian AF in 12/21. Canx.
G-EBAJ	Avro 548	-	E3043	.12.21	Crashed at Brooklands on 9.4.28. Canx 5/28.
G-EBAK	Bristol F.2b Fighter	5008	H1291	21.12.21	To Belgian AF in 12/21. Canx.
G-EBAL	Bristol F.2b Fighter	5009	H1292	21.12.21	To Belgian AF in 2/22. Canx.
G-EBAM	Bristol F.2b Fighter	4957	H1240	21.12.21	To Belgian AF in 2/22. Canx.
G-EBAN	Airco DH.9A	-	F2867	21.12.21	To Spanish AF in 3/22. Canx.
G-EBAO	Airco DH.9	-	H5716	31.12.21	To Belgian AF in 1/22. Canx.
G-EBAP	Airco DH.9	-	H5741	31.12.21	To Belgian AF in 1/22. Canx.
G-EBAQ	Airco DH.9	-	H5753	31.12.21	To Belgian AF in 1/22. Canx.
G-EBAR	Airco DH.9	-	H5747	31.12.21	To Belgian AF in 1/22. Canx.
G-EBAS	Airco DH.9	-	H5662	31.12.21	To Belgian AF in 1/22. Canx.
G-EBAT	Bristol F.2b Fighter	4959	H1242	31.12.21	Crashed at Croydon on 28.1.22 (Was on delivery flight to Belgian AF). Canx.
G-EBAU	Bristol F.2b Fighter	4961	H1244	31.12.21	To Belgian AF in 2/22. Canx 15.2.22.
G-EBAV	Avro 504K	-	F9783	2. 1.22	Crashed at Slough on 20.8.22. Canx.
G-EBAW	Airco DH.9B	25		5. 1.22	Canx 10.9.23.
G-EBAX	Airco DH.9C	26		5. 1.22	WFU 25.3.24. Canx 23.4.24.
G-EBAY	Avro 504K	-		. 1.22	Canx 7/23.
G-EBAZ	Sopwith Pup	-	C1524	9. 1.22	Scrapped at Stag Lane in 1924. Canx.
G-EBBA	Airco DH.9	-	H5735	9. 1.22	To Belgian AF in 1/22. Canx.
G-EBBB	Airco DH.9	-	H5709	9. 1.22	To Belgian AF in 1/22. Canx.
G-EBBC	Avro 548	-	H2212	. 1.22	WFU on 26.8.24. Canx 25.11.25.
G-EBBD	Bristol F.2b Fighter	3492	D7842	12. 1.22	To Belgian AF in 1/22. Canx.
G-EBBE	Sopwith 7F.1 Snipe	-	J461	13. 1.22	No CofA issued. To Belgian AF in 3/22. Canx 2.3.22.
G-EBBF	Avro 504K	-	E1843	. 1.22	WFU on 5.7.24. Canx.
G-EBBG	Handley Page W.8B	W.8/2		. 1.22	Wrecked in gales after forced-landing at Abbeville, France on 15.2.28. Canx.
G-EBBH	Handley Page W.8B	W.8/3		. 1.22	WFU on 2.4.29. Canx.
G-EBBI	Handley Page W.8B	W.8/4		. 1.22	WFU on 24.3.32. Canx.
G-EBBJ	Airco DH.9	-	H5711	21. 2.22	To Belgian AF in 1/22. Canx.
G-EBBK	Airco DH.9	-	H5719	21. 2.22	To Belgian AF in 1/22. Canx.
G-EBBL	Vickers 61 Vulcan	1		24. 2.22	WFU on 30.5.24. Scrapped at Croydon in 5/24. Canx.
G-EBBM	Short 184	-	N9096	27. 2.22	WFU on 11.8.23. Canx.
G-EBBN	Short 184	-	N9118	27. 2.22	WFU on 16.5.23. Canx.
G-EBBO	Bristol F.2b Fighter	4975	H1258	27. 2.22	To Belgian AF in 2/22. Canx.
G-EBBP	Avro 504K	-	H6653	27. 2.22	To Belgian AF in 2/22. Canx.
G-EBBQ	DH.34	27		6. 3.22	Crashed at Rotterdam on 27.8.23. Canx 29.11.23.
G-EBBR	DH.34	28		6. 3.22	Crashed on take-off from Ostend, Belgium on 19.5.24. Canx.
G-EBBS	DH.34	29		6. 3.22	Fatal crash near Ivinghoe Beacon, Bucks. on 14.9.23. Canx.
G-EBBT	DH.34B (Originally regd as DH.34, converted in 1925)	30		6. 3.22	Canx as WFU 31.3.26. Dismantled in 3/26.
G-EBBU	DH.34	31		6. 3.22	Crashed at Harrow Weald on 3.11.22. Canx.
G-EBBV	DH.34	32		6. 3.22	WFU & dismantled on 31.3.26. Canx.
G-EBBW	DH.34	34		6. 3.22	WFU & dismantled on 30.3.26. Canx.
G-EBBX	DH.34B (Originally regd as DH.34, converted by 2/24)	35		6. 3.22	Fatal crash at Purley, near Croydon, Surrey on 24.12.24. Canx.
G-EBBY	DH.34B (Originally regd as DH.34, converted in 1925)	36		6. 3.22	WFU & dismantled on 31.3.26. Canx.
G-EBBZ	Vickers 60 Viking IV	15		14. 3.22	Crashed during a test flight at Brooklands on 13.4.22. Canx.
G-EBCA	SE.5A	-	E5956	. 3.22	WFU on 24.7.28. Canx 12/30.
G-EBCB	Avro 504K	-	H221	16. 3.22	Destroyed in gales in 11/28. Canx in 2/29.
G-EBCC	Avro 504K	-	H6656	21. 3.22	To Belgian AF in 5/22. Canx.
G-EBCD	Avro 504K	-	H7487	21. 3.22	To Belgian AF in 5/22. Canx.
G-EBCE	SE.5A	1160	C9208	30. 3.22	Canx as sold abroad 7.4.27. In USA with smoke-writing apparatus in 1931.
G-EBCF	Avro 504K	-	H2065	1. 4.22	To Belgian AF in 5/22. Canx.
G-EBCG	Airco DH.9A	-	F2868	1. 4.22	WFU on 10.7.24. Canx 5.1.27.
G-EBCH	Airco DH.9	-	H5836	1. 4.22	To Belgian AF in 4/22. Canx.
G-EBCI	Airco DH.9	-	H5742	1. 4.22	To Belgian AF in 4/22. Canx.
G-EBCJ	Airco DH.9	-	H5820	1. 4.22	To Belgian AF in 4/22. Canx.
G-EBCK	Avro 504K	PL.6126	E3379	. 4.22	WFU on 1.2.28. Canx.
G-EBCL	Avro 504K	-	E9227	6. 4.22	Crashed at Rogerstone, near Newport on 6.5.22. Canx.
G-EBCM	Parnall Panther	5845	N7530	8. 4.22	WFU in 1922. Canx.
G-EBCN	Bristol Type 17A Fighter	6223	N8957	10. 4.22	To SABCA as pattern aircraft. Canx 24.7.23.
G-EBCO	Avro 504K	-	H7482	12. 4.22	To Belgian AF in 4/22. Canx.
G-EBCP	Vickers 170 Vanguard (Originally regd as Type 62, then Type 103)	1	J6924	19. 4.22	Tail unit overstressed, dived into ground near Shepperton, Middx., on 16.5.29 & DBF. Canx.
G-EBCQ	Avro 504K	-	H6547	. 4.22	Crashed at Barrow-in-Furness on 24.8.23. Canx.
G-EBCR	Avro 504K	-	H7474	25. 4.22	To Belgian AF in 5/22. Canx.
G-EBCS	Avro 504K	-	H2062	25. 4.22	To Belgian AF in 5/22. Canx.
G-EBCT	Avro 504K	-	H2071	25. 4.22	To Belgian AF in 5/22. Canx.
G-EBCU	Bristol F.2b Fighter	-	E2058	25. 4.22	To Belgian AF in 5/22. Canx.

Regn	Type	c/n	Previous identity	Regn date	Fate or immediate subsequent identity (if known)
G-EBCV	Bristol F.2b Fighter	4998	H1281	25. 4.22	To Belgian AF in 7/22. Canx.
G-EBCW	Bristol F.2b Fighter	4962	H1245	25. 4.22	To Belgian AF in 7/22. Canx.
G-EBCX	DH.34	40		28. 4.22	Crashed at Croydon on 23.9.24. Canx.
G-EBCY	DH.34	41		28. 4.22	NTU - Believed not completed. Canx.
G-EBCZ	Airco DH.9C	38		28. 4.22	Crashed at Newcastle on 4.7.23. Canx.
G-EBDA	Avro 534 Baby	5064		28. 4.22	To Russia in 6/22. Canx.
G-EBDB	Bristol F.2b Fighter	-	E5219	1. 5.22	To Belgian AF in 7/22. Canx.
G-EBDC	Avro 504K	-	H2060	1. 5.22	To Belgian AF in 5/22. Canx.
G-EBDD	Airco DH.9C	39		18. 5.22	W/o in 1925. Canx 6.11.25.
G-EBDE	Airco DH.9	-	H5738	19. 5.22	Crashed near Istres, France on 28.5.22. Canx.
G-EBDF	Airco DH.9	-	H5652	23. 5.22	To Canada in 1922 - regd as G-CAEU on 12.1.25. Canx.
G-EBDG	Airco DH.9	"4890"		. 5.22	WFU on 12.7.26. Scrapped in 1930. Canx in 12/30.
G-EBDH	Vickers 61 Vulcan	2		. 6.22	WFU on 14.7.23. Canx.
G-EBDI	Fairey III	F.333	N9253	12. 6.22	Crashed in Gulf of Assam on 25.8.22. Canx.
G-EBDJ	Avro 504K	-	H2052	12. 6.22	To Belgian AF in 6/22. Canx.
G-EBDK	Martinsyde F.6	-		16. 6.22	Scrapped at Brooklands in 4/30. Canx.
G-EBDL	Airco DH.9	-	H5678	17. 6.22	Flown to India as "G-EBDE" in 8/22 and donated to the University of Benares, Calcutta, India on 13.11.22. Canx.
G-EBDM	Martinsyde F.4	-	H7692	19. 6.22	To Portuguese AF in 6/23. Canx.
G-EBDN	Bristol F.2b Fighter	-	H927	21. 6.22	To Belgian AF in 7/22. Canx.
G-EBDO	DH.37A (Originally regd as DH.37, converted to DH.37A in 1927)	43		22. 6.22	Crashed during Bournemouth races on 4.6.27. Canx.
G-EBDP	Avro 504K	-	F2284	22. 6.22	WFU on 24.7.25. Canx.
G-EBDQ	Felixstowe F.3	-	N4177	26. 6.22	Canx 13.11.22.
G-EBDR	Bristol 172 Racer Monoplane	6148		27. 6.22	Development abandoned 1922. Scrapped in 1924. Canx.
G-EBDS	SE.5A	-		28. 6.22	CofA expired 22.11.24. Canx 5.1.26. Scrapped at Hendon.
G-EBDT	SE.5A	-		28. 6.22	To Germany as D-1636 in 5/29. CofA expired 15.2.35.
G-EBDU	SE.5A	-		28. 6.22	CofA expired 7.10.23. Canx 2.6.24. Scrapped at Hendon.
G-EBDV	SE.5A	1699	F7997	28. 6.22	CofA expired 4.10.23. Canx 5.1.26. Scrapped at Hendon.
G-EBDW	SE.5A	717	C8675	28. 6.22	CofA expired 29.9.24. Canx 29.9.24. Scrapped at Hendon.
G-EBDX	SE.5A	1693	F7991	28. 6.22	Canx 7.4.27 as sold abroad. In USA with smoke-writing apparatus in 1931.
G-EBDY	SE.5A	1071	C9029	28. 6.22	CofA expired 7.1.24. Canx 2.6.24. Scrapped at Hendon.
G-EBDZ	SE.5A	744	C8702	28. 6.22	Canx 7.4.27 as sold abroad. In USA with smoke-writing apparatus in 1931.
G-EBEA	Vickers 61 Vulcan (Originally regd as Vickers 71 Vulcan)	3		. 7.22	WFU on 20.7.23. Canx.
G-EBEB	Airco DH.6 (Built from spares)	-		11. 7.22	WFU in 9/30. Canx in 12/35. Stored at Hesketh Park, burned c.1940
G-EBEC	Vickers 124 Vixen V (Originally regd as Type 71 Vixen I, later to Type 87 Vixen II, then Type 105 Vixen IV)	1		12. 7.22	WFU in 2/30. Canx.
G-EBED	Vickers 67 Viking IV (Originally regd as Type 60)	17		. 7.22	WFU on 30.7.27. Canx.
"G-EBED"	Vickers 60 Viking IV Replica	-	BAPC.114 "R4"/"NC144"	----	On display 10/96 at Brooklands Museum. (Static replica built for the film "The People Time Forgot")
G-EBEE	Bristol F.2b Fighter	-	H926	13. 7.22	To Belgian AF in 7/22. Canx.
G-EBEF	Airco DH.9	-	H5775	13. 7.22	Sold Abroad. Canx 18.9.22.
G-EBEG	Airco DH.9	-	D1347	13. 7.22	Sold Abroad. Canx 18.9.22.
G-EBEH	Airco DH.9	-	D5777	13. 7.22	Sold Abroad. Canx 13.11.22.
G-EBEI	Airco DH.9	-	F1286	13. 7.22	Sold Abroad. Canx 18.9.22.
G-EBEJ	Airco DH.9	-	F1216	13. 7.22	Sold Abroad. Canx 18.9.22.
G-EBEK	Vickers 63 Vulcan	4		20. 7.22	WFU on 1.11.23. Canx.
G-EBEL	Avro 504K	PL.6038	E3291	22. 7.22	Sold Abroad. Canx 8.1.23.
G-EBEM	Vickers 61 Vulcan (Built as cargo carrier, converted to 8-seater in 1922)	5		. 7.22	Crashed in sea off Nice, France on 7.5.26. Canx.
G-EBEN	Airco DH.9	-	H5688	24. 8.22	To Egypt 11/24. Canx 3.12.24.
G-EBEO	Avro 504K	-	C691	2. 8.22	Canx 8/24.
G-EBEP	Airco DH.9	-	D5799	. 8.22	Crashed at West Hill, Sanderstead, Surrey in 17.11.28. Canx.
G-EBEQ	Boulton & Paul P.9 (C/n quoted as P.9/7 - this c/n belonged to G-AUCB (regn used from 31.8.21 until it was burned out on 5.11.21))	?		. 8.22	Crashed in Switzerland on 10.2.29; Rebuilt & to Switzerland as CH-259 on 4.9.30. Canx 1/32.
G-EBER	Sopwith 1F.1 Camel	-	F6302	8. 8.22	Fatal crash when it flew into buildings during low-level stunting at Abu Sueir on 4.11.22. Canx.
G-EBES	Vickers 61 Vulcan	6		11. 8.22	NTU - Not completed. Canx.
G-EBET	Vickers 61 Vulcan Note: Shipped to Australia in 1/23, for sale to QANTAS Ltd on the condition that it was able to meet some of their specific requirements. It was assembled at Point Cook, Victoria and flown to Longreach, where the tests were carried out. It failed in this venture and returned to the UK with fate given above.	7		11. 8.22	Scrapped c 1923. Canx.
G-EBEU	Armstrong Whitworth Siskin II (Built as 2-seater, coverted to single-seater in 1923)	AW.10		21. 8.22	WFU in 11/24. Canx 11.8.25.
G-EBEV	Bristol 75 Ten-Seater (Converted to Type 75A freighter in 2/24)	6145		22. 8.22	WFU in 1926. Canx 3.1.27.
G-EBEW	Bristol 83A Lucifer (Originally regd as Type 73 Taxiplane)	6153		23.10.22	WFU on 12.7.25. Scrapped in 7/25. Canx.
G-EBEX	Lowe Marlburian	HL(M)9		7.11.22	Crashed near Gosforth on 19.11.22. Canx 25.11.22.
G-EBEY	Bristol 73 Taxiplane	6154	(G-EBFX) G-EBEY	10.11.22	Dismantled at Filton in 5/25. Canx 6.1.26.
G-EBEZ	Airco DH.9J (Originally regd as DH.9, converted in 1926)	66		12.12.22	WFU in 4/33. Scrapped in 1933. Canx.
G-EBFA	Martinsyde F.4	-	H7688	9. 1.23	To Portuguese AF in 1/27. Canx 5.1.27.
G-EBFB	Avro 504N	-	H2518	24. 1.23	Canx 7.1.25.
G-EBFC	Vickers 74 Vulcan	8		25. 1.23	WFU on 22.12.25. Burnt at Croydon in 1927. Canx.

Regn	Type	c/n	Previous identity	Regn date	Fate or immediate subsequent identity (if known)
G-EBFD	Bristol F.2b Fighter	6223	E2354	25. 1.23	To Serbian Army in 3/23. Canx 27.3.23.
G-EBFE	Avro 554 Antartic Baby	5040		1. 2.23	Scrapped in Newfoundland, Canada during in 1927. Canx.
G-EBFF	SE.5A	646/2404	F896	12. 2.23	Canx 7.4.27 as sold abroad. In USA with smoke-writing apparatus in 1931.
G-EBFG	SE.5A	682/2404	F932	12. 2.23	Canx 7.4.27 as sold abroad. In USA with smoke-writing apparatus in 1931.
G-EBFH	SE.5A	685/2404	F935	12. 2.23	Crashed at Nashville, Tennessee, USA on 16.9.23. Canx 17.10.23.
G-EBFI	SE.5A	1680	F7978	12. 2.23	Canx 7.4.27 as sold abroad. In USA with smoke-writing apparatus in 1931.
G-EBFJ	Sopwith Pup	-	C242	22. 2.23	Scrapped in 1924. Canx.
G-EBFK	Supermarine Sea Eagle	1163		12. 3.23	Crashed Southampton Water on 30.11.23. Canx 21.5.24.
G-EBFL	Avro 548	-	H2053	29. 3.23	Crashed on 24.7.23. Canx.
G-EBFM	Avro 548	-	H2070	29. 3.23	Crashed at Brooklands on 20.9.28. Canx.
G-EBFN	DH.50	73		. 4.23	To Australia in 2/26 - reserved as G-AUEX on 17.3.36 - NTU, regd as G-AUEY on 13.4.26. Canx.
G-EBFO	DH.50J (Originally regd as DH.50, converted in 1925)	74		. 4.23	Damaged at Stag Lane in 1926; was dismantled and stored in such state. Fuselage only to Australia in 1929. Canx.
	Note: Fuselage only was purchased by Norman Brearley of Weatern Australian Airlines and had it shipped to Perth, Western Australia. As that airline had been operating the type for some time, it was fitted with wings, tail, undercarriage and a spare Nimbus engine from stock and recorded as a DH.50A, and then regd as VH-UMC on 19.9.29.				
G-EBFP	DH.50	75		. 4.23	Crashed at Semkah, Iraq on 24.11.32. Scrapped in 1933. Canx.
G-EBFQ	DH.9J (Originally regd as DH.9, converted in 1926)	76		11. 4.23	WFU on 28.7.32. Canx.
G-EBFR	Bristol 81 Puma Trainer	6239		19. 4.23	Crashed at Filton in 6/23. No CofA issued. Canx.
G-EBFS	Bristol 81 Puma Trainer	6240		19. 4.23	Scrapped in 5/24. Canx 7.5.24.
G-EBFT	Bristol 81 Puma Trainer	6241		19. 4.23	Crashed at Filton on 10.3.25. Canx.
G-EBFU	Bristol 81 Puma Trainer	6242		19. 4.23	Crashed at Filton on 8.7.28. Canx 1/29.
G-EBFV	Avro 504K	-		19. 4.23	Crashed at Long Sutton, Lincs on 24.9.23. Canx.
G-EBFW	Avro 504K	-	E1850	1. 5.23	Crashed at Mudford, near Yeovil on 17.9.26. Canx.
G-EBFX	Bristol 73 Taxiplane	6154	G-EBEY	3. 5.23	NTU - Registered in error, remained as G-EBEY. Canx 12.6.23.
G-EBFY	Bristol 73 Taxiplane	6155		3. 5.23	Dismantled at Filton 18.5.24 and used for spares. Canx.
G-EBFZ	Bristol 83A Lucifer	6373		3. 5.23	WFU in 6/31. Scrapped in 12/31. Canx.
G-EBGA	Bristol 83D Lucifer (Originally regd as Type 83A, converted to Type 83B in 1926 & modified to Type 83D in 1928)	6374		3. 5.23	WFU in 10/33. Scrapped in 12/33. Canx.
G-EBGB	Bristol 83A Lucifer	6375		3. 5.23	Destroyed in mid-air collision with Bristol Type 89 G-EBIH over Filton on 20.8.29. Canx.
G-EBGC	Bristol 83A Lucifer	6376		3. 5.23	WFU in 6/31. Scrapped in 12/31. Canx.
G-EBGD	Bristol 83A Lucifer	6377		3. 5.23	WFU in 6/31. Scrapped in 12/31. Canx.
G-EBGE	Bristol 83A Lucifer	6378		3. 5.23	WFU in 6/31. Scrapped in 12/31. Canx.
G-EBGF	Bristol 76 Jupiter Fighter	6379		3. 5.23	Engine seizure at 20,000ft and crashed at Filton on 23.11.23. Canx.
G-EBGG	Bristol 84 Bloodhound (Mod) (Originally regd as Type 78 Fighter C, converted to Type 84 in 1925 with new c/n 6710)	6222	J7236 G-EBGG	3. 5.23	WFU in 1928. Canx 1/29. Scrapped at Filton in 1931.
G-EBGH	Avro 504K	-	H6602	8. 5.23	Crashed near Brigg on 5.6.23. Canx.
G-EBGI	Avro 504K	-	H2416	15. 5.23	WFU on 29.5.24. Canx.
G-EBGJ	SE.5A	716	C8674	23. 5.23	Canx 7.4.27 as sold abroad. In USA with smoke-writing apparatus in 1931.
G-EBGK	SE.5A	1062	C9020	23. 5.23	Canx 7.4.27 as sold abroad. In USA with smoke-writing apparatus in 1931.
G-EBGL	SE.5A	1662	F7960	23. 5.23	Canx 7.4.27 as sold abroad. In USA with smoke-writing apparatus in 1931.
G-EBGM	SE.5A	1678	F7976	23. 5.23	Canx 2.6.24. Reported dismantled for spares in the USA.
G-EBGN	Gnosspelius Gull	1		29. 5.23	WFU c 1924. Canx.
G-EBGO	Vickers 78 Vulture I	1		1. 6.23	Crashed Komandorski Islands, Aleutians on 2.8.24. Canx.
G-EBGP	Short 184	-	N2996	1. 6.23	NTU - Not converted. Canx.
G-EBGQ	Airco DH.9	-	H5632	4. 6.23	Crashed at Renfrew on 30.10.24. Canx.
G-EBGR	Supermarine Sea Eagle	1164		5. 6.23	Canx as WFU in 1929. Hull painted as "G-EBGS" stored at Hythe, then at Heston until burnt on 13.2.54.
G-EBGS	Supermarine Sea Eagle	1165		5. 6.23	Rammed by a ship & sank in St.Peter Port, Guernsey on 14.12.26. Canx.
G-EBGT	DH.9J (Originally regd as DH.9, converted in 1926)	82		7. 6.23	Crashed at Hatfield on 16.10.32. Canx.
G-EBGU	DH.9	83		7. 6.23	Sold Abroad in 11/24. Canx.
G-EBGV	Avro 504K	-	E9358	13. 6.23	Sold Abroad. Canx 26.6.24.
G-EBGW	RAE Zephyr	1		13. 6.23	Scrapped in 1925. Canx.
G-EBGX	Airco DH.9A	-	F2872	16. 6.23	WFU c 1924. Canx.
G-EBGY	Avro 504K	R/LE/10390		28. 6.23	Crashed 12.6.24. Canx 6/24.
G-EBGZ	Avro 504K	R/LE/10407		28. 6.23	Dismantled & scrapped at Hooton in 2/34. Canx.
G-EBHA	Gloster 12A Grebe I	-		29. 6.23	CofA expired 29.7.29 & WFU. Scrapped in 1930. Canx.
G-EBHB	Avro 504K	-		17. 7.23	Canx in 8/24.
G-EBHC	Avro 504N	R3/LY/10331		20. 7.23	Crashed at Whitley on 3.8.23. Canx.
G-EBHD	Avro 504N	R3/LY/10348		20. 7.23	WFU on 2.3.33. Canx in 9/36.
G-EBHE	Avro 504K (Originally regd as Avro 504N, modified in 1932)	R3/LY/10365		20. 7.23	Crashed at Maylands on 10.10.33. Canx.
G-EBHF	Blackburn Pellet Seaplane	-	N56	23. 7.23	Sank in a take-off accident at Cowes, IoW on 27.9.23. Canx.
G-EBHG	Bristol 76B Fighter	6380		25. 7.23	To Swedish Army as 4300 in 5/24. Canx 26.5.24.
G-EBHH	Bristol 89A Jupiter Fighter (Originally regd as Type 76A)	6381		25. 7.23	Destroyed in mid-air collision with Bristol Type 89 G-EBJA over Filton on 23.9.25. Canx.
G-EBHI	Armstrong Whitworth Wolf	AW.18		25. 7.23	W/o on 15.1.31. Scrapped in 1931. Canx.

Regn	Type	c/n	Previous identity	Regn date	Fate or immediate subsequent identity (if known)
G-EBHJ	Armstrong Whitworth Wolf	AW.28	J6921	25. 7.23	Canx on 19.5.30. Scrapped in 1931.
G-EBHK	Avro 548	-	H7488	28. 7.23	Sold Abroad on 12.8.25. Canx 1.1.26.
G-EBHL	Avro 548	-	H2067	28. 7.23	W/o after accident on 6.11.25. Canx 11/25.
G-EBHM	Avro 504K	-	E3794	30. 7.23	Damaged at Port Talbot on 31.5.27 and subsequently DBF. Canx 15.6.27.
G-EBHN	Vickers 89 Viget	1	Lympne 1923	3. 8.23	WFU in 1928. Canx.
G-EBHO	Vickers 95 Vulture I (Originally regd as Vulture II)	2		9. 8.23	Crashed off Akyab, Burma on 24.5.24. Canx.
G-EBHP	Airco DH.9	-	H9203	29. 8.23	Canx as WFU 18.1.26. Canx.
G-EBHQ	Salmon Tandem Monoplane	-		16. 8.23	Scrapped in 1925. Canx.
G-EBHR	ANEC I	-	Lympne 1923 No.18	29. 8.23	To Australia in 8/24 - regd as G-AUEQ on 16.10.24. Canx in 9/32.
G-EBHS	RAE Hurricane	2		10. 9.23	Canx 12.1.27.
G-EBHT	Avro 504N	R3/LY/10382		. 9.23	Crashed Locks Common, Porthcawl 25.6.32. Canx 12/32.
G-EBHU	Gloster 14A Gannet (Originally regd as a Gloster 14)	1	Lympne 1923 No.7	15. 9.23	Canx 25.1.28.
G-EBHV	Airco DH.9J (Originally regd as DH.9, converted in 1926)	-	H5844	19. 9.23	WFU on 28.9.28. Canx.
G-EBHW	Avro 558	5089	Lympne 1923 No.11	19. 9.23	WFU at Hendon in 1924. Canx.
G-EBHX	DH.53 Humming Bird	98	Lympne 1923 No.8	22. 9.23	(On display 3/96 Old Warden)
G-EBHY	Armstrong Whitworth Siskin II (Built as single-seater)	AW.11		1.10.23	To R.Swedish AF in 9/25. Canx 2.9.25.
G-EBHZ	DH.53 Humming Bird	99		. 9.23	Crashed at Lympne on 18.9.26. Canx.
G-EBIA	SE.5A	654/2404	F904 "F703"/"D7000"/G-EBIA/F904	26. 9.23	The Shuttleworth Trust, Old Warden
G-EBIB	SE.5A (Regd with c/n 688/2404)	687/2404	"F939" G-EBIB/F937	26. 9.23	CofA expired 8.8.35 & WFU. Canx 1.12.46. (On display 8/97 South Kensington, London)
G-EBIC	SE.5A (Regd with c/n 687/2404) (Also allotted 9208M)	688/2404	"B4563" G-EBIC/F938	26. 9.23	WFU in 9/30. Canx 31.12.38. (On display 10/95 Hendon)
G-EBID	SE.5A	326/2329	C6376 ?	26. 9.23	CofA expired 9.6.28 & WFU. Canx in 2/32. Scrapped in 1932 at Hounslow.
G-EBIE	SE.5A	328/2329	C6378 ?	26. 9.23	CofA expired 9.6.28 & WFU. Canx in 2/32. Scrapped in 1932 at Hounslow.
G-EBIF	SE.5A	1398	E5683	26. 9.23	To Germany as D-1633 in 5/29. CofA expired 15.2.35. Canx 16.5.29.
G-EBIG	Airco DH.9C (Originally regd as DH.9)	-	H5886	.10.23	WFU on 17.4.30. Scrapped in 1931. Canx.
G-EBIH	Bristol 89 Puma Trainer (Originally laid down as Type 81A, completed as Type 89)	6382		15.10.23	Destroyed in mid-air collision with Bristol type 83A Lucifer G-EBGB over Filton on 20.8.29. Canx.
G-EBII	Avro 504K	-	E1826	15.10.23	WFU on 5.11.24. Canx.
G-EBIJ	Sperry M-1 Messenger	12		9.11.23	Fatal crash in forced landing in the English Channel off Fairlight, Sussex on 13.12.23. Canx.
G-EBIK	Armstrong Whitworth Siskin IV	-		10.11.23	NTU. Not completed. Canx.
G-EBIL	ANEC IA (Originally regd as Mk.I, converted to Mk.IA in 7/25)	1	Lympne 1925 No.15/G-EBIL/Lympne 1923 No.17/J7506	21.11.23	Canx 22.1.26.
G-EBIM	DH.51A (Originally regd as DH.51, converted to DH.51A in 1924)	100		.11.23	To Australia in 4/27 - regd as G-AUIM on 28.7.27. Canx.
G-EBIN	Avro 504K	-		28.11.23	Crashed at Plymouth on 25.7.24. Canx.
G-EBIO	Bristol F.2b Fighter	4971	H1254	.11.23	CofA expired 4.9.32 & WFU. Scrapped in 1935. Canx.
G-EBIP	Vickers 106 Vixen III (Originally regd as Type 91 Vixen III)	1		. 1.24	To G-EBPY in 6/28. Canx.
G-EBIQ	DH.51	101		. 1.24	WFU on 5.7.30. Scrapped at Hanworth in 1933. Canx.
G-EBIR	DH.51	102	VP-KAA G-KAA/G-EBIR	22. 1.24	(The Shuttleworth Trust)
G-EBIS	Avro 504K	R/LE/12663		. 1.24	Crashed at Rainhill on 22.4.35. Canx.
G-EBIT	Avro 548A	5100		. 2.24	Crashed Kingstown, Carlisle on 25.9.30. Canx in 3/38.
G-EBIU	Avro 548A	5101		. 2.24	DBR at Rhyl on 17.5.37. Canx.
G-EBIV	Avro 548A	5102		. 2.24	Canx in 3/38.
G-EBIW	DH.50A	116		11. 3.24	To Australia in 7/24 - regd as G-AUER on 15.10.24. Canx.
G-EBIX	Handley Page W.8G Hamilton (Originally regd as W.8F)	W.8/7		3. 4.24	Crashed near Neufchatel, France on 30.10.30. Canx.
G-EBIY	Westland Woodpigeon II (Originally regd as Woodpigeon I)	WP.1		. 4.24	WFU on 8.9.30. (In scrapyard at Ferrybridge, Yorks in 1949)
G-EBIZ	Avro 504K	-		29. 4.24	WFU in 1933. Canx in 8/35.
G-EBJA	Bristol 89 Trainer	6522		8. 5.24	Destroyed in mid-air collison with Bristol Type 89 G-EBHH over Filton on 23.9.25. Canx.
G-EBJB	Bristol 89 Trainer	6523		8. 5.24	Crashed & DBF near Filton on 15.12.25. Canx.
G-EBJC	Bristol 89 Trainer	6524		8. 5.24	NTU - Not completed. Canx 11.5.25.
G-EBJD	Avro 504Q Seaplane	5103		12. 6.24	Abandoned at Liefde Bay, Spitzbergen on 16.8.24. Canx in 6/25.
G-EBJE	Avro 504K (Includes components of Avro 548A G-EBKN ex E449; allotted 9205M .94)	927		7.24	(On display 10/95 Hendon)
G-EBJF	Vickers 98 Vagabond	1	Lympne 1924 No.16	1. 7.24	Scrapped in 1927. Canx.
G-EBJG	Parnall Pixie III	-	Lympne 1926 No.14/G-EBJG/Lympne 1924 No.18/(No.17)	. 7.24	Midland Air Museum (Components only remain for long term rebuild 4/96)
G-EBJH	Hawker Cygnet (Originally c/n 1)	2	Lympne 1924 No.15	. 7.24	Crashed on take-off from Lympne on 27.8.27. Canx.

Regn	Type	c/n	Previous identity	Regn date	Fate or immediate subsequent identity (if known)
G-EBJI(1)	Hawker Hedgehog	T.2		8. 7.24R	NTU - To G-EBJN 7/24. Canx.
G-EBJI(2)	Hawker Cygnet Replica	PFA/77-10240		9. 8.77	(Under construction 12/96)
G-EBJJ	Beardmore WB.XXIV Wee Bee I	WB.XXIV		14. 7.24	To Australia in 1933 - regd as VH-URJ on 26.4.33. Canx.
G-EBJK	Bristol 91B Brownie (Originally regd as Type 91, modified in 1926)	6526		14. 7.24	Crashed on take-off from at Farnborough on 21.3.28. Canx.
G-EBJL	Bristol 91A Brownie (Converted to Type 91A single-seater in 1927)	6527		14. 7.24	WFU on 24.11.32. Canx.
G-EBJM	Bristol 91A Brownie	6528		14. 7.24	CofA expired 17.7.26 & WFU. Canx 16.7.28.
G-EBJN	Hawker Hedgehog	T.2	(G-EBJI)	16. 7.24	NTU - To RAF as N187 in 9/24. Canx.
G-EBJO	ANEC II	2	Lympne 1924 No.7	. 7.24	The Shuttleworth Trust (On rebuild by Don Cashmore at Radcliffe on Trent 10/97)
G-EBJP	Supermarine Sparrow II (Originally regd as Sparrow I)	1211		. 7.24	Canx 3.1.30.
G-EBJQ	Armstrong Whitworth Siskin III	AW.66	J6981	29. 7.24	No CofA issued. Restored to RAF as J6981 in 11/24. Canx 24.11.20.
G-EBJR	Airco DH.9 Seaplane	158	H9289	22. 7.24	To Egypt. Canx 3.11.24.
G-EBJS	Armstrong Whitworth Siskin III	AW.67	J6982	29. 7.24	No CofA issued. Restored to RAF as J6982 in 11/24. Canx 24.11.20.
G-EBJT	Westland Widgeon II (Originally regd as Woodpigeon I with c/n WA.1570)	WA.1671		. 7.24	Crashed near Detling on 19.10.30. Canx.
G-EBJU	Short S.4 Satellite	S.644	Lympne 1926 No.15/G-EBJU/Lympne 1924 No.8	30. 7.24	WFU in late 1926. Canx in 1/28.
G-EBJV	Westland Woodpigeon II	WP.2		. 8.24	WFU in 1933. Canx.
G-EBJW	Airco DH.9	-	H9333	. 8.24	WFU on 5.7.28. Canx.
G-EBJX	Airco DH.9	-	H9147	. 8.24	WFU on 5.6.27. Canx.
G-EBJY	Supermarine Swan Seaplane	1173	N175	23. 8.24	Scrapped in 1927. Canx.
G-EBJZ	Gloster II Seaplane (1924 Schneider Trophy Race No.1)	2	(J7504)	3. 9.24	Float strut collapsed alighting on rough water after first flight during trials and sank at Felixstowe on 19.9.24 & w/o. Canx.
G-EBKA	Short S.1 Stellite	S.638		3. 9.24	To RAF as N193 in 7/25. Canx 22.7.25.
G-EBKB	Avro 504K	-	E2969	. 9.24	Crashed in sea off Scarborough on 13.9.31. Canx.
G-EBKC	Cranwell C.L.A.2	CLA.2		19. 9.24	Crashed at Martlesham Heath. Canx 20.5.25.
G-EBKD	Blackburn L.1 Bluebird I	9803/1		27. 9.24	Fatal crash & DBF after mid-air collision with Widgeon G-EBPW at Bournemouth on 6.6.27. Canx.
G-EBKE	Fairey IIID	F.576		4.10.24	Scrapped in 1929. Canx.
G-EBKF	Blackburn T.2 Dart Seaplane	8312/1		20.10.24	DBR near Digby, Lincs on 7.1.32. Canx.
G-EBKG	Blackburn T.2 Dart Seaplane	8312/2		20.10.24	WFU at Brough on 25.1.28. Canx.
G-EBKH	Blackburn T.2 Dart Seaplane	8312/3		20.10.24	CofA expired 9.5.33 & WFU. Scrapped at Hatfield, Yorks in 1952. Canx.
G-EBKI	DH.54 Highclere	151		17.11.24	DBR when hangar collapsed in heavy snow at Croydon on 2.2.27. Canx.
G-EBKJ	DH.50A	132		21.11.24	To Czechoslovakian Government as L-BALG in 1/25. Canx.
G-EBKK	Parnall Pixie III	-	Lympne 1924 No.19	.11.24	Crashed at Woodford on 16.7.30. Canx in 9/30.
G-EBKL	Martinsyde ADC.1	K501		28.11.24	WFU on 21.4.27. Burnt at Croydon in 1930. Canx.
G-EBKM	Parnall Pixie II	-	J7324 (G-EBKM)	1.12.24	Crashed at Coswarth Farm, Colan, Cornwall on 19.4.39. Canx.
G-EBKN	Avro 548A	-	E449	.12.24	WFU on 29.6.28. Allotted 9205M in 1994. (Components to Avro 504K G-EBJE in 1969)
G-EBKO	Airco DH.9	-	H9319	.12.24	WFU on 15.2.29. Scrapped in 1930. Canx.
G-EBKP	Avro 562 Avis	5105	Lympne 1924 No.10	19.12.24	WFU on 20.11.28. Scrapped in 1932. Canx.
G-EBKQ	Avro 504O (Originally regd as Avro 504N Floatplane, converted to Avro 582 in 1927, modified to Avro 504O in 6/30)	5104	K-8 G-EBKQ	.12.24	WFU on 12.6.31. To Instructional Airframe. Canx in 11/35.
G-EBKR	Avro 504K	PL.6129	E3382	.12.24	Crashed at Church Lawton, Cheshire on 22.7.32. Canx.
G-EBKS	Avro 504K	-		.12.24	WFU at Brooklands on 9.6.27. Canx.
G-EBKT	DH.60 Moth (Cirrus I)	168		10. 2.25	Crashed at Stanmore, Middlesex on 21.8.27. Canx.
G-EBKU	DH.60 Moth (Cirrus I)	169		10. 2.25	Crashed at Lahore on 22.7.27. Canx.
G-EBKV	Airco DH.9 (C/n quoted as "853")	-	H9337	11. 2.25	To Australia - regd as G-AUFB on 24.9.26. Canx 5.1.27.
G-EBKW	Avro 563 Andover	5097	J7264	27. 2.25	Restored to RAF as J7264 in 1/27. Canx.
G-EBKX	Avro 504K	PL.6133	E3386	. 2.25	Crashed at Crosby, Lancs on 21.7.34. Canx.
G-EBKY	Sopwith Dove (Converted to Sopwith Pup)	3004/14	"N5180" "N5184"/G-EBKY	27. 3.25	(The Shuttleworth Trust)
G-EBKZ	DH.50A	133		2. 4.25	Crashed at Roborough, Plymouth on 23.10.28. Canx.
G-EBLA	Avro 504K	R/LE/18615		. 4.25	Crashed into sea off Weymouth on 29.5.28. Canx.
G-EBLB	Vickers 74 Vulcan	9		. 4.25	Crashed at Little Woodcote, near Croydon on 13.7.28. Canx.
G-EBLC	Airco DH.9A	-	E8781	14. 4.25	WFU at Croydon on 6.8.29. Canx.
G-EBLD	Vickers 119 Vespa II (Originally regd as Type 113 Vespa I)	1		14. 4.25	To O-5/G-ABIL as Type 210 Vespa VI in 1/31. Canx.
G-EBLE	Handley Page W.9 Hampstead	W.9/1		6. 5.25	To Australia in 1/29 - regd as VH-ULK on 5.8.29. Canx.
G-EBLF	Armstrong Whitworth Argosy II (Originally regd as Argosy I)	AW.154		16. 5.25	WFU at Croydon in 9/34. Canx.
G-EBLG	Bristol 93 Boarhound	6805		28. 5.25	WFU at Filton in 4/27. Canx 2.4.27.
G-EBLH	DH.9J (Originally regd as DH.9, converted in 1926)	181		29. 5.25	Crashed near Maidenhead on 12.5.27. Canx.
G-EBLI	DH.60 Moth (Cirrus I)	183		29. 5.25	Crashed at Stanmore, Middlesex on 9.10.27. Canx.
G-EBLJ	Gloster IIIA Seaplane (Originally regd as Gloster III, converted in 1927)	III	N195	3. 6.25	Restored to RAF as N195 in 1927. Canx 31.8.26.
G-EBLK	Armstrong Whitworth Atlas I (Rebuilt with c/n AW.278 in 8/26)	AW.139		4. 6.25	To RAF as J8675 in 11/27. Canx as WFU 3.2.28.

Regn	Type	c/n	Previous identity	Regn date	Fate or immediate subsequent identity (if known)
G-EBLL	Armstrong Whitworth Siskin IV	AW.143		4. 6.25	No recorded CofA issued. WFU in 1926. Canx.
G-EBLM	Armstrong Whitworth Atlas II	AW.141		4. 6.25	To RAF as J9128 in 6/28. Canx.
G-EBLN	Armstrong Whitworth Siskin V	AW.97	(Roumanian AF)	4. 6.25	DBR on landing at Town Moor. Canx 1.1.27.
G-EBLO	Armstrong Whitworth Argosy II (Originally regd as Argosy I)	AW.155		4. 6.25	Crashed at Aswan, Egypt in 16.6.31. Canx
G-EBLP	Supermarine S.4	1215	N197	9. 6.25	Crashed at Baltimore, USA on 22.10.25. Canx.
G-EBLQ	Armstrong Whitworth Siskin V	AW.102	(Roumanian AF)	25. 6.25	Destroyed in fatal crash at Whitley on 19.7.26. Canx.
G-EBLR	DH.60 Moth (Cirrus I)	184		22. 6.25	Crashed at Sale, Cheshire on 11.6.27. Canx.
G-EBLS	DH.60 Moth (Cirrus I)	185		22. 6.25	Crashed at Sherburn-in-Elmet on 5.2.28. Canx.
G-EBLT	DH.60 Moth (Cirrus I)	186		22. 6.25	DBF at Witney on 27.10.36. Canx in 11/36.
G-EBLU	DH.60 Moth (Cirrus I)	187		22. 6.25	Crashed on landing at Stag Lane on 8.1.26. Canx.
G-EBLV	DH.60 Moth (Cirrus III)	188		22. 6.25	(On loan to The Shuttleworth Trust)
G-EBLW	DH.60 Moth (Cirrus I)	189		22. 6.25	Crashed at Shirley, near Birmingham on 3.11.29. Canx.
G-EBLX	DH.60 Moth (Cirrus I)	190		22. 6.25	Crashed at Blyth, Northumberland on 20.5.31. Canx.
G-EBLY	DH.60 Moth (Cirrus I)	191		22. 6.25	Crashed at Cramlington on 22.2.27. Canx.
G-EBLZ	Fairey Freemantle Seaplane	F.420		22. 6.25	NTU - Completed for RAF as N173 in 1926. Canx in 1/27.
G-EBMA	Hawker Woodcock II	-	J7515	1. 7.25	Landed in fog & spun round near Luton on 3.7.25 during King's Cup Race. Repaired & returned to RAF as J7515. Canx.
G-EBMB	Hawker Cygnet I (Originally Cygnet c/n 2)	1	Lympne 1924 No.14	29. 7.25	Canx 30.11.61. (On display RAF Museum, Hendon)
G-EBMC	Cranwell C.L.A.3 Parasol	CLA.3		30. 7.25	DBR in 7/26. Scrapped in 1929. Canx.
G-EBMD	Blackburn RT.1 Kangaroo (Converted to dual trainer in 1924)	-	B8837	13. 8.25	CofA expired 7.2.29 & WFU. Scrapped at Sherburn-in-Elmet in 1929. Canx.
G-EBME	DH.60 Moth (Cirrus I)	193		21. 8.25	To Australia in 9/27 - regd as G-AUME on 26.1.28. Canx 22.9.27.
G-EBMF	DH.60 Moth (Cirrus I)	194		21. 8.25	WFU in 3/35. Scrapped at Gatwick in 1948. Canx.
G-EBMG	Saunders A.4 Medina Seaplane	A.4/1	N214	10.10.25	Scrapped in 1929. Canx.
G-EBMH	Martinsyde ADC.1	K.502		22.10.25	To Latvian AF in 7/26. Canx.
G-EBMI	Martinsyde F.4	-	D4295	.10.25	Crashed at Woodley on 24.8.30. Canx.
G-EBMJ	Short S.7 Mussel I	S.678		30.10.25	Capsized on landing on the River Medway, near Rochester on 24.8.28. Wreck to RAF Halton. Canx.
G-EBMK	Bristol 99A Badminton (Originally regd as Type 99, modified in 1927)	6921		16.11.25	Fatal crash on take-off from Filton on 28.7.27. Canx.
G-EBML	Bristol 89 Trainer	6918		19.11.25	W/o on 14.5.27. Canx.
G-EBMM	Handley Page W.10	W.10/1		.11.25	Crashed at Aston Clinton, Bucks on 22.9.34. Canx.
G-EBMN	Bristol 89 Trainer	6919		19.11.25	W/o on 17.3.27. Canx.
G-EBMO	DH.60 Moth (Cirrus I)	197		27.11.25	Crashed at Shellong, Assam on 18.7.27. Canx.
G-EBMP	DH.60 Moth (Cirrus I)	198		27.11.25	To Sweden as S-AACD/SE-ACD in 11/29. Canx.
G-EBMQ	DH.60 Moth (Cirrus I)	201		27.11.25	Crashed prior to CofA lapsed 28.8.34. Canx in 4/35.
G-EBMR	Handley Page W.10	W.10/2		25.11.25	DBR at Hal Far, Malta on 22.9.34. Canx in 11/34.
G-EBMS	Handley Page W.10	W.10/3		25.11.25	Crashed into the English Channel on 21.10.26. Canx.
G-EBMT	Handley Page W.10	W.10/4		25.11.25	Fatal crash into the English Channel off Dungeness on 17.6.29. Canx.
G-EBMU	DH.60 Moth (Cirrus I)	234		11.12.25	To Canada as CF-AEN in 4/29. Canx.
G-EBMV	DH.60 Moth (Cirrus I)	235		11.12.25	Crashed in 8/29. Canx 8/29.
G-EBMW	DH.66 Hercules	236		11.12.25	DBR near Koepang, Timor on 19.4.31. Canx.
G-EBMX	DH.66 Hercules	237		11.12.25	To South African AF as 262 in 11/34. Canx.
G-EBMY	DH.66 Hercules	238		11.12.25	WFU & broken up at Kisumu, Kenya in 1933. Canx.
G-EBMZ	DH.66 Hercules	239		11.12.25	DBF after stalling on approach to Jask, Persia on 6.9.29. Canx.
G-EBNA	DH.66 Hercules	240		11.12.25	DBR in forced landing at Gaza, Egypt on 14.2.30. Canx.
G-EBNB	Bristol 83B Lucifer	6922		14.12.25	To Hungary in 2/26. Canx 15.2.26.
G-EBNC	Bristol 83B Lucifer	6923		14.12.25	To Hungary in 2/26. Canx 15.2.26.
G-EBND	Avro 567 Avenger II (Originally regd as Avro 566 Avenger I)	5109		24.12.25	WFU in 28.6.29. To instructional airframe at Hamble in 5/31. Canx.
G-EBNE	Avro 504R Gosport	5110	K-6 G-EBNE	24.12.25	To Instructional Airframe at Hamble in 1930. Canx in 2/33.
G-EBNF	Avro 504R Gosport	5111		24.12.25	Crashed at Cheadle Hulme, Cheshire on 21.10.28. Canx.
G-EBNG	Beardmore Inflexible (Rohrbach Ro.VIII)	WB		29.12.25	NTU - To RAF as J7557 in 3/28. Canx 12.7.27.
G-EBNH	Avro 504K	-		. 1.26	Crashed at Bridgend, Glamorgan on 7.5.28. Canx.
G-EBNI	Armstrong Whitworth Atlas I	AW.142		11. 1.26	To RAF as J9129 in 5/28. Canx.
G-EBNJ	DH.65A Hound (Originally regd as DH.65, converted in 1927)	250		15. 1.26	To RAF as J9127 in 1/28. Canx.
G-EBNK	DH.65J Hound	251		15. 1.26	NTU - Not completed. Canx.
G-EBNL	RAE Sirocco	3		26. 1.26	NTU - Not completed. Canx in 1/29.
G-EBNM	DH.60 Moth (Cirrus I)	249		19. 2.26	To Denmark as T-DMOL in 1/28. Canx.
G-EBNN	DH.60 Moth (Cirrus I)	260		19. 2.26	Crashed near Lympne on 27.3.29. Canx.
G-EBNO	DH.60 Moth (Cirrus I)	261		19. 2.26	To Sweden as S-AABS in 7.28. Canx 26.7.28.
G-EBNP	DH.60X Moth (Cirrus II)	280		19. 2.26	Crashed at Stag Lane on 22.11.26. Canx.
G-EBNQ	Vickers 141 (Originally regd as Vickers 123 Scout)	1		25. 2.26	Scrapped in 1930. Canx.
G-EBNR	Avro 504K	-	F8864	1. 3.26	WFU on 13.2.30. Canx.
G-EBNS	Handley Page HP.32 Hamlet (Originally three Lucifer IV 120hp engines, modified to two Lynx 220hp in 1927, then three Mongoose 150hp in 1928)	1		15. 3.26	Scrapped at Farnborough in 1929. Canx in 1/30.
G-EBNT	Gloster 17 Gamecock I	95/12877		17. 3.26	To RAF as J8033 in 3/27. Canx 27.4.27.
G-EBNU	Avro 504K	-	E448	19. 3.26	To Finnish AF as AV-57 in 9/26. Canx.
G-EBNV	English Electric S.1 Wren (Now composite aircraft - principally c/n 3 rebuilt 1955/56)	4	(BAPC 11)	9. 4.26	(On display 3/96 Old Warden)

Regn	Type	c/n	Previous identity	Regn date	Fate or immediate subsequent identity (if known)
G-EBNW	Avro 572 Buffalo II (Originally regd as Avro 571 Buffalo I, converted in 1927, modified to seaplane in 7/28)	R3/BTC/30021		19. 4.26	To RAF as N239 in 1/29. Canx.
G-EBNX	DH.60 Moth (Cirrus II)	262		22. 4.26	To USA as NC1686 in 9/27. Canx 22.9.27.
G-EBNY	DH.60 Moth (Cirrus I)	263		22. 4.26	Crashed prior to CofA lapsed 15.11.29. Wreckage at Woodley in 4/32. Canx.
G-EBNZ	Bristol 89 Trainer	6963		26. 4.26	WFU on 21.10.29. Canx 14.1.30.
G-EBOA	Bristol 89 Trainer	6964		26. 4.26	Crashed at Moorpark, Renfrew on 10.3.27. Canx 15.3.27.
G-EBOB	Avro 504K	-	F8865	10. 5.26	WFU on 3.3.29. Canx.
G-EBOC	Bristol 89A Trainer	6965		14. 5.26	Destroyed in mid-air collision with Bristol Type 89A G-AAWJ over Filton on 7.7.31. Canx.
G-EBOD	Bristol 89A Trainer	6966		14. 5.26	Crashed on railway embankment near Pollockshaws Station, Glasgow on 26.5.27. Canx 14.1.30.
G-EBOE	Gloster 27 Gamecock	-		20. 5.26	Originally not completed. Canx 19.3.28. Was later completed for the RAF as J9248 in 6/29.
G-EBOF	Avro 536	-		31. 5.26	WFU on 5.3.29. Canx.
G-EBOG	SE.5A (Rebuilt as Dudley Watt D.W.1 1927-1932)	-		5. 6.26	DBF at Whitchurch in 1932. Canx as sold 12/32.
G-EBOH	DH.60 Moth (Cirrus I)	269		8. 6.26	DBR at Ewshott, Surrey on 15.5.30. Canx.
G-EBOI	DH.60 Moth (Cirrus I)	270		8. 6.26	To RAF as 2061M in 5/40. Canx 2.3.40.
G-EBOJ	Martinsyde Nimbus	K.1001		9. 6.26	WFU on 18.7.29. Burnt at Croydon in 1930. Canx.
G-EBOK	Avro 548	R/R3/Re/70022		12. 6.26	Crashed at Milnrow Aerodrome, Lancs on 2.6.34. Canx 1/37.
G-EBOL	Martinsyde F.4	K.1002		. 6.26	Crashed on Epsom Downs on 7.10.27. Remains burnt at Croydon in 1930. Canx.
G-EBOM	Blackburn RT.1 Kangaroo (Converted to dual trainer in 1924)	-	B8839	18. 6.26	Crashed at Brough on 25.9.28. Canx.
G-EBON	Parnall Plover	-	N9705	19. 6.26	W/o in 1/29. Canx in 1/29.
G-EBOO	Halton HAC.II Minus (Originally regd HAC.1 Mayfly (2-seater), converted to HAC.II Minus (single-seater) in 1927)	1		23. 6.26	WFU on 26.9.29. Lower wings used in construction of Clarke Cheetah Biplane G-AAJK in 1929. Remainder dismantled at Halton in 1930. Canx.
G-EBOP	DH.50J (Originally regd as DH.50A)	281		5. 7.26	DBR at Kisumu, Kenya on 17.10.27. Canx.
G-EBOQ	DH.9J	282		5. 7.26	Crashed near Coventry on 9.7.29. Canx.
G-EBOR	DH.9J	283		5. 7.26	WFU on 10.8.29. Canx.
G-EBOS	DH.60 Moth (Cirrus I)	268		5. 7.26	Spun in from low altitude on to Mote Mount Golf Course, Mill Hill, Middlesex on 20.10.28. Canx.
G-EBOT	DH.60 Moth (Cirrus I)	272		5. 7.26	Crashed at Broxbourne on 13.12.31. Canx.
G-EBOU	DH.60 Moth (Genet I)	271	Lympne 1926 No.2	5. 7.26	To Germany as D-1651 in 6/29. Canx 7.6.29.
G-EBOV	Avro 581E Avian (Originally regd as Avro 581, converted to Avro 581A in 1927, then modified to Avro 581E)	5116	Lympne 1926 No.9	7. 7.26	Canx 14.1.30 as sold in Australia: did not attain registration. On display Queensland Cultural Centre, Brisbane, Australia 2/96.
G-EBOW	Bristol Type 101	7019		17. 7.26	Broke up during a steep dive at Filton on 29.11.29. Canx.
G-EBOX	Avro 504R Gosport	R3/G/80086		20. 7.26	Sold Abroad. Canx 16.8.26.
G-EBOY	Avro 536	P.8	G-EAKL	23. 7.26	WFU on 11.4.29. Canx.
G-EBOZ	Armstrong Whitworth Argosy II (Originally regd as Argosy I)	AW.156		. 7.26	WFU at Almaza, Egypt on 2.6.34. Canx in 10/34.
G-EBPA	SE.5A	-	D7016	30. 7.26	CofA expired 11.4.28 & WFU. Scrapped. Canx 3/32.
G-EBPB	Cranwell C.L.A.4A	CLA.4A/1		17. 8.26	Scrapped at Heston in 1933. Canx.
G-EBPC	Cranwell C.L.A.4A	CLA.4A/2		18. 8.26	Crashed on 4.3.27. Canx.
G-EBPD	SE.5A	-	D7022	31. 8.26	W/o? Canx 27.4.27.
G-EBPE	DH.9 Seaplane	284		2. 9.26	WFU in Northern Rhodesia on 20.12.27. Canx.
G-EBPF	DH.9 Seaplane	285		2. 9.26	WFU in Northern Rhodesia on 20.12.27. Canx.
G-EBPG	DH.60 Moth (Cirrus II)	359		2. 9.26	Crashed at Worthy Down on 4.6.27. Canx in 1/28.
G-EBPH	Avro 585 (Originally regd as Avro 504R Gosport)	R3/R/70000		23. 9.26	WFU at Hamble on 25.11.29. Canx in 1/30.
G-EBPI	ANEC IV Missel Thrush (Converted to a Genet II)	1		. 9.26	Fatal crash near Peebles, Scotland on 20.7.28. Canx.
G-EBPJ	Avro 548	-	E9337	25.10.26	Crashed at Maylands on 31.7.28. Canx in 12/30.
G-EBPK	Blackburn RT.1 Kangaroo (Converted to dual trainer in 1924)	-	B8840	29.10.26	CofA expired 2.7.29 & WFU at Sherburn-in-Elmet. Scrapped in 1929. Canx.
G-EBPL	Fokker F.VIIA	4938	H-NADH	30.10.26	Sold to Holland; Crashed near Estaires, France on 21.1.27 whilst on delivery. Cannibalized with fuselage going to H-NAEB and a wing to H-NADX. Canx.
G-EBPM	DH.60 Moth (Cirrus II)	353		18.11.26	Crashed near Lympne on 27.2.30. Canx.
G-EBPN	Airco DH.6	-	C7823	.11.26	WFU on 6.7.28. Scrapped in 7/28. Canx.
G-EBPO	Avro 548 (C/n also quoted as P1/8133)	PL.6134	E3387	23.11.26	Canx 9/31.
G-EBPP	DH.60 Moth (Cirrus II)	355		1.12.26	To Australia in 2/27 - regd as G-AUPP on 14.3.27. Canx in 5/27.
G-EBPQ	DH.60 Moth (Cirrus II)	357		1.12.26	Crashed at Newhaven on 20.6.32. Canx.
G-EBPR	DH.60 Moth (Cirrus II)	358		1.12.26	Crashed at Halton on 22.10.30. Canx.
G-EBPS	DH.60 Moth (Cirrus II)	360		1.12.26	Spun in close to at Duxford on 20.1.29. Canx.
G-EBPT	DH.60 Moth (Cirrus II)	361		1.12.26	Crashed at Cramlington on 1.12.29. Canx.
G-EBPU	DH.60 Moth (Cirrus II)	373		1.12.26	CofA lapsed 24.3.30 & WFU. Canx.
G-EBPV	Fokker F.VIIA/3m	4982	H-NADS	1.12.26	To Italy as I-BBEC in 3/27. Canx 18.3.27.
G-EBPW	Westland Widgeon III	WA.1677		. 4.27	Fatal crash after mid-air collision with Blackburn Bluebird G-EBKD at Bournemouth on 6.6.27. Canx.
G-EBPX	Vickers 157 Vendace II (Originally regd as Type 133)	1		3. 1.27	To Brazil in 6/28. Canx 6.6.28.
G-EBPY	Vickers 146 Vivid Seaplane (Originally regd as Type 130 Vivid, then as Type 142)	1	G-EBIP	. 6.28	DBF at Broomfield aerodrome, Chelsford whilst on overhaul & engine change on 17.9.32. Canx.
G-EBPZ	Fairey IIID	F.814	S1076	18. 1.27	DBR when it sank at Kisumu, Lake Victoria on 13.3.27. Canx.
G-EBQA	SE.5A	-		18. 1.27	CofA expired 9.6.28 & WFU. Canx 2/32. Scrapped at Hounslow.

Regn	Type	c/n	Previous identity	Regn date	Fate or immediate subsequent identity (if known)
G-EBQB	SE.5A	-		18. 1.27	CofA expired 10.6.30 & WFU. Scrapped at Hendon. Canx 5/35.
G-EBQC	SE.5A	-		18. 1.27	To Germany as probably D-2081 in 6/31. CofA expired 15.2.35. Canx in 6/31.
G-EBQD	Airco DH.9	-	H9205	. 1.27	WFU in Southern Rhodesia on 10.5.29. Scrapped in 1930. Canx.
G-EBQE	DH.60 Moth (Cirrus II)	370		26. 1.27	Crashed at Bastia, Corsica in 7/31. Canx.
G-EBQF	Bristol 93A Beaver	7123		2. 2.27	WFU at Filton in 4/27. Canx 3.2.28.
G-EBQG	Parnall (Cierva) C.11 Autogyro	P1/5281		4. 2.27	Never flown; WFU at Yate in 1928. To instructional airframe Hamble in 1931. Canx in 12/31.
G-EBQH	DH.60X Moth	276		. 4.27	CofA lapsed on 3.9.37 & WFU. Canx.
G-EBQI	DH.50A	136		. 5.27	Crashed at Ecclestone, near Chorley on 2.8.31. Canx.
G-EBQJ	DH.60 Moth (Cirrus II)	371		22. 2.27	Crashed at Aurangabad, India on 4.8.27. Canx.
G-EBQK	SE.5A	-	F9130	19. 3.27	WFU on 31.7.29. Scrapped at Hendon. Canx in 2/32.
G-EBQL	Avro 594 Avian IV (Originally regd as Avian I, converted in 1927)	R3/AV/117		. 4.27	Crashed at Barton on 18.11.33. Canx.
G-EBQM	SE.5A	-	D7020	22. 3.27	CofA expired 4.11.30. WFU & dismantled. Canx 12/32.
G-EBQN	Avro 594 Avian I	R3/AV/100		. 4.27	To RAF as 2081M in 1/40. Canx 4.1.40.
G-EBQO	Dornier Do.J Wal	37	N-25 R.Norwegian AF	2. 4.27	To Germany as D-1422 in 10/28. Canx.
G-EBQP	DH.53 Humming Bird	114	J7326	. 5.27	Fatal crash after it stalled from 60 ft at Hamble on 21.7.34. (On rebuild 3/97 - based on wings ex Martin Monoplane G-AEYY)
G-EBQQ	SE.5A	-	C1091	4. 4.27	Fatal crash at Brooklands on 9.11.28. Canx in 1/29.
G-EBQR	Avro 504K	-		. 4.27	WFU on 26.6.31. Canx in 4/37.
G-EBQS	Bristol 89A Trainer	6967		. 4.27	WFU on 17.6.29. Canx as w/o 14.1.30.
G-EBQT	Bristol 89A Trainer	7124		. 4.27	Crashed at Tewkesbury, Gloucester on 23.8.28. Canx.
G-EBQU	DH.71 Tiger Moth	323		5. 4.27	To Australia in 11/29 - regd as VH-UNH on 20.1.30. Canx.
G-EBQV	DH.60 Moth (Cirrus II)	375		. 4.27	Canx in 10/36.
G-EBQW	DH.60 Moth (Cirrus II)	378		12. 4.27	Canx in 12/30.
G-EBQX	DH.60 Moth (Cirrus II)	385		12. 4.27	WFU in 10/37. Scrapped at Beddington, Surrey in 6/51. Canx.
G-EBQY	DH.60 Moth (Cirrus II)	376		. 5.27	WFU on 2.6.28. Canx in 1/29.
G-EBQZ	DH.60 Moth (Cirrus II)	386		31. 5.27	WFU on 31.7.35. Canx.
G-EBRA	DH.53 Humming Bird	109	J7270	26. 4.27	Canx in 12/29 as sold abroad, believed as spares.
G-EBRB	Avro 536	-		27. 4.27	Crashed at Barry on 28.5.28. Canx 12.6.28.
G-EBRC	Avro 594 Avian II	R3/AV/118		30. 4.27	Crashed in sea off Ventnor, IoW on 6.9.27. Canx.
G-EBRD	Avro 548	-		1. 6.27	Scrapped in South Africa in 1928. Canx as WFU 2.6.28.
G-EBRE	Blackburn L.1A Bluebird II	9803/2		11. 5.27	DBR at Hadleigh on 6.1.30. Canx.
G-EBRF	Blackburn L.1A Bluebird II	9803/3		11. 5.27	Burned at Gravesend on 3.8.37. Canx.
G-EBRG	Blackburn L.1A Bluebird II	9803/4		11. 5.27	Crashed at Sherburn-in-Elmet, Yorks on 5.2.28. Canx.
G-EBRH	DH.60X Moth Seaplane	404		18. 5.27	Crashed on landing at Kastrup, Denmark on 4.9.27. Canx.
G-EBRI	DH.60X Moth	405		18. 5.27	To RAF as X5128 12/39. Canx 19.12.39.
G-EBRJ	DH.53 Humming Bird	108	J7269	20. 5.27	WFU on 27.11.28. Scrapped at Woodley in 1930. Canx.
G-EBRK	DH.53 Humming Bird	112	J7273	23. 5.27	Crashed in 3/32. Canx.
G-EBRL	Westland Widgeon III	WA.1679		11. 7.27	Crashed at Yeovil on 3.6.31. Canx.
G-EBRM	Westland Widgeon IIIA	WA.1680		7. 9.27	Canx in 12.31. Scrapped at Brooklands in 1931.
G-EBRN	Westland Widgeon III	WA.1724		. 9.27	WFU at Stranraer on 9.2.49. Burnt in 1951. Canx.
G-EBRO	Westland Widgeon III	WA.1682		. 8.27	WFU on 23.3.38. Scrapped. Canx.
G-EBRP	Westland Widgeon III	WA.1694		. 8.27	To India as G-IAAW in 1/28. Canx.
G-EBRQ	Westland Widgeon III	WA.1684		11. 7.27	WFU on 2.1.36. Canx.
G-EBRR	Avro 594 Avian III	R3/AV/119		. 7.27	Crashed in 1/29. Canx.
G-EBRS	Avro 594 Avian III	R3/AV/120		. 7.27	To Switzerland as CH-202 in 8/27. Canx.
G-EBRT	DH.60X Moth	410		31. 5.27	Crashed at Ashingdon, Essex on 20.6.36. Canx.
G-EBRU	DH.60 Moth (Cirrus II)	387		8. 6.27	DBR at Rakos, Budapest, Hungary on 6.8.27. Canx.
G-EBRV	DH.71 Tiger Moth	324		1. 6.27	WFU on 7.8.28. Preserved at Hatfield, DBR by enemy bombing in 1940. Canx.
G-EBRW	DH.53 Humming Bird	107	J7268	. 6.27	CofA expired 19.6.34 & WFU. Canx.
G-EBRX	DH.60 Moth (Cirrus II)	388		10. 6.27	To Holland as PH-KLG in 3/34. Canx.
G-EBRY	DH.60 Moth (Cirrus II)	389		12. 8.27	To RAF as AW147 in 6/40. Canx 23.6.40.
G-EBRZ	DH.60X Moth	413		30. 6.27	Crashed near Sherburn-in-Elmet on 23.9.27. Canx.
G-EBSA	DH.60X Moth	414		28. 6.27	Crashed at Crockerwell, Devon on 8.4.31. Canx.
G-EBSB	Bristol 89A Trainer	7156		13. 6.27	WFU on 30.7.29. Canx 14.1.30.
G-EBSC	Avro 548	-		23. 6.27	Crashed in South Africa in 5/28. Canx.
G-EBSD	Avro 594A Avian III (Modified to Avro 594C with Alpha engine 10/27)	R3/AV/121		. 6.27	Crashed in 12/32. Scrapped in 3/33. Canx.
G-EBSE	Avro 504K	-	H2234	4. 7.27	WFU on 11.4.32. Canx.
G-EBSF	DH.60X Moth	415		7. 7.27	Crashed at Tabora, Tanganyika on 8.4.28 & sold in South Africa. Canx.
G-EBSG	Avro 504K	-	H257	11. 7.27	WFU on 28.7.28. Canx in 11/34.
G-EBSH	Bristol 89A Trainer	7157		8. 7.27	WFU on 28.11.33. Canx.
G-EBSI	DH.60X Moth	416		14. 7.27	To Denmark as T-DALF on 9/27. Canx.
G-EBSJ	Avro 504K	-	H2365	. 7.27	Canx in 5/35.
G-EBSK	DH.60X Moth	417		14. 7.27	Crashed at Hucknall on 22.8.28. Canx.
G-EBSL	Avro 504K	-	D6330	. 7.27	Crashed on 9.5.32. Canx in 5/32.
G-EBSM	Avro 504K	-	H9859	. 7.27	WFU on 17.5.29. Canx.
G-EBSN	DH.60X Moth	418		23. 7.27	Crashed at Filton on 6.5.28. Canx.
G-EBSO	DH.60X Moth	419		25. 7.27	Crashed at Brooklands on 28.5.32. Canx.
G-EBSP	DH.60X Moth	420		6. 8.27	Crashed at Woodley on 3.8.33. Canx.
G-EBSQ	DH.60X Moth	421		. 8.27	Crashed at Nairobi, Kenya on 12.3.28. Canx.
G-EBSR	DH.60X Moth	422		11. 8.27	To South Africa as G-UAAO in 8/28. Canx.
G-EBSS	DH.60X Moth	423		2. 8.27	Crashed at Selby Farm near Lympne on 13.10.28. Canx.
G-EBST	DH.60X Moth	427		8. 8.27	To RAF as AX793 in 7/40. Canx 9.7.40.
G-EBSU	DH.60X Moth	428		8. 8.27	To Norway as N-38 but crashed at Calais, France during delivery flight on 19.3.29. Canx 19.3.29.

Regn	Type	c/n	Previous identity	Regn date	Fate or immediate subsequent identity (if known)
G-EBSV	Blackburn L.1A Bluebird II	9803/5		. 8.27	WFU in 12/31. Dismantled at Spikins' Garage, Twickenham in 1932. Canx.
G-EBSW	Blackburn L.1A Bluebird II (Converted to seaplane in 1927, modified back to landplane in 6/30)	9803/6		. 8.27	WFU at Whitchurch on 26.1.34. Canx.
G-EBSX	Blackburn L.1A Bluebird II	9803/7		17. 8.27	To Brazil in 10/27. Canx 11.11.27.
G-EBSY	Blackburn L.1A Bluebird II	9803/8		6.10.27	To Brazil in 10/27. Canx 11.11.27.
G-EBSZ	Blackburn L.1A Bluebird II	9803/9		. 8.27	WFU on 15.3.32. Dismantled in 1936. Canx.
G-EBTA	Blackburn L.1A Bluebird II	9803/10		.10.27	Crashed at Brough in 12/30. Canx.
G-EBTB	Blackburn L.1A Bluebird II	9803/11		. .28	Crashed in 3/29. Canx.
G-EBTC	Blackburn L.1A Bluebird II	9803/12		. .28	Crashed in 3/30. Canx.
G-EBTD	DH.60X Moth	430		30. 7.27	To RAF as AW153 in 6/40. Canx 24.6.40.
G-EBTE	Parnall Imp	-		. 8.27	Scrapped in 12/33. Canx.
G-EBTF	Avro 536	-		. 8.27	WFU in 12/30. Canx.
G-EBTG	DH.60X Moth	469		. 8.27	DBR on landing at Maylands on 24.8.38. Canx.
G-EBTH	DH.60X Moth	429		8. 8.27	To 2030 ATC Sqdn at Sheldon, Birmingham in 1940 and burned in 1951. Canx.
G-EBTI	DH.60X Moth	431		10. 8.27	To Johore in 8/34 - but allocated marks VR-SAD were NTU; to Kuala Lumpur as VR-RAB in 1934. Canx in 8/34.
G-EBTJ	DH.60X Moth	432		13. 9.27	To South Africa as G-UAAD in 10/27. Canx.
G-EBTK	SE.5A	-		9. 8.27	Scrapped at Kingswood Knoll in 11/34. Canx.
G-EBTL	DH.61 Giant Moth	325		12. 8.27	To Australia in 3/28 - regd as G-AUTL on 6.3.28. Canx.
G-EBTM	SE.5A	-		20. 8.27	To Germany as D-1634 in 5/29. CofA expired 1.4.34. Canx 16.5.29.
G-EBTN	DH.9J	326		29. 8.27	WFU in 1.4.33. Scrapped. Canx.
G-EBTO	SE.5A	-		17. 8.27	WFU in 12/29. Canx 10/30.
G-EBTP	Avro 594 Avian III	R3/AV/124		17. 8.27	To South Africa as G-UAAN/ZS-AAN in 2/29. Canx.
G-EBTQ	Fokker F.VIIA	5023	H-NAEC	22. 8.27	Missing on transatlantic flight on 31.8.27. Canx.
G-EBTR	Airco DH.9 (Nimbus engine demonstrator)	-	H9369	26. 8.27	To South Africa in 9/30. Canx.
G-EBTS	Fokker F.VIIA	4953	H-NADK	. 9.27	Scrapped in 3/37. Canx.
G-EBTT	DH.53 Humming Bird	111	J7272	5. 9.27	Conversion abandoned. Canx in 7/28.
G-EBTU	Avro 594 Avian III	R3/AV/125		. 9.27	To Australia in 3/28 (arrived 19.3.28) - regd as G-AUTU on 30.5.28. Canx in 5/28.
G-EBTV	DH.60X Moth	436		12. 9.27	Crashed into sea off Skegness on 23.4.33. Canx.
G-EBTW	Avro 587 Cierva C.8R (Originally regd as Cierva C.6D, converted in 1928)	5114	J8068	9. 9.27	Scrapped in 1929. Canx.
G-EBTX	Avro 552A (Originally regd as Avro 586 Cierva C.8V, modified in 1930)	5113	G-EAPR H2323	9. 9.27	To G-ABGO in 11/30. Canx.
G-EBTY	Avro 594 Avian III	R3/AV/128		12. 9.27	To RAF as 2077M in 12/39. Canx 20.12.39.
G-EBTZ	DH.60X Moth	437		12. 9.27	To RAF as AW146 in 6/40. Canx 11.6.40.
G-EBUA	DH.60X Moth	438		12. 9.27	To Denmark as T-DALP in 10/27. Canx.
G-EBUB	Westland Widgeon III	WA.1695		12. 3.28	To Australia in 1928 - regd as G-AUHU on 30.7.28. Canx in 8/28.
G-EBUC	Westland Widgeon III	WA.1696		. .27R	NTU - Sold abroad. Canx.
G-EBUD	Westland Widgeon III	WA.1697		. .27R	NTU - To Australia in 8/28 - regd as G-AUIN on 26.9.28. Canx.
G-EBUE	Westland Widgeon III	WA.1698		. .27R	NTU. Canx.
G-EBUF	DH.60X Moth	441		19. 9.27	To France as F-ANHN in 1/35. Canx.
G-EBUG	Avro 594 Avian III	R3/CN/101		. 9.27	To USA as NC7083 in 6/28. Canx.
G-EBUH	Blackburn L.1A Bluebird II	9803/13		. 9.27	WFU on 26.6.31. Canx.
G-EBUI	Blackburn L.1A Bluebird II	9803/14		30. 9.27	Crashed in 3/29. Canx.
G-EBUJ	DH.60X Moth Seaplane	450		27. 9.27	To Royal Singapore Flying Club in 1929 - regd as VR-SAG in 7/34. Canx 1.9.34.
G-EBUK	DH.60X Moth Seaplane	451		27. 9.27	To Royal Singapore Flying Club in 1929 - regd as VR-SAF in 7/34. Canx 1.9.34.
G-EBUL	DH.60X Moth	443		29. 9.27	WFU at Nairobi, Kenya on 9.10.28. Canx.
G-EBUM	Airco DH.9C	"8370"	O-BATA (RAF)	29. 9.27	To India as VT-AAK in 1/28. Canx.
G-EBUN	Airco DH.9C	-	O-BELG F1223	29. 9.27	To India as VT-AAL in 1/28. Canx.
G-EBUO	DH.60X Moth	452		29. 9.27	To Southern Rhodesia as VP-YAB in 8/30. Canx.
G-EBUP	Short S.5 Singapore I	S.677	N179	6.10.27	Restored as RAF as N179 in 10/28. Canx.
G-EBUQ	Not allocated.				
G-EBUR	DH.60X Moth	446		18.10.27	Crashed at Detling on 20.7.30. Canx.
G-EBUS	DH.60X Moth	444	NC9706 G-EBUS	19.10.27	Crashed at Fareham on 27.7.39. Canx 5.11.45.
G-EBUT	Atlantic Model 4 Universal (Regd as a Fokker F.XI Universal)	422	VP-KAB G-EBUT/NC3199	19.10.27	To Australia in 1935 - regd as VH-UTO on 9.6.35. Canx in 12/35.
G-EBUU	DH.60X Moth	471		27.10.27	Crashed at Renfrew on 1.5.28. Canx.
G-EBUV	DH.60X Moth Seaplane	474		3.11.27	Crashed in Grand Bahamas in 8/28. Canx.
G-EBUW	DH.60X Moth	475		3.11.27	Fatal crash when it dived into the ground at Odsey, Cambs on 18.5.29. Canx.
G-EBUX	DH.60X Moth	476		3.11.27	Crashed at Brooklands on 22.3.31. Canx.
G-EBUY	Avro 504R Gosport	R3/CN/100		3.11.27	To RAF as J9175 in 1/29. Canx.
G-EBUZ	DH.60X Moth	478		.11.27	To India as VT-AEE in 2/34. Canx.
G-EBVA	Avro 594 Avian IIIA	R3/CN/104		.11.27	DBF at Brooklands on 24.10.36. Canx.
G-EBVB	SE.5A	-		12.11.27	CofA expired 14.4.34. Scrapped at Hendon in 1934. Canx.
G-EBVC	DH.60X Moth	483		16.11.27	Crashed at Woodley on 14.6.30. Canx.
G-EBVD	DH.60 Moth (Cirrus II)	247	J8031	30.11.27	WFU in 7/39. Scrapped at Coulsdon, Surrey in 1949. Canx.
G-EBVE	Avro 548	-		.11.27	DBR at Brooklands in 11/28. Canx.
G-EBVF	Henderson HSF.1	HSF.1		.11.27	Scrapped in 1930. Canx.
G-EBVG	Short S.8 Calcutta	S.712	(N214)	.11.27	Capsized in storm at Mirabella, Crete on 28.12.36. Canx.

Regn	Type	c/n	Previous identity	Regn date	Fate or immediate subsequent identity (if known)
G-EBVH	Short S.8/2 Calcutta	S.713	(N215)	.11.27	WFU at Hamble on 29.9.37. Broken up in 1937. Canx.
G-EBVI	Avro 594 Avian III	R3/CN/107		.12.27	Crashed at Stevenage on 1.6.34. Canx.
G-EBVJ	DH.60X Moth	501		3.12.27	To Southern Rhodesia as VP-YAE in 10/30. Canx.
G-EBVK	DH.60X Moth	467		13.12.27	Crashed at Broxbourne on 6.7.37. Canx.
G-EBVL	Avro 504K	-		.12.27	WFU on 13.3.37. Scrapped in 1939. Canx.
G-EBVM	Vickers 147 Valiant (Originally regd as Type 131)	1		15.12.27	To Chilean AF. Canx 12.12.28.
G-EBVN	DH.60 Genet Moth	-		. .27R	NTU. Canx.
G-EBVO	Blackburn F.2 Lincock I	9906		. 1.28	Crashed at Cleveland, Ohio on 28.8.31. Canx.
G-EBVP	Blackburn F.1 Turcock I	9725		6. 1.28	DBF after hitting a tree during speed trials at Martlesham Heath on 13.2.28. Canx.
G-EBVQ	Not allocated.				
G-EBVR	Bristol 89A Trainer	7234		11. 1.28	W/o on 14.1.30. Canx.
G-EBVS	Airco DH.6	4443	(ex)	. 1.28	WFU on 26.4.29. Scrapped in 4/29. Canx.
G-EBVT	DH.60X Moth	537		16. 1.28	Crashed at Lenzie, near Glasgow on 10.2.29. Canx.
G-EBVU	Avro 594 Avian III	R3/CN/111		. 1.28	Crashed near Elizabethville, Congo on 18.10.28. Canx 12/28.
G-EBVV	DH.75 Hawk Moth	327		18. 1.28	No CofA issued. Scrapped in 1930. Canx.
G-EBVW	Avro 504K	-		. 1.28	Dismantled at Hooton in 12/31. Canx.
G-EBVX	DH.60X Moth	538		23. 1.28	Crashed on the beach of the Bay of Sollum, Egypt on 17.5.28. Canx.
G-EBVY	Avro 504N	R3/CN/126		. 1.28	Crashed at Tooting, London on 30.1.35. Canx.
G-EBVZ	Avro 594 Avian III	R3/CN/112		. 1.28	Crashed at Scarcliffe, Derby on 19.5.34. Canx.
G-EBWA	DH.60X Moth	539		23. 1.28	Crashed near Buxton, Derbyshire on 11.10.34. Canx.
G-EBWB	Blackburn T.3A Velos	9593/1		26. 1.28	To scrap yard in York Road, Leeds in 12/33, was still present in 1939. Canx.
G-EBWC	DH.60X Moth	553		2. 3.28	Collided with hangar at Lympne on 7.7.28. Was to have been re-regd G-EBZN. Canx.
G-EBWD	DH.60X Moth	552		2. 3.28	(The Shuttleworth Trust)
G-EBWE	Blackburn L.1B Bluebird III (Originally regd as L.1A Bluebird II with 9803/15)	629/15		. 2.28	Crashed at Nivelles, Belgium on 8.9.31. Canx.
G-EBWF	Avro 504K	-		. 2.28	Scrapped at Hornchurch in 12/32. Canx.
G-EBWG	Airco DH.6	-	B2791	6. 2.28	WFU in 4/31. Burned c.1940. Canx.
G-EBWH	Avro 548	-		7. 2.28	DBR at Canvey Island, Essex on 22.7.28. Canx.
G-EBWI	DH.60X Moth	557		15. 2.28	WFU in 5/36 after crash. Canx.
G-EBWJ	Avro 548	-		. 2.28	WFU on 4.5.32. Scrapped in 1932. Canx.
G-EBWK	Avro 594 Avian III	R3/CN/114		7. 3.28	WFU on 18.12.40 & sold as spares. Canx.
G-EBWL	DH.60X Moth	556		2. 3.28	Crashed at Hanworth on 16.7.31. Canx in 12/31.
G-EBWM	Avro 608 Hawk	5125		29. 2.28	NTU - Completed as Avro 627 Mailplane regd G-ABTM with c/n 502 in 1931. Canx.
G-EBWN	Bristol 89A Trainer (Assembled by Renfrew School of Flying)	R.58		1. 3.28	WFU on 30.7.29. Canx.
G-EBWO	Avro 504K	-		. 3.28	Destroyed in gales at Caversham Bridge, Reading on 1.4.29. Canx.
G-EBWP	Avro 594 Avian III	R3/CN/113		7. 3.28	To South Africa as G-UAAR in 7/28. Canx.
G-EBWQ	Not allocated.				
G-EBWR	Avro 594 Avian III	R3/CN/116		. 3.28	To Argentina in 12/30. Canx.
G-EBWS	DH.60X Moth	558		7. 3.28	Sold Abroad in 1/29 (possibly to Spain). Canx.
G-EBWT	DH.60X Moth	590		10. 3.28	Crashed at Nazeing, Essex on 24.3.34. Canx.
G-EBWU	Avro 594 Avian IV	R3/CN/117		. 3.28	WFU in 8/44, to National Studios, Elstree as stage property. Canx.
G-EBWV	DH.60G Moth	566		28. 3.28	Lost at sea 18.10.28, left St.John's Newfoundland on Atlantic flight on 17.10.28. Canx.
G-EBWW	Avro 594 Avian III	R3/CN/118		7. 3.28	To India as VT-AAW 3/29. Canx 20.3.29.
G-EBWX	DH.60X Moth	583		10. 3.28	WFU on 16.4.31. Canx.
G-EBWY	DH.60X Moth	584		10. 3.28	Crashed on 26.6.32. Canx 6.10.32.
G-EBWZ	DH.60X Moth	509		13. 3.28	Crashed at Addlestone, Surrey on 18.1.30. Canx.
G-EBXA	Avro 504K	-		. 3.28	WFU on 18.12.33. Canx in 12/33.
G-EBXB	DH.60X Moth	592		22. 3.28	To Argentina in 4/28. Canx.
G-EBXC	SE.5A	1347		29. 3.28	To Germany as D-1635 in 5/29. Canx 16.5.29.
G-EBXD	Avro 594 Avian IIIA	R3/CN/121		. 3.28	Crashed near Weybridge on 2.8.37. Canx in 12/37.
G-EBXE	Avro 594 Avian IIIA	R3/CN/123		. 3.28	DBF at Brooklands on 24.10.36. Canx.
G-EBXF	DH.60X Moth	609		31. 3.28	Sold Abroad in 12/34. Canx.
G-EBXG	DH.60X Moth	615		4. 4.28	Crashed at Chilwell, Notts. on 3.11.34. Canx.
G-EBXH	Supermarine Seagull III	-	N9653	3. 4.28	Scrapped in 1930. Canx in 1/37.
G-EBXI	Supermarine Seagull III	-	N9654	3. 4.28	Not converted. To spares use. Canx 15.6.28.
G-EBXJ	Avro 594 Avian IIIA	R3/CN/133		. 4.28	To Sweden as SE-AEM in 10/35. Canx.
G-EBXK	Westland IV	WA.1771		. 4.28	WFU on 3.5.36. Canx.
G-EBXL	SE.5A	-		17. 4.28	To Germany as D-1632 in 5/29. Canx 16.5.29.
G-EBXM	DH.53 Humming Bird	113	J7325	19. 4.28	WFU at Brooklands in 8/31. Rebuilt by College of Engineering in 1936. Canx.
G-EBXN	DH.53 Humming Bird	110	J7271	. 4.28	DBF in hangar fire at Hooton Park Racecourse on 8.7.40. Canx.
G-EBXO	Avro 594 Avian IIIA	R3/CN/124		. 5.28	CofA expired 6.2.35 & WFU. Canx 12/35.
G-EBXP	DH.60X Moth	626		7. 5.28	To Canada as G-CAXP in 7/28. Canx in 11/28.
G-EBXQ	Not allocated.				
G-EBXR	Airco DH.9	-	H9276	24. 4.28	To Australia in 11/28 - regd as G-AUJA on 8.11.28. Canx.
G-EBXS	DH.60X Moth	593		24. 4.28	Crashed at Tadcaster on 7.6.36. Canx.
G-EBXT	DH.60X Moth	548		. 5.28	To RAF as AW157 in 6/40. Canx 28.6.40.
G-EBXU(1)	DH.60X Moth Seaplane	627		2. 5.28	Crashed near Sao Paulo, Brazil in 1930. Canx in 12/31.
G-EBXU(2)	DH.60X Moth (Rebuilt from components .96)	"627"		31.12.92	
G-EBXV	Avro 504K	-		. 5.28	CofA expired 22.3.33 & WFU. Canx in 4/37.
G-EBXW	DH.60X Moth	594		2. 5.28	To Portugal as C-PAAB in 8/29. Canx.
G-EBXX	Avro 594 Avian IIIA	R3/CN/233		. 5.28	WFU on 29.3.34. Canx in 12/34.

Regn	Type	c/n	Previous identity	Regn date	Fate or immediate subsequent identity (if known)
G-EBXY	Avro 594 Avian IIIA	R3/CN/234		. 5.28	To RAF as 2078M in 12/39. Canx 20.12.39.
G-EBXZ	Avro 594 Avian IIIA	R3/CN/235		11. 5.28	To Australia in 6/28 - regd as G-AUHX on 31.7.28. Canx.
G-EBYA	Avro 594 Avian IIIA	R3/CN/134		. 5.28	WFU on 4.7.29. Canx in 4/31.
G-EBYB	Avro 504K	-		. 5.28	WFU on 2.10.31. Dismantled in 2/33. Canx in 2/35.
G-EBYC	Hawker Heron (First Hawker metal aircraft)(Originally regd with c/n 1A)	1B	J6989	15. 5.28	Collided with a car at Hendon on 20.7.28 before start of King's Cup Race. Canx 1/30.
G-EBYD	DH.60X Moth	672		17. 5.28	Broke up in mid-air and crashed 3 miles from Stag Lane on 3.8.28. Canx.
G-EBYE	Avro 504K	-		. 5.28	Crashed at Brixton, London on 2.2.31. Canx.
G-EBYF	Armstrong Whitworth Atlas I	AW.346		23. 5.28	WFU in 11/32. Rebuilt as G-ACAI with new c/n 830. Canx.
G-EBYG	DH.60X Moth	337		29. 5.28	DBF in African bush in 4/30. Canx in 3/33.
G-EBYH	DH.60X Moth	338		29. 5.28	Crashed at Theydon Bois, Essex on 25.5.37. Canx.
G-EBYI	Fokker F.VIIB/3m	5063	H-NAEK	30. 5.28	DBR near Mongala, Sudan in 7/29. Canx.
G-EBYJ	DH.60X Moth	647		4. 6.28	Crashed near Lyons, France on 25.9.29. Canx.
G-EBYK	DH.60G Gipsy Moth	825		. 6.28	Crashed at Arborfield, Berks on 18.7.31. Canx.
G-EBYL	Bristol 89A Trainer	7265		4. 6.28	WFU on 3.10.33. Canx in 12/34.
G-EBYM	Avro 594 Avian IIIA	R3/CN/151		11. 6.28	To Spain as M-CAAE in 7/28. Canx.
G-EBYN	Avro 594 Avian IIIA	R3/CN/152		11. 6.28	To Spain as M-CDDD in 7/28. Canx.
G-EBYO	Avro 594 Avian IIIA	R3/CN/153		. 6.28	Crashed at St.Lythans, Cardiff on 13.12.31. Canx.
G-EBYP	Avro 594 Avian IIIA	R3/CN/154		. 6.28	Crashed at Ashford, Kent on 18.8.32. Canx 1/37.
G-EBYQ	Not allocated.				
G-EBYR	Avro 594 Avian IIIA	R3/CN/155		. 6.28	To Australia - regd as G-AUJY on 24.1.29. Canx in 1930.
G-EBYS	DH.60G Gipsy Moth	829		23. 7.28	To South Africa as ZS-ABO in 11/29. Canx.
G-EBYT	Bristol 83E	7266		15. 6.28	Scrapped in 12/30. Canx.
G-EBYU	Simmonds Spartan	1		23. 6.28	Crashed near Bury St.Edmunds on 10.3.29. Canx.
G-EBYV	DH.60G Gipsy Moth (Originally regd as DH.60X Moth Seaplane, modified to landplane in 1928, converted to DH.60G in 1931)	648	EI-AAG G-EBYV	23. 6.28	Crashed at Medomsley, Durham on 30.6.36. Canx.
G-EBYW	Avro 504K	-		. 6.28	WFU on 11.6.35. Canx in 3/38.
	Note: The fate given above is as quoted, but this aircraft was, in fact, shipped out to Australia sometime late in 1934, by Major E.G.Clark and was never registered there, although an application to have it registered was made on 16.1.35. The aircraft encountered down-draft and force-landed in an apple orchard at The Summit, Stanthorpe, Queensland, Australia on 30.1.35 and was w/o.				
G-EBYX	Vickers 166 Vellore I (Originally regd as Type 134)	1	J8906	31. 7.28	W/o after it pancaked on trees at Cape Don on the Cobourg Peninsula, approx. 100 miles northeast of Darwin, Australia on 18.5.29. Canx.
	Note: It is alleged that parts from "the Vickers Vellore which crashed at Cape Don", along with components from another two aircraft, were used in the construction of the "Fremantle Monoplane", also known as the "Evans Monoplane" built between 1930 and 1935 but was condemned, being scrapped a few years later having never been registered.				
G-EBYY	Avro 617 Cierva C.8L Mk.II	-		21. 6.28	On display Musee de l'Air et de l'Espace, Le Bourget, Paris in 1/95. Canx.
G-EBYZ	DH.60G Gipsy Moth	801		. 6.28	Crashed near Cambridge on 20.9.32. Canx.
G-EBZA	Avro 504K	-		. 6.28	WFU in 12/31. Canx.
G-EBZB	Avro 504K	-	H2262	. 6.28	WFU in 10/33. Canx.
G-EBZC	DH.60X Moth	678		3. 7.28	To RAF as AW158 in 6/40. Canx 28.6.40.
G-EBZD	Avro 594 Avian IIIA	R3/CN/161		. 7.28	Crashed at Wallington on 2.4.31. Canx.
G-EBZE	DH.60X Moth	643		6. 7.28	Crashed prior to 4/33. Canx.
G-EBZF	DH.60X Moth	644		6. 7.28	To Spain as M-CAAK in 12/29. Canx.
G-EBZG	DH.60X Moth	676		6. 7.28	WFU at Abu Sueir, Egypt on 28.2.37. Canx.
G-EBZH	DH.60X Moth	679		9. 7.28	To Germany as D-2298 in 7/32. Canx.
G-EBZI	DH.60X Moth	650		6. 7.28	Crashed near Witney on 12.8.37. Canx.
G-EBZJ	Fokker F.VIIB/3m	5087	H-NAEL	4. 7.28	Lost over the sea on 4.9.29. Canx as WFU 15.9.30.
G-EBZK	Bristol Type 109	7268	R-2 G-EBZK	4. 7.28	Scrapped in 1931. Canx in 12/31.
G-EBZL	DH.60X Moth	682		9. 7.28	To RAF as AW159 in 6/40. Canx 28.6.40.
G-EBZM	Avro 594A Avian IIIA	R3/CN/160		. 7.28	On loan to Manchester Museum of Science & Industry. (Fitted with parts from G-ABEE) (On display 3/96)
G-EBZN(1)	DH.60X Moth	553	G-EBWC	9. 7.28	NTU - W/o at Lympne on 7.7.28 still as G-EBWC. Canx.
G-EBZN(2)	DH.60G Moth	608	VP-NAB VP-YAA/ZS-AAP/G-UAAP	28.10.88	(On rebuild from some original components)
G-EBZO	DH.60X Moth	683		14. 7.28	Crashed at Auchterarder on 18.7.29. Canx.
G-EBZP	DH.60X Moth	681		14. 7.28	DBF at Witney on 27.10.36. Canx.
G-EBZQ	Not allocated.				
G-EBZR	DH.60G Gipsy Moth	844		. 7.28	To Southern Rhodesia as VP-YAM in 6/33. Canx.
G-EBZS	DH.60X Moth	684		23. 7.28	Crashed near Radlett on 18.7.29. Canx.
G-EBZT	DH.60X Moth	685		23. 7.28	To Denmark as OY-DUD in 5/31. Canx.
G-EBZU	DH.60X Moth	686		23. 7.28	Crashed at Irlam, Lancs on 9.10.32. Canx.
G-EBZV	Junkers F.13fe	2024		12. 7.28	To Sweden as SE-AFW in 4/37. Canx.
G-EBZW	DH.60X Moth	687		23. 7.28	Crashed at Mousehold on 19.5.32. Canx.
G-EBZX	DH.60X Moth	649		26. 7.28	To Polish AF as "6" in 8/28. Canx 31.8.28.
G-EBZY	DH.60X Moth	806		28. 7.28	To New Zealand as ZK-ABV in 2/33. Canx.
G-EBZZ	DH.60X Moth	691		1. 8.28	Crashed at Stansted Abbots, Essex on 23.6.34. Canx 12/34.

SPECIAL MARKS - Used for the Director of Civil Aviation

Regn	Type	c/n	Previous identity	Regn date	Fate or immediate subsequent identity (if known)
G-EDCA(1)	DH.60 Moth (75hp Genet I)	379	J8818	13.10.27	Restored to RAF as J8818 in 2/28. Canx.
G-EDCA(2)	DH.60X Moth	529	J9122	22. 2.28	CofA expired 18.4.30 & WFU. To RAF in 4/30. Canx.

SECTION 4 - SECOND AND CURRENT SEQUENTIAL UK REGISTER - G-AAAA ONWARDS

Regn	Type	c/n	Previous identity	Regn date	Fate or immediate subsequent identity (if known)
G-AAAA	DH.60G Gipsy Moth	805		30. 7.28	To RAF as X5038 in 11/39. Canx.
G-AAAB	Supermarine Solent (Nanok)	1244	99 Danish Navy	7. 8.28	WFU on 17.7.31. Scrapped in 1934. Canx.
G-AAAC	DH.60X Moth	694		10. 8.28	To RAF as DG587 in 1/41. Canx 25.1.41.
G-AAAD	DH.60X Moth	696		15. 8.28	Canx in 2/34.
G-AAAE	DH.60G Gipsy Moth	826		31. 8.28	Sold in USA as NC9707 in 1929. Canx.
G-AAAF	Avro 504K	-		. 8.28	WFU in 17.5.36. Canx.
G-AAAG	DH.60X Moth	697		. 8.28	Crashed in sea off Spithead on 7.11.34. Canx.
G-AAAH	DH.60G Moth	804		30. 8.28	Canx in 12/31. (On display at South Kensington, London)
	(A full-size reproduction aircraft is also displayed at the Gatwick Hilton Hotel and is allocated BAPC.168)				
G-AAAI	DH.60G Gipsy Moth	817		30. 8.28	To Egypt as SU-ABK in 8/33. Canx.
G-AAAJ	DH.60G Gipsy Moth	803		31. 8.28	To South Africa as ZS-ABN in 8/29. Canx.
G-AAAK	DH.60G Gipsy Moth	807		31. 8.28	Sold abroad in 1/30. Canx.
G-AAAL	DH.60G Gipsy Moth	809		30. 8.28	Crashed on take-off from Lea, IoW on 21.8.39. Canx.
G-AAAM	DH.60G Gipsy Moth	814		31. 8.28	To USA as NC9704 in 10/28. Canx.
G-AAAN	DH.61 Giant Moth	331		. 8.28	To Australia in 1/32 - regd as VH-UQJ on 25.2.32. Canx.
G-AAAO	DH.60G Gipsy Moth	808		31. 8.28	To RAF as X5019 in 11/39. Canx 1.11.39.
G-AAAP	Avro 594 Avian IIIA	R3/CN/169		23. 8.28	To USA as NX6663 in 9/28. Canx.
G-AAAR	DH.60M Moth	339		30. 8.28	To Canada as G-CAVX in 11/28. Canx.
G-AAAS	DH.60G Gipsy Moth Seaplane	810		31. 8.28	Sold abroad in 2/37. Canx.
G-AAAT	Avro 594 Avian IV	R3/CN/172		. 8.28	Crashed at Cheltenham on 21.9.35. Canx.
G-AAAU	Avro 594 Avian IIIA	R3/CN/177		29. 8.28	NTU. Canx.
G-AAAV	DH.60G Gipsy Moth	815		30. 8.28	To RAF as BK826 in 8/40. Canx 31.8.40.
G-AAAW	Blackburn T.3 Velos	1440/1		30. 8.28	WFU on 22.1.34. Broken up at Old Warden Aerodrome in 1935. Canx.
G-AAAX	Blackburn T.3 Velos	1440/2		30. 8.28	CofA expired 10.5.33. To scrap yard in York Road, Leeds. Still present in 1939. Canx.
G-AAAY	Blackburn T.3 Velos	1440/3		30. 8.28	CofA expired 31.3.33. Scrapped at Bentley in 1933. Canx.
G-AAAZ	Blackburn T.3 Velos	1440/4		30. 8.28	CofA expired 15.3.32. Scrapped in 1932. Canx.
"G-AAB"	DH.82A Tiger Moth	"84971"	ZS-NWJ (ZS-BUY)	----	Based on quoted c/n original p.i. would be T6671 which was exported to the SAAF. Noted painted end 1998 for a film.
G-AABA	DH.60X Moth	700		6. 9.28	Crashed in North Sea on 9.3.29. The wreckage was picked up by the German steamer "Margot" in the North Sea, some 60 miles west of Terschelling. Canx.
G-AABB	Blackburn L.1B Bluebird III	1450/1		. 9.28R	NTU - To New Zealand as ZK-AAQ in 8/29. Canx.
G-AABC	Blackburn L.1B Bluebird III	1450/2		. 9.28R	NTU - To Spain in 8/29. Canx.
G-AABD	Blackburn L.1B Bluebird III	1450/3		. 3.29	Crashed at Bridlington on 26.10.30. Canx.
G-AABE	Blackburn L.1B Bluebird III	1450/4		. 3.29	Crashed near Lichfield on 22.3.36. Canx.
G-AABF	Blackburn L.1B Bluebird III	1450/5		. 3.29	Crashed at Hatfield on 18.6.31. Canx.
G-AABG	Blackburn L.1B Bluebird III Seaplane	1450/6		17. 5.29	Not completed. Canx.
G-AABH	DH.60X Moth	699		11. 9.28	To RAF as V4738 in 1/40. Canx 16.2.40.
G-AABI	DH.60G Gipsy Moth	845		. 9.28	To RAF as DG658 in 2/41. Canx 26.2.41.
G-AABJ	DH.60G Gipsy Moth	827		14. 9.28	To RAF as X5034 in 11/39. Canx 11.11.39.
G-AABK	DH.60G Gipsy Moth (Converted to Gipsy III)	811		14. 9.28	To RAF as X5031 in 11/39. Canx 3.11.39.
G-AABL	DH.60X Moth	702		14. 9.28	Crashed at Kingsbury, Middlesex on 15.10.30. Canx.
G-AABM	DH.60G Gipsy Moth	816		17. 9.28	To Shanghai in 12/28. Canx 19.12.28.
G-AABN	DH.60G Gipsy Moth	802		14. 9.28	Crashed at Stanmore, Middlesex on 3.6.31. Canx.
G-AABO	DH.60G Gipsy Moth	865		14. 9.28	Sold abroad in 4/32. Canx.
G-AABP	Avro 612 Cierva C.17 Mk.I	-		14. 9.28	Broken up in 1931. Canx.
G-AABR	Avro 616 Avian IV	R3/CN/178	K-1	14. 9.28	To B-Class marks as K-1 in 9/30. Canx.
G-AABS	Avro 616 Avian IV	R3/CN/179	K-2	14. 9.28	To B-Class marks as K-2 in 5/31. Canx.
G-AABT	Avro 616 Avian IV	R3/CN/180	K-3	14. 9.28	To B-Class marks as K-3 in 10/30. Canx.
G-AABU	Avro 594 Avian IIIA	R3/CN/181		14. 9.28	NTU. Canx.
G-AABV	Blackburn L.1C Bluebird IV	1430/1		14. 9.28	Crashed at Hedon, Hull on 6.3.34. Canx.
G-AABW	Avro 548	G516		17. 9.28	Crashed near Welling, Kent on 19.9.29. Canx.
G-AABX	Avro 594 Avian IV	R3/CN/183		25. 9.28	To RAF as 2080M in 2/40. Canx 17.2.40.
G-AABY	Fairey IIIF	F.1129		. 9.28	To Australia (arrived in 10/34) - regd as VH-UTT on 13.3.35. Canx in 4/35.
G-AABZ	Avro 594 Avian IIIA	R3/CN/173		25. 9.28	To Tanganyika as VR-TAG in 6/32. Canx.
G-AACA	Avro 504K	-		28. 9.28	WFU on 26.6.33. Canx.
"G-AACA"	Avro 504K Static Replica	-	BAPC.177 "G1381"	--	(On display 10/96 Brooklands)
G-AACB	Blackburn L.1C Bluebird IV	1730/1		11.10.28	To Norway as N-40 in 10/29. Canx.
G-AACC	Blackburn L.1C Bluebird IV	1730/2		.10.28	WFU on 16.10.37. DBF in hangar fire at Hooton on 11.7.40. Canx.
G-AACD	DH.60M Moth	340		16.10.28	Crashed at Fen Ditton, Cambridge on 24.6.37. (Rebuilt but stored .89)
G-AACE	Avro 594 Avian IV	R3/CN/236		.10.28	To RAF as 2082M in 1/40. Canx 4.1.40.
G-AACF	Avro 594 Avian IV	R3/CN/237		.10.28	Was captured in Guernsey by Germans in 3/41. Canx.
G-AACG	Avro 504K	-	F8811	19.10.28	WFU in Guernsey on 11.11.29. Canx.
G-AACH	Armstrong Whitworth Argosy II	AW.362		24.10.28	Crashed & burned out at Croydon Airport on 22.4.31. Canx.
G-AACI	Armstrong Whitworth Argosy II	AW.363		24.10.28	Fatal crash & burned out near Dixmunde, Belgium on 28.3.33. Canx.
G-AACJ	Armstrong Whitworth Argosy II	AW.364		24.10.28	WFU in 12/36. Canx.
G-AACK	DH.60G Gipsy Moth	831		27.10.28	To Spain as M-CDAA in 12/28. Canx.
G-AACL	DH.60G Gipsy Moth	887		7.11.28	Lost in English Channel on 1.3.31. Canx.

Regn	Type	c/n	Previous identity	Regn date	Fate or immediate subsequent identity (if known)
G-AACM	DH.60G Gipsy Moth	991	SP-ACT G-AACM	.11.28	Crashed at South Farnborough on 7.3.33. Canx.
G-AACN	Handley Page HP.39 Gugnunc	1	K1908 G-AACN	2.11.28	(On display at Wroughton)
G-AACO	DH.60G Gipsy Moth	874		2.11.28	Crashed at Malton, Yorks on 24.6.34. Canx.
G-AACP	Airco DH.9	-	H9248	7.11.28	Dismantled at Hanworth in 1938. Canx.
G-AACR	Airco DH.9	-	H9324	7.11.28	WFU on 21.6.33. Canx in 9/33..
G-AACS	Airco DH.9	-	H9327	7.11.28	NTU - Conversion abandoned. Possibly to G-AADU. Canx.
G-AACT	Avro 504R Gosport	R3/CN/238		9.11.28	W/o in 1/30. Canx.
G-AACU	DH.60M Moth	342		14.11.28	To RAF as AV995 in 6/40. Canx 9.6.40.
G-AACV	Avro 616 Avian IVM	R3/CN/239	J9783 G-AACV	.11.28	Sold abroad in 12/34. Canx.
G-AACW	Avro 504K	-		19.11.28	Crashed near Gatwick on 25.1.31. Canx.
G-AACX	Avro 504K	-		19.11.28	W/o in 4/29. Canx.
G-AACY	DH.60G Gipsy Moth	841		.21.11.28	To RAF as AV991 in 5/40. Canx 27.5.40.
G-AACZ	DH.60G Gipsy Moth	1021		29.11.28	CofA lapsed on 12.7.39 & WFU. Scrapped in 1942. Canx.
G-AADA	DH.60G Gipsy Moth	1019		28.11.28	Crashed at Walberton, Sussex on 17.2.36. Canx.
G-AADB	DH.60 Moth (Cirrus II)	372	BuA.7564	30.11.28	Crashed near Eastleigh on 29.6.37. Canx.
G-AADC	DH.60G Gipsy Moth Coupe	917		29.11.28	Crashed at Chipping Warden on 14.4.30. Canx.
G-AADD	DH.60G Gipsy Moth	1017		6.11.28	To Canada as CF-ANY in 7/30. Canx.
G-AADE	Westland Widgeon III	WA.1778		3.12.28	Crashed at Beaulieu, Hants on 10.7.32. Canx.
G-AADF	Avro 594 Avian IV	R3/CN/204		.12.28	To RAF as 2074M in 2/40. Canx 28.2.40.
G-AADG	Monocoupe 70	154	NC6751	6.12.28	WFU on 29.4.39. Broken up at Gatwick in 1947. Canx.
G-AADH	DH.60G Gipsy Moth	889		17.12.28	To RAF as X5028 in 11/39. Canx 3.11.39.
G-AADI	DH.60G Gipsy Moth	970		.12.28	Crashed at Middlesbrough on 10.2.35. Canx.
G-AADJ	DH.60X Moth Seaplane	920		19.12.28	To Royal Singapore Flying Club in 1929 - regd as VR-SAH in 9/34. Canx 1.9.34.
G-AADK	DH.60X Moth Seaplane	921		19.12.28	To Royal Singapore Flying Club in 1929 - regd as VR-SAE in 9/34. Canx.
G-AADL	Avro 594 Avian IV	R3/CN/182		20.12.28	WFU on 10.8.38. Canx.
G-AADM	Avro 618 Ten	241		17.12.28	To Australia in 8/29 - regd as VH-UMF on 13.11.29. Canx.
G-AADN	Short S.8/1 Calcutta	S.748		17.12.28	Forced landed off Spezia, Italy and sank whilst under tow on 26.10.29. Canx.
G-AADO	Gloster A.S.31 Survey Biplane	1		31.12.28	To South African AF as 250 in 3/33. Canx.
G-AADP	DH.60G Gipsy Moth	1022		21. 1.29	Hit clubhouse and crashed at Abridge Aerodrome, Essex on 8.9.34. Canx.
G-AADR	Moth Corporation DH.60GM Moth	138	NC939M	2. 6.86	
G-AADS	DH.60G Gipsy Moth	1028		21. 1.29	To South Africa as ZS-ABF in 11/29. Canx.
G-AADT	Avro 548	-	F8767	. 1.29	WFU on 20.10.31. Canx in 12/31.
G-AADU	Airco DH.9 (Possibly ex.G-AACS)	-		. 1.29	Canx in 1/38. Scrapped between 1939 and 1945.
G-AADV	DH.60G Gipsy Moth (Amphibian)	998		21. 1.29	Capsized off Folkestone on 24.12.29. Canx.
G-AADW	DH.60G Gipsy Moth	988		21. 1.29	Crashed in Greece on 23.3.31. Canx.
G-AADX	DH.60G Gipsy Moth Coupé	1002		21. 1.29	Crashed at Dagenham, Essex on 2.2.31. Canx.
G-AADY	Avro 504K	61370	J8373	. 1.29	CofA expired 21.3.31. Canx as WFU in 12/31.
G-AADZ(1)	Fokker F.VIIb-3m	5105	PH-ADP	. 2.29	Badly damaged taxying at Dum Dum Airport, Calcutta on 10.6.29. Canx.
G-AADZ(2)	Fokker F.VIIb-3m	5195	PH-AGP	. 1.30	To Switzerland as CH-165 in 2/31. Canx.
G-AAEA	DH.60G Gipsy Moth	1030		4. 2.29	To Ireland as EI-AAR in 5/33. Canx.
G-AAEB	DH.60G Gipsy Moth	1003		. 2.29	Sold abroad in 10/32. Canx.
G-AAEC	Avro 594 Avian IV	R3/CN/223		. 2.29	To RAF as 2076M in 12/39. Canx 20.12.39.
G-AAED	Avro 504K	-		28. 1.29	Crashed at Stag Lane on 4.7.29. Canx.
G-AAEE	DH.60G Gipsy Moth Coupé	981		. 2.29	WFU on 25.1.41 & donated to Sheffield ATC. Canx.
G-AAEF	DH.60G Gipsy Moth	1059		4. 2.29	Sold abroad in 2/37. Canx.
G-AAEG	DH.60G Gipsy Moth	1027	D-EUPI D-1599/G-AAEG	4. 2.29	(On rebuild .94) (Provenance unconfirmed)
G-AAEH	DH.60G Gipsy Moth	1083		4. 2.29	To RAF as X5025 in 11/39. Canx 3.11.39.
G-AAEI	DH.60G Gipsy Moth	993		4. 2.29	Crashed near Stag Lane on 1.11.30. Canx.
G-AAEJ	Armstrong Whitworth Argosy II	AW.400		. 2.29	WFU on 8.5.35. Dismantled at Croydon in 1935. Canx.
G-AAEK	Ryan B.1 Brougham	167	7719(USA)	. 2.29	Not certified. WFU in 1933. Broken up in 10/33. Canx.
G-AAEL	DH.60G Gipsy Moth	994		. 2.29	Crashed at Armthorpe on 1.8.32. Canx.
G-AAEM	Avro 504K	-		. 2.29	Crashed at Somerton, near Cowes on 16.8.29. Canx.
G-AAEN	DH.60G Gipsy Moth	990		27. 2.29	Crashed on landing near Blandford on 16.11.31. Canx.
G-AAEO	DH.60G Gipsy Moth	1079		26. 2.29	To Northern Rhodesia as VP-RAF in 7/36. Canx.
G-AAEP	DH.60G Gipsy Moth	1096		. 2.29	To Brazil as P-BABM in 2/30. Canx.
G-AAER	DH.60G Gipsy Moth	1097		26. 2.29	To Germany as D-1612 in 4/29. Canx.
G-AAES	Avro 504K	-		21. 2.29	WFU on 28.3.30. Burnt at Hooton Park in 1935. Canx.
G-AAET	DH.60G Gipsy Moth	1080		. 2.29	To RAF as AW126 in 6/40. Canx 18.6.40.
G-AAEU	DH.60G Gipsy Moth	916		21. 2.29	Crashed near Charing, Kent on 2.9.34. Canx.
G-AAEV	DH.61 Giant Moth	335		. 2.29	Crashed at Broken Hill, Northern Rhodesia on 19.1.30. Canx.
G-AAEW	DH.60G Gipsy Moth	1043		26. 2.29	To RAF on 2.6.40, crashed near Netheravon in 11/41. Canx.
G-AAEX	DH.60G Gipsy Moth	997		. 2.29	To RAF as X5021 in 11/39. Canx 1.11.39.
G-AAEY	HSF.2 Gadfly II	1		27. 2.29	WFU on 15.9.30. Scrapped in 6/34. Canx. (Wheels and axle reportedly used in construction of Pou-du-Ciel G-ADSE)
G-AAEZ	Avro 504K	-		. 2.29	Crashed at Burscough, near Ormskirk on 11.3.34. Canx.
G-AAFA	DH.80A Puss Moth	2038		23. 5.30	To Sweden as SE-AFH in 10/36. Canx.
G-AAFB	DH.60M Moth	1336		12. 3.29	To Germany as D-1600 in 3/29. Canx.
G-AAFC	DH.60G Gipsy Moth	1037		25. 3.29	To France as F-ALHI in 1/32. Canx.
G-AAFD	Westland Widgeon IIIA	WA.1782		. 3.29	Crashed into the English Channel off Cap d'Alprecht, France on 6.6.33. Canx.
G-AAFE	Avro 504K	-		. 3.29	WFU on 30.5.30. Canx.
G-AAFF	DH.60M Moth	1338		15. 3.29	To Yugoslavia as UN-PDH in 4/29. Canx.

Regn	Type	c/n	Previous identity	Regn date	Fate or immediate subsequent identity (if known)
G-AAFG	Bristol 110A	7348	R-4	12. 3.29	Damaged on landing at Filton in 2/30. Canx.
G-AAFH	Parnall Elf I	1		. 3.29	DBR in force landing at Herongate, Rickmansworth on 20.3.34. Canx.
G-AAFI	DH.60G Gipsy Moth	1095		. 3.29	To RAF as DG579 in 1/41. Canx 13.1.41.
G-AAFJ	Avro 504K	-	J8375	. 3.29	WFU on 29.5.31. Canx.
G-AAFK	DH.60G Gipsy Moth	1040		. 3.29	To India as VT-AEZ in 2/33. Canx.
G-AAFL	DH.60G Gipsy Moth	1005		. 3.29	Ditched into the sea off Bournemouth on 11.8.29. Canx.
G-AAFM	DH.60G Gipsy Moth	1006		. 3.29	Destroyed by bombs at Gatwick in 1940. Canx 14.5.42.
G-AAFN	Westland Widgeon IIIA	WA.1779		20. 3.29	W/o in 1/30. Canx.
G-AAFO	DH.60G Gipsy Moth	989		21. 3.29	To RAF as X5053 in 11/39. Canx 17.11.39.
G-AAFP	Simmonds Spartan	11		20. 3.29	DBR in 3/30. Canx.
G-AAFR	Simmonds Spartan	12		. 3.29	Crashed into Hamble River, near Bursledon on 27.3.30. Canx.
G-AAFS	DH.60G Gipsy Moth	1012		. 3.29	To RAF on 18.2.41 with marks DG589 allotted but NTU, became 2569M in 1941. Canx.
G-AAFT	Avro 504K	-	J8379	25. 3.29	WFU in 3/31. Canx.
G-AAFU	Klemm L.25-1	129	D-1565	23. 3.29	DBF in hangar fire at Maylands on 6.2.40. Canx.
G-AAFV	Klemm L.25	136		26. 3.29	WFU on 16.2.30. Scrapped in 1931. Canx.
G-AAFW	DH.75A Hawk Moth	343		11. 4.29	To Canada as G-CYVD in 11/29 / CF-CCA 7/30. Canx.
G-AAFX	DH.75A Hawk Moth	348		11. 4.29	To Australia in 1930 - regd as VH-UNW on 24.4.30. Canx in 12/30.
G-AAFY	DH.60G Gipsy Moth	999		5. 4.29	To South Africa as ZS-AKV in 10/37. Canx.
G-AAFZ	Short S.7 Mussel II	S.750	M-1 G-AAFZ	6. 4.29	Scrapped in 1/34. Canx.
G-AAGA	DH.60G Gipsy Moth	1058		8. 4.29	To RAF as BK834 in 9/40. Canx 3.9.40.
G-AAGB	Avro 504K	-		. 4.29	Crashed at Telscombe, near Newhaven in 11.7.34. Canx.
G-AAGC	Koolhoven FK.41	4102		16. 4.29	To South Africa as ZS-ADX in 1930. Canx.
G-AAGD	DH.60G Gipsy Moth	1008		11. 4.29	To Germany as D-1628 in 5/29. Canx.
G-AAGE	DH.60M Moth	1332		. 4.29	To Germany in 2/34. Canx.
G-AAGF	Bristol 76 Jupiter	7350		11. 4.29	WFU on 19.6.33. Canx.
G-AAGG	Avro 504K	-		. 4.29	CofA expired 4.5.33 & WFU. Canx in 12/35.
G-AAGH	Westland Widgeon IIIA	WA.1866		15. 4.29	DBF after colliding with a hangar whilst running amok on start-up at Merryfield Aerodrome, Somerset on 27.7.48. Canx.
G-AAGI	DH.60G Gipsy Moth	1010		16. 4.29	To South Africa in 11/32. Canx.
G-AAGJ	Avro 620 Cierva C.17 Autogiro Mk.II	5129		19. 4.29	To instructional airframe at Hamble in 1931. To G-ADEO in 1935. Canx.
G-AAGK	Avro 620 Cierva C.17 Autogiro Mk.II	5130		19. 4.29	Sold abroad in 1/30. Canx.
G-AAGL	Avro 620 Cierva C.17 Autogiro Mk.II	5131		19. 4.29	Crashed at Haldon Aerodrome, Teignmouth on 21.9.29. Canx.
G-AAGM	DH.60G Gipsy Moth	1009	HB-OLA CH-346/A-63/G-AAGM	22. 4.29	Broken up on 19.12.40. Canx.
G-AAGN	Simmonds Spartan	14		22. 4.29	Crashed at Ratcliffe Aerodrome, Leicester on 6.9.30. Canx. Rear fuselage and tail unit used in building Blake Bluetit (BAPC.37)/G-BXIY.
G-AAGO	Simmonds Spartan	29		. 4.29	WFU on 4.8.33. Canx.
G-AAGP	Avro 594 Avian IV	R3/CN/304		23. 4.29	To Spain as M-CFAF/EC-FAF in 1/30. Canx.
G-AAGR	Avro 594 Avian IV	R3/CN/232		23. 4.29	To RAF as 2071M in 1/40. Canx 18.1.40.
G-AAGS	DH.60G Gipsy Moth	1042		. 4.29	Crashed at Barmouth on 30.8.33. Canx.
G-AAGT	DH.60G Gipsy Moth Coupe	1052		. 4.29	WFU on 27.3.37. Canx.
G-AAGU	Junkers F.13ge	2047		. 4.29	To South Africa as ZS-AEN in 12/32. Canx.
G-AAGV	Simmonds Spartan	27		. 4.29	W/o in 9/30. Rebuilt as G-ABXO with same c/n. Canx.
G-AAGW	Westland Wessex (Originally regd as a Westland IV)	WA.1867		. 4.29	WFU at Watchfield on 16.8.40. Canx.
G-AAGX	Handley Page HP.42E (Originally c/n E.1)	HP.42/1		30. 4.29	Crashed in the Gulf of Oman on 1.3.40. Canx.
G-AAGY	Simmonds Spartan	15		. 4.29	WFU on 15.3.39. Scrapped at Redhill in 8/47. Canx.
G-AAGZ	DH.60G Gipsy Moth	1007		. 5.29	To South Africa as ZS-ABW in 6/30. Canx.
G-AAHA	Simmonds Spartan	23		6. 5.29	To South Africa as ZS-ADC in 3/32. Canx.
G-AAHB	DH.60M Moth	1352		10. 5.29	Crashed at Hambrook, Bristol on 23.9.29. Rebuilt as G-AASR with new c/n 1441. Canx.
G-AAHC	Armstrong Whitworth AW.14 Starling	AW.277	J8027	10. 5.29	Last flown on 14.3.31. Canx in 12/31.
G-AAHD	Avro 594 Avian IV	R3/CN/318		. 5.29	To Sweden as SE-ADT in 8/33. Canx.
G-AAHE	Avro 594 Avian IV	R3/CN/319		. 5.29	WFU on 1.9.39. Scrapped between 1939 and 1945. Canx.
G-AAHF	DH.60G Gipsy Moth	1051		21. 5.29	Crashed at Croydon (possibly on 11.1.30). Canx in 3/30.
G-AAHG	DH.60G Gipsy Moth	1085		21. 5.29	To RAF as DG580/2547M in 1/41. Canx 13.1.41.
G-AAHH	Bristol 105A Bulldog II	7331		15. 5.29	WFU on 14.6.30. Scrapped at Filton in 1935. Canx.
G-AAHI	DH.60G Moth (Gipsy I) (Rebuild from components left over from G-AAWO rebuild)	1082		. 5.29	
G-AAHJ	Avro 616 Avian IVM	R3/CN/316		. 5.29	Crashed Newmarket Road, Cambridge on 13.6.31. Canx.
G-AAHK	Avro 594 Avian IV	R3/CN/317		. 5.29	WFU on 3.1.39. Canx in 12/46.
G-AAHL	Klemm L.25-I	144	D-1589	. 5.29	Crashed at Whitchurch on 27.2.32. Canx.
G-AAHM	Cierva C.19 Autogiro Mk.IV (Originally regd as Mk.I)	5132		21. 5.29	Crashed at White City Stadium, London on 29.9.32. Canx.
G-AAHN	Avro 594 Avian IV	R3/CN/320		22. 5.29	To RAF as 2079M in 12/39. Canx 20.12.39.
G-AAHO	DH.60G Gipsy Moth	1056		24. 5.29	To India as VT-AGZ in 1/35. Canx.
G-AAHP	DH.60G Gipsy Moth	1067		. 5.29	WFU on 21.6.36. Canx.
G-AAHR	DH.60G Gipsy Moth	1068		. 5.29	Stalled off a loop and spun in at Sunbury on 1.10.33. Canx in 12/34.
G-AAHS	DH.60G Gipsy Moth	1011		31. 5.29	To Argentina as R155 in 2/30. Canx.
G-AAHT	DH.60G Gipsy Moth	1089		. 5.29	To India as VT-ABN in 12/29. Canx.
G-AAHU	DH.60G Gipsy Moth	1099		27. 5.29	To RAF as BK827 as 8/40. Canx 26.8.40.

Regn	Type	c/n	Previous identity	Regn date	Fate or immediate subsequent identity (if known)
G-AAHV	Simmonds Spartan	44		. 5.29	WFU on 16.7.38. Spares use at Denham in 7/59. Canx.
G-AAHW	Klemm L.25-1a	152	D-ELFK G-AAHW	. 5.29	To Germany as D-EFTE(3) in 7/98. Canx 2.6.98.
G-AAHX	DH.60G Gipsy Moth	1062		. 5.29	Fatal crash near Purley Way, Waddon, near Croydon on 29.6.30. Canx.
G-AAHY	DH.60M Moth	1362	HB-AFI G-AAHY	. 5.29	
G-AAHZ	DH.80 Puss Moth	396		30. 5.29	NTU - No CofA issued. To 'B'-class marks E-1 and converted to engine test bed in 1930/31 at Stag Lane. Canx in 1/32.
G-AAIA	DH.60G Gipsy Moth	1090		1. 6.29	To RAF as X5037 in 11/39. Canx 12.11.39.
G-AAIB	DH.60G Gipsy Moth	1110		. 6.29	Crashed at Renfrew on 15.5.30. Canx.
G-AAIC	DH.60G Gipsy Moth	1100		. 6.29	To Holland as PH-AJM(2) in 4/34. Canx.
G-AAID	ABC Robin	1		6. 6.29	WFU on 26.6.31. Scrapped at Brooklands in 1932. Canx.
G-AAIE	DH.60G Gipsy Moth	1094		. 6.29	To RAF as AW160 in 6/40. Canx 28.6.40.
G-AAIF	DH.60M Moth	1363		. 6.29	To India as VT-ADH in 1/32. Canx.
G-AAIG	Hendy 281 Hobo	1		7. 6.29	WFU on 17.8.38. Destroyed by bombs at Lympne in 8/40. Canx.
G-AAIH	Weymann/Lepère/Cierva C.18	18		5. 6.29	To USA in 1929. Canx.
G-AAII	Southern Martlet	2/SH200		. 6.29	To Ireland as EI-ABG in 6/36. Canx.
G-AAIJ	Avro 594 Avian IV	R3/CN/325		11. 6.29	To Spain as M-CIAA in 6/29. Canx.
G-AAIK	Avro 594 Avian IV	R3/CN/326		11. 6.29	To Spain as M-CAIA in 6/29. Canx.
G-AAIL	Civilian C.A.C.1 Coupe	0.1		8. 6.29	To Ireland as EI-AAV in 5/35. Canx.
G-AAIM	DH.60G Gipsy Moth	1153		. 6.29	CofA lapsed on 24.9.39. Canx in 12/46.
G-AAIN	Parnall Elf II	2 & J.6		11. 6.29	(The Shuttleworth Trust)
G-AAIO	Parnall Elf II	3 & J.5		. 6.29	Crashed at Daglingworth, near Cirencester on 13.1.34. Canx.
G-AAIP	Saunders-Roe A.17 Cutty Sark	A.17/1		. 6.29	WFU on 9.5.34. Scrapped in 1935. Canx.
G-AAIR	Blackburn L.1C Bluebird IV	SB.202	(G-AAJD)	. 6.29	Crashed at Agades, Nigeria on 17.4.35. Canx.
G-AAIS	Hinkler Ibis	1		11. 6.29	Scrapped at Lee-on-Solent in 1959. Canx.
G-AAIT	Boulton Paul P.41 Phoenix II (Originally regd as Phoenix I)	P.41/1		11. 6.29	Canx in 11/35.
G-AAIU	DH.60G Gipsy Moth	1055		. 6.29	Crashed at Walmore Common, Glos on 24.1.39. Canx.
G-AAIV	DH.60G Gipsy Moth	1104		. 6.29	To RAF as AW127 in 6/40. Canx 23.6.40.
G-AAIW	DH.60G Gipsy Moth	1081		. 6.29	To RAF as X5030 in 12/39. Canx 15.12.39.
G-AAIX	Avro 594 Avian IV	R3/CN/330		. 6.29	WFU on 5.11.36. Scrapped at Southend in 1940. Canx.
G-AAIY	Armstrong Whitworth Wolf	AW.428		14. 6.29	WFU in 1931 - To Instructional Airframe at Hamble. Canx.
G-AAIZ	Supermarine Seagull IV	-	N9605	. 6.29	WFU on 9.7.30 & burnt at Brooklands in 12/33. Canx.
G-AAJA	DH.60G Gipsy Moth	1106		. 6.29	Crashed at Gosport on 2.5.36. Canx.
G-AAJB	Simmonds Spartan	19		19. 6.29	WFU on 24.6.30. Forward bulkhead used in building Blake Bluetit (BAPC.37)/G-BXIY. Canx.
G-AAJC	Blackburn L.1C Bluebird IV	SB.207		18. 6.29	To Southern Rhodesia as VP-YAI in 6/32. Canx.
G-AAJD	Blackburn L.1C Bluebird IV	SB.202		18. 6.29	NTU - To G-AAIR in 6/29. Canx 1/30.
G-AAJE	Blackburn L.1C Bluebird IV	SB.203		18. 6.29	NTU - To G-AAOB in 10/29. Canx.
G-AAJF	Westland Widgeon IIIA	WA.1776		. 6.29	Crashed at Bad Reichenball, Germany on 17.5.31. Canx.
G-AAJG	DH.60G Gipsy Moth	1130		. 6.29	WFU in 1.7.37. Canx.
G-AAJH	DH.66 Hercules	393		19. 6.29	To South African AF as 260 in 4/34. Canx.
G-AAJI(1)	Westland IV	WA.1897	P-1 (VP-KAD)	19. 6.29	NTU - To G-ABAJ in 5/30. Canx.
G-AAJI(2)	Avro 619 Five	288		. .29R	NTU - To Kenya as VP-KAE in 1929. Canx.
G-AAJJ	DH.60G Gipsy Moth	1105	EI-ABA G-AAJJ	. 6.29	To RAF as BD164 in 8/40. Canx 8.8.40.
G-AAJK	Clarke Cheetah (Convertable Monoplane/Biplane)	CC.1 (Built using the lower wings of Halton Mayfly G-EBOO and some DH.53 components)		. 6.29	WFU on 3.7.34. Scrapped in 1937. Canx.
G-AAJL	DH.60G Gipsy Moth	1054		. 6.29	To RAF as DG657 in 2/41. Canx 18.2.41.
G-AAJM	DH.60G Gipsy Moth	1091		. 6.29	To India as VT-AFH in 3/34. Canx.
G-AAJN	DH.60G Gipsy Moth	1049		. 6.29	Crashed near Brooklands on 3.10.36. Canx.
G-AAJO	DH.60G Gipsy Moth	1101		. 6.29	To New Zealand as ZK-ADT. Canx 12/34.
G-AAJP	DH.60G Gipsy Moth	1123		. 6.29	To RAF as W7947 in 2/40. Canx 3.2.40.
G-AAJR	DH.60G Gipsy Moth	1050		. 6.29	Lost in Bristol Channel on 20.9.31. Canx.
G-AAJS	DH.60G Gipsy Moth	1139		. 7.29	To RAF as X5055 in 1/40. Canx 12.1.40.
G-AAJT	DH.60G Gipsy Moth	1084		4. 7.29	To USA as NC947M in 1/30. Canx.
G-AAJU	DH.60G Gipsy Moth	1103		5. 7.29	Destroyed in mid-air collision with DH.60G Gipsy Moth G-AAKL over Stag Lane 29.7.29. Canx.
G-AAJV	DH.60G Gipsy Moth	1108		. 7.29	To Kenya as VP-KAL in 4/31. Canx.
G-AAJW	DH.60G Gipsy Moth	1135		. 7.29	To RAF as X5040 in 11/39. Canx 12.11.40.
G-AAJX	DH.60M Moth	1374		16. 7.29	Crashed at Hyde, Manchester on 14.5.31. Canx.
G-AAJY	Short S.11 Valetta	S.747	(N242)	18. 7.29	WFU at Martlesham Heath on 16.7.32. Canx.
G-AAJZ	DH.60G Gipsy Moth	1134		. 7.29	To RAF as DG586 in 1/41. Canx 25.1.41.
G-AAKA	Avro 616 Avian IVM	R3/CN/324		. 7.29	Crashed en-route Moulmein-Rangoon on 12.8.32. Canx in 12/32.
G-AAKB	DH.60M Moth	1365		2. 8.29	To France as F-AJOA in 1/30. Canx.
G-AAKC	DH.60G Gipsy Moth	1149		. 7.29	To South Africa as ZS-AKJ in 3/37. Canx.
G-AAKD	DH.60G Gipsy Moth	1150		. 7.29	Sold abroad in 8/34. Canx.
G-AAKE	DH.60G Gipsy Moth	1151		. 7.29	WFU at Barton-in-the-Clay, Beds. on 15.7.39. Canx.
G-AAKF	DH.60G Gipsy Moth	1127		25. 7.29	To New Zealand as ZK-ABM in 11/29. Canx.
G-AAKG	DH.60G Gipsy Moth	1126		. 7.29	Sold abroad in 12/34. Canx.
G-AAKH	Hawker Hawfinch	-	J8776	24. 7.29	NTU - Remained with RAF as J8776. Canx 7/29.
G-AAKI	DH.60G Gipsy Moth	1152		. 7.29	To RAF as AX789 in 7/40. Canx 14.7.40.
G-AAKJ	DH.60X Moth	1162		. 7.29	Crashed at Southall, Middlesex on 18.10.35. Canx.
G-AAKK	DH.60G Gipsy Moth	1093		23. 7.29	To New Zealand as (ZK-ACK)/ZK-AKK in 3/31. Canx.
G-AAKL	DH.60G Gipsy Moth	1029		23. 7.29R	NTU. Destroyed over Stag Lane in mid-air collision with DH.60G Gipsy Moth G-AAJU on 29.7.29 before registration and certification details were completed. Canx.
G-AAKM	DH.60G Gipsy Moth	1142	EI-ABB G-AAKM	. 7.29	To India as VT-APU in 6/41. Canx.

Regn	Type	c/n	Previous identity	Regn date	Fate or immediate subsequent identity (if known)
G-AAKN	DH.60G Gipsy Moth	1136		27. 7.29	Crashed in Langstone Harbour, Portsmouth on 15.10.36. Canx.
G-AAKO	DH.60G Gipsy Moth	1045		. 7.29	To RAF as X5035 in 11/39. Canx 4.11.39.
G-AAKP	DH.60M Moth (Cirrus III)	1394		30. 7.29	To RAF as AW148 in 6/40. Canx 24.6.40.
G-AAKR	DH.60M Moth (Cirrus III)	1395		30. 7.29	Crashed near Lympne on 18.9.31. Canx.
G-AAKS	DH.60M Moth (Cirrus III)	1396		30. 7.29	Crashed at Hessenthal am Main, Germany on 24.3.30. Canx.
G-AAKT	Avro 621 Tutor	321		26. 7.29	To RAF in 1930, possibly as K2893. Canx.
G-AAKU	DH.60G Gipsy Moth	1092		. 7.29	To RAF as X5047 in 11/39. Canx 15.11.39.
G-AAKV	DH.60M Moth	1369		. 7.29	To India as VT-AEX in 1/34. Canx.
G-AAKW	DH.60M Moth	1380	D-EKIV G-AAKW	. 7.29	To Switzerland as HB-AFU in 4/37. Canx.
G-AAKX	DH.60G Gipsy Moth	1154		. 8.29	Lost in Thames Estuary on 1.6.33. Canx.
G-AAKY	Avro 620 Cierva C.19 Autogiro Mk.II	5133		9. 8.29	To USA as NC311V in 12/29. Canx.
G-AAKZ	Avro 620 Cierva C.19 Autogiro Mk.II	5134		9. 8.29	Crashed at Sherburn-in-Elmet, Yorks on 31.5.31. Canx.
G-AALA	Avro 620 Cierva C.19 Autogiro Mk.III (Originally regd as Mk.II)	5135		9. 8.29	Crashed in 5/32. Canx.
G-AALB	Westland Widgeon IIIA	WA.1783		9. 8.29	To Canada as CF-AIQ in 5/30. Canx.
G-AALC	Fokker F.III	1558	T-DOFF	17. 8.29	Crashed near Croydon Aerodrome on 11.9.29. Canx.
G-AALD	DH.60G Gipsy Moth	1137		16. 8.29	To Kenya as VP-KAG in 1/30. Canx.
G-AALE	DH.60G Gipsy Moth	1140		. 8.29	Crashed Isle of Islay on 4.9.32. Canx.
G-AALF	DH.60M Moth	1402		. 8.29	To Denmark as OY-DEG in 12/31. Canx.
G-AALG	DH.60G Gipsy Moth (Originally built as DH.60M Moth)	1411	HA-AAB G-AALG	. 8.29	To RAF as X5104 in 1/40. Canx 10.1.40.
G-AALH	Blackburn F.2A Lincock	2050/1		. 8.29	CofA expired 27.3.35. Broken up in 1935. Canx.
G-AALI	Koolhoven FK.41	4103		. 8.29	To Australia in 1929 - regd as VH-ULX on 17.9.29. Canx in 10/29.
G-AALJ	DH.60G Gipsy Moth	1087		. 8.29	Crashed near West Malling on 8.12.34. Canx.
G-AALK	DH.60G Gipsy Moth Coupe	1174		. 8.29	Crashed near Hawick on 3.4.37. Canx.
G-AALL	Hawker Tomtit	41H/26478 & 9		. 8.29	Scrapped in 1937. Canx.
G-AALM	DH.60G Gipsy Moth	1160		. 8.29	Crashed near Poix, France on 21.4.30. Canx.
G-AALN	DH.60G Gipsy Moth	1047	F-AJJV G-AALN	. 8.29	To RAF as X5041 in 11/39. Canx 12.11.39.
G-AALO	Bristol 89A Trainer	7351		29. 8.29	WFU on 9.12.33. Canx.
G-AALP	Surrey Flying Services AL-1	AL-1		29. 8.29	(Stored 1/98)
G-AALR	DH.60G Gipsy Moth	1159		. 9.29	To Brazil as PP-TAD in 12/31. Canx.
G-AALS	DH.60M Moth	1409		. 9.29	To Nyasaland as VP-NAA in 9/34. Canx.
G-AALT	DH.60G Gipsy Moth	1184		. 9.29	WFU on 6.2.38. Canx.
G-AALU	DH.60G Gipsy Moth	1178		6. 9.29	Crashed at Witley on 10.3.30. Canx.
G-AALV	DH.60G Gipsy Moth	1179		. 9.29	To RAF as X5032 in 11/39. Canx 11.11.39.
G-AALW	DH.60G Gipsy Moth	1180		. 9.29	To RAF as X5027 in 11/39. Canx 3.11.39.
G-AALX	DH.60M Moth	1410		. 9.29	Crashed off Shoreham Harbour on 24.9.37. Canx.
G-AALY	DH.60G Gipsy Moth	1175		9. 9.29	To France as F-AJKM in 11/29. Canx.
G-AALZ	DH.60G Gipsy Moth	1177		6. 9.29	Crashed Velika Gorica, near Sisak, Yugoslavia on 22.9.30. Canx.
G-AAMA	Simmonds Spartan	17		29. 5.29	WFU in 12/32. Canx.
G-AAMB	Simmonds Spartan	21		29. 5.29	Ditched in sea off Southend on 26.2.39. Canx.
G-AAMC	Simmonds Spartan	20		29. 5.29	Crashed at Hanworth on 28.7.29. Canx.
G-AAMD	Simmonds Spartan	24		19. 7.29	NTU - To G-ABHH in 1930. Canx.
G-AAME	Simmonds Spartan	26		19. 7.29	Crashed near Hamble on 26.3.30. Rebuilt as G-AAML(2). Canx.
G-AAMF	Simmonds Spartan	33		19. 7.29	Crashed at Weston on 28.7.29. Not delivered. Canx.
G-AAMG	Simmonds Spartan	34		19. 7.29	Crashed near Ratcliffe, Leicester on 6.9.30. Canx.
G-AAMH	Simmonds Spartan	22		. 8.29	Crashed in forest, 12 miles from Kutahya, Turkey on 15.10.33. Canx.
G-AAMI	Simmonds Spartan	35		2. 8.29	To Norway as N-43 in 4/30. Canx.
G-AAMJ	Simmonds Spartan	36		2. 8.29	NTU - Not delivered. Canx in 12/30.
G-AAMK	Simmonds Spartan	37		2. 8.29	NTU - Not delivered. Canx in 12/30.
G-AAML(1)	Simmonds Spartan	38		. .30	Crashed at Croydon in 6/31. Rebuilt as G-AAML(2) in 1931. Canx.
G-AAML(2)	Simmonds Spartan (Rebuild of c/n 38 with parts from G-AAME c/n 26)	26	G-AAME	. 7.31	Crashed at Croydon on 3.10.31. Canx.
G-AAMM	DH.60X Moth	1228		. .30	DBF at Witney on 27.10.36. Canx.
G-AAMN	DH.60X Moth	1229		26. 3.30	CofA lapsed on 23.4.32. Canx.
G-AAMO	DH.60X Moth	1281		2. 7.30	Crashed at Port Meadow, Oxford on 4.9.32. Canx.
G-AAMP	DH.60X Moth	1279		. 7.30	To Brough ATC Sqdn in 1941. Scrapped near Brough in 1950. Canx.
G-AAMR	DH.60X Moth	1280		. 7.30	DBF in hangar fire at Maylands on 6.2.40. Canx.
G-AAMS	DH.60X Moth	1285		. 7.30	To RAF as X5018 in 2/40. Canx 11.11.39.
G-AAMT	DH.60X Moth	1809		16. 9.30	Crashed at Cotgrave, Tollerton on 9.11.30. Canx.
G-AAMU	DH.60X Moth	1826		. .30	WFU on 19.12.40. Scrapped at Hanworth in 11/46. Canx.
G-AAMV	DH.60X Moth	1828		. .30	To RAF as BK844 in 9/40. Canx 10.9.40.
G-AAMW	DH.60X Moth	1831		. .30	WFU in 1.2.40. Canx.
G-AAMX(1)	DH.60X Moth	-		. .29R	NTU - Not built. Canx.
G-AAMX(2)	Moth Corporation DH.60GM Moth	125	NC926M	11. 9.86	Canx as WFU 19.8.95. (On display at RAF Cosford)
G-AAMY(1)	DH.60X Moth	-		. .29R	NTU - Not built. Canx.
G-AAMY(2)	Moth Corporation DH.60GMW Moth	86	N585M NC585M	2. 5.80	
G-AAMZ(1)	DH.60X Moth	-		. .29R	NTU - Not built. Canx.
G-AAMZ(2)	DH.60G Moth	1293	EC-ABX EC-BAU/Spanish AF 30-52/EC-NAN/M-CNAN/MW-134	13. 7.87	To USA as N60MZ in 9/98. Canx 4.9.98.
G-AANA	Desoutter I	D.14		. .29	Crashed near Stansted on 8.4.35. Canx.
G-AANB	Desoutter I	D.15		. .29	To RAF as HM508 in 12/41. Canx 9.12.41.
G-AANC	Desoutter I	D.16		29. 1.30	Crashed at Leith Hill, near Ockley, Surrey 12.9.31. Canx.

Regn	Type	c/n	Previous identity	Regn date	Fate or immediate subsequent identity (if known)
G-AAND	Desoutter I	D.20		4. 3.30	WFU on 28.7.33. Canx.
G-AANE(1)	Desoutter I	D.24		. .30	Crashed at Plaxton, Kent on 5.7.30. Rebuilt as G-AANE(2) in 1930. Canx.
G-AANE(2)	Desoutter I	D.26	(G-AANF)	. .30	Canx in 12/35.
	(Rebuild of G-AANE(1) with parts from (G-AANF))				
G-AANF(1)	Desoutter	-		. .29R	NTU - Not built. Parts used in rebuild of G-AANE c/n D.24 in 1930. Canx.
G-AANF(2)	Moth Corporation DH.60GMW Moth	49	N298M N237K/NC237K	3. 2.87	Badly damaged by fire following forced landing in a field 1 mile southeast of Popham on 8.8.89. Canx as TWFU 19.9.90. (On rebuild 2/91 at Mandeville, New Zealand)
G-AANG(1)	Desoutter	-		. .29R	NTU - Not built. Canx.
G-AANG(2)	Bleriot Type XI (1910 original)	14	(BAPC 3)	29.11.81	The Shuttleworth Trust (No external marks) (On display 5/97 Old Warden)
G-AANH(1)	Desoutter	-		. .29R	NTU - Not built. Canx.
G-AANH(2)	Deperdussin Monoplane (Possibly c/n 143)	43	(BAPC 4)	29.10.81	The Shuttleworth Trust (No external marks) (On display 3/96 Old Warden)
G-AANI(1)	Desoutter	-		. .29R	NTU - Not built. Canx.
G-AANI(2)	Blackburn 1912 Monoplane No.9	725	(BAPC 5)	29.10.81	The Shuttleworth Trust (No external marks)
G-AANJ(1)	Desoutter	-		. .29R	NTU - Not built. Canx.
G-AANJ(2)	Luft-Verkehrs Gesellschaft C.VI		C7198/18	29.10.81	
	(Composite aircraft including	4503	"1594"/C7198/18		
	parts from LVG 1594, captured 1916/17 and was allotted RFC "serial" XG7)				
G-AANK	Desoutter	-		. .29R	NTU - Not built. Canx.
G-AANL(1)	Desoutter	-		. .29R	NTU - Not built. Canx.
G-AANL(2)	DH.60M Moth (Composite rebuild)	1446	OY-DEH R.Danish AF S-357/S-107	26. 6.87	
G-AANM(1)	Desoutter	-		. .29R	NTU - Not built. Canx.
G-AANM(2)	Bristol F2b Fighter (Regd with c/n "67634")	"67626"	BAPC.166	16. 7.87	(Complete but dismantled engineless 2/99 Sandown as D7889)
G-AANN	Desoutter	-		. .29R	NTU - Not built. Canx.
G-AANO(1)	Desoutter	-		. .29R	NTU - Not built. Canx.
G-AANO(2)	Moth Corporation DH.60GMW Moth (Composite rebuild)	165	N590N NC590N	3. 3.88	(On rebuild 11/91)
G-AANP	Desoutter	-		. .29R	NTU - Not built. Canx.
G-AANR	Desoutter	-		. .29R	NTU - Not built. Canx.
G-AANS	Desoutter	-		. .29R	NTU - Not built. Canx.
G-AANT	Desoutter	-		. .29R	NTU - Not built. Canx.
G-AANU	Desoutter	-		. .29R	NTU - Not built. Canx.
G-AANV(1)	Desoutter	-		. .29R	NTU - Not built. Canx.
G-AANV(2)	Morane Saulnier DH.60M Moth	13	HB-OBU CH-349/F-AJNY	8. 3.84	
G-AANW	Desoutter	-		. .29R	NTU - Not built. Canx.
G-AANX	Desoutter	-		. .29R	NTU - Not built. Canx.
G-AANY	Desoutter	-		. .29R	NTU - Not built. Canx.
G-AANZ	Desoutter	-		. .29R	NTU - Not built. Canx.
G-AAOA	Blackburn L.1C Bluebird IV	SB.200		10.10.29	Crashed at Feltham on 6.4.30. Canx.
G-AAOB	Blackburn L.1C Bluebird IV	SB.203	G-AAJE	10.10.29	Broken up at Hanworth in 12/30. Canx.
G-AAOC	Blackburn L.1C Bluebird IV	SB.204		10.10.29	To Spain as EC-UUU in 12/33. Canx.
G-AAOD	Blackburn L.1C Bluebird IV	SB.205		10.10.29	Broken up at Hanworth in 12/30. Canx.
G-AAOE	Blackburn L.1C Bluebird IV	SB.206		10.10.29	Sold abroad in 12/34. Canx.
G-AAOF	Blackburn L.1C Bluebird IV	SB.209		9.12.29	To Iceland as TF-LOA in 1937, NTU & scrapped in 1939. Canx.
G-AAOG	Blackburn L.1C Bluebird IV	SB.213		9.12.29	Crashed at Oulton, near Leeds on 13.4.30. Canx in 12/30.
G-AAOH	Blackburn L.1C Bluebird IV	SB.214		9.12.29	Crashed at Bushey Park on 27.1.31. Canx.
G-AAOI	Blackburn L.1C Bluebird IV	SB.221		4. 2.30	Crashed at Sherburn on 20.1.34. Canx.
G-AAOJ	Blackburn L.1C Bluebird IV	SB.222		4. 2.30	WFU on 6.7.34. Broken up at Gatwick in 3/37. Canx.
G-AAOK(1)	Blackburn L.1C Bluebird IV	-		. .30R	NTU - Not built. Canx.
G-AAOK(2)	Curtiss-Wright Travel Air CW-12Q	12Q-2026	N370N NC370N/NC352M	18.11.81	Badly damaged in gales at Rijeka, Yugoslavia on 21.10.83. (On rebuild 11/98 at Biggin Hill)
G-AAOL	Blackburn L.1C Bluebird IV	-		. .30R	NTU - Not built. Canx.
G-AAOM	Blackburn L.1C Bluebird IV	-		. .30R	NTU - Not built. Canx.
G-AAON	Blackburn L.1C Bluebird IV	-		. .30R	NTU - Not built. Canx.
G-AAOO	Blackburn L.1C Bluebird IV	-		. .30R	NTU - Not built. Canx.
G-AAOP	Blackburn L.1C Bluebird IV	-		. .30R	NTU - Not built. Canx.
G-AAOR(1)	Blackburn L.1C Bluebird IV	-		. .30R	NTU - Not built. Canx.
G-AAOR(2)	DH.60G Moth	1075	EC-AAO	15. 4.85	
	(Original identity uncertain and probably composite)				
G-AAOS	Blackburn L.1C Bluebird IV	-		. .30R	NTU - Not built. Canx.
G-AAOT	Blackburn L.1C Bluebird IV	-		. .30R	NTU - Not built. Canx.
G-AAOU	Blackburn L.1C Bluebird IV	-		. .30R	NTU - Not built. Canx.
G-AAOV	Blackburn L.1C Bluebird IV	-		. .30R	NTU - Not built. Canx.
G-AAOW	Blackburn L.1C Bluebird IV	-		. .30R	NTU - Not built. Canx.
G-AAOX	Blackburn L.1C Bluebird IV	-		. .30R	NTU - Not built. Canx.
G-AAOY	Blackburn L.1C Bluebird IV	-		. .30R	NTU - Not built. Canx.
G-AAOZ	Blackburn L.1C Bluebird IV	-		. .30R	NTU - Not built. Canx.
G-AAPA	DH.60X Moth	1164		15. 8.29	Crashed at Hedon, Hull on 17.7.35. Canx.
G-AAPB	DH.60X Moth	1165		15. 8.29	Crashed near Sheffield on 28.3.30. Canx.
G-AAPC	DH.60X Moth	1166		15. 8.29	Crashed at Yeadon on 22.3.36. Canx.
G-AAPD	DH.60X Moth	1167		15. 8.29	Crashed pre-8/30. Canx.
G-AAPE	DH.60X Moth	1168		15. 8.29	Crashed in 1930. Canx.
G-AAPF	DH.60X Moth	1169		15. 8.29	Crashed in 1932. Canx.
G-AAPG	DH.60X Moth	1170		15. 8.29	To RAF as AV996 in 6/40. Canx 3.6.40.
G-AAPH	DH.60X Moth	1171		15. 8.29	To RAF as X5020 in 11/39. Canx 1.11.39.
G-AAPI	DH.60X Moth	1172		15. 8.29	Crashed in 1930. Canx.

Regn	Type	c/n	Previous identity	Regn date	Fate or immediate subsequent identity (if known)
G-AAPJ	DH.60X Moth	1173		15. 8.29	Crashed at Chilworth, Oxon on 16.8.36. Canx.
G-AAPK	Desoutter I	D.1		. .29	WFU on 2.5.40. Canx.
G-AAPL	DH.60X Moth	1198		26. 9.29	Crashed at Waltham, Grimsby on 18.5.32. Canx.
G-AAPM	DH.60X Moth	1199		26. 9.29	Crashed at Tollerton on 23.3.32. Canx.
G-AAPN	DH.60X Moth	1200		26. 9.29	Crashed at Hampton, Middlesex on 6.5.30. Canx.
G-AAPO	DH.60X Moth	1201		26. 9.29	Crashed at Hanworth on 20.2.32. Canx.
G-AAPP	Desoutter I	D.2		. .29	DBR at Cape Town, South Africa on 21.11.31. Canx.
G-AAPR	Desoutter I	D.3		11.11.29	To Belgium as OO-ALF in 6/30. Canx.
G-AAPS	Desoutter I	D.4		.11.29	To RAF as ES946 in 7/41. Canx 14.7.41.
G-AAPT	Desoutter I	D.5		.11.29	WFU on 24.6.38. Scrapped. Canx in 12/46.
G-AAPU	Desoutter I	D.6		.11.29	WFU at Cambridge on 29.7.37. Canx.
G-AAPV	DH.60X Moth	1215		.11.29	Crashed at Truro on 21.4.35. Canx.
G-AAPW	DH.60X Moth	1216		.11.29	To RAF as W7945 in 2/40. Canx 3.2.40.
G-AAPX	Desoutter I	D.8		20.12.29	CofA expired 31.12.30 & WFU. Canx.
G-AAPY	Desoutter I	D.9		.12.29	Crashed at Pinner, Middlesex on 31.10.34. Canx 12/46.
G-AAPZ	Desoutter I	D.25		. .30	(On rebuild at Old Warden)
G-AARA	DH.60G Gipsy Moth	1186		. 9.29	To RAF as X5046 in 11/39. Canx 12.11.39.
G-AARB	DH.60M Moth	1412		. 9.29	DBF in hangar fire at Maylands on 6.2.40. Canx.
G-AARC	DH.60G Gipsy Moth	1187		. 9.29	To RAF as DG584 in 1/41. Canx 25.1.41.
G-AARD	DH.60M Moth	1414		. 9.29	Sold abroad in 1/36. Canx.
	(Rebuilt in 2/31 as a DH.60G with new c/n 1833)				
G-AARE	DH.60G Gipsy Moth	1176		18. 9.29	Crashed on Cross Fell, Penrith on 21.4.36. Canx.
G-AARF	DH.80A Puss Moth	2059	SU-ACN	25. 7.30	To RAF as HK866 in 2/41. Canx 1.12.46 in census.
			VP-KBO/(VP-KBM)/VP-KAT/G-AARF		
G-AARG	Fokker F.III	1561	T-DOFC	. 9.29	WFU on 1.2.30. Canx.
G-AARH	DH.60M Moth	1417		. 9.29	To RAF as AV997 in 6/40. Canx 4.6.40.
G-AARI	DH.60M Moth	1413		. 9.29	Sold abroad in 1/33. Canx.
G-AARJ	Henderson-Glenny HSF.2 Gadfly II	2		17. 9.29	To Canada as CF-AMG in 4/30. Canx.
G-AARK	Henderson-Glenny GH.3 Gadfly III	1		17. 9.29	WFU in 1930. Canx.
G-AARL	DH.60M Moth	1416		. 9.29	To South Africa in 9/31. Canx.
G-AARM	DH.60X Moth	477	C-PAAA	26. 9.29	Crashed in Port Meadow, Oxford on 3.11.29. Canx.
G-AARN	Airco DH.6	3868	(RAF)	24. 9.29	Not converted. Scrapped in 1933. Canx.
G-AARO(1)	Klemm L.25-I	-		. 9.29R	NTU - Canx.
G-AARO(2)	Arrow Sport A2-60	341	N932S	17. 9.79	To USA as N280AS in 6/83. Canx.
			NC932S		
G-AARP	Gloster/GAL Monospar ST.3	SS.1		26. 9.29	WFU on 20.7.32. Scrapped at Hanworth in 1932. Canx.
G-AARR	DH.9J	397		. 9.29	WFU on 25.12.32. Scrapped in 1936. Canx in 1/37.
G-AARS	DH.9J	398		. 9.29	Crashed in a field near Hamble on 9.9.34. Canx.
G-AART	DH.9J	399		. 9.29	WFU on 8.5.33. Scrapped in 1936. Canx in 1/37.
G-AARU	DH.60M Moth	1424		12.10.29	To RAF as X5119 in 11/39. Canx 29.11.39.
G-AARV	Avro 504K	R/R3/SP/312		8.10.29	Crashed at Berksbourne on 2.1.31. Canx.
G-AARW	DH.60G Gipsy Moth	1209		16.10.29	To South Africa in 9/30. Canx.
G-AARX	Comper CLA.7 Swift	CLA.7/1		12.10.29	WFU on 15.4.31. Scrapped in 12/31. Canx.
G-AARY	DH.66 Hercules	703		14.10.29	WFU on 9.2.35. Canx.
G-AARZ	Avro 621 Tutor	322	K-4	29.10.29	Crashed at Vincennes, France on 10.6.34. Canx.
			G-AARZ		
G-AASA	DH.60M Moth	1438		.10.29	To New Zealand as ZK-ACK in 3/31. Canx.
G-AASB	DH.60G Gipsy Moth	1053		.10.29	To Sweden as SE-AFP in 12/36. Canx.
G-AASC	DH.9J	704		1.11.29	Scrapped in 1931. Canx 12/31.
G-AASD	DH.60M Moth	1440		6.11.29	To Iraq as YI-ASD in 3/32. Canx.
G-AASE	Supermarine Air Yacht	1285		.11.29	Crashed into sea near Capri, Italy on 25.1.33. Canx.
G-AASF	DH.60M Moth	1439		.11.29	To India as VT-ADE in 12/31. Canx.
G-AASG	DH.60G Gipsy Moth	1203		.11.29	CofA lapsed on 15.11.30. Canx as destroyed 13.3.39.
G-AASH	Supermarine Southampton II	-	S1235	8.11.29	Restored to RAF as S1235 in 3/30. Canx.
G-AASI	Hawker Tomtit	12		.11.29	WFU on 26.5.39. Scrapped between 1939 and 1945. Canx.
G-AASJ	Short S.8/I Calcutta	S.752		11.11.29	Fatal crash at Alexandria, Egypt on 31.12.35. Canx.
G-AASK	Fairey IIIF	F.1272		12.11.29	WFU on 12.5.31. Canx.
G-AASL	DH.60M Moth	1430		18.11.29	To RAF as X5127 in 12/39. Canx 6.12.39.
G-AASM	DH.60M Moth	1433		.11.29	Crashed at Cheam, Surrey on 22.4.34. Canx.
G-AASN	DH.60G Gipsy Moth Seaplane	839		14.11.29	To Malaya as VR-RAA in 9/34. Canx.
			Sarawak Govt		
G-AASO	Avro 619 Five	383		.11.29	Crashed at Broken Hill, Northern Rhodesia on 18.1.32. Canx.
G-AASP	Avro 618 Ten	384		19.11.29	WFU on 20.11.39. Destroyed at Whitchurch on 3.4.40. Canx.
G-AASR	DH.60M Moth	1441	G-AAHB	.11.29	To RAF as AW110 in 6/40. Canx 3.6.40.
G-AASS	Avro 504K	-	F2540	.11.29	Crashed at Swansea Aerodrome on 1.8.31. Canx.
G-AAST	Avro 504K	-	F9819	26.11.29	WFU on 10.1.31. Canx.
G-AASU	Blackburn L.1C Bluebird IV	SB.208		9.12.29	Crashed at Hendon on 7.6.30. Canx.
G-AASV	Blackburn L.1C Bluebird IV	SB.211		14.12.29	CofA expired 21.1.36 & WFU. Canx at census in 12/37.
G-AASW	Vickers 172 Vellore III	1		5.12.29	To B-Class marks O-4 in 3/32; scrapped in 1934. Canx.
G-AASX	Avro 504K	-		.12.29	WFU on 13.11.30. Canx.
G-AASY	DH.60G Gipsy Moth	1048	EI-ABE	.12.29	To RAF as AW128 in 6/40. Canx 18.6.40.
			G-AASY		
G-AASZ	DH.60G Gipsy Moth	1434		.12.29	To RAF as X5043 in 11/39. Canx 12.11.39.
	(Rebuilt as a DH.60M)				
G-AATA	DH.60M Moth	1460		.12.29	To Egypt as SU-AAF in 9/32. Canx.
G-AATB	DH.60M Moth	1467		.12.29	To India as VT-ABY in 8/31. Canx.
G-AATC	DH.80A Puss Moth	2001		23.12.29	To Australia in 8/30 - regd as VH-UON on 11.8.30. Canx in 12/30.
G-AATD	Klemm L.25-I	163		.12.29	WFU on 26.5.39. Canx.
G-AATE	Blackburn L.1C Bluebird IV	SB.210		31.12.29	Scrapped at Hamsey Green in 12/47. Canx.
G-AATF	Desoutter I	D.19		. 1.30	DBR in accident at Hanworth on 9.5.34. Canx.
G-AATG	Fokker F.VIIb/3m	5206	PH-AGW	4. 1.30	To Italy as I-AAIG in 6/35. Canx.
G-AATH	Junkers A.50 Junior	3512		24. 3.30	To Germany as D-2155 in 2/31. Canx.

Regn	Type	c/n	Previous identity	Regn date	Fate or immediate subsequent identity (if known)
G-AATI	Desoutter I	D.10		14. 1.30	To New Zealand as ZK-ACJ in 12/30. Canx.
G-AATJ	Desoutter I	D.11		17. 1.30	DBR in crash at Shoreham on 2.9.34. Canx 8/45.
G-AATK	Desoutter I	D.12		. 1.30	To RAF as HH980 in 8/41. Canx 31.8.41.
G-AATL	Avro 616 Avian IVM	R3/CN/415		. 1.30	WFU on 12.2.35. Canx.
G-AATM	Blackburn L.1C Bluebird IV	SB.217		4. 2.30	Crashed at Coal Aston on 27.8.32. Canx.
G-AATN	Blackburn L.1C Bluebird IV	SB.218		25. 2.30	To India as VT-ACR in 9/32. Canx.
G-AATO	Blackburn L.1C Bluebird IV	SB.219		4. 2.30	Fatal crash at Broomfield, near Brough on 4.8.32. Canx.
G-AATP	Blackburn L.1C Bluebird IV	SB.220		24. 2.30	Crashed and burned at Sherburn-in-Elmet on 2.5.34. Canx.
G-AATR	Bristol 105 Bulldog III	7397	J9591	13. 1.30	Restored to RAF as J9591 in 1/31. Canx 20.1.31.
G-AATS	Blackburn L.1C Bluebird IV	SB.215		30. 1.30	WFU on 4.5.34. Canx in 12/36.
G-AATT	Fairey IIIF	F.1315		16. 1.30	Crashed at Gweri, Uganda on 10.7.31. Canx.
G-AATU	Avro 621 Tutor	437		20. 1.30	WFU in 10/31. Canx.
G-AATV	Avro 616 Avian IVM	R3/CN/435	SU-AAG G-AATV	. 1.30	To New Zealand as ZK-ADQ in 3/35. Canx.
G-AATW	Desoutter I	D.13		29. 1.30	To Belgium as OO-ALG in 6/30. Canx.
G-AATX	Desoutter I	D.18		. 1.30	Crashed at Edenbridge, Kent on 1.10.32. Canx.
G-AATY	Avro 504K	-		22. 1.30	Crashed at Bridlington on 28.8.33. Remains scrapped at Driffield in 1937. Canx.
G-AATZ	Short S.8/I Calcutta	S.754		. 1.30	Scrapped at Hamble in 1939. Canx.
G-AAUA	Avro 620 Cierva C.19 Mk.IIA	5136		25. 1.30	Sold abroad in 3/31 (possibly to Spain). Canx.
G-AAUB	Vickers 220 Viastra VIII	1		29. 1.30	Broken up at Brooklands in 1933. Canx.
	(Originally regd as Type 160 Viastra I in 1930, then Type 199 Viastra III in 1931)				
G-AAUC	Handley Page HP.42E	42/4		30. 1.30	To RAF as AS981 in 5/40. Canx 29.5.40.
G-AAUD	Handley Page HP.42E	42/3		30. 1.30	DBR in gales at Whitchurch on 19.3.40. Canx.
G-AAUE	Handley Page HP.42E	42/2		30. 1.30	To RAF as AS982 in 5/40. Canx 29.5.40.
G-AAUF	Blackburn L.1C Bluebird IV	SB.223		31. 3.30	DBR at Brough on 16.7.32. Canx.
G-AAUG	Blackburn L.1C Bluebird IV	SB.224		4. 2.30	Crashed at High Post on 20.3.38. Sold as scrap. Canx.
G-AAUH	DH.60M Moth	1462		. 2.30	DBF in hangar fire at Gravesend on 3.8.37. Canx.
G-AAUI	DH.60M Moth	1495		. 2.30	Canx in 1/33.
G-AAUJ	Avro 504K	KAS.1		7. 2.30	Fatal crash when it span into the ground at Harrogate on 5.10.32. Canx.
G-AAUK	Avro 504K	KAS.2		7. 2.30	Crashed near Epsom Racecourse on 3.6.31. Canx.
G-AAUL	Avro 504K	KAS.3		7. 2.30	Crashed Dovercourt Aerodrome, Harwich on 2.8.31. Canx.
G-AAUM	Blackburn T.3 Velos	9762/1		7. 2.30	CofA expired 22.1.34. Scrapped in 1934. Canx.
	(Fitted with metal floats for trials)				
G-AAUN	Avro 616 Avian IVM	R3/CN/438		11. 2.30	To Tanganyika as VR-TAA in 9/31. Canx.
G-AAUO	Robinson Redwing I	RA.1		11. 2.30	Crashed at Shoreham on 11.3.33. Canx.
G-AAUP	Klemm L.25-Ia	145		19. 2.30	(Stored 6/95 Denford Manor, Hungerford)
G-AAUR	DH.60G Gipsy Moth	1245		5. 3.30	Rebuilt as G-ACCY in 2/33. Canx.
G-AAUS	DH.60M Moth	1477		. 3.30	To Australia (departed UK on 3.8.32) - regd as VH-UQT on 21.12.32. Canx 3/33.
G-AAUT	Blackburn L.1C Bluebird IV	SB.225		8. 5.30	Sank off Felixstowe on 12.1.31. Canx.
	(Converted to Floatplane in 12/30)				
G-AAUU	Blackburn L.1C Bluebird IV	SB.226		4. 4.30	Sold abroad in 6/35. Canx.
G-AAUV	Blackburn L.1C Bluebird IV	SB.227		5. 5.30	WFU on 1.4.32. Canx in 12/32.
G-AAUW	Blackburn L.1C Bluebird IV	SB.228		20. 5.30	WFU on 13.7.32. Canx in 12/32.
G-AAUX	Blackburn L.1C Bluebird IV	SB.229		26. 5.30	Crashed at Waltham, Grimsby on 29.4.37. Canx.
G-AAUY	Blackburn L.1C Bluebird IV	SB.230		18. 6.30	Sold abroad in 7/30. Canx.
G-AAUZ	DH.75A Hawk Moth	705		. 3.30	Sold abroad in 12/38. Canx.
G-AAVA	DH.80A Puss Moth	2002		5. 6.30	To Holland as PH-ATI in 5/38. Canx in 6/38.
G-AAVB	DH.80A Puss Moth	2003	SU-AAB G-AAVB	. 6.30	Canx 12.5.41. To RAF as DR755 in 5/41, NTU - crashed on landing at Kenley on 4.9.41 still as G-AAVB.
G-AAVC	DH.60G Gipsy Moth (Amphibian)	1238		7. 3.30	Crashed in 11/30. Canx.
G-AAVD	Southern Martlet	201		. 3.30	WFU on 11.8.39. Derelict at Turnhouse in 1944. Canx.
G-AAVE	DH.60M Moth	1493		. 3.30	To India as VT-ANS in 1/41. Canx.
G-AAVF	Blackburn L.1C Bluebird IV	SB.231		24. 6.30	Crashed in 9/36. Canx.
G-AAVG	Blackburn L.1C Bluebird IV	SB.232		24. 6.30	To Australia in 1933 - regd as VH-UQZ on 31.5.33. Canx in 3/36.
G-AAVH	Blackburn L.1C Bluebird IV	SB.233		5. 8.30	WFU on 2.10.33. Canx in 12/34.
G-AAVI	Blackburn L.1C Bluebird IV	SB.234		29. 8.30	To India as VT-ADI on 13.4.32. Canx.
G-AAVJ(1)	Blackburn L.1C Bluebird IV	SB.235		. 8.30R	NTU - (Possibly crated for shipment to Japan) Canx.
G-AAVJ(2)	DH.60GM Gipsy Moth	157	N573N NC573N	17. 8.83	Restored in USA as N573N 8/94. Canx 1.3.94.
G-AAVK	Blackburn L.1C Bluebird IV	SB.236		. 8.30R	NTU - (Possibly crated for shipment to Japan) Canx.
G-AAVL	Breda 15	1419		. 3.30	WFU on 6.11.35. Broken up in 1937. Canx.
G-AAVM	Avro 616 Avian IVM	R3/CN/416		. 3.30	WFU on 26.2.40. Canx in 12/46.
G-AAVN	Breda 15	1414		. 3.30	WFU on 1.6.32. Broken up in 1932. Canx.
G-AAVO	Desoutter I	D.22		. 3.30	WFU on 5.10.34. Canx in 12/36.
G-AAVP	Avro 616 Avian IVM	R3/CN/417		. 3.30	WFU on 22.4.38. Canx in 8/45.
G-AAVR	DH.60M Moth	1482		. 3.30	Destroyed in mid-air collision with Hawker Hart K5800 over Horley, Sussex on 8.5.39. Canx.
G-AAVS	Klemm L.26a-II	197		. 3.30	To Germany as D-1804 in 12/34. Canx.
G-AAVT	Hendy 302	1		. 3.30	WFU at Gravesend in 14.3.38. Canx.
	(Rebuilt in 1933 by CS Napier to become Hendy 302A with 130hp Cirrus Hermes IV)				
G-AAVU	DH.60M Moth	1485		. 3.30	Crashed at Hendon on 8.11.31. Rebuilt as PK-SAI 7/32. Canx.
G-AAVV	DH.60M Moth	1486		. 3.30	To RAF as DG581 in 1/41. Canx 24.1.41.
G-AAVW	Avro 504K	-	F9720	. 3.30	WFU on 24.6.35. Canx.
G-AAVX	Saunders-Roe A.17 Cutty Sark	A.17/4		. 3.30	To Singapore as VR-SAA in 10/34. Canx.
"G-AAVX"	SNCAN Stampe SV-4C	360	G-AWXZ F-BHMZ/French Mil/F-BCOI	----	Wore false marks for a Hercule Poirot mystery film in 1990. Also noted in these false marks at Booker 23.4.95
G-AAVY	DH.60G Gipsy Moth	1230		. 4.30	To RAF as X5023 in 11/39. Canx 3.11.39.
G-AAVZ	DH.60M Moth	1480		. 4.30	To Holland as PH-ARS in 9/37. Canx.
G-AAWA	Westland (P.V.6) Wapiti V	WA/1822		4. 4.30	To P-6 in 1932 and rebuilt as Wallace G-ACBR. Canx.

Regn	Type	c/n	Previous identity	Regn date	Fate or immediate subsequent identity (if known)
G-AAWB	Avro 504K	-		4. 4.30	Not converted. Canx.
G-AAWC	Avro 504K	KAS.5		. 4.30	WFU on 20.5.31. Canx.
G-AAWD	Avro 504K	KAS.4		. 4.30	WFU on 3.4.35. Broken up in 10/36. Canx.
G-AAWE	Klemm L.25-I	181		. 4.30	WFU at Broxbourne in 12/33. Canx.
G-AAWF	Avro 616 Avian IVM	R3/CN/354		. 4.30	Crashed at Thursley on 22.7.34. Canx.
G-AAWG	Vickers 196 Jockey III	1		8. 4.30	NTU - Not completed. Canx.
G-AAWH	Avro 616 Avian IVM	R3/CN/418		. 4.30	To RAF as 2083M in 2/40. Canx 13.2.40.
G-AAWI	Avro 616 Avian Sport	R3/CN/454		. 4.30	To South Africa as ZS-ANP in 2/37. Canx.
G-AAWJ	Bristol 89A Trainer	7352		9. 4.30	Destroyed in mid-air collision with Bristol Type 89A G-EBOC over Filton 7.7.31. Canx.
G-AAWK	Dudley-Watt DW.II	1		. 4.30	Dismantled at Kingswood Knoll, Surrey in 12/34. Canx.
G-AAWL	DH.60G Gipsy Moth	1231		14. 4.30	To Portugal as CS-AAG in 12/30. Canx.
G-AAWM	Simmonds Spartan	10		11. 4.30	DBR in 12/30. Canx.
G-AAWN	DH.60G Gipsy Moth	1234		2. 5.30	To New Zealand as ZK-ACY in 6/32. Canx.
G-AAWO	DH.60G Gipsy Moth (Composite 1953 rebuild including parts of G-AAHI c/n 1082)	1235		2. 5.30	
G-AAWP	DH.60G Gipsy Moth	1236		. 5.30	Sold in Egypt in 6/32. Canx.
G-AAWR	DH.60G Gipsy Moth	1237		. 5.30	To RAF as BD166 in 8/40. Canx 6.8.40.
G-AAWS	DH.60G Gipsy Moth	1239		. 5.30	Crashed at Nursling, Hants on 31.3.36. Canx.
G-AAWT	Desoutter I	D.23		. 4.30	To Dutch East Indies as PK-SAN in 10/33. Canx.
G-AAWU	DH.60M Moth	1474	E-2	. 4.30	To India as VT-AEW in 1/34. Canx.
G-AAWV	DH.60M Moth	1476		17. 4.30	Crashed at Tomas, Burma on 3.7.30. Canx.
G-AAWW	Klemm L.27a-III	196		. 4.30	Crashed near Rochdale on 20.5.32. Canx in 2/33.
G-AAWX	DH.60G Gipsy Moth	1241		. 4.30	Crashed at Charing, Kent on 3.5.33. Canx.
G-AAWY	Spartan Arrow	51		. 4.30	Broken up in 1940. Canx.
G-AAWZ	Spartan Arrow	52		. 4.30	WFU on 12.2.40. Scrapped between 1940 and 1945. Canx.
G-AAXA	DH.60G Gipsy Moth	1246		8. 5.30	To G-AAZE in 6/30. Canx.
G-AAXB	Junkers A.50 Junior	3523		22. 5.30	WFU on 16.4.31. Canx.
G-AAXC	Handley Page HP.42W	42/5		23. 4.30	DBR in gales at Whitchurch on 19.3.40. Canx.
G-AAXD	Handley Page HP.42W	42/6		23. 4.30	DBR in forced landing at Tiverton on 7.11.39. Canx.
G-AAXE	Handley Page HP.42W	42/7		23. 4.30	DBF at Karachi, Pakistan on 31.5.37. Canx.
G-AAXF	Handley Page HP.42W	42/8		23. 4.30	To RAF as AS983 in 5/40. Canx 29.5.40.
G-AAXG	DH.60M Moth	1542	F-AJZB G-AAXG	. 4.30	To New Zealand as (ZK-ADF)/ZK-AEJ in 9/35. Canx.
G-AAXH	Avro 616 Avian Sport	R3/CN/456		. 4.30	WFU on 23.4.40. Scrapped in 1/49. Canx.
G-AAXI	DH.80A Puss Moth	2024		26. 5.30	Crashed on take-off from Lester Field, St.John's, Newfoundland on 6.7.30 & DBF. Canx in 2/31.
G-AAXJ	DH.80A Puss Moth	2006		. 5.30	To India as VT-ACZ in 6/31. Canx as PWFU 10.7.31.
G-AAXK	Klemm L.25-1a	182		. 4.30	(On rebuild by P.Smith after damage in hangar collapse at White Waltham in 3/62) Canx by CAA 18.3.91. (Stored 3/96)
G-AAXL	DH.80A Puss Moth	2010		. 5.30	DBR in forced-landing on a mud bank at Dogs Head Sand, The Wash, 5 miles off Hunstanton on 26.5.32. The airframe was eventually set on fire to attact rescuers and the aircraft was destroyed as a consequence and by the rising tide. Some wreckage, including the engine, was salvaged on 28.5.32. Canx in 1/33.
G-AAXM	DH.80A Puss Moth	2011		16. 5.30	To Belgium as OO-ANH in 9/33. Canx in 3/33.
G-AAXN	DH.80A Puss Moth	2012		16. 5.30	Crashed in the sea, Goodwin Sands in the English Channel on 22.6.30. Canx in 6/30.
G-AAXO	DH.80A Puss Moth	2041		. 5.30	To RAF as X9404 in 5/40. Canx 4.4.40.
G-AAXP	Saunders-Roe A.22 Segrave Meteor I	1		1. 5.30	Canx as WFU in 9/32. Mainplane noted at Redhill in 1947.
G-AAXR	DH.80A Puss Moth	2007		. 4.30	To RAF as DG661 in 2/41. Canx 18.2.41.
G-AAXS	DH.80A Puss Moth	2009		. 5.30	Destroyed in a fire which started in a lock-up at Hatfield on 9.7.35. Canx in 7/35.
G-AAXT	DH.80A Puss Moth	2013		. 5.30	To France as F-APZX in 6/37. Canx in 1/37.
G-AAXU	DH.80A Puss Moth	2014		14. 6.30	To Egypt as SU-ABE in 1932. Canx in 3/32.
G-AAXV	DH.80A Puss Moth	2026		. 6.30	To South Africa as ZS-AIB in 10/36. Canx in 3/37.
G-AAXW	DH.80A Puss Moth	2027		. 6.30	Crashed in fog into hillside near Ruvo di Puglia, Apulia, Italy on 19.2.32. Airframe returned to UK. CofA expired 22.7.32. Canx as WFU in 4/37.
G-AAXX	DH.80A Puss Moth	2028		. 6.30	To Argentina as R290 in 10/35. Canx in 12/34.
G-AAXY	DH.80A Puss Moth	2029		. 6.30	To RAF as DJ711 in 3/41. Canx 25.3.41.
G-AAXZ	DH.80A Puss Moth	2030		. 6.30	CofA lapsed on 27.9.36 in Southern Rhodesia. Canx as WFU in 5/37.
G-AAYA	DH.80A Puss Moth	2031		. 6.30	DBR when hangar collapsed following enemy raid at Brooklands on 4.9.40. Canx 14.11.45 in census.
G-AAYB	DH.80A Puss Moth	2033		. 6.30	Crashed on take-off from frozen lake at St.Moritz, Switzerland on 31.1.33. Canx in 12/33.
G-AAYC	DH.80A Puss Moth	2035		27. 5.30	Crashed some time after 9.5.39. Canx 1.12.46 in census.
G-AAYD	DH.80A Puss Moth	2036		. 5.30	Crashed at Crawthorne, Edgworth Homes, near Bolton on 15.11.35. Canx in 12/35.
G-AAYE	DH.80A Puss Moth	2037		26. 5.30	Canx as sold in 11/32 (probably overseas).
G-AAYF	DH.60M Moth	1535		. 5.30	Crashed at Eltham on 4.7.31. Canx.
G-AAYG	DH.60M Moth	1546		. 5.30	To RAF as X5126 in 12/39. Canx 6.12.39.
G-AAYH	Avro 504K	-	H9833	5. 5.30	To Ireland as EI-AAM in 3/32. Canx.
G-AAYI	Avro 504K	-	H9861	5. 5.30	WFU on 28.5.31. Canx.
G-AAYJ	DH.60G Gipsy Moth	1248		. 5.30	Crashed 40 miles SW of Nairobi on 14.1.33. Canx.
G-AAYK	DH.80A Puss Moth	2034		. 5.30	Crashed on landing at Heston on 1.4.32. Canx in 1/33.
G-AAYL	DH.60G Gipsy Moth	1252		. 5.30	To RAF as BK835 in 9/40. Canx 3.9.40.
G-AAYM	Avro 504K	-	J8370	. 5.30	WFU in 12/34. Canx.
G-AAYN	Avro 620 Cierva C.19 Autogiro Mk.III	5137		9. 5.30	Sold abroad in 10/30 (possibly to Argentina). Canx.

Regn	Type	c/n	Previous identity	Regn date	Fate or immediate subsequent identity (if known)
G-AAYO	Avro 620 Cierva C.19 Autogiro Mk.III	5138		9. 5.30	To RAF as K1696 in 9/30. Canx 6.11.30.
G-AAYP	Avro 620 Cierva C.19 Autogiro Mk.IV (Originally regd as Mk.III)	5139		9. 5.30	Scrapped in 1932. Canx.
G-AAYR	Avro 624 Six	457	K-5	10. 5.30	To Hong Kong as VR-HAQ 12/31. Canx.
G-AAYS	DH.60X Moth	1232		19. 5.30	Crashed in Southampton Water on 4.12.32. Canx.
G-AAYT	DH.60G Gipsy Moth	1233		. 5.30	To RAF as DR606 in 3/41. Canx 27.3.41.
G-AAYU	Avro 616 Avian Sport	R3/CN/419		. 5.30	Crashed at Charlton Abbots, Glos. on 21.9.36. Canx.
G-AAYV	Avro 625 Avian Monoplane	R3/CN/459		. 5.30	WFU on 18.4.39. Canx.
G-AAYW	Avro 625 Avian Monoplane	R3/CN/460		. 5.30	WFU on 17.2.40. Scrapped between 1939 and 1945. Canx.
G-AAYX	Southern Martlet	202		14. 5.30	(On long term rebuild at Old Warden)
G-AAYY	DH.60G Gipsy Moth	1251		. 5.30	To Ceylon as VP-CAC in 12/36. Canx.
G-AAYZ	Southern Martlet	203		. 5.30	WFU on 23.1.36. Scrapped in 1937. Canx.
G-AAZA	Comper CLA.7 Swift	S.30/2		. 6.30R	NTU - To Argentina as R-222 in 1931. Canx.
G-AAZB	Comper CLA.7 Swift	S.30/3		4. 6.30	Scrapped in 2/31. Canx.
G-AAZC	Comper CLA.7 Swift	S.30/4		. 6.30	WFU on 28.5.38. Canx.
G-AAZD	Comper CLA.7 Swift	S.30/5	SU-AAJ G-AAZD	. 6.30	Crashed at Witney on 31.7.38. Canx.
G-AAZE(1)	Comper CLA.7 Swift	S.30/6		. 6.30R	NTU - To Argentina as R-232. Canx.
G-AAZE(2)	DH.60G Gipsy Moth	1246	G-AAXA	. 6.30	To RAF as BK843 in 9/40. Canx 10.9.40.
G-AAZF	Comper CLA.7 Swift	S.30/7		4. 6.30	WFU on 25.7.33. Scrapped in Coley and Atkinson's yard at Hounslow, Middlesex in 1937. Canx.
G-AAZG	DH.60G Gipsy Moth	1253		23. 5.30	To Spanish AF as MW-133/M-CMMA in 6/30. Canx.
G-AAZH	Klemm L.25a-I	180	D-1776	. 5.30	To RAF as X5009 in 4/40. Canx 9.4.40.
G-AAZI	Desoutter II	D.27		. 5.30	To RAF as HM507 in 11/41. Canx 9.11.41.
G-AAZJ	DH.60M Moth	1538		. 5.30	Sold abroad in 4/33. Canx.
G-AAZK	Junkers F.13ge	2052		26. 5.30	Crashed near Meopham, Kent on 21.7.30 after structural failure in the air. Canx.
G-AAZL	DH.60G Gipsy Moth	1254		23. 5.30	To Yugoslavia as UN-PAH in 8/30. Canx.
G-AAZM	DH.80A Puss Moth	2042		. 5.30	To Argentina as R-258 in 3/34. Canx 27.7.33.
G-AAZN	DH.80A Puss Moth	2043		. 6.30	Fatal crash in thick fog at Rough Stone Farm, between Bradnop and Ipstones, near Leek, Staffs., on 23.11.34. Canx in 11/34.
G-AAZO	DH.80A Puss Moth	2045		. 6.30	To RAF as AX870 in 7/40. Canx 23.7.40.
G-AAZP	DH.80A Puss Moth	2047	HL537 G-AAZP/SU-AAC/G-AAZP	4. 6.30	
G-AAZR	DH.60G Gipsy Moth	1275		. 6.30	WFU in 10.10.37, components at Clifton, York until 6/51. Canx.
G-AAZS	DH.80A Puss Moth	2061		. 6.30R	NTU - To Kenya as VP-KAH in 8/30; Later to G-ABNV. Canx.
G-AAZT	DH.80A Puss Moth	2063		. 7.30	To RAF as 2063M in 7/40. Canx 2.3.40.
G-AAZU	DH.80A Puss Moth	2076		. 7.30	To Tanganyika as VR-TAI in 2/33. CofA expired 13.7.32. Canx in 2/33.
G-AAZV	DH.80A Puss Moth	2077		. 8.30	To RAF as X9402 in 5/40. Canx 4.4.40.
G-AAZW	DH.80A Puss Moth	2090		. 7.30	To RAF as ES916 in 5/41. Canx 31.5.41.
G-AAZX	DH.80A Puss Moth	2101		. 7.30	To RAF as X9401 in 5/40. Canx 4.4.40.
G-AAZY	DH.80A Puss Moth	2025		10. 6.30	Fatal crash at Petit Clamart, near Villacoublay, France on 5.7.30. Canx in 12/30.
G-AAZZ	DH.60G Gipsy Moth	1255		27. 5.30	To South Africa as ZS-ADA in 7/31. Canx.
G-ABAA	Avro 504K	-	"H2311" G-ABAA	11. 9.30	(On loan to Manchester Museum of Science & Industry & on display)
G-ABAB	Avro 504K	-		. 5.30	WFU on 6.7.33. Canx 15.8.45.
G-ABAC	Bristol 105 Bulldog II	7399	R-1	30. 5.30	Crashed at Filton on 4.6.30. Canx.
G-ABAD	DH.60G Gipsy Moth	1256		. 5.30	To Egypt as SU-ABD in 6/32. Canx.
G-ABAE	DH.60G Gipsy Moth	1257		. 5.30	To RAF as AW129 in 6/40. Canx 18.6.40.
G-ABAF	DH.60G Gipsy Moth	1258		. 5.30	Crashed at Brooklands on 24.2.35. Canx.
G-ABAG	DH.60G Gipsy Moth	1259		. 5.30	The Shuttleworth Trust.
G-ABAH	DH.60G Gipsy Moth	1262		2. 7.30	To Ireland as EI-AAF in 6/31. Canx.
G-ABAI	DH.60M Moth	1472		. 5.30	To RAF as W7948 in 2/40. Canx 10.2.40.
G-ABAJ	Westland Wessex	WA/1897	OO-AGC G-ABAJ/(G-AAJI)/P-1/(VP-KAD)	. 5.30	WFU on 24.8.38. Canx.
G-ABAK	DH.60G Gipsy Moth	1265		11. 6.30	Crashed at Voi, Kenya on 14.5.31. Canx.
G-ABAL	DH.60G Gipsy Moth	1264		. 6.30	To RAF as X5118 in 11/39. Canx 20.11.39.
G-ABAM	DH.60G Gipsy Moth	1263		. 6.30	Crashed at Borough Green, Kent on 18.8.39. Canx 10.9.39.
G-ABAN	DH.60M Moth	1549		13. 6.30	To New Zealand as ZK-ACC in 9/30. Canx.
G-ABAO	DH.60X Moth	1247		. 6.30	To RAF as BD163 in 8/40. Canx 11.8.40.
G-ABAP	Avro 621 Tutor	461		29. 5.30	To Tanganyika as VR-TAB in 2/32. Canx.
G-ABAR	Avro 621 Tutor	462		29. 5.30	To Tanganyika as VR-TAC in 2/32. Canx.
"G-ABAR"	Monocoupe 90	5W40	D-2609	. 6.30	Painted incorrectly - To G-ABBR in 6/30. Canx.
G-ABAS	DH.60M Moth	1539		4. 6.30	Crashed near Redhill on 20.3.35. Canx.
G-ABAT	DH.60M Moth	1540		. .30	To RAF as DG588 in 1/41. Canx 25.1.41.
G-ABAU	Avro 504K	-	J8553	2. 6.30	DBF in hangar fire at Broomfield, Chelmsford, Essex on 8.9.32. Canx.
G-ABAV	Avro 504K	-	J8348	2. 6.30	Crashed at Holyhead in 9/30. Canx.
G-ABAW	Avro 504K	-	J8347	2. 6.30	WFU on 14.7.32. Canx.
G-ABAX	Hawker Tomtit	27		. 6.30	WFU on 27.7.39. Canx 7.11.45.
G-ABAY	Avro 504K	-		3. 6.30	WFU on 12.7.34. Canx.
G-ABAZ	Spartan 3-Seater	53		. 6.30	WFU on 25.6.39. Canx in 12/46.
G-ABBA	DH.60G Gipsy Moth	1261		. 6.30	To RAF as AW130 in 6/40. Canx 23.6.40.
G-ABBB	Bristol 105A Bulldog IIA	7446	"K2227" G-ABBB/R-11/G-ABBB	12. 6.30	Badly damaged in crash Farnborough 13.9.64. (On display at RAF Museum as K2227)
G-ABBC	Saunders-Roe A.17 Cutty Sark	A.17/5		. 6.30	WFU on 10.4.34. Canx.
G-ABBD	DH.60X Moth	1266		. 6.30	To RAF as W9367 in 2/40. Canx 12.2.40.
G-ABBE	Spartan Arrow	75		. 6.30	To New Zealand as ZK-ACQ in 5/31. Canx.

Regn	Type	c/n	Previous identity	Regn date	Fate or immediate subsequent identity (if known)
G-ABBF	Avro 504K	-	H202	. 6.30	WFU on 27.7.34. Canx.
G-ABBG	DH.60G Gipsy Moth	1260		11. 6.30	To Yugoslavia as UN-PAV in 4/31. Canx.
G-ABBH	DH.80A Puss Moth	2005		. 6.30	Fatal crash when spun in during gale at Verneuil-sur-Avre, France on 14.6.31. Canx 26.8.31.
G-ABBI	DH.60G Gipsy Moth	1267		19. 6.30	To Yugoslavia as UN-PAS in 4/31. Canx.
G-ABBJ	DH.60G Gipsy Moth	1268		. 6.30	To RAF as X9303 in 4/40. Canx 4.4.40.
G-ABBK	DH.60G Gipsy Moth	1270		. 6.30	To RAF as DG659 in 2/41. Canx 20.2.41.
G-ABBL	DH.60M Moth	1547		19. 6.30	To India as VT-ACU in 4/31. Canx.
G-ABBM	DH.60G Gipsy Moth	1271		19. 6.30	To Kenya as VP-KBC in 1/34. Canx.
G-ABBN	Southern Martlet	204		. 6.30	WFU on 30.4.34. Scrapped in 1935. Canx.
G-ABBO	DH.60G Gipsy Moth	1272		. 6.30	Sold abroad in 10/33. Canx.
G-ABBP	DH.60G Gipsy Moth	1273		19. 6.30	To Belgium as OO-AAA as 7/30. Canx.
G-ABBR	Monocoupe 90	5W40	"G-ABAR" D-2609	. 6.30	Returned to Germany as D-2609 in 7/33. Canx.
G-ABBS	DH.80A Puss Moth	2020		4. 7.30	To Iraq as YI-ABB in 5/35. Canx in 12/34.
G-ABBT	Klemm L.25a-I	216	D-1776	. 6.30	WFU on 12.4.34. Canx in 5/36.
G-ABBU	Klemm L.26a-III	225	(VR-HCY) G-ABBU	. 6.30	WFU on 28.7.38. Canx.
G-ABBV	DH.60G Gipsy Moth	1276	EI-AAK G-ABBV	. 6.30	Crashed near Brockworth on 15.7.39. Canx.
G-ABBW	DH.60G Gipsy Moth	1277		. 6.30	Ditched into sea off Shoreham on 27.6.39. Canx.
G-ABBX	DH.60G Gipsy Moth	1278		. 6.30	To RAF as AW131 in 6/40. Canx 23.6.40.
G-ABBY	Avro 619 Five	458		. 6.30	Scrapped in 3/41. Canx.
"G-ABBY"	Auster 6	-		----	False marks worn by an instructional airframe used by the Airwork engineering school at Perth in 9/61.
G-ABBZ	Breda 15	1638		17. 7.30	No CofA issued. Canx in 12/32.
G-ABCA	Breda 15	1639		17. 7.30	No CofA issued. Canx in 12/32.
G-ABCB	Breda 15	1640		17. 7.30	No CofA issued. Canx in 12/32.
G-ABCC	Breda 15 (Ugo Antoni Wing)	1641		17. 7.30	DBR at Chosen Hill, Churchdown, Glos. on 1.12.33. Canx.
G-ABCD	Avro 616 Avian IVM	R3/CN/420		. 6.30	Crashed at Perry Barr on 8.3.38. Canx.
G-ABCE	Avro 616 Avian Sport	R3/CN/421		. 6.30	To Holland as PH-OVG in 6/35. Canx.
G-ABCF	Avro 616 Avian IVA	R3/CN/467		20. 6.30	To Australia in 10/30 - was allocated marks VH-UPT, but NTU as crashed at Mascot, New South Wales, Australia on 12.4.31. Canx.
G-ABCG	DH.60G Gipsy Moth	1288		. 6.30	Sold abroad in 3/39. Canx 7.3.39.
G-ABCH	DH.60M Moth	1553		. 6.30	To Holland as PH-AJE in 5/33. Canx.
G-ABCI	Klemm L.26a III	226		. 7.30	To Holland as PH-APA(2) in 10/37. Canx.
G-ABCJ	Saunders-Roe A.19B Cloud (Originally regd with c/n A.19/1)	A.19/1A	CF-ARB G-ABCJ/L4	. 7.30	WFU on 18.7.36. Canx.
G-ABCK	Avro 620 Cierva C.19 Autogiro Mk.III	5140		8. 7.30	To New Zealand as ZK-ACL in 12/30. Canx.
G-ABCL	Avro 620 Cierva C.19 Autogiro Mk.III	5142		8. 7.30	Struck a tree during take off from Hounslow Heath and crashed on 29.11.30. Canx.
G-ABCM	Avro 620 Cierva C.19 Autogiro Mk.III	5141		8. 7.30	To RAF as K1948 in 1/31. Canx.
G-ABCN	Fairey Firefly IIM	F.1130		9. 7.30	WFU on 9.7.31. Canx.
G-ABCO	Avro 616 Avian IVM	R3/CN/422		. 7.30	W/o in 12/37. Canx.
G-ABCP	DH.66 Hercules	347	G-AUJR	10. 7.30	Crashed in swamp near Entebbe, Uganda on 23.11.35. Canx.
G-ABCR	DH.80A Puss Moth	2083		. 8.30	To RAF as DD820 in 1/40. Canx 18.11.40.
G-ABCS	DH.60G Gipsy Moth	1282		. 7.30	To RAF as X5039 in 11/39. Canx 12.11.39.
G-ABCT	DH.60G Gipsy Moth	1286		. 7.30	To RAF as X5048 in 11/39. Canx 15.11.39.
G-ABCU	Desoutter II	D32		. 7.30	Ditched in Mediterranean Sea off Belmonte, Calabria, Italy on 3.12.30. Wreck salvaged by the Italian AF and dumped at the Naples Aero Club. Eventually the wreck was shipped back to Heston and burned in 5/31. Canx.
G-ABCV	Desoutter II	D33		. 7.30R	NTU - To Canada as CF-CBZ in 11/30. Canx.
G-ABCW	DH.60M Moth	1552		. 7.30	To India as VT-AEC in 4/33. Canx.
G-ABCX	DH.80A Puss Moth	2040		. 7.30	Canx as sold in 4/38 (probably abroad).
G-ABCY	Klemm L.25a-I	215		. 7.30	WFU on 16.6.39. Canx.
G-ABCZ	DH.60M Moth	1555		18. 7.30	To Kenya as VP-KAO in 8/31. Canx.
G-ABDA	DH.60G-III Moth Major (Originally regd as DH.60G Gipsy Moth)	1284	2595M DG583/G-ABDA	. 7.30	To USA as N1284A 12/98. Canx 2.11.98.
G-ABDB	DH.60M Moth	1557		. 7.30	To Norway as LN-BAU in 8/35. Canx.
G-ABDC	Junkers F.13ge	2074		. 7.30	To Sweden as SE-AEC in 12/34. Canx.
G-ABDD	Junkers F.13ge	2095		16. 7.30	To Germany as D-1949 in 9/30. Canx.
G-ABDE	DH.60G Gipsy Moth	1827		. 7.30	To India as VT-ADX in 1/33. Canx.
G-ABDF	DH.80A Puss Moth	2057		. 7.30	Fatal crash & DBF at Easton Lodge, Dunmow on 29.5.55. Canx 28.2.56
G-ABDG	DH.80A Puss Moth	2070		. 7.30	To RAF as AX869 in 7/40. Canx 23.7.40.
G-ABDH	DH.80A Puss Moth	2081		25. 7.30	Fatal crash at Kettlebury Hill, Churt, near Hindhead on 27.7.32, following structural failure in a thunderstorm. Canx in 12/32.
G-ABDI	DH.80A Puss Moth	2091		. 7.30	Fatal crash at Horne, near Horley, Surrey on 23.12.37. Canx in 5/38.
G-ABDJ	DH.80A Puss Moth	2065		. 7.30R	NTU - To South Africa as ZS-ACF in 12/30. Canx.
G-ABDK	DH.60G Gipsy Moth	1804		. .30	To RAF as X5033 in 2/40. Canx 11.11.39.
G-ABDL	DH.80A Puss Moth	2106		. 7.30	To RAF as BD181 in 8/40. Canx 6.8.40.
G-ABDM	DH.80A Puss Moth	2105		. 7.30	To RAF as ES953 in 7/41. Canx 31.7.41.
G-ABDN	Avro 616 Avian IVM	R3/CN/423		. 7.30	Crashed at Skegness on 6.6.33. Canx.
G-ABDO	Robinson Redwing II	RAC.2		. 7.30	DBF at Gravesend in 8/37. Canx.
G-ABDP	Avro 616 Avian IVM	R3/CN/472		. 7.30	WFU on 2.11.39. Canx in 12/46.
G-ABDR	DH.60G Gipsy Moth	1287		25. 7.30	Crashed at Erdington, Birmingham on 12.7.31. Canx.
G-ABDS	Blackburn L.1C Bluebird IV	SB.245		26. 7.30	WFU on 22.9.31. Canx.

Regn	Type	c/n	Previous identity	Regn date	Fate or immediate subsequent identity (if known)
G-ABDT	DH.60M Moth	1543		5. 8.30	To Brazil in 3/32. Canx.
G-ABDU	DH.60G Gipsy Moth	1290		. 8.30	To RAF as X5024 in 11/39. Canx 3.11.39.
G-ABDV	DH.60G Gipsy Moth	1291		. 8.30	Crashed near Nevers, France on 5.1.34. Canx.
G-ABDW	DH.80A Puss Moth	2051	VH-UQB G-ABDW	23. 8.30	Canx as PWFU 21.1.82. On display East Fortune as VH-UQB.
G-ABDX	DH.60G Gipsy Moth	1294	HB-UAS G-ABDX	. 8.30	
G-ABDY	Armstrong Whitworth Atlas Trainer	AW.536		16. 8.30	WFU on 24.9.31. Scrapped in 1938. Canx.
G-ABDZ	Desoutter II	D.34		16. 8.30	To Hungary as H-MAAA in 10/30. Canx.
G-ABEA	Avro 616 Avian Sport	R3/CN/424		19. 8.30	To Kenya as VP-KAN in 10/31. Canx.
G-ABEB	DH.60G Gipsy Moth	1298		30. 8.30	Sold abroad in 12/30. Canx.
G-ABEC	DH.80A Puss Moth	2055		. 8.30	To France as F-ANEC in 4/34. CofA expired 15.7.33. Canx in 3/34.
G-ABED	Avro 616 Avian Sport	R3/CN/474		. 8.30	DBF in hangar fire at Hooton Park on 8.7.40. Canx.
G-ABEE	Avro 616 Avian Sport	R3/CN/473		. 8.30	WFU on 21.8.53. Canx. (Parts to G-EBZM) Stored incomplete in Australia.
G-ABEF	Ford 4-AT-E	4-AT-61	NC9678	. 8.30	To Australia in 1934 - regd as VH-UDY on 7.10.34. Canx in 6/35.
	Note: Aircraft was flown for a brief period as G-ABEF in New Guinea before marks VH-UDY was applied.				
G-ABEG	Westland Wessex	WA.1901		. 8.30	DBR at Chirindu, Northern Rhodesia in 1936. Canx.
G-ABEH	DH.80A Puss Moth	2072	HH981 G-ABEH/VP-KAV/G-ABEH	. 9.30	DBR on landing at Thruxton on 15.8.48. Canx as WFU 20.3.49. Parts used in restoration of G-AAZP in early 1950s. Remains on dump at Thruxton in 10/55.
G-ABEI	DH.80A Puss Moth	2073		. 9.30	To RAF as BK846 in 9/40. Canx 12.9.40.
G-ABEJ	DH.80A Puss Moth	2074		30. 8.30	To India as VT-ACJ in 12/30. Canx in 12/30.
G-ABEK	DH.60G Gipsy Moth	1289		15. 9.30	CofA lapsed on 25.3.39. Canx 8.11.45.
G-ABEL	DH.80A Puss Moth	2075		. 9.30	To Belgium as OO-AEL in 3/35. Canx.
G-ABEM	DH.80A Puss Moth	2109		. 9.30	To Holland as PH-ATL in 5/38. Canx.
G-ABEN	DH.60G Gipsy Moth	1812		30. 8.30	To Australia (departed UK on 5.10.30, arrived 10.12.30) - regd as VH-UPV on 21.4.31. Canx in 1/31.
G-ABEO	DH.60G Gipsy Moth	1813		. 8.30	To RAF as BK828 in 8/40. Canx 31.8.40.
G-ABEP	DH.60G Gipsy Moth	1292		. 8.30	Ditched into the English Channel on 7.3.33, whilst crossing from St.Inglevert and Lympne. Canx.
G-ABER	DH.60G Gipsy Moth	1296		. 8.30	To RAF as W7946 in 2/40. Canx 13.2.40.
G-ABES	DH.60G Gipsy Moth	1299		. 9.30	To RAF as AX792 in 7/40. Canx 9.7.40.
G-ABET	Spartan 3-Seater	54		. 9.30	WFU on 16.5.40. Canx in 12/46.
G-ABEU	Blackburn L.1C Bluebird IV	SB.246		10. 9.30	To Switzerland as CH-345 in 7/32. Canx.
G-ABEV(1)	Blackburn L.1C Bluebird IV	SB.238		. .30R	NTU - To G-ABPN 9/31. Canx.
G-ABEV(2)	DH.60G Gipsy Moth	1823	N4203E G-ABEV/HB-OKI/CH-217	10. 3.77	
G-ABEW(1)	Blackburn L.1C Bluebird IV	SB.239		. .30R	To India as VT-ADK on 23.6.32. Canx.
G-ABEW(2)	DH.60G-III Moth	5018	SE-ADN	23. 8.79	NTU - Not Imported. Remained as SE-ADN. Canx 23.7.86.
G-ABEX	Blackburn L.1C Bluebird IV	SB.240		. .30R	NTU - To G-ABVZ 4/32. Canx.
G-ABEY	Blackburn L.1C Bluebird IV	SB.241		. .30R	NTU - To G-ABZX 9/32. Canx.
G-ABEZ	Bristol 118	7561	R-3	12. 9.30	To RAF as K2873 in 2/32. Canx.
G-ABFA	Short S.17 Kent	S.758		11. 9.30	Crashed at Mirabella Bay, Crete on 22.8.36. Canx.
G-ABFB	Short S.17 Kent	S.759		11. 9.30	DBF at Brindisi, Italy on 9.11.35. Canx.
G-ABFC	Short S.17 Kent	S.760		11. 9.30	WFU on 19.7.38. Scrapped at Hythe in 6/38. Canx.
G-ABFD	DH.60G Gipsy Moth	1800		. 9.30	To RAF as BK845 in 9/40. Canx 17.9.40.
G-ABFE	Lockheed 5 Vega	155	NC372E	30. 9.30	To G-ABGK in 1/31. Canx.
G-ABFF	Ford 5-AT-C	5-AT-68	NC409H	14.10.30	To G-ABHF in 1/31. Canx.
G-ABFG	Fairey Fox IIM	F.1138	J9834	17. 9.30	WFU in 11/32. Canx.
	(Converted to demonstration 2-seater fighter in 1931)				
G-ABFH	Fairey Firefly III	F.1137	S1592	17. 9.30	Restored to RN as S1592 c.1932. Canx.
G-ABFI	Civilian CAC Coupé II	0.2.1		27. 9.30	To Holland as PH-BBC in 4/33. Canx.
G-ABFJ	Civilian CAC Coupé II	0.2.2		27. 9.30	Forced landed at Sandbach on 8.7.31 & WFU. Canx.
G-ABFK	Blackburn F.2D Lincock III	2920/2		27. 9.30	CofA expired 2.6.34. WFU & used as instructional airframe at Brooklands until at least 6/36, engineless. Canx.
G-ABFL	Avro 626 Trainer	477		3.10.30	Crashed at Courtrai, Belgium in 1/31. Canx.
G-ABFM	Avro 626 Trainer	478		3.10.30	To Argentina in 9/31. Canx.
G-ABFN	Sikorsky S-39A	908	NC806W	13.10.30	Restored in USA as NC806W in 7/35. Canx.
G-ABFO	Desoutter II	D38		15.10.30	Struck a hill and crashed on the coast 10 miles south of Stranraer, Wigtownshire in fog on 22.5.32. Canx.
G-ABFP	Blackburn B-1 Segrave I	3169/1	B-1 G-ABFP	14.10.30	CofA expired 10.3.34. Scrapped in 3/34. Canx.
G-ABFR	Blackburn B-1 Segrave I	3169/2		14.10.30	Crashed at Heston on 27.5.37. Remains at Redhill in 2/38. Canx.
G-ABFS	Klemm L.26a-II	208	D-1833	16.10.30	Sold abroad in 9/33. Canx.
G-ABFT	DH.60G Gipsy Moth	1817		23.10.30	To RAF as BK836 in 9/40. Canx 10.9.40. To 2067 ATC Sqdn at Derby from 10.8.43 until 17.1.46.
G-ABFU	DH.80A Puss Moth	2123		19.11.30	Fatal crash when it struck HT pylon in Dauphine Alps and crashed near La Balme de Retournel, Isere, nr.Grenoble, France on 29.10.32 (or 30.10.32?). Canx in 12/32.
G-ABFV	DH.80A Puss Moth	2122		.10.30	To RAF as 2067M in 7/40. Canx 24.1.40.
G-ABFW	DH.60G Gipsy Moth	1820		4.11.30	Crashed at Sabzawar, Persia on 2.5.31. Canx.
G-ABFX	Caudron C.193	6479/7	F-AJSI	3.11.30	To France as F-ALLJ in 6/31. Canx.
G-ABFY	DH.80A Puss Moth	2115		.11.30	To South Africa as ZS-ADT in 7/32. Canx 11/32.
G-ABFZ	Avro 620 Cierva C.19 Autogiro Mk.IVP	5143		.11.30	WFU on 23.5.36. Scrapped in 1937. Canx.
G-ABGA	Avro 620 Cierva C.19 Autogiro Mk.IVP	5145		5.11.30	WFU in 12/31. Canx.

Regn	Type	c/n	Previous identity	Regn date	Fate or immediate subsequent identity (if known)
G-ABGB	Avro 620 Cierva C.19 Autogiro Mk.IVP	5144		.11.30	Crashed in display at Cape Town on 17.2.33. Canx.
G-ABGC	DH.60G Gipsy Moth	1802		8.11.30	To Mexico as X-BAFA in 12/30. Canx.
G-ABGD	DH.80A Puss Moth	2104		7.11.30	Canx as sold in 12/33. CofA renewed 13.1.34. Presumably sold overseas.
G-ABGE	Vickers 216 Vildebeest VII (Originally regd as Type 132 Vildebeest I, then Type 192 Vildebeest II, then Type 209 Vildebeest V (for Paris Show))	1	N230	11.11.30	To B-Class marks as O-3 in 1931, then to Spain as EC-W11. Canx.
G-ABGF	Blackburn L.1C Bluebird IV (Converted to Seaplane in 3/31)	SB.252		7.11.30	DBR in Sierra Leone through acid corrosion in 5/31. Canx.
G-ABGG	Avro 626	476	K-8	8.11.30	Sold abroad in 1/37. Canx.
G-ABGH	Avro 646 Sea Tutor	485		8.11.30	To RAF as K2893 in 12/32. Canx.
G-ABGI	Avro 504K	-		10.11.30	WFU on 21.7.34. Canx in 1/36.
G-ABGJ	Avro 504K	-		10.11.30	Not converted. Canx in 12/34.
G-ABGK	Lockheed 5 Vega	155	G-ABFE NC372E	.11.30	Crashed at Aleppo, Syria on 21.10.34. Rebuilt in 1936 and regd as VH-UVK on 23.6.36. Canx.
G-ABGL	DH.60G Gipsy Moth	1808		.11.30	To Ireland as EI-AAH in 8/31. Canx.
G-ABGM	DH.60G Gipsy Moth	1811		.11.30	To RAF as X5112 in 12/39. Canx 20.12.39.
G-ABGN	DH.60G Gipsy Moth	1814		.11.30	WFU in Kenya on 21.12.32. Canx.
G-ABGO	Avro 552A Viper	5113	G-EBTX G-EAPR/H2323	13.11.30	Crashed at Coal Aston, Sheffield on 25.10.33. Canx.
G-ABGP	DH.60G Gipsy Moth	1816		.11.30	Sold abroad in 3/32. Canx.
G-ABGR	DH.80A Puss Moth	2116		.11.30	Sold abroad, probably to Africa. CofA expired 31.12.31. Canx 11/32.
G-ABGS	DH.80A Puss Moth	2117		.11.30	To RAF as AX872 in 7/40. Canx 28.7.40.
G-ABGT	DH.80A Puss Moth	2120		.11.30	CofA expired 6.11.36. To Nyasaland in 1936. Canx 1.12.46 in census. (The Gipsy III engine from this aircraft was discovered in Zambia in the 90s and is now in the UK awaiting a suitable aircraft to fit it to).
G-ABGU	DH.60G Gipsy Moth	1819		21.11.30	To Malaya in 12/31 - regd as VR-RAD in 8/34. Canx.
G-ABGV	DH.60G Gipsy Moth	1822		21.11.30	To Malaya in 12/31 - regd as VR-RAC in 8/34. Canx.
G-ABGW	Spartan Arrow	77		14.11.30	W/o in 10/34. Canx.
G-ABGX	DH.80A Puss Moth	2121		.11.30	To France as F-AMRX 1/35. CofA expired 6.1.34. Canx in 12/34.
G-ABGY	DH.60G Gipsy Moth	1807		.11.30	To Kenya as VP-KAQ in 2/32. Canx.
G-ABGZ	DH.80A Puss Moth	2071	UN-PAI	21.11.30	Restored to Yugoslavia as UN-PAI in 6/31. Canx 26.6.31.
G-ABHA	Avro 621 Tutor	487		26.11.30	To Tanganyika as VR-TAE in 6/32. Canx.
G-ABHB	DH.80A Puss Moth	2113		.11.30	To RAF as X9405 in 5/40. Canx 4.4.40.
G-ABHC	DH.80A Puss Moth	2125		.11.30	To New Zealand Permanent Air Force as 2125 in 8/31. Canx in 12/32.
G-ABHD	Spartan Arrow	80		26.11.30	To Australia in 1931 - regd as VH-UQD on 25.6.31. Canx in 2/32.
G-ABHE	Aeronca C.2 (Converted to glider in 1937)	A.100		.11.30	DBR by gales at Maiden Newton, Dorset in 11/38. Canx.
G-ABHF	Ford 5-AT-C	5-AT-68	G-ABFF NC409H	7. 1.31	To Australia in 10/34 - regd as VH-UTB on 10.12.34. Canx.
G-ABHG	Saunders-Roe A.19 Cloud	A.19/2		3.12.30	DBR at Ibsley in 5/41 & WFU at Hythe in 6/41. To St.Leonards, near Ringwood, Hampshire by 1952 and converted into a caravan! Canx.
G-ABHH	Simmonds Spartan	24	(G-AAMD)	6.12.30	Crashed Tunis, Tunisia on 3.2.31. Rebuilt in 3/32 as ZS-ADI. Canx.
G-ABHI	Avro 504K	-	J8342	9.12.30	WFU on 24.5.33. Canx.
G-ABHJ	Avro 504K	-	J8343	9.12.30	Crashed at Hooton in 1933. Canx.
G-ABHK	Avro 504K	-	J8351	9.12.30	Crashed at Hooton in 1933. Canx.
G-ABHL	Avro 616 Avian IVM	R3/CN/489		8.12.30	Canx in 9/31.
G-ABHM	DH.60G Gipsy Moth	1830		.12.30	To RAF as BK841 in 9/40. Canx 10.9.40.
G-ABHN	DH.60M Moth	1680		.12.30	To RAF as X5130 in 12/39. Canx 6.12.39.
G-ABHO	Ford 5-AT-C	5-AT-60	NC401H	.12.30	To Australia in 10/35 - regd as VH-UBI on 26.10.35. Canx.
G-ABHP	Avro 504K	-	J8371	17.12.30	To Ireland as EI-AAN in 3/32. Canx.
G-ABHR	Spartan Arrow	81		.12.30	WFU on 3.6.37. Canx.
G-ABHS	DH.60G Gipsy Moth	1824		31.12.30	To Poland as SP-ALK in 9/33. Canx.
G-ABHT	Armstrong Whitworth Siskin III (2-seater)	AW.651		24.12.30	Crashed at Sarisbury, Hants on 8.6.31. Canx.
G-ABHU	Armstrong Whitworth Siskin III (2-seater)	AW.652		. 1.31	WFU on 17.5.37. Canx.
G-ABHV	Armstrong Whitworth Atlas Trainer	AW.653		. 1.31	WFU on 27.5.37. Scrapped in 1938. Canx.
G-ABHW	Armstrong Whitworth Atlas Trainer	AW.654		. 1.31	WFU on 12.4.34. Scrapped in 1938. Canx.
G-ABHX	Armstrong Whitworth Atlas Trainer	AW.655		. 1.31	Scrapped in 1938. Canx.
G-ABHY	DH.60M Moth	1685		9. 3.31	To Australia (departed UK 1.4.31 & arrived 10.4.31) - became VH-UQH on 7.9.31. Canx in 12/31.
G-ABHZ	Fenton Cheel	F.Mk.1		5. 1.31	Construction abandoned. Canx 15.8.45.
G-ABIA	DH.80A Puss Moth	2127		. 1.31	To RAF as ES917 in 5/41. Canx 19.5.41.
G-ABIB	Avro 616 Avian Sport	R3/CN/490		. 1.31	To India as VT-AEV in 11/33. Canx.
G-ABIC	Avro 616 Avian IVM	R3/CN/486		8. 1.31	To Tanganyika as VR-TAD in 6/32. Canx.
G-ABID	DH.60G Moth	514	J9107	12. 1.31	To India as VT-AGJ in 3/35. Canx.
G-ABIE	Avro 616 Avian IVM	R3/CN/491		. 1.31	Crashed near Avellino, Italy on 23.10.34. Canx.
G-ABIF	Southern Martlet	205		. 1.31	WFU on 17.3.40. Donated to an ATC Sqdn in the Hatfield area (possibly 2203 ATC Sqdn) in 1940. Canx 1.12.45.
G-ABIG	Desoutter II	D.39		15. 1.31	To OO-CAB in 6/33. Canx.
G-ABIH	DH.80A Puss Moth	2140		17. 2.31	To USA as NC770N in 11/31. Canx in 11/31.

Regn	Type	c/n	Previous identity	Regn date	Fate or immediate subsequent identity (if known)
G-ABII	Hawker Tomtit	54		21. 1.31	Crashed at Cowes, IoW on 10.4.48. Canx.
G-ABIJ	DH.80A Puss Moth	2141		26. 1.31	To India as VT-AGM in 3/35. Canx early 1935.
G-ABIK	Angus Aquila	1		23. 1.31	Fatal crash when it stalled and dived into the ground at Hanworth on 21.3.31. Canx.
G-ABIL	Vickers 210 Vespa VI	6/1	O-5 G-EBLD	23. 1.31	To RAF as K3588 in 5/33. Canx 4.5.33.
G-ABIM	Avro 616 Avian Sport	R3/CN/501		. 1.31	WFU on 1.5.40. Canx 1.12.46.
G-ABIN	DH.80A Puss Moth	2135		. 1.31	To RAF as DJ712 in 2/41. Canx 25.1.41.
G-ABIO	DH.60G Gipsy Moth	1846		2. 2.31	To Sweden as SE-ABG in 4/35. Canx.
G-ABIP	Handley Page HP.35 Clive II	HP.35/1	J9948	2. 2.31	NTU - Restored to RAF as J9948. Canx.
G-ABIR	Avro 621 Tutor	497		. 2.31	To RAF as HM504 in 10/41, then to 1403 ATC Sqdn at Radford, Notts in 4/42 as 3065M. Canx 31.10.41.
G-ABIS	Avro 621 Tutor	498		. 2.31	To RAF as HM505 in 10/41, then to 1493 ATC Sqdn at Leeds as 3064M in 12/41. Canx 31.10.41.
G-ABIT	DH.80A Puss Moth	2137		. 2.31	To Belgium as OO-EIT in 9/35. Canx in 9/35.
G-ABIU	DH.80A Puss Moth	2139	ZS-ADO G-ABIU	. 2.31	To RAF as DR608 in 5/41. Canx 31.5.41.
G-ABIV	Armstrong Whitworth Atlas II	AW.696	A-3	13. 2.31	WFU on 11.10.32. Canx in 12/34.
G-ABIW	Avro 616 Avian IVM	R3/CN/500		. 2.31	WFU on 19.9.39. Canx.
G-ABIX	Arrow Active I	1		. 2.31	DBF & crashed at Markschapel, near Louth, Lincs. on 30.12.35. Canx.
G-ABIY	DH.80A Puss Moth	2134		26. 2.31	Crashed at Portsmouth Aerodrome on 28.3.35. Canx as PWFU in 3/35.
G-ABIZ	DH.80A Puss Moth	2136		. 2.31	To RAF as W9369 in 3/40. Canx 16.1.40.
G-ABJA	Blackburn L.1C Bluebird IV	SB.249		25. 2.31	To Ireland as EI-AAO in 5/32. Canx.
G-ABJB	DH.80A Puss Moth	2147		9. 3.31	To Czechoslovakia as OK-OFK in 3/32. Canx in 4/32.
G-ABJC	DH.60G Gipsy Moth	1825		. 3.31	To India as VT-AEO in 12/33. Canx.
G-ABJD	DH.80A Puss Moth	2144		9. 3.31	To France as F-APFZ in 12/36. Canx.
G-ABJE	DH.60G Gipsy Moth	1841		7. 3.31	To France as F-ALQA in 9/31. Canx.
G-ABJF	Avro 504K	KAS.6		. 3.31	WFU on 16.5.33. Canx.
G-ABJG	Avro 626	496		5. 3.31	To B-Class marks as K-10 in 1933 as Avro 637. Canx 1.12.46.
G-ABJH	DH.60G Gipsy Moth	1838		. 3.31	To RAF as X5111 in 12/39. Canx 20.12.39.
G-ABJI	DH.60G Gipsy Moth	1839		. 3.31	To RAF as X5036 in 11/39. Canx 12.11.39.
G-ABJJ	DH.60G Gipsy Moth	1840	BK842 G-ABJJ	. 3.31	To Canada as CF-AAA in 7/62. Canx.
G-ABJK	Vickers 204 Vildebeest IV (Originally regd as Type 194 Vildebeest III)	-	O-1	10. 3.31	Crashed at Farnborough in 1932. Canx. (Was to have been modified to Type 217 - not proceeded with)
G-ABJL	DH.60G Gipsy Moth	1837		. 3.31	Crashed at Findon, near Worthing on 21.5.34. Canx.
G-ABJM	Avro 627 Mailplane (Rebuild of Avro 608 G-EBWM c/n 5125)	502		. 3.31	Converted to Armstrong Siddeley Tiger VI testbed in 6/33. Dismantled at Woodford in 1934. Canx.
G-ABJN	DH.60G Gipsy Moth	1851		. 3.31	To RAF as AW119 in 6/40. Canx 11.6.40.
G-ABJO	DH.80A Puss Moth	2145		. 3.31	Crashed in 12/35? Canx as PWFU in 12/35.
G-ABJP	Saunders-Roe A.21 Windover	A.21/2		. 3.31	WFU on 1.3.37. Canx.
"G-ABJP"	BN-2A-8 Islander	313		----	NTU - Painted in error. To G-BAJP 12/72. Canx.
G-ABJR	Comper CLA.7 Swift	S.31/1		. 3.31	Crashed at Brooklands on 28.1.34. Canx.
G-ABJS	Spartan 3-Seater	56		. 3.31	To Australia in 1934 - regd as VH-UUU on 20.7.35. Canx in 12/35.
G-ABJT	DH.60G Gipsy Moth	1244	SP-ABT	. 3.31	To RAF as AW132 in 6/40. Canx 23.6.40.
G-ABJU	DH.80A Puss Moth	2156		30. 3.31	To RAF as ES918 in 5/41. Canx 27.3.41.
G-ABJV	DH.80A Puss Moth	2154		. 3.31	To Kenya as VP-KBW in 10/35. Canx 6.10.35.
G-ABJW	Southern Metal Martlet	31/1		19. 3.31	Not certified. Scrapped in 11/32. Canx.
G-ABJX	Klemm L.27a-III	247		. 3.31	WFU on 23.11.39. Scrapped at Burton in 1946. Canx.
G-ABJY	DH.80A Puss Moth	2155		. 3.31	Crashed near Horsham, Sussex on 22.10.36. Canx as PWFU in 12/37.
G-ABJZ	DH.60G Gipsy Moth	1842		. 3.31	Collided with Hawker Hind K5418 and crashed at Tilmanstone, near Deal, Kent on 21.7.39. Canx.
G-ABKA	Avro 616 Avian IVM	R3/CN/503		23. 3.31	DBF at Hamble on 11.6.32. Canx.
G-ABKB	Avro 616 Avian IVM	R3/CN/504		23. 3.31	To RAF as 2073M in 2/40. Canx 28.2.40.
G-ABKC	Vickers 173 Vellore IV	1		23. 3.31	To RAF as K2133 in 8/31. Canx.
G-ABKD	DH.80A Puss Moth	2143		28. 3.31	To RAF as X9403 in 4/40. Canx 10.5.40.
G-ABKE	Armstrong Whitworth Atlas II	AW.697		24. 3.31	No CofA issued. Canx in 5/36.
G-ABKF	Armstrong Whitworth AW.16	AW.722	A-2	24. 3.31	WFU on 30.12.32. Canx in 1/37.
G-ABKG	DH.80A Puss Moth	2157		. 3.31	To RAF as W6416 in 3/40. Canx 2.1.40.
G-ABKH	Martinsyde AV.1	AV.1		. 3.31	Crashed at Bekesbourne on 5.2.33. Canx.
G-ABKI	Avro 616 Avian Sport	R3/CN/505		. 3.31	To Sweden as SE-AEN in 10/35. Canx.
G-ABKJ	Spartan 3-Seater	55		. 3.31	WFU on 25.5.40. Canx 1.12.46.
G-ABKK	Spartan 3-Seater	58		. 3.31	DBR on 10.5.36 at Coventry after colliding with Avro 504N G-AECR. Canx.
G-ABKL	Spartan 3-Seater	76		. 3.31	DBF in hangar fire at Hooton Park on 8.7.40. Canx.
G-ABKM	DH.60T Moth Trainer	1700		20. 4.31	To Swedish AF as Fv5103 in 6/31. Canx.
G-ABKN	DH.60T Moth Trainer	1701		20. 4.31	To Swedish AF as Fv5104 in 6/31. Canx.
G-ABKO	DH.60T Moth Trainer	1702		20. 4.31	To Swedish AF as Fv5105 in 6/31. Canx.
G-ABKP	DH.60T Moth Trainer	1703		20. 4.31	To Swedish AF as Fv5106 in 6/31. Canx.
G-ABKR	DH.60T Moth Trainer	1704		20. 4.31	To Swedish AF as Fv5107 in 6/31. Canx.
G-ABKS	DH.60T Moth Trainer	1705		20. 4.31	To 'B'-Class marks as E-4 & scrapped in 12/31. Canx.
G-ABKT	Spartan 3-Seater	57		. 3.31	Canx in 12/46.
G-ABKU	DH.60M Moth	1672		1. 4.31	To 'B'-Class marks E-3 & scrapped in 12/31. Canx.
G-ABKV	Blackburn CA.15C Monoplane	2780/1		1. 4.31	To RAF as K4241 in 3/34. Canx.
G-ABKW	Blackburn CA.15C Biplane	2781/1		1. 4.31	Canx in 1/34.
G-ABKX	Aeronca C.2	A.114		2. 4.31	Sold abroad in 5/31. Canx.
G-ABKY	Vickers 212 Vellox	1		. 4.31	Crashed at Wallington, Surrey on 10.8.36. Canx.
G-ABKZ	DH.80A Puss Moth	2132	DR607 G-ABKZ	. 4.31	CofA expired 10.5.49. Scrapped at Southend in 5/49. Canx as WFU 18.1.50.

Regn	Type	c/n	Previous identity	Regn date	Fate or immediate subsequent identity (if known)
G-ABLA	Robinson Redwing II	3		2. 4.31	Crashed near Salisbury on 12.10.32. Canx.
G-ABLB	DH.80A Puss Moth	2149		. 4.31	To RAF as X9400 in 5/40. Canx 4.4.40.
G-ABLC	DH.80A Puss Moth	2150		. 4.31	Canx as sold abroad in 2/38.
G-ABLD	DH.80A Puss Moth	2158		. 4.31	To Holland as PH-ATB in 5/35. Canx in 6/35.
G-ABLE(1)	Supermarine 179 Monoplane Flying-boat	1316		7. 4.31	Not completed, hull construction was well advanced. Canx 19.1.32.
G-ABLE(2)	Cessna 170A	170-19903	VR-NAH N1327D	. 2.61	Sold by Jack Benson on 12.3.72, this had lain at Hurn ever since. CofA expired 5.2.73. Canx as WFU 24.8.73.
G-ABLF	Avro 616 Avian Sport	R3/CN/522		. 4.31	To Australia in 1936 - regd as VH-UVX on 26.6.36. Canx in 8/36.
G-ABLG	DH.80A Puss Moth	2159		. 4.31	To RAF as DG662 in 2/41. Canx 13.2.41.
G-ABLH	DH.60G Gipsy Moth	1848		. 4.31	Crashed in 3/40. Canx.
G-ABLI	Spartan A.24 Mailplane	A.24/1		17. 4.31	WFU on 23.2.33. Scrapped in 1933. Canx.
G-ABLJ	Spartan 3-Seater	59		. 4.31	WFU & donated to No.1F ATC Sqdn at Leicester in 1944. Canx.
G-ABLK	Avro 616 Avian V	R3/CN/523	VH-UQG G-ABLK	. 4.31	Crashed south of Reggane, in the Sahara on 12.4.33. Canx.
G-ABLL	Avro 504K	-	J8333	. 4.31	Crashed at Lowton Moor, Lancs on 30.8.34. Canx.
G-ABLM	Cierva C.24	710		22. 4.31	(On display in De Havilland Aircraft Museum 3/96 Salisbury Hall, London Colney)
G-ABLN	DH.60G Gipsy Moth	1850		. 4.31	CofA lapsed on 16.9.39. Canx 7.3.46.
G-ABLO	DH.80A Puss Moth	2167		. 5.31	To France as F-AMUY in 1/34. Canx in 11/33.
G-ABLP	DH.80A Puss Moth	2162		7. 5.31	To RAF as EM995 in 5/41. Canx 31.5.41.
G-ABLR	DH.80A Puss Moth	2163		7. 5.31	To RAF as BK871 in 10/40. Canx 27.10.40.
G-ABLS	DH.80A Puss Moth	2164		7. 5.31	
G-ABLT	DH.60G Gipsy Moth	1852		. 4.31	To RAF as X5113 in 12/39. Canx 20.12.39.
G-ABLU	Avro 618 Ten	528		. 4.31	Crashed at Ruysselede, Belgium on 30.12.33. Canx.
G-ABLV	Avro 504K	-	H3086	2. 5.31	WFU on 15.5.32. Scrapped in 1936. Canx.
G-ABLW	Avro 504K	-	H3087	. 5.31	Not converted. Canx in 1/34.
G-ABLX	DH.80A Puss Moth	2173		. 5.31	To RAF as EM996 in 5/41. Canx 20.5.41.
G-ABLY	DH.80A Puss Moth	2189	ES919 G-ABLY	21. 7.31	Not re-converted. Canx 16.3.48.
G-ABLZ	DH.60G Gipsy Moth	1853		. 5.31	To RAF as BD162 in 8/40. Canx 8.8.40.
G-ABMA	DH.60G Gipsy Moth	1854		. 5.31	To Mozambique as CR-AAI in 10/37. Canx.
G-ABMB	Avro 548	-	H2232	7. 5.31	WFU on 17.5.35. Scrapped in 1940. Canx.
G-ABMC	DH.80A Puss Moth	2160		. 5.31	To RAF as DP849 in 3/41. Canx 20.3.41.
G-ABMD	DH.80A Puss Moth	2168		. 5.31	DBF in hangar fire at Hooton Park on 8.7.40. Canx 8.7.40.
G-ABME	Avro 616 Avian IVM	R3/CN/529		. 5.31	To Australia in 1936 - regd as VH-UVR on 3.11.36. Canx in 11/36.
G-ABMF	Robinson Redwing II	5		. 5.31	To RAF as 2114M in 1940. Canx.
G-ABMG	DH.80A Puss Moth	2172		. 5.31	To France as F-ANEZ in 9/34. Canx 12.7.34.
G-ABMH	DH.80A Puss Moth	2174		15. 5.31	To France as F-ANBR in 4/34. Canx in 4/34.
G-ABMI	Blackburn L.1C Bluebird IV	SB.254		11. 5.31	Crashed in 2/33. Canx.
G-ABMJ	Robinson Redwing II	4		15. 5.31	To Ireland as EI-ABC in 4/35. Canx in 12/34.
G-ABMK	Spartan Arrow	82	S-1	. 5.31	To Norway as LN-BAS in 7/35. Canx.
G-ABML	Avro 504K	-	E438	18. 5.31	Not converted. Canx in 1931.
G-ABMM	Southern Metal Martlet	31/2		19. 5.31	Not completed. Canx in 12/32.
G-ABMN	DH.80A Puss Moth	2176		17. 6.31	To India as VT-ADN in 7/32. Canx in 6/32.
G-ABMO	Avro 616 Avian IVM	R3/CN/532		. 5.31	To RAF as 2070M in 1/40. Canx 4.1.40.
G-ABMP	DH.80A Puss Moth	2185		. 6.31	To RAF as DP850 on 25.3.41 but NTU - Somersaulted on night-time forced landing near Beaconsfield, Bucks on 26.3.41 whilst on delivery. Canx 21.3.41.
G-ABMR	Hawker Hart II	H.H-1	"J9941" G-ABMR/"J9933"/G-ABMR	28. 5.31	(On display at RAF Museum Hendon as J9941)
G-ABMS	DH.80A Puss Moth	2166		. 5.31	To RAF as DP854 in 3/41. Canx 23.3.41.
G-ABMT	DH.66 Hercules	346	G-AUJQ	9. 6.31	To South African AF as 261 in 7/34. Canx.
G-ABMU	Robinson Redwing II	6		. 5.31	Crashed at Ipswich on 5.1.33. Canx.
G-ABMV	Robinson Redwing II	7		. 5.31	To New Zealand as ZK-ADD in 4/33. Canx.
G-ABMW	Desoutter I	D28		. 6.31	To RAF as HM560 in 5/42. Canx 18.5.42.
G-ABMX	DH.60M Moth	1698		. 6.31	Damaged at Lydda on 25.6.38. To ground instructional airframe at Lydda until 1948.
G-ABMY	Comper CLA.7 Swift	S.31/2		17. 6.31	To Tanganyika as VR-TAF in 6/32. Canx.
G-ABMZ	DH.60M Moth	1420	VT-ABM	. 6.31	To India as VT-ANT in 1/41. Canx.
G-ABNA	DH.60M Moth	1711		10. 6.31	To India as VT-ACW in 12/31. Canx.
G-ABNB	Potez 36/15	2359	F-ALJC	9. 6.31	NTU. Marks not used - remained as F-ALJC /31. Canx.
G-ABNC	DH.80A Puss Moth	2170		. 6.31	To France as F-AQOR in 6/38. Canx in 3/38.
G-ABND	DH.60G Gipsy Moth	1845		. 6.31	To Egypt as SU-ABF in 5/33. Canx.
G-ABNE	DH.60M Moth	1384	OK-ATH D-2296/G-ABNE/J9922	. 6.31	To Czechoslovakia as OK-ATT in 1/36. Canx.
G-ABNF	DH.80A Puss Moth	2188		. 6.31R	NTU - To US Air Attache, then G-ADOC in 1935. Canx.
G-ABNG	DH.60T Moth Trainer	1725		25. 6.31	To Shanghai in 10/31. Canx.
G-ABNH	Comper CLA.7 Swift	S.31/4		20. 6.31	To South Africa as ZS-AEU in 12/31. Canx.
G-ABNI	DH.60T Tiger Moth	1726		25. 6.31	To Canada as CF-APL in 9/31. Canx.
G-ABNJ	DH.60T Tiger Moth	1727	E-5	25. 6.31	To Swedish AF as Fv.562 in 12/31. Canx.
G-ABNK	DH.60T Moth Trainer	1728		25. 6.31	To Shanghai in 10/31. Canx.
G-ABNL	DH.60T Moth Trainer	1729		25. 6.31	To Shanghai in 10/31. Canx.
G-ABNM	DH.60T Moth Trainer	1730		25. 6.31	To Shanghai in 10/31. Canx.
G-ABNN	DH.80A Puss Moth	2190		. 6.31	Sold abroad in 5/35. Canx.
G-ABNO	DH.80A Puss Moth	2161		. 6.31	Crashed near Denbigh on 6.9.33. Canx in 11/33.
G-ABNP	Robinson Redwing II	8		. 6.31	W/o at Frinton in 1934. Rebuilt as G-ABRM. Canx.
G-ABNR	DH.60M Moth	1706		. 6.31	To RAF as X9296 in 2/40. Canx 7.2.40.
G-ABNS	DH.80A Puss Moth	2178		. 6.31	CofA expired 4.4.40. Destroyed by bombs at Manston in 8/40. Canx 5.11.45 in census.

Regn	Type	c/n	Previous identity	Regn date	Fate or immediate subsequent identity (if known)
G-ABNT	Civilian CAC.1 Coupe (C/n also quoted as 0.3)	0.2.3		23. 6.31	
G-ABNU	Simmonds Spartan	25		. 6.31	WFU on 14.10.33. Scrapped at Brooklands in 1948. Canx.
G-ABNV	DH.80A Puss Moth	2061	VP-KAH (G-AAZS)	. 7.31	CofA expired 15.11.37. To Italy as I-BIGA in 9/38. Canx in 7/38.
G-ABNW	Bellanca Pacemaker	167	I-AAPI	. 6.31	To RAF as DZ209 in 7/41. Canx 18.7.41.
G-ABNX	Robinson Redwing II	9		. 6.31	(Stored 8/97)
G-ABNY	DH.60T Moth Trainer	1724		24. 7.31	To Shanghai in 9/31. Canx.
G-ABNZ	DH.80A Puss Moth	2200	EI-ABM G-ABNZ	. 7.31	To RAF as 2065M in 1/40. Canx 18.1.40.
G-ABOA	DH.60G Gipsy Moth	1859		. 7.31	Sold abroad in 4/37. Canx.
G-ABOB	Spartan Arrow	83		. 7.31	WFU on 19.5.39. Canx.
G-ABOC	DH.80A Puss Moth	2201		. 7.31	To Kenya as VP-KCN in 5/38. Canx.
G-ABOD	Hawker Tomtit	55		. 7.31	WFU on 3.2.36. Scrapped between 1939 and 1945. Canx 1.1.47.
G-ABOE	DH.60G Gipsy Moth	1856		. 7.31	To RAF as X5017 in 11/39. Canx 11.11.37.
G-ABOF	DH.80A Puss Moth	2191		. 7.31	To RAF as 2066M in 10/40. Canx 20.10.40.
G-ABOG	DH.60G Gipsy Moth	1857		. 7.31	To RAF as AW149 in 6/40. Canx 24.6.40.
G-ABOH	PB Scarab	5		16. 7.31	Scrapped in 1945. Canx 1.12.46.
G-ABOI	Wheeler Slymph	AHW.1		17. 7.31	(Loaned to Midland Air Museum) (Dismantled components stored 4/96 Baginton)
G-ABOJ	Klemm L.26a-III	325		. 7.31	WFU on 27.7.39. Scrapped at Knowle, Birmingham in 1945. Canx.
G-ABOK	Robinson Redwing II	10		. 7.31	Crashed at Gatwick in 1936. Canx.
G-ABOL	Avro 504K	KAS.7		23. 7.31	Not converted. Canx in 12/32.
G-ABOM	Desoutter II	D.30	EI-AAD	. 7.31	To Australia (departed UK on 29.12.31, arrived in Australia in 2/32) - regd as VH-UEE on 11.3.32. Canx in 3/32.
G-ABON	DH.60G Gipsy Moth	1865		31. 7.31	To South Africa as ZS-ADY in 5/33. Canx.
G-ABOO	Armstrong Whitworth Atlas Trainer	AW.739		24. 7.31	WFU on 27.3.34. Scrapped in 1938. Canx.
G-ABOP	Klemm L.27a-VIII	307		. 7.31	WFU at Bristol on 2.3.39. Scrapped in 1939. Canx.
G-ABOR	Klemm L.27a-IX	330		. 7.31	To Australia in 1936 - regd as VH-USZ on 17.6.36. Canx in 6/36.
G-ABOS	Klemm L.25a-I	214		. 7.31	WFU at Gravesend in 3/37. Canx.
G-ABOT	Blackburn L.1C Bluebird IV	SB.237		30. 7.31	Sank off Kirkmichael, Isle of Man on 26.5.39. Remains to local ATC on 3.6.39 (either 440 (1st Isle of Man) ATC Sqdn or 506 (Isle of Man Schools) Sqdn). Canx.
G-ABOU	DH.60G Gipsy Moth	1862		. 8.31	To RAF as W6415 in 1/40. Canx 3.3.40.
G-ABOV	DH.60G Gipsy Moth	1868		. 8.31	Crashed near Wye, Kent on 10.11.38. Canx.
G-ABOW	DH.60G Gipsy Moth	1860		11. 8.31	To Ireland as EI-AAI in 8/31. Canx.
G-ABOX(1)	[Type not known]	-		. 8.31R	NTU. Canx.
G-ABOX(2)	Sopwith Pup	-	N5195	12. 9.84	Permit to Fly expired 22.4.93. (On display in Museum of Army Flying, Middle Wallop)
G-ABOY	DH.60G Gipsy Moth	1863		. 8.31	To RAF as X5022 in 11/39. Canx 3.11.39.
G-ABOZ	DH.60G Gipsy Moth	1866		11. 8.31	To Ireland as EI-AAJ in 8/31. Canx.
G-ABPA	DH.60M Moth	1712		14. 8.31	Crashed in TransJordan in 1931. Canx.
G-ABPB	DH.80A Puss Moth	2196		. 8.31	To RAF as 2064M in 1/40. Canx 9.1.40.
G-ABPC	DH.60G Gipsy Moth	1867		13. 8.31	To RAF as AX784 in 4/40. Canx 19.4.40.
G-ABPD	DH.60G Gipsy Moth	1869		. 8.31	To RAF as AW133 in 6/40. Canx 23.6.40.
G-ABPE	Comper CLA.7 Swift	S.31/3		. 8.31	Crashed at St.Albans on 26.4.47. Canx.
G-ABPF	DH.80A Puss Moth	2207		. 8.31	To Malaya as VR-RAF in 8/34. Canx.
G-ABPG	DH.9J	1990		26. 8.31	Scrapped in 1933. Canx in 12/33.
G-ABPH	DH.60T Tiger Moth	1732		26. 8.31	To Portuguese Government in 12/31. Canx.
G-ABPI	Armstrong Whitworth AW.15 Atalanta	AW.740		26. 8.31	To India as VT-AEF in 8/33. Canx.
G-ABPJ	DH.60M Moth	1556	EI-AAE	. 8.31	To RAF as X5026 in 11/39. Canx 3.11.39.
G-ABPK	DH.60G Gipsy Moth	1871		. 8.31	Crashed at Exeter on 14.11.37. Canx.
G-ABPL	Bristol 89A Jupiter	7711		2. 9.31	WFU on 23.10.33. Canx.
G-ABPM	Bristol 89A Jupiter	7712		2. 9.31	WFU on 6.11.32. Canx.
G-ABPN	Blackburn L.1C Bluebird IV	SB.238	(G-ABEV)	. 9.31	Crashed at Waltham, Grimsby on 16.10.35. Canx.
G-ABPO	DH.60G Gipsy Moth	1879		10. 9.31	To Belgium as OO-AMO in 10/31. Canx.
G-ABPP	[Type not known]	-		. 9.31R	NTU. Canx.
G-ABPR	Comper CLA.7 Swift	S.31/5		. 9.31	DBF in hangar fire at Broxbourne on 23.6.47. Canx.
G-ABPS	DH.53 Humming Bird	-		8. 9.31	Possibly ex.G-EBTT/J7272 c/n 111. Canx as NTU.
G-ABPT	DH.60G Gipsy Moth	1874		. 9.31	To India as VT-AEH in 6/33. Canx.
G-ABPU	Avro 594B Avian IIIA	R3/CN/170	EI-AAA	10. 9.31	To India as VT-AGC in 12/34. Canx.
G-ABPV	Blackburn L.1C Bluebird IV	SB.253		14. 9.31	Crashed at Tatoi, Athens, Greece on 24.10.31. Canx.
G-ABPW	Civilian CAC.1 Coupe II	0.2.5		16. 9.31	To Germany as D-.... in 10/32. Canx.
G-ABPX	Darmstadt D.22 Biplane	-		25. 9.31	NTU. Canx.
G-ABPY	Comper CLA.7 Swift	S.31/6		. 9.31	To Australia - regd as VH-UZB on 25.3.39. Canx in 8/37.
G-ABPZ	Spartan 3-Seater	60		30. 9.31	To South Africa as ZS-ADP in 11/32. Canx.
G-ABRA	Spartan 3-Seater	61		30. 9.31	To Ireland as EI-AAT in 6/33. Canx.
G-ABRB	Spartan 3-Seater	62		30. 9.31	To Tanganyika as VR-TAJ in 11/32. Canx.
G-ABRC	DH.82 Tiger Moth	1733	E-6	28. 9.31	To RAF as BB723 in 10/40. Canx 30.10.40.
G-ABRD	DH.60G Gipsy Moth	1877		. 9.31	To RAF as AW134 in 6/40. Canx 23.6.40.
G-ABRE	Comper CLA.7 Swift	S.31/8		. 9.31	Crashed at St.Malo, France on 16.12.32. Canx.
G-ABRF	DH.60M Moth	1794		.10.31	Crashed at Norwich in 2.9.37. Canx.
G-ABRG	Klemm L.25b VII	358		12.10.31	To Germany as D-2393 in 1/33. Canx.
G-ABRH	Armstrong Whitworth AW.16	AW.765		8.10.31	To Chinese AF in 11/32. Canx
G-ABRI	Armstrong Whitworth AW.16	AW.766		8.10.31	To Chinese AF in 11/32. Canx
G-ABRJ	Armstrong Whitworth AW.16	AW.767		8.10.31	To Chinese AF in 11/32. Canx.
G-ABRK	Avro 626	553		.10.31	Sold abroad in 9/37. Canx.
G-ABRL	Robinson Redwing III	11		15.10.31	DBR at Cotonou, Dahomey on 2.2.35. Canx.
G-ABRM	Robinson Redwing II	12		15.10.31	Crashed on landing at Frinton in 12/35. Canx.

Regn	Type	c/n	Previous identity	Regn date	Fate or immediate subsequent identity (if known)
G-ABRN	Desoutter I	D29		.10.31	WFU on 9.3.40. Canx in 12/46.
G-ABRO	DH.60G Gipsy Moth	1870		21.10.31	To RAF as X5129 in 12/39. Canx 19.12.39.
G-ABRP	Klemm L.26a-X	350		.10.31	WFU at Heston on 31.3.37. Canx.
G-ABRR	DH.80A Puss Moth	2209		. 8.31	To RAF as X9378 in 3/40. Canx 31.3.40.
G-ABRS	Avro 631 Cadet	558		26.10.31	To Hong Kong as VR-HCS in 10/34. Canx.
G-ABRT	DH.60G Gipsy Moth	1884		24.10.31	To India as VT-ACO in 1/32. Canx.
G-ABRU	Armstrong Whitworth Atlas II	AW.768		23.10.31	To Kwangsi AF in 12/32. Canx.
G-ABRV	Armstrong Whitworth Atlas II	AW.769		23.10.31	To Kwangsi AF in 12/32. Canx.
G-ABRW	Armstrong Whitworth Atlas II	AW.770		23.10.31	To Kwangsi AF in 12/32. Canx.
G-ABRX	Armstrong Whitworth Atlas II	AW.771		23.10.31	To Kwangsi AF in 12/32. Canx.
G-ABRY	Armstrong Whitworth Atlas II	AW.772		23.10.31	To Kwangsi AF in 12/32. Canx.
G-ABRZ	Armstrong Whitworth Atlas II	AW.773		23.10.31	To Kwangsi AF in 12/32. Canx.
G-ABSA	DH.80A Puss Moth	2203		10.11.31	Crashed in 10/32. Canx.
G-ABSB	DH.80A Puss Moth	2213		19.11.31	Crashed at Clacton on 7.5.33. Canx in 1/36.
G-ABSC	Avro 616 Avian IVM	R3/CN/562		16.11.31	WFU on 18.9.39. Scrapped between 1939 and 1945. Canx.
G-ABSD(1)	DH.60G Gipsy Moth	1883		21.11.31	Crashed at Bungendore, New South Wales, Australia on 14.10.32. Canx in 2/33.
G-ABSD(2)	DH.60G Gipsy Moth (C/n as quoted - Identity suspect)	"1883"	A7-96 VH-UTN	3. 2.86	(On rebuild following import from USA in 1985 as basket case)
	Note: G-ABSD(1) did not become VH-UTN - whilst the paperwork for VH-UTN shows the c/n 1883, it was virtually a new aircraft, incoporating parts from G-ABSD(1) and other dead Moths, and quite a lot of new components. VH-UTN was impressed as A7-96 on 22.7.40, and the RAAF record card (Form E/E.88) clearly shows that it did not survive a ballooned landing at Parafield, South Australia on 12.12.40, and was "Converted to components and produce". The original Gipsy I engine from G-ABSD(1) is reportedly to be used in the building of G-ABSD(2).				
G-ABSE	Hawker Fury I	HF.4		7.12.31	WFU on 11.3.37. Scrapped in 1938. Canx.
G-ABSF	DH.60M Moth	1337	(US Army)	27.11.31	To Denmark as OY-DAG in 12/31. Canx.
G-ABSG	Comper C.97 Trimaster	3097		7.12.31	NTU - Construction abandoned. Canx.
G-ABSH	DH.60G Gipsy Moth	1885		.12.31	Crashed at Langstone Harbour, Portsmouth on 2.1.39. Canx.
G-ABSI	Airspeed AS.4 Ferry	4		.12.31	To RAF as AV968 in 4/40. Canx 18.4.40. To 474 ATC Sqdn at Long Eaton as 2758M in 11/40.
G-ABSJ	Airspeed AS.4 Ferry	5		.12.31	To India as VT-AFO in 8/34. Canx.
G-ABSK	DH.82 Tiger Moth	1796		15.12.31	To Portugal in 12/32. Canx.
G-ABSL	Avro 504K	-		.12.31	WFU on 26.6.34. Canx in 8/36.
G-ABSM	Avro 504K	-	H1986	.12.31	WFU on 12.1.37. Canx in 12/37.
G-ABSN	Avro 504K	-	H2965	.12.31	WFU on 5.2.35. Canx 7.4.38.
G-ABSO	DH.80A Puss Moth	2217		.12.31	To RAF as X9439 in 4/40. Canx 1.4.40.
G-ABSP	Avro 618 Ten	525		22.12.31	To Egyptian AF as F200. Canx.
G-ABSR	Avro 618 Ten	526		22.12.31	To Egyptian AF as F201. Canx.
G-ABSS	Avro 616 Sports Avian	576		.12.31	Crashed into River Mersey, near Speke on 1.2.36. Canx.
G-ABST	Spartan Arrow	87		.12.31	WFU on 20.4.34. Broken up in 1936. Canx.
G-ABSU	Stinson Junior S	8066	NC10897	.12.31	To Sweden as SE-AFE in 7/36. Canx.
G-ABSV	Avro 548	-		22.12.31	WFU on 31.8.35. Scrapped in 1940. Canx 1.12.46.
G-ABSW	DH.82 Tiger Moth	3102		6. 1.32	To India as VT-AOI in 3/41. Canx.
G-ABSX	DH.82 Tiger Moth	3103		6. 1.32	To India as VT-AOE in 2/41. Canx.
G-ABSY	DH.82 Tiger Moth	3104		6. 1.32	To India as VT-ANX in 2/41. Canx.
G-ABSZ	DH.82 Tiger Moth	3105		6. 1.32	To India as VT-AOF in 2/41. Canx.
G-ABTA	DH.82 Tiger Moth	3106		6. 1.32	To India as VT-AOO in 4/41. Canx.
G-ABTB	DH.82 Tiger Moth	3101	PH-AJO G-ABTB	8. 1.32	To RAF as BD153 in 8/40. Canx 8.8.40.
G-ABTC	Comper CLA.7 Swift	S.32/1		1. 1.32	Permit expired 18.7.84. Stored 11/93 Lalant. Canx by CAA 22.2.99.
G-ABTD	DH.80A Puss Moth	2216		. 1.32	To RAF as HK861 in 2/41. Canx 1.2.41.
G-ABTE	Klemm L.25b-II	360		. 1.32	To Sweden as SE-AGI in 1/38. Canx.
G-ABTF	DH.60M Moth	1798		. 1.32	To RAF as BK829 in 8/40. Canx 31.8.40.
G-ABTG	Armstrong Whitworth AW.15 Atalanta	AW.785		14. 1.32	Fatal crash into hillside on take-off from Kisumu, Kenya on 27.7.38. Canx.
G-ABTH	Armstrong Whitworth AW.15 Atalanta	AW.741		14. 1.32	Wing damaged in Egypt in 6/39 & WFU. Broken up. Canx.
G-ABTI	Armstrong Whitworth AW.15 Atalanta	AW.742		14. 1.32	To RAF as DG451 in 4/41. Canx 5.4.41.
G-ABTJ	Armstrong Whitworth AW.15 Atalanta	AW.743		14. 1.32	To RAF as DG452 in 4/41. Canx 5.4.41.
G-ABTK	Armstrong Whitworth AW.15 Atalanta	AW.744		14. 1.32	DBF in hangar fire at Willingdon Airport, Delhi, India on 29.9.36. Canx.
G-ABTL	Armstrong Whitworth AW.15 Atalanta	AW.784		14. 1.32	To RAF as DG450 in 4/41. Canx 7.4.41.
G-ABTM	Armstrong Whitworth AW.15 Atalanta	AW.786		14. 1.32	To India as VT-AEG in 8/33. Canx.
G-ABTN	Hawker Hart	H.H-3		25. 1.32	Lost over the English Channel off Ostend on 30.11.32 on return journey from Paris Aero Show. Canx.
G-ABTO	Comper/Cierva C.25 Autogiro	G.31/1		25. 1.32	Dismantled at Heston in 12/33. Canx.
G-ABTP	DH.60G Gipsy Moth	1891		. 1.32	To RAF as DG660 in 2/41. Canx 18.2.41.
G-ABTR	Spartan 3-Seater II	101		. 1.32	WFU on 5.5.38. Burnt at Gatwick in 1947. Canx.
G-ABTS	DH.60G Gipsy Moth	1900		. 2.32	To RAF as AW135 in 6/40. Canx 23.6.40.
G-ABTT	Spartan 3-Seater II	64		4. 2.32	Crashed at Stanton, Suffolk on 21.5.32. Canx.
G-ABTU	Spartan 3-Seater II	65		. 2.32	To Malaya as VR-RAQ in 1938. Canx.
G-ABTV	DH.80A Puss Moth	2218		. 2.32	To RAF as DP846 in 3/41. Canx 16.3.41.
G-ABTW	DH.60G Gipsy Moth	1893		9. 2.32	To Poland as SP-AHD in 3/32. Canx.
G-ABTX	Avro 504K	-		9. 2.32	NTU - Not converted. Canx.
G-ABTY	Spartan Cruiser I	24M		. 2.32	Crashed into the English Channel off Le Treport, France on 11.5.35. Canx.
G-ABTZ	Stinson Junior S	8050	NC10879	. 2.32	WFU on 11.4.38. Scrapped in 1940. Canx.
G-ABUA	Comper CLA.7 Swift	S.32/2		. 2.32	To Dutch East Indies as PK-SAQ in 11/34. Canx.

Regn	Type	c/n	Previous identity	Regn date	Fate or immediate subsequent identity (if known)
G-ABUB	DH.60G Gipsy Moth	363	VH-UFT G-AUFT	20. 2.32	To RAF as X5029 in 11/39. Canx 3.11.39.
G-ABUC	Avro 620 Cierva C.19 Autogiro Mk.IVP	5148		19. 2.32	To Singapore as VR-SAR in 11/36. Canx.
G-ABUD	Avro 620 Cierva C.19 Autogiro Mk.IVP	5149		19. 2.32	W/o in 3/33 (possibly at Hanworth). Canx.
G-ABUE	Avro 620 Cierva C.19 Autogiro Mk.IVP	5150		19. 2.32	Sold abroad in 5/32 (possibly to Germany). Canx.
G-ABUF	Avro 620 Cierva C.19 Autogiro Mk.IVP	5151		19. 2.32	Scrapped in 5/35 (possibly at Hanworth). Canx.
G-ABUG	Avro 620 Cierva C.19 Autogiro Mk.IVP	5152		19. 2.32	To Sweden as SE-ADU in 12/35. Canx.
G-ABUH	Avro 620 Cierva C.19 Autogiro Mk.IVP	5153		19. 2.32	To Australia in 1934 - regd as VH-USO on 5.11.34. Canx in 12/34.
G-ABUI	DH.60G-III Moth	5000		. 2.32	Crashed and burned at Nacton, Suffolk on 11.6.37. Canx.
G-ABUJ	DH.80A Puss Moth	2219		4. 3.32	Ditched into sea off Seaview, IoW on 15.7.33. Canx.
G-ABUK	Avro 504K	-	J8365	1. 3.32	Crashed at Hedon, Hull on 3.9.32. Canx.
G-ABUL	DH.82 Tiger Moth	3107		4. 3.32	To RAF as BB792 in 9/40. Canx 17.9.40.
"G-ABUL"	DH.82A Tiger Moth	83805	XL717 G-AOXG/T7291	----	(On display as such at RNAS Yeovilton)
G-ABUM	Not allocated.				
G-ABUN	Avro 616 Avian IVM	R3/CN/587		. 3.32	WFU on 8.9.39. Canx in 12/46.
G-ABUO	DH.83 Fox Moth	4000		19. 3.32	To Canada as CF-API in 1/33. Canx.
G-ABUP	DH.83 Fox Moth	4001		. 3.32	Crashed at Ashby, near Scunthorpe on 24.8.33. Canx.
G-ABUR	Percival P.1A Gull Four	D.20		. 3.32	Crashed at Luwinga, Northern Rhodesia on 26.8.35. Canx.
G-ABUS	Comper CLA.7 Swift	S.32/4		27. 2.32	Permit expired 19.6.79. (On rebuild .89)
G-ABUT	DH.83 Fox Moth	4002		. 3.32	To RAF as X9304 in 4/40. Canx 2.4.40.
G-ABUU	Comper CLA.7 Swift	S.32/5		7. 3.32	To 131 (City of Newcastle) ATC Sqdn at Jessmond Barracks, Newcastle from 1942 until 1951. To the Fundacion Infante de Orleans, Cuatro Vientos, Spain as EC-HAM 2/99. Canx 18.1.99.
G-ABUV	Percival P.1A Gull Four	3 & D.22		. 3.32	Crashed at Nice, France on 2.11.36. Canx.
G-ABUW	Blackburn B.2	3580/1	(B-2)	7. 3.32	To an ATC Sqdn at Blackburn Olympia Works, Leeds as 2887M in 2/42 (possibly 1493 or 2168 ATC Sqdn). Canx 17.2.42.
G-ABUX	DH.80A Puss Moth	2220		11. 3.32	To RAF as DD821 in 12/40. Canx 15.12.40.
G-ABUY	Westland Wapiti I	WA.2298C		9. 3.32	NTU - To RAF. Canx.
G-ABUZ	General Aircraft Monospar ST.4 Mk.I	GAL/ST4/1		. 3.32	WFU on 5.7.36. Canx in 12/46.
G-ABVA	DH.60G Gipsy Moth	1894		11. 3.32	To France as F-ALVV in 3/32. Canx.
G-ABVB	Westland Wessex	WA.2156		. 3.32	Crashed at Ryde, IoW on 8.6.36. Canx.
G-ABVC	Avro 504K	-	F8841	11. 3.32	WFU on 25.5.36. Canx in 11/45.
G-ABVD	Romeo Ro.5	145	I-AAVT	19. 3.32	Not certified. WFU in 1933. Canx.
G-ABVE	Arrow Active II	2		19. 3.32	
G-ABVF	Saunders-Roe A.17 Cutty Sark	A.17/9		21. 3.32	To Japan in 1932. Canx.
G-ABVG	Miles (Parnall) M.1 Satyr	001 & J.7		. 3.32	Crashed into telephone wires in 9/36. Canx.
G-ABVH	Avro 504N	-	J8372	. 3.32	WFU on 1.8.36. Canx in 12/46.
G-ABVI	DH.83 Fox Moth	4004		. 3.32	DBF in hangar fire at Maylands on 6.2.40. Canx.
G-ABVJ	DH.83 Fox Moth	4006		. 3.32	DBF at Brooklands on 24.10.36. Canx.
G-ABVK	DH.83 Fox Moth	4005		. 3.32	To RAF as X2867 in 12/39. Canx 29.12.39.
G-ABVL	Avro 616 Sport Avian IVM	R3/CN/588		. 3.32	To Sweden as SE-AEZ in 7/36. Canx.
G-ABVM	Vickers 203 Viastra VI	1	N1 (VH-UON)	23. 3.32	NTU - To O-6 in 5/31 & broken up at Brooklands in 12/32. Canx.
	Note: The marks VH-UON may have only been tentatively allotted. The marks were subsequently used by a Puss Moth.				
G-ABVN	General Aircraft Monospar ST.4 Mk.I	GAL/ST4/2		. 3.32	To Australia (departed UK on 19.12.36, arrived at Darwin, Australia 11.1.37) but not regd - aircraft sat around Mascot, New South Wales and believed used during World War II as an instructional airframe by the RAAF. Reportedly derelict at Bankstown, Sydney in 1954. Canx.
G-ABVO	General Aircraft Monospar ST.4 Mk.I	GAL/ST4/4		. 3.32	To India as VT-ADT in 4/34. Canx.
G-ABVP	General Aircraft Monospar ST.4 Mk.I	GAL/ST4/3		. 3.32	To RAF as X9434 in 4/40. Canx 8.4.40.
G-ABVR	General Aircraft Monospar ST.4 Mk.I	GAL/ST4/5		1. 4.32	To Switzerland as CH-347 in 11/32. Canx.
G-ABVS	General Aircraft Monospar ST.4 Mk.I	GAL/ST4/6	EI-AAQ G-ABVS	. 4.32	WFU on 21.8.37. Canx in 7/39.
G-ABVT	DH.80A Puss Moth	2223		. 3.32	To Spain as EC-AAV in 3/34. Canx.
G-ABVU	Avro 631 Cadet	592		. 4.32	WFU on 7.9.38. Scrapped at Barton in 1951. Canx.
G-ABVV	Avro 631 Cadet	589		5. 4.32	Crashed at Kirkbymoorside on 30.5.39. Canx.
G-ABVW	DH.60G-III Moth	5003		. 4.32	To Holland as PH-ART in 8/37. Canx.
G-ABVX	DH.80A Puss Moth	2228		18. 4.32	To RAF as X5044 in 11/39. Canx 15.11.39.
G-ABVY	Avro 504N	-	H2524	21. 5.32	Crashed at Nuneaton on 4.5.34. Canx in 10/36.
G-ABVZ	Blackburn L.1C Bluebird IV	SB.240	(G-ABEX)	19. 4.32	To Germany as D-2536 in 12/32. Canx.
G-ABWA	DH.80A Puss Moth	2229		. 4.32	Crashed at Le Havre, France on 30.12.36. Canx.
G-ABWB	DH.83 Fox Moth	4007		. 4.32	To India as VT-AKV in 12/38. Canx.
G-ABWC	Not allocated.				
G-ABWD	DH.83 Fox Moth	4009		16. 7.32	To Switzerland as CH-344 in 7/32. Canx.
G-ABWE	Comper CLA.7 Swift	S.32/7		. 4.32	Sold abroad in 2/40. Canx.
G-ABWF	DH.83 Fox Moth	4008		. 4.32	Crashed near Belgaum, India on 28.3.35. Canx.
G-ABWG	DH.80A Puss Moth	2232		. 4.32	To RAF as 2069M in 1/40. Canx 19.1.40.
G-ABWH	Comper CLA.7 Gipsy Swift	GS.32/2	NC27K G-ABWH	. 4.32	To Australia in 7/39 - regd as VH-ACG on 19.7.39. Canx.
G-ABWI	Blackburn B.2	4700/1		9. 5.32	Fatal crash at Ellerton, Selby on 9.10.36. Canx.

Regn	Type	c/n	Previous identity	Regn date	Fate or immediate subsequent identity (if known)
G-ABWJ	Avro 631 Cadet	597		30. 4.32	To Brazil as PP-TJC in 1/37. Canx.
G-ABWK	Avro 504K	-	E9353	. 4.32	To Australia in 1934 - did not attain registration. UK CofA expired 11.8.35. Canx in 12/35.
	Note: Shipped to Australia sometime late in 1934, by Major E.G.Clerk of Toowoomba, Queensland. A fate has not been established, although it was still extant at 27.3.35, when Major Clerk applied for registration in Australia for it.				
G-ABWL	DH.60G Gipsy Moth	1896		. 4.32	Crashed near Shoreham on 23.5.36. Canx 31.12.38.
G-ABWM	DH.60G Gipsy Moth	1898		. 4.32	To South Africa as ZS-AMX in 11/37. Canx.
G-ABWN	DH.60G Gipsy Moth	1897	PH-AJF G-ABWN	. 4.32	CofA lapsed on 6.10.39. Canx 1.12.46.
G-ABWO	Spartan 3-Seater I	66		. 4.32	DBF in hangar fire at Maylands on 6.2.40. Canx.
G-ABWP	Spartan Arrow 1	78		. 4.32	(Stored 3/99 Redhill)
G-ABWR	Spartan Arrow	79		. 4.32	To Denmark as OY-DOO in 8/38. Canx.
G-ABWS	Avro 631 Cadet	606		19. 5.32	To ATC at Stroud, Glos. as 2957M in 9/41. Canx 6.9.41.
G-ABWT	DH.60G-III Moth	5004		30. 5.32	To Kenya as VP-KAR in 6/32. Canx.
G-ABWU	Spartan 3-Seater I	67		. 4.32	DBF in hangar fire at Hooton Park on 8.7.40. Canx.
G-ABWV	Spartan 3-Seater I	68		. 4.32	Crashed at Little Ponton, near Grantham on 28.9.33. Canx.
G-ABWW	Comper CLA.7 Gipsy Swift	GS.32/1		. 4.32	To 2520 ATC Sqdn at Tonbridge, Kent in 1943 & WFU. Canx.
G-ABWX	Spartan 3-Seater I	69		. 5.32	Crashed at Tinwald Downs, near Dumfries on 12.9.32. Canx.
G-ABWY	DH.60G Gipsy Moth	1899		26. 5.32	Crashed at Croydon on 13.1.35. Canx in 11/40.
G-ABWZ	DH.80A Puss Moth	2236		. 5.32	Crashed near Chipping Norton on 17.12.38. Canx in 11/40.
G-ABXA	Bristol 96 Fighter (F.2b)	7059	J8258	. 5.32	WFU on 30.6.33. Canx in 11/34.
G-ABXB	DH.60G Gipsy Moth	1902		. 5.32	To RAF as BK848 in 8/40. Canx 8.8.40.
G-ABXC	DH.60G Gipsy Moth	1903		4. 6.32	To France as F-AMAR in 6/32. Canx.
G-ABXD	Avro 620 Cierva C.19 Autogiro Mk.IVP	5154		1. 6.32	To Japan in 8/32. Canx.
G-ABXE	Avro 620 Cierva C.19 Autogiro Mk.IVP	5155		1. 6.32	To Japan in 8/32. Canx.
G-ABXF	Avro 620 Cierva C.19 Autogiro Mk.IVP	5156		1. 6.32	To Japan as J-BAYA in 12/32. Canx.
G-ABXG	Avro 620 Cierva C.19 Autogiro Mk.IVP	5157		1. 6.32	Crashed at Hanworth on 25.4.37. Canx.
G-ABXH	Avro 620 Cierva C.19 Autogiro Mk.IVP	5158		1. 6.32	To Spain as EC-W13/EC-ATT in 12/32. Canx.
G-ABXI	Avro 620 Cierva C.19 Autogiro Mk.IVP	5159		1. 6.32	To Spanish AF as 49-1 in 12/32. Canx.
G-ABXJ	DH.80A Puss Moth	2238		11. 6.32	To Ceylon in 7/33. Canx.
G-ABXK	Breda 33	3208		29. 6.32	To Italy in 10/32. Canx.
G-ABXL	Granger Archeopteryx	3A		3. 6.32	(On display at Old Warden)
G-ABXM	DH.60M Moth	3028		6. 6.32	To Yugoslavia as UN-SAI/YU-SAI in 7/32. Canx.
G-ABXN	Airspeed AS.5 Courier	7		7. 6.32	To RAF as X9427 on 12.6.40; NTU and scrapped at White Waltham in 9/40. Canx.
G-ABXO	Spartan 3-Seater	27	G-AAGV	7. 6.32	WFU on 23.7.38. Canx 1.12.46.
G-ABXP	Cierva C.19 Autogiro Mk.V	-		13. 6.32	Scrapped in 1935 (possibly at Hanworth). Canx.
G-ABXR	DH.60G Gipsy Moth	1905		. 6.32	To RAF as AW111 in 6/40. Canx 6.6.40.
G-ABXS	DH.83 Fox Moth	4015		. 6.32	To Australia in 8/35 - regd as VH-UVL on 6.9.35. Canx.
G-ABXT	DH.60G Gipsy Moth	1901		. 6.32	To South Africa in 4/33. Canx.
G-ABXU	Avro 631 Cadet	607		16. 6.32	To 1821 ATC Sqdn at Oakdale, Wales as 2958M in 1/42. Canx 11.1.42.
G-ABXV	Bristol 96 Fighter (F.2b)	6464	F4711	15. 6.32	Crashed at Capenoch, Dumfriesshire on 17.9.33. Canx.
	(Originally c/n 4697, rebuilt c.1924 with present c/n)				
G-ABXW	Saunders-Roe A.19 Cloud	A.19/4		. 6.32	Fatal crash into sea off Jersey, Channel Islands on 31.7.36. Canx.
G-ABXX	DH.60G-III Moth	5005		28. 6.32	To Colombia in 11/32. Canx.
G-ABXY	DH.80A Puss Moth	2241		. 6.32	Crashed near Genholac, Gevennes, France on 28.3.34. Canx.
G-ABXZ	DH.60G Gipsy Moth	1904		. 6.32	To RAF as X5052 in 11/39. Canx 17.11.39.
G-ABYA	DH.60G Gipsy Moth	1906		. 6.32	Crashed near Biggin Hill on 21.5.72. Canx by CAA 3.4.89. (Stored 2/95 Biggin Hill)
G-ABYB	Avro 504K	-		. 6.32	WFU on 28.2.33. Canx in 6/33.
G-ABYC	Avro 631 Cadet	621		. 7.32	WFU at Barton on 4.8.39. Scrapped in 5/51. Canx.
G-ABYD	Bristol 96 Fighter (F.2b)	7574	J8446	4. 7.32	Scrapped in 3/33. Canx.
G-ABYE	Bristol 96 Fighter (F.2b)	7559	F4721	. 7.32	WFU on 17.12.34. Canx in 4/38.
	(Originally c/n 4707, rebuilt c.1924 with new c/n 6680, again c.1925 with new c/n 6874, again c.1927 with c/n 7116, then again c.1930 with present c/n)				
G-ABYF	Bristol 96 Fighter (F.2b)	7573	J8429	. 7.32	WFU at Redhill on 12.8.35. Broken up in 1939. Canx.
G-ABYG	Spartan 3-Seater I	70		. 7.32	WFU on 26.8.38. Canx in 12/46.
G-ABYH	Spartan 3-Seater I	71		. 7.32	Crashed at Hayling Island on 20.7.35. Canx.
G-ABYI	DH.60G Gipsy Moth	1907		. 7.32	To India as VT-AFK in 10/34. Canx.
G-ABYJ	DH.82 Tiger Moth	3137		14. 7.32	Crashed at Winkfield on 13.7.36. Canx.
G-ABYK	Boulton & Paul P.64 Mailplane	P64		14. 7.32	Fatal crash when it struck the ground during third test flight of the Martlesham trials on 21.10.33. Canx.
G-ABYL	Bristol 96 Fighter (F.2b)	7579	J8444	21. 7.32	Scrapped in 1933. Canx.
G-ABYM	Avro 626	622		22. 7.32	WFU on 17.8.38. Scrapped in 1939. Canx.
G-ABYN	Spartan 3-Seater II	102	EI-ABU G-ABYN	. 7.32	(On rebuild by Croydon Aviation Co 1995-1998) Canx by CAA 31.3.99. Reserved as ZK-ARH.
G-ABYO	DH.83 Fox Moth	4012		. 7.32	Crashed at Caerwent, Monmouth on 16.6.34. Canx.
G-ABYP	DH.80A Puss Moth	2233	BK870 G-ABYP	. 7.32	Crashed at Eaton Bray, Beds. on 31.8.47. Canx.
G-ABYR	DH.83 Fox Moth	4017		11. 8.32	To Australia in 11/32 - regd as VH-UQR on 21.3.33. Canx.
G-ABYS	Sikorsky S-38B	314/19	NC15V	. 7.32	To France as F-AOUC in 2/36. Canx.
G-ABYT	Bristol 96 Fighter (F.2b)	7568	J8434	3. 8.32	Scrapped in 1936 after collision with barbed wire fence at Lympne in 1935. Canx.
G-ABYU	DH.80A Puss Moth	2234		. 8.32	To France as F-AQCE in 6/37. Canx.

Regn	Type	c/n	Previous identity	Regn date	Fate or immediate subsequent identity (if known)
G-ABYV	DH.60G-III Moth	5007		. 8.32	To Austria as OE-DAC in 6/35. Canx.
G-ABYW	DH.80A Puss Moth	2240		. 8.32	To Spanish Nationalists in 2/37. Canx.
G-ABYX	Handley Page HP.33 Clive I	HP.33	J9126	13. 8.32	Scrapped in 1935. Canx.
G-ABYY	Fairey Fox III	F.1842		13. 8.32	To Chinese AF in 1933. Canx.
G-ABYZ	DH.60G-III Moth	5008		. 8.32	Sold abroad in 8/37. Canx.
G-ABZA	DH.83 Fox Moth	4014	(ZS-ADE)	26. 8.32	To Yugoslavia as UN-SAK in 9/32. Canx.
G-ABZB(1)	DH.60G-III Moth	5011		30. 8.32	To Sweden as SE-AIA in 5/39. Canx.
G-ABZB(2)	DH.60G-III Moth Major (Regd as ex.SE-AIA in error)	5138	SE-AEL OY-DAK	11. 9.80	
G-ABZC	Avro 504K	-		. 8.32	Crashed at Chard on 30.4.33. Canx.
G-ABZD	DH.83 Fox Moth	4026		26. 9.32	To USA as NC12739 in 12/32. Canx.
G-ABZE	DH.60G Gipsy Moth	1908		. 9.32	To RAF as DG585 in 1/41. Canx 25.1.41.
G-ABZF	Avro 631 Cadet	623		. 9.32	Crashed at Liverpool on 10.6.36. Canx.
G-ABZG	Bristol 96 Fighter (F.2b)	7043	J8245	. 9.32	WFU on 8.8.34. Scrapped 5/38. Canx.
G-ABZH	Spartan 3-Seater II	103		. 9.32	Crashed near Drogheda, Ireland on 1.10.33. Canx as WFU 2.10.33.
G-ABZI	Spartan 3-Seater II	104	YI-AAB G-ABZI	. 9.32	Crashed at Farnborough on 7.8.36. Canx.
G-ABZJ	Blackburn B-1 Segrave	3854/1		17. 9.32	NTU - To G-ACMI 11/33. Canx at census in 12/32.
G-ABZK	DH.60G-III Moth	5012		. 9.32	CofA lapsed on 16.5.40. Scrapped in 11.45. Canx.
G-ABZL	Armstrong Whitworth AW.16	AW.823		22. 9.32	To China in 2/34. Canx.
G-ABZM	DH.83 Fox Moth	4018		23. 9.32	To Norway as LN-ABP in 1/33 but crashed in North Sea during delivery flight on 23.1.33. Canx.
G-ABZN	DH.83 Fox Moth	4022	SU-ABA G-ABZN	. 9.32	To Sweden as SE-AFL in 9/36. Canx.
G-ABZO	Klemm L.25c-XI	413	D-7	. 9.32	To Ireland as EI-ABJ in 1/37. Canx.
G-ABZP	Avro 621 Tutor	624		26. 9.32	WFU on 13.7.39 at Pengam Moors, Cardiff. Scrapped in 1940. Canx.
G-ABZR	Avro 621 Tutor	625		26. 9.32	Crashed at Cape Town, South Africa on 17.2.33. Canx.
G-ABZS	DH.60G-III Moth	5014		7.10.32	To RAF as BD177 in 8/40. Canx 23.8.40.
G-ABZT	DH.60G-III Moth	5015		7.10.32	Crashed on Isle of Islay on 24.5.36. Canx.
G-ABZU	DH.60G-III Moth	5016		7.10.32	To RAF as BD178 in 8/40. Canx 23.8.40.
G-ABZV	DH.60G-III Moth	5017		7.10.32	To RAF as BD179 in 8/40. Canx 23.8.40.
G-ABZW	Bristol 105 Bulldog IV	7745	R-7	3.10.32	NTU - To RAF as K4292 in 7/34. Canx 26.7.34.
G-ABZX	Blackburn L.1C Bluebird IV	SB.241	(G-ABEY)	29. 9.32	To G-ADXG in 11/35. Canx.
G-ABZY	Stinson Junior S	8093	NC12141	20.10.32	Sold abroad in 1/34. Canx.
G-ABZZ	Comper CLA.7 Swift	S.32/8		10. 8.32	To Yugoslavia as YU-PDS in 8/36. Canx.
G-ACAA(1)	Bristol 96 Fighter (F.2b)	7434	F4516	.10.32	
G-ACAA(2)	Bristol F.2b Fighter	-		25.10.91	(On rebuild 7/97)
	(Regd as "original" G-ACAA with c/n 7434 ex F4516 but in fact rebuilt from various components including ex Weston-on-the-Green fuselage frame)				
G-ACAB	DH.80A Puss Moth	2247		.10.32	DBF in hangar fire at Hooton on 8.7.40. Canx.
G-ACAC	Bristol 96 Fighter (F.2b)	7571	J8437	1.11.32	WFU at Hooton on 11.4.34. Scrapped in 1/36. Canx.
G-ACAD	Spartan 3-Seater II	105		.10.32	WFU on 12.5.39. Scrapped between 1939 and 1945. Canx 1.12.46.
G-ACAE	Ford 5-AT-D	5-AT-107	NC440H	.10.32	To RAF as X5000 in 4/40. Canx 26.4.40.
G-ACAF	Spartan 3-Seater II	106		.10.32	Scrapped in 1938. Canx in 1/39.
G-ACAG	Comper CLA.7 Swift	S.32/10		1.11.32	To Australia in 1934 - regd as VH-UVC on 9.10.34. Canx in 12/34.
G-ACAH	Blackburn B.2	4700/2		1.11.32	To 1187 ATC Sqdn at Hemel Hempstead as 2907M in 2/42. Canx 17.2.42.
G-ACAI	Armstrong Whitworth Atlas II (Rebuild of Atlas I G-EBYF)	AW.830		1.11.32	To Hong Kong as VR-HCD in 12/35. Canx.
G-ACAJ	DH.83 Fox Moth	4033		19.11.32	To G-ACDD in 2/33. Canx.
G-ACAK	Ford 4-AT-E	4-AT-68	EC-KKA M-CKAA/NC8406	7.11.32	To Australia in 5/35 - regd as VH-USX on 24.5.35. Canx.
G-ACAL	Percival P.1B Gull Four	D.21		10.11.32	Crashed at Sandhurst, Kent on 1.10.33. Canx.
G-ACAM	DH.60G Gipsy Moth	1915		.11.32	To India as VT-AFJ in 6/34. Canx.
G-ACAN	DH.84 Dragon I	6000	E-9	16.11.32	Crashed near Dunbeath on 21.5.41 due to engine failure. Canx.
G-ACAO	DH.84 Dragon I	6001		16.11.32	To RAF as X9398 in 4/40. Canx 2.4.40.
G-ACAP	DH.84 Dragon I	6002		16.11.32	Fatal crash at Lyndhurst on 26.3.36. Canx.
G-ACAR	[Reservation]	-		. .32R	NTU. Canx.
G-ACAS	Fairey Fox I (Also c/n FA.35756)	F.3575		24.11.32	Caught fire in the air & burnt out on landing at Ford on 14.7.33. Canx.
G-ACAT	Percival P.1B Gull Four	D.24		20. 3.33	To Australia in 4/33 - regd as VH-UQW on 18.5.33. Canx.
G-ACAU	Avro 504K	-		16.11.32	Crashed at Epping on 22.5.33. Canx.
G-ACAV	Avro 504K	-		16.11.32	WFU on 28.5.34. Canx.
G-ACAW	Avro 504K	-		16.11.32	WFU on 1.3.37. Canx in 9/37.
G-ACAX	Avro 552	12		16.11.32	Crashed at Sandridge, near Hatfield on 27.3.36. Canx.
G-ACAY	Avro 638 Club Cadet	626		.11.32	Scrapped at Horton Kirby in 1940. Canx.
G-ACAZ	Westland P.V.3	WA.2419	P-3	22.11.32	To RAF as K4048 in 11/33. Canx.
G-ACBA	DH.82 Tiger Moth	3152		20.12.32	Collided with Hawker Hart K4372 at Filton on 3.5.39 & DBR. Canx.
G-ACBB	DH.82 Tiger Moth	3153		20.12.32	Destroyed in mid-air collision with DH.82A G-ACBE over Yate on 25.6.34. Canx.
G-ACBC	DH.82 Tiger Moth	3154		20.12.32	Crashed at Shepperdine on 11.3.40. Canx.
G-ACBD	DH.82 Tiger Moth	3155		20.12.32	To India as VT-ANY in 2/41. Canx.
G-ACBE	DH.82 Tiger Moth	3156		20.12.32	Destroyed in mid-air collision with DH.82A G-ACBB over Yate on 25.6.34. Canx.
G-ACBF	DH.82 Tiger Moth	3157		20.12.32	To India as VT-AOP in 4/41. Canx.
G-ACBG	DH.82 Tiger Moth	3158		20.12.32	To India as VT-AOM in 4/41. Canx.

Regn	Type	c/n	Previous identity	Regn date	Fate or immediate subsequent identity (if known)
G-ACBH	Blackburn B.2 (Probably now a composite with G-ADFO c/n 5920/2 w/o in 1940)	4700/3	(2895M) G-ACBH	1.12.32	Crashed 4 miles west of Brough on 16.3.40. Fuselage impressed 17.2.42 as 2895M, but was regd as G-ACBH when used by the 692 ATC Sqdn at Brentwood Institute, Essex from 2/42 until c.1945. (Stored 1/96 for possible refurbishment)
G-ACBI	Blackburn B.2	4700/4		1.12.32	Fatal crash at Brough Haven, East Yorks on 30.7.37. Canx.
G-ACBJ	Blackburn B.2	4700/5		1.12.32	To 1069 ATC Sqdn at Wimborne Minster, Dorset as 2900M in 2/42. Canx 17.2.42.
G-ACBK	Blackburn B.2	4700/6		1.12.32	To 218 ATC Sqdn at Rotherham, Yorks as 2906M in 2/42. Canx 17.2.42.
G-ACBL	DH.80A Puss Moth	2246		17.12.32	To Spain as EC-VAA in 1/33. Canx.
G-ACBM	Spartan Cruiser II	2	YI-AAA G-ACBM	.12.32	Scrapped in 11/37. Canx.
G-ACBN	DH.82A Tiger Moth	3148		5.12.32	To Spanish AF as 33-1 in 12/32. Canx.
G-ACBO	DH.83 Fox Moth	4036		.12.32	To Kenya as VP-KBH in 11/34. Canx.
G-ACBP	Shackleton-Murray SM.1	8		.12.32	Landed in sea off Isle of Wight in 1937. Broken up in 1937. Canx.
G-ACBR	Westland Wallace (Originally regd as PV.6/1)	WA.1822	P-6 G-AAWA	28.12.32	To RAF as K3488 in 12/33. Canx.
G-ACBS	Heinkel He.64c	427	K3596 G-ACBS/D-2305	.12.32	To Southern Rhodesia as VP-YBI in 1/37. Canx.
G-ACBT	Airspeed AS.4 Ferry	6		21.12.32	WFU on 17.2.35. Dismantled at Renfrew in 1941. Canx.
G-ACBU	DH.60G Gipsy Moth	1849	ZS-ADB	26. 1.33	To Ireland as EI-AAW in 5/34. Canx.
G-ACBV	Avro 594B Avian IV	R3/AV/423		.12.32	WFU on 30.4.37. Canx 1.12.46.
G-ACBW	DH.84 Dragon I	6009		13. 1.33	To RAF as BS816 in 10/40. Canx 27.10.40.
G-ACBX	DH.60G-III Moth	5020		. 1.33	To RAF as X5132 in 12/39. Canx 11.12.39.
G-ACBY	Comper CLA.7 Gipsy Swift	GS.32/3		10. 1.33	Crashed at Moulton, Northants during King's Cup Race on 8.7.33. Canx.
G-ACBZ	DH.83 Fox Moth	4040		24. 1.33	To Australia in 12/36 - regd as VH-UZD on 1.4.37. Canx.
G-ACCA	DH.83 Fox Moth	4041		24. 1.33	To Australia in 1935 - regd as VH-UTY on 4.6.35. Canx in 6/35.
G-ACCB	DH.83 Fox Moth	4042		24. 1.33	Ditched in sea off Southport on 25.9.56 - Salvaged. (On rebuild 10/95)
G-ACCC	Vickers 259 Viastra X	1		19. 1.33	To RAF as L6102 in 5/35. Canx.
G-ACCD	Armstrong Whitworth AW.35 Scimitar	AW.828		13. 1.33	WFU on 31.7.35. Scrapped in 1936. Canx.
G-ACCE	DH.84 Dragon I	6010		24. 3.33	Crashed on take-off from Kirkwall on 29.8.34. Canx.
G-ACCF	DH.83 Fox Moth	4046		2. 2.33	Impressed into RAF on 31.8.41 (no serial known). Canx.
G-ACCG	Bristol 96 Fighter (F.2b)	7576	J6790	. 2.33	WFU on 10.6.38. Scrapped in 7/39. Canx.
G-ACCH	Avro 631 Cadet	627		6. 2.33	WFU on 18.4.40. Broken up for spares in 12/41. Canx.
G-ACCI	Avro 631 Cadet	628		6. 2.33	To 1431 ATC Sqdn at Newbiggin-by-the-Sea as 2945M in 7/41. Canx 25.7.41.
G-ACCJ	Avro 631 Cadet	629		6. 2.33	To 1084 ATC Sqdn at Market Harborough as 2946M in 7/41. Canx 25.7.41.
G-ACCK	Avro 631 Cadet	630		6. 2.33	To 473 ATC Sqdn at Hartlepool as 2952M in 8/41. Canx 31.8.41.
G-ACCL	Avro 631 Cadet	631		6. 2.33	WFU on 11.1.40. Scrapped in 8/42. Canx 4.3.42.
G-ACCM	Avro 631 Cadet	632		6. 2.33	Crashed in River Thames at Purfleet on 18.4.36. Canx.
G-ACCN	Avro 631 Cadet	633		6. 2.33	Damaged when hit by Hawker Hart Special K4415 which had crashlanded at Hamble on 16.6.38. To 392 ATC Sqdn at Newmarket as ground instructional airframe 2939M in 7/41. Canx 23.7.41.
G-ACCO	General Aircraft Monospar ST.6 (Originally regd as ST.4 Mk.II)	GAL/ST4/8	X9376 G-ACCO	2. 2.33	To RAF as DR849 in 8/41. Canx.
G-ACCP	General Aircraft Monospar ST.4 Mk.II	GAL/ST4/10		2. 2.33	WFU on 10.8.39. Canx.
G-ACCR	DH.84 Dragon I	6011		28. 2.33	Ditched into the English Channel off Le Treport, France on 22.1.36. Canx.
G-ACCS	DH.83 Fox Moth	4044		13. 2.33	To Australia in 8/36 - regd as VH-UUS on 18.2.37. Canx.
G-ACCT	DH.83 Fox Moth	4047		13. 2.33	To Australia in 11/37 - regd as VH-ABU on 20.1.38. Canx.
G-ACCU	DH.83 Fox Moth	4048		13. 2.33	To Australia in 12/36 - regd as VH-UZC on 23.3.37. Canx.
G-ACCV	DH.84 Dragon I	6014		7. 2.33	Crashed at Bridgeport, Connecticut, USA on 24.7.33. Canx.
G-ACCW	DH.60G-III Moth	5022		13. 2.33	To RAF as X5114 in 12/39. Canx 11.12.39.
G-ACCX	Avro 504K	-		8. 2.33	Crashed at Stewkley, Leighton Buzzard on 19.6.34. Canx.
G-ACCY	DH.60G Gipsy Moth Coupe	1245	G-AAUR	. 2.33	Crashed at Redhill on 20.6.38. Canx.
G-ACCZ	DH.84 Dragon I	6015		21. 4.33	To RAF as AW154 in 7/40. Canx 1.7.40.
G-ACDA	DH.82 Tiger Moth (Note : DH.82A N3529, based Old Rhinebeck, New York is painted as G-ACDA)	3175	BB724 G-ACDA	6. 2.33	(Crashed & burned out near Cirencester 27.6.79 - rebuild probably composite with G-ANOR) (On rebuild by Skysport off-site 1/96)
G-ACDB	DH.82 Tiger Moth	3176		6. 2.33	To RAF as BB725 in 10/40. Canx 30.10.40.
G-ACDC	DH.82 Tiger Moth (Now composite airframe after several major rebuilds)	3177	BB726 G-ACDC	6. 2.33	
G-ACDD	DH.83 Fox Moth	4033	OO-ENC G-ACDD/(G-ACAJ)	.12.32	To New Zealand as ZK-AEK in 10/35. Canx in 7/35.
G-ACDE	DH.82 Tiger Moth	3178		6. 2.33	To RAF as BB727 in 10/40. Canx 30.10.40.
G-ACDF	DH.82 Tiger Moth	3179		6. 2.33	To RAF as BB741 in 10/40. Canx 30.10.40.
G-ACDG	DH.82 Tiger Moth	3180	BB728 G-ACDG	6. 2.33	To Holland as PH-UAY in 3/47. Canx.
G-ACDH	DH.82 Tiger Moth	3181		6. 2.33	Crashed near White Waltham on 25.2.38. Canx.
G-ACDI	DH.82 Tiger Moth (Composite rebuild)	3182	BB742 G-ACDI	6. 2.33	Crashed at Christchurch on 10.7.54. (On rebuild 8/97)

Regn	Type	c/n	Previous identity	Regn date	Fate or immediate subsequent identity (if known)
G-ACDJ	DH.82 Tiger Moth	3183	BB729 G-ACDJ	6. 2.33	
G-ACDK	DH.82 Tiger Moth	3184		6. 2.33	To RAF as BB730 in 10/40. Canx 10.10.40.
G-ACDL	DH.84 Dragon I	6016		21. 4.33	To Spanish Republicans in 8/36. Canx.
G-ACDM	DH.84 Dragon I	6017		21. 4.33	To South Africa as ZS-AEI in 11/33. Canx.
G-ACDN	DH.84 Dragon I	6018		21. 4.33	To RAF as AW170 in 7/40. Canx 7.7.40.
G-ACDO	Handley Page W.8e	1	OO-AHJ	. 2.33R	NTU - Scrapped at Ford in 1934. Canx.
G-ACDP	Saro A.17 Cutty Sark	A.17/10		13. 2.33	CofA expired 10.4.39 & WFU at Hamble. Scrapped. Canx.
G-ACDR	Saro A.17 Cutty Sark	A.17/11		13. 2.33	WFU at Hamble on 11.4.37. Broken up in 1938. Canx.
"G-ACDR"	DH.82A Tiger Moth	86536	N9295	----	Was painted in fictitious marks at Denton, Texas 6/91.
G-ACDS	Comper CLA.7 Swift	S.33/2		13. 2.33	Delivered to France on 16.4.33; crashed in 1/34; rebuilt as F-AOTP in 1936. Canx.
G-ACDT	Comper CLA.7 Swift	S.33/3		13. 2.33	Destroyed in a German air raid on Paris in 6/40. Canx.
G-ACDU	DH.80A Puss Moth	2142	UN-SAA	. 2.33	Crashed at Aston Clinton, Bucks. on 13.6.36. Canx as PWFU in 7/38.
G-ACDV	DH.60G-III Moth	5023		21. 2.33	To RAF as BD174 in 8/40. Canx 23.8.40.
G-ACDW	Spartan Cruiser II	3		20. 2.33	To Egypt as SU-ABL in 4/34. Canx.
G-ACDX	Spartan Cruiser II	4		20. 2.33	DBR in forced landing at Gosport on 9.10.35. Canx.
G-ACDY	DH.82A Tiger Moth	3189		20. 3.33	Crashed in River Don, Aberdeen on 26.8.33. Canx.
G-ACDZ	DH.83 Fox Moth	4054		15. 3.33	To RAF as X2865 in 12/39. Canx 29.12.39.
G-ACEA	DH.83 Fox Moth	4055		15. 3.33	To RAF as AW124 in 6/40. Canx 23.6.40.
G-ACEB	DH.83 Fox Moth	4058		15. 3.33	To Australia in 1935 - regd as VH-USJ on 9.7.35. Canx.
G-ACEC	DH.83 Fox Moth	4059		15. 3.33	To Australia in 4/37 - regd as VH-AAX on 23.7.37. Canx.
G-ACED	DH.83 Fox Moth	4064		12. 4.33	To Australia in 1937 - regd as VH-UZL on 27.5.37. Canx.
G-ACEE	DH.83 Fox Moth	4065		12. 4.33	Crashed at Riverside Park, Dundee, Angus on 31.7.34. Canx.
G-ACEF	Spartan 3-Seater II	107		. 2.33	WFU on 13.4.39. Scrapped between 1939 and 1945. Canx.
G-ACEG	Spartan Clipper (ST-5 Wing)	201	S-5	24. 2.33	Destroyed in air raid at Cowes, IoW on 4.5.42. Canx.
G-ACEH	DH.82 Tiger Moth	3185		28. 2.33	To Poland as SP-AMX in 2/34. Canx.
G-ACEI	DH.83 Fox Moth	4068		21. 4.33	Crashed & DBF at Alva, Clackmannanshire on 1.7.33. Canx.
G-ACEJ	DH.83 Fox Moth	4069		21. 4.33	
G-ACEK	DH.84 Dragon I	6019		2. 5.33	To RAF as AX867 in 7/40. Canx 21.7.40.
G-ACEL	Handley Page HP.34 Hare	HP.34/1	J8622	27. 2.33	Not converted. WFU at Hanworth in 3/33, progressively broken up by vandals until the remains were scrapped in 1937. Canx.
G-ACEM	Blackburn B.2	5093/1		28. 2.33	To 438 ATC Sqdn at Thanet, Kent as 2890M in 2.42. Canx 17.2.42.
G-ACEN	Blackburn B.2	5093/2		28. 2.33	Fatal crash at Osgodby, Selby on 26.12.40. Canx.
G-ACEO	Blackburn B.2	5093/3		28. 2.33	To 1028 (Eden Valley) ATC Sqdn at Cumberland as 2899M in 2/42. Canx 17.2.42.
G-ACEP	Blackburn B.2	5093/4		28. 2.33	WFU on 1.10.41. Canx 11.9.42.
G-ACER	Blackburn B.2	5093/5		28. 2.33	Crashed at Brough on 11.9.40. Canx.
G-ACES	Blackburn B.2	5093/6		28. 2.33	To 1283 ATC Sqdn at Gelligaer, Wales as 2904M in 2/42. Canx 17.2.42.
G-ACET	DH.84 Dragon I (Composite based on original wings)	6021	2779M AW171/G-ACET	21. 4.33	(On rebuild .95)
G-ACEU	DH.84 Dragon I	6022		24. 3.33	Sold abroad in 3/37. Canx.
G-ACEV	DH.84 Dragon I	6023		8. 5.33	To Spanish Republicans in 8/36. Canx.
G-ACEW	General Aircraft Monospar ST.4 Mk.II	GAL/ST4/11		2. 3.33	DBF at Croydon on 13.12.37. Canx.
G-ACEX	DH.83 Fox Moth	4056		. 3.33	To RAF as X2866 in 12/39. Canx 29.12.39.
G-ACEY	DH.83 Fox Moth	4057		. 3.33	DBF in hangar fire at Hooton on 8.7.40. Canx.
G-ACEZ	DH.82 Tiger Moth	3186	BB790 G-ACEZ	. 3.33	Crashed near Andover on 23.8.61. Canx.
G-ACFA	DH.82 Tiger Moth	3187		. 3.33	To India as VT-AGD in 1/35. Canx.
G-ACFB	Airspeed AS.4 Ferry	9		6. 3.33	To 1037 (Meir) ATC Sqdn, near Stoke as DJ715 in 2/41. Canx 18.2.41.
G-ACFC	DH.83 Fox Moth	4053		23. 3.33	To RAF as AX859 in 5/40. Canx 10.5.40.
G-ACFD	Comper CLA.7 Swift	S.33/5	(CH-353)	8. 3.33	To France as F-ANIY in 9/34. Canx.
G-ACFE	DH.80A Puss Moth	2259		. 3.33	To France as F-AMYR in 5/34. Canx.
G-ACFF	DH.83 Fox Moth	4060		24. 3.33	To RAF as X9305 in 4/40. Canx 2.4.40.
G-ACFG	DH.84 Dragon I	6027		3. 5.33	To Australia in 2/37 - allotted regn VH-UZG but NTU as aircraft crashed about 22 miles north of Cairns, Queensland on 7.5.37 and was w/o. Canx.
G-ACFH	Avro 640 Cadet	640		18. 3.33	DBF in hangar fire at Hooton on 8.7.40. Canx.
G-ACFI	Avro 671 Cierva C.30A Autogiro	1		21. 3.33	No CofA issued. Scrapped in 1938. Canx.
G-ACFJ	Percival P.1C Gull Four	D.23		21. 3.33	To France as F-AOZS in 1/36. Canx.
G-ACFK	Bristol Fighter F.2b	7431	J8285	22. 3.33	No CofA issued. Scrapped in 5/36. Canx.
G-ACFL	Bristol Fighter F.2b	7570	C4897	22. 3.33	Not converted. Scrapped in 5/36. Canx.
G-ACFM	Not allocated.				
G-ACFN	Bristol Fighter F.2b (Originally c/n 4528, rebuilt c.1923 with new c/n 6282, reconditioned c.1928 with present c/n)	7144	F4542	22. 3.33	Not converted. Scrapped in 5/36. Canx.
G-ACFO	Bristol Fighter F.2b	7137	C4750	22. 3.33	Not converted. Scrapped in 5/36. Canx.
G-ACFP	Bristol Fighter F.2b (Originally c/n 4420, rebuilt c.1925 with new c/n 6865, reconditioned c.1931 with present c/n)	7581	F4434	22. 3.33	WFU on 12.4.34. Scrapped in 1/38. Canx.
G-ACFR	General Aircraft Monospar ST.4 Mk.II	GAL/ST4/12		30. 3.33	WFU on 3.7.36. Canx.
G-ACFS	Avro 640 Cadet	644		12. 4.33	DBF in hangar fire at Hooton on 8.7.40. Canx.
G-ACFT	Avro 640 Cadet	645		12. 4.33	DBF in hangar fire at Hooton on 8.7.40. Canx.
G-ACFU	Avro 640 Cadet	646		12. 4.33	Crashed at Crawcott, near Buckingham on 18.10.37. Canx.
G-ACFV	Avro 642-IIM Eighteen	642		. 4.33	Crashed on 4.6.34; Rebuilt and sold to Australia in 1936 - regd as VH-UXD on 28.9.36. Canx.
G-ACFW	Avro 626	648		5. 4.33	WFU on 1.7.38. Scrapped in 1950. Canx.
G-ACFX	Avro 640 Cadet	647		12. 4.33	To Malaya as VR-RAJ in 11/36. Canx.

Regn	Type	c/n	Previous identity	Regn date	Fate or immediate subsequent identity (if known)
G-ACFY	Percival P.1C Gull Four	D.26		8. 4.33	Sold abroad in 6/37. Canx.
G-ACFZ	Avro 626 Seaplane	643		12. 4.33	To Brazil in 9/36. Canx.
G-ACGA	Avro 639 Cabin Cadet	639	K-14	12. 4.33	No CofA issued. Scrapped at Woodford in 1936. Canx.
G-ACGB	DH.83 Fox Moth	4007		21. 4.33	To India as VT-AGI in 3/35. Canx.
G-ACGC	Percival P.1C Gull Four	D.25		8. 4.33	To Brazil as PP-BAA in 1/37. Canx.
G-ACGD	DH.60G-III Moth	5025		21. 4.33	Crashed on Broad Law on 25.7.36. Canx.
G-ACGE	DH.82A Tiger Moth	3155	PH-AJD G-ACGE	21. 4.33	To India as VT-AJV in 1/38. Canx.
G-ACGF	Avro 618 Ten	527		11. 4.33	WFU on 5.4.35. Canx in 12/46.
G-ACGG	DH.84 Dragon I	6025		3. 5.33	To Australia in 12/37 - regd as VH-AAC on 18.2.38. Canx.
G-ACGH	Miles M.2 Hawk	H.101		19. 4.33	Canx in 12/33.
G-ACGI	General Aircraft Monospar ST.6	GAL/ST6/14		24. 4.33	To RAF as AV979 in 5/40. Canx 6.5.40.
G-ACGJ	Waco UIC	3749		19. 6.33	To Australia in 1935 - regd as VH-UAX on 12.10.35. Canx.
G-ACGK	DH.84 Dragon I	6033		1. 6.33	Ditched into sea off Inverness on 8.1.35. Canx.
G-ACGL	Comper CLA.7 Swift	S.33/6		30. 5.33	WFU on 22.3.40. Broken up in 1942. Canx.
G-ACGM	General Aircraft Monospar ST.4 Mk.II	GAL/ST4/17		. 5.33	To France in 10/33. Canx.
G-ACGN	DH.83 Fox Moth	4063		9. 5.33	To Australia in 1/36 - regd as VH-UDD on 14.1.36. Canx.
G-ACGO	Saunders-Roe A.19 Cloud	A.19/5		8. 5.33	To Czechoslovakia as OK-BAK in 7/34. Canx.
G-ACGP	Percival P.1C Gull Four (Originally regd as P.1B)	D.28		11. 5.33	WFU on 21.5.38. Scrapped at Thame in 1946. Canx.
G-ACGR	Percival P.1C Gull Four IIA (Originally regd as P.1B)	D.29		11. 5.33	Canx in 12/34. On display 8/97 Brussels, Belgium.
G-ACGS	DH.85 Leopard Moth	7002	AX858 G-ACGS/PH-ALM/G-ACGS	14. 6.33	Broken up and canx in 8/47. Parts to G-APKH.
G-ACGT	Avro 594B Avian IIIA (Originally regd as Avro 594A)	R3/CN/171	EI-AAB	8. 5.33	Yorkshire Light Aircraft Ltd (On long term rebuild 1/97)
G-ACGU	DH.84 Dragon I	6034		1. 6.33	Crashed & DBF on take-off from Heston on 16.7.35. Canx.
G-ACGV	Avro 616 Avian Sport	R3/CN/649		12. 5.33	To RAF as 2235M in 8/40. Canx 25.8.40.
G-ACGW	DH.83 Fox Moth	4067		24. 5.33	Crashed & DBF at Jersey Racecourse on 1.10.33. Canx.
G-ACGX	DH.60G-III Moth	5029		23. 5.33	To RAF as X5131 in 12/39. Canx 11.12.39.
G-ACGY	Avro 638 Club Cadet	650		. 5.33	To Mozambique as CR-AAS in 2/39. Canx.
G-ACGZ	DH.60G-III Moth	5030		30. 5.33	To India as VT-AFW in 10/34. Canx.
G-ACHA	Percival P.3 Gull Six (Originally regd as P.1C Gull Four II, converted in 1934)	D.30		17. 6.33	To Australia in 1935 - regd as VH-UTP on 9.6.35. Canx.
G-ACHB	DH.85 Leopard Moth	7001		14. 6.33	To RAF as BD144 in 7/40. Canx 24.7.40.
G-ACHC	DH.85 Leopard Moth	7003		14. 6.33	To RAF as BD167 in 8/40. Canx 23.8.40.
G-ACHD	DH.85 Leopard Moth	7000	E-1	14. 6.33	Scrapped at Hatfield in 1940. Canx 1.12.46.
G-ACHE	Spartan Arrow	84		13. 5.33	Crashed at Horsham on 28.4.35. Canx.
G-ACHF	Spartan Arrow	85		13. 5.33	DBF in hangar fire at Maylands, Romford on 6.2.40. Canx.
G-ACHG	Spartan Arrow	86		13. 5.33	To Denmark as OY-DUK in 10/35. Canx.
G-ACHH	DH.60G-III Moth	5026		23. 5.33	To Angola as CR-LAG in 2/38. Canx.
G-ACHI	Westland Wessex	WA.2151A		23. 5.33	CofA expired 23.5.40 & WFU at Hamble. Canx.
G-ACHJ	Miles M.2 Hawk	3		25. 5.33	Crashed at Clyst St.George, Devon on 20.7.38. Canx.
G-ACHK	Miles M.2 Hawk	4		25. 5.33	Crashed at Cherangani, Kenya on 16.12.33. Canx.
G-ACHL	Miles M.2 Hawk	5		25. 5.33	To RAF as AX838 in 11/40. Canx.
G-ACHM	Percival P.1C Gull Four	D.32		24. 5.33	To France as F-AQLZ in 5/36. Canx.
G-ACHN	Avro 638 Club Cadet	651		1. 6.33	WFU on 21.2.40. Canx.
G-ACHO	Avro 638 Club Cadet	652		1. 6.33	Sold abroad in 6/41. Canx.
G-ACHP	Avro 638 Club Cadet	653	HM570 G-ACHP	1. 6.33	Crashed at Denham on 1.1.56. Canx.
G-ACHR	Bristol 96 Fighter (F.2b) (Originally c/n 4328, rebuilt c.1924 with new c/n 6830, reconditioned c.1927 with new c/n 7127 and again c.1931 with present c/n)	7578	F4342	6. 6.33	Crashed at Guigmes, Seine-et-Marne, France on 19.9.33. Canx.
G-ACHS	General Aircraft Monospar ST.4 Mk.II	GAL/ST4/15		28. 4.33	Damaged at Shaibah, Persia on 10.11.33, not repaired. Canx.
G-ACHT	Percival P.1C Gull Four	D.31		14. 6.33	Sold abroad in 12/36. Canx.
G-ACHU	General Aircraft Monospar ST.6 (Originally regd as ST.4 Mk.II)	GAL/ST4/18		6. 6.33	WFU on 26.5.39. Canx.
G-ACHV	DH.84 Dragon I	6035		14. 6.33	To RAF as X9379 in 3/40. Canx 30.3.40.
G-ACHW	Avro 638 Club Cadet	654		. 6.33	Scrapped at Southend in 1940. Canx.
G-ACHX	DH.84 Dragon I	6036		7. 7.33	Crashed at Purley, Surrey on 25.4.38. Canx.
G-ACHY	Avro 640 Club Cadet	655		12. 6.33	NTU - Not completed. Canx.
G-ACHZ	Miles M.2 Hawk	6		. 6.33	Crashed at Bekesbourne on 25.6.39. Canx.
G-ACIA	DH.60G-III Moth	5033		22. 6.33	Sold abroad in 7/36. Canx.
G-ACIB	DH.60G-III Moth	5034		22. 6.33	To RAF as BD175 in 8/40. Canx 23.8.40.
G-ACIC	General Aircraft Monospar ST.6 (Built as ST.4 Mk.II)	GAL/ST4/20		26. 6.33	WFU on 22.12.38. DBF in hangar fire at Maylands, Romford on 6.2.40. Canx.
G-ACID	DH.83 Fox Moth	4039	D-2408	23. 6.33	To Australia in 1935 - regd as VH-UTF on 9.7.35. Canx.
G-ACIE	DH.84 Dragon I	6032	OK-ATO G-ACIE/OK-ATO/G-ACIE	28. 6.33	To Egypt as SU-ABZ in 3/39. Canx.
G-ACIF	Avro 616 Avian IVM	R3/CN/656		3. 7.33	WFU in Nigeria on 27.8.40. Canx in 12/46.
G-ACIG	DH.83 Fox Moth	4072		10. 7.33	To RAF as X9299 in 3/40. Canx 14.3.40.
G-ACIH	Avro 643 Club Cadet	657		. 7.33	To Ireland as EI-ALU in 4/61. Canx.
G-ACII	DH.60G-III Moth	5036		12. 7.33	Sold abroad in 3/34. Canx.
G-ACIJ	Westland Wessex	WA.2152A		7. 7.33	To Egyptian AF as W202 in 5/34. Canx.
G-ACIK	DH.60G-III Moth	5037		12. 7.33	To South Africa in 3/40. Canx.
G-ACIL	Avro 638 Club Cadet	661	K-11	10. 7.33	Crashed at Thundersley, Essex on 22.12.35. Canx.
G-ACIM	Avro 671 Cierva C.30P Autogiro	658		20. 7.33	Sold abroad in 3/34. Canx.
G-ACIN	Avro 671 Cierva C.30P Autogiro	659		20. 7.33	WFU on 12.12.36. Scrapped in 1938. Canx.
G-ACIO	Avro 671 Cierva C.30P Autogiro	660		20. 7.33	WFU on 14.1.38. Scrapped in 1939. Canx.

Regn	Type	c/n	Previous identity	Regn date	Fate or immediate subsequent identity (if known)
G-ACIP	Percival P.1B Gull Four	D.33		20. 7.33	To Holland as PH-HCA in 12/35. Canx.
G-ACIR	Percival P.1C Gull Four	D.34		. 7.33	Crashed & DBF on take-off from Heston on 20.2.35. Canx.
G-ACIS	Percival P.1C Gull Four	D.35		20. 7.33	To India as VT-AFU in 11/34. Canx.
G-ACIT	DH.84 Dragon I	6039		24. 7.33	CofA expired 25.5.74. (On display 9/93 Wroughton)
G-ACIU	DH.84 Dragon I	6041		25. 7.33	To RAF as X9395 in 4/40. Canx 2.4.40.
G-ACIV	DH.80A Puss Moth	2131	ZS-ACH	. 7.33	To RAF as ES954 in 7/41. Canx 31.7.41.
G-ACIW	DH.84 Dragon I	6038		28. 7.33	To France as F-ANGE in 7/34. Canx.
G-ACIX	Comper Mouse	M.33/1		13. 7.33	WFU on 21.5.35. Canx.
G-ACIY	DH.83 Fox Moth	4077		9. 8.33	To RAF as DZ213 in 6/41. Canx 20.6.41.
G-ACIZ	Miles M.2 Hawk	7		. 7.33	Crashed at Tollerton on 30.6.36. Canx in 12/36.
G-ACJA	DH.82 Tiger Moth	3191		1. 8.33	To Austria as A-81 in 9/34. Canx.
G-ACJB	DH.60G-III Moth	5035		12. 7.33	To RAF as BD176 in 8/40. Canx 23.8.40.
G-ACJC	Miles M.2 Hawk	8		29. 7.33	To Denmark as OY-DAK in 3/35. Canx.
G-ACJD	Miles M.2 Hawk	9		29. 7.33	Crashed near Wimbourne, Dorset on 9.8.34. Canx in 12/34.
G-ACJE	General Aircraft Monospar ST.4 Mk.II	GAL/ST4/21		2. 8.33	To Italian AF as MM.245 in 8/33. Canx.
G-ACJF	General Aircraft Monospar ST.4 Mk.II	GAL/ST4/19		3. 8.33	WFU at Heston on 21.3.39. Destroyed on 16.3.47. Canx.
G-ACJG	DH.60G Gipsy Moth	1921		3. 8.33	To RAF as AW136 in 6/40. Canx 23.6.40.
G-ACJH	DH.84 Dragon I	6040		9. 8.33	To France as F-AMTM in 11/33. Canx.
G-ACJI	Short S.16 Scion	S.766		. 8.33	To RAF as X9375 in 3/40. Canx 19.3.40.
G-ACJJ	Short S.17/L Scylla	S.768		16. 8.33	Wrecked in gales at Drem on 1.4.40. Canx.
G-ACJK	Short S.17/L Scylla	S.769		15. 8.33	WFU at Exeter on 17.12.39. Broken up in 1940. Canx.
G-ACJL	Airspeed AS.5 Courier	10		9. 8.33	To Australia in 10/34 - regd as VH-UUF on 9.10.35. Canx.
	Note: Was one of the London-Melbourne Air Race entries, and arrived in Australia in 10/34. Little is known of this aircraft other than certainly the engine and probably the airframe were shipped back to the UK in late 1936 and/or early 1937 - its final fate is not clear.				
G-ACJM	DH.84 Dragon I	6049		. 8.33	DBR on landing at Hamble on 12.8.34. Canx.
G-ACJN	Bristol 105 Bulldog IVA	7808	R-8	16. 8.33	NTU - Remained as R-8 (B-Class marks). Scrapped at Filton in 1938. Canx.
G-ACJO	Spartan Cruiser II	5		27. 8.33	To Yugoslavia as YU-SAN in 9/33. Canx.
G-ACJP	Percival P.1C Gull Four	D.36		22. 8.33	To Japan as J-BASC in 3/34. Canx.
G-ACJR	Percival P.1C Gull Four	D.37		22. 8.33	Crashed into the English Channel on 1.5.34. Canx.
G-ACJS	DH.84 Dragon I	6042		2. 8.33	Canx in 11/36.
G-ACJT	DH.84 Dragon I	6043		24. 8.33	Crashed on take-off from Weston-super-Mare on 20.12.39. Canx.
G-ACJU	Westland Wallace	WA.2302E		1. 9.33	To RAF as K5116 in 6/35. Canx 6/35.
G-ACJV	Percival P.1C Gull Four	D.39		. 9.33	To Australia in 1933 - regd as VH-CKS on 8.12.33. Canx.
	(Made record flight to Australia in 12/33 piloted by Sir Charles Kingsford Smith)				
G-ACJW	Percival P.1C Gull Four	D.38		7. 9.33	To Australia in 11/34 - regd as VH-UTC on 30.1.35. Canx.
G-ACJX	Avro 640 Cadet	666		4. 9.33	Broken up at Heston in 11/34. Canx.
G-ACJY	Miles M.2 Hawk	10		1. 9.33	DBR after striking a telegraph pole whilst landing at Woodley on 25.9.33. Canx.
G-ACJZ	Avro 638 Club Cadet	667		. 9.33	WFU at Southend on 15.11.39. Scrapped in 1940. Canx.
G-ACKA	Airwork/Cierva C.30P Autogiro Mk.II	AH.1		1. 9.33	WFU on 19.12.34. Scrapped in 1938. Canx.
G-ACKB	DH.84 Dragon I	6055		. 9.33	To RAF as AX863 in 7/40. Canx 7.7.40.
G-ACKC	DH.84 Dragon I	6056		. 9.33	To Spanish Republicans in 8/36. Canx.
G-ACKD	DH.84 Dragon I	6052		. 9.33	Sold abroad to Ethiopian Red Cross in 12/35 and crashed on take-off at Akaki on 23.3.36 & burnt out. Canx.
G-ACKE	Avro 616 Avian IVM	R3/CN/414	VH-UOB	13. 9.33	DBR in ground collision with DH.82A G-AHKZ at Baginton on 26.7.50. Engine & other parts to G-ABEE. Canx.
G-ACKF	DH.60G-III Moth Major	5042		28. 9.33	To Dutch East Indies as PK-SAO in 10/33. Canx.
G-ACKG	Spartan Cruiser II	7		. 9.33R	NTU - To India as VT-AER in 11/33. Canx.
G-ACKH	Fairey Fox III	F.1925 & A.F.3032		13.10.33	To Belgian AF in 3/34. Canx.
G-ACKI	Miles M.2 Hawk	11		13.10.33	Crashed at Morston, Norfolk on 25.8.34. Canx in 12/34.
G-ACKJ	DH.85 Leopard Moth	7006		.10.33	To France as F-AMXQ in 12/33. Canx.
G-ACKK	DH.85 Leopard Moth	7008		16.11.33	To South Africa as ZS-ALL in 7/37. Canx.
G-ACKL	DH.85 Leopard Moth	7009		.11.33	To RAF as BD169 in 12/40. Canx 23.8.40.
G-ACKM	DH.85 Leopard Moth	7026		. 1.34	To RAF as AW169 in 12/40. Canx 21.6.40.
G-ACKN	DH.85 Leopard Moth	7013		.11.33	To RAF as AV975 in 12/40. Canx 8.5.40.
G-ACKO	DH.85 Leopard Moth	7014		27.11.33	To Belgium as OO-GEJ in 4/38. Canx.
G-ACKP	DH.85 Leopard Moth	7200		16.11.33	To RAF as BK867 in 10/40. Canx 22.10.40.
G-ACKR	DH.85 Leopard Moth	7023		.11.33	To RAF as X9294 in 3/40. Canx 31.3.40.
G-ACKS	DH.85 Leopard Moth	7033		.11.33	To RAF as AW120 in 6/40. Canx 16.6.40.
G-ACKT	General Aircraft Monospar ST.4 Mk.II	GAL/ST4/29		27.10.33	Hit power cables and crashed at Thrupp's Farm, Lidlington on 5.12.33. Canx.
G-ACKU	DH.84 Dragon II	6066		.10.33	To RAF as AW172 in 7/40. Canx 7.7.40.
G-ACKV	DH.60G-III Moth Major	5024	SE-ADO	.10.33	Sold abroad in 9/36 - possibly Spain. Canx.
G-ACKW	Miles M.2B Hawk	12		.10.33	To India as VT-AES but crashed near Paris on 20.1.34 whilst on delivery. Canx.
G-ACKX	Miles M.2 Colonial Hawk	13		18.10.33	To Dutch East Indies as PK-SAL in 10/33. Canx.
G-ACKY	DH.85 Leopard Moth	7016		.10.33	To Australia in 12/37 - regd as VH-ADV on 22.2.38. Canx.
G-ACKZ	DH.83 Fox Moth	4083		27.10.33	To India as VT-AJW in 1/38. Canx.
G-ACLA	Miles M.2 Hawk	15		24.10.33	Sold abroad in 12/33. Canx.
G-ACLB	Miles M.2 Hawk	16		24.10.33	WFU on 7.11.34. Canx 12/35.
G-ACLC	Blackburn B.2	5290/1		24.10.33	Fatal mid-air collision with Blackburn B.2 G-ADFS over the River Humber on 24.6.40. Canx.
G-ACLD	Blackburn B.2	5290/2	(2885M) G-ACLD	24.10.33	Crashed at Rawcliffe, York on 16.6.51. Parts to G-AEBJ. Canx.
G-ACLE	DH.84 Dragon I	6044	YI-AAC	31.10.33	To RAF as X9397 in 4/40. Canx 2.4.40.

Regn	Type	c/n	Previous identity	Regn date	Fate or immediate subsequent identity (if known)
G-ACLF	Airspeed AS.5B Courier (Originally regd as Airspeed AS.5A)	12		.10.33	To RAF as X9342 in 3/40. Canx 18.3.40.
G-ACLG	Percival P.1C Gull Four	D.27		27. 4.33	To India as VT-AFV in 11/34. Canx.
G-ACLH	Klemm L.32-X	668	CH-360	2.11.33	To Ireland as EI-ABF in 12/36. Canx.
G-ACLI	Miles M.2A Hawk	14		18.10.33	DBF in hangar fire at Brooklands on 24.10.36. Canx.
G-ACLJ	Percival P.1C Gull Four	D.40		.10.33	To India as VT-AGO in 6/35. Canx.
G-ACLK	DH.85 Leopard Moth	7027		. 1.34	To RAF as W9370 in 12/39. Canx 15.12.39.
G-ACLL	DH.85 Leopard Moth	7028	AW165 G-ACLL	16. 1.34	Permit expired 6.12.95. (Stored 10/96)
G-ACLM	DH.85 Leopard Moth	7032		. 1.34	To RAF as X9380 in 3/40. Canx 27.3.40.
G-ACLN	DH.85 Leopard Moth	7044		29. 3.34	To Spanish Republicans in 12/37. Canx.
G-ACLO	DH.85 Leopard Moth	7048		. 3.34	To Angola as CR-LAI in 3/38. Canx.
G-ACLP	DH.84 Dragon I	6057		7.11.33	To France as F-AMTR in 11/33. Canx.
G-ACLR	Airspeed AS.5A Courier	11		.11.33	To RAF as X9344 3/40. Canx 18.3.40.
G-ACLS	Airspeed AS.5A Courier	15		.11.33	Crashed at Grenoble, France on 17.10.34. Canx.
G-ACLT	Airspeed AS.5A Courier	14		.11.33	To RAF as X9394 3/40. Canx 29.3.40.
G-ACLU	Avro 640 Cadet	679		.11.33	Sold abroad in 4/39. Canx.
G-ACLV	Avro 504N	-	J8573	.11.33	WFU on 10.1.39. Canx in 12/46.
G-ACLW	DH.85 Leopard Moth	7046		. 3.34	To RAF as AX862 in 6/40. Canx 15.6.40.
G-ACLX	DH.85 Leopard Moth	7036		. 3.34	Crashed near Tukuyu, Tanganyika on 23.8.34. Canx.
G-ACLY	DH.85 Leopard Moth	7012		.12.33	To RAF as AW166 in 7/40. Canx 9.7.40.
G-ACLZ	DH.85 Leopard Moth	7040	AW121 G-ACLZ	. 3.34	Not re-converted & broken up in 1947. Parts used in rebuild of G-ACTJ. Canx.
G-ACMA	DH.85 Leopard Moth	7042	BD148 G-ACMA	14. 3.34	(Stored 2/95)
G-ACMB	DH.60G Gipsy Moth	526	J9119	21. 4.34	To RAF as X9302 in 4/40. Canx 4.4.40.
G-ACMC	DH.84 Dragon I	6053		.11.33	To Australia in 7/36 - regd as VH-UXK on 1.10.36. Canx in 8/36.
G-ACMD(1)	Avro 639 Cabin Cadet	686		22.11.33	NTU - To G-ACNY 2/34. Canx.
G-ACMD(2)	DH.82A Tiger Moth	3195	N182DH EC-AGB/Spanish AF 33-5	20. 1.88	
G-ACME	Comper Kite	K.34/42		11. 5.34	Scrapped at Heston in 1935. Canx.
G-ACMF	DH.60G-III Moth Major	5047		.11.33	To Sweden as SE-AGD in 9/37. Canx.
G-ACMG	Avro 631 Cadet	682		21.11.33	WFU on 13.2.40. Canx.
G-ACMH	Miles M.2 Hawk	17		.11.33	Sold abroad in 9/34. Canx.
G-ACMI	Blackburn B-1 Segrave I (Fitted with Duncanson wing)	3854/1	(G-ABZJ)	28.12.33	Broken up in 10/35. Canx.
G-ACMJ	DH.84 Dragon I	6058		.12.33	To RAF as X9396 in 4/40. Canx 2.4.40.
G-ACMK	British Klemm L.25c-Ia Swallow	1		.12.33	To Ireland as EI-ADS in 3/48. Canx.
G-ACML	Comper CLA.7 Swift	S.33/10		.12.33	To Belgium as OO-OML in 4/35. Canx.
G-ACMM	Miles M.2 Hawk	18		.12.33	Scrapped at Stoke-on-Trent between 1939 and 1945. Canx.
G-ACMN	DH.85 Leopard Moth	7050	X9381 G-ACMN	. 4.34	
G-ACMO	DH.84 Dragon II	6062		.11.33	To Australia in 3/38 - regd as VH-ABK on 27.10.38. Canx in 3/38.
G-ACMP	DH.84 Dragon II	6063		.11.33	Crashed on mudflats near Splott, Cardiff on 22.7.35. Canx.
G-ACMR	Pickering-Pearson KP.2	2		1.12.33	Scrapped in 1935. Canx.
G-ACMS	DH.85 Leopard Moth	7024		29.12.33	To India as VT-AGN in 4/35. Canx.
G-ACMT	Airspeed AS.6G Envoy II	17		30.12.33	To Spanish AF as 41-1 in 9/36. Canx.
G-ACMU	Airspeed AS.8 Viceroy	18		30.12.33	To Spanish Republicans in 8/36. Canx.
G-ACMV	DH.85 Leopard Moth	7025		19. 1.34	W/o in 12/35. Canx.
G-ACMW	Spartan Cruiser II	6		19.12.33	To Yugoslavia as YU-SAO in 4/34. Canx.
G-ACMX	Miles M.2 Hawk	23	(EI-AAV) G-ACMX	8. 1.34	To Ireland as EI-ABQ in 12/38. Canx.
G-ACMY	DH.60G-III Moth Major	5055		. 1.34	To Italy as I-RAFF in 1/35. Canx.
G-ACMZ	British Klemm L.25c-Ia Swallow	2		22. 1.34	WFU at Old Warden on 4.12.39. Derelict in 1958. Burnt at Clothall Common on 7.11.64. Canx.
G-ACNA	DH.84 Dragon II	6067		25. 1.34	To Spanish Republicans in 8/36. Canx.
G-ACNB	Avro 504K (Real identity obscure)	R3/LE/61400	"E3404"	29.12.82	To G-ADEV(2) in 4/84. Canx.
G-ACNC	Comper Streak	ST33/1		11. 1.34	WFU at Heston on 9.7.36. Scrapped in 1937. Canx.
G-ACND(1)	Percival P.2 Mew Gull	E.20		26. 1.34	Crashed near Angouleme, France in 10.35. Canx.
G-ACND(2)	Percival P.2 Mew Gull	E.20A		. .	WFU at Luton & burnt on 7.7.45. Canx.
G-ACNE	Avro 631 Cadet	692		30. 1.34	DBR on take-off from Hamble on 10.7.40. Canx.
G-ACNF	Avro 631 Cadet	693		30. 1.34	To 273 (1st Wallasey) ATC Sqdn at Wallasey, Cheshire as 2953M in 8/41. Canx 31.8.41.
G-ACNG	DH.84 Dragon II	6069		. 1.34	Crashed at Hatston, Kirkwall on 19.4.40. Canx.
G-ACNH	DH.84 Dragon II	6070		. 1.34	Canx in 1/37.
G-ACNI	DH.84 Dragon II	6071		. 1.34	To Irish Air Corps as DH-18 in 3/37. Canx.
G-ACNJ	DH.84 Dragon II	6072		. 1.34	CofA lapsed 28.5.43 & WFU at Dyce. Broken up in 1946 for spares. Canx.
G-ACNK	Avro 616 Avian IVM	R3/CN/479	ZS-...	6. 2.34	To RAF as 2072M in 2/40. Canx 28.2.40.
G-ACNL	DH.60G-III Moth Major	5061		. 1.34	Sold abroad in 8/37. Canx.
G-ACNM	DH.60G-III Moth Major	5062		. 1.34	To Southern Rhodesia as VP-YBP in 7/37. Canx.
G-ACNN	DH.85 Leopard Moth	7011		16.11.33	To RAF as AX861 in 5/40. Canx 12.5.40.
G-ACNO	Spartan Cruiser II	8		9. 2.34	To Czechoslovakia as OK-ATQ in 5/34. Canx.
G-ACNP	DH.60G-III Moth Major	5057		16. 2.34	To Yugoslavia as YU-PCH in 3/34. Canx.
G-ACNR	DH.60G-III Moth Major	5067		. 2.34	To South Africa in 5/40. Canx.
G-ACNS	DH.60G-III Moth Major	5068		. 2.34	To South Africa in 3/40. Canx.
G-ACNT	Avro 641 Commodore	691		. 2.34	WFU at Woodford on 27.8.37. Dismantled on 13.10.39. Believed scrapped in 1950. Canx.
G-ACNU	British Klemm L.25c-Ia Swallow	5		19. 2.34	Sold abroad on 19.4.40. Canx.
G-ACNV	Avro 504N	R3/LY/93598	K1808	. 2.34	WFU on 10.4.35. Canx in 3/37.

Regn	Type	c/n	Previous identity	Regn date	Fate or immediate subsequent identity (if known)
G-ACNW	Miles M.2 Hawk	26		19. 2.34	Crashed at Woodley on 23.9.35. Canx.
G-ACNX	Miles M.2 Hawk	24	EI-AAX G-ACNX	. 2.34	To RAF as DG578 in 1/41, then to 1211 ATC Sqdn at Swadlincote as 2617M in 4/42. Canx 7.1.41.
G-ACNY	Avro 639 Cabin Cadet	686	(G-ACMD)	. 2.34	Sold abroad in 6/41. Canx.
G-ACNZ	Airspeed AS.5C Courier	20		. 2.34	To RAF as X9346 in 3/40. Canx 18.3.40.
G-ACOA	DH.60M Moth	1566	VH-UQA	. 2.34	Undercarriage struck pylon on take-off from Hanworth, then stalled and crashed into Elmgate Ave., Feltham on 20.8.36. Canx in 12/36.
G-ACOB	Miles M.2C Hawk	19		2. 3.34	To France as F-AMZW in 5/34. Canx.
G-ACOC	Miles M.2 Hawk	25		. 3.34	Sold abroad in 1/38. Canx in 3/44.
G-ACOD	Avro 504N	-	F8713	. 3.34	Fatal mid-air collision with Westland Wessex G-ADFZ over Blackpool on 7.9.35. Canx.
G-ACOE	British Klemm L.25c-Ia Swallow	6		9. 3.34	To Germany as D-ECOE in 5/36. Canx.
G-ACOF	DH.60G-III Moth Major	5058		14. 3.34	Sold abroad in 5/34. Canx.
G-ACOG	DH.60G-III Moth Major	5070		29. 3.34	To India as VT-ANK in 11/40. Canx.
G-ACOH	DH.60G-III Moth Major	5071		29. 3.34	Destroyed in mid-air collision with a Hawker Hart K3887 over Castle Bromwich Aerodrome on 9.12.34. Canx.
G-ACOI	DH.60G-III Moth Major	5072		29. 3.34	To India as VT-ANL in 11/40. Canx.
G-ACOJ(1)	Parnall Peto	-	N182	23. 3.34	Not completed. Canx.
G-ACOJ(2)	DH.85 Leopard Moth	7035	F-AMXP	5. 6.87	
G-ACOK	Avro 504N	-	F2588	24. 4.34	Crashed at Rhyl on 14.8.38. Canx.
G-ACOL	DH.85 Leopard Moth	7045	HB-OXO CH-368	21.12.83	Not rebuilt and absorbed into G-ACUS. Canx by CAA 2.9.91.
G-ACOM	Avro 504N	-	E430	. 3.34	WFU on 14.4.40. Scrapped in 1940. Canx.
G-ACON	British Klemm L.25c-Ia Swallow	7		. 3.34	Crashed near Retford on 6.9.34. Canx.
G-ACOO	DH.85 Leopard Moth	7054		. 3.34	To RAF as BD172 in 8/40. Canx 28.8.40.
G-ACOP	Miles M.2 Hawk	41		28. 5.34	Crashed at Woodley on 4.8.35. Canx.
G-ACOR	DH.84 Dragon II	6073		. 3.34	To Australia in 2/38 - regd as VH-AEA on 23.6.38. Canx.
G-ACOS	DH.85 Leopard Moth	7038		12. 3.34	To Belgian Congo as (OO-BOB)/OO-CAA in 3/34. Canx.
G-ACOT	DH.85 Leopard Moth	7057		. 3.34	To South Africa as ZS-AFN in 1/35. Canx.
G-ACOU	Spartan Cruiser II	9		23. 3.34	To Czechoslovakia as OK-ATM in 7/34. Canx.
G-ACOV	Avro 621 Tutor	95001	K1791	21. 3.34	Crashed at Stretton, Burton-on-Trent on 17.6.34. Canx.
G-ACOW	British Klemm L.25c-Ia Swallow	8		. 3.34	To RAF as X5010 in 4/40. Canx 9.4.40.
G-ACOX	Boulton & Paul P.71A	P.71A/1		22. 3.34	Lost in the English Channel on 25.9.36. Canx.
G-ACOY	Boulton & Paul P.71A	P.71A/2		22. 3.34	Crashed & DBR on landing at Haren Aerodrome, Brussels, Belgium on 25.10.35. Canx.
G-ACOZ	Avro 640 Cadet	697		. 3.34	WFU on 5.4.37. Scrapped in 1941. Canx.
G-ACPA	Percival P.1C Gull Four (Later modified to P.3 Gull Six standard)	D.44		. 3.34	Crashed near Avignon, France on 2.10.35. Canx.
G-ACPB	Avro 640 Cadet	696		. 3.34	DBF in hangar fire at Hooton on 8.7.40. Canx.
G-ACPC	Miles M.2D Hawk 3-Seater	20	U-1	26. 3.34	WFU on 2.4.35. Scrapped in 5/37. Canx.
G-ACPD	Miles M.2D Hawk	30		26. 3.34	DBR in collision with Avro 504N G-ACLV at Clayhury, Woodford, Essex on 30.9.34. Canx.
G-ACPE	Bristol 96 Fighter (F.2b)	7577	J8448	. 3.34	WFU on 8.10.35. Scrapped in 1/39. Canx.
G-ACPF	DH.85 Leopard Moth	7049		. 4.34	To RAF as AW123 in 5/40. Canx 23.6.40.
G-ACPG	DH.85 Leopard Moth	7051		. 4.34	To RAF as AV988 in 5/40. Canx 16.5.40.
G-ACPH	DH.60G-III Moth Major	5073		. 4.34	To Singapore as VR-SAZ in 9/37. Canx.
G-ACPI	DH.60G-III Moth Major	5077		. 4.34	To South Africa in 5/40. Canx.
G-ACPJ	British Klemm L.25c-Ia Swallow	10		. 4.34	WFU on 30.10.47. Scrapped at Cowes, IoW in 1949. Canx.
G-ACPK	DH.85 Leopard Moth	7056		. 4.34	To RAF as X9382 in 3/40. Canx 27.3.40.
G-ACPL	DH.86	2300	E-2	23. 4.34	To RAF as HK844 in 12/41. Canx 13.12.41.
G-ACPM	DH.89 Dragon Rapide	6251		7. 6.34	Fatal crash in sea 4 miles off Folkestone on 2.10.34. Canx.
G-ACPN	DH.89 Dragon Rapide	6252		12. 8.34	To Spanish Nationalists in 8/36. Canx.
G-ACPO	DH.89 Dragon Rapide	6253		12. 7.34	To Australia in 1936 - regd as VH-UBN on 17.8.36. Canx in 8/36.
G-ACPP	DH.89 Dragon Rapide	6254		20. 2.35	To Canada as CF-PTK in 6/61. Canx.
G-ACPR	DH.89 Dragon Rapide	6255		20. 2.35	DBR at Burford on 19.2.40. Canx.
G-ACPS	DH.82A Tiger Moth	1993		7. 4.34	To France as F-AQDP in 6/37. Canx.
G-ACPT	DH.60G-III Moth Major	5080		. 4.34	To RAF as AW161 in 6/40. Canx 28.6.40.
G-ACPU	British Klemm BK.1 Eagle I	2		. 4.34	To RAF as DR609/2679M in 4/41. Canx 10.4.41.
G-ACPV	Avro 504N	-	K1250	13. 4.34	To RAF as BV209 in 1/41. Canx 16.1.41.
G-ACPW	Miles M.2D Hawk	33		13. 4.34	Sold abroad in 4/35. Canx.
G-ACPX	DH.84 Dragon II	6075		. 4.34	To RAF as X9399 in 4/40. Canx 2.4.40.
G-ACPY	DH.84 Dragon II	6076	EI-ABI G-ACPY	. 4.34	Shot down by a German fighter off Scilly Isles on 3.6.41. Canx.
G-ACPZ	Blackburn B.2	5290/3		17. 4.34	To 1098 ATC Sqdn at RNAS Gosport, Hants as 2902M in 2/42. Canx 17.2.42.
G-ACRA	Blackburn B.2	5290/4	(2905M) G-ACRA	17. 4.34	To 1345 (Malden & Coombe) ATC Sqdn in Surrey as 2905M in 2/42. Canx 17.2.42.
G-ACRB	Miles M.2 Hawk	27	U-11	. 4.34	Sold abroad in 1/37. Canx in 2/43.
G-ACRC	DH.85 Leopard Moth	7058		. 4.34	To RAF as AW168 in 6/40. Canx 21.6.40.
G-ACRD	British Klemm L.25c-Ia Swallow	11		. 4.34	To RAF as X5011 in 4/40. Canx 9.4.40.
G-ACRE	Avro 504N	-	E9408	7. 5.34	Fatal crash at Gamlingay, Cambs on 13.2.38. Canx.
G-ACRF	DH.84 Dragon II	6077		30. 4.34	To Australia in 2/36 - regd as VH-UXG on 27.4.36. Canx.
G-ACRG	British Klemm BK.1 Eagle I	1		23. 4.34	W/o in 6/38. Canx.
G-ACRH	DH.84 Dragon II	6078		16. 6.34	Crashed & DBF after take-off from Dyce on 13.7.34. Canx.
G-ACRI	DH.60G-III Moth Major	5079		. 4.34	To RAF as BK833 in 8/40. Canx 26.8.40.
G-ACRJ	DH.85 Leopard Moth	7052		. 5.34	To India as VT-AKH in 7/38. Canx.
G-ACRK	DH.83 Fox Moth	4090	E-10	10. 7.34	To Australia in 1935 - regd as VH-UBB on 7.10.35. Canx.
G-ACRL	Parmentier Wee Mite	1		24. 4.34	Broken up in 3/36. Canx.
G-ACRM	Avro 652	698		2. 5.34	To RAF as DG655 in 3/41. Canx 14.2.41.
G-ACRN	Avro 652	699		2. 5.34	To RAF as DG656 in 3/41. Canx 14.2.41.

Regn	Type	c/n	Previous identity	Regn date	Fate or immediate subsequent identity (if known)
G-ACRO	DH.84 Dragon II	6079		3. 5.34	To Kenya as VP-KBG in 10.34. Canx.
G-ACRP	Avro 552	9		. 4.34	WFU on 2.7.35. Canx in 3/36.
G-ACRR	DH.60G-III Moth Major	5082		. 4.34	To RAF as W7949 in 2/40. Canx 27.2.40.
G-ACRS	Avro 504N	-	K1802	2. 5.34	Crashed at Cove, near Farnborough on 30.6.34. Canx.
G-ACRT	Miles M.2 Hawk	31		2. 5.34	WFU on 1.9.39. Derelict at Kidlington in 1956. Canx.
G-ACRU	DH.83 Fox Moth	4089		28. 5.34	To Australia in 1937 - regd as VH-AAZ on 20.11.37. Canx.
G-ACRV	DH.85 Leopard Moth	7060		. 5.34	To RAF as AV986 in 5/40. Canx 12.5.40.
G-ACRW	DH.85 Leopard Moth	7061	AX873 G-ACRW	2. 6.34	To Norway as LN-TVT in 5/52. Canx.
G-ACRX	Avro 641 Commodore	700		4. 5.34	To Egypt as SU-AAS in 1936. Canx.
G-ACRY	Avro 631 Club Cadet	701		4. 5.34	Crashed into the Solent off Hillhead on 4.6.34. Canx.
G-ACRZ	Avro 631 Club Cadet	702		4. 5.34	To 696 ATC Sqdn at Stroud, Glos. as 2962M in 2/42. Canx 10.2.42.
G-ACSA	DH.60G-III Moth Major	5087		15. 6.34	Sold abroad in 11/34. Canx.
G-ACSB	DH.80A Puss Moth	2053	VH-UPJ	7. 5.34	To Holland as PH-AMN in 3/35. Canx.
G-ACSC	Miles M.2D Hawk	35		. 5.34	WFU on 17.7.36. Canx 1.12.46.
G-ACSD	Miles M.2 Hawk	28		11. 5.34	Crashed in severe snow storm at Kelshall, near Royston on 4.4.35. Canx.
G-ACSE	DH.85 Leopard Moth	7062		. 5.34R	NTU - To Austrian Aero Club as A-145 in 1934. Canx.
G-ACSF	DH.85 Leopard Moth	7065		. 5.34	To RAF as BD147 in 7/40. Canx 28.7.40.
G-ACSG	DH.85 Leopard Moth	7066		. 5.34	To India as VT-AHO in 5/36. Canx.
G-ACSH	DH.85 Leopard Moth	7067		10. 7.34	To RAF as X9384 in 6/40. Canx 27.6.40.
G-ACSI	DH.85 Leopard Moth	7068		15. 6.34	To India as VT-AJC in 6/37. Canx.
G-ACSJ	DH.85 Leopard Moth	7070		15. 6.34	To RAF as AW117 in 6/40. Canx 9.6.40.
G-ACSK	DH.82 Tiger Moth	3223		15. 5.34	To R.New Zealand AF as NZ731 in 5/40. Canx.
G-ACSL	Miles M.2 Hawk	29	U-1	. 5.34	Canx in 12/36.
G-ACSM	Spartan Cruiser II	10		. 5.34	To RAF as X9433 in 4/40. Canx 2.4.40.
G-ACSN	British Klemm L.25c-Ia Swallow	9		17. 5.34	To Spain as EC-XXA in 1/35. Canx.
G-ACSO	British Klemm L.25c-Ia Swallow	12		. 5.34	Destroyed in hangar collapse at Bourn in 1952. Canx.
G-ACSP	DH.88 Comet (New build based on some original components)	1994	CS-AAJ G-ACSP/E-1	21. 8.34	(On rebuild 10/96)
G-ACSR	DH.88 Comet	1995		23. 8.34	To France as F-ANPY in 4/35. Canx.
G-ACSS	DH.88 Comet	1996	K5084 G-ACSS	4. 9.34	(On display at Old Warden)
"G-ACSS"	DH.88 Comet	-		----	A static replica of G-ACSS, built in Australia for film purposes, is owned by Graham Gaywood - is also BAPC.216.
"G-ACSS"	DH.88 Comet	-		----	A "second" flying replica was built in 1993 by Repeat Aircraft, Riverside, CA for Tom Wathen and is regd N88XD.
G-ACST	DH.60G-III Moth Major	5088		15. 6.34	To Singapore as VR-SBA in 11/37. Canx.
G-ACSU	DH.85 Leopard Moth	7071		15. 6.34	To RAF as AV984 in 5/40. Canx 12.5.40.
G-ACSV	Stinson SR.5 Reliant	8779	NC13824	. 5.34	For RAF as X8518 in 2/40. NTU, crashed on 9.6.40. Canx.
G-ACSW	DH.83 Fox Moth	4091		29. 5.34	To India as VT-AFT in 9/34. Canx.
G-ACSX	Miles M.2D Hawk	42		17. 5.34	Crashed into ground in mist at Bilsdale, Yorks on 5.6.34. Canx.
G-ACSY	Airspeed AS.5A Courier	16		17. 5.34	Crashed near Sevenoaks, Kent on 29.9.34. Canx.
G-ACSZ	Airspeed AS.5A Courier	19		. 5.34	Crashed at Doncaster on 29.5.37. Canx.
G-ACTA	DH.87A Hornet Moth (Built as a DH.87)	1997	E-6	14. 6.34	Scrapped at Hatfield in 2/46. Canx.
G-ACTB	Avro 638 Club Cadet	704		. 5.34	Scrapped at Southend in 1940. Canx.
G-ACTC	Parnall Hendy Heck (Westland-built as Hendy 3308 Heck with c/n 341)	-	P(B-Class)	23. 5.34	CofA expired on 29.4.37. Scrapped in 1937. Canx.
G-ACTD	Miles M.2F Hawk Major	36		24. 5.34	Crashed at Doncaster Airport on 31.8.36. Canx.
G-ACTE	Miles M.2E Hawk Speed Six	43		24. 5.34	To Spanish Republicans in 9/37. Canx.
G-ACTF	Comper CLA.7 Swift	S.32/9	VT-ADO	24. 5.34	
G-ACTG	DH.85 Leopard Moth	7073		15. 6.34	To RAF as BD140 in 5/40. Canx 12.5.40.
G-ACTH	DH.85 Leopard Moth	7074		12. 7.34	To Italy as I-ACIH in 2/36. Canx.
G-ACTI	Miles M.2 Hawk	37		. 6.34	Damaged at Gabes, Egypt in 2/37. Canx in 2/43.
G-ACTJ	DH.85 Leopard Moth (Parts from G-ACLZ used in rebuild .47)	7075	BD146 G-ACTJ	20. 8.34	To Switzerland as HB-UAB in 5/50. Canx.
G-ACTK	DH Technical School TK.1	1	E-3	8. 6.34	Scrapped in 1936. Canx.
G-ACTL	DH.85 Leopard Moth	7076		12. 7.34	To RAF as AW125 in 6/40. Canx 17.6.40.
G-ACTM	Miles M.3 Falcon	102	U-3	11. 6.34	Crashed at Mersa Matruh, Egypt on 18.7.35. Canx.
G-ACTN	Miles M.2 Colonial Hawk	103		. 6.34	Crashed whilst trying to land at Meir, Stoke-on-Trent in a severe snowstorm on 15.12.35. Canx.
G-ACTO	Miles M.2 Hawk	32		. 6.34	To RAF as AW152 in 6/40. Canx 26.6.40.
G-ACTP	British Klemm L.25c-Ia Swallow	22		14. 6.34	WFU on 2.9.39. Scrapped in 1940 Canx.
G-ACTR	British Klemm BK.1 Eagle I	25		14. 6.34	To Australia in 9/34 - regd as VH-USI on 14.12.34. Canx.
G-ACTS	General Aircraft Monospar ST.10	GAL/ST10/32	T-5	11. 6.34	To RAF as X9453 in 4/40. Canx 2.4.40.
G-ACTT	DH.89 Dragon Rapide	6257		. 6.34	To RAF as X8509 in 3/40. Canx 8.3.40.
G-ACTU	DH.89 Dragon Rapide	6258		3. 9.34	To RAF as AW115 in 6/40. Canx 8.6.40.
G-ACTV	DH.80A Puss Moth	2080	VT-ACA	30. 5.34	To RAF as AX868 in 7/40. Canx 23.7.40.
G-ACTW	DH.60G-III Moth Major	5091		. 5.34	To India as VT-AIO in 2/37. Canx.
G-ACTX	Avro 638 Club Cadet	718		. 6.34	Scrapped at Horton Kirby in 1940. Canx.
G-ACTY	Avro 638 Club Cadet	719		11. 6.34	NTU - Not completed. Canx.
G-ACTZ	Avro 638 Club Cadet	720		11. 6.34	To Malaya as VR-RAW in 6/41. Canx.
G-ACUA	Avro 641 Commodore	721		11. 6.34	To Egypt as SU-AAU in 1936. Canx.
G-ACUB	British Klemm L.25c-Ia Swallow	15		14. 6.34	W/o on 22.2.38. Canx.
G-ACUC	DH.60G-III Moth Major	5084		11. 6.34	To Australia (departed UK 28.9.34, arrived on 6.11.34) - regd as VH-UUC on 25.9.35. Canx in 5/35.
G-ACUD	Miles M.2 Hawk	38		11. 6.34	Crashed at West Woodhay on 5.6.36. Canx in 12/36.

Regn	Type	c/n	Previous identity	Regn date	Fate or immediate subsequent identity (if known)
G-ACUE	Blackburn B.2	5290/5		11. 6.34	Struck HT cables & crashed at Little Weighton, East Yorks. on 12.11.35. Canx.
G-ACUF	British Klemm L.25c-Ia Swallow	16		26. 6.34	Scrapped in 1940. Canx.
G-ACUG	Avro 641 Commodore	722		14. 6.34	To RAF as DJ710 in 2/41. Canx 15.2.41.
G-ACUH	Avro 631 Cadet	724		13. 6.34	Crashed near Southampton on 10.9.34. Canx.
G-ACUI	Avro 671 Cierva C.30A Autogiro	705		12. 6.34	To RAF as HM581 in 9/42. Canx 2.9.42.
G-ACUJ	DH.85 Leopard Moth	7079		10. 8.34	To India as VT-AJP in 8/37. Canx.
G-ACUK	DH.85 Leopard Moth	7080		12. 9.34	To RAF as X9295 in 4/40. Canx 11.4.40.
G-ACUL	Percival P.3 Gull Six (Originally regd as P.1D Gull Four)	D.45		. 7.34	To New Zealand as ZK-AES in 11/36. Canx.
G-ACUM	British Klemm L.25c-Ia Swallow	17		13. 7.34	Crashed & DBF at Beenham, Berks. on 23.7.34. Canx.
G-ACUN	Avro 660	723		14. 6.34	NTU - Not completed. Canx.
G-ACUO	DH.85 Leopard Moth	7081		3. 9.34	To RAF as AX865 in 7/40. Canx 11.7.40.
G-ACUP	Percival P.3 Gull Six	D.46		. 7.34	To Australia in 5/39 - regd as VH-ACM on 31.7.39. Canx.
G-ACUR	DH.60G-III Moth Major	5097		16. 7.34	Lost in the North Sea off Great Yarmouth on 22.3.37. Canx.
G-ACUS	DH.85 Leopard Moth (Composite including parts from HB-OXO (G-ACOL) c/n 7045)	7082	HB-OXA (G-ACUS)	17.11.77	
G-ACUT	Avro 671 Cierva C.30A Autogiro	725		19. 6.34	WFU on 8.3.37. Canx in 12/37.
G-ACUU	Avro 671 Cierva C.30A Autogiro	726	(G-AIXE) HM580/G-ACUU	26. 6.34	WFU at Elmdon in 4/60. Canx as WFU 14.11.88. (On display 7/99 at Duxford)
G-ACUV	Short S.16 Scion 1	S.774		26. 6.34	WFU on 27.4.40. Scrapped between 1940 and 1945. Canx 23.3.46.
G-ACUW	Short S.16 Scion 1	S.775		26. 6.34	To RAF as AV981 in 5/40. Canx 2.5.40.
G-ACUX	Short S.16 Scion 1	S.776	VH-UUP G-ACUX	26. 6.34	Not rebuilt following import. Canx in 7/81. Stored at Ulster Folk & Transport Museum.
G-ACUY	Short S.16 Scion 1	S.777		26. 6.34	To RAF as AV974 in 4/40. Canx 27.4.40.
G-ACUZ	Short S.16 Scion 2	S.778		26. 6.34	To RAF as W7419 in 3/40. Canx 8.3.40.
G-ACVA	Kay Gyroplane 33/1	1002		26. 6.34	Canx in 9/58. (On display at Kelvin Hall, Glasgow)
G-ACVB	Kay Gyroplane 33/1	1003		26. 6.34	NTU - Not completed. Canx.
G-ACVC	Avro 671 Cierva C.30A Autogiro	706		26. 6.34	Sold abroad in 8/34. Canx.
G-ACVD	DH.84 Dragon II	6084		29. 6.34	Intended for Australia as VH-UZX (allotted on 27.9.37), but crashed 800 yards west of Waddon Station, Beddington, Surrey on 26.2.38 prior to delivery. Canx.
G-ACVE	Airspeed AS.5A Courier	22		. 6.34	Crashed on take-off at Portsmouth Airport on 20.8.36. Canx.
G-ACVF	Airspeed AS.5A Courier (Originally regd as AS.5B)	23	X9437 G-ACVF	. 6.34	WFU at Southend on 18.12.47. Scrapped in 6/51. Canx.
G-ACVG	Airspeed AS.5J Courier	24		3. 7.34	To India as VT-AFY in 11/34. Canx.
G-ACVH	Airspeed AS.6A Envoy I	28		. 7.34	Forced-landing in Langstone Harbour, Hants in 5/36. Canx.
G-ACVI	Airspeed AS.6H Envoy I	29		. 7.34	To Australia in 8/36 - regd as VH-UXM on 22.10.36. Canx.
G-ACVJ	Airspeed AS.6A Envoy I	30		. 7.34	To Spanish Republicans in 8/36. Canx.
G-ACVK	DH.82 Tiger Moth	3224		12. 7.34	To India as VT-ANV in 2/41. Canx.
G-ACVL	DH.82 Tiger Moth	3225		12. 7.34	To India as VT-AOG in 2/41. Canx.
G-ACVM	Miles M.2F Hawk Major	109		. 7.34	Crashed at Hurst, near Woodley on 2.6.36. Canx.
G-ACVN	Miles M.2F Hawk Major	39		3. 7.34	To Brazil in 8/34. Canx.
G-ACVO	Miles M.2 Hawk	106		. 7.34	Crashed at Flamstead, near Harpenden on 15.11.34. Canx.
G-ACVP	Miles M.2 Hawk	107		4. 7.34	To Denmark as OY-DEI in 11/34. Canx.
G-ACVR	Miles M.2D Hawk	108		. 7.34	WFU on 15.8.36. Canx in 11/45.
G-ACVS	DH.85 Leopard Moth	7064		5. 7.34	To Poland as SP-BSZ in 10/34. Canx.
G-ACVT	Spartan Cruiser II	11		4. 7.34	Crashed at Ronaldsway, Isle of Man on 23.3.36. Canx.
G-ACVU	British Klemm BK.1 Eagle I	30		13. 7.34	Crashed in the Mediterranean Sea off Corsica on 13.4.36. Canx.
G-ACVV	British Klemm L.25c-Ia Swallow	14		17. 7.34	WFU on 6.5.39. Derelict at Old Warden in 1958. Burnt at Clothall Common on 7.11.64. Canx.
G-ACVW	British Klemm L.25c-Ia Swallow	3		16. 7.34	Impounded in Russia on 13.11.38. Canx.
G-ACVX	Avro 671 Cierva C.30A Autogiro	707		13. 7.34	To Holland as PH-ASA in 10/37. Canx.
G-ACVY	DH.86B (Built as a DH.86)	2302		21. 7.34	Spar failed in 8/46 and scrapped at Langley in 1948. Canx.
G-ACVZ	DH.86	2303		21. 7.34	Crashed at Elsdorf, near Cologne, Germany on night of 15/16.3.37. Canx.
G-ACWA	British Klemm L.25c-Ia Swallow	18		19. 7.34	To RAF as X5008 in 4/40. Canx 9.4.40.
G-ACWB	DH.82 Tiger Moth	3226		21. 7.34	To R.New Zealand AF as NZ737 in 1/40. Canx.
G-ACWC	DH.86	2304		29. 1.35	Crashed at Minna, Nigeria on 17.6.41. Canx.
G-ACWD	DH.86	2305		29. 1.35	To RAF as HK829 in 11/41. Canx 22.11.41.
G-ACWE	DH.86	2306		. 1.35R	NTU - To Australia in 1/35 - regd as VH-UUA on 22.1.35. Canx.
G-ACWF	Avro 671 Cierva C.30A Autogiro	708		24. 7.34	To RAF as DR624 in 6/41. Canx 1.6.41.
G-ACWG	Avro 671 Cierva C.30A Autogiro	709		24. 7.34	To France as F-AOHY in 9/34. Canx.
G-ACWH	Avro 671 Cierva C.30A Autogiro	710		24. 7.34	To RAF as DR623 in 6/41. Canx 1.6.41.
G-ACWI	Avro 671 Cierva C.30A Autogiro	711		24. 7.34	To France as F-AOIO in 9/34. Canx.
G-ACWJ	Avro 671 Cierva C.30A Autogiro	712		24. 7.34	To Holland as PH-HHH in 1/35. Canx.
G-ACWK	Avro 671 Cierva C.30A Autogiro	713		24. 7.34	To Germany as D-EKOM in 11/34. Canx.
G-ACWL	Avro 671 Cierva C.30A Autogiro	714		24. 7.34	To Germany as D-EKOP in 11/34. Canx.
G-ACWM	Avro 671 Cierva C.30A Autogiro	715	(G-AHMK) AP506/G-ACWM	24. 7.34	Not re-converted postwar. (Frame on display 4/98 Weston-super-Mare)
G-ACWN	Avro 671 Cierva C.30A Autogiro	716		24. 7.34	Sold abroad in 2/37. Canx.
G-ACWO	Avro 671 Cierva C.30A Autogiro	717	V1187 G-ACWO	24. 7.34	To Belgium in 1949 as spares for OO-ADK. Canx.
G-ACWP	Avro 671 Cierva C.30A Autogiro	728	AP507 G-ACWP	24. 7.34	(On display 8/97 South Kensington, London)
G-ACWR	Avro 671 Cierva C.30A Autogiro	731		24. 7.34	To RAF as V1186 in 12/39. Canx 17.12.39.
G-ACWS	Avro 671 Cierva C.30A Autogiro	732		24. 7.34	To RAF as AP509 in 6/40. Canx 1.6.40.
G-ACWT	Avro 671 Cierva C.30A Autogiro	733		24. 7.34	To France as F-AOLK in 12/34. Canx.

Regn	Type	c/n	Previous identity	Regn date	Fate or immediate subsequent identity (if known)
G-ACWU	Avro 671 Cierva C.30A Autogiro	736		24. 7.34	To Switzerland as HB-MAB in 1/35. Canx.
G-ACWV	Miles M.2F Hawk Major	110		. 7.34	WFU on 9.11.38. Scrapped between 1939 and 1945. Canx.
G-ACWW	Miles M.2F Hawk Major	111		. 7.34	To Malaya as VR-RAV in 6/40. Canx.
G-ACWX	Miles M.2F Hawk Major	112		. 7.34	WFU on 3.11.35. Canx in 6/36.
G-ACWY	Miles M.2F Hawk Major	113		. 7.34	To RAF as NF748 in 2/43. Canx 18.2.43.
G-ACWZ	Avro 671 Cierva C.30A Autogiro	752		. .34	WFU at Redhill on 10.1.37. Canx.
G-ACXA	Avro 671 Cierva C.30A Autogiro	753		4. 4.35	To Italy as I-CIER in 8/35. Canx.
G-ACXB(1)	Avro 671 Cierva C.30A Autogiro	754		. 4.35R	NTU - Not completed. Canx.
G-ACXB(2)	DH.60G-III Moth Major	5098	EC-ABY EC-BAX/Spanish AF 30-53/EC-YAY	24. 1.89	(On rebuild)
G-ACXC	Avro 671 Cierva C.30A Autogiro	755		. .35R	NTU - Not completed. Canx.
G-ACXD	British Klemm L.25c-Ia Swallow	20		21. 8.34	To Denmark as OY-DOL in 5/37. Canx.
G-ACXE	British Klemm L.25c-Ia Swallow	21		29.10.34	(Long term rebuild by J.G.Wakeford .89)
G-ACXF	DH.60G Gipsy Moth	425	VH-UGX G-AUGX	1. 8.34	To RAF as HM582 in 8/42. Canx 5.8.42.
G-ACXG	Avro 671 Cierva C.30A Autogiro	743		2. 8.34	To Holland as PH-ARA 5.6.37 (& written off at Waalhaven next day). Remains sold to UK. Canx.
G-ACXH	DH.85 Leopard Moth	7077		4. 9.34	To RAF as BD173 in 8/40. Canx 28.8.40.
G-ACXI	DH.84 Dragon II	6087		16. 8.34	To Turkish AF in 12/35. Canx.
G-ACXJ	Avro 643 Cadet	758		3. 8.34	WFU on 23.2.40. Scrapped between 1939 and 1945. Canx.
G-ACXK	DH.60G-III Moth Major	5095		18. 8.34	Abandoned at Bucharest on German invasion in 9/39. Canx in 11/45.
G-ACXL	Miles M.2F Hawk Major	114		21. 8.34	WFU on 22.4.38. Scrapped between 1939 and 1945. Canx.
G-ACXM	Miles M.2F Hawk Major	115		21. 8.34	To India as VT-AGX in 11/35. Canx.
G-ACXN	Miles M.2F Hawk Major	116		21. 8.34	To Kenya as VP-KBL in 10/34. Canx.
G-ACXO	Fairey Fox I	F.856	J7950	20. 8.34	To Australia in 10/34 - regd as VH-UTR on 27.2.36. Canx in 3/35.
	Note: Was one of the London-Melbourne Air Race entries, arriving in 10/34.				
G-ACXP	Avro 671 Cierva C.30A Autogiro	772		21. 8.34	To Australia in 12/34 - regd as VH-USQ on 23.1.35. Canx.
G-ACXR	Avro 671 Cierva C.30A Autogiro	760		24. 8.34	WFU on 14.12.35. Canx in 5/38.
G-ACXS	British Klemm L.25c-Ia Swallow	23		10. 9.34	WFU at Walsall on 23.9.39. Derelict in 1947. Canx.
G-ACXT	Miles M.2F Hawk Major	118		10. 9.34	To RAF as DG577 in 1/41. Canx 7.1.41.
G-ACXU	Miles M.2F Hawk Major	119		31. 8.34	To New Zealand as ZK-ADJ in 9/34. Canx.
G-ACXV	Avro 671 Cierva C.30A Autogiro	744		6. 9.34	To Czechoslovakia as OK-IEA in 12/35. Canx.
G-ACXW	Avro 671 Cierva C.30A Autogiro	737	BV999 G-ACXW	5. 9.34	CofA expired on 10.7.47 & WFU at White Waltham. Donated to the Twickenham ATC Sqdn. Canx.
G-ACXX	Fairey Fox I	F.876	J8424	8.10.34	DBF in forced landing near Foggia, near Apulia, Italy on 22.10.34. Canx.
G-ACXY	Percival P.3 Gull Six (Originally regd as P.1C Gull Four)	D.42		14. 9.34	To France as F-OAXY in 2/36. Canx.
G-ACXZ	Miles M.2 Hawk	104		10. 9.34	Sold abroad in 3/37. Canx.
G-ACYA	Miles M.2 Hawk	105		10. 9.34	DBF in hangar fire at Hooton on 8.7.40. Canx.
G-ACYB	Miles M.2G Hawk Major	120		10. 9.34	To Switzerland as HB-OAS in 10/34. Canx.
G-ACYC	Avro 671 Cierva C.30A Autogiro	776		13. 9.34	To France as F-AOHZ in 9/35. Canx.
G-ACYD	DH.60G-III Moth Major	5100		27. 9.34	To Kenya as VP-KCP in 3/38. Canx.
G-ACYE	Avro 671 Cierva C.30A Autogiro	775	AP510 G-ACYE	11. 9.34	WFU at Eastleigh on 25.7.47. Used for spares. Canx.
G-ACYF	DH.86	2313		7.12.34	To Singapore as VR-SBD in 6/38. Canx.
G-ACYG	DH.86	2314		7.12.34	To RAF as AX840 in 7/40. Canx 21.7.40.
G-ACYH	Avro 671 Cierva C.30A Autogiro	771		13. 9.34	To RAF as DR622 in 6/41. Canx 1.6.41.
G-ACYI	Westland CL.20 Autogiro	WA.2351F		24. 9.34	No CofA issued. Broken up at Hanworth in 1938. Canx.
G-ACYJ	Airspeed AS.6J Envoy I	31		24. 9.34	Intended for Australia and was regd as VH-UXY on 13.11.34, but disappeared somewhere in the vicinity of Hawaii whilst on delivery to Australia. Canx.
G-ACYK	Spartan Cruiser III	101		2. 5.35	Crash at Largs, Ayrshire on 14.1.38. (Remains recovered 7.73 - Front fuselage only, on display 3/96 East Fortune)
G-ACYL	Spartan Cruiser II	12		.10.34	To RAF as X9431 in 4/40. Canx 2.4.40.
G-ACYM	DH.89 Dragon Rapide	6269		10. 1.35	For RAF as X9320 in 3/40. NTU as crashed at Mayenneville, France on 12.2.40. Destroyed in 5/40. Canx.
G-ACYN	DH.82 Tiger Moth	3314		15.10.34	Crashed near Afikim, Jordan Valley, Palestine in mid-1939. (Marks VQ-PAN NTU). Canx.
G-ACYO	Miles M.2H Hawk Major	121	NF752 G-ACYO	24. 9.34	Crashed at Elstree on 28.11.54. Canx.
G-ACYP	Avro 671 Cierva C.30A Autogiro	745		24. 9.34	To Poland as SP-ANN in 10/34. Canx.
G-ACYR	DH.89 Dragon Rapide	6261		15.10.34	CofA lapsed 23.8.47 & WFU at Desford; to Spain by sea on 11.6.57 for museum. (On display at Cuatro Vientos, Spain)
G-ACYS	Percival P.3 Gull Six	D.47		12.10.34	To India as VT-AGY in 10/34. Canx.
G-ACYT	DH.80A Puss Moth	2231	E-8	24.10.34	To RAF as ES920 in 5/41. Canx 31.5.41.
G-ACYU	Klemm L.32-V	402	D-2299	.10.34	To Australia in 1935 - regd as VH-UVE on 12.12.35. Canx.
G-ACYV	Vickers 252 Vildebeest XI	1	O-7	5.10.34	Scrapped in 1938. Canx.
G-ACYW	Miles M.2X Hawk	117		24.10.34	To Spain as EC-W25/EC-ZZA in 11/34. Canx.
G-ACYX	Miles M.2H Hawk Major	129		16.10.34	To France as F-BCEX in 9/46. Canx.
G-ACYY	British Klemm L.25c-Ia Swallow	26		3.11.34	WFU at Maylands on 20.11.39. Derelict in 1940. Canx.
G-ACYZ	Miles M.2H Hawk Major	123		16.10.34	To Australia in 1938 - regd as VH-ACC on 9.12.38. Canx.
G-ACZA	Avro 643 Cadet	794		18.10.34	To Malaya as (VR-SAM)/VR-RAR in 3/38. Canx.
G-ACZB	Avro 641 Commodore	729		18.10.34	To RAF as HH979 in 8/41. Canx 27.8.41.
G-ACZC	Avro 504N	-	K1802	24.10.34	To RAF as AX854 in 6/40. Canx 9.6.40.
G-ACZD	Miles M.2 Hawk	130		30.10.34	To Sweden as SE-AFS in 5/37. Canx.
G-ACZE	DH.89 Dragon Rapide	6264	(N.....) G-AJGS/G-ACZE/Z7266/G-ACZE	20.11.34	(Stored 8/97 Henstridge)
G-ACZF	DH.89 Dragon Rapide	6268		20.11.34	CofA lapsed 18.5.47. Scrapped at Whitney in 8/48. Canx.
G-ACZG	Short S.22 Scion Senior	S.779	VT-AGU	25.10.34	Restored to India as VT-AGU in 1/36. Canx.

Regn	Type	c/n	Previous identity	Regn date	Fate or immediate subsequent identity (if known)
G-ACZH	Blackburn B.2	5290/6		31.10.34	To 1375 ATC Sqdn at Napier Road School, East Ham, London as 2886M in 2/42. Canx 17.2.42.
G-ACZI	Miles M.2H Hawk Major	132		2.11.34	To South Africa as ZS-AFM in 11/36. Canx.
G-ACZJ	Miles M.2H Hawk Major	122		.11.34	To India as VT-AIR in 6/37. Canx.
G-ACZK	British Klemm L.25c-Ia Swallow	28		22.11.34	To Ireland as EI-ABD in 3/35. Canx.
G-ACZL	Airspeed AS.5A Courier	25		14.11.34	To RAF as X9345 in 3/40. Canx 18.3.40.
G-ACZM	Spartan Cruiser II	14		14.11.34	WFU at Renfrew on 9.1.40. Scrapped in 4/42. Canx.
G-ACZN	DH.86	2316		7.12.34	Crashed at Jersey Airport on 4.11.38. Canx.
G-ACZO	DH.86	2318		7.12.34	For RAF as AX841 in 7/40 but NTU; Destroyed in an air raid at Lee-on-Solent on 16.7.40. Canx.
G-ACZP	DH.86B (Originally regd as DH.86)	2321	AX843 G-ACZP	7.12.34	DBR at Barajas, Madrid on 21.9.58. Canx.
G-ACZR	DH.86	2322		7.12.34	To RAF as AX844 in 7/40. Canx 21.7.40.
G-ACZS	Avro 638 Club Cadet	797		13.11.34	Sold abroad in 6/41. Canx.
G-ACZT	British Klemm BK.I Eagle	107		19.11.34	Destroyed by enemy action at Ards on 5.5.41. Canx.
G-ACZU	DH.89 Dragon Rapide	6274		20. 3.35	Sold abroad in 7/37. Canx.
G-ACZV	Avro 671 Cierva C.30A Autogiro	791		20.11.34	To France as F-BDDA in 4/37. Canx.
G-ACZW	Miles M.2 Hawk	136		19.11.34	Sold abroad in 12/34. Canx.
G-ACZX	DH.60G-III Moth Major	5113		.11.34	Crashed at Mansfield, Notts. on 21.8.37. Canx.
G-ACZY	DH.82 Tiger Moth	3315		12.12.34	To India as VT-ANZ in 2/41. Canx.
G-ACZZ	DH.82 Tiger Moth	3316		12.12.34	Crashed at Filton on 30.7.36. Canx.
G-ADAA	DH.85 Leopard Moth	7087		12.12.34	To India as VT-AKX in 2/39. Canx.
G-ADAB	Miles M.2H Hawk Major	137		29.11.34	WFU on 25.5.40. Scrapped at Walsall in 12/47. Canx.
G-ADAC	Miles M.2F Hawk Major	134		29.11.34	To India as VT-AGT in 9/35. Canx.
G-ADAD	Heston Phoenix 1	1/1		29.11.34	To Greece as SX-AAH in 10/36. Canx.
G-ADAE	DH.89 Dragon Rapide	6272	OY-DIN G-ADAE	20. 2.35	CofA lapsed on 28.7.47. Scrapped at Ronaldsway, IoM in 8/48. Canx.
G-ADAF	Saro A.17 Cutty Sark	A17/12		6.12.34	To Mexico in 12/35. Canx.
G-ADAG	DH.89 Dragon Rapide	6266		30. 1.35	To RAF as Z7264 in 7/40. Canx 15.7.40.
G-ADAH	DH.89 Dragon Rapide	6278		30. 1.35	WFU at Booker in 1969. (On display at Manchester Museum of Science & Industry)
G-ADAI	DH.89 Dragon Rapide	6287		. 1.35	To RAF as Z7262 in 7/40. Canx 15.7.40.
G-ADAJ	DH.89 Dragon Rapide	6276		. 1.35	To France as F-BEDY in 4/48. Canx.
G-ADAK	DH.89 Dragon Rapide	6881		. 1.35	To RAF as AW155 in 7/40. Canx 6.7.40.
G-ADAL	DH.89 Dragon Rapide	6863		30. 1.35	To RAF as X9448 in 4/40. Canx 9.4.40.
G-ADAM	Pitcairn PA.19	H.89		11.12.34	Crashed at Newtownards, Northern Ireland in 1935. WFU on 26.12.35. Canx.
G-ADAN	DH.60G-III Moth Major	5122		2. 1.35	To RAF as W7976 in 4/40. Canx 17.4.40.
G-ADAO	DH.89 Dragon Rapide	6275		16. 2.35	To Spanish Nationalists in 9/36. Canx.
G-ADAP	DH.85 Leopard Moth	7090	VP-KBU G-ADAP	10. 4.35	To RAF as AV989 in 5/40. Canx 20.5.40.
G-ADAR	DH.85 Leopard Moth	7091		2. 1.35	Crashed at Bennetts Bridge, Co.Kilkenny on 10.7.35. Canx.
G-ADAS	Miles M.2H Hawk Major	138		19.12.34	To Spanish Republicans in 8/36. Canx in 1/37.
G-ADAT	DH.60G-III Moth Major	5019	VP-KAU	. 1.35	To RAF as X5124 in 12/39. Canx 6.12.39.
G-ADAU	Avro 631 Cadet	806		27.12.34	To 36F ATC Sqdn at Enfield, Middlesex as 2970M in 2/42. Canx 10.2.42.
G-ADAV	Avro 631 Cadet	805		27.12.34	To 1178 ATC Sqdn at Wigan, Lancs as 2954M in 8/41. Canx 31.8.41.
G-ADAW	Miles M.2H Hawk Major	139		28.12.34	Crashed near Woodley on 3.5.36. Canx.
G-ADAX	Airspeed AS.5A Courier	26		. 1.35	To RAF as X9347 in 3/40. Canx 18.3.40.
G-ADAY	Airspeed AS.5A Courier	27		. 1.35	To RAF as X9343 in 3/40. Canx 18.3.40.
G-ADAZ	Airspeed AS.6J Envoy I	32		16. 1.35	To RAF as DG663 in 2/41. Canx 14.2.41.
G-ADBA	Airspeed AS.6J Envoy I	33		16. 1.35	To RAF as P5778 in 11/38. Canx 14.2.39.
G-ADBB	Airspeed AS.6J Envoy I	34		16. 1.35	To Spanish Nationists in 9/36. Canx.
G-ADBC	Avro 638 Club Cadet	807		1. 1.35	To France as F-AQCJ in 4/37. Canx.
G-ADBD	Avro 504N	-	K1245	. 1.35	Crashed at Southend on 22.7.36. Canx.
G-ADBE	Pitcairn PA.19	H.87	NC2503	16. 1.35	WFU on 24.4.40. Scrapped at Kenley in 1950. Canx.
G-ADBF	Miles M.3A Falcon	131		9. 1.35	To Italy as I-ZENA in 6/35. Canx.
G-ADBG	Miles M.2H Hawk Major	143		9. 1.35	To Argentina in 1/35. Canx in 12/36.
G-ADBH	DH.85 Leopard Moth	7030	F-AMXR	. 1.35	To RAF as AV983 in 5/40. Canx 12.5.40.
G-ADBI	Miles M.3A Falcon	140		. 1.35	To Southern Rhodesia as VP-YBN in 3/37. Canx.
G-ADBJ	Avro 671 Cierva C.30A Autogyro	798		16. 1.35	WFU on 20.6.36. Canx 1.1.40.
G-ADBK	Miles M.2 Hawk	146		24. 1.35	Crashed at Bekesbourne on 9.8.37. Canx.
G-ADBL	Armstrong Whitworth AW.35 Scimitar	AW.460	A-2	24. 1.35	No CofA issued & scrapped at Baginton in 1958. Canx.
G-ADBM	Avro 504N	-	K1055	. 1.35	To RAF as AX871 in 6/40. Canx 21.6.40.
G-ADBN	General Aircraft Monospar ST.12	GAL/ST12/35	HB-AIR G-ADBN/T-6	. 1.35	To RAF as BD150 in 8/40. Canx 5.8.40.
G-ADBO	Avro 504N	-	K2354	29. 1.35	WFU on 14.4.40. Canx in 12/46.
G-ADBP	Avro 504N	-	K2353	29. 1.35	To RAF as AX874 in 6/40. Canx 21.6.40.
G-ADBR	Avro 504N	-	K1819	29. 1.35	WFU on 2.6.39. Canx in 12/46.
G-ADBS	Avro 504N	-	K1251	29. 1.35	Fatal crash at Lancarffe Farm, Bodmin on 15.8.35. Canx.
G-ADBT	Miles M.2H Hawk Major	145		31. 1.35	WFU on 5.6.40. Canx 1.12.46.
G-ADBU	DH.89 Dragon Rapide	6280		27. 4.35	DBR in 11/36. Canx.
G-ADBV	DH.89 Dragon Rapide	6286		. 2.35	To RAF as X8511 in 3/40. Canx 2.3.40.
G-ADBW	DH.89 Dragon Rapide	6288		. 2.35	To RAF as Z7265 in 7/40. Canx 15.7.40.
G-ADBX	DH.89 Dragon Rapide	6289		. 2.35	Crashed whilst landing at Ronaldsway, IoM on 16.5.36. Canx.
G-ADBY	General Aircraft Monospar ST.4 Mk.II	GAL/ST4/26		20. 2.35	To South Africa as ZS-AHE in 6/36. Canx.
G-ADBZ	Airspeed AS.6J Envoy I	35		. 2.35	Crashed at Titsey Hill, Surrey on 22.1.37. Canx.
G-ADCA	Airspeed AS.6A Envoy I	36		. 2.35	Crashed near Ales, France on 28.8.36. Canx.
G-ADCB	Airspeed AS.6A Envoy I	37		1. 2.35	To Japan as J-BDDO in 8/35. Canx.

Regn	Type	c/n	Previous identity	Regn date	Fate or immediate subsequent identity (if known)
G-ADCC	Airspeed AS.6A Envoy I	38		1. 2.35	To Japan as J-BDAO in 5/35. Canx.
G-ADCD	Airspeed AS.6D Envoy III	39		1. 2.36	To South Africa as ZS-AGA in 7/36. Canx.
G-ADCE	Airspeed AS.6A Envoy I	40		1. 2.35	To Japan as J-BDEO in 8/35. Canx.
G-ADCF	Miles M.2H Hawk Major	153		6. 2.35	WFU on 28.4.40. Canx in 11/45. (Noted dismantled in the open at Squires Gate in 1949)
G-ADCG	DH.82 Tiger Moth	3318	A2126 A728/BB731/G-ADCG	11. 2.35	To Belgium as OO-TGM in 6/93. Canx 2.6.93.
G-ADCH	DH.82 Tiger Moth	3319		11. 2.35	To RAF as BB732 in 10/40. Canx 30.10.40.
G-ADCI	Miles M.2F Hawk Major	147		8. 2.35	To New Zealand as ZK-AFM in 5/37. Canx.
G-ADCJ	Miles M.2F Hawk Major	154		13. 2.35	WFU on 12.3.40. Canx.
G-ADCK	Avro 671 Cierva C.30A Autogiro	780		5. 2.35	To Australia in 1935 - regd as VH-UUQ on 2.7.35. Canx.
G-ADCL	DH.89 Dragon Rapide	6277		16. 4.35	To Spanish Nationalists as 40-2 in 8/36. Canx.
G-ADCM	DH.86	2317		15. 2.35	Crashed at Zwettl, Austria on 22.10.35. Canx.
G-ADCN	DH.86	2319		15. 2.35	DBF during engine tests at Donmuang airport, Bangkok, Thailand on 3.12.38. Canx.
G-ADCO	DH.85 Leopard Moth	7093		20. 2.35	To RAF as X9383 in 3/40. Canx 27.3.40.
G-ADCP	DH.84 Dragon II	6092		8. 3.35	To RAF as X9440 in 4/40. Canx 4.4.40.
G-ADCR	DH.84 Dragon II	6094		6. 3.35	Crashed on landing at St.Just, near Penzance on 25.6.38. Canx.
G-ADCS	Martin-Baker MB.1	MB.1		11. 2.35	DBF in 3/38. Canx.
G-ADCT	DH.84 Dragon II	6095		21. 3.35	Crashed at Longman Aerodrome, Inverness on 14.2.40. Canx.
G-ADCU	Miles M.2H Hawk Major	162		18. 2.35	WFU on 10.8.40. Canx 1.12.46.
G-ADCV	Miles M.2H Hawk Major	156		20. 2.35	DBR when a wall collapsed on it at Croydon on 4.2.50. Canx.
G-ADCW	Miles M.2H Hawk Major	152		19. 2.35	Crashed at Manston on 28.4.35. Canx.
G-ADCX	Avro 631 Cadet	813		18. 2.35	To Seaford ATC Sqdn, Sussex as 2956M in 9/41. Canx 1.9.41.
G-ADCY	Miles M.2H Hawk Major	158		20. 2.35	To RAF as BD141 in 6/40. Canx 30.6.40.
G-ADCZ	Bristol Type 142	7838	R-12	25. 2.35	NTU - To RAF as K7557 in 7/35. Canx.
	(Transport prototype developed as Bristol 142M Blenheim)				
G-ADDA	Avro 504N	-	K1810	27. 2.35	WFU on 5.5.39. Canx in 12/46.
G-ADDB	BK Swallow II	32		25. 2.35	WFU on 14.5.40. Canx.
G-ADDC	Miles M.2H Hawk Major	164		12. 3.35	To Spanish Republicans in 10/36. Canx.
G-ADDD	DH.89 Dragon Rapide	6283		4. 3.35	To RAF as AW116 in 6/40. Canx 4.6.40.
"G-ADDD"	DH.89A Dragon Rapide	6835	G-AJHO NR747	----	Briefly painted as such in 1986 by special permission of CAA. Restored as G-AJHO in 1986.
G-ADDE	DH.89 Dragon Rapide	6282		7. 5.35	To RAF as X9386 in 3/40. Canx 21.3.40.
G-ADDF	DH.89 Dragon Rapide	6284		. 5.35	To Spanish Republicans in 10/36. Canx.
G-ADDG	Stinson SR.5 Reliant	9326A		9. 5.35	To RAF as X8519 in 2/40. Canx 10.2.40.
G-ADDH	Beechcraft B.17L Staggerwing	23		13. 3.35	DBR at Orpington, Kent on 21.10.36; Wreck to France. Canx.
G-ADDI	DH.84 Dragon II	6096		18. 3.35	To USA as N34DH in 11/70. Canx 18.11.70.
G-ADDJ	DH.84 Dragon II	6097		18. 3.35	To Australia in 3/37 - regd as VH-UZZ on 21.6.37. Canx.
G-ADDK	Miles M.2P Hawk Major	190		21. 5.35	To RAF as BD180 in 8/40. Canx 5.8.40.
G-ADDL	De-Bruyne DB.2 Snark	DB.2		12. 3.35	To RAF as L6103 in 5/36. Canx.
G-ADDM	Miles M.2H Hawk Major	142		5. 3.35	Canx in 12/36.
G-ADDN	Short S.16 Scion II	S.785		13. 6.35	To RAF as X9364 in 3/40. Canx 15.3.40.
G-ADDO	Short S.16 Scion II	S.786		10. 7.35	To RAF as AX864 in 7/40. Canx 6.7.40.
G-ADDP	Short S.16 Scion II	S.787		12. 7.35	To RAF as X9374 in 3/40. Canx 19.3.40.
G-ADDR	Short S.16 Scion II	S.788	M-3	9. 4.36	To RAF as X9366 in 3/40. Canx 20.3.40.
G-ADDS	Short S.16 Scion II	S.789		. .35R	NTU - To Australia in 8/35 - regd as VH-UUT on 24.10.35; later to G-AEOY. Canx.
G-ADDT	Short S.16 Scion II	S.790		17. 8.35	Crashed at Porthcawl on 26.7.36. Canx.
G-ADDU	Miles M.2H Hawk Major	180		15.11.35	To Spanish Republicans in 10/36. Canx.
G-ADDV	Short S.16 Scion II	S.792		22. 5.36	To RAF as X9456 in 4/40. Canx 11.4.40.
G-ADDW(1)	Short S.16 Scion II	S.793		. 3.36R	NTU - To Australia as VH-UTV in 5/36. Canx.
G-ADDW(2)	Proctor/HM.14 Pou du Ciel	TP.1		19. 9.36	WFU on 30.3.37. Canx.
G-ADDX	Short S.16 Scion II	S.794		11. 5.36	To RAF as X9430 in 4/40. Canx 3.4.40.
G-ADDY	General Aircraft Monospar ST.12	GAL/ST12/39		12. 3.35	To Spanish Nationalists as 31-3 in 8/36. Canx.
G-ADDZ	General Aircraft Monospar ST.12	GAL/ST12/40		4. 4.35	To Estonia as ES-AXY in 6/37. Canx.
G-ADEA	DH.86	2323		18. 5.35	To Singapore as VR-SBC in 6/38. Canx.
G-ADEB	DH.86	2324		18. 5.35	Crashed at Altenkirchen, Germany on 12.8.36. Canx.
G-ADEC	DH.86	2325		18. 5.35	To Uruguay as CX-AAH in 9/38. Canx.
G-ADED	DH.84 Dragon II	6098		13. 4.35	Crashed on take-off from Ronaldsway, IoM on 1.7.35. Canx.
G-ADEE	DH.84 Dragon II	6099		15. 4.35	Crashed on slopes of Fairsnape Fell, near Blackpool on 26.10.35. Canx.
G-ADEF	DH.88 Comet	2261		20. 6.35	Crashed north of Khartoum, Sudan on 23.9.35. Canx.
G-ADEG	Avro 643 Cadet	817		14. 3.35	WFU on 10.8.40. Canx.
G-ADEH	Avro 638 Club Cadet	816		14. 3.35	WFU on 22.3.40. Canx.
G-ADEI	Avro 504N	-	E3460	21. 3.35	Crashed at Hanworth on 16.5.39. Canx.
G-ADEJ	BK Eagle II	110		27. 3.35	Crashed in 12/35. Canx.
G-ADEK	Bristol Type 143	7839	R-14	22. 3.35	NTU - Remained as R-14 (B-Class marks). Scrapped between 1939 and 1945. Canx.
G-ADEL	Spartan Cruiser III	102		14. 3.35	To RAF as X9432 in 4/40. Canx 2.4.40.
G-ADEM	Spartan Cruiser III	103		14. 3.35	Crashed at Stanley Park on 20.11.36. Canx.
G-ADEN	Miles M.2H Hawk Major	161		22. 3.35	To Portugal as CS-AAL in 3/35. Canx.
G-ADEO	Avro 594 Avian IV	A25/1	G-AAGJ	22. 3.35	To RAF as 2075M in 1/40. Canx 17.1.40.
G-ADEP	Percival P.3 Gull Six	D.49		11. 3.35	Sold abroad in 8/36. Canx.
G-ADER	Miles M.3A Falcon Major	157		16. 4.35	To France as F-AQER in 2/37. Canx.
G-ADES	BK Eagle II	111		. 3.35	To Switzerland as HB-DES in 1/36. Canx.
G-ADET	Avro 504N	-	J8533	29. 4.35	To RAF as AX875 in 6/40. Canx 21.6.40.
G-ADEU	Percival P.3 Gull Six	D.48		25. 3.35	To France as F-AQNA in 2/38. Canx.
G-ADEV(1)	Avro 504N	-	H5199	14. 8.35	To RAF as BK892 in 2/41. Canx 7.9.40.

Regn	Type	c/n	Previous identity	Regn date	Fate or immediate subsequent identity (if known)
G-ADEV(2)	Avro 504K (Real identity obscure although originally an Avro 504N. If correct, p.i. was 3118M/BK892/G-ADEV/H5199 - but this is unlikely)	R3/LE/61400	G-ACNB "E3404"	18. 4.84	
G-ADEW	Westland Wessex	WA.1899	OO-AGE	22. 3.35	Fatal crash into the English Channel, off Christchurch, Hants on 3.7.35. Canx.
G-ADEX	Avro 643 Cadet	820		20. 3.35	Sold abroad in 9/37. Canx.
G-ADEY	Pobjoy Pirate	101		29. 3.35	Scrapped in 1936. Canx.
G-ADEZ	DH.60M Moth	1669	VP-KAI	. 3.35	To RAF as AX794 in 7/40. Canx 20.7.40.
G-ADFA	Percival P.3 Gull Six	D.50		12. 4.35	Scrapped in 11/45. Canx.
G-ADFB	BK Eagle II	112		12. 4.35	To Japan in 8/35. Canx.
G-ADFC	Miles M.2H Hawk Major	167		22. 3.35	To India as VT-AKG in 6/38. Canx.
G-ADFD	Avro 643 Cadet	819		1. 4.35	WFU on 8.7.40. Canx.
G-ADFE	Miles M.4A Merlin	151	U-8	5. 4.35	WFU on 5.4.40. Canx 1.12.46.
G-ADFF	DH.86B (Originally built as DH.86A)	2328		7.11.35	To RAF as AX760 in 8/41. Canx 15.8.41.
G-ADFG	DH.85 Leopard Moth	7100		11. 5.35	To France as F-AREP in 7/38. Canx.
G-ADFH	Miles M.3A Falcon Major	196	HM496 G-ADFH	21. 5.35	WFU at Redhill in 8/54. Canx.
G-ADFI	DH.84 Dragon II	6100		5. 9.35	Crashed at Thurso, Caithness on 3.7.37. Canx.
G-ADFJ	DH.85 Leopard Moth	7103		10. 5.35	To France as F-AOCS in 6/40. Canx.
G-ADFK	DH.60G-III Moth Major	5143		11. 4.35	To RAF as AW162 in 6/40. Canx 28.6.40.
G-ADFL	DH.60G-III Moth Major	5144		12. 4.35	To Austria as OE-TAT in 12/35. Canx.
G-ADFM	DH.60G-III Moth Major	5145		12. 4.35	To Austria as OE-TET in 12/35. Canx.
G-ADFN	Blackburn B.2	5920/1		3. 4.35	To 734 ATC Sqdn at Cambridge Technical School, Durham as 2897M in 2/42. Canx 17.2.42.
G-ADFO	Blackburn B.2	5920/2		3. 4.35	DBR in forced landing at Newport, Yorks on 3.9.40. Canx.
G-ADFP	Blackburn B.2	5920/3		3. 4.35	To 463 ATC Sqdn at 'Pontefract Secondary Modern Boys School', Pontefract, Yorks as 2892M in 2/42. Canx 17.2.42.
G-ADFR	Blackburn B.2	5920/4		3. 4.35	To 628 ATC Sqdn at Pinner Grammer School, Middlesex as 2894M in 2/42. Canx 17.2.42.
G-ADFS	Blackburn B.2	5920/5		3. 4.35	Fell into the River Humber following an air collision with Blackburn B.2 G-ACLC on 24.6.40. Canx.
G-ADFT	Blackburn B.2	5920/6		3. 4.35	To 1176 ATC Sqdn at Bexhill, Surrey as 2908M in 2/42. Canx 17.2.42.
G-ADFU	Blackburn B.2	5920/7		3. 4.35	To 1415 ATC Sqdn at King Edward School, Birmingham as 2903M in 2/42. Canx 17.2.42.
G-ADFV	Blackburn B.2	5920/8		3. 4.35	To 574 ATC Sqdn at Caterham School, Surrey as 2893M on 17.2.42. Cut up in 1950, rear fuselage preserved in HQ building, rest buried nearby. Reconstruction attempted in 1967 - failed? (Forward fuselage for rebuild 4/96)
G-ADFW	Avro 504N	-	K1061	4. 4.35	WFU on 13.5.37. Canx in 11/45.
G-ADFX	DH.89 Dragon Rapide	6290		17. 6.35	To RAF as X9457 in 4/40. Canx 27.4.40.
G-ADFY	DH.89 Dragon Rapide	6291		28. 6.35	To Spanish Nationalists in 8/36. Canx.
G-ADFZ	Westland Wessex	WA.1900	OO-AGF	. 4.35	Destroyed in mid-air collision with Avro 504N G-ACOD over Blackpool on 7.9.35. Canx 1.12.46.
G-ADGA	Miles M.2F Hawk Major	169		12. 4.35	To India in 9/39. Canx in 5/41.
G-ADGB	Avro 504N	-	J8758	. 4.35	WFU on 18.6.36. Canx.
G-ADGC	Avro 504N	-	J9689	. 4.35	Not converted. Canx in 1/36.
G-ADGD	Miles M.2H Hawk Major	165		18. 4.35	W/o on 22.6.35. Canx.
G-ADGE	Miles M.2H Hawk Major	135		30. 4.35	To Kenya as VP-KCM in 12/37. Canx.
G-ADGF	DH.82 Tiger Moth	3345		23. 5.35	To RAF as BB704 in 9/40. Canx 17.9.40.
G-ADGG	DH.82 Tiger Moth	3346		23. 5.35	To RAF as BB695 in 9/40. Canx 17.9.40.
G-ADGH	DH.82 Tiger Moth	3347		23. 5.35	To RAF as BB696 in 9/40. Canx 17.9.40.
G-ADGI	Miles M.2 Hawk	175		30. 4.35	To RAF as AW150 in 6/40. Canx 26.6.40.
G-ADGJ	BA Eagle II	121		7. 5.35	To India as VT-AHT in 7/36. Canx.
G-ADGK	Percival P.10 Gull Four	D.51		7. 5.35	Crashed at Baden-Baden, Germany on 6.6.35. Canx.
G-ADGL	Miles M.2H Hawk Major	166		24. 5.35	Destroyed by bombs at Lympne in 6/40. Canx.
G-ADGM	Avro 504N	-	K1962	. 5.35	DBF at Brooklands on 24.10.36. Canx.
G-ADGN	Avro 504N	-	H2962	7. 5.35	WFU on 9.8.36. Canx in 3/38.
G-ADGO	DH.82 Tiger Moth	2262		10. 5.35	W/o in 3/40. Canx.
G-ADGP	Miles M.2L Hawk Speed Six	160	(N.....) G-ADGP	20. 5.35	
G-ADGR	Miles M.2 Hawk	192		8. 4.35	Crashed at Evere, Belgium on 18.7.37. Canx.
G-ADGS	DH.82 Tiger Moth	3337		23. 5.35	To RAF as BB705 in 9/40. Canx 17.9.40.
G-ADGT	DH.82 Tiger Moth	3338	BB697 G-ADGT	23. 5.35	WFU at Ludham prior to CofA expiry on 8.5.67. Broken up to provide spares for G-APIG and others. Wreck at Ludham in 8/69.
G-ADGU	DH.82 Tiger Moth	3339		23. 5.35	To RAF as BB693 in 9/40. Canx 17.9.40.
G-ADGV	DH.82 Tiger Moth	3340	(D-E...) G-ADGV/(G-BACW)/BB694/G-ADGV	23. 5.35	
G-ADGW	DH.82 Tiger Moth	3341		23. 5.35	To RAF as BB706 in 9/40. Canx 17.9.40.
G-ADGX	DH.82 Tiger Moth	3342	BB698 G-ADGX	23. 5.35	Crashed at Thruxton on 11.7.53. Canx.
G-ADGY	DH.82 Tiger Moth	3343		23. 5.35	To RAF as BB699 in 9/40. Canx 17.9.40.
G-ADGZ	DH.82 Tiger Moth	3344		23. 5.35	To RAF as BB700 in 9/40. Canx 17.9.40.
G-ADHA(1)	DH.82 Tiger Moth	3348		. 5.35R	NTU - To Canada as CF-AVG in 7/35. Canx.
G-ADHA(2)	DH.83 Fox Moth	4097	N83DH ZK-ASP/R.New Zealand AF NZ566/ZK-ADI	3.12.84	Restored to New Zealand as ZK-ADI in 2/97. Canx 3.2.97.
G-ADHB	DH.85 Leopard Moth	7104		24. 5.35	To RAF as W9371 in 12/39. Canx 15.12.39.
G-ADHC	Miles M.3A Falcon Major	163		22. 5.35	To Italy as I-ZENA in 3/36. Canx.
G-ADHD(1)	DH.85 Leopard Moth	7106		. 5.35R	NTU - To South Africa (as spares?). Canx.

Regn	Type	c/n	Previous identity	Regn date	Fate or immediate subsequent identity (if known)
G-ADHD(2)	DH.60G-III Moth Major (Rebuild of ex Spanish components acquired from USA)	5105	EC-... Spanish AF 34-5/EC-W32	17. 2.88	(On rebuild at Henlow)
G-ADHE	DH.60G-III Moth Major	5147		23. 5.35	Crashed at Rickmansworth, Herts on 22.3.58. Canx.
G-ADHF	Miles M.2H Hawk Major	173		11. 5.35	To Dutch East Indies as PK-SAR in 9/35. Canx.
G-ADHG	Miles M.3A Falcon Major	193		5. 6.35	To Australia in 5/37 - regd as VH-AAT in /37. Canx.
G-ADHH	Miles M.3A Falcon Major	181		16. 5.35	To Palestine as VQ-PAO in 3/40. Canx.
G-ADHI	Miles M.3A Falcon Major	189		14. 5.35	To RAF as X9300 in 3/40. Canx 14.3.40.
G-ADHJ	Short S.20 Mayo Composite	S.796		17. 6.35	Broken up at Rochester on 21.8.41. Canx.
G-ADHK	Short S.21 Mayo Composite	S.797		17. 6.35	Destroyed by enemy action at Poole on 11.5.41. Canx.
G-ADHL	Short S.23 Empire	S.795		17. 6.35	Broken up at Hythe in 11/46. Canx.
G-ADHM	Short S.23 Empire	S.804		17. 6.35	Broken up at Hythe in 1947. Canx.
G-ADHN	DH.82 Tiger Moth	3471		9.12.35	To RAF as BB811 in 10/40. Canx 17.10.40.
G-ADHO	Airspeed AS.23 (Douglas DC-2-115F)	-		25. 5.35	NTU - Not built. Canx.
G-ADHP	Avro 636	821		27. 5.35	NTU - Not completed. Canx.
G-ADHR	DH.82 Tiger Moth	3371		6. 8.35	To RAF as BB743 in 10/40. Canx 30.10.40.
G-ADHS	DH.82 Tiger Moth	3372		6. 8.35	To RAF as BB744 in 10/40. Canx 30.10.40.
G-ADHT	DH.82 Tiger Moth	3373		8. 8.35	To RAF as BB733 in 10/40. Canx 30.10.40.
G-ADHU	DH.82 Tiger Moth	3374		8. 8.35	To RAF as BB734 in 10/40. Canx 30.10.40.
G-ADHV	DH.82 Tiger Moth	3375		8. 8.35	To RAF as BB735 in 10/40. Canx 30.10.40.
G-ADHW	DH.82 Tiger Moth	3376		8. 8.35	Fatal crash after collision with Gauntlet II K5303 emerging from cloud over Smallford, Herts on 21.1.38. Canx.
G-ADHX	DH.82 Tiger Moth	3377		. 8.35	Was to have become BB793 with RAF but crashed at Sywell on 27.8.40. Canx.
G-ADHY	DH.82 Tiger Moth	3366		13. 8.35	To RAF as BB745 in 10/40. Canx 30.10.40.
G-ADHZ	DH.82 Tiger Moth	3367		13. 8.35	To RAF as BB746 in 10/40. Canx 30.10.40.
G-ADIA	DH.82 Tiger Moth	3368	BB747 G-ADIA	13. 8.35	
G-ADIB	DH.82 Tiger Moth	3369	BB748 G-ADIB	13. 8.35	To France as F-BGZU in 5/54. Canx.
G-ADIC	DH.82 Tiger Moth	3370		13. 8.35	Crashed at Littlewick Green, Berks on 23.2.40. Canx.
G-ADID	BA Eagle II	118		29. 5.35	To RAF as HM500 in 10/41. Canx 6.10.41.
G-ADIE	Avro 643 Cadet	848		31. 5.35	To Ireland as EI-ALP in 9/60. Canx.
G-ADIF	Fairey Fantome	F.2118	F-6	5. 6.35	Crashed at Evere, Brussels on 18.7.35. Canx.
G-ADIG	Miles M.2P Hawk Major	204		31. 5.35	Crashed after propellor failure resulting in the engine being torn out whilst en route Budapest to Hamburg on 8.6.36. Canx.
G-ADIH	DH.82A Tiger Moth	3349	3654M BB789/G-ADIH	17. 6.35	Crashed at Broadstairs, near Ramsgate Airport on 20.11.52. Canx.
G-ADII	DH.82A Tiger Moth	3350		17. 6.35	To RAF as BB701 in 9/40. Canx 17.9.40.
G-ADIJ	DH.82A Tiger Moth	3351	BB788 G-ADIJ	17. 6.35	To New Zealand as ZK-BBS in 9/52. Canx.
G-ADIK	General Aircraft Monospar ST.4 Mk.II	GAL/ST4/27		30. 5.35	Crashed at Godstone, Surrey on 6.4.36. Canx.
G-ADIL	DH.60G Gipsy Moth	522	J9115	3. 6.35	To RAF as X5050 in 11/39. Canx 15.11.39.
G-ADIM	DH.89 Dragon Rapide	6293		25. 7.35	To RAF as Z7263 in 7/40. Canx 15.7.40.
G-ADIN	Gloster Gamecock (Special)	1	J8047	3. 6.35	W/o when undercarriage collapsed & overturned at Sywell in 5/36. Canx.
G-ADIO	DH.60G-III Moth Major (Built by D.H. Technical School)	2263		6. 6.35	(Last ex-works Moth) To Austria as OE-DIO in 7/35. Canx.
G-ADIP	Short S.22 Scion Senior	S.810		. .35R	NTU - To India as VT-AHI in 8/36. Canx.
G-ADIR	DH.87B Hornet Moth (Built as a DH.87A)	8000	E-1	11. 6.35	To RAF as W9387 in 2/40. Canx 29.2.40.
G-ADIS	DH.87B Hornet Moth (Built as a DH.87A)	8001	E-2	11. 6.35	To RAF as W9391 in 2/40. Canx 29.2.40.
G-ADIT	Miles M.2H Hawk Major	168		12. 6.35	To 1851 ATC Sqdn at Norton, Suffolk as X5126 in 12/39. Canx 19.12.39.
G-ADIU	Miles M.3A Falcon Major	202		13. 6.35	To Australia as VH-ACE in 1/37. Canx.
G-ADIV	General Aircraft Monospar ST.25 Jubilee	GAL/ST25/46		13. 6.35	Crashed into Wigtown Bay on 11.8.36. Canx.
G-ADIW	DH.82A Tiger Moth	3352		1. 7.35	To India in 9/40. Canx.
G-ADIX	DH.82A Tiger Moth	3353		1. 7.35	To India in 9/40. Canx.
G-ADIY	DH.82A Tiger Moth	3354		1. 7.35	To India in 9/40. Canx.
G-ADIZ	DH.82A Tiger Moth	3355		1. 7.35	To India in 9/40. Canx.
G-ADJA	DH.82A Tiger Moth	3356		1. 7.35	To India in 9/40. Canx.
G-ADJB	DH.82A Tiger Moth	3378		29. 8.35	Crashed near Woodley on 12.3.36. Canx.
G-ADJC	DH.82A Tiger Moth	3379		29. 8.35	To RAF as BB815 in 10/40. Canx 9.10.40.
G-ADJD	DH.82A Tiger Moth	3380		29. 8.35	To RAF as BB816 in 10/40. Canx 9.10.40.
G-ADJE	DH.82A Tiger Moth	3381		29. 8.35	To RAF as W5015 in 11/39. Canx 17.11.39.
G-ADJF	DH.82A Tiger Moth	3382		29. 8.35	To RAF as BB791 in 10/40. Canx 9.10.40.
G-ADJG	DH.82A Tiger Moth	3383		29. 8.35	To RAF as BB817 in 10/40. Canx 9.10.40.
G-ADJH	DH.82A Tiger Moth	3384		29. 8.35	To RAF as X5045 in 11/39. Canx 17.11.39.
G-ADJI	DH.82A Tiger Moth	3385	BB818 G-ADJI	29. 8.35	To France as F-BHII in 9/55. Canx.
G-ADJJ	DH.82A Tiger Moth	3386	BB819 G-ADJJ	29. 8.35	WFU on 20.3.75. (Stored 4/95 Great Eversden)
G-ADJK	Stinson SR.6A Reliant	9613		26. 9.35	Sold abroad in 7/37. Canx.
G-ADJL	BA Swallow II	400		13. 6.35	WFU on 29.12.39. Broken up at Elstree in 1953. Canx.
G-ADJM	BA Swallow II	401		13. 6.35	Force-landed in the English Channel, off Dover on 14.5.38, aircraft was towed to Dover but later scrapped. Canx.
G-ADJN	BA Swallow II	402		13. 6.35	WFU on 16.9.39 & destroyed at Lympne in 9/40. Canx.
G-ADJO	BA Eagle II	122		13. 6.35	To France as F-ARIO in 9/38. Canx.

Regn	Type	c/n	Previous identity	Regn date	Fate or immediate subsequent identity (if known)
G-ADJP	General Aircraft Monospar ST.4 Mk.II	GAL/ST4/28		25. 6.35	To RAF as X9367 in 3/40. Canx 18.3.40.
G-ADJR	Bristol 96 Fighter (F.2b)	7580	J8455	18. 6.35	WFU on 8.6.37. Scrapped in 1/38. Canx.
G-ADJS	BA Eagle II	119		. 6.35	To RAF as (DR610)/2680M in 4/41. Canx 10.4.41.
G-ADJT	Avro 643 Cadet II	849		24. 6.35	To France as F-AQMX in 3/38. Canx.
G-ADJU	DH.87B Hornet Moth (Built as a DH.87A)	8002		3. 8.35	To Hong Kong as VR-HCX in 10/37. Canx.
G-ADJV	DH.87B Hornet Moth (Built as a DH.87A)	8003	AX857 G-ADJV	29. 7.35	Crashed at Fairoaks on 13.10.51. Canx.
G-ADJW	DH.87A Hornet Moth	8004		29. 7.35	To France as F-AOVY in 4/36. Canx.
G-ADJX	DH.87A Hornet Moth	8005		30. 8.35	To RAF as X9443 in 5/40. Canx 10.5.40.
G-ADJY	DH.87B Hornet Moth (Built as a DH.87A)	8006		29. 7.35	Crashed at Chwilog on 6.4.37. Canx.
G-ADJZ	DH.87A Hornet Moth	8008		3. 9.35	To RAF as X9444 in 5/40. Canx 10.5.40.
G-ADKA	DH.87A Hornet Moth	8007		4. 9.35	To RAF as W5746 in 1/40. Canx 13.1.40.
G-ADKB	DH.87B Hornet Moth (Built as a DH.87A)	8012		3. 9.35	To RAF as W6421 in 1/40. Canx 7.1.40.
G-ADKC	DH.87B Hornet Moth	8064	X9445 G-ADKC	27. 3.36	
G-ADKD	DH.87B Hornet Moth (Built as a DH.87A)	8016	X9321 G-ADKD	.10.35	WFU at Croft on 23.10.47. Canx.
G-ADKE	DH.87B Hornet Moth (Built as a DH.87A)	8018		8.10.35	To RAF as W5830 in 10/39. Canx 3.10.39.
G-ADKF	DH.87A Hornet Moth	8019		5.10.35	To Australia in 6/37 - regd as VH-AAV in /37. Canx.
G-ADKG	DH.82A Tiger Moth	3361		6. 8.35	To RAF as BB749 in 10/40. Canx 30.10.40.
G-ADKH	DH.87B Hornet Moth	8068		20. 2.36	To RAF as W5747 in 1/40. Canx 19.1.40.
G-ADKI	DH.87A Hornet Moth	8029		30.10.35	To RAF as AV951 in 7/40. Canx 3.7.40.
G-ADKJ	DH.87A Hornet Moth	8032		5.11.35	To RAF as W5748 in 1/40. Canx 20.1.40.
G-ADKK	DH.87B Hornet Moth (Built as a DH.87A)	8033	W5749 G-ADKK	9.11.35	
G-ADKL	DH.87B Hornet Moth (Built as a DH.87A)	8035	F-BCJO G-ADKL/W5750/G-ADKL	18.12.35	
G-ADKM	DH.87B Hornet Moth (Built as a DH.87A)	8037	W5751 G-ADKM	12.11.35	
G-ADKN	DH.87B Hornet Moth	8073		22. 2.36	To RAF as W6422 in 1/40. Canx 2.1.40.
G-ADKO	DH.87A Hornet Moth	8042		21.11.35	W/o in 3/38. Canx.
G-ADKP	DH.87B Hornet Moth	8081		. .36	To RAF as X9322 in 2/40. Canx 24.2.40.
G-ADKR	DH.87B Hornet Moth (Built as a DH.87A)	8045		23.11.35	To RAF as W5752 in 1/40. Canx 20.1.40.
G-ADKS	DH.87B Hornet Moth	8046		16. 4.36	To RAF as X9458 in 3/40. Canx 12.3.40.
G-ADKT	DH.87B Hornet Moth (Built as a DH.87A)	8014		2.10.35	To Austraia as VH-ABO in 12/37. Canx.
G-ADKU	DH.87B Hornet Moth	8051		4. 1.36	To RAF as W9386 in 2/40. Canx 21.2.40.
G-ADKV	DH.87B Hornet Moth (Built as a DH.87A)	8054		28.12.35	To RAF as W9372 in 3/40. Canx 2.3.40.
G-ADKW	DH.87B Hornet Moth	8074	W5754 G-ADKW	10. 3.36	WFU at Panshanger on 14.7.48. Broken up for spares in 1950. Canx.
G-ADKX	Percival P.3 Gull Six	D.52		10. 7.35	To RAF as AX698 in 11/40. Canx 18.11.40.
G-ADKY	Avro 671 Cierva C.30A Autogiro	749		29. 6.35	Sold abroad in 8/35. Canx.
G-ADKZ	Avro 626	862		2. 7.35	To Czechoslovkia in 12/35. Canx.
G-ADLA	Miles M.2H Hawk Major	176		8. 7.35	To South Africa as ZS-APX in 2/39. Canx.
G-ADLB	Miles M.2H Hawk Major	210		9. 7.35	Sold abroad in 7/36. Canx.
G-ADLC	Miles M.3B Falcon Six	213		10. 7.35	Crashed near Totnes on 28.7.38. Canx.
G-ADLD	BA Swallow II	404		2. 7.35	Destroyed by bombs at Lympne in 9/40. Canx.
G-ADLE	Beechcraft B.17R	50		. 7.35	Crashed on Isle of Laaland, Denmark on 20.1.39. Canx 29.6.40.
G-ADLF	Blackburn B.2	5920/9		10. 7.35	To 449 ATC Sqdn at Port Talbot as 2891M in 2/42. Canx 17.2.42.
G-ADLG	Blackburn B.2	5920/10		10. 7.35	To 358 (Welling) ATC Sqdn in Kent as 2888M in 2/42. Canx 17.2.42.
G-ADLH	Miles M.2S Hawk Major	194		10. 7.35	Crashed near Rouen, France on 28.10.37. Canx.
G-ADLI	Miles M.3A Falcon Major	206		10. 7.35	Crashed at Elstree on 10.7.52. Canx.
G-ADLJ	DH.60M Moth	1514	K1202	8. 7.35	CofA expired 2.3.38. Canx in 8/45.
G-ADLK	DH.60M Moth	1661	K1828	8. 7.35	To India as VT-AJO in 7/37. Canx.
G-ADLL	General Aircraft Monospar ST.12	GAL/ST12/45		19. 7.35	To RAF as X9341 in 3/40. Canx 15.3.40.
G-ADLM	General Aircraft Monospar ST.4 Mk.II	GAL/ST4/30		12. 7.35	Crashed on take-off from Croydon on 16.5.36. Canx.
G-ADLN	Miles M.2R Hawk Major	211		13. 7.35	To RAF as DG664 in 2/41. Canx 18.2.41.
G-ADLO	Miles M.2P Hawk Major	220		15. 7.35	To New Zealand as ZK-AFL in 5/37. Canx.
G-ADLP	DH.80A Puss Moth	2111	VT-ACI	10. 7.35	Crashed at Sliders Farm, Ashdown Forest, near Dane Hill, Sussex on 5.9.36. Canx 10/36.
G-ADLR	BA III Cupid	701		17. 7.35	To South Africa in 1936. Canx.
G-ADLS	Miles M.3C Falcon Six	231		15. 7.35	To Spanish Republicans in 8/36. Canx.
G-ADLT	General Aircraft Monospar ST.25 Jubilee	ST25/50		2. 8.35	To France as F-AQAC in 5/37. Canx.
G-ADLU	DH.82A Tiger Moth	3357		29. 7.35	To R.New Zealand AF as NZ735 in 1/40. Canx.
G-ADLV	DH.82A Tiger Moth	3364		6. 8.35	To RAF as BB750 in 10/40. Canx 30.10.40.
G-ADLW	DH.82A Tiger Moth	3365		6. 8.35	To RAF as BB751 in 10/40. Canx 30.10.40.
G-ADLX	DH.82A Tiger Moth	3360		6. 8.35	Crashed at White Waltham on 1.7.39. Canx.
G-ADLY	DH.87B Hornet Moth (Built as a DH.87A)	8020	W9388 G-ADLY	5.10.35	
G-ADLZ	DH.82A Tiger Moth	3362		6. 8.35	To RAF as BB752 in 10/40. Canx 30.10.40.

Regn	Type	c/n	Previous identity	Regn date	Fate or immediate subsequent identity (if known)
G-ADMA	DH.82A Tiger Moth	3363	BB753 G-ADMA	6. 8.35	To Australia as VH-PCG in 12/56. Canx.
G-ADMB	BA Swallow II	405		16. 7.35	Canx in 12/36.
G-ADMC	General Aircraft Monospar ST.25 Jubilee	GAL/ST25/47		25. 7.35	To South Africa as ZS-APC in 10/38. Canx.
G-ADMD	General Aircraft Monospar ST.25 Jubilee	GAL/ST25/49		23. 7.35	Crashed at Lomasco, Italy on 2.1.37. Canx.
G-ADME	Appleby/HM.14 Pou du Ciel	SVA.1		26. 7.35	WFU on 3.12.36. Canx 31.12.38 in census.
G-ADMF	BA L.25C Swallow II	406		22. 7.35	To Ireland as EI-AFF in 5/49. Canx.
G-ADMG	Avro 621 Tutor	795		20. 7.35	To Greek AF as E-69 in 12/35. Canx.
G-ADMH	Appleby/HM.14 Pou du Ciel	SVA.2		23. 7.35	WFU on 26.8.37. Canx 31.7.38.
	(Damaged at Heston 29.7.35; rebuilt 8/35 as prototype Abbott-Baynes Cantilever Pou)				
G-ADMI	Percival P.3 Gull Six	D.54		19. 8.35	To France as F-APEI 8/36. Canx.
G-ADMJ	DH.87B Hornet Moth	8066	W9389 G-ADMJ	7. 3.36	To Australia as VH-AMJ 9/51. Canx.
G-ADMK	DH.87B Hornet Moth	8067		. .36R	NTU - To G-AEIY in 5/36. Canx.
G-ADML	DH.87B Hornet Moth	8069		17. 2.36	To RAF as X9323 in 2/40. Canx 24.2.40.
G-ADMM	DH.87B Hornet Moth	8072		5. 3.36	To RAF as W5755 in 1/40. Canx 22.1.40.
G-ADMN	DH.87B Hornet Moth	8076		29. 2.36	To RAF as W5770 in 1/40. Canx 15.1.40.
G-ADMO	DH.87B Hornet Moth	8086	(OY-DTI) AV969/G-ADMO	15. 5.36	To Falkland Islands as VP-FAE in 9/49. Canx.
G-ADMP	DH.87B Hornet Moth	8082		10. 3.36	To RAF as BK837 in 9/40. Canx 5.9.40.
G-ADMR	DH.87B Hornet Moth	8087		18. 5.36	To RAF as X9310 in 4/40. Canx 27.4.40.
G-ADMS	DH.87B Hornet Moth (Built as a DH.87A)	8044		23.11.35	To RAF as W5771 in 1/40. Canx 22.1.40.
G-ADMT	DH.87B Hornet Moth	8093		8. 5.36	
G-ADMU	BAC Drone	5		26. 7.35	Crashed at Braunstone on 15.1.39. Canx.
G-ADMV	Hafner AR.3 Mk.II Gyroplane	AR.III		26. 7.35	To RAF as DG670 in 4/41. Canx 28.4.41.
G-ADMW	Miles M.2H Hawk Major	177	DG590 G-ADMW	30. 7.35	CofA expired 30.7.65 & WFU. Repainted as DG590. To RAF Museum. Allotted 8379M. Canx by CAA 16.9.86. (Stored at Cardington)
G-ADMX	BA Swallow II	408		29. 7.35	WFU on 29.9.38. Scrapped in 1940. Canx.
G-ADMY	DH.86	2327		9. 8.35	To RAF as X9442 in 4/40. Canx 4.4.40.
G-ADMZ	General Aircraft Monospar ST.25 Jubilee	GAL/ST25/53		29. 7.35	To Spain as EC-AFF in 6/36. Canx.
G-ADNA	DH.90 Dragonfly	7500	E-2	15. 8.35	To RAF as X9452 in 4/40. Canx 17.4.40.
G-ADNB	DH.87B Hornet Moth	8080	W5772 G-ADNB	15. 4.36	To USA as N36DH in 10/71. Canx 5.10.71.
G-ADNC	DH.87B Hornet Moth	8084		6. 5.36	To RAF as W5773 in 1/40. Canx 22.1.40.
G-ADND	DH.87B Hornet Moth	8097	W9385 G-ADND	4. 8.36	
G-ADNE	DH.87B Hornet Moth	8089	X9325 G-ADNE	10. 3.36	
G-ADNF	DH.83 Fox Moth	4024	SU-ABG	13. 8.35	To Australia as VH-ABQ in 10/38. Canx.
G-ADNG	DH.89 Dragon Rapide	6297		15. 8.35	Crashed near Rutba on 10.3.36. Canx.
G-ADNH	DH.89 Dragon Rapide	6300		15. 8.35	To RAF as W6423 in 1/40. Canx 7.1.40.
G-ADNI	DH.89 Dragon Rapide	6301		15. 8.35	To RAF as W9365 in 4/40. Canx 12.4.40.
G-ADNJ	Miles M.2S Hawk Major	203		12. 8.35	Crashed into the Irish Sea off Malin Head on 6.9.35. Canx.
G-ADNK	Miles M.2S Hawk Major	222		12. 8.35	Sold abroad in 10/35. Canx.
G-ADNL	Miles M.5 Sparrowhawk	239		12. 8.35	(On rebuild from components discarded from reconstruction .53 as M.77 Sparrowjet)
	(Rebuilt as M.77 Sparrowjet G-35-2 with c/n FGM.77/1006 in 1953)				
G-ADNM	General Aircraft Monospar ST.25 Jubilee	GAL/ST25/51	(PH-IPM)	12. 8.35	To Holland as PH-IPM on 9/35. Canx.
G-ADNN	General Aircraft Monospar ST.25 Jubilee	GAL/ST25/52		12. 8.35	To Kenya as VP-KCB in 7/36. Canx.
G-ADNO	DH Technical School T.K.2	1998	E-3	16. 8.35	WFU at Hatfield on 14.10.47. Canx in 1948.
G-ADNP	DH.82A Tiger Moth	3411		4.10.35	To India as VT-AOA in 2/41. Canx.
G-ADNR	DH.82A Tiger Moth	3412		4.10.35	To India as VT-ANU in 2/41. Canx.
G-ADNS	DH.82A Tiger Moth	3413		4.10.35	Crashed at Yatesbury on 23.8.40. Canx.
G-ADNT	DH.82A Tiger Moth	3414		4.10.35	Crashed near Avebury, Wilts on 24.8.38. Canx.
G-ADNU	DH.82A Tiger Moth	3415		4.10.35	To India as VT-AOL in 3/41. Canx.
G-ADNV	DH.82A Tiger Moth	3416		4.10.35	To RAF as BD155 in 8/40. Canx 8.8.40.
G-ADNW	DH.82A Tiger Moth	3417		4.10.35	Collided with DH.82A G-ADNY near Avebury, Wilts on 3.12.38. Canx in 3/41.
G-ADNX	DH.82A Tiger Moth	3418		4.10.35	To India as VT-ANW in 2/41. Canx.
G-ADNY	DH.82A Tiger Moth	3419		4.10.35	To India as VT-AOB in 2/41. Canx.
G-ADNZ(1)	DH.82A Tiger Moth	3420		4.10.35	To India as VT-AOC in 2/41. Canx.
G-ADNZ(2)	DH.82A Tiger Moth	85614	6948M DE673	10.10.74	
G-ADOA	DH.82A Tiger Moth	3421		4.10.35	Crashed at Manton Down, near Farnborough on 26.9.39. Canx.
G-ADOB	DH.82A Tiger Moth	3422		4.10.35	To India as VT-AOJ in 3/41. Canx.
G-ADOC	DH.80A Puss Moth	2188	US Embassy (G-ABNF)	. 8.35	Crashed prior to 9/37. Canx in 5/41.
G-ADOD	Miles M.2U Hawk Speed Six	195		24. 8.35	Crashed at Gwelo, Southern Rhodesia on 1.10.36. Canx.
G-ADOE	Percival P.1E Gull Four	D.53		24. 8.35	Ditched into the English Channel off Ferring, Sussex on 7.10.47. Canx.
G-ADOF	DH.82A Tiger Moth	3399		19. 9.35	To RAF as BB672 in 9/40. Canx 19.9.40.
G-ADOG	DH.82A Tiger Moth	3400		19. 9.35	To RAF as BB673 in 9/40. Canx 19.9.40.
G-ADOH	DH.82A Tiger Moth	3401		19. 9.35	To RAF as BB674 in 9/40. Canx 19.9.40.
G-ADOI	DH.82A Tiger Moth	3402		19. 9.35	To RAF as BB675 in 9/40. Canx 19.9.40.
G-ADOJ	DH.82A Tiger Moth	3403		19. 9.35	To RAF as BB676 in 9/40. Canx 19.9.40.
G-ADOK	DH.82A Tiger Moth	3404	BB677 G-ADOK	19. 9.35	To Holland as PH-UEX 7/51. Canx.

Regn	Type	c/n	Previous identity	Regn date	Fate or immediate subsequent identity (if known)
G-ADOL	DH.82A Tiger Moth	3405		19. 9.35	To RAF as BB678 in 9/40. Canx 19.9.40.
G-ADOM	DH.82A Tiger Moth	3406		19. 9.35	To RAF as BB679 in 9/40. Canx 19.9.40.
G-ADON	DH.82A Tiger Moth	3407		19. 9.35	To RAF as BB680 in 9/40. Canx 19.9.40.
G-ADOO	DH.82A Tiger Moth	3408		19. 9.35	To RAF as BB681 in 9/40. Canx 19.9.40.
G-ADOP	DH.82A Tiger Moth	3409		19. 9.35	To RAF as BB682 in 9/40. Canx 19.9.40.
G-ADOR	DH.82A Tiger Moth	3410	(G-AJKF) BB687/(BB683)/G-ADOR	19. 9.35	To Pakistan AF in 11/48. Canx.
G-ADOS	DH.84 Dragon II	6103	E-4	21.10.35	To RAF as HM569 in 6/42. Canx 6.6.42.
G-ADOT	DH.87B Hornet Moth (Built as DH.87A)	8027	X9326 G-ADOT	6.10.35	WFU at Stapleford on 15.10.59. (On display at Salisbury Hall, London Colney)
G-ADOU	Hills/HM.14 Pou du Ciel (Also c/n quoted as Hills.1)	FH.1		23. 9.35	(Reportedly crashed near Cheadle, Cheshire on 5.4.36) Canx 19.6.36.
G-ADOV	Perman/HM.14 Pou du Ciel	GAP/SS.50		1.10.35	WFU on 23.8.36. Canx.
G-ADOW	DH.82A Tiger Moth	3387		24. 9.35	To RAF as BB856 in 1/41. Canx 3.1.41.
G-ADOX	DH.82A Tiger Moth	3388		24. 9.35	To RAF as BB857 in 1/41. Canx 3.1.41.
G-ADOY	DH.82A Tiger Moth	3389		24. 9.35	To RAF as BB858 in 1/41. Canx 3.1.41.
G-ADOZ	DH.82A Tiger Moth	3390		24. 9.35	To RAF as BB859 in 1/41. Canx 3.1.41.
G-ADPA	DH.82A Tiger Moth	3391		24. 9.35	To RAF as BB851 in 1/41. Canx 3.1.41.
G-ADPB	DH.82A Tiger Moth	3392		24. 9.35	Crashed at Stoughton, Leicester on 27.5.40. Canx.
G-ADPC	DH.82A Tiger Moth (Now composite rebuild)	3393	BB852 G-ADPC	24. 9.35	
G-ADPD	DH.82A Tiger Moth	3394		24. 9.35	Crashed near Peterborough on 24.3.36. Canx.
G-ADPE	DH.82A Tiger Moth	3395		24. 9.35	To RAF as BB853 in 1/41. Canx 3.1.41.
G-ADPF	DH.82A Tiger Moth	3396		24. 9.35	DBR at Braunstone on 22.7.40. Canx.
G-ADPG	DH.82A Tiger Moth	3397		24. 9.35	Crashed at Desford on 27.9.40, with marks BB854 NTU. Canx.
G-ADPH	DH.82A Tiger Moth	3398		24. 9.35	To RAF as BB855 in 1/41. Canx 3.1.41.
G-ADPI	General Aircraft Monospar ST.25 Jubilee	GAL/ST25/54		. 8.35	To Spanish Republicans in 8/36. Canx.
G-ADPJ	BAC Super Drone	7		. 8.35	Crashed at Leicester on 3.4.55. (On rebuild 4/96 using parts from G-AEJR c/n 22 and G-AEKU c/n 29)
G-ADPK	General Aircraft Monospar ST.25 Jubilee	GAL/ST25/55		30. 8.35	To RAF as X9348 on 16.3.40, NTU as crashed at Ringway sameday; rebuilt & to RAF as DR848 in 1941. Canx.
G-ADPL	General Aircraft Monospar ST.25 Jubilee	GAL/ST25/56		3. 9.35	To RAF as X9369 in 3/40. Canx 21.3.40.
G-ADPM	General Aircraft Monospar ST.25 Jubilee	GAL/ST25/57		3. 9.35	DBF at Hooton Park on 8.7.40. Canx.
G-ADPN	BA Eagle II	124		28. 8.35	Crashed at Cardiff on 20.9.36. Canx.
G-ADPO	BA Eagle II	125		. 8.35	Scrapped at Hanworth in 1940. Canx.
G-ADPP	Brook/HM.14 Pou du Ciel	CB/HS/4		24. 9.35	Damaged at Sherburn on 6.10.35. Not repaired & WFU on 23.8.36. Canx 5.11.45.
G-ADPR	Percival P.3 Gull Six	D.55	AX866 G-ADPR	29. 8.35	To ZK-DPR. (On display at Auckland International Airport, New Zealand) Canx 14.3.95.
G-ADPS	BA Swallow II	410		4. 9.35	
G-ADPT	BA Swallow II	411		6. 9.35	WFU on 30.1.40. Canx.
G-ADPU	Perman/HM.14 Pou du Ciel	EGP.51		. 8.35R	NTU. Canx.
G-ADPV	Perman/HM.14 Pou du Ciel	EGP.52		24. 1.36	WFU on 12.1.37. Canx.
G-ADPW	Perman/HM.14 Pou du Ciel	GAP/SS.53		18.10.35	WFU on 3.10.36. Canx.
G-ADPX	Perman/HM.14 Pou du Ciel	EGP.54		2. 2.36	Canx in 7/36.
G-ADPY	Perman/HM.14 Pou du Ciel	EGP.55		14. 2.36	WFU on 21.11.36. Canx.
G-ADPZ	Priest/HM.14 Pou du Ciel	PP/H/300		3. 9.35	Canx in 3/36.
G-ADRA	Pietenpol Air Camper	PFA/1514		10. 4.78	
G-ADRB	Not allocated.				
G-ADRC	K & S Jungster J-1	PFA/44-10453		14. 2.79	Canx as TWFU 25.1.88.
G-ADRD	Not allocated.				
G-ADRE	Not allocated.				
G-ADRF	Not allocated.				
G-ADRG	Not allocated.				
"G-ADRG"	Mignet HM.14 Pou-Du-Ciel (Modern reproduction with fictitious marks)	-	BAPC.77	----	(On rebuild to taxy status 10/93)
G-ADRH	DH.87B Hornet Moth (Originally regd with c/n IMC/8164, amended in 20.5.85)	8038	F-AQBY HB-OBE	6. 8.82	Shipped to Gore, New Zealand 16.5.91 for rebuild. (On rebuild .98) Reserved as ZK-ANR.
G-ADRI	Not allocated.				
G-ADRJ	Not allocated.				
G-ADRK	Not allocated.				
G-ADRL	Not allocated.				
G-ADRM	Not allocated.				
G-ADRN	Not allocated.				
G-ADRO	Not allocated.				
G-ADRP	Not allocated.				
G-ADRR	Aeronca C.3	A.734	N17423 NC17423	6. 9.88	(Stored Roughay Farm, Bishops Waltham .92)
G-ADRS	Not allocated.				
G-ADRT	Not allocated.				
G-ADRU	Not allocated.				
G-ADRV	Not allocated.				
G-ADRW	Piper Aerostar 601P	61P-0442-167	N99RW	25. 6.79	To USA as N8497S in 8/80. Canx 29.8.80.
G-ADRX	Not allocated.				
"G-ADRX"	Mignet HM.14 Pou-Du-Ciel (Rebuilt from original remains acquired from Torver, Lake District)	-	BAPC.231	----	(On display 3/96 Haverigg)
G-ADRY	Not allocated.				
"G-ADRY"	Mignet HM.14 Pou-Du-Ciel (Fictitious marks - built by P.D.Roberts, Swansea 60s-.78)	-	BAPC.29	----	(On display 10/96 Brooklands)

Regn	Type	c/n	Previous identity	Regn date	Fate or immediate subsequent identity (if known)
G-ADRZ	Not allocated.				
G-ADSA	BAC Drone	6		. 9.35	DBF at St.Columb, Cornwall in 1938. Canx.
G-ADSB	BAC Drone (Rebuild of BAC.VII c/n 132)	3	BGA.197	. 9.35	WFU on 19.10.39. Canx. (Converted from Drone to glider BGA.607 in 1948)
G-ADSC	Mignet HM.14 Pou du Ciel	NAD.1		26.11.35	WFU on 30.9.35. Canx in 12/36.
G-ADSD	Mignet HM.14 Pou du Ciel	NAD.2		14.11.35	Canx 3.3.36.
G-ADSE	Griffin/HM.14 Pou du Ciel	CFRG.2		3. 9.35	Authorisation to Fly expired on 18.10.36. Air Ministry Category E & stored at Cornerpods, Thames Ditton on 31.8.39. Canx 1.12.46.
G-ADSF	BA Swallow II	413		9. 9.35	WFU on 1.9.39 & destroyed at Lympne in 9/40. Canx.
G-ADSG	Percival P.3 Gull Six	D.58		6. 9.35	To India as VT-ALT in 8/39. Canx.
G-ADSH	DH.82A Tiger Moth	3424		11. 9.35	To RAF as BB754 in 10/40. Canx 30.10.40.
G-ADSI	DH.82A Tiger Moth	3423		11. 9.35	Crashed near Dumfries on 1.7.38. Canx.
G-ADSJ	DH.87B Hornet Moth	8096		. 9.35R	NTU - To New Zealand as ZK-ACP in 5/36. Canx.
G-ADSK	DH.87B Hornet Moth (Now on rebuild from components)	8091	D-EJOM AP-AES/G-ADSK/ AV952/G-ADSK	9. 4.36	CofA expired 14.3.70. Broken up for spares in 1974 at Woking with parts used on rebuild of G-ADKL. Canx by CAA 15.9.86 (On rebuild at Gore, New Zealand .93)
G-ADSL	DH.87B Hornet Moth	8098		. 9.35R	NTU - To South Africa as ZS-AII in 8/36. Canx.
G-ADSM	Percival P.3 Gull Six	D.59		13. 9.35	For RAF as BD165 in 8/40, NTU - Destroyed in 1940 before being impressed. Canx 11.8.40.
G-ADSN	General Aircraft Monospar ST.25 Jubilee	GAL/ST25/58		. 9.35	To Spanish Republicans in 7/36. Canx.
G-ADSO	Aeronca C.3	A.579	CF-CYC	. 9.35	WFU on 11.2.38. Used by 16F Wood Green & Hornsey ATC Sqdn, London from 1939 until 1955. Canx.
G-ADSP	Aeronca C.3	A.580	CF-CYB	. 9.35	WFU on 10.10.39. Scrapped between 1939 and 1945. Canx.
G-ADSR	Armstrong Whitworth AW.27 Ensign II (Originally regd as Mk.I)	AW.1156		3.10.35	WFU at Almaza, Cairo in 9/44. Scrapped on 3.1.45. Canx.
G-ADSS	Armstrong Whitworth AW.27 Ensign II (Originally regd as Mk.I)	AW.1157	(VT-AJE) G-ADSS	3.10.35	Scrapped at Hamble on 26.3.47. Canx.
G-ADST	Armstrong Whitworth AW.27 Ensign II (Originally regd as Mk.I)	AW.1158		3.10.35	Scrapped at Hamble on 28.3.47. Canx.
G-ADSU	Armstrong Whitworth AW.27 Ensign II (Originally regd as Mk.I)	AW.1159	(VT-AJF) G-ADSU	3.10.35	WFU in 2/45. Scrapped at Almaza, Cairo in 3/46. Canx.
G-ADSV	Armstrong Whitworth AW.27 Ensign II (Originally regd as Mk.I)	AW.1160		3.10.35	Scrapped at Hamble on 23.3.47. Canx.
G-ADSW	Armstrong Whitworth AW.27 Ensign II (Originally regd as Mk.I)	AW.1161		3.10.35	Scrapped at Hamble on 21.4.47. Canx.
G-ADSX	Armstrong Whitworth AW.27 Ensign II (Originally regd as Mk.I)	AW.1162		3.10.35	Abandoned at Le Bourget, France on 1.6.40, to Luftwaffe. Canx.
G-ADSY	Armstrong Whitworth AW.27 Ensign II (Originally regd as Mk.I)	AW.1163		3.10.35	Scrapped at Hamble on 26.3.47. Canx.
G-ADSZ	Armstrong Whitworth AW.27 Ensign II (Originally regd as Mk.I)	AW.1164		3.10.35	Shot down by fighters at Merville, France on 23.5.40. Canx.
G-ADTA	Armstrong Whitworth AW.27 Ensign II (Originally regd as Mk.I)	AW.1165	(VT-AJG) G-ADTA	3.10.35	DBR on landing at Lympne on 23.5.40. To Hamble for spares use. Canx.
G-ADTB	Armstrong Whitworth AW.27 Ensign II (Originally regd as Mk.I)	AW.1166		3.10.35	Scrapped at Hamble on 20.3.47. Canx.
G-ADTC	Armstrong Whitworth AW.27 Ensign II (Originally regd as Mk.I)	AW.1167	(VT-AJH) G-ADTC	3.10.35	DBR by German aircraft at Whitchurch on 24.11.40. Canx.
G-ADTD	Miles M.3D Falcon Six (Originally regd as M.3B)	255		. 9.35	Crashed into sea off Angmering, Sussex on 21.9.62. Canx.
G-ADTE	General Aircraft Monospar ST.25 Jubilee	GAL/ST25/59		30. 9.35	Crashed at Addis Alum. Ethiopia on 26.12.35. Canx.
G-ADTF	Avro 643 Cadet II	870		20. 9.35	To 1102 ATC Sqdn at Melksham as 2950M in 8/41. Canx 28.8.41.
G-ADTG	Avro 643 Cadet II	871		20. 9.35	To 1478 ATC Sqdn at Golders Green, Middx as 2943M in 7/41. Canx 23.7.41.
G-ADTH	Avro 643 Cadet II	872		20. 9.35	Crashed in sea off Milford-on-Sea on 9.7.39. Canx 4.3.42.
G-ADTI	Avro 643 Cadet II	873		20. 9.35	Crashed at Filton on 17.2.37. Canx.
G-ADTJ	Avro 643 Cadet II	874		20. 9.35	To 303 ATC Sqdn at Worksop as 2960M in 12/41. Canx 13.12.41.
G-ADTK	Avro 643 Cadet II	875		20. 9.35	To 227 ATC Sqdn at Dagenham, Essex as 2971M in 2/42. Canx 10.2.42.
G-ADTL	Avro 643 Cadet II	876		20. 9.35	To 1131 ATC Sqdn at Olney as 2961M in 2/42. Canx 10.2.42.
G-ADTM	Avro 643 Cadet II	877		20. 9.35	Crashed at Westend, near Southampton on 6.2.36. Canx.
G-ADTN	Avro 643 Cadet II	878		20. 9.35	To an ATC Sqdn in Shropshire as 2972M in 12/41. Canx 18.12.41.
G-ADTO	Avro 643 Cadet II	879		20. 9.35	Crashed at Leicester on 8.8.39. Canx.
G-ADTP	Avro 643 Cadet II	880		20. 9.35	To 68 ATC Sqdn at Holywell as 2949M in 8/41. Canx 26.8.41.
G-ADTR	Avro 643 Cadet II	881		20. 9.35	Dived into ground at Radcot Bridge, Bampton, Oxon. on 15.8.40. Canx.
G-ADTS	Avro 643 Cadet II	882		20. 9.35	To 522 ATC Sqdn at Lays School, Dundee as 2948M in 8/41. Canx 11.8.41.
G-ADTT	Avro 643 Cadet II	883		20. 9.35	To 973 ATC Sqdn at Southgate, Middx as 2944M in 7/41. Canx 23.7.41.
G-ADTU	Avro 643 Cadet II	884		20. 9.35	To 1417 ATC Sqdn at Leeds as 2947M in 7/41. Canx 23.7.41.
G-ADTV	Avro 643 Cadet II	885		20. 9.35	To 444 (Shoreditch) ATC Sqdn in London as 2942M in 7/41. Canx 23.7.41.
G-ADTW	Avro 643 Cadet II	886		20. 9.35	To 499 ATC Sqdn at Port Talbot as 2955M in 9/41. Canx 1.9.41.
G-ADTX	Avro 643 Cadet II	887		20. 9.35	To 291 (Westminster & Chelsea) ATC Sqdn at Chelsea, London as 2940M in 7/41. Canx 23.7.41.

Regn	Type	c/n	Previous identity	Regn date	Fate or immediate subsequent identity (if known)
G-ADTY	Avro 643 Cadet II	888		20. 9.35	To 437 ATC Sqdn at Poplar, London as 2941M in 7/41. Canx 23.7.41.
G-ADTZ	Avro 643 Cadet II	889		20. 9.35	Crashed at Walgrave, near Coventry on 7.12.38. Canx in 11/45.
G-ADUA	BAC Super Drone	8		26. 9.35	Crashed at Caxton Gibbet, Cambs on 20.12.36. Canx.
G-ADUB	Lazars-Bieber/HM.14 Pou du Ciel	ML.1		26. 9.35	Canx in 9/36.
G-ADUC	DH.82A Tiger Moth	3425		10.10.35	To RAF as BB812 in 10/40. Canx 12.10.41.
G-ADUD	Not allocated.				
G-ADUE	DH.86B (Originally regd as DH.86A)	2333		19.12.35	To RAF as AX762 in 4/40, but painted as AX672. Canx 20.9.41.
G-ADUF	DH.86B (Originally regd as DH.86A)	2334	SU-ACR G-ADUF/HK828/G-ADUF	19.12.35	CofA lapsed 3.5.52. Canx.
G-ADUG	DH.86B (Originally regd as DH.86A)	2335		19.12.35	To RAF as HK831 in 11/41. Canx 5.11.41.
G-ADUH	DH.86B (Originally regd as DH.86A)	2336	EI-ABT G-ADUH	19.12.35	Destroyed in ground collision with Auster YI-ABO (c/n 2149, formerly G-AIBO) at Bahrein in 5/51. Canx.
G-ADUI	DH.86B (Originally regd as DH.86A)	2337		19.12.35	To RAF as HK830 in 11/41. Canx 5.11.41.
G-ADUJ	Avro 626	868		27. 9.35	To Austria in 12/35. Canx.
G-ADUK	DH.82A Tiger Moth	3426		2.10.35	To R.New Zealand AF as NZ732 in 1/40. Canx.
G-ADUL	DH.85 Leopard Moth	7072	D-EGYV	.10.35	Crashed on take-off from Alicante, Spain on 23.1.36. Canx.
G-ADUM	DH.89 Dragon Rapide	6315		16. 3.36	To Turkey as TC-ARI in 5/36. Canx.
G-ADUN	DH.89 Dragon Rapide	6316		16. 3.36	To Turkey as TC-BAY in 5/36. Canx.
G-ADUO	DH.89 Dragon Rapide	6317		16. 3.36	To Turkey as TC-CAN in 5/36. Canx.
G-ADUP	DH.89 Dragon Rapide	6319		. 3.36R	NTU - To Australia as VH-UVT /36. Canx.
G-ADUR	DH.87B Hornet Moth	8085		10. 3.36	(Stored 4/94 Chalmington)
G-ADUS	Lockheed 8D Altair	152	VH-USB	7.10.35	Crashed into the Bay of Bengal on 7.11.35. Canx.
G-ADUT	Short S.23 Empire	S.811		7.10.35	To R.Australian AF as A18-10 in 9/39. Canx.
G-ADUU	Short S.23 Empire	S.812		7.10.35	Forced to alight in Atlantic due to carburettor icing and sank 285 miles southeast of Port Washington, USA on 21.1.39. Canx.
G-ADUV	Short S.23 Empire	S.813		7.10.35	WFU at Hythe on 26.1.47. Broken up in 1947. Canx.
G-ADUW	Short S.23 Empire	S.814		7.10.35	Broken up at Hythe in 1947. Canx.
G-ADUX	Short S.23 Empire	S.815		7.10.35	Crashed on take-off from Sabang, Sumatra, Netherlands East Indies on 29.12.41. Canx.
G-ADUY	Short S.23 Empire	S.816		7.10.35	Badly damaged taxying at Tandjong, Batavia, Java, Netherlands East Indies on 12.3.39. Canx.
G-ADUZ	Short S.23 Empire	S.817		7.10.35	Crashed at Brindisi, Italy on 15.12.37. Canx.
G-ADVA	Short S.23 Empire	S.818		7.10.35	Fatal crash in Beaujolais Mts., near Ouroux, France on 24.3.37. Canx.
G-ADVB	Short S.23 Empire	S.819		7.10.35	Scrapped at Hythe in 1947. Canx.
G-ADVC	Short S.23 Empire	S.820		7.10.35	Crashed on alighting in Phaleron Bay, Athens, Greece on 1.10.37. Canx.
G-ADVD	Short S.23 Empire	S.821		7.10.35	Crashed on landing in Mozambique Harbour on 1.5.39. Canx.
G-ADVE	Short S.23 Empire	S.822		7.10.35	Caught in gust whilst alighting on River Hooghly, Calcutta, India on 12.6.39, capsized and sunk. Canx.
G-ADVF	Miles M.2W Hawk Trainer	217		10.10.35	CofA expired 7.10.39 & WFU. Scrapped. Canx.
G-ADVG	General Aircraft Monospar ST.25 Jubilee	GAL/ST25/61		17.10.35	To Spanish Republicans in 8/36. Canx.
G-ADVH	General Aircraft Monospar ST.25 Jubilee	GAL/ST25/62		17.10.35	To RAF as X9365 in 3/40; NTU & crashed at Saighton Camp on 4.4.40. Canx.
G-ADVI	Haddow/HM.14 Pou du Ciel	WBH.1		22.10.35	Authorisation to Fly expired on 26.9.36 & WFU. Canx in 1/38.
G-ADVJ	DH.86B (Originally regd as DH.86A)	2338	EI-ABK G-ADVJ	4. 2.36	WFU on 30.7.52. Derelict at Bahrein in 8/52. Canx.
G-ADVK	DH.86B (Originally regd as DH.86A)	2339		4. 2.36	Abandoned at Jersey Airport in 6/40. Destroyed during German invasion of the Channel Isles. Canx.
G-ADVL	Paterson/HM.14 Pou du Ciel	RHP.1		24.10.35	Fatal crash at Renfrew on 20.4.36. Canx.
G-ADVM	Bowen/HM.14 Pou du Ciel	B.9		15.10.35	WFU on 7.10.36. Canx in 9/45.
G-ADVN	DH.82A Tiger Moth	3427		25.10.35	To RAF as BB684 in 9/40. Canx 19.9.40.
G-ADVO	DH.82A Tiger Moth	3428		25.10.35	Collided with DH.82A G-ADOK at Perth on 8.2.36. Canx.
G-ADVP	DH.82A Tiger Moth	3429		25.10.35	To RAF as BB685 in 9/40. Canx 19.9.40.
G-ADVR	Miles M.2 Hawk	171	(YR-ITR)	.10.35	Crashed at Bekesbourne on 30.8.39. Canx.
G-ADVS	Gregory/HM.14 Pou du Ciel	CCLG.1		22.10.35	Authoration to Fly expired on 14.1.37 & WFU. Canx 31.12.38 in census.
G-ADVT	BA Eagle II	130		.10.35	To RAF as DP847 in 3/41. Canx 14.3.41.
G-ADVU	Mignet HM.14 Pou du Ciel	-		.10.35R	NTU - Not completed. Canx.
"G-ADVU"	Mignet HM.14 Pou du Ciel (Built by Ken Fern/Vintage & Rotary Wing Collection .93)	-	BAPC.211	----	(On display in North East Aircraft Museum 4/96)
G-ADVV	BA IV Double Eagle	901	Y-1	.10.35	To RAF as ES949 in 7/41. Canx 31.7.41.
G-ADVW	Baker/HM.14 Pou du Ciel	RLB.1		25.10.35	WFU in 1939. Canx 1.12.46 in census.
G-ADVX	DH.82A Tiger Moth	3441		9.12.35	To RAF as BB799 in 10/40. Canx 12.10.40.
G-ADVY	DH.82A Tiger Moth	3442		9.12.35	To RAF as BB795 in 10/40. Canx 12.10.40.
G-ADVZ	DH.82A Tiger Moth	3443	BB796 G-ADVZ	9.12.35	To Norway as LN-BDL in 9/54. Canx.
G-ADWA	DH.82A Tiger Moth	3444		9.12.35	To RAF as BB797 in 10/40. Canx 12.10.40.
G-ADWB	DH.82A Tiger Moth	3445		9.12.35	To RAF as BB798 in 10/40. Canx 12.10.40.
G-ADWC	DH.82A Tiger Moth	3446		9.12.35	To RAF as BB794 in 10/40. Canx 12.10.40.
G-ADWD	DH.82A Tiger Moth	3447		9.12.35	W/o in 1/40. Canx.
G-ADWE	DH.82A Tiger Moth	3448		9.12.35	To RAF as BB800 in 10/40. Canx 12.10.40.
G-ADWF	DH.82A Tiger Moth	3449		9.12.35	To RAF as BB801 in 10/40. Canx 12.10.40.
G-ADWG	DH.82A Tiger Moth	3492		3. 3.36	To India as VT-AMA in 1/40. Canx.

Regn	Type	c/n	Previous identity	Regn date	Fate or immediate subsequent identity (if known)
G-ADWH	General Aircraft Monospar ST.25 Jubilee	GAL/ST25/63		2.11.35	To France as F-AQAD in 5/37. Canx.
G-ADWI	General Aircraft Monospar ST.25 Jubilee (Modified to GAL.26 in 1936, converted back before sale to France)	GAL/ST25/64	T-6 G-ADWI	1.11.35	To France as F-AQCL in 6/37. Canx.
G-ADWJ	DH.82A Tiger Moth	3450	BB803 G-ADWJ	9.12.35	(On rebuild 3/96 Shobdon)
G-ADWK	DH.82A Tiger Moth	3451		9.12.35	To RAF as BB802 in 10/40. Canx 12.10.40.
G-ADWL	DH.82A Tiger Moth	3452	BB804 G-ADWL	9.12.35	To West Germany as D-ECUT in 4/57. Canx.
G-ADWM	DH.82A Tiger Moth	3453		9.12.35	To RAF as BB805 in 10/40. Canx 12.10.40.
G-ADWN	DH.82A Tiger Moth	3454		9.12.35	To RAF as BB808 in 10/40. Canx 12.10.40.
G-ADWO	DH.82A Tiger Moth (Now composite rebuild including components from G-AOAC and G-AOJJ, also fitted with parts from G-ADXT/BB860 in 1950/51 rebuild)	3455	BB807 G-ADWO	9.12.35	Badly damaged at Christchurch on 31.7.58. (On display at Southampton Hall of Aviation)
G-ADWP	DH.82A Tiger Moth	3456		9.12.35	To RAF as BB806 in 10/40. Canx 12.10.40.
G-ADWR	Tomkins/HM.14 Pou du Ciel	JA.1		31.10.35	WFU on 30.10.36. Canx in 1/37.
G-ADWS	Whyteleafe Motors/HM.14 Pou du Ciel	MW.1		1.11.35R	NTU. WFU c.1939. Canx.
G-ADWT	Miles M.2W Hawk Trainer	215	NF750 G-ADWT	6.11.35	To Canada as CF-NXT in 6/64. Canx.
G-ADWU	Miles M.2W Hawk Trainer	224		6.11.35	Rebuilt with c/n 483. CofA expired 3.8.40 & WFU. Canx.
G-ADWV	Miles M.2W Hawk Trainer	228		6.11.35	CofA expired on 23.1.40 & WFU. Canx.
G-ADWW	Miles M.5A Sparrowhawk	264		.11.35	To USA as NC191M in 11/36. Canx.
G-ADWX	Fraser/HM.14 Pou du Ciel	FB.1		7.11.35	Damaged in a hard landing c.1938. WFU at Conor Bridge, Ross-shire by 8/39. Canx in 11/45 in census.
G-ADWY	DH.85 Leopard Moth	7117		20.11.35	To RAF as X9385 in 3/40. Canx 21.3.40.
G-ADWZ	DH.89 Dragon Rapide	6309	F-APEZ G-ADWZ	8.11.35	To RAF as X9449 in 4/40. Canx 12.4.40.
G-ADXA	Miles M.7 Nighthawk	263	U-5	7.11.35	Crashed near Woodley on 22.1.36. Canx.
G-ADXB	DH.82A Tiger Moth	3430		13.11.35	To RAF as BB736 in 10/40. Canx 30.10.40.
G-ADXC	DH.82A Tiger Moth	3431		13.11.35	Crashed at Parndon, Essex on 16.11.36. Canx.
G-ADXD	DH.82A Tiger Moth	3432		13.11.35	To RAF as BB737 in 10/40. Canx 30.10.40.
G-ADXE	DH.82A Tiger Moth	3433		13.11.35	To RAF as BB755 in 10/40. Canx 30.10.40.
G-ADXF	Chambers/HM.14 Pou du Ciel	EHC.1		18.11.35	WFU on 3.11.36. Canx 31.12.37 in census.
G-ADXG	Blackburn L.1C Bluebird IV	SB.241	G-ABZX (G-ABEY)	15.11.35	NTU - To B-Class marks as B-10 in 1/36. Canx.
G-ADXH	BA Swallow II	415		21.11.35	DBF at Maylands, Essex on 6.2.40. Canx.
G-ADXI	DH.82A Tiger Moth	3434		25.11.35	To RAF as BB756 in 10/40. Canx 30.10.40.
G-ADXJ	DH.82A Tiger Moth	3435		25.11.35	To RAF as BB738 in 10/40. Canx 30.10.40.
G-ADXK	DH.82A Tiger Moth	3457		3.12.35	To RAF as BB686 in 9/40. Canx 19.9.40.
G-ADXL	Praga E.114 Air Baby	107	OK-PGC	27.11.35	To South Africa as ZS-AHL in 5/36. Canx 6.5.36.
G-ADXM	DH.90 Dragonfly	7509	(G-AEDU)	9. 5.36	To RAF as X9327 in 2/40. Canx 29.2.40.
G-ADXN	DH.82A Tiger Moth	3458		3.12.35	To RAF as (BB687)/BB683 in 9/40. Canx 19.9.40.
G-ADXO	DH.82A Tiger Moth	3459		3.12.35	To RAF as BB688 in 10/40. Canx 30.10.40.
G-ADXP	DH.82A Tiger Moth	3460		3.12.35	To RAF as BB689 in 10/40. Canx 30.10.40.
G-ADXR	DH.82A Tiger Moth	3461		3.12.35	To RAF as BB690 in 10/40. Canx 30.10.40.
G-ADXS	Story/HM.14 Pou-Du-Ciel	CLS.1		18.11.35	WFU on 1.12.36. (On rebuild Winthorpe 9/97)
G-ADXT	DH.82A Tiger Moth (Despite "restoration" of BB860/G-ADXT this was mainly a rebuild of various components)	3436	BB860 G-ADXT	9.12.35	
G-ADXU	DH.82A Tiger Moth	3437		9.12.35	To RAF as BB861 in 1/41. Canx 3.1.41.
G-ADXV	DH.82A Tiger Moth	3438		9.12.35	To RAF as BB862 in 1/41. Canx 3.1.41.
G-ADXW	DH.82A Tiger Moth	3439		9.12.35	Crashed near Desford on 18.6.37. Canx.
G-ADXX	DH.82A Tiger Moth	3440		9.12.35	To RAF as BB863 in 1/41. Canx 3.1.41.
G-ADXY	Goodall/HM.14 Pou du Ciel	JG.1		28.11.35	Fatal accident whilst taxying at Aberdeen Aerodrome on 30.9.36. Canx 2.10.36.
G-ADXZ	DH.82A Tiger Moth	3475		9.12.35	Crashed at Croy, Ayrshire on 25.6.38. Canx.
G-ADYA	DH.82A Tiger Moth	3476		9.12.35	To RAF as BB810 in 10/40. Canx 12.10.40.
G-ADYB	DH.82A Tiger Moth	3477		9.12.35	To RAF as BB809 in 10/40. Canx 12.10.40.
G-ADYC	DH.86B (Originally regd as DH.86A)	2340		29. 2.36	To RAF as L8037 in 8/38. Canx.
G-ADYD	DH.86B (Originally regd as DH.86A)	2341		29. 2.36	To RAF as L8040 in 8/38. Canx.
G-ADYE	DH.86B (Originally regd as DH.86A)	2346		29. 2.36	To Uruguay as CX-ABG in 11/37. Canx.
G-ADYF	DH.86A	2347		29. 2.36	Crashed on night take-off from Gatwick on 15.9.36. Canx.
G-ADYG	DH.86B (Originally regd as DH.86A)	2343		21. 5.36	To RAF as N6246 in 6/38. Canx.
G-ADYH	DH.86B (Originally regd as DH.86A)	2344		21. 5.36	To AURI Indonesia as RI-008 in 5/48. Canx.
G-ADYI	DH.86B (Originally regd as DH.86A)	2345		21. 5.36	To RAF as AX795 in 7/40. Canx 21.7.40.
G-ADYJ	DH.86B (Originally regd as DH.86A)	2348		15. 5.36	To RAF as L7596 in 10/37. Canx.
G-ADYK	DH.89 Dragon Rapide	6310		2.12.35	To Spanish AF in 2/36. Canx.
G-ADYL(1)	DH.89 Dragon Rapide	6311		2.12.35	To Spanish AF in 2/36. Canx.
G-ADYL(2)	DH.89 Dragon Rapide	6895	4X-AEI Israeli AF/DF 1306/VP-KED/PH-RAD/NR831	. 8.55	WFU at Fairoaks on 16.12.58. Broken up at Luton in 1964. Canx.
G-ADYM	DH.89 Dragon Rapide	6312		2.12.35	To Spanish AF in 2/36. Canx.
G-ADYN	General Aircraft Monospar ST.25 Universal	GAL/ST25/73		29.11.35	To RAF as X9373 in 3/40. Canx 19.3.40.
G-ADYO	Park/HM.14 Pou du Ciel	BHP.1		3.12.35	WFU on 14.11.36. Canx in 1/37.

Regn	Type	c/n	Previous identity	Regn date	Fate or immediate subsequent identity (if known)
G-ADYP	Aeronca C.3	A.596		.12.35	WFU on 20.1.37. Scrapped between 1939 and 1945. Canx.
G-ADYR	Aeronca C.3	A.597		.12.35	WFU in 10/36. Canx.
G-ADYS	Aeronca C.3	A.600		.12.35	
G-ADYT	Aeronca C.3	A.601		.12.35	Sold abroad in 12/37. Canx.
G-ADYU	C.L.W. Curlew	CLW.1		6.12.35	WFU on 6.11.39. Scrapped at Gravesend in 1948. Canx.
G-ADYV	Mignet HM.14 Pou du Ciel	JSB.1		.11.35R	NTU. Canx in 11/35.
"G-ADYV"	Mignet HM.14 Pou du Ciel (Modern reproduction built .95 by Bill Francis)	-	BAPC.243	----	(Stored 8/95 Malvern Wells)
G-ADYW	Avro 621 Tutor	-	K1231	6.12.35	WFU on 18.8.39. Canx in 12/46.
G-ADYX	Luton Buzzard II	LAB/1		9.12.35	Crashed at Great West Aerodrome on 8.5.38. Canx.
G-ADYY	BA Eagle II	116		9.12.35	To Trinidad as VP-TAM in 7/45. Canx.
G-ADYZ	Miles M.2X Hawk Trainer	235		5.12.35	CofA expired on 18.8.40. Scrapped. Canx.
G-ADZA	Miles M.2X Hawk Trainer	241		5.12.35	To 1887 ATC Sqdn at Lewisham, London as DG665 in 2/41. Canx 18.2.41.
G-ADZB	Miles M.2X Hawk Trainer	242		6.12.35	Rebuilt in 2/37 with new fuselage c/n 481. WFU on 4.7.40. Scrapped in 7/40. Canx.
G-ADZC	Miles M.2X Hawk Trainer	249		6.12.35	WFU 17.11.39. Scrapped in 1940. Canx.
G-ADZD	Miles M.2Y Hawk Trainer	253	U-2	6.12.35	CofA expired 4.4.40 & WFU. Scrapped. Canx.
G-ADZE	Miles M.2X Hawk Trainer	254		6.12.35	Crashed in 1936. Canx.
G-ADZF	Heinkel He.70G	1692	D-UBOF	18.12.35	WFU on 1.4.40. Scrapped in 1944. Canx.
G-ADZG	Perman/HM.14 Pou du Ciel	SS.16		.12.35R	NTU. Canx.
G-ADZH	Fokker F.XII	5284	PH-AFV	23. 3.36	To Spanish Nationalists as 20-5 in 8/36. Canx.
G-ADZI	Fokker F.XII	5285	PH-AFU(2)	. 1.36	Crashed at Biarritz on delivery flight to Spain on 15.8.36 and burnt out. Canx.
G-ADZJ	Fokker F.XII	5292	PH-AIE	29. 1.36	To Spanish Nationalists as 20-6 in 8/36. Canx.
G-ADZK	Fokker F.XII	5301	PH-AII	7. 2.36	DBR at La Rochelle, France on 16.8.36 whilst on delivery to Spain. Canx.
G-ADZL	Miles M.3B Falcon Six	262		12.12.35	WFU on 13.12.44. Canx.
G-ADZM	Blackburn B.2	6300/1		12.12.35	To 702 ATC Sqdn at Vaughan Road School, West Harrow, Middx as 2896M in 2/42. Canx 17.2.42.
G-ADZN	Blackburn B.2	6300/2		12.12.35	To 387 ATC Sqdn at Airedale, Yorks as 2889M in 2/42. Canx 17.2.42.
G-ADZO	Percival P.3 Gull Six	D.63		12.12.35	CofA expired 7.2.39 & WFU. Scrapped. Canx.
G-ADZP	Plant/HM.14 Pou du Ciel	JBP.1		16.12.35	WFU on 2.12.36. Donated to 663 ATC Sqdn at Audenshaw Grammar School, Gt.Manchester between 1939 and 1945. Canx.
G-ADZR	Miles M.3A Falcon	209		13.12.35	To Australia as VH-AAS in 6/36. Canx.
G-ADZS	Little/HM.14 Pou du Ciel	1101 No.684		13.12.35	Canx in 1939.
G-ADZT	Miles/HM.14 Pou du Ciel	SSM.1		.12.35R	NTU. WFU c.1939. Canx.
G-ADZU	Miles M.2H Hawk Major	184		.12.35	Crashed at Linz, Vienna, Austria on 15.5.37. Canx.
G-ADZV	Dodson-Caunse/HM.14 Pou du Ciel	AC.1		23.12.35	Damaged on turning over at Hooton on 2.5.36. Not repaired & broken up. Canx.
G-ADZW	Perman/HM.14 Pou du Ciel	EGP.55		.12.35R	NTU. Canx.
"G-ADZW"	Mignet HM.14 Pou du Ciel (Built by H.Shore, Isle of Wight '90s)	-	BAPC.253	----	(On display 2/99 Sandown)
G-ADZX	Perman Parasol	EGP.57		2. 5.36	WFU & burnt at Gravesend, Kent in 7/37. Canx.
G-ADZY	Dover-Beck/HM.14 Pou du Ciel	LRDB.1		4. 1.36	Canx in 3/37.
G-ADZZ	Aeronca C.3	A.599		. 1.36	Crashed at Hythe, Kent on 15.8.36. Canx.
G-AEAA	Avro 504N	14		1. 1.36	WFU on 2.6.37. Canx in 9/38.
G-AEAB	Percival P.10 Vega Gull	K.20		28. 2.36	Crashed at Mpulungu, Northern Rhodesia on 30.9.36. Canx.
G-AEAC	Aeronca C.3	A.603		5. 1.36	To South Africa as ZS-AGX in 3/36. Canx.
G-AEAD	Kendrew/HM.14 Pou du Ciel	EWK.1		24. 1.36	WFU on 17.12.36. Canx 11.12.38.
G-AEAE	Aeronca C.3	A.604		. 1.36	WFU in 12/36. Canx.
G-AEAF	Aeronca C.3	A.598		18. 1.36	To Holland as PH-ALG in 6/36. Canx.
G-AEAG	Miles M.3D Falcon Six	266		13. 1.36	To Australia as VH-ABT in 6/38. Canx 31.12.38.
G-AEAH	BA Swallow II	433		17. 1.36	To India as VT-AIK in 10/36. Canx.
G-AEAI	Cessna C.34 Airmaster	314	HM502 G-AEAI	. 1.36	DBF on ground at Squires Gate on 20.9.50. Canx.
G-AEAJ	DH.89 Dragon Rapide	6320		22. 2.36	To RAF as W6425 in 1/40. Canx 4.1.40.
G-AEAK	DH.89 Dragon Rapide	6324		22. 2.36	Crashed at Speke on 25.4.39. Canx.
G-AEAL	DH.89 Dragon Rapide	6325	(SE-BAL) G-AEAL	22. 2.36	To France as F-OAUE in 4/56. Canx.
G-AEAM	DH.89 Dragon Rapide	6326		22. 2.36	To RAF as W6424 in 1/40. Canx 4.1.40.
G-AEAN	BAC Super Drone	9		20. 1.36	Crashed at Southend Airport on 22.7.36. Canx.
G-AEAO	Miles M.3B Falcon Six	269	PH-EAO G-AEAO	18. 1.36	To RAF as R4071 in 11/39. Canx.
G-AEAP	DH.86B (Originally regd as DH.86A)	2349		27. 1.36	To RAF as HK843 in 10/41. Canx 22.10.41.
G-AEAR	Avro 643 Cadet II	922		14. 3.36	To 1203 ATC Sqdn at Bridgnorth as 2959M in 12/41. Canx 11.12.41.
G-AEAS	Percival P.10 Vega Gull	K.23		. 1.36	Crashed at Mbeya, Tanganyika on 28.6.36. Canx in 12/36.
G-AEAT	General Aircraft Monospar ST.25 Universal	GAL/ST25/75		3. 2.36	Crashed near Brasted on 16.3.38. Canx.
G-AEAU	BA Swallow II	416		29. 1.36	WFU at Exeter on 13.6.40. Derelict. Canx.
G-AEAV	BA Swallow II	418		29. 1.36	Scrapped at Christchurch in 9/50. Canx.
G-AEAW	Miles M.2X Hawk Trainer	246		29. 1.36	Sold abroad in 12/36. Canx.
G-AEAX	Miles M.2X Hawk Trainer	260		29. 1.36	To RAF as DG666 in 2/41. Canx 18.2.41.
G-AEAY	Miles M.2Y Hawk Trainer	261		29. 1.36	WFU in 20.9.39. Scrapped. Canx.
G-AEAZ	Miles M.2X Hawk Trainer	270		29. 1.36	WFU in 1937. Canx.
G-AEBA	Oliver/HM.14 Pou-du-Ciel	AO.1		24. 1.36	Damaged at Kennford, Devon. WFU on 1.1.37. Canx 19.11.45.
G-AEBB	Owen/HM.14 Pou-du-Ciel	KWO.1		24. 1.36	WFU on 31.5.39. To 424 ATC Sqdn at Southampton (from 1941 until 1968). (On display at Old Warden)
G-AEBC	BAC Super Drone	10		8. 2.36	Fatal crash at Hereford on 1.5.36. Canx.

Regn	Type	c/n	Previous identity	Regn date	Fate or immediate subsequent identity (if known)
G-AEBD	Hawker Osprey	S0.1		3. 2.36	To Spanish Government as EA-KAJ in 6/36. Canx.
G-AEBE	Blackburn B.2	6300/3		3. 2.36	To 1233 ATC Sqdn at Chipping Sodbury, Glos. as 2898M in 2/42. Canx 17.2.42.
G-AEBF	Blackburn B.2	6300/4		3. 2.36	Crashed at Sunbury on 9.9.37. Canx.
G-AEBG	Blackburn B.2	6300/5		4. 2.36	To 1223 ATC Sqdn at Caerphilly, Wales as 2938M in 2/42. Canx 17.2.42.
G-AEBH	Blackburn B.2	6300/6		4. 2.36	Crashed at Kingsbury on 17.8.36. Canx.
G-AEBI	Blackburn B.2	6300/7		4. 2.36	Damaged in ground collision with Hawker Hart K4434 at Hanworth on 31.1.38. Canx.
G-AEBJ	Blackburn B.2	6300/8	2887M G-AEBJ	4. 2.36	
G-AEBK	Blackburn B.2	6300/9		4. 2.36	To 1155 ATC Sqdn at Cheshunt Grammar School, Herts as 2901M in 2/42. Canx 17.2.42.
G-AEBL	Blackburn B.2	6300/10		4. 2.36	To 1086 ATC Sqdn at Hawick, Roxburghshire as 2973M in 2/42. Canx 17.2.42.
G-AEBM	Blackburn B.2	6795/1		5. 2.36	To RAF as L6891 in 6/37. Canx.
G-AEBN	Blackburn B.2	6795/2		5. 2.36	To RAF as L6892 in 6/37. Canx.
G-AEBO	Blackburn B.2	6795/3		5. 2.36	To RAF as L6893 in 6/37. Canx.
G-AEBP	Miles M.7A Nighthawk	282		3. 2.36	To U6 in 1936/L6846 in 5/37. Canx.
G-AEBR	Bacon-Butts/HM.14 Pou-du-Ciel	A.1		10. 2.36	Damaged in 2/37 and not flown again. Wings given to "a young Flea builder" and fuselage given away post-war to "a chap at Ramsgate for a Hydrofoil?". WFU on 21.9.37. Canx 31.7.38.
G-AEBS	Davidson/HM.14 Pou-du-Ciel	CRD.1		4. 2.36	Fatal crash at Digby on 21.5.36. Canx 19.6.36.
G-AEBT	Wood-Vaugh/HM.14 Pou-du-Ciel	W & V.1		20. 2.36	Scrapped in 1951. Canx.
G-AEBU	DH.90 Dragonfly	7501		8. 2.36	To France as F-AQEU in 3/38. Canx.
G-AEBV	Airspeed AS.6J Envoy III	52		12. 2.36	To Spanish Republicans in 8/36. Canx.
G-AEBW	DH.89 Dragon Rapide	6327		22. 2.36	Abandoned at Bordeaux, France on 18.6.40. Canx.
G-AEBX	DH.89 Dragon Rapide	6328		22. 2.36	Crashed at Belfast Harbour, Northern Ireland on 3.7.38. Canx.
G-AEBY	DH.82A Tiger Moth	3485		13. 2.36	To RAF as BB702 in 9/40. Canx 17.9.40.
G-AEBZ	DH.82A Tiger Moth	3486		13. 2.36	To RAF as BB703 in 9/40. Canx 17.9.40.
G-AECA	BA Swallow II	417		11. 2.36	To South Africa as ZS-DAV in 8/46. Canx.
G-AECB	General Aircraft Monospar ST.18 Croydon	GAL/ST.18/501	T-22	14. 2.36	Force landed on coral reef in Timor Sea off Australia on 7.10.36 & abandoned. Canx.
G-AECC	Miles M.3D Falcon Six	280	DG576 G-AECC	10. 2.36	Crashed into the sea off Bembridge, IoW on 8.5.59. Canx.
G-AECD	Smedley-Bell/HM.14 Pou-du-Ciel	WVS.1		11. 2.36	WFU on 17.2.37. Canx.
G-AECE	Stubbs/HM.14 Pou-du-Ciel	JS.1		13. 2.36	WFU on 26.2.37. Canx in 12/37.
G-AECF	Percival P.10 Vega Gull	K.21		17. 2.36	To France as F-AQCF in 4/37. Canx.
G-AECG	DH.82A Tiger Moth	3488		21. 2.36	Crashed at Desford on 29.5.37. Canx.
G-AECH	DH.82A Tiger Moth	3489		21. 2.36	To RAF as BB864 in 1/41. Canx 3.1.41.
G-AECI	DH.82A Tiger Moth	3490		21. 2.36	To RAF as BB865 in 1/41. Canx 3.1.41.
G-AECJ	DH.82A Tiger Moth	3491		21. 2.36	To RAF as BB866 in 1/41. Canx 3.1.41.
G-AECK	Perman/HM.14 Pou du Ciel	EGP.58		. 2.36R	NTU. Canx.
G-AECL	Perman/HM.14 Pou du Ciel	EGP.59		. 2.36R	NTU. Canx.
G-AECM	Perman/HM.14 Pou du Ciel	EGP.60		14. 2.36	WFU on 8.4.37. Canx 1.12.46.
G-AECN	Mignet HM.14 Pou du Ciel	DCB.1		17. 2.36	Cartwheeled at Leamington on 10.5.36. Post-war it was pulled by ponies around a field, as a family plaything, until it was destroyed. Canx 13.11.45.
"G-AECN"	Burgoyne-Stirling Dicer Mk.1	-		----	WFU in 1948. Noted flying at RAF Station, Wymeswold in late-1949. Not officially regd.
G-AECO	Fairchild 24C8-C	2718		14. 4.36	To RAF as BK869 in 12/40. Canx 4.12.40.
G-AECP	BAC Super Drone	11		4. 3.36	WFU on 20.1.39. Canx in 12/46.
G-AECR	Avro 504N	-	K2396	17. 2.36	Sold abroad in 3/38. Canx.
G-AECS	Avro 504N	-	J8548	17. 2.46	WFU on 26.5.39. Broken up at Christchurch in 1940. Canx.
G-AECT	Miles M.11A Whitney Straight	290		18. 2.46	To RAF as BS755 in 10/40. Canx 21.10.40.
	(Originally regd as M.11 Straight Special)				
G-AECU	Short S.22 Scion Senior	S.834		19. 2.36	To RAF as HK868 in 2/42. Canx.
G-AECV	Clyde Battery Company/HM.14 Pou-du-Ciel	CV.1		17. 2.36	WFU on 24.2.37. Canx 31.12.37 in census.
G-AECW	DH.90 Dragonfly	7504		29. 2.36	WFU on 10.10.44. Scrapped in 11/45. Canx.
G-AECX	DH.90 Dragonfly	7505	VT-AKC G-AECX	28. 4.36	To RAF as AX855 in 6/40. Canx 2.6.40.
G-AECY	BA Swallow II	419		24. 2.36	WFU on 15.3.39. Canx in 12/46.
G-AECZ	DH.84 Dragon II	6105	AV982 G-AECZ	11. 3.36	To Ireland as EI-AFK in 3/50. Canx.
G-AEDA	BAC Super Drone	12		23. 3.36	WFU on 8.4.39. Canx in 12/46.
G-AEDB	BAC Super Drone	13		18. 3.36	(Stored 7/96)
	(Also registered under BGA system as BGA.2731 3.81)				
	(Now composite with wings of G-AEJH and tail end of G-AEEN)				
G-AEDC	BAC Super Drone	14		23. 3.36	WFU on 29.4.37. Canx in 12/46.
G-AEDD	Avro 504N	-	K1823	4. 5.36	Crashed at Walsall on 13.3.39. Canx.
G-AEDE	Miles M.8 Peregrine	300	U-9	21. 2.36	Dismantled in 12/37. Canx.
G-AEDF	Rose/HM.14 Pou-du-Ciel	AR.1		24. 2.36	W/o in 11/36. Canx.
G-AEDG	DH.90 Dragonfly	7516		29. 7.36	To Australia as VH-ADG on 12.10.37. Canx.
G-AEDH	DH.90 Dragonfly	7510		. .36	To RAF as AV987 in 5/40. Canx 10.5.40.
G-AEDI	DH.90 Dragonfly	7511		14. 5.36	To Singapore as VR-SAX in 10/36. Canx.
G-AEDJ	DH.90 Dragonfly	7515		. .36	To RAF as AV992 in 6/40. Canx 22.6.40.
G-AEDK	DH.90 Dragonfly	7517		3. 7.36	To RAF as AW164 in 6/40. Canx 29.6.40.
G-AEDL	Miles M.3B Falcon Six	259		3. 3.36	Crashed on 3.9.39. Canx.

Regn	Type	c/n	Previous identity	Regn date	Fate or immediate subsequent identity (if known)
G-AEDM	Bullock/HM.14 Pou-du-Ciel	RB.1		29. 2.36	Severly damaged in a crash at White Cross, near Indian Queens, near Bodmin in early-1937. WFU 10.3.37. Canx 4/37.
G-AEDN	Pearce/HM.14 Pou-du-Ciel	PHS.1		10. 3.36	WFU at Sudbury on 29.4.38. Scrapped between 1939 and 1945. Canx.
G-AEDO	Watson/HM.14 Pou-du-Ciel	CS.1		29. 2.36	Canx 15.8.45.
G-AEDP	Wardley/HM.14 Pou-du-Ciel	WHW.1		29. 2.36	WFU on 23.2.37. Canx 31.12.38.
G-AEDR	Dutton/HM.14 Pou-du-Ciel	ED.1		29. 2.36	Canx 12/36 in census. Stored & then scrapped.
G-AEDS	Wright/HM.14 Pou-du-Ciel	FGW.1		29. 2.36	Canx 31.12.38.
G-AEDT	DH.90 Dragonfly	7508	N2034 G-AEDT/VH-AAD/G-AEDT/(VH-ABM)/G-AEDT	9. 5.36	To New Zealand as ZK-AYR in 4/98. Canx 23.3.98.
G-AEDU(1)	DH.90 Dragonfly	7509		. 5.36R	NTU - To G-ADXM 5/36. Canx.
G-AEDU(2)	DH.90A Dragonfly	7526	N190DH G-AEDU/ZS-CTR/CR-AAB	4. 6.79	
G-AEDV	DH.90 Dragonfly	7524		. .36	To RAF as X9389 in 3/40. Canx 27.3.40.
G-AEDW	DH.90 Dragonfly	7503		10. 3.36	To Rhodesia as VP-YBR in 2/38. Canx.
G-AEDX	BA Swallow II	421		13. 3.36	To RAF as ES952 in 7/41. Canx 31.7.41.
G-AEDY	General Aircraft Monospar ST.25 Universal	GAL/ST25/72		9. 3.36	Crashed near Hanworth on 10.1.40. Canx.
G-AEDZ	DH.60G Gipsy Moth	1031	D-EONA D-1644	. 3.36	Crashed prior to 26.2.37. Canx.
G-AEEA	DH.82A Tiger Moth	3495		17. 3.36	To RAF as BB691 in 9/40. Canx 19.9.40.
G-AEEB	DH.80A Puss Moth	2089	VH-UQO	6. 3.36	CofA expired 2.10.39. Presumed scrapped between 1939 and 1945. Canx 28.11.45 in census.
G-AEEC	Putnam/HM.14 Pou-du-Ciel	PAC.5		9. 3.36	Sold abroad in 12/36. Canx.
G-AEED	Putnam/HM.14 Pou-du-Ciel	PAC.6		. 3.36R	NTU. Canx.
G-AEEE	Putnam/HM.14 Pou-du-Ciel	PAC.7		. 3.36R	NTU. Canx.
G-AEEF	Dunning-Ferguson/HM.14 Pou-du-Ciel	HJD.1		13. 3.36	Reported as "destroyed" on 22.2.39. WFU on 28.2.37. Canx 9.3.39 in census.
G-AEEG	Miles M.3A Falcon Major	216	SE-AFN Swedish AF Fv.913/SE-AFN/G-AEEG	14. 3.36	
G-AEEH	Davis/HM.14 Pou-Du-Ciel	EGD.1		13. 3.36	WFU on 15.5.38. Canx 8/46 in census. (On display 3/96 RAF Cosford)
G-AEEI	Cooper's Garage/HM.14 Pou-du-Ciel	CG.1		11. 3.36	WFU on 31.3.37. Broken up. Canx 14.11.45 in census.
G-AEEJ	Ipswich & District Pou Club/HM.14 Pou-du-Ciel	IDPC.1		11. 3.36	Scrapped in 11/36. Canx.
G-AEEK	DH.90 Dragonfly	7518		26. 6.36	Crashed at Beeding, Sussex on 17.8.37. Canx.
G-AEEL	Miles M.2X Hawk Trainer	271		14. 3.36	WFU on 25.5.40. Canx.
G-AEEM	Percival P.10 Vega Gull	K.22		23. 3.36	To Sweden as SE-AHR in 5/39. Canx.
G-AEEN	BAC Super Drone	16		16. 5.36	Crashed at Ramsgate on 24.8.37. Tail end to G-AEDB. Canx.
G-AEEO	BAC Super Drone	15		1. 4.36	DBF at Hooton Park on 8.7.40. Canx.
G-AEEP	BAC Super Drone	17		17. 3.36	WFU on 30.4.39. Canx in 12/46.
G-AEER	BA Eagle II	126		21. 3.36	Crashed at Breedon-on-the-Hill on 2.10.37. Canx.
G-AEES	Hawker 41H Tomtit	-	K1782	23. 3.36	DBF in hangar fire at Maylands, Essex on 6.2.40. Canx.
G-AEET	DH.87B Hornet Moth	8092	X9319 G-AEET	18. 3.36	To Canada as CF-EEJ in 6/69. Canx 6.6.69.
G-AEEU	Hillson Praga	HA.2		21. 4.36	WFU on 2.2.40. Used as spares at Gosport for G-AEUT in 1/51. Canx.
G-AEEV	Hillson Praga	HA.3		21. 4.36	WFU on 6.9.39. Burnt at Yeadon in 1955. Canx.
G-AEEW	Doig/HM.14 Pou-du-Ciel	RGD/A/22		31. 3.36	Fatal crash when it dived into ground out of control during a test flight at Penshurst, Kent on 4.5.36. Canx 31.7.36.
G-AEEX	Howitt/HM.14 Pou-du-Ciel	H.32C		24. 3.36	No Authorisation to Fly issued. (At one time stored at the Oxford University Air Squadron headquarters, St.Cross Road, Oxford). Canx 31.12.38 in census. (Tailwheels to G-AEOH).
G-AEEY	Butler/HM.14 Pou-du-Ciel	RB.1		25. 3.36	WFU on 31.3.37. Canx.
G-AEEZ	Miles M.2H Hawk Major	179		25. 3.36	Crashed at Barton on 8.3.39. Canx in 12/46.
G-AEFA	Miles M.2H Hawk Major	183		30. 3.36	To South Africa as ZS-AHH in 4/36. Canx.
G-AEFB	Miles M.3A Falcon Major	229		30. 3.36	To RAF as X9301 in 3/40. Canx 14.3.40.
G-AEFC	Thorn/HM.14 Pou-du-Ciel	RLT.1		26. 3.36	Canx in 3/37.
G-AEFD	Biggs/HM.14 Pou-du-Ciel	GFB.1		26. 3.36	WFU on 7.4.37. Canx 5.11.45 in census.
G-AEFE	Barrow/HM.14 Pou-du-Ciel	LVGB.1		27. 3.36	Hit a rabbit burrow during trials from Ipswich and tipped onto its side (date?). Not flown again and stored - perhaps at Ipswich, later burnt in fire at Colchester. WFU on 2.3.37. Canx 22.1.39 in census.
G-AEFF	Crossley/HM.14 Pou-du-Ciel	EC.1		27. 3.36	Canx in 12/36.
G-AEFG	Nolan/HM.14 Pou-du-Ciel	JN.1		27. 3.36	WFU on 31.3.38. (On rebuild 7/96) (Also BAPC.75)
G-AEFH	DH.86B (Originally regd as DH.86A)	2350		15. 4.36	Abandoned during evacuation of France at Bordeaux on 18.6.40. Canx.
G-AEFI	Motram/HM.14 Pou-du-Ciel	LEM.1		28. 3.36	Crashed at Leamington on 16.6.36. Canx in 12/36.
G-AEFJ	Curtis/HM.14 Pou-du-Ciel	MLC.1		30. 3.36	Canx 31.9.38.
G-AEFK	Scott/HM.14 Pou-du-Ciel	SFD.1		30. 3.36	WFU on 30.9.36. Canx in 3/37.
G-AEFL	Shoults/HM.14 Pou-du-Ciel	CRS.1		30. 3.36	CofA expired in 12/40. Canx.
G-AEFM	BA Swallow II	437		1. 4.36	WFU on 18.5.40. Canx in 6/46.
G-AEFN	DH.90 Dragonfly	7507		28. 4.36	To RAF as X9390 in 3/40. Canx 27.3.40.
G-AEFO	Turner/HM.14 Pou-du-Ciel	WT.1		1. 4.36	Canx in 1/46.
G-AEFP	Glasgow Corporation Tramway/HM.14 Pou-du-Ciel	GCT.1		1. 4.36	Authorisation to Fly expired on 15.10.36 & WFU. Canx 31.12.36.
G-AEFR	DH.85 Leopard Moth	7125		23. 4.36	To RAF as AV985 in 5/40. Canx 12.5.40.
G-AEFS	Miles M.2F Hawk Major	124	VT-AFR	8. 4.36	To Australia as VH-AAH in 12/36. Canx.
G-AEFT	Aeronca C.3 (Rebuilt in 1976 with major parts of G-AETG and carries c/n AB.110 thereof)	A.610		17. 4.36	
G-AEFU	Aeronca C.3	A.609		14. 4.36	To Ireland as EI-ABN in 4/37. Canx.
G-AEFV	Mercer/HM.14 Pou-du-Ciel	A2.51		26. 3.36	Canx in 2/38.

Regn	Type	c/n	Previous identity	Regn date	Fate or immediate subsequent identity (if known)
G-AEFW	Aero/HM.14 Pou-du-Ciel	A8/CB.1		14. 4.36	Force-landed near Lympne during cross-Channel attempt on 17.5.36. Canx 15.8.46 in census.
G-AEFX	DH.84 Dragon II	6106		23. 4.36	To Australia in 4/36 - regd as VH-UVN on 10.7.36. Canx in 5/36.
G-AEFY	Stinson SR-7B Reliant	9691		20. 6.36	To RAF as W7979 in 2/40. Canx 21.2.40.
G-AEFZ	BA Eagle II	133		15. 4.36	To RAF as ES944 in 6/41. Canx 30.6.41.
G-AEGA	Avro 626	923		14. 4.36	To Austria in 5/36. Canx.
G-AEGB	Avro 626	924		14. 4.36	To Austria in 5/36. Canx.
G-AEGC	Avro 626	925		14. 4.36	To Austria in 6/36. Canx.
G-AEGD	Abbot/HM.14 Pou du Ciel	CP.1		15. 4.36	Canx 31.1.37.
G-AEGE	Miles M.2P Hawk Major	267		17. 4.36	To RAF as HL538 in 9/41. Fuselage moved at Redhill in 1949. Canx 6.9.41.
G-AEGF	Airspeed AS.6J Envoy III (Originally regd as Envoy II)	55		1. 5.36	Not completed. Canx in 1/37.
G-AEGG	Airspeed AS.6J Envoy III (Originally regd as Envoy II)	56		1. 5.36	Not completed. Canx in 1/37.
G-AEGH	Parnall Hendy Heck IIC	J.10		29. 4.36	To RAF as NF749 in 3/43. Canx 8.3.43.
G-AEGI	Parnall Hendy Heck IIC	J.11		29. 4.36	DBR after ground collision with Spitfire G-AISU on 17.6.50. Stored at Wolverhampton until mid-1953 and burnt. Canx.
G-AEGJ	Parnall Hendy Heck IIC	J.12		19. 9.36	Not completed. To spares use. Canx.
G-AEGK	Parnall Hendy Heck IIC	J.13		. 4.36R	NTU - To G-AEMR. Canx.
G-AEGL	Parnall Hendy Heck IIC	J.14		. 4.36R	NTU - To RAF as K8853 in 1936. Canx.
G-AEGM	BA Swallow II	436		28. 4.36	DBF at Hooton on 27.6.36. Canx.
G-AEGN	BA Swallow II	438		28. 4.36	Scrapped in 8/50. Canx.
G-AEGO	BA Eagle II	127		28. 4.36	To RAF as HM506 in 8/41. Canx 6.8.41.
G-AEGP	Miles M.2H Hawk Major	186		24. 4.36	To 1889 ATC Sqdn at Faringdon, Berks as DP851 in 3/41. Canx 10.3.41.
G-AEGR	Miles M.2H Hawk Major	188		24. 4.36	Crashed at Bucklebury Place on 27.4.37. Canx.
G-AEGS	DH.89A Dragon Rapide	6335		13. 5.36	Crashed at Affule, Palestine on 30.12.36. Canx.
G-AEGT	Hartley/HM.14 Pou-du-Ciel	RPH.1		30. 4.36	Air Ministry Category E noted as housed at the Brown House Inn, Winster, Windermere on 1.9.39. Canx 1.12.46 in census.
G-AEGU	Essex/HM.14 Pou-du-Ciel	GAE.1		22. 4.36	WFU on 14.5.37. Canx in 12/46 in census.
G-AEGV	East Midlands Aviation Co/HM.14 Pou-du-Ciel (Rebuild with some original components)	EMAC.1		22. 4.36	WFU on 26.5.37. Canx in 12/37. Midland Air Museum (On display 4/96)
G-AEGW	Avro 504N	-	J9702	22. 4.36	DBF in hangar fire at Hooton Park on 8.7.40. Canx.
G-AEGX	General Aircraft Monospar ST.25 Ambulance	GAL/ST25/80		29. 4.36	To Spanish Republicans in 3/37. Canx.
G-AEGY	General Aircraft Monospar ST.25 Universal	GAL/ST25/93		29. 4.36	To RAF as X9377 in 4/40. Canx 9.4.40.
G-AEGZ	British Marine BM-1 (Was to have been licence built Sikorsky S-42A)	1		23. 4.36	Not built. Canx.
G-AEHA	Percival P.10 Vega Gull	K.24		28. 4.36	To France as F-AQEA in 6/37. Canx.
G-AEHB	BA Swallow II	425		. 4.36	Ditched into the sea on 3.7.36. Canx.
G-AEHC	DH.90 Dragonfly	7514		. 4.36	Crashed at Darnaw, Kircudbrightshire on 2.2.37. Canx.
G-AEHD	Litchfield-Price/HM.14 Pou du Ciel	LPM.1		27. 4.36	Sold in 1/37. Canx.
G-AEHE	Fokker F.VIIa	4984	PH-ADN H-NADN	2. 6.36	To Holland as PH-EHE in 6/36. Canx.
G-AEHF	Fokker F.VIIa	4952	PH-ADX H-NADX	2. 6.36	To Sweden as (PH-EHF)/(SE-AGF)/SE-AGH in 12/36. Canx.
G-AEHG	Leicestershire Flying Club/HM.14 Pou-du-Ciel	LFPC.1		28. 4.36	Canx in 5/37.
G-AEHH	Cooper/HM.14 Pou-du-Ciel	CHC.1		28. 4.36	Crashed in 1937 and dismantled. Stored at Spondon in 9/39. Canx 1.12.46 in census.
G-AEHI	BA Swallow II	424		30. 4.36	WFU on 20.8.47. Broken up in 6/48. Canx.
G-AEHJ	Heston Phoenix	1/3		29. 4.36	Crashed into the River Mersey, Liverpool on 13.2.40. Canx.
G-AEHK	BA Swallow II	426		5. 5.36	To RAF as X5007 in 4/40. Canx 9.4.40.
G-AEHL	BA Swallow II	427		5. 5.36	To RAF as BK895 in 8/40. Canx 1.8.40.
G-AEHM	Dolman/HM.14 Pou-Du-Ciel	HJD.1		30. 4.36	Canx in 3/39 in census. (On display at Wroughton)
G-AEHN	Miles M.7 Nighthawk	283		6. 5.36	To Romanian AF in 8/36. Canx.
G-AEHO	Miles M.7 Nighthawk	284		6. 5.36	To Romanian AF in 8/36. Canx.
G-AEHP	Miles M.2Z Hawk Trainer	258	U3	6. 5.36	To Romanian AF in 12/36. Canx.
G-AEHR	Miles M.2Y Hawk Trainer	237		6. 5.36	To Romanian AF in 12/36. Canx.
G-AEHS	Miles M.2Y Hawk Trainer	245		6. 5.36	To Romanian AF in 12/36. Canx.
G-AEHT	Miles M.2Y Hawk Trainer	265		6. 5.36	To Romanian AF in 12/36. Canx.
G-AEHU	Miles M.2Y Hawk Trainer	292		6. 5.36	To Romanian AF in 12/36. Canx.
G-AEHV	Miles M.2Y Hawk Trainer	293		6. 5.36	To Romanian AF in 12/36. Canx.
G-AEHW	Miles M.2Y Hawk Trainer	294		6. 5.36	To Romanian AF in 12/36. Canx.
G-AEHX	Miles M.2Y Hawk Trainer	295		6. 5.36	To Romanian AF in 12/36. Canx.
G-AEHY	Miles M.2Y Hawk Trainer	296		6. 5.36	To Romanian AF in 12/36. Canx.
G-AEHZ	Miles M.2Y Hawk Trainer	297		6. 5.36	To Romanian AF in 12/36. Canx.
G-AEIA	Bouskill/HM.14 Pou-du-Ciel	HFB.1		30. 4.36	WFU 23.4.37. Burnt when the type was 'banned'. Canx 31.12.37 in census. Engine survived until at least 1953.
G-AEIB	BA Swallow II	441		8. 5.36	WFU on 21.7.39. To Doncaster Aero Club. Canx.
G-AEIC	BA Swallow II	428		8. 5.36	WFU on 6.3.40. Scrapped at Tollerton in 1948. Canx.
G-AEID	DH.82A Tiger Moth	3498		11. 5.36	Crashed at Desford on 27.9.40. Canx.
G-AEIE	Abbot/HM.14 Pou-du-Ciel	WB.1		5. 5.36	Canx 1.12.37.
G-AEIF	Percival P.10 Vega Gull	K.25		11. 5.36	To France as F-AQMZ in 4/38. Canx.
G-AEIG	BA Swallow II	429		. 5.36	Destroyed in collision with G-AFER over Cotgrove on 16.2.39. Remains stored at Knowle in 1952. Canx as WFU 26.7.39.
G-AEIH	BA Swallow II	430		. 5.36	To RAF as X5006 in 4/40. Canx 3.4.40.

Regn	Type	c/n	Previous identity	Regn date	Fate or immediate subsequent identity (if known)
G-AEII	Killick/HM.14 Pou-du-Ciel	1A		13. 5.36	Canx in 6/36.
G-AEIJ	Avro 504N	-	J8507	. 5.36	Crashed into the Irish Sea on 21.1.37. Canx.
G-AEIK	Taylor J/2 Cub	S.556		11. 5.36	WFU on 5.10.39. Broken up between 1939 and 1945. Canx.
G-AEIL	Pobjoy/Short S.16/1 Scion II	PA.1003		11. 5.36	To RAF as Z7187 in 1940. Canx.
G-AEIM	Short S.8/8 Rangoon	S.757	S1433	11. 5.36	WFU at Hamble on 19.4.40. Canx.
G-AEIN	BA Double Eagle IV	902		. 5.36	To RAF as ES950 in 7/41. Canx 31.7.41.
G-AEIO	Squires/HM.14 Pou-du-Ciel	JSS.1		11. 5.36	WFU on 10.5.37. Canx in 12/37.
G-AEIP	Phoenix Aircraft Corp/HM.14 Pou-du-Ciel	PACCO.1		15. 5.36	WFU on 3.4.37. Canx in 12/38.
G-AEIR	Avro 643 Cadet II	926		13. 5.36	Crashed into sea off Hamble on 8.6.40. Canx.
G-AEIS	DH.84 Dragon II	6107		14. 5.36	To Turkish AF in 12/36. Canx.
G-AEIT	DH.84 Dragon II	6108		14. 5.36	To Turkish AF in 12/36. Canx.
G-AEIU	DH.84 Dragon II	6109		14. 5.36	To Turkish AF in 12/36. Canx.
G-AEIV	DH.80A Puss Moth	2067	VH-UQK	. 5.36	To RAF as DP853 in 3/41. Canx 19.3.41.
G-AEIW	BA Swallow II	431		26. 5.36	To Ireland as EI-ABY in 8/39. Canx.
G-AEIX	Green/HM.14 Pou-du-Ciel	JCCG.1		9. 6.36	No Authorisation to Fly issued. Canx 31.12.38 in census.
G-AEIY	DH.87B Hornet Moth	8067	(G-ADMK)	22. 5.36	To RAF as AW114 in 6/40. Canx 4.6.40.
G-AEIZ	Birkenhead Flying Club/HM.14 Pou-du-Ciel	BFC.1		20. 5.36	Flew poorly and was abandoned after a crash - though DBR. Canx 1.12.37.
G-AEJA	Oldham Welding Co/HM.14 Pou-du-Ciel	OWCM.1		21. 5.36	WFU on 19.5.37. Canx in 12/38.
G-AEJB	General Aircraft Monospar ST.25 Universal	GAL/ST25/82		22. 5.36	To Free French AF in Ethiopia in 1/42. Canx.
G-AEJC	Abbot/HM.14 Pou-du-Ciel	CP.3		27. 7.36	WFU on 21.4.37. Canx 1.12.37.
G-AEJD	Abbot/HM.14 Pou-du-Ciel	CP.4		27. 7.36	WFU on 21.4.37. Canx 1.12.37.
G-AEJE	Abbot/HM.14 Pou-du-Ciel	CP.5		27. 7.36R	NTU - Canx.
G-AEJF	Abbot/HM.14 Pou-du-Ciel	CP.6		27. 7.36R	NTU - Canx.
G-AEJG	Abbot/HM.14 Pou-du-Ciel	CP.7		27. 7.36R	NTU - Canx.
G-AEJH	BAC Super Drone	18		2. 6.36	Broken up at Knowle, Birmingham in 9/48. Wings to G-AEDB. Canx.
G-AEJI	Stinson SR.8D Reliant	9728		3. 9.36	To RAF as X8520 in 2/40. Canx 10.2.40.
G-AEJJ	Percival P.10 Vega Gull	K.27		25. 5.36	To RAF as X9455 in 4/40. Canx 2.4.40.
G-AEJK	BAC Super Drone	19		2. 6.36	Crashed on 17.4.51. Scrapped by Otley Motors, London. Canx.
G-AEJL	BAC Super Drone	20		9. 6.36	Crashed at Monkmoor in 1937. Canx in 3/37.
G-AEJM	DH.86B (Originally regd as DH.86A)	2351		6. 7.36	To RAF as X9441 in 4/40. Canx 4.4.40.
G-AEJN	Pobjoy/Short S.16/1 Scion II	PA.1004		2. 9.36	To RAF as AV990 in 5/40. Canx 25.5.40.
G-AEJO	Tuckett/HM.14 Pou-du-Ciel	HJT.1		9. 6.36	Canx in 8/39.
G-AEJP	BAC Super Drone	21		15. 7.36	To France in 6/39. Canx.
G-AEJR	BAC Super Drone	22		15. 7.36	Canx as WFU 26.10.84; Wings to BAC VII Replica BGA.2878.
G-AEJS	BAC Super Drone	23		7. 7.36	Crashed at Gerrards Cross on 27.4.47. Canx.
G-AEJT	Stinson SR.6A Reliant	9646	NC15169	. 7.36	To Tanganyika in 5/37. Canx.
G-AEJU	Baker/HM.14 Pou du Ciel	CEB.1		18. 6.36	WFU on 26.5.37. Canx 31.12.38 in census.
G-AEJV	General Aviation Monospar ST.25 Universal	GAL/ST25/83		10. 6.36	Crashed at Lympne on 12.3.38. Canx.
G-AEJW	General Aircraft Monospar ST.25 Universal	GAL/ST25/84		10. 6.36	To New Zealand as ZK-AFF in 12/36. Canx.
G-AEJX	Small & Hardie/HM.14 Pou du Ciel	SH.1		4. 6.36	WFU at Perth on 11.6.37. Canx.
G-AEJY	Fleet F.7C-2	69		7. 5.38	WFU on 13.3.47. Scrapped at Altrincham in 7/59. Canx.
G-AEJZ	Crosland/HM.14 Pou-du-Ciel (Also allotted BAPC.120)	TLC.1		9. 6.36	Canx 31.12.38 in census. To 1323 (Ryedale) ATC Sqdn at Brough 1.5.71 until 1983. Bomber County Aviation Museum (Stored 4/97 Hemswell)
G-AEKA	Gray/HM.14 Pou du Ciel	EHG.1		10. 6.36	No Authorisation to Fly issued. Canx 31.12.38 in census.
G-AEKB	BA Swallow II	444		9. 6.36	To RAF as 3568M in 11/42. Canx 30.11.42.
"G-AEKB"	Wackett Widgeon II	-		----	Launched 7.7.25 carrying these markings, said to stand for E.K.Bowden, Minister of Defence in Australia at the time. Regn G-AUKB was reserved but NTU. Transferred to the R.Australian AF.
G-AEKC	BA Swallow II	443		25. 6.36	WFU on 10.10.39. Canx in 12/46.
G-AEKD	Percival P.10 Vega Gull	K.28		15. 6.36	Fatal crash at Sanganer aerodrome, between Bombay and Jaipur, India on 12.10.37. Canx.
G-AEKE	Percival P.10 Vega Gull	K.29		16. 6.36	Crashed near Oxted, Surrey on 24.1.38. Canx.
G-AEKF	DH.89A Dragon Rapide	6332		15. 6.36	To Yugoslavia as YU-SAS in 6/36. Canx.
G-AEKG	BA Swallow II	442		25. 6.36	WFU on 3.11.39. Derelict at Maylands, Essex. Canx.
G-AEKH	Berrington/HM.14 Pou du Ciel	CLB.1		29. 6.36	WFU on 17.7.37. Canx 5.11.45 in census.
G-AEKI	BA Eagle II	131		26. 6.36	To RAF as ES948 in 7/41. Canx 31.7.41.
G-AEKJ	Miles M.2H Hawk Major	185		23. 6.36	To Brazil in 7/36. Canx.
G-AEKK	Miles M.3B Falcon Six	248		23. 6.36	To RAF as W9373 in 1/40. Canx 6.1.40.
G-AEKL	Percival P.6 Mew Gull	E.21		. 6.36	Damaged in air raid at Lympne in 6/40. WFU at Lympne on 12.7.40. Canx.
G-AEKM	BAC Super Drone	24		7. 7.36	To RAF for research in 1/41. Canx 6.1.41.
G-AEKN	BAC Super Drone	25		14. 1.37	WFU on 17.1.38. Scrapped in 1945. Canx.
"G-AEKN"	Miles M.12 Mohawk	298		----	Marked in error - became G-AEKW.
G-AEKO	BAC Super Drone	26		28. 7.36	Scrapped in 1945/46. Canx.
G-AEKP	DH.87B Hornet Moth	8101		2. 7.36	To RAF as AV972 in 4/40. Canx 28.4.40.
G-AEKR	Claybourn Co/HM.14 Pou-Du-Ciel (Rebuilt using original engine after DBF at Finningley on 4.9.70. Also BAPC.121)	CAC.1		26. 6.36	Canx 31.7.38. (On display at Doncaster Museum)
G-AEKS	DH.87B Hornet Moth	8100		17. 7.36	To RAF as W5753 in 1/40. Canx 21.1.40.
G-AEKT	BAC Super Drone	28		9.11.36	Crashed (as "PR-?") on 16.4.41. Canx in 12/46.

Regn	Type	c/n	Previous identity	Regn date	Fate or immediate subsequent identity (if known)
G-AEKU	BAC Super Drone	29		24.11.36	Scrapped between 1939 and 1945. Canx.
G-AEKV	BAC Drone de luxe (Also allotted BGA.2510 5/79)	30		13. 1.37	Permit expired on 6.10.60. On display in Brooklands Museum 3/97. Canx as WFU 14.1.99.
G-AEKW	Miles M.12 Mohawk	298	HM503 G-AEKW/"G-AEKN"/U8	14. 7.36	Crashed in Spain in late-1949. Sold to the USA in 11/75. (On rebuild Fort Union, Virginia, USA)
G-AEKX	Miles M.12 Mohawk	301		14. 7.36	Not completed. Canx in 12/37.
G-AEKY	DH.87B Hornet Moth	8102	W9383 G-AEKY	14. 7.36	WFU at White Waltham on 28.8.53. Canx.
G-AEKZ	DH.84 Dragon I	6028	SU-ABH	. 7.36	To RAF as AW163 in 6/40. Canx 30.6.40.
G-AELA	DH.82A Tiger Moth	3509		24. 7.36	Crashed near Woolsington on 6.3.37. Canx.
G-AELB	DH.82A Tiger Moth	3510		21. 7.36	To RAF as AX781 in 7/40. Canx 22.7.40.
G-AELC	DH.82A Tiger Moth	3511		21. 7.36	To RAF as AX782 in 7/40. Canx 22.7.40.
G-AELD	DH.82A Tiger Moth	3512		21. 7.36	Crashed near Prestatyn on 11.4.37. Canx.
G-AELE	Percival P.10 Vega Gull	K.26		21. 5.36	Ditched in the Bay of Canche, off Le Touquet, France on 26.6.39. Canx.
G-AELF	Percival P.10 Vega Gull	K.30		16. 7.36	To India as VT-AJZ in 3/38. Canx.
G-AELG	BA Swallow II	449		15. 7.36	To Ireland as EI-AMU in 8/62. Canx.
G-AELH	BA Swallow II	446		15. 7.36	To RAF as BK896 in 8/40. Canx 1.8.40.
G-AELI	BA Swallow II	445		25. 7.36	Crashed near Lympne on 21.9.38. Canx.
G-AELJ	BA Swallow II	448		19. 8.36	WFU on 21.10.39. Canx.
G-AELK	Hillson Praga	HA.13		17. 9.36	Crashed at Aldwark, Yorks on 9.4.37. Canx.
G-AELL	Hillson Praga	HA.14		2.11.36	WFU at Barton on 4.1.39. Broken up between 1939 and 1945. Canx.
G-AELM	North Liverpool Light Plane Club/ HM.14 Pou du Ciel	NLLPC.1		22. 7.36	WFU on 31.7.37. Canx.
G-AELN	Cheltenham Light Aero Club/HM.14 Pou du Ciel	CLAC.1		28. 7.36	WFU on 29.7.37. Canx 1.12.37.
G-AELO	DH.87B Hornet Moth	8105	AW118 G-AELO	30. 7.36	
G-AELP	DH.82A Tiger Moth	3513		27. 7.36	To RAF as BB757 in 10/40. Canx 30.10.40.
G-AELR	Dart Pup	2		28. 7.36	Crashed on take-off in 8/38. Canx.
G-AELS	Percival P.10 Vega Gull	K.31		22. 7.36	To RAF as W9376 in 3/40. Canx 31.3.40.
G-AELT	Miles M.5A Sparrowhawk	275		28. 7.36	To South Africa as ZS-ANO in 3/38. Canx.
G-AELU	Stinson SR.8D Reliant	9759		8. 9.36	To RAF as X9596 in 5/40. Canx 1.5.40.
G-AELV	BA Swallow II	447		31. 7.36	Destroyed at Hanworth on 24.5.39. Canx.
G-AELW	Percival P.10 Vega Gull	K.32		28. 7.36	To RAF as X9349 in 3/40. Canx 11.3.40.
G-AELX	Aeronca C.3	A.663		. 7.36	Fatal crash into Irish Sea on 9.6.51. Canx.
G-AELY	Aeronca C.3	A.664		. 7.36	Crashed at Hanworth on 9.10.37. Canx.
G-AELZ	Dart Flittermouse	HNB.1		30. 7.36	Scrapped at Blackbushe in 1951. Canx.
G-AEMA	GAL.42 Cygnet I (Built as CW Cygnet c/n 0001)	GAL/42/108		30. 7.36	WFU on 2.7.43. Canx.
G-AEMB	Percival P.10 Vega Gull	K.33		31. 7.36	To RAF as X9371 in 3/40. Canx 16.3.40.
G-AEMC	Stinson SR.8B Reliant	9758	NC16175	9.10.36	WFU on 20.1.39. Canx.
G-AEMD	BA Swallow II	452		12. 8.36	WFU on 20.4.40. Canx.
G-AEME	Weaver/HM.14 Pou du Ciel	WB.1		7. 8.36	WFU on 25.8.37. Canx in 12/37.
G-AEMF	DH.82A Tiger Moth	3514		12. 8.36	To RAF as BB758 in 10/40. Canx 30.10.40.
G-AEMG	DH.87B Hornet Moth	8071		18. 8.36	To India as VT-AKA in 3/38. Canx.
G-AEMH	DH.89A Dragon Rapide	6336	X9387 G-AEMH	. 8.36	WFU at Ipswich in 7/60. Broken up in 1961. Canx as destroyed 14.2.73. (Parts to G-AIUL c/n 6837 for rebuild in 7/97)
G-AEMI	DH.84 Dragon II	6110		14. 8.36	To RAF as AW173 in 7/40. Canx 6.7.40.
G-AEMJ	DH.84 Dragon II	6111		14. 8.36	To Portuguese AF as 504 in 4/37. Canx.
G-AEMK	DH.84 Dragon II	6112		14. 8.36	To Australia in 3/38 - regd as VH-AAO on 15.2.40. Canx in 6/38.
G-AEML	DH.89 Dragon Rapide	6337	X9450 G-AEML	1. 9.36	
G-AEMM	DH.89 Dragon Rapide	6339		31. 8.36	Crashed on 3.5.40. Canx in 3/46.
G-AEMN	General Aircraft Monospar ST.25 Universal	GAL/ST25/88		15. 8.36	To Spanish Republicans in 11/36. Canx.
G-AEMO	Percival P.6 Mew Gull	E.23		17. 8.36	To South Africa as ZS-AHO in 9/36. Canx.
G-AEMP	Avro 504N	-	J9017	. 8.36	To RAF as BV208 in 1/41. Canx 16.1.41.
G-AEMR	Parnall Hendy Heck IIC	J.13	G-AEGK	4. 7.39	Scrapped at Cardiff in 1948. Canx.
G-AEMS	BA Swallow II	453		25. 8.36	Crashed at Eastham, Cheshire on 1.5.38. Canx.
G-AEMT	Heston Phoenix II	1/4		25. 8.36	To RAF as X9393 in 3/40. Canx 29.3.40.
G-AEMU	DH.82A Tiger Moth	3516		28. 8.36	To India as VT-ANM in 11/40. Canx.
G-AEMV	BA Swallow II	454		28. 8.36	WFU on 6.2.40. Canx.
G-AEMW	BA Swallow II	456		. 8.36	Crashed at Clothall Common on 29.12.63. Canx.
G-AEMX	DH.92 Dolphin	6400		27. 8.36	Regn never painted on aircraft. To E-6 in 9.9.36. Scrapped at Hatfield in 10/36. Canx.
G-AEMY	Bird/HM.14 Pou-Du-Ciel	NMB.1		25. 8.36	Canx 31.7.37. (Major parts stored 3/96 Leeds)
G-AEMZ	Lockheed 12A	1206		. 8.36	To RAF as R8987 in 9/39. Canx 8.9.39.
G-AENA	Airspeed AS.6J Envoy III	60		10. 9.36	Crashed at Abercorn, Northern Rhodesia on 1.10.36. Canx.
G-AENB	DH.85 Leopard Moth	7128		4. 9.36	To Yugoslavia as YU-PEA in 9/36. Canx.
G-AENC	BA Swallow II	455		5. 9.36	W/o in 3/37. Canx.
G-AEND	Toy & Riley/HM.14 Pou du Ciel	TR.1		1. 9.36	WFU on 16.9.37. Canx in 9/38.
G-AENE	BA Eagle II	132		16. 9.36	To France as F-AQNE in 5/37. Canx.
G-AENF	Tipsy S.2	28	OO-ASA	. 9.36	WFU on 26.7.39. Canx.
G-AENG	Miles M.3A Falcon Major	234		10. 9.36	Crashed at Scarborough on 10.9.37. Canx.
G-AENH	Miles M.11A Whitney Straight	303		10. 9.36	To Australia as VH-ABN in 12/37. Canx.
G-AENI	Brown/HM.14 Pou du Ciel	FWB.1		5. 9.36	Wrecked on the ground in a storm at Walton, Peterborough in 1939. Canx 8.9.42.
G-AENJ	Patson/HM.14 Pou du Ciel	JP/1		5. 9.36	Canx in 10/37.
G-AENK	DH.82A Tiger Moth	3517		22. 9.36	To India as VT-AON in 4/41. Canx.

Regn	Type	c/n	Previous identity	Regn date	Fate or immediate subsequent identity (if known)
G-AENL	Avro 643 Cadet II	949		16. 9.36	To 580 ATC Sqdn at Dauntey's School, Wilts as 2951M in 8/41. Canx 28.8.41.
G-AENM	Broughton-Blayney Brawney	BB.50		19. 9.36	Crashed near Hanworth on 21.3.37. Canx.
G-AENN	DH.89A Dragon Rapide	6340		22. 9.36	To RAF as W6455 in 1/40. Canx 23.1.40.
G-AENO	DH.89A Dragon Rapide	6341	EI-ABP G-AENO	22. 9.36	To Ireland and restored as EI-ABP in 2/38. Canx.
G-AENP	Hawker Afghan Hind	41H/81902	(BAPC 78) R.Afghan AF	29.10.81	
G-AENR	DH.86B	2352	(AX842) G-AENR	. 9.36	CofA lapsed 21.7.46. Scrapped at Langley in 11/48. Canx.
G-AENS	Miles M.2H Hawk Major	198		18. 9.36	To RAF as DP848 in 3/41. Canx 10.3.41.
G-AENT	Miles M.2X Hawk Trainer	328		18. 9.36	Crashed near Woodbridge in 19.12.36. Canx.
G-AENU	Foster-Wikner FW.2 Wicko (Originally regd as FW.1)	1		18. 9.36	WFU at Plymouth in 1952. Canx.
G-AENV	Appleby/HM.18 Pou du Ciel	HM.18		17. 9.36	To France in 9/37. Canx in 12/37.
G-AENW	Aeronca 100	AB.101		22. 9.36	WFU on 8.11.37. Scrapped between 1939 and 1945. Canx.
G-AENX	Short S.22 Scion Senior	S.835		15. 7.36	Sank at moorings at Bathurst, West Africa in 8/39. Canx.
G-AENY	Beechcraft C.17R Staggerwing	114		16.12.36	Crashed at Biarritz, France in 9/37. Canx.
G-AENZ	BAC Drone	PGC.4	BGA.198	26. 9.36	Canx in 1946.
	(Rebuild of Planette No.4 and BAC VII c/n 137)				
G-AEOA	DH.80A Puss Moth	2184	ES921 G-AEOA/YU-PAX/UN-PAX	1.10.36	
G-AEOB	Tipsy S.2 (Originally regd with c/n T.51)	101		.10.36	Scrapped at Hanworth in 12/37. Canx.
G-AEOC	Miles M.9 Kestrel Trainer (Miles Master prototype)	330	U-5	6.10.36	Remained as U-5 (B-Class marks), then to RAF as N3300 in 5/38. Canx.
G-AEOD	Reid & Seigrist RS.1 Snargasher	1		9.10.36	Scrapped in 1944. Canx.
G-AEOE	DH.82A Tiger Moth	3521		19.10.36	To South African AF as SAAF 1494 in 6/40. Canx.
G-AEOF	Rearwin 8500 Sportster	462	N15863 NC15863	1.12.81	(Stored 8/97)
"G-AEOF"	Millon HM.14 Pou-Du-Ciel	WM.1		---	(Loaned to Aviodome and stored .92 Schiphol, Netherlands)
	(Fictitious marks adopted on aircraft in 1964; allotted BAPC.22)				
G-AEOG	Hordern-Richmond Autoplane	1		16.10.36	WFU on 11.4.40. Scrapped between 1940 and 1945. Canx.
G-AEOH	Streather/HM.14 Pou-Du-Ciel (Now reproduction using original wings)	RCS.1		15.10.36	(Extant .95 Dieme, France)
G-AEOI	Lockheed 12A	1212	X9316 G-AEOI	2. 3.37	To Venezuela as YV-P-AED in 4/48. Canx.
G-AEOJ	Armour/HM.14 Pou du Ciel	MDSA.1		21.10.36	Air Ministry category E at Cellardyke, Anstruther, Fife in 1939. WFU on 4.8.39. Canx in 11/45. Reportedly broken up.
G-AEOK	Porterfield 35-70	246		10.12.36	WFU on 13.7.40. Scrapped at Gatwick in 1949. Canx.
G-AEOL	Hillson Praga	HA.15		21.12.36	WFU on 8.2.39. Broken up at Barton in 1947. Canx.
G-AEOM	Hillson Praga	HA.16		20. 1.37	WFU on 4.1.38. Broken up at Barton between 1939 and 1945. Canx.
G-AEON	Hillson Praga	HA.20		3.11.36	Sold abroad in 12/36. Canx.
G-AEOO	Aeronca C.3	A.709		26.10.36	Not certificated. Scrapped at Denham in 1949. Canx.
G-AEOP	Aeronca C.3	A.711		26.10.36	Not certificated. Scrapped at Denham in 1949. Canx.
G-AEOR	Stinson SR.8B Reliant	9820		31.12.36	To RAF as HM593 in 12/42. Canx 31.12.42.
G-AEOS	Fokker F.XII	5291	PH-AID	29.10.36	WFU in 3/40 due to lack of spares. Scrapped in 6/40. Canx.
G-AEOT	Fokker F.XII	5300	PH-AIH	29.10.36	Crashed near Crawley, Sussex on 19.11.36. Canx.
G-AEOU	Fairchild 24C8-F	3126		9.11.36	To RAF as BS817 in 10/40. Canx 14.10.40.
G-AEOV	DH.89A Dragon Rapide	6342	E-4	.11.36	To RAF as W6456 in 1/40. Canx 10.1.40.
G-AEOW	BA Swallow II	457		5.11.36	DBR at Heston on 16.3.47. Canx.
G-AEOX	Miles M.2H Hawk Major	205		5.11.36	To France as F-APOY in 1/37. Canx.
G-AEOY	Short S.16/1 Scion II	S.789	VH-UUT (G-ADDS)	.11.36	Crashed at Terim on 17.12.37. Canx.
G-AEOZ	BA Swallow II	458		.11.36	WFU on 8.1.40. Canx in 12/46.
G-AEPA	General Aircraft Monospar ST.25 Universal	GAL/ST25/94		6.11.36	To RAF as X9372 in 3/40. Canx 19.3.40.
G-AEPB	DH.83 Fox Moth	134		5.11.36	No CofA issued. Canx in 11/38.
G-AEPC	Bellanca 28-70	902	NR190M EI-AAZ	7.11.36	To Spanish AF as LB.1 in 1937. Canx.
G-AEPD	Luton LA.4 Minor	LA.3		11.11.36	WFU on 23.4.40. Canx.
G-AEPE	DH.89A Dragon Rapide	6344		. 2.37	To RAF as BD143 in 7/40. Canx 24.7.40.
G-AEPF	DH.89A Dragon Rapide	6353		10. 3.37	Abandoned at Bordeaux, France on 18.6.40. Canx.
G-AEPG	General Aircraft Monospar ST.25 Universal	GAL/ST25/87		14.11.36	To France as F-AQOM in 6/38. Canx.
G-AEPH	Bristol 96 Fighter (F.2b) (Original c/n 3746, rebuilt	7575	D8096 G-AEPH/D8096	13.11.36	
	c.1925 with new c/n 6848, rebuilt again c.1931 with present c/n)				
G-AEPI	Hillson Praga	HA.12		20. 1.37	WFU on 4.1.39. Scrapped between 1939 and 1945. Canx.
G-AEPJ	Hillson Praga	HA.25		. 1.37	WFU on 18.6.40. Scrapped between 1939 and 1945. Canx.
G-AEPK	Hillson Praga	HA.26		6. 3.37	WFU on 14.3.40. Scrapped between 1939 and 1945. Canx.
G-AEPL	Hillson Praga	HA.23		26. 1.37	To Singapore in 1937. Canx.
G-AEPM	Hillson Praga	HA.24		26. 1.37	To Singapore as VR-SAU in 1937. Canx.
G-AEPN	Lockheed 10A Electra	1080A		17.12.36	To RAF as W9105 in 4/40. Canx 14.4.40.
G-AEPO	Lockheed 10A Electra	1081A		17.12.36	To RAF as W9106 in 4/40. Canx 12.4.40.
G-AEPP	Lockheed 10A Electra	1082A		17.12.36	Crashed during night landing in a blizzard at Croydon on 13.12.37. Canx.
G-AEPR	Lockheed 10A Electra	1083A		17.12.36	Crashed at Almaza, Egypt on 14.4.44. Canx.
G-AEPS	Percival P.10 Vega Gull	K.45		.11.36	To Egypt as SU-AAX in 10/38. Canx.
G-AEPT	Fokker F.VIII	5043	PH-AEF H-NAEF	25.11.36	WFU on 12.1.38. Broken up in 5/38. Canx.

Regn	Type	c/n	Previous identity	Regn date	Fate or immediate subsequent identity (if known)
G-AEPU	Fokker F.VIII	5046	PH-AEI H-NAEI	25.11.36	To SE-AHA in 4/39. Canx.
G-AEPV	DH.87B Hornet Moth	8106		11.12.36	To RAF as W5774 in 1/40. Canx 21.1.40.
G-AEPW	DH.89A Dragon Rapide	6350		1.12.36	To RAF as X8510 in 3/40. Canx 4.3.40.
G-AEPX	Taylor HW Experimental	TE.2		7.12.36	Crashed at Hamsey Green on 7.1.37. Canx.
G-AEPY	Taylor LW Experimental	TE.3		7.12.36	Not built. Canx.
G-AEPZ	Taylor LW Experimental	TE.4		7.12.36	Not built. Canx.
G-AERA	Taylor Experimental	-		.12.36R	NTU - Not built. Canx.
G-AERB	BA Eagle II	137		.11.36	To France as F-ARRB in 5/38. Canx.
G-AERC	Miles M.11A Whitney Straight (Originally regd as M.11B)	305		.11.36	To RAF as AV971 in 4/40. Canx 26.4.40.
G-AERD	Percival P.3 Gull Six	D.65	HB-OFU	16. 9.77	Canx 28.11.86 on sale to Australia.
G-AERE	DH.89A Dragon Rapide	6355		. .37	Crashed at Forest-in-Teesdale, Co.Durham on 20.6.39. Canx.
G-AERF	Broughton-Blayney Brawney	BB.51		2.12.36	Fatal crash at Bromley Hill, Kent on 6.6.37. Canx.
G-AERG	Broughton-Blayney Brawney	BB.52		2.12.36	CofA expired 22.12.37 & WFU. Canx.
G-AERH	Percival P.10 Vega Gull	K.41		2.12.36	Crashed into a house and burned out on take-off from Hanworth in Isle of Man Race on 29.5.37. Canx.
G-AERI	BA Swallow II	465		5.12.36	WFU on 20.12.39. Canx.
G-AERJ	Millichamp/HM.14 Pou du Ciel	WBM.1		1.12.36	WFU on 30.11.37. Canx.
G-AERK	BA Swallow II	466		16.12.36	WFU at Weston on 28.3.40. Broken up in 3/40. Canx.
G-AERL	Percival P.10 Vega Gull	K.42		3.12.36	To RAF as X1033 in 4/40. Canx 16.4.40.
G-AERM	DH.82A Tiger Moth	3280	K4284	16.12.36	Restored to RAF as K4284 in 10/37. Canx 7.10.37.
G-AERN	DH.89A Dragon Rapide	6345		13. 1.37	To Spain as EC-AKO in 12/54. Canx.
G-AERO(1)	C.W.A. Swan	1		. 1.37R	NTU - Not built. Canx.
G-AERO(2)	Auster J/1 Autocrat	1994	(G-AHHE)	. 5.46	To New Zealand as ZK-AUX in 7/50. Canx.
G-AERP	Dart Kitten I	121		14.12.36	Crashed at Broxbourne on 23.11.52. Canx.
G-AERR	BA Swallow II	468		.12.36	To Ireland as EI-AFD in 6/48. Canx.
G-AERS	Miles M.11A Whitney Straight	304		.12.36	To RAF as ES922 in 5/41. Canx 6.5.41.
G-AERT	Airspeed AS.6J Envoy III	68		6. 1.37	To Military Governor of Lui Chow, South China in 1/37. Canx.
G-AERU	Junkers Ju.52/3mge	5440	SE-AER	5. 1.37	WFU in 4/41 & used for spares in the Belgian Congo. Canx.
G-AERV	Miles M.11A Whitney Straight	307	EM999 G-AERV	30.12.36	CofA expired 9.4.66. Canx by CAA 7.9.81. (On rebuild 4/96)
G-AERW	DH.82A Tiger Moth	3543		18. 1.37	Canx in 12/37.
G-AERX	Junkers Ju.52/3mge	5518	SE-AES	26. 1.37	To Belgium as OO-CAP in 9/41. Canx.
G-AERY	Miles M.11A Whitney Straight	309		. 1.37	To India as VT-AKF in 4/38. Canx.
G-AERZ	DH.89A Dragon Rapide	6356		10. 3.37	Crashed on golf course at Craigarad, Co.Down on 1.4.46. Canx.
G-AESA	DH.82A Tiger Moth	3544		18. 1.37	To RAF as BD161 in 8/40. Canx 8.8.40.
G-AESB	Aeronca C.3	A.638	N15742 NC15742	5. 8.88	(On rebuild .97)
G-AESC	DH.82A Tiger Moth	3545		18. 1.37	Crashed at Weybridge on 6.9.37. Canx.
G-AESD	DH.82A Tiger Moth	3552		18. 1.37	To RAF as BD156 in 8/40. Canx 8.8.40.
G-AESE	DH.87B Hornet Moth (Was restored ex.RAF on 11.5.46 with Short conversion c/n SH.44C)	8108	W5775 G-AESE	13. 1.37	
G-AESF	BAC Super Drone	31		19. 2.37	Broken up in 11/45. Canx.
G-AESG	Kronfeld Monoplane	33		. 2.37	DBF at Gerrards Cross in 1943. Canx.
G-AESH	Kronfeld Monoplane	-		. 2.37R	NTU - Not completed; DBF in 1943. Canx.
G-AESI	BA Swallow II	473		21. 1.37	W/o in 6/38. Canx.
G-AESJ	Beechcraft C.17R	118		. 1.37	To RAF as DS180 in 5/41. Canx 31.5.41.
G-AESK	Taylor J/2 Cub	957		. 1.37	WFU in 5/38. Canx.
G-AESL	BA Swallow II	471		20. 1.37	To 1834 ATC Sqdn at Hayle, Cornwall as 3412M in 10/42. Canx 28.10.42.
G-AESM	DH.82A Tiger Moth	3582		18. 3.37	To India as VT-AOK in 3/41. Canx.
G-AESN	DH.82A Tiger Moth	3586		18. 3.37	To India as VT-AOH in 2/41. Canx.
G-AESO	DH.82A Tiger Moth	3587		18. 3.37	Crashed near Avebury, Wilts on 30.3.40. Canx.
G-AESP	Aeronca 100	AB.109		18. 1.37	WFU for spares use in 1953. Parts to G-AEXD. Canx.
G-AESR	DH.89A Dragon Rapide	6363		18. 3.37	Crashed at Gerdes el Abid, Libya on 22.7.56. Canx.
G-AESS	General Aircraft Monospar ST.25 Universal	GAL/ST25/79		19. 1.37	Crashed at Burntisland Beach, Fife on 20.7.38. Canx in 1943.
G-AEST	Mosscraft M.A.1	MA.1		18. 1.37	Crashed at Newport, Staffs on 17.6.50. Canx.
G-AESU	Tipsy S.2	102		27. 4.37	Crashed at Walsall on 2.5.37. Canx.
G-AESV	Heston Phoenix II	1/5	X2891 G-AESV	. 1.37	Crashed in the French Alps in 4/52. Canx.
G-AESW	DH.90 Dragonfly	7544		3. 2.37	To RAF as AV976 in 5/40. Canx 10.5.40.
G-AESX	Aeronca 100	AB.106		. 2.37	WFU on 2.2.38. Scrapped between 1939 and 1945. Canx.
G-AESY	Lockheed 10A Electra	1102		17. 3.37	Crashed into the sea in Storstroem Straits, near Vondingborg, off Copenhagen, Denmark on 15.8.39. Canx.
G-AESZ	Chilton DW.1 (Long term rebuild project using some original components)	DW.1/1		. 1.37	Crashed near Felixstowe on 24.5.53.
G-AETA	Caudron G.III (Also reported as c/n 5019 or 5021; allotted 9203M .94)	7487	OO-ELA O-BELA	29. 1.37	Sold to RAF in 1972. (On display RAF Museum)
G-AETB	Miles M.11A Whitney Straight	310		4. 2.37	Crashed near Beauvais, France on 21.6.37. Canx.
G-AETC	DH.87B Hornet Moth	8109		10. 2.37	To RAF as W5776 in 1/40. Canx 17.1.40.
G-AETD	Percival P.10 Vega Gull	K.46		. 2.37	To Belgium as OO-ANC in 3/39. Canx.
G-AETE	Percival P.10 Vega Gull	K.47		. 2.37	To Belgium as OO-ATY in 2/39. Canx.
G-AETF	Percival P.10 Vega Gull	K.48		1. 2.37	To RAF as W9378 in 3/40. Canx 18.3.40.
G-AETG	Aeronca 100	AB.110		. 2.37	Crashed on take-off from Booker on 7.4.69. Canx as destroyed 29.2.72. (Major parts to G-AEFT in 1976 - on rebuild with parts from G-AEWV 4/96)
G-AETH	Short S.22 Scion Senior	S.836		. 2.37R	NTU - To RAF as L9786 in 10/39. Canx.

Regn	Type	c/n	Previous identity	Regn date	Fate or immediate subsequent identity (if known)
G-AETI	Saro A.17 Cutty Sark	A.17/8	VR-HAY	4. 2.37	WFU on 14.2.40. Scrapped. Canx.
G-AETJ	Miles M.14A Hawk Trainer III	331	U-2	15. 2.37	To New Zealand as ZK-AEX in 2/38. Canx.
G-AETK	DH Technical School TK.4	2265	E-4	26. 7.37	Crashed near Hatfield on 1.10.37. Canx.
G-AETL	Miles M.14A Hawk Trainer III	332		15. 2.37	To New Zealand as ZK-AEY in 2/38. Canx.
G-AETM	DH.86B	2353		6. 4.37	To Finland as (OH-SLA)/OH-IPA in 12/39. Canx.
G-AETN	Miles M.3A Falcon Major	226		15. 2.37	Crashed at Star Cross, Devon on 17.5.37. Canx.
G-AETO	DH.82A Tiger Moth	3561		11. 3.37	To Australia as VH-ACP in 5/40. Canx.
G-AETP	DH.82A Tiger Moth	3574		18. 3.37	To Holland as PH-UCA on 1.6.46. Canx.
G-AETR	Aeronca 100	AB.112		. 2.37	Fatal crash at Strangford Lough, Co.Down on 2.3.47. Canx.
G-AETS	Miles M.11A Whitney Straight	312		16. 2.37	To RAF as DR611 in 5/41, but mispainted as DR617. Canx 20.5.41.
G-AETT	Pobjoy-Short S.16/1 Scion II	PA.1005		24. 2.37	Crashed at Barnstaple, Devon on 13.2.40. Canx.
G-AETU	Gordon Dove	S.C.B. III		. 2.37	Destroyed in hangar fire at Maylands on 6.2.40. Canx.
G-AETV	Short S.23 Empire	S.838		1. 3.37	To Australia as VH-ABG on 12.9.42. Canx 9/42.
G-AETW	Short S.23 Empire	S.839		1. 3.37	Crashed landing on Lake Ramadi, 12 miles from Lake Habbaniyah, near Baghdad, Iraq on 27.11.38 in sandstorm. Canx.
G-AETX	Short S.23 Empire	S.840		1. 3.37	Destroyed by sabotage at Congella, Durban, South Africa on 1.12.42. Canx.
G-AETY	Short S.23 Empire	S.841		1. 3.37	To RAF as AX659 in 7/40. Canx 9.7.40.
G-AETZ	Short S.23 Empire	S.842		1. 3.37	Shot down by the Japanese between Java, Netherlands East Indies and Broome, Western Australia on 28.2.42. Canx.
G-AEUA	Short S.23 Empire	S.843		1. 3.37	To R.Australian AF as A18-11 in 9/39. Canx.
G-AEUB	Short S.23 Empire	S.844		1. 3.37	To Australia in 2/42 - regd as VH-ADU on 12.8.42. Canx.
G-AEUC	Short S.23 Empire	S.845		1. 3.37	Destroyed in air raid at Broome, Western Australia on 3.3.42. Canx.
G-AEUD	Short S.23 Empire	S.846	AX660 G-AEUD	1. 3.37	Broken up at Hythe on 6.3.47. Canx.
G-AEUE	Short S.23 Empire	S.847		1. 3.37	Scrapped at Hythe in 1947. Canx.
G-AEUF	Short S.23 Empire	S.848		1. 3.37	Crashed on night landing at Port Darwin, Northern Territories, Australia on 22.3.42, planing bottom broke up and aircraft capsized. Canx.
G-AEUG	Short S.23 Empire	S.849		1. 3.37	To Australia in 7/38 - regd as VH-ABC on 26.9.38. Canx.
G-AEUH	Short S.23 Empire	S.850	VH-ABD G-AEUH	1. 3.37	Shot down off Koepang, Timor, Netherland East Indies on 30.1.42. Canx.
G-AEUI	Short S.23 Empire	S.851	VH-ABE G-AEUI	1. 3.37	Broken up at Hythe in 1947. Canx.
G-AEUJ	Miles M.11A Whitney Straight	313		19. 2.37	(Stored 6/92 RAF Cosford)
G-AEUK	Hillson Praga	HA.27		19. 3.37	Crashed near Rochdale on 29.5.39. Canx.
G-AEUL	Hillson Praga	HA.28		19. 3.37	WFU on 13.4.39. Scrapped between 1939 and 1945. Canx in 12/46.
G-AEUM	Hillson Praga	HA.29		. 3.37	WFU on 16.10.39. Scrapped between 1939 and 1945. Canx in 12/46.
G-AEUN	Hillson Praga	HA.30		. 3.37	WFU on 1.8.40. Scrapped between 1939 and 1945. Canx in 12/46.
G-AEUO	Hillson Praga	HA.31		. 3.37	WFU on 11.9.39. Scrapped between 1939 and 1945. Canx.
G-AEUP	Hillson Praga	HA.32		24. 5.37	Crashed & DBF in mountains in Turkey on 23.7.47. Canx.
G-AEUR	Hillson Praga	HA.33		24. 5.37	W/o on 1.4.39. Canx.
G-AEUS	Hillson Praga	HA.34		18. 8.37	Crashed at Barton on 22.6.39. Canx.
G-AEUT	Hillson Praga	HA.35		. .37	Crashed at Sinalunga, Siena, Italy on 19.6.57. Canx.
G-AEUU	Hillson Praga	HA.36		. .37	Scrapped between 1939 and 1945. Canx.
G-AEUV	DH.82A Tiger Moth	3599		18. 3.37	To RAF as BB692 in 9/40. Canx 19.9.40.
G-AEUW	Aeronca 100	AB.108		. 2.37	WFU on 22.2.38. Canx.
G-AEUX	Miles M.11A Whitney Straight	314	DJ713 G-AEUX	23. 2.37	To Kenya as VP-KHO in 12/49. Canx.
G-AEUY	Miles M.11A Whitney Straight	315		. 2.37	To RAF as W7422 in 3/40. Canx 4.3.40.
G-AEUZ	Miles M.11A Whitney Straight	316		5. 3.37	To Kenya as VP-KKF in 10/52. Canx.
G-AEVA	Miles M.11A Whitney Straight	318	DR612 G-AEVA	. 3.37	Crashed on Mt.Moutier, Switzerland on 2.7.54. Canx.
G-AEVB	DH.82A Tiger Moth	2264		2. 3.37	To RAF as BB739 in 10/40. Canx 30.10.40.
G-AEVC	BA Swallow II	474		4. 3.37	To 304 ATC Sqdn at Hastings & destroyed in air raid at Hastings in 1943. Canx.
G-AEVD	BA Swallow II	460		. 3.37	DBF at Maylands, Essex on 6.2.40. Canx.
G-AEVE	Aeronca II Srs.500 (Later mod to Ely 700)	AB.120		. 3.37	Dismantled at Warton in 1947. (Remains near Warton in 9/49) Wings used for G-AEVT. Canx.
G-AEVF	Miles M.11A Whitney Straight	317		2. 3.37	To RAF as BS814 in 9/40. Canx 21.9.40.
G-AEVG	Miles M.11A Whitney Straight	319	DP854 (DP845)/G-AEVH	2. 3.37	To Australia as VH-EVG in 5/55. Canx.
G-AEVH	Miles M.11A Whitney Straight	321		. 3.37	Crashed near Newbury on 28.1.39. Canx.
G-AEVI	Avro 626	982		3. 3.37	To Austria in 6/37. Canx.
G-AEVJ	Avro 626	983		3. 3.37	To Austria in 6/37. Canx.
G-AEVK	Avro 626	984		3. 3.37	To Austria in 6/37. Canx.
G-AEVL	Miles M.11A Whitney Straight	322	NF751 DP855/G-AEVL	9. 3.37	To New Zealand as ZK-AZX in 10/51. Canx 14.10.51.
G-AEVM	Miles M.11A Whitney Straight	324		10. 3.37	To RAF as BS815 in 9/41. Canx 21.9.41.
G-AEVN	General Aircraft Monospar ST.25 Ambulance	GAL/ST25/77		. 3.37	To Spanish Republicans in 6/37. Canx.
G-AEVO	Hawker 41H Tomtit	-	K1451	. 3.37	WFU 9.3.40. Canx.
G-AEVP	Hawker 41H Tomtit	13	J9782	. 3.37R	NTU - To G-AFFL 3/38. Canx.
G-AEVR	Aeronca 100	AB.111		. 3.37	WFU on 30.3.38. Canx.
G-AEVS	Aeronca 100 (Now composite including parts of original G-AEXD)	AB.114		3.37	(On display 3/99 at Breighton)

Regn	Type	c/n	Previous identity	Regn date	Fate or immediate subsequent identity (if known)
G-AEVT	Aeronca 100	AB.115		. 3.37	Crashed at Loughborough on 11.7.50. Parts to G-AEFT. Canx.
G-AEVU	DH.87B Hornet Moth	8112		. 3.37	To India as VT-AKE in 3/38. Canx.
G-AEVV	DH.91 Albatross	6800	(K8618) E-2	3. 1.38	To RAF as AX903 in 9/40. Canx 1.9.40.
G-AEVW	DH.91 Albatross	6801	(K8619) F-5	3. 1.38	To RAF as AX904 in 9/40. Canx 1.9.40.
G-AEVX	Stinson SR.9B Reliant	5156		11. 5.37	To RAF as W7980 in 2/40. Canx 21.2.40.
G-AEVY	Stinson SR.9D Reliant	5253		18. 5.37	To RAF as W7984 in 2/40. Canx 21.2.40.
G-AEVZ	BA L.25c Swallow II	475		19. 3.37	
G-AEWA	Miles M.11A Whitney Straight	320	DJ714 G-AEWA	9. 3.37	Crashed near Neufchatel, France on 3.3.61. Canx.
G-AEWB	BA Swallow II	476		. 3.37	WFU on 1.8.40. Donated to 252 (Bridlington) ATC Sqdn at Driffield in 1949. Canx.
G-AEWC	Carden-Baynes Bee	1		11. 3.37	Scrapped in 1939. Canx.
G-AEWD	Curtiss T-32 Condor	29	NC12367	7. 5.37	To RAF as P5723 in 10/38. Canx.
G-AEWE	Curtiss T-32 Condor	30	NC12368	7. 5.37	To RAF as P5725 in 10/38. Canx.
G-AEWF	Curtiss T-32 Condor	36	NC12375	7. 5.37	To RAF as P5726 in 10/38. Canx.
G-AEWG	DH.82A Tiger Moth	3589		1. 4.37	To RAF as X5105 in 1/40. Canx 5.1.40.
G-AEWH	BA Swallow II	477		24. 3.37	Crashed into Shepperton Reservoir on 23.8.37. Canx.
G-AEWI	BA Swallow II	478		. 3.37	Scrapped in 10/39. Canx.
G-AEWJ	Tipsy S.2	103		. 3.37R	NTU - Crashed at Ramsgate, Kent on 6.6.37. Canx.
G-AEWK	Miles M.11A Whitney Straight	325		24. 3.37	To RAF as AV970 in 4/40. Canx 19.4.40.
G-AEWL	DH.89A Dragon Rapide	6367		. 3.37	To France as F-OATT in 1/56. Canx.
G-AEWM	DH.87B Hornet Moth	8114		. 3.37	To South Africa as ZS-AOS in 7/38. Canx.
G-AEWN	General Aircraft Monospar ST.25 Ambulance	GAL/ST25/78		. 3.37	Crashed into the sea off Cannes on 5.8.37. Canx in 12/37.
G-AEWO	Percival P.10 Vega Gull	K.49		23. 3.37	To Switzerland as HB-UTU in 4/39. Canx.
G-AEWP	Percival P.10 Vega Gull	K.51		23. 3.37	Crashed at Johnstone, near Renfrew on 3.7.37. Canx.
G-AEWR	DH.86B	2354		7. 5.37	Abandoned in evacuation of France at Bordeaux on 18.6.40. Canx.
G-AEWS	Percival P.10 Vega Gull	K.52		. 3.37	To RAF as X9435 in 4/40. Canx 2.4.40.
G-AEWT	Miles M.11A Whitney Straight	326		30. 3.37	To France as F-APPZ in 10/37. Canx.
G-AEWU	Aeronca 100	AB.116		. 3.37	DBR when portable hangar collapsed at Farnborough in 2/55. Canx.
G-AEWV	Aeronca 100	AB.117		. 3.37	Crashed at Dunstable in 6/64. Canx as WFU in 1967.
G-AEWW	Aeronca 100	AB.118		. 3.37	Not certificated. Scrapped between 1939 and 1945. Canx.
G-AEWX	Aeronca 100	AB.119		. 3.37	Not certificated. Scrapped between 1939 and 1945. Canx.
G-AEWY	DH.87B Hornet Moth	8116	W5777 G-AEWY	7. 4.37	Crashed at Barton on 18.4.64. Canx.
G-AEWZ	DH.90A Dragonfly	7556	DJ716 G-AEWZ	10. 4.37	DBR at Elmdon on 3.3.61. Canx.
G-AEXA	Aeronca 100	AB.113		. 4.37	WFU 19.4.38. Scrapped between 1939 and 1945. Canx.
G-AEXB	Aeronca 100	AB.134		9. 4.37	Fatal crash into the Irish Sea on 8.7.37. Canx.
G-AEXC	Hawker 41H Tomtit	26481 & 11	J9781	. 4.37	Scrapped between 1939 and 1945. Canx.
G-AEXD	Aeronca 100 (Mostly comprises parts of G-AESP after rebuild in 1958)	AB.124		1. 4.37	(On rebuild 1/91) (Sold to Cox '97)
G-AEXE	Airspeed AS.6J Envoy III	67		12. 4.37	To Military Governor of Lui Chow, South China in 7/37. Disappeared without trace en route. Canx.
G-AEXF	Percival P.6 Mew Gull (Rebuild c/n PFA/13-10020)	E.22	ZS-AHM	18. 5.37	
G-AEXG	DH.82A Tiger Moth	3584		29. 4.37	To RAF as AX786 in 7/40. Canx 22.7.40.
G-AEXH	BA Swallow II	479		. 4.37	WFU & presented to 1423 ATC Sqdn as 3636M in 3/43. Canx 16.3.43.
G-AEXI	DH.90A Dragonfly	7554		20. 5.37	To Kenya as VP-KCS in 11/38. Canx.
G-AEXJ	Miles M.11A Whitney Straight	501		20. 4.37	To RAF as BS818 in 10/40. Canx 29.10.40.
G-AEXK	Tipsy S.2	104		. 4.37	Scrapped at Hooton in 8/37. Canx.
G-AEXL	Tipsy S.2	105		. 4.37R	NTU - WFU in 1937. Canx.
G-AEXM	DH.87B Hornet Moth	8122		28. 4.37	To Uruguay as CX-ABD in 10/37. Canx.
G-AEXN	DH.90A Dragonfly	7559		. 4.37	Crashed in Hampden Woods, near High Wycombe, Bucks., on 21.7.39. Canx 29.3.40.
G-AEXO	DH.89A Dragon Rapide	6368		19. 5.37	To RAF as X8507 in 3/40. Canx 26.3.40.
G-AEXP	DH.89A Dragon Rapide	6369		19. 5.37	To RAF as X8505 in 3/40. Canx.
G-AEXR	Northrop 1C Delta	/	SE-ADI NC13755	. 5.37R	NTU - To Iraq as YI-OSF in 1937. Canx.
G-AEXS	Howitt Monoplane	H.32D		26. 4.37	Stored at Abingdon 1939 - 1945. Canx.
G-AEXT	Dart Kitten IIA	123		30. 4.37	
G-AEXU	Percival P.10 Vega Gull	K.56		1. 5.37	To RAF as X1032 in 4/40. Canx 26.4.40.
G-AEXV	Percival P.10 Vega Gull	K.57	X9391 G-AEXV	1. 5.37	Broken up at Southend in 4/50. Canx.
G-AEXW	Stinson SR.9D Reliant	5262		5. 7.37	To RAF as W7982 in 2/40. Canx 22.2.40.
G-AEXX	Airspeed AS.6J Envoy III	66	L7270 G-AEXX	26. 5.37	To Sweden as SE-ASN in 6/46. Canx 19.6.46.
G-AEXY	Piper J/2 Cub	971		23. 6.37	To Spain as EC-ALB 3/53. Canx.
G-AEXZ	Piper J/2 Cub	997		5. 2.38	(On rebuild off airfield)
G-AEYA	Miles M.11A Whitney Straight	342		20. 5.37	To RAF as DP237 in 4/41. Canx 17.4.41.
G-AEYB	Miles M.11A Whitney Straight	500		20. 5.37	To Italy as I-BONA in 12/37. Canx.
G-AEYC	Percival P.10 Vega Gull	K.59	W6464 G-AEYC	28. 5.37	DBF at Gatwick on 14.8.60. Canx.
G-AEYD	Percival P.10 Vega Gull	K.60		28. 5.37	To Southern Rhodesia as VP-YBV in 5/38. Canx.
G-AEYE	Percival P.16A Q-Six	Q.20	X9328 G-AEYE	26. 5.37	WFU on 14.5.49. Canx.
G-AEYF	General Aircraft Monospar ST.25 Ambulance	GAL/ST25/95		31. 5.37	To Denmark as OY-DAZ in 3/39. Canx.

Regn	Type	c/n	Previous identity	Regn date	Fate or immediate subsequent identity (if known)
G-AEYG	Tipsy S.2	106		. 5.37R	NTU. Canx.
G-AEYH	Tipsy S.2	107		. 5.37R	NTU. Canx.
G-AEYI	Miles M.11C Whitney Straight	341	U-4	31. 5.37	Crashed near Hounslow on 28.6.38. Canx.
G-AEYJ	Miles M.11A Whitney Straight	343		. 5.37	To Belgium as OO-ZUT in 12/38. Canx.
G-AEYK	Hillson Praga	HA.37		12.11.37	DBR at Barton on 8.8.39. Canx.
G-AEYL	Hillson Praga	HA.38		. .37	Scrapped between 1939 and 1945. Canx.
G-AEYM	Hillson Praga	HA.39		. .37	Crashed at Weston-super-Mare on 1.9.39. Canx.
G-AEYN	Hillson Praga	HA.40		. 6.37R	NTU - Not completed. Canx.
G-AEYO	Hillson Praga	HA.41		. 6.37R	NTU - Not completed. Canx.
G-AEYP	Hillson Praga	HA.42		. 6.37R	NTU - Not completed. Canx.
G-AEYR	Hillson Praga	HA.43		. 6.37R	NTU - Not completed. Canx.
G-AEYS	Hillson Praga	HA.44		. 6.37R	NTU - Not completed. Canx.
G-AEYT	Hillson Praga	HA.45		. 6.37R	NTU - Not completed. Canx.
G-AEYU	Hillson Praga	HA.46		. 6.37R	NTU - Not completed. Canx.
G-AEYV	BA Swallow II	480		. 6.37	Canx in 11/45.
G-AEYW	BA Swallow II	481		7. 6.37	Destroyed in air raid at Lympne in 9/40. Canx.
G-AEYX	Heston Phoenix II	1/6		8. 6.37	To RAF as X9338 in 3/40. Canx 5.3.40.
G-AEYY	Martin Monoplane (See comments on G-EBQP)	1	G-AAJK	6. 7.37	CofA expired 3.11.39. (On long term rebuild .89) Canx by CAA 3.6.98.
G-AEYZ	Stinson SR.9D Reliant	5265		16. 7.37	To RAF as X8521 in 2/40. Canx 10.2.40.
G-AEZA	Gordon Dove	S.B.IV		21. 6.37	Scrapped in 5/39. Canx.
G-AEZB	Gordon Dove	3		20. 6.37	DBR at Tilbury, Essex on 9.9.37. Canx.
G-AEZC	DH.82A Tiger Moth	3624		28. 7.37	To RAF as BD152 in 8/40. Canx 8.8.40.
G-AEZD	Martin Baker MB.2	M.B.2	"M-B-1"	15. 6.37	To RAF as P9594 in 3/39. Canx.
G-AEZE	Curtiss T-32 Condor	28	NC12366	11. 8.37	To RAF as P5724 in 10/38. Canx.
G-AEZF	Pobjoy-Short S.16/1 Scion 2 (Converted to landplane in 11/41)	PA.1008	M-5 G-AEZF	18. 6.37	WFU in 5/54. (On rebuild to static condition 10/96)
G-AEZG	DH.87B Hornet Moth	8131	BK830 G-AEZG	1. 7.37	To Australia as VH-UXY in 4/79. Canx 20.4.79.
G-AEZH	DH.87B Hornet Moth	8132		28. 6.37	To RAF as W9381 in 3/40. Canx 30.4/40.
G-AEZI	DH.85 Leopard Moth	7113	I-NENO VP-KBV	26. 6.37	To RAF as AW122 in 6/40. Canx 15.6.40.
G-AEZJ	Percival P.10 Vega Gull	K.65	SE-ALA D-IXWD/PH-ATH/G-AEZJ	2. 7.37	
G-AEZK	Percival P.10 Vega Gull	K.66		2. 7.37	To RAF as X9339 in 3/40. Canx 5.3.40.
G-AEZL	Percival P.10 Vega Gull	K.67		2. 7.37	To RAF as X9436 in 5/40. Canx 10.5.40.
G-AEZM	BA Swallow II	434	VT-AHJ	. 7.37	DBF at Bluebell Hill, Rochester on 15.3.54. Canx.
G-AEZN	Shapley Kittiwake Mk.1	ESS/1		8. 7.37	WFU on 28.6.38. Canx.
G-AEZO	Miles M.11A Whitney Straight	347		12. 7.37	Crashed south of Malakal, Sudan on 9.10.37. Canx.
G-AEZP	Miles M.14B Hawk Trainer II	494		17. 7.37	Sold abroad in 10/38. Canx.
G-AEZR	Miles M.14B Hawk Trainer II	495		. 7.37	Sold abroad in 10/38. Canx.
G-AEZS	Miles M.14 Hawk Trainer III (Fitted with M.18 wing in 1940/41)	538	U-0229 U-6/G-AEZS	12. 7.37	Canx in 12/46.
G-AEZT	DH.87B Hornet Moth	8133		20. 7.37	To RAF as W5778 in 1/40. Canx 21.1.40.
G-AEZU	General Aircraft Monospar ST.25 Jubilee	GAL/ST25/67		. 7.37R	NTU - To France as F-AQOL in 5/38. Canx.
G-AEZV	Tipsy S.2	108		. 7.37R	NTU - Canx.
G-AEZW	Tipsy S.2	109		. 7.37R	NTU - Canx.
G-AEZX	Bucker Bu.133C Jungmeister	1018	N5A PP-TDP	10. 5.88	Crashed in a field soon after take-off from Grantham Lodge on 21.6.88. Canx.
G-AEZY	DH.87B Hornet Moth	8138		26. 7.37	To RAF as W9384 in 3/40. Canx 31.3.40.
G-AEZZ	Foster-Wikner GM.1 Wicko (Originally regd as a FW.3)	2		22. 7.37	To RAF as ES943 in 7/41. Canx 10.7.41.
G-AFAA	Percival P.6 Mew Gull	E.24	X-2	14. 7.37	DBF at Luton on 7.7.45. Canx.
G-AFAB	Miles M.11A Whitney Straight	346		20. 7.37	To RAF as BD145 in 7/40. Canx 24.7.40.
G-AFAC	Premier Gordon Dove	-		. 7.37R	NTU - Not built. Canx.
G-AFAD	Premier Gordon Dove	-		. 7.37R	NTU - Not built. Canx.
G-AFAE	Premier Gordon Dove	-		. 7.37R	NTU - Not built. Canx.
G-AFAF	Premier Gordon Dove	-		. 7.37R	NTU - Not built. Canx.
G-AFAG	Premier Gordon Dove	-		. 7.37R	NTU - Not built. Canx.
G-AFAH	DH.89A Dragon Rapide	6377		24. 8.37	To RAF as X8508 in 3/40, but NTU & DBF at Merville, France on 21.5.40. Canx.
G-AFAI	DH.82A Tiger Moth	3602		26. 7.37	To Turkey as TC-KUR in 9/37. Canx.
G-AFAJ	DH.86B	2355		22. 7.37	To Turkey as TC-ERK in 9/37. Canx.
G-AFAK	DH.86B	2356		22. 7.37	To Turkey as TC-FER in 9/37. Canx.
G-AFAL	DH.86B	2357		22. 7.37	To Turkey as TC-GEN in 9/37. Canx.
G-AFAM	DH.86B	2358		22. 7.37	To Turkey as TC-HEP in 12/37. Canx.
G-AFAN	DH.90A Dragonfly	7556		21. 7.37	To Turkey as TC-IDE in 9/37. Canx.
G-AFAO	DH.89A Dragon Rapide	6372		21. 7.37	To Turkey as TC-DAG in 9/37. Canx.
G-AFAP	Junkers Ju52/3m	5881		13. 8.37	Captured by German military forces at Oslo, Norway on 9.4.40. Canx.
"G-AFAP"	CASA 352L (Junkers Ju52/3m)	163	T2B-272 Spanish AF	----	(On display at Cosford)
G-AFAR	DH.82A Tiger Moth	3627		16. 8.37	To RAF as BB867 in 1/41. Canx 3.1.41.
G-AFAS	DH.82A Tiger Moth	3628		16. 8.37	To RAF as BB868 in 1/41. Canx 3.1.41.
G-AFAT	DH.87B Hornet Moth	8137		11. 8.37	Crashed at Lympne on 7.7.39. Canx.
G-AFAU	Percival P.10 Vega Gull	K.69		22. 7.37	To RAF as X9332 in 2/40. Canx 26.2.40.
G-AFAV	Percival P.10 Vega Gull	K.76		23. 7.37	To RAF as X1034 in 5/40. Canx 29.5.40.
G-AFAW	Miles M.13 Hobby	1Y	U-2	26. 7.37	To RAF as L9706 in 5/38. Canx.
G-AFAX	BA Eagle 2	138	VH-ACN G-AFAX	29. 7.37	
G-AFAY	Miles M.3B Falcon Six	233	OE-DBB	29. 7.37	Scrapped at Heston in 1946. Canx.
G-AFAZ	Foster-Wikner Wicko GM.1	4		. 7.37	To RAF as ES924 in 5/41. Canx 21.5.41.

Regn	Type	c/n	Previous identity	Regn date	Fate or immediate subsequent identity (if known)
G-AFBA	Deekay Knight	237/1		3. 8.37	Scrapped between 1939 and 1945. Canx.
G-AFBB	BA Swallow II	461		11. 8.37	To India as VT-AIG 10/37. Canx.
G-AFBC	Percival P.10 Vega Gull	K.75	X9340 G-AFBC	9. 8.37	Crashed at Eastleigh on 12.7.54. Canx.
G-AFBD	Percival P.10 Vega Gull	K.70		. 8.37R	NTU. To G-AFBO in 8/37. Canx.
G-AFBE	Hillson Praga	-		18. 8.37R	NTU. Canx.
G-AFBF	Miles M.3B Falcon Six	256	AV973 G-AFBF/D-EGYV	14.10.37	Crashed in France in 1948 & used for spares. Canx.
G-AFBG	DH.87B Hornet Moth	8140		. 8.37R	NTU - To France as F-AQEB in 11/37. Canx.
G-AFBH	DH.87B Hornet Moth	8141		7.10.37	To RAF as X9324 in 2/40. Canx 29.2.40.
G-AFBI	Stinson SR-9D Reliant	5400		26.10.37	To RAF as W5791 in 12/39. Canx 1.12.39.
G-AFBJ	Short S.23 Empire	S.876	VH-ABA G-AFBJ/VH-ABA/G-AFBJ	26. 8.37	Scrapped at Hythe in 1947. Canx.
G-AFBK	Short S.23 Empire	S.877	VH-ABB G-AFBK	26. 8.37	Restored to Australia as VH-ABB in 3/38. Canx.
G-AFBL	Short S.23 Empire	S.878	VH-ABF G-AFBL	26. 8.37	Scrapped at Hythe in 1947. Canx.
G-AFBM	General Aircraft Monospar ST.25 Universal	GAL/ST25/96		28. 7.37	To Turkey in 10/37. Canx.
G-AFBN	General Aircraft Monospar ST.25 Universal	GAL/ST25/97		28. 7.37	To Turkey in 10/37. Canx.
G-AFBO	Percival P.10 Vega Gull	K.70	(G-AFBD)	27. 8.37	Abandoned at Berlin, Germany on 3.9.39 & to Luftwaffe. Canx.
G-AFBP	Luton LA-4A Minor	LA.4		6. 9.37	WFU, fuselage stored in two parts on Isle of Wight. Canx.
G-AFBR	Percival P.10 Vega Gull	K.79		8. 9.37	Crashed at Luton on 1.6.38. Canx.
G-AFBS	Miles M.14A Hawk Trainer III	539	(G-AKKU) BB661/G-AFBS	17. 9.37	CofA expired in 1963. Canx by CAA 22.12.95. (On rebuild 7/99 Duxford)
G-AFBT	Northrop 2L Gamma	347		20. 9.37	Broken up at Filton in 11/45. Canx.
G-AFBU	Shaw/HM.14 Pou du Ciel	NHS.1		27.10.37	Canx as WFU 27.10.38.
G-AFBV	Miles M.11A Whitney Straight	497		2.10.37	Crashed at Ipswich on 15.6.39. Canx.
G-AFBW	Percival P.10 Vega Gull	K.82		11.10.37	To RAF as W9377 in 1/40. Canx 19.1.40.
G-AFBX	Hillson Pennine	HA.100		27.10.37	Not completed. Canx 19.11.45.
G-AFBY	Cessna C.34 Airmaster	319	NC16409	15.10.37	Scrapped at Cowes, IoW in 11/51. Canx.
G-AFBZ	Kronfeld Drone	35		24. 8.37	Destroyed between 1939 and 1945. Canx in 12/46.
G-AFCA	DH.82A Tiger Moth	3637		24. 9.37	To RAF as BD154 in 8/40. Canx 8.8.40.
G-AFCB	BA Swallow II	482		13.10.37	To RAF as BJ575 in 9/40. Canx 10.9.40.
G-AFCC	Miles M.11A Whitney Straight	499		14.10.37	To Chile in 12/37. Canx.
G-AFCD	SCAL FB.30 Avion Bassou	2	F-APDT	11.11.37	Crashed at Hanworth on 12.6.38. Canx.
G-AFCE	Bristol 142M Blenheim I	8814		2.11.37	To Yugoslav AF in 11/37. Canx.
G-AFCF	Bristol 142M Blenheim I	8815		2.11.37	To Yugoslav AF in 11/37. Canx.
G-AFCG	Currie Wot	CPA.1/1		28.10.37	Destroyed in German air raid on Lympne in 5/40. Canx.
G-AFCH	Grumman G.21A Goose	1009		26.10.37	To Dutch East Indies as PK-AER in 7/38. Canx.
G-AFCI	Short S.26 (G-Class) (Later issued new c/n SH.42C)	S.871	X8275 G-AFCI	6.12.41	DBR in gales at Isle of Sheppey in 3/54. Canx.
G-AFCJ	Short S.26 (G-Class)	S.872		. .41R	NTU - To RAF as X8274 in 7/40. Canx.
G-AFCK	Short S.26 (G-Class)	S.873	X8273 (G-AFCK)	6.12.41	Crashed into River Tagus, Lisbon, Portugal on 9.1.43. Canx.
G-AFCL	BA L.25c Swallow II	462		3.11.37	
G-AFCM	Tipsy B	503	OO-DOS	3.11.37	Burnt at Slough in 8/52. Canx.
G-AFCN	Miles M.11A Whitney Straight	502		8.11.37	To RAF as V4739 in 10/39. Canx 12.10.39.
G-AFCO	Lockheed 12A	1238		18.11.37	To India as VT-AJS in 3/38. Canx.
G-AFCP	Miles M.3E Falcon Six	289		17.11.37	Broken up for spares in 4/38. Canx.
G-AFCR	Miles M.17 Monarch	638	W6461 G-AFCR/U-1	17.11.37	Crashed at Este, near Venice on 2.7.57. Canx.
G-AFCS	Lockheed 10A Electra	1025	NC14936	8. 2.38	Crashed at Almaza, Egypt on 19.11.43. Canx.
G-AFCT	Short S.30 Empire	S.879		15.11.37	Scrapped at Hythe in 1947. Canx.
G-AFCU	Short S.30 Empire	S.880		15.11.37	To RAF as V3137 in 3/40. Canx 16.3.40.
G-AFCV	Short S.30 Empire	S.881		15.11.37	To RAF as V3138 in 3/40. Canx 16.3.40.
G-AFCW	Short S.30 Empire	S.882		15.11.37	DBF at Hythe on 19.6.39. Canx.
G-AFCX	Short S.30 Empire	S.883		15.11.37	Sunk by hurricane while moored in River Tagus, Lisbon, Portugal on 15.2.41. Canx.
G-AFCY	Short S.30 Empire	S.884	(VH-...)	15.11.37	To New Zealand as ZK-AMC in 3/40. Canx.
G-AFCZ	Short S.30 Empire	S.885	(ZK-AMB) G-AFCZ/(VH-...)	15.11.37	Crashed into the sea off Bathurst, Gambia on 14.9.42. Canx.
G-AFDA	Short S.30 Empire	S.886	(VH-...)	15.11.37	To New Zealand as ZK-AMA in 3/40. Canx.
G-AFDB	Miles M.14A Hawk Trainer III	542		27.11.37	To RAF as BB662 in 9/40. Canx 17.9.40.
G-AFDC	DH.82A Tiger Moth	3594	(ZS-ANR)	19.11.37	To South Africa as ZS-ARK in 12/37. Canx.
G-AFDD	DH.82A Tiger Moth	3595	(ZS-ANS)	19.11.37	To South Africa as ZS-ARL in 12/37. Canx.
G-AFDE	General Aircraft Monospar ST.25 Universal	GAL/ST25/98		2.12.37	Sold abroad in 1/38. Canx.
G-AFDF	DH.87B Hornet Moth	8145		. 2.38	To RAF as W9382 in 3/40. Canx 31.3.40.
G-AFDG	DH.87B Hornet Moth	8146		28. 3.38	To RAF as W9390 in 3/40. Canx 31.3.40.
G-AFDH	DH.80A Puss Moth	2054	ZK-ABR	.12.37	CofA expired 23.7.40 and to ground instructional airframe. Scrapped at Redhill on 20.5.54 and burnt. Canx 1.12.46 in census.
G-AFDI	DH.91 Albatross	6802	E-2	28. 6.38	Destroyed by arson at Whitchurch, Bristol on 20.10.40. Canx.
G-AFDJ	DH.91 Albatross	6803		28. 6.38	Scrapped in 9/43. Canx.
G-AFDK	DH.91 Albatross	6804		28. 6.38	Crash landed near Shannon Airport, Ireland on 16.7.43. Canx.
G-AFDL	DH.91 Albatross	6805		3. 4.39	Destroyed in forced landing near Pucklechurch, Glos., on 6.10.40. Canx.
G-AFDM	DH.91 Albatross	6806		4. 4.39	Scrapped in 9/43. Canx.

Regn	Type	c/n	Previous identity	Regn date	Fate or immediate subsequent identity (if known)
G-AFDN	Taylorcraft Model A	406		19. 1.38	To RAF on 31.7.41; became instructional airframe until WFU on 1.12.41. Canx.
G-AFDO	Piper J3C-65 Cub (Frame no.2633)	2593	N21697 NC21697	7. 6.88	
G-AFDP	Cierva C.40	1001		18.12.37	To RAF as P9636 in 6/40. Canx.
G-AFDR	Cierva C.40	1002		18.12.37	To RAF as T1419 in 6/40. Canx.
G-AFDS	Currie Wot	CPA.1/2		4. 1.38	Destroyed in German air raid on Lympne in 5/40. Canx.
G-AFDT	DH.87B Hornet Moth	8150	W5779 G-AFDT	. 5.38	Crashed near Penarth, Wales on 20.12.51. Canx.
G-AFDU	DH.87B Hornet Moth	8160		1. 7.38	To RAF as W9379 in 1/40. Canx 11.1.40.
G-AFDV	DH.85 Leopard Moth	7120	VH-AHB	26. 7.38	To RAF as W5783 in 1/40. Canx 20.1.40.
G-AFDW	DH.87B Hornet Moth	8154		24. 6.38	To RAF as W9380 in 3/40. Canx 31.3.40.
G-AFDX	Hanriot HD.1	"HD.1"	OO-APJ Belgian AF H-1/ Belgian AF N75	4. 5.38	DBR on landing at Old Warden on 17.6.39. Wings destroyed in air raid on Brooklands in 1940, fuselage survived and sold in USA in 1963, rebuilt in 1968 as N75 & on display at RAF Museum. Canx.
G-AFDY	DH.87B Hornet Moth	8149		. 5.38	To RAF as W5780 in 1/40. Canx 14.1.40.
G-AFDZ	DH.60G Gipsy Moth	1924		29. 7.38	To RAF as X5056 in 1/40. Canx 10.1.40.
G-AFEA	Percival P.10 Vega Gull	K.84		7. 1.38	Sold abroad in 7/52. Canx.
G-AFEB	Lockheed 10A Electra	1122		1. 2.38	To RAF as W9104 in 4/40. Canx 12.4.40.
G-AFEC	DH.87B Hornet Moth	8157		11. 5.38	To RAF as X9446 in 4/40. Canx 3.4.40.
G-AFED	DH.87B Hornet Moth	8162		23. 8.38	To Kenya as KAAU K37 in 9/39. Canx.
G-AFEE	DH.87B Hornet Moth	8155		. .38	To RAF as W5781 in 1/40. Canx 13.1.40.
G-AFEF	DH.87B Hornet Moth	8156		5. 5.38	To RAF as X9447 in 3/40. Canx 11.3.40.
G-AFEG	De Bruyne-Maas Ladybird	D.B.3/M.1		18. 1.38	WFU & stored in a barn near Peterborough in 1960, then at Shortlands, Kent in 1964. Canx.
G-AFEH	Percival P.10 Vega Gull	K.100	(G-AHVN) X9315/G-AFEH	24. 1.38	WFU on 20.4.51. Scrapped at Squires Gate in 4/53. Canx.
G-AFEI	Tipsy B2	506	OO-DOV	21. 1.38	DBF at Hooton Park on 8.7.40. Canx.
G-AFEJ	DH.82A Tiger Moth	3664		25. 1.38	To India as VT-AMC in 3/40. Canx 21.3.40.
G-AFEK	Percival P.10 Vega Gull	K.89		24. 1.38	To RAF as X9392 in 3/40. Canx 26.3.40.
G-AFEL	Monocoupe 90A	A.782	N19432 NC19432	7. 6.82	
G-AFEM	Percival P.10 Vega Gull	K.91		24. 1.38	To RAF as X9368 in 3/40. Canx 12.3.40.
G-AFEN	DH.89A Dragon Rapide	6399	(TJ-AAI) HK864/G-AFEN/(Z7188)/VQ-PAC/G-AFEN	13. 4.38	To Argentina as LV-AGV in 12/48. Canx 30.12.48.
G-AFEO	DH.89A Dragon Rapide	6405		11. 4.38	To RAF as X8506 in 3/40. Canx 26.3.40.
G-AFEP	DH.89A Dragon Rapide	6406	X9388 G-AFEP	11. 4.38	To Kenya as VP-KFV in 6/48. Canx.
G-AFER	BA Swallow II	484		11. 4.38	Fatal crash in a field, near the Grantham Canal on 16.2.39 after collision with BA Swallow G-AEIG. Canx 1.1.46.
G-AFES	BA Swallow II	464		10. 2.38	To Ireland as EI-ABX in 7/39. Canx 20.3.39.
G-AFET	Miles M.14A Hawk Trainer III	556		3. 2.38	To RAF as AV978 in 5/40. Canx 1.3.40.
G-AFEU	Miles M.14A Hawk Trainer III	557		5. 2.38	Crashed into the sea off Cliftonville on 17.7.38. Canx.
G-AFEV	Miles M.14A Hawk Trainer III	558		5. 2.38	Crashed at Lyme Regis on 30.8.39. Canx.
G-AFEW	Miles M.14A Hawk Trainer III	559		5. 2.38	W/o in 1938. Canx.
G-AFEX	Taylorcraft Model A	-		. 2.38R	NTU. Canx.
G-AFEY	DH.89A Dragon Rapide	6402		7. 3.38	Crashed at Wideford, Orkney on 18.3.40. Canx.
G-AFEZ	DH.89A Dragon Rapide	6408	X9451 G-AFEZ	31. 5.38	To Laos as F-LAAL in 11/56. Canx.
G-AFFA	DH.82A Tiger Moth	3706		23. 8.38	To RAF as BB813 in 10/40. Canx 12.10.40.
G-AFFB	DH.89A Dragon Rapide	6409		12. 4.38	CofA lapsed 23.6.62 & WFU at Baginton. Canx.
G-AFFC	DH.89A Dragon Rapide	6410		12. 4.38	To RAF as HK862 in 2/42. Canx 15.2.42.
G-AFFD	Percival P.16A Q-Six	Q.21	(G-AIEY) X9407/G-AFFD	12. 2.38	(On rebuild by Aeroservice (IoM) Ltd)
G-AFFE	Percival P.16A Q-Six	Q.23		12. 2.38	To RAF as W9374 in 9/39. Canx 24.9.39.
G-AFFF	DH.89A Dragon Rapide	6386		24. 2.38	Crashed into Craighton Hill, Milngavie, near Renfrew on 27.9.46. Canx.
G-AFFG	Helmy Aerogypt IV (Originally regd as Mk.1, then Mk.II)	3		17. 2.38	Crashed at Northolt on 26.11.46. Canx.
G-AFFH	Piper J/2 Cub	1166	EC-ALA G-AFFH	26. 3.38	(On rebuild .97)
G-AFFI	Not allocated.				
"G-AFFI"	Mignet HM.14 Pou-Du-Ciel	YA.1	BAPC.76	----	Yorkshire Air Museum (Modern reproduction with fictitious marks) (On display 5/97)
G-AFFJ	Piper J3 Cub	1165		. 3.38	To West Germany as (D-EDIX)/D-EJUM(3)in 1/56. Canx.
G-AFFK	Fairchild 24C8-F	3120	NC16819	31. 3.38	To RAF as EF523 in 7/41. Canx 17.7.41.
G-AFFL	Hawker Tomtit	13	(G-AEVP) J9782	9. 3.38	Broken up at Southend in 9/39. Remains dumped at Newmarket in 1941. Canx.
G-AFFM	Airspeed AS.40 Oxford	75	L4538	29. 8.38	Fatal crash & DBF after striking a barrage balloon cable over Camshall, near Fareham on 20.11.39. Canx.
G-AFFN	Tipsy S.2	36	OO-ASJ	8. 3.38	Scrapped at Blackbushe in 2/53. Canx.
G-AFFO	DH.82A Tiger Moth	3674		17. 3.38	To South Africa as ZS-AIY in 5/38. Canx 11.5.38.
G-AFFP	Bristol 142M Blenheim I	8157		8. 3.38	To Turkish AF as 2503 in 3/38. Canx.
G-AFFR	Bristol 142M Blenheim I	8158		8. 3.38	To Turkish AF as 2504 in 3/38. Canx.
G-AFFS	Bristol 142M Blenheim I	8159		8. 3.38	To Turkish AF as 2505 in 3/38. Canx.
G-AFFT	Bristol 142M Blenheim I	8160		8. 3.38	To Turkish AF as 2506 in 4/38. Canx.
G-AFFU	Bristol 142M Blenheim I	8161		8. 3.38	To Turkish AF as 2507 in 4/38. Canx.
G-AFFV	Bristol 142M Blenheim I	8162		8. 3.38	To Turkish AF as 2508 in 4/38. Canx.
G-AFFW	Bristol 142M Blenheim I	8163		8. 3.38	To Turkish AF as 2509 in 5/38. Canx.
G-AFFX	Bristol 142M Blenheim I	8164		8. 3.38	To Turkish AF as 2510 in 5/38. Canx.
G-AFFY	Bristol 142M Blenheim I	8165		8. 3.38	To Turkish AF as 2511 in 5/38. Canx.
G-AFFZ	Bristol 142M Blenheim I	8166		8. 3.38	To Turkish AF as 2512 in 5/38. Canx.

Regn	Type	c/n	Previous identity	Regn date	Fate or immediate subsequent identity (if known)
G-AFGA	Miles M.5A Sparrowhawk	273		. 3.38	Canx 1.1.39.
G-AFGB	Arpin A-2 (Originally regd as A-1 Mk.2)	1		17. 3.38	Scrapped in 1946. Canx.
G-AFGC	BA L.25c Swallow II	467	BK893 G-AFGC	4. 4.38	(Stored 1/98)
G-AFGD	BA L.25c Swallow II	469	BK897 G-AFGD	4. 4.38	
G-AFGE	BA L.25c Swallow II	470	BK894 G-AFGE	4. 4.38	
G-AFGF	Tipsy B	1		. 3.38	Burned at Slough in 8/52. Canx.
G-AFGG	Marendaz Mk.III	2		23. 3.38	Sold for scrap at Barton-in-the-Clay on 19.12.40. Canx.
G-AFGH	Chilton DW.1	DW.1/2		30. 3.38	(On rebuild by Newbury Aeroplane Co 6/95)
G-AFGI	Chilton DW.1	DW.1/3		30. 3.38	
G-AFGJ	DH.82 Tiger Moth	3679		11. 4.38	To RAF as (AX791)/AX787. Canx 21.7.40.
G-AFGK	Miles M.11A Whitney Straight	509	U-1	6. 4.38	To USA as N72511 in 9/77. Canx 13.9.77.
G-AFGL	Miles M.17 Monarch	786		12. 4.38	To France as F-ARPE in 3/39. Canx.
G-AFGM(1)	Miles M.64	-	U-0253	. .45R	NTU. Remained as U-0253. Canx.
G-AFGM(2)	Piper J/4A Cub Coupe	4-943	N26895 NC26895	30.12.81	
G-AFGN	Lockheed 14-WF62 Super Electra	1467		20. 6.38	DBF in forced landing at Luxeuil, France on 11.8.39. Canx.
G-AFGO	Lockheed 14-WF62 Super Electra	1468		20. 6.38	Crashed near Portishead, Bristol on 22.11.38. Canx.
G-AFGP	Lockheed 14-WF62 Super Electra	1469		20. 6.38	Crashed at Khartoum, Sudan on 4.8.41. Canx.
G-AFGR	Lockheed 14-WF62 Super Electra	1470		20. 6.38	Crashed at El Fasher, Sudan on 19.1.41. Canx.
G-AFGS	BA Swallow II	483		. 4.38	Stalled and crashed into sea off Folkestone Beach during a forced landing on 6.7.38 & DBR. Canx.
G-AFGT	DH.82A Tiger Moth	3681	(G-AMEA) W7955/G-AFGT	25. 4.38	To R.Thailand Navy in 1/51. Canx.
G-AFGU	Percival P.10 Vega Gull	K.92		19. 4.38	Crashed & burned at Brundholme, Ghyll, Westmoreland on 14.5.38. Canx.
G-AFGV	BA Swallow II	485		22. 4.38	To Ireland as EI-AFN in 8/50. Canx.
G-AFGW	DH.82A Tiger Moth	3684		5. 5.38	Sold abroad in 2/40. Canx.
G-AFGX	Percival P.16A Q-Six	Q.27		9. 5.38	To RAF as X9336 in 3/40. Canx 8.3.40.
G-AFGY	DH.82A Tiger Moth	3699		9. 5.38	To RAF as BB740 in 10/40. Canx 30.10.40.
G-AFGZ	DH.82A Tiger Moth	3700	G-AMHI BB759/G-AFGZ	9. 5.38	
G-AFHA	Mosscraft MA.1	MA.1/2		27. 2.67	Not built. (Small components only stored)
G-AFHB	Stinson SR-10B Reliant (Restored 12/45 as SR-10J)	5819	W7981 G-AFHB	22. 7.38	To Kenya as VP-KDK in 10/46. Canx.
G-AFHC	BA L.25c Swallow II	486		17. 5.38	(Stored 1/98)
G-AFHD	BA Swallow II	487		17. 5.38	Scrapped at Tollerton in 12/46. Canx.
G-AFHE	DH.87B Hornet Moth	8158		17. 6.38	To South Africa AF as SAAF 1586 in 2/40. Canx.
G-AFHF	Taylorcraft Model A	X458		23. 5.38	DBF at Ely, Cambs on 21.1.39. Canx.
G-AFHG	Percival P.16A Q-Six	Q.26		10. 5.38	To RAF as X9329 in 2/40. Canx 26.2.40.
G-AFHH	BA Swallow II	488		24. 5.38	To Ireland as EI-AGH 10/53. Canx.
G-AFHI	DH.82A Tiger Moth	3682		21. 5.38	To RAF as BD151 in 8/40. Canx 7.8.40.
G-AFHJ	Bristol F.2b Fighter (Originally c/n 4573, rebuilt c.1923 with new c/n 6331, and again c.1928 with present c/n)	7146	F4587	23. 5.38	Destroyed by enemy action between 1939 and 1945. Canx.
G-AFHK	BA Swallow II	491		1. 6.38	Scrapped at Hanworth in 12/46. Canx.
G-AFHL	BA Swallow II	492		1. 6.38	Scrapped at Hanworth in 12/46. Canx.
G-AFHM	BA Swallow II	493		1. 6.38	To Ireland as EI-AEC in 7/48. Canx 17.7.48.
G-AFHN	BA Swallow II	494		7. 6.38	Crashed at Feltham on 15.7.39. Canx.
G-AFHO	BA Swallow II	495		7. 6.38	Scrapped at Hanworth in 12/46. Canx.
G-AFHP	BA Swallow II	496		7. 6.38	Scrapped at Hanworth in 12/46. Canx.
G-AFHR	BA Swallow II	489		7. 6.38	To New Zealand as ZK-AGO in 6/38. Canx.
G-AFHS	BA Swallow II	490		7. 6.38	Crashed at Merstham, Surrey on 24.7.60. Canx.
G-AFHT	DH.82A Tiger Moth	3695		30. 6.38	To RAF as BD142 in 7/40. Canx 22.7.40.
G-AFHU	BA Swallow II	497		8. 6.38	Scrapped at Hanworth in 12/46. Canx.
G-AFHV	BA Swallow II	498		8. 6.38	Scrapped at Hanworth in 12/46. Canx.
G-AFHW	BA Swallow II	499		8. 6.38	Scrapped at Hanworth in 12/46. Canx.
G-AFHX	DH.87A Hornet Moth	8022	OE-DKS	9. 6.38	To France as F-ARAS in 6/38. Canx 21.6.38.
G-AFHY	DH.89A Dragon Rapide	6417		1. 7.38	To Belgium in 6/50 for spares use. Canx 9.6.50.
G-AFHZ	DH.89A Dragon Rapide	6418		1. 7.38	To Uganda as VP-UAX in 9/47. Canx.
G-AFIA	DH.89A Dragon Rapide	6419		1. 7.38	DBF at Abadan, Iraq on 20.8.42. Canx.
G-AFIB	Hawker Tomtit	-	K1781	18. 6.38	Destroyed by enemy action in 10/43. Later used as a road block. Canx.
G-AFIC	BA Eagle II	141		23. 6.38	To India as VT-AKO in 10/38. Canx.
G-AFID	Barnwell BSW Mk.1 (BSW = Barnwell Scott Whitchurch)	1		20. 6.38	Fatal crash at Whitchurch on 2.8.38. Canx.
G-AFIE	Percival P.10 Vega Gull	K.99		30. 6.38	Destroyed in air raid at Hendon on 7.10.40. Canx.
G-AFIF	Douglas DC-1-109	1137	N233Y NS233Y/NR233Y/NX233Y	25. 6.38	To Spain as EC-AGJ in 9/38. Canx in 10/38.
G-AFIG	BA Swallow II	472		28. 6.38	Crashed at Sleaford, Lincs on 19.9.38. Canx.
G-AFIH	BA Swallow II	500		28. 6.38	To Ireland as EI-AGA in 6/52. Canx 9.6.52.
G-AFII	BA Swallow II	501		28. 6.38	Scrapped at Hanworth in 12/46. Canx.
G-AFIJ	BA Swallow II	502		28. 6.38	To Switzerland as HB-AKI in 6/39. Canx 19.6.39.
G-AFIK	BA Swallow II	503		28. 6.38	Scrapped at Hanworth in 12/46. Canx.
G-AFIL	BA Swallow II	504		28. 6.38	Scrapped at Hanworth in 12/46. Canx.
G-AFIM	Percival P.10 Vega Gull	K.93		28. 6.38	Abandoned at Le Bourget, France in 5/40. Canx.
G-AFIN	Chrislea LC.1 Airguard	LC.1		7. 7.38	Scrapped in 2/46. (New fuselage built by K.Fern combined with original wings/tail etc) (Stored 3/96)
G-AFIO	Piper J3 Cub	2348		19. 7.38	Scrapped between 1939 & 1945. Canx.
G-AFIP	General Aircraft Monospar ST.25 Universal	GAL/ST25/99		7. 7.38	To RAF as X9333 in 3/40. Canx 6.3.40.

Regn	Type	c/n	Previous identity	Regn date	Fate or immediate subsequent identity (if known)
G-AFIR	Luton LA-4 Minor	JSS.2		7. 7.38	
G-AFIS	BA Eagle II	143		8. 7.38	To India as VT-AKP in 1/39. Canx.
G-AFIT	Percival P.10 Vega Gull	K.90		18. 7.38	To RAF as W9375 in 9/39. Canx 28.9.39.
G-AFIU	Parker CA-4 Parasol Monoplane (Despite 1982 regn date, this is a pre-war Luton Minor type built under these reserved marks in 1938)	CA-4		19.10.82	No Permit to Fly issued. (Stored by N.H.Ponsford 3/96) Canx by CAA 31.3.99.
G-AFIV	General Aircraft Monospar ST.25 Universal	GAL/ST25/100		28. 7.38	To RAF as X9334 in 3/40. Canx 6.3.40.
G-AFIW	Percival P.16A Q-Six	Q.30		27. 7.38	Broken up for spares at Luton in 9/49. Canx.
G-AFIX	Percival P.16A Q-Six	Q.31	X9406 G-AFIX	. 7.38	Crashed on landing at Broomhall on 6.5.49. Canx.
G-AFIY	Piper J3C Cub	2425		27. 8.38	Broken up at Bury St.Edmunds, Suffolk in 12/41. Canx.
G-AFIZ	Piper J3C-50 Cub	2424		. 8.38	To Ireland as EI-ADR in 11/47. Canx 15.11.47.
G-AFJA	Taylor-Watkinson Dingbat	DB.100		2. 8.38	Damaged on take-off from Headcorn on 19.5.75 and partially rebuilt. (Stored 4/94 Berkswell, Coventry)
G-AFJB	Foster-Wikner GM.1 Wicko	5	DR613 G-AFJB	15. 8.38	(Stored at Berkeswell, near Coventry /96)
G-AFJC	Aeronca 50C Chief	C1028		29. 8.38	Scrapped in 5/49. Canx.
G-AFJD	Airspeed AS.6J Envoy III	76		2. 8.38	To RAF as N9107 in 8/38. Canx.
G-AFJE	Airspeed AS.6J Envoy III	77		2. 8.38	To RAF as N9108 in 8/38. Canx.
G-AFJF	DH.82A Tiger Moth	3722		22. 8.38	To R.New Zealand AF as NZ734 in 1/40. Canx.
G-AFJG	DH.82A Tiger Moth	3724		23. 8.38	To RAF as (AX787)/AX791. Canx 22.7.40.
G-AFJH	DH.82A Tiger Moth	3725		23. 8.38	To RAF as AX788 in 7/40. Canx 22.7.40.
G-AFJI	DH.82A Tiger Moth	3747		22. 8.38	To R.New Zealand AF as NZ733 in 1/40. Canx.
G-AFJJ	Miles M.11A Whitney Straight	306	OO-UMK	19. 8.38	To RAF as BD168 in 8/40. Canx 14.8.40.
G-AFJK	DH.82A Tiger Moth	3748	BB760 G-AFJK	22. 8.38	DBR at Squires Gate on 16.4.54. Canx.
G-AFJL	DH.82A Tiger Moth	3749		22. 8.38	To R.New Zealand AF as NZ730 in 1/40. Canx.
G-AFJM	DH.82A Tiger Moth	3766		23. 8.38	To RAF as BD170 in 8/40. Canx 23.9.40.
G-AFJN	DH.82A Tiger Moth	3767		23. 8.38	To RAF as BD171 in 8/40. Canx 23.8.40.
G-AFJO	Taylorcraft Model A	X568		22. 8.38	Crashed at Staverton on 15.6.52. Canx.
G-AFJP	Taylorcraft Model A	X585		17. 8.38	Crashed on take-off from a field 1 mile west of RAF Woodbridge, Suffolk on 3.10.53. Canx.
G-AFJR	Tipsy Trainer I (Was converted to Belfair)(For static rebuild as Trainer I with remains of G-AFRV)	2		20. 8.38	Canx as TWFU 12.4.89. To Musee Royal de L'Armee (Stored .92 Brussels)
G-AFJS	Tipsy Trainer I	3		. 8.38	Crashed at St.Mellons, Cardiff on 3.7.55. Canx.
G-AFJT	Tipsy Trainer I	4		. 8.38	To Finland as OH-SVA in 8/50. Canx 28.8.50.
G-AFJU	Miles M.17 Monarch	789	X9306 G-AFJU	25. 8.38	Aircraft Preservation Society of Scotland (On display at East Fortune)
G-AFJV	Mosscraft MA.2	MA.2/2		27. 2.67	Not built. (Small components only stored)
G-AFJW	Taylorcraft Model A	X619		. 8.38	Crashed at Rearsby in 1939. Canx.
G-AFJX	Miles M.11A Whitney Straight	507	BD183 G-AFJX	30. 8.38	To New Zealand as ZK-AUK in 4/50. Canx 21.3.50.
G-AFJY	McClure	-		. 9.38R	NTU - Not built. Canx.
G-AFJZ	Miles M.17 Monarch	790		5. 9.38	To RAF as W6462 in 11/39. Canx 1.11.39.
G-AFKA	DH.60G Gipsy Moth	1000	EI-AAC	27. 9.38	To RAF as DG582 in 1/41. Canx 25.1.41. Then to 292 ATC Sqdn at Eccles, Manchester as 2592M (stored at Education Offices, Clarendon Road, Manchester).
G-AFKB	Hawker Tomtit	-	K1785	. 9.38	Crashed at Braunstone, Leics on 13.7.39. Canx.
G-AFKC	Percival P.16A Q-Six	Q.33		10. 9.38	To RAF as W6085 in 2/40. Canx 3.2.40.
G-AFKD	Lockheed 14-WF62 Super Electra	1484		20.10.38	Crashed on a mountain near Loch Lomond on 22.4.40. Canx.
G-AFKE	Lockheed 14-WF62 Super Electra	1485		20.10.38	To RAF as HK982 in 11/43. Canx 19.11.43.
G-AFKF	Parnall 382 Heck III	T.20	J-1	14. 9.39	To RAF as R9138 in 6/41. Canx 16.6.41.
G-AFKG	Percival P.16A Q-Six	Q.32		24. 9.38	To RAF as X9363 in 3/40. Canx 4.3.40.
G-AFKH	BA Eagle II	142		28. 9.38	To Switzerland as HB-EBE in 1939. Canx.
G-AFKI	DH.83 Fox Moth	4003	EI-AAP (ZS-ADE)	27. 9.38	To RAF in 8/41. Canx 31.8.41.
G-AFKJ	Grumman G.21A Goose	1049		30. 9.38	To RAF as MV993 in 2/41. Canx.
G-AFKK	Foster-Wikner Wicko GM.1	8		6.10.38	To RAF as ES913 in 5/41. Canx 3.5.41.
G-AFKL	Miles M.2H Hawk Major	221		5.10.38	Crashed at Woodley on 29.3.39. Canx.
G-AFKM	DH.60M Moth	1509	K1227	4.10.38	To India as VT-ANT in 8/40. Canx 17.8.40.
G-AFKN	Taylorcraft Model A	X628		29.10.38	Crashed at Bury St.Edmunds, Suffolk on 11.3.39. Canx.
G-AFKO	Taylorcraft Model BC	X1091		15.12.38	WFU in 1943 and converted to Taylorcraft H Glider. Canx.
G-AFKP	Tipsy Trainer I	5	F-0222 G-AFKP	29.10.38	Crashed at Gedaref, Sudan on 4.6.52. Canx.
G-AFKR	Lockheed 12A	1267		10.11.38	To France as F-ARQA in 4/39. Canx 29.4.39.
G-AFKS	Foster-Wikner Wicko GM.1	6		5.11.38	To RAF as HM574 in 6/42. Canx 30.6.42.
G-AFKT	Hillson Helvellyn	HA.200		7.11.38	Broken up in 11/42. Canx.
G-AFKU	Foster-Wikner Wicko GM.1	7		9.11.38	To RAF as ES947 in 8/41. Canx 24.8.41.
G-AFKV	DH.80A Puss Moth	2118	VP-KAK	9.11.38	To Sweden as SE-AHO in 12/38. Canx 7.12.38.
G-AFKW	Fairchild F.24C8-E	2817	VH-AAW	4.10.38	To RAF as BK868 in 12/40. Canx 4.12.40.
G-AFKX	Hawker Hurricane Mk.I	5436	L1606	29.10.38	Last recorded flight was on 4.5.41 & WFU. Canx.
G-AFKY	DH.60G Gipsy Moth	1887	OO-AMR	24.10.38	To RAF as X5042 in 11/39. Canx 12.11.39.
G-AFKZ	Short S.30 Empire	S.1003		10.11.38	Scrapped at Hythe in 1947. Canx.
G-AFLA	Bristol 142M Blenheim I	9222		20.10.38	To Turkish AF as 397 in 11/38. Canx.
G-AFLB	Bristol 142M Blenheim I	9223		20.10.38	To Turkish AF as 398 in 11/38. Canx.
G-AFLC	Bristol 142M Blenheim I	9224		20.10.38	To Turkish AF as 399 in 11/38. Canx.
G-AFLD	Bristol 142M Blenheim I	9225		20.10.38	To Turkish AF as 400 in 12/38. Canx.
G-AFLE	Bristol 142M Blenheim I	9226		20.10.38	To Turkish AF as 401 in 12/38. Canx.
G-AFLF	Bristol 142M Blenheim I	9227		20.10.38	To Turkish AF as 402 in 12/38. Canx.
G-AFLG	Bristol 142M Blenheim I	9228		20.10.38	To Turkish AF as 403 in 1/39. Canx.
G-AFLH	Bristol 142M Blenheim I	9229		20.10.38	To Turkish AF as 404 in 1/39. Canx.
G-AFLI	Bristol 142M Blenheim I	9230		20.10.38	To Turkish AF as 405 in 1/39. Canx.

Regn	Type	c/n	Previous identity	Regn date	Fate or immediate subsequent identity (if known)
G-AFLJ	Bristol 142M Blenheim I	9231		20.10.38	To Turkish AF as 406 in 1/39. Canx.
G-AFLK	Bristol 142M Blenheim I	9232		20.10.38	To Turkish AF as 407 in 1/39. Canx.
G-AFLL	Bristol 142M Blenheim I	9233		20.10.38	To Turkish AF as 408 in 1/39. Canx.
G-AFLM	Bristol 142M Blenheim I	9234		20.10.38	To Turkish AF as 485 in 2/39. Canx.
G-AFLN	Bristol 142M Blenheim I	9235		20.10.38	To Turkish AF as 486 in 2/39. Canx.
G-AFLO	Bristol 142M Blenheim I	9236		20.10.38	To Turkish AF as 487 in 2/39. Canx.
G-AFLP	Bristol 142M Blenheim I	9237		20.10.38	To Turkish AF as 488 in 2/39. Canx.
G-AFLR	Bristol 142M Blenheim I	9238		20.10.38	To Turkish AF as 489 in 2/39. Canx.
G-AFLS	Bristol 142M Blenheim I	9239		20.10.38	To Turkish AF as 490 in 2/39. Canx.
G-AFLT(1)	Aeronca Ely 700	AB.131		31.10.38	Not certificated. Scrapped in 1941. Canx 10.2.41.
G-AFLT(2)	Miles M.65 Gemini 1A	6520	EI-ADM	14.11.47	Crashed at Burpham, near Guildford on 10.1.54. Canx.
G-AFLU	Aeronca Ely 700	AB.130		31.10.38	WFU at Farnborough in 11/52. Cannibalised. Canx.
G-AFLV	DH.60G Gipsy Moth	1847	OO-ARG	11. 3.39	To RAF as AW145 in 6/40. Canx 23.6.40.
G-AFLW	Miles M.17 Monarch	792		2.11.38	
G-AFLX	DH.82A Tiger Moth	3790		11.11.38	To India as VT-AOD in 9/40. Canx.
G-AFLY	DH.89A Dragon Rapide	6426		22.11.38	To RAF as Z7253 in 7/40. Canx 13.7.40.
G-AFLZ	DH.89A Dragon Rapide	6429		22.11.38	To RAF as Z7254 in 7/40. Restored as G-AHPX in 5/46. Canx 15.7.40.
G-AFMA	DH.89A Dragon Rapide	6430	UN-73 G-AFMA/Z7255/G-AFMA	22.11.38	To Portugal as CS-AEB in 4/50. Canx 13.4.50.
G-AFMB	Cunliffe-Owen Flying Wing	OA.1		22.11.38	To Free French AF in West Africa in 5/41. Canx.
G-AFMC	DH.82A Tiger Moth	3793		6.12.38	To RAF as AX783 in 7/40. Canx 22.7.40.
G-AFMD	DH.82A Tiger Moth	3794		6.12.38	To RAF as AX785 in 7/40. Canx 22.7.40.
G-AFME	DH.89A Dragon Rapide	6431		9.12.38	To RAF as Z7257 in 7/40. Canx 15.7.40.
G-AFMF	DH.89A Dragon Rapide (Rebuilt in 1949 with parts from G-AHXY)	6432	Z7256 G-AFMF	9.12.38	Crashed near Hexham on 19.2.54. Canx.
G-AFMG	DH.89A Dragon Rapide	6433	Z7259 G-AFMG	9.12.38	To Ireland as EI-AEA in 5/48. Canx 21.5.48.
G-AFMH	DH.89A Dragon Rapide	6434		9.12.38	To RAF as Z7258 in 7/40. Canx 15.7.40.
G-AFMI	DH.89A Dragon Rapide	6435		9.12.38	To RAF as Z7260 in 7/40. Canx 15.7.40.
G-AFMJ	DH.89A Dragon Rapide	6436	Z7261 G-AFMJ	9.12.38	To Paraguay as ZP-TDH in 9/56. Canx 17.9.56.
G-AFMK	Short S.32	S.1022		19.12.38	Not completed & order canx 17.10.39. Canx 1.1.46 in census.
G-AFML	Short S.32	S.1023		19.12.38	Not completed & order canx 17.10.39. Canx 1.1.46 in census.
G-AFMM	Short S.32	S.1024		19.12.38	Not completed & order canx 17.10.39. Canx 1.1.46 in census.
G-AFMN	Tipsy Trainer I	6		15.12.38	DBF at Hooton Park on 8.7.40. Canx.
G-AFMO(1)	Lockheed 14-WF62 Super Electra	1490		3. 1.39	Crashed at Heston on 15.1.40. Canx.
G-AFMO(2)	Lockheed B.14	1761		21. 3.40	Canx 22.11.45.
G-AFMP	DH.87B Hornet Moth	8120	EI-ABO	2. 1.39	To RAF as W5782 in 1/40. Canx 22.1.40.
G-AFMR	Lockheed 14-WF62 Super Electra	1491		3. 1.39	To RAF as HK984 in 10/43. Canx.
G-AFMS	Mosscraft MA.2	2	CF-BUB G-AFMS	2. 1.39	Crashed at Builth Wells on 7.7.58. Canx.
G-AFMT	Percival P.16A Q-Six	Q.25	(VH-ABL)	2. 1.39	To RAF as X9454 in 4/40. Canx 9.4.40.
G-AFMU	Luton LA-5 Major	LA.5/1		3. 1.39	DBF at Gerrards Cross in 1943. Canx.
G-AFMV	Percival P.16A Q-Six	Q.37		10. 1.39	To RAF as HK838 in 12/41. Canx 4.12.41.
G-AFMW	Zlin XII-38 Srs.2	1001	OK-LZX	18. 1.39	Scrapped at Gravesend between 1939 and 1945. Canx.
G-AFMX	Zlin XII-2 Srs.1	153	OK-TBK	18. 1.39	Scrapped at Gravesend between 1939 and 1945. Canx.
G-AFMY	DH.60M Moth	1657	K1907	16. 1.39	To RAF as X5051 in 11/39. Canx 18.11.39.
G-AFMZ	DH.94 Moth Minor	94029		10. 7.39	To RAF as AW151 in 6/40. Canx 26.6.40.
G-AFNA	DH.94 Moth Minor	94058		21. 7.39	To South Africa 9/39 - no known marks allotted. To R.Australian AF as A21-1 in 1/40. Canx.
G-AFNB	DH.94 Moth Minor	94066		19. 8.39	NTU - To R.Australian AF as A21-7 in 2/40. Canx.
G-AFNC	DH.94A Dragon Rapide	6442	V4724 G-AFNC	1. 2.39	To Belgium as OO-CCD in 8/46. Canx 14.8.46.
G-AFND	DH.89A Dragon Rapide	6443	V4725 G-AFND	1. 2.39	To TransJordan as TJ-AAP in 7/48. Canx 13.7.48.
G-AFNE	DH.94 Moth Minor	94009		23. 5.39	Sold abroad in 1/40. Canx 25.1.40.
G-AFNF	DH.94 Moth Minor	94010	BK838 G-AFNF	1. 5.39	To France as F-BFYR in 10/51. Canx 18.10.51.
G-AFNG	DH.94 Moth Minor Coupé	94014	AW112 G-AFNG	2. 5.39	
G-AFNH	DH.94 Moth Minor	94023	BK839 G-AFNH	9. 5.39	Crashed in Isle of Skye on 15.4.49. Canx.
G-AFNI	DH.94 Moth Minor (Cabin)	94035	W7972 G-AFNI	11. 5.39	(On rebuild 6/94)
G-AFNJ	DH.94 Moth Minor	94038	AW113 G-AFNJ	15. 5.39	To France as F-BAOG in 7/54. Canx 17.7.54.
G-AFNK	DH.94 Moth Minor	94048		31. 7.39	To RAF as BK847 in 9/40. Canx 12.9.40.
G-AFNL	DH.82A Tiger Moth	82185		28. 6.39	To R.New Zealand AF as NZ736 in 1/40. Canx.
G-AFNM	DH.82A Tiger Moth	82186		22. 6.39	To Australia as VH-ADO (allotted 21.2.40) - NTU; To R.Australian AF as A17-684 in 7/40. Canx 9.2.40.
G-AFNN	DH.94 Moth Minor	94067		23. 8.39	NTU - To R.Australia AF, but NTU - regd as VH-ACR on 17.1.40. Canx.
G-AFNO	DH.94 Moth Minor	94060		. 7.39R	NTU - To R.Australian AF as A21-4 in 2/40. Canx.
G-AFNP	DH.82A Tiger Moth	3881		30. 1.39	To India as VT-AMH in 5/40. Canx 27.5.40.
G-AFNR	DH.82A Tiger Moth	3882		30. 1.39	To RAF as W7952 in 1/40. Canx 15.1.40.
G-AFNS	DH.82A Tiger Moth	3883		30. 1.39	To South African AF as SAAF 1496 in 6/40. Canx 10.6.40.
G-AFNT	DH.82A Tiger Moth	3884		30. 1.39	To South African AF as SAAF 1495 in 6/40. Canx 10.6.40.
G-AFNU	DH.82A Tiger Moth	3885		30. 1.39	To South Africa in 5/40. Canx 6.5.40.
G-AFNV	DH.82A Tiger Moth	3886		30. 1.39	To South Africa as ZS-ATN in 5/40. Canx 6.5.40.
G-AFNW	Taylorcraft Plus C	100		11. 1.39	To RAF as ES956 in 7/41. Canx 31.7.41.

Regn	Type	c/n	Previous identity	Regn date	Fate or immediate subsequent identity (if known)
G-AFNX	DH.94 Moth Minor	94072		. 7.39R	NTU - To R.Australia AF in 1939, but NTU - regd as VH-ACQ on 16.1.40. Canx.
G-AFNY	DH.94 Moth Minor Coupé	9401		13. 4.39	Believed destroyed at Lee-on-Solent by a German bomb raid on 16.8.40. Canx.
G-AFNZ	DH.94 Moth Minor	94050		24. 7.39	To R.Australian AF as A21-5 in 2/40. Canx in 10/39.
G-AFOA	DH.94 Moth Minor	94074		10. 8.39	NTU - To R.Australian AF as A21-11 in 2/40. Canx.
G-AFOB	DH.94 Moth Minor	94018	X5117 G-AFOB	16. 5.39	(Stored 4/94 Chalmington)
G-AFOC	DH.94 Moth Minor	94042		16. 5.39	To RAF as X5115 in 11/39. Canx 21.11.39.
G-AFOD	DH.94 Moth Minor	94022	X5120 G-AFOD	9. 5.39	WFU on 20.6.47. Broken up for spares at Eastleigh in 1949.
G-AFOE	DH.94 Moth Minor	94024		9. 5.39	To RAF as X5121 in 12/39. Canx 16.12.39.
G-AFOF	DH.94 Moth Minor	94056		31. 7.39	To R.Australian AF as A21-2 in 2/40. Canx in 1939.
G-AFOG	DH.94 Moth Minor	94063		23. 8.39	To R.Australian AF as A21-6 in 2/40. Canx.
G-AFOH	Cessna C-145 Airmaster	463	N19495 NC19495	17. 8.81	Restored as N19495 11/83. Canx 28.10.83.
"G-AFOH"	Handley Page HP.70 Halifax C.VIII	1369	G-AJNW PP296	----	In 12/50 these marks was used by this aircraft in the film "No Highway" and converted to the fictitious Reindeer aircraft with tricycle undercarriage, four "jets" and a single fin and rudder. See G-AJNW.
G-AFOI	DH.89A Dragon Rapide	6450		28. 7.39	CofA lapsed 20.9.57 & WFU at Sywell. Scrapped. Canx.
G-AFOJ	DH.94 Moth Minor Coupé	9407	E-1 E-0236/G-AFOJ	21. 7.39	(To De Havilland Aircraft Museum) (On display at Salisbury Hall, London Colney)
G-AFOK	Heston Type 5 Racer	1		23. 1.39	DBR at Heston on 12.6.40. Canx.
G-AFOL	Heston Type 5 Racer	2		23. 1.39	NTU - Not completed. Canx.
G-AFOM	DH.94 Moth Minor	94008		24. 4.39	To Singapore as VR-SBJ 2/40; To Australia as VH-AED on 22.10.42. Canx.
G-AFON	DH.94 Moth Minor	94012		24. 4.39	To Australia 2/40 - no marks allotted; To New Zealand as ZK-AHK in 9/41. Canx 21.2.40.
G-AFOO	DH.94 Moth Minor	94033		11. 5.39	To Singapore as VR-SBI in 9/41; To Australia as VH-AEE on 21.3.45. Canx.
G-AFOP	DH.94 Moth Minor	94041		15. 5.39	To Holland as PH-AZG 9.4.40. Canx 7.3.40.
G-AFOR	DH.94 Moth Minor Coupé	9404		29. 8.39	To R.Australian AF as A21-14 in 2/40. Canx.
G-AFOS	DH.94 Moth Minor	94078		10. 8.39	To R.Australian AF as A21-13 in 2/40. Canx.
G-AFOT	DH.94 Moth Minor	94021		6. 5.39	To RAF as AV977 in 5/40. Canx 6.5.40.
G-AFOU	DH.94 Moth Minor	94039		16. 5.39	To RAF as X9298 in 2/40. Canx 29.2.40.
G-AFOV	DH.94 Moth Minor	94053		19. 7.39	To R.Australia AF, but NTU - regd as VH-ADJ on 24.1.40. Canx in 1939.
G-AFOW	DH.94 Moth Minor	94047		16. 5.39	To R.Australia AF 10/39, but NTU - regd as VH-ACS on 23.1.40. Canx 16.5.39.
G-AFOX	DH.94 Moth Minor	94027		9. 5.39	To RAF as W7973 in 1/40. Canx 26.1.40.
G-AFOY	DH.94 Moth Minor	94043		19. 5.39	To RAF as W7974 in 1/40. Canx 26.1.40.
G-AFOZ	DH.94 Moth Minor	94055	W7975 G-AFOZ	21. 7.39	Crashed during an aerobatic display at Turnhouse on 3.5.75. Canx 9.6.75 as destroyed.
G-AFPA	DH.94 Moth Minor	94065		16. 8.39	NTU - To R.Australian AF as A21-8 in 2/40. Canx.
G-AFPB	DH.94 Moth Minor	94015		5. 5.39	To RAF as W7971 in 1/40. Canx 26.1.40.
G-AFPC	DH.94 Moth Minor	94007		25. 4.39	To RAF as W6458 in 12/39. Canx 19.12.39.
G-AFPD	DH.94 Moth Minor	94034	W6459 G-AFPD	16. 5.39	To Ireland as EI-AKU in 6/59. Canx 25.6.59.
G-AFPE	DH.94 Moth Minor	94070		. 5.39R	NTU - To R.Australian AF as A21-10 in 2/40. Canx 29.8.39.
G-AFPF	Lockheed 12A	1270		1. 3.39	To France as F-ARPP in 5/39. Canx 20.5.39.
G-AFPG	DH.94 Moth Minor	94009		24. 4.39	To 1220 ATC Sqdn at March, Cambs as BD182 in 8/40. Canx 18.8.40.
G-AFPH	DH.94 Moth Minor	94016	X5133 G-AFPH	2. 5.39	To Singapore as VR-SDI in 1/52. Canx 26.11.51.
G-AFPI	DH.94 Moth Minor	94057		21. 7.39	To RAF as X5116 in 11/39. Canx 21.11.39.
G-AFPJ	DH.94 Moth Minor	94030		12. 5.39	To Egypt as SU-ACP in 11/41. Canx.
G-AFPK	DH.94 Moth Minor	94013		7. 7.39	To 650 ATC Sqdn at Uppingham as AX790 in 7/40. Canx 28.7.40.
G-AFPL	DH.94 Moth Minor Coupé	9408		24. 7.39	To RAF as HM584 in 10/42. Canx 3.2.42.
G-AFPM	DH.94 Moth Minor	94032	BK840 G-AFPM	31. 7.39	Crashed at Kirby Overblow, Harrogate on 12.5.51. Canx.
G-AFPN	DH.94 Moth Minor	94044	X9297 G-AFPN	23. 5.39	
G-AFPO	DH.94 Moth Minor	94052	HM544 G-AFPO	19. 7.39	Crashed at Prauthoy, France on 30.1.48. Canx.
G-AFPP	Piper J-4 Cub Coupé	4-441		1. 2.39	To West Germany as D-EDED in 6/56. Canx 21.6.56.
G-AFPR	DH.94 Moth Minor (Now small original components only)	94031	X5122 G-AFPR	16. 5.39	WFU on 15.4.56. Wings stored at Hamble in 1984. Reserved as ZK-AJN. (On rebuild .98 Gore, New Zealand) Canx 19.3.99 on sale to New Zealand.
G-AFPS	DH.94 Moth Minor	94059		31. 7.39	To RAF as W6460 in 12/39. Canx 14.12.39.
G-AFPT	DH.94 Moth Minor	94026	BK831 2611M/BK831/G-AFPT	10. 5.39	Crashed at White Waltham on 17.9.47. Canx.
G-AFPU	DH.94 Moth Minor	94045		19. 5.39	To RAF as BK832 in 8/40. Canx 26.8.40.
G-AFPV	Comper	-		. .39R	NTU. Canx.
G-AFPW	DH.94 Moth Minor	94064		18. 8.39	To R.Australian AF as A21-16 in 2/40. Canx.
G-AFPX	Willoughby Delta F	1		25. 1.39	Crashed at Calcott, near Bicester on 10.7.39. Canx.
G-AFPY	DH.60G Gipsy Moth (Reconstructed by Southern Aircraft)	RC/SA/1		17. 3.39	To RAF as X5049 in 11/39. Canx 15.11.39.
G-AFPZ	Short S.33 Empire	S.1025		27. 1.39	To Australia as A18-14, then regd as VH-ACD on 1.7.43. Canx 13.7.42.
G-AFRA	Short S.33 Empire	S.1026		27. 1.39	Scrapped at Hythe in 11/46. Canx.
G-AFRB	Short S.33 Empire	S.1027		27. 1.39	Construction abandoned in 5/40. Canx.

Regn	Type	c/n	Previous identity	Regn date	Fate or immediate subsequent identity (if known)
G-AFRC	Carine-Luton LA-4A Minor	JRC.1		30. 1.39	Crashed at Closelake Airport, IoM on 12.3.39. Canx.
G-AFRD(1)	DH.94 Moth Minor	94001	E-4	4. 4.39	Crashed at Wheathamstead on 11.4.39. Canx.
G-AFRD(2)	DH.94 Moth Minor	94006		15. 5.39	To Australia in 1940 - allotted regn as VH-AAQ on 22.5.40; regd in New Zealand as ZK-AHI in 9/41. Canx.

Note: The crash of G-AFRD (c/n 94001) has been confirmed by John Cunningham's log book, and before the end of the month c/n 94006 had been substituted with the same registration, although the paperwork, naturally, continued to refer to c/n 94001. A problem then arises when on arrival in Australia, unless the maker's plate bearing the orginal c/n 94001 had been affixed to this alleged later airframe, some considerable difficulty would have occurred when it did arrive - from the Customs Department, the local de Havilland factory, and certainly the Department of Civil Aviation. Any of the Australian-standard inspections that would have taken place at this time in its history would have revealed this anomally immediately, under the then prevailing rigidity of these standards. In Australia de Havilland applied for registration of this aircraft on 16.5.40, and VH-AAQ was re-allotted on the 22nd (originally being allotted on 17.4.39 for believed intended use on c/n 94076) but with all paperwork showing the c/n as 94001!

Regn	Type	c/n	Previous identity	Regn date	Fate or immediate subsequent identity (if known)
G-AFRE	DH.87B Hornet Moth	8107	W5784 G-AFRE/EI-ABL	9. 2.39	To Gold Coast as VP-AAC in 3/52. Canx.
G-AFRF	DH.90 Dragonfly	7519	F-AOZC	9. 3.39	To RAF as AV993 in 6/40. Canx 22.6.40.
G-AFRG	Handley Page HP.54 Harrow I	6595	K6933	15. 2.39	To R.Canadian AF as 794 in 10/40. Canx 21.10.40.
G-AFRH	Handley Page HP.54 Harrow I	-	K7029	15. 2.39	To R.Canadian AF as 795 in 10/40. Canx 21.10.40.
G-AFRI	DH.90 Dragonfly	7536	F-APAX	27. 3.39	To RAF as AV994 in 6/40. Canx 26.6.40.
G-AFRJ	DH.94 Moth Minor	94068		31. 7.39	NTU - To R.Australian AF as A21-9 in 2/40. Canx.
G-AFRK	DH.89A Dragon Rapide	6441		9. 3.39	CofA lapsed 10.3.59. Broken up at Christchurch in 3/59. Canx.
G-AFRL	Handley Page HP.54 Harrow I	-	K7027	6. 3.39	Restored to RAF as K7027 on 21.10.40. Canx.
G-AFRM	Avro 504N	-	K1964	15. 3.39	DBF at Hooton Park on 8.7.40. Canx.
G-AFRN(1)	Messerschmitt Bf.108B-1 Taifun	2039		27. 3.39	To RAF as DK280 in 4/41. Canx 17.4.41.
G-AFRN(2)	Messerschmitt Bf.108B-1 Taifun	1660	ES995 (ES955)/G-AFZO/D-IDBT	19. 9.46	To Switzerland as HB-ESL in 4/50. Canx.
G-AFRO	Miles M.18 Mk.1	1075	U-2	11. 3.39	NTU - To U-0222 (B-Class marks) in 1940. Canx.
G-AFRP	Shapley Kittiwake Mk.II	ESS.2		23. 3.39	Crashed on Dartmoor in 12/46. Canx.
G-AFRR	DH.94 Moth Minor Coupé	9403	HM579 G-AFRR	13. 4.39	To New Zealand as ZK-BFP in 3/54. Canx 30.3.54.
G-AFRS	Stinson SR-10C Reliant	5904		21. 6.39	To RAF as W7978 in 2/40. Canx 21.2.40.
G-AFRT	Tipsy Trainer I	8		4. 5.39	Burned at Slough, Berks in 1952. Canx.
G-AFRU	Tipsy Trainer I	9		15. 7.39	Scrapped at Redhill in 1954. Canx.
G-AFRV	Tipsy Trainer I	10		15. 7.39	Struck cables on approach to Herrings Farm at Cross-in-Hand, Sussex on 15.9.79. Used for spares for rebuild of G-AFJR. Canx by CAA 10.2.87.
G-AFRW	Gunton Special	TFWG-1		21. 3.39	Construction not completed. Sold 5/45 and converted to Pivot Parasol as G-AGOO.
G-AFRX	Armstrong Whitworth AW.23	AW.1251	K3585	3. 4.39	Destroyed in German air raid while in storage at Ford on 18.8.40. Canx.
G-AFRY	DH.94 Moth Minor Coupé	9402	X5123 G-AFRY	15. 6.39	WFU at Perth on 10.12.51. Canx.
G-AFRZ	Miles M.17 Monarch	793	G-AIDE W6463/G-AFRZ	24. 3.39	(Stored 6/92)
G-AFSA	General Aircraft Monospar ST.25 Universal	GAL/ST25/101		24. 3.39	To RAF as X9331 in 3/40. Canx 6.3.40.
G-AFSB	General Aircraft Monospar ST.25 Universal	GAL/ST25/102		24. 3.39	To RAF as X9330 in 3/40. Canx 6.3.40.
G-AFSC	Tipsy Trainer 1	11		15. 7.39	
G-AFSD	DH.94 Moth Minor Coupé	9400	E-6	30. 3.39	To India as VT-AMF 5/40. Canx 30.5.40.
G-AFSE	DH.94 Moth Minor	94089		. 7.39R	NTU - To R.Australian AF as A21-25 in 3/40. Canx.
G-AFSF	DH.94 Moth Minor	94100		. 7.39R	NTU - To R.Australian AF as A21-35 in 4/40. Canx.
G-AFSG	DH.82A Tiger Moth	82097		20. 4.39	To RAF as W7954 in 2/40. Canx 15.1.40.
G-AFSH	DH.82A Tiger Moth	82139	X5106 G-AFSH	20. 4.39	To New Zealand as ZK-BAT in 3/52. Canx 23.3.52.
G-AFSI	DH.82A Tiger Moth	82142		20. 4.39	To RAF as X5107 in 2/40. Canx 5.1.40.
G-AFSJ	DH.82A Tiger Moth	82182	X5108 G-AFSJ	20. 4.39	Crashed near Warrington on 26.6.55. Canx.
G-AFSK	DH.82A Tiger Moth	82140		20. 4.39	Crashed near Wooler, Northumberland on 27.6.39. Canx.
G-AFSL	DH.82A Tiger Moth	82141		20. 4.39	To RAF as W7950 in 2/40. Canx 15.1.40.
G-AFSM	DH.82A Tiger Moth	82183	(G-AKTF) X5109/G-AFSM	20. 4.39	To Pakistan AF in 11/48. Canx 23.11.48.
G-AFSN	DH.82A Tiger Moth	82184		20. 4.39	To RAF as X5110 in 1/40. Canx 5.1.40.
G-AFSO	DH.89A Dragon Rapide	6445		21. 4.39	To RAF as W6457 in 1/40. Canx 23.1.40.
G-AFSP	DH.82A Tiger Moth	82584		22. 4.39	To RAF as W7951 in 2/40. Canx 15.1.40.
G-AFSR	DH.82A Tiger Moth	82585		22. 4.39	To RAF as W7953 in 2/40. Canx 15.1.40.
G-AFSS	DH.82A Tiger Moth	82586		22. 4.39	To RAF as X9318 in 3/40. Canx 2.3.40.
G-AFST	DH.82A Tiger Moth	82587		22. 4.39	To RAF as W7956 in 2/40. Canx 15.1.40.
G-AFSU	DH.82A Tiger Moth	82588		22. 4.39	To RAF as W7970 in 2/40. Canx 15.1.40.
G-AFSV	Chilton DW.1A	DW.1A/1		5. 4.39	(Rebuild nearing completion 12/93)
G-AFSW	Chilton DW.2	DW.2/1		6. 4.39	Not completed. (Fuselage box stored - possibly beyond rebuild)
G-AFSX	DH.82A Tiger Moth	82004	N6731	14. 4.39	To RAF as AX856 in 7/40. Canx 1.7.40.
G-AFSY	Piper J-4A Cub Coupé	4-510		27. 4.39	To RAF as HM565 in 5/42. Canx 30.5.42.
G-AFSZ	Piper J-4A Cub Coupé	4-538	BT440 G-AFSZ	30. 5.39	Crashed at Fairoaks on 30.5.62. Canx.
G-AFTA	Hawker 41 Tomtit	30380	K1786 G-AFTA/K1786	26. 4.39	
G-AFTB	Piper J-4A Cub Coupé	4-541		14. 6.39	To RAF as BV989 in 12/40. Canx 14.12.40.
G-AFTC	Piper J-4A Cub Coupé	4-525	BV990 G-AFTC	30. 5.39	To France as F-BFQS in 11/49. Canx.
G-AFTD	Piper J-4A Cub Coupé	4-542		14. 6.39	To RAF as HL531 in 10/41. Canx 15.10.41.

Regn	Type	c/n	Previous identity	Regn date	Fate or immediate subsequent identity (if known)
G-AFTE	Piper J-4A Cub Coupé	4-537		26. 5.39	Crashed at Leicester on 8.8.39. Canx.
G-AFTF	DH.90 Dragonfly	7533	VH-UXA	15. 4.39	To RAF as BD149 in 8/40. Canx 5.8.40.
G-AFTG	DH.60G Gipsy Moth	1927		1. 5.39	To RAF as X5054 in 11/39. Canx 17.11.39.
G-AFTH	DH.94 Moth Minor	94040		24. 7.39	To RAF as HM585 in 10/42. Canx 30.10.42.
G-AFTI	DH.82A Tiger Moth	82233		22. 8.39	To Dutch East Indies in 5/40. Canx 7.5.40.
G-AFTJ	DH.82A Tiger Moth	82575		4. 5.39	To Malaya as VR-RAU in 5/40. Canx 21.1.40.
G-AFTK	DH Technical School TK.5	2266		30. 3.39	Not flown. Scrapped at Hatfield in 1940. Canx.
G-AFTL	Lockheed 12A	1203	NC16077	15. 5.39	Extensively damaged in an air raid at Heston on 19.9.40. To Burbank, USA & rebuilt as NX21707, then Trinidad & Tobago as VP-TAI in 11/42. Canx 5.1.43.
G-AFTM	Stinson SR-9C Reliant	5160	NC2217	28. 7.39	To RAF as W7983 in 2/40. Canx 21.2.40.
G-AFTN	Taylorcraft Plus C/2 (Originally regd as Plus C)	102	HL535 G-AFTN	2. 5.39	CofA expired 1.11.57. On rebuild 10/97 for Leicestershire County Council Museums. Canx by CAA 13.1.99.
G-AFTO	Taylorcraft Plus C	103		2. 5.39	To RAF as HL533 in 9/41. Canx 30.9.41.
G-AFTP	Taylorcraft Plus C	104		2. 5.39	To RAF in 7/41. Canx 31.7.41.
G-AFTR	Miles M.14B Hawk Trainer II	1078		4. 5.39	To RAF as BB663 in 9/40. Canx 17.9.40.
G-AFTS	Miles M.14B Hawk Trainer II	1079		4. 5.39	To RAF as BB664 in 9/40. Canx 17.9.40.
G-AFTT	Taylorcraft Plus C	101		2. 5.39	To RAF in 7/41. Canx 21.7.41.
G-AFTU	Avro 652A Anson I	1111	N5150	15. 5.39	To Greek AF as TT51 in 5/39. Canx 27.5.39.
G-AFTV	Avro 652A Anson I	1112	N5155	15. 5.39	To Greek AF as TT52 in 5/39. Canx 27.5.39.
G-AFTW	Avro 652A Anson I	1113	N5160	15. 5.39	To Greek AF as TT53 in 5/39. Canx 27.5.39.
G-AFTX	Miles M.17 Monarch	795		11. 5.39	To F-ARRL in 11/39. Canx 27.7.39.
G-AFTY	Taylorcraft Plus C	105		19. 5.39	To RAF as HL536 in 9/41. Canx 30.9.41.
G-AFTZ	Taylorcraft Plus C	106		19. 5.39	To RAF as HH987 in 8/41. Canx 31.8.41.
G-AFUA	Taylorcraft Plus C/2 (Originally regd as Plus C)	107		19. 5.39	Crashed at Northaw, Middlesex on 18.10.48. Canx.
G-AFUB	Taylorcraft Plus D (Originally regd as Plus C, then C/2)	108	HL534 G-AFUB	19. 5.39	To Ireland as EI-AGD 6/53. Canx.
G-AFUC	Not allocated.				
G-AFUD	Taylocraft Plus C	109		19. 5.39	To RAF as HH986 in 8/41. Canx 31.8.41.
G-AFUE	DH.95 Flamingo	95001		18. 5.39	To RAF as T5357 in 10/39. Canx 21.10.39.
G-AFUF	DH.95 Flamingo	95002	E-1	8. 6.39	To RAF as X9317 in 3/40. Canx 2.3.40.
G-AFUG	Henry-Luton LA-4 Minor	WSH.1		18. 5.39	Not completed. Canx 1.12.46.
G-AFUH	Avro 652A Anson I	1114	N5165	19. 5.39	To Greek AF as TT54 in 6/39. Canx 10.6.39.
G-AFUI	Avro 652A Anson I	1115	N5170	19. 5.39	To Greek AF as TT55 in 6/39. Canx 10.6.39.
G-AFUJ	Avro 652A Anson I	1116	N5175	19. 5.39	To Greek AF as TT56 in 6/39. Canx 10.6.39.
G-AFUK	Not allocated.				
G-AFUL	Fouldes/HM.14 Pou du Ciel	THF/1		20. 5.39	Canx 12/46 in census.
G-AFUM	Avro 652A Anson I	1117	N5185	23. 5.39	To Greek AF as TT57 in 6/39. Canx 10.6.39.
G-AFUN	Avro 652A Anson I	1118	N5190	23. 5.39	To Greek AF as TT58 in 6/39. Canx 24.6.39.
G-AFUO	Avro 652A Anson I	1119	N5200	23. 5.39	To Greek AF as TT59 in 6/39. Canx 24.6.39.
G-AFUP	Luscombe 8A Master	1246	N25370 NC25370	7. 6.88	
G-AFUR	Avro 652A Anson I	1120	N5205	23. 5.39	To Greek AF as TT60 in 6/39. Canx 24.6.39.
G-AFUS	Avro 652A Anson I	1121	N5210	23. 5.39	To Greek AF as TT61 in 7/39. Canx 10.7.39.
G-AFUT	Avro 652A Anson I	1122	N5215	23. 5.39	To Greek AF as TT62 in 7/39. Canx 10.7.39.
G-AFUU	DH.94 Moth Minor	94084		. 7.39R	NTU - To R.Australian AF as A21-20 in 3/40. Canx.
G-AFUV	DH.94 Moth Minor	94085		. 7.39R	NTU - To R.Australian AF as A21-22 in 3/40. Canx.
G-AFUW	Stinson Junior R	8510	OO-HVS NC12157	22. 5.39	To RAF as X8522 in 2/40. Canx 10.2.40.
G-AFUX	Taylorcraft Plus C	111		13. 6.39	To RAF as HH988 in 8/41. Canx 31.8.41.
G-AFUY	Taylorcraft Plus C	112		13. 6.39	To RAF as ES957 in 7/41. Canx 31.7.41.
G-AFUZ	Taylorcraft Plus C	113		23. 6.39	To RAF as ES960 in 7/41. Canx 31.7.41.
G-AFVA	Taylorcraft Plus C	114		23. 6.39	To RAF as HH982 in 8/41. Canx 31.8.41.
G-AFVB	Taylorcraft Plus C	115		23. 6.39	To RAF as HH985 in 8/41. Canx 31.8.41.
G-AFVC	Percival P.16A Q-Six	Q.24	F-AQOK	30. 6.39	To RAF as AX860 in 5/40. Canx 10.5.40.
G-AFVD	Piper J-4A Cub Coupé	-		. 6.39R	NTU. Not Imported. Canx.
G-AFVE(1)	Piper J-4A Cub Coupé	-		. 6.39R	NTU. Not Imported. Canx.
G-AFVE(2)	DH.82A Tiger Moth	83720	T7230	1. 2.78	
G-AFVF	Piper J-4A Cub Coupé	4-586	BV991 G-AFVF	4. 7.39	Crashed at Gatwick on 24.6.48. Canx.
G-AFVG	Piper J-4A Cub Coupé	4-588		4. 7.39	To RAF as BV987 in 12/40. Canx 14.12.40.
G-AFVH	Tipsy S.2	29	OO-ASB	7. 6.39	To Belgium as OO-TIP in 7/49. Canx 27.7.49.
G-AFVI	Percival P.10 Vega Gull	K.109	P5992	9. 6.39	Crashed at Tortosa, Spain on 18.5.44. Canx.
G-AFVJ	DH.90 Dragonfly	7521	F-AOYK	12. 6.39	To RAF as X9337 in 3/40. Canx 6.3.40.
G-AFVK	Foster-Wikner Wicko GM.1	09		13. 6.39	To RAF as HM499 in 10/41. Canx 31.10.41.
G-AFVL	Piper J-4A Cub Coupé	4-543		21. 6.39	To RAF as BT441 in 11/40. Canx 21.11.40.
G-AFVM	Piper J-4A Cub Coupé	4-554		21. 6.39	To RAF as BV988 in 12/40. Canx 14.12.40.
G-AFVN	Tipsy Trainer I	12		15. 7.39	Permit expired 7.6.97. (Stored 8/97)
G-AFVO	Tipsy Trainer I	15		31. 8.39	To Belgium as OO-DAU in 9/46. Canx 5.9.46.
G-AFVP	Tipsy Trainer I	14		23. 8.39	Scrapped between 6/40 and 1945. Canx.
G-AFVR	GAL.42 Cygnet II	GAL/42/109	HL539 G-AFVR	14. 6.39	Crashed near Woerth, France on 26.8.69. Canx.
G-AFVS	Airspeed AS.46 Oxford	83		17. 6.39	Believed sunk in SS Athenia in transit to Canada 3.9.39. Canx.
G-AFVT	Stinson SR-10J Reliant (Originally regd as SR-10C)	5911		23. 8.39	To USA as N5913 in 9/68. Canx 30.9.68.
G-AFVU	Taylorcraft Plus C	116		5. 7.39	DBF at Maylands, Essex on 6/7.2.40. Canx.
G-AFVV	Hawker Tomtit	-	K1784	4. 7.39	Canx in 11/45.
G-AFVW	Taylorcraft Plus C/2 (Originally regd as Plus C)	117		5. 7.39	To RAF as HL532 in 9/41. Canx 30.9.41.
G-AFVX	Taylorcraft Plus C/2 (Originally regd as Plus C)	118		5. 7.39	To RAF as HM501 in 10/41. Canx 31.10.41.

Regn	Type	c/n	Previous identity	Regn date	Fate or immediate subsequent identity (if known)
G-AFVY	Taylorcraft Plus C/2 (Originally regd as Plus C)	119		5. 7.39	To RAF as HH984 in 8/41. Canx 31.8.41.
G-AFVZ	Taylorcraft Plus C/2 (Originally regd as Plus C)	120		5. 7.39	To RAF as HH983 in 8/41. Canx 31.8.41.
G-AFWA	Piper J-4A Cub Coupé	4-558		4. 7.39	To RAF as BV180 in 3/41. Canx 3.4.41.
G-AFWB	Piper J-4A Cub Coupé	4-559		4. 7.39	To RAF as BV181 in 3/41. Canx 3.4.41.
G-AFWC	DH.82A Tiger Moth	82589		13. 7.39	To RAF as W6417 in 2/40. Canx 24.4.40.
G-AFWD	DH.82A Tiger Moth	82590		13. 7.39	To RAF as W6418 in 2/40. Canx 24.4.40.
G-AFWE	DH.82A Tiger Moth	82591		13. 7.39	To RAF as W6419 in 2/40. Canx 24.4.40.
G-AFWF	DH.82A Tiger Moth	82592		13. 7.39	To RAF as W6420 in 2/40. Canx 24.4.40.
G-AFWG	Percival P.10 Vega Gull	K.71	L7272	3. 7.39	CofA expired in 12/46. (Was based at Buenos Aires, Argentina) Canx.
G-AFWH	Piper J/4A Cub Coupé	4-1341	N33093 NC33093	14. 1.82	
G-AFWI	DH.82A Tiger Moth	82187	8218M BB814/G-AFWI	19. 7.39	
G-AFWJ	DH.60M Moth	1600	K1860	17. 7.39	To RAF as W9368 in 2/40. Canx 17.7.40.
G-AFWK	Taylorcraft Plus C	121		1. 8.39	To RAF as ES958 in 7/41. Canx 10.9.41.
G-AFWL	Taylorcraft Plus C	122		1. 8.39	Dismantled at Rearsby on 29.5.40; rebuilt as G-AGBF c/n 131 in 6/40. Canx.
G-AFWM	Taylorcraft Plus C/2 (Originally regd as Plus C)	123	ES959 G-AFWM	1. 8.39	WFU in 8/56. Scrapped in 1961. Canx.
G-AFWN	Auster J/1 Autocrat (Originally regd as Taylorcraft Plus D, converted in 1945)	124		1. 8.39	To West Germany as D-EKOM in 9/56. Canx 23.7.56.
G-AFWO	Taylorcraft Plus D	125	X7534 G-AFWO	1. 8.39	Crashed at Willesden, North London on 29.5.63. Canx.
G-AFWP	General Aircraft Monospar ST.25 Universal	GAL/ST25/103		19. 7.39	To RAF as X9335 in 3/40. Canx 24.4.40.
G-AFWR	Piper J-4A Cub Coupé	4-589	NC23471	11. 8.39	To RAF as BT442 in 11/40. Canx 27.12.40.
G-AFWS	Piper J-4A Cub Coupé	4-612	ES923 G-AFWS/NC23491	2. 8.39	To Finland as OH-CPB in 7/51. Canx.
G-AFWT	Tipsy Trainer 1	13		1. 8.39	
G-AFWU	Piper J-4A Cub Coupé	4-619	NC24531	2. 8.39	Scrapped between 1939 and 1945. Canx.
G-AFWV	Piper J-4A Cub Coupé	4-622	NC24530	2. 8.39	Sold to RAF as spares in 5/41. Canx 13.6.41.
G-AFWW	Piper J-4A Cub Coupé	4-618	NC24532	2. 8.39	Sold to RAF as spares in 5/41. Canx 13.6.41.
G-AFWX	DH.60G-III Moth	5032	EI-AAU	5. 8.39	Scrapped at Gatwick in 1945. Canx 12/46.
G-AFWY	Miles M.14A Hawk Trainer III	1080		27. 7.39	To RAF as BB665 in 9/40. Canx 19.9.40.
G-AFWZ	Airspeed AS.6K Envoy III	59	VT-AIC	1. 8.39	To RAF as X9370 in 3/40. Canx 17.7.40.
G-AFXA	Miles M.14A Hawk Trainer III	1081	(G-ALOG) BB666/G-AFXA	11. 8.39	Not re-converted. Scrapped in 1956. Canx.
G-AFXB	Miles M.14A Hawk Trainer III	1082		11. 8.39	To RAF as BB667 in 9/40. Canx 19.9.40.
G-AFXC	Aeronca Ely F.C.1	F.C.1		. 8.39R	NTU - Project abandoned. Canx.
G-AFXD	Bristol 149 Blenheim IV	9392	(P4910)	4. 8.39	To Greek AF in 1939/40. Canx.
G-AFXE	Bristol 149 Blenheim IV	9393	(P4911)	4. 8.39	To Greek AF in 1939/40. Canx.
G-AFXF	Bristol 149 Blenheim IV	9397	(P4915)	4. 8.39	To Greek AF in 1939/40. Canx.
G-AFXG	Bristol 149 Blenheim IV	9398	(P4916)	4. 8.39	To Greek AF in 1939/40. Canx.
G-AFXH	Bristol 149 Blenheim IV	9403	(P4921)	4. 8.39	To Greek AF in 1939/40. Canx.
G-AFXI	Bristol 149 Blenheim IV	9404	(P4922)	4. 8.39	To Greek AF in 1939/40. Canx.
G-AFXJ	Bristol 149 Blenheim IV	9416	(P6891)	4. 8.39	To Greek AF in 1939/40. Canx.
G-AFXK	Bristol 149 Blenheim IV	9417	(P6892)	4. 8.39	To Greek AF in 1939/40. Canx.
G-AFXL	Bristol 149 Blenheim IV	9422	(P6897)	4. 8.39	To Greek AF in 1939/40. Canx.
G-AFXM	Bristol 149 Blenheim IV	9423	(P6898)	4. 8.39	To Greek AF in 1939/40. Canx.
G-AFXN	Bristol 149 Blenheim IV	9428	(P6903)	4. 8.39	To Greek AF in 1939/40. Canx.
G-AFXO	Bristol 149 Blenheim IV	9429	(P6904)	4. 8.39	To Greek AF in 1939/40. Canx.
G-AFXP	Lockheed 12A	1274		12. 8.39	To India as VT-AMB in 3/40. Canx 6.3.40.
G-AFXR	Fokker F.XXII	5360	PH-AJR	9. 8.39	To RAF as HM159 in 10/41. Canx 15.10.41.
G-AFXS	Piper J-4A Cub Coupé	4-647	DG667 G-AFXS/NC24641	22. 8.39	To Finland as OH-CPF in 7/53. Canx 20.7.53.
G-AFXT	Piper J-4A Cub Coupé	4-653	NC24651	12.10.39	To RAF as DP852 in 3/41. Canx 26.4.41.
G-AFXU	Piper J-4A Cub Coupé	4-672	NC24731	12.10.39	To RAF as BV984 in 12/40. Canx.
G-AFXV	Piper J-4A Cub Coupé	4-693	NC24741	12.10.39	To RAF as BV986 in 12/40. Canx.
G-AFXW	Piper J-4A Cub Coupé	4-612	NC23491	. .39R	NTU - Already allocated G-AFWS 8/39. Canx.
G-AFXX	Piper J-4A Cub Coupé	4-696	NC24761	. .39R	To RAF as BV985 in 12/40. Canx.
G-AFXY	Piper J-4A Cub Coupé (Was possibly to become EI-ABZ but impressed into the RAF)	4-689	NC24771	. .39R	NTU - To RAF as HL530 in 10/40. Canx.
G-AFXZ	DH.82A Tiger Moth	82234		22. 8.39	To Dutch East Indies in 5/40. Canx 8.5.40.
G-AFYA	DH.82A Tiger Moth	82235		22. 8.39	To South African AF as 1546 in 6/40. Canx 25.6.40.
G-AFYB	DH.82A Tiger Moth	82593		22. 8.39	To Dutch East Indies in 5/40. Canx 8.5.40.
G-AFYC	DH.82A Tiger Moth	82594		22. 8.39	To Dutch East Indies in 5/40. Canx 8.5.40.
G-AFYD	Luscombe 8AF Silvaire (Originally regd as a 8E)	1044	N25120 NC25120	29. 7.75	
G-AFYE(1)	Lockheed 14-H2	1507		. .39R	NTU - Canx 14.9.39 as Not Imported. To CR-AAV.
G-AFYE(2)	DH.95 Flamingo	95007		31. 5.40	Dived vertically into the ground at Asmara, Eritrea on 15.2.43. Canx.
G-AFYF(1)	Lockheed 14-H2	1508		. .39R	NTU - Canx 14.9.39 as Not Imported. To CR-AAX.
G-AFYF(2)	DH.95 Flamingo	95009		31. 5.40	Scrapped at Redhill in 1950. Canx.
G-AFYG(1)	Douglas DC-5-5..	422		30. 8.39R	NTU - Cancelled order tranferred to Pennsylvania Central Airlines as a DC-5-518, but again NTU and components used in construction of c/ns 606 (BuA.1901) & 607 (BuA.1902). Canx 14.9.39.
G-AFYG(2)	DH.95 Flamingo	95010		31. 5.40	Crashed at Asmara, Eritrea on 5.4.43. Canx.

Regn	Type	c/n	Previous identity	Regn date	Fate or immediate subsequent identity (if known)
G-AFYH(1)	Douglas DC-5-5..	423		30. 8.39R	NTU - Cancelled order tranferred to Pennsylvania Central Airlines as a DC-5-518, but again NTU and components used in construction of c/ns 606 (BuA.1901) & 607 (BuA.1902). Canx 14.9.39.
G-AFYH(2)	DH.95 Flamingo	95011	BT312 G-AFYH	31. 5.40	Scrapped at Redhill in 5/54. Canx.
G-AFYI(1)	Douglas DC-5-5..	424		30. 8.39R	NTU - Cancelled order tranferred to KLM as PH-AXA, but due to situation in Europe was delivered to KLM (West Indies Division) as PJ-AIW in 5/40 as a DC-5-510. Canx 14.9.39.
G-AFYI(2)	DH.95 Flamingo	95012		1. 6.40	Crashed in landing accident at Adana, Turkey on 13.9.42. Canx.
G-AFYJ(1)	Douglas DC-5-5..	425		30. 8.39R	NTU - Cancelled order tranferred to Columbian Airline S.C.A.D.T.A. as a DC-5-535, but again NTU and components used in construction of c/ns 608 (BuA.1903). Canx 14.9.39.
G-AFYJ(2)	DH.95 Flamingo	95013	E-16	1. 6.40	Scrapped at Redhill in 1950. Canx.
G-AFYK(1)	Douglas DC-5-5..	426		30. 8.39R	NTU - Cancelled order tranferred to KLM as PH-AXB, but due to situation in Europe was delivered to KLM (West Indies Division) as PJ-AIZ in 5/40 as a DC-5-510. Canx 14.9.39.
G-AFYK(2)	DH.95 Flamingo	95014	E-17	31. 5.40	Scrapped at Redhill in 1950. Canx.
G-AFYL(1)	Douglas DC-5-5..	427		30. 8.39R	NTU - Cancelled order tranferred to Pennsylvania Central Airlines as a DC-5-518, but again NTU and components used in construction of c/ns 609 (BuA.1904). Canx 14.9.39.
G-AFYL(2)	DH.95 Flamingo	95015		31. 5.40	Scrapped at Redhill in 1950. Canx.
G-AFYM(1)	Douglas DC-5-5..	428		30. 8.39R	NTU - Cancelled order tranferred to KLM as PH-AXE, but due to the situation in Europe was delivered to K.N.I.L.M. as PK-ADB in 1940 as a DC-5-511. Canx 14.9.39.
G-AFYM(2)	Bristol 130 Bombay	SH.10	L5817	. .39R	NTU - Remained with RAF as L5817. Canx.
G-AFYN(1)	Douglas DC-5-5..	429		30. 8.39R	NTU - Cancelled order tranferred to Pennsylvania Central Airlines as a DC-5-518, but again NTU and components used in construction of c/ns 610 (BuA.1905). Canx 14.9.39.
G-AFYN(2)	Bristol 130 Bombay	SH.7	L5814	. .39R	NTU - Remained with RAF as L5814. Canx.
G-AFYO(1)	Douglas DC-5-5..	430		30. 8.39R	NTU - Cancelled order tranferred to KLM as PH-AXG, but due to the situation in Europe was delivered to K.N.I.L.M. as PK-ADA in 1940 as a DC-5-511. Canx 14.9.39.
G-AFYO(2)	Bristol 130 Bombay	-		. .39R	NTU - Canx.
G-AFYO(3)	Consolidated-Vultee CV.32 (B-24D-70-CO) Liberator	-	42-40551	. 3.44	(Marks used for one flight only) To NC18649 3/44. Canx.
G-AFYO(4)	Stinson HW-75 Model 105 Voyager (Probably also ex French Mil with identity "22586")	7039	F-BGQP NC22586	25. 4.77	
G-AFYP	DH.94 Moth Minor	94082		15. 8.39R	NTU - To R.Australia AF as A21-37 in 4/40. Canx.
G-AFYR	DH.94 Moth Minor	94083		15. 8.39R	NTU - To R.Australia AF as A21-23 in 3/40. Canx.
G-AFYS	DH.94 Moth Minor	94086		15. 8.39R	NTU - To R.Australia AF as A21-21 in 3/40. Canx.
G-AFYT	DH.94 Moth Minor Coupé	94101		15. 8.39R	NTU. To E-2. Canx.
G-AFYU	Lockheed 14-WF62 Super Electra	1444	PH-ASL	18. 8.39	Ditched in the sea off Catavia, Sicily on 21.12.39. Canx.
G-AFYV	Miles M.14A Hawk Trainer III	1083		22. 8.39	NTU - Allocated to RAF as BB668; not built. Canx.
G-AFYW	Miles M.14A Hawk Trainer III	1084		22. 8.39	NTU - Allocated to RAF as BB669; not built. Canx.
G-AFYX	Miles M.14A Hawk Trainer III	1085		22. 8.39	NTU - Allocated to RAF as BB670; not built. Canx.
G-AFYY	Miles M.14A Hawk Trainer III	1086		22. 8.39	NTU - Allocated to RAF as BB671; not built. Canx.
G-AFYZ	DH.95 Flamingo	95016		. 8.39R	NTU - Not built. Canx.
G-AFZA(1)	DH.95 Flamingo	95017		. 8.39R	NTU - Not built. Canx.
G-AFZA(2)	Piper J/4A Cub Coupe	4-873	N26198 NC26198	27. 6.84	
G-AFZB	DH.60M Moth	1595	K1845	22. 8.39	No CofA issued. To RAF as X9438 in 4/40. Canx 10.5.40.
G-AFZC	DH.82A Tiger Moth	83392		. 8.39R	NTU - To Australia as VH-ACT in 2/40. Canx.
G-AFZD	DH.82A Tiger Moth	82595		22. 8.39	To South African AF as 1547 in 6/40. Canx 22.6.40.
G-AFZE	Heath Parasol	PA.1		25. 8.39	(Stored 11/93 at Horsley) Canx by CAA 11.6.96.
G-AFZF	DH.82A Tiger Moth	3524	W5014 G-AFZF/D-EDIK/OE-DIK	29. 8.39	To West Germany as D-EDER in 10/55. Canx.
G-AFZG	DH.85 Leopard Moth	7062	D-EABC OE-ABC/A-145/(G-ACSE)	29. 8.39	To RAF as AW156 in 7/40. Canx 12.7.40.
G-AFZH	Taylorcraft Plus D	126		7.11.39	To RAF as W5740 in 7/40. Canx 1.8.40.
G-AFZI	Taylorcraft Plus D	127	W5741 G-AFZI	27. 2.40	Crashed at Bembridge, IoW on 21.10.63. Canx.
G-AFZJ	Taylorcraft Plus D	128		7.11.39	WFU at Rearsby on 17.7.41. Canx as WFU 28.11.39.
G-AFZK(1)	Taylorcraft Plus D	129		. .39R	NTU - Not built. Canx.
G-AFZK(2)	Luscombe 8A Master	1042	N25118 NC25118	24.10.88	
G-AFZL(1)	Taylorcraft Plus D	130		. .39R	NTU - Not built. Canx.
G-AFZL(2)	Porterfield CP-50	581	N25401 NC25401	18. 3.82	
G-AFZM	DH.94 Moth Minor	94105		. 8.39R	NTU - To R.Australian AF. Not completed. Canx.
G-AFZN(1)	DH.94 Moth Minor	94106		. 8.39R	NTU - To R.Australian AF. Not completed. Canx.
G-AFZN(2)	Luscombe 8A Master	1186	N25279 NC25279	5.10.81	
G-AFZO(1)	Messerschmitt Bf.108B-1 Taifun	1660	D-IDBT	28. 9.39	To RAF as (ES955)/ES995 in 9/41. Canx 10.6.41.
G-AFZO(2)	Messerschmitt Bf.108B-1 Taifun	370114	AW167 D-IJHW	19. 9.46	To Switzerland as HB-ESM in 4/50. Canx.
G-AFZP	Fokker F.XXII	5357	HM160 G-AFZP/PH-AJP	15. 8.39	WFU at Prestwick on 10.8.47. Broken up in 7/52. Canx.
G-AFZR	Fokker F.XXXVI	5348	PH-AJA	15. 8.39	Impressed 30.11.39 as HM161, but marks not worn. Burned out in take-off accident at Prestwick on 21.5.40. Canx.

Regn	Type	c/n	Previous identity	Regn date	Fate or immediate subsequent identity (if known)
G-AFZS	Saro A.37 Shrimp	A.37/1		22. 9.39	To RAF as TK580 in 1944. Canx 1.1.46. Broken up at Felixstowe in 1949.
G-AFZT	Peterborough Guardian	G.1		12.10.39	NTU - Not completed. Sold 14.1.41. Canx.
G-AFZU	Armstrong Whitworth AW.27 Ensign II	AW.1821		20.10.39	Scrapped at Hamble on 16.4.47. Canx.
G-AFZV	Armstrong Whitworth AW.27 Ensign II	AW.1822		20.10.39	Forced landed near Cape Mirik, Mauritania on 3.2.42; Rebuilt in France as F-AFZV. Canx.
G-AFZW	Avro 621 Tutor	-	K3237	14.11.39	To RAF as AV980 in 4/40. Canx 17.7.40.
G-AFZX	Marendaz Trainer	ABT.1		31.10.39	WFU in 1940. To Halton ATC. Canx.
G-AFZY	Miles M.11A Whitney Straight	506	NF747 G-AFZY/U-0227/G-AFZY	9.11.39	To New Zealand as ZK-AXD in 9/50. Canx.
G-AFZZ	Lockheed 14H Super Electra	1493	SP-BPL	7.11.39	NTU - Crashed at Bucharest, Romania on 24.7.40 still marked as SP-BPL. Canx.
G-AGAA	Lockheed 14H Super Electra	1492	SP-BPK	7.11.39	Not delivered. Crashed at Bucharest on 24.7.40. Canx.
G-AGAB	Lockheed 14H Super Electra	1490	SP-BNE	7.11.39	Not delivered. Seized during German invasion of Budapest in 1940. Canx 1/46. Remained as SP-BNE.
G-AGAC	Lockheed 14H Super Electra	1423	SP-BNH	7.11.39	Not delivered. Seized during German invasion of Budapest in 1940. Canx 1/46. Remained as SP-BNH.
G-AGAD	Douglas DC-2-115F	1378	SP-ASL	7.11.39	Not delivered. Seized during German invasion of Budapest in 1940. Canx 1/46. Remained as SP-ASL.
G-AGAE	Junkers Ju52/3m	5588	SP-AKX	7.11.39	WFU in 1940. Restored to Poland as SP-AKX. Canx in 1/46.
G-AGAF	Lockheed 10A Electra	1087	SP-BGG	7.11.39	Not delivered. Seized during German invasion of Budapest in 1940. Canx 1/46. Remained as SP-BGG.
G-AGAG	Lockheed 10A Electra	1047	SP-AYC	7.11.39	Not delivered. Seized during German invasion of Budapest in 1940. Canx 1/46. Remained as SP-AYC.
G-AGAH	Lockheed 10A Electra	1086	SP-BGF	7.11.39	Not delivered. Seized during German invasion of Budapest in 1940. Canx 1/46. Remained as SP-BGF.
G-AGAI	Lockheed 10A Electra	1085	SP-BGE	7.11.39	Not delivered. Seized during German invasion of Budapest in 1940. Canx 1/46. Remained as SP-BGE.
G-AGAJ	Lockheed 10A Electra	1088	SP-BGH	7.11.39	Not delivered. Seized during German invasion of Budapest in 1940. Canx 1/46. Remained as SP-BGH.
G-AGAK	Hirtenberg HS.9A	001	D-EDJH OE-DJH	20.11.39	(Stored at Filton during 1939/46) Crashed at Petersfield on 15.2.58. Canx.
G-AGAL	GAL.42 Cygnet II	GAL/42/110		26. 2.40	To RAF as DG566 in 3/41. Canx 3.5.41.
G-AGAM	DH.94 Moth Minor Coupe	9405	E-7	21. 2.40	To India as VT-AMD in 5/40. Canx 3.5.40.
G-AGAN	DH.94 Moth Minor Coupe	9406		21. 2.40	To India as VT-AME in 5/40. Canx 30.5.40.
G-AGAO	DH.94 Moth Minor	94103	E-14	21. 2.40	To India as VT-AMG in 5/40. Canx 30.5.40.
G-AGAP	DH.82 Tiger Moth	3688	F-AQOX	19. 2.40	To Australia as VH-ADK in 3/40. Canx 8.3.40.
G-AGAR	Lockheed 414 Hudson III	1766	N7364	21. 3.40	Destroyed by enemy action at Le Luc, France on 29.3.41. Canx.
G-AGAS	GAL.42 Cygnet II	GAL/42/117		2. 4.40	To Argentina as LV-KGA in 8/41. Canx 8.8.41.
G-AGAT	Piper J3F-50 Cub	4062	N26126 NC26126	17. 7.87	
G-AGAU	GAL.42 Cygnet II	GAL/42/118	ES914 G-AGAU	2. 4.40	Crashed at Somerton, IoW on 28.8.49. Canx.
G-AGAV	Lockheed 14H Super Electra	1425	SP-LMK	11. 4.40	Overhaul abandoned at Croydon in 3/44 due to corrosion & WFU. Scrapped in 2/46. Canx.
G-AGAW	GAL.42 Cygnet 2	GAL/42/112		16. 4.40	To Brasil as PP-TDY in 1940. Canx 30.3.41.
G-AGAX	GAL.42 Cygnet 2	GAL/42/114	ES915 G-AGAX	25. 4.40	Crashed near Barnsley, Yorks on 4.4.55. Canx.
G-AGAY	Focke-Wulf FW.200B Condor	2894	OY-DAM	15. 5.40	To RAF as DX177 in 1/41. Canx 9.1.41.
G-AGAZ	DH.95 Flamingo	95005	E-16	20. 5.40	To RAF as AE444 in 6/40. Canx 14.8.40.
G-AGBA	GAL.42 Cygnet 2	GAL/42/113	HM495 G-AGBA	21. 5.40	Not converted. Scrapped at Squires Gate on 16.1.57. Canx.
G-AGBB	Douglas DC-3-178	1590	PH-ALI	24. 7.40	Shot down over Bay of Biscay on 1.6.43 by a Ju88. Canx.
G-AGBC	Douglas DC-3-194B	1939	PH-ALR	1. 8.40	Crashed at Heston Airfield on 21.9.40. Canx.
G-AGBD	Douglas DC-3-194C	1980	PH-TBD G-AGBD/NL202/G-AGBD/PH-ARB	25. 7.40	To Yugoslavia as YU-ABM in 5/53. Canx.
G-AGBE	Douglas DC-3-194D	2022	PH-TBE NL201/G-AGBE/PH-ARZ	1. 8.40	Crashed at Lons-le-Saunlier, France on 18.11.46. Canx.
G-AGBF	Taylorcraft Plus D (Rebuild of Plus C G-AFWL c/n 122)	131		6. 6.40	To RAF as X7533 in 8/40. Canx 9.8.40.
G-AGBG	Lockheed 14H Super Electra	1421	SP-BWF	19. 6.40	To Sweden as SE-BTN in 3/51. Canx.
G-AGBH	Douglas DC-2-115L	1584	(PH-TBB) NL203/G-AGBH/PH-ALE	1. 8.40	Destroyed at Luqa, Malta on 3.10.46. Canx.
G-AGBI(1)	Miles M.5 Sparrowhawk	-	U-5	. .40R	NTU & allocation unconfirmed - Remained as U-5 (B-Class marks). Canx.
G-AGBI(2)	Douglas DC-3-194D Dakota	2019	PH-ARW	1. 8.40	Destroyed in air raid at Whitchurch on 24.11.40. Canx.
G-AGBJ	Consolidated-Vultee CV.28-3 Catalina	C-3	AM258 NC777	12.12.40	To RAF as SM706 in 1/44. Canx.
G-AGBK	General Aircraft GAL.45 Owlet	GAL/45/134		8. 8.40	To RAF as DP240 in 5/41. Canx 12.1.42.
G-AGBL	General Aircraft GAL.47	GAL/47/135	T-47	8. 8.40	NTU - To T-0224 (B-Class marks). Destroyed on 2.4.42. Canx 11/45.
G-AGBM	Tipsy BC	BRC-502	HM494 F-0222/G-AGBM/OO-DOP	21. 9.40	Restored to Belgium as OO-DOP in 1/47. Canx 2.1.47.
G-AGBN	General Aircraft GAL.42 Cygnet 2	GAL/42/111	ES915 G-AGBN	4.10.40	Canx as WFU 15.11.88. (On display 3/96 East Fortune)
G-AGBO	Lockheed 18-07 Lodestar	2018		6. 3.41	To RAF as HK973 in 11/43. Canx 19.11.43.
G-AGBP	Lockheed 18-07 Lodestar	2024		6. 3.41	To RAF as HK980 in 11/43. Canx 19.11.43.
G-AGBR	Lockheed 18-07 Lodestar	2070		6. 3.41	To Kenya as VP-KFE in 4/48. Canx 19.4.48.
G-AGBS	Lockheed 18-07 Lodestar	2071		6. 3.41	To Kenya as VP-KFB in 3/48. Canx 17.3.48.
G-AGBT	Lockheed 18-56 Lodestar	2076		6. 3.41	To Kenya as VP-KFA in 2/48. Canx 23.2.48.

Regn	Type	c/n	Previous identity	Regn date	Fate or immediate subsequent identity (if known)
G-AGBU	Lockheed 18-56 Lodestar	2090		6. 3.41	To Australia as (VH-BKH)/VH-FAD in 6/49. Canx 15.6.49.
G-AGBV	Lockheed 18-56 Lodestar	2091		6. 3.41	To Kenya as VP-KFC in 3/48. Canx 17.3.48.
G-AGBW	Lockheed 18-56 Lodestar	2094		6. 3.41	Crashed into Kinangop Peak, Aberdare Mountains, Kenya on 5.1.44. Canx.
G-AGBX	Lockheed 18-56 Lodestar	2095		6. 3.41	To Kenya as VP-KFF in 4/48. Canx 22.4.48.
G-AGBY	DH.95 Flamingo	95020	(BK822)	8. 2.41	Scrapped at Whitney, Oxon in 12/44. Canx.
G-AGBZ	Boeing 314A Clipper	2081	NC18607	24. 4.41	Restored to USA as NC18607 in 4/48. Canx.
G-AGCA	Boeing 314A Clipper	2082	NC18608	24. 4.41	Restored to USA as NC18608 in 4/48. Canx.
G-AGCB	Boeing 314A Clipper	2084	NC18610	24. 4.41	Restored to USA as NC18610 in 4/48. Canx.
G-AGCC	DH.95 Flamingo	95008	R2766	12. 7.40	Restored to RAF as R2766 in 2/41. Canx 14.2.41.
G-AGCD	Consolidated-Vultee CV.32-2 (LB-30A) Liberator I	2	AM259	19. 4.41	Restored to RAF as AM259 in 7/44. Canx 1/46.
G-AGCE	Lockheed 414 Hudson V	2789	AM707	29. 5.41	Restored to RAF as AM707 in 8/41. Canx 15.8.41.
G-AGCF(1)	Douglas DC-2-120	1310	NC14277	. 7.41R	NTU - To RAF on 5.7.41, reportedly as AX769. Canx.
G-AGCF(2)	Armstrong Whitworth AW.38 Whitley V	AW.2694	BD360	16. 4.42	Restored to RAF as BD360 in 8/43. Canx 26.8.43.
G-AGCG(1)	Douglas DC-2-120	1311	NC14278	. 7.41R	NTU - For RAF as HK867, but collided with Hurricane Z4257 while landing at Hastings Site, Freetown, Sierra Leone on 7.9.41, whilst on delivery. Canx.
G-AGCG(2)	Armstrong Whitworth AW.38 Whitley V	AW.2695	BD361	16. 4.42	Restored to RAF as BD361 in 7/43. Canx 22.7.43.
G-AGCH(1)	Douglas DC-2-120	1312	NC14279	. 7.41R	NTU - DBR at Bathurst, Gambia on 2.8.41. Canx.
G-AGCH(2)	Armstrong Whitworth AW.38 Whitley V	AW.2696	BD362	16. 4.42	Restored to RAF as BD362 in 3/43. Canx 5.3.43.
G-AGCI(1)	Douglas DC-2-112	1239	NC13713	. 7.41R	NTU - To USAAC as 42-53527 (C-32A) on 28.5.42. Canx.
G-AGCI(2)	Armstrong Whitworth AW.38 Whitley V	AW.2716	BD382	16. 4.42	Crashed into Bay of Gibraltar on 29.6.42. Canx 3.11.42.
G-AGCJ(1)	Douglas DC-2-112	1249	NC13723? XA-BJM/NC13723	. 7.41R	NTU - To USAAC as 42-53528 (C-32A) on 26.5.42. Canx.
G-AGCJ(2)	Armstrong Whitworth AW.38 Whitley V	AW.2717	BD383	16. 4.42	Restored to RAF as BD383 in 10/43. Canx 17.10.43.
G-AGCK(1)	Douglas DC-2-118B	1367	NC14295? XA-BJG/NC14295	. 7.41R	NTU - To USAAC as 42-53532 (C-32A) on 28.5.42. Canx.
G-AGCK(2)	Armstrong Whitworth AW.38 Whitley V	AW.2718	BD384	16. 4.42	Restored to RAF as BD384 in 10/43. Canx 16.10.43.
G-AGCL	Lockheed 18-07 (C-56C-LO) Lodestar	2092	(AX757) 42-53502/NC33616	7.10.41	NTU - Not delivered. To Free French AF as FL-AZM, then F-BAML. Canx 11/41.
G-AGCM	Lockheed 18-56 (C-56C-LO) Lodestar	2093	AX759 42-53503/NC33617	29. 9.41	To RAF as VR955 in 10/46. Canx 2.10.46.
G-AGCN	Lockheed 18-56 (C-56D-LO) Lodestar	2020	AX756 42-53504/NC25630	29. 9.41	Restored to RAF as AX756 in 11/47. Canx 19.11.47.
G-AGCO	Lockheed 18-56 (C-56D-LO) Lodestar	2021	AX758 42-53505/NC25631	29. 9.41	Scrapped at RAF Kasfareet in 11/47. Canx 19.11.47.
G-AGCP	Lockheed 18-56 (C-56D-LO) Lodestar	2022	AX721 42-53506/NC25632	24. 7.41	Scrapped at RAF Kasfareet in 11/47. Canx 19.11.47.
G-AGCR	Lockheed 18-56 (C-56C-LO) Lodestar	2072	AX718 42-53500/NC3138	24. 7.41	Crashed on take-off in Malta on 13.5.42. Canx.
G-AGCS	Lockheed 18-08 (C-56C-LO) Lodestar	2031	AX723 42-53497/NC25640	7.10.41	NTU - Not delivered. Remained with RAF as AX723. Canx 7/42.
G-AGCT	Lockheed 18-08 (C-56C-LO) Lodestar	2001	AX722 42-53495/NC25604	24. 7.41	To RAF as HK974 in 11/43. Canx 19.11.43.
G-AGCU	Lockheed 18-56 (C-56C-LO) Lodestar	2068	AX720 42-53499/NC34900	24. 7.41	Restored to RAF as AX720 in 26.11.47. Canx 16.11.47. To Spanish AF as T.4-2 in 1949.
G-AGCV	Lockheed 18-56 (C-56C-LO) Lodestar	2042	AX717 42-53498/NC6175	24. 7.41	Restored to RAF as AX717 in 10/46. Canx 2.10.46.
G-AGCW	Lockheed 18-08 (C-56C-LO) Lodestar	1956	AX719 42-53494/NC18993	24. 7.41	To RAF as HK975 in 9/43. Canx 18.9.43.
G-AGCX	Lockheed 18-08 (C-56C-LO) Lodestar	2012	AX764 42-53496/NC3030	29.11.41	To RAF as HK981 in 9/43. Canx 21.9.43.
G-AGCY	Lockheed 18-08 (C-56C-LO) Lodestar	2077	AX765 42-53501/NC1611	7.10.41	WFU in 1947. Canx 19.11.47. To Spanish AF in 1949.
G-AGCZ	Lockheed 18-08 (C-56D-LO) Lodestar	2023	AX763 42-53507/NC25633/NX25633	29. 9.41	Crashed in Western Desert, North Africa on 23.2.43. Canx.
G-AGDA	Consolidated-Vultee CV.28-5ME (PBY-5) Catalina I	122	AH563	24. 6.41	DBF in landing accident in Poole Harbour, Dorset on 23.3.43. Canx.
G-AGDB	Taylorcraft Plus D	132		18. 6.41	WFU in 1941. To RAF as Auster 1 LB267 c/n 137 in 9/41. Canx.
G-AGDC	Lockheed 414 Hudson III	2585	V9061 BuA.39639	5. 7.41	To RAF as VJ416 in 8/45. Canx 29.8.45.
G-AGDD	Lockheed 18-08 Lodestar	2087	2087 R.Norwegian AF/G-AGDD/NX34901	21. 7.41	Canx 9.7.45. To R.Norwegian AF 2087/T-AC
G-AGDE	Lockheed 18-08 Lodestar	2086	2086 R.Norwegian AF/NX33669	9. 8.41	To R.Norwegian AF as 2086 on 16.11.43. Crashed into sea off Leuchars, Fife on 17.12.43.
G-AGDF	Lockheed 414 Hudson III	3772	V9167	4. 9.41	Crashed into sea off Skredewick, Sweden on 23.6.42. Canx.
G-AGDG	DH.89A Dragon Rapide	6547	X7387	11. 9.41	To France as F-BEDX in 4/48. Canx 21.11.47.
G-AGDH	DH.89A Dragon Rapide	6548	X7388	11. 9.41	Destroyed in gales at Stornoway on 25.11.41. Canx.
G-AGDI	Curtiss Wright CW.20	101	41-21041 NX19436	24. 9.41	Scrapped at Filton in 10/43. Canx.
G-AGDJ	Fane F1/40	F.1	T1788	11. 9.41	Scrapped between 1941 and 1945. Canx in 12.46.
G-AGDK	Lockheed 414 Hudson III	3757	V9152	22.10.41	To RAF as VJ421 in 8/45. Canx 29.8.45.
G-AGDL	Miles M.5A Sparrowhawk	276	U-0223 U-3	22.10.41	Crashed at Tollerton on 19.6.48. Canx.
G-AGDM	DH.89A Dragon Rapide	6584		11.11.41	To France as F-OAXK in 3/57. Canx 30.3.57.

Regn	Type	c/n	Previous identity	Regn date	Fate or immediate subsequent identity (if known)
G-AGDN	General Aircraft Monospar ST.25 Universal	ST25/89	CF-BAH	12.11.41	WFU on 16.7.44. Scrapped. Canx in 1/47.
G-AGDO	Lockheed 414 Hudson III	-	AE581	9. 1.42	Restored to RAF as AE581 in 4/42. Canx 17.4.42.
G-AGDP	DH.89A Dragon Rapide	6403	F-AQOH	26.11.41	CofA expired 24.7.58 & WFU at Elmdon. Dismantled at Wolverhampton in 10/61. Burnt in 8/69. Canx.
G-AGDR	Consolidated-Vultee CV.32-2 (LB-30B) Liberator I	9	AM918 40-2357	5. 1.42	Shot down by RAF near Eddystone Lighthouse on 16.2.42 in error. Canx.
G-AGDS	Consolidated-Vultee CV.32-2 (LB-30A) Liberator I	6	AM263 G-AGDS/AM263	26. 1.42	Restored to RAF as AM263 in 8/44. Canx.
G-AGDT	Lockheed 12A	1285	HM573 G-AGDT/Y-0233	12. 9.42	To Sweden as SE-BTO in 5/51. Canx.
G-AGDU	Armstrong Whitworth AW.38 Whitley V	AW.1126	Z9208 G-AGDU/Z9208	17. 3.42	DBR at Whitchurch on 12.8.42. Canx 20.8.42.
G-AGDV	Armstrong Whitworth AW.38 Whitley V	AW.1134	Z9216	17. 3.42	Restored to RAF as Z9216 in 4/42. Canx 15.4.42.
G-AGDW	Armstrong Whitworth AW.38 Whitley V	AW.2106	Z6660	17. 3.42	Restored to RAF as Z6660 in 4/42. Canx 15.4.42.
G-AGDX	Armstrong Whitworth AW.38 Whitley V	AW.2719	BD385	16. 4.42	Restored to RAF as BD385 in 7/43. Canx 22.7.43.
G-AGDY	Armstrong Whitworth AW.38 Whitley V	AW.2720	BD386	16. 4.42	Restored to RAF as BD386 in 4/43. Canx 20.4.43.
G-AGDZ	Armstrong Whitworth AW.38 Whitley V	AW.2721	BD387	16. 4.42	Restored to RAF as BD387 in 1/43. Canx 27.1.43.
G-AGEA	Armstrong Whitworth AW.38 Whitley V	AW.2722	BD388	16. 4.42	Restored to RAF as BD388 in 1/43. Canx 27.1.43.
G-AGEB	Armstrong Whitworth AW.38 Whitley V	AW.2723	BD389	16. 4.42	Restored to RAF as BD389 in 1/43. Canx 27.1.43.
G-AGEC	Armstrong Whitworth AW.38 Whitley V	AW.2724	BD390	16. 4.42	Restored to RAF as BD390 in 7/43. Canx 22.7.43.
G-AGED	DH.89A Dragon Rapide	6621	X7504	21. 4.42	Crashed at Renfrew on 2.2.43. Canx.
G-AGEE	DH.89A Dragon Rapide	6622	X7505	16. 4.42	To Iceland as TF-KAA in 7/53. Canx 1.7.53.
G-AGEF	Hawker Tomtit	-	K1783	8. 7.42	Badly damaged in accident on 18.10.43. Canx.
G-AGEG	DH.82A Tiger Moth	82710	N9146 D-EDIL/R.Netherlands AF A-32/PH-UFK/R.Netherlands AF A-32/R4769	16. 8.82	
G-AGEH	Lockheed 18-56 Lodestar	2147	HK851 (EW985)/41-29635	21. 5.42	Canx 19.11.47. To Spanish AF as T.4-4 in 1949.
G-AGEI	Lockheed 18-56 Lodestar	2084	42-38262 CF-BTY/NC18818	24. 7.42	To R.Norwegian AF as 2084/T-AB in 7/45. Canx 9.7.45.
G-AGEJ	Lockheed 18-56 Lodestar	2085	CF-BTZ NC18819	24. 7.42	Ditched in North Sea off Smogen, Sweden on 4.4.43. Canx.
G-AGEK	Miles M.27 Master III	-	DL670	3. 7.42	To Irish Air Corps for demonstrations in 11/42, restored to RAF as DL670. Canx in 12/46.
G-AGEL	Consolidated-Vultee CV.32-3 (LB-30) Liberator II	10	AL512	31. 7.42	NTU - operated as AL512. DBR on hitting a snow bank at Gander, Newfoundland on 27.12.43. Canx.
G-AGEM	Consolidated-Vultee CV.32-3 (LB-30) Liberator II	26	AL528	31. 7.42	NTU - Operated as AL528. Crashed at Charlottetown, Prince Edward Island, Canada on 21.2.46. Canx.
G-AGEN	Douglas DC-3-277D Dakota (C-49H)	4118	42-38251 NC33655	17. 7.42	NTU - To RAF as MA943 in 8/42. Canx 1.8.42.
G-AGEO(1)	Miles M.27 Master III	-		. .42R	NTU. Canx.
G-AGEO(2)	Miles M.14A Hawk Trainer III	333		9.10.47	Scrapped at Thruxton in 1/49. Canx.
G-AGEP	Miller-Luton LA-4 Minor	LRM.1 & PFA/538B		21. 9.42	Not completed. Canx in 1/63. Wings used for G-ASRF.
G-AGER	Short S.25 Sunderland III	-	JM660	12.11.42	Scrapped at Hamble in 7/56. Canx.
G-AGES	Short S.25 Sunderland III	-	JM661	12.11.42	Crashed near Brandon Head, Co.Kerry, Eire on 28.7.43. Canx.
G-AGET	Short S.25 Sunderland III	-	JM662	12.11.42	DBF on River Hooghly, Calcutta, India on 15.2.43. Canx 20.2.46.
G-AGEU	Short S.25 Sunderland III	-	JM663	12.11.42	WFU at Hamble in 3/53. Scrapped in 8/53. Canx.
G-AGEV	Short S.25 Sunderland III	-	JM664	12.11.42	DBR in heavy landing Poole Harbour on 4.3.46. Beached on Brownsea Island. Canx.
G-AGEW	Short S.25 Sunderland III	-	JM665	12.11.42	Overturned on take-off & sank at Sourabaya, Java on 5.9.48. Canx.
G-AGEX	Vickers 456 Warwick C.1	-	BV243	30.11.42	No CofA issued. Restored to RAF as BV243 in 5/43. Canx 1.8.43.
G-AGEY	Vickers 456 Warwick C.1	-	BV244	30.11.42	No CofA issued. Restored to RAF as BV244 in 11/43. Canx 1.8.43.
G-AGEZ	Vickers 456 Warwick C.1	-	BV245	30.11.42	No CofA issued. Restored to RAF as BV245 in 11/43. Canx 1.8.43.
G-AGFA	Vickers 456 Warwick C.1	-	BV246	30.11.42	No CofA issued. Restored to RAF as BV246 in 10/43. Canx 1.8.43.
G-AGFB	Vickers 456 Warwick C.1	-	BV247	30.11.42	No CofA issued. Restored to RAF as BV247 in 7/43. Canx 1.8.43.
G-AGFC	Vickers 456 Warwick C.1	-	BV248	30.11.42	No CofA issued. Restored to RAF as BV248 in 9/43. Canx 1.8.43.
G-AGFD	Vickers 456 Warwick C.1	-	BV249	30.11.42	No CofA issued. Restored to RAF as BV249 in 10/43. Canx 1.8.43.
G-AGFE	Vickers 456 Warwick C.1	-	BV250	30.11.42	No CofA issued. Restored to RAF as BV250 in 10/43. Canx 1.8.43.
G-AGFF	Vickers 456 Warwick C.1	-	BV251	30.11.42	No CofA issued. Restored to RAF as BV251 in 8/43. Canx 1.8.43.
G-AGFG	Vickers 456 Warwick C.1	-	BV252	30.11.42	No CofA issued. Restored to RAF as BV252 in 10/43. Canx 1.8.43.
G-AGFH	Vickers 456 Warwick C.1	-	BV253	30.11.42	No CofA issued. Restored to RAF as BV253 in 10/43. Canx 1.8.43.

Regn	Type	c/n	Previous identity	Regn date	Fate or immediate subsequent identity (if known)
G-AGFI	Vickers 456 Warwick C.1	-	BV254	30.11.42	No CofA issued. Restored to RAF as BV254 in 10/43. Canx 1.8.43.
G-AGFJ	Vickers 456 Warwick C.1	-	BV255	30.11.42	No CofA issued. Restored to RAF as BV255 in 7/43. Canx 1.8.43.
G-AGFK	Vickers 456 Warwick C.1	-	BV256	30.11.42	No CofA issued. Restored to RAF as BV256 in 11/43. Canx 1.8.43.
G-AGFL	Consolidated-Vultee CV.28-5B Catalina IB	808	FP221 G-AGFL/FP221	27.10.42	Scuttled of Fremantle, Western Australia on 28.11.45. Canx 6.6.46.
G-AGFM	Consolidated-Vultee CV.28-5B Catalina IB	831	FP244 G-AGFM/FP244	27.10.42	Scuttled of Fremantle, Western Australia on 28.11.45. Canx 6.6.46.
G-AGFN	Consolidated-Vultee CV.32-4 (B-24D-CO) Liberator III	-	FL909	27.10.42	Restored to RAF as FL909 in 1/45. Canx 19.2.45.
G-AGFO	Consolidated-Vultee CV.32-4 (B-24D-CO) Liberator III	-	FL915	9. 9.43	Restored to RAF as FL915 on 30.3.45. Canx 3.3.45.
G-AGFP	Consolidated-Vultee CV.32-4 (B-24D-CO) Liberator III	-	FL917	9. 9.44	Restored to RAF as FL917 in 1/45. Canx 31.1.45.
G-AGFR	Consolidated-Vultee CV.32-4 (B-24D-CO) Liberator III	-	FL918 41-11738	9. 9.43	Restored to RAF as FL918 in 1/45. Canx 31.1.45.
G-AGFS	Consolidated-Vultee CV.32-4 (B-24D-CO) Liberator III	-	FL920 41-11683	9. 9.43	Restored to RAF as FL920 in 1/45. Canx 31.1.45.
G-AGFT(1)	Avro 685 York C.1	-	(LV633)	5.11.42R	NTU. To RAF as LV633 4/43. Canx.
G-AGFT(2)	Avia FL-3	176	I-TOLB MM.....	21. 8.84	
G-AGFU	DH.89A Dragon Rapide	6463	R5926	26.11.42	Sold to Belgium in 6/50. WFU at Brussels, Belgium in 1952. Canx.
G-AGFV	DH.98 Mosquito FB.VI	98421	DZ411	23.12.42	Destroyed at Stockholm, Sweden on 4.7.44. Canx.
G-AGFW	Miles M.17 Monarch	787	TP819 G-AGFW/U-0226/OO-UMK(2)	29.12.42	Restored to Belgium as OO-UMK(2) in 2/47. Canx.
G-AGFX	Douglas C-47-DL Dakota	6223	ZS-DAI G-AGFX/FD769/42-5635	23. 2.43	To South Africa as ZS-DCZ in 6/49. Canx 14.6.49.
G-AGFY	Douglas C-47-DL Dakota	6224	FD770 42-5636	8. 3.43	To South Africa as ZS-DAH in 7/48. Canx 12.7.48.
G-AGFZ	Douglas C-47-DL Dakota	6225	FD771 42-5637	8. 3.43	Crashed while landing at Bromma, Sweden on 21.4.44. Canx.
G-AGGA	Douglas C-47-DL Dakota	6241	AP-AAB (VT-CPB)/G-AGGA/FD777/VT-CPB/FD777/42-5653	8. 3.43	To France as F-OACA in 5/49. Canx 28.5.49.
G-AGGB	Douglas C-47-DL Dakota	6227	(ZS-DAJ) G-AGGB/FD773/42-5639	8. 3.43	To South Africa as ZS-DDJ in 9/49. Canx 6.9.49.
G-AGGC	DH.98 Mosquito FB.VI	98723	HJ680	15. 4.43	Restored to RAF as HJ680 in 1/46. Canx 4.1.46.
G-AGGD	DH.98 Mosquito FB.VI	98730	HJ681	15. 4.43	DBR when overshot landing at Sarenas, Sweden on 3.1.44. Canx.
G-AGGE	DH.98 Mosquito FB.VI	98740	HJ718	15. 4.43	Restored to RAF as HJ718 in 6/45. Canx 16.6.45.
G-AGGF	DH.98 Mosquito FB.VI	98742	HJ720	15. 4.43	Crashed onto Glen Esk at 2550ft, near Leuchars on 17.8.43. Canx.
G-AGGG	DH.98 Mosquito FB.VI	98743	HJ721	15. 4.43	Crashed near Leuchars on 25.10.43. Canx.
G-AGGH	DH.98 Mosquito FB.VI	98750	HJ723	15. 4.43	Restored to RAF as HJ723 in 6/45. Canx 16.6.45.
G-AGGI	Douglas C-47-DL Dakota	9050	(ZS-DAG) G-AGGI/FD796/42-32824	26. 4.43	To South Africa as ZS-DCY in 5/49. Canx 5.49.
G-AGGJ	Avro 652A Anson I	1152	LT191	17. 5.43	Ferry marks used for delivery to RAF Aboukir, Egypt in 7/43. Restored to RAF as LT191 7/43. Canx 10.6.44.
G-AGGK	Avro 652A Anson I	1153	LT192	17. 5.43	Ferry marks used for delivery to RAF Aboukir, Egypt in 7/43. Restored to RAF as LT192 7/43. Canx 10.6.44.
G-AGGL	Avro 652A Anson I	1154	LT203	17. 5.43	Ferry marks used for delivery to RAF Aboukir, Egypt in 7/43. Restored to RAF as LT203 7/43. Canx 10.6.44.
G-AGGM	Avro 652A Anson I	1155	LT204	17. 5.43	Ferry marks used for delivery to RAF Aboukir, Egypt in 7/43. Restored to RAF as LT204 7/43. Canx 10.6.44.
G-AGGN	Avro 652A Anson I	1156	LT236	17. 5.43	Ferry marks used for delivery to RAF Aboukir, Egypt in 7/43. Restored to RAF as LT236 7/43. Canx 10.6.44.
G-AGGO	Avro 652A Anson I	1157	LT255	17. 5.43	Ferry marks used for delivery to RAF Aboukir, Egypt in 7/43. Restored to RAF as LT255 7/43. Canx 10.6.44.
G-AGGP	Avro 652A Anson I	1158	LT256	17. 5.43	Ferry marks used for delivery to RAF Aboukir, Egypt in 7/43. Restored to RAF as LT256 7/43. Canx 10.6.44.
G-AGGR	Avro 652A Anson I	1159	LT257	17. 5.43	Ferry marks used for delivery to RAF Aboukir, Egypt in 7/43. Restored to RAF as LT257 7/43. Canx 10.6.44.
G-AGGS	Avro 652A Anson I	1160	LT307	17. 5.43	Ferry marks used for delivery to RAF Aboukir, Egypt in 7/43. Restored to RAF as LT307 7/43. Canx 10.6.44.
G-AGGT	Avro 652A Anson I	1161	LT340	17. 5.43	Ferry marks used for delivery to RAF Aboukir, Egypt in 7/43. Restored to RAF as LT340 7/43. Canx 10.6.44.
G-AGGU	Avro 652A Anson I	1162	EG677	17. 5.43	Ferry marks used for delivery to RAF Aboukir, Egypt in 7/43. Restored to RAF as EG677 7/43. Canx 10.6.44.
G-AGGV	Avro 652A Anson I	1163	LS995	17. 5.43	Ferry marks used for delivery to RAF Aboukir, Egypt in 7/43. Restored to RAF as LS995 7/43. Canx 10.6.44.
G-AGGW	Avro 652A Anson I	1164	LT279	17. 5.43	Ferry marks used for delivery to RAF Aboukir, Egypt in 7/43. Restored to RAF as LT279 7/43. Canx 10.6.44.
G-AGGX	Avro 652A Anson I	1165	LT115	17. 5.43	Ferry marks used for delivery to RAF Aboukir, Egypt in 7/43. Restored to RAF as LT115 7/43. Canx 10.6.44.
G-AGGY	Avro 652A Anson I	1166	LT176	17. 5.43	Ferry marks used for delivery to RAF Aboukir, Egypt in 7/43. Restored to RAF as LT176 7/43. Canx 10.6.44.
G-AGGZ	Avro 652A Anson I	1167	LT234	17. 5.43	Ferry marks used for delivery to RAF Aboukir, Egypt in 7/43. Restored to RAF as LT234 7/43. Canx 10.6.44.
G-AGHA	Avro 652A Anson I	1168	LT276	17. 5.43	Ferry marks used for delivery to RAF Aboukir, Egypt in 7/43. Restored to RAF as LT276 7/43. Canx 10.6.44.

Regn	Type	c/n	Previous identity	Regn date	Fate or immediate subsequent identity (if known)
G-AGHB(1)	Avro 652A Anson I	1169	LT281	17. 5.43	Ferry marks used for delivery to RAF Aboukir, Egypt in 7/43. Restored to RAF as LT281 7/43. Canx 10.7.44 as written o
G-AGHB(2)	Hawker Sea Fury FB.XI (Parts sold to USA & incorporated into rebuild as N4434P, using identity of WH589) (On rebuild 3/94 using major sections of wreck plus original centre section of TF956, rear fuselage of R.Netherlands Navy 10 11, ex 6-14/VX715 and parts from G-FURY/WJ244)	41H-636336	CF-CHB RAN WH589/WH589	9. 5.74	Badly damaged in forced landing at Munster, West Germany on 24.6.79. Remains to Elstree on 26.7.79. Canx as WFU 9.9.81.
G-AGHC	Avro 652A Anson I	1170	EG651	17. 5.43	Ferry marks used for delivery to RAF Aboukir, Egypt in 7/43. Restored to RAF as EG651 in 7/43. Canx 10.6.44.
G-AGHD	Avro 652A Anson I	1171	LS989	17. 5.43	Ferry marks used for delivery to RAF Aboukir, Egypt in 7/43. Restored to RAF as LS989 in 7/43. Canx 10.6.44.
G-AGHE	Douglas C-47A-DL Dakota	9189	FD827 42-23327	5. 5.43	To Singapore as VR-SCR in 8/48. Canx 8.8.48.
G-AGHF	Douglas C-47A-DL Dakota	9186	FD824 42-23324	10. 5.43	To USA as N9994F in 3/50. Canx 12.3.50.
G-AGHG	Consolidated-Vultee CV.32-2 (LB-30A) Liberator I	5	AM262	8. 6.43	NTU - Flew marked as AM262. Restored to RAF in 9/44. Canx 1.1.46.
G-AGHH	Douglas C-47A-DL Dakota	9187	FD825 42-23325	14. 5.43	To Greece as SX-BAN in 11/49. Canx 9.11.49.
G-AGHI	DH.89A Dragon Rapide	6455	P9588	2.12.43	WFU at Croydon on 31.8.50. Remains to Portsmouth. Canx.
G-AGHJ	Douglas C-47A-25-DL Dakota	9413	YI-GHJ G-AGHJ/FD867/42-23551	24. 8.43	WFU at Beirut, Lebanon in 8/65. Canx.
G-AGHK	Douglas C-47A-25-DL Dakota	9406	FD860 42-23544	1. 6.43	Crashed attempting a single engined landing at Oviedo, Spain on 17.4.46. Canx.
G-AGHL	Douglas C-47A-25-DL Dakota	9407	FD861 42-23545	14. 6.43	To Ghana as 9G-AAF in 4/60. Canx 5.4.60.
G-AGHM	Douglas C-47A-30-DL Dakota	9623	VP-KGI G-AGHM/FD901/42-23761	15. 9.43	To Cyprus as 5B-CBD in 5/69. Canx 18.4.69.
G-AGHN	Douglas C-47A-25-DL Dakota	9414	FD868 42-23552	3. 8.43	To Australia as VH-BZB on 9.8.50. Canx 21.11.49.
G-AGHO	Douglas C-47A-40-DL Dakota	9862	FD941 42-24000	10. 8.43	To USA as N9993F in 3/51. Canx 12.3.51.
G-AGHP	Douglas C-47A-25-DL Dakota	9408	VR-HDO G-AGHP/FD862/42-23546	25. 8.43	Port wing failed & crashed at Chatenoy, near Nemours, France on 16.5.58. Canx.
G-AGHR	Douglas C-47A-50-DL Dakota	10097	FL514 42-24235	15. 9.43	Crashed on take-off Luqa, Malta on 24.10.45. Canx.
G-AGHS	Douglas C-47A-50-DL Dakota	10099	FL516 42-24237	15. 9.43	To Cyprus as 5B-CBA in 4/69. Canx 18.4.69.
G-AGHT	Douglas C-47A-50-DL Dakota	10103	FL520 42-24241	16. 9.43	DBR in heavy landing Luqa, Malta on 14.8.46. Canx.
G-AGHU	Douglas C-47A-40-DL Dakota	9863	FD942 42-24001	5.10.43	To Hong Kong as VR-HDQ in 2/48. Canx 12.2.48.
G-AGHV	Short S.25 Sunderland III	S.1154	JM722	1. 7.43	Capsized during storm at Rod-el-Faraq on 9/10.3.46. Canx.
G-AGHW	Short S.25 Sunderland III	S.1606	ML725	1. 7.43	Crashed into Brightstone Down, IoW on 19.11.47. Canx.
G-AGHX	Short S.25 Sunderland III	S.1607	ML726	1. 7.43	Scrapped at Hamble in 10/48. Canx.
G-AGHY	DH.82A Tiger Moth (Composite rebuild from ex Rollason airframe/components)	82292	N9181	17. 2.88	(On rebuild)
"G-AGHY"	Douglas C-47A-75-DL Dakota	19347	G-DAKS TS423/42-100884	----	Marks used in film work in 1980/81.
G-AGHZ	Short S.25 Sunderland III	S.1608	ML727	1. 7.43	WFU at Hamble in 1949. Scrapped in 1/52. Canx 1/52.
G-AGIA	Short S.25 Sunderland III	S.1609	ML728	1. 7.43	WFU at Hythe in 2/51. Scrapped in 7/52. Canx.
G-AGIB	Short S.25 Sunderland III	S.1610	ML729	1. 7.43	Crashed near Sollum, 130 miles S of Tobruk on 5/6.11.43. Canx.
G-AGIC	DH.89A Dragon Rapide	6522	X7349	6. 7.43	To France as F-BEDZ in 11/47. Canx 20.11.47.
G-AGID	Consolidated-Vultee CV.28-5 (PBY-5) Catalina IVA	1109	JX575 (BuA.08215)	5. 7.43	Scuttled of Fremantle, Western Australia on 28.11.45. Canx 28.11.45.
G-AGIE	Consolidated-Vultee CV.28-5 (PBY-5) Catalina IVA	1111	JX577 (BuA.08217)	5. 7.43	Scuttled of Fremantle, Western Australia on 28.11.45. Canx 28.11.45.
G-AGIF	DH.89A Dragon Rapide	6509	X7336	15. 7.43	Scrapped at Newtownards, Northern Ireland on 24.1.50, remains burnt in 4/54. Canx 13.10.50.
G-AGIG	Lockheed 18-56 Lodestar	2151	EW980 41-29630	15. 7.43	Restored to RAF as EW980 in 11/47, and to Spanish AF as T.4-7 in 1/49. Canx 26.11.47.
G-AGIH(1)	Lockheed 18-56 Lodestar	2491	RR997 (FS737)/42-56018	. 7.43R	Crashed on test flight on 13.12.43. Canx. Canx.
G-AGIH(2)	Lockheed 18-56 Lodestar	2619	43-16459	21. 8.43	Crashed into hill-top at Kinnekulle, Sweden on 29.8.44. Canx.
G-AGII	Lockheed 18-56 Lodestar	2492	RR998 (FS738)/42-56019	21. 8.43	To R.Norwegian AF as 2492/T-AD in 7/45. Canx 9.7.45.
G-AGIJ	Lockheed 18-56 Lodestar	2593	43-16433	4. 3.44	To R.Norwegian AF as 2593/T-AE in 7/45. Canx 9.7.45.
G-AGIK	Lockheed 18-56 Lodestar	2594	43-16434	4. 3.44	To R.Norwegian AF as 2594/T-AF in 7/45. Canx 9.7.45.
G-AGIL	Lockheed 18-56 Lodestar	2143	HK855 (EW976)/41-29626	17. 9.43	Returned to RAF as (HK855)/EW976 in 11/47 & to Spanish AF in 1/49. Canx 19.11.47.
G-AGIM	Lockheed 18-56 Lodestar	2144	EW977 41-29627	27. 9.43	Returned to RAF as EW977 in 11/47 & to Spanish AF as T.4-3 in 1/49. Canx 26.11.47.
G-AGIN	Lockheed 18-56 Lodestar	2146	EW979 41-29629	27. 9.43	Returned to RAF as EW979 in 12/47 & to Spanish AF as T.4-9 in 1/49. Canx 3.12.47.
G-AGIO	Douglas C-47A-1-DK Dakota	11907	FL548 42-92140	8.11.43	To Hong Kong as VR-HDO(2) in 12/47. Canx 19.8.47.
G-AGIP	Douglas C-47A-1-DK Dakota	11903	FL544 42-92136	20.12.43	To Moroccan AF as CN-ALI in 10/63. Canx 12.8.63.
G-AGIR	Douglas C-47A-1-DK Dakota	11932	FL568 42-92162	20.12.43	Crashed at Telmest, near Casablanca in Atlas Mountains, Morocco on 28.8.44. Canx.

Regn	Type	c/n	Previous identity	Regn date	Fate or immediate subsequent identity (if known)
G-AGIS	Douglas C-47A-1-DK Dakota	12017	FZ607 42-92239	28.12.43	To France as F-OAOE in 11/53. Canx 11.11.53.
G-AGIT	Douglas C-47A-1-DK Dakota	11921	FL560 42-92152	27.12.43	To Hong Kong as VR-HDP in 12/47. Canx 9.10.47.
G-AGIU	Douglas C-47A-1-DK Dakota	12096	FZ561 42-92310	9. 1.44	To Mali as (CT-ABB)/TZ-ABB in 3/61. Canx 23.3.61.
G-AGIV	Piper J3C-65 Cub (L-4J-PI) (Frame No. 12506)	12676	OO-AFI OO-GBA/44-80380	13. 8.82	
"G-AGIV"	Douglas C-47A-85-DL Dakota	19975	G-BHUB Spanish AF T3-29/N51V/N9985F/SE-BBH/43-15509	----	Regn applied for film work in 1981.
G-AGIW	Douglas C-47A-1-DK Dakota	12186	FZ630 42-92391	2. 2.44	Crashed at Mill Hill, London on 17.10.50. Canx.
G-AGIX	Douglas C-47A-1-DK Dakota	12053	FZ628 42-92271	7. 2.44	Crashed near Sywell on 31.7.48. Canx.
G-AGIY	Douglas C-47A-1-DK Dakota	12102	FZ567 42-92315	7. 2.44	DBR on landing at El Adem, Libya on 23.3.46. Canx.
G-AGIZ	Douglas C-47A-1-DK Dakota	12075	FL647 42-92291	21. 2.44	To France as F-OAQJ in 5/54. Canx 11.5.54.
G-AGJA	Avro 685 York C.1	1207	WW508 G-AGJA/WW541/G-AGJA/MW103	8. 1.44	WFU at Stansted on 7.1.59. Broken up in 8/59. Canx.
G-AGJB	Avro 685 York C.1	1208	WW503 G-AGJB/MW108	21. 1.44	WFU & broken up at Stansted in 9/55. Canx in 4/59.
G-AGJC	Avro 685 York C.1	1209	WW504 G-AGJC/MW113	17. 4.44	WFU at Stansted on 19.12.57. Broken up. Canx.
G-AGJD	Avro 685 York C.1	1210	MW121	5. 7.44	DBR when swung on take-off Castle Benito, Tripoli, Libya on 1.2.49. Canx.
G-AGJE	Avro 685 York C.1	1211	WW580 G-AGJE/MW129	11. 9.44	WFU at Stansted in 6/56. Broken up in 10/56. Canx.
G-AGJF	DH.89A Dragon Rapide	6499	X7326	25.10.43	Crashed at Barra, Hebrides on 6.8.47. Canx.
G-AGJG	DH.89A Dragon Rapide	6517	X7344	25.10.43	(On rebuild 7/99 Duxford)
G-AGJH	Lockheed 18-56 Lodestar	2153	EW982 41-29632	1.11.43	Restored to RAF as EW982 in 12/47. To Spanish AF in 1948. Canx 3.12.47.
G-AGJI	Avro 683 Lancaster B.II	-	DV379	11.11.43	Restored to RAF as DV379 on 24.12.46. Canx.
G-AGJJ	Short S.25 Sunderland III	-	ML751	24.11.43	Scrapped at Hamble in 1/52. Canx.
G-AGJK	Short S.25 Sunderland III	-	ML752	24.11.43	Scrapped at Hamble in 1/52. Canx.
G-AGJL	Short S.25 Sunderland III	-	ML753	24.11.43	Scrapped at Hamble in 1/52. Canx.
G-AGJM	Short S.25 Sunderland III	-	ML754	24.11.43	Scrapped at Hamble in 1/52. Canx.
G-AGJN	Short S.25 Sunderland III	-	ML755	24.11.43	DBR when struck rocks in Funchal Harbour, Madeira on 21.1.53. Canx as destroyed /53.
G-AGJO	Short S.25 Sunderland III	-	ML756	24.11.43	Struck by ship & DBR at Hythe on 21.2.49. Canx.
G-AGJP	Consolidated-Vultee CV.32-3 (LB-30) Liberator II	12	AL514	11.11.43	To France as F-BEFX in 4/51. Canx 6.4.51.
G-AGJR	Douglas C-47A-1-DK Dakota	11995	PH-AZR FL587/42-92219	14. 2.44	To The Netherlands as PH-TAY in 2/46. Canx 5.2.46.
G-AGJS	Douglas C-47A-1-DK Dakota	12173	PH-AZS FZ618/42-92379	2. 3.44	To The Netherlands as NL-204/PH-TAZ in 1/46. Canx 25.1.46.
G-AGJT	Douglas C-47A-1-DK Dakota	12172	PH-AZT FZ617/42-92378	15. 5.44	To The Netherlands as PH-TBA in 2/46. Canx 5.2.46.
G-AGJU	Douglas C-47A-1-DK Dakota	12169	FZ614 42-92375	2. 6.44	DBR on landing at Whitchurch on 3.1.47. Canx.
G-AGJV	Douglas C-47A-1-DK Dakota	12195	FZ638 42-92399	2. 6.44	To British Virgin Islands as VP-LVM in 3/80. Canx 3.3.80.
G-AGJW	Douglas C-47A-1-DK Dakota	12199	FZ641 42-92402	2. 6.44	To Ghana as 9G-AAD in 7/59. Canx 9.7.59.
G-AGJX	Douglas C-47A-1-DK Dakota	12014	FL604 42-92236	25. 7.44	Crashed into high ground at Stowting, Kent 11.1.47. Canx.
G-AGJY	Douglas C-47A-1-DK Dakota	12019	FL608 42-92240	25. 7.44	To Hong Kong as VR-HDN in 10/47. Canx 9.10.47.
G-AGJZ	Douglas C-47A-1-DK Dakota	12054	FL629 42-92272	25. 7.44	To Ghana as 9G-AAE in 4/60. Canx 5.4.60.
G-AGKA	Douglas C-47B-1-DK Dakota	14141/25586	KJ802 43-48325	21. 9.45	To Aden as VR-AAA in 2/50. Canx 1.2.50.
G-AGKB	Douglas C-47B-1-DK Dakota	14143/25588	KJ804 43-48327	21. 9.44	To Brazil as PP-XEM/PP-VBT in 6/50. Canx 2.6.50.
G-AGKC	Douglas C-47B-1-DK Dakota	14146/25591	KJ807 43-48330	21. 9.44	To France as F-VNAE in 2/51. Canx.
G-AGKD	Douglas C-47B-1-DK Dakota	14150/25595	KJ811 43-48334	21. 9.44	Destroyed at Malta on 23.12.46. Canx.
G-AGKE	Douglas C-47B-1-DK Dakota	14361/25806	5B-CAZ G-AGKE/VR-AAB/JY-ABN/TJ-ABN/VR-AAB/G-AGKE/KJ867/43-48545	21. 9.44	To USA as N27AA 2/72. Canx. Derelict at Bahrain marked as G-AMZZ.
G-AGKF	Douglas C-47B-1-DK Dakota	14362/25807	KJ868 43-48546	21. 9.44	To France as F-BEFQ in 6/49. Canx 22.6.49.
G-AGKG	Douglas C-47B-1-DK Dakota	14373/25818	KJ879 43-48557	21. 9.44	To Burma as XY-ACL in 3/50. Canx 8.3.50.
G-AGKH	Douglas C-47B-1-DK Dakota	14365/25810	YI-GKH G-AGKH/KJ871/43-48549	21. 9.44	To Aden as VR-AAC in 2/50. Canx 1.2.50.
G-AGKI	Douglas C-47B-5-DK Dakota	14654/26099	KJ928 43-48838	7.11.44	To Kenya as VP-KHK in 10/49. Canx 6.10.49.
G-AGKJ	Douglas C-47B-5-DK Dakota	14660/26105	KJ933 43-48844	7.11.44	To Aden as VR-AAD in 2/50. Canx 1.2.50.
G-AGKK	Douglas C-47B-5-DK Dakota	14655/26100	KJ929 43-48839	7.11.44	To France as F-OAFQ in 4/49. Canx 4.4.49.

Regn	Type	c/n	Previous identity	Regn date	Fate or immediate subsequent identity (if known)
G-AGKL	Douglas C-47B-5-DK Dakota	14662/26107	EI-ADW G-AGKL/KJ935/43-48846	7.11.44	To France as F-OADA in 6/49. Canx 22.6.49.
G-AGKM	Douglas C-47B-10-DK Dakota	14986/26431	KJ992 43-49170	18.11.44	DBR when u/c collapsed on take-off at El Adem, Libya on 8.4.45. Canx.
G-AGKN	Douglas C-47B-10-DK Dakota	14984/26429	KJ990 43-49168	9.12.44	Crashed into cliffs at Cape Cicie, near Toulon on 14.7.48. Canx in 8/48.
G-AGKO	DH.98 Mosquito FB.VI	-	HJ667	18. 4.44	Restored to RAF as HJ667 in 6/45. Canx 16.6.45.
G-AGKP	DH.98 Mosquito FB.VI	-	LR296	18. 4.44	Crashed into the North Sea 5 miles off Scottish coast near Leuchars on 17.8.44. Canx.
G-AGKR	DH.98 Mosquito FB.VI	-	HJ792	18. 4.44	Missing between Gothenburg & Leuchars on 29.8.44. Canx.
G-AGKS	Consolidated-Vultee CV.28 (PB2B-1) Catalina IVB	-	(JX287)	6. 4.44	Scuttled off Mascot, Sydney, Australia in 3/46. Canx 3/46.
G-AGKT	Consolidated-Vultee CV.32-3 (LB-30) Liberator II	117	AL619	9. 5.44	Broken up at Mascot, Sydney, Australia for spares in 12/47. Canx 12/47.
G-AGKU	Consolidated-Vultee CV.32-3 (LB-30) Liberator II	45	AL547	24. 7.44	Broken up at Mascot, Sydney, Australia for spares in 12/47. Canx 12/47.
G-AGKV	Short S.25 Sunderland III	-	ML786	28. 6.44	Scrapped at Belfast, Northern Ireland in 1949. Canx 18.5.51.
G-AGKW	Short S.25 Sunderland III	-	ML787	28. 6.44	Scrapped at Belfast, Northern Ireland in 1949. Canx 18.5.51.
G-AGKX	Short S.25 Sunderland III	-	ML788 G-AGKX/ML788	28. 6.44	WFU at Hamble in 3/53. Canx 8/53.
G-AGKY	Short S.25 Sunderland III	-	ML789	28. 6.44	DBR during night take-off near Cowes, IoW on 28.1.53. Sank between Fawley & Calshot when being towed to Calshot.
G-AGKZ	Short S.25 Sunderland III	-	ML790	28. 6.44	Scrapped at Hythe in 5/49. Canx 5/49.
G-AGLA	Short S.25 Sunderland III	-	ML791	28. 6.44	Scrapped at Hamble in 9/49. Canx 8/49.
G-AGLB	Avro XIX Srs.1 (Originally regd as Anson XII, to Avro XIX 10/45)	1205	NL152	28.11.44	Restored to the RAF as NL152 in 11/48. Canx 17.11.48.
G-AGLC	Percival P.34 Proctor III	H.111	DX198	11.10.44	NTU - Remained as DX198 in 10/44. Canx.
G-AGLD	Vickers 474 Warwick GR.V	-	PN703	22. 8.44	Scrapped Wisley in 1/46. Derelict 1949. Canx 15.7.46.
G-AGLE	DH.89A Dragon Rapide	6784	NR685	14.12.44	Crashed at Morden, Surrey on 17.3.49. Remains to Portsmouth. Canx 8/59.
G-AGLF	Avro 691 Lancastrian 1	Set.1 & 1172	VB873 (PD140)	1.12.44	Crashed at Landing Ground H3, Syrian Desert on 11.5.47. Canx.
G-AGLG	Lockheed 18-56 Lodestar	2615	43-16455	2. 9.44	To R.Norwegian AF as 2615/T-AG in 7/45. Canx 9.7.45.
G-AGLH	Lockheed 18-56 Lodestar	2616	43-16456	2. 9.44	To R.Norwegian AF as 2616/T-AH in 7/45. Canx 9.7.45.
G-AGLI	Lockheed 18-56 Lodestar	2620	43-16460	2. 9.44	Lost in the sea north of Umea, Sweden on 1/2.5.45. Canx.
G-AGLJ	Percival P.34 Proctor III	H.406	LZ599	25. 8.44	Lost in the English Channel on 1.4.51. Canx.
G-AGLK	Taylorcraft Auster 5D (Originally regd as Auster 5)	1137	RT475	25. 8.44	
G-AGLL	Taylorcraft Auster 5	1138	RT476	25. 8.44	DBR in 10/49. Canx in 1/50.
G-AGLM	Avro 652A Anson XI	1204	NL246	17.10.44	Restored to RAF as NL246 in 2/46. Canx 12.2.46.
G-AGLN	DH.89A Dragon Rapide	6795	NR696	2.10.44	Crashed at Abadan, Persia in 15.12.46. Canx.
G-AGLO	DH.89A Dragon Rapide	6779	NR680	27.10.44	NTU - Remained as NR680, then to G-AKSC 1/48. Canx in 11/44.
G-AGLP	DH.89A Dragon Rapide	6780	NR681	28.10.44	WFU at Croydon on 17.10.50. Canx 8/59.
G-AGLR	DH.89A Dragon Rapide	6781	NR682	28.10.44	Crashed at Four Oaks Cross Roads, Berkswell, near Coventry on 7.10.56. Canx.
G-AGLS	Avro 691 Lancastrian 1	Set.2 & 1173	VD238 (PD141)	1.12.44	WFU at Hurn on 10.9.50. Scrapped. Canx 8.1.51.
G-AGLT	Avro 691 Lancastrian 1	Set.3 & 1174	VD241 (PD142)	1.12.44	Scrapped at Hurn in 1/50. Canx 1/51.
G-AGLU	Avro 691 Lancastrian 1	Set.4 & 1175	VD253 (PD143)	1.12.44	DBR on take-off at Hurn on 15.8.46. Canx.
G-AGLV	Avro 691 Lancastrian 1	Set.5 & 1176	VP-KGT G-AGLV/VF163/(PD144)	1.12.44	Scrapped at Dunsfold in 3/52. Canx 24.3.52.
G-AGLW	Avro 691 Lancastrian 1	Set.6 & 1177	VF164 (PD145)	1.12.44	WFU at Hurn on 1.9.50. Scrapped in 1/51. Canx 22.1.51.
G-AGLX	Avro 691 Lancastrian 1	Set.7 & 1178	VF165 (PD146)	1.12.44	Missing in Indian Ocean, north of Cocos Islands on 23.3.46. Canx.
G-AGLY	Avro 691 Lancastrian 1	Set.8 & 1179	VF166 (PD159)	1.12.44	Scrapped at Hurn in 1/51. Canx 1/51.
G-AGLZ	Avro 691 Lancastrian 1	Set.9 & 1180	VF167 (PD160)	1.12.44	To Australia as VH-EAU in 11/47. Canx 2.11.47.
G-AGMA	Avro 691 Lancastrian 1	Set.10 & 1181	VF152 (PD161)	1.12.44	Scrapped at Hurn on 13.1.51. Canx 22.1.51.
G-AGMB	Avro 691 Lancastrian 1	Set.11 & 1182	VF153 (PD162)	1.12.44	Crashed on landing Tengah, Singapore on 27.8.48. Canx.
G-AGMC	Avro 691 Lancastrian 1	Set.12 & 1183	VF154 (PD163)	1.12.44	Undercarriage collapsed on landing at Mascot, Sydney, Australia on 2.5.46. Canx 3.7.46.
G-AGMD	Avro 691 Lancastrian 1	Set.13 & 1184	VF155 (PD164)	1.12.44	To Austalia as VH-EAS in 7/47. Canx 16.7.47.
G-AGME	Avro 691 Lancastrian 1	Set.14 & 1185	VF156 (PD165)	1.12.44	Scrapped at Hurn in 2/50. Canx 21.12.49.
G-AGMF	Avro 691 Lancastrian 1	Set.15 & 1186	VF160 (PD166)	1.12.44	Crashed when struck ground at St.Aubin du Ternay, France on 20.8.46. Canx.
G-AGMG	Avro 691 Lancastrian 1	Set.17 & 1187	VF161 (PD167)	1.12.44	Scrapped at Hurn on 4.11.50. Canx 8.1.51.
G-AGMH	Avro 691 Lancastrian 1	Set.18 & 1188	VF162 (PD168)	1.12.44	DBR in heavy landing at Karachi, Pakistan on 17.5.46. Canx.
G-AGMI	Luscombe 8A Master	1569	N28827 NC28827	15.11.88	Badly damaged in crash on take-off from Biggin Hill on 26.3.94 (On rebuild 5/95)

Regn	Type	c/n	Previous identity	Regn date	Fate or immediate subsequent identity (if known)
G-AGMJ	Avro 691 Lancastrian 1	Set.19 & 1189	VF145 (PD169)	1.12.44	Scrapped at Hurn on 15.1.51. Canx 22.1.51.
G-AGMK	Avro 691 Lancastrian 1	Set.20 & 1190	VF146 (PD170)	1.12.44	Scrapped at Hurn on 15.1.51. Canx 22.1.51.
G-AGML	Avro 691 Lancastrian 1	Set.21 & 1191	VF147 (PD171)	1.12.44	To Australia as VH-EAT in 9/47. Canx 15.8.47.
G-AGMM	Avro 691 Lancastrian 1	Set.22 & 1192	VF148 (PD172)	1.12.44	DBR at Castel Benito, Tripoli, Libya on 7.11.49. Canx.
G-AGMN	Avro 691 Lancastrian 1	Set.23 & 1193	VF149 (PD173)	1.12.44	NTU - To RAF as Lancastrian II as VM701. Canx 15.2.46.
G-AGMO	Avro 691 Lancastrian 1	Set.24 & 1194	VF150 (PD174)	1.12.44	NTU - To RAF as Lancastrian II as VM702. Canx 15.2.46.
G-AGMP	Avro 691 Lancastrian 1	Set.25 & 1195	VF151 (PD175)	1.12.44	NTU - To RAF as Lancastrian II as VM703. Canx 15.2.46.
G-AGMR	Avro 691 Lancastrian 1	Set.26 & 1196	VF137 (PD176)	1.12.44	NTU - To RAF as Lancastrian II as VM704. Canx 15.2.46.
G-AGMS	Avro 691 Lancastrian 1	Set.27 & 1197	VF138 (PD177)	1.12.44	NTU - To RAF as Lancastrian II as VM725. Canx 15.2.46.
G-AGMT	Avro 691 Lancastrian 1	Set.28 & 1198	VF139 (PD178)	1.12.44	NTU - To RAF as Lancastrian II as VM726. Canx 15.2.46.
G-AGMU	Avro 691 Lancastrian 1	Set.29 & 1199	VF140 (PD179)	1.12.44	NTU - To RAF as Lancastrian II as VM727. Canx 15.2.46.
G-AGMV	Avro 691 Lancastrian 1	Set.31 & 1200	VF141 (PD180)	1.12.44	NTU - To RAF as Lancastrian II as VM728. Canx 15.2.46.
G-AGMW	Avro 691 Lancastrian 1	Set.32 & 1201	VF142 (PD181)	1.12.44	NTU - To RAF as Lancastrian II as VM729. Canx 15.2.46.
G-AGMX	Avro 691 Lancastrian 1	Set.33 & 1202	VF143 (PD182)	1.12.44	NTU - To RAF as Lancastrian II as VM730. Canx 15.2.46.
G-AGMY	Avro 691 Lancastrian 1	Set.34 & 1203	VF144	1.12.44	NTU - To RAF as Lancastrian II as VM731. Canx 15.2.46.
G-AGMZ	Douglas C-47B-10-DK Dakota	14978/26423	AP-AAA VT-CPA/G-AGMZ/KJ985/43-49162	9.12.44	To Aden as VR-AAE in 2/50. Canx 1.2.50.
G-AGNA	Douglas C-47B-10-DK Dakota	14967/26412	KJ976 43-49151	8.12.44	Crashed at Basra, Iraq on 1.5.45. Canx.
G-AGNB	Douglas C-47B-15-DK Dakota	15274/26719	YI-GNB G-AGNB/KK137/43-49458	26. 1.45	To Aden as VR-AAF in 2/50. Canx 1.2.50.
G-AGNC	Douglas C-47B-15-DK Dakota	15283/26728	EI-ADX G-AGNC/KK145/43-49467	26. 1.45	To France as F-OAFR in 4/49. Canx 4.4.49.
G-AGND	Douglas C-47B-15-DK Dakota	15280/26725	KK142 43-49464	26. 1.45	To Bahamas as VP-BBT in 1/61. Canx 4.1.61.
G-AGNE	Douglas C-47B-15-DK Dakota	15276/26721	KK139 43-49460	14. 2.45	To Kenya as VP-KHN in 11/49. Canx 21.11.49.
G-AGNF	Douglas C-47B-15-DK Dakota	15534/26979	KK201 43-49461	14. 2.45	To Burma as XY-ACM in 3/50. Canx 8.3.50.
G-AGNG	Douglas C-47B-15-DK Dakota	15552/26997	EI-ADY G-AGNG/KK216/43-49736	14. 2.45	To Canada as CF-GVZ in 2/51. Canx 26.1.51.
G-AGNH	DH.89A Dragon Rapide	6803	VP-KCT VG764/G-AGNH/NR715	9. 1.45	To Aden as VR-AAP in 3/56. Canx 6.7.56.
G-AGNI	Avro 652A 19 Srs.1 (Originally regd as Anson XII, to Avro XIX .45)	1214	MG159	17. 1.45	Crashed in Port Erin Bay, off Brodda Head, IoM on 11.6.48. Canx as PWFU 30.6.48.
G-AGNJ(1)	Portsmouth Aerocar Minor	1		19. 2.45	Construction abandoned. Canx 10.10.47.
G-AGNJ(2)	DH (Aust) 82A Tiger Moth	660	VP-YOJ ZS-BGF/SAAF 2366	21. 2.89	(On rebuild)
G-AGNK	Douglas C-47B-15-DK Dakota	15540/26985	KK206 43-49724	14. 2.45	WFU at Southend on 14.12.63. Scrapped in 1966. Canx.
G-AGNL	Avro 685 York C.1	1213	WW581 G-AGNL/TS789	19. 3.45	Scrapped at Stansted in 3/54. Canx.
G-AGNM	Avro 685 York C.1	1215	WW511 G-AGNM/XA192/G-AGNM/TS790	22. 3.45	WFU at Stansted in 1/58. Broken up in 12/58. Canx.
G-AGNN	Avro 685 York C.1	1216	WW465 G-AGNN/ZS-BGU/G-AGNN/TS791	12. 4.45	WFU at Stansted in 5/57. Broken up in 7/57. Canx.
G-AGNO	Avro 685 York C.1	1217	WW576 WW577/G-AGNO/TS792	9. 6.45	WFU at Stansted in 3/60. Canx.
G-AGNP	Avro 685 York C.1	1218	OD-ABT G-AGNP/WW509/G-AGNP/ZS-BRA/G-AGNP/TS793	27. 6.45	To Lebanon as OD-ACZ in 6/57. Canx 3.6.57.
G-AGNR	Avro 685 York C.1	1219	ZS-ATP G-AGNR/TS794	9. 7.45	Crashed at Az-Zubair, Basra, Iraq on 16.7.47. Canx.
G-AGNS	Avro 685 York C.1	1220	WW466 G-AGNS/ZS-BTT/G-AGNS/TS795	20. 8.45	DBR at Idris El Alwal, Tripoli on 22.4.56. Broken up in 9/57 at Heathrow. Canx.
G-AGNT	Avro 685 York C.1	1221	WW514 G-AGNT/ZS-ATU/G-AGNT/TS796	20. 8.45	WFU & broken up at Stansted in 12/56. Canx.
G-AGNU	Avro 685 York C.1	1222	XD670 G-AGNU/ZS-ATR/G-AGNU/TS797	20. 8.45	To Lebanon as OD-ACO in 12/56. Canx 12.12.56.
G-AGNV	Avro 685 York C.1	1223	"MW100" "LV633"/G-AGNV/TS798	20. 8.45	WFU on 9.10.64. (On display 3/96 Cosford Aerospace Museum)
G-AGNW	Avro 685 York C.1	1224	WW581 G-AGNW/ZS-ATS/G-AGNW/TS799	20. 8.45	To Iran as EP-ADB in 2/55. Canx 6.2.55.
G-AGNX	Avro 685 York C.1	1225	WW582 G-AGNX/TS800	20. 8.45	WFU at Stansted in 6/53. Broken up in 2/55. Canx.
G-AGNY	Avro 685 York C.1	1226	WW510 G-AGNY/TS801	20. 8.45	Crashed at Kyritz Brandenburg, near Berlin on 26.6.54. Canx.
G-AGNZ	Avro 685 York C.1	1227	ZS-BRB G-AGNZ/TS802	20. 8.45	DBF on landing at Gatow, West Berlin on 24.8.52. Canx.

Regn	Type	c/n	Previous identity	Regn date	Fate or immediate subsequent identity (if known)
G-AGOA	Avro 685 York C.1	1228	WW542 G-AGOA/TS803	20. 8.45	Scrapped at Squires Gate in 1/54. Canx in 4/59.
G-AGOB	Avro 685 York C.1	1229	WW501 G-AGOB/TS804	20. 8.45	WFU at Stansted in 2/62. Broken up at Luton in 11/63. Canx
G-AGOC	Avro 685 York C.1	1230	TS805	20. 8.45	Scrapped at Hurn in 11/49. Canx in 11/49.
G-AGOD	Avro 685 York C.1	1231	WW577 WW576/G-AGOD/TS806	20. 8.45	To Iran as EP-ADC in 10/55. Canx 1.10.55.
G-AGOE	Avro 685 York C.1	1232	TS807	20. 8.45	WFU at Stansted in 1/55. Broken up in 2/55. Canx in 4/56.
G-AGOF	Avro 685 York C.1	1233	WW579 G-AGOF/ZS-ATT/G-AGOF/TS808	20. 8.45	WFU at Squires Gate in 1/55. Scrapped in 2/55. Canx.
G-AGOG	Percival P.34 Proctor III	H.337	HM460	9. 3.45	To Egypt in 4/50. Canx 4.4.50.
G-AGOH	Auster J/1 Autocrat	1442		19. 4.45	Leicestershire County Council Museums (On loan to Newark Air Museum - on display 9/97) CofA expired 24.8.95.
G-AGOI	Westland Whirlwind I	WA.7048	P7048	29. 3.45	Dismantled at Yeovil in 5/47. Canx in 5/47.
G-AGOJ	DH.89A Dragon Rapide	6850	NR774	27. 4.45	Crashed at Lympne on 1.5.61. Canx.
G-AGOK	Vickers 491 Viking 1A	1 & 101	(TT194)	18. 5.45	DBR in forced-landing at Effingham on 23.4.46. Remains to Shoeburyness Gunnery Ranges in 1/47. Canx.
G-AGOL	Vickers 495 Viking 1A	2 & 102	(TT197)	4. 7.45	To RAF as VX238 in 2/50. Canx 28.2.50.
G-AGOM	Vickers 496 Viking 1A	3 & 103	(TT181)	4. 7.45	To RAF as VX141 in 12/47. Canx 11.12.47.
G-AGON	Vickers 498 Viking 1A	4 & 104	VW214 G-AGON	11. 2.45	WFU at Southend in 12/55. Scrapped in 1956. Canx.
G-AGOO	Pivot S/S Parasol Monoplane	1	(G-AFRW)	14. 5.45	Not completed. Scrapped at Gorleston in 2/47. Canx 12/46.
G-AGOP	DH.89A Dragon Rapide	6873	NR797	25. 5.45	Crashed at Mile Post 100 on Syrian oil pipeline on 25.6.48 Canx.
G-AGOR	DH.89A Dragon Rapide	6877	NR801	25. 5.45	To Kenya as VP-KLB in 4/53. Canx 29.4.53.
G-AGOS	Reid & Sigrist RS.4 Bobsleigh (Originally RS.3 Desford Trainer)	3	VZ728 G-AGOS	. 4.45	WFU 9.11.81. (Leicester Museum of Science & Industry) (Stored 4/96)
G-AGOT	DH.89A Dragon Rapide	6876	NR800	31. 5.45	To Kenya as VP-KCX in 8/45. Canx 2.8.45.
G-AGOU	DH.89A Dragon Rapide	6875	NR799	31. 5.45	To Kenya as VP-KCW in 8/45. Canx 2.8.45.
G-AGOV	DH.89A Dragon Rapide	6874	NR798	31. 5.45	To Kenya as VP-KCY in 8/45. Canx 2.8.45.
G-AGOW	DH.89A Dragon Rapide	6849	VP-KCV G-AGOW/NR773	31. 5.45	Scrapped at Croydon in 12/57 still marked as VP-KCV. Canx.
G-AGOX	DH.89A Dragon Rapide	6848	NR772	31. 5.45	To Kenya as VP-KCU in 8/45. Canx 2.8.45.
G-AGOY	Miles M.38 Messenger 3	4690	EI-AGE G-AGOY/HB-EIP/G-AGOY/U-0247	5. 6.45	(On rebuild 4/92)
G-AGOZ	Miles M.57 Aerovan 1	4700	U-0248	5. 6.45	WFU at Woodley in 1947. Broken up in 11/49. Fuselage used as a caravan 6/50. Canx.
G-AGPA	Percival P.31 Proctor V (Originally regd as Proctor IV)	H.764	RM161	19. 6.45	DBR at Plympton St.Mary on 4.8.47. Scrapped at Gatwick in 7/48. Canx.
G-AGPB	Avro 652A Anson 19 Srs.1 (Originally regd as Anson XII, then as Anson XIX 11/45)	1271	PH828	3. 9.45	DBR in overshoot at Bovingdon on 22.9.50. Canx.
G-AGPC(1)	Douglas C-47 Dakota	-		. 6.45R	NTU. Canx.
G-AGPC(2)	Handley Page HP.70 Halifax C.VIII	1360	PP287	25.10.47	To France as F-BCJS in 10/47. Canx 25.10.47.
G-AGPD	Miles M.60 Marathon I	6265	U-10	5. 6.45	Crashed near Amesbury on 10.5.48. Canx.
G-AGPE	Foster-Wikner Wicko G.M.1A	II	HM497	8. 6.45	WFU at Eastleigh on 1.7.48. Scrapped in 3/49. Canx 5/49.
G-AGPF	Avro 688 Tudor 1	1234	TT176	20. 8.45	To MoS as VX192 in 3/49. Canx 16.3.49.
G-AGPG	Avro 652A Anson 19 Srs.2 (Originally regd as Anson XII, to Anson XIX in 1/47, to 19 Srs.2 in 5/52)	1212		15. 6.45	CofA expired 13.2.71 & WFU at Southend. Canx 5.11.75. (Stored 3/97 Chadderton)
G-AGPH	DH.89A Dragon Rapide	6889	NR813	13. 6.45	DBR at Barra, Hebrides on 6.12.51. Canx.
G-AGPI	DH.89A Dragon Rapide	6885	NR809	13. 6.45	Overshot landing and crashed at Somerton, IoW on 16.6.49. Canx.
G-AGPJ	DH.104 Dove 1B (Originally regd as a Srs.1)	04000/P1	WJ310 G-AGPJ	22. 6.45	To Cape Verde Islands as CR-CAC in 3/56. Canx 27.3.56.
G-AGPK(1)	Avro 691 Lancastrian 1	Set.35		1. 8.45	NTU - To RAF as Lancastrian II as VM732. Canx 15.2.46.
G-AGPK(2)	DH.82A Tiger Moth	86566	N657DH F-BGDN/French AF/PG657	27.10.88	
G-AGPL	Avro 691 Lancastrian 1	Set.36		1. 8.45	NTU - To RAF as Lancastrian II as VM733. Canx 15.2.46.
G-AGPM	Avro 691 Lancastrian 1	Set.37		1. 8.45	NTU - To RAF as Lancastrian II as VM734. Canx 15.2.46.
G-AGPN	Avro 691 Lancastrian 1	Set.38		1. 8.45	NTU - To RAF as Lancastrian II as VM735. Canx 15.2.46.
G-AGPO	Avro 691 Lancastrian 1	Set.39		1. 8.45	NTU - To RAF as Lancastrian II as VM736. Canx 15.2.46.
G-AGPP	Avro 691 Lancastrian 1	Set.41		1. 8.45	NTU - To RAF as Lancastrian II as VM737. Canx 15.2.46.
G-AGPR	Avro 691 Lancastrian 1	Set.42		1. 8.45	NTU - To RAF as Lancastrian II as VM738. Canx 15.2.46.
G-AGPS	Auster J/2 Arrow	1660	Z-1	10. 7.45	DBR in gales at Rearsby on 16.3.47. Canx.
G-AGPT	Short S.25/V Sandringham II	SH.2C	DD834	19. 7.45	To Argentina as LV-AAP in 5/46. Canx 21.11.45.
G-AGPU	Avro 652A Anson 19 Srs.1 (Originally regd as Anson XII, to Anson XIX in 11/45)	1241	PH816	4. 8.45	Restored to RAF as PH816 in 2/48. Canx 4.2.48.
G-AGPV	Bristol 170 Freighter II (Originally regd as a Mk.I)	12730	(G-APIO) VR380/G-AGPV/(VK900)	27. 6.45	WFU at Baginton with CofA expired in 7/63. To Gatwick in 6/64. Broken up in 10/65. Canx.
G-AGPW	Bristol 167 Brabazon 1 (Was the largest landplane ever built in Britain and cost some £3 million in 1949)	12759	VX206 G-AGPW	27. 6.45	Scrapped at Filton in 10/53. Canx 10/53.
G-AGPX	Miles M.38 Messenger IIB	6266	U-0273	28. 6.45	WFU at Stapleford on 25.3.62. Canx.
G-AGPY	Short S.25/V Sandringham III	SH.3C	DD841	19. 7.45	To Argentina as LV-AAR in 11/45 with c/n SH.54C. Canx 24.11.45.
G-AGPZ	Short S.25/V Sandringham II	SH.1C	DV964	19. 7.45	To Argentina as LV-AAQ in 11/45. Canx 17.11.45.
G-AGRA	DH.82A Tiger Moth	86173	NL690	30. 6.45	To Ireland as EI-AGG in 9/53. Canx 4.9.53.
G-AGRB	DH.82A Tiger Moth	86348	NL905	30. 6.45	To Belgium as OO-EVN in 4/53. Canx 15.4.53.
G-AGRC	Avro 688 Tudor 4C (Originally regd Tudor 1)	1251	(TS866)	5. 9.45	Scrapped at Woodford in 12/48. Canx 12/48.
G-AGRD	Avro 688 Tudor 4C (Originally regd Tudor 1)	1252	(TS867)	5. 9.45	Scrapped at Woodford in 12/48. Canx 3/49.

Regn	Type	c/n	Previous identity	Regn date	Fate or immediate subsequent identity (if known)
G-AGRE	Avro 688 Tudor 4B (Originally regd Tudor 1)	1253	(TS868)	5. 9.45	Fatal crash into Atlantic Ocean, off Bermuda on 17.1.49. Canx.
G-AGRF	Avro 688 Tudor 4B (Originally regd Tudor 1)	1254	(TS869)	5. 9.45	WFU at Hurn. Scrapped at Southend in 9/53. Canx.
G-AGRG	Avro 688 Super Trader 4C (Originally regd as Tudor 1, then as Tudor 4C)	1255	(TS870)	5. 9.45	DBF after undercarriage collapsed at Brindisi on 27.1.59. Canx.
G-AGRH	Avro 688 Super Trader 4B (Originally regd as Tudor 1, then as Tudor 4B)	1256	(TS871)	5. 9.45	Crashed into Mount Suphan Dag, Turkey on 23.4.59. Canx.
G-AGRI	Avro 688 Tudor 4 (Originally regd as Tutor I)	1257	XF739 G-AGRI/(TS872)	5. 9.45	Scrapped at Stansted in 10/54. Canx.
G-AGRJ	Avro 688 Tudor I	1258	(TS873)	5. 9.45	Scrapped at Stansted in 8/56. Canx.
G-AGRK	Avro 688 Tudor I	1259	(TS874)	5. 9.45	Not completed. Scrapped at Woodford in 12/50. Canx 12/50.
G-AGRL	Avro 688 Tudor I	1260	(TS875)	5. 9.45	Not completed. Scrapped at Woodford in 12/50. Canx 12/50.
G-AGRM	Vickers 498 Viking 1A	5 & 105		11. 2.46	To RAF as VW215 in 8/47. Canx 15.8.47.
G-AGRN	Vickers 498 Viking 1A	6 & 106		11. 2.46	To RAF as VW216 in 8/47. Canx 23.8.47.
G-AGRO	Vickers 498 Viking 1A	7 & 107		11. 2.46	Scrapped at Tollerton in 2/49. Canx.
G-AGRP	Vickers 639 Viking 1 (Originally regd as 498 Viking 1A)	8 & 108	XF639 G-AGRP	11. 2.46	WFU at Gatwick in 3/62. Scrapped in 6/62. Canx.
G-AGRR	Vickers 657 Viking 1 (Originally regd as 498 Viking 1A)	9 & 109	XB-QEX G-AGRR	11. 2.46	To West Germany as D-AIDA in 4/57. Canx 11.4.57.
G-AGRS	Vickers 657 Viking 1 (Originally regd as 498 Viking 1A)	110	VP-TAV G-AGRS	8. 5.46	Scrapped at Southend in 5/63. Canx.
G-AGRT	Vickers 657 Viking 1 (Originally regd as 498 Viking 1A)	111	VP-TAW G-AGRT	8. 5.46	DBF on ground at El Adem, Libya on 26.2.58. Parts salvaged and remains shipped to Blackbushe on 26.5.58. Canx.
G-AGRU	Vickers 657 Viking 1 (Originally regd as 498 Viking 1A)	112	VP-TAX G-AGRU	8. 5.46	WFU & stored at Southend in 9/63. Later used as a hot-dog stall at Soesterberg, The Netherlands in 1/64. On display at Brooklands Museum in 1/99. Canx.
G-AGRV	Vickers 639 Viking 1 (Originally regd as 498 Viking 1A)	114	VP937 G-AGRV	8. 5.46	WFU at Southend in 3/61. Canx 7/61. Broken up in 6/63.
G-AGRW	Vickers 639 Viking 1 (Originally regd as 498 Viking 1A)	115	XF640 G-AGRW	8. 5.46	CofA expired 9.7.68. WFU & stored at Luton in 8/64. Later used as a Coffee Bar at Soesterberg, The Netherlands. On display at Vienna Airport, Austria 8/96.
G-AGRX	Avro 689 Tudor VII (Originally regd as Tudor II)	1261	VX199 G-AGRX/(TS883)	24. 9.45	Scrapped at Tarrant Rushton in 3/54. Canx 4/59.
G-AGRY	Avro 689 Tudor II	1262	XF537 G-AGRY/VX202/G-AGRY/(TS884)	24. 9.45	Scrapped at Stansted 7/59. Canx 4/59.
G-AGRZ	Avro 689 Tudor II	1263	VZ366 G-AGRZ/(TS885)	24. 9.45	Scrapped at Southend in 7/59. Canx.
G-AGSA	Avro 689 Tudor II	1264	(TS886)	24. 9.45	To MoS as VZ720 in 12/48. Canx.
G-AGSB	Avro 689 Tudor II	1265	(TS887)	24. 9.45	Intended as Avro 711A Trader. Not built. Canx 10.1.49.
G-AGSC	Avro 689 Tudor II	1266	(TS888)	24. 9.45	Intended as Avro 711A Trader. Not built. Canx 10.1.49.
G-AGSD	Avro 689 Tudor II	1267	(TS889)	24. 9.45	Intended as Avro 711A Trader. Not built. Canx 10.1.49.
G-AGSE	Avro 689 Tudor II	1268	(TS890)	24. 9.45	Intended as Avro 711A Trader. Not built. Canx 10.1.49.
G-AGSF	Avro 689 Tudor II	1269	(TS891)	24. 9.45	Intended as Avro 711A Trader. Not built. Canx 10.1.49.
G-AGSG	Avro 689 Tudor II	1270	(TS892)	24. 9.45	Intended as Avro 711A Trader. Not built. Canx 10.1.49.
G-AGSH	DH.89A Dragon Rapide 6	6884	EI-AJO G-AGSH/NR808	25. 7.45	
G-AGSI	DH.89A Dragon Rapide	6886	NR810	25. 7.45	To Australia as VH-BFS in 2/55. Canx 26.10.54.
G-AGSJ	DH.89A Dragon Rapide	6888	NR812	25. 7.45	To Denmark as OY-ACZ in 12/49. Canx 2.12.49.
G-AGSK	DH.89A Dragon Rapide	6887	NR811	25. 7.45	To Transjordan as TJ-ABP in 10/53. Canx 2.10.53.
G-AGSL	Avro 685 York C.1	1236	WW579 G-AGSL/TS809	1. 8.45	Scrapped at Squires Gate in 6/54. Canx 5/54.
G-AGSM	Avro 685 York C.1	1237	WW540 G-AGSM/TS810	1. 8.45	WFU at Stansted in 3/50. Broken up in 3/54. Canx 8/54.
G-AGSN	Avro 685 York C.1	1238	WW578 G-AGSN/TS811	1. 8.45	Crashed Fayid, Egypt in 8/51, to Stansted & scrapped in 1/52. Canx.
G-AGSO	Avro 685 York C.1	1239	WW467 G-AGSO/TS812	1. 8.45	Scrapped at Stansted in 4/58. Canx 1/59.
G-AGSP	Avro 685 York C.1	1240	TS813	1. 8.45	Scrapped at Heathrow in 5/55. Canx 4/55.
G-AGSR	Benes Mraz Be.550 Bibi	2	OK-BET	30. 7.45	(Imported in 1939 & stored until 1945) Fatal crash near White Waltham on 25.10.51. Canx.
G-AGSS	Handley Page HP.68 Hermes I	HP68/1		20. 8.45	Crashed at Kendalls Hall, near Radlett on 3.12.45. Canx.
G-AGST	Avro 688 Tudor 8 (Originally regd as Tudor I, then Tudor 4)	1249	(TT181)	20. 8.45	To MoS as VX195 in 1/51. Canx 8.1.51.
G-AGSU	Avro 689 Tudor II	1235		20. 8.45	Crashed near Woodford on take-off when a wing struck the ground on 23.8.47. Canx.
G-AGSV	Avro 689 Tudor II	1250		20. 8.45	Construction abandoned. Was intended as Avro 711A Trader prototype. Canx 1/49.
G-AGSW	Percival P.31 Proctor IV	As.1 & H.796	RM193	10. 9.45	Crashed at Porquis, Ontario, Canada on 19.7.46. Canx.
G-AGSX	Percival P.31 Proctor IV	As.2 & H.799	RM196	13.11.45	DBR at Haren, Belgium on 17.5.47. Scrapped at Tollerton in 3/52. Canx.
G-AGSY	Percival P.31 Proctor IV	Ae.1 & H.800	RM197	10. 9.45	To Australia as VH-ARV in 11/46. Canx 6.11.46.
G-AGSZ	Percival P.44 Proctor V	As.3	RM191	13.11.45	To Australia as VH-ADP in 7/51. Canx 17.7.51.
G-AGTA	Percival P.44 Proctor V	Ae.10		8.12.45	Sold in Brazil on 28.1.46. Canx.
G-AGTB	Percival P.44 Proctor V	Ae.8		8.12.45	To Australia in 10/47 - regd as VH-BCM in 11/47. Canx 5.11.47.
G-AGTC	Percival P.44 Proctor V	Ae.3		8.12.45	Crashed on beach near Malaga Airport, Spain on 2.5.69. Canx.
G-AGTD	Percival P.44 Proctor V	Ae.9		17.12.45	Crashed on take-off Kingstown, Carlisle on 18.10.48. Canx.
G-AGTE	Percival P.44 Proctor V	Ae.14		19. 2.46	To France as F-OAMV in 2/53. Canx 10.2.53.
G-AGTF	Percival P.44 Proctor V	Ae.16		19. 2.46	WFU at Martlesham Heath in 7/64. Canx.

Regn	Type	c/n	Previous identity	Regn date	Fate or immediate subsequent identity (if known)
G-AGTG	Portsmouth Aerocar Major	2001		10. 9.45	Scrapped at Portsmouth in 10/50. Canx 2/51.
G-AGTH	Percival P.34 Proctor III	H.291	HM397	11. 9.45	To France as F-DAAO in 8/51. Canx 1.8.51.
G-AGTI	Consolidated-Vultee CV.32-3 (LB-30) Liberator II	39	AL541	25. 9.45	To Australia as VH-EAI in 7/47. Canx 2.7.47.
G-AGTJ	Consolidated-Vultee CV.32-3 (LB-30) Liberator II	22	AL524	25. 9.45	To Australia as VH-EAJ in 7/47 (originally allotted VH-EAE c 3/47). Canx 2.7.47.
G-AGTK(1)	Scottish Aviation SAL.50 Concord	77		. 9.45R	NTU - Not built. Canx.
G-AGTK(2)	Handley Page HP.70 Halifax C.VIII	1347	PP274	25. 6.47	To France as F-BCJX(2) in 8/47. Canx 29.7.47.
G-AGTL	Lockheed 12A (R30-2)	1287	BuA.02947 NC33615	19. 9.45	To France as F-BJJY in 3/63. Canx 22.12.60.
G-AGTM	DH.89A Dragon Rapide 6	6746	JY-ACL OD-ABP/G-AGTM/NF875	19. 9.45	
G-AGTN	DH.89A Dragon Rapide	6749	NF878	19. 9.45	To TransJordan as TJ-ABJ in 2/52. Canx 20.2.52.
G-AGTO	Auster J/1 Autocrat	1822		2.10.45	
G-AGTP	Auster J/1N Alpha (Originally regd as J/1 Autocrat)	1823		2.10.45	Fatal crash on take-off from Enstone on 31.5.78. Canx as destroyed 16.6.78.
G-AGTR	Auster J/1 Autocrat	1824		2.10.45	To West Germany as D-ENUM in 12/58. Canx 9.12.58.
G-AGTS	Auster J/1 Autocrat	1825		2.10.45	Crashed at Denham on 25.11.47. Canx in 1948.
G-AGTT	Auster J/1 Autocrat	1826		2.10.45	
G-AGTU	Auster J/1 Autocrat	1837		2.10.45	To Southern Rhodesian AF as SR-28 in 8/47. Canx.
G-AGTV	Auster J/1 Autocrat	1838		2.10.45	To Ireland as EI-AMK in 9/62. Canx 22.5.62.
G-AGTW	Auster J/1 Autocrat	1839		2.10.45	To France as F-OAJK in 7/51. Canx 24.7.51.
G-AGTX	Auster J/1 Autocrat	1840		2.10.45	CofA expired 27.1.65 & WFU at Southend. Scrapped in 1968.
G-AGTY	Auster J/1 Autocrat	1841		9.11.45	Crashed at Denham on 19.7.54. Canx.
G-AGTZ	Short S.25 Sandringham III	SH.4C	EJ170	25. 9.45	To Argentina as LV-AAQ in 2/46. Canx 24.11.45.
G-AGUA	Airspeed AS.57 Ambassador 1	61	RT665 G-AGUA/(RT665)	27. 9.45	WFU at Christchurch in 1951, fuselage to Heathrow in 1954. Scrapped at Stansted in 6/63. Canx.
G-AGUB	Handley Page HP.74 Hermes II	HP.74/1	(PW943)	21. 8.47	To RAF as VX234 in 10/53. Canx.
G-AGUC	DH.104 Dove 1 (Originally c/n 4002)	04000/P2		8.10.45	Crashed at West Howe, near Bournemouth on 14.8.46. Canx 17.1.47.
G-AGUD	Avro 652A Anson 19 Srs.1	1275	VL360	9.11.45	To USA as N9951F in 1/55. Canx 23.9.54.
G-AGUE	Avro 652A Anson 19 Srs.1	1276	VL361	9.11.45	Crashed & DBF during overshoot at Speke on 16.8.46. Canx as WFU 3.12.46.
G-AGUF	DH.89A Dragon Rapide	6855	NR779	18.10.45	Crashed at Ramsgate on 29.6.57. Canx.
G-AGUG	DH.89A Dragon Rapide	6859	AP-AGL G-AGUG/NR783	18.10.45	To France as F-OCAG in 12/62. Canx 10.1.63.
G-AGUH	Avro 652A Anson 19 Srs.1	1273	120 Ethiopian AF/G-AGUH/VL358	23.10.45	WFU at Baginton in 9/60. Scrapped at Filton in 11/60. Canx as PWFU 19.9.60.
G-AGUI	Avro 652A Anson 19 Srs.1	1274	121 Ethiopian AF/G-AGUI/VL359	23.10.45	Used for spares & burnt at Croydon on 21.2.53. Canx 4.9.56.
G-AGUJ(1)	Avro 683 Lancaster B.III	-	PB418	. .45R	NTU - Remained with RAF as PB418. Canx.
G-AGUJ(2)	Avro 683 Lancaster B.III	-	PP689	27.10.45	Scrapped at Langley in 12/49. Canx 14.12.49.
G-AGUK(1)	Avro 683 Lancaster B.III	-	ME549	. .45R	NTU - Ramained with RAF as ME549. Canx.
G-AGUK(2)	Avro 683 Lancaster B.III	-	PP688	27.10.45	Scrapped at Langley in 1/47. Canx 1/47.
G-AGUL(1)	Avro 683 Lancaster B.III	-	RF270	. .45R	NTU - Remained with RAF as RF270. Canx.
G-AGUL(2)	Avro 683 Lancaster B.III	-	PP690	27.10.45	Crashed on landing Heathrow on 23.10.47. Remains scrapped in 2/48. Canx.
G-AGUM(1)	Avro 683 Lancaster B.III	-	RF250	. .45R	NTU - Remained with RAF as RF250. Canx.
G-AGUM(2)	Avro 683 Lancaster B.III	-	PP751	27.10.45	Scrapped at Dunsfold in 12/49. Canx 14.12.49.
G-AGUN(1)	Avro 683 Lancaster B.III	-	RF214	. .45R	NTU - Remained with RAF as RF214. Canx.
G-AGUN(2)	Avro 683 Lancaster B.III	-	PP744	27.10.45	NTU - Not delivered. To G-AHVN in 7/46. Canx 3.7.46.
G-AGUO(1)	Avro 683 Lancaster B.III	-	RF246	. .45R	NTU - Remained with RAF as RF246. Canx.
G-AGUO(2)	Avro 683 Lancaster B.III	-	PP746	27.10.45	NTU - Not delivered. Canx 7/46. Scrapped in 5/47.
G-AGUP	DH.89A Dragon Rapide	6911	NR847	24.10.45	To France as F-OBGY in 2/58. Canx 26.2.58.
G-AGUR	DH.89A Dragon Rapide	6910	NR846	9.11.45	Crashed at Rhein Main, Frankfurt, West Germany on 2.8.54. Canx.
G-AGUS	Miles M.65 Gemini I Prototype (Converted to Mk.II in 1949)	4701	U-0249	29.10.45	To Sweden as SE-BUY in 7/52. Canx 11.7.52.
G-AGUT	Bristol 170 Freighter I (Originally regd as Mk.IIA)	12733	(G-APIP) VR382/G-AGUT	29.10.45	Not converted. WFU at Blackbushe. Broken up in 6/59. Canx.
G-AGUU	DH.89A Dragon Rapide	6908	NR844	30.10.45	To North Borneo as VR-OAA in 8/52. Canx 1.8.52.
G-AGUV	DH.89A Dragon Rapide	6912	NR848	30.10.45	Crashed at Taif, Bahrein on 26.4.54. Canx.
G-AGUW	Miles M.38 Messenger IIC	6267	U-0274	30.10.45	To Belgium as OO-CCM in 8/46. Canx 26.8.46.
G-AGUX	Avro 652A Anson 19 Srs.1	1277		9.11.45	Crashed at Rio de Oro, 25m E of Villa Cisneros, Spanish Sahara on 15.12.51. Canx as destroyed 4.1.52. Rebuilt as EC-ALF in 1955.
G-AGUY	Stinson L-5 Sentinel	-		1.11.45R	NTU - Not converted. Canx 21.10.47.
G-AGUZ	Nord 1000	NORD/1000/15		1.11.45	Not converted. Scrapped at Gatwick in 1946. Canx in 10/47.
G-AGVA	Avro 652A Anson 19 Srs.1	1278		9.11.45	To West Germany as D-IGOR in 4/56. Canx 6.4.56.
G-AGVB	Bristol 170 Freighter 21 (Originally regd as Mk.IIB)	12731	XF656 G-AGVB/G-18-1/(VK903)	5.11.45	Crashed at Le Touquet, France on 4.11.58. Canx.
G-AGVC	Bristol 170 Freighter 21 (Originally regd as Mk.1, then Mk.31)	12732	XF657 G-AGVC/G-18-2/G-AGVC	5.11.45	DBR on landing at Ronaldsway, IoM on 30.6.62. Canx.
G-AGVD	Short S.40 Shetland II	S.1313	DX171 G-AGVD/DX171	16.11.45	WFU at Belfast, Northern Ireland in 11/49. Scrapped in 1951. Canx.
G-AGVE	Percival P.34 Proctor III	H.524	LZ724	7.11.45	To New Zealand as ZK-APG in 5/47. Canx 6.5.47.
G-AGVF	Auster J/1N Alpha (Originally regd as J/1 Autocrat)	1857		7.12.45	Badly damaged in severe gales at Enstone on 2.1.76. Rebuilt and sold to Australia. Canx 7.8.78.
G-AGVG	Auster J/1 Autocrat	1858		7.12.45	Badly damaged by severe gales at Hull/Paull on 2.1.76. (On rebuild as J/1U Workmaster 11/95 off airfield)
G-AGVH	Auster J/1 Autocrat	1859		7.12.45	To Malaya as VR-RBO in 11/50. Canx 14.11.50.

Regn	Type	c/n	Previous identity	Regn date	Fate or immediate subsequent identity (if known)
G-AGVI	Auster J/1 Autocrat (Converted to Rover Turbine-powered in 1965, de-converted in 1968)	1860		7.12.45	Crashed at Portadown on 4.11.72. Canx as WFU 20.10.75.
G-AGVJ	Auster J/1N Alpha (Originally regd as J/1 Autocrat)	1861		7.12.45	WFU in 8/64. Canx as WFU 29.9.71 at Tollerton. (Donated various components to G-AIBY in 1970)
G-AGVK	Auster J/1 Autocrat	1844		7.12.45	To France as F-BFYS in 12/48. Canx 15.12.48.
G-AGVL	Auster J/1 Autocrat	1871		10. 1.46	Crashed at Panshanger on 22.1.67. Canx.
G-AGVM	Auster J/1N Alpha (Originally regd as J/1 Autocrat)	1872		1. 2.46	Crashed at Lulsgate on 19.9.59. Canx.
G-AGVN	Auster J/1 Autocrat	1873	EI-CKC G-AGVN	18. 1.46	
G-AGVO	Auster J/1 Autocrat	1874		18. 1.46	To Australia as VH-AJE in 4/52. Canx 12.2.52.
G-AGVP	Auster J/1 Autocrat	1875		1. 2.46	To Trinidad & Tobago as VP-TBV in 6/57. Canx 20.12.56.
G-AGVR	Auster J/1 Autocrat	1876		18. 1.46	To Australia as VH-WRB in 2/51. Canx 28.2.51.
G-AGVS	Auster J/1 Autocrat	1877		19. 1.46	To Nyasaland as VP-NAJ in 4/48. Canx 21.4.38.
G-AGVT	Auster J/1 Autocrat	1878		1. 2.46	DBR in gales Heston 16.3.47. Rebuilt as Z-1/G-AICA. Canx.
G-AGVU	Auster J/1 Autocrat	1879		18. 1.46	To France as F-BBRU in 2/52. Canx 19.2.52.
G-AGVV	Piper J3C-65 Cub (L-4H-PI)	11163	F-BCZK(2) French AF/43-29872	19. 2.81	
G-AGVW	Miles M.14A Hawk Trainer III	1748	P6380 U-0259	15.11.45	Destroyed in mid-air collision with Auster OY-DGA off Copenhagen on 21.4.46. Canx.
G-AGVX	Miles M.28 Mercury IV	4685	HB-EED G-AGVX/U-0243	16.11.45	To Australia as VH-AKH in 12/52. Canx 31.12.52.
G-AGVY	Airspeed AS.40 Oxford (Converted to AS.65 Consul)	3204	V3679	30.11.45	Missing on Beirut-Amman flight on 11.2.49, wreckage found near Hairture, Lebanon on 21.2.49. Canx 28.3.49.
G-AGVZ	Lockheed 12A (UC-40D-LO)	1277	LA621 42-38349/NC18900	7.12.45	To USA as NC79820 in 2/47. Canx 13.2.47.
G-AGWA	Avro 652A Anson 19 Srs.1	1332	D-IDEK N9923F/G-AGWA	6. 5.46	Used for spares, still marked as D-IDEK 1963. Canx as PWFU 17.6.64. Nose & tail sections to Wealden Park County School, Cuckfield, Sussex as Instructional Airframe. Scrapped in 1979.
G-AGWB(1)	Avro 652A Anson 19	-		.12.45R	NTU. Canx.
G-AGWB(2)	Percival P.34 Proctor III	H.504	LZ734 G-AGWB/LZ734	19. 3.46	Caught fire in the air while competing in the National Air Races on 5.8.67, and was destroyed by fire immediately after forced-landing near Moulton Station, nine miles south-west of Middleton St.George. Was in full service livery as LZ734 as it was engaged in filming "Devils Brigade" at Henlow at the time. Canx.
G-AGWC	DH.89A Dragon Rapide	6916	NR852	13.12.45	To Pakistan as AP-ADM in 7/52. Canx 9.7.52.
G-AGWD	Avro 652A Anson C.19 Srs.2	1285	PH860	28.12.45	To RAF/Egypt as VN889/SU-ADN in 2/46. Canx as PWFU 26.2.46.
G-AGWE	Avro 652A Anson C.19 Srs.2	1286	TX201	28.12.45	Canx as sold 17.5.73. Used for spares for G-BFIR in 1980. Dismantled & noted 16.4.98 at Titusville, FL, USA.
G-AGWF	Avro 652A Anson C.19 Srs.2	1287	TX202	28.12.45	WFU at Croydon on 20.9.57. Scrapped. Canx.
G-AGWG	Avro 691 Lancastrian III	Set.40 & 1279	TX274	28.11.45	Crashed on landing Kindley Field, Bermuda on 13.11.47. Canx.
G-AGWH	Avro 691 Lancastrian III	Set.58 & 1280	TX275	28.11.45	Lost in Andes approx. 40 miles from Santiago, Chile on 2.8.47. Canx.
G-AGWI	Avro 691 Lancastrian III	Set.59 & 1281	TX276	28.11.45	Scrapped at Tarrant Rushton on 26.9.51. Canx.
G-AGWJ	Avro 691 Lancastrian III	Set.60 & 1282	TX280	28.11.45	Crashed on take-off from Bathurst, Gambia on 30.8.46. Canx.
G-AGWK	Avro 691 Lancastrian III	Set.61 & 1283	TX281	28.11.45	Crashed on landing at Kindley Field, Bermuda on 5.9.47. Canx.
G-AGWL	Avro 691 Lancastrian III	Set.62 & 1284	TX282	28.11.45	Scrapped at Tarrant Rushton on 26.9.51. Canx.
G-AGWM	Lockheed 12A (UC-40D-LO)	1211 & SH.49C	LA620 42-38352/NC17311	19. 2.46	To Belgium as OO-AFA in 3/47. Canx 31.3.47.
G-AGWN	Lockheed 12A (UC-40D-LO)	1275 & SH.50C	LA623 42-38348/NC1....	19. 2.46	To Australia as VH-BHH in 10/52. Canx 31.10.53.
G-AGWO	Miles M.57 Aerovan II	6432	U-8	19. 2.46	Crashed in gale Newtownards, Northern Ireland on 5.4.47. Canx.
G-AGWP	DH.89A Dragon Rapide	6918	UN-71 G-AGWP/RL936	8.12.45	To Belgian Congo as OO-CJE in 11/60. Canx 28.9.60.
G-AGWR	DH.89A Dragon Rapide	6917	NR853	8.12.45	To Denmark as OY-DYA in 4/54. Canx 30.5.54.
G-AGWS	Douglas C-47-DL Dakota	6208	WZ984 G-AGWS/41-38749	28.12.45	To Canada as CF-FCQ in 7/52. Canx 1.5.52.
G-AGWT	Miles M.7A Nighthawk	286	VR-TCM VP-KMM/G-AGWT U-0225/U5	28.12.45	Sold to Singapore but seized at Marseilles-Marignane Airport & sold for scrap at Lignane, near Aix-en-Provence. (Noted at Lignane on 29.6.65 in advance state of decomposition) Canx as WFU in 3/63.
G-AGWU	Short S.45 Seaford I	S.1293	NJ201	31.12.45	Restored to RAF as NJ201 in 2/47. Canx 1.7.47.
G-AGWV	Percival P.28 Proctor 1	K.256	P6197	14. 1.46	Crashed at Benina, Libya on 27.7.52. Canx.
G-AGWW	Short S.25 Sandringham 3	SH.5C	EJ156	3. 1.46	To Uruguay as CX-AFA in 5/46. Canx 26.2.46.
G-AGWX	Short S.25 Sandringham 3	SH.6C	(LV-AAS) G-AGWX/ML876	3. 1.46	To Uruguay as CX-AKF in 4/46. Canx 26.2.46.
G-AGWY	Auster J/1 Autocrat	1880		21. 1.46	To West Germany as D-ELYM in 2/56. Canx 28.2.56.
G-AGWZ	Auster J/1 Autocrat	1881		24. 1.46	Crashed on take-off at Haddington, East Lothian on 20.5.47. Canx.
G-AGXA	Handley Page HP.60A Halifax B.III	-	NR169	4. 1.46	To Australia as VH-BDT in 2/47. Canx 17.2.47.
G-AGXB	Auster J/1 Autocrat	1892		21. 1.46	DBR in gales at Tollerton on 16.12.62. Canx.
G-AGXC	Auster J/1 Autocrat	1893		21. 1.46	Crashed at Denham on 16.1.52. Canx.
G-AGXD	Auster J/1 Autocrat	1894		21. 1.46	To Australia as VH-DDY in 4/55. Canx 20.4.55.
G-AGXE	Auster J/1 Autocrat	1895		21. 1.46	To South Africa as ZS-BPM in 4/47. Canx 2.4.47.

Regn	Type	c/n	Previous identity	Regn date	Fate or immediate subsequent identity (if known)
G-AGXF	Auster J/1 Autocrat	1896		21. 1.46	Crashed into White Horse Hill, Litton Cheney, near Bridport on 5.4.52. Canx.
G-AGXG	Auster J/1 Autocrat	1897		21. 1.46	DBR when struck by DH.82A G-ANDA at Denham on 6.3.55. Canx.
G-AGXH	Auster J/1N Alpha (Originally regd as J/1 Autocrat)	1898		21. 1.46	Derelict at Lympne in 12/71. Canx as WFU at Shoreham 15.12.72 after CofA expiry on 25.4.69.
G-AGXI	Auster J/1 Autocrat	1899		21. 1.46	To South Africa as ZS-DDM in 11/48. Canx 27.11.48.
G-AGXJ	Auster J/1 Autocrat	1900		1. 2.46	To France as F-BGRX in 3/53. Canx 1.3.53.
G-AGXK	Auster J/1 Autocrat	1951		24. 1.46	Crashed at Midland, near Staverton on 20.8.53. Canx.
G-AGXL	Auster J/1 Autocrat	1961		24. 1.46	Crashed in France on 26.6.47. Canx.
G-AGXM	Auster J/1 Autocrat	1962		22. 1.46	Crashed at Loch Leven on 12.7.53. Canx.
G-AGXN	Auster J/1N Alpha (Originally regd as J/1 Autocrat)	1963		22. 1.46	
G-AGXO	Auster J/1 Autocrat	1964		1. 2.46	To Spain as EC-AJS in 12/53. Canx 2.12.53.
G-AGXP	Auster J/1 Autocrat	1965		21. 1.46	WFU on 4.2.71. Stored dismantled at Ipswich and DBF on 4.10.73. Canx 25.4.72.
G-AGXR	Auster J/1 Autocrat	1966		1. 2.46	To Uganda as VP-UAL in 8/46. Canx 6.8.46.
G-AGXS	Auster J/1 Autocrat	1967		24. 1.46	To Spain as EC-ALD in 8/55. Canx 12.5.55.
G-AGXT	Auster J/1N Alpha (Originally regd as J/1 Autocrat)	1968		1. 2.46	Hit hedge on landing at Bickmarsh after engine failure on 7.6.69. Wreck to South Wales. Canx.
G-AGXU	Auster J/1N Alpha (Originally regd as J/1 Autocrat)	1969		24. 1.46	
G-AGXV	Auster J/1 Autocrat	1970		1. 2.46	
G-AGXW	Auster J/1 Autocrat	1971		25. 1.46	To New Zealand as ZK-AUB in 2/50. Canx 17.2.50.
G-AGXX	Auster J/1 Autocrat	1982		1. 2.46	Crashed at Cambridge on 16.12.51. Canx.
G-AGXY	Auster J/1 Autocrat	1983	YI-ABM G-AGXY	1. 2.46	Scrapped at Perth in 9/54. Canx 7.2.54.
G-AGXZ	Auster J/1 Autocrat	1984		24. 1.46	To South Africa as ZS-DAE in 7/48. Canx 22.7.48.
G-AGYA	Percival P.28 Proctor 1	K.247	P6188	6. 2.46	To Australia as VH-BQQ in 8/51. Canx 27.8.51.
G-AGYB	Percival P.28 Proctor 1	K.265	P6231	6. 2.46	Derelict at Cowes, IoW in 4/53. Canx 4/59.
G-AGYC	Percival P.28 Proctor 1	K.241	P6182	21. 5.46	Scrapped at Croydon in 2/52. Canx.
G-AGYD	Auster J/1N Alpha (Originally regd as J/1 Autocrat)	1985		4. 2.46	(On rebuild by B.Ellis 4/94)
G-AGYE	Auster J/1 Autocrat	1986		4. 2.46	Crashed at Le Baule, France on 28.7.48. Canx.
G-AGYF	Auster J/1 Autocrat	1987		4. 2.46	Crashed at Southend on 29.8.54. Canx.
G-AGYG	Auster J/1 Autocrat	1988	F-BDAX G-AGYG	4. 2.46	Crashed at Sherrington on 18.9.65. Canx.
G-AGYH	Auster J/1N Alpha (Originally regd as J/1 Autocrat)	1989		4. 2.46	(On rebuild)
G-AGYI	Auster J/1N Alpha (Originally regd as J/1 Autocrat)	1990		4. 2.46	Crashed at Teg Down, Brighton on 3.9.58. Canx.
G-AGYJ	Auster J/1 Autocrat	1991		19. 1.46	To Australia as VH-BGB in 1/52. Canx 9.1.52.
G-AGYK	Auster J/1 Autocrat	2002		4. 2.46	(Stored dismantled 10/97 Bidgord)
G-AGYL	Auster J/1 Autocrat	2003		4. 2.46	Crashed at Llyswen, Brecon on 6.7.64. Canx.
G-AGYM	Auster J/1N Alpha (Originally regd as J/1 Autocrat)	2004		4. 2.46	CofA expired 30.4.72. Canx as WFU 14.11.72.
G-AGYN	Auster J/1 Autocrat	2005		4. 2.46	To Norway as (LN-BFT)/LN-BFV in 4/56. Canx 6.4.56.
G-AGYO	Auster J/1 Autocrat	2006		4. 2.46	Crashed at Kemsing, Sevenoaks on 24.8.51. Canx.
G-AGYP	Auster J/1N Alpha (Originally regd as J/1 Autocrat)	2007		7. 2.46	Crashed at East Didsbury, Manchester on 14.4.61. Canx.
G-AGYR	Auster J/1 Autocrat	2008		8. 2.46	Crashed at Kirkburton on 11.12.50. Canx.
G-AGYS	Auster J/1 Autocrat	1866	(VR-LAA) G-AGYS	18. 1.46	Crashed at Sherbo Island on 28.4.49. Canx in 2/50. Rebuilt as F-BGXX in 1953.
G-AGYT	Auster J/1N Alpha (Originally regd as J/1 Autocrat)	1862		18. 1.46	CofA expired 27.2.91. (On overhaul at Lightwater, Surrey)
G-AGYU	DH.82A Tiger Moth	85265	DE208	10. 1.46	(Stored 10/96)
G-AGYV	DH.82A Tiger Moth	82029	N6751	10. 1.46	To Belgium as OO-TWD in 7/46. Canx 11.7.46.
G-AGYW	DH.82A Tiger Moth	3857	N6544	10. 1.46	To Pakistan as AP-AEP in 2/49. Canx 9.2.49.
G-AGYX	Douglas C-47A-10-DK Dakota	12472	KG437 42-92648	15. 1.46	To The Netherlands as PH-MAG in 7/65. Canx 1.7.65.
G-AGYY	Ryan ST-3KR (PT-21-RY)	1167	N56792 41-1942	15. 6.83	
G-AGYZ	Douglas C-47A-5-DK Dakota	12278	FZ681 42-108843	6. 2.46	To Ethiopia as ET-AGQ in 6/77. Canx 8.6.77.
G-AGZA	Douglas C-47A-10-DK Dakota	12455	KG420 42-92633	18. 2.46	Crashed into house-roof on take-off from Northolt, South Ruislip on 19.12.46. Canx.
G-AGZB	Douglas C-47A-1-DK Dakota	12180	FZ624 42-92385	21. 2.46	Crashed near Ventnor, IoW on 6.5.62. Canx.
G-AGZC	Douglas C-47A-5-DK Dakota	12222	AP-AAN (VT-CPN)/G-AGZC/FZ662/42-92423	25. 2.46	To Mali as (CT-AAA)/TZ-ABA in 3/61. Canx 6.3.61.
G-AGZD	Douglas C-47A-10-DK Dakota	12450	KG415 42-92628	27. 2.46	To Bahamas as VP-BCC in 5/63. Canx 14.5.63.
G-AGZE	Douglas C-47A-10-DK Dakota	12416	KG386 42-92598	18. 3.46	To France as F-BEFS in 4/49. Canx 4.4.49.
G-AGZF	Douglas C-47A-1-DL Dakota	9172	WZ984 G-AGZF/42-23310	11. 1.46	To French AF as 42-23310/F-RAFC in 10/52. Canx 5.10.52.
G-AGZG	Douglas C-47A-35-DL Dakota	9803	WZ985 G-AGZG/42-93941	11. 1.46	To French AF as 42-23941 in 10/52. Canx 5.10.52.
G-AGZH	Consolidated-Vultee CV.32-3 (LB-30) Liberator II	69	AL571	11. 1.46	Scrapped at Prestwick in 4/50. Canx.
G-AGZI	Consolidated-Vultee CV.32-3 (LB-30) Liberator II	55	AL557	11. 1.46	To Greece as SX-DAA in 2/48. Canx 24.2.48.
G-AGZJ	DH.89A Dragon Rapide	6936	RL954	12. 1.46	WFU at Cardiff on 30.6.50. Canx.

Regn	Type	c/n	Previous identity	Regn date	Fate or immediate subsequent identity (if known)
G-AGZK	DH.89A Dragon Rapide	6937	RL955	12. 1.46	WFU at Beirut, Lebanon in 12/51. DBF at Amman, Jordan on 9.5.53. Canx.
G-AGZL	Percival P.28 Proctor I	K.285	P6251	14. 1.46	DBF in hangar fire at Broxbourne on 23.6.47. Canx.
G-AGZM	Percival P.28 Proctor I	K.293	P6259	14. 1.46	Crashed near Stapleford on 29.1.57. Canx.
G-AGZN	Taylorcraft Plus D	178	LB319	23. 1.46	Crashed into pylon near Rearsby on 1.2.48. Canx.
G-AGZO	DH.89A Dragon Rapide	6913	NR849	26. 1.46	To France as F-BGZJ in 5/62. Canx 24.5.62.
G-AGZP(1)	DH.98 Mosquito PR.IX	-		. 1.46R	NTU. Canx.
G-AGZP(2)	Handley Page HP.70 Halton II	1398	ZS-BTA G-AGZP/PP336	14. 3.46	Emergency landing at Stansted on 10.4.51. CofA expired 1.4.52 & WFU at Bovingdon. Canx 27.2.53.
G-AGZR(1)	DH.98 Mosquito PR.IX	-		. 1.46R	NTU. Canx.
G-AGZR(2)	Miles M.14A Hawk Trainer III	902	U-0252 N3856	26. 2.46	To Siam Navy in 11/47. Canx 12.11.47.
G-AGZS	Avro 652A Anson 19 Srs.1	1330	TX236	6. 5.46	Crashed into Bell Hill, near Petersfield, Hants on 4.1.52. Canx as destroyed 4.1.52.
G-AGZT	Avro 652A Anson 19 Srs.1	1331	TX255	6. 5.46	Damaged on landing at Croydon on 3.1.57, not repaired and scrapped at Croydon in 3/60. Canx as PWFU 21.3.63.
G-AGZU	DH.89A Dragon Rapide	6773	NR674	22. 1.46	To South Africa as ZS-DLS in 4/55. Canx 23.4.55.
G-AGZV	Stinson SR.10C Reliant	5902	VP-KDV G-AGZV/BS803/NC21133	21. 1.46	To New Zealand as ZK-BDV in 8/53. Canx 27.8.53.
G-AGZW	Stinson 105 Voyager	7504	X1050	21. 1.46	To Sweden as SE-BYI in 6/53. Canx 17.4.53.
G-AGZX	Miles M.3B Falcon Six	269	R4071 G-AEAO/PH-EAO/G-AEAO	22. 1.46	To Belgium as OO-FLY in 12/46. Canx 23.12.46.
G-AGZY	DH.82A Tiger Moth	82287	N9176	25. 1.46	To India as VT-DBC in 2/49. Canx 2.2.49.
G-AGZZ	DH(Aust).82A Tiger Moth	T256 & 926	N3862 VH-BTU/VH-RNM/VH-BMY/R.Australian AF A17-503	14. 5.82	
G-AHAA	Miles M.28 Mercury 6	6268		26. 1.46	To West Germany as D-EHAB in 9/56. Canx 31.8.56.
G-AHAB	Percival P.28 Proctor I	K.301	P6267	26. 1.46	Burnt at Panshanger on 5.11.63. Canx.
G-AHAC	Airspeed AS.6J Envoy III	79	P5626	24. 1.46	Scrapped at Tollerton in 5/50. Canx.
G-AHAD	Taylorcraft Plus D	154	LB283	24. 1.46	To Ireland as EI-ALJ in 4/59. Canx 7.9.59.
G-AHAE	Taylorcraft Plus C/2	114	HH982 G-AFVA	28. 1.46	WFU at Panshanger in 10/52. Scrapped in 1957. Canx.
G-AHAF	Taylorcraft Plus C/2	110	T9120	26. 1.46	DBR when Taylorcraft G-AHUG landed on top of it at Thruxton on 29.5.48. Cannibalised to service G-AHUG. Canx.
G-AHAG	DH.89A Dragon Rapide	6926	RL944	31. 1.46	CofA expired 15.7.73. (Stored 9/97)
G-AHAH	Taylorcraft Plus D	199	LB340	1. 2.46	Crashed at Musbury, Devon on 10.7.47. Canx.
G-AHAI	Taylorcraft Plus D	202	LB343	1. 2.46	Crashed at Moselle, France on 8.11.59. Canx.
G-AHAJ	Taylorcraft Plus D	221	LB374	1. 2.46	Crashed at Cranleigh on 20.11.47. Canx.
G-AHAK	Taylorcraft Plus D	177	LB318	1. 2.46	Crashed at Speke on 16.6.57. Canx.
G-AHAL	Auster J/1N Alpha (Originally regd as J/1 Autocrat)	1870		31. 1.46	
G-AHAM	Auster J/1 Autocrat	1885		21. 1.46	
G-AHAN	DH.82A Tiger Moth	86553	N90406 F-BGDG/French AF/PG644	31. 5.85	
G-AHAO	Auster J/1 Autocrat	1886		7. 2.46	To Sweden as SE-BYU in 12/53. Canx 21.11.53.
G-AHAP	Auster J/1 Autocrat	1887		8. 2.46	Permit to Fly expired 20.2.91. (Being modified with Rover V-8 by Classic Parts & Panels Ltd, Aylesbury 8/91, but reported at Farley Farm, Romsey 1/97)
G-AHAR	Auster J/1 Autocrat	1888	F-BGRZ G-AHAR	7. 2.46	(Fuselage frame stored at Mavis Enderby in 9/98)
G-AHAS	Auster J/1 Autocrat	1889		7. 2.46	To Sweden as SE-ART in 3/46. Canx.
G-AHAT	Auster J/1N Alpha (Originally regd as J/1 Autocrat)	1849	(HB-EOK)	11. 2.46	Crashed at Old Sarum on 31.8.74. CofA expired 6.2.75. Canx as WFU 7.7.75. (Frame at Dumfries in 9/98)
G-AHAU	Auster J/1-160 Autocrat	1850	(HB-EOL)	11. 2.46	
G-AHAV	Auster J/1 Autocrat	1863	(HB-EOM)	13. 2.46	WFU on 1.3.72. CofA expired 21.6.75. (Stored 4/96 Headcorn) Canx by CAA 22.2.99.
G-AHAW	Auster J/1 Autocrat	1865	(HB-EUK)	5. 3.46	To New Zealand as ZK-AWH in 8/50. Canx 7.9.50.
G-AHAX	Auster J/1B Aiglet	1955		12. 3.46	To New Zealand as ZK-AUO in 5/50. Canx 1.5.50.
G-AHAY	Auster J/1 Autocrat	1956		12. 3.46	Sold to Israel 10.3.83 for preservation. Canx.
G-AHAZ	Percival P.28 Proctor I	K.229	P6170	6. 2.46	Crashed near Zurich, Switzerland on 17.9.46. Canx.
G-AHBA	Percival P.44 Proctor V	Ae.17		19. 2.46	WFU in 11/63. Canx.
G-AHBB	Percival P.44 Proctor V	Ae.18		19. 3.46	To Argentina as LV-NEH in 10/46. Canx 31.10.46.
G-AHBC	Percival P.44 Proctor V	Ae.26		23. 3.46	Crashed at Ocana, near Madrid, Spain on 21.9.54. Canx.
G-AHBD	Percival P.44 Proctor V	Ae.27		21. 3.46	CofA expired 22.3.68 & WFU at Baginton. Broken up at Blackbushe in 1974. Engine to G-AEXF. Canx as WFU 5.5.70.
G-AHBE	Percival P.44 Proctor V	Ae.28		3. 4.46	To Indian as VT-CEP in 1/47. Canx 7.1.47.
G-AHBF	Percival P.44 Proctor V	Ae.31		3. 4.46	To Indian as VT-CFP in 1/47. Canx 7.1.47.
G-AHBG	Percival P.44 Proctor V	Ae.32		3. 4.46	To Indian as VT-CFQ in 1/47. Canx 7.1.47.
G-AHBH	Percival P.44 Proctor V	Ae.37		15. 4.46	Crashed at Jersey on 4.8.65. Canx.
G-AHBI	Percival P.44 Proctor V	Ae.38		15. 4.46	To Turkey as TC-TUL in 7/53. Canx 9.7.53.
G-AHBJ	Percival P.44 Proctor V	Ae.39		18. 4.46	WFU at Croydon on 13.12.57. Canx.
G-AHBK	General Aircraft Monospar ST.25 Jubilee	GAL/ST25/71	K8308	6. 2.46	Crashed near Cirencester on 2.6.47. Canx.
G-AHBL	DH.87B Hornet Moth	8135	P6786 CF-BFN	6. 2.46	
G-AHBM	DH.87B Hornet Moth	8126	P6785 CF-BFJ/(CF-BFO)/CF-BFJ	6. 2.46	
G-AHBN	Avro 652A Anson I	-	NK270	28. 2.46	To Italy as I-AHBN in 7/48. Canx 26.7.48.
G-AHBO	Taylorcraft Plus C/2	109	HH986 G-AFUD	13. 2.46	Crashed at Weston Favell, Northampton on 24.5.52. Canx.
G-AHBP	Junkers Ju52/3m (Converted by Short Bros.)	6750 & SH.7C	VM908 D-APZX	20. 8.46	Broken up at Castle Bromwich in 2/48. Canx.
G-AHBR	Percival P.34 Proctor III	H.400	LZ593	21. 2.46	Crashed into sea off Paignton on 10.11.46. Canx.
G-AHBS	Percival P.28 Proctor I	K.162	P6062	21. 2.46	DBR taxying at Little Snoring on 3.3.60. Canx.

Regn	Type	c/n	Previous identity	Regn date	Fate or immediate subsequent identity (if known)
G-AHBT	Avro 691 Lancastrian III	Set.71 & 1288		20. 2.46	WFU at Dunsfold in 3/52. Canx 24.3.52.
G-AHBU	Avro 691 Lancastrian III	Set.72 & 1289		20. 2.46	Crashed on take off at Nutts Corner, Belfast, Northern Ireland on 3.10.47. Canx.
G-AHBV	Avro 691 Lancastrian III	Set.73 & 1290		20. 2.46	WFU at Dunsfold in 3/52. Canx 7.3.52.
G-AHBW	Avro 691 Lancastrian III	Set.74 & 1291		20. 2.46	To Australia as VH-EAV in 2/48. Canx 21.1.48.
G-AHBX	Avro 691 Lancastrian III	Set.75 & 1292		20. 2.46	To Italy as I-AHBX in 2/48. Canx 13.2.48.
G-AHBY	Avro 691 Lancastrian III	Set.76 & 1293		20. 2.46	To Italy as I-AHBY in 11/47. Canx 12.11.47.
G-AHBZ	Avro 691 Lancastrian III	Set.77 & 1294		20. 2.46	To Pakistan as AP-ACQ in 3/49. Canx 8.3.49.
G-AHCA	Avro 691 Lancastrian III	Set.78 & 1295		20. 2.46	Burnt in hangar fire at Dunsfold on 8.12.46. Canx.
G-AHCB	Avro 691 Lancastrian III	Set.79 & 1296		20. 2.46	To Italy as I-AHCB in 7/47. Canx 21.7.47.
G-AHCC	Avro 691 Lancastrian III	Set.80 & 1297		20. 2.46	Scrapped at Dunsfold in 3/52. Canx 24.3.52.
G-AHCD	Avro 691 Lancastrian III	Set.81 & 1298		20. 2.46	To Italy as I-AHCD in 12/47. Canx 17.12.47.
G-AHCE	Avro 691 Lancastrian III	Set.82 & 1299		20. 2.46	To Italy as I-DALR in 8/47. Canx 7.8.47.
G-AHCF	Auster J/1 Autocrat	1960		11. 3.46	To Spain as EC-DAZ in 10/48. Canx 1.1.51.
G-AHCG(1)	Auster J/1 Autocrat	-		. .46R	NTU - Canx.
G-AHCG(2)	Taylorcraft Plus D	206	LB347	12. 3.46	To Ireland as EI-ANA in 8/63. Canx 1.6.63.
G-AHCH(1)	Auster J/1 Autocrat	-		. .46R	NTU - Canx.
G-AHCH(2)	Taylorcraft Plus D	164	LB293	12. 3.46	DBR at Rearsby on 16.3.47. Canx.
G-AHCI(1)	Auster J/1 Autocrat	-		. .46R	NTU - Canx.
G-AHCI(2)	Taylorcraft Plus D	159	LB288	12. 3.46	DBF at Shoreham on 18.9.51. Canx.
G-AHCJ	Auster J/1 Autocrat	1972		25. 3.46	Crashed at Speeton on 5.9.48. Canx.
G-AHCK	Auster J/1N Alpha (Originally regd as J/1 Autocrat)	1973		25. 3.46	Damaged in arson attack at Ingoldmells on 14.9.91. Canx by CAA 22.4.94. (Stored at Mavis Enderby in 9/98)
G-AHCL	Auster J/1N Alpha (Originally regd as J/1 Autocrat)	1977	G-OJVC G-AHCL	13. 5.46	CofA expired 10.10.91. (On rebuild 8/92)
G-AHCM	Auster J/1N Alpha (Originally regd as J/1 Autocrat)	1979		25. 3.46	To The Netherlands as PH-AAF in 1/63. Canx 1.1.63.
G-AHCN	Auster J/1N Alpha (Originally regd as J/1 Autocrat)	1980	OY-AVM G-AHCN	25. 3.46	Restored as OY-AVM. Canx 12.11.79.
G-AHCO	Auster J/1 Autocrat	1992		25. 3.46	To West Germany as D-EGEH in 5/58. Canx.
G-AHCP	Auster J/1 Autocrat	1993		25. 3.46	Crashed at Sywell on 28.6.47. Canx.
G-AHCR(1)	Auster J/1 Autocrat	-		. .46R	NTU - Canx.
G-AHCR(2)	Gould-Taylorcraft Plus D Special (Originally regd as a Taylorcraft Plus D)	211	LB352 G-AHCR	15. 4.46	
G-AHCS	Douglas C-47A-5-DK Dakota	12348	KG341 42-108850	21. 3.46	Crashed near Oslo, Norway on 7.8.46. Canx.
G-AHCT	Douglas C-47A-5-DK Dakota	12308	KG313 42-108846	21. 3.46	WFU on 19.1.72. Canx 18.8.72. To fire dump at Ringway in 6/73.
G-AHCU	Douglas C-47-25-DK Dakota	13381	KG621 42-93466	29. 3.46	WFU at Southend on 16.10.66. Broken up in 1/70. Canx 24.2.70.
G-AHCV	Douglas C-47A-10-DK Dakota	12443	KG408 42-92622	24. 4.46	WFU at Southend on 28.3.66. Broken up in 1/70. Canx.
G-AHCW	Douglas C-47A-25-DK Dakota	13308	KG585 42-108946	24. 4.46	DBR in collision with RAF Anson VV243 and crashed near Exhall, Coventry on 19.2.49. Canx.
G-AHCX	Douglas C-47A-25-DK Dakota	13335	KG604 42-93425	24. 4.46	To Yemen as YE-ABC in 7/62. Canx 19.6.62.
G-AHCY	Douglas C-47A-5-DK Dakota	12355	KG348 42-92543	1. 5.46	Fatal crash into hillside at Wimberry Stones, Saddleworth, Oldham on 19.8.49. Canx.
G-AHCZ	Douglas C-47A-1-DK Dakota	11924	YI-HCZ G-AHCZ/FL563/42-92155	9. 5.46	To Cyprus as 5B-CBC 5/69. Canx 18.4.69.
G-AHDA	Douglas C-47A-1-DK Dakota	12177	FZ622 42-92383	13. 5.46	Not converted. Broken up for spares at Speke in 1946. Canx 8.4.47.
G-AHDB	Douglas C-47A-1-DK Dakota	12077	FL649 42-92293	31. 5.46	Not converted. Broken up for spares at Speke in 1946. Canx.8.4.47.
G-AHDC	Douglas C-47A-25-DK Dakota	13481	DG664 42-93556	16. 6.46	Not converted. To spares use at Speke on 8.4.47. Canx.
G-AHDD	DH.82A Tiger Moth	86051	EM849	21. 2.46	Crashed near Calais, France on 6.8.55. Canx.
G-AHDE	DH.82A Tiger Moth	86113	EM919	21. 2.46	To France as F-OAGR in 4/50. Canx 1.4.50.
G-AHDF	DH.82A Tiger Moth	86164	EM981	21. 2.46	To Hong Kong as VR-HEM in 3/49. Canx 9.3.49.
G-AHDG	DH.82A Tiger Moth	85213	DE143	27. 2.46	Crashed near Casablanca on 16.4.50. Canx.
G-AHDH	Percival P.28 Proctor I	K.236	P6177	26. 2.46	Not converted. Broken up at Panshanger in 12/50. Canx.
G-AHDI	Percival P.28 Proctor I	K.253	P6194	26. 2.46	To Australia as VH-AUC in 6/51. Canx 1.6.51.
G-AHDJ	Percival P.28 Proctor I	K.298	P6264	26. 2.46	Crashed at Great Barford, near Bedford on 18.6.54. Canx.
G-AHDK	Percival P.28 Proctor I	K.146	P6034	27. 2.46	To Belgium as OO-AVG in 5/46. Canx 17.5.46.
G-AHDL	Handley Page HP.70 Halton I	1308 & SH.23C	PP224	19. 3.46	Destroyed in belly landing at Gatow, East Germany on 1.4.49. Canx 1.4.49.
G-AHDM(1)	Handley Page HP.70 Halton I	1312 & SH.20C	PP228	19. 3.46	WFU at Blackbushe on 7.5.50. Scrapped in 9/50. Canx 18.9.50.
G-AHDM(2)	Miles HDM.105 Aerovan (Rebuild of M.57 Aerovan G-AJOF c/n 6403 in 1957 with Hurel-Dubois high aspect ratio wing)	105/1009	G-35-3 G-AJOF	18. 4.57	WFU at Shoreham on 28.6.58. Canx.

Regn	Type	c/n	Previous identity	Regn date	Fate or immediate subsequent identity (if known)
G-AHDN	Handley Page HP.70 Halton I	1318 & SH.24C	PP234	19. 3.46	Scrapped at Southend in 11/50. Canx 20.11.50.
G-AHDO	Handley Page HP.70 Halton I	1310 & SH.29C	(ZS-DAT) G-AHDO/PP226	19. 3.46	Scrapped at Southend in 11/50. Canx 11.11.50.
G-AHDP	Handley Page HP.70 Halton I	1341 & SH.25C	PP268	19. 3.46	Crashed at Schleswigland, near Berlin, East Germany on 4.4.49. Canx 27.3.51.
G-AHDR	Handley Page HP.70 Halton I	1342 & SH.26C	PP269	19. 3.46	To France as F-BECK(2) in 6/48. Canx 28.5.48.
G-AHDS	Handley Page HP.70 Halton I	1350 & SH.22C	PP277	19. 3.46	CofA expired 22.2.50 & WFU at Southend. Broken up in 3/51. Canx 27.3.51.
G-AHDT	Handley Page HP.70 Halton I	1370 & SH.27C	PP308	19. 3.46	Scrapped for spares use in 11/49 at Schleswigland, Germany. Canx 11.11.49.
G-AHDU	Handley Page HP.70 Halton I	1372 & SH.18C	PP310	19. 3.46	Scrapped at Southend in 11/50. Canx as WFU 25.3.54.
G-AHDV	Handley Page HP.70 Halton I	1376 & SH.21C	PP314	19. 3.46	DBR by gales at Squires Gate on 17.12.52 & damaged Halifax C.VIII G-AKEC. Canx 4.3.53.
G-AHDW	Handley Page HP.70 Halton I	1377 & SH.19C	PP315	19. 3.46	Scrapped at Southend in 11/50. Canx 20.11.50.
G-AHDX	Handley Page HP.70 Halton I	1378 & SH.28C	PP316	19. 3.46	Crashed into Mount Hohgart, in Swiss Alps on 16.4.50. Canx 16.4.50.
G-AHDY	Consolidated-Vultee CV.32-4 (B-24D-CO) Liberator III	1941	LV337 41-1087	27. 2.46	Broken up at Prestwick in 10/50. Canx.
G-AHDZ	Airspeed AS.40 Oxford II	PAC/397	ED190	27. 2.46	To France as F-BBIU in 7/54. Canx 8.7.54.
G-AHEA	DH.89A Dragon Rapide	6946	RL964	27. 2.46	To France as F-BHCF in 1/55. Canx 21.1.55.
G-AHEB	DH.89A Dragon Rapide	6945	EI-ADP G-AHEB/RL963	27. 2.46	To France as F-BHVQ in 3/57. Canx 8.2.57.
G-AHEC	Luscombe 8A Silvaire	3428	N72001 NC72001	28.10.88	
G-AHED	DH.89A Dragon Rapide 6	6944	RL962	27. 2.46	WFU on 17.4.68. Canx 3.3.69. (In store 10/95 RAF Cardington)
G-AHEE	Percival P.30 Proctor II	H.206	BV649	4. 3.46	WFU at Luton in 4/50. Canx.
G-AHEF	Airspeed AS.65 Consul	4044	PH191	5. 3.46	WFU on 13.9.58. Scrapped at Christchurch in 8/60. Canx.
G-AHEG	Airspeed AS.65 Consul	1052	T1206	5. 3.46	WFU at Shoreham on 10.5.61. Scrapped in 7/63. Canx.
G-AHEH	Airspeed AS.65 Consul	3362	TJ-ABB G-AHEH/LX641	5. 3.46	To Spain as EC-AJX in 6/54. Canx 19.6.54.
G-AHEI	Taylorcraft Plus D	126	W5740 G-AFZH	5. 3.46	To France as F-OAQP in 3/54. Canx 17.3.54.
G-AHEJ	Lockheed L.049D-46-25 Constellation	1975	N2740A G-AHEJ/N90902/42-94554	6. 4.46	WFU at Biggin Hill in 7/61. Broken up in 2/63. Canx.
G-AHEK	Lockheed L.049D-46-25 Constellation	1976	N90903 42-94555	6. 4.46	To USA as N2737A in 6/55. Canx 28.2.55.
G-AHEL	Lockheed L.049D-46-25 Constellation	1977	N2736A G-AHEL/N90604/42-94556	6. 4.46	To Kenya as 5Y-ABF in 12/64. Canx 30.12.64.
G-AHEM	Lockheed L.049D-46-25 Constellation	1978	N90605 42-94557	6. 4.46	To USA as N2735A in 6/55. Canx 11.10.54.
G-AHEN	Lockheed L.049D-46-25 Constellation	1980	HB-IED 4X-AKD/N74192/G-AHEN/N90606/42-94559	6. 4.46	WFU at Luton on 21.4.65. Scrapped in 11/65. Canx.
G-AHEO	Short S.25 Sunderland III	-	JM716	20. 3.46	Broken up for spares at Hamble in 11/49. Canx.
G-AHEP	Short S.25 Sunderland III	-	DD860 G-AHEP/DD860	20. 3.46	WFU at Hamble on 11.9.52. Canx.
G-AHER	Short S.25 Sunderland III	-	PP142	20. 3.46	Scrapped at Hamble in 1/52. Canx.
G-AHES	Percival P.28 Proctor I	H.6	R7490	13. 3.46	Scrapped at Thruxton in 9.55. (Wings used for G-AEYC) Canx.
G-AHET	Percival P.10C Vega Gull	K.105	P5989	14. 3.46	DBR in forced landing at Kirby Trading Estate, near Liverpool on 2.5.60. Canx.
G-AHEU	Percival P.28 Proctor I	H.17	R7521	15. 3.46	WFU at Gatwick in 9/56. Canx.
G-AHEV	Percival P.28 Proctor I	H.25	R7529	15. 3.46	WFU at Cardiff in 12/54. Burnt at Portsmouth. Canx.
G-AHEW	Avro 685 York C.1	1300		20. 3.46	Fatal crash on take off from Bathurst, Gambia on 6.9.46. Canx.
G-AHEX	Avro 685 York C.1	1301		20. 3.46	Crashed near Caravellas Bay, Brazil on 5.1.49. Canx.
G-AHEY	Avro 685 York C.1	1302	HZ-CAA JY-ABZ/G-AHEY/WW506/G-AHEY	20. 3.46	Scrapped at Stansted in 8/62. Canx.
G-AHEZ	Avro 685 York C.1	1303		20. 3.46	Crashed on landing at Dakar, Senegal on 13.4.47. Canx.
G-AHFA	Avro 685 York C.1	1304	WW504 G-AHFA	20. 3.46	Crashed in Atlantic Ocean off Newfoundland on 2.2.52. Canx.
G-AHFB	Avro 685 York C.1	1305	JY-AAC G-AHFB/WW586/WW499/G-AHFB	20. 3.46	Scrapped at Luton in 4/63. Canx.
G-AHFC	Avro 685 York C.1	1306	(HZ-CAA) G-AHFC/WW507/G-AHFC	20. 3.46	To Lebanon as OD-ACJ in 10/55. Canx 13.10.55.
G-AHFD	Avro 685 York C.1	1307	WW500 G-AHFD	20. 3.46	To Lebanon as OD-ADB in 6/57. Canx 13.6.57.
G-AHFE	Avro 685 York C.1	1308	WW578 G-AHFE	20. 3.46	WFU at Stansted in 1959. Broken up in 2/60. Canx.
G-AHFF	Avro 685 York C.1	1309	WW503 G-AHFF	20. 3.46	WFU at Stansted in 9/59. Broken up in 3/60. Canx.
G-AHFG	Avro 685 York C.1	1310	WW468 G-AHFG	20. 3.46	WFU at Stansted in 10/56. Broken up in 2/59. Canx.
G-AHFH	Avro 685 York C.1	1311	WW502 G-AHFH	20. 3.46	To Lebanon as OD-ADA in 6/57. Canx 3.6.57.
G-AHFI	Avro 685 York C.1	1316		22. 3.46	Fatal crash near Schleswigland, East Germany on 15.3.49. Canx.
G-AHFJ	DH.89A Dragon Rapide	6545	X7385	25. 3.46	To Kenya as VP-KFW, but crashed in Mauritius whilst on delivery on 8.8.48. Canx 26.6.48.

Regn	Type	c/n	Previous identity	Regn date	Fate or immediate subsequent identity (if known)
G-AHFK	Percival P.34 Proctor III	H.538	LZ768	25. 3.46	Derelict at Nairobi, Kenya in 2/64. Canx in 12/63 on sale to East Africa.
G-AHFL	Vickers-Supermarine 236 Walrus I	6S/26388	L2246	23. 3.46	To Norway as LN-TAK in 7/48. Canx 1.7.48.
G-AHFM	Vickers-Supermarine 236 Walrus I	-	W3070	23. 3.46	Scrapped at Cowes, IoW in 7/50. Canx.
G-AHFN	Vickers-Supermarine 236 Walrus I	6S/35698	L2336	1. 4.46	DBR in gales at Loch Ryan, Stranraer on 3.7.55. Canx.
G-AHFO	Vickers-Supermarine 236 Walrus I	-	L2282	1. 4.46	Scrapped at Cowes, IoW in 7/50. Canx.
G-AHFP	Miles M.38 Messenger 4 (Originally regd as Messenger 3)	6332		12. 4.46	To Ireland as EI-AGB in 1/53. Canx 1.10.52.
G-AHFR	Percival P.44 Proctor V (Originally regd as Proctor IV)	H.775	RM172	25. 3.46	WFU at Hucknall in 5/61. Canx.
G-AHFS	Airspeed AS.65 Consul	2942	HN769	25. 3.46	To Sweden as SE-BTU in 8/51. Canx 2.8.51.
G-AHFT	Airspeed AS.65 Consul	2593	UN-99 G-AHFT/HN423	25. 3.46	Ditched in the English Channel, south of Brighton on 14.6.52. Canx.
G-AHFU	Percival P.28 Proctor I	K.246	P6187	29. 3.46	To Australia as VH-DUL in 2/58. Canx 28.2.58.
G-AHFV(1)	Percival P.28 Proctor I	-		. 3.46R	NTU - Canx.
G-AHFV(2)	Avro 652A Anson I	-	AW966	27. 7.46	Fatal crash in English Channel off Isle of Wight, SSW of Brook on 3.7.47. Canx as PWFU 10.11.47.
G-AHFW	Percival P.28 Proctor I	K.296	P6262	26. 3.46	Scrapped at Beirut, Lebanon in 6/51. Canx.
G-AHFX	Percival P.28 Proctor I	K.249	P6190	29. 3.46	To Australia as VH-AYV in 10/46. Canx 18.10.46.
G-AHFY	Percival P.28 Proctor I	K.259	P6200	29. 3.46	WFU at Lympne in 2/62. Canx.
G-AHFZ	Percival P.28 Proctor I	H.8	R7492	29. 3.46	To South Africa as ZS-BMK in 11/46. Canx 11.11.46.
G-AHGA	Percival P.34 Proctor III	H.486	LZ704	29. 3.46	WFU at Elstree in 9/63. Canx.
G-AHGB	Percival P.34 Proctor III	H.560	LZ799	29. 3.46	To South Africa as ZS-BGD, but crashed on delivery as G-AHGB. Canx 20.1.47.
G-AHGC	DH.89A Dragon Rapide	6583	X7442	28. 3.46	WFU on 4.7.68. Components for possible use in G-ALAX c/n 6930 rebuild. Canx.
G-AHGD	DH.89A Dragon Rapide	6862	NR786	1. 4.46	Destroyed in fatal crash near Audley End House on 30.6.91.
G-AHGE	Miles M.38 Messenger 4	6330		2. 4.46	Crashed at Tugela, South Africa on 25.10.46. Canx.
G-AHGF	DH.89A Dragon Rapide	6903	NR839	2. 5.46	To New Zealand as (ZK-BCP)/ZK-BFK in 4/54. Canx 1.5.54.
G-AHGG	DH.89A Dragon Rapide	6902	NR838	2. 5.46	To Liberia as EL-AAA in 4/52. Canx 10.4.52.
G-AHGH	DH.89A Dragon Rapide	6934	RL952	2. 5.46	To Sweden as SE-BXZ in 6/53. Canx 10.6.53.
G-AHGI	DH.89A Dragon Rapide	6935	RL953	2. 5.46	To France as F-OANF in 11/52. Canx 13.11.52.
G-AHGJ	Percival P.44 Proctor V	Ae.41		10. 4.46	WFU at Cranfield in 9/63. Canx.
G-AHGK	Percival P.44 Proctor V	Ae.45		18. 5.46	DBR at Mezze Airport, Damascus, Syria on 5.2.47. Canx as WFU in 1948.
G-AHGL	Percival P.44 Proctor V	Ae.47		27. 5.46	Crashed at Jersey on 9.9.60. Canx.
G-AHGM	Percival P.44 Proctor V	Ae.48		18. 5.46	Scrapped at Croydon in 2/52. Canx.
G-AHGN	Percival P.44 Proctor V	Ae.44		18. 5.46	To USA as N588E in 3/50. Canx 30.3.50.
G-AHGO	Percival P.44 Proctor V	Ae.23		9. 5.46	To New Zealand as ZK-ARA in 6/48. Canx 3.6.48.
G-AHGP	Percival P.44 Proctor V	Ae.42		27. 5.46	Crashed at Belvedere in 1949. Rebuilt in Rhodesia as VP-YKR in 1954. Canx 10.11.49.
G-AHGR	Percival P.44 Proctor V	Ae.56		24. 6.46	Crashed on take-off from Hamburg, West Germany on 15.4.61. Canx.
G-AHGS	Percival P.44 Proctor V	Ae.57		22. 5.46	To Iceland as TF-HGS in 5/54. Canx 10.5.54.
G-AHGT	Percival P.44 Proctor V	Ae.25	(SU-ADO)	4. 6.46	To Ethiopia as ET-P-4 in 1/51. Canx 13.1.51.
G-AHGU	Airspeed AS.40 Oxford II	3277	V3815	3. 4.46	DBR at Fairoaks on 11.10.60. Canx.
G-AHGV	Taylorcraft Auster 5	757	MT191	2.12.46	Forced landed at Humberstone, Leics. on 14.5.49. Canx.
G-AHGW	Taylorcraft Plus D	222	LB375	2. 9.46	
G-AHGX	Taylorcraft Plus D	162	LB291	24. 8.46	To Finland as OH-AUG in 9/52. Canx 30.9.52.
G-AHGY	Taylorcraft Plus D	204	LB345	24. 4.46	WFU at Denham in 7/48. Canx.
G-AHGZ	Taylorcraft Plus D	214	LB367	24. 4.46	(Nearing complete after rebuild 1/99 Old Sarum)
G-AHHA	Taylorcraft Plus D	160	LB289	24. 4.46	To Switzerland as HB-EOR in 6/46. Canx 22.6.46.
G-AHHB	Taylorcraft Plus D	156	LB285	24. 4.46	To Belgium as OO-DCL in 8/59. Canx 17.6.59.
G-AHHC	Taylorcraft Plus D	136	LB266	24. 4.46	To Finland as OH-AUD in 11/51. Canx 3.11.51.
G-AHHD	Auster J/1 Autocrat	1976		9. 4.46	To Holland as PH-FCB in 2/48. Canx 16.1.48.
G-AHHE	Auster J/1 Autocrat	1994		9. 4.46	NTU - To G-AERO in 5/46. Canx.
G-AHHF	Auster J/1 Autocrat	2009		11. 5.46	To Denmark as OY-DGO in 6/46. Canx 14.6.46.
G-AHHG	Auster J/1 Autocrat	2010		11. 5.46	To Denmark as (LN-BAO)/OY-DGI in 7/46. Canx 14.6.46.
G-AHHH	Auster J/1 Autocrat (Type changed from J/1A Alpha to J/1 Autocrat with effect from 1.12.70)	2011	F-BAVR G-AHHH	11. 5.46	
G-AHHI	Auster J/1 Autocrat	2012	OO-PIT OO-ANL/G-AHHI	11. 5.46	DBF at Squires Gate on 4.1.59. Canx.
G-AHHJ	Auster J/1 Autocrat	2013		11. 5.46	To Egypt as SU-AGR in 12/49. Canx 10.12.49.
G-AHHK	Auster J/1 Autocrat	2014		11. 5.46	CofA expired 22.3.70. (Last known on rebuild at Shobdon) Canx as WFU 3.4.89.
G-AHHL	Auster J/1 Autocrat	2015		11. 5.46	Crashed near Avranches, France on 27.9.61. Canx.
G-AHHM	Auster J/1 Autocrat	2016		11. 5.46	Crashed off Cromer on 31.12.59. Canx.
G-AHHN	Auster J/1 Autocrat	2017		11. 5.46	CofA expired 6.12.81. (Last known at Mullagmore) Canx as WFU 3.4.89.
G-AHHO	Auster J/1 Autocrat	2018		11. 5.46	To West Germany as D-EGUT in 10/56. Canx 9.5.56.
G-AHHP	Auster J/1N Alpha (Originally regd as J/1 Autocrat)	2019	G-SIME G-AHHP	11. 5.46	Damaged in gales mid-1980s. CofA expired 8.3.86. (On rebuild .92 Meppershall) Canx by CAA 22.2.99.
G-AHHR	Auster J/1 Autocrat	2020		11. 5.46	Crashed at Rochester on 12.3.55 - Rebuilt as G-AOXR 10/52. Canx.
G-AHHS	Auster J/1 Autocrat	2021		11. 5.46	Ditched into sea off Berck, France on 15.4.63. Canx.
G-AHHT	Auster J/1N Alpha (Originally regd as J/1 Autocrat)	2022		11. 5.46	
G-AHHU	Auster J/1N Alpha (Originally regd as J/1 Autocrat)	2023		11. 5.46	Crashed at Soria, Spain on 10.6.63. (On rebuild 12/91)
G-AHHV	Auster J/1 Autocrat	2024		11. 5.46	To Palestine VQ-PAS in 7/46. Canx 29.7.46.

Regn	Type	c/n	Previous identity	Regn date	Fate or immediate subsequent identity (if known)
G-AHHW	Auster J/1N Alpha (Originally regd as J/1 Autocrat)	1995		16. 5.46	To France as F-BKGX in 8/62. Canx.
G-AHHX	Taylorcraft Plus D	173	LB314	20. 5.46	To West Germany as D-ELUS in 1/57. Canx.
G-AHHY	Taylorcraft Plus D	216	LB369	20. 5.46	To Rhodesia as VP-YPX in 12/58. Canx.
G-AHHZ	Taylorcraft Plus D	229	LB382	12. 6.46	Crashed at Snarford, Lincs on 15.10.50. Canx.
G-AHIA	DH.89A Dragon Rapide	6948	RL966	8. 4.46	DBR whilst taxying at Maritse, Rhodes on 5.3.51. Canx.
G-AHIB	Avro 652A Anson C.19 Srs.1	1317	TX240	30. 4.46	WFU at Wymeswold in 2/60. Canx as PWFU 6.3.63.
G-AHIC	Avro 652A Anson C.19 Srs.2 (Originally regd as Srs.1, converted in 10/61)	1318	TX241	30. 4.46	CofA expired 20.1.73. Used as spares for G-BFIR & scrapped early 1980s. Canx as PWFU 30.5.84.
G-AHID	Avro 652A Anson C.19 Srs.2 (Originally regd as Srs.1, converted in 1950)	1319	TX242	30. 4.46	To Kenya as VP-KKK in 2/51. Canx 15.5.50.
G-AHIE	Avro 652A Anson C.19 Srs.1	1320	TX243	30. 4.46	WFU at Squires Gate on 23.6.47. Remains burnt by Squires Gate Fire Service in 3/59. Canx as PWFU 10.5.63.
G-AHIF	Avro 652A Anson C.19 Srs.1	1321	TX244	30. 4.46	To Sweden as SE-BRS in 9/50. Canx 11.9.50.
G-AHIG	Avro 652A Anson C.19 Srs.1	1322	TX245	30. 4.46	Ditched off Calshot 6.8.55, salvaged and conveyed to Jersey where broken up for spares in 1/57. Canx as PWFU 9.8.56.
G-AHIH	Avro 652A Anson C.19 Srs.1	1323	N9924F G-AHIH/TX247	30. 4.46	To West Germany as D-IDEL in 2/56. Canx 20.2.56.
G-AHII	Avro 652A Anson C.19 Srs.1	1324	TX250	30. 4.46	To Sweden as SE-BTM in 4/51. Canx 30.3.51.
G-AHIJ	Avro 652A Anson C.19 Srs.1	1325	TX251	30. 4.46	To Pakistan as AP-AGA in 12/52. Canx 13.12.52.
G-AHIK	Avro 652A Anson C.19 Srs.1	1326	TX252	30. 4.46	To Sweden as SE-BUI in 2/52. Canx 15.1.52.
G-AHIL	Short S.45 Solent III	S.1300		23. 4.46	Scrapped in 1954 at Solway Morgan's Boatyard, Hamworthy, Hants. Canx.
G-AHIM	Short S.45 Solent III	S.1301		23. 4.46	Scrapped at Belfast, Northern Ireland in 1952. Canx.
G-AHIN	Short S.45 Solent III	S.1302		23. 4.46	Sold to Portugal on 15.12.58 & used in UK marks until WFU at Lisbon on 18.12.59. Canx.
G-AHIO	Short S.45 Solent III	S.1303		23. 4.46	To Australia as VH-TOD in 11/51. Canx 30.10.51.
G-AHIP	Piper J3C-65 Cub (L-4H-PI) (Frame no.11950; official c/n is 12008 - see comments under G-AJAD)	12122	OO-GEJ(2) OO-ALY/44-79826	3. 7.85	
G-AHIR	Short S.45 Solent III	S.1304		23. 4.46	Scrapped at Belfast, Northern Ireland in 1952. Canx.
G-AHIS	Short S.45 Solent III	S.1305		23. 4.46	Scrapped at Belfast, Northern Ireland in 1952. Canx.
G-AHIT	Short S.45 Solent III	S.1306		23. 4.46	WFU at Belfast, Northern Ireland in 12/49. Canx.
G-AHIU	Short S.45 Solent II	S.1307		23. 4.46	Scrapped in 1954 at Solway Morgan's Boatyard, Hamworthy, Hants. Canx.
G-AHIV	Short S.45 Solent II	S.1308		23. 4.46	To Australia as VH-TOC in 7/51. Canx 22.6.51.
G-AHIW	Short S.45 Solent II	S.1309		23. 4.46	Scrapped at Belfast, Northern Ireland in 1952. Canx.
G-AHIX	Short S.45 Solent III	S.1310		23. 4.46	Sank at Netley on 1.2.50. Canx.
G-AHIY	Short S.45 Solent III	S.1311		23. 4.46	Scrapped at Belfast, Northern Ireland in 1952. Canx.
G-AHIZ	DH.82A Tiger Moth (Regd with fuselage no. MCO/DH/4610)	86533	PG624	23. 4.46	
G-AHJA	DH.89A Dragon Rapide	6486	R9558	8. 4.46	DBR at Halfpenny Green in 1969. Canx as WFU 9.4.70. Sold to Australia in 1978.
G-AHJB	Bristol 170 Freighter IIA	12734		30. 5.46	To Brasil as PP-YPF but crashed on 4.7.46 in sea 198kms E of Aracaju, Brasil whilst on delivery. Canx.
G-AHJC	Bristol 170 Freighter 21E (Originally regd as Mk.IIA, then Mk.I)	12735		30. 5.46	To Australia in 9/49 - regd as VH-INK on 23.9.49. Canx 8.9.49.
G-AHJD	Bristol 170 Freighter 21 (Originally regd as Mk.IIA, then Mk.I)	12736	VR-NAK G-AHJD	30. 5.46	WFU at Yeadon in 9/62. Scrapped in 1963. Canx.
G-AHJE	Bristol 170 Freighter 1A	12737		24. 7.46	To Argentina as LV-XII in 10/46. Canx 30.11.46.
G-AHJF	Bristol 170 Freighter 21 (Originally regd as Mk.II, then Mk.IA)	12738		24. 7.46	To France as F-BENF in 4/48. Canx 1.4.48.
G-AHJG	Bristol 170 Freighter 21 (Originally regd as Mk.II then Mk.IIA)	12739	ZS-BOM G-AHJG	24. 7.46	To Ecuador as HC-SBU in 8/48. Canx 29.8.48.
G-AHJH	Bristol 170 Freighter IIA	12740		24. 7.46	To Brasil as PP-YPD in 10/46. Canx 6.10.46.
G-AHJI	Bristol 170 Freighter 21E (Originally regd as Mk.IIA)	12741	F-DABI EC-AES/G-AHJI/VT-CHK/G-AHJI	24. 7.46	CofA expired 4.12.64 & WFU at Southend. Broken up in 11/65. Canx as WFU 6.12.65.
G-AHJJ	Bristol 170 Freighter 21 (Originally regd as Mk.IIA)	12742	VT-CHL G-AHJJ	24. 7.46	Crashed near Cowbridge, Glamorgan on 21.3.50. Canx.
G-AHJK	Bristol 170 Freighter IIA	12743		8. 8.46	To Brasil as PP-YPE in 12/46. Canx 6.10.46.
G-AHJL	Bristol 170 Freighter 21P (Originally regd as Mk.IIC then Mk.IIA)	12744	VT-CGV G-AHJL	8. 8.46	To G-18-13/Pakistan AF as G778 in 8/49. Canx.
G-AHJM	Bristol 170 Freighter 21P (Originally regd as Mk.IIC)	12745	VT-CGW G-AHJM	8. 8.46	To Pakistan AF as G779 in 8/49. Canx 4.8.49.
G-AHJN	Bristol 170 Freighter 21E (Originally regd as Mk.IIA)	12746	VT-CGX G-AHJN	8. 8.46	To G-18-15/MoS as WW378 in 8/51. Canx 28.8.51.
G-AHJO	Bristol 170 Freighter 21P (Originally regd as Mk.IIA)	12747		8. 8.46	To Pakistan AF as G781 in 8/49. Canx 4.8.49.
G-AHJP	Bristol 170 Freighter 21E	12748	XF658 G-AHJP/F-BENH/G-AHJP	8. 8.46	To France as F-DABJ in 11/53. Canx 28.11.53.
G-AHJR(1)	De Schelde Scheldemusch	53	PH-AMG	. 4.46R	NTU - Remained as PH-AMG. Canx.
G-AHJR(2)	Short S.25 Sunderland MR.5	SH1552	SZ584	27. 6.46	Restored to RAF as SZ584 in 4/48. Canx 15.5.48.
G-AHJS	DH.89 Dragon Rapide	6967	TX309	16. 4.46	WFU at Blackbushe on 20.5.66. Canx 13.7.73. Components for possible use in G-ALAX c/n 6930 rebuild.
G-AHJT	Avro 683 Lancaster B.III	AW.3496 & S4/VA2505	LL809	25. 4.46	Scrapped at Tarrant Rushton in 1/50. Canx.
G-AHJU	Avro 683 Lancaster B.III	S4/VA3094	LM681	25. 4.46	Scrapped at Tarrant Rushton in 9/51. Canx 26.9.51.
G-AHJV	Avro 683 Lancaster B.III	S4/VA30257	LM639	25. 4.46	Scrapped at Tarrant Rushton in 1/50. Canx 25.1.50.
G-AHJW	Avro 683 Lancaster B.III	RS/VALB127336	ED866	25. 4.46	Fatal crash into high ground at Connaught Park, near Andover on 22.11.48. Canx.
G-AHJX	Airspeed AS.65 Consul	541	LB529	16. 4.46	Crashed at Guernsey, Channel Islands on 12.5.50. Canx.
G-AHJY	Airspeed AS.65 Consul	2647	HN471	16. 4.46	To Iceland as TF-RPM but crashed at Deepcar 12.4.51 whilst on delivery flight. Canx.

Regn	Type	c/n	Previous identity	Regn date	Fate or immediate subsequent identity (if known)
G-AHJZ	Airspeed AS.65 Consul	2686	HN494	16. 4.46	To France as F-BFAT in 4/57. Canx 4.4.57.
G-AHKA	DH.89A Dragon Rapide	6839	NR751	16. 4.46	To France as F-OAQL in 7/55. Canx 17.12.53.
G-AHKB	DH.89A Dragon Rapide	6596	X7454	16. 4.46	To France as F-BEKB in 10/61. Canx 16.10.61.
G-AHKC	Avro 652A Anson 19 Srs.1	1327	SU-ADQ G-AHKC/TX246	29. 4.46	Restored as Egypt as SU-ADQ in 5/48. Canx 31.5.48.
G-AHKD	Avro 652A Anson 19 Srs.1	1328	SU-ADP G-AHKD/TX248	29. 4.46	Restored as Egypt as SU-ADP in 5/48. Canx 31.5.48.
G-AHKE	Avro 652A Anson 19 Srs.1	1329	SU-ADO G-AHKE/TX249	29. 4.46	Restored as Egypt as SU-ADO in 5/48. Canx 31.5.48.
G-AHKF	Avro 652A Anson I	-	NK602	17. 4.46	To Kenya as VP-KDW in 4/47. Canx.
G-AHKG	Avro 652A Anson I	-	EG499	17. 4.46	To Kenya as VP-KEO in 10/47. Canx 28.10.47.
G-AHKH	Avro 652A Anson I	-	EG526	21. 5.46	To Singapore as VR-SDL in 4/52. Canx 6.4.52.
G-AHKI	Avro 652A Anson I	-	MG771	21. 5.46	To Kenya as VP-KEM in 8/47. Canx 7.8.47.
G-AHKJ	Avro 652A Anson I	-	EG413	21. 5.46	Crashed at Croydon on 12.2.47. Canx as PWFU 13.3.47.
G-AHKK(1)	Avro 652A Anson I	-		. .46R	NTU. Canx.
G-AHKK(2)	Handley Page HP.70 Halifax C.VIII	1371	PP309	25. 6.47	To France as F-BCJV in 7/47. Canx 9.7.47.
G-AHKL	Miles M.65 Gemini 1A	6305		17. 4.46	WFU at Lympne on 15.2.66. CofA expired 26.2.66. Canx 3.4.69.
G-AHKM	Miles M.16 Mentor	462	L4420	18. 4.46	Crashed at Clayhildon, Devon on 1.4.50. Canx.
G-AHKN	Taylorcraft Plus D	180	LB321	24. 4.46	DBF at Thruxton on 26.2.47. Canx.
G-AHKO	Taylorcraft Plus D	228	LB381	24. 4.46	To West Germany as D-ECOD in 3/56. Canx 10.3.56.
G-AHKP	Miles M.14A Hawk Trainer III	1832	R1831	24. 4.46	Crashed at Greenock on 4.8.54. Canx.
G-AHKR	DH.89A Dragon Rapide	6824	NR736	23. 4.46	Crashed near Mt.Slieau Ruy, IoM on 15.4.57. Canx.
G-AHKS	DH.89A Dragon Rapide	6812	NR724	23. 4.46	To Borneo as VR-OAC in 6/55. Canx 2.6.55.
G-AHKT	DH.89A Dragon Rapide 6	6811	NR723	23. 4.46	To France as F-OAUG in 2/58. Canx 17.2.58.
G-AHKU	DH.89A Dragon Rapide 6	6810	NR722	23. 4.46	WFU at Biggin Hill on 12.8.70. Canx as WFU 16.5.72.
G-AHKV	DH.89A Dragon Rapide	6792	NR693	23. 4.46	CofA expired 3.12.68 & WFU at Elmdon. Canx as WFU 9.9.69.
G-AHKW	Percival P.28 Proctor I	H.21	R7525	24. 4.46	WFU at Stansted in 6/49. Canx.
G-AHKX	Avro 652A Anson 19 Srs.2	1333		18. 4.46	(On rebuild 4/97 by Avro Heritage Society)
G-AHKY	Miles M.18 Srs.2	4426	HM545 U-0224/U-8	26. 4.46	Permit expired 20.9.89 & WFU at Perth. Canx as WFU 19.3.92. (On display 3/96 East Fortune)
G-AHKZ	DH.82A Tiger Moth	83636	T7170	8. 5.46	DBR in ground collision with Avian G-ACKE at Baginton on 26.7.50. Canx.
G-AHLA	DH.82A Tiger Moth	84103	T7726	8. 5.46	To Portugal as CS-AAB in 6/51. Canx 1.6.51.
G-AHLB	DH.82A Tiger Moth	82691	R4750	26. 4.46	To New Zealand as ZK-BJN in 11/54. Canx 22.11.54.
G-AHLC	DH.82A Tiger Moth	83822	T5892	26. 4.46	Crashed at Fairoaks on 22.8.48. Canx.
G-AHLD	DH.82A Tiger Moth	85111	T6864	26. 4.46	To New Zealand as ZK-AUY in 7/50. Canx 21.7.50.
G-AHLE	Avro 671 Cierva C.30A Autogiro	710	DR623 G-ACWH	26. 4.46	WFU at Eastleigh in 6/47. Scrapped by 1440 ATC Sqdn at Shoreham in 2/52, with engine going to Hendon Museum. Canx.
G-AHLF	DH.89A Dragon Rapide	6494	X7321	26. 4.46	WFU at Portsmouth on 22.2.60. Scrapped in 12/62. Canx.
G-AHLG	Chrislea LC.III Ace I	100		26. 4.46	WFU at Exeter in 1/49. Scrapped in 4/52. Canx.
G-AHLH	Lockheed 12A	1226	NC18130	21. 5.46	To Ireland as EI-ALV in 3/61. Canx 16.3.61.
G-AHLI	Taylorcraft Auster III	540	NJ911	21. 5.46	CofA expired 26.4.73. Canx by CAA 23.2.99.
G-AHLJ	Taylorcraft Plus C/2	106	HH987 G-AFTZ	1. 5.46	To Ireland as EI-ALH in 5/60. Canx 28.4.60.
G-AHLK	Taylorcraft Auster III	700	NJ889	1. 5.46	(On rebuild 2/99 Leicester)
G-AHLL	DH.89A Dragon Rapide	6576	X7416	8. 5.46	Crashed at St.Just, Cornwall on 21.5.59. Remains used for spares in 1960. Canx.
G-AHLM	DH.89A Dragon Rapide	6708	HG723	8. 5.46	Crashed at St.Marys, Scilly Isles on 20.7.63. Canx.
G-AHLN	DH.89A Dragon Rapide	6754	NF883	8. 5.46	To France as F-BGOQ in 4/53. Canx 1.12.53.
G-AHLO	DH.80A Puss Moth	2187	HM534 (DR630)/Bu.A8877	1. 5.46	To Canada as CF-PEI in 10/69. Canx 26.9.69.
G-AHLP	DH.82A Tiger Moth	83041	R5179	2. 5.46	Crashed at Fairoaks on 2.9.47. Canx.
G-AHLR	DH.82A Tiger Moth	83885	T7461	2. 5.46	To New Zealand as ZK-AUU in 6/50. Canx 15.6.50.
G-AHLS	DH.82A Tiger Moth	3799	N6462	2. 5.46	DBF in hangar fire at Broxbourne on 23.6.47. Canx.
G-AHLT	DH.82A Tiger Moth	82247	N9128	2. 5.46	
G-AHLU	DH.89A Dragon Rapide	6633	X7516	2. 5.46	To Australia as VH-AHI in 12/49. Canx 14.12.49.
G-AHLV	Avro 685 York I	1340	(VR-HFE) G-AHLV	3. 6.46	WFU & broken up at Stansted in 2/52. Canx.
G-AHLW	Percival P.28 Proctor I	K.227	P6168	7. 6.46	DBF in hangar fire at Broxbourne on 23.6.47. Canx.
G-AHLX	Douglas C-47A-30-DK Dakota	14035/25480	KG803 43-48219	8. 5.46	To Yugoslavia as YU-ABG in 12/47. Canx 23.12.47.
G-AHLY	Douglas C-47A-30-DK Dakota	13849/25294	KG750 43-48033	8. 5.46	To Yugoslavia as YU-ABF in 12/47. Canx 23.12.47.
G-AHLZ	Douglas C-47A-30-DK Dakota	14008/25453	KG776 43-48192	8. 5.46	To Yugoslavia as YU-ABI in 12/47. Canx 23.12.47.
G-AHMA	Airspeed AS.65 Consul	3428	LX732	4. 5.46	Crashed at Villemoireau, Isere, France on 23.12.46. Canx.
G-AHMB	Airspeed AS.65 Consul	3112	LX281	4. 5.46	To Israel as 4X-ACO / Israeli DF/AF as 2809? in 8/49. Canx 26.8.49.
G-AHMC	Airspeed AS.65 Consul	2778	HN583	4. 5.46	Believed broken up for spares at Croydon. Canx.
G-AHMD	Airspeed AS.65 Consul	3545	NM329	4. 5.46	Burned at Squires Gate on 20.4.56. Canx.
G-AHME	DH.82A Tiger Moth	84163	T7790	4. 5.46	WFU at Apethorpe on 22.10.52. Canx.
G-AHMF	DH.82A Tiger Moth	83904	T7475	4. 5.46	DBF in hangar fire at Broxbourne on 23.6.47. Canx.
G-AHMG	Percival P.28 Proctor 1	K.303	P6269	8. 5.46	To Australia as VH-AYU in 10/48. Canx 17.8.48.
G-AHMH	Percival P.48 Merganser	AU.1	X-2	13. 5.46	Scrapped at Luton in 8/48. Canx.
G-AHMI	Avro 671 Cierva C.30 Autogiro	708	DR624 G-ACWF	8. 5.46	WFU at White Waltham in 1950. Canx.
G-AHMJ	Avro 671 Cierva C.30A Autogiro (Avro 671 Rota I)	- R3/CA/43	K4235	8. 5.46	Dismantled in 7/47 and given to Hayes and Harlington Sea Cadets. WFU at White Waltham in 1950. Canx 12.11.98 on sale to USA.
G-AHMK(1)	Avro 681 Cierva C.30A Autogiro	715	AP506 G-ACWM	. 7.46R	NTU - Restored as G-ACWM 7/46. Canx 8/46.

Regn	Type	c/n	Previous identity	Regn date	Fate or immediate subsequent identity (if known)
G-AHMK(2)	DH.82A Tiger Moth	82077	N6807	19. 8.46	To Holland as PH-UAX 3/47. Canx 8/46.
G-AHML	DH.82A Tiger Moth	84316	T7963	8. 5.46	Crashed at Sywell on 13.6.48. Canx.
G-AHMM	DH.82A Tiger Moth	86072	EM870	8. 5.46	Crashed near Newport Pagnell on 10.7.54. Canx.
G-AHMN	DH.82A Tiger Moth	82223	N6985	8. 5.46	
G-AHMO	Finch-Luton LA-4A Minor	RSF.1 & PFA/815		8. 5.46	DBR while taking-off at Sandown, IoW on 22.10.66. Parts to G-ATWS. Canx.
G-AHMP	Percival P.30 Proctor II	H.170	BV631	9. 5.46	WFU at Levesden in 4/63. Canx.
"G-AHMP"	Scottish Aviation Pioneer Srs.1	101	VL515	----	Marks used for publicity to record aircrafts first flight on 5.11.47. Remained as VL515, then to G-AKBF(2). Canx.
G-AHMR	Percival P.28 Proctor I	K.307	P6273	9. 5.46	Crashed at South Mimms, Herts on 30.5.51. Canx.
G-AHMS	Percival P.28 Proctor I	K.248	P6189	9. 5.46	Crashed at Tonerre, France on 14.5.47. Canx.
G-AHMT	Percival P.28 Proctor I	H.24	R7528	9. 5.46	WFU at Prestwick in 8/48. Broken up in 2/59. Canx.
G-AHMU	Percival P.28 Proctor I	H.1	R7485	9. 5.46	To New Zealand as ZK-AJY in 7/46. Canx 2.7.46.
G-AHMV	Percival P.34 Proctor III	H.547	LZ789	9. 5.46	WFU at Perth in 8/51. Canx.
G-AHMW	Percival P.28 Proctor I	K.314	P6305	9. 5.46	To Belgium as OO-CCZ in 7/46. Canx 2.7.46.
G-AHMX	Percival P.28 Proctor I	K.260	P6226	9. 5.46	Wrecked in forced landing at Lausanne, Switzerland on 3.3.49. Canx.
G-AHMY	Percival P.30 Proctor II	H.82	BV637	9. 5.46	DBR in forced landing 15m SE of Boulogne, France on 21.1.47. Wreck to Hanworth in 9/47. Canx as destroyed in 1948.
G-AHMZ	Avro 652A Anson I	-	EG637	9. 5.46	To Kenya as VP-KHP in 2/50. Canx 23.1.50.
G-AHNA	Percival P.28 Proctor I	H.2	R7486	9. 5.46	Crashed on forced-landing in a ploughed field at High Hall Farm, Tolleshunt D'Arcy, Essex on 27.12.67. Canx.
G-AHNB	Percival P.30 Proctor II	H.186	BV639	9. 5.46	WFU at Lympne in 6/59. Canx.
G-AHNC	DH.82A Tiger Moth	85881	DF132	23. 5.46	WFU at Lasham on 28.1.65. Used for spares for G-APIG. Canx.
G-AHND	DH.82A Tiger Moth	85142	T6913	23. 5.46	Crashed near Biggin Hill on 8.4.66. Canx.
G-AHNE	Miles M.14A Hawk Trainer III	2170	T9977	27. 5.46	To New Zealand as ZK-BBA in 11/52. Canx 9.10.52.
G-AHNF	Percival P.28 Proctor I	H.12	G-AKBX G-AHNF/R7496	9. 5.46	Not converted. Canx as WFU 19.8.47.
G-AHNG	Taylorcraft Plus D	200	LB341	13. 5.46	Crashed in Dorset in 8/71. Canx as destroyed 30.5.84.
G-AHNH(1)	Avro 688 Tudor 4B (Originally regd as Tudor 1)	1341		20. 5.46	NTU - Construction abandoned. Canx 29.12.50.
G-AHNH(2)	Bucker Bu.181 Bestmann (Huggland built)	25083	D-EBOH Swedish AF Fv.25083	17. 5.88	Canx 7.2.94 on sale to Australia. (Possibly the unidentified ex.UK Bu.181 noted at Gunnedah, New South Wales, Australia on 18.10.96)
G-AHNI	Avro 688 Super Trader 4B (Originally regd as Tudor 1, then as Tudor 4B)	1342		20. 5.46	Scrapped at Stansted in 6/59. Canx.
G-AHNJ	Avro 688 Tudor 4B (Originally regd as Tudor 1)	1343		20. 5.46	Broken up at Ringway in 1953. Canx as WFU.
G-AHNK	Avro 688 Tudor 4B (Originally regd as Tudor 1)	1344		20. 5.46	Broken up at Ringway in 1953. Canx as WFU.
G-AHNL	Avro 688 Super Trader 4B (Originally regd as Tudor 1, then as Tudor 4B)	1345		20. 5.46	WFU at Southend on 7.11.59. Scrapped in 2/60. Canx.
G-AHNM	Avro 688 Super Trader 4B (Originally regd as Tudor 1, then as Tudor 4B)	1346		20. 5.46	WFU at Stansted on 27.6.59. Scrapped in 6/59. Canx.
G-AHNN	Avro 688 Tudor 4B (Originally regd as Tudor 1)	1347		20. 5.46	Broken up at Ringway in 1953. Canx as WFU.
G-AHNO	Avro 688 Super Trader 4B (Originally regd as Tudor 1, then as Tudor 4B)	1348		20. 5.46	WFU at Stansted on 3.8.59. Scrapped in 8/59. Canx.
G-AHNP	Avro 688 Tudor 4B (Originally regd as Tudor 1)	1349		20. 5.46	Fatal crash north-east of Bermuda, in Atlantic Ocean on 30.1.48. Canx.
G-AHNR(1)	Avro 688 Tudor 4B (Originally regd as Tudor 1)	1350		20. 5.46	NTU - Construction abandoned. Canx 10.12.48.
G-AHNR(2)	Taylorcraft BC-12D	7204	N43545 NC43545	15.11.88	
G-AHNS	Avro 652A Anson I	-	MG634	13. 5.46	To France as F-DAEJ in 10/55. Canx 23.6.55.
G-AHNT	Avro 652A Anson I	-	MG866	13. 5.46	To Ireland as EI-AHO in 2/56 - Not delivered & scrapped in 3/58 at Portsmouth. Canx 6.2.56.
G-AHNU	Miles M.14A Hawk Trainer III	2033	T9766	10. 5.46	Crashed near Sandbach, Cheshire on 7.2.51. Canx.
G-AHNV	Miles M.14A Hawk Trainer III	1949	R1978	10. 5.46	Crashed at Wolverhampton on 25.7.52. Canx.
G-AHNW	Miles M.14A Hawk Trainer III	1921	R1950	10. 5.46	Crashed at Elstree on 2.6.57. Canx.
G-AHNX	DH.82A Tiger Moth	83622	T7163	18. 5.46	Crashed at Luton on 30.5.48. Canx.
G-AHNY	DH.82A Tiger Moth	82172	N6928	18. 5.46	WFU at Lympne on 8.9.48. Broken up for spares. Canx.
G-AHNZ	Taylorcraft Plus D	208	LB349	17. 5.46	To France as F-BAVU. Canx 12.9.50.
G-AHOA	Miles M.18 Mk.5 (Originally regd as a Mk.3)	4432	U-3 U-0238	13. 5.46	Crashed at Littondale, Yorks on 25.5.50. Canx.
G-AHOB	Miles M.19 Master II	6434	U-5 U-0246/W8515	13. 5.46	Scrapped in 1950. Canx.
G-AHOC	Junkers Ju52/3mg10e	SH.16C & 501441	VM923 Luftwaffe	21. 5.46	Scrapped at Warrington in 2/48. Canx as WFU in 1948.
G-AHOD	Junkers Ju52/3mg8e	SH.10C & 131150	VN740 Luftwaffe	21. 5.46	Scrapped at Warrington in 2/48. Canx as WFU in 1948.
G-AHOE	Junkers Ju52/3mg8e	SH.8C	VN723 Luftwaffe	21. 5.46	Scrapped at Warrington in 2/48. Canx as WFU in 1948.
G-AHOF	Junkers Ju52/3mg10e	SH.9C	VN729 Luftwaffe	21. 5.46	Scrapped at Warrington in 2/48. Canx as WFU in 1948.
G-AHOG	Junkers Ju52/3mg8e	SH.17C & 3317	VM979 Luftwaffe KI+LZ	21. 5.46	Scrapped at Warrington in 2/48. Canx as WFU in 1948.
G-AHOH	Junkers Ju52/3mg8e	SH.14C & 641364	VN746 Luftwaffe	21. 5.46	Scrapped at Warrington in 2/48. Canx as WFU in 1948.
G-AHOI	Junkers Ju52/3mg8e	SH.13C & 641227	VN744 Luftwaffe	21. 5.46	Scrapped at Warrington in 2/48. Canx as WFU in 1948.

Regn	Type	c/n	Previous identity	Regn date	Fate or immediate subsequent identity (if known)
G-AHOJ	Junkers Ju52/3mg8e	SH.15C & 500138	VN756 Luftwaffe	21. 5.46	Scrapped at Warrington in 2/48. Canx as WFU in 1948.
G-AHOK	Junkers Ju52/3mg8e	SH.12C & 2998	VN742 Luftwaffe	21. 5.46	Crashed at Renfrew on 26.1.47. Canx.
G-AHOL	Junkers Ju52/3mg8e	SH.11C & 641213	VN741 Luftwaffe	21. 5.46	Scrapped at Warrington in 2/48. Canx as WFU in 1948.
G-AHOM	Percival Q.6	Q.43	P5637	21. 5.46	WFU at Thruxton on 28.7.58. Broken up in 1961. Canx.
G-AHON	Vickers 498 Viking 1A	116	WZ973 G-AHON	27. 6.46	DBR at Luqa, Malta on 27.5.52. Shipped to Southend where it was blown off its trestle by a gale in 12/52 & suffered further damage. Moved to Blackbushe. Canx.
G-AHOO(1)	Vickers 498 Viking 1A	-		. .46R	NTU. Canx.
G-AHOO(2)	DH.82A Tiger Moth (Regd with c/n 86149)	86150	6940M EM967	6. 6.85	
G-AHOP	Vickers 498 Viking 1A	117	WZ972 G-AHOP	27. 6.46	CofA expired 10.7.67 & WFU at Hurn. Scrapped in 8/67. Canx.
G-AHOR	Vickers 498 Viking 1A	118	ZS-DNU G-AHOR/XD637/G-AHOR	27. 6.46	Crashed at Tarbes, France on 29.5.60. Canx.
G-AHOS	Vickers 657 Viking 1 (Originally regd as a 498)	119	VP-TAT G-AHOS	27. 6.46	WFU & stored at Hurn in 5/62. Broken up in 8/62. Canx.
G-AHOT	Vickers 498 Viking 1A	121	XD635 G-AHOT	27. 6.46	To South Africa as ZS-DKH in 10/54. Canx 26.9.54.
G-AHOU	Vickers 657 Viking 1 (Originally regd as a 498)	122	VP-TAU G-AHOU	27. 6.46	WFU & stored at Southend in 5/62. Broken up in 6/63. Canx.
G-AHOV	Vickers 498 Viking 1A	123		27. 6.46	Broken up for spares at Southend in 1952. Canx.
G-AHOW	Vickers 498 Viking 1A (Converted to Viking 1 in 8/60)	124	ZS-DKI G-AHOW/XD636/G-AHOW	27. 6.46	WFU & stored at Manston in 9/67. CofA expired 19.3.68. Canx as WFU 3.2.69.
G-AHOX	Vickers 614 Viking 1	125		27. 6.46	To RAF as VW218 7/48. Canx.
G-AHOY	Vickers 639 Viking 1 (Originally regd as a 614)	128	XF765 G-AHOY	27. 6.46	CofA expired 15.3.68 & WFU at Manston. Broken up. Canx as WFU 3.2.69.
G-AHOZ	Vickers 657 Viking 1 (Originally regd as a 614)	129	VP-YJA VP-TAZ/G-AHOZ	27. 6.46	WFU & stored at Southend in 1/63. Broken up in 4/64. Canx.
G-AHPA	Vickers 614 Viking 1	130	VW217 G-AHPA	4. 9.46	Used as spares at Croydon. Broken up at Wymeswold in 1958. Canx.
G-AHPB	Vickers 639 Viking 1 (Originally regd as a 614)	132	XF638 G-AHPB	4. 9.46	CofA expired 20.5.68. (Wore marks "D-BABY" whilst displayed at Dusseldorf, Germany) (Displayed at Technorama Museum, Winterthur, Switzerland) Broken up some date between 1988 and 1993. Canx.
G-AHPC	Vickers 639 Viking 1 (Originally regd as a 614)	133	XF764 G-AHPC	4. 9.46	WFU & stored at Hurn. Broken up in 7/62. Canx.
G-AHPD	Vickers 639 Viking 1 (Originally regd as a 614)	134		4. 9.46	DBR in forced landing at Beutre, France on 8.5.51. Canx.
G-AHPE	Vickers 657 Viking 1 (Originally regd as a 614)	137	VP-TBB(2) G-AHPE	4. 9.46	WFU & used for spares at Southend. Broken up in 6/61. Canx.
G-AHPF	Vickers 657 Viking 1 (Originally regd as a 614)	138	VP-YJB VP-TBC(2)/G-AHPF	4. 9.46	To Austria as OE-FAE in 4/58. Canx 17.4.58.
G-AHPG	Vickers 614 Viking 1	139	VP-YHJ ZS-DDO/VP-YHJ/G-AHPG	4. 9.46	WFU & used as a snack bar at Blantyre, Malawi. Canx as WFU 18.1.62.
G-AHPH	Vickers 643 Viking 1 (Originally regd as a 614)	141	VP-YIR ZS-DEP/VP-YIR/ZS-BSB/G-AHPH	4. 9.46	DBR on landing at Southend on 28.7.59. Canx.
G-AHPI	Vickers 639 Viking 1 (Originally regd as a 614)	142		4. 9.46	Crashed at Monte la Cinta, Sicily on 16.2.52. Canx.
G-AHPJ	Vickers 614 Viking 1	147	XF763 G-AHPJ	4. 9.46	To France as F-OCEU in 5/65. Canx.
G-AHPK	Vickers 610 Viking 1B	148		30. 9.46	Crashed at Finebush Lane, Ruislip on 6.1.48. Canx.
G-AHPL	Vickers 610 Viking 1B	149	VP-YKK G-AHPL	30. 9.46	DBR on take-off from Manston on 2.8.65. WFU & stored at Manston in 8/65. CofA expired 8.5.67. Canx as WFU 3.2.69.
G-AHPM	Vickers 610 Viking 3B (Originally regd as Srs.1B)	152	XG349 G-AHPM/XF632/G-AHPM	30. 9.46	Crashed into Mount Holteheia near Holthei 46 kms NE of Stavanger, Norway on 9.8.61. Canx.
G-AHPN	Vickers 610 Viking 1B	155		30. 9.46	Fatal crash in fog at Heathrow on 31.10.50. Canx.
G-AHPO	Vickers 610 Viking 1B	157	XF631 G-AHPO	30. 9.46	DBR after overunning runway at Nuremberg, West Germany on 20.12.53. Broken up in 12/55. Canx.
G-AHPP	Vickers 610 Viking 1B	160	(D-AGID) (D-CABO)/G-AHPP	30. 9.46	To Portuguese India as CR-IAC in 3/55. Canx 29.2.55.
G-AHPR	Vickers 610 Viking 1B	164		30. 9.46	WFU & stored at Hurn in 3/62. Broken up in 3/62. Canx.
G-AHPS	Vickers 610 Viking 1B	167	(D-CEDU) G-AHPS	30. 9.46	To West Germany as D-ABOM in 4/56. Canx 21.1.56.
G-AHPT	DH.89A Dragon Rapide	6478	R9550	22. 5.46	Crashed at St.Albans on 7.7.59. Canx.
G-AHPU	DH.89A Dragon Rapide	6963	TX305	25. 5.46	To Sierra Leone as VR-LAD in 4.58. Canx 5.3.58.
G-AHPV	DH.89A Dragon Rapide	6759	NF888	22. 5.46	To South Africa as ZS-AYG in 8/46. Canx 12.8.46.
G-AHPW	DH.89A Dragon Rapide	6678	HG693	22. 5.46	To South Africa as ZS-BCO in 9/46. Canx 12.8.46.
G-AHPX	DH.89A Dragon Rapide	6429	Z7254 G-AFLZ	22. 5.46	To South Africa as ZS-AYF in 8/46. Canx 12.8.46.
G-AHPY	DH.89A Dragon Rapide	6561	X7401	22. 5.46	To South Africa as ZS-BCP in 8/46. Canx 12.8.46.
G-AHPZ	DH.82A Tiger Moth	83794	EI-AFJ G-AHPZ/T7280	22. 5.46	
G-AHRA	DH.104 Dove 1	04003		11. 6.46	Fatal crash on Chewton Common, New Milton on 13.3.47. Canx.
G-AHRB	DH.104 Dove 1B (Originally regd as Dove 1)	04005	VR-NAJ G-AHRB	21. 6.46	To Cape Verde as CR-CAD in 10/57. Canx 1.10.57.
G-AHRC	DH.82A Tiger Moth	84555	T6064	28. 5.46	Ditched in sea 8 miles north of Anglesey on 23.8.71. Canx.
G-AHRD	Avro 652A Anson I	-	EG633	27. 5.46	To Kenya as VP-KDX 10/47. Canx 21.10.47.
G-AHRE	Short S.25 Sandringham 2	SH.43C	ML843	21. 5.46	To Argentina as LV-ACT in 12/46. Canx 13.7.46.
G-AHRF	Vickers 630 Viscount	1	VX211 G-AHRF	23. 5.46	Crashed near Khartoum, Sudan on 27.8.52. Canx.

Regn	Type	c/n	Previous identity	Regn date	Fate or immediate subsequent identity (if known)
G-AHRG	Vickers 663 Tay Viscount	2		23. 5.46	NTU - To MoS as VX217 in 7/49. Canx.
G-AHRH	DH.89A Dragon Rapide	6823	NR735	22. 5.46	To France as F-OBOH in 2/60. Canx 12.2.60.
G-AHRI	DH.104 Dove 1B (Originally regd as Dove 1)	04008	4X-ARI G-AHRI	11. 7.46	Canx as WFU 18.5.72 after a long sojourn at Little Staughton. (On display 2/99 Winthorpe)
G-AHRJ	DH.104 Dove 1	04004	SN-AAA G-AHRJ/SN-AAA/G-AHRJ	25. 9.46	To Iraq as YI-ACT in 6/55. Canx 22.7.55.
G-AHRK	Airspeed AS.65 Consul	3096	VP-RBM G-AHRK/LX265	18. 6.46	To Spain as EC-WGI/EC-AGI in 4/52. Canx 5.3.52.
G-AHRL	DH.82A Tiger Moth	84736	T6362	28. 5.46	To New Zealand as ZK-AZH in 6/52. Canx 12.12.51.
G-AHRM	DH.82A Tiger Moth	3861	N6548	28. 5.46	DBR at Fairoaks on 18.8.58. Canx.
G-AHRN	DH.82A Tiger Moth	83553	T5841	28. 5.46	Crashed near Newbury, Berks on 24.5.52. Canx.
G-AHRO	Cessna 140	8069	N89065 NC89065	25. 1.82	
G-AHRP	Avro 671 Cierva C.30A Autogiro	771	DR622 G-ACYH	28. 5.46	WFU at White Waltham on 24.7.48. Canx.
G-AHRR	DH.82A Tiger Moth	85753	DE855	28. 5.46	To New Zealand as ZK-BBH in 5/52. Canx 9.5.52.
G-AHRS	DH.82A Tiger Moth	85035	T6748	28. 5.46	DBR at Broxbourne on 27.2.47. Canx.
G-AHRT	DH.82A Tiger Moth	84957	T6643	28. 5.46	To Malaya as VR-RBJ in 6/49. Canx 29.6.49.
G-AHRU	DH.82A Tiger Moth	84258	T7883	28. 5.46	To India as VT-DBZ in 2/49. Canx 11.2.49.
G-AHRV	DH.82A Tiger Moth	82104	N6849	28. 5.46	To Denmark as OY-DNR in 1/69. Canx 28.6.68.
G-AHRW	DH.82A Tiger Moth	85189	T6980	28. 5.46	To Holland as PH-NEB 4/50. Canx 13.3.50.
G-AHRX	DH.82A Tiger Moth	83669	T7359	28. 5.46	Crashed at Kidlington on 23.7.53. Canx.
G-AHRY	Percival P.30 Proctor II	H.192	BV642	29. 5.46	Broken up at Broxbourne in 4/54. Canx.
G-AHRZ	Avro 626 Prefect I	-	K5069	30. 5.46	Scrapped at Gatwick in 1949. Canx.
G-AHSA	Avro 621 Tutor	-	K3215 G-AHSA/K3215	30. 5.46	
G-AHSB	Taylorcraft Plus D	174	LB315	1. 7.46	DBR in ground collision at Gatwick on 11.4.55. Canx.
G-AHSC	Taylorcraft Plus D	192	LB333	1. 7.46	To Ireland as EI-ACP in 10/46. Canx 19.7.46.
G-AHSD	Taylorcraft Plus D	182	LB323	1. 7.46	CofA expired 10.9.62. (On rebuild 2/99 near Shipdham)
G-AHSE	Taylorcraft Plus D	194	LB335	24. 8.46	Not converted. Broken up at Rearsby in 10/47. Canx.
G-AHSF	Taylorcraft Plus D	224	LB377	1. 7.46	DBR at Rearsby on 2.9.47. Canx.
G-AHSG	Taylorcraft Plus D	217	LB370	1. 7.46	Crashed in 1952. Scrapped at Stapleford in 1959. Canx.
G-AHSH	Auster J/1 Autocrat	2028		12. 6.46	To France as F-DAAV in 9/52. Canx 7.8.52.
G-AHSI	Auster J/1 Autocrat	2029		22. 6.46	To Spain as EC-AMB in 2/55. Canx 22.2.55.
G-AHSJ	Taylorcraft Plus D	172	LB313	22. 7.46	DBR at Chingford, Essex on 25.8.56. Canx.
G-AHSK	Taylorcraft Plus D	213	LB366	22. 7.46	WFU at Perth in 8/50. Scrapped in 10/51. Canx.
G-AHSL	Taylorcraft Plus D	189	LB330	22. 7.46	Crashed off Longniddry, MacMerry on 23.7.48. Canx.
G-AHSM	Auster J/1 Autocrat	2107		8. 8.46	To France as F-OAJG in 3/51. Canx 1.7.51.
G-AHSN	Auster J/1 Autocrat	2105		8. 8.46	Crashed at Denham on 11.7.55. Canx.
G-AHSO	Auster J/1N Alpha (Originally regd as J/1 Autocrat)	2123		8. 8.46	(On rebuild at Mavis Enderby in 9/98)
G-AHSP	Auster J/1 Autocrat	2134	F-BGRO G-AHSP	8. 8.46	
G-AHSR	Auster J/1 Autocrat	2135		8. 8.46	To Australia as VH-AIH in 8/50. Canx 6.5.52.
G-AHSS	Auster J/1N Alpha (Originally regd as J/1 Autocrat)	2136		8. 8.46	
G-AHST	Auster J/1N Alpha (Originally regd as J/1 Autocrat)	2137		8. 8.46	
G-AHSU	Auster J/1 Autocrat	2138		8. 8.46	To Egypt as SU-AGS in 11/49. Canx 30.11.49.
G-AHSV	Auster J/1 Autocrat	2139		8. 8.46	To France as F-BENL in 12/47. Canx 3.12.47.
G-AHSW	Auster J/1 Autocrat	2140		8. 8.46	Canx by CAA 24.6.87. To USA as N47DN.
G-AHSX	Auster J/1 Autocrat	2141		8. 8.46	To Liberia as EL-AAD in 9/52. Canx 27.8.52.
G-AHSY	Auster J/3 Atom	2250		10. 9.46	Dismantled Rearsby in 1950. Rebuilt as Auster J-4 G-AJYX with c/n 2941 in 9/50. Canx.
G-AHSZ	Auster J/1 Autocrat	2112		19. 8.46	To France as F-OAGT in 3/50. Canx 15.2.50.
G-AHTA	Percival P.14A Q-Six	Q.46	P5640	31. 5.46	To Belgium as OO-PQA in 11/46. Canx 29.11.46.
G-AHTB	Percival P.14A Q-Six	Q.39	P5634	31. 5.46	Crashed at Almaza on 26.9.47; Rebuilt & to Egypt as SU-AEQ in 8/48. Canx 2.11.47.
G-AHTC	Percival P.31 Proctor 1	K.251		31. 5.46	Crashed in Uganda on 28.12.47. Canx in 1948.
G-AHTD	Percival P.44 Proctor 5	Ae.60		24. 6.46	Crashed at Flushing, Belgium on 20.12.47. Fuselage abandoned in blister hangar, Woolsington in 1949. Canx.
G-AHTE	Percival P.44 Proctor 5	Ae.58		26. 6.46	CofA expired 10.8.61 & WFU at Elmdon. rebuild 1/97 at Nayland)
G-AHTF	Percival P.44 Proctor 5	Ae.59		26. 6.46	To Finland as OH-PPB in 12/53. Canx 1.2.53.
G-AHTG	Percival P.44 Proctor 5	Ae.61		26. 6.46	To Australia as VH-BDA in 1/51. Canx 15.1.51.
G-AHTH	Percival P.44 Proctor 5	Ae.62		26. 6.46	Crashed at Redditch on 8.3.48. Canx.
G-AHTI	Percival P.44 Proctor 5	Ae.66		26. 6.46	To Spain as EC-AHX in 1/53. Canx 28.2.52.
G-AHTJ	Percival P.44 Proctor 5	Ae.67		24. 6.46	To India as VT-CTF in 5/48. Canx 15.4.48.
G-AHTK	Percival P.44 Proctor 5	Ae.68		24. 6.46	Crashed into sea off Ostend, Belgium on 4.8.57. Canx.
G-AHTL	Percival P.44 Proctor 5	Ae.70		24. 6.46	To France as F-OAOZ in 2/54. Canx 20.12.53.
G-AHTM	Percival P.44 Proctor 5	Ae.71		17. 7.46	To Finland as OH-PPA in 10/51. Canx 23.8.51.
G-AHTN	Percival P.28 Proctor I	K.279	P6245	29. 5.46	To Australia as VH-BLC in 6/48. Canx 22.6.48.
G-AHTO	Vickers-Supermarine 236 Walrus I	-	W2688	3. 6.46	Scrapped at Cowes, IoW in 7.50. Canx.
G-AHTP	Vickers-Supermarine 236 Walrus II	-	Z1763	3. 6.46	Scrapped at Cowes, IoW in 7.50. Canx.
G-AHTR	DH.89A Dragon Rapide	6964	TX306	3. 6.46	DBF at Abadan, Iran in 1950. Canx.
G-AHTS	DH.89A Dragon Rapide	6962	TX304	3. 6.46	DBR in the Middle East on 29.4.47. Canx.
G-AHTT	DH.89A Dragon Rapide	6966	TX308	3. 6.46	To Iran as EP-AAX in 10/51. Canx 29.10.51.
G-AHTU	Percival P.34 Proctor III	H.559	LZ798	6. 6.46	DBR in forced landing in a field near Rivabolo, Turin, Italy on 17.9.47. Canx.
G-AHTV	Percival P.28 Proctor I	K.305	P6271	5. 6.46	To Australia as VH-BCX in 12/53. Canx 3.12.53.
G-AHTW	Airspeed AS.40 Oxford 1	3083	V3388	6. 6.46	CofA expired 15.12.60 & WFU. Canx by CAA 3.4.89. (On display 7/99 Duxford)
G-AHTX	Miles M.57 Aerovan 3	6380		11. 6.46	DBF at Baalbeck, Lebanon on 9.11.51. Canx.

Regn	Type	c/n	Previous identity	Regn date	Fate or immediate subsequent identity (if known)
G-AHTY	DH.89A Dragon Rapide	6608	X7491	5. 6.46	To France as F-BGIS in 8/52. Canx 21.7.52.
G-AHTZ	Avro 671 Cierva C.30A Autogiro	705	HM581 G-ACUI	11. 6.46	Crashed & burned out at Elmdon on 4.3.58. Canx.
G-AHUA	Taylorcraft Plus D	193	LB334	13. 6.46	To Finland as OH-AUB in 3/50. Canx 26.3.50.
G-AHUB	DH.82A Tiger Moth (Fuselage No. MCO/DH/4311)	86234	NL763	6. 6.46	To New Zealand as ZK-BFM in 3/54. Canx 17.3.54.
G-AHUC	Avro 671 Cierva C.30A Autogiro	732	AP509 G-ACWS	11. 6.46	To Sweden as SE-AZA in 7/46. Canx 17.7.46.
G-AHUD	Avro 652A Anson I	RY/LW/11945	LT766	12. 6.46	WFU at White Waltham in 6/47. Broken up. Canx as PWFU 17.2.49.
G-AHUE	DH.82A Tiger Moth	84240	T7868	12. 6.46	Fatal crash after collision with Olympia 463 glider BGA.1305 near Meir on 5.4.70. Canx as WFU 27.2.73.
G-AHUF	DH.82A Tiger Moth	86221	A2123 NL750	26. 2.85	
G-AHUG	Taylorcraft Plus D (Fitted with parts from G-AHAF in 1948)	153	LB282	6. 6.46	CofA expired 12.7.70. (On rebuild Panshanger 1/92)
G-AHUH	Taylorcraft Plus D	150	LB279	5. 6.46	Engine failed in a loop and crashed near Ballard Down, Swanage on 17.7.49. Canx.
G-AHUI(1)	Auster	-		. 6.46R	NTU - Canx.
G-AHUI(2)	Miles M.38 Messenger 2A	6335		19. 7.46	WFU in 9/60.
G-AHUJ	Miles M.14A Hawk Trainer III	1900	R1914	6. 6.46	
G-AHUK	Miles M.14A Hawk Trainer III	1959	T9672	6. 6.46	Sold abroad in 9/49. Canx 19.8.49.
G-AHUL	Miles M.14A Hawk Trainer III	677	L8210	6. 6.46	Not converted. Scrapped at Weston in 2/47. Canx.
G-AHUM	Taylorcraft Plus D	157	LB286	11. 6.46	CofA expired 16.6.55 & WFU at Fairoaks. (Wings and c/n used in building of G-ARRK in 6/61) Canx.
G-AHUN(1)	DH.82A Tiger Moth	85903	DF154	. 6.46R	NTU - To G-AHZH 6/46. Canx.
G-AHUN(2)	Temco Globe GC-1B Swift	3536/766	EC-AJK OO-KAY/NC77764	24. 7.86	
G-AHUO	DH.82A Tiger Moth	83688	T7218	13. 6.46	Crashed at Eastleigh on 15.7.53. Canx.
G-AHUP	DH.82A Tiger Moth	84211	T7846	13. 6.46	To Holland as PH-UAU in 5/47. Canx 24.1.47.
G-AHUR	DH.82A Tiger Moth	83856	T7452	13. 6.46	To Holland as PH-UAT in 3/47. Canx 24.10.46.
G-AHUS	DH.82A Tiger Moth	85006	T6706	13. 6.46	To Holland as PH-UCC in 11/46. Canx 14.10.46.
G-AHUT	DH.82A Tiger Moth	85606	DE665	19. 6.46	Crashed at Dyeford, near Woking on 9.1.55. Canx.
G-AHUU	Globe GC-1B Swift	1003		24. 6.46	To Norway as LN-BDE in 5/54. Canx.
G-AHUV	DH.82A Tiger Moth	3894	N6593	24. 6.46	
G-AHUW	Percival P.28 Proctor I	K.294	P6260	17. 6.46	To New Zealand as ZK-AKQ in 9/46. Canx 10.9.46.
G-AHUX	Percival P.28 Proctor I	K.244	P6185	17. 6.46	To Australia as VH-BGY in 5/55. Canx 13.5.55.
G-AHUY	Percival P.28 Proctor I	K.254	P6195	17. 6.46	To Belgium as OO-USA in 7/46. Canx 22.7.46.
G-AHUZ	Percival P.28 Proctor I	K.302	P6268	17. 6.46	To Australia in 10/51. Canx 31.10.51.
G-AHVA	Percival P.28 Proctor I	H.10	R7494	17. 6.46	Scrapped at Denham in 7/62. Canx.
G-AHVB	Percival P.28 Proctor I	K.292	P6258	14. 6.46	To France as F-BBSM in 9/50. Canx 22.9.50.
G-AHVC	Percival P.28 Proctor I	K.324	P6315	17. 6.46	Broken up at Redhill in 1951. Canx.
G-AHVD	Percival P.28 Proctor I	H.7	R7491	17. 6.46	To France as F-BFPN in 11/49. Canx 17.11.49.
G-AHVE	Percival P.28 Proctor I	H.13	R7497	14. 6.46	To New Zealand as ZK-AKP in 8/46. Canx 21.8.46.
G-AHVF	Percival P.30 Proctor II	H.194	BV654	14. 6.46	Crashed in Egypt on 23.10.46. Canx.
G-AHVG	Percival P.30 Proctor II	H.224	BV658	17. 6.46	To Australia as VH-AVG 5/58. Canx 25.3.57.
G-AHVH	Percival P.28 Proctor I	K.242	P6183	17. 6.46	To Iceland as TF-TUK in 7/46. Canx 22.7.46.
G-AHVI	Percival P.28 Proctor I	K.269	P6235	17. 6.46	To South Africa as ZS-BXH in 9/47. Canx 24.9.47.
G-AHVJ	Percival P.28 Proctor I	K.209	P6130	17. 6.46	To Southern Rhodesia as VP-YGJ in 9/47. Canx 24.9.47.
G-AHVK	Percival P.30 Proctor II	H.58	BV551	17. 6.46	To France as F-BFKB(2) in 3/54. Canx 22.3.54.
G-AHVL	Percival P.30 Proctor II	H.216	BV645	14. 6.46	To New Zealand as ZK-AHQ in 12/46. Canx 15.10.46.
G-AHVM	Percival P.34 Proctor III	H.509	LZ739	24. 6.46	Scrapped at Croydon in 2/49. Canx.
G-AHVN(1)	Percival P.10 Vega Gull	K.100	X9315 G-AFEH	14. 6.46R	NTU - Restored as G-AFEH in 6/46. Canx.
G-AHVN(2)	Avro 683 Lancaster B.III	-	(G-AGUN) PP744	17. 7.46	Scrapped at Tarrant Rushton in 1/50. Canx 26.9.51.
G-AHVO	Avro 626 Prefect	-	K5066	24. 6.46	Scrapped at Hastings in 1950. Canx.
G-AHVP	Taylorcraft Plus D	146	LB276	13. 6.46	Crashed at Elmdon on 15.4.51. Canx.
G-AHVR	Taylorcraft Plus D	170	LB311	13. 6.46	Crashed near Torrington, Devon on 24.4.60. Canx.
G-AHVS	Taylorcraft Plus D	201	LB342	13. 6.46	Crashed at Sleap on 12.8.61. Canx.
G-AHVT	Handley Page HP.70 Halifax C.VIII	1351	PP278	25. 6.47	To France as F-BCJR in 9/47. Canx 24.10.47.
G-AHVU	DH.82A Tiger Moth	84728	T6313	14. 8.46	
G-AHVV	DH.82A Tiger Moth	86123	EM929	24. 6.46	Written-off after dive into ground following aerobatic manoeuvre at Lympne on 12.12.71. (On rebuild 1/94)
G-AHVW	DH.82A Tiger Moth	84626	T6178	24. 6.46	To New Zealand for spares in 11/51 & used in rebuild of ZK-AQD. Canx 19.11.51.
G-AHVX	DH.82A Tiger Moth	86127	EM944	14. 6.46	To France as F-OAPE in 2/54. Canx 23.1.54.
G-AHVY	DH.82A Tiger Moth	83315	T5617	14. 6.46	Crashed at Christchurch on 12.10.58. Canx.
G-AHVZ	DH.82A Tiger Moth	86433	NM113	14. 6.46	Crashed at Hamble on 26.11.47. Canx.
G-AHWA	DH.82A Tiger Moth	85711	DE813	14. 6.46	DBR at Dusseldorf, West Germany on 7.8.53. Canx.
G-AHWB	DH.82A Tiger Moth	85710	DE812	14. 6.46	Crashed near Winchester on 24.4.55. Canx.
G-AHWC	DH.82A Tiger Moth	83880	T7456	14. 6.46	Crashed at Old Warden on 29.6.58. Canx.
G-AHWD	Taylorcraft Plus D	230	LB383	17. 6.46	WFU at Elstree in 4/52. Scrapped at Gatwick in 1955. Canx.
G-AHWE	DH.82A Tiger Moth	86427	NL995	14. 6.46	Crashed into a radio mast on take-off from Exeter on 17.8.55. Canx.
G-AHWF	DH.89A Dragon Rapide	6965	TX307	25. 6.46	To Iran as EP-AAW in 10/51. Canx 29.10.54.
G-AHWG	Globe GC-1B Swift (Was to have been Helliwells-built)	1		29. 6.46R	NTU - Not built. Canx.
G-AHWH	Globe GC-1B Swift	1243	NC3250K	17. 1.47	WFU at Wombleton in 6/61. Canx.
G-AHWI	Taylorcraft Plus D	166	LB296	20. 6.46	Destroyed after ground collision with a Spitfire at Gatwick on 8.5.53. Canx.
G-AHWJ	Taylorcraft Plus D	165	LB294	20. 6.46	(On rebuild 1/97)

Regn	Type	c/n	Previous identity	Regn date	Fate or immediate subsequent identity (if known)
G-AHWK	Taylorcraft Plus D	220	LB373	20. 6.46	WFU at Lulsgate in 9/52. Canx.
G-AHWL	Handley Page HP.70 Halifax C.VIII	1393	PP331	25.10.47	To France as F-BCJT in 10/47 (French CofA issued 18.5.48 & w/o two days later). Canx 25.10.47.
G-AHWM	Handley Page HP.70 Halifax C.VIII	1322	PP238	21. 6.46	NTU - To G-AJZY in 6/47. Canx.
G-AHWN	Handley Page HP.70 Halifax C.VIII	1314	PP230 G-AHWN/PP230	21. 6.46	DBR when u/c collapsed on landing at Schleswigland, West Germany on 6.7.49. Returned to Bovingdon to be broken up by 8/50. CofA expired 30.9.49. Canx as WFU 1.5.50.
G-AHWO	Percival P.44 Proctor 5	Ae.72		22. 7.46	Crashed at Collinstown, Dublin on 5.5.59. Rebuild as EI-ALY 6/61 not completed.
G-AHWP	Percival P.44 Proctor 5	Ae.69		2. 7.46	Crashed into the sea off Margate on 6.1.48. Canx.
G-AHWR	Percival P.44 Proctor 5	Ae.73		10. 7.46	Crashed near Baginton on 18.6.54. Canx.
G-AHWS	Percival P.44 Proctor 5	Ae.74		15. 7.46	To France as F-OATM in 10/55. Canx 6.10.55.
G-AHWT	Percival P.44 Proctor 5	Ae.75		10. 7.46	WFU at Luton in 4/51. Burnt in fire fighting display at Stansted on 20.9.52. Canx.
G-AHWU	Percival P.44 Proctor 5	Ae.36		4. 7.46	Crashed at Elmdon on 24.6.54. Canx.
G-AHWV	Percival P.44 Proctor 5	Ae.77		17. 7.46	WFU at Biggin Hill in 3/63. Burnt in 9/64. Canx.
G-AHWW	Percival P.44 Proctor 5	Ae.78		15. 7.46	To New Zealand as ZK-AVW in 8/50. Canx 20.9.50.
G-AHWX	Percival P.44 Proctor 5	Ae.80		23. 9.46	To Italy as I-ADOH in 11/48. Canx 11.11.48.
G-AHWY	Percival P.44 Proctor 5	Ae.81		19. 8.46	Crashed on take-off from Bembridge, IoW on 9.9.48. Canx.
G-AHWZ	Percival P.44 Proctor 5	Ae.82		31. 8.46	To Trinidad & Tobago as VP-TBR in 4/57. Canx 18.9.56.
G-AHXA	Airspeed AS.40 Oxford	-	V3870	1. 7.46	To Egypt as SU-AER in 8/47. Canx 9.8.47.
G-AHXB	DH.82A Tiger Moth	84114	T5978	27. 6.46	To New Zealand as ZK-BFL in 3/54. Canx 17.3.54.
G-AHXC	DH.82A Tiger Moth	85032	T6745	26. 6.46	Crashed at Hatfield Park, Herts on 28.6.52. Canx.
G-AHXD	DH.82A Tiger Moth	85856	DE996	1. 7.46	Crashed at St.Mellons on 24.7.49. Canx.
G-AHXE	Taylorcraft Plus D	171	LB312	9. 7.46	
G-AHXF	Taylorcraft Plus D	184	LB325	25. 6.46	To Finland as OH-AUH in 1/53. Canx 29.11.52.
G-AHXG	Taylorcraft Plus D	181	LB322	25. 6.46	DBR in gales at Sleap on 12.2.61. (Sundry pieces used in building G-ARRK) Canx.
G-AHXH	Miles M.57 Aerovan 4 (Originally regd as an Aerovan 3)	6382		28. 6.46	To Holland as (PH-NKA)/PH-EAB in 3/59. Canx 28.1.59.
G-AHXI	Avro 671 Cierva C.30A Autogiro	R3/CA/41	K4233	29. 6.46	To Belgium as OO-ADK in 7/48. Canx 5.7.48.
G-AHXJ	Beechcraft D-17S Traveller (UC-43-BH)	6686	FT465	1. 7.46	Destroyed at Ypenburg, Holland in ground collision with DH.82A PH-UAX on 24.6.47. Canx.
G-AHXK	Avro 652A Anson 19 Srs.2 (Originally regd as Srs.1, converted to Srs.2 in 9/54)	1351		5. 7.46	To Australia as VH-RCC in 9/62. Canx 10.9.62.
G-AHXL	Avro 652A Anson 19 Srs.1	1352		5. 7.46	To Sweden as SE-BRP in 8/50. Canx 25.7.50.
G-AHXM	Avro 652A Anson 19 Srs.1	1353		5. 7.46	Undercarriage collapsed on landing at Blackbushe on 5.11.51. Canx 31.10.52 as sold for spares.
G-AHXN(1)	Avro 685 York 1	1354		. 7.46R	NTU - To LV-XGN. Canx.
G-AHXN(2)	DH.82A Tiger Moth	82339	N9244	22. 7.46	Crashed near Caxton, Cambridge on 22.4.62. Canx.
G-AHXO(1)	Avro 685 York 1	1355		. 7.46R	NTU - To LV-XGO. Canx.
G-AHXO(2)	DH.82A Tiger Moth	86151	EM966	22. 7.46	Crashed at Pulborough, Sussex on 16.1.47. Canx.
G-AHXP(1)	Avro 685 York 1	1356		. 7.46R	NTU - To LV-XGP. Canx.
G-AHXP(2)	Airspeed AS.65 Consul	2996	HN840	29. 7.46	To Israel as 4X-ACV / Israeli DF/AF as 2807 in 10/49. Canx 23.10.49.
G-AHXR	Miles M.38 Messenger 2A	6333	YI-HRH G-AHXR	10. 7.46	WFU at Sywell on 14.1.62. Canx.
G-AHXS	Avro 652A Anson I	-	N9531	2. 7.46	CofA expired 10.3.55 & WFU. Canx 2.11.55.
G-AHXT	Avro 652A Anson I	RY/LW/4394	EG265 ?	2. 7.46	CofA expired 8.3.49. Canx as WFU 21.2.50. Stored and finally scrapped at Squires Gate in 1957.
G-AHXU	Miles M.69 Marathon 2	6544		10. 7.46	To MoS as VX231 in 4/50. Canx 9.5.51.
G-AHXV	DH.89A Dragon Rapide	6747	NF876	11. 7.46	Crashed at Ronaldsway, Isle of Man on 15.1.49. Canx.
G-AHXW	DH.89A Dragon Rapide	6782	NR683	11. 7.46	To USA as N683DH in 3/71. Canx 16.3.71.
G-AHXX	DH.89A Dragon Rapide	6800	NR701	11. 7.46	To Borneo as VR-OAB in 9/52. Canx 1.8.52.
G-AHXY	DH.89A Dragon Rapide	6808	NR720	11. 7.46	Crashed at Renfrew on 27.12.48. Canx.
G-AHXZ	DH.89A Dragon Rapide	6825	NR737	11. 7.46	DBF at Renfrew on 28.8.51. Canx.
G-AHYA	Fairey Firefly T.1	F.7661	F-1 MB750	5. 7.46	Restored to Royal Navy as MB750 in 2/47. Canx 13.10.47.
G-AHYB	Consolidated-Vultee CV.32-2 (LB-30B) Liberator I	11	AM920 40-2359	19. 8.46	To France as F-BEFR in 4/51. Canx 6.3.51.
G-AHYC	Consolidated-Vultee CV.32-3 (LB-30) Liberator II	5	AL507	19. 8.46	DBR on landing at Prestwick on 13.11.48. Canx.
G-AHYD	Consolidated-Vultee CV.32-3 (LB-30) Liberator II	20	AL522	19. 8.46	To France as F-BFGJ in 5/51. Canx 6.4.51.
G-AHYE	Consolidated-Vultee CV.32-3 (LB-30) Liberator II	27	AL529	19. 8.46	Broken up at Prestwick in 12/48. Canx.
G-AHYF	Consolidated-Vultee CV.32-3 (LB-30) Liberator II	90	AL592	19. 8.46	To France as F-BEFY in 4/51. Canx 6.4.51.
G-AHYG	Consolidated-Vultee CV.32-3 (LB-30) Liberator II	101	AL603	29. 8.46	To France as F-BFGK in 4/51. Canx 6.4.51.
G-AHYH(1)	Consolidated-Vultee CV.32-3 (LB-30) Liberator II	122	AL614	29. 8.46	NTU - Unservicable on 28.8.46. Canx.
G-AHYH(2)	Handley Page HP.70 Halifax C.VIII	1334	PP261 G-AHYH/PP261	24. 9.46	WFU at Woolsington in 1949. Broken up in 10/49. Canx 1.11.49.
G-AHYI(1)	Consolidated-Vultee CV.32-3 (LB-30) Liberator II	123	AL615	29. 8.46	NTU - Reduced to spares use on 29.8.46. Canx.
G-AHYI(2)	Handley Page HP.70 Halifax C.VIII	1373	PP311 G-AHYI/PP311	24. 9.46	WFU at Bovingdon in 10/49. Canx as WFU 20.3.50.
G-AHYJ	Consolidated-Vultee CV.32-3 (LB-30) Liberator II	125	AL627	29. 8.46	Not converted. Broken up for spares in 2/47. Canx.
G-AHYK	Miles M.14A Hawk Trainer III	868	N3822	12. 7.46	Crashed at Croydon on 7.9.47. Canx.

Regn	Type	c/n	Previous identity	Regn date	Fate or immediate subsequent identity (if known)
G-AHYL	Miles M.14A Hawk Trainer III	2071	T9834	12. 7.46	DBR in 1960. Canx in 5/67.
G-AHYM	Miles M.14A Hawk Trainer III	2085	T9848	12. 7.46	Crashed at Lee-on-Solent on 6.10.51. Canx.
G-AHYN	Avro 652A Anson 19 Srs.1	1359		27. 7.46	CofA expired 24.4.68 & WFU at Thruxton. Canx as PWFU 21.5.68. Remains scrapped in late 1968.
G-AHYO	Avro 652A Anson 19 Srs.1	1360		10. 8.46	Crashed near Lubushi Mission, 40m W of Kasama, Northern Rhodesia on 31.10.46. Canx as PWFU 21.1.47.
G-AHYP	DH.82A Tiger Moth	84487	T8195	17. 7.46	To France as F-BDJM in 8/50. Canx 10.8.50.
G-AHYR	DH.82A Tiger Moth	83639	T7173	17. 7.46	To Holland as PH-UCD 11/46. Canx 15.10.46.
G-AHYS	DH.82A Tiger Moth	82022	N6744	17. 7.46	To Holland as PH-UAV 3/47. Canx 1.11.46.
G-AHYT	DH.82A Tiger Moth	82076	N6806	16. 7.46	To Syrian AF as SR-D2 in 10/46. Canx 1.10.46.
G-AHYU	DH.82A Tiger Moth	83887	T5897	16. 7.46	To Syrian AF as SR-D1 in 10/46. Canx 1.10.46.
G-AHYV	DH.82A Tiger Moth	83398	T5683	16. 7.46	To India as VT-DBF in 2/49. Canx 16.2.49.
G-AHYW	Airspeed AS.65 Consul	3923	PG936	15. 7.46	DBR in forced-landing northeast of Salisbury, Southern Rhodesia on 16.10.46. Canx.
G-AHYX	DH.104 Dove 1	04018		15. 6.46	Crashed at Isfahan, Persia on 24.9.49. Canx 19.10.49.
G-AHYY	Short S.25 Sandringham 5	SH.31C	ML838	15. 7.46	WFU in 11/55 at Solway Morgan's Boatyard, Hamworthy, Hants. Scrapped in 3/59. Canx.
G-AHYZ	Short S.25 Sandringham 5	SH.35C	ML784	15. 7.46	DBF at Belfast, Northern Ireland on 18.1.47, during conversion. Canx.
G-AHZA	Short S.25 Sandringham 5	SH.34C	ML783	15. 7.46	Scrapped in 3/59 at Solway Morgan's Boatyard, Hamworthy, Hants. Canx.
G-AHZB	Short S.25 Sandringham 5	SH.38C	NJ171	15. 7.46	Crashed into sea off Bahrein Island on 23.8.47. Canx.
G-AHZC	Short S.25 Sandringham 5	SH.39C & SH.1159	NJ253	15. 7.46	Scrapped in 3/59 at Solway Morgan's Boatyard, Hamworthy, Hants. Canx.
G-AHZD	Short S.25 Sandringham 5	SH.40C & SH.1195	NJ257	15. 7.46	To Australia as VH-EBV in 7/51. Canx 10.8.51.
G-AHZE	Short S.25 Sandringham 5	SH.36C & SH.1018	ML818	15. 7.46	WFU in 11/55 at Solway Morgan's Boatyard, Hamworthy, Hants. Scrapped in 3/59. Canx.
G-AHZF	Short S.25 Sandringham 5	SH.41C	NJ188	15. 7.46	To Australia as VH-EBY in 7/51. Canx 3.7.51.
G-AHZG	Short S.25 Sandringham 5	SH.37C	ML828	15. 7.46	To Australia as VH-EBZ in 7/51. Canx 3.7.51.
G-AHZH	DH.82A Tiger Moth	85903	(G-AHUN) DF154	16. 7.46	Crashed at Portsmouth on 24.3.57. Canx.
G-AHZI	Vickers Supermarine 329 Spitfire Mk.IIB	CBAF/960	P8727	16. 7.46	Crashed at Copenhagen, Denmark on 15.4.47. Canx.
G-AHZJ	Handley Page HP.70 Halifax C.VIII	1331	PP247	17. 7.46	Crashed on take-off from Bergamo, near Milan, Italy on 31.7.47. Canx 19.8.47.
G-AHZK	Handley Page HP.70 Halifax C.VIII	1330	PP246	17. 7.46	WFU at Stansted in 1949. Broken up in 1950. Canx 7.10.49.
G-AHZL	Handley Page HP.70 Halifax C.VIII	1326	PP242	17. 7.46	WFU at Stansted in 12/48. Broken up in 6/49. Canx 23.12.48.
G-AHZM	Handley Page HP.70 Halifax C.VIII	1333	PP260	17. 7.46	Undercarriage collapsed at Elstree on 16.9.46 and used for spares. Canx 31.10.52.
G-AHZN	Handley Page HP.70 Halifax C.VIII	1328	PP244	17. 7.46	Ditched in sea off Le Zoute, Belgium 26.9.46. Canx 1.1.47.
G-AHZO	Handley Page HP.70 Halifax C.VIII	1323	PP239	17. 7.46	WFU at Stansted in 1949. Broken up in 6/49. Canx 7.10.49.
G-AHZP	Consolidated-Vultee CV.32-3 (LB-30) Liberator II	14	AL516	19. 7.46	Crashed at Speke on 13.10.48. Canx.
G-AHZR	Consolidated-Vultee CV.32-3 (LB-30) Liberator II	50	AL552	19. 7.46	To Greece as SX-DAB in 12/49. Canx 9.12.49.
G-AHZS	Miles M.38 Messenger 2A	6331		19. 7.46	WFU at Ramsgate in 8/62. Canx.
G-AHZT	Miles M.38 Messenger 2A	6334		19. 7.46	CofA expired 24.7.70. Canx as WFU 9.9.81.
G-AHZU	Miles M.38 Messenger 2A	6337		19. 7.46	Crashed near Invergowrie, in Firth of Tay on 10.6.57. Canx.
G-AHZV	Airspeed AS.65 Consul	4397	RR356	19. 7.46	WFU at Stansted on 7.12.50. Scrapped in 3/56. Canx.
G-AHZW	Airspeed AS.65 Consul	3091	LX260	19. 7.46	WFU on 28.3.58. Canx.
G-AHZX	Percival P.44 Proctor 5	Ae.83		31. 8.46	Crashed into sea west of St.John-sur-Mer, France on 16.4.47. Canx.
G-AHZY	Percival P.44 Proctor 5	Ae.84		14. 8.46	To Belgium as OO-ARM in 9/57. Canx 25.7.57.
G-AHZZ	Percival P.44 Proctor 5	Ae.85	(OO-BUP) G-AHZZ	23. 8.46	To South Africa as ZS-BUP in 2/48. Canx 3.2.48.
G-AIAA	Percival P.44 Proctor 5	Ae.20	(OO-CCD)	29. 8.46	Crashed at Burnaston, Derby on 26.11.61. Canx.
G-AIAB	Percival P.44 Proctor 5	Ae.43	(ZS-AVP)	3. 8.46	Crashed at Luton on 20.11.47. Canx.
G-AIAC	Percival P.44 Proctor 5	Ae.51		14. 8.46	DBF at Broxbourne on 23.6.47. Canx.
G-AIAD	Percival P.44 Proctor 5	Ae.24		13. 8.46	Crashed into sea off Nice, France on 18.5.48. Canx.
G-AIAE	Percival P.44 Proctor 5 (Converted to a Junkers Ju-87 replica)	Ae.86		4. 9.46	DBR at Hurn on 31.5.66. Canx.
G-AIAF	Percival P.44 Proctor 5	Ae.87		4. 9.46	Crashed at Stanton Harcourt, Oxon on 19.11.61. Canx.
G-AIAG	Percival P.44 Proctor 5	Ae.88		4. 9.46	Crashed at Naples, Italy on 30.6.64. Canx.
G-AIAH	Airspeed AS.65 Consul	4316	PK252	22. 7.46	WFU on 24.2.59. Burned at Portsmouth on 2.11.61. Canx.
G-AIAI	Miles M.14A Hawk Trainer III	- PP.38384		27. 7.46	Scrapped at Northolt in 6/49. Canx.
G-AIAJ	Miles M.38 Messenger 2A	6338	EI-AHL G-AIAJ	24. 7.46	Scrapped at Stapleford in 6/65. Canx.
G-AIAK	DH.82A Tiger Moth	85130	T6901	25. 7.46	To PH-UAW 5/47. Canx 24.1.47.
G-AIAL	DH.82A Tiger Moth	83642	T7176	25. 7.46	To HB-UBE 9/46. Canx 23.9.46.
G-AIAM	DH.82A Tiger Moth	84259	T7884	25. 7.46	To PH-UCB 6/47. Canx 24.1.47.
G-AIAN	Handley Page HP.70 Halifax C.VIII	1344	PP271	2. 9.46	Restored to RAF as PP271 in 4/47. Canx 25.4.47.
G-AIAO	Handley Page HP.70 Halifax C.VIII	1345	PP272	2. 9.46	Restored to RAF as PP272 in 4/47. Canx 25.4.47.
G-AIAP	Handley Page HP.70 Halifax C.VIII	1354	PP281 G-AIAP/PP281	2. 9.46	Crashed on take-off from Dum Dum, Calcutta, India on 20.11.50 hitting a building 1/2 mile from the runway. Canx 25.11.50.

Regn	Type	c/n	Previous identity	Regn date	Fate or immediate subsequent identity (if known)
G-AIAR	Handley Page HP.70 Halifax C.VIII	1388	PP326 G-AIAR/PP326	2. 9.46	CofA expired 6.10.50 & WFU at Thame. Canx 23.4.51.
G-AIAS	Handley Page HP.70 Halifax C.VIII	1389	PP327 G-AIAS/PP327	2. 9.46	Possible spares use since major accident at Aldermaston in 11/46 whilst as PP327. Scrapped in 4/49. Canx 1.4.49.
G-AIAT	Airspeed AS.40 Oxford	3589	NM387	30. 8.46	WFU at Christchurch on 15.4.60. Scrapped in 1964. Canx.
G-AIAU	Airspeed AS.40 Oxford	3645	NM457	30. 8.46	WFU on 14.7.53. Scrapped at Nicosia, Cyprus in 6/54. Canx.
G-AIAV	Airspeed AS.40 Oxford	3704	NM536	30. 8.46	To VR-HFC 9/51. Canx 17.7.51.
G-AIAW	Airspeed AS.40 Oxford	3784	SE-CAM G-AIAW/NM649	30. 8.46	To EC-APF 9/56. Canx 13.9.56.
G-AIAX	Airspeed AS.40 Oxford	-	DF356	30. 8.46	WFU at Christchurch on 25.5.60. Scrapped in 1964. Canx.
G-AIAY	Airspeed AS.40 Oxford	-	DF521	30. 8.46	Not converted. Scrapped Hurn in 5/47. Canx.
G-AIAZ	Douglas C-47A-25-DK Dakota	13459	KG647 42-93536	. 6.46	Restored to RAF as KG647 on 31.7.46. Canx 18.10.46.
G-AIBA	Douglas C-47A-40-DL Dakota	9860	FD939 42-23998	. 6.46	Restored to RAF as FD939 in 7/46. Canx.
G-AIBB	DH.89A Dragon Rapide	6813	NR725	25. 9.46	To F-OBVJ 8/61. Canx.
G-AIBC	Airspeed AS.65 Consul	4399	RR358	29. 7.46	WFU at Southend on 19.5.50. Scrapped in 6/52. Canx.
G-AIBD	Miles M.38 Messenger 2A	6336		29. 7.46	WFU at Portsmouth in 7/63. Canx.
G-AIBE	Fairey Fulmar II	F.3707	N1854 G-AIBE/N1854	29. 7.46	CofA expired 6.7.59. (On display 3/96 RNAS Yeovilton)
G-AIBF	Airspeed AS.65 Consul	3422	LX726	30. 7.46	WFU at Blackbushe on 6.11.53. Scrapped in 4/54. Canx.
G-AIBG(1)	Douglas C-47A-30-DK Dakota	14022/25467	KG790 43-48206	. 8.46R	NTU - To VT-CGA 9/46. Canx.
G-AIBG(2)	Handley Page HP.61 Halifax B.VI	-	RG790	17.11.47	Broken up at Stansted in 1948. Canx 20.7.50 as scrapped.
G-AIBH	Auster J/1N Alpha (Originally regd as J/1 Autocrat)	2113		19. 8.46	Crashed on landing at Little Gransden on 16.8.87.
G-AIBI	Auster J/1 Autocrat	2122		19. 8.46	Crashed into Marguerite Bay, Graham Land, Antarctica on 15.9.47. Canx.
G-AIBJ	Auster J/1 Autocrat	2145		2. 9.46	To PT-ADI 1/48. Canx.
G-AIBK	Auster J/1 Autocrat	2146		2. 9.46	To EI-ACY 5/47. Canx 9.4.47.
G-AIBL	Auster J/1 Autocrat	2147		2. 9.46	To VH-BDQ 3/53. Canx 18.12.52.
G-AIBM	Auster J/1 Autocrat	2148		2. 9.46	
G-AIBN	DH.82A Tiger Moth	84320	T7967	3. 8.46	To EI-AOP 9/65. Canx 20.9.65.
G-AIBO	Auster J/1 Autocrat	2149		2. 9.46	To YI-ABO 3/48. Canx 1.3.48.
G-AIBP	Auster J/1 Autocrat	2150		2. 9.46	To VH-ASI 5/52. Canx 6.5.52.
G-AIBR	Auster J/1 Autocrat	2151		2. 9.46	
G-AIBS	Auster J/1 Autocrat	2154		2. 9.46	Crashed near Peterborough on 22.5.51. Canx.
G-AIBT	Auster J/1 Autocrat	2155		2. 9.46	To VH-AYO 9/51. Canx 3.9.51.
G-AIBU	Auster J/1 Autocrat	2156		2. 9.46	To VT-CIR 1/47. Canx 1.1.47.
G-AIBV	Auster J/1N Alpha (Originally regd as J/1 Autocrat)	2157		2. 9.46	To ZK-ATS 9/49. Canx 9.8.49.
G-AIBW	Auster J/1N Alpha (Originally regd as J/1 Autocrat)	2158		2. 9.46	
G-AIBX	Auster J/1 Autocrat	2159		2. 9.46	
G-AIBY	Auster J/1 Autocrat	2160		2. 9.46	WFU at Wickenby on 4.4.75. CofA expired 13.4.81. (Stored 6/97)
G-AIBZ	Auster J/1N Alpha (Originally regd as J/1 Autocrat)	2161		2. 9.46	Canx as WFU 21.7.75. To VH-OLZ 1/91.
G-AICA	Auster J/2 Arrow	1878/1	Z-1 G-AGVT	9. 9.46	To F-BAVS 10/50. Canx 7.9.50.
G-AICB	Auster J/1 Autocrat	2133		12. 9.46	Crashed at Tollerton on 21.3.48. Canx.
G-AICC	Auster J/1 Autocrat	2163		12. 9.46	To SU-AEX 10/46. Canx 20.10.46.
G-AICD	Miles M.14A Hawk Trainer III	1734	P6366	13. 8.46	Not converted. Destroyed at Christchurch on 22.6.52. Canx.
G-AICE	Miles M.14A Hawk Trainer III	2049	T9812	13. 8.46	To F-OAPJ 4/53. Canx 22.2.54.
G-AICF	Bristol 170 Freighter Mk.1A	12749		26. 8.46	To LV-XIJ/LV-AEV 1/47. Canx 19.12.46.
G-AICG	Bristol 170 Freighter Mk.1A	12750		26. 8.46	To LV-XIL/LV-AEW 2/47. Canx 19.12.46.
G-AICH	Bristol 170 Freighter Mk.1A	12751		26. 8.46	To LV-XIM/LV-AEY 2/47. Canx 19.12.46.
G-AICI	Bristol 170 Freighter Mk.1A	12752		26. 8.46	To LV-XIN 4/47. Canx 16.1.47.
G-AICJ	Bristol 170 Freighter Mk.1A	12753		26. 8.46	To LV-XIO/LV-AEZ 4/47. Canx 16.1.47.
G-AICK	Bristol 170 Freighter Mk.1A	12754		26. 8.46	To LV-XIP/LV-AEX 4/47. Canx 16.1.47.
G-AICL	Bristol 170 Freighter Mk.21E	12755		26. 8.46	To Australia 3/49 - regd as VH-INJ on 23.11.49. Canx 29.3.49.
G-AICM	Bristol 170 Freighter Mk.21 (Originally regd as a Mk.I, then Mk.1A)	12756		26. 8.46	Crashed near Templehof, West Berlin, East Germany on 19.1.53. Canx.
G-AICN	Bristol 170 Freighter Mk.21	12757		26. 8.46	To EC-ADI 5/48. Canx 7.4.48.
G-AICO	Bristol 170 Freighter Mk.1A	12758		26. 8.46	To LV-XIQ/LV-AFB 5/47. Canx 8.4.47.
G-AICP	Bristol 170 Freighter Mk.1A	12760		26. 8.46	To LV-XIR/LV-AFC 6/47. Canx 16.4.47.
G-AICR	Bristol 170 Freighter 21E (Originally regd as Mk.1A)	12761		26. 8.46	To HC-SBM 3/47. Canx 6.10.47.
G-AICS	Bristol 170 Freighter 21E (Originally regd as Mk.I)	12762	XF659 G-AICS/HC-SBZ/G-AICS/HC-SBN/G-AICS	26. 8.46	Fatal crash on Winter Hill, Horwich, near Bolton on 27.2.58. Canx.
G-AICT	Bristol 170 Freighter 21E (Originally regd as Mk.IIA)	12763	VR-NAL G-AICT/G-18-40/R-40/G-AICT	26. 8.46	WFU at Southend in 10/65. Scrapped in 1966. Canx.
G-AICU	Bristol 170 Freighter Mk.1A	12764		26. 8.46	To LV-XIS 5/47. Canx 16.4.47.
G-AICV	Douglas DC-3-194B	1943	PH-TBF D-ARPF/Luftwaffe NA+LC/PH-ALV	16. 8.46	Broken up at Dunsfold in 5/48. Canx.
G-AICW	Bristol 170 Freighter Mk.1A	12765		26. 8.46	To LV-XIT 6/47. Canx 16.4.47.
G-AICX(1)	Wren Goldcrest	1		13. 8.46	NTU - Not completed. Scrapped in 1947. Canx.
G-AICX(2)	Luscombe 8A Silvaire	2568	N71141 NC71141	27. 1.88	
G-AICY	DH.104 Dove 1	04019	OE-FAB G-AICY	22. 6.46	(Conversion to Riley Dove abandoned due to corrosion) WFU in 1965. (Fuselage at Luton 1968) Canx as WFU 15.3.77.
G-AICZ	Airspeed AS.65 Consul	4317	PK253	16. 8.46	To Israel DF/AF as 2801 in 4/49. Canx 26.6.49.

Regn	Type	c/n	Previous identity	Regn date	Fate or immediate subsequent identity (if known)
G-AIDA	DH.82A Tiger Moth	83311	T7030	19. 8.46	To PH-UFF 7/52. Canx 15.7.52.
G-AIDB	DH.82A Tiger Moth	85839	DE979	19. 8.46	To D-ECOF 11/57. Canx 3.10.57.
G-AIDC	Gloster G.41F Meteor F.4	-		19. 8.46	Seriously damaged by a Belgian pilot at Melsbroek, Belgium on 5.5.47. Canx. (Parts used for G-AKPK).
G-AIDD	DH.82A Tiger Moth	83224	T5491	20. 8.46	Crashed at Roborough, Plymouth on 18.9.57. Canx.
G-AIDE	Miles M.17 Monarch	793	W6463 G-AFRZ	23. 8.46	Reverted as G-AFRZ 10/82. Canx.
G-AIDF	Miles M.14A Hawk Trainer III	1766	P6411	21. 8.46	Wrecked in gales at Southend on 5.9.67. Canx as WFU 6.7.73.
G-AIDG	Miles M.65 Gemini 1A	6308		27. 8.46	To ET-P-14 in 12/49. Canx 12.12.49.
G-AIDH	Miles M.38 Messenger 2A	6340		27. 8.46	To VH-ALN 11/51. Canx 5.11.51.
G-AIDI	Miles M.57 Aerovan 3	6383		27. 8.46	Scrapped at Beirut, Lebanon in 2/51. Canx.
G-AIDJ	Miles M.57 Aerovan 4	6387	VP-YGC G-AIDJ	6. 9.46	Crashed near Rutbah, Iraq on 22.11.48. Canx.
G-AIDK	Miles M.38 Messenger 2A	6355		30. 8.46	WFU - Remains at Tredegar. Canx as destroyed 17.6.81.
G-AIDL	DH.89A Dragon Rapide 6	6968	TX310	23. 8.46	
G-AIDM	Vickers-Supermarine 507 Sea Otter ASR.I	014352	309	22. 8.46	To YV-P-AEO 11/47. Canx 13.11.47.
G-AIDN	Vickers Supermarine 502 Spitfire Trainer VIII	6S/729058	N32 MT818	22. 8.46	To N58JE 8/86. Canx 3.7.86.
G-AIDO	Miles M.65 Gemini 1A	6306		30. 8.46	To SE-BUG 5/52. Canx 9.1.52.
G-AIDP	DH.82A Tiger Moth	86180	NL697	22. 8.46	DBF at Broxbourne on 23.6.47. Canx.
G-AIDR	DH.82A Tiger Moth	83323	T5625	22. 8.46	To ZK-BEF 1/54. Canx 6.11.53.
G-AIDS	DH.82A Tiger Moth	84546	T6055	22. 8.46	
G-AIDT	DH.82A Tiger Moth	84717	T6302	22. 8.46	To D-EJOM 12/57. Canx 9.10.57.
G-AIDU	DH.82A Tiger Moth	84485	T8193	23. 8.46	DBF at Broxbourne on 23.6.47. Canx.
G-AIDV	DH.82A Tiger Moth	83489	T5832	23. 8.46	WFU on 3.2.49. Canx.
G-AIDW	Airspeed AS.65 Consul	2956	HN783	23. 8.46	WFU at Southend on 18.10.50. Scrapped on 11.9.51. Canx.
G-AIDX	Airspeed AS.65 Consul	4318	PK254	28. 8.46	To HB-LAT 10/56. Canx 27.6.55.
G-AIDY	Airspeed AS.65 Consul	3094	LX263	2. 9.46	DBR at Berck-sur-Mer, France on 14.6.48. Canx.
G-AIDZ	Airspeed AS.65 Consul	4404	RR363	28. 8.46	To F-BFVS 7/51. Canx 8.6.51.
G-AIEA	Airspeed AS.65 Consul	4320	PK256	28. 8.46	To F-OAHJ 10/50. Canx 16.10.50.
G-AIEB	Percival P.28 Proctor I	H.9	R7493	4. 9.46	To VH-AHY 2/52. Canx 24.1.52.
G-AIEC	Percival P.28 Proctor I	K.318	P6309	4. 9.46	To ZK-ALS 12/46. Canx 4.12.46.
G-AIED	Percival P.28 Proctor I	K.331	P6322	4. 9.46	CofA expired 15.10.65 & WFU at Shoreham. (Removed by road to Pinewood film studios) Canx.
G-AIEE	Percival P.28 Proctor I	K.280	P6246	4. 9.46	To F-BGRY in 1950. Canx 16.2.50.
G-AIEF	Percival P.28 Proctor I	K.325	P6316	4. 9.46	To VH-SMS 5/47. Canx 26.11.47.
G-AIEG	Percival P.30 Proctor II	H.196	BV644	4. 9.46	To F-BFYV 11/51. Canx 14.11.51.
G-AIEH	Percival P.30 Proctor II	H.68	BV556	4. 9.46	WFU at Baginton in 3/63. Canx.
G-AIEI	Percival P.30 Proctor II	H.188	BV640	4. 9.46	To ZS-BPZ 8/47. Canx 18.8.47.
G-AIEJ	Vickers-Supermarine 236 Walrus II	S2/10761	HD903	24. 8.46	Broken up at Renfrew in 12/48. Canx.
G-AIEK	Miles M.38 Messenger 2A	6339	U-9	27. 8.46	
G-AIEL	DH.82A Tiger Moth	3957	N6653	27. 8.46	Crashed at Sherburn-in-Elmet on 15.9.51. Canx.
G-AIEM	Percival P.44 Proctor 5	Ae.90		18.10.46	To VP-KGJ 8/48. Canx 30.8.48.
G-AIEN	Percival P.44 Proctor 5	Ae.96		22. 2.47	To VH-BSH 5/56. Canx 29.9.55.
G-AIEO	Percival P.44 Proctor 5	Ae.97		28. 9.46	To ZK-ARP 8/48. Canx 24.11.48.
G-AIEP	Percival P.44 Proctor 5	Ae.98		17. 9.46	WFU at Cambridge on 12.4.59. Canx.
G-AIER	Percival P.44 Proctor 5	Ae.99		14.10.46	To VH-AAH 4/52. Canx 24.4.52.
G-AIES	Percival P.44 Proctor 5	Ae.102		25.10.46	WFU in 8/65. Burnt on bonfire at White Waltham on 5.11.65. Canx.
G-AIET	Percival P.44 Proctor 5	Ae.103		14.10.46	To EI-AMV 11/62. Canx 27.10.62.
G-AIEU	Percival P.44 Proctor 5	Ae.105		8. 3.47	To ZS-DCO 12/48. Canx 29.12.48.
G-AIEV	Percival P.44 Proctor 5	Ae.106		2.11.46	To VH-ALR 3/52. Canx 12.3.52.
G-AIEW	Percival P.44 Proctor 5	Ae.55	(LV-NKI)	1.11.46	To TJ-AAK 6/48. Canx 8.6.48.
G-AIEX	Percival P.28 Proctor I	K.233	P6174	28. 8.46	To D-EFAG 7/56. Canx 10.7.56.
G-AIEY(1)	Percival P.16A Q-Six	Q.21	X9407 G-AFFD	28. 8.46	NTU - Restored as G-AFFD 8/46. Canx.
G-AIEY(2)	Percival P.28 Proctor 1	K.261	P6227	14.11.46	WFU at Henlow on 18.5.67. Converted to Junkers Ju-87 replica for the "Battle of Britain" film in 1968. Canx as WFU 14.3.73.
G-AIEZ	Avro 652A Anson I (C/n also quoted as RY/LW/23942)	RY/LW/29942		3. 9.46	Illegally flown to Israel but force landed at Rhodes en route. Noted derelict at Rhodes in 1952. Canx 25.5.49. Eventually delivered to Israeli DF/AF as 2909 in 1953.
G-AIFA	Avro 652A Anson I	RY/LW/5183		3. 9.46	To VR-TAT 3/48. Canx 3.3.48.
G-AIFB	Avro 652A Anson I	RY/LW/8315		3. 9.46	To Israeli DF/AF as 4X-FHL/2901 in 3/49. Canx 26.4.48.
G-AIFC	Avro 652A Anson I	RY/LW/7274		3. 9.46	To Israeli DF/AF as 4X-FHM/2902 in 3/49. Canx 26.4.48.
G-AIFD	Avro 652A Anson I	RY/LW/2356		3. 9.46	To (VR-AAH)/ET-P-18 10/53. Canx 14.7.52.
G-AIFE	Percival P.34 Proctor III	H.115	DX200	3. 9.46	To VH-BVW 6/56. Canx 1.6.56.
G-AIFF	Bristol 170 Freighter 31 (Originally regd as Mk.II, then Mk.21)	12766	R-42	11.10.46	Crashed in English Channel, 12 miles southeast of Portland on 6.5.49. Canx.
G-AIFG	Bristol 170 Freighter 21E	12767		11.10.46	To SA-AAD 8/49. Canx 30.8.49.
G-AIFH	Bristol 170 Freighter 1A	12768		11.10.46	To LV-XIU 6/47. Canx 16.4.47.
G-AIFI	Bristol 170 Freighter 1A	12769		11.10.46	To LV-XIV 7/47. Canx 16.4.47.
G-AIFJ	Bristol 170 Freighter 1A	12770		11.10.46	To LV-XIW 7/47. Canx 16.4.47.
G-AIFK	Bristol 170 Freighter 1A	12771		11.10.46	To LV-XIX 8/47. Canx 16.4.47.
G-AIFL	Bristol 170 Freighter 21E	12772		11.10.46	To SA-AAC 8/49. Canx 8.8.49.
G-AIFM	Bristol 170 Freighter 21E	12773	F-DABK G-AIFM/XF660/G-AIFM/F-BEND/G-AIFM	11.10.46	WFU at Lydd in 11/63. Scrapped on 15.5.64. Canx.
G-AIFN	Bristol 170 Freighter 21	12774		11.10.46	To F-BENC 8/48. Canx 25.8.48.
G-AIFO	Bristol 170 Freighter 21E	12775	VR-NAA(2) VP-YHZ/G-AIFO	11.10.46	WFU at Southend in 6/65. Canx.
G-AIFP	Bristol 170 Wayfarer 21E	12776		11.10.46	To EC-ADH 5/48. Canx 7.4.48.

Regn	Type	c/n	Previous identity	Regn date	Fate or immediate subsequent identity (if known)
G-AIFR	Bristol 170 Wayfarer 21E	12777		11.10.46	To EC-ADK 7/48. Canx 16.6.48.
G-AIFS	Bristol 170 Wayfarer 21E	12778	(G-ATOC) EC-ADL/G-AIFS	11.10.46	WFU at Luton in 5/66. Broken up 1/68. Canx as WFU 3.1.68.
G-AIFT	Bristol 170 Wayfarer 21E	12779		11.10.46	To VP-YHW 7/48. Canx 29.6.48.
G-AIFU	Bristol 170 Wayfarer 21E	12780	R-53	11.10.46	To Pakistan AF as G-775 in 8/48. Canx 4.8.48.
G-AIFV	Bristol 170 Wayfarer 21 (Originally regd as Mk.2A)	12781	XF661 G-AIFV/VT-CID/G-AIFV	11.10.46	WFU at Lydd in 10/61. Broken up 5/62. Canx.
G-AIFW	Bristol 170 Wayfarer 21	12782		11.10.46	To F-BECR 10/48. Canx 1.10.48.
G-AIFX	Bristol 170 Wayfarer 21E	12783		11.10.46	To SA-AAB 6/49. Canx 22.6.49.
G-AIFY	Bristol 170 Freighter 21E	12784	G-18-62 G-AIFY	11.10.46	To VR-NAX 4/49. Canx 12.4.49.
G-AIFZ	Auster J/1N Alpha (Originally regd as J/1 Autocrat)	2182		2.11.46	
G-AIGA	Auster J/1 Autocrat	2183		2.11.46	Crashed Higher Brixham, Devon on 6.8.47. Canx.
G-AIGB	Auster J/1 Autocrat	2184		2.11.46	To HB-EOZ in 1947. Canx 5.12.46.
G-AIGC	Auster J/1 Autocrat	2185		2.11.46	To D-EBOT 12/58. Canx 1.10.58.
G-AIGD	Auster J/1N Alpha (Originally regd as J/1 Autocrat)	2186		2.11.46	
G-AIGE	Auster J/1 Autocrat	2187		5.11.46	WFU at Southend in 4/55. Canx.
G-AIGF	Auster J/1N Alpha (Originally regd as J/1 Autocrat)	2188		5.11.46	CofA expired 19.5.85. (On overhaul 9/96)
G-AIGG	Auster J/1 Autocrat	2189		5.11.46	To VH-AVW 7/53. Canx 27.4.53.
G-AIGH	Auster J/1 Autocrat	2190		5.11.46	To EC-AIS 11/54. Canx 9.9.53.
G-AIGI	Auster J/1 Autocrat	2191		5.11.46	To F-DADG 1/54. Canx 17.7.53.
G-AIGJ	Auster J/1 Autocrat	2153		4.10.46	Crashed at Haren Airfield, Antwerp, Belgium on 27.11.48. Canx.
G-AIGK	Auster J/1 Autocrat	2173	(LN-NAJ)	12.10.46	DBR on landing at Drayton Home Farm, Lowick, Northants on 10.10.68. Canx as destroyed 1.4.69.
G-AIGL	Auster J/1 Autocrat	2174		12.10.46	To VH-AIK 2/53. Canx 8.10.52.
G-AIGM	Auster J/1N Alpha (Originally regd as J/1 Autocrat)	2177		2.10.46	Badly damaged in a hangar collapse at Wickenby in 1/87. Canx as destroyed 13.10.93.
G-AIGN	Auster J/2 Arrow	2351		4.10.46	To VH-BNP 2/50. Canx 16.11.49.
G-AIGO	Auster J/1B Aiglet	2164		12.10.46	To VH-ALO 5/54. Canx 24.7.51.
G-AIGP	Auster J/1 Autocrat	2165		12.10.46	CofA expired 19.6.72. Canx as WFU 30.10.73. (On rebuild at Mavis Enderby 9/98)
G-AIGR	Auster J/1N Alpha (Rebuilt 1953 with spare fuselage no. TAY/R/308G) (The original frame stored by C.J.Baker at Carr Farm, Newark 10/88, was reported at Taylors, Sywell 3/90 and 6/91)	2172		12.10.46	Damaged in gales at Cranfield in 3.86. CofA expired 25.4.88. Canx by CAA 20.1.96. (Stored 9/96 Newark)
G-AIGS	Auster J/1 Autocrat	2175		12.10.46	To ZK-AUI 8/51. Canx 20.6.51.
G-AIGT	Auster J/1N Alpha (Originally regd as J/1 Autocrat)	2176		12.10.46	CofA expired 22.10.76. Canx by CAA 23.2.99.
G-AIGU	Auster J/1N Alpha (Originally regd as J/1 Autocrat)	2180		12.10.46	CofA expired 5.9.74. Canx as TWFU 1.7.92. (On rebuild 3/96)
G-AIGV	Auster J/1 Autocrat	2207		12.10.46	To TF-ACC 9/55. Canx 19.9.55.
G-AIGW	Auster J/2 Arrow	2352		22.10.46	To VH-BDE 1/48. Canx 21.2.47.
G-AIGX	Auster J/1 Autocrat	2167	(OY-DRI)	22.10.46	Crashed at Beziers, France on 9.8.48. Canx.
G-AIGY	Auster J/1 Autocrat	2168	(OY-DRE)	22.10.46	Crashed at Pwllheli on 1.8.50. Canx.
G-AIGZ	Auster J/4 Archer	2066		13.11.46	To VH-AAL 9/51. Canx 19.9.51.
G-AIHA	Vickers 616 Viking 3B (Originally regd as 1A, then 1B)	146	VP-YEW G-AIHA	10. 9.46	Broken up at Heathrow in 8/60. Canx.
G-AIHB	Percival P.30 Proctor II	H.166	BV629	4. 9.46	Crashed at Benghazi, Libya in 1/49. Canx.
G-AIHC	Airspeed AS.65 Consul	4312	PK248	4. 9.46	To OO-GVP 9/46. Canx 10.9.46.
G-AIHD	Percival P.34 Proctor III	H.171	DX241	6. 9.46	WFU at Woolsington on 30.9.63. Canx.
G-AIHE	Percival P.28 Proctor I	K.282	P6248	6. 9.46	Crashed at Maulden, Beds on 18.11.51. Canx.
G-AIHF	Percival P.28 Proctor I	H.11	R7495	6. 9.46	Crashed at Chemchemal, Iraq in 11/56. Canx.
G-AIHG	Percival P.28 Proctor I	H.4	R7488	6. 9.46	WFU at White Waltham on 16.4.60. Canx.
G-AIHH	Percival P.28 Proctor I	K.245	P6186	6. 9.46	Scrapped at Squires Gate in 9/56. Canx.
G-AIHI	Miles M.65 Gemini 1A	6283		16. 9.46	To F-BENP 2/48. Canx 20.2.48.
G-AIHJ	Miles M.57 Aerovan 4	6388		16. 9.46	To F-BENO 5/48. Canx 5.3.48.
G-AIHK	Miles M.57 Aerovan 3	6384		17. 9.46	Crashed at Airstrip K.1, Iraq on 2.10.49. Canx.
G-AIHL	Miles M.57 Aerovan 3	6385		17. 9.46	Crashed Kastrup, Denmark on 29.10.46. Canx.
G-AIHM	Miles M.65 Gemini 1A	6307		17. 9.46	DBR in crash on take-off Le Touquet, France on 18.11.62. Canx.
G-AIHN	DH.89A Dragon Rapide 4	6498	X7325	5. 9.46	To ZS-DJT 7/54. Canx 23.7.54.
G-AIHO	DH.82A Tiger Moth	3383	BB817 G-ADJG	6. 9.46	Crashed at Baginton on 6.9.53. Canx.
G-AIHP	DH.82A Tiger Moth	84880	T6551	6. 9.46	To Pakistan AF in 11/48. Canx 25.11.48.
G-AIHR	DH.82A Tiger Moth	84129	T7747	6. 9.46	To Syrian AF as SR-D4 in 11/46. Canx 17.10.46.
G-AIHS	DH.82A Tiger Moth	84681	T6255	6. 9.46	To Syrian AF as SR-D3 in 11/46. Canx 17.10.46.
G-AIHT	DH.82A Tiger Moth	85237	DE167	6. 9.46	To VT-DBE 2/49. Canx 18.2.49.
G-AIHU	Handley Page HP.70 Halifax C.VIII	1306	PP222	6. 9.46	Flew into a hill 4 miles Cwm, St.Asaph, Wales on 5.12.47. Canx 5.12.47.
G-AIHV	Handley Page HP.70 Halifax C.VIII	1335	PP262	6. 9.46	Broken up at Stansted in 1952. Canx as WFU 27.2.53.
G-AIHW	Handley Page HP.70 Halifax C.VIII	1357	PP284	6. 9.46	Crashed on night landing at Heathrow on 5.6.47 returning from Spain with 6 tons of Apricots. Canx 3.7.47.
G-AIHX	Handley Page HP.70 Halifax C.VIII	1367	PP294	6. 9.46	Crashed in night landing at Squires Gate on 3.9.48. Canx 3.9.48.
G-AIHY	Handley Page HP.70 Halifax C.VIII	1325	PP241	6. 9.46	Damaged in landing accident at Le Bourget, France on 28.12.49. Canx 18.1.50.
G-AIHZ	Beechcraft D-17S Traveller (UC-43-BH)	6905	FT535 44-67799	17. 9.46	To South Africa in 6/48. Canx 1.6.48.
G-AIIA	Avro 652A Anson 19 Srs.2	-	PH858	7.10.46	Restored to RAF as PH858. Canx as PWFU 1.3.48.

Regn	Type	c/n	Previous identity	Regn date	Fate or immediate subsequent identity (if known)
G-AIIB	Vickers-Supermarine 236 Walrus I	-	X9467	10. 9.46	DBR by gale at Weston-super-Mare in 1947. Canx.
G-AIIC	Avro 652A Anson I	-	EG492	13. 9.46	DBR in forced landing at Tanganyika on 13.11.46. Canx 15.4.47.
G-AIID	Handley Page HP.70 Halifax C.VIII	1379	PP317 G-AIID/PP317	24. 9.46	Mispainted as G-AHYI at one stage. Not converted. Canx 7.10.49. Scrapped on 20.3.50.
G-AIIE	Miles M.65 Gemini 2A	6310		17. 9.46	To F-DFPP 2/50. Canx 10.3.50.
G-AIIF	Miles M.65 Gemini 2A	6312		17. 9.46	CofA expired 16.4.71 & WFU at Lulsgate. Canx 1.5.71.
G-AIIG	Miles M.57 Aerovan 3	6386		18. 9.46	To I-VALF 10/53. Canx 20.10.53.
G-AIIH	Piper J3C-65 Cub (L-4H-PI)	11945	44-79649	14. 9.46	
G-AIII	Percival P.34 Proctor III	H.561	LZ800	17. 9.46	To F-DAAS 5/52. Canx 22.4.52.
G-AIIJ	Percival P.28 Proctor I	K.328	P6319	17. 9.46	To EI-ACX 1/47. Canx 9.12.46.
G-AIIK	Percival P.28 Proctor I	K.286	P6252	17. 9.46	Not converted. Canx 22.4.49.
G-AIIL	Percival P.34 Proctor III	H.548	LZ790	17. 9.46	To VH-AYQ 11/51. Canx 25.2.52.
G-AIIM	Airspeed AS.65 Consul	4342	PK290	17. 9.46	To Turkish AF in 9/46. Canx 25.9.46.
G-AIIN	Airspeed AS.65 Consul	4344	PK292	17. 9.46	To VP-YIC 11/49. Canx 4.11.49.
G-AIIO	Airspeed AS.65 Consul	4349	PK297	17. 9.46	Crashed in mountains near Lumbreras, Spain on 15.7.47. Canx 17.7.48.
G-AIIP	Percival P.28 Proctor I	K.232	P6173	31.10.46	WFU at Elstree in 10/52. Canx.
G-AIIR	Percival P.34 Proctor III	H.237	HM315	17. 9.46	WFU at Elmdon on 12.4.63. Canx.
G-AIIS	Airspeed AS.65 Consul	4398	RR357	17. 9.46	DBR at Normanton, Yorks on 1.11.49. Scrapped Croydon in 2/51. Canx.
G-AIIT	Percival P.10 Vega Gull	K.69	X9332 G-AFAU	17. 9.46	WFU at Croydon on 25.11.47. Scrapped in 12/50. Canx.
G-AIIU	Taylorcraft Plus D	196	LB337	19. 9.46	DBR at Denham on 28.12.58. (To Rearsby in 5/61, fuselage & tailplane fitted to G-ARRK) Canx.
G-AIIV	DH.82A Tiger Moth	86172	EM989	16.10.46	To VR-NAE 8/49. Canx 9.2.50.
G-AIIW(1)	DH.104 Dove 1	-		. .46R	NTU - Canx.
G-AIIW(2)	Percival P.28 Proctor I	K.321	P6312	24. 9.46	To VH-BQH 11/54. Canx 11.9.54.
G-AIIX	DH.104 Dove 1	04010		25. 9.46	To SN-AAB 9/47. Canx 31.8.47.
G-AIIY	DH.104 Dove 1B (Originally regd as Dove 1)	04016	ST-AAC SN-AAC/G-AIIY	25. 9.46	WFU at Coventry in 5/71. Canx 17.5.71.
G-AIIZ	DH.82A Tiger Moth	84959	T6645	19. 9.46	To SE-AMH 8/87. Canx 20.8.87.
G-AIJA	DH.82A Tiger Moth	85520	DE553	19. 9.46	Crashed at Sandown, IoW on 22.8.57. Canx.
G-AIJB	DH.82A Tiger Moth	84734	T6319	19. 9.46	To PH-UDB 3/47. Canx 29.11.46.
G-AIJC	DH.82A Tiger Moth	3729	5356M N5461	19. 9.46	To PH-UDA 3/47. Canx 29.11.46.
G-AIJD	Douglas C-47-DL Dakota	9049	FD795 42-32823	17. 9.46	To YV-C-AVK 1/51. Canx 29.1.51.
G-AIJE	Vickers 621 Viking 2	127	VL226 G-AIJE/VL226/G-AIJE	19. 9.46	Crashed at Southall, Middx on 9.9.58. Canx.
G-AIJF	Auster J/1 Autocrat	2304		15. 4.47	Crashed at West Hartlepool on 29.8.49. Canx.
G-AIJG	Auster J/1 Autocrat	2305		15. 4.47	Destroyed in mid-air collision with DH.87B G-AFDT over Dinas, Powis, Wales on 20.12.51. Canx.
G-AIJH	Auster J/1 Autocrat	2306		15. 4.47	To OH-AUC 11/51. Canx 31.10.51.
G-AIJI	Auster J/1N Alpha (Originally regd as J/1 Autocrat)	2307		15. 4.47	Damaged in gales Kirmington on 12.1.75. Canx as WFU 12.3.75. (Frame only for spares use 9/96)
G-AIJJ	Auster J/1 Autocrat	2217	(ZS-BMN)	28. 3.47	To XY-ABE 9/47. Canx 13.9.47.
G-AIJK	Auster J/4 Archer	2067		13.11.46	CofA expired 24.8.68 & WFU. (On rebuild off-site 4/96)
G-AIJL	Auster J/4 Archer	2068		13.11.46	To VH-AAG 5/51. Canx 28.5.51.
G-AIJM	Auster J/4 Archer	2069	EI-BEU G-AIJM	13.11.46	Damaged in forced landing near Tring 5.1.97. CofA expired 28.3.97. (Stored pending overhaul/repairs)
G-AIJN	Auster J/4 Archer	2070		13.11.46	To VH-AAO 6/51. Canx 20.6.51.
G-AIJO	Auster J/4 Archer	2071		13.11.46	To LX-REX 5/50. Canx 10.5.50.
G-AIJP	Auster J/4 Archer	2072		13.11.46	To VH-AET 11/51. Canx 19.9.51.
G-AIJR	Auster J/4 Archer	2073		13.11.46	To EI-CPN 4/98. Canx 18.7.97.
G-AIJS	Auster J/4 Archer	2074		13.11.46	CofA expired 14.12.71. Broken up for spares. Canx as WFU 1.9.81. (Remains stored 5/96)
G-AIJT	Auster J/4 Srs.100 (Originally regd as J/4 Archer)	2075	(F-....) G-AIJT	13.11.46	
G-AIJU	Auster J/2 Arrow	2361		29.11.46	To VH-BNQ 11/49. Canx 16.11.49.
G-AIJV	Auster J/2 Arrow	2362		29.11.46	To VP-JAR 12/49. Canx 18.8.49.
G-AIJW	Auster J/1 Autocrat	2192		5.11.46	To F-OAJI 7/51. Canx 7.2.51.
G-AIJX	Auster J/1 Autocrat	2193		5.11.46	Ditched off St.David's Head, Pembroke on 15.8.47. Canx.
G-AIJY	Auster J/1 Autocrat	2194		5.11.46	Crashed at Speeton on 5.9.48. Canx.
G-AIJZ	Auster J/1 Autocrat	2195		5.11.46	Crashed at Kingsland, Hereford on 25.10.70. CofA expired 17.6.71. (Frame stored 11/95)
G-AIKA	Taylorcraft Auster 5	889	MT188	24.10.46	To ZK-AVU 7/50. Canx 12.7.50.
G-AIKB	Taylorcraft Auster 5	1408	TJ341	13.11.46	Crashed near Ruabon, Wrexham on 26.3.48. Canx.
G-AIKC	Taylorcraft Auster 5	1078	NJ699	13.11.46	To ZP-TDK 4/57. Canx 25.4.57.
G-AIKD	Auster J/1 Autocrat	2120	(OY-DPO)	13.11.46	To F-BEXT 1/50. Canx 13.1.50.
G-AIKE	Taylorcraft Auster 5 (Frame no. TAY 2450)	1097	"G-ANIA" G-AIKE/NJ728	15.11.46	Blown over by gales at Luton on 1.9.65. CofA expired 3.2.66. (On rebuild 9/96)
G-AIKF	Fairey Gyrodyne	F.B.1 & F.8465		20. 9.46	Fatal crash at Ufton, near Reading on 17.4.49. Canx.
G-AIKG	Percival P.28 Proctor I	K.255	P6196	23. 9.46	To EC-AGX 7/52. Canx 25.6.52.
G-AIKH	Percival P.28 Proctor I	K.231	P6172	23. 9.46	Crashed at Shoreham on 25.7.47. Canx.
G-AIKI	Percival P.28 Proctor I	K.238	EI-AJR G-AIKI/P6179	23. 9.46	WFU on 18.6.57. Broken up at Kidlington in 10/61. Canx.
G-AIKJ	Percival P.34 Proctor III	H.31	R7532	23. 9.46	DBR near Tonbridge on 16.11.58. Canx.
G-AIKK	Percival P.28 Proctor I	H.5	R7489	23. 9.46	DBR at Le Touquet, France on 1.4.54. Canx.
G-AIKL	Vickers-Supermarine 236 Walrus II	S2/12325	HD915	23. 9.46	Not converted. Scrapped at Weston-super-Mare in 10/47. Canx.
G-AIKM	Avro 652A Anson 19 Srs.2	1364		30. 9.46	Crashed near Luton Airport on 21.4.49. Canx 21.4.49.

Regn	Type	c/n	Previous identity	Regn date	Fate or immediate subsequent identity (if known)
G-AIKN	Vickers 621 Viking 1B	131	VL227 G-AIKN	30. 9.46	WFU on 22.6.60. Donated to Southend Airport Fire Service in 11/65. Broken up in 1969. Canx.
G-AIKO	Airspeed AS.65 Consul	4339	TJ-ABE G-AIKO/PK287	25. 9.46	To EC-AJV 5/54. Canx 22.5.54.
G-AIKP	Airspeed AS.65 Consul	4323	PK259	3.10.46	To ZS-BJX 10/47. Canx 6.10.47.
G-AIKR	Airspeed AS.65 Consul	4338	PK286	25. 9.46	CofA expired 14.5.65 & WFU. (On display 1997 Rockcliffe, Canada)
G-AIKS	Airspeed AS.65 Consul	4340	PK288	25. 9.46	WFU on 14.10.50. Burned at Squires Gate on 20.4.56. Canx.
G-AIKT	Airspeed AS.65 Consul	4356	PK304	25. 9.46	WFU at Croydon on 6.3.58. Canx.
G-AIKU	Airspeed AS.65 Consul	4348	PK296	25. 9.46	To TJ-AAX 5/51. Canx 23.4.51.
G-AIKV	Miles M.57 Aerovan 4	6389		1.10.46	DBR in forced landing at Fermandville Beach, near Cherbourg, France on 12.1.47. Canx.
G-AIKW	Miles M.65 Gemini 1A	6309		30. 9.46	Crashed off Isle of Rum, Scotland on 7.9.47. Canx.
G-AIKX	Airspeed AS.65 Consul	4354	PK302	26. 9.46	WFU at Croydon on 15.3.56. Scrapped in 9/56. Canx.
G-AIKY	Airspeed AS.65 Consul	4324	VR-SCD G-AIKY/PK260	26. 9.46	To 4X-AEK 5/53. Canx 5.5.53.
G-AIKZ	Airspeed AS.65 Consul	4325	PK261	26. 9.46	To I-VALH 5/56. Canx 3.4.55.
G-AILA	Airspeed AS.65 Consul	4322	PK258	26. 9.46	To Turkish AF in 9/46. Canx 27.9.46.
G-AILB	Miles M.57 Aerovan 4	6391		5.10.46	To EC-EAK 11/47. Canx 14.11.47.
G-AILC	Miles M.57 Aerovan 4	6392		5.10.46	To EC-EAL/EC-ABA 11/47. Canx 17.11.47.
G-AILD	Miles M.57 Aerovan 4	6393		5.10.46	To EC-EAM/EC-ABB 11/47. Canx 14.11.47.
G-AILE	Miles M.57 Aerovan 4	6394		5.10.46	To EC-EAN/EC-ACQ 11/47. Canx 17.11.47.
G-AILF	Miles M.57 Aerovan 4	6400		14.10.46	DBR at Guernsey on 20.8.50. Canx.
G-AILG	Miles M.65 Gemini 1A	6311		18.10.46	To F-BGPR in 1952. Canx 18.4.52.
G-AILH	Miles M.60 Marathon 1	6430		18.10.46	To RAF as VX229 in 1952. Canx.
G-AILI	Miles M.38 Messenger 2A	6362		25.10.46	Crashed at Beauvais, France on 23.5.64. Canx.
G-AILJ	Miles M.71 Merchantman	6695	G-21-1 U-21	31.10.46	Scrapped in 1948. Canx.
G-AILK	Miles M.65 Gemini 1A	6453		31.10.46	To VH-BJZ in 1947. Canx 4.12.47.
G-AILL	Miles M.38 Messenger 2A	6341		14.11.46	CofA expired 11.4.73 & WFU at Rush Green. Canx as WFU 30.3.89. (Major components stored 3/96 with parts from G-AISL)
G-AILM	Miles M.57 Aerovan IV	6398		22.11.46	To SX-BDA(2) 6/55. Canx 5.5.55.
G-AILN	Percival P.28 Proctor I	K.264	P6230	2.10.46	WFU at Tollerton in 10/50. Broken up. Canx.
G-AILO	Handley Page HP.70 Halifax C.VIII	1353	PP280	14.10.46	CofA expired 31.8.51 & WFU at Bovingdon. Scrapped. Canx 1.2.52.
G-AILP	Percival P.28 Proctor I	K.250	P6191	2.10.46	WFU at Elstree in 3/56. Canx.
G-AILR	DH.82A Tiger Moth	83634	T7168	3.10.46	DBF in hangar fire at Broxbourne on 23.6.47. Canx.
G-AILS	DH.82A Tiger Moth	84958	T6644	3.10.46	DBF in hangar fire at Broxbourne on 23.6.47. Canx.
G-AILT	DH.82A Tiger Moth	85857	DE997	3.10.46	DBF in hangar fire at Broxbourne on 23.6.47. Canx.
G-AILU	Bristol 170 Freighter 21	12785		3.12.46	To Pakistan AF as G776 in 8/48. Canx 4.4.48.
G-AILV	Bristol 170 Freighter 21E (Originally regd as Mk.21)	12786		3.12.46	To EC-AEH 12/48. Canx 27.11.48.
G-AILW	Bristol 170 Freighter 21 (Originally regd as Mk.1A)	12787	F-BCJM G-AILW	3.12.46	To OO-FAH(2) 8/63. Canx 14.8.63.
G-AILX	Bristol 170 Freighter 1	12788		3.12.46	To F-BCJN 5/47. Canx 7.5.47.
G-AILY	Bristol 170 Freighter 2	12789	R-37	3.12.46	NTU - Remained as R-37 (B-Class marks). Canx.
G-AILZ	Bristol 170 Freighter 21E	12790		3.12.46	To SA-AAA 8/49. Canx 22.6.49.
G-AIMA	Bristol 170 Freighter 21	12791	D-BODO D-AHOI/G-AIMA/VR-NAZ/G-AIMA/G-18-63	3.12.46	To (OO-ABG)/OO-FAG(2) 4/62. Canx 4.4.62.
G-AIMB	Bristol 170 Freighter 2	12792		3.12.46	To SE-BNG 8/47. Canx 26.7.47.
G-AIMC	Bristol 170 Freighter 1A	12793		3.12.46	DBR after parking brake failed and it rolled down the airstrip into Little Wau Creek, Papua New Guinea on 23.10.47. Canx 18.12.47.
G-AIMD	Bristol 170 Freighter 21E	12794		3.12.46	To SA-AAE 9/49. Canx.
G-AIME	Bristol 170 Freighter 21E (Originally regd as a Mk.IIA)	12795	XF662 G-AIME/R-38/ZS-BVI/G-AIME	3.12.46	WFU at Lydd in 10/63. Broken up at Southend 5/64. Canx.
G-AIMF	Bristol 170 Wayfarer 21P	12796		3.12.46	To Pakistan AF as G789 in 7/50. Canx 7.7.50.
G-AIMG	Bristol 170 Freighter 21	12797		3.12.46	To EC-AEG 12/48. Canx 21.10.46.
G-AIMH	Bristol 170 Freighter 21	12798	XF663 G-AIMH/F-BECT/G-AIMH	3.12.46	WFU at Lydd in 12/62. Broken up in 1963. Canx.
G-AIMI	Bristol 170 Freighter 21E	12799		3.12.46	To RAF as WB482 on 30.3.49, then R.Australian AF as A81-1 on 14.4.49. Canx 24.1.49.
G-AIMJ	Bristol 170 Wayfarer 21P	12800		3.12.46	To Pakistan AF as G790 in 7/50. Canx 7.7.50.
G-AIMK	Bristol 170 Wayfarer 21E	12801		3.12.46	To F-BENX 6/48. Canx 21.4.48.
G-AIML(1)	Bristol 170 Wayfarer 21	12802		3.12.46	NTU - To F-BCJA 12/46. Canx in 1.47.
G-AIML(2)	Bristol 167 Brabazon 2	12870	(VX343)	18. 7.47	Broken up at Filton in 10/53 when half completed. Canx.
G-AIMM	Bristol 170 Wayfarer 21P	12803		3.12.46	To Pakistan AF as G780 in 11/49. Canx 15.8.49.
G-AIMN	Bristol 170 Wayfarer 21P	12804		3.12.46	To Pakistan AF as G782 in 12/49. Canx 15.8.49.
G-AIMO	Bristol 170 Freighter 21E	12805		3.12.46	To RAF as WB483 on 24.1.49, then R.Australian AF as A81-2 on 14.4.49. Canx.
G-AIMP	Bristol 170 Wayfarer 21P	12806		3.12.46	To Pakistan AF as G777 in 11/49. Canx 30.8.49.
G-AIMR	Bristol 170 Freighter 21E	12807		3.12.46	To RAF as WB484 on 14.2.49, then R.Australian F as A81-3 on 5.5.49. Canx.
G-AIMS	Bristol 170 Wayfarer 21P	12808		3.12.46	To Pakistan AF as G791 in 7/50. Canx 7.7.50.
G-AIMT	Bristol 170 Freighter 21E	12809		3.12.46	To F-BENV 5/48. Canx 21.4.48.
G-AIMU	Bristol 170 Wayfarer 21P	12810		3.12.46	To Pakistan AF as G783 in 12/49. Canx 15.8.49.
G-AIMV	Bristol 170 Wayfarer 21P	12811		3.12.46	To Pakistan AF as G784 in 12/49. Canx 15.8.49.
G-AIMW	Bristol 170 Freighter 21E	12812		27. 1.47	To F-BENG 3/48. Canx 27.2.48.
G-AIMX	Bristol 170 Wayfarer 21P	12813		27. 1.47	To Pakistan AF as G785 in 1/50. Canx 15.8.49.
G-AIMY	Bristol 170 Wayfarer 21P	12814		27. 1.47	To Pakistan AF as G786 in 1/50. Canx 15.8.49.
G-AIMZ	Bristol 170 Wayfarer 21P	12815		27. 1.47	To Pakistan AF as G787 in 2/50. Canx 30.1.50.
G-AINA	Bristol 170 Wayfarer 21P	12816		27. 1.47	To Pakistan AF as G788 in 7/50. Canx 7.7.50.

Regn	Type	c/n	Previous identity	Regn date	Fate or immediate subsequent identity (if known)
G-AINB	Bristol 170 Wayfarer 21P	12817		27. 1.47	To Pakistan AF as G792 in 7/50. Canx 7.7.50.
G-AINC	Bristol 170 Wayfarer 21P	12818		27. 1.47	To Pakistan AF as G793 in 5/51. Canx 17.7.51.
G-AIND	Bristol 170 Wayfarer 21P	12819		27. 1.47	To Pakistan AF as G794 in 6/51. Canx 17.7.51.
G-AINE	Bristol 170 Wayfarer 21P	12820		27. 1.47	To Pakistan AF as G795 in 6/51. Canx 17.7.51.
G-AINF	Bristol 170 Wayfarer 21P	12821		27. 1.47	To Pakistan AF as G796 in 6/51. Canx 17.7.51.
G-AING	Bristol 170 Wayfarer 21P	12822		27. 1.47	To Pakistan AF as G797 in 7/51. Canx 17.7.51.
G-AINH	Bristol 170 Wayfarer 21P	12823		27. 1.47	To Pakistan AF as G798 in 7/51. Canx 17.7.51.
G-AINI	Bristol 170 Wayfarer 21P	12824		27. 1.47	To Pakistan AF as G799 in 8/51. Canx 17.7.51.
G-AINJ	Bristol 170 Wayfarer 21P	12825		27. 1.47	To Pakistan AF as G800 in 9/51. Canx 17.7.51.
G-AINK	Bristol 170 Freighter 31 (Originally regd as a Mk.21)	12826	WH575 G-AINK/G-18-92/G-AINK	27. 1.47	To ZK-AYG 4/51. Canx.
G-AINL	Bristol 170 Freighter 31E (Originally regd as a Mk.21)	12827	WJ320 G-AINL/EI-AFP/G-AINL/WJ320/G-AINL/G-18-93/G-AINL	27. 1.47	To CF-YDO 2/69. Canx 7.11.68.
G-AINM	Bristol 170 Freighter 31	12828		27. 1.47	To ZK-AYH 5/51. Canx 30.4.51.
G-AINN	Bristol 170 Freighter 31MC	12829	G-18-95	27. 1.47	To R.Canadian AF as 9696 11/51. Canx 9.11.51.
G-AINO	Bristol 170 Freighter 31MC	12830		27. 1.47	To R.Canadian AF as 9697 11/51. Canx 9.11.51.
G-AINP	Bristol 170 Freighter 30	12831	(RCAF) G-18-97/G-AINP	27. 1.47	To CF-GBT 12/51. Canx 14.12.51.
G-AINR	Bristol 170 Freighter 31MNZ	12832	G-18-98	27. 1.47	To R.New Zealand AF as NZ5901 11/51. Canx 17.4.52.
G-AINS	Bristol 170 Freighter 31MNZ	12833	G-18-99	27. 1.47	To R.New Zealand AF as NZ5902 11/51. Canx 17.4.52.
G-AINT	Bristol 170 Freighter 31MNZ	12834	G-18-100	27. 1.47	To R.New Zealand AF as NZ5903 2/52. Canx 17.4.52.
G-AINU	DH.82A Tiger Moth	82330	N9213	8.10.46	Crashed near Faversham, Kent on 23.5.48. Canx.
G-AINV	DH.82A Tiger Moth	82107	N6852	8.10.46	To AP-ACJ 2/49. Canx 16.2.49.
G-AINW	DH.82A Tiger Moth	83011	R5129	8.10.46	To VT-DBI 2/49. Canx 16.2.49.
G-AINX	DH.82A Tiger Moth	85764	DE879	8.10.46	Not converted. To spares at Tollerton in 1949. Canx.
G-AINY	DH.82A Tiger Moth	83812	T7416	8.10.46	To ZK-AYC 11/51. Canx 3.4.51.
G-AINZ	Avro 652A Anson I	-	MG218	7.10.46	CofA expired 18.1.49 & WFU. Broken up. Canx 19.2.52.
G-AIOA	Avro 652A Anson I	-	NK601	7.10.46	CofA expired 16.2.48 & WFU. Broken up. Canx 19.2.52.
G-AIOB	Avro 652A Anson I	-	NK843	7.10.46	To SE-BRW 5/50. Canx 27.4.50.
G-AIOC	Avro 671 Cierva C.30A Autogiro	R3/CA/47	K4239	16.10.46	DBR at Elstree on 10.7.49. Canx.
G-AIOD	Douglas C-47A-30-DK Dakota	13847/25292	LX-LAB G-AIOD/KG748/43-48031	14.10.46	To OO-APB(3) 10/48. Canx 12.11.48.
G-AIOE	Douglas C-47A-5-DK Dakota	12373	LX-LAC G-AIOE/KG364/42-92559	14.10.46	To SX-BBA 3/48. Canx 1.3.48.
G-AIOF	Douglas C-47A-5-DK Dakota	12332	KG333 42-92522	14.10.46	To SX-BBB 3/48. Canx 9.3.48.
G-AIOG	Douglas C-47A-10-DK Dakota	12482	KG447 42-92657	14.10.46	To TF-ISG 1/47. Canx 6.12.46.
G-AIOH	Handley Page HP.70 Halifax C.VIII	1324	PP240	4.11.46	Crashed on landing at Barcelona, Spain on 30.5.47. Canx 13.9.48.
G-AIOI	Handley Page HP.70 Halifax C.VIII	1327	PP243	4.11.46	DBER in a taxying accident at Tegel, West Berlin, East Germany on 15.2.49. Canx 15.2.49.
G-AIOJ	Miles M.14A Hawk Trainer III	2105	T9888	18.10.46	To ZK-ATE 6/49. Canx 21.6.49.
G-AIOK	Miles M.14A Hawk Trainer III	2148	T9955	18.10.46	Crashed at Burnaston on 23.8.50. Canx.
G-AIOL	Airspeed AS.65 Consul	4321	PK257	16.10.46	To 4X-ACR 11/49 / Israeli DF/AF as 2808. Canx 7.11.49.
G-AIOM	Airspeed AS.65 Consul	4347	PK295	16.10.46	Forced-landed in field 6m N of Lyons, France on 24.1.48 & DBR. Canx.
G-AION	Airspeed AS.65 Consul	4352	PK300	16.10.46	To F-BCJD 12/46. Canx 11.11.46.
G-AIOO	Airspeed AS.65 Consul	4357	(ZS-BNT) G-AIOO/PK305	16.10.46	Crashed at Perpignan, France on 27.11.47. Canx.
G-AIOP	Airspeed AS.65 Consul	671	(OO-MAB) HM643	30. 1.47	To SE-BTB 4/51. Canx 22.3.51.
G-AIOR	Airspeed AS.65 Consul	4341	PK289	4.11.46	To 4X-ACP 9/49 / Israeli DF/AF as 2809?. Canx 1.9.49.
G-AIOS	Airspeed AS.65 Consul	4329	PK265	9.11.46	WFU on 26.5.58 & used as a film prop. Canx.
G-AIOT	Airspeed AS.65 Consul	4330	UN-97 G-AIOT/PK266	9.11.46	WFU at Thruxton on 17.8.55. Canx.
G-AIOU	Airspeed AS.65 Consul	4355	PK303	9.11.46	Crashed in Egyptian desert near Cairo 24.5.48. Canx.
G-AIOV	Airspeed AS.65 Consul	4361	PK309	25.11.46	To I-VALZ 5/56. Canx 31.8.54.
G-AIOW	Airspeed AS.65 Consul	4353	PK301	9.11.46	WFU on 14.4.54. Dismantled at Croydon in 12/54. Canx.
G-AIOX	Airspeed AS.65 Consul	2188	EB748	9.12.46	To TJ-ABD 12/50. Canx 12.11.50.
G-AIOY	Airspeed AS.65 Consul	4334	PK282	9.12.46	To SE-BTD 8/50. Canx 16.8.50.
G-AIOZ	Airspeed AS.65 Consul	4335	PK283	9.12.46	Crashed near Limpsfield, Surrey on 29.4.47. Canx.
G-AIPA	Avro 652A Anson I	-	EF866	22.10.46	CofA expired 21.4.60 & WFU at Burnaston. Scrapped in 1961. Canx as PWFU 14.2.63.
G-AIPB	Avro 652A Anson I	-	LT288	7.11.46	Conversion abandoned when longerons found to be corroded. Canx as PWFU 13.4.48. Used for spares & remains still at Cranfield in 6/51.
G-AIPC	Avro 652A Anson I (Believed converted by Avro with c/n 1385)	-	MG588	18.11.46	CofA expired 26.8.55 & WFU at Cranfield. Canx as PWFU 4.4.61. Remains scrapped at Cranfield in 1961/62.
G-AIPD	Avro 652A Anson I	-	NK616	13.12.46	To OY-DYY 12/53. Canx 17.10.53.
G-AIPE	Taylorcraft Auster 5	1416	TJ347	17.12.46	To PH-NET(2) 6/52. Canx 22.5.52.
G-AIPF	Taylorcraft Auster 5	1039	NJ638	17.12.46	To TC-ALIS 4/52. Canx 26.3.52.
G-AIPG	Auster J/4 Archer	2076		17.12.46	To VP-KNB 7/55. Canx 21.1.55.
G-AIPH	Auster J/4 Archer Srs.100 (Originally regd as J/4 Archer) (Used as Rolls-Royce Continental O-200A test-bed in 1966)	2077	G-37-5 G-AIPH	17.12.46	Crashed shortly after take-off from Hucknall on 8.4.72. Canx.
G-AIPI	Auster J/4 Archer	2078		17.12.46	To F-OAMY 1/51. Canx 17.1.51.
G-AIPJ	Auster J/4 Archer	2079		17.12.46	To VH-AAK 5/51. Canx 28.8.51.
G-AIPK	Auster J/4 Archer	2080		17.12.46	To ZK-AXC 9/50. Canx 6.10.50.
G-AIPL	Auster J/4 Archer	2081		17.12.46	To VH-AEA 5/51. Canx 26.5.51.
G-AIPM	Auster J/4 Archer	2082		9. 1.47	To VH-AEC 10/51. Canx 18.10.51.
G-AIPN	Taylorcraft Auster 5	1151	RT488	20.12.46	To F-BGPD 2/52. Canx 13.2.52.

Regn	Type	c/n	Previous identity	Regn date	Fate or immediate subsequent identity (if known)
G-AIPO	Taylorcraft Auster 5	1544	TJ543	20.12.46	To F-DAAI 8/51. Canx 18.7.51.
G-AIPP	Auster J/4 Archer	2083		9. 1.47	To HB-EOX 7/47. Canx.
G-AIPR	Auster J/4 Archer	2084	D-EDGE G-AIPR	9. 1.47	
G-AIPS	Auster J/4 Archer	2085		9. 1.47	Crashed at Denham on 15.6.51. Canx.
G-AIPT	Auster J/1 Autocrat	2200		9. 1.47	To ZS-DBN 11/47. Canx 1.11.47.
G-AIPU	Auster J/1 Autocrat	2202		9. 1.47	To F-BFXO 7/51. Canx 23.5.51.
G-AIPV	Auster J/1 Autocrat	2203		9. 1.47	
G-AIPW	Taylorcraft Auster 5A Srs.160 (Originally regd as J/1 Autocrat)	2204		9. 1.47	To Amman Museum and painted in Arab Legion AF c/s as A-430. Canx 13.11.95 on sale to Jordan.
G-AIPX	Auster J/1 Autocrat	2205		13. 1.47	Crashed at Somerford on 18.9.49. Canx.
G-AIPY	Auster J/1 Autocrat	2206		13. 1.47	To VH-AJQ 11/50. Canx 25.6.50.
G-AIPZ	Auster J/1 Autocrat	2208		13. 1.47	To EI-AGJ 11/53. Canx 30.10.53.
G-AIRA	Auster J/1 Autocrat	2209		13. 1.47	To VQ-BAA 4/52. Canx 8.4.52.
G-AIRB	Auster J/1 Autocrat	2214		13. 1.47	Fatal crash at Tump Farm, Coleford, Hereford on 11.4.71. Canx.
G-AIRC	Auster J/1 Autocrat	2215		13. 1.47	
G-AIRD	Auster J/4 Archer	2086		15. 1.47	Crashed at Stainfield, Lincs on 5.1.58. Canx.
G-AIRE	Taylorcraft Plus D	223	LB376	18.10.46	Crashed off Spurn Head on 30.4.66. Canx.
G-AIRF	Percival P.28 Proctor I	K.426	Z7251	22.10.46	To EI-ACV 12/46. Canx 12.11.46.
G-AIRG	Douglas C-47A-30-DK Dakota	13843/25288	KG744 43-48027	19.10.46	To XY-ABF 3/48. Canx.
G-AIRH	Douglas C-47A-10-DK Dakota	12445	(ZS-DBB) G-AIRH/KG410/42-92624	19.10.46	To ZS-DDC 7/49. Canx.
G-AIRI	DH.82A Tiger Moth	3761	N5488	22.10.46	CofA expired 9.11.81. Canx as WFU 3.4.89. (Stored 3/97)
G-AIRJ	DH.82A Tiger Moth	84326	T7973	22.10.46	WFU at White Waltham in 8/52. Canx.
G-AIRK	DH.82A Tiger Moth	82336	N9241	22.10.46	
G-AIRL	Avro 652A Anson I	-	MG970	22.10.46	Not converted & used for spares. Canx 16.8.49 as scrapped.
G-AIRM	Avro 652A Anson I	-	MG585	22.10.46	To VP-YLC 3/54. Canx 24.2.54.
G-AIRN	Avro 652A Anson I	-	NK667	22.10.46	DBR when forced landed at Piadena, Northern Italy on 22.2.52, whilst on delivery to Hong Kong. Canx as PWFU 28.7.52.
G-AIRO	Avro 652A Anson I	-	N9895	22.10.46	Not converted & used for spares. Canx 16.8.49 as scrapped.
G-AIRP	Airspeed AS.65 Consul	4400	RR359	21.10.46	Dismantled at Langley in 5/51. Canx.
G-AIRR	DH.82A Tiger Moth	84086	T7692	24.10.46	Crashed near Newtownards, Northern Ireland on 3.4.60. Canx.
G-AIRS	Miles M.65 Gemini 1A	6315		14.10.46	Crashed on Oxley Golf Course, Watford 11.3.56. Canx.
G-AIRT	DH.98 Mosquito PR.XVI	-	NS812	23.10.46	To Israeli AF/DF as D-160 in 7/48. Canx 5.7.48.
G-AIRU	DH.98 Mosquito PR.XVI	-	NS811	23.10.46	To Israeli AF/DF in 7/48 (possible to 2102!). Canx 5.7.48.
G-AIRV	Avro 652A Anson C.19 Srs.2	-	PH830	22.10.46	Returned to RAF as PH830 in 3/49. Canx 21.3.49.
G-AIRW	Avro 652A Anson I	-	MH167	23.10.46	To VP-KHS 4/52. Canx 5.7.50.
G-AIRX	Avro 652A Anson I	-	AX232	23.10.46	To VP-KJK 4/52. Canx 9.6.52.
G-AIRY	Miles M.38 Messenger 2A	6343		2.12.46	To ZK-ATT 4/50. Canx 28.3.50.
G-AIRZ	Airspeed AS.40 Oxford	2816	HN610	31.10.46	Crashed near Luxembourg on 18.7.52. Canx.
G-AISA	Tipsy B Trainer Srs.1	17		24. 4.47	
G-AISB	Tipsy B Trainer Srs.1	18		24. 4.47	To OO-EOT. Canx 21.11.89.
G-AISC	Tipsy B Trainer Srs.1	19		24. 4.47	Permit to Fly expired 23.5.79. (Fuselage only stored 3/99 Cumbernauld)
G-AISD	Miles M.65 Gemini 1A	6285	OO-RLD VP-KDH/G-AISD	26.11.46	Restored as OO-RLD. Canx 7.1.88.
G-AISE	Miles M.57 Aerovan 4	6395		2.12.46	WFU at Tollerton on 12.11.47. Scrapped. Canx.
G-AISF	Miles M.57 Aerovan 4	6396		2.12.46	Crashed at Ringway on 29.4.57. Canx.
G-AISG	Miles M.57 Aerovan 4	6405		9.12.46	Crashed at Croydon on 14.6.47. Canx.
G-AISH	Miles M.28 Mercury 3	4684	PW937 U-0242	9.12.46	NTU - Scrapped at Woodley in 2/48. Canx.
G-AISI	Miles M.57 Aerovan 4	6397		23.12.46	To OO-MAP 8/50. Canx 19.8.50.
G-AISJ	Miles M.57 Aerovan 5	6404		8. 1.47	Crashed at Woodley on 15.7.47. Canx.
G-AISK	Miles M.65 Gemini 1A	6319		10. 1.47	To F-BFVH 12/50. Canx 27.10.50.
G-AISL	Miles M.38 Messenger 2A	6346		18. 1.47	CofA expired 13.6.67. Broken up in 7/67 at Panshanger. (Parts to G-AILL) Canx as WFU 12.4.73.
G-AISM	Miles M.65 Gemini 1A	6454		27. 1.47	Crashed at Lelant, near St.Ives, Cornwall on 7.7.60. Canx.
G-AISN	Miles M.65 Gemini 1A	6323		29. 1.47	To F-BDJD(2) 2/53. Canx 28.1.53.
G-AISO	Miles M.65 Gemini 1A	6326		29. 1.47	To VH-BJP 4/50. Canx 31.3.50.
G-AISP	Piper J3C-65 Cub (L-4H-PI)	11691	43-30400	28.10.46	To EC-AKD 10/54. Canx 7.5.53.
G-AISR	DH.82A Tiger Moth	84559	T6068	24.10.46	To I-GIVI 2/65. Canx 7.1.65.
G-AISS	Piper J3C-65 Cub (L-4H-PI) (Frame no.11904)	12077	D-ECAV SL-AAA/44-79781	3. 9.85	
G-AIST	Vickers Supermarine 300 Spitfire Mk.Ia (Westland-built) (Also has c/n HA1 6S/5 139 - Heston Aircraft Company issued c/n)	WASP/20/2	AR213	25.10.46	
G-AISU	Vickers Supermarine 349 Spitfire LF.Vb	CBAF/1061	AB910	25.10.46	
G-AISV	Piper J3C-85 Cub (L-4H-PI)	11810	43-30519	28.10.46	To NC74137 10/47. Canx 8.10.47.
G-AISW	Piper J3C-85 Cub (L-4H-PI)	11780	43-30489	28.10.46	Crashed in North Sea off North Foreland on 16.2.48. Canx.
G-AISX	Piper J3C-85 Cub (L-4H-PI) (Frame No. 11489)	11663	43-30372	28.10.46	
G-AISY	DH.82A Tiger Moth	82018	VT-CZV G-AISY/N6740	30.10.46	To PH-CRO 9/97. Canx 8.9.97.
G-AISZ	DH.82A Tiger Moth	83661	T7294	30.10.46	To VP-CBB 5/48. Canx 22.5.48.
G-AITA	DH.82A Tiger Moth	84859	T6518	30.10.46	Crashed near Welwyn on 27.6.48. Canx in 1948.
G-AITB	Airspeed AS.40 Oxford 1	-	MP425	1.11.46	CofA expired on 24.5.61 & WFU at Perth. (On display Hendon)
G-AITC	Handley Page HP.70 Halifax C.VIII	1382	PP320	1.11.46	DBER on landing at Brindisi, Italy on 20.1.50. Canx 20.1.50.
G-AITD	DH.82A Tiger Moth	85617	DE676	31.10.46	Crashed near Yeadon on 7.7.59. Canx.

Regn	Type	c/n	Previous identity	Regn date	Fate or immediate subsequent identity (if known)
G-AITE	DH.82A Tiger Moth	85202	DE132	31.10.46	Crashed at Speeton, Yorks on 15.8.52. Canx.
G-AITF	Airspeed AS.40 Oxford 1	-	ED290	1.11.46	CofA expired 8.6.60 & WFU at Perth. (On rebuild to flying condition 3/92 Port Elizabeth, South Africa)
G-AITG	Fairchild F.24W-41A Argus II (UC-61-FA)	356	FK347 42-32131	31.10.46	Ditched near Silloth, in Solway Firth on 11.11.46. Canx.
G-AITH	DH.82A Tiger Moth	85525	DE558	11.11.46	DBR in hangar collapse at Taif, Saudi Arabia on 2.4.49. Canx.
G-AITI	DH.82A Tiger Moth	84000	T7603	11.11.46	To Saudi Arabia in 10/50. Canx 18.10.50.
G-AITJ	Avro 652A Anson I	-	MG874	4.11.46	CofA expired 11.12.51 & WFU at Bahrein. Canx 2.1.52 as reduced to produce.
G-AITK	Avro 652A Anson I	-	W2628	4.11.46	To SE-BRT 4/50. Canx 3.4.50.
G-AITL	Avro 652A Anson I	-	EG324	4.11.46	CofA expired 18.10.49 & WFU at Croydon. Scrapped in 1951. Canx as PWFU 12.12.52.
G-AITM	Miles M.11A Whitney Straight (RAF serial mispainted in service)	312	"DR617" DR611/G-AETS	11.11.46	Not converted. Scrapped at Weston-super-Mare in 3/48. Canx.
G-AITN	Miles M.14A Hawk Trainer III	1826	R1825	11.11.46	WFU at Fairoaks in 11/62. Canx.
G-AITO	Miles M.14A Hawk Trainer III	1842	R1841	11.11.46	Crashed at Shoreham on 3.11.51. Canx.
	(Crashed at Tollerton in 1948, rebuilt with fuselage from c/n 1786 ex.P6443)				
G-AITP	Piper J3C-65 Cub	10951	OO-AAO 43-30401	4.10.83	To SE-BEL. Canx 13.6.88.
G-AITR	Miles M.14A Hawk Trainer III	1845	R1844	11.11.46	To Egyptian AF in 6/49. Canx 8.6.49.
G-AITS	Miles M.14A Hawk Trainer III	1997	T9730	11.11.46	Crashed at Hurstpierpoint, Sussex on 16.8.55. Canx.
G-AITT	Miles M.14A Hawk Trainer III	1658	P2436	11.11.46	To Egyptian AF in 2/49. Canx 25.2.49.
G-AITU	Miles M.14A Hawk Trainer III	423	L5991	11.11.46	To Egyptian AF in 9/49. Canx 2.9.49.
G-AITV	Miles M.14A Hawk Trainer III	595	L8086	11.11.46	To Egyptian AF in 9/49. Canx 20.9.49.
G-AITW	Miles M.14A Hawk Trainer III	1884	R1898	11.11.46	To Egyptian AF in 2/49. Canx 18.2.49.
G-AITX	Miles M.14A Hawk Trainer III	1843	R1842	11.11.46	To Egyptian AF in 2/49. Canx 18.2.49.
G-AITY	Miles M.14A Hawk Trainer III	616	L8138	11.11.46	To I-AITY 6/49. Canx 23.6.49.
G-AITZ	Miles M.14A Hawk Trainer III	1074	N5438	11.11.46	Scrapped at Thruxton in 9/49. Canx.
G-AIUA	Miles M.14A Hawk Trainer III	2035	T9768	11.11.46	Crashed on landing at Roborough on 26.9.65. CofA expired 13.7.67. (Stored 1995 with parts from G-ANWO)
G-AIUB	Miles M.14A Hawk Trainer III	613	L8135	11.11.46	Crashed at Cowes, IoW on 18.7.50. Canx.
G-AIUC	Miles M.14A Hawk Trainer III	843	N3795	11.11.46	To F-OAGQ 6/50. Canx 24.3.50.
G-AIUD	Miles M.14A Hawk Trainer III	606	L8128	11.11.46	To Egyptian AF in 10/49. Canx 2.9.49.
G-AIUE	Miles M.14A Hawk Trainer III	995	N3962	11.11.46	Crashed at Seething on 26.8.52. Canx.
G-AIUF	Miles M.14A Hawk Trainer III	1782	P6438	11.11.46	To US Army Flying Club, West Germany in 1956. Canx.
G-AIUG	Miles M.14A Hawk Trainer III	988	N3955	11.11.46	Scrapped at Croydon in 9/51. Canx.
G-AIUH	Airspeed AS.40 Oxford 1	3507	NM277	13.10.47	To VP-KOX in 9/58. Canx 20.9.58.
G-AIUI	DH.89A Dragon Rapide	6675	HG690	8.11.46	Crashed into sea off Dalby, near Peel, Isle of Man on 10.6.48. Canx.
G-AIUJ	DH.89A Dragon Rapide	6724	NF853	8.11.46	To VT-CHZ 1/47. Canx.
G-AIUK	DH.89A Dragon Rapide	6640	X7523	8.11.46	To VP-KND 2/55. Canx 14.2.55.
G-AIUL	DH.89A Dragon Rapide 6	6837	NR749	8.11.46	CofA expired 29.9.67. Canx as WFU 6.4.73.
	(On rebuild 7/97 with parts from G-AEMH/G-AKRN; parts possibly consumed since in rebuild of G-AJBJ - fuselage still present 3/98 Ley Farm, Chirk)				
G-AIUM	DH.89A Dragon Rapide	6519	X7346	20.11.46	To SE-BTA 7/50. Canx 25.7.50.
G-AIUN	DH.89A Dragon Rapide	6602	X7485	20.11.46	To Israeli DF/AF as S-75 in 9/48. Canx 16.5.50.
G-AIUO	DH.89A Dragon Rapide	6467	R5930	20.11.46	To SE-BTT 7/51. Canx 19.7.51.
G-AIUP	Avro 685 York C.1	1374		12.11.46	DBR on landing at Heathrow on 25.7.47. Canx.
G-AIUR	Airspeed AS.65 Consul	967	UN-95 G-AIUR/HN174	10.12.46	WFU in 2/49. Canx.
G-AIUS	Airspeed AS.65 Consul	750	HM757	10.12.46	To CN-TEJ 1/61. Canx.
G-AIUT	Airspeed AS.65 Consul	3375	LX666	10.12.46	To VP-YID 11/49. Canx 4.11.49.
G-AIUU	Airspeed AS.65 Consul	5104	UN-102 G-AIUU/W6562	14. 2.47	Dismantled at Croydon in 10/50. Canx.
G-AIUV	Airspeed AS.65 Consul	5098	HN191	7. 2.47	To Israel AF/DF as 2805 in 4/50. Canx 4.4.50.
G-AIUW	Airspeed AS.65 Consul	5100		7. 2.47	To 4X-ACQ 5/50 / Israeli DF/AF as 2810. Canx 22.2.50.
G-AIUX	Airspeed AS.65 Consul	5106	LB527	14. 2.47	To VP-KMI 5/54. Canx 7.4.54.
G-AIUY	Airspeed AS.65 Consul	5116	HN323	7. 2.47	To I-VALC 4/55. Canx 6.1.55.
G-AIUZ	Airspeed AS.65 Consul	5105	V4125	7. 2.47	Crashed near Berne, Switzerland on 2.9.48. Scrapped at Croydon. Canx.
G-AIVA	Airspeed AS.65 Consul	5102	BG152	7. 2.47	To EC-AHU 2/53. Canx 2.2.53.
G-AIVB	Vickers 610 Viking 1B	215		18.11.46	To CR-IAD 2/56. Canx 7.2.56.
G-AIVC	Vickers 649 Viking 1B (Originally regd as Type 610)	216	WZ353 G-AIVC	18.11.46	To D-AGAD 3/57. Canx 20.3.57.
G-AIVD	Vickers 610 Viking 3B (Originally regd as Viking 1B)	217	HB-AAR D-ADAM/G-AIVD	18.11.46	WFU at Manston on 3.4.65. Broken up. Canx.
G-AIVE	Vickers 610 Viking 1B	218		18.11.46	Crashed into northern slope of Irish Law mountain, near Largs, Ayrshire on 21.4.48. Canx.
G-AIVF	Vickers 610 Viking 3B (Originally regd as Viking 1B, reverted back to Viking 1B in 5/67)	219	HB-AAN D-BARI/D-AGIL/G-AIVF	18.11.46	WFU at Manston on 19.5.68. Canx as WFU 3.2.69.
G-AIVG	Vickers 610 Viking 1B	220		18.11.46	Crashed at Le Bourget, France on 12.8.53. CofA expired 12.2.54. (Fuselage stored 4/95 Mulhouse, France)
G-AIVH	Vickers 610 Viking 1B	221	XG896 G-AIVH	18.11.46	WFU at Blackbushe on 14.1.59. Broken up in 2/60. Canx.
G-AIVI	Vickers 610 Viking 1B	222		18.11.46	To D-ABEL 12/55. Canx 28.12.55.
G-AIVJ	Vickers 610 Viking 1B	223		18.11.46	To D-ABIR 2/56. Canx 13.2.56.
G-AIVK	Vickers 610 Viking 1B	224		18.11.46	WFU & stored at Gatwick in 5/61. Scrapped in 1962. Canx.
G-AIVL	Vickers 610 Viking 3B (Originally regd as Viking 1B)	225		18.11.46	WFU & Broken up at Heathrow in 6/61. Canx.
G-AIVM	Vickers 610 Viking 1B	226		18.11.46	To (D-CADA)/D-ADEL in 12/55. Canx 15.12.55.
G-AIVN	Vickers 610 Viking 1B	227		18.11.46	To VP-YMO in 9/54. Canx 10.9.54.

Regn	Type	c/n	Previous identity	Regn date	Fate or immediate subsequent identity (if known)
G-AIVO	Vickers 610 Viking 3B (Originally regd as Viking 1B)	228	XG568 XF630/G-AIVO	18.11.46	WFU & used for spares at Nice, France in 11/62. Broken up in 1963. Canx.
G-AIVP	Vickers 610 Viking 1B	229		18.11.46	Fatal crash after mid-air collision with a Soviet AF Yak-3 fighter over Berlin, Germany on 5.4.48. Canx.
G-AIVR	Vickers 644 Viking 1B	230		18.11.46	NTU - To YI-ABP 10/47. Canx.
G-AIVS	Vickers 644 Viking 1B	231		18.11.46	NTU - To YI-ABQ 12/47. Canx.
G-AIVT	Vickers 644 Viking 1B	232		18.11.46	NTU - To YI-ABR 1/48. Canx.
G-AIVU	DH.82A Tiger Moth	85244	DE174	14.11.46	Crashed at Woolsington on 19.6.49. Canx.
G-AIVV	DH.82A Tiger Moth	85103	T6856	14.11.46	Crashed at Grange-over-Sands in 9/49. WFU in 11/50. Canx.
G-AIVW	DH.82A Tiger Moth Seaplane (Converted to Seaplane in 7/63)	83135	T5370	14.11.46	CofA expired 20.7.85.
	(On long term rebuild 3/96 following w/o nr.Camber 27.8.82. Mainly comprises airframe of G-ANLR c/n 82111 ex N6856)				
G-AIVX	Short SA.6 Sealand	SH1555		7.11.46	Scrapped at Belfast, Northern Ireland in 4/55. Canx.
G-AIVY	Airspeed AS.40 Oxford	891	HM965	9.11.46	WFU at Nicosia, Cyprus on 7.9.55. Scrapped in 9/56. Canx.
G-AIVZ	DH.82A Tiger Moth	82291	N9180	14.11.46	To ZK-BCN 3/53. Canx 10.3.53.
G-AIWA	Percival P.28B Proctor I	H.20	R7524	14.11.46	Crashed at Le Ferte Alais, France on 9.6.84. Canx as destroyed 2.6.89.
G-AIWB	Percival P.34 Proctor III	H.541	LZ771	14.11.46	To HB-UMI 1/47. Canx 7.1.47.
G-AIWC	Douglas C-47A-25-DK Dakota	13474	VR-AAK G-AIWC/KG657/42-93550	14.11.46	To OO-SBI 2/52. Canx 12.2.62.
G-AIWD	Douglas C-47A-25-DK Dakota	13475	KG658 42-93551	14.11.46	Canx 4.3.67 on sale to Lebanon. To VR-ABF 3/67.
G-AIWE	Douglas C-47A-25-DK Dakota	13479	KG662 42-93554	14.11.46	To EC-AGS 4/52. Canx 19.4.52.
G-AIWF	DH.104 Dove 1B (Originally regd as Dove 1)	04023	ZS-DFA G-AIWF	20.11.46	To TF-BPD 5/64. Canx 19.5.64.
G-AIWG	DH.89A Dragon Rapide	6497	X7324	20.11.46	To VH-AIK 2/50. Canx 25.1.50.
G-AIWH	Avro 652A Anson X (Officially regd as ex.NK787)	-	NK727	14.11.46	To VR-AAG 6/52. Canx 18.6.52.
G-AIWI	Handley Page HP.70 Halifax C.VIII	1302	PP218	18.11.46	CofA expired 12.5.49 & WFU at Bovingdon. Scrapped in 5/49. Canx 20.3.50.
G-AIWJ	Handley Page HP.70 Halifax C.VIII	1359	PP286	18.11.46	WFU at Stansted in 1949. Canx 19.12.50 on sale to Ministry of Civil Aviation Fire School at Stansted. Still substantially complete on 6.6.51 but dismantled by 10/51.
G-AIWK	Handley Page HP.70 Halifax C.VIII	1368	PP295	18.11.46	Damaged by vandals while parked at Mascot, Sydney, Australia during 12/47 & scrapped. Canx 30.12.52.
G-AIWL	Handley Page HP.70 Halifax C.VIII	1364	PP291	18.11.46	Not converted. Canx 19.12.50 on sale to Ministry of Civil Aviation Fire School at Stansted. Still substantially complete on 6.6.51, but gone by 2.10.51.
G-AIWM	Handley Page HP.70 Halifax C.VIII	1339	PP266	18.11.46	Canx 19.12.50 on sale to Ministry of Civil Aviation Fire School at Stansted. Still substantially on 6.6.51 but to Cardiff by 2.10.51, for MCA Fire School, Pengam Moors.
G-AIWN	Handley Page HP.70 Halifax C.VIII	1319	PP235	18.11.46	CofA expired 15.5.50 & WFU at Southend. Scrapped. Canx 25.5.51.
G-AIWO	Handley Page HP.70 Halifax C.VIII	1363	PP290	18.11.46	Not converted. Used for spares at Stansted. Canx 18.6.48.
G-AIWP	Handley Page HP.70 Halifax C.VIII	1361	PP299	18.11.46	WFU at Stansted. Sold as scrapped in 3/50. Canx 20.3.50.
G-AIWR	Handley Page HP.70 Halifax C.VIII	1329	PP245	18.11.46	To ZS-BUL 12/47. Canx 16.12.47.
G-AIWS	Miles M.65 Gemini 1A	6327		14. 1.47	WFU at Shoreham on 11.5.49. Scrapped. Canx.
G-AIWT	Handley Page HP.70 Halifax C.VIII	1338	PP265	18.11.46	DBR at Bovingdon 5.9.47. Scrapped. Canx 14.2.51.
G-AIWU	Vickers-Supermarine 236 Walrus III	-	HD867	16.11.46	WFU & scrapped in 7/50. Canx.
G-AIWV	Avro 652A Anson X	-	NK668	18.11.46	To VR-SDM 8/52. Canx 7.8.52.
G-AIWW	Avro 652A Anson I	-	MG569	18.11.46	Fatal crash at St.Doniface Down, Isle of Wight on 20.11.47. Canx 16.12.47.
G-AIWX	Avro 652A Anson I	-	AX360	18.11.46	Scrapped at Bahrein in 1950. CofA expired 25.4.51. Canx 2.1.52.
" -AIWX"	Avro 652A Anson C.21	"3634"		----	False marks worn for Paris Air Show in 6/99. Reverted to G-VROE in 6/99.
G-AIWY	DH.89A Dragon Rapide	6775	NR676	22.11.46	To OY-AAO 1/47. Canx 7.1.47.
G-AIWZ	DH.89A Dragon Rapide	6867	NR791	21.11.46	Crashed on landing at Brough on 30.7.49. Canx.
G-AIXA	Taylorcraft Plus D	134	LB264	13. 1.47	
G-AIXB	Taylorcraft Plus D	225	LB378	22.11.46	To VP-YNM 2/56. Canx 1.2.56.
G-AIXC	Fairchild F.24W-41A Argus II (UC-61-FA)	836	HB599 43-14872	26.11.46	To YI-ABN 3/48. Canx 6.3.48.
G-AIXD	DH.82A Tiger Moth	82224	N6986	25.11.46	DBF after striking a low voltage cable and crashed while on a local flight from Rendcomb on 20.7.95. Canx by CAA 14.11.95.
G-AIXE(1)	Avro 671 Cierva C.30A Autogiro	726	HM580 G-ACUU	.11.46R	NTU - Restored as G-ACUU 11/46. Canx.
G-AIXE(2)	Avro 652A Anson C.19 Srs.2	1376		4.12.46	Forced landed near Knutsford Road, Chelford, Cheshire on 7.1.48. Canx as PWFU 27.4.48. Remains as spares at Barton, still present in 10/49.
G-AIXF	DH.82A Tiger Moth	84956	T6642	28.11.46	To Pakistan AF in 11/48. Canx 25.11.48.
G-AIXG	DH.82A Tiger Moth	85430	DE422	28.11.46	Crashed at Thruxton on 3.11.51. Canx.
G-AIXH	DH.82A Tiger Moth	85652	N5445 VR-HFH/VR-HEL/G-AIXH/DE722	28.11.46	To D-EHXH(2) 6/87. Canx 25.3.87.
G-AIXI	DH.82A Tiger Moth	83129	T5364	28.11.46	Crashed at Cranfield on 21.10.51. Canx.
G-AIXJ	DH.82A Tiger Moth	85434	DE426	28.11.46	
	(Probably now composite airframe, rebuilt by Newbury Aeroplane Co .91)				
G-AIXK	DH.82A Tiger Moth	86118	EM924	28.11.46	To Pakistan AF in 11/48. Canx 25.11.48.

Regn	Type	c/n	Previous identity	Regn date	Fate or immediate subsequent identity (if known)
G-AIXL	DH.82A Tiger Moth	82999	R5117	30.11.46	Crashed at Portsmouth on 2.7.55. Canx.
G-AIXM	Fairchild F.24W-41A Argus II (UC-61-FA)	856	HB619 43-14892	9.12.46	To VH-BLB 9/52. Canx 18.2.52.
G-AIXN	Benes-Mraz M.1C Sokol	112	OK-BHA	22. 4.47	CofA expired 13.4.77. (On rebuild Barton 2/99)
G-AIXO	Avro 652A Anson I (Officially regd with c/n RY/LW/248)	-	MG248	30.11.46	To Israeli DF/AF as 4X-FHR/2907 in 1/53. Canx 23.10.52.
G-AIXP	Percival P.28 Proctor I	H.15	R7499	3.12.46	To ZK-AOA 2/47. Canx 22.2.47.
G-AIXR	Vickers 627 Viking 1B	233	WZ355 G-AIXR	30.11.46	WFU & stored at Southend on 22.9.63. Broken up in 2/65. Canx.
G-AIXS	Vickers 627 Viking 1B	234	WZ354 G-AIXS	30.11.46	DBR after stalling on approach to Blackbushe on 15.8.54. Canx.
G-AIXT	Avro 652A Anson I (Originally regd with c/n RY/LW/8349, then RY/LW/20037)	RY/LW/20520	MH236	30.11.46	Crashed at Croydon on 18.7.47. Canx as PWFU 18.7.47.
G-AIXU	Avro 652A Anson I	-	NK823	30.11.46	CofA expired 2.6.50 & WFU at Bahrein. Broken up in 11/50. Canx 16.11.50.
G-AIXV	Avro 652A Anson I (Officially regd as ex.MG241)	RY/LW/15583	MG341	30.11.46	To OY-FAD 7/54. Canx 26.4.54.
G-AIXW	Avro 652A Anson I	RY/LW/25904	NK648	30.11.46	Crashed on a house at Mons, Belgium on 26.4.50. Canx as WFU 26.4.50.
G-AIXX	Avro 652A Anson I (Regd as ex.P9695)	RY/LW/48305	R9695	30.11.46	To F-BEDZ 6/48. Canx.
G-AIXY	Avro 652A Anson I	RY/LW/20181	MG966	30.11.46	CofA expired 13.9.49 & WFU in Saudi Arabia. Canx as PWFU 13.12.49.
G-AIXZ	Avro 652A Anson I	RY/LW/8344	EG646	30.11.46	Crashed in Jersey on 5.2.51. Canx as destroyed 15.5.57.
G-AIYA	Avro 688 Tudor 3 (Converted from Tudor I on 1.5.54)	1367	VP301 G-AIYA	30.11.46	WFU & stored at Stansted in 5/55. Canx.
G-AIYB	Miles M.14A Hawk Trainer III	1840	R1839	4.12.46	Crashed at Redhill on 16.1.52. Canx.
G-AIYC	Miles M.14A Hawk Trainer III	2087	T9870	4.12.46	Crashed near East Grinstead on 4.8.50. Canx.
G-AIYD	Miles M.14A Hawk Trainer III	2132	T9915	4.12.46	Crashed Nutfield, near Redhill on 29.11.53. Canx.
G-AIYE	DH.89A Dragon Rapide	6815	NR727	12.12.46	To F-OAYS 3/57. Canx 20.3.57.
G-AIYF	Percival P.34 Proctor III	H.550	LZ792	5.12.46	To ZK-ANZ 2/47. Canx 6.2.47.
G-AIYG(1)	Percival P.28 Proctor I	K.232	P6173	5.12.46	NTU - Registered in error, to G-AIIP 12/46. Canx.
G-AIYG(2)	SNCAN Stampe SV-4B	21	OO-CKZ F-BCKZ/French Mil	31. 8.89	
G-AIYH	Percival P.28 Proctor I	K.276	P6242	5.12.46	WFU at Luton in 7/52. Canx.
G-AIYI	Beechcraft C-18S Expeditor (AT-7B)	-	FR883 (FE883)/42-43487	23.12.46	Crashed on take off at Sherburn on 24.8.49. Canx.
G-AIYJ	DH.90A Dragonfly	7553	SU-ABW	5.12.46	WFU at Gatwick on 17.2.48. Canx in 3/49.
G-AIYK	Avro 652A Anson C.19 Srs.2	1375	EI-AGW G-AIYK	4.12.46	To F-OBAG 4/57. Canx 16.4.57.
G-AIYL	Miles M.14A Hawk Trainer	517	L6896	9.12.46	To F-DADV 7/53. Canx 9.6.53.
G-AIYM	Avro 621 Tutor	-	K3363	5.12.46	Not converted. Scrapped in 1949. Canx.
G-AIYN	Armstrong-Whitworth AW.55 Apollo	AW.3137		10.12.46	To MoS as VX220 in 9/52. Canx 16.7.53.
G-AIYO	Fairchild F.24W-41A Argus II (UC-61-FA)	850	HB613 43-14886	10.12.46	WFU at White Waltham in 2/58. Canx.
G-AIYP	DH.89A Dragon Rapide	6456	P9589	9.12.46	Crashed at Pentre Uchaf, near Pwllheli on 5.7.53. Canx.
G-AIYR	DH.89A Dragon Rapide	6676	HG691	11.12.46	
G-AIYS	DH.85 Leopard Moth	7089	YI-ABI SU-ABM	16.12.46	
G-AIYT	Douglas C-47A-10-DK Dakota	12486	KG451 42-92661	20.12.46	To ZS-BCJ 4/47. Canx 12.3.47.
G-AIYU	Piper J3C-65 Cub (L-4H-PI)	10710	43-29419	2. 4.47	To PH-NIL 2/58. Canx 1.10.57.
G-AIYV	Piper J3C-65 Cub (L-4H-PI)	11295	43-30004	2. 4.47	To (N9830F)/N9829F 7/58. Canx 22.5.58.
G-AIYW(1)	Piper J3C-65 Cub	-		. .47R	NTU - Canx.
G-AIYW(2)	Stinson AT-19 Reliant I	1410	FB682	22. 3.47	To VP-KEH 10/47. Canx 17.10.47.
G-AIYX	Piper J3C-65 Cub (L-4H-PI)	10993	43-29702	2. 4.47	To D-EHAL 1/56. Canx 19.8.55.
G-AIYY	DH.84A Dragon Rapide	6854	NR778	19.12.46	WFU at Rochester on 30.4.64. Canx.
G-AIYZ	Percival P.44 Proctor V	Ae.108		20.12.46	To ZS-DCV 3/49. Canx 12.3.49.
G-AIZA	Percival P.44 Proctor V	Ae.122		7. 2.47	Crashed at Hurn on 20.4.58. Canx.
G-AIZB	Percival P.44 Proctor V	Ae.49		1. 4.47	To F-OAPR 5/54. Canx 1.3.54.
G-AIZC	Percival P.44 Proctor V	Ae.104		17. 4.47	Scrapped at Croydon in 7/50. Canx.
G-AIZD	Percival P.44 Proctor V	Ae.101		23. 6.47	To TJ-AAN 10/48. Canx 8.10.48.
G-AIZE	Fairchild F.24W-41A Argus II (UC-61A-FA)	565	N9996F G-AIZE/43-14601	18.12.46	WFU on 6.3.73. Canx 6.4.73. (On rebuild by Medway Aircraft Preservation Group of Rochester 11/97)
G-AIZF	DH.82A Tiger Moth	83635	T7169	23.12.46	Crashed at Oldfield Farm, Gaydon on 21.2.64. Canx.
G-AIZG	Vickers-Supermarine 236 Walrus 1	6S/21840	EI-ACC IAC N-18/(L2301)/N-18	20.12.46	WFU at Thame in 1949. Canx in 1963. (On display 3/96 RNAS Yeovilton as 'L2301')
G-AIZH	Avro 652A Anson I	-	MG472	20.12.46	Not converted & used for spares. Canx 16.8.49 as scrapped.
G-AIZI	DH.89A Dragon Rapide	6861	NR785	30.12.46	Crashed at Wallington on 14.9.52. Canx.
G-AIZJ	Miles M.14A Hawk Trainer III	1645	P2408	30.12.46	Not converted. Scrapped at Gatwick in 1949. Canx.
G-AIZK	Miles M.14A Hawk Trainer III	1706	P2506	30.12.46	WFU at Foulsham on 14.11.56. Scrapped in 1963. Canx.
G-AIZL	Miles M.14A Hawk Trainer III	592	L8083	30.12.46	Crashed in 1952. Scrapped at Speke in 1955. Canx.
G-AIZM(1)	Miles M.14A Hawk Trainer III	-		. .46R	NTU - Canx.
G-AIZM(2)	Miles M.19 Master II	-	EM300	30.12.46	Not converted. Scrapped at Gatwick in 1949. Canx.
G-AIZN(1)	Miles M.14A Hawk Trainer III	-		. .46R	NTU - Canx.
G-AIZN(2)	Miles M.19 Master II	-	DM442	30.12.46	Not converted. Scrapped at Gatwick in 1949. Canx.
G-AIZO	Handley Page HP.70 Halifax C.VIII	1366	PP293	1. 1.47	Crash landed at Studham, near Dunstable on 23.5.48. Canx 23.5.48.
G-AIZP	Auster J/4 Archer	2087		14. 1.47	Crashed at Shardlow, near Derby on 19.11.49. Canx.
G-AIZR	Auster J/4 Archer	2088		14. 1.47	To F-OAKI 2/51. Canx 8.2.51.
G-AIZS	Auster J/4 Archer	2089		14. 1.47	To F-OALT 9/51. Canx 27.9.51.
G-AIZT	Auster J/4 Archer	2090		14. 1.47	Crashed & burned at Gaddesby, Leics on 2.12.56. Canx.

Regn	Type	c/n	Previous identity	Regn date	Fate or immediate subsequent identity (if known)
G-AIZU	Auster J/1 Autocrat	2228		31. 1.47	
G-AIZV	Auster J/1N Alpha	2229	ST-ABP	31. 1.47	To ST-ABP 2/62. Canx 27.3.62.
	(Originally regd as J/1 Autocrat)		G-AIZV		
G-AIZW	Auster J/1 Autocrat	2230		31. 1.47	To SE-CGR 8/58. Canx 14.8.58.
G-AIZX	Auster J/1 Autocrat	2231		31. 1.47	To F-BFPQ 6/50. Canx 10.4.50.
G-AIZY	Auster J/1 Autocrat	2233		31. 1.47	Badly damaged by vandals Portskewett, Caldicot, Gwent in 8/89 following rebuild. (On rebuild at Brunel Technical College, Ashley Down, Bristol in 6/91)
G-AIZZ	Auster J/1 Autocrat	2234		31. 1.47	Substantially damaged after hitting power cables and crashing into a field at Whitehall Farm, Watton-at-Stone on 14.2.91. Canx by CAA 29.4.91.
G-AJAA	DH.104 Dove 1	04031		30. 1.47	To ET-T-23 in 1/48. Canx 12.1.48.
G-AJAB	Auster J/1N Alpha	2235		4. 2.47	CofA expired 3.10.75. WFU & stored at Tongham.
	(Originally regd as a J/1 Autocrat)				Canx as WFU 9.12.88.
G-AJAC	Auster J/1N Alpha	2236		4. 2.47	Crashed on 14.5.78. (On rebuild 6/94) Canx as PWFU 28.1.99.
	(Originally regd as a J/1 Autocrat)				
G-AJAD	Piper J3C-65 Cub (L-4H-PI)	12008	(G-AISX)	26. 6.84	
	(Frame No.11835)		OO-GEJ/44-79712		
	(Regd with c/n 11700 - the history of this airframe is complex. It has the original fuselage of OO-GEJ discarded in its rebuild in 1970's. OO-GEJ was rebuilt using frame no 11950 (c/n 12122) ex OO-ALY/44-79826 and is now G-AHIP. OO-ALY was then rebuilt from c/n 11700 ex OO-TON/43-30409)				
G-AJAE	Auster J/1N Alpha	2237		4. 2.47	
	(Originally regd as a J/1 Autocrat)				
G-AJAF	Auster J/1B Aiglet	2238		4. 2.47	To ZK-AUF 5/50. Canx 8.3.50.
	(Originally regd as a J/1 Autocrat)				
G-AJAG	Auster J/1 Autocrat	2239		4. 2.47	To VH-ABB 4/52. Canx 20.12.51.
G-AJAH	Auster J/1 Autocrat	2240		4. 2.47	WFU at Ipswich on 17.11.69. Canx.
G-AJAI	Auster J/1 Autocrat	2241		4. 2.47	To OE-AAH 10/55. Canx 30.9.55.
G-AJAJ	Auster J/1N Alpha	2243		4. 2.47	(Stored 5/97)
	(Originally regd as a J/1 Autocrat)				
G-AJAK	Taylorcraft Auster 5	1021	EI-AKN	13. 2.47	Crashed at Ramsgate on 16.2.67. Canx.
			F-BIAU/G-AJAK/NJ625		
G-AJAL	Auster J/1 Autocrat	2216		13. 2.47	To EC-ADG 6/48. Canx 26.6.48.
G-AJAM	Auster J/2 Arrow	2371		8. 2.47	
G-AJAN	Taylorcraft Auster 5	1248	RT618	8. 2.47	To F-BEEI 9/50. Canx 26.9.50.
G-AJAO	Piper J3C-65 Cub (L-4H-PI)	12162	OO-RAM	17. 5.85	
	(Frame no.11990)		ALAT/44-79866		
G-AJAP	Luscombe 8A Silvaire	2305	N45778	26. 1.89	
			NC45778		
G-AJAR	Auster J/1 Autocrat	2232		11. 2.47	DBR in 1963. Canx as WFU 3.6.69.
G-AJAS	Auster J/1N Alpha	2319		14. 3.47	(On rebuild 9/96)
	(Originally regd as a J/1 Autocrat)				
G-AJAT	Fairchild F.24W-41A Argus II	300	EV792	24. 1.47	To D-EJES 12/55. Canx 1.10.55.
	(UC-61-FA)		41-38856		
G-AJAU	Douglas C-47A-10-DK Dakota	12433	KG398	9. 1.47	To VR-SCP 10/47. Canx 28.10.47.
			42-92613		
G-AJAV	Douglas C-47A-5-DK Dakota	12386	KG377	9. 1.47	To N19E 9/50. Canx 6.9.50.
			42-92571		
G-AJAW	Lockheed 18-07 Lodestar	1954	VP-TAE	18. 1.47	To SE-BTL 10/51. Canx 29.8.51.
	(Formerly Lockheed 14H c/n 1404)		TI-54/NX17385/NC17385		
G-AJAX	Airspeed AS.65 Consul	3331	(MC-ABA)	10. 1.47	To Israeli DF/AF as 2804 in 4/49. Canx 8.4.49.
			LX599		
G-AJAY	Douglas C-47A-25-DK Dakota	13375	KG616	13. 1.47	To EC-AET 6/50. Canx 5.6.50.
			42-93461		
G-AJAZ	Douglas C-47A-50-DL Dakota	10100	FL517	13. 1.47	To EC-ADR 12/48. Canx 3.12.48.
			42-24238		
G-AJBA	Avro 652A Anson I	-	AX409	14. 1.47	DBF at Montge, France on 10.2.50. Canx 10.2.50 as destroyed
G-AJBB	Douglas C-47A-10-DK Dakota	12477	KG442	22. 1.47	To VT-CJH 3/47. Canx 28.6.47.
			42-92653		
G-AJBC	Douglas C-47A-5-DK Dakota	12304	FZ698	15. 1.47	To SX-BBC 2/48. Canx 13.2.48.
			42-92497		
G-AJBD	Douglas C-47A-20-DK Dakota	13012	KG529	15. 1.47	To SX-BBD 3/48. Canx 13.2.48.
			42-93134		
G-AJBE(1)	Piper J3C-65 Cub (L-4H-PI)	12109	44-79813	17. 1.47	NTU - To NC6400N/G-AKNC 1/48. Canx.
G-AJBE(2)	Handley Page HP.61 Halifax B.VI	-	RG785	17.11.47	To Pakistan AF in 10/49. Canx 21.10.49.
G-AJBF	Fairchild F.24W-41A Argus II	869	HB632	17. 1.47	To OH-FCH 11/51. Canx 1.11.51.
	(UC-61-FA)		43-14905		
G-AJBG	Douglas C-47A-30-DK Dakota	14003/25448	KG771	18. 1.47	Fatal crash prior to landing at Bovingdon on 20.5.48. Canx.
			43-48187		
G-AJBH	Douglas C-47A-30-DK Dakota	14015/25460	KG783	18. 1.47	To French AF as 48199/F-RAVQ 10/52. Canx 17.10.52.
			43-48199		
G-AJBI	DH.104 Dove 6	04026	XY-ACE	20. 1.47	WFU at Gatwick on 12.4.67. (To Southend by road on 23.9.67)
	(Originally regd as Dove 1, then 1B)		G-AJBI/XY-ACE/G-AJBI/AP-AHC/G-AJBI/AP-AFT/		Canx as WFU 21.8.68.
			G-AJBI/XY-ACE/G-AJBI/XY-ACE/G-AJBI		Scrapped at Southend in 4/70.
G-AJBJ	DH.89A Dragon Rapide	6765	NF894	20. 1.47	Canx by CAA 16.12.91. (Under rebuild 3/98 at Chirk)
G-AJBK	Handley Page HP.70 Halifax C.VIII	1337	PP264	17. 2.47	To F-BCJZ 10/47. Canx 18.10.47.
G-AJBL	Handley Page HP.70 Halifax C.VIII	1349	PP276	17. 2.47	CofA expired 6.7.49 & WFU at Bovingdon. Canx 27.12.49. Broken up.
G-AJBM	Vickers 610 Viking 1B	239		3. 6.47	To Argentine AF as T-92 in 1/56. Canx 26.1.56.
G-AJBN	Vickers 610 Viking 1B	240		3. 6.47	WFU & used for fire practice at Heathrow in 5/60. Broken up in 9/60. Canx.

Regn	Type	c/n	Previous identity	Regn date	Fate or immediate subsequent identity (if known)
G-AJBO	Vickers 610 Viking 1B	241	XG895 XF629/G-AJBO	3. 6.47	Crashed into Star Hill, west of Blackbushe on 1.5.57. Canx.
G-AJBP	Vickers 610 Viking 1B	242		3. 6.47	To F-BJAH 12/58. Canx 5.12.58.
G-AJBR	Vickers 610 Viking 1B	243		3. 6.47	To D-AHAF 1/57. Canx 5.1.57.
G-AJBS	Vickers 610 Viking 1B	244		3. 6.47	To Argentine AF as T-93 in 1/56. Canx 26.1.56.
G-AJBT	Vickers 610 Viking 1B	245	VP-YNF G-AJBT	3. 6.47	WFU & stored at Luton in 2/62. Scrapped in 2/62. Canx.
G-AJBU	Vickers 610 Viking 1B	246	XF532 G-AJBU	3. 6.47	WFU & stored at Hurn in 3/60. Broken up with remains going to Overseas Aviation for spares in 3/61. Canx.
G-AJBV	Vickers 610 Viking 1B	247		3. 6.47	To YI-ACJ 5/53. Canx 22.5.53.
G-AJBW	Vickers 649 Viking 1B (Originally regd as 610 Viking)	248		3. 6.47	To F-BFDN 6/58. Canx 25.6.58.
G-AJBX	Vickers 610 Viking 1B	249	(D-BABA) (D-BFIX)/D-AFIX/(D-AMEN)/G-AJBX	3. 6.47	WFU at Manston on 9.5.65. Canx.
G-AJBY	Vickers 610 Viking 1B	250		17. 9.47	To (D-AFUS)/D-BELA 3/56. Canx 26.1.56.
G-AJBZ	Vickers 610 Viking 1B	251		17. 9.47	NTU - To VT-CRB 2/48. Canx 1.3.48.
G-AJCA	Vickers 610 Viking 1B	252	SU-AIF G-AJCA	17. 9.47	WFU & used for spares at Hurn in 1/61. Broken up in 1962. Canx.
G-AJCB	Vickers 610 Viking 1B	253		17. 9.47	NTU - To VT-CRC 2/48. Canx.
G-AJCC	Vickers 610 Viking 1B	254		17. 9.47	NTU - To VT-CSP 4/48. Canx 12.4.48.
G-AJCD	Vickers 610 Viking 3B (Originally regd as Viking 1B)	255	XG350 XF633/G-AJCD	17. 9.47	WFU at Nice, France in 11/62. Broken up for spares in 1963. Canx.
G-AJCE	Vickers 610 Viking 3B (Originally regd as Viking 1B)	256	D-AHOF G-AJCE	17. 9.47	DBR after forced landing at Lyons, France on 14.8.61. Canx.
G-AJCF	Vickers 616 Viking 1B	257		17. 9.47	To VP-YHT 5/48. Canx 28.2.48.
G-AJCG(1)	Vickers 610 Viking 1B	258		. .47R	NTU - To G-AJDI 2/49. Canx.
G-AJCG(2)	Handley Page HP.70 Halifax C.VIII	1390	LN-OAS PP328	17. 8.48	Canx 22.10.58. Possibly abandoned at Lydda in 6/49.
G-AJCH(1)	Vickers 610 Viking 1B	259		. .47R	NTU - To G-AJDJ 2/49. Canx.
G-AJCH(2)	Taylorcraft Auster 5	2054	TW510	18. 8.48	To VP-FAA 9/49. Canx 26.9.49.
G-AJCI(1)	Vickers 610 Viking 1B	260		. .47R	NTU - To G-AJDK 3/49. Canx.
G-AJCI(2)	Taylorcraft Auster 5	817	MS951	18. 8.48	To VP-FAB 9/49. Canx 26.9.49.
G-AJCJ(1)	Vickers 610 Viking 1B	261		. .47R	NTU - To Pakistan AF J-750 on 14.6.48 as type 649. Canx.
G-AJCJ(2)	Cierva W.14 Skeeter 1	W.14/1		26. 8.48	Broken up at Eastleigh in 11/52. Canx.
G-AJCK(1)	Vickers 610 Viking 1B	262		. .47R	NTU - To G-AJDL 3/49. Canx.
G-AJCK(2)	Heath Parasol	SH.1		27.10.48	WFU in 1953. Canx.
G-AJCL(1)	Vickers 610 Viking 1B	263		. .47R	NTU - To G-AKBG 3/49. Canx.
G-AJCL(2)	DH.89A Dragon Rapide	6722	NF851	7. 9.48	WFU at Shobdon on 11.1.71. Broken up. Canx 24.5.71.
G-AJCM(1)	Vickers 610 Viking 1B	264		. .47R	NTU - To G-AKBH 4/49. Canx.
G-AJCM(2)	Miles M.14A Hawk Trainer III	1934	R1963	20. 9.48	Crashed at Tupton, Chesterfield on 11.5.53. Canx.
G-AJCN(1)	Vickers 610 Viking 1B	265		. .47R	NTU - Not built. Canx in 2/48.
G-AJCN(2)	Percival P.34 Proctor III	H.211	HM296	26.10.48	To OO-RLD 3/51. Canx 6.3.51.
G-AJCO(1)	Vickers 610 Viking 1B	266		. .47R	NTU - Not built. Canx in 2/48.
G-AJCO(2)	Avro 652A Anson I	-	NK370	17. 9.48	Not converted. Canx as PWFU 4.3.52.
G-AJCP(1)	Vickers 610 Viking 1B	267		. .47R	NTU - Not built. Canx in 2/48.
G-AJCP(2)	Avro 652A Anson I	-	MG829	17. 9.48	Not converted. Canx as PWFU 4.3.52.
G-AJCP(3)	Rollason-Druine D.31 Turbulent	PFA/512		9. 2.59	(Stored 10/95)
G-AJCR(1)	Vickers 610 Viking 1B	268		. .47R	NTU - Not built. Canx in 2/48.
G-AJCR(2)	Avro 652A Anson I	-	NK878	17. 9.48	Not converted. Canx 4.3.52 as destroyed.
G-AJCS(1)	Vickers 610 Viking 1B	269		. .47R	NTU - Not built. Canx in 2/48.
G-AJCS(2)	Avro 652A Anson I	-	NK947	20. 9.48	Not converted. Canx 9.1.51 as destroyed.
G-AJCT(1)	Vickers 610 Viking 1B	270		. .47R	NTU - Not built. Canx in 2/48.
G-AJCT(2)	Avro 652A Anson I	-	NK957	20. 9.48	Not converted. Canx 9.1.51 as destroyed.
G-AJCU(1)	Vickers 610 Viking 1B	271		. .47R	NTU - Not built. Canx in 2/48.
G-AJCU(2)	Percival P.34 Proctor III	H.261	HM351	20. 9.48	Crashed at Tosside, Yorks on 25.6.50. Canx.
G-AJCV(1)	Vickers 610 Viking 1B	272		. .47R	NTU - Not built. Canx in 2/48.
G-AJCV(2)	Percival P.34 Proctor III	H.218	BV655	20. 9.48	To F-BFYZ 11/51. Canx 20.10.51.
G-AJCW(1)	Vickers 610 Viking 1B	273		. .47R	NTU - Not built. Canx in 2/48.
G-AJCW(2)	Percival P.34 Proctor III	H.423	LZ633	22. 9.48	Not converted. To Chingford ATC in 1953. Canx.
G-AJCX(1)	Vickers 610 Viking 1B	274		. .47R	NTU - Not built. Canx in 2/48.
G-AJCX(2)	Percival P.34 Proctor III	H.184	BV638	22. 9.48	Scrapped at Portsmouth in 1958. Canx.
G-AJCY(1)	Vickers 610 Viking 1B	275		. .47R	NTU - Not built. Canx in 2/48.
G-AJCY(2)	Percival P.34 Proctor III	H.525	LZ755	20. 9.48	WFU at Kidlington in 1/54. Canx.
G-AJCZ(1)	Vickers 610 Viking 1B	276		. .47R	NTU - Not built. Canx in 2/48.
G-AJCZ(2)	Percival P.34 Proctor III	H.534	LZ764	27. 9.48	To EC-AGT 3/52. Canx 17.3.52.
G-AJDA(1)	Vickers 610 Viking 1B	277		. .47R	NTU - Not built. Canx in 2/48.
G-AJDA(2)	Percival P.34 Proctor III	'4976'		23. 9.48	Not converted. Canx 20.8.59.
G-AJDB(1)	Vickers 610 Viking 1B	278		. .47R	NTU - Not built. Canx in 2/48.
G-AJDB(2)	Percival P.34 Proctor III	K.407	Z7218	28. 9.48	Not converted. Scrapped at Chessington in 9/50. Canx.
G-AJDC(1)	Vickers 610 Viking 1B	279		. .47R	NTU - Not built. Canx in 2/48.
G-AJDC(2)	Fairchild F.24W-41A Argus (UC-61-FA)	-		. .49R	NTU - Canx.
G-AJDC(3)	Douglas DC-3-277B (C-49H)	2205	ZS-BTO NC25660/42-65582/NC25660	20.10.49	To SE-BWD 3/53. Canx 20.2.53.
G-AJDD(1)	Vickers 610 Viking 1B	280		. .47R	NTU - Not built. Canx in 2/48.
G-AJDD(2)	Fairchild F.24W-46A Argus III (UC-61-FA)	1130	KK512 44-83168	31. 3.49	DBF on ground at Bahrein on 18.4.49. Canx.
G-AJDE(1)	Vickers 610 Viking 1B	281		. .47R	NTU - Not built. Canx in 2/48.
G-AJDE(2)	Douglas C-47A-25-DK Dakota	13182	ZS-DBV VP-KGL/G-AJDE/ZS-BCA/42-93287	27. 9.48	To PH-SSM 2/61. Canx 6.1.61.
G-AJDF(1)	Vickers 610 Viking 1B	282		. .47R	NTU - Not built. Canx in 2/48.
G-AJDF(2)	Miles M.38 Messenger 4A	-	RH370	24. 9.48	CofA expired 21.6.68. Canx as WFU 6/68.

Regn	Type	c/n	Previous identity	Regn date	Fate or immediate subsequent identity (if known)
G-AJDG(1)	Vickers 610 Viking 1B	283		. .47R	NTU - Not built. Canx in 2/48.
G-AJDG(2)	Douglas DC-3-277B	2199	ZS-BTN NC21794	1.11.49	To N90C 7/55. Canx 25.7.55.
G-AJDH(1)	Vickers 610 Viking 1B	284		. .47R	NTU - Not built. Canx in 2/48.
G-AJDH(2)	Avro 652A Anson C.19 Srs.2	-	VL336	9. 3.50	Restored to RAF as VL336 in 6/54. Canx 30.7.59.
G-AJDI(1)	Vickers 610 Viking 1B	285		. .47R	NTU - Not built. Canx in 2/48.
G-AJDI(2)	Vickers 610 Viking 1B	258	(G-AJCG)	24. 2.49	To Argentine AF as T-91 in 1/56. Canx 26.1.56.
G-AJDJ(1)	Vickers 610 Viking 1B	286		. .47R	NTU - Not built. Canx in 2/48.
G-AJDJ(2)	Vickers 610 Viking 1B	259	(G-AJCH)	24. 2.49	To SU-AIG 6/54. Canx 9.6.54.
G-AJDK(1)	Vickers 610 Viking 1B	287		. .47R	NTU - Not built. Canx in 2/48.
G-AJDK(2)	Vickers 610 Viking 1B	260	(G-AJCI)	9. 3.49	To Arab Legion AF as VK500 in 10/53. Canx 23.10.53.
G-AJDL(1)	Vickers 610 Viking 1B	288		. .47R	NTU - Not built. Canx in 2/48.
G-AJDL(2)	Vickers 610 Viking 1B	262	(G-AJCK)	16. 3.49	Crashed after hitting a marker beacon at Nutts Corner, Belfast, Northern Ireland on 5.1.53. Canx.
G-AJDM	Miles M.38 Messenger 2A	6347		27. 1.47	Broken up at Stapleford in 2/62. Canx.
G-AJDN	DH.89A Dragon Rapide	6860	NR784	27. 1.47	To F-OBIV 8/58. Canx 29.8.58.
G-AJDO	Fairchild F.24W-41A Argus II (UC-61-FA)	284	EV776 41-38840	25. 1.47	To VH-AKY 5/50. Canx 1.5.50.
G-AJDP	DH.104 Dove 6 (Originally regd as Dove 1)	04028	5N-ABU G-AJDP/XY-ACW/G-AJDP/XY-ACW/G-AJDP/AP-AER/G-AJDP	27. 1.47	CofA expired 30.1.69. Canx as WFU 13.3.70.
G-AJDR	Miles M.14A Hawk Trainer III	2169	T9976	27. 1.47	CofA expired 14.9.64. WFU at New Milton. Canx.
"G-AJDR"	Miles M.14A Hawk Trainer III (Composite aircraft which flew as such 1.54 - 3.71)	1750	G-AJRS P6382	. 1.54	Restored to RAF marks as P6382 in 3/71. Canx 1.3.71.
G-AJDS	Piper J3C-65 Cub (L-4H)	11658	43-30367	29. 1.47	To D-EJYD 11/58. Canx 9.8.58.
G-AJDT	Fairchild F.24W-41A Argus II (UC-61-FA)	350	FK341 42-32125	29. 1.47	To OH-FCL 3/52. Canx 28.2.52.
G-AJDU	DH.82A Tiger Moth	82045	N6781	27. 1.47	To R.Pakistan AF in 11/48. Canx 25.11.48.
G-AJDV	Auster J/1N Alpha (Originally regd as Auster J/1 Autocrat)	2244		28. 2.47	Crashed at Bisley on 13.4.63. Canx.
G-AJDW	Auster J/1N Alpha (Originally regd as Auster J/1 Autocrat)	2320		14. 3.47	CofA expired 17.11.77 & stored as Caddington. Damaged by goats in 1991. Canx by CAA 20.11.96. (On rebuild to Beagle Husky standard at Mavis Enderby 9/98 with wings of Husky G-AVOD)
G-AJDX	Auster J/1 Autocrat	2321		14. 3.47	To XY-ABU 6/49. Canx 6.6.49.
G-AJDY	Auster J/1 Autocrat	2322		14. 3.47	CofA expired 9.7.71. (On rebuild 7/95 Sywell) Canx by CAA 13.1.99.
G-AJDZ	Auster J/1 Autocrat	2323		14. 3.47	To VP-TBG 11/52. Canx 4.11.52.
G-AJEA	Auster J/1 Autocrat	2324		14. 3.47	Ditched off Lundy Island on 20.8.55. Canx.
G-AJEB	Auster J/1N Alpha (Originally regd as Auster J/1 Autocrat)	2325		14. 3.47	Canx as WFU 9.6.81. (On rebuild 11/96 at Manchester Museum of Science & Industry)
G-AJEC	Auster J/1 Autocrat	2327		14. 3.47	To ZK-BJL 1/55. Canx 18.11.54.
G-AJED	Auster J/1 Autocrat	2308		14. 3.47	Crashed near Uckfield on 19.7.51. Canx.
G-AJEE	Auster J/1 Autocrat	2309		14. 3.47	Canx by CAA 21.1.80. (Stored 8/92)
G-AJEF	Auster J/1N Alpha (Originally regd as Auster J/1 Autocrat)	2310		14. 3.47	To ZK-AUL 5/50. Canx 24.5.50.
G-AJEG	Auster J/1 Autocrat	2311		14. 3.47	Crashed at Merville, France on 11.12.48. Canx.
G-AJEH	Auster J/1N Alpha (Originally regd as Auster J/1 Autocrat)	2312		14. 3.47	CofA expired 28.5.90.
G-AJEI	Auster J/1N Alpha (Originally regd as Auster J/1 Autocrat)	2313		14. 3.47	CofA expired 13.8.94. (Stored 1/97) (Composite, rebuilt in 1976, including fuselage of F-BFUT c/n 3357; original fuselage stored by Crofton Aeroplane Services, Stubbington 1/95)
G-AJEJ	Auster J/1 Autocrat	2314		14. 3.47	Crashed at Potten End, near Luton on 18.2.49. Canx.
G-AJEK	Auster J/1 Autocrat	2315		14. 3.47	To F-BCUZ 3/52. Canx 26.2.52.
G-AJEL	Auster J/1 Autocrat	2316		14. 3.47	Crashed at Borrisokane, Eire on 10.8.48. Canx.
G-AJEM	Auster J/1 Autocrat	2317	F-BFPB G-AJEM	14. 3.47	CofA expired 18.2.72. (On rebuild .94)
G-AJEN	Auster J/1 Autocrat	2328		14. 3.47	Crashed at Puncknowle, Dorset on 31.8.52. Canx.
G-AJEO	Auster J/1 Autocrat	2329		14. 3.47	DBR in ground collision at Southend on 22.4.60. Canx.
G-AJEP	Auster J/1N Alpha (Originally regd as Auster J/1 Autocrat)	2330		14. 3.47	Crashed at Christchurch on 22.11.59. Canx.
G-AJER	Auster J/5A	2093		17. 2.47	To VH-KSB 3/49. Canx 3.6.47.
G-AJES(1)	Auster J/5	2094		17. 2.47	NTU. To R.New Zealand AF as NZ1701. Canx.
G-AJES(2)	Piper J3C-65 Cub (L-4H-PI) (Regd with frame No.11602)	11776	OO-ACB 43-30485	21. 9.84	
G-AJET	Auster J/1 Autocrat	2242		22. 2.47	To ZS-DAD 6/48. Canx 26.5.48.
G-AJEU	Auster J/1 Autocrat	2301		1. 4.47	To EC-AHF 8/52. Canx 28.5.52.
G-AJEV	Auster J/1 Autocrat	2247		2. 4.47	To ZS-DCP 1/49. Canx 28.1.49.
G-AJEW	Auster J/1 Autocrat	2302		2. 4.47	To D-EDIG 5/57. Canx 29.4.57.
G-AJEX	Miles M.65 Gemini 1A	6324		3. 2.47	Crashed at Panshanger on 4.3.59. Canx.
G-AJEY	Miles M.38 Messenger 2A	6359		3. 2.47	Crashed near Bait, France on 28.6.47. Canx.
G-AJEZ	Miles M.38 Messenger 2A	6360		3. 2.47	To (EC-EAL)/EC-ACU in 11/47. Canx 17.11.47.
G-AJFA	Miles M.65 Gemini 1A	6287		3. 2.47	To EC-ACT in 11/47. Canx 17.11.47.
G-AJFB	Miles M.65 Gemini 1A	6288		3. 2.47	To EC-ACS in 11/47. Canx 17.11.47.
G-AJFC	Miles M.38 Messenger 2A	6349		7. 2.47	Crashed at Bognor Regis on 7.7.63. Canx.
G-AJFD	Miles M.65 Gemini 1A	6325		7. 2.47	CofA expired 18.10.64 and WFU at Exeter. Canx.
G-AJFE	Miles M.28 Mercury 5	6697	HB-EEF G-AJFE	20. 3.47	Crashed at West Hyde, near Denham on 13.3.55. Canx.
G-AJFF	Miles M.38 Messenger 2A	6363		26. 3.47	WFU on 16.3.68. Canx 16.4.73.
G-AJFG	Miles M.38 Messenger 2A	6364	EI-ADT G-AJFG	26. 3.47	Dismantled for inspection after arrival from Ireland in 12/66; found to be beyond economical repair & WFU at Swanton Morley. Scrapped 12/66. Fuselage & wings in a car breaker's yard at Scarning, near East Dereham in 1968. Canx

Regn	Type	c/n	Previous identity	Regn date	Fate or immediate subsequent identity (if known)
G-AJFH	Miles M.38 Messenger 2A	6365		31. 3.47	To Liberia in 1/61. Canx 17.1.61.
G-AJFI	Taylorcraft Auster 5	1557	TJ531	28. 1.47	To OH-AUA 3/50. Canx 23.3.50.
G-AJFJ	DH.89A Dragon Rapide	6587	X7445	29. 1.47	WFU at Croydon on 26.6.48. Broken up in 6/51. Canx.
G-AJFK	DH.89A Dragon Rapide	6552	X7392	29. 1.47	To AP-AFN 3/52. Canx 21.2.52.
G-AJFL	DH.89A Dragon Rapide	6631	X7514	29. 1.47	To VP-UAW 3/47. Canx 28.3.47.
G-AJFM	DH.89A Dragon Rapide	6496	X7323	29. 1.47	To VP-KEE 1/47. Canx 15.4.47.
G-AJFN	DH.89A Dragon Rapide	6520	(OO-CDE) G-AJFN/X7347	29. 1.47	DBF at Kosti Airfield, Sudan on 4.12.47. Canx.
G-AJFO	DH.89A Dragon Rapide	6756	(OO-CDF) G-AJFO/NF885	29. 1.47	DBF at Kosti Airfield, Sudan on 4.12.47. Canx.
G-AJFP	Vickers 627 Viking 1B	235		3. 2.47	To VT-DAP 12/48. Canx 12.12.48.
G-AJFR	Vickers 627 Viking 1B	236		3. 2.47	WFU & stored at Southend in 9/64. Broken up in 1966. Canx as WFU 7.3.69.
G-AJFS	Vickers 627 Viking 1B	237	WZ311 G-AJFS	3. 2.47	WFU at Southend in 5/64. Broken up in 2/65. Canx.
G-AJFT	Vickers 627 Viking 1B	238	WZ306 G-AJFT	3. 2.47	WFU in 9/63 & to Gatwick Airport Fire Service. Canx.
G-AJFU	Vickers-Supermarine 507 Sea Otter ASR.I	-	JM747	3. 2.47	Scrapped at Blackbushe in 1950. Canx.
G-AJFV	Vickers-Supermarine 507 Sea Otter ASR.I	-	JM959	3. 2.47	To XY-ABT 4/49. Canx 1.12.48.
G-AJFW	Vickers-Supermarine 507 Sea Otter ASR.I	-	JM957	3. 2.47	Not converted. Scrapped at Blackbushe in 1950. Canx.
G-AJFX	Avro 652A Anson I	-	NK826	3. 2.47	DBR after forced landing and colliding with a donkey at Gizeh, nr.Cairo, Egypt 10.7.51. Canx 7.8.52 as sold & WFU.
G-AJFY	Fairchild F.24W-41A Argus II (UC-61-FA)	368	FK359 42-32163	25. 3.47	To VP-KES 11/47. Canx 12.11.47.
G-AJFZ	Airspeed AS.65 Consul	5097	T1013	7. 2.47	Dismantled at Portsmouth in 7/49. Canx.
G-AJGA	Airspeed AS.65 Consul	5117	X6740	10. 3.47	WFU at Stansted on 13.12.54. Scrapped in 3/56. Canx.
G-AJGB	Airspeed AS.65 Consul	5110	LX156	25. 3.47	WFU in 2/51. Scrapped at Croydon. Canx.
G-AJGC	Airspeed AS.65 Consul	5119	LW833	25. 3.47	Crashed in forced-landing near La Rochelle, France on 13.11.47. Canx.
G-AJGD	Airspeed AS.65 Consul	5120	HM633	25. 3.47	DBR in forced-landing Dukes Meadows, Chiswick on 15.7.49. Scrapped at Croydon. Canx.
G-AJGE	Airspeed AS.65 Consul	5121	R5973	15. 4.47	Missing in the Mediterranean between Benina and Castle Benito on 27.2.48. Canx.
G-AJGF	Airspeed AS.65 Consul	5122	HN199	29. 3.47	To Israeli DF/AF as 2806 in 8/49. Canx 25.8.49.
G-AJGG	Airspeed AS.65 Consul	5123	TJ-ABG G-AJGG/HN733	25. 3.47	To F-BGOP in 3/53. Canx 25.2.53.
G-AJGH	Airspeed AS.65 Consul	5124	AT676	29. 3.47	To OO-... 6/50. Canx 9.6.50.
G-AJGI	Airspeed AS.65 Consul	5125	LW832	14. 4.47	DBR in forced-landing near Chalons, France on 14.11.47. Canx.
G-AJGJ	Taylorcraft Auster 5	1147	RT486	31. 1.47	(On rebuild at Popham)
G-AJGK	Miles M.14A Hawk Trainer III	1941	R1970	5. 2.47	To Egyptian AF in 9/49. Canx 2.9.49.
G-AJGL	Miles M.14A Hawk Trainer III	1933	R1962	5. 2.47	To Egyptian AF in 9/49. Canx 2.9.49.
G-AJGM	Miles M.14A Hawk Trainer III	589	L8080	5. 2.47	DBR at Denham on 21.9.48. Canx.
G-AJGN	Miles M.14A Hawk Trainer III	896	N3850	5. 2.47	To Egyptian AF in 9/49. Canx 2.9.49.
G-AJGO	Percival P.28 Proctor I	K.268	P6234	5. 2.47	Scrapped at Gatwick in 5/51. Canx.
G-AJGP	Miles M.14A Hawk Trainer III	753	L8327	5. 2.47	Not converted. Scrapped at White Waltham in 1947. Canx.
G-AJGR	Airspeed AS.40 Oxford I	3290	LX533	12. 2.47	Scrapped in 2/52. Canx.
G-AJGS	DH.89A Dragon Rapide	W1001	G-ACZE	24.10.47	To USA on 28.8.70 (no US-reg issued). Canx 15.11.73. Restored as G-ACZE 1/85.
G-AJGT	DH.104 Dove 7XC (Originally regd as Dove 2, then converted to Dove 5X in 1951)	04034		3. 3.47	CofA expired 28.10.76 & WFU at Biggin Hill. Broken up in 9/79. Canx by CAA 15.9.86.
G-AJGU	Bristol 171 Sycamore Mk.2	12869		10. 2.47	NTU - To RAF as VW905 in 9/49. Canx.
G-AJGV	DH.89A Dragon Rapide	6589	X7447	11. 2.47	To Paraguay in 5/55. Canx 5.5.55.
G-AJGW	Fairchild F.24W-41A Argus II (UC-61-FA)	322	FK313 42-32117	10. 4.47	To OO-ACF 8/53. Canx 24.7.53.
G-AJGX	Douglas C-47A-1-DK Dakota	12162	FZ607 42-92369	24. 2.47	To SX-BAI 11/47. Canx 5.11.47.
G-AJGY	PA-12 Super Cruiser	12-1118		25. 2.47	To F-BGQY 1/53. Canx 26.12.52.
G-AJGZ	DH.89A Dragon Rapide	6883	NR807	12. 2.47	DBF on ground at Agha Jari, Persia on 16.7.49. Canx.
G-AJHA	Miles M.14A Hawk Trainer III	1972	T9685	11. 2.47	WFU at Elmdon in 4/56. Canx.
G-AJHB	Miles M.14A Hawk Trainer III	628	N2259	11. 2.47	WFU in 6/48. Scrapped at Sherburn in 1957. Canx.
G-AJHC	Miles M.14A Hawk Trainer III	876	N3830	11. 2.47	WFU on 13.8.48. Scrapped at Croft, Darlington in 1952. Canx.
G-AJHD	Miles M.14A Hawk Trainer III	650	L8160	11. 2.47	WFU in 4/60. Broken up at Woolsington in 11/60. Canx.
G-AJHE	Miles M.14A Hawk Trainer III	825	N3777	11. 2.47	To F-OAFU 12/49. Canx 21.12.49.
G-AJHF	Miles M.14A Hawk Trainer III	2081	T9844	11. 2.47	Crashed at Croft, Darlington on 15.2.48. Canx.
G-AJHG	Miles M.14A Hawk Trainer III	1984	T9697	11. 2.47	Crashed near Glasgow on 22.6.54. Canx.
G-AJHH	Miles M.14A Hawk Trainer III	1000	N3967	11. 2.47	To F-OAFV 5/49. Canx 29.3.49.
G-AJHI	DH.82A Tiger Moth	86344	NL897	10. 2.47	Crashed at Haddington, East Lothian on 26.4.51. Canx.
G-AJHJ	Taylorcraft Auster 5	1067	NJ676	10. 2.47	WFU at Haldon Moor in 6/49. (Stored 1/98)
G-AJHK	Avro 652A Anson I	-	NK842	10. 2.47	CofA expired 5.5.48. Scrapped at Tollerton in 1949. Canx 22.2.50 as "abandoned in South Africa in 1947 and w/o".
G-AJHL	DH.104 Dove 2	04043		12. 2.47	Crashed & DBR in the Ionian Sea, near Lochri, Southern Italy on 9.2.48. Canx.
G-AJHM	SAI KZ.VII UA Laerke	148	OY-AAN	24. 4.47	To F-BFXA 7/49. Canx 15.7.49.
G-AJHN	DH.82A Tiger Moth	85664	DE734	12. 2.47	Crashed at Elstree on 15.9.47. Canx.
G-AJHO	DH.89A Dragon Rapide	6835	"G-ADDD" G-AJHO/NR747	14. 2.47	Forced landed in a field 5 miles south of Oxford on 5.2.89 and overturned, caught fire and burnt out. Canx as destroyed 31.3.89.
G-AJHP	DH.89A Dragon Rapide	6770	NR671	14. 2.47	To F-OBOI 5/60. Canx 12.3.60.

Regn	Type	c/n	Previous identity	Regn date	Fate or immediate subsequent identity (if known)
G-AJHR	DH.82A Tiger Moth	85349	DE315	12. 2.47	To ZK-AUZ 8/50. Canx 28.7.50.
G-AJHS	DH.82A Tiger Moth	82121	N6866	12. 2.47	
G-AJHT	DH.82A Tiger Moth	83734	T7393	12. 2.47	To ZK-BEE 12/53. Canx 1.12.53.
G-AJHU	DH.82A Tiger Moth	83900	T7471	12. 2.47	Failed to become airborne and crashed into a tree on take-off from Thatcham, Berks on 4.6.86. Canx.
G-AJHV	Taylorcraft Auster 5	806	MS941	14. 2.47	Crashed at Hanover, Germany on 30.12.53. Canx.
G-AJHW	Sikorsky S-51	51-17	WB220 G-AJHW	27. 2.47	To CF-JTO 6/57. Canx 22.5.57.
G-AJHX	DH.104 Dove 1B (Originally regd as Srs.1)	04037		18. 2.47	WFU on 29.1.70. (Sold to Vernair 1.10.70 & delivered to Speke on 8.12.70) Canx 16.7.73.
G-AJHY	Douglas C-47A-25-DK Dakota	13388	KG628 42-108954	18. 2.47	To TN-AAF 5/65. Canx 6.10.64.
G-AJHZ	Douglas C-47A-10-DK Dakota	12421	EC-ASQ G-AJHZ/KG391/42-92602	18. 2.47	Canx 14.9.66 as sold abroad. Derelict at Lisbon in 1968.
G-AJIA	Douglas C-47A-1-DK Dakota	12208	FZ664 42-108836	18. 2.47	To (CT-AAC)/TZ-ABC 3/61. Canx 23.3.61.
G-AJIB	Douglas C-47A-30-DL Dakota	9624	FD902 42-23762	18. 2.47	WFU at Southend on 13.10.65. Broken up in 1/70. Canx.
G-AJIC	Douglas C-47A-30-DL Dakota	9487	FD869 42-23625	18. 2.47	CofA expired 24.8.66. Derelict at Benina Airport, Libya in 8/66. Canx as WFU 26.2.69.
G-AJID	Auster J/1 Autocrat	2218	(ZS-BMO)	28. 3.47	To F-PAGD 9/96 / F-AZJN. Canx 28.5.91.
G-AJIE	Auster J/1 Autocrat	2219	(ZS-BMP)	28. 3.47	Ditched off Jersey on 10.5.59. Canx.
G-AJIF	Auster J/1 Autocrat	2248		28. 3.47	To ZS-BWK 12/47. Canx 5.12.47.
G-AJIG	Auster J/1 Autocrat	2249		28. 3.47	To D-EGAD 7/56. Canx 11.7.56.
G-AJIH	Auster J/1 Autocrat	2318		2. 4.47	(Stored 6/97)
G-AJII	Taylorcraft Auster 5	1588	F-BFXG G-AJII/TJ537	16. 4.47	Canx 4.10.79 on sale to Canada.
G-AJIJ(1)	Taylorcraft Auster 5	-		. .47R	NTU - Canx.
G-AJIJ(2)	Auster J/3 Atom	2401		10. 4.47	Construction abandoned. Canx 11.1.49.
G-AJIK	Taylorcraft Auster 5	1161	RT498	24. 4.47	To Lebanon in 2/52. Canx 8.2.52.
G-AJIL	Taylorcraft Auster 5	1086	NJ702	24. 4.47	To F-BECZ(2) 12/47. Canx.
G-AJIM	Auster J/1 Autocrat	2331	(G-ARSB) OY-AAK/G-AJIM	24. 4.47	To VH-AUO 9/78. Canx 10.1.78.
G-AJIN	Auster J/1 Autocrat	2332		24. 4.47	To D-EJYN 6/57. Canx 14.6.57.
G-AJIO	Auster J/1 Autocrat	2333		30. 4.47	Crashed into sea off Clacton on 9.3.55. Canx.
G-AJIP	Auster J/1N Alpha (Originally regd as Auster J/1 Autocrat)	2334		30. 4.47	Crashed after hitting trees in valley 2 miles West of Longbridge Deverill on 21.1.73. Canx as WFU 16.8.73.
G-AJIR	Auster J/1 Autocrat	2335		30. 4.47	To F-OAKY 5/51. Canx 1.5.51.
G-AJIS	Auster J/1N Alpha (Originally regd as Auster J/1 Autocrat)	2336		30. 4.47	
G-AJIT	Auster J/1 Kingsland (Originally regd as Auster J/1 Autocrat)(Modified with Cont O-200-A)	2337		30. 4.47	
G-AJIU	Auster J/1 Autocrat	2338		30. 4.47	
G-AJIV	Auster J/1 Autocrat	2339		30. 4.47	DBR at Portreath, Cornwall on 3.11.51. Canx.
G-AJIW	Auster J/1N Alpha (Originally regd as Auster J/1 Autocrat)	2340		30. 4.47	
G-AJIX	Auster J/1 Autocrat	2341		30. 4.47	To VH-AQN 10/51. Canx 29.10.51.
G-AJIY	Auster J/1 Autocrat	2342		30. 4.47	DBF in fatal crash on landing at Tredegar on 23.8.77. Canx as destroyed 21.6.85.
G-AJIZ	Auster J/1 Autocrat	2343		30. 4.47	To F-OAKL 6/52. Canx 22.4.52.
G-AJJA	Taylorcraft Auster 5 (Modified to J/1A in 1949)	1211	RT576	17. 2.47	Crashed at Elmdon on 18.1.48. Canx.
G-AJJB	Taylorcraft Auster 5	1563	TJ520	17. 3.47	To VP-KKL 12/52. Canx 24.11.52.
G-AJJC	Vickers-Supermarine Walrus II	S2/8474	HD917	18. 2.47	To LN-SUK 9/49. Canx 19.9.49.
G-AJJD	Vickers-Supermarine Walrus II	-	HD916	18. 2.47	Not converted. Scrapped at Gravesend in 1949. Canx 3/49.
G-AJJE	Beechcraft D-17S Traveller (UC-43-BH)	4925	FZ435 43-10877	19. 2.47	To VP-YIT 5/51. Canx 1.5.51.
G-AJJF	DH.104 Dove 5 (Originally regd as Dove 1, then to Dove 1B)	04041		28. 2.47	To YI-AGB 5/73. Canx 1.5.73.
G-AJJG	Taylorcraft Auster 5	1107	NJ732	19. 2.47	To F-OAHS 8/50. Canx.
G-AJJH	Taylorcraft Auster 5A (Originally regd as Auster 5, converted in 1950)	1014	NJ617	21. 2.47	To F-BGOX 12/52. Canx 10.12.52.
G-AJJI	Miles M.14A Hawk Trainer III	1985	T9698	25. 2.47	Crashed at Elstree on 19.8.56. Canx.
G-AJJJ	Beechcraft D-17S Traveller (UC-43-BH)	4922	FZ432 43-10874	27. 2.47	To VH-MJE 12/52. Canx 8.12.52.
G-AJJK	Miles M.25 Martinet TT.1	-	HP145	27. 2.47	To SE-BCP 5/47. Canx 23.5.47.
G-AJJL	Miles M.25 Martinet TT.1	-	EM646	27. 2.47	To SE-BCO 5/47. Canx 23.5.47.
G-AJJM	Miles M.68	6696		4. 3.47	Scrapped at Woodley in 1948. Canx.
G-AJJN	Vickers 610 Viking 1B (Originally regd as Type 636)	289		28. 2.47	WFU in 12/61 & stored at Southend. Broken up in 4/64. Canx.
G-AJJO	Miles M.25 Martinet TT.1	-	HN913	27. 2.47	To SE-BCN 5/47. Canx 23.5.47.
G-AJJP	Fairey FB.2 Jet Gyrodyne	F.9420 & FB.2		1. 3.47	To RAF as XD759 in 11/50. Canx 9.11.50.
G-AJJR	Taylorcraft Auster 5	1050	NJ667	4. 3.47	To VH-ABA 8/51. Canx 17.9.51.
G-AJJS(1)	Avro 711A Trader (Originally regd as Avro 689 Tudor 2)	1392	(TS893)	14. 3.47	NTU - Not completed. Canx 10.1.49.
G-AJJS(2)	Cessna 120	13047	8R-GBO VP-GBO/VP-TBO/N1106M/YV-T-CTA/NC2786N	7. 1.87	
G-AJJT(1)	Avro 711A Trader (Originally regd as Avro 689 Tudor 2)	1393	(TS894)	14. 3.47	NTU - Not completed. Canx 10.1.49.
G-AJJT(2)	Cessna 120	12881	N2621N NC2621N	27. 1.88	

Regn	Type	c/n	Previous identity	Regn date	Fate or immediate subsequent identity (if known)
G-AJJU(1)	Avro 711A Trader (Originally regd as Avro 689 Tudor 2)	1394	(TS895)	14. 3.47	NTU - Not completed. Canx 10.1.49.
G-AJJU(2)	Luscombe 8E Silvaire	2295	N45768 NC45768	10. 1.89	
G-AJJV	Avro 689 Tudor 2	1395	(TS896)	14. 3.47	NTU - Built as Avro 706 Ashton for RAF as WB490. Canx 10.1.49.
G-AJJW	Avro 689 Tudor 2	1396	(TS897)	14. 3.47	NTU - Built as Avro 706 Ashton for RAF as WB491. Canx 10.1.49.
G-AJJX	Avro 689 Tudor 2	1397	(TS898)	14. 3.47	NTU - Built as Avro 706 Ashton for RAF as WB492. Canx 10.1.49.
G-AJJY	Avro 689 Tudor 2	1398	(TS899)	14. 3.47	NTU - Built as Avro 706 Ashton for RAF as WB493. Canx 10.1.49.
G-AJJZ	Avro 689 Tudor 2	1399	(TS900)	14. 3.47	NTU - Built as Avro 706 Ashton for RAF as WB494. Canx 10.1.49.
G-AJKA	Avro 689 Tudor 2	1400	(TS901)	14. 3.47	NTU - Built as Avro 706 Ashton for RAF as WE670. Canx 10.1.49.
G-AJKB(1)	Avro 689 Tudor 2	1401	(TS902)	14. 4.47	NTU - Not built. Canx 10.1.49.
G-AJKB(2)	Luscombe 8E Silvaire	3058	N71631 NC71631	4. 1.89	
G-AJKC	Avro 689 Tudor 3	1368	VP312 G-AJKC	6. 3.47	Scrapped at Southend in 8/56. Canx.
G-AJKD	DH(Aust).82A Tiger Moth	233	VH-AUU R.Australian AF A17-232	17. 3.47	Crashed at Dorridge, near Elmdon on 5.8.51. Canx.
G-AJKE	DH.89A Dragon Rapide	6555	X7395	12. 3.47	To F-BEFU in 5/52. Canx 20.5.52.
G-AJKF(1)	DH.82A Tiger Moth	3410	BB687 (BB683)/G-ADOR	. 3.47R	NTU - Restored as G-ADOR 5/47. Canx.
G-AJKF(2)	DHA.84 Dragon III	2081	A34-92 R.Australian AF	28. 3.47	NTU - Not Imported. Remained in Australia - Regd as VH-BDS on 28.4.48. Canx.
G-AJKG(1)	DH.82A Tiger Moth	-		. 3.47R	NTU - Canx.
G-AJKG(2)	Miles M.38 Messenger 2A	6373		30. 5.47	To VH-AVQ in 8/53. Canx 17.8.53.
G-AJKH	DH.89A Dragon Rapide	6763	NF892	19. 3.47	To EP-AAV in 10/54. Canx 29.10.54.
G-AJKI	DH.89A Dragon Rapide	6768	NR792	19. 3.47	To EP-AAY in 10/54. Canx 29.10.54.
G-AJKJ	Miles M.57 Aerovan 4	6406		26. 3.47	Crashed off Southport on 25.3.48. Canx.
G-AJKK	Miles M.38 Messenger 2A	6366		9. 4.47	CofA expired 3.10.69 & WFU near Penzance. Canx by CAA 15.9.86.
G-AJKL	Miles M.38 Messenger 2A	6358		9. 3.47	WFU at Luton on 31.7.69. Canx.
G-AJKM	Miles M.57 Aerovan 4	6402		15. 5.47	DBR in gales at Lympne on 3.5.49. Broken up at Southend in 1949. Canx.
G-AJKN	Miles M.65 Gemini 1A	6286		29. 3.47	To EC-ACR 11/47. Canx 17.11.47.
G-AJKO	Miles M.57 Aerovan 4	6408		29. 3.47	To VP-KEN 9/47. Canx 17.9.47.
G-AJKP	Miles M.57 Aerovan 4	6401		29. 3.47	Fatal crashed on Spaldings' Factory at Whiteheath, Oldbury, on 17.12.57. Canx.
G-AJKR	Miles M.65 Gemini 1A	6455		29. 3.47	To I-AJKR 10/54. Canx 18.10.54.
G-AJKS	Miles M.65 Gemini 1A	6289	CF-EMW	8. 4.47	CofA expired in 4/64. Broken up at White Waltham in 10/65. Canx.
G-AJKT	Miles M.38 Messenger 2A	6379		14. 4.47	WFU on 11.10.62. Scrapped at Sywell in 1965. Canx as WFU 22.2.73.
G-AJKU	Miles M.57 Aerovan 4	6407		14. 4.47	WFU in 7/50. Burnt at Squires Gate in 11/57. Canx.
G-AJKV	Miles M.65 Gemini 1A	6328		28. 4.47	CofA expired 29.10.65 and WFU. Canx.
G-AJKW	DH.89A Dragon Rapide	6539	X7379	22. 3.47	Crashed at Halfpenny Green on 7.5.67. Canx.
G-AJKX	DH.89A Dragon Rapide	6457	R5921	22. 3.47	To AP-AGI 5/53. Canx 7.1.53.
G-AJKY	DH.89A Dragon Rapide	6553	X7393	22. 3.47	To F-OAQZ 6/54. Canx 23.6.54.
G-AJKZ	Stinson AT-19 Reliant	1404		22. 3.47	Not converted. Canx 27.10.47.
G-AJLA	Beechcraft D-17S Traveller (UC-43-BH)	4935	FZ439 43-10887	27. 3.47	To HB-KID 12/48. Canx 31.12.48.
G-AJLB	Fairchild F.24W-41A Argus II (UC-61-FA)	842	HB605 43-14884	2. 4.47	Not converted. Canx in 7/47.
G-AJLC	Douglas C-53 Dakota II	4930	6252M TJ167/42-6478	2. 4.47	To NC74139 12/47. Canx 10.11.47.
G-AJLD	Beechcraft D-17S Traveller (UC-43-BH)	4921	FZ431 43-10873	2. 4.47	Not converted. To NC66402 in 10/48. Canx 6.10.48.
G-AJLE	Taylorcraft Auster 5	1550	TJ541	21. 3.47	To SE-BZC 11/53. Canx 16.10.53.
G-AJLF	Taylorcraft Auster 5	844	MT110	21. 3.47	Not converted. Scrapped at Squires Gate in 2/49. Canx.
G-AJLG	Taylorcraft Auster 5	742	MT175	21. 3.47	To SE-BZA 10/53. Canx.
G-AJLH	Airspeed AS.65 Consul	5126	NJ376	22. 4.47	DBR at Seaton on 25.10.50. Scrapped at Bovingdon in 5/51. Canx.
G-AJLI	Airspeed AS.65 Consul	5127	LX760	25. 4.47	To EC-AGK 2/52. Canx 16.2.52.
G-AJLJ	Airspeed AS.65 Consul	5128	UN-96 G-AJLJ/HM627	1. 5.47	DBR on 11.11.48. Scrapped at Croydon in 1950. Canx.
G-AJLK	Airspeed AS.65 Consul	5129	(TJ-ABF) G-AJLK/HN780	25. 4.47	To TJ-AAY 7/51. Canx.
G-AJLL	Airspeed AS.65 Consul	5130	HN479	29. 4.47	To F-BCJE 1/49. Canx 7.1.49.
G-AJLM	Airspeed AS.65 Consul	5131	LW899	25. 4.47	To TC-GOK 8/52. Canx 22.7.52.
G-AJLN	Airspeed AS.65 Consul	5132	V4159	29. 4.47	To 4X-AEN 5/53. Canx 8.4.53.
G-AJLO	Airspeed AS.65 Consul	5133	X6859	15. 5.47	To Belgium Congo AF as C-34 in 10/48. Canx 4.10.48.
G-AJLP	Airspeed AS.65 Consul	5135	DF402	21. 5.47	To TJ-ABC 9/50. Canx 28.9.50.
G-AJLR	Airspeed AS.65 Consul	5136	R6029	25. 5.47	Canx as WFU 26.2.73. Stored Cardington as "VH-SCO" 1988.
G-AJLS	Percival P.28 Proctor I	K.271	P6237	25. 3.47	WFU at Blackbushe in 4/64. Canx.
G-AJLT	Vickers-Supermarine 507 Sea Otter ASR.1	181716	JM982	25. 3.47	Not converted. Broken up at Langley in 1949. Canx.
G-AJLU	Vickers-Supermarine 507 Sea Otter ASR.1	129893	JM985	25. 3.47	Not converted. Broken up at Langley in 1949. Canx.

Regn	Type	c/n	Previous identity	Regn date	Fate or immediate subsequent identity (if known)
G-AJLV	DH.104 Dove 6 (Originally regd as Dove 1)	04063		3. 4.47	WFU on 24.10.70. Canx as WFU 14.11.72.
G-AJLW(1)	DH.104 Dove 2	04059		23. 3.47	NTU - To G-AJZT 19.6.47. Canx 4.47.
G-AJLW(2)	DH.104 Dove 2B (Originally regd as prototype Dove 2)	04033		12. 5.47	DBR in forced landing 8 miles west of Droitwich on 26.4.65. Canx 2.6.65.
G-AJLX	Douglas C-47A-30-DK Dakota	14038/25483	KG806 43-48222	31. 3.47	To VT-DDK 4/50. Canx 6.4.50.
G-AJLY	Douglas C-47A-25-DK Dakota	13452	KG640 42-93530	31. 3.47	To VP-CBA 5/48. Canx 24.5.48.
G-AJLZ	Douglas C-47A-50-DL Dakota	10101	FL518 42-24239	31. 3.47	To LX-LAA 12/47. Canx 31.12.47.
G-AJMA	DH.104 Dove 1	04053		1. 4.47	To ET-T-24 in 1/48. Canx 31.1.48.
G-AJMB	Bristol 156 Beaufighter TF.X	-	RD135	10. 4.47	To Israeli DF/AF (serial in D170 to D173 range) in 1948. Canx 28.5.49.
G-AJMC	Bristol 156 Beaufighter TF.X	-	RD448	10. 4.47	To Israeli DF/AF (serial in D170 to D173 range) in 1948. Canx 28.5.49.
G-AJMD	Bristol 156 Beaufighter TF.X	-	RD427	10. 4.47	To Israeli DF/AF (serial in D170 to D173 range) in 1948. Canx 28.5.49.
G-AJME	Bristol 156 Beaufighter TF.X	-	ND929	10. 4.47	Fatal crash on approach to Thame on 28.7.48 prior to expected delivery to Israeli DF/AF. Canx 28.5.49.
G-AJMF	Bristol 156 Beaufighter TF.X	-	NV306	10. 4.47	Not converted. Scrapped in 1948 at Ringway. Canx 28.5.49.
G-AJMG	Bristol 156 Beaufighter TF.X	-	LZ185	10. 4.47	To Israeli DF/AF (serial in D170 to D173 range) in 1948. Canx 28.5.49.
G-AJMH	Percival P.31C Proctor IV	H.633	NP327	31. 3.47	To VH-GBW 11/54. Canx 1.9.54.
G-AJMI	Percival P.31C Proctor IV	H.596	NP189	31. 3.47	Scrapped at Sherburn. Canx 18.10.55.
G-AJMJ	Percival P.31C Proctor IV	H.610	NP214	31. 3.47	To VP-KGB 6/48. Canx 29.6.48.
G-AJMK	Percival P.31 Proctor IV	H.643	NP247	31. 3.47	Scrapped at Tollerton in 7/50. Canx.
G-AJML	Percival P.31C Proctor IV	H.763	RM160	31. 3.47	Crashed at Ivinghoe on 14.1.49. Canx.
G-AJMM	Percival P.31 Proctor IV	H.595	NP188	31. 3.47	WFU at Tollerton on 15.10.51. Canx.
G-AJMN	Percival P.31C Proctor IV	H.745	NP386	31. 3.47	To VP-KGC 6/48. Canx 29.6.48.
G-AJMO	Percival P.31 Proctor IV	H.601	NP194	31. 3.47	Not converted. Canx 22.10.48.
G-AJMP	Percival P.31C Proctor IV	H.742	NP383	31. 3.47	WFU in 2/57. Canx.
G-AJMR	Percival P.31 Proctor IV	H.582	NP175	31. 3.47	Not converted. Scrapped at Tollerton. Canx 22.10.48.
G-AJMS	Percival P.31 Proctor IV	H.749	NP390	31. 3.47	Not converted. Canx 22.10.48.
G-AJMT	Percival P.31 Proctor IV	H.650	NP254	31. 3.47	Not converted. Canx 22.10.48.
G-AJMU	Percival P.31C Proctor IV	H.724	NP353	31. 3.47	Crashed at Tok, Alaska, USA on 21.11.48. Canx.
G-AJMV	Percival P.31 Proctor IV	H.759	NP400	31. 3.47	To F-BEEH 10/50. Canx 9.10.50.
G-AJMW	Percival P.31 Proctor IV	H.629	NP233	31. 3.47	Scrapped at Rochester in 10/54. Canx.
G-AJMX	Percival P.31 Proctor IV	H.773	RM170	31. 3.47	DBR at Rochester on 13.7.52. Canx.
G-AJMY(1)	Fairchild F.24W Argus	-		. .47R	NTU - Canx.
G-AJMY(2)	DH.89A Dragon Rapide	6511	X7338	13. 6.47	To CR-GAK /52. Canx 21.8.52.
G-AJMZ	Short S.25 Sandringham 5	SH.56C	JM681	1. 4.47	Scrapped in 3/59 at Solway Morgan's Boatyard, Hamworthy, Hants. Canx.
G-AJNA	DH.89A Dragon Rapide	6516	X7343	8. 5.47	To F-BEDI 12/47. Canx 10.12.47.
G-AJNB	DH.86B	2342	SU-ABV E-2	8. 4.47	Canx as sold abroad in Sudan 9/48. WFU in 1949 & derelict at Wadi Haifa.
G-AJNC	Airspeed AS.40 Oxford	5137	ED251	1. 5.47	To VP-YIY 11/51. Canx 31.10.51.
G-AJND	Airspeed AS.65 Consul	5138	EB718	27. 5.47	To XY-ABJ 11/47. Canx 4.11.47.
G-AJNE	Airspeed AS.65 Consul	5139	LW900	27. 5.47	WFU at Scone, Perth in 5/61. Canx 23.5.61.
G-AJNF	Airspeed AS.65 Consul	5145	HM847	27. 5.47	To VT-CRG 1/48. Canx 22.1.48.
G-AJNG	Airspeed AS.65 Consul	5146	DF522	27. 5.47	To SE-BUP 2/52. Canx 7.3.52.
G-AJNH	Airspeed AS.65 Consul	5150	HM915	16. 6.47	To F-BDPY 7/47. Canx 24.7.47.
G-AJNI	Airspeed AS.65 Consul	5157	DF515	16. 6.47	To F-BDPV 7/47. Canx 24.7.47.
G-AJNJ	Airspeed AS.65 Consul	5158	EB908	16. 6.47	To Burmese AF in 11/47. Canx.
G-AJNK	Airspeed AS.65 Consul	5159	MP347	16. 6.47	To VT-CZQ 1/48. Canx 27.1.48.
G-AJNL	Airspeed AS.65 Consul	5160	HN831	16. 6.47	To XY-ABK 11/47. Canx 4.11.47.
G-AJNM	Republic RC.3 Seabee	200		10. 4.47	To OY-ABZ 12/48. Canx 26.1.49.
G-AJNN	Fairchild F.24W-41A Argus II	325	FK316 42-32100	10. 4.47	Scrapped at Elstree in 4/52. Canx.
G-AJNO	Vickers-Supermarine Walrus II	S2/23642		10. 4.47	Scrapped at Prestwick on 28.8.59. Canx.
G-AJNP	Vickers-Supermarine Walrus II	S2/8757		10. 4.47	Not converted. Canx.
G-AJNR	Douglas C-47A-1-DK Dakota	12095	FZ560 42-92309	10. 4.47	To VT-COK 8/47. Canx 27.8.47.
G-AJNS	DH.104 Dove 2	04057		14. 4.47	To VT-CRT 9/47. Canx 8.9.47.
G-AJNT	Handley Page HP.70 Halifax C.VIII	1332	PP259	14. 4.47	To F-BCQX 6/47 (marks allocated to SV-4C on 5.8.47 - almost certainly intended as F-BCJY but probably written off on delivery and marks re-allocated later). Canx 19.6.47.
G-AJNU	Handley Page HP.70 Halifax C.VIII	1352	PP279	14. 4.47	To AP-ACH 5/48. Canx 18.5.48.
G-AJNV	Handley Page HP.70 Halifax C.VIII	1365	PP292	14. 4.47	To HB-AIF 8/47. Canx 20.8.47.
G-AJNW	Handley Page HP.70 Halifax C.VIII	1369	PP296	14. 4.47	CofA expired 26.4.50. WFU at Blackbushe. Canx 23.10.50. In 12/50 it was used in the film "No Highway" and converted to the fictitious Reindeer aircraft with tricycle undercarriage, four "jets" and a single fin and rudder. For the film the regn "G-AFOH" was applied.
G-AJNX	Handley Page HP.70 Halifax C.VIII	1374	PP312	14. 4.47	To AP-ABZ 5/48. Canx 5.5.48. Delivered to Pakistan ex-Bovingdon 9.5.48. Ran out of fuel next day and force-landed at 30.10 N/46.10 E some 30m NW of Shaibah.
G-AJNY	Handley Page HP.70 Halifax C.VIII	1384	PP322	14. 4.47	To AP-ACG 5/48. Canx 5.5.48.

Regn	Type	c/n	Previous identity	Regn date	Fate or immediate subsequent identity (if known)
G-AJNZ	Handley Page HP.70 Halifax C.VIII	1385	PP323	14. 4.47	While en route Nutts Corner, Belfast to Squires Gate on milk run on 28.9.48 it flew into high ground at Cronk-ny-Irree Laa some 4½ miles NNW of Port St.Mary on the Isle of Man. Canx 21.10.48.
G-AJOA	DH.82A Tiger Moth	83167	T5424	29. 4.47	
G-AJOB	Miles M.57 Aerovan 4	6409		23. 4.47	Crashed into sea off Southrock Lighthouse, Northern Ireland on 27.6.57. Canx.
G-AJOC	Miles M.38 Messenger 2A	6370		23. 4.47	Canx as WFU 5.1.82. (Stored 4/96 at Cultra Manor, Holywood)
G-AJOD	Miles M.38 Messenger 2A	6698		23. 4.47	Crashed Sangher, Dumfries on 26.9.52. Canx.
G-AJOE	Miles M.38 Messenger 2A	6367		28. 4.47	
G-AJOF	Miles M.57 Aerovan 4	6403		28. 4.47	WFU in 1/55. To G-35-3 in 3/57 and rebuilt as HDM.105 - To G-AHDM 4/57. Canx.
G-AJOG	Miles M.57 Aerovan 4	6410	OO-ERY G-AJOG	28. 4.47	Scrapped at Chivenor in 1963. Burnt on 5.11.63. Canx.
G-AJOH	Miles M.65 Gemini 1A	6456		6. 5.47	To CF-HVK 4/55. Canx 26.4.55.
G-AJOI	Miles M.57 Aerovan 4	6411		6. 5.47	DBR in gales at Elmdon on 7.12.50. Canx.
G-AJOJ	Miles M.65 Gemini 1A	6280		9. 5.47	WFU on 7.9.68. Burnt at Ford in 10/70. Canx.
G-AJOK	Miles M.65 Gemini 1A	6281		9. 5.47	To HB-EEE 7/51. Canx 25.7.51.
G-AJOL	Miles M.65 Gemini 1A	6321		9. 5.47	Crashed on take off at Cowfold, near Horsham, Sussex on 29.8.49. Wreakage to Lea, Isle of Wight. Canx.
G-AJOM	Miles M.65 Gemini 1A	6282		13. 5.47	To PT-AHT 1/51. Canx 22.1.51.
G-AJON(1)	Sikorsky S-51	-		. .47R	NTU - Canx.
G-AJON(2)	Aeronca 7AC Champion	7AC-2633	OO-TWH	3. 1.86	
G-AJOO	Sikorsky S-51	51-21		20. 4.47	DBR at Fawar, Sudan on 16.10.49. Canx.
G-AJOP	Sikorsky S-51 (Erected by Westland with c/n WA/H/1)	51-26		22. 7.47	NTU - To RN as VW209 on 7/47. Canx 6.8.47.
G-AJOR	Sikorsky S-51	51-32	G-28-1 G-AJOR	23. 8.47	To CF-JTP 6/57. Canx 22.5.57.
G-AJOS	DH.104 Dove 5 (Originally regd as Dove 1, converted to Dove 5 by 23.5.68)	04036	ST-AAD G-AJOS/ST-AAD/SN-AAD/G-AJOS	17. 4.47	To 6V-ACQ 12/71. Canx 17.11.71.
G-AJOT(1)	DH.104 Dove 1	04072		17. 4.47	NTU - To YI-ABJ 10/47. Canx in 4/47.
G-AJOT(2)	DH.104 Dove 1 (Originally regd as Dove 1, converted to Srs.1B in 1954, converted back in 1958)	04051		3. 5.47	To 6V-ABL 10/68. Canx 1.10.68.
G-AJOU(1)	DH.104 Dove 1	04079		17. 4.47	NTU - To ZS-BCC 11/47. Canx in 5/47.
G-AJOU(2)	DH.104 Dove 1	04058		9. 6.47	Fatal crash into Mount Coron, near Privas, France on 13.5.48. Canx.
G-AJOV	Sikorsky S-51	51-35		10.10.47	To CF-JTQ 6/57. Canx 22.5.57.
"G-AJOV"	Westland WS-51 Dragonfly HR.3	WA/H/80	WP495	----	(On display at RAF Cosford)
G-AJOW	Fairchild F.24W-41A Argus II (UC-61-FA)	298	EV790 41-38854	21. 4.47	To I-AJOW 11/53. Canx 12.11.53.
G-AJOX	Fairchild F.24W-41A Argus II (UC-61-FA)	361	FK352 42-32156	21. 4.47	To OH-FCE 5/52. Canx 23.4.52.
G-AJOY	Fairchild F.24W-41A Argus II (UC-61-FA)	367	FK358 42-32162	21. 4.47	DBR in forced landing at Colebrook, Devon on 20.12.49. Canx.
G-AJOZ	Fairchild F.24W-41A Argus I (UC-61-FA)	347	FK338 42-32142	21. 4.47	Crashed at Rennes, France on 16.8.62. (On loan to The Thorpe Camp Preservation Group) (Stored 3/96)
G-AJPA	Fairchild F.24W-41A Argus II (UC-61-FA)	352	FK343 42-32147	21. 4.47	To ZK-AUW 7/50. Canx 10.7.50.
G-AJPB	Fairchild F.24W-41A Argus II (UC-61-FA)	290	EV782 41-38846	21. 4.47	To SE-BRU 5/50. Canx 25.4.50.
G-AJPC	Fairchild F.24W-41A Argus II (UC-61-FA)	324	FK315 42-32119	21. 4.47	To OH-FCJ 1/52. Canx 11.1.52.
G-AJPD	Fairchild F.24W-41A Argus II (UC-61-FA)	366	FK357 42-32161	21. 4.47	To PH-NFW 6/50. Canx 15.5.50.
G-AJPE	Fairchild F.24W-41A Argus II (UC-61-FA)	344	FK335 42-32139	21. 4.47	WFU at Elstree in 7/53. Canx.
G-AJPF	Douglas C-47A-25-DK Dakota	13456	KG644 42-93534	18. 4.47	To CF-IOC 9/51. Canx 5.2.51.
G-AJPG	Handley Page HP.60A Halifax B.III	-	NA684	23. 4.47	Made emergency landing at Cranfield 25.3.45 (as NA684) and remained there. To College of Aeronautics, Cranfield 4/47. No CofA issued and civilian marks not used. Became ground instructional airframe ans static test-bed. Canx 31.12.48. Still present 5/54.
G-AJPH	Vickers 618 Viking 3B (Was Nene Viking as VX856)	207	XJ304 G-AJPH/VX856/G-AJPH	30. 4.47	WFU & stored at Heathrow in 1961. Broken up in 9/62 with remains to gravel pit at Bedfont, Middlesex. Canx.
G-AJPI	Fairchild F.24R-46A Argus III (UC-61A-FA)	851	HB614 43-14887	26. 4.47	
G-AJPJ	Handley Page HP.70 Halifax C.VIII	1336	PP263	26. 4.47	To Israel & crashed on landing at Lydda on 20.7.48 whilst on delivery flight. Canx 17.7.48.
G-AJPK	Handley Page HP.70 Halifax C.VIII	1375	PP313	29. 4.47	CofA expired 3.10.48 & WFU at Thame. Still present in 5/50. Canx 23.3.59.
G-AJPL	Douglas C-54A-1-DO Skymaster	7464	PH-TAK NL309/41-107445	25. 6.47	Crashed at Castel Benito, Tripoli, Libya on 4.2.49. Canx.
G-AJPM	Douglas C-54A-15-DC Skymaster	10376	PH-TBS NL314/42-72271	10. 7.47	To F-BELS 4/50. Canx 5.4.50.
G-AJPN	Douglas C-54A-15-DC Skymaster	10375	PH-TAL NL310/42-72270	5.11.47	To F-BELR 5/50. Canx 12.5.50.
G-AJPO	Douglas C-54A-DO Skymaster	3094	PH-TAB NL300/41-37303	22.10.47	To F-BELQ 6/50. Canx 8.6.50.
G-AJPP(1)	Douglas C-54A Skymaster	-		.10.47R	NTU. Canx.

Regn	Type	c/n	Previous identity	Regn date	Fate or immediate subsequent identity (if known)
G-AJPP(2)	Avro 691 Lancastrian C.2 (Also c/n R3/CB/485418)	Set.55	G-AKFI VL979	21. 1.48	To AP-ACN 7/48. Canx 14.7.48.
G-AJPR	DH.104 Dove 1B (Originally regd as Dove 1)	04029		30. 4.47	CofA expired 14.9.68 & WFU at Biggin Hill. Canx as WFU 30.10.69. Fuselage to Leavesden as test-bed.
G-AJPS	Auster J/2 Arrow	2389		12. 5.47	To VH-ABF 7/51. Canx 30.7.51.
G-AJPT	Auster J/2 Arrow	2390		12. 5.47	To VH-ACD 5/50. Canx 16.5.50.
G-AJPU	Auster J/2 Arrow	2392		12. 5.47	WFU at Rearsby in 1/58 and rebuilt as J/4 Archer G-APJM with c/n 2091. Canx.
G-AJPV	Auster J/2 Arrow	2393		12. 5.47	To VH-KAE 5/50. Canx 29.3.50.
G-AJPW	Auster J/1 Autocrat	2345		12. 5.47	To SN-ABA 1/52. Canx 18.1.52.
G-AJPX	Auster J/1B Aiglet	2346		12. 5.47	To VH-AYJ 11/51. Canx 1.8.51.
G-AJPY	Auster J/1 Autocrat	2347		12. 5.47	To VH-PAB 11/51. Canx 1.5.51.
G-AJPZ	Auster J/1 Autocrat	2348	F-BFPE G-AJPZ	12. 5.47	Badly damaged in gales at Thruxton on 2.3.84. Canx as WFU 18.11.88. (On rebuild 2/96)
G-AJRA	Auster J/1 Autocrat	2349		12. 5.47	To CS-ACI 12/48. Canx 28.9.48.
G-AJRB	Auster J/1 Autocrat	2350		12. 5.47	
G-AJRC	Auster J/1 Autocrat	2601		12. 5.47	
G-AJRD	Auster J/1 Autocrat	2602		12. 5.47	Ditched into sea off Shanklin, IoW on 29.8.47. Canx.
G-AJRE	Auster J/1 Autocrat	2603		12. 5.47	
G-AJRF	Auster J/1 Autocrat	2604	PH-NFC(2) G-AJRF	12. 5.47	To PH-NGC 8/55. Canx.
G-AJRG	Auster J/1 Autocrat	2605		12. 5.47	To F-BDRP 5/50. Canx 16.5.50.
G-AJRH	Auster J/1N Alpha (Originally regd as J/1 Autocrat)	2606		12. 5.47	CofA expired 5.6.69. (Leicestershire County Council Museums 1984) Preserved on pole 4/99 Charnwood Museum. Canx by CAA 18.1.99.
G-AJRI	Auster J/1 Autocrat	2607		12. 5.47	Crashed in the Belgian Congo on 1.10.48. Canx.
G-AJRJ	Auster J/1 Autocrat	2608		12. 5.47	To VT-CYR 10/48. Canx 1.10.48.
G-AJRK	Auster J/1 Autocrat	2609		12. 5.47	Fatal crash behind Northcote Hill, near Shorwell, IoW on 22.5.76. Canx.
G-AJRL	Auster J/2 Arrow	2365		23. 5.47	To VH-BYZ 5/50. Canx 16.5.50.
G-AJRM	Auster J/1 Autocrat	2611		23. 5.47	To F-BDPR 3/48. Canx 18.7.47.
G-AJRN	Auster J/1 Autocrat	2612	(PH-...) G-AJRN	23. 5.47	To EI-AUM 9/70. Canx 10.9.70.
G-AJRO	Auster J/1 Autocrat	2613		23. 5.47	Crashed at Colyton, Devon on 20.11.51. Canx.
G-AJRP	Auster J/1 Autocrat	2615		23. 5.47	To VH-AMK 10/52. Canx 21.3.52.
G-AJRR	Auster J/2 Arrow	2372	(ZS-BNN)	3. 6.47	To VH-KBR 5/50. Canx 16.5.50.
G-AJRS	Miles M.14A Hawk Trainer III (Composite aircraft which flew as G-AJDR 1.54 - 3.71)	1750	P6382 G-AJDR/G-AJRS/P6382	3. 6.47	
G-AJRT	Miles M.14A Hawk Trainer III	744	L8288	30. 4.47	Crashed at Waltham, Grimsby on 15.8.59. Canx.
G-AJRU	Miles M.14A Hawk Trainer III	352	L5921	30. 4.47	Not converted. Burnt at Redhill on 21.5.54. Canx.
G-AJRV	Miles M.14A Hawk Trainer III	1774	P6419	30. 4.47	Crashed near Alexandria, Dumbarton on 29.9.55. Canx.
G-AJRW	Douglas C-47A-80-DL Dakota	19569	TS426 43-15103	9. 6.47	To VR-SCM 8/47. Canx 2.8.47.
G-AJRX	Douglas C-47A-1-DK Dakota	12209	FZ690 42-92411	9. 6.47	To VR-SCO 8/47. Canx 28.7.47.
G-AJRY(1)	Douglas C-47A-25-DK Dakota	13366	KG607 42-93453	9. 6.47	To VR-SCN 8/47. Canx 6.8.47.
G-AJRY(2)	Douglas C-47A-25-DK Dakota	13331	(G-ASDX) N702S/CU-P702/N96U/RCAF A601B/KG600/42-93421	19.11.62	To ZS-PTG 4/74. Canx 1.4.74.
G-AJRZ	Fairchild F.24W-41A Argus II (UC-61-FA)	722	FZ782 43-14758	2. 5.47	WFU in 1959. Derelict at Southend. Canx.
G-AJSA	Fairchild F.24W-41A Argus II (UC-61-FA)	218	HM174 EV710/41-38774	5. 5.47	W/o in 1949. Canx.
G-AJSB	Fairchild F.24W-41A Argus II (UC-61-FA)	318	EV810 41-13582	5. 5.47	DBR in forced landing on Dartmoor on 20.3.48. Canx.
G-AJSC	Avro 652A Anson I (Regd as ex.DG696)	-	VH-ALY AX261	5. 5.47	WFU in 7/50. Canx 26.4.48. Fate unknown.
G-AJSD	Avro 652A Anson I	-	VH-AKI DJ165	6. 5.47	CofA lapsed 8.5.48. Scrapped at Southend in 1949. Canx as PWFU 13.7.50.
G-AJSE	Avro 652A Anson I (Regd as ex.AX261)	-	VH-ALX DG696	5. 5.47	Sold 31.5.48. WFU in 7/50. Canx 31.5.48 as not re-regd. CofA lapsed on 24.2.49. Fate unknown.
G-AJSF	Miles M.14A Hawk Trainer III	1932	R1961	5. 5.47	Crashed at Kinder Low, Derbyshire on 28.7.57. Canx.
G-AJSG	Fairchild F.24W-41A Argus II (UC-61-FA)	837	HB600 43-14873	15. 5.47	To VH-DDG 1/55. Canx 27.9.54.
G-AJSH	Fairchild F.24W-41A Argus II (UC-61-FA)	845	HB608 43-14881	15. 5.47	Crashed at Fairoaks on 30.3.58. Canx.
G-AJSI	Avro 652A Anson I	-	VP-KDH EG135	6. 5.47	CofA expired on 8.4.49. WFU at Squires Gate in 1950. Canx as PWFU 21.2.50.
G-AJSJ	DH.89A Dragon Rapide	6826	NR738	8. 5.47	Crashed in Tunisia on 18.9.47. Canx.
G-AJSK	DH.89A Dragon Rapide	6500	X7327	8. 5.47	To VP-KMD 2/54. Canx 14.2.54.
G-AJSL	DH.89A Dragon Rapide	6801	NR713	8. 5.47	Canx as WFU in 12/70. Stored at Usworth in 1/71. To VH-UXZ 1/95.
G-AJSM	Fairchild F.24W-41A Argus II (UC-61-FA)	859	HB622 43-14895	8. 5.47	To ZK-ASZ 12/48. Canx 1.12.48.
G-AJSN	Fairchild F.24W-41A Argus II (UC-61-FA)	849	HB612 43-14885	8. 5.47	Damaged in heavy landing at Cork on 10.6.67. Canx as WFU 12.3.73. (Stored 2/95)
G-AJSO	Fairchild F.24W-41A Argus II (UC-61-FA)	854	HB617 43-14890	8. 5.47	To VH-AKZ 12/50. Canx 1.5.50.
G-AJSP	Fairchild F.24W-41A Argus II (UC-61-FA)	872	HB635 43-14908	8. 5.47	To PH-NGY 8/57. Canx 30.8.57.
G-AJSR	Fairchild F.24W-41A Argus II (UC-61-FA)	858	HB621 43-14894	8. 5.47	To OH-FCG 11/51. Canx 22.8.51.

Regn	Type	c/n	Previous identity	Regn date	Fate or immediate subsequent identity (if known)
G-AJSS	Fairchild F.24W-41A Argus II (UC-61-FA)	870	HB633 43-14906	8. 5.47	To OH-VSE 2/52. Canx 6.2.52.
G-AJST	Fairchild F.24W-41A Argus II (UC-61-FA)	342	FK333 42-32137	8. 5.47	To OO-ACK 8/53. Canx 22.7.53.
G-AJSU	Fairchild F.24W-41A Argus II (UC-61-FA)	229	HM185 EV721/41 38704	8. 5.47	To OO-CDM 5/48. Canx 20.5.48.
G-AJSV	Fairchild F.24W-41A Argus II (UC-61-FA)	306	EV798 41-38852	8. 5.47	Crashed on Mont Carvel, near Montreuil, France on 1.11.47. Canx.
G-AJSW	Fairchild F.24W-41A Argus II (UC-61-FA)	280	EV772 41-38826	8. 5.47	To OO-DER 8/48. Canx 12.8.48.
G-AJSX	Fairchild F.24W-41A Argus II (UC-61-FA)	293	EV785 41-38839	8. 5.47	DBR in gales at Biggin Hill in 1961. Canx as WFU in 5/63.
G-AJSY	Fairchild F.24W-41A Argus II (UC-61-FA)	263	EV755 41-38809	8. 5.47	Crashed near Coquilhatville, Belgian Congo on 25.9.47. Canx as DBR in 1948.
G-AJSZ	Handley Page HP.61 Halifax B.VI	-	RG722	14. 5.47	Not converted. Broken up for spares at Bovingdon in 1948. Canx 19.6.47.
G-AJTA	Miles M.65 Gemini 1A	6329		19. 5.47	To HB-EEA 6/47. Canx 27.6.47.
G-AJTB	Miles M.65 Gemini 1A	6457		19. 5.47	Crashed at Berck-Plage, France 29/30.1.51; remains to Croydon. Canx.
G-AJTC	Miles M.57 Aerovan 4	6414		27. 5.47	DBR at Dachau, near Munich, West Germany on 23.9.55. Canx.
G-AJTD	Miles M.57 Aerovan 4	6415		29. 5.47	DBR in gales at Newtownards, Northern Ireland on 3.11.48. Canx.
G-AJTE	Miles M.65 Gemini 1A	6302		29. 5.47	To VP-KEG 11/47. Canx 8.11.47.
G-AJTF	Miles M.65 Gemini 1A	6303		2. 6.47	To (ZS-BSP)/OO-CDJ 1/48. Canx.
G-AJTG	Miles M.65 Gemini 3B (Originally regd as Gemini 1B)	6459		2. 6.47	WFU at Exeter in 11/60. Scrapped in 1964. Canx.
G-AJTH	Miles M.65 Gemini 1A	6304	VP-KFL VP-UAY/G-AJTH	2. 6.47	CofA expired 20.2.75. Proposed rebuild abandoned & scrapped at Banstead. Canx by CAA 15.9.86.
G-AJTI	Miles M.65 Gemini 1A	6444		2. 6.47	To (ZS-BRV)/OO-CDO 10/47. Canx 8.10.47.
G-AJTJ	Miles M.65 Gemini 1A	6445		2. 6.47	To OO-CDW 5/48. Canx 3.5.48.
G-AJTK	Miles M.57 Aerovan 4	6416		2. 6.47	Scrapped at Tollerton in 1/47. Canx as WFU 12.11.47.
G-AJTL	Miles M.65 Gemini 1A	6461		2. 6.47	WFU at Jersey in 3/63. Canx prior to CofA expiry 28.4.63.
G-AJTM	Taylorcraft Auster 5	1445	TJ402	20. 5.47	To VP-KNE 3/55. Canx 3.3.55.
G-AJTN	Taylorcraft Auster 5	1052	NJ668	20. 5.47	To HB-EUA 6/50. Canx 16.6.50.
G-AJTO	Douglas C-47A-15-DK Dakota	12647	42-92806	20. 5.47	To Australia 3/48 - regd as VH-INF 15.12.48. Canx 4.3.48.
G-AJTP	Percival P.31 Proctor IV	H.665	NP281	21. 5.47	Ditched into the sea off Singapore on 17.9.58. Canx.
G-AJTR	Fairchild F.24W-41A Argus II (UC-61-FA)	224	HM180 EV716/41-38780	14. 5.47	To OH-FCI 11/51. Canx 8.1.52.
G-AJTS	Percival P.30 Proctor II	H.32	BV538	21. 5.47	To ZK-ATW 12/49. Canx 20.12.49.
G-AJTT	Percival P.34 Proctor III	H.83	DX184	21. 5.47	Not converted. Scrapped at Gatwick in 1949. Canx 27.5.49.
G-AJTU	DH.89A Dragon Rapide	6558	X7398	21. 5.47	To VP-KGS 12/48. Canx 31.12.48.
G-AJTV	Taylorcraft Auster 5	1433	TJ367	22. 5.47	To TC-URER 4/52. Canx 26.3.52.
G-AJTW	DH.82A Tiger Moth	82203	N6965	21. 5.47	Struck crops and overturned while landing at Raydon, near Ipswich on 7.6.99 and extensively damaged.
G-AJTX	Handley Page HP.61 Halifax B.VI	-	RG720	27. 5.47	Not converted. Broken up for spares at Bovington in 1948. Canx 30.7.47.
G-AJTY	Handley Page HP.61 Halifax B.VI	-	RG756	27. 5.47	Not converted. Broken up for spares at Bovington in 1948. Canx 5.8.47.
G-AJTZ	Handley Page HP.61 Halifax B.VI	-	RG757	27. 5.47	Not converted. Broken up for spares at Bovington in 1948. Canx 19.6.47.
G-AJUA	Handley Page HP.61 Halifax B.VI	-	RG824	27. 5.47	Not converted. Broken up for spares at Bovington in 1948. Canx 3.7.47.
G-AJUB	Handley Page HP.61 Halifax B.VI	-	RG825	27. 5.47	Not converted. Broken up for spares at Bovington in 1948. Canx 30.7.47.
G-AJUC	Auster J/1 Autocrat	2303		2. 6.47	To VP-UBA 8/47. Canx 22.8.47.
G-AJUD	Auster J/1 Autocrat	2614		5. 6.47	Suffered severe gale damage. CofA expired 18.5.74. (On rebuild 8/92) Canx by CAA 31.3.99.
G-AJUE	Auster J/1 Autocrat	2616		5. 6.47	
G-AJUF	Auster J/1 Autocrat	2617		5. 6.47	To LN-ORF 3/52. Canx 14.3.52.
G-AJUG	Auster J/1 Autocrat	2619		5. 6.47	To VR-RBL 1/50. Canx 23.12.49.
G-AJUH	Auster J/1 Autocrat	2620		5. 6.47	To ZK-AWI 12/50. Canx 2.11.50.
G-AJUI	Auster J/1 Autocrat	2621		5. 6.47	To PH-NDM 7/48. Canx 29.6.48.
G-AJUJ	Auster J/1 Autocrat	2622		5. 6.47	Crashed at Liskeard on 12.4.52. Rebuilt as G-AMTM c/n 3101 7/52 by Auster Aircraft. Canx.
G-AJUK	Auster J/1 Autocrat	2623		5. 6.47	Crashed at Spalding on 6.5.51. Canx.
G-AJUL	Auster J/1N Alpha (Converted from J/1 Autocrat)	2624		18. 6.47	(On rebuild 12/90)
G-AJUM	Auster J/1 Autocrat	2625		18. 6.47	Crashed at Kingsbury Episcopi, Somerset on 6.10.58. Canx.
G-AJUN	Auster J/1 Autocrat	2626		18. 6.47	To VH-ALM 1/52. Canx 9.10.51.
G-AJUO	Auster J/1N Alpha (Converted from J/1 Autocrat)	2627		18. 6.47	Destroyed after being blown into the next field in severe gales at Shawdene on 2.1.76. Canx.
G-AJUP	Auster J/1 Autocrat	2628		18. 6.47	Crashed at Harwich on 5.4.53. Canx.
G-AJUR	Auster J/1 Autocrat	2629		18. 6.47	Crashed at Maurepas, near Toussus, France on 15.10.53. Canx.
G-AJUS	Auster J/1 Autocrat	2630		18. 6.47	Broken up & used as spares at Rearsby in 1951. Canx.
G-AJUT	Auster J/1 Autocrat	2631	EI-AFG G-AJUT	18. 6.47	To VP-KMN 8/54. Canx 28.6.54.
G-AJUU	Auster J/1 Autocrat	2632		18. 6.47	Broken up & used as spares at Rearsby in 1951. Canx.
G-AJUV	Auster J/1 Autocrat	2633		18. 6.47	Broken up & used as spares at Rearsby in 1951. Canx.
G-AJUW	Auster J/1N Alpha (Converted from J/1B Aiglet)	2634		18. 6.47	To EI-AMY 3/63. Canx 30.3.63.
G-AJUX	Auster J/1 Autocrat	2635		18. 6.47	To ZK-AUG 2/50. Canx 7.2.50.
G-AJUY	Auster J/1 Autocrat	2636		18. 6.47	To ZK-AWT 12/50. Canx 7.2.50.

Regn	Type	c/n	Previous identity	Regn date	Fate or immediate subsequent identity (if known)
G-AJUZ	Auster J/1 Autocrat	2637		30. 9.47	To ZK-AXO 5/51. Canx 13.2.51.
G-AJVA	DH.82A Dragon Rapide	6600	X7483	29. 5.47	To TJ-ABM 10/52. Canx.
G-AJVB	DH.89A Dragon Rapide	6753	NF882	29. 5.47	To TJ-AAZ 12/51. Canx 30.12.51.
G-AJVC	Miles M.38 Messenger 2A	6371		30. 5.47	Crashed at Munchen-Gladbach, West Germany on 19.11.56. Canx.
G-AJVD	DHC.1A-1 Chipmunk 22	10		26. 5.47	To G-ARFW 10/60. Canx.
G-AJVE	DH.82A Tiger Moth	85814	DE943	28. 5.47	
	(Composite 1981 rebuild - including substantial parts of G-APGL c/n 86460/NM140)				
G-AJVF	DH.82A Tiger Moth	83911	T5901	28. 5.47	To New Zealand for spares in 11/51. Canx 19.11.51.
G-AJVG	Beechcraft 35 Bonanza	D-1098		18.11.47	To 4X-AER in 1949. Canx.
G-AJVH	Fairey Swordfish II	-	LS326	28. 5.47	Restored to RN as LS326 in 4/59. Canx 30.4.59.
G-AJVI	Fairchild F.24W-41A Argus I (UC-61-FA)	208	HM164 EV700/41-38764	30. 5.47	To F-BBIO(2) 10/53. Canx 21.9.53.
G-AJVJ	Percival P.34 Proctor III	H.510	LZ740	2. 6.47	DBF at Cowes, IoW on 20.4.49. Canx.
G-AJVK	Taylorcraft Auster 5	1537	TJ514	2. 6.47	To F-OAEF 9/49. Canx 23.9.49.
G-AJVL	Miles M.38 Messenger 2A	6372		30. 5.47	To VH-BJM 11/49. Canx 1.12.49.
G-AJVM	Fairchild F.24W-41A Argus II (UC-61-FA)	861	HB624 43-14897	3. 6.47	Not converted. Broken up at Exeter in 1952. Canx.
G-AJVN	Taylorcraft Auster 5	1435	TJ372	4. 6.47	To ZK-AVX 9/50. Canx 26.10.50.
G-AJVO	Republic RC-3 Seabee	645		5. 6.47	To LN-TSN 5/49. Canx 12.3.49.
G-AJVP	Republic RC-3 Seabee	644		5. 6.47	To LN-PAM 5/48. Canx 18.5.48.
G-AJVR	Vickers-Supermarine 507 Sea Otter ASR.I	-	JM966	4. 6.47	NTU - To G-AKYH 4/48. Canx.
G-AJVS	DH.82A Tiger Moth	84257	T7882	3. 6.47	To PH-UDC 8/47. Canx 10.7.47.
G-AJVT	Taylorcraft Auster 5	1495	TJ478	4. 6.47	CofA expired 25.8.70. (Frame/wings stored 5/86 at Sproatley) Canx as WFU 3.4.89.
G-AJVU	Taylorcraft Auster 5	1834	TW502	4. 6.47	To ZK-AUH 9/50. Canx 22.8.50.
G-AJVV	Taylorcraft Auster 5	1817	TW478	4. 6.47	Crashed at Denham on 18.9.52. Canx as destroyed /53.
G-AJVW	Taylorcraft Auster 5	1833	TW503	4. 6.47	To CR-ACK in 7/48. Canx.
G-AJVX	Miles M.28 Mercury II	-	HM583 U-0237	5. 6.47	To VH-BBK 3/50. Canx 2.2.50.
G-AJVY	Douglas C-47A-5-DK Dakota	12358	KG351 42-108851	4. 6.47	To F-OAGZ 7/50. Canx 11.7.50.
G-AJVZ	Douglas C-47A-75-DL Dakota	19361	TS432 42-100898	4. 6.47	Crashed at Ringway Airport, Manchester on 27.3.51. Canx.
G-AJWA	Miles M.65 Gemini 1A	6290		16. 6.47	Sold to Denmark 1/66 but not regd; WFU 1967. Remains to Egeskov Castle Museum, Denmark on 29.6.65.
G-AJWB	Miles M.38 Messenger 2A	6699		17. 6.47	Crashed at Doncaster, Yorks on 23.3.70. (On rebuild .96)
G-AJWC	Miles M.65 Gemini 1A	6295		16. 6.47	Static tests on glued joints; WFU at Cranfield in 10/63. Canx in 9/63.
G-AJWD	Miles M.57 Aerovan 4	6412		14. 6.47	Crashed near Dunkirque, France on 26.8.56. Canx.
G-AJWE	Miles M.65 Gemini 1A	6452		7. 6.47	Crashed on take-off from Biggin Hill on 11.4.64. Canx.
G-AJWF	Miles M.65 Gemini 1A	6291	EI-AGF G-AJWF	16. 6.47	WFU at Cranfield in 9/63. Canx.
G-AJWG	Miles M.65 Gemini 1A	6292		16. 6.47	CofA expired 13.3.65. Scrapped for spares at Sleap in 3/65. Burnt on 5.11.66. Canx as WFU 8.10.81.
G-AJWH	Miles M.65 Gemini 1A	6293		13. 6.47	To F-BJEP 8/59. Canx 29.6.59.
G-AJWI	Miles M.57 Aerovan 4	6418		13. 6.47	To Israeli AF/DF as 17 in 1948. Canx 6.11.50.
G-AJWJ	Airspeed AS.41 Oxford	460	U-7 G-AJWJ/X7265	18. 6.47	Scrapped at Woodley in 12/48. Canx.
G-AJWK	Miles M.57 Aerovan 4	6417		20. 6.47	To YI-ABV 3/48. Canx 17.3.48.
G-AJWL	Miles M.65 Gemini 1A	6460		24. 6.47	To (OO-CDR)/OO-ODR 6/50. Canx 26.6.50.
G-AJWM	Avro 683 Lancaster B.I	-	PP741	4. 6.47	To Italy for spares use in 11/48. Canx 30.11.48.
G-AJWN	Percival P.34 Proctor III	H.195	HM288	9. 6.47	To OO-INT 1/50. Canx 20.1.50.
G-AJWO	Airspeed AS.65 Consul	5148	AT760	17. 6.47	To F-OAFD 10/49. Canx 27.10.49.
G-AJWP	Airspeed AS.65 Consul	5161	NM642	25. 6.47	To F-BDPX 9/47. Canx 24.7.47.
G-AJWR	Airspeed AS.65 Consul	5162	HN829	18. 7.47	To F-BEDP 10/47. Canx 1.10.47.
G-AJWS	Airspeed AS.65 Consul	5170	G-5-21 F-OAGD/G-AJWS/HM756	16. 7.47	To I-SAFI 6/63. Canx 12.12.62.
G-AJWT	Airspeed AS.65 Consul	5169	HN713	25. 7.47	To VR-TAR 3/48. Canx 19.4.48.
G-AJWU	Airspeed AS.65 Consul	5180	HM917	14. 8.47	To XY-ABI 11/47. Canx 26.8.47.
G-AJWV	Airspeed AS.65 Consul	5172	UB339 Burmese AF/G-AJWV/HM636	14. 8.47	To Turkish AF as 123 in 1949. Canx.
G-AJWW	Airspeed AS.65 Consul	5173	HN717	14. 8.47	To F-BEDT 12/47. Canx 29.10.47.
G-AJWX	Airspeed AS.65 Consul	5174	NJ302	14. 8.47	To VR-TAS 12/47. Canx 3.11.47.
G-AJWY	Airspeed AS.65 Consul	5175	VR-TAU G-AJWY/EB974	14. 8.47	To TJ-ABA 9/50. Canx 2.9.50.
G-AJWZ	Airspeed AS.65 Consul	5176	AT657	14. 8.47	To F-OABU 6/48. Canx 28.4.48.
G-AJXA	Fairchild F.24W-41A Argus II (UC-61-FA)	360	FK351 42-32156	5.11.47	To VH-CMB 6/54. Canx 20.11.51.
G-AJXB	DH.89A Dragon Rapide	6530	X7370	14. 6.47	To SE-CBU 8/56. Canx 4.3.56.
G-AJXC	Taylorcraft Auster 5	1409	TJ343	11. 6.47	Damaged at Hook, Hants in gales on 16.10.87. CofA expired 2.8.82. Canx by CAA 3.4.89. (Stored 9/94)
G-AJXD	Handley Page HP.70 Halifax C.VIII	1392	PP330	9. 6.47	To F-BCJQ 6/47. Canx 10.6.47.
G-AJXE	Airspeed AS.65 Consul	5164	HN734	16. 6.47	DBR at Elstree on 21.11.59. Canx.
G-AJXF	Airspeed AS.65 Consul	5165	NM314	16. 6.47	WFU on 6.8.60. Scrapped at Squires Gate. Canx.
G-AJXG	Airspeed AS.65 Consul	5166	NM334	16. 6.47	WFU on 5.3.59. Burnt at Southend on 19.6.60. Canx.
G-AJXH	Airspeed AS.65 Consul	5167	HN719	16. 6.47	To EC-ANL 4/57. Canx 28.1.57.
G-AJXI	Airspeed AS.65 Consul	5168	V4283	16. 6.47	To F-BHVY 2/57. Canx 16.1.57.
G-AJXJ	DH.82A Tiger Moth	DHP.26		3. 7.47	To PH-UDE 8/47. Canx 10.7.47.
G-AJXK(1)	Auster J/1 Autocrat	2638		. .47R	NTU - Not built. Canx.
G-AJXK(2)	Miles M.57 Aerovan 4	HPR/144		4.10.47	Crashed at Woodley on 3.12.50. Canx.

Regn	Type	c/n	Previous identity	Regn date	Fate or immediate subsequent identity (if known)
G-AJXL(1)	Auster J/1 Autocrat	2639		. .47R	NTU - Not built. Canx.
G-AJXL(2)	Douglas C-47A-30-DL Dakota	9628	ZS-DDV SAAF 6802/FD906/42-23766	19.10.50	To G-AMGD 11/50. Canx.
G-AJXM(1)	Auster J/1 Autocrat	2640		. .47R	NTU - To ZK-ATO as a J/1B. Canx.
G-AJXM(2)	DH.82A Tiger Moth	3711	N5448	12.10.50	To R.Thailand Navy as "No.4" in 1/51. Canx 17.1.51.
G-AJXN(1)	Auster J/1 Autocrat	2641		. .47R	NTU - To VP-TAY. Canx.
G-AJXN(2)	DH.82A Tiger Moth	3915	N6614	12.10.50	To R.Thailand Navy as "No.5" in 9/51. Canx 29.9.51.
G-AJXO	Auster J/1 Autocrat	2642		21. 5.48	To F-OAIA 7/46. Canx 21.8.50.
G-AJXP(1)	Auster J/1 Autocrat	2643		. .47R	NTU - To VH-KAC as a J/1B. Canx.
G-AJXP(2)	DH.82A Tiger Moth	3938	N6634	12.10.50	To R.Thailand Navy in 2/51. Canx 19.2.51.
G-AJXR(1)	Auster J/1 Autocrat	2644		. .47R	NTU - To VH-KAB as a J/1B. Canx.
G-AJXR(2)	DH.82A Tiger Moth	82457	N9387	12.10.50	To R.Thailand Navy in 2/51. Canx 19.2.51.
G-AJXS	Auster J/1 Autocrat	2645		13.10.48	DBF at Shoreham on 5.9.51. Canx.
G-AJXT(1)	Auster J/1 Autocrat	2646		. .47R	NTU - To G-AJYR 5/50 as a J/1B. Canx.
G-AJXT(2)	DH.82A Tiger Moth	82816	R4899	12.10.50	To R.Thailand Navy in 2/51. Canx 19.2.51.
G-AJXU	Auster J/1 Autocrat	2618		19. 6.47	To CS-ACN 7/47. Canx.
G-AJXV	Taylorcraft Auster 5	1065	F-BEEJ G-AJXV/NJ695	8. 9.47	
G-AJXW	Auster P Avis 1	2838	Z-2	17. 2.48	Canx as WFU on 4.2.49 - rebuilt as G-AJYF 7/49.
G-AJXX	Taylorcraft Auster 4	875	MT104	4. 5.48	To F-DAAK 3/52. Canx 9.2.52.
G-AJXY	Taylorcraft Auster 4	792	MT243	4. 5.48	(On rebuild .93)
G-AJXZ	Auster J/2 Arrow	2386	OO-AXE	27. 5.48	To VH-AFD 9/52. Canx 8.5.51.
G-AJYA	Auster J/5A (Originally built as a Auster J/1)	2226	VP-YGP	10. 8.48	To SU-AGA 3/49. Canx 10.3.49.
G-AJYB	Auster J/1N Alpha (Originally regd as Taylorcraft Auster 4)	847	MS974	3. 2.49	
G-AJYC	Taylorcraft Auster 4	1193	(HB-EOG) RT553	9. 9.48	To VP-KGD 8/49. Canx 12.6.49.
G-AJYD	Taylorcraft Auster 5	1105	NJ731	9. 9.48	To ZK-AWD 11/50. Canx 7.11.50.
G-AJYE	Auster J/5	2874		18.10.48	To VP-AAB 11/49. Canx 4.3.50.
G-AJYF	Auster P Avis 2 (Rebuild of G-AJXW c/n 2838)	2907	G-AJXW Z-2	19. 7.49	DBR in forced-landing at Queenborough, Leics on 2.8.50. Canx.
G-AJYG	Auster J/5	2876		17. 1.49	To CS-ADZ 2/49. Canx 3.2.49.
G-AJYH	Taylorcraft Auster 5	1400	TJ352	2. 3.49	To PH-NAD 11/49. Canx 15.9.49.
G-AJYI	Taylorcraft Auster 4	977	MT343	8. 3.49	To F-BFXF in 1951. Canx 9.9.50.
G-AJYJ(1)	Auster	-		. .47R	NTU - Canx.
G-AJYJ(2)	DH.82A Tiger Moth	84621	T6173	24.10.50	Not converted. Broken up at Croydon in 12/50. Canx.
G-AJYK	Auster J/5B Autocar	2908		3. 8.49	Crashed 4 miles N of Leicester on 18.9.50. Canx.
G-AJYL	Auster J/5A	2889		24.10.49	To AP-AFI 10/51. Canx 2.10.51.
G-AJYM	Auster J/5B Autocar	2909		14.11.49	Crashed at Boston, Lincs on 7.4.50. Canx.
G-AJYN	Auster J/5B Autocar (Converted to J/5P Autocar in 1/57, prior to sale to Spain)	2910		10.11.49	To EC-ANK 3/57. Canx 28.1.57.
G-AJYO	Auster J/5B Autocar	2913	OY-ACI	11. 3.50	Crashed into power cables near Sheraton, Durham on 21.4.76. Canx.
G-AJYP	Taylorcraft Auster 5	804	MS939	20. 4.50	To VR-SDQ 7/52. Canx 27.6.52.
G-AJYR	Auster J/1B Aiglet	2646	(G-AJXT)	24. 5.50	Crashed near Boston, Lincs on 6.7.64. Canx.
G-AJYS	Auster J/5E Autocar	2917		1. 6.50	Dismantled in 1951, fuselage stored until 1961, modified to J-5B standard then sold as a spare airframe. Canx.
G-AJYT	Auster J/1B Aiglet	2660		29. 6.50	Crashed near Skegness on 4.7.63. Canx.
G-AJYU	Taylorcraft Auster 5D (Prototype converted from TW453 c/n 1793)	2666		18. 7.50	To OY-ACI 8/51. Canx 13.7.51.
G-AJYV	Auster J/5B Autocar	2927		19. 7.50	To EC-AIR 9/53. Canx 19.9.53.
G-AJYW	Auster J/1B Aiglet	2663		28. 8.50	To ZK-BAQ 4/52. Canx 3.1.52.
G-AJYX	Auster J/4 Archer (Rebuild of Auster J-3 Atom G-AHSY c/n 2250)	2941		20. 9.50	Crashed near Melton Mowbray on 22.4.51. Canx.
G-AJYY	Auster J/5B Autocar	2928		4.10.50	To VH-DYY 4/55. Canx 31.3.55.
G-AJYZ(1)	Auster	-		. .47R	NTU - Canx.
G-AJYZ(2)	Miles M.38 Messenger 2A	HPR.146	EI-AGU G-AJYZ	31.10.50	WFU on 4.10.68. Canx as WFU 26.2.73.
G-AJZA	Percival P.31 Proctor IV	H.754	NP395	17. 6.47	Not converted. Broken up at Tollerton in 1948. Canx.
G-AJZB	Miles M.25 Martinet TT.1	-	MS836	18. 6.47	Not converted. Scrapped at Bovingdon in 3/48. Canx.
G-AJZC	Miles M.25 Martinet TT.1	-	MS871	18. 6.47	Not converted. Scrapped at Bovingdon in 3/48. Canx.
G-AJZD	Douglas C-47A-5-DK Dakota	12333	KG334 42-92523	18. 6.47	To PK-AKG 11/50. Canx 29.11.50.
G-AJZE	DH.98 Mosquito PR.34	-	RG231	1.11.47	Returned to RAF as RG231 in 8/49. Canx 19.10.50.
G-AJZF	DH.98 Mosquito PR.34	-	RG238	1.11.47	Returned to RAF as RG238 in 8/49. Canx 19.10.50.
G-AJZG	Miles M.57 Aerovan 4	6413		3. 7.47	To I-VALT in 1/54. Canx 18.1.54.
G-AJZH	Miles M.14A Hawk Trainer III	1641	P2404	4. 7.47	Crashed at Nuthamstead, Herts on 22.8.57. Canx.
G-AJZI	Miles M.65 Gemini 1A	6462		4. 7.47	Crashed at Ridge Park, near Croydon on 27.2.48. Canx.
G-AJZJ	Miles M.65 Gemini 1A	6465		25. 7.47	CofA expired 10.1.65; WFU at Baginton and fuselage used as spares for G-AMME in 1967 at Biggin Hill. Canx.
G-AJZK	Miles M.65 Gemini 1A	6466		30. 7.47	Crashed near Usumbura, Belgian Congo on 10.7.48. Canx.
G-AJZL	Miles M.65 Gemini 1A	6467		16. 9.47	To VH-ALJ in 10/51. Canx 17.8.51.
G-AJZM	Miles M.65 Gemini 1A	6468		16. 9.47	To VH-BLN in 8/48. Canx 25.8.48.
G-AJZN	Miles M.57 Aerovan 4	6420		30. 7.47	WFU at Tollerton in 2/52. Canx.
G-AJZO	Miles M.65 Gemini 1A	6446		30. 7.47	Crashed at Margate in 4/69. Canx 26.10.73 as destroyed.
G-AJZP	Miles M.57 Aerovan 4	6421		30. 7.47	To F-OACN in 6/49. Canx 27.5.49.
G-AJZR	Miles M.57 Aerovan 4	6422		30. 7.47	To TC-VAN in 1/49. Canx 16.1.48.
G-AJZS	Miles M.65 Gemini 1A	6297		30. 7.47	CofA expired 28.3.64; WFU at White Waltham. Used by 136 ATC Sqdn at Chipping Norton in an attempt to build a simulator for Navigational training, abandoned and it was buried on site by 11/73. Canx.

Regn	Type	c/n	Previous identity	Regn date	Fate or immediate subsequent identity (if known)
G-AJZT	DH.104 Dove 2	04059	(G-AJLW)	19. 6.47	Fatal crash into trees while circling fete at Banstead, Surrey on 9.6.51. Canx 12.2.52.
G-AJZU	DH.104 Dove 1	04054		24. 6.47	To OO-CFC 8/47. Canx 29.8.47.
G-AJZV	SAI KZ.VII Laerke	151		26. 8.47	Crashed near Manston on 20.12.47. Canx.
G-AJZW	Vickers 640 Viscount	3		25. 6.47	NTU - Construction abandoned. C/n used again on G-AMAV. Canx 9.4.48.
G-AJZX	Douglas C-47-DL Dakota (R4D-1)	9051	BuA.91104 FD797/42-32825	23. 6.47	To PK-PAB 3/51. Canx 6.1.51.
G-AJZY	Handley Page HP.70 Halifax C.VIII	1322	PP238 G-AHWM/PP238	23. 6.47	Crashed at Hyde Lane, Great Missenden on 8.3.51 and burnt out. Canx 8.3.51.
G-AJZZ	Handley Page HP.70 Halifax C.VIII	1396	PP334	23. 6.47	Struck high ground in night approach to Schleswigland, West Germany at 0300 hrs on 21.3.49. Canx 21.3.49.
G-AKAA	Piper J3C-65 Cub (L-4H-PI)	10780	43-29489	23. 6.47	To EC-GQE 10/96. Canx 31.10.96.
G-AKAB	Avro 683 Lancaster B.I	-	PP739	20. 6.47	Broken up at Dunsfold in 11/48. Canx.
G-AKAC	Handley Page HP.70 Halifax C.VIII	1340	PP267	24. 6.47	Fatal crash & DBF near Nauren, 9 miles from Oranienburg, East Germany on 30.4.49. Canx 30.4.49.
G-AKAD	Handley Page HP.70 Halifax C.VIII	1356	PP283	24. 6.47	DBR in crash at Rennes, France on 17.5.48. Canx 19.5.48.
G-AKAE	Percival P.30 Proctor II	H.208	BV650	23. 6.47	Not converted. Canx 31.10.49.
G-AKAF	Percival P.34 Proctor III	H.276	HM366	23. 6.47	Not converted. Canx 31.10.49.
G-AKAG	Consolidated CV.32 (C-87-CF) Liberator C.VII	-	EW611 44-39219	25. 6.47	Marks used for ferry flight only. Used as instructional airframe at Cranfield from 1947 until 1958. Canx 6.10.49. Scrapped at Aylesbury in 1959.
G-AKAH	Miles M.38 Messenger 2A	6375		24. 6.47	To PH-NDR 11/48. Canx 10.9.48.
G-AKAI	Miles M.38 Messenger 2A	6376		24. 6.47	To VH-AVD 3/52. Canx 19.2.52.
G-AKAJ	Avro 683 Lancaster B.I	-	HK557	1. 7.47	Not converted. Broken up at Tarrant Rushton. Canx 25.1.50.
G-AKAK	Avro 683 Lancaster B.I	-	PP743	1. 7.47	Not converted. Broken up at Tarrant Rushton. Canx 25.1.50.
G-AKAL	Avro 683 Lancaster B.I	-	PP742	1. 7.47	Not converted. Broken up at Tarrant Rushton. Canx 25.1.50.
G-AKAM	Avro 683 Lancaster B.I	-	PP734	1. 7.47	Not converted. Broken up at Tarrant Rushton. Canx 25.1.50.
G-AKAN	Miles M.38 Messenger 2A	6702		27. 6.47	To F-BGPU 2/52. Canx 26.2.52.
G-AKAO	Miles M.38 Messenger 2A	6703		27. 6.47	To SE-BYY 9/53. Canx 7.9.53.
G-AKAP	Handley Page HP.61 Halifax B.VI	-	(OO-XAB) RG763	1. 7.47	Belgian marks allocated but not officially registered in Belgium, nevertheless was noted wearing these marks at Gatwick on 13.5.47. No CofA issued & broken up for spares at Thame. Canx 19.3.48.
G-AKAR	Douglas C-47B-20-DK Dakota	15444/26889	KK191 43-49628	3. 7.47	To PP-VBV 6/51. Canx 1.1.51.
G-AKAS	Miles M.14A Hawk Trainer III	1971	T9684	2. 7.47	Crashed at Croydon on 7.5.57. Canx.
G-AKAT	Miles M.14A Hawk Trainer III	2005	F-AZOR G-AKAT/T9738	2. 7.47	
G-AKAU	Miles M.14A Hawk Trainer III	1947	R1976	2. 7.47	WFU at Bicester on 27.10.63. Canx.
G-AKAV	Miles M.38 Messenger 2A	6374		7. 7.47	WFU at Elstree in 2/64. Canx.
G-AKAW(1)	Erco Ercoupe 415	-		. .47R	NTU - Canx.
G-AKAW(2)	Handley Page HP.61 Halifax B.VI	-	RG784	17.11.47	To Pakistan AF in 10/49. Canx 21.10.49.
G-AKAX	Bucker Bu.181 Bestmann	120417	122 Air Min/Luftwaffe	10. 7.47	Never flown, stored in open at Denham until broken up in 1950. Canx.
G-AKAY	Douglas C-47A-1-DK Dakota	12006	FL597 42-92229	11. 7.47	To VR-SCG 4/51. Canx 10.4.51.
G-AKAZ	Piper J3C-65 Cub (L-4A-PI) (Frame no.8616)	AN.1 & 8499	F-BFYL French Mil/42-36375	19. 4.82	
G-AKBA	Handley Page HP.70 Halifax C.VIII	1303	PP219	11. 7.47	Crashed on take-off from Albacete, Spain on 25.5.48 & DBR. Canx 25.5.48.
G-AKBB	Handley Page HP.70 Halifax C.VIII	1321	PP237	11. 7.47	DBR when undercarriage collapsed on landing at Schleswigland, West Germany on 11.2.49. Canx 11.2.49.
G-AKBC	Newbury EoN AP.4 Mk.2	EoN/1		11. 7.47	DBR in pilotless take-off at Lympne on 14.4.50. Canx.
G-AKBD	Vickers-Supermarine 502 Spitfire Trainer VIII	6S/730847		14. 7.47	Not completed. Canx in 5/48.
G-AKBE	Cunliffe-Owen COA-19 Concordia 1	2		14. 7.47	Scrapped c.1948. Canx.
G-AKBF(1)	Cunliffe-Owen COA-19 Concordia 1	3		. 7.47R	Was to have become VT-CQT but construction suspended on 18.11.47. Scrapped at Eastleigh. Canx.
G-AKBF(2)	Scottish Aviation Pioneer Srs.1	101	G-31-1 VL515/"G-AHMP"/VL515	14. 8.48	To XE512 in 6.53. Canx.
G-AKBG(1)	Cunliffe-Owen COA-19 Concordia 1	4		. 7.47R	NTU - Construction suspended on 18.11.47. Canx.
G-AKBG(2)	Vickers 610 Viking 1B	263	(G-AKCL)	31. 3.49	WFU & stored at Hurn in 6/62. Broken up in 1962. Canx.
G-AKBH(1)	Cunliffe-Owen COA-19 Concordia 1	5		. 7.47R	NTU - Construction suspended on 18.11.47. Canx.
G-AKBH(2)	Vickers 610 Viking 3B (Originally regd as Viking 1B)	264	XG567 G-AKBH/(G-AJCM)	20. 4.49	To F-BJRS 4/61. Canx 1.4.61.
G-AKBI(1)	Cunliffe-Owen COA-19 Concordia 1	6		. 7.47R	NTU - Construction suspended on 18.11.47. Canx.
G-AKBI(2)	Handley Page HP.61 Halifax B.VI	-	RG716	4.10.48	Not converted. Broken up at Bovingdon in 5/48. Canx 2.5.49.
G-AKBJ(1)	Cunliffe-Owen COA-19 Concordia 1	7		. 7.47R	NTU - Construction suspended on 18.11.47. Canx.
G-AKBJ(2)	Handley Page HP.70 Halifax C.VIII	1317	PP233	29. 9.48	Crashed on landing at Tegel, Germany & DBR on 1.6.49. Canx 1.6.49.
G-AKBK(1)	Cunliffe-Owen COA-19 Concordia 1	8		. 7.47R	NTU - Construction suspended on 18.11.47. Canx.
G-AKBK(2)	Handley Page HP.70 Halifax C.VIII	1315	PP231	29. 9.48	CofA expired 10.1.50 & WFU at Bovingdon. Still present in 8/50. Canx 28.12.51.
G-AKBL	Miles M.38 Messenger 2A	6701	EI-AFH G-AKBL	15. 7.47	Crashed into Irish Sea on 1.4.53. Canx.
G-AKBM	Miles M.38 Messenger 2A	6704		15. 7.47	WFU on 22.5.61 & dismantled at Weston-super-Mare. Parts used for spares in rebuild of G-AIEK. Canx.
G-AKBN	Miles M.38 Messenger 2A	6377	EI-AFM G-AKBN	15. 7.47	CofA expired 12.7.73. Canx as WFU 25.3.75.
G-AKBO	Miles M.38 Messenger 2A	6378		15. 7.47	

Regn	Type	c/n	Previous identity	Regn date	Fate or immediate subsequent identity (if known)
G-AKBP	Handley Page HP.71 Halifax C.VIII	1362	PP289	16. 7.47	To HB-AIL 9/47. Canx 3.9.47.
G-AKBR	Handley Page HP.71 Halifax C.VIII	1391	G-AKIE (HB-AIM)/G-AKBR/PP329	16. 7.47	CofA expired 22.12.49. Scrapped in West Germany in 1950. Canx 20.3.50.
G-AKBS	Piper J3C-65 Cub	21967		29. 9.47	To EI-AEB 8/48. Canx 4.8.48.
G-AKBT	Piper J3C-65 Cub	21984		29. 9.47	To CS-AAP 2/49. Canx 27.11.48.
G-AKBU	Piper J3C-65 Cub	22021		29. 9.47	To CS-AAQ 2/49. Canx 23.12.48.
G-AKBV	Piper J3C-65 Cub	21962		29. 9.47	To EC-AJI 7/56. Canx 19.10.51.
	(C/ns of above believed to be frame numbers and built up from spares)				
G-AKBW	DH.89A Dragon Rapide	6585	X7443	18. 7.47	Not converted. Scrapped in 5/48. Canx.
G-AKBX	Percival P.28 Proctor I	H.12	G-AHNF R7496	16. 7.47	Registered in error; remained as G-AHNF. Canx 19.8.47.
G-AKBY	Avro 689 Tudor 5 (Built as Tudor 2)	1417	(TS903)	16. 8.47	Fatal crash in field near Llandow Airport, Cardiff on 19.3.50. Canx.
G-AKBZ	Avro 689 Tudor 5 (Built as Tudor 2)	1418	(TS904)	16. 8.47	WFU & stored at Stansted. Broken up in 7/59. Canx.
G-AKCA	Avro 689 Tudor 5 (Built as Tudor 2)	1419	CF-FCY G-AKCA/(TS905)	16. 8.47	Broken up at Stansted in 2/57 still marked as CF-FCY. Canx.
G-AKCB	Avro 689 Tudor 5 (Built as Tudor 2)	1420	(TS906)	16. 8.47	WFU & stored at Stansted. Broken up in 7/59. Canx.
G-AKCC	Avro 689 Tudor 5 (Built as Tudor 2)	1421	(TS907)	16. 8.47	DBR on landing at Bovingdon on 26.10.51. Canx.
G-AKCD	Avro 689 Tudor 5 (Built as Tudor 2)	1422	(TS908)	16. 8.47	WFU & stored at Stansted. Broken up in 1956. Canx.
G-AKCE	Lockheed L.049E-46-26 Constellation (Originally regd as L.049, then as L.049D)	1971	NX54212 42-94550	12. 8.47	To N2741A in 6/55. Canx 27.6.55.
G-AKCF	DH.104 Dove 1	04030	PH-MAD G-AKCF/CF-DJI	28. 7.47	To TJ-ACE 10/67. Canx 2.10.67.
G-AKCG	DH(Aust).82A Tiger Moth	124	VH-AVD R.Australian AF A17-127	25. 7.47	Destroyed in hangar collapse at Taif, Saudi Arabia on 18.10.50. Canx.
G-AKCH	DH.82A Tiger Moth	83043	VH-BDJ R.Australian AF R5181/R5181	25. 7.47	Crashed near Stirling on 29.8.57. Canx.
G-AKCI	DH(Aust).82A Tiger Moth	229	VH-BDK R.Australian AF A17-228	25. 7.47	WFU on 28.6.52. Broken up at Perth in 2/56. Canx.
G-AKCJ	Fairchild F.24W-41A Argus II (UC-61-FA)	308	EV798 41-38862	23. 7.47	To VH-AZL 1/56. Canx 26.9.51.
G-AKCK(1)	Beechcraft D-18S	-		. .47R	NTU - Not Imported. Canx.
G-AKCK(2)	Airspeed AS.65 Consul	5177	HM827	14. 8.47	To F-OABT 9/49. Canx 28.4.48.
G-AKCL	DH.82A Tiger Moth	85928	DF192	2. 8.47	To VT-DCA 2/49. Canx 16.2.49.
G-AKCM	DH.82A Tiger Moth	83303	T5610	2. 8.47	To Saudi Arabia in 10/50. Canx 18.10.50.
G-AKCN	Miles M.38 Messenger 2A	6705		29. 7.47	To ZK-AUM 7/50. Canx 21.6.50.
G-AKCO	Short S.25 Sandringham 7 (Sunderland GR.3 c/n SB2022 conv.)	SH57C	JM719	29. 7.47	To VH-APG 10/54. Canx 10.5.55.
G-AKCP	Short S.25 Sandringham 7	SH58C	EJ172	29. 7.47	To CX-ANI 3/51. Canx 1.3.51.
G-AKCR	Short S.25 Sandringham 7	SH59C	ML840	29. 7.47	To CX-ANA 12/50. Canx 12.12.50.
G-AKCS	DHC.1A-1 Chipmunk	18		1. 8.47	To VH-AFR 6/50. Canx 14.6.50.
G-AKCT	Handley Page HP.71 Halifax C.VIII	1346	HB-AIK G-AKCT/PP273	1. 8.47	To Egyptian AF 12/48. Canx 4.9.47.
G-AKCU	Sikorsky S-51	51-028		9.10.47	Crashed at Croesor Dam, Merionethshire on 24.5.49, due to engine failure. Canx.
G-AKCV	Airspeed AS.65 Consul	5178	NM593	14. 8.47	To Belgian AF as C-32 in 12/48. Canx 4.10.48.
G-AKCW	Airspeed AS.65 Consul	5179	NJ318	14. 8.47	To MoS as VX587 in 12/48. Canx 16.12.48.
G-AKCX	Bell 47B	49	NC129B	12. 8.47	DBR at Heathfield, near Prestwick on 7.2.49. Canx.
G-AKCY	Percival P.44 Proctor 5	Ae.121		18. 8.47	Crashed near Bagdhad Airport, Iraq on 24.12.49. Canx.
G-AKCZ	Beechcraft C-18S Expeditor (UC-45B)	6116	HB178 43-35616	12. 8.47	To VP-RCA 11/50. Canx 14.8.50.
G-AKDA	Miles M.65 Gemini 1A	6296		6. 8.47	To SE-AYM 11/50. Canx 9.10.50.
G-AKDB	Miles M.65 Gemini 1A	6294		6. 8.47	WFU on 27.3.70. Broken up at Tollerton 11/70 and used for spares. Canx 1.11.70.
G-AKDC	Miles M.65 Gemini 3C (Originally regd as a Gemini 3, then as a Gemini 3A)	6496	G-21-2 U-23	6. 8.47	To VR-TBP 9/57. Canx 28.12.57.
G-AKDD	Miles M.65 Gemini 1A	6284		16. 9.47	Crashed into sea off Warden Point, Isle of Sheppey on 5.3.61. Canx.
G-AKDE	Miles M.65 Gemini 1A	6298		18. 8.47	To VP-TBI 2/53. Canx 20.2.53.
G-AKDF	Miles M.38 Messenger 2A	6706		16. 8.47	WFU on 28.10.66. Canx 27.4.73.
G-AKDG	Miles M.65 Gemini 1A	6450		20. 8.47	To F-BBSL 9/50. Canx 9.9.50.
G-AKDH	Miles M.65 Gemini 1A	6449		20. 8.47	To VH-AJW 9/50. Canx 27.7.50.
G-AKDI	Miles M.65 Gemini 1A	6451		20. 8.47	To F-BGTM 8/53. Canx 17.7.53.
G-AKDJ	Miles M.65 Gemini 1A	6448		20. 8.47	Crashed during forced-landing on Bispham Sands, Lancs 5.1.61. Canx.
G-AKDK	Miles M.65 Gemini 1A	6469		22. 8.47	CofA expired 27.3.70. Canx as WFU 5.11.73. (Stored Egeskov Castle, Denmark in 1992) (For rebuild with parts from G-AJWA c/n 6290)
G-AKDL	Miles M.65 Gemini 1A	6300		20. 8.47	To ZK-AUA 10/50. Canx 23.3.50.
G-AKDM	Piper PA-12 Super Cruiser	12-3966		26. 9.47	To ZS-DFI 1/51. Canx 8.6.51.
G-AKDN	DHC.1A Chipmunk 10	11		14. 8.47	
G-AKDO	Avro 691 Lancastrian Mk.10-PP	-	CF-CMV KB729	17. 9.47	WFU at Tarrant Ruston in 5/51. Broken up. Canx.
G-AKDP	Avro 691 Lancastrian Mk.10-PP	-	CF-CMY FM185	17. 9.47	Forced landed & DBR 7 miles W of Ludwigslust, West West Germany on 10.4.49. Canx.

Regn	Type	c/n	Previous identity	Regn date	Fate or immediate subsequent identity (if known)
G-AKDR	Avro 691 Lancastrian Mk.10-PP	-	CF-CMZ FM186	17. 9.47	WFU at Tarrant Ruston in 5/51. Broken up. Canx.
G-AKDS	Avro 691 Lancastrian Mk.10-PP	-	CF-CNA FM187	17. 9.47	WFU at Tarrant Ruston in 5/51. Broken up. Canx.
G-AKDT	Douglas C-47B-1-DK Dakota	14161/25606	KJ822 43-48345	19. 8.47	To VP-KIF 6/50. Canx 23.6.50.
G-AKDU	Avro 652A Anson 19 Srs.2	1423		12. 9.47	Damaged after engine failure near Heany, Bulwayo on 30.7.50. Reportedly broken up in 1953. Canx 16.12.53 as reduced to spares.
G-AKDV	Avro 652A Anson 19 Srs.2	1424		12. 9.47	Crashed at Sombula, S.Rhodesia on 2.3.50. Canx 20.6.50. Wreck at Heany in 8/50.
G-AKDW	DH.89A Dragon Rapide	6897	F-BCDB G-AKDW/YI-ABD/NR833	25. 8.47	(On rebuild 3/96)
G-AKDX	DH.89A Dragon Rapide	6898	YI-ABE NR834	25. 8.47	To VP-KIO 2/51. Canx 5.2.51.
G-AKDY	Percival P.44 Proctor V	Ae.113		20. 8.47	To VP-KEW 12/47. Canx 23.12.47.
G-AKDZ	Percival P.44 Proctor V	Ae.117		4. 9.47	Crashed near Addis Ababa, Eithiopia on 14.7.59. Canx.
G-AKEA	Percival P.44 Proctor V	Ae.127		23. 9.47	Crashed at Cherbourg, France on 25.6.57. Canx.
G-AKEB	Percival P.44 Proctor V	Ae.100		22. 9.47	To F-BHCM 11/54. Canx 11.11.54.
G-AKEC	Handley Page HP.71 Halifax C.VIII	1355	PP282	15. 8.47	DBR by Halton I G-AHDV in gales at Squires Gate on 17.12.52. Canx 4.3.53.
G-AKED	DH.89A Dragon Rapide	6487	R9559	25. 8.47	To F-DABY 3/56. Canx 26.11.55.
G-AKEE	DH.82A Tiger Moth	-	"T7179"	18. 8.47	To VP-CAW 9/47. Canx 25.9.47.
G-AKEF	Percival P.31 Proctor IV	H.671	NP287	19. 8.47	WFU at Wolverhampton in 1/53. Canx.
G-AKEG	Miles M.65 Gemini 3C	6299		21. 8.47	CofA expired 30.6.63 & WFU at Yeadon. Broken up at Baginton in 1964. Canx.
G-AKEH	Miles M.65 Gemini 1A	6473		25. 8.47	To VR-SDC. Canx 22.10.51.
G-AKEI	Miles M.65 Gemini 1A	6470	EI-AHN G-AKEI	28. 8.47	CofA expired 23.11.63 & WFU at Renfrew. Canx.
G-AKEJ	Miles M.65 Gemini 1A	6482		8. 9.47	WFU at Baginton in 8/65; cannibalised. Canx.
G-AKEK	Miles M.65 Gemini 3A (Originally regd as Gemini 1A)	6483		8. 9.47	Canx as WFU 20.11.74; fuselage at Squires Gate. (On long term rebuild 12/94).
G-AKEL	Miles M.65 Gemini 1A	6484		8. 9.47	Canx as WFU 30.5.84. To Ulster Folk & Transport Museum. (Components only 4/96 - for rebuild with G-AKGE)
G-AKEM	Miles M.65 Gemini 1A	6485		8. 9.47	CofA expired 10.4.65 & WFU at Lympne. Scrapped in 1967.
G-AKEN	Miles M.65 Gemini 1A	6486		8. 9.47	To VH-BTP 1/54. Canx.
G-AKEO	Miles M.65 Gemini 1A	6487	VP-KET G-AKEO	8. 9.47	CofA expired 7.5.62 & WFU at Shoreham; burnt after 1964. Canx.
G-AKEP	Miles M.65 Gemini 1A	6493		8. 9.47	To Israeli DF/AF / 4X-ACK 7/49. Canx.
G-AKER	Miles M.65 Gemini 1A	6491		8. 9.47	CofA expired 18.9.65 & WFU at Baginton; cannibalised at Biggin Hill; cockpit section to Berks Aviation Group. Canx as WFU 20.8.73.
G-AKES	Miles M.65 Gemini 1A	6447		8. 9.47	To YV-P-AED 3/53. Canx 16.10.52.
G-AKET	DH.104 Dove 1B (Originally regd as Dove 1)	04056	PH-KLS G-AKET/I-AKET/G-AKET	21. 8.47	CofA expired 31.12.65 & WFU at Exeter. Used for spares at Baginton in 1968. Canx as WFU 28.2.73.
G-AKEU	DH.89A Dragon Rapide	6672	HG673	5. 9.47	To OO-ABL 7/51. Canx 21.6.51.
G-AKEV	DHC.1 Chipmunk 10	1	G-5-3 G-AKEV/CF-DIO-X	27. 8.47	WFU at Panshanger in 1/51. Broken up. Canx.
G-AKEW	Avro 652A Anson I	-	DJ168	25. 8.47	To VP-KHL 1/50. Canx 20.10.49.
G-AKEX	Percival P.34 Proctor III	H.549	LZ791	26. 8.47	To SE-BTR 12/50, but crashed on 11.1.51 at Eslov, Sweden whilst on delivery. Canx 27.12.50.
G-AKEY	Slingsby T.29B Motor Tutor	WN.544	G-26-1 AB-1	27. 8.47	Sold to the Bahamas. Canx 1.11.62.
G-AKEZ	Miles M.38 Messenger 2A	6707		27. 8.47	CofA expired 15.11.68. (Sold in 1997 and based New Zealand)
G-AKFA	Bell 47B-3	69		11. 9.47	DBR on landing at Gatwick on 4.1.55. Canx.
G-AKFB	Bell 47B-3	73		11. 9.47	Canx as destroyed in 1968.
G-AKFC	Ercoupe 415CD	4784	VX147 G-AKFC/NC7465H	29. 8.47	Struck a tree and crashed while practising an engine-off emergency landing at Halfpenny Green on 13.8.67. Canx 2.4.73.
G-AKFD	Chrislea CH.3 Super Ace 2	101		27. 8.47	Crated for Australia as VH-BRP in 3/49, but burned out in a ship's fire as deck cargo at Port Said, Egypt in 1949. Canx 8.6.49.
G-AKFE	Avro 652A Anson C.19 Srs.2	-	VP512	6. 9.47	Restored to RAF as VP512 in 4/56. Canx 18.4.56.
G-AKFF	Avro 691 Lancastrian C.4	Set.64 & R3/LB/374179	TX284	29. 8.47	WFU in 4/51 at Tarrant Rushton. Scrapped in 9/51 Canx 21.9.51.
G-AKFG	Avro 691 Lancastrian C.4 (C/n also quoted as RY/LC/59774)	Set.66 & 59884	TX286	29. 8.47	WFU in 4/51 at Tarrant Rushton. Scrapped in 9/51. Canx.
G-AKFH	Avro 691 Lancastrian C.4 (Also c/n R3/LB/485422)	Set.63	VP-KFD G-AKFH/TX283	29. 8.47	DBF on landing at Gatow, Berlin, East Germany on 26.6.49. Canx.
G-AKFI	Avro 691 Lancastrian C.2 (Also c/n R3/CB/485418)	Set.55	VL979	29. 8.47	To G-AJPP(2) 1/48. Canx.
G-AKFJ	Avro 621 Tutor	-	K6105	29. 8.47	Crashed on take off at Doncaster on 30.7.49. Canx.
G-AKFK	Avro 652A Anson I	-	NK770	29. 8.47	WFU at Tollerton in 12/52. Canx.
G-AKFL	Avro 652A Anson I	-	NK674	29. 8.47	Crashed on beach near Beirut, Lebanon on 18.12.49. Canx 18.12.49 as destroyed.
G-AKFM	Avro 652A Anson I	-	MG495	29. 8.47	To VP-KME 12/53. Canx 30.12.53.
G-AKFN	Fairchild F.24W-41A Argus II (UC-61-FA)	839	HB602 43-14875	5. 9.47	To VH-UEL 9/60. Canx 16.10.60.
G-AKFO	DH.89A Dragon Rapide	6460	R5924	3. 9.47	Not converted. Broken up in 8/49. Canx.
G-AKFP	Handley Page HP.81 Hermes 4	HP.81/1	XD632 G-AKFP	12. 9.47	DBR after colliding with DC-3 VT-AUA on landing at Dum Dum, Calcutta, India on 1.9.57. Canx.

Regn	Type	c/n	Previous identity	Regn date	Fate or immediate subsequent identity (if known)
G-AKFR	Percival P.31 Proctor IV	H.666	NP282	2. 9.47	NTU - To G-AKLC 10/47. Canx.
G-AKFS	Percival P.31 Proctor IV	H.605	NP198	2. 9.47	NTU - To G-AKLB 10/47. Canx.
G-AKFT	Percival P.31 Proctor IV	H.660	NP276	2. 9.47	NTU - To G-AKLD 10/47. Canx.
G-AKFU	Miles M.65 Gemini 1A	6494		8. 9.47	Crashed during forced landing 60 miles from Goose Bay, Labrador, Canada on 14.8.65. Canx.
G-AKFV	Miles M.65 Gemini 1A	6495		10. 9.47	To VP-KEX /47. Canx 2.1.48.
G-AKFW	Miles M.65 Gemini 1A	6501		10. 9.47	To VP-RBK 10/48. Canx 28.9.48.
G-AKFX	Miles M.65 Gemini 1A	6502		10. 9.47	Crashed on take-off from Shoreham on 26.10.60. Canx.
G-AKFY	Miles M.65 Gemini 1A	6503	HB-EEF G-AKFY	10. 9.47	CofA expired 11/63 & WFU at Biggin Hill. Canx.
G-AKFZ	Miles M.65 Gemini 1A	6476		11. 9.47	To OO-CDX 2/48. Canx 6.2.48.
G-AKGA	Miles M.65 Gemini 1A	6474		11. 9.47	To OO-CMA 6/50. Canx 26.6.50.
G-AKGB	Miles M.65 Gemini 1A	6504		16. 9.47	To VH-BMW /49. Canx 2.8.49.
G-AKGC	Miles M.65 Gemini 1A	6489		16. 9.47	Crashed during forced landing Anjou, Grenoble, France on 3.7.61. Canx.
G-AKGD	Miles M.65 Gemini 1A	6492		11. 9.47	Canx as WFU 22.11.73. (Parts only stored off-site 3/96)
G-AKGE	Miles M.65 Gemini 3C	6488	EI-ALM G-AKGE	18.10.47	Canx 30.5.84. Parts to Ulster Folk & Transport Museum, Belfast. (Stored 4/96) (For rebuild with components from G-AKEL)
G-AKGF	DH.82A Tiger Moth	85916	DF180	16. 9.47	Crashed at Thruxton on 28.7.62. Canx 31.8.62.
G-AKGG	DH.82A Tiger Moth	3959	N6655	16. 9.47	To Thailand Navy as "No.1" in 10/50. Canx 27.10.50.
G-AKGH	Boeing 377-10-32 Stratocruiser	15974		15. 6.49	To (N137A)/N402Q 8/58. Canx 4.8.58.
G-AKGI	Boeing 377-10-32 Stratocruiser	15975		15. 6.49	To (N100Q)/N405Q 1/59. Canx 8.1.59.
G-AKGJ	Boeing 377-10-32 Stratocruiser	15976		15. 6.49	To (N102Q)/N407Q 1/59, but broken up still marked as G-AKGJ. Canx 26.1.59.
G-AKGK	Boeing 377-10-32 Stratocruiser	15977		15. 6.49	To (N104Q)/N409Q 3/59. Canx 12.3.59.
G-AKGL	Boeing 377-10-32 Stratocruiser	15978		15. 6.49	To (N86Q)/N404Q 9/58. Canx 15.9.58.
G-AKGM	Boeing 377-10-32 Stratocruiser	15979		15. 6.49	To (N105Q)/N410Q 3/59. Canx 15.3.59.
G-AKGN	Handley Page HP.70 Halifax C.VIII	1395	PP333	16. 9.47	CofA expired 25.10.49. Suffered gale damage at Thame on 17.12.49. Scrapped. Canx. Still present in 4/50.
G-AKGO	Handley Page HP.70 Halifax C.VIII	1386	PP324	10. 9.47	Not converted. Canx 2.1.48. At Stansted by 5/48 with Ministry of Civil Aviation Fire School. Transferred to MCA Fire premises at Pengam Moors, Cardiff by 1952.
G-AKGP	Handley Page HP.70 Halifax C.VIII	1307	PP223	10. 9.47	To F-BESE 6/48. Canx 15.6.48.
G-AKGR	Miles M.14A Hawk Trainer III	1982	T9695	8. 9.47	Crashed at Lympne on 1.4.56. Canx.
G-AKGS	Miles M.14A Hawk Trainer III	1765	P6410	8. 9.47	Crashed in Granada, Spain on 1.4.54. Canx.
G-AKGT	DH.82A Tiger Moth	83095	R5236	8. 9.47	To VT-DBB 2/49. Canx 2.2.49.
G-AKGU	DH.82A Tiger Moth	83750	T5852	8. 9.47	To VT-DBK 1/49. Canx 19.1.49.
G-AKGV	DH.89A Dragon Rapide	6796	F-BFPU G-AKGV/NR697	9.10.47	To C-GXFJ 6/76. Canx 21.6.76.
G-AKGW	Fairchild F.24W-41A Argus II (UC-61-FA)	343	FK334 42-32118	16. 9.47	To OH-VSD 8/51. Canx 25.5.51.
G-AKGX	Douglas C-47A-40-DL Dakota	9874	FD953 42-24012	17. 9.47	To VR-NCS 1/58. Canx 28.1.58.
G-AKGY	DH.89A Dragon Rapide	6723	NF852	29. 9.47	To F-BFEH 1/57. Canx 5.12.56.
G-AKGZ	Handley Page HP.70 Halifax C.VIII	1400	PP338	17. 9.47	Crashed on take-off from Gatow, East Germany on 8.10.48. Canx 21.10.48.
G-AKHA	Miles M.65 Gemini 1A	6507		16. 9.47	Crashed at Haditha, Kirkup, Iraq on 25.1.49. Canx.
G-AKHB	Miles M.65 Gemini 1A	6508		16. 9.47	CofA expired 12.4.65 & WFU at White Waltham. Canx.
G-AKHC	Miles M.65 Gemini 3A (Originally regd as Gemini 1A)	6490		10.10.47	DBER when blown over onto a parked car at White Waltham in 9/65. Broken up in 10/65. Canx.
G-AKHD	Miles M.57 Aerovan 4	6425		23. 9.47	To F-BFPF 9/49. Canx 12.9.49.
G-AKHE	Miles M.65 Gemini 1A	6509		23. 9.47	Crashed at Hilsea, Portsmouth on 22.7.53. Canx.
G-AKHF	Miles M.57 Aerovan 4	6399		26. 9.47	To I-VALK 4/54. Canx 13.5.54.
G-AKHG	Miles M.57 Aerovan 4	6424		26. 9.47	Crashed at Hama, Syria on 21.2.52. Canx.
G-AKHH	Miles M.65 Gemini 1A	6511		3.10.47	To F-BFPG 1/50. Canx 22.11.49.
G-AKHI	Miles M.65 Gemini 1A	6512		3.10.47	To SU-AGG 12/49. Canx 9.12.49.
G-AKHJ	Miles M.65 Gemini 1A	6513		3.10.47	CofA expired 19.12.63 & WFU at Shobdon. Scrapped 1965. Canx.
G-AKHK	Miles M.65 Gemini 1A	6514		3.10.47	Crashed on take-off from Montpellier, France on 30.8.59. Canx.
G-AKHL	Miles M.65 Gemini 1A	6515		3.10.47	To F-BDAF 3/48. Canx 10.2.48.
G-AKHM	Miles M.65 Gemini 1A	6516		3.10.47	To F-BDAG 3/48. Canx 10.2.48.
G-AKHN	Miles M.65 Gemini 1A	6517		3.10.47	To F-BDAH 3/48. Canx 10.2.48.
G-AKHO	Miles M.65 Gemini 1A	6518		3.10.47	To F-BDAI 3/48. Canx 10.2.48.
G-AKHP	Miles M.65 Gemini 1A	6519		3.10.47	
G-AKHR	Miles M.65 Gemini 1A	6477		3.10.47	To VT-CQZ 12/47. Canx 30.12.47.
G-AKHS	Miles M.65 Gemini 1A	6510		10.10.47	To OO-GAR 11/53. Canx 16.11.53.
G-AKHT	Miles M.65 Gemini 3A (Originally regd as Gemini 1A)	6521		18.10.47	To VH-BMT /49. Canx 25.1.49.
G-AKHU	Miles M.65 Gemini 1A	6522		18.10.47	To VH-BMV /49. Canx 2.8.49.
G-AKHV	Miles M.65 Gemini 1A	6523	(F-BDAJ) G-AKHV	18.10.47	WFU at Biggin Hill in 6/66. Canx as destroyed 28.3.67.
G-AKHW	Miles M.65 Gemini 1A	6524		21.10.47	Shipped to New Zealand 16.5.91. To ZK-KHW. Canx 9.12.94.
G-AKHX	Miles M.65 Gemini 1A	6525		21.10.47	To OO-RVE 3/55. Canx 8.2.55.
G-AKHY	Miles M.65 Gemini 1A	6526		21.10.47	DBR in forced landing at Shebbear, Devon on 4.4.65. Canx.

Regn	Type	c/n	Previous identity	Regn date	Fate or immediate subsequent identity (if known)
G-AKHZ	Miles M.65 Gemini 7 (Originally regd as Gemini 1A, conv. in 1957)	6527		21.10.47	CofA expired 8.1.64 & WFU at Kidlington. (On rebuild by Miles Aircraft Collection for Museum of Berkshire Aviation 3/96 - Received Parts from G-AMME at some stage and the rear fuselage of G-ALUG) Canx.
G-AKIA	Vickers-Supermarine 236 Walrus II	-	HD929	8. 1.48	NTU - Not converted. Scrapped at Redhill. Canx.
G-AKIB(1)	Vickers-Supermarine 236 Walrus II	-	HD925	9. 9.47	NTU - Allocated in error. To G-AKJE 1/48. Canx.
G-AKIB(2)	Piper J3C-90 Cub (L-4H-PI) (Frame No.12139)	12311	OO-RAY 44-80015	18. 4.84	
G-AKIC	Vickers-Supermarine 507 Sea Otter ASR.I	-	JM826	8. 1.48	NTU - Not converted. Broken up at Redhill as spares for Dutch Navy. Canx.
G-AKID	Vickers-Supermarine 507 Sea Otter ASR.I	-	JM764	8. 1.48	Broken up at Redhill in 3/50 as spares for Dutch Navy. Canx.
G-AKIE	Handley Page HP.71 Halifax C.VIII	1391	(HB-AIM) G-AKBR/PP329	15. 9.47	Registered in error - restored as G-AKBR 10/47. Canx 24.10.47.
G-AKIF	DH.89A Dragon Rapide	6838	LN-BEZ G-AKIF/NR750	24. 9.47	
G-AKIG	DH.82A Tiger Moth	85888	DF139	26. 9.47	WFU at Blackbushe on 25.4.49. Canx in 2/53.
G-AKIH	Percival P.44 Proctor V	Ae.124		20.11.47	To TC-PAR 5/52. Canx 24.9.52.
G-AKII	Douglas C-47A-5-DK Dakota	12299	FZ693 42-92492	18. 9.47	To VP-BBR 2/60. Canx 1.2.60.
G-AKIJ	Douglas C-47A-25-DK Dakota	13304	KG581 42-93397	18. 9.47	To VR-NCP 1/58. Canx 28.1.58.
G-AKIK	Douglas C-47A-25-DK Dakota	13487	KG670 42-93562	18. 9.47	To French AF as 13487 in 3/57. Canx 1.3.57.
G-AKIL	Douglas C-47A-30-DK Dakota	13837/25282	KG738 43-48021	18. 9.47	To N9988F 10/51. Canx 21.10.51.
G-AKIM	Miles M.38 Messenger 2A	6709		19. 9.47	WFU at Stapleford on 28.1.66. Canx as WFU 19.2.73.
G-AKIN	Miles M.38 Messenger 2A	6728		19. 9.47	
G-AKIO	Miles M.38 Messenger 2A	6729	PH-NIR G-AKIO	19. 9.47	WFU at Barton on 16.7.70 & burnt 26.5.71. Canx as destroyed 7.5.73.
G-AKIP	Miles M.38 Messenger 2A	6727		19. 9.47	To HB-EEC in 1/49. Canx 30.12.47.
G-AKIR	Miles M.38 Messenger 2A	6726		19. 9.47	DBR at Leverton, Outgate on 5.6.71. Canx as WFU 2.11.71 at Portland.
G-AKIS	Miles M.38 Messenger 2A	6725		19. 9.47	Damaged in Belgium. Canx as WFU 24.2.70. (Stored .92)
G-AKIT	Percival P.44 Proctor 5	Ae.128		15. 1.48	To PT-AAS 8/49. Canx 10.8.48.
G-AKIU	Percival P.44 Proctor 5	Ae.129		20. 2.48	(Under rebuild Houghton-on-the-Hill 11/92)
G-AKIV	Percival P.44 Proctor 5	Ae.139		9. 3.48	To VH-BLU 8/48. Canx 14.8.48.
G-AKIW	Percival P.44 Proctor 5	Ae.131		6. 4.48	To VH-DIW 10/50. Canx 10.10.50.
G-AKIX	Percival P.44 Proctor 5	Ae.130		16. 4.48	WFU in Egypt in 10/51. Canx.
G-AKIY	DH.82A Tiger Moth	82799	VH-AQZ R4882	22. 9.47	To AP-ACK 5/49. Canx 19.5.49.
G-AKIZ	Fairchild F.24R-41A Argus II (UC-61-FA)	287	EV779 41-38843	23. 9.47	To OH-FCK 1/52. Canx 10.1.52.
G-AKJA	Fairchild F.24R-41A Argus II (UC-61-FA)	304	EV796 41-38860	23. 9.47	To OH-FCO 7/52. Canx 20.6.52.
G-AKJB	Fairchild F.24R-41A Argus II (UC-61-FA)	285	EV777 41-38841	23. 9.47	To ZS-DCX 4/49. Canx 26.4.49.
G-AKJC	PA-12 Super Cruiser	12-3994		29. 9.47	To F-BCPP 10/47. Canx 23.10.47.
G-AKJD	Slingsby T.29 Motor Tutor	599		2.10.47	Crashed at Dunstable on 21.6.64. Canx.
G-AKJE	Vickers-Supermarine 236 Walrus II	-	(G-AKIB) HD925	8. 1.48	Not converted. Scrapped at Redhill in 1952. Canx.
G-AKJF	Handley Page HP.70 Halifax C.VIII	1301	PP217	26. 9.47	Not converted. Canx 19.12.50 on sale to MCA Fire School at Stansted. Parts still identifiable in 5/52.
G-AKJG	DH.104 Dove 2B (Originally regd as Srs.2)	04071	VP-YGP G-AKJG	23.10.47	DBR in a belly-landing at Old, Northamptonshire as the result of an engine fire on 20.1.65. Canx.
G-AKJH	Douglas C-47A-20-DK Dakota	13164	EI-ARR G-AKJH/KG572/42-93271	2.10.47	To (ZS-FKK)/VQ-ZJB 8/68. Canx 10.68.
G-AKJI	Handley Page HP.61 Halifax B.VI	-	RG695	6.10.47	Not converted. Scrapped at Doncaster in 1948. Canx 23.9.48.
G-AKJJ	Handley Page HP.61 Halifax B.VI	-	RG698	6.10.47	Not converted. Scrapped at Doncaster in 1948. Canx 23.9.48.
G-AKJK	Fairchild F.24W-41A Argus II (UC-61-FA)	309	EV801 42-13573	8.10.47	To VR-RBE 2/48. Canx 26.2.48.
G-AKJL	Fairchild F.24W-41A Argus II (UC-61-FA)	339	FK330 42-32134	8.10.47	To VH-ALF 7/51. Canx 13.12.50.
G-AKJM	Fairchild F.24W-41A Argus II (UC-61-FA)	314	EV806 42-13578	8.10.47	To VH-AVN 6/51. Canx 29.6.51.
G-AKJN	Douglas C-47A-10-DK Dakota	12489	KG454 42-92663	9.10.47	To F-OAIG 2/51. Canx 3.2.51.
G-AKJO	Avro 691 Lancastrian C.4	Set.70 & RY/LB/59112	TX290	15.10.47	To AP-ACO 7/48. Canx 14.7.48.
G-AKJP	DH.104 Dove 5 (Originally regd as Dove 1, then Dove 1B in 1958)	04064		21.10.47	To YI-AGC 5/73. Canx 1.5.73.
G-AKJR	DH.104 Dove 2B (Originally regd as Dove 1B, then 2)	04084	AP-AGJ G-AKJR	23.10.47	WFU at Southend in 8/68. (Was to have been converted to Carstedt Jet Liner 600J Dove but project aborted) Scrapped in 5/70. Canx.
G-AKJS	DH.89A Dragon Rapide	W.1002	E-0228	3.11.47	Sold to France (spares) 6/65. Canx 21.6.65.
G-AKJT	Taylorcraft Auster 5	1583	TJ530	16.12.47	To VT-DGB 4/52. Canx 24.3.52.
G-AKJU	Auster J/1N Alpha (Originally regd as Auster 5)	2058	TW513	16.12.47	While towing Schleicher Ka-7 BGA.1031 from Barrards Hall, Wattisham the undercarriage hooked onto some standing corn and it crashed 3 miles S of RAF Wattisham 15.8.71. Remains taken to Shipham and officially WFU on 1.11.71. Rebuilt as G-TENT 1/90. Canx.
G-AKJV	Miles M.14A Hawk Trainer III	1762	P6407	17.12.47	WFU at Redhill in 2/54. Burnt on 24.5.54. Canx.
G-AKJW	Miles M.14A Hawk Trainer III	528	L6907	17.12.47	Crashed at East Grinstead on 19.7.48. Canx.

Regn	Type	c/n	Previous identity	Regn date	Fate or immediate subsequent identity (if known)
G-AKJX	Miles M.14A Hawk Trainer III	560	L8051	17.12.47	WFU at Lympne in 6/50. Scrapped in 7/54. Canx.
G-AKJY	DH.89A Dragon Rapide	6447	R2486	22.12.47	To F-OAPT 5/54. Canx 7.4.54.
G-AKJZ	DH.89A Dragon Rapide	6880	NR804	17.12.47	WFU at Biggin Hill on 13.7.59. Canx.
G-AKKA	Miles M.65 Gemini 1A	6528		21.10.47	To LN-TAH 4/48. Canx 27.4.48.
G-AKKB	Miles M.65 Gemini 1A	6537		28.10.47	
G-AKKC	Miles M.38 Messenger 2A	6369		3.12.47	DBR in overshoot on landing on an airstrip at St.Crowland, Lincs., on 25.7.67. Canx.
G-AKKD	Miles M.65 Gemini 1A	6531		14. 2.48	To VT-CTQ 4/48. Canx 14.4.48.
G-AKKE	Miles M.65 Gemini 1A	6317		8. 4.48	To CR-LCD 5/49. Canx 27.5.49.
G-AKKF	Miles M.65 Gemini 1A	6532		3. 5.48	To VP-KJC 11/51. Canx 11.10.51.
G-AKKG	Miles M.38 Messenger 4	6700	HB-EEC	30. 4.48	Fatal crash & DBF while landing at Round Wood, Eder Farm, Partridge Green, Sussex on 1.6.68. Canx.
G-AKKH	Miles M.65 Gemini 1A	6479	OO-CDO	23. 7.48	CofA expired 21.9.89. (Stored 7/96)
G-AKKI	Miles M.38 Messenger 2A	6713		4. 6.48	Mid-air collision with Auster 5 G-APAH over Danbury, East Essex and crashed at East Hanningfield, Chelmsford on 16.3.58. Canx.
G-AKKJ	Miles M.57 Aerovan 4	6423		12. 3.49	To CR-LCL 3/51. Canx 6.1.52.
G-AKKK	Miles M.38 Messenger 2A	6712		24. 3.49	To F-DADU/F-BFOU 8/54. Canx 16.8.54.
G-AKKL	Miles M.38 Messenger 2A	6717		24. 3.49	To ZK-AWE 1/51. Canx 1.8.50.
G-AKKM	Miles M.38 Messenger 2A	6714		5. 8.49	Crashed at Wolverhampton on 5.2.58. Canx.
G-AKKN	Miles M.38 Messenger 2A	6709		22. 9.49	WFU on 25.4.69. Canx as WFU 20.2.73.
G-AKKO	Miles M.38 Messenger 2A	6716		3. 3.50	WFU at Shipdham on 27.8.70. Canx 5.4.73.
G-AKKP(1)	Miles (unknown type)	-		. .49R	NTU - Canx.
G-AKKP(2)	Handley Page HP.71 Halifax A.IX	1548	RT885	9. 3.50	Not converted. Used for spares. Canx 20.11.50.
G-AKKR	Miles M.14A Hawk Trainer III (Identity could in fact be ex T9967 c/n 2160 from 1943 rebuild)	1995	"T9967" G-AKKR/T9708	23. 6.48	CofA expired 10.4.65. (Allotted 8378M as T9707) (On display 3/96 Manchester Museum of Science & Industry)
G-AKKS	Miles M.14A Hawk Trainer III	1790	P6446	23. 6.48	WFU at Renfrew in 10/54. Canx.
G-AKKT	Miles M.14A Hawk Trainer III	405	L5973	23. 6.48	Not converted. Scrapped at Denham in 1951. Canx.
G-AKKU(1)	Miles M.14A Hawk Trainer III	539	BB661 G-AFBS	23. 6.48	NTU - restored as G-AFBS 6/48. Canx.
G-AKKU(2)	Handley Page HP.71 Halifax A.IX	1555	RT892	9. 3.50	Not converted. Used for spares. Canx 20.11.50.
G-AKKV	Miles M.14A Hawk Trainer III	987	N3954	23. 6.48	Crashed at Hemswell on 13.6.60. Canx.
G-AKKW	Miles M.14A Hawk Trainer III	1776	P6421	23. 6.48	WFU at Denham on 22.3.50. Canx.
G-AKKX	Miles M.14A Hawk Trainer III	2039	T9802	23. 6.48	Crashed at Denham on 28.3.51. Canx.
G-AKKY	Miles M.14A Hawk Trainer III (Also allotted BAPC.44 to reflect rebuild status from various parts)	2078	T9841	23. 6.48	WFU at Renfrew in 11/60. Canx as WFU 12.4.73. (On display 4/97 Woodley)
G-AKKZ	Miles M.14A Hawk Trainer III	2227	V1074	23. 6.48	WFU at Denham in 9/55. Burnt at Northolt. Canx.
G-AKLA	DH.89A Dragon Rapide	6764	NF893	23.10.47	DBR at Jodhpur, India on 15.6.54. Canx.
G-AKLB	Percival P.31 Proctor IV	H.605	(G-AKFS) NP282	27.10.47	Broken up at Squires Gate in 11/50. Canx.
G-AKLC	Percival P.31 Proctor IV	H.666	(G-AKFR) NP198	27.10.47	Crashed at Hollis Hill, near Shipley on 19.8.49. Canx.
G-AKLD	Percival P.31 Proctor IV	H.660	(G-AKFT) NP276	27.10.47	Broken up at Perth in 1954. Canx.
G-AKLE	Avro 691 Lancastrian C.4	Set.65	TX285	31.10.47	No CofA issued. Scrapped at Dunsfold in 9/48. Canx.
G-AKLF	Percival P.40 Prentice T.1	PAC/033	VR209	15.11.47	Returned to RAF as VR209 in 1949. Canx.
G-AKLG	Percival P.40 Prentice T.1	PAC/034	VR210	15.11.47	Returned to RAF as VR210 in 1949. Canx.
G-AKLH	Taylorcraft Auster 5	791	MT269	8.11.47	Not converted. Used for spares 7/48. Canx.
G-AKLI	Handley Page HP.61 Halifax B.VI	-	RG783	17.11.47	To Pakistan AF in 10/49. Canx 21.10.49.
G-AKLJ	Handley Page HP.61 Halifax B.VI	-	RG781	17.11.47	To Pakistan AF in 10/49. Canx 21.10.49.
G-AKLK	Handley Page HP.61 Halifax B.VI	-	RG779	17.11.47	To Pakistan AF in 10/49. Canx 21.10.49.
G-AKLL	Douglas C-47A-30-DK Dakota	14005/25450	KG773 43-48189	18.11.47	To EC-AEU 6/50. Canx 6.6.50.
G-AKLM	Short SA.6 Sealand I	SH1562		26.11.47	DBF following crash into mountainside at Lindesnes, Southern Norway on 15.10.49. Canx.
G-AKLN	Short SA.6 Sealand I	SH1563		26.11.47	To LN-SUF 6/52. Canx 1.5.52.
G-AKLO	Short SA.6 Sealand I	SH1564		26.11.47	To VR-SDS 10/52. Canx.
G-AKLP	Short SA.6 Sealand I	SH1565	G-14-4 G-AKLP/VP-TBA/G-AKLP	26.11.47	To VR-SDV 9/54. Canx 5.5.54.
G-AKLR	Short SA.6 Sealand I	SH1566	VP-TBB G-AKLR	26.11.47	To YU-CFJ 9/51. Canx 7.5.51.
G-AKLS	Short SA.6 Sealand I	SH1567	G-14-2 G-AKLS/(VP-TBC)/G-AKLS	26.11.47	To YU-CFK 9/51. Canx 7.3.51.
G-AKLT	Short SA.6 Sealand I	SH1568	G-14-3 G-AKLT	26.11.47	To PK-CMA 1/51. Canx 6.3.50.
G-AKLU	Short SA.6 Sealand I	SH1569		26.11.47	To LN-SUH 5/51. Canx 16.4.51.
G-AKLV	Short SA.6 Sealand I	SH1570	AP-AFM G-AKLV	26.11.47	WFU at Rochester in 4/60. Canx.
G-AKLW	Short SA.6 Sealand I	SH1571	(USA) R.Saudi AF/SU-AHY/G-AKLW	26.11.47	(Stored 1/99 Ulster Folk & Transport Museum)
G-AKLX	Short SA.6 Sealand I	SH1572		26.11.47	To AP-AGB 12/52. Canx 20.10.52.
G-AKLY	Short SA.6 Sealand I	SH1573		26.11.47	To AP-AGC 12/52. Canx 20.10.52.
G-AKLZ	Short SA.6 Sealand I	SH1574		26.11.47	To Indian Navy as INS-101 in 1/53. Canx 8.8.52.
G-AKMA	Short SA.6 Sealand I	SH1575		26.11.47	To Indian Navy as INS-102 in 2/53. Canx 8.8.52.
G-AKMB	Taylorcraft Auster 5	1529	TJ480	24.11.47	To SE-BUR 4/52. Canx 4.4.52.
G-AKMC	Taylorcraft Auster 5	1516	(OH-AUA) G-AKMC/TJ458	24.11.47	To ZK-AVF 7/50. Canx 19.7.50.
G-AKMD	DH.89A Dragon Rapide	6802	NR714	2. 3.48	To F-OAKD 1/52. Canx 17.12.51.
G-AKME	DH.89A Dragon Rapide	6767	NF896	1. 3.48	DBF at Lympne on 30.6.50. Canx.
G-AKMF	DH.89A Dragon Rapide	6617	X7500	23. 2.48	To Israeli DF/AF as S-74 in 5/50. Canx in 11/48.

Regn	Type	c/n	Previous identity	Regn date	Fate or immediate subsequent identity (if known)
G-AKMG	DH.89A Dragon Rapide	6635	X7518	24. 2.48	To F-BGPI 6/52. Canx 23.4.52.
G-AKMH	DH.89A Dragon Rapide	6704	HG719	28. 2.48	To 9Q-CJK in 10/64. Canx 22.10.64.
G-AKMI	Taylorcraft Auster 5	1530	TJ741	26.11.47	To F-BGPB 2/52. Canx 29.1.52.
G-AKMJ	Miles M.14A Hawk Trainer III	777	L8351	26.11.47	To ZS-DBF 12/48. Canx 8.12.48.
G-AKMK	Miles M.14A Hawk Trainer III	897	N3851	27.11.47	To ZK-ATD 7/49. Canx 12.6.49.
G-AKML	Miles M.14A Hawk Trainer III	335	L5914	27.11.47	To Egyptian AF in 9/49. Canx 2.9.49.
G-AKMM	Miles M.14A Hawk Trainer III	1712	P6344	27.11.47	To Egyptian AF in 9/49. Canx 9.9.49.
G-AKMN	Miles M.14A Hawk Trainer III	424	L5992	27.11.47	Fatal crash ¼ mile east of Wheaton Aston Airfield, near Wolverhampton on 26.2.53. Canx as destroyed /53.
G-AKMO	Miles M.14A Hawk Trainer III	395	L5963	27.11.47	To Egyptian AF in 9/49. Canx 2.9.49.
G-AKMP	Miles M.14A Hawk Trainer III	601	L8092	27.11.47	To Egyptian AF in 9/49. Canx 2.9.49.
G-AKMR	Miles M.14A Hawk Trainer III	1820	R1819	27.11.47	Not converted. Scrapped at Lympne in 1954. Canx.
G-AKMS	Miles M.14A Hawk Trainer III	1650	P2428	27.11.47	To Egyptian AF in 9/49. Canx 2.9.49.
G-AKMT	Miles M.14A Hawk Trainer III	730	L8274	27.11.47	To Egyptian AF in 9/49. Canx 2.9.49.
G-AKMU	Miles M.14A Hawk Trainer III	775	L8349	27.11.47	DBR at Weston-super-Mare on 4.11.49. Canx.
G-AKMV	Avro 652A Anson I	-	EG239	27.11.47	To VP-KHT 1/51. Canx 27.7.50.
G-AKMW	Avro 691 Lancastrian C.2	Set.53	VL977	28.11.47	WFU at Dunsfold in 5/51. Scrapped. Canx.
G-AKMX	DH.82A Tiger Moth	83474	T7089	28.11.47	Not Converted. Broken up at Broxbourne in 4/49. Canx.
G-AKMY	Miles M.14A Hawk Trainer III	2191	V1018	29.11.47	Not converted. Scrapped at Southport in 1956. Canx.
G-AKMZ	Miles M.14A Hawk Trainer III	1775	P6420	29.11.47	Not converted. Burnt at Squires Gate in 1956. Canx.
G-AKNA	Miles M.14A Hawk Trainer III	534	L6913	29.11.47	Reduced to spares at Broxbourne. Canx in 10/56.
G-AKNB	Douglas C-47-DL Dakota	9043	EI-BDU	5.12.47	To N59NA 7/85. Canx 22.7.85.
			G-AKNB/XY-ACN/G-AKNB/FD789/42-32817		
G-AKNC	Piper J3C-65 Cub (L-4H-PI)	12109	NC6400N	5. 1.48	To OH-CPC. Canx 13.12.48.
			(G-AJBE)/44-79813		
G-AKND	DH.89A Dragon Rapide	6515	X7342	29.11.47	To VP-KGE 8/48. Canx 12.8.48.
G-AKNE	DH.89A Dragon Rapide	6591	X7449	29.11.47	To F-OBDV 9/57. Canx 23.9.57.
G-AKNF	DH.89A Dragon Rapide	6518	X7345	29.11.47	To EP-ADP 7/55. Canx 18.7.55.
G-AKNG	Handley Page HP.61 Halifax B.VI	-	RG658	29.11.47	Broken up at Bovingdon in 5/48. Canx 9.2.48.
G-AKNH	Handley Page HP.61 Halifax B.VI	-	RG700	29.11.47	Broken up at Bovingdon in 5/48. Canx 9.2.48.
G-AKNI	Handley Page HP.61 Halifax B.VI	-	RG717	29.11.47	Broken up at Bovingdon in 5/48. Canx 9.2.48.
G-AKNJ	Handley Page HP.61 Halifax B.VI	-	RG759	29.11.47	Broken up at Bovingdon in 5/48. Canx 18.2.48.
G-AKNK	Handley Page HP.61 Halifax B.VI	-	RG712	29.11.47	Broken up at Bovingdon in 5/48. Canx 9.2.48.
G-AKNL	Handley Page HP.61 Halifax B.VI		PP171	29.11.47	Broken up at Bovingdon in 5/48. Canx 8.3.48.
		1270			
G-AKNM	Douglas C-47B-1-DK Dakota		OO-CBU	2.12.47	Broken up at Castle Donnington on 5.1.73. Canx.
		14354/25799	G-AKNM/CF-GON/KJ860/43-48538		
G-AKNN	DH.89A Dragon Rapide	6598	X7456	8.12.47	WFU at Castle Donnington on 29.8.69. Canx 10.9.73.
G-AKNO	Short S.45 Solent 3	S.1294	NJ202	2.12.47	To VH-TOA, but sank at Malta on 28.1.51 whilst on delivery. Canx 20.12.50.
G-AKNP	Short S.45 Solent 3	S.1295	NJ203	2.12.47	To VH-TOB 1/51. Canx 20.3.51.
G-AKNR	Short S.45 Solent 3	S.1296	NJ204	2.12.47	To ZK-AMQ 11/51. Canx 6.11.51.
G-AKNS	Short S.45 Solent 3	S.1297	WM759	2.12.47	WFU at Poole in 1956. Canx.
			G-AKNS/NJ205		
G-AKNT	Short S.45 Solent 3	S.1298	NJ206	2.12.47	To N9947F 11/55. Canx 15.11.55.
G-AKNU	Short S.45 Solent 3	S.1299	NJ207	2.12.47	Fatal crash at Chessell Down, IoW on 15.11.57. Canx.
G-AKNV	DH.89A Dragon Rapide	6458	EI-AGK	2.12.47	To OO-AFG 9/55. Canx 27.9.55.
			G-AKNV/R5922		
G-AKNW	DH.89A Dragon Rapide	6469	R5932	2.12.47	To LR-ABH 6/50. Canx 23.6.50.
G-AKNX	DH.89A Dragon Rapide	6629	X7512	4.12.47	To F-OATD 9/55. Canx 13.9.55.
G-AKNY	DH.89A Dragon Rapide	6470	R5933	11.12.47	To F-OBRX 10/60. Canx 3.10.60.
G-AKNZ	DH.89A Dragon Rapide	6550	X7390	11.12.47	To LV-AGY 12/48. Canx 30.12.48.
G-AKOA	DH.89A Dragon Rapide	6618	X7501	11.12.47	To EP-ADO 7/55. Canx 15.6.55.
G-AKOB	DH.89A Dragon Rapide	6492	R9564	11.12.47	To VP-KNS 12/55. Canx 30.11.55.
G-AKOC	DH.89A Dragon Rapide	6814	NR726	18. 3.48	To VH-CFA 7/49. Canx 10.6.49.
G-AKOD	DH.89A Dragon Rapide	6566	X7406	3.12.47	To F-OAQY 6/54. Canx 23.6.54.
G-AKOE	DH.89A Dragon Rapide 4	6601	X7484	3.12.47	CofA expired 25.7.82 & WFU. (Stored 3/98 at Chirk)
G-AKOF	DH.89A Dragon Rapide	6538	X7378	4.12.47	Crashed into River Mersey on 11.11.48. Canx.
G-AKOG	DH.89A Dragon Rapide	6878	NR802	19. 5.48	To VP-RCH 10/51. Canx 8.10.51.
G-AKOH	DH.89A Dragon Rapide	6582	X7441	4.12.47	To F-BGXH 6/53. Canx 12.5.53.
G-AKOI	DH.89A Dragon Rapide	6546	X7386	4.12.47	To TJ-AAQ 7/48. Canx 7.7.48.
G-AKOJ	DH.89A Dragon Rapide	6580	X7439	4.12.47	To TJ-AAJ 5/48. Canx 14.5.48.
G-AKOK	DH.89A Dragon Rapide	6474	R5946	4.12.47	To F-BGPK 4/52. Canx 20.3.53.
G-AKOL	Miles M.14A Hawk Trainer III	923	N3882	4.12.47	DBF at Dyce on 12.5.49. Canx.
G-AKOM	DH.89A Dragon Rapide	6758	OO-DCB	8.12.47	To F-OGAU 5/56. Canx 12.4.55.
			G-AKOM/NF887		
G-AKON	DH.89A Dragon Rapide	6620	X7503	8.12.47	To VP-KFX 7/48. Canx 8.7.48.
G-AKOO	DH.89A Dragon Rapide	6468	R5931	8.12.47	To CC-CIC-0034 in 4/52. Canx 13.12.48.
G-AKOP	DH.89A Dragon Rapide	6636	X7519	9.12.47	To Israel AF/DF in 5/48. Canx 3.5.48.
G-AKOR	DH.89A Dragon Rapide	6577	X7417	31.12.47	To VQ-FAN 12/52. Canx 4.12.52.
G-AKOS	Miles M.37 Martinet Trainer	-	JN668	22.12.47	NTU - Not converted. Derelict at Staverton in 1949. Canx.
G-AKOT	Taylorcraft Auster 5	1469	TJ433	23.12.47	Crashed at Gorlestone on 9.9.62. Canx.
G-AKOU	Taylorcraft Auster 5	1412	TJ342	23.12.47	To ZK-AVH 9/50. Canx 14.7.50.
G-AKOV	DH.89A Dragon Rapide	6612	X7495	17.12.47	To VP-KNC 2/55. Canx 7.2.55.
G-AKOW	Taylorcraft Auster 5	1579	PH-NAD(2)	23.12.47	CofA expired 26.6.82. Canx as WFU 5.8.87. (On display at
	(Regd with c/n TJ569A following Dutch rebuild)		PH-NEG(2)/G-AKOW/TJ569		AAC Middle Wallop as TJ569)
G-AKOX	Taylorcraft Auster 5	1264	RT637	23.12.47	To PH-NEP(2) 4/52. Canx 17.3.52.
G-AKOY	DH.89A Dragon Rapide	6504	X7331	31.12.47	To AP-AGM 6/53. Canx 11.4.53.
G-AKOZ	Douglas C-47B-20-DK Dakota		KN259	2. 1.48	To French AF as 49927 in 11/52. Canx 12.11.52.
		15743/27188	43-49927		
G-AKPA	DH.89A Dragon Rapide	6709	HG724	12. 1.48	To EI-AML 6/62. Canx 8.6.62.
G-AKPB	Percival P.44 Proctor V	Ae.65	SU-ACH	14. 2.48	To SU-AFG 2/48. Canx 2.6.48.

Regn	Type	c/n	Previous identity	Regn date	Fate or immediate subsequent identity (if known)
G-AKPC	Short S.29 Stirling V	-	(OO-XAM) G-AKPC/PK148	6. 1.48	Scrapped at Thame in 11/48. Canx.
G-AKPD	Lockheed 14-08-2 Lodestar	1429	CF-TCD	8. 1.48	Crashed in sea off Elba on 29.10.48. Canx in 1949.
G-AKPE	Miles M.14A Hawk Trainer III	823	N3775	27. 1.48	WFU at Crosby-on-Eden on 8.5.65. Canx.
G-AKPF	Miles M.14A Hawk Trainer III (Magister I)(Composite with fuselage of N3788/G-ANLI c/n 836 from 1955 rebuild)	2228	V1075	27. 1.48	Permit expired 30.8.96. (On display ?/99 Sandown)
G-AKPG	Miles M.14A Hawk Trainer III	356	L5925	31. 1.48	Crashed at Cranfield on 12.11.64. Canx.
G-AKPH	Taylorcraft Auster 5	1099	NJ719	27. 1.48	WFU on 25.6.60. Dismantled at Rutherglen in 1/61. Canx.
G-AKPI	Taylorcraft Auster 5	1088	NJ703	27. 1.48	CofA expired 1.12.85. (To J.Allen 1/91 and stored 5/93 Croft, near Skegness)
G-AKPJ	Taylorcraft Auster 5	1586	TJ567	27. 1.48	To ZK-AXP 9/50. Canx 30.9.50.
G-AKPK	Gloster Meteor T.7 (Constructed from wings, rear fuselage and tail unit of Meteor 4 G-AIDC)	G5/201		9. 1.48	To Belgian AF as ED-1 in 11/48. Canx 23.11.48.
G-AKPL	Miles M.14A Hawk Trainer III	871	N3825	12. 1.48	Crashed at Strabane, Ireland on 26.1.64. Canx.
G-AKPM	Miles M.14A Hawk Trainer III	591	L8082	12. 1.48	DBR at Lympne on 22.10.50. Canx.
G-AKPN	Vickers-Supermarine 507 Sea Otter ASR.I	-	JN139	10. 1.48	To Egyptian AF in 2/49. Canx 2.5.49.
G-AKPO	Vickers-Supermarine 507 Sea Otter ASR.I	-	JN114	10. 1.48	To Egyptian AF in 2/49. Canx 2.5.49.
G-AKPP	Vickers-Supermarine 507 Sea Otter ASR.I	-	JM989	10. 1.48	To Egyptian AF in 2/49. Canx 2.5.49.
G-AKPR	Vickers-Supermarine 507 Sea Otter ASR.I	-	JN197	10. 1.48	To Egyptian AF in 2/49. Canx 2.5.49.
G-AKPS	Vickers-Supermarine 507 Sea Otter ASR.I	-	JN187	10. 1.48	To Egyptian AF in 2/49. Canx 2.5.49.
G-AKPT	Vickers-Supermarine 507 Sea Otter ASR.I	-	JN138	10. 1.48	To Egyptian AF in 2/49. Canx 2.5.49.
G-AKPU	Vickers-Supermarine 507 Sea Otter ASR.I	-	JN137	10. 1.48	To Egyptian AF in 2/49. Canx 2.5.49.
G-AKPV	Vickers-Supermarine 507 Sea Otter ASR.I	-	JN194	10. 1.48	To Egyptian AF in 2/49. Canx 2.5.49.
G-AKPW	Douglas C-47A-25-DK Dakota	13729	KG728 42-93779	17. 1.48	To VR-SCQ 3/48. Canx 3.3.48.
G-AKPX	Fairchild F.24R-46R Argus III (UC-61K-FA)	960	HB722 43-14986	12. 1.48	To OH-FCA 6/50. Canx 6.6.50.
G-AKPY	Avro 691 Lancastrian C.4	Set.47	VL971	19. 1.48	WFU at Hurn on 22.8.49. Scrapped in 2/50. Canx 21.12.49.
G-AKPZ	Avro 691 Lancastrian C.4	Set.48	VL972	19. 1.48	WFU at Hurn on 25.10.49. Scrapped in 2/50. Canx 21.12.49.
G-AKRA(1)	Avro 691 Lancastrian C.2	-		. 1.48R	NTU. Canx.
G-AKRA(2)	Piper J3C-65 Cub (L-4H-PI) (Frame No 11080)	11255	I-FIVI 43-29964	15. 6.84	(On rebuild 8/97)
G-AKRB	Avro 691 Lancastrian C.4	Set.41 & 1248	VM737 (G-AGPP)	19. 1.48	WFU at Hurn on 14.8.49. Scrapped in 2/50. Canx 21.12.49.
G-AKRC	Taylorcraft Auster 4	856	MT100	16. 1.48	To OH-AUF 5/52. Canx 24.5.52.
G-AKRD	Airspeed AS.57 Ambassador 1 (Modified to Tyne Ambassador in 1958, then Dart Ambassador)	62	G-37-3 G-AKRD/(RT668)	9. 2.48	Scrapped at Hucknall in 10/69. Canx.
G-AKRE	DH.89A Dragon Rapide	6606	X7489	21. 1.48	To F-OABH 1/49. Canx 7.1.49.
G-AKRF	Vickers-Supermarine 507 Sea Otter ASR.I	S2/04991	JM977	14. 1.48	To R.Netherlands Navy as 18-1. Canx 4.6.49.
G-AKRG	Vickers-Supermarine 507 Sea Otter ASR.I	-	JN134	14. 1.48	Scrapped at Burnaston in 1957. Canx.
G-AKRH	Miles M.14A Hawk Trainer III	785	L8359	20. 1.48	WFU in 11/56. Broken up ay Squires Gate in 1963. Canx.
G-AKRI	Miles M.14A Hawk Trainer III	623	L8145	20. 1.48	To EI-ADU 5/48. Canx 14.5.48.
G-AKRJ	Miles M.14A Hawk Trainer III	1862	R1876	20. 1.48	Crashed into sea off Shoreham on 29.1.49. Canx.
G-AKRK	Miles M.14A Hawk Trainer III	1860	R1859	20. 1.48	Not converted. Scrapped at Croydon in 1949. Canx.
G-AKRL	Miles M.14A Hawk Trainer III	2042	T9805	17. 1.48	To OO-PAB 3/49. Canx 8.3.49.
G-AKRM	Miles M.14A Hawk Trainer III	2104	T9887	17. 1.48	Crashed near Chester on 8.4.53. Canx.
G-AKRN	DH.89A Dragon Rapide	6513	X7340	17. 1.48	WFU at Ipswich on 27.6.60. Canx as destroyed 14.2.73. Parts used in rebuilt of G-AIUL in 7/97.
G-AKRO	DH.89A Dragon Rapide	6480	R9552	17. 1.48	To F-OAOY 2/54. Canx 6.1.54.
G-AKRP	DH.89A Dragon Rapide	6940	CN-TTO F-DAFS/G-AKRP/RL958	26. 1.48	(On rebuild 5/98 at Sywell)
G-AKRR	DH.89A Dragon Rapide	6950	SN-ABB G-AKRR/RL968	26. 1.48	To SN-ABB in 11/52. Canx 8.11.52.
G-AKRS	DH.89A Dragon Rapide	6952	RL981	21. 1.48	To Israeli DF/AF Museum as 4X-970/002 in 5/78. Canx 29.2.84.
G-AKRT	Miles M.14A Hawk Trainer III	2100	T9883	24. 1.48	Crashed at Elstree on 8.11.53. Canx.
G-AKRU	Miles M.14A Hawk Trainer III	1874	R1888	24. 1.48	WFU at Rochester in 5/53. Burnt in 9/54. Canx.
G-AKRV	Miles M.14A Hawk Trainer III	2113	T9896	24. 1.48	To VP-KNW, but crashed in Tanganyika on 22.3.56 before re-regd. Canx.
G-AKRW	Miles M.14A Hawk Trainer III	931	N3890	24. 1.48	DBR on landing at Hawkhurst on 11.7.53. Canx.
G-AKRX	Vickers-Supermarine 507 Sea Otter ASR.I	1806/C/206	JM968	20. 1.48	Not converted. Scrapped at Langley in 1949. Canx.
G-AKRY	Hawker Fury F.1	-	NX798	29. 1.48	Crashed in Egypt in 10/48 whilst on delivery. Canx /49.
G-AKRZ	Hawker Fury F.1	-	LA610	29. 1.48	NTU - Seized by the Egyptians in 1948. Canx in 1949.
G-AKSA	Airspeed AS.65 Consul	5188		26. 1.48	To Burmese AF as UB-102 in 8/49. Canx 11.8.49.
G-AKSB	DH.89A Dragon Rapide	6951	RL980	27. 1.48	To VP-AAA 2/50. Canx 17.2.50.
G-AKSC	DH.89A Dragon Rapide	6779	NR680 (G-AGLO)/NR680	27. 1.48	To F-OATC 9/55. Canx 3.8.55.
G-AKSD	DH.89A Dragon Rapide	6949	RL967	27. 1.48	To F-OBVI 9/61. Canx 24.8.61.
G-AKSE	DH.89A Dragon Rapide	6870	EI-AKH G-AKSE/NR794	27. 1.48	To F-BLHE 4/63. Canx 7.4.63.
G-AKSF	DH.89A Dragon Rapide	6490	R9562	14. 2.48	DBF on ground at Prestwick on 23.7.49. Canx.

Regn	Type	c/n	Previous identity	Regn date	Fate or immediate subsequent identity (if known)
G-AKSG	DH.89A Dragon Rapide	6931	RL949	28. 1.48	To F-BHAF 7/56. Canx 10.5.56.
G-AKSH	DH.89A Dragon Rapide	6471	R5934	31. 1.48	To VQ-FAM 1/52. Canx 22.11.51.
G-AKSI	Taylorcraft Auster 5	1159	RT497	9. 2.48	To HB-EON 5/48. Canx 20.4.48.
G-AKSJ	Taylorcraft Auster 5	1448	TJ401	31. 1.48	NTU - To G-AKSP 2/48. Canx.
G-AKSK	DH.104 Dove 1B (Originally regd as Srs.1)	04116		12. 2.48	Crashed in Sloden Enclosure, New Forest, 1½ miles west of Fritham, Hants on 23.7.55. Canx 27.2.56.
G-AKSL	DH.89A Dragon Rapide	6865	NR789	4. 2.48	To F-BGPL 4/52. Canx 1.4.52.
G-AKSM	Douglas C-47A-40-DL Dakota	9860	FD939 G-AIBA/FD939/42-23998	4. 2.48	To TF-ISB 3/51. Canx 7.3.51.
G-AKSN	Avro 691 Lancastrian C.2	Set.49	VL973	10. 2.48	WFU at Dunsfold in 5/51. Broken up. Canx.
G-AKSO	Avro 691 Lancastrian C.2	Set.50	VL974	10. 2.48	WFU at Dunsfold in 5/51. Broken up. Canx.
G-AKSP	Taylorcraft Auster 5	1448	(G-AKSJ) TJ401	6. 2.48	To F-BDAY 7/49. Canx 27.7.49.
G-AKSR	DH.104 Dove 1B (Originally regd as Dove 1)	04121	(VR-B..) G-AKSR/Pakistan AF P1301/AP-AKS/G-AKSR	12. 2.48	To TJ-ACC(2) 8/65. Canx 22.7.65.
G-AKSS	DH.104 Dove 1B (Originally regd as Dove 1)	04122	ZS-DFC G-AKSS	12. 2.48	CofA expired 28.2.75. Canx as destroyed 4.11.76.
G-AKST	DH.104 Dove 1B (Originally regd as Dove 1)	04125	XY-ACV G-AKST/AP-AFE/G-AKST/XY-ACV/G-AKST	8. 3.48	DBR when hangar collapsed in cyclone at Chittagong, Burma and tidal wave swept through on 31.10.60. Canx.
G-AKSU	DH.104 Dove 1	04126		8. 3.48	To VR-TBB 6/48. Canx 14.6.48.
G-AKSV	DH.104 Dove 1B (Originally regd as Dove 1)	04161		17. 4.48	To YI-AEH 8/66. Canx 25.8.66.
G-AKSW	DH.104 Dove 6 (Originally regd as Dove 2)	04166		12. 5.48	To CR-CAR 7/68. Canx 11.7.68.
G-AKSX	Tipsy M Trainer	1	G-6-1 OO-POM	24. 2.48	NTU - Broken up in 3/48 as G-6-1. Canx.
G-AKSY	Taylorcraft Auster 5D	1567	F-BGOO G-AKSY/TJ534	10. 2.48	(On rebuild .92) Canx as TWFU 31.2.92.
G-AKSZ	Taylorcraft Auster 5C (Gipsy Major 1)	1503	F-BGPQ G-AKSZ/TJ457	10. 2.48	
G-AKTA	Taylorcraft Auster 5	1319	TJ227	10. 2.48	To F-BFXX(2) 6/51. Canx 25.5.61.
G-AKTB	Avro 691 Lancastrian C.2	Set.42 & 1247	VM738 (G-AGPR)	17. 2.48	WFU at Tarrant Rushton in 4/51. Scrapped 26.9.51. Canx.
G-AKTC	Avro 691 Lancastrian C.2	Set.54	VL978	17. 2.48	No CofA issued. Broken up for spares at Langley in 6/48. Canx 27.8.48.
G-AKTD	DH.89A Dragon Rapide	6791	NR692	19. 2.48	To F-BFVM 5/51. Canx 4.5.51.
G-AKTE	DH.82A Tiger Moth	3848	5431M N6535	16. 3.48	To OO-RMU 2/50. Canx 22.5.50.
G-AKTF	Taylorcraft Auster 5	1443	TJ399	1. 3.48	Crashed off Beachy Head, in English Channel on 7.2.60. Canx.
G-AKTG	Avro 691 Lancastrian C.2	Set.43 & RY/LB/485398	VL967	24. 1.48	No CofA issued. Broken up for spares at Langley in 8/48. Canx 27.8.48.
G-AKTH(1)	Avro 689 Tudor 2	1425	(TS909)	20. 2.48R	NTU - Not built. Canx 23.4.51.
G-AKTH(2)	Piper J3C-65 Cub (L-4J-PI) (Frame No 13041) (Regd with incorrect c/n 13047)	13211	OO-AGL PH-UCR/45-4471	14. 7.86	
G-AKTI(1)	Avro 689 Tudor 2	1426	(TS910)	20. 2.48R	NTU - Not built. Canx 23.4.51.
G-AKTI(2)	Luscombe 8A Silvaire	4101	N1374K NC1374K	27. 5.87	
G-AKTJ(1)	Avro 689 Tudor 2	1427	(TS911)	20. 2.48R	NTU - Not built. Canx 23.4.51.
G-AKTJ(2)	Piper J3C-85 Cub	22288	N3595K NC3595K	16. 5.88	To EI-BYY 4/90. Canx 14.8.89.
G-AKTK(1)	Avro 689 Tudor 2	1428	(TS912)	20. 2.48R	NTU - Not built. Canx 23.4.51.
G-AKTK(2)	Aeronca 11AC Chief	11AC-1017	N9379E NC9379E	13. 3.89	
G-AKTL(1)	Avro 689 Tudor 2	1429		20. 2.48R	NTU - Not built. Canx 23.4.51.
G-AKTL(2)	Luscombe 8A Silvaire	2581	N71154 NC71154	8. 4.88	To G-SAGE 8/90. Canx.
G-AKTM(1)	Avro 689 Tudor 2	1430		20. 2.48R	NTU - Not built. Canx 23.4.51.
G-AKTM(2)	Luscombe 8F Silvaire 90	6174	C-GGMZ N1547B	2. 6.88	Badly damaged on landing at Sandford Hall, near Oswestry on 21.9.97. Canx as destroyed 12.1.98.
G-AKTN(1)	Avro 689 Tudor 2	1431		20. 2.48R	NTU - Not built. Canx 23.4.51.
G-AKTN(2)	Luscombe 8A Silvaire	3540	N77813 NC77813	22. 7.88	Permit expired 22.10.98.
G-AKTO(1)	Avro 689 Tudor 2	1432		20. 2.48R	NTU - Not built. Canx 23.4.51.
G-AKTO(2)	Aeronca 7BCM Champion (Modified from 7AC standard in 8/50)	7AC-940	N8515X N82311/NC82311	19. 5.88	
G-AKTP(1)	Avro 689 Tudor 2	1433		20. 2.48R	NTU - Not built. Canx 23.4.51.
G-AKTP(2)	PA-17 Vagabond	17-82	N4683H NC4683H	24. 6.88	
G-AKTR(1)	Avro 689 Tudor 2	1434		20. 2.48R	NTU - Not built. Canx 23.4.51.
G-AKTR(2)	Aeronca 7AC Champion	7AC-3017	N58312 NC58312	19. 6.89	
G-AKTS(1)	Avro 689 Tudor 2	1435		20. 2.48R	NTU - Not built. Canx 23.4.51.
G-AKTS(2)	Cessna 120	11875	N77434 NC77434	26. 5.88	
G-AKTT(1)	Avro 689 Tudor 2	1436		20. 2.48R	NTU - Not built. Canx 23.4.51.
G-AKTT(2)	Luscombe 8A Silvaire	3279	N71852 NC71852	21. 7.88	Damaged in take-off crash at Chelford, Cheshire on 6.7.91. (On repair 1/96)
G-AKTU	Vickers 634 Viking 1B	211	WZ356 G-AKTU/EI-ADI	15. 3.48	WFU on 23.6.62. Broken up at Hurn in 9/62. Canx 27.6.62.
G-AKTV(1)	Cierva W.11 Air Horse	W.11/2		. .47R	NTU - To G-ALCW 9/48. Canx.

Regn	Type	c/n	Previous identity	Regn date	Fate or immediate subsequent identity (if known)
G-AKTV(2)	Vickers 634 Viking 1B	208	WZ357 G-AKTV/EI-ADF	15. 3.48	WFU & stored at Southend in 9/63. Broken up in 8/64. Canx.
G-AKTW	Westland-Sikorsky S-51 Widgeon 2 (Built as WS-51 Mk.1A)	WA/H/001	XD649 G-AKTW	27. 2.48	To G-APPR 11/58 as Mk.2. Canx.
G-AKTX	DH.89A Dragon Rapide	6639	X7522	1. 3.48	To Israeli DF/AF as S-72. Canx 17.5.50.
G-AKTY	DH.89A Dragon Rapide	6563	X7403	3. 3.48	To F-BFVR 8/51. Canx 11.5.51.
G-AKTZ	DH.89A Dragon Rapide	6482	R5954	3. 3.48	DBR near Benghazi, Libya on 27.5.57. Canx.
G-AKUA	Miles M.14A Hawk Trainer III	1021	N3988	2. 3.48	Crashed at Burnaston on 21.7.57. Canx.
G-AKUB	DH.89A Dragon Rapide 4	6488	R9560	3. 3.48	To EP-ADN 7/55. Canx 11.6.55.
G-AKUC	DH.89A Dragon Rapide 4	6565	X7405	3. 3.48	To EP-ADM 7/55. Canx 13.6.55.
G-AKUD	Avro 652A Anson 19 Srs.2	1449	VM373 G-AKUD/VM373	31. 3.48	To EL-ABC 8/55. Canx 3.8.55.
G-AKUE(1)	Avro 689 Tudor 2	1437		20. 2.48R	NTU - Not Built. Canx 23.4.51.
G-AKUE(2)	OGMA DH.82A Tiger Moth	P.68	ZS-FZL CR-AGM/FAP...	12. 2.86	Badly damaged in take-off crash from Bryngwynbach Farm, St.Asaph on 2.1.89. CofA expired 6.6.91. (Wreck at Kemble 5/98)
G-AKUF(1)	Avro 689 Tudor 2	1438		20. 2.48R	NTU - Not Built. Canx 23.4.51.
G-AKUF(2)	Luscombe 8F Silvaire	4794	N2067K NC2067K	1. 8.88	
G-AKUG(1)	Avro 689 Tudor 2	1439		20. 2.48R	NTU - Not Built. Canx 23.4.51.
G-AKUG(2)	Luscombe 8A Silvaire	3689	N77962 NC77962	21. 7.88	
G-AKUH(1)	Avro 689 Tudor 2	1440		20. 2.48R	NTU - Not Built. Canx 23.4.51.
G-AKUH(2)	Luscombe 8E Silvaire	4644	N1917K NC1917K	24.10.88	
G-AKUI(1)	Avro 689 Tudor 2	1441		20. 2.48R	NTU - Not Built. Canx 23.4.51.
G-AKUI(2)	Luscombe 8E Silvaire	2464	N45937 NC45937	24.10.88	Badly damaged on take-off from Old Sarum on 26.3.89 and caught by crosswind. Permit expired 17.1.90. (On rebuild 11/96)
G-AKUJ(1)	Avro 689 Tudor 2	1442		20. 2.48R	NTU - Not Built. Canx 23.4.51.
G-AKUJ(2)	Luscombe 8E Silvaire	5282	N2555K NC2555K	4. 8.88	
G-AKUK(1)	Avro 689 Tudor 2	1443		20. 2.48R	NTU - Not Built. Canx 23.4.51.
G-AKUK(2)	Luscombe 8A Silvaire	5793	N1166B NC1166B	28.10.88	
G-AKUL(1)	Avro 689 Tudor 2	1444		20. 2.48R	NTU - Not Built. Canx 23.4.51.
G-AKUL(2)	Luscombe 8A Silvaire	4189	N1462K NC1462K	9. 2.89	Permit expired 21.5.90. (Rebuild nearing completion 3/99)
G-AKUM(1)	Avro 689 Tudor 2	1445		20. 2.48R	NTU - Not Built. Canx 23.4.51.
G-AKUM(2)	Luscombe 8F Silvaire	6452	N2025B	17. 2.88	
G-AKUN(1)	Avro 689 Tudor 2	1446		20. 2.48R	NTU - Not Built. Canx 23.4.51.
G-AKUN(2)	Piper J3C-85 Cub	6914	N38304 NC38304	13. 1.89	
G-AKUO(1)	Avro 689 Tudor 2	1447		20. 2.48R	NTU - Not Built. Canx 23.4.51.
G-AKUO(2)	Aeronca 11AC Chief	11AC-1376	N9730E NC9730E	16. 1.89	
G-AKUP(1)	Avro 689 Tudor 2	1448		20. 2.48R	NTU - Not Built. Canx 23.4.51.
G-AKUP(2)	Luscombe 8E Silvaire (To be floatplane)	5501	N2774K NC2774K	9. 5.89	(Stored 12/96)
G-AKUR	Cessna 140	13819	N1647V NC1647V	26. 1.89	
G-AKUS	DH.89A Dragon Rapide	6805	NR717	11. 3.48	To Israeli DF/AF as S-77. Canx 16.5.50.
G-AKUT	Handley Page HP.61 Halifax B.VI	-	RG736	25. 2.49	To Pakistan AF in 10/49. Canx 21.10.49.
G-AKUU	Handley Page HP.61 Halifax B.VI	-	RG813	25. 2.49	Not converted. Canx 20.7.50 as scrapped.
G-AKUV	Chrislea CH.3 Super Ace Srs.2	104		8. 3.48	Crashed at Thruxton on 26.3.53. Canx.
G-AKUW	Chrislea CH.3 Super Ace Srs.2	105		8. 3.48	
G-AKUX	Chrislea CH.3 Super Ace Srs.2	106		8. 3.48	WFU at Beirut, Lebanon on 3.5.52. Scrapped in 4/66. Canx.
G-AKUY	Chrislea CH.3 Super Ace Srs.2	107		8. 3.48	To LV-XAX/LV-RXV in 9/48. Canx 20.9.48.
G-AKUZ	Chrislea CH.3 Super Ace Srs.2	108		8. 3.48	To LV-XAY/LV-RXW in 9/48. Canx 20.9.48.
G-AKVA	Chrislea CH.3 Super Ace Srs.2	109		8. 3.48	To VP-AAE in 9/54. Canx 31.12.53.
G-AKVB	Chrislea CH.3 Super Ace Srs.2	110		8. 3.48	Crashed at Rettenden, Essex on 22.5.55. Canx.
G-AKVC	Chrislea CH.3 Super Ace Srs.2	111		8. 3.48	To VR-RBI in 4/49. Canx 20.4.49.
G-AKVD	Chrislea CH.3 Super Ace Srs.2	112	(VH-BRP) G-AKVD	8. 3.48	To JA3062 in 2/53. Canx 10.2.53.
G-AKVE	Chrislea CH.3 Super Ace Srs.2	113		8. 3.48	To PT-AJG in 5/50. Canx 10.5.50.
G-AKVF	Chrislea CH.3 Super Ace Srs.2	114	AP-ADT G-AKVF	8. 3.48	Permit expired 17.7.95. (Stored 4/97)
G-AKVG	Chrislea CH.3 Super Ace Srs.2	115		8. 3.48	To HB-EAA in 12/50. Canx 22.4.50.
G-AKVH	Chrislea CH.3 Super Ace Srs.2	116		8. 3.48R	NTU - Construction completed by 4/49, but never flown. Canx 24.2.59.
G-AKVI	Chrislea CH.3 Super Ace Srs.2	117		8. 3.48R	NTU - Construction completed by 4/49, but never flown. Canx 24.2.59.
G-AKVJ	Chrislea CH.3 Super Ace Srs.2	118		8. 3.48R	NTU - Construction completed by 4/49, but never flown. Canx 24.2.59.
G-AKVK	Chrislea CH.3 Super Ace Srs.2	119		8. 3.48R	NTU - Construction completed by 4/49, but never flown. Canx 24.2.59.
G-AKVL	Chrislea CH.3 Super Ace Srs.2	120		8. 3.48R	NTU - Construction completed by 4/49, but never flown. Canx 24.2.59.
G-AKVM(1)	Chrislea CH.3 Super Ace Srs.2	121		8. 3.48R	NTU - Partially completed, construction abandoned. Canx 24.2.59.
G-AKVM(2)	Cessna 120	13431	N3173N NC3173N	10. 1.89	

Regn	Type	c/n	Previous identity	Regn date	Fate or immediate subsequent identity (if known)
G-AKVN(1)	Chrislea CH.3 Super Ace Srs.2	122		8. 3.48R	NTU - Partially completed, construction abandoned. Canx 24.2.59.
G-AKVN(2)	Aeronca 11AC Chief	11AC-469	N3742B NC3742B	13. 1.89	
G-AKVO(1)	Chrislea CH.4 Skyjeep 4	123		8. 3.48R	NTU - Partially completed, construction abandoned. Canx 24.2.59.
G-AKVO(2)	Taylorcraft BC-12D	9845	N44045 NC44045	10. 1.89	
G-AKVP(1)	Chrislea CH.4 Skyjeep 4	124		8. 3.48R	NTU - Partially completed, construction abandoned. Canx 24.2.59.
G-AKVP(2)	Luscombe 8A Silvaire	5549	N2822K NC2822K	21. 7.88	
G-AKVR	Chrislea CH.4 Skyjeep 4	125	VH-OLD VH-RCD/VH-BRP/G-AKVR	8. 3.48	
G-AKVS	Chrislea CH.4 Skyjeep 4	126		8. 3.48	To F-OAMP in 10/52. Canx 2.10.52.
G-AKVT	Chrislea CH.4 Skyjeep 4	127		8. 3.48	To CX-AMR in 1/51. Canx 26.7.50.
G-AKVU	DH.89A Dragon Rapide	6476	R9548	10. 3.48	To F-BGPM in 6/52. Canx 1.4.52.
G-AKVV	Percival P.28 Proctor I	K.267	P6233	30. 3.48	WFU at Blackbushe in 11/50. Canx.
G-AKVW	Avro 652A Anson I (Quoted as ex.L7909 but is possibly ex.MG292 sold to British Air Transport on 18.8.47)	"7909"		10. 3.48	To (VR-AAI) in 1/53 and probably scrapped at Bahrein. Canx 27.1.53.
G-AKVX	Douglas C-47A-10-DK Dakota	12587	KG475 42-92752	16. 3.48	To ZS-BYX in 3/48. Canx 9.6.48.
G-AKVY	DH.82A Tiger Moth	85789	DE904	18. 3.48	To VT-DBJ in 1/49. Canx 19.1.49.
G-AKVZ	Miles M.38 Messenger 4B	6352	RH427	25. 6.48	
G-AKWA	Vickers-Supermarine 507 Sea Otter ASR.I	-	JM739	2. 7.48	Not converted. Scrapped at Langley in 1949. Canx.
G-AKWB	Percival P.34 Proctor III	H.320	HM426	20. 7.48	To VP-AAD 2/53. Canx 12.8.52.
G-AKWC	Percival P.34 Proctor III	H.375	LZ568	20. 7.48	Not converted. Scrapped. Canx 21.3.51.
G-AKWD	Percival P.34 Proctor III	H.381	LZ574	20. 7.48	To VH-ABN 11/51. Canx 9.11.51.
G-AKWE	Percival P.34 Proctor III	H.303	HM409	23. 3.48	WFU at Staverton in 4/52. Canx.
G-AKWF	Percival P.34 Proctor III	H.123	DX217	23. 3.48	To EC-AGL 6/52. Canx 12.4.52.
G-AKWG	Taylorcraft Auster 5	1134	RT471	23. 3.48	Crashed at Gosport on 19.4.50. Canx.
G-AKWH	Taylorcraft Auster 5	2051	TW507	25. 3.48	To VP-KID 11/49. Canx 23.5.50.
G-AKWI	Taylorcraft Auster 5	984	MT346	25. 3.48	Sold abroad 5/48. Canx.
G-AKWJ	Percival P.34 Proctor III	H.45	R7539	25. 3.48	WFU at Biggin Hill on 28.3.62. Broken up in 1962. Canx.
G-AKWK	Taylorcraft Auster 5	1375	TJ299	25. 3.48	To TC-AYLA 4/52. Canx 17.3.52.
G-AKWL	Percival P.31C Proctor IV	H.682	NP298	30. 3.48	WFU at Blackbushe in 9/56. Canx.
G-AKWM	Percival P.34 Proctor III	H.429	LZ639	31. 3.48	Not converted. Scrapped at Thame. Canx.
G-AKWN	Percival P.34 Proctor III	H.426	LZ636	31. 3.48	Not converted. Scrapped at Thame. Canx.
G-AKWO	Percival P.30 Proctor II	H.44	BV544	31. 3.48	To VH-SCC 5/55. Canx 4.10.54.
G-AKWP	Percival P.34 Proctor III	H.37	R7535	31. 3.48	WFU at Denham in 2/61. Canx.
G-AKWR	Percival P.34 Proctor III	H.498	LZ716	31. 3.48	DBR at Shannon, Ireland on 7.7.63. Canx.
G-AKWS	Taylorcraft Auster 5A-160	1237	RT610	1. 4.48	
G-AKWT	Taylorcraft Auster 5	998	MT360	1. 4.48	Crashed at Tollerton in 7.8.48. CofA expired 22.7.49. (Stored 9/96 Newark)
G-AKWU	Percival P.34 Proctor III	H.537	LZ767	9. 4.48	To France in 11/49. Canx.
G-AKWV	Percival P.34 Proctor III	H.260	HM350	9. 4.48	Collided with Proctor G-AIKJ at Sutton, near Southend on 20.6.53. Canx.
G-AKWW	Percival P.34 Proctor III	H.471	LZ689	9. 4.48	Crashed in the Italian Alps on 14.11.48. Canx.
G-AKWX	DH.82A Tiger Moth	3739	N5471	8. 4.48	To OO-TMB 10/48. Canx 13.10.48.
G-AKWY	DH.82A Tiger Moth	83138	T5371	8. 4.48	Crashed at Petersfield on 27.8.57. Canx.
G-AKWZ	DH.82A Tiger Moth	86253	NL782	6. 4.48	WFU at Barton. Scrapped in 10/49. Canx.
G-AKXA	DH.82A Tiger Moth	85141	T6912	6. 4.48	Crashed at Barton on 8.10.49. Canx.
G-AKXB	DH.82A Tiger Moth	85754	DE856	10. 4.48	To OO-TMA 10/48. Canx 13.10.48.
G-AKXC	DH.82A Tiger Moth	82040	N6776	10. 4.48	To ZK-BCE 1/53. Canx 3.11.52.
G-AKXD	DH.82A Tiger Moth	84136	T7749	10. 4.48	DBR in forced landing in Lincolnshire on 10.2.60. Canx.
G-AKXE	DH.82A Tiger Moth	82065	N6795	14. 6.51	To ZK-BAI 10/51. Canx 5.10.51.
G-AKXF	DH.82A Tiger Moth	84742	T6368	10. 4.48	To OO-AJM 6/50. Canx 6.5.50.
G-AKXG	DH.82A Tiger Moth	84572	T6105	10. 4.48	To VH-KYA 3/55. Canx 30.3.55.
G-AKXH	DH.82A Tiger Moth	84568	T6101	10. 4.48	To ZK-AVB 9/50. Canx 22.9.50.
G-AKXI	Percival P.30 Proctor II	K.405	Z7216	9. 4.48	To VH-BQO 8/51. Canx 29.8.51.
G-AKXJ	Percival P.34 Proctor III	H.209	HM295	9. 4.48	To PT-ALZ 7/52. Canx 9.7.52.
G-AKXK	Percival P.34 Proctor III	H.252	HM342	9. 4.48	Crashed at Beirut, Lebanon on 19.6.58. Canx.
G-AKXL	Percival P.34 Proctor III	H.311	HM417	9. 4.48	Not converted. Canx.
G-AKXM	Miles M.14A Hawk Trainer III	864	N3816	12. 4.48	To Egyptian AF in 9/49. Canx 2.9.49.
G-AKXN	Miles M.14A Hawk Trainer III	364	L5932	12. 4.48	To Egyptian AF in 9/49. Canx 2.9.49.
G-AKXO	DH.82A Tiger Moth	83548	T7121	5. 4.48	Crashed at Shoreham on 13.3.64. Canx.
G-AKXP	Taylorcraft Auster 5	1017	NJ633	13. 4.48	Crashed on take off St.Mary's, Isles of Scilly on 9.4.70. CofA expired 19.12.70. (On long term rebuild by Classic Vintage Aircraft Svs 6/95)
G-AKXR	Taylorcraft Auster 5	1289	TJ200	13. 4.48	To SE-CGL 8/58. Canx 28.7.58.
G-AKXS	DH.82A Tiger Moth	83512	T7105	13. 4.48	
G-AKXT	Handley Page HP.70 Halifax C.VIII	1304	PP220	20. 4.48	CofA expired 28.12.49. WFU at Bovingdon. Canx 28.12.51.
G-AKXU	DH.82A Tiger Moth	86247	NL776	13. 4.48	Not converted. Broken up at Hamble in 1948. Canx.
G-AKXV	DH.82A Tiger Moth	85648	DE718	13. 4.48	Not converted. Broken up at Hamble in 1948. Canx.
G-AKXW	DH.82A Tiger Moth	83820	T7441	13. 4.48	Not converted. To Instructional Airframe at Perth in 9/61. Canx. - See "G-ERTY".
G-AKXX	Avro 652A Anson I	-	AX256	13. 4.48	No CofA issued, used as instructional airframe. Canx 4.2.49 as reduced to produce.
G-AKXY	Avro 652A Anson I	-	LV201	13. 4.48	No CofA issued, used for spares and insured for ground risks only wef 18.5.52. Canx 4.2.49 as reduced to produce.
G-AKXZ	Percival P.34 Proctor III	H.147	DX229	7. 4.48	Crashed at Kosti, Sudan on 2.8.52. Canx.

Regn	Type	c/n	Previous identity	Regn date	Fate or immediate subsequent identity (if known)
G-AKYA	Percival P.44 Proctor V	Ae.112	X-1	20. 8.48	To JY-ACM 9/62. Canx 4.8.62.
G-AKYB	Percival P.44 Proctor V	Ae.116		16. 8.48	WFU at Biggin Hill in 3/64. Burnt in 9/65. Canx.
G-AKYC	Percival P.44 Proctor V	Ae.114		6.12.48	WFU at Lympne in 4/55. Canx.
G-AKYD	Percival P.44 Proctor V	Ae.119		16.11.48	Crashed off Flushing, Holland on 14.8.58. Canx.
G-AKYE	Percival P.50 Prince	P.50/11		18.12.50	To PP-NBF 5/51. Canx 4.5.51.
G-AKYF	Stinson L-5 Sentinel	-	42-90552	8. 4.48	To VP-KHM 9/49. Canx 16.9.49.
G-AKYG	Percival P.34 Proctor III	H.294	HM400	16. 4.48	Not converted. Broken up at Squires Gate in 1957. Canx.
G-AKYH	Vickers-Supermarine 507 Sea Otter ASR.I	-	(G-AJVR) JM966	16. 4.48	To R.Netherlands Navy as 18-3. Canx 6.10.49.
G-AKYI	Percival P.31 Proctor IV	H.718	NP347	16. 4.48	Not converted. Scrapped at Squires Gate in 1949. Canx.
G-AKYJ	Percival P.31 Proctor IV	H.789	RM186	16. 4.48	To D-EJUT 1/58. Canx 2.1.58.
G-AKYK	Percival P.31 Proctor IV	H.807	RM225	16. 4.48	Broken up at Squires Gate in 11/50. Canx.
G-AKYL	DH(Aust).82A Tiger Moth	225	VH-BCY R.Australian AF A17-224	27. 4.48	To ZK-AXT 12/50. Canx 16.11.50.
G-AKYM	DH(Aust).82A Tiger Moth	T137 & DHA.329	VH-AUE R.Australian AF A17-310	27. 4.48	To ZK-AXU 12/50. Canx 16.12.50.
G-AKYN	DH.82A Tiger Moth	85072	T6803	23. 4.48	Not converted. Broken up at Croydon in 1949. Canx.
G-AKYO	DH.82A Tiger Moth	83899	T7470	23. 4.48	To D-EMUT 6/56. Canx 4.6.65.
G-AKYP	DH.82A Tiger Moth	84068	T7679	23. 4.48	To CR-LCN 8/51. Canx 1.8.51.
G-AKYR	DH.82A Tiger Moth	83022	R5140	28. 4.48	Crashed near Stapleford on 4.6.58. Canx.
G-AKYS	DH.104 Dove 2B (Originally regd as Dove 1)	04135	I-ORIF G-AKYS	29. 4.48	To "6-VPRD"/6V-PRD 8/64. Canx 18.3.65.
G-AKYT	Taylorcraft Auster 4A (Originally regd as an Auster 4)	891	MT165	30. 4.48	To F-BECV 8/51. Canx.
G-AKYU	Taylorcraft Auster 5	2057	TW512	11. 5.48	To F-DADS 11/54. Canx 5.11.54.
G-AKYV	Beechcraft 35 Bonanza	D-446	ZS-BPX	12. 5.48	To VP-YGS 4/48. Canx.
G-AKYW	DH.89A Dragon Rapide	6581	X7440	18. 5.48	To LV-AGR 11/48. Canx 23.11.48.
G-AKYX	DH.89A Dragon Rapide	6864	NR788	18. 5.48	To LV-AEN 11/48. Canx 14.9.48.
G-AKYY	DH.89A Dragon Rapide	6822	NR734	18. 5.48	To LV-AES 11/48. Canx 23.11.48.
G-AKYZ	DH.89A Dragon Rapide	6789	NR690	18. 5.48	To LV-AEO 11/48. Canx 23.11.48.
G-AKZA	DH.89A Dragon Rapide	6892	NR828	18. 5.48	To LV-AEP 12/48. Canx 18.10.48.
G-AKZB	DH.89A Dragon Rapide	6790	NR691	18. 5.48	Crashed at St.Just Airport, Lands End on 12.12.61. Canx.
G-AKZC	Miles M.38 Messenger 4A	-	RH372	14. 5.48	WFU at Stapleford in 5/59. Canx.
G-AKZD	Percival P.34 Proctor III	H.249	HM339	5. 8.48	Not converted. Scrapped at Squires Gate in 1948. Canx.
G-AKZE	Percival P.34 Proctor III	H.405	LZ598	5. 8.48	Not converted. Scrapped at Squires Gate in 1948. Canx.
G-AKZF	Percival P.34 Proctor III	H.439	LZ649	5. 8.48	Not converted. Scrapped at Squires Gate in 1948. Canx.
G-AKZG	Percival P.34 Proctor III	H.530	LZ760	5. 8.48	To VH-KZG 1/57. Canx 17.1.57.
G-AKZH	DH.89A Dragon Rapide	6529	X7369	19. 5.48	To CR-GAJ 5/52. Canx 7.5.52.
G-AKZI	DH.89A Dragon Rapide	6536	X7376	19. 5.48	To Israeli DF/AF as S-76 in 9/48. Canx in 5/50.
G-AKZJ	DH.89A Dragon Rapide	6549	X7389	19. 5.48	To Israeli DF/AF; to 4X-ACU in 5/49. Canx 6/50.
G-AKZK	DH.82A Tiger Moth	83815	T7436	22. 5.48	To F-OATP 9/55. Canx 15.9.55.
G-AKZL	DH.82A Tiger Moth	85750	DE852	22. 5.48	To F-OASJ 8/55. Canx 27.9.54.
G-AKZM	DH.82A Tiger Moth	85909	DF173	22. 5.48	To ZK-BES 10/53. Canx 22.9.53.
G-AKZN	Percival P.34A Proctor III	K.386	Z7197	24. 5.48	CofA expired 29.11.63. (Allotted 8380M) (On display 10/95 Hendon)
G-AKZO	DH.89A Dragon Rapide	6575	X7415	20. 5.48	To F-BHFM 4/61. Canx 9.8.60.
G-AKZP	DH.89A Dragon Rapide	6882	NR806	20. 5.48	Crashed near Hammamet, Tunis on 16.3.57. Canx.
G-AKZR	Percival P.34 Proctor III	H.159	DX235	20. 5.48	WFU at Denham in 7/53. Canx.
G-AKZS	Percival P.34 Proctor III	H.257	HM347	20. 5.48	To VH-BEG 1/54. Canx 15.9.53.
G-AKZT	DH.89A Dragon Rapide	6894	LR-AAE NR830	28. 5.48	To CY-AAK 4/52. Canx 9.4.52.
G-AKZU	Miles M.38 Messenger 4A	-	RH369	21. 5.48	To F-BGOM 8/52. Canx 15.7.52.
G-AKZV	DH.89A Dragon Rapide	6843	LR-AAD NR755	24. 5.48	To LV-AGW 3/49. Canx.
G-AKZW	DH.89A Dragon Rapide	6896	LR-AAF NR832	24. 5.48	To CR-GAI 5/52. Canx 26.4.52.
G-AKZX	Miles M.38 Messenger 4A	-	RH424	21. 5.48	Crashed on take-off from Rochester on 24.7.65. Canx.
G-AKZY	Messerschmitt Bf.108D-1 Taifun	3059	Luftwaffe D-ERPN	7. 6.48	To HB-DUB 1/50. Canx.
G-AKZZ(1)	Percival P.44 Proctor V	-		. .48R	NTU. Canx.
G-AKZZ(2)	DH.82A Tiger Moth	84105	T7728	4. 4.51	Crashed in sea off Bournemouth Pier on 30.5.53. Canx.
G-ALAA(1)	Percival P.44 Proctor V	-		. .48R	NTU. Canx.
G-ALAA(2)	DH.82A Tiger Moth	86284	NL825	17. 4.51	To ZK-AZI in 7/51. Canx.
G-ALAB(1)	Percival P.44 Proctor V	-		. .48R	NTU. Canx.
G-ALAB(2)	Auster J/1B Aiglet	2708		1. 5.51	Crashed off Caguari, Tunisia on 10.11.53. Canx.
G-ALAC(1)	Percival P.44 Proctor V	-		. .48R	NTU. Canx.
G-ALAC(2)	Miles M.38 Messenger 4A (Converted to Messenger 5 by 9/51)	6345	G-2-1 G-ALAC/(RH420)	2. 5.51	Crashed at Faversham on 22.9.51. Canx.
G-ALAD(1)	Percival P.44 Proctor V	-		. .48R	NTU. Canx.
G-ALAD(2)	DH.82A Tiger Moth	-	"T6296"	14. 6.51	To ZK-BAW 11/52. Canx.
G-ALAE	Miles M.38 Messenger 4A (Originally regd as Messenger 1)	6346	RH421	28. 5.48	DBR whilst landing at Epping Upland on 2.8.58. Canx.
G-ALAF	Miles M.38 Messenger 4A (Originally regd as Messenger 1)	6350	RH425	28. 5.48	To ZK-BED 2/54. Canx 19.2.54.
G-ALAG	Miles M.38 Messenger 4A (Originally regd as Messenger 1)	6347	F-BGQZ G-ALAG/RH422	28. 5.48	Crashed at Gittelde Harz, West Germany on 30.12.57. Canx.
G-ALAH	Miles M.38 Messenger 4A (Originally regd as Messenger 1)	-	RH377	28. 5.48	CofA expired 18.4.65. WFU on 18.4.65. (Stored as G-ALAH in 3/95 at Sabadella, Barcelona, Spain)
G-ALAI	Miles M.38 Messenger 4A (Originally regd as Messenger 1)	6348	RH423	19. 7.48	Canx as WFU 6.6.70.
G-ALAJ	Miles M.38 Messenger 4A	6354	RH429	27. 5.48	DBR in gales at Christchurch on 29.7.56. Canx.
G-ALAK	Lockheed L.749A-79-32 Constellation	2548	(CX-BHD) (N1489)/G-ALAK/EI-ACR/(VP-C..)/(NC86534)	22. 6.48	To CP-797 1/68. Canx 8.8.67.

Regn	Type	c/n	Previous identity	Regn date	Fate or immediate subsequent identity (if known)
G-ALAL	Lockheed L.749A-79-32 Constellation	2549	EI-ACS (NC86535)	22. 6.48	To OB-R-899(1) 4/67. Canx.
G-ALAM	Lockheed L.749A-79-32 Constellation	2554	EI-ADA (NC.....)	22. 6.48	Crashed after overshooting landing at Kallang Airport, Singapore on 13.3.54. Canx.
G-ALAN	Lockheed L.749A-79-32 Constellation	2555	EI-ADD (NC.....)	22. 6.48	To N1554V 3/59. Canx 20.3.59.
G-ALAO	Lockheed L.749A-79-32 Constellation	2566	EI-ADE (F-....)	22. 6.48	To N4902C 9/58. Canx 26.9.58.
G-ALAP	Miles M.38 Messenger 4A (Originally regd as Messenger 1)	-	RH368	28. 5.48	Crashed at Bark Island gliding site, near Halifax on 24.5.61. Canx.
G-ALAR	Miles M.38 Messenger 4A	-	RH371	28. 5.48	To VP-KJL 2/52. Canx 8.1.52.
G-ALAS	DH.89A Dragon Rapide	6484	R9556	1. 6.48	NTU - To G-ALEJ 6/48. Canx.
G-ALAT	DH.89A Dragon Rapide	6851	NR775	26. 5.48	To F-BHCE 1/55. Canx 24.1.55.
G-ALAU	DH.89A Dragon Rapide	6609	X7492	26. 5.48	To LV-AER 12/48. Canx 15.10.48.
G-ALAV	Miles M.38 Messenger 4A (Originally regd as Messenger 1)	6353	RH428	28. 5.48	WFU at Skegness in 3/58. Canx.
G-ALAW	Miles M.38 Messenger 4A (Originally regd as Messenger 1)	6351	RH426	1. 6.48	CofA expired 21.4.67. WFU & dismantled at Elstree. Canx.
G-ALAX	DH.89A Dragon Rapide (Fuselage stored .94 with components from G-AFRK, G-AHGC, G-AHJS and G-ASRJ)	6930	RL948	27. 5.48	CofA expired 8.3.67 & WFU. Rebuilding abandoned at Luton.
G-ALAY	DH.89A Dragon Rapide	6942	RL960	27. 5.48	To LV-AGX 3/49. Canx 30.12.48.
G-ALAZ	DH.89A Dragon Rapide	6932	RL950	27. 5.48	To OO-CFI 7/48. Canx 27.7.48.
G-ALBA	DH.89A Dragon Rapide	6821	NR733	27. 5.48	WFU at Baginton on 29.9.61. Canx.
G-ALBB	DH.89A Dragon Rapide	6829	NR741	27. 5.48	Crashed at Heathrow on 1.8.52. Canx.
G-ALBC	DH.89A Dragon Rapide	6572	X7412	27. 5.48	Crashed on high ground near Edale, Derbyshire on 30.12.63. Canx.
G-ALBD	DH.82A Tiger Moth	84130	T7748	27. 5.48	Hit trees on landing at Leopoldsburg, Belgium on 24.5.81. CofA expired 31.10.81. (Stored in Holland pending rebuild)
G-ALBE	Miles M.38 Messenger 4A (Originally regd as Messenger 1)	4691	RG327	26. 5.48	WFU at Newtownards, Northern Ireland in 11/65. Derelict at Gortin, Co.Londonderry in 1969. Canx.
G-ALBF	DH.104 Dove 5 (Originally regd as Dove 1, then Dove 1B in 1957, then Dove 5 in 4/68)	04152		9. 6.48	To YI-AGA 5/73. Canx 1.5.73.
G-ALBG	Douglas C-47B-30-DK Dakota	14014/25459	KG782 43-48198	8. 6.48	To French AF as 48198 in 5/49. Canx 11.5.49.
G-ALBH	DH.89A Dragon Rapide	6607	(LX-LAC) G-ALBH/X7490	7. 6.48	To OO-CJD 9/60. Canx 28.9.60.
G-ALBI	DH.89A Dragon Rapide	6525	LX-LAD G-ALBI/X7352	7. 6.48	To F-OBRV 8/60. Canx 16.8.60.
G-ALBJ	Taylorcraft Auster 5	1831	TW501	3. 6.48	
G-ALBK	Taylorcraft Auster 5	1273	RT644	3. 6.48	
G-ALBL	Fairey Primer 1	F.8455	G-6-4	7. 6.48	Broken up in 1949. Canx.
G-ALBM	DH.104 Dove 5 (Originally regd as Srs.1, then to Dove 1B, then Dove 5B)	04171	G-5-1 G-ALBM	28. 6.48	WFU on 17.2.73. Broken up by Spooner Aviation, Shoreham. Canx 19.7.74.
G-ALBN	Bristol 173 Mk.1	12871		22. 7.48	To RAF as XF785 in 1953. Canx.
G-ALBO	Bristol 175 Britannia Srs.101	12873	(WB470) (VX442)	11. 6.48	To RAF as Instructional Airframe as 7708M in 10/60. DBF at St.Athan on 21.5.68. Canx.
G-ALBP	Miles M.38 Messenger 4A (Originally regd as Messenger 1)	-	RH376	18. 6.48	To VH-WYN 4/55. Canx 7.7.55.
G-ALBR	Miles M.38 Messenger 4A (Originally regd as Messenger 1)	-	RH378	18. 6.48	Crashed on take off from Elstree on 2.7.49. Canx.
G-ALBS	Handley Page HP.70 Halifax C.VIII	1313	PP229	14. 6.48	Not converted. Scrapped at Bovingdon in 8/50. Canx 5.3.52.
G-ALBT	Handley Page HP.70 Halifax C.VIII	1343	PP270	14. 6.48	Not converted. Scrapped at Bovingdon in 8/50. Canx 5.3.52.
G-ALBU	Handley Page HP.70 Halifax C.VIII	1381	PP319	14. 6.48	Not converted. Scrapped at Bovingdon in 8/50. Canx 1.5.50.
G-ALBV	Handley Page HP.70 Halifax C.VIII	1383	PP321	14. 6.48	Not converted. Scrapped at Bovingdon in 8/50. Canx 30.8.49.
G-ALBW	Taylorcraft Auster 5	1470	TJ410	16. 6.48	Crashed near Booker on 24.7.52. Canx.
G-ALBX	Avro 685 York C.1	PC.4494	FM400	15. 6.48	Crashed shortly after take-off from Wunstorf, West Germany on 19.6.49. Canx.
G-ALBY	DH.104 Dove 1	04171		28. 6.48	To Indian AF as HW526 in 12/48. Canx 26.12.48.
G-ALBZ	Handley Page HP.70 Halifax C.VIII	1348	PP275	29. 9.48	Destroyed in collision with Halifax C.VIII G-AHWN on landing at Schleswigland on 10.5.49. Canx 12.6.49.
G-ALCA	Douglas C-47A-1-DK Dakota	12159	AP-ABW G-ALCA/South African AF 6817/FZ604/42-92366	23. 6.48	Restored as AP-ABW 10/48. Canx 2.10.48.
G-ALCB	Douglas C-47A-40-DL Dakota	9878	AP-ADH G-ALCB/South African AF 6806/FD957/42-24016	20. 7.48	Broken up at Tollerton in 12/50. Canx.
G-ALCC	Douglas C-47A-50-DL Dakota	10106	6808 South African AF/FL523/42-24244	11.10.48	To (5B-CBE)/5B-CAW in 3/69. Canx 6.3.69.
G-ALCD(1)	Douglas C-47A Dakota III	-		. .48R	NTU. Canx.
G-ALCD(2)	Handley Page HP.70 Halifax C.VI	-	ST808	2. 5.49	Used for spares and broken up at Bovingdon in 1949. Canx 27.7.49.
G-ALCE	Percival P.34 Proctor III	H.266	HM356	28. 6.48	To I-ADOG 8/48. Canx 28.8.48.
G-ALCF	Percival P.34 Proctor III	H.466	LZ684	28. 6.48	To VH-AHR 6/49. Canx 14.6.49.
G-ALCG	Percival P.34 Proctor III	H.368	LZ561	28. 6.48	To I-MARG 2/49. Canx 13.9.48.
G-ALCH	Percival P.34 Proctor III	H.447	LZ657	18. 6.48	WFU at Squires Gate in 5/50. Canx.
G-ALCI	Percival P.34 Proctor III	H.113	DX199	18. 6.48	Not converted. Scrapped at Squires Gate in 1949. Canx.
G-ALCJ	Percival P.34 Proctor III	H.389	LZ582	18. 6.48	Scrapped at Squires Gate in 5/50. Canx.
G-ALCK	Percival P.34A Proctor III	H.536	LZ766	18. 6.48	CofA expired 19.6.63 & WFU at Woolsington. (On display 7/99 at Duxford)
G-ALCL	Percival P.34 Proctor III	H.284	HM390	7. 7.48	WFU at Newtownards, Northern Ireland in 4/54. Canx.

Regn	Type	c/n	Previous identity	Regn date	Fate or immediate subsequent identity (if known)
G-ALCM	Percival P.50 Prince I	P.50/1	G-23-1	14. 8.48	Broken up at Luton in 7/56. Canx.
G-ALCN	Percival P.34 Proctor III	H.386	LZ579	20. 7.48	To LR-ABJ. Canx 12.12.50.
G-ALCO	Percival P.34 Proctor III	H.464	LZ682	20. 7.48	WFU at Croydon in 6/55. Canx.
G-ALCP	Percival P.34 Proctor III	H.470	LZ688	20. 7.48	Not converted. Canx.
G-ALCR	Percival P.34 Proctor III	H.145	DX228	19. 7.48	To F-BFPS 5/50. Canx 11.5.50.
G-ALCS(1)	Saab 91A Safir	91-120	SE-BNH	. .48R	NTU - To VT-CYU /48. Canx.
G-ALCS(2)	Miles M.65 Gemini 3C (Originally regd as Series 3A with c/n 6534)	WAL/C/1001		7.11.49	WFU in 1983. Canx by CAA 30.5.84.
G-ALCT	Taylorcraft Auster 5	1532	TJ513	28. 7.48	To SE-BZB 10/53. Canx 22.9.53.
G-ALCU	DH.104 Dove 2B	04022	(EI-...) G-ALCU/VT-CEH	3. 8.48	CofA expired 16.3.73. Canx as WFU 8.9.78. (On display 4/96 Baginton)
G-ALCV	Cierva W.11 Air Horse	W.11/1	VZ724 G-ALCV	11. 8.48	Restored to RAF as VZ724 10/48. Canx.
G-ALCW	Cierva W.11 Air Horse	W.11/2	(G-AKTV)	23. 9.48	NTU - To RAF as WA555 in 1/51. Canx 8.1.51.
G-ALCX	Handley Page HP.70 Halifax C.VIII	1397	PP335	29. 9.48	WFU at Bovingdon in 11/49. Scrapped in 1952. Canx.
G-ALCY	Handley Page HP.61 Halifax B.VI	-	RG719	4.10.48	Not converted. Broken up at Bovingdon in 5/49. Canx 2.5.49.
G-ALCZ	Handley Page HP.61 Halifax B.VI	-	RG774	4.10.48	Not converted. Broken up at Bovingdon in 5/49. Canx 2.5.49.
G-ALDA	Handley Page HP.81 Hermes IV (Conv. to Mk.IVA, then back)	HP.81/2	WZ838 G-ALDA	6. 9.49	WFU at Southend in 12/64. Scrapped in 1965. Canx.
G-ALDB	Handley Page HP.81 Hermes IVA (Originally regd as Mk.IV)	HP.81/3	WZ839 G-ALDB	27.10.49	Crashed at St.Pithiviers, France on 23.7.52. Canx.
G-ALDC	Handley Page HP.81 Hermes IV (Conv. to Mk.IVA, then back)	HP.81/4	WZ840 G-ALDC	27.10.49	DBR on landing at Southend on 9.10.60. Broken up in 3/62. Canx.
G-ALDD	Handley Page HP.81 Hermes IVA (Originally regd as Mk.IV)	HP.81/5		27.10.49	WFU at Stansted on 19.3.59. Broken up. Canx as WFU 17.7.59.
G-ALDE	Handley Page HP.81 Hermes IVA (Originally regd as Mk.IV)	HP.81/6	VP-BBO G-ALDE	27.10.49	WFU at Hurn in 10/61. Scrapped at Hurn in 5/62. Canx.
G-ALDF	Handley Page HP.81 Hermes IVA (Originally regd as Mk.IV)	HP.81/7	WZ841 G-ALDF	27.10.49	Crashed in sea off Trapani, Sicily on 25.8.52. Canx.
G-ALDG	Handley Page HP.81 Hermes IV (Conv. to Mk.IVA, then back)	HP.81/8		27.10.49	WFU at Gatwick in 9/62. CofA expired 9.1.63. (Fuselage only on display 7/99 at Duxford)
G-ALDH	Handley Page HP.81 Hermes IVA (Originally regd as Mk.IV)	HP.81/9		27.10.49	DBR on landing at Heathrow on 8.3.60. Canx.
G-ALDI	Handley Page HP.81 Hermes IV (Conv. to Mk.IVA, then back)	HP.81/10	XJ309 G-ALDI	27.10.49	WFU at Stansted. Scrapped in 10/62. Canx.
G-ALDJ	Handley Page HP.81 Hermes IVA (Originally regd as Mk.IV)	HP.81/11		27.10.49	Crashed into forest & DBF on approach to Blackbushe on 5.11.56. Canx.
G-ALDK	Handley Page HP.81 Hermes IVA (Originally regd as Mk.IV)	HP.81/12	XJ281 G-ALDK	27.10.49	DBR landing on Drigh Road, Karachi, Pakistan on 5.8.56. Scrapped locally. Canx.
G-ALDL	Handley Page HP.81 Hermes IV (Conv. to Mk.IVA, then back)	HP.81/13	VP-BBP G-ALDL	27.10.49	Broken up at Southend in 1962. Canx.
G-ALDM	Handley Page HP.81 Hermes IV (Conv. to Mk.IVA, then back)	HP.81/14		27.10.49	WFU at Hurn on 23.11.60. Scrapped in 5/68. Canx.
G-ALDN	Handley Page HP.81 Hermes IV	HP.81/15		27.10.49	DBR on forced landing 110 kms SE of Atar, Sahara Desert on 26.5.52. Canx.
G-ALDO	Handley Page HP.81 Hermes IVA (Originally regd as Mk.IV)	HP.81/16		27.10.49	WFU at Blackbushe. Scrapped in 3/59. Canx.
G-ALDP	Handley Page HP.81 Hermes IV (Conv. to Mk.IVA, then back)	HP.81/17	XJ269 G-ALDP	27.10.49	WFU at Stansted. Scrapped in 10/62. Canx.
G-ALDR	Handley Page HP.81 Hermes IV (Conv. to Mk.IVA, then back)	HP.81/18		27.10.49	WFU at Stansted on 4.6.59. Broken up. Canx.
G-ALDS	Handley Page HP.81 Hermes IV (Conv. to Mk.IVA, then back)	HP.81/19		27.10.49	CofA expired 30.1.60 & WFU at Stansted. Broken up. Canx.
G-ALDT	Handley Page HP.81 Hermes IVA (Originally regd as Mk.IV)	HP.81/20	VP-BBQ G-ALDT/OD-ACB/G-ALDT	27.10.49	CofA expired in 1/62 & WFU. Broken up at Southend in 6/62. Canx.
G-ALDU	Handley Page HP.81 Hermes IV (Conv. to Mk.IVA, then back)	HP.81/21	XJ288 G-ALDU	27.10.49	WFU at Southend in 10/62. Scrapped in 11/62. Canx.
G-ALDV	Handley Page HP.81 Hermes IVA (Originally regd as Mk.IV)	HP.81/22		27.10.49	DBF on crashing near Bishops Stortford on 1.4.58. Canx.
G-ALDW	Handley Page HP.81 Hermes IV (Conv. to Mk.IVA, then back)	HP.81/23		27.10.49	DBR after bomb explosion at Nicosia, Cyprus on 4.3.56. Canx.
G-ALDX	Handley Page HP.81 Hermes IV (Conv. to Mk.IVA, then back)	HP.81/24	XJ267 G-ALDX	27.10.49	WFU at Blackbushe on 30.11.59. Broken up. Canx.
G-ALDY	Handley Page HP.81 Hermes IV (Conv. to Mk.IVA, then back)	HP.81/25	OD-ACC G-ALDY	27.10.49	WFU at Stansted in 12/58. Broken up. Canx.
G-ALDZ	Handley Page HP.61 Halifax B.VI	-	RG822	4.10.48	Not converted. Broken up at Bovingdon in 5/49. Canx 2.5.49.
G-ALEA	Handley Page HP.61 Halifax B.VI	-	RG826	4.10.48	Not converted. Broken up at Bovingdon in 5/49. Canx 2.5.49.
G-ALEB	Handley Page HP.61 Halifax B.VI	-	RG827	4.10.48	Not converted. Broken up at Bovingdon in 5/49. Canx 2.5.49.
G-ALEC(1)	Handley Page HP.61 Halifax B.VI	-	RG847	4.10.48	Not converted. Broken up at Bovingdon in 5/49. Canx 2.5.49.
G-ALEC(2)	DH.104 Dove 6B (Originally regd as Dove 2A)	04402	(G-APPD) XB-SUU	25.11.58	Fatal crash into North Road, Cardiff on 6.5.59. Canx.
G-ALED	Handley Page HP.61 Halifax B.VI	-	RG853	4.10.48	Not converted. Broken up at Bovingdon in 5/49. Canx 2.5.49.
G-ALEE	Handley Page HP.61 Halifax B.VI	-	RG877	4.10.48	Not converted. Broken up at Bovingdon in 5/49. Canx 2.5.49.
G-ALEF	Handley Page HP.70 Halifax C.VIII	1399	LN-OAT PP337	9.10.48	CofA expired on 20.11.50 & WFU at Luton. Scrapped. Canx 7.8.51.
G-ALEG	Westland-Sikorsky S-51 Mk.1A	WA/H/002		6.10.48	To RAF as WZ749 3/52. Canx 9.11.51.
G-ALEH	PA-17 Vagabond	17-87	N4689H NC4689H	17. 8.81	
G-ALEI	Westland-Sikorsky S-51 Mk.1A	WA/H/004		6.10.48	Crashed at Sion, Switzerland on 4.5.50. Canx.

Regn	Type	c/n	Previous identity	Regn date	Fate or immediate subsequent identity (if known)
G-ALEJ	DH.89A Dragon Rapide	6484	(G-ALAS) R9556	1. 6.48	Crashed at Eccleshall in 14.9.56. Canx.
G-ALEK	Avro 652A Anson I	-	NK242	5.10.48	To OO-SRA 3/49. Canx 25.2.49.
G-ALEL	Avro 652A Anson I	-	MG247	5.10.48	Not converted. Scrapped at Croydon in 1/49. Canx 6.1.49 as reduced to produce.
G-ALEM	Avro 652A Anson I	-	MG756	5.10.48	Not converted. Scrapped at Croydon in 1/49. Canx 26.7.49 as broken up.
G-ALEN	Avro 652A Anson I	-	EG435	5.10.48	Not converted. Scrapped at Croydon in 1/49. Canx 5.8.49 as broken up.
G-ALEO	Percival P.31C Proctor IV	H.672	NP288	5.10.48	Crashed at Nuremburg, West Germany on 30.8.55. Canx.
G-ALEP	Douglas C-54B-5-DO Skymaster	18327	ZS-BYO N74628/43-17217	13.12.48	To (VH-INY) on 26.1.51/VH-INX on 12.2.51. Canx 4/51.
G-ALER	Percival P.34 Proctor III	H.455	LZ673	6.10.48	WFU at Stapleford on 17.3.55. Canx.
G-ALES	Percival P.34 Proctor III	H.77	DX181	8.10.48	WFU at Biggin Hill in 6/63. Canx.
G-ALET	DH.89A Dragon Rapide	6832	NR744	15.10.48	To F-OALD 9/51. Canx 10.9.51.
G-ALEU	Handley Page HP.82 Hermes V	HP.82/1		25. 8.49	DBR on forced landing at Chilbolton on 10.4.51. Canx.
G-ALEV	Handley Page HP.82 Hermes V	HP.82/2		25. 8.49	Broken up at Farnborough in 9/53. Canx as WFU /53.
G-ALEW	Fairey Primer	F.8456	G-6-5	14.10.48	Not completed. Broken up in 1951. Canx as WFU 19.3.51.
G-ALEX	Percival P.31C Proctor IV	H.854	NP177	12.10.48	Not converted. Canx.
G-ALEY	Taylorcraft Auster 5	895	MT124	12.10.48	To ZK-AYB 11/50. Canx 14.11.50.
G-ALEZ	Douglas C-47A-1-DK Dakota	12066	ZS-BVF FL639/42-92283	14.10.48	To ZS-DBP 10/59. Canx.
G-ALFA	Taylorcraft Auster 5	1236	RT607	20.10.48	
	(Identity uncertain, since c/n 1236 also reported as sold as HB-EOC 4/48. Also reported as c/n 826 ex.MS958 but unlikely)				
G-ALFB	Percival P.34 Proctor III	H.540	LZ770	20.10.48	To F-OAJZ 6/51. Canx 16.6.51.
G-ALFC	Percival P.34 Proctor III	H.472	LZ690	20.10.48	Not converted. Scrapped at Croydon in 1/51. Canx.
G-ALFD	Avro 652A Anson I	-	EG689	20.10.48	Crashed into airport buildings on landing in fog at Melsbroek, Brussels on 17.2.52. Canx 17.2.52 as destroyed.
G-ALFE	Miles M.14A Hawk Trainer III	2239	V1086	22.10.48	DBR at Ford in 2/56. Remains scrapped at Portsmouth in 1957. Canx.
G-ALFF	Percival P.34 Proctor III	H.63	R7567	26.10.48	WFU at Lympne in 3/50. Canx.
G-ALFG	DH.82A Tiger Moth	83038	R5176	4. 4.49	To SE-COT 5/61. Canx 20.11.60.
G-ALFH	Miles M.14A Hawk Trainer III	2063	T9826	25.11.48	Not converted. Scrapped at Northolt in 1951. Canx.
G-ALFI	Miles M.14A Hawk Trainer III	2110	T9893	25.11.48	Not converted. Scrapped at Northolt in 1951. Canx.
G-ALFJ	Avro 652A Anson I	-	NL116	11.11.48	Crashed into a hangar at Croydon on 8.3.49. Canx 8.3.49.
G-ALFK	Percival P.34 Proctor III	H.79	DX182	13.12.48	To F-BAVQ 11/50. Canx 16.11.50.
G-ALFL	DH.98 Mosquito NF.36	-	RL150	26.11.48	Restored to RAF as RL150 in 11/49. Canx.
G-ALFM	DH.104 Dove 4	04211	VP961 G-ALFM/VP961	15.12.48	To G-HBBC 1/96. Canx.
G-ALFN	Avro 652A Anson 19 Srs.2	1508	VM336	2.12.48	Restored to RAF as VM336 in 5/50. Canx.
G-ALFO	Douglas C-47A-90-DL Dakota	20401	VH-BHC 43-15935	30.12.48	To (N300A)/N94529 12/50. Canx 22.12.50.
G-ALFP	Avro 652A Anson I	-	NK971	17.12.48	To Israeli DF/AF as 4X-FHS/2908 in 5/53. Canx 23.10.52.
G-ALFR	Airspeed AS.57 Ambassador 2	5210		10.10.49	CofA expired 31.3.67 & WFU at Lasham. Scrapped. Canx as WFU 26.2.73.
G-ALFS	Percival P.34 Proctor III	H.479	LZ697	13.12.48	DBF at Wadi Halfa, Sudan on 14.6.49. Canx.
G-ALFT	DH.104 Dove 6 (Originally regd as Dove 2, then Dove 2B)	04233		14.12.48	CofA expired 13.6.73. Canx as WFU 11.2.77. (On display 2/97 Caernarfon Air World)
G-ALFU	DH.104 Dove 6 (Originally regd as Dove 2, then Dove 2B)	04234		14.12.48	CofA expired 4.6.71. Canx as WFU 14.11.72. (On display 7/99 Duxford)
G-ALFV	Percival P.34 Proctor III	H.221	HM301	20.12.48	To F-DAAB 3/51. Canx 17.3.51.
G-ALFW	Percival P.34 Proctor III	H.416	LZ626	20.12.48	To F-OAIS 1/51. Canx 18.1.51.
G-ALFX	Percival P.34 Proctor III	H.477	(OO-...) G-ALFX/LZ695	20.12.48	WFU at Yeadon in 12/62. Canx.
G-ALFY	Percival P.34 Proctor III	H.181	HM281	30.12.48	Not converted. Scrapped at Staverton. Canx /53.
G-ALFZ	Percival P.50 Prince 2	P50/2		10. 1.49	To PP-XEG/PP-NBA in 8/50. Canx 30.6.50.
G-ALGA(1)	Slingsby Kirby Kitten	1		11. 1.49	NTU - Not completed. Dismantled at Denham in 1949. Scrapped in 7/51. Canx.
G-ALGA(2)	PA-15 Vagabond	15-348	N4575H NC4575H	3.12.86	
G-ALGB	DH.89A Dragon Rapide	6706	HG721	17.12.48	To F-BHCD in 10/54. Canx.
G-ALGC	DH.89A Dragon Rapide	6906	YI-ABF NR842	3. 1.49	DBR at Biggin Hill on 9.3.64. Canx as WFU 21.7.66.
G-ALGD	DH.82A Tiger Moth	3819	N6482	6. 1.49	To France in 9/49. Canx 6.9.49.
G-ALGE	DH.89A Dragon Rapide	6907	YI-ABG NR843	5. 1.49	To EI-AMN 7/62. Canx 5.7.62.
G-ALGF	DH.82A Tiger Moth	83127	T5362	6. 1.49	DBF at Twinholme, Kirkudbrightshire on 11.12.49. Canx.
G-ALGG	Percival P.34 Proctor III	H.180	BV636	18. 1.49	To LN-TVM 3/49. Canx 30.3.49.
G-ALGH	Piper J3C-65 Cub (L-4H-PI) (Regd with c/n 12156)	12328	44-80545(2) 44-80032	4. 4.49	To TF-KAP 10/52. Canx 8.7.52.
G-ALGI	DH.89A Dragon Rapide	6909	YI-ABH NR845	13. 1.49	To F-OAND 9/53. Canx 21.9.53.
G-ALGJ	Miles M.14A Hawk Trainer III	2106	T9889	15. 1.49	Crashed at Egremont, Cumberland on 22.7.52. Canx.
G-ALGK	Miles M.14A Hawk Trainer III	1742	P6374	15. 1.49	Ditched into River Crouch, off Burnham on 21.1.51. Canx.
G-ALGL(1)	Miles M.14A Hawk Trainer III	1933	R1962	. .49R	NTU - To Egyptian AF in 9/49. Canx.
G-ALGL(2)	Percival P.31 Proctor IV	H.581	NP174	2. 2.49	Not converted. Broken up in 1951. Canx.
G-ALGM	DH.89A Dragon Rapide	6559	X7339	17. 2.49	To F-BGOL 7/52. Canx 21.7.52.
G-ALGN	DH.89A Dragon Rapide	6943	RL961	17. 2.49	To F-OAKE 1/52. Canx 28.1.52.
G-ALGO	DH.89A Dragon Rapide	6830	NR742	17. 2.49	Crashed at Abadan, Iran on 10.7.51. Canx.
G-ALGP	Percival P.34 Proctor III	H.232	HM310	17. 2.49	Not converted. Scrapped at Croydon in 1953. Canx.
G-ALGR	Percival P.34 Proctor III	H.258	HM348	17. 2.49	To Belgium in 10/50. Canx 12.10.50.
G-ALGS	Percival P.34 Proctor III	H.554	LZ796	9. 2.49	To West Germany in 8/53. Canx 7.8.53.

Regn	Type	c/n	Previous identity	Regn date	Fate or immediate subsequent identity (if known)
G-ALGT	Vickers Supermarine 379 Spitfire F.XIVc	6S/432263	"RM619" RM689	9. 2.49	Destroyed in fatal crash at Woodford on 27.6.92. Canx by CAA 2.4.93.
G-ALGU	DH.98 Mosquito NF.XIX	-	TA299	16. 2.49	WFU at Tarrant Rushton. Scrapped in 4/52. Canx.
G-ALGV	DH.98 Mosquito NF.XIX	-	TA343	16. 2.49	Scrapped at Tarrant Rushton in 4/52. Canx.
G-ALGW	Auster 6	1928	TW562	17. 2.49	Not converted. Broken up at Croydon in 1953. Canx.
G-ALGX	DH.82A Tiger Moth	83147	T5300	1. 3.49	Crashed at Grennteith-Mann, West Germany on 2.3.54. Canx.
G-ALGY	Percival P.34 Proctor III	H.492	LZ710	11. 1.49	WFU at Lympne in 3/52. Canx as WFU 12.4.73.
G-ALGZ	Miles M.14A Hawk Trainer III	2150	T9957	17. 2.49	Not converted. Scrapped at Croydon in 1950. Canx.
G-ALHA	Miles M.14A Hawk Trainer III	1879	R1893	17. 2.49	Not converted. Scrapped at Croydon in 1950. Canx.
G-ALHB	Miles M.14A Hawk Trainer III	971	N3933	17. 2.49	Not converted. Scrapped at Croydon in 1950. Canx.
G-ALHC	Canadair DC4-M2 Argonaut	145	RRAF-601 R.Rhodesian AF-180/G-ALHC	23. 2.49	WFU at Redhill in 8/64. Scrapped 7-10/65. Canx.
G-ALHD	Canadair DC4-M2 Argonaut	146	VP-KOY G-ALHD	23. 2.49	To OY-AFC 5/61. Canx 29.3.61.
G-ALHE	Canadair DC4-M2 Argonaut	151		23. 2.49	Crashed into trees 3 miles after take-off from Kano, Nigeria on 24.6.56. Canx.
G-ALHF	Canadair DC4-M2 Argonaut	152	VP-KOI G-ALHF	23. 2.49	WFU at Redhill in 8/64. Broken up in 1964. Canx.
G-ALHG	Canadair DC4-M2 Argonaut	153		23. 2.49	Fatal crash into centre of Stockport at the junction of Waterloo Road and Upper Brook Street on approach to Ringway Airport on 4.6.67. Canx.
G-ALHH	Canadair DC4-M2 Argonaut	154	RRAF-602 R.Rhodesian AF-181/G-ALHH	23. 2.49	WFU at Redhill in 1964. Scrapped in 7/65. Canx.
G-ALHI	Canadair DC4-M2 Argonaut	155	RRAF-603 R.Rhodesian AF-182/G-ALHI	23. 2.49	WFU at Redhill in 10/65. To Stansted Fire School in 1/66. Canx.
G-ALHJ	Canadair DC4-M2 Argonaut	156	VP-KOT G-ALHJ	23. 2.49	WFU at Heathrow in 12/58. Scrapped in 1967. Canx.
G-ALHK	Canadair DC4-M2 Argonaut	157		23. 2.49	To OY-AFB 1/61. Canx 31.1.61.
G-ALHL	Canadair DC4-M2 Argonaut	158		23. 2.49	Hit trees & crashed 1200 yards short of runway when landing at Idris, Tripoil, Libya on 21.9.55. Canx.
G-ALHM	Canadair DC4-M2 Argonaut	159	VP-KOJ G-ALHM	23. 2.49	WFU at Castle Donington. Broken up in 3/66. Canx.
G-ALHN	Canadair DC4-M2 Argonaut	160	OY-AFA G-ALHN	23. 2.49	WFU for spares at Burnaston. Broken up in 5/62. Canx.
G-ALHO	Canadair DC4-M2 Argonaut	161		23. 2.49	To VP-KNY 3/57. Canx 29.3.57.
G-ALHP	Canadair DC4-M2 Argonaut	162		23. 2.49	WFU for spares at Burnaston. Broken up in 10/61. Canx.
G-ALHR	Canadair DC4-M2 Argonaut	163		23. 2.49	To VR-AAR 2/60. Canx 18.2.60.
G-ALHS	Canadair DC4-M2 Argonaut	164		23. 2.49	WFU at Castle Donington on 14.4.68. Scrapped in 5/70. Canx as WFU 25.9.68.
G-ALHT	Canadair DC4-M2 Argonaut	165	OY-AAH G-ALHT	23. 2.49	WFU at Gatwick on 24.3.65. Scrapped at Redhill in 10/65. Canx.
G-ALHU	Canadair DC4-M2 Argonaut	166		23. 2.49	To OY-AAI 4/60. Canx 24.4.60.
G-ALHV	Canadair DC4-M2 Argonaut	167		23. 2.49	To VR-AAT 6/60. Canx 15.7.60.
G-ALHW	Canadair DC4-M2 Argonaut	168	RRAF-600 R.Rhodesian AF-179/G-ALHW	23. 2.49	WFU at Redhill on 1.10.65. Scrapped at Castle Donnington in 3/66. Canx.
G-ALHX	Canadair DC4-M2 Argonaut	169		23. 2.49	To VR-AAS 4/60. Canx 30.4.60.
G-ALHY	Canadair DC4-M2 Argonaut	170		23. 2.49	WFU at Castle Donington in 11/67. Scrapped in 1970. Canx as WFU 25.9.68.
G-ALHZ	Avro 652A Anson I	-	NK451	16. 2.49	Not converted. Canx as PWFU 11.8.51. Probably broken up for spares at Kingstown, Carlisle.
G-ALIA	Avro 652A Anson I	-	NK862	16. 2.49	Not converted. Canx as PWFU 20.12.50. Probably broken up for spares at Kingstown, Carlisle.
G-ALIB	Avro 652A Anson I	-	NK489	16. 2.49	Not converted. Canx as WFU 18.1.51. Probably broken up for spares at Kingstown, Carlisle.
G-ALIC	Avro 652A Anson I	-	NK933	16. 2.49	Not converted. Canx as WFU 20.12.50. Probably broken up for spares at Kingstown, Carlisle.
G-ALID	Avro 652A Anson I	-	NK873	16. 2.49	Not converted. Canx as WFU 20.12.50. Probably broken up for spares at Kingstown, Carlisle.
G-ALIE	Avro 652A Anson I	-	NL186	16. 2.49	Not converted. Canx as WFU 20.12.50. Probably broken up for spares at Kingstown, Carlisle.
G-ALIF	Avro 652A Anson I	-	NL132	16. 2.49	Not converted. Canx as PWFU 19.5.53. Probably broken up for spares at Kingstown, Carlisle.
G-ALIG	Avro 652A Anson I	-	NL182	16. 2.49	Not converted. Canx 26.4.50 as reduced to produce. Probably broken up for spares at Kingstown, Carlisle.
G-ALIH	Avro 652A Anson I	-	NL229	16. 2.49	CofA expired 21.9.67 & WFU at Southend. Canx as PWFU 6.5.68. DBF by vandals at Winthorpe on 11.5.71.
G-ALII	Avro 652A Anson I	-	NK996	16. 2.49	Not converted. Scrapped at Squires Gate in 1954. Canx as WFU 20.12.50.
G-ALIJ(1)	Short S.45 Seaford I	S.1292	NJ200	17. 2.49R	NTU. Canx in 10/49.
G-ALIJ(2)	PA-17 Vagabond	17-166	N4866H NC4866H	13. 2.87	
G-ALIK	Westland-Sikorsky S-51 Widgeon Mk.2 (Built as S-51 Mk.1A)	WA/H/003		16. 2.49	To G-APPS 11/58. Canx.
G-ALIL	Westland-Sikorsky S-51 Mk.1A	WA/H/005		16. 2.49	To RAF as WB810 3/49. Canx 28.3.49.
G-ALIM	Miles M.14A Hawk Trainer III	640	N4557	21. 2.49	Crashed at Kerriemuir, near Perth on 14.9.56. Canx.
G-ALIN	Miles M.14A Hawk Trainer III	2027	T9760	21. 2.49	Not converted. Burnt at Rochester in 3/54. Canx.
G-ALIO	Miles M.14A Hawk Trainer III	1700	P2500	21. 2.49	Crashed near Sevenoaks on 6.7.58. Canx.
G-ALIP	Miles M.14A Hawk Trainer III	1825	R1824	21. 2.49	Not converted. Burnt at Rochester in 3/54. Canx.
G-ALIR	Handley Page HP.71 Halifax A.IX	1479	RT791	9. 3.50	Not converted. Used for spares and broken up at Southend in 11/50. Canx 3.4.59.
G-ALIS	Percival P.34A Proctor II	K.392	Z7203	21. 2.49	To VH-BQR 2/52. Canx 21.2.52.
G-ALIT	Percival P.34 Proctor III	H.169	DX240	21. 2.49	DBR at Panshanger on 17.5.56. Canx.

Regn	Type	c/n	Previous identity	Regn date	Fate or immediate subsequent identity (if known)
G-ALIU	DH.82A Tiger Moth	84623	T6175	28. 2.49	To PH-UEY 9/51. Canx 30.8.51.
G-ALIV	DH.82A Tiger Moth	84673	T6247	28. 2.49	Conversion to Thruxton Jackaroo abandoned in 6/62. Canx.
G-ALIW	DH.82A Tiger Moth	82901	N27WB ZK-ATI/R.New Zealand AF NZ899/R5006	17. 8.81	
G-ALIX	DH.82A Tiger Moth	84576	T6109	28. 2.49	To PH-NGO 4/56. Canx 15.3.56.
G-ALIY	DH.82A Tiger Moth	3951	N6647	28. 2.49	To F-OAJS 8/51. Canx 16.5.51.
G-ALIZ	DH.82A Tiger Moth	82439	N9369	28. 2.49	To EI-AFI 9/49. Canx 1.9.49.
G-ALJA	Percival P.50 Prince 2	P.50/3		7. 3.49	To VR-SDB in 7/50. Canx 27.7.50.
G-ALJB	Taylorcraft Auster 5	1557	TJ545	2. 3.49	Crashed at Harraton Hall, Co.Durham on 13.5.51. Canx.
G-ALJC	Taylorcraft Auster 5	1829	TW500	2. 3.49	To Morocco 4/51. Canx 21.4.51.
G-ALJD	Taylorcraft Auster 5	1079	NJ691	2. 3.49	To F-DAAG 8/51. Canx 4.6.51.
G-ALJE	Taylorcraft Auster 4	918	MT186	2. 3.49	To F-DAAY 12/50. Canx 6.12.50.
G-ALJF	Percival P.34A Proctor III	K.427	Z7252	3. 3.49	
G-ALJG	Percival P.34 Proctor III	H.425	LZ635	12. 3.49	Severely damaged at Nova Ligure, Italy on 6.10.49. Canx.
G-ALJH	Percival P.34 Proctor III	H.103	DX194	7. 3.49	To EC-AJA 4/53. Canx 16.3.53.
G-ALJI	Percival P.34 Proctor III	H.234	HM312	7. 3.49	To F-BENS 9/51. Canx 14.9.51.
G-ALJJ	Beechcraft C-18S Expeditor	8468	VR-HED PI-C80/44-87209	2. 1.50	To VH-KFD 5/52. Canx 24.12.50.
G-ALJK	Percival P.34 Proctor III	H.513	LZ743	7. 3.49	Crashed on take-off at Sydney, Australia on 27.12.49. Canx.
G-ALJL	DH.82A Tiger Moth	84726	T6311	7. 3.49	CofA expired 28.9.50. (On long term rebuild from components 11/92)
G-ALJM	Vickers Supermarine 509 Spitfire Trainer IX	6S/735189	G-15-92	4. 3.49	To Egyptian AF as 684 in 4/50. Canx 17.3.50.
G-ALJN	EoN-Chilton Olympia 1	EoN/O/030 & CAH/OL/7	BGA.434	16. 3.49	To Ireland as IGA.103. Canx.
G-ALJO	EoN AP.5 Olympia 1	EoN/O/008	BGA.507	5. 3.49	Reverted to BGA.507 in 1/64. Canx.
G-ALJP	EoN AP.5 Olympia 1	EoN/O/003	BGA.503	16. 3.49	Reverted to BGA.503 in 1/64. Canx.
G-ALJR	Carden-Baynes Scud III	2	BGA.283	16. 3.49	To BGA.684 in 1/53. Canx.
G-ALJS	EoN AP.5 Olympia 2	EoN/O/047	BGA.545	30. 3.49	Crashed on 10.4.49. Canx.
G-ALJT	EoN AP.5 Olympia 1	EoN/O/038	BGA.553	18. 3.49	Canx c.1950. To ZS-GCM 8/54.
G-ALJU	Slingsby T.21B Sedbergh TX.1	540	BGA.573	18. 3.49	Reverted to BGA.573 in 1/64. Canx.
G-ALJV	EoN AP.5 Olympia 2	EoN/O/006	BGA.505	18. 3.49	Reverted to BGA.505 in 1/64. Canx.
G-ALJW	Schewiyer DFS 108-68 Weihe	000348	BGA.448 Luffwaffe LO+WQ	8. 4.49	Reverted to BGA.448 in 1/64. Canx.
G-ALJX	EoN AP.5 Olympia 1	EoN/O/021	BGA.549	8. 4.49	Crashed at Bolsover on 2.8.53. Canx.
G-ALJY	EoN AP.5 Olympia 2	EoN/O/031	BGA.550	8. 4.49	Crashed at Firle Beacon on 13.10.52. Canx.
G-ALJZ	EoN AP.5 Olympia 1	EoN/O/037	BGA.562	8. 4.49	Crashed near Lasham on 20.7.58. Canx.
G-ALKA	EoN AP.5 Olympia 1	EoN/O/039	BGA.537	8. 4.49	Crashed at Sutton Bridge on 16.10.70. Canx.
G-ALKB	Martin-Hearn/Slingsby T.8 Kirby Tutor	MHL/RT.9	BGA.468	8. 4.49	Reverted to BGA.468 in 1/64. Canx.
G-ALKC	Slingsby T.8 Kirby Tutor	SSK/FF 935	BGA.610	8. 4.49	CofA expired in 10/58. Reverted to BGA.610 in 1/64. Canx.
G-ALKD	Martin-Hearn/Slingsby T.7 Kirby Cadet	MHL/RC.3	BGA.437	8. 4.49	Reverted to BGA.437 in 1/63. Canx.
G-ALKE	Martin-Hearn/Slingsby T.7 Kirby Cadet	MHL/RC.22	BGA.496	8. 4.49	Reverted to BGA.496. Canx 26.1.51.
G-ALKF	Slingsby T.21B Sedbergh TX.1	552	BGA.631	8. 4.49	Crashed at Lasham on 23.5.70. Canx.
G-ALKG	DFS 68 Weihe (built by Jacobs-Schweyer, rebuilt by Slingsby)	535	BGA.433	18. 3.49	To ZK-GAE 10/52. Canx in 1964.
G-ALKH	DFS/30 Kranich II (Mraz-built)	828	BGA.494 (Germany)	21. 3.49	To Ireland as IAC.104. Canx.
G-ALKI	Taylorcraft Auster 5C	1272	TJ187	13. 5.49	To ZK-AZF 12/51. Canx 22.10.51.
G-ALKJ	Taylorcraft Auster 5	2052	TW508	13. 5.49	To VH-AJD 3/50. Canx 18.1.50.
G-ALKK	Taylorcraft Auster 5	1652	TJ638	19. 5.49	To ZK-AXQ 11/50. Canx 8.11.50.
G-ALKL	Westland-Sikorsky S-51 Mk.1B	WA/H/011	G-17-1	23. 3.49	To Egyptian AF as 105 in 11/49. Canx 23.11.49.
G-ALKM	EoN AP.5 Olympia 2 (Originally regd as Olympia 1)	EoN/O/015	BGA.514	29. 3.49	Reverted to BGA.514. Canx.
G-ALKN	EoN AP.5 Olympia 1	EoN/O/032	BGA.561	30. 4.49	Reverted to BGA.561. Canx.
G-ALKO	EoN AP.5 Olympia 1	EoN/O/010	BGA.508	1. 6.49	Reverted to BGA.508. Canx.
G-ALKP	Martin-Hearn/Slingsby T.8 Kirby Tutor	MHL/RT.10	BGA.469	3. 5.49	Reverted to BGA.469. Canx.
G-ALKR	DFS/14 S.G.38 Schulgeiter	061404	BGA.613	3. 5.49	Reverted to BGA.613. Canx.
G-ALKS	Slingsby T.21B Sedbergh TX.1	536		3. 5.49	To BGA.646 6/50. Canx.
G-ALKT	Martin-Hearn/Slingsby T.7 Kirby Cadet (Modified to T.8 Tutor in 6/51)	MHL/RC.4	BGA.438	3. 5.49	W/o on 9.7.59. Canx.
G-ALKU	DFS/49 Grunau Baby 2 (built by F.Coleman)	-	BGA.277	3. 5.49	To RAFGSA.270. Canx.
G-ALKV	EoN AP.7 Primary	EoN/P/010	BGA.587	3. 5.49	CofA expired in 3/53. Reverted to BGA.587. Canx.
G-ALKW	Slingsby T.7 Kirby Cadet 1	-	BGA.617	12. 4.49	CofA expired in 1/55. Reverted to BGA.617. Canx.
G-ALKX	Slingsby T.21B Sedbergh TX.1	543	BGA.601	14. 4.49	Restored as BGA.601. Canx.
G-ALKY	Schleicher Ka.2B Rhönbussard	485	BGA.395	4. 7.49	Restored as BGA.395. Canx.
G-ALKZ	Abbott-Baynes Scud II	-	BGA.123(2)	23. 3.49	Canx in 3/50. CofA expired 3/52.
G-ALLA	EoN AP.5 Olympia 1	EoN/O/011	BGA.509	26. 3.49	Reverted to BGA.509. Canx.
G-ALLB	EoN AP.5 Olympia 2	EoN/O/078	BGA.606	30. 4.49	To BGA.703 3/54. Canx.
G-ALLC	Slingsby T.12 Gull 1	320A	BGA.380	1. 4.49	CofA expired in 7/53. Reverted to BGA.380. Canx.
G-ALLD	EoN AP.5 Olympia 2	EoN/O/018	BGA.530	24. 3.49	Canx in 4/49 as destroyed.
G-ALLE	Slingsby T.8 Kirby Tutor	598		6. 4.49	WFU at Sherburn-in-Elmet in 3/58. Canx in 2/63 as destroyed.
G-ALLF	Slingsby T.30A Kirby Prefect	548	BGA.599 (Holland) PH-1/BGA.599/G-ALLF/BGA.599	29. 3.49	
G-ALLG	Slingsby T.21B Sedbergh TX.1	553	BGA.636	29. 3.49	Reverted to BGA.636. Canx.
G-ALLH	Slingsby T.21B Sedbergh TX.1	554	BGA.637	29. 3.49	To RAF as WB919 in 6/49. Canx 9.6.49.

Regn	Type	c/n	Previous identity	Regn date	Fate or immediate subsequent identity (if known)
G-ALLI	Douglas C-47A-75-DL Dakota	19351	TS433 42-100888	30. 3.49	To VP-YRX 3/60. Canx 9.3.60.
G-ALLJ	Grumman G.73 Mallard	J-41		26. 3.49	To PK-AKE in 5/49. Canx 14.5.49.
G-ALLK	DHA.3 Drover 2	3	VH-EBQ	31. 3.49	NTU - Not Imported. Remained as VH-EBQ. Canx 5/51.
G-ALLL	Sproule-Ivanoff Camel 1 (built by Scott Light Aircraft in 1939)	-		30. 3.49	Crashed at Dunstable on 19.8.51 after mid-air collision. Canx as WFU 24.1.52.
G-ALLM	EoN AP.5 Olympia 1	EoN/O/005	BGA.511	2. 4.49	Reverted to BGA.511. Canx.
G-ALLN	Slingsby T.30B Kirby Prefect	568	BGA.638	2. 4.49	Crashed at Cambridge on 2.9.54. WFU 3/63. Canx.
G-ALLO	Martin-Hearn/Slingsby T.7 Kirby Cadet	MHL/RC.13	BGA.451	2. 4.49	Crashed on 12.9.54. Canx as WFU in 8/63.
G-ALLP	Martin-Hearn/Slingsby T.7 Kirby Cadet	MHL/RC.12	BGA.450	2. 4.49	Reverted to BGA.450. Canx.
G-ALLR	EoN AP.7 Primary 1	EoN/P/017	BGA.594	2. 4.49	CofA expired in 5/53. To BGA.630. Canx.
G-ALLS	EoN AP.5 Olympia 1	EoN/O/002	BGA.502	2. 4.49	Crashed on 11.5.50. Canx.
G-ALLT	Slingsby T.21B Sedbergh TX.1	549	BGA.614	4. 4.49	WFU 1/64. To RNGSA. Canx.
G-ALLU	EoN AP.8 Baby	EoN/B/001	BGA.608	4. 4.49	Restored to BGA.608. Canx.
G-ALLV	EoN AP.7 Primary 1	EoN/P/001	BGA.577	4. 4.49	Restored to BGA.577. Canx.
G-ALLW	EoN AP.7 Primary 1	EoN/P/005	BGA.582	4. 4.49	To India in 7/49. Canx 9.7.49.
G-ALLX	EoN AP.7 Primary 1	EoN/P/006	(BGA.656) BGA.583	4. 4.49	To India in 7/49. Canx 9.7.49.
G-ALLY	EoN AP.7 Primary 1	EoN/P/007	BGA.584	4. 4.49	To India in 7/49. Canx 9.7.49.
G-ALLZ	Göppingen III Minimoa	158	BGA.338	14. 4.49	To TF-SOM in 1951. Canx.
G-ALMA	Piper J3C-90 Cub (L-4H-PI) (Regd with Frame no. 12042 as c/n)	12214	44-79918	25. 4.49	Canx as sold in West Germany. To N9865F 2/57.
G-ALMB	Westland-Sikorsky S-51 Mk.1A	WA/H/006		29. 3.49	To I-MCOM 4/51. Canx 13.4.51.
G-ALMC	Westland-Sikorsky S-51 Mk.1A	WA/H/007		29. 3.49	To RAF as WF308 in 3/50. Canx 15.11.50.
G-ALMD	Westland-Sikorsky S-51 Mk.1B	WA/H/012	G-17-2	29. 3.49	NTU - To Egyptian AF in 12/49. Canx 23.11.49.
G-ALME	Schleicher Ka.2B Rhönbussard	620	BGA.337	28. 3.49	Reverted to BGA.337. Canx.
G-ALMF	Hawkridge Venture 1	V.1149	BGA.640	28. 3.49	To BGA.688 in 3/53. Canx.
G-ALMG	DFS/68 Weihe	000078	BGA.639	28. 3.49	To BGA.642 8/49. Canx 24.8.49.
G-ALMH	Martin-Hearn/Slingsby T.8 Kirby Tutor	MHL/RT.19	BGA.480	28. 3.49	Reverted to BGA.480. Canx.
G-ALMI	Slingsby T.12 Gull 1	304A	BGA.353	28. 3.49	Damaged at Ballykelly on 14.10.62. Canx as destroyed.
G-ALMJ	EoN AP.5 Olympia 1	EoN/O/046	BGA.544	28. 3.49	Reverted to BGA.544. Canx.
G-ALMK	Martin-Hearn/Slingsby T.7 Kirby Cadet	MHL/RC.21	BGA.459	28. 3.49	Crashed at RAF Odiham on 21.8.49. Canx.
G-ALML	Martin-Hearn/Slingsby T.7 Kirby Cadet	MHL/RC.24	BGA.498	28. 3.49	Reportedly to RNGSA. Canx.
G-ALMM	DFS/49 Grunau Baby 2B (Built by Hawkridge)	G-4848	BGA.615	28. 3.49	Restored as BGA.615. Canx.
G-ALMN	EoN AP.7 Primary 1	EoN/P/012	BGA.589	28. 3.49	CofA expired in 4/51. Reverted to BGA.591. Canx.
G-ALMO	EoN AP.7 Primary 1	EoN/P/004	BGA.581	28. 3.49	Reverted to BGA.581. Canx.
G-ALMP	Zlin Z.24 Krajanak	101	OK-8592	28. 3.49	To BGA.655 in 4/50. Canx.
G-ALMR	DH.104 Dove 1B (Originally regd as Srs.1)	04099	VT-CSO	13. 5.49	Forced landed on Lytham Marsh, near Warton on 12.4.60. Canx as destroyed 4.7.60.
G-ALMS	Percival P.30 Proctor II	K.383	Z7194	16. 5.49	Collided with Auster at Shoreham in 1951. Scrapped at Croydon. Canx.
G-ALMT	EoN AP.5 Olympia 2	EoN/O/085	BGA.603	27. 4.49	Reverted to BGA.603. Canx.
G-ALMU(1)	EoN AP.7 Primary	-		. .49R	NTU. Canx.
G-ALMU(2)	WAC/Miles M.65 Gemini 3A	WAL/C/1004		21. 4.51	WFU at Biggin Hill on 3.5.67. Canx 12.3.73.
G-ALMV(1)	EoN AP.7 Primary	-		. .49R	NTU. Canx.
G-ALMV(2)	DH.82A Tiger Moth	3256	K4260	23. 4.52	To ZK-BCD 11/52. Canx 7.11.52.
G-ALMW	EoN AP.5 Olympia 1	EoN/O/007	BGA.506	28. 3.49	To ZK-GBI 9/57. Canx.
G-ALMX	Martin-Hearn/Slingsby T.7 Kirby Cadet	MHL/RC.8	BGA.442	7. 4.49	Reverted to BGA.442. Canx.
G-ALMY	EoN AP.5 Olympia 2	EoN/O/020	BGA.532	2. 5.49	Reverted to BGA.532. Canx.
G-ALMZ	EoN AP.7 Primary 1	EoN/P/008	BGA.585	6. 5.49	Reverted to BGA.585. Canx.
G-ALNA	DH.82A Tiger Moth	85061	T6774	11. 4.49	Extensively damaged in forced landing in a disused gravel pit near Clacton on 26.1.86 & was submerged. Canx.
G-ALNB	EoN AP.5 Olympia 1	EoN/O/014	BGA.513	8. 4.49	Reverted to BGA.513. Canx.
G-ALNC	EoN AP.7 Primary 1	EoN/P/016	BGA.593	23. 5.49	Reverted to BGA.593. Canx 3/50.
G-ALND	DH.82A Tiger Moth	82308	N9191	12. 4.49	Crashed at Panshanger on 8.3.81. (On rebuild 3/96)
G-ALNE	EoN AP.5 Olympia 2	EoN/O/040	BGA.538	26. 4.49	Reverted to BGA.538. Canx.
G-ALNF	EoN AP.5 Olympia 2 (Later modified to Olympia Mk.4 prototype, then Olympia 402)	EoN/O/096		12. 4.49	Crashed in France during World Championships in 7/56. Canx in 9/56.
G-ALNG	EoN AP.5 Olympia 2	EoN/O/001	BGA.501	12. 4.49	Crashed near Barnet, Herts on 11.4.55. Canx.
G-ALNH	Slingsby T.6 Kirby Kite 1	247A	BGA.285	13. 4.49	Reverted to BGA.285. Canx.
G-ALNI	Slingsby T.6 Kirby Kite 1	253A	BGA.291	13. 4.49	Reverted to BGA.291. CofA expired in 12/66. Canx.
G-ALNJ	Slingsby T.21B Sedbergh TX.1	533	BGA.570	13. 4.49	Reverted to BGA.570. Canx.
G-ALNK	Martin-Hearn/Slingsby T.8 Kirby Tutor	MHL/RT.13	BGA.474	13. 4.49	Reverted to BGA.474. Canx.
G-ALNL	EoN AP.5 Olympia 1	EoN/O/036	BGA.560	13. 4.49	Reverted to BGA.560. Canx.
G-ALNM	EoN AP.5 Olympia 1	EoN/O/033	BGA.552	23. 4.49	Reverted to BGA.552. Canx.
G-ALNN	Beechcraft D-17S Traveller	6699	(LN-HAK) FT473/44-67722/Bu.23687	14. 4.49	To F-OACT 4/49. Canx 17.5.49.
G-ALNO	Slingsby T.7 Kirby Cadet	508	BGA.429	20. 4.49	Reverted to BGA.429. Canx.
G-ALNP	Slingsby T.13 Petrel 1	348A	BGA.418	20. 4.49	Reverted to BGA.418. Canx.
G-ALNR	Slingsby T.2 Falcon 2	2	BGA.163	11. 5.49	DBF at Long Mynd in 1955. Canx.
G-ALNS	DH.89A Dragon Rapide	6778	NR679	21. 4.49	To 9Q-CJK 10/64. Canx 22.10.64.
G-ALNT	DH.89A Dragon Rapide	6713	HG728	21. 4.49	To VH-CFA(2) 11/52. Canx 26.2.52.

Regn	Type	c/n	Previous identity	Regn date	Fate or immediate subsequent identity (if known)
G-ALNU	Taylorcraft Auster 4	819	MS952	21. 4.49	To F-BFXZ 9/51. Canx 7.8.51.
G-ALNV	Taylorcraft Auster 5	1216	RT578	21. 4.49	WFU at Squires Gate. Dismantled at Leicester East in 10/59. (Stored 9/96)
G-ALNW	Taylorcraft Auster 5	1606	TJ585	21. 4.49	To OO-VAV 8/52. Canx 24.7.52.
G-ALNX	Miles M.14A Hawk Trainer III	678	L8211	25. 4.49	Not converted. Scrapped at Elstree in 10/52. Canx.
G-ALNY	Miles M.14A Hawk Trainer III	584	L8075	25. 4.49	Not converted. Scrapped at Elstree on 5.11.53. Canx.
G-ALNZ	Miles M.14A Hawk Trainer III	426	L5993	25. 4.49	Not converted. Scrapped at Elstree in 10/52. Canx.
G-ALOA	Miles M.14A Hawk Trainer III	567	L8058	25. 4.49	Not converted. Scrapped at Elstree in 10/52. Canx.
G-ALOB	Miles M.14A Hawk Trainer III	1044	N5408	25. 4.49	Not converted. Scrapped at Elstree in 6/52. Canx.
G-ALOC	Miles M.14A Hawk Trainer III	1054	N5418	25. 4.49	Sold abroad in 2/50. Canx 24.2.50.
G-ALOD	Cessna 140	14691	N2440V	14.10.83	
G-ALOE	Miles M.14A Hawk Trainer III	964	N3926	25. 4.49	To OO-ACH in 1952. Canx 12.9.52.
G-ALOF	Miles M.14A Hawk Trainer III	1066	N5430	25. 4.49	Not converted. Burnt at Elstree on 5.11.53. Canx.
G-ALOG(1)	Miles M.14A Hawk Trainer III	1081	BB666 G-AFXA	. 4.49R	NTU. Allocated in error - Restored to G-AFXA 4/49. Canx.
G-ALOG(2)	Miles M.14A Hawk Trainer III	732	L8276	25. 4.49	Crashed at Speke on 29.7.55. Canx.
G-ALOH	Miles M.14A Hawk Trainer III	2025	T9758	25. 4.49	Not converted. Scrapped at Croydon in 1949. Canx.
G-ALOI	Planet Satellite	1		26. 4.49	Broken up at Redhill in 1958. Canx.
G-ALOJ	Percival P.34 Proctor III	H.422	LZ632	27. 5.49	To F-BBTH in 4/50. Canx 20.4.50.
G-ALOK	Percival P.34 Proctor III	H.396	LZ589	27. 5.49	WFU on 25.4.64. Converted to resemble a Stuka for the film "Battle of Britain" in 1968 and thought to have been destroyed. Canx by CAA 9.9.81.
G-ALOL	Percival P.34 Proctor III	H.462	LZ680	27. 5.49	Not converted. Scrapped at Croydon. Canx.
G-ALOM	Handley Page HP.61 Halifax B.VI	-	ST801	27. 4.49	Used for spares & broken up at Southend in 11/49. Canx 11.11.49.
G-ALON	Handley Page HP.71 Halifax A.IX	1451	RT763	27. 4.49	CofA expired 31.5.50 & WFU at Southend. Canx 21.6.50.
G-ALOO	Handley Page HP.71 Halifax A.IX	1475	RT787	27. 4.49	To Egyptian AF as 1158 in 2/50. Canx 15.2.50.
G-ALOP	Handley Page HP.71 Halifax A.IX	1520	RT846	27. 4.49	To Egyptian AF as 1155 in 12/49. Canx 21.12.49.
G-ALOR	Handley Page HP.71 Halifax A.IX	1551	RT888	27. 4.49	To Egyptian AF as 1157 in 2/50. Canx 3.2.50.
G-ALOS	Handley Page HP.71 Halifax A.IX	1589	RT937	27. 4.49	CofA expired 14.6.50 & WFU at Southend. Canx 21.6.50.
G-ALOT	Abbott-Baynes Scud 2 (built by Slingsby)	215B	BGA.231	25. 4.49	Reverted to BGA.231. Canx.
G-ALOU	Bristol 171 Sycamore Srs.1	12836	VL963	25. 4.49	Restored to RAF as VL963 in 8/49. Canx 8.1.51.
G-ALOV	DH.89A Dragon Rapide	6638	X7521	29. 4.49	To F-OAPS in 3/54. Canx 1.3.54.
G-ALOW	DHC-2 Beaver 1	36		29. 4.49	To VP-YKA in 11/52. Canx 17.10.52.
G-ALOX	DH.82A Tiger Moth	82704	6083M R4763	28. 4.49	Crashed at Wimbledon Common on 31.7.54. Canx.
G-ALOY	Martin-Hearn/Slingsby T.7 Kirby Cadet	MHL/RC.9	BGA.443	5. 5.49	Reverted to BGA.443. Canx.
G-ALOZ	RFD Dagling Primary (built by Hawkridge)	D.12478	BGA.567	5. 5.49	Reverted to BGA.567. Canx.
G-ALPA	Slingsby T.12 Gull 1	316A	BGA.379	5. 5.49	To RAF as VW912. Canx.
G-ALPB	Slingsby T.25 Gull 4	505	BGA.565	5. 5.49	Reverted to BGA.565. Canx.
G-ALPC	Slingsby T.30B Kirby Prefect	567	BGA.625	5. 5.49	Reverted to BGA.625. Canx.
G-ALPD	Martin-Hearn/Slingsby T.8 Kirby Tutor	MHL/RT.4	BGA.463	5. 5.49	CofA expired in 11/57. Wings to BGA.836. Canx as WFU 1/64.
G-ALPE	Slingsby T.8 Tutor	513	BGA.485	5. 5.49	Crashed at Dunstable on 2.4.63. Canx.
G-ALPF	Avro 694 Lincoln B.2	-	RE290	28. 4.49	Not converted. Broken up at Southend in 1952. Canx.
G-ALPG	DFS/49 Grunau Baby 2B	105	BGA.446	28. 4.49	Reverted to BGA.446. Canx.
G-ALPH	Slingsby T.6 Kirby Kite 1	220A	BGA.239	28. 4.49	W/o on 10.5.52. Canx.
G-ALPI	Slingsby T.7 Kirby Cadet	512	BGA.432	28. 4.49	Reverted to BGA.432. Canx.
G-ALPJ	Slingsby T.12 Gull 1	312A	BGA.378	28. 4.49	Reverted to BGA.378. Canx.
G-ALPK	DH.89A Dragon Rapide	6757	NF886	3. 5.49	CofA expired 4.6.66 & WFU. Broken up in 7/68 for spares at Netheravon. Canx.
G-ALPL	DFS 68 Weihe (built by Jacobs-Schweyer)	000376	BGA.489	2. 5.49	Taken abroad by owner, prior to 9/51. Canx.
G-ALPM	Douglas C-47A-80-DL Dakota	19566	ZS-BRX TS435/43-15100	3. 5.49	NTU - Remained as ZS-BRX. Canx.
G-ALPN	Douglas C-47A-1-DK Dakota	12158	ZS-DDZ SAAF6827/FZ603/42-108831	19.10.50	CofA expired 14.3.68 & WFU at Ronaldsway, IoM. Broken up in 1968. Canx as WFU 5.11.68.
G-ALPO	EoN AP.5 Olympia 1	EoN/O/022	BGA.551	6. 5.49	Crashed at Doncaster on 3.3.66. Canx.
G-ALPP	Slingsby T.13 Petrel 1	361A		6. 5.49	To BGA.651 in 7/50. Canx.
G-ALPR	Slingsby T.6 Kirby Kite 1	285A	BGA.327	6. 5.49	Restored as BGA.327. Canx.
G-ALPS	EoN AP.7 Primary	EoN/P/003	BGA.580	6. 5.49	WFU in 1955. (Wreck at Twinwood Farm on 2.4.74)
G-ALPT	DFS/49 Grunau Baby 2B	BA.240	BGA.604	6. 5.49	Crashed at Sandown, IoW on 13.9.56. Canx as WFU 3/63.
G-ALPU	Martin-Hearn/Slingsby T.7 Kirby Cadet	MHL/RC.12	BGA.473	6. 5.49	Reverted to BGA.473. Canx.
G-ALPV	EoN AP.5 Olympia 1	EoN/O/065	BGA.568	6. 5.49	Reverted to BGA.568. Canx.
G-ALPW	EoN AP.7 Primary	EoN/P/009	BGA.586	17. 5.49	Reverted to BGA.586. Canx in 2/50.
G-ALPX	Martin-Hearn/Slingsby T.7 Kirby Cadet	MHL/RC.11	BGA.445	18. 5.49	Reverted to BGA.445. Canx in 2/50.
G-ALPY	Martin-Hearn/Slingsby T.7 Kirby Cadet (Modified to T.8 Tutor)	MHL/RC.18	BGA.456	18. 5.49	Crashed at Nympsfield on 17.3.60. Canx.
G-ALPZ	Martin-Hearn/Slingsby T.7 Kirby Cadet	MHL/RC.23	BGA.497	18. 5.49	W/o prior to 2/51. Canx.
G-ALRA	DFS/49 Grunau Baby 2B	450	BGA.447	24. 5.49	Reverted to BGA.447. Canx in 2/50.
G-ALRB	EoN AP.5 Olympia 1	EoN/O/087	BGA.618	17. 5.49	Reverted to BGA.618. Canx in 2/50.

Regn	Type	c/n	Previous identity	Regn date	Fate or immediate subsequent identity (if known)
G-ALRC	DFS/49 Grunau Baby 2B	-	BGA.217	25. 5.49	Reverted to BGA.217. Canx.
G-ALRD	Scott Viking 1	114	BGA.416	1. 4.49	Reverted to BGA.416. Canx.
G-ALRE	Martin-Hearn/Slingsby T.7 Kirby Cadet	MHL/RC.6	BGA.440	18. 5.49	CofA expired in 5/66. Reverted to BGA.440. Canx.
G-ALRF	Martin-Hearn/Slingsby T.7 Kirby Cadet	MHL/RC.7	BGA.441	18. 5.49	To Ireland in 1954. Canx in WFU 11/62.
G-ALRG	Martin-Hearn/Slingsby T.8 Kirby Tutor	MHL/RT.3	BGA.462	18. 5.49	CofA expired in 1/60. Reverted to BGA.462. Canx as WFU 11/62.
G-ALRH	EoN AP.8 Baby	EoN/B/005	BGA.629 G-ALRH/BGA.629	18. 4.49	
G-ALRI	DH.82A Tiger Moth	83350	ZK-BAB G-ALRI/T5672	2. 5.51	CofA expired 19.8.94.
G-ALRJ	Slingsby T.8 Kirby Tutor	299A	BGA.346	18. 5.49	Canx in 4/52. CofA expired in 4/53. Reverted to BGA.346.
G-ALRK	Hutter H.17A Nimbus (built by D.Campbell)	-	BGA.490	25. 5.49	Reverted to BGA.490. Canx.
G-ALRL	EoN AP.5 Olympia 2 (Originally regd as Olympia 1)	EoN/O/009	BGA.515	17. 5.49	Reverted to BGA.515. Canx.
G-ALRM	Scott-Hutter H.17 Nimbus (Built by Zander & Scott)	107	BGA.352	25. 5.49	CofA expired in 4/52. Reverted to BGA.352. Canx.
G-ALRN	Martin-Hearn/Slingsby T.8 Kirby Tutor	MHL/RT.8	BGA.467	21. 6.49	Reportedly to RNGSA. Canx.
G-ALRO	DFS/49 Grunau Baby 2B (built by RNAS Fleetlands)	FL.001		21. 6.49	To BGA.653 in 8/50. Canx as WFU 3/63.
G-ALRP	DFS/49 Grunau Baby 2B (built by RNAS Fleetlands)	FL.002		21. 6.49	To BGA.648 in 6/50. Canx as WFU 3/63.
G-ALRR	DFS/49 Grunau Baby 2B (built by RNAS Fleetlands)	FL.003		21. 6.49	To (BGA.670)/RNGSA in 1951. Canx as WFU 3/63.
G-ALRS	EoN AP.8 Baby	EoN/B/002	BGA.626	19. 5.49	To ZK-GAF 11/52. Canx.
G-ALRT	Hutter H.17 Nimbus	-	BGA.598	24. 5.49	Scrapped in 1970 at Lasham. Canx by CAA 15.9.86.
G-ALRU	EoN AP.8 Baby	EoN/B/004	BGA.628 (BGA.645)	25. 5.49	Crashed at Bardney on 28.5.71. Canx.
G-ALRV	EoN AP.8 Baby	EoN/B/003	BGA.627 (BGA.644)	25. 5.49	Crashed on 24.9.57. Canx.
G-ALRW	DH.89A Dragon Rapide	6941	RL959	16. 5.49	To F-BGXT in 10/53. Canx 25.9.53.
G-ALRX	Bristol 175 Britannia Srs.101	12874	(WB473) (VX447)	25. 6.51	DBR on landing at Littleton-upon-Servern, near Severn Estuary on 4.2.54. Fuselage to instructional airframe at Filton, front fuselage later to Brize Norton. Canx.
G-ALRY	Percival P.54 Survey Prince 1	P.54/8	F-BJAJ G-ALRY/F-BJAJ/G-ALRY/F-BJAJ/G-ALRY/F-BJAJ/G-ALRY/VP-KNN/G-ALRY	11. 8.49	WFU at Leavesden after CofA expired on 28.3.66. Canx.
G-ALRZ	Abbot-Baynes Scud II	-		23. 5.49	Crashed at Cranfield on 5.6.49. Canx.
G-ALSA	Boeing 377-10-28 Stratocruiser	15943	(SE-BDP)	15. 6.49	Crashed on approach to Prestwick on 25.12.54. Canx.
G-ALSB	Boeing 377-10-28 Stratocruiser	15944	(OY-DFY)	15. 6.49	To (N103Q)/N408Q 2/59. Canx 7.2.59.
G-ALSC	Boeing 377-10-28 Stratocruiser	15945	(LN-LAF)	15. 6.49	To (N101Q)/N406Q 12/58. Canx 8.1.59.
G-ALSD	Boeing 377-10-28 Stratocruiser	15946	(SE-BDR)	15. 6.49	To (N85Q)/N403Q 9/58. Canx 10.9.58.
G-ALSE	DH.82A Tiger Moth	85812	DE941	20. 5.49	To PH-UDX 5/49. Canx 20.11.49. (The UK CofA No.10748 shows G-ALSE ex.DE941 became PH-UDX, but the identities of PH-UDX and PH-UDZ may be reversed).
G-ALSF	DH.82A Tiger Moth	83157	T5414	20. 5.49	To PH-UDY 5/49. Canx 20.11.49.
G-ALSG	DH.82A Tiger Moth	83607	T7148	20. 5.49	To PH-UDZ 5/49. Canx 20.11.49. (The UK CofA No.10749 shows G-ALSG ex.T7148 became PH-UDZ, but the identities of PH-UDX and PH-UDZ may be reversed).
G-ALSH	DH.82A Tiger Moth	85786	DE901	20. 5.49	Crashed at Thruxton on 6.8.60. Canx.
G-ALSI	Letov XL-107 Lunak	-		28. 6.49	Crashed at Grenoble, France on 2.7.50. Canx.
G-ALSJ(1)	EoN AP.5 Olympia 1	-		. .49R	NTU. Canx.
G-ALSJ(2)	Bristol 170 Freighter 31E	12937	EI-AFQ G-ALSJ/G-18-111	19. 6.49	To ZK-BMA 11/55. Canx.
G-ALSK(1)	Hawkridge Dagling	-		. .49R	NTU. Canx.
G-ALSK(2)	Handley Page HP.71 Halifax A.IX	1506	RT832	9. 3.50	Not converted. Scrapped at Southend. Canx 20.12.51.
G-ALSL(1)	DFS/14 S.G.38	-		. .49R	NTU. Canx.
G-ALSL(2)	Handley Page HP.71 Halifax A.IX	1542	RT879	9. 3.50	Broken up at Hawarden in 11/50. Canx 20.11.50.
G-ALSM	Percival P.34 Proctor III	H.465	LZ683	31. 5.50	Lost over the Timor Sea on 11.5.52. Canx.
G-ALSN	Slingsby T.21P	502		25. 5.49	To BGA.675 in 3/52. Canx as WFU 1/64.
G-ALSO	DFS/49 Grunau Baby 2B (built by Hawkridge)	G.3348	BGA.578	25. 5.49	Reverted to BGA.578. Canx.
G-ALSP	Bristol 171 Sycamore 3	12900		17.11.50	NTU - To RAF as WV783 in 4/52. Canx 26.3.52.
G-ALSR	Bristol 171 Sycamore 3	12886		11.12.50	To RAF as XH682 in 7/54. Canx.
G-ALSS	Bristol 171 Sycamore 3	12887		9. 6.49	NTU - To RAF as WA576. Canx 17.11.50.
G-ALST	Bristol 171 Sycamore 3	12888		9. 6.49	NTU - To RAF as WA577. Canx 17.11.50.
G-ALSU	Bristol 171 Sycamore 3	12889		9. 6.49	NTU - To AAC as WA578. Canx 7.11.50.
G-ALSV	Bristol 171 Sycamore 3	12890		17.11.50	NTU - To RAF as WT923 in 5/51. Canx 26.3.52.
G-ALSW	Bristol 171 Sycamore 3	12891		17.11.50	NTU - To RAF as WT933 in 4/52. Canx 26.3.52.
G-ALSX	Bristol 171 Sycamore 3	12892	G-48-1 G-ALSX/VR-TBS/G-ALSX	17.11.50	CofA expired 24.9.65 & WFU. (Open store pending rebuild 3/96 Weston-super-Mare)
G-ALSY	Bristol 171 Sycamore 3	12893		17.11.50	NTU - To RAF as WT924 in 10/51. Canx 26.3.52.
G-ALSZ	Bristol 171 Sycamore 3	12894		17.11.50	NTU - To RAF as WV695. Canx 26.3.52.
G-ALTA	Bristol 171 Sycamore 3	12895		17.11.50	NTU - To RAF as WT925 in 4/52. Canx 26.3.52.
G-ALTB	Bristol 171 Sycamore 3	12896		17.11.50	NTU - To RAF as WT939 in 4/52. Canx 22.2.53.

Regn	Type	c/n	Previous identity	Regn date	Fate or immediate subsequent identity (if known)
G-ALTC	Bristol 171 Sycamore 3	12897		17.11.50	To RAF as WT926 in 4/52. Canx 26.3.52.
G-ALTD	Bristol 171 Sycamore 3	12898		17.11.50	NTU - To RAF as WV781 in 4/52. Canx 26.3.52.
G-ALTE	Bristol 171 Sycamore 3	12899		17.11.50	NTU - To RAF as WV782 in 4/52. Canx 26.3.52.
G-ALTF	Percival P.34 Proctor III	H.158	DX234	8. 7.49	Not converted. Scrapped at Croydon in 1951. Canx.
G-ALTG	Percival P.30 Proctor II	K.413	Z7238	8. 7.49	To VH-BQP 11/51. Canx 31.10.51.
G-ALTH	Slingsby T.25 Gull 4	547	BGA.612	26. 5.49	To RAFGSA.219. Canx.
G-ALTI	Martin-Hearn/Slingsby T.26 Kite 2	MHL/RK.4	BGA.520	27. 5.49	Canx as WFU in 1/64. Burnt at Hunslet in 2/71.
G-ALTJ	Dunstable-Dart Cambridge 1	-	BGA.263	22. 6.49	Destroyed in mid-air collision with Olympia G-ALLM at Camphill on 15.6.52. Canx as WFU 1/53.
G-ALTK	Slingsby T.7 Kirby Cadet 1	511	BGA.428	22. 6.49	DBR at Thruxton. Canx as WFU in 3/63.
G-ALTL	Slingsby T.6 Kirby Kite 1	296A	BGA.343	31. 5.49	Reverted to BGA.343. Canx in 3/50. CofA expired in 11/53.
G-ALTM	DH.104 Dove 2	04236		18. 6.49	DBR in forced landing at Heathrow on 22.6.55. (Remains to Croydon and painted with fictitious reg "N764JN" for a film) Canx as WFU 8.12.55.
G-ALTN	DFS/49 Grunau Baby 2B	-		22. 6.49	Canx as WFU in 1/64.
G-ALTO	Cessna 140	14253	N2040V	19. 1.82	
G-ALTP	Airspeed AS.40 Oxford 1	4151	PH321	31. 5.49	DBF at Christchurch on 1.1.62. Canx.
G-ALTR	Airspeed AS.40 Oxford 1	4187	PH368	31. 5.49	DBR on take-off from Bordeaux, France on 14.8.61. Canx.
G-ALTS	DH.104 Dove 4	04260	VP977	10. 6.49	Restored to RAF as VP977 in 10/49. Canx 16.11.49.
G-ALTT	Douglas C-47A-1-DK Dakota	12000	TF-FIS G-ALTT/ZS-DBZ/(ZS-BXJ)/South African AF 6860/FL591/42-92223	16. 6.49	To ET-ABI 2/64. Canx 7.2.64.
G-ALTU	Slingsby T.8 Tutor (built by D.C.Burgoyne)	-		21. 6.49	To BGA.657 in 10/50. Canx as WFU 1/64.
G-ALTV	EoN AP.5 Olympia 1	EoN/0/004	BGA.504	21. 6.49	Reverted to BGA.504. Canx as WFU 1/64.
G-ALTW	DH.82A Tiger Moth	84177	T7799	13. 6.49	Crashed at Panshanger on 5.11.69. CofA expired 8.6.70. Canx by CAA 7.9.81. (On rebuild 10/91)
G-ALTX	Vickers-Supermarine 507 Sea Otter ASR.I	S2/0802	JM827	29. 6.49	To the Royal Dutch Navy as spares in 3/50. Canx 6.3.50.
G-ALTY	Slingsby T.7 Kirby Cadet 1	510	BGA.427	22. 6.49	Crashed on 24.8.57. Rebuilt as RAFGSA.258. Canx.
G-ALTZ	Airspeed AS.65 Consul	5134	EI-ADB HN844	21. 6.49	Damaged at Leopoldville in the Belgian Congo on 4.6.57. Canx 13.11.57.
G-ALUA	Brunswick LF-1 Zaunkoenig	V-2	VX190 D-YBAR	28. 6.49	To EI-AYU 5/74. Canx 16.4.74.
G-ALUB	Handley Page HPR.1 Marathon 1	101		24. 6.49	To RAF as XA249 in 3/52. Canx 9.9.52.
G-ALUC	DH.82A Tiger Moth	83094	R5219	28. 6.49	
G-ALUD	Slingsby T.6 Kirby Kite 1	27A	BGA.236 (BGA.222)	4. 7.49	Restored as BGA.236. Canx.
G-ALUE	Auster J/1 Autocrat	2104	EI-ACO	6. 7.49	Crashed at Buxton on 20.9.52. Dismantled remains to Barton. Rebuilt as G-AMVN 10/52. Canx.
G-ALUF	Cierva W.14 Skeeter 2	W.14/2		18. 7.49	Broken up by vibration due to ground resonance at Eastleigh on 26.6.50. Canx.
G-ALUG	Miles M.65 Gemini 1A	6320	EI-ACW	13. 7.49	WFU at Sywell on 15.6.64. Scrapped in 1967. (Rear fuselage to G-AKHZ) Canx.
G-ALUH	Vickers 478 Wellington T.10 (Marks used whilst on tail boom radar device tests)	-	RP468	22. 7.49	Restored to RAF as RP468 in 10/49. Canx 11.10.49.
G-ALUI	Percival P.34 Proctor III	H.521	LZ751	28. 7.49	Not converted. Broken up at Croft in 1954. Canx.
G-ALUJ	Percival P.34 Proctor III	H.111	F-DADK G-ALUJ/DX198/(G-AGLC)/DX198	28. 7.49	Crashed at Roseberry Topping, Yorks on 10.2.60. Canx.
G-ALUK	Percival P.34 Proctor III	H.165	DX238	28. 7.49	Not converted. Scrapped at Croydon. Canx.
G-ALUL	DHC.1 Chipmunk 22 (Fuselage no. DHH/f/54)	C1/0101	OY-ATV Denmark AF P-122	3.12.82	To VH-LBW 7/85. Canx 19.7.85.
G-ALUM	Avro 652A Anson I	-	MG901	29. 7.49	To OY-DYC 5/54. Canx 6.3.54.
G-ALUN	Saro SR.45 Princess	SR.901		15.10.49	WFU in 1958. Scrapped at Cowes, IoW in 1967. Canx.
G-ALUO	Saro SR.45 Princess	SR.902		15.10.49	Not completed. Scrapped at Cowes, IoW in 1967. Canx.
G-ALUP	Saro SR.45 Princess	SR.903		15.10.49	Not completed. Scrapped at Cowes, IoW in 1967. Canx.
G-ALUR	Avro 652A Anson X	RY/LW/17436	MG471	5. 8.49	To OH-ANA 7/52. Canx 20.6.52.
G-ALUS	Avro 652A Anson X	-	NK737	8. 8.49	Scrapped at Southend in 10/50. Canx 27.10.50 as reduced to spares.
G-ALUT	Handley Page HP.71 Halifax A.IX	1576	RT924	10. 8.49	Not converted. Scrapped at Southend in 11/50. Canx 20.11.50.
G-ALUU	Handley Page HP.71 Halifax A.IX	1522	RT848	10. 8.49	Not converted. Scrapped at Southend in 11/50. Canx 20.11.50.
G-ALUV	Handley Page HP.71 Halifax A.IX	1536	RT873	10. 8.49	Not converted. Scrapped at Southend in 11/50. Canx 21.6.50.
G-ALUW	Miles M.14A Hawk Trainer III	1693	P2493	10. 8.49	To OO-AJT in 1952. Canx 13.3.52.
G-ALUX	Miles M.14A Hawk Trainer III	1649	P2427	10. 8.49	WFU at Fairoaks in 4/63. Burnt in 1967. Canx.
G-ALUY	Percival P.30 Proctor II	H.220	BV656	10. 6.49	Not converted. Scrapped at Blackbushe. Canx 21.7.59.
G-ALUZ	Felce-Luton LA-4A Minor	DEF.1		. .49R	WFU & stored at Hinckley. Canx.
G-ALVA	Percival P.34 Proctor III	H.383	LZ576	28. 8.49	To F-BBCQ(2) 4/50. Canx 26.4.50.
G-ALVB	Vickers-Supermarine 507 Sea Otter ASR.I	S2/0807	JM818	22. 8.49	To the Royal Dutch Navy as 18-2 in 10/49. Canx 3.10.49.
G-ALVC	Avro 683 Lancaster B.VII	-	NX726	24. 8.49	Not converted. Broken up at Luton in 1949. Canx.
G-ALVD(1)	Beechcraft 35 Bonanza	-		. .49R	NTU. Canx.
G-ALVD(2)	DH.104 Dove 2B (Originally regd as Dove 2)	04277		24.11.49	To AP-AJB 5/57. Canx 22.5.57.
G-ALVE	Percival P.34 Proctor III	H.482	LZ700	30. 8.49	Not converted. Scrapped at Blackbushe. Canx 21.7.59.
G-ALVF(1)	Lockheed 18-40 Lodestar	2008	ZS-BAJ V-188	. .49R	NTU. To N54549. Canx.
G-ALVF(2)	DH.104 Dove 1B (Originally regd as Dove 1)	04168		29. 9.49	To TJ-ACD(2) 3/65. Canx 25.3.65.
G-ALVG	DH.106 Comet 1 Prototype	06001	G-5-1	1. 9.49	Broken up at RAE Farnborough in 7/53. Canx.

Regn	Type	c/n	Previous identity	Regn date	Fate or immediate subsequent identity (if known)
G-ALVH	Handley Page HP.71 Halifax A.IX	1476	RT788	12. 9.49	To Egyptian AF as 1163. Canx 8.5.50.
G-ALVI	Handley Page HP.71 Halifax A.IX	1481	RT793	12. 9.49	To Egyptian AF as 1156. Canx 19.1.50.
G-ALVJ	Handley Page HP.71 Halifax A.IX	1526	RT852	12. 9.49	To Egyptian AF as 1159. Canx 25.2.50.
G-ALVK	Handley Page HP.71 Halifax A.IX	1564	RT901	12. 9.49	To Egyptian AF as 1160. Canx 9.3.50.
G-ALVL	Handley Page HP.71 Halifax A.IX	1570	RT907	12. 9.49	To Egyptian AF as 1162. Canx 5.4.50.
G-ALVM	Handley Page HP.71 Halifax A.IX	1590	RT938	12. 9.49	To Egyptian AF as 1161. Canx 22.3.50. (This was the 6,176th & last Cricklewood-built Halifax delivered to RAF 20.11.46)
G-ALVN	Avro 652A Anson I	-	LT452	20. 9.49	To Israeli DF/AF as 4X-FHN/2903 in 11/49. Canx 24.5.50.
G-ALVO	Avro 652A Anson I	-	LV320	20. 9.49	To Israeli DF/AF as 4X-FHO/2904 in 12/49. Canx 24.5.50.
G-ALVP	DH.82A Tiger Moth	82711	R4770	26. 9.49	CofA expired 15.2.61 & WFU at Shoreham. (Stored for rebuild)
G-ALVR	Piper J3C-65 Cub (L-4H-PI)	11535	NC73100	16. 5.50	To D-EKYR 9/57. Canx 29.8.57.
G-ALVS	DH.104 Dove 6 (Originally regd as Dove 2, then converted to Srs.2B)	04199		24.10.49	WFU at Stansted on 19.11.70. Canx as WFU 14.11.72.
G-ALVT	DH.104 Dove 2	04206		24.10.49	To RAF as WX958 in 7/51. Canx 18.7.51.
G-ALVU	DH.89A Dragon Rapide	6526	X7353	27.10.49	Not converted. Burnt at Squires Gate in 1962. Canx.
G-ALVV	Taylorcraft Auster 4	865	MT143	27.10.49	To EC-AKU 6/55. Canx 4.3.55.
G-ALVW	Handley Page HPR.1 Marathon 1	102	VX249	15.11.49	To RAF as XA250 in 3/52. Canx 13.6.52.
G-ALVX	Handley Page HPR.1 Marathon 1	103		15.11.49	To RAF as XA251 in 3/52. Canx 13.6.52.
G-ALVY	Handley Page HPR.1 Marathon 1	104	XA252 G-ALVY	15.11.49	Not converted. Broken up at Shoreham in 2/62. Canx as WFU 6.2.62.
G-ALVZ	Douglas C-47B-35-DK Dakota	16675/33423	VR-SDD G-ALVZ/KP211/44-77091	9.11.49	WFU on 18.4.70. Broken up at Bahrein. Canx.
G-ALWA	Avro 701 Athena T.2	1519	VR569	19.12.49	Restored to RAF as VR569 in 1/51. Canx 11.7.50.
G-ALWB	DHC.1 Chipmunk 22A (Fuselage no. DHH/f/41)	C1/0100	Lebanese Army/G-ALWB/OE-ABC/G-ALWB	28.12.49	
G-ALWC	Douglas C-47A-25-DK Dakota	13590	(F-GBOL) G-ALWC/KG723/42-93654	10. 1.50	CofA expired 6.2.83. Canx by CAA 3.4.89. (Open storage 6/95 Toulouse-Blagnac, France)
G-ALWD	Douglas C-47A-20-DK Dakota	12911	KG507 42-93043	10. 1.50	To G-AMDZ 11/50. Canx.
G-ALWE	Vickers 701 Viscount	4		2. 1.50	Fatal crash into houses at Shadow Moss Road, Wythenshawe, Manchester on 14.3.57 whilst on approach to Ringway. Canx.
G-ALWF	Vickers 701 Viscount	5		2. 1.50	CofA expired 16.4.72 & WFU at Speke. Canx as WFU 18.4.72. (On display 7/99 Duxford)
G-ALWG	Percival P.50 Prince 2	P.50/7		26. 1.50	To YV-P-AEO in 4/50. Canx 18.4.50.
G-ALWH	Percival P.50 Prince 2A	P.50/10	YV-P-AEQ G-ALWH	26. 1.50	To N206UP 11/76. Canx 15.11.76.
G-ALWI	DH.89A Dragon Rapide (Wore incorrect temporary marks G-ALWJ on ferry flight for conversion 3.2.50)	6703	HG718	21. 1.50	To F-BGPJ 3/52. Canx 19.3.52.
G-ALWJ	DH.89A Dragon Rapide (Wore incorrect temporary marks G-ALWI on ferry flight for conversion 3.2.50)	6777	NR678	21. 1.50	To VP-KLL 11/53. Canx 12.10.53.
G-ALWK	DH.89A Dragon Rapide	6856	NR780	26. 1.50	To F-OBAL 4/57. Canx 15.4.57.
G-ALWL	DH.89A Dragon Rapide	6845	NR769	30. 1.50	To F-BGPH 3/52. Canx 5.3.52.
G-ALWM	DH.89A Dragon Rapide	6755	NF884	30. 1.50	To F-OAGP 6/50. Canx 20.6.50.
G-ALWN	DH.89A Dragon Rapide	6729	NF858	30. 1.50	To F-BGPG 3/52. Canx 5.3.52.
G-ALWO	DH.89A Dragon Rapide	6840	NR752	23. 1.50	To VP-YHE 6/51. Canx 1.6.51.
G-ALWP	DH.89A Dragon Rapide	6707	HG722	23. 1.50	To VQ-FAL 6/51. Canx 28.6.51.
G-ALWR	Percival P.34 Proctor III	H.253	HM343	24. 1.50	Not converted. Scrapped at Hamble. Canx 5.2.51.
G-ALWS	DH.82A Tiger Moth	82415	N9328	24. 1.50	Not (yet) converted. (Frame stored 5/99 Welshpool)
G-ALWT	DH.82A Tiger Moth	85106	T6859	24. 1.50	To ZK-BCF 1/53. Canx 10.12.52.
G-ALWU	DH.82A Tiger Moth	83717	T7227	24. 1.50	To VH-BTC 11/55. Canx 20.10.55.
G-ALWV	DH.82A Tiger Moth	85973	EM742	24. 1.50	Not converted. Scrapped at Hamble. Canx in 2/51.
G-ALWW	DH.82A Tiger Moth	86366	NL923	24. 1.50	
G-ALWX	Avro 652A Anson I	-	EG674	16. 1.50	Reduced to spares at Croydon in 5/53. Canx 19.5.53.
G-ALWY	DH.89A Dragon Rapide	6741	NF870	18. 1.50	Crashed at Port Ellen, Isle of Islay on 19.4.52. Canx.
G-ALWZ	DH.82A Tiger Moth	82245	N9126	19. 1.50	To ZK-AUV 6/50. Canx 21.6.50.
G-ALXA	DH.89A Dragon Rapide	6727	NF866	16. 1.50	DBF at Gai-Lam, Hanoi, French Indio China on 4.6.52. Canx.
G-ALXB	Avro 652A Anson I	-	LV273	16. 1.50	To F-DAEK 1/56. Canx 17.10.55.
G-ALXC	Avro 652A Anson I	-	EI-AGQ G-ALXC/MH182	16. 1.50	DBR at Speke on 22.1.58. CofA expired 21.3.61. Canx as PWFU 26.5.63. To Southend Airport Fire Services 1964. Scrapped in 1968.
G-ALXD	Avro 652A Anson I	-	LT959	16. 1.50	No CofA issued. Reduced to spares at Croydon in 7/50. Canx 13.7.50.
G-ALXE	Avro 652A Anson I (Regd as ex.R9785)	-	N9785	16. 1.50	To Israeli DF/AF as 4X-FHP/2905 4/50. Canx 1.5.50.
G-ALXF	Avro 652A Anson I	-	EG436	16. 1.50	To VR-SDK 3/52. Canx 25.3.52.
G-ALXG	Avro 652A Anson I	-	N9904	16. 1.50	No CofA issued. Used for spares at Blackpool in 1953. Canx as WFU 27.2.56. Finally scrapped late 1956.
G-ALXH	Avro 652A Anson XI (Rebuilt 10/55 to Anson 19 standard using fuselage of PH808)	-	W1731	16. 1.50	Crashed near Guiseley, Yorkshire on 9.4.63 after engine failure. Canx 14.5.63 as destroyed.
G-ALXI	DH.89A Dragon Rapide	6690	HG705	31. 1.50	To OE-FAA in 11/55. Canx 15.10.55.
G-ALXJ	DH.89A Dragon Rapide	6863	NR787	31. 1.50	Crashed into sea off Laxey Head, IoM on 10.7.51. Canx.
G-ALXK	Douglas C-47B-25-DK Dakota	16080/32828	KN404 44-76496	17. 1.50	CofA expired 21.5.67 & WFU at Lasham. Canx as WFU 14.11.69. Broken up.
G-ALXL	Douglas C-47B-35-DK Dakota	16487/33235	KN595 44-76903	16. 1.50	To (5B-CBB)/(N94717). Burnt on fire dump at Bahrein. Canx 18.4.69.
G-ALXM	Douglas C-47B-35-DK Dakota	16465/33213	KN582 44-76881	16. 1.50	To PH-MAA 7/60. Canx 1.7.60.

Regn	Type	c/n	Previous identity	Regn date	Fate or immediate subsequent identity (if known)
G-ALXN	Douglas C-47B-5-DK Dakota (Fitted with Dart engines in 1951, then refitted with R-1830s)	14661/26106	G-37-1 G-ALXN/KJ934/43-48845	19. 1.50	WFU at Southend on 18.6.63. Broken up in 1964. Canx 21.3.73.
G-ALXO	Douglas C-47B-35-DK Dakota	16699/33447	KP228 44-77115	19. 1.50	To EI-AFL 6/50. Canx 18.4.50.
G-ALXP	Firth FH.01/4 Atlantic	FH.01/4		18. 1.50	Not completed. Airframe presented to the museum of the College of Aeronautics, Cranfield in 1955. Canx 8.12.53.
G-ALXR	Handley Page HPR.1 Marathon 1	105		25. 1.50	To RAF as XA253 in 3/52. Canx 13.6.52.
G-ALXS	DH.89A Dragon Rapide	6715	(TJ-AAU) G-ALXS/HG730	24. 1.50	To F-OAIH 8/51. Canx 22.5.51.
G-ALXT	DH.89A Dragon Rapide	6736	4R-AAI CY-AAI/G-ALXT/NF865	24. 1.50	(On display 9/93 Wroughton)
G-ALXU	DH.89A Dragon Rapide	6797	NR698	24. 1.50	To TJ-AAV 5/50. Canx 20.5.50.
G-ALXV	Airspeed AS.40 Oxford 1	203	X6811	26. 1.50	Not converted. Scrapped Squires Gate in 6/50. Canx.
G-ALXW	Airspeed AS.40 Oxford 1	-	NJ352	26. 1.50	Not converted. Scrapped Squires Gate in 6/50. Canx.
G-ALXX	Airspeed AS.40 Oxford 1	-	EB759	26. 1.50	Not converted. Scrapped Squires Gate in 6/50. Canx.
G-ALXY	Airspeed AS.40 Oxford 1	3829	AT660	26. 1.50	Not converted. Scrapped Squires Gate in 6/50. Canx.
G-ALXZ	Taylorcraft Auster 5/150 (Frame No. TAY24070)	1082	D-EGOF PH-NER(2)/G-ALXZ/NJ689	1. 2.50	
G-ALYA	Hants & Sussex HS.1 Herald	HSAC/001		3. 2.50	Not completed. Broken up in 1954. Canx 6.5.59.
G-ALYB	Taylorcraft Auster 5	1173	RT520	3. 2.50	CofA expired 26.5.63. Canx by CAA 29.2.84. (On rebuild 5/97 South Yorkshire Aviation Museum)
G-ALYC	Percival P.34 Proctor III	H.139	DX225	9. 2.50	Not converted. Canx 19.10.50.
G-ALYD	Taylorcraft Auster 5	824	MS957	10. 2.50	Canx as WFU 30.8.73.
G-ALYE	Avro 652A Anson I (It is reliably reported that DJ669 (G-AMBF) was in fact converted as G-ALYE, possibly in error)	-	LV280	22. 2.50	To Israeli DF/AF as 4X-FHQ/2906 in 6/50. Canx 26.6.50.
G-ALYF	Douglas C-47A-75-DL Dakota	19350	TS424 42-100887	6. 3.50	Dismantled at Prestwick in 6/67 to provide spares for G-AOGZ. Used for rescue training at Abbotsinch in 8/71. Remains destroyed in filming "Airline" in 1981. Canx.
G-ALYG	Taylorcraft Auster 5D (Regd with incorrect identity MT968)	835	MS968	14. 3.50	CofA expired 19.1.70. (Frame stored 9/95) (For ultimate rebuild as Auster 5)
G-ALYH	Taylorcraft Auster 4	849	MT107	24. 2.50	To D-EBYW (reportedly for spares use). Canx 1.7.59.
G-ALYI	Handley Page HP.71 Halifax A.IX	1547	RT884	9. 3.50	Not converted. Scrapped at Southend in 5/51. Canx 24.5.51.
G-ALYJ	Handley Page HP.71 Halifax A.IX	1464	RT776	9. 3.50	Not converted. Scrapped at Southend in 1950. Canx 20.12.51.
G-ALYK	Handley Page HP.71 Halifax A.IX	1473	RT785	9. 3.50	Not converted. Scrapped at Southend in 1950. Canx 3.4.50.
G-ALYL	Handley Page HP.71 Halifax A.IX	1511	RT837	9. 3.50	Not converted. Scrapped at Southend in 1950. Canx 20.12.51.
G-ALYM	Handley Page HP.71 Halifax A.IX	1460	RT772	9. 3.50	Not converted. Scrapped at Southend in 1950. Canx 20.12.51.
G-ALYN	Handley Page HP.71 Halifax A.IX	1450	RT762	9. 3.50	Not converted. Scrapped at Southend in 1950. Canx 20.12.51.
G-ALYO	DH.104 Devon C.1	04261	VP978	14. 3.50	Restored to RAF as VP978 in 12/52. Canx 16.6.53.
G-ALYP	DH.106 Comet 1	06003		18. 9.51	Fatal crash into sea off near Elba, Italy on 10.1.54. Canx.
G-ALYR	DH.106 Comet 1	06004		18. 9.51	Crashed at Calcutta, India on 25.7.53. Remains to Farnborough for water tank tests. Canx.
G-ALYS	DH.106 Comet 1	06005		18. 9.51	WFU in 4/54. Broken up RAE Farnborough in 1955. Canx.
G-ALYT(1)	DH.106 Comet 1	06007		. .50R	NTU - To G-ALYU(2) 9/51. Canx.
G-ALYT(2)	DH.106 Comet 2X	06006		29.11.51	WFU at Hatfield on 22.6.54. To instructional airframe at RAF Halton in 5/59 as 7610M. Broken up in 9/67. Canx.
G-ALYU(1)	DH.106 Comet 1	06008		. .50R	NTU - To G-ALYV(2) 9/51. Canx.
G-ALYU(2)	DH.106 Comet 1	06007	(G-ALYT)	18. 9.51	WFU in 4/54. Destroyed in tank tests at Farnborough. Broken up Stansted in 1963. Canx. (Fuselage to Pengham Moors)
G-ALYV(1)	DH.106 Comet 1	06009		. .50R	NTU - To G-ALYW(2) 9/51. Canx.
G-ALYV(2)	DH.106 Comet 1	06008	(G-ALYU)	18. 9.51	Fatal crash near Jalalogori, West Bengal, India on 2.5.53. Canx.
G-ALYW(1)	DH.106 Comet 1	06010		. .50R	NTU - To G-ALYX(2) 9/51. Canx.
G-ALYW(2)	DH.106 Comet 1 (Fuselage converted to "Nimrod" exhibition airframe - marked XV238)	06009	(G-ALYV)	18. 9.51	CofA expired 14.6.54. Broken up at Heathrow in 6/55, remains to Farnborough. Canx. To RAF Exhibition Unit (Extant 9/96)
G-ALYX(1)	DH.106 Comet 1	06011		. .50R	NTU - To G-ALYY(2) 9/51. Canx.
G-ALYX(2)	DH.106 Comet 1	06010	(G-ALYW)	18. 9.51	WFU in 4/54. CofA expired 21.7.54. Broken up RAE Farnborough 6/55. Canx. Nose section to Lasham 3/93. Fuselage centre-section stored by DRA 3/93; possibly since scrapped.
G-ALYY(1)	DH.106 Comet 1	06012		. .50R	NTU - To G-ALYZ 11/51. Canx.
G-ALYY(2)	DH.106 Comet 1	06011	(G-ALYX)	18. 9.51	Fatal crash into Tyrrhenian sea near Stromboli, Italy on 8.4.54. Canx.
G-ALYZ	DH.106 Comet 1	06012		27.11.51	Crashed when taking-off from Rome-Ciampino, Italy on 26.10.52. Canx as destroyed /53.
G-ALZA	DH.82A Tiger Moth	83589	ZK-BAH T5853	19. 1.53	Restored as ZK-BAH 8/53. Canx.
G-ALZB	DH.104 Dove 2A	04381	(N1577V)	21. 1.53	To XB-SUC 3/53. Canx 11.3.53.
G-ALZC	DH.104 Dove 2A	04384	(N1579V)	21. 1.53	To N1579V 5/53. Canx 20.5.53.
G-ALZD	DH.104 Dove 2A	04389	(N1559V)	21. 1.53	To N1559V 4/53. Canx 11.5.53.
G-ALZE	Britten-Norman BN-1F (Reconstructed in 1951 after engine failed on take-off)	1		16. 3.50	WFU at Bembridge, IoM in 4/53. Canx as WFU 8.6.89. (On display at Southampton)
G-ALZF	DH.89A Dragon Rapide	6541	X7381	24. 3.50	To F-BGON 9/52. Canx.
G-ALZG	HP/Miles M.65 Gemini 3C (Originally regd as a Series 3)	HPR.141		24. 3.50	To EI-BHJ 8/79. Canx 16.8.79.
G-ALZH	DH.89A Dragon Rapide	6448	R2487	24. 3.50	To F-OAKF 4/52. Canx 2.4.52.

Regn	Type	c/n	Previous identity	Regn date	Fate or immediate subsequent identity (if known)
G-ALZI	DH.82A Tiger Moth	84013	T7611	24. 3.50	To ZK-AZO 11/51. Canx 9.11.51.
G-ALZJ	DH.89A Dragon Rapide	6573	X7413	27. 3.50	To F-OAME 6/56. Canx 30.4.56.
G-ALZK	DH.106 Comet 1	06002	G-5-2	28. 3.50	WFU at Hatfield in 4/53. Broken up in 7/57. Canx.
G-ALZL	DH.114 Heron Srs.1	10903	LN-BDH G-ALZL	30. 3.50	To OY-DGS 12/66. Canx 2.12.66.
G-ALZM	Taylorcraft Auster 5D	1035	NJ635	31. 3.50	To ZK-BMD 11/55. Canx 5.8.55.
G-ALZN	Airspeed AS.57 Ambassador 2	5212	(G-ALZO)	5. 4.50	CofA expired 24.5.68 & WFU at Lasham. Scrapped. Canx as WFU 25.3.70.
G-ALZO(1)	Airspeed AS.57 Ambassador 2	5212		. .50R	NTU - To G-ALZN 4/50. Canx.
G-ALZO(2)	Airspeed AS.57 Ambassador 2	5226	108 R.Jordanian AF/G-ALZO/(G-AMAD)	5. 4.50	CofA expired 14.5.71. Canx as WFU 10.9.81. (On rebuild 7/99 Duxford)
G-ALZP	Airspeed AS.57 Ambassador 2	5213	(ZK-DFC) G-ALZP/CN-MAK/G-ALZP/(R.Jordanian AF 109)/G-ALZP	5. 4.50	WFU on 28.6.71. Broken up at West Malling in 1974. Canx 13.9.74.
G-ALZR	Airspeed AS.57 Ambassador 2 (Modified to Tyne Ambassador in 1959)	5214	G-37-4 G-ALZR	5. 4.50	WFU at Lasham on 25.11.69. Canx as WFU 26.2.73.
G-ALZS	Airspeed AS.57 Ambassador 2	5215	HB-IEK G-ALZS/(LN-BWE)/G-ALZS	5. 4.50	Overshot & DBR on landing at Luton on 14.9.67. Canx.
G-ALZT	Airspeed AS.57 Ambassador 2	5216		5. 4.50	WFU at Woolsington, Newcastle on 10.8.68. Canx.
G-ALZU	Airspeed AS.57 Ambassador 2	5217		5. 4.50	Fatal crash on take-off from Munich-Riem, West Germany on 6.2.58. Canx.
G-ALZV	Airspeed AS.57 Ambassador 2	5218	HB-IEM G-ALZV	5. 4.50	WFU at Luton on 28.1.68. Scrapped in 1968. Canx as WFU 5.6.68.
G-ALZW	Airspeed AS.57 Ambassador 2	5219		5. 4.50	CofA expired 26.5.67. Broken up at Southend in 4/68. Canx.
G-ALZX	Airspeed AS.57 Ambassador 2	5220	VH-BUI G-ALZX	5. 4.50	DBR at Beauvais, France on 14.4.66. Canx.
G-ALZY	Airspeed AS.57 Ambassador 2	5221	107 R.Jordanian AF/G-ALZY	5. 4.50	WFU at Lasham in 11/67. CofA expired 13.6.68. Scrapped. Canx as WFU 20.1.69.
G-ALZZ	Airspeed AS.57 Ambassador 2	5222	HB-IEL G-ALZZ/(LN-BWF)/G-ALZZ	5. 4.50	WFU at Luton on 22.4.69. Scrapped at Luton in 6/69. CofA expired 9.9.69. Canx.
G-AMAA	Airspeed AS.57 Ambassador 2	5223		5. 4.50	CofA expired 1.2.67. WFU at Lasham, spares use 2/67. Canx.
G-AMAB	Airspeed AS.57 Ambassador 2	5224		5. 4.50	DBR in forced-landing 4 miles southwest of Dusseldorf, Germany on 8.4.55. Canx.
G-AMAC	Airspeed AS.57 Ambassador 2	5225		5. 4.50	CofA expired 22.7.68. Canx as WFU 2.12.68 at Southend. Scrapped in 4/69. Canx.
G-AMAD(1)	Airspeed AS.57 Ambassador 2	5226		. .50R	NTU - To G-ALZO 4/50. Canx.
G-AMAD(2)	Airspeed AS.57 Ambassador 2	5211		5. 4.50	Swung off the runway and crashed into the central terminal area while landing at Heathrow on 3.7.68. Canx.
G-AMAE	Airspeed AS.57 Ambassador 2	5227	VH-BUK G-AMAE	5. 4.50	WFU at Lasham on 2.6.71. Canx 14.1.72.
G-AMAF	Airspeed AS.57 Ambassador 2	5228	(HB-IEI) G-AMAF	5. 4.50	Dismantled at Wymeswold in 1962. Remains to Luton for spares use in 11/63.
"G-AMAF"	Cessna 150	?		----	False marks applied by the Mission Aviation Fellowship. Noted at Carmarthen in 1997 and on a lorry north of Bournemouth on 4.12.98. Possibly is G-BOWC (w/o 10.7.94).
G-AMAG	Airspeed AS.57 Ambassador 2	5229		5. 4.50	DBR in wheels-up landing at Manston on 30.9.68. Canx as WFU 26.11.68.
G-AMAH	Airspeed AS.57 Ambassador 2	5230	VH-BUJ G-AMAH	5. 4.50	WFU at Lasham on 31.10.70. Canx 14.1.72.
G-AMAI	DH.89A Dragon Rapide	6879	D-ILIT "G-RCYR"/EC-AGP/G-AMAI/NR803	4. 4.50	To D-I... Canx 19.4.99.
G-AMAJ	DH.82A Tiger Moth	83256	T5537	1.12.51	To ZK-BAM 7/52. Canx 28.3.52.
G-AMAK	Westland-Sikorsky S-51 Mk.1A	WA/H/020		13. 4.50	NTU - Crashed at Yeovil on 7.6.50 as G-17-1. Canx.
G-AMAL	Percival P.34A Proctor III	H.47	R7559	28. 4.50	Crashed at Peebles on 1.10.50. Canx.
G-AMAM	DH.89A Dragon Rapide	6571	X7411	11. 4.50	WFU at Wymeswold on 20.11.60. Canx.
G-AMAN	Percival P.34A Proctor III	H.533	LZ763	14. 4.50	DBR at Silverstone on 19.7.52. Canx.
G-AMAO	Taylorcraft Auster 5	1095	NJ721	21. 4.50	Not converted. Dismantled at Croydon in 4/53. Canx.
G-AMAP	Taylorcraft Auster 5	1417	TJ351	21. 4.50	To France 7/51 as a spares source. Canx 13.7.51.
G-AMAR	DH.82A Tiger Moth	82119	N6864	21. 4.50	To HB-UBF 9/53. Canx 30.7.53.
G-AMAS	Westland-Sikorsky S-51 Mk.1A	WA/H/026	G-17-2	13. 4.50	NTU - To R.Thailand AF 8/50. Canx 5.6.50.
G-AMAT	Westland-Sikorsky S-51 Mk.1A	WA/H/027	G-17-3	13. 4.50	NTU - To R.Thailand AF 8/50. Canx 5.6.50.
G-AMAU	Hawker Hurricane Mk.IIc (12,780th & final Hurricane built)	-	PZ865	1. 5.50	Restored as PZ865 in 1963. Transferred to Military Marks on 19.12.72.
G-AMAV	Vickers 700 Viscount (Second use of c/n - see comments under G-AJZW)	3		19. 6.50	WFU at Wisley on 1.4.58. Fuselage to Stansted Fire School in 8/63. Canx.
G-AMAW	Luton LA-4 Minor (Also known as Swalesong SA.I)	JRC.1 & SA.I		29. 4.50	(Dismantled 3/99 Breighton)
G-AMAX	Handley Page HPR.1 Marathon 1	106		29. 4.50	To RAF as XA254 in 3/52. Canx 13.6.52.
G-AMAY	Handley Page HPR.1 Marathon 1	107		29. 4.50	To RAF as XA255 in 3/52. Canx 13.6.52.
G-AMAZ	Fairchild F.24W-41A Argus II	756	NC79922 FZ816/43-14792	11. 5.50	No CofA issued. Broken up at Bahrein in 3/52. Canx.
G-AMBA	Fairchild F.24W-46A Argus III	1146	NC79925 KK528/44-83184	11. 5.50	Not converted. Scrapped at Bahrein in 3/52. Canx.
G-AMBB	DH.82A Tiger Moth (Composite rebuild - parts to "G-MAZY")	85070	T6801	1. 5.50	Not converted. (On rebuild /97)
G-AMBC	Avro 652A Anson XI	-	NL231	2. 5.50	Not converted, used for spares at Kingstown, Carlisle in 1953. Canx as PWFU 19.5.53.
G-AMBD	DH.82A Tiger Moth	'8286'		1. 5.50	Crashed at Le Touquet, France on 24.6.55. Canx.
G-AMBE	Avro 652A Anson I	-	EG228	2. 5.50	CofA expired 4.12.61 & WFU at Southend. Canx as PWFU 27.7.62. Broken up for spares at Southend 1.11.62.

Regn	Type	c/n	Previous identity	Regn date	Fate or immediate subsequent identity (if known)
G-AMBF	Avro 652A Anson I	-	DJ669	2. 5.50	No CofA issued. Canx 13.7.50 as reduced for spares.
G-AMBG	Avro 652A Anson I	-	MH124	2. 5.50	No CofA issued. Canx 18.8.50 as reduced for spares.
G-AMBH	Miles M.65 Gemini 3A (Originally regd as a Gemini 3)	65/1001		9. 5.50	To OO-COA 8/58. Canx 6.6.58.
G-AMBI	DH.82A Tiger Moth	86426	NL994	5. 5.50	DBR in forced-landing at Stourpaine, Dorset on 14.2.61. Canx.
G-AMBJ	DH.82A Tiger Moth	3950	N6646	5. 5.50	To AP-AEB 8/50. Canx 1.8.50.
G-AMBK	DH.82A Tiger Moth	86435	NM115	5. 5.50	Crashed at Charmy Down, near Gloucester on 22.7.52. Canx.
G-AMBL	Youngman-Baynes High Lift (Percival P.46)	001	VT789	10. 5.50	WFU in 10/54 and presented to Aeronautical College, Cranfield. Canx.
G-AMBM	Miles M.14A Hawk Trainer III	1625	P2388	10. 5.50	Crashed at Deols, France on 14.9.54. Canx.
G-AMBN	Miles M.14A Hawk Trainer III	752	L8326	10. 5.50	Crashed at Wightwick, near Wolverhampton on 25.4.54. Canx.
G-AMBO	Miles M.14A Hawk Trainer III	1956	T9669	10. 5.50	Not converted. Scrapped at Fairoaks in 6/51. Canx.
G-AMBP	Miles M.14A Hawk Trainer III	1757	P6402	10. 5.50	Crashed at Fairoaks on 2.6.51. Canx.
G-AMBR	DH.82A Tiger Moth	85447	DE451	17. 5.50	To VP-CBG 9/50. Canx 14.9.50.
G-AMBS	Percival P.34A Proctor III	H.241	HM319	16. 5.50	DBR at Woolsington on 16.8.59. Canx.
G-AMBT	Airspeed AS.65 Consul	5202		19. 5.50	To F-OAHG 7/50. Canx 29.6.50.
G-AMBU	Airspeed AS.65 Consul	5243		19. 5.50	To F-OAHH 7/50. Canx 29.6.50.
G-AMBV	Avro 652A Anson I	-	EG316	17. 5.50	No CofA issued. Canx 13.7.50 as reduced for spares.
G-AMBW	Douglas C-47A-30-DK Dakota	13830/25275	XB246 G-AMBW/HC-SBS/KG731/43-48014	24. 4.50	To Vietnam as F-VNAU 12/53. Canx 21.10.53.
G-AMBX	Handley Page HP.71 Halifax A.IX	1447	RT759	23. 5.50	Not converted. Scrapped at Hawarden in 2/51. Canx 6.2.51.
G-AMBY	Beechcraft D-17S (YC-43) Traveler	295	NC91397 DR628/39-139	24. 5.50	To VP-YIV 8/51. Canx 15.9.51.
G-AMBZ	Taylorcraft Auster 5	1036	NJ636	24. 5.50	To ZK-AVG 7/50. Canx 17.7.50.
G-AMCA	Douglas C-47B-30-DK Dakota	16218/32966	KN487 44-76634	1. 6.50	
G-AMCB	Handley Page HP.71 Halifax A.IX	1558	RT895	7. 6.50	Not converted. Reduced to spares at Southend in 1950. Canx 20.11.50.
G-AMCC	Handley Page HP.71 Halifax A.IX	1510	RT836	7. 6.50	Not converted. Reduced to spares at Southend in 1950. Canx 20.11.50.
G-AMCD	Handley Page HP.71 Halifax A.IX	1556	RT893	7. 6.50	Not converted. Reduced to spares at Southend in 1950. Canx 20.11.50.
G-AMCE	Handley Page HP.71 Halifax A.IX	1553	RT890	7. 6.50	Not converted. Reduced to spares at Southend in 1950. Canx 20.11.50.
G-AMCF	Handley Page HP.71 Halifax A.IX	1587	RT935	7. 6.50	Not converted. Reduced to spares at Southend in 1950. Canx 25.3.54.
G-AMCG	Handley Page HP.71 Halifax A.IX	1490	RT816	7. 6.50	Not converted. Reduced to spares at Southend in 1950. Canx 25.3.54.
G-AMCH	Armstrong Whitworth AW.55 Apollo	AW.3138		10. 6.50	Marks not used. To RAF as VX224 in 12/52. Canx.
G-AMCI	Avro 652A Anson XI	-	NK987	1. 6.50	No CofA issued - not converted. Canx as WFU 20.12.50. Scrapped at Kingstown in 1953.
G-AMCJ	Gloster Meteor F.8	G5/1210		19. 6.50	To (R.Danish AF as 490)/(Egyptian AF as 1424)/G-7-1 in 1951. Rebuilt as G-ANSO in 1954. Canx.
G-AMCK	DH.82A Tiger Moth	84641	N65N C-GBBF/SLN-05/D-EGXY/HB-UAC/G-AMCK/T6193	15. 6.50	
G-AMCL	DH.82A Tiger Moth	84884	T6555	28. 6.50	To ZK-AVC 10/50. Canx 22.9.50.
G-AMCM	DH.82A Tiger Moth	85295	DE249	14.12.50	(On long term rebuild from components following crash near Somerton, Hants on 25.9.55)
G-AMCN	DH.82A Tiger Moth	84236	T7864	30. 6.50	Crashed at Gosport, Hants on 29.7.54. Canx.
G-AMCO	Percival P.34A Proctor III	H.463	LZ681	27. 6.50	To EC-AHB 8/52. Canx 12.4.52.
G-AMCP	Percival P.44 Proctor 5	Ae.150		10. 7.50	To F-BEAK 3/55. Canx 13.5.54.
G-AMCR	Bristol 173 Freighter 31MNZ	12927		11. 7.50	To G-18-101/R.New Zealand AF as NZ5904 4/52. Canx 17.4.52.
G-AMCS	Vickers-Supermarine 236 Walrus I	4501		12. 7.50	Not converted. Dismantled for spares 11/50. Canx.
G-AMCT	DH.89A Dragon Rapide	6714	HG729	13. 7.50	To F-BHTH 8/56. Canx 13.8.56.
G-AMCU	Airspeed AS.40 Oxford	5244	PH305	19. 7.50	Not converted. Burned at Christchurch 1952/3. Canx.
G-AMCV	Airspeed AS.40 Oxford	5245	NM803	19. 7.50	Not converted. Burned at Christchurch 1952/3. Canx.
G-AMCW	Airspeed AS.40 Oxford	5246	BG571	19. 7.50	Not converted. Burned at Christchurch 1952/3. Canx.
G-AMCX	Airspeed AS.40 Oxford	5247	PH517	19. 7.50	To EC-WGE/EC-AGE 9/51. Canx 20.7.51.
G-AMCY	Airspeed AS.40 Oxford	5248	PH373	19. 7.50	Not converted. Burned at Christchurch 1952/3. Canx.
G-AMCZ	Airspeed AS.40 Oxford	5249	HN786	19. 7.50	Not converted. Burned at Christchurch 1952/3. Canx.
G-AMDA	Avro 652A Anson I	-	N4877	20. 7.50	Damaged on landing at Staverton 2.11.72 & rebuilt to static condition. Canx by CAA 9.9.81. (On rebuild 7/99 Duxford)
G-AMDB	Douglas C-47B-10-DK Dakota (Fitted with Dart 504/505 engines in 1951, then with R-1830s)	14987/26432	G-37-2 G-AMDB/KJ993/(G-AMTN)/KJ993/43-49171	3. 8.50	WFU at Lympne on 15.12.67. Canx as WFU 12.4.73.
G-AMDC	Cierva W.14 Skeeter 5	-		31. 7.50	NTU - To G-AMTZ 8/52. Canx 20.8.52.
G-AMDD	DH.104 Dove 6 (Originally regd as Srs.2, then 2B)	04292		8. 8.50	To VQ-ZJC 9/68. Canx 26.9.68.
G-AMDE	Miles M.65 Gemini 3A	WAL/C/1001		9. 8.50	Crashed at Sibson on 24.9.67. Canx.
G-AMDF	DH.82A Tiger Moth	83838	T7327	18. 8.50	To R.Thailand Navy as "No.3" in 1/51. Canx 15.11.50.
G-AMDG	DH.89A Dragon Rapide	6818	NR730	17. 8.50	To F-OAIR 4/51. Canx 8.3.51.
G-AMDH	Handley Page HPR.1 Marathon 1	108		19. 8.50	To RAF as XA256 in 3/52. Canx 13.6.52.
G-AMDI	DH.82A Tiger Moth	85216	DE146	21. 8.50	To R.Thailand Navy as "No.2" in 1/51. Canx 1.11.50.
G-AMDJ	Miles M.75 Aries 1	75/1002	G-35-1	22. 8.50	To VH-FAV 5/54. Canx 1.3.55.
G-AMDK	DH.82A Tiger Moth	82207	N6969	24. 8.50	To R.Thailand Navy as "No.7" in 10/50. Canx 14.11.50.
G-AMDL	DH.82A Tiger Moth	82727	R4783	24. 8.50	To R.Thailand Navy as "No.5" in 10/50. Canx 27.10.50.
G-AMDM	DH.82A Tiger Moth	82939	R5038	24. 8.50	To R.Thailand Navy as "No.6" in 11/50. Canx 1.11.50.
G-AMDN	Hiller 360 UH-12A	166	N8166H	2.10.50	To N3878B 1/80. Canx 21.1.80.
G-AMDO	Hiller 360 UH-12A	172	N8172H	2.10.50	Crashed at Armuelles, Panama on 3.3.58. Canx.

Regn	Type	c/n	Previous identity	Regn date	Fate or immediate subsequent identity (if known)
G-AMDP	DH.82A Tiger Moth	3980	N6707	2. 9.50	To ZK-AXZ 1/51. Canx 3.1.51.
G-AMDR	DH.82A Tiger Moth	3708	N5445	2. 9.50	To F-OAIQ 1/53. Canx 9.10.50.
G-AMDS	Taylorcraft Auster 5	1115	NJ738	5. 9.50	To VH-ASP 5/51. Canx 20.12.50.
G-AMDT	DH.82A Tiger Moth	84564	T6097	5. 9.50	To R.Thailand Navy as "No.8" in 12/50. Canx 20.12.50.
G-AMDU	DH.82A Tiger Moth	82057	N6787	5. 9.50	To R.Thailand Navy as "No.9" in 12/50. Canx 20.12.50.
G-AMDV	DH.82A Tiger Moth	83578	T7127	5. 9.50	To R.Thailand Navy as "No.13" in 12/50. Canx 20.12.50.
G-AMDW	DH.82A Tiger Moth	83479	T7094	5. 9.50	To R.Thailand Navy in 12/50. Canx 20.12.50.
G-AMDX	DH.82A Tiger Moth	84173	T6025	5. 9.50	To R.Thailand Navy as "No.11" in 12/50. Canx 20.12.50.
G-AMDY	DH.82A Tiger Moth	85883	DF134	5. 9.50	To R.Thailand Navy as "No.10" in 12/50. Canx 20.12.50.
G-AMDZ	Douglas C-47A-20-DK Dakota	12911	G-ALWD KG507/42-93043	23.11.50	WFU at Southend in 9/67. Broken up in 1/70. Canx.
G-AMEA(1)	DH.82A Tiger Moth	3681	W7955 G-AFGT	. 9.50R	NTU - Restored as G-AFGT 9/50. Canx.
G-AMEA(2)	DH.82A Tiger Moth	85315	DE269	31.10.50	To OY-ACD 2/51. Canx 29.1.51.
G-AMEB	DH.82A Tiger Moth	85667	DE737	15. 9.50	To R.Thailand Navy as "No.14" in 2/51. Canx.
G-AMEC	DH.82A Tiger Moth	86052	EM850	15. 9.50	To ZK-BAJ 10/51. Canx 5.10.51.
G-AMED	Percival P.44 Proctor V	Ae.115		16.11.50	To F-OAMF 10/52. Canx 4.10.52.
G-AMEE	DH.82A Tiger Moth	82722	R4778	20. 9.50	To R.Thailand Navy in 2/51. Canx 19.2.51.
G-AMEF	DH.82A Tiger Moth	85149	T6920	20. 9.50	To R.Thailand Navy in 2/51. Canx 19.2.51.
G-AMEG	DH.82A Tiger Moth	84187	T7809	20. 9.50	To R.Thailand Navy in 2/51. Canx 18.1.51.
G-AMEH	DH.82A Tiger Moth	83613	T7154	20. 9.50	To R.Thailand Navy in 2/51. Canx 19.2.51.
G-AMEI	DH.104 Dove 2	04296		17.10.50	To HB-LAR 6/51. Canx 22.6.51.
G-AMEJ	Miles M.65 Gemini 1A	HPR.145		27. 9.50	DBR at Ouville, near Dieppe, France on 20.6.55. CofA expired 6/55. Scrapped Southend 12/57. Canx.
G-AMEK	Handley Page HPR.1 Marathon 1	109		28. 9.50	To RAF as XA257 in 3/52. Canx 13.6.52.
G-AMEL	Handley Page HPR.1 Marathon 1A (Originally regd as a Marathon 1)	110		28. 9.50	To RAF as XA258 in 3/52. Canx 13.6.52.
G-AMEM	Handley Page HPR.1 Marathon 1	111		28. 9.50	To RAF as XA259 in 3/52. Canx 13.6.52.
G-AMEN	PA-18-95 Super Cub (L-18C-PI) (Frame no 18-1963 - also Italian rebuild c/n OMA.71-08)	18-1998	(G-BJTR) Italian AF MM52-2398 "EI.71"/I-EIAM/MM52-2398/52-2398	29.12.81	
G-AMEO	Handley Page HPR.1 Marathon 1A	112	VR-NAI G-AMEO	28. 9.50	To D-CFSA 7/55. Canx 11.6.55.
G-AMEP	Handley Page HPR.1 Marathon 1	113		28. 9.50	To RAF as XA260 in 3/52. Canx 13.6.52.
G-AMER	Handley Page HPR.1 Marathon 1	114		28. 9.50	To RAF as XA261 in 3/52. Canx 13.6.52.
G-AMES	DH.82A Tiger Moth	83424	T5703	11.12.59	To USA as N5300 in 4/66. Canx 24.1.66.
G-AMET	Handley Page HPR.1 Marathon 1	115		28. 9.50	To RAF as XA262 in 3/52. Canx 13.6.52.
G-AMEU	Handley Page HPR.1 Marathon 1	116		28. 9.50	To RAF as XA263 in 3/52. Canx 13.6.52.
G-AMEV	Handley Page HPR.1 Marathon 1	117		28. 9.50	To RAF as XA264 in 3/52. Canx 13.6.52.
G-AMEW	Handley Page HPR.1 Marathon 1	118	XA265 G-AMEW	28. 9.50	WFU at Burnaston, near Derby on 27.9.60. Canx.
G-AMEX	DH.82A Tiger Moth	83346	T5639	20.10.50	To ZK-AYA 5/51. Canx 3.1.51.
G-AMEY	DH.82A Tiger Moth	85545	DE578	19.10.50	Crashed on take-off from Little Snoring after being stolen from its hangar on 16.5.68. Canx as WFU in 1969. (It was transported to Kirkbymoorside on 16.12.68 and was transmogrified into a Rumpler for a "Biggles" film as G-AXAL)
G-AMEZ	DH.82A Tiger Moth	85828	DE957	19.10.50	Crashed at Verden-Scharnhorst, West Germany on 16.8.64. Canx.
G-AMFA	DH.82A Tiger Moth	83296	T5603	17.10.50	To R.Thailand Navy in 1/51. Canx 18.1.51.
G-AMFB	DH.82A Tiger Moth	84212	T6033	17.10.50	To R.Thailand Navy in 1/51. Canx.
G-AMFC	DH.82A Tiger Moth	3822	N6485	19.10.50	To R.Thailand Navy in 2/51. Canx 19.2.51.
G-AMFD	DH.82A Tiger Moth	85440	DE432	18.10.50	Sold abroad in 11/50. Canx 30.11.50.
G-AMFE	DH.82A Tiger Moth	83475	T7090	17.10.50	Sold abroad in 11/50. Canx 30.11.50.
G-AMFF	DH.82A Tiger Moth	82883	R4973	17.10.50	Sold abroad in 11/50. Canx 30.11.50.
G-AMFG	DH.82A Tiger Moth	84630	T6182	19.10.50	Sold abroad in 11/50. Canx 30.11.50.
G-AMFH	DH.82A Tiger Moth	86283	NL824	18.10.50	Sold abroad in 11/50. Canx 30.11.50.
G-AMFI	DH.82A Tiger Moth	82377	N9276	18.10.50	Sold abroad in 11/50. Canx 30.11.50.
G-AMFJ	Airspeed AS.40 Oxford	3615	HM413	19.10.50	To Israel DF/AF as 2813 in 1951. Canx 15.12.51.
G-AMFK	Airspeed AS.40 Oxford	796	DF276	19.10.50	To Israel DF/AF as 2812 in 1951. Canx 19.12.51.
G-AMFL	Airspeed AS.40 Oxford	-	HM831	19.10.50	To Israel DF/AF as 2814 in 1952. Canx 28.2.51.
G-AMFM	Airspeed AS.40 Oxford	-	LB417	19.10.50	Not converted. Broken up at Kirkbridge as spares for Israeli DF/AF in 1951. Canx 17.1.51.
G-AMFN	DH.82A Tiger Moth	83454	T5819	20.10.50	To ZK-BJQ 8/54. Canx 18.8.54.
G-AMFO	Auster J/5B Autocar	2932		18.10.50	Crashed at Kirkaldy, Fife on 8.7.55. Canx.
G-AMFP	Auster J/5B Autocar	2933		21.10.50	Crashed near St.Julien, France on 10.8.72. Canx 3.10.72.
G-AMFR	Taylorcraft Auster 5	1828	TW499	23.10.50	To ZK-AWU 1/51. Canx 31.10.50.
G-AMFS	Taylorcraft Auster 5	1802	TW464	23.10.50	To PH-NEO 4/52. Canx 1.4.52.
G-AMFT	Taylorcraft Auster 5	1827	TW498	23.10.50	To VH-ARX 11/50. Canx 14.1.51.
G-AMFU	DH.104 Dove 6 (Originally regd as a Dove 1)	04117	VP-KDE	30.10.50	To OO-SCD 8/69. Canx 7.8.69.
G-AMFV	Douglas C-47A-50-DL Dakota	10105	ZS-DEF South African AF 6810/FL522/42-24243	15.11.50	CofA expired 8.6.73 & WFU at Baginton. Scrapped for spares at Lympne in 8/73. Canx as WFU 5.12.83.
G-AMFW	DH.82A Tiger Moth	83557	T5845	1.11.50	To ZK-AZY 9/51. Canx 29.8.51.
G-AMFX	DH.82A Tiger Moth	86286	NL827	7.11.50	To OO-AAS 1/51. Canx 12.12.50.
G-AMFY	DH.82A Tiger Moth	3986	N6713	11.11.50	To R.Thailand Navy in 1/51. Canx 17.1.51.
G-AMFZ	DH.82A Tiger Moth	84680	T6254	11.11.50	To R.Thailand Navy as "No.17" in 1/51. Canx 17.1.51.
G-AMGA	DH.82A Tiger Moth	82175	N6931	11.11.50	To R.Thailand Navy in 2/51. Canx 19.2.51.
G-AMGB	DH.82A Tiger Moth	82794	R4877	11.11.50	To R.Thailand Navy in 1/51. Canx 17.1.51.
G-AMGC	DH.82A Tiger Moth	83677	T7191	14.11.50	DBR near Hawarden, Chester on 10.11.63. Canx.
G-AMGD	Douglas C-47A-30-DL Dakota	9628	G-AJXL ZS-DDV/SAAF6802/FD906/42-23766	16.11.50	To VP-YTT 11/61. Canx 30.11.61.
G-AMGE	Percival P.34 Proctor III	H.377	LZ570	23.11.50	DBR at Woolsington on 10.5.63. Canx.

Regn	Type	c/n	Previous identity	Regn date	Fate or immediate subsequent identity (if known)
G-AMGF	Miles M.65 Gemini 7 (Originally regd as a Gemini 3A)	WAL/C/1003		29.11.50	WFU at Heathrow in 11/63 and broken up. Canx.
G-AMGG	Vickers 635 Viking 1B	290	ZS-BNE	19.12.50	Crashed at Agadir, Morocco on 22.12.59. Canx.
G-AMGH	Vickers 635 Viking 1B	293	D-BOBY (D-BEDO)/D-AEDO/D-CEDO/G-AMGH/ZS-BNH	19.12.50	WFU & stored at Cambridge in 10/60. Broken up at Southend in 7/61. Canx.
G-AMGI	Vickers 635 Viking 1B	297	XA192 G-AMGI/ZS-BNL	19.12.50	WFU & used as a cabin crew trainer at Heathrow in 6/60. Broken up. Canx.
G-AMGJ	Vickers 635 Viking 1B	295	ZS-BNJ	19.12.50	To D-AHUF in 4/57. Canx 16.4.57.
G-AMGK	Avro 685 York 1	1356	OD-ABV G-AMGK/XA191/WW512/G-AMGK/LV-AFZ/LV-XGP/(G-AHXP)	28.12.50	CofA expired 26.7.61 & WFU at Stansted. Broken up in 7/61. Canx.
G-AMGL	Avro 685 York 1	1354	LV-AFV LV-XGN/(G-AHXN)	28.12.50	To RAF as XA192 & crashed near Hamburg on 11.3.52. Canx.
G-AMGM	Avro 685 York 1	1355	LV-AFY LV-XGO/(G-AHXO)	28.12.50	DBR on landing at Lyneham on 27.11.52. Wreck transferred to Stansted. Canx as destroyed /53.
G-AMGN	Handley Page HPR.1 Marathon 1	119		29.12.50	To RAF as XA266 in 3/52. Canx 13.6.52.
G-AMGO	Handley Page HPR.1 Marathon 1	120		29.12.50	To RAF as XA267 in 3/52. Canx 13.6.52.
G-AMGP	Handley Page HPR.1 Marathon 1	121		29.12.50	To RAF as XA268 in 3/52. Canx 13.6.52.
G-AMGR	Handley Page HPR.1 Marathon 1	122	XA269 G-AMGR	29.12.50	Not converted. Stored at Shoreham in 5/59. Broken up at Havant in 2/62. Canx.
G-AMGS	Handley Page HPR.1 Marathon 1	123		29.12.50	To RAF as XA270 in 3/52. Canx 13.6.52.
G-AMGT	Handley Page HPR.1 Marathon 1	124		29.12.50	To RAF as XA271 in 3/52. Canx 13.6.52.
G-AMGU	Handley Page HPR.1 Marathon 1	125		29.12.50	To RAF as XA272 in 3/52. Canx 13.6.52.
G-AMGV	Handley Page HPR.1 Marathon 1	126		29.12.50	To RAF as XA273 in 3/52. Canx 13.6.52.
G-AMGW	Handley Page HPR.1 Marathon 1A (Originally regd as a Marathon 1)	127	VR-NAN G-AMGW	29.12.50	WFU & stored at Burnaston in 7/60. Scrapped in 1962. Canx.
G-AMGX	Handley Page HPR.1 Marathon 1A (Originally regd as a Marathon 1)	128	VR-NAO G-AMGX	29.12.50	WFU & stored in 8/56. Broken up at Southend in 1959. Canx.
G-AMGY	Hiller 360 UH-12A	165	N8165H	16. 1.51	Broken up at Redhill in 6/63. Canx.
G-AMGZ	DH.82A Tiger Moth	86477	NM157	15. 1.51	To ZK-AYD 5/51. Canx 1.3.51.
G-AMHA	DH.82A Tiger Moth	85304	DE258	19. 1.51	Sold abroad in 6/51. Canx 1.6.51.
G-AMHB	Westland-Sikorsky S-51 Mk.1B	WA/H/030		18. 1.51	To OO-CWA 5/51. Canx 12.5.51.
G-AMHC	Westland-Sikorsky S-51 Mk.1B	WA/H/029		18. 1.51	To OO-CWB 10/51. Canx 30.1.52.
G-AMHD	Westland-Sikorsky S-51 Mk.1B	WA/H/048		18. 1.51	To OO-CWC 10/51. Canx 7.2.52.
G-AMHE	Airspeed AS.40 Oxford	-	LX427	29. 1.51	To Israel DF/AF as 2815 in 5/52. Canx 30.5.52.
G-AMHF	DH.82A Tiger Moth (Rebuilt with components from G-BABA c/n 86584 ex F-BGDT/PG687)	83026	R5144	6. 2.51	
G-AMHG	DH.82A Tiger Moth	86448	NM128	6. 2.51	WFU at Portsmouth on 11.7.54. Canx.
G-AMHH	DH.82A Tiger Moth	84275	T6045	29. 1.51	To R.Thailand Navy in 2/51. Canx 19.2.51.
G-AMHI	DH.82A Tiger Moth	3700	BB759 G-AFGZ	30. 1.51	Crashed at East Meon, Petersfield on 25.7.58. Canx. Rebuilt & restored as G-AFGZ 2/89.
G-AMHJ	Douglas C-47A-25-DK Dakota	13468	SU-AZI G-AMHJ/ZS-BRW/KG651/42-108962	6. 2.51	
G-AMHK	Sikorsky S-55 Srs.1	55-016	XA842 G-AMHK/WW339/G-AMHK	6. 2.51	To LN-ORK 9/53. Canx 1.9.53.
G-AMHL	DH.82A Tiger Moth	84006	T7609	22. 2.51	Not converted. Canx 6.3.51.
G-AMHM	DH.104 Dove 6 (Originally regd as Dove 2)	04300		2. 3.51	To Katangan AF in 7/63. Canx 25.7.63.
G-AMHN	DH.82A Tiger Moth	3757	N5484	22. 3.51	To F-OAJQ 5/51. Canx 4.5.51.
G-AMHO	DH.82A Tiger Moth	84607	T6159	9. 3.51	To ZK-AYI 9/51. Canx 10.7.51.
G-AMHP	DH.82A Tiger Moth	85326	DE280	9. 3.51	Crashed at Thruxton on 23.4.57. Canx.
G-AMHR	Handley Page HPR.1 Marathon 1A (Originally regd as a Marathon 1)	129	VR-NAR G-AMHR	2. 3.51	WFU & stored at Burnaston in 7/60. Broken up. Canx.
G-AMHS	Handley Page HPR.5 Marathon 1A	130	XJ830 G-AMHS/VR-NAS/G-AMHS	2. 3.51	Not converted; stored at Hurn in 1959. Scrapped in 2/62. Canx.
G-AMHT	Handley Page HPR.1 Marathon 1A	131	XA274 G-AMHT	2. 3.51	Not converted; stored at Shoreham in 4/62. Broken up in 5/64. Canx.
G-AMHU	Handley Page HPR.1 Marathon 1A	132		2. 3.51	To RAF as XA275 in 3/52. Canx 13.6.52.
G-AMHV	Handley Page HPR.5 Marathon 1A	133	XJ831 G-AMHV/VR-NAT/G-AMHV	2. 3.51	To CF-NUH 3/61. Canx 11.3.61.
G-AMHW	Handley Page HPR.1 Marathon 1A	134	VR-NAU G-AMHW	2. 3.51	To R.Jordanian AF as VK501 9/54. Canx.
G-AMHX	Handley Page HPR.1 Marathon 1A	135		2. 3.51	To RAF as XA276 in 3/52. Canx 13.6.52.
G-AMHY	Handley Page HPR.1 Marathon 1A	136	XA277 G-AMHY	2. 3.51	To JA6009 in 7/54. Canx 21.7.54.
G-AMHZ	Handley Page HPR.1 Marathon 1A	137	XA278 G-AMHZ	2. 3.51	To JA6010 in 8/54. Canx 5.8.54.
G-AMIA	Handley Page HPR.1 Marathon 1A	138		2. 3.51	To XY-ACX 7/52. Canx 9.7.52.
G-AMIB	Handley Page HPR.1 Marathon 1A	139		2. 3.51	To XY-ACY 7/52. Canx 9.7.52.
G-AMIC	Handley Page HPR.1 Marathon 1A	140		2. 3.51	To XY-ACZ 7/52. Canx 9.7.52.
G-AMID	Airspeed AS.65 Consul	5250		10. 3.51	To F-BGPF 3/52. Canx 25.2.52.
G-AMIE	DH.82A Tiger Moth	84647	T6199	16. 3.51	DBR in forced landing at Finedon, near Wellingborough on 30.9.51. Canx 30.9.51.
G-AMIF	DH.82A Tiger Moth	3841	N6528	22. 3.51	To F-OAJR 8/51. Canx 30.5.51.
G-AMIG	DH.82A Tiger Moth	82405	N9318	22. 3.51	To ZK-AYM 5/51. Canx 24.4.51.
G-AMIH	Auster J/1B Aiglet	2706		28. 3.51	To F-OAMZ 2/53. Canx 28.1.53.
G-AMII	Taylorcraft Auster 5	1013	NJ626	29. 3.51	To VH-AZI 3/52. Canx 29.10.51.
G-AMIJ	DH.82A Tiger Moth	84702	T6287	9. 4.51	Not converted. Canx. Broken up at Portsmouth in 1951.
G-AMIK	DH.82A Tiger Moth	84709	T6294	9. 4.51	Not converted. Canx. Broken up at Croydon in 7/53.
G-AMIL	DH.82A Tiger Moth	84930	T6616	9. 4.51	Not converted. Canx. Broken up at Croydon in 7/53.
G-AMIM	DH.82A Tiger Moth	84953	T6639	9. 4.51	Not converted. Canx. Broken up at Portsmouth in 1951.

Regn	Type	c/n	Previous identity	Regn date	Fate or immediate subsequent identity (if known)
G-AMIN	DH.82A Tiger Moth	84986	T6686	9. 4.51	Not converted. Canx. Burnt at Hamsey Green on 5.11.56.
G-AMIO	DH.82A Tiger Moth	84135	T5984	9. 4.51	Not converted. Canx. Burnt at Hamsey Green on 5.11.56.
G-AMIP	DH.82A Tiger Moth	84053	T5963	9. 4.51	Not converted. Canx. Broken up at Croydon in 1954.
G-AMIR	DH.82A Tiger Moth	83591	T5855	9. 4.51	Not converted. Canx. Broken up at Portsmouth in 1951.
G-AMIS	DH.82A Tiger Moth	83347	T5669	9. 4.51	Not converted. Canx. Burnt at Hamsey Green on 5.11.56.
G-AMIT	DH.82A Tiger Moth	83257	T5538	9. 4.51	Not converted. Canx. Burnt at Hamsey Green on 5.11.56.
G-AMIU	DH.82A Tiger Moth	83228	T5495	9. 4.51	Cartwheeled on landing at Booker on 15.10.69. Canx.
G-AMIV	DH.82A Tiger Moth	83105	R5246	9. 4.51	WFU at Boxted 12.11.65. Canx as WFU 15.6.73. (Stored 1998)
G-AMIW	DH.82A Tiger Moth	3996	N6723	9. 4.51	Not converted. Canx. Burnt at Hamsey Green on 5.11.56.
G-AMIX	DH.82A Tiger Moth	85208	DE138	9. 4.51	To ZK-BFA 3/54. Canx 24.3.54.
G-AMIY	DH.82A Tiger Moth	85128	T6899	9. 4.51	Not converted. Canx. Burnt at Hamsey Green on 5.11.56.
G-AMIZ	DH.82A Tiger Moth	85143	T6914	9. 4.51	Not converted. Canx. Broken up at Portsmouth in 1951.
G-AMJA	DH.82A Tiger Moth	85169	T6960	9. 4.51	Not converted. Canx. Burnt at Hamsey Green on 5.11.56.
G-AMJB	DH.82A Tiger Moth	85177	T6968	9. 4.51	Not converted. Canx. Burnt at Hamsey Green on 5.11.56.
G-AMJC	DH.82A Tiger Moth	84610	T6162	9. 4.51	Not converted. Canx. Burnt at Hamsey Green on 5.11.56.
G-AMJD	DH.82A Tiger Moth	83728	T7238	9. 4.51	To OO-SOI 10/52. Canx 11.11.52.
G-AMJE	Auster J/1B Aiglet	2707		14. 4.51	Crashed at Fahl in the Sudan on 11.10.52. Canx.
G-AMJF	DH.82A Tiger Moth	84712	T6297	30. 4.51	DBR at Dunstable on 5.8.62. Canx.
G-AMJG	DH.82A Tiger Moth	84674	T6248	7. 5.51	To ZK-AYS 8/51. Canx 5.6.51.
G-AMJH	Bournemouth Non-Rigid Airship No.1	001		15. 5.51	WFU on 15.8.52. Canx 22.6.60.
G-AMJI	Bristol 173 Mk.2	12872	XH379 G-AMJI	5. 6.51	Crashed at Filton on 16.9.56. Wreck broken up at Old Mixon. Canx.
G-AMJJ	DH.104 Dove 4	04267	WB532	19. 6.51	Restored to RAF as WB532 in 6/56. Canx 15.12.56.
G-AMJK	DH.89A Dragon Rapide	6657	VT-ARV HG658	17. 5.51	To F-OBVL 10/61. Canx 9.10.61.
G-AMJL	DH.82A Tiger Moth	82070	N6800	28. 5.51	Crashed near Woolsington on 30.4.52. Canx.
G-AMJM	Taylorcraft Auster 5	1792	TW452	18. 5.51	To F-BBSO 9/51. Canx 8.8.51.
G-AMJN	DH.82A Tiger Moth	85212	DE142	21. 5.51	To D-EJIF 10/55. Canx 20.8.55.
G-AMJO	DH.82A Tiger Moth	84192	T6029	21. 5.51	Not converted. Scrapped at Gatwick in 12/52. Canx.
G-AMJP	Dart Kitten III	131		25. 5.51	Crashed at Hillington, King's Lynn on 5.6.66. Canx.
G-AMJR	DH.82A Tiger Moth	85167	T6958	23. 5.51	To OH-ELA 9/51. Canx 20.9.51.
G-AMJS	DH.82A Tiger Moth	84570	T6103	23. 5.51	To ZK-AXW 1/52. Canx 28.9.51.
G-AMJT	Westland-Sikorsky S-55 Whirlwind Srs.1	WA/1	G-17-1	25. 5.51	To RN as XA862 3/53. Canx 13.3.53.
G-AMJU	Douglas C-47B-5-DK Dakota	14480/25925	XF757 G-AMJU/KJ894/43-48664	25. 5.51	To 9Q-CIR 1/70. Canx 4.1.70.
G-AMJV	Taylorcraft Auster 4	976	MT340	11. 6.51	To F-DABR 1/53. Canx 28.1.53.
G-AMJW	Westland-Sikorsky S-51 Mk.1A	WA/H/120	G-17-2	9. 1.52	To R.Thailand AF as 305-53 in 5/53. Canx 22.5.53.
G-AMJX	Douglas C-47B-20-DK Dakota	15635/27080	KN214 43-49819	2. 6.51	To Moroccan AF as 49819/CN-ALJ in 8/63. Canx 12.8.63.
G-AMJY	Douglas C-47B-40-DK Dakota	16808/33556	KP254 44-77224	2. 6.51	To 4R-ACI 11/59. Canx 11.11.59.
G-AMJZ	DH.104 Dove 1B (Originally regd as a Dove 1)	04118	VP-KDF	13. 6.51	CofA expired on 18.9.60 & WFU at Bahrein. Canx as WFU 12.2.61.
G-AMKA	DH.104 Dove 2	04328		11. 6.51	NTU - To N4963N 7/51. Canx 19.6.51.
G-AMKB	DH.104 Dove 2	04329		11. 6.51	NTU - To N4266C 7/51. Canx 19.6.51.
G-AMKC	DH.104 Dove 2	04331		11. 6.51	NTU - To XB-REW 9/51. Canx 19.6.51.
G-AMKD	DH.104 Dove 2	04336		11. 6.51	NTU - To N1515V 9/51. Canx 19.6.51.
G-AMKE	Douglas C-47B-5-DK Dakota	14483/25928	KJ897 43-48667	23. 6.51	To VP-YUU 10/62. Canx 16.10.62.
G-AMKF	Auster J/5F Aiglet Trainer	2709	G-25-1	27. 6.51	To VH-AFS 1/52. Canx 7.12.51.
G-AMKG	Auster J/5G Cirrus Autocar	2982		27. 6.51	To VH-ADX 7/52. Canx 1.2.52.
G-AMKH	DH.82A Tiger Moth	3554	L6921	3. 7.51	Crashed at Fairoaks on 8.9.53. Canx.
G-AMKI	DH.82A Tiger Moth	84643	(OH-ELB) G-AMKI/T6195	3. 7.51	To EI-AGC 5/53. Canx 24.4.53.
G-AMKJ	DH.82A Tiger Moth	85892	DF143	27. 6.51	To OH-ELB 5/52. Canx 8.4.52.
G-AMKK	Percival P.50 Prince 3	P50/37		13. 7.51	To VR-SDR 6/52. Canx 10.6.52.
G-AMKL	Auster B.4	2983	XA177 G-AMKL/G-25-2	3. 7.51	Dismantled at Rearsby in 1956. Canx 24.9.58.
G-AMKM	Percival P.44 Proctor 5	Ae.138		6. 7.51	To F-BFVP 8/51. Canx 27.7.51.
G-AMKN	DH.82A Tiger Moth	84803	T6564	9. 7.51	To ZK-BAA 12/51. Canx 25.7.51.
G-AMKO	DH.82A Tiger Moth	84772	T6398	9. 7.51	To ZK-BBD 8/51. Canx 25.7.51.
G-AMKP	DH.82A Tiger Moth	84031	T5956	9. 7.51	To New Zealand in 7/51. Canx 25.7.51.
G-AMKR	DH.82A Tiger Moth	84194	T6031	9. 7.51	To New Zealand in 7/51. Canx 25.7.51.
G-AMKS	DH.104 Dove 1B (Originally regd as a Dove 1)	04290	ZS-DFJ G-AMKS	18. 7.51	CofA expired 10.11.72. Broken up as spares for G-AWFM. Canx as destroyed 4.11.76.
G-AMKT	DH.104 Dove 1B (Originally regd as a Dove 1)	04291		18. 7.51	Crashed in forced landing 5 miles from Walton Airport, Lahore, Pakistan on 19.2.60. Canx as destroyed 24.5.60.
G-AMKU	Auster J/1B Aiglet (Mod to J/1S standard)	2721	ST-ABD SN-ABD/G-AMKU	10. 7.51	
G-AMKV	DH.82A Tiger Moth	84551	T6060	25. 7.51	Not converted. Canx 5.6.59.
G-AMKW	Percival P.54 Prince 6B (Originally regd as a P.50 Prince 3B)	P50/34		17. 8.51	WFU on 7.8.70. To Stansted Fire School in 1971. Canx.
G-AMKX	Percival P.54 Prince 6B (Originally regd as a P.50 Prince 3B)	P50/35		17. 8.51	WFU on 22.12.69. To Stansted Fire School in 1971. Canx.
G-AMKY	Percival P.54 Prince 6B (Originally regd as a P.50 Prince 3B)	P50/36		17. 8.51	WFU on 16.10.70. To Stansted Fire School compound 3/71. Canx.
G-AMKZ	Miles M.65 Gemini 3A	WAL/C/1005		2. 8.51	To SE-CMX 8/61. Canx 9.8.61.
G-AMLA	DH.82A Tiger Moth	83076	R5214	8. 8.51	To ZK-BAP 3/52. Canx 16.1.52.
G-AMLB	DH.82A Tiger Moth	3724	AX791 (AX787)/G-AFJG	10. 8.51	Not converted. Scrapped at Wolverhampton in 1953. Canx.

Regn	Type	c/n	Previous identity	Regn date	Fate or immediate subsequent identity (if known)
G-AMLC	DHC.1 Chipmunk 21	C1/0414		22. 8.51	To VH-MLO 8/54. Canx 29.5.54.
G-AMLD	DH.82A Tiger Moth	84723	T6308	7. 8.51	To ZK-AZG 4/52. Canx 27.11.51.
G-AMLE	DH.82A Tiger Moth	84899	T6570	17. 8.51	To ZK-AXX 3/52. Canx 24.1.52.
G-AMLF	DH.82A Tiger Moth	86572	PG675	18. 8.51	To N675LF 7/71. Canx 21.7.71.
G-AMLG	DH.82A Tiger Moth	85686	DE772	23. 8.51	To ZK-AZV 3/52. Canx 1.10.51.
G-AMLH	DH.82A Tiger Moth	85534	DE567	22. 8.51	Crashed at Woolsington on 14.11.53. Canx.
G-AMLI	Auster J/5B Autocar	2954		22. 8.51	To ZK-BAE 2/52. Canx 9.1.52.
G-AMLJ	Bristol 170 Freighter 31E	13072	OD-ACM	23. 8.51	To EI-APC 3/66. Canx 2.3.66.
			G-AMLJ/EI-AFR/G-18-116/G-AMLJ		
G-AMLK(1)	Bristol 170 Freighter 31E	13073	G-18-112	23. 8.51R	NTU - To G-AMWA 8/51. Canx.
G-AMLK(2)	Bristol 170 Freighter 31M	13060	ZK-EPD	10. 9.82	Restored as ZK-EPD 4/84. Canx 4.4.84.
			R.New Zealand AF NZ5907/G-18-114		
G-AMLL	Bristol 170 Freighter 31E	13074	EI-AFS	23. 8.51	To CF-UME 5/66. Canx 25.4.66.
			G-AMLL		
G-AMLM	Bristol 170 Freighter 31E	13075	G-41-2-66	23. 8.51	To ZK-CQD 8/66. Canx 10/66.
			EC-AHN/EC-WHN/G-AMLM		
G-AMLN	Bristol 170 Freighter 31E	13076		23. 8.51	To EI-AFT 1/53. Canx 9.9.52.
G-AMLO	Bristol 170 Freighter 31E	13077		23. 8.51	To EC-WHO/EC-AHO 2/53. Canx 17.10.52.
G-AMLP	Bristol 170 Freighter 32	13078		23. 8.51	To CF-QWJ 7/71. Canx 9.6.71.
	(Originally regd as a Freighter 31E)				
G-AMLR	Bristol 170 Freighter 31MC	13079	G-18-120	23. 8.51R	NTU - To R.Canadian AF as 9698 in 2/53. Canx 1.4.53.
G-AMLS	Bristol 170 Freighter 31MNZ	13080		23. 8.51R	NTU - To R.New Zealand AF as NZ5909 in 6/53. Canx 29.6.53.
G-AMLT	Bristol 170 Freighter 31MI	13081	G-18-124	23. 8.51R	NTU - To Iraq AF as 330 in 4/53. Canx 4.4.53.
G-AMLU	Taylorcraft Auster 4	756	MT193	24. 8.51	DBF at Wyberton on 6.4.52. Canx.
G-AMLV	DH.82A Tiger Moth	83754	T7244	29. 8.51	Not converted. Broken up at Gatwick in 3/55. Canx.
G-AMLW	Percival P.50 Prince 4	P50/43	F-BJAI	23.11.51	Restored as F-BJAI in 4/61. Canx 16.6.60.
	(Originally regd as a Prince 3)		G-AMLW/VH-AGF(3)/G-AMLW/YV-P-AEB/G-AMLW		
G-AMLX	Percival P.50 Prince 4	P50/44		3.12.51	To VR-UDA in 3/55. Canx 26.3.55.
	(Originally regd as a Prince 3)				
G-AMLY	Percival P.50 Prince 4	P50/45	YV-P-AEC	3.12.51	To VR-UDC 8/58. Canx 11.7.58.
	(Originally regd as a Prince 3)		G-AMLY		
G-AMLZ	Percival P.50 Prince 6E	P50/46	(VR-TBN)	23.11.51	CofA expired 18.6.71 & WFU at Baginton. Canx as WFU
	(Originally regd as a Prince 3)		G-AMLZ		9.10.84. (On display at Caernarfon Air World 2/97)
G-AMMA	DHC.1 Chipmunk 21	C1/0470		21. 9.51	To OY-DHJ 7/69. Canx 23.4.69.
G-AMMB	Percival P.50 Prince 2	P50/13		21. 9.51	To ZS-DGX 11/52. Canx 15.12.52.
	(Originally allocated as a Prince 3)				
G-AMMC	Miles M.14A Hawk Trainer III	779	L8353	15. 9.51	To ZK-AYW 11/53. Canx 1.10.53.
G-AMMD	Miles M.14A Hawk Trainer III	741	L8285	15. 9.51	To ZK-AWX 12/52. Canx 16.11.52.
G-AMME	Miles M.65 Gemini 3A	WAL/C/1006		18. 9.51	Canx as WFU 10.4.71. CofA expired 21.4.71 & WFU at Baginton. (Parts to G-AKHZ).
G-AMMF	DH.82A Tiger Moth	85225	DE155	21. 9.51	To ZK-AZW 10/52. Canx 4.3.52.
G-AMMG	DH.82A Tiger Moth	82793	R4876	21. 9.51	To ZK-BAL 6/52. Canx 18.1.52.
G-AMMH	DH.82A Tiger Moth	83644	T7178	21. 9.51	To ZK-BAK 4/52. Canx 18.1.52.
G-AMMI	Auster J/5	2901		17. 9.51	To VH-KAG 1/52. Canx 1/52.
G-AMMJ	Douglas C-47B-40-DK Dakota		VP-BAU	1.10.51	To CF-FAX 4/52. Canx 13.3.52.
		16770/33518	KP233/44-77186		
G-AMMK	DH.82A Tiger Moth	82521	N9494	2.10.51	To ZK-AYY 3/52. Canx 12.10.51.
G-AMML	DH.82A Tiger Moth	84134	T5983	2.10.51	To ZK-AYX 7/52. Canx 12.10.51.
G-AMMM	Auster J/1B Aiglet	2719		1.10.51	To F-OAJV 11/51. Canx 12.11.51.
G-AMMN(1)	DH.82A Tiger Moth	83713	T7392	. .51R	NTU - To ZK-BJO 3/55. Canx.
G-AMMN(2)	DH.82A Tiger Moth	83707	T7386	4.10.51	To ZK-BCB 11/52. Canx 18.10.52.
G-AMMO	DH.82A Tiger Moth	85151	T6942	4.10.51	To ZK-BAX 11/52. Canx 21.2.52.
G-AMMP	DH.82A Tiger Moth	85184	T6975	6.10.51	To ZK-BCA 11/52. Canx 18.10.52.
G-AMMR	Auster J/1B Aiglet	2744		11.10.51	CofA expired 19.4.60 & WFU. Canx.
G-AMMS	Auster J/5K Aiglet Trainer	2745		11.10.51	
	(Originally J/5F with c/n 2720)				
G-AMMT	DH.82A Tiger Moth	84153	T6020	11.10.51	To ZK-AZP 5/52. Canx 29.1.52.
G-AMMU	Auster J/5	2902		12.10.51	To AP-AFP 2/52. Canx 15.2.52.
G-AMMV	DH.82A Tiger Moth	3985	N6712	17.10.51	To ZK-AZQ 5/52. Canx 8.1.52.
G-AMMW	DH.82A Tiger Moth	82215	N6977	17.10.51	To ZK-BBL 8/52. Canx 4.3.52.
G-AMMX	DH.82A Tiger Moth	83478	T7093	17.10.51	To ZK-BAN 7/52. Canx 28.3.52.
G-AMMY	Hiller 360 UH-12A	148	OO-MAT	26.10.51	Crashed at Grantchester, near Cambridge on 20.11.56. Canx.
			N8148H		
G-AMMZ	Auster J/5B Autocar	2948		24.10.51	Crashed at Brough-under-Stainmore on 28.10.60. Canx.
G-AMNA	Avro 652A Anson 19 Srs.1	-	VL298	30.10.51	Restored to RAF as VL298 in 4/53. Canx 6.3.53.
G-AMNB	Auster J/5B Autocar	2950		1.11.51	To ZK-BET 12/53. Canx 10.11.53.
G-AMNC	Auster J/5P Autocar	2953		1.11.51	To ZK-BVL 9/57. Canx 21.8.57.
	(Originally regd as a J/5B)				
G-AMND	DH.82A Tiger Moth	85383	DE361	7.11.51	To ZK-BAV 3/52. Canx 1.2.52.
G-AMNE	DH.82A Tiger Moth	84526	T8253	18. 4.52	To ZK-BBK 8/52. Canx 3.6.52.
G-AMNF	DH.82A Tiger Moth	84648	T6200	13.11.51	To ZK-BAD 7/52. Canx 25.2.52.
G-AMNG	DH.82A Tiger Moth	84649	T6201	13.11.51	To ZK-BAC 7/52. Canx 24.1.52.
G-AMNH	DH.82A Tiger Moth	86451	NM131	16.11.51	To ZK-BAO 3/52. Canx 11.12.51.
G-AMNI	Taylorcraft Auster 5	1030	NJ637	21.11.51	To F-BGPC 4/52. Canx 16.4.52.
G-AMNJ	Vickers 635 Viking 1B	296	ZS-BNK	27.11.51	To D-CEDA 11/55. Canx 2.11.55.
G-AMNK	Vickers 634 Viking 1B	210	SU-AFM	26.11.51	Crashed into sea after take-off from Heraklion, Crete
			EI-ADH		on 24.8.60. Canx.
G-AMNL	Douglas C-47B-35-DK Dakota		XF767	30.11.51	To I-TAVO 1/62. Canx 23.11.61.
		16644/33392	G-AMNL/KN682/44-77060		
G-AMNM	Auster J/5F Aiglet Trainer	2731		18.12.51	To VT-DGD 4/52. Canx 2.4.52.
G-AMNN	DH.82A Tiger Moth	86457	NM137	24.12.51	(Crashed at Redhill on 27.5.64)
	(Composite from unidentified airframe; the "real" G-AMNN may have been absorbed into G-BPAJ)				
G-AMNO	DH.82A Tiger Moth	3709	N5446	1. 1.52	Crashed at Turnhouse on 24.3.57. Canx.

Regn	Type	c/n	Previous identity	Regn date	Fate or immediate subsequent identity (if known)
G-AMNP	DH.82A Tiger Moth	84775	T6401	5. 2.52	To VR-RBY 6/52. Canx 4.4.52.
G-AMNR	Vickers 635 Viking 1B	291	ZS-BNF	4. 1.52	CofA expired 13.4.61 & WFU at Cambridge. Broken up. Canx.
G-AMNS	Vickers 635 Viking 1B	294	ZS-BNI	4. 1.52	To Argentine AF as T-90 in 1/56. Canx 26.1.56.
G-AMNT	Percival P.50 Prince 3A	P50/41		18. 2.52	To R.Thailand AF as Q1-1/98 in 4/52. Canx 4.4.52.
G-AMNU	Taylorcraft Auster 5	1603	TJ587	11. 1.52	To D-EFIR 10/56. Canx 12.9.56.
G-AMNV	Douglas C-47D-40-DK Dakota	16833/33581	6V-AAM(2) G-AMNV/SE-EDI/G-AMNV/EC-ATM/G-AMNV/KP279/44-77249	16. 1.52	To VQ-ZEA 11/65. Canx 11.11.65.
G-AMNW	Douglas C-47B-1-DK Dakota	14177/25622	KJ838 43-48361	16. 1.52	WFU at Southend on 14.2.66. Broken up in 1/70. Canx.
G-AMNX	Vickers 635 Viking 3B (Originally regd as Viking 1B)	292	ZS-BNG	15. 1.52	WFU in 2/61 & stored at Heathrow. Broken up in 10/61. Canx.
G-AMNY	Vickers 701 Viscount	6		23. 5.52	DBR on landing at Luqa Airport, Malta on 5.1.60.
G-AMNZ(1)	Vickers 701 Viscount	7		. .52R	NTU - To G-AMOG 5/52. Canx.
G-AMNZ(2)	Vickers 701 Viscount	20	(G-AMOG)	25. 5.52	WFU at Cardiff-Rhoose 6/71. CofA expired 23.9.71. Broken up in 10/71. Canx.
G-AMOA	Vickers 701 Viscount	9		23. 5.52	DBR at Bristol-Lulsgate on 19.1.70. CofA expired 14.11.70. Stored engineless in 1971. Canx as WFU 6.5.71.
G-AMOB	Vickers 701 Viscount	11		23. 5.52	To PP-SRI 10/62. Canx 26.2.63.
G-AMOC	Vickers 701 Viscount	13	VP-BCH G-AMOC	23. 5.52	WFU & stored 9.10.70. Broken up in 10/71 at Cardiff-Rhoose.
G-AMOD	Vickers 701 Viscount	15		23. 5.52	To PP-SRJ 10/62. Canx 26.2.63.
G-AMOE	Vickers 701 Viscount	17		23. 5.52	WFU on 6.1.72. Used for cabin crew training in 1/72. Half of fuselage mated to G-AOHJ in 1976. Preserved at Lampton Pleasure Park in 4/77, marked as "G-WHIZ". Broken up in 3/93. Canx.
G-AMOF	Vickers 701 Viscount	19		23. 5.52	To PP-SRM 10/62. Canx 26.2.63.
G-AMOG(1)	Vickers 701 Viscount	20		. .52R	NTU - To G-AMNZ 5/52. Canx.
G-AMOG(2)	Vickers 701 Viscount	7	(G-AMNZ)	23. 5.52	WFU at Cardiff in 1971. On display since 4/76 at RAF Cosford Museum. Canx as WFU 17.5.76.
G-AMOH	Vickers 701 Viscount	21		23. 5.52	WFU & stored on 9.11.71. Broken up in 9/72 at Rhoose Airport, Cardiff. Canx as WFU 1.9.72.
G-AMOI	Vickers 701 Viscount	22		23. 5.52	To (PP-SRK)/PP-SRL 10/62. Canx 23.3.63.
G-AMOJ	Vickers 701 Viscount	23		23. 5.52	WFU & stored 19.12.70. Broken up in 12/71 at Cardiff. Canx.
G-AMOK	Vickers 701X Viscount	24		23. 5.52	To YV-C-AMB 4/63. Canx 2.4.63.
G-AMOL	Vickers 701 Viscount	25		23. 5.52	Crashed at Speke Airport on 20.7.65. Canx.
G-AMOM	Vickers 701 Viscount	26		23. 5.52	Crashed on take-off at Blackbushe on 20.1.56 and was destroyed in the subsequent fire. Canx.
G-AMON	Vickers 701 Viscount	27		23. 5.52	WFU & stored at Rhoose Airport in 12/70. Broken up at Cardiff in 5/79. Canx as WFU 10.5.76.
G-AMOO	Vickers 701 Viscount	28		23. 5.52	WFU & stored at Rhoose Airport on 19.12.70. Broken up in 10/71 at Cardiff. Canx.
G-AMOP	Vickers 701 Viscount	29		23. 5.52	WFU & stored at Rhoose Airport in 8/71. Broken up in 9/72. Canx as WFU 13.4.72.
G-AMOR	Taylorcraft Auster 5	1781	(PH-NER) TW451	24. 1.52	To OH-AUE 5/52. Canx 22.3.52.
G-AMOS	Auster J/5F Aiglet Trainer (Built as single seater with Gipsy Major 1G engine)	2718		28. 1.52	Crashed in Austrian Alps, 20 miles from Salzburg, Austria on 10.4.53. Canx.
G-AMOT	Percival P.50 Prince 4D (Originally regd as a Prince 3)	P50/47		5. 2.52	Stalled & crashed in forced-landing in dence bush 4 miles southwest of Mackinnon Road airstrip, about 70 miles north of Mombasa, Kenya on 6.6.58. Canx.
G-AMOU	DH.82A Tiger Moth	84695	N200D 9M-ALJ/VR-RBZ/G-AMOU/T6269	5. 2.52	Canx 18.11.93 on sale to Thailand. Operated at Don Muang by Thai AF Museum as "21" - no civil regn.
G-AMOV	Auster J/5F Aiglet Trainer	2768		4. 2.52	To VH-BTQ 6/54. Canx 29.4.54.
G-AMOW	Westland-Sikorsky S-51 Mk.1A	WA/H/122	G-17-3	13. 2.52	NTU - To Italian AF as MM80038 in 2/53. Canx 2/53.
G-AMOX	Westland-Sikorsky S-51 Mk.1A	WA/H/123	G-17-6	13. 2.52	To Italian AF as MM80040 in 2/53. Canx.
G-AMOY	Auster J/5G Cirrus Autocar	2985		6. 2.52	Crashed near Khartoum, Sudan on 12.10.54. Canx.
G-AMOZ	Auster J/5G Cirrus Autocar	2986		6. 2.52	To SN-ABI 3/56. Canx 17.1.56.
G-AMPA	Auster J/5G Cirrus Autocar	2987		6. 2.52	To SN-ABE 3/56. Canx 17.1.56.
G-AMPB	Auster J/5G Cirrus Autocar	2988		6. 2.52	To SN-ABF 3/56. Canx 17.1.56.
G-AMPC	Auster J/5G Cirrus Autocar	2989	SN-ABC G-AMPC	6. 2.52	To SN-ADG 3/56. Canx 17.1.56.
G-AMPD	DH.82A Tiger Moth	85874	DF125	20. 2.52	To ZK-BAS 7/52. Canx 23.3.52.
G-AMPE(1)	Bristol 170 Freighter 31	13127	G-18-128	. .52R	NTU - To G-AMWB 2/52. Canx.
G-AMPE(2)	SNCAN NC.854S Chardonneret	54	G-BIUP F-BFSC	. 8.82R	NTU - Remained as G-BIUP. Canx.
G-AMPF(1)	Bristol 170 Freighter 31	13128	G-18-129	. .52R	NTU - To G-AMWC 2/52. Canx.
G-AMPF(2)	PA-18-95 Super Cub	18-2048	D-EMVY R.Netherlands AF R-52/52-2448	1. 2.85	Fatal crash when aircraft ditched in the sea 10 miles north of Dinard, France on 10.4.87. Canx by CAA 5.2.92.
G-AMPG(1)	Bristol 170 Freighter 31	13131	G-18-132	. .52R	NTU - To G-AMWD 2/52. Canx.
G-AMPG(2)	PA-12 Super Cruiser	12-985	N2647M NC2647M	25. 3.85	
G-AMPH	Bristol 170 Freighter 31	13132	G-18-133	. .52R	NTU - To G-AMWE 2/52. Canx.
G-AMPI(1)	Bristol 170 Freighter 31	13133	G-18-134	. .52R	NTU - To G-AMWF 2/52. Canx.
G-AMPI(2)	SNCAN Stampe SV-4C	213	N6RA F-BCFX	13. 2.84	(Frame stored Staverton 3/92)
G-AMPJ	Auster J/5A Cropduster	2905		21. 2.52	Crashed at Langworth, near Lincoln on 26.6.56. Canx.
G-AMPK	Auster J/5A Cropduster	2906		21. 2.52	To F-OAKN 4/52. Canx 19.3.52.
G-AMPL	Percival P.34A Proctor III	H.421	LZ631	22. 2.52	Not converted. Scrapped at Croydon. Canx.
G-AMPM	DH.82A Tiger Moth	86128	EM945	23. 2.52	To ZK-BBF 4/52. Canx 31.3.52.
G-AMPN	DH.82A Tiger Moth	85829	DE969	23. 2.52	To ZK-BBG 7/52. Canx 31.3.52.

Regn	Type	c/n	Previous identity	Regn date	Fate or immediate subsequent identity (if known)
G-AMPO	Douglas C-47B-30-DK Dakota (Regd with c/n 33186/16438)	16437/33185	LN-RTO G-AMPO/KN566/44-76853	25. 2.52	(Stored 5/98 Coventry)
G-AMPP	Douglas C-47B-15-DK Dakota	15272/26717	XF756 G-AMPP/KK136/43-49456	4. 3.52	WFU at Lasham. Canx 7.2.71. Used marks G-AMSU in Dan-Air Museum. To Euro-Disney, France in 1993.
G-AMPR	Percival P.50 Prince 4E (Originally regd as a Prince 3)	P50/48		12. 3.52	To VR-TBN 2/56. Canx 2.11.55.
G-AMPS	Douglas C-47B-25-DK Dakota	15993/32741	KN371 44-76409	4. 3.52	To VP-YKN 5/53. Canx 13.3.53.
G-AMPT	Douglas C-47B-30-DK Dakota	16187/32935	KN462 44-76603	4. 3.52	To VP-YKM 5/53. Canx 14.5.53.
G-AMPU	Auster J/5	2903	VQ-CAA G-AMPU	1. 4.52	DBF at Kosti, Sudan on 3.1.61. Canx.
G-AMPV	Auster J/5	2904	VQ-CAB G-AMPV	1. 4.52	Crashed at Ringway Airport, Manchester on 10.6.61. Canx.
G-AMPW	Auster J/5B Autocar	2961		28. 3.52	DBR near Bonnybridge on 23.4.74. Canx 30.5.84.
G-AMPX	Auster J/5A Cropduster	3000		20. 3.52	To ZK-BDW 2/54. Canx 1.1.54.
G-AMPY	Douglas C-47B-15-DK Dakota	15124/26569	(EI-BKJ) G-AMPY/N15751/G-AMPY/TF-FIO/G-AMPY/JY-ABE/"JY-AAE"/G-AMPY/KK116/43-49308	8. 3.52	
G-AMPZ	Douglas C-47B-30-DK Dakota	16124/32872	EI-BDT(2) G-AMPZ/TF-AIV/G-41-3-66/(PH-RIC)/(OD-AEQ)/G-AMPZ/OD-AEQ/G-AMPZ/KN442/44-76540	8. 3.52	
G-AMRA	Douglas C-47B-15-DK Dakota	15290/26735	XE280 G-AMRA/KK151/43-49474	8. 3.52	
G-AMRB	Douglas C-47B-35-DK Dakota	16670/33418	KN701 44-77086	8. 3.52	Crashed near Largs, Ayr on 28.3.56. Canx.
G-AMRC	DH.82A Tiger Moth	3406	BB679 G-ADOM	14. 3.52	To ZK-BBB 6/52. Canx 22.4.52.
G-AMRD	DH.82A Tiger Moth	3695	BD142 G-AFHT	14. 3.52	To ZK-BBC 6/52. Canx 22.4.52.
G-AMRE	Westland-Sikorsky S-51 Mk.1A	WA/H/121	LN-ORG G-AMRE	18. 3.52	Crashed at Yeovil, Somerset on 29.4.57. Canx.
G-AMRF	Auster J/5F Aiglet Trainer	2716	VT-DHA G-AMRF	20. 3.52	
G-AMRG	Miles M.65 Gemini 1A	6313	VR-SDJ VR-RGG/VR-GGG	22. 3.52	To HB-EEH 8/58. Canx 13.9.58.
G-AMRH	DH.82A Tiger Moth	86411	NL979	24. 3.52	To OO-SOG 5/52. Canx 18.4.52.
G-AMRI	Avro 685 York C.1	-	XF739 G-AMRI/MW138	26. 3.52	To OD-ACD 6/55. Canx 24.6.55.
G-AMRJ	Avro 685 York C.1	-	XG897 G-AMRJ/MW326	26. 3.52	To OD-ACE 7/55. Canx 19.7.55.
G-AMRK	Gloster Gladiator 1	-	L8032 "K8032"/G-AMRK/L8032	16. 5.52	
G-AMRL	Auster J/5F Aiglet Trainer	2779		3. 4.52	To EI-AUS 11/70. Canx.
G-AMRM	DH.82A Tiger Moth	83513	T7106	18. 4.52	To ZK-BBI 8/52. Canx 3.6.52.
G-AMRN	DH.104 Dove 6 (Originally regd as a Dove 1, then Dove 2, then Dove 6B)	04024	ZS-AVH (ZS-BSA)	4. 4.52	To TF-EVM 8/64. Canx 10.8.64.
G-AMRO	Bristol 170 Freighter 31M	13124	G-18-125	1. 4.52	NTU - To Iraqi AF as 331 in 5/53. Canx 25.5.53.
G-AMRP	Bristol 170 Freighter 31E	13125	G-44-1-66 EC-AHH/EC-WHH/(G-AMRP)/G-18-126	1. 4.52	To ZK-CPU 7/66. Canx 23.7.66.
G-AMRR	Bristol 170 Freighter 31 (Originally regd as Mk.31E)	13126	EC-AHI EC-WHI/(G-AMRR)/G-18-127	1. 4.52	To ZK-CPT 5/66. Canx 7.5.66.
G-AMRS	Bristol 170 Freighter 31E	13129	G-18-130	1. 4.52R	NTU - To EC-WHJ/EC-AHJ 6/53. Canx 14.11.52.
G-AMRT	Bristol 170 Freighter 31E	13130	G-18-131	1. 4.52R	NTU - To EC-WHK/EC-AHK 7/53. Canx 14.11.52.
G-AMRU	Bristol 170 Freighter 31	13136		1. 4.52R	NTU - To CF-FZU 1/53. Canx 10.3.53.
G-AMRV	Bristol 170 Freighter 31	13137		1. 4.52R	NTU - To CF-TFX 9/53. Canx 4.9.53.
G-AMRW	Bristol 170 Freighter 31	13138		1. 4.52R	NTU - To CF-TFY 10/53. Canx 4.9.53.
G-AMRX	Bristol 170 Freighter 31	13139		1. 4.52R	NTU - To CF-TFZ 10/53. Canx 4.9.53.
G-AMRY	Bristol 170 Freighter 31	13140	G-18-142	1. 4.52R	NTU - To F-VNAR 10/53. Canx 2.9.53.
G-AMRZ	Bristol 170 Freighter 31	13141	G-18-143	1. 4.52R	NTU - To F-VNAS 10/53. Canx 2.9.53.
G-AMSA	Bristol 170 Freighter 32 (Originally regd as Mk.31E)	13142	XH385 G-AMSA	1. 4.52	WFU at Lydd on 30.6.65. Scrapped in 4/67. Canx.
G-AMSB	Bristol 170 Freighter 31MB	13143		1. 4.52	To Burmese AF as UB721 in 3/54. Canx 5.10.53.
G-AMSC	DH.82A Tiger Moth	84676	T6250	9. 4.52	To F-OAMB 7/53. Canx 31.5.52.
G-AMSD	DH.82A Tiger Moth	84738	T6364	9. 4.52	To F-OAMC 7/53. Canx 31.5.52.
G-AMSE	DH.82A Tiger Moth	85005	T6705	9. 4.52	To PH-UFG 7/52. Canx 10.7.52.
G-AMSF	Douglas C-47B-5-DK Dakota	14380/25825	XF646 G-AMSF/KJ880/43-48564	21. 4.52	Crashed at Elmdon Airport, Birmingham on 5.3.60. Canx.
G-AMSG	SIPA 903	77	OO-VBL F-BGHB	25.11.81	(On overhaul Kintbury 8/97)
G-AMSH	Douglas C-47B-35-DK Dakota	16583/33331	XF667 G-AMSH/XF648/G-AMSH/KN642/44-76999	21. 4.52	Canx 13.12.66 on sale to Lebanon. To VR-ABE 3/67.
G-AMSI	Douglas C-47B-5-DK Dakota	14642/26087	KJ919 43-48826	24. 4.52	To ZS-DHW 5/53. Canx.
G-AMSJ	Douglas C-47B-35-DK Dakota	16477/33225	XF768 G-AMSJ/KN590/44-76893	24. 4.52	To I-TAVI 11/61. Canx 23.11.61.
G-AMSK	Douglas C-47B-30-DK Dakota	16206/32954	XF769 G-AMSK/KN477/44-76622	24. 4.52	To VP-YNH 8/55. Canx.
G-AMSL	Douglas C-47B-10-DK Dakota	14966/26411	XF766 G-AMSL/KJ975/43-49150	26. 4.52	Destroyed on ground at Dukhan, Arabia on 18.2.56. Canx.
G-AMSM	Douglas C-47B-20-DK Dakota	15764/27209	KN274 43-49948	28. 4.52	Ground-looped on take-off from Lydd Airport on 17.8.78. Canx as WFU 11.9.78.

Regn	Type	c/n	Previous identity	Regn date	Fate or immediate subsequent identity (if known)
G-AMSN	Douglas C-47B-35-DK Dakota	16631/33379	N3455 G-AMSN/EI-BSI/SU-BFZ/N3455/G-AMSN/KN673/44-77047	28. 4.52	(Stored 10/97 North Weald)
G-AMSO	Douglas C-47B-40-DK Dakota	16820/33568	KP266 44-77236	29. 4.52	To VP-KKH 10/52. Canx 21.10.52.
G-AMSP	DH.114 Heron 1B	14009		15. 5.52	To CF-EYX 7/53. Canx 13.7.53.
G-AMSR	Douglas C-47B-10-DK Dakota	14799/26244	KJ952 44-48983	1. 5.52	To ZS-DJZ 7/54. Canx.
G-AMSS	Douglas C-47B-25-DK Dakota	16092/32840	KN415 44-76508	5. 5.52	To EP-AIQ 11/68. Canx 2.11.68.
G-AMST	Douglas C-47B-30-DK Dakota	16207/32955	KN478 44-76623	29. 4.52	To VP-KKI 9/52. Canx 30.9.52.
G-AMSU	Douglas C-47B-40-DK Dakota	16800/33548	KP246 44-77216	16. 5.52	WFU at Lasham on 6.2.69. Scrapped. Canx as WFU 26.2.73.
"G-AMSU"	Douglas C-47B-15-DK Dakota	15272/26717	G-AMPP XF756/G-AMPP/KK136/43-49456	-----	Marks used for Dan-Air Museum - See G-AMPP. Canx.
G-AMSV	Douglas C-47B-25-DK Dakota	16072/32820	F-BSGV G-AMSV/KN397/44-76488	15. 5.52	
G-AMSW	Douglas C-47B-30-DK Dakota	16171/32919	KN449 44-76587	15. 5.52	Crashed into Mt.Canigou, near Perpignan, France on 7.10.61. Canx.
G-AMSX	Douglas C-47B-35-DK Dakota	16448/33196	KN573 44-76864	15. 5.52	To VP-GCF 3/66. Canx 12.1.66.
G-AMSY	DH.82A Tiger Moth	82205	N6967	16. 5.52	DBR on landing at Southend on 6.11.55. Canx.
G-AMSZ	Taylorcraft Auster 5	838	N34DW G-AMSZ/MS971	22. 5.52	Canx as WFU 30.1.80. Marks G-HOLS issued in 7/79 for proposed rebuild as a Warner Special with a Bonner engine.
G-AMTA	Auster J/5F Aiglet Trainer	2780		24. 5.52	
G-AMTB	Auster J/5F Aiglet Trainer	2781		24. 5.52	WFU on 12.9.65 & used as instructional airframe. Sold as spares in 9/68. Canx.
G-AMTC	Auster J/5F Aiglet Trainer	2782	D-EFEP G-AMTC	24. 5.52	DBR at Manaccan, Cornwall on 11.6.65. Canx.
G-AMTD	Auster J/5F Aiglet Trainer	2783	EI-AVL G-AMTD	24. 5.52	Badly damaged on landing at Hayrish Farm, Okehampton on 7.8.93. (Wings only present 5/96) Canx as WFU 15.1.99.
G-AMTE	Auster J/5F Aiglet Trainer	2784		24. 5.52	To VH-WKY 2/78. Canx 24.2.78.
G-AMTF	DH.82A Tiger Moth	84207	ZK-AVE G-AMTF/T7842	11. 6.52	
G-AMTG	DH.82A Tiger Moth	3787	N6457	11. 6.52	To ZK-BBW 10/52. Canx 22.9.52.
G-AMTH	DH.82A Tiger Moth	85325	DE279	11. 6.52	To ZK-AVZ 6/53. Canx 14.1.53.
G-AMTI	Percival P.44 Proctor 5	Ae.151		14. 6.52	To TC-GUN 7/52. Canx 24.7.52.
G-AMTJ	Percival P.44 Proctor 5	Ae.152		14. 6.52	Broken up at Boscombe Down in 9/61. Canx.
G-AMTK	DH.82A Tiger Moth	3982	N6709	18. 6.52	CofA expired 27.5.66. (On rebuild)
G-AMTL	DH.82A Tiger Moth	82592	W6420 G-AFWF	24. 6.52	To OO-SOF 7/52. Canx 28.7.52.
G-AMTM	Auster J/1 Autocrat (Auster Aircraft rebuild - originally c/n 2622 which crashed in 4/52)	3101	G-AJUJ	3. 7.52	
G-AMTN	Douglas C-47A-1-DK Dakota	11979	SAAF6818 FL572/42-92204	. .52R	To ZS-DHO 4/53. Canx.
G-AMTO	DH.82A Tiger Moth	84655	T6229	17. 7.52	WFU & stored at Rush Green in 1970. Canx as WFU 6.3.73.
G-AMTP	DH.82A Tiger Moth	84875	T6534	17. 7.52	To OO-ETP 7/53. Canx 29.8.52.
G-AMTR	Auster J/5F Aiglet Trainer	2789		18. 7.52	Crashed at Lybster, Caithness on 29.1.64. Canx.
G-AMTS	DH.114 Heron 2	14007	XL961 G-AMTS	18. 7.52	Fatal crash at Biggin Hill on 16.7.61. Canx 19.1.62.
G-AMTT	DH.82A Tiger Moth	83420	T5699	22. 7.52	To ZK-BCO 7/53. Canx 19.2.53.
G-AMTU	DH.82A Tiger Moth	82698	R4757	22. 7.52	To ZK-BEJ 2/54. Canx 12.9.53.
G-AMTV	DH.82A Tiger Moth	3858	OO-SOE G-AMTV/N6545	5. 8.52	
G-AMTW	DH.82A Tiger Moth	84730	T6315	5. 8.52	To OO-SOH 10/52. Canx 2.10.52.
G-AMTX	DH.82A Tiger Moth	83850	T7446	6. 8.52	Not converted. To G-APJV 1/58. Canx.
"G-AMTX"	Thruxton Jackaroo	-		----	Non-flying mock-up built from spares.
G-AMTY	DH.82A Tiger Moth	84256	T7881	6. 8.52	NTU - To G-ANNP 2/54. Canx.
G-AMTZ	Saro W.14 Skeeter Mk.6	SR.907	(G-AMDC)	20. 8.52	To RAF as XG303 3/54. Canx.
G-AMUA	DH.82A Tiger Moth	84675	T6249	16. 8.52	To ZK-BBQ 10/52. Canx 9.9.52.
G-AMUB	DH.82A Tiger Moth	3975	N6671	18. 8.52	Not converted. Derelict at Squires Gate in 1956. Canx.
G-AMUC	DHC.1 Chipmunk 21 (Fuselage no. DHB/f/668)	C1/0824		2. 9.52	To N99856 3/76. Canx 15.3.76.
G-AMUD	DHC.1 Chipmunk 21 (Fuselage no. DHB/f/669)	C1/0825		2. 9.52	Crashed at Porchfield, IoW on 22.3.53. Canx.
G-AMUE	DHC.1 Chipmunk 21 (Fuselage no. DHB/f/673)	C1/0831		2. 9.52	Destroyed in a night mid-air collision with RAF Balliol WG184 near Middle Wallop on 22.10.56. Canx.
G-AMUF	DHC.1 Chipmunk 21 (Fuselage no. DHB/f/682)	C1/0832		2. 9.52	
G-AMUG	DHC.1 Chipmunk 21 (Fuselage no. DHB/f/686)	C1/0833		2. 9.52	Fatal crash at Derwent Farm, near Yedingham, Yorks. on 30.5.74. Canx as destroyed 30.11.84.
G-AMUH	DHC.1 Chipmunk 21 (Fuselage no. DHB/f/688)	C1/0834		2. 9.52	To ZK-MUH 7/87. Canx 9.1.87.
G-AMUI	Auster J/5F Aiglet Trainer	2790		29. 8.52	CofA expired 15.2.66 & WFU at Crowland. (On rebuild Garston, Liverpool 10/98)
G-AMUJ	Auster J/5F Aiglet Trainer	2791		29. 8.52	Crashed at South Rauceby, Sleaford on 8.6.60. (Stored 9/96)
G-AMUK	DH.114 Heron 1B	14006	(VR-B..) G-AMUK/VH-AHB/G-AMUK	5. 9.52	WFU at Southend on 25.5.68. Broken up and remains taken to Staravia dump at Lasham in 7/72. Canx.
G-AMUL	Avro 685 York C.1	-	XF284 G-AMUL/MW308	18. 9.52	Crashed during take-off from Stansted on 30.4.56. Canx.
G-AMUM	Avro 685 York C.1	-	XF285 G-AMUM/MW332	18. 9.52	DBR on landing at Luqa, Malta on 13.4.54. Canx.

Regn	Type	c/n	Previous identity	Regn date	Fate or immediate subsequent identity (if known)
G-AMUN	Avro 685 York C.1	-	XD667 G-AMUN/MW321	18. 9.52	Fatal crash at Mole Hill Green on approach to Stansted on 23.12.57. Canx.
G-AMUO	DH.82A Tiger Moth	84631	T6183	16. 9.52	To PH-UFH 10/52. Canx 10.10.52.
G-AMUP	Lockheed L.049E-46-27 Constellation	2051	N2738A (G-ARHJ)/N2738A/G-AMUP/N90921/NC90921	6. 2.53	WFU at Luton. Canx as WFU 5.8.65. Broken up in 11/65.
G-AMUR	Lockheed L.049E-46-27 Constellation	2065	N90927 NC90927	6. 3.53	To N2739A 5/55. Canx 28.4.55.
G-AMUS	Avro 685 York C.1	-	XF919 G-AMUS/MW110	22. 9.52	WFU in 12/56 & broken up for spares at Heathrow in 5/58. Canx.
G-AMUT	Avro 685 York C.1	-	CF-HTM G-AMUT/MW185	22. 9.52	DBR on landing at Luqa, Malta on 20.5.58. Canx.
G-AMUU	Avro 685 York C.1	-	XD668 G-AMUU/MW183	22. 9.52	WFU at Heathrow in 2/59. Broken up in 5/59. Canx.
G-AMUV	Avro 685 York C.1	-	XD669 G-AMUV/XD623/G-AMUV/MW226	22. 9.52	DBR in forced landing at Badshahpur, near Gurgaon, 28 miles from Delhi, India on 25.5.58. Canx.
G-AMUW	Luton LA-4 Minor	WP.1		22. 9.52	Construction abandoned. Canx as WFU 13.4.73.
G-AMUX	Blackburn & General C.3/46 Freighter 1 (GAL.60 Universal Mk.1)	1000	WF320	24.10.52	Marks not used. Remained with RAF as WF320. Canx 11.12.58.
G-AMUY	DH.82A Tiger Moth	85291	DE245	1.10.52	To OO-SOD 11/52. Canx 11.11.52.
G-AMUZ	DH.104 Dove 1B	04386		1.10.52	Sold to Vernair on 1.10.70 & transported by road to Speke on 31.12.70. Broken up for spares. Canx as WFU 16.7.73.
G-AMVA	Douglas C-47B-30-DK Dakota	16415/33163	EP-ABE(2) G-AMVA/KN552/44-76831	4.10.52	To EP-AML 5/72. Canx as WFU 3.5.72.
G-AMVB	Douglas C-47B-5-DK Dakota	14637/26082	XF647 G-AMVB/KJ915/43-48821	4.10.52	DBF at Masjid-I-Sulaiman, Iran on 22.10.58. Canx.
G-AMVC	Douglas C-47B-35-DK Dakota	16642/33390	XF645 G-AMVC/KN681/44-77058	4.10.52	Crashed at Croglin Fell, 4m NE of Kirkoswald, Cumberland on 17.10.61. Canx.
G-AMVD	Taylorcraft Auster 5	1565	F-BGTF G-AMVD/TJ565	6.10.52	
G-AMVE	DH.82A Tiger Moth	84581	T6114	6.10.52	To ZK-BCG 2/53. Canx 7.1.53.
G-AMVF	DH.82A Tiger Moth	84660	T6234	6.10.52	To VH-SCI 9/59. Canx 26.6.59.
G-AMVG	DH.82A Tiger Moth	84663	T6237	6.10.52	To ZK-BEY 5/54. Canx 22.9.53.
G-AMVH	DH.82A Tiger Moth	84671	T6245	6.10.52	To ZK-BEN 2/54. Canx 12.10.53.
G-AMVI	DH.82A Tiger Moth	85010	T6710	6.10.52	To ZK-BEP 2/54. Canx 12.10.53.
G-AMVJ	DH.82A Tiger Moth	83413	T7043	6.10.52	To F-OANB 1/54. Canx 28.5.53.
G-AMVK	Douglas C-47B-20-DK Dakota	15530/26975	KK197 43-49714	7.10.52	To VR-AAM 6/55. Canx 16.6.53.
G-AMVL	Douglas C-47B-35-DK Dakota	16660/33408	XF746 G-AMVL/KN694/44-77076	7.10.52	To ZS-DKR 12/54. Canx 28.1.55.
G-AMVM	Auster J/5F Aiglet Trainer	2758		8.10.52	To OO-CHT 2/53. Canx 9.2.53.
G-AMVN	Auster J/1S	3102	VP-KKG G-AMVN	8.10.52	Destroyed in mid-air collision with Forney F-1A G-AROP over Fyfield, Essex on 24.4.69. Canx.
G-AMVO	DH.82A Tiger Moth	85547	DE580	10.10.52	To ZK-BCH 2/53. Canx 7.1.53.
G-AMVP	Tipsy Junior	J.111	OO-ULA	23.10.52	Damaged in forced landing with engine failure at Wroughton on 4.7.93. (Under repair 12/95)
G-AMVR	DH.104 Dove 2B	04394		30.10.52	To JA5005 2/53. Canx 23.2.53.
G-AMVS	DH.82A Tiger Moth	82784	OO-SOJ G-AMVS/R4852	12.11.52	(On rebuild Shobdon 8/92)
G-AMVT	DH.104 Dove 1B	04375		20.11.52	To JA5003 1/53. Canx 10.2.53.
G-AMVU	DHC-2 Beaver 1	190	XH455 G-AMVU/CF-GCR	21.11.52	To VR-LAB 9/56. Canx in 9.56.
G-AMVV	DH.104 Dove 1	04020	VP-YEU (ZS-AWB)	8.12.52	To PH-MAC 5/58. Canx 28.5.58.
G-AMVW	Blackburn & General C.3/46 Freighter 1 (GAL.65 Universal Mk.2)	1001	(WZ889)	19.12.52	Marks not used. To RAF as WZ889 1/53. Canx.
G-AMVX	DH.82A Tiger Moth	82060	N6790	11.12.52	WFU at Stapleford in 12/59. Canx 15.1.61.
G-AMVY	Avro 685 York C.1	-	MW292	8. 1.53	NTU - Not converted. Broken up at Bovingdon in 4/54. Canx.
G-AMVZ	Avro 685 York C.1	-	MW302	8. 1.53	NTU - Not converted. Broken up at Bovingdon in 8/54. Canx.
G-AMWA	Bristol 170 Freighter Mk.32	13073	XF650 G-AMWA/(G-AMLK)/G-18-112	23. 8.51	Crashed on take off from Guernsey on 24.9.63. Canx.
G-AMWB	Bristol 170 Freighter Mk.31E	13127	XF651 G-AMWB/(G-AMPE)/G-18-128	21. 2.52	CofA expired 15.6.67. WFU at Lydd. Broken up on 4/5.4.68. Canx.
G-AMWC	Bristol 170 Freighter Mk.31E	13128	XF652 G-AMWC/(G-AMPF)/G-18-129	21. 2.52	WFU at Lydd in 12/64. Broken up in 4/67. Canx as WFU in 1967.
G-AMWD	Bristol 170 Freighter Mk.32	13131	F-BKBD G-AMWD/XF653/G-AMWD/(G-AMPG)/G-18-132	21. 2.52	WFU at Lydd 12/65. Broken up at Southend in 4/67. Canx as WFU in 1/66.
G-AMWE	Bristol 170 Freighter Mk.32	13132	XF654 G-AMWE/(G-AMPH)/G-18-133	21. 2.52	CofA expired 25.6.66. WFU at Lydd. Scrapped in 1967. Canx.
G-AMWF	Bristol 170 Freighter Mk.32	13133	XF655 G-AMWF/(G-AMPI)/G-18-134	21. 2.52	CofA expired 1.11.67. WFU at Lydd. Broken up in 4/68. Canx.
G-AMWG	Bristol 171 Sycamore 3A	13068		1.12.52	To VH-INQ 9/59. Canx 2.7.58.
G-AMWH	Bristol 171 Sycamore 3A	13069		1.12.52	DBR on landing at Cowes, IoW on 15.8.64. Canx.
G-AMWI	Bristol 171 Sycamore 4	13070		1.12.52	To RN as "XN635"/XR595 6/61. Canx /58.
G-AMWJ	Bristol 171 Sycamore 4	13071		1.12.52	To R.Australian AF as XD653 3/54. Canx 30.9.53.
G-AMWK	Bristol 171 Sycamore 4	13194		1.12.52	NTU - To RAF as XE313 in 10/53. Canx.
G-AMWL	Bristol 171 Sycamore 4	13195		1.12.52	NTU - To RAF as XE314 in 10/53. Canx.
G-AMWM	Bristol 171 Sycamore 4	13196		1.12.52	NTU - To RAF as XE315 in 10/53. Canx.
G-AMWN	Bristol 171 Sycamore 4	13197		1.12.52	NTU - To RAF as XE316 in 10/53. Canx.
G-AMWO	Bristol 171 Sycamore 4	13198		1.12.52	NTU - To RAF as XE317 in 10/53. Canx.
G-AMWP	Bristol 171 Sycamore 4	13199		1.12.52	NTU - To Belgium AF as B1/OT-ZKA in 3/54. Canx.
G-AMWR	Bristol 171 Sycamore 4	13200		1.12.52	NTU - To Belgium AF as B2/OT-ZKB in 3/54. Canx.
G-AMWS	Bristol 171 Sycamore 4	13201		1.12.52	NTU - To Belgium AF as B3/OT-ZKC in 3/54. Canx.
G-AMWT	Bristol 171 Sycamore 4	13202		1.12.52	NTU - To R.Australian AF as A91-2 in 8/54. Canx.

Regn	Type	c/n	Previous identity	Regn date	Fate or immediate subsequent identity (if known)
G-AMWU	Bristol 171 Sycamore 4	13203		1.12.52	NTU - To RAF as XJ361 in 4/56. Canx.
G-AMWV	Douglas C-47B-1-DK Dakota	14155/25600	EI-APB G-AMWV/KJ816/43-48339	4.12.52	WFU & scrapped at Prestwick on 20.5.69. To Fire dump in 8/71. Canx.
G-AMWW	Douglas C-47B-30-DK Dakota	16262/33010	(N3102Q) G-AMWW/EI-ARP/G-AMWW/KN492/44-76678	5.12.52	To N2685W 12/81. Canx 2.11.81.
G-AMWX	Douglas C-47B-25-DK Dakota	15846/32594	XF792 G-AMWX/KN310/44-76262	5.12.52	Forced landed on beach at Mers-les-Bains, France on 17.12.65, destroyed by immersion. Canx.
G-AMWY	DH.104 Dove 1B	04407		1. 1.53	To JA5006 3/53. Canx 1.4.53.
G-AMWZ	DH.104 Dove 2A	04388	(N4282C)	5. 1.53	To CF-HGT 2/53. Canx 9.11.53.
G-AMXA	DH.106 Comet 2	06023		8. 1.53	To RAF as XK655 in 3/56. Canx 2.3.55.
G-AMXB	DH.106 Comet 2	06024		8. 1.53	To RAF as XK669 in 11/55. Canx 2.3.55.
G-AMXC	DH.106 Comet 2	06025		8. 1.53	To RAF as XK659 in 5/56. Canx 2.3.55.
G-AMXD	DH.106 Comet 2E (Originally regd as a Comet 2)	06026		8. 1.53	To RAF as XN453 in 4/59. Canx 2.3.55.
G-AMXE	DH.106 Comet 2	06027		8. 1.53	NTU - To RAF as XK663 in 7/55. Canx 2.3.55.
G-AMXF	DH.106 Comet 2	06028		8. 1.53	NTU - To RAF as XK670 in 3/56. Canx 2.3.55.
G-AMXG	DH.106 Comet 2	06029		8. 1.53	NTU - To RAF as XK671 in 8/56. Canx 2.3.55.
G-AMXH	DH.106 Comet 2	06030		8. 1.53	NTU - To RAF as XK695 in 8/56. Canx 2.3.55.
G-AMXI	DH.106 Comet 2	06031		8. 1.53	NTU - To RAF as XK696 in 9/56. Canx 2.3.55.
G-AMXJ	DH.106 Comet 2	06032		8. 1.53	NTU - To RAF as XK697 in 11/56. Canx 2.3.55.
G-AMXK	DH.106 Comet 2E (Originally regd as a Comet 2)	06033		8. 1.53	To RAF as XV144 in 8/66. Canx 24.10.66.
G-AMXL(1)	DH.106 Comet 2	06034		8. 1.53	NTU - To RAF as XK698 in 2/56. Canx 2.3.55.
G-AMXL(2)	DHC.1 Chipmunk 22 (Fuselage no. DHB/f/127)	C1/0242	OH-HCA WD301	26. 5.60	Spun into ground at Dartford Salt Marshes, Kent on 5.3.78. Canx in 6.78.
G-AMXM	Avro 685 York C.1	-	MW323	8. 1.53	To OO-ADM 5/59. Canx 27.5.59.
G-AMXN	DH.104 Dove 2A	04391	(N4283C)	5. 1.53	To CF-HGQ 2/53. Canx 16.11.53.
G-AMXO	DH.104 Dove 2A	04414		5. 1.53	To CF-HGR 4/53. Canx 4.11.53.
G-AMXP	DH.104 Dove 2A	04420	XJ319 G-AMXP	5. 1.53	To VH-DVE 10/92. Canx by CAA 22.12.95.
G-AMXR	DH.104 Dove 2B	04379	(N4280C)	21. 1.53	To D-CFSB 7/54. Canx 22.7.54.
G-AMXS	DH.104 Dove 2A	04382	(N4281C)	21. 1.53	To YV-T-FTQ 8/53. Canx 28.8.53.
G-AMXT	DH.104 Dove 6 (Originally regd as Dove 2A)	04392	(G-BJXI) XJ347/G-AMXT/(N1561V)	21. 1.53	Dismantled in 1/98 at Sandown. To Cowes Scrapyard. Canx by CAA 12.2.98.
G-AMXU	DH.104 Dove 2A	04393	G-5-19 G-AMXU/(N1562V)	21. 1.53	To CR-AHT in 3/55. Canx 1.3.55.
G-AMXV	DH.104 Dove 2B (Originally regd as Dove 2A)	04400		22. 1.53	To VH-DHD 10/54. Canx 29.11.54.
G-AMXW	DH.104 Dove 6 (Originally regd as Dove 2A)	04401	(G-ARLE) XJ349/G-AMXW	22. 1.53	To N11XW 3/75. Canx 3.3.75.
G-AMXX	DH.104 Dove 2A	04406		22. 1.53	To RN as XJ348 10/54. Canx 21.10.54.
G-AMXY	DH.104 Dove 6 (Originally regd as Dove 2A)	04409	XJ323 G-AMXY	22. 1.53	To 9J-AAE 1/69. Canx 16.1.69.
G-AMXZ	DH.104 Dove 2A	04410		22. 1.53	To RN as XJ324 in 9/54. Canx 23.9.54.
G-AMYA(1)	Miles M.57 Aerovan 4	HPR.29		10. 2.53R	NTU - Construction abandoned in 10/54. Canx 18.9.59. Fuselage burnt at Stapleford on 26.11.69.
G-AMYA(2)	Zlin Z.381 Bestmann (Czech-built Bucker Bu.181 Bestmann)	461	OO-AVC OK-AVC	17. 6.87	Permit expired 21.2.96. Canx by CAA 31.10.96. On display 10/97 at Polk City, Florida, USA.
G-AMYB	Douglas C-47B-35-DK Dakota	16598/33346	(5N-AJE) G-AMYB/(G-AZDF)/ST-AAK/SN-AAK/G-AMYB/KN652/44-77014	29. 1.53	To N6CA 1/73. Canx 4.1.73.
G-AMYC	Miles M.57 Aerovan 4	HPR.47 & 6647		10. 2.53	NTU - Construction abandoned in 10/54. Canx 28.5.54.
G-AMYD	Auster J/5L Aiglet Trainer	2773		13. 2.53	
G-AMYE	Auster J/5F Aiglet Trainer	2775		13. 2.53	To ZK-BDO 8/53. Canx 15.7.53.
G-AMYF	Bristol 173 Mk.3	13204		4. 3.53	NTU - To RAF as XE286 in 6/53. Canx.
G-AMYG	Bristol 173 Mk.3	13205		4. 3.53	NTU - To RAF as XE287 in 6/53. Canx.
G-AMYH	Bristol 173 Mk.3	13206		4. 3.53	NTU - To RAF as XE288 in 6/53. Canx.
G-AMYI	Auster J/8L Aiglet Trainer (Originally regd as a J/5K)	3151		23. 2.53	To VH-UYQ 10/77. Canx 5.10.77.
G-AMYJ	Douglas C-47B-25-DK Dakota	15968/32716	SU-AZF G-AMYJ/XF747/G-AMYJ/KN353/44-76384	23. 2.53	(Stored 5/98 Coventry)
G-AMYK	Bristol 175 Britannia Srs.200	13207		25. 2.53	NTU - Not built. To (G-AOFA)/G-AOVA. Canx.
G-AMYL(1)	Bristol 175 Britannia Srs.300	13208		25. 2.53	NTU - Not built. To (G-AOFB). Canx 11.3.55.
G-AMYL(2)	PA-17 Vagabond	17-30	N4613H NC4613H	24. 4.87	(Stored 9/97)
G-AMYM	DH.104 Dove 1B	04403		9. 3.53	To JA5007 4/53. Canx 19.5.53.
G-AMYN	Westland-Sikorsky S-55 Whirlwind Srs.1	WA/A/4	G-17-3	13. 3.53	NTU - To French Navy 4/54. Canx.
G-AMYO	DH.104 Dove 1B (Originally regd as Srs.1)	04086	VP-YEV	18. 3.53	To Senegal 6/69. Canx 4.6.69.
G-AMYP	DH.104 Dove 2A	04421	XJ322 G-AMYP	2. 4.53	Crashed at Shoreham on 9.7.83. Canx.
G-AMYR	Auster J/5G Cirrus Autocar	3052		28. 3.53	To YE-AAM 11/56. Canx 20.4.56.
G-AMYS	Douglas C-47B-15-DK Dakota	15109/26554	KK104 43-49293	1. 4.53	To VP-YKO 6/53. Canx 12.6.53.
G-AMYT	Douglas C-47B-1-DK Dakota	14360/25805	KJ866 43-48544	1. 4.53	To VP-YKL 7/53. Canx 16.7.53.
G-AMYU	DH.114 Heron 1B	14017		31. 3.53	Overshot and crashed into a glasshouse landing at Guernsey on 15.8.58. Canx 25.9.58.
G-AMYV	Douglas C-47B-30-DK Dakota	16195/32943	XF623 G-AMYV/KN469/44-76611	1. 4.53	To G-41-4-67/South Arabian Federation AF as 204 in 9/67. Canx 6.9.67.
G-AMYW	Douglas C-47B-30-DK Dakota	16272/33020	KN497 44-76688	1. 4.53	DBR at 80 miles southwest of Hail, Saudi Arabia on 8.4.67. Canx.

Regn	Type	c/n	Previous identity	Regn date	Fate or immediate subsequent identity (if known)
G-AMYX	Douglas C-47B-30-DK Dakota	16294/33042	XF619 G-AMYX/KN509/42-76710	1. 4.53	To EI-APJ 7/66. Canx 8.7.66.
G-AMYY	Douglas C-47B-10-DK Dakota	14992/26437	KJ998 43-49176	11. 4.53	To VP-YKP 5/53. Canx 28.5.53.
G-AMYZ	Douglas C-47B-40-DK Dakota	16823/33571	KP269 44-77239	16. 4.53	Not converted. Broken up for spares at Croydon on 20.7.53. Canx.
G-AMZA	Douglas C-47B-40-DK Dakota	16821/33569	KP267 44-77237	16. 4.53	Not converted. Broken up for spares at Croydon on 10.7.53. Canx.
G-AMZB	Douglas C-47B-20-DK Dakota	15535/26980	KK202 43-49719	26. 3.53	To OO-SBK 3/62. Canx 6.3.62.
G-AMZC	Douglas C-47B-35-DK Dakota	16522/33270	KN620 44-76938	7. 4.53	Fatal crash at Ratingen on final approach at Dusseldorf, West Germany on 22.12.55 and burnt out. Canx.
G-AMZD	Douglas C-47B-25-DK Dakota	16112/32860	XF281 G-AMZD/KN431/44-76528	10. 4.53	Crashed in Montseny Mountains, near Barcelona, Spain on 19.8.59. Canx.
G-AMZE	Douglas C-47B-1-DK Dakota	14368/25813	KJ874 43-48552	15. 4.53	Broken up for spares at Burnaston on 1.2.64. Canx.
G-AMZF	Douglas C-47B-20-DK Dakota	15633/27078	XF749 G-AMZF/KN212/43-49817	24. 4.53	To CF-RTY 1/66. Canx 1.6.66.
G-AMZG	Douglas C-47B-35-DK Dakota	16668/33416	XF748 G-AMZG/KN700/44-77084	24. 4.53	To TF-AIO 6/66. Canx 4.6.66.
G-AMZH	Douglas C-47B-20-DK Dakota	15665/27110	KN421 43-49849	2. 5.53	To VH-SBW on 22.5.65. Canx 20.5.65.
G-AMZI	Auster J/5F Aiglet Trainer	3104		4. 5.53	
G-AMZJ	DH.104 Dove 1B (Originally regd as a Dove 1)	04429	(6V-AAM) G-AMZJ	28. 4.53	WFU on 24.4.65. Seized in 1967 at Benina, Libya for non-payment of debts. Later noted derelict. Canx 30.7.73.
G-AMZK	DH.104 Dove 1B	04430		28. 4.53	To JA5008 in 6/53. Canx 20.6.53.
G-AMZL	DHC.1 Chipmunk 21 (Fuselage no. DHH/f/4)	C1/0004	WB552	3. 6.53	Restored to RAF as WB552 in 7/53. Canx 20.4.54.
G-AMZM	Percival P.56 Provost T.1 (Also c/n PAC/F/20)	P56/20	(WV437)	23. 5.53	To G-23-6/Malaysian AF as FM1036 in 5/61 as mark T.51. Canx 27.4.61.
G-AMZN	DH.104 Dove 6 (Prototype)	04437		15. 5.53	To SE-GRA 6/72. Canx 30.5.72.
G-AMZO	DH.87B Hornet Moth	8040	SE-ALD OY-DEZ/VR-RAI	15. 5.53	Restored as OY-DEZ 5/74. Canx 14.2.74.
G-AMZP	Taylorcraft Auster 5	1312	TJ219	22. 5.53	To F-OANT 8/53. Canx 30.6.53.
G-AMZR	Douglas C-47B-30-DK Dakota	16335/33083	KN531 44-76751	27. 5.53	To SN-AAJ 5/54. Canx 11.5.54.
G-AMZS	Douglas C-47B-15-DK Dakota	15137/26582	(5N-AJF) G-AMZS/(G-AZDG)/ST-AAI/SN-AAI/G-AMZS/KK127/43-49321	27. 5.53	To N7CA 1/73. Canx 4.1.73.
G-AMZT	Auster J/5F Aiglet Trainer	3107		28. 5.53	
G-AMZU	Auster J/5F Aiglet Trainer	3108		28. 5.53	
G-AMZV	Auster J/5G Cirrus Autocar	3065		28. 5.53	Crashed at Weston-super-Mare on 28.8.66. Canx.
G-AMZW	Douglas C-47B-20-DK Dakota	15654/27099	KN231 43-49838	29. 5.53	To SN-AAH 7/53. Canx 1.7.53.
G-AMZX	Douglas C-47B-15-DK Dakota	15287/26732	KK149 43-49471	29. 5.53	To SN-AAG 9/53. Canx 14.9.53.
G-AMZY	DH.104 Dove 8XC (Originally regd as Srs.2B, then Srs.1B in 1959, then Srs.6 in 1959)	04431		1. 6.53	WFU at Exeter in 7/74 for spares. Canx as WFU 24.7.74.
G-AMZZ	Douglas C-47B-35-DK Dakota	16592/33340	EP-ABD G-AMZZ/KN648/44-77008	8. 6.53	CofA expired 13.4.70. Canx as WFU 26.5.71. Derelict at Bahrain by 10/78.
"G-AMZZ"	Douglas C-47B-1-DK Dakota	14361/25806	G-AGKE (N27AA)/5B-CAZ/G-AGKE/VR-AAB/JY-ABN/TJ-ABN/VR-AAB/G-AGKE/KJ867/43-48545	----	Derelict at Bahrain marked as such. Is really N94718.
G-ANAA	Avro 685 York C.1	-	MW100	8. 6.53	Not converted. Broken up for spares at Stansted in 9/55. Canx.
G-ANAB	Avro 685 York C.1	-	MW104	8. 6.53	Not converted. Broken up for spares at Stansted in 9/55. Canx.
G-ANAC	Avro 685 York C.1	-	MW236	8. 6.53	Not converted. Broken up for spares at Stansted in 9/55. Canx.
G-ANAD	Douglas C-47B-20-DK Dakota	15770/27215	KN279 43-49954	23. 6.53	To VR-AAI 5/54. Canx 17.3.54.
G-ANAE	Douglas C-47B-5-DK Dakota	14656/26101	TF-VON TF-SUM/G-ANAE/"TF-SUO"/"TF-SUN"/G-ANAE/XF791/G-ANAE/KJ930/43-48840	15. 6.53	To VR-ABH 1/68. Canx 21.2.68.
G-ANAF	Douglas C-47B-35-DK Dakota	16688/33436	N170GP G-ANAF/KP220/44-77104	17. 6.53	
G-ANAG	DHC.1 Chipmunk 21 (Fuselage no. DHB/f/802)	C1/0944		24. 6.53	To (JA3060)/JA3090 2/54. Canx 11.1.54.
G-ANAH	DH.89A Dragon Rapide	6786	NR687	24. 6.53	To CX-API 9/54. Canx 26.8.54.
G-ANAI	DH.104 Dove 1B	04422		25. 6.53	To JA5011 in 9/53. Canx 14.9.53.
G-ANAJ	Short S.45 Solent 4	S.1293	NJ201 G-AGWU/NJ201	25. 6.53	Bad weather drove it onto the beach at Santa Margherita, Genoa, Italy on 26.9.56. Dismantled on site for spares and scrapped. Canx.
G-ANAK	Short S.25 Sunderland 5	-	PP162	25. 6.53	Not converted. DBR in gales at Hamble on 27.11.54. Canx.
G-ANAL	Westland-Sikorsky S-51 Mk.1A	WA/H/090		27. 6.53	To G-ANZL 3/55. Canx 11.2.55.
G-ANAM	Westland-Sikorsky S-51 Mk.1A	WA/H/091		29. 6.53	To JA7014 in 10/53. Canx 17.7.53.
G-ANAN	DH.104 Dove 1B (Originally regd as a Dove 1)	04062	XY-ADE G-ANAN/EP-ACH	8. 7.53	To 6V-ABT 6/69. Canx 4.6.69.
G-ANAO	Auster J/5F Aiglet Trainer	3109		9. 7.53	To ZK-BDY 11/53. Canx 21.10.53.
G-ANAP	DH.104 Dove 6 (Originally regd as Dove 1B)	04433		17. 7.53	Canx as WFU 31.8.73. Instructional Airframe 1/97 at Bristol/Lulsgate - to fire dump by 1/99.
G-ANAR	DHC-2 Beaver 2	80	XN142 G-ANAR/XH463/G-ANAR/CF-GQE	24. 7.53	To CF-CNR 8/71. Canx 6.8.71.

Regn	Type	c/n	Previous identity	Regn date	Fate or immediate subsequent identity (if known)
G-ANAS	Douglas C-47B-35-DK Dakota	16509/33257	KN611 44-76925	15. 7.53	NTU - To ZS-DHY 7/53. Canx.
G-ANAT	Percival P.44 Proctor 5	Ae.92	VN895	18. 7.53	DBR at Elmdon Airport on 30.3.58. Canx.
G-ANAU	Auster J/5F Aiglet Trainer	3110		29. 7.53	To ZK-BRA 10/56. Canx 24.7.56.
G-ANAV	DH.106 Comet 1A	06013	CF-CUM	15. 8.53	Broken up at RAE Farnborough in 1955. Canx. (Nose section to Science Museum).
G-ANAW	Avro 685 York C.1	-	MW139	28. 7.53	Not converted. Scrapped at Stansted in 9/55. Canx.
G-ANAX	DH.114 Heron 1B	14024		21. 8.53	To JA6151 in 9/53. Canx 4.11.53.
G-ANAY	DH.82A Tiger Moth	83890	T5900	15. 8.53	DBF after crashing on take-off from Fairoaks on 8.10.53. Canx.
G-ANAZ	Scottish Aviation Pioneer CC.1	SA/A2/102 & 103	VL516	21. 8.53	Returned to RAF as XE514 in 9/53. Canx 30.4.54.
G-ANBA	Bristol 175 Britannia Srs.102	12902		7. 1.54	WFU at Luton on 20.11.69. Canx as WFU 10.3.70.
G-ANBB	Bristol 175 Britannia Srs.102	12903		7. 1.54	Fatal crash near Ljubljana Airport, Yugoslavia on 1.9.66. Canx.
G-ANBC	Bristol 175 Britannia Srs.102	12904		7. 1.54	DBR on landing at Khartoum, Sudan on 11.11.60. Canx.
G-ANBD	Bristol 175 Britannia Srs.102	12905		7. 1.56	WFU on 12.1.70. Broken up in 5/70 at Southend. Canx as WFU 24.4.70.
G-ANBE	Bristol 175 Britannia Srs.102	12906		18. 1.56	WFU in 12/70. Broken up in 6/72 at Luton. Canx as WFU 2.10.81.
G-ANBF	Bristol 175 Britannia Srs.102	12907		18. 1.56	WFU on 26.10.69. Broken up in 4/70 at Luton. Canx as WFU 10.3.70.
G-ANBG	Bristol 175 Britannia Srs.102	12908		18. 1.56	To G-APLL 3/58. Canx 19.3.58.
G-ANBH	Bristol 175 Britannia Srs.102	12909		18. 1.56	WFU in 28.10.68. Broken up in 9/69 at Southend. Canx as WFU 24.4.70.
G-ANBI	Bristol 175 Britannia Srs.102	12910		4. 3.56	WFU in 27.9.69. Broken up in 2/70 at Luton. Canx as WFU 10.4.70.
G-ANBJ	Bristol 175 Britannia Srs.102	12911		4. 3.56	WFU on 13.10.70. Broken up in 2/71 at Luton. Canx.
G-ANBK	Bristol 175 Britannia Srs.102	12912		4. 3.56	WFU at Woolsington on 31.12.71. Broken up in 3/72. Canx.
G-ANBL	Bristol 175 Britannia Srs.102	12913		4. 3.56	WFU on 29.12.70. Broken up in 7/72 at Luton. Canx.
G-ANBM	Bristol 175 Britannia Srs.102	12914		4. 3.56	To PK-ICA 1/69. Canx 10.1.69.
G-ANBN	Bristol 175 Britannia Srs.102	12915		4. 3.56	To PK-ICB 1/69. Canx 10.1.69.
G-ANBO	Bristol 175 Britannia Srs.102	12916		4. 3.56	WFU on 15.10.70. Broken up in 5/71 at Luton. Canx.
G-ANBP	DH.104 Dove 6A	04438	G-5-16	28. 8.53	To N1584V 10/53. Canx 21.10.53.
G-ANBR	DH.104 Dove 6A	04439	G-5-14	31. 8.53	To N1585V 10/53. Canx 21.10.53.
G-ANBS	Auster J/5G Cirrus Autocar	3068		28. 8.53	To SN-ABH 1/56. Canx 17.1.56.
G-ANBT	DH.82A Tiger Moth	83626	T7167	1. 9.53	To ZK-BEC 11/53. Canx 22.10.53.
G-ANBU	DH.82A Tiger Moth	3882	W7952 G-AFNR	1. 9.53	To OO-BYL 1/54. Canx.
G-ANBV	DH.82A Tiger Moth	3375	D-EHYB G-ANBV/BB735/G-ADHV	1. 9.53	Canx as sold in Spain on 2.6.64. Derelict at Las Palmas in 3/67 as G-ANBV.
G-ANBW	DH.82A Tiger Moth	83564	T5807	1. 9.53	To ZK-BFF 4/54. Canx 20.1.54.
G-ANBX	DH.82A Tiger Moth	85644	DE714	1. 9.53	To ZK-BEB 11/53. Canx 22.10.53.
G-ANBY	DH.82A Tiger Moth	86042	EM840	2. 9.53	Not converted. Scrapped at Rochester in 4/60. Canx.
G-ANBZ	DH.82A Tiger Moth	85621	DE680	2. 9.53	To SL-AAF 1/55. Canx 3.12.54.
G-ANCA	Bristol 175 Britannia Srs.301	12917		11. 3.55	Fatal crash into a wood at Downend, 3 miles from Filton airport on 6.11.57. Canx.
G-ANCB	Bristol 175 Britannia Srs.302	12918	G-18-1	20. 1.56	Marks not used. To XA-MEC 11/57. Canx 15.8.57.
G-ANCC	Bristol 175 Britannia Srs.308F (Originally regd as Srs.302)	12919	XA-MED G-18-2/(G-14-1)/G-ANCC	8. 1.57	WFU at Gatwick on 12.6.69. Broken up in 8/70 at Biggin Hill. Canx 27.4.73.
G-ANCD	Bristol 175 Britannia Srs.307F (Originally regd as Srs.305)	12920	4X-AGE (N6595C)/G-ANCD/G-18-3	3. 1.58	To 5Y-AYR 5/75. Canx 13.5.75.
G-ANCE	Bristol 175 Britannia Srs.307F (Originally regd as Srs.305) (First to be fitted with Aviation Traders extra-wide freight door in 10/65 - designated ATL.99)	12921	(N6596C) G-ANCE	3. 1.58	To EI-BAA 5/74. Canx 21.5.74.
G-ANCF	Bristol 175 Britannia Srs.308F (Originally regd as Srs.305)	12922	5Y-AZP G-ANCF/LV-GJB/LV-PPJ/ (G-ANCF)/G-14-1/G-18-4/G-ANCF/(N6597C)	3. 1.58	WFU at Manston on 12.12.81. Broken up at Manston. Fuselage stored 6/97 at Kemble. Canx as WFU 21.2.84.
G-ANCG	Bristol 175 Britannia Srs.308F (Originally regd as Srs.305)	12923	LV-GJC LV-PPL/G-14-2/G-ANCG/(N6598C)	3. 1.58	DBR at Manston on 20.4.67. Canx.
G-ANCH	Bristol 175 Britannia Srs.309 (Originally regd as Srs.305)	12924	9G-AAG G-ANCH/G-41/9G-AAG/G-ANCH/(N6599C)	3. 1.58	Broken up in 8/73 at Biggin Hill. Canx.
G-ANCI(1)	Bristol 175 Britannia Srs.300	12925		. .53R	NTU - To G-AOVH 2/57. Canx.
G-ANCI(2)	DH.114 Heron 1B	14043	OO-BIA (G-ANCI)/4X-ARL/G-ANCI/G-5-13	6. 6.55	WFU at Southend on 13.11.69. Broken up and remains taken to Staravia dump at Lasham by 1/73. Canx.
G-ANCJ(1)	Bristol 175 Britannia Srs.300	12926		. .53R	NTU - To G-AOVI 2/57. Canx.
G-ANCJ(2)	DH.114 Heron 2C	14082		7. 6.55	To VP-LIB 11/59. Canx 29.1.60.
G-ANCK	DH.82A Tiger Moth	82301	N9184	2. 9.53	To ZK-BFC 7/54. Canx 12.3.54.
G-ANCL	DH.82A Tiger Moth	84593	T6126	2. 9.53	To ZK-BFZ 8/54. Canx 12.3.54.
G-ANCM	DHC.3 Otter	17		3. 9.53	To Indian AF as IM-1057 in 3/57. Canx in 7/56.
G-ANCN	DH.82A Tiger Moth	85674	DE744	4. 9.53	To OO-NCN 4/55. Canx.
G-ANCO	DH.104 Dove 6A	04440	G-5-15	9. 9.53	To N1586V 5/54. Canx 4.6.54.
G-ANCP	DH.82A Tiger Moth	86475	NM155	4. 9.53	To ZK-BJK 12/54. Canx 20.4.54.
G-ANCR	DH.82A Tiger Moth	86147	EM964	4. 9.53	To ZK-BFW 7/54. Canx 6.4.54.
G-ANCS	DH.82A Tiger Moth	82824	R4907	12. 9.53	
G-ANCT	DH.82A Tiger Moth	85467	DE471	9. 9.53	DBR in gales at Wyberton on 7.2.61. Canx.
G-ANCU	DH.82A Tiger Moth	84692	T6266	9. 9.53	Not converted. Scrapped at Christchurch in 1956. Canx.
G-ANCV	DH.82A Tiger Moth	85009	T6709	9. 9.53	Crashed at South Fambridge, Essex on 15.3.63. Canx.
G-ANCW	DH.82A Tiger Moth	84349	T7996	9. 9.53	Not converted. Scrapped at Christchurch in 1956. Canx.
G-ANCX	DH.82A Tiger Moth	83719	T7229	15. 9.53	
G-ANCY	DH.82A Tiger Moth	85234	DE164	12. 9.53	To OO-DLA 5/55. Canx 1.3.55.
G-ANCZ	DH.82A Tiger Moth	82588	W7970 G-AFSU	16. 9.53	Crashed at Panshangar on 16.1.59. Canx.

Regn	Type	c/n	Previous identity	Regn date	Fate or immediate subsequent identity (if known)
G-ANDA	DH.82A Tiger Moth	83768	T7269	24. 9.53	Crashed in forced-landing at Hook Heath Golf Course, near Woking on 21.3.67. Canx.
G-ANDB	DH.82A Tiger Moth	83343	T7035	28.11.53	To ZK-BFH 4/54. Canx 1.3.54.
G-ANDC	DH.82A Tiger Moth	82814	R4897	31. 8.53	To LX-JON 12/53. Canx 4.12.53.
G-ANDD	DH.82A Tiger Moth	85668	DE738	30. 9.53	To RCAF Gliding Club in France as SLN-04 in 8/56. Canx 1.12.55.
G-ANDE	DH.82A Tiger Moth	85957	EM726	23. 9.53	
	(Aircraft rebuilt several times)				
G-ANDF	DH.82A Tiger Moth	85530	DE563	21. 9.53	Crashed at Onslow, Surrey on 5.7.55. Canx.
G-ANDG	DH.82A Tiger Moth	82472	N9402	21. 9.53	Destroyed in collision with D.31 Turbulent G-APBZ at Fairoaks on 6.9.59. Canx.
G-ANDH	DH.82A Tiger Moth	3579	L6944	21. 9.53	Crashed in West Germany in 1954. Canx.
			(2259M)/(2256M)/L6944		
G-ANDI(1)	DH.82A Tiger Moth	3946	N6642	22. 9.53R	NTU - To G-ANDM 9/53. Canx.
G-ANDI(2)	DH.82A Tiger Moth	82335	N40DH	22. 9.53	To D-ENDI(3) 10/88. Canx 8.9.88.
			G-ANDI/(G-ANDM)/N9240		
G-ANDJ	DH.82A Tiger Moth	82437	N9367	22. 9.53	Crashed near Theale, Berks on 5.5.56. Canx.
G-ANDK	DH.82A Tiger Moth	83554	T5842	22. 9.53	Not converted. Scrapped at White Waltham in 3/56. Canx.
G-ANDL	DH.82A Tiger Moth	85339	DE305	22. 9.53	Crashed near Waltham St.Lawrence on 10.1.58. Canx.
G-ANDM(1)	DH.82A Tiger Moth	82335	N9240	23. 9.53R	NTU - To G-ANDI 9/53. Canx.
G-ANDM(2)	DH.82A Tiger Moth	3946	EI-AGP	23. 9.53	
			G-ANDM/EI-AGP/G-ANDM/(G-ANDI)/N6642		
G-ANDN	DH.82A Tiger Moth	85882	DF133	22. 9.53	To SE-COY 6/61. Canx 16.11.60.
G-ANDO	DH.82A Tiger Moth	84841	T6500	22. 9.53	To N9921F 3/55. Canx.
G-ANDP	DH.82A Tiger Moth	82868	D-EBEC	22. 9.53	(Damaged mid .95)
			N9920F/G-ANDP/R4960		
G-ANDR	DH.82A Tiger Moth	82089	N6840	23. 9.53	To (N9922F) 3/55 /(D-EBOC) 7/55 /D-EGOH 8/57. Canx.
G-ANDS	DH.82A Tiger Moth	86358	NL915	22. 9.53	To ZK-BEA 11/53. Canx 20.10.53.
G-ANDT	DH.82A Tiger Moth	86428	NL996	22. 9.53	To ZK-BDZ 11/53. Canx 20.10.53.
G-ANDU	Taylorcraft Auster 5	1510	TJ459	8.10.53	To SE-CAO 6/55. Canx 17.12.53.
G-ANDV	DH.82A Tiger Moth	83771	T7272	30. 9.53	DBR on take-off from Wisley on 5.6.66. Canx.
G-ANDW	DH.82A Tiger Moth	84739	T6365	30. 9.53	Not converted. Canx on 19.7.54.
G-ANDX	DH.104 Dove 7XC	04435	XG496	28. 9.53	WFU at Newcastle 3/95. Permit expired 3.4.86. (Stored 5/99 at Kemble) Canx by CAA 24.2.99.
	(Originally regd as Dove 1B)		G-ANDX		
G-ANDY	DH.104 Dove 6	04441	XJ320	28. 9.53	DBR after crashing on take-off in field near Juniper Green, Edinburgh on 29.5.62. Canx.
	(Originally regd as Dove 6A)		G-ANDY		
G-ANDZ	DH.82A Tiger Moth	85689	DE775	24. 9.53	Not converted. To mock-up agricultural conversion at Rochester in 12/59. Canx.
G-ANEA	DH.82A Tiger Moth	85611	DE670	24. 9.53	Crashed at New Romney, Kent on 24.6.60. Canx.
G-ANEB	DH.82A Tiger Moth	82326	N9209	24. 9.53	To SE-CGB 4/57. Canx 15.4.57.
G-ANEC	DH.82A Tiger Moth	86102	EM908	24. 9.53	Crashed at Letterkenny, Eire on 21.6.60. Canx.
G-ANED	DH.82A Tiger Moth	82913	R5018	24. 9.53	Not converted. Dismantled at Perth in 1956. Canx.
G-ANEE	DH.82A Tiger Moth	83161	T5418	28. 9.53	To EI-ANN 10/64. Canx 19.7.64.
G-ANEF	DH.82A Tiger Moth	83226	T5493	28. 9.53	Struck trees during climb out after take-off at RAF Cranwell on 17.9.88, sold to Sweden in 1991 for rebuild. Canx by CAA 10.9.96. To SE-AMM 4/98.
G-ANEG	Douglas C-47B-35-DK Dakota	16696/33444	(N99886)	28. 9.53	Derelict at Bahrain still marked as G-ANEG. Canx in 12/82.
			G-ANEG/(9M-AUJ)/G-ANEG/(N26AA)/G-ANEG/(5B-CAY)/G-ANEG/(OD-AEP)/G-ANEG/44-7711		
G-ANEH	DH.82A Tiger Moth	82067	N6797	24. 9.53	
G-ANEI	DH.82A Tiger Moth	82960	R5065	29. 9.53	To USA as N523R 10/64. Canx 20.8.64.
G-ANEJ	DH.82A Tiger Moth	85592	DE638	1.10.53	DBR on landing at Owstwich, Yorks on 15.5.65. Canx as WFU 10.9.73. Sold to R.Malaysian AF for museum in 2/89. (On display at Sungei Besi Air Base, Kuala Lumpur)
G-ANEK	DH.82A Tiger Moth	82303	N9186	1.10.53	Crashed at Frankfurt, West Germany on 10.3.54. Canx.
G-ANEL	DH.82A Tiger Moth	82333	N9238	1.10.53	
G-ANEM	DH.82A Tiger Moth	82943	EI-AGN	1.10.53	
			G-ANEM/R5042		
G-ANEN	DH.82A Tiger Moth	85418	OO-ACG	2.10.53	
			G-ANEN/DE410		
G-ANEO	DH.82A Tiger Moth	85549	EI-AGL	2.10.53	Crashed at Keston, Kent on 16.4.61. Canx.
			G-ANEO/DE582		
G-ANEP	Taylorcraft Auster 5	1368	TJ307	2.10.53	DBF at Dusseldorf, West Germany on 12.3.54. Canx.
G-ANER	DH.82A Tiger Moth	82041	N6777	2.10.53	Crashed at Staverton on 16.6.60. Canx.
G-ANES	DH.82A Tiger Moth	82911	R5016	2.10.53	WFU at Ipswich on 26.10.54. Canx 20.2.59.
G-ANET	DH.89A Dragon Rapide	6700	HG715	5.10.53	To VR-AAL 6/55. Canx 29.5.55.
G-ANEU	DH.89A Dragon Rapide	6836	NR748	5.10.53	To F-OAQU 9/54. Canx 26.8.54.
G-ANEV	DH.82A Tiger Moth	83813	T7417	6.10.53	Crashed at Pengham Moors, Cardiff on 22.7.58. Canx.
G-ANEW	DH.82A Tiger Moth	86458	NM138	6.10.53	WFU at Thruxton on 18.6.62. (Stored 4/98 Henstridge)
G-ANEX	DH.82A Tiger Moth	84541	T6050	10.10.53	Crashed into sea off Margate, Kent on 3.9.54. Canx.
G-ANEY	DH.82A Tiger Moth	85964	EM733	10.10.53	Canx as WFU on 22.12.59. Canx 16.11.60
G-ANEZ	DH.82A Tiger Moth	84218	T7849	20.10.53	
G-ANFA	DH.82A Tiger Moth	83824	T7297	9.10.53	To ZK-BGJ 8/54. Canx 6.4.54.
G-ANFB	DH.82A Tiger Moth	82032	N6754	9.10.53	To ZK-BFG 4/54. Canx 1.3.54.
G-ANFC(1)	DH.82A Tiger Moth	85385	DE363	13.10.53	DBF at Dunstable on 25.1.71. Canx as WFU 26.1.82.
G-ANFC(2)	DH.82A Tiger Moth	-	"DE363"	30. 3.89	(Fuselage on restoration 5/99 Welshpool)
	("Restored" with identity of G-ANFC(1) but unlikely)				
G-ANFD	DH.104 Dove 6A	04444		16.10.53	To N1588V 11/53. Canx 9.12.53.
G-ANFE	DH.114 Heron 1B	14034	(VR-B..)	16.10.53	To Liechtenstein but became TN-ABA 4/68. Canx 5.4.68.
			G-ANFE/VH-ARB/G-ANFE		
G-ANFF	DH.114 Heron 1B	14036		16.10.53	To JA6152 1/54. Canx 25.1.54.
G-ANFG	DH.114 Heron 1B	14037		16.10.53	To JA6153 3/54. Canx 1.3.54.
G-ANFH	Westland-Sikorsky S-55 Whirlwind Srs.1	WA/15		27.10.53	CofA expired 17.7.71 & WFU at North Denes. Canx as WFU 2.9.77. (Stored 5/97 Weston-super-Mare)

Regn	Type	c/n	Previous identity	Regn date	Fate or immediate subsequent identity (if known)
G-ANFI	DH.82A Tiger Moth	85577	DE623	16.10.53	
	(Note: a Tiger Moth painted as DE623 is on display at the Auto Und Technik Museum, Sinsheim. This is actually D-EDON)				
G-ANFJ	DH.82A Tiger Moth	82822	R4905	16.10.53	Crashed at Walsgrave, near Coventry on 6.4.57. Canx.
G-ANFK	DH.82A Tiger Moth	84231	T7862	22.10.53	Crashed during 1957. Canx as destroyed 6.4.60.
G-ANFL	DH.82A Tiger Moth	84617	T6169	22.10.53	
G-ANFM	DH.82A Tiger Moth	83604	T5888	22.10.53	
G-ANFN	DH.82A Tiger Moth	83375	T5678	22.10.53	Crashed at South Petherton, Somerset on 17.6.60. Canx.
G-ANFO	DH.82A Tiger Moth	86357	NL914	22.10.53	Crashed at Little Snoring on 17.3.62. Canx.
G-ANFP	DH.82A Tiger Moth	82530	N9503	28.10.53	Dismantled at Rush Green on 1.7.63. (Stored 3/96)
G-ANFR	DH.82A Tiger Moth	85299	DE253	27.10.53	To HB-UBL 5/54. Canx 30.4.54.
G-ANFS	DH.82A Tiger Moth	83569	T5812	27.10.53	Crashed near Port Talbot on 22.12.53. Canx.
G-ANFT	DH.82A Tiger Moth	84206	T7841	27.10.53	Crashed at Hurga Cotton Scheme, Sudan on 6.11.60. Canx.
G-ANFU	Taylorcraft Auster 5	1748	TW385	31.10.53	
	(Composite, cockpit section on rebuild 5/93 with frame from unidentified Auster 6; to be painted as NJ719 using identity of starboard wing ex G-AKPH)				
G-ANFV	DH.82A Tiger Moth	85904	DF155	1.12.53	
G-ANFW	DH.82A Tiger Moth	85660	DE730	5.11.53	(Stored 7/99 Duxford)
	(Regd with fuselage no. 3737)				
G-ANFX	DH.82A Tiger Moth	85238	DE168	9.11.53	To F-OAPF 2/54. Canx 12.2.54.
G-ANFY	DH.82A Tiger Moth	86349	NL906	13.11.53	WFU on 25.5.68. Canx as WFU 22.2.73. (Stored in poor condition 1/96 Ashford, Kent)
	(Converted to Thruxton Jackaroo in 11/57)				
G-ANFZ	DH.82A Tiger Moth	82013	N6735	13.11.53	To OO-ZAC 4/56. Canx 29.4.56.
G-ANGA	Taylorcraft Auster 5	1807	TW468	9.11.53	To VH-BGN 2/56. Canx 27.5.55.
G-ANGB	Percival P.34 Proctor III	H.404	LZ597	20.11.53	To VH-GGB 5/56. Canx 29.5.56.
G-ANGC	Percival P.34 Proctor III	H.565	LZ804	20.11.53	To VH-BXQ 5/58. Canx 11.4.58.
G-ANGD	DH.82A Tiger Moth	83683	T7213	24.11.53	To D-EKAL 8/56. Canx.
G-ANGE	DH.104 Dove 2	04167	VT-CVA	13.11.53	DBR at Libya's airstrip No.12 on 26.2.64. Broken down into its major components at Benina, Libya in 1967. Canx on 21.5.64.
G-ANGF	Avro 685 York C.1	-	MW254	19.11.53	To OD-ADL 4/59. Canx 21.4.59.
G-ANGG	Percival P.44 Proctor V	Ae.95	VN898	20.11.53	To SE-BZW 7/54. Canx 3.7.54.
G-ANGH	Percival P.31 Proctor IV	H.740	NP369	20.11.53	Not converted. Canx 2.11.54.
G-ANGI	Percival P.31 Proctor IV	H.689	NP269	20.11.53	Not converted. Canx 2.11.54.
G-ANGJ	DH.82A Tiger Moth	84771	T6397	24.11.53	To ZK-BEW 4/54. Canx 28.12.53.
G-ANGK(1)	Bristol 175 Britannia Srs.250	13234		23.11.53	NTU - To 4X-AGC. Canx.
G-ANGK(2)	Cessna 140A	15396	N9675A	10. 3.89	
G-ANGL	Avro 685 York C.1	-	MW231	23.11.53	To EP-ADA 2/55. Canx 26.1.55.
G-ANGM	Percival P.31 Proctor IV	H.583	NP176	23.11.53	WFU at Southend in 10/57. Canx as WFU in 10/57.
G-ANGN	Percival P.31 Proctor IV	H.587	NP180	23.11.53	Not converted. Broken up at Southend in 4/59. Canx.
G-ANGO	Percival P.31 Proctor IV	H.684	NP300	23.11.53	Not converted. Burnt at Southend in 4/60. Canx.
G-ANGP	Percival P.31 Proctor IV	H.689	NP305	23.11.53	Not converted. Broken up at Southend in 2/57. Canx.
G-ANGR	Westland-Sikorsky S-51 Mk.1A	WA/H/130	G-17-1	23.11.53	NTU - To Japanese Navy as 8832 in 2/54. Canx.
G-ANGS	Westland-Sikorsky S-51 Mk.1A	WA/H/131	G-17-2	23.11.53	NTU - To Japanese Navy as 8833 in 2/54. Canx.
G-ANGT	DH.82A Tiger Moth	83829	T7302	24.11.53	To ZK-BEX 4/54. Canx 28.12.53.
G-ANGU	DH.104 Dove 6	04446	G-5-15	26.11.53	To EI-AUK 8/70. Canx 5.8.70.
G-ANGV	Auster J/1B Aiglet	3122		30.11.53	To ZK-BDX 3/54. Canx 23.3.54.
G-ANGW	Taylorcraft Auster 5	845	MS980	5.12.53	To OE-AAT 11/55. Canx 12.3.56.
G-ANGX	Taylorcraft Auster 4	881	MT108	5.12.53	To VH-AZJ 11/54. Canx 12.10.54.
	(Also c/n "TAY/38799" quoted)				
G-ANGY	DH.82A Tiger Moth	85314	DE268	4.12.53	Not converted. Canx in 7/56.
G-ANGZ	DH.82A Tiger Moth	85949	DF213	4.12.53	To F-BHIX 11/55. Canx.
G-ANHA	Vickers 701C Viscount	61		12.12.53	To PP-SRP 12/62. Canx 23.5.63.
G-ANHB	Vickers 701C Viscount	62		12.12.53	To PP-SRN 8/62. Canx 23.4.63.
G-ANHC	Vickers 701C Viscount	63		12.12.53	Crashed at Anzio, Italy on 22.10.58, after a mid-air collision with an Italian AF F-86K. Canx.
G-ANHD	Vickers 701C Viscount	64		12.12.53	To PP-SRO 8/62. Canx 23.4.63.
G-ANHE	Vickers 701C Viscount	65		12.12.53	To PP-SRQ 8/62. Canx 23.5.63.
G-ANHF	Vickers 701C Viscount	66		12.12.53	To PP-SRR 8/62. Canx 25.7.63.
G-ANHG	DH.82A Tiger Moth	3763	N5490	4.12.53	To F-BHIN 1/56. Canx 22.7.55.
G-ANHH	DH.82A Tiger Moth	3865	N6552	4.12.53	To F-BHAN 10/54. Canx 26.5.54.
G-ANHI	DH.82A Tiger Moth	83002	R5120	4.12.53	Crashed at Lutterworth, Leics. on 2.10.65. Canx.
G-ANHJ	DH.82A Tiger Moth	84230	T7861	4.12.53	To F-BHIT 11/55. Canx 22.7.55.
G-ANHK	DH.82A Tiger Moth	82442	F-BHIM G-ANHK/N9372	4.12.53	
G-ANHL	Taylorcraft Auster 4	902	MT133	5.12.53	Crashed at Dinard, France on 12.12.61. Canx as WFU in 10/65.
G-ANHM	Taylorcraft Auster 4	846	MT137	5.12.53	To VH-AZO 11/54. Canx 12.10.54.
G-ANHN	Taylorcraft Auster 4	900	MT163	5.12.53	To D-EGUK 5/58. Canx 25.7.58.
G-ANHO	Taylorcraft Auster 5	899	MT169	5.12.53	Crashed at Biggin Hill on 9.5.64. Canx.
G-ANHP	Taylorcraft Auster 4	906	MT170	5.12.53	To D-ELIT 11/55. Canx 18.11.55.
G-ANHR	Taylorcraft Auster 5	759	MT192	5.12.53	(On rebuild 6/96)
G-ANHS	Taylorcraft Auster 4	737	MT197	5.12.53	
G-ANHT	Taylorcraft Auster 5	764	MT218	5.12.53	To OO-DBA 11/54. Canx 12.10.54.
G-ANHU	Taylorcraft Auster 4	799	EC-AXR G-ANHU/MT255	5.12.53	(On rebuild 9/96)
G-ANHV	Taylorcraft Auster 5	922	MT277	5.12.53	To SE-CAP 2/55. Canx 12.10.54.
G-ANHW	Taylorcraft Auster 5D	1396	TJ320	5.12.53	Forced landed at Carlton Manor, Norfolk in 1970, taken dismantled to Shipdam and WFU there 15.12.71. (On rebuild 9/96)
	(Originally regd as a Auster 5)				
G-ANHX	Taylorcraft Auster 5D	2064	TW519	5.12.53	(Stored 9/96)
	(Originally regd as a Auster 5)				

Regn	Type	c/n	Previous identity	Regn date	Fate or immediate subsequent identity (if known)
G-ANHY	Taylorcraft Auster 5D (Originally regd as a Auster 5)	1757	TW387	5.12.53	To ZK-BGU 4/55. Canx 8.2.55.
G-ANHZ	Taylorcraft Auster 5	1753	TW384	5.12.53	Canx 18.1.95 on sale to Switzerland.
G-ANIA	Taylorcraft Auster 5	2050	D-EHUV G-ANIA/HB-EUB/ G-ANIA/TW506	5.12.53	This aircraft is actually G-AIKE which was restored to the register as such on 2.9.88. Canx as WFU 26.11.91.
G-ANIB	Taylorcraft Auster 5	1818	TW475	5.12.53	To F-BHCO 7/54. Canx.
G-ANIC	Taylorcraft Auster 5	1816	TW474	5.12.53	Not converted. To spares use Caen, France in 7/54. Canx.
G-ANID	Taylorcraft Auster 5	1811	TW471	5.12.53	Crashed at Stonor, near Oxford on 13.2.58. Canx.
G-ANIE	Taylorcraft Auster 5	1809	TW467	5.12.53	
G-ANIF	Taylorcraft Auster 5	1709	TW460	5.12.53	To SE-CGO 1/58. Canx.
G-ANIG	Taylorcraft Auster 5	1795	TW457	5.12.53	To EC-AJJ 7/54. Canx 15.6.54.
G-ANIH	Taylorcraft Auster 5	1779	TW449	5.12.53	Canx 8.8.73 on sale to Singapore.
G-ANII	Taylorcraft Auster 5D (Originally regd as a Auster 5)	1739	TW374	5.12.53	To F-OARN 11/55. Canx 28.7.54.
G-ANIJ	Taylorcraft Auster 5D (Originally regd as a Auster 5)	1680	(EI-...) G-ANIJ/TJ672	5.12.53	(Stored 5/99 at Kemble)
G-ANIK	Taylorcraft Auster 5	1674	TJ657	5.12.53	Crashed at Guiseley, near Leeds on 4.3.62. Canx.
G-ANIL	Taylorcraft Auster 5	1575	TJ527	5.12.53	To D-ECIL 6/57. Canx 10.5.57.
G-ANIM	Taylorcraft Auster 5	1542	TJ515	5.12.53	To LN-BDK 6/54. Canx 2.6.54.
G-ANIN	Taylorcraft Auster 5	1494	TJ506	5.12.53	DBR at Great Ness, Ulverston on 19.11.59. Canx.
G-ANIO	Taylorcraft Auster 5	1425	TJ422	5.12.53	To LN-BNB 4/60. Canx 20.2.60.
G-ANIP	Taylorcraft Auster 5	1453	TJ394	5.12.53	To SX-ADA 1/55. Canx 28.6.56.
G-ANIR	Taylorcraft Auster 5	1438	TJ380	5.12.53	To 7Q-YDG 7/67. Canx.
G-ANIS	Taylorcraft Auster 5	1429	TJ375	5.12.53	CofA expired 19.9.76. Canx by CAA 8.10.81. (Stored in garage 6/97 Longford, Ireland)
G-ANIT	Taylorcraft Auster 5	1407	TJ339	5.12.53	Crashed off Hastings on 2.7.54. Canx.
G-ANIU	Taylorcraft Auster 5	841	MS977	5.12.53	To LN-BDU 2/55. Canx 12.10.55.
G-ANIV(1)	DH.82A Tiger Moth	84764	T6390	3.12.53R	NTU -To G-ANIX(2) 12/53. Canx.
G-ANIV(2)	DH.82A Tiger Moth	86109	(G-ANIX) EM915	3.12.53	To ZK-BGW 10/54. Canx 9.7.54.
G-ANIW	DH.82A Tiger Moth	85450	DE454	3.12.53	To ZK-BGV 12/54. Canx 9.7.54.
G-ANIX(1)	DH.82A Tiger Moth	86109	EM915	3.12.53R	NTU - To G-ANIV(2) 12/53. Canx.
G-ANIX(2)	DH.82A Tiger Moth (Now composite rebuild of unidentified Tiger in Germany .90/92 which used paperwork of D-ELOM, the former G-ANIX/T6390)	84764	D-EFTF(2) G-ANIX(2)/(G-ANIV)/T6390	3.12.53	
G-ANIY	DH.82A Tiger Moth	84137	T7750	7.12.53	Crashed at Doncaster on 27.6.61. Canx.
G-ANIZ	DH.82A Tiger Moth	83896	T7467	7.12.53	To USA as N9714 in 12/67. Canx 6.12.67.
G-ANJA	DH.82A Tiger Moth	82459	N9389	7.12.53	
G-ANJB	DH.104 Dove 6A	04448		14.12.53	To YV-P-DPK 4/55. Canx 22.3.55.
G-ANJC	DH.104 Dove 6A	04449		14.12.53	To N1563V 1/54. Canx 15.2.54.
G-ANJD	DH.82A Tiger Moth	84652	T6226	8.12.53	WFU on 6.9.81. (On rebuild 7/97)
G-ANJE	DH.82A Tiger Moth	82014	N6736	8.12.53	Crashed at Roborough, Plymouth on 27.2.60. Canx.
G-ANJF	DH.82A Tiger Moth	85802	DE931	9.12.53	To D-EMAX 1/56. Canx 18.1.56.
G-ANJG	DH.82A Tiger Moth	83875	T7349	12.12.53	To F-BGZT 6/54. Canx 26.5.54.
G-ANJH	DH.82A Tiger Moth	85887	DF138	12.12.53	To F-BGZX 5/54. Canx 26.5.54.
G-ANJI	DH.82A Tiger Moth	85099	T6830	12.12.53	To F-BHIQ 11/55. Canx 22.7.55.
G-ANJJ	DH.82A Tiger Moth	84766	T6392	12.12.53	To F-BHIC 8/55. Canx 22.7.55.
G-ANJK	DH.82A Tiger Moth	84557	T6066	12.12.53	CofA expired 12.5.85. (Stored 5/94) Canx by CAA 1.3.96.
G-ANJL	DH.82A Tiger Moth	84910	T6581	12.12.53	To F-BHAM 3/55. Canx 26.5.54.
G-ANJM	DH.82A Tiger Moth	84078	T7684	12.12.53	To F-BGZR 5/54. Canx 26.5.54.
G-ANJN	DH.82A Tiger Moth	86453	NM133	12.12.53	To F-BHIY 8/55. Canx 22.7.54.
G-ANJO	DH.82A Tiger Moth	86511	NM203	12.12.53	To F-BHIZ 9/55. Canx 22.7.54.
G-ANJP	DH.82A Tiger Moth	85783	DE898	12.12.53	To F-BHIV 10/55. Canx 22.7.55.
G-ANJR	DH.89A Dragon Rapide	6816	NR728	12.12.53	To F-OAKX 11/54. Canx 8.7.54.
G-ANJS	Westland-Sikorsky S-55 Whirlwind Srs.1	WA/18		14.12.53	Ditched 6 miles from the "Southern Harvester" oil refinery vessel off the Brazilian coast on 5.11.55. Canx.
G-ANJT	Westland-Sikorsky S-55 Whirlwind Srs.1	WA/19		14.12.53	Ditched off Antarctica on 29.1.58. Canx.
G-ANJU	Westland-Sikorsky S-55 Whirlwind Srs.1	WA/23		14.12.53	Ditched into the South Atlantic Ocean on 20.12.56. Canx.
G-ANJV	Westland-Sikorsky S-55 Whirlwind Srs.3	WA/24	VR-BET G-ANJV	14.12.53	(Stored - unmarked 5/97 Weston-super-Mare)
G-ANJW	DH.82A Tiger Moth	85233	DE163	19.12.53	To F-BGZS 6/54. Canx 26.5.54.
G-ANJX	DH.82A Tiger Moth	85585	DE631	19.12.53	Not converted. DBR at Croydon on 16.1.54. Canx.
G-ANJY	DH.82A Tiger Moth	86098	EM904	19.12.53	To F-BHAO 6/54. Canx 26.5.54.
G-ANJZ	DH.82A Tiger Moth	86176	NL693	19.12.53	To F-BHIF 9/55. Canx 22.7.55.
G-ANKA	DH.82A Tiger Moth	3742	N5474	19.12.53	To I-LUNI 2/60. Canx 8.2.60.
G-ANKB	DH.82A Tiger Moth	82155	N6911	19.12.53	To CF-CJW 3/72. Canx 31.3.72.
G-ANKC	DH.82A Tiger Moth	82163	N6919	19.12.53	To F-BHIJ 8/55. Canx 22.7.55.
G-ANKD	DH.82A Tiger Moth	82289	N9178	19.12.53	To F-BHIK 9/55. Canx 22.7.55.
G-ANKE	DH.82A Tiger Moth	84627	T6179	19.12.53	To F-BHIP 10/55. Canx 22.7.55.
G-ANKF	DH.82A Tiger Moth	83803	T7289	19.12.53	To F-BHIE 8/55. Canx 22.7.55.
G-ANKG	DH.82A Tiger Moth	86154	EM971	19.12.53	Crashed at Ipswich on 11.9.58. Canx.
G-ANKH	DH.82A Tiger Moth	82323	N9206	24.12.53	To PH-NIG 9/57. Canx 10.9.57.
G-ANKI	Taylorcraft Auster 5	1790	TW446	21.12.53	To D-ELYD 8/56. Canx 11.8.56.
G-ANKJ	DH.82A Tiger Moth	86372	NL929	30.12.53	To SE-COO 5/63. Canx 21.10.62.
G-ANKK	DH.82A Tiger Moth	83590	T5854	24.12.53	
G-ANKL	DH.82A Tiger Moth	85470	OO-JIM G-ANKL/DE474	24.12.53	To New Zealand for rebuild in 1994. Canx by CAA 8.3.99.
G-ANKM	DH.82A Tiger Moth	3989	N6716	24.12.53	To F-BGZV 6/54. Canx 26.5.54.
G-ANKN	DH.82A Tiger Moth	82700	R4759	24.12.53	To CF-JJI 8/57. Canx 5.8.57.
G-ANKO	DH.82A Tiger Moth	82995	R5113	24.12.53	To F-BGZP 5/54. Canx 26.5.54.

Regn	Type	c/n	Previous identity	Regn date	Fate or immediate subsequent identity (if known)
G-ANKP	DH.82A Tiger Moth	83006	R5124	24.12.53	To F-BHIB 8/55. Canx 22.7.55.
G-ANKR	DH.82A Tiger Moth	82114	N6859	24.12.53	Not converted. Canx in 9/56.
G-ANKS	DH.82A Tiger Moth	84659	T6233	24.12.53	To F-BHIH 8/55. Canx 22.7.55.
G-ANKT	DH.82A Tiger Moth	85087	T6818	24.12.53	
G-ANKU	DH.82A Tiger Moth	85866	DF117	24.12.53	Crashed on take off from Kilpadder, Co.Wicklow, Eire on 10.8.65. Canx.
G-ANKV	DH.82A Tiger Moth (Provenence uncertain; static rebuild by Acebell Avn early .94)	84166	T7793	30.12.53	Not converted. Canx 9/56. (On display in former Terminal Building at Croydon Airport)
G-ANKW	DH.82A Tiger Moth	86101	EM907	30.12.53	To F-BHAQ 6/55. Canx 26.5.54.
G-ANKX	DH.82A Tiger Moth	82438	"G-ANMM" N9368	30.12.53	To F-BGZQ 2/55. Canx 26.5.54.
G-ANKY	DH.82A Tiger Moth	84110	T7733	30.12.53	To SE-CGE 4/57. Canx 4.4.57.
G-ANKZ	DH.82A Tiger Moth	3803	(N.....) F-BHIO/G-ANKZ/N6466	30.12.53	
G-ANLA	DH.82A Tiger Moth	83000	R5118	30.12.53	To F-BHIG 8/55. Canx 22.7.55.
G-ANLB	DH.82A Tiger Moth	83857	T7453	30.12.53	DBR at Southam, Warks. on 17.3.62. Canx.
G-ANLC	DH.82A Tiger Moth	85154	T6945	30.12.53	Converted to Rumpler C.V replica at Croydon in 1961 and WFU in Jordan. Canx 22.7.55.
G-ANLD	DH.82A Tiger Moth	85990	OO-DPA G-ANLD/EM773	30.12.53	
G-ANLE	DH.82A Tiger Moth	86462	NM142	30.12.53	Crashed at Tillington, Essex on 20.2.64. Canx.
G-ANLF	Douglas C-47A-1-DK Dakota	11979	F-OAOR G-ANLF/ZS-DHO/(G-AMTN)/SAAF 6818/FL572/42-92204	6. 1.54	To OO-SBH 9/61. Canx 1.9.61.
G-ANLG	DH.82A Tiger Moth	86248	NL777	4. 1.54	Crashed at Luton on 11.5.58. Canx.
G-ANLH	DH.82A Tiger Moth (Fuselage No. MCO/DH/4623)	86546	N3744F OO-EVO/G-ANLH/PG637	4. 1.54	
G-ANLI	Douglas C-47B-25-DK Dakota	16013/32761	H-712 Pakistan AF/KN387/44-76429	11. 1.54	To F-OAPB 2/54. Canx 19.2.54.
G-ANLJ	Douglas C-47A-10-DK Dakota	12498	H-706 Pakistan AF/VP906/KG463/42-108865	11. 1.54	To F-OAQE 4/54. Canx 21.4.54.
G-ANLK	Douglas C-47B-1-DK Dakota	14357/25802	H-713 Pakistan AF/KJ863/43-48541	11. 1.54	To N1592V 3/54. Canx 9.3.54.
G-ANLL	Douglas C-47B-40-DK Dakota	16816/33564	H-716 Pakistan AF/KP262/44-77232	11. 1.54	To F-OAPP 3/54. Canx 23.3.54.
G-ANLM	Douglas C-47B-20-DK Dakota	15669/27114	AP-ACD Pakistan AF H-710/KN244/43-49853	11. 1.54	To F-OAQD 3/54. Canx 5.4.54.
G-ANLN	DH.114 Heron 1B	14035		8. 1.54	To 6Y-JCZ 9/63. Canx 30.7.63.
G-ANLO	DH.106 Comet 3B (Originally regd as a Comet 3)	06100		6. 1.54	To RAF as XP915 6/61. Canx 25.1.61.
G-ANLP	DH.82A Tiger Moth	85872	DF123	7. 1.54	Crashed at Brookbridge, Worcs on 23.8.58. Canx.
G-ANLR	DH.82A Tiger Moth	82111	N6856	7. 1.54	Crashed at Syderstone, Norfolk on 23.4.66. Canx. (Airframe for rebuild of G-AIVW in 11/68)
G-ANLS	DH.82A Tiger Moth	85862	DF113	7. 1.54	
G-ANLT	Miles M.14A Hawk Trainer III (Magister I)	836	N3788	7. 1.54	Not converted. Fuselage used in 1955 rebuild of G-AKPF c/n 2228. Remains burnt at Burnaston in 1957. Canx.
G-ANLU	Taylorcraft Auster 5	1780	TW448	8. 1.54	(Stored by Crofton Aeroplane Services 1/95)
G-ANLV	Westland-Sikorsky S-51 Mk.1A	WA/H/132		23. 3.54	Crashed at Montfort L'Armory, France on 14.6.57. Canx.
G-ANLW	Westland-Sikorsky S-51 Widgeon Mk.2 (Originally regd as Mk.1A)	WA/H/133	"MD497" G-ANLW	23. 3.54	(Stored 8/97 Sywell)
G-ANLX	DH.82A Tiger Moth	84165	T7792	8. 1.54	Crashed near Luton Airport on 31.12.55. (Minor components held for composite rebuild)
G-ANLY	Douglas C-47B-5-DK Dakota	14644/26089	H-701 Pakistan AF/KJ920/43-48828	11. 1.54	To XY-ADD 6/54. Canx 2.6.54.
G-ANLZ	Douglas C-47B-40-DK Dakota	16769/33517	AP-AFL Pakistan AF (H-704 or H-714)/KP232/44-77185	11. 1.54	To XY-ADB 6/54. Canx 2.6.54.
G-ANMA	Douglas C-47B-30-DK Dakota	16197/32945	H-717 Pakistan AF/KN470/44-76613	11. 1.54	To VH-MML on 20.4.54. Canx 18.2.54.
G-ANMB	Douglas C-47B-20-DK Dakota	15663/27108	H-718 Pakistan AF/KN239/43-49847	11. 1.54	To F-BGSM 3/54. Canx 12.4.54.
G-ANMC	Douglas C-47B-1-DK Dakota	14348/25793	H-719 Pakistan AF/KJ854/43-48532	11. 1.54	To XY-ADC 6/54. Canx 2.6.54
G-ANMD	Percival P.44 Proctor V	Ae.94	VN897	9. 1.54	To OO-ADS 5/54. Canx 13.5.54.
G-ANME	DH.82A Tiger Moth	82866	R4958	11. 1.54	WFU at Wolverhampton in 5/62. Canx.
G-ANMF	Bristol 170 Freighter 31	13216	G-18-192	12. 1.54	WFU on 31.8.67 at Lydd. Broken up in 8/70. Canx.
G-ANMG(1)	Bristol 170 Freighter 21	13211	G-18-187	. .54R	NTU - To G-ANWG 1/54. Canx.
G-ANMG(2)	Saro W.14 Skeeter 6	SR.904		1. 5.54	To RAF as XK773 11/55. Canx 7.8.55.
G-ANMH(1)	Bristol 170 Freighter 21	13212	G-18-188	. .54R	NTU - To G-ANWH 1/54. Canx.
G-ANMH(2)	Saro W.14 Skeeter 6	SR.905		1. 5.54	To RAF as XJ355 11/54. Canx 17.8.53.
G-ANMI(1)	Bristol 170 Freighter 21	13213	G-18-189	. .54R	NTU - To G-ANWI 1/54. Canx.
G-ANMI(2)	Saro W.14 Skeeter 7 (Originally regd as Skeeter 5)	SR.906	XK964 G-ANMI	1. 5.54	WFU at Eastleigh. Canx in 9/58.
G-ANMJ	DH.104 Devon 1B (Converted from Srs.1 in 1968)	04006	VP-YES	15. 1.54	WFU at Baginton on 25.6.69. Canx as WFU 17.5.71.
G-ANMK	DH.82A Tiger Moth	82440	N9370	18. 1.54	To VH-BQM 7/55. Canx 21.7.55.
G-ANML	DH.82A Tiger Moth	84553	T6062	22. 1.54	To F-BHIR 11/55. Canx 22.7.55.
G-ANMM	DH.82A Tiger Moth	83552	"G-ANMN" T5840	22. 1.54	To F-BGZZ 6/54. Canx 26.5.54.
G-ANMN	DH.82A Tiger Moth	83299	"G-ANOY" T5606	22. 1.54	To F-BHIS 11/55. Canx 22.7.55.
G-ANMO	DH.82A Tiger Moth	3255	F-BHIU G-ANMO/K4259	22. 1.54	

Regn	Type	c/n	Previous identity	Regn date	Fate or immediate subsequent identity (if known)
G-ANMP	DH.82A Tiger Moth	86126	EM943	22. 1.54	Crashed into Langstone Harbour, Portsmouth on 29.7.57. Canx.
G-ANMR	DH.82A Tiger Moth	84817	T6463	22. 1.54	To F-BGZN 5/54. Canx 26.5.54.
G-ANMS	DH.82A Tiger Moth	84876	T6547	22. 1.54	To VH-SCD 5/57. Canx 1.12.56.
G-ANMT	DH.82A Tiger Moth	85058	T6771	22. 1.54	To F-BGZO 5/54. Canx 26.5.54.
G-ANMU	DH.82A Tiger Moth	85132	T6903	22. 1.54	To D-ECOR 8/57. Canx 31.7.57.
G-ANMV	DH.82A Tiger Moth	83745	F-BHAZ G-ANMV/T7404	22. 1.54	
G-ANMW	DH.82A Tiger Moth	82173	N6929	22. 1.54	To F-BHAX 6/54. Canx 26.5.54.
G-ANMX	DH.82A Tiger Moth	82433	N9346	22. 1.54	To F-BHIL 9/55. Canx 22.7.55.
G-ANMY	DH.82A Tiger Moth	85466	OO-SOL "OO-SOC"/G-ANMY/DE470	22. 1.54	
G-ANMZ	DH.82A Tiger Moth	85588	DE634	22. 1.54	Crashed at Challock on 22.5.69. Canx as destroyed 11.5.81.
G-ANNA	DH.82A Tiger Moth	83598	T5882	22. 1.54	To F-OASE 2/55. Canx 7.9.54.
G-ANNB	DH.82A Tiger Moth	84233	N6037 D-EGYN/G-ANNB/T6037	22. 1.54	(On rebuild)
G-ANNC	DH.82A Tiger Moth	84569	T6102	22. 1.54	To OO-SOM(2) 4/58. Canx 9.4.58.
G-ANND	DH.82A Tiger Moth	83689	T7219	22. 1.54	To SE-CPW 10/62. Canx 16.10.62.
G-ANNE(1)	DH.82A Tiger Moth	83814	T7418	22. 1.54	To OO-CCI 8/57. Canx 2.7.57.
G-ANNE(2)	DH.82A Tiger Moth	"83814"		15. 4.94	(On rebuild 3/96)
	(Composite airframe, unlikely to have any connection with original G-ANNE)				
G-ANNF	DH.82A Tiger Moth	83028	R5146	22. 1.54	Converted to Rumpler C.V replica at Croydon in 1961 & WFU in Jordan. Canx 22.7.55.
G-ANNG	DH.82A Tiger Moth	85504	"G-ANKX" DE524	22. 1.54	
G-ANNH	DH.82A Tiger Moth	83102	R5243	22. 1.54	To D-ECOB 10/57. Canx 27.10.57.
G-ANNI	DH.82A Tiger Moth	85162	T6953	22. 1.54	
G-ANNJ	DH.82A Tiger Moth	83764	T7265	22. 1.54	To F-BHAR 6/54. Canx 26.5.54.
G-ANNK	DH.82A Tiger Moth	83804	F-BFDO(2) G-ANNK/T7290	22. 1.54	WFU on 25.9.87. (On rebuild Cranfield 5/92)
G-ANNL	DH.82A Tiger Moth	83826	T7299	22. 1.54	To HB-UBX 1/57. Canx.
G-ANNM	DH.82A Tiger Moth	85148	T6919	22. 1.54	To F-BHAP 5/54. Canx 26.5.54.
G-ANNN	DH.82A Tiger Moth	84073	T5968	2. 2.54	Not converted. (On rebuild .96)
G-ANNO	DH.114 Heron 1B/C	14049	G-5-7	12. 2.54	To HS-EOB 3/80. Canx 12.3.80.
G-ANNP	DH.82A Tiger Moth	84256	G-AMTY T7881	2. 2.54	Crashed at Munich, West Germany on 12.8.55. Canx.
G-ANNR	DH.82A Tiger Moth	86490	NM182	2. 2.54	To ZK-BFI 5/54. Canx 1.3.54.
G-ANNS	DH.82A Tiger Moth	85712	DE814	2. 2.54	To ZK-BFJ 5/54. Canx 1.3.54.
G-ANNT(1)	Douglas C-47A-1-DK Dakota	12090	ZS-DCA (ZS-DBL)/SAAF 6866/FZ555/42-92304	. .54R	NTU - To F-OAPH 3/54. Canx 25.3.54.
G-ANNT(2)	Lockheed L.749A-79-52 Constellation	2671	N6025C	13. 8.54	To N4901C 3/58. Canx.
G-ANNU	DH.82A Tiger Moth	86156	EM973	5. 2.54	To ZK-BFB 6/54. Canx 24.3.54.
G-ANNV	Auster J/5F Aiglet Trainer	3113		15. 2.54	To K-AAAD/9K-AAD 8/60. Canx 25.6.60.
G-ANNW	Auster J/5F Aiglet Trainer	3120		15. 2.54	To K-AAAE/9K-AAE 8/60. Canx 25.6.60.
G-ANNX	Auster J/5B Autocar	3075		15. 2.54	To K-AAAF/9K-AAF 8/60. Canx 25.6.60.
G-ANNY	Auster J/5B Autocar	3076		15. 2.54	Crashed in low water, Kuwait on 25.10.54. Canx.
G-ANNZ	Auster J/1B Aiglet	3128		16. 2.54	To I-UEST 5/61. Canx 27.3.61.
G-ANOA	Hiller 360 UH-12A	170	F-BEEG N8170H	12. 2.54	CofA expired 12.6.70. Stored at Redhill, later becoming an instructional airframe. Canx as WFU 28.8.79.
G-ANOB	Hiller 360 UH-12A	120	F-BGGZ HB-XAI/I-ELAM/N8120H	4. 5.54	DBR at Barton, Cambs on 30.5.61. Canx.
G-ANOC	Hiller 360 UH-12A	115	F-BFGY N8115H	16. 3.54	Crashed at Glentham, Lincs on 23.8.55. Canx.
G-ANOD	DH.82A Tiger Moth	84588	T6121	16. 2.54	CofA expired 7.2.60. (On long term rebuild 6/94)
G-ANOE	Fiat G.212PW	10	F-BCUX I-ENEA/(MM61636)	17. 2.54	WFU on 12.1.56. Broken up at Beirut in 1964. Canx.
G-ANOF	DH.82A Tiger Moth	86252	NL780	19. 2.54	Crashed at Boxted, Essex on 23.6.59. Canx.
G-ANOG	DH.82A Tiger Moth	83327	T7021	22. 2.54	Not converted. Derelict at Panshangar in 1958. Canx.
G-ANOH	DH.82A Tiger Moth	86040	EM838	22. 2.54	
G-ANOI	DH.82A Tiger Moth	82864	R4956	22. 2.54	Not converted. Scrapped at Panshangar in 1956. Canx.
G-ANOJ	DH.82A Tiger Moth	86031	EM814	22. 2.54	To F-OAVT 11/56. Canx 2.12.55.
G-ANOK	SAAB 91C Safir	91311	(SE-CAH)	22. 2.54	CofA expired 5.2.73. Canx by CAA 15.10.81. (Stored at Museum of Flight, East Fortune)
G-ANOL	DH.114 Heron 2B	14052		26. 2.54	To VP-BAO(2) 8/55. Canx 20.8.55.
G-ANOM	DH.82A Tiger Moth	82086	N6837	2. 3.54	(On rebuild 12/95)
G-ANON	DH.82A Tiger Moth	84270	T7909	4. 3.54	
G-ANOO	DH.82A Tiger Moth	85409	DE401	11. 3.54	
G-ANOP	DH.82A Tiger Moth	85446	DE450	4. 3.54	To VH-BFW 2/56. Canx 6.4.55.
G-ANOR	DH.82A Tiger Moth	85635	DE694	4. 3.54	
G-ANOS	DH.82A Tiger Moth	85461	DE465	4. 3.54	To CF-JNF 8/72. Canx 31.8.72.
G-ANOT	DH.82A Tiger Moth	84242	T7870	4. 3.54	To ZK-BGD 8/54. Canx 18.5.54.
G-ANOU	DH.82A Tiger Moth	82862	R4954	4. 3.54	To ZK-BFS 10/54. Canx 18.5.54.
G-ANOV	DH.104 Dove 6 (Originally regd as Dove 5)	04445	G-5-16	11. 3.54	WFU at Stansted in 1978. Canx as WFU 6.7.81. (On display 3/96 East Fortune)
G-ANOW	DHC.1 Chipmunk 21 (Fuselage no. DHB/f/840)	C1/0972		8. 3.54	To CX-BGH 9/68. Canx 19.7.68.
G-ANOX	DH.82A Tiger Moth	84155	T6022	8. 3.54	To EC-AMF 4/56. Canx 26.10.55.
G-ANOY	DH.82A Tiger Moth	84069	"G-ANNG" T7680	8. 3.54	To F-BHAS 6/54. Canx 26.5.54.
G-ANOZ	DH.82A Tiger Moth	3983	N6710	18. 3.54	Crashed at Yeovil, Somerset on 17.8.56. Canx.
G-ANPA	DH.114 Heron 2B	14053		16. 3.54	To CF-HLI 6/54. Canx 3.7.54.
G-ANPB	DH.82A Tiger Moth	82485	N9431	19. 3.54	Crashed near Fairoaks, Surrey on 24.7.57. Canx.

Regn	Type	c/n	Previous identity	Regn date	Fate or immediate subsequent identity (if known)
G-ANPC	DH.82A Tiger Moth	82858	R4950	19. 3.54	Crashed into hillside at Scotlandwell, near Loch Leven on 2.1.67. Canx. (Stored 4/96 Castlemoate House, Dublin)
G-ANPD	DH.82A Tiger Moth	86482	NM174	27. 3.54	To F-BHAU 6/54. Canx 26.5.54.
G-ANPE	DH.82A Tiger Moth	83738	G-IESH G-ANPE/F-BHAT/G-ANPE/T7397	27. 3.54	
G-ANPF	DH.82A Tiger Moth	82378	N9277	27. 3.54	To F-BHID 8/55. Canx 11.7.55.
G-ANPG	Taylorcraft Auster 5	1000	MT363	26. 3.54	WFU at Croydon on 31.3.55. Canx.
G-ANPH	DH.104 Dove 6	04450		1. 4.54	Canx as WFU 29.1.75.
G-ANPI	DH.82A Tiger Moth	85219	DE149	26. 3.54	Crashed at Mursley, Bucks on 12.4.57. Canx.
G-ANPJ	DH.82A Tiger Moth	82503	N9449	8. 4.54	NTU - To G-ANUL 8/54. Canx.
G-ANPK	DH.82A Tiger Moth	3571	L6936	5. 4.54	Badly damaged in forced landing on Jaywick Sands, Clacton on 18.8.96. (Stored 1/97 Great Waltham)
G-ANPL	DH.82A Tiger Moth	85624	DE683	5. 4.54	WFU in West Germany in 2/64. Canx.
G-ANPM	DH.82A Tiger Moth	82322	N9205	20. 4.54	To D-EGUR 10/56. Canx 29.9.56.
G-ANPN	DH.82A Tiger Moth	82391	N9310	20. 4.54	To D-EGUP 6/56. Canx 6.6.56.
G-ANPO	DH.82A Tiger Moth	85309	DE263	8. 4.54	Not converted. Scrapped at Thruxton. Canx 18.6.69.
G-ANPP	Percival P.34 Proctor III	H.264	HM354	8. 4.54	CofA expired 5.5.69. Canx by CAA 3.4.89.
G-ANPR	Percival P.34 Proctor III	H.325	HM431	8. 4.54	To VH-BPR 6/55. Canx 16.6.55.
G-ANPS	DH.82A Tiger Moth	83168	T5425	15. 4.54	To F-BHAY 6/54. Canx 26.5.54.
G-ANPT	DH.82A Tiger Moth	82536	N9509	15. 4.54	To F-BHAV 6/54. Canx 26.5.54.
G-ANPU	DH.82A Tiger Moth	86155	EM972	15. 4.54	Crashed at Dyheld Down, near Netheravon on 2.7.56. Canx.
G-ANPV(1)	DH.114 Heron 2D	14055		27. 4.54	NTU - To Congo Government as CGG 5/54. Canx 12.2.54.
G-ANPV(2)	DH.114 Heron 2D	14098	G-5-24 (G-ANPV)	20.11.56	To VH-CLX 1/71. Canx 5.1.71.
G-ANPW	DH.82A Tiger Moth	85557	DE603	15. 4.54	Not converted. Canx 10.12.55 on sale to Australia as spares.
G-ANPX	DH.82A Tiger Moth	85378	DE356	15. 4.54	Not converted. Reduced to spares at Croydon in 7/56. Canx on sale to Australia as spares.
G-ANPY	DH.82A Tiger Moth	85358	DE336	15. 4.54	Not converted. Reduced to spares at Croydon in 7/56.
G-ANPZ	DH.82A Tiger Moth	83145	T5378	26. 4.54	To ZK-BFX 6/54. Canx 16.6.54.
G-ANRA	DH.82A Tiger Moth	83096	R5237	26. 4.54	To SE-CGC 4/57. Canx 15.4.57.
G-ANRB	DH.82A Tiger Moth	85487	DE507	26. 4.54	To ZK-BFY 6/54. Canx 16.6.54.
G-ANRC	Avro 685 York C.1	-	XG898 G-ANRC/MW327	30. 4.54	DBR in take-off accident at Stansted on 22.9.54 & burnt out. Canx.
G-ANRD	DH.82A Tiger Moth	3860	N6547	4. 5.54	Crashed at Palmers Farm, Coolham, Sussex on 20.4.58. Remains to White Waltham by 7/59. Canx.
G-ANRE	DH.82A Tiger Moth	82106	N6851	3. 5.54	Crashed in South Cameroons on 12.9.57. Canx.
G-ANRF	DH.82A Tiger Moth	83748	T5850	24. 5.54	
G-ANRG	Scottish Aviation Pioneer 2	SAL/PP/105	XH469 G-ANRG	17. 5.54	WFU at Prestwick in 8/59. Broken up in 1/62. Canx.
G-ANRH	DH.82A Tiger Moth	86033	EM816	4. 6.54	Crashed in South Cameroons on 29.11.57. Canx.
G-ANRI	DH.82A Tiger Moth	83036	R5174	4. 6.54	To D-EGAL 12/55. Canx 1.11.55.
G-ANRJ	DH.82A Tiger Moth	85400	DE378	20. 5.54	Not converted & WFU at Bembridge. Canx 22.12.56.
G-ANRK	DH.82A Tiger Moth	85215	DE145	4. 6.54	To D-ENOX 8/57. Canx 16.7.57.
G-ANRL	DH.82A Tiger Moth	84536	T8263	14. 6.54	CofA expired 12.8.60 & WFU. Canx.
G-ANRM	DH.82A Tiger Moth	85861	DF112	8. 6.54	
G-ANRN	DH.82A Tiger Moth	83133	T5368	24. 5.54	
G-ANRO	DH.82A Tiger Moth	84281	T7917	24. 5.54	WFU at Foulsham on 20.9.61. Canx.
G-ANRP	Taylorcraft Auster 5	1789	TW439	21. 5.54	
G-ANRR	Vickers 732 Viscount	74	OD-ACF G-ANRR	2. 3.54	Crashed at Frimley, Surrey on 2.12.58. Canx.
G-ANRS	Vickers 732 Viscount	75	SU-AKY G-ANRS/OD-ACH/ G-ANRS/OD-ACH/G-ANRS	2. 3.54	WFU on 10.7.69 & used as cabin crew trainer at Rhoose, Cardiff painted as "G-WHIZ". Broken up in 2/96. Canx.
G-ANRT	Vickers 732 Viscount	76	YI-ADM G-ANRS/OD-ACG/G-ANRT	2. 3.54	To SU-AKX 7/59. Canx.
G-ANRU	DH.82A Tiger Moth	82036	N6772	24. 5.54	Crashed near Morbihan, France on 17.5.58. Canx.
G-ANRV	DH.82A Tiger Moth	82381	N9300	24. 5.54	WFU at North Luffenham on 10.6.55. Canx.
G-ANRW	DH.82A Tiger Moth	86029	EM812	24. 5.54	Not converted. Broken up for spares at Stapleford in 1961. Canx.
G-ANRX	DH.82A Tiger Moth	3863	N6550	25. 5.54	WFU at Boxted on 20.6.61. On display 3/96 Salisbury Hall, London Colney.
G-ANRY	DH.82A Tiger Moth	85240	DE170	25. 5.54	Crashed at Croydon on 3.1.57. Canx.
G-ANRZ	DH.82A Tiger Moth	83097	R5238	25. 5.54	To OO-SOG 6/54. Canx 7.7.54.
G-ANSA	DH.82A Tiger Moth	82194	N6944	26. 5.54	Crashed into the River Mersey, near Speke on 30.3.58. Canx.
G-ANSB	DH.82A Tiger Moth	85328	DE282	28. 5.54	To LN-BDN 9/54. Canx 24.9.54.
G-ANSC	DH.82A Tiger Moth	85294	DE248	28. 5.54	To LN-BDM 11/54. Canx 24.9.54.
G-ANSD	DH.82A Tiger Moth	82229	N9116	28. 5.54	To (LN-BDP) in 1954 but used for spares. Canx 10.6.59.
G-ANSE	DH.82A Tiger Moth	85738	DE840	29. 5.54	To LN-BDO 6/54. Canx 24.6.54.
G-ANSF	Boulton & Paul P.108 Balliol T.2	BP.6C	VR595	1. 6.54	WFU at Wolverhampton in 9/56. Canx.
G-ANSG	DH.82A Tiger Moth	85569	DE615	2. 6.54	Crashed near Caen, France on 15.6.57. Canx.
G-ANSH	DH.82A Tiger Moth	86320	NL873	3. 6.54	To SE-CHH 9/59. Canx 6.7.59.
G-ANSI	DH.82A Tiger Moth	86120	EM926	10. 6.54	To ZK-BQF 5/56. Canx 1.5.56.
G-ANSJ	DH.82A Tiger Moth	85071	T6802	10. 6.54	To ZK-BLV 10/55. Canx 7.10.56.
G-ANSK	DH.82A Tiger Moth	83740	T7399	10. 6.54	To ZK-BKF 3/55. Canx 31.5.55.
G-ANSL	DH.82A Tiger Moth	84120	T7738	10. 6.54	To ZK-BLQ 9/55. Canx.
G-ANSM	DH.82A Tiger Moth	82909	R5014	3. 6.54	
G-ANSN	DH.82A Tiger Moth	85781	DE896	3. 6.54	Crashed at Glan-y-Mor, Wales on 23.9.56. Canx.
G-ANSO	Gloster Meteor T.7 (Originally built as Meteor F.8 G-AMCJ)	G5/1525	G-7-1	12. 6.54	To SE-DCC 8/59. Canx 11.8.59.
G-ANSP	DH.82A Tiger Moth	85762	DE877	16. 6.54	To ZS-JVZ 4/70. Canx 2.2.70.
G-ANSR	DH.82A Tiger Moth	83861	T7335	17. 6.54	Crashed in Studland Bay, Dorset on 4.3.61. Canx.

Regn	Type	c/n	Previous identity	Regn date	Fate or immediate subsequent identity (if known)
G-ANSS	Auster J/5L Aiglet Trainer	3123		25. 6.54	To VP-YNK 11/55. Canx 11.9.55.
G-ANST	DH.82A Tiger Moth	85826	DE955	29. 6.54	To ZK-BGX 11/54. Canx 15.8.54.
G-ANSU	DH.82A Tiger Moth	85768	DE883	29. 6.54	To ZK-BGY 11/54. Canx 15.8.54.
G-ANSV	Auster J/5F Aiglet Trainer	3124		5. 7.54	Crashed at Hockley Heath, Warks on 11.8.65. Canx.
G-ANSW	Auster J/5G Cirrus Autocar	3091		1. 7.54	To VH-BYT 6/55. Canx 31.8.54.
G-ANSX	DH.82A Tiger Moth	83610	T7151	13. 7.54	To (PH-NGO(2))/PH-NIS 8/58. Canx 21.7.58.
G-ANSY	Avro 685 York C.1	-	XG929 G-ANSY/MW193	14. 7.54	Fatal crash near Zurrieg, Malta on 18.2.56 whilst as XG929. Canx.
G-ANSZ	DH.114 Heron 1B	14047	J6-LBC G-ANSZ/9L-LAI/G-ANSZ/G-5-16	21. 7.54	DBR in hurricane at St.Lucia in 2/83. (Probably used as spares) Canx by CAA 15.9.86.
G-ANTA	DH.82A Tiger Moth	86466	NM146	15. 7.54	To F-OASD 10/55. Canx 7.9.54.
G-ANTB	Douglas C-47B-20-DK Dakota	15762/27207	KN273 43-49946	22. 7.54	Crashed at Oak Walk, St.Peter, Jersey on 14.4.65. Canx.
G-ANTC	Douglas C-47B-5-DK Dakota	14666/26111	C-GOZA G-ANTC/KJ938/43-48850	22. 7.54	To N4261P 6/83. Canx 2.6.83.
G-ANTD	Douglas C-47A-10-DK Dakota	14969/26414	TJ-ACF G-ANTD/KJ977/43-49153	27. 7.54	CofA expired 15.4.73 & WFU at Norwich Airport. Broken up. Canx.
G-ANTE	DH.82A Tiger Moth	84891	T6562	20. 9.54	
G-ANTF	Lockheed L.749A-79-22 Constellation (Conv. to freighter in 1960)	2504	N9816F G-ANTF/VH-EAF/VT-CQS/(N86521)	16. 8.54	DBF at Baginton on 1.2.70. Remains broken up in 1971. Canx.
G-ANTG	Lockheed L.749A-79-22 Constellation	2505	VH-EAE VT-CQR/(N86522)	10. 9.54	To N1552V 11/58. Canx 2.12.58.
G-ANTH	Avro 685 York C.1	-	MW177	26. 7.54	Not converted. Scrapped at Stansted in 10/55. Canx.
G-ANTI	Avro 685 York C.1	-	MW143	23. 7.54	WFU at Lasham in 12/62. Broken up in 5/63. Canx.
G-ANTJ	Avro 685 York C.1	-	MW149	23. 7.54	WFU at Lasham in 12/62. Broken up in 10/64. Canx 3.9.64.
G-ANTK	Avro 685 York C.1	-	MW232	23. 7.54	WFU at Lasham on 30.4.64. (On rebuild 7/99 Duxford)
G-ANTL	DH.82A Tiger Moth	82884	R4974	23. 7.54	To D-EHAG 8/56. Canx 18.8.56.
G-ANTM	DH.82A Tiger Moth	83329	T7023	23. 7.54	To Bavaria. Canx 17.4.56.
G-ANTN	DH.82A Tiger Moth	85878	DF129	30. 7.54	To ZK-BLJ 8/55. Canx 16.5.55.
G-ANTO	DH.104 Dove 6A	04451		16. 8.54	To N1565V 8/54. Canx 9.4.54.
G-ANTP	Scottish Aviation Twin Pioneer Srs.3 (Originally regd as Srs.1)	501		5. 7.54	DBR on take-off from Jorhat, Assam, India on 10.3.60. Canx.
G-ANTR	DH.82A Tiger Moth	85676	DE746	26. 7.54	To D-ECEB 4/56. Canx 23.1.56.
G-ANTS	DH.82A Tiger Moth	3845	N6532	26. 7.54	Not converted. Exported to Sweden for rebuild in 1988. Canx by CAA 2.9.91.
G-ANTT	DH.82A Tiger Moth	82462	N9392	26. 7.54	Canx as destroyed 24.5.56.
G-ANTU	DH.82A Tiger Moth	82489	N9435	26. 7.54	To D-ENYG 8/59. Canx 15.5.59.
G-ANTV	DH.82A Tiger Moth	84589	T6122	26. 7.54	To D-EKUR 11/55. Canx 24.10.55.
G-ANTW	DH.82A Tiger Moth	83580	T7129	26. 7.54	To D-EGIT 4/56. Canx 21.3.56.
G-ANTX	Boeing 377-10-34 Stratocruiser	15965	N31225	3. 1.55	To (N107Q)/N412Q 7/59. Canx 27.7.59. Broken up at Oakland still marked as G-ANTX.
G-ANTY	Boeing 377-10-34 Stratocruiser	15966	N31226	27.10.54	To (N108Q)/N413Q 7/59. Canx 31.7.59. Broken up at Oakland still marked as G-ANTY.
G-ANTZ	Boeing 377-10-34 Stratocruiser	15967	N31227	16.12.54	To (N106Q)/N411Q 5/59. Canx 14.4.59. Broken up at Oakland still marked as G-ANTZ.
G-ANUA	Boeing 377-10-34 Stratocruiser	15968	N31228	29.12.54	To (N109Q)/N414Q 8/59. Canx 3.8.59.
G-ANUB	Boeing 377-10-34 Stratocruiser	15969	N31229	22. 9.54	WFU at Stansted in 1/60. Broken up. Canx.
G-ANUC	Boeing 377-10-34 Stratocruiser	15971	N31231	1.12.54	WFU at Stansted in 1/60. Broken up. Canx.
G-ANUD	DH.82A Tiger Moth	83435	T5714	4. 8.54	Crashed at Fairoaks, Surrey on 29.7.60. Canx.
G-ANUE	DH.82A Tiger Moth	83757	T7247	4. 8.54	Crashed near Stapleford, Essex on 7.1.62. Canx.
G-ANUF	DH.82A Tiger Moth	84156	T7783	4. 8.54	WFU at Roborough, Plymouth in 8/55. Canx.
G-ANUG	DH.82A Tiger Moth	84523	T8250	4. 8.54	Crashed at Mop End, near High Wycombe on 17.9.55. Canx.
G-ANUH	DH.82A Tiger Moth	85410	DE402	9. 8.54	Crashed at Kings Norton, Birmingham on 16.6.59. Canx.
G-ANUI	DH.82A Tiger Moth	85532	DE565	9. 8.54	To VH-BQN 7/55. Canx 20.4.55.
G-ANUJ	DH.82A Tiger Moth	85942	DF206	3. 9.54	Crashed at Aslacton, near Norwich on 18.11.61. Canx.
G-ANUK	Westland-Sikorsky S-55 Whirlwind Srs.3	WA/39		14. 8.54	Crashed on 4.8.72. Canx as WFU 23.11.72.
G-ANUL	DH.82A Tiger Moth	82503	(G-ANPJ) N9449	16. 8.54	To VH-RSF 7/56. Canx 20.7.56.
G-ANUM	Boeing 377-10-26 Stratocruiser	15927	N1027V	31. 8.54	To (N1027V)/N401Q 7/58. Canx 7.7.58.
G-ANUN	Avro 685 York C.1	-	MW253	6. 9.54	NTU - To G-ANVO 11/54. Canx.
G-ANUO	DH.114 Heron 2D (Originally regd as Heron 2C)	14062		17. 9.54	Stored at Biggin Hill with CofA expired 12.9.86. Canx as WFU 9.8.96. (On display 12/96, Croydon Airport)
G-ANUP	Lockheed L.749A-79-31 Constellation	2562	VH-EAA	15. 2.55	To OE-IFO 5/63. Canx 1.5.63.
G-ANUR	Lockheed L.749A-79-31 Constellation	2565	VH-EAB	26. 2.55	To N1949 3/67. Canx 23.2.67.
G-ANUS	Not allotted.				
G-ANUT	DH.104 Dove 6	04454		25. 2.55	CofA expired 24.4.76. Canx as WFU 11.2.77.
G-ANUU	DH.104 Dove 6	04455		30. 3.55	CofA expired 17.5.76. Canx as WFU 11.2.77.
G-ANUV	Lockheed L.749A-76-33 Constellation	2551	N90607 PH-TDC	28. 6.55	To N9830F 2/58. Canx 8.1.58.
G-ANUW	DH.104 Dove 6	04458		16. 5.55	WFU at Stansted on 31.3.81. Canx as WFU 5.6.96. (Stored 2/97 at North Weald)
G-ANUX	Lockheed L.749A-76-33 Constellation	2556	N90623 PH-TDD/(NC.....)	3.12.54	To N1593V 4/57. Canx 6.5.57.
G-ANUY	Lockheed L.749A-76-33 Constellation	2557	N90625 PH-TDE/(NC.....)	28. 1.55	To N6688N/HK-651 in 5/59. Canx 13.5.59.

Regn	Type	c/n	Previous identity	Regn date	Fate or immediate subsequent identity (if known)
G-ANUZ	Lockheed L.749A-76-33 Constellation	2559	N90621 PH-TDG	28. 2.55	To N9812F 4/58. Canx 14.3.58.
G-ANVA	Lockheed L.749A-76-33 Constellation	2564	N90608 PH-TDH	28. 5.55	To N6687N/HK-652 4/59. Canx 29.4.59.
G-ANVB	Lockheed L.749A-76-33 Constellation	2589	N90624 PH-TDI	28. 3.55	To N9813F 3/58. Canx 11.3.58.
G-ANVC	DH.104 Dove 1B (Originally regd as Dove 1)	04128	XY-ADI G-ANVC/XY-ADI/ G-ANVC/XY-ADI/G-ANVC/AP-AGT/G-ANVC/VR-NIT	13. 9.54	WFU at Gatwick on 13.2.66. (To Southend by road on 23.9.67) Scrapped at Southend. Canx as WFU 21.8.68.
G-ANVD	Lockheed L.749A-76-33 Constellation	2544	N90622 PH-TDB	28. 4.55	To N6689N/HK-650 in 5/59. Canx 27.5.59.
G-ANVE	DH.82A Tiger Moth	83223	T5490	14. 9.54	To D-EBUN 12/55. Canx 15.5.55.
G-ANVF	DH.115 Vampire T.55	15485		23. 9.54	To Finnish AF as VT-1 in 4/55. Canx 18.4.55.
G-ANVG	Auster J/5G Cirrus Autocar	3095		29. 9.54	To VH-AZK 1/55. Canx 3.12.54.
G-ANVH	DH.114 Heron 2	14074		29. 9.54	To CF-IJR 8/55. Canx 9.9.55.
G-ANVI	DH.82A Tiger Moth	82028	N6750	30. 9.54	To OE-AAF 8/55. Canx 26.8.55.
G-ANVJ(1)	Auster J/8F Aiglet Trainer	3152		23.11.54	Construction Abandoned. Canx 12/54.
G-ANVJ(2)	Percival P.31C Proctor IV	H.709	NP338	6. 4.55	To F-BIGR 8/57. Canx 29.8.57.
G-ANVK	Percival P.31 Proctor IV	H.621	NP225	8.10.54	To F-BEKN(2) 2/56. Canx 17.2.56.
G-ANVL	Beechcraft C18S	6395	N714A	19.10.54	To F-BHCJ 12/54. Canx.
"G-ANVL"	Blackburn Beverley	-		-----	Marks applied for some publicity photographs. Canx.
G-ANVM	Auster J/5G Cirrus Autocar	3158		19.10.54	To VH-KCA 9/55. Canx 13.9.55.
G-ANVN	Auster J/5G Cirrus Autocar	3153	XJ941 G-ANVN	19.10.54	To VR-TBR 10/57. Canx 31.10.57.
G-ANVO	Avro 685 York C.1	-	XJ264 G-ANVO/(G-ANUN)/MW253	18.11.54	WFU at Luton in 6/63. Broken up in 10/63. Canx.
G-ANVP	Convair CV.540 Napier-Eland Convair (Originally regd as CV.340-42C)	153	N8458H PI-C344	25. 1.55	To N340EL 11/57. Canx 9.10.57.
G-ANVR	Bristol 170 Freighter 32	13251		23.10.54	WFU at Baginton on 12.5.71. Broken up in 3/74. Canx.
G-ANVS	Bristol 170 Freighter 32	13252		23.10.54	WFU at Lydd on 28.11.67. Broken up in 7/70. Canx.
G-ANVT	Auster J/5G Cirrus Autocar	3159		2.11.54	To VH-KCE 9/55. Canx 29.8.55.
G-ANVU	DH.104 Dove 1B (Originally regd as Srs.1)	04082	VR-NAP	12.11.54	CofA expired 14.9.77 & WFU at Southend. Canx 16.9.86 on sale to Sweden. (Stored .92 Malmslatt, Linkoping, Sweden)
G-ANVV	DH.82A Tiger Moth	83098	R5239	15.11.54	To OO-ACI 6/55. Canx 7.12.54.
G-ANVW	Percival P.31 Proctor IV	H.594	NP187	23.11.54	DBR at Olivares de Jucar, Spain on 17.6.56. Canx.
G-ANVX	Percival P.31C Proctor IV	H.771	RM168	23.11.54	Not converted. Broken up at Gatwick in 2/56. Canx.
G-ANVY	Percival P.31C Proctor IV	H.772	RM169	23.11.54	To SE-CEA in 12/56. Canx 16.11.56.
G-ANVZ	Percival P.31C Proctor IV	H.797	RM194	23.11.54	WFU at Luqa, Malta in 7/56. Canx.
G-ANWA	Percival P.31 Proctor IV	H.725	NP354	23.11.54	Crashed on beach at Propriano, Corsica on 13.2.62. Canx.
G-ANWB	DHC.1 Chipmunk 21 (Fuselage no. DHB/f/858) (Originally regd with c/n C1/0986)	C1/0987	G-5-17	15. 2.55	CofA expired 8.3.91. (On rebuild 6/96 Blackpool) Canx by CAA 26.2.99.
G-ANWC	Percival P.31 Proctor IV	H.634	NP238	23.11.54	Not converted. Scrapped at White Waltham in 1956. Canx 22.12.60.
G-ANWD	Percival P.31 Proctor IV	H.655	NP271	23.11.54	To OE-ACB 8/58. Canx 30.6.58.
G-ANWE	Percival P.31 Proctor IV	H.691	NP307	23.11.54	Not converted. Scrapped at White Waltham in 1957. Canx 2.12.63.
G-ANWF	Percival P.31 Proctor IV	H.700	NP329	23.11.54	To OO-ARL 4/57. Canx 15.4.57.
G-ANWG	Bristol 170 Superfreighter 32	13211	(G-ANMG) G-18-187	12. 1.54	To F-BKBG 5/61. Canx 3.5.61.
G-ANWH	Bristol 170 Superfreighter 32	13212	(G-ANMH) G-18-188	12. 1.54	To F-BLHH 12/62. Canx 7.1.63.
G-ANWI	Bristol 170 Superfreighter 32	13213	(G-ANMI) G-18-189	12. 1.54	To F-BKBI 6/61. Canx 31.5.61.
G-ANWJ	Bristol 170 Superfreighter 32	13254		31. 1.56	WFU at Lydd on 3.3.68. CofA expired 30.5.68. Broken up in 7/70. Canx as WFU 5.2.71.
G-ANWK	Bristol 170 Superfreighter 32	13259		31. 1.56	WFU at Lydd on 20.10.69. CofA expired 18.6.70. Broken up in 8/70. Canx as WFU 5.2.71.
G-ANWL	Bristol 170 Superfreighter 32	13260		31. 1.56	Crashed at Les Prevosts, St.Saviour, Guernsey on 1.11.61. Canx.
G-ANWM	Bristol 170 Superfreighter 32	13261	F-BPIM G-ANWM/G-18-208	31. 1.56	WFU at Lydd in 8/70. CofA expired 26.11.70. Broken up. Canx as WFU 5.2.71.
G-ANWN	Bristol 170 Superfreighter 32	13262	G-18-209	31. 1.56	To F-BPIN 3/68. Canx 2.1.68.
G-ANWO(1)	Bristol 170 Superfreighter 32	-		. .56R	NTU. Canx.
G-ANWO(2)	Miles M.14A Hawk Trainer III	718	L8262	31.12.58	(Stored at West Chiltington, nr.Pulborough 11/92)
G-ANWP	Percival P.31 Proctor IV	K.435	MX451	23.11.54	Not converted. Broken up at Gatwick in 2/56. Canx.
G-ANWR	Percival P.31 Proctor IV	H.556	NP157	23.11.54	Not converted. Broken up at Panshangar in 12/57. Canx.
G-ANWS	Percival P.31 Proctor IV	H.580	NP173	23.11.54	Not converted. Broken up at Panshangar in 12/57. Canx.
G-ANWT	Percival P.31 Proctor IV	H.624	NP228	23.11.54	To OO-ACJ 8/55. Canx.
G-ANWU	Percival P.31 Proctor IV	H.642	NP246	23.11.54	To OO-ARJ 4/57. Canx 15.4.57.
G-ANWV	Percival P.31 Proctor IV	H.696	NP325	23.11.54	To OO-ARK 4/57. Canx 15.4.57.
G-ANWW	Avro 652A Anson 19 Srs.2 (Originally regd as Anson 20)	-	VP-YOF G-ANWW/VS512	25.11.54	Crashed at Maidenhead Thicket, Berks on 8.7.58. Canx as destroyed 4.9.58.
G-ANWX	Auster J/5L Aiglet Trainer	3131		25.11.54	Badly damaged when overturned on landing at Fenland 1.8.93. Canx as WFU 24.9.93. (On rebuild 9/96)
G-ANWY	Percival P.30 Proctor II	K.401	Z7212	30.11.54	To VH-BXU 6/58. Canx 11.4.58.
G-ANWZ	DH.114 Heron 1B	14081		1.12.54	WFU at Gatwick on 7.3.70 due to corrosion. Dismantled and roaded to Coventry for spares. Canx as WFU 17.5.71.
G-ANXA	DH.114 Heron 1B	14044	G-5-11	3.12.54	To ZK-EKO 6/77. Canx 24.6.77.
G-ANXB	DH.114 Heron 1B	14048	G-5-14	3.12.54	WFU at Biggin Hill in 1959. Canx 2.11.81. (On display 2/99 at Winthorpe, Newark)
G-ANXC	Auster J/5R Alpine (Originally regd as J/5L)	3135	5Y-UBD VP-UBD/G-ANXC/(AP-AHG)/G-ANXC	4.12.54	
G-ANXD	Percival P.31 Proctor IV	H.611	NP215	9.12.54	Not converted. Scrapped at Exeter in 9/58. Canx.

Regn	Type	c/n	Previous identity	Regn date	Fate or immediate subsequent identity (if known)
G-ANXE	Percival P.31 Proctor IV	H.652	NP268	9.12.54	Not converted. DBF at Exeter on 24.9.59. Canx.
G-ANXF	Percival P.31 Proctor IV	H.706	NP335	9.12.54	Not converted. DBF at Exeter on 24.9.59. Canx.
G-ANXG	Percival P.31 Proctor IV	H.722	NP351	9.12.54	Not converted. Scrapped at Exeter in 9/58. Canx.
G-ANXH	Percival P.31C Proctor IV	H.784	RM181	9.12.54	Not converted. Scrapped at Exeter in 7/60. Canx.
G-ANXI	Percival P.31 Proctor IV	K.437	LA589	9.12.54	Not converted. DBF at Exeter on 24.9.59. Canx.
G-ANXJ	Avro 685 York C.1	-	MW141	10.12.54	Not converted. Broken up at Stansted in 10/56. Canx.
G-ANXK	Avro 685 York C.1	-	MW178	10.12.54	Not converted, Broken up at Thame in 7/55. Canx.
G-ANXL	Avro 685 York C.1	-	MW196	10.12.54	Not converted. Broken up at Thame in 7/55. Canx.
G-ANXM	Avro 685 York C.1	-	MW227	10.12.54	Not converted. Broken up at Southend in 4/55. Canx.
G-ANXN	Avro 685 York C.1	-	MW258	10.12.54	WFU at Lasham in 2/63. Canx as WFU 6/63. Broken up in 8/63.
G-ANXO	Avro 685 York C.1	-	MW318	10.12.54	Not converted. Scrapped in 4/55 at Thame, Oxon. Canx.
G-ANXP	Piper J3C-65 Cub (L-4H-PI)	12192	N79819 NC79819/44-79896	13.12.54	To D-EGUL 10/55. Canx 14.10.55.
G-ANXR	Percival P.31C Proctor IV	H.803	RM221	14.12.54	
G-ANXS	DH.82A Tiger Moth	85623	DE682	18.12.54	To VH-BEY 9/55. Canx 6.4.55.
G-ANXT	DH.82A Tiger Moth	83110	R5251	18.12.54	To VH-BIC 6/55. Canx 17.3.55.
G-ANXU	DH.82A Tiger Moth	84646	T6198	18.12.54	To VH-BEW 7/55. Canx 17.3.55.
G-ANXV	Vickers 747 Viscount	97		21.12.54	To VH-BAT 9/55. Canx 19.10.55.
G-ANXW	Auster J/5L Aiglet Trainer	3132		30.12.54	To K-AAAG/9K-AAG 8/60. Canx 25.6.60.
G-ANXX	Auster J/5L Aiglet Trainer	3133		30.12.54	To K-AAAH/9K-AAH 8/60. Canx 25.6.60.
G-ANXY	Auster J/5L Aiglet Trainer	3134		30.12.54	To K-AAAI/9K-AAI 8/60. Canx 25.6.60.
G-ANXZ	Auster J/5P Autocar	3161		30.12.54	To K-AAAJ/9K-AAJ 8/60. Canx 25.6.60.
G-ANYA	Avro 685 York C.1	-	MW210	4. 1.55	WFU at Stansted in 8/59. Broken up in 8/62. Canx.
G-ANYB	Aviation Traders ATL-98 Carvair (Originally regd as Douglas C-54B-1-DC)	10528/1	N59952 N88723/42-72423	31. 1.55	WFU & stored at Lydd, Kent on 5.3.67. Broken up in 7/70. Canx.
G-ANYC	Percival P.31C Proctor IV	H.804	RM222	8. 1.55	WFU at Elstree in 8/61. Canx.
G-ANYD	Percival P.31C Proctor IV	H.788	RM185	8. 1.55	To OO-ACL 2/55. Canx 18.2.55.
G-ANYE	Auster J/5P Autocar	3165		30.12.54	To K-AAAK/9K-AAK 8/60. Canx 25.6.60.
G-ANYF	Douglas C-47B-20-DK Dakota	15555/27000	ZS-DIY SAAF6865/KK218/43-49739	17. 1.55	To CF-HTH 2/55. Canx 8.2.55.
G-ANYG	Auster B.8 Agricola 1	B/101	G-25-3	12. 1.55	Canx on sale as ZK-BMI on 30.11.55 but not delivered.
G-ANYH	Vickers 747 Viscount	145		15. 1.55	To VH-BUT 10/56. Canx 13.9.56.
G-ANYI	Short S.45 Solent 4	S.1558	ZK-AMN	17. 1.55	WFU near Tagus River, near Lisbon, Portugal in 11/58. Broken up on 24.8.71. Canx.
G-ANYJ	DH.114 Heron 2	14080		19. 1.55	To LN-SUB 2/57. Canx 11.2.57.
G-ANYK	DH.90A Dragonfly	7529	F-OAMS OO-PET(2)/EC-AAQ/EC-BAA/Spanish AF AF.756/F-APDE	20. 1.55	Crashed on landing at La Baule, France on 22.6.61. Canx.
G-ANYL	Boulton & Paul P.108 Balliol T.2	BP.7C	WN164	22. 1.55	To Ceylon AF as CA306 in 4/55. Canx 11.3.55.
G-ANYM	Boulton & Paul P.108 Balliol T.2	BP.8C	WN166	22. 1.55	To Ceylon AF as CA307 in 4/55. Canx 11.3.55.
G-ANYN	DH.82A Tiger Moth	85083	T6814	22. 2.55	Crashed at Le Touquet, France on 30.7.60. Canx.
G-ANYO	Percival P.34 Proctor III (Regd with c/n HB.400)	H.410	LZ603	27. 1.55	Not converted. Canx 14.8.59. (See G-AOCD)
G-ANYP	Percival P.31 Proctor IV	H.591	NP184	28. 1.55	Canx by CAA 22.12.95; reportedly to Australia (possibly the one marked as "NP184" noted at Gunnedah, New South Wales, Australia on 18.10.96).
G-ANYR	Percival P.31 Proctor IV	H.592	NP185	28. 1.55	WFU at Thruxton in 12/56. Canx in 10/61.
G-ANYS	Percival P.31 Proctor IV	H.646	NP250	28. 1.55	Crashed near Enniskillen on 3.2.63. Canx.
G-ANYT	Percival P.31 Proctor IV	H.695	NP324	28. 1.55	To West Germany in 7/55. Written off in West Germany on 28.8.55. Canx.
G-ANYU	Percival P.31 Proctor IV	H.705	NP334	28. 1.55	CofA expired 1.5.67 & WFU at Staverton. Burnt in 12/67.
G-ANYV	Percival P.31 Proctor IV	H.692	NP308	31. 1.55	WFU at Portsmouth in 6/60. Burnt on 2.11.61. Canx.
G-ANYW	Percival P.31 Proctor IV	H.726	NP355	31. 1.55	Not converted. Broken up at Biggin Hill in 6/62. Canx 10.10.60.
G-ANYX	DH.82A Tiger Moth	3888	N6587	4. 3.55	Crashed at Thruxton on 24.11.57. Canx.
G-ANYY	Percival P.31 Proctor IV	H.739	NP368	3. 2.55	Not converted. Broken up at Gatwick in 12/55. Canx.
G-ANYZ	Percival P.31C Proctor IV	H.793	RM190	10. 2.55	Crashed into English Channel on 23.10.58. Canx.
G-ANZA	Percival P.31 Proctor IV	H.613	NP217	10. 2.55	Not converted. To 1216 ATC Sqdn at Eastleigh in 1958. Canx.
G-ANZB	Percival P.31 Proctor IV	H.676	NP292	10. 2.55	Not converted. Broken up at Portsmouth in 2/56. Canx.
G-ANZC	Percival P.31 Proctor IV	H.693	NP309	10. 2.55	WFU at Thruxton in 3/60. Canx.
G-ANZD	Percival P.31 Proctor IV	H.732	NP361	10. 2.55	Not converted. Broken up at Eastleigh in 4/57. Canx.
G-ANZE	Douglas C-47B-30-DK Dakota	13864/25309	C-406 Pakistan AF/KG765/43-48048	22. 2.55	To Burmese AF as UBT-714/XY-URT 8/55. Canx 6.8.55.
G-ANZF	Douglas C-47B-15-DK Dakota	15125/26570	H-704 ? Pakistan AF/KK117/43-49309	22. 2.55	To Burmese AF as UBT-713 6/55. Canx 30.6.55.
G-ANZG	Douglas C-47B-35-DK Dakota	16498/33246	AP-AFH Pakistan AF C-407/KN603/44-76914	22. 2.55	To Swedish AF as Fv.79005 4/55. Canx 14.4.55.
G-ANZH	Beechcraft A35 Bonanza	D.2108	N8698A	14. 2.55	To F-DABZ 2/56. Canx 21.2.56.
G-ANZI	Percival P.31 Proctor IV	H.600	NP193	8. 2.55	Not converted. Burnt at Rhoose on 13.6.59. Canx.
G-ANZJ	Percival P.31 Proctor IV (Received wings from G-AOBW in rebuild post-1971)	H.687	NP303	8. 2.55	WFU at Baginton on 10.3.67. Canx as WFU 6.3.73.
G-ANZK	Vickers 621 Viking C.2	145	VL230	14. 2.55	Not converted. Broken up for spares at Bovingdon in 7/55. Canx.
G-ANZL	Westland-Sikorsky S-51 Mk.1A	WA/H/090	G-ANAL	14. 2.55	Crashed near Netheravon on 2.10.59. Canx.
G-ANZM	Hiller 360 UH-12A (Rebuild with parts from c/n 122 ex.LN-FOH/LN-ORH/F-BFPR/N8122H)	106	OO-APR(2) N8106H	18. 2.55	CofA expired 21.11.62 & WFU at Redhill. Broken up in 1962. Canx.
G-ANZN	Westland-Sikorsky S-55 Whirlwind Srs.1A	WA/54	G-17-3	22. 2.55	To VP-BAF(2) 7/55. Canx 14.7.55..

Regn	Type	c/n	Previous identity	Regn date	Fate or immediate subsequent identity (if known)
G-ANZO	Westland-Sikorsky S-55 Whirlwind Srs.1	WA/55	G-17-4	22. 2.55	To VP-BAG 8/55. Canx 14.7.55.
G-ANZP	DH.89A Dragon Rapide	6682	HG697	22. 2.55	WFU at Speke on 30.7.62. Sold to France for spares in 1965. Canx.
G-ANZR(1)	DH.82A Tiger Moth	82997	R5115	4. 3.55	To D-EGER 6/56. Canx 10.1.56.
G-ANZR(2)	DH.82A Tiger Moth (Rebuild from unidentified airframe)	"5115"		15. 2.74	Used in rebuild of G-ANDE in 1978. Canx as WFU 6.8.86.
G-ANZS	DH.82A Tiger Moth	85082	T6813	4. 3.55	To VH-DCH 2/60. Canx 18.6.59.
G-ANZT	DH.82A Tiger Moth (Converted to Thruxton Jackaroo in 7/57)	84176	T7798	4. 3.55	
G-ANZU	DH.82A Tiger Moth	3583	L6938	9. 3.55	(Stored .94)
G-ANZV	Boulton & Paul P.108 Balliol T.2	BP.9C	WN147	8. 3.55	To Ceylon AF as CA308 in 5/55. Canx 10.5.55.
G-ANZW	Boulton & Paul P.108 Balliol T.2	BP.10C	WN148	8. 3.55	To Ceylon AF as CA309 in 5/55. Canx 10.5.55.
G-ANZX	Agusta-Bell 47G	017		18. 3.55	Crashed at Conington, Hunts on 25.7.62. Canx.
G-ANZY	DH.82A Tiger Moth	85242	DE172	14. 3.55	To VR-NCJ 8/57. Canx 4.8.57.
G-ANZZ	DH.82A Tiger Moth	85834	DE974	14. 3.55	(On rebuild)
G-AOAA	DH.82A Tiger Moth	85908	DF159	14. 3.55	Came off runway and cartwheeled on landing at Redhill on 4.6.89. CofA expired 8.12.91.
G-AOAB	DH.82A Tiger Moth	86354	NL911	14. 3.55	To SE-CGD 4/57. Canx 15.4.57.
G-AOAC	DH.82A Tiger Moth	82216	N6978	14. 3.55	Crashed at Lessay, France on 22.6.74. Canx as WFU 9.4.75.
G-AOAD	DH.82A Tiger Moth	82533	N9506	14. 3.55	WFU in Sudan in 6/60. Canx.
G-AOAE	DH.82A Tiger Moth	82015	N6737	14. 3.55	Crashed near Tadcaster, Yorks on 21.1.59. Canx.
G-AOAF	DH.82A Tiger Moth	82812	R4895	14. 3.55	To ZK-BLK 8/55. Canx 16.5.55.
G-AOAG	DH.104 Dove 6	04457		14. 3.55	To VH-DHF 8/55. Canx 15.7.55.
G-AOAH	DH.82A Tiger Moth	85980	EM749	15. 3.55	To VH-BTD 7/56. Canx 21.11.55.
G-AOAI	Blackburn Beverley C.1	1002	XB259	15. 3.55	Restored to RAF as XB259 in 1/55. Canx 30.3.55.
G-AOAJ	Westland-Sikorsky S-51 Mk.1A	WA/H/134	G-17-1	18. 3.55	Crashed at Yeovil, Somerset on 25.10.56. Canx.
G-AOAK	Percival P.34A Proctor III	H.61	R7566	21. 3.55	To OO-DOC 5/55. Canx 3.6.55.
G-AOAL	Douglas C-47B-30-DK Dakota	16426/33174	F-OAQA AP-ADA/KN559/44-76842	21. 3.55	To Burmese AF as UBT-712 in 7/55. Canx 19.7.55.
G-AOAM	Beechcraft A35 Bonanza	D-1990	VR-ABA	21. 3.55	To OO-ALU(2) 5/56. Canx 7.5.56.
G-AOAN	Avro 685 York C.1	-	MW199	26. 3.55	Not converted. WFU & stored at Tollerton in 7/56. Broken up in 3/57. Canx.
G-AOAO	DH.89A Dragon Rapide	6844	NR756	22. 3.55	To F-BHGR 1/56. Canx 4.1.56.
G-AOAP	Percival P.31C Proctor IV	H.585	NP178	24. 3.55	Not converted. Scrapped at Panshangar in 11/57. Canx.
G-AOAR	Percival P.31C Proctor IV	H.588	NP181	24. 3.55	WFU at Biggin Hill in 10/65. Canx.
G-AOAS	Percival P.31C Proctor IV	H.593	NP186	24. 3.55	Not converted. Burnt at Panshangar on 5.11.57. Canx.
G-AOAT	Percival P.31C Proctor IV	H.808	RM226	24. 3.55	Not converted. Burnt at Panshangar on 5.11.57. Canx.
G-AOAU	Percival P.31C Proctor IV	H.623	NP227	24. 3.55	Not converted. Burnt at Panshangar on 5.11.57. Canx.
G-AOAV	Percival P.31C Proctor IV	H.812	RM230	24. 3.55	Not converted. Burnt at Panshangar on 5.11.57. Canx.
G-AOAW	Percival P.31C Proctor IV	H.653	NP269	24. 3.55	Not converted. Burnt at Panshangar on 5.11.57. Canx.
G-AOAX	Percival P.31C Proctor IV	H.657	NP273	24. 3.55	Not converted. Burnt at Panshangar on 5.11.57. Canx.
G-AOAY	Percival P.31C Proctor IV	H.673	NP289	24. 3.55	Not converted. Dumped at Croydon by 9/59, then Biggin Hill in 10/59. Canx.
G-AOAZ	Percival P.31C Proctor IV	H.697	NP326	24. 3.55	Not converted. Burnt at Panshangar on 5.11.57. Canx.
G-AOBA	Percival P.31C Proctor IV	H.698	NP327	24. 3.55	Not converted. Burnt at Panshangar on 5.11.57. Canx.
G-AOBB	Percival P.31C Proctor IV	H.713	NP342	24. 3.55	Not converted. Scrapped at Squires Gate by 9/60. Canx.
G-AOBC	Percival P.31C Proctor IV	H.734	NP363	24. 3.55	Not converted. Burnt at Panshangar on 5.11.57. Canx.
G-AOBD	Percival P.31C Proctor IV	H.744	NP385	24. 3.55	Not converted. Burnt at Panshangar on 5.11.57. Canx.
G-AOBE	Percival P.31C Proctor IV	H.762	NP403	24. 3.55	Not converted. Burnt at Panshangar on 5.11.57. Canx.
G-AOBF	Percival P.34A Proctor III	H.476	LZ694	24. 3.55	WFU at White Waltham in 9/56. Canx.
G-AOBG	Somers-Kendall SK-1	1		30. 3.55	WFU after engine turbine failure 11.7.57. Stored at Cranfield, then stored in rafters 10/97 Breighton.
G-AOBH	DH.82A Tiger Moth	84350	T7997	31. 3.55	
G-AOBI	Percival P.31C Proctor IV	H.729	NP358	1. 4.55	WFU at Halfpenny Green in 8/64. Used to rebuild Proctor IV NP294. Canx.
G-AOBJ	DH.82A Tiger Moth	85830	N10RM D-EBIG/G-AOBJ/DE970	9. 7.55	Destroyed in crash on take-off from Cardiff 20.8.97. Canx by CAA 23.11.98.
G-AOBK	DH.82A Tiger Moth	82152	N6908	7. 4.55	To D-EKYN 10/55. Canx 18.9.55.
G-AOBL	Short S.45 Solent 4	S.1556	ZK-AML	12. 4.55	WFU in 11/58 & scrapped Tagus Estuary, Lisbon, Portugal. Canx.
G-AOBM	Bristol 171 Sycamore Mk.4	13267		12. 4.55	To CF-HVX in 5/55. Canx.
G-AOBN	Douglas C-53D-DO Dakota 4	11711	F-OAIF SE-BAU/42-68784	20. 4.55	To ET-AGR 7/77. Canx 20.7.77.
G-AOBO	DH.82A Tiger Moth	3810	N6473	23. 4.55	
G-AOBP	DH.82A Tiger Moth	82795	R4878	23. 4.55	To D-EDIR 10/55. Canx.
G-AOBR	DH.82A Tiger Moth	85133	T6904	23. 4.55	To D-EDAR 7/55. Canx.
G-AOBS	DH.82A Tiger Moth	84768	T6394	5. 5.55	To PH-UFN 3/56. Canx.
G-AOBT	DH.82A Tiger Moth	86598	PG701	5. 5.55	To PH-UFO 2/56. Canx.
G-AOBU	Hunting Percival P.84 Jet Provost T.1	P84/006	(XM129) G-42-1/G-AOBU	2. 5.55	
G-AOBV	Auster J/5P Autocar	3171		9. 5.55	Canx by CAA 14.11.91. (Stored 10/97 Cheshunt)
G-AOBW	Percival P.31C Proctor IV	H.710	NP339	26. 4.55	WFU at Elstree in 7/64. Canx.
G-AOBX	DH.82A Tiger Moth	83653	T7187	26. 4.55	
G-AOBY	Vickers 626 Viking C.2	179	VL248	27. 4.55	To XB-FIP 5/55. Canx.
G-AOBZ	DH.104 Dove 1B (Originally regd as a Dove 1)	04127	VR-NIL	2. 5.55	WFU at Southend in 1967. Scrapped in 4/70. Canx as WFU 19.3.73.
G-AOCA	Vickers 755D Viscount	91		17. 5.55	NTU - To CU-T603 5/56. Canx.
G-AOCB	Vickers 755D Viscount	92	VR-BBL CU-T604/(G-AOCB)	17. 5.55	WFU at Castle Donington on 31.10.69. Canx as WFU 16.4.70.

Regn	Type	c/n	Previous identity	Regn date	Fate or immediate subsequent identity (if known)
G-AOCC	Vickers 755D Viscount	93	VR-BBM CU-T605/G-AOCC)	17. 5.55	WFU at Castle Donington on 21.4.69. Broken up in 8/69. CofA expired 11.9.69. Canx.
G-AOCD	Percival P.34A Proctor III	H.410	LZ603	29. 4.55	To OO-DYM 2/56. Canx 12.2.55.
G-AOCE	DH.104 Dove 1	04044	VR-NAB	9. 5.55	Fatal crash in force landed on the beach at Dungeness Point on 15.1.58. Canx as DBR 7.1.59.
G-AOCF	Westland-Sikorsky S-55 Whirlwind Srs.3	WA/58	5A-DBA 5A-BDA/G-AOCF	9. 5.55	To VR-BDB 12/68. Canx 18.12.68.
	(Originally regd as a Srs.1, became Srs.3 with effect from 29.10.68)				
G-AOCG	DH.82A Tiger Moth	83369	T7039	9. 5.55	To VH-KYC 3/56. Canx 8.7.55.
G-AOCH	Vickers 621 Viking 1 (Modified to Viking 3, reverted to Viking 1 in 1967)	150	D-BABY (D-BONA)/D-AMOR/G-AOCH/VL231/R.Australian AF A82-1/VL231	13. 5.55	WFU & stored at Manston on 7.7.68. CofA expired 7.7.68. Canx as WFU 3.2.69.
G-AOCI	DH.98 Mosquito PR.34	-	NS639	18. 5.55	Not converted. Burnt at Thruxton 10/60. Canx.
G-AOCJ	DH.98 Mosquito PR.34	-	NS742	18. 5.55	To Israeli DF/AF as 4X-FDG/2190 in 8/56. Canx 10.10.56.
G-AOCK	DH.98 Mosquito PR.34	-	NS753	25. 5.55	Not converted. Burnt at Thruxton 10/60. Canx.
G-AOCL	DH.98 Mosquito PR.34	-	RG173	25. 5.55	Not converted. Burnt at Thruxton 10/60. Canx.
G-AOCM	DH.98 Mosquito PR.34	-	RG174	25. 5.55	To Israeli DF/AF as 4X-FDF/90 (ferry marks only!). Canx 31.10.56.
G-AOCN	DH.98 Mosquito PR.34	-	TA614	25. 5.55	To Israeli DF/AF as (4X-FDI/2192) in 8/56 & 4X-FDL/2192 in 12/56. Canx 29.11.56.
G-AOCO	DH.98 Sea Mosquito Mk.33	-	TW246	18. 8.55	Not converted. Scrapped at Lossiemouth in 1957. Canx.
G-AOCP(1)	DH.98 Mosquito PR.34	-	(ex)	. 5.55R	NTU - Canx.
G-AOCP(2)	Taylorcraft Auster 5	1800	TW462	25. 5.56	WFU at Hemswell on 22.6.68. (On rebuild 9/96)
G-AOCR(1)	DH.98 Mosquito PR.34	-	(ex)	. 5.55R	NTU - Canx.
G-AOCR(2)	Taylorcraft Auster 5D (Originally regd as an Auster 5)	1060	EI-AJS G-AOCR/NJ673	25. 5.56	
G-AOCS(1)	DH.98 Mosquito PR.34	-	(ex)	. 5.55R	NTU - Canx.
G-AOCS(2)	DH.82A Tiger Moth	86476	T-201 R.Jordanian AF/TJ-AAG/NM156	3. 7.56	Not converted & WFU at RAF Amman, Jordan. Canx 25.4.60.
G-AOCT(1)	DH.98 Mosquito PR.34	-	(ex)	. 5.55R	NTU - Canx.
G-AOCT(2)	Douglas C-47A-20-DK Dakota	12813	400 Pakistan AF/VP908/KG492/42-92955	6. 7.56	To F-OAYR 11/56. Canx 23.10.56.
G-AOCU(1)	DH.98 Mosquito PR.34	-	(ex)	. 5.55R	NTU - Canx.
G-AOCU(2)	Taylorcraft Auster 5	986	MT349	8. 6.56	
G-AOCV(1)	DH.98 Mosquito PR.34	-	(ex)	. 5.55R	NTU - Canx.
G-AOCV(2)	DH.82A Tiger Moth	3974	N6670	11. 6.56	DBF at Dunstable on 25.1.71. Canx 30.5.74.
	[Note: Originally allocated to R4961 c/n 82869, which became G-APJP. When G-APJP was being overhauled in 1973, it was briefly "restored" to G-AOCV until error discovered]				
G-AOCW(1)	DH.98 Mosquito PR.34	-	(ex)	. 5.55R	NTU - Canx.
G-AOCW(2)	DH.82A Tiger Moth	83172	T5429	14. 6.56	To D-ECEF 10/56. Canx 8.10.56.
G-AOCX(1)	DH.98 Mosquito PR.34	-	(ex)	. 5.55R	NTU - Canx.
G-AOCX(2)	DH.82A Tiger Moth	84661	T6235	18. 6.56	To SE-CGI 7/57. Canx 11.7.57.
G-AOCY(1)	DH.98 Mosquito PR.34	-	(ex)	. 5.55R	NTU - Canx.
G-AOCY(2)	Auster J/5P Autocar	3258		19. 6.56	Crashed at Bampton, Devon on 30.6.62. Canx.
G-AOCZ	Westland-Sikorsky S-55 Whirlwind Srs.3 (Originally regd as a Srs.1)	WA/115	EP-HAE G-AOCZ	16. 5.55	To VR-BDF 2/69. Canx 18.2.69.
G-AODA	Westland-Sikorsky S-55 Whirlwind Srs.3 (Originally regd as a Srs.1)	WA/113	9Y-TDA EP-HAC/G-AODA	13. 5.55	Canx by CAA 23.9.93. (On display 4/98 Weston-super-Mare)
G-AODB	Westland-Sikorsky S-55 Whirlwind Srs.3 (Originally regd as a Srs.1)	WA/114		13. 5.55	To VR-BDH 2/69. Canx 18.2.69.
G-AODC	Auster J/5P Autocar	3187		23. 5.55	To OE-DAC 7/55. Canx 30.11.55.
G-AODD	Douglas C-47A-60-DL Dakota	10239	OD-AAO LR-AAO/NC36412/42-24377	27. 5.55	To Burmese AF as UBT-715 in 9/55. Canx 5.9.55.
G-AODE	Handley Page HPR.7 Dart Herald 100 (Built as a HPR.3 Herald)	147		14. 6.55	Crashed near Godalming, Surrey on 30.8.58. Canx.
G-AODF	Handley Page HPR.7 Dart Herald 200 (Built as a HPR.3 Herald)	148		14. 6.55	To G-ARTC 8/61. Canx 22.8.61.
G-AODG	Vickers 736 Viscount	77	OD-ACR G-AODG/(LN-FOF)	22. 7.55	DBR on landing at Castle Donington on 20.2.69. Canx.
G-AODH	Vickers 736 Viscount	78	VP-TBY G-AODH/(LN-FOL)	22. 7.55	Crashed at Frankfurt on 30.10.61. Canx.
G-AODI	Agusta-Bell 47G-1	042		1. 7.55	Fatal crash near Luton airport shortly after take-off on 25.2.59. Canx.
G-AODJ	Agusta-Bell 47G-1	044		30. 9.55	Crashed at Scone, near Perth on 12.7.60. Canx.
G-AODK	Agusta-Bell 47G-1	045		3.11.55	Crashed at Kennoway, Fife on 9.8.65. Canx.
G-AODL	Bristol 171 Sycamore 4	13403		29. 6.55	To VH-INO 5/56. Canx 11.5.56.
G-AODM	DH.104 Dove 6A	04460	G-5-11	15. 7.55	To N1509V 9/55. Canx 26.8.55.
G-AODN	DH.104 Dove 6B (Originally regd as Dove 2B)	04338	F-OAKG	22. 7.55	To HB-LAQ 4/60. Canx 31.3.60.
G-AODO	Westland-Sikorsky S-55 Whirlwind Srs.3 (Originally regd as a Srs.1)	WA/116		25. 7.55	To VR-BBZ 6/63. Canx 6.2.63.
G-AODP	Westland-Sikorsky S-55 Whirlwind Srs.3 (Originally regd as a Srs.1)	WA/117	(PH-THB) G-AODP/VP-TCN/G-AODP/5N-ABP/VR-NDL/G-AODP	25. 7.55	Restored as 5N-ABP 11/68. Canx 25.10.68.
G-AODR	DH.82A Tiger Moth	86251	NL779	4. 8.55	Crashed at Nympsfield on 18.9.61. To G-ISIS 12/83.
G-AODS	DH.82A Tiger Moth	82942	R5041	4. 8.55	Extensively damaged on landing at Sherburn on 5.7.70. Canx.
G-AODT	DH.82A Tiger Moth	83109	R5250	4. 8.55	

Regn	Type	c/n	Previous identity	Regn date	Fate or immediate subsequent identity (if known)
G-AODU	DH.82A Tiger Moth	85835	DE975	2. 8.55	Crashed near Laindon, Essex on 17.11.68. (Rebuilt at Kirkbymoorside in 12/68 as a Rumpler G-AXAM for a "Biggles" film) Canx as WFU 9.1.69.
G-AODV	DH.104 Dove 6A	04461		9. 8.55	To N2066A 12/55. Canx 29.12.55.
G-AODW	DH.82A Tiger Moth	86493	NM185	9. 8.55	To D-EMOR 3/56. Canx 13.3.56.
G-AODX	DH.82A Tiger Moth	83437	T5716	10. 8.55	DBF at Nympsfield on 7.5.73. Canx.
G-AODY	DH.114 Heron 2	14089	OY-ADU LN-SUA/G-AODY	5. 9.55	To N576PR 7/71. Canx 20.7.71.
G-AODZ	Scottish Aviation Pioneer Srs.2	SAL/PP/115		19. 8.55	WFU at Prestwick in 1/59. Broken up for spares. Canx.
G-AOEA	DH.82A Tiger Moth	85436	DE428	22. 8.55	To D-EFYN 11/55, but crashed at Ostend, Belgium on delivery 27.11.55. Canx 11.11.55.
G-AOEB	DH.82A Tiger Moth	83524	T5838	22. 8.55	To ZK-BNF 1/56. Canx 14.10.55.
G-AOEC	DH.82A Tiger Moth	82078	N6808	22. 8.55	To ZK-BNG 3/56. Canx 14.10.55.
G-AOED	DH.82A Tiger Moth	83091	R5216	24. 8.55	To D-EKIF 8/56. Canx 4.6.56.
G-AOEE	DH.82A Tiger Moth	84186	T7808	24. 8.55	To D-EKUL 4/56. Canx 21.3.56.
G-AOEF	DH.82A Tiger Moth	85138	T6909	24. 8.55	To D-EMUS 1/56. Canx 23.1.56.
G-AOEG	DH.82A Tiger Moth	83547	T7120	7. 9.55	To G-TIGA 6/85. Canx.
G-AOEH	Aeronca 7AC Champion	7AC-2144	N79854 OO-TWF	8. 9.55	DBR at Newtownards on 22.3.79. Canx.
G-AOEI	DH.82A Tiger Moth	82196	N6946	14. 9.55	
G-AOEJ	Percival P.34A Proctor III	H.268	HM358	15. 9.55	Crashed at Denham on 19.3.63. Canx.
G-AOEK	Blackburn Beverley C.1	1003	XB260	20. 9.55	Restored to RAF as XB260 in 11/55. Canx 30.9.57.
G-AOEL	DH.82A Tiger Moth	82537	N9510	27. 9.55	WFU on 18.7.72. On display 3/96 East Fortune.
G-AOEM	DH.82A Tiger Moth	84554	T6063	11.10.55	Canx 6.12.55 on sale to West Germany.
G-AOEN	Scottish Aviation Twin Pioneer Srs.3 (Originally regd as a Srs.1)	502		1.10.55	DBR after force landing in River Zambesi, Luabo, Mozambique on 12.12.59. Canx.
G-AOEO	Scottish Aviation Twin Pioneer Srs.3 (Originally regd as a Srs.1)	503		1.10.55	Port wing failed in flight and crashed 300 miles SW of Tripoli, Libya on 8.12.57. Canx.
G-AOEP	Scottish Aviation Twin Pioneer Srs.1	504		1.10.55	To VH-BHJ 5/57. Canx 17.7.57.
G-AOER	Scottish Aviation Twin Pioneer Srs.1	505		1.10.55	To XC-CUJ 8/62. Canx 26.8.62.
G-AOES	DH.82A Tiger Moth	84547	T6056	6.10.55	
G-AOET	DH.82A Tiger Moth	85650	DE720	7.10.55	
G-AOEU	DH.82A Tiger Moth	86187	NL704	8.10.55	To D-EFYN 5/56. Canx 7.5.56.
G-AOEV	DH.82A Tiger Moth	82765	R4833	8.10.55	To D-EKUN 12/55. Canx 29.11.55.
G-AOEW	DH.82A Tiger Moth	86519	NM211	8.10.55	To D-EDOR 11/55. Canx 8.12.55.
G-AOEX	Thruxton Jackaroo	86483	NM175	10.10.55	CofA expired 3.2.68. WFU at Thruxton in 1968. (On rebuild 5/90)
G-AOEY	Thruxton Jackaroo	85899	DF150	10.10.55	To VR-NCY 9/58. Canx 26.8.57.
G-AOEZ	Auster J/5L Aiglet Trainer	3141		14.10.55	Crashed while making a forced-landing near Sandown, Isle of Wight on 30.7.66. Wreck removed to Kidlington in 1/67, and to Staverton in 4/67. Canx.
G-AOFA(1)	Bristol 175 Britannia Srs.312	13207	(G-AMYK)	. .55R	NTU - To G-AOVA 2/57. Canx.
G-AOFA(2)	Hiller 360 UH-12C	785		30. 8.56	Crashed at Crowland on 25.8.61. Canx.
G-AOFB(1)	Bristol 175 Britannia Srs.312	13208	(G-AMYL)	. .55R	NTU - Not built. Canx in 1/56.
G-AOFB(2)	DH.82A Tiger Moth	83170	6728M T5427	30. 8.56	To F-OBAJ 8/57. Canx 28.12.56.
G-AOFC(1)	Bristol 175 Britannia Srs.312	13231		. .55R	NTU - To G-AOVC 2/57. Canx.
G-AOFC(2)	Convair CV.240-56	64	JA5048 G-AOFC/N9853F/VH-TAQ	12. 9.56	Canx on sale JA5048 on 8.7.58, but only delivered as far as Beirut then returned to the UK. To (N5550A)/LN-LAU in 6/59.
G-AOFD(1)	Bristol 175 Britannia Srs.312	13235		. .55R	NTU - To G-AOVD 2/57. Canx.
G-AOFD(2)	DH.82A Tiger Moth	85930	DF194	11. 9.56	Crashed at Tewin, Herts on 16.9.62. Canx.
G-AOFE(1)	Bristol 175 Britannia Srs.312	13236		. .55R	NTU - To G-AOVE 2/57. Canx.
G-AOFE(2)	DHC.1 Chipmunk 22A (Fuselage no. DHB/f/53) (Originally regd as a Mk.22)	C1/0150	WB702	13. 9.56	
G-AOFF(1)	Bristol 175 Britannia Srs.312	13237		. .55R	NTU - To G-AOVF 2/57. Canx.
G-AOFF(2)	DHC.1 Chipmunk 22 (Fuselage no. DHB/f/82)	C1/0196	OH-HCE G-AOFF/WB749	13. 9.56	To N9246Z 12/75. Canx 19.12.75.
G-AOFG(1)	Bristol 175 Britannia Srs.312	13238		. .55R	NTU - To G-AOVG 2/57. Canx.
G-AOFG(2)	DH.82A Tiger Moth	84529	T8256	17. 9.56	To VH-AWI 11/57. Canx 28.11.56.
G-AOFH(1)	Bristol 175 Britannia Srs.312	-		. .55R	NTU. Canx.
G-AOFH(2)	DH.82A Tiger Moth	82996	7043M R5114	2.10.56	Crashed at Wolverhampton on 20.10.57. Canx.
G-AOFI(1)	Bristol 175 Britannia Srs.312	-		. .55R	NTU. Canx.
G-AOFI(2)	DH.104 Dove 6 (Originally regd as Dove 2B)	04477		24. 9.56	CofA expired 3.6.70 & WFU. Scrapped at Baginton. Canx.
G-AOFJ(1)	Bristol 175 Britannia Srs.312	13418		. .55R	NTU - To G-AOVJ 2/57. Canx.
G-AOFJ(2)	Auster 5 Alpha	3401		3.10.56	CofA expired 20.9.79. Canx by CAA 3.4.89. (On rebuild Perth-Scone 5/98)
G-AOFK	Hiller 360 UH-12B	745		8. 6.55	Crashed at Hamble on 4.10.55. Canx.
G-AOFL	Hiller 360 UH-12B	746		8. 6.55	Crashed at Bourn on 13.12.65. Canx.
G-AOFM	Auster J/5P Autocar	3178		16. 6.55	
G-AOFN	Piaggio P.136-L1	195	I-RAIA	12. 7.55	Canx 3.8.58 on sale to Italy. Broken up by Piaggio without gaining an Italian registration.
G-AOFO	DH.82A Tiger Moth	82120	N6865	17.10.55	Crashed at Tollerton on 29.9.62. Canx.
G-AOFP	DH.82A Tiger Moth	84185	T7807	18.10.55	To D-EMEC 10/57. Canx 1.9.57.
G-AOFR	DH.82A Tiger Moth	86425	NL993	27.10.55	To SE-COX 9/61. Canx 20.11.60.
G-AOFS	Auster J/5L Aiglet Trainer	3143	EI-ALN G-AOFS	28.10.55	
G-AOFT	Auster J/5P Autocar	3193		28.10.55	To ZK-BLZ 12/55. Canx 21.11.55.

Regn	Type	c/n	Previous identity	Regn date	Fate or immediate subsequent identity (if known)
G-AOFU	Edgar Percival EP.9 (Became Prospector 1 in 1959)(Originally identified in documentation as c/n 920 - until about 20.10.56)	20		1.11.55	Crashed whilst crop-spraying at Maturabi, Sudan on 3.11.62. Canx.
G-AOFV	Hiller 360 UH-12B	748		3.11.55	Crashed at Ludham, Norfolk on 6.4.65. Canx.
G-AOFW	Aviation Traders ATL-98 Carvair (Originally regd as a Douglas C-54A-15-DC)	10351/12	EC-AVD EC-WVD/EC-AVD/G-AOFW/N1436V/I-DALV/N88919/42-72246	9.11.55	WFU & stored at Southend in 1978. Broken up in 12/83. Canx.
G-AOFX(1)	Douglas DC-6A (Line No. 648)	44889	N6813C	. .55R	NTU - Remained as N6813C. Canx.
G-AOFX(2)	Vickers 701C Viscount	182		20.12.55	To PP-SRS 8/63. Canx 25.7.63.
G-AOFY(1)	Douglas DC-6A (Line No. 662)	45058	N6814C	. .55R	NTU - Remained as N6814C. Canx.
G-AOFY(2)	DH.114 Heron 1B	14099		3. 2.56	Fatal crash when it overshot on landing in a gale at Port Ellen on the Isle of Islay on 28.9.57 and crashed at Glenmachrie. Canx.
G-AOFZ	Douglas C-47-DL Dakota	9131	VP-YON G-AOFZ/XY-ACP/ZS-BJZ/FD814/42-32905	25.11.55	Crashed at Azaiba, Muscat on 17.8.66. Canx.
G-AOGA	Miles M.75 Aries 1	75/1007	EI-ANB G-AOGA	9.11.55	Damaged at Cork on 8.8.69. Canx 30.5.84. (Stored 4/96 at Castlemoate House, Dublin)
G-AOGB	DH.82A Tiger Moth	83140	T5373	17.11.55	Crashed at Uffington on 19.4.62. Canx.
G-AOGC	DH.114 Heron 2C	14094	PH-ILO G-AOGC	24.11.55	To N17600 4/67. Canx 21.3.67.
G-AOGD	Percival P.30 Proctor II	K.403	Z7214	24.11.55	CofA expired 17.1.59 & WFU. Scrapped. Canx 31.3.59.
G-AOGE	Percival P.34A Proctor III	H.210	BV651	24.11.55	CofA lapsed 21.5.84. (Stored 8/97 Biggin Hill) Canx by CAA 19.1.99.
G-AOGF	Scottish Aviation Pioneer Srs.2	SAL/PP/118		5.12.55	To EP-AHD 3/58. Canx 27.3.58.
G-AOGG	Vickers 759D Viscount	140		3. 1.56	To TF-ISN 4/57. Canx 19.3.57.
G-AOGH	Vickers 759D Viscount	149		3. 1.56	To TF-ISU 4/57. Canx 19.3.57.
G-AOGI	DH.82A Tiger Moth	85922	(N.....) OO-SOA/G-AOGI/DF186	14.12.55	WFU on 23.8.91. (Stored Ingoldmells 10/92)
G-AOGJ	DH.82A Tiger Moth	83283	T7025	15.12.55	To OO-SOB 3/56. Canx 16.1.56.
G-AOGK	Scottish Aviation Pioneer Srs.2	SAL/PP/125		16. 1.56	To RAF as XL517 in 3/56. Canx 3.4.56.
G-AOGL	Olympia DFS/70 Meise	00117		6. 1.56	To D-5508 12/56. Canx as WFU in 10/63.
G-AOGM	Auster J/5P Autocar	3197		10. 1.56	DBR at Squires Gate, Blackpool on 19.9.70. Canx.
G-AOGN	Auster J/5R Alpine	3301		16. 1.56	To VH-BTI 11/56. Canx 19.11.56.
G-AOGO	DH.114 Heron 2D	14096		19. 1.56	To N585PR 6/76. Canx 6.7.76.
G-AOGP	DH.82A Tiger Moth	85586	DE632	20. 1.56	To VR-RBQ 7/56. Canx 12.3.56.
G-AOGR	DH.82A Tiger Moth	84566	XL714 G-AOGR/T6099	20. 1.56	(Stored 10/97)
G-AOGS	DH.82A Tiger Moth	3815	N6478	30. 1.56	To N82TM 3/71. Canx 1.3.71.
G-AOGT	DH.82A Tiger Moth	83594	T5878	30. 1.56	Canx 1.5.56 on sale to Spain. Scrapped in UK marks 1960.
G-AOGU	DH.114 Heron 2E (Originally regd as a Heron 2D)	14097	OY-DPO D-CASI/G-AOGU	1. 2.56	To D-CAHA 7/70. Canx 23.7.70.
G-AOGV	Auster J/5R Alpine	3302		2. 2.56	CofA expired 17.7.72. (Stored in garage 3/97)
G-AOGW	DH.114 Heron 2E	14095		2. 2.56	To C-GCML 9/72. Canx 14.2.73.
G-AOGX	Douglas C-47B-1-DL Dakota	20777	AP-AED 43-16311	14. 2.56	To F-OAYM 9/56. Canx 27.9.56.
G-AOGY	DH.82A Tiger Moth	82918	R5023	8. 2.56	To VH-RSE 7/56. Canx 6.7.56.
G-AOGZ	Douglas C-47B-35-DK Dakota	16534/33282	KN628 44-76950	18. 2.56	To N4849 in 1/69. Canx 19.3.69.
G-AOHA(1)	Vickers 802 Viscount	150		. .56R	NTU - To G-AOJA 1/56. Canx.
G-AOHA(2)	Taylorcraft Auster 5	1796	TW456	7. 3.56	To ZP-TDL 4/57. Canx 24.4.57.
G-AOHB(1)	Vickers 802 Viscount	151		. .56R	NTU - To G-AOJB 1/56. Canx.
G-AOHB(2)	DH.114 Heron 2D	14100		8. 3.56	To TF-AIN 5/65. Canx 10.5.65.
G-AOHC(1)	Vickers 802 Viscount	152		. .56R	NTU - To G-AOJC 1/56. Canx.
G-AOHC(2)	DH.82A Tiger Moth	82591	W6419 G-AFWE	15. 3.56	Crashed at Holywell, Flintshire on 26.5.56. Canx.
G-AOHD(1)	Vickers 802 Viscount	153		. .56R	NTU - To G-AOJD 1/56. Canx.
G-AOHD(2)	Hunting Percival P.84 Jet Provost T.2	P.84/12	A99-001 R.Australian AF/G-AOHD	26. 3.56	(Stored .95 Point Cook, Victoria)
G-AOHE(1)	Vickers 802 Viscount	154		. .56R	NTU - To G-AOJE 1/56. Canx.
G-AOHE(2)	Westland-Sikorsky S-55 Whirlwind Srs.3	WA/126		21. 3.56	Crashed on 12.6.69. Canx as destroyed 18.6.69.
G-AOHF(1)	Vickers 802 Viscount	155		. .56R	NTU - To G-AOJF 1/56. Canx.
G-AOHF(2)	Auster J/5P Autocar	3191	EI-AJH G-AOHF/(D-EFOR)	15. 5.56	To VH-EDF 1/71. Canx 20.3.70.
G-AOHG	Vickers 802 Viscount	156		2. 1.56	WFU on 30.4.75. Broken up at Rhoose 10/75. Canx as WFU 30.5.75.
G-AOHH	Vickers 802 Viscount	157		2. 1.56	Stored at Yeadon 20.11.75. Canx as WFU 12.12.75. Broken up.
G-AOHI	Vickers 802 Viscount	158		2. 1.56	Fatal crash Ben More, Perth on 19.1.73. Canx.
G-AOHJ	Vickers 802 Viscount	159		2. 1.56	WFU & stored in 4/76. Broken up in 7/76. Mated with half of fuselage from G-AMOE to become "G-WHIZ". Canx as WFU 7.5.76
G-AOHK	Vickers 802 Viscount	160		2. 1.56	WFU & stored at Yeadon 4/76. Broken up. Canx as WFU 7.5.76.
G-AOHL	Vickers 802 Viscount	161		2. 1.56	WFU on 6.2.81 & used as cabin services trainer at Southend. Canx 27.3.81. Used for spares in 1992. Derelict by 1/94. (Extant 2/99)
G-AOHM	Vickers 802C Viscount	162		2. 1.56	WFU & stored 1/99 at Southend. Sold to Kenya 21.5.99. To 3D-OHM 9/99. Canx 25.8.99.
G-AOHN	Vickers 802 Viscount	163		2. 1.56	Canx as WFU 1.10.75 & stored at Rhoose. Broken up at Cardiff.
G-AOHO	Vickers 802 Viscount	164		2. 1.56	WFU & stored at Rhoose 31.3.76. Fuselage to Hotel de France, St.Helier, Jersey. Canx as WFU 7.5.76.

Regn	Type	c/n	Previous identity	Regn date	Fate or immediate subsequent identity (if known)
G-AOHP	Vickers 802 Viscount	165		2. 1.56	DBR on crash-landing at Ballerup, Copenhagen, Denmark on 17.11.57. Canx.
G-AOHR	Vickers 802 Viscount	166		2. 1.56	Canx as WFU 1.10.75 & stored at Rhoose. Broken up in 6/76 at Cardiff. Nose to 192 ATC Sqdn at TAVR Centre, Bridgend.
G-AOHS	Vickers 802 Viscount	167		2. 1.56	WFU & stored in 6/75. Canx as WFU 11.7.76. Broken up for spares at Cardiff, remains to fire dump.
G-AOHT	Vickers 802 Viscount	168	ZS-SKY G-AOHT	2. 1.56	WFU & stored in 7/87. Broken up at Southend in 3/91. Canx at destroyed 21.7.94.
G-AOHU	Vickers 802 Viscount	169		2. 1.56	DBR at Heathrow on 7.1.60. Canx.
G-AOHV	Vickers 802C Viscount	170		2. 1.56	To G-BLNB 6/84. Canx.
G-AOHW(1)	Vickers 802 Viscount	171		. .55R	NTU - To G-AORD 5/56. Canx.
G-AOHW(2)	Vickers 802 Viscount	253	(G-AORC)	2. 1.56	Canx as WFU 17.11.75 & stored at Newcastle. Used for spares. To Fire Service in 5/76. Scrapped in 8/83.
G-AOHX	Westland-Sikorsky S-51 Mk.1A	WA/H/139		13. 1.56	To JA7025 5/56. Canx 21.5.56.
G-AOHY	DH.82A Tiger Moth	3850	N6537	23. 2.56	WFU on 20.8.60. (On rebuild 2/96 Middle Wallop)
G-AOHZ	Auster J/5P Autocar	3252		28. 2.56	
G-AOIA	Douglas DC-7C (Line No. 727)	45111		27. 8.56	To N90803 4/64. Canx 25.5.64.
G-AOIB	Douglas DC-7C (Line No. 736)	45112		27. 8.56	To N90802 3/64. Canx 23.3.64.
G-AOIC	Douglas DC-7C (Line No. 739)	45113		27. 8.56	To N90801 2/64. Canx 10.2.64.
G-AOID	Douglas DC-7C (Line No. 740)	45114		27. 8.56	To N90778 5/63. Canx 29.5.63.
G-AOIE	Douglas DC-7C (Line No. 746)	45115	PH-SAX G-AOIE	27. 8.56	To Shannon for spares use in 11/69. Canx as WFU 31.3.70. Scrapped 10/97 at Waterford, Ireland.
G-AOIF	Douglas DC-7C (Line No. 750)	45116		27. 8.56	To N90804 5/64. Canx 29.5.64.
G-AOIG	Douglas DC-7C (Line No. 751)	45117		27. 8.56	To N90773 4/63. Canx 17.6.63.
G-AOIH	Douglas DC-7C (Line No. 756)	45118		27. 8.56	To N90774 5/63. Canx 6.5.63.
G-AOII	Douglas DC-7C/F (Line No. 760) (Converted to DC-7C/F in 1960)	45119		27. 8.56	To OY-KNE 5/65. Canx 1.1.65.
G-AOIJ	Douglas DC-7C/F (Line No. 795) (Converted to DC-7C/F in 1960)	45120		27. 8.56	To N16465 5/65. Canx 15.5.65.
G-AOIK	DH.82A Tiger Moth	85403	DE395	20. 8.56	To RN as XL715 in 9/56. Canx 4.9.56.
G-AOIL	DH.82A Tiger Moth	83673	XL716 G-AOIL/T7363	20. 8.56	
G-AOIM	DH.82A Tiger Moth	83536	T7109	27. 8.56	
G-AOIN	DH.82A Tiger Moth	3964	N6660	13. 1.56	Crashed at Wattisham, Norfolk on 4.9.65. Canx.
G-AOIO	Thruxton Jackaroo	82151	N6907	13. 1.56	Canx 27.2.78 on sale to Australia.
G-AOIP	DH.82A Tiger Moth	82706	R4765	13. 1.56	Crashed near Fakenham on 31.5.60. Canx.
G-AOIR	Thruxton Jackaroo	82882	R4972	13. 1.56	
G-AOIS	DH.82A Tiger Moth	83034	R5172	13. 1.56	
G-AOIT	Thruxton Jackaroo	83190	T5465	13. 1.56	WFU at Renfrew in 7/65. Canx 16.7.73.
G-AOIU	DH.82A Tiger Moth	84615	T6167	13. 1.56	To D-EDUF 5/56, but destroyed in ground accident at Borkenberge on 1.8.56 prior to formal regn. Canx 25.6.56.
G-AOIV	Thruxton Jackaroo	85146	T6917	13. 1.56	To Argentina 7/59 and WFU at Don Torcuate Airport, Buenos Aires. Canx 21.7.59.
G-AOIW	Thruxton Jackaroo	85147	T6718	13. 1.56	Crashed at Thruxton on 23.4.64. Canx.
G-AOIX	Thruxton Jackaroo	83472	T7087	13. 1.56	WFU on 22.4.67. Canx 24.6.69. Rebuilt as Tiger Moth & regd as G-BPAJ on 5.11.80.
G-AOIY	Auster J/5V-160 Autocar (Originally regd as a J/5G Cirrus Autocar, then as J/5D Warden)	3199		1. 3.56	(On rebuild 3/98)
G-AOIZ	DH.104 Dove 1	04257	VP964	7. 3.56	Restored to RAF as VP964 6/58. CofA expired 17.6.58. Canx as WFU 23.9.61.
G-AOJA	Vickers 802 Viscount	150	(G-AOHA)	2. 1.56	Fatal crash when it overshot on landing in fog at Nutts Corner, Belfast on 23.10.57. Canx.
G-AOJB	Vickers 802 Viscount	151	(G-AOHB)	2. 1.56	WFU & stored in 4/76. To Liverpool Fire Service in 10/76. Canx as WFU 7.5.76.
G-AOJC	Vickers 802 Viscount	152	(G-AOHC)	2. 1.56	Canx as WFU 31.10.75 & stored at Rhoose. Broken up in 1996 at Cardiff. Fuselage stored 7/96 Enstone.
G-AOJD	Vickers 802 Viscount	153	(G-AOHD)	2. 1.56	Canx as WFU 7.5.76. Used by Jersey Airport Fire Service. (Extant 12/96)
G-AOJE	Vickers 802 Viscount	154	(G-AOHE)	6. 3.56	WFU & stored in 3/80. Broken up in 8/81 at Cardiff. Canx.
G-AOJF	Vickers 802 Viscount	155	(G-AOHF)	6. 3.56	WFU & stored in 2/80. Broken up in 8/81. Canx.
G-AOJG	Hunting-Percival P.66 President I (Also c/n P66/79) (Originally regd as a Hunting-Percival Prince 5)	HPAL/PEM/79		27. 3.56	To Danish AF as 697 in 7/59. Canx 4.7.59.
G-AOJH	DH.83C Fox Moth	FM.42	AP-ABO	29. 3.56	
G-AOJI	Douglas C-47B-30-DK Dakota	16411/33159	VR-AAO G-AOJI/KN550/44-76827	4. 4.56	To VP-BAH(2) 12/58. Canx 16.12.58.
G-AOJJ	DH.82A Tiger Moth	85877	DF128	5. 4.56	
G-AOJK	DH.82A Tiger Moth	82813	R4896	5. 4.56	
G-AOJL	Taylorcraft Auster 5	1791	TW455	6. 4.56	To SE-CMB 5/59. Canx 20.2.59.
G-AOJM	DHC.1 Chipmunk 22 (Fuselage no. DHB/f/12)	C1/0079	WB633	9. 4.56	To D-ECEM 8/56. Canx 23.8.56.
G-AOJN	DHC.1 Chipmunk 22 (Fuselage no. DHB/f/133)	C1/0248	WD306	9. 4.56	To D-EFOM 10/56. Canx 17.10.56.
G-AOJO	DHC.1 Chipmunk 22 (Fuselage no. DHB/f/27)	C1/0113	D-EDUG G-AOJO/WB665	9. 4.56	To VR-NBH 1/60. Canx 18.1.60.

Regn	Type	c/n	Previous identity	Regn date	Fate or immediate subsequent identity (if known)
G-AOJP	DHC.1 Chipmunk 22 (Fuselage no. DHB/f/84)	C1/0199	D-EFOL G-AOJP/WB751	9. 4.56	Restored as D-EFOL 1/58. Canx 13.1.58.
G-AOJR	DHC.1 Chipmunk 22 (Fuselage no. DHB/f/89)	C1/0205	SE-BBS OY-DFB/D-EGIM/G-AOJR/D-EGIM/G-AOJR/WB756	9. 4.56	
G-AOJS	DHC.1 Chipmunk 22 (Fuselage no. DHB/f/78)	C1/0192	5N-AAE VR-NBI/G-AOJS/D-EHOF/G-AOJS/WB745	9. 4.56	Canx 6.9.96 on sale to Australia.
G-AOJT	DH.106 Comet 1XB	06020	F-BGNX	11. 5.56	Broken up in fatigue tests at Farnborough 10/56. Canx. (Fuselage at London Colney 3/96).
G-AOJU	DH.106 Comet 1A (Originally regd as a Comet 1XB)	06021	XM829 G-AOJU/F-BGNY	11. 5.56	To RAF as XM829 in 1958. Canx 14.6.61.
G-AOJV	DHC.1 Chipmunk 22 (Fuselage no. DHB/f/51)	C1/0147	WB699	13. 4.56	To D-EJAN 8/56. Canx 23.8.56.
G-AOJW	DHC.1 Chipmunk 22 (Fuselage no. DHH/f/97)	C1/0171	WB719	13. 4.56	To D-EFUS 9/56. Canx 12.9.56.
G-AOJX	DH.82A Tiger Moth	3272	K4276	18. 4.56	To OO-EVS 7/56. Canx 5.6.56.
G-AOJY	DHC.1 Chipmunk 22 (Fuselage no. DHB/f/10)	C1/0077	WB631	16. 4.56	Blown into a road roller at Lulsgate on 24.6.66. Canx. (Remains to Hamble in 1967)
G-AOJZ	DHC.1 Chipmunk 22 (Fuselage no. DHB/f/68)	C1/0181	WB732	16. 4.56	Crashed 7 miles southwest of Perth, Scotland on 31.5.66. Canx. (Instructional Airframe 12/95 Perth marked as "G-ASTD" - for sale 1996)
G-AOKA	Percival P.40 Prentice T.1	PAC/156	VR306	28. 3.56	Not converted. Scrapped at Southend in 4/57. Canx.
G-AOKB	Percival P.40 Prentice T.1	PAC/166	VR310	28. 3.56	Not converted. Scrapped at Southend. Canx.
G-AOKC	Percival P.40 Prentice T.1	PAC/334	VS732	11. 4.56	Not converted. Scrapped at Stansted. Canx.
G-AOKD	Percival P.40 Prentice T.1	5840/12	VS390	11. 4.56	Not converted. To instructional airframe at Perth in 7/61. Canx.
G-AOKE	Percival P.40 Prentice T.1	PAC/189	VR316	11. 4.56	Not converted. Scrapped at Southend. Canx.
G-AOKF	Percival P.40 Prentice T.1	PAC/130	VR284	11. 4.56	To EL-AFJ in 3/66. Canx 5.3.66.
G-AOKG	Percival P.40 Prentice T.1	PAC/147	VR301	11. 4.56	Not converted. Scrapped at Southend. Canx.
G-AOKH	Percival P.40 Prentice T.1 (Regd with c/n 5800/11)	PAC/212	VS251	11. 4.56	Stored at Biggin Hill. CofA expired 2.8.73. Canx by CAA 17.6.92. (Stored 8/97)
G-AOKI	Percival P.40 Prentice T.1	PAC/018	VR193	28. 3.56	Not converted. Scrapped at Southend. Canx.
G-AOKJ	Percival P.40 Prentice T.1	PAC/065	VR239	11. 4.56	Not converted. Scrapped at Southend. Canx.
G-AOKK	Percival P.40 Prentice T.1	PAC/069	VR243	11. 4.56	Not converted. Scrapped at Southend. Canx.
G-AOKL	Percival P.40 Prentice T.1	PAC/208	VS610	13. 4.56	
G-AOKM	Percival P.40 Prentice T.1	PAC/343	VS741	13. 4.56	Not converted. Scrapped at Stansted. Canx.
G-AOKN	Percival P.40 Prentice T.1	PAC/277	VS642	13. 4.56	Not converted. Scrapped at Stansted. Canx.
G-AOKO	Percival P.40 Prentice T.1	PAC/234	VS621	13. 4.56	CofA expired 23.10.72 & WFU at Baginton. Canx as WFU 9.10.84. (Stored for spares 5/96)
G-AOKP	Percival P.40 Prentice T.1	PAC/260	VS635	13. 4.56	Not converted. Scrapped at Southend. Canx.
G-AOKR	Percival P.40 Prentice T.1	PAC/295	VS649	13. 4.56	Not converted. Scrapped at Southend. Canx.
G-AOKS	Percival P.40 Prentice T.1	PAC/357	VS755	13. 4.56	Not converted. Scrapped at Southend. Canx.
G-AOKT	Percival P.40 Prentice T.1	5840/4	VS382	13. 4.56	Scrapped at Southend in 11/62. Canx.
G-AOKU	Percival P.40 Prentice T.1	5840/5	VS383	13. 4.56	Not converted. Scrapped at Southend. Canx.
G-AOKV	Percival P.40 Prentice T.1	PAC/199	VR321	13. 4.56	Not converted. Scrapped at Southend. Canx.
G-AOKW	Percival P.40 Prentice T.1	PAC/315	VS690	20. 4.56	Not converted. Scrapped at Southend. Canx.
G-AOKX	Percival P.40 Prentice T.1	5820/14	VS329	20. 4.56	Not converted. Scrapped at Southend. Canx.
G-AOKY	Percival P.40 Prentice T.1	PAC/250	VS630	20. 4.56	Not converted. Scrapped at Southend. Canx.
G-AOKZ	Percival P.40 Prentice T.1	PAC/238	VS623	20. 4.56	Not converted. To instructional airframe at Redhill in 7/61. (Stored 4/96 Baginton)
G-AOLA	Percival P.40 Prentice T.1	5820/9	VS324	20. 4.56	Not converted. Scrapped at Southend. Canx.
G-AOLB	Percival P.40 Prentice T.1	5840/8	VS386	20. 4.56	Not converted. Scrapped at Southend. Canx.
G-AOLC	Percival P.40 Prentice T.1	5840/17	VS395	20. 4.56	Not converted. Scrapped at Southend. Canx.
G-AOLD	Percival P.40 Prentice T.1	PAC/317	VS692	20. 4.56	Not converted. Scrapped at Southend. Canx.
G-AOLE	Percival P.40 Prentice T.1	5830/22	VS375	20. 4.56	Not converted. Scrapped at Southend. Canx.
G-AOLF	Percival P.40 Prentice T.1	PAC/201	VR322	20. 4.56	Not converted. Scrapped at Southend. Canx.
G-AOLG	Percival P.40 Prentice T.1	PAC/346	VS744	25. 4.56	Not converted. Scrapped at Southend. Canx.
G-AOLH	Percival P.40 Prentice T.1	PAC/331	VS729	25. 4.56	Not converted. Scrapped at Southend. Canx.
G-AOLI	Percival P.40 Prentice T.1	PAC/320	VS695	25. 4.56	Not converted. Scrapped at Southend. Canx.
G-AOLJ	Percival P.40 Prentice T.1	PAC/286	VS644	25. 4.56	Not converted. Scrapped at Southend. Canx.
G-AOLK	Percival P.40 Prentice T.1	PAC/225	VS618	25. 4.56	
G-AOLL	Percival P.40 Prentice T.1	5840/23	VS412	25. 4.56	Not converted. Scrapped at Southend. Canx.
G-AOLM	Percival P.40 Prentice T.1	5840/18	VS396	25. 4.56	To OO-LUC 3/60. Canx 28.1.60.
G-AOLN	Percival P.40 Prentice T.1	5840/13	VS391	25. 4.56	Not converted. Scrapped at Southend. Canx.
G-AOLO	Percival P.40 Prentice T.1	5840/10	VS388	25. 4.56	To OO-CIM 10/58. Canx 11.12.58.
G-AOLP	Percival P.40 Prentice T.1	5840/7	VS385	25. 4.56	To N1041P 3/79. Canx 5.3.79.
G-AOLR(1)	Percival P.40 Prentice T.1	5830/21	VS374	25. 4.56	To G-AOMK(2) /59. Canx.
G-AOLR(2)	Percival P.40 Prentice T.1	PAC/153	G-AOMK(1) VR304	. .59	Crashed at Kilsythe on 30.7.61. Canx.
G-AOLS	Percival P.40 Prentice T.1	5830/12	VS365	25. 4.56	Not converted. Scrapped at Southend. Canx.
G-AOLT	Percival P.40 Prentice T.1	5830/6	VS359	25. 4.56	Not converted. Scrapped at Southend. Canx.
G-AOLU	Percival P.40 Prentice T.1 (Also c/n 5830/3)	B3/1A/PAC/283	EI-ASP G-AOLU/VS356	25. 4.56	(On rebuild 8/95)
G-AOLV	Percival P.40 Prentice T.1	5820/25	VS353	25. 4.56	Not converted. Scrapped at Southend. Canx.
G-AOLW	Percival P.40 Prentice T.1	5820/12	VS327	25. 4.56	Not converted. Scrapped at Southend. Canx.
G-AOLX	Percival P.40 Prentice T.1	5820/5	VS320	3. 5.56	Not converted. Scrapped at Southend. Canx.
G-AOLY	Percival P.40 Prentice T.1	5820/4	VS319	3. 5.56	Not converted. Scrapped at Southend. Canx.
G-AOLZ	Percival P.40 Prentice T.1	5820/3	VS318	3. 5.56	Not converted. Scrapped at Southend. Canx.
G-AOMA	Percival P.40 Prentice T.1	5810/21	VS286	3. 5.56	Not converted. Scrapped at Southend. Canx.
G-AOMB	Percival P.40 Prentice T.1	5810/18	VS283	3. 5.56	Not converted. Scrapped at Southend. Canx.
G-AOMC	Percival P.40 Prentice T.1	5810/1	VS266	3. 5.56	Not converted. Scrapped at Southend. Canx.
G-AOMD	Percival P.40 Prentice T.1	5800/15	VS255	3. 5.56	Not converted. Scrapped at Southend. Canx.
G-AOME	Percival P.40 Prentice T.1	5800/12	VS252	3. 5.56	Not converted. Scrapped at Southend. Canx.

Regn	Type	c/n	Previous identity	Regn date	Fate or immediate subsequent identity (if known)
G-AOMF	Percival P.40 Prentice T.1 (Regd with c/n 5820/1)	PAC/252	(VH-...) G-AOMF/VS316	3. 5.56	To ZK-DJC 6/72. Canx.
G-AOMG	Percival P.40 Prentice T.1	PAC/096	VR268	3. 5.56	NTU - Not converted. (Was delivered by road) Scrapped at Southend. Canx.
G-AOMH	Percival P.40 Prentice T.1	PAC/190	VR317	22. 5.56	Not converted. Scrapped at Southend. Canx.
G-AOMI	Percival P.40 Prentice T.1	PAC/187	VR315	22. 5.56	Not converted. Scrapped at Stansted. Canx.
G-AOMJ	Percival P.40 Prentice T.1	PAC/186	VR314	22. 5.56	Not converted. Scrapped at Stansted. Canx.
G-AOMK(1)	Percival P.40 Prentice T.1	PAC/153	VR304	22. 5.56	To G-AOLR(2) /59. Canx.
G-AOMK(2)	Percival P.40 Prentice T.1	5830/21	G-AOLR(1) VS374	. .59	CofA expired 6.9.65 & WFU at Baginton, later to Wellesbourne Mountford. Canx.
G-AOML	Percival P.40 Prentice T.1	PAC/150	VR303	22. 5.56	Not converted. Scrapped at Stansted. Canx.
G-AOMM	Percival P.40 Prentice T.1	PAC/142	VR295	22. 5.56	Not converted. Scrapped at Southend. Canx.
G-AOMN	Percival P.40 Prentice T.1	PAC/140	VR294	22. 5.56	Not converted. Scrapped at Stansted. Canx.
G-AOMO	Percival P.40 Prentice T.1	PAC/138	VR292	22. 5.56	Not converted. Scrapped at Stansted. Canx.
G-AOMP	Percival P.40 Prentice T.1	PAC/135	VR289	22. 5.56	Not converted. Scrapped at Stansted. Canx.
G-AOMR	Percival P.40 Prentice T.1	PAC/134	VR288	22. 5.56	Not converted. Scrapped at Stansted. Canx.
G-AOMS	Percival P.40 Prentice T.1	PAC/132	VR286	22. 5.56	Not converted. Scrapped at Stansted. Canx.
G-AOMT	Percival P.40 Prentice T.1	PAC/131	VR285	22. 5.56	Not converted. Scrapped at Southend. Canx.
G-AOMU	Percival P.40 Prentice T.1	PAC/112	VR276	22. 5.56	Not converted. Scrapped at Stansted. Canx.
G-AOMV	Percival P.40 Prentice T.1	PAC/110	VR274	22. 5.56	Not converted. Scrapped at Stansted. Canx.
G-AOMW	Percival P.40 Prentice T.1	PAC/108	VR272	22. 5.56	Not converted. Scrapped at Stansted. Canx.
G-AOMX	Percival P.40 Prentice T.1	PAC/098	VR270	22. 5.56	Not converted. Scrapped at Southend. Canx.
G-AOMY	Percival P.40 Prentice T.1	PAC/093	VR265	22. 5.56	Not converted. Scrapped at Stansted. Canx.
G-AOMZ	Percival P.40 Prentice T.1	PAC/091	VR263	22. 5.56	Not converted. Scrapped at Stansted. Canx.
G-AONA	Percival P.40 Prentice T.1	PAC/071	VR245	22. 5.56	Not converted. Scrapped at Stansted. Canx.
G-AONB	Percival P.40 Prentice T.1	PAC/070	VR244	22. 5.56	WFU at Rochester in 3/62. Canx 16.4.70.
G-AONC	Percival P.40 Prentice T.1	PAC/066	VR240	22. 5.56	Not converted. Scrapped at Stansted. Canx.
G-AOND	Percival P.40 Prentice T.1	PAC/042	VR221	22. 5.56	Not converted. Scrapped at Stansted. Canx.
G-AONE	Percival P.40 Prentice T.1	PAC/041	VR220	22. 5.56	Not converted. Scrapped at Stansted. Canx.
G-AONF	Percival P.40 Prentice T.1	PAC/033	VR208	22. 5.56	Not converted. Scrapped at Stansted. Canx.
G-AONG	Percival P.40 Prentice T.1	PAC/032	VR207	22. 5.56	Not converted. Scrapped at Southend. Canx.
G-AONH	Percival P.40 Prentice T.1	PAC/019	VR196	22. 5.56	Not converted. Scrapped at Stansted. Canx.
G-AONI	Percival P.40 Prentice T.1	PAC/355	VS753	22. 5.56	Not converted. Scrapped at Southend. Canx.
G-AONJ	Percival P.40 Prentice T.1	PAC/353	VS751	22. 5.56	Not converted. Scrapped at Southend. Canx.
G-AONK	Percival P.40 Prentice T.1	PAC/342	VS740	22. 5.56	Not converted. Scrapped at Stansted. Canx.
G-AONL	Percival P.40 Prentice T.1	PAC/339	VS737	22. 5.56	Not converted. Scrapped at Southend. Canx.
G-AONM	Percival P.40 Prentice T.1	PAC/335	VS733	22. 5.56	Not converted. Scrapped at Southend. Canx.
G-AONN	Percival P.40 Prentice T.1	PAC/330	VS728	22. 5.56	Not converted. Scrapped at Stansted. Canx.
G-AONO	Percival P.40 Prentice T.1	PAC/329	VS727	22. 5.56	Not converted. Scrapped at Southend. Canx.
G-AONP	Percival P.40 Prentice T.1	PAC/328	VS726	22. 5.56	Not converted. Scrapped at Stansted. Canx.
G-AONR	Percival P.40 Prentice T.1	PAC/325	VS724	22. 5.56	Not converted. Scrapped at Stansted. Canx.
G-AONS	Percival P.40 Prentice T.1	PAC/312	VS687	22. 5.56	To VH-BAO 3/58. Canx.
G-AONT	Percival P.40 Prentice T.1	PAC/310	VS684	22. 5.56	Not converted. Scrapped at Stansted. Canx.
G-AONU	Percival P.40 Prentice T.1	PAC/305	VS681	22. 5.56	Not converted. Scrapped at Stansted. Canx.
G-AONV	Percival P.40 Prentice T.1	PAC/291	VS648	22. 5.56	Not converted. Scrapped at Stansted. Canx.
G-AONW	Percival P.40 Prentice T.1	PAC/285	VS643	22. 5.56	Not converted. Scrapped at Stansted. Canx.
G-AONX	Percival P.40 Prentice T.1	PAC/273	VS639	22. 5.56	Not converted. Scrapped at Southend. Canx.
G-AONY	Percival P.40 Prentice T.1	PAC/259	VS634	22. 5.56	Not converted. Scrapped at Stansted. Canx.
G-AONZ	Percival P.40 Prentice T.1	5800/2	VS242	22. 5.56	Not converted. Scrapped at Southend. Canx.
G-AOOA	Percival P.40 Prentice T.1	5800/3	VS243	30. 5.56	Not converted. Scrapped at Stansted. Canx.
G-AOOB	Percival P.40 Prentice T.1	5800/4	VS244	30. 5.56	Not converted. Scrapped at Southend. Canx.
G-AOOC	Percival P.40 Prentice T.1	5800/6	VS246	30. 5.56	Not converted. Scrapped at Southend. Canx.
G-AOOD	Percival P.40 Prentice T.1	5800/13	VS253	30. 5.56	Not converted. Scrapped at Stansted. Canx.
G-AOOE	Percival P.40 Prentice T.1	5800/16	VS256	30. 5.56	Not converted. Scrapped at Stansted. Canx.
G-AOOF	Percival P.40 Prentice T.1	5800/17	VS257	30. 5.56	Not converted. Scrapped at Southend. Canx.
G-AOOG	Percival P.40 Prentice T.1	5810/4	VS269	30. 5.56	Not converted. Scrapped at Stansted. Canx.
G-AOOH	Percival P.40 Prentice T.1	5810/8	VS273	30. 5.56	Not converted. Scrapped at Stansted. Canx.
G-AOOI	Percival P.40 Prentice T.1	5810/11	VS276	30. 5.56	Not converted. Scrapped at Stansted. Canx.
G-AOOJ	Percival P.40 Prentice T.1	5810/12	VS277	30. 5.56	Not converted. Scrapped at Stansted. Canx.
G-AOOK	Percival P.40 Prentice T.1	5810/24	VS289	30. 5.56	Not converted. Scrapped at Stansted. Canx.
G-AOOL	Percival P.40 Prentice T.1	5820/2	VS317	30. 5.56	Not converted. Scrapped at Stansted. Canx.
G-AOOM	Percival P.40 Prentice T.1	5820/6	VS321	30. 5.56	Not converted. Scrapped at Stansted. Canx.
G-AOON	Percival P.40 Prentice T.1	5820/7	VS322	30. 5.56	Not converted. Scrapped at Southend. Canx.
G-AOOO	Percival P.40 Prentice T.1	5820/8	VS323	30. 5.56	Not converted. Scrapped at Stansted. Canx.
G-AOOP	Percival P.40 Prentice T.1	5820/10	VS325	30. 5.56	Not converted. Scrapped at Stansted. Canx.
G-AOOR	Percival P.40 Prentice T.1	5820/13	VS328	30. 5.56	Not converted. Scrapped at Southend. Canx.
G-AOOS	Percival P.40 Prentice T.1	5820/17	VS332	30. 5.56	Not converted. Scrapped at Southend. Canx.
G-AOOT	Percival P.40 Prentice T.1	5820/18	VS333	30. 5.56	Not converted. Scrapped at Stansted. Canx.
G-AOOU	Percival P.40 Prentice T.1	5820/19	VS334	30. 5.56	Not converted. Scrapped at Stansted. Canx.
G-AOOV	Percival P.40 Prentice T.1	5820/22	VS338	30. 5.56	Not converted. Scrapped at Stansted. Canx.
G-AOOW	Percival P.40 Prentice T.1	5820/24	VS352	30. 5.56	Not converted. Scrapped at Stansted. Canx.
G-AOOX	Percival P.40 Prentice T.1	5830/1	VS354	30. 5.56	Not converted. Scrapped at Stansted. Canx.
G-AOOY	Percival P.40 Prentice T.1	5830/2	VS355	30. 5.56	Not converted. Scrapped at Stansted. Canx.
G-AOOZ	Percival P.40 Prentice T.1	5830/4	VS357	30. 5.56	Not converted. Scrapped at Stansted. Canx.
G-AOPA	Percival P.40 Prentice T.1	5830/9	VS362	30. 5.56	Not converted. Scrapped at Stansted. Canx.
G-AOPB	Percival P.40 Prentice T.1	5830/10	VS363	30. 5.56	Not converted. Scrapped at Stansted. Canx.
G-AOPC	Percival P.40 Prentice T.1	5830/11	VS364	30. 5.56	Not converted. Scrapped at Stansted. Canx.
G-AOPD	Percival P.40 Prentice T.1	5830/20	VS373	30. 5.56	Not converted. Scrapped at Stansted. Canx.
G-AOPE	Percival P.40 Prentice T.1	5830/24	VS377	30. 5.56	Not converted. Scrapped at Stansted. Canx.
G-AOPF	Percival P.40 Prentice T.1	5830/25	VS378	30. 5.56	Not converted. Scrapped at Stansted. Canx.
G-AOPG	Percival P.40 Prentice T.1	5840/6	VS384	30. 5.56	Not converted. DBR in gales at Southend 3.11.57. Canx.
G-AOPH	Percival P.40 Prentice T.1	5840/9	VS387	30. 5.56	Not converted. Scrapped at Stansted. Canx.
G-AOPI	Percival P.40 Prentice T.1	5840/14	VS392	30. 5.56	Not converted. Scrapped at Stansted. Canx.

Regn	Type	c/n	Previous identity	Regn date	Fate or immediate subsequent identity (if known)
G-AOPJ	Percival P.40 Prentice T.1	5840/15	VS393	30. 5.56	Not converted. Scrapped at Southend. Canx.
G-AOPK	Percival P.40 Prentice T.1	5840/22	VS411	30. 5.56	Not converted. Scrapped at Southend. Canx.
G-AOPL	Percival P.40 Prentice T.1	PAC/207	VS609	30. 5.56	To ZS-EUS 5/67. Canx 24.4.67.
G-AOPM	Percival P.40 Prentice T.1	PAC/211	VS611	30. 5.56	Not converted. Scrapped at Stansted. Canx.
G-AOPN	Percival P.40 Prentice T.1	PAC/214	VS612	30. 5.56	Not converted. Scrapped at Southend. Canx.
G-AOPO	Percival P.40 Prentice T.1	PAC/215	VS613	30. 5.56	To OO-OPO 4/58. Canx 11.9.58.
G-AOPP	Percival P.40 Prentice T.1	PAC/216	VS614	30. 5.56	Not converted. Scrapped at Stansted. Canx.
G-AOPR	Percival P.40 Prentice T.1	PAC/220	VS615	30. 5.56	Not converted. Scrapped at Stansted. Canx.
G-AOPS	Percival P.40 Prentice T.1	PAC/223	VS616	30. 5.56	Not converted. Scrapped at Stansted. Canx.
G-AOPT	Percival P.40 Prentice T.1	PAC/226	VS619	30. 5.56	Not converted. Scrapped at Southend. Canx.
G-AOPU	Percival P.40 Prentice T.1	PAC/237	VS622	30. 5.56	Not converted. Scrapped at Southend. Canx.
G-AOPV	Percival P.40 Prentice T.1	PAC/240	VS625	30. 5.56	Not converted. Scrapped at Stansted. Canx.
G-AOPW	Percival P.40 Prentice T.1	PAC/244	(OO-CDR) G-AOPW/VS628	30. 5.56	Fatal crash & DBF when it struck the ground while being demonstrated in an air display at Barton on 9.8.59. Canx.
G-AOPX	Percival P.40 Prentice T.1	PAC/252	VS631	30. 5.56	Not converted. Scrapped at Stansted. Canx.
G-AOPY	Percival P.40 Prentice T.1	PAC/255	VS633	30. 5.56	Not converted. Scrapped at Stansted. Canx. (In a playgroun at Basildon New Town fitted with a dummy nose in 1967)
G-AOPZ	DHC.1 Chipmunk 22A (Fuselage no. DHB/f/60) (Originally regd as a Mk.22)	C1/0161	WB713	16. 4.56	DBR at Netherthorpe on 8.4.62. Canx.
G-AORA	DH.82A Tiger Moth	3364	BB750 G-ADLV	17. 5.56	To SE-CWG 8/63. Canx 21.6.63.
G-AORB(1)	Bristol 173 Mk.3	13206	XE288 (G-AMYH)	20. 4.56	NTU - Not completed. Canx.
G-AORB(2)	Cessna 170B	20767	OO-SIZ N2615D	13. 2.84	
G-AORC(1)	Vickers 802 Viscount	253		. .56R	NTU - To G-AOHW. Canx.
G-AORC(2)	Vickers 802 Viscount	254	(G-AORD)	14. 5.56	Hit power lines and crashed at Craigie, 4½ miles ENE of Prestwick on 28.4.58 & DBF. Canx.
G-AORD(1)	Vickers 802 Viscount	254		. .56R	NTU - To G-AORC. Canx.
G-AORD(2)	Vickers 802 Viscount	171	(G-AOHW)	14. 5.56	WFU & stored in 12/75 at Birmingham. To Fire service & DBF by 1976. Canx as WFU 19.1.76.
G-AORE	DHC.1 Chipmunk 22 (Fuselage no. DHB/f/90)	C1/0206	WB757	24. 4.56	Canx 14.7.71 on sale to USA.
G-AORF	DHC.1 Chipmunk 22 (Fuselage no. DHH/f/..)	C1/0089	WB648	30. 4.56	Crashed on take-off from White Waltham on 21.7.68. Canx.
G-AORG	DH.114 Heron 2B	14101	XR441 G-AORG/G-5-16	1. 5.56	
G-AORH	DH.114 Heron 2B	14102		1. 5.56	To Royal Navy as XR442. Canx 17.4.61.
G-AORI	Taylorcraft Auster 5	1154	RT489	26. 4.56	Crashed at Stagsend, Bedfordshire on 7.12.56. Canx.
G-AORJ	DH.114 Heron 2E	14104		27. 4.56	To PH-ILA(2) 1/59. Canx 15.1.59.
G-AORK	DHC.1 Chipmunk 22 (Fuselage no. DHB/f/123)	C1/0238	WD298	27. 4.56	To N8345 1/69. Canx in 11.68.
G-AORL	DHC.1 Chipmunk 22 (Fuselage no. DHB/f/39)	C1/0131	WB683	27. 4.56	To VH-DCZ 2/87. Canx 8.9.86.
G-AORM	DH.104 Dove 6A	04468		28. 4.56	To N70L 6/56. Canx.
G-AORN	Auster J/1N Alpha	3352		30. 4.56	Crashed near Boston, Lincs on 6.7.58. On scrap-heap at Rearsby by 9/59. Canx.
G-AORO	PA-22-150 Tri-Pacer	22-2098	VP-KMY N3277B	2. 5.56	WFU at Stapleford in 10/64. Canx.
G-AORP	DHC.1 Chipmunk 22 (Fuselage no. DHH/f/40)	C1/0134	WB686	1. 5.56	Crashed on landing at Petticoe Wick Bay, Berwick on 8.5.60 Noted at Perth marked as "G-PDWO" in 9/67 (until 1974/5). Canx.
G-AORR	DHC.1 Chipmunk 22 (Fuselage no. DHH/f/19)	C1/0018	HB-TUB G-AORR/WB566	7. 5.56	To ZK-TNR 2/84. Canx 17.2.84.
G-AORS	DHC.1 Chipmunk 22 (Fuselage no. DHB/f/106)	C1/0223	WD284	7. 5.56	To D-EHUM 12/56. Canx 14.11.56.
G-AORT	Westland-Sikorsky S-55 Whirlwind Srs.1	WA/173	G-17-1	7. 5.56	To HZ-ABE 12/56. Canx 19.11.56.
G-AORU	DHC.1 Chipmunk 22 (Fuselage no. DHH/f/..)	C1/0170	WB718	10. 5.56	To HB-TUD 8/57. Canx 1.6.57.
G-AORV	DHC.1 Chipmunk 22 (Fuselage no. DHH/f/117)	C1/0177	WB725	15. 5.56	Crashed at Crowcombe, Somerset on 9.11.60. Canx.
G-AORW	DHC.1 Chipmunk 22A (Fuselage no. DHB/f/38) (Originally regd as a Mk.22)	C1/0130	WB682	28. 5.56	
G-AORX	DH.82A Tiger Moth	83866	T7340	22. 5.56	To HB-UBB 8/56. Canx 8.8.56.
G-AORY	DH.82A Tiger Moth	85508	DE528	22. 5.56	To SE-CGA 5/57. Canx 14.4.57.
G-AORZ	DH.82A Tiger Moth	84122	T7740	22. 5.56	To F-OAZV 7/57. Canx 14.8.56.
G-AOSA	DHC.1 Chipmunk 22 (Fuselage no. DHB/f/165)	C1/0285	WD348	5. 7.56	Crashed into trees at Coupar Angus, Fife on 4.12.66. Canx.
G-AOSB	DHC.1 Chipmunk 22 (Fuselage no. DHB/f/166)	C1/0287	WD349	5. 7.56	To VH-RSN 7/58. Canx 31.3.58.
G-AOSC	DHC.1 Chipmunk 22 (Fuselage no. DHB/f/3)	C1/0057	WB616	5. 7.56	To VH-MOE 4/57. Canx 22.11.56.
G-AOSD	DH.82A Tiger Moth	83483	T5826	25. 6.56	Crashed at Syerston on 30.3.58. Canx.
G-AOSE	DH.104 Dove 6	04470		18. 6.56	Scrapped in 1974 at Coventry. Canx as WFU 30.5.84.
G-AOSF	DHC.1 Chipmunk 22 (Fuselage no. DHH/f/27)	C1/0023	D-EIIZ G-AOSF/HB-TUA/G-AOSF/WB571	25. 6.56	
G-AOSG	PA-18-135 Super Cub	18-4036	OO-ALH (OO-LVV)/Italian AF MM54-2436/I-EIVT/MM54-2436/54-2436	. .84R	NTU - To G-BLFB 2/84. Canx.
G-AOSH	DHC.1 Chipmunk 22 (Fuselage no. DHH/f/26)	C1/0022	WB570	27. 6.56	To HB-TUC. Canx 1.3.57.
G-AOSI	DHC.1 Chipmunk 22 (Fuselage no. DHH/f/62)	C1/0054	WB613	27. 6.56	To VR-SDW 5/57. Canx 2.4.57.

Regn	Type	c/n	Previous identity	Regn date	Fate or immediate subsequent identity (if known)
G-AOSJ	DHC.1 Chipmunk 22 (Fuselage no. DHH/f/70)	C1/0071	WB628	27. 6.56	Crashed near Kidlington on 26.2.61. Canx.
G-AOSK	DHC.1 Chipmunk 22A (Fuselage no. DHH/f/121) (Originally regd as a Mk.22)	C1/0178	WB726	26. 6.56	
G-AOSL	Taylorcraft Auster 5M (Originally regd as an Auster 5)	1815	TW477	9. 7.56	To D-ENIR 3/60. Canx 19.12.59
G-AOSM	DH.82A Tiger Moth	84896	T6567	23. 6.56	Crashed at Fishtoft, near Boston on 30.1.60. Canx.
G-AOSN	DHC.1 Chipmunk 22 (Fuselage no. DHH/f/28)	C1/0026	WB574	26. 6.56	Crashed at Church Hill, Harefield on 19.2.77 & DBR. Canx.
G-AOSO	DHC.1 Chipmunk 22 (Fuselage no. DHB/f/112)	C1/0227	(F-AZDN) G-AOSO/WD288	26. 6.56	
G-AOSP	DHC.1 Chipmunk 22 (Fuselage no. DHH/f/108)	C1/0174	WB722	26. 6.56	To VH-BTL. Canx.
G-AOSR	DHC.1 Chipmunk 22 (Fuselage no. DHH/f/68)	C1/0062	WB621	26. 6.56	To VH-BSV 7/60. Canx.
G-AOSS	DH.98 Mosquito B.35	-	TK655	26. 6.56	Not converted. Scrapped at Burnaston in 1960. Canx.
G-AOST	DHC.1 Chipmunk 22 (Fuselage no. DHB/f/41)	C1/0135	WB687	6. 7.56	To N2790 6/70. Canx 20.5.70.
G-AOSU	DHC.1 Chipmunk 22 (Fuselage no. DHB/f/100) (Lyc O-360)	C1/0217	WB766	28. 6.56	
G-AOSV	DHC.1 Chipmunk 22 (Fuselage no. DHH/f/16)	C1/0016	WB564	28. 6.56	To OH-HCD 10/56. Canx 1.9.56.
G-AOSW	DHC.1 Chipmunk 22 (Fuselage no. DHB/f/104)	C1/0221	WD283	28. 6.56	To ZK-BSV 12/59. Canx 19.10.59.
G-AOSX	DHC.1 Chipmunk 22 (Fuselage no. DHB/f/393)	C1/0512	OH-HCC G-AOSX/WG462	29. 6.56	Flew into wires at Walpole St.Peter, Norfolk on 3.11.64. Canx.
G-AOSY	DHC.1 Chipmunk 22 (Fuselage no. DHH/f/39)	C1/0037	WB585	29. 6.56	
G-AOSZ	DHC.1 Chipmunk 22A (Fuselage no. DHB/f/13) (Originally regd as a Mk.22)	C1/0080	WB635	29. 6.56	To G-TRIC 12/89. Canx.
G-AOTA	DHC.1 Chipmunk 22 (Fuselage no. DHH/f/109)	C1/0127	WB679	29. 6.56	To VH-BSU 12/57. Canx.
G-AOTB	DHC.1 Chipmunk 22 (Fuselage no. DHB/f/47)	C1/0143	WB695	29. 6.56	To VH-WFD. Canx.
G-AOTC	DHC.1 Chipmunk 22 (Fuselage no. DHH/f/98)	C1/0158	WB712	29. 6.56	Damaged in heavy landing at Scone, Perthshire on 31.1.58. (Dented fuselage at Burnaston in 8/58) Canx.
G-AOTD	DHC.1 Chipmunk 22 (Fuselage no. DHH/f/44)	C1/0040	WB588	30. 6.56	
G-AOTE	DH.104 Dove 6	04471	G-5-17	2. 7.56	To VH-DHE 10/56. Canx 28.9.56.
G-AOTF	DHC.1 Chipmunk 23 (Fuselage no. DHH/f/16) (Lyc O-360)	C1/0015	WB563	2. 7.56	
G-AOTG	DHC.1 Chipmunk 22 (Fuselage no. DHB/f/426)	C1/0541	WG491	2. 7.56	To N88GF 12/68. Canx 7.12.68.
G-AOTH	DHC.1 Chipmunk 22 (Fuselage no. DHH/f/59)	C1/0052	Lebanese Army/G-AOTH/WB611	3. 7.56	Fatal crash at Fawley Green, Henley on 6.2.70. Canx.
G-AOTI	DH.114 Heron 2D	14107	G-5-19	25. 7.56	CofA expired 24.6.87 and WFU at Biggin Hill. (On display 5/96 Salisbury Hall, London Colney) Canx as WFU 17.10.95.
G-AOTJ	Taylorcraft Auster 5	1760	TW388	9. 7.56	Crashed River Esk, Langholm, Dumfries on 7.10.63. Canx.
G-AOTK	Druine D.53 Turbi	1 & PFA/230		1.11.56	
G-AOTL	DHC.1 Chipmunk 22 (Fuselage no. DHH/f/86)	C1/0122	WB674	11. 7.56	To VH-RVR. Canx.
G-AOTM	DHC.1 Chipmunk 22A (Fuselage no. DHH/f/758) (Originally regd as a Mk.22)	C1/0862	WP988	11. 7.56	To N65312 4/76. Canx 26.4.76.
G-AOTN	DHC.1 Chipmunk 22 (Fuselage no. DHH/f/25)	C1/0024	WB572	13. 7.56	To VH-BON 9/57. Canx 11.6.57.
G-AOTO	DHC.1 Chipmunk 22 (Fuselage no. DHB/f/88)	C1/0204	WB755	13. 7.56	To R.Jordanian AF as T-212 10/56. Canx.
G-AOTP	DHC.1 Chipmunk 22 (Fuselage no. DHH/f/33)	C1/0034	WB582	12. 7.56	Crashed in forced-landing at Merry Hill Farm, Bushey Heath, Herts., on 11.6.59. Remains to Elstree by 7/59. Canx.
G-AOTR	DHC.1 Chipmunk 22 (Fuselage no. DHH/f/50)	C1/0045	HB-TUH D-EGOG/G-AOTR/WB604	12. 7.56	
G-AOTS	DHC.1 Chipmunk 22 (Fuselage no. DHH/f/55)	C1/0046	WB605	12. 7.56	To D-EMID 10/56. Canx 17.10.56.
G-AOTT	DHC.1 Chipmunk 22A (Fuselage no. DHH/f/58) (Originally regd as a Mk.22)	C1/0053	WB612	12. 7.56	To (D-EMEF)/D-EMUM 12/58. Canx 18.12.58.
G-AOTU	DHC.1 Chipmunk 22A (Fuselage no. DHB/f/102) (Originally regd as a Mk.22)	C1/0219	WB768	12. 7.56	To 5N-AGO 11/62. Canx 14.11.62.
G-AOTV	DHC.1 Chipmunk 22 (Fuselage no. DHB/f/349) (Originally regd as a Mk.22)	C1/0482	WG408	12. 7.56	To N19547 6/76. Canx 1.6.76.
G-AOTW	DHC.1 Chipmunk 22 (Fuselage no. DHB/f/92)	C1/0208	WB759	12. 7.56	To D-ELEF 10/56. Canx 17.10.56.
G-AOTX	DHC.1 Chipmunk 22A (Fuselage no. DHH/f/5) (Originally regd as a Mk.22)	C1/0005	WB553	12. 7.56	To HB-TUL 11/69. Canx 11.11.69.
G-AOTY	DHC.1 Chipmunk 22A (Fuselage no. DHB/f/403) (Originally regd as a Mk.22)	C1/0522	WG472	12. 7.56	
G-AOTZ	DHC.1 Chipmunk 22A (Fuselage no. DHB/f/340) (Originally regd as a Mk.22)	C1/0475	WG401	12. 7.56	To OO-FFT 4/72. Canx 24.3.72.
G-AOUA	DH.104 Dove 6A	04475		12. 7.56	To N435T 9/56. Canx 25.9.56.
G-AOUB	DHC.1 Chipmunk 22 (Fuselage no. DHB/f/61)	C1/0162	WB714	16. 7.56	To VH-RNE. Canx 4.10.56.
G-AOUC	DHC.1 Chipmunk 22 (Fuselage no. DHB/f/354)	C1/0486	WG412	16. 7.56	To VH-RNJ. Canx 4.10.56.

Regn	Type	c/n	Previous identity	Regn date	Fate or immediate subsequent identity (if known)
G-AOUD	Douglas C-47B-1-DL Dakota	14128/25573	I-LILI 43-48312	10. 8.56	To N4848 in 2/69. Canx 30.1.69.
G-AOUE	Scottish Aviation Pioneer 2	SAL/PP/119		25. 7.56	DBR at Fort Bragg, USA on 6.11.56. Canx.
G-AOUF	DH.104 Dove 6	04476		19. 7.56	To D-IBYW 7/68. Canx 23.4.68.
G-AOUG	DH.104 Dove 6	04478	302 KAF-AB 9K-AAB/K-AAAB/G-AOUG	25. 7.56	CofA expired 21.3.61. Probably destroyed in the fighting i the Lebanon. Canx by CAA 15.9.86.
G-AOUH	DH.104 Dove 6	04479	301 KAF-AC 9K-AAC/K-AAAC/G-AOUH	25. 7.56	CofA expired 10.4.61. Probably destroyed in the fighting i the Lebanon. Canx by CAA 15.9.86.
G-AOUI	DH.82A Tiger Moth	85374	DE352	10. 8.56	To I-CEDI 3/65. Canx 18.2.65.
G-AOUJ	Fairey Ultralight Helicopter	F.9424	XJ928	1. 8.56	CofA expired 29.9.59 & WFU at White Waltham. (Stored 8/97 Weston-super-Mare)
G-AOUK	Fairey Ultralight Helicopter	F.9426	XJ936	1. 8.56	NTU. Canx in 1958.
G-AOUL	Taylorcraft Auster 5D	1755	TW389	7. 8.56	Crashed at Baldock, Herts on 16.5.61. Canx.
G-AOUM	DHC.1 Chipmunk 22 (Fuselage no. DHB/f/494)	C1/0616	WK607	8. 8.56	To ZK-BSS 5/57. Canx.
G-AOUN	DHC.1 Chipmunk 22 (Fuselage no. DHB/f/43)	C1/0137	WB689	10. 8.56	To OO-NCL 2/70. Canx 14.8.69.
G-AOUO	DHC.1 Chipmunk 22 (Fuselage no. DHB/f/66) (Lyc O-360)	C1/0179	WB730	10. 8.56	
G-AOUP	DHC.1 Chipmunk 22 (Fuselage no. DHB/f/67)	C1/0180	WB731	10. 8.56	
G-AOUR	DH.82A Tiger Moth	86341	NL898	14. 8.56	Crashed at Newtownards on 6.6.65. (Stored 4/96 Cultra Manor, Holywood)
G-AOUS	Hunting Percival P.84 Jet Provost T.2B (Originally regd as a T.2)	P.84/14		16. 8.56	Crashed at Biggleswade, Beds on 16.11.60. Canx.
G-AOUT	Airspeed AS.40 Oxford I	-	O-6 Belgian AF/MP301	27. 8.56	Not converted. Burned in 8/56 at Ringway. Canx.
G-AOUU	Bristol 170 Freighter 32	13257	G-18-204	24. 8.56	WFU on 15.6.65 at Lydd. Broken up in 5/67. Canx.
G-AOUV	Bristol 170 Freighter 32	13258	G-18-205	24. 8.56	CofA expired 20.5.67. WFU at Lydd. Broken up in 4/68. Canx
G-AOUW	DH.82A Tiger Moth	82356	N9255	25. 9.56	To F-BDVJ 4/57. Canx 28.1.57.
G-AOUX	DH.82A Tiger Moth	3956	N6652	25. 9.56	To HB-UBC 10/56. Canx 2.11.56.
G-AOUY	DH.82A Tiger Moth	3796	N6459	25. 9.56	Crashed at Nelson, Glam on 24.5.62. Canx.
G-AOUZ	DH.82A Tiger Moth	85348	EI-AJP G-AOUZ/DE314	25. 9.56	To F-OAQF 11/57. Canx 14.8.57.
G-AOVA	Bristol 175 Britannia Srs.319 (Originally regd as a Srs.312)	13207	9G-AAH G-AOVA/(G-AOFA)/(G-AMYK)	21.11.55	WFU on 5.5.70 & used for spares 10/71 at Baginton. Canx.
G-AOVB	Bristol 175 Britannia Srs.312F (Originally regd as Srs.312)	13230		28. 1.57	To LV-PNJ/LV-JNL 10/69. Canx 3.10.69.
G-AOVC	Bristol 175 Britannia Srs.312	13231	(G-AOFC)	13. 2.57	Used by Dept of Trade & Industry fire school in 11/70 at Stansted. CofA expired 2.6.70. Canx as WFU 17.11.70.
G-AOVD	Bristol 175 Britannia Srs.312	13235	(G-AOFD)	13. 2.57	Crashed & DBF at Sopley Farm, Winkton, near Christchurch, Hants., on 24.12.58. Canx.
G-AOVE	Bristol 175 Britannia Srs.312	13236	(G-AOFE)	13. 2.57	To EC-WFK/EC-BFK in 11/66. Canx 30.11.66.
G-AOVF	Bristol 175 Britannia Srs.312F (Originally regd as Srs.312)	13237	9Q-CAZ G-AOVF/(G-AOFF)	13. 2.57	WFU at Manston. Flown to Cosford 31.5.84. Canx as WFU 21.11.84. (On display RAF Cosford)
G-AOVG	Bristol 175 Britannia Srs.312	13238	(G-AOFG)	13. 2.57	WFU on 30.1.74. Broken up in 8/74 at Luton. Canx.
G-AOVH	Bristol 175 Britannia Srs.312	12925	(G-ANCI)	13. 2.57	WFU & used as a cabin trainer in 11/71. Canx as destroyed 26.5.72 and broken up at Luton.
G-AOVI	Bristol 175 Britannia Srs.312	12926	(G-ANCJ)	13. 2.57	WFU in 1/72. Canx as destroyed 26.5.72 & broken up at Luto
G-AOVJ	Bristol 175 Britannia Srs.312	13418	(G-AOFJ)	13. 2.57	WFU & used for spares in 12/70 at Stansted until DBF. Canx
G-AOVK	Bristol 175 Britannia Srs.312	13419		13. 2.57	Broken up in 2/70 at Luton. Canx as WFU 27.2.70.
G-AOVL	Bristol 175 Britannia Srs.312	13420		21. 5.57	Broken up in 7/71 at Luton. Canx as destroyed 26.5.72.
G-AOVM	Bristol 175 Britannia Srs.312F (Converted to Srs.312F in 1968)	13421		21. 5.57	To EC-BSY 12/69. Canx 1.12.69.
G-AOVN	Bristol 175 Britannia Srs.312	13422		21. 5.57	WFU in 11/73. Broken up in 2/74 at Luton. Canx.
G-AOVO	Bristol 175 Britannia Srs.312	13423		21. 5.57	Fatal crash on 29.2.64 into mountain 10m ESE of Innsbruck, Austria. Canx.
G-AOVP	Bristol 175 Britannia Srs.312F (Converted to Srs.312F in 1968)	13424		21. 5.57	CofA expired 6.8.75 & WFU. Broken up at Biggin Hill. Canx as WFU 5.12.83.
G-AOVR	Bristol 175 Britannia Srs.317 (Originally regd as a Srs.312)	13429		21. 5.57	To EC-WFJ/EC-BFJ in 10/66. Canx 17.10.66.
G-AOVS	Bristol 175 Britannia Srs.312F	13430		28. 2.58	Broken up in 10/79 at Luton. To cabin trainer at East Midlands Airport. Canx.
G-AOVT	Bristol 175 Britannia Srs.317 (Originally regd as a Srs.312)	13427		23. 6.58	WFU at Luton 10.3.75. Canx as WFU 21.9.81. (On display 7/99 Duxford)
G-AOVU	DH.106 Comet 4C	6424	(G-APMD) (G-APDN)	22.10.59	To XA-NAR 3/60. Canx 25.3.60.
G-AOVV	DH.106 Comet 4C	6425	(G-APME)	12.11.59	To XA-NAS 1/60. Canx 11.1.60.
G-AOVW	Taylorcraft Auster 5 (Mod)	894	MT119	16.11.59	
G-AOVX	Luton LA-5 Major	PAL/1207		18.11.59	Incorporated into G-ARAF late-1960. Canx as WFU 23.2.73.
G-AOVY	DH.104 Dove 1 (Converted to Dove 1B in 1961) (Reverted to Dove 1 in 1967)	04009	ZS-CAG ZS-BCB	22. 1.60	WFU at Luton on 3.4.68. Canx as WFU 16.1.69. Chopped up & remains removed from Denham in 4/69.
G-AOVZ	Jodel D.140 Mousquetaire	42		23. 3.60	DBR at Castlebridge, Wexford on 14.9.75. Canx as destroyed 27.11.75.
G-AOWA	Percival P.40 Prentice T.1	PAC/043	VR222	1.10.56	Not converted. Scrapped at Southend. Canx.
G-AOWB	Percival P.40 Prentice T.1	PAC/095	VR267	1.10.56	Not converted. Scrapped at Stansted. Canx.
G-AOWC	Percival P.40 Prentice T.1	PAC/149	VR302	1.10.56	Not converted. Scrapped at Stansted. Canx.
G-AOWD	Percival P.40 Prentice T.1	PAC/154	VR305	1.10.56	Not converted. Scrapped at Stansted. Canx.
G-AOWE	Percival P.40 Prentice T.1	PAC/179	VR312	1.10.56	Not converted. Scrapped at Stansted. Canx.
G-AOWF	Percival P.40 Prentice T.1	PAC/194	VR318	1.10.56	Not converted. DBR in gales at Stansted on 3.11.57. Canx.

Regn	Type	c/n	Previous identity	Regn date	Fate or immediate subsequent identity (if known)
G-AOWG	Percival P.40 Prentice T.1	PAC/205	VR324	1.10.56	Not converted. Scrapped at Stansted. Canx.
G-AOWH	Percival P.40 Prentice T.1	5800/1	VS241	1.10.56	Not converted. Scrapped at Stansted. Canx.
G-AOWI	Percival P.40 Prentice T.1	5800/7	VS247	1.10.56	Not converted. Scrapped at Stansted. Canx.
G-AOWJ	Percival P.40 Prentice T.1	5800/8	VS248	1.10.56	Not converted. Scrapped at Stansted. Canx.
G-AOWK	Percival P.40 Prentice T.1	5800/9	VS249	1.10.56	Not converted. Scrapped at Stansted. Canx.
G-AOWL	Percival P.40 Prentice T.1	5810/7	VS272	1.10.56	Not converted. Scrapped at Stansted. Canx.
G-AOWM	Percival P.40 Prentice T.1	5820/20	VS335	1.10.56	Not converted. Scrapped at Stansted. Canx.
G-AOWN	Percival P.40 Prentice T.1	5820/21	VS336	1.10.56	Not converted. Scrapped at Stansted. Canx.
G-AOWO	Percival P.40 Prentice T.1	5830/18	VS371	1.10.56	Not converted. Scrapped at Stansted. Canx.
G-AOWP	Percival P.40 Prentice T.1	5830/23	VS376	1.10.56	Not converted. Scrapped at Stansted. Canx.
G-AOWR	Percival P.40 Prentice T.1	5840/2	VS380	1.10.56	Not converted. Scrapped at Stansted. Canx.
G-AOWS	Percival P.40 Prentice T.1	5840/11	VS389	1.10.56	Not converted. Scrapped at Stansted. Canx.
G-AOWT	Percival P.40 Prentice T.1	5840/19	VS397	1.10.56	To OD-ACQ 12/58. Canx 19.12.58.
G-AOWU	Percival P.40 Prentice T.1	5840/20	VS409	1.10.56	Not converted. Scrapped at Southend. Canx.
G-AOWV	Percival P.40 Prentice T.1	5840/21	VS410	1.10.56	Not converted. Scrapped at Stansted. Canx.
G-AOWW	Percival P.40 Prentice T.1	PAC/290	VS646	1.10.56	Not converted. Scrapped at Stansted. Canx.
G-AOWX	Percival P.40 Prentice T.1	PAC/318	VS693	1.10.56	Not converted. Scrapped at Stansted. Canx.
G-AOWY	Percival P.40 Prentice T.1	PAC/319	VS694	1.10.56	Not converted. Scrapped at Stansted. Canx.
G-AOWZ	Percival P.40 Prentice T.1	PAC/321	VS696	1.10.56	Not converted. Scrapped at Stansted. Canx.
G-AOXA	Percival P.40 Prentice T.1	PAC/322	VS697	1.10.56	Not converted. Scrapped at Stansted. Canx.
G-AOXB	Percival P.40 Prentice T.1	PAC/336	VS734	1.10.56	Not converted. Scrapped at Stansted. Canx.
G-AOXC	Percival P.40 Prentice T.1	PAC/338	VS736	1.10.56	Not converted. Scrapped at Southend. Canx.
G-AOXD	Percival P.40 Prentice T.1	PAC/341	VS739	1.10.56	Not converted. Scrapped at Stansted. Canx.
G-AOXE	Percival P.40 Prentice T.1	PAC/356	VS754	1.10.56	Not converted. Scrapped at Stansted. Canx.
G-AOXF	DH.82A Tiger Moth	85454	DE458	3.10.56	To F-OBAK 6/57. Canx 1.1.57.
G-AOXG	DH.82A Tiger Moth	83805	T7291	3.10.56	To RN as XL717 in 10/56. Canx.
G-AOXH	DH.115 Vampire T.55	15798	G-5-11	4.10.56	To Chilean AF as J-01 in 4/57. Canx 16.4.57.
G-AOXI	Douglas C-47B-1-DK Dakota (Fitted with Dart engines in 1957)	14168/25613	KJ829 G-AOXI/G-37-2/G-AOXI/KJ829/43-48352	17.10.56	Not converted and used for spares at Usworth in 11/64. Canx.
G-AOXJ	DH.82A Tiger Moth	84542	T6051	23.10.56	Crashed at Bawdsey, Suffolk on 23.4.60. Canx.
G-AOXK	Douglas DC-4-1009	42931	OY-DFI	15.10.56	To 5H-AAH 7/63. Canx 24.6.63.
G-AOXL	DH.114 Heron 1B	14015	(LN-BFY) G-AOXL/PK-GHB	5. 4.57	To LN-BFY 2/72. Canx 11.10.71.
"G-AOXL"	DH.114 Heron 2. See G-ANUO				
G-AOXM	DH.114 Heron 1B	14016	PK-GHC	5. 4.57R	NTU - Remained as PK-GHC. Canx.
G-AOXN	DH.82A Tiger Moth	85958	EM727	31.10.56	
G-AOXO	Tipsy Belfair	537	(OO-TIG)	7.11.56	Crashed at Eastbach Farm on 26.8.75. Canx.
G-AOXP	Scottish Aviation Pioneer Srs.2	SAL/PP/120		6.11.56	To EP-AHE 3/58. Canx 2.3.58.
G-AOXR	Auster J/1N Alpha (Rebuild of G-AHHR c/n 2020)	AUS.327FM		31.10.56	To CR-CAJ 7/62. Canx 19.6.62.
G-AOXS	DH.82A Tiger Moth	85425	DE417	9.11.56	Crashed near Reigate Heath on 28.2.60. Canx.
G-AOXT	Taylorcraft Auster 5	1756	TW386	20.11.56	To VP-TBZ 5/57. Canx 13.5.57.
G-AOXU	Vickers 804 Viscount	248		20.11.56	To SP-LVC 12/62. Canx 15.11.62.
G-AOXV	Vickers 804 Viscount	249		20.11.56	To SP-LVA 11/62. Canx 1.10.62.
G-AOXW	Miles M.65 Gemini 1A	6478	VP-KFJ VP-UAZ	20.11.56	CofA expired 3.1.60 and WFU at Foulsham. Canx.
G-AOXX	DH.82A Tiger Moth	84797	T6443	20.11.56	Scrapped at Rochester in 7/60. Canx.
G-AOXY(1)	Cessna 180	32554	N7657A	. .56R	NTU - To 5Y-AAK. Canx 1/58.
G-AOXY(2)	DH.82A Tiger Moth	84762	T6388	12.11.57	Struck overhead cables and DBF in resulting crash at Hesters Way Lane, Cheltenham on 6.7.59. Canx.
G-AOXZ	DH.114 Heron 2D	14109	G-5-11	21.11.56	To VP-BAN(2) 1/57. Canx 21.12.56.
G-AOYA	Taylorcraft Auster 5	2055	6799M TW515	26.11.56	To VP-AAG 8/57. Canx 11.7.57.
G-AOYB	Westland-Sikorsky S-55 Whirlwind Srs.3 (Originally regd as a Srs.1)	WA/191	VR-BBN G-AOYB	3.12.56	To D-HOBI 12/64. Canx 1.1.65.
G-AOYC	DH.104 Dove 6 (Originally regd as Srs.1, then 1B)	04065	(PK-...) G-AOYC/VT-COW	7.12.56	To PK-ICS 9/69. Canx 7.9.69.
G-AOYD	DH.104 Dove 2	04092	VT-CKE	1. 3.57	To N13114 6/67. Canx 10.4.67.
G-AOYE	Douglas C-47A-50-DL Dakota	10028	FL510 42-24166	17.12.56	To French AF as 24166 in 4/57. Canx 9.5.57.
G-AOYF	Vickers 806A Viscount	255		20.12.56	DBR on landing at Johannesburg, South Africa on 26.10.57. Shipped back to the UK. Some of the remains used in the building of G-APOX c/n 418. Canx.
G-AOYG	Vickers 806 Viscount	256		20.12.56	Broken up in 1/94 at Southend. Canx as destroyed 7.3.94.
G-AOYH(1)	Vickers 806 Viscount	257		. .56R	NTU - To G-AOYI 12/56. Canx.
G-AOYH(2)	Vickers 806 Viscount	311		20.12.56	To C-GWPY 7/83. Canx 21.7.83.
G-AOYI(1)	Vickers 808 Viscount	258		. .56R	NTU - To G-APDW 7/57. Canx.
G-AOYI(2)	Vickers 806 Viscount	257	G-LOND G-AOYI/(G-AOYH)	20.12.56	Restored as G-LOND 2/87. Canx.
G-AOYJ	Vickers 806 Viscount	259		20.12.56	To G-BLOA 8/84. Canx.
G-AOYK	Vickers 806 Viscount	260		20.12.56	To PK-RVK 5/70. Canx 11.4.70.
G-AOYL	Vickers 806 Viscount	261		20.12.56	WFU in 9/87. Used for spares. Broken up in 2/93 at Southend. Canx as destroyed 22.6.94.
G-AOYM	Vickers 806 Viscount	262		20.12.56	To EC-DYC 10/85. Canx 29.10.85.
G-AOYN	Vickers 806 Viscount	263		20.12.56	To G-OPAS 10/94. Canx.
G-AOYO	Vickers 806 Viscount	264		20.12.56	To EC-DXU 10/85. Canx 24.9.85.
G-AOYP	Vickers 806 Viscount	265		20.12.56	To G-PFBT 3/94. Canx.
G-AOYR	Vickers 806 Viscount	266		20.12.56	WFU 20.4.94 at Southend. Broken up in 6/96. Canx as destroyed 7.7.98.

Regn	Type	c/n	Previous identity	Regn date	Fate or immediate subsequent identity (if known)
G-AOYS	Vickers 806 Viscount	267		20.12.56	Broken up in 2/85 as Southend. Canx as WFU 30.11.88.
G-AOYT	Vickers 806 Viscount	268		20.12.56	To B-3001 4/69. Canx 12.5.69.
G-AOYU	DH.82A Tiger Moth	82270	N9151	27.12.56	Canx 14.7.71 on sale to USA. To C-GABB in 9/78.
G-AOYV	Vickers 827 Viscount (Originally regd as a Viscount 810, then as a 812)	316		20.12.56	To PP-SRH 10/60. Canx 21.3.60.
G-AOYW	Vickers 950 Vanguard	703		27.12.56	WFU & stored in 1962. Broken up in 1964 at Wisley.
G-AOYX	DHC.3 Otter	204		12. 4.57	Canx 27.6.61 on sale to Portugal. To TR-LLZ.
G-AOYY	Westland-Sikorsky S-55 Whirlwind Srs.2	WA/192		3. 1.57	To CF-KAD 7/57. Canx 8.7.57.
G-AOYZ	Westland-Sikorsky S-55 Whirlwind Srs.2	WA/193		3. 1.57	To CF-KAE 7/57. Canx 8.7.57.
G-AOZA	Douglas C-47B-25-DK Dakota	15800/32548	KN297 44-76216	8. 1.57	To French AF as 76216 in 11/57. Canx 29.7.57.
G-AOZB	DH.82A Tiger Moth	3917	N6616	9. 1.57	Mid-air collision with PA-28-181 G-BNNP on 19.5.90 resulting in a fatal crash at Gatton Bottom, nr.Reigate. Canx as destroyed 20.10.94.
G-AOZC	DH.82A Tiger Moth	84635	T6187	9. 1.57	To PH-EAA 12/57. Canx 10.9.57.
G-AOZD	Westland-Sikorsky S-51 Widgeon Mk.2	WA/H/140		11. 1.57	To 5N-AGL 11/66. Canx 11.11.66.
G-AOZE	Westland-Sikorsky S-51 Widgeon Mk.2	WA/H/141	5N-ABW G-AOZE	11. 1.57	Canx. (On display 4/98 Weston-super-Mare)
G-AOZF	DH.104 Dove 5	04482		14. 1.57	To JA5038 in 2/57. Canx 1.3.57.
G-AOZG	DH.89A Dragon Rapide 4	6603	X7486	23. 1.57	To VR-LAC 1/58. Canx 10.12.57.
G-AOZH	DH.82A Tiger Moth	86449	NM129	18. 1.57	
G-AOZI	Douglas C-47B-25-DK Dakota	16119/32867	PakistanAF KN437/44-76535	21. 1.57	To N9848F 7/57. Canx 4.3.57.
G-AOZJ	DHC.1 Chipmunk 22A (Fuselage no. DHB/f/139) (Originally regd as a Mk.22)	C1/0256	EI-AHV WD319	23. 1.57	To HB-TUE 11/57. Canx 11.11.57.
G-AOZK	Westland-Sikorsky S-55 Whirlwind Srs.3 (Originally regd as a Srs.1)	WA/240	5N-ABO VR-NDK/G-AOZK/Yugoslavia H-11/G-17-1	31. 1.57	To VR-BEQ 1/74. Canx 8.1.74.
G-AOZL	Auster J/5Q Alpine	3202		5. 2.57	(Stored 1/98)
G-AOZM	DH.114 Heron 1B	14002	4X-ARK G-AOZM/I-AOZM/G-AOZM/LN-PSG	6. 5.57	WFU at Southend on 21.2.70. Scrapped in 7/72. Canx.
G-AOZN	DH.114 Heron 1B	14005	9L-LAL G-AOZN/LN-SUD	15. 3.57	To ZK-EJM 9/76. Canx 8.9.76.
G-AOZO	Edgar Percival EP.9 (Became Propector 1 in 9/59)	29	G-43-8	12. 2.57	Fatal crash on take-off from Lympne on 2.7.80 and burnt out. Canx as destroyed 5.5.81.
G-AOZP	DHC.1 Chipmunk 22A (Fuselage no. DHB/f/70) (Originally regd as a Mk.22)	C1/0183	WB734	14. 2.57	
G-AOZR	Hiller 360 UH-12C	847		27. 2.57	To N9739C 5/62. Canx 1.3.62.
G-AOZS	Hiller 360 UH-12C	848		27. 2.57	WFU on 18.1.66 after accident. Canx.
G-AOZT	PA-18A-150 Super Cub	18-5503	N6976D	27. 2.57	To VP-JBQ 6/60. Canx 18.3.60.
G-AOZU	DHC.1 Chipmunk 22A (Fuselage no. DHB/f/63) (Originally regd as a Mk.22)	C1/0164	5N-AGP G-AOZU/EI-AHP/WB728	21. 2.57	To VH-RWI(4) 7/97. Canx 9.7.97.
G-AOZV	DHC.1 Chipmunk 22A (Fuselage no. DHB/f/115) (Originally regd as a Mk.22)	C1/0230	EI-AHT WD290	21. 2.57	To (N6EA)/N83778 9/73. Canx 10.9.73.
G-AOZW	DH.104 Dove 1B	04098	VR-NET	7. 3.57	CofA lapsed 21.12.66. WFU at Biggin Hill in 1967 & used to keep G-ALCU flying. Canx as WFU 27.4.70.
G-AOZX	DH.114 Heron 2D	14112	G-5-15	21. 2.57	To CN-MAA 3/57. Canx 26.2.57.
G-AOZY	Edgar Percival EP.9	23	G-43-2	4. 3.57	DBR at Mesmerode, near Wunsdorf, West Germany on 6.5.57 in a flying accident while spraying. Canx.
G-AOZZ	Armstrong-Whitworth 650 Argosy Srs.100	AW.6651		12. 3.57	To G-11-1 in 11/68 / N896U in 12/68. Canx 1.10.68.
G-APAA	Auster J/5R Alpine	3303		23. 6.56	Crashed on landing at Badminton on 9.8.75. Canx as WFU 20.10.75. Wings to G-ARLY.
G-APAB	DHC.1 Chipmunk 22A (Fuselage no. DHB/f/28)(Originally regd as a Mk.22)	C1/0115	WB667	5. 3.57	To VR-RCF 1/58. Canx 20.2.58.
G-APAC	DHC.1 Chipmunk 22 (Fuselage no. DHH/f/..)	C1/0167	WB715	5. 3.57	Crashed on landing at Luton on 8.5.62. Wreck to Rush Green in 10/65 for rebuild as a crop-sprayer. Project abandoned and parts used in G-ATVF. Canx.
G-APAD	Edgar Percival EP.9	27	G-43-6	18. 3.57	To VH-SSW on 8.9.58 (CofR No. 2400), then VH-SSX sameday. Canx 1.8.58.
G-APAE	Auster J/1N Alpha	3372		25. 3.57	To SE-CGN in 7/57. Canx 23.7.57.
G-APAF	Auster 5 Alpha	3404	G-CMAL G-APAF	25. 3.57	
G-APAG	DH.104 Dove 1B (Originally regd as Srs.1)	04114	VR-NIB	25. 3.57	CofA expired 9.6.66. Derelict at Benina Airport, Libya. Canx as WFU 22.7.70.
G-APAH	Auster 5 Alpha	3402		29. 3.57	
G-APAI	Thruxton Jackaroo	85838	DE978	3. 4.57	Crashed at Chilbolton on 8.4.64. Canx.
G-APAJ	Thruxton Jackaroo	83314	T5616	3. 4.57	To VH-KRK 1/79. Canx 21.8.78.
G-APAK	Thruxton Jackaroo	84286	T7922	3. 4.57	To VT-DOF 1/62. Canx 18.6.69.
G-APAL	DH.82A Tiger Moth (Converted to/from Thruxton Jackaroo 5/59 - 7/84)	82102	N6847	4. 4.57	
G-APAM	DH.82A Tiger Moth (Converted to/from Thruxton Jackaroo 10/59 - 1987)	3874	N6580	3. 4.57	
G-APAN	Not allotted [Note: 'APAN' is emergency radar code]				
G-APAO	DH.82A Tiger Moth (Converted to/from Thruxton Jackaroo 5/59 - 3/81)	82845	R4922	3. 4.57	

Regn	Type	c/n	Previous identity	Regn date	Fate or immediate subsequent identity (if known)
G-APAP	DH.82A Tiger Moth (Converted to/from Thruxton Jackaroo 9/59 - 8/86)	83018	R5136	3. 4.57	Badly damaged on take-off from Kingston Deverill, Warminster on 4.9.94. (Fuselage awaiting rebuild 7/99 at Duxford)
G-APAR	Auster J/1N Alpha	3370		4. 4.57	Crashed into Sullington Hill, near Arundel on 16.4.63. Canx.
G-APAS	DH.106 Comet 1A	06022	8351M XM823/G-APAS/G-5-23/F-BGNZ	23. 5.57	(On display 3/96 RAF Cosford)
G-APAT	Vickers 621 Viking C.2	153	VL232	4. 4.57	WFU at Hurn 5/61. Scrapped at Cranfield. Canx.
G-APAU	Bristol 170 Freighter 32	13256	G-18-203	4. 4.57	WFU at Lasham in 13.8.73. Scrapped in 5/75. Canx.
G-APAV	Bristol 170 Freighter 32	13263	G-18-210	9. 4.57	WFU at Lasham in 1974. Scrapped in 5/75. Canx.
G-APAW	DH.82A Tiger Moth	85263	DE206	11. 4.57	Crashed in forced-landing at Redhill on 20.12.59. Wreck at Croydon 2/60. Canx.
G-APAX	DH.82A Tiger Moth	3813	N6476	11. 4.57	To HB-UBF 7/57. Canx 22.8.57.
G-APAY	DH.82A Tiger Moth	85200	T6991	11. 4.57	To I-SUDD 7/60. Canx 29.7.60.
G-APAZ	Vickers 668 Varsity T.1	561	WF415	15. 4.57	Crashed into house roof at Gloucester on 27.3.63. Canx.
G-APBA	DH.104 Dove 6A	04487	(ZP-TDE) G-APBA	15. 4.57	To LV-PKY-283 6/58. Canx.
G-APBB	DH.104 Dove 2	04219	VT-DBG	29. 4.57	NTU - Remained as VT-DBG. Canx.
G-APBC	Douglas C-47B-20-DK Dakota	15676/27121	KN250 43-49860	25. 4.57	To N26932 in 11/81. Canx 23.9.81.
G-APBD(1)	Rollason-Druine D.31 Turbulent	-		. 1.57R	NTU - Canx.
G-APBD(2)	PA-23-160 Aztec	23-1781	EI-ALD	29.10.59	DBR on 7.11.81. Canx.
G-APBE	Auster 5 Alpha	3403		7. 5.57	
G-APBF	Edgar Percival EP.9	26	G-43-5	7. 5.57	To D-EDUV in 10/57. Canx 24.10.57.
G-APBG	DH.104 Dove 5	04490		13. 5.57	To JA5046 in 12/57. Canx 26.12.57.
G-APBH	Vickers 798D Viscount	226	N7464	14. 5.57	To N6599C in 2/59. Canx 26.1.59.
G-APBI	DH.82A Tiger Moth	86097	EM903	16. 5.57	Damaged at Audley End on 7.7.80. CofA expired 19.4.82. (On rebuild 12/90)
G-APBJ	DH.89A Dragon Rapide	6872	V-2 R.Netherlands AF/PH-VNB/R.Netherlands AF V-2/NR796	14. 5.57	To F-OBGE in 3/58. Canx 6.9.57.
G-APBK	Westland-Sikorsky S-51 Mk.1A	WA/H/145		14. 5.57	To VR-BFL in 10/57. Canx 6.12.57.
G-APBL	Westland-Sikorsky S-51 Mk.1A	WA/H/146		14. 5.57	To VR-BFM in 11/57. Canx 6.12.57.
G-APBM	DH.89A Dragon Rapide	6748	V-1 R.Netherlands AF/PH-VNA/R.Netherlands AF V-1/NF877	13. 5.57	To F-OBRU in 8/60. Canx 21.7.60.
G-APBN	DH.89A Dragon Rapide	6787	OO-ARI(2) Belgium AF D-5/NR688	16. 5.57	NTU - Remained as OO-ARI 12/57 / F-OBIA in 4/58. Canx.
G-APBO	Druine D.53 Turbi	PFA/229		3. 6.57	
G-APBP	Douglas C-47A-20-DK Dakota	13173	D-CABA F-BAXJ/42-93279	17. 5.57	To VP-TBW in 3/58. Canx 28.1.58.
G-APBR	Edgar Percival EP.9	28	G-43-7	23. 5.57	To VH-SSC on 4.9.57 (CofR No. 2892) - NTU; To VH-SSV on 22.10.57 (CofR No. 2375). Canx 22.10.57.
G-APBS	Percival P.40 Prentice T.1	PAC/074	VR248	22. 5.57	Not converted. Scrapped at Stansted. Canx in 8/61.
G-APBT	Percival P.40 Prentice T.1	PAC/133	VR287	22. 5.57	Not converted. Scrapped at Stansted. Canx in 8/61.
G-APBU	Percival P.40 Prentice T.1	PAC/079	VR253	22. 5.57	Not converted. Scrapped at Stansted. Canx in 8/61.
G-APBV	Percival P.40 Prentice T.1	5840/3	VS381	22. 5.57	Not converted. Scrapped at Stansted. Canx in 8/61.
G-APBW	Auster 5A Alpha	3405		23. 5.57	
G-APBX	Beechcraft C-18S	269	VT-ANJ	28. 5.57	DBF at Hurn on 5.8.59. Wreck on dump at Biggin Hill 12/59. Canx.
G-APBY	DH.82A Tiger Moth	82166	N6922	31. 5.57	To OO-SOK 8/57. Canx 24.7.57.
G-APBZ	Druine D.31 Turbulent	PFA/440		31. 5.57	Crashed on beach at Berck, France 15.4.63. Canx.
G-APCA	Avro 685 York 1	-	MW295	5. 6.57	To OD-ACQ 6/57. Canx 11.6.57.
G-APCB	Auster J/5Q Alpine	3204		5. 6.57	
G-APCC	DH.82A Tiger Moth	86549	PG640	11. 6.57	
G-APCD	Vickers 754D Viscount	243		2. 4.57	To OD-ADD 11/57. Canx 5.11.57.
G-APCE	Vickers 754D Viscount	244		2. 4.57	To OD-ADE 12/57. Canx 5.11.57.
G-APCF	Avro 652A Anson 19 Srs.2 (T.20)	-	VS514	5. 6.57	To F-OBIJ 8/58. Canx 21.7.58.
G-APCG	Avro 652A Anson 19 Srs.2 (T.20)	-	VS519	5. 6.57	To F-OBAI 12/57. Canx 6.12.57.
G-APCH	Avro 652A Anson 19 Srs.2 (T.20)	-	VS558	5. 6.57	To F-OBHB 6/58. Canx 20.6.58.
G-APCI	Avro 652A Anson 19 Srs.2 (T.20)	-	VS559	5. 6.57	To F-OBMP 5/59. Canx 14.5.59.
G-APCJ	Avro 652A Anson 19 Srs.2 (T.20)	-	VS561	5. 6.57	To F-OBAH 11/57. Canx 17.10.57.
G-APCK	Avro 652A Anson 19 Srs.2 (T.20)	-	VV866	5. 6.57	To F-OBGO 2/58. Canx 28.1.58.
G-APCL	PA-23-150 Apache	23-1159	EI-ANI G-APCL	27. 8.57	Crashed on landing at Shoreham on 6.7.72. Canx.
G-APCM	Druine D.31 Turbulent	PFA/163		22. 1.57	Destroyed during start-up at Aldergrove on 29.11.64. Canx.
G-APCN	Boulton & Paul P.108 Balliol T.2	BPA.10C(2)	WG224	12. 5.57	To Ceylon AF as CA310 in 8/57. Canx 13.8.57.
G-APCO	Boulton & Paul P.108 Balliol T.2	BPA.11C	WG230	12. 5.57	To Ceylon AF as CA311 in 8/57. Canx 13.8.57.
G-APCP	Boulton & Paul P.108 Balliol T.2	BPA.12C	G-3-2 WN132	12. 5.57	To Ceylon AF as CA312 in 8/57. Canx 13.8.57.
G-APCR	Edgar Percival EP.9	21	G-43-1	11. 7.57	Destroyed on take-off from Fezen, Libya on 19.8.58. Canx as destroyed 8.10.58.
G-APCS	Edgar Percival EP.9	24	G-43-3	11. 7.57	Crashed into Gibraltar Harbour on 24.8.62 whilst engaged in filming of "The Running Man". Canx as destroyed 30.11.62.
G-APCT	Edgar Percival EP.9	25	G-43-4	11. 7.57	To EC-ASO 4/62. Canx 16.4.62.
G-APCU	DH.82A Tiger Moth	82535	(PH-...) G-APCU/N9588	18. 6.57	Reserved as PH-TGR(2) on 10.5.84. Canx by CAA 16.5.85. To PH-TYG 5/86.
G-APCV	DHC.1 Chipmunk 22 (Fuselage no. DHH/f/112)(Originally regd as a Mk.22)	C1/0176	WB724	19. 6.57	To VH-FBB 2/58. Canx 7.2.58.
G-APCW	Douglas C-54A-5-DC Skymaster	10299	N93266 NC93266/YV-C-AHU/YV-AHU/42-72194	5. 7.57	To 9Q-PCW 4/62. Canx 28.3.62.

Regn	Type	c/n	Previous identity	Regn date	Fate or immediate subsequent identity (if known)
G-APCX	Auster J/5R Alpine	3304		26. 6.57	To VH-KBV 2/79. Canx 10.1.79.
G-APCY	Auster J/1N Alpha	3377	5N-ACX VR-NDQ/G-APCY	26. 6.57	Crashed in Muang District, Phangnnga Province, Thailand on 19.3.77 while en-route to Australia. To VH-PCY in 5/84. Canx 11.1.84.
G-APCZ	DH.104 Dove 6	04313	F-BFVL F-OANL/F-BFVL	28. 8.57	To VH-MJD 9/67. Canx 23.9.67.
G-APDA	DH.106 Comet 4	6401	9V-BAS 9M-AOA/G-APDA	2. 2.57	Broken up Lasham in 9/72. Canx.
G-APDB	DH.106 Comet 4	6403	9M-AOB G-APDB	2. 2.57	Canx as WFU 18.2.74. (On display 7/99 Duxford)
G-APDC	DH.106 Comet 4	6404	9V-BAT 9M-AOC/G-APDC	2. 2.57	Broken up Lasham 4/75. Canx.
G-APDD	DH.106 Comet 4	6405	5Y-AMT G-APDD/9M-AOD/G-APDD	2. 2.57	Scrapped Lasham 3/73. WFU 2.4.73.
G-APDE	DH.106 Comet 4	6406	5Y-ALF G-APDE/9V-BAU/9M-AOE/G-APDE	2. 2.57	Scrapped Lasham 3/73. WFU 2.4.73.
G-APDF	DH.106 Comet 4	6407		2. 2.57	To RAF as XV814 in 3/67. Canx.
G-APDG(1)	DH.106 Comet 4	6408		. .57R	NTU - To LV-PLM/LV-AHN. Canx.
G-APDG(2)	DH.106 Comet 4	6427	9K-ACI G-APDG	2. 2.57	WFU on 11.1.74. Broken up Lasham in 6/74. Canx as WFU 2.12.77.
G-APDH	DH.106 Comet 4	6409		2. 2.57	Crashed Singapore 22.3.64. Canx.
G-APDI(1)	DH.106 Comet 4	6410		. .57R	NTU - To LV-PLO/LV-AHO. Canx.
G-APDI(2)	DH.106 Comet 4	6428		2. 2.57	To HC-ALT 3/66. Canx.
G-APDJ(1)	DH.106 Comet 4	6411		. .57R	NTU - To LV-PLP/LV-AHP. Canx.
G-APDJ(2)	DH.106 Comet 4	6429		2. 2.57	Broken up Lasham in 6/74. Canx.
G-APDK	DH.106 Comet 4	6412	5Y-ALD G-APDK	2. 2.57	Broken up Lasham in 9/80. Canx. (Displayed Air Scout Activity Centre, Lasham 1975)
G-APDL	DH.106 Comet 4	6413	5Y-ADD G-APDL	2. 2.57	DBR in wheels-up landing at Woolsington on 7.10.70. Stripped for spares. Canx as WFU 1.4.71.
G-APDM	DH.106 Comet 4	6414	9V-BBJ G-APDM/OD-AEV/G-APDM	2. 2.57	WFU 2.5.74. (Ground trainer at Gatwick).
G-APDN(1)	DH.106 Comet 4C	6424		. .57R	NTU - To (G-APMD)/G-AOVU. Canx.
G-APDN(2)	DH.106 Comet 4	6415		2. 2.57	Fatal crash near Arbucias, Gerona, Spain on 4.7.70. Canx as destroyed 6.7.70.
G-APDO	DH.106 Comet 4	6416		2. 2.57	Broken up at Lasham in 6/74. Canx.
G-APDP	DH.106 Comet 4	6417	9V-BBH G-APDP	2. 2.57	To RAE as XX944 in 7/73. Canx 8.6.73.
G-APDR	DH.106 Comet 4	6418	XA-NAP XA-NAZ/G-APDR	2. 2.57	Broken up at Stansted. Canx.
G-APDS	DH.106 Comet 4	6419		2. 2.57	To RAF as XW626. Canx 24.2.69.
G-APDT	DH.106 Comet 4	6420	XA-NAB XA-POW/G-APDT	2. 2.57	Broken up 8/90. Canx. (Fire-training Heathrow).
G-APDU	Hiller 360 UH-12C	849	N9736C G-APDU	12. 7.57	
G-APDV	Hiller 360 UH-12C	856	9Y-TCE VP-TCE/G-APDV	12. 7.57	CofA expired 14.2.80. Canx in 2/85 on sale to USA. To N912WC 2/85.
G-APDW	Vickers 805 Viscount	258	(G-AOYI)	4. 7.57	To VR-BAX 4/58. Canx 8.4.58.
G-APDX	Vickers 805 Viscount	312		4. 7.57	To VR-BAY 2/59. Canx 12.12.59.
G-APDY	Westland-Sikorsky S-55 Whirlwind Srs.3 (Originally regd as a Srs.2)	WA/241		9. 7.57	To Nigerian AF as NAF-502 9/67. Canx 27.9.67.
G-APDZ	DH.82A Tiger Moth	83699	T7369	23. 7.57	Fatal crash during aerobatics practice at Little Snoring on 12.5.60. Canx.
G-APEA	Vickers 951 Vanguard	704		9. 9.57	WFU at Heathrow in 12/72. Broken up in 5/73. Canx.
G-APEB	Vickers 951 Vanguard	705		9. 9.57	WFU at Heathrow on 31.3.73. Broken up. Canx 4.6.73.
G-APEC	Vickers 951 Vanguard	706		9. 9.57	Fatal crash on 2.10.71 nr.Aarsele, 30kms SW of Ghent, Belgium. Canx.
G-APED	Vickers 951 Vanguard Merchantman	707		9. 9.57	WFU at Heathrow on 24.2.71. Canx 5.1.73. Broken up in 5/73.
G-APEE	Vickers 951 Vanguard	708		9. 9.57	Crashed and burnt out in fog while attempting to land at Heathrow on 27.10.65. Canx.
G-APEF	Vickers 951 Vanguard Merchantman	709		9. 9.57	To PK-MVJ 5/72. Canx 15.5.72.
G-APEG	Vickers 953C Vanguard Merchantman	710		9. 9.57	CofA expired 18.5.83 & WFU. Stored 3/96 East Midlands. Canx as WFU 18.2.92. Broken up 5/97.
G-APEH	Vickers 953 Vanguard	711		9. 9.57	To PK-MVF 3/74. Canx 31.3.74.
G-APEI	Vickers 953 Vanguard	712		9. 9.57	To PK-MVD 3/75. Canx 22.3.75.
G-APEJ	Vickers 953C Vanguard Merchantman	713		9. 9.57	WFU 24.12.92. Broken up 1.6.95. Used for spares. Canx 15.11.96 as WFU. Stored 12/96 East Midlands Airport.
G-APEK	Vickers 953C Vanguard Merchantman	714		9. 9.57	WFU & stored engineless 6/95 at Perpignan, France. CofA expired 16.12.89. Canx 7.11.96 as WFU.
G-APEL	Vickers 953C Vanguard Merchantman	715		9. 9.57	To F-BYCF 8/76. Canx 24.8.76.
G-APEM	Vickers 953C Vanguard Merchantman	716	F-BYCE G-APEM	9. 9.57	Preserved at East Midlands Airport. Broken up in 7/95. Canx 7.11.96 as WFU.
G-APEN	Vickers 953 Vanguard	717		9. 9.57	To PK-MVE 1/74. Canx 2.1.74.
G-APEO	Vickers 953C Vanguard Merchantman	718		9. 9.57	WFU at Prestwick on 6.5.75. Broken up in 11/77. Canx as WFU 5.12.77.
G-APEP	Vickers 953C Vanguard Merchantman	719		9. 9.57	On display 2/99 Brooklands Museum. Canx as WFU 28.2.97.
G-APER	Vickers 953 Vanguard	720		9. 9.57	CofA expired 9.12.74. WFU Heathrow 25.4.75. Broken up 6/75.
G-APES	Vickers 953C Vanguard Merchantman	721		9. 9.57	WFU 6.2.95 East Midlands, then to Prestwick 6.5.75. Canx as WFU 28.2.97. Broken up in 5/97.

Regn	Type	c/n	Previous identity	Regn date	Fate or immediate subsequent identity (if known)
G-APET	Vickers 953C Vanguard Merchantman	722		9. 9.57	WFU & stored in 6/92 East Midlands. CofA expired 6.7.91. Canx 7.11.96 as WFU. Broken up in 5/97.
G-APEU	Vickers 953 Vanguard	723		9. 9.57	CofA expired 10.3.75. WFU Heathrow 25.4.75. Broken up 6/75.
G-APEV	DH.114 Heron 2D	14125		26. 7.57	To I-AOVE 12/60. Canx 18.9.61.
G-APEW	EoN AP.6 Olympia 403	EoN/4/001		26. 7.57	To RAFGSA as 306 in 1962. Canx.
G-APEX	Vickers 806 Viscount	381		16. 8.57	WFU at Southend in 3/84. CofA expired 12.5.84. Broken up. Canx as WFU 14.2.90.
G-APEY	Vickers 806 Viscount	382		15. 8.57	
G-APEZ	Douglas DC-4-1009	42921	N33682 NC33682	23. 9.57	WFU at Baginton after CofA expired 8.7.66. Broken up in 5/67 at Coventry. Canx.
G-APFA	Druine D.52 Turbi	PFA/232		5. 2.57	
G-APFB	Boeing 707-436 (Line No. 35)	17703	N31241	7. 8.59	WFU Kingman, AZ 11/76. Broken up 9/79 with part of the fuselage used in E-3A programme at Renton, WA. Canx as WFU 26.11.76.
G-APFC	Boeing 707-436 (Line No. 101)	17704	N5088K	7. 8.59	WFU Wichita, KS 5/75 & tested to destruction. Canx 12.6.75.
G-APFD	Boeing 707-436 (Line No. 112)	17705	N5091K	7. 8.59	To N888NW 11/80. Canx 20.11.80.
G-APFE	Boeing 707-436 (Line No. 113)	17706	N5092K	7. 8.59	Fatal crash on lower slopes of Mount Fuji, Japan after breaking up in severe turbulence on 5.3.66. Canx.
G-APFF	Boeing 707-436 (Line No. 127)	17707		7. 8.59	WFU Boeing Field, WA 5/81. Broken up 5/81. Canx.
G-APFG	Boeing 707-436 (Line No. 128)	17708	N5094K	7. 8.59	WFU 11/80 at Stansted. Broken up 3/89. Fuselage used for fire suppression trials Cardington. (Extant 2/97)
G-APFH	Boeing 707-436 (Line No. 144)	17709		7. 8.59	WFU Wichita, KS 5/75. Broken up in 1977 at Wichita, KS. Canx 12.6.75.
G-APFI	Boeing 707-436 (Line No. 145)	17710		7. 8.59	WFU Kingman, AZ 11/76. Broken up 9/79. Canx 26.11.76.
G-APFJ	Boeing 707-436 (Line No. 163)	17711		7. 8.59	WFU and preserved at RAF Cosford on 12.6.81. Canx. (On display 3/96)
G-APFK	Boeing 707-436 (Line No. 164)	17712		7. 8.59	Written-off during simulated engine failure on take-off at Prestwick on 17.3.77. All then engines were torn off and aircraft DBF. Canx.
G-APFL	Boeing 707-436 (Line No. 169)	17713	5X-CAU 9Q-CRW/G-APFL	7. 8.59	Not restored - Allocated N9149M, but remained as 5X-CAU and transferred to Uganda Government in 10/83.
G-APFM	Boeing 707-436 (Line No. 170)	17714		7. 8.59	WFU Kingman, AZ 11/76. Broken up 9/79. Canx 26.11.76.
G-APFN	Boeing 707-436 (Line No. 171)	17715		7. 8.59	WFU Kingman, AZ 4/76. Broken up 9/79.
G-APFO	Boeing 707-436 (Line No. 175)	17716		7. 8.59	WFU Kingman, AZ 3/81. Canx 31.3.81 on sale to USA. Dismantled with derelict fuselage with no tail still present 2/85.
G-APFP	Boeing 707-436 (Line No. 176)	17717		7. 8.59	To Franklin Institute, Philadelphia, PA, USA in 5/75. Broken up in 10/88. Canx 12.6.75.
G-APFR	Vickers 745D Viscount	229	N7467	2. 9.57	To CF-DTA 3/58. Canx 12.3.58.
G-APFS	DH.82A Tiger Moth	3741	N5473	27. 8.57	Crashed at Woodbridge, Suffolk on 4.7.63. Canx.
G-APFT	DH.82A Tiger Moth	83584	T7145	27. 8.57	To PH-NIK 2/58. Canx 22.11.57.
G-APFU	DH.82A Tiger Moth	86081	EM879	28. 8.57	
G-APFV(1)	DH.115 Vampire T.55	15802	G-5-13	. 8.57R	NTU - To Lebanese AF as L160 in 12/57. Canx.
G-APFV(2)	PA-23-160 Apache	23-1686	EI-ALK	11.12.59	To EI-BAW 5/75. Canx 1.5.75.
G-APFW	Auster J/5R Alpine	3307		29. 8.57	Ditched in English Channel off Le Touquet on 7.2.61. Canx.
G-APFX	DH.82A Tiger Moth	82353	N9252	29. 8.57	Crashed into Langstone Harbour, Portsmouth on 29.4.58. Canx.
G-APFY	Edgar Percival EP.9	32	G-43-2	11. 8.57	To VH-SSB on 4.9.57 (CofR No. 2893) - NTU; To VH-SSW on 22.10.57 (CofR No. 2376). Canx 22.10.57.
G-APFZ	Auster B.8 Agricola	B.118		17. 9.57	To ZK-CCV in 7/62. Canx 4.7.62.
G-APGA	Percival P.40 Prentice T.1	PAC/051	VR232	30. 7.57	Not converted. Scrapped at Stansted. Canx in 2/61.
G-APGB	Percival P.40 Prentice T.1	PAC/087	VR260	30. 7.57	Not converted. Scrapped at Stansted. Canx in 11/61.
G-APGC	Percival P.40 Prentice T.1	PAC/088	VR261	30. 7.57	Not converted. Scrapped at Stansted. Canx in 11/61.
G-APGD	Percival P.40 Prentice T.1	PAC/197	VR320	30. 7.57	Not converted. Scrapped at Stansted. Canx in 11/61.
G-APGE	Percival P.40 Prentice T.1	5810/5	VS270	30. 7.57	Not converted. Scrapped at Stansted. Canx in 11/61.
G-APGF	Percival P.40 Prentice T.1	5810/16	VS281	30. 7.57	Not converted. Scrapped at Stansted. Canx in 11/61.
G-APGG	Percival P.40 Prentice T.1	5810/20	VS285	30. 7.57	Not converted. Scrapped at Stansted. Canx in 11/61.
G-APGH	Percival P.40 Prentice T.1	PAC/303	VS651	30. 7.57	Not converted. Scrapped at Stansted. Canx in 8/61.
G-APGI	Percival P.40 Prentice T.1	PAC/311	VS686	30. 7.57	Not converted. Scrapped at Stansted. Canx in 8/61.
G-APGJ	Percival P.40 Prentice T.1	PAC/313	VS688	30. 7.57	Not converted. Scrapped at Stansted. Canx in 11/61.
G-APGK	Percival P.40 Prentice T.1	PAC/332	VS730	30. 7.57	Not converted. Scrapped at Stansted. Canx in 11/61.
G-APGL	DH.82A Tiger Moth	86460	NM140	6. 9.57	(On rebuild 3/97)
G-APGM	DH.82A Tiger Moth	86550	EI-AHM (EI-AHH)/PG641	9. 1.86	To I-JJOY 7/88. Canx 13.5.88.
G-APGN	Percival P.40 Prentice T.1	PAC/055	VR236	18. 6.57	Not converted. Scrapped at Stansted. Canx in 11/61.
G-APGO	Percival P.40 Prentice T.1	PAC/084	VR257	18. 6.57	Not converted. Scrapped at Stansted. Canx in 2/61.
G-APGP	Percival P.40 Prentice T.1	PAC/106	VR271	18. 6.57	Not converted. Scrapped at Stansted. Canx in 8/61.
G-APGR	Percival P.40 Prentice T.1	PAC/125	VR279	18. 6.57	Not converted. Scrapped at Stansted. Canx in 8/61.
G-APGS	Percival P.40 Prentice T.1	5810/19	VS248	18. 6.57	Not converted. Scrapped at Stansted. Canx in 11/61.
G-APGT	Percival P.40 Prentice T.1	PAC/185	VR313	18. 6.57	To OO-CDR 9/59. Canx 15.9.59.
G-APGU	Percival P.40 Prentice T.1	5820/23	VS337	18. 6.57	Not converted. Scrapped at Stansted. Canx in 8/61.
G-APGV	Percival P.40 Prentice T.1	5830/5	VS358	18. 6.57	Not converted. Scrapped at Stansted. Canx in 2/61.
G-APGW	Percival P.40 Prentice T.1	5830/8	VS361	18. 6.57	Not converted. Scrapped at Stansted. Canx in 8/61.
G-APGX	Percival P.40 Prentice T.1	5840/25	VS414	18. 6.57	Not converted. Scrapped at Stansted. Canx in 8/61.
G-APGY	Percival P.40 Prentice T.1	PAC/232	VS620	18. 6.57	Not converted. Scrapped at Stansted. Canx in 11/61.
G-APGZ	Percival P.40 Prentice T.1	PAC/271	VS637	18. 6.57	Not converted. Scrapped at Stansted. Canx in 8/61.
G-APHA	Percival P.40 Prentice T.1	PAC/272	VS638	18. 6.57	Not converted. Scrapped at Stansted. Canx in 2/61.

Regn	Type	c/n	Previous identity	Regn date	Fate or immediate subsequent identity (if known)
G-APHB	Percival P.40 Prentice T.1	PAC/276	VS641	18. 6.57	Not converted. Scrapped at Stansted. Canx in 8/61.
G-APHC	Percival P.40 Prentice T.1	PAC/292	VS647	18. 6.57	Not converted. Scrapped at Stansted. Canx in 11/61.
G-APHD	Percival P.40 Prentice T.1	PAC/301	VS650	18. 6.57	Not converted. Scrapped at Stansted. Canx in 8/61.
G-APHE	Percival P.40 Prentice T.1	PAC/309	VS683	18. 6.57	Not converted. Scrapped at Stansted. Canx in 8/61.
G-APHF	Percival P.40 Prentice T.1	PAC/308	VS685	18. 6.57	Not converted. Scrapped at Stansted. Canx in 8/61.
G-APHG	Percival P.40 Prentice T.1	PAC/316	VS691	18. 6.57	Not converted. Scrapped at Stansted. Canx in 8/61.
G-APHH	Percival P.40 Prentice T.1	PAC/326	VS725	18. 6.57	Not converted. Scrapped at Stansted. Canx in 8/61.
G-APHI	Percival P.40 Prentice T.1	PAC/324	VS723	18. 6.57	Not converted. Scrapped at Stansted. Canx in 11/61.
G-APHJ	Percival P.40 Prentice T.1	PAC/333	VS731	18. 6.57	Not converted. Scrapped at Stansted. Canx in 11/61.
G-APHK	Percival P.40 Prentice T.1	PAC/337	VS735	18. 6.57	Not converted. Scrapped at Stansted. Canx in 8/61.
G-APHL	Percival P.40 Prentice T.1	PAC/340	VS738	18. 6.57	Not converted. Scrapped at Stansted. Canx in 8/61.
G-APHM	Percival P.40 Prentice T.1	PAC/348	VS746	18. 6.57	Not converted. Scrapped at Stansted. Canx in 2/61.
G-APHN	Percival P.40 Prentice T.1	PAC/349	VS747	18. 6.57	Not converted. Scrapped at Stansted. Canx in 8/61.
G-APHO	Percival P.40 Prentice T.1	PAC/350	VS748	18. 6.57	Not converted. Scrapped at Stansted. Canx in 8/61.
G-APHP	Percival P.40 Prentice T.1	PAC/359	VS757	18. 6.57	Not converted. Scrapped at Stansted. Canx in 8/61.
G-APHR	Percival P.40 Prentice T.1	PAC/358	VS756	18. 6.57	Not converted. Scrapped at Stansted. Canx in 8/61.
G-APHS	Percival P.40 Prentice T.1	PAC/354	VS752	18. 6.57	Not converted. Scrapped at Stansted. Canx in 11/61.
G-APHT	Auster C.6 Atlantic	3447	G-25-5	26. 8.57	NTU - Marks were worn at SBAC Show Farnborough in 9/57. Development of type abandoned. Canx as WFU.
G-APHU	Auster 5 Alpha	3407		3. 9.57	To OE-DBZ 1/60. Canx 28.1.60.
G-APHV	Avro 652A Anson C.19 Srs.2	-	VM360	19. 9.57	CofA lapsed 15.6.73. Canx as PWFU 21.1.82. (On display 3/96 East Fortune)
G-APHW	DH.114 Heron 2C (Originally regd as a Heron 2D)	14118		26. 9.57	To XB-ZIP 10/57. Canx 16.12.59.
G-APHX	Scottish Aviation Twin Pioneer Srs.1	507	9K-ACB G-APHX/VR-OAE	2.10.57	Canx as WFU 5.3.73. Stored at Staverton in 3/73. Broken up in 8/78.
G-APHY	Scottish Aviation Twin Pioneer Srs.1	508	9K-ACC G-APHY/VR-OAF	2.10.57	To C-FSTX 8/74. Canx 16.8.74.
G-APHZ	Thruxton Jackaroo	82168	N6924	3.10.57	To CF-QOT 5/71. Canx 25.12.70.
G-APIA	Edgar Percival EP.9	33	G-43-3	15.10.57	To VH-FBY 2/58. Canx 24.3.58.
G-APIB	Edgar Percival EP.9	34	G-43-1	15.10.57	To VH-FBZ 2/58. Canx 24.3.58.
G-APIC	Taylorcraft Auster 5	1668	TJ651	1.11.57	To VR-SED 10/58. Canx 7.10.58.
G-APID	Douglas C-54A-15-DC Skymaster	10408	N75337 YV-C-EVB/N54305/42-72303	7.11.57	To Seville, Spain as a Cafe 8/67. Canx 14.8.67 on sale to Spain.
G-APIE	Tipsy Belfair B	535	(OO-TIE)	22.10.57	
G-APIF	Percival P.40 Prentice 1	PAC/306	VS652	24.10.57	Not converted. Scrapped at Croydon in 7/58. Fuselage to Castle Bromwich, wings to Biggin Hill.
G-APIG	DH.82A Tiger Moth	84882	T6553	25.10.57	To F-AZEI 12/87. Canx 15.9.86.
G-APIH	DH.82A Tiger Moth	82981	N111DH OY-DGJ/D-EMEX/G-APIH/R5086	25.10.57	
G-APII	Vickers 651 Valetta C.1	302	VL275	12.11.57	Not converted. WFU Manchester, to Blackbushe 1/59 & scrapped.
G-APIJ	Vickers 651 Valetta C.1	491	WD162	12.11.57	Not converted. WFU Manchester, to Blackbushe 1/59 & scrapped.
G-APIK	Auster J/1N Alpha	3375		11.11.57	
G-APIL	Auster J/1N Alpha	3386		11.11.57	Fatal crash when struck overhead cables at Tombel, South Cameroons on 30.9.59. Canx.
G-APIM	Vickers 806 Viscount	412		19.11.57	DBR while parked at Southend when struck by Short SD.3-30 G-BHWT on 11.1.88. Remains on display 3/97 at Brooklands.
G-APIN	Douglas C-54D-5-DC Skymaster	10736	N2750A 42-72631	12. 1.58	Destroyed in air attack by Katangan AF Fouga Magister at Kamina, Congo on 16.9.61. Canx.
G-APIO(1)	Bristol 170 Freighter I	12730	VR380 G-AGPV	.11.57R	NTU - Reverted to G-AGPV 11/57. Canx.
G-APIO(2)	DH.82A Tiger Moth	84005	T7608	9.12.57	Not converted. Canx as WFU 2.4.73.
G-APIP(1)	Bristol 170 Freighter I	12733	VR382 G-AGUT	.11.57R	NTU - Reverted to G-AGUT 11/57. Canx.
G-APIP(2)	DH.82A Tiger Moth	83555	T5843	9.12.57	Crashed at Hayes Common on 28.7.63. Canx.
G-APIR	Scottish Aviation Twin Pioneer Srs.3 (Originally regd as Srs.1)	521		9.12.57	To Nepal as 9N-RF6 in 5/65. Canx 24.3.65.
G-APIS	Not allocated.				
G-APIT	Percival P.40 Prentice T.1	PAC/016	VR192	28.11.57	CofA expired 7.9.67. Canx as WFU 8.11.79. (On display 3/96 Lasham)
G-APIU	Percival P.40 Prentice T.1	PAC/024	VR200	28.11.57	CofA expired 23.3.67. Derelict in 1972 at Coventry. Canx as WFU 9.10.84. (Spares use 5/96)
G-APIV	Percival P.40 Prentice T.1	PAC/047	VR227	28.11.57	Not converted. Scrapped at Stansted. Canx in 2/61.
G-APIW	Percival P.40 Prentice T.1	PAC/049	VR229	28.11.57	Not converted. Scrapped at Stansted. Canx in 11/61.
G-APIX	Percival P.40 Prentice T.1	PAC/054	VR235	28.11.57	Not converted. Scrapped at Stansted. Canx in 2/61.
G-APIY	Percival P.40 Prentice T.1	PAC/075	VR249	28.11.57	WFU on 18.3.67. Canx 19.4.73. (On display 2/99 Winthorpe as VR249)
G-APIZ	Rollason-Druine D.31 Turbulent	PFA/478		22.11.57	Crashed at Wells House Farm, West Clandon, near Guildford on 26.5.63. Remains to Croydon & broken up on 30.10.63.
G-APJA	Percival P.40 Prentice T.1	PAC/076	VR250	28.11.57	Not converted. Scrapped at Stansted. Canx in 11/61.
G-APJB	Percival P.40 Prentice T.1	PAC/086	VR259	28.11.57	
G-APJC	Percival P.40 Prentice T.1	PAC/124	VR277	28.11.57	Not converted. Scrapped at Stansted. Canx in 11/61.
G-APJD	Percival P.40 Prentice T.1	5810/13	VS278	28.11.57	Not converted. Scrapped at Southend. Canx in 7/62.
G-APJE	Percival P.40 Prentice T.1	5810/17	VS282	28.11.57	WFU on 3.8.64 at Ingoldmells. Canx.
G-APJF	Percival P.40 Prentice T.1	PAC/347	VS745	28.11.57	Not converted. Scrapped at Stansted. Canx in 11/61.
G-APJG	Percival P.40 Prentice T.1	PAC/351	VS749	28.11.57	Not converted. Destroyed in gales 19.10.59 Southend. Canx.
G-APJH	Percival P.40 Prentice T.1	PAC/307	VS682	28.12.57	Not converted. Scrapped at Stansted. Canx in 2/61.
G-APJI	Percival P.40 Prentice T.1	5810/15	VS280	28.12.57	Not converted. Scrapped at Southend. Canx in 7/62.
G-APJJ(1)	Scottish Aviation Twin Pioneer Srs.1	523		. .57R	NTU - To (G-APJM)/G-APLM in 2/58. Canx.

Regn	Type	c/n	Previous identity	Regn date	Fate or immediate subsequent identity (if known)
G-APJJ(2)	Fairey Ultralight Helicopter	F.9428		4.12.57	WFU at White Waltham on 1.4.59. Canx as WFU 2.3.73. (On display 4/96 Baginton)
G-APJK(1)	Scottish Aviation Twin Pioneer Srs.1	526		. .57R	NTU - To (G-APJN)/G-APLN in 2/58. Canx.
G-APJK(2)	DH.82A Tiger Moth	86231	NL760	13.12.57	To I-RIBI 8/58. Canx.
G-APJL	DH.82A Tiger Moth	85642	DE712	2.12.57	To N126B 7/69. Canx 25.7.69.
G-APJM(1)	Scottish Aviation Twin Pioneer Srs.1	523	(G-APJJ)	. .57R	NTU - To G-APLM in 2/58. Canx.
G-APJM(2)	Auster J/4 Archer (Rebuild of J/2 Arrow G-AJPU c/n 2392)	2091		17.12.57	Ditched off Varne Lightship on 27.5.61. Canx.
G-APJN(1)	Scottish Aviation Twin Pioneer Srs.1	526	(G-APJK)	. .57R	NTU - To G-APLN in 2/58. Canx.
G-APJN(2)	Hiller 360 UH-12B	686	HB-XAH	23.12.57	To N38772 2/83. Canx.
G-APJO	DH.82A Tiger Moth	86446	NM126	23.12.57	Crashed at Ross-on-Wye on 5.8.58. (On rebuild; may really be parts of G-APJR - c/n quoted as "17712")
G-APJP	DH.82A Tiger Moth	82869	(G-AOCV) R4961	30. 7.57	To SE-GXO 7/80. Canx 30.10.79.
G-APJR	DH.82A Tiger Moth	83712	T7391	11.11.57	Crashed on take-off from a field at Southview Farm, Princethorpe, Warwickshire on 28.5.61.
G-APJS	DH.114 Heron 1B	14001	ZK-AYV	21.12.57	Crashed into Mt.Saraceno, Italy on 19.2.58 on delivery from New Zealand. (Wreck found on 10.5.58) Canx.
G-APJT	Scottish Aviation Twin Pioneer Srs.1	529		18.12.57	To Malaysian AF as FM1001 on 4/58. Canx 18.4.58.
G-APJU	Vickers 806 Viscount	413		30.12.57	To PK-RVM 5/70. Canx 14.8.70.
G-APJV	Thruxton Jackaroo	83850	(G-AMTX) T7446	1. 1.58	Crashed at Rhoose on 18.4.60. Canx.
G-APJW	DH.89A Dragon Rapide 4	6578	"G-AZZZ" X7437	2. 1.58	To F-BHOB 10/62. Canx 9.8.62.
G-APJX	Taylorcraft Auster 5	1439	TJ373	3. 1.58	DBR by gales at Inverness on 28.9.69. Canx as WFU in 1970.
G-APJY	Auster J/1N Alpha	3380		3. 1.58	Crashed at Walney Island on 10.10.65. Canx.
G-APJZ	Auster J/1N Alpha	3382	5N-ACY (VR-NDR)/G-APJZ	3. 1.58	Overturned on landing at Thornicombe on 10.11.75. (On rebuild 8/90)
G-APKA	DH.89A Dragon Rapide	6827	NR739	7. 1.58	To VR-LAE 7/58. Canx 8.2.58.
G-APKB	PA-18A-150 Super Cub	18-6250	N8590D	19. 2.58	Crashed at Nuthampstead, near Royston, Herts., on 25.5.59. Canx.
G-APKC	Westland-Sikorsky S-55 Whirlwind Srs.1	WA/250	VP-TCG G-APKC	14. 1.58	To D-HODY 4/64. Canx.
G-APKD	Auster J/1N Alpha	3384		16. 1.58	To EI-AVW 8/72. Canx 27.7.72.
G-APKE	DH.82A Tiger Moth	86421	NL989	7. 2.58	Crashed & burnt while landing near Rearsby on 22.8.64. Canx.
G-APKF	Vickers 806 Viscount	396		28. 1.58	To XW-TDN 9/69. Canx 25.9.69.
G-APKG	Vickers 804 Viscount	395		22. 1.58	To SP-LVB 11/62. Canx.
G-APKH	DH.85 Leopard Moth (Built from spares from G-ACGS/G-ACLZ)	PPS.85/1/DH7131		23. 1.58	
G-APKI	Auster J/5P Autocar	3274		24. 1.58	Destroyed in take-off crash from Perranporth on 16.5.71. Canx.
G-APKJ	Vickers 744 Viscount	88	(YV-C-ANJ) G-APKJ/N7402	31. 1.58	Destroyed in heavy landing at Itami, Japan 12.6.61. Remains to Ansett-ANA. Canx.
G-APKK	Vickers 744 Viscount	89	(YV-C-ANK) G-APKK/N7403	6. 2.58	To RAF as XR801 1/62. Canx.
G-APKL	Auster J/1N Alpha	3383		27. 1.58	Crashed at Le Touquet, France on 8.7.63. Canx.
G-APKM	Auster J/1N Alpha	3385		27. 1.58	CofA expired 9.1.89. (Stored at owner's house 4/90) Canx as TWFU 9.10.91.
G-APKN	Auster J/1N Alpha	3387		27. 1.58	
G-APKO(1)	Douglas DC-3A-197E	4123	N33644 NC33644/(41-7701)	. 3.58R	NTU - Remained as N33644 3/58. Canx 1/60.
G-APKO(2)	PA-23-150 Apache	23-154	VP-KOO ZS-DLD	23. 2.60	To ZK-BWJ 4/60. Canx 17.5.60.
G-APKP	Auster J/1U Workmaster	3497	(F-OBHP)	30. 1.58	Crashed whilst spraying at Mongenu, Nigeria on 10.10.63. Canx.
G-APKR	Vickers 651 Valetta C.1	338	VW802	10. 2.58	Undercarriage collapsed and destroyed on landing Gatwick 21.9.63. To spares Biggin Hill. Canx.
G-APKS	Vickers 637 Valetta C.1	165	VL263	10. 2.58	Not converted. Scrapped at Biggin Hill in 1/59 to provide spare parts for G-APKR. Canx.
G-APKT	DH.114 Heron 1B	14019	CX-AOR	7. 2.58	To 9L-LAG 12/64. Canx 3.12.64.
G-APKU	DH.114 Heron 1B	14025	9L-LAT (G-APKU)/9L-LAD/G-APKU/CX-AOS	17. 3.58	Canx as destroyed 26.3.79.
G-APKV	DH.114 Heron 1B	14045	CX-AOU	17. 3.58	WFU at Shobdon on 21.3.67. Broken up at Southend 7/72 and remains taken to Staravia dump at Lasham by 1/73. Canx.
G-APKW	DH.114 Heron 1B/C	14046	5B-CCD G-APKW/9Q-CRL/G-APKW/CX-AOV	12. 2.58	To HS-EAA 2/80. Canx 12.3.80.
G-APKX	Hiller 360 UH-12A	337	CF-HAP N64C	14. 2.58	Crashed near Chilbolton, Hants on 4.7.66. Rebuilt as N93219 in 1974. Canx.
G-APKY	Hiller 360 UH-12B	673	PH-NFL(2)	4. 3.58	CofA expired 7.5.74. Canx. (Stored 5/96)
G-APKZ	Rollason-Druine D.31 Turbulent	PFA/479		17. 1.58	Fatal crash at Cudham Lane, near Green Street, Green, Farnborough, Kent on 6.12.60. Canx.
G-APLA	Hiller 360 UH-12A	137	F-BFLX	14. 2.58	Crashed at High Roding, near Dunmow, Essex on 28.5.58. Canx.
G-APLB	DH.82A Tiger Moth	86099	EM905	24. 2.58	Crashed into sea off Bembridge on 8.5.58. Canx.
G-APLC	DH.82A Tiger Moth	3277	K4281	24. 2.58	Crashed after striking overhead cables while spraying at Wyke Farm, near Sherborne, Dorset on 15.7.60. Wreck to Portsmouth in 8/60. Canx.
G-APLD	EoN AP.6 Olympia 419	EoN/4/002		24. 2.58	To BGA.1022 in 5/61. Canx 11.4.59.

Regn	Type	c/n	Previous identity	Regn date	Fate or immediate subsequent identity (if known)
G-APLE	Westland WS-59 Westminster 1	WA/1		27. 2.58	Canx as WFU 29.9.60. Dismantled at Yeovil in 9/60.
G-APLF	Westland-Sikorsky S-58 Wessex Srs.2	WA/53		27. 2.58	NTU - Not completed. Canx 24.10.63.
G-APLG	Auster J/5L Aiglet Trainer	3148		4. 3.58	WFU 6/68. CofA expired 26.10.68. (On rebuild by Solway Aviation Society 5/97) Canx by CAA 11.2.99.
G-APLH	Bristol 170 Freighter 31	13250	G-18-197	10. 3.58	To CF-YDP 12/68. Canx 28.3.69.
G-APLI	DH.82A Tiger Moth	85593	DE639	7. 3.58	To SE-COG 9/60. Canx 15.6.60.
G-APLJ	PA-23-160 Apache E	23-1366	5N-ABS VR-NDG/G-APLJ	16. 6.58	To VH-DRR 7/63. Canx 9.7.63.
G-APLK	Miles M.100 Student 2 (Originally regd with c/n 100/1008)	M.1008	G-MIOO G-APLK/XS941/G-APLK/G-35-4	11. 3.58	Restored as G-MIOO in 11/96. Canx.
G-APLL	Bristol 175 Britannia Srs.102	12908	G-ANBG	19. 3.58	CofA expired 4.3.69. Stored at Woolsington in 4/69. Canx as WFU 24.4.70.
G-APLM	Scottish Aviation Twin Pioneer Srs.1	523	5N-ABQ VR-NDM/G-APLM/(G-APJM)/(G-APJJ)	12. 2.58	Restored as 5N-ABQ 7/63. Canx 19.7.63.
G-APLN	Scottish Aviation Twin Pioneer Srs.1	526	5N-ABR VR-NDN/G-APLN/(G-APJN)/(G-APJK)	12. 2.58	Crashed into sea off Chepbica, Morocco on 16.1.63. Canx.
G-APLO	DHC.1 Chipmunk 22A (Fuselage no. DHB/f/48) (Originally regd as a Mk.22)	C1/0144	EI-AHU WB696	15. 4.58	
G-APLP	Edgar Percival EP.9 (Became Propector 1 in 7/59)	35	G-43-8	18. 3.58	Forced landing on the beach near South Pier, Blackpool and submerged by the tide on 15.7.59. Canx. (Airframe in scrapyard at Takeley on 3.8.63)
G-APLR	DH.82A Tiger Moth	84682	T6256	26. 3.58	To I-JENA 1/59. Canx 6.8.58.
G-APLS	EoN AP.6 Olympia 415 (Originally regd as an Olympia 419)	EoN/4/003		26. 3.58	WFU. Canx 6.9.65.
G-APLT	EoN AP.6 Olympia 419X	EoN/4/004		23. 3.58	To Ireland as IGA.105 in 1/65. Canx 9.1.65.
G-APLU	DH.82A Tiger Moth	85094	VR-AAY F-OBKK/G-APLU/T6825	2. 4.58	
G-APLV	DH.82A Tiger Moth	86562	PG653	2. 4.58	To I-RIBU 12/59. Canx 12.2.59.
G-APLW	Scottish Aviation Twin Pioneer Srs.1	532	VR-OAG G-APLW	10. 1.58	To 9M-ANO 5/64. Canx 21.5.64.
G-APLX	Vickers 745D Viscount	230	G-16-6 N7468	15. 4.58	To N6595C 7/58. Canx 19.7.58.
G-APLY	PA-18A-150 Super Cub	18-6459		12. 5.58	Crashed while spraying near Herne Bay, Kent on 3.2.66. Canx.
G-APLZ	Rollason-Druine D.31 Turbulent	PFA/480		9. 4.58	Crashed at Grange Farm, Lower Burnham Road. Latchington, near Maldon, Essex on 23.4.74. Canx.
G-APMA	DH.106 Comet 4B	6421		15. 4.58	WFU at Heathrow 25.1.72. Broken up 7/72.
G-APMB	DH.106 Comet 4B	6422		15. 4.58	CofA expired 18.5.79. Canx as WFU 19.1.79. (Crew-trainer Gatwick) (Extant 10/97)
G-APMC	DH.106 Comet 4B	6423		15. 4.58	WFU on 19.9.74, CofA expiry 10.11.74. Broken up Lasham in 4/75. Canx.
G-APMD(1)	DH.106 Comet 4C	6424	(G-APDN)	. .58R	NTU - To G-AOVU 10/59. Canx.
G-APMD(2)	DH.106 Comet 4B	6435		15. 4.58	WFU on 31.3.75. Broken up Lasham in 1978. Canx as WFU 23.3.77.
G-APME(1)	DH.106 Comet 4C	6425		. .58R	NTU - To G-AOVV 11/59. Canx.
G-APME(2)	DH.106 Comet 4B	6436		15. 4.58	WFU on 2.5.78. Broken up Lasham 6/79. Canx as WFU 29.11.78
G-APMF	DH.106 Comet 4B	6426		15. 4.58	WFU on 14.8.75. Broken up Lasham 2/76. Canx as WFU 23.3.77
G-APMG(1)	Bell 47D-1	13	LN-ORA SE-HAF/N159B/NC159B	. 4.58R	NTU - Damaged at Sudbury on 3.8.58 & restored as LN-ORA. Canx.
G-APMG(2)	DH.106 Comet 4C	6440	G-APZM	. 1.60R	NTU - Remained as G-APZM. Canx.
G-APMG(3)	DH.106 Comet 4B	6442		4. 1.60	Broken up Lasham 4/78. Canx.
G-APMH	Auster J/1U Workmaster	3502	F-OBOA G-APMH	15. 4.58	
G-APMI	Auster J/1U Workmaster (Originally regd with c/n 3503)	3506		15. 4.58	To F-OBOB 7/59. Canx 21.7.59.
G-APMJ	Auster J/1U Workmaster	3504		15. 4.58	Crashed into Dudgeon Hill, Kirkcudbrightshire on 18.10.63. Canx.
G-APMK	Auster J/1U Workmaster	3505		15. 4.58	Destroyed in an accident in 9/69. Canx.
G-APML	Douglas C-47B-1-DK Dakota	14175/25620	KJ836 43-48359	17. 4.58	(On overhaul 7/97)
G-APMM	DH.82A Tiger Moth	85427	DE419	18. 4.58	WFU at Southend on 19.9.74. Canx 26.3.90 on sale to Sweden (At Alvesta, Sweden in 1998)
G-APMN	DHC.1 Chipmunk 23 (Fuselage no. DHB/f/36)	C1/0128	WB680	21. 4.58	Crashed at Foxes Farm, Potterhanworth Fen, Lincs on 27.7.58. Wreck to Croydon by 9/59, then Biggin Hill in 10/59. Canx.
G-APMO	Hunting P.66 President 2 (Also c/n P66/108)	1031	SudanAF 11 G-23-3/EC-APB	24. 4.58	WFU 10.7.70. Canx. Aircraft moved from Fire School compoun at Stansted to 1163 Sqdn ATC HQ Earls Colne, Essex in 1973 less outer wings and other parts. Reportedly broken up in 1976 & stored off site at Hayhouse Farm.
G-APMP(1)	Hiller 360 UH-12C	1036		. .58R	NTU - Canx.
G-APMP(2)	Hiller 360 UH-12C	1041		26. 6.58	CofA expired 23.7.76 & WFU at Southend. Used for spares. Canx as WFU 29.2.84.
G-APMR	Hiller 360 UH-12C	1037		4. 6.58	To N38767 4/83. Canx 21.1.80.
G-APMS	Hiller 360 UH-12C	1038	N9778C G-APMS/N9778C/G-APMS	4. 6.58	To N812WC 2/85. Canx 13.2.85.
G-APMT	Scottish Aviation Twin Pioneer Srs.3 (Originally regd as a Srs.1)	537	EP-AGG G-APMT	6. 5.58	To 9L-LAC 8/61. Canx 12.7.62.
G-APMU	Auster J/1B Aiglet	2793	VP-KKS	6. 5.58	Crashed into the Mediterranean on delivery 12.7.58. Canx.
G-APMV	DH.114 Heron 2E	14128		5. 5.58	To N579PR 2/72. Canx 18.2.72.
G-APMW	DHC.1 Chipmunk 22 (Fuselage no. DHB/f/11)	C1/0078	EI-AJA WB632	12. 5.58	Crashed at Bishophill Farm, Stanley, Perthshire on 27.6.62 Canx.

Regn	Type	c/n	Previous identity	Regn date	Fate or immediate subsequent identity (if known)
G-APMX(1)	DH.82A Tiger Moth	85496	DE516	9. 5.58R	NTU - To G-APOC 7/58. Canx.
G-APMX(2)	DH.82A Tiger Moth	85645	DE715	9. 5.58	
G-APMY	PA-23-160 Apache	23-1258	EI-AJT	15. 5.58	WFU at Halfpenny Green on 1.11.81. (On loan to South Yorkshire Aviation Museum 5/97)
G-APMZ	Rollason-Druine D.31 Turbulent	PFA/401		17. 4.58	Crashed at Clements Farm, Newtownards on 1.2.64. Canx.
G-APNA	Bristol 175 Britannia Srs.317	13425		9. 5.58	WFU in 5/72. Broken up in 6/73 at Baginton. Canx as WFU 19.12.73.
G-APNB	Bristol 175 Britannia Srs.317	13426		9. 5.58	WFU on 31.1.71 at Luton. Broken up in 11/71 for spares use. Canx.
G-APNC	DHC.1 Chipmunk 22 (Fuselage no. DHB/f/425)	C1/0540	WG490	16. 5.58	To D-EGAP 8/58. Canx 20.8.58.
G-APND	Vickers 831 Viscount	402	(4X-AVF) G-APND/JY-ADB/G-APND	20. 5.58	To G-16-20/4X-AVF 11/73. Canx 7.11.73.
G-APNE	Vickers 831 Viscount	403	JY-ADA G-APNE	20. 5.58	To 4X-AVE 9/72. Canx 9.9.72.
G-APNF	Vickers 776 Viscount (Originally regd as Viscount 745D)	225	9K-ACD G-APNF/EI-AJW/G-16-4/(N7463)	3. 6.58	WFU on 21.3.70 at Woolsington. Remains burnt in 9/70 Canx as WFU 23.4.70.
G-APNG	Vickers 745D Viscount	228	EI-AJV G-16-3/(N7466)	24. 6.58	To CF-RBC 4/59. Canx 26.3.59.
G-APNH	Aviation Traders ATL-98 Carvair (Originally regd as Douglas C-54B-5-DO; converted in 1/65)	18333/11	(PH-EUR) G-APNH/(D-ANET)/N37477/43-17133	17. 6.58	Damaged on landing at Le Bourget, France on 18.3.71. Canx as WFU 2.6.71.
G-APNI	Hiller 360 UH-12C	1039		26. 6.58	Crashed while taking off at Armuelles Airport, Panama in 4/59. Canx.
G-APNJ	Cessna 310A	35335	EI-AJY N3635D	2. 6.58	CofA expired 28.11.74 & WFU. Canx as WFU 5.12.83. Instructional Airframe 1/99 Shoreham.
G-APNK	Douglas C-47B-1-DK Dakota	14178/25623	KJ839 43-48362	4. 6.58	To VP-BAB(4) 12/58. Canx 2.11.58.
G-APNL	Percival P.66 Pembroke C.1 (Also c/n K66/13)	P66/13	WV710	11. 6.58	Not converted. Derelict Blackpool 1960. Scrapped 3/65. Canx.
G-APNM	Auster 5 Alpha	3409		11. 6.58	To SE-CFN 2/59. Canx 3.2.59.
G-APNN	Auster 5 Alpha	3410		10. 6.58	To SE-CME 10/59. Canx 20.8.59.
G-APNO	Douglas DC-6A/B (Line No. 1015)	45531		11. 7.58	To HB-IBS 1/69. Canx 11.1.69.
G-APNP	Douglas DC-6A/B (Line No. 1025)	45532		11. 7.58	To HB-IBT 1/69. Canx 11.1.69.
G-APNR	Hiller 360 UH-12C	784	F-BHTG N38770	26. 6.58	To N38770 /83. Canx 21.1.80.
G-APNS	Garland-Bianchi Linnet 1	001		17. 6.58	(Stored 6/95)
G-APNT	Bellamy Currie Wot (Also regd with c/n P.6/399)	HAC/3		18. 6.58	
G-APNU	Saunders-Roe P.531-1	S2/5267		24. 6.58	NTU. WFU at Eastleigh in 1960. Canx in 9/64. Scrapped at Hayes in 1964.
G-APNV	Saunders-Roe P.531-1	S2/5268		24. 6.58	To Royal Navy as XN332 in 10/59. Canx 1.10.59.
G-APNW	Scottish Aviation Pioneer	149		2. 7.58	To R.Ceylon AF as CC603 in 9/58. Canx 1.8.59.
G-APNX	Scottish Aviation Pioneer	150		2. 7.58	To R.Ceylon AF as CC604 in 9/58. Canx 1.8.59.
G-APNY	Piaggio P.136L-2	242		4. 7.58	To HB-LAV 8/59. Canx 8.7.59.
G-APNZ	Rollason-Druine D.31 Turbulent	PFA/482		17. 4.58	Badly damaged when crashed into River Rother, near Iden, East Sussex on 3.9.95. (On rebuild .95)
G-APOA	Auster J/1N Alpha	3381		10. 7.58	Destroyed in fatal crash at Oxenden Wood, Chelsfield, near Orpington on 15.11.93. Canx as destroyed 10.5.94.
G-APOB	RFD Free Balloon "Small World"	S.372		10. 7.58	Ditched in mid-Atlantic during attempted Atlantic crossing on 15.12.58. Canx 22.2.60.
G-APOC	DH.82A Tiger Moth	85496	(G-APMX) DE516	11. 7.58	To I-PUMA 1/59. Canx 1.11.58.
G-APOD	Tipsy Belfair	536	(OO-TIF)	16. 7.58	(On rebuild 4/97)
G-APOE	DHC.1 Chipmunk 22A (Fuselage no. DHB/f/575)(Originally regd as a Mk.22)	C1/0685	WP793	17. 7.58	To N2533 1/70. Canx 8.1.70.
G-APOF	Hiller 360 UH-12C	776	F-BBDZ F-BBNZ(2)/PH-NGP	24. 7.58	Crashed at Redhill on 25.5.68. Canx.
G-APOG	DH.82A Tiger Moth	82499	N9445	28. 7.58	To HB-UBH 3/59. Canx 4.5.59.
G-APOH	Hunting H.107 (Later renamed as the BAC.107)	H.107/1		30. 7.58	NTU - Not built. Canx 4.5.59.
G-APOI	Saunders-Roe P.502 Skeeter Srs.8	S2/5081		29. 7.58	WFU on 30.3.61. (Stored 1/94)
G-APOJ	Saunders-Roe P.502 Skeeter Srs.8	S2/5091		29. 7.58	NTU - Construction abandoned. Canx 21.11.58.
G-APOK	Saunders-Roe P.502 Skeeter Srs.8	S2/5111		29. 7.58	NTU - Construction abandoned. Canx 21.11.58.
G-APOL	Druine D.31 Turbulent (Converted from D.36 to D.31 in 1968)	PFA/439		31. 7.58	Badly damaged on take-off Charterhall 24.7.93. (Stored 3/94)
G-APOM	Douglas DC-6A (Line No. 1003)	45519	N7821C	22. 8.58	Crashed at Shannon Airport on 26.3.61 & DBF, undercarriage collapsed. Canx.
G-APON	Douglas DC-6A (Line No. 662)	45058	N6814C (G-AOFY)	10. 9.58	Restored as N6814C 6/64. Canx 8.6.64.
G-APOO	Vickers 621 Viking 2	156	VL233	6. 8.58	WFU at Southend 18.8.64. CofA expired 3.4.65. Broken up. Canx.
G-APOP	Vickers 623 Viking 2	177	VL246	6. 8.58	WFU at Southend & used as a cabin trainer 4.1.65. CofA expired 27.3.65. Scrapped in 1/70. Canx.
G-APOR	Vickers 623 Viking 2	178	VL247	6. 8.58	WFU at Southend 5/64. Broken up 2/65. Canx.
G-APOS	DHC.1 Chipmunk 23 (Fuselage no. DHB/f/662)(Originally regd as a Mk.22)	C1/0763	WP893	8. 8.58	To N8345 8/69. Canx 18.8.69.

Regn	Type	c/n	Previous identity	Regn date	Fate or immediate subsequent identity (if known)
G-APOT	Hiller 360 UH-12C	1040		8. 8.58	To N9755C 2/62. Canx 2.2.62.
G-APOU	DH.82A Tiger Moth	85867	DF118	15. 8.58	To SE-CHG 9/59. Canx 20.5.59.
G-APOV	Rollason Thruxton Jackaroo	83012	R5130	15. 8.58	Crashed at Hawkenbury Farm, Staplehurst, Kent on 3.7.61. Canx.
G-APOW	Vickers 702 Viscount	72	VP-BCD G-APOW/VP-TBL	5. 9.58	WFU & stored in 5/69. Broken up in 2/70 East Midlands Airport. Canx as WFU 6.4.70.
G-APOX	Vickers 806 Viscount	418		10. 9.58	To PK-RVL 6/70. Canx 24.6.70.
G-APOY	DHC.1 Chipmunk 22A (Originally regd as Mk.22) (Fuselage no. DHB/f/787)	C1/0898	7439M WZ867	11. 9.58	Stored dismantled in Norway since 7/71. Canx 8.9.72 on sale to Norway.
G-APOZ	SAN Jodel D.117	846		10. 9.58	Destroyed in forced-landing at Wembury, Devon on 13.8.65.
G-APPA	DHC.1 Chipmunk 22 (Fuselage no. DHB/f/699)	C1/0792	N5073E G-APPA/WP917	11. 9.58	(On rebuild 7/97)
G-APPB	DH.82A Tiger Moth	82062	N6792	24. 9.58	Crashed at St.Lawrence Bay, Essex during take-off on 21.2.64. Canx.
G-APPC	Vickers 810 Viscount	362	N250V G-APPC/(N250V)	30. 9.58	WFU at Southend on 29.9.68. Broken up in 6/72. Canx.
G-APPD(1)	DH.104 Dove 6B	04402	XB-SUU	. 9.58R	NTU - To G-ALEC(2) 11/58. Canx 9/58.
G-APPD(2)	DH.114 Heron 2D	14127	H-106 R.Jordanian AF/G-APPD/R.Jordanian AF H-106	1.12.58	To LN-NPH 2/66. Canx 24.1.66.
G-APPE	Bristol 175 Britannia Srs.252	13450		31.10.58	To RAF as XN392 3/59. Canx 28.10.59.
G-APPF	Bristol 175 Britannia Srs.252	13451		28.11.58	To RAF as XN398 3/59. Canx 19.3.59.
G-APPG	Bristol 175 Britannia Srs.252	13452		28.11.58	To RAF as XN404 3/59. Canx 27.3.59.
G-APPH	Scottish Aviation Twin Pioneer Srs.3 (Converted from Srs.1 in 6/60)	540		29. 9.58	To VH-AIS 8/62. Canx 30.7.62.
G-APPI	PA-18A-150 Super Cub	18-6575		2.10.58	Crashed whilst spraying near Devizes, Wiltshire on 13.4.65. Wreck to Thruxton.
G-APPJ	Douglas C-47B-40-DK Dakota	16861/33609	44-77277	3.10.58	To 9G-AAC 3/59. Canx 9.3.59.
G-APPK	DHC.1 Chipmunk 22 (Fuselage no.DHB/f/97)	C1/0214	EI-AJE WB764	8.10.58	To N4998T 9/77. Canx 12.9.77.
G-APPL	Percival P.40 Prentice 1	PAC/013	VR189	7.10.58	
G-APPM	DHC.1 Chipmunk 22 (Fuselage no. DHB/f/59)	C1/0159	WB711	14.10.58	
G-APPN	DH.82A Tiger Moth	83839	T7328	17.10.58	Crashed near Mendlesham, Suffolk on 14.7.64. (On rebuild by R.Souch at Hill Farm, Durley 6/96)
G-APPO	Douglas C-47A-90-DL Dakota	20453	VR-TBT EI-AFB/OY-DDO/OY-DDI/43-15987	22.10.58	WFU at Luton in 2/70 & used for spares. Canx.
G-APPP	DHA.3 Drover 2	5002	(VH-CAT) VH-BMU	. 3.59R	NTU - Not Imported - Remained as VH-BMU. Canx 9/59.
G-APPR	Westland-Sikorsky S-51 Widgeon Mk.2	WA/H/001	G-AKTW XD649/G-AKTW	3.11.58	To 5N-ABV 5/62. Canx 20.6.62.
G-APPS	Westland-Sikorsky S-51 Widgeon Mk.2	WA/H/003	VP-TCM G-APPS/G-ALIK	3.11.58	To 5N-AGA 7/63. Canx.
G-APPT	DH.82A Tiger Moth	84567	T6100	24.10.58	To (OO-SOK)/OO-SOW 1/59. Canx 2.1.59.
G-APPU	Vickers 812 Viscount	364	N252V G-APPU/(N252V)	7.11.58	DBR on landing at Southend on 4.5.68. Canx.
G-APPV	Auster J/1N Alpha	3389		31.10.58	To SE-CMA 11/58. Canx 2.4.59.
G-APPW	Scottish Aviation Twin Pioneer Srs.2	533	(PI-C430)	20. 8.58	WFU & stored at Prestwick in 11/59. Canx as WFU 4.6.64. Fuselage to Army for parachute training in 4/62.
G-APPX	Vickers 702 Viscount	73	VP-BBV G-APPX/VP-TBM	14.11.58	WFU at East Midlands on 15.7.73. Broken up by 10/77. Canx.
G-APPY	Westland-Sikorsky S-55 Whirlwind Srs.2	WA/268		6.11.58	To EP-BSK 4/59. Canx 2.4.59.
G-APPZ	Westland-Sikorsky S-55 Whirlwind Srs.2	WA/269		6.11.58	To EP-CSK 4/59. Canx 2.4.59.
G-APRA	DH.82A Tiger Moth	85347	DE313	11.11.58	Crashed on take-off near Kells, Co.Meath, Eire on 23.6.63. Rebuilt as EI-AHI 9/93. Canx.
G-APRB	Thruxton Jackaroo	3971	N6667	25.11.58	Not converted. Dismantled at Thruxton. Canx 18.6.69.
G-APRC	Thruxton Jackaroo	84489	T8197	25.11.58	Conversion abandoned. Canx 18.6.69.
G-APRD	Hiller 360 UH-12C	777	N9738C G-APRD/N5319V	9.12.58	To LN-ORX 9/69. Canx 20.6.69.
G-APRE	Auster 5 Alpha	3411		5.12.58	To SE-CGK 2/59. Canx 20.1.59.
G-APRF	Auster 5 Alpha	3412	VR-LAF G-APRF	8.12.58	
G-APRG	DH.82A Tiger Moth	82332	N9215	8.12.58	To OH-ELC 9/60. Canx 13.9.60.
G-APRH	Garland-Bianchi Linnet	002		15. 1.59	Destroyed in heavy landing in Jersey on 5.5.67. Canx.
G-APRI	DH.114 Heron 2D	14126	H-105 R.Jordanian AF/G-APRI/R.Jordanian AF H-105	30.12.58	To N782R 12/65. Canx 1.11.65.
G-APRJ	Avro 694 Lincoln B.2	-	RF342 G-36-3/G-29-1/G-APRJ/RF342	29.12.58	(Remains in open storage 10/97 North Weald)
G-APRK	DH.114 Heron 2D	14050	5N-AGM(2) G-APRK/OY-DGK/G-APRK/OY-DPN/PH-VLA/G-APRK/SA-R-5	12. 1.59	Restored as OY-DGK 1/68. Canx 19.1.68.
G-APRL	Armstrong-Whitworth 650 Argosy Srs.101	AW.6652	N890U N602Z/N6507R/G-APRL	2. 1.59	Flown from East Midlands Airport to Coventry on 20.2.87 & WFU. Canx as WFU 19.11.87. On display 3/96 Baginton.
G-APRM	Armstrong-Whitworth 650 Argosy Srs.102	AW.6653		2. 1.59	CofA expired 1.4.82 & WFU at Exeter. Broken up for spares. Canx as destroyed 12.8.85.
G-APRN	Armstrong-Whitworth 650 Argosy Srs.102	AW.6654	N897U G-APRN/G-11-2	2. 1.59	WFU on 27.8.82. Broken up. Canx.
G-APRO	Auster 6A Tugmaster (Remains painted up as G-APRO in the hands of John Morris, Marblehead, Massachusetts .91)	-	WJ370	21. 1.59	To N370WJ. Canx 29.5.84.
G-APRP	Avro 694 Lincoln B.2	-	RF402	22. 1.59	Not converted. Broken up for spares for G-APRJ in 1960. Canx 6/59.

Regn	Type	c/n	Previous identity	Regn date	Fate or immediate subsequent identity (if known)
G-APRR	CZL Super Aero 45 Srs.04	04-014	OK-KFQ	5. 1.59	
G-APRS	Scottish Aviation Twin Pioneer Srs.3	561	G-BCWF XT610/G-APRS/(PI-C430)	9. 1.59	
G-APRT	Taylor JT.1 Monoplane	PFA/537		15. 1.59	
G-APRU	Morane-Saulnier MS.760 Paris 1A	8	G-36-2 F-WJAC	15. 1.59	Canx 31.3.86 on sale to Canada. To N60GT 4/86.
G-APRV	Westland-Sikorsky S-55 Whirlwind Srs.1	WA/295		13. 1.59	To VR-BBE 2/59. Canx 23.3.59.
G-APRW	Westland-Sikorsky S-55 Whirlwind Srs.3 (Originally Srs.1, converted in 1967)	WA/296	D-HODA VR-BBF/G-APRW	13. 1.59	To ZS-HDX 12/73. Canx 3.12.73.
G-APRX	DH.82A Tiger Moth	85302	DE256	16. 1.59	Crashed at Compton Abbas on 6.10.68. Canx as destroyed 15.7.69.
G-APRY	DH.82A Tiger Moth	85482	DE486	16. 1.59	To I-BANG 7/59. Canx 21.5.59.
G-APRZ	NHI H.3 Kolibrie 1	3009	PH-ACD	6. 2.59	To 4X-BDB 8/61. Canx.
G-APSA	Douglas DC-6A (Line No. 995)	45497	4W-ABQ HZ-ADA/G-APSA/CF-MCK/CF-CZY	23. 1.59	
G-APSB	DHC.1 Chipmunk 22A (Fuselage no. DHB/f/820) (Originally regd as a Mk.22)	C1/0930	WZ883	21. 1.59	To N111PR 3/71. Canx 11.3.71.
G-APSC	DHC.1 Chipmunk 22 (Fuselage no. DHB/f/561)	C1/0673	WP782	21. 1.59	To N12158 7/71 with c/n JC-1. Canx 14.7.71.
G-APSD	DH.89A Dragon Rapide	6556	X7396	4. 2.59	WFU on 10.7.64. Burnt at Shoreham on 4.5.66. Canx.
G-APSE	Brantly B.2	14		9. 6.59	To N511R 11/60. Canx 23.11.60.
G-APSF	Brantly B.2	15		9. 6.59	To N511Z 11/60. Canx 23.11.60.
G-APSG	Not allocated.				
G-APSH	Hiller 360 UH-12B	747	N5313V	1. 4.59	To N3877W 3/83. Canx 21.1.80.
G-APSI	EoN AP.6 Olympia 401	EoN/4/005		24. 2.59	To RAFGSA.252 in 5/59. Canx.
G-APSJ	Piaggio P.166	354		11. 3.59	To (VH-SMF)/VH-ACV 11/63. Canx 25.11.63.
G-APSK	DH.104 Dove 5	04504		9. 2.59	CofA expired 18.9.75 & WFU at Levesden. Broken up. Canx.
G-APSL	Hiller 360 UH-12B	555	N5300V	16. 2.59	Overturned and DBF in a forced-landing at Yolanda Farm, 36 miles from Santiago, Dominican Republic on 19.4.60. Canx.
G-APSM	Auster J/1N Alpha	3388		11. 2.59	To TS-AAA 3/59. Canx 23.3.59.
G-APSN	Auster J/1N Alpha	3390		11. 2.59	To TS-AAB 3/59. Canx 23.3.59.
G-APSO	DH.104 Dove 5	04505	(N1046T) G-APSO	16. 2.59	(Stored dismantled 3/99 Cumbernauld)
G-APSP	Auster J/1U Workmaster	3498	(F-OBHQ)	22. 4.59	Destroyed at Ebona, Cameroons on 21.11.64. Canx as destroyed 17.12.68.
G-APSR	Auster J/1U Workmaster	3499	OO-HXA G-APSR/VP-JCD/(F-OBHR)/G-APSR	22. 4.59	
G-APSS	DH.82A Tiger Moth	84653	T6227	18. 2.59	CofA expired 10.6.66. Canx 4.4.67.
G-APST	Druine D.31 Turbulent	PFA/472		10. 3.59	Destroyed in gales at Lydd on 2.5.76. Canx as destroyed 14.9.76.
G-APSU	Thruxton Jackaroo	3879	N6585	20. 2.59	Conversion abandoned at Thruxton 1962. Canx 18.6.69.
G-APSV	Thruxton Jackaroo (Identity unconfirmed; regd as "DE636")	85358	(G-ANPY) DE336	20. 2.59	Conversion abandoned at Thruxton 1962. Canx.
G-APSW	DH.114 Heron 2D	14132		24. 2.59	To CR-TAI 5/59. Canx 30.5.59.
G-APSX	EoN AP.6 Olympia 419X	EoN/4/007		24. 2.59	To BGA.1052 in 4/62. Canx as WFU in 9/59.
G-APSY	Bensen B.7Mc Gyrocopter	JH/001 & 2		22. 2.59	Crashed at Biggin Hill on 19.9.59 & DBR. Canx as WFU 13.4.73. (Stored)
G-APSZ	Cessna 172	172-46472	N6372E	21. 5.59	Damaged in gales at Barton on 2.3.84. Canx as TWFU 8.1.85. (Stored 4/91)
G-APTA	Vickers 702 Viscount	71	VP-BBW G-APTA/VP-BBW/G-APTA/VP-TBK	7. 8.59	WFU & stored at Southend. CofA expired 13.7.69. Broken up in 2/70. Canx 24.2.70.
G-APTB	Vickers 833 Viscount	424		2. 3.59	To 4X-AVB 12/69. Canx 17.12.69.
G-APTC	Vickers 833 Viscount	425		2. 3.59	To 4X-AVC 10/69. Canx 14.10.69.
G-APTD	Vickers 833 Viscount	426	JY-ADC G-APTD	2. 3.59	To 4X-AVD 2/70. Canx 20.2.70.
G-APTE	Westland-Sikorsky WS-51 Widgeon 2	WA/H/149	(5N-AGM) G-APTE	3. 3.59	WFU on 20.10.67. Canx as WFU 2.3.73.
G-APTF	DHC.1 Chipmunk 22 (Fuselage no. DHB/f/280)	C1/0392	WG320	4. 3.59	To Irish Air Corps in 3/65 & parts used in 199 (C1/0013). Canx 17.2.65.
G-APTG	DHC.1 Chipmunk 22A (Fuselage no. DHB/f/303)(Originally regd as a Mk.22)	C1/0440	WG353	4. 3.59	DBR on landing at Elstree on 3.10.65. Wreck to East Midlands. Canx.
G-APTH	Agusta-Bell 47J Ranger	1058	5N-ACP G-APTH	17. 4.59	To D-HELT 3/92. Canx 5.2.92.
G-APTI	DH.82A Tiger Moth	82783	R4851	10. 3.59	Crashed on landing at Vinon, Southern France on 17.8.63. Canx.
G-APTJ	PA-22-135 Tri-Pacer	22-1025	N1207C	10. 3.59	To VP-YRE 4/59. Canx 17.8.59.
G-APTK	Cessna 310	35453	OO-DST N5253A	10. 4.59	Crashed whilst on approach to Norwich on 25.10.74. Canx as destroyed 6.11.74.
G-APTL	Avro 652A Anson 19 Srs.2	-	VM305	2. 4.59	To EP-CAA 3/60. Canx 18.3.60.
G-APTM	Hiller 360 UH-12B	674	PI-C364	2. 4.59	To N3877L 2/83. Canx 21.1.80.
G-APTN	Hiller 360 UH-12B	680	PI-C365	2. 4.59	To N9742F 8/62. Canx 8.8.62.
G-APTO	Auster J/1N Alpha	3391		15. 4.59	To D-EGIV 4/59. Canx 4.5.59.
G-APTP	PA-22-150 Tri-Pacer (Conv. to PA-20 Pacer standard)	22-5009	EI-AJN	20. 3.59	
G-APTR	Auster J/1N Alpha	3392		15. 4.59	(On rebuild 9/96)
G-APTS	DHC.1 Chipmunk 22A (Fuselage no. DHB/f/573) (Originally regd as a Mk.22)	C1/0683	WP791	21. 4.59	To VH-ZIZ 7/94. Canx 1.7.93.
G-APTT	Douglas DC-4-1009	42916	N5518V VH-ANE/NC6406	1. 5.59	To TJ-ABD 11/61. Canx 22.9.61.
G-APTU	Auster 5	3413		20. 4.59	
G-APTV	DH.82A Tiger Moth	83790	T7276	27. 4.59	To I-MOMI 8/59. Canx 2.7.59.

Regn	Type	c/n	Previous identity	Regn date	Fate or immediate subsequent identity (if known)
G-APTW	Westland-Sikorsky S-51 Widgeon Srs.2	WA/H/150		24. 4.59	WFU at Southend on 26.9.75. Canx as WFU 24.8.77. (On display 5/97 at Helston)
G-APTX	Westland WS-59 Westminster 1	WA/2		5. 5.59	WFU in 1960. Dismantled at Yeovilton in 8/62. Canx 6/64.
G-APTY	Beechcraft G35 Bonanza	D-4789	EI-AJG	4. 6.59	
G-APTZ	Rollason-Druine D.31 Turbulent	PFA/508		18. 3.59	
G-APUA	Auster J/1N Alpha	3393		6. 5.59	To SE-CMD 6/59. Canx 10.6.59.
G-APUB	Beechcraft 95 Travel Air	TD-240		5. 6.59	To N2620U 9/81. Canx 23.9.81.
G-APUC	Douglas C-47A-20-DK Dakota	12893	EI-ACH 42-93027	3. 6.59	To 9N-AAM 4/64. Canx 3.4.64.
G-APUD	Wallis-Bensen B-7Mc Gyrocopter	1		11. 5.59	WFU on 27.9.60 at Biggin Hill. Canx as WFU 27.2.70. (Loaned to Manchester Museum of Science and Industry) (On display 3/96)
G-APUE	CZL L-40 Meta-Sokol	150708	OK-NMB	2. 6.59	
G-APUF	Cessna 310C	35960	N1860H	9. 6.59	Crashed near Vieira do Minho, Portugal on 18.11.70. Canx.
G-APUG	Luton LA-5A Major	PAL.1203 & PFA/1205		13. 5.59	(Under construction Camberley 1963-75) Construction abandoned. Canx as WFU 5.8.87.
G-APUH	Hiller 360 UH-12B	744	D-HABA	14. 5.59	Destroyed when overturned and burnt out at Setar, French Sahara on 19.12.59. Canx.
G-APUI	PA-18A-150 Super Cub	18-6670	EI-AKS	21. 5.59	Crashed after striking cables at Good Easter, Essex on 25.7.63. Canx.
G-APUJ	PA-18A-150 Super Cub	18-6644	N9377D	9. 6.59	Crashed, struck cables on take-off at Dunholme, Lincs on 2.8.62. Canx.
G-APUK	Auster J/1 Autocrat	1843	5N-ADW VR-NDJ/G-APUK/D-EGEG/SE-ARA	16. 6.59	CofA expired 8.10.75. Canx by CAA 3.4.89. (Stored .95 at owner's home)
G-APUL	Auster 5 Alpha	3414		2. 6.59	To D-ECUZ 11/59. Canx 2.11.59.
G-APUM	Scottish Aviation Twin Pioneer Srs.3	547		3. 6.59	To Nepal as 9N-RF7 in 5/65. Canx 4.5.65.
G-APUN	Phoenix-Luton LA-5A Major	PFA/1201		10. 6.59	Construction abandoned. Canx as WFU 26.11.74.
G-APUO	Aviamilano F.8L Falco Srs.III	209		19. 6.59	Crashed on take-off from Denham on 31.1.60. Canx.
G-APUP	Sopwith Pup (Used most parts of Pup N5182)	B.5292 & PFA/1582	N5182	13. 2.59	WFU at Blackbushe on 28.6.78. (On display 10/95 Hendon) (Also allotted 9213M .94)
G-APUR	PA-22-160 Tri-Pacer	22-6711		3. 7.59	
G-APUS	DHC.1 Chipmunk T.10 (Fuselage no. DHB/f/175)	C1/0297	WD358	8. 6.59	Conversion abandoned at Biggin Hill in 1960. Canx 1.9.60.
G-APUT	PA-22-160 Tri-Pacer	22-6673		31. 7.59	To VH-PUT 7/77. Canx 22.7.77.
G-APUU	Breguet 905PS Fauvette	P.S.5	F-CCIE	19. 6.59	Restored as F-CCIE in 2/64. Canx 10.1.64.
G-APUV	Bensen B-7MC Gyrocopter	3		16. 6.59	Badly damaged in a crash at Manby on 2.9.60 & WFU. Canx 12.6.68.
G-APUW	Auster J/5V Srs.160 Autocar	3273	(VH-...)	23. 6.59	
G-APUX	Hawker Hunter T.66A (Nose section from Indian Hunter T.66 BS369 & fuselage of Belgian Hunter F.6 IF.19) (Converted to T.72 version prior to going to Chile)	8763 & H/IF/19	L-581 Lebanon AF/G-APUX/Iraqi AF 567(1)/G-APUX	24. 6.59	To G-9-232/Chilean AF as J-718 in 8/67 as a T.72. Canx 9.8.67.
G-APUY	Rollason-Druine D.31 Turbulent	PFA/509		24. 6.59	(On rebuild .95) (Wings at Barton 12/97)
G-APUZ	PA-24-250 Comanche	24-1094	N6000P	3. 7.59	
G-APVA	PA-22-160 Tri-Pacer	24-6741		1. 9.59	Forced landing at Crosland Moor on 20.9.73. (Remains to Bodmin later). Canx by CAA 15.9.86.
G-APVB	NHI H.3 Kolibrie	H.3011	PH-NIW	. 6.59R	NTU - Reservation only. Crashed at St.Andrew's, Fife on 6.6.59 still as PH-NIW. Canx 7.59.
G-APVC	Cessna 310C	35948	N1848H	3. 7.59	Restored as N1848H 3/62. Canx 12.3.63.
G-APVD	Westland-Sikorsky S-51 Widgeon Srs.2	WA/H/151		30. 6.59	WFU at Southend on 13.10.69. Canx as WFU 24.8.77.
G-APVE	Piaggio P.166	355		10. 6.59	To VH-SMF 9/63. Canx 4.7.63.
G-APVF(1)	Hunting-Percival P.84 Jet Provost	-		. 7.59R	NTU - Canx.
G-APVF(2)	Putzer Elster B	006	D-EEQX West German AF 97+04/D-EJUH	29.12.83	
G-APVG(1)	Mooney M.20A	1474	N8164E	. 7.59R	NTU - To G-APVV 7/59. Canx.
G-APVG(2)	Auster J/5L Aiglet Trainer	3306	(ZK-BQW)	10. 7.59	
G-APVH	Armstrong-Whitworth 650 Argosy Srs.101	AW.6655		3. 7.59	To N6504R 11/60. Canx.
G-APVI	Phoenix-Luton LA-4A Minor	PAL.1101		7. 7.59	Not completed. Canx 15.5.81. Completed as ZK-FSU in 2/89 with c/n AACA/713.
G-APVJ	Hunting P.66 President 2	114	EC-APC	24. 8.59	To Sudanese AF as 12 in 3/60. Canx 4.12.59.
G-APVK	PA-23-160 Apache	23-1719		12.10.59	Destroyed in forced landing near Dewsbury on 25.7.76. Canx as destroyed 9.10.84.
G-APVL	Saunders-Roe P.531-2	S2/5311		23. 7.59	To Army Air Corps as XP166 in 4/61. Canx.
G-APVM	Saunders-Roe P.531-2	S2/5312		23. 7.59	To Army Air Corps as XR493 in 9/61. Canx.
G-APVN	Druine D.31 Turbulent	PFA/511		24. 7.59	(Stored 3/97)
G-APVO	Garland Bianchi Linnet	003		6. 8.59	NTU - Not completed. Canx 21.2.61. Parts used for G-ASFW.
G-APVP	DH.82A Tiger Moth	85758	DE873	29. 7.59	Fatal crash & burnt out after colliding with overhead cables at Dulles Farm, Ellingham, Norfolk on 21.7.68. Canx.
G-APVR	PA-18A-150 Super Cub	18-7062	N10P	10. 8.59	Crashed at Sunk Island, Hull on 1.9.65. Canx.
G-APVS	Cessna 170B (Converted back to its 1954 tailwheel configuration in 1968)	170-26156	N2512C	7. 8.59	
G-APVT	DH.82A Tiger Moth	3250	K4254	7. 8.59	Fatal crash after colliding with Beta G-ATLY near Tollerton on 29.9.73 and destroyed. Canx.
G-APVU	CZL L-40 Meta-Sokol	150706	OK-NMI	21. 8.59	Damaged on landing at Ringway on 12.9.78. (On rebuild .93)
G-APVV	Mooney M.20A	1474	(G-APVG) N8164E	30. 7.59	Crashed at Barton on 11.1.81. Canx by CAA 3.4.89. (Fuselage stored 2/99 Winthorpe)
G-APVW	Beechcraft A35 Bonanza	D-1168	EI-BIL G-APVW/N9866F/4X-ACI/Israli DF/AF 0604/ZS-BTE	5. 2.60	To G-NEWT 2/90. Canx.

Regn	Type	c/n	Previous identity	Regn date	Fate or immediate subsequent identity (if known)
G-APVX(1)	Scottish Aviation Twin Pioneer Srs.3	548		. 9.59R	NTU - To G-ARBA 4/60. Canx.
G-APVX(2)	DH.104 Dove 6	04509	G-5-12	10.12.59	To VH-WST 4/72. Canx 25.4.72.
G-APVY	PA-25-150 Pawnee	25-168		31. 5.60	CofA expired 2.7.87. Canx by CAA 22.3.91.
G-APVZ	Rollason-Druine D.31 Turbulent	PFA/545		23. 7.59	
G-APWA	Handley Page HPR.7 Dart Herald 100	149	PP-SDM G-APWA/PP-SDM/PP-ASV/G-APWA	28. 9.59	CofA expired 13.8.82 & WFU at Southend. Canx as WFU 29.1.87. (On display 4/97 Woodley)
G-APWB	Handley Page HPR.7 Dart Herald 101	150		28. 9.59	To HK-718 11/70. Canx 5.11.70.
G-APWC	Handley Page HPR.7 Dart Herald 101	151		28. 9.59	To HK-715 10/70. Canx 26.10.70.
G-APWD	Handley Page HPR.7 Dart Herald 101	152		28. 9.59	To HK-721 11/70. Canx 24.11.70.
G-APWE	Handley Page HPR.7 Dart Herald 201	153		28. 9.59	WFU in 11/82 at Norwich. CofA expired 30.3.83. Broken up in 11/85. Canx as destroyed 14.11.84.
G-APWF	Handley Page HPR.7 Dart Herald 201	154		28. 9.59	WFU & stored in 7/81 at Jersey Airport. Broken up in 4/84. Canx as WFU 9.2.84.
G-APWG	Handley Page HPR.7 Dart Herald 201	155		28. 9.59	WFU & stored in 7/81 at Jersey Airport. Broken up in 4/84. Canx as WFU 9.2.84.
G-APWH	Handley Page HPR.7 Dart Herald 201	156		28. 9.59	WFU in 11.7.80 at Norwich. Broken up in 4/82. Canx. Fuselage to Norwich Fire Service.
G-APWI	Handley Page HPR.7 Dart Herald 201	157		28. 9.59	To B-2009 8/68. Canx 6.12.68.
G-APWJ	Handley Page HPR.7 Dart Herald 201	158		28. 9.59	WFU at Norwich in 6/85, then to Duxford 7.7.85. Canx as WFU 10.7.85. (On display 7/99 Duxford)
G-APWK	Westland-Sikorsky S-51 Widgeon Srs.2	WA/H/152		26. 8.59	WFU at Yeovil on 22.5.70. Canx 10.9.73.
G-APWL	EoN AP.10 460 Standard Srs.1A	EoN/S/001	BGA.1172 RAFGSA.268/G-APWL	2. 9.59	
G-APWM	Westland-Sikorsky S-55 Whirlwind Srs.1	WA/297	9K-BHD G-APWM	8. 9.59	No CofA issued since being restored in 12/73. Canx as destroyed 30.4.85.
G-APWN	Westland-Sikorsky S-55 Whirlwind Srs.3 (Originally regd as a Srs.1)	WA/298	VR-BER G-APWN/5N-AGI/G-APWN	8. 9.59	CofA expired 17.5.78 & WFU at Redhill. Canx as WFU 25.6.81. (On display 3/96 Baginton)
G-APWO	Westland-Sikorsky S-55 Whirlwind Srs.3 (Originally regd as a Srs.1)	WA/299		8. 9.59	To EP-HAG 3/66. Canx 30.3.66.
G-APWP	Druine D.31 Turbulent	PFA/497		14. 9.59	WFU at Little Gransden in 10/70. (Status uncertain)
G-APWR	PA-22-160 Tri-Pacer	22-6666	EI-AKP	10. 9.59	Crashed in the sea off Isle of Wight on 7.7.91. Canx by CAA 21.10.91.
G-APWS	Vickers 621 Viking C.2	140	VL229	17. 9.59	Not converted. To spares use at Southend in 1961. Canx in 12/64.
G-APWT	Bellamy Currie Wot	HAC/4		28. 9.59	To N67247 7/75. Canx 8.7.75.
	(Made its first turbine-powered flight at Eastleigh on 26.1.60)				
G-APWU	Thurston Tawney Owl	TA.1-1		23. 9.59	Damaged on first flight at Stapleford on 22.4.60. (Stored 8/95 - for possible rebuild) Canx by CAA 15.9.86.
G-APWV	CZL L.40 Meta-Sokol	150707		3.11.59	Crashed on take-off from Stapleford on 17.7.65. Canx.
G-APWW	Armstrong-Whitworth 650 Argosy Srs.101	AW.6656	N895U N6503R/G-APWW/G-1-3	29. 9.59	To VH-BBA 4/74. Canx 9.4.74.
G-APWX	Lancashire EP.9 Prospector I	41		23. 9.59	To N8395 in 11/68. Canx 29.11.68. Derelict at Tutwiler, Mississippi, USA in 1975 still marked as G-APWX. Canx 29.11.68.
G-APWY	Piaggio P.166	362		16.12.59	(On display 9/93 Wroughton)
G-APWZ	Lancashire EP.9 Prospector I	42		5.11.59	Damaged in gales at Goodwood on 7/8.2.84. Canx as WFU 1.10.84. (On rebuild 7/93) Parts to G-APXW.
G-APXA	Westland-Sikorsky S-55 Whirlwind Srs.2 (Originally regd as Srs.1)	WA/318		28.10.59	To 9K-BHA 5/60. Canx 25.6.60.
G-APXB	Westland-Sikorsky S-55 Whirlwind Srs.2 (Originally regd as Srs.1)	WA/319		28.10.59	To 9K-BHB 6/60. Canx 25.6.60.
G-APXC	EoN AP.5 Olympia 2B	EoN/O/136		6.11.59	To BGA.1125 6/63. Canx 17.8.63.
G-APXD	Aeromere F.8L Falco 3	216		9.11.59	To EI-BBT 6/76. Canx 4.6.76.
G-APXE	Auster J/1U Workmaster	3500	(F-OBHS)	18.11.59	Damaged in the Sudan in 12/66. Canx as WFU 18.4.72.
G-APXF	Westland-Sikorsky S-55 Whirlwind Srs.2 (Originally regd as Srs.1)	WA/320	9K-BHC G-APXF	13.11.59	No CofA issued since being restored in 12/73. Canx as destroyed 30.4.85.
G-APXG	DH.114 Heron 2D	14137		20.11.59	To (K-ABAA)/9K-BAA 1/60. Canx 25.6.60.
G-APXH	Helio H.391B Courier	61	VP-YTP G-APXH/N7805B	10.12.59	Crashed on landing at Athens, Greece on 8.11.64 & DBR. Fuselage at Herzlia, Israel in 1978. Canx.
G-APXI	Westland-Sikorsky S-55 Whirlwind Srs.1	WA/321		3.12.59	NTU - Not built. Canx 4.6.64.
G-APXJ	PA-24-250 Comanche	24-291	VR-NDA	11.12.59	Canx by CAA 25.6.87.
G-APXK	Piaggio P.166	364		8. 3.60	To 5N-ADQ 11/69. Canx 26.11.69.
G-APXL	Scottish Aviation Twin Pioneer Srs.2	566	(PI-C433)	15.12.59	Restored as PI-C433 6/60. Canx 21.6.60.
G-APXM	PA-22-160 Tri-Pacer	22-7055		21. 1.60	Crashed at Sheldon, near Dunkeswell, Devon on 7.10.78 and used for spares at Tredegar. Canx as WFU 7.11.96.
G-APXN	PA-23-250 Aztec	27-119	TF-OBE G-APXN	3. 5.60	Crashed near Gleneagles on 24.6.71. Canx.
G-APXO	PA-22-150 Caribbean	22-7056		21. 1.60	Crashed about 30 miles from Burgos, Spain on 15.5.70. Canx.

Regn	Type	c/n	Previous identity	Regn date	Fate or immediate subsequent identity (if known)
G-APXP	PA-22-160 Tri-Pacer (Rebuilt in 1972 with fuselage from G-ARBT c/n 22-3870)	22-7111		29. 1.60	Crashed near Turriff, Aberdeen on 30.7.78. Canx by CAA 15.9.86.
G-APXR	PA-22-160 Tri-Pacer	22-7172		29. 1.60	
G-APXS	PA-22-150 Caribbean	22-7057		21. 1.60	Fatal crash & DBF 3 miles SSE of Sittingbourne, Kent on 8.6.71. Canx.
G-APXT	PA-22-150 Tri-Pacer (Badly damaged in storm Southend 26.12.85 & on rebuild to PA-20 Pacer status)	22-3854	N4545A	16. 2.60	
G-APXU	PA-22-150 Tri-Pacer (Mod)	22-474	N1723A	10. 2.60	(On rebuild Perth-Scone 5/98)
G-APXV	PA-22-160 Tri-Pacer	22-6411	N9437D	8. 1.60	To EI-AWD 12/72. Canx 19.12.72.
G-APXW	Lancashire Acft EP-9 Prospector (Composite rebuild from G-APWZ and others)	43		22.12.59	Crashed near Gartley, Aberdeenshire on 30.9.73 & DBR. Canx 20.5.82. (On display 3/96 Middle Wallop)
G-APXX	DHA.3 Drover 2	5014	VH-EAS VH-EAZ	15.12.59	Not converted. To Southend Museum in 5/67. Canx as WFU 26.11.73. (On display 3/96 Lasham)
G-APXY	Cessna 150	150-17711	N7911E	15. 1.60	
G-APXZ	Payne Knight Twister	BKT-001 & PFA/1307		7. 1.60	Not completed. Dismantled at Biggin Hill in 1967. Canx 26.3.73.
G-APYA	Cessna 175A	175-56444	N6944E	25. 1.60	To EI-AND 8/63. Canx 28.8.63.
G-APYB	Tipsy T.66 Nipper 3	T.66/S.39	(OO-NID)	28. 1.60	(Stored 4/97)
G-APYC	DH.106 Comet 4B	6437	SX-DAK G-APYC	21. 1.60	WFU at Lasham on 11.12.78. Broken up at RAF Kemble in 1979. Canx as WFU 11.12.78.
G-APYD	DH.106 Comet 4B	6438	SX-DAL G-APYD	21. 1.60	CofA expired 3.11.79. Canx as WFU 23.11.79. (On display 9/93 Wroughton)
G-APYE	DH.104 Dove 8 (Originally regd as a Dove 8A)	04515	G-5-11	22. 1.60	To N6533D 5/62. Canx 17.5.62.
G-APYF	Saunders-Roe XROE-1 Rotorcycle (Also Hiller c/n 9)	S2/7592	G-46-1	22. 1.60	NTU. Canx as WFU 27.12.63.
G-APYG(1)	Hawker Sea Hawk Executive	-		. .60R	NTU - Canx.
G-APYG(2)	Jodel	-		.10.60R	NTU - Canx.
G-APYG(3)	DHC.1 Chipmunk 22 (Fuselage no. DHH/f/66)	C1/0060	OH-HCB WB619	11.11.60	
G-APYH	Britten-Norman CC.1 Cushioncraft	C.1		9. 2.60	To Inter-Service Hovercraft Trials Unit in 1961. WFU and presented to Royal Military College of Science. Canx.
G-APYI	PA-22-135 Tri-Pacer (Converted to Pacer standard)	22-2218	N8031C	8. 2.60	
G-APYJ	Cessna 180A	180-50012	EI-ALO G-APYJ/N347TC/N9714B	26. 2.60	To VH-EDM 12/61. Canx 19.11.61.
G-APYK	Douglas C-54A-1-DC Skymaster	10279	N56006 42-72174	10. 3.60	Fatal crash into Mt.Canigou, near Roussillon, France while on approach to Perpignan on 3.6.67. Canx.
G-APYL	Bell 47D-1	LfS 1-1953	SE-HAG	6. 5.60	Destroyed in forced-landing near Perth on 18.7.63. Canx.
G-APYM	Cessna 172	172-46690	N7090T	19. 2.60	Crashed at Sarsden, Oxfordshire on 11.8.62. Wreck to Thruxton. Canx.
G-APYN	PA-22-160 Tri-Pacer	22-6797	N2804Z	24. 2.60	
G-APYO	Fairey Gannet T.5	F.9137	'AS-14' Indonesian Navy/WN365	17. 2.60	To RN as XT752 in 8/66. Canx.
G-APYP	Piaggio P.166	365		8. 3.60	To VH-MMP 1/64. Canx 30.1.64.
G-APYR	PA-18A-150 Super Cub (Rebuilt using spares fuselage no. 18-8017S)	18-4466	N2999P	26. 4.60	To PH-AAS 4/66. Canx 31.12.65.
G-APYS	Champion 7FC Tri-Traveler	7FC-386		. 2.60	NTU - Damaged 5.60 prior to delivery. Seen "serviceable" at Biggin Hill in 5/62 marked as G-APYS. To N8952R in 6/63. Canx.
G-APYT	Champion 7FC Tri-Traveler	7FC-387		9. 5.60	
G-APYU	Champion 7FC Tri-Traveler	7FC-388		12. 5.60	Crashed on landing at Old Warden on 23.4.72. Canx by CAA 3.4.89. (Stored 5/96)
G-APYV(1)	DH.82A Tiger Moth	85287	6746M DE241	. 2.60R	NTU - To G-AREH 7/60. Canx.
G-APYV(2)	Phoenix-Luton LA-4 Minor	PAL/1117 & PFA/820		26. 5.60	NTU - Not completed. Canx by CAA 2.9.91.
G-APYW	PA-22-150 Tri-Pacer	22-4994	N7131D	3. 3.60	CofA expired 6.7.88. (Present status and location uncertain) Canx by CAA 12.7.93.
G-APYX	PA-23-250 Aztec	27-105		28. 4.60	Canx as destroyed on 14.4.85.
G-APYY	Bristol 175 Britannia Srs.318	13432	CU-T668 CU-P668	25. 3.60	Restored as CU-T668 9/60. Canx 15.9.60.
G-APYZ	Rollason-Druine D.31 Turbulent	PFA/546		2. 2.60	Crashed at Little Snoring, Norfolk on 15.6.74, wreckage stored. Canx by CAA 24.8.81.
G-APZA	Consolidated 28-5A (PBY-5A) Catalina IIIA	1619	N94574 BuA.48257	14. 1.60	Not converted. Scrapped at Southend in 11/60. Canx as WFU 28.6.61.
G-APZB	Vickers 707 Viscount	30	EI-AFV	1. 2.60	WFU & stored in 5/68. CofA expired 12.5.68. Broken up in 2/70 at Southend. Canx as destroyed 26.2.70.
G-APZC	Vickers 707 Viscount	34	EI-AGI	29. 1.60	WFU & stored in 5/68. CofA expired 24.6.69. Broken up in 2/70 at Southend. Canx as destroyed 23.2.70.
G-APZD	PA-23-160 Aztec	23-1869		29. 1.60	Crashed into the railway embankment at Turnhouse while attempting an emergency landing due to engine failure shortly after take-off for Abbotsinch on 3.5.68. Canx.
G-APZE	PA-23-160 Aztec	23-1870		29. 1.60	WFU at Bansted in 12/81. Canx 4.10.84.
G-APZF	PA-24-250 Comanche (Officially regd with c/n 24-1190)	24-1205	EI-AKV	21. 1.60	Crashed at Peniarth on 1.6.69. Canx as destroyed 12.7.69.
G-APZG	PA-24-250 Comanche (Officially regd with c/n 24-1197)	24-1190	EI-AKW	19. 1.60	To G-DISK 8/89. Canx.
G-APZH	PA-24-250 Comanche	24-1557	N6893P	24. 1.60	NTU - Canx 5.2.60 as Not Imported. To D-ENOQ 5/60.
G-APZI	PA-24-250 Comanche	24-1605	N6894P	29. 1.60	NTU - Canx 5.2.60 as Not Imported. To N6894P/I-AIRC.
G-APZJ	PA-18-150 Super Cub (Rebuilt .86 following accident 12.6.83 using unidentified new fuselage frame; original frame in open store Membury 9/89)	18-7233		29. 1.60	

Regn	Type	c/n	Previous identity	Regn date	Fate or immediate subsequent identity (if known)
G-APZK	PA-18-160 Super Cub	18-7248		29. 1.60	To EI-CKH 6/94. Canx 3.6.94.
G-APZL	PA-22-160 Tri-Pacer	22-7054	EI-ALF	27. 1.60	
G-APZM	DH.106 Comet 4C	6440	SX-DAN G-APZM/(G-APMG)/G-APZM	3. 2.60	WFU at Lasham on 10.1.79. Broken up in 9/80. Canx as WFU 10.1.79.
G-APZN	Vickers 761D Viscount	190	XY-ADH 9Q-CRH/XY-ADH/G-APZN/XY-ADH	31. 3.60	WFU. Broken up in 1/80 at Eastleigh. Canx.
G-APZO	Hiller 360 UH-12A	167	N8167H	20. 4.60	To SU-ALK 2/61. Canx 15.2.61.
G-APZP	Vickers 779D Viscount	250	LN-FOH OE-LAB/LN-FOH	28. 3.60	Restored as LN-FOH 3/61. Canx 1.3.61.
G-APZR	Cessna 150	150-17861	N6461T	31. 3.60	Damaged in gales at Biggin Hill on 14.1.81. Canx. (Front fuselage only used as engine test-bed 2/95)
G-APZS	Cessna 175A Skylark	175-56677	N7977T	31. 3.60	(Badly damaged after being caught by a gust of wind and overturned taxying at Turnhouse on 29.6.94)
G-APZT	Douglas DC-6B (Line No. 176)	43263	N90751	28. 4.60	To 9K-ABB 7/62. Canx 7.7.62.
G-APZU(1)	PA-22-150 Tri-Pacer	22-5181	N7420D	. .60R	NTU - To G-APZX 4/60. Canx.
G-APZU(2)	DH.104 Dove 6	04511		13. 4.60	WFU at Exeter but believed taken to The Netherlands for destruction in the making of a film. Canx as WFU 14.4.89.
G-APZV	Avro 748 Srs.1/100	1534		24. 3.60	Converted to HS.780/748MF c/n 1548 - To G-ARRV 5/63. Canx 9.5.63.
G-APZW	Champion 7FC Tri-Traveler	7FC-393		12. 9.60	To EI-BBE 9/75. Canx 18.9.75.
G-APZX	PA-22-150 Tri-Pacer (Converted to taildragger)	22-5181	(G-APZU) N7420D	28. 4.60	
G-APZY	PA-22-150 Tri-Pacer	22-5123	N7334D	11. 4.60	Crashed at Naneby Hall on 25.7.64. Canx.
G-APZZ	Druine D.31 Turbulent	PFA/552		10. 3.60	Crashed into English Channel on 10.7.64. Canx.
G-AQAA	The series from G-AQAA to G-AQZZ were not allocated.				
G-ARAA	Cessna 182C Skylane	182-52646	N8746T	21. 4.60	Fatal crash into St.Catherine's Hill, Blackgang, Isle of Wight on 5.5.61. Remains at Panshanger by 2.6.61. Canx.
G-ARAB	Cessna 150C	150-17885	N6485T	29. 4.60	Badly damaged when blown over by high winds at Elstree on 26.1.87. Canx by CAA 25.6.87.
G-ARAC(1)	Cessna 180	180-50816		. 3.60R	NTU - Canx.
G-ARAC(2)	Cessna 180C	180-50827	N9327T	. 4.60R	NTU - To G-ARAT 5/60. Canx.
G-ARAC(3)	Cessna 310D	39154	N6854T	21. 6.60	Crashed at Perth, Scotland on 24.6.64. Canx.
G-ARAD	Phoenix Luton LA-5A Major	PAL/1204 & PFA/836		29. 4.60	(Completed but not flown) (Stored Lennox Plunton, Borgue 3/94)
G-ARAE	PA-22-150 Tri-Pacer	22-4114	PH-RAC N6818B	13. 5.60	Crashed while making a forced-landing at Stapleford Abbotts, 2 miles SE of Stapleford Tawney on 4.3.67. Canx.
G-ARAF	Phoenix Luton LA-5 Major (Incorporating LA-5 G-AOVX)	PAL/1209		24. 3.60	Construction abandoned. Canx as WFU 28.2.73.
G-ARAG	PA-22-160 Tri-Pacer	22-7348		28. 4.60	Clipped trees while taking-off from a private strip at Kenton Cross, Devon on 14.6.70. Canx.
G-ARAH	PA-22-160 Tri-Pacer	22-7423		28. 6.60	To G-HALL 11/79. Canx.
G-ARAI	PA-22-160 Tri-Pacer	22-7421		17. 5.60	
G-ARAJ	PA-22-160 Tri-Pacer	22-7393		17. 5.60	Forced landing near Skipsea, Yorks on 15.6.76. (Remains moved to Usworth by 7/76) Canx by CAA 14.7.86.
G-ARAK	PA-22-160 Tri-Pacer	22-7405		17. 5.60	To EL-ADW. Canx 18.10.62.
G-ARAL	PA-22-160 Tri-Pacer	22-7419		17. 5.60	To OO-DLH 7/63. Canx 20.6.63.
G-ARAM	PA-18-150 Super Cub	18-7312		17. 5.60	
G-ARAN	PA-18-150 Super Cub	18-7307		28. 4.60	
G-ARAO	PA-18-95 Super Cub	18-7327		17. 5.60	
G-ARAP	Champion 7EC Tri-Traveler (Originally regd as a 7FC)	7FC-394		12. 9.60	Damaged in crash at Eglinton, Northern Ireland on 22.9.81. (On rebuild 12/92)
G-ARAR	Champion 7FC Tri-Traveler	7FC-395		12. 9.60	Crashed at Sywell on 27.3.70 & DBR. Canx as WFU 30.7.70.
G-ARAS	Champion 7FC Tri-Traveler	7FC-396		12. 9.60	Extensively damaged after stalling 4.5.98 on approach to Headcorn.
G-ARAT	Cessna 180C	180-50827	(G-ARAC) N9327T	18. 5.60	
G-ARAU	Cessna 150	150-17894	N6494T	29. 4.60	CofA expired 14.9.84. Canx by CAA 3.4.89. (Stored unmarked 9/96 at Willingham)
G-ARAV(1)	Cessna 172A Skylark	172-47508	N9708T	. 3.60R	NTU - Canx. To VH-RGH 7/60.
G-ARAV(2)	Cessna 172A Skylark	172-47571	N9771T	29. 4.60	To EI-BAG 8/74. Canx 29.7.74.
G-ARAW	Cessna 182C Skylane	182-52843	N8943T	18. 5.60	
G-ARAX	PA-22-150 Tri-Pacer	22-3830	N4523A	22. 4.60	
G-ARAY	Avro 748 Srs.1A/200	1535	OY-DFV G-11/G-ARAY/PI-C784/G-ARAY/VP-LIO/ G-ARAY/PP-VJQ/G-ARAY/YV-C-AMC/G-ARAY	21. 4.60	WFU 17.10.89. CofA expired 16.6.90. Broken up in 5/92 at Lasham with fuselage going to fire services 12/95. Canx as WFU 2.11.95.
G-ARAZ	DH.82A Tiger Moth	82867	R4959	25. 3.60	
G-ARBA	Scottish Aviation Twin Pioneer Srs.3	548	(G-APVX)	29. 4.60	DBR 44 kms SE of Basra, Iraq on 10.1.71. Remains to Prestwick. Canx as WFU 5.8.71.
G-ARBB	DH.106 Comet 4C	6443	(XA-NAT)	27. 4.60	To XA-NAT(1) 11/60. Canx 25.11.60.
G-ARBC	Cessna 310D	39234	N6934T	5. 9.60	Canx as WFU 3.8.76. CofA expired 25.6.77. (On fire dump 12/95 Perth)
G-ARBD	DH.104 Dove 8A	04516		6. 5.60	To N6532D 6/61. Canx 22.5.61.
G-ARBE	DH.104 Dove 8 (Originally regd as a Dove 8A)	04517		6. 5.60	
G-ARBF	Bensen B.7M Gyrocopter	004		6. 5.60	Crashed at Tangmere on 29.4.61. Canx.
G-ARBG	Fairey Tipsy T.66 Nipper 2 (VW 1834)	ABAC.1 & T.66/S.57		11. 5.60	(Damaged on landing at Felthorpe on 16.5.84) (On rebuild off airfield 5/91)
G-ARBH	DH.104 Dove 1 (Originally regd as Srs.1, converted to Srs.1B in 1960, converted back to Srs.1)	04196	XY-ABS	14. 7.60	Canx 30.5.84. (Open storage 11/88 Zaragoza, Spain)
G-ARBI	Cessna 310C	35011	N2611C	18. 5.60	W/o 2.8.72. Canx as WFU 23.11.73. Wreck at Staverton 9/74.

Regn	Type	c/n	Previous identity	Regn date	Fate or immediate subsequent identity (if known)
G-ARBI	Cessna 310C	35011	N2611C	18. 5.60	W/o 2.8.72. Canx as WFU 23.11.73. Wreck at Staverton 9/74.
G-ARBJ	Slingsby T.43 Skylark 3F	WN1028	BGA.738	18. 5.60	To N5563V. Canx 15.8.60.
G-ARBK	Bensen B.7Mc Gyrocopter	005		30. 5.60	No CofA or Permit issued. Canx as WFU 5.3.73.
G-ARBL	Druine D.31 Turbulent	PFA/533		24. 5.60	Destroyed in hangar fire at Old Sarum on 16.1.87. Canx as destroyed 12.2.87.
G-ARBM	Auster J/1B Aiglet	2792	EI-AMO G-ARBM/VP-SZZ/VP-KKR	8. 6.60	
G-ARBN	PA-23-160 Apache	23-1385	EI-AKI N3421P	1. 6.60	Damaged at Sibson in 8/86. CofA expired 25.8.86. Canx as WFU 5.1.89. (Stored 5/98 at Sibson)
G-ARBO	PA-24-250 Comanche	24-2117		15. 6.60	Damaged in forced landing on a beach near Morecambe Bay on 27.4.83 & submerged by the tide. (Noted stored in a shed in a back garden of a house in Crudwell, Wilts in 1986)
"G-ARBO"	Airspeed AS.40 Oxford 1	-	DF425	----	False marks worn by an instructional airframe used by Air Service Training Ltd at Hamble in 1949, then Perth in 7/60.
"G-ARBO"	DH.82A Tiger Moth	-		----	False marks worn by an instructional airframe used by the Airwork engineering school at Perth in 9/61.
G-ARBP	Tipsy T.66S Nipper Srs.2	54		7. 6.60	
G-ARBR	PA-23-250 Aztec	27-170	N.....	15. 6.60	To F-BOES. Canx 21.8.66.
G-ARBS	PA-22-160 Tri-Pacer (Converted to PA-20 Pacer standard)	22-6858	N2868Z	24. 8.60	
G-ARBT	PA-22-150 Tri-Pacer	22-3870	N4559A	9. 9.60	DBR in landing accident at Fairoaks on 20.10.62. Fuselage used in rebuild of G-APXP c/n 22-7111 in 1972. Canx.
G-ARBU	PA-22-150 Tri-Pacer	22-4011	N4855A	18. 8.60	Fatal crash in the Leiza Navarre Mountains, Spain after taking-off from San Sebastian for Madrid on 19.5.68. Canx.
G-ARBV	PA-22-160 Tri-Pacer (Rebuilt 1983/84 using fuselage of G-ARDP c/n 22-4254)	22-5836	N8633D	29. 6.60	
G-ARBW	Vickers 779D Viscount	247	LN-FOM OE-LAE/LN-FOM	22. 6.60	Restored as LN-FOM. Canx 6.1.61.
G-ARBX	PA-18-95 Super Cub	18-7355		10. 6.60	DBF at St.Angelo on 9.4.81. Canx.
G-ARBY	Vickers 708 Viscount	10	F-BOEC G-ARBY/F-BGNL	27. 6.60	DBR in crash at Ottery St.Mary, near Exeter Airport on 17.7.80. Canx.
G-ARBZ	Rollason-Druine D.31 Turbulent	PFA/553		6. 5.60	
G-ARCA	PA-22-160 Tri-Pacer	22-7432		16. 6.60	Crashed at Maidstone, Kent on 8.1.67. Canx as WFU 5.3.73.
G-ARCB	PA-22-150 Caribbean	22-7470		16. 6.60	To 5B-CAQ /67. Canx 1.5.67.
G-ARCC	PA-22-150 Caribbean	22-4006	N4853A	23. 6.60	
G-ARCD	PA-22-160 Tri-Pacer	22-7478		16. 6.60	DBR at Squires Gate on 1.2.68. CofA expired 6.7.68. Canx as WFU 24.8.70. (Remains stored at Squires Gate 2/70)
G-ARCE	PA-20-135 Pacer	20-1107	F-BLLA CN-TDJ/F-DADR	28. 4.83	NTU - To G-PAXX 20.5.83. Canx.
G-ARCF	PA-22-150 Caribbean	22-4563	N5902D	28. 6.60	
G-ARCG	PA-22-160 Tri-Pacer	22-4443	N5743D	28. 6.60	Blown over by another aircraft and DBR at Luton 5.10.69. Canx as destroyed 4.12.69.
G-ARCH	Cessna 310D	39253	N6953T	19.10.60	DBR at Perth, Scotland on 16.2.70. Canx.
G-ARCI	Cessna 310D	39266	N6966T	21.10.60	Damaged in belly landing Sandtoft on 22.8.86 following first flight after rebuild. CofA expired 25.4.84. Canx by CAA 3.1.89. (Engineless & in open store Squires Gate 5/98)
G-ARCJ	Cessna 175A Skylark	175-56744	N8044T	14.10.60	DBR whilst taking-off from Sibson, Warwickshire on 23.8.66. Canx.
G-ARCK	Cessna 175A Skylark	175-56745	N8045T	7.11.60	DBR at Lympne, Kent on 25.10.72. Canx as WFU 29.10.73.
G-ARCL	Cessna 175A Skylark	175-56746	N8046T	15. 9.60	Badly damaged by severe gales at Withybush on 2.1.76. Canx 30.5.84.
G-ARCM	Cessna 172B Skyhawk	172-47852	N6952X	16.12.60	To G-TOBY 4/81. Canx.
G-ARCN	Percival P.66 President 2A (Originally c/n P66/106)	2/1040	10 Sudan AF/G-ARCN/EC-APA	27. 6.60	CofA expired 28.1.70 & WFU. Scrapped in 10/70 at Filton. Canx as destroyed 6.10.70.
G-ARCO	DH.106 Comet 4B	6449		15. 7.60	Fatal crash into Mediterannean Sea near the Island of Kastellorizon, east of Rhodes, Greece on 12.10.67. Canx.
G-ARCP	DH.106 Comet 4B	6451		15. 7.60	To G-BBUV 12/73. Canx.
G-ARCR(1)	Cessna 182C Skylane	182-52925	N9025T	. .60R	NTU - To (VP-KSH)/VR-TBW /60. Canx.
G-ARCR(2)	DHC.1 Chipmunk 22 (Fuselage no. DHB/f/158)	C1/0277	EI-AJF WD336	4. 8.60	Fatal crash at Church Road, Windlesham on 2.9.73. Canx as destroyed 13.2.75.
G-ARCS	Auster D.6/180	3703		4. 7.60	(Status uncertain)
G-ARCT	PA-18-95 Super Cub	18-7375	EI-AVE G-ARCT	6. 7.60	Damaged in hangar fire at Mullaghmore on 29.3.87. (Stored .96)
G-ARCU	PA-22-150 Caribbean	22-7471		6. 7.60	Damaged in a forced landing near Naples, Italy on 6.9.71. (Probably sold for spares or scrapped) CofA expired 15.10.72. Canx as WFU 5.12.77. (Remains noted in a scrapyard outside Rome in 1986)
G-ARCV	Cessna 175A Skylark	175-56757	N8057T	7.11.60	
G-ARCW	PA-23-160 Apache (Mod)	23-796	N2187P	7. 7.60	Canx by CAA 5.10.93. (Stored 8/96 Water Leisure Park, Skegness)
G-ARCX	Gloster Meteor NF.14 (Built by AWA)	AW.2163	WM261	8. 9.60	WFU at Turnhouse in 2/69. Canx as WFU 25.10.73. (On display 3/96 East Fortune)
G-ARCY	Auster 6A Tugmaster	2482	G-25-9 7433M/TW624	6. 7.60	Fatal crash on approach to Lasham on 9.9.60. Canx.
"G-ARCY"	Auster 6A Tugmaster	1905	TW524	----	Painted in error - To G-ARDX 8/60.
G-ARCZ	Rollason-Druine D.31 Turbulent	PFA/554		23. 6.60	Crashed onto the M11 Motorway on 1.6.84. Canx.
G-ARDA	Auster J/5G Cirrus Autocar	3157	VR-NBB	26. 7.60	Crashed at Squires Gate on 6.2.66. Canx.
G-ARDB	PA-24-250 Comanche	24-2166	PH-RON G-ARDB/N7019P	15. 8.60	
G-ARDC	Cessna 210 Centurion	210-57007	N7307E	15. 6.60	To SX-AJW 5/83. Canx 5.7.82.

Regn	Type	c/n	Previous identity	Regn date	Fate or immediate subsequent identity (if known)
G-ARDD	Scintex Piel CP.301C-1 Emeraude	549		4. 7.60	
	(Rebuilt by EMK Aeroplanes with c/n EMK.004)				
G-ARDE	DH.104 Dove 6	04469	I-TONY	15.11.60	(Stored 7/97)
G-ARDF	DHC.1 Chipmunk 22	C1/0314	(7643M)	25.11.60	DBR in accident at Thruxton on 11.7.71.
	(Fuselage no. DHB/f/193)		WD375		Canx as WFU 14.6.72.
G-ARDG	Edgar Percival EP.9 Prospector 2	47		14 7.60	Canx as WFU 28.5.82. To Museum of Army Flying, Middle Wallop. (Stored 7/93 with parts from G-APWZ/APXW)
G-ARDH	DH.104 Riley Dove 400	04519		20. 6.60	To OY-DRP 9/71. Canx 21.6.71.
	(Originally regd as Dove 8X for display at the 21st SBAC, Farnborough on 5-11.9.60)				
G-ARDI	DH.106 Comet 4B	6447	SX-DAO	15. 7.60	WFU on 21.9.71. Reduced to spares at Southend in 10/71.
			G-ARDI		Canx as WFU 16.5.72.
G-ARDJ	Auster D.6/180	3704		15. 7.60	Force-landed in a field 1½ miles south-east of Leicester on 30.5.86 & went through a hedge onto a road and overturned. (On rebuild 5/98 Leicester)
G-ARDK(1)	Aero Commander 560F	560F-892-.		9. 1.61R	NTU - Not Imported. Canx.
G-ARDK(2)	Aero Commander 560F	560F-882-.		. 4.61R	NTU - Not Imported. Canx.
G-ARDK(3)	Aero Commander 560F	560F-992-6		. 5.61	Canx 10.11.71 on sale to Portugal. To CS-AJL 10/72. (Open storage 3/95 Lisbon Airport - marks CS-AJL not applied)
G-ARDL	PA-24-250 Comanche	24-2161		28. 9.60	Force landed at Keighley on 4.8.70. Canx as WFU 27.5.71.
G-ARDM	DH.104 Dove 1B	04175	XY-ABN	22. 4.61	To 6V-PRB 2/64. Canx 30.7.65.
	(Originally regd as Dove 1)				
G-ARDN	DH.104 Dove 1B	04184	PH-VLC	23.11.60	To HB-LAX 11/66. Canx 25.11.66.
	(Originally regd as Dove 1)		"PH-VLA"/G-ARDN/XY-ABQ		
G-ARDO	Wassmer Jodel D.112	146	F-PBTE	22. 8.60	
	(Built by Ets Couesnon)		F-BBTE/F-WBTE		
	(Composite with fuselage of G-AYEO c/n 684 ex F-BIGG)				
G-ARDP	PA-22-160 Tri-Pacer	22-4254	N7004B	11. 8.60	CofA expired 12.12.79 & WFU at Southend. Fuselage used in rebuild of G-ARBV c/n 22-5836 in 1993/94. Canx.
G-ARDR	PA-24-180 Comanche	24-1053	N5963P	27. 7.60	Crashed near Monk's Myre Loch, Blairgowrie, Perthshire on 12.4.68. (Remains deposited at Goodwood) Canx.
G-ARDS	PA-22-150 Caribbean	22-7154	N3214Z	4. 9.60	
G-ARDT	PA-22-160 Tri-Pacer	22-6210	N9158D	15. 9.60	
G-ARDU	PA-22-150 Tri-Pacer	22-4950	N7053D	15. 9.60	Crashed near Lands End on 8.9.73. Canx as destroyed 9.9.74, and last reported at St.Just.
G-ARDV	PA-22-160 Tri-Pacer	22-7487	EI-APA	28. 7.60	Damaged at Ballymena, Northern Ireland on 10.7.98. CofA
			G-ARDV		expired 2.1.99. (Stored 2/99 Northrepps Village, Norfolk)
G-ARDW	DHC.1 Chipmunk 22	C1/0848	WP982	29. 7.60	Fatal crash & DBF while engaged in aerobatics practice at
	(Fuselage no. DHB/f/751)				Netherthorpe on 11.5.68. Canx.
G-ARDX	Auster 6A Tugmaster	1905	"G-ARCY"	2. 8.60	Badly damaged by fire at Lasham on 1.1.64. CofA expired
			TW524		29.8.64. (Frame stored 3/96)
G-ARDY	Tipsy T.66 Nipper 2	55		10. 8.60	
G-ARDZ	SAN Jodel D.140A Mousquetaire	49	(N.....)	10.11.60	CofA expired 29.11.91. (Stored 9/97 Monewden)
	(Originally regd as a D.140)		G-ARDZ		Canx by CAA 24.2.99.
G-AREA	DH.104 Dove 8	04520		3. 8.60	(Stored 3/96 at Hatfield)
	(Originally regd as a Dove 8A, converted to Dove 8 in mid-6/61)				
G-AREB	Cessna 175B Skylark	175-56818	N8118T	29.12.60	Damaged pre 3/90. (Stored 6/90) CofA expired 6.4.91. Canx by CAA 9.3.99.
G-AREC	DH.114 Heron 2D	14140		11. 8.60	To N562PR 12/68. Canx 5.12.68.
G-ARED(1)	PA-23-160 Apache	23-1887		. .60R	NTU - Canx.
G-ARED(2)	PA-23-160 Apache G	23-1886		28. 9.60	WFU at Biggin Hill on 29.10.79. Canx.
G-AREE(1)	PA-22-1..	22-....		. .60R	NTU - Canx.
G-AREE(2)	PA-23-250 Aztec	27-329		5.12.60	CofA expired 6.6.81. (Last known of in open storage at Stapleford) Canx by CAA 16.12.91.
G-AREF(1)	PA-22-1..	22-....		. .60R	NTU - Canx.
G-AREF(2)	PA-23-250 Aztec	27-285		28. 9.60	WFU at Biggin Hill on 3.9.85. Canx as WFU 30.9.85.
G-AREG	DH.104 Dove 1B	04061	OY-AAJ	9. 9.60	Seized against debts at Benina in 12/67, since noted as
			EP-ACG		derelict. Canx 31.12.67 as sold to Libya.
G-AREH	DH.82A Tiger Moth	85287	(G-APYV)	4. 7.60	(On long-term rebuild 5/94)
			6746M/DE241		
G-AREI(1)	DH.106 Comet 4B	6453		. 8.60R	NTU - To G-ARGM 8/60. Canx.
G-AREI(2)	Taylorcraft Auster III	518	9M-ALB	14.12.60	
			VR-RBM/VR-SCJ/MT438		
G-AREJ	Beechcraft B95 Travel Air	TD-123		5. 9.60	DBR at Stapleford on 15.8.80. CofA expiry 28.6.81. Canx as WFU 15.10.81.
G-AREK	Aviation Traders ATL-98 Carvair		F-BMHV	20. 9.60	To F-BYCL 7/77. Canx 6.7.77.
	(Initially Douglas	10365/5	LX-IOG/LX-IOH/G-41-1-73/N9757F/G-AREK/D-ADAL/N5520V/		
	C-54A-15-DC, converted in 11/62)		VH-INY/CY-CAC/VP-CBD/VH-ANG/NC57777/NC58003/BuA.50843/42-72260		
G-AREL(1)	Douglas C-54D-1-DC Skymaster	10563	D-AMIR	. 8.60R	NTU - To OO-RIC 12/60. Canx 16.12.80.
			N6874C/Bu.50877/42-72458		
G-AREL(2)	PA-22-150 Caribbean	22-7284	N3344Z	14. 9.60	
G-AREM	PA-22-150 Tri-Pacer	22-2714	N2303P	26. 8.60	Fatal crash at Bircher Common, Herefordshire on 23.9.67. Canx.
G-AREN	PA-22-150 Tri-Pacer	22-6196	N9056D	26. 8.60	Fatal crash at sea south of Littlehampton, Sussex, while on a photographic flight from Lympne to the Isle of Wight on 27.5.61. Canx.
G-AREO	PA-18-150 Super Cub	18-7407		24. 8.60	
G-AREP	Douglas DC-6B	43846	N90769	23. 9.60	To 9K-ABC 9/63. Canx 19.6.63.
	(Line No. 335)				
G-ARER	Vickers 708 Viscount	12	F-BGNM	19. 9.60	To F-BOEA in 8/66. Canx 27.6.66.
G-ARES	PA-22-150 Caribbean	22-7469	N3558Z	2. 9.60	To OY-DCR 3/64. Canx 1.2.64.
G-ARET	PA-22-160 Tri-Pacer	22-7590		2. 9.60	CofA expired 20.5.83. (On rebuild 10/97)
G-AREU	PA-18-95 Super Cub	18-7152	N3096Z	27. 9.60	To EI-ANY 11/64. Canx 11.11.64.
G-AREV	PA-22-160 Tri-Pacer	22-6540	N9628D	25.10.60	

Regn	Type	c/n	Previous identity	Regn date	Fate or immediate subsequent identity (if known)
G-AREW	PA-23-150 Apache	23-250	N1230P	7. 9.60	Restored as N1230P. Canx 11.2.63.
G-AREX	Aeronca 15AC Sedan	15AC-61	CF-FNM	12. 9.60	
G-AREY	Bellanca 14-13-2 Cruisair	1564	N9962F OO-DVL/NC74451	5. 6.61	Caught fire in the early hours of 8.8.69 and was destroyed at Blackbushe. Canx.
G-AREZ	Rollason-Druine D.31 Turbulent	PFA/561		22. 9.60	
G-ARFA	PA-22-150 Caribbean	22-7482	N3566Z	8. 9.60	To F-BLOD 1/64. Canx 6.8.63.
G-ARFB	PA-22-150 Caribbean	22-7518	N3625Z	8. 9.60	
G-ARFC	PA-22-150 Caribbean	22-7531	N3636Z	8. 9.60	Crashed at Fairoaks on 17.5.64. Canx.
G-ARFD	PA-22-160 Tri-Pacer	22-7565	N3667Z	8. 9.60	
G-ARFE	Bensen B.8M Gyrocopter	006		13. 9.60	No CofA or Permit issued. WFU at Yeovil 5/65. Canx.
G-ARFF	Beechcraft 65 Queen Air	LC-50		30. 9.60	To OO-AWA 4/76. Canx 29.4.76.
G-ARFG	Cessna 175AX Skylark (Rebuilt in 1988 to Cessna 172 standard)	175-56505	N7005E	15.11.60	
G-ARFH	PA-24-250 Comanche	24-2240	N7087P	13.10.60	
G-ARFI	Cessna 150A	150-59100	N41836 G-ARFI/N7000X	1. 2.61	
G-ARFJ	Cessna 172B Skyhawk	172-48306	N7806X	23. 3.61	Crashed near Yeadon on 30.7.64. Canx.
G-ARFK	Cessna 172B Skyhawk	172-48211	N7711X	23. 3.61	To EI-AYH 11/73. Canx 13.9.73.
G-ARFL	Cessna 175B Skylark	175-56868	N8168T	2. 2.61	
G-ARFM	Cessna 175B Skylark	175-56876	N8176T	2. 2.61	Dismantled at Newtownards, Northern Ireland. CofA expired 23.10.79. Canx by CAA 14.7.86.
G-ARFN	Cessna 150A	150-59172	N7072X	23. 3.61	Struck a tree and crashed after engine failure while taking-off at Crosby-on-Eden on 23.9.67. Canx.
G-ARFO	Cessna 150A	150-59174	N7074X	23. 3.61	
G-ARFP	Vickers 668 Varsity T.1	546	WF387	21. 9.60	CofA expired 20.9.67. Restored to RAF as WF387 in 9/67. Canx.
G-ARFR	PA-23-250 Aztec	27-5	N4503P	5.12.60	Crashed at Fontanes, Loire, France on 16.5.63. Canx.
G-ARFS	PA-22-150 Caribbean	22-7322	N3409Z	15.11.60	DBR 15.6.84. Canx.
G-ARFT	SAN Jodel DR.1050 Ambassadeur	170		27.10.60	Damaged when jumped chocks on being started Prestwick 15.6.84.
G-ARFU(1)	Douglas DC-6 (Line No. 6)	42856	N90703 NX90703	5.10.60	NTU - To JY-ACF 12/60. Canx 31.12.60.
G-ARFU(2)	EoN AP.10 Standard 460 Srs.1B	EoN/S/003		7. 3.61	To BGA.1177 in 6/64. Canx 20.1.65.
G-ARFV	Fairey Tipsy T.66 Nipper 2	44		5.10.60	Damaged in forced landing near West Malling on 25.9.90. (On rebuild .97)
G-ARFW	DHC.1A-1 Chipmunk 22	10	G-AJVD	12.10.60	Crashed 13 miles east of Cherbourg, France on 20.6.66. Canx.
G-ARFX	Saab 91A Safir	91-136	PH-UEC	12.10.60	Crashed at Home Farm, near Elstree on 15.7.62. Canx.
G-ARFY	PA-24-250 Comanche	24-2035	N6901P	25.10.60	Crashed near Cork, Ireland on 8.8.64. Canx.
G-ARFZ(1)	PA-22-150 Caribbean	22-7585	N3714Z	10. 7.61	NTU - Not Imported. To N10335. Canx.
G-ARFZ(2)	DH.104 Dove 8	04526	G-ARSI	17. 1.62	Burnt out at Biggin Hill on 24.2.73. Canx.
G-ARGA	Percival P.40 Prentice T.1	PAC/035	VR211	13.10.60	Not converted. Sold as scrap to International Alloys Ltd. at Aylesbury. Dumped by 4/61. Canx in 1961.
G-ARGB	Auster 6A Tugmaster	2593	VF635	12.10.60	CofA expired 21.6.74 at Southend. (Frame only stored 9/96)
G-ARGC	Cessna 180D (Robertson STOL conversion)	180-50931	N6431X	25.11.60	DBR on landing at Cockerham, near Lancaster on 26.4.80. Canx.
G-ARGD	Cessna 182D Skylane	182-53088	N9988T	2. 2.61	To CR-LDS 7/61. Canx 18.7.61.
G-ARGE	PA-22-160 Tri-Pacer	22-7606		17.10.60	To CR-LEL 2/62. Canx 18.12.61.
G-ARGF	PA-22-160 Tri-Pacer	22-7615		17.10.60	To CR-LEM 12/61. Canx 18.12.61.
G-ARGG	DHC.1 Chipmunk 22 (Fuselage no. DHB/f/132)	C1/0247	WD305	19.10.60	
G-ARGH	DHC.1 Chipmunk 22 (Fuselage no. DHB/f/72)	C1/0185	WB736	20.10.60	Crashed while landing at Ingoldmells, Skegness on 18.7.66. Remains sold for spares to Farm Aviation at Rush Green and used to rebuild G-APOS. Canx as WFU 23.2.73.
G-ARGI(1)	Saro P.531 Mk.2 Scout	S2/8441	XP189	. .60R	NTU - Remained with Army Air Corps as XP189. Canx.
G-ARGI(2)	Auster 6A Tugmaster	2299	VF530	8.12.60	WFU in 7/73. Canx. (Stored 9/96)
G-ARGJ	Payne-Knight Twister	BKT/002 & PFA/1308		28.10.60	Not completed. Canx as WFU 25.7.73.
G-ARGK	Cessna 210 Centurion	210-57427	N9627T	14. 3.61	CofA expired 19.9.77 & WFU. Abandoned at Palma, Majorca (still present in 8/83). Canx by CAA 9.10.84.
G-ARGL	PA-22-160 Tri-Pacer	22-5898	N8717D	22.11.60	Crashed at Horwich, near Bolton on 21.1.78. Canx.
G-ARGM	DH.106 Comet 4B	6453	(G-AREI)	31. 8.60	Canx as WFU 19.9.74 at Lasham. CofA expired on 6.10.74. Broken up in 9/74.
G-ARGN(1)	PA-22-108 Colt	22-8150		. .60R	NTU - Not Imported. To N4633Z. Canx.
G-ARGN(2)	DH.104 Dove 1	04001	N73795 CF-BNU	24. 1.62	CofA expired on 6.12.67. Canx as WFU 31.12.70 at Cranfield.
G-ARGO	PA-22-108 Colt	22-8034		18. 1.61	(Stored 3/98 Liverpool)
G-ARGP	Cessna 310	310-35260	N311EG CF-ILF/N3060D	2. 2.61	To F-BKBS 6/62. Canx 12.4.62.
G-ARGR	Vickers 708 Viscount	14	F-BOEB G-ARGR/F-BGNN	20.12.60	To 9Q-CAN(3) 3/85. Canx 26.11.84.
G-ARGS	PA-24-250 Comanche	24-898	N5817P	2.12.60	DBR at Mayenne, France on 19.4.65. Canx.
G-ARGT	Auster J/1N Alpha (Originally regd as J/1 Autocrat, modified in 1968)	2199	VP-YLT VP-RCF/VP-YGB	2. 1.61	To VH-EUD 3/73. Canx 5.3.73.
G-ARGU	PA-18-150 Super Cub	18-7544		20.12.60	To 5N-AEF 8/61. Canx 21.8.61.
G-ARGV	PA-18-180 Super Cub	18-7559	N10F	20.12.60	(Damaged in forced landing during take-off from Aboyne on 23.8.96)
G-ARGW	Aero Commander 500B	981-22		28.11.60	To N721LA 2/79. Canx 15.2.79.
G-ARGX	PA-22-160 Tri-Pacer	22-7616		20.12.60	Crashed near Newbury on 16.12.71. Canx as WFU 2.2.73.

Regn	Type	c/n	Previous identity	Regn date	Fate or immediate subsequent identity (if known)
G-ARGY	PA-22-160 Tri-Pacer (Converted to taildragger in 1/89)	22-7620	G-JEST G-ARGY	20.12.60	(Badly damaged in crash at Flecknoe on 4.10.91 whilst as G-JEST) (Stored pending rebuild 7/95)
G-ARGZ	Rollason-Druine D.31 Turbulent	PFA/562		7.11.60	(Heavy landing on landing at Rochester on 10.4.88)
G-ARHA	Forney F.1A Aircoupe	5725	N3030G	16.12.60	CofA expired on 20.3.70 & WFU at White Waltham. Canx as WFU 5.11.73. To G-ONHH 12/89.
G-ARHB	Forney F.1A Aircoupe	5733		17. 4.61	
G-ARHC	Forney F-1A Aircoupe	5734		26. 5.61	
G-ARHD	Forney F.1A Aircoupe	5735		22. 2.61	Caught in snowstrom and force-landed 10 miles south of St.Angelo on 25.11.73. Canx 21.12.73 as destroyed.
G-ARHE	Forney F.1A Aircoupe	5736		22. 2.61	Crashed at Kelvedon Hatch, Essex on 4.6.65. Canx.
G-ARHF	Forney F.1A Aircoupe	5737		26. 5.61	Canx by CAA 10.11.95. (Stored 2/99 Shipdham)
G-ARHG	Forney F.1A Aircoupe	5738		29. 3.61	Crashed at Biggin Hill on 3.6.64. Canx.
G-ARHH	PA-22-150 Caribbean	22-7626		20.12.60	To OY-AEI 3/63. Canx 20.3.63.
G-ARHI	PA-24-180 Comanche	24-2260		20.12.60	
G-ARHJ(1)	Lockheed L.049E-46-27 Constellation	2051	N2738A G-AMUP/N90921/NC90921	.12.60R	NTU - Restored as G-AMUP 1/61. Canx.
G-ARHJ(2)	PA-23-150 Apache	23-369	N1326P	9. 3.61	Fatal crash into Hilfield Reservoir immediately after take-off from Elstree on 27.1.68. Canx.
G-ARHK	Lockheed L.049-46-21 Constellation	2036	CU-T547 (4X-AKF)/CU-T547/N88836/NC88836	9. 2.61	NTU - Seized at Charlotte, NC in 1/61. To 4X-AOK 7/62. Canx 30.4.62.
G-ARHL	PA-23-250 Aztec	27-402		3. 3.61	(On overhaul 1/96)
G-ARHM	Auster 6A Tugmaster	2515	VF557	5. 1.61	
G-ARHN	PA-22-150 Caribbean (Rebuilt with parts from G-ATXB)	22-7514	N3622Z	10. 1.61	
G-ARHO	PA-22-150 Caribbean	22-7538	N3643Z	10. 1.61	To OY-ACW 7/62. Canx 6.3.62.
G-ARHP	PA-22-160 Tri-Pacer	22-7549	N3652Z	10. 1.61	
G-ARHR	PA-22-150 Caribbean	22-7576	N3707Z	10. 1.61	
G-ARHS	PA-22-160 Tri-Pacer	22-7582	N3711Z	10. 1.61	Struck overhead cable and crashed while attempting a forced landing near Ashwood pumping station on the Kidderminster-Wolverhampton road on 22.10.67. Canx.
G-ARHT	PA-22-150 Caribbean	22-7583	N3712Z	10. 1.61	Canx as WFU on 6.6.84.
G-ARHU	PA-22-160 Tri-Pacer	22-7602	N3726Z	10. 1.61	Crashed at Breighton on 24.5.98. Wreck present still in 7/98, removed by late-3/99. Canx by CAA 3.12.98.
G-ARHV	PA-22-160 Tri-Pacer	22-7614	N3734Z	10. 1.61	CofA expired 22.6.66 & WFU at Luton. Canx as WFU 13.9.73.
G-ARHW	DH.104 Dove 8	04512		10. 1.61	
G-ARHX	DH.104 Dove 8	04513		11. 1.61	WFU on 8.9.78 at Leavesden. Used by Southgate ATC. Canx 6.12.78. (On display 5/97)
G-ARHY	Vickers 745D Viscount	118	N7420	20. 1.61	To PI-C773 5/61. Canx 23.1.61.
G-ARHZ	Rollason-Druine D.62A Condor	PFA/247 & RAE/602		13.12.60	Badly damaged on landing at Damyns Hall, Upminster on 4.9.94.
G-ARIA	Bell 47D (Modified to a Bell 47G)	D-6	N4929V YI-ABY/NC152B	20. 1.61	To F-GFDP 7/87. Canx 27.3.87.
G-ARIB	PA-22-160 Tri-Pacer	22-7559	N3661Z	18. 1.61	Crashed near Strathallan on 27.5.70. Canx as WFU 27.8.70.
G-ARIC	Douglas C-54A-10-DC Skymaster	10306	N53487 Bu.39162/42-72201	18. 7.61	To 9Q-RIC 4/62. Canx 28.3.62.
G-ARID	Cessna 172B Skyhawk	172-48209	N7709X	2. 2.61	
G-ARIE	PA-24-250 Comanche	24-1888	ZS-CNL	25. 5.61	To F-OBPO. Canx.
G-ARIF	Ord-Hume O-H 7 Minor Coupe (Modified Phoenix Luton LA-4C Minor, also had c/n PAL/1026)	O-H 7 & PAL/1401		22. 8.60	No CofA or Permit issued. Canx. (Stored incomplete 3/96)
G-ARIG	Cessna 310B	35578	EI-AOS G-ARIG/N5378A	20. 1.61	Restored as EI-AOS 8/75. Canx 20.8.75.
G-ARIH	Auster 6A Tugmaster	2463	TW591	23. 1.61	
G-ARII	Beechcraft 65 Queen Air	LC-85		26. 1.61	To VH-CTE 5/68. Canx 10.2.68.
G-ARIJ	PA-22-160 Tri-Pacer	22-7552	N3655Z	26. 1.61	Ditched into the sea off Wimereux, France on 13.6.65. Canx.
G-ARIK	PA-22-150 Caribbean	22-7570	N3701Z	26. 1.61	
G-ARIL	PA-22-150 Caribbean	22-7574	N3705Z	26. 1.61	(On rebuild .92)
G-ARIM	Druine D.31 Turbulent	PFA/510		27. 2.61	Not completed. (Parts incorporated in G-AWBM)(Extant 4/97)
G-ARIN	PA-24-250 Comanche	24-1182	N6084P	10. 2.61	Crashed in a field near Bodmin on 20.5.90 on take-off. Canx as WFU 29.8.90.
G-ARIO	Bellamy Hilborne BH.1 Halcyon (Light twin all-wooden three/four seater machine)	HAC.5		30. 1.61	DBR during taxying trials at Eastleigh on 17.2.62. Project abandoned. Canx.
G-ARIP	Not allocated.				
G-ARIR	Vickers 708 Viscount	36	F-BLHI G-ARIR/F-BGNS	22. 3.61	To 9Q-CAH(2) 3/85. Canx 26.11.84.
G-ARIS	PA-22-108 Colt	22-8102		22. 2.61	Crashed at Kidlington on 5.11.61. Canx.
G-ARIT	Temco D.16 Twin Navion	NAV-4-1832	N4832K	8. 2.61	To TF-AIP 5/65. Canx 10.4.65.
G-ARIU	Cessna 172B Skyhawk	172-48449	(G-ARLT) N7949X	27. 6.61	CofA expired 17.11.76 & WFU at Baginton. Canx 5.2.82.
G-ARIV	Cessna 172B Skyhawk	172-48452	(G-ARLU) N7952X	24. 5.61	Canx as destroyed 16.3.95.
G-ARIW	Rousseau Piel CP.301B Emeraude	112	F-BIRQ	25. 4.61	To EI-CFG 6/91. Canx 21.1.91.
G-ARIX	SCAN 30/1 Widgeon	19	EI-ALE VP-KNV/F-BGTD	13. 2.60	Crashed while landing on Southampton Water, off Calshot on 19.5.61. Canx.
G-ARIY	Douglas C-54A Skymaster	3116	N88747 42-32941	2. 2.61	WFU at Speke on 23.7.64. Broken up for spares /65. Remains to Liverpool Airport Fire Service 1/66. Canx.
G-ARIZ	Rollason Druine D.31 Turbulent	PFA/563		30.12.60	Fatal crash on the Prospect estate, Limerick, Ireland after a mid-air collision with Plus D EI-ALJ on 25.8.62. Canx.
G-ARJA	Aero Commander 520	150	N2638B	15. 5.61	To SE-EFY 11/63. Canx 21.10.63.
G-ARJB	DH.104 Dove 8	04518		29. 9.60	WFU on 10.12.73. Canx 8.2.82. (Stored dismantled 3/99 Cumbernauld)
G-ARJC(1)	DH.106 Comet 4B	6452		. .61R	NTU - To G-ARJK 2/61. Canx.

Regn	Type	c/n	Previous identity	Regn date	Fate or immediate subsequent identity (if known)
G-ARJC(2)	PA-22-108 Colt	22-8154		21. 3.61	WFU on 28.11.75. Canx 2.2.82. (On rebuild)
G-ARJD(1)	DH.106 Comet 4B	6455		. .61R	NTU - To G-ARJL 2/61. Canx.
G-ARJD(2)	PA-22-108 Colt	22-8262		12. 4.61	DBR at Thruxton 17.11.71, used as spares at White Waltham. Canx 15.6.72 as destroyed. Frame stored 4/98 at Henstridge.
G-ARJE(1)	DH.106 Comet 4B	6456		. .61R	NTU - To G-ARJM 2/61. Canx.
G-ARJE(2)	PA-22-108 Colt	22-8184		29. 3.61	CofA expired 29.4.73. Fuselage parts at Hamble in 1984. (On rebuild .93)
G-ARJF(2)	DH.106 Comet 4B	6459		. .61R	NTU - To G-ARJN 2/61. Canx.
G-ARJF(2)	PA-22-108 Colt	22-8199		23. 3.61	CofA expired 9.2.80. (On rebuild 6/93 Warminster) Canx by CAA 11.12.96.
G-ARJG(1)	PA-23 Apache	-		. .61R	NTU - Canx.
G-ARJG(2)	PA-22-108 Colt	22-8226		12. 4.61	WFU at Blackbushe on 8.6.72. Canx 30.5.84.
G-ARJH(1)	PA-23 Apache	-		. .61R	NTU - Canx.
G-ARJH(2)	PA-22-108 Colt	22-8249		29. 3.61	
G-ARJI	PA-24-180 Comanche	24-2666		17. 4.61	Crashed at Fairoaks on 19.1.65. Canx.
G-ARJJ	Aero Commander 520	16	N4115B	3. 5.61	DBF on ground at Fairoaks on 19.8.69. Canx.
G-ARJK	DH.106 Comet 4B	6452	(G-ARJC)	13. 2.61	WFU & stored at Lasham in 11/76. Broken up in 10/77. Canx as WFU 2.12.77.
G-ARJL	DH.106 Comet 4B	6455	(G-ARJD)	13. 2.61	WFU & stored at Lasham in 11/73. CofA expired 29.7.74. Canx as WFU 19.9.74. Broken up in 9/74.
G-ARJM	DH.106 Comet 4B	6456	(G-ARJE)	13. 2.61	Fatal crash shortly after take off from Esenborga Airport, Ankara, Turkey on 21.12.61. Canx.
G-ARJN	DH.106 Comet 4B	6459	(G-ARJF)	13. 2.61	WFU & stored at Lasham in 12/77. Broken up in 11/78. Canx as WFU 24.8.81.
G-ARJO	CZL L-40 Meta-Sokol	150704		6. 4.61	Crashed at Biggin Hill on 4.6.65. Canx.
G-ARJP	PA-22-108 Colt	22-8129		21. 3.61	To ZS-IGX 1/71. Canx 19.6.70.
G-ARJR	PA-23-160 Apache G	23-1966	N4447P	1. 3.61	DBR at Little Berkhampstead on 22.7.78. (Instructional Airframe 5/95 Kidlington)
G-ARJS	PA-23-160 Apache G	23-1977		3. 3.61	
G-ARJT	PA-23-160 Apache G	23-1981		3. 3.61	(Stored 8/96)
G-ARJU	PA-23-160 Apache G	23-1984		3. 3.61	
G-ARJV	PA-23-160 Apache G	23-1985		3. 3.61	
G-ARJW	PA-23-160 Apache G	23-1986		3. 3.61	WFU & used for spares for G-ARJV at Lulsgate. (Noted dismantled 5/86) Canx as WFU 22.11.88.
G-ARJX	PA-23-160 Apache G	23-1987		3. 3.61	To TF-JEP 8/70. Canx 9.8.70.
G-ARJY	Douglas C-54A Skymaster	10288	N30068 42-72183	17. 2.61	Overshot and DBR while landing at Collinstown, Dublin, Ireland on 19.9.61. Remains to East Anglian Flying Services for spares use. Canx.
G-ARJZ	Rollason-Druine D.31 Turbulent (Converted to seaplane in 1966-74)	PFA/564		8. 2.61	(Stored 9/97)
G-ARKA	Bristol 175 Britannia Srs.324	13516	(HB-ITF) G-ARKA/CF-CPD/G-18-8	15. 2.61	Broken up in 10/71 at Baginton for spares. Canx.
G-ARKB	Bristol 175 Britannia Srs.324	13517	(HB-ITG) G-ARKB/CF-CPE	13. 4.61	WFU in 11/69. Broken up in 10/71 at Baginton for spares. Canx.
G-ARKC	Auster 6A Tugmaster	2261	VF492	15. 2.61	Crashed at Bidford-on-Avon on 12.6.71. Canx.
G-ARKD	Commonwealth CAC.17 (P-51D) Mustang Mk.20	1330	VH-BVM R.Australian AF A68-5	24. 2.61	DBR after an outbreak of fire in its cockpit at Athens, Greece on 7.9.61. (At Athens in damaged state 10/62)
G-ARKE	Beagle A.109 Airedale (Modified to A.109X, then A.111 status in 9/61) (Originally regd with c/n A.109-X)	B.501	G-25-11	24. 2.61	WFU at Rearsby in 4/63. Scrapped. Canx.
G-ARKF	Beagle A.109Y Airedale (Originally regd with c/n A.109-Y)	B.502		24. 2.61	Broken up at Rearsby in 6/62. Canx.
G-ARKG	Auster J/5G Cirrus Autocar	3061	AP-AHJ VP-KKN	22. 2.61	
G-ARKH	Vickers 707 Viscount	31	VR-BBJ G-ARKH/VR-BBJ/EI-AFW	9. 3.61	To VP-BCF 1/64. Canx 17.2.64.
G-ARKI	Vickers 707 Viscount	32	VR-BBH G-ARKI/VR-BBH/EI-AFY	9. 5.61	To VP-BCE 1/64. Canx 23.1.64.
G-ARKJ	Beechcraft N35 Bonanza	D-6736		5. 5.61	
G-ARKK	PA-22-108 Colt	22-8290		12. 4.61	
G-ARKL	PA-22-108 Colt	22-8297		12. 4.61	Crashed at Fairoaks on 10.8.68. CofA expired 8.9.69. Canx as WFU 18.9.73. Broken up for spares at Sandown in 1974.
G-ARKM	PA-22-108 Colt	22-8313		12. 4.61	
G-ARKN	PA-22-108 Colt	22-8327	N10F	9. 5.61	
G-ARKO	PA-22-108 Colt	22-8347		26. 4.61	To EI-BAV 4/75. Canx 14.4.75.
G-ARKP	PA-22-108 Colt	22-8364		19. 5.61	(On overhaul 4/96)
G-ARKR	PA-22-108 Colt	22-8376		9. 5.61	
G-ARKS	PA-22-108 Colt	22-8422		7. 6.61	
G-ARKT	PA-22-108 Colt	22-8448		7. 6.61	To EI-AYS 6/74. Canx 12.6.74.
G-ARKU	DH.114 Heron 2	14072	VR-NAQ	17. 3.61	To RN as XR445 3/61. Canx 28.3.61.
G-ARKV	DH.114 Heron 2	14091	VR-NCE	17. 3.61	To RN as XR443 3/61. Canx 28.3.61.
G-ARKW	DH.114 Heron 2	14092	VR-NCF	17. 3.61	To RN as XR444 3/61. Canx 28.3.61.
G-ARKX	Vickers 828 Viscount	443		23. 3.61	To JA8201 7/61. Canx 26.7.61.
G-ARKY	Vickers 828 Viscount	444		23. 3.61	To JA8202 7/61. Canx 27.7.61.
G-ARKZ	Vickers 828 Viscount	445		23. 3.61	To JA8203 7/61. Canx 7.9.61.
G-ARLA	PA-22-160 Tri-Pacer	22-7200	N3252Z	23. 3.61	DBF at Kirkbymoorside on 17.11.68. Canx.
G-ARLB	PA-24-250 Comanche	24-2352		21. 3.61	To G-BUTL 4/84. Canx.
G-ARLC	Cessna 180C	180-50663	N9163T	29. 3.61	To VP-UBK 2/64. Canx 18.1.64.
G-ARLD	Helio H.395 Super Courier	522	N1890B N13B	25. 4.61	DBR due to engine fire on start up at Tilstock on 19.4.88. Canx as destroyed 18.10.88.
G-ARLE(1)	DH.104 Dove 2A	04401	XJ349 G-AMXW	28. 6.61R	NTU - Restored as G-AMXW 6/61. Canx.

Regn	Type	c/n	Previous identity	Regn date	Fate or immediate subsequent identity (if known)
G-ARLE(2)	Lancashire EP.9 Prospector I	44	G-47-1	3. 8.61	DBR Umsenita Block, Managil Cotton Scheme, in the Sudan on 10.10.64 while crop spraying. Canx 3.66.
G-ARLF	Douglas C-54A-1-DC Skymaster	10278	TF-RVH N50787/42-72173	29. 3.61	DBF on the ground at Malaga, Spain on 8.10.61. Canx.
G-ARLG	Beagle-Auster D.4/108	3606		4. 4.61	
G-ARLH	Beagle A.61 Terrier 1	3720	EI AMD G-ARLH/VX109	4. 4.61	Dismantled at White Waltham. Canx as WFU 10.9.73.
G-ARLI	PA-23-150 Apache	23-120	N1109P	5. 4.61	CofA expired 10.11.73 & WFU. Scrapped at Sandown in 4/83. Canx by CAA 15.9.86.
G-ARLJ	PA-23-150 Apache	23-127	N1117P	8. 6.61	Crashed at Biggin Hill on 10.3.63. Canx.
G-ARLK	PA-24-250 Comanche	24-2433	EI-ALW G-ARLK/N7257P/N10F	25. 5.61	
G-ARLL	PA-24-250 Comanche	24-2463		25. 5.61	Ditched into the sea off Hastings on 20.7.85. (Salvaged & taken to Lydd) Canx as destroyed 30.7.86.
G-ARLM(1)	Beagle A.61 Terrier 2 (Conversion of Auster 6 c/n 1936)	B.646	TW568	. 4.61R	NTU - To G-AYDW 5/70. Canx.
G-ARLM(2)	Beagle A.61 Terrier 1 (Conversion of Auster AOP.6 c/n 2573)	B.702	(G-ARLP) VF631	11. 4.61	To G-ASDK 10/62. Canx 24.10.62.
G-ARLN(1)	Beagle A.61 Terrier 1 (Conversion of Auster AOP.6 c/n 2487)	B.645	TW629	. 4.61R	NTU - To EI-ARO 6/67. Canx.
G-ARLN(2)	Beagle A.61 Terrier 1 (Also given c/n's 3727(1) & B.632(1))	B.703	WE558	11. 4.61	To G-ASDL 10/62. Canx 24.10.62.
G-ARLO	Beagle A.61 Terrier 1 (Conversion of Auster AOP.6)	2500	TW642	11. 4.61	Damaged in forced landing in sea off Shoreham 10.7.79. (Stored 3/96 - for rebuild as Auster AOP.6)
G-ARLP(1)	Beagle A.61 Terrier 2 (Conversion of Auster AOP.6 c/n 2573)	B.702	VF631	. 4.61R	To G-ARLM(2) 4/61. Canx.
G-ARLP(2)	Beagle A.61 Terrier 1 (C/n officially quoted as 2573 which was VF631 and which became G-ARLM(2)/G-ASDK)	3724(1)	VX123	11. 4.61	(Badly damaged in landing crash Truleigh Farm, Edburton 4.8.91) (On rebuild .92)
G-ARLR	Beagle A.61 Terrier 2 (Conversion of Auster AOP.6)	3721 & B.601	VW996	11. 4.61	
G-ARLS	PA-23-250 Aztec	27-431		7. 4.61	Ditched in sea off Isle of Wight in position 50:39N 01:00W and subsequently sank on 29.7.75. Canx.
G-ARLT(1)	Cessna 172B	172-48449	N7949X	. .61R	NTU - To G-ARIU 6/61. Canx.
G-ARLT(2)	Cessna 172B	172-48505	N8005X	16. 6.61	Badly damaged in forced landing at Dulverton, Somerset on 21.9.86. Canx as WFU 5.8.87.
G-ARLU(1)	Cessna 172B	172-48452	N7952X	. .61R	NTU - To G-ARIV 5/61. Canx.
G-ARLU(2)	Cessna 172B	172-48502	N8002X	14. 6.61	DBR at Biggin Hill on 30.10.77. Fuselage only as an Instructional Airframe 8/93 Baldonnel. Canx as WFU 6.8.80.
G-ARLV	Cessna 172B	172-48497	N7997X	27. 6.61	Crashed on take-off from Newbury Racecourse on 23.10.92. Canx as WFU 1.3.93.
G-ARLW	Cessna 172B	172-48499	N7999X	15. 6.61	Damaged in heavy landing at Barton on 20.2.90. Parts used for spares in rebuild of G-ARMR. (Open store 1/96 Barton) Canx by CAA 21.1.99.
G-ARLX	SAN Jodel D.140B Mousquetaire II	66		12. 4.61	(Stored 8/97)
G-ARLY	Auster J/5P Autocar	3271	(VH-...)	14. 4.61	CofA lapsed 6.6.71. Sold in Switzerland 11.87. (On rebuild to D.6/180 standard using parts from Airedale G-ARNR and J/5R G-APAA wings) Canx by CAA 25.2.99.
G-ARLZ	Rollason-Druine D.31A Turbulent	RAE/578		7. 4.61	
G-ARMA	PA-23-160 Apache G	23-1967	N4448P	8. 5.61	CofA expired 22.7.77. (Instructional Airframe 9/96 Kidlington) Canx by WFU 29.10.91.
G-ARMB	DHC.1 Chipmunk 22A (Fuselage no. DHB/f/25)	C1/0099	WB660	26. 4.61	
G-ARMC	DHC.1 Chipmunk 22A (Fuselage no. DHH/f/107)	C1/0151	WB703	26. 4.61	
G-ARMD	DHC.1 Chipmunk 22A (Fuselage no. DHB/f/122)	C1/0237	WD297	26. 4.61	WFU at Hamble on 5.6.76. Canx 2.2.82. Fuselage with Ross Aviation in 1995.
G-ARME	DHC.1 Chipmunk 22A (Fuselage no. DHB/f/199)	C1/0320	WD381	26. 4.61	Crashed at Adgestone, near Sandown, Isle of Wight on 29.3.66. Canx.
G-ARMF	DHC.1 Chipmunk 22A (Fuselage no. DHB/f/282)	C1/0394	WG322	26. 4.61	(Damaged in ground loop at Top Farm, Tadlow on 19.6.96)
G-ARMG	DHC.1 Chipmunk 22A (Fuselage no. DHB/f/460)	C1/0575	WK558	26. 4.61	
G-ARMH	PA-23-250 Aztec	27-443		26. 5.61	Ditched into the sea 40 miles south of Tangiers on 7.8.83. Canx.
G-ARMI	PA-23-160 Apache G	23-1980	N4460P	9. 5.61	CofA expired 4.10.82 & WFU at Stapleford. Believed scrapped; removed from Stapleford mid-1987. Canx as WFU 1.3.89.
G-ARMJ	Cessna 185 Skywagon	185-0100	N9900X	12. 7.61	CofA expired 16.6.84. Sold to Australia in 7/85. Canx by CAA 10.2.87. Became VH-FFC in 3/93.
G-ARMK	Cessna 310F	310F-0136	N5836X	6. 7.61	Fatal crash into high ground 3 miles NW of Capel Curig, Carnarvonshire on 29.9.68. Canx.
G-ARML	Cessna 175B Skylark	175-56995	N8295T	12. 7.61	
G-ARMM	Cessna 175B Skylark	175-56996	N8296T	26. 7.61	Crashed on take-off from Sibson on 11.4.76. Canx.
G-ARMN(1)	Cessna 175B Skylark	175-56998	N8298T	. 4.61R	NTU - To G-AROD 10/61. Canx.
G-ARMN(2)	Cessna 175B Skylark	175-56994	N8294T	18. 8.61	
G-ARMO	Cessna 172B Skyhawk	172-48560	N8060X	12. 6.61	
G-ARMP	Cessna 172B	172-48563	N8063X	27. 7.61	Blown over in a thunderstorm at Birmingham on 6.7.89. Canx as destroyed 10.11.89.
G-ARMR	Cessna 172B Skyhawk (Rebuilt using parts from G-ARLW)	172-48566	N8066X	12. 6.61	

Regn	Type	c/n	Previous identity	Regn date	Fate or immediate subsequent identity (if known)
G-ARMS	DH.82A Tiger Moth	85698	DE784	25. 4.61	Struck trees and crashed while low-flying at George airfield, George, South Africa on 27.5.61. (Wreck on rebuild at Krugersdorp 7/96).
G-ARMT	DH.104 Dove 6	04514		25. 4.61	To VH-DHA 6/71. Canx 21.1.71.
G-ARMU	Helio H.395 Super Courier	523	EI-ATG G-ARMU/N4172D/N13B	25. 5.61	Crashed into trees on take-off from a private strip at Ormesby Hall, near Caister, Norfolk on 30.8.70, broke into four sections on impact with the ground. Canx.
G-ARMV	Avro 748 Srs.1/101	1536		28. 4.61	Crashed & DBR at Lympne on 11.7.65. Canx 18.11.65.
G-ARMW	Avro 748 Srs.1A/101	1537	G-FBMV G-ARMW/V2-LVO/G-ARMW/VP-LII/G-ARMW	28. 4.61	To G-ERMV 3/92. Canx.
G-ARMX	Avro 748 Srs.1A/101	1538	VP-LVN G-ARMX	28. 4.61	Broken up in 9/90, still marked as VP-LVN. (Canx 21.10.92 to VP-L.. !) Fuselage on fire dump 1/98 Ringway.
G-ARMY	Douglas DC-6A (Line No. 969)	45457	VR-BBP N660NA/N7818C	16. 5.61	To HZ-ADB 3/64. Canx 26.3.64.
G-ARMZ	Rollason-Druine D.31 Turbulent	PFA/565		2. 5.61	(On rebuild Rushett Farm, Chessington 8/97)
G-ARNA	Mooney M.20B	1806		26. 6.61	CofA expired 14.8.81. Canx as WFU 16.12.91. (Stored 3/94 Casablanca-Anfa, Morocco)
G-ARNB	Auster J/5G Cirrus Autocar	3169	AP-AHL VP-KNL	18. 5.61	(Status uncertain - possibly on rebuild .95)
G-ARNC	PA-22-108 Colt	22-8466		9. 6.61	To EI-BDA 4/77. Canx 29.4.77.
G-ARND	PA-22-108 Colt	22-8484		6. 6.61	
G-ARNE	PA-22-108 Colt	22-8502		15. 6.61	
G-ARNF(1)	PA-22-108 Colt	22-8525		. 6.61R	NTU - Not Imported. To N4933Z. Canx.
G-ARNF(2)	PA-22-108 Colt	22-8523		16. 6.61	Crashed at Woolaston, Glos. on 1.9.62. Canx.
G-ARNG	PA-22-108 Colt	22-8547		26. 6.61	CofA expired 12.10.73. (On rebuild 8/97 Shoreham)
G-ARNH	PA-22-108 Colt	22-8558		5. 9.61	DBR at Blackbushe on 1.9.72. Canx as WFU 24.5.73. (Fuselage on rebuild off-site 4/96)
G-ARNI	PA-22-108 Colt	22-8575		26. 7.61	
G-ARNJ	PA-22-108 Colt	22-8587		3. 8.61	
G-ARNK	PA-22-108 Colt (Mod to tail-dragger and Lyc O-320 as "Super Colt")	22-8622		5. 9.61	Damaged on landing at RAF Coltishall on 30.3.97. (On rebuild Framlingham 8/97)
G-ARNL	PA-22-108 Colt	22-8625		3. 8.61	
G-ARNM	PA-22-108 Colt	22-8643		5. 9.61	To PH-RRL 8/62. Canx 12.10.62.
G-ARNN	Globe GC-1B Swift	1272	VP-YMJ VP-RDA/ZS-BMX/NC3279K	11. 5.61	Crashed at Hucknall on 1.9.73. (Rebuild nearing completion Tatenhill 5/89)
G-ARNO	Beagle A.61 Terrier 1	3722	VX113	8. 5.61	CofA expired 19.8.81, Canx as WFU 17.12.91. (On rebuild 7/97)
G-ARNP	Beagle A.109 Airedale (Originally regd with c/n A.109-P1)	B.503		10. 5.61	
G-ARNR	Beagle A.109 Airedale (Originally regd with c/n A.109-P2)	B.504		10. 5.61	Canx as WFU 12.7.63. Reduced to spares at Rearsby.
G-ARNS	Beagle A.109 Airedale (Originally regd with c/n A.109-P3)	B.505		10. 5.61	To HB-EUE 9/62. Canx 8.11.62.
G-ARNT	Beagle A.109 Airedale (Originally regd with c/n A.109-P4)	B.506		10. 5.61	To OY-DRT 6/72. Canx 6.3.72.
G-ARNU	Cessna 310F	310F-0142	N5842X	17. 7.61	Fatal crash in wooded country near Munsbach, Germany on 9.1.62. Canx.
G-ARNV	Proacaer F.15B Picchio 3	18		26. 5.61	Crashed off Ramsey, IoM on 9.9.69. Canx.
G-ARNW	Proacaer F.15B Picchio 3	19	(G-ARUE)	26. 5.61	NTU - To I-PROE 9/62. (Carried a plate proclaiming it to be G-ARUE when seen at Hanover Show in 1962) Canx 13.9.62.
G-ARNX	SAN Jodel D.117	296	F-BHGE	13. 6.61	CofA expired 24.8.68 & WFU at Redhill. Canx as WFU 13.9.73.
G-ARNY	SAN Jodel D.117	595	F-BHXQ	13. 6.61	
G-ARNZ	Rollason-Druine D.31 Turbulent	PFA/579		28. 6.61	
G-AROA	Cessna 172B Skyhawk	172-48628	N8128X	19. 9.61	
G-AROB	Cessna 172B Skyhawk	172-48631	N8131X	7.12.61	Crashed near Barton Airport, Manchester on 25.4.65. Canx.
G-AROC	Cessna 175BX Skylark (Modified to 172 standard)	175-56997	G-OTOW G-AROC/N8297T	2.10.61	
G-AROD	Cessna 175B Skylark	175-56998	N28814 G-AROD/(G-ARMN)/N8298T	2.10.61	DBR at Nantwich on 16.8.83. Canx 30.5.84.
G-AROE(1)	Orlican L-40 Meta-Sokol	15....		. 5.61R	NTU - Canx.
G-AROE(2)	CZL Aero 145 Super Aero	19-014	(D-GONE) G-AROE/OK-NHF	4. 7.61	To D-GASA(2) 8/97. Canx 17.4.97.
G-AROF	Orlican L-40 Meta-Sokol	150905		10. 7.61	To OK-... 2/98. Canx 10.2.98.
G-AROG	DH.104 Dove 1B (Originally regd as a Dove 1)	04207	VR-NOB	24. 5.61	WFU at Biggin Hill on 14.10.64. (Transported to Coventry by road in 1967) Canx as WFU 3.3.69.
G-AROH	DH.104 Dove 5	04415	XJ321 (XB-TAN)	24. 5.61	CofA expired on 23.3.70 & WFU at Biggin Hill. Canx as WFU 21.11.73.
G-AROI	DH.104 Dove 5	04474	N2401J G-AROI/XK897	24. 5.61	To OY-AJR 6/80. Canx.
G-AROJ	Beagle A.109 Airedale (Originally regd with c/n A.109-1)	B.508	HB-EUC G-AROJ	17. 5.61	CofA expired 8.1.76 & WFU. Canx 21.1.80. (On rebuild 9/96)
G-AROK	Cessna 310F	310F-0148	N5848X	19. 7.61	Damaged in a wheels-up landing at Manston on 11.3.79. Removed to Blackbushe by 7/84. Re-regd G-OITD 9/85. Canx.
G-AROL(1)	PA-22-108 Colt	22-8663		. 5.61R	NTU - Not Imported. To TF-KAX. Canx.
G-AROL(2)	PA-22-108 Colt	22-8796		7.11.61	Broken up for spares at Kidlington in 7/62.
G-AROM(1)	PA-22-108 Colt	22-8689		. 5.61R	NTU - Not Imported. To OH-CPL 9/61. Canx.
G-AROM(2)	PA-22-108 Colt	22-8805		7.11.61	Damaged in forced landing at Gibraltar Barracks, Aldershot on 30.7.89. Parts used in the construction of G-GGLE in 5/93. Canx as WFU 15.11.96
G-ARON(1)	PA-22-108 Colt	22-8703		. 5.61R	NTU - Not Imported. To I-SANF 12/61. Canx.
G-ARON(2)	PA-22-108 Colt	22-8822		23.11.61	

Regn	Type	c/n	Previous identity	Regn date	Fate or immediate subsequent identity (if known)
G-AROO	Forney F.1A Aircoupe	5750	N25B	3.11.61	
G-AROP	Forney F.1A Aircoupe	5751	N25B	31. 7.61	Fatal crash after colliding in mid-air with Auster J/1S G-AMVN near Stapleford Tawney, Essex on 24.4.69. Canx.
G-AROR	Forney F.1A Aircoupe 415	5752	N25B	21. 7.61	To D-ELWS 9/79. Canx.
G-AROS(1)	Forney F.1A Aircoupe	5...		. 5.61R	NTU - Not Imported. Canx.
G-AROS(2)	DH.114 Heron 2	14077	4X-ARJ G-AROS/D-CASA/G-AROS/I-AOGO/VR-NAW	5.12.61	To N13663 3/67. Canx 2.3.67.
G-AROT	Aeromere F.8L Falco Srs.3	224		23. 6.61	To G-FALC 2/81. Canx.
G-AROU(1)	Forney F.1A Aircoupe	5...		. 5.61R	NTU - Not Imported. Canx.
G-AROU(2)	Beechcraft 65 Queen Air	LC-114		9.10.61	To N1277C. Canx 5.2.69.
"G-AROU"	PA-24-180 Comanche	24-2427	N7251P	----	Delivered with registration painted incorrectly. To G-ARUO.
G-AROV(1)	Forney F.1A Aircoupe	5...		. 5.61R	NTU - Not Imported. Canx.
G-AROV(2)	DH.106 Comet 4C	6460	LV-AIB LV-PTS/G-AROV	11. 8.61	WFU at Lasham 3.10.77. Broken up in 11/78. Canx.
G-AROW	SAN Jodel D.140B Mousquetaire II	71		13. 9.61	
G-AROX	Cessna 310B	35505	N5305A	7. 6.61	To SE-ETU. Canx 11.10.65.
G-AROY	Boeing-Stearman A75N1 (PT-17) Kaydet	75-4775	N56418 42-16612	6. 6.61	
G-AROZ	SNCAN Stampe SV-4C	508	F-BDGQ	11. 6.61	Crashed at Bigin Hill on 15.5.65. Canx.
G-ARPA	DH.121 Trident 1C	2101		13. 4.61	WFU & stored at Prestwick on 28.2.75. Scrapped 9.4.76. Canx as WFU 1.4.76.
G-ARPB	DH.121 Trident 1C	2102		13. 4.61	WFU & stored at Prestwick on 28.2.75. To Fire School in 1/78. Canx as WFU 1.4.76.
G-ARPC	DH.121 Trident 1C	2103		13. 4.61	Burnt in cabin fire at Heathrow on 28.12.75. Canx as WFU 1.4.76.
G-ARPD	DH.121 Trident 1C	2104		13. 4.61	WFU at Heathrow on 30.4.81. To fire dump at Teesside on 27.8.81. Canx as WFU 30.9.81.
G-ARPE	DH.121 Trident 1C	2105		13. 4.61	WFU & stored at Prestwick on 5.4.75. Scrapped 4.5.76. Canx as WFU 1.4.76.
G-ARPF	DH.121 Trident 1C	2106		13. 4.61	WFU & stored at Prestwick on 7.4.75. Scrapped 10.5.76. Canx as WFU 1.4.76.
G-ARPG	DH.121 Trident 1C	2107		13. 4.61	WFU & stored at Prestwick on 8.4.75. Scrapped 11.5.76. Canx as WFU 1.4.76.
G-ARPH	DH.121 Trident 1C	2108		13. 4.61	WFU on 26.3.82. (On display 3/96 RAF Cosford)
G-ARPI	DH.121 Trident 1C	2109		13. 4.61	Fatal crash soon after take-off from Heathrow on 18.6.72 and crashed near Staines. Canx.
G-ARPJ	DH.121 Trident 1C	2110		13. 4.61	WFU & stored at Prestwick on 9.4.75. Scrapped 25.5.76. Canx as WWFU 1.4.76.
G-ARPK	DH.121 Trident 1C	2111		13. 4.61	WFU on 24.5.82. To Fire School Ringway. Canx. (On fire dump 1/98 Ringway)
G-ARPL	DH.121 Trident 1C	2112		13. 4.61	WFU on 24.5.82. To fire dump at Edinburgh. Canx. Remains scrapped in 2/96.
G-ARPM	DH.121 Trident 1C	2113		13. 4.61	WFU & stored at Prestwick on 11.4.75. Scrapped 26.5.76. Canx as WFU 1.4.76.
G-ARPN(1)	DH.121 Trident 1C	2114		13. 4.61R	NTU - To G-ASWU 10/64. Canx.
G-ARPN(2)	DH.121 Trident 1C	2115	(G-ARPO)	23. 3.64	WFU on 24.5.82. To fire dump at Aberdeen. Canx.
G-ARPO(1)	DH.121 Trident 1C	2115		13. 4.61R	NTU - To G-ARPN 3/64. Canx.
G-ARPO(2)	DH.121 Trident 1C	2116	(G-ARPP)	23. 3.64	WFU. To Teesside Fire School on 12.12.83. (Extant 4/99 Teesside)
G-ARPP(1)	DH.121 Trident 1C	2116		13. 4.61R	NTU - To G-ARPO 3/64. Canx.
G-ARPP(2)	DH.121 Trident 1C	2117	(G-ARPR)	23. 3.64	WFU. To Fire School at Glasgow in 2/83. Canx. (Extant 12/95 Glasgow)
G-ARPR(1)	DH.121 Trident 1C	2117		13. 4.61R	NTU - To G-ARPP 3/64. Canx.
G-ARPR(2)	DH.121 Trident 1C	2119	(G-ARPT)	23. 3.64	WFU at Heathrow. Canx as WFU 30.9.81. To Teesside Fire School on 16.9.81.
G-ARPS(1)	DH.121 Trident 1C	2118		13. 4.61R	NTU - To G-ASWV 10/64. Canx.
G-ARPS(2)	DH.121 Trident 1C	2120	(G-ARPU)	23. 3.64	Destroyed in cabin fire at Heathrow on 29.7.69. Canx.
G-ARPT(1)	DH.121 Trident 1C	2119		13. 4.61R	NTU - To G-ARPR 3/64. Canx.
G-ARPT(2)	DH.121 Trident 1C	2121	(G-ARPW)	23. 3.64	Destroyed by Ambassador 2 G-AMAD when it swung off the runway and crashed into the central terminal area while landing at Heathrow on 3.7.68. Canx.
G-ARPU(1)	DH.121 Trident 1C	2120		13. 4.61R	NTU - To G-ARPS 3/64. Canx.
G-ARPU(2)	DH.121 Trident 1C	2122	(G-ARPX)	23. 3.64	WFU at Heathrow in 11/74. Broken up on 17.11.75. Nose & tail sections to Hatfield for fatigue tests. Canx.
G-ARPV	Not allocated. [Was reserved by de Havilland Engine Co. Ltd. in 11/59]				
G-ARPW(1)	DH.121 Trident 1C	2121		13. 4.61R	NTU - G-ARPT 3/64. Canx.
G-ARPW(2)	DH.121 Trident 1C	2123	(G-ARPY)	23. 3.64	WFU on 31.3.81. To Teesside Fire School on 26.3.82. Canx.
G-ARPX(1)	DH.121 Trident 1C	2122		13. 4.61R	NTU - G-ARPU 3/64. Canx.
G-ARPX(2)	DH.121 Trident 1C	2124	(G-ARPZ)	23. 3.64	WFU at Perth on 29.11.82. Scrapped in 1997. Canx.
G-ARPY(1)	DH.121 Trident 1C	2123		13. 4.61R	NTU - G-ARPW 3/66. Canx.
G-ARPY(2)	DH.121 Trident 1C	2126		23. 3.64	Crashed at Felthorpe, Norfolk on 3.6.66. Canx.
G-ARPZ(1)	DH.121 Trident 1C	2124		13. 4.61R	NTU - G-ARPX 3/66. Canx.
G-ARPZ(2)	DH.121 Trident 1C	2128		23. 3.64	WFU at Dunsfold on 7.4.83. Canx. (Escape systems test airframe) (Extant 6/97 Dunsfold)
G-ARRA	Boeing 707-436 (Line No. 266)	18411		17. 1.62	WFU at Stansted on 1.11.80. To N4465D 8/83. Canx 24.8.83.
G-ARRB	Boeing 707-436 (Line No. 330)	18412		17. 1.62	WFU & stored at Kingman, AZ, USA in 1/76. Broken up in 9/79. Canx.
G-ARRC	Boeing 707-436 (Line No. 334)	18413		17. 1.62	Sold on 2.3.81 & stored at Perpignan, France. To N4465C in 9/83. Canx 24.8.83.
G-ARRD	SAN Jodel DR.1050 Ambassadeur	274		20. 7.61	
G-ARRE	SAN Jodel DR.1050 Ambassadeur	275		20. 7.61	

Regn	Type	c/n	Previous identity	Regn date	Fate or immediate subsequent identity (if known)
G-ARRF	Cessna 150A	150-59297	N7197X	15. 9.61	Damaged at Henscott Farm, near Holsworthy on 11.3.88. (On rebuild at Banbury) Canx by CAA 11.12.96.
G-ARRG	Cessna 175B Skylark	175-56999	N8299T	5.10.61	Damaged in gales at North Denes on 3.11.70. Canx as destroyed 7.12.70. (Stored unmarked 9/96)
G-ARRH	Cessna 175B Skylark	175-57000	N8300T	5.10.61	Ditched into the sea off Southsea on 26.1.82. Canx.
G-ARRI	Cessna 175B Skylark	175-57001	N8301T	5.10.61	CofA expired 13.8.77. Canx by CAA 9.10.84.
G-ARRJ	Saucer P.4S Srs.2	P4S Ser.2		30. 8.62	Construction abandoned. Canx as WFU 1/78.
G-ARRK	Taylorcraft Plus D (Fitted with fuselage and tailplane from G-AIIU, with sundry pieces from G-AHXG plus wings and c/n from G-AHUM)	157	G-AHUM LB286	14. 6.61	To EI-AMF 4/62. Canx 1.4.62.
G-ARRL	Auster J/1N Alpha	2115	VP-KFK VP-KPF/VP-KFK/VP-UAK	13. 6.61	CofA expired 7.6.68. Canx as WFU 3.4.89.
G-ARRM	Beagle B.206X (Originally regd as Beagle B.2 Srs.1 with c/n B2/1010, re-designated in 9/61)	B.001		23. 6.61	CofA expired 28.12.64. WFU at Shoreham. (Stored 5/99 at Kemble)
G-ARRN	Beagle A.61 Terrier 2 (Conversion of Auster 6 c/n 2296)	B.630	(OH-BEA) G-ARRN/VF527	16. 6.61	To D-EDTU 9/64. Canx.
G-ARRO	Beagle A.109 Airedale (Originally regd with c/n A.109-P5)	B.507	(EI-AVP) G-ARRO	16. 6.61	To EI-AYL(2) 3/74. Canx 8.3.74.
G-ARRP(1)	PA-28-160 Cherokee	28-54		. 6.61R	NTU - Not Imported. To D-EGRI. Canx.
G-ARRP(2)	PA-28-160 Cherokee	28-52		25. 8.61	To G-LIZI 1/89. Canx.
G-ARRR	Cessna 310 (Riley 65)	35416	N5216A	25. 8.61	To HB-LBN. Canx 14.6.62.
G-ARRS	Menavia Piel CP.301A Emeraude	226	F-BIMA	29. 6.61	
G-ARRT	Wallis WA-116/Mc Gyroplane Srs.1	2 & B.201		28. 6.61	Permit expired 26.5.83. (Stored 2/99 Reymerston)
G-ARRU	Druine D.31 Turbulent	PFA/502		28. 6.61	(Badly damaged in forced landing at Spelmonden Road, Goudhurst, Kent on 8.7.96)
G-ARRV	Avro 780/748MF Srs.1 (Conversion of Avro 748 c/n 1534)	1548	G-APZV	29. 6.61	CofA expired 3.9.65. WFU at Woodford. To instructional airframe with RAF as 8669M in 1981. Canx as WFU 3.4.69.
G-ARRW	Avro 748 Srs.1/105	1549	EI-BSE G-ARRW	29. 6.61	Canx by CAA 11.10.91. To G-MRRV 28.2.92.
G-ARRX	Auster 6A Tugmaster	2281	VF512	4. 7.61	
G-ARRY	SAN Jodel D.140B Mousquetaire II	72		13. 9.61	
"G-ARRY"	DHC.1 Chipmunk T.10 (Fuselage no. DHB/f/121)	C1/0236	WD296	----	Taxied into bowser at Middle Wallop on 19.7.57, to Perth for ground instruction with false marks. Noted painted as such at Perth in 9/61 & 9/67.
G-ARRZ	Rollason-Druine D.31 Turbulent	PFA/580		21. 8.61	Badly damaged in crash at Horley, Surrey on 21.7.90. Permit expired 21.12.90. (On rebuild 2/99 at Hingham, Norfolk)
G-ARSA	Bristol 170 Freighter 31M	13169	S4409 Pakistan AF/G-18-161	5. 7.61	Not converted and imported for spares. WFU at Southend in 8/61. Broken up in 9/68. Canx 22.6.64.
G-ARSB(1)	Auster J/1 Autocrat	2331	OY-AAK G-AJIM	. 7.61R	NTU - Restored as G-AJIM 7/61. Canx.
G-ARSB(2)	Cessna 150A	150-59337	N7237X	25. 9.61	CofA expired 10.6.88. (Open storage 9/96 at Sibson) Canx by CAA 1.8.94.
G-ARSC	PA-24-180 Comanche	24-2620		14. 7.61	Crashed at Auston End Farm, near Hitchin on 15.12.78. Canx 5.12.80.
G-ARSD	Aviation Traders ATL-98 Carvair (Conv. Douglas C-54A-10-DC)	10311/2	N57670 42-72206	14. 7.61	WFU at Lydd, Kent on 4.10.67. Broken up in 8/70. CofA expired 13.4.68. Canx as destroyed 26.8.70.
G-ARSE	Not allocated.				
"G-ARSE"	Beagle A.61 Terrier 2	2539	VF581	----	Wore marks "G-ARSE" on the starboard side on 21.7.61, corrected to G-ARSL by 22.7.61.
G-ARSF	Aviation Traders ATL-98 Carvair (Conv. Douglas C-54B-5-DO)	18339/3	N88709 43-17139	17. 7.61	Crashed whilst on approach near Rotterdam Airport, The Netherlands on 28.12.62. Canx.
G-ARSG	Roe Triplane Type IV Replica (ADC Cirrus III) (Also c/n TRI.1)	HAC.1	(BAPC.1)	29.10.81	(Carries no external marks)
G-ARSH	Aviation Traders ATL.98 Carvair (Conv. Douglas C-54A-10-DC)	10338/4	G-41-2 N65142/42-72233	17. 7.61	Marks not used - To N9758F. Canx 4.9.62.
G-ARSI	DH.104 Dove 8	04526		10. 7.61	To G-ARFZ 1/62. Canx.
G-ARSJ	Scintex CP.301C-2 Emeraude	581		28. 7.61	(On overhaul 6/96)
G-ARSK	PA-24-250 Comanche	24-2751		14. 7.61	To N8500C. Canx 22.8.80.
G-ARSL	Beagle A.61 Terrier 2	2539	VF581	13. 7.61	(On rebuild 7/97)
G-ARSM	Britten-Norman CC.2 Cushioncraft	7 & 001		12. 2.61	To RN as XR814 9/62. Canx.
G-ARSN	DH.104 Dove 8A	04525	201 Irish Air Corps/EI-ARV/G-ARSN	13. 7.61	To G-LIDD 6/83. Canx.
G-ARSO	Orlican L-40 Meta-Sokol	150906		20. 7.61	DBR at Dinard, France on 29.9.71. Canx as destroyed 14.3.72.
G-ARSP	Orlican L-40 Meta-Sokol	150907		20. 7.61	To OK-NPM 7/93. Canx 5.7.93.
G-ARSR	PA-18-150 Super Cub	18-7605		20. 7.61	To ST-ABR 9/61. Canx 1.2.62.
G-ARSS	PA-18-150 Super Cub	18-7606		20. 7.61	To ST-ABS 9/61. Canx 1.2.62.
G-ARST	PA-22-108 Colt	22-8823	(ZK-BXZ)	23.11.61	Crashed at Squires Gate on 13.2.69. Canx as WFU 15.4.70.
G-ARSU	PA-22-108 Colt	22-8835	EI-AMI G-ARSU	23.11.61	
G-ARSV	PA-22-108 Colt	22-8844		23.11.61	Struck a tree and crashed in a forced-landing at Whitchurch Hill, Berks on 4.3.67. Canx.
G-ARSW	PA-22-108 Colt	22-8858		23.11.61	
G-ARSX	PA-22-160 Tri-Pacer	22-6712	N2907Z	8. 8.61	(Stored 6/97)
G-ARSY	PA-28-160 Cherokee	28-103		11.12.61	DBF at Southend on 27.6.68. Canx as destroyed 13.2.70.
G-ARSZ	Houston Gyroplane (built by P.J.Houston)	03		25. 8.61	Construction abandoned. Canx as WFU 31.7.84.
G-ARTA	Vickers VC-10 Srs.1109 (Originally regd as Srs.1100, converted by 4/69)	803	OD-AFA G-ARTA	10. 8.61	DBR on landing at Gatwick on 28.1.72. Canx as WFU 12.8.74.

Regn	Type	c/n	Previous identity	Regn date	Fate or immediate subsequent identity (if known)
"G-ARTA"	Percival P.28 Proctor 1	-		----	False marks worn by an instructional airframe used by Air Service Training Ltd at Ansty in 1949.
G-ARTB	Mooney M.20B Mark 21	1866		30. 8.61	To G-JDIX 11/85. Canx.
G-ARTC	Handley Page HPR.7 Dart Herald 200	148	G-AODF	. 8.61	WFU & stored in 5/62. Broken up in 1970 at Radlett.
G-ARTD	PA-23-160 Apache	23-1530	N4053P	25. 8.61	Destroyed in fatal crash at Moel Hebogdeddgelert, near Porthmadog on 2.8.99.
G-ARTE	EoN AP.10 Standard 460 Srs.1D	EoN/S/004		30. 8.61	To BGA.1178 in 7/64. Canx.
G-ARTF	Druine D.31 Turbulent	PFA/161		14. 9.61	Crashed & DBR at Little Gransden on 26.2.92. Canx as destroyed 13.3.92.
G-ARTG	Hiller 360 UH-12C	936	HP-262	21. 9.61	CofA expired 9.8.75 & WFU at Bourn. Preserved at Stockbridge. Canx as WFU 5.12.83.
G-ARTH	PA-12 Super Cruiser	12-3278	EI-ADO	22. 9.61	(Stored 6/96)
G-ARTI	DH.114 Heron 2D	14143		14. 9.61	To F-BRSK 2/70. Canx 19.1.70.
G-ARTJ	Bensen B.8M Gyrocopter (Originally regd with c/n 8-104-100)	7		22. 9.61	Canx as WFU 6.6.75. (Stored 6/95)
G-ARTK	Cessna 310 (Riley 65)	35044	N2644C	7.11.61	To VP-YYK /65. Canx 9.8.65.
G-ARTL	DH.82A Tiger Moth	-	"T7281"	22. 9.61	
	(Considerable doubt as to true identity - if correct - c/n is 83795 which became AP-AEV in 1951)				
G-ARTM	Beagle A.61 Terrier 1	3723	WE536	9.10.61	Crashed at Priory Farm, Turvey, Beds on 28.5.70. CofA expired 13.11.71 & WFU at Sywell. Canx as WFU 12.9.73. (On rebuild 9/96)
G-ARTN	Campbell-Bensen B.7Mc Gyrocopter (Originally regd with c/n DC/61/008)	8		26. 9.61	DBR & WFU in 4/68. Permit expired 23.6.68. Rebuilt as G-AVXB. Canx.
G-ARTO	Douglas DC-6B (Line No. 382)	44083	N90962	6.10.61	To 9K-ABA 7/62. Canx 7.7.62.
G-ARTP	DHC.1 Chipmunk 22A (Fuselage no. DHB/f/4)	C1/0061	EI-AMH G-ARTP/EI-AJC/WB620	3.10.61	To Irish Air Corps as 200. Canx 17.2.65.
G-ARTR	DHC-2 Beaver 1	25	ZS-DCG	5.10.61	To ZK-CKH 12/64. Canx 7.8.64.
G-ARTS	DH.104 Dove 6 (Originally regd as a Dove 2A)	04369	5N-ACJ 5N-ACW/PH-SAA/G-ARTS/N6532D/N20R/N1572V	18. 1.62	DDB in ground incident on 23.2.75. Scrapped at Biggin Hill in 1977. Canx.
G-ARTT	Morane-Saulnier MS.880B Rallye Club	008		11.12.61	(On rebuild 11/96)
G-ARTU	Edgar Percival EP.9	38	XM797	20.11.61	Crashed at Old Warden on 2.9.69. Canx.
G-ARTV	Edgar Percival EP.9	39	(OO-...) G-ARTV/D-ELSA/G-ARTV/XM819	20.11.61	Canx 1.2.77 on sale to USA. To N747JC 24.10.88.
G-ARTW	Cessna 150B	150-59471	N7371X	23. 2.62	CofA expired 6.11.69 & WFU at Perth. Canx as WFU 11.11.69.
G-ARTX	Cessna 150B	150-59477	N7377X	23. 2.62	Badly damaged at Roborough on 14.9.72. Canx as WFU 12.1.73.
G-ARTY	Cessna 150B	150-59482	N7382X	23. 2.62	Canx as WFU 4.12.68 at Perth. (Instructional Airframe 5/96 Perth)
G-ARTZ(1)	McCandless M.2 Gyrocopter	M2/1		.10.61	(At the Ulster Folk & Transport Museum, Cultra Manor, Holywood; on display unmarked 6/97)
G-ARTZ(2)	McCandless M.4 Gyrocopter	M4/1		24.10.61	
G-ARUA	DH.114 Heron 2D	14114	I-BKET	29. 1.62	To OY-DGR 12/66. Canx 2.12.66.
G-ARUB(1)	PA-18-150 Super Cub	18-7756	N3932Z	. .62R	NTU - Not Imported. Remained as N3932Z. Canx.
G-ARUB(2)	EoN AP.10 460 Standard Srs.1B	EoN/S/005		23. 1.62	To BGA.1154 3/64. Canx 17.6.64.
G-ARUC	PA-22-108 Colt	22-9175		21. 3.62	Overturned in gales at Ringway on 29.2.76. Canx as destroyed 18.5.76.
G-ARUD	Douglas DC-7C (Line No. 754)	45160	OO-SFD EP-ADU/OO-SFD	29.11.61	Fatal crash into a swamp and burnt out immediately after take-off from Douala, Cameroon on 4.3.62. Canx.
G-ARUE(1)	Proacaer F.15 Picchio	19		.11.61R	NTU - To G-ARNW/I-PROE. Carries a plate proclaiming it to be G-ARUE when seen at the Hanover show in 1962. Canx in 1962 as registration NTU.
G-ARUE(2)	DH.104 Dove 7	04530	IAC-194 Irish Air Corps/(G-ARUE)	7.10.80	To D-IKER 10/83. Canx by CAA 17.7.86.
G-ARUF	Hiller 360 UH-12C	903	HP-263 N5324V	21. 9.61	Ditched into Loch Awe, Crinan Pier, Argyll on 6.7.63. Canx.
G-ARUG	Auster J/5G Cirrus Autocar	3272	G-25-9 (VH-...)	2. 1.62	
G-ARUH	SAN Jodel DR.1050 Ambassadeur	284		5.12.61	(Stored Denham 3/89)
G-ARUI	Beagle A.61 Terrier 1	2529	(G-ASAA) VF571	9. 3.62	
G-ARUJ	Piaggio P.166	376		12.12.61	CofA expired 26.5.71 & WFU at Yeadon. Canx as WFU 25.2.72.
G-ARUK	Commonwealth CAC.18 P-51 Mustang Mk.22	1498	VH-UWB (VH-JWB)/R.Australian AF A68-113	5. 4.62	Fatal crash into high ground near Kallista, in the Dandenong Ranges, Victoria, Australia on 12.4.62. Canx.
G-ARUL	LeVier Cosmic Wind	103	N22C	28.11.61	
	(Rebuilt 1973 under c/n PFA/1511; original components on rebuild by John Tempest at Kingscliffe, Peterborough 12/95)				
G-ARUM	DH.104 Dove 8	04528		29.11.61	To G-DDCD 1/84. Canx.
G-ARUN	Bensen B.7M Gyrocopter	9		5.12.61	Not completed. Canx 14.4.62.
G-ARUO	PA-24-180 Comanche	24-2427	"G-AROU" N7251P	16. 1.62	
G-ARUP	PA-28-160 Cherokee	28-127		11.12.61	Crash-landed in a backgarden in Rayleigh Road, Eastwood, near Southend on 6.6.76. Canx as WFU 12.8.76.
G-ARUR	PA-28-160 Cherokee	28-133		16. 1.62	Damaged in forced landing nr.Redhill Aerodrome on 14.9.92. Canx as destroyed 27.11.92. (Fuselage stored 8/97)
G-ARUS	PA-28-160 Cherokee	28-159		16. 1.62	Undershot at Bembridge on 25.6.72 following engine failure on approach. Canx as destroyed 9.1.73.
G-ARUT	Auster J/5G Cirrus Autocar	2974	AP-AJW AP-AHI/VP-KKM/(PT-ANM)	29.11.61	DBR in forced-landing near Barnet, Herts on 13.8.65. Canx.
G-ARUU	Vickers 745D Viscount	198	N7442	11.12.61	To Empire Test Pilots School as XR802 in 1/62. Canx 5.1.62.

Regn	Type	c/n	Previous identity	Regn date	Fate or immediate subsequent identity (if known)
G-ARUV(1)	PA-28-160 Cherokee	28-206		.11.61	To EI-AME 1/62. Canx.
G-ARUV(2)	Piel CP.301 Emeraude Srs. 1	PFA/700		2. 2.62	
G-ARUW	PA-24-250 Comanche	24-2913		29.12.61	DBR on landing at Scothes Farm, Hurstpierpoint on 24.7.76. Canx as destroyed 21.4.77.
G-ARUX	Beagle A.61 Terrier 1	3729	WE611	14.12.61	DBR at Luton on 18.8.63. Canx.
G-ARUY	Auster J/1N Alpha	3394		2. 2.62	
G-ARUZ	Cessna 175C Skylark	175-57080	N8380T	23. 2.62	
G-ARVA	Vickers VC-10 Srs.1101	804		16. 1.63	To 5N-ABD 9/69. Canx 29.9.69.
G-ARVB	Vickers VC-10 Srs.1101	805		16. 1.63	WFU at Heathrow on 25.7.74. Broken up in 10/76. Canx 7.10.76 as sold to USA.
G-ARVC	Vickers VC-10 Srs.1101	806		16. 1.63	To A40-VC. Canx 7.10.75.
G-ARVD	Not allocated.				
G-ARVE	Vickers VC-10 Srs.1101	807		16. 1.63	WFU at Heathrow on 31.10.74. Broken up in 10/76. Canx 7.10.76 as sold to USA.
G-ARVF	Vickers VC-10 Srs.1101	808		16. 1.63	WFU on 11.4.83. (On display 4/99 Hermeskeil Museum, near Trier, Germany) Canx.
G-ARVG	Vickers VC-10 Srs.1101	809		16. 1.63	To A40-VG. Canx 7.10.75.
G-ARVH	Vickers VC-10 Srs.1101	810		16. 1.63	WFU at Heathrow on 31.10.74. Broken up in 10/76. Canx 7.10.76 as sold to USA.
G-ARVI	Vickers VC-10 Srs.1101	811		16. 1.63	To A40-VI. Canx 7.10.75.
G-ARVJ(1)	Vickers VC-10 Srs.1101	815		. 1.63	NTU - To G-ARVM(2) 1/63. Canx.
G-ARVJ(2)	Vickers VC-10 Srs.1101	812	(G-ARVK)	16. 1.63	To RAF as ZD493 in 9/82. Canx 20.9.82.
G-ARVK(1)	Vickers VC-10 Srs.1101	812		. 1.63	NTU - To G-ARVJ(2) 1/63. Canx.
G-ARVK(2)	Vickers VC-10 Srs.1101	813	(G-ARVL)	16. 1.63	To A40-VK. Canx 7.10.75.
G-ARVL(1)	Vickers VC-10 Srs.1101	813		. 1.63	NTU - To G-ARVK(2) 1/63. Canx.
G-ARVL(2)	Vickers VC-10 Srs.1101	814	(G-ARVM)	16. 1.63	To A40-VL. Canx 7.10.75.
G-ARVM(1)	Vickers VC-10 Srs.1101	814		. 1.63	NTU - To G-ARVL(2) 1/63. Canx.
G-ARVM(2)	Vickers VC-10 Srs.1101	815	(G-ARVJ)	16. 1.63	WFU on 22.10.79. (On display at RAF Cosford) Canx.
G-ARVN(1)	Vickers VC-10 Srs.1101	816		. .62R	NTU - Not built. Canx.
G-ARVN(2)	Servotec Rotorcraft Grasshopper 1 (There are two airframes which were G-ARVN; the other was stored by J.Wilkie at Squires Gate)	1		16. 2.63	WFU at Hanworth in 5/63. Canx as WFU 14.3.77. (Stored 8/97 Weston-super-Mare)
G-ARVO(1)	Vickers VC-10 Srs.1101	817		. .62R	NTU - Not built. Canx.
G-ARVO(2)	Forney F.1A Aircoupe	5931		. .62R	NTU - Not Imported. Canx.
G-ARVO(3)	PA-18-95 Super Cub	18-7252	D-ENFI N3376Z	18. 1.83	
G-ARVP(1)	Vickers VC-10 Srs.1101	818		. .62R	NTU - Not built. Canx.
G-ARVP(2)	Lockheed L.049D-46-19 Constellation	1967	HB-IEB 4X-AKB/N90828/RX-123/NC90828/43-10315	13. 2.62	CofA expired 2.4.65 & WFU at Luton. Broken up in 5/65. Canx.
G-ARVR	PA-28-160 Cherokee	28-280		1. 3.62	DBR at Wolverhampton on 26.9.65. Canx.
G-ARVS	PA-28-160 Cherokee	28-339		12. 3.62	To G-JAKS 7/99. Canx.
G-ARVT	PA-28-160 Cherokee	28-379		21. 3.62	
G-ARVU	PA-28-160 Cherokee	28-410	PH-ONY G-ARVU	30. 3.62	
G-ARVV	PA-28-160 Cherokee	28-451		11. 7.62	
G-ARVW	PA-28-160 Cherokee	28-502		11. 7.62	Substantially damaged on a failed take-off at Bodmin on 26.9.90. Canx as WFU 14.11.90.
G-ARVX	DH.114 Heron 2	14086	I-AOBI VR-NCC	15. 1.62	To OY-ADF 10/62. Canx 5.9.62.
G-ARVY	Brantly B.2	145	N5998X	30. 1.62	DBR in an autorotative landing near Kidlington on 28.8.64. Dismantled for spares at Kidlington in 9/64. Canx.
G-ARVZ	Rollason-Druine D.62A Condor (Converted to D.62B in 1977)	RAE/606		6.12.61	
G-ARWA	Agusta-Bell 47J-2 Ranger	2005	9J-RCZ G-ARWA/EC-AUA/G-ARWA/SE-HAZ	19. 1.62	To I-CIEM 5/68. Canx 13.6.68.
G-ARWB	DHC.1 Chipmunk 22A (Fuselage no. DHB/f/498) (Converted to a Mk.22A in 9/67)	C1/0621	WK611	2. 1.62	
G-ARWC	Cessna 150B	150-59515	N1115Y	18. 4.62	DBR at Exeter on 28.4.84. Canx as destroyed 23.11.88.
G-ARWD	Boeing 707-465 (Line No. 271)	18372	VR-BBW (G-ARWD)	26. 1.62	WFU & stored at Kingman, AZ in 5/82, later broken up. Canx.
G-ARWE	Boeing 707-465 (Line No. 302)	18373	(VR-BBZ) (G-ARWE)	26. 1.62	Crashed at Heathrow on 8.4.68. (Nose used to repair Boeing 707-331B N776TW) Canx.
G-ARWF	Cessna 310G	310G-0050	N8950Z	8. 3.62	To EI-ATC 10/69. Canx 3.2.69.
G-ARWG	Druine D.61 Condor (Reportedly originally reserved in 12/58)	PFA/600		6. 1.61	Not completed. Canx 15.9.62.
G-ARWH	Cessna 172C Skyhawk	172-49166	N1466Y	18. 4.62	WFU & displayed on restaurant at Golders Green. Canx as WFU 29.11.88. (Stored for spares 3/96)
G-ARWI	Douglas C-54B-10-DO Skymaster	18349	N90450 NC90450/43-17149	22. 2.62	To Nigerian AF as NAF311 in 1971. Canx 13.12.68.
G-ARWJ	Douglas DC-6B (Line No. 334)	43844	VR-BBQ CF-CUQ	24. 1.62	Restored as CF-CUQ 12/62. Canx 2.1.63.
G-ARWK	Douglas C-54G-1-DO Skymaster	35936	N904 45-483	3. 5.62	To D-ADAD 11/67. Canx 3.10.67.
G-ARWL	Cessna 182E	182-53895	N2895Y	13. 4.62	Crashed at Ashbourne on 18.10.75. Canx.
G-ARWM	Cessna 175C Skylark	175-57109	N8509X	24. 5.62	Fatal crash at Chilgrove, 6 miles from Goodwood on 10.3.91. Canx as destroyed 4.7.91.
G-ARWN	Cessna 150B	150-59523	N1123Y	17. 4.62	Fatal crash at Llangyseleca, about 10 miles NE of Swansea on 2.5.70. Canx.
G-ARWO	Cessna 172C Skyhawk	172-49187	N1487Y	10. 4.62	
G-ARWP	Cessna 172C	172-49192	N1492Y	6. 6.62	Overturned & DBR through overshooting while landing at Biggin Hill on 23.7.67. Canx.
G-ARWR	Cessna 172C Skyhawk	172-49172	N1472Y	13. 4.62	
G-ARWS	Cessna 175C Skylark	175-57102	N8502X	12. 4.62	

Regn	Type	c/n	Previous identity	Regn date	Fate or immediate subsequent identity (if known)
G-ARWT	Vickers 828 Viscount	448		23. 1.62	To JA8205. Canx 30.3.62.
G-ARWU	Vickers 828 Viscount	449		23. 1.62	To JA8206. Canx 7.5.62.
G-ARWV	Vickers 828 Viscount	450		23. 1.62	To JA8207. Canx 9.6.62.
G-ARWW	Bensen B.8M Gyrocopter (Built by S.J.Bartlam)	SJB.1	N10171	7. 2.62	Permit expired 1.4.82. Canx as WFU 17.12.91.
G-ARWX	Phoenix Luton LA-5A Major	PAL/1208		1. 2.62	Not completed - To G-BENH 2/77. Canx 30.5.84.
G-ARWY	Mooney M.20A	1305	N1079B	16. 3.62	WFU on 6.8.80. Canx 4.2.82.
G-ARWZ	Bristol 175 Britannia Srs.313	13233	4X-AGB	13. 2.62	Restored as 4X-AGB. Canx 26.3.65.
G-ARXA	Bristol 175 Britannia Srs.313	13234	4X-AGC G-ARXA/4X-AGC/(G-ANGK)	13. 2.62	Stored as 4X-AGC in 11/68 and broken up for spares in 11/70 at Luton. Canx.
G-ARXB	Beagle A.109 Airedale (Originally regd with c/n A.109-2)	B.509	(EI-ATE) G-ARXB	5. 2.62	To EI-BBK 11/75. Canx 16.10.75.
G-ARXC	Beagle A.109 Airedale (Originally regd with c/n A.109-3)	B.510	EI-ATD G-ARXC	9. 4.62	WFU at Leicester in 11/76. Canx as WFU 12.4.89. (Stored 9/96)
G-ARXD	Beagle A.109 Airedale (Originally regd with c/n A.109-4)	B.511		9. 4.62	(Stored 6/95)
G-ARXE	Lockheed L.149-46-10 Constellation	1965	(HB-IEA) 4X-AEA/N90827/RX-121/NC90827/43-10313	13. 2.62	WFU at Luton in 5/65. Broken up. Canx.
G-ARXF	PA-23-250 Aztec	27-2015		21. 2.62	Impounded at Tripoli, Libya. CofA expired 24.9.82. Canx by CAA 17.7.86.
G-ARXG	PA-24-250 Comanche	24-3154		21. 2.62	
G-ARXH	Bell 47G (Built as Bell 47B)	40	(F-....) G-ARXH/N120B/NC120B	13. 2.62	(Stored Luton 6/92)
G-ARXI	PA-24-250 Comanche	24-2748	N7542P	27. 3.62	To SE-FFG 7/68. Canx 9.7.68.
G-ARXJ	Douglas C-54B-10-DO Skymaster	18370	N100J N4270/N8344C/XT-100/XT-T-103/43-17170	29. 5.62	To HP-451 6/67. Canx 21.6.67.
G-ARXK	PA-22-160 Tri-Pacer	22-6689	EI-AKY	20. 2.62	Crashed into sea off Alderney on 26.8.66. Canx.
G-ARXL	Beagle A.61 Terrier 1	3726	WE555	20. 2.62	Crashed at Chatteris, Cambs on 15.6.70. Canx as WFU 6.7.70.
G-ARXM	Beagle B.206Y	B.002	G-35-5	19. 2.62	Crashed at Wisborough Green, Sussex on 25.5.64. Canx.
G-ARXN	Cobelavia Tipsy T.66 Nipper Srs.2	77		3. 7.62	CofA expired 19.8.80. Canx by CAA 12.4.89. (Stored 5/96 Hucknall)
G-ARXO	Brantly B.2	175		16. 2.62	Crashed in the course of an instructional flight at Kidlington on 14.7.62. Canx.
G-ARXP	Phoenix Luton LA-4A Minor	PAL/1119 & PFA/816		23. 2.62	(Stored 8/97)
G-ARXR	Forney F.1A Aircoupe	5762	N3059G	28. 6.62	Crashed immediately after take-off from Biggin Hill on 29.4.67. Canx.
G-ARXS	Forney F.1A Aircoupe	5731	D-EBSA N3037G	23. 7.62	To EI-AUT 12/70. Canx 29.10.70.
G-ARXT	SAN Jodel DR.1050 Ambassadeur	355		14. 3.62	
G-ARXU	Auster 6A Tugmaster	2295	VF526	5. 3.62	
G-ARXV(1)	PA-23 Apache	-		. 3.62R	NTU. Canx.
G-ARXV(2)	Hiller 360 UH-12E	2193	EP-HAJ G-ARXV/5N-AGG/VR-BCA/5N-ABX/G-ARXV	24. 5.62	To ZS-HCT. Canx 17.1.69.
G-ARXW	Morane MS.885 Super Rallye	100		30. 3.62	
G-ARXX	Morane MS.880B Rallye Club	106		30. 3.62	Last known on rebuild near Southampton with CofA expired 17.1.83. (Reportedly to Spain for rebuild .91) Canx by CAA 20.4.94.
G-ARXY	Morane MS.880B Rallye Club	108		30. 3.62	DBR on landing at Widdrington, near Morpeth on 31.3.84. Canx as WFU 28.12.84.
G-ARXZ	Douglas DC-6A/B (Line No. 803)	45326	CF-CZS	19. 3.62	Restored as CF-CZS 9/64. Canx 16.10.64.
G-ARYA	DH.125 Srs.1	25001		1. 3.62	CofA expired 1.10.65. WFU at Kelsterton College, Chester as instructional airframe in 4/68. Canx.
G-ARYB	DH.125 Srs.1	25002		1. 3.62	WFU at BAe Hatfield. CofA expired 11.1.68. Canx 4.3.69. Preserved 4/96 at Midland Air Museum, Coventry.
G-ARYC	DH.125 Srs.1	25003		1. 3.62	WFU at Hatfield on 1.8.73. Canx as WFU 31.3.76. (To Mosquito Museum, London Colney)
G-ARYD	Auster 6A	-	WJ358	8. 3.62	Conversion abandoned at Perth in 9/63. Canx as WFU 5.8.87. (On display 3/96 AAC Middle Wallop)
G-ARYE	Douglas DC-7C (Line No. 937)	45308	OO-SFG	5. 4.62	To D-ABAR 3/66. Canx 8.2.66.
G-ARYF	PA-23-250 Aztec B	27-2065		11. 4.62	
G-ARYG	PA-23-250 Aztec B	27-2093		11. 4.62	Crashed into Craig Dunan Hill, Inverness on 22.1.66. Wreck stored at Dalcross in 1967. Canx.
G-ARYH	PA-22-160 Tri-Pacer	22-7039	N3102Z	9. 3.62	
G-ARYI	Cessna 172C	172-49260	N1560Y	13. 7.62	
G-ARYJ	LET L-200A Morava	170804	OK-PLT	2. 4.62	Restored as OK-PLT. Canx 2.10.62.
G-ARYK	Cessna 172C	172-49288	N1588Y	13. 7.62	
G-ARYL	CZL Aero 145	20-003		2. 4.62	To OK-... Canx 14.9.62.
G-ARYM	DH.104 Dove 8	04529		10. 4.62	WFU at Exeter 30.6.78. Broken up. Canx 15.2.82.
G-ARYN	Bolkow F.207	212		19. 3.62	To D-EHUK(2) 7/63. Canx 1.11.63.
G-ARYO	PA-28-180 Cherokee	28-679	N5572W	12. 7.62	NTU - Not Imported. Remained as N5572W. Canx.
G-ARYP	PA-28-180 Cherokee	28-693	N5586W	12. 7.62	NTU - Not Imported. Remained as N5586W. Canx.
G-ARYR	PA-28-180 Cherokee B	28-770		12. 7.62	
G-ARYS	Cessna 172B Skyhawk	172-49291	N1591Y	13. 7.62	
G-ARYT	PA-25-235 Pawnee	25-662		22. 2.62	Crashed at Downham Market on 15.6.64. Canx.
G-ARYU	Cessna 320 Skyknight	320-0109	N5209X	21. 5.62	Canx 3.12.75 on sale to the United Arab Emirates. To 5B-CDL 10/77.
G-ARYV	PA-24-250 Comanche	24-2516	N7337P	17. 4.62	(Stored 5/97)
G-ARYW	SAN Jodel D.117	639	F-BIBS	21. 5.62	Fatal crash immediately after take-off from Rhoose on 16.8.62. Canx.

Regn	Type	c/n	Previous identity	Regn date	Fate or immediate subsequent identity (if known)
G-ARYX	Brantly B.2	182	N2134U	10. 5.62	Crashed at East Berks Golfcourse, Crowthorne on 15.6.64. Canx.
G-ARYY	Douglas DC-4-1009	42907	N33679 NC33679	18. 4.62	WFU on 1.7.68. Broken up at Southend in 1/70. Canx as destroyed 23.2.70.
G-ARYZ	Beagle A.109 Airedale	B.512		9. 4.62	
G-ARZA	Wallis WA.116/F (Built as Beagle-Wallis WA.116 Srs.1)	B.202	XR942 G-ARZA	18. 4.62	To CS-GAA. Canx 16.8.88.
G-ARZB	Beagle-Wallis WA.116 Srs.1 (Another Wallis is on display 10/93 in Planet Hollywood, Leicester Square, London W1 as G-ARZB and is an unidentified aircraft owned by D.Worrall t/a James Bond Collectors Club)	B.203	XR943 G-ARZB	18. 4.62	Permit expired 29.6.93. (Stored 2/99 Reymerston Hall)
G-ARZC(1)	Wallis WA.116	B.204		. .62R	NTU - To XR944/G-ASDY. Canx.
G-ARZC(2)	Wallis WA.116	B.205		18. 4.62	DBR at Swanton Morley on 7.11.65. Rebuilt as G-ATTB c/n 214. Canx.
G-ARZD	Cessna 172C	172-49389	N1689Y	22. 6.62	Crashed at St.Marys, Isles of Scilly on 28.5.77. Canx 1.2.82. (Stored 11/93)
G-ARZE	Cessna 172C	172-49388	N1688Y	22. 6.62	Blown over by high winds at Brawdy on 11.9.76 & DBR. Canx. (Training Airframe 3/95)
G-ARZF	Cessna 150B	150-59610	N1210Y	22. 6.62	CofA expired 17.7.84. Canx as WFU 17.11.88.
G-ARZG	Aermacchi-Lockheed AL.60B-1	6219/39		21. 6.62	DBR in ground collision with Viking G-AGRW at Squires Gate on 7.7.65. Canx.
G-ARZH	PA-25-235 Pawnee	25-2026		4. 7.62	Crashed near Downham Market on 2.8.69. (Remains at Stapleford late-1969)
G-ARZI	Brantly B.2A	165	N2117U	30. 5.62	CofA expired 27.2.69. Canx as WFU 5.12.83.
G-ARZJ	Brantly B.2A	170	N2122U	30. 5.62	Crashed at Llanfairfechan, Wales on 12.4.64. Dismantled for spares at Kidlington in 9/64. Canx.
G-ARZK	Brantly B.2A	171	N2123U	30. 5.62	Crashed at Kidlington on 24.4.67. Canx.
G-ARZL	Bensen B.7M Gyrocopter	9		7. 5.62	Canx as WFU on 30.5.84.
G-ARZM	Rollason-Druine D.31 Turbulent	PFA/581		23. 3.62	Badly damaged in forced landing at Boughton Monchelsea, Kent on 23.6.91. (Small pieces only remain stored 1/96) Canx as PWFU 4.2.99.
G-ARZN	Beechcraft N35 Bonanza	D-6795	N215DM	23. 5.62	(On rebuild 5/97)
G-ARZO	Douglas DC-6A/B (Line No. 722)	45078	CF-CZQ OD-ADP/CF-CZQ	25. 5.62	Restored as CF-CZQ 12/62. Canx 31.12.62.
G-ARZP	Beagle A.109 Airedale	B.513		11. 5.62	Canx as WFU 30.8.84.
G-ARZR	Beagle A.109 Airedale	B.514		11. 5.62	Crash into sea off Folkestone after involvement in a mid-air collision with D.62B Condor G-AVRV on 6.7.68. Canx.
G-ARZS	Beagle A.109 Airedale	B.515		11. 5.62	To EI-BAL 10/74. Canx 15.10.74.
G-ARZT	Beagle A.61 Terrier 2	B.602	WE604	28. 5.62	Fatal crash at Home Farm, Leigh, Kent on 15.8.73. Canx.
G-ARZU	Beagle A.61 Terrier 2	B.603	WE535	28. 5.62	WFU on 31.8.69. Canx 14.3.73 and badly damaged in hangar collapse at Enstone on 2.1.76.
G-ARZV	Aviation Traders ATL.98 Carvair (Conv. Douglas C-54A-5-DO)	7480/6	N75298 YV-C-AVH/NC90431/41-107461	8. 6.62	To EI-AMP 12/62. Canx 21.1.63.
G-ARZW	Currie Wot	1 & HAC/5		25. 5.62	Badly damaged in crash into a field north of Headcorn airfield on 12.2.88. (On rebuild 10/95 as Pfalz D.VII scale replica)
G-ARZX	Cessna 150B	150-59642	N1242Y	13. 7.62	Canx by CAA 16.9.98.
G-ARZY	PA-25-235 Pawnee	25-2087		4. 7.62	Crashed at Bishops Itchington, Rugby on 20.3.63. Canx.
G-ARZZ(1)	PA-25-235 Pawnee	25-2106		12. 7.62R	NTU - Not Imported. To AN-AOU 6/62. Canx 10.8.62.
G-ARZZ(2)	PA-25-235 Pawnee	25-2180		10. 8.62R	NTU - Not Imported. To F-OBXY. Canx 31.8.62.
G-ARZZ(3)	PA-25-235 Pawnee	25-2073	N6567Z	31. 8.62	Crashed at Quaik, Sudan on 28.10.63. Canx.
G-ASAA(1)	Beagle A.61 Terrier 1	2529	VF571	. 3.62R	NTU - Allocated in error. To G-ARUI 3/62. Canx.
G-ASAA(2)	Phoenix Luton LA-4A Minor	0-H/4		19. 4.62	
G-ASAB	Jodel DR.105A Ambassadeur	87	F-BIVS	1.11.62	Crashed after take-off from Fairoaks on 14.6.67. Canx.
G-ASAC	Beagle A.61 Terrier 2 (Converted from Auster 6 c/n 3728)	B.606	WE587	1. 6.62	Crashed on landing Roborough, Plymouth on 4.9.64. Canx.
G-ASAD	Beagle A.61 Terrier 2 (Converted from Auster 6 c/n 3731)	B.610	WE559	1. 6.62	Ditched and sank in the English Channel 9 miles SE of Lympne on 30.8.70. Canx.
G-ASAE	Beagle A.61 Terrier 2	B.611	WE606	1. 6.62	Fatal crash at Sobney Pumping Station, near Reading on 4.11.62 after a mid-air collision with RAF Chipmunk WD372. Canx.
G-ASAF	Beagle A.109 Airedale	B.517		26. 6.62	To OY-AOM 7/62. Canx 27.7.62.
G-ASAG	Beagle A.61 Terrier 2 (Converted from Auster 6 c/n 2508)	B.607	VF550	26. 6.62	Crashed near Halfpenny Green on 11.9.66. Canx as WFU 26.6.70.
G-ASAH	Beagle A.109 Airedale	B.518	(9H-A..) G-ASAH	26. 6.62	Crashed at Bergues, France on 23.7.72. Canx.
G-ASAI	Beagle A.109 Airedale	B.516		26. 6.62	(On rebuild 6/95)
G-ASAJ	Beagle A.61 Terrier 2 (Converted from Auster 6 c/n 3732)	B.605	WE569	26. 6.62	
G-ASAK	Beagle A.61 Terrier 2	B.604	WE591	26. 6.62	
G-ASAL(1)	Scottish Aviation Twin Pioneer Srs.3	599		23. 5.62	Airframe not completed. Sold as scrap 5/76. Canx as WFU 5.3.69.
G-ASAL(2)	Scottish Avn Bulldog Srs.120/124	BH120-239	(G-BBHF) G-31-17	5. 9.73	CofA expired 30.11.89. Stored at Prestwick.
G-ASAM	Rollason-Druine D.31 Turbulent	PFA/595		25. 4.62	Badly damaged in forced landing at Coxheath, Kent on 23.6.91. (Stored 8/96) Canx as PWFU 4.2.99.
G-ASAN	Beagle A.61 Terrier Srs.2	B.608	VX928	26. 6.62	(On rebuild 4/97)
G-ASAO	Morane MS.885 Super Rallye	139		21. 6.62	Ditched into the English Channel off Worthing, Sussex on 20.1.67. Canx.
G-ASAP	Morane MS.885 Super Rallye	140		21. 6.62	Fatal crash 15.6.75, ditched in Channel and sunk, en route from Le Touquet to Lydd. Canx.
G-ASAR	Morane MS.880B Rallye Club	177		21. 6.62	Canx as WFU 18.6.76.
G-ASAS	Bolkow Bo.208A-1 Junior	514	D-ENCY	27. 8.62	To D-EKMY 4/65. Canx 1.2.64.

Regn	Type	c/n	Previous identity	Regn date	Fate or immediate subsequent identity (if known)
G-ASAT	Morane MS.880B Rallye Club	178		21. 6.62	
G-ASAU	Morane MS.880B Rallye Club	179		21. 6.62	
G-ASAV	Morane MS.880B Rallye Club	180		21. 6.62	CofA expired 20.1.89. Dismantled for spares at Barton. Canx as WFU 13.3.89.
G-ASAW	Bolkow/Klemm Kl.107C	150	D-ELOQ	7. 6.62	Crashed into sea off Littlehampton, Sussex on 5.1.65. Canx.
G-ASAX	Beagle A.61 Terrier 2 (Converted from Auster 6 c/n 1911)	B.609	TW533	12. 6.62	
G-ASAY	Bolkow F.207	257	D-EGLU	7. 6.62	DBR in a forced landing at Libin, Belgium on 17.12.62. Rebuilt & restored as D-EGLU in 10/63. Canx.
G-ASAZ	Hiller 360 UH-12E-4	2070	N5372V	18. 6.62	(Stored dismantled with engine damaged 4/99 Gamlingay, Five Acres Farm)
G-ASBA	Phoenix Currie Wot	AE.1 & PFA/3005		16. 8.62	
G-ASBB	Beechcraft 23 Musketeer	M-15		21. 6.62	
G-ASBC	Forney F-1A Aircoupe	5760	N3057G	27. 8.62	Crashed and burnt out after striking a tree on approach to Stapleford on 7.9.66. Canx.
G-ASBD	Hughes 269A	52-0081	G-17-2 XS684/G-ASBD	11. 7.62	Crashed at Redmoor House Farm, Menthorpe, near Driffield on 1.8.81. Canx.
G-ASBE	Vickers 634 Viking 1B	214	SU-AFL EI-ADL	18. 6.62	Broken up for spares at Luton in 3/63. Canx.
G-ASBF	Handley Page HPR.7 Dart Herald 204	163		22. 6.62	NTU - To G-ASBP 6/62. Canx.
G-ASBG	Handley Page HPR.7 Dart Herald 203	164	I-TIVA G-ASBG	26. 6.62	WFU at Norwich on 23.9.81. Canx 13.6.83. Broken up in 8/84.
G-ASBH	Beagle A.109 Airedale	B.519		26. 6.62	
G-ASBI	Beagle A.109 Airedale	B.520		26. 6.62	To VH-UEM(2) 7/63. Canx 2.8.63.
G-ASBJ	Beagle A.109 Airedale	B.521		26. 6.62	To 9M-AMT 9/63. Canx 11.10.63.
G-ASBK	Beagle A.109 Airedale	B.522		26. 6.62	To CF-POL 2/63. Canx 26.2.63.
G-ASBL	Hughes 269A	42-0066	G-17-1 XS349/G-ASBL	29. 6.62	Crashed at Fairlop, Essex on 27.10.64. Canx.
G-ASBM	Vickers 828 Viscount	457		4. 7.62	To JA8208 10/62. Canx 10.10.62.
G-ASBN	Mooney M.20C	2183	N6436U	28. 6.62	To VH-MOZ 11/77. Canx 26.7.77.
G-ASBO	Vickers 828 Viscount	458		4. 7.62	To JA8209 11/62. Canx 7.11.62.
G-ASBP	Handley Page HPR.7 Dart Herald 204	163	PI-C869 G-ASBP/(G-ASBF)	22. 6.62	Restored as PI-C869 10/66. Canx.
G-ASBR	Vickers 828 Viscount	459		4. 7.62	To JA8210 2/63. Canx 8.2.63.
G-ASBS	Coopavia CP.301A Emeraude	236	F-BIMJ	23. 7.62	CofA expired 6.1.87. Canx as destroyed 23.1.87.
G-ASBT	Beagle A.61 Terrier 2	B.612	WE603	12. 7.62	To (D-ECXO)/D-EBMU 8/62. Canx 27.7.62.
G-ASBU	Beagle A.61 Terrier 2 (Converted from Auster 6 c/n 3733(1))	B.613	WE570	12. 7.62	Damaged at Netherley on 12.8.80. CofA expired 5.7.82. Canx as WFU 16.10.85. (Stored for spares 12/95)
G-ASBV	Beagle-Auster D.5/180 Husky	3677		12. 7.62	Struck the ground and crashed during a demonstration flight at Ecuvillens, near Fribourg, Switzerland on 20.10.63. (Was fitted with skis for demonstrations to the Swiss Army) Canx
G-ASBW	Druine D.31 Turbulent	PFA/404		20. 7.62	Crashed near Stonehaven on 11.10.75. Canx.
G-ASBX	Beagle A.109 Airedale	B.524	(F-....) G-ASBX	16. 7.62	To AP-ANP 12/62. Canx 28.1.63.
G-ASBY	Beagle A.109 Airedale	B.523		23. 7.62	CofA expired 22.3.80. (Stored 5/92)
G-ASBZ	Beagle A.109 Airedale	B.525		23. 7.62	To VH-UEP 8/62. Canx 22.8.62.
G-ASCA	Beagle A.109 Airedale	B.526		23. 7.62	To VH-UEH 8/62. Canx 22.8.62.
G-ASCB	Beagle A.109 Airedale	B.527		23. 7.62	Crashed into the River Douro at Barqueiros do Douro, Portugal on 26.7.64 while taking-off after a forced-landing on a nearby beach. Rebuilt as CS-AIB 6/68. Canx.
G-ASCC	Beagle E.3 Mk.11	B.701	(G-25-12) XP254	23. 7.62	Damaged on landing at Long Marston on 5.11.95. (On rebuild 9/97)
G-ASCD	Beagle A.61 Terrier 2	B.615	PH-SFT (PH-SCD) G-ASCD/VW993	23. 7.62	Broken up for spares and various parts departed Blackbushe in opposite directions c 1974. Fuselage only to Nymsfield. Canx as WFU 5.10.89. (On display 5/97 Elvington)
G-ASCE	Beagle A.61 Terrier 2	B.616	WE571	23. 7.62	To HB-EUD 8/62. Canx 31.7.62.
G-ASCF	Beagle A.61 Terrier 2	B.617	WE548	23. 7.62	To SE-ELO 9/67. Canx 10.4.67.
G-ASCG	Beagle A.61 Terrier 2 (Converted from Auster 6 c/n 2575)	B.618	VF633	23. 7.62	To VH-UPS 6/68. Canx 16.1.69.
G-ASCH	Beagle A.61 Terrier 2 (Converted from Auster 6 c/n 2523)	B.619	VF565	23. 7.62	CofA expired 20.7.81 & WFU at Enstone. Canx by CAA 12.6.91. (Stored un-regd 2/99 at Fakenham, Norfolk)
G-ASCI	Beagle A.61 Terrier 2 (Converted from Auster 6 c/n 2571)	B.620	VF629	23. 7.62	To D-ENZO 11/62. Canx 9.11.62.
G-ASCJ	PA-24-250 Comanche	24-2368	5N-AEB N7197P	2. 8.62	DBR in forced landing at Hurn on 10.9.86. Canx as WFU 8.1.87.
G-ASCK	Beagle B.218X (Originally regd as Beagle-Miles M.218)	B.051	G-35-6	26. 7.62	Rebuilt as M.242 G-ASTX in 1964. Canx as marks withdrawn 3.6.64.
G-ASCL	Beechcraft 23 Musketeer	M-107		7. 8.62	Crashed on take-off at Kirkbymoorside on 24.6.66. Parts used in rebuild of PH-MUS which became G-AWIK. Canx.
G-ASCM	Isaacs Fury II	PFA/2002/1B & 1		1. 8.62	
G-ASCN	Short SC.7 Skyvan 1A (Originally regd as Skyvan 1, converted in 10/63)	SH1828		7. 8.62	Last flew on 15.8.66 & WFU. Used for mock-up purposes 2/68. Broken up in 11/76 at Sydenham. Canx.
G-ASCO	Short SC.7 Skyvan 2	SH1829		7. 8.62	WFU at Sydenham, Northern Ireland on 21.5.68. Broken up in 10/72. Canx as destroyed 5.3.73.
G-ASCP	PA-23-250 Aztec B	27-2194	N5177Y	8. 8.62	NTU - Canx 28.1.63 as Not Imported. Remained as N5177Y, then to 9Q-CQJ.
G-ASCR	PA-23-250 Aztec B	27-2215		8. 8.62	Crashed into the garden of an observatory at Worlesbury Hill near Weston-super-Mare on 28.4.63. Canx.
G-ASCS	Grumman G.73 Mallard	J-55	CF-PQE CF-HAV/N2985	7. 8.62	To CF-YQC 4/69. Canx 18.4.69.
G-ASCT	Bensen B.7Mc Gyrocopter	DC.3		14. 8.62	CofA expired 11.11.66 & WFU. (Stored dismantled 8/97 Weston-super-Mare)

Regn	Type	c/n	Previous identity	Regn date	Fate or immediate subsequent identity (if known)
G-ASCU	PA-18A-150 Super Cub	18-6797	VP-JBL	31. 8.62	
G-ASCV	DFS Weihe (built by AB Flygindustri)	224	SE-STN	20. 8.62	To BGA.1297 in 3/66. Canx.
G-ASCW	Bolkow Bo.207	256	D-EGLO	27. 8.62	NTU - Canx as Not Imported 1.11.63. Stored at Laupheim. Restored as D-EGLO 7/64.
G-ASCX	DH.114 Heron 2D	14124	CA+002 West German AF	30. 8.62	To VH-CLV 5/70. Canx 7.5.70.
G-ASCY	Phoenix Luton LA-4A Minor	PAL/1124		5. 9.62	To EI-ATP 8/69. Canx.
G-ASCZ	Menavia Piel CP.301A Emeraude	233	F-BIMG	1.10.62	
G-ASDA	Beechcraft 65-80 Queen Air	LD-64		2.10.62	CofA expired 8.11.69 & WFU. Canx by CAA 31.1.89. (Front section only extant 2/95 Biggin Hill)
G-ASDB	Rollason-Druine D.31 Turbulent	PFA/1600		23. 8.62	Fatal crash at Shoreham on 11.8.68. (Parts stored 2/99 at Hingham, Norfolk)
G-ASDC	Aviation Traders ATL-98 Carvair (Conv. Douglas C-54-DC)	10273/7	LX-BNG N54373/42-72168	11. 1.63	To N80FA 4/79. Canx 30.4.79.
G-ASDD	DH.104 Dove 5	04452	I-ALGJ G-ASDD/OY-FAL	10.10.62	WFU at Biggin Hill on 27.7.75. Canx 8.2.82.
G-ASDE	Rollason-Druine D.31 Turbulent	PFA/1601		23. 8.62	To N69M 9/64. Canx 22.9.64.
G-ASDF	Edwards Gyrocopter (Mod. Adams-Wilson XH-1 Hobbycopter)	NAFE.1		17.10.62	Canx in 1963 as not completed. (Under restoration 11/98 Innsworth, Glos.)
G-ASDG	PA-23-160 Apache	23-2044		17.10.62	To TF-EGG 6/69. Canx 12.6.69.
G-ASDH	PA-23-160 Apache	23-2045		17.10.62	Crashed on take-off into Royal Victoria Hospital, Netley, near Hamble on 10.1.67. Canx.
G-ASDI	PA-23-160 Apache	23-2046		17.10.62	DBR near Kettering on 6.10.74. Canx.
G-ASDJ	Cessna 320A Skyknight	320A-0032	N3032R	25.10.62	Fatal crash ½ mile off-shore between Arbroath and Carnoustie on 4.2.70. Canx.
G-ASDK	Beagle A.61 Terrier 2 (Converted from Auster AOP.6 c/n 2573)	B.702	G-ARLM(2) (G-ARLP)/VF631	26.10.62	
G-ASDL	Beagle A.61 Terrier 2 (Also given c/n's 3727(1) & B.632(1))	B.703	G-ARLN(2) WE558	26.10.62	
G-ASDM	Bell 47G	B-16	N21H	8.11.62	Crashed at Middle Erg sand dunes, 15 miles south of El Bourma, Tunisia on 8.3.66. Canx as WFU 17.8.73.
G-ASDN	PA-24-250 Commanche	24-3280	N8033P	31.10.62	To 3D-JKB 11/82. Canx 23.2.82.
G-ASDO	Beechcraft 95-A55 Baron	TC-401		5.11.62	CofA expired 16.4.83 & WFU. To 2498 (Island of Jersey) ATC Sqdn at Jersey. Canx as WFU 27.1.89. (Extant 11/93)
G-ASDP	Vickers 843 Viscount	451		8.11.62	To China as 84301 in 7/63. Canx 16.7.63.
G-ASDR	Vickers 843 Viscount	452		8.11.62	To China as 84302 in 8/63. Canx 24.8.63.
G-ASDS	Vickers 843 Viscount	453		8.11.62	To China as 84303 in 8/63. Canx 19.9.63.
G-ASDT	Vickers 843 Viscount	454		8.11.62	To China as 84304 in 11/63. Canx 27.12.63.
G-ASDU	Vickers 843 Viscount	455		8.11.62	To China as 84305 in 1/64. Canx 9.2.64.
G-ASDV	Vickers 843 Viscount	456		8.11.62	To China as 84306 in 2/64. Canx 16.4.64.
G-ASDW	Rousseau Aviation CP.301B Emeraude	119	F-BJEY	6.12.62	Swung on touchdown at Long Marston on 21.10.75 during a cross-wind landing and on trying to become airborne again from the adjacent grass area, struck a cow and crashed. Canx as destroyed 4.12.75. Parts to CP.301A G-BIDE.
G-ASDX(1)	Douglas C-47A-25-DK Dakota	13331	N702S CU-P702/N96U/RCAF A601B/KG600/42-93421	19.11.62R	NTU - To G-AJRY 11/62. Canx 12/62.
G-ASDX(2)	PA-24-250 Comanche	24-3367		6.12.62R	NTU - To G-ASEO 1/63. Canx 12/62.
G-ASDX(3)	PA-23-250 Aztec B	27-2281		.12.62R	NTU - Not Imported. To SE-ECM 5/63. Canx 2/63.
G-ASDY	Beagle-Wallis WA-116/F (Built as WA.116 Srs.1)	B.204	XR944 (G-ARZC)	9.11.62	Permit expired 28.10.97. (Stored 2/99 Reymerston Hall)
G-ASDZ	DH.106 Comet 4C	6457	ST-AAW G-ASDZ/(XA-NAD(3))	13.11.62	Broken up at Lasham in 10/75. Canx.
G-ASEA	Phoenix Luton LA-4A Minor	PAL/1154		14.11.62	Damaged in forced landing at Mendlesham on 8.4.89. (Wings at Waits Farm, Belchamp Walter 5/93) (On rebuild 1/97)
G-ASEB	Phoenix Luton LA-4A Minor	PAL/1149		26.11.62	(On overhaul 4/96)
G-ASEC	DH.125 Srs.1/521 (Used for trials work on HS.136 project until 10/68, then as Srs.600 prototype)	25004		29.11.62	To G-FIVE 6/79. Canx.
G-ASED	Vickers 831 Viscount	419	EC-AZK EC-WZK/G-ASED/ST-AAN	10.12.62	To 4X-AVG 3/74. Canx 6.3.74.
G-ASEE	Auster J/1N Alpha	3359	I-AGRI	1. 2.63	Overturned on landing at RAE Bedford on 9.2.74 and badly damaged. Canx by CAA 29.11.89. (Wreck stored 8/92)
G-ASEF	Auster 6A Tugmaster	-	VW985	17.12.62	Damaged & dismantled at Bicester in 1966. Canx 13.1.67. (Stored 11/92)
G-ASEG	Auster 6A Tugmaster	2506	VF548	17.12.62	(Damaged in gales at Chesil Beach, near Bovington Camp on 13.2.97) (Noted hangared with no fabric at Haverfordwest in 5/99)
G-ASEH	Brantly B.2A	303	(XS682) G-ASEH	2. 1.63	WFU at Kidlington on 15.12.70. Canx.
G-ASEI	Brantly B.2A	304		2. 1.63	Crashed near Bladon, Oxon on 19.10.65. Canx.
G-ASEJ	PA-28-180 Cherokee B	28-1049		10. 1.63	To EI-BBC 6/75. Canx 16.6.75.
G-ASEK	PA-28-180 Cherokee	28-1082		10. 1.63	Fatal crash into high ground at Eskdale, Cumberland on 17.9.66. Canx.
G-ASEL	Beagle A.109 Airedale	B.534		17. 1.63	To I-CINA 5/63. Canx 8.5.63.
G-ASEM	Beagle A.109 Airedale	B.536		17. 1.63	To I-COSO 5/63. Canx 8.5.63.
G-ASEN	Douglas C-54A Skymaster	10412	TF-FIM G-ASEN/VR-HFF/CF-CPD/N88936/42-72307	17. 1.63	To ZS-IJT 2/71. Canx 4.2.71.
G-ASEO	PA-24-250 Comanche	24-3367	(G-ASDX)	23. 1.63	
G-ASEP	PA-23-235 Apache	27-541		28. 1.63	
G-ASER	PA-23-250 Aztec B	27-2283		28. 1.63	Crashed into Nigg Bay, near Cromarty, Aberdeen on 14.9.72. Canx as WFU 24.11.72. (Used as children's plaything 2/97)
G-ASES	DH.82A Tiger Moth	86465	NM145	6. 2.63	Not converted at Croydon. Canx as WFU 23.2.73.

Regn	Type	c/n	Previous identity	Regn date	Fate or immediate subsequent identity (if known)
G-ASET	DH.82A Tiger Moth	86246	NL775	8. 2.63	To CF-FDQ 2/72. Canx 3.3.72.
G-ASEU	Rollason-Druine D.62A Condor	RAE/607		12. 2.63	
G-ASEV	PA-23-250 Aztec B	27-2298		12. 2.63	WFU at Stapleford. Canx by CAA 7.2.83.
G-ASEW	Brantly B.2B	308		13. 2.63	CofA expired 17.12.73 & WFU at Kidlington. Canx as WFU 11.7.75.
G-ASEX	Not allocated.				
G-ASEY	Beagle A.61 Terrier 2	B.632		18. 2.63	Canx as WFU 19.1.77.
G-ASEZ	Hunting Percival Jet Provost T.52	PAC/P84/1093		18. 2.63	To Sudan AF as 181 in 3/63. Canx.
G-ASFA	Cessna 172D Skyhawk	172-50182	N2582U	21. 2.63	
G-ASFB	Beechcraft 23 Musketeer	M-231		25. 2.63	Crashed at Ash House Farm, Winsford on 23.5.81. Canx.
G-ASFC	DH.89A Dragon Rapide	6679	HG694	25. 2.63	CofA expired on 27.8.65 & WFU. Burnt at Weston-on-the-Green in 11/79. Canx.
G-ASFD	LET L-200A Morava	170808	OK-PHH	26. 2.63	(Stored 7/95)
G-ASFE	DHC.1 Chipmunk 22 (Fuselage no. DHB/f/767)	C1/0875	WZ853	28. 2.63	Struck on the ground and DBR by the Chipmunk G-AOST at Tollerton, Notts. on 16.8.64. Canx.
G-ASFF	PA-23-235 Apache	27-556		4. 3.63	Ditched into sea off Bournemouth on 24.9.80. Canx.
G-ASFG	PA-23-250 Aztec B	27-2311		4. 3.63	To 5B-CFM 9/83. Canx 21.9.83.
G-ASFH	PA-24-180 Comanche	24-3239	EI-AMM	1. 3.63	To N51867 1/78. Canx 25.1.78.
G-ASFI	DH.114 Heron 2D	14108	(N4661T) G-ASFI/West German AF CA+001/G-5-15	4. 3.63	To CR-GAT 8/64. Canx 15.9.64.
G-ASFJ	Beechcraft P35 Bonanza	D-7171		6. 3.63	To G-REST 12/82. Canx.
G-ASFK	Auster J/5G Cirrus Autocar	3276		7. 3.63	
G-ASFL	PA-28-180 Cherokee B	28-1170		7. 3.63	
G-ASFM	Beagle A.61 Terrier 2	B.623		8. 3.63	Fatal crash at Rearsby after take-off on a glider-towing flight on 23.5.64. Canx.
G-ASFN	Bensen B.7 Gyrocopter	B1/1		12. 3.63	WFU at Spennymoor on 28.10.69. Canx as WFU 28.10.69.
G-ASFO(1)	Bolkow Bo.208A-1 Junior	515	D-ENDA	. 3.63	NTU - Remained as D-ENDA. Canx.
G-ASFO(2)	Bolkow Bo.208A-1 Junior	517	(G-ASFR) D-ENDI	12. 3.63	CofA expired 6.11.71. Dumped at Hurn. Canx as WFU 22.3.77.
G-ASFP(1)	Bolkow Bo.208A-1 Junior	516	D-ENDE	. 3.63	NTU - To G-ASFS(2). Canx.
G-ASFP(2)	Bolkow Bo.208A-1 Junior	523	D-EGMU	12. 3.63	NTU - Not Imported. Remained as D-EGMU 7/63. Canx.
G-ASFR(1)	Bolkow Bo.208A-1 Junior	517	D-ENDI	. 3.63	NTU - To G-ASFO(2). Canx.
G-ASFR(2)	Bolkow Bo.208A-1 Junior	522	D-EGMO	12. 3.63	Permit to Fly expired 29.3.90. (Wreck stored 9/98 at Redcar, Yearby)
G-ASFS(1)	Bolkow Bo.208A Junior	518	D-ENDO	. 3.63	NTU - Not Imported. To OO-RMU 7/63. Canx.
G-ASFS(2)	Bolkow Bo.208A-1 Junior	516	(G-ASFP) D-ENDE	12. 3.63	Crashed at Biggin Hill on 29.1.66. Canx.
G-ASFT(1)	Bolkow Bo.208A Junior	519	D-ENDU	. 3.63	NTU - Not Imported. Remained as D-ENDU. Canx.
G-ASFT(2)	Bolkow Bo.208A-1 Junior	521	D-EGMI	12. 3.63	Fatal crash into trees after take-off at Panshanger on 5.3.73. Canx.
G-ASFU	Bristol 175 Britannia Srs.313	13431	4X-AGD	18. 3.63	Restored as 4X-AGD 3/63. Canx 8.4.63.
G-ASFV	Bristol 175 Britannia Srs.313	13232	4X-AGA	19. 3.63	Restored as 4X-AGA 3/63. Canx 1.4.63.
G-ASFW	Fairtravel Linnet 2	003	(G-APVO)	15. 3.63	Crashed at Biggin Hill on 25.10.69. Canx as WFU 9.11.69.
G-ASFX	Druine D.31 Turbulent	PFA/513		18. 3.63	
G-ASFY	Douglas C-54A Skymaster	10335	HB-ILC N88922/42-72230	19. 3.63	To N3454 11/68. Canx 26.11.68.
G-ASFZ	PA-25-235 Pawnee	25-6309	N6672Z	20. 3.63	Rebuilt with new frame c/n 25-2246 ex.N6277Z and re-regd as G-BSFZ 10/79. Canx.
G-ASGA	Vickers Super VC-10 Srs.1151	851		11. 4.63	To RAF as ZD230 4/81. Canx 24.4.81.
G-ASGB	Vickers Super VC-10 Srs.1151	852		11. 4.63	To RAF as ZD231 4/81. Canx 27.4.81.
G-ASGC	Vickers Super VC-10 Srs.1151	853		11. 4.63	WFU on 15.4.80. Canx. (On display 7/99 Duxford)
G-ASGD	Vickers Super VC-10 Srs.1151	854		11. 4.63	To RAF as ZD232 5/81. Canx 27.5.81.
G-ASGE	Vickers Super VC-10 Srs.1151	855		11. 4.63	To RAF as ZD233 5/81. Canx 19.5.81.
G-ASGF	Vickers Super VC-10 Srs.1151	856		11. 4.63	To RAF as ZD234 4/81. Canx 10.4.81.
G-ASGG	Vickers Super VC-10 Srs.1151	857		11. 4.63	To RAF as ZD235 4/81. Canx 27.4.81.
G-ASGH	Vickers Super VC-10 Srs.1151	858		11. 4.63	To RAF as ZD236 4/81. Canx 27.4.81.
G-ASGI	Vickers Super VC-10 Srs.1151	859		11. 4.63	To RAF as ZD237 5/81. Canx 27.5.81.
G-ASGJ	Vickers Super VC-10 Srs.1151	860		11. 4.63	To RAF as ZD238 5/81. Canx 27.5.81.
G-ASGK	Vickers Super VC-10 Srs.1151	861		11. 4.63	To RAF as ZD239 4/81. Canx 27.4.81.
G-ASGL	Vickers Super VC-10 Srs.1151	862		11. 4.63	To RAF as ZD240 4/81. Canx 10.4.81.
G-ASGM	Vickers Super VC-10 Srs.1151	863		11. 4.63	To RAF as ZD241 4/81. Canx 27.4.81.
G-ASGN	Vickers Super VC-10 Srs.1151	864		11. 4.63	Hijacked near Beirut on 9.9.70 and blown up by PFLP guerillas on 12.9.70 at Dawsons Field, 40 miles NE of Amman, Jordan. Canx.
G-ASGO	Vickers Super VC-10 Srs.1151	865		11. 4.63	Destroyed by hijackers on 3.3.74 at Amsterdam-Schiphol, Netherlands. Displayed at Netherlands National Aerospace Museum. Canx.
G-ASGP	Vickers Super VC-10 Srs.1151	866		11. 4.63	To RAF as ZD242 4/81. Canx 27.4.81.
G-ASGR	Vickers Super VC-10 Srs.1151	867		11. 4.63	To RAF as ZD243 6/81. Canx 15.6.81.
G-ASGS	Vickers Super VC-10 Srs.1151	868		11. 4.63	NTU - Aircraft not completed. Marks canx as WFU 19.6.72.
G-ASGT	Vickers Super VC-10 Srs.1151	869		11. 4.63	NTU - Aircraft not completed. Marks canx as WFU 19.6.72.
G-ASGU	Vickers Super VC-10 Srs.1151	870		11. 4.63	NTU - Aircraft not completed. Marks canx as WFU 19.6.72.
G-ASGV	Vickers Super VC-10 Srs.1151	871		11. 4.63	NTU - Aircraft not completed. Marks canx as WFU 19.6.72.
G-ASGW	Vickers Super VC-10 Srs.1151	872		11. 4.63	NTU - Aircraft not completed. Marks canx as WFU 19.6.72.
G-ASGX	Vickers Super VC-10 Srs.1151	873		11. 4.63	NTU - Aircraft not completed. Marks canx as WFU 19.6.72.
G-ASGY	Vickers Super VC-10 Srs.1151	874		11. 4.63	NTU - Aircraft not completed. Marks canx as WFU 19.6.72.
G-ASGZ	Vickers Super VC-10 Srs.1151	875		11. 4.63	NTU - Aircraft not completed. Marks canx as WFU 19.6.72.
G-ASHA	Reims Cessna F.172D Skyhawk (Wichita c/n 50131)	0008	F-WLIK (N2531U)	26. 3.63	Fatal crash on take-off from Sheepwash on 4.10.92. Canx as destroyed 22.12.92.
"G-ASHA"	Cessna 182F Skylane	182-54633	N3233U	----	Delivered wearing incorrect registration on 9.4.63. To G-ASHB. Canx.

Regn	Type	c/n	Previous identity	Regn date	Fate or immediate subsequent identity (if known)
G-ASHB	Cessna 182F Skylane	182-54633	"G-ASHA" N3233U	26. 3.63	To G-WARP 6/95. Canx.
G-ASHC	PA-23-160 Apache (Originally regd with c/n 23-1312)	23-1319	5N-ACK VR-NDE/PH-NIO	27. 3.63	Crashed at Aintree on 21.3.64. (Parts at Luton 9/64) Canx.
G-ASHD	Brantly B.2A	314		2. 4.63	Crashed into River Colne, off Brightlingsea, Essex on 19.2.67. (Components stored 5/97 Weston-super-Mare)
G-ASHE	Reims Cessna F.172D	0004		8. 4.63	Fatal crash into a car park immediately after take-off from Old Warden on 26.6.66. Canx.
G-ASHF	Cessna 150C	150-59908	N7808Z	22. 3.63	Fatal crash into sea off Swanage on 24.6.73 after apparent break-up in flight. Aircraft sank.
G-ASHG	BAC One-Eleven Srs.200AB	004		25. 3.63	Crashed and burnt out at Stonehill Copse, Chicklade, Wiltshire on 22.10.63. Canx.
G-ASHH	PA-23-250 Aztec	27-63	N455SL N4557P	25. 3.63	CofA expired 27.9.85. Canx by CAA 3.2.95. (Stored 5/98 at Sibson)
G-ASHI	Aero Commander 680	658-255	HB-GOB	8. 4.63	Crashed on M2 Motorway shortly after take-off from Rochester on 19.2.75. Remains to Elstree and officially canx as destroyed 25.3.75.
G-ASHJ	Brantly B.2B	319	XS683 G-ASHJ	9. 4.63	CofA expired 14.10.75. Canx as WFU 26.9.84.
G-ASHK	Brantly B.2A	315	XS681 G-ASHK	9. 4.63	Crashed at Wood Farm, Newport Pagnall on 18.12.75. Canx.
G-ASHL	Douglas DC-7C (Line No. 974)	45495	OO-SFK	9. 4.63	Restored as OO-SFK 11/65. Canx 3.10.65.
G-ASHM	LET L-200D Morava	171207		10. 4.63	Fatal crash into power cables 7 miles north-east of Norwich Airport on 21.12.69 whilst on approach. Canx.
G-ASHN	Scottish Aviation Twin Pioneer Srs.1	513	EP-AGB	16. 4.63	To HC-AHT 6/63. Canx 8.6.63.
G-ASHO	Cessna 182F Skylane	182-54832	N3432U	18. 4.63	To G-PICS 6/81. Canx.
G-ASHP	EoN A.10 460 Srs.1	EoN/S/017		26. 4.63	To ZK-GDK 9/63. Canx 6.11.63.
G-ASHR	Beechcraft 35-A33 Debonair	CD-214	EI-ALI	25. 4.63	To G-DEBY 6/86. Canx.
G-ASHS	SNCAN Stampe SV-4C	265	F-BCFN	23. 4.63	
	(Original fuselage used for spares in rebuild of G-AWEF in 1980; rebuilt 1984 using fuselage of G-AZIR c/n 452 ex F-BCXR)				
G-ASHT	Rollason-Druine D.31 Turbulent	PFA/1610		23. 4.63	
G-ASHU	PA-15 Vagabond	15-46	N4164H NC4164H	1. 5.63	
G-ASHV	PA-23-250 Aztec B	27-2347	(N5281Y)	1. 5.63	CofA expired 22.7.85 & stored at Guernsey. Canx as WFU 20.6.88. (On fire dump 1/99 Alderney)
G-ASHW	DH.104 Dove 8	04532	VQ-LAZ G-ASHW	2. 5.63	Crashed on take-off from Cherbourg, France on 20.11.80. Canx by CAA 22.11.84.
G-ASHX	PA-28-180 Cherokee B	28-1266		3. 5.63	
G-ASHY	Auster 6A Tugmaster	3724(2)	VX110	6. 5.63	To SE-ELA 4/64. Canx 1.4.64.
G-ASHZ	Aviation Traders ATL-98A Carvair (Conv. Douglas C-54B-20-DO)	27249/9	N9326R CP-682/N9326R/HP-268/HP-256/XA-MAA/N88816/44-9023	6. 5.63	To N89FA 5/79. Canx 14.5.79.
G-ASIA	DH.89A Dragon Rapide	6718	NF847	6. 5.63	Not converted. Dismantled at Abingdon in 1963. Canx 11/65.
G-ASIB	Reims Cessna F.172D Skyhawk (Wichita c/n 50091)	0006	F-WLIR (N2491U)	9. 5.63	
G-ASIC	Beechcraft 65-80 Queen Air	LD-102		. 5.63R	NTU - To G-ASIU 5/63. Canx.
G-ASID	Douglas DC-7C (Line No. 757)	45161	OO-SFE G-ASID/OO-SFE	13. 5.63	Belly-landed and DBR after hitting an obstruction while landing at Yesilkoy Airport, Istanbul, Turkey on 28.9.64. Canx.
G-ASIE	Beagle A.61 Terrier 2	B.626	G-35-11 VX924	15. 5.63	To SE-ELR 7/64. Canx 29.7.64.
G-ASIF	Auster 6A Tugmaster	2556	VF615	14. 5.63	WFU at Bicester on 10.8.69. Canx as WFU 4.5.73.
G-ASIG	Hiller 360 UH-12E	2190		20. 5.63	To ZK-HCN 7/68. Canx 11.7.68.
G-ASIH	Hiller 360 UH-12E	2192		20. 5.63	Crashed into hillside at Shinnel Head, Tynron, Dumfriesshire 11.3.71. Canx as WFU 6.12.71.
G-ASII	PA-28-180 Cherokee B	28-1264		21. 5.63	
G-ASIJ	PA-28-180 Cherokee B	28-1333		21. 5.63	
G-ASIK	Not allocated.				
G-ASIL	PA-28-180 Cherokee B	28-1350		21. 5.63	
G-ASIM	Moravan Zlin Z.326T Trener Master	838	OK-SNA	22. 5.63	Crashed at Seething on 22.8.71. Canx.
G-ASIN	Not allocated.				
G-ASIO	Aero Commander 500A	1113-55	N4441 N444H/N6236X	22. 5.63	To N1527T 10/77. Canx 14.10.77.
G-ASIP	Auster 6A Tugmaster	2549	VF608	22. 5.63	Damaged by fire at Nympsfield on 7.5.73. (Stored 6/97 Kemble)
G-ASIR	Beechcraft D95A Travel Air	TD-543		23. 5.63	Crashed into the Irish Sea off Valley on 25.8.78 and beached at Holyhead. Canx 23.2.82.
G-ASIS	Wassmer Jodel D.112	1166	F-BKNR	24. 2.81	To EI-CKX 12/94. Canx 17.11.94.
G-ASIT	Cessna 180	180-32567	N7670A	24. 5.63	
G-ASIU	Beechcraft 65-80 Queen Air	LD-102	(G-ASIC)	24. 5.63	Canx 9.9.81 on sale to West Germany. To 5X-SAM.
G-ASIV	Douglas DC-7C (Line No. 960)	45310	N8299H OO-CFJ/G-ASIV/OO-CFJ/OO-SFJ	28. 5.63	To D-ABAK 3/66. Canx 8.2.66.
G-ASIW	Vickers VC-10 Srs.1103	819		29. 5.63	To 7Q-YKH 11/74. Canx 12.11.74.
G-ASIX	Vickers VC-10 Srs.1103	820		29. 5.63	To A40-AB 10/74. Canx 10.10.74.
G-ASIY	PA-25-235 Pawnee	25-2446		30. 5.63	
G-ASIZ	Beechcraft 35 Bonanza	D-161	N2769V NC2769V	5. 6.63	Crashed at Sleap on 9.7.72. Canx as WFU 5.9.72.
G-ASJA	BAC One-Eleven Srs.201AC	BAC.005		6. 6.63	To G-52-1/N734EB 3/70. Canx 14.10.69.

Regn	Type	c/n	Previous identity	Regn date	Fate or immediate subsequent identity (if known)
G-ASJB	BAC One-Eleven Srs.201AC	BAC.006		6. 6.63	DBR on heavy landing at Wisley on 18.3.64. Remains moved by road to Hurn on 29.3.64. Canx.
G-ASJC	BAC One-Eleven Srs.201AC	BAC.007	EI-BWI N101EX/G-ASJC	6. 6.63	Broken up in 1/94 at Southend. Canx as destroyed 14.3.94.
G-ASJD	BAC One-Eleven Srs.201AC	BAC.008		6. 6.63	To RAF as XX105 in 10/71. Canx 1.10.71.
G-ASJE	BAC One-Eleven Srs.201AC	BAC.009		6. 6.63	To (N29967)/N102EX 6/82. Canx 1.6.82.
G-ASJF	BAC One-Eleven Srs.201AC	BAC.010		6. 6.63	To N103EX 4/82. Canx 26.4.82.
G-ASJG	BAC One-Eleven Srs.201AC	BAC.011		6. 6.63	To N104EX 3/82. Canx 24.3.82.
G-ASJH	BAC One-Eleven Srs.201AC	BAC.012		6. 6.63	To N105EX 3/82. Canx 1.3.82.
G-ASJI	BAC One-Eleven Srs.201AC	BAC.013		6. 6.63	To N106EX 1/82. Canx 25.1.82.
G-ASJJ	BAC One-Eleven Srs.201AC	BAC.014		6. 6.63	Crashed into a sand quarry south of Milan-Linate, Italy shortly after take-off on 14.1.69. Canx 14.1.69.
G-ASJK	PA-25-235 Pawnee	25-2486		7. 6.63	To 5Y-AZA 10/75. Canx 3.10.75.
G-ASJL	Beechcraft H35 Bonanza	D-5132	N5582D	14. 6.63	
G-ASJM	PA-30-160 Twin Comanche	30-33		17. 6.63	Canx as WFU on 30.9.82.
G-ASJN	Campbell-Bensen B.8 Gyrocopter	CA/1		17. 6.63	DBR at Sherburn-in-Elmet on 28.9.69. Canx as WFU 28.8.81.
G-ASJO(1)	Beechcraft 23 Musketeer	M-482		. 6.63R	NTU - Canx.
G-ASJO(2)	Beechcraft 23 Musketeer	M-518		18. 6.63	
G-ASJP	PA-23-250 Aztec B	27-2364		25. 6.63	To 9J-RIA 3/68. Canx 30.4.68.
G-ASJR	Cessna 182F Skylane	182-54939	N3539U	26. 6.63	Crashed and DBF at Brayfield, Northants on 23.9.77. Canx.
G-ASJS	Scottish Aviation Twin Pioneer Srs.2	515	EP-AGC	28. 6.63	To LN-BFK 9/63. Canx 5.9.63.
G-ASJT	HS.748 Srs.1/107	1559		4. 7.63	To RAE Farnborough as XW750 1/70. Canx 20.1.70.
G-ASJU	Aero Commander 520	82	N4176B	2. 7.63	CofA expired 22.7.73 & WFU at Biggin Hill. Canx by CAA 30.11.84.
G-ASJV	Vickers Supermarine 361 Spitfire LF.IXB	CBAF.IX.552	OO-ARA Belgiun AF SM-41/Fokker B-13/R.Neth AF H-68/R.Neth AF H-105/MH434	3. 7.63	(Stored engineless 7/99 Duxford)
G-ASJW	Bell 47D-1	D.12	N158B	3. 7.63	Crashed at Saxilby, Lincs on 19.7.71. Canx as destroyed 17.8.73.
G-ASJX	Brantly B.2B	325		9. 7.63	Crashed into a back garden in Dalhousie Street, Perth on 4.7.68. Canx.
G-ASJY	Gardan GY-80-160 Horizon (Originally regd as a GY-80-150 model)	13	F-BLOY	9. 7.63	Crashed into Hillfield Reservoir, near Elstree on 21.6.76. Canx 6.76.
G-ASJZ	SAN Jodel D.117A	826	F-BITD	5. 7.63	
G-ASKA	DH.98 Mosquito TT.35	-	RS709	8. 7.63	To N9797 8/69. Canx 18.8.69.
G-ASKB	DH.98 Mosquito TT.35	-	N35MK G-ASKB/RS712	8. 7.63	To N35MK 3/88. Canx 20.10.87.
G-ASKC	DH.98 Mosquito TT.35	-	TA719	8. 7.63	Crashed after an engine failure while approaching to land at Staverton on 27.7.64. (On display 7/99 Duxford)
G-ASKD	Aviation Traders ATL.98 Carvair (Conv. Douglas C-54B-1-DC)	10458/14	CF-EPW EI-ANJ/G-ASKD/D-ANEK/(D-ABIB)/OO-SBO/F-BHVR/OO-SBO/N88721/42-72353	9. 7.63	To LN-NAA 11/74. Canx 11.11.74.
G-ASKE	Short SC.5 Belfast C.1	SH.1816	XR362 G-ASKE	10. 7.63	To RAF as XR362 in 8/66. Canx.
G-ASKF	PA-25-235 Pawnee	25-2231	N6636Z	10. 7.63	Collided with overhead cables and crashed at Branston, Lincs., on 9.7.68. Canx.
G-ASKG	Aviation Traders ATL-98 Carvair (Conv. Douglas C-54A-15-DC)	10382/10	F-BRPT G-ASKG/LX-BBP/N1221V/LN-HAU/N12491/42-72277	12. 7.63	To TR-LUP 2/75. Canx 25.2.75.
G-ASKH	DH.98 Mosquito T.3	-	RR299	12. 7.63	Fatal crash into woodlands about 1 mile west of Barton on 21.7.96. Canx as destroyed 16.12.96.
G-ASKI	DH.89A Dragon Rapide	6858	NR782	12. 7.63	To I-BOBJ 3/65. Canx 16.2.65.
G-ASKJ	Beagle A.61 Terrier 2	3730	(EI-AMC) VX926	16. 7.63	WFU following undercarriage collapse at Redhill on 20.6.84. (On rebuild Gamlingay 1/96)
G-ASKK	Handley Page HPR.7 Dart Herald 211	161	PP-ASU G-ASKK/(PI-C910)/CF-MCK	17. 7.63	WFU on 30.3.85. Canx as WFU 29.4.85. (On display 10/97 Norwich)
G-ASKL	SAN Jodel D.150A Mascaret	27		18. 7.63	
G-ASKM	Beechcraft 65-80 Queen Air	LD-116		18. 7.63	To G-TUBS 3/85. Canx.
G-ASKN	Aviation Traders ATL.98A Carvair (Conv. Douglas C-54-DO)	3058/13	D-ADAM N79000/NC79000/41-37272	22. 7.63	To TR-LWP 6/76. Canx 10.6.76.
G-ASKO	DH.89A Dragon Rapide	6735	NF864	22. 7.63	To F-OCHF 8/67. Canx 17.1.66.
G-ASKP	DH.82A Tiger Moth	3889	N6588	22. 7.63	
G-ASKR	Rousseau Aviation CP.301B Emeraude	110	F-BIPO	22. 7.63	Crashed and burnt out while taking off at Couplaw Farm, Strathaven on 11.6.64. Canx.
G-ASKS	Cessna 336 Skymaster	336-0070	N1770Z	24. 7.63	Destroyed in fatal crash 7 miles NE of Douglas, IoM on 13.10.95. Canx as destroyed 13.10.95.
G-ASKT	PA-28-180 Cherokee B	28-1410		24. 7.63	
G-ASKU	Reims Cessna F.172E (Wichita c/n 50579)	0024	(N2979U)	29. 7.63	To OO-NZC 2/73. Canx 22.1.73.
G-ASKV	PA-25-235 Pawnee	25-2272	9Q-CHV G-ASKV/ST-ACW/G-ASKV/ST-ACW/G-ASKV/ST-ACF/G-ASKV/N6700Z	31. 7.63	
G-ASKW	PA-23-235 Apache	27-576		31. 7.63	Ditched and sank 17½ miles SE of Southwold, Suffolk on 25.2.71. Canx.
G-ASKX	Omnipol L-13 Blanik	172803		31. 7.63	To BGA.1459 in 4/68. Canx as WFU 5.4.83.
G-ASKY	Omnipol L-13 Blanik	172802		31. 7.63	To RAFGSA as 326 in 9/63. Canx 2.10.63 as marks withdrawn.
G-ASKZ	Armstrong-Whitworth 650 Argosy Srs.220 (Originally regd as a Srs.200)	AW.6799		31. 7.63	CofA expired 24.11.65 & WFU at Bitteswell. Broken up in 9/67 for spares. Canx as WFU.
G-ASLA	PA-25-235 Pawnee (Originally regd with c/n 25-2380, fitted with new fuselage with old being used in rebuild of G-BCBJ)	25-5544	N6802Z	1. 8.63	To PH-WAT 4/84. Canx 9.5.84.
G-ASLB	Cessna 150C	150-59971	N7871Z	1. 8.63	WFU at Biggin Hill on 30.7.72. Canx 12.9.74.
G-ASLC	Reims Cessna F.172E Rocket	0028		2. 8.63	DBR in crash on take-off from near Shiplake College, Henley on 2.9.70. Canx as destroyed 30.12.70.
G-ASLD	PA-30-160 Twin Comanche	30-58	(ZS-...) G-ASLD	9. 8.63	Crashed at Bembridge, IoW on 5.5.72. Canx.

Regn	Type	c/n	Previous identity	Regn date	Fate or immediate subsequent identity (if known)
G-ASLE	PA-30-160 Twin Comanche	30-88		9. 8.63	To N30885 7/85. Canx 16.7.85.
G-ASLF	Bensen B.8 Gyrocopter	10		12. 8.63	Not completed. Canx by CAA 9.8.91.
G-ASLG	Beechcraft 95-A55 Baron	TC-495		16. 8.63	To N18JH 12/70. Canx 1.12.70.
G-ASLH	Cessna 182F Skylane	182-54905	N3505U	19. 8.63	
G-ASLI	Bucker Bu.131 Jungmann	20	HB-EVA Swiss AF A-92	20. 8.63	To ZS-BUC(2) 11/73. Canx 13.7.73.
G-ASLJ	PA-23-235 Pawnee	25-2264	ST-ADS G-ASLJ/ST-ACH/G-ASLJ/N6694Z	20. 8.63	To (PH-VOW)/PH-VBC 3/70. Canx 24.11.69.
G-ASLK	PA-25-235 Pawnee	25-2370	9Q-CFK G-ASLK/ST-ADT/G-ASLK/ST-ACG/G-ASLK/N6801Z	20. 8.63	
G-ASLL	Cessna 336 Skymaster	336-0074	N1774Z	23. 8.63	CofA expired 6.1.74 & WFU. Canx as WFU 6.12.77. (Fuselage cabin stored 3/92)
G-ASLM	PA-28-180 Cherokee	28-1244		26. 8.63	Crashed near Corinth, Greece on 21.3.65. Wreckage found on 24.5.65. Canx.
G-ASLN	Forney F-1A Aircoupe	5729	N3035G	26. 8.63	Crashed on take-off from Bodmin on 22.11.74. Canx as destroyed 29.2.84.
G-ASLO	Brantly B.2B	330	EI-AVK G-ASLO/N2168U	3. 9.63	DBF at Newton-le-Willows on 15.6.74. Canx 7.5.81.
G-ASLP	Bensen B.8 Gyrocopter	11		3. 9.63	Canx as WFU 4.9.73. (Stored dismantled 2/99)
G-ASLR	Agusta-Bell 47J-2 Ranger	2057		3. 9.63	Damaged on take-off Lulsgate 31.1.96. Canx as WFU 28.2.97.
G-ASLS	Auster J/5F Aiglet Trainer	2767	OD-APA Arab Legion AF A-408	4. 9.63	Crashed near Sevenoaks on 3.4.65. Scrapped at Weston in 1982. Canx by CAA 15.9.86.
G-ASLT	Auster J/5F Aiglet Trainer	2771	OD-APB Arab Legion AF A-409	4. 9.63	CofA expired on 12.3.69. DBF at Herzlia, Israel on 17.3.72. Canx as WFU 8.11.73.
G-ASLU	Bensen B.8 Gyrocopter (built by D.P.Reason)	D.P.R.1		6. 9.63	Crashed at Burtonwood on 11.4.66. Canx.
G-ASLV	PA-28-235 Cherokee	28-10048		11. 9.63	
G-ASLW	Armstrong-Whitworth Meteor NF.14	AW.5814	WS829	12. 9.63	Crashed into sea between Madeira and Cape Verde on 28.10.69. Canx as destroyed 6.11.69.
G-ASLX	Menavia Piel CP.301A Emeraude	292	F-BISV	12. 9.63	
G-ASLY	Reims Cessna F.172E Rocket	0019		13. 9.63	Crashed at Squires Gate on 7.7.68. Canx.
G-ASLZ	Mooney M.20C Ranger Mk.21	2596	N6892U	16. 9.63	To F-BVVZ 6/74. Canx 3.6.74.
G-ASMA	PA-30-160 Twin Comanche (Originally regd with c/n 30-145) (Mod to C/R status)	30-143		17. 9.63	
G-ASMB	CEA Jodel DR.1050 Ambassadeur	127	F-BKMN F-OBMN	19. 9.63	Suffered engine failure and crashed into a tree immediately after take-off from Dinard/Pleurtuit, France for Jersey on 18.7.67. Canx.
G-ASMC	Hunting-Percival P.56 Provost T.1	PAC/F/417	XF908	19. 9.63	CofA expired 14.2.72. Canx by CAA 22.11.91. (Stored 5/86 Moenchengladbach, Germany)
G-ASMD	Cessna 310D	39163	N6863T	20. 9.63	To F-BRSE 1/70. Canx 3.8.69.
G-ASME	Bensen B.8M Gyrocopter	12		24. 9.63	
G-ASMF	Beechcraft D95A Travel Air	TD-565		26. 9.63	
G-ASMG	DH.104 Dove 8	04533		10.10.63	To VH-JGZ 4/89. Canx 6.12.88.
G-ASMH	PA-30-160 Twin Comanche	30-180		16.10.63	Crashed at Kidbrooke Park Road, Greenwich, London SE3 on 29.11.81. Canx as WFU 29.2.84.
G-ASMI	PA-30-160 Twin Comanche	30-112		16.10.63	Fatal crash on take-off from Gander, Newfoundland on 27.11.63 while on delivery flight to the UK. Canx.
G-ASMJ	Reims Cessna F.172E Rocket (Wichita c/n 50584)	0029		25.10.63	
G-ASMK	Beagle B.206 Srs.2X (Originally regd as Srs.1, later to B.206S Srs.2)	B.005		25.10.63	WFU at Shoreham on 18.7.66. Canx as WFU 17.11.72.
G-ASML	Phoenix Luton LA-4A Minor	PAL/1148 & PFA/802		28.10.63	Crashed at Grummock on 25.4.82. Canx.
G-ASMM	Rollason-Druine D.31 Turbulent	PFA/611		31.10.63	
G-ASMN	PA-23-160 Apache G	23-1989	5N-AAT 5N-ADA/N4464P	30.10.63	To N772MM 9/89. Canx 14.9.89.
G-ASMO	PA-23-160 Apache G	23-1995	5N-AAU 5N-ADB/N4473P	30.10.63	WFU at Bournemouth on 2.9.81. Canx 17.11.82.
G-ASMP	EoN 460 Olympia Srs.1	EoN/S/021		4.11.63	To BGA.1242 /65. Canx as WFU 5.5.69.
G-ASMR	PA-30-160 Twin Comanche	30-227		7.11.63	To SE-FLH 8/75. Canx 2.6.75.
G-ASMS	Cessna 150A	150-59204	N7104X	18.11.63	
G-ASMT	Fairtravel Linnet 2	004		20.11.63	
G-ASMU	Cessna 150C	150-60252	N4252U	26.11.63	Damaged in gales at Barton on 13.2.89. (On rebuild .91) Canx by CAA 17.12.93.
G-ASMV	Scintex CP.1310-C3 Super Emeraude	919		22.11.63	(Stored 10/97)
G-ASMW	Cessna 150D	150-60247	N4247U	26.11.63	
G-ASMX	DH.104 Dove 5	04486	I-ALGO G-ASMX/PH-ION	2.12.63	To VH-DHN 2/66. Canx 14.2.66.
G-ASMY	PA-23-160 Apache H	23-2032	N4309Y	3.12.63	(Stored 9/97)
G-ASMZ	Beagle A.61 Terrier 2 (Converted from Auster 10 c/n 2285)	B.629	G-35-11 VF516	4.12.63	
G-ASNA	PA-23-250 Aztec B	27-2451		6.12.63	WFU at Glasgow in 3/82 & used for spares. Broken up in 2/87. Canx as WFU 11.7.88.
G-ASNB	Auster 6A Tugmaster	3725(2)	VX118	6.12.63	
G-ASNC	Beagle D.5/180 Husky	3678		9.12.63	
G-ASND	PA-23-250 Aztec	27-134	N4800P	10.12.63	
G-ASNE	PA-28-180 Cherokee B	28-1509		11.12.63	To ZK-SNE 4/79. Canx 2.6.78.
G-ASNF	Erco Ercoupe 415-CD	4754	PH-NCF NC94647	11.12.63	Crashed on landing at Bodmin on 15.6.73. CofA expired 2.7.73. (On rebuild .93 with major parts from OO-JPB c/n 4777)

Regn	Type	c/n	Previous identity	Regn date	Fate or immediate subsequent identity (if known)
G-ASNG	DH.104 Dove 6	04485	(HB-LFF) G-ASNG/(HB-LFF)/G-ASNG/PH-IOM	16.12.63	To EI-BJW 11/80. Canx 7.11.80. (On fire dump 8/93 Waterford still painted as G-ASNG)
G-ASNH	PA-23-250 Aztec B	27-2486		17.12.63	To N818MJ. Canx 2.8.99.
G-ASNI	Scintex CP.1310-C3 Super Emeraude	925		20.12.63	
G-ASNJ	Aero Commander 500A	1272-95	N78352	23.12.63	To OE-FPZ 3/69. Canx 3.3.69.
G-ASNK	Cessna 205	205-0400	N8400Z	27.12.63	
G-ASNL	Sikorsky S-61N Mk.II	61-220	PH-SBH G-ASNL/N4604G	31.12.63	Ditched in North Sea on 11.3.83 en route to Aberdeen; Rebuilt as N4503E 10/83. Canx.
G-ASNM	Sikorsky S-61N Mk.II	61-221	PH-SBC G-ASNM/N4605G	31.12.63	Ditched and sank in North Sea 52 miles NE of Aberdeen on 15.11.70. Canx.
G-ASNN	Cessna 182F Skylane	182-55012	N3612U	27.12.63	Damaged in forced landing in a field 300 yards short of the runway at Prees, near Whitchurch, Shropshire on 5.1.85. CofA expired 3.5.85. Canx as destroyed 13.6.85. (Para-trainer use 5/97)
G-ASNO	Beechcraft 95-B55 Baron	TC-574		3. 1.64	To N9164N 7/81. Canx 9.7.81.
G-ASNP	Mooney M.20C Ranger	2689		3. 1.64	To N85NP 9/84. Canx 21.9.84.
G-ASNR	Mooney M.20E Super 21	278		7. 1.64	Fatal crash in English Channel on 10.10.71, en route Le Touquet to Biggin Hill.
G-ASNS	Cessna 310 (Riley 65)	35073	LN-FAD N2673C	7. 1.64	To VT-EDK 4/74. Canx.
G-ASNT	Beagle A.61 Terrier 2 (Conversion of Auster 6 c/n 2560)	B.624	(PH-SFR) G-35-11/VF618	8. 1.64	Crashed near Goring-on-Sea on 10.4.65. Canx.
G-ASNU	DH.125 Srs.1	25005	D-COMA (D-CFKG)/G-ASNU	9. 1.64	WFU by 12/82. Impounded at Lagos through ownership dispute Lagos, Nigeria. Canx by CAA 18.11.91.
G-ASNV	Agusta-Bell 47J-2 Ranger	2061		13. 1.64	To G-EURA 7/83. Canx.
G-ASNW	Reims Cessna F.172E (Wichita c/n 50613)	0031		13. 1.64	
G-ASNX	Beechcraft Super H-18	BA-663		13. 1.64	To 9Q-CSP 12/69. Canx 29.12.69.
G-ASNY	Campbell-Bensen B.8M Gyrocopter	RCA/203		15. 1.64	Permit expired 16.3.70. Canx as WFU 17.12.91.
G-ASNZ	Benson B.7M Gyrocopter	13		22. 1.64	No Permit to Fly issued. Canx by CAA 17.6.91.
G-ASOA	PA-30-160 Twin Comanche (Originally regd with c/n 30-390)	30-285		21. 1.64	Overshot and crashed while landing at St.Mary's, Isles of Scilly on 10.5.64. Canx.
G-ASOB	PA-30-160 Twin Comanche	30-279		21. 1.64	To G-MAAG 4/85. Canx.
G-ASOC	Auster 6A Tugmaster	2544	VF603	21. 1.64	
G-ASOD	Not allocated.				
G-ASOE	Hiller 360 UH-12C	778	N5318V	23. 1.64	DBR on start-up at Tollerton on 26.7.67. Canx as WFU 16.12.68.
G-ASOF	Beagle B.206 Srs.1	B.007		28. 1.64	To N163 in 12/80. Canx 29.12.80.
G-ASOG	Douglas C-54A-15-DC Skymaster	10359	N9760F HB-ILB/N75415/42-72254	30. 1.64	Crashed 5 kms short of Frankfurt Airport, West Germany on 21.1.67. Canx.
G-ASOH	Beechcraft 95-B55A Baron	TC-656		31. 1.64	
G-ASOI	Beagle A.61 Terrier 2	B.627	G-35-11 WJ404	31. 1.64	
G-ASOJ	Reims Cessna F.172E	0046		31. 1.64	Fatal crash into a house at Aldridge, Staffs on 16.4.66. Canx.
G-ASOK	Reims Cessna F.172E	0057	(G-AZWT) G-ASOK	31. 1.64	
G-ASOL	Bell 47D-1	4	N146B	31. 1.64	CofA expired 6.9.71 & WFU. Canx as WFU 5.12.83. (Stored 8/97 Weston-super-Mare)
G-ASOM	Beagle A.61 Terrier 2 (Conversion of Auster AOP.6 c/n 2274)	B.622	G-JETS G-ASOM/G-35-11/VF505	3. 2.64	
G-ASON	PA-30-160 Twin Comanche	30-312	(N7273Y)	4. 2.64	CofA expired 30.11.91. Canx by CAA 9.7.92. (Stored WFU 3/99 at Elstree)
G-ASOO	PA-30-160 Twin Comanche	30-334		4. 2.64	To G-LADI 4/94. Canx.
G-ASOP	Sopwith Camel F.1 (Restoration of genuine 1917 Kingston-upon-Thames built Camel, rescued as derelict from Lincolnshire in 1962)	TS-01	B6291	8. 2.89	Sold in USA early .94. Canx by CAA 27.1.99.
G-ASOR	PA-30-160 Twin Comanche	30-344		4. 2.64	To F-BMRO 9/64. Canx 13.9.64.
G-ASOS	Not allocated.				
G-ASOT	Not allocated.				
G-ASOU	Westland Sikorsky WS-55 Whirlwind Srs.3	WA/402	5N-AGK G-ASOU/D-HODE/G-ASOU/(Ghana AF G-605)	11. 2.64	To VR-BDG 2/69. Canx 18.2.69.
G-ASOV	PA-25-235 Pawnee	25-2657		12. 2.64	To SE-ITY 11/85. Canx 4.11.85.
G-ASOW	Not allocated.				
G-ASOX	Cessna 205A	205-0556	N4856U	13. 2.64	CofA expired 1.8.92 & WFU.
G-ASOY	Beagle A.61 Terrier 2	B.621	G-35-11 WE551	17. 2.64	Crashed at Traben-Trabach, West Germany on 20.7.65. Canx.
G-ASOZ	Vickers Supermarine 509 Spitfire Trainer IX	CBAF/7122	158 Irish Air Corps/G-15-171/MJ627	19. 2.64	Not converted, dismantled at Elstree in 12/64. To G-BMSB 5/78. Canx.
G-ASPA	DH.104 Dove 8	04536		20. 2.64	WFU at Chalgrove on 27.8.82. Canx 18.1.83. Used for spares for G-AVVF.
G-ASPB	Jodel D.117	596	F-BHXR	21. 2.64	Crashed at Market Drayton on 26.10.66. Canx.
G-ASPC	Piaggio P.166B	412		21. 2.64	WFU at Luton on 8.5.71. Canx 1.6.72. Scrapped at Luton in 9/72.
G-ASPD	Beagle A.61 Terrier 2 (Originally regd with c/n 2502)	B.640	VF644	25. 2.64	Fatal crash into trees near Leuchars while flying through a snowstorm on 1.4.68. Canx.
G-ASPE	PA-24-250 Comanche	24-3639		26. 2.64R	NTU - Not Imported. To N8380P/HR-212 in 9/64. Canx.
G-ASPF	Wassmer Jodel D.120 Paris-Nice	02	F-BFNP	26. 2.64	
G-ASPG	Jodel D.150 Mascaret	41		26. 2.64	Crashed on a hillside at Midnight Farm, Ingleby Greenhow, Yorks on 10.6.66 & burnt out. Canx.
G-ASPH	Maule Bee Dee M.4	45	N4702T	26. 2.64	To OY-BAD 8/64. Canx 14.8.64.
G-ASPI	Reims Cessna F.172E	0050		26. 2.64	

Regn	Type	c/n	Previous identity	Regn date	Fate or immediate subsequent identity (if known)
G-ASPJ	Handley Page HPR.7 Dart Herald 210	173	(HB-AAI)	26. 2.64	To HB-AAK 3/64. Canx 6.3.64.
G-ASPK	PA-28-140 Cherokee	28-20051		28. 2.64	
G-ASPL	HS.748 Srs.2A/108	1560		28. 2.64	Crashed at Nailstone, Leics on 26.6.81. Canx as destroyed 19.5.83.
G-ASPM	Douglas C-54B Skymaster	10543	HZ-AAI N66644/42-72438	28. 2.64	To ZS-IRK 9/72. Canx 8.9.72.
G-ASPN	Douglas C-54E Skymaster	10337	HZ-AAG N49288/AP-ADL/NC49288/BuA.39175/42-72232	28. 2.64	To ZS-IRE 4/72. Canx 18.4.72.
G-ASPO	Cessna 210D Centurion	210-58383	N3883Y	2. 3.64	Fatal crash at Rothersthorpe, 3 miles SW of Northampton on 6.12.67. Canx.
G-ASPP	Bristol Boxkite Replica (Also c/n BOX.1) (Built by Miles)	BM.7279	(BAPC.2)	29.10.81	(Carries no external registration)
G-ASPR	Schempp-Hirth Standard Austria	34		2. 3.64	WFU at Lasham in 4/75; No BGA certificate. Canx 12.2.82.
G-ASPS	Piper J3C-90 Cub (Frame No. 21971)	22809	N3571N NC3571N	2. 3.64	
G-ASPT	Cessna 172D Skyhawk	172-49675	CF-OYN N2175Y	3. 3.64	Crashed on landing at Christchurch, Hants on 16.7.69. Canx as PWFU 7.8.84.
G-ASPU	Druine D.31 Turbulent	PFA/1623		4. 3.64	(Damaged in forced landing at Hurst Green, East Sussex on 8.10.95)
G-ASPV	DH.82A Tiger Moth (Identity obscure - real G-ASPV to Norway 7.75 & rebuilt as LN-MAX)	84167	T7794	5. 3.64	
G-ASPW	DHC.1 Chipmunk 23 (Fuselage no. DHB/f/79) (Regd with c/n C1/0602/WK580/7155M; Composite)	C1/0193	WB746	6. 3.64	Struck overhead cables and crashed at Wheathampstead, Herts., on 1.7.67. Canx.
G-ASPX	Campbell Bensen B.8S Gyrocopter	CA/204		9. 3.64	Fatal crash on beach at Morfa Bychan, Wales on 16.11.89. Canx by CAA 16.7.90.
G-ASPY	Scheibe SF-24A Motorspatz	4010/V10	D-KEBU	10. 3.64	Stalled on take-off from North Hill Gliding Site on 27.8.76 & DBR. Canx.
G-ASPZ	DH.82A Tiger Moth	83666	D-EDUM T7356	10. 3.64	To D-EDUM 4/67. Canx.
G-ASRA	PA-24-250 Comanche	24-1285	N6183P	10. 3.64	Crashed at Alvechurch, near Redditch on 23.2.78. (Wreck moved to Bovingdon via Baginton) Canx.
G-ASRB	Rollason-Druine D.62B Condor	RAE/608		11. 3.64	(Stored 1/99 at Shoreham)
G-ASRC	Rollason-Druine D.62C Condor (Originally regd as a D.62B)	RAE/609		11. 3.64	
G-ASRD	Downer Bellanca 14-19-3	4125	EI-AKR	11. 3.64	Fatal crash at Oakley Farm, Welshampton, near Oswestry on 12.8.66. Canx.
G-ASRE	PA-23-250 Aztec C	27-2520		12. 3.64	WFU at Ipswich on 4.11.82. Scrapped in 1995.
G-ASRF	Gowland GWG.2 Jenny Wren (Used modified Luton Minor wings once fitted to G-AGEP)	GWG.2 & PFA/1300		18. 3.64	Permit expired 4.6.71. (Stored Brookmans Park) Canx by CAA 11.12.96.
G-ASRG	Beagle A.61 Terrier 2	B.633	WE599	18. 3.64	To EI-ASU 1/68. Canx 5.12.67.
G-ASRH	PA-30-160 Twin Comanche	30-368		19. 3.64	
G-ASRI	PA-23-250 Aztec B	27-2352	N5287Y	24. 3.64	CofA expired 30.8.87. Canx as WFU 19.11.87. (Instructional Airframe 1/96 Witney)
G-ASRJ	DH.89A Dragon Rapide	6959	JY-ACG JY-ACE/TJ-ACE/TJ-AAD/TX301	25. 3.64	Canx as destroyed 16.2.70.
G-ASRK	Beagle A.109 Airedale	B.538		26. 3.64	
G-ASRL	Beagle A.61 Terrier 2	B.631	WE609	18. 3.64	Crashed at Kota, Malawi on 18.4.69. Canx as WFU 18.9.69. Repaired as VP-WDN in 1970.
G-ASRM	DH.89A Dragon Rapide	6961	JY-AAE TJ-AAE/TX303	26. 3.64	Canx 27.7.64 on sale to the Belgian Congo.
G-ASRN	PA-30-160 Twin Comanche	30-381		31. 3.64	Fatal crash after take-off from Newbury Racecourse on 18.6.72 and DBF in crash.
G-ASRO	PA-30-160 Twin Comanche	30-395		31. 3.64	
G-ASRP	SAN Jodel DR.1050 Ambassadeur	64	F-BITI	1. 4.64	Ditched in Swanbister Bay, Orkney on 17.3.86 soon after take-off from Swanbister Farm. Aircraft later beached. (On rebuild by K.Wood 10/94) Canx as PWFU 20.1.99.
G-ASRR	Cessna 182G Skylane	182-55135	(G-CBIL) EI-ATF/G-ASRR/N3735U	2. 4.64	
G-ASRS	Douglas C-54E-15-DO Skymaster	27353	HZ-AAW SA-R4/N90901/44-9127	2. 3.64	To OO-FAI 8/64. Canx 20.7.64.
G-ASRT	SAN Jodel D.150 Mascaret	45		6. 4.64	
G-ASRU	PA-30-160 Twin Comanche	30-376		6. 4.64	To N2627Y 10/81. Canx 7.10.81.
G-ASRV	Beechcraft 95-B55 Baron	TC-677		17. 4.64	To OO-GRK 1/72. Canx 22.12.71.
G-ASRW	PA-28-180 Cherokee B	28-1606		21. 4.64	
G-ASRX	Beechcraft 65-A80 Queen Air	LD-159		21. 4.64	CofA expired 30.4.84 & WFU at Exeter. Canx by CAA 14.12.88. Scrapped in 1994.
G-ASRY	Tipsy Nipper T.66 Srs.2	T.66/25	OY-AEK	21. 4.64	NTU - Not Imported. To SE-CWH. Canx 27.5.64.
G-ASRZ	Douglas DC-6B (Line No. 450)	44176	OO-CTN	22. 4.64	Restored as OO-CTN 11/64. Canx 13.11.64.
G-ASSA	PA-30-160 Twin Comanche	30-421		22. 4.64	To N99135 1/77. Canx 24.1.77.
G-ASSB	PA-30-160 Twin Comanche	30-432		22. 4.64	Canx as WFU 25.8.92. (Instructional Airframe 3/94 at Brooklands)
G-ASSC	DH.82A Tiger Moth	82720	R4776	27. 4.64	To N81DH 9/71. Canx 14.9.71.
G-ASSD	Vickers Supermarine 361 Spitfire Mk.IXc	CBAF.IX.1514	OO-ARB Belgium AF SM-43/Belgium AF B-15/R.Neth AF H-55/R.Neth AF H-116/MK297	28. 4.64	To N1882 5/69. Canx 18.4.69.
G-ASSE	PA-22-108 Colt	22-9832	N5961Z	28. 4.64	
G-ASSF	Cessna 182G Skylane	182-55593	N2493R	5. 5.64	
G-ASSG	Not allocated.				
G-ASSH(1)	DH.125 Srs.1	25007		. .64R	NTU - To HB-VAH 6/64. Canx.

Regn	Type	c/n	Previous identity	Regn date	Fate or immediate subsequent identity (if known)
G-ASSH(2)	HS.125 Srs.1A	25017	N3060 G-ASSH	5. 5.64	To N3060 in 12/64. Canx 20.12.64.
G-ASSI	DH.125 Srs.1	25008		5. 5.64	To 5N-AWD 11/82. Canx 12.11.82.
G-ASSJ	HS.125 Srs.1A	25013		5. 5.64	To N125J 9/64. Canx 15.9.64.
G-ASSK	HS.125 Srs.1A	25014		5. 5.64	To N125G 1/65. Canx 13.1.65.
G-ASSL	HS.125 Srs.1A	25016		5. 5.64	To CF-RWA 12/64. Canx 18.12.64.
G-ASSM	DH.125 Srs.1/522	25010	5N-AMK G-ASSM	5. 5.64	(On display 8/97 South Kensington)
G-ASSN	Champion 7GCBA Challenger	7GCBA-14	N9873Y	4. 5.64	Crashed at Boreham, Essex on 27.7.65. Canx.
G-ASSO	Cessna 150D	150-60536	N4536U	7. 5.64	To G-SAMZ 4/84. Canx.
G-ASSP	PA-30-160 Twin Comanche	30-458		7. 5.64	
G-ASSR	PA-30-160 Twin Comanche	30-467		7. 5.64	Force landed in boggy ground at Llangennech, near Swansea on 17.3.92. Canx by CAA 21.7.92.
G-ASSS	Cessna 172E Skyhawk	172-51467	N5567T	7. 5.64	
G-ASST	Cessna 150D	150-60630	N5930T	7. 5.64	
G-ASSU	Menavia CP.301A Emeraude	230	F-BIME	8. 5.64	Canx as WFU 23.3.81.
G-ASSV	Kensinger KF (Built by R.F.Ferguson)	02	N23S	11. 5.64	Fatal crash on take-off from Halfpenny Green on 2.7.69. Permit expired 30.7.69. (On rebuild 9/97)
G-ASSW	PA-28-140 Cherokee	28-20055		11. 5.64	
G-ASSX	Cessna 172E Skyhawk	172-51470	N5570T	11. 5.64	Crashed into a hillside near Mold, Clwyd on 19.5.81. Canx as destroyed 9.10.84.
G-ASSY	Druine D.31 Turbulent	PFA/586		12. 5.64	Badly damaged when struck by Terrier G-ASKJ at Redhill 8.5.83. (Wings & fuselage stored 5/93 Dunkeswell)
G-ASSZ	Cessna 310A (Riley 65)	35407	N5207A	12. 5.64	To OY-DRH 4/69. Canx 2.2.69.
G-ASTA	Druine D.31 Turbulent	152	F-PJGH	12. 5.64	
G-ASTB	Agusta-Bell 47G-3B-1 (Originally regd with c/n 1535)	1542		13. 5.64	Missing in the English Channel on 1.7.66 whilst flying from Lympne to Le Touquet, France. Canx.
G-ASTC	PA-28-150 Cherokee	28-458	N6596D (N5390W)	13. 5.64	After landing at Stapleford on 13.4.73, Cherokee G-ATVO landed on top of it and it was DBR. Canx 30.5.73 as destroyed.
G-ASTD	PA-23-250 Aztec C	27-2549		14. 5.64	Canx 15.8.85 on sale to USA. Reserved as N64P. (Noted engineless at Aberdeen in 12/85 and marked as 'STD')
"G-ASTD"	DHC.1 Chipmunk 22 (Fuselage no. DHB/f/68)	C1/0181	G-AOJZ WB732	----	Used at Perth for ground instruction until offered for sale in 1996.
G-ASTE	PA-E23-250 Aztec C	27-2557		14. 5.64	Fatal crash into Yeadon cemetery whilst on approach to Yeadon on 20.1.69. Canx.
G-ASTF	Bristol 175 Britannia Srs.314	13453	CF-CZW G-ASTF/CF-CZW	20. 5.64	CofA expired 2.3.70. Broken up in 10/70 at Gatwick. Canx as WFU 30.10.70.
G-ASTG	Nord 1002 Pingouin II	183	F-BGKI French AF 183	21. 5.64	Broken up for spares for G-ATBG in 10/70. (Dismantled 7/99 at Duxford)
G-ASTH	Mooney M.20C	2701	N6906U	22. 5.64	Crashed at Dinard, France on 16.11.66. Canx.
G-ASTI	Auster 6A Tugmaster	3745	WJ359	27. 5.64	
G-ASTJ	BAC One-Eleven Srs.201AC	BAC.085		27. 5.64	To N107EX 12/81. Canx 30.12.81.
G-ASTK	DHC.2 Beaver 1	1502	VR-AAX ST-ACA/CF-OSQ	27. 5.64	To (EP-...)/N9747F 5/66. Canx 1.2.66.
G-ASTL	Fairey Firefly TT.1	F.5607	SE-BRD Z2033	1. 6.64	WFU on 3.2.82. (On display 7/99 Duxford)
G-ASTM	Hiller 360 UH-12B	538	XB478 BuA.134728	2. 6.64	To N3877K in 2/83. Canx 21.1.80.
G-ASTN	Nord 1101 Noralpha	54	F-BLTR French Mil	2. 6.64	Suffered engine failure and crashed at Oldenburg, West Germany on 5.8.64. Canx.
G-ASTO	Pilatus PC-6/H2 Porter	541	HB-FAM G-ASTO/HB-FAM	3. 6.64	Restored as HB-FAM 8/66. Canx 7.3.67.
G-ASTP	Hiller 360 UH-12C	1045	N9750C	4. 6.64	Canx by CAA 24.1.90. To International Helicopter Museum on 12.10.89. (Cockpit on rebuild 4/98 Weston-super-Mare)
G-ASTR	Hiller 360 UH-12B	542	XB513 BuA.134732	4. 6.64	To N3877F in 1982. Canx 21.1.80.
G-ASTS	Douglas DC-6B (Line No. 363)	43831	OO-CTK	9. 6.64	Restored as OO-CTK 11/64. Canx 11.11.64.
G-ASTT	Orlican L-40 Meta-Sokol	150908		10. 6.64	Crashed at Bembridge, IoW on 6.6.71. Canx.
G-ASTU	CZL Aero 145 Super Aero	172012		10. 6.64	DBR at Sherburn on 16.8.71. Scrapped at Yeadon. Canx 29.10.73.
G-ASTV	Cessna 150D	150-60705	N6005T	17. 6.64	WFU on 18.10.75. Canx 2.5.83. Fuselage used in rebuild of G-AWAX 94/96.
G-ASTW	Douglas DC-6A/B (Line No. 323)	43826	N91306	16. 6.64	Canx 6.4.66 on sale to USA. To OO-GER(2) 4/66.
G-ASTX	Beagle B.242X (Rebuild of M.218 G-ASCK c/n B.051) (Originally regd with c/n B.053, changed in 3/66)	B242-001	G-ASCK G-35-6	18. 6.64	CofA expired 17.6.66. DBF at Shoreham in 8/69. Canx.
G-ASTY	DH.125 Srs.1A	25007	HB-VAH (G-ASSH)	19. 6.64	Restored as HB-VAH 1/65. Canx 8.1.65.
G-ASTZ	Hughes H.269B	54-0085		23. 6.64	WFU on 22.11.75. Canx 3.2.82.
G-ASUA	Nord 1002 Pingouin	248	F-BFDY F-SEEL/F-SCCJ	23. 6.64	Crashed on landing Elstree 30.7.64. (In store)
G-ASUB	Mooney M.20E Super 21	397	N7158U	24. 6.64	
G-ASUC	Mooney M.20C Ranger Mk.21	2768		24. 6.64	To VH-CYG 5/67. Canx 5.11.69.
G-ASUD	PA-28-180 Cherokee B	28-1654		29. 6.64	
G-ASUE	Cessna 150D (New fuselage fitted in 1965)	150-60718	N6018T	30. 6.64	(Stored 6/94)
G-ASUF	BAC One-Eleven Srs.203AE	BAC.015	N1541	30. 6.64	Restored as N1541 in 5/65. Canx 23.2.65.
G-ASUG	Beechcraft E.18S-9700 (Originally regd as E.18S, became -9700 with effect from 11.2.69)	BA-111	N575C N555CB/N24R	3. 7.64	WFU at Abbotsinch on 12.5.75. (On display East Fortune)

Regn	Type	c/n	Previous identity	Regn date	Fate or immediate subsequent identity (if known)
G-ASUH	Reims Cessna F.172E	0070		6. 7.64	CofA expired 14.4.78 & WFU at Norwich. Later noted dismantled at Felthorpe. Canx as WFU 22.3.89. (Fuselage in open store 7/95)
G-ASUI	Beagle A.61 Terrier 2 (Conversion of Auster 10 c/n 2570)	B.641	VF628	6. 7.64	
G-ASUJ	Hiller 360 UH-12E	2317		6. 7.64	Crashed at Platy, Thessalonika, Greece on 15.5.65. Canx.
G-ASUK	Hiller 360 UH-12E	2339		6. 7.64	Crashed at Spilsby, Lincs on 15.3.66. Canx.
G-ASUL	Cessna 182G Skylane	182-55077	N3677U	9. 7.64	
G-ASUM(1)	Brantly B.2B	419		14. 7.64	NTU - To G-ASUN(2) 7/64. Canx.
G-ASUM(2)	Brantly 305 (Originally regd with c/n 1004)	1005	(G-ASXF) (G-ASUN)/N2236U	14. 7.64	To N16616 9/66. Canx 23.9.66.
G-ASUN(1)	Brantly 305	"1004"		14. 7.64	NTU - To (G-ASXF)/G-ASUM(2) 7/64. Canx.
G-ASUN(2)	Brantly B.2B	419	(G-ASUM)	14. 7.64	Crashed at Shipdon-on-Cherwell, Oxon, while on a training flight from Kidlington on 6.5.67. Canx as WFU 23.2.73.
G-ASUO	Bolkow Bo.208A-2 Junior	537	D-EGQU	17. 7.64	To OY-DST 9/72. Canx 8.7.72.
G-ASUP	Reims Cessna F.172E	0071		22. 7.64	
G-ASUR	Dornier Do.28A-1	3051	D-IBOM	28. 7.64	
G-ASUS	Jurca MJ.2B Tempete	PFA/2001		28. 7.64	Crashed at Weston-super-Mare on 18.5.80. Canx.
G-ASUT	PA-30-160 Twin Comanche	30-347	N7303Y	30. 7.64	To OY-BKO 8/68. Canx 9.8.68.
G-ASUU	DH.114 Heron 2B	14087	121 South African AF	30. 7.64	To C-FYBM 3/71. Canx 31.3.71.
G-ASUV	DH.104 Riley Dove 400 (Converted from Dove 5)	04246	105 South African AF	30. 7.64	To 5N-AGF 9/65. Canx 17.3.65.
G-ASUW	DH.104 Riley Dove 1 (British prototype Riley Dove, converted from Dove 5)	04256	OO-BPL G-ASUW/South African AF 108	30. 7.64	To N99254 2/77. Canx 17.2.77.
G-ASUX	DH.104 Riley Dove 1 (Converted from Dove 5)	04250	107 South African AF	30. 7.64	To N668R 11/65. Canx 1.11.65.
G-ASUY	DH.114 Heron 2B	14085	OY-DPR G-ASUY/South African AF 120	30. 7.64	To N554PR 5/68. Canx 1.4.68.
G-ASUZ	DH.114 Heron 2D	14116	EC-ANY	31. 7.64	To N565PR 11/68. Canx 16.10.68.
G-ASVA	DH.114 Heron 2D	14121	EC-AOB	31. 7.64	To N564PR 11/68. Canx 16.10.68.
G-ASVB	DH.114 Heron 2D	14122	EC-AOC	31. 7.64	To VQ-FAE 10/64. Canx 1.10.64.
G-ASVC	DH.114 Heron 2D	14123	EC-AOF	31. 7.64	To VQ-FAF 10/64. Canx 1.10.64.
G-ASVD	Not allocated.				
G-ASVE	Beechcraft 65-A80 Queen Air	LD-185		31. 7.64	To 7Q-YFQ 3/80. Canx 17.3.80.
G-ASVF	Cessna 150E	150-60799	N6099T	31. 7.64	WFU at Luton on 10.6.67. Canx.
G-ASVG	Rousseau Piel CP.301B Emeraude	109	F-BILV	7. 8.64	
G-ASVH	Hiller 360 UH-12B	510	XB474 BuA.134724	11. 8.64	To SE-HNU 6/85. Canx 28.6.85.
G-ASVI	Hiller 360 UH-12B	536	XB476 BuA.134726	11. 8.64	To N3877E 2/83. Canx 21.1.80.
G-ASVJ	Hiller 360 UH-12B (Rebuilt with parts from XB519 c/n 548)	537	XB477 BuA.134727	11. 8.64	Crashed at Middle Wallop while on a training flight on 4.8.66. Canx.
G-ASVK	Hiller 360 UH-12B (Rebuilt with parts from XB522 c/n 551)	539	XB479 BuA.134729	11. 8.64	To N38769 2/83. Canx 21.1.80.
G-ASVL	Hiller 360 UH-12B (Rebuilt with parts from XB523 c/n 552)	541	XB481 BuA.134731	11. 8.64	To N3877A 2/83. Canx 21.1.80.
G-ASVM	Reims Cessna F.172E	0077		11. 8.64	
G-ASVN	Cessna 206 Super Skywagon	206-0275	N5275U	12. 8.64	
G-ASVO	Handley Page HPR.7 Dart Herald 214	185	PP-SDG G-ASVO/G-8-3	13. 8.64	WFU after collision with a floodlight on 8.4.97 at Hurn whilst taxiing. Stored at Hurn in 6/97, nose in grounds of Valley Nurseries, Beech, near Alton in 4/99. Forward fuselage outside Shoreham airport information centre 5/99.
G-ASVP	PA-25-235 Pawnee	25-2978		17. 8.64	
G-ASVR	PA-25-235 Pawnee	25-2979	ST-ADK G-ASVR	17. 8.64	Badly damaged in gales at Southend on 2.1.76. Canx.
G-ASVS	Omnipol L-13 Blanik	172604	OK-3840	19. 8.64	To BGA.2991 in 8/84. Canx 20.4.89.
G-ASVT	BAC One-Eleven Srs.200AT	BAC.095		19. 8.64	NTU - Planned rebuild of c/n 006 (G-ASJB) - Not proceded with. Canx 20.7.71.
G-ASVU	Reims Cessna F.172E	0075		19. 8.64	CofA expired on 25.2.73 & WFU.
G-ASVV	Cessna 310I	310I-0052	N8052M	24. 8.64	To G-ROGA 4/83. Canx.
G-ASVW	PA-25-235 Pawnee	25-2805	N7068Z	24. 8.64	Crashed near Wadi Medni, Sudan on 25.10.65. Canx.
G-ASVX	PA-25-235 Pawnee	25-2895	N7112Z	24. 8.64	Fatal collision with RAF Phantom XV493 over Denver Sluice, Fordham Fen on 9.8.74. Canx as WFU 16.9.74.
G-ASVY	PA-23-235 Pawnee	25-2923	N7138Z	24. 8.64	To ST-ADL 10/67. Canx 9.9.67.
G-ASVZ	PA-28-140 Cherokee	28-20357		24. 8.64	
G-ASWA	PA-28-140 Cherokee	28-20349		24. 8.64	WFU at Southend on 4.5.77. Canx 1.2.82.
G-ASWB	Beagle A.109 Airedale	B.543		25. 8.64	CofA expired 27.6.97. In open storage Antwerp 1997/8 without prop. Canx by CAA 10.6.98.
G-ASWC	Not allocated.				
G-ASWD	Reims Cessna F.172F	0089		25. 8.64	Fatal crash into Berriw Mountain, 15 miles West of Oswestry on 7.9.68. Canx.
G-ASWE	Bolkow Bo.208A-2 Junior	561	D-EFHE	26. 8.64	To G-CLEM 9/81. Canx.
G-ASWF	Beagle A.109 Airedale	B.537		26. 8.64	CofA expired 24.7.83. Canx by CAA 3.2.89.
G-ASWG	PA-25-235 Pawnee	25-2900	ST-ADM G-ASWG/N7113Z	28. 8.64	To SE-IXI 12/86. Canx 9.12.86.
G-ASWH	Phoenix Luton LA-5A Major	PAL/1225		31. 8.64	Damaged in forced landing near Turnworth, Dorset on 3.7.77 (On rebuild .91)
G-ASWI	Westland-Sikorsky S-58 Wessex 60 Srs.2	WA/199	VR-BDS G-ASWI/VR-BDS/G-ASWI/G-17-1	2. 9.64	Crashed into the North Sea, 11 miles east of Bacton on 13.8.81. Canx as destroyed 5.12.83.
G-ASWJ	Beagle B.206C Srs.1	B.009		9. 9.64	WFU at Filton on 18.1.73. To RAF Halton as 8449M in 1976. (On loan to Brunel Technical College 11/95)

Regn	Type	c/n	Previous identity	Regn date	Fate or immediate subsequent identity (if known)
G-ASWK	CZL Aero 145 Super Aero Srs.20	172003		10. 9.64	Overturned and DBR in a forced-landing due to engine failure while taking-off at Thruxton on 24.4.68. Canx.
G-ASWL	Reims Cessna F.172F Rocket	0087		10. 9.64	
G-ASWM	Beagle A.61 Terrier 2 (Conversion of Auster AOP.6 c/n 2592)	B.628	G-35-11 VF634	14. 9.64	WFU on 10.9.75. Canx 10.7.78. To VH-WFM 3/81.
G-ASWN	Bensen B.8M Gyrocopter	14		15. 9.64	(Status uncertain)
G-ASWO	Cessna 210D Centurion	210-58502	N2302F	17. 9.64	Crashed onto a Motorway at Rogliano, near Cosenza, Italy on 13.11.80. Canx.
G-ASWP	Beechcraft A23 Musketeer II	M-587		22. 9.64	Damaged on landing at Sedlescombe on 5.3.94.
G-ASWR	Agusta-Bell 47J-2 Ranger	2078		22. 9.64	Crashed in 1966. Canx as destroyed 6.4.73.
G-ASWS	CZL Aero 145 Super Aero Srs.20	172004		22. 9.64	Crashed on take-off from Lydd on 9.7.78. Canx as destroyed 7.2.84.
G-ASWT	CZL Aero 145 Super Aero Srs.20	172005		22. 9.64	Broken up for spares at Elstree. Canx 11.7.84.
G-ASWU	DH.121 Trident 1E	2114	5B-DAD G-ASWU/9K-ACF/G-ASWU/(G-ARPN)	1.10.64	WFU at Heathrow on 1.8.80. Canx 19.5.81.
G-ASWV	DH.121 Trident 1E	2118	(G-ARPS)	1.10.64	To 9K-ACG 5/66. Canx 23.11.65.
G-ASWW	PA-30-160 Twin Comanche	30-556	N7531Y	1.10.64	
G-ASWX	PA-28-180 Cherokee B	28-1932		1.10.64	
G-ASWY	PA-28-180 Cherokee B	28-1941		1.10.64	NTU - Not Imported. To TG-GUZ 11/64. Canx 12.11.64.
G-ASWZ	Landon-Chacksfield L.C.1 Tean	L.C.1-190-01		1.10.64	Not completed. Canx 13.9.73.
G-ASXA	DH.114 Heron 2	14065	VT-DHD G-5-11	6.10.64	To N16720 7/66. Canx 8.6.66.
G-ASXB	DH.82A Tiger Moth	3852	7152M N6539	6.10.64	To N555XB 10/90. Canx 11.3.88.
G-ASXC	SIPA 903	8	F-BEYK	6.10.64	(Being reassembled 1/99 Andrewsfield)
G-ASXD	Brantly B.2B	435		7.10.64	
G-ASXE(1)	Brantly B.2B	436		.10.64R	NTU - To N2271U /64. Canx.
G-ASXE(2)	Brantly B.2B	445		7.10.64	To G-WASP 2/77. Canx.
G-ASXF(1)	Brantly 305	1005	N2236U	.10.64R	NTU - To (G-ASUN)/G-ASUM(2) 7/64. Canx.
G-ASXF(2)	Brantly 305	1014		7.10.64	CofA expired 16.2.79 & WFU at Biggin Hill. Canx 24.5.82.
G-ASXG	McKinnon G.21C Turbo Goose (Originally regd as Grumman G.21A Super Goose, converted in 1968)	1083	N3692 N36992/CF-BZY/R.Canadian AF 926	8.10.64	To CF-AWH 9/73. Canx 6.9.73.
G-ASXH	Bensen B.8M Gyrocopter	15		8.10.64	WFU at Wooburn Green. Canx as WFU 22.8.73. (Stored 3/96)
G-ASXI	Cobelavia Tipsy T.66 Nipper 3	56	OO-KOC VH-CGH/(VH-CGC)	13.10.64	
G-ASXJ	Phoenix Luton LA-4A Minor	PFA/801		14.10.64	
G-ASXK	Dunmow-Coleman Aircopta	01		14.10.64	NTU - Not completed. Canx as WFU 5.12.77.
G-ASXL	Armstrong-Whitworth 650 Argosy Srs.222	AW.6800		14.10.64	Crashed near Piacenza, Italy on 4.7.65. Canx.
G-ASXM	Armstrong-Whitworth 650 Argosy Srs.222	AW.6801		14.10.64	To CF-TAG 6/70. Canx 22.6.70.
G-ASXN	Armstrong-Whitworth 650 Argosy Srs.222	AW.6802		14.10.64	To CF-TAJ 1/70. Canx 31.1.70.
G-ASXO	Armstrong-Whitworth 650 Argosy Srs.222	AW.6803		14.10.64	To CF-TAX 4/70. Canx 4.4.70.
G-ASXP	Armstrong-Whitworth 650 Argosy Srs.222	AW.6804		14.10.64	Crashed and DBF on take-off at Stansted on 4.12.67. Canx.
G-ASXR	Cessna 210 Centurion	210-57532	5Y-KPW VP-KPW/N6532X	16.10.64	(On rebuild 12/97)
G-ASXS	SAN Jodel DR.1050 Ambassadeur	133	F-BJNG	19.10.64	
G-ASXT	Grumman G.159 Gulfstream I	135	N755G	19.10.64	Canx 9.8.82 on sale to USA. Broken up at Denver, CO, USA in 9/83.
G-ASXU	Wassmer Jodel D.120A Paris-Nice	196	F-BKAG	19.10.64	
G-ASXV	Beechcraft 65-A80 Queen Air	LD-205	OO-ATO(2) G-ASXV	21.10.64	To EC-EEO 6/87. Canx 4.6.87.
G-ASXW	Omnipol L-13 Blanik	173145		21.10.64	To BGA.1306 in 4/66. Canx 30.3.69.
G-ASXX	Avro 683 Lancaster B.VII (Also allotted 8375M)	-	WU-15 French Navy/NX611	22.10.64	Canx as WFU 16.2.79. (On display 5/99 East Kirkby)
G-ASXY	SAN Jodel D.117A	914	F-BIVA	27.10.64	
G-ASXZ	Cessna 182G Skylane	182-55738	N3238S	28.10.64	
G-ASYA	Aero Commander 560F	1283-56	N1015	30.10.64	To N36JH 11/77. Canx 10.10.77.
G-ASYB	PA-23-250 Aztec C	27-2641	N5568Y	30.10.64	WFU on 30.12.78. Canx as WFU 14.12.79.
G-ASYC(1)	Cessna 337 Super Skymaster	337-0027	N2127X	.10.64R	NTU - Not Imported. Remained as N2127X. Canx.
G-ASYC(2)	Cessna 337 Super Skymaster	337-0033	N2133X	30.10.64	NTU - Not Imported. Remained as N2133X. Canx 31.5.65.
G-ASYD	BAC One-Eleven Srs.475EZ (Originally regd as Srs.400AM; Converted to prototype Srs.500 in 1967; To Srs.475EM in 1970)	BAC.053		9.11.64	WFU. Displayed 11/96 at Brooklands. Canx as WFU 25.7.94.
G-ASYE	BAC One-Eleven Srs.410AQ	BAC.054		9.11.64	To (N4111X)/N3939V 9/66. Canx 8.9.66.
G-ASYF	Lockheed L.749A-79-50 Constellation	2630	ZS-DBS	3.11.64	To N1939 6/67, but marks NTU; Scrapped at Miami, FL, USA in 7/69 still marked as G-ASYF. Canx 10.8.67.
G-ASYG	Beagle A.61 Terrier 2	B.637	VX927	3.11.64	CofA expired 19.12.70 & WFU at East Midlands. (On rebuild 1/95)
G-ASYH(1)	Cessna 150E	150-60987	N6287T	4.11.64R	NTU - Not Imported. Remained as N6287T. Canx.
G-ASYH(2)	Cessna 150E	150-60978	N6278T	9.12.64	Fatal crash into Black Combe, near Millom, Cumberland on 22.2.66. Wreckage remained undiscovered until 12.3.66. Canx.
G-ASYI	Cessna 180H	180-51485	N4785U	4.11.64	Canx as destroyed 17.4.73.
G-ASYJ	Beechcraft D95A Travel Air	TD-595	N8675Q	6.11.64	
G-ASYK	PA-30-160 Twin Comanche	30-573	N7543Y	6.11.64	Crashed on take-off from Sandown, IoW on 11.5.96. Canx as WFU 30.10.96.

Regn	Type	c/n	Previous identity	Regn date	Fate or immediate subsequent identity (if known)
G-ASYL	Cessna 150E	150-60795	N6095T	10.11.64	Badly damaged on landing at Bagby on 16.8.91. Canx as WFU 14.10.91.
G-ASYM	Laverda F.8L Super Falco Srs.IV	404	D-ECFA	12.11.64	Badly damaged in wheels-up landing at Linton on 6.9.75. Canx as WFU 19.3.76. Rebuilt & regd as D-EOEA in 9/77.
G-ASYN	Beagle A.61 Terrier 2 (Converted from Auster 6 c/n 2288)	B.634	VF519	16.11.64	Badly damaged by severe gales at Netherthorpe on 2.1.76. CofA expired 28.3.76. (Stored 2/96)
G-ASYO	PA-30-160 Twin Comanche	30-570	N7532Y	17.11.64	Restored as N7532Y 8/79. Canx 20.8.79.
G-ASYP	Cessna 150E	150-60794	N6094T	23.11.64	
G-ASYR	DH.104 Dove 8	04537	803 Ethiopian AF	20.11.64	Restored as Ethiopian AF as 803 in 2/65. Canx 20.4.65.
G-ASYS	Lockheed L.749A-79-50 Constellation	2623	ZS-DBR (4X-AOL)/ZS-DBR	24.11.64	Broken up in 3/67 at Baginton. Canx on sale to Germany 13.2.67.
G-ASYT	Lockheed L.749A-79-50 Constellation	2631	ZS-DBT (4X-AOM)/ZS-DBT	24.11.64	Broken up in 6/67 at Baginton. Canx as WFU 20.5.69.
G-ASYU	Lockheed L.749A-79-50 Constellation	2632	ZS-DBU	14.11.64	CofA never issued. WFU & stored at Woensdrecht, The Netherlands 12/64. Broken up in 4/67 at Baginton. Canx.
G-ASYV	Cessna 310G	310G-0048	HB-LBY N8948Z	24.11.64	Rebuilt with parts from Cessna 310F G-OITD & re-regd as G-XITD 10/87. Canx.
G-ASYW	Bell 47G-2	2219	VR-BBA CP-704/VP-TCF/CP-671/VR-BBA	26.11.64	To (F-GMPZ 5/98)/F-GIZV 6/99. Canx 12.12.97.
G-ASYX	HS.125 Srs.1A	25019		30.11.64	To N1125G 2/65. Canx 12.2.65.
G-ASYY	CZL Super Aero 45	51-186	F-BKGY	7.12.64	To N145SA 11/78. Canx 10.11.78.
G-ASYZ	Victa Airtourer 100	78		8.12.64	Canx as TWFU 6.9.91.
G-ASZA	Victa Airtourer 100	83		8.12.64	Crashed at Trecyndd Road, near Caerphilly, Wales on 26.5.66. Canx.
G-ASZB	Cessna 150E	150-61113	N3013J	16.12.64	
G-ASZC	Beechcraft B95A Travel Air	TD-532	OY-AOP N9985R	17.12.64	To OH-BTB 12/69. Canx 29.12.69.
G-ASZD	Bolkow Bo.208A-2 Junior	563	D-ENKI	16.12.64	
G-ASZE	Beagle A.61 Terrier 2 (Conversion of Auster 6 c/n 2510)	B.636	VF552	17.12.64	
G-ASZF	Boeing 707-336C (Line No. 448) (Converted to cargo version in 11/76)	18924	N2978G	21.12.64	To 5N-ARO 6/83. Canx 20.5.83.
G-ASZG	Boeing 707-336C (Line No. 452)	18925		21.12.64	To LX-FCV(2) 11/83. Canx 26.5.83.
G-ASZH	SAN Jodel D.117	705	F-BIDP	21.12.64	DBR on take-off from Ashbourne on 9.10.77. Canx.
G-ASZI	Short SC.7 Skyvan 3 (Originally regd as a Skyvan 2)	SH1830		31.12.64	Crashed at Sydenham on 30.12.68. Used as Skyliner mock-up. Broken up on 18.3.72. Canx 11.1.71.
G-ASZJ	Short SC.7 Skyvan 3A-100-9 (Originally regd as a Skyvan 2)	SH1831		31.12.64	To 9U-... Canx 16.3.99.
G-ASZK	Omnipol L-13 Blanik	173202		31.12.64	To RAFGSA.357/BGA.1397 in 5/67. Canx.
G-ASZL	Omnipol L-13 Blanik	173206		31.12.64	To BGA.1347 in 8/66. Canx.
G-ASZM	HS.125 Srs.1A	25020		1. 1.65	To N167J 2/65. Canx 25.2.65.
G-ASZN	HS.125 Srs.1A	25021		1. 1.65	To N575DU 3/65. Canx 10.3.65.
G-ASZO	HS.125 Srs.1A	25022		1. 1.65	To CF-SDA 2/65. Canx 11.1.65.
G-ASZP	HS.125 Srs.1A	25023		1. 1.65	To N1125 in 3/65. Canx 27.4.65.
G-ASZR	Fairtravel Linnet 2	005		5. 1.65	
G-ASZS	Gardan GY-80-160 Horizon	70		6. 1.65	
G-ASZT	Douglas C-54D-1-DC Skymaster	10640	9J-RBL VP-YYR/G-ASZT/VP-MAA/D-AMAX/N4043A/BuA.91997/42-72535/KL982/42-72535	12. 1.65	To VQ-ZEE/TN-ABC 5/68. Canx 15.5.68.
G-ASZU	Cessna 150E	150-61152	N3052J	13. 1.65	
G-ASZV	Tipsy T.66 Nipper Srs.2	45	5N-ADE 5N-ADY/VR-NDD	14. 1.65	Permit to Fly expired 23.5.90. (Stored 3/97)
G-ASZW	Reims Cessna F.172F	0138		15. 1.65	To G-ENOA 9/81. Canx.
G-ASZX	Beagle A.61 Terrier 1	3742	(SE-ELO) WJ368	18. 1.65	Damaged in forced landing at Verdun, France c.6.89. CofA expired 24.2.90. (On rebuild by R.Webber 7/97)
G-ASZY	Clutton-Tabenor FRED Srs.2	EC/ES/1A & PFA/1311		19. 1.65	To N4499Y 10/83. Canx 28.10.83.
G-ASZZ	Cessna 310J	310J-0077	N3077L	17. 3.65	To G-TUBY 6/83. Canx.
G-ATAA	PA-28-180 Cherokee B	28-2055	(OO-...) G-ATAA/(CN-...)/G-ATAA	20. 1.65	Badly damaged in crash 2km east of Melan, France on 12.9.86. Canx by CAA 24.11.86. (Open store 9/94 Southend)
G-ATAB	Douglas DC-7CF (Line No. 876)	45361	N6348C	21. 1.65	WFU at Lasham on 23.3.70. Canx 2.3.73. Broken up in 8/73.
G-ATAC	Cessna 185D Skywagon	185-0807		21. 1.65	To TZ-ABW 3/65. Canx 11.2.65.
G-ATAD	Mooney M.20C Ranger	2863	N79394	21. 1.65	Damaged on take-off from Coal Aston on 1.6.91. Canx as destroyed 2.9.91.
G-ATAE	PA-24-250 Comanche	24-1322	N6220P	22. 1.65	Crashed near Redditch on 12.6.71. Canx.
G-ATAF	Reims Cessna F.172F	0135		25. 1.65	
G-ATAG	CEA Jodel DR.1050 Ambassadeur	226	F-BKGG	25. 1.65	
G-ATAH	Cessna 336 Skymaster	336-0007	N1707Z	26. 1.65	CofA expired 5.12.76. (Open storage 3/92 at Farley Farm, Romsey) Canx by CAA 25.7.96.
G-ATAI	DH.104 Dove 8	04538		26. 1.65	CofA expired 8.9.84. Scrapped at Exeter in 11/84. Canx as WFU 23.3.89.
G-ATAJ	Hunting P.84 Jet Provost T.4 (Was in fact an interim T.5 version based at Luton)	BAC.166	XS231	27. 1.65	NTU - Remained with RAF as XS231. Canx 10.3.65.
G-ATAK	Aeromilano F.8L Falco 3	204	D-ENYB	28. 1.65	To EI-BCJ 11/76. Canx 23.11.76.
G-ATAL	Dornier Do.28B-1	3067		28. 1.65	To (F-OCYT) 3/77 / D-IKHD 11/77. Canx.
G-ATAM	HS.748 Srs.2A/214LFD	1576	ZS-HSA G-ATAM/9J-ABL/G-ATAM/OY-DFS/G-ATAM/9G-ABV/G-ATAM/PI-C1020/G-ATAM/XA-SEI/G-ATA	28. 1.65	To TR-LQY 10/72. Canx 26.9.72.
G-ATAN	Cessna U.206 Super Skywagon	U206-0358	N2158F	29. 1.65	Crashed at Bath Racecourse on 23.5.69. Canx 24.6.69.

Regn	Type	c/n	Previous identity	Regn date	Fate or immediate subsequent identity (if known)
G-ATAO	PA-24-260 Comanche	24-4053	N8634P	29. 1.65	Ditched into the English Channel 30 miles south of Bournemouth on 3.12.81. Canx as destroyed 5.12.83.
G-ATAP	DH.104 Dove 6	04496	HB-LAP	1. 2.65	To SE-EUR 7/65. Canx 3.5.65.
G-ATAR	PA-23-250 Aztec C	27-2748	N5634Y	4. 2.65	To OO-MAR(2) 5/68. Canx.
G-ATAS	PA-28-180 Cherokee C	28-2137		4. 2.65	
G-ATAT	Cessna 150E	150-61141	N3041J	9. 2.65	Canx by CAA 15.8.85. (Stored for rebuild .92)
G-ATAU	Rollason-Druine D.62B Condor	RAE/610		10. 2.65	
G-ATAV	Rollason-Druine D.62C Condor (Originally regd as D.62B)	RAE/611		10. 2.65	(Stored 4/97)
G-ATAW	Beagle A.109 Airedale	B.541		12. 2.65	WFU in 8/79. Canx.
G-ATAX	Taylorcraft Auster III (Frame no.TAY/1524)	546	PH-UFP (PH-RAF)/G-ATAX/PH-UFP/R.Netherlands Navy 21-33/MLD 1-33/KLu R-13/NJ916	12. 2.65	To VH-KRL 12/80. Canx 11.4.78.
G-ATAY	HS.125 Srs.1A	25026	G-5-11	16. 2.65	To N225KJ 3/65. Canx 27.3.65.
G-ATAZ	HS.125 Srs.1A	25029		22. 2.65	To N10122 5/65. Canx 15.5.65.
G-ATBA	HS.125 Srs.1A	25030		22. 2.65	To N413GH 5/65. Canx 19.5.65.
G-ATBB	HS.125 Srs.1A	25031		22. 2.65	To N1923M 6/65. Canx 6.6.65.
G-ATBC	HS.125 Srs.1A	25032		22. 2.65	To N65MK 6/65. Canx 3.6.65.
G-ATBD	HS.125 Srs.1A	25033		22. 2.65	To N125G 6/65. Canx 25.9.65.
G-ATBE	Douglas C-47A-35-DL Dakota	9813	EI-ANK 5N-AAO/VR-NCO/VH-AFA(2)/"VHC-HM"/42-23951	23. 2.65	To CF-CQT 5/70. Canx 1.4.70.
G-ATBF(1)	Canadair F-86E Sabre 4	377	MM19477 FU-19477/XB546/R.Canadian AF 19477	. .65R	NTU - Canx.
G-ATBF(2)	Canadair F-86E Sabre 4	507	MM19607 FU-19607/XB733/R.Canadian AF 19607	24. 3.66	Canx as WFU 16.2.79.
G-ATBG	Nord 1002 Pingouin II	121	F-BGVX F-OTAN-5/French Mil F-SCCO	24. 2.65	
G-ATBH	CZL Aero 145 Srs.20	172015		24. 2.65	(On rebuild .97)
G-ATBI	Beechcraft A23 Musketeer II	M-696		26. 2.65	
G-ATBJ	Sikorsky S-61N (Possibly ex N10043)	61-269		12. 3.65	
G-ATBK	Reims Cessna F.172F	0137		2. 3.65	To G-EWUD 5/87. Canx.
G-ATBL	DH.60G Moth	1917	HB-OBA CH-353	2. 3.65	
G-ATBM(1)	PA-25-235 Pawnee B	25-3168		. .65R	NTU - Not Imported. To N7270Z/YI-AEE. Canx.
G-ATBM(2)	PA-25-235 Pawnee B	25-3133		3. 3.65	Crashed/DBF at Kalamitsi Apokoronou, Crete on 22.7.65. Canx.
G-ATBN	PA-28-140 Cherokee	28-20597	(N6518W) N11C	3. 3.65	Crashed on take-off from Brocks Farm, Stock, Essex on 2.12.84. Canx by CAA 12.9.86.
G-ATBO	PA-28-140 Cherokee	28-20778		3. 3.65	Overturned on take-off from Newhouse Farm, Elmley Lovett, near Droitwich on 28.9.70. Canx as WFU 8.10.73.
G-ATBP	Alpavia Fournier RF-3 (Originally regd with c/n 55)	59		11. 3.65	
G-ATBR	CEA Jodel DR.1050/M1 Sicile Record	625		12. 3.65	To 5A-CAA 1/68. Canx.
G-ATBS	Druine D.31 Turbulent	PFA/1620		16. 3.65	
G-ATBT	Reims Cessna F.172F	0119		16. 3.65	Crashed into a peat bog on Winter Hill, Pennines on 2.10.68. Canx.
G-ATBU	Beagle A.61 Terrier 2 (Conversion of Auster 6 c/n 2552)	B.635	VF611	17. 3.65	
G-ATBV	PA-23-250 Aztec C	27-2777	N5661Y	18. 3.65	To N3859D 3/83. Canx 30.3.83.
G-ATBW	Cobelavia Tipsy T.66 Nipper 2	52	OO-MAG	19. 3.65	
G-ATBX	PA-20-135 Pacer	20-904	VP-KRX VR-TCH/VP-KKE	19. 3.65	CofA expired 13.6.91. (Stored 5/92)
G-ATBY	Westland-Sikorsky S-58 Wessex 60 Srs.1	WA/460	VR-BDT G-ATBY	22. 3.65	To 5N-AJM 2/75. Canx 4.2.75.
G-ATBZ	Westland-Sikorsky S-58 Wessex 60 Srs.1	WA/461		22. 3.65	CofA expired & WFU at Weston-super-Mare on 5.12.81. To G-17-4. (On display Weston-super-Mare) Canx as TWFU 23.11.82.
G-ATCA	Westland-Sikorsky S-58 Wessex 60 Srs.1	WA/462	(PH-THA) G-ATCA	22. 3.65	Crashed and burnt out at Rhoose-Cardiff on 9.9.72. Canx
G-ATCB	Westland-Sikorsky S-58 Wessex 60 Srs.1	WA/463	7S-HSL G-ATCB	22. 3.65	To 5N-AJP 10/77. Canx 4.10.77.
G-ATCC	Beagle A.109 Airedale	B.542		25. 3.65	
G-ATCD	Beagle D.5/180 Husky	3683		25. 3.65	
G-ATCE	Cessna U.206 Super Skywagon	U206-0380	N2180F	25. 3.65	
G-ATCF	Campbell-Bensen B.8S Gyrocopter	CA/300		26. 4.65	Canx as WFU 10.3.69.
G-ATCG	Omnipol L-13 Blanik	173214		31. 3.65	To BGA.1500 in 10/68. Canx 3.6.81.
G-ATCH	Omnipol L-13 Blanik	173215		31. 3.65	To BGA.1301 in 2/66. Canx.
G-ATCI	Victa Airtourer 100	91	ZK-CHB	5. 4.65	Crashed near Esh Winning on 25.8.81. Canx.
G-ATCJ	Phoenix Luton LA-4A Minor	RMS.1 & PAL/1163 & PFA/812		5. 4.65	
G-ATCK	Victa Airtourer 100	92		5. 4.65	Fatal crash just outside the boundary of Biggin Hill on on 25.8.74. Canx 25.6.75 as destroyed.
G-ATCL	Victa Airtourer 100	93		5. 4.65	
G-ATCM	PA-23-250 Aztec C	27-2834	N5712Y	5. 4.65	Crashed while landing at Guipavas airfield, Brest, France on 26.6.68. Canx.
G-ATCN	Phoenix Luton LA-4A Minor	PAL/1118		7. 4.65	
G-ATCO	HS.125 Srs.1A	25035		7. 4.65	To N1515P 6/65. Canx 26.6.65.
G-ATCP	HS.125 Srs.1A	25038		7. 4.65	To N926G 7/65. Canx 12.7.65.

Regn	Type	c/n	Previous identity	Regn date	Fate or immediate subsequent identity (if known)
G-ATCR	Cessna 310	35311	SE-CXX N3611D	13. 4.65	CofA expired 7.5.77. Dismantled at Fosse Way Farm, Ashorne in early 1983. (Stored dismantled at the Holy Hill Service Station, south of Swanton Novers, Norfolk on the B1110 road by 23.4.83). Canx as WFU 9.10.84.
G-ATCS	Cessna E310J	310J-0145	N3145L	13. 4.65	Fatal crash at Fraignot, north of Dijon, France on 10.11.72. Canx.
G-ATCT	BN-2A Islander (Prototype)	1		15. 4.65	Fatal crash into a lake at Wymbritseradeel, near Sneek, Holland on 9.11.66. Canx.
G-ATCU	Cessna 337 Super Skymaster	337-0133	N2233X	22. 4.65	
G-ATCV	Wallis WA.117 Autogyro Srs.1	301	N5640Y	26. 4.65	Major components used to build G-AVJV c/n K/402/X in 1967. Canx as WFU in 3/67 at Reymerston Hall.
G-ATCW	Cessna 182H Skylane	182-56203	N2303X	26. 4.65	To 5Y-ADN 1/66. Canx 10.1.66.
G-ATCX	Cessna 182H Skylane	182-55848	N3448S	26. 4.65	
"G-ATCX"	Cessna 182A Skylane	182-34078	G-OLSC G-ATNU/EI-ATC/N6078B	----	Painted as such for film use in mid .90s. Is G-OLSC really.
G-ATCY	PA-E23-250 Aztec C	27-2754	N5640Y	26. 4.65	To EI-BOO 4/84. Canx 10.4.84.
G-ATCZ	DH.114 Heron 2C	14076	OY-BAO I-AOLO/VR-NAV	27. 4.65	To N12333 3/66. Canx 16.2.66.
G-ATDA	PA-28-160 Cherokee	28-206	EI-AME G-ARUV	27. 4.65	
G-ATDB	SNCAN Nord 1101 Noralpha (Note: A Nord 1101 marked as "F-OTAN-6" was reported at Barton 8/96, but is believed to be G-BAYV)	186	F-OTAN-6 French Mil	27. 4.65	(On rebuild 8/93)
G-ATDC	PA-E23-250 Aztec C	27-2751	N5668Y	27. 4.65	Canx as WFU 11.7.84.
G-ATDD	Beagle B.206 Srs.1 (Originally regd as B.206R, re-designated as a Srs.1 in 1966)	B.013		27. 4.65	WFU after undercarriage collapsed at Sherburn in 6/73. Canx as PWFU 9.4.74. (Stored 5/99 at Kemble)
G-ATDE	DHC.1 Chipmunk 22 (Fuselage no. DHB/f/69)	C1/0182	WB733	28. 4.65	Restored to RAF as WB733 in 1/68. Canx 19.1.68.
G-ATDF	DHC.1 Chipmunk 22 (Fuselage no. DHB/f/628)	C1/0735	WP850 G-ATDF/WP850	28. 4.65	To N735DH 4/76. Canx 13.4.76.
G-ATDG	Gardan GY-80-160 Horizon	101		28. 4.65	Crashed at Whitton Hill, Ramsbottom on 28.10.77. Canx.
G-ATDH	Gardan GY-80-160 Horizon	105		28. 4.65	Ditched in the sea 2½ miles southwest of Porthcawl on 10.4.78. Canx as destroyed 29.2.84.
G-ATDI	DHC.1 Chipmunk 22 (Fuselage no. DHB/f/412)	C1/0527	WG477	28. 4.65	NTU - To G-ATDP 5/65. Canx.
G-ATDJ	Vickers VC-10 Srs.1103	825	(9G-ABQ)	4. 5.65	To RAF as XX914 in 4/73. Canx 5.4.73.
G-ATDK	Warm-Air Airship (built by Vacuum Reflex Ltd)	V.R.1		4. 5.65	Construction abandoned. Canx as WFU 21.4.69.
G-ATDL	Cessna 310J	310J-0146	N3146L	5. 5.65	Crashed on landing at Abbotsinch on 5.9.77. Canx 14.11.77.
G-ATDM	Hiller 360 UH-12E	2288		5. 5.65	Crashed near Longcourse Farm, Duckmanton, near Chesterfield on 29.7.75. Canx.
G-ATDN	Beagle A.61 Terrier 2 (Conversion of Auster 6 c/n 2499)	B.638	TW641	7. 5.65	
G-ATDO	Bolkow Bo.208C-1 Junior 3	576	D-EGZU	10. 5.65	
G-ATDP	DHC.1 Chipmunk 22 (Fuselage no. DHB/f/412)	C1/0527	(G-ATDI) WG477	14. 5.65	Restored to RAF as WG477 in 1/68. Canx 15.1.68.
G-ATDR	Vickers 739A Viscount	393	SU-AKN	11. 5.65	WFU at Blackbushe in 11/69. Broken up in 5/70 at Speke. Canx as WFU 19.2.73.
G-ATDS	Handley Page HPR.7 Dart Herald 209	189	4X-AHT G-ATDS	12. 5.65	WFU at Hurn on 10.1.91. To Airport Fire Service in 10/95. Canx as WFU 7.2.96. Scrapped in 4/96.
G-ATDT	Sud SA.318C Alouette Astazou	1901		13. 5.65	NTU - Not Imported. To N4675/Senegal AF. Canx.
G-ATDU	Vickers 739 Viscount	87	SU-AIE	13. 5.65	Broken up at Speke Airport in 4/69. Canx as WFU 10.7.69.
G-ATDV	PA-24-400 Comanche	26-111	N8530P	14. 5.65	To N3983D 7/83. Canx 21.7.83.
G-ATDW	Hiller 360 UH-12E-4	2030	N5350V VP-YXR	18. 5.65	To ZK-HCQ 8/68. Canx 5.8.68.
G-ATDX	DHC.1 Chipmunk 22 (Fuselage no. DHB/f/394)	C1/0513	WG463	20. 5.65	Restored to RAF as WG463 in 1/68. Canx 3.1.68.
G-ATDY	DHC.1 Chipmunk 22 (Fuselage no. DHB/f/360)	C1/0492	WG418	20. 5.65	Restored to RAF as WG418 in 1/68. Canx 19.1.68.
G-ATDZ	Moravan Zlin Z.326T Trener-Master	304	OK-LHC	20. 5.65	To VH-ILZ 8/85. Canx 14.2.85.
G-ATEA	DHC.1 Chipmunk 22 (Fuselage no. DHB/f/395)	C1/0514	WG464	21. 5.65	Restored to RAF as WG464 in 1/68. Canx 3.1.68.
G-ATEB	DHC.1 Chipmunk 22 (Fuselage no. DHB/f/785)	C1/0896	WZ866	21. 5.65	Restored to RAF as WZ866 in 1/68. Canx 3.1.68.
G-ATEC	PA-25-235 Pawnee	25-3407		24. 5.65	Crashed at Wyberton on 1.9.66. Canx.
G-ATED	Hiller 360 UH-12E	2342		24. 5.65	Crashed whilst spraying at Lutton Grange Farm, near Holbeach on 19.7.84. Canx as destroyed 29.9.86.
G-ATEE	Luton Beta Srs.1	PFA/247		25. 5.65	Built as Rollason Beta B.2 with c/n RAE/04, regn NTU and became G-AWHX 4/68. Canx as WFU 8.4.70.
G-ATEF	Cessna 150E	150-61378	N3978U	25. 5.65	
G-ATEG	Cessna 150E	150-61383	N3983U	25. 5.65	To 5B-CIW 7/95. Canx 5.7.95.
G-ATEH	HS.748 Srs.2A/222	1585	HP-416 G-ATEH	26. 5.65	To VP-LIW 6/68. Canx 21.6.68.
G-ATEI	HS.748 Srs.2/222	1586	CF-TAX G-ATEI/VP-LIN/G-ATEI	26. 5.65	To PI-C1029 in 9/70. Canx 28.8.70.
G-ATEJ	HS.748 Srs.2/222	1587		26. 5.65	To CF-MAL 12/67. Canx 23.12.67.
G-ATEK	HS.748 Srs.2/222	1588	6V-AFX CS-TAV/G-ATEK/RP-C1041/V2-LIV/VP-LIV/G-ATEK	26. 5.65	Broken up at Southend, still marked as 6V-AFX in 7/91. Canx by CAA 17.6.92.
G-ATEL	Aviation Traders ATL.90 Accountant I	ATL.90	G-41-1	30. 8.57	WFU in 1/58. Development abandoned. Broken up in 2/60 at Southend. Canx 8.10.58.
G-ATEM	PA-28-180 Cherokee C	28-2329		26. 5.65	

Regn	Type	c/n	Previous identity	Regn date	Fate or immediate subsequent identity (if known)
G-ATEN	PA-30-160 Twin Comanche	30-544	N7483Y	27. 5.65	To N41BA 1/77. Canx 24.1.77.
G-ATEO	Slingsby T.51 Dart 15/17	1471		28. 5.65	To N179E 8/65. Canx 9.8.65.
G-ATEP	EAA Sport Biplane (built by E.L. Martin)	PFA/1301		28. 5.65	Dismantled & stored at Castel Farm, Guernsey with CofA expired 18.6.73. Canx by CAA 14.7.86. (Stored in very poor condition 8/96 at Guernsey)
G-ATER	PA-25-235 Pawnee B	25-3405		31. 5.65	DBR on take-off from a strip at Frampton Farm, near Boston, Lincs on 27.7.69. Canx. (Remains at Ludham 8/69)
G-ATES	PA-32-260 Cherokee Six	32-20		31. 5.65	Crashed near Kinglassie on 8.2.81 during a forced landing. Canx as WFU 22.10.84. (Front fuselage used as Para-trainer 9/92 at Ipswich)
G-ATET	PA-30-160 Twin Comanche	30-770	N230ET G-ATET/N7749Y	31. 5.65	
G-ATEU	Beagle B.206R Srs.1	B.015		31. 5.65	Crashed on take-off from Ndola, Zambia on 17.1.66. Canx.
G-ATEV	CEA Jodel DR.1050 Ambassadeur	18	F-BJHL	31. 5.65	(On rebuild .97)
G-ATEW	PA-30-160 Twin Comanche	30-719	N7640Y	3. 6.65	
G-ATEX	Victa Airtourer 100/RR (Fitted with Rolls Royce Continental O-240-A engine in 1970 to become a Srs.100/RR from a Srs.100)	110	(VH-MTU)	3. 6.65	
G-ATEY	Cessna 411	411-0087	N7387U	3. 6.65	To N34JH 9/75. Canx 29.9.75.
G-ATEZ	PA-28-140 Cherokee	28-21044		8. 6.65	
G-ATFA	Bensen B.8 Gyrocopter	WHE.III		9. 6.65	Canx as WFU 30.5.84.
G-ATFB	PA-25-235 Pawnee B	25-3155	N7266Z	11. 6.65	To 4X-AIF 6/66. Canx 10.6.66.
G-ATFC	Sud SE.3160 Alouette III	1258		14. 6.65	To EP-HAD 8/65. Canx 25.8.65.
G-ATFD	CEA Jodel DR.1050 Ambassadeur	311	F-BKIM	14. 6.65	
G-ATFE	DH.114 Heron 2	14067	VT-DHE	15. 6.65	To VH-CLS 6/65. Canx 28.6.65.
G-ATFF(1)	PA-23-250 Aztec C	27-2848	N5725Y	. .65R	NTU - Crashed at Gander on 16.5.65 whilst on delivery. Canx.
G-ATFF(2)	PA-23-250 Aztec C	27-2898	N5769Y	16. 6.65	
G-ATFG	Brantly B.2B	448		16. 6.65	(Stored in 1983 in damaged condition at Newport Pagnell) CofA expired 25.3.85. Canx as WFU 25.9.87. (On rebuild 9/90) (On display in Museum of Flight 3/96)
G-ATFH	Brantly B.2B	449		16. 6.65	Exploded in flight & crashed at Highfield Farm, Empingham, Leics on 10.4.76. Canx.
G-ATFI(1)	Alpavia Fournier RF-3	67		. 6.65	NTU - Not Imported. Canx.
G-ATFI(2)	Alpavia Fournier RF-3	83		16. 6.65	NTU - Not Imported. To F-BMTV 2/66. Canx 16.6.65.
G-ATFJ	Hiller 360 UH-12E	2349		16. 6.65	Crashed at Thorney on 1.3.66. To USA & rebuilt as N7755 in 1968. Canx.
G-ATFK	PA-30-160 Twin Comanche	30-721	N7642Y	17. 6.65	Damaged on landing at White Waltham on 12.6.89. Canx by CAA 21.10.92.
G-ATFL	Reims Cessna F.172F	0171		17. 6.65	Canx as WFU 31.3.87. CofA expired 28.1.88.
G-ATFM	Sikorsky S-61N Mk.II (Possibly initially N10052)	61-270	CF-OKY	21. 6.65	
G-ATFN	Vickers 739A Viscount	394	SU-AKO	23. 6.65	Fatal crash near Langenbruck, N of Munich, West Germany on 9.8.68. Canx.
G-ATFO	HS.125 Srs.1B	25037	D-CAFI	23. 6.65	To D-CAFI 12/66. Canx.
G-ATFP	Ercoupe 415CD	2168	N99545 NC99545	28. 6.65	DBF at Southend on 27.6.68. Canx as WFU 16.8.73.
G-ATFR	PA-25-150 Pawnee	25-135	OY-ADJ	28. 6.65	
G-ATFS	PA-24-180 Comanche	24-56	N5052P	28. 6.65	Restored as N5052P 5/77. Canx 23.5.77.
G-ATFT	PA-23-250 Aztec C	27-2970	N5839Y	30. 6.65	To ST-ACY 4/66. Canx 6.4.66.
G-ATFU	DH.85 Leopard Moth	7007	HB-OTA CH-366	30. 6.65	Canx by CAA 7.11.96. On rebuild in New Zealand as ZK-ARG in 1998.
G-ATFV	Agusta-Bell 47J-2A Ranger	2093	9J-ACX G-ATFV/Italian AF MM80417	1. 7.65	Canx by CAA 22.12.92. (Stored 9/93)
G-ATFW	Phoenix Luton LA-4A Minor	PFA/811		2. 7.65	
G-ATFX	Reims Cessna F.172G	0196		8. 7.65	Damaged in gales Booker 25.1.90. Canx by CAA 22.3.91. On display in Redhill shopping centre 7/97, Woking Shopping Centre 7.3.98 & on a trailer at Popham on 15.3.98 all-red without marks for raising money for AMAF ("Leprosy Awareness"/"Flight Aid").
G-ATFY	Reims Cessna F.172G	0199		8. 7.65	
G-ATFZ	PA-23-160 Apache	23-1314	D-GIGI OE-FIM	8. 7.65	Crashed near Godalming, Surrey on 1.9.66. Canx.
G-ATGA	HS.125 Srs.1A	25043		9. 7.65	To N125J 8/65. Canx 21.8.65.
G-ATGB	Beechcraft 65-90 King Air	LJ-80		9. 7.65	NTU - Not Imported. To N774K 11/65. Canx in 1/66.
G-ATGC	Victa Airtourer 100	115		9. 7.65	Crashed on take-off from Eglinton on 29.2.76. Canx.
G-ATGD	Bristol 175 Britannia Srs.314	13393	CF-CZA	9. 7.65	To 5X-UVT 9/69. Canx 4.9.69.
G-ATGE	SAN Jodel DR.1050 Ambassadeur	114	F-BJJF	9. 7.65	
G-ATGF	Morane-Saulnier MS.892A Rallye Commodore 150	10547		9. 7.65	Ran into a hedge on landing at Seaton, Devon on 1.8.78. Canx by CAA 14.7.86.
G-ATGG	Morane-Saulnier MS.885 Super Rallye	144	F-BKLR	14. 7.65	CofA expired 14.10.83 & WFU at Southend. Canx by CAA 3.4.89.
G-ATGH	Brantly B.2B	451		14. 7.65	To N199BB 12/97. Canx 6.11.97.
G-ATGI	DH.104 Riley Dove 5 (Originally regd as DH.104 Dove 5B)	04097	D-100 R.Jordanian AF/TJ-ACA/YI-ABK	12. 7.65	To VH-ABM 7/74. Canx 21.5.74.
G-ATGJ	DH.104 Riley Dove 5 (Originally regd as DH.104 Dove 5B)	04113	D-101 R.Jordanian AF/TJ-ACB/YI-ABL	12. 7.65	To VH-ABK 3/74. Canx 20.3.74.
G-ATGK	DH.104 Riley Dove 400 (Originally regd as Dove 5B)	04288	F-BORJ G-ATGK/R.Jordanian AF D-102/TJ-ACC/(TJ-ABG)	12. 7.65	To JY-AEU 11/75. Canx 19.12.75.
G-ATGL	DH.104 Dove 5B	04289	D-103 R.Jordanian AF/TJ-ACD/(TJ-ABH)	12. 7.65	Not converted to Riley Dove. Canx as WFU 14.9.71 at Luton.
G-ATGM	Helio H.395 Super Courier	593	N4199D	12. 7.65	Crashed on take-off from Gwaensgor, Flint, Gwent on 29.6.71. Scrapped at Stockport in 12/75. Canx.
G-ATGN	Thorn K-800 Coal Gas Balloon	2		12. 7.65	Canx as WFU 23.6.81. (Stored)

Regn	Type	c/n	Previous identity	Regn date	Fate or immediate subsequent identity (if known)
G-ATGO	Reims Cessna F.172G	0181		12. 7.65	
G-ATGP	SAN Jodel DR.1050 Ambassadeur	122	F-BJNB	14. 7.65	
G-ATGR	Beechcraft 95-B55 Baron	TC-841	N6146V	14. 7.65	To N28375 6/76. Canx 28.6.76.
G-ATGS	HS.125 Srs.1A	25046		19. 7.65	To N48UC 9/65. Canx 19.6.65.
G-ATGT	HS.125 Srs.1A	25047		19. 7.65	To N778SM 9/65. Canx 25.9.65.
G-ATGU	HS.125 Srs.1A	25051		19. 7.65	To N9300 10/65. Canx 4.10.65.
G-ATGV	Miles SE.5A Replica	SEM.7282		20. 7.65	To EI-ARA 6/67. Canx.
G-ATGW	Miles SE.5A Replica	SEM.7283		20. 7.65	To EI-ARB 6/67. Canx.
G-ATGX	Wassmer Jodel D.120 Paris-Nice	134	F-BIXQ	20. 7.65	Fatal crash whilst landing at Wombleton on 3.1.66. Canx.
G-ATGY	Gardan GY-80-160 Horizon	121		20. 7.65	
G-ATGZ	Griffiths GH-4 Gyroplane	G.1		20. 7.65	(Stored Shardlow, Derby 7/91)
G-ATHA	PA-23-235 Apache	27-610	N4326Y	21. 7.65	Canx as WFU 7.6.86. (Instructional Airframe 6/91)
G-ATHB	Handley Page HPR.7 Dart Herald 210	162	HB-AAG CF-MCM	22. 7.65	To B-2001 in 2/66. Canx 24.2.66.
G-ATHC	DHC.1 Chipmunk 22 (Fuselage no. DHB/f/731)	C1/0835	WP969	26. 7.65	Restored to RAF as WP969 in 1/68. Canx 3.1.68.
G-ATHD	DHC.1 Chipmunk 22 (Fuselage no. DHB/f/734)	C1/0837	WP971 G-ATHD/WP971	26. 7.65	
G-ATHE	Handley Page HPR.7 Dart Herald 207	165	D-BOBO G-ATHE/JY-ACR/R.Jordanian AF 109/(CF-EPA)	26. 7.65	To B-2011 in 3/69. Canx 4.3.69.
G-ATHF	Cessna 150F	150-61592	N6292R	26. 7.65	DBR on landing at Teversham, Cambridge on 7.9.83. Canx.
G-ATHG	Cessna 150F	150-61719	N8119S	26. 7.65	Canx as destroyed 29.4.91.
G-ATHH	SNCAN 1101 Noralpha	162	F-BLQS F-UJGH	28. 7.65	To N208K 7/83. Canx 20.7.83.
G-ATHI	PA-28-180 Cherokee C	28-2545		2. 8.65	DBR in crash at Castlebar, Co.Mayo, Ireland on 9.5.74. Canx 8.7.74. (Instructional Airframe 5/92)
G-ATHJ	PA-23-250 Aztec C	27-2757	N5643Y	2. 8.65	To A6-ZAZ 1/85. Canx 21.1.85.
G-ATHK	Aeronca 7AC Champion	7AC-971	N82339 NC82339	2. 8.65	Permit expired on 17.6.86. Damaged by gales at Hook on 16.10.87.
G-ATHL	Wallis WA-116/F Srs.1	401 & 212		3. 8.65	Damaged in a forced landing 1½ miles from Shipdham on 5.3.85. Canx as WFU 25.5.89.
G-ATHM	Wallis WA-116/F Srs.1 (Also quoted as c/n 213)	402 & 211	4R-ACK G-ATHM	3. 8.65	Permit expired 23.5.93. (Stored 2/99 Reymerston Hall)
G-ATHN	SNCAN 1101 Noralpha	84	F-BFUZ(2) French Mil F-UIXE/F-SCSM	5. 8.65	CofA expired 23.6.75. Canx by CAA 16.12.91. (Stored in crate in laundry 1/99 Guernsey)
G-ATHO	Beagle B.206 Srs.1	B.019		5. 8.65	To OO-VRH 7/76. Canx 26.7.76.
G-ATHP	Druine D.31 Turbulent	PFA/432	VT-XAG	6. 8.65	Fatal crash when it struck overhead power cables while landing at Membury on 5.10.68. Canx.
G-ATHR	PA-28-180 Cherokee C	28-2343	EI-AOT	11. 8.65	
G-ATHS	PA-28-180 Cherokee C	28-2800	(ST-...) G-ATHS	12. 8.65	To ST-ADU 12/68. Canx 23.11.68.
G-ATHT	Victa Airtourer 115	120		16. 8.65	
G-ATHU	Beagle A.61 Terrier 1 (Originally regd as a Auster 7)	AUS/127/FM	7435M WE539	16. 8.65	
G-ATHV	Cessna 150F	150-62019	N8719S	16. 8.65	
G-ATHW	Mooney M.20E Chapparal Mk.21	805	N5881Q	16. 8.65	To G-RAFW 11/84. Canx.
G-ATHX	SAN Jodel DR.100A Ambassadeur	74	F-OBMM	17. 8.65	
G-ATHY	Cessna 150F	150-62059	N8759S	19. 8.65	NTU - Not Imported. Remained as N8759S. Canx 27.9.65.
G-ATHZ	Cessna 150F	150-61586	(EI-AOP) N6286R	20. 8.65	
G-ATIA	PA-24-260 Comanche	24-4049	N8650P	20. 8.65	
G-ATIB	Bensen B.8M Gyrocopter	16		23. 8.65	Not completed. Canx by CAA 9.8.91.
G-ATIC	CEA Jodel DR.1050 Ambassadeur	6	F-BJCJ	23. 8.65	Veered off the runway when landing at Leicester on 30.6.95 and collided with a parked aircraft.
G-ATID	Cessna 337 Super Skymaster	337-0239	N6239F	24. 8.65	Canx by CAA 7.7.97. (Based in Portugal)
G-ATIE	Cessna 150F	150-61591	N6291R	24. 8.65	Overturned in forced-landing 2 miles east of Shobdon on 28.7.79 after engine failure, substantially damaged. (Fuselage used as para-trainer 4/97; abandoned?)
G-ATIF	Pfalz D.III Replica	PPS/PFALZ/1		24. 8.65	To EI-ARC 5/67. Canx 17.5.67.
G-ATIG	Handley Page HPR.7 Dart Herald 214	177	PP-SDI G-ATIG	25. 8.65	WFU & stored at Norwich in 4/95. Canx as WFU 29.10.96. (On fire dump 2/99 at Norwich)
G-ATIH	PA-22-108 Colt	22-9086	N5360Z	28. 8.65	NTU - Not Imported. Remained as N5360Z. Canx.
G-ATII	Beechcraft S35 Bonanza	D-7693	VR-BCD	3. 9.65	To N77GR 3/81. Canx 4.3.81.
G-ATIJ	Pfalz D.III Replica	PT.16		3. 9.65	To EI-ARD 5/67. Canx 17.5.67.
G-ATIK	HS.125 Srs.1A	25052		8. 9.65	To N816M 11/65. Canx 9.11.65.
G-ATIL	HS.125 Srs.1A	25057		8. 9.65	To N188K 11/65. Canx 26.11.65.
G-ATIM	HS.125 Srs.1A	25060		8. 9.65	To N2601 12/65. Canx 7.12.65.
G-ATIN	SAN Jodel D.117	437	F-BHNV	8. 9.65	(Stored 4/97)
G-ATIO	Caudron C.276H Luciole	7207/26	F-PHQM F-AOFD	9. 9.65	Destroyed in Ireland whilst making "Blue Max" film. Canx 23.11.65.
G-ATIP	Caudron C.277 Luciole	7546/135	F-AQFB	9. 9.65	To F-BNMB 11/65. Canx.
G-ATIR	AIA Stampe SV-4C	1047	F-BNMC G-ATIR/F-BMKQ/Aeronavale/F-BCDM/Aeronavale	9. 9.65	
G-ATIS	PA-28-160 Cherokee C	28-2713		9. 9.65	
G-ATIT	Not allocated.				
G-ATIU	Westland-Sikorsky S-55 Whirlwind Srs.3	WA/412	EP-HAF G-ATIU	10. 9.65	To 5N-AIV 8/71. Canx 26.8.71.
G-ATIV	PA-28-140 Cherokee	28-21211		13. 9.65	To PH-NLU 1/66. Canx 29.12.65.
G-ATIW	GEMS MS.892A Rallye Commodore 150	10561		14. 9.65	To EI-BCH 9/76. Canx 23.8.76.
G-ATIX	SNCAN 1101 Noralpha	154	F-BLYO French AF	14. 9.65	To N2685N 1/82. Canx 5.1.82.

Regn	Type	c/n	Previous identity	Regn date	Fate or immediate subsequent identity (if known)
G-ATIY	Fokker DR.1 Triplane Replica (built by John Bitz GmbH)	001		15. 9.65	To EI-APW 5/67. Canx.
G-ATIZ	SAN Jodel D.117	636	F-BIBR	15. 9.65	Damaged in a crash at Leicester on 30.6.95. (Sold as a "wreck" 5/96)
G-ATJA	SAN Jodel DR.1050 Ambassadeur	378	F-BKHL	15. 9.65	
G-ATJB	Victa Airtourer 100 T.3	122		16. 9.65	Fatal crash into mountainside at Champagney, France while en route from Southend to Basle on 16.3.74. Canx.
G-ATJC	Victa Airtourer 100	125		16. 9.65	
G-ATJD	PA-28-140 Cherokee	28-21235		20. 9.65	Fatal crash on landing at Markyate on 16.4.83 & DBF. Canx as destroyed 29.2.84.
G-ATJE	PA-28-140 Cherokee	28-21243		20. 9.65	Crashed on landing at Biggin Hill on 10.9.72. Canx.
G-ATJF	PA-28-140 Cherokee	28-21283		20. 9.65	Crashed on a beach near Corcubion, Spain on 29.8.79. (Fuselage stored 3/89 Sabadell, Spain)
G-ATJG	PA-28-140 Cherokee (Rebuilt with spares from G-BBSO in 80s)	28-21299		20. 9.65	
G-ATJH	PA-28-140 Cherokee	28-21315		20. 9.65	DBR in crash in mountains, near Cilcain, near Mold, Flintshire on 15.10.66. Fuselage stored at Fornebu airport, Sweden in 1967. Canx.
G-ATJI	DHC.1 Chipmunk 22 (Fuselage no. DHB/f/646)	C1/0750	WP863	21. 9.65	Restored to RAF as WP863 in 1/68. Canx.
G-ATJJ	DHC.1 Chipmunk 22 (Fuselage no. DHB/f/706)	C1/0797	WP921	21. 9.65	Restored to RAF as WP921 in 1/68. Canx.
G-ATJK	DHC.1 Chipmunk 22 (Fuselage no. DHB/f/716)	C1/0805	WP927	21. 9.65	Restored to RAF as WP927 in 1/68. Canx.
G-ATJL	PA-24-260 Comanche	24-4203	N8752P	23. 9.65	
G-ATJM	Fokker DR.1 Triplane Replica (built by John Bitz GmbH)	002	N78001 EI-APY/G-ATJM	23. 9.65	(Stored 10/97)
G-ATJN	Dormois Jodel D.125	863	F-PINZ	23. 9.65	
G-ATJO	Cessna 337A Super Skymaster	337-0281	N6281F	24. 9.65	Destroyed in mid-air collision with Varsity WF334 near Immingham, Lincs on 14.6.66. Canx.
G-ATJP	PA-23-160 Apache	23-1736	5N-ADX VR-NDC	27. 9.65	WFU at Ipswich in 1976 - Believed to be one of the hangar casualities at Biggin Hill in 1987. Canx as destroyed 27.5.87.
G-ATJR	PA-E23-250 Aztec C	27-3033	N5881Y	30. 9.65	CofA expired 23.7.95. Canx as WFU 21.3.96. Fuselage noted dumped in 1/98 at Ringway.
G-ATJS	Aermacchi-Lockheed AL.60B-2	6227/47		1.10.65	NTU - Not Imported. To I-VARH 8/68. Canx.
G-ATJT	Gardan GY-80-160 Horizon	108		4.10.65	
G-ATJU	Cessna 150F	150-61865	N8265S	7.10.65	Crashed 2 miles north of Durham on 9.11.82. Canx 20.4.83.
G-ATJV	PA-32-260 Cherokee Six (Originally regd with c/n 32-102)	32-103	TF-GOS G-ATJV	7.10.65	(Stored 9/97)
G-ATJW	SNCAN 1101 Noralpha	167	F-BLQP French Mil	12.10.65	To N5337M 6/84. Canx 5.6.84.
G-ATJX	Bucker Bu.131 Jungmann	36	D-EDMI HB-AFE/Swiss AF A-88	12.10.65	Restored as HB-AFE 12/86. Canx 17.12.86.
G-ATJY	Brantly B.2B	455		13.10.65	Crashed at Kidlington on 4.11.72. Canx as WFU 17.7.73.
G-ATJZ	PA-E23-250 Aztec C	27-2967	N5819Y	13.10.65	WFU at Shoreham on 5.9.81. Canx 22.4.82.
G-ATKA	PA-23-150 Apache	23-596	5N-ABG VR-NBG	18.10.65	To TF-BAR 8/70. Canx 6.8.70.
G-ATKB	Beagle Auster D.5/180 Husky	3682		18.10.65	To 5H-MMU 11/66. Canx.
G-ATKC	SNCAN Stampe SV-4B	1081	F-BFRK French AF	19.10.65	Fatal crash in a field at Shinhay, near Royston on 2.8.87. Canx as destroyed 8.3.88.
G-ATKD	Cessna 150F	150-62551	N8451G	20.10.65	Destroyed when crashed into trees at Lavendon, near Orkney, Bucks on 21.4.84. Canx by CAA 14.7.86.
G-ATKE	Cessna 150F	150-62364	N3564L	20.10.65	Crashed on take-off from Ingoldmels on 24.3.84 & used for spares at Wyberton. Canx as WFU 16.11.84.
G-ATKF	Cessna 150F	150-62386	N3586L	20.10.65	
G-ATKG	Hiller 360 UH-12B	496	103 R.Thailand AF	21.10.65	WFU on 28.11.69. Canx 21.1.80.
G-ATKH	Phoenix Luton LA-4A Minor	PFA/809		25.10.65	(Stored 1/96)
G-ATKI	Piper J3C-75 Cub	17545	N70536 NC70536	25.10.65	(Damaged when overturned taxying Enstone 14.11.93) (On rebuild 8/97)
G-ATKJ	Beagle A.61 Terrier 2 (Converted from Auster 6 c/n 2533)	B.639	VF575	25.10.65	Crashed on take-off from Rearsby on 27.12.65. Canx.
G-ATKK	HS.125 Srs.1A	25064		28.10.65	To N230H 12/65. Canx 16.12.65.
G-ATKL	HS.125 Srs.1A	25065		28.10.65	To N631SC 12/65. Canx 30.12.65.
G-ATKM	HS.125 Srs.1A/522	25066		28.10.65	To N925CT 2/66. Canx 16.2.66.
G-ATKN	HS.125 Srs.1A/522	25070		28.10.65	To N520M 1/66. Canx 20.1.66.
G-ATKO	Beagle B.206 Srs.1	B.022		2.11.65	To N6862 6/72. Canx 21.6.72.
G-ATKP	Beagle B.206 Srs.1	B.026		2.11.65	To OO-EEL 6/73. Canx 14.6.73.
G-ATKR	Druine D.31 Turbulent	PFA/1615		3.11.65	Crashed at Shoreham on 10.8.75. Canx as destroyed 20.9.84.
G-ATKS	Reims Cessna F.172G	0201		9.11.65	To OK-XKG 4/95. Canx 11.4.95.
G-ATKT	Reims Cessna F.172G	0206		9.11.65	
G-ATKU	Reims Cessna F.172G	0232		9.11.65	Blown over and wrecked at Cranfield on 20.1.97. (On rebuild 1/97)
G-ATKV	Westland-Sikorsky S-55 Whirlwind Srs.3	WA/493	EP-HAN(1) G-ATKV	11.11.65	To VR-BEU 1/74. Canx 8.1.74.
G-ATKW	PA-E23-250 Aztec C	27-2997	N5846Y	15.11.65	DBF in hangar fire at Exeter on 12/13.1.81. Canx.
G-ATKX	SAN Jodel D.140C Mousquetaire III	163		19.11.65	
G-ATKY	Cessna 150F	150-62613	N8513G	23.11.65	Destroyed in storm at Chalbury Grange, Dorset on 15/16.12.79. Canx.
G-ATKZ	Cobelavia Tipsy T.66 Nipper 2 (Originally regd with c/n 69)	72		24.11.65	

Regn	Type	c/n	Previous identity	Regn date	Fate or immediate subsequent identity (if known)
G-ATLA	Cessna 182J Skylane	182-56923	N2823F	24.11.65	
G-ATLB	SAN Jodel DR.1050/M1 Excellence (Built originally as a Jodel DR.100A in 1959)	78	F-BIVG	29.11.65	
G-ATLC	PA-E23-250 Aztec C	27-3058	N5903Y	29.11.65	CofA expired 30.9.78 & WFU at Hurn. Canx by CAA 14.7.86.
G-ATLD	Cessna E310K	310K-0068	N6968L	30.11.65	To 5B-CGL 10/86. Canx 31.10.86.
G-ATLE	Bristol 175 Britannia Srs.314	13395	CF-CZC	30.11.65	WFU at Gatwick on 11.12.68. Canx 16.3.70. Used for fire training at Gatwick; Broken up in 3/84.
G-ATLF	Beagle B.206 Srs.2	B.023		1.12.65	To VH-UNC 5/66. Canx.
G-ATLG	Hiller 360 UH-12B	505	105 R.Thailand AF	2.12.65	Canx as WFU 21.1.80.
G-ATLH	Fewsdale Tigercraft Gyro-Glider	FT.5		6.12.65	DBF in 7/78. Canx as WFU 10.2.82. (Stored 6/97)
G-ATLI	HS.125 Srs.1A/522	25073		6.12.65	To N372CM 2/66. Canx 24.1.66.
G-ATLJ	HS.125 Srs.1A/522	25075		6.12.65	To N666M 2/66. Canx 11.2.66.
G-ATLK	HS.125 Srs.1A/522	25078		6.12.65	To N40DC 3/66. Canx 3.3.66.
G-ATLL	HS.125 Srs.1A/522	25079		6.12.65	To N440DC 3/66. Canx 9.3.66.
G-ATLM	Reims Cessna F.172G	0252		6.12.65	
G-ATLN	Reims Cessna F.172G	0257		6.12.65	Blown over in a gale & DBR after landing at Calais on 17.10.67. Canx as WFU 26.4.83.
G-ATLO(1)	Brantly 305	1021		7.12.65	NTU - To N2214U. Canx.
G-ATLO(2)	Brantly 305	1027		3. 3.66	NTU - To N2219U. Canx.
G-ATLO(3)	Brantly 305	1028		. 4.66	Crashed & DBF at Stourport-on-Severn, Worcs on 1.10.76. Canx as destroyed 5.12.83.
G-ATLP	Bensen B.8M Gyrocopter	17		9.12.65	
G-ATLR	Reims Cessna F.172G	0204		13.12.65	Stalled and crashed at Walkeridge Farm, near Overton on 3.10.81. Canx as WFU on 6.12.88.
G-ATLS	Cessna 150F (Was officially regd with c/n 150-62924)	150-62954	(N8854G)	13.12.65	Canx 5.5.70 on sale to Switzerland. To F-BSEP 9/70.
G-ATLT(1)	Cessna U.206A Super Skywagon	U206-0509		13.12.65	NTU - Not Imported. Canx.
G-ATLT(2)	Cessna U.206A Super Skywagon	U206-0523	N4823F	21.12.65	
G-ATLU	Turner HAFB	1		13.12.65	DBR on maiden flight at Dunstable on 29.8.66. Canx by CAA 22.7.86. (Some parts to Balloon Museum at Marsh Benham)
G-ATLV	Jodel Wassmer D.120 Paris-Nice	224	F-BKNQ	15.12.65	
G-ATLW	PA-28-180 Cherokee C	28-2877		17.12.65	(Damaged when struck by D.117 G-ATIZ landing at Leicester 30.6.95)
G-ATLX	Beechcraft D95A Travel Air	TD-538	N7714N N771W	21.12.65	Crashed at Zurich, Switzerland on 7.11.69. Canx.
G-ATLY	Rollason-Luton Beta	RAE/01		22.12.65	Fatal crash after collision with Tiger Moth G-APVT near Tollerton on 29.9.73. Canx.
G-ATLZ	Westland-Sikorsky S-55 Whirlwind Srs.3	WA/125	EP-HAK G-ATLZ/French AF F-8/(XK933)	22.12.65	To 5N-AJH 10/71. Canx 18.10.71.
G-ATMA	Bristol 175 Britannia Srs.314	13428	5Y-ANS G-ATMA/CF-CZX	28.12.65	Canx as WFU 1.6.73. Broken up in 1974 at Biggin Hill.
G-ATMB	Reims Cessna F.150F (Wichita c/n 62648)	0012		28.12.65	Struck high ground northeast of Sligo, Ireland on 5.7.88 & DBR. Canx as destroyed 9.11.88.
G-ATMC	Reims Cessna F.150F (Wichita c/n 62849)	0020		28.12.65	
G-ATMD	PA-25-235 Pawnee	25-2595	SE-EIP N6908Z	28.12.65	To ZS-FEW 12/67. Canx.
G-ATME	PA-25-235 Pawnee	25-2802	SE-EMF	28.12.65	To ZS-FEV 12/67. Canx.
G-ATMF	Douglas DC-7CF (Line No. 656)	44873	N7314 N731PA	30.12.65	To F-BTDJ 4/72. Canx 13.4.72.
G-ATMG	Socata MS.893A Rallye Commodore 180 (Originally regd as MS.892 Rallye Commodore with same c/n, re-designated on 4.1.66)	10567		3. 1.66	CofA expired 13.5.93. Canx by CAA 12.12.96.
G-ATMH	Beagle D.5/180 Husky	3684		3. 1.66	
G-ATMI	HS.748 Srs.2A/225	1592	VP-LIU G-ATMI/VP-LIU/G-ATMI/VP-LIU/G-ATMI/VP-LIU/G-ATMI	4. 1.66	
G-ATMJ	HS.748 Srs.2A/225	1593	VP-LAJ G-ATMJ/6Y-JFJ/G-ATMJ	4. 1.66	
G-ATMK	Reims Cessna F.150F (Wichita c/n 62671)	0013		6. 1.66	To EI-BHW 11/79. Canx 9.11.79.
G-ATML	Reims Cessna F.150F (Wichita c/n 62722)	0014		6. 1.66	
G-ATMM	Reims Cessna F.150F (Wichita c/n 62775)	0016		6. 1.66	
G-ATMN(1)	Reims Cessna F.150F (Wichita c/n 63455)	0054		. 1.66	NTU - To G-ATRN 3/66. Canx.
G-ATMN(2)	Reims Cessna F.150F (Wichita c/n 63526)	0060	(G-ATNE)	6. 1.66	Ditched off the Isle of Grain on 11.5.84. (Later salvaged) Canx as destroyed 22.8.85. (Stored 9/95)
G-ATMO	Reims Cessna F.172G	0269		6. 1.66	Crashed at Roborough, Plymouth on 15.5.66. Canx.
G-ATMP	Cessna 210F Centurion	210-58735	N1835F F-BIFU(2)/N1835F	6. 1.66	To (EI-BNO)/EI-BOD 6/83. Canx 23.5.83.
G-ATMR	Cessna 310K	310K-0098	N6998L	6. 1.66	NTU - Not Imported. To OO-SIK. Canx.
G-ATMS	Beagle A.61 Terrier 2	2562/B.643	VF620	10. 1.66	Fatal crash & burnt on take-off at Saltby airfield whilst glider-towing on 18.8.73. Canx 21.8.73 as destroyed.
G-ATMT	PA-30-160 Twin Comanche	30-439	XW938 G-ATMT/N7385Y	10. 1.66	
G-ATMU	PA-23-160 Apache G	23-2000	N4478P	11. 1.66	(Stored 10/97)
G-ATMV	PA-28-140 Cherokee	28-21465		11. 1.66	Crashed near Aldergrove, Northern Ireland on 17.5.74. Canx as destroyed 12.6.74.

Regn	Type	c/n	Previous identity	Regn date	Fate or immediate subsequent identity (if known)
G-ATMW	PA-28-140 Cherokee	28-21486		11. 1.66	
G-ATMX	Cessna 150F	150-62372	SE-ETC N3572L	13. 1.66	Canx by CAA 8.7.94.
G-ATMY	Cessna 150F	150-62642	SE-ETD N8542G	13. 1.66	
G-ATMZ	Moravan Zlin Z.226 Trener	130	OO-MDB OE-CKW/OK-LLT	14. 1.66	Crashed at Redhill on 8.4.67. Canx. (Remains at Farnborough in 1/68)
G-ATNA	DH.121 Trident 1E-103	2130	AP-ATK	14. 1.66	Restored as AP-ATK 3/66. Canx 2.3.66.
G-ATNB	PA-28-180 Cherokee C	28-3057		20. 1.66	
G-ATNC(1)	Reims Cessna F.150F (Wichita c/n 63381)	0049		. 1.66	NTU - To G-ATRK 3/66. Canx.
G-ATNC(2)	Reims Cessna F.150F	0055		20. 1.66	DBR whilst landing at Pudsey on 28.12.71. Canx as WFU 16.8.73.
G-ATND(1)	Reims Cessna F.150F	0059		. 1.66	NTU - To G-ATNJ 1/66. Canx.
G-ATND(2)	Reims Cessna F.150F	0041		20. 1.66	Force-landed due to fog near Haisthorpe while flying from Grindale on 9.12.72. Canx as WFU 24.8.73. Parts to G-BELT.
G-ATNE(1)	Reims Cessna F.150F (Wichita c/n 63526)	0060		. 1.66	NTU - To G-ATMN(2) 1/66. Canx.
G-ATNE(2)	Reims Cessna F.150F (Wichita c/n 63252)	0042		20. 1.66	
G-ATNF	Reims Cessna F.150F (Wichita c/n 63540)	0061		20. 1.66	NTU - Not Imported. To OH-CEN 7/66. Canx.
G-ATNG	Reims Cessna F.150F (Wichita c/n 63568)	0062		20. 1.66	NTU - To G-ATPM 2/66. Canx.
G-ATNH	Reims Cessna F.172G	0278		20. 1.66	To EI-BAO 2/75. Canx 27.1.75.
G-ATNI(1)	Reims Cessna F.150F (Wichita c/n 63384)	0052		. 1.66	NTU - To G-ATNX(2) 1/66. Canx.
G-ATNI(2)	Reims Cessna F.150F (Wichita c/n 63499)	0058	(G-ATOG)	24. 1.66	To G-NSTG 8/89. Canx.
G-ATNJ(1)	Reims Cessna F.150F (Wichita c/n 63454)	0053		. 1.66	NTU - To G-ATRM 3/66. Canx.
G-ATNJ(2)	Reims Cessna F.150F	0059	(G-ATND)	24. 1.66	Collided with F.150F G-ATOG on approach to Scone/Perth on 24.9.74. Canx.
G-ATNK	Reims Cessna F.150F (Wichita c/n 63638)	0065		25. 1.66	W/o in 11/86. Canx by CAA 9.7.87.
G-ATNL	Reims Cessna F.150F (Wichita c/n 63652)	0066		25. 1.66	
G-ATNM	HS.125 Srs.1A/522	25082		27. 1.66	To N909B in 3/66. Canx 17.3.66.
G-ATNN	HS.125 Srs.1A/522	25084		27. 1.66	To N1125G in 4/66. Canx 5.4.66.
G-ATNO	HS.125 Srs.1A/522	25088		27. 1.66	To N1230B in 5/66. Canx 6.5.66.
G-ATNP	HS.125 Srs.1A/522	25091		27. 1.66	To N1230G in 5/66. Canx 16.5.66.
G-ATNR	HS.125 Srs.1A/522	25096		27. 1.66	To N235KC in 6/66. Canx 28.6.66.
G-ATNS	HS.125 Srs.1A/522	25098		27. 1.66	To N10121 in 7/66. Canx 13.7.66.
G-ATNT	HS.125 Srs.1A/522	25100		27. 1.66	To N125J in 7/66. Canx 17.7.66.
G-ATNU	Cessna 182A Skylane	182-34078	EI-ANC N6078B	27. 1.66	To G-OLSC 8/87. Canx.
G-ATNV	PA-24-260 Comanche B	24-4350	N8896P	28. 1.66	(Stored 4/99 Bourn)
G-ATNW(1)	Reims Cessna F.150F (Wichita c/n 63582)	0063		. 1.66	NTU - To G-ATOF 2/66. Canx.
G-ATNW(2)	Reims Cessna F.150F (Wichita c/n 63383)	0051		31. 1.66	To 4X-CEZ 6/77. Canx 21.6.77.
G-ATNX(1)	Reims Cessna F.150F	0064		. 1.66	NTU - To G-ATOG 2/66. Canx.
G-ATNX(2)	Reims Cessna F.150F (Wichita c/n 63384)	0052	(G-ATNI)	31. 1.66	Damaged at Coventry on 2.4.88. Canx by CAA 2.8.96.
G-ATNY	Cessna 337A Super Skymaster	337A-0364	N6364F	31. 1.66	Destroyed in fatal crash into high ground at Moch Siabod, near Betws-y-Coed, Wales on 8.6.79. Canx.
G-ATNZ	Bristol 175 Britannia Srs.314	13396	CF-CZD	31. 1.66	WFU on 16.2.70. Broken up in 6/72 at Biggin Hill. Canx as WFU 6.5.71.
G-ATOA	PA-23-160 Apache G	23-1954	N4437P	31. 1.66	
G-ATOB	Douglas DC-7CF (Line No. 668)	44875	N7334 N733PA	31. 1.66	To VR-BCT 10/67. Canx 12.68.
G-ATOC(1)	Bristol 170 Freighter 21	12778	EC-ADL	31. 1.66	NTU - Restored as G-AIFS 1/66. Canx.
G-ATOC(2)	Bolkow Bo.208C-1 Junior 3	600	D-ECGU	3. 2.66	To EI-AUR 11/70. Canx 20.10.70.
G-ATOD	Reims Cessna F.150F (Wichita c/n 62342)	0003		1. 2.66	
G-ATOE	Reims Cessna F.150F (Wichita c/n 63096)	0031		1. 2.66	
G-ATOF(1)	Reims Cessna F.150F (Wichita c/n 63485)	0057		. .66R	NTU - Not Imported. To D-EFVL 6/66. Canx.
G-ATOF(2)	Reims Cessna F.150F (Wichita c/n 63582)	0063	(G-ATNW)	1. 2.66	Crashed in forced landing 2 miles N of Perth 25.11.71. Canx as destroyed 1.12.71. (On fire dump 2/96 Perth)
G-ATOG(1)	Reims Cessna F.150F (Wichita c/n 63499)	0058		. .66R	NTU - To G-ATNI 1/66. Canx.
G-ATOG(2)	Reims Cessna F.150F	0064	(G-ATNX)	1. 2.66	Crashed on landing at Perth on 27.1.81. To instructional airframe. Canx.
G-ATOH	Rollason-Druine D.62B Condor	RAE/612	(EC-...) G-ATOH	3. 2.66	
G-ATOI	PA-28-140 Cherokee	28-21556		3. 2.66	
G-ATOJ	PA-28-140 Cherokee	28-21584		3. 2.66	
G-ATOK	PA-28-140 Cherokee	28-21612		3. 2.66	
G-ATOL	PA-28-140 Cherokee	28-21626		3. 2.66	
G-ATOM	PA-28-140 Cherokee	28-21640		3. 2.66	
G-ATON	PA-28-140 Cherokee	28-21654		3. 2.66	

Regn	Type	c/n	Previous identity	Regn date	Fate or immediate subsequent identity (if known)
G-ATOO	PA-28-140 Cherokee	28-21668		3. 2.66	CofA expired 24.9.84. (To Carlisle 5.3.99 for restoration)
G-ATOP	PA-28-140 Cherokee	28-21682		3. 2.66	
G-ATOR	PA-28-140 Cherokee	28-21696		3. 2.66	(Stored 9/96)
G-ATOS	PA-28-140 Cherokee	28-21710		3. 2.66	To G-DENE 2/98. Canx.
G-ATOT	PA-28-180 Cherokee C	28-3061		3. 2.66	
G-ATOU	Mooney M.20E Chapparel Super 21	961	N5946Q	3. 2.66	
G-ATOV	HS.125 Srs.1A/522	25074		4. 2.66	To N400NW 2/66. Canx 23.2.66.
G-ATOW	HS.125 Srs.1A/522	25083		4. 2.66	To (N16777)/N43ST in 3/66. Canx 29.3.66.
G-ATOX	HS.125 Srs.1A/522	25087		4. 2.66	To CF-ALC 5/66. Canx 21.3.66.
G-ATOY	PA-24-260 Comanche B	24-4346	N8893P	7. 2.66	Crashed on take-off from Elstree on 6.3.79. (Fuselage on display 3/96 East Fortune)
G-ATOZ	Bensen B.8M Gyrocopter (Substantially rebuilt in 1986, original airframe stored at Wimborne)	18		7. 2.66	
G-ATPA	PA-25-235 Pawnee B	25-3720		8. 2.66	Crashed 6 miles north of Ruthin, Denbighshire on 18.8.73. Canx.
G-ATPB	HS.125 Srs.1B/522	25089		8. 2.66	To OO-SKJ 6/75. Canx 23.6.75.
G-ATPC	DH.125 Srs.1	25009		11. 2.66	To RAF as XW930 on 7.12.70. Canx 3.5.71.
G-ATPD	HS.125 Srs.1B/522	25085	5N-AGU G-ATPD	11. 2.66	
G-ATPE	HS.125 Srs.1B/522	25092		11. 2.66	CofA expired 1.4.87. Canx as WFU 14.3.90.
G-ATPF	Short SC.7 Skyvan 2-100-2	SH1833		14. 2.66	WFU at Sydenham on 27.1.69. Canx 5.3.73. Broken up in 11/76 at Belfast.
G-ATPG	Short SC.7 Skyvan 2-200-2	SH1835		14. 2.66	To N731R 5/67. Canx.
G-ATPH	BAC One-Eleven Srs.304AX	BAC.110		16. 2.66	To CF-QBN 4/69. Canx 1.4.69.
G-ATPI	BAC One-Eleven Srs.304AX	BAC.112		16. 2.66	To CF-QBO 4/69. Canx 1.4.69.
G-ATPJ	BAC One-Eleven Srs.304AG	BAC.033	(9K-ACI)	16. 2.66	To CC-CYF 11/90. Canx 19.11.90.
G-ATPK	BAC One-Eleven Srs.304LAG (Originally regd as Srs.304AG)	BAC.034	VP-BCP G-ATPK/(9K-ACJ)	16. 2.66	To 5N-OMO 5/91. Canx 1.5.91.
G-ATPL	BAC One-Eleven Srs.304AG	BAC.035	9K-ACO G-ATPL/(9K-ACK)	16. 2.66	To CC-CYI 12/90. Canx 17.12.90.
G-ATPM	Reims Cessna F.150F (Wichita c/n 63568)	0062	(G-ATNG)	18. 2.66	Fatal crash & DBF north of Winchester and west of the A34 road on 27.12.90. Canx as destroyed 21.2.91.
G-ATPN	PA-28-140 Cherokee	28-21899		18. 2.66	
G-ATPO	Not allocated.				
G-ATPP	PA-28-180 Cherokee	28-21906		18. 2.66	Crashed near Booker on 16.5.77. Canx 16.5.77.
G-ATPR	PA-E23-250 Aztec C	27-3082	N5923Y	21. 2.66	To N9190T 7/81. Canx 9.7.81.
G-ATPS	Cessna 310K	310K-0090	N6990L	21. 2.66	To OH-CDH 11/69. Canx 7.11.69.
G-ATPT	Cessna 182J Skylane	182-57056	N2956F	22. 2.66	
G-ATPU	Cessna 337A Super Skymaster	337A-0397	F-OCLP G-ATPU/N6397F	22. 2.66	To TF-SKY 12/76. Canx 7.12.76.
G-ATPV	Barritault JB.01 Minicab (Rebuild of GY-20 F-PHUC c/n A.155)	01	F-PJKA	22. 2.66	(Stored 6/97)
G-ATPW	Wallis WA.118 Meteorite	401		23. 2.66	WFU at Reymerston Hall in 3/66. Major components used to build G-AVJW c/n K/502/X in 1967. Canx as WFU in 3/67.
G-ATPX	Omnipol L-13 Blanik	173301		23. 2.66	To BGA.1321 in 5/66. Canx.
G-ATPY	Omnipol L-13 Blanik	173302		23. 2.66	To BGA.1322 in 5/66. Canx.
G-ATPZ	Omnipol L-13 Blanik	173303		23. 2.66	To BGA.1324 in 5/66. Canx.
G-ATRA	Omnipol L-13 Blanik	173304		23. 2.66	To BGA.1325 in 5/66. Canx.
G-ATRB	Omnipol L-13 Blanik	173305		23. 2.66	To BGA.1326 in 6/66. Canx.
G-ATRC	Beechcraft B95A Travel Air	TD-504	EI-AMC	23. 2.66	Badly damaged in forced landing nr.Le Mans, France 13.6.97. Canx as destroyed 19.3.98.
G-ATRD	Reims Cessna F.150F	0043		28. 2.66	Forced landing in a field near Bedley, near Elmdon on 14.4.78. Canx as destroyed 19.2.79.
G-ATRE	Reims Cessna F.172G	0288		28. 2.66	Overturned on landing at Bridlington on 28.2.77. Canx as destroyed 28.3.77.
G-ATRF	Omnipol L-13 Blanik	173324		1. 3.66	To BGA.1327 in 6/66. Canx.
G-ATRG	PA-18-180 Super Cub	18-7764	5B-CAB N4985Z	1. 3.66	
G-ATRH	PA-18-150 Super Cub	18-7830	5B-CAD	3. 3.66	Crashed on take-off from Sutton Bank on 24.11.69. Canx as WFU 7.11.73.
G-ATRI	Bolkow Bo.208C-1 Junior	602	D-ECGY	3. 3.66	
G-ATRJ	Reims Cessna F.150F	0044		4. 3.66	Crashed while taking-off in long grass at Honeydon airstrip, Bedfordshire on 25.7.67. (Wreckage to Biggin Hill) Canx.
G-ATRK	Reims Cessna F.150F (Wichita c/n 63381)	0049	(G-ATNC)	4. 3.66	
G-ATRL	Reims Cessna F.150F (Wichita c/n 63382)	0050		4. 3.66	WFU at Shoreham with parts, including wings, used in rebuild of G-AVHM. Canx. (Redundant fuselage stored 1/99 at Shoreham)
G-ATRM	Reims Cessna F.150F (Wichita c/n 63454)	0053	(G-ATNJ)	4. 3.66	
G-ATRN	Reims Cessna F.150F (Wichita c/n 63455)	0054	(G-ATMN)	4. 3.66	To G-SCAT 9/86. Canx.
G-ATRO	PA-28-140 Cherokee	28-21871		4. 3.66	
G-ATRP	PA-28-140 Cherokee	28-21885		4. 3.66	Damaged on landing at Boughton Monchelsea on 16.10.81. CofA expired 20.9.84. Canx as WFU 10.11.86. (Fuselage stored 1/98 Southend)
G-ATRR	PA-28-140 Cherokee	28-21892		4. 3.66	
G-ATRS	PA-28-140 Cherokee	28-21913		4. 3.66	DBR at Squires Gate on 28.7.70. Canx 15.6.81.
G-ATRT	PA-28-140 Cherokee	28-21920		4. 3.66	Crashed at Clacton on 15.8.69. Canx as WFU 14.10.69.
G-ATRU	PA-28-180 Cherokee C	28-3219		4. 3.66	Substationally damaged when struck a fence on approach to Old Warden on 11.8.86. Canx as WFU 25.10.90.

Regn	Type	c/n	Previous identity	Regn date	Fate or immediate subsequent identity (if known)
G-ATRV	Aviation Traders ATL.98 Carvair (Conv. Douglas C-54E-5-DO)	27311/15	OD-ADW N88886/44-9085	7. 3.66	To F-BOSU 5/67. Canx 7.5.67.
G-ATRW	PA-32-260 Cherokee Six	32-360	N11C	8. 3.66	
G-ATRX	PA-32-260 Cherokee Six	32-390		8. 3.66	
G-ATRY	Alon A-2 Aircoupe	A-140		11. 3.66	Crashed on take-off from Sandown, IoW on 10.7.79. Remains scrapped in 1981. Canx by CAA 14.7.86.
G-ATRZ	DH.114 Heron 2	14069	VT-DHG	7. 7.66	To N16721 9/66. Canx 27.7.66.
G-ATSA	DH.114 Heron 2	14073	VT-DHK	7. 7.66	To N16722 9/66. Canx.
G-ATSB	PA-E23-250 Aztec C	27-3405	G-ATZJ N6179Y	18.11.76	To EI-BML 3/82. Canx 4.3.82.
G-ATSC	Westland Wessex 60 Srs.1	WA/544	HC-ASD G-ATSC/PH-THZ/G-ATSC	11. 3.66	Ditched 3 miles west of BP platform WC in Sole Field in the North Sea on 8.3.76. Canx.
G-ATSD	Beagle B.206S Srs.2	C.10/B.027		11. 3.66	To EC-BES 8/66. Canx 16.5.66.
G-ATSE	PA-30-160 Twin Comanche B	30-983	N7896Y	11. 3.66	Crashed into the River Tay, off Dundee on 5.2.78. Canx.
G-ATSF	Agusta-Bell 47D-1	031	N6064C Pakistan/I-FINT	11. 3.66	Crashed/DBF near Brigg, Lincs on 31.5.66. Canx.
G-ATSG	Not allocated.				
G-ATSH	Bell 47D-1	183	N237B	11. 3.66	Crashed/DBF near Cranbrook, Kent on 11.6.71. Canx.
G-ATSI	Bolkow Bo.208C-1 Junior	605	D-EFNU	14. 3.66	
G-ATSJ	Brantly 305	1024		14. 3.66	Crashed at Sutton Bank on 24.6.77. Canx as destroyed 30.9.81.
G-ATSK	Druine D.62B Condor	RAE/613		14. 3.66	Fatal crash on northern boundary of Fairoaks on 20.7.73. Canx 30.7.73.
G-ATSL	Reims Cessna F.172G	0260		16. 3.66	
G-ATSM	Cessna 337A Super Skymaster (Originally regd with c/n 337-0343 - probably a clerical error)	337A-0434	N5334S	23. 3.66	
G-ATSN	HS.125 Srs.1A/522	25093		28. 3.66	To N77D 5/66. Canx 27.5.66.
G-ATSO	HS.125 Srs.1A/522	25095		28. 3.66	To N125Y 6/66. Canx 10.6.66.
G-ATSP	HS.125 Srs.1A/522	25097		28. 3.66	To LN-NPE 4/68. Canx 25.11.67.
G-ATSR	Beechcraft M35 Bonanza	D-6236	EI-ALL	29. 3.66	
G-ATSS	Reims Cessna F.150F	0017		4. 4.66	Crashed at Selkirk Racecourse on 1.8.69. Canx as WFU 12.2.73.
G-ATST	Socata MS.893A Rallye Commodore 180	10618		4. 4.66	CofA expired 17.11.84. Canx as WFU on 2.7.85.
G-ATSU	SAN Jodel D.140B Mousquetaire II	80	F-BKSA	4. 4.66	To G-OBAN 2/92. Canx.
G-ATSV	Cessna 310C	35795	9L-LAE ZS-CKA/VP-YSB/N6695B	4. 4.66	Crashed in France on 19.10.72. Canx as WFU 8.2.73.
G-ATSW	Brookland Mosquito Mk.I Gyroplane	1		5. 4.66	Canx as WFU 15.6.67.
G-ATSX	Bolkow Bo.208C-1 Junior	608	D-EJUC(2)	7. 4.66	
G-ATSY	Wassmer WA.41 Super Baladou IV	117		12. 4.66	
G-ATSZ	PA-30-160 Twin Comanche B	30-1002	EI-BPS (EI-BBS)/G-ATSZ/(AN-...)/G-ATSZ/N7912Y	13. 4.66	
G-ATTA	Vickers 745D Viscount	124	N7426	19. 4.66	WFU at Yeadon in 1/70. Broken up in 11/71. Canx as WFU 24.4.70.
G-ATTB	Wallis WA-116/F Gyroplane (Rebuild of WA-116 G-ARZC(2) c/n B.205)	214		19. 4.66	Permit expired 18.5.98. (Stored 2/99 Reymerston Hall)
G-ATTC	Armstrong-Whitworth 650 Argosy Srs.222	AW.6805		19. 4.66	To CF-TAZ 4/70. Canx 30.4.70.
G-ATTD	Cessna 182J Skylane	182-57229	N3129F	19. 4.66	
G-ATTE	PA-28-140 Cherokee	28-21935		25. 4.66	Suffered fuel starvation and crashed while making a forced-landing beside the A10 road south of Royston, Herts., on 11.5.67. Canx.
G-ATTF	PA-28-140 Cherokee	28-21939		25. 4.66	
G-ATTG	PA-28-140 Cherokee	28-21943		25. 4.66	(Stored 2/99 Shipdham)
G-ATTH	PA-28-140 Cherokee	28-21947		25. 4.66	To (A6-...)/AP-AWR /71. Canx 20.6.70.
G-ATTI	PA-28-140 Cherokee	28-21951		24. 4.66	
G-ATTJ	PA-28-140 Cherokee	28-21955		25. 4.66	To (A6-...)/AP-AWS /71. Canx 20.6.70.
G-ATTK	PA-28-140 Cherokee	28-21959		25. 4.66	(Active 7/96)
G-ATTL	Beagle B.206 Srs.2	B.028		25. 4.66	To LV-DMR 11/67. Canx 10.10.67.
G-ATTM	CEA Jodel DR.250/160 Quadriplace	65		26. 4.66	
G-ATTN	Piccard HAFB (62,000 cu ft)	15 & 1352		27. 4.66	Canx as WFU 5.12.77. (Envelope/basket stored 6/94 South Kensington, London)
G-ATTO	Agusta-Bell 47J-2 Ranger	2012	OY-HAW G-ATTO/HB-XAR	27. 4.66	Ditched in sea off Fernando Po Island, in the Gulf of Guinea on 2.11.68. Canx as WFU 21.4.69.
G-ATTP	BAC One-Eleven Srs.207AJ	039	9J-RCH 7Q-YKE/9J-RCH/G-ATTP/VP-YXA	28. 4.66	To CC-CYM 11/91. Canx 19.11.91.
G-ATTR	Bolkow Bo.208C-1 Junior	612	D-EHEH(2)	29. 4.66	
G-ATTS(1)	DHC.1 Chipmunk 22 (Fuselage no. DHB/f/678)	C1/0779	WP906	. 4.66	NTU - Remained with RAF as WP906. Canx.
G-ATTS(2)	DHC.1 Turbo Chipmunk 21 (Fuselage no. DHB/f/664)(Rover TP-90)	C1/0765	7650M WP895	29. 4.66	To N2247 10/69. Canx 20.10.69.
G-ATTT	Not allocated.				
G-ATTU	PA-28-140 Cherokee	28-21987		2. 5.66	Damaged in collision with AA-5A G-OCPL at Elstree on 27.6.92. Canx as WFU 4.9.92. (To Hotel for display in foyer .93 Geneva, Switzerland)
G-ATTV	PA-28-140 Cherokee	28-21991		2. 5.66	
G-ATTW	PA-28-140 Cherokee	28-21983		2. 5.66	Crashed on approach at Bishops Lydeard, near Taunton on 24.1.71. Canx 9.2.82.
G-ATTX	PA-28-180 Cherokee C	28-3390	PH-VDP (G-ATTX)/N11C	2. 5.66	Canx by CAA 3.12.92.
G-ATTY	PA-32-260 Cherokee Six	32-460	N11C	2. 5.66	To G-RAYE 5/96. Canx.
G-ATTZ	PA-25-235 Pawnee B	25-3746		2. 5.66	To 5Y-TAD 6/75. Canx 18.6.75.

Regn	Type	c/n	Previous identity	Regn date	Fate or immediate subsequent identity (if known)
G-ATUA	PA-25-235 Pawnee B	25-3738		2. 5.66	WFU on 31.8.75. Canx 9.2.82.
G-ATUB	PA-28-140 Cherokee	28-21971		2. 5.66	
G-ATUC	PA-28-140 Cherokee	28-21975		2. 5.66	Crashed into a hill near Ratlinghope, Salop on 2.4.88. Canx as WFU 28.3.95.
G-ATUD	PA-28-140 Cherokee	28-21979		2. 5.66	
G-ATUE	Vickers 812 Viscount	357	N244V	3. 5.66	WFU & stored in 5/72. Broken up in 1/74 at East Midlands Airport. Nose to 1122 Marmion (Tamworth) ATC Sqdn in 3/78. Canx as destroyed 17.1.78.
G-ATUF	Reims Cessna F.150F (Wichita c/n 63229)	0040		4. 5.66	
G-ATUG	Rollason-Druine D.62B Condor	RAE/614		4. 5.66	
G-ATUH	Tipsy T.66 Nipper 1	6	OO-NIF	4. 5.66	
G-ATUI	Bolkow Bo.208C-1 Junior	611	D-EHEF	4. 5.66	
G-ATUJ	Beagle B.206S Srs.2	B.029	ZS-EMI 9J-ABB/ZS-EMI/G-ATUJ	5. 5.66	To N61JH 5/80. Canx 29.5.80.
G-ATUK	Beagle B.206S Srs.2	B.032		5. 5.66	To ST-ADA 11/66. Canx 29.11.66.
G-ATUL	PA-28-180 Cherokee C	28-3033	N9007J	6. 5.66	
G-ATUM	Beechcraft D.18S	A-850	D-IANA N20S	10. 5.66	To N15750 3/69. Canx.
G-ATUN	Reims Cessna F.172G	0285		12. 5.66	Damaged when it overran into an embankment at North Denes on 7.4.69. Canx as WFU 30.5.69.
G-ATUO	PA-30-160 Twin Comanche	30-1063	N7965Y	12. 5.66	Fatal crash into the Massif du Sancy, near Super Bresse, 20 miles from Issoire, France on 22.3.68. Canx.
G-ATUP	Victa Airtourer 115	152	(ZK-CMF)	13. 5.66	Crashed into sea off St.Catherines Down, Isle of Wight on 24.6.68. Canx.
G-ATUR	Brantly 305 (Originally regd as c/n 1025 (became N2217U))	1029	N12H	13. 5.66	CofA expired 6.11.70. Canx 21.3.73. To TF-DEV 2/75.
G-ATUS	Brantly 305 (Originally regd as c/n 1026 (became N2218U))	1030		13. 5.66	Damaged in landing at Barton on 14.3.70. Canx as destroyed 25.5.70.
G-ATUT	Cessna 182J	182-57231	N3131F	17. 5.66	DBR in forced-landing at Beaumont Manor, Hoddesdon, Herts on 19.9.67. Remains sold to Roger Aviation at Cranfield.
G-ATUU	HS.125 Srs.1A/522	25102		17. 5.66	To N756 in 8/66. Canx 24.8.66.
G-ATUV	HS.125 Srs.1A/522	25103		17. 5.66	To N533 in 9/66. Canx 2.9.66.
G-ATUW	HS.125 Srs.1A/522	25104		17. 5.66	To N257H in 8/66. Canx 1.9.66.
G-ATUX	HS.125 Srs.1A/522	25107		17. 5.66	To N7125J in 9/66. Canx.
G-ATUY	HS.125 Srs.1A/522	25108		17. 5.66	To N1025C in 9/66. Canx 14.9.66.
G-ATUZ	HS.125 Srs.1A/522	25109		17. 5.66	To N201H in 9/66. Canx 26.9.66.
G-ATVA	PA-30-160 Twin Comanche B	30-1001	N7126G	18. 5.66	Restored as N7126G in 12/68. Canx.
G-ATVB	Bolkow Bo.208C-1 Junior	614	D-EHEM(2)	18. 5.66	Fatal crash into high ground at Rockshill, near Hambleton on 6.1.72. Canx.
G-ATVC	PA-32-260 Cherokee Six	32-99	N3269W	20. 5.66	To EI-BDV 1/78. Canx 8.12.77.
G-ATVD	Not allocated.				
G-ATVE	Vickers 812 Viscount	366	N254V	25. 5.66	WFU at Southend on 26.10.69. Broken up in 6/72. Canx as WFU 22.11.72.
G-ATVF	DHC.1 Chipmunk 22 (Lyc AEIO-360) (Fuselage no. DHB/f/147)	C1/0265	WD327	25. 5.66	
G-ATVG	Hiller 360 UH-12E	2191	EP-HAL G-ATVG/5N-ABX/VP-YVP/5N-ABX	26. 5.66	DBF at Cambridge on 13.7.74. Canx 3.2.82.
G-ATVH	BAC One-Eleven Srs.207AJ	BAC.040	9J-RCI G-ATVH/9J-RCI/VP-YXB	26. 5.66	To CC-CYL 12/91. Canx 4.12.91.
G-ATVI	SIPA 903	89	F-BGHN	27. 5.66	CofA expired 24.4.74 & WFU at Elstree. Canx as WFU 6.10.81.
G-ATVJ	PA-28-140 Cherokee	28-21999		27. 5.66	To PH-VRH 9/66. Canx.
G-ATVK	PA-28-140 Cherokee	28-22006		27. 5.66	(On rebuild 1/98 Southend)
G-ATVL	PA-28-140 Cherokee	28-22013		27. 5.66	
G-ATVM	Hiller 360 UH-12E	2123	EP-HAI G-ATVM/5N-AGH/VP-YXS/VR-BBR	27. 5.66	Wrecked in autorotative descent upon rocky terrain 50 miles north of Agadir, Morocco on 16.7.68. Canx as destroyed.
G-ATVN	Hiller 360 UH-12E	2133	5N-AGC VR-BBV	27. 5.66	Fatal crash at Spring Lane, Balderton, near Newark on 28.2.72. Canx 20.8.81.
G-ATVO	PA-28-140 Cherokee	28-22020		27. 5.66	
G-ATVP	Vickers FB.5 Gunbus Replica	VAFA-01 & FB.5		31. 5.66	Canx as WFU 27.2.69. (On display Hendon, painted in RFC c/s 2345)
G-ATVR	Vickers 812 Viscount	365	N253V	1. 6.66	WFU at Stansted on 15.6.70. To Stansted Fire School. Canx as WFU 14.3.77.
G-ATVS	PA-28-180 Cherokee C	28-3041	N9014J	1. 6.66	
G-ATVT	Beagle 206S Srs.2	C.14/B.035		9. 6.66	To EC-BFR 9/66. Canx 20.9.66.
G-ATVU	BAC One-Eleven Srs.401AK	074	N5032	2. 6.66	Restored as N5032 in 6/66. Canx.
G-ATVV	Reims Cessna F.172G	0221	SE-ESK	6. 6.66	Ran out of fuel and force-landed short of Woolsington on 17.5.74. Canx 31.5.74.
G-ATVW	Rollason-Druine D.62B Condor	RAE/615		7. 6.66	
G-ATVX	Bolkow Bo.208C-1 Junior	615	D-EHER(2)	9. 6.66	
G-ATVY	Grumman G.164 Agcat	287	6Y-JDP N725Y/N11E	9. 6.66	To N8285/D-FADA 11/68. Canx.
G-ATVZ	Grumman G.164 Agcat	288	6Y-JDR N726Y	9. 6.66	To N8286/D-FACU 11/68. Canx.
G-ATWA	SAN Jodel DR.1050 Ambassadeur	296	F-BKHA	10. 6.66	
G-ATWB	SAN Jodel D.117	423	F-BHNH	10. 6.66	Stalled and crashed while landing at Goodwood on 10.3.68.
G-ATWC	Not allocated.				
G-ATWD	SIPA 903	74	F-BGBY	10. 6.66	Crashed into the estuary of the River Humber, near Cleethorpes after stalling at low altitude on 20.8.67. Canx.

Regn	Type	c/n	Previous identity	Regn date	Fate or immediate subsequent identity (if known)
G-ATWE	Morane-Saulnier MS.892A Rallye Commodore 150	10634		13. 6.66	Badly damaged in forced landing west of Taunton on 29.3.81. (For rebuild .89 Newport, Gwent area) Canx by CAA 17.2.99.
G-ATWF	PA-22-150 Tri-Pacer	22-5216	6Y-JBJ VP-JBJ	14. 6.66	DBR when struck wall at Little Dinham, Cornwall on 3.7.71. Canx.
G-ATWG	PA-30-160 Twin Comanche B	30-1094	N7990Y	15. 6.66	To N114RS 9/83. Canx 22.9.83.
G-ATWH	HS.125 Srs.1B/R522 (Originally regd as Srs.1B/522, re-designated after fitting of the long range ventral fuel tank)	25094	HZ-B01 G-ATWH	15. 6.66	To G-YUGO 8/88. Canx.
G-ATWI	DH.82A Tiger Moth	83741	F-BGZY (F-OAPT)/T7400	15. 6.66	NTU - Not Imported. Remained as F-BGZY. Canx 14.3.73.
G-ATWJ	Reims Cessna F.172F	0095	EI-ANS	21. 6.66	
G-ATWK	Boeing-Stearman A75N1 (PT-17) Kaydet	75-1697	N55322 41-8138	21. 6.66	NTU - Not Imported. Canx 8.11.67.
G-ATWL	Wassmer-Jodel D.120 Paris Nice	209	F-OBUF	22. 6.66	Destroyed in fatal crash at Niddery Castle, near Edinburgh on 16.5.79. Canx as destroyed 29.2.84.
G-ATWM	Montgolfier HAFB Replica	B.100		23. 6.66	Damaged at Dunstable on 28.8.66. Canx as WFU 3.4.69.
G-ATWN	Aero Commander 680F	943-14	N390GA N6116X	23. 6.66	To ZS-KAU 4/77. Canx 25.4.77.
G-ATWO	PA-28-180 Cherokee C	28-3049	N9021J	28. 6.66	To G-KERY 10/83. Canx.
G-ATWP	Alon A-2 Aircoupe	A.188		28. 6.66	To G-HARY 3/93. Canx.
G-ATWR	PA-30-160 Twin Comanche B	30-1134	N8025Y	30. 6.66	Damaged in crash at Crosland Moor on 14.9.93. (Stored 8/94) Canx as TWFU 18.4.95.
G-ATWS	Phoenix Luton LA-4A Minor	PAL/1195 & PFA/818		30. 6.66	WFU at Kirklangley on 26.3.69. Canx 8.2.82. (On rebuild 4/97)
G-ATWT	Napier-Bensen Gyrocopter	21102	G-29-3	5. 7.66	WFU in 10/70. Canx as WFU 31.1.77.
G-ATWU	BN-2A Mk.III Trislander (Originally built as BN-2 Islander; Converted to Trislander in 1970)	2		6. 7.66	WFU at Bembridge, IoW on 10.10.68. To Static Test Rig. Canx as WFU 23.11.70.
G-ATWV	Boeing 707-336C (Line No. 645)	19498		6. 7.66	To 9G-ACX 2/82. Canx 17.2.82.
G-ATWW	Omnipol L-13 Blanik	173328		6. 7.66	To Ireland as IGA.110 in 8/66. Canx 11.8.66.
G-ATWX	Omnipol L-13 Blanik	173329		6. 7.66	To BGA.1345 in 9/66. Canx.
G-ATWY	Omnipol L-13 Blanik	173340		6. 7.66	To BGA.1384 in 4/67. Canx 17.11.69.
G-ATWZ	GEMS MS.892A Rallye Commodore 150	10636		7. 7.66	Canx as WFU 10.11.89.
G-ATXA	PA-22-150 Tri-Pacer (PA-20 Super Pacer standard)	22-3730	N4403A	8. 7.66	
G-ATXB	PA-22-150 Tri-Pacer	22-5616	N8125D	8. 7.66	DBR when nosewheel collapsed near Crediton, Devon on 26.8.74. Canx as WFU 20.1.75. Parts used in rebuilt of G-ARHN.
G-ATXC	Aeronca 7AC Champion	7AC-1304	N82661 NC82661	8. 7.66	Stalled and crashed while taking-off at Biggin Hill on 24.1.67. Canx 3.4.67. Wings fitted to Volmer VJ-22 G-BAHP by 11/72.
G-ATXD	PA-30-160 Twin Comanche B	30-1166	N8053Y	12. 7.66	
G-ATXE	HS.125 Srs.1A/522	25101	G-5-11	12. 7.66	To N142B 7/66. Canx 26.7.66.
G-ATXF	Gardan GY-80-150 Horizon	40	F-BLOX	14. 7.66	Ditched in sea 2 miles north of Alderney on 7.6.97. Canx as destroyed 29.7.97.
G-ATXG	PA-E23-250 Aztec C	27-3345	N6133Y	14. 7.66	Crashed at Peters Green, near Luton on 9.2.77 on landing. Canx.
G-ATXH	Handley Page 137 Jetstream 200 (Production No. 01) (Originally regd as Srs.1 - converted to Srs.200 in 1/70)	198		15. 7.66	WFU in 2/70 at Filton. Broken up in 10/72.
G-ATXI	Handley Page 137 Jetstream 3M (Production No. 02) (Originally regd as Srs.1 - converted to Srs.3 in 5/69)	199		15. 7.66	Broken up at Radlett in 12/70. Canx as WFU 17.1.74.
G-ATXJ	Handley Page 137 Jetstream 300 (Production No. 03) (Originally regd as Srs.1)	200		15. 7.66	WFU at Luton in 3/70. Canx 11.4.72. Sold as spares to USA in 5/73.
G-ATXK	Handley Page 137 Jetstream 1 (Production No. 04)	201		15. 7.66	To N2958F 6/76. Canx 5.5.70.
G-ATXL	Avro 504K Replica	HAC.1		19. 7.66	To N2939 in 8/71. Canx 6.8.71.
G-ATXM	PA-28-180 Cherokee C	28-2759	N8809J	19. 7.66	
G-ATXN	Mitchell-Procter Kittiwake 1	1 & PFA/1306		19. 7.66	
G-ATXO	SIPA 903	41	F-BGAP	19. 7.66	
G-ATXP	PA-18A-150 Super Cub	18-7860	5B-CAE	21. 7.66	To (ZS-...)/VP-WAU. Canx 23.11.66.
G-ATXR	Abingdon Free Balloon HAFB	A.F.B.1		22. 7.66	Permit expired 1.9.76 & WFU. Canx by CAA 14.7.86.
G-ATXS	Douglas DC-3A-228F Dakota	4103	PP-ASJ PT-ASJ/PP-PCJ/NC33612	26. 7.66	NTU - Not Imported. Canx 27.8.68. Stored at Ft.Lauderdale, FL, USA for spares.
G-ATXT	Douglas R4D-1 Dakota	4306	PP-ASP PP-ANC/NC95481/Bu.4699	26. 7.66	NTU - Not Imported. To N950FA 3/68. Canx.
G-ATXU	Douglas C-47A-70-DL Dakota	19176	PP-ASR PT-BEJ/PP-YPP/NC54325/42-100713	26. 7.66	NTU - Not Imported. To CP-820 in 8/67. Canx 27.8.68.
G-ATXV	Curtiss C-46A Commando	430	PP-SLK PP-ITH/43-47360	26. 7.66	NTU - Not Imported. To CP-826. Canx 27.8.68.
G-ATXW	McCandless M.4 Gyrocopter (Originally regd as M.2)	M4/2		27. 7.66	WFU on 5.10.71. Canx 2.6.80.
G-ATXX	McCandless M.4 Gyrocopter	M4/3		27. 7.66	Canx as WFU 9.9.70. (On display 6/97 Cultra Manor, Holywood)
G-ATXY	McCandless M.4/T.1 Gyrocopter (Re-designated from M.4 to M.4/T.1 on 16.8.68)	M4/4		27. 7.66	WFU on 2.5.72. Canx 3.7.80.
G-ATXZ	Bolkow Bo.208C-1 Junior	624	D-ELNE(2)	28. 7.66	
G-ATYA	PA-25-235 Pawnee	25-2579	5B-CAA(3) N6885Z	29. 7.66	To SE-IUR 1/86. Canx 6.1.86.
G-ATYB	Brantly 305	1035	N12H	29. 7.66	To EI-ARU 9/67. Canx 17.8.67.
G-ATYC	Beagle B.206 Srs.1	B.039		1. 8.66	CofA expired 14.6.73 & WFU at Yeadon. Canx 20.9.73.
G-ATYD	Beagle B.206 Srs.2	B.040		1. 8.66	To N81CA 1/73. Canx 4.1.73.

Regn	Type	c/n	Previous identity	Regn date	Fate or immediate subsequent identity (if known)
G-ATYE	Beagle B.206 Srs.1	B.041		1. 8.66	To N38JH 2/78. Canx 17.2.78.
G-ATYF	PA-30-160 Twin Comanche B	30-1205	N8089Y	2. 8.66	To N47KB 5/76. Canx 4.5.76.
G-ATYG	Campbell-Bensen B.8MG Gyrocopter	CA/304		3. 8.66	To D-HTYG 12/66. Canx.
G-ATYH	HS.125 Srs.3A	25111		10. 8.66	To N1041B 10/66. Canx 6.10.66.
G-ATYI	HS.125 Srs.3A	25112		10. 8.66	To N2525 1/67. Canx 15.2.67.
G-ATYJ	HS.125 Srs.3A	25114		10. 8.66	To N425K 10/66. Canx 20.10.66.
G-ATYK	HS.125 Srs.3A	25115		10. 8.66	To N229P 10/66. Canx 31.10.66.
G-ATYL	HS.125 Srs.3A	25118		10. 8.66	To N743UT 11/66. Canx 8.11.66.
G-ATYM	Reims Cessna F.150G	0074		15. 8.66	
G-ATYN	Reims Cessna F.150G	0076		15. 8.66	(Badly damaged on take-off from Stewton on 30.6.95)
G-ATYO	Taylor JT.2 Titch	JFT.1		15. 8.66	Fatal crash at Rochford, Essex shortly after take-off from Southend on 16.5.67. Canx.
G-ATYP	Bolkow Bo.208C-1 Junior	617	D-EHUW(2)	16. 8.66	To OY-POK 7/76. Canx 28.7.76.
G-ATYR	PA-30-160 Twin Comanche B	30-1183	N8069Y	16. 8.66	Crashed into Saulmore Bay, opposite Solmore Farm, near Oban Bay on 17.10.74. Canx as destroyed 31.10.74.
G-ATYS	PA-28-180 Cherokee C	28-3296	N9226J	19. 8.66	
G-ATYT(1)	Socata MS.892A Rallye Commodore 150	10656		. 8.66	NTU - Not Imported. To F-OCIR in 1967. Canx.
G-ATYT(2)	Socata MS.893A Rallye Commodore 150	10637		22. 8.66	Crashed into the English Channel and sank 2 miles southwest of Lessay, France on 21.5.70. Canx.
G-ATYU	Sikorsky S-61D-2 Sea King	61-393		23. 8.66	To Royal Navy as XV370 in 10/66. Canx.
G-ATYV	Bell 47G-4	177	9L-LAJ G-ATYV/F-BDRU	25. 8.66	To I-VFEE. Canx.
G-ATYW	Beagle B.206 Srs.1	B.038		26. 8.66	To N26857 in 9/81. Canx 22.9.81.
G-ATYX	Beagle B.206S Srs.2	C.18/B.043		26. 8.66	To EC-BJF 2/67. Canx 6.2.67.
G-ATYY	Morane-Saulnier MS.893A Rallye Commodore 180	10674		2. 9.66	NTU - Not Imported. To F-BOTE 3/67. Canx.
G-ATYZ	Morane-Saulnier MS.880B Rallye Club	848		2. 9.66	Forced landed at Netherthorpe on 14.7.74 and subsequently damaged in gales in 1/76. Canx by CAA 6.12.84.
G-ATZA	Bolkow Bo.208C-1 Junior	629	D-ENFA(2)	2. 9.66	Crashed and burnt-out at Clip Gate Farm on 25.7.98. Canx as destroyed 19.8.98.
G-ATZB	Hiller 360 UH-12B	497	102 R.Thailand AF	12. 9.66	Canx 21.1.80. To N38763 in 1/83.
G-ATZC	Boeing 707-365C (Line No. 556)	19416	PH-TRW N737AL/(G-ATZC)	14. 9.66	To C-GFLG 11/81. Canx 27.11.81.
G-ATZD	Boeing 707-365C (Line No. 654)	19590	VR-BCP (OD-APA)/VR-BCP/G-ATZD	14. 9.66	Canx in 5/83 as sold to Leichtenstein. To 5A-DLV 6/85.
G-ATZE	HS.125 Srs.1A/522	25110	G-5-11	15. 9.66	To N3125B 9/66. Canx 11.1.67.
G-ATZF	Douglas C-47A-5-DK Dakota	12324	OE-LBC SE-CFM/LN-NAB/KG32//42-92515	16. 9.66	Canx 6.10.66 on sale to Hong Kong. To VR-ABD(2) 10/66.
G-ATZG	Abingdon Free Balloon HAFB	A.F.B.2		19. 9.66	WFU without having received a permit. Canx by CAA 17.7.86.
G-ATZH	Canadair CL-44D4-2	21	N452T (G-ATZH)/N452T/CF-NNE-X	20. 9.66	Crashed into the sea off Hong Kong on 2.9.77. Canx.
G-ATZI	Canadair CL-44D4-2	25	N455T (G-ATZI)/N455T	20. 9.66	To HB-IEN 3/74. Canx 22.3.74.
G-ATZJ	PA-E23-250 Aztec C	27-3405	N6179Y	20. 9.66	To G-ATSB 11/76. Canx.
G-ATZK	PA-28-180 Cherokee C	28-3128	D-EFUN N9090J	21. 9.66	
G-ATZL	CEA Jodel DR.250/160 Quadriplace	87		22. 9.66	To G-BCGG(2) 11/81. Canx.
G-ATZM	Piper J3C-90 Cub (Frame No. 21310)	20868	N2092M NC2092M	26. 9.66	
G-ATZN	HS.125 Srs.3B	25116	G-5-11	28. 9.66	Canx 16.12.74 on sale to Zambia. To N93TC in 2/75.
G-ATZO	Beagle B.206C Srs.1	B.044	EI-APO G-ATZO	28. 9.66	Canx on sale to USA 11.12.81 (no regn issued). (Stored 7/91 Coldwater, Michigan, USA)
G-ATZP	Beagle B.206S Srs.2	B.046	9J-ABB G-ATZP/G-35-34	28. 9.66	To 9J-AAM 7/69. Canx 28.7.69.
G-ATZR	Beagle B.206 Srs.2	B.047		28. 9.66	To VH-UNL 12/67. Canx 21.12.68.
G-ATZS	Wassmer WA.41 Super Baladou IV	128		30. 9.66	
G-ATZT	Air & Space 18A Gyroplane	18-36	N6127S	30. 9.66	NTU - Not Imported. Canx 12.3.68.
G-ATZU	PA-30-160 Twin Comanche B	30-1271	N8158Y	5.10.66	Badly damaged on landing at Brussels, Belgium on 16.10.84. Canx as destroyed 10.10.86.
G-ATZV	PA-30-160 Twin Comanche B	30-1278	N8165Y	5.10.66	To N54483 in 9/84. Canx 7.9.84.
G-ATZW	English Electric Canberra B.2	71018	WD937	5.10.66	WFU at Samlesbury. CofA expired 16.12.67. Scrapped. Canx as WFU 16.12.68.
G-ATZX	Bell 47G-2	1469	HB-XAT	5.10.66	Crashed at Redhill on 27.2.75. Canx as WFU 27.6.75.
G-ATZY	Reims Cessna F.150G	0135		14.10.66	
G-ATZZ	Reims Cessna F.150G	0136		14.10.66	To G-DENB 12/95. Canx.
G-AUAA	The series from G-AUAA to G-AUTU was allocated to Australia from 6/21 until 1928.				
G-AUTO	Cessna 441 Conquest II	441-0078	(N88842)	8. 1.79	To G-HOSP 10/89. Canx.
G-AVAA	Reims Cessna F.150G	0164		14.10.66	Canx by CAA 16.4.96.
G-AVAB	Reims Cessna F.150G	0165		14.10.66	Collided in mid-air with Cessna F.150H G-AVSS and crashed about 5 miles N of Scone, nr Guildtown, Perth on 22.11.75.
G-AVAC	Reims Cessna F.150G	0192		14.10.66	Forced landing into a hillside near Scone, Perth on 11.10.77. Canx as WFU 13.12.77.
G-AVAD	HS.125 Srs.3A	25119	G-5-11	17.10.66	To N231H 11/66. Canx 21.11.66.
G-AVAE	HS.125 Srs.3A	25121		17.10.66	To N795J 2/67. Canx 16.3.67.
G-AVAF	HS.125 Srs.3A	25122		17.10.66	To N12225 3/67. Canx 25.5.67.
G-AVAG	HS.125 Srs.3A	25123		17.10.66	To N700M 2/67. Canx 6.3.67.
G-AVAH	HS.125 Srs.3A	25124		17.10.66	To N125J 4/67. Canx 8.5.67.

Regn	Type	c/n	Previous identity	Regn date	Fate or immediate subsequent identity (if known)
G-AVAI	HS.125 Srs.F3B/RA (Originally regd as Srs.3B)	25125	LN-NPA(2) G-AVAI	17.10.66	To F-GFMP 11/85. Canx 29.10.85.
G-AVAJ	Hiller 360 UH-12B	726	116 R.Thailand AF	18.10.66	Canx as TWFU 11.8.87. To N5025J.
G-AVAK	Socata MS.893A Rallye Commodore 180	10664	FI-AWJ G-AVAK	19.10.66	DBR in forced landing in a field at Buttergask Farm, Coupar Angus on 6.3.85. Canx by CAA 12.9.86.
G-AVAL	Beagle B.206 Srs.2	B.048		26.10.66	Crashed at St.Jean de Suaves, near Tours, France on 6.3.71. Canx.
G-AVAM	Beagle B.206 Srs.2	B.049		26.10.66	Fatal crash when engine failed on take-off and crashed 2 miles S of Jersey on 6.8.70. Canx.
G-AVAN	Beagle B.206 Srs.2	B.050		26.10.66	To VH-FDA 6/67. Canx 12.12.67.
G-AVAO	PA-30-160 Twin Comanche	30-1132	N8023Y	26.10.66	To N29951 6/82. Canx 24.4.81.
G-AVAP	Reims Cessna F.150G	0107		27.10.66	To G-DENC 12/95. Canx.
G-AVAR	Reims Cessna F.150G	0122		27.10.66	
G-AVAS	Reims Cessna F.172H	0370		27.10.66	Crashed at Halfpenny Green on 19.12.82. Canx by CAA 15.8.85.
G-AVAT	Van den Bemden Free Balloon (Gas)	81	OO-BDO	31.10.66	Exploded and burnt out after landing at Halland, Sussex on 20.7.68. Canx.
G-AVAU	PA-30-160 Twin Comanche B	30-1328	N8230Y	8.11.66	
G-AVAV	Vickers Supermarine 509 Spitfire Trainer IX	CBAF/7269	159 Irish Air Corps/G-15-172/MJ772	8.11.66	To N8R 5/75. Canx 18.5.75.
G-AVAW	Rollason-Druine D.62C Condor (Originally regd as a D.62B)	RAE/617		10.11.66	
G-AVAX	PA-28-180 Cherokee C	28-3798		11.11.66	
G-AVAY(1)	PA-28-180 Cherokee C	28-3812		.11.66	NTU - Canx.
G-AVAY(2)	PA-28-180 Cherokee C	28-3793		11.11.66	To Dodson Aviation Scrapyard, Ottawa, KS, USA. To N54592 7/84. Canx 11.7.84.
G-AVAZ(1)	PA-28-180 Cherokee C	28-3819		.11.66	NTU - To N9635J. Canx.
G-AVAZ(2)	PA-28-180 Cherokee C	28-3794		11.11.66	To G-OIBO 1/87. Canx.
G-AVBA(1)	PA-28-180 Cherokee C	28-3833		.11.66	NTU - Canx.
G-AVBA(2)	PA-28-180 Cherokee C	28-3795		11.11.66	WFU at Hamble on 21.12.83. Sold to USA. To Dodson Aviation Scrapyard, Ottawa, KS, USA.
G-AVBB(1)	PA-28-180 Cherokee C	28-3854		.11.66	NTU - Canx.
G-AVBB(2)	PA-28-180 Cherokee C	28-3796		11.11.66	To Dodson Aviation Scrapyard, Ottawa, KS, USA. To N54590 7/84. Canx 11.7.84.
G-AVBC(1)	PA-28-180 Cherokee C	28-3868		.11.66	NTU - Canx.
G-AVBC(2)	PA-28-180 Cherokee C	28-3797		11.11.66	To Dodson Aviation Scrapyard, Ottawa, KS, USA. To N5459X 7/84. Canx 11.7.84.
G-AVBD(1)	PA-28-180 Cherokee C	28-3882		.11.66	NTU - Canx.
G-AVBD(2)	PA-28-180 Cherokee C	28-3799		11.11.66	Fatal crash after mid-air collision with PA-28 G-AVBI approximately ½ mile NE of Hamble Airport on 27.2.70. Canx.
G-AVBE(1)	PA-28-180 Cherokee C	28-3896		.11.66	NTU - Canx.
G-AVBE(2)	PA-28-180 Cherokee C	28-3800		11.11.66	To N5460N 7/84. Canx 11.7.84.
G-AVBF	Not allocated.				
G-AVBG(1)	PA-28-180 Cherokee C	28-3903		.11.66	NTU - Canx.
G-AVBG(2)	PA-28-180 Cherokee C	28-3801		11.11.66	
G-AVBH(1)	PA-28-180 Cherokee C	28-3910		.11.66	NTU - Canx.
G-AVBH(2)	PA-28-180 Cherokee C	28-3802		11.11.66	
G-AVBI(1)	PA-28-180 Cherokee C	28-3917		.11.66	NTU - Canx.
G-AVBI(2)	PA-28-180 Cherokee C	28-3803		11.11.66	Fatal crash after mid-air collision with PA-28 G-AVBD approximately ½ mile NE of Hamble Airport on 27.2.70. Canx.
G-AVBJ(1)	PA-28-180 Cherokee C	28-3924		.11.66	NTU - Canx.
G-AVBJ(2)	PA-28-180 Cherokee C	28-3806		11.11.66	Collided with PA-28 G-AXZC over Hamble on 30.4.81. Canx 18.3.83.
G-AVBK	Scheibe SF-25A Motor Falke	4544	D-KANO	11.11.66	Badly damaged by severe gales at Rattlesden, Suffolk on 2.1.76. Canx as WFU 15.1.81. Used for spares for G-BECF.
G-AVBL	PA-30-160 Twin Comanche B	30-1362	N8236Y	14.11.66	To G-COMB 9/84. Canx.
G-AVBM	PA-28-140 Cherokee	28-22527		14.11.66	Fatal crash at Home Farm on the Tetbury-Dursley road on 6.8.73 while outbound from Staverton. Canx 26.11.73.
G-AVBN	PA-28-140 Cherokee	28-22562		14.11.66	Fatal crash & DBF when it crashed at Ruxley Green, Sidcup, Kent on 30.8.70. Canx.
G-AVBO	Not allocated.				
G-AVBP	PA-28-140 Cherokee	28-22582		14.11.66	Badly damaged in forced landing at Godmanchester on 14.8.96. Scrapped. Canx as destroyed 6.1.97
G-AVBR	PA-28-180 Cherokee C	28-3931	N9679J	14.11.66	NTU - Canx 18.1.67 on sale to Switzerland. To F-BOSO 1/67.
G-AVBS	PA-28-180 Cherokee C	28-3938		14.11.66	
G-AVBT	PA-28-180 Cherokee C	28-3945		14.11.66	
G-AVBU	PA-32-260 Cherokee Six	32-733		14.11.66	Crashed on landing at Cork, Ireland on 28.2.81. Canx.
G-AVBV	PA-32-260 Cherokee Six	32-743		14.11.66	NTU - Not Imported. To 4X-ANG 1/67. Canx.
G-AVBW	BAC One-Eleven Srs.320L-AZ	BAC.107		15.11.66	To G-BKAU 4/82. Canx.
G-AVBX	BAC One-Eleven Srs.320L-AZ	BAC.109		15.11.66	To G-BKAV 4/82. Canx.
G-AVBY	BAC One-Eleven Srs.320L-AZ	BAC.113		15.11.66	To G-BKAW 4/82. Canx.
G-AVBZ	Reims Cessna F.172H	0387		18.11.66	
G-AVCA	Brantly B.2B (Originally regd as c/n 446)	466		18.11.66	Destroyed in landing accident at Strumpshaw Inn Field, near Norwich on 8.2.80. Canx by CAA 14.7.86.
G-AVCB	CEA Jodel DR.1051 Sicile	411	F-BLAK	18.11.66	Crashed at Whitecross Farm, near Wallingford on 9.10.77. Canx.
G-AVCC	Reims Cessna F.172H	0365		28.11.66	Badly damaged by severe gales at East Midlands on 2.1.76. Canx as destroyed 8.3.88.
G-AVCD	Reims Cessna F.172H	0385		28.11.66	To G-SACD 6/83. Canx.
G-AVCE	Reims Cessna F.172H	0389		28.11.66	Canx as destroyed 6.1.99.
G-AVCF	DH.114 Heron Srs.2E	14110	5Y-KVC VP-KVC	30.11.66	To N714R 10/68. Canx 12.7.67.

Regn	Type	c/n	Previous identity	Regn date	Fate or immediate subsequent identity (if known)
G-AVCG	Beagle B.206 Srs.2	B.051		30.11.66	To N206GB 1/76. Canx 7.1.76.
G-AVCH	Beagle B.206 Srs.2	B.052		30.11.66	To VH-FDB 7/67. Canx.
G-AVCI	Beagle B.206 Srs.2	B.053		30.11.66	To N85JH 5/76. Canx 19.5.76.
G-AVCJ	Beagle B.206 Srs.2	C.30/B.054		30.11.66	To N102JD 10/77. Canx 10.10.77.
G-AVCK	Avro 652A Anson 19 Srs.2	33749	TX157	30.11.66	Not converted, no CofA issued. Scrapped at Halfpenny Green late 1969. Canx by CAA 16.9.72.
G-AVCL	PA-24-260 Comanche B	24-4213	N8763P	2.12.66	NTU - Damaged near Gander on 21.1.67 on delivery. To OO-YET 9/68. Canx.
G-AVCM	PA-24-260 Comanche B	24-4520	N9054P	5.12.66	
G-AVCN	BN-2A-8 Islander (Originally regd as BN-2)	3		6.12.66	To F-OGHG 2/76. Canx 3.2.76.
G-AVCO	AIA Stampe SV-4C	1040	F-BBGN French AF	6.12.66	To VH-WEF 11/76. Canx 23.10.75.
G-AVCP	PA-30-160 Twin Comanche B	30-1197	N8082Y	9.12.66	To G-LUCY 11/81. Canx.
G-AVCR	Beagle A.61 Terrier 1 (Originally regd as Auster 7)	-	WE572	12.12.66	DBR on 20.10.74. Canx as WFU 10.7.75. Damaged in hangar collapse at Enstone on 2.1.76.
G-AVCS	Beagle A.61 Terrier 1 (Originally regd as Auster 7; but actually an Auster 10)	"109FM"	WJ363	12.12.66	Damaged in heavy landing at Finmere on 18.10.81. CofA expired 28.6.82. Canx by CAA 3.4.89. (On rebuild 11/95)
G-AVCT	Reims Cessna F.150G	0128		12.12.66	(On rebuild Fownhope, Hereford 3/96) Canx as WFU 1.5.98.
G-AVCU	Reims Cessna F.150G	0129		12.12.66	To G-OSTY 3/97. Canx.
G-AVCV	Cessna 182J Skylane	182-57492	N3492F	15.12.66	
G-AVCW	PA-30-160 Twin Comanche B	30-1375	N8249Y	16.12.66	To ZS-LKC 3/83. Canx 14.1.83.
G-AVCX	PA-30-160 Twin Comanche B	30-1302	N8185Y	16.12.66	
G-AVCY	PA-30-160 Twin Comanche B	30-1367	N8241Y	16.12.66	Landing gear accidentally retracting on take-off from Cardiff on 9.3.91. Canx as WFU 17.7.91.
G-AVCZ	Rollason-Druine D.62B Condor	RAE/618		16.12.66	To EI-BCP 1/77. Canx 24.1.77.
G-AVDA	Cessna 182K Skylane	182-57959	N2759Q	16.12.66	
G-AVDB	Cessna 310L	310L-0079	N2279F	20.12.66	WFU at Perth on 8.7.79. Canx 6.8.79. (Fuselage only stored 7/98 at Popham)
G-AVDC	Reims Cessna F.172H	0382		21.12.66	Wrecked in the slipstream of a DC-4 at Manston on 31.3.67. To Yeadon 22.5.67 and fuselage used in rebuild of G-AVKG. Canx.
G-AVDD	PA-28-140 Cherokee	28-21528	OE-DPD (OE-APD)/N11C	22.12.66	To OO-DPD 5/67. Canx.
G-AVDE	Turner Gyro-Glider Mk.1	1		23.12.66	Canx by CAA 9.8.91.
G-AVDF	Beagle B.121 Pup Srs.100 (Originally regd as B.121C c/n B.151, became B.121 Srs.100 with effect from 6.2.69)	B121-001		28.12.66	WFU at Shoreham on 22.5.68. (On rebuild Cambridge Airport)
G-AVDG	Wallis WA-116 Srs.1 Agile	215		28.12.66	Permit expired 23.5.92. (Stored 2/99 Reymerston Hall)
G-AVDH	Wallis WA-116 Srs.1 Agile	216		28.12.66	Not completed. Major components to G-AXAS c/n 217. Canx 19.2.69.
G-AVDI	PA-23-150 Apache	23-1111	N223Z	29.12.66	To N64742 5/77. Canx.
G-AVDJ	Vickers Supermarine 361 Spitfire HF.IXb (Also c/n CBAF/5542 is quoted)	CBAF.IX.533	OO-ARD Belgium AF SM-40/Belgium AF B-12/R.Neth AF H-65/R.Neth AF H-108/MH415	29.12.66	To N415MH 11/68. Canx.
G-AVDK	Slingsby Nipper T.66 Srs.2	9	OO-NIK	30.12.66	WFU at Kirkbymoorside in 4/68 for conversion to Srs.3 (as G-AWIZ c/n S.100). Upon inspection, the airframe proved to be non-standard and the wings non-aerobatic, and conversion was abandoned, the machine being broken up for spares and then destroyed in the fire at Kirkbymoorside on 18.11.68. Canx.
G-AVDL	HS.125 Srs.3A	25126	G-5-11	2. 1.67	To N510X 5/67. Canx 4.5.67.
G-AVDM	HS.125 Srs.3A	25129	G-5-12	2. 1.67	To N521M 2/67. Canx 2.3.67.
G-AVDN	Fokker F-27 Friendship 200	10316	PH-FKL	3. 1.67	To A40-FN 10/75. Canx 16.10.75.
G-AVDO	Bell 47G-2	804	N62K 51-14039	5. 1.67	To N7739 5/73. Canx 2.5.73.
G-AVDP	Beechcraft A23-19 Musketeer	MB-229	N3274R N62K	5. 1.67	Crashed on to a railway line near Le Bourget, France on 5.10.68. Canx.
G-AVDR	Beechcraft 65-B80 Queen Air (Originally regd with c/n LD-333)	LD-339	A40-CR G-AVDR	5. 1.67	CofA expired 30.6.86. Canx as WFU 18.5.90. (Instructional airframe at Brunel Technical College, Bristol)
G-AVDS	Beechcraft 65-B80 Queen Air	LD-337	A40-CS G-AVDS	5. 1.67	CofA expired 26.8.77. Canx as WFU 1.3.89. (Instructional airframe at Brunel Technical College, Bristol)
G-AVDT	Aeronca 7AC Champion	7AC-6932	N3594E NC3594E	5. 1.67	Permit expired 10.7.90. (Stored 6/97 at Rathfriland, Co.Down)
G-AVDU	Champion 7EC Traveler	7EC-739	N9837Y	5. 1.67	To EI-BHV 10/79. Canx 8.10.79.
G-AVDV	PA-22-150 Tri-Pacer (Modified to PA-20 Super Pacer standard)	22-3752	N4423A	5. 1.67	
G-AVDW	Rollason-Druine D.62B Condor	RAE/619		5. 1.67	To G-OPJH 4/97. Canx.
G-AVDX	HS.125 Srs.3B/RA (Originally regd as Srs.3B, converted in 1970)	25113	G-5-13	10. 1.67	To 5N-AVZ 5/83. Canx 27.5.83.
G-AVDY	Phoenix Luton LA-4A Minor	PAL/1183 & PFA/808		10. 1.67	
G-AVDZ	PA-25-235 Pawnee C	25-3982		11. 1.67	Crashed & DBF at White Horse Farm, South Kyme, Lincs on 10.3.87. Canx as destroyed 26.3.87.
G-AVEA	Malmo MFI-9 Junior	04	SE-EBO	11. 1.67	Restored as SE-EBO 6/69, then to OY-DZL 7/69. Canx 22.6.69.
G-AVEB	Morane-Saulnier MS.230Et2	1076	F-BGJT	13. 1.67	To N230EB 7/96. Canx 19.6.96.
G-AVEC	Reims Cessna F.172H	0405		13. 1.67	
G-AVED	Vickers 798D Viscount	286	YS-07C N746HA/N6593C/(N7475)	13. 1.67	WFU & stored in 4/70. Broken up in 11/70 at Woolsington. Canx as WFU 22.4.70.
G-AVEE	SNIAS SE.3130 Alouette II	1203	F-BNKZ F-WNKZ/Dutch AF H-3/F-WIEP	16. 1.67	Overturned and broke up 4 miles N of Snettisham in the Wash during seal-culling exercise on 7.7.73. Canx.
G-AVEF	SAN Jodel 150 Mascaret	16	F-BLDK	19. 1.67	

Regn	Type	c/n	Previous identity	Regn date	Fate or immediate subsequent identity (if known)
G-AVEG	SIAI-Marchetti S.205-18F	225	(OO-HAN)	20. 1.67	To G-IPEC 5/84. Canx.
G-AVEH	SIAI-Marchetti S.205-20R	346		20. 1.67	
G-AVEI	SAN Jodel D.117	294	F-BHGI	23. 1.67	Fatal crash into house at Brixham, Devon while en route from Roborough to Booker on 3.9.73. Canx.
G-AVEJ	BAC One-Eleven Srs.402AP	BAC.094	G-16-1 PI-C1141	23. 1.67	Restored as PI C1141 11/67. Canx 30.11.67.
G-AVEK	Cessna 411A (Originally regd with c/n 411A-0277)	411A-0274	N3274R	23. 1.67	To EI-BCT 8/77. Canx 24.8.77.
G-AVEL	Reims Cessna F.150G	0176		23. 1.67	Crashed at Fourdoun on 29.3.70. Canx.
G-AVEM	Reims Cessna F.150G	0198		23. 1.67	
G-AVEN	Reims Cessna F.150G	0202		23. 1.67	
G-AVEO	Reims Cessna F.150G	0204	EI-BOI G-AVEO	23. 1.67	To G-DENA 12/95. Canx.
G-AVEP	Reims Cessna F.150G	0205		23. 1.67	Force-landed and hit fence 6 miles west of Scone on 4.7.73. Canx as destroyed 25.7.73.
G-AVER	Reims Cessna F.150G	0206		23. 1.67	
G-AVES	SNCAN Stampe SV-4C	476	F-BDBM	23. 1.67	To N3956 10/70. Canx 22.10.70.
G-AVET	Beechcraft 95-C55A Baron	TE-362	N34BM G-AVET	26. 1.67	To N362RH 5/93. Canx 10.5.93.
G-AVEU	Wassmer WA.41 Super Baladou IV	136		27. 1.67	
G-AVEV	Avro 652A Anson 19 Srs.2	"33787"	VV297	27. 1.67	Not converted. Broken up for spares at Baginton in 2/67. Canx as destroyed 17.2.67.
G-AVEW	Westland-Sikorsky S-58 Wessex 60 Srs.1	WA/562	G-17-1	27. 1.67	To VH-BHL 4/68. Canx.
G-AVEX	Rollason-Druine D.62B Condor	RAE/616		31. 1.67	
G-AVEY	Phoenix Currie Super Wot	SE.100 & PFA/3006		31. 1.67	Permit expired 4.8.97. (Stored 10/97)
G-AVEZ	Handley Page HPR.7 Dart Herald 210	169	PP-ASW G-AVEZ/HB-AAH	31. 1.67	WFU on 5.1.81 at Norwich. Canx 4.1.83. To Rescue training at Norwich. (On fire dump 2/99 Norwich)
G-AVFA	HS.121 Trident 2E	2140		1. 2.67	WFU at Heathrow on 29.3.83. Scrapped in 1/84. Canx as WFU 20.2.84.
G-AVFB	HS.121 Trident 2E	2141	5B-DAC G-AVFB	1. 2.67	WFU at Heathrow on 27.3.82. Canx 9.7.82. (On display 7/99 Duxford)
G-AVFC	HS.121 Trident 2E	2142		1. 2.67	WFU at Heathrow on 24.10.81. Canx 12.5.82.
G-AVFD	HS.121 Trident 2E	2143		1. 2.67	WFU at Heathrow on 22.3.82. Canx 9.7.82.
G-AVFE	HS.121 Trident 2E	2144		1. 2.67	Flown to Belfast on 13.2.85 for the Belfast Airport Authority. Canx as WFU 20.3.85. (Extant 4/96 Aldergrove)
G-AVFF	HS.121 Trident 2E	2145		1. 2.67	WFU at Heathrow on 29.1.85. Scrapped at Southend. Canx as destroyed 29.1.85.
G-AVFG	HS.121 Trident 2E	2146		1. 2.67	WFU at Heathrow on 24.5.85. Used for ground training. Canx as WFU 19.1.89. (Extant 12/97 Heathrow)
G-AVFH	HS.121 Trident 2E	2147		1. 2.67	WFU at Heathrow on 24.10.81. Canx 12.5.82.
G-AVFI	HS.121 Trident 2E	2148		1. 2.67	WFU at Heathrow on 11.9.81. Canx 12.5.82.
G-AVFJ	HS.121 Trident 2E	2149		1. 2.67	WFU at Teesside on 24.6.82. Canx 9.7.82. (Extant 4/99)
G-AVFK	HS.121 Trident 2E	2150		1. 2.67	WFU at Heathrow on 31.12.81. Canx 12.5.82.
G-AVFL	HS.121 Trident 2E	2151		1. 2.67	WFU at Heathrow on 6.12.84. Flown to Southend on 31.1.85. Scrapped. Canx as destroyed 8.3.85.
G-AVFM	HS.121 Trident 2E	2152		1. 2.67	WFU on 30.3.83. Instructional Airframe 1/99 at Bristol/Lulsgate.
G-AVFN	HS.121 Trident 2E	2153		1. 2.67	WFU at Heathrow on 8.12.84. Scrapped at Southend in 1/85. Canx as destroyed 29.1.85.
G-AVFO(1)	HS.121 Trident 2E	2154		1. 2.67R	NTU - To 5B-DAA 9/69. Canx.
G-AVFO(2)	HS.121 Trident 2E	2156		24. 2.69	Flown to Southend 13.2.85 for scrapping. Canx as WFU 20.3.85.
G-AVFP	PA-28-140 Cherokee	28-22652		31. 1.67	
G-AVFR	PA-28-140 Cherokee	28-22747		31. 1.67	
G-AVFS	PA-32-300 Cherokee Six	32-40038		31. 1.67	Damaged in forced landing at Crosland Moor on 28.9.90. CofA expired 12.7.91. (On rebuild 1/97)
G-AVFT	PA-32-300 Cherokee Six	32-40108		31. 1.67	To EI-ASY 6/68. Canx.
G-AVFU	PA-32-300 Cherokee Six	32-40182	(G-AXZX) G-AVFU	31. 1.67	
G-AVFV	PA-30-160 Twin Comanche B	30-1404	N8275Y	31. 1.67	Fatal crash into Mount Snowdon, North Wales on 22.10.72. Canx.
G-AVFW	PA-30-160 Twin Comanche B	30-1410	N8278Y	31. 1.67	To N160MJ. Canx 29.4.85.
G-AVFX	PA-28-140 Cherokee	28-22757		31. 1.67	
G-AVFY	PA-28-140 Cherokee	28-22762		31. 1.67	To G-OHOG 5/91. Canx.
G-AVFZ	PA-28-140 Cherokee	28-22767		31. 1.67	
G-AVGA	PA-24-260 Comanche B	24-4489	"G-AVKH" N9027P	31. 1.67	
G-AVGB	PA-28-140 Cherokee	28-22772	N11C	31. 1.67	To EC-FUZ /94. Canx 29.4.93.
G-AVGC	PA-28-140 Cherokee	28-22777		31. 1.67	
G-AVGD	PA-28-140 Cherokee	28-22782		31. 1.67	
G-AVGE	PA-28-140 Cherokee	28-22787		31. 1.67	
G-AVGF	PA-28-140 Cherokee	28-22792		31. 1.67	To LN-SAS 12/75. Canx 19.11.75.
G-AVGG	PA-28-140 Cherokee	28-22797		31. 1.67	Crashed at Papplewick, Notts. on 10.8.70. Canx as WFU 16.3.73. (Cabin at Duxford 4/98 - Wreck still present 7/99)
G-AVGH	PA-28-140 Cherokee	28-22802		31. 1.67	WFU at Rhoose on 5.12.91. Canx as WFU 19.2.92. (Wreck stored 1/97 Cardiff)
G-AVGI	PA-28-140 Cherokee	28-22822		31. 1.67	
G-AVGJ	SAN Jodel DR.1050 Ambassadeur	265	F-BJYJ	31. 1.67	WFU with glue failure in 1985. Canx by CAA 10.6.93. (On rebuild off-site 6/95)
G-AVGK	PA-28-180 Cherokee C	28-3639	N9516J	2. 2.67	

Regn	Type	c/n	Previous identity	Regn date	Fate or immediate subsequent identity (if known)
G-AVGL	Reims Cessna F.150G	0157		3. 2.67	To G-HUNY 6/83. Canx.
G-AVGM	Reims Cessna F.150G	0158		3. 2.67	To EI-BFE 8/78. Canx 4.7.78.
G-AVGN	PA-24-260 Comanche B	24-4514	N9049P	3. 1.67	To OE-KGW 5/83. Canx 31.5.83.
G-AVGO	Short SC.7 Skyvan 2-200	SH1837	N4906	6. 2.67	To N4906 4/67. Canx 10.4.67.
G-AVGP	BAC One-Eleven Srs.408EF	BAC.114	(HI-148) G-AVGP	7. 2.67	To ZS-OAF. Canx 4.12.96.
G-AVGR	Avro 652A Anson 19 Srs.2	"33751"	TX176	7. 2.67	Not converted. Scrapped at Staverton in 3/69. Canx as PWFU 21.6.71.
G-AVGS	SAAB 91D Safir	91-308	(SE-...) G-AVGS/SE-CFZ/SE-XAT	8. 2.67	Restored as SE-CFZ 9/75. Canx 17.9.75.
G-AVGT	PA-30-160 Twin Comanche	30-123	EI-AVS G-AVGT/N7105Y	8. 2.67	To VH-KNT 3/78. Canx 17.11.77.
G-AVGU	Reims Cessna F.150G	0199		8. 2.67	Badly damaged on landing at Southend on 25.5.83. Canx by CAA 14.10.86. (Stored dismantled 5/98 at Little Staughton)
G-AVGV	Reims Cessna F.150G	0149		8. 2.67	Badly damaged in a heavy landing at Bagby on 8.5.95. Canx as WFU 19.7.95.
G-AVGW	HS.125 Srs.3B	25120		8. 2.67	Fatal crash into the roof of Vauxhall Motors' factory at Luton on 23.12.67. Canx.
G-AVGX	Bolkow Bo.208C-1 Junior 3	630	D-ENNA(2)	13. 2.67	Crashed at Lintfort, near Kamp, West Germany on 12.11.72. Canx by CAA 9.9.81. Wreck to Biggin Hill.
G-AVGY(1)	Vickers 812 Viscount	363	N251V	14. 2.67	NTU - To G-AVHE 2/67. Canx.
G-AVGY(2)	Cessna 182K Skylane	182-58112	N3112Q	17. 2.67	
G-AVGZ	CEA Jodel DR.1051 Sicile (Converted to DR.1050 in 1967 with a Continental O-200-A engine)	341	F-BKPR	14. 2.67	CofA expired 13.7.97. (Stored 4/97)
G-AVHA	HS.125 Srs.3A/RA (Originally regd as Srs.3A)	NA700 & 25134	G-5-11	15. 2.67	To N514V 4/68. Canx 8.4.68.
G-AVHB	HS.125 Srs.3A/RA (Originally regd as Srs.3A)	NA701 & 25136		15. 2.67	To N501W 5/68. Canx 7.5.68.
G-AVHC	Brookland Mosquito II Gyroplane	5		16. 2.67	WFU on 27.4.68. Canx 3.6.80.
G-AVHD	Mooney M.20F Executive 21	670260	N9700M	17. 2.67	NTU - Not Imported. To F-BOSJ 6/67. Canx 13.4.67.
G-AVHE	Vickers 812 Viscount	363	(G-AVGY) N251V	20. 2.67	WFU on 30.3.70. Broken up in 8/72 at Southend. Canx as destroyed 14.2.73.
G-AVHF	Beechcraft A23-19 Musketeer Sport III	MB-236		20. 2.67	Crashed on landing at Spanhoe on 1.8.90. Canx as destroyed 13.9.90.
G-AVHG	Beechcraft 35-C33 Debonair	CD-1090		20. 2.67	To OO-GEM 4/75. Canx 7.4.75.
G-AVHH	Reims Cessna F.172H Skyhawk	0337		20. 2.67	(Stored 8/97)
G-AVHI	Reims Cessna F.172H Skyhawk	0343		20. 2.67	Fatal crash in forced-landing in sea 50 miles from Wick and sank 11.12.72; was blown off course in strong wind whilst en-route from Dyce to Ringway and ran out of fuel.
G-AVHJ	Wassmer WA.41 Baladou	138		21. 2.67	CofA expired 9.4.87. Donated to Jersey Fire School. Canx as WFU 29.11.90.
G-AVHK	Vickers 812 Viscount	359	N246V	21. 2.67	WFU on 5.4.70. Broken up in 7/72 at Southend. Canx as WFU 21.3.73.
G-AVHL	SAN Jodel DR.105A Ambassadeur	90	F-BIVY	23. 2.67	
G-AVHM	Reims Cessna F.150G (Rebuilt using parts & wings from G-ATRL)	0181		24. 2.67	
G-AVHN	Reims Cessna F.150G	0182		24. 2.67	Damaged on 28.1.85. Later used as an instructional airframe at Brunel College, Lulsgate. Canx as destroyed 5.8.94.
G-AVHO	Beagle B.206 Srs.2	B.058	VQ-LAY G-AVHO	24. 2.67	To N97JH 3/77. Canx 11.3.77.
G-AVHP	Beagle B.206 Srs.2	B.057	G-35-33 G-AVHP	24. 2.67	To N966B 7/67. Canx 24.7.67.
G-AVHR	Beagle B.206 Srs.2	B.056		24. 2.67	To N12CR 4/74. Canx 16.4.74.
G-AVHS	Beagle B.206S Srs.2	B.055	G-35-16 G-35-14	24. 2.67	To N1008B 9/67. Canx 4.9.67.
G-AVHT	Beagle E.3 (Originally regd as Auster AOP.9M; re-designated in 1974)	-	WZ711	1. 3.67	
G-AVHU	Avro 652A Anson 19 Srs.2	"33783"	TX211	3. 3.67	Not converted and eventually scrapped in 7/72 at Southend. Canx as PWFU 30.5.84.
G-AVHV	DH.104 Dove 8	04542		6. 3.67	Fatal crash on final approach to Wolverhampton on 9.4.70. Canx.
G-AVHW	PA-30-160 Twin Comanche B	30-1414	N8280Y	7. 3.67	Crashed at Scatsta, Shetlands on 18.9.74. Canx 24.3.80.
G-AVHX	DH.104 Dove 1	04132	ST-AAE SN-AAE/VP-YHU	9. 3.67	Not converted & WFU at Baginton. Canx as WFU 17.5.71.
G-AVHY	Sportavia-Putzer Fournier RF-4D	4009		10. 3.67	(Stored 4/97)
G-AVHZ	PA-30-160 Twin Comanche B	30-1424	N8287Y	10. 3.67	To G-VIST 6/83. Canx.
G-AVIA(1)	Reims Cessna F.150G	0126		. 3.67R	NTU - To F-BOGR. Canx.
G-AVIA(2)	Reims Cessna F.150G	0184		10. 3.67	
G-AVIB	Reims Cessna F.150G	0180		10. 3.67	
G-AVIC	Reims Cessna F.172H	0320	N17011	10. 3.67	
G-AVID	Cessna 182K	182-57734	N2534Q	10. 3.67	
G-AVIE	Reims Cessna F.172H	0326	N17014	10. 3.67	Overturned by a gust of wind while taxiing at Coventry on 4.2.89. Later used for spares at Sibson. Canx as WFU 18.1.95.
G-AVIF	Omnipol L-13 Blanik	173348		10. 3.67	To BGA.1385 8/67. Canx as marks withdrawn in 8/67.
G-AVIG	Agusta-Bell 206B JetRanger (Originally 206A; later modified)	8004	VR-BGC G-AVIG/9Y-TDM/9Y-TCZ/G-AVIG	10. 3.67	Crashed after striking ice in the Weddell Sea, in the Antartica on 5.1.85. Canx as destroyed 25.3.85.
G-AVIH	Agusta-Bell 206A JetRanger	8007	VR-BFH G-AVIH/5N-AIW/G-AVIH/ZS-HDI/VR-BCM/G-AVIH	10. 3.67	To VH-LED. Canx 28.8.84.
G-AVII	Agusta-Bell 206B JetRanger (Originally 206A; later modified)	8011		10. 3.67	

Regn	Type	c/n	Previous identity	Regn date	Fate or immediate subsequent identity (if known)
G-AVIJ	Avro 652A Anson 19 Srs.2	"33755"	TX182	10. 3.67	Not converted and scrapped at Halfpenny Green in 1968. Canx by CAA 16.9.72.
G-AVIK	Campbell-Bensen B.7MC Gyrocopter	DC/61/009	VP-KRI	14. 3.67	Canx as destroyed 15.10.74.
G-AVIL	Alon A.2 Aircoupe	A.5	N5471E	14. 3.67	
G-AVIM	Socata MS.880B Rallye Club	880		14. 3.67	To EI-AWU 1/74. Canx 11.7.73.
G-AVIN	Socata MS.880B Rallye Club	884		14. 3.67	
G-AVIO	Socata MS.880B Rallye Club (Originally regd with c/n 885)	901		14. 3.67	To EI-CHN 2/93. Canx 12.1.93.
G-AVIP	Brantly B.2B	471		14. 3.67	
G-AVIR	Reims Cessna F.172H Skyhawk	0423		14. 3.67	Damaged in a storm at Norwich on 16.10.87. Canx as WFU 13.6.88.
G-AVIS(1)	Reims Cessna F.172H Skyhawk	0460		. 3.67R	NTU - Not Imported. To EC-WNE/EC-BNE 5/68. Canx.
G-AVIS(2)	Reims Cessna F.172H Skyhawk	0413		14. 3.67	
G-AVIT	Reims Cessna F.150G	0217		14. 3.67	
G-AVIU	CEA Jodel DR.1050 Ambassadeur	134	F-BJJN	14. 3.67	Crashed and burnt out at Sandown Golfcourse on 14.6.80. Canx by CAA 6.8.86.
G-AVIV	CEA Jodel DR.250/160 Quadriplace	92		16. 3.67	Crashed at Carneod Daffydd, near Bangor, Wales on 23.8.69. Canx.
G-AVIW	Vickers 812 Viscount	358	N245V	17. 3.67	To B-2031 1/75. Canx 31.1.75.
G-AVIX	Cessna 337B Super Skymaster	337-0554	N5454S	17. 3.67	To G-RORO 1/80. Canx.
G-AVIY	Vickers 786D Viscount	333	YS-11C AN-AKP/(HK-946X)	20. 3.67	WFU at Yeadon in 4/70. Broken up in 6/70 at Wymeswold. Canx as WFU 24.4.70.
G-AVIZ	Scheibe SF-25A Motor Falke (Originally regd with c/n 4551)	4552	D-KOFY	21. 3.67	CofA expired 19.9.91. (Stored 1/99 at Brunton, Northumberland) (Regd to Spilsby Gliding Trust on 12.4.99)
G-AVJA	Vickers 815 Viscount	336	AP-AJD	21. 3.67	Crashed on take-off from Ringway on 20.3.69. Canx.
G-AVJB	Vickers 815 Viscount	375	AP-AJF	21. 3.67	To SE-IVY. Canx 28.10.86.
G-AVJC	Reims Cessna F.172H Skyhawk	0363		22. 3.67	Blown over & DBR in high winds during night 5-6.7.69 at Dinard, France.
G-AVJD	HS.125 Srs.3A/RA (Originally regd as Srs.3A)	NA702 & 25137	G-5-11	28. 3.67	To CF-AAG 5/68. Canx.
G-AVJE	Reims Cessna F.150G	0219		29. 3.67	
G-AVJF	Reims Cessna F.172H Skyhawk	0393		31. 3.67	
G-AVJG	Cessna 337B Super Skymaster	337-0715	N2415S	31. 3.67	CofA expired 31.5.92. (Open storage at Farley Farm, Romsey) Canx by CAA 30.7.96.
G-AVJH	Druine D.62 Condor	PFA/603		31. 3.67	Crashed on landing Nefyn, Gwynedd 31.7.83. Permit expired 4.11.83. Canx as destroyed 5.1.89. (On rebuild 12/95)
G-AVJI	Reims Cessna F.172H Skyhawk	0442		31. 3.67	Badly damaged on landing at Croft Farm, Defford on 8.10.95. (Wings with Northbrook College, Shoreham 9/98)
G-AVJJ	PA-30-160 Twin Comanche B	30-1420	N8285Y	7. 4.67	
G-AVJK	SAN Jodel DR.1050/M1 Excellence	453	F-BLJH	7. 4.67	
G-AVJL	Vickers 812 Viscount	389	N247V	7. 4.67	To B-2033 4/75. Canx 16.5.75.
G-AVJM	Reims Cessna F.172H Skyhawk	0372		12. 4.67	Hit high ground at Ingleby Greenhow on 2.7.72 and written off. Canx by CAA 20.8.81.
G-AVJN	Brantly B.2B	473		12. 4.67	To G-OMAX 8/87. Canx.
G-AVJO	Fokker E.III Replica (Regd with c/n PPS/FOK/6) (built by D.E.Bianchi)	PPS/FOK/1 & PPS/REP/6		12. 4.67	
G-AVJP	Campbell-Bensen B.8M Gyrocopter (Originally regd with c/n CA/304, changed on 3.5.67)	CA/305		12. 4.67	Canx as WFU 16.8.73.
G-AVJR	Abingdon Free Balloon HAFB	A.F.B.3		12. 4.67	Canx as destroyed 28.2.78.
G-AVJS	Nord 1002 Pingouin	196	F-BKFA French AF	12. 4.67	Canx 24.3.76 on sale to the USA.
G-AVJT	PA-30-160 Twin Comanche B	31-1415	N8281Y	12. 4.67	To F-GALF 5/76. Canx 1.3.76.
G-AVJU	PA-24-260 Comanche B	24-4657	N9199P	12. 4.67	To G-ENIU 7/87. Canx.
G-AVJV	Wallis WA-117 Srs.1 (Used major components of G-ATCV c/n 301)	K/402/X		12. 4.67	Permit expired 21.4.89. (Stored 2/99 Reymerston Hall)
G-AVJW	Wallis WA-118/M Meteorite (Used major components of G-ATPW c/n 401)	K/502/X		12. 4.67	Permit expired 21.4.83. (Stored 2/99 Reymerston Hall) (It is reliably reported that two gyros have carried the marks G-AVJW)
G-AVJX	Short SC.7 Skyvan 3-300-1 (Originally regd as Skyvan 2-201)	SH1838	VH-EJR	12. 4.67	To VH-FSG 10/68. Canx 7.10.68.
G-AVJY	Champion 7FC Tri-Traveler	7FC-372	N8913R	17. 4.67	WFU at Rush Green on 17.4.70. Canx 25.7.73.
G-AVJZ	Vickers 812 Viscount	360	N248V	17. 4.67	Crashed and burnt out while taking-off for an air test at Southend on 3.5.67. Canx.
G-AVKA	Boeing 707-399C (Line No. 601)	19415	N319F G-AVKA/N319F	17. 4.67	To CS-TBH 5/73. Canx 7.5.73.
G-AVKB	Brochet MB.50 Pipistrelle	02	F-PFAL F-WFAL	17. 4.67	
G-AVKC	BN-2A-21 Islander (Originally regd as BN-2)	4	(F-BUFX) G-AVKC	17. 4.67	To N43MJ 6/79. Canx 14.5.79.
G-AVKD	Sportavia-Putzer Fournier RF-4D	4024		19. 4.67	
G-AVKE	Gadfly HDW-1	HDW-1		19. 4.67	Canx as WFU 12.10.81. (Stored 8/97 Weston-super-Mare)
G-AVKF	Reims Cessna F.172H Skyhawk	0366		21. 4.67	Crashed & DBF near Worthing on 19.3.78. Canx as WFU 20.10.81.
G-AVKG	Reims Cessna F.172H Skyhawk (Rebuilt with fuselage of G-AVDC c/n 0382 in 1986)	0345		21. 4.67	
G-AVKH	Slingsby Nipper T.66 RA.45 Srs.3 (Tipsy c/n 27)	S.101/1585		24. 4.67	Crashed and DBF at Newby Grange Park Farm, Yorks 26.10.74. Canx as destroyed 29.11.74. Rebuilt & re-regd as G-BRIK in 4/77 with c/n PFA/25-10174.
"G-AVKH"	PA-24-260 Comanche B	24-4489	N9027P	----	NTU - To G-AVGA in 1/67. Canx.

Regn	Type	c/n	Previous identity	Regn date	Fate or immediate subsequent identity (if known)
G-AVKI	Slingsby Nipper T.66 RA.45 Srs.3 (Tipsy c/n 31)	S.102/1586		24. 4.67	
G-AVKJ	Slingsby Nipper T.66 RA.45 Srs.3 (Tipsy c/n 32)	S.103/1587		24. 4.67	
G-AVKK	Slingsby Nipper T.66 RA.45 Srs.3 (Tipsy c/n 74)	S.104/1588	EI-BJH G-AVKK	24. 4.67	
G-AVKL	PA-30-160 Twin Comanche B	30-1418	OY-DHL G-AVKL/N8284Y	25. 4.67	
G-AVKM	Rollason-Druine D.62B Condor	RAE/620		26. 4.67	Badly damaged in gales Wilkieston Farm, Cupar, Angus on 2/3.3.82. CofA expired 30.6.82. (Stored 2/96)
G-AVKN	Cessna 401	401-0082	(N3282Q)	26. 4.67	
G-AVKO	Gloster Non-Rigid Airship	001		26. 4.67	Construction abandoned. Parts used for G-AWVR. Canx by CAA 14.10.86.
G-AVKP	Beagle A.109 Airedale	B.540	SE-EGA	26. 4.67	
G-AVKR	Bolkow Bo.208C-1 Junior 3	648	D-EGRA(2)	28. 4.67	
G-AVKS	Bell 47G-2	689	9J-RDE F-BHMH/HB-XAE	28. 4.67	To F-GDPD 6/84. Canx 10.1.84.
G-AVKT	Tipsy Nipper T.66 Srs.3 (Cobelavia-built)	70	OO-HEL OO-DEL	1. 5.67	Fatal crash when dived into ground at Constable Burton, Paull, Yorks on 19.9.72. Canx as destroyed 14.2.73.
G-AVKU	Wassmer WA.41 Super Baladou IV	144		1. 5.67	NTU - Not Imported. Canx 5.12.77.
G-AVKV	PA-28-140 Cherokee	28-23243	N9759W	1. 5.67	NTU - Not Imported. Remained as N9759W. Canx 3.5.67.
G-AVKW	SNCAN Stampe SV-4B	561	F-BDDG	1. 5.67	Crashed at Tilburstow Hill, Godstone, Surrey on 29.10.67. Canx as destroyed 29.6.70.
G-AVKX	Hiller 360 UH-12E	2103	CN-MAO	3. 5.67	Crashed into power cables near RAF Waddington on 4.7.80. Canx as WFU 17.10.86.
G-AVKY	Hiller 360 UH-12E	2104	CN-MAP	3. 5.67	Crashed at Stennings Farm, Sulhampstead, near Newbury on 26.6.84. Canx as destroyed 7.7.94.
G-AVKZ	PA-23-250 Aztec C	27-3658	N6448Y	3. 5.67	CofA expired 29.10.90. Canx as WFU 3.6.92. (Stored at Little Snoring 5/93)
G-AVLA	PA-28-140 Cherokee	28-22932	N11C (N9509W)	8. 5.67	To G-PIKK 8/88. Canx.
G-AVLB	PA-28-140 Cherokee	28-23158		8. 5.67	
G-AVLC	PA-28-140 Cherokee	28-23178		8. 5.67	
G-AVLD	PA-28-140 Cherokee	28-23193		8. 5.67	
G-AVLE	PA-28-140 Cherokee	28-23223		8. 5.67	
G-AVLF	PA-28-140 Cherokee	28-23268		8. 5.67	
G-AVLG	PA-28-140 Cherokee	28-23358		8. 5.67	
G-AVLH	PA-28-140 Cherokee	28-23368		8. 5.67	
G-AVLI	PA-28-140 Cherokee	28-23388		8. 5.67	
G-AVLJ	PA-28-140 Cherokee	28-23393	9H-AAZ G-AVLJ	8. 5.67	
G-AVLK	Beagle 206 Srs.2	B.059		8. 5.67	To N15JP 4/74. Canx 16.4.74.
G-AVLL	Beagle 206S Srs.2	C.36/B.060	5N-AGW G-AVLL/G-35-15	8. 5.67	To N850EX. Canx 20.12.76.
G-AVLM	Beagle B.121 Pup Srs.160 (Originally regd as Srs.150, modified in 1968)	B121-003		8. 5.67	(On rebuild 6/98 at Egginton)
G-AVLN	Beagle B.121 Pup Srs.150	B121-004		8. 5.67	(Stored 6/96)
G-AVLO	Bolkow Bo.208C-1 Junior	650	D-EGUC(2)	8. 5.67	
G-AVLP	PA-23-250 Aztec C	27-3633	N6337Y	9. 5.67	To 5N-AWR(2) 11/87. Canx 9.11.87.
G-AVLR	PA-28-140 Cherokee	28-23288		9. 5.67	
G-AVLS	PA-28-140 Cherokee	28-23303	N11C	9. 5.67	To G-OKYM 5/88. Canx.
G-AVLT	PA-28-140 Cherokee	28-23328		9. 5.67	
G-AVLU	PA-28-140 Cherokee	28-23343		9. 5.67	To G-LTFB 2/97. Canx.
G-AVLV	PA-23-250 Aztec C	27-3619	N6352Y	9. 5.67	To G-OIOO 8/81. Canx.
G-AVLW	Sportavia-Putzer Fournier RF-4D	4025		9. 5.67	
G-AVLX	Luton LA-4A Minor	PFA/814		9. 5.67	Crashed at Newtownards, Northern Ireland on 27.10.68. Canx.
G-AVLY	Wassmer Jodel D.120A Paris-Nice	331		11. 5.67	
G-AVLZ	Wassmer Jodel D.120A Paris-Nice	333		11. 5.67	NTU - Not Imported. To F-BOYL. Canx 13.12.67.
G-AVMA	Socata GY-80-180 Horizon	196		12. 5.67	
G-AVMB	Rollason-Druine D.62B Condor	RAE/621		12. 5.67	(On rebuild by C.Dray 10/97; possibly with new fuselage)
G-AVMC	Westland-Sikorsky S-58 Wessex 60 Srs.1	WA/561	G-17-3	. 5.67R	NTU - To G-AVNE 5/67. Canx.
G-AVMD	Cessna 150G	150-65504	N2404J	16. 5.67	
G-AVME	PA-28-140 Cherokee (Rebuilt with spare fuselage c/n 28-22700S in 3-7/67)	28-21203	N4507R	16. 5.67	To 9G-ACS. Canx 17.1.79.
G-AVMF	Reims Cessna F.150G	0203		17. 5.67	
G-AVMG	Reims Cessna F.150G	0068		17. 5.67	NTU - DBF at Brussels, Belgium on 22.5.67 - prior to delivery. To N17015. Canx in 1967.
G-AVMH	BAC One-Eleven Srs.510ED	BAC.136		11. 5.67	
G-AVMI	BAC One-Eleven Srs.510ED	BAC.137		11. 5.67	
G-AVMJ	BAC One-Eleven Srs.510ED	BAC.138		11. 5.67	WFU 6/94. Dismantled in 6/95 at Filton; fuselage used as cabin trainer at Hurn 8/96.
G-AVMK	BAC One-Eleven Srs.510ED	BAC.139		11. 5.67	
G-AVML	BAC One-Eleven Srs.510ED	BAC.140		11. 5.67	
G-AVMM	BAC One-Eleven Srs.510ED	BAC.141		11. 5.67	(Stored 12/95 at Hurn)
G-AVMN	BAC One-Eleven Srs.510ED	BAC.142		11. 5.67	(Stored 2/99 at Hurn)
G-AVMO	BAC One-Eleven Srs.510ED	BAC.143		11. 5.67	Canx as WFU 12.7.93. (On display at Cosford)
G-AVMP	BAC One-Eleven Srs.510ED	BAC.144		11. 5.67	
G-AVMR	BAC One-Eleven Srs.510ED	BAC.145		11. 5.67	(Stored 3/96 at Hurn)
G-AVMS	BAC One-Eleven Srs.510ED	BAC.146		11. 5.67	
G-AVMT	BAC One-Eleven Srs.510ED	BAC.147		11. 5.67	

Regn	Type	c/n	Previous identity	Regn date	Fate or immediate subsequent identity (if known)
G-AVMU	BAC One-Eleven Srs.510ED	BAC.148		11. 5.67	Canx as WFU 12.7.93. (On display 7/99 at Duxford)
G-AVMV	BAC One-Eleven Srs.510ED	BAC.149		11. 5.67	(Stored 9/96 at Hurn)
G-AVMW	BAC One-Eleven Srs.510ED	BAC.150		11. 5.67	
G-AVMX	BAC One-Eleven Srs.510ED	BAC.151	5N-USE G-AVMX	11. 5.67	(Stored 9/97 at Hurn)
G-AVMY	BAC One-Eleven Srs.510ED	BAC.152		11. 5.67	
G-AVMZ	BAC One-Eleven Srs.510ED	BAC.153	5N-OSA G-AVMZ	11. 5.67	
G-AVNA	Beechcraft A65 Queen Air	LC-267		18. 5.67	To N48133 6/75. Canx 3.6.75.
G-AVNB	Reims Cessna F.150G	0216		18. 5.67	To G-JWDS 12/88. Canx.
G-AVNC	Reims Cessna F.150G	0200		18. 5.67	
G-AVND	Partenavia P.64 Oscar	16	I-PAKK	18. 5.67	To ZS-FCH 6/67. Canx 26.7.67.
G-AVNE	Westland-Sikorsky S-58 Wessex 60 Srs.1	WA/561	G-17-3 G-AVNE/5N-AJL/G-AVNE/9M-ASS/VH-BHC(2)/PK-HBQ/G-AVNE/(G-AVMC)/G-17-3	15. 5.67	(On display 5/97 - painted as G-17-3 Weston-super-Mare)
G-AVNF	Douglas C-47-DL Dakota	9004	PP-AND PP-BRA/42-5697	19. 5.67	Canx 23.6.67. To JY-ADE 8.7.67 but not delivered, stored at Le Bourget 29.8.67 until 1969 for spares use. Broken up.
G-AVNG	Beechcraft 65-A80 Queen Air	LD-176	D-ILBO	22. 5.67	To G-REXY 1/85. Canx.
G-AVNH	Bolkow Bo.208C-1 Junior	655	D-EJME	23. 5.67	Crashed at Steyning, near Shoreham on 10.3.68. Canx in 4/71.
G-AVNI	PA-30-160 Twin Comanche B	30-1430	N8292Y	24. 5.67	CofA expired 29.4.79. Canx by CAA 29.2.84.
G-AVNJ	Vickers 812 Viscount	361	N249V	26. 5.67	WFU & stored at Southend on 23.10.69. Broken up in 6/72. Canx as WFU 22.11.72.
G-AVNK	PA-23-250 Aztec C	27-3355	N6142Y	26. 5.67	To G-FOYL 8/79. Canx.
G-AVNL	PA-23-250 Aztec C	27-3363	N6147Y	26. 5.67	WFU at Biggin Hill on 5.1.83.
G-AVNM	PA-28-180 Cherokee C	28-4033	N11C	26. 5.67	To G-SOOT 8/88. Canx.
G-AVNN	PA-28-180 Cherokee C	28-4049		26. 5.67	
G-AVNO	PA-28-180 Cherokee C	28-4105		26. 5.67	
G-AVNP	PA-28-180 Cherokee C	28-4113		26. 5.67	
G-AVNR	PA-28-180 Cherokee C	28-4121		26. 5.67	
G-AVNS	PA-28-180 Cherokee C	28-4129		26. 5.67	
G-AVNT	PA-28-180 Cherokee C	28-4145		26. 5.67	To Dodson Aviation Scrapyard, Ottawa, KS, USA. To N5459N. Canx 11.7.84.
G-AVNU	PA-28-180 Cherokee C	28-4153		26. 5.67	
G-AVNV	PA-28-180 Cherokee C	28-4206		26. 5.67	To Dodson Aviation Scrapyard, Ottawa, KS, USA. To N5458U. Canx 11.7.84.
G-AVNW	PA-28-180 Cherokee C	28-4210		26. 5.67	
G-AVNX	Sportavia-Putzer Fournier RF-4D	4026		26. 5.67	
G-AVNY	Sportavia-Putzer Fournier RF-4D	4029		26. 5.67	To G-IVEL 6/95. Canx.
G-AVNZ	Sportavia-Putzer Fournier RF-4D	4030		26. 5.67	
G-AVOA	SAN Jodel DR.1050 Ambassadeur	195	F-BJYY	31. 5.67	
G-AVOB	CEA DR.250/160 Captaine	52	F-OCIB	2. 6.67	Ditched in English Channel on 6.7.69 between Boulogne and Dover. Wreckage found on 13.7.69. Canx as destroyed 15.7.69
G-AVOC	CEA Jodel DR.221 Dauphin	67		2. 6.67	Crashed at Framfield on 7.3.71. (On rebuild Enstone 8/97)
G-AVOD	Beagle D.5/180 Husky	3688		6. 6.67	Crashed on take-off at Crosland Moor on 31.7.92. Canx as destroyed 8.9.92. (Wreck stored 6/96 at Spilsby) Wings to G-AJDW 9/98.
G-AVOE	BAC One-Eleven Srs.416EK	BAC.129	G-SURE G-AVOE	6. 6.67	To N390BA. Canx 21.6.84.
G-AVOF	BAC One-Eleven Srs.416EK	BAC.131	G-BMAN G-16-32/G-BMAN/G-AVOF	6. 6.67	To N392BA. Canx 15.3.85.
G-AVOG	Campbell-Bensen B.8MB Gyrocopter	CA/306		6. 6.67	Canx as WFU 29.7.68. (Stored at Membury in 7/68)
G-AVOH	Rollason-Druine D.62B Condor	RAE/622		6. 6.67	
G-AVOI	HS.125 Srs.3B	25128	G-5-13	6. 6.67	To F-GECR 1/85. Canx 17.12.84.
G-AVOJ	HS.125 Srs.3A/RA	NA703 & 25139	G-5-11	6. 6.67	To N612G. Canx 30.5.68.
G-AVOK	HS.125 Srs.3A/RA	NA704 & 25141	G-5-12	6. 6.67	To N75C. Canx 21.6.68.
G-AVOL	HS.125 Srs.3A/RA	NA705 & 25142		6. 6.67	To N7055/N9040. Canx 2.7.68.
G-AVOM	CEA Jodel DR.221 Dauphin	65		6. 6.67	
G-AVON	Phoenix-Luton LA-5 Major	PFA/1234		6. 6.67	Not completed. Canx by CAA 2.8.91.
G-AVOO	PA-18-180 Super Cub	18-8511		7. 6.67	
G-AVOP	Jodel D.11	PFA/900		8. 6.67	DBR at Slinford on 8.8.91. Canx.
G-AVOR	Lockspeiser Lord Development Aircraft LDA-01	LDA.01 & PFA/1346		8. 6.67	To G-UTIL 8/86. Canx.
G-AVOS	BN-2A Islander	5		8. 6.67	To N584JA 9/67. Canx 28.9.67.
G-AVOT	Slingsby T.56 SE.5A Currie Wot (Scale Replica)	1590		8. 6.67	To EI-ARH 6/67. Canx.
G-AVOU	Slingsby T.56 SE.5A Currie Wot (Scale Replica)	1591		8. 6.67	To EI-ARI 6/67. Canx.
G-AVOV	Slingsby T.56 SE.5A Currie Wot (Scale Replica)	1592		8. 6.67	To EI-ARJ 6/67. Canx.
G-AVOW	Slingsby T.56 SE.5A Currie Wot (Scale Replica)	1593		8. 6.67	To EI-ARK 6/67. Canx.
G-AVOX	Slingsby T.56 SE.5A Currie Wot (Scale Replica)	1594		8. 6.67	To EI-ARM 6/67. Canx.
G-AVOY	Slingsby T.56 SE.5A Currie Wot (Scale Replica)	1595		8. 6.67	To EI-ARL 6/67. Canx.
G-AVOZ	PA-28-180 Cherokee C	28-3711	N9574J	13. 6.67	(Overshot on landing at Gunton Park, Cromer on 4.9.99)
G-AVPA	Sopwith Pup Replica (built by C.J.Warrilow)	CJW.1		13. 6.67	

Regn	Type	c/n	Previous identity	Regn date	Fate or immediate subsequent identity (if known)
G-AVPB	Boeing 707-336C	19843	(9G-ACZ)	14. 6.67	To SU-DAC 2.84. Canx 2.2.84.
	(Line No. 735)		G-AVPB		
G-AVPC	Druine D.31 Turbulent	PFA/544		15. 6.67	
G-AVPD	McKay-Jodel D.92 Bebe			15. 6.67	(Stored 2/96)
		521 & MAC.1 & PFA/927			
	(built by S.McKay)(Originally regd as Jodel D.9 Bebe)				
G-AVPE	HS.125 Srs.3B	25127		15. 6.67	To G-5-623/G-KASS 3/89. Canx.
	(Type amended to Srs.F.3B on 29.6.84)				
G-AVPF	PA-30-160 Twin Comanche B	30-1427	N8289Y	15. 6.67	To N206RG 5/77. Canx 9.5.77.
G-AVPG	Reims Cessna F.150G	0195		20. 6.67	Fatal crash at Denham on 19.12.68. (Remains dumped in a hangar at Denham until mid-2/69, when it was given to the local dustmen!) Canx.
G-AVPH	Reims Cessna F.150G	0197		20. 6.67	
G-AVPI	Reims Cessna F.172H Skyhawk	0409		20. 6.67	
G-AVPJ	DH.82A Tiger Moth	86326	NL879	20. 6.67	
G-AVPK	Socata MS.892A Rallye Commodore 150	10736		20. 6.67	CofA expired 10.1.92. (Stored 8/92) Canx by CAA 13.4.99.
G-AVPL	Socata MS.894A Rallye Commodore 150	10737		20. 6.67	To G-FOAM 6/82. Canx.
G-AVPM	SAN Jodel D.117	593	F-BHXO	20. 6.67	
G-AVPN	Handley Page HPR.7 Dart Herald 213	176	I-TIVB	22. 6.67	WFU on 20.10.97. (On display at Elvington) Canx as WFU 8.12.97.
			G-AVPN/D-BIBI/(HB-AAK)		
G-AVPO	Hindustan HAL-26 Pushpak 1	PK-127	9M-AOZ	31. 3.83	
			VT-DWL		
G-AVPP	Avro 652A Anson 19 Srs.2	"34370"	VM330	27. 6.67	Not converted and scrapped in 7/68 at Halfpenny Green. Canx by CAA 16.9.72.
G-AVPR	PA-30-160 Twin Comanche B	30-1511	N8395Y	27. 6.67	
G-AVPS	PA-30-160 Twin Comanche B	30-1548	N8393Y	27. 6.67	
G-AVPT	PA-18-150 Super Cub	18-8513	N4267Z	27. 6.67	Badly damaged in forced landing at Headcorn on 10.2.91. Canx by CAA 6.2.97.
G-AVPU	PA-18-150 Super Cub	18-8533	N4292Z	27. 6.67	Fatal crash and burnt out at Portmoak on 25.10.84. Canx by CAA 14.10.86.
G-AVPV	PA-28-180 Cherokee C	28-2705	9J-RBP	27. 6.67	
G-AVPW	Douglas C-47A-10-DK Dakota	12476	KG441	29. 6.67	To YV-25CP 6/75. Canx 17.6.75.
			(RCAF)/42-92652		
G-AVPX	Taylor JT.1 Monoplane	PFA/1410 & AJP.1		5. 7.67	Destroyed in fatal crash 1 mile north of Fenland on 4.8.86. Canx as destroyed 22.10.86.
G-AVPY	PA-25-235 Pawnee C	25-4330	N4636Y	7. 7.67	Crashed spraying at Lower Radbourne Farm, Ladbroke, Warwickshire on 25.6.76. Canx.
G-AVPZ	Moravan Zlin Z.526 Trener Master	1015	OK-VRE	7. 7.67	Overshot and crashed into the roof of a hangar while landing at Kidlington on 5.5.68. Canx.
G-AVRA	BN-2A-8 Islander	6	F-BUOQ	7. 7.67	Restored as F-BUOQ 9/74. Canx 25.3.74.
	(Originally regd as BN-2)		(F-BUFV)/G-AVRA		
G-AVRB	BN-2A-26 Islander	7		7. 7.67	To YV-T-MTM(2) 12/67. Canx 8/68.
G-AVRC	BN-2A-26 Islander	8	(TF-REJ)	7. 7.67	To N28BN 6/78. Canx 6.6.78.
			G-AVRC/OO-AST/OO-ARI(2)/G-4-8/I-TRAM/G-51-1/G-AVRC		
G-AVRD	HS.125 Srs.3B	25130	G-5-14	7. 7.67	To HB-VAZ 2/68. Canx 4.3.68.
G-AVRE	HS.125 Srs.3B	25131	G-5-11	7. 7.67	To F-BPMC 5/68. Canx 13.5.68.
G-AVRF	HS.125 Srs.3B	25133		7. 7.67	To G-ILLS 8/89. Canx.
G-AVRG	HS.125 Srs.3B/RA	25144	G-5-12	7. 7.67	To G-OHEA 11/86. Canx.
	(Converted from Srs.3A to Srs.3B/RA in 1968)				
G-AVRH	HS.125 Srs.3A/RA	NA706 & 25146		7. 7.67	To N77167 7/68. Canx 22.7.68.
	(Originally regd as Srs.3A)				
G-AVRI	HS.125 Srs.3A/R	25148	G-5-13	7. 7.67	To N8125J 8/67. Canx 10.8.67.
	(Originally regd as Srs.3A)				
G-AVRJ	HS.125 Srs.3A/R	25149		7. 7.67	To N1125E 8/67. Canx 14.8.67.
	(Originally regd as Srs.3A)				
G-AVRK	PA-28-180 Cherokee C	28-4041		11. 7.67	
G-AVRL	Boeing 737-204	19709		14. 7.67	To N311XV 4/86. Canx 3.4.86.
	(Line No. 38)				
G-AVRM	Boeing 737-204	19710		14. 7.67	To N312XV 1/86. Canx 30.1.86.
	(Line No. 54)				
G-AVRN	Boeing 737-204	19711	N281LF	14. 7.67	To N172PL 6/94. Canx 29.10.93.
	(Line No. 155)		G-AVRN/PH-TVG/G-AVRN		
G-AVRO	Boeing 737-204	19712	B-2605	14. 7.67	To N313VA 5/86. Canx 2.5.86.
	(Line No. 162)		G-AVRO/B-2605/G-AVRO		
G-AVRP	PA-28-140 Cherokee	28-23153		14. 7.67	
G-AVRR	HS.748 Srs.2A/239	1635	ZS-HSI	14. 7.67	To TR-LQJ 10/71. Canx 22.10.71.
	(Originally regd as Srs.2)		G-AVRR/9J-ABM/G-AVRR/ZS-IGI/G-AVRR/CF-YQD/G-AVRR		
G-AVRS	Gardan GY-80-180 Horizon	224		14. 7.67	(Struck a hedge on landing at Throstle Nest Farm, Cleveland on 12.9.99)
G-AVRT	PA-28-140 Cherokee	28-23143		17. 7.67	
G-AVRU	PA-28-180 Cherokee C	28-4025		17. 7.67	
G-AVRV	Rollason-Druine D.62B Condor	RAE/623		18. 7.67	Fatal crash into sea off Folkestone after mid-air collision with Airedale G-ARZR on 6.7.68. Canx.
G-AVRW	Barritault JB-01 Minicab	OH-1549 & PFA/1800		18. 7.67	
G-AVRX	PA-E23-250 Aztec C	27-3646	N6438Y	20. 7.67	To G-BTCG 6/82. Canx.
G-AVRY	PA-28-180 Cherokee C	28-4089		24. 7.67	
G-AVRZ	PA-28-180 Cherokee C	28-4137		24. 7.67	
G-AVSA	PA-28-180 Cherokee C	28-4184		24. 7.67	
G-AVSB	PA-28-180 Cherokee C	28-4191		24. 7.67	
G-AVSC	PA-28-180 Cherokee C	28-4193		24. 7.67	
G-AVSD	PA-28-180 Cherokee C	28-4195		24. 7.67	

Regn	Type	c/n	Previous identity	Regn date	Fate or immediate subsequent identity (if known)
G-AVSE	PA-28-180 Cherokee C	28-4196		24. 7.67	Canx by CAA 18.5.99.
G-AVSF	PA-28-180 Cherokee C	28-4197		24. 7.67	
G-AVSG	PA-28-180 Cherokee C	28-4377		24. 7.67	Crashed at Fawkham Green, Kent on 1.4.76. Canx.
G-AVSH	PA-28-180 Cherokee D	28-4395		24. 7.67	To G-HOCK 5/86. Canx.
G-AVSI	PA-28-140 Cherokee	28-23148		24. 7.67	
G-AVSJ	PA-30-160 Twin Comanche	30-1327	N8229Y	25. 7.67	Fatal crash when flown into hill at Col du Mont, Verdun near Limonest, France on 24.4.72.
G-AVSK	Bell 47G-4A	7576	N7178S	26. 7.67	Crashed & DBF at Glentrool Forest, Wigtown on 14.2.73 and used for spares. Canx as WFU 12.10.81.
G-AVSL	Lebaudy Replica Airship	1		28. 7.67	Destroyed in gales in 1967. Canx as destroyed 15.4.77.
G-AVSM	Piaggio P.166L-B2	416		1. 8.67	WFU at Luton on 9.9.71. Canx as WFU 1.6.72. To I-PJAG 9/72.
G-AVSN	Agusta-Bell 206A JetRanger	8008		1. 8.67	Destroyed in mid-air collision with Tiger Moth G-ANDE at Biggin Hill on 15.5.77. Canx by CAA 24.8.81.
G-AVSO	PA-23-250 Aztec C	27-2794	N5679Y	1. 8.67	Crashed into hills north-east of Loch Leven on 1.10.79. Canx.
G-AVSP	PA-28-180 Cherokee C	28-3952	(PJ-ACT)	8. 8.67	
G-AVSR	Beagle D.5/180 Husky	3689		8. 8.67	
G-AVSS	Reims Cessna F.150H	0233		8. 8.67	Collided in mid-air with Cessna F.150G G-AVAB and crashed about 5 miles north of Scone, near Guildtown on 22.11.75.
G-AVST	Bensen B.7 Seaplane	B.7		8. 8.67	Canx as WFU 5.3.69.
G-AVSU	Hughes 269A	62-0102	N8778F	8. 8.67	Crashed at Eastleigh on 30.10.68. Canx as WFU 23.9.74.
G-AVSV(1)	Agusta-Bell 206A JetRanger	8021		. .67R	NTU - To (G-AVSX(1))/F-BNPS 11/68. Canx.
G-AVSV(2)	Agusta-Bell 206A JetRanger	8014	VR-BCU G-AVSV	8. 8.67	Fatal crash into the sea 18 miles W of Accra, Ghana while returning from a coastal oil rig on 22.7.70. Canx.
G-AVSW(1)	Agusta-Bell 206A JetRanger	8022		. .67R	NTU - To (G-ASVY(3))/G-AVZH 12/67. Canx.
G-AVSW(2)	Agusta-Bell 206B JetRanger II (Originally 206A; later modified)	8016	5N-AHW G-AVSW	8. 8.67	To VH-UOA 6/94. Canx 20.4.94.
G-AVSX(1)	Agusta-Bell 206A JetRanger	8023		. .67R	NTU - To (G-AVSY(2))/(G-AVSZ(2))/R.Saudi Arabian AF as 1205. Canx.
G-AVSX(2)	Agusta-Bell 206A JetRanger	8021	(G-AVSV)	. .67R	NTU - To F-BNPS 11/68. Canx.
G-AVSX(3)	Agusta-Bell 206A JetRanger	8027		8. 8.67	To EP-HAO 3/68. Canx.
G-AVSY(1)	Agusta-Bell 206A JetRanger	8024		. .67R	NTU - To Iran AF as 5-57. Canx.
G-AVSY(2)	Agusta-Bell 206A JetRanger	8023	(G-AVSX)	. .67R	NTU - To (G-AVSZ(2))/R.Saudi Arabian AF as 1205. Canx.
G-AVSY(3)	Agusta-Bell 206A JetRanger	8022	(G-AVSW)	. .67R	NTU - To G-AVZH 12/67. Canx.
G-AVSY(4)	Agusta-Bell 206A JetRanger	8031		8. 8.67	To VR-BCQ 3/68. Canx 12.3.68.
G-AVSZ(1)	Agusta-Bell 206A JetRanger	8025		. .67R	NTU - To G-AVYX 11/67. Canx.
G-AVSZ(2)	Agusta-Bell 206A JetRanger	8023	(G-AVSY) (G-AVSX)	. .67R	NTU - To R.Saudi Arabian AF as 1205. Canx.
G-AVSZ(3)	Agusta-Bell 206B JetRanger (Originally 206A; later modified)	8032	VH-BEQ PK-HBZ/VR-BCR/PK-HBD/VR-BCR/G-AVSZ	8. 8.67	
G-AVTA	Avro 652A Anson 19 Srs.2	"33418"	PH845	8. 8.67	Not converted and scrapped at Halfpenny Green in 1968. Canx by CAA 16.9.72.
G-AVTB(1)	Slingsby Nipper T.66 RA.45 Srs.3	S.105/1565	(9J-...)	9. 8.67	Crashed into trees while on approach to West Tanfield, near Wath, Yorks., on 8.6.68. Rebuilt as G-AVTB(2). Canx.
G-AVTB(2)	Slingsby Nipper T.66 RA.45 Srs.3 (Rebuild from S.105/1565)	S.129/1676	G-AVTB(1) (9J-...)	.10.68	To G-CORD 3/88. Canx.
G-AVTC	Slingsby Nipper T.66 RA.45 Srs.3	S.106/1583		9. 8.67	Crashed at Redhill on 17.5.78. Canx by CAA 16.12.91.
G-AVTD	Slingsby Nipper T.66 RA.45 Srs.3	S.107/1604		9. 8.67	NTU - To ZS-UDT 3/68. Canx 30.11.67.
G-AVTE	Bell 206A JetRanger	66		11. 8.67	Crashed 3 miles northeast of New Galloway on 25.9.83. Canx 5.10.83.
G-AVTF	BAC One-Eleven Srs.420EL	BAC.122	"G-AVTR" LV-IZR/G-AVTF/LV-IZR/"LY-IZR"	11. 8.67	Restored as LV-PID/LV-IZR 10/67. Canx.
G-AVTG	Fairchild-Hiller FH.1100	10	N517FH	14. 8.67	Fatal crash at Paris Air Show, Le Bourget, France on 5.6.69 after structural failure. Canx as WFU 23.2.73.
G-AVTH	CEA Jodel DR.1051 Sicile	243	F-BKGT	14. 8.67	Destroyed in fatal accident at Woodplumpton, near Preston on 12.4.80. Canx as WFU 15.6.81.
G-AVTI	PA-30-160B Twin Comanche B	30-1337	N8210Y	14. 8.67	To N65374 7/76. Canx 19.7.76.
G-AVTJ	PA-32-260 Cherokee Six (Rebuild using spare frame no.32-860S)	32-219	N3373W	14. 8.67	
G-AVTK	PA-32-260 Cherokee Six (Rebuild using spare frame no.32-856S)	32-223	(I-....) G-AVTK/N3266W	14. 8.67	To I-GOES 4/98. Canx 20.4.98.
G-AVTL	Brighton Ax7-65 HAFB (Originally regd as Hot-Air Group 1/4 Free Balloon with c/n 1)	01		17. 8.67	Retired from active flying and stored. Canx as WFU 11.9.81. (Inflated 8/92)
G-AVTM	Reims Cessna F.150H Commuter	0238		17. 8.67	To SE-IOD 5/84. Canx 23.5.84.
G-AVTN	Reims Cessna F.150H Commuter	0245		17. 8.67	Crashed off Isle of Mull on 24.12.75.
G-AVTO	Reims Cessna F.150H Commuter	0252		17. 8.67	To CN-TCV 5/84. Canx 11.10.83.
G-AVTP	Reims Cessna F.172H Skyhawk	0458		17. 8.67	
G-AVTR	Reims Cessna F.172H Skyhawk	0470		17. 8.67	Believed to have crashed into the Thames between Canvey Island and the Kent Coast on 26.12.69. Canx.
"G-AVTR"	BAC One-Eleven Srs.420EL	BAC.122	LV-IZR G-AVTF/LV-IZR/"LY-IZR"	17. 8.67	Reportedly painted in these marks in error. Restored as G-AVTF. Canx.
G-AVTS	PA-23-250 Aztec C	27-3489	N6251Y	21. 8.67	To N4241N 5/81. Canx 6.5.81.
G-AVTT	Ercoupe 415D	4399	SE-BFZ NC3774H	21. 8.67	(Stored 9/97; for sale)
G-AVTU	DH.114 Heron 2D	14148		22. 8.67	To R.Malaysian AF as FM1060 1/74. Canx 21.1.74.
G-AVTV	Socata MS.893A Rallye Commodore 180	10725		24. 8.67	
G-AVTW	Boeing 707-399C (Line No. 659)	19767		25. 8.67	To CS-TBI 4/73. Canx 11.4.73.
G-AVTX	Taylor JT.1 Monoplane	PFA/1408		25. 8.67	Construction abandoned. Parts believed used in the construction of G-BDEV. Canx by CAA 14.10.86.

Regn	Type	c/n	Previous identity	Regn date	Fate or immediate subsequent identity (if known)
G-AVTY	HS.125 Srs.3A/RA	25151		30. 8.67	To N125F 9/67. Canx 5.2.68.
G-AVTZ	HS.125 Srs.3A/RA	25152		30. 8.67	To CF-QNS 12/67. Canx.
G-AVUA	Reims Cessna F.172H	0464		5. 9.67	Damaged in high winds at Compton Abbas on 27.2.90. Canx as WFU 11.4.90. (Stored 2/99 North Walsham, Norfolk)
G-AVUB	BN-2A-6 Islander (Converted to BN-2S in 1968, then reverted back)	9		5. 9.67	To OO-ARI(1) 6/71 but NTU - To G-4-9, then CF-YZF in 12/73 . Canx 21.6.71.
G-AVUC	BN-2A-6 Islander	10		5. 9.67	To N671JA 12/67. Canx 15.1.68.
G-AVUD	PA-30-160 Twin Comanche B	30-1515	N8422Y	5. 9.67	
G-AVUE	Ballon Fabrik K-1260/3-RI HAFB	8828		11. 9.67	To HB-BOZ 6/72. Canx 8.6.72.
G-AVUF	Reims Cessna F.172H	0477		11. 9.67	Crashed on take-off from Bembridge, IoW on 21.4.75 & DBR. Canx 31.5.77.
G-AVUG	Reims Cessna F.150H	0234		11. 9.67	(On rebuild at Sturgate 6/96)
G-AVUH	Reims Cessna F.150H	0244		11. 9.67	
G-AVUI	Reims Cessna F.150H	0247		11. 9.67	Crashed at Netherthorpe on 17.12.78. Used for spares. Canx as WFU 29.2.84.
G-AVUJ	Laverda F.8L Super Falco Srs.IV	412		12. 9.67	DBF at Doncaster prior on 6.9.79.
G-AVUK	Enstrom F-28A	12	N4460	14. 9.67	Crashed at Thruxton on 3.12.75. Canx 20.7.83.
G-AVUL	Reims Cessna F.172H	0448		15. 9.67	To 5B-CIY 10/95. Canx 23.10.95.
G-AVUM	Hughes 269B	67-0317		15. 9.67	To G-PLOW 9/83. Canx.
G-AVUN	PA-30-160 Twin Comanche B	30-1329	N8231Y	20. 9.67	To N7HU 4/83. Canx 29.4.83.
G-AVUO	Phoenix Luton LA.4A Minor	PAL/1313		21. 9.67	(Not completed and parts used in construction of G-AXKH - possible long-term build project)
G-AVUP	PA-28-140 Cherokee	28-24120		25. 9.67	To EI-ATK 10/68. Canx.
G-AVUR	PA-28-140 Cherokee	28-24060		25. 9.67	DBR in gale at Andrewsfield on 4.2.74. Canx as destroyed 28.10.74.
G-AVUS(1)	PA-28-140 Cherokee	28-24100		. .67R	NTU - To G-AVUU 9/67. Canx.
G-AVUS(2)	PA-28-140 Cherokee	28-24065	(G-AVUT)	25. 9.67	
G-AVUT(1)	PA-28-140 Cherokee	28-24065		. .67R	NTU - To G-AVUS 9/67. Canx.
G-AVUT(2)	PA-28-140 Cherokee (Fitted with wings of G-ATRS & parts of G-BCPV during rebuild)	28-24085	(G-AVUU)	25. 9.67	
G-AVUU(1)	PA-28-140 Cherokee	28-24085		. .67R	NTU - To G-AVUT 9/67. Canx.
G-AVUU(2)	PA-28-140 Cherokee	28-24100	(G-AVUS)	25. 9.67	
G-AVUV	Cessna 310N	310N-0013	N4113Q	25. 9.67	To N39710 5/83. Canx 10.5.83.
G-AVUW	Schleicher Ka.6E	4135		26. 9.67	To N1342 4/68. Canx.
G-AVUX	Reims Cessna F.172H Skyhawk	0476		26. 9.67	To EI-BKF 12/80. Canx 6.11.80.
G-AVUY	PA-32-300 Cherokee Six	32-40305		29. 9.67	To OH-PCV 4/70. Canx 3.3.70.
G-AVUZ	PA-32-300 Cherokee Six	32-40302		29. 9.67	
G-AVVA	HS.125 Srs.3B	25138	G-5-16 (G-5-12)	29. 9.67	To HB-VBN 4/68. Canx.
G-AVVB	HS.125 Srs.3B/RA (Originally regd as Srs.3B)	25140	G-5-17 (G-5-16)	29. 9.67	To G-DJLW 1/89. Canx.
G-AVVC	Reims Cessna F.172H Skyhawk	0443		29. 9.67	
G-AVVD	Not allocated.				
G-AVVE	Reims Cessna F.150H	0230		29. 9.67	Crashed at East Fortune on 16.5.83. CofA expired 8.9.85. T Tattershall for spares. Canx as WFU 5.12.83.
G-AVVF	DH.104 Dove 8	04541		2.10.67	WFU at Staverton on 11.2.88. Broken up in 4/91. Canx as WF 26.6.91. Wreck on fire dump 6/97 Staverton.
G-AVVG	PA-28-180 Cherokee C (Rebuilt using spare frame c/n 28-3807S)	28-2909	N7517W	3.10.67	To G-NITA 1/84. Canx.
G-AVVH	Agusta-Bell 206B JetRanger (Originally 206A; later modified)	8026	HP-644 G-AVVH	3.10.67	To EI-BEV 5/78. Canx 15.5.78.
G-AVVI	PA-30-160 Twin Comanche B	30-1613	EI-AVD G-AVVI/N8454Y	5.10.67	Damaged in crash at Shipdham on 6.4.91. (On rebuild 8/93) Canx as WFU 29.9.97.
G-AVVJ	Socata MS.893A Rallye Commodore 180	10752		6.10.67	
G-AVVK	Socata MS.880B Rallye Club (Originally regd with c/n 11043)	1143		6.10.67	To EI-AUP 9/70. Canx 23.9.70.
G-AVVL	Reims Cessna F.150H	0257		6.10.67	(Under development 7/97 Cranfield with experimental Wankel MWAE 100R engine)
G-AVVM	SAN Jodel D.117	624	F-BIBF	6.10.67	Destroyed in fatal crash on landing at Brunton on 30.7.82. Canx by CAA 14.10.86.
G-AVVN	Rollason-Druine D.62C Condor (Originally regd as D.62B)	RAE/624		6.10.67	Fatal crash in the grounds of the Oaksmere Country Club, Brome, Suffolk on 31.7.87. Canx as destroyed 17.3.88.
G-AVVO	Avro 652A Anson 19 Srs.2	"34219"	VL348	6.10.67	Not converted. Canx by CAA 16.9.72. (On display 2/99 Winthorpe as VL348)
G-AVVP	Avro 652A Anson 19 Srs.2	"34520"	VP509	6.10.67	Not converted. WFU at Halfpenny Green in 1/68. Broken up for spares at Shawbury in 3/68. Canx as PWFU 6.2.68.
G-AVVR	Avro 652A Anson 19 Srs.2	"34530"	VP519	6.10.67	Not converted. To Elmdon 13.7.68 & scrapped - nose section to The Aeroplane Collection in early 1970s. Canx by CAA 16.9.72.
G-AVVS	Hughes H.269B	116-0284	EI-APN N8907F	9.10.67	To I-SCVB. Canx 7.1.88.
G-AVVT	PA-23-250 Aztec C	27-3486	N6495Y	12.10.67	CofA expired 15.4.85. (Taken by road to IoW in 4/87) Canx by CAA 3.4.89.
G-AVVU	Beechcraft A23A Musketeer Custom III	M-1092		17.10.67	Crashed into field near Goodwood, Sussex on 20.9.81. Canx as destroyed 29.2.84.
G-AVVV	PA-28-180 Cherokee C (Rebuilt in 1967 using spare frame 28-3808S)	28-2853	N8880J	19.10.67	To EI-CIF 6/93. Canx 24.5.93.
G-AVVW	Reims Cessna F.150H	0258		19.10.67	WFU on 31.5.82. Canx as WFU 4.6.82. (To Instructional Airframe)
G-AVVX	Reims Cessna F.150H	0259		19.10.67	Damaged at Franklyn's Field on 12.12.97. Canx as destroye 17.3.98.
G-AVVY	Reims Cessna F.150H	0264		19.10.67	To G-UFLY 9/89. Canx.

Regn	Type	c/n	Previous identity	Regn date	Fate or immediate subsequent identity (if known)
G-AVVZ	Reims Cessna F.172H	0475		19.10.67	To LN-HHB 5/76. Canx 7.5.76.
G-AVWA	PA-28-140 Cherokee	28-23660		19.10.67	
G-AVWB	PA-28-140 Cherokee	28-23680		19.10.67	Crashed at Chigwell 3.3.81.
G-AVWC	Not allocated.				
G-AVWD	PA-28-140 Cherokee	28-23700		19.10.67	
G-AVWE	PA-28-140 Cherokee	28-23720		19.10.67	CofA expired 22.4.82 & WFU. (Later in open storage at Biggin Hill) Canx by CAA 8.6.89. (On rebuild 4/93)
G-AVWF	PA-28-140 Cherokee	28-23740	PH-VRK (G-AVWF)	19.10.67	CofA expired 23.5.81. Used for spares at Caernarfon in 1985. Canx as WFU 19.11.85.
G-AVWG	PA-28-140 Cherokee	28-23760		19.10.67	Badly damaged in forced landing Tal-y-Fan, Conwy, Gwynedd on 11.12.88. (Only wings remained 6/96) (Components used to rebuild G-BBEF in 1998)
G-AVWH	PA-28-140 Cherokee	28-23780		19.10.67	To G-OSOW 6/94. Canx.
G-AVWI	PA-28-140 Cherokee	28-23800		19.10.67	
G-AVWJ	PA-28-140 Cherokee	28-23940		19.10.67	
G-AVWK	PA-28-140 Cherokee	28-23945		19.10.67	Crashed during a practice forced-landing at Needless Hall, near Morpeth on 23.6.68. Canx.
G-AVWL	PA-28-140 Cherokee	28-24000		19.10.67	(Stored 7/97)
G-AVWM	PA-28-140 Cherokee	28-24005		19.10.67	
G-AVWN	PA-28R-180 Cherokee Arrow	28R-30170		19.10.67	
G-AVWO	PA-28R-180 Cherokee Arrow	28R-30205		19.10.67	
G-AVWP	PA-28R-180 Cherokee Arrow	28R-30219		19.10.67	To EI-ASV 2/68. Canx 17.2.68.
G-AVWR	PA-28R-180 Cherokee Arrow	28R-30242		19.10.67	
G-AVWS	PA-28R-180 Cherokee Arrow	28R-30326		19.10.67	DBER in forced landing in a field at Creon, France on 14.10.71. Canx as destroyed 20.8.73.
G-AVWT	PA-28R-180 Cherokee Arrow	28R-30362		19.10.67	
G-AVWU	PA-28R-180 Cherokee Arrow	28R-30380		19.10.67	
G-AVWV	PA-28R-180 Cherokee Arrow	28R-30404		19.10.67	
G-AVWW	Mooney M.20F Executive	670501	N6422Q	19.10.67	DBF at Chase Farm, Little Burstead, Essex on 15.9.79. Canx by CAA 14.10.86.
G-AVWX	Cessna 310L	310L-0186	N3336X	19.10.67	To VH-EDK 12/70. Canx 25.11.70.
G-AVWY	Sportavia-Putzer Fournier RF-4D	4031		26.10.67	(On rebuild Barton 2/99)
G-AVWZ	Sportavia-Putzer Fournier RF-4D	4032		26.10.67	Crashed on take-off from Shoreham on 11.1.81. Canx 2.2.81.
G-AVXA	PA-25-235 Pawnee C (Rebuilt using new frame)	25-4244	N4576Y	26.10.67	
G-AVXB	Bensen B.8 Gyrocopter (Rebuild of G-ARTN (c/n DC/61/008) and designates Lovegrove PL.1 Gyrocopter 6/80)	PCL-1		26.10.67	Permit expired 23.6.87. Canx by CAA 4.12.90.
G-AVXC	Slingsby Nipper T.66 RA.45 Srs.3	S.108/1605		26.10.67	
G-AVXD	Slingsby Nipper T.66 RA.45 Srs.3	S.109/1606		26.10.67	
G-AVXE	Slingsby Nipper T.66 RA.45 Srs.3	S.110/1607		26.10.67	To 9J-RID 2/68. Canx 1.2.68.
G-AVXF	PA-28R-180 Cherokee Arrow	28R-30044		26.10.67	
G-AVXG	Luton LA-5A Major	001		26.10.67	Fatal crash shortly after take-off from Trafford Farm, Benendon on 19.2.76. Canx 15.7.76.
G-AVXH	Douglas DC-7CF (Line No. 692)	44881	N7398A N739PA	30.10.67	Restored as N7398A 4/69. Canx 12.4.69.
G-AVXI	HS.748 Srs.2A/238	1623		2.11.67	
G-AVXJ	HS.748 Srs.2A/238	1624		2.11.67	(Stored 3/99 at Exeter)
G-AVXK	HS.125 Srs.3B/RA (Originally regd as Srs.3B)	25143	D-CHTH G-AVXK/G-5-18	2.11.67	To 5N-AOG 1/83. Canx 24.1.83.
G-AVXL	HS.125 Srs.3B	25145	LN-APC G-AVXL/G-5-20	2.11.67	To I-SNAF 1/78. Canx 20.1.78.
G-AVXM	HS.125 Srs.3A/RA (Originally regd as Srs.3A)	25153	G-5-19	2.11.67	To N30F 1/68. Canx 19.1.68.
G-AVXN	HS.125 Srs.3A/RA (Originally regd as Srs.3A)	25155		2.11.67	To N32F 1/68. Canx 26.1.68.
G-AVXO	BN-2A Islander	11		2.11.67	To N672JA 12/67. Canx.
G-AVXP	BN-2A Islander	12		2.11.67	To (N681VK)/N581JA 1/68. Canx.
G-AVXR	BN-2A Islander	13	G-51-2	2.11.67	NTU - To G-51-2/TR-LNG 1/68. Canx.
G-AVXS	BN-2A Islander	14	G-51-3	2.11.67	To TI-1063C 2/68. Canx 1.2.68.
G-AVXT	BN-2A Islander	15		2.11.67	To VH-AIA 3/68. Canx 7.3.68.
G-AVXU	BN-2A Islander	16	G-51-4	2.11.67	NTU - To G-51-4/TR-LNF 3/68. Canx.
G-AVXV	Blériot XI	225		2.11.67	To F-AZIN. Canx 16.7.92.
G-AVXW	Rollason-Druine D.62B Condor	RAE/625		3.11.67	
G-AVXX	Reims Cessna FR.172E Rocket	0013		7.11.67	Struck a hillside and came to rest inverted at St.Johns-in-the-Vale, Cumbria on 11.1.92. Canx as destroyed 7.1.94.
G-AVXY	Auster AOP.9 (Regd with c/n AUS/120)	B5/10/120	XK417	7.11.67	
G-AVXZ	PA-28-180 Cherokee C	28-4340		13.11.67	Overshot on landing at Lelant, near St.Ives on 8.9.73. Remains donated to 1907 ATC Sqdn at Hayle, Cornwall.
G-AVYA	DH.121 Trident 1E-140	2135		13.11.67	NTU - To 4R-ACN 7/69. Canx 11.11.68.
G-AVYB	DH.121 Trident 1E-140	2136		13.11.67	WFU at Heathrow on 31.8.80. Canx 19.5.81.
G-AVYC	DH.121 Trident 1E-110 (Originally regd as Srs.1E-140, became Srs.1E-110 on 22.1.69)	2137		13.11.67	WFU at Heathrow on 31.7.80. Canx 19.5.81.
G-AVYD	DH.121 Trident 1E-110	2138		13.11.67	Damaged at Bilbao on 15.9.75. Canx as WFU 5.12.75.
G-AVYE	DH.121 Trident 1E-140	2139		13.11.67	WFU on 24.4.81. Canx 19.5.81. (Cabin fire suppression research; extant 1/93 Hatfield)
G-AVYF(1)	Beechcraft A23-24 Musketeer	MA-333		.67R	NTU - Canx.

Regn	Type	c/n	Previous identity	Regn date	Fate or immediate subsequent identity (if known)
G-AVYF(2)	Beechcraft A23-24 Musketeer	MA-316		14.11.67	Damaged in forced landing 2 miles south of Usworth on 4.7.81. Canx by CAA 14.10.86.
G-AVYG	SNCAN Stampe SV-4C	537	F-BDCH	14.11.67	To N14SV 9/70. Canx 11.9.70.
G-AVYH	Cessna U206 Super Skywagon	206-0075	5Y-KTT VP-KTT/N5075U	15.11.67	Stolen & DBR in fatal crash in Rhodesia whilst 5Y-KTT, which was then canx 19.10.67. Ownership passed to London & Edinburgh Insurance as one of the interested parties to whom the owner presumably owed money - hence no CofA issued. Canx as WFU 26.10.70.
G-AVYI	Reims Cessna FR.172E Rocket	0018		17.11.67	NTU - Not Imported. To D-EDLP 5/68. Canx 13.12.67.
G-AVYJ	Reims Cessna FR.172E Rocket	0017	F-WLIS	17.11.67	NTU - Not Imported. To OH-CCZ 3/68. Canx 13.12.67.
G-AVYK	Beagle A.61 Terrier 3	B.642	WJ357	20.11.67	(Stored 8/98 at Aboyne)
G-AVYL	PA-28-180 Cherokee D	28-4622		24.11.67	
G-AVYM	PA-28-180 Cherokee D	28-4638		24.11.67	
G-AVYN	PA-28-180 Cherokee D	28-4662		24.11.67	Crashed 10 miles west of Ripon on 23.9.69. Canx.
G-AVYO	PA-28-140 Cherokee	28-24186		24.11.67	Crashed near Sandown, IoW on 8.7.84. Canx as destroyed 8.10.85.
G-AVYP	PA-28-140 Cherokee	28-24211		24.11.67	
G-AVYR	PA-28-140 Cherokee	28-24226		24.11.67	
G-AVYS	PA-28R-180 Cherokee Arrow	28R-30456		24.11.67	
G-AVYT	PA-28R-180 Cherokee Arrow	28R-30472		24.11.67	
G-AVYU	Beagle Auster A.61 Terrier 1 (Is actually an Auster 10 converted from a Mk.6)	3746	WJ401	24.11.67	Canx as WFU 6.5.75. Shipped to Australia 8/78.
G-AVYV	Wassmer Jodel D.120A Paris-Nice	252	F-BMAM	27.11.67	(Stored 4/96)
G-AVYW	Brookland Mosquito Mk.II Gyroplane	4		27.11.67	Crashed at Teesside on 9.3.69. Canx.
G-AVYX(1)	Agusta-Bell 206A JetRanger	8030		. .67R	NTU - To Saudia Arabian AF as 1405. Canx.
G-AVYX(2)	Agusta-Bell 206A JetRanger	8025	(G-AVSZ)	27.11.67	To VH-JOY 11/91. Canx 12.11.91.
G-AVYY	SNCAN Stampe SV-4C	548	F-BDCS	29.11.67	To CF-AYF 3/70. Canx 17.3.70.
G-AVYZ	BAC One-Eleven Srs.320L-AZ	BAC.133		29.11.67	To G-BKAX 4/82. Canx.
G-AVZA	IMCO Callair A-9	1200	SE-EUA N26D	30.11.67	Damaged at Pinchbeck on 4.8.73. Rebuild & re-regd as G-TDFS 10/86. Canx.
G-AVZB	LET Z-37 Cmelak	04-08	OK-WKQ	30.11.67	Canx as WFU 21.12.88. (On display 9/93 Wroughton)
G-AVZC	Hughes H.269B	45-0189	EI-AOU	5.12.67	Crashed in a field near the A63 road on 28.3.90. Canx by CAA 16.7.90. Wreck at Barton 30.8.90.
G-AVZD	HS.748 Srs.2/228	1601	A10-601	6.12.67	To R Australian AF as A10-601 8/68. Canx 9.8.68.
G-AVZE	Rollason Druine D.62B Condor	RAE/626		8.12.67	To EI-BXT 8/88. Canx 23.8.88.
G-AVZF	Bell 47G-2	2225	9L-LAM G-AVZF/LN-ORO/N6731D	12.12.67	To OO-BEM 3/72. Canx.
G-AVZG(1)	Agusta-Bell 206A JetRanger	8040		. .67R	NTU - To Turkish Army as J-040. Canx.
G-AVZG(2)	Agusta-Bell 206A JetRanger	8017		12.12.67	Canx 8.4.76 on sale to Canada.
G-AVZH(1)	Agusta-Bell 206A JetRanger	8002		. .67R	NTU - To SE-HPB. Canx.
G-AVZH(2)	Agusta-Bell 206A JetRanger	8022	(G-AVSY) (G-AVSW)	14.12.67	Crashed at South Cerney on 4.10.72. Canx as WFU 22.2.73.
G-AVZI	Bolkow Bo.208C-1 Junior	673	D-EGZF	19.12.67	CofA expired 24.7.76. Stored at Park Farm. (Status uncertain)
G-AVZJ	HS.125 Srs.3A/RA	25156		19.12.67	To N522M 1/68. Canx 5.2.68.
G-AVZK	HS.125 Srs.3A/RA	25158		19.12.67	To XB-PUE 5/68. Canx 12.3.68.
G-AVZL	HS.125 Srs.3A/RA	25159	G-5-19	19.12.67	To CF-WOS 3/68. Canx 6.3.68.
G-AVZM	Beagle B.121 Pup Srs.100	B121-005		19.12.67	CofA expired 18.10.81. Canx as WFU 5.12.83.
G-AVZN	Beagle B.121 Pup Srs.100	B121-006		19.12.67	
G-AVZO	Beagle B.121 Pup Srs.100	B121-007		19.12.67	CofA expired 12.7.85 & WFU at Benedon.
G-AVZP	Beagle B.121 Pup Srs.100	B121-008		19.12.67	
G-AVZR	PA-28-180 Cherokee C	28-4114	N4779L	19.12.67	
G-AVZS	Cessna 310B	35660	SE-ETW ST-AAV/VP-YPT/N5460A	27.12.67	Crashed on landing at Elstree on 24.5.83. Canx 21.7.83.
G-AVZT	PA-31 Navajo	31-86	N9059Y	27.12.67	To N27337 5/82. Canx 5.5.82.
G-AVZU	Reims Cessna F.150H	0283		29.12.67	
G-AVZV	Reims Cessna F.172H Skyhawk	0511		29.12.67	
G-AVZW	EAA Model P Biplane	PFA/1314		29.12.67	Overturned and badly damaged on landing at Goodwood on 26.4.85 when starboard wheel brake jammed. CofA expired 12.3.86. (Status uncertain)
G-AVZX	Socata MS.880B Rallye Club	1165		29.12.67	
G-AVZY	Socata MS.880B Rallye Club	1166		29.12.67	Canx as WFU 30.5.84.
G-AVZZ	Boeing 707-138B (Line No. 54)	17699	VH-EBD	4. 1.68	To N500JJ 11/78. Canx 10.11.78.
G-AWAA	Morane Saulnier MS.880B Rallye Club	1174		29.12.67	CofA expired 4.8.91. (Stored 10/95 at St.Just) Canx by CAA 4.3.99.
G-AWAB	Morane Saulnier MS.893A Rallye Commodore 180	10786		29.12.67	Fatal crash on take-off from Lansdown race-course strip, near Bath on 2.8.69, engine failed and crashed into nearby woods. (Wreckage to Farnborough on 4.8.69)
G-AWAC	Gardan GY-80-180 Horizon	234		29.12.67	
G-AWAD	Beechcraft 95-D55 Baron	TE-548		1. 1.68	To G-MOSS 6/95. Canx.
G-AWAE	Beechcraft 95-D55 Baron	TE-546		1. 1.68	To N55BE 1/85. Canx 13.11.84.
G-AWAF	Beechcraft 95-D55 Baron	TE-544		1. 1.68	Canx 11.7.84 on sale to USA. To Dodson Aviation Scrapyard.
G-AWAG	Beechcraft 95-D55 Baron	TE-542		1. 1.68	Canx 11.7.84 on sale to USA. To Dodson Aviation Scrapyard.
G-AWAH	Beechcraft 95-D55 Baron	TE-540		1. 1.68	
G-AWAI	Beechcraft 95-D55 Baron	TE-538		1. 1.68	To N63RC 2/93. Canx 19.2.93.
G-AWAJ	Beechcraft 95-D55 Baron	TE-536		1. 1.68	
G-AWAK	Beechcraft 95-D55 Baron	TE-534		1. 1.68	To N5357G. Canx 1.6.84.
G-AWAL	Beechcraft 95-D55 Baron	TE-532		1. 1.68	Canx 11.7.84 on sale to USA. To Dodson Aviation Scrapyard.
G-AWAM	Beechcraft 95-D55 Baron	TE-530		1. 1.68	Canx 11.7.84 on sale to USA. To Dodson Aviation Scrapyard.

Regn	Type	c/n	Previous identity	Regn date	Fate or immediate subsequent identity (if known)
G-AWAN	Beechcraft 95-D55 Baron	TE-528		1. 1.68	CofA expired 14.3.83 & WFU at Hamble. Canx as WFU 11.7.84. To Dodson Aviation Scrapyard in USA.
G-AWAO	Beechcraft 95-D55 Baron	TE-524		1. 1.68	To N95SB 4/86. Canx 24.1.86.
G-AWAP	Aerospatiale SA.318C Alouette Astazou	1966	F-BOSD	3. 1.68	Crashed on Gat Sand, in The Wash on 26.6.83. Canx as destroyed 11.7.84.
G-AWAR	Moravan Zlin Z.526A Akrobat	1036		4. 1.68	DBR on landing after the port wing failed in a flight from Hullavington on 5.6.70. Canx.
G-AWAS	Campbell-Bensen B.8Mc Gyrocopter	CA/307		5. 1.68	Canx as WFU 10.7.73. (Stored Borgo San Laurenz, Florence, Italy - noted still marked as G-AWAS in 1983)
G-AWAT	Rollason-Druine D.62B Condor	RAE/627		8. 1.68	
G-AWAU	Vickers FB.27A Vimy Replica	VAFA-02	"H651"	8. 1.68	Canx as WFU 19.7.73. (On display 10/95 RAF Museum, Hendon)
G-AWAV	Reims Cessna F.150F (Wichita c/n 62476)	0007	OY-DKL	5. 1.68	Damaged when undercarriage collapsed at Ipswich on 10.10.83. (Fuselage in open store 3/95 at Southend)
G-AWAW	Reims Cessna F.150F (Wichita c/n 63167)	0037	OY-DKJ	5. 1.68	Canx as WFU 16.5.90. (On display in Flight Lab gallery 8/97 South Kensington, London)
G-AWAX	Cessna 150D (Rebuilt 94/96 with fuselage from G-ASTV - original fuselage stored 11/94)	150-60153	OY-TRJ N4153U	5. 1.68	
G-AWAY	PA-28R-180 Cherokee Arrow	28R-30496		8. 1.68	Crashed on take-off from Atarot Airport, Jerusalem on 25.11.75. Canx.
G-AWAZ	PA-28R-180 Cherokee Arrow	28R-30512		8. 1.68	
G-AWBA	PA-28R-180 Cherokee Arrow	28R-30528		8. 1.68	
G-AWBB	PA-28R-180 Cherokee Arrow	28R-30552		8. 1.68	
G-AWBC	PA-28R-180 Cherokee Arrow	28R-30572		8. 1.68	
G-AWBD	PA-28-140 Cherokee	28-24241		8. 1.68	Crashed into Scafell Pike in Lake District on 28.3.78.
G-AWBE	PA-28-140 Cherokee	28-24266		8. 1.68	
G-AWBF	Not allocated.				
G-AWBG	PA-28-140 Cherokee	28-24286		8. 1.68	Forced landing on Hayle Sands, near St.Ives, Cornwall on 3.11.90, and subsequently immersed by the tide.
G-AWBH	PA-28-140 Cherokee	28-24306		8. 1.68	(Stored 5/95)
G-AWBI	Douglas DC-7CF (Line No. 698)	44884	N7421 N742PA	11. 1.68	Restored as N7421 4/69. Canx 21.4.69.
G-AWBJ	Sportavia-Putzer Fournier RF-4D	4055		12. 1.68	
G-AWBK	Cessna 421 Golden Eagle (Originally regd with c/n 421-0124 (became N3150K))	421-0125	(N3151K)	12. 1.68	To F-GAJJ 10/76. Canx 4.10.76.
G-AWBL	BAC One-Eleven Srs.416EK	BAC.132		17. 1.68	To ZS-NYZ 7/96. Canx 23.7.96.
G-AWBM	Druine D.31A Turbulent (Incorporates parts of G-ARIM)	PFA/1647		17. 1.68	
G-AWBN	PA-30-160 Twin Comanche B	30-1472	N8517Y	18. 1.68	
G-AWBO	Bensen B.8M Gyrocopter (Originally regd with c/n 17)	19		18. 1.68	Fatal crash at Druidale, IoM on 15.9.69. Canx 4.11.69.
G-AWBP	Cessna 182L Skylane	182-58831	N42051	18. 1.68	To ZS-NOI 7/94. Canx 20.6.94.
G-AWBR	Handley Page 137 Jetstream 3M (Production No. 05) (Originally ordered as first C-10A for USAF until contract cancelled)	258		22. 1.68	WFU in 10/69. Broken up at Radlett in 5/70. Nose to 1163 ATC Sqdn at Earls Colne & reportedly scrapped by 1978. Canx as WFU 17.1.74.
G-AWBS	PA-28-140 Cherokee	28-24331		22. 1.68	
G-AWBT	PA-30-160 Twin Comanche B	30-1668	N8508Y	22. 1.68	Damaged in landing at Kirmington on 10.3.88. Canx as WFU 15.7.88. (Instructional Airframe 7/97 Cranfield)
G-AWBU	Morane-Saulnier Type N Replica	PPS/REP/7		22. 1.68	
G-AWBV	Cessna 182L Skylane	182-58815	(VH-...) G-AWBV/N42024	22. 1.68	To VH-TRS(3) 7/97. Canx 15.7.97.
G-AWBW	Reims Cessna F.172H	0486		22. 1.68	Crashed on landing at Compton Abbas on 20.5.73. Canx as WFU 23.5.74. (Instructional Airframe 6/91)
G-AWBX	Reims Cessna F.150H	0286		22. 1.68	
G-AWBY	BN-2A-6 Islander (Originally regd as BN-2)	17		22. 1.68	To I-LACO 10/73. Canx 20.9.72.
G-AWBZ	BN-2A-8 Islander (Originally regd as BN-2)	18		22. 1.68	To VH-ISG 4/73. Canx 17.4.73.
G-AWCA	BN-2A Islander	19		22. 1.68	To N582JA 4/68. Canx.
G-AWCB	BN-2A Islander	20		22. 1.68	To N585JA 4/68. Canx.
G-AWCC	BN-2A Islander	21		22. 1.68	To D-IOLT 4/68. Canx.
G-AWCD	CEA Jodel DR.253 Regent	113		24. 1.68	To F-GFLU 12/87. Canx 10.12.87.
G-AWCE	Slingsby Nipper T.66 RA.45 Srs.3	S.111/1617		24. 1.68	Canx 20.6.70 on sale to Norway, but crashed on 28.6.70 at Groenoera, Snaasa, Norway whilst on delivery.
G-AWCF	Slingsby Nipper T.66 RA.45 Srs.3	S.112/1618		24. 1.68	NTU - To VP-WCC 3/68. Canx 20.3.68.
G-AWCG	Slingsby Nipper T.66 RA.45 Srs.3	S.113/1619		24. 1.68	NTU - To 9J-AAJ 4/68. Canx.
G-AWCH	Reims Cessna F.172H Skyhawk	0522		25. 1.68	To G-HILS 12/88. Canx.
G-AWCI	Cessna 337C Super Skymaster	337-0863	N2563S	25. 1.68	Crashed at Orsett Hall, Essex on 7.11.70. Canx in 8/73.
G-AWCJ	Reims Cessna F.150H	0314		25. 1.68	Crashed in 2/83. Believed used for spares. Canx by CAA 14.10.86.
G-AWCK	Reims Cessna F.150H	0278		25. 1.68	Undercarriage collapse at Baginton on 30.9.75. (Fuselage in open store 9/94)
G-AWCL	Reims Cessna F.150H	0276		25. 1.68	Canx as destroyed 2.2.88.
G-AWCM	Reims Cessna F.150H	0281		25. 1.68	
G-AWCN	Reims Cessna FR.172E Rocket	0020		25. 1.68	
G-AWCO	Reims Cessna F.150H (Originally regd with c/n 0347)	0338		29. 1.68	Used for spares at Biggin Hill in 1983. CofA expired 29.8.75. Canx by CAA 14.10.86. (Wreck in open storage 2/95)

Regn	Type	c/n	Previous identity	Regn date	Fate or immediate subsequent identity (if known)
G-AWCP	Reims Cessna F.150H (Converted to tail-wheel configuration)	0354		29. 1.68	
G-AWCR	Piccard Ax6 HAFB	6204		29. 1.68	Canx as WFU 24.5.78. (Extant 2/97)
G-AWCS	Short SC.7 Skyvan 3-300-1 (Originally a Skyvan 2-200)	SH1839	(VH-EJS)	31. 1.68	To N33VC 4/73. Canx 23.2.73.
G-AWCT	Short SC.7 Skyvan 3-300-11 (Originally a Skyvan 2-200)	SH1842	(VH-EJT)	31. 1.68	To CR-LJF 10/68. Canx.
G-AWCU	Aero Grand Commander 680FP	1377-142	HB-GBW	1. 2.68	To N46832 6/73. Canx 22.6.73.
G-AWCV	Vickers 760D Viscount	186	VR-AAW (VR-AAU)/9M-ALY/(VR-RCH)/VR-HFI	5. 2.68	WFU & stored 4/70. Broken up 5/70 at Teesside. Canx as WFU 16.4.70.
G-AWCW	Beechcraft E95 Travel Air	TD-717		7. 2.68	To HB-GIX. Canx 4.9.92.
G-AWCX	PA-32-260 Cherokee Six (Rebuilt with spare fuselage c/n 32-859S)	32-206	(N3360W)	7. 2.68	Crashed at Borsbeke, Belgium on 1.7.78. To OO-APS(2). Canx.
G-AWCY	PA-32-260 Cherokee Six (Rebuilt with spare fuselage c/n 32-858S)	32-211	(N3365W)	7. 2.68	To G-ETBY 7/89. Canx.
G-AWCZ	PA-32-260 Cherokee Six (Rebuilt with spare fuselage c/n 32-857S)	32-225	(N3294W)	7. 2.68	Crashed at Gough Farm, Blackpark Forest, Chirk on 24.4.76. Remains to Cranfield later. Canx as destroyed 29.2.84.
G-AWDA	Slingsby Nipper T.66 RA.45 Srs.3	S.117/1624		7. 2.68	
G-AWDB	Slingsby Nipper T.66 RA.45 Srs.3	S.118/1625		7. 2.68	To HB-SPQ /77. Canx 5.5.75.
G-AWDC	Slingsby Nipper T.66 RA.45 Srs.3	S.119/1626		7. 2.68	CofA expired 5.6.70. Canx as WFU 20.9.73.
G-AWDD	Slingsby Nipper T.66 RA.45 Srs.3	S.120/1627		7. 2.68	To G-NIPA 6/96. Canx.
G-AWDE	AESL Airtourer T.2 (115)	504		9. 2.68	Crashed at Stapleford on 23.3.75. Canx as WFU 5.6.75. (Fuselage in open store 8/96)
G-AWDF	BAC One-Eleven Srs.204AF	BAC.134	N1124J	13. 2.68	Restored as N1124J 3/68. Canx.
G-AWDG	Boeing 707-138B (Line No. 64)	17702	VH-EBG	7. 3.68	To N600JJ 12/78. Canx 10.11.78.
G-AWDH	Druine D.31 Turbulent	PFA/1633 & RH-01		15. 2.68	Crashed on take-off from Haworth on 8.7.74. Canx.
G-AWDI	PA-23-250 Aztec C	27-3811	N6520Y	15. 2.68	CofA expired 21.6.85. Canx as WFU on 4.3.88. (Stored 2/97 Willington Village, near Cardington)
G-AWDJ	Cessna 411	411-0184	N4984T	15. 2.68	To N124AC 4/81. Canx 12.5.81.
G-AWDK	Canadair CL-44D4-1	23	N125SW CF-NNM-X	19. 2.68	To PK-BAZ 8/79. Canx 14.8.79.
G-AWDL	PA-25-235 Pawnee C	25-4511		20. 2.68	To 5B-CEZ 6/82. Canx 29.6.82.
G-AWDM	Cessna 401	401-0204	N7836F	21. 2.68	DBR after crashing on Bognor Regis Golf Course shortly after take-off from Lec Refrigeration's airstrip at Bognor on 7.5.71. Canx 24.3.72. Rebuilt as D-IAMG 5/73.
G-AWDN	PA-18-135 Super Cub	18-2151	5N-ADS F-OBKI/N2535A	21. 2.68	Damaged in gales in Morocco on 20.3.69 and also on shipment to UK. Parts used for G-ARTH. Canx as destroyed 20.3.69.
G-AWDO	Druine D.31 Turbulent	PFA/1649		21. 2.68	
G-AWDP	PA-28-180 Cherokee D	28-4870		21. 2.68	(Extant 2/99)
G-AWDR	Reims Cessna FR.172E Rocket	0004		21. 2.68	
G-AWDS	Pilatus PC-6/B1-H2 Turbo-Porter	616	(ST-ADF) HB-FCK	22. 2.68	To ST-AEU 4/73. Canx 12.4.73.
G-AWDT	DH.114 Heron 2D	14147	OY-AFO	22. 2.68	To "N557PR"/N577PR 10/71. Canx 2.10.71.
G-AWDU	Brantly B.2B	481		23. 2.68	
G-AWDV	Slingsby T.49C Capstan	1559	N5551 G-AWDV	26. 2.68	Destroyed in the fire at Slingsby's factory at Kirkbymoorside on 18.11.68. Canx.
G-AWDW	Bensen CB.8M Gyrocopter	DS.1330		26. 2.68	(Stored - status uncertain)
G-AWDX	Beagle B.121 Pup Srs.100	B121-009		28. 2.68	To D-EKDX. Canx 5.6.85.
G-AWDY	Beagle B.121 Pup Srs.150	B121-010	G-35-010 HB-NAA/G-AWDY/G-35-010	28. 2.68	Restored as HB-NAA 8/70. Canx 5.8.70.
G-AWDZ	Beagle B.121 Pup Srs.100	B121-011		28. 2.68	Crashed at Netherthorpe on 3.9.78. Canx.
G-AWEA	Beagle B.121 Pup Srs.100	B121-012		28. 2.68	To OO-WEA 4/69. Canx 3.4.69.
G-AWEB	Beagle B.121 Pup Srs.100	B121-013		28. 2.68	To N556MA 9/68. Canx.
G-AWEC	Beagle B.121 Pup Srs.100	B121-014		28. 2.68	To VR-HGT 10/74. Canx 18.9.74.
G-AWED	PA-31 Turbo Navajo	31-109	N9076Y	28. 2.68	To G-VICK 11/83. Canx.
G-AWEE	Sud SA.318C Alouette II Astazou	1971		29. 2.68	Fatal crash after collision in mid-air with SE.5A Replica EI-ARB over sea 1½ miles North of Wicklow Head, Ireland while filming on 18.8.70. Canx.
G-AWEF	SNCAN Stampe SV-4C	549	F-BDCT	29. 2.68	
G-AWEG	Cessna 172G Skyhawk	172-54322	N4253L	29. 2.68	Broken up at Usworth in 1984. Canx by CAA 3.4.89.
G-AWEH	Campbell-Bensen B.8M Gyrocopter	CA/308		1. 3.68	Canx as WFU 2.3.73. Shipped to Australia in 1968.
G-AWEI	Rollason-Druine D.62B Condor	RAE/628		6. 3.68	
G-AWEJ	BAC One-Eleven Srs.408EF	BAC.115		5. 3.68	To G-BBMG 9/73. Canx.
G-AWEK	Sportavia-Putzer Fournier RF-4D	4071		6. 3.68	
G-AWEL	Sportavia-Putzer Fournier RF-4D	4077		7. 3.68	
G-AWEM	Sportavia-Putzer Fournier RF-4D	4078		7. 3.68	
G-AWEN	SAN Jodel DR.1050 Ambassadeur	67	F-BIVD	8. 3.68	Crashed on landing at Crosland Moor on 11.8.83. Parts incorporated in rebuild of G-AYKK. Canx by CAA 28.11.91.
G-AWEO	Reims Cessna F.150H	0342		11. 3.68	Overturned whilst taxying at Baginton on 22.11.89 & extensively damaged. Canx as destroyed 30.1.90. (On rebuild 3/96)
G-AWEP	Barritault JB-01 Minicab	PFA/1801		12. 3.68	

Regn	Type	c/n	Previous identity	Regn date	Fate or immediate subsequent identity (if known)
G-AWER	PA-23-250 Aztec C	27-3852	N6556Y	12. 3.68	To G-OSNI 7/98. Canx.
G-AWES	Cessna 150H (Originally regd with c/n 68628)	150-68626	N22933	20. 3.68	WFU after gale damage at Glenrothes on 2.10.81. (On rebuild 1/97 Yeadon)
G-AWET	PA-28-180 Cherokee D	28-4871		21. 3.68	
G-AWEU	PA-28-140 Cherokee	28-24456		21. 3.68	To G-PAWL 9/02. Canx.
G-AWEV	PA-28-140 Cherokee	28-24460		21. 3.68	
G-AWEW	PA-28-140 Cherokee	28-24468		21. 3.68	To EI-ATN 8/69. Canx 25.4.69.
G-AWEX	PA-28-140 Cherokee	28-24472		21. 3.68	
G-AWEY	PA-28R-180 Cherokee Arrow	28R-30612		21. 3.68	Crashed at Fermoy, near Cork, Ireland on 25.7.69. Canx as destroyed 29.2.84.
G-AWEZ	PA-28R-180 Cherokee Arrow	28R-30592		21. 3.68	
G-AWFA	PA-28R-180 Cherokee Arrow	28R-30691		21. 3.68	To N23653 7/69. Canx 3.7.69.
G-AWFB(1)	PA-28R-180 Cherokee Arrow	28R-30746		21. 3.68	NTU - Not Imported. Canx.
G-AWFB(2)	PA-28R-180 Cherokee Arrow	28R-30689		2. 4.68	
G-AWFC(1)	PA-28R-180 Cherokee Arrow	28R-30701		21. 3.68	NTU - Not Imported. To PT-DIB. Canx.
G-AWFC(2)	PA-28R-180 Cherokee Arrow	28R-30670		2. 4.68	
G-AWFD(1)	PA-28R-180 Cherokee Arrow	28R-30697		21. 3.68	NTU - Not Imported. To N4951J. Canx.
G-AWFD(2)	PA-28R-180 Cherokee Arrow	28R-30669		2. 4.68	
G-AWFE	SAN Jodel D.140E Mousquetaire IV	166	F-BNIP	22. 3.68	Crashed at Fairwood Common on 15.6.80. Canx 17.3.82.
G-AWFF	Reims Cessna F.150H	0280		25. 3.68	
G-AWFG	Reims Cessna FR.172E Rocket	0028		25. 3.68	NTU - To F-BPER. Canx.
G-AWFH	Reims Cessna F.150H	0274		25. 3.68	Crashed at Swanton Morley on 16.12.79. CofA expired 17.12.81. (Now fitted with tail from G-AWTX & stored with Cheshire Fire Brigade Training School, Winsford)
G-AWFI	PA-30-160 Twin Comanche B	30-1697	N8536Y	26. 3.68	Hit a cow on landing at Crimond on 7.5.74. Canx 14.12.79.
G-AWFJ	PA-28R-180 Cherokee Arrow	28R-30688		26. 3.68	
G-AWFK	PA-28R-180 Cherokee Arrow	28R-30690		26. 3.68	Crashed on landing Hinton-in-the-Hedges 20.6.96. CofA expired 28.9.96. Canx as destroyed 14.10.96.
G-AWFL	Sud SA.318C Alouette Astazou	1997		26. 3.68	To EI-AWC 1/73. Canx 29.1.73.
G-AWFM	DH.104 Dove 6	04079	9J-RHX VP-YLX/VP-RCL/ZS-BCC/(G-AJOU)	27. 3.68	To ZS-BCC 10/78. Canx 26.8.81.
G-AWFN	Rollason-Druine D.62B Condor	RAE/629		27. 3.68	
G-AWFO	Rollason-Druine D.62B Condor	RAE/630		27. 3.68	
G-AWFP	Rollason-Druine D.62B Condor	RAE/631		27. 3.68	
G-AWFR	Druine D.31 Turbulent	SU.001 & PFA/1652		27. 3.68	(Under construction .93)
G-AWFS	PA-25-235 Pawnee C	25-4368	N4648Y	29. 3.68	Crashed at Scotland Farm, Lincs on 27.4.73. Canx as destroyed 15.2.74.
G-AWFT	Jodel D.9 Bebe	PFA/932		29. 3.68	(Stored 8/94)
G-AWFU	Fokker F-27 Friendship 400	10325	PH-SAR PH-FKV	2. 4.68	To A40-FU 10/75. Canx 2.10.75.
G-AWFV	Agusta-Bell 206A JetRanger	8042		2. 4.68	To 5N-AHN 6/68. Canx.
G-AWFW	SAN Jodel D.117	599	PH-VRE F-BHXU	2. 4.68	
G-AWFX	Sikorsky S-61N	61-216	AP-AOB N653X	3. 4.68	Canx 12.5.88 as sold to Canada. To N7011M.
G-AWFY	Sud SA.318C Alouette Astazou II	2007		3. 4.68	To I-MADR. Canx 8.5.84.
G-AWFZ	Beechcraft A23-19A Musketeer Sport	MB-323	N2811B	3. 4.68	(Stored 9/97)
G-AWGA	Beagle A.109 Airedale	B.535	EI-ATA G-AWGA/D-ENRU	3. 4.68	WFU on 3.7.86. Canx as WFU 30.9.86. (Roaded out of Biggin Hill 12/93)
G-AWGB	Vickers Supermarine 509 Spitfire Trainer IX (Also quoted as CBAF/4494)	CBAF/11432	163 Irish Air Corp/G-15-176/TE308	4. 4.68	To CF-RAF 9/70. Canx 7.7.70.
G-AWGC	Reims Cessna F.172H	0500		5. 4.68	To G-GUNN 10/81. Canx.
G-AWGD	Reims Cessna F.172H	0503		5. 4.68	
G-AWGE	Reims Cessna F.172H	0510		5. 4.68	Crashed at Toussus le Noble, France on 10.4.72. Canx.
G-AWGF	Ballon Fabrik Free Balloon	8879		5. 4.68	DBF at Swindon. Canx as destroyed 8.5.69.
G-AWGG	BAC One-Eleven Srs.413FA (Changed designation from Srs.408EF on 18.6.68, c/n changed to 128 on 15.5.68, and back to 116 on 11.6.68)	BAC.116		8. 4.68	To D-ALLI 4/69. Canx 26.2.69.
G-AWGH	Cessna 310N	310N-0141	N5041Q	8. 4.68	NTU - Not Imported. Canx in 1968 on sale to Belgium. To I-ALCC 7/68.
G-AWGI	Cessna 210H Centurion	210-59001	N6101F	8. 4.68	NTU - Not Imported. Canx 9.8.68. To D-EMMN 2/69.
G-AWGJ	Reims Cessna F.172H	0531		8. 4.68	Damaged in gales at Headcorn on 16.10.87. CofA expired 7.9.90. (Wreck stored 1/96 at Headcorn)
G-AWGK	Reims Cessna F.150H	0347		8. 4.68	
G-AWGL	Bensen B.8 Gyrocopter	RGG.1		9. 4.68	Not completed. Canx by CAA 14.10.86.
G-AWGM	Mitchell-Procter Kittiwake II (Now called Arkle Kittiwake II)	002 & PFA/1329		9. 4.68	Damaged in heavy landing at Halton on 18.1.86. Permit expired 13.10.86. (Open store 9/95 in garden near Shrewsbury) Canx by CAA 4.3.99.
G-AWGN	Sportavia-Putzer Fournier RF-4D	4084		9. 4.68	
G-AWGO	Sportavia-Putzer Fournier RF-4D	4085		9. 4.68	Collided with RF-5 G-AYBS off Needles, IoW 24.6.72, broke up and crashed onto Yarmouth beach.
G-AWGP	Cessna T.210H Turbo Centurion	T210-0337	EI-BLJ G-AWGP/N6937R	9. 4.68	Canx by CAA 14.10.91. To ZS-NOS 9/94.
G-AWGR	Reims Cessna F.172H Skyhawk	0484		9. 4.68	
G-AWGS	Canadair CL-44D4-1	27	N127SW	10. 4.68	To N907L 3/80. Canx 5.3.80.

Regn	Type	c/n	Previous identity	Regn date	Fate or immediate subsequent identity (if known)
G-AWGT	Canadair CL-44D4-1	30	N128SW N123SW	10. 4.68	To 5B-DAN 6/79. Canx 8.6.79.
G-AWGU	Agusta-Bell 206B JetRanger II (Originally 206A; later modified)	8044		10. 4.68	To A40-DC. Canx 3.9.84.
G-AWGV	Vickers 745D Viscount	116	I-LIRE N7418	11. 4.68	WFU & stored in 4/70. Broken up in 5/70 at Tees-side. Canx as WFU 16.4.70.
G-AWGW	Reims Cessna F.172H Skyhawk	0482		11. 4.68	To 5B-CCC 11/76. Canx 30.11.76.
G-AWGX	Reims Cessna F.172H Skyhawk	0492		11. 4.68	Crashed 3 miles southwest of Devils Elbow, near Perth, Scotland on 9.6.76. Canx as WFU 5.12.83.
G-AWGY	Reims Cessna F.150H	0306		11. 4.68	Crashed on landing at Dunkeswell on 9.4.82. Canx.
G-AWGZ	Taylor JT.1 Monoplane	M.1 & PFA/1406		17. 4.68	(Damaged in heavy landing at Sleap on 14.7.92)
G-AWHA	CASA C.2111D (He.111H-16)	025	B2I-77 Spanish AF	14. 5.68	To D-CAGI 8/70. Canx 15.8.70.
G-AWHB	CASA C.2111D (He.111H-16) (Officially quoted as c/n 167 - ex B2I-37)	049	B2I-57 Spanish AF	14. 5.68	(On rebuild 12/98 North Weald)
G-AWHC	Hispano HA-1110-M4L	40/2	C4K-112 Spanish AF	14. 5.68	To N1109G 2/69. Canx 20.2.69.
G-AWHD	Hispano HA-1112-M1L	190	C4K-126 Spanish AF	14. 5.68	To N90603 2/69. Canx 20.2.69.
G-AWHE	Hispano HA-1112-M1L (Regd incorrectly with c/n 64, error was discovered when stripped down by the American owner)	67	C4K-31 Spanish AF	14. 5.68	To N109ME 2/69. Canx 20.2.69.
G-AWHF	Hispano HA-1112-M1L	129	C4K-61 Spanish AF	14. 5.68	DBR through undercarriage collapse while landing at Duxford on 21.5.68. Canx.
G-AWHG	Hispano HA-1112-M1L	139	C4K-75 Spanish AF	14. 5.68	Canx 25.10.74 on sale to USA. Marks D-FWME reserved on 6.11.98.
G-AWHH	Hispano HA-1112-M1L	145	C4K-105 Spanish AF	14. 5.68	To N6036 10/68. Canx.
G-AWHI	Hispano HA-1112-M1L	166	C4K-106 Spanish AF	14. 5.68	To N90607 2/69. Canx 20.2.69.
G-AWHJ	Hispano HA-1112-M1L	171	C4K-100 Spanish AF	14. 5.68	To N90605 2/69. Canx 20.2.69.
G-AWHK	Hispano HA-1112-M1L (Regd with c/n 172 - c/n 223 should be C4K-155)	223	C4K-102 Spanish AF	14. 5.68	To N9938 10/68. Canx.
G-AWHL	Hispano HA-1112-M1L	186	C4K-122 Spanish AF	14. 5.68	Canx 17.2.69 on sale to Spain.
G-AWHM	Hispano HA-1112-M1L	187	C4K-99 Spanish AF	14. 5.68	To N90604 2/69. Canx 20.2.69.
G-AWHN	Hispano HA-1112-M1L	193	C4K-130 Spanish AF	14. 5.68	To N90602 2/69. Canx 20.2.69.
G-AWHO	Hispano HA-1112-M1L	199	C4K-127 Spanish AF	14. 5.68	To N90601 2/69. Canx 20.2.69.
G-AWHP	Hispano HA-1112-M1L	208	C4K-144 Spanish AF	14. 5.68	To N8575 2/69. Canx 20.2.69.
G-AWHR	Hispano HA-1112-M1L	220	C4K-152 Spanish AF	14. 5.68	To N4109G 10/68. Canx.
G-AWHS	Hispano HA-1112-M1L (Fitted with DB.605D engine)	228	C4K-170 Spanish AF	14. 5.68	Canx 17.2.69 on sale to Spain. To N170BG. (On display 9/97 Sinsheim, Germany)
G-AWHT	Hispano HA-1112-M1L	234	C4K-169 Spanish AF	14. 5.68	To N9939 10/68. Canx.
G-AWHU	Boeing 707-379C (Line No. 718)	19821	VN-83415 VN-B3415/9Q-CKI/G-AWHU/N762U	11. 4.68	To 5X-JEF 8/90. Canx 31.7.90.
G-AWHV	Rollason Beta B.2A (Originally regd as B.2)	RAE/02		17. 4.68	DBF on a strip near Bristol during 1995. Canx as destroyed 17.10.95.
G-AWHW	Rollason Beta B.2 (re-designated B4 on fitment of a Continental C90-8F engine)	RAE/03		17. 4.68	Destroyed in fatal crash at RAF Wattisham on 17.12.87. Canx by CAA 12.2.92.
G-AWHX	Rollason Beta B.2	RAE/04	(G-ATEE)	17. 4.68	(On rebuild 3/91)
G-AWHY	Falconar F-11-3	PEB.02 & PFA/1322	G-BDPB (G-AWHY)	17. 4.68	
G-AWHZ	BN-2 Islander	22		17. 4.68	NTU - To G-51-5/D-IJAN 4/68. Canx.
G-AWIA	BN-2A-26 Islander	23		17. 4.68	To CF-XYK 5/68. Canx.
G-AWIB	BN-2A Islander	24		17. 4.68	To N586JA 7/68. Canx.
G-AWIC	BN-2A Islander	25		17. 4.68	To N589JA 7/68. Canx.
G-AWID	BN-2A Islander	26		17. 4.68	To R.Thailand AF as 501 in 10/68. Canx.
G-AWIE	BN-2A Islander	27		17. 4.68	To N457SA 9/68. Canx.
G-AWIF	Brookland Mosquito	3 & LC.1		17. 4.68	Canx as WFU 30.5.84. (Stored 5/98 at St.Merryn)
G-AWIG	Wassmer Jodel D.112	1067	F-BKAA	23. 4.68	To EI-BSB 6/87. Canx 8.11.85.
G-AWIH	Mooney M.20C Ranger	680107		24. 4.68	To N87992 6/77. Canx 24.6.77.
G-AWII	Vickers-Supermarine 349 Spitfire LF.Vc	WASP/20/223	AR501	25. 4.68	
G-AWIJ	Vickers Supermarine 329 Spitfire Mk.IIa	CBAF/14	P7350	25. 4.68	Returned to RAF as P7350. Canx to MOD 29.2.84.
G-AWIK	Beechcraft 23 Musketeer (Rebuilt with parts from G-ASCL)	M-534	PH-MUS N8746M	25. 4.68	Destroyed in fatal crash at Little Downham, Cambs on 3.4.83. Canx by CAA 22.11.84.
G-AWIL	Agusta-Bell 206A JetRanger	8049	(VH-...) G-AWIL	30. 4.68	To VH-BHV 8/68. Canx 9.8.68.
G-AWIM	Agusta-Bell 206A JetRanger	8050	(VH-...) G-AWIM	30. 4.68	To VH-BHW 8/68. Canx 9.8.68.
G-AWIN	Campbell-Bensen B.8Mc Gyrocopter	CA/309		30. 4.68	Crashed near Cheltenham pre 1977. Canx as destroyed 7.2.90

Regn	Type	c/n	Previous identity	Regn date	Fate or immediate subsequent identity (if known)
G-AWIO	Brantly B.2B	483	G-OBPG G-AWIO	30. 4.68	Canx by CAA 29.11.95.
G-AWIP	Phoenix Luton LA-4A Minor	PAL/1308 & PFA/830		30. 4.68	Badly damaged in crash near Holme-on-Spalding Moor on 20.7.88. Permit expired 8.5.89. (Status uncertain)
G-AWIR	Bushby-Long Midget Mustang I	PFA/1315		30. 4.68	(On overhaul at owner's home .91)
G-AWIS	PA-28-180 Cherokee D	28-4979		30. 4.68	Crashed near Elstree on 10.7.73. Canx as destroyed 24.9.73.
G-AWIT	PA-28-180 Cherokee D	28-4987		30. 4.68	
G-AWIU	PA-28R-180 Cherokee Arrow	28R-30717		30. 4.68	Crashed at Conway, North Wales on 11.6.71.
G-AWIV	Airmark TSR.3 (built by T.M.Storey) (Originally regd as Storey TSR.3)	PFA/1325		30. 4.68	(On overhaul)
G-AWIW	SNCAN Stampe SV-4B	532	F-BDCC	2. 5.68	(On rebuild 3/95)
G-AWIX	PA-30-160 Twin Comanche B	30-1704	N8557Y	2. 5.68	To N80BL 11/76. Canx 3.11.76.
G-AWIY	PA-23-250 Aztec C	27-3823	N6599Y	2. 5.68	To G-ESKU 4/96. Canx.
G-AWIZ	Slingsby Nipper T.66 RA.45 Srs.3 (Belgian-built Mk.II as c/n 9) (Rebuild of G-AVDK)	S.100		2. 5.68	Construction abandoned. Canx in 1968. DBF at Kirkbymoorside on 18.11.68.
G-AWJA	Cessna 182L Skylane	182-58883	N1658C	3. 5.68	CofA expired 21.4.85. (Last known of stored at Movenis, Northern Ireland) Canx as destroyed 29.11.88.
G-AWJB	Brighton MAB-65 HAFB	MAB-3		3. 5.68	Canx 4.12.70 on sale to Italy. To HB-BOU(1) 2/73.
G-AWJC	Brighton Gas Balloon	MAB-4		3. 5.68	CofA expired 20.8.78. Canx by CAA 16.12.91.
G-AWJD	Campbell-Bensen B.8M Gyrocopter	CA/310		3. 5.68	Canx as WFU 3.1.74.
G-AWJE	Slingsby Nipper T.66 RA.45 Srs.3	S.121/1628		8. 5.68	
G-AWJF	Slingsby Nipper T.66 RA.45 Srs.3	S.122/1629		8. 5.68	Permit to Fly expired 7.6.88. Canx by CAA 17.9.91. (Stored off-site 6/95)
G-AWJG	Slingsby Nipper T.66 RA.45 Srs.3	S.123/1630		8. 5.68	To VH-EOK 4/69. Canx 8.68.
G-AWJH	Slingsby Nipper T.66 RA.45 Srs.3	S.124/1631		8. 5.68	Canx as WFU 15.7.74.
G-AWJI	Socata MS.880B Rallye Club	1217		15. 5.68	CofA expired 26.11.84. Canx by CAA 3.4.89.
G-AWJJ	Socata MS.893A Rallye Commodore 180	10918		15. 5.68	Collided with a car at Dunstable on 16.3.73. Canx as destroyed 4.5.73. Remains removed to Biggin Hill.
G-AWJK	Socata MS.880B Rallye Club	1218		15. 5.68	To G-MONA 4/79. Canx.
G-AWJL	Bell 206A JetRanger	181		16. 5.68	Crashed near Croughton, Northants on 22.7.69. Canx 17.9.69.
G-AWJM	Short SC.7 Skyvan 3-300-3	SH1853	VH-FSH G-AWJM	16. 5.68	To N60DA 6/73. Canx 19.4.73.
G-AWJN	Tigercraft Gyro-Glider Tiger Mk.II	FT.6		17. 5.68	Not built. Canx as WFU 18.8.81.
G-AWJO	Tigercraft Gyro-Glider Tiger Mk.II	FT.7		17. 5.68	Sold on 1.9.81. Canx as WFU 23.4.82.
G-AWJP	Tigercraft Gyro-Glider Tiger Mk.III	FT.8		17. 5.68	Not built. Canx by CAA 14.10.86.
G-AWJR	Tigercraft Gyro-Glider Tiger Mk.I	FT.9		17. 5.68	Not completed. Canx as WFU 14.10.81.
G-AWJS	Tigercraft Gyro-Glider Mosquito Mk.I	FT.10		17. 5.68	Not built. Canx by CAA 14.10.86.
G-AWJT	Tigercraft Gyro-Glider Tiger Mk.I	FT.11		17. 5.68	Not built. Canx as WFU 11.7.84.
G-AWJU	Cessna 421 Golden Eagle	421-0114	N4914T	20. 5.68	Canx 10.7.68 on sale to Belgium. To SE-FEE 6/68.
G-AWJV	DH.98 Mosquito TT.35	-	TA634	21. 5.68	Canx as WFU 19.10.70. (On display 3/96 Salisbury Hall, London Colney)
G-AWJW	Agusta-Bell 206B JetRanger II (Originally 206A; later modified)	8052		22. 5.68	To G-FSDA 1/83. Canx.
G-AWJX	Moravan Zlin Z.526 Trener Master	1049		22. 5.68	(On rebuild 12/93)
G-AWJY	Moravan Zlin Z.526 Trener Master	1050		22. 5.68	
G-AWJZ	Reims Cessna F.150H	0356		23. 5.68	To G-OJVH 3/81. Canx.
G-AWKA	Reims Cessna F.172H	0529		23. 5.68	Crashed near Bordeaux-Merignac, France on 26.5.72. Canx as destroyed 3.4.74.
G-AWKB	Jurca MJ.5 Sirocco Type F.2 Srs.39	PFA/2204		24. 5.68	To G-CLAX 4/99. Canx.
G-AWKC	Hughes H.269B	16-0234	EI-APH	23. 5.68	To OE-AXG 3/77. Canx 31.1.77.
G-AWKD	PA-17 Vagabond	17-192	F-BFMZ N4892H/NC4892H	27. 5.68	
G-AWKE	Cessna 337C Super Skymaster	337-0939	N2639S	27. 5.68	Crashed in Jaizkibel Mountain, on landing at San Sebastian, Spain on 28.4.76. Canx 4.76.
G-AWKF	PA-30-160 Twin Comanche B	30-1712	N8565Y	29. 5.68	To OY-AJW 2/77. Canx 25.1.77.
G-AWKG	Hiller 360 UH-12B	669	0-35 Belgium AF/51-16414	4. 6.68	To N99437 2/77. Canx 1.2.77.
G-AWKH	HS.125 Srs.3A/RA	NA707 & 25160	G-5-15	7. 6.68	To N350NC 7/68. Canx.
G-AWKI	HS.125 Srs.3A/RA	NA708 & 25161		7. 6.68	To N9149 8/68. Canx.
G-AWKJ	BAC One-Eleven Srs.408EF	BAC.128		11. 6.68	To G-BIII 1/74. Canx.
G-AWKK	Beagle B.121 Pup Srs.100	B121-015		11. 6.68	To N557MA 10/68. Canx.
G-AWKL	Beagle B.121 Pup Srs.150	B121-016	G-35-016	11. 6.68	To VH-EPA 2/69. Canx.
G-AWKM	Beagle B.121 Pup Srs.100	B121-017		11. 6.68	Damaged in ground accident at Fairwood Common in 7/91. Stored at Swansea and suffered further damage when a forklift truck backed into the fin area in late 1991. Had suffered corrosion damage by 3/92 whilst still at Swansea. Moved & stored dismantled 1/99 Bourne Park.
G-AWKN	Beagle B.121 Pup Srs.150	B121-018	G-35-018	11. 6.68	To HB-NAD 11/68. Canx 10.10.68.

Regn	Type	c/n	Previous identity	Regn date	Fate or immediate subsequent identity (if known)
G-AWKO	Beagle B.121 Pup Srs.100	B121-019		11. 6.68	
G-AWKP	CEA Jodel DR.253 Regent	130		14. 6.68	Forced landed southeast of Waterford, Ireland on 8.6.98. Canx by CAA 13.10.98.
G-AWKR	Cessna 337C Super Skymaster	337-0960	N2660S	14. 6.68	To 4X-AYD 11/68. Canx 28.11.68.
G-AWKS	Socata MS.880B Rallye Club	1225		17. 6.68	WFU at Staverton on 31.5.81. Canx 2.2.82.
G-AWKT	Socata MS.880B Rallye Club	1235		17. 6.68	
G-AWKU	Beechcraft A23-19A Musketeer	MB-352		17. 6.68	DBR on landing at Lympne on 16.4.69. Canx as WFU 8.7.69.
G-AWKV	Short SC.7 Skyvan 3-200-2 (Originally regd as Srs.2-200)	SH1847	N735R	21. 6.68	Restored as N735R 12/68. Canx.
G-AWKW	PA-24-180 Comanche	24-1344	N6239P	21. 6.68	To G-NUNN 3/85. Canx.
G-AWKX	Beechcraft A65 Queen Air	LC-303		21. 6.68	CofA expired 25.10.89. Canx as WFU 19.12.90. (Instructional Airframe 8/97 Shoreham)
G-AWKY	Beechcraft B80 Queen Air	LD-393		21. 6.68	NTU - To G-AWOI 6/68. Canx.
G-AWKZ	PA-23-160 Apache	23-1708	OY-AIV N4215P	26. 6.68	Damaged when undercarriage collapsed on landing at Ipswich on 31.1.77. Canx as WFU 29.2.84.
G-AWLA	Reims Cessna F.150H	0269	N13175	27. 6.68	
G-AWLB	Druine D.31 Turbulent (built by A.E.Shoulder)	AES.1		27. 6.68	Not completed. Canx by CAA 10.7.91.
G-AWLC	Sud SA.318C Alouette II Astazou	2014		27. 6.68	CofA expired 1.7.71 and rebuilt in 1972 as SA.315B Lama G-AZNI. Canx.
G-AWLD	Reims Cessna F.172H Skyhawk	0517		27. 6.68	Crashed 1 mile East of Tomintoul, 35 miles East of Inverness on 3.12.74. Canx 14.2.75 as destroyed.
G-AWLE	Reims Cessna F.172H Skyhawk	0525		27. 6.68	CofA expired 28.11.85. Canx as WFU 17.7.86.
G-AWLF	Reims Cessna F.172H Skyhawk	0536		27. 6.68	
G-AWLG	SIPA 903	82	F-BGHG	27. 6.68	(Stored .97)
G-AWLH	PA-22-135 Tri-Pacer	22-977	N1141C	1. 7.68	To 4X-ANJ 4/69. Canx 29.4.69.
G-AWLI	PA-22-150 Tri-Pacer	22-5083	N7256D	1. 7.68	
G-AWLJ	Reims Cessna F.150H	0328		3. 7.68	Crashed on landing at Tillingham on 20.11.84. (Remains later in open storage at Southend) Canx by CAA 3.8.94.
G-AWLK	Brookland Mosquito Mk.II Gyroplane	7		5. 7.68	To F-WMEF/F-PMEF 10/68. Canx.
G-AWLL	Agusta-Bell 206B JetRanger II (Originally 206A; later modified)	8076		5. 7.68	To (PH-HXH)/PH-HWH. Canx 31.8.93.
G-AWLM	Campbell-Bensen B.8MS Gyrocopter	CA/311	EI-ATE(2) G-AWLM	8. 7.68	Permit expired 20.3.80. Canx by CAA 16.12.91. (Stored .92)
G-AWLN	Beagle B.206 Srs.3 (Originally a Srs.2, officially became Srs.3 on 27.8.69)	B.080		8. 7.68	To PT-IQH 9/72. Canx 25.9.72.
G-AWLO	Boeing Stearman E75 (PT-13D) Kaydet (Originally regd with c/n 75-8375, which should have been N2S-5 BuA.43281)	75-5563	5Y-KRR VP-KRR/42-17400	9. 7.68	
G-AWLP	Mooney M.20F Executive 21	680200		9. 7.68	
G-AWLR	Slingsby Nipper T.66 RA.45 Srs.3	S.125/1662		9. 7.68	
G-AWLS	Slingsby Nipper T.66 RA.45 Srs.3	S.126/1663		9. 7.68	Badly damaged on take-off from Stapleford on 14.1.88. (On rebuild .95)
G-AWLT	Slingsby Nipper T.66 RA.45 Srs.3	S.127/1674		9. 7.68	Destroyed in the fire at Slingsby's factory at Kirkbymoorside on 18.11.68. (Was for export to Kenya) Canx.
G-AWLU	Slingsby Nipper T.66 RA.45 Srs.3	S.128/1675		9. 7.68	Destroyed in the fire at Slingsby's factory at Kirkbymoorside on 18.11.68. (F/f on 5.11.68) Canx.
G-AWLV	Agusta-Bell 206B JetRanger (Originally 206A; later modified)	8072		10. 7.68	To VH-BHL 5/72. Canx.11.5.72.
G-AWLW	Hawker Hurricane Mk.XII (built by CCF)	42012	CF-SMI RCAF 5588	10. 7.68	To C-GCWH. Canx 30.4.84.
G-AWLX	Auster J/2 Arrow	2378	F-BGJQ OO-ABZ	10. 7.68	WFU at Ipswich on 23.4.70. Canx 14.4.73. (On rebuild 11/93)
G-AWLY	Reims Cessna F.150H	0364		16. 7.68	Forced landing in the Scafell area of the Lake District on 11.7.88. Canx as destroyed 20.3.89.
G-AWLZ	Sportavia-Putzer Fournier RF-4D	4099		12. 7.68	
G-AWMA	PA-25-235 Pawnee	25-4682	N4878Y	15. 7.68	Crashed & DBF near Erith, Cambs. on 27.7.77. Canx.
G-AWMB	PA-30-160 Twin Comanche B	30-1716	N8569Y	18. 7.68	To OY-DLC 10/75. Canx 2.10.75.
"G-AWMB"	Reims Cessna F.172H	0488		----	(Delivered painted as such in error) To G-AWMP 7/68.
G-AWMC	Campbell-Bensen B.8MS Gyrocopter	CA/312		18. 7.68	Not completed. Canx as WFU 10.6.85.
G-AWMD	Jodel D.11	PFA/904		19. 7.68	
G-AWME	Hiller 360 UH-12E	2130	5N-AIP G-AWME/VR-BBU/G-AWME/5N-AGB/VR-BBU	23. 7.68	To ZS-HED 7/74. Canx 12.7.74.
G-AWMF	PA-18-150 Super Cub	18-8674	N4356Z	23. 7.68	
G-AWMG	Avro 652A Anson 19 Srs.2	"276926"	VV958	23. 7.68	Crashed at Uzuakoli Leprosy Settlement, near Umuahia, Biafra on 3.9.68. Canx as destroyed 3.9.68.
G-AWMH	Avro 652A Anson 19 Srs.2	"38002"	TX227	23. 7.68	Ditched in sea off Liberia coast near River Cess on 20.6.69 after engine failure. Canx as destroyed 20.6.69. (Was marked as "K516" for film work at Bovingdon in 7/68)
G-AWMI	AESL Airtourer T2 (115)	505		24. 7.68	
G-AWMJ	Reims Cessna F.172H Skyhawk	0550		24. 7.68	Crashed on take-off from Biggin Hill on 13.1.79. Canx.
G-AWMK	Agusta-Bell 206B JetRanger (Originally 206A; later modified)	8073	9Y-TFC G-AWMK/(VR-BCV)/G-AWMK	25. 7.68	
G-AWML	Avro 652A Anson 19 Srs.2	-	TX166	25. 7.68	Scrapped at Weston-super-Mare in 5/70. Canx as PWFU 6.8.70.
G-AWMM	Socata MS.893A Rallye Commodore 180	10924		25. 7.68	Canx by CAA 8.5.92.
G-AWMN	Phoenix Luton LA-4A Minor (Originally regd with c/n PFA/807)	PFA/827		30. 7.68	

Regn	Type	c/n	Previous identity	Regn date	Fate or immediate subsequent identity (if known)
G-AWMO	Omega 84 HAFB	01		31. 7.68	To OY-BOB 5/69. Canx 13.5.69.
G-AWMP	Reims Cessna F.172H Skyhawk	0488	"G-AWMB"	31. 7.68	
G-AWMR	Druine D.31 Turbulent	43 & PFA/1661		1. 8.68	(Stored 4/97)
G-AWMS	HS.125 Srs.3B	25150	G-5-13	1. 8.68	To N511BX 8/81. Canx 12.8.81.
G-AWMT	Reims Cessna F.150H	0360		1. 8.68	
G-AWMU	Reims Cessna F.172H Skyhawk	0487		1. 8.68	To G-OBHX 8/86. Canx.
G-AWMV	HS.125 Srs.3A/RA	NA709 & 25163	G-5-16	1. 8.68	To N208H 11/68. Canx.
G-AWMW	HS.125 Srs.400A	NA710 & 25170		1. 8.68	To N1259K 9/68. Canx.
G-AWMX	HS.125 Srs.400A	NA711 & 25173		2. 8.68	To N125J 9/68. Canx.
G-AWMY	HS.125 Srs.400A	NA712 & 25174		2. 8.68	To N1199M 11/68. Canx.
G-AWMZ	Reims Cessna F.172H Skyhawk	0554		2. 8.68	Hit ground at Bucknarrowbridge, 2 miles NE of Bootle on 18.1.76. Canx as WFU 1.9.81. Used as training aid at Cark 10/97.
G-AWNA	Boeing 747-136 (Line No. 23)	19761	N1799B	30. 7.68	WFU at Bruntingthorpe 11/98. Canx 15.12.98 on sale to USA.
G-AWNB	Boeing 747-136 (Line No. 41)	19762	N1798B	30. 7.68	WFU & stored 9/98 at Roswell, NM, USA. Canx 30.9.98 on sale to USA. Being dismantled 7/99 at Roswell, NM, USA.
G-AWNC	Boeing 747-136 (Line No. 48)	19763		30. 7.68	WFU & stored 8/99 at Chateauroux, France.
G-AWND	Boeing 747-136 (Line No. 107)	19764		30. 7.68	Detained by Iraqi forces at Kuwait City, Kuwait 1.8.90 and DBR 27.2.91 by shelling. Canx as destroyed 17.4.91.
G-AWNE	Boeing 747-136 (Line No. 109)	19765		30. 7.68	
G-AWNF	Boeing 747-136 (Line No. 111)	19766		30. 7.68	
G-AWNG	Boeing 747-136 (Line No. 150)	20269		29. 1.69	WFU & stored 12/98 at Roswell, NM, USA. Canx 16.12.98 on sale to USA. Being dismantled 7/99 Roswell, NM, USA.
G-AWNH	Boeing 747-136 (Line No. 169)	20270		29. 1.69	Stored 6/99 at Albuquerque. Canx 18.6.99 on sale to USA.
G-AWNI	Boeing 747-136 (Line No. 172)	20271		29. 1.69	To (N125TW)/N17125 3/81. Canx 23.3.81.
G-AWNJ	Boeing 747-136 (Line No. 183)	20272		29. 1.69	WFU & stored 12/98 at Roswell, NM, USA. Canx 18.12.98 on sale to USA. Being dismantled 7/99 at Roswell, NM, USA.
G-AWNK	Boeing 747-136 (Line No. 184)	20273		29. 1.69	To (N126TW)/N17126 3/81. Canx 30.3.81.
G-AWNL	Boeing 747-136 (Line No. 187)	20284		29. 1.69	WFU & stored 11/98 at Roswell, NM, USA. Canx 1.12.98 on sale to USA. Being dismantled 7/99 at Roswell, NM, USA.
G-AWNM	Boeing 747-136 (Line No. 210)	20708		29. 3.73	
G-AWNN	Boeing 747-136 (Line No. 220)	20809		13. 8.73	Canx 13.5.99 on sale to USA. Being dismantled 7/99 at Roswell, NM, USA.
G-AWNO	Boeing 747-136 (Line No. 222)	20810		13. 8.73	
G-AWNP	Boeing 747-136 (Line No. 246)	20952		18. 9.74	
G-AWNR	BN-2A-8 Islander	30		2. 8.68	To N30BN 2/78. Canx.
G-AWNS	BN-2A Islander	31		2. 8.68	NTU - To G-51-6/N676SA 11/68. Canx 7.10.68.
G-AWNT	BN-2A Islander	32		2. 8.68	
G-AWNU	BN-2A-9 Islander	33		2. 8.68	To 8P-ASD 2/76. Canx 23.4.76.
G-AWNV	BN-2A Islander	34		2. 8.68	To Abu Dhabi AF as 201 in 11/68. Canx 6.11.68.
G-AWNW	BN-2A Islander	35		2. 8.68	NTU - To CF-RDI 12/68. Canx 24.10.68.
G-AWNX	BN-2A-26 Islander	36		2. 8.68	NTU - To VH-ATS. Canx 1.11.68.
G-AWNY	BN-2 Islander (Originally regd as a BN-2A)	37		2. 8.68	To F-OGDR 1/70. Canx 22.8.69.
G-AWNZ	BN-2A Islander	38		2. 8.68	NTU - To G-51-7/N589SA 12/68. Canx 15.11.68.
G-AWOA	Socata MS.880B Rallye Club	1258		2. 8.68	
G-AWOB	Socata MS.880B Rallye Club	1270		2. 8.68	To EI-BDH 7/77. Canx 8.7.77.
G-AWOC	Socata MS.892A Rallye Commodore 150	10926		2. 8.68	Taxied into Cessna 182 G-ASLH at Shobdon 13.6.74. Canx 6.11.74 as destroyed.
G-AWOD	BN-2A-8 Islander	39		2. 8.68	NTU - To G-51-8/N583JA 12/68. Canx 15.11.68.
G-AWOE	Aero Grand Commander 680E	753-41	N3844C	5. 8.68	
G-AWOF	PA-15 Vagabond	15-227	F-BETF	6. 8.68	
G-AWOG	PA-30-160 Twin Comanche B	30-1401	5N-APW N8272Y	7. 8.68	To JA5191 8/71. Canx.
G-AWOH	PA-17 Vagabond	17-191	F-BFMY N4891H	6. 8.68	
G-AWOI	Beechcraft 65-B80 Queen Air	LD-393	(G-AWKY)	6. 8.68	To LN-TST 10/74. Canx 8.10.74.
G-AWOJ	Reims Cessna F.172H Skyhawk	0535		6. 8.68	
G-AWOK	Sussex Gas (Free) Balloon	SARD.1		7. 8.68	WFU in 1970. (Stored at Balloon Museum) Canx as WFU 29.2.84
G-AWOL	Bell 206B JetRanger (Originally 206A; later modified)	239	N4085G	7. 8.68	To G-REVS 6/90. Canx.
G-AWOM	Bell 206B JetRanger (Originally 206A; later modified)	280		7. 8.68	To N37738. Canx 15.3.74.
G-AWON	English Electric Lightning F.53	95291	G-27-56	9. 8.68	To R.Saudi AF as 53-686 4/69. Canx 9.68.
G-AWOO	English Electric Lightning F.53	95293	G-27-57	9. 8.68	To R.Saudi AF as 53-687 4/69. Canx 9.68.
G-AWOP	Not allocated.				
G-AWOR	BAC 167 Strikemaster Mk.80	PS.102	G-27-9	9. 8.68	To R.Saudi AF as 902. Canx 9.68.
G-AWOS	BAC 167 Strikemaster Mk.80	PS.106	G-27-13	9. 8.68	To R.Saudi AF as 906. Canx 9.68.
G-AWOT	Reims Cessna F.150H	0389		14. 8.68	(Stored 4/97)
G-AWOU	Cessna 170B	170-25829	VQ-ZJA ZS-CKY/CR-ADU/N3185A	16. 8.68	

Regn	Type	c/n	Previous identity	Regn date	Fate or immediate subsequent identity (if known)
G-AWOV	Canadair CL-44D4-1	32	N429SW	21. 8.68	To HB-IEO. Canx 15.12.77.
			G-AWOV/N229SW		
G-AWOW	PA-31 Turbo Navajo	31-229	N9172Y	21. 8.68	To OY-DLY 12/75. Canx 3.11.75.
G-AWOX	Westland-Sikorsky S-58 Wessex 60		G-17-2	28. 8.68	(Extant 5/93 - see G-AZBY)
	Srs.1	WA/686	G-AWOX/5N-AJO/G-AWOX/9Y-TFB/G-AWOX/VH-BHE(3)/G-AWOX/VR-BCV/G-AWOX/G-17-1		
G-AWOY	Agusta-Bell 206B JetRanger	8094		29. 8.68	To SE-HEP 5/74. Canx 18.1.74.
	(Originally 206A; later modified)				
G-AWOZ	AESL Airtourer T.2 (115)	507		30. 8.68	Fatal crash during aerobatic display at fate near Chew Magna, southeast of Lulsgate 7.6.75. Canx.
G-AWPA	Druine D.31A Turbulent	RAE/100 & PFA/1612		3. 9.68	DBF at Thruxton on 30.9.78. Canx.
G-AWPB	Druine D.31A Turbulent	RAE/101		3. 9.68	Fatal crash at Sleap on 25.5.70. Canx.
G-AWPC	HS.125 Srs.400A	NA713 & 25175		3. 9.68	To N217F 11/68. Canx 12.68.
G-AWPD	HS.125 Srs.400A	NA714 & 25176		3. 9.68	To CF-NER 11/68. Canx.
G-AWPE	HS.125 Srs.400A	NA715 & 25179		3. 9.68	To N778S 12/68. Canx.
G-AWPF	HS.125 Srs.400A	NA716 & 25180		3. 9.68	To N196KC 1/69. Canx 12.68.
G-AWPG	Moravan Zlin Z.526 Trener Master			5. 9.68	Destroyed in fatal crash at Seething on 6.6.81.
	(Originally regd with c/n 1057)	1061			Canx as destroyed 29.2.84.
G-AWPH	Percival P.56 Provost T.1	PAC/F/003	WV420	6. 9.68	
	(Also c/n P56/003)				
G-AWPI	Percival P.56 Provost T.1	PAC/F/330	XF685	6. 9.68	Not converted. WFU at Baginton 3.6.69. Broken up. Canx.
	(Also c/n P56/330)				
G-AWPJ	Reims Cessna F.150H	0376		9. 9.68	
G-AWPK	PA-23-250 Aztec	27-3947	N6635Y	11. 9.68	To N62RS. Canx 25.5.83.
G-AWPL	Bensen B.8 Gyrocopter	NFH.1		11. 9.68	Not completed. Canx as WFU 11.7.84.
	(built by N.F.Higgins)				
G-AWPM	Beechcraft B90 King Air	LJ-417		12. 9.68	To N29TC. Canx 20.5.74.
G-AWPN	Shield Xyla	2 & PFA/1320		13. 9.68	(Damaged on landing Finmere 16.8.80) (Rebuilt 3/96) (For sale 10/97)
G-AWPO	Not allocated.				
G-AWPP	Reims Cessna F.150H	0348		13. 9.68	(Fuselage in hangar at Cranfield on 17.6.99 & wings dumped)
G-AWPR	Camco Mk.IIA V-Liner	1657		16. 9.68	Half completed airframe seriously damaged in a factory fire at Slingsby, Kirkbymoorside on 18.11.68. Remains scrapped. Canx as WFU 11.7.73.
G-AWPS	PA-28-140 Cherokee	28-20196	5N-AEK	16. 9.68	
G-AWPT	IMCO Callair B-1	10002	SE-EWA	16. 9.68	To ET-ADE 7/69. Canx 3.7.69.
G-AWPU	Reims Cessna F.150J	0411		18. 9.68	
G-AWPV	Reims Cessna F.172H Skyhawk	0585		18. 9.68	Canx as destroyed 17.10.79.
G-AWPW	PA-12 Super Cruiser	12-3947	N78572	23. 9.68	
			NC78572		
G-AWPX	Cessna 150E	150-60906	5N-AFR	19. 9.68	To EC-FCR. Canx 15.1.91.
			N11B/N6206T		
G-AWPY	Campbell-Bensen B.8M Gyrocopter	CA/314		20. 9.68	(Extant 5/95)
G-AWPZ	Bjorn Andreasson BA-4B	1	SE-XBS	24. 9.68	
G-AWRA	Beagle B.121 Pup Srs.150	B121-020	G-35-020	24. 9.68	Canx in 10/68 on sale to Australia. To ZK-CYP but damaged in transit 12/68 (London Docks) & broken up at Sywell in 1971.
G-AWRB	Beagle B.121 Pup Srs.100	B121-021	(LV-...)	24. 9.68	To D-EKRB. Canx 22.5.85.
			G-AWRB/G-35-021		
G-AWRC	Beagle B.121 Pup Srs.150	B121-022	G-35-022	24. 9.68	NTU - To EI-ATF 12/68. Canx.
G-AWRD	Beagle B.121 Pup Srs.150	B121-023	G-35-023	24. 9.68	NTU - To HB-NAH 1/69. Canx.
G-AWRE	Beagle B.121 Pup Srs.150	B121-024	G-35-024	24. 9.68	Canx 22.6.69 on sale to Iraq.
G-AWRF	Beagle B.121 Pup Srs.150	B121-025	G-35-025	24. 9.68	NTU - To LX-NIT 1/69. Canx.
G-AWRG	DH.104 Dove (Sea Devon C.1)	04073	VP954	25. 9.68	WFU unconverted at Leavesden. Scrapped in 12/69. Canx as WFU 30.10.69.
G-AWRH	PA-18-95 Super Cub (L-18C-PI)		OO-HMI	2.10.68	NTU - Not Imported. To OO-SPS 4/69. Canx 18.4.69.
	(Frame no. 18-1527)	18-1555	ALAT 51-15555		
G-AWRI(1)	Bell 206A JetRanger	289		2.10.68R	NTU - Not Imported. To EP-HAY. Canx.
G-AWRI(2)	Bell 206A JetRanger	306		4. 3.69	To F-BXPF 3/76. Canx 14.1.76.
G-AWRJ	Cessna 421 Golden Eagle	421-0192		8.10.68	To N96192. Canx 8.9.76.
G-AWRK	Reims Cessna F.150J	0410		8.10.68	
G-AWRL	Reims Cessna F.172H	0581		8.10.68	Canx as WFU 4.2.91.
G-AWRM	Beagle B.206S Srs.2	B.070	(LV-PLE)	10.10.68	To N54JH. Canx 23.9.79.
			G-AWRM/G-35-24		
G-AWRN	Beagle B.206S Srs.2	B.071	G-35-25	10.10.68	To (LV-PLF)/G-35-25/PT-DYW. Canx 28.10.68.
G-AWRO	Beagle B.206S Srs.2	B.072	(LV-PLG)	10.10.68	To N60JH. Canx 21.6.79.
			G-AWRO/G-35-26		
G-AWRP	Cierva Rotorcraft CR.LTH.1			14.10.68	CofA expired 12.5.72 & WFU at Redhill. Canx as WFU 5.12.83.
	Grasshopper III	GB.1			(On display 4/98 Weston-super-Mare)
	(Originally regd as Servotec Grasshopper Srs.3 with same c/n)				
G-AWRR	Beagle B.121 Pup Srs.150	B121-030	G-35-030	14.10.68	To EP-BAD(2) 3/69. Canx 6.3.69.
G-AWRS	Avro 652A Anson 19 Srs.2	"33785"	TX213	14.10.68	WFU 5.2.73. Canx as PWFU 30.5.84. (On rebuild 5/97)
G-AWRT	AESL Airtourer T4 (115)	508		14.10.68	DBR at Biggin Hill on 23.11.73. Canx.
G-AWRU	Cessna 172 Skyhawk	172-36788	N9188B	14.10.68	DBF at the Whatfield private strip, Suffolk on 29.12.68. Canx.
G-AWRV	Agusta-Bell 206A JetRanger	8095		16.10.68	To F-GAJL. Canx 28.5.76.
G-AWRW	Beagle B.121 Pup Srs.150	B121-027	G-35-027	16.10.68	Damaged at Southend on 19.12.78. Canx as WFU 7.9.81.
G-AWRX	Beagle B.121 Pup Srs.150	B121-028	G-35-028	16.10.68	DBR on landing at Swansea on 18.10.69. Canx.
G-AWRY	Hunting-Percival P.56 Provost T.1		8043M	29.10.81	Damaged in forced landing near Newbury on 28.7.87.
	(Also c/n P.56/339)	PAC/F/339	XF836		(On rebuild 6/94)
G-AWRZ	Bell 47G-5	7832	HB-XCK	17.10.68	Damaged in crash while spreading fertiliser at Fillingham on 26.4.86. Canx by CAA 10.1.91. To 5B-CGM.
			N1344X		

Regn	Type	c/n	Previous identity	Regn date	Fate or immediate subsequent identity (if known)
G-AWSA	Avro 652A Anson 19 Srs.2	"293483"	VL349	21.10.68	Canx 18.8.69 as sold in USA. To N5054 but not delivered. (On display 7/97 Flixton as VL349)
G-AWSB	Avro 652A Anson 19 Srs.2	"266324"	VM351	21.10.68	To USA as N7522. Canx 5.11.68.
G-AWSC	Canadair CL-44D4-1	26	N126SW G-AWSC/N126SW	21.10.68	Nose-wheel collapsed on landing Lusaka, Zambia 22.12.74 and propellors on 3 engines damaged. Canx 28.2.75 as destroyed.
G-AWSD	Reims Cessna F.150J	0406		21.10.68	Damaged by storm at Denham on 16.10.87. Canx as WFU 8.4.92. (Stored 5/98 at Sibson)
G-AWSE	Handley Page 137 Jetstream 1 (Production No. 1)	202		22.10.68	To N1039S. Canx 19.8.69.
G-AWSF	Cessna 401	401-0166	N4066Q	22.10.68	To G-BZFL 1/81. Canx.
G-AWSG	Short SC.7 Skyvan 3-100-13	SH1851	G-14-1	23.10.68	Canx 29.1.71 on sale to Hong Kong. To (PK-PSB)/PK-XSA/PK-PSE 12/72.
G-AWSH	Moravan Zlin Z.526 Trener Master	1052	OK-XRH G-AWSH	23.10.68	
G-AWSI	Agusta-Bell 47J-3 Ranger	2008	D-HEFA	24.10.68	To D-HAKU 11/72. Canx.
G-AWSJ	Agusta-Bell 47G-2	971/218	3B-XD Austrian AF	28.10.68	To F-BUXD(2) 4/76. Canx 2.4.76.
G-AWSK	Agusta-Bell 47G-2	687/211	3B-XB Austrian AF/OE-UXA	28.10.68	To F-BVFY 3/82. Canx 5.2.82.
G-AWSL	PA-28-180 Cherokee D	28-4907		30.10.68	
G-AWSM	PA-28-235 Cherokee C	28-11125		30.10.68	
G-AWSN	Rollason-Druine D.62B Condor	RAE/632		31.10.68	
G-AWSO	Rollason-Druine D.62B Condor	RAE/633		31.10.68	DBF. Canx 30.5.84.
G-AWSP	Rollason-Druine D.62B Condor	RAE/634		31.10.68	(Stored 10/97)
G-AWSR	Rollason-Druine D.62B Condor	RAE/635		31.10.68	Crashed at Holne, Devon on 18.8.73. Canx.
G-AWSS	Rollason-Druine D.62C Condor (Originally regd as D.62B)	RAE/636		31.10.68	(Stored 10/95)
G-AWST	Rollason-Druine D.62B Condor	RAE/637		31.10.68	
G-AWSU	Aeromere-Laverda F.8L Super Falco Srs.IV	416		31.10.68	To EI-BMF 1/82. Canx 25.1.82.
G-AWSV	Saro Skeeter AOP.12	S2/5107	XM553	31.10.68	Canx as TWFU 23.5.95.
G-AWSW	Beagle D.5/180 Husky	3690	XW635 G-AWSW	4.11.68	
G-AWSX	Schiebe SF-27M-A	6306	D-KIMK	4.11.68	To D-KANN 12/81. Canx 18.10.79.
G-AWSY	Boeing 737-204 (Line No. 166)	20236		4.11.68	To N173PL 6/94. Canx 12.10.93.
G-AWSZ	Socata MS.894A Rallye Minerva 220	11005	F-BPSO	6.11.68	DBR in forced landing at Mullaghmore on 20.10.78. Canx by CAA 14.10.86.
G-AWTA	Cessna E.310N	310N-0054	EI-ATB N4154Q	8.11.68	To N510PS 12/96. Canx 13.11.96.
G-AWTB	Percival P.56 Provost T.1 (Also c/n PAC/F/342)	P56/342	XF838	8.11.68	To Rhodesian AF in 1973. Canx.
G-AWTC	Percival P.56 Provost T.1 (Also c/n PAC/F/338)	P56/338	XF693	8.11.68	To Rhodesian AF as 3616 in 1973. Canx.
G-AWTD	Percival P.56 Provost T.1 (Also c/n PAC/F/285)	P56/285	XF554	8.11.68	To Rhodesian AF as 3614 in 1973. Canx.
G-AWTE	Percival P.56 Provost T.1 (Also c/n PAC/F/336)	P56/336	XF691	8.11.68	To Rhodesian AF as 3165 in 1973. Canx.
G-AWTF	Percival P.56 Provost T.1 (Also c/n PAC/F/004)	P56/004	WV421	8.11.68	To Rhodesian AF in 1973. Canx.
G-AWTG	Percival P.56 Provost T.1 (Also c/n PAC/F/086)	P56/086	WV540	8.11.68	To Rhodesian AF as 6307 in 1973. Canx.
G-AWTH	Reims Cessna F.172H Skyhawk	0626	F-WLIT	8.11.68	NTU - Not Imported. To PH-VDW 6/69. Canx 14.1.69.
G-AWTI	Reims Cessna F.172H Skyhawk	0580		8.11.68	Canx in 6/72. Rebuilt & re-regd as G-MELT in 9/83.
G-AWTJ	Reims Cessna F.150J	0419		8.11.68	
G-AWTK	Boeing 707-349C (Line No. 445) (Originally regd as 707-320C, upgraded on 16.1.69)	18975	N322F	11.11.68	To G-BDCN 5/75. Canx.
G-AWTL	PA-28-180 Cherokee D	28-5068		12.11.68	
G-AWTM	PA-28-140 Cherokee B	28-25128	N11C	12.11.68	To G-KEAN 12/85. Canx.
G-AWTN	PA-28-140 Cherokee B	28-25206		12.11.68	NTU - Not Imported. To N7299F. Canx 19.11.68.
G-AWTO	PA-28-140 Cherokee B	28-25212		12.11.68	NTU - Not Imported. To N7298F. Canx 19.11.68.
G-AWTP	Schleicher Ka.6E Rhonsegler	4123		12.11.68	To N29JG. Canx 17.12.69.
G-AWTR	Beechcraft A23-19A Musketeer Sport	MB-411	N2758B	14.11.68	Canx as WFU 5.12.88. To EI-CCA 7/90.
G-AWTS	Beechcraft A23-19A Musketeer Sport	MB-412	OO-BGN G-AWTS/N2763B	14.11.68	
G-AWTT	Beechcraft A23-19A Musketeer Sport	MB-418	N2766B	14.11.68	DBR on take-off from a private strip at Northiam, near Rye on 7.5.70. Canx as destroyed 16.7.70.
G-AWTU	Beechcraft A23-19A Musketeer Sport	MB-423	AP-AWT (A6-...)/G-AWTU/N2769B	14.11.68	Overhaul abandoned on return from Pakistani regn in 7/80 & used for spares at Deanland. Canx as WFU 21.5.85
G-AWTV	Beechcraft A23-19A Musketeer Sport	MB-424	N2770B	14.11.68	
G-AWTW	Beechcraft 95-B55 Baron	TC-1200		14.11.68	To N9074H 9/95. Canx 10.8.95.
G-AWTX	Reims Cessna F.150J	0404		18.11.68	Tail fitted to G-AWFH. (On overhaul 5/98 at Sywell)
G-AWTY	Reims Cessna F.150J	0407		18.11.68	NTU - To (G-AXBL)/PK-DCB 12/69. Canx 14.1.69.
G-AWTZ	Brookland Mosquito Mk.II Gyroplane	8		19.11.68	Crashed at Woodford on 27.6.70. Canx.

Regn	Type	c/n	Previous identity	Regn date	Fate or immediate subsequent identity (if known)
G-AWUA	Cessna P.206D Super Skylane	P206-0550	N8750Z	21.11.68	Damaged in gales at Thruxton on 16.10.87. Canx as destroyed 11.8.88. (Stored 6/96)
G-AWUB	Gardan GY-201 Minicab	A.205	F-PERX	22.11.68	WFU on 8.12.81. (Fuselage stored 9/91)
G-AWUC	Bell 206A JetRanger	323		22.11.68	To F-BXPE 12/75. Canx 27.10.75.
G-AWUD	Canadair CL-44D4-1	14	N124SW / C-FMYO-X	22.11.68	NTU - Not Imported. Remained as N124SW. Canx 19.12.68.
G-AWUE	SAN Jodel DR.1050 Ambassadeur	299	F-BKHE	22.11.68	(Rebuild completed at Insch by 7/99)
G-AWUF	HS.125 Srs.1B/522 (Originally regd as Srs.1B)	25106	5N-ALY / G-AWUF/HZ-BIN	22.11.68	To G-DJMJ 1/84. Canx.
G-AWUG	Reims Cessna F.150H	0299		25.11.68	(Damaged by gales at Edinburgh on 26.12.98)
G-AWUH	Reims Cessna F.150H	0307		25.11.68	CofA expired 16.7.94. Stored 9/96 Bournemouth. Canx as WFU 8./.97.
G-AWUI	Reims Cessna F.150H	0318		25.11.68	To 5B-CCY in 4/77. Canx 22.4.77.
G-AWUJ	Reims Cessna F.150H	0332		25.11.68	
G-AWUK	Reims Cessna F.150H	0344		25.11.68	Crashed at Shoreham on 4.9.71. Canx as WFU 13.4.73. (Stored 4/95)
G-AWUL	Reims Cessna F.150H	0346		25.11.68	
G-AWUM	Reims Cessna F.150H	0362		25.11.68	Scrapped and removed from Biggin Hill on 12.7.80 after an accident (details?). CofA expired 22.5.81. Canx by CAA 27.2.87.
G-AWUN	Reims Cessna F.150H	0377		25.11.68	
G-AWUO	Reims Cessna F.150H	0380		25.11.68	
G-AWUP	Reims Cessna F.150H	0381		25.11.68	DBR in Ireland in 1983. (Last known stored at Shannon) Canx by CAA 9.1.89.
G-AWUR	Reims Cessna F.150J	0390		25.11.68	Crashed at Peplow, near Market Drayton, Salop on 22.5.73. Canx by CAA 14.10.86.
G-AWUS	Reims Cessna F.150J	0394		25.11.68	Damaged at Popham on 22.11.86. (Present status unknown) Canx by CAA 4.7.94.
G-AWUT	Reims Cessna F.150J	0405		25.11.68	
G-AWUU	Reims Cessna F.150J	0408	EI-BRA / G-AWUU	25.11.68	
G-AWUV	Reims Cessna F.150J	0409		25.11.68	Rebuilt as G-BELT 1/77. Canx.
G-AWUW	Reims Cessna F.172H Skyhawk	0576		25.11.68	Canx as WFU 11.4.90.
G-AWUX	Reims Cessna F.172H Skyhawk	0577		25.11.68	
G-AWUY	Reims Cessna F.172H Skyhawk	0578		25.11.68	
G-AWUZ	Reims Cessna F.172H Skyhawk	0587		25.11.68	
G-AWVA	Reims Cessna F.172H Skyhawk	0597		25.11.68	
G-AWVB	SAN Jodel D.117	604	F-BIBA	26.11.68	
G-AWVC	Beagle B.121 Pup Srs.100	B121-026	(OE-CUP) / G-35-026	27.11.68	
G-AWVD	Not allocated.				
G-AWVE	CEA Jodel DR.1050/M1 Sicile Record	612	F-BMPQ	27.11.68	
G-AWVF	Hunting-Percival P.56 Provost T.1 (Also c/n P56/375)	PAC/F/375	XF877	28.11.68	(Open store 7/98 Brimpton)
G-AWVG	AESL Airtourer T2 (115)	513	OO-WIC / G-AWVG	29.11.68	
G-AWVH	AESL Airtourer T2 (115)	512		29.11.68	Crashed at Goodwood, Sussex on 15.3.81. Remains to 2243 (Laindon & Basildon) ATC Sqdn in Essex. Scrapped in 1991. Canx as destroyed 5.12.83.
G-AWVI	Handley Page 137 Jetstream 1 (Production No. 3)	204		29.11.68	To N1040S. Canx 17.9.69.
G-AWVJ	Handley Page 137 Jetstream 1 (Production No. 5)	206	(N1036S) / G-AWVJ	29.11.68	To RN as XX475 7/73. Canx.
G-AWVK	Handley Page 137 Jetstream 200 (Originally regd as Srs.1) (Production No. 7)	208	N1035S / G-AWVK	29.11.68	To G-RAVL 12/86. Canx.
G-AWVL	Hughes 269A	63-0234	ZS-HCN / VP-YWB	2.12.68	Crashed at Heacham, Norfolk on 1.5.72. Canx as WFU 5.2.73.
G-AWVM	Short SC.7 Skyvan 3-200-20	SH1852	N33BB / PP-SDO/G-AWVM/G-14-1	2.12.68	To N50DA 4/73. Canx 19.4.73.
G-AWVN	Aeronca 7AC Champion	7AC-6005	N2426E / NC2426E	4.12.68	
G-AWVO	Agusta-Bell 206B JetRanger (Originally 206A; later modified)	8111	VH-BHI(5) / PK-HCA/G-AWVO/9Y-TDN/PK-HBG/G-AWVO	4.12.68	To G-DBHH 5/96. Canx.
G-AWVP	Brookland Mosquito Mk.II Gyroplane	9		6.12.68	Canx as WFU 11.7.84.
G-AWVR	Skyship Non-Rigid Airship (Parts from G-AVKO used during construction)	1		6.12.68	Last known stored at Wroughton. Canx as WFU 21.8.81.
G-AWVS	Cessna 337D Super Skymaster (Robertson STOL conversion)	337-0991	N2691S	6.12.68	To OY-BZO. Canx 16.4.85.
G-AWVT	Cessna 411A	411A-0256	N3265R	6.12.68	To N87615 5/75. Canx 16.5.75.
G-AWVU	Brookland Mosquito Mk.II Gyroplane	10		6.12.68	Canx 13.5.70 on sale to France.
G-AWVV	Schleicher ASK-14	14008	D-KOBB	6.12.68	To EI-APS 11/69. Canx 24.11.69.
G-AWVW	PA-E23-250 Aztec D	27-4054	OY-RPF / G-AWVW/N6799Y	9.12.68	To G-TAPE 10/83. Canx.
G-AWVX	BN-2A Islander	47		9.12.68	To Abu Dhabi AF as 202 in 2/69. Canx 13.2.69.
G-AWVY	BN-2A-26 Islander	48	N48BN / G-AWVY	9.12.68	To SE-IIA 3/81. Canx 26.1.81.
G-AWVZ	Jodel D.112	898	F-PKVL	12.12.68	
G-AWWA	Westland-Sikorsky S-55 Whirlwind Srs.3	WA/397	VR-BDD / G-AWWA/Ghana AF G-601/G-17-1	12.12.68	To 5N-AJG 10/71. Canx 11.10.71.

Regn	Type	c/n	Previous identity	Regn date	Fate or immediate subsequent identity (if known)
G-AWWB	Canadair CL-44D4-2	17	VR-HHC G-AWWB/N448T	12.12.68	To N908L 4/80. Canx 23.4.80.
G-AWWC	Not allocated.				
G-AWWD	Boeing 707-349C (Line No. 553)	19355	N325F G-AWWD/N325F	12.12.68	To D2-TAD 12/77. Canx 30.11.77.
G-AWWE	Beagle B.121 Pup Srs.150	B121 032	G-35-032	12.12.68	
G-AWWF	Beagle B.121 Pup Srs.100	B121-033	G-35-033	12.12.68	To G-JIMB 4/94. Canx.
G-AWWG	Beagle B.121 Pup Srs.150	B121-034	YI-AEK G-AWWG/G-35-034	12.12.68	To YI-AEK 3/69. Canx 3.4.69.
G-AWWH	Beagle B.121 Pup Srs.100	B121-035	G-35-035	12.12.68	Blown over in gales at Dyce on 21.9.69 & DBR. Scrapped at Cranfield in 9/71. Canx as destroyed 30.10.69.
G-AWWI	SAN Jodel D.117	728	F-BIDU	13.12.68	
G-AWWJ	Piaggio P.166	406	9L-LAF	18.12.68	Canx 29.5.69 on sale to Switzerland. To 5N-ADP 2/70.
G-AWWK	Beechcraft 65-B90 King Air	LJ-446		18.12.68	To G-BHGT 10/79. Canx.
G-AWWL	HS.125 Srs.3B/RA	25169	N3AL VH-BBJ/G-AWWL/G-5-17	24.12.68	To N84TF. Canx 19.4.82.
G-AWWM	Gardan GY-201 Minicab	A.195	F-BFOQ	1. 1.69	
G-AWWN	SAN Jodel DR.1051 Sicile	398	F-BLJA	8. 1.69	
G-AWWO	CEA Jodel DR.1050 Ambassadeur	552	F-BLOI	8. 1.69	
G-AWWP	Aerosport Woody Pusher Mk.3 (Originally regd as Woodsbird Woody Pusher Mk.1)	WA/163 & PFA/1323		7. 1.69	(Complete and flown) (Stored 6/93)
G-AWWR	SNCAN Stampe SC-4C	1073	F-BAUT	9. 1.69	To N31034 12/70. Canx.
G-AWWS	Short SC.7 Skyvan 3-200-15	SH1854	N7978 CF-VAN/G-AWWS/G-14-2	10. 1.69	To EI-BNN 3/83. Canx 23.5.83.
G-AWWT	Druine D.31 Turbulent	PFA/1653		15. 1.69	(Badly damaged on landing at Andrewsfield on 7.10.96)
G-AWWU	Reims Cessna FR.172F Rocket	0111		15. 1.69	
G-AWWV	Reims Cessna FR.172F Rocket	0076		15. 1.69	DBR at Strathallen on 29.6.80. Canx.
G-AWWW	Cessna 401	401-0294	N8446F	19.12.68	
G-AWWX	BAC One-Eleven Srs.509EW	BAC.184		15. 1.69	To (G-OBWG 4/93)/5N-... Stored since 11/92 at Southend. Scrapped at Southend in 9/98.
G-AWWY	BAC One-Eleven Srs.509EW	BAC.185	LV-JNU LV-PSW/G-AWWY/(G-AXMK(1))	15. 1.69	To LV-LHT. Canx 13.10.75.
G-AWWZ	BAC One-Eleven Srs.509EW	BAC.186	EI-CCW G-BSYN/G-AWWZ	15. 1.69	To ZS-NMS 12/94. Canx 28.11.94.
G-AWXA	Cessna 182M Skylane	182-59403	EI-BOW G-AWXA/N70877	16. 1.69	Ditched in sea off Rome, Italy on 3.2.96. Canx as destroyed 14.6.96.
G-AWXB	HS.125 Srs.400A	NA717 & 25183	G-5-18	17. 1.69	To N162A. Canx 13.2.69.
G-AWXC	HS.125 Srs.400A	NA718 & 25187		17. 1.69	To N600L. Canx 27.2.69.
G-AWXD	HS.125 Srs.400A	NA719 & 25188		17. 1.69	To N545S. Canx 18.3.69.
G-AWXE	HS.125 Srs.400A	NA720 & 25185		17. 1.69	To N140C. Canx 16.4.69.
G-AWXF	HS.125 Srs.400A	NA721 & 25186		17. 1.69	To N125G. Canx 25.4.69.
G-AWXG	Aerospatiale SE.316B Alouette III	1517	F-WIEQ	20. 1.69	To EI-ATO /69. Canx 7.7.70.
G-AWXH	Reims Cessna F.150H	0353		21. 1.69	Crashed near Conglesbury on 17.2.81. Canx.
G-AWXI	Vickers 814 Viscount	339	D-ANOL	21. 1.69	DBF on take-off from Heathrow on 22.1.70. Remains to East Midlands Airport in 3/70 as scrap. Canx as WFU 16.3.70.
G-AWXJ	BAC One-Eleven Srs.416EK	BAC.166	HB-ITK G-AWXJ	22. 1.69	Canx 17.9.71 on sale to Hong Kong. To 9V-BEF 12/71.
G-AWXK	Aero Commander 680V/TU (Originally regd as a 680T, then a 680TA)	1540-6	N6300	22. 1.69	To F-WSTM 10/70. Canx 10.11.70.
G-AWXL	Aero Commander 680T	1532-2	N1186Z	22. 1.69	To HB-GEK 8/69. Canx 29.8.69.
G-AWXM	Cessna 401	401-0165	N4065Q	23. 1.69	To G-CAFE(2) 7/79. Canx.
G-AWXN	HS.125 Srs.400B	25177		23. 1.69	To South African AF as 02 in 7/70. Canx.
G-AWXO	HS.125 Srs.400B	25178		23. 1.69	To 5N-BUA. Canx 27.1.93.
G-AWXP	Scintex CP.301-C1 Emeraude	565	F-BJFZ	24. 1.69	Ditched into sea off Dymchurch on 24.6.71. Finally WFU on 1.6.72 after laying in the car park at Denham airfield for some months.
G-AWXR	PA-28-180 Cherokee D	28-5171		24. 1.69	
G-AWXS	PA-28-180 Cherokee D	28-5283		24. 1.69	
G-AWXT	Morane-Saulnier MS.880B Rallye Club	835	F-BNXU	24. 1.69	Canx as destroyed 5.2.78.
G-AWXU	Reims Cessna F.150J	0492		24. 1.69	To G-INGR 8/96. Canx.
G-AWXV	Reims Cessna F.172H	0619		24. 1.69	Forced landing at Crossens, near Southport on 21.3.91. Canx as WFU 18.11.91.
G-AWXW	PA-23-250 Aztec D	27-4096	N6765Y	27. 1.69	Canx as WFU 1.12.83.
G-AWXX	Westland-Sikorsky S-58 Wessex 60 Srs.1	WA/694	G-17-6 G-AWXX/VH-BHX/G-AWXX	29. 1.69	Used for spares for G-AYNC. Scrapped in 5/90. Canx 16.12.91.
G-AWXY	Morane-Saulnier MS.885 Super Rallye	5097	EI-AMG	29. 1.69	
G-AWXZ	SNCAN Stampe SV-4C	360	"G-AAVX" G-AWXZ/F-BHMZ/French Mil/F-BCOI	30. 1.69	
G-AWYA	BN-2A Islander	54		30. 1.69	NTU - To 6Y-JFL 5/69. Canx 24.2.69.
G-AWYB	Reims Cessna FR.172F Rocket	0075		30. 1.69	
G-AWYC	Reims Cessna FR.172F Rocket	0101		30. 1.69	NTU - Not Imported. Canx 7.7.69 as marks WFU. To LN-IKQ 6/69.
G-AWYD	Cessna 337D Super Skymaster	337D-1076	N86095	30. 1.69	NTU - Not Imported. To OY-AKP 1/69. Canx 30.1.70.
G-AWYE	HS.125 Srs.1B/522 (Originally regd as Srs.1B)	25090	HB-VAT	30. 1.69	To N102TW. Canx 18.5.90.
G-AWYF	Gulfstream G.159 Gulfstream I	48	N302K VR-BBY/N748G	30. 1.69	To N213GA 6/94. Canx 13.6.94.
G-AWYG	Short SC.7 Skyvan 3-200-26	SH1856	G-14-28	4. 2.69	To N28TC 6/74. Canx 21.6.74.

Regn	Type	c/n	Previous identity	Regn date	Fate or immediate subsequent identity (if known)
G-AWYH	Aero Commander 200D	338	N2965T	5. 2.69	To N200HS 12/81. Canx 7.12.81.
G-AWYI	BE.2c Replica	001		5. 2.69	To N1914B. Canx 17.6.71.
G-AWYJ	Beagle B.121 Pup Srs.100	B121-038	G-35-038	10. 2.69	
G-AWYK	Reims Cessna FR.172F Rocket	0106		10. 2.69	To VP-YIS(2) 10/72. Canx 13.10.72.
G-AWYL	CEA Jodel DR.253B Regent	143		11. 2.69	
G-AWYM	Handley Page 137 Jetstream 1 (Production No. 9)	210		11. 2.69	To N62BS. Canx 10.6.69.
G-AWYN	Handley Page 137 Jetstream 1 (Production No. 11)	212		11. 2.69	To N340. Canx 17.6.69.
G-AWYO	Beagle B.121 Pup Srs.100	B121-041	G-35-041	11. 2.69	
G-AWYP	Handley Page 137 Jetstream 1 (Production No. 12)	213		11. 2.69	To N137HP. Canx 27.6.69.
G-AWYR	BAC One-Eleven Srs.501EX	BAC.174	EI-CID G-AWYR	11. 2.69	To "5N-ESB"/"5N-ES_"/5N-ESA 12/98. Canx 23.12.98.
G-AWYS	BAC One-Eleven Srs.501EX	BAC.175		11. 2.69	To 5N-ESB 10/98. Canx 23.9.98.
G-AWYT	BAC One-Eleven Srs.501EX	BAC.176	EI-CIE G-AWYT/(G-AXMH(1))	11. 2.69	To 9Q-CKY 10/94. Canx 14.10.94.
G-AWYU	BAC One-Eleven Srs.501EX	BAC.177	EI-CIC G-AWYU/(G-AXHI(1))	11. 2.69	To 9Q-CKI 11/94. Canx 2.12.94.
G-AWYV	BAC One-Eleven Srs.501EX	BAC.178		11. 2.69	
G-AWYW	BN-2A Islander	55		11. 2.69	To 5A-BBA 6/69. Canx 19.7.69.
G-AWYX	Morane-Saulnier MS.880B Rallye Club	1311		11. 2.69	CofA expired 27.6.86. (Open storage 4/98 Henstridge)
G-AWYY	Slingsby T.57 Sopwith Camel F.1 Replica (Clerget)	1701	"C1701" N1917H/G-AWYY	14. 2.69	Permit expired 1.9.85. Canx as WFU 25.11.91. (On display 3/96 RNAS Yeovilton)
G-AWYZ	HS.121 Trident 3B Srs.101	2301		14. 1.69	WFU at Heathrow on 16.10.83. Scrapped in 6/84. Canx as WFU 20.2.84.
G-AWZA	HS.121 Trident 3B Srs.101	2302		14. 1.69	WFU at Heathrow on 23.10.82. Scrapped in 1/84. Canx as WFU 20.2.84.
G-AWZB	HS.121 Trident 3B Srs.101	2303		14. 1.69	WFU at Heathrow on 25.11.83. Scrapped in 8/84. Canx as WFU 20.2.84.
G-AWZC	HS.121 Trident 3B Srs.101	2304		14. 1.69	To 9Q-CTM(2) 11/84. Canx 14.11.84.
G-AWZD	HS.121 Trident 3B Srs.101	2305		14. 1.69	To 9Q-CTI. Canx 26.7.85.
G-AWZE	HS.121 Trident 3B Srs.101	2306		14. 1.69	WFU at Heathrow on 22.5.83. Scrapped in 6/84. Canx as WFU 20.2.84.
G-AWZF	HS.121 Trident 3B Srs.101	2307		14. 1.69	To 9Q-CTE. Canx 8.3.85.
G-AWZG	HS.121 Trident 3B Srs.101	2308		14. 1.69	To (9Q-CTY)/9Q-CTD(2) 9/85. Canx 12.9.85.
G-AWZH	HS.121 Trident 3B Srs.101	2309		14. 1.69	WFU at Heathrow on 6.9.85. Broken up in 6/86. Canx as destroyed 27.6.86.
G-AWZI	HS.121 Trident 3B Srs.101	2310		14. 1.69	WFU at Heathrow on 1.5.85. Broken up in 6/87. Canx as destroyed 9.7.87. (Fuselage used by Surrey County Fire Brigade HQ as an Instructional Airframe - extant 1/94)
G-AWZJ	HS.121 Trident 3B Srs.101	2311		14. 1.69	Canx as WFU 7.3.86. (Used by Prestwick Fire Dept - Extant 4/97)
G-AWZK	HS.121 Trident 3B Srs.101	2312		14. 1.69	WFU at Heathrow on 1.11.85. Canx as WFU 29.5.90. (Used as instructional airframe for anti-terrorist training) (Extant 4/97)
G-AWZL	HS.121 Trident 3B Srs.101	2313		14. 1.69	WFU at Heathrow on 23.11.83. Broken up in 6/86. Canx as destroyed 30.7.86.
G-AWZM	HS.121 Trident 3B Srs.101	2314		14. 1.69	WFU at Heathrow on 13.12.85. Flown to Wroughton on 28.2.86. Canx as WFU 18.3.86. (On display 9/93 Wroughton)
G-AWZN	HS.121 Trident 3B Srs.101	2315		14. 1.69	WFU at Heathrow on 22.12.85. Flown to Cranfield on 17.3.86. Canx as WFU 18.3.86. Scrapped at Cranfield by 10/95.
G-AWZO	HS.121 Trident 3B Srs.101	2316		14. 1.69	WFU at Heathrow on 31.12.85. Flown to Hatfield on 18.4.86 for BAe non-destructive training/preservation. Canx as WFU 27.5.86. (Stored 3/96 Hatfield)
G-AWZP	HS.121 Trident 3B Srs.101	2317		14. 1.69	WFU at Heathrow on 13.12.85. Broken up in 6/86 - Nose section to Manchester Museum of Science & Industry. Canx as destroyed 27.6.86.
G-AWZR	HS.121 Trident 3B Srs.101	2318		14. 1.69	WFU at Heathrow on 27.9.85. To Teesside for fire-training. Canx as WFU 26.3.86. (Extant 4/99 Teesside)
G-AWZS	HS.121 Trident 3B Srs.101	2319		14. 1.69	WFU at Heathrow on 5.12.85. To Teesside for fire-training. Canx as WFU 18.3.86. (Extant 4/99 Teesside)
G-AWZT	HS.121 Trident 3B Srs.101	2320		14. 1.69	Fatal crash near Gaj, Hrvatska, Yugoslavia after midair collision with DC-9-31 YU-AJR on 10.9.76. Canx.
G-AWZU	HS.121 Trident 3B Srs.101	2321		14. 1.69	Flown to Stansted for fire practice on 7.3.86. Canx as WFU 18.3.86. (Open storage 10/97 Stansted)
G-AWZV	HS.121 Trident 3B Srs.101	2322		14. 1.69	To 9Q-CTZ(2) 5/86. Canx 30.5.86.
G-AWZW	HS.121 Trident 3B Srs.101	2323		14. 1.69	WFU at Heathrow on 19.10.83. Scrapped in 6/84. Canx as WFU 20.2.84.
G-AWZX	HS.121 Trident 3B Srs.101	2324		14. 1.69	Flown to Gatwick on 1.10.84. Canx as WFU 29.11.84. (Fire Services Airframe at Gatwick) (Extant 12/95)
G-AWZY	HS.121 Trident 3B Srs.101	2325		14. 1.69	NTU - To G-AYVF 4/71. Canx.
G-AWZZ	HS.121 Trident 3B Srs.101	2326		14. 1.69	Flown to Birmingham on 4.11.84. Canx as WFU 23.11.84. (Used by Birmingham Airport Fire Service as a Training Airframe 3/97 at Elmdon)
G-AXAA	Canadair CL-44D4-2	18	N449T	14. 2.69	To N122AE. Canx 25.9.81.
G-AXAB	PA-28-140 Cherokee	28-20238	EI-AOA N6206W	17. 2.69	
G-AXAC	SNCAN Stampe SV-4C	616	F-BDFL	17. 2.69	To N31627 6/72. Canx 12.6.72.
G-AXAD	Short SC.7 Skyvan 3-200-12	SH1857	G-14-29	17. 2.69	To N20CK 6/69. Canx 12.6.69.
G-AXAE	Short SC.7 Skyvan 3-200-12	SH1858	G-14-30	17. 2.69	To N3748 4/69. Canx 11.4.69.
G-AXAF	Short SC.7 Skyvan 3-200-12	SH1859	G-14-31	17. 2.69	To N22CK 6/69. Canx 12.6.69.

Regn	Type	c/n	Previous identity	Regn date	Fate or immediate subsequent identity (if known)
G-AXAG	Short SC.7 Skyvan 3-200-18	SH1861	G-14-33	17. 2.69	To N123PA 9/69. Canx 5.9.69.
G-AXAH	SIAI-Marchetti SF-260	103	OO-HAY I-SIAY	18. 2.69	To N1039S 4/79. Canx 28.4.79.
G-AXAI	Aviation Traders ATL.98A Carvair (Conv. Douglas C-54B-5-DO)	18342/17	LX-IOF N30042/43-17142	19. 2.69	To F-BVEF 1/76. Canx 27.1.76.
G-AXAJ	AESL Airtourer T4 (150)	522		20. 2.69	Crashed on take-off from Staverton on 10.8.76. Canx.
G-AXAK	Socata MS.880B Rallye Club	1304		20. 2.69	
G-AXAL	Slingsby Rumpler C.5 Replica (Built using DH.82A G-AMEY)	1704		20. 2.69	To N1915E 3/71. Canx 31.3.71.
G-AXAM	Slingsby Rumpler C.5 Replica (Built using DH.82A G-AODU)	1705		20. 2.69	To N1916E 3/71. Canx 31.3.71.
G-AXAN	DH.82A Tiger Moth (Officially regd with c/n EM720-85)	85951	F-BDMM French AF/EM720	21. 2.69	
G-AXAO	Omega O-56 HAFB (Rebuilt as Western O-65 c/n 021)	02		25. 2.69	(Extant 12/90) Canx by CAA 19.5.93.
G-AXAP	Agusta-Bell 206A JetRanger	8116		25. 2.69	To PK-HBH 4/69. Canx 14.4.69.
G-AXAR	Wallis WA-117 Autogyro	G/403/X		25. 2.69	Fatal crash during display at SBAC Show, Farnborough on 11.9.70. Canx.
G-AXAS	Wallis WA-116-T/Mc Autogyro (Used major components from G-AVDH c/n 216)	217		25. 2.69	
G-AXAT	SAN Jodel D.117A	836	F-BITJ	26. 2.69	
G-AXAU	PA-30-160 Twin Comanche C	30-1753	N8613Y	25. 2.69	CofA expired 8.3.86. (Stored 2/96 Bournemouth)
G-AXAV	PA-30-160 Twin Comanche C	30-1793	N8656Y	25. 2.69	CofA expired 24.6.84. (Last reported at Guernsey) Canx as WFU 18.11.85.
G-AXAW	Cessna 421A Golden Eagle	421A-0038	(EI-TCK) G-AXAW/N2238Q	28. 2.69	To EI-TCK 11/91. Canx 4.11.91.
G-AXAX	PA-23-250 Aztec D	27-4155	N6816Y	3. 3.69	To 9G-ZAR 9/98. Canx 23.9.98.
G-AXAY	Bell 206B JetRanger (Originally 206A; later modified)	332		3. 3.69	Crashed at Inkpen Ridge, near Hungerford on 7.3.74. Canx.
G-AXAZ	PA-31 Turbo Navajo	31-245	N9184Y	5. 3.69	To G-BXAZ 7/85. Canx.
G-AXBA	BN-2A Islander	51	G-51-15	5. 3.69	To F-OGEB 5/70. Canx 22.8.69.
G-AXBB	BAC One-Eleven Srs.409AY	BAC.162	A40-BB G-AXBB/TI-1055C/G-AXBB/YR-BCP/G-AXBB/G-16-6	6. 3.69	To 5N-AYR. Canx 24.10.89.
G-AXBC	PA-32-300 Cherokee Six C	32-40685	N11C	7. 3.69	To ZS-JUK 3/76. Canx 24.2.76.
G-AXBD	PA-25-235 Pawnee C	25-4888		7. 3.69	Crashed while spraying at Parsonage Farm, Norfolk on 2.7.76. Canx as WFU 3.8.94.
G-AXBE	Beagle B.121 Pup Srs.100	B121-039	G-35-039	12. 3.69	Fuselage broke in two places in force-landed & overturned S of Basingstoke golf-course 15.3.70. Canx as WFU 17.9.73.
G-AXBF	Beagle D.5/180 Husky	3691	OE-DEW	17.10.84	
G-AXBG	Curtiss-Bensen B.8M Gyrocopter	RC.1		12. 3.69	
G-AXBH	Reims Cessna F.172H Skyhawk	0571		12. 3.69	
G-AXBI	Reims Cessna F.172H Skyhawk	0572		12. 3.69	NTU - Not Imported. Marks canx as WFU 7.7.69. To LN-LJF 9/69.
G-AXBJ	Reims Cessna F.172H Skyhawk	0573		12. 3.69	
G-AXBK	Reims Cessna F.172H Skyhawk	0579		12. 3.69	Fatal crash at Ize, Houdrie, France on 11.4.70. Canx.
G-AXBL	Reims Cessna F.150J	0407	(G-AWTY)	12. 3.69R	NTU - Not Imported. Marks canx as WFU 7.7.69. To PK-DCB 12/69.
G-AXBM	Reims Cessna F.150J	0425		12. 3.69R	NTU - Not Imported. Marks canx as WFU 7.7.69. To D-EGHF 9/69.
G-AXBN	Reims Cessna F.150J	0430		12. 3.69R	NTU - Not Imported. Marks canx as WFU 7.7.69. To HB-CUV 10/69.
G-AXBO	Not allocated.				
G-AXBP	Reims Cessna F.150J	0434		12. 3.69R	NTU - Not Imported. Marks canx as WFU 7.7.69. To I-ALPP 7/69.
G-AXBR	Reims Cessna F.150J	0443		12. 3.69R	NTU - Not Imported. Marks canx as WFU 7.7.69. To I-RAVU 10/69.
G-AXBS	Reims Cessna F.150J	0445		12. 3.69R	NTU - Not Imported. Marks canx as WFU 7.7.69. To D-EGHD 9/69.
G-AXBT	Reims Cessna FR.172F Rocket	0062		12. 3.69R	NTU - Not Imported. Marks canx as WFU 7.7.69. To D-EEAT 7/69.
G-AXBU	Reims Cessna FR.172F Rocket	0073		12. 3.69	Crashed near Priestland, Darvel on 13.10.74. Canx in 12/79. (Wreck in store 2/96)
G-AXBV	Cessna 337D Super Skymaster	337-1077	N86098	12. 3.69R	NTU - To G-AXRX 11/69. Canx.
G-AXBW	DH.82A Tiger Moth	83595	6854M T5879	12. 3.69	
G-AXBX	SNCA SO.1221S Djinn	1043/FR.93	F-BIUA	12. 3.69	To F-BSEZ 3/70. Canx 12.3.70.
G-AXBY	Cessna 401A	401A-0032	N6232Q	13. 3.69	To N70SC 5/82. Canx 13.5.82.
G-AXBZ	DH.82A Tiger Moth	86552	F-BGDF French AF/PG643	14. 3.69	
G-AXCA	PA-28R-200 Cherokee Arrow	28R-35053		18. 3.69	
G-AXCB	Beagle B.206S Srs.2	B.061	G-35-15	18. 3.69	To VH-FDF 4/69. Canx 11.4.69.
G-AXCC	Bell 47G-2	1413	EP-HBD G-AXCC/Austrian AF 3B-XA/OE-BXA/N985B	18. 3.69	Substantially damaged on landing at Fount Hill, Newick, East Sussex on 18.10.81. Canx by CAA 4.12.86.
G-AXCD	Agusta-Bell 47G-2	220	EP-HBC G-AXCD/Austrian AF 3B-XF	18. 5.69	To F-GANT 1/83. Canx 3.2.82.
G-AXCE	Agusta-Bell 47G-2	234	3B-XG Austrian AF	18. 5.69	To EP-HBB 5/69. Canx 20.5.69.
G-AXCF	Agusta-Bell 47G-2	244	EP-HBA G-AXCF/Austrian AF 3B-XK	18. 5.69	To F-GANS 5/82. Canx 3.2.82.
G-AXCG	SAN Jodel D.117	510	PH-VRA F-BHXI	19. 3.69	

Regn	Type	c/n	Previous identity	Regn date	Fate or immediate subsequent identity (if known)
G-AXCH	Morane-Saulnier MS.885 Super Rallye	265	F-BKUT	19. 3.69	Canx as WFU 7.10.74.
G-AXCI	Bensen B.8M Gyrocopter	CEW.1		20. 3.69	Canx as WFU 7.2.74. (Stored 9/93)
G-AXCJ	Beechcraft A23-24 Musketeer Super III	MA-352		24. 3.69	To EI-BFF 8/78. Canx 13.7.78.
G-AXCK	BAC One-Eleven Srs.401AK	090	N5044	24. 3.69	To N164W. Canx 4.2.83.
G-AXCL	Socata MS.880B Rallye Club	1321		25. 3.69	
G-AXCM	Socata MS.880B Rallye Club	1322		25. 3.69	
G-AXCN	Socata MS.880B Rallye Club	1328		25. 3.69	(Damaged in gales at Thruxton on 16.10.87) (On rebuild .92)
G-AXCO	PA-30-160 Twin Comanche C	30-1802	N8660Y	26. 3.69	To OY-DLV 10/75. Canx 29.10.75.
G-AXCP	BAC One-Eleven Srs.401AK	087	N5041	26. 3.69	To N173FE. Canx 1.12.86.
G-AXCR	North American AT-16 Harvard IIB	14-324	U-322 Swiss AF/FE590/42-787	27. 3.69	To D-FHGK 11/69. Canx 1.9.69.
G-AXCS	Short SC.7 Skyvan 2-101	SH1834	I-CESA	28. 3.69	Broken up in 10/72 at Sydenham. Canx.
G-AXCT	Short SC.7 Skyvan 3-100-18	SH1862	G-14-34	28. 3.69	To CF-YQY. Canx 12.6.69.
G-AXCU	Short SC.7 Skyvan 3-100-17	SH1863	G-14-35	28. 3.69	To N100LV. Canx 5.9.69.
G-AXCV	Beagle B.121 Pup Srs.150	B121-044	G-35-044	31. 3.69	Canx 2.4.69 on sale to Australia. To ZK-CYP 7/69.
G-AXCW	Beagle B.121 Pup Srs.150	B121-045	G-35-045	31. 3.69	To SE-FOG 9/75. Canx 4.7.75.
G-AXCX	Beagle B.121 Pup Srs.150	B121-046	G-35-046	31. 3.69	
G-AXCY	SAN Jodel D.117A	499	F-BHXB	31. 3.69	
G-AXCZ	SNCAN Stampe SV-4C	186	F-BCFG	31. 3.69	To ZS-VFW 8/84. Canx 9.1.84.
G-AXDA	Reims Cessna FR.172F Rocket	0123		3. 4.69	NTU - Not Imported. To D-EBMR 10/69. Canx.
G-AXDB	Piper J3C-65 Cub (L-4B-PI) (C/n quoted is same as G-BBLH)	10006	F-BMSJ F-BFQY/43-1145	9. 4.69	Damaged by gales at Bembridge on 12/13.12.72 & later stored. Canx by CAA 24.9.91.
G-AXDC	PA-23-250 Aztec D	27-4169	N6829Y	8. 4.69	
G-AXDD	PA-31-310 Turbo Navajo	31-376	N9284Y	8. 4.69	To G-NMAN 7/81. Canx.
G-AXDE	Bensen B.8 Gyrocopter	THJ-001		9. 4.69	NTU - Not Imported. Canx 19.2.70.
G-AXDF	PA-25-235 Pawnee	25-3780	OH-PIC	9. 4.69	DBF after hitting overhead cables and crashed at Horkstow, nr Barton-on-Humber on 8.4.72. Canx.
G-AXDG	CEA Jodel DR.253B Regent	147		14. 4.69	NTU - Not Imported. Marks canx as WFU 1.7.69. To D-EBAE 10/69.
G-AXDH	BN-2A Islander (First BN-2A Series 2)	70		14. 4.69	To VP-LMG(2) 9/90. Canx 24.8.90.
G-AXDI	Reims Cessna F.172H	0574		14. 4.69	
G-AXDJ	Reims Cessna F.150J	0455		14. 4.69	Crashed on landing at Baginton on 2.4.78. Canx as WFU 19.8.81.
G-AXDK	CEA Jodel DR.315 Petit Prince	378		16. 4.69	
G-AXDL	PA-30-160 Twin Comanche C	30-1856	N8707Y	17. 4.69	To G-RNTV 9/87. Canx.
G-AXDM	HS.125 Srs.400B	25194		17. 4.69	
G-AXDN	BAC/Aerospatiale Concorde SST (first production a/c)	13522 & 01		16. 4.69	WFU on 20.8.77 at Duxford. Canx as WFU 10.11.86. (On display 7/99 Duxford)
G-AXDO	HS.125 Srs.400A	NA722 & 25190		16. 4.69	To N1393 5/69. Canx 20.5.69.
G-AXDP	HS.125 Srs.400A	NA723 & 25191		16. 4.69	To N511YP. Canx 20.5.69.
G-AXDR	HS.125 Srs.400A	NA726 & 25195		16. 4.69	To N111MB. Canx 21.7.69.
G-AXDS	HS.125 Srs.400A	NA727 & 25196		16. 4.69	To N814M. Canx 5.8.69.
G-AXDT	Omega 84 HAFB	003		18. 4.69	To F-WOHE/F-BOHE. Canx 16.6.69.
"G-AXDT"	Omega 84 HAFB	04		----	Initially flown marked as such - corrected to G-AXJB 7/69.
G-AXDU	Beagle B.121 Pup Srs.150	B121-048	G-35-048	18. 4.69	Slewed off the runway on landing at Old Warden on 22.10.96 & struck a hedge. Canx as destroyed 12.1.98.
G-AXDV	Beagle B.121 Pup Srs.100	B121-049	G-35-049	18. 4.69	
G-AXDW	Beagle B.121 Pup Srs.100	B121-053	G-35-053	18. 4.69	
G-AXDX	Wassmer Jodel D.120 Paris-Nice	328	F-BOBL	21. 4.69	Crashed at Manor Farm, near Masham on 20.10.79. Canx 20.8.81.
G-AXDY	Falconair F-11-3	PFA/906		21. 4.69	(Incorporated redundant parts from Jodel D.112 G-AYBR) Canx 26.9.84. (Fuselage stored 9/91)
G-AXDZ	Airmark Cassutt Speed One (Originally regd as Cassutt Racer Srs.IIIM with same c/n)	PFA/1341		21. 4.69	Canx by CAA 26.2.99.
G-AXEA	Cassutt Racer Srs.IIIM	PFA/1342		21. 4.69	Crashed & DBF at Shobdon on 20.5.78. Canx.
G-AXEB	Cassutt Racer Srs.IIIM	PFA/1343		21. 4.69	Canx as WFU 10.5.85.
G-AXEC	Cessna 182M Skylane	182-59491	N71088	22. 4.69	Fatal crash near Belfast City Airport on 28.1.93. Canx as WFU 17.6.93.
G-AXED	PA-25-235 Pawnee B	25-3586	OH-PIM OH-CPY/N7540Z	24. 4.69	
G-AXEE	English Electric Lightning F.53	95311	G-27-86	24. 4.69	To Kuwaiti AF as 418. Canx 10.6.69.
G-AXEF	BAC 167 Strikemaster Mk.81 (Also c/n EEP/JP/165)	PS.128	G-27-35	24. 4.69	To South Yemen AF as 503. Canx 10.6.69.
G-AXEG	HS.125 Srs.3B/RA (Originally regd as Srs.3A/RA)	25172	ZS-CAL(2) G-AXEG	24. 4.69	Restored as ZS-CAL(2) 5/86. Canx 11.4.86.
G-AXEH	Beagle B.125 Bulldog 1	B.125-001		25. 4.69	Canx as WFU 15.1.77. (On display 3/96 East Fortune)
G-AXEI	Ward P.45 Gnome (built by M.Ward)	P.45		25. 4.69	Canx as WFU 30.5.84. (On display 6/99 at Breighton)
G-AXEJ	Hughes 369HS (500HS) (Originally regd with c/n 69-0102S)	69-0101S		25. 4.69	To G-IDWR 5/81. Canx.
G-AXEK	Handley Page 137 Jetstream 1 (Production No. 2)	203	G-8-4	28. 4.69	To N1FY 3/72. Canx 16.3.72.
G-AXEL	Handley Page 137 Jetstream 1 (Production No. 6)	207	G-8-6	28. 4.69	DBR on landing at Courtyard Farm, near Hunstanton on 29.9.69. Canx 6.1.70. (Remains to Radlett 10/69, fuselage to Kidlington in late 1/70)
G-AXEM	Handley Page 137 Jetstream 1 (Production No. 4)	205	D-INAH G-AXEM/G-8-5	28. 4.69	To D-INAH /69. Canx 10.10.69.
G-AXEN	Beechcraft 60 Duke	P-94	N7204D	28. 4.69	To D-ICAV 10/70. Canx 27.8.70.
G-AXEO	Scheibe SF-25B Falke	4645	D-KEBC	1. 5.69	

Regn	Type	c/n	Previous identity	Regn date	Fate or immediate subsequent identity (if known)
G-AXEP	Handley Page 137 Jetstream 1 (Production No. 8)	209	G-8-7	2. 5.69	To N5V. Canx 27.5.69.
G-AXER	PA-30-160 Twin Comanche C	30-1820	EI-ANU(2) G-AXER/N8676Y	7. 5.69	To N44278. Canx 29.7.83.
G-AXES	Beagle B.121 Pup Srs.150	B121-056	5Y-AKG G-AXES/G-35-056	6. 6.69	Badly damaged on landing at Nairobi on 19.1.87. (Present status unknown) Canx as WFU 13.7.94.
G-AXET	Beagle B.121 Pup Srs.150	B121-057	G-35-057	6. 5.69	DBF near Calvi, Corsica on 28.5.79. Canx.
G-AXEU	Beagle B.121 Pup Srs.150	B121-062	(5N-AJC) G-35-062	6. 5.69	To G-OPUP 10/84. Canx.
G-AXEV	Beagle B.121 Pup Srs.150	B121-070	G-35-070	6. 5.69	
G-AXEW	Beagle B.121 Pup Srs.100	B121-061	G-53-061	6. 5.69	Stalled on landing at Andrewsfield on 8.7.84 & DBER. Canx by CAA 12.9.86.
G-AXEX	Beagle B.121 Pup Srs.100	B121-063	G-35-063	6. 5.69	DBR after crashing into a tree in a field 1 mile west of Donnington Hall on 28.5.85. Canx as destroyed 18.11.85.
G-AXEY	Beagle B.121 Pup Srs.100	B121-065	G-35-065	6. 5.69	To OY-BFZ 2/74. Canx 5.7.72.
G-AXEZ	Aermacchi-Lockheed AL.60B-1	6144/2	OY-AFR	6. 5.69	Ditched off Yarmouth, IoW on 30.8.69. Canx.
G-AXFA	PA-E23-250 Aztec D	27-4177	N6837Y	8. 5.69	To N4517W. Canx 2.11.83.
"G-AXFA"	Beagle B.121 Pup Srs.150	B121-050	YI-AEL G-AXFZ/G-35-050	----	Incorrectly painted as such in 1969. To G-AXFZ.
G-AXFB	Britten-Norman BN-3 Nymph	5001		8. 5.69	Rebuilt as Norman NAC-1 Freelance 180 G-NACI 6/84 with c/n NAC.001. Canx 20.6.84.
G-AXFC	BN-2A Islander	76	(D-IAFC) G-AXFC	8. 5.69	To VH-WGQ. Canx 28.11.73.
G-AXFD	PA-25-235 Pawnee	25-4018	OH-PIK	8. 5.69	To OY-CYY. Canx 2.3.90.
G-AXFE	Beechcraft 65-B90 King Air	LJ-481		13. 5.69	To G-KJET 5/88. Canx.
G-AXFF	Cessna A.188 Agwagon	188-0366	N8116V	13. 5.69	Crashed at Pinchbeck, Lincs on 1.4.81. Canx by CAA 7.1.87.
G-AXFG	Cessna 337D Super Skymaster	337-1070	(EI-...) G-AXFG/OY-BVP/G-AXFG/N86081	14. 5.69	
G-AXFH	DH.114 Heron 1B/C	14022	J6-LBD G-AXFH/JA6161/PK-GHG	14. 5.69	CofA expired 28.1.83. (Stored at Southend) Canx by CAA 19.12.90.
G-AXFI	Short SC.7 Skyvan 3-200-17	SH1865	N200LV G-AXFI/G-14-37	14. 5.69	To A40-SI. Canx 4.11.75.
G-AXFJ	Campbell Curlew	CA/316		14. 5.69	(Mock-up only) Canx as WFU 3.3.72.
G-AXFK	Reims Cessna F.172H Skyhawk	0613		16. 5.69	Forced landing at Egypt Farm, Rushlake on 18.2.76. Canx as destroyed 19.3.76.
G-AXFL	BN-2A-26 Islander	73	9H-AAB G-AXFL/G-51-17	19. 5.69	To (VH-AAB)/VH-MKN. Canx 1.3.71.
G-AXFM	Cierva Rotorcraft CR.LTH.1 Grasshopper III (Completed only as ground-running rig)	GB.2		19. 5.69	Canx as WFU 5.12.83. (Stored 3/96 at Redhill)
G-AXFN	Jodel D.119	980	F-PHBU	19. 5.69	
G-AXFO	SNCA SO.1221S Djinn	1001/FR.7	F-BHOI F-WHOI	20. 5.69	To F-BSES 12/70. Canx 12.3.70.
G-AXFP	SNCA SO.1221 Djinn	1041/FR.91	F-BIFP	20. 5.69	To F-BSEX 4/71. Canx 12.3.70.
G-AXFR	SNCA SO.1221 Djinn	1042/FR.92	F-BIFQ	20. 5.69	To F-BSEY. Canx 12.3.70.
G-AXFS	SNCA SO.1221S Djinn	1015/FR.51	F-BIEU West German AF PB+156/PB+124	20. 5.69	To F-BSEU 5/71. Canx 12.3.70.
G-AXFT	SNCA SO.1221S Djinn	1105/FR.72	F-BMLH ALAT-50	20. 5.69	To F-BSEV 1/75. Canx 12.3.70.
G-AXFU	SNCA SO.1221S Djinn	1106/FR.18	F-BMLO ALAT-14	20. 5.69	To F-BSET 1/75. Canx 12.3.70.
G-AXFV	Handley Page 137 Jetstream 200 (Production No. 10) (Originally regd as Srs.1)	211	G-8-8	20. 5.69	To 9Q-CTC 12/73. Canx 23.12.73.
G-AXFW	English Electric Lightning F.53	95312	G-27-87	21. 5.69	To Kuwaiti AF as 419. Canx 10.6.69.
G-AXFX	BAC 167 Strikemaster Mk.81 (Also c/n EEP/JP/168)	PS.129	G-27-36	21. 5.69	To South Yemen AF as 504 in 6/69. Canx 10.6.69.
G-AXFY	HS.125 Srs.400B	25189	G-5-20	22. 5.69	NTU - To R.Malaysian AF as FM1200 in 6/69. Canx 16.6.69.
G-AXFZ	Beagle B.121 Pup Srs.150	B121-050	"G-AXFA" YI-AEL/G-AXFZ/G-35-050	23. 5.69	To YI-AEL 6/69. Canx 3.6.69.
G-AXGA	PA-18-95 Super Cub (L-18C-PI) (Frame no. 10-2059)	18-2047	PH-NLE (PH-CUB)/ R.Netherlands AF R-51/8A-51/52-2447	22. 5.69	Damaged on landing at Felthorpe on 26.12.86. Canx as WFU 29.5.87. (Stored at Tattershall Thorpe 8/90)
G-AXGB	BN-2A-8 Islander	75	G-51-18	23. 5.69	To HS-SKA. Canx 10.7.69.
G-AXGC	Socata MS.880B Rallye Club	1349		23. 5.69	CofA expired 12.5.88. (Stored Elstree 9/95)
G-AXGD	Socata MS.880B Rallye Club	1352		23. 5.69	CofA expired 8.7.85 & stored at Stapleford. Canx as WFU 22.1.86.
G-AXGE	Socata MS.880B Rallye Club	1353		23. 5.69	
G-AXGF	Cessna A.188 Agwagon	188-0344	N8094V	27. 5.69	DBF after crashing on take-off from a private field at Forest Lodge, near Dyfynog, Breconshire on 11.8.70. Canx 1.9.70.
G-AXGG	Reims Cessna F.150J	0440		28. 5.69	
G-AXGH	Piccard HAFB	DP-1	HB-BOG	28. 5.69	WFU 27.4.73. Canx.
G-AXGI	Cessna 337D Super Skymaster	337D-1095	N86141	28. 5.69	Crashed at Laycock Farm, Waterston, Dorchester on 6.8.69. Remains moved to Yeadon for possible repair but Canx as WFU 22.1.70. (Later used for spares)
G-AXGJ	Cessna 337D Super Skymaster	337D-1088	N86127	29. 5.69	To G-ORAV 6/80. Canx.
G-AXGK	Handley Page 137 Jetstream 200 (Production No. 15) (Originally regd as Srs.1)	215		29. 5.69	To N200PA. Canx 16.7.69.
G-AXGL	Handley Page 137 Jetstream 1 (Production No. 16)	216	N1037S G-AXGL	29. 5.69	To RN as XX476 7/73. Canx.

Regn	Type	c/n	Previous identity	Regn date	Fate or immediate subsequent identity (if known)
G-AXGM	Handley Page 137 Jetstream III (Production No. 18) (Originally regd as Srs.1)	218		29. 5.69	To N12218. Canx 2.12.69.
G-AXGN	Handley Page 137 Jetstream 1 (Production No. 19)	220		29. 5.69	To N1038S. Canx 30.7.69.
G-AXGO	Bell 206A JetRanger	416		30. 5.69	Crashed into the Severn Estuary on 2.3.78. Canx.
G-AXGP	Piper J3C-90 Cub (L-4J-PI) (Officially quoted as c/n 9542 and 43-28251. Frame no. is 12374)	12544	F-BGPS F-BDTM/44-80248	2. 6.69	Permit expired 5.5.94. (Active 7/95)
G-AXGR	Phoenix Luton LA-4A Minor	PAL/1125		2. 6.69	CofA expired 10.4.91. (Stored at Eshott in 4/94)
G-AXGS	Rollason-Druine D.62B Condor	RAE/638		3. 6.69	
G-AXGT	Rollason-Druine D.62B Condor	RAE/639		3. 6.69	Destroyed after failing to gain height on take-off from Harvest Farm, Milden on 16.8.92 and struck Reims Cessna FR.172J G-LOYA (0352). Canx as destroyed 7.9.92.
G-AXGU	Rollason-Druine D.62B Condor	RAE/640		3. 6.69	Crashed near Godalming, Surrey on 31.3.75. Canx as WFU 8.3.88. (Stored 9/94)
G-AXGV	Rollason-Druine D.62B Condor	RAE/641		3. 6.69	
G-AXGW	Boeing 707-336C (Line No. 838)	20374		3. 6.69	To 7O-ACO 12/81. Canx 22.12.81.
G-AXGX	Boeing 707-336C (Line No. 841)	20375		3. 6.69	To A7-AAC 7/84. Canx 19.7.84.
G-AXGY	Rollason-Druine D.62C Condor (Originally regd as D.62B)	RAE/642		3. 6.69	Destroyed in fatal crash at Bessacarr, near Doncaster on 25.2.71. Canx.
G-AXGZ	Rollason-Druine D.62B Condor	RAE/643		3. 6.69	
G-AXHA	Cessna 337A Super Skymaster	337-0484	(EI-ATH) N5384S	5. 6.69	
G-AXHB	Handley Page 137 Jetstream 1 (Production No. 13)	214		5. 6.69	To CF-QJB. Canx 27.6.69.
G-AXHC	SNCAN Stampe SV-4C	293	F-BCFU	6. 6.69	
G-AXHD	SNCAN Stampe SV-4C	522	F-BDIK	6. 6.69	To N527R. Canx 10.8.70.
G-AXHE	BN-2A Islander	86	4X-AYV G-AXHE/"F-CXFR"/G-AXHE	6. 6.69	DBR on landing at Cark on 5.2.94. Canx as WFU 31.3.94. Rear fuselage at Strathallan 8/98 - wing at Cumbernauld 2/99.
G-AXHF	Socata MS.880B Rallye Club	1370	F-BNGV F-WNGV	6. 6.69	To EI-AUJ 6/70. Canx 9.6.70.
G-AXHG	Socata MS.880B Rallye Club	1371	F-BNGX F-WNGX	6. 6.69	CofA expired 26.5.85. Canx as WFU 24.6.85. (Spares use 4/95)
G-AXHH(1)	Socata MS.880B Rallye Club	1375		6. 6.69R	NTU - Not Imported. To OH-SCX 10/69. Canx.
G-AXHH(2)	Socata MS.880B Rallye Club	1515		. 8.69R	NTU - Not Imported. To F-BRYU 1/70. Canx.
G-AXHH(3)	Socata MS.880B Rallye Club	1555		.10.69R	NTU - Not Imported. To F-BSAM 3/70. Canx.
G-AXHH(4)	Socata MS.880B Rallye Club	1616	F-BNGU F-WNGU	14.10.69	To EI-AUN 6/70. Canx 9.6.70.
G-AXHI(1)	Socata MS.880B Rallye Club	1376		6. 6.69R	NTU - Not Imported. To D-EBSO /69. Canx.
G-AXHI(2)	Socata MS.880B Rallye Club	1516		. 8.69R	NTU - Not Imported. To F-BRYM 12/69. Canx.
G-AXHI(3)	Socata MS.880B Rallye Club	1556		.10.69R	NTU - Not Imported. To F-BSAY 3/70. Canx.
G-AXHI(4)	Socata MS.880B Rallye Club	1617		14.10.69	Stored at Sandown with CofA expired 7.6.87. Canx by CAA 4.5.90.
G-AXHJ	Handley Page 137 Jetstream 1 (Production No. 17)	217		9. 6.69	To N12217. Canx 3.10.69.
G-AXHK	Beagle B.121 Pup Srs.100	B121-071	G-35-071	9. 6.69	Overshot on landing at Teesside on 10.1.70. Remains taken to Yeadon. Canx as WFU 5.5.70.
G-AXHL	Beagle B.121 Pup Srs.150	B121-072	G-35-072	9. 6.69	To YI-AEM. Canx 4.7.69.
G-AXHM	Beagle B.121 Pup Srs.150	B121-073	(YI-AEN) G-AXHM/G-35-073	9. 6.69	DBR at Warminster on 2.3.74. At Elstree 4/74 in use for spares. Canx 14.6.74 as destroyed.
G-AXHN	Beagle B.121 Pup Srs.150	B121-074	G-35-074	9. 6.69	To YI-AEO. Canx 4.7.69.
G-AXHO	Beagle B.121 Pup Srs.150	B121-077	G-35-077	9. 6.69	
G-AXHP	Piper J3C-65 Cub (L-4J-PI) (Regd with c/n "AF36506" which is a USAAC contract number - frame no. 12762)	12932	F-BETT NC74121/44-80636	9. 6.69	
G-AXHR	Piper J3C-65 Cub (L-4H-PI)	10892	F-BETI 43-29601	9. 6.69	
G-AXHS	Socata MS.880B Rallye Club	1357		9. 6.69	
G-AXHT	Socata MS.880B Rallye Club	1358		9. 6.69	
G-AXHU	Socata MS.880B Rallye Club	1359		9. 6.69	To EI-AUE 4/70. Canx 26.3.70.
G-AXHV	SAN Jodel D.117A	695	F-BIDF	9. 6.69	
G-AXHW	Agusta-Bell 47G-4	2517	9L-LAK	10. 6.69	To F-BXXT 6/76. Canx 25.5.76.
G-AXHX	Socata MS.893A Rallye Commodore 150	11424		10. 6.69	CofA expired 6.7.86. Stored at Burnaston. Canx by CAA 14.3.90.
G-AXHY	BN-2A-1 Islander (Constructed from c/n 85, became first Romanian built Islander, became BN-2A-1 in mid-1970)	601		10. 6.69	To 5Y-AMG 8/70. Canx 5.8.70.
G-AXHZ	McCandless M.4 Gyroplane	M.4/5		12. 6.69	To EI-ASR 9/69. Canx 17.9.69.
G-AXIA	Beagle B.121 Pup Srs.100	B121-078	G-35-078	17. 6.69	
G-AXIB	Beagle B.121 Pup Srs.100	B121-080	G-35-080	17. 6.69	Fatal crash on landing at Squires Gate on 16.5.70. Canx.
G-AXIC	Beagle B.121 Pup Srs.100	B121-082	G-35-082	17. 6.69	Crashed near Dewent Water on 31.7.73. Canx as WFU 28.2.74.
G-AXID	Beagle B.121 Pup Srs.150	B121-086	G-35-086	17. 6.69	To SE-FOK 12/76. Canx 9.12.76.
G-AXIE	Beagle B.121 Pup Srs.150	B121-087	G-35-087	17. 6.69	
G-AXIF	Beagle B.121 Pup Srs.150	B121-088	(SE-FGV) G-35-088	17. 6.69	
G-AXIG	Scottish Avn Bulldog Srs.100/104 (Originally regd as Beagle B.125 with c/n B125-002)	BH120-002		24. 6.69	

Regn	Type	c/n	Previous identity	Regn date	Fate or immediate subsequent identity (if known)
G-AXIH	Bucker Bu.133C Jungmeister (Dornier-built)	11	HB-MIP Swiss AF U-64	25. 6.69	To D-EGDS(2) 1/85. Canx 4.7.84.
G-AXII	Bensen B.8 Gyrocopter (Mod)	PCL-4		25. 6.69	Canx as WFU 20.8.73.
G-AXIJ	AIA Stampe SV-4C	1077	F-BJDV	25. 6.69	To N1322T. Canx 28.8.70.
G-AXIK	Handley Page 137 Jetstream III (Production No. 21) (Originally regd as Srs.1)	221		26. 6.69	To N12221. Canx 2.10.69.
G-AXIL	Handley Page 137 Jetstream 1 (Production No. 24)	223		25. 6.69	To N12223. Canx 2.10.69.
G-AXIM	Handley Page 137 Jetstream III (Production No. 25) (Originally regd as Srs.1)	224		25. 6.69	To N12224. Canx 2.10.69.
G-AXIN	BN-2A Islander	79	G-51-20	26. 6.69	To VH-RTP 2/71. Canx 20.11.70.
G-AXIO	PA-28-140 Cherokee B	28-25764		26. 6.69	
G-AXIP	PA-28-140 Cherokee B	28-25790	N11C	26. 6.69	To 5B-CDP 10/81. Canx 16.10.81.
G-AXIR	PA-28-140 Cherokee B	28-25795		26. 6.69	
G-AXIS	PA-31-300 Turbo Navajo	31-466	N6551L	26. 6.69	To F-BXMM 9/75. Canx 27.6.75.
G-AXIT	Socata MS.893A Rallye Commodore 180	11430		27. 6.69	(Damaged on colliding unmanned with a fence after start-up at Seighford on 7.11.98)
G-AXIU	Socata MS.894A Rallye Minerva 220	11065		27. 6.69	To EI-AYT 8/74. Canx 30.7.74.
G-AXIV	PA-23-250 Aztec D	27-4166	N6826Y	2. 7.69	To EI-BDM 10/77. Canx 6.10.77.
G-AXIW	Scheibe SF-25B Falke	4657	(D-KABJ)	3. 7.69	Crashed into the ground at Halesend on 27.4.91.
G-AXIX	AESL Airtourer T4 (150)	A.527		3. 7.69	
G-AXIY	Bird Gyrocopter	GB.001		3. 7.69	Canx 9.8.91. (On display at Chudleigh Motor Museum)
G-AXIZ	PA-28-180 Cherokee D	28-5391		4. 7.69	Canx 12.7.69 on sale to Switzerland. To TU-TFB 8/69.
G-AXJA	Omega 56 HAFB	05		4. 7.69	To EI-ANP 1/70. Canx 13.1.70.
G-AXJB	Omega 84 HAFB (Initially flown as G-AXDT)	04		9. 7.69	CofA expired 20.8.73. (Extant 2/97)
G-AXJC	Bell 206A JetRanger	417		9. 7.69	To 9M-ARA /72. Canx 24.11.72.
G-AXJD	HS.125 Srs.400A	NA728 & 25198		9. 7.69	To N24CH. Canx 10.9.69.
G-AXJE	HS.125 Srs.400A	NA729 & 25200		9. 7.69	To N702S. Canx 18.9.69.
G-AXJF	HS.125 Srs.400A	NA730 & 25201		9. 7.69	To N220T. Canx 30.9.69.
G-AXJG	HS.125 Srs.400A	NA731 & 25202		9. 7.69	To N65LT. Canx 15.10.69.
G-AXJH	Beagle B.121 Pup Srs.150	B121-089	G-35-089	11. 7.69	
G-AXJI	Beagle B.121 Pup Srs.150	B121-090	G-35-090	11. 7.69	
G-AXJJ	Beagle B.121 Pup Srs.150	B121-091	G-35-091	11. 7.69	Badly damaged on overrun of runway after brakes failed at Crosland Moor (date?). (Stored 5/99 Crosland Moor)
G-AXJK	BAC One-Eleven Srs.501EX	BAC.191	EI-CIB G-AXJK	18. 7.69	To 9Q-CKP 10/94. Canx 14.10.94.
G-AXJL	BAC One-Eleven Srs.501EX	BAC.209		18. 7.69	To RP-C1188 3/77. Canx.
G-AXJM	BAC One-Eleven Srs.501EX	BAC.214	7Q-YKI G-AXLM	18. 7.69	To 5N-OAL 9/93. Canx 23.7.93.
G-AXJN	Beagle B.121 Pup Srs.150	B121-092	G-35-092	11. 7.69	Canx by CAA 1.10.91. To VH-YJN /92.
G-AXJO	Beagle B.121 Pup Srs.150	B121-094	G-35-094	11. 7.69	
G-AXJP	Beagle B.121 Pup Srs.150	B121-095	G-35-095	11. 7.69	To OE-DUP 8/70. Canx 1.8.70.
G-AXJR	Scheibe SF-25B Falke	4652	D-KICD	14. 7.69	
G-AXJS	Sportavia-Putzer Fournier RF-4D	4148		14. 7.69	Fatal crash into sea 1/2 mile off Newtownhill, Kincardineshire on 14.10.72. Canx as destroyed 11.7.73.
G-AXJT	SNCAN Stampe SV-4C	418	F-BCTB	14. 7.69	To N12SV. Canx 21.9.70.
G-AXJU	Douglas C-47B-30-DK Dakota	16175/32923	KN452 44-76591	14. 7.69	To 5Y-AKB. Canx 5.12.83.
G-AXJV	PA-28-140 Cherokee B	28-25572	N11C	14. 7.69	
G-AXJW	PA-28-140 Cherokee B	28-25656	N11C	14. 7.69	To G-RECK 3/88. Canx.
G-AXJX	PA-28-140 Cherokee B	28-25990		14. 7.69	
G-AXJY	Cessna U.206D Skywagon (Robertson STOL conversion)	U206-1368	N72326	15. 7.69	(Damaged on take-off Shobdon 7.9.86) (Rebuild finished at Ipswich 1/98) To N72127 2/97. Canx 25.2.97.
G-AXJZ	Handley Page 137 Jetstream 1 (Production No. 28)	227		15. 7.69	To N12227 9/69. Canx 3.10.69.
G-AXKA	SIAI-Marchetti SF-260	1-22	OO-HEI	16. 7.69	To VH-SFN 2/70. Canx 18.2.70.
G-AXKB	BN-2A Islander	95	G-51-30	16. 7.69	To N95BN 1/78. Canx.
G-AXKC	BN-2A Islander	97	G-51-32	16. 7.69	NTU - To YR-BNB. Canx 29.8.69.
G-AXKD	PA-23-250 Aztec D	27-4293	N6936Y	18. 7.69	To G-OART 11/93. Canx.
G-AXKE	Agusta-Bell 206A JetRanger	8166	PK-HBJ G-AXKE	18. 7.69	To VR-BFS 10/75. Canx 21.10.75.
G-AXKF	Agusta-Bell 206B JetRanger II (Originally 206A; later modified)	8170	PK-HBL G-AXKF	18. 7.69	To PK-HCC. Canx 30.6.76.
G-AXKG	Handley Page 137 Jetstream 1 (Production No. 29)	229		21. 7.69	To N10EA. Canx 16.2.70.
G-AXKH	Phoenix Luton LA-4A Minor	PAL/1316 & PFA/823		21. 7.69	(Parts of G-AVUO used in construction) (Status uncertain)
G-AXKI	Jodel D.9 Bebe	SAS/001 & PFA/928A & PFA/940		22. 7.69	To TF-... Canx 13.10.98.
G-AXKJ	Jodel D.9 Bebe	SAS/002 & PFA/928B & PFA/941		22. 7.69	
G-AXKK	Westland-Bell 47G-4A	WA/716	G-17-1	22. 7.69	To G-OEMH 6/93. Canx.
G-AXKL	Westland-Bell 47G-4A	WA/717	G-17-2	22. 7.69	Crashed at South Kinsey on 30.7.83. Canx 19.5.86 on sale to West Germany (possibly as spares).
G-AXKM	Westland-Bell 47G-4A	WA/718	G-17-3	22. 7.69	Badly damaged in a heavy landing at Redhill on 7.4.83. Canx as destroyed 17.10.85.
G-AXKN	Westland-Bell 47G-4A	WA/719	EC-EDF (D-H...)/G-AXKN/G-17-4	22. 7.69	Canx by CAA 9.2.99.
G-AXKO	Westland-Bell 47G-4A	WA/720	G-17-5	22. 7.69	
G-AXKP	Westland-Bell 47G-4A	WA/721	G-17-6	22. 7.69	Crashed at Middle Wallop (date?). Canx as destroyed 18.1.72.

Regn	Type	c/n	Previous identity	Regn date	Fate or immediate subsequent identity (if known)
G-AXKR	Westland-Bell 47G-4A	WA/722	G-17-7	22. 7.69	To VH-ULL(3) 6/96. Canx 13.12.95.
G-AXKS	Westland-Bell 47G-4A	WA/723	G-17-8	22. 7.69	CofA expired 21.9.82. Canx as WFU 22.4.82. (On display at Museum of Army Flying, Middle Wallop)
G-AXKT	Westland-Bell 47G-4A	WA/724	G-17-9	22. 7.69	Struck a Westland Scout on landing at Middle wallop and destroyed in crash on 6.10.81.
G-AXKU	Westland-Bell 47G-4A	WA/725	G-17-10	22. 7.69	To G-MASH 11/89. Canx.
G-AXKV	Westland-Bell 47G-4A	WA/726	G-17-11	22. 7.69	Crashed at Tidworth Training Area, Wilts on 31.11.74. Canx as destroyed 5.12.83.
G-AXKW	Westland-Bell 47G-4A	WA/727	G-17-12	22. 7.69	
	(See also comments under G-AYOE)				
G-AXKX	Westland-Bell 47G-4A	WA/728	G-17-13	22. 7.69	
G-AXKY	Westland-Bell 47G-4A	WA/729	G-17-14	22. 7.69	
G-AXKZ	Westland-Bell 47G-4A	WA/730	G-17-15	22. 7.69	Canx 19.5.86 on sale to West Germany.
G-AXLA	Westland-Bell 47G-4A	WA/731	G-17-16	22. 7.69	Canx 19.5.86 on sale to West Germany.
G-AXLB	Short SC.7 Skyvan 3-100-24	SH1869	G-14-41	23. 7.69	To SX-BBN 6/70. Canx 30.5.70.
G-AXLC	Short SC.7 Skyvan 3-100-24	SH1870	G-14-42	23. 7.69	To SX-BBO 6/70. Canx 30.5.70.
G-AXLD	Short SC.7 Skyvan 3-200-19	SH1872	G-14-44	23. 7.69	To CF-NAS. Canx 9.10.69.
G-AXLE	Short SC.7 Skyvan 3-200-23	SH1873	G-14-45	23. 7.69	To N10DA. Canx 16.1.70.
G-AXLF	Campbell-Bensen B.8MG Gyrocopter	CA/318		23. 7.69	Canx as WFU 9.6.70.
G-AXLG	Cessna 310K	310K-0204	N3804X	25. 7.69	
G-AXLH	Slingsby Nipper T.66 RA.45 Srs.3	S.130/1706	9M-APH G-AXLH	25. 7.69	Crashed near Hurn on 12.5.79. Canx.
G-AXLI	Slingsby Nipper T.66 RA.45 Srs.3	S.131/1707		25. 7.69	
G-AXLJ	Slingsby Nipper T.66 RA.45 Srs.3	S.132/1708		25. 7.69	To HB-SPN 8/70. Canx 1.6.70.
G-AXLK	Sud Aviation SE.3160 Alouette III	1061	EP-HBH	29. 7.69	Abandoned in Iran. Canx 4.4.79 as Not Imported.
			VP-BEC/ZS-HDA/(G-AXLK)/South Vietnam AF 1061		
G-AXLL(1)	BAC One-Eleven Srs.523FJ	BAC.198		29. 7.69R	NTU - To G-16-12/(VP-BCQ)/VP-LAN as Srs.517FE. Canx.
G-AXLL(2)	BAC One-Eleven Srs.523FJ	BAC.193	OB-R-1173	8.10.69	
			OB-R1137/PP-SDT/G-AXLL/G-16-8		
G-AXLM	BAC One-Eleven Srs.523FJ	BAC.199	PP-SDV G-AXLM	29. 7.69	To G-16-23/4X-BAS. Canx 20.5.78.
G-AXLN	BAC One-Eleven Srs.523FJ	BAC.211	VR-CAL	29. 7.69	To G-EKPT 4/90. Canx.
			TG-AYA/PP-SDU/G-AXLN		
G-AXLO	Handley Page 137 Jetstream 1 (Production No. 32)	231		29. 7.69	To N10DG. Canx 1.12.69.
G-AXLP	Handley Page 137 Jetstream 1 (Production No. 33)	233		29. 7.69	To N8943. Canx 8.12.69.
G-AXLR	Vickers VC-10 Srs.1106/C.1 (Flying test-bed for RB-211 engine)	829	(G-37-6) (G-1-1)/XR809	30. 7.69	Canx 1.6.76 as returned to RAF. Broken up at RAF Kemble in 10/82.
G-AXLS	SAN Jodel DR.105A Ambassadeur	86	F-BIVR	31. 7.69	
G-AXLT	Campbell-Bensen B.8MG Gyrocopter	CA/317		31. 7.69	CofA expired 15.1.71. Canx as WFU 2.8.73.
G-AXLU	HS.125 Srs.400B	25181	(G-5-13)	31. 7.69	To South African AF as 01 in 3/70. Canx 13.3.70.
G-AXLV	HS.125 Srs.400B	25182		31. 7.69	To South African AF as 03 in 4/70. Canx 13.4.70.
G-AXLW	HS.125 Srs.400B	25184		31. 7.69	To South African AF as 04 in 5/70. Canx 5.5.70.
G-AXLX	HS.125 Srs.400B	25199	HB-VBW G-AXLX	31. 7.69	To (HB-VGU)/HB-VBW 5/80. Canx 8.5.80.
G-AXLY	BN-2A Islander	91	G-51-27	31. 7.69	To JA5175. Canx 16.10.69.
G-AXLZ	PA-18-95 Super Cub (L-18C-PI)(Frame No 18-2065)	18-2052	PH-NLB	31. 7.69	(Badly damaged on landing at Low Farm, South Walsham on 14.8.97)
			R.Netherlands AF R-45/8A-45/52-2452		
G-AXMA	PA-24-180 Comanche	24-3467	N8214P	5. 8.69	
G-AXMB	Slingsby T.7 Motor Cadet Mk.2 (Originally regd as a Mk.1)	-	BGA.805 VM590	5. 8.69	Permit expired 9.7.82 & WFU. Canx by CAA 9.1.92. (On rebuild in 1992)
G-AXMC	SNCAN Stampe SV-4C	278	F-BBHA(2)	5. 8.69	NTU - To OY-DSW 3/73. Canx 9.3.73.
			F-BCKP/French Mil		
G-AXMD	Omega O-20 HAFB	06		7. 8.69	Canx as WFU 7.12.89. (Inflated 4/93; extant 2/97) (To British Balloon Museum)
	(Also second envelope c/n 07 - it is not know which is held)				
G-AXME	SNCAN Stampe SV-4C	545	(CS-...)	13. 8.69	(Stored in Portugal). Canx by CAA 3.4.89.
			G-AXME/F-BDCP		
G-AXMF(1)	BAC One-Eleven Srs. -	BAC.171		14. 8.69	NTU - Not built. Canx.
G-AXMF(2)	BAC One Eleven Srs.518FG	BAC.200	PT-TYV G-AXMF	26. 8.69	NTU - To LV-MEX. Canx 23.3.78.
G-AXMG(1)	BAC One-Eleven Srs. -	BAC.173		14. 8.69	NTU - Not built. Canx.
G-AXMG(2)	BAC One-Eleven Srs.518FG	BAC.201	EI-CDO	26. 8.69	To ZS-NMT 1/95. Canx 20.1.95.
			(EI-CCV)/G-FLRU/G-AXMG/5B-DAF/G-AXMG		
G-AXMH(1)	BAC One-Eleven Srs.501EX	BAC.176		14. 8.69	NTU - To G-AWYT 2/69. Canx.
G-AXMH(2)	BAC One-Eleven Srs.518FG	BAC.202		26. 8.69	To G-BDAS 2/75. Canx.
G-AXMI(1)	BAC One-Eleven Srs.501EX	BAC.177		14. 8.69	NTU - To G-AWYU 2/69. Canx.
G-AXMI(2)	BAC One-Eleven Srs.518FG	BAC.203		26. 8.69	To G-BDAE 2/75. Canx.
G-AXMJ(1)	BAC One-Eleven Srs.208AF	BAC.180		14. 8.69	NTU - To N1127J. Canx.
G-AXMJ(2)	BAC One-Eleven Srs.518FG	BAC.204		26. 8.69	To G-BCWG 2/75. Canx.
G-AXMK(1)	BAC One-Eleven Srs.509EW	BAC.185		14. 8.69	NTU - To G-AWWY 1/69. Canx.
G-AXMK(2)	BAC One-Eleven Srs.518FG	BAC.205	VP-LAK	26. 8.69	To G-BCWA 1/75. Canx.
			G-AXMK/TG-ARA/G-AXMK		
G-AXML(1)	BAC One-Eleven Srs.515FB	BAC.187		14. 8.69	NTU - To D-ALAT. Canx.
G-AXML(2)	BAC One-Eleven Srs.518FG	BAC.206	AN-BHJ G-AXML	26. 8.69	To PT-TYW 10/74. Canx 15.10.74.
G-AXMM	Bell 206B JetRanger (Originally 206A; later modified)	405	N1469W	14. 8.69	To G-ROGR 1/82. Canx.
G-AXMN	Auster J/5B Autocar	2962	F-BGPN	14. 8.69	

Regn	Type	c/n	Previous identity	Regn date	Fate or immediate subsequent identity (if known)
G-AXMO	Short SC.7 Skyvan 3M-400-5	SH1871	G-14-43	15. 8.69	NTU - To Indonesian AF as T-701 in 8/69. Canx 31.7.70.
G-AXMP	PA-28-180 Cherokee D	28-5436		19. 8.69	
G-AXMR	PA-31-310 Turbo Navajo	31-473	N6558L	19. 8.69	To ST-AHZ 12/81. Canx 16.11.81.
G-AXMS	PA-30-160 Twin Comanche C	30-1974	N8816Y	19. 8.69	Restored as N8816Y 10/96. Canx 17.10.96.
G-AXMT	Dornier Bucker Bu.133C Jungmeister	46	N133SJ G-AXMT/HB-MIY/Swiss AF U-99	19. 8.69	
G-AXMU	BAC One-Eleven Srs.432FD	BAC.157	A40-BU G-AXMU/G-16-14/PI-C1151/G-AXMU/VP-BCZ	19. 8.69	To 5N-AXQ. Canx 8.10.90.
G-AXMV	Beagle B.121 Pup Srs.100	B121-099	G-35-099	19. 8.69	Presumed to have hit high-tension cables at Thamesmead and crashed into River Thames on 14.4.74. Canx.
G-AXMW	Beagle B.121 Pup Srs.100	B121-101	G-35-101	19. 8.69	
G-AXMX	Beagle B.121 Pup Srs.150	B121-103	VH-UPT G-AXMX/G-35-103	19. 8.69	
G-AXMY	PA-30-160 Twin Comanche C	30-1879	N8726Y	21. 8.69	To G-SOOO 12/81. Canx.
G-AXMZ	BN-2A Islander	105	7Q-YKC G-AXMZ/G-51-38	22. 8.69	To OB-R-1272 4/83. Canx.
G-AXNA	Boeing 737-204 (Line No. 245)	20282	PH-TVF G-AXNA	25. 8.69	To F-GGPC 10/90. Canx 21.9.90.
G-AXNB(1)	Boeing 737-204	20289		. .69R	NTU - Not built - C/n used on Boeing 727-251 N267US. Canx.
G-AXNB(2)	Boeing 737-204 (Line No. 251)	20389		25. 8.69	To F-GGPB 3/90. Canx 23.2.90.
G-AXNC	Boeing 737-204 (Line No. 255)	20417		25. 8.69	Restored as TF-ABD 1/93. Canx 12.1.93.
G-AXND	BN-2A-26 Islander	602		27. 8.69	To 9M-APK 1/70. Canx 31.12.69.
G-AXNE	Gloster Meteor NF.14 (Built by AWA)	-	WS804	28. 8.69	Abandoned at Bissau, Portugese Guinea in 9/69. Canx as WFU 14.3.77.
G-AXNF	BN-2A Islander	96	G-51-31	29. 8.69	To 4X-AYT. Canx 8.9.69.
G-AXNG	Agusta-Bell 206A JetRanger	8173	(VR-B..) G-AXNG	29. 8.69	To CR-ALJ. Canx 10.10.69.
G-AXNH	SNCAN Stampe SV-4C	185	F-BCFF	29. 8.69	Ditched into sea 3 1/2 miles from Hythe Beach on 10.4.72. Canx.
G-AXNI	Bucker Bu.133 Jungmeister (built by Bucker-Flugzeugebau)	1001	HB-MIM Swiss AF U-51/HB-HAP	29. 8.69	To (N72493)/N133WK. Canx 25.7.77.
G-AXNJ	Jodel Wassmer D.120 Paris-Nice	52	F-BHYO	29. 8.69	
G-AXNK	Reims Cessna F.150J	0415	N13722	2. 9.69	Force-landed near White Waltham on 28.5.90. Canx as destroyed 3.6.92.
G-AXNL	Beagle B.121 Pup Srs.100	B121-113	G-35-113	3. 9.69	
G-AXNM	Beagle B.121 Pup Srs.100	B121-114	G-35-114	3. 9.69	CofA expired 27.5.97.
G-AXNN	Beagle B.121 Pup Srs.150	B121-104	G-35-104	3. 9.69	
G-AXNO	Beagle B.121 Pup Srs.150	B121-105	G-35-105	3. 9.69	To LN-HHC 6/76. Canx 7.5.76.
G-AXNP	Beagle B.121 Pup Srs.150	B121-106	G-35-106	3. 9.69	
G-AXNR	Beagle B.121 Pup Srs.150	B121-108	G-35-108	3. 9.69	
G-AXNS	Beagle B.121 Pup Srs.150	B121-110	G-35-110	3. 9.69	
G-AXNT	Vickers 952F Vanguard	737	CF-TKN	5. 9.69	To F-BXOO(2). Canx 28.10.75.
G-AXNU	Campbell Cricket	CA/319		8. 9.69	Crash landed near Lambourne on 7.8.70. CofA expired 17.12.70. Canx as WFU 24.10.73.
G-AXNV	Short SC.7 Skyvan 3M-400 (Originally regd as 3-200-12)	SH1868	N23CK G-14-40	8. 9.69	To Ecuador AF as SAE-T-100/HC-AXH. Canx 16.3.71.
G-AXNW	SNCAN Stampe SV-4C (Mod)	381	F-BFZX French Mil	11. 9.69	
G-AXNX	Cessna 182M Skylane	182-59322	N70606	16. 9.69	
G-AXNY	Flixter Pixie	S.B.S.1		16. 9.69	No CofA or Permit issued. (Stored at Spalding) Canx as WFU 7.12.83.
G-AXNZ	Pitts S-1C Special (Also quoted c/n EB.2)	EB.1 & PFA/1383		16. 9.69	Permit expired 30.8.91. (Stored 3/97)
G-AXOA	HS.125 Srs.400A	NA732 & 25203		16. 9.69	To N500AG. Canx 20.10.69.
G-AXOB	HS.125 Srs.400A	NA733 & 25204		16. 9.69	To N380X. Canx 30.10.69.
G-AXOC	HS.125 Srs.400A	NA734 & 25205		16. 9.69	To N125J. Canx 7.11.69.
G-AXOD	HS.125 Srs.400A	NA736 & 25207		16. 9.69	To N30PR. Canx 5.12.69.
G-AXOE	HS.125 Srs.400A	NA737 & 25208		16. 9.69	To N2500W. Canx 17.12.69.
G-AXOF	HS.125 Srs.400A	NA738 & 25210		16. 9.69	To N702D. Canx 2.1.70.
G-AXOG	PA-E23-250 Aztec D	27-4330	N6965Y	17. 9.69	
G-AXOH(1)	Socata MS.894A Rallye Minerva 220	11070		17. 9.69	NTU - To F-BRYO 1/69. Canx.
G-AXOH(2)	Socata MS.894A Rallye Minerva 220	11062	D-EAGU	20.10.69	
G-AXOI	Jodel D.92 Bebe	PFA/930		22. 9.69	Fatal crash on landing at Shoreham on 2.3.96. Permit expired 25.9.96. Canx as WFU 7.10.96.
G-AXOJ	Beagle B.121 Pup Srs.150	B121-109	G-35-109	24. 9.69	
G-AXOK	SNCAN Stampe SV-4C	232	F-BCGG	24. 9.69	Badly damaged in crash shortly after take-off from Sibson 18.6.72. Canx.
G-AXOL	Phoenix Currie Wot	PFA/3012		26. 9.69	To ZK-WOT 11/94. Canx 2.11.94.
G-AXOM	Penn-Smith Gyroplane	DJPS.1		26. 9.69	Permit expired 24.2.71. Canx as WFU 11.10.74. (On display at Stondon Transport Museum & Garden Centre, Lower Stondon)
G-AXON	Handley Page 137 Jetstream 1 (Production No. 26)	225	G-8-10	29. 9.69	To N10AB. Canx 1.12.69.
G-AXOO	Vickers 952 Vanguard	733	PK-ICC G-AXOO/CF-TKJ	30. 9.69	WFU Manston in 5/73. Used for spares /75. Broken up in /77. Canx 5.12.77.
G-AXOP	Vickers 952 Vanguard	745	CF-TKV	30. 9.69	Fatal crash into Jura mountains, near Hochwald, Solothurn, Switzerland on 10.4.73. Canx.
G-AXOR	PA-28-180 Cherokee D	28-5453		30. 9.69	
G-AXOS(1)	Socata MS.894A Rallye Minerva 220	11082		3.10.69R	NTU - Not Imported. Canx.

Regn	Type	c/n	Previous identity	Regn date	Fate or immediate subsequent identity (if known)
G-AXOS(2)	Socata MS.894A Rallye Minerva 220	11079		20.10.69	
G-AXOT	Socata MS.893A Rallye Commodore 180	11433		3.10.69	
G-AXOU	Agusta-Bell 206A JetRanger	8179		6.10.69	To VR-BEW 1/74. Canx 8.1.74.
G-AXOV	Beechcraft 95-B55A Baron	TC-1307		6.10.69	To N1307 10/93. Canx 6.7.93.
G-AXOW	PA-23-250 Aztec D	27-4306	EI-BDN G-AXOW/N6946Y	6.10.69	CofA expired. (Was stored at Hurn) Canx 4.12.86.
G-AXOX	BAC One-Eleven Srs.432FD	BAC.121	A40-BX G-AXOX/VP-BCY/G-16-5	6.10.69	To 5N-AXT. Canx 11.7.90.
G-AXOY	Vickers 952 Vanguard	727	TF-JEJ G-AWOY/TF-AVA/G-AWOY/CF-TKD	6.10.69	To F-BXOH. Canx 11.11.75.
G-AXOZ	Beagle B.121 Pup Srs.100	B121-115	N70290 G-AXOZ/G-35-115	7.10.69	
G-AXPA	Beagle B.121 Pup Srs.100	B121-116	D-EATL G-AXPA/G-35-116	7.10.69	
G-AXPB	Beagle B.121 Pup Srs.100	B121-117	G-35-117	7.10.69	
G-AXPC	Beagle B.121 Pup Srs.100	B121-119	PH-VRS G-AXPC/G-35-119	7.10.69	
G-AXPD	Beagle B.121 Pup Srs.100	B121-121	G-35-121	7.10.69	DBR by storms at Manston on 16.10.87. Canx as destroyed 14.7.88.
G-AXPE	BN-2A Islander	117	G-51-44	7.10.69	To Abu Dhabi AF as 203. Canx 30.10.69.
G-AXPF	Reims Cessna F.150K	0543		14.10.69	
G-AXPG	Mignet HM.293	PFA/1333		14.10.69	Permit expired 20.1.77. (Stored 3/97)
G-AXPH	BAC One-Eleven Srs.521FH	BAC.194	G-16-9	15.10.69	To LV-JNS. Canx 13.11.69.
G-AXPI	Cessna P.172D	P172-57173	9M-AMR N11B/(N8573X)	16.10.69	To G-WPUI 6/80. Canx.
G-AXPJ	Westland-Sikorsky S-58 Wessex 60 Srs.1	WA/696		16.10.69	To PK-HBR 8/70. Canx 11.8.70.
G-AXPK	SNCAN Stampe SV-4C	266	F-BCLY	16.10.69	Crashed at Leicester East on 15.6.71. Canx.
G-AXPL	Hughes H.369HS (500HS)	89-0112S		20.10.69	To VH-PMY. Canx 10.10.75.
G-AXPM	Beagle B.121 Pup Srs.150	B121-122	G-35-122	20.10.69	
G-AXPN	Beagle B.121 Pup Srs.150	B121-123	G-35-123	20.10.69	
G-AXPO	Beagle B.121 Pup Srs.150	B121-124	G-35-124	20.10.69	NTU - To VH-EPG. Canx 10.11.69.
G-AXPP	Beagle B.121 Pup Srs.150	B121-125	G-35-125	20.10.69	To VH-EPH. Canx 10.11.69.
G-AXPR	Beagle B.121 Pup Srs.150	B121-127	G-35-127	20.10.69	NTU - To VH-EPJ. Canx 10.11.69.
G-AXPS	HS.125 Srs.3B	25135	HB-VAY G-5-14	20.10.69	Crashed on take-off and caught fire at Turnhouse on 20.7.70 after port wing hit runway. Canx.
G-AXPT(1)	Hughes H.269B	16-0228	N9451F	. .69R	NTU - To G-AXXD 2/70. Canx.
G-AXPT(2)	Short SC.7 Skyvan 3M-100-27	SH1867	G-14-39	24.10.69	To G-14-39/Royal AF of Oman as 911. Canx 28.3.74.
G-AXPU	HS.125 Srs.3B/RA	25171	G-IBIS G-AXPU/HB-VBT/G-5-19	24.10.69	To G-BXPU 3/83. Canx.
G-AXPV	Beagle 206S Srs.3	B.074	G-35-28	28.10.69	To N206BC 7/75. Canx 31.7.75.
G-AXPW	AIA Stampe SV-4C	1098	F-BFUI	28.10.69	To N15SV. Canx 24.3.77.
G-AXPX	HS.125 Srs.400A	NA735 & 25206		28.10.69	To VP-BDH 2/70. Canx 20.11.69.
G-AXPY	BN-2A Islander	111	G-51-41	3.11.69	To (PH-KJF)/PH-NVA 6/70. Canx 16.6.70.
G-AXPZ	Campbell Cricket	CA/320		3.11.69	
G-AXRA	Campbell Cricket	CA/321A		3.11.69	No current Permit to Fly. (See G-AYDJ) Canx by CAA 25.10.90.
G-AXRB	Campbell Cricket	CA/322		3.11.69	Canx as WFU 11.7.84.
G-AXRC	Campbell Cricket	CA/323		3.11.69	
G-AXRD	Campbell Cricket	CA/324		3.11.69	Crashed at Rhoose on 10.6.70. Canx.
G-AXRE	Handley Page 137 Jetstream III (Production No. 36) (Originally regd as Srs.1)	235		3.11.69	To N10GA. Canx 6.1.70.
G-AXRF	Handley Page 137 Jetstream 1 (Production No. 37)	237		3.11.69	To N2527. Canx 6.1.70.
G-AXRG	Handley Page 137 Jetstream III (Production No. 38) (Originally regd as Srs.1)	238		3.11.69	To N11360. Canx 17.2.70.
G-AXRH	Handley Page 137 Jetstream III (Production No. 40) (Originally regd as Srs.1)	240		3.11.69	To N4770. Canx 26.2.70.
G-AXRI	Handley Page 137 Jetstream 200 (Production No. 41) (Originally regd as Srs.1)	241		3.11.69	Canx as WFU 12.6.74, but re-regd G-BCGU same day.
G-AXRJ	BN-2A Islander	123	(N862JA) G-51-49	4.11.69	DBR on landing at Rawalpindi, Pakistan on 7.4.70. Canx as WFU 6.7.70.
G-AXRK	Practavia Pilot Sprite 115	15 & PFA/1381		4.11.69	Canx by CAA 26.7.91. (Under construction 7/95)
G-AXRL	PA-28-160 Cherokee	28-324	PH-CHE D-EFRI/N11C	5.11.69	WFU at Headcorn as DBER in 8/84 due to corrosion. Canx by CAA 12.8.94.
G-AXRM	BN-2A-8 Islander	128	G-51-51	5.11.69	To N158MA. Canx 31.10.75.
G-AXRN	BN-2A-26 Islander	129	G-51-52	5.11.69	To C-GGYY 12/75. Canx.
G-AXRO	PA-30-160 Twin Comanche C	30-1978	N8820Y	5.11.69	
G-AXRP	SNCAN Stampe SV-4C (Regd G-BLOL 2/85 but restored in 9/94 and stored at Rotary Farm, Hatch 7/95)	554	G-BLOL G-AXRP/F-BDCZ	7.11.69	Crashed on landing at Little Gransden on 19.10.74. A proposed restoration as G-BLOL (with c/n 'SS-SV-R1') in 1985 did not proceed either.
G-AXRR	Auster AOP.9	AUS.178 & B5/10/178	XR241 G-AXRR/XR241	7.11.69	(Forced landed near Penshurst on 1.2.99; at Duxford 4/99)
G-AXRS	Boeing 707-355C (Line No. 643)	19664	N526EJ PH-TRF/N526EJ	7.11.69	To 5N-AOQ 7/84. Canx 23.7.84.
G-AXRT	Reims Cessna FA.150K Aerobat (Tail-wheel conversion)	0018		12.11.69	
G-AXRU	Reims Cessna FA.150K Aerobat	0020		12.11.69	CofA expired 10.12.87. (Stored 6/97 at Kemble) Canx by CAA 2.3.99.
G-AXRV	Bell 47G-4A	7690		12.11.69	To 9L-LAO 5/70. Canx 1.12.69.

Regn	Type	c/n	Previous identity	Regn date	Fate or immediate subsequent identity (if known)
G-AXRW	PA-30-160 Twin Comanche C	30-1774	5N-ADM N8633Y	12.11.69	Fatal crash 300 yards from Shipdham on 23.1.73 whilst inbound from Dyce. Canx.
G-AXRX	Cessna 337D Super Skymaster	337-1077	(G-AXBV) N86098	12.11.69	To EI-BFY 9/78. Canx 27.9.78.
G-AXRY	Agusta-Bell 206A JetRanger	8188		13.11.69	To 5N-AIO 8/70. Canx 19.8.70.
G-AXRZ	Reims Cessna FA.150K Aerobat	0014		13.11.69	Force-landed at Flixton on 11.10.74. Canx as WFU 27.11.74.
G-AXSA	Beagle B.121 Pup Srs.150	B121-133	G-35-133	13.11.69	To HB-NAG /71. Canx 17.2.71.
G-AXSB	Beagle B.121 Pup Srs.150	B121-135	G-35-135	13.11.69	To D-EKAK(2) 12/71. Canx 14.5.71.
G-AXSC	Beagle B.121 Pup Srs.100	B121-138	G-35-138	13.11.69	
G-AXSD	Beagle B.121 Pup Srs.100	B121-139	G-35-139	13.11.69	
G-AXSE	Beagle B.121 Pup Srs.100	B121-142	G-35-142	13.11.69	To D-EBBZ 5/70. Canx 9.3.70.
G-AXSF	Procter Nash Petrel	PFA/1516 & P.003		17.11.69	Permit expired 7.4.94. (Stored 10/95)
	(Double allocation of PFA c/n - no connection with G-BACA)				
G-AXSG	PA-28-180 Cherokee E	28-5605		17.11.69	Damaged in crash on landing at Cumbernauld on 14.4.94. CofA expired 5.7.94. (Stored by R.Everett 5/97)
G-AXSH	PA-28-140 Cherokee C	28-26404		17.11.69	To G-TIMW 3/85. Canx.
	(Originally regd as a PA-28-140B with c/n 28-26405, was amended on 16.1.70)				
G-AXSI	Reims Cessna F.172H Skyhawk	0687	G-SNIP G-AXSI	19.11.69	
G-AXSJ	Reims Cessna FA.150K Aerobat	0029		19.11.69	To G-BUTT 8/86. Canx.
G-AXSK	Reims Cessna FA.150K Aerobat	0051		19.11.69	Struck sea-wall while practising forced landings at Tollesbury, near Goldhanger, Essex 17.8.71. Remains to Stapleford, then Southend. Canx as destroyed 29.10.71.
G-AXSL	Cessna 310P	310P-0167	N5867M	19.11.69	To N9110V. Canx 1.9.81.
G-AXSM	CEA Jodel DR.1051 Sicile	512	F-BLRH	20.11.69	
G-AXSN	BN-2A-26 Islander	81	N870JA G-51-22	21.11.69	To VH-ROV. Canx 23.1.70.
G-AXSO	Reims Cessna F.172H Skyhawk	0570		21.11.69	To HB-CDN 5/73. Canx 23.2.73.
G-AXSP	PA-30-160 Twin Comanche C	30-1982	N8824Y	21.11.69	To G-BKCL 1/81. Canx.
G-AXSR	Brantly B.2B	474	G-ROOF G-AXSR/N2237U	24.11.69	
G-AXSS	BN-2A-26 Islander	603		24.11.69	To S7-AAE. Canx 19.6.79.
	(Originally regd as BN-2A)				
G-AXST	BN-2A Islander	604	7Q-YKD G-AXST	24.11.69	To OB-R-1271. Canx 15.4.83.
G-AXSU	BN-2A-26 Islander	605		24.11.69	To VH-EQZ 7/70. Canx 3.8.70.
	(Originally regd as BN-2A)				
G-AXSV	CEA Jodel DR.340 Major	335	F-BRCC	24.11.69	Damaged in forced landing at Rossington, Yorks on 21.7.90. Canx as WFU 2.1.97.
G-AXSW	Reims Cessna FA.150K Aerobat	0003		25.11.69	
G-AXSX	Beechcraft C23 Musketeer	M-1287		25.11.69	
G-AXSY	BAC One-Eleven Srs.524FF	BAC.195	D-AMUR	26.11.69	Restored as D-AMUR. Canx 12.12.69.
G-AXSZ	PA-28-140 Cherokee B	28-26188		26.11.69	
G-AXTA	PA-28-140 Cherokee B	28-26301		26.11.69	
G-AXTB	PA-28-140 Cherokee B	28-26194		26.11.69	Crashed at Gallens End Farm, Lambourne End on 13.7.80. Canx as WFU 19.8.81.
G-AXTC	PA-28-140 Cherokee B	28-26265		26.11.69	(Stored 9/97)
G-AXTD	PA-28-140 Cherokee B	28-26206		26.11.69	Extensively damaged when it struck a lampost on the A2 road on take-off from the strip at Dunkirk, near Canterbury on 29.4.98 and crashed into nearby woods. Canx as destroyed 9.7.98.
G-AXTE	PA-28-140 Cherokee B	28-26277		26.11.69	To A6-ACE. Canx 3.7.85.
G-AXTF	PA-28-140 Cherokee B	28-26224		26.11.69	Crashed on take-off from Litton Farm, Dorset on 23.6.79. Canx.
G-AXTG	PA-28-140 Cherokee B	28-26253	N11C	26.11.69	To 5B-CFO 2/84. Canx 3.2.84.
G-AXTH	PA-28-140 Cherokee B	28-26283		26.11.69	Damaged in a forced landing near Compton Abbas on 28.2.88. The wreck was stored at Caterham late in 1990 but was later scrapped. Canx by CAA 13.7.95.
G-AXTI	PA-28-140 Cherokee B	28-26259		26.11.69	To G-LTFC 6/94. Canx.
G-AXTJ	PA-28-140 Cherokee B	28-26241		26.11.69	
G-AXTK	PA-28-140 Cherokee B	28-26235		26.11.69	DBR on overshoot at Clacton on 6.9.81. CofA expired 25.6.84. Canx as destroyed 26.3.85. (Wreck stored 1/94)
G-AXTL	PA-28-140 Cherokee B	28-26247		26.11.69	
G-AXTM	PA-28-140 Cherokee B	28-26295		26.11.69	Crashed at Treadgear on 21.2.81. Canx as destroyed 29.2.84.
G-AXTN	PA-28-140 Cherokee B	28-26307		26.11.69	Crashed into hillside 44 kms NNE of Geneva, Switzerland on 31.7.76. Canx as destroyed 29.2.84.
G-AXTO	PA-24-260 Comanche C	24-4900	N9449P	28.11.69	
G-AXTP	PA-28-180 Cherokee C	28-3791	OH-PID	1.12.69	
G-AXTR	HS.125 Srs.400A	NA739 & 25211		3.12.69	To N125DH. Canx 6.4.70.
G-AXTS	HS.125 Srs.400A	NA740 & 25212		3.12.69	To N702P. Canx 13.2.70.
G-AXTT	HS.125 Srs.400A	NA741 & 25213		3.12.69	To CF-CFL. Canx 14.1.70.
G-AXTU	HS.125 Srs.400B	NA742 & 25214	N60QA N60PC/N40PC/G-AXTU	3.12.69	To G-5-20/N731HS. Canx 29.12.77.
	(Originally regd as Srs.400A)				
G-AXTV	HS.125 Srs.400A	NA743 & 25216		3.12.69	To N9138. Canx 20.4.70.
G-AXTW	HS.125 Srs.400A	NA744 & 25218		3.12.69	To N575DU. Canx 25.3.70.
G-AXTX	Wassmer Jodel D.112	1077	F-BKCA	3.12.69	
G-AXTY	DH.82A Tiger Moth	85970	F-BDMP EM739	3.12.69	To N16645. Canx 12.12.72.
G-AXTZ	Beagle B.121 Pup Srs.100	B121-148	G-35-148	4.12.69	Crashed at Andrewsfield on 30.3.75. CofA expired 14.2.76. (On rebuild 10/96 Withybush) Canx by CAA 11.3.99.
G-AXUA	Beagle B.121 Pup Srs.100	B121-150	G-35-150	4.12.69	

Regn	Type	c/n	Previous identity	Regn date	Fate or immediate subsequent identity (if known)
G-AXUB	BN-2A Islander	121	5N-AIJ G-AXUB/N859JA/G-51-47	4.12.69	
G-AXUC	PA-12 Super Cruiser	12-621	5Y-KFR VP-KFR/ZS-BIN	5.12.69	(On rebuild 5/98 Maypole Farm)
G-AXUD	BN-2A Islander	132	VH-ATZ	5.12.69	To VH-ATZ. Canx 13.1.70.
G-AXUE	CEA Jodel DR.105A Ambassadeur	59	F-BKFX F-OBFX	9.12.69	Cought by a gust of wind on approach and crashed at Bagby on 11.6.89. Canx as WFU 23.4.90.
G-AXUF	Reims Cessna FA.150K Aerobat	0043		9.12.69	
G-AXUG	Reims Cessna F.150J/RR	0497	F-BRBF	9.12.69	To F-WLIT/HB-CVZ 9/71. Canx 27.9.71.
G-AXUH	PA-31-300 Navajo	31-501	N6576L	11.12.69	To CR-LKO 5/70. Canx 1.5.70.
G-AXUI	Handley Page 137 Jetstream 1 (Production No. 22)	222	G-8-9	11.12.69	To G-NFLC 12/95. Canx.
G-AXUJ	Auster J/1 Autocrat	1957	PH-OTO	11.12.69	To G-OSTA 7/99. Canx.
G-AXUK	SAN Jodel DR.1050 Ambassadeur	292	F-BJYU	11.12.69	
G-AXUL	Canadair CL-44D4-2	24	N454T	12.12.69	To N104BB. Canx 7.7.81.
G-AXUM	Handley Page 137 Jetstream 1 (Production No. 44)	245		12.12.69	Canx as PWFU 20.1.99.
G-AXUN	Handley Page 137 Jetstream 1 (Production No. 45)	246		12.12.69	To G-BCWW 7/74. Canx.
G-AXUO	Handley Page 137 Jetstream 1 (Production No. 46)	248		12.12.69	To F-BTMI 8/72. Canx 20.4.72.
G-AXUP	Handley Page 137 Jetstream 1 (Production No. 49)	251		12.12.69	To RN as XX481 6/74. Canx 17.1.74.
G-AXUR	Handley Page 137 Jetstream 1	259		12.12.69	To RN as XX479 5/74. Canx 17.1.74.
G-AXUS	BN-2A Islander	606		12.12.69	To VT-DYZ 7/70. Canx 20.11.70.
G-AXUT	BN-2A Islander	607		12.12.69	To 9Q-CTS 6/70. Canx 3.6.70.
G-AXUU	BN-2A Islander	608		12.12.69	To VT-EAN 11/70. Canx 21.12.70.
G-AXUV(1)	Reims Cessna F.172H Skyhawk	0740		12.12.69	NTU - Not Imported. To D-ECFW 8/70. Canx.
G-AXUV(2)	Reims Cessna F.172K Skyhawk	0731		17.12.69	
G-AXUW	Reims Cessna FA.150K Aerobat	0045		17.12.69	DBR at Leicester East on 17.1.80. Canx as WFU 5.12.83.
G-AXUX	Beechcraft B95 Travel Air	TD-417	OE-FAD D-GINU	18.12.69	To G-EDIT 3/87. Canx.
G-AXUY	SAN Jodel DR.100A Ambassadeur	51	F-BIZI	18.12.69	Crashed at Ash House Farm, Winsford on 3.9.78. CofA expired 3.11.78. (Instructional Airframe 1/96 with 162 ATC Sqdn, Stockport)
G-AXUZ	Practavia Pilot Sprite S.125	PFA/1337		22.12.69	Not completed. Canx 11.7.84.
G-AXVA	Cessna 401B	401B-0009	N7909Q	22.12.69	To OH-CGW 1/76. Canx 28.10.75.
G-AXVB	Reims Cessna F.172H Skyhawk	0703		22.12.69	
G-AXVC	Reims Cessna FA.150K Aerobat	0047		22.12.69	To N922SZ 7/92. Canx 24.4.92.
G-AXVD	Not allocated.				
G-AXVE	Cessna 210K Centurion	210-59257	N8257M	29.12.69	To OO-FKT 3/72. Canx 3.3.72.
G-AXVF	Handley Page 137 Jetstream 1 (Production No. 30) (Originally a Srs.2 but not regd as such)	230	G-8-11	31.12.69	To N85230 2/70. Canx 6.9.73.
G-AXVG	HS.748 Srs.2A/226	1589	RP-C1301 G-AXVG/OE-LHS	31.12.69	To C-FGGE. Canx 17.7.89.
G-AXVH	Campbell Cricket	CA/330		1. 1.70	To LN-GGI. Canx 25.6.70.
G-AXVI	Campbell Cricket	CA/325		1. 1.70	To 9M-APY 11/70. Canx 1.4.70.
G-AXVJ	Campbell Cricket	CA/326		1. 1.70	Canx 24.7.70 on sale to Denmark.
G-AXVK	Campbell Cricket	CA/327		1. 1.70	Went out of control and crashed at St.Merryn, Cornwall on 16.7.87. Permit expired 8.3.89. Canx by CAA 6.1.97. (Under restoration 2/99)
G-AXVL	Campbell Cricket	CA/328		1. 1.70	Canx 25.6.70 on sale to Kuwait. (On display 3/96 at Syrian Military Museum, Tekkiye Mosque, Damascus, Syria)
G-AXVM	Campbell Cricket	CA/329		1. 1.70	
G-AXVN	McCandless M.4 Gyrocopter	M4/6		5. 1.70	(Extant 10/95)
G-AXVO	BAC One-Eleven Srs.515FB	BAC.197	G-16-11	5. 1.70	To (D-AMUR)/(D-ANOR)/D-AMOR. Canx 27.2.70.
G-AXVP	BN-2A-8 Islander	127	G-51-50	6. 1.70	To (F-BUIB)/F-BUID 6/73. Canx 23.3.73.
G-AXVR	BN-2A-8 Islander	139	G-51-65 N865JA	6. 1.70	To N139BN. Canx 1.12.78.
G-AXVS	SAN Jodel DR.1050 Ambassadeur	155	F-BJNL	6. 1.70	To G-SPOG 9/95. Canx.
G-AXVT	Cessna A.185F Skywagon	01617		7. 1.70	To TZ-APR 4/70. Canx 19.3.70.
G-AXVU	Omega 84 HAFB	09		7. 1.70	Canx as WFU 22.8.89. (To British Balloon Museum) (Extant 6/97)
G-AXVV	Piper J3C-65 Cub (L-4H-PI)	10863	F-BBQB 43-29572	7. 1.70	CofA expired 16.6.73. (Stored 4/96 Rathcoole, Ireland) Canx by CAA 12.4.99.
G-AXVW	Reims Cessna F.150K	0548		9. 1.70	To G-IANJ 5/98. Canx.
G-AXVX	Reims Cessna F.172H Skyhawk	0664		9. 1.70	To CS-AUT 4/90. Canx 2.2.90.
G-AXVY	SIAI Marchetti SF.260	227	OO-HEV	12. 1.70	Crashed on take-off from Fairoaks on 11.4.70. CofA expired 25.1.71. WFU 23.1.74.
G-AXVZ	HS.748 Srs.2A/253	1671	9N-AAU	12. 1.70	Restored as 9N-AAU 1/70. Canx 26.1.70.
G-AXWA	Auster AOP.9	B5/10/133	XN437	13. 1.70	(Status uncertain - thought exported .94)
G-AXWB	Omega 65 HAFB	06		20. 1.70	Canx by CAA 19.5.93.
G-AXWC	Not allocated.				
G-AXWD	Jurca MJ.10 Spitfire XIV Replica	PFA/1345		13. 1.70	Construction abandoned. Canx by CAA 12.9.86.
G-AXWE	Reims Cessna F.150K	0530	(HB-CUA) F-WLIS	16. 1.70	Badly damaged by severe gales at Barton on 2.1.76. Dismantled at Barton with CofA expired 13.6.81. Canx as WFU 23.10.86.
G-AXWF	Reims Cessna F.172H Skyhawk	0697		16. 1.70	Badly damaged in gales at Clacton on 26/27.11.83. Canx by CAA 3.4.89. (Stored in scrapyard 7/95)
G-AXWG	BN-2A Islander	135	5N-AIK G-AXWG/N862JA/G-51-55	16. 1.70	Crashed in Greenland on 8.8.79. Canx.

Regn	Type	c/n	Previous identity	Regn date	Fate or immediate subsequent identity (if known)
G-AXWH	BN-2A Islander	137	VR-BBI 5N-AIL/G-AXWH/N864JA/G-51-58	16. 1.70	To N137MW 2/98. Canx 23.7.97.
G-AXWI	BN-2A-9 Islander (Originally regd as BN-2A)	609		16. 1.70	To F-OCRA 11/70. Canx 15.10.70.
G-AXWJ	BN-2A-9 Islander (Originally regd as BN-2A)	610		16. 1.70	To 8R-GDS 9/70. Canx 31.7.70.
G-AXWK	BN-2A Islander	124	VH-FLF(2)	20. 1.70	To VH-EQT. Canx 27.2.70.
G-AXWL	Beechcraft D-18S (3TM)	CA-167	N6685 Canadian AF 1567	22. 1.70	Restored as N6685 7/72. Canx 21.7.72.
G-AXWM	DH.82A Tiger Moth	86501	F-BGCK NM193	26. 1.70	To N5984. Canx 24.11.70.
G-AXWN	Reims Cessna F.337E Super Skymaster (Wichita c/n 337-01218)	0005		26. 1.70	To EC-CCO 3/73. Canx 2.2.73.
G-AXWO	BN-2A-26 Islander (Originally regd as BN-2A)	140	G-4-10 G-AXWO/G-51-59	26. 1.70	To JA5193 4/72. Canx 21.4.72.
G-AXWP	BN-2A-26 Islander (Originally regd as BN-2A)	147	G-51-66	26. 1.70	To VP-LMH. Canx 17.11.93.
G-AXWR	BN-2A-26 Islander (Originally regd as BN-2A)	149	G-51-68	26. 1.70	To YV-921C 1/95. Canx 9.1.95.
G-AXWS	BN-2A-26 Islander (Originally regd as BN-2A)	152	G-51-152	26. 1.70	To VH-RTV. Canx 11.3.70.
G-AXWT	Jodel D.11	PFA/911		26. 1.70	
G-AXWU	Short SC.7 Skyvan 3M-200-21	SH1866	SX-BBT G-AXWU/G-14-38	30. 1.70	To G-14-38/Royal AF of Oman as 912 in 4/74. Canx 29.4.74.
G-AXWV	CEA DR.253B Regent	104	F-OCKL	2. 2.70	
G-AXWW	Cessna 180H	180-52109	N9009M	3. 2.70	To CR-LKM 9/70. Canx 4.6.70.
G-AXWX	Cessna 180H	180-52110	N9010M	3. 2.70	To CR-LKN 9/70. Canx 4.6.70.
G-AXWY	Taylor JT.2 Titch	PFA/3212		30. 1.70	Not completed. Parts to G-CWOT. Canx 30.5.84.
G-AXWZ	PA-28R-200 Cherokee Arrow	28R-35605		3. 2.70	
G-AXXA	PA-28-180 Cherokee E	28-5606		3. 2.70	Crashed at White Waltham on 31.5.82. Canx.
G-AXXB	PA-31-300 Navajo (Panther conversion)	31-583	N7XB N6645L/G-AXXB/N6645L	3. 2.70	To N77XB. Canx 23.7.81.
G-AXXC	Rousseau Piel CP.301B Emeraude	117	F-BJAT	4. 2.70	Extensively damaged on take-off from North Cowton, Yorks on 13.9.81. (On rebuild .97)
G-AXXD	Hughes H.269B	16-0228	(G-AXPT) N9451F	4. 2.70	Crashed into the Thames near Battersea in 10/73. Salvaged but used for spares. Canx as WFU 26.8.81.
G-AXXE	DH.82A Tiger Moth	86535	F-BGDD PG626	4. 2.70	To D-EOPR 6/75, but crashed in Belgium whilst on delivery flight. Canx 24.6.75.
G-AXXF	BN-2A-20 Islander	134	(N863JA) G-51-54	5. 2.70	To VH-BPV. Canx 29.7.70.
G-AXXG	BN-2A-2 Islander	143	G-51-62	5. 2.70	To 5X-BEE 4/89. Canx 20.4.89.
G-AXXH	BN-2A-26 Islander	144	G-51-64	5. 2.70	To ST-AIY 8/84. Canx 17.8.84.
G-AXXI	BN-2A Islander	148	G-51-67	5. 2.70	To 8R-GDJ 7/70. Canx 2.6.70.
G-AXXJ	BN-2A-26 Islander	150	OO-ARI(3) G-AXXJ/G-51-150	5. 2.70	To G-PASW 5/90. Canx.
G-AXXK	BN-2A Islander	151	EI-AUF G-AXXK/G-51-151	5. 2.70	To F-BPTT. Canx 18.8.75.
G-AXXL	Westland S-58 Wessex 60 Srs.1	WA/732		10. 2.70	To 5N-AIR 12/70. Canx 10.12.70.
G-AXXM	Coopavia-Menavia CP.301A Emeraude	220	F-BIJT	10. 2.70	No UK CofA issued. (Possibly only used for spares) Canx by CAA 4.12.86.
G-AXXN	McCandless M.4 Gyroplane	1002		13. 2.70	To G-BNFL 8/85 as a WHL Airbuggy with same c/n. Canx.
G-AXXO	Bell 206A JetRanger	420		16. 2.70	To N67219. Canx 22.9.75.
G-AXXP	Bradshaw HAB-76 (Ax7) HAFB	RB.001		20. 2.70	WFU at Markyate in 2/77. Canx 9.9.81. (Stored British Balloon Museum, Newbury)
G-AXXR	Beechcraft 95-B55A Baron	TC-1347		23. 2.70	To G-BNBY 2/83. Canx.
G-AXXS	Handley Page 137 Jetstream 1 (Production No. 48)	249	G-8-14	23. 2.70	To RAF as XX477 9/73. Canx 2.5.73.
G-AXXT	Handley Page 137 Jetstream 1 (Production No. 51)	261		23. 2.70	To RAF/RN as XX478 12/73. Canx by CAA 5.12.83.
G-AXXU	Handley Page 137 Jetstream 1 (Production No. 52)	262		23. 2.70	To RAF/RN as XX480 3/74. Canx by CAA 5.12.83.
G-AXXV	DH.82A Tiger Moth	85852	F-BGJI French AF/DE992	24. 2.70	
G-AXXW	SAN Jodel D.117 (Mod)	632	F-BIBN	26. 2.70	
G-AXXX	Not allocated.				
G-AXXY	Boeing 707-336C (Line No. 851) (Originally regd as Srs.336B)	20456		11. 2.70	To 4X-BMC 7/84. Canx 26.7.84.
G-AXXZ	Boeing 707-336C (Line No. 853) (Originally regd as Srs.336B)	20457		11. 2.70	To 9G-ADB 9/83. Canx 24.6.83.
G-AXYA	PA-31-300 Turbo Navajo	31-632	N6731L	27. 2.70	To OY-FRE. Canx 14.11.88.
G-AXYB	PA-31-300 Turbo Navajo	31-641	5N-AEQ G-AXYB/N6736L	27. 2.70	To G-BXYB 1/80. Canx.
G-AXYC	PA-31-310 Turbo Navajo	31-642	N6737L	27. 2.70	To G-BSFT 6/79. Canx.
G-AXYD	BAC One-Eleven Srs.509EW	BAC.210		27. 2.70	To (G-OWBF 4/93)/5N-... Stored since 11/92 at Southend as G-AXYD. Stripped for spares in 9/98. Scrapped in 12/98.
G-AXYE	HS.125 Srs.400A	NA745 & 25220		27. 2.70	To N41BH 3/70. Canx 23.3.70.
G-AXYF	HS.125 Srs.400A	NA747 & 25222		27. 2.70	To N43BH 3/70. Canx 23.3.70.
G-AXYG	HS.125 Srs.400A	NA748 & 25224		27. 2.70	To N44BH 3/70. Canx 23.3.70.
G-AXYH	HS.125 Srs.400A	NA749 & 25225		27. 2.70	To N45BH 3/70. Canx 23.3.70.
G-AXYI	HS.125 Srs.400A	NA750 & 25226		27. 2.70	To N46BH 3/70. Canx 23.3.70.
G-AXYJ	HS.125 Srs.403B	25217	G-5-14	27. 2.70	To 9Q-CGM/9Q-CHD 5/73. Canx 1.5.73.

Regn	Type	c/n	Previous identity	Regn date	Fate or immediate subsequent identity (if known)
G-AXYK	Taylor JT.1 Monoplane	PFA/1409		2. 3.70	(Badly damaged in forced landing at Couhe, France on 30.6.95) (On repair 11/95)
G-AXYL	BN-2A Islander	155	G-51-155	3. 3.70	To 5Y-DLC 12/73. Canx 8.1.73.
G-AXYM	BN-2A Islander	156	5N-AIQ G-AXYM/G-51-156	3. 3.70	To G-BSPY 6/90. Canx.
G-AXYN	BN-2A Islander	157	G-51-157	3. 3.70	To 9Q-CRF 11/70. Canx.
G-AXYO	PA-25-235 Pawnee C	25-5157	N8706L	5. 3.70	Crashed into cables & DBR while crop-spraying at Hillbourne Farm, Brandeston, Suffolk 4.7.81. Canx as destroyed 12.8.81
G-AXYP	BN-2A Islander	158	G-51-158	5. 3.70	To VH-FLD. Canx 8.5.70.
G-AXYR	BN-2A-26 Islander	159	G-51-159	5. 3.70	To VH-ISA 4/70. Canx 28.4.70.
G-AXYS	BN-2A Islander	164	G-51-164	5. 3.70	To VH-EQX. Canx 16.6.70.
G-AXYT	BN-2A Islander	165	G-51-165	5. 3.70	To VH-RUT 8/70. Canx 18.5.70.
G-AXYU	Jodel D.9 Bebe	547	EI-BVE G-AXYU	5. 3.70	
G-AXYV	Luton Beta Srs.2 (C/n is actually the PFA Membership number of the owner!)	PFA/2202/6		9. 3.70	Not completed. Canx by CAA 5.12.83.
G-AXYW	SNCAN Stampe SV-4C	163	F-BBPF	10. 3.70	To VH-BVU(2) 6/81. Canx 25.1.77.
G-AXYX	WHE Airbuggy (Originally regd as McCandless M.4 Gyroplane)	1003		10. 3.70	Badly damaged in heavy landing at Melbourne, York on 30.7.83. Canx as destroyed 28.8.87. (On rebuild/spares for G-AXYZ 7/94)
G-AXYY	WHE Airbuggy (Originally regd as McCandless M.4 Gyroplane)	1004		10. 3.70	Permit expired 8.11.87. Canx by CAA 11.2.97.
G-AXYZ	WHE Airbuggy (Originally regd as McCandless M.4 Gyroplane)	1005		10. 3.70	Permit expired 22.12.82. (Extant 5/95)
G-AXZA	WHE Airbuggy (Originally regd as McCandless M.4 Gyroplane)	1006		10. 3.70	Permit expired 15.8.96. (Based at Hoofdoorp, The Netherlands)
G-AXZB	WHE Airbuggy (Originally regd as McCandless M.4 Gyroplane)	1007		10. 3.70	Permit expired 18.11.86. Canx by CAA 19.2.97.
G-AXZC	PA-28-180 Cherokee E	28-5700		12. 3.70	Collided with PA-28 G-AVBJ over Hamble on 30.4.81. Canx.
G-AXZD	PA-28-180 Cherokee E	28-5609		12. 3.70	
G-AXZE	PA-28-180 Cherokee E	28-5676		12. 3.70	To N5458J. Canx 11.7.84.
G-AXZF	PA-28-180 Cherokee E	28-5688		12. 3.70	
G-AXZG	Schempp-Hirth Standard Cirrus	18		12. 3.70	To BGA.1621/CLE in 1/71. Canx.
G-AXZH	Glasflugel Standard Libelle 15	82		12. 3.70	To RAFGSA-16 in 1971. Canx.
G-AXZI	Schleicher ASW-12	12011	BGA.1545	12. 3.70	To N145T in 1971. Canx.
G-AXZJ	Reims Cessna F.172K	0706		12. 3.70	Crashed at Ledbury on 12.12.76. Canx.
G-AXZK	BN-2A-26 Islander	153	V2-LAD VP-LAD/G-AXZK/G-51-153	12. 3.70	
G-AXZL	Beagle B.206S Srs.2	B.062	(YI-AMA) G-AXZL/(PT-DIP)/G-35-16	16. 3.70	To N87631 6/75. Canx 16.6.75.
G-AXZM	Slingsby Nipper T.66 RA.45 Srs.3A (Slingsby kit c/n S.133/1709)	PFA/1378		16. 3.70	Badly damaged in forced landing near Eshott on 21.8.89. (Possibly on rebuild off airfield 5/90)
G-AXZN	Thruston Teal Amphibian Srs.TSC-1A (Damaged in USA & fitted with replacement fuselage c/n 18, but c/n plate on fin remained as 8)	8		16. 3.70	Damaged near Sddington on 13.1.73. Canx as destroyed 26.1.73. Destroyed by vandalism in a field near Biggin Hill on 27/28.1.73.
G-AXZO	Cessna 180	31137	N3639C	17. 3.70	
G-AXZP	PA-E23-250 Aztec D	27-4464	N13819	17. 3.70	
G-AXZR	Taylor JT.2 Titch	PFA/1503		17. 3.70	Not completed. Canx by CAA 2.9.91.
G-AXZS	Westland-Sikorsky S-55 Whirlwind Srs.3	WA/492	VR-BDM AMDB-102	17. 3.70	To 9Y-TDJ 7/70. Canx 26.6.70.
G-AXZT	SAN Jodel D.117A	607	F-BIBD	17. 3.70	
G-AXZU	Cessna 182N Skylane	182-60104	N92233	19. 3.70	
G-AXZV	Mooney M.20F	680129	N3848N	20. 3.70	To D-EGAX. Canx 12.7.76.
G-AXZW	Ercoupe 415C	2654	N2031H	23. 3.70	To N49918. Canx 29.6.77.
G-AXZX	PA-32-300 Cherokee Six	32-40182	G-AVFU	23. 3.70R	NTU - Remained as G-AVFU. Canx 23.3.70.
G-AXZY	BN-2A-9 Islander	611		23. 3.70	To F-OCRB 11/70. Canx 15.10.70.
G-AXZZ	BN-2A Islander	612		23. 3.70	To 8R-GDT 9/70. Canx 31.8.70.
G-AYAA	PA-28-180 Cherokee E	28-5799		24. 3.70	
G-AYAB	PA-28-180 Cherokee E	28-5804		24. 3.70	
G-AYAC	PA-28R-200 Cherokee Arrow B	28R-35606		24. 3.70	
G-AYAD	PA-30-160 Twin Comanche C	30-1996	N8838Y	24. 3.70	To N38760. Canx 6.4.83.
G-AYAE	Bell 47G-4A	7682	N1489W	26. 3.70	To SX-HBU 5/85. Canx 28.5.85.
G-AYAF	PA-30-160 Twin Comanche C	30-2000	N8842Y	26. 3.70	CofA expired 8.5.77 & WFU at Shipdham. Canx as WFU 24.11.86. (Stored 9/95)
G-AYAG	Boeing 707-321 (Line No. 217)	18085	N759PA	26. 3.70	To G-41-372 then VP-BDF 12/72. Canx 8.12.72.
G-AYAH	Beechcraft D-18S (3TM)	CA-159	N6123 RCAF 1559	31. 3.70	To N96240. Canx 18.8.76.
G-AYAI	Sportavia-Putzer Fournier RF-5	5071		31. 3.70	Fatal accident at Cranfield on 7.7.90. Canx as destroyed 17.10.90.
G-AYAJ	Cameron O-84 HAFB	11		31. 3.70	Canx as WFU 1.2.90. To British Balloon Museum & Library. (Extant 10/97)
G-AYAK	Yakovlev Yak C.11	172701	OK-KIE	31. 3.70	To N11YK 6/84. Canx 7.6.84.
G-AYAL	Omega 56 HAFB	10		2. 4.70	CofA expired 25.8.76. To British Balloon Museum & Library. Canx by CAA 18.10.84. (Extant 2/97)
G-AYAM	Cameron O-84 HAFB	12		2. 4.70	Canx 27.4.73 on sale to Japan.
G-AYAN	Slingsby Cadet III Motor Glider (Converted from T.31B frame no. SSK/FF776)	003 & PFA/1385	BGA1224 RAFGSA 223	6. 4.70	Permit expired 26.2.93. (Stored 5/97 at Brunton, Northumberland).
G-AYAO	Reims Cessna F.172H	0695		7. 4.70	To OO-YAO. Canx 14.8.85.
G-AYAP	PA-28-180 Cherokee E	28-5794		8. 4.70	To G-GALA 7/89. Canx.

Regn	Type	c/n	Previous identity	Regn date	Fate or immediate subsequent identity (if known)
G-AYAR	PA-28-180 Cherokee E	28-5797		8. 4.70	
G-AYAS	PA-28-180 Cherokee E	28-5800		8. 4.70	To G-GRUB 3/86. Canx.
G-AYAT	PA-28-180 Cherokee E	28-5801		8. 4.70	
G-AYAU	PA-28-180 Cherokee E	28-5802		8. 4.70	To G-ONET 6/98. Canx.
G-AYAV	PA-28-180 Cherokee E	28-5803		8. 4.70	Canx as TWFU 18.10.96. To G-DLTR 15.3.98.
G-AYAW	PA-28-180 Cherokee E	28-5805		14. 4.70	
G-AYAX	BN-2A-6 Islander	613		6. 4.70	Canx 27.10.70 on sale to Australia. To VP-PAM.
G-AYAY	BN-2A-6 Islander	614		6. 4.70	To VQ-FBP. Canx 16.12.70.
G-AYAZ	BN-2A-7 Islander	615	(9V-BDW) G-AYAZ	6. 4.70	To R.Hong Kong AuxAF as HKG-7 in 12/71. Canx.
G-AYBA	BN-2A Islander	616		6. 4.70	To 4X-AYN. Canx 4.3.71.
G-AYBB	BN-2A Islander	617		6. 4.70	To 9Q-CYA 4/71. Canx 11.3.71.
G-AYBC	Reims Cessna F.150K	0549		7. 4.70	Destroyed at Biggin Hill overnight 22/23.2.75. Canx as WFU 18.7.75.
G-AYBD	Reims Cessna F.150K	0583		7. 4.70	
G-AYBE	Agusta-Bell 206A JetRanger	8192		9. 4.70	To F-GALU 6/77. Canx 18.5.77.
G-AYBF	Mooney M.20F Executive 21	670383	N3290F	13. 4.70	To D-EBYE 7/76. Canx 12.7.76.
G-AYBG	Scheibe SF-25B Falke	4696	(D-KECJ)	13. 4.70	
G-AYBH	HS.125 Srs.600B (Originally regd as Srs.400B, changed with effect from 21.10.70)	25256	G-5-13 RP-C111/G-AYBH	10. 4.70	To Irish Air Corps as 236. Canx 12.6.79.
G-AYBI	BN-2A-9 Islander	145	G-51-63	14. 4.70	To VH-ISD 11/71. Canx 19.5.71.
G-AYBJ	Boeing 707-321 (Line No. 68)	17597	N719PA	16. 4.70	To N431MA 4/78. Canx 6.2.78.
G-AYBK	PA-28-180 Cherokee E	28-5806	N11C	14. 4.70	To G-TEMP 5/89. Canx.
G-AYBL	BN-2A Islander	154	G-51-154	15. 4.70	To D-INYL 8/70. Canx 31.7.70.
G-AYBM	BN-2A Islander	162	G-51-162	15. 4.70	To CR-ALQ 6/70. Canx 27.3.72.
G-AYBN	BN-2A Islander	167	G-51-167	15. 4.70	To CR-ALR 6/70. Canx 27.3.72.
G-AYBO	PA-23-250 Aztec D	27-4510	N13874	15. 4.70	
G-AYBP	Wassmer Jodel D.112	1131/17	F-PMEK HB-SOV	16. 4.70	
G-AYBR	Wassmer Jodel D.112	1259	F-BMIG	16. 4.70	
G-AYBS	Sportavia-Putzer Fournier RF-5	5074		20. 4.70	Collided with RF-4D G-AWGO off Needles, IoW 24.6.72. Aircraft beached but was salt-water immersed. Canx 4.10.73.
G-AYBT	PA-28-180 Cherokee E	28-5809		24. 4.70	To N5458N. Canx 11.7.84.
G-AYBU	Omega/Western O-84 HAFB	001		20. 4.70	Canx by CAA 22.4.92.
G-AYBV	Chasle YC-12 Tourbillon	MA.001W & PFA/1335		20. 4.70	Not completed. Canx as WFU 11.7.91. (stored 10/91)
G-AYBW	Reims Cessna FA.150K Aerobat	0044		22. 4.70	Stalled and hit rising ground at Glen Almond Home Farm, 12 miles WNW of Perth on 8.10.72. Canx 24.10.72. (Stored 5/97)
G-AYBX	Campbell Cricket	CA/331		20. 4.70	Canx 1.9.70 on sale to Kuwait.
G-AYBY	Campbell Cricket	CA/332		20. 4.70	Canx 1.9.70 on sale to Kuwait.
G-AYBZ	Campbell Cricket	CA/333		20. 4.70	Canx 1.9.70 on sale to Kuwait.
G-AYCA	Campbell Cricket	CA/334		20. 4.70	Canx 1.9.70 on sale to Kuwait.
G-AYCB	Campbell Cricket	CA/335		20. 4.70	Canx 1.9.70 on sale to Kuwait.
G-AYCC	Campbell Cricket	CA/336		20. 4.70	
G-AYCD	BN-2A Islander	168	G-51-168	22. 4.70	To VH-EQY. Canx 27.5.70.
G-AYCE	Scintex CP.301C-1 Emeraude	530	F-BJFH	20. 4.70	
G-AYCF	Reims Cessna FA.150K Aerobat	0055		22. 4.70	
G-AYCG	SNCAN Stampe SV-4C	59	F-BOHF(2) F-BBAE/French Mil	24. 4.70	
G-AYCH	Hiller 360 UH-12B (H-23B)	687	O-26 Dutch AF/54-872	27. 4.70	Not converted & WFU at Thruxton. Canx as WFU 2.9.74.
G-AYCI	Hiller 360 UH-12B (H-23B)	736	O-8 Dutch AF/54-2942	27. 4.70	Not converted & WFU at Thruxton. Canx as WFU 2.9.74.
G-AYCJ	Cessna TP.206D Turbo Super Skylane	P206-0552	N8752Z	27. 4.70	
G-AYCK	AIA Stampe SV-4C	1139	G-BUNT G-AYCK/F-BANE(2)	28. 4.70	
G-AYCL	Cessna T.210K Turbo Centurion	T210-59306	(N9406M)	28. 4.70	To SE-FTC. Canx 1.3.76.
G-AYCM	Bell 206A JetRanger	529		28. 4.70	Damaged on take-off at Hapton Valley Colliery, near Burnley on 2.10.88. Wreck at Barton 30.8.90. Canx as WFU 23.11.90.
G-AYCN	Piper J3C-65 Cub (C/n as quoted but this became PH-UCM in 11/46. Identity obscure)	"13365"	F-BCPO(2)	28. 4.70	(Stored 4/91)
G-AYCO	CEA Jodel DR.360 Chevalier	362	F-BRFI	29. 4.70	
G-AYCP	Jodel D.112	67	F-BGKO	30. 4.70	
G-AYCR	Morane-Saulnier MS.880B Rallye Club	70	F-BKDX	30. 4.70	Force landed in a field at Rye Errish Farm, Southleigh, Devon on 9.10.70. Canx as destroyed 10.11.70.
G-AYCS	Short SC.7 Skyvan 3M-400-4	SH1876	G-14-48	1. 5.70	To Royal AF of Oman as 903. Canx 9.10.70.
G-AYCT	Reims Cessna F.172H	0724		1. 5.70	
G-AYCU	BN-2A-27 Islander	169	G-51-169	1. 5.70	To CF-CMY. Canx 1.9.70.
G-AYCV	BN-2A-26 Islander	170	G-51-170	1. 5.70	To "VP-LVE"/VP-LVD 9/74. Canx 18.9.74.
G-AYCW	BN-2A-6 Islander	171	G-51-171 (N111VA)/G-AYCW/G-51-171	1. 5.70	To 4X-AYA /73. Canx 28.10.71.
G-AYCX	BN-2A Islander	172	G-51-172	1. 5.70	To VH-EQV. Canx 15.7.70.
G-AYCY	BN-2A-8 Islander	173	G-51-173	1. 5.70	To VH-EQW. Canx 15.7.70.
G-AYCZ	Slingsby Glasflugel (H-401) T.59B Kestrel	19		1. 5.70	To N23FV. Canx 31.7.70.
G-AYDA	PA-25-235 Pawnee C	25-4254	OH-PIW	4. 5.70	DBR near Stamford, Lincs on 23.6.71. Canx as WFU 23.8.73.
G-AYDB	Brighton HAFB	MAB-5		4. 5.70	To D-Westphalia 12/73. Canx 5.12.73.

Regn	Type	c/n	Previous identity	Regn date	Fate or immediate subsequent identity (if known)
G-AYDC	Reims Cessna F.172H Skyhawk	0718		4. 5.70	Fatal crash 400 meters E of Humphrey Head, near Grange-over Sands, Morecombe Bay on 9.12.72. Canx as destroyed 9.7.73.
G-AYDD	SIAI-Marchetti SF-260	2-28	OO-HEL	5. 5.70	To N260GF. Canx 5.5.77.
G-AYDE	PA-23-250 Aztec C	27-3807	N6516Y	5. 5.70	Hit by BAC One-Eleven G-AXMJ at Luton on 18.4.74. Canx as destroyed 9.8.74.
G-AYDF	Cessna 414	414-0091	N8191Q	5. 5.70	To HB-LFS 9/70. Canx 24.7.70.
G-AYDG	Socata MS.894A Rallye Minerva 220	11620		7. 5.70	
G-AYDH	HS.748 Srs.2A/264	1678	F-BSRA G-AYDH/G-11-2	13. 5.70	Broken up for spares in 8/92. Canx as destroyed 25.11.92.
G-AYDI	DH.82A Tiger Moth	85910	F-BDOE(2) French AF/DF174	7. 5.70	
G-AYDJ	Campbell Cricket	CA/321		7. 5.70	Permit expired 13.4.72 & WFU at Enstone. (See G-AXRA)
G-AYDK	Bell 206A JetRanger	337		11. 5.70	To 9J-ACT /71. Canx 5.5.71.
G-AYDL	BN-2A-6 Islander	174	G-51-174	11. 5.70	To CR-ALS 6/70. Canx.
G-AYDM	BN-2A-27 Islander	179	G-51-179	11. 5.70	To LN-VIW 7/70. Canx 1.7.70.
G-AYDN	PA-18-150 Super Cub	18-8874		13. 5.70	To 5Y-ANH /70. Canx 1.12.70.
G-AYDO	Short SC.7 Skyvan 3-200-25	SH1874	(VR-H..) G-AYDO/G-14-46	13. 5.70	Canx 6.9.71 on sale to Hong Kong. To PK-PSA 10/71.
G-AYDP	Short SC.7 Skyvan 3M-400-4	SH1879	G-14-51	13. 5.70	To Royal AF of Oman as 901. Canx 8.6.70.
G-AYDR	SNCAN Stampe SV-4C	307	F-BCLG	13. 5.70	Damaged in an incident on 16.6.73 and WFU 17.8.73. (On rebuild 8/93)
G-AYDS	Snow S.2D-600 Commander	1370D	VH-SNC	15. 5.70	To 4X-ASK. Canx 15.6.71.
G-AYDT	PA-28-140 Cherokee C	28-26558		18. 5.70	Crashed into the Severn Estuary on 24.10.76. Canx.
G-AYDU	AJEP Wittman W.8 Tailwind	AJEP/2 & PFA/1363		18. 5.70	To G-CIPI 7/87. Canx.
G-AYDV	Swalesong SA.II Srs.1	PFA/1353		18. 5.70	Canx as TWFU 11.12.91.
G-AYDW	Beagle A.61 Terrier 2 (Conversion of Auster 6 c/n 1936)	B.646	G-ARLM(1) TW568	20. 5.70	CofA expired 1.7.73. Dismantled at Blackbushe in 1974 prior to its removal. Canx by CAA 1.7.85. (On rebuild in Kings Lynn area in 1999)
G-AYDX	Beagle A.61 Terrier 2	B.647	VX121	20. 5.70	Canx by CAA 24.8.99.
G-AYDY	Phoenix Luton LA-4A Minor	PAL/1302 & PFA/817		21. 5.70	
G-AYDZ	CEA Jodel DR.200	01	F-BLKV F-WLKV	21. 5.70	
G-AYEA	SAN Jodel DR.1050 Ambassadeur	369	F-BKHG	21. 5.70	Crashed into the Bristol Channel off the North Devon coast on 26.3.72. Canx as WFU 11.12.72.
G-AYEB	Wassmer Jodel D.112	586	F-BIQR	26. 5.70	
G-AYEC	Menavia Piel CP.301A Emeraude	249	F-BIMV	26. 5.70	Badly damaged on take-off from Netherthorpe on 6.3.97. Permit expired 10.6.97.
G-AYED	PA-24-260 Comanche C	24-4923	N9417P	28. 5.70	
G-AYEE	PA-28-180 Cherokee E	28-5813		28. 5.70	
G-AYEF	PA-28-180 Cherokee E	28-5815		28. 5.70	
G-AYEG	Falconar F-9	PFA/1321		29. 5.70	
G-AYEH	SAN Jodel DR.1050 Ambassadeur	455	F-BLJB	8. 6.70	
G-AYEI	PA-31-300 Turbo Navajo	31-631	N6730L	29. 5.70	CofA expired 11.5.89. Canx as WFU 5.6.92. Remains on fire dump 9/98 at Southend.
G-AYEJ	SAN Jodel DR.1050 Ambassadeur	253	F-BJYG	1. 6.70	
G-AYEK	SAN Jodel DR.1050 Ambassadeur	282	F-BJYL	1. 6.70	Forced landing in a playing field at Hollins County Primary School, Pilsworth, Bury on 18.10.91. Canx as destroyed 6.11.91.
G-AYEL	Bell 47G-5	25007	N8139J	4. 6.70	To 5B-CFS 1/84. Canx 13.12.83.
G-AYEM	PA-23-250 Aztec D	27-4411	N13762	4. 6.70	Crashed at Glenrothes on 14.3.77. Canx.
G-AYEN	Piper J3C-65 Cub (L-4H-PI) (Frame No 12012; official identity is c/n 9696/43-835 but fuselages probably swopped with F-BGQA on conversion 1952/53)	12184	F-BGQD (F-BGQA)/French AF/44-79888	4. 6.70	
G-AYEO	Dormois Jodel D.112	684	F-BIGG	4. 6.70	Canx as WFU 5.11.74. Fuselage to G-ARDO c/n 146.
G-AYEP	HS.125 Srs.F400B	25219	G-5-14	4. 6.70	To 4W-ACA 1/77. Canx.
G-AYER	HS.125 Srs.400B	25238	9K-ACR G-AYER	4. 6.70	To G-TOPF 7/84. Canx.
G-AYES	Socata MS.892A Rallye Commodore 150	10513	F-BMVJ	8. 6.70	CofA expired 7.8.82. Canx by CAA 12.9.86.
G-AYET	Socata MS.892A Rallye Commodore 150	10565	F-BNBR	8. 6.70	CofA expired 15.9.96. Canx by CAA 22.10.96. (Stored 3/97)
G-AYEU	Brookland Hornet 3 Gyroplane	12		8. 6.70	DBR in heavy landing at St.Merryn, Cornwall on 10.8.81. Canx.
G-AYEV	SAN Jodel DR.1050 Ambassadeur	179	F-BERH(2) F-OBTH/F-OBRH	10. 6.70	
G-AYEW	CEA Jodel DR.1051 Sicile	443	F-BLMJ	11. 6.70	
G-AYEX	Boeing 707-355C (Line No. 582)	19417	N525EJ	12. 6.70	Restored as N525EJ 1/85. Canx 28.12.84.
G-AYEY	Reims Cessna F.150K	0553		15. 6.70	Overturned in forced landing at East Hill Farm, Exbury on 24.6.88. (Stored 8/95 Bournemouth) Canx by CAA 2.3.99.
G-AYEZ	Cessna 180C Skywagon	180-50695	TR-LLP F-OBOG/N9195T	15. 6.70	Crashed at junction of landing strip and Fifield/Bavant Road, near Salisbury on 12.5.74. Wreck moved to Ford.
G-AYFA	Scottish Aviation Twin Pioneer Mk.3 (Originally regd as a CC.2)	538	G-31-15 XM285	15. 6.70	CofA expired 24.5.82. Stored Shobdon. Canx as WFU 16.5.91.
G-AYFB	Reims Cessna F.337E Super Skymaster (Wichita c/n 01242)	0009	EI-AWF G-AYFB	16. 6.70	To 4X-AYX. Canx 17.10.75.
G-AYFC	Rollason-Druine D.62B Condor	RAE/644		19. 6.70	
G-AYFD	Rollason-Druine D.62B Condor	RAE/645		19. 6.70	

Regn	Type	c/n	Previous identity	Regn date	Fate or immediate subsequent identity (if known)
G-AYFE	Rollason-Druine D.62C Condor	RAE/646		19. 6.70	
G-AYFF	Rollason-Druine D.62B Condor	RAE/647		19. 6.70	
G-AYFG	Rollason-Druine D.62C Condor	RAE/648		19. 6.70	Canx by CAA 6.7.87.
G-AYFH	Rollason-Druine D.62B Condor	RAE/649		19. 6.70	To G-YNOT 11/83. Canx.
G-AYFI	PA-39-160 Twin Comanche C/R	39-67	N8922Y N9705N	19. 6.70	To PH-GAD 4/75. Canx 25.3.75.
G-AYFJ	Morane-Saulnier MS.880B Rallye Club	5333	F-BKZR (ZS-CDE)	19. 6.70	CofA expired 18.5.92. (Stored 6/94)
G-AYFK	SIAI-Marchetti SF-260	2-39	OO-HEZ	19. 6.70	To OO-CNL 10/71. Canx 25.9.71.
G-AYFL	HS.748 Srs.2A/269	1679	G-11-1 G-11	22. 6.70	To CF-CSE. Canx 2.10.70.
G-AYFM	HS.125 Srs.403B	25227		22. 6.70	To G-MKOA 6/82. Canx.
G-AYFN	Vickers 952F Vanguard	725	SE-FTK G-41-1-72/G-AYFN/TF-JES/G-AYFN/CF-TKB	23. 6.70	To F-BXAJ. Canx 10.9.75.
G-AYFO	Dornier Bucker Bu.133 Jungmeister	4	HB-MIO Swiss AF U-57	24. 6.70	To N40BJ. Canx 28.4.71. (On rebuild by PPS at Booker 3/96, still painted as G-AYFO)
G-AYFP	SAN Jodel D.140 Mousquetaire	18	F-BMSI F-OBLH/F-WNDO	24. 6.70	
G-AYFR	SNCAN Nord 262A-22 Fregate	29	F-WNDD 4R-ACL/F-BNKX	24. 6.70	To F-BTDQ 2/72. Canx 22.2.72.
G-AYFS	Brookland Hornet Gyroplane	17		25. 6.70	Not completed. Canx 11.7.84.
G-AYFT	PA-39-160 Twin Comanche C/R	39-66	N8911Y	25. 6.70	Restored as N8911Y 8/98. Canx 19.8.98.
G-AYFU	Crosby Andreasson Super BA.4B	001 & PFA/1358		26. 6.70	Spun in at Parham Park, Storrington on 3.6.78. (Wreck to Bovington in 1979) Canx.
G-AYFV	Crosby Andreasson Super BA.4B	002 & PFA/1359		26. 6.70	
G-AYFW	Crosby Andreasson Super BA.4B	003		26. 6.70	Crashed west of Chateauroux, France on 28.7.78. Canx as WFU 24.8.81.
G-AYFX	American Aviation AA-1 Yankee Clipper	AA1-0318	N6118L	26. 6.70	CofA expired 8.7.94. (On rebuild 12/95) Canx as WFU 29.3.96
G-AYFY	EAA Biplane	PFA/1319		26. 6.70	Canx 11.7.84. (Stored, unfinished Tattershall Thorpe 7/91 - since sold to a Public House for display)
G-AYFZ	PA-31-300 Turbo Navajo	31-679	N6771L	30. 6.70	To G-OWLC 6/91. Canx.
G-AYGA	SAN Jodel D.117	436	F-BHNU	30. 6.70	
G-AYGB	Cessna 310Q	310Q-0111	N7611Q	2. 7.70	CofA expired 23.10.87. (Instructional Airframe 10/97) Canx by CAA 23.6.94.
G-AYGC	Reims Cessna F.150K	0556		2. 7.70	
G-AYGD	CEA Jodel DR.1051 Sicile	515	F-BLRE	3. 7.70	
G-AYGE	SNCAN Stampe SV-4C	242	F-BCGM	6. 7.70	(Stored dismantled 7/99 Duxford)
G-AYGF	BN-2A-8 Islander	193	G-51-193	9. 7.70	To VP-LVB 6/72. Canx 16.6.72.
G-AYGG	Wassmer Jodel D.120A Paris-Nice	184	F-BJPH	10. 7.70	
G-AYGH	BN-2A-3 Islander	618		9. 7.70	To EP-AFQ 1/72. Canx 10.1.72.
G-AYGI	BN-2A Islander	619		9. 7.70	To A2-ZFY. Canx 27.4.71.
G-AYGJ	BN-2A-6 Islander	620		9. 7.70	To VH-BAY. Canx 22.6.71.
G-AYGK	IRMA BN-2A-6 Islander	621	SX-BBS G-AYGK	9. 7.70	
G-AYGL	BN-2A-27 Islander	622	SX-BBV G-AYGL	9. 7.70	To C-GKES. Canx 23.5.74.
G-AYGM	Cessna T.210K Turbo Centurion	T210-59338	N9438M	13. 7.70	To G-MIST 12/80. Canx.
G-AYGN	Cessna 210K Centurion	210-59329	N9429M	13. 7.70	To EI-CDX 8/91. Canx 22.7.91.
G-AYGO	Reims Cessna FR.172G Rocket	0146	N10146	14. 7.70	Crashed at Ennistymon, Eire on 1.7.76. The wreck was subsequently taken to Shannon. Canx as WFU 24.8.81.
G-AYGP	PA-25-235 Pawnee	25-5210	N8756L	14. 7.70	Crashed while crop-spraying at East Keal, Lincs on 6.7.77. Canx.
G-AYGR	SNCAN Stampe SV-4C	641	F-BMMI	14. 7.70	Collided with Tiger Moth G-ANMO at Weston-super-Mare 30.7.72 and written-off. Canx.
G-AYGS	BN-2A-7 Islander	182	G-51-182	14. 7.70	To ZS-IJA. Canx 10.8.70.
G-AYGT	BN-2A-7 Islander	183	G-51-183	14. 7.70	To CF-ZUT. Canx 22.2.71.
G-AYGU	BN-2A-6 Islander	190	G-51-190	14. 7.70	To XU-BAE 4/72. Canx 9.12.70.
G-AYGV	BN-2A-6 Islander	191	G-51-191	14. 7.70	To N88CA 4/72. Canx 24.4.72.
G-AYGW	BN-2A-7 Islander	192	ZS-IJB C9-AMO/CR-AMO/ZS-IJB/G-AYGW/G-51-192	14. 7.70	To VP-WHX /78. Canx 3.9.77.
G-AYGX	Reims Cessna FR.172G Rocket	0208		15. 7.70	
G-AYGY	Beechcraft 65-100 King Air	B-79		20. 7.70	To N104TB. Canx 16.10.79.
G-AYGZ	Beechcraft 95-B58 Baron	TH-112		20. 7.70	To F-GEPO 3/87. Canx 16.1.87.
G-AYHA	American Aviation AA-1 Yankee Clipper	AA1-0396	N6196L	21. 7.70	
G-AYHB	American Aviation AA-1 Yankee	AA1-0397		21. 7.70	Fatal crash at Preesall, near Fleetwood on 1.1.71. Canx.
G-AYHC	American Aviation AA-1 Yankee	AA1-0398		21. 7.70	DBR at Perpignan, France on 12.5.71. Canx.
G-AYHD	American Aviation AA-1 Yankee	AA1-0399		21. 7.70	Fatal crash on aproach to Denham at Beverley Nurseries, Denham on 26.4.73. Canx.
G-AYHE	Campbell Cricket	CA/337		21. 7.70	Canx 4.3.72 on sale to Kuwait.
G-AYHF	Campbell Cricket	CA/338		21. 7.70	DBR at Elstree on 30.9.72. Canx as WFU 24.8.81.
G-AYHG	Campbell Cricket	CA/339		21. 7.70	To LN-GGI 4/72. Canx 4.4.72.
G-AYHH	Campbell Cricket	CA/340		21. 7.70	To G-TVSI 4/82. Canx.
G-AYHI	Campbell Cricket	CA/341		21. 7.70	Permit expired 19.8.86. Canx by CAA 2.3.99.

Regn	Type	c/n	Previous identity	Regn date	Fate or immediate subsequent identity (if known)
G-AYHJ	Campbell Cricket	CA/342		21. 7.70	To F-WSYR 7/71R. Canx 21.12.70.
G-AYHK	BN-2A-26 Islander	194	G-51-194	22. 7.70	To VH-RTK. Canx 19.8.70.
G-AYHL	BN-2A-6 Islander	195	G-51-195	22. 7.70	To VH-ISB. Canx 27.10.70.
G-AYHM	BAC One-Eleven Srs.402AP	BAC.161	EC-BQF PI-C1151	22. 7.70	To (D-AFWA)/YR-BCH 8/72. Canx 2.8.72.
G-AYHN	Bell 206A JetRanger	225	N4702R	22. 7.70	To N4802R. Canx 18.12.75.
G-AYHO	English Electric Canberra B.62	HP.183B	G-27-111 WJ616	22. 7.70	To Argentina AF as B101. Canx 28.9.70.
G-AYHP	English Electric Canberra B.62	71234	G-27-112 WJ714	22. 7.70	To Argentina AF as B102. Canx 28.9.70.
G-AYHR	BAC 167 Strikemaster Mk.87 (Regd with c/n "601")	PS.164	OJ4 Botswana	22. 7.70	To G-UNNY 3/98. Canx. DF/Kenyan AF 601/G-27-191/G-AYHR/G-27-191
G-AYHS	BAC 167 Strikemaster Mk.84 (Also c/n EEP/JP/1934)	PS.151	G-27-143	22. 7.70	To Singapore AF as 314 in 9/70. Canx 28.9.70.
G-AYHT	BAC 167 Strikemaster Mk.84 (Also c/n EEP/JP/1935)	PS.152	G-27-144	22. 7.70	To Singapore AF as 315 in 10/70. Canx 28.9.70.
G-AYHU	DH.82A Tiger Moth	86321	F-BGEU NL875	23. 7.70	To N5050C. Canx 19.8.70.
G-AYHV	SNCAN Stampe SV-4C	609	F-BDFE F-ZJFF/F-BDFE	23. 7.70	WFU at Shipdam. Canx as WFU 11.9.74.
G-AYHW	Reims Cessna F.337E Super Skymaster (Wichita c/n 01291)	0019		31. 7.70	To G-SKYM 9/80. Canx.
G-AYHX	SAN Jodel D.117A	903	F-BIVE	23. 7.70	
G-AYHY	Sportavia-Putzer Fournier RF-4D	4156		24. 7.70	
G-AYHZ	PA-28R-200 Cherokee Arrow	28R-35737		28. 7.70	Crashed into Mediterranean Sea on 20.11.76. Canx.
G-AYIA	Hughes 369HS (500)	99-0120S		29. 7.70	Badly damaged in heavy landing in S.France on 1.6.88. CofA expired 16.7.88. (To March Helicopters - stored for spares use 8/97)
G-AYIB	Cessna 182N	182-60366	N92807	30. 7.70	Struck pheasant coop on landing at East Church Farm, Isle of Sheppey on 18.7.90. Canx as WFU 14.12.90.
G-AYIC	PA-28-180 Cherokee E	28-5822		31. 7.70	Canx 1.1.73 on sale to Malta but was lost en route Luqa to Catania 20.12.72 and presumed crashed.
G-AYID	Beechcraft 95-B55A Baron	TC-1283	SE-EXK	27. 7.70	Canx 16.9.75 on sale to West Germany. To SE-GRC 9/75.
G-AYIE	PA-28-180 Cherokee E	28-5843		31. 7.70	Canx 29.9.70 on sale to Switzerland. To I-ALPY 12/70.
G-AYIF	PA-28-140 Cherokee C	28-26877		31. 7.70	
G-AYIG	PA-28-140 Cherokee C	28-26878		31. 7.70	
G-AYIH	PA-28-140 Cherokee C	28-26910		31. 7.70	Fatal crash in a garden of a house in Bedford Road, Cranfield on 7.7.90. Canx as destroyed 25.10.90. (Wreck at AIU Farnborough on 24.5.91)
G-AYII	PA-28R-200 Cherokee Arrow	28R-35736		4. 8.70	
G-AYIJ	SNCAN Stampe SV-4B	376	F-BCOM	4. 8.70	
G-AYIK	Beechcraft B80 Queen Air	LD-370	8P-BAR VQ-BAR(2)	11. 8.70	To N24CA. Canx 9.11.70.
G-AYIL	Scheibe SF-25B Falke	46108	D-KMAC	11. 8.70	Lost power on take-off from Waldershare Park, near Dover on 6.9.87, struck some trees and crashed. Canx by CAA 11.8.88.
G-AYIM	HS.748 Srs.2A/270	1687	G-11-687 CS-TAG/G-AYIM/G-11-5	11. 8.70	
G-AYIN	Cessna 310Q	310Q-0107	N7607Q	12. 8.70	NTU - Not Imported. To D-ICAH 5/71. Canx 1.1.71.
G-AYIO	PA-28-140 Cherokee C	28-26879	N5525U	13. 8.70	Fatal crash into Horseshoe Hill, near Consett on 7.4.92. Canx as destroyed 7.7.92.
G-AYIP	PA-39 Twin Comanche C/R	39-65	N8910Y	14. 8.70	Impounded in Morocco for drug smuggling. Canx 11.4.84 on sale to Morocco.
G-AYIR	HS.748 Srs.2A/264	1681	ZS-LHN 7P-LAI/ZS-LHN/A2-ABC/F-BSRU/CS-TAF/G-AYIR/G-11-3	17. 8.70	To C-FTTW 1/86. Canx 23.1.86.
G-AYIS	BN-2A-6 Islander	205	G-51-205	19. 8.70	To PT-DYL. Canx 18.10.71.
G-AYIT	DH.82A Tiger Moth	86343	F-BGEZ French AF/NL896	20. 8.70	
G-AYIU	Cessna 182N Skylane	182-60411	N92885	24. 8.70	To HB-CGG 9/82. Canx 29.9.82.
G-AYIV	BN-2A-6 Islander	118	(8R-GDN) G-51-45	28. 8.70	To CR-AME 11/70. Canx 3.3.72.
G-AYIW	BN-2A-9 Islander	125	(8R-GDQ) G-51-49	28. 8.70	To CS-AJO 3/72. Canx 2.3.72.
G-AYIX	Short SC.7 Skyvan 3-100-30	SH1884	G-14-56	1. 9.70	To 9N-RAA. Canx 30.11.70.
G-AYIY	Agusta-Bell 206A JetRanger	8199		2. 9.70	To VR-BDR 1/71. Canx 26.1.71.
G-AYIZ	HS.125 Srs.403B (Regd as Srs.400 until 4/79)	25223	F-BSSL PJ-SLB/G-AYIZ/G-5-15	7. 9.70	To G-TACE 1/81. Canx.
G-AYJA	SAN Jodel DR.1050 Ambassadeur	150	F-BJJJ	8. 9.70	
G-AYJB	SNCAN Stampe SV-4C	560	F-BDDF	8. 9.70	
G-AYJC	Stinton-Warren S.31-2	S.31-2/001		8. 9.70	Not built. Canx 5.12.77.
G-AYJD	Alpavia Fournier RF-3	11	F-BLXA	8. 9.70	Permit expired 19.5.95. (Stored 9/97)
G-AYJE	BN-2A-26 Islander (Originally regd as BN-2A-6)	623	CR-CAS G-AYJE/(EI-AVE)/G-AYJE	10. 9.70	To EC-844/EC-FIP. Canx 4.10.91.
G-AYJF	BN-2A-3 Islander	624		10. 9.70	To CR-AOV 1/73. Canx 8.1.74.
G-AYJG	BN-2A-8 Islander	625		10. 9.70	To CR-AOH 1/73. Canx 8.1.74.
G-AYJH	BN-2A-8 Islander	626		10. 9.70	To F-OCQH 8/71. Canx 5.7.71.
G-AYJI	BN-2A-7 Islander	627		10. 9.70	Canx 23.9.71 on sale to USA. To HP-566 10/71.
G-AYJJ	BN-2A-7 Islander	628		10. 9.70	To A40-DJ. Canx 23.10.75.
G-AYJK	BN-2A-7 Islander	629		10. 9.70	To A40-DK. Canx 16.10.75.
G-AYJL	BN-2A-8 Islander	630		10. 9.70	To 9Q-CAE 12/71. Canx 23.12.71.
G-AYJM	Cessna A.188B Agwagon	A188-0444	CN-TEN N8194V	10. 9.70	DBF after crashing nr Bridgwater, Somerset, whilst crop-spraying at Clayhill Farm 9.5.72. Canx.
G-AYJN	Short SC.7 Skyvan 3-100-32	SH1885	G-14-57	14. 9.70	To A40-SN. Canx 2.10.75.

Regn	Type	c/n	Previous identity	Regn date	Fate or immediate subsequent identity (if known)
G-AYJO	Short SC.7 Skyvan 3-100-32	SH1886	G-14-58	14. 9.70	To A40-SO. Canx 23.10.75.
G-AYJP	PA-28-140 Cherokee C	28-26403		15. 9.70	
G-AYJR	PA-28-140 Cherokee C	28-26694		15. 9.70	
G-AYJS	PA-28-140 Cherokee C	28-26916		15. 9.70	To G-SMTH 9/90. Canx.
G-AYJT	PA-28-140 Cherokee C	28-26928	N11C	15. 9.70	To G-MLUA 12/91. Canx.
G-AYJU	Cessna TP.206A Turbo Super Skywagon	P206-0241	N17GWM (N4641F)	16. 9.70	To CS-DAH. Canx 14.4.93.
G-AYJV	DH.82A Tiger Moth	86456	F-BDOC(2) French AF/NM136	17. 9.70	To N88816 5/73. Canx 24.4.73.
G-AYJW	Reims Cessna FR.172G Rocket	0225		17. 9.70	
G-AYJX	Reims Cessna FA.150L Aerobat	0118		23. 9.70	Crashed near Wick on 11.10.76. Canx.
G-AYJY	Isaacs Fury II	PFA/1373		23. 9.70	
G-AYJZ	Cameron (Ax8) O-84 HAFB	16		30. 9.70	To EI-BAY 5/75. Canx 21.5.75.
G-AYKA	Beechcraft 95-B55A Baron	TC-523	HB-GEW G-AYKA/D-IKUN/N8683M	30. 9.70	Badly damaged on landing Elstree 18.6.89. Canx by CAA 28.2.90. (Instructional Airframe 1/99 Shoreham)
G-AYKB	Bede BD-4E-150	151 & BD4E/2		30. 9.70	NTU - Not completed. Parts used to build G-BEKL. Canx by CAA 18.10.84.
G-AYKC	DH.82A Tiger Moth	85729	F-BGEO French AF/DE831	30. 9.70	WFU on 26.10.73. Canx 9.1.84 on sale in USA.
G-AYKD	SAN Jodel DR.1050 Ambassadeur	351	F-BKHR	30. 9.70	
G-AYKE	Socata MS.880B Rallye Club	1783		30. 9.70	To EI-BCW 4/77. Canx 13.4.77.
G-AYKF	Socata MS.880B Rallye Club	1784		30. 9.70	Destroyed in fatal crash on take off from Barton on 26.8.96. Canx by CAA 18.2.97.
G-AYKG	Socata ST-10 Diplomate	117		30. 9.70	Damaged at Crowland on 4.3.75. Canx as WFU 27.6.75.
G-AYKH	Socata MS.880B Rallye Club	1785		30. 9.70	Damaged on take-off from a farm near Winsham, Chard, Somerset 4.10.73. Canx as destroyed 12.11.73.
G-AYKI	Morane-Saulnier MS.500 Criquet	43	F-BJQB French AF	2.10.70	Force landed at Briare, France on delivery. To N44FS. Canx 17.11.70.
G-AYKJ	SAN Jodel D.117A	730	F-BIDX	6.10.70	
G-AYKK	SAN Jodel D.117	378	F-BHGM F-BHDZ	6.10.70	CofA expired 22.5.85. (On rebuild 5/99 Crosland Moor with parts from G-AWEN)
G-AYKL	Reims Cessna F.150L	0676		6.10.70	
G-AYKM	Reims Cessna FA.150L Aerobat	0084		6.10.70	Fatal crash Chevening House, Knockholt, Kent on 25.8.72 & burnt out. Canx.
G-AYKN	BAC One-Eleven Srs.527FK	BAC.215	PI-C1171	7.10.70	Restored as PI-C1171 12/70. Canx 19.5.71.
G-AYKO	PA-39 Twin Comanche C/R	39-80	N8921Y	7.10.70	To N14473 4/73. Canx 10.4.73.
G-AYKP	BN-2A-3 Islander	207	G-51-207	7.10.70	To VH-ISC. Canx 20.11.70.
G-AYKR	BN-2A-2 Islander	217	G-51-217	7.10.70	To VH-MIB. Canx 20.11.70.
G-AYKS	Leopoldoff L.7 Colibri	125	F-PCZX F-APZQ	8.10.70	
G-AYKT	SAN Jodel D.117	507	F-BGYY F-OAYY	9.10.70	
G-AYKU	PA-23-250 Aztec D	27-4521	N13885	12.10.70	To G-CSFT 9/84. Canx.
G-AYKV	PA-28-140 Cherokee C	28-26850		12.10.70	To G-LFSI 7/89. Canx.
G-AYKW	PA-28-140 Cherokee C	28-26931		12.10.70	Badly damaged on landing at Old Warden on 24.7.97. (Stored engineless at Bourn in 4/99)
G-AYKX	PA-28-140 Cherokee C	28-26933		12.10.70	
G-AYKY	PA-28-140 Cherokee C	28-26939		12.10.70	Crashed on landing at Crosby (Carlisle) on 21.3.77. Canx by CAA 20.8.81.
G-AYKZ	SAI KZ-VIII	202	HB-EPB OY-ACB	13.10.70	Permit expired 17.7.81. (Stored 3/95)
G-AYLA	AESL Airtourer T2 (115)	524		12.10.70	
G-AYLB	PA-39 Twin Comanche C/R	39-63	N8908Y	12.10.70	
G-AYLC	CEA Jodel DR.1051 Sicile	536	F-BLZG	12.10.70	
G-AYLD	Vickers 952F Vanguard	730	SE-FTH G-AYLD/CF-TKG	14.10.70	To F-BUFT. Canx 16.11.73.
G-AYLE	Morane-Saunlier MS.880B Rallye Club	1123	F-BPBJ	14.10.70	Fatal crash in farmland shortly after take-off from Dunkeswell on 16.6.95. Canx as destroyed 14.11.95.
G-AYLF	CEA Jodel DR.1051 Sicile	547	F-BLZQ	14.10.70	
G-AYLG	HS.125 Srs.F400B (Originally regd as Srs.400B, series amended on 22.4.85)	25254	3D-AVL G-AYLG	15.10.70	To G-5-624/G-VJAY 3/89. Canx.
G-AYLH	DH.114 Heron 2E	14054	OY-ADV LN-SUL/LN-NPI	15.10.70	To CF-LOL 5/72. Canx 19.5.72.
G-AYLI	HS.125 Srs.400B	25240	G-5-11	15.10.70	To I-GJBO 12/75. Canx 10.11.75.
G-AYLJ	PA-31-300 Turbo Navajo	31-693	N6783L	22.10.70	To N555AV 5/83. Canx 10.5.83.
G-AYLK	SNCAN Stampe SV-4C	673	F-BDNR	22.10.70	Crashed in Ireland in 1971. CofA expired 28.2.74. Canx by CAA 4.12.86.
G-AYLL	CEA Jodel DR.1050 Ambassadeur	11	F-BJHK	27.10.70	
G-AYLM	American Aviation AA-1 Yankee	AA1-0442		21.10.70	To G-SEXY 6/81. Canx.
G-AYLN	American Aviation AA-1 Yankee	AA1-0443		21.10.70	Crashed through a hedge on landing at Shotteswell on 26.1.78. Canx as destroyed 26.11.79.
G-AYLO	American Aviation AA-1 Yankee	AA1-0444		21.10.70	DBR on landing at Rhoose on 23.9.84. Canx by CAA 28.3.85.
G-AYLP	American Aviation AA-1 Yankee	AA1-0445	EI-AVV G-AYLP	21.10.70	
G-AYLR	BN-2A-6 Islander	197	G-51-197	22.10.70	To VP-LAQ 11/70. Canx 3.2.71.
G-AYLS	BN-2A-20 Islander	227	G-51-227	22.10.70	To VH-EDI. Canx 23.2.71.
G-AYLT	Boeing 707-336C (Line No. 854)	20517		23.10.70	To 9Q-CLY 11/81. Canx 17.11.81.
G-AYLU	Pitts S-1S Special	370-H & PFA/1526		23.10.70	To SE-XGU. Canx 17.4.86.

Regn	Type	c/n	Previous identity	Regn date	Fate or immediate subsequent identity (if known)
G-AYLV	Wassmer Jodel D.120 Paris-Nice	300	F-BNCG	27.10.70	Permit expired 13.9.83. (Departed Stapleford pre .88) (Status uncertain)
G-AYLW	Beechcraft 100 King Air	B-80		27.10.70	To N9021J 11/78. Canx 7.11.78.
G-AYLX	Hughes 269C	90-0041		28.10.70	
G-AYLY	PA-23-250 Aztec C	27-3498	N6258Y	28.10.70	Canx by CAA 20.11.90. To G-BXPS 10.12.90.
G-AYLZ	SPP CZL Super Aero 45 Srs.04	06-014	9M-AOF F-BILP	2.11.70	
G-AYMA	Stolp SA.300 Starduster Too	EAA/50553 & PFA/35-10076		5.11.70	To G-BTGS(2) 9/87. Canx.
G-AYMB	BN-2A-27 Islander	200	G-51-200	5.11.70	To F-BTGO 11/72. Canx 22.2.72.
G-AYMC	BN-2A-6 Islander	204	N36JA G-51-204	5.11.70	To HP-556 11/70. Canx.
G-AYMD	Socata MS.880B Rallye Club	1734		5.11.70	Forced-landing at foot of Salt Box Hill on 21.11.72. CofA expired 26.11.72. Canx as WFU 8.8.73.
G-AYME	Sportavia-Putzer Fournier RF-5	5089		6.11.70	
G-AYMF	AESL Airtourer T6/24	B.557		10.11.70	Fatal crash after spinning in near St.Just aerodrome 9.6.72. (Wreck stored 4/96)
G-AYMG	Handley Page HPR.7 Dart Herald 213	179	D-BEBE	13.11.70	WFU 7.7.92. Broken up in 8/94 at Hurn. Canx as WFU 10.1.97.
G-AYMH	Bell 206A JetRanger	586	N7052J	16.11.70	To VR-BEV 1/74. Canx 8.1.74.
G-AYMI	Gulfstream G.1159 Gulfstream II	91	N17586	17.11.70	To VH-ASM 4/73. Canx 10.4.73.
G-AYMJ	PA-28-140 Cherokee C	28-26749		17.11.70	Crashed on take off from Crosby (Carlisle) on 28.11.78 & DBF. Canx by CAA 20.8.81.
G-AYMK	PA-28-140 Cherokee C	28-26772	(PT-DPU)	17.11.70	
G-AYML	PA-28-140 Cherokee C	28-26784		17.11.70	Crashed on take-off from Dunkeswell on 8.9.91. Canx as destroyed 7.11.91.
G-AYMM	Cessna 421B Golden Eagle II	421B-0033	N8033Q	18.11.70	
G-AYMN	PA-28-140 Cherokee C	28-26754	(PT-DPT)	18.11.70	Badly damaged in forced landing near Whitwell, Isle of Wight on 18.9.88. Canx as destroyed 10.11.88. (Fuselage stored 3/95 near Shipdam)
G-AYMO	PA-23-250 Aztec C	27-2995	5Y-ACX N5845Y	18.11.70	
G-AYMP	Phoenix Currie Wot Special	PFA/3014		18.11.70	
G-AYMR	Lederlin 380L Ladybug	EAA/55189 & PFA/1513		19.11.70	(Under construction .92)
G-AYMS	Owl Racer OR65-2	PFA/1519 & OR65-2-1		19.11.70	Fatal crash into River Thames at Greenwich on 31.5.71. Canx.
G-AYMT	SAN Jodel DR.1050 Ambassadeur	454	F-BKHY	19.11.70	Struck power cable in thunderstorm and crashed on the runway of the disused Dalby airfield on 2.6.89. (Stored 8/90) Canx as destroyed 27.1.97.
G-AYMU	Wassmer Jodel D.112	1015	F-BJPB	23.11.70	Badly damaged on landing at Westfield Farm strip, Hailsham, East Sussex on 7.1.92. (On rebuild Eastbourne 7/92)
G-AYMV	Western 20 HAFB	002		23.11.70	(Active 11/95)
G-AYMW	Bell 206B JetRanger (Originally 206A; later modified)	587	EI-BJR G-AYMW	25.11.70	
G-AYMX	Bell 206A JetRanger	605		25.11.70	To G-ONOW 8/88. Canx.
G-AYMY	Bell 47G-5	25023		25.11.70	To 5B-CEQ 2/82. Canx 15.2.82.
G-AYMZ	PA-28-140 Cherokee C	28-26796	N11C	25.11.70	To EI-COZ 11/97. Canx 30.10.97.
G-AYNA	Phoenix Currie Wot	PFA/3016		25.11.70	DBR at Redhill on 17.6.79. Canx.
G-AYNB	PA-31-300 Turbo Navajo	31-688	N6778L	26.11.70	To G-BOIS 11/84. Canx.
G-AYNC	Westland S-58 Wessex 60 Srs.1	WA/739	G-17-1 G-AYNC/VH-SJD/G-AYNC	30.11.70	To 9G-DAN 5/93. Canx 17.8.93.
G-AYND	Cessna 310Q	310Q-0110	N7610Q	2.12.70	
G-AYNE	MBB Bo.209B Monsun 160RV	114	D-EBPC	2.12.70	Not Imported - Crash landed after first flight as D-EBPC. Rebuilt and remained as D-EBPC. Canx 2.12.70.
G-AYNF	PA-28-140 Cherokee C	28-26778	(PT-DPV)	3.12.70	
G-AYNG	PA-28-140 Cherokee C	28-26790		3.12.70	DBF at Elstree on 2.11.81. Canx.
G-AYNH	BN-2A-6 Islander	213	N39JA G-51-213	7.12.70	To CR-AMG. Canx 20.1.71.
G-AYNI	BN-2A-6 Islander	216	G-51-216	7.12.70	To PT-IAS 1/72. Canx 12.1.72.
G-AYNJ	PA-28-140 Cherokee C	28-26810		8.12.70	
G-AYNK	Hughes H.369HE (500HE)	59-0102E	EI-AUA N9012F	9.12.70	To D-HCAB. Canx 13.12.76.
G-AYNL	Cessna 175	175-56094	N6594E	10.12.70	Crashed on take-off from Duck End Farm, Wilstead on 27.12.71. Canx.
G-AYNM	Beechcraft D95A Travel Air	TD-629	N5887J	10.12.70	Fatal crash onto Ullenwood Golf Course, near Cheltenham on 26.8.76. Canx.
G-AYNN	Cessna 185B Skywagon	185-0518	8R-GCC VP-GCC/N2518Z	11.12.70	
G-AYNO	Hughes 269C	100-0054		14.12.70	Crashed near Marsh Brook, north of Ludlow on 22.3.73. Canx.
G-AYNP	Westland WS.55 Whirlwind Srs.3	WA/71	ZS-HCY G-AYNP/XG576	14.12.70	Was stored at Redhill with CofA expired 27.10.85. Delivered to the International Helicopter Museum at Weston-super-Mare by road from Redhill on 14.2.94. Canx by CAA 22.2.94. (To Hubschrauber Museum, Germany 6/95)
G-AYNR	HS.125 Srs.400B	25235	HB-VCE G-5-18	21.12.70	To G-BKAJ 4/82. Canx.
G-AYNS	H2-B1 Helicopter (built by D.J.Fry)	1		21.12.70	CofA expired 13.2.73 & WFU. Canx.
G-AYNT	BN-2A-3 Islander	631		21.12.70	To 9Q-CRP 3/72. Canx.
G-AYNU	BN-2A-3 Islander	632		21.12.70	To 9V-BDH 6/71. Canx 15.7.71.
G-AYNV	BN-2A-7 Islander	633		21.12.70	To 9Q-CYB 9/71. Canx 24.9.71.
G-AYNW	BN-2A-3 Islander	634		21.12.70	To 9V-BEB 12/71. Canx 30.9.71.

Regn	Type	c/n	Previous identity	Regn date	Fate or immediate subsequent identity (if known)
G-AYNX	BN-2A-8 Islander	635		21.12.70	To VP-LVA 10/71. Canx.
G-AYNY	BN-2A-3 Islander	636		21.12.70	To CR-AMX 10/71. Canx 23.10.71.
G-AYNZ	BN-2A-3 Islander	637		21.12.70	To CR-AMU 9/71. Canx 3.9.71.
G-AYOA	BN-2A-7 Islander	638		21.12.70	To 9Q-CYC 9/71. Canx 24.9.71.
G-AYOB	BN-2A-3 Islander	639		21.12.70	To 9V-BFC 1/72. Canx 30.11.71.
G-AYOC	BN-2A-8 Islander	640	CR-CAT G-AYOC	21.12.70	To 4X-CAY. Canx 11.3.88.
G-AYOD	Cessna 172 Skyhawk	172-28379	F-OARV N5779A	21.12.70	Canx 25.3.92 on sale to Sweden. To SE-KYX (Permit reserved 21.5.96).
G-AYOE	Bell 47G	1515	F-OCBF F-BKQZ/D-HEBO	21.12.70	Crashed at Bondon Estate, Exmouth on 16.7.77. (Composite static rebuild, wearing "G-AXKW" and used as heliport marker 3/97) CofA expired 5.5.79.
G-AYOF	Agusta-Bell 47G-2	122	F-OCGB French Mil F-SFN.	21.12.70	To (OE-AXI)/OE-AXT. Canx 13.8.76.
G-AYOG	Agusta-Bell 47G-3	119	F-BIFO French Mil	21.12.70	Crashed at Probus, near Truro on 17.5.78. Used for spares at Thruxton. Canx as destroyed 5.12.83.
G-AYOH	Bell 47G-2A	1637	Gabon Army French AF/N2856B	21.12.70	To OE-AXI. Canx 14.6.76.
G-AYOI	HS.125 Srs.400B	25243	G-5-14	21.12.70	NTU - To PT-DTY(2). Canx 16.2.71.
G-AYOJ	HS.125 Srs.400B	25246	(G-5-16) 9Q-COH/G-AYOJ	21.12.70	To G-LORI 7/83. Canx.
G-AYOK	HS.125 Srs.403B	25250	TR-LQU G-AYOK	21.12.70	To N20S. Canx 22.2.77.
G-AYOL	Gardan GY-80-180 Horizon	176	N3788 F-BNQU	21.12.70	CofA expired 29.6.83 & WFU at Jersey. Canx.
G-AYOM	Sikorsky S-61N Mk.II (Also Mitsubishi c/n M61-001)	61-143	N4585 JA9506/N94565	30.12.70	To EI-SAR 6/98. Canx 26.6.98.
G-AYON	BN-2A-6 Islander	226	G-51-226	4. 1.71	To HP-572 2/71. Canx 5.7.71.
G-AYOO	BN-2A-3 Islander	247	G-51-247	4. 1.71	To CR-AMS 1/71. Canx.
G-AYOP	BAC One-Eleven Srs.530FX	BAC.233		4. 1.71	
G-AYOR	BAC One-Eleven Srs.518FG	BAC.232		4. 1.71	To G-BDAT 2/75. Canx.
G-AYOS	BAC One-Eleven Srs.527FK	BAC.213	PI-C1161	4. 1.71	Restored as PI-C1161. Canx 19.5.71.
G-AYOT	Schiebe SF-27M-A	6310	D-KOBG	6. 1.71	Crashed while turning onto finals at Peron, on the Somme, France on 26.7.78. Canx.
G-AYOU	Cessna 401B	401B-0112	N7972Q	6. 1.71	To N4488A. Canx 24.8.83.
G-AYOV	Reims Cessna FA.150L Aerobat	0104		6. 1.71	DBR at Honiley on 11.2.79. Canx.
G-AYOW	Cessna 182N Skylane	182-60481	N8941G	6. 1.71	
G-AYOX	Vickers 814 Viscount	370	4X-AVA G-AYOX/D-ANAC	6. 1.71	WFU & stored at Teesside in 1/84. CofA expired 14.11.84. Dismantled in 1986 & taken by road to Southend via East Midlands. Canx as WFU 24.2.87.
G-AYOY	Sikorsky S-61N Mk.II	61-476		7. 1.71	
G-AYOZ	Reims Cessna FA.150L Aerobat	0085		7. 1.71	
G-AYPA	Beechcraft A24R Sierra	MC-91		8. 1.71	To G-USTO 10/83. Canx.
G-AYPB	Beechcraft C23 Musketeer	M-1319		8. 1.71	Crashed on the beach at Langney Point, near Eastbourne on 20.6.89. Canx as destroyed 22.8.89.
G-AYPC	Beechcraft 65-70 Queen Air	LB-35		8. 1.71	To G-REXP 9/85. Canx.
G-AYPD	Beechcraft 95-B55A Baron	TC-1389		8. 1.71	To LY-ARA. Canx 23.8.99.
G-AYPE	MBB Bo.209C Monsun 160RV	123	(C-....) G-AYPE/D-EFJA	11. 1.71	
G-AYPF	Reims Cessna F.177RG Cardinal (Wichita c/n 00098)	0006		11. 1.71	To G-OAMP 11/93. Canx.
G-AYPG	Reims Cessna F.177RG Cardinal (Wichita c/n 00102)	0007		11. 1.71	
G-AYPH	Reims Cessna F.177RG Cardinal (Wichita c/n 00146)	0018		11. 1.71	
G-AYPI	Reims Cessna F.177RG Cardinal (Wichita c/n 00177)	0025		11. 1.71	
G-AYPJ	PA-28-180 Cherokee E	28-5821		12. 1.71	
G-AYPK	Reims Cessna FA.150L	0106		12. 1.71	Fatal crash into St.Roche's Hill, near Goodwood on 12.2.80. Canx as destroyed 30.4.80.
G-AYPL	BN-2A-3 Islander	253	ZS-IJC G-AYPL/G-51-253	12. 1.71	To C-GZKG. Canx 24.10.77
G-AYPM	PA-18-95 Super Cub (L-18C-PI) (Frame No. 18-1282)	18-1373	ALAT 18-1373/51-15373	13. 1.71	
G-AYPN	PA-18-95 Super Cub (L-18C-PI)	18-1600	ALAT 18-1600/51-15600	13. 1.71	Crashed at Petersfield on 28.8.71. Canx.
G-AYPO	PA-18-95 Super Cub (L-18C-PI) (Rebuilt 1984 using OO-TSJ c/n 18-1398 (Frame No. 18-1325) - ex (LN-TSJ)/OO-HMH/51-15398) (Old frame possibly to G-BRRL)	18-1615	ALAT 18-1615/51-15615	13. 1.71	
G-AYPP	PA-18-95 Super Cub (L-18C-PI)	18-1626	ALAT 18-1626/51-15626	13. 1.71	Crashed at Stoke St.Mary, Norfolk on 29.12.83. CofA expired 31.8.85. Canx by CAA 30.7.84. (Stored 8/97)
G-AYPR	PA-18-95 Super Cub (L-18C-PI)	18-1631	ALAT 18-1631/51-15631	13. 1.71	
G-AYPS	PA-18-95 Super Cub (L-18C-PI)	18-2092	ALAT 18-2092/52-2492	13. 1.71	
G-AYPT	PA-18-95 Super Cub (L-18C-PI) (Frame No 18-1508)	18-1533	(D-EALX) ALAT 18-1533/51-15533	13. 1.71	
G-AYPU	PA-28R-200 Cherokee Arrow D	28R-7135005		13. 1.71	
G-AYPV	PA-28-140 Cherokee D	28-7125039		13. 1.71	
G-AYPW	PA-28R-200 Cherokee Arrow D	28R-35791		13. 1.71	Fatal crash after take-off at Halfpenny Green on 28.8.72. Canx.

Regn	Type	c/n	Previous identity	Regn date	Fate or immediate subsequent identity (if known)
G-AYPX	BN-2A-21 Islander	271	G-51-271	13. 1.71	To ZS-IRC 3/72. Canx 8.3.72.
"G-AYPX"	BN-2A Mk.III Trislander	245		----	NTU - Painted in error. To G-51-245/G-AYTU. Canx.
G-AYPY	Slingsby T.61D Falke (Originally registered as a Slingsby Scheibe SF-25B Falke)	1723		13. 1.71	To NEJSGSA 9. Canx 9.11.73.
G-AYPZ	Campbell Cricket	CA/343		13. 1.71	Permit expired 20.8.87.
G-AYRA	Campbell Cricket	CA/344		13. 1.71	Badly damaged near Great Billingham School, Norfolk on 28.3.98. Permit expired 31.8.83.
G-AYRB	Campbell Cricket	CA/345		13. 1.71	Canx 26.11.84 on sale to Hong Kong.
G-AYRC	Campbell Cricket	CA/346	Nassau G-AYRC	13. 1.71	Permit expired 17.8.77. Canx as WFU 11.7.84. (Stored at private house 1/96)
G-AYRD	Campbell Cricket	CA/347		13. 1.71	Canx 1.7.71 on sale to Morocco.
G-AYRE	Campbell Cricket	CA/348		13. 1.71	Canx 11.7.84 - possilby on sale in France.
G-AYRF	Reims Cessna F.150L	0665		14. 1.71	
G-AYRG	Reims Cessna F.172K	0761		14. 1.71	
G-AYRH	GEMS MS.892A Rallye Commodore 150	10558	F-BNBX	14. 1.71	CofA expired 28.9.95.
G-AYRI	PA-28R-200 Cherokee Arrow D	28R-7135004		15. 1.71	
G-AYRJ	LeVier Cosmic Wind	101	N20C NX67888	18. 1.71	To N289A. Canx 25.8.78.
G-AYRK	Cessna 150J	150-70856	5N-AII N61170	19. 1.71	CofA expired 25.4.76. Canx by CAA 3.4.89. (Fuselage in ope store 9/94 at Southend)
G-AYRL	Sportavia-Putzer Fournier SFS-31 Milan	6606	D-KIRL	19. 1.71	Damaged on landing in a field at Old Station Road, Bincombe, near Weymouth on 14.6.86. Canx as WFU 26.3.87.
G-AYRM	PA-28-140 Cherokee D	28-7125049		19. 1.71	
G-AYRN	Schleicher ASK-14	14050	D-KISA	20. 1.71	To F-CALG(2) 8/92. Canx 11.8.92.
G-AYRO	Reims Cessna FA.150L Aerobat	0102		21. 1.71	
G-AYRP	Reims Cessna FA.150L Aerobat	0101		21. 1.71	Overturned on landing at Andrewsfield on 2.8.87. Canx as WFU 28.11.89.
G-AYRR(1)	HS.125 Srs.F400	25258		. 1.71R	NTU - To G-AZHS 10/71. Canx.
G-AYRR(2)	HS.125 Srs.403B	25247	G-5-672 9Q-CCF(2)/G-AYRR	21. 1.71	To 9Q-CSN(3). Canx 27.7.93.
G-AYRS	Wassmer Jodel D.120A Paris-Nice	255	F-BMAV	22. 1.71	
G-AYRT	Reims Cessna F.172K	0777		22. 1.71	
G-AYRU	BN-2A-6 Islander	181	G-51-181 OH-BNA/G-51-181	22. 1.71	
G-AYRV	BN-2A-7 Islander	233	G-51-233	26. 1.71	NTU - To CF-ZWF 4/71. Canx.
G-AYRW	BN-2A-3 Islander	272		26. 1.71	NTU - To G-51-272/TC-KUN 8/72. Canx 14.8.72.
G-AYRX	BN-2A-3 Islander	273	G-51-273	26. 1.71	To EP-PAC 5/71. Canx 28.5.71.
G-AYRY	DH 125 Srs.1B/522	25105	D-CKCF (D-CKOW)	29. 1.71	To HZ-FMA. Canx 4.3.81.
G-AYRZ	Boeing 707-321 (Line No. 212)	18084	N758PA	29. 1.71	To G-41-3-72 then VP-BDG 12/72. Canx 8.12.72.
G-AYSA	PA-23-250 Aztec C	27-3799	N6509Y	1. 2.71	
G-AYSB	PA-30-160 Twin Comanche C	30-1916	N8760Y	1. 2.71	
G-AYSC	BAC One-Eleven Srs.524FF	BAC.235		4. 2.71	NTU - To D-AMAT 5/71. Canx 30.3.71.
G-AYSD	Slingsby T.61A Falke	1726		4. 2.71	CofA expired 29.4.94. (Stored 1/95)
G-AYSE	PA-31-300 Turbo Navajo	31-323	9Q-CSO	4. 2.71	To N9248Y. Canx 12.2.76.
G-AYSF	PA-23-250 Aztec D	27-3996	N6777Y	9. 2.71	Crashed near Taala Beacon, near Loch Skeen on 27.7.76. Canx.
G-AYSG	Reima Cessna F.172K	0758		9. 2.71	To EI-BPL 3/85. Canx 18.3.85.
G-AYSH	Taylor JT.1 Monoplane	PFA/1413		10. 2.71	
G-AYSI	Boeing 707-373C (Line No. 349)	18707	N375WA	24. 2.71	To (N3751Y)/HK-2401X 4/80. Canx 1.4.80.
G-AYSJ	Dornier Bucker Bu.133C Jungmeister	38	D-EHVP G-AYSJ/HB-MIW/Swiss AF U-91	12. 2.71	
G-AYSK	Phoenix Luton LA-4A Minor	PFA/832		17. 2.71	
G-AYSL	Boeing 707-321 (Line No. 71)	17599	N721PA	4. 3.71	N80703 11/79. Canx 1.11.79.
G-AYSM	BN-2A-6 Islander	641		16. 2.71	To YR-BNG. Canx 30.6.71.
G-AYSN	BN-2A-9 Islander	642		16. 2.71	To PT-JJI 11/73. Canx 22.11.73.
G-AYSO	BN-2A-21 Islander	643	D-IOLG G-AYSO	16. 2.71	To C-GPAB. Canx 1.2.78.
G-AYSP	BN-2A-9 Islander	644		16. 2.71	To PT-KAC 2/74. Canx 25.2.74.
G-AYSR	BN-2A-9 Islander	645		16. 2.71	To PT-JQF 3/74. Canx 20.3.74.
G-AYSS	BN-2A-8 Islander	646		16. 2.71	To VH-WGT 8/74. Canx 1.8.74.
G-AYST	BN-2A-9 Islander	647		16. 2.71	To (F-OCSB)/F-OCTB 2/73. Canx 20.2.73.
G-AYSU	BN-2A-9 Islander	648		16. 2.71	To Abu Dhabi AF as 204 1/72. Canx 25.1.72.
G-AYSV	BN-2A-9 Islander	649		16. 2.71	To F-BTGH 9/72. Canx 13.4.72.
G-AYSW	BN-2A-9 Islander	650		16. 2.71	To PP-FBU 5/72. Canx 19.5.72.
G-AYSX	Reims Cessna F.177RG Cardinal II (Wichita c/n 00175)	0024		17. 2.71	
G-AYSY	Reims Cessna F.177RG Cardinal II (Wichita c/n 00180)	0026		17. 2.71	
G-AYSZ	Reims Cessna FA.150L Aerobat	0092		19. 2.71	Canx as destroyed 24.4.92. (Possibly to USA for spares)
G-AYTA	Socata MS.880B Rallye Club	1789		19. 2.71	CofA expired 7.11.88. Donated to Manchester Museum of Science & Industry as an instructional airframe in 1991. Canx as wfu 12.5.93.
G-AYTB	Socata MS.880B Rallye Club	1790		19. 2.71	DBR in gales at Newtownards on 25.11.80. Remains sold as spares and removed by road on 15.3.81. Canx by CAA 4.12.86
G-AYTC	PA-E23-250 Aztec C	27-2725	5Y-ABL	19. 2.71	CofA expired 16.11.79 & WFU at Castle Donington. Canx.
G-AYTD	PA-23-250 Aztec C	27-2850	5Y-ACA	19. 2.71	CofA expired 24.2.83 & WFU at Southend. Canx.
G-AYTE	Fairchild-Hiller FH-1100	45	EI-ART	19. 2.71	DBR at Southampton Heliport in 6/71. Canx as WFU 13.9.74.

Regn	Type	c/n	Previous identity	Regn date	Fate or immediate subsequent identity (if known)
G-AYTF	Bell 206A JetRanger	385	N1453W	19. 2.71	To OO-COB. Canx 30.7.86.
G-AYTG	Reims Cessna F.177RG Cardinal II (Wichita c/n 00117)	0010		23. 2.71	To EI-BHC 7/79. Canx 11.7.79.
G-AYTH	Reims Cessna FR.172H Rocket (Regd as a FR.172E, plate on a/c proclaimed it to be a FR.172H - 1st in UK)	0245		23. 2.71	Forced landed and damaged at Warton Sands, Carnforth on 10.8.80. Canx by CAA 18.8.81. Rebuilt & re-regd as G-HANK in 12/82.
G-AYTI	Reims Cessna F.172K	0780		23. 2.71	NTU - Not Imported. To D-ECMC 3/71. Canx.
G-AYTJ	Cessna 207 Super Skywagon	207-00191	N1591U	24. 2.71	To ZS-ODC 8/97. Canx 14.8.96.
G-AYTK	Westland-Sikorsky S-55 Whirlwind Srs.3	WA/65	XJ401	24. 2.71	To VR-BFG 10/74. Canx 11.10.74.
G-AYTL	Gray Free Balloon (Hot-Air)	RFG.1		26. 2.71	NTU - Construction abandoned. Canx 11.7.84.
G-AYTM(1)	Grumman G.164A AgCat	672	N6555	2. 3.71R	NTU - Not Imported. To ZS-AVX(2) 2/72. Canx.
G-AYTM(2)	Grumman G.164A AgCat	797	N6555	23.12.71	To G-WOLL 2/81. Canx.
G-AYTN	Cameron O-65 HAFB	18		3. 3.71	CofA expired 9.5.81. Canx by CAA 22.11.91.
G-AYTO	PA-23-250 Aztec D	27-4568	N14004	3. 3.71	Damaged in flooding of Piper Lock Haven factory on 23.6.72. Canx on sale to USA 1.3.74 & rebuilt as N2799S.
G-AYTP	PA-E23-250 Aztec E	27-4585	N13970	3. 3.71	To ZK-FHO 3/84. Canx 6.3.84.
G-AYTR	Menavia Piel CP.301A Emeraude	229	F-BIMD	3. 3.71	
G-AYTS	BN-2A-7 Islander	235	G-51-235	3. 3.71	To 9V-BDT 12/71. Canx 25.11.71.
G-AYTT	Phoenix PM-3 Duet (Regd as Luton LA-4A Minor III)	PFA/841		4. 3.71	
G-AYTU	BN-2A Mk.III Trislander	245	G-51-245 "G-AYPX"	9. 3.71	To TR-LQL 5/72. Canx 25.1.72.
G-AYTV	Jurca MJ.2D Tempete	PFA/2002		10. 3.71	
G-AYTW	Vickers 803 Viscount	175	(Oman 506) G-AYTW/EI-AOL/PH-VID	11. 3.71	DBF in fire fighting exhibition at Hurn on 12.10.75. Canx.
G-AYTX	Aero Commander 680V	1709-84	9J-RGD	11. 3.71	To ZS-HSA 2/72. Canx 14.2.72.
G-AYTY	Bensen B.8 Gyrocopter	JHW.1 & G/01-1127		11. 3.71	Canx as WFU 29.8.96.
G-AYTZ	Cessna T.210K Turbo Centurion (Wichita-built)	210-59360	N9460M	12. 3.71	NTU - Remained as N9460M, then D-ECGS. Canx.
G-AYUA	Auster AOP.9	B5/10/119	7855M XK416	12. 3.71	(Stored Bruntingthorpe 3/96)
G-AYUB	CEA Jodel DR.253B Regent	185		15. 3.71	
G-AYUC	Reims Cessna F.150L	0706		17. 3.71	Fatal crash in woods 4 miles north-east of Market Rasen on 3.6.85. Canx as destroyed 17.6.85.
G-AYUD	PA-25-235 Pawnee	25-3717	OH-PIH N4477Y/N4457Y/HC-ALB	17. 3.71	Crashed at St.Ives Farm, East Grinstead on 17.6.81. Canx.
G-AYUE	Air & Space 18A Gyroplane	18-61	N6150S	17. 3.71	DBR after overturning at Membury on 21.5.71. Canx.
G-AYUF	PA-31-310 Turbo Navajo	31-700	EI-BAE G-AYUF/N6790L	17. 3.71	To G-SUZE 10/82. Canx.
G-AYUG	PA-28-140 Cherokee D	28-7125139		17. 3.71	To G-JIMY 5/81. Canx.
G-AYUH	PA-28-180 Cherokee F	28-7105042		17. 3.71	
G-AYUI	PA-28-180 Cherokee F	28-7105043	N8557 G-AYUI	17. 3.71	CofA expired 5.11.93. Semi-derelict and in open storage at Andrewsfield with parts missing 3/99. Canx by CAA 27.10.98.
G-AYUJ	Evans VP-1	PFA/1538		17. 3.71	Damaged in forced landing off Ainsdale Beach, Southport on 16.6.96. Permit expired 28.2.97.
G-AYUK	Western-Brighton M-B65 HAFB	003		17. 3.71	To D-Westfalen II in 12/73. Canx 10.12.73.
G-AYUL	PA-23-250 Aztec E	27-4611	N13992	19. 3.71	To N139DB. Canx 17.10.91.
G-AYUM	Slingsby T.61A Falke	1730		19. 3.71	
G-AYUN	Slingsby T.61A Falke	1731		19. 3.71	
G-AYUO	Slingsby T.61A Falke	1732		19. 3.71	Crashed on approach to Booker on 17.2.73. Canx.
G-AYUP	Slingsby T.61A Falke	1735	XW983 G-AYUP	19. 3.71	CofA expired 15.7.96. (Stored 2/97 RAF Bicester)
G-AYUR	Slingsby T.61A Falke	1736		19. 3.71	
G-AYUS	Taylor JT.1 Monoplane	PFA/1412		19. 3.71	Overturned on landing at Coombe Down, Salisbury on 3.11.92. Permit expired 8.10.93.
G-AYUT	SAN Jodel DR.1050 Ambassadeur	479	F-BLJZ	22. 3.71	
G-AYUU	PA-23-250 Aztec C	27-3640	N6367Y	26. 3.71	To 4X-AJM. Canx 10.10.75.
G-AYUV	Reims Cessna F.172H	0752		26. 3.71	
G-AYUW	BAC One-Eleven Srs.476FM (Originally regd as a Srs.475EZ)	BAC.239	OB-R-953 G-16-17/G-AYUW	26. 3.71	Overhaul abandoned at Luton & WFU. Stored at Luton; Broken up in 6/88 - Fuselage at Hurn for water sprinkler trials; departed 8.8.94. Canx as WFU 8.11.88.
G-AYUX	DH.82A Tiger Moth	86560	F-BDOQ French AF/PG651	26. 3.71	To I-EDAI. Canx 6.5.88.
G-AYUY	Reims Cessna FA.150K Aerobat	0081		26. 3.71	To G-POTS 11/91. Canx.
G-AYUZ	Reims Cessna FA.150L Aerobat	0114		26. 3.71	NTU - Canx 6.12.71 as not imported. To D-ECPP 10/71.
G-AYVA	Cameron O-84 HAFB	17		30. 3.71	(Non-airworthy) Canx by CAA 19.5.93. (On loan to The Balloon Preservation Group 7/98)
G-AYVB	Reims Cessna F.172K	0792		30. 3.71	To G-TOBI 1/84. Canx.
G-AYVC	PA-23-250 Aztec E	27-4607	N13989	30. 3.71	To N29226. Canx 21.4.82.
G-AYVD	Not allocated.				
G-AYVE	Boeing 707-321 (Line No. 209)	18083	N757PA	2. 4.71	To (N757PA)/N423MA 1/78. Canx.
G-AYVF	HS.121 Trident 3B Srs.101	2325	(G-AWZY)	14. 4.71	WFU at Heathrow 1.2.85; Broken up at Southend. Canx as destroyed 29.1.85.
G-AYVG	Boeing 707-321 (Line No. 70)	17598	N720PA	5. 4.71	To N3791G 7/80. Canx 22.7.80.
G-AYVH	DH.82A Tiger Moth	86621	F-BGEG PG735	30. 3.71	To N45TM. Canx 17.5.71.
G-AYVI	Cessna T.210H Turbo Centurion	T210-0351		31. 3.71	Crashed at Dods Farm, Lauder, Berwicks on 24.11.89 & DBR. Canx 25.7.90 on sale in the USA. To Dodson Aviation Scrapyard and probably for spares use.

Regn	Type	c/n	Previous identity	Regn date	Fate or immediate subsequent identity (if known)
G-AYVJ	PA-23-250 Aztec D	27-4020	N6747Y	2. 4.71	To OY-BSY. Canx 13.7.83.
G-AYVK	BAC 167 Strikemaster Mk.83 (C/n also reported as 168)	PS.174	G-27-189	5. 4.71	To G-27-189 6/71 / Kuwaiti AF as 120 in 7/71. Canx.
G-AYVL	BAC 167 Strikemaster Mk.83 (C/n also reported as 169)	PS.175	G-27-190	5. 4.71	To G-27-190 6/71 / Kuwaiti AF as 121 in 7/71. Canx.
G-AYVM	PA-31-300 Turbo Navajo	31-516	N6589L	5. 4.71	To N91RS. Canx 12.8.83.
G-AYVN	Luton LA-5A Major	PFA/1204		6. 4.71	Fatal crash between Goborne and Culcheth (Warrington) on 31.5.81. Canx.
G-AYVO	Wallis WA-120 Srs.1	K/602/X		6. 4.71	Permit expired 31.12.75. (Stored 2/99 Reymerston Hall)
G-AYVP	Aerosport Woody Pusher	181 & PFA/1344		6. 4.71	(Stored incomplete)
G-AYVR	HS.748 Srs.2A/216	1700	G-11-5 PK-IHD/G-AYVR/G-11-7	8. 4.71	Restored as PK-IHD 1/73. Canx 9.1.73.
G-AYVS	DH.106 Comet 4C	6474	9K-ACE	8. 4.71	WFU at Lasham on 6.1.77. Broken up in 4/78. Canx as WFU 13.10.78.
G-AYVT	Maurice Brochet MB.84	9	F-BGLI	13. 4.71	Damaged 28.6.77 and later stored at Tattershall Thorpe. Canx as WFU 3.9.81. (Stored 8/90)
G-AYVU	Cameron O-56 HAFB	19		14. 4.71	Canx by CAA 1.4.92.
G-AYVV	Socata ST.10 Diplomate	126		14. 4.71	Crashed near Wooley Service Station, Yorks on the M.1 Motorway on 30.9.79. Canx as WFU 9.8.81.
G-AYVW	Socata MS.894A Rallye Minerva 220	11836		14. 4.71	NTU - To D-EAHL(2) 2/72. Canx 12.1.73 as not imported.
G-AYVX	Socata MS.893A Rallye Commodore 180	11637	F-BSFJ	14. 4.71	To G-GIGI 9/81. Canx.
G-AYVY	DH.82A Tiger Moth	86526	F-BGCZ French AF/PG617	14. 4.71	Substantially damaged when caught by a gust of wind on landing at Liverpool on 22.5.87. Canx 21.2.89 on sale to Sweden. To SE-AMI 7/90.
G-AYVZ	Jodel D.11	PFA/902		14. 4.71	DBF whilst under construction at Rochester in 6/71. Canx as destroyed 21.3.73.
G-AYWA	Avro 652A Anson 19 Srs.2	1361	OO-VIT OO-DFA/OO-CFA	14. 4.71	Transferred to the Will Roberts collection at Auchterarder. Canx as PWFU 22.8.73. (Stored 5/95)
G-AYWB	BAC One-Eleven Srs.531FS	BAC.237	EI-CCU G-DJOS/G-AYWB/VR-CAB/TI-LRL/TI-LRF/TI-1084C/G-AWYB	14. 4.71	To ZS-NUG 7/95. Canx 25.5.95.
G-AYWC	Not allocated.				
G-AYWD	Cessna 182N Skylane	182-60468	N8928G	15. 4.71	
G-AYWE	PA-28-140 Cherokee C	28-26826	N5910U	16. 4.71	
G-AYWF	PA-23-250 Aztec C	27-3911	N6606Y	16. 4.71	Canx 27.6.85 on sale to USA. To Dodson Aviation Scrapyard in the USA. Regd as N250BH in 7/85.
G-AYWG	PA-E23-250 Aztec C	27-3926	N6620Y	16. 4.71	CofA expired 9.11.85. Canx as WFU 2.12.86. Used for spares at Shoreham.
G-AYWH	SAN Jodel D.117A	844	F-BIVU	16. 4.71	
G-AYWI	BN-2A Mk.III-1 Trislander	262	G-51-262	19. 4.71	To G-OCME 5/86. Canx.
G-AYWJ	BN-2A-10 Islander	276	(HP-547) G-AYWJ/G-51-276	19. 4.71	To CR-LMW 3/73. Canx 25.1.73.
G-AYWK	PA-32-300 Cherokee Six D	32-7140008	N8616N	19. 4.71	To G-LADA 1/80. Canx.
G-AYWL	Taylor Monoplane Mk.2	PFA/1435		20. 4.71	NTU - Construction abandoned. Canx 5.12.83.
G-AYWM	AESL Airtourer T5 (Super 150)	A.534		16. 4.71	
G-AYWN	Scottish Aviation Bulldog Srs.100	BH.100-101		19. 4.71	To Swedish Army as Fv61001 7/71. Canx 29.7.71.
G-AYWO	Scottish Aviation Bulldog Srs.100	BH.100-102		19. 4.71	To Swedish Army as Fv61002 7/71. Canx 29.7.71.
G-AYWP	Scottish Aviation Bulldog Srs.100	BH.100-103		19. 4.71	To Swedish Army as Fv61003 8/71. Canx 7.8.71.
G-AYWR	Handley Page 137 Jetstream 200 (Production No. 42)	243	G-8-13	20. 4.71	Canx 31.1.74 as WFU. To G-BBYM 13.2.74.
G-AYWS	Beechcraft C23 Musketeer	M-1351		20. 4.71	DBF in ground collision with DH.83 G-ACEJ at Old Warden on 17.7.82. Canx as destroyed 5.12.83.
G-AYWT	AIA Stampe SV-4C	1111	F-BLEY(2) F-BAGL(2)	21. 4.71	
G-AYWU	Cessna 150G	150-65352	N4052J	21. 4.71	CofA expired 22.6.72 & WFU.
G-AYWV	PA-39-160 Twin Comanche C/R	39-84	N8927Y	21. 4.71	To N289WW 3/81. Canx 6.3.81.
G-AYWW	PA-28R-200 Cherokee Arrow D	28R-7135049	N11C	21. 4.71	To G-GYMM 2/90. Canx.
G-AYWX	DH.106 Comet 4C	6465	9K-ACA	22. 4.71	Canx as WFU 2.5.78. Broken up Lasham 10/79.
G-AYWY	PA-E23-250 Aztec D	27-4069	EI-ATI N6735Y	22. 4.71	Crashed on landing at Castlebridge, Wexford on 15.10.75. Canx as destroyed 26.3.76. (Instructional airframe 5/92 Dublin College of Technology)
G-AYWZ	PA-39-160 Twin Comanche C/R	39-85	N8928Y	22. 4.71	Canx 10.8.81 on sale to USA; Became G-SJAB 9/81.
G-AYXA	PA-39-160 Twin Comanche C/R	39-86	N8929Y	22. 4.71	To N4225N. Canx 10.2.81.
G-AYXB	BAC One-Eleven Srs.521EH	BAC.192	LV-JNR PP-SDP/LV-JNR/G-16-7	22. 4.71	Restored as LV-JNR. Canx 8.10.71.
G-AYXC	IRMA BN-2A-20 Islander	651		26. 4.71	To CS-AJU 4/75. Canx 21.4.75.
G-AYXD	IRMA BN-2A-9 Islander	652		26. 4.71	To "PP-FBY"/PP-FBV 5/72. Canx 19.5.72.
G-AYXE	IRMA BN-2A-8 Islander	653		26. 4.71	To EI-AWM 5/73. Canx 24.8.73.
G-AYXF	IRMA BN-2A-3 Islander	654	CS-AGH G-AYXF	26. 4.71	Restored as CS-AGH 8/72. Canx 24.8.72.
G-AYXG	BN-2A-2 Islander	655		26. 4.71	To EP-PAF 10/72. Canx 23.10.72.
G-AYXH	BN-2A-8 Islander	656		26. 4.71	To CR-ANJ 1/74. Canx 8.1.74.
G-AYXI	BN-2A-8 Islander	657		26. 4.71	To F-BTOY 10/72. Canx 19.7.72.
G-AYXJ	BN-2A-8 Islander	658		26. 4.71	To CR-ANH 9/72. Canx 8.9.72.
G-AYXK	BN-2A-26 Islander	659		26. 4.71	To D-IAJW. Canx 12.6.80.
G-AYXL	BN-2A-21 Islander	660		26. 4.71	To ZS-VIS(2) 1/73. Canx 16.1.73.

Regn	Type	c/n	Previous identity	Regn date	Fate or immediate subsequent identity (if known)
G-AYXM	Campbell Cricket	CA/349		27. 4.71	To I-NANO 3/76. Canx 17.9.75.
G-AYXN	Campbell Cricket	CA/350		27. 4.71	To VR-HGV 2/72. Canx 25.2.72.
G-AYXO	Phoenix Luton LA-5A Major	PFA/1211		27. 4.71	No Permit issued. (Believed completed and flown in 1977)
	(Flown in 1971 with 65hp Walter Minor but not certified)				Canx by CAA 2.9.91. (Stored 1/96)
G-AYXP	SAN Jodel D.117A	693	F-BIDD	27. 4.71	
G-AYXR	Boeing 707-321	17608	N730PA	7. 5.71	To N37681 4/80. Canx 6.6.80.
	(Line No. 122)				
G-AYXS	SIAI-Marchetti S.205-18R	4-165	OY-DNG	28. 4.71	
G-AYXT(1)	Westland-Sikorsky S-55 Whirlwind		XK906	. 4.71R	NTU - Broken up. Canx.
	HAS.7	WA/153			
G-AYXT(2)	Westland-Sikorsky S-55 Whirlwind		XK940	28. 4.71	(On rebuild 3/97)
	HAS.7 (Srs.2)	WA/167			
G-AYXU	Champion 7KCAB Citabria	232-70	N7587F	28. 4.71	
G-AYXV	Reims Cessna FA.150 Aerobat	0117		29. 4.71	Extensively damaged after hitting cables on overshoot from Popham on 5.9.79. (Stored at Popham). Canx as WFU 24.9.79.
G-AYXW	Evans VP-1	PFA/1544		30. 4.71	
G-AYXX	Reims Cessna F.172H Skyhawk	0656		3. 5.71	DBF on 31.12.82. Canx.
G-AYXY	PA-39-160 Twin Comanche C/R	39-87	N8930Y	4. 5.71	To G-OGET 3/83. Canx.
G-AYXZ	PA-39-160 Twin Comanche C/R	39-88	N8931Y	4. 5.71	To N289ZZ 2/81. Canx 2.12.80.
G-AYYA	BN-2A-27 Islander	278	G-51-278	6. 5.71	To VH-ISE. Canx 22.10.71.
G-AYYB	BN-2A-20 Islander	281	G-51-281	6. 5.71	To VH-ISF 5/72. Canx 30.5.72.
G-AYYC	Taylor JT.1 Monoplane	PFA/1421		7. 5.71	To EI-BKK 2/81. Canx 9.1.81.
G-AYYD	Socata MS.894A Rallye Minerva 220	11826		7. 5.71	Canx 20.6.91 on sale to Ireland. (Badly damaged Isle of Eigg 5/75)
G-AYYE	Reims Cessna F.150L	0715		10. 5.71	DBR at Staverton on 26.4.78. (Wreck in open store 12/93)
G-AYYF	Reims Cessna F.150L	0716		10. 5.71	Destroyed in forced landing at Aber Farm, Talybont-on-Usk, Dyfed on 27.11.90. Canx as destroyed 18.5.99.
G-AYYG	HS.748 Srs.2A/275	1697	ZK-MCF	10. 5.71	To G-OSOE 11/97. Canx.
			C-GRCU/ZK-MCF/G-AYYG/ZK-MCF/G-AYYG/ZK-MCF/G-AYYG/G-11-9		
G-AYYH	HS.748 Srs.2A/266LFD	1701	G-11-8	10. 5.71	To 5W-FAN 1/72. Canx 22.11.71.
G-AYYI	Westland WS-55 Whirlwind 3	WAH/82	XG587	10. 5.71	To 5N-AIS 7/71. Canx 28.7.71.
G-AYYJ	Slingsby T.61A Falke	1733		10. 5.71	To SE-TMD 7/71. Canx 14.6.71.
G-AYYK	Slingsby T.61A Falke	1737		10. 5.71	
G-AYYL	Slingsby T.61A Falke	1738		10. 5.71	Damaged in a gale at Manston on 15.12.82. (On rebuild 7/90)
G-AYYM	Bede BD-4	29		10. 5.71	Canx as WFU 6.12.71. (Probably completed in Pittsburgh, USA where the owner lived)
G-AYYN	PA-28R-200 Cherokee Arrow D	28R-7135054		10. 5.71	Collided with Bo.209 G-AZVC on 19.8.84 and crashed at The Street, Cobham, Kent. Canx as destroyed 25.2.85.
G-AYYO	CEA Jodel DR.1050/M1 Sicile Record	622	EI-BAI	11. 5.71	
			G-AYYO/F-BMPZ		
G-AYYP	BN-2A-6 Islander	243	G-51-243	11. 5.71	To N119DW. Canx 29.9.71.
G-AYYR	Short SC.7 Skyvan 3-100-19	SH1864	G-14-36	12. 5.71	To 9M-AQG /71. Canx 16.8.71.
			CF-TAI/G-14-36		
G-AYYS	Mooney M.20C Ranger	2002	YV-T-RTG	12. 5.71	To N222YS 7/73. Canx 20.7.73.
			(N78968)		
G-AYYT	CEA Jodel DR.1050/M1 Sicile Record	587	F-BMGU	13. 5.71	
G-AYYU	Beechcraft C23 Musketeer Custom	M-1353		14. 5.71	
G-AYYV	BN-2A-6 Islander	219	G-51-219	17. 5.71	To CR-AMV 7/71. Canx.
G-AYYW	BN-2A-2 Islander	277	D-IOLA	17. 5.71	
			G-AYYW/G-51-277		
G-AYYX	Socata MS.880B Rallye Club	1812		18. 5.71	
G-AYYY	Socata MS.880B Rallye Club	1849		18. 5.71	CofA expired 28.4.86. (Stored Panshangar) Canx by CAA 21.2.97.
G-AYYZ	Socata MS.880B Rallye Club	1850		18. 5.71	To G-OLFS 4/88. Canx.
G-AYZA	Short SC.7 Skyvan 3-100-34	SH1892	G-14-64	18. 5.71	Canx 6.9.71 on sale to Hong Kong. To PK-PSD 10/71.
G-AYZB	Short SC.7 Skyvan 3-100-34	SH1893	G-14-65	18. 5.71	Canx 6.9.71 on sale to Hong Kong. To PK-PSC 10/71.
G-AYZC	PA-E23-250 Aztec D	27-4570	N13955	19. 5.71	To 5B-CGC(2). Canx 22.4.86.
G-AYZD	Short SC.7 Skyvan 3M-400-9	SH1894	G-14-66	20. 5.71	To Nepalese Army as RA-N14. Canx 20.9.71.
G-AYZE	PA-39-160 Twin Comanche C/R	39-92	N8934Y	20. 5.71	
G-AYZF	Western O-65 HAFB	004		20. 5.71	To F-WTEI/F-BTEI 4/72. Canx 4.4.72.
G-AYZG	Cameron O-84 HAFB	21		21. 5.71	To OO-BAP 5/77. Canx 25.5.77.
G-AYZH	Taylor JT.2 Titch	PFA/1316		21. 5.71	No Permit issued - probably not completed. Canx by CAA 23.2.99.
G-AYZI	SNCAN Stampe SV-4C	15	(EI-...)	24. 5.71	(On rebuild 6/98 at Spanhoe)
			G-AYZI/F-BBAA(2)/French Mil		
G-AYZJ	Westland WS-55 Whirlwind HAS.7	WA/263	XM685	24. 5.71	Marks were NTU. Canx as WFU 29.12.80. (On display 2/99 Winthorpe as XM685)
	(Also c/n WAG/34)				
G-AYZK	CEA Jodel DR.1050/M1 Sicile Record	590	F-BMGY	24. 5.71	
G-AYZL	Scottish Aviation Bulldog Srs.101	BH.100-104		25. 5.71	To Swedish Army as Fv61004 8/71. Canx 27.8.71.
G-AYZM	Scottish Aviation Bulldog Srs.101	BH.100-105		25. 5.71	To Swedish Army as Fv61005 8/71. Canx 2.9.71.
G-AYZN	PA-E23-250 Aztec D	27-4220	N6874Y	26. 5.71	To 5N-... 6/95. Canx 28.6.95.
G-AYZO	PA-E23-250 Aztec C	27-3321	N6112Y	26. 5.71	To EI-BLA 4/81. Canx 3.4.81.
			CF-THZ/N6112Y		
G-AYZP	PA-39-160 Twin Comanche C/R	39-91	N8933Y	28. 5.71	To EI-AYG 2/74. Canx 7.1.74.
G-AYZR	BN-2A Mk.III Trislander	279	G-51-279	3. 6.71	To N85CA. Canx 27.8.71.
G-AYZS	Rollason-Druine D.62B Condor	RAE/650		4. 6.71	

Regn	Type	c/n	Previous identity	Regn date	Fate or immediate subsequent identity (if known)
G-AYZT	Rollason-Druine D.62B Condor	RAE/651		4. 6.71	While towing a glider at Whatfield on 25.6.89 the engine failed, the glider released itself but the aircraft went into a spin and crashed near the strip. Canx as destroyed 14.8.89.
G-AYZU	Slingsby T.61A Falke	1740		4. 6.71	
G-AYZV	Slingsby T.61A Falke	1741		4. 6.71	To OY-VXD 4/73. Canx 10.4.73.
G-AYZW	Slingsby T.61A Falke	1743		4. 6.71	
G-AYZX	Sportavia-Putzer Fournier RF-5	5100		7. 6.71	DBF in hangar fire at Kenley on 23.10.78. Canx.
G-AYZY	PA-30-160 Twin Comanche C/R	30-89	N8949Y	7. 6.71	To N111DS 7/84. Canx 18.7.84.
G-AYZZ	Boeing 707-323C (Line No. 741)	20089	N8417 G-AYZZ/N8417	8. 6.71	Restored as N8417 12/73. Canx 31.12.73.
G-AZAA	Cameron O-84 HAFB	22		8. 6.71	To SE-ZZT 8/73. Canx 29.6.73.
G-AZAB	PA-30-160 Twin Comanche B	30-1475	5H-MNM 5Y-AGB	8. 6.71	
G-AZAC	PA-31-310 Navajo B	31-701	N6791L	8. 6.71	To F-BSGU 3/76. Canx 25.3.76.
G-AZAD	CEA Jodel DR.1051 Sicile	501	F-BLMX	10. 6.71	Fatal crash near Rosemarkie Mast, near Fortrose on 9.5.99. (Wreck at Inverness 6/99)
G-AZAE	HS.748 Srs.2A/274	1695	G-11-10 PK-MHD	14. 6.71	To PK-MHM 12/71. Canx 13.12.71.
G-AZAF	HS.125 Srs.400B	25249	G-5-16	16. 6.71	To N51993 12/76. Canx 3.12.76.
G-AZAG	Agusta Bell 206A JetRanger	8101	HB-XCY	18. 6.71	Crashed on sands near Cark, Flookburgh on 30.10.79. Canx as destroyed 5.12.83.
G-AZAH	CEA Jodel DR.1050/M1 Sicile Record	580	OY-DFM F-BMGP	18. 6.71	Fatal crash into Ivinghoe Beacon, near Tring on 5.4.75. Canx.
G-AZAI	PA-28-140 Cherokee D	28-7125362		18. 6.71	Fatal crash into Loch Tay on take-off from a field adjacent to Ardeonaig Hotel, Kenmore on 8.3.75. Canx.
G-AZAJ	PA-28R-200 Cherokee Arrow B	28R-7135116		18. 6.71	
G-AZAK	Scottish Aviation Bulldog Srs.101	BH.100-106		18. 6.71	To Swedish Army as Fv61006 9/71. Canx 17.9.71.
G-AZAL	Scottish Aviation Bulldog Srs.101	BH.100-107		18. 6.71	To Swedish Army as Fv61007 9/71. Canx 26.9.71.
G-AZAM	Scottish Aviation Bulldog Srs.101	BH.100-108		18. 6.71	To Swedish Army as Fv61008 10/71. Canx 3.10.71.
G-AZAN	Scottish Aviation Bulldog Srs.101	BH.100-109		18. 6.71	To Swedish Army as Fv61009 10/71. Canx 12.10.71.
G-AZAO	Scottish Aviation Bulldog Srs.101	BH.100-110		18. 6.71	To Swedish Army as Fv61010 10/71. Canx 18.10.71.
G-AZAP	Scottish Aviation Bulldog Srs.101	BH.100-111		18. 6.71	To Swedish Army as Fv61011 11/71. Canx 1.11.71.
G-AZAR	Scottish Aviation Bulldog Srs.101	BH.100-112		18. 6.71	To Swedish Army as Fv61012 11/71. Canx 7.11.71.
G-AZAS	Scottish Aviation Bulldog Srs.101	BH.100-113		18. 6.71	To Swedish Army as Fv61013 11/71. Canx 13.11.71.
G-AZAT	Scottish Aviation Bulldog Srs.101	BH.100-114		18. 6.71	To Swedish Army as Fv61014 11/71. Canx 7.11.71.
G-AZAU	Cierva CR. LTH-1 Rotorcraft Grasshopper III (Incomplete - only floor pan, panel, power and lift group)	GB.3		21. 6.71	Not completed. Canx as WFU 5.12.83. (Stored 3/96 Weston-super-Mare) (Orig. regd as an Servotec Grasshopper 02 with same c/n)
G-AZAV	Cessna 337F Super Skymaster	337-01388	N1788M	22. 6.71	To 9L-L.. 4/97. Canx 10.4.97.
G-AZAW	Gardan GY-80-160 Horizon	104	F-BMUL	24. 6.71	
G-AZAX	BN-2A-7 Islander	241	CF-QPM G-51-241	28. 6.71	Restored as CF-QPM 7/71. Canx 14.7.71.
G-AZAY	Aeromere F.8L Falco 3	230	D-EFAK	30. 6.71	To HB-UOG 6/73. Canx 12.3.76.
G-AZAZ	Bensen B.8M Gyrocopter	RNEC.1		2. 7.71	(Stored 3/96 Wroughton)
G-AZBA	Tipsy T.66 Nipper Srs.3B (Slingsby-built kit)	ESJT.1 & PFA/1390		30. 6.71	Not completed. Canx as WFU 19.9.75. (Preserved Yeovilton Museum)
G-AZBB	MBB Bo.209C Monsun 160FV	137	D-EFJO	1. 7.71	
G-AZBC	PA-39-160 Twin Comanche C/R	39-111	N8951Y	1. 7.71	
G-AZBD	PA-39-160 Twin Comanche C/R	39-112	N8952Y	1. 7.71	To N289XX. Canx 9.7.81.
G-AZBE	AESL Airtourer T5 (Super 150)	A.535		5. 7.71	
G-AZBF	PA-39-160 Twin Comanche C/R	39-113	N8953Y	8. 7.71	To N125AC. Canx 27.5.81.
G-AZBG	PA-31-310 Turbo Navajo	31-569	N6633L	6. 7.71	To A2-CAM 1/77. Canx 30.12.76.
G-AZBH	Cameron O-84 HAFB	23		8. 7.71	Canx as WFU 30.8.85.
G-AZBI	SAN Jodel 150 Mascaret	43	F-BMFB	12. 7.71	
G-AZBJ	Reims Cessna FRA.150L Aerobat	0121	F-BSHP	12. 7.71	NTU - Not Imported. To F-WLIO/F-BTFA 12/71. Canx 10.10.71.
G-AZBK	PA-23-250 Aztec D	27-4683	N14077	12. 7.71	To EI-WAC 5/95. Canx 23.2.95.
G-AZBL	Jodel D.9 Bebe	PFA/938		12. 7.71	(Status uncertain - on rebuild .93?)
G-AZBM	Beechcraft C90 King Air	LJ-532		12. 7.71	To N900TB /77. Canx 13.1.77.
G-AZBN	Noorduyn AT-16-ND Harvard IIB	14A-1431	PH-HON R.Netherlands AF B-97/FT391/43-13132	13. 7.71	
G-AZBO	Not allocated.				
G-AZBP	PA-31-300 Turbo Navajo	31-551	N6617L	14. 7.71	To N1AL 9/76. Canx 20.9.76.
G-AZBR	Bell 47G-4A	7756	9L-LAS G-AZBR	15. 7.71	To SX-HAZ 10/78. Canx 29.9.78.
G-AZBS	Bell 47G-5	25045		15. 7.71	To SX-HBM 8/80. Canx 25.7.80.
G-AZBT	Western O-65 HAFB	005		15. 7.71	Canx by CAA 19.5.93. (Extant 3/96)
G-AZBU	Auster AOP.9 (Also c/n B5/10/183)	AUS.183	7862M XR246	15. 7.71	
G-AZBV	BN-2A-2 Islander	285	(EI-AVO) G-AZBV/G-51-285	16. 7.71	To 4X-AYK 5/72. Canx 16.3.72.

Regn	Type	c/n	Previous identity	Regn date	Fate or immediate subsequent identity (if known)
G-AZBW	PA-39-160 Twin Comanche C/R	39-114	N8954Y	16. 7.71	To N4297A. Canx 19.5.83.
G-AZBX	Western O-65 HAFB	006		16. 7.71	CofA expired 23.8.78. Canx as WFU 5.12.83.
G-AZBY	Westland S-58 Wessex 60 Srs.1 (Helicopter may actually be G-AWOX)	WA/740	G-17-5 G-AZBY/5N-ALR/G-AZBY	21. 7.71	(Painted in USMC c/s as "EM-16" for film use) (Stored 4/99 Honey Crock Farm, Redhill) CofA expired 14.12.82. Canx as TWFU 23.11.82.
G-AZBZ	Westland S-58 Wessex 60 Srs.1	WA/741	G-17-7 G-AZBZ/5N-AJI/G-AZBZ	21. 7.71	Canx as TWFU 23.11.82.
G-AZCA	Westland S-58 Wessex 60 Srs.1	WA/742		21. 7.71	To 9M-ATA 1/74. Canx 8.1.74.
"G-AZCA"	Beagle B.121 Pup Srs.100	B121-168	G-35-168	----	Incorrectly marked as G-AZCA in 10/71 in error. To G-AZDA.
G-AZCB	SNCAN Stampe SV-4C	140	F-BBCR	21. 7.71	
G-AZCC	Cessna 210J Centurion	210-59067	(EI-AWH) G-AZCC/5N-AIE/N1734C/(N6167F)	21. 7.71	To EI-AWH 1/73. Canx 18.1.73.
G-AZCD	Reims Cessna FR.172G Rocket	0206	F-BRXE	28. 7.71	To OO-WCD 5/73. Canx 16.5.73.
G-AZCE	Pitts S-1C Special	373.H & PFA/1527		26. 7.71	Crashed at Eastbach Farm on 2.9.75. (On rebuild as a S-1D) (Sold in Canada 15.7.76)
G-AZCF	Sikorsky S-61N Mk.II	61-488		26. 7.71	To VR-UDQ. Canx 1.3.82.
G-AZCG	BN-2A-3 Islander	288	G-51-288	28. 7.71	To ZS-IJD 12/71. Canx 3.11.71.
G-AZCH	HS.125 Srs.3B/RA	25154	EP-AHK G-5-11	29. 7.71	CofA expired 16.8.81. Broken up 12/82 at Luton due to corrosion. Rear fuselage/fin used on c/n 25270. Canx.
G-AZCI	Cessna 320A Skyknight	320A-0021	CF-PKY N3021R	29. 7.71	Stored in wrecked condition 7/91 Kano, Nigeria. CofA expired 29.6.83. Canx by CAA 16.12.91.
G-AZCJ	Beagle B.121 Pup Srs.100	B121-152	G-35-152	30. 7.71	DBR at Cranleigh strip on 18.8.78. Canx.
G-AZCK	Beagle B.121 Pup Srs.100	B121-153	G-35-153	30. 7.71	
G-AZCL	Beagle B.121 Pup Srs.150	B121-154	G-35-154	30. 7.71	
G-AZCM	Beagle B.121 Pup Srs.150	B121-155	G-35-155	30. 7.71	To HB-NAV 5/72. Canx 4.5.72.
G-AZCN	Beagle B.121 Pup Srs.150	B121-156	HB-NAY G-AZCN/G-35-156	30. 7.71	
G-AZCO	Beagle B.121 Pup Srs.150	B121-157	G-35-157	30. 7.71	To HB-NAU 5/72. Canx 4.5.72.
G-AZCP	Beagle B.121 Pup Srs.100	B121-158	(D-EKWA) G-AZCP/G-35-158	30. 7.71	
G-AZCR	Beagle B.121 Pup Srs.100	B121-159	G-35-159	30. 7.71	To D-EKWH 3/73. Canx 12.5.73.
G-AZCS	Beagle B.121 Pup Srs.100B	B121-160	G-35-160	30. 7.71	To OO-NAR 5/73. Canx 27.4.73.
G-AZCT	Beagle B.121 Pup Srs.100	B121-161	G-35-161	30. 7.71	
G-AZCU	Beagle B.121 Pup Srs.100	B121-162	G-35-162	30. 7.71	
G-AZCV	Beagle B.121 Pup Srs.150	B121-163	HB-NAR G-AZCV/G-35-163	30. 7.71	
G-AZCW	Beagle B.121 Pup Srs.150	B121-164	G-35-164	30. 7.71	To HB-NAS 3/72. Canx 10.3.72.
G-AZCX	Beagle B.121 Pup Srs.150	B121-165	G-35-165	30. 7.71	To HB-NAT 3/72. Canx 29.2.72.
G-AZCY	Beagle B.121 Pup Srs.150	B121-166	HB-NAW G-AZCY/G-35-166	30. 7.71	
G-AZCZ	Beagle B.121 Pup Srs.150	B121-167	G-35-167	30. 7.71	
G-AZDA	Beagle B.121 Pup Srs.100	B121-168	"G-AZCA" G-35-168	30. 7.71	
G-AZDB	Beagle B.121 Pup Srs.100	B121-169	G-35-169	30. 7.71	Crashed into Mt. Carraghan, IoM on 8.10.77. Canx.
G-AZDC	Sikorsky S-61N	61-424	C-GSPI G-AZDI/I-EVMA/N6956R	3. 8.71	Canx 22.4.87 on sale to France. To N91158 9/87.
G-AZDD	MBB Bo.209B Monsun 150FF	143	D-EBJC	3. 8.71	
G-AZDE	PA-28R-200 Cherokee Arrow B	28R-7135141		3. 8.71	
G-AZDF(1)	Douglas C-47B-35-DK Dakota	16598/33346	ST-AAK SN-AAK/G-AMYB/KN652/44-77014	3. 8.71	NTU - Restored as G-AMYB 8/71. Canx.
G-AZDF(2)	Cameron O-84 HAFB	24		18. 8.71	Canx as WFU 22.4.98. (Based in Germany)
G-AZDG(1)	Douglas C-47B-15-DK Dakota	15137/26582	ST-AAI SN-AAI/G-AMZS/KK127/43-49321	3. 8.71	NTU - Restored as G-AMZS 8/71. Canx.
G-AZDG(2)	BAC One-Eleven Srs.414EG	BAC.127	D-ANDY G-16-3	. 8.71R	NTU - To G-AZED 8/71. Canx.
G-AZDG(3)	Beagle B.121 Pup Srs.100	B121-145	(G-BLYM) HB-NAM/(VH-EPT)/G-35-145	17. 6.85	
G-AZDH	PA-31-300 Turbo Navajo	31-728	N7215L	5. 8.71	To N4433L. Canx 12.8.83.
G-AZDI	AESL Airtourer T4 (Super 150)	A.539		9. 8.71	Crashed at Balloc near Glasgow on 12.6.72. Canx as destroyed 27.7.73.
G-AZDJ	PA-32-300 Cherokee Six D	32-7140068	OY-AJK G-AZDJ/N5273S	23. 8.71	
G-AZDK	Beechcraft 95-B55 Baron	TC-1406		23. 8.71	
G-AZDL	BN-2A-26 Islander	661		23. 8.71	To ZK-KHA 11/73. Canx 1.11.73.
G-AZDM	BN-2A-3 Islander	662		23. 8.71	To 9XR-KA 1/73. Canx 30.1.73.
G-AZDN	BN-2A-3 Islander	663		23. 8.71	To PK-KNC 8/73. Canx 23.8.73.
G-AZDO	BN-2A-3 Islander	664		23. 8.71	To 9XR-KG 1/73. Canx 4.1.73.
G-AZDP	BN-2A-3 Islander	665		23. 8.71	To EP-PAG 12/72. Canx 18.12.72.
G-AZDR	BN-2A-8 Islander	666		23. 8.71	To HI-213 6/73. Canx 9.8.73.
G-AZDS	BN-2A-8 Islander	667		23. 8.71	To CS-AJF 9/72. Canx 18.9.72.
G-AZDT	BN-2A-9 Islander	668		23. 8.71	To PT-IKA 11/72. Canx 24.11.72.
G-AZDU	BN-2A-9 Islander	669		23. 8.71	To PT-ILB 8/73. Canx 9.8.73.
G-AZDV	BN-2A-8 Islander	670		23. 8.71	To PT-IMI 8/73. Canx 9.8.73.
G-AZDW	PA-28-180 Cherokee F	28-7105174		25. 8.71	Crashed in forced landing on Hayling Island on 18.2.85. Canx as destroyed 22.4.85.
G-AZDX	PA-28-180 Cherokee F	28-7105186		25. 8.71	
G-AZDY	DH.82A Tiger Moth	86559	F-BGDJ French AF/PG650	25. 8.71	
G-AZDZ	Cessna 172K Skyhawk	172-58501	5N-AIH N1647C/N84508	25. 8.71	Forced landing at Delapre Golf Course, Northants on 19.9.81 and extensively damaged. Canx as destroyed 5.12.83. (Extant 10/95)

Regn	Type	c/n	Previous identity	Regn date	Fate or immediate subsequent identity (if known)
G-AZEA	Cessna 182N Skylark	182-60466	N8926G	26. 8.71	To G-WACV 8/86. Canx.
G-AZEB	BAC One-Eleven Srs.517FE	BAC.188	VP-LAP G-AZEB/VP-BCN	26. 8.71	To RP-C1186 9/75. Canx 25.11.75.
G-AZEC	BAC One-Eleven Srs.517FE	BAC.189	VP-LAR G-AZEC/VP-BCO	26. 8.71	To RP-C1187 11/75. Canx 25.11.75.
G-AZED	BAC One-Eleven Srs.414EG	BAC.127	(N174FE) G-AZED/(G-AZDG)/D-ANDY/G-16-3	26. 8.71	To N174FE. Canx 15.3.88.
G-AZEE	Morane-Saulnier MS.880B Rallye Club (Composite including fuselage of G-AZNJ c/n 5375 in 1980; original fuselage stored in rafters South Scarle 9/94)	74	F-BKKA	1. 9.71	
G-AZEF	Wassmer Jodel D.120 Paris-Nice	321	F-BNZS	1. 9.71	
G-AZEG	PA-28-140 Cherokee D	28-7125530		1. 9.71	
G-AZEH	BN-2A-2 Islander	289	G-51-289	7. 9.71	To VQ-SAJ 12/75. Canx 27.10.75.
G-AZEI	BN-2A-3 Islander	291	G-51-291	7. 9.71	To PK-OAB 5/75. Canx 20.5.75.
G-AZEJ	Hughes 269C	100-0059		7. 9.71	To ZS-HJD. Canx 2.10.80.
G-AZEK	HS.125 Srs.400B	25259		7. 9.71	To South African AF as 05 in 1/72. Canx 28.1.72.
G-AZEL	HS.125 Srs.400B	25260		7. 9.71	To South African AF as 06 in 1/72. Canx 28.1.72.
G-AZEM	HS.125 Srs.400B	25269		7. 9.71	To South African AF as 07 in 1/72. Canx 28.1.72.
G-AZEN	Scottish Aviation Bulldog Srs.101	BH.100-117		9. 9.71	To Swedish Army as Fv61015 11/71. Canx 13.11.71.
G-AZEO	Scottish Aviation Bulldog Srs.101	BH.100-118		9. 9.71	To Swedish Army as Fv61016 11/71. Canx 20.11.71.
G-AZEP	Scottish Aviation Bulldog Srs.101	BH.100-119		9. 9.71	To Swedish Army as Fv61017 12/71. Canx 7.12.71.
G-AZER	Cameron O-42 (Ax5) HAFB	26		9. 9.71	CofA expired 15.5.81. Canx by CAA 25.3.92. (Inflated 9/93 at Attringham Park Balloon Meet)
G-AZES	Scottish Aviation Bulldog Srs.101	BH.100-121		9. 9.71	To Swedish Army as Fv61018 11/71. Canx 27.11.71.
G-AZET	Scottish Aviation Bulldog Srs.101	BH.100-122		9. 9.71	To Swedish Army as Fv61019 12/71. Canx 14.12.71.
G-AZEU	Beagle B.121 Pup Srs.150	B121-130	(VH-EPL) G-35-130	15. 9.71	
G-AZEV	Beagle B.121 Pup Srs.150	B121-131	(VH-EPM) G-35-131	15. 9.71	
G-AZEW	Beagle B.121 Pup Srs.150	B121-132	(VH-EPN) G-35-132	15. 9.71	
G-AZEX	Beagle B.121 Pup Srs.150	B121-134	(VH-EPO) G-35-134	15. 9.71	To HB-NAX 5/72. Canx 19.5.72.
G-AZEY	Beagle B.121 Pup Srs.150	B121-136	HB-NAK G-AZEY/(VH-EPP)/G-35-136	15. 9.71	
G-AZEZ	Beagle B.121 Pup Srs.150	B121-137	(VH-EPQ) G-35-137	15. 9.71	To HB-NAN 3/72. Canx 23.3.72.
G-AZFA	Beagle B.121 Pup Srs.150	B121-143	(VH-EPR) G-35-143	15. 9.71	
G-AZFB	Boeing 720-051B (Line No. 222)	18381	N730US N791TW	16. 9.71	To N2464C 6/83. Canx 15.3.83.
G-AZFC	PA-28-140 Cherokee D	28-7125486		16. 9.71	
G-AZFD	Fokker F-27 Friendship 600	10323	HB-AAW PH-FKT	17. 9.71	To A40-FD 10/75. Canx 9.10.75.
G-AZFE	PA-E23-250 Aztec D	27-4577	EI-BPA G-AZFE/N13962	17. 9.71	To G-BZFE 10/87. Canx.
G-AZFF	Wassmer Jodel D.112	1175	F-BLFI	17. 9.71	
G-AZFG	BN-2A Mk.III-1 Trislander	299	G-51-299	17. 9.71	To N60JA 11/71. Canx 17.2.72.
G-AZFH	Western O-65 HAFB	008		20. 9.71	Canx 1.5.72 on sale to Australia.
G-AZFI	PA-28R-200 Cherokee Arrow D	28R-7135160		21. 9.71	
G-AZFJ	Cessna T.310Q	310Q-0234	(F-....) G-AZFJ/N7734Q	21. 9.71	To N9RV. Canx 19.3.79.
G-AZFK	SAN Jodel D.117	602	F-BHXY	22. 9.71	Fatal crash on landing at Doncaster on 14.4.73. Canx as destroyed 11.2.75.
G-AZFL	Cessna E.310P II	310P-0221	N5921M	23. 9.71	To G-FLIX 3/81. Canx.
G-AZFM	PA-28R-200 Cherokee Arrow D	28R-7135218		24. 9.71	
G-AZFN	Cameron O-56 HAFB	25		28. 9.71	Stolen. Canx as destroyed 13.7.78.
G-AZFO	PA-30-160 Twin Comanche C (Mod. to PA-39 C/R Status)	30-1917	N8761Y	28. 9.71	To G-CALV(2) 1/89. Canx.
G-AZFP	Reims Cessna F.177RG Cardinal (Wichita c/n 00194)	0031		29. 9.71	To G-FIJJ 4/99. Canx.
G-AZFR	Cessna 401B	401B-0121	N7981Q	30. 9.71	
G-AZFS	Beechcraft 65-B80 Queen Air	LD-322	N900KQ N900KC/N7822L	29. 9.71	To N65GC 4/85. Canx 10.4.85.
G-AZFT	HS.121 Trident 2E Srs.102	2157		29. 9.71	To China as 240 12/72. Canx 15.12.72.
G-AZFU	HS.121 Trident 2E Srs.102	2158		29. 9.71	To China as 242 3/73. Canx 16.3.73.
G-AZFV	HS.121 Trident 2E Srs.102	2159		29. 9.71	To China as 244 7/73. Canx 23.7.73.
G-AZFW	HS.121 Trident 2E Srs.102	2160		29. 9.71	To China as 246 9/73. Canx 6.9.73.
G-AZFX	HS.121 Trident 2E Srs.102	2161		29. 9.71	To China as 248 11/73. Canx 7.11.73.
G-AZFY	HS.121 Trident 2E Srs.102	2162		29. 9.71	To China as 250 1/74. Canx 16.1.74.
G-AZFZ	Cessna 414 RAM	414-0175	N8245Q	30. 9.71	To N414FZ 7/96. Canx 26.7.96.
G-AZGA	Jodel Wassmer D.120 Paris-Nice	144	F-BIXV	30. 9.71	
G-AZGB	PA-23-250 Aztec D	27-4099	N878SH N10F	4.10.71	To G-ODIR 8/89. Canx.
G-AZGC	SNCAN Stampe SV-4C	120	F-BCGE	4.10.71	Damaged taxying at Folly Farm, Hungerford on 28.5.90. (Stored 5/93)

Regn	Type	c/n	Previous identity	Regn date	Fate or immediate subsequent identity (if known)
G-AZGD	SNCAN Stampe SV-4C	413	F-BGRL F-BCQV	4.10.71	Crashed near Touloun, France on 4.7.76. Canx.
G-AZGE	SNCAN Stampe SV-4C	576	F-BDDV	6.10.71	(Stored 3/97)
G-AZGF	Beagle B.121 Pup Srs.150	B121-076	PH-KUF G-35-076	6.10.71	
G-AZGG	Beechcraft 65-C90 King Air	LJ-543		6.10.71	To N29791. Canx 9.12.82.
G-AZGH	Socata MS.880B Rallye Club	1895		7.10.71	Badly damaged at Gransha, near Newry, Northern Ireland on 20.4.83. Canx by CAA 4.12.86.
G-AZGI	Socata MS.880B Rallye Club	1896		7.10.71	(Stored 6/97)
G-AZGJ	Socata MS.880B Rallye Club	1897		7.10.71	Components used in composite rebuild of G-BIOR. Canx as WFU 29.9.86.
G-AZGK	Socata MS.880B Ralyye Club	1901		7.10.71	Crashed at Trevethoe House, Lelant, St.Ives on 16.8.74. Canx as WFU 25.8.81.
G-AZGL	Socata MS.894A Rallye Minerva 220	11929		7.10.71	
G-AZGM	PA-28R-180 Cherokee Arrow D	28R-30411	N4550J	7.10.71	To G-MAST 9/80. Canx.
G-AZGN	BN-2A-9 Islander	671		11.10.71	To PT-ILC 8/73. Canx 9.8.73.
G-AZGO	BN-2A-8 Islander	672		11.10.71	To HI-215 6/73. Canx 8.1.74.
G-AZGP	BN-2A-3 Islander	673		11.10.71	To (5Y-ARZ(1))/F-BUFV 12/73. Canx 8.1.74.
G-AZGR	BN-2A-9 Islander	674		11.10.71	To (F-BUTN)/5U-AAN 5/74. Canx 7.5.74.
G-AZGS	BN-2A-3 Islander	675		11.10.71	To PK-KNE 3/74. Canx 6.3.74.
G-AZGT	BN-2A-9 Islander	676	EC-CFX G-AZGT	11.10.71	To DQ-FCN. Canx 30.9.77.
G-AZGU	BN-2A-9 Islander	677	EC-CFY G-AZGU	11.10.71	To 8R-GFI. Canx 3.11.80.
G-AZGV	BN-2A-2 Islander	678		11.10.71	To CR-LOQ 4/75. Canx 11.4.75.
G-AZGW	BN-2A-8 Islander	679		11.10.71	To HI-214 6/73. Canx 8.1.74.
G-AZGX	BN-2A-8 Islander	680		11.10.71	To (HI-216)/F-OGGL /73. Canx 8.1.74.
G-AZGY	Rousseau-Piel CP.301B Emeraude	122	F-BRAA	12.10.71	
G-AZGZ	DH.82A Tiger Moth	86489	F-BGCF French AF/NM181	13.10.71	
G-AZHA	PA-E23-250 Aztec E	27-4735	N14172	14.10.71	To OH-PTV. Canx 30.9.85.
G-AZHB	Robin HR.100/200B Royal	118		14.10.71	
G-AZHC	Wassmer Jodel D.112	585	F-BIQQ	18.10.71	
G-AZHD	Slingsby T.61A Falke	1753		18.10.71	
G-AZHE	Slingsby T.61B Falke (Originally regd as T.61A)	1755	N61TB G-AZHE	18.10.71	Damaged on 17.6.88. (Stored 7/95 Tatenhill) Canx by CAA 14.3.99.
G-AZHF	Cessna 150L	150-72575	N1275Q	18.10.71	Crashed onto a factory roof at Kackadown Lane, Kitts Green, nr.Birmingham airport on 21.3.85. Canx as destroyed 31.7.85
G-AZHG	Cessna 421B Golden Eagle II	421B-0107	N8077Q	18.10.71	To F-BRGR 10/75. Canx 3.10.75.
G-AZHH	K & S SA.102.5 Cavalier	69194 & PFA/1393		20.10.71	
G-AZHI	AESL Airtourer T5 (Super 150)	A.540		20.10.71	
G-AZHJ	Scottish Aviation Twin Pioneer Srs.3	577	G-31-16 XP295	20.10.71	WFU & stored in 9/91. (Stored 7/97) Canx as TWFU 23.7.97.
G-AZHK	Robin HR.100/200B Royal	113	G-ILEG G-AZHK	22.10.71	
G-AZHL	PA-31-300 Turbo Navajo	31-760	N7238L	22.10.71	Lost height and crashed soon after take-off at Teesside on 15.7.87 & severely damaged. Canx as destroyed 17.3.88.
G-AZHM	Cassutt Racer IIIM	PFA/1379		22.10.71	Badly damaged in an accident near Halton cum Beckering on 21.4.86. Canx as destroyed 23.2.89.
G-AZHN	AW.650 Argosy Srs.101	AW.6657	N893U N600Z/N6505R/G-1-4	25.10.71	Canx as WFU 29.11.76. Broken up at Castle Donington in 5/77.
G-AZHO	SAN Jodel DR.1050 Ambassadeur	157	F-BJNK	26.10.71	Canx as WFU 4.2.81.
G-AZHP	Short SC.7 Skyvan 3M-400-9	SH1898	G-14-70	26.10.71	To R.Nepalese AF as 9N-RF15/RAN-15 in 1/72. Canx 20.1.72.
G-AZHR	Piccard Ax6 HAFB	617	N17US	27.10.71	
G-AZHS	HS.125 Srs.F600 (Originally regd as Srs.F400)	25258	(G-AYRR)	27.10.71	To G-BFAN 5/76. Canx.
G-AZHT	AESL Airtourer T3	525		29.10.71	Badly damaged in forced landing at Glen Forsa, Mull on 29.4.88. (Stored off-site 6/95)
G-AZHU	Phoenix Luton LA-4A Minor	PFA/839		1.11.71	
G-AZHV	Scottish Aviation Bulldog Srs.100	BH.100/124		4.11.71	To Swedish Army as Fv61020 12/71. Canx 11.12.71.
G-AZHW	Scottish Aviation Bulldog Srs.100	BH.100/125		4.11.71	To Swedish Army as Fv61021 12/71. Canx 31.12.71.
G-AZHX	Scottish Aviation Bulldog Srs.100	BH.100/126		4.11.71	To Swedish Army as Fv61022 12/71. Canx 31.12.71.
G-AZHY	Scottish Aviation Bulldog Srs.100	BH.100/128		4.11.71	To Swedish Army as Fv61023 12/71. Canx 31.12.71.
G-AZHZ	Scottish Aviation Bulldog Srs.100	BH.100/129		4.11.71	To Swedish Army as Fv61024 1/72. Canx 13.1.72.
G-AZIA	PA-39-160 Twin Comanche C/R	39-129	N8966Y	4.11.71	To LN-BIA. Canx by CAA 22.10.81 & 25.10.90.
G-AZIB	Socata ST-10 Diplomate	141		4.11.71	(Made a wheels-up landing at Tollerton on 13.6.99)
G-AZIC	Sud MS.894A Rallye Minerva 220	11888		4.11.71	NTU - Not imported - To F-BTHZ 1/72. Canx.
G-AZID	Reims Cessna FA.150L Aerobat	0083	N9447	8.11.71	
G-AZIE	PA-25-235 Pawnee C	25-5303	N84P	8.11.71	To 5B-CEY /82. Canx 5.7.82.
G-AZIF	PA-23-250 Aztec E	27-4633	N14019	9.11.71	Fatal crash near Great Sampford, Essex on 5.1.72 whilst on approach. Canx.
G-AZIG	Sportavia-Putzer Fournier RF-4D	4033	OO-WAC	10.11.71	Crashed on take-off from Little Farringdon, Glos. on 11.6.76. Canx by CAA 9.10.84.

Regn	Type	c/n	Previous identity	Regn date	Fate or immediate subsequent identity (if known)
G-AZIH	Auster J/1N Alpha	3395		11.11.71	To G-BLPG 5/82. Canx.
G-AZII	SAN Jodel D.117A	848	F-BNDO F-OBFO	12.11.71	
G-AZIJ	Robin DR.360 Knight	634		15.11.71	
G-AZIK	PA-34-200 Seneca II	34-7250018	N2392T	15.11.71	
G-AZIL	Slingsby T.61A Falke	1756		16.11.71	
G-AZIM	PA-31-310 Turbo Navajo B	31-776	N7250L	19.11.71	To EI-BOL 9/83. Canx 16.9.83.
G-AZIN	Canadair CL-44D4-2	19	N450T CF-NBP-X	19.11.71	To PK-BAW 6/82. Canx 28.6.82.
G-AZIO	SNCAN Stampe SV-4C	389	F-BACB	24.11.71	Canx as WFU 1.10.86. (On rebuild at Booker)
G-AZIP	Cameron O-65 HAFB	29		24.11.71	(Non-airworthy - stored 2/97)
G-AZIR	SNCAN Stampe SV-4C (Fuselage used in rebuild of G-ASHS c/n 265 in .84)	452	F-BCXR	24.11.71	Canx as WFU 1.10.86.
G-AZIS	Scottish Aviation Bulldog Srs.100	BH.100/130		25.11.71	To Swedish Army as Fv61025 1/72. Canx 13.1.72.
G-AZIT	Scottish Aviation Bulldog Srs.100	BH.100/132		25.11.71	To Swedish Army as Fv61026 1/72. Canx 24.1.72.
G-AZIU	Scottish Aviation Bulldog Srs.100	BH.100/133		25.11.71	To Swedish Army as Fv61027 1/72. Canx 24.1.72.
G-AZIV	Scottish Aviation Bulldog Srs.100	BH.100/134		25.11.71	To Swedish Army as Fv61028 2/72. Canx 4.2.72.
G-AZIW	Scottish Aviation Bulldog Srs.100	BH.100/135		25.11.71	To Swedish Army as Fv61029 1/72. Canx 31.1.72.
G-AZIX	American Aviation AA-1A Trainer 2	AA1A-0302		25.11.71	Somersaulted in forced landing near Henley on 2.4.73. Canx as destroyed 13.1.76.
G-AZIY	DH.106 Comet 4	6434	LV-AHU LV-PPA	26.11.71	WFU at Lasham 26.11.73. Canx as WFU 29.10.75. Broken up Lasham in 3/77.
G-AZIZ	Sud MS.894A Rallye-Minerva 220	11883		29.11.71	To 5Y-AYX 9/75. Canx 4.9.75.
G-AZJA	BN-2A Mk.III-1 Trislander	305	G-51-305	26.11.71	To HP-946. Canx 30.3.82.
G-AZJB	PA-34-200-2 Seneca	34-7250017	N1036U	26.11.71	To OY-FRA. Canx 16.1.87.
G-AZJC	Sportavia-Putzer Fournier RF-5	5108		30.11.71	
G-AZJD	North American AT-6D-NT Harvard IIA	88-14948	F-BJBF Belgium AF H-9/SAAF 7509/EX959/41-33932	30.11.71	To F-WZDU .84/F-AZDU 6/85. Canx 9.10.84.
G-AZJE	Barritault JB.01 Minicab (Originally regd as an Garden GY-20 Minicab and Ord-Hume JB.01 Minicab with same c/n)	JBE.1 & PFA/1806		1.12.71	(Stored 12/95)
G-AZJF	Cameron O-65 HAFB	30		1.12.71	To D-BRANDBLASE 12/76. Canx 7.12.76.
G-AZJG	Western O-65 HAFB	009		1.12.71	To SE-ZZC 1/73. Canx 28.12.72.
G-AZJH	HS.748 Srs.2A/271LFD	1698		1.12.71	To 9N-RAC 1/75. Canx 20.1.75.
G-AZJI	Western O-65 HAFB	007		2.12.71	Canx by CAA 19.5.93. (Active 9/94)
G-AZJJ	Bell 47D-1	147	I-MAGR	3.12.71	Scrapped at Southampton Heliport. Canx as WFU 2.9.74.
G-AZJK	Agusta-Bell 47G-2	001	I-SIAP	3.12.71	Broken up at Southampton in 1973. Canx as WFU 11.9.81.
G-AZJL	Agusta-Bell 47G-2	221	I-CIEB	3.12.71	Broken up at Southampton in 1973. Canx as WFU 11.9.81.
G-AZJM	Boeing 707-324C (Line No. 430)	18886	N17323	10.12.71	Restored as N17323 12/80. Canx 22.12.80.
G-AZJN	Robin DR.300/140 Major	642		6.12.71	
G-AZJO	Scottish Aviation Bulldog Srs.100	BH.100/137		8.12.71	To Swedish Army as Fv61030 2/72. Canx 7.2.72.
G-AZJP	Scottish Aviation Bulldog Srs.100	BH.100/138		8.12.71	To Swedish Army as Fv61031 2/72. Canx 11.2.72.
G-AZJR	Scottish Aviation Bulldog Srs.100	BH.100/139		8.12.71	To Swedish Army as Fv61032 2/72. Canx 28.2.72.
G-AZJS	Scottish Aviation Bulldog Srs.100	BH.100/141		8.12.71	To Swedish Army as Fv61033 2/72. Canx 28.2.72.
G-AZJT	Scottish Aviation Bulldog Srs.100	BH.100/142		8.12.71	To Swedish Army as Fv61034 3/72. Canx 3.3.72.
G-AZJU	Scottish Aviation Bulldog Srs.100	BH.100/143		8.12.71	To Swedish Army as Fv61035 3/72. Canx 6.3.72.
G-AZJV	Reims Cessna F.172L Skyhawk	0810		8.12.71	
G-AZJW	Reims Cessna F.150L Commuter	0752		8.12.71	To G-SADE 5/91. Canx.
G-AZJX	Reims Cessna F.150L Commuter	0756		8.12.71	To 5B-CFF. Canx 23.12.82.
G-AZJY	Reims Cessna FRA.150L Aerobat (This aircraft was officially rebuilt at Sleap in 7.81 following ditching off Isle of Man 18.9.72; its true pedigree is thus unconfirmed)	0126		8.12.71	
G-AZJZ	PA-23-250 Aztec E	27-4744	N14179	8.12.71	Fatal crash drug-running at Sierra de lo Almijara, Spain on 11.3.96. Canx by CAA 12.6.96.
G-AZKA	Socata MS.880B Rallye Club	1911		8.12.71	Destroyed in a gale at Clenrothes on the night of 2/3.3.82 Canx.
G-AZKB	Socata MS.880B Rallye Club	1913		8.12.71	To EI-BGB 1/79. Canx 28.11.78.
G-AZKC	Socata MS.880B Rallye Club	1914		8.12.71	
G-AZKD	Socata MS.880B Rallye Club	1949		8.12.71	Damaged at Franklinsfield on 4.9.92. Canx as WFU 25.8.93.
G-AZKE	Socata MS.880B Rallye Club	1950		8.12.71	
G-AZKF	Socata MS.880B Rallye Club	1951		8.12.71	To EI-BBU 7/76. Canx 26.7.76.
G-AZKG	Reims Cessna F.172L Skyhawk	0825		8.12.71	To G-BPRM 4/88. Canx.
G-AZKH	Reims Cessna F.177RG Cardinal	0049	(PH-LTH) G-AZKH	8.12.71	Damaged at Doncaster Racecourse on 5.7.79. Rebuilt & re-regd as G-OADE 5/82. Canx.
G-AZKI	Noorduyn AT-16 Harvard IIB	14A-1269	PH-SKM R.Netherland AF B-45/FT229/43-12970	8.12.71	To F-WZDS .84/F-AZDS 12/87. Canx 11.7.86.
G-AZKJ	Canadair CL-44D4-2	37	N1001T CF-PZZ-X	13.12.71	To G-BRED 8/80. Canx.
G-AZKK	Cameron O-56 HAFB	32		13.12.71	
G-AZKL	Short SC.7 Skyvan 3M-400-11	SH1897	G-14-69	13.12.71	To R.Thailand Police as 21897 in 7/73. Canx 6.7.73.

Regn	Type	c/n	Previous identity	Regn date	Fate or immediate subsequent identity (if known)
G-AZKM	Boeing 720-051B (Line No. 223)	18382	N731US N792TW	15.12.71	To N2464K 3/83. Canx 14.4.83.
G-AZKN	Avions Pierre Robin Jodel HR.100/200B	122		20.12.71	Damaged in force-landing near Long Watton, Leics. on 1.9.95. Canx as WFU 31.5.96. (Dismantled wreck stored at Hinton-in-the-Hedges in 1/99)
G-AZKO	Reims Cessna F.337F Super Skymaster (Wichita c/n 01380)	0041		20.12.71	
G-AZKP	SAN Jodel D.117	419	F-BHND	20.12.71	
G-AZKR	PA-24-180 Comanche	24-2192	N7044P	23.12.71	
G-AZKS	American Aviation AA-1A Trainer (Originally AA-1 standard; fuselage damaged and replaced by AA-1A version)	AA1-0334	N6134L	23.12.71	
G-AZKT	Reims Cessna F.177RG Cardinal	0039		23.12.71	Crashed on landing at Newbury Racecourse on 7.11.79. Canx.
G-AZKU	Reims Cessna F.177RG Cardinal	0050		23.12.71	To LX-RST 11/76. Canx 26.11.76.
G-AZKV	Reims Cessna FRA.150L Aerobat	0127		23.12.71	Badly damaged in forced landing into a hedge at Redlake, Lostwithiel on 15.9.91. Canx as destroyed 30.10.91. (Status uncertain - only small parts and wings stored 8/96)
G-AZKW	Reims Cessna F.172L Skyhawk	0836		23.12.71	
G-AZKX	Reims Cessna FR.172H	0331		23.12.71	NTU - Not Imported. To I-BZAN 11/72. Canx 8.8.72.
G-AZKY	Reims Cessna F.150L Commuter	0804		23.12.71	NTU - Not Imported. To D-EEZM 9/72. Canx 1.8.72.
G-AZKZ	Reims Cessna F.172L Skyhawk	0814		23.12.71	
G-AZLA	Taylor JT.2 Titch	PFA/3218		23.12.71	Construction abandoned. Canx 5.12.83.
G-AZLB	Western O-65 HAFB	012		23.12.71	To F-GAZD 5/79. Canx 9.1.78.
G-AZLC	Cessna 182P Skylane II	182-60867	N9327G	24.12.71	To EI-BDP 11/77. Canx 3.11.77.
G-AZLD	Cessna 182P Skylane II	182-60868	N9328G	24.12.71	To 5B-CDU /80. Canx 4.6.80.
G-AZLE	Boeing-Stearman E75 (N2S-5) Kaydet	75-8543	CF-XRD N5619N/BuA.43449	29.12.71	
G-AZLF	Wassmer Jodel D.120 Paris-Nice	230	F-BLFL	30.12.71	
G-AZLG	Beechcraft 95-55 Baron 58	TH-195		30.12.71	To F-BXAC 9/74. Canx 26.6.74.
G-AZLH	Reims Cessna F.150L	0757		31.12.71	
G-AZLI	BN-2A-3 Islander	297	G-51-297	31.12.71	To EP-PAE 3/72. Canx 6.3.72.
G-AZLJ	BN-2A Mk.III-1 Trislander	319	G-OREG SX-CBN/G-OREG/G-OAVW/G-AZLJ/G-51-319	31.12.71	
G-AZLK	Reims Cessna F.150L	0743		31.12.71	To G-SACE 3/84. Canx.
G-AZLL	Reims Cessna FRA.150L	0135		31.12.71	Fatal crash at Turweston on 4.2.99 & DBR. Canx as destroyed 21.7.99.
G-AZLM	Reims Cessna F.172L	0842		31.12.71	Crashed on take off from Badminton on 23.3.91. Canx as destroyed 15.4.91. (Fuselage stored 9/97 Flixton)
G-AZLN	PA-28-180 Cherokee F	28-7105210		3. 1.72	
G-AZLO	Reims Cessna F.337F Super Skymaster (Wichita c/n 01347)	0029		4. 1.72	WFU & stored at St.Just after CofA expiry 22.4.82. Canx by CAA 4.12.86. (Noted dismantled at Bourn in 3/91 & 7/95) (Unmarked fuselage stored 4/99 at Bourn)
G-AZLP	Vickers 813 Viscount	346	ZS-CDT (ZS-SBT)/ZS-CDT	4. 1.72	CofA expired 3.4.82 & WFU. To CAA Fire School at Tees-side. Canx as WFU 19.12.86. (Extant 4/99 Tees-side)
G-AZLR	Vickers 813 Viscount	347	ZS-CDU (ZS-SBU)/ZS-CDU	4. 1.72	CofA expiry 31.3.83 & WFU at Tees-side. To East Midlands Airport & used as cabin trainer 11/96. Canx as WFU 26.4.90. Broken up 3/97.
G-AZLS	Vickers 813 Viscount	348	ZS-CDV (ZS-SBV)/ZS-CDV	4. 1.72	CofA expired 9.6.83 & WFU. To CAA Fire School at Tees-side. Canx as WFU 19.12.86. (Extant 4/99 Tees-side)
G-AZLT	Vickers 813 Viscount	349	ZS-CDW (ZS-SBW)/ZS-CDW	4. 1.72	Damaged at Leeds-Bradford on 6.10.80 - Repaired & re-regd as G-BMAT 3/81. Canx.
G-AZLU(1)	Vickers 813 Viscount	350	ZS-CDX (ZS-SBX)/ZS-CDX	. .71R	NTU - To G-AZNA 2/72. Canx.
G-AZLU(2)	DHC.2 Beaver Mk.1	1558	VH-IDS	6. 1.72	To C-GMAM 4/75. Canx 1.4.75.
G-AZLV(1)	Vickers 813 Viscount	351	ZS-CDY (ZS-SBY)/ZS-CDY	. .71R	NTU - To G-AZNB 2/72. Canx.
G-AZLV(2)	Cessna 172K Skyhawk	172-57908	4X-ALM N79138	10. 1.72	
G-AZLW(1)	Vickers 813 Viscount	352	ZS-CDZ (ZS-SBZ)/ZS-CDZ	. .71R	NTU - To G-AZNC 2/72. Canx.
G-AZLW(2)	DH.106 Comet 4	6432	LV-AHS LV-POZ	10. 1.72	WFU 2.3.73. Whilst awaiting scrapping at Lasham 3/73 a fire from the old seats from G-APDE caused it to be burnt out.
G-AZLX	Western O-65 HAFB	010		10. 1.72	To N3AF 6/73. Canx 4.6.73.
G-AZLY	Reims Cessna F.150L Commuter	0771		10. 1.72	
G-AZLZ	Reims Cessna F.150L Commuter	0772		10. 1.72	
G-AZMA	SAN Jodel D.140B Mousquetaire	65	PH-SBB	10. 1.72	Destroyed by arson at Mullaghmore on 29.3.87. Canx as destroyed 20.11.87.
G-AZMB	Bell 47G-5	2639	CF-NJW	12. 1.72	To G-SOLH 3/97. Canx.
G-AZMC	Slingsby T.61A Falke	1757		12. 1.72	(Sold - stored 8/90)
G-AZMD	Slingsby T.61A Falke	1758		12. 1.72	Canx as WFU 15.8.75.
G-AZME	PA-31-300 Turbo Navajo	31-754	N7232L	14. 1.72	To N105RS. Canx 22.8.83.
G-AZMF	BAC One-Eleven Srs.530FX	BAC.240	7Q-YKJ G-AZMF/PT-TYY/G-AZMF	14. 1.72	
G-AZMG	PA-23-250 Aztec C	27-3500	5Y-APA (5Y-AMA)/5X-UVF/5Y-AFS	18. 1.72	To G-COMM 1/81. Canx.
G-AZMH	Morane-Saulnier MS.500	637	EI-AUU F-BJQG/French Mil	20. 1.72	Canx 25.6.97 on sale to Germany. (On display 3/99 at Gatow Museum, Berlin, Germany, marked 7A-WN)
G-AZMI	BAC One-Eleven Srs.401AK	066	N5026	20. 1.72	To G-16-19/G-BBME 3/74. Canx 19.2.73.
G-AZMJ	American Aviation AA-5 Traveler	AA5-0019	N5819L	27. 1.72	
G-AZMK	PA-23-250 Aztec E	27-4715	OY-AJA G-AZMK/N14152	28. 1.72	Restored as N14152. Canx 20.11.91.

Regn	Type	c/n	Previous identity	Regn date	Fate or immediate subsequent identity (if known)
G-AZML	Canadair CL-44D4-2	38	N1002T CF-RSL-X	28. 1.72	To N121AE. Canx 30.10.80.
G-AZMM	Sud ST-10 Diplomate	144		28. 1.72	To OO-TVM. Canx 6.7.76.
G-AZMN	AESL Airtourer T5 (Super 150)	A.550		28. 1.72	Crashed into a field half a mile north of Glasgow Airport on 23.6.87 and badly damaged. Canx by CAA 14.9.88. (Stored 6/97)
G-AZMO	PA-32-260 Cherokee Six	32-499	SE-EYN	28. 1.72	To G-OSIX 8/86. Canx.
G-AZMP	Scottish Aviation Bulldog Srs.100	BH.100/145		1. 2.72	To Swedish Army as Fv61036 3/72. Canx 14.3.72.
G-AZMR	Scottish Aviation Bulldog Srs.100	BH.100/146		1. 2.72	To Swedish Army as Fv61037 3/72. Canx 20.3.72.
G-AZMS	Scottish Aviation Bulldog Srs.100	BH.100/148		1. 2.72	To Swedish Army as Fv61038 3/72. Canx 20.3.72.
G-AZMT	Scottish Aviation Bulldog Srs.100	BH.100/149		1. 2.72	To Swedish Army as Fv61039 3/72. Canx 27.3.72.
G-AZMU	Scottish Aviation Bulldog Srs.100	BH.100/151		1. 2.72	To Swedish Army as Fv61040 3/72. Canx 27.3.72.
G-AZMV	Rollason D.62C Condor	RAE/652		1. 2.72	Fatal crash at Tibenham on 28.4.90. Canx as WFU 4.9.90.
G-AZMW	PA-39-160 Twin Comanche C/R	39-54	(D-GMWV) N8897Y	4. 2.72	To F-GCTF 9/80. Canx.
G-AZMX	PA-28-140 Cherokee D	28-24777	SE-FLL LN-LMK	7. 2.72	CofA expired 9.1.82. (Instructional Airframe 3/96 North East Wales Institute of Higher Education, Connah's Quay)
G-AZMY	SIAI-Marchetti SF-260	2-50	OO-HOA	7. 2.72	To N260TV 12/84. Canx 20.12.84.
G-AZMZ	Socata MS.893A Rallye Commodore 180	11927		8. 2.72	
G-AZNA	Vickers 813 Viscount	350	(G-AZLU) ZS-CDX/(ZS-SBX)/ZS-CDX	8. 2.72	WFU & stored at Waarschoot. On display in car park 7/97 Zomergem, Belgium. Canx by CAA 17.6.92.
G-AZNB	Vickers 813 Viscount	351	(G-AZLV) ZS-CDY/(ZS-SBY)/ZS-CDY	8. 2.72	CofA expired 8.5.83. Broken up at Teesside. Canx as WFU 19.12.86.
G-AZNC	Vickers 813 Viscount	352	(G-AZLW) ZS-CDZ/(ZS-SBZ)/ZS-CDZ	8. 2.72	WFU & stored in 2/82. Painted green/unmarked and used for non-destructive training at Teesside in 5/97. Canx as WFU 27.10.88.
G-AZND	DH.121 Trident 1E	2134	9K-ACH	8. 2.72	To 5B-DAE 4/73. Canx 11.4.73.
G-AZNE	Sikorsky S-61N	61-467	VR-BDU I-EVME	9. 2.72	Crashed alongside drilling platform Glomar North Sea some 120 miles E of Dyce 4.4.73. Canx.
G-AZNF	AIA Stampe SV-4C	1101	F-BGJM French Mil	9. 2.72	To G-HJSS 9/92. Canx.
G-AZNG	Vickers 952 Vanguard	744	PK-MVC G-AZNG/SE-FTI/G-AZNG/CF-TKU	10. 2.72	To F-BVUY 9/74. Canx 27.9.74.
G-AZNH	Vickers 814 Viscount	342	503 Oman AF/G-AZNH/D-ANUR	14. 2.72	To 9G-ACL 9/77. Canx 2.11.77.
G-AZNI	Sud SA.315B Lama	2014/06	G-AWLC	14. 2.72	Crashed at Tambobamba on 23.12.94. Canx 22.2.95 on sale to USA. To N2128Z 4/95.
G-AZNJ	Morane-Saulnier MS.880B Rallye Club	5375	F-BKZS	14. 2.72	CofA expired 4.5.77 & WFU at Southend. Canx as WFU 5.12.83. Fuselage to G-AZEE c/n 74 in 1980.
G-AZNK	SNCAN Stampe SV-4A	290	F-BKXF F-BCGZ	15. 2.72	
G-AZNL	PA-28R-200 Cherokee Arrow D II	28R-7235006		16. 2.72	
G-AZNM	PA-39-160 Twin Comanche C/R	39-130	N8967Y	16. 2.72	To D-GHSH 8/72. Canx 24.8.72.
G-AZNN	SNCAN Stampe SV-4A	500	F-BDGI	17. 2.72	To G-OODE 5/77. Canx.
G-AZNO	Cessna 182P Skylane	182-61005	N7365Q	18. 2.72	
G-AZNP	Vickers 814 Viscount	343	D-ANEF	18. 2.72	Crashed on landing at Hurn 28.1.72 whilst on delivery, still marked as D-ANEF. Canx 24.2.72 as WFU. (Was intended for Oman AF as 504)
G-AZNR	Cameron O-56 HAFB	31		21. 2.72	To OO-BML 3/72. Canx 23.3.72.
G-AZNS	Cameron O-84 HAFB	33		21. 2.72	To ZS-HAC(2) 8/72. Canx 16.5.75.
G-AZNT	Cameron O-84 HAFB	34		21. 2.72	
G-AZNU	Cameron O-84 HAFB	35		21. 2.72	To SE-ZZX 6/73. Canx 27.4.73.
G-AZNV	Cameron O-65 HAFB	37		21. 2.72	To F-WOHO/F-BOHO 7/72. Canx 1.7.72.
G-AZNW	Cameron O-84 HAFB	38		21. 2.72	To LN-ASI 8/73. Canx 29.6.73.
G-AZNX	Boeing 720-051B (Line No. 230)	18383	N732US N793TW	21. 2.72	To N24666 3/83. Canx 10.3.83.
G-AZNY	PA-E23-250 Aztec E	27-4668	N14058	21. 2.72	Damaged taxying at Norwich on 15.7.82. Canx 23.2.83. To Dodson Aviation Scrapyard, Ottawa, KS, USA.
G-AZNZ	Boeing 737-222 (Line No. 95)	19074	N9036U	1. 3.72	To N144AW. Canx 25.4.85.
G-AZOA	MBB Bo.209 Monsun 150FF	183	D-EAAY	21. 2.72	
G-AZOB	MBB Bo.209 Monsun 150FF	184	D-EAAZ	21. 2.72	(Crashed on take-off from Droitwich on 21.8.83) (Stored 8/92)
G-AZOC	MBB Bo.209 Monsun 150FF	185	D-EAIA	8. 3.72	Fatal crash into high ground at Killhope Law, near Allenheads, Northumberland 14.4.75. Canx.
G-AZOD	PA-E23-250 Aztec D	27-4344	N697RC N6976Y	21. 2.72	To G-OXTC 5/89. Canx.
G-AZOE	AESL Airtourer T2 (115)	A.528		21. 2.72	
G-AZOF	AESL Airtourer T5 (Super 150)	A.549		21. 2.72	
G-AZOG	PA-28R-200 Cherokee Arrow D II	28R-7235009		21. 2.72	
G-AZOH	Beechcraft B80 Queen Air	LD-410	N7891R	28. 2.72	To CN-TKS 27.3.95. Canx 22.9.93.
G-AZOI	Boeing 707-321 (Line No. 83)	17602	N724PA	13.11.71R	NTU - Remained as N724PA 11/71. Canx.
G-AZOJ	Beechcraft 56TC Baron	TG-10	N5443U G-AZOJ/N5443U	28. 2.72	To OO-FAN 5/76. Canx 10.5.76.

Regn	Type	c/n	Previous identity	Regn date	Fate or immediate subsequent identity (if known)
G-AZOK	Slingsby T.61A Falke	1766		28. 2.72	Crashed near Loch Leven on 24.9.74. Canx 7.11.74. To RAFGSA for spares use 1975.
G-AZOL	PA-34-200-2 Seneca	34-7250075	N4348T	28. 2.72	
G-AZOM	MBB Bo.105C (Converted to Bo.105D)	S.21	EI-AWB G-AZOM/D-HDAD	1. 3.72	Ditched near Burnham Ridge Buoy on 24.7.84 & w/o. Canx as destroyed 20.2.86.
G-AZON	PA-34-200-2 Seneca	34-7250081	N4381T	1. 3.72	DBR near Elstree on 27.3.84. Canx by CAA 20.1.92.
G-AZOO	Western O-65 HAFB	015		1. 3.72	(Extant 2/97)
G-AZOP	Aerostar Mooney M.20E Chapparel	21-0023	N9617V	1. 3.72	Fatal crash at Lawrence End Estate, Dane Street, near Peters Green shortly after take-off from Luton on 30.9.76. Canx.
G-AZOR	MBB Bo.105DB	S.20	EC-DOE G-AZOR/D-HDAC	1. 3.72	
G-AZOS	Jurca MJ.5-H1 Sirocco	001 & PFA/2206		1. 3.72	
G-AZOT	PA-34-200-2 Seneca	34-7250073	N4340T	3. 3.72	To Dodson Aviation Scrapyard, Ottawa, KS, USA. (Wings only at Andrewsfield 1/99 - fuselage being rebuilt elsewhere)
G-AZOU	SAN Jodel DR.1051 Sicile	354	F-BJYX	7. 3.72	
G-AZOV	Vickers 837 Viscount	439	OE-LAH	7. 3.72	To Taiwan as B-2029 12/72. Canx 13.12.72.
G-AZOW	Robin DR.253 Regent	200		7. 3.72	Hit tree on approach to Headcorn, Kent on 26.5.75. Canx as destroyed 27.6.75.
G-AZOX	Robin DR.360 Major 160	657		7. 3.72	Crashed at Biggin Hill on 21.7.73. Canx as destroyed 20.11.75.
G-AZOY	Slingsby T.59D Kestrel 19	1771		7. 3.72	To ZS-GID 5/73. Canx 5.2.73.
G-AZOZ	Reims Cessna FRA.150L Aerobat	0136		7. 3.72	
G-AZPA	PA-25-235 Pawnee C	25-5223	N8797L	7. 3.72	
G-AZPB	PA-25-235 Pawnee C	25-5160	N8709L	7. 3.72	Crashed while spraying at Bayons Manor, Tealby on 5.7.76. Canx.
G-AZPC	Slingsby T.61C Falke	1767		7. 3.72	
G-AZPD	AESL Airtourer T.6-24	B.569	(ZK-DDS)	7. 3.72	To ZK-DKU 10/73. Canx 10.10.73.
G-AZPE	BAC One-Eleven Srs.515FB	BAC.208	D-ALAS	9. 3.72	To TI-LRK 10/73. Canx 17.10.73.
G-AZPF	Sportavia-Putzer Fournier RF-5	5001	D-KOLT	10. 3.72	
G-AZPG	DH.104 Dove 5	04462	HB-LAS	13. 3.72	CofA expired 24.11.76 & WFU. Broken up at Southend & removed in 1979. Canx as WFU 29.2.84.
G-AZPH	Craft-Pitts S-1S Special	S1S-001-C	N11CB	13. 3.72	Ground-looped on landing at Little Snoring on 10.5.91. Canx as WFU 8.1.97. On display at the Science Museum, London.
G-AZPI	Scottish Aviation Bulldog Srs.100	BH.100/152		13. 3.72	To Swedish Army as Fv61041 4/72. Canx 17.4.72.
G-AZPJ	Scottish Aviation Bulldog Srs.100	BH.100/154		13. 3.72	To Swedish Army as Fv61042 4/72. Canx 18.4.72.
G-AZPK	Scottish Aviation Bulldog Srs.100	BH.100/155		13. 3.72	To Swedish Army as Fv61043 4/72. Canx 25.4.72.
G-AZPL	Scottish Aviation Bulldog Srs.100	BH.100/156		13. 3.72	To Swedish Army as Fv61044 5/72. Canx 1.5.72.
G-AZPM	Scottish Aviation Bulldog Srs.100	BH.100/157		13. 3.72	To Swedish Army as Fv61045 5/72. Canx 8.5.72.
G-AZPN	Scottish Aviation Bulldog Srs.100	BH.100/158		13. 3.72	To Swedish Army as Fv61046 5/72. Canx 15.5.72.
G-AZPO	Scottish Aviation Bulldog Srs.100	BH.100/162		13. 3.72	To Swedish Army as Fv61047 5/72. Canx 22.5.72.
G-AZPP	Scottish Aviation Bulldog Srs.100	BH.100/163		13. 3.72	To Swedish Army as Fv61048 5/72. Canx 22.5.72.
G-AZPR	Scottish Aviation Bulldog Srs.100	BH.100/164		13. 3.72	To Swedish Army as Fv61049 6/72. Canx 8.6.72.
G-AZPS	Scottish Aviation Bulldog Srs.100	BH.100/165		13. 3.72	To Swedish Army as Fv61050 6/72. Canx 15.6.72.
G-AZPT	Cessna 421B Golden Eagle II	421B-0233	N5990M	14. 3.72	To F-BTDY 7/72. Canx 15.6.72.
G-AZPU	BN-2A-7 Islander	298	G-51-298	14. 3.72	To YI-AFZ 5/73. Canx 1.5.73.
G-AZPV	Phoenix-Luton LA-4A Minor	PFA/833		14. 3.72	
G-AZPW	Boeing 707-340C (Line No. 844)	20275	AP-AWB	20. 3.72	Restored as AP-AWZ 10/72. Canx 1.10.72.
G-AZPX	Western O-31 HAFB	011		20. 3.72	(Extant 2/97)
G-AZPY	BAC One-Eleven Srs.515FB	BAC.187	D-ALAT	21. 3.72	To D-AMAS 5/72. Canx 1.5.72.
G-AZPZ	BAC One-Eleven Srs.515FB	BAC.229	D-AMAM G-AZPZ/D-ALAQ	21. 3.72	To 5N-IMO. Canx 17.3.94.
G-AZRA	MBB Bo.209 Monsun 150FF	192	D-EAIH	21. 3.72	
G-AZRB	Cessna 340	340-0056	N5856M	22. 3.72	To N4085C. Canx 5.8.81.
G-AZRC	Cessna 340	340-0062	N5891M	22. 3.72	To N3947A. Canx 13.5.83.
G-AZRD	Cessna 401B	401B-0218	N7999Q	22. 3.72	
G-AZRE	Vickers 952 Vanguard	729	CF-TKF	23. 3.72	Canx 12.9.75 on sale to France. Marks F-BXOF NTU. (Stored at Perpignan still marked as G-AZRE)
G-AZRF	Sikorsky S-61N	61-473	PK-HBT	7. 5.72	Canx 22.4.87 on sale to France. To N9115Z 9/87.
G-AZRG	PA-23-250 Aztec D	27-4386	N6536Y	23. 3.72	Canx as WFU 19.10.93. (On fire dump 4/97 Ronaldsway)
G-AZRH	PA-28-140 Cherokee D (Mod) (Modified in 1999)	28-7125585		23. 3.72	
G-AZRI	Payne HAFB (56,500 cu.ft)	GFP.1		21. 3.72	(Active 4/93)
G-AZRJ	BN-2A-8 Islander	681		23. 3.72	To XA-DIM 6/73. Canx.
G-AZRK	Sportavia-Putzer Fournier RF-5	5112		23. 3.72	
G-AZRL	PA-18-95 Super Cub (L-18C-PI)(Frame No 18-1213)	18-1331	OO-SBR OO-HML/ALAT 18-1331/51-15331	23. 3.72	
G-AZRM	Sportavia-Putzer Fournier RF-5	5111		24. 3.72	
G-AZRN	Cameron O-84 HAFB	28		28. 3.72	(Extant 4/93)

Regn	Type	c/n	Previous identity	Regn date	Fate or immediate subsequent identity (if known)
G-AZRO	Boeing 707-340C (Line No. 849)	20488	AP-AWA	28. 3.72	To AP-AXG 11/73. Canx 1.11.73.
G-AZRP	AESL Airtourer T2 (115)	A.529		28. 3.72	
G-AZRR	Cessna 310Q	310Q-0490	N9923F	28. 3.72	
G-AZRS	PA-22-150 Tri-Pacer	22-5141	XT-AAH F-OCGZ/ALAT 22-5141/"F-MKAC"	28. 3.72	
G-AZRT	Cessna 182P Skylane	182-61063	N7423Q	28. 3.72	To ZK-EJO 12/76. Canx 29.11.76.
G-AZRU	Agusta-Bell 206B JetRanger II	8304	EI-BES G-AZRU	28. 3.72	Badly damaged in forced landing whilst spraying near Sutton-in-Ashfield, Notts. on 19.6.84. Canx by CAA 27.7.89.
G-AZRV	PA-28R-200 Cherokee Arrow B	28R-7135191	N2309T	4. 4.72	
G-AZRW	Cessna T.337C Turbo Super Skymaster	337-0914	9XR-DB N2614S	4. 4.72	CofA expired 7.6.82. Canx by CAA 3.4.89. (Stored 7/94)
G-AZRX	Gardan GY-80-160 Horizon	14	F-BLIJ	4. 4.72	Badly damaged on landing at Sandtoft on 14.8.91. Canx by CAA 21.10.91. (On display in crazy golf course on seafront 6/99 at Marine Parade, Southend-on-Sea)
G-AZRY	Short SC.7 Skyliner Executive	SH1901	G-14-73	4. 4.72	To LN-NPA 7/73. Canx 4.7.73.
G-AZRZ	Cessna U.206F Stationair	U206-01803	N9603G	4. 4.72	
G-AZSA	Stampe et Renard SV-4B (Officially regd in error as c/n "64")	1203	V-61 Belgium AF	5. 4.72	
G-AZSB	CEA Jodel DR.250/160 Captaine	18	F-OCGL	5. 4.72	Crashed on landing at Barton on 9.6.74. Canx as WFU 6.1.75.
G-AZSC	Noorduyn AT-16-ND Harvard IIB	14A-1363	PH-SKK (N.....)/PH-SKK/R.Netherlands AF B-19/FT323/43-13064	7. 4.72	
G-AZSD	Slingsby T.29B Motor Tutor (Rebuild of Slingsby c/n 561 by R.G.Boyton)	RGB 01/72 & PFA/1574		7. 4.72	
G-AZSE	PA-28R-200 Cherokee Arrow B II	28R-7235044		10. 4.72	Crashed near Castle Bay, Barra, Outer Hebrides on 16.6.84. Canx by CAA 4.12.86.
G-AZSF	PA-28R-200 Cherokee Arrow B II	28R-7235048		10. 4.72	
G-AZSG	PA-28-180 Cherokee F	28-7205166		10. 4.72	Crashed on take-off at Netherthorpe on 11.7.91. Canx as destroyed 11.5.92.
G-AZSH	PA-28R-180 Cherokee Arrow B	28R-30461	N4612J	18. 4.72	To G-WWAL 10/98. Canx.
G-AZSI	Douglas DC-4-1009	42987	LN-TUR Belgium AF KX-2\'OT-CWV'/OO-SBL/OY-DFO	11. 4.72	WFU & used for spares at Stansted in 6/72. Canx as WFU 14.3.77.
G-AZSJ	Cessna 414	414-0253	N8248Q	12. 4.72	To D-INGA 2/75. Canx 6.2.75.
G-AZSK	Taylor JT.1 Monoplane	PFA/1436		12. 4.72	Not completed. Canx by CAA 2.9.91.
G-AZSL	SEEMS MS.890B Rallye Commodore 145	10324	F-BLBB (ZS-CDA)	13. 4.72	CofA expired 3.8.77 & WFU at Sherburn-in-Elmet. Canx as WFU 5.12.83.
G-AZSM	PA-28R-180 Cherokee Arrow D	28R-30684	5Y-AIQ N4942J	14. 4.72	Destroyed when crashed shortly after take-off from Annemasse, in the French Alps on 2.9.85. Canx by CAA 4.12.86.
G-AZSN	PA-28R-200 Cherokee Arrow D	28R-35642	N3083R	17. 4.72	Forced landing near the A38 road at Axbridge on 2.10.88 & DBR. Canx by CAA 3.2.89.
G-AZSO	DH.114 Heron 2/1P	14051	ZS-DIG	18. 4.72	To C-GCAT 4/74. Canx 2.4.74.
G-AZSP	Cameron O-84 HAFB	43		18. 4.72	Canx as WFU 11.1.82. (Extant 2/97)
G-AZSR	Short SC.7 Skyvan 3M-400-11	SH1902	G-14-74	19. 4.72	To R.Thai Police as 21902 in 6/72. Canx 30.6.72.
G-AZSS	Jodel D.9	PFA/939		20. 4.72	Not completed. Canx 11.7.84.
G-AZST	Western O-65 HAFB	016		20. 4.72	To N3AF 9/72. Canx 10.9.72.
G-AZSU	HS.748 Srs.2A/232	1612	A2-ABB G-AZSU/VP-BCM	20. 2.72	To F-GPDC 5/95. Canx 25.4.95.
G-AZSV	Hiller 360 UH-12E	2114	EP-HAH (5N-AGJ)/ZS-HAV/VR-BBO	21. 4.72	Crashed near Wingate Farm, near Lynton, Devon on 28.7.80. Canx.
G-AZSW	Beagle B.121 Pup Srs.100	B121-140	PH-VRT G-35-140	24. 4.72	
G-AZSX	Beagle B.121 Pup Srs.100	B121-141	PH-VRU G-35-141	24. 4.72	Crashed near Booker on 3.8.83. Canx by CAA 4.12.86.
G-AZSY	PA-24-260 Comanche	24-4438	N8979P	24. 4.72	To N59RG. Canx 19.10.82.
G-AZSZ	PA-23-250 Aztec D	27-4194	N6851Y	25. 4.72	
G-AZTA	MBB Bo.209 Monsun 150FF	190	D-EAIF	25. 4.72	
G-AZTB	MBB Bo.209 Monsun 150FF	159	D-EBJS	28. 4.72	Crashed at Usworth on 13.2.80. Canx.
G-AZTC	MBB Bo.209 Monsun 150FF	172	D-EAAL	28. 4.72	To D-EFTC 1/77. Canx 5.7.76.
G-AZTD	PA-32-300 Cherokee Six D	32-7140001	N8611N	26. 4.72	(Open storage at Enstone in 6/98)
G-AZTE	Reims Cessna FRA.150L Aerobat	0143		28. 4.72	To EI-BJA 3/80. Canx 3.3.80.
G-AZTF	Reims Cessna F.177RG Cardinal	0054		28. 4.72	
G-AZTG	Boeing 707-321 (Line No. 75)	17600	N722PA	3. 5.72	Canx as WFU 27.11.78 at Lasham. Broken up in 4/82.
G-AZTH	Bensen B.8 Gyroplane	EH.1		28. 4.72	No CofA or Permit issued. Dismantled and the parts dispersed. Canx as WFU 5.12.83.
G-AZTI	MBB Bo.105DBS-4 (Originally regd as an Bo.105C)	S.34	EI-BTE G-AZTI/EC-DRY/G-AZTI/D-HDAN	27. 4.72	Rebuilt with new pod S.912 in 1993 - To G-BUTN 1/93. Canx as WFU 26.1.93.
G-AZTJ	Fuji FA.200-180 Aero Subaru	FA200-166		28. 4.72	Fatal crash into Liverpool Bay on 4.2.75. Canx.
G-AZTK	Reims Cessna F.172F Skyhawk	0116	PH-CON OO-SIR	27. 4.72	(Badly damaged in forced landing in a field ½ mile SW of Guildford on 3.12.93)
G-AZTL	PA-31-300 Navajo	31-589	N6650L	28. 4.72	Hit tree on approach to Stapleford 3.1.73 and destroyed. Canx.
G-AZTM	AESL Airtourer T2 (115)	A.530		28. 4.72	(Status uncertain; departed by road from Staverton in 1985) Canx as WFU 30.5.84.
G-AZTN	AESL Airtourer T2 (115)	A.531		28. 4.72	Crashed at Puriton, Somerset on 27.6.77. Canx as WFU 30.3.83. (Wreck stored 9/95)

Regn	Type	c/n	Previous identity	Regn date	Fate or immediate subsequent identity (if known)
G-AZTO	PA-34-200-2 Seneca	34-7250141	N4516T	28. 4.72	Overran runway and went into a ditch on landing at Beverley 27.8.92. Canx by CAA 15.2.93. (Wings at Stapleford in 5/98)
G-AZTP	SNCAN Stampe SV-4C	90	F-BBNH	28. 4.72	To CF-DJQ 9/72. Canx 4.9.72.
G-AZTR	SNCAN Stampe SV-4C	596	F-BDEQ	28. 4.72	(Stored in Blue Max Movie Aircraft Museum 3/96)
G-AZTS	Reims Cessna F.172L Skyhawk	0066		28. 4.72	
G-AZTT	PA-28R-200 Cherokee Arrow D	28R-7135205	N2316T	27. 4.72	Crashed into trees in fog at Bayleys Hill, Kent on 9.1.77. Canx by CAA 4.12.86.
G-AZTU	Cessna 177 Cardinal	00543	N3243T	28. 4.72	To LN-HHD 4/79. Canx 4.9.79.
G-AZTV	Stolp SA.500 Starlet	SSM.2 & PFA/1584		19. 5.72	Damaged in forced landing at Manor Farm, Grateley, Hants on 4.7.92. (Status uncertain)
G-AZTW	Reims Cessna F.177RG Cardinal	0043		28. 4.72	
G-AZTX	Scottish Aviation Bulldog Srs.100	BH.100/166		28. 4.72	To Swedish Army as Fv61051 6/72. Canx 19.6.72.
G-AZTY	Scottish Aviation Bulldog Srs.100	BH.100/167		28. 4.72	To Swedish Army as Fv61052 6/72. Canx 26.6.72.
G-AZTZ	Scottish Aviation Bulldog Srs.100	BH.100/171		28. 4.72	To Swedish Army as Fv61053 7/72. Canx 17.7.72.
G-AZUA	Scottish Aviation Bulldog Srs.100	BH.100/172		28. 4.72	To Swedish Army as Fv61054 7/72. Canx 10.7.72.
G-AZUB	Scottish Aviation Bulldog Srs.100	BH.100/173		28. 4.72	To Swedish Army as Fv61055 8/72. Canx 1.8.72.
G-AZUC	Scottish Aviation Bulldog Srs.100	BH.100/174		28. 4.72	To Swedish Army as Fv61056 8/72. Canx 10.8.72.
G-AZUD	Scottish Aviation Bulldog Srs.100	BH.100/175		28. 4.72	To Swedish Army as Fv61057 8/72. Canx 1.8.72.
G-AZUE	Scottish Aviation Bulldog Srs.100	BH.100/176		28. 4.72	To Swedish Army as Fv61058 8/72. Canx 22.8.72.
G-AZUF	HS.125 Srs.600A	256001		4. 5.72	To N82BH 8/72. Canx 30.8.72.
G-AZUG	American Aviation AA-5 Traveler	AA5-0083		8. 5.72	To G-KASH 9/83. Canx.
G-AZUH	PA-31-310 Navajo	31-780	N7403L	8. 5.72	To N126AC. Canx 24.8.81.
G-AZUI	Vickers 952 Vanguard	740	CF-TKQ	9. 5.72	WFU at Southend 20.3.74. Canx.
G-AZUJ	Beechcraft 95-B55 Baron	TC-1454		9. 5.72	Destroyed in a fatal crash at Elmdon on 29.11.75. Canx as destroyed 5.12.83.
G-AZUK	BAC One-Eleven Srs.476FM	BAC.241	OB-R-1080 G-AZUK/G-16-16/OB-R-1080	9. 5.72	To 5N-ECI. Canx 25.11.94.
G-AZUL	Stampe et Renard SV-4B (Regd with c/n 27)	1169	V-27 (Belgian AF)	10. 5.72	To D-EIHD 11/85. Canx 24.8.83.
G-AZUM	Reims Cessna F.172L Skyhawk	0863		11. 5.72	
G-AZUN	Reims Cessna F.172L Skyhawk	0839	(OO-FCB)	11. 5.72	To G-OFCM 10/81. Canx.
G-AZUO	Reims Cessna F.177RG Cardinal II	0056		11. 5.72	To 9H-ACG. Canx 4.11.92.
G-AZUP	Cameron O-65 HAFB	36		11. 5.72	(Extant 9/94)
G-AZUR	BN-2A-2 Islander	302	G-51-302 (N57JA)	11. 5.72	To JA5195 8/72. Canx 24.7.72.
G-AZUS	BN-2A-2 Islander	303	G-51-303 (N58JA)	11. 5.72	To D-IHVH 6/72. Canx 8.6.72.
G-AZUT	Socata MS.893A Rallye Commodore 180	10963	VH-TCH	12. 5.72	
G-AZUU	Sportavia-Putzer Fournier RF-4D	4095	F-BPLD	12. 5.72	Crashed at Cleeve Hill Golf Course, Cheltenham on 25.7.82. Canx.
G-AZUV	Cameron O-65 HAFB	41		12. 5.72	Damaged & WFU at Rendharn Green, Suffolk. Canx 6.1.82. (Stored - no longer airworthy)
G-AZUW	Cameron A-140 HAFB	45		12. 5.72	To F-BTVO 6/73. Canx 7.6.73.
G-AZUX	Western O-56 HAFB	017		15. 5.72	(Extant 6/97)
G-AZUY	Cessna 310L	310L-0012	SE-FEC LN-LMH/N2212F	15. 5.72	
G-AZUZ	Reims Cessna FRA.150L Aerobat	0146		16. 5.72	
G-AZVA	MBB Bo.209 Monsun 150FF	177	(D-EAAQ)	16. 5.72	
G-AZVB	MBB Bo.209 Monsun 150FF	178	(D-EAAS)	16. 5.72	
G-AZVC	MBB Bo.209 Monsun 150FF	188	D-EAID	18. 5.72	Collided with PA-28R-200 G-AYYN during the Kent Messenger Air Race on 19.8.84 and crashed at Bretts Bridge, Cobham. Canx as destroyed 22.1.85.
G-AZVD	Not allocated.				
G-AZVE	American Aviation AA-5 Traveler	AA5-0074	N5847L	16. 5.72	Canx as destroyed 20.10.97.
G-AZVF	Socata MS.894A Rallye Minerva 220	11999	(F-OCSR)	16. 5.72	
G-AZVG	American Aviation AA-5 Traveler	AA5-0075	N5875L	16. 5.72	
G-AZVH	Socata MS.894A Rallye Minerva 220	12017		16. 5.72	
G-AZVI	Socata MS.892A Rallye Commodore 150	12039		16. 5.72	
G-AZVJ	PA-34-200 Seneca II	34-7250125	N4529T	16. 5.72	
G-AZVK	Reims Cessna F.177RG Cardinal	0058		18. 5.72	To F-GAJE 1/77. Canx 8.6.76.
G-AZVL	Jodel D.119 (Valladeau built)	794	F-BILB	19. 5.72	
G-AZVM	Hughes 369HS (500C)	61-0326S	N9091F	19. 5.72	
G-AZVN	Bell 206B JetRanger II	759		22. 5.72	DBR near Kippen, Stirling on 30.6.78. Canx.
G-AZVO	Cameron O-84 HAFB	39		22. 5.72	To N14446 3/73. Canx 12.3.73.
G-AZVP	Reims Cessna F.177RG Cardinal	0057		22. 5.72	
G-AZVR	Reims Cessna F.150L	0798		25. 5.72	To G-HFCB 2/87. Canx.

Regn	Type	c/n	Previous identity	Regn date	Fate or immediate subsequent identity (if known)
G-AZVS	HS.125 Srs.3B	25132	OY-DKP	25. 5.72	To G-MRFB 8/85. Canx.
G-AZVT	Cameron O-84 HAFB	40		30. 5.72	CofA expired 2.6.78. (Extant with Jenny Robinson .94) (Extant 2/97) Canx by CAA 4.8.98.
G-AZVU	Cessna TU.206D Turbo Super Skywagon	U206-1311	4X-ALK N72180	30. 5.72	To EC-CEI 9/73. Canx 11.7.73.
G-AZVV	PA-28-180 Cherokee G	28-7205171		30. 5.72	Fatal crash when struck trees on take-off from a private strip at Drumlaig Castle, Dumfries on 8.11.85. Canx as WFU 8.8.86.
G-AZVW	Bell 47G-5A	25084	N14811	30. 5.72	To 5B-CFX 4/84. Canx 3.2.84.
G-AZVX	Bell 47G-5A	25085	N14812	30. 5.72	To 5B-CFY 4/84. Canx 3.2.84.
G-AZVY	Cessna 310Q	310Q-0040	SE-FKV N7540Q	31. 5.72	To G-EGEE 11/83. Canx.
G-AZVZ	PA-28-140 Cherokee E	28-7225250		5. 6.72	To EC-DYL 1/86. Canx 2.1.86.
G-AZWA	Boeing 707-321 (Line No. 98)	17605	N727PA	22. 6.72	To (N727PA)/N70798 10/77. Canx 7.11.77.
G-AZWB	PA-28-140 Cherokee E	28-7225244		5. 6.72	
G-AZWC	Not allocated.				
G-AZWD	PA-28-140 Cherokee E	28-7225298		6. 6.72	
G-AZWE	PA-28-140 Cherokee E	28-7225303		6. 6.72	
G-AZWF	SAN Jodel DR.1050 Ambassadeur (Composite including fuselage of DR.1050M F-BLJX c/n 492)	130	F-BJJT	7. 6.72	
G-AZWG	Bell 47G-5	25044	SE-HEB	8. 6.72	Restored as SE-HEB 2/74. Canx 20.9.73.
G-AZWH	Scottish Aviation Bulldog Srs.101	BH.100/179		8. 6.72	To Swedish Army as Fv61061 8/72. Canx 29.8.72.
G-AZWI	Scottish Aviation Bulldog Srs.101	BH.100/180		8. 6.72	To Swedish Army as Fv61062 9/72. Canx 11.9.72.
G-AZWJ	Scottish Aviation Bulldog Srs.101	BH.100/181		8. 6.72	To Swedish Army as Fv61063 9/72. Canx 12.9.72.
G-AZWK	Scottish Aviation Bulldog Srs.101	BH.100/182		8. 6.72	To Swedish Army as Fv61064 9/72. Canx 19.9.72.
G-AZWL	Scottish Aviation Bulldog Srs.101	BH.100/183		8. 6.72	To Swedish Army as Fv61065 9/72. Canx 26.9.72.
G-AZWM	Scottish Aviation Bulldog Srs.101	BH.100/184	Fv61066 Swedish Army/G-AZWM	8. 6.72	Restored as Swedish Army as Fv61066 4/73. Canx 17.4.73.
G-AZWN	Scottish Aviation Bulldog Srs.101	BH.100/185	Fv61067 Swedish Army/G-AZWN	8. 6.72	Restored as Swedish Army as Fv61067 4/73. Canx 17.4.73.
G-AZWO	Scottish Aviation Bulldog Srs.101	BH.100/186		8. 6.72	To Swedish Army as Fv61068 10/72. Canx 19.10.72.
G-AZWP	Scottish Aviation Bulldog Srs.101	BH.100/187		8. 6.72	To Swedish Army as Fv61069 4/73. Canx 17.4.73.
G-AZWR	Scottish Aviation Bulldog Srs.101	BH.100/188		8. 6.72	To Swedish Army as Fv61070 4/73. Canx 17.4.73.
G-AZWS	PA-28R-200 Cherokee Arrow D	28R-30749	N4993J	8. 6.72	
G-AZWT(1)	Reims Cessna F.172E	0057	G-ASOK	. 6.72	NTU - Allocated in error. Remained as G-ASOK. Canx.
G-AZWT(2)	Westland Lysander Mk.IIIA	Y1536	RCAF 1582 V9552	9. 6.72	(On overhaul Duxford 10/97)
G-AZWU	Reims Cessna F.150L	0815		9. 6.72	DBR at Husbands Bosworth on 3.4.80. Canx.
G-AZWV	Cessna U.206D Super Skywagon	206-1183	5Y-AIH N29235	9. 6.72	Destroyed in fatal take-off crash from Dubai, UAE on 29.9.77. (Wreck next to runway at Dubai in 8/80) Canx as destroyed 5.12.83.
G-AZWW	PA-23-250 Aztec E	27-4727	N14161	14. 6.72	To F-GOPR. Canx 23.6.95.
G-AZWX	Short SC.7 Skyvan 3-100-39	SH1906	G-14-78	14. 6.72	To R.Thai Highways Dept as U-01/HS-DOH 11/72. Canx 8.11.72.
G-AZWY	PA-24-260 Comanche C	24-4806	N9310P	16. 6.72	
G-AZWZ	McCulloch J-2	066	N4356G	19. 6.72	Ditched in sea off Worthing Pier on 21.9.75. Canx as destroyed 28.10.75.
G-AZXA	Beechcraft 95-C55 Baron	TE-72	SE-EKZ	19. 6.72	
G-AZXB	Cameron O-65 HAFB	48		20. 6.72	CofA expired 6.5.81. (Extant 2/97)
G-AZXC	Reims Cessna F.150L	0793		20. 6.72	
G-AZXD	Reims Cessna F.172L Skyhawk	0878		20. 6.72	
G-AZXE	Wassmer Jodel D.120A Paris-Nice	296	F-BNCL	20. 6.72	Fatal crash near Cotgrove on 28.3.88. Canx as destroyed 6.2.89.
G-AZXF	Reims Cessna FRA.150L Aerobat	0144		20. 6.72	Crashed into the River Humber on 14.7.74. Wreck lying sunk in position 324 degrees from Chalk Tower at 1225 metres distance. Canx.
G-AZXG	PA-23-250 Aztec D	27-4328	N6963Y	23. 6.72	Crashed on landing at Little Snoring on 25.10.91 & DBR. Canx by CAA 6.5.93. (Instructional Airframe 7/97)
G-AZXH	PA-34-200 Seneca II	34-7250215	N5068T	23. 6.72	Damaged on landing at Le Mans, France (date?). Remains to Booker in 8/86 and scrapped in 11/86. Canx as destroyed 13.7.87.
G-AZXI	Hughes 269C	41-0110		28. 6.72	To HB-XNH. Canx 13.4.82.
G-AZXJ	BAC 167 Strikemaster Mk.88 (Also c/n EEP/JP/3235)	PS.303	G-27-199	28. 6.72	To RNZAF as NZ6363 in 7/72. Canx 10.7.72.
G-AZXK	BAC 167 Strikemaster Mk.88 (Also c/n EEP/JP/3236)	PS.304	G-27-200	28. 6.72	To RNZAF as NZ6364 in 9/72. Canx 12.9.72.
G-AZXL	BAC 167 Strikemaster Mk.89	PS.311	G-27-207	28. 6.72	To Ecuador AF as T-243 in 7/72. Canx 10.7.72.
G-AZXM	HS.121 Trident Srs.2E	2154	5B-DAA	28. 6.72	Flown to Southend on 4.2.85 for scrapping. Broken up. Canx as destroyed 8.3.85.
G-AZXN	BN-2A-2 Islander	682		29. 6.72	To OB-T-1035 10/73. Canx 8.10.73.
G-AZXO	BN-2A-9 Islander	683		29. 6.72	To CR-APD. Canx 8.5.75.
G-AZXP	BN-2A-8 Islander	684		29. 6.72	To 9M-ASL 6/73. Canx 29.5.73.
G-AZXR	BN-2A-9 Islander	685	CR-CAU G-AZXR	29. 6.72	To N143FS 7/93. Canx 7.7.93.

Regn	Type	c/n	Previous identity	Regn date	Fate or immediate subsequent identity (if known)
G-AZXS	BN-2A-27 Islander	686		29. 6.72	To DQ-FCA 9/73. Canx 19.9.73.
G-AZXT	BN-2A-2 Islander	687		29. 6.72	To CR-APO. Canx 8.5.75.
G-AZXU	BN-2A-9 Islander	688	F-BUFX (F-OCTB)/G-AZXU	29. 6.72	To F-OGSM. Canx 8.5.75.
G-AZXV	BN-2A-9 Islander	689		29. 6.72	To PT-KAB. Canx 8.5.75.
G-AZXW	BN-2A-9 Islander	690		29. 6.72	To PT-JNT. Canx 8.5.75.
G-AZXX	BN-2A-8 Islander	691	C9-APT CR-APT/G-AZXX	29. 6.72	To EC-DBK 12/77. Canx 18.11.77.
G-AZXY	BN-2A-3 Islander	692		29. 6.72	To PK-KND 12/73. Canx 6.12.73.
G-AZXZ	BN-2A-3 Islander	693		29. 6.72	To 9M-ATM 5/74. Canx 29.5.74.
G-AZYA	Gardan GY-80-160 Horizon	57	F-BLPT	7. 7.72	
G-AZYB	Bell 47H-1	1538	LN-OQG SE-HBE/OO-SHW	4. 7.72	Crashed at St.Mary Bourne, near Thruxton on 21.4.84. Canx as destroyed 22.4.85. (Cockpit on rebuild 4/98 Weston-super-Mare)
G-AZYC	Cessna A188B Agwagon	188-00875	N4475Q	30. 6.72	DBR at Hardwick prior to CofA expiry on 24.3.79 (date?) and subsequently used for spares. Canx as destroyed 5.12.83.
G-AZYD	GEMS MS.893A Rallye Commodore 180	10645	F-BNSE	30. 6.72	
G-AZYE	PA-32-260 Cherokee Six	32-646	5Y-AEA N3732N	26. 6.72	To OO-SAN 1/77. Canx 26.11.76.
G-AZYF	PA-28-180 Cherokee D	28-5227	5Y-AJK	23. 6.72	To N7813M 4/94. Canx 8.4.94.
G-AZYG	PA-E23-250 Aztec C	27-2647	5Y-AAU	26. 6.72	Accident prior to 11.8.79. (Wreck noted at Elstree on 11.3.81) Canx as WFU 11.7.84.
G-AZYH	Cameron O-84 HAFB	44		4. 7.72	To SE-ZZY 8/73. Canx 28.8.73.
G-AZYI	Cessna E.310Q	310Q-0129	N7629Q	6. 7.72	DBF at Bandirran Farm, near Perth on 1.11.83. Canx.
G-AZYJ	WSK PZL-104 Wilga 35	62153	SP-WEA(2)	6. 7.72	To G-WILG 4/97. Canx.
G-AZYK	Cessna 310Q	310Q-0491	N4182Q	7. 7.72	To G-IMLI 4/86. Canx.
G-AZYL	Portslade School HAFB	MK17		10. 7.72	Canx as WFU 25.4.85.
G-AZYM	Cessna 310Q	310Q-0507	N5893M N4592L	6. 7.72	
G-AZYN	BAC 167 Strikemaster Mk.88 (Also c/n EEP/JP/3237)	PS.305	G-27-201	13. 7.72	To RNZAF as NZ6365 in 9/72. Canx 12.9.72.
G-AZYO	PA-28R-200 Cherokee Arrow II	28R-7235205		7. 7.72	NTU - To G-BAAP 8/72. Canx as marks WFU 7.7.72.
G-AZYP	PA-28-140 Cherokee C	28-7125289	LN-MTP	7. 7.72	Fatal crash into Illgill Head, Wastwater, Cumberland 25.3.73. Canx 26.11.73 as destroyed.
G-AZYR	Cessna 340	340-0063	N5893M	12. 7.72	To G-REEN 2/84. Canx.
G-AZYS	Scintex CP.301C-1 Emeraude	568	F-BJAY	7. 7.72	
G-AZYT	Fairchild-Hiller FH-1100	79	5N-AGX N579FH	12. 7.72	To N96118 3/75. Canx 13.3.75.
G-AZYU	PA-23-250 Aztec E	27-4601	N13983	13. 7.72	
G-AZYV	Burns HAFB (O-77)	PRB-01		3. 7.72	CofA expired 12.8.81. (Active in Italy 5/91) Canx by CAA 18.4.97.
G-AZYW	Short SC.7 Skyvan 3A-100-40	SH1903	G-14-75	12. 7.72	To LN-NPG 5/75. Canx 9.5.75.
G-AZYX	GEMS MS.893A Rallye Commodore 180	10640	F-BNXJ	12. 7.72	Crashed at Talgarth, near Brecon on 13.6.81. Canx 17.3.82.
G-AZYY	Slingsby T.61A Falke	1770		12. 7.72	
G-AZYZ	Wassmer WA.51A Pacific	30	F-OCSE	14. 7.72	
G-AZZA	PA-E23-250 Aztec D	27-4016	(PT-DIU) N6743Y	12. 7.72	CofA expired 13.8.82. Broken up at Glenrothes in early-1983. Canx by CAA 21.1.87. To Dodson Aviation Scrapyard in the USA.
G-AZZB	Agusta-Bell 206B JetRanger II	8327		14. 7.72	DBF after landing at Inglestone, Edinburgh on 19.8.84. Canx in 4/86.
G-AZZC	Douglas DC-10-10 (Line No. 47)	46905		14. 7.72	To N902CL 10/82. Canx 1.10.82.
G-AZZD	Douglas DC-10-10 (Line No. 50)	46906		14. 7.72	To N916CL 10/82. Canx 30.4.82.
G-AZZE	Beechcraft A23-19 Musketeer Sport III	MB-200	LN-TVH	14. 7.72	To G-DJHB 8/82. Canx.
G-AZZF	Morane-Saulnier MS.880B Rallye Club	174	F-BKKO	18. 7.72	CofA expired 8.7.84. Canx as destroyed 6.12.88.
G-AZZG	Cessna 188 Agwagon 230	188-0279	OY-AHT N8029V	12. 7.72	CofA expired 1.5.81. (On rebuild 5/92)
G-AZZH	Practavia Pilot Sprite 115	PFA/1532		13. 7.72	No CofA. (Stored in back garden Dagenham .92)
G-AZZI	Cessna U.206F Stationair	U206-01857	N9657G	17. 7.72	To OO-VDD(3) 5/76. Canx 7.5.76.
G-AZZJ	Beechcraft 95-B55 Baron	TC-1171	N7728R	21. 7.72	Flew into high ground at Paynes End Farm, Hastoe, near Tring, Herts on 4.1.74 and completely destroyed. Canx by CAA 11.9.81.
G-AZZK	Cessna 414 Chancellor	414-0277	(3A-...) G-AZZK/N1562T	17. 7.72	To F-GNZK 6/95. Canx 6.4.95.
G-AZZL	PA-E23-250 Aztec E	27-4720	N14156	19. 7.72	Crashed on landing at Grindale, North Yorks on 2.4.80. Canx.
G-AZZM	BN-2A Mk.III Trislander	321		20. 7.72	To HK-2481 in 5/80. Canx 27.5.80.
G-AZZN	PA-28-140 Cherokee	28-23674	N3658K	18. 7.72	Crashed when overshoot landing at Stapleford on 6.5.77. Canx.
G-AZZO	PA-28-140 Cherokee	28-22887	N4471J	18. 7.72	
G-AZZP	Reims Cessna F.172H Skyhawk	0730	LN-RTA	23. 7.72	Badly damaged in forced landing near Smarden, Kent on 8.6.97. Canx by CAA 20.10.97.
G-AZZR	Reims Cessna F.150L Commuter	0690	LN-LJX	24. 7.72	
G-AZZS	PA-34-200-2 Seneca	34-7250221	EI-BDD G-AZZS/N5212T	17. 7.72	CofA expired 15.11.86. Canx as WFU 17.9.87. To Dodson Aviation Scrapyard, Ottawa, KS, USA.

Regn	Type	c/n	Previous identity	Regn date	Fate or immediate subsequent identity (if known)
G-AZZT	PA-28-180 Cherokee D	28-4604	N5302L	19. 7.72	Crashed on landing at Stapleford on 2.3.80. Canx as destroyed 5.12.83. (Used for crash investigation work/ instructional airframe at Cranfield)
G-AZZU	AESL Airtourer Super T4 (150)	A.555		19. 7.72	To OY-ARF 12/77. Canx 10.1.78.
G-AZZV	Reims Cessna F.172L Skyhawk	0883		18. 7.72	
G-AZZW	Sportavia-Putzer Fournier RF-5	5113		20. 7.72	To LN-GRY 5/97. Canx 25.4.97.
G-AZZX	Reims Cessna FRA.150L Aerobat	0152		27. 7.72	Overturned on landing at Newtownards on 28.2.87. CofA expired 16.8.88. (On rebuild Maypole Farm, Chislet 12/93)
G-AZZY	Robin HR.100/210D Royale	144		25. 7.72	NTU - Not imported. Canx 7.8.72. To (D-EMSH)/F-BUPZ 6/73.
G-AZZZ	DH.82A Tiger Moth	86311	F-BGJE French AF/NL864	27. 7.72	
"G-AZZZ"	DH.89A Dragon Rapide	6578	X7437	----	Unofficially painted as such in 6/55 - To G-APJW 1/58.
G-BAAA	Lockheed L.1011-385-1 Tristar 1	193N-1024	N7852Q	27. 7.72	To VR-HHV 3/77. Canx 11.3.77.
G-BAAB	Lockheed L.1011-385-1 Tristar 1	193N-1032		27. 7.72	To VR-HHW 10/77. Canx 14.10.77.
G-BAAC	Reims Cessna FRA.150L Aerobat	0141		27. 7.72	Crashed at Bodmin on 31.7.77. Canx.
G-BAAD	Evans VP-1 Super	PFA/1540		27. 7.72	
G-BAAE	BN-2A-3S Islander	308	G-51-308	28. 7.72	To (N21JA)/PK-KNA 10/73. Canx 28.8.73.
G-BAAF	Manning-Flanders MF.1 Replica	PPS/REP/8		27. 7.72	Permit expired 6.8.96. (To Blue Max Movie Aircraft Museum) (Carries no external marks)
G-BAAG	Beechcraft 95-B55 Baron	TC-1472		31. 7.72	To G-RICK 5/84. Canx.
G-BAAH	Coates Swalesong S.A.III	SA.III & PFA/1590		31. 7.72	Canx by CAA 2.9.91.
G-BAAI	Socata MS.893A Rallye Commodore 180	10705	F-BOVG	31. 7.72	
G-BAAJ	PA-23-250 Aztec C	27-2569	SE-EIU	31. 7.72	To G-OBEY 5/79. Canx.
G-BAAK	Cessna 207 Skywagon	207-00061	(G-BBYG) G-BAAK/4X-ALQ/N91078	31. 7.72	To ZK-JFJ 6/95. Canx 3.5.95.
G-BAAL	Cessna 172A	172-47678	PH-KAP D-ELGU/N9878T	31. 7.72	
G-BAAM	Beechcraft E90 King Air	LW-28		4. 8.72	To N56MC 12/74. Canx 10.12.74.
G-BAAN	Hughes 269C (300C)	42-0136		3. 8.72	To PH-EPL 4/74. Canx 17.4.74.
G-BAAO	PA-28-180 Cherokee C	28-3980	LN-AEL (SE-FAG)	3. 8.72	To EI-BDR 12/77. Canx 29.11.77.
G-BAAP	PA-28R-200 Cherokee Arrow II	28R-7235205	(G-AZYO)	4. 8.72	To CS-DBK 3/96. Canx 11.3.96.
G-BAAR	PA-28R-200 Cherokee Arrow D II	28R-7235197	N11C	4. 8.72	To EI-BPB 11/84. Canx 15.11.84.
G-BAAS	Reims Cessna FR.172E Rocket	0040	SE-FBW OY-DKN	4. 8.72	To EI-BJI 5/80. Canx 20.5.80.
G-BAAT	Cessna 182P Skylane	182-60835	N399JF G-BAAT/N9295G	10. 8.72	
G-BAAU	Enstrom F-28C-UK	092		10. 8.72	CofA expired 13.7.85. (Stored at Bournemouth)
G-BAAV	Reims Cessna FRA.150L Aerobat	0155		10. 8.72	Crashed at Baldoon, Wigtown on 10.2.80. Canx 8.10.80.
G-BAAW	Jodel D.119 (Valladeau built)	366	F-BHMY	11. 8.72	
G-BAAX	Cameron O-84 HAFB	50		8. 8.72	Canx as WFU 11.5.93.
G-BAAY	Valtion Lentokonetehdar Viima II	VI-3	OH-VIG Finnish AF VI-3	12. 8.72	To OO-EBL. Canx 28.11.89.
G-BAAZ	PA-28R-200 Cherokee Arrow B	28R-7135146	N2388T (XB-VOC)	15. 8.72	(Damaged when struck by taxying PA-23 G-ESKY at Guernsey on 13.9.97)
G-BABA	DH.82A Tiger Moth	86584	F-BGDT French AF/PG687	11. 8.72	Components used in rebuild of G-AMHF in 1985. Canx by CAA 13.6.96. (On rebuild in Italy as I-BABA)
G-BABB	Reims Cessna F.150L Commuter	0830		15. 8.72	
G-BABC	Reims Cessna F.150L Commuter	0831		15. 8.72	
G-BABD	Reims Cessna FRA.150L Aerobat (Mod)	0153		3. 8.72	
G-BABE	Taylor JT.2 Titch	PEB/01 & PFA/1394		3. 8.72	Permit expired 7.5.98.
G-BABF	Not allocated.				
G-BABG	PA-28-180 Cherokee C	28-2031	PH-APU N7978W	15. 8.72	
G-BABH	Reims Cessna F.150L Commuter	0820	EI-CCZ G-BABH	15. 8.72	
G-BABI	Hughes 269C (300C)	72-0149		16. 8.72	To D-HACA 4/76. Canx 6.4.76.
G-BABJ	HS.748 Srs.2A/248	1718	G11-1	18. 8.72	To South Korean AF as 1718 in 7/75. Canx 14.7.75.
G-BABK	PA-34-200-2 Seneca	34-7250219	PH-DMN G-BABK/N5203T	18. 8.72	
G-BABL	HS.125 Srs.400B	25271	XX506 G-BABL/G-5-14	18. 8.72	To EC-CMU 2/75. Canx 13.2.75.
G-BABM	Hawker Hunter FGA.74B	S4/R/S4/U/3308	G-9-363 XF432	21. 8.72	To Singapore AF as 526 in 10/72. Canx 16.10.72.
G-BABN	Hughes 269C (300C)	72-0140		16. 8.72	Fatal crash 5 miles south of Bawtry on 15.1.75. Canx.
G-BABO	Not allocated.				
G-BABP	HS.121 Trident 2E Srs.107	2163		21. 8.72	To China as 252 in 10/74. Canx 30.10.74.
G-BABR	HS.121 Trident 2E Srs.107	2164		21. 8.72	To China as 254 in 10/74. Canx 30.10.74.
G-BABS	HS.121 Trident 2E Srs.107	2165		21. 8.72	To China as 256 in 1/75. Canx 20.1.75.
G-BABT	HS.121 Trident 2E Srs.107	2166		21. 8.72	To China as 258 in 1/75. Canx 7.3.75.
G-BABU	HS.121 Trident 2E Srs.107	2167		21. 8.72	To China as 260 in 4/75. Canx 11.4.75.
G-BABV	HS.121 Trident 2E Srs.107	2168		21. 8.72	To China as 262 in 6/75. Canx 3.6.75.
G-BABW	Beechcraft E90 King Air	LW-25		18. 8.72	To N4406W 6/83. Canx 20.6.83.

Regn	Type	c/n	Previous identity	Regn date	Fate or immediate subsequent identity (if known)
G-BABX	Beechcraft A100 King Air	B-141		18. 8.72	Crashed on landing at Sturgate on 12.1.77. Canx as WFU 19.1.77.
G-BABY	Taylor JT.2 Titch	JRB-2 & PFA/3204		21. 8.72	Permit expired 10.10.91. Canx by CAA 4.12.96.
G-BABZ	Beechcraft 35-C33 Debonair	CD-890	SE-EKI	23. 8.72	To OO-ABZ 11/76. Canx 24.11.76.
G-BACA	BAC Procter Petrel	PFA/1516		21. 8.72	WFU at Warton. Scrapped at Blackpool in mid-1987. Canx as destroyed 6.12.88.
G-BACB	PA-34-200-2 Seneca	34-7250251	N5354T	25. 8.72	
G-BACC	Reims Cessna FRA.150L Aerobat	0157		16. 8.72	
G-BACD	Reims Cessna FRA.150L Aerobat	0156		22. 8.72	Fatal crash at Musden Head Moor, near Accrington on 31.5.81. Canx as destroyed 5.12.83.
G-BACE	Sportavia-Putzer Fournier RF-5	5102	(PT-DVZ) D-KCID	25. 8.72	
G-BACF	Reims Cessna F.337F Super Skymaster (Wichita c/n 01402)	0048		3. 8.72	Extensively damaged on landing at Newtownards on 5.10.83. Canx as destroyed 2.12.83.
G-BACG	PA-31 Navajo	31-46	5Y-AFY	29. 8.72	To TF-ERR(2) 12/73. Canx 27.12.73.
G-BACH	Enstrom F-28A-UK	094		29. 8.72	Force landed in lake near Frimley, Surrey on 15.7.81. Stored near Coventry in 1985. Canx as WFU 12.7.94. Parts used for fund-raising near Somersham with parts from G-BATU and G-JDHI, and now wears the marks "G-BACH".
G-BACI	HS.125 Srs.403B	NA776 & 25283	N73BH	29. 8.72	To XA-LOV(2) 11/81. Canx 9.11.81.
G-BACJ	Wassmer Jodel D.120 Paris-Nice	315	F-BNZC	1. 9.72	Permit expired 28.2.98.
G-BACK	DH.82A Tiger Moth	85879	F-BDOB French AF/DF130	4. 9.72	Sold to Chilean AF Museum in 12/87. Canx 25.1.89 on sale to Chile. To CC-DMC in 1995.
G-BACL	SAN Jodel D.150 Mascaret	31	F-BSTY CN-TYY	4. 9.72	
G-BACM	Reims Cessna FRA.150L Aerobat	0160		4. 9.72	To EI-BRX 1/86. Canx 8.1.86.
G-BACN	Reims Cessna FRA.150L Aerobat	0161		4. 9.72	
G-BACO	Reims Cessna FRA.150L Aerobat	0163		4. 9.72	
G-BACP	Reims Cessna FRA.150L Aerobat (Mod to F.150L standard in 1983/85)	0164		4. 9.72	
G-BACR	Scottish Aviation Bulldog Srs.100	BH.100/189		30. 8.72	To Swedish AF as 61071 12/72. Canx.
G-BACS	Scottish Aviation Bulldog Srs.100	BH.100/190		30. 8.72	To Swedish AF as 61072 1/73. Canx.
G-BACT	Scottish Aviation Bulldog Srs.100	BH.100/191		30. 8.72	To Swedish AF as 61073 12/72. Canx.
G-BACU	Scottish Aviation Bulldog Srs.100	BH.100/192		30. 8.72	To Swedish AF as 61074 1/73. Canx.
G-BACV	Scottish Aviation Bulldog Srs.100	BH.100/193		30. 8.72	To Swedish AF as 61075 1/73. Canx.
G-BACW	DH.82A Tiger Moth	3340	BB694 G-ADGV	. 8.72R	NTU - Restored as G-ADGV 9/72. Canx.
G-BACX	Scottish Aviation Bulldog Srs.100	BH.100/194		30. 8.72	To Swedish AF as 61076 1/73. Canx.
G-BACY	Scottish Aviation Bulldog Srs.100	BH.100/195		30. 8.72	To Swedish AF as 61077 1/73. Canx.
G-BACZ	Scottish Aviation Bulldog Srs.100	BH.100/196		30. 8.72	To Swedish AF as 61078 1/73. Canx.
G-BADA	Scottish Aviation Bulldog Srs.100	BH.100/197		30. 8.72	To Swedish AF as 61079. Canx 17.4.73.
G-BADB	Scottish Aviation Bulldog Srs.100	BH.100/198		30. 8.72	To Swedish AF as 61080. Canx 17.4.73.
G-BADC	Rollason-Luton Beta B.2A	JJF.1 & PFA/1384		7. 9.72	Permit expired 31.1.85. (On overhaul Barton 5/95)
G-BADD	PA-E23-250 Aztec C	27-3122	5Y-ADL	25. 7.72	NTU - To G-BALU 1/73. Canx.
G-BADE	PA-23-250 Aztec D	27-4205	5Y-AJM N6860Y	5. 9.72	To 5H-BOC 12/87. Canx 14.12.87.
G-BADF	PA-34-200-2 Seneca	34-7250257	N5446T	4. 9.72	To OY-SUW 11/84. Canx 23.11.84.
G-BADG	Cameron O-84 HAFB	42		6. 9.72	To 5Y-ARU 9/72. Canx 22.11.72.
G-BADH	Slingsby T.61A Falke	1774		6. 9.72	
G-BADI	PA-23-250 Aztec D	27-4235	N6885Y	5. 9.72	CofA expired 29.10.92. (Fuselage in open storage 12/98 North Weald)
G-BADJ	PA-E23-250 Aztec E	27-4841	N14279	11. 9.72	
G-BADK	BN-2A-8 Islander	309	G-51-309	8. 9.72	To F-ODYF 8/91. Canx 24.6.91.
G-BADL	PA-34-200-2 Seneca	34-7250247	N5307T	4. 9.72	Damaged on landing at Turnhouse on 21.10.95. Canx as WFU 15.8.96.
G-BADM	Rollason-Druine D.62B Condor	RAE/653 & PFA/49-11442		8. 9.72	
G-BADN	Wassmer WA.52 Europa	54		11. 9.72	To G-BDSN 3/76. Canx.
G-BADO	PA-32-300 Cherokee Six E	32-7240011	N8664N	15. 9.72	
G-BADP	Boeing 737-204ADV (Line No. 316)	20632		15. 9.72	To CC-CSH 11/92. Canx 10.11.92.
G-BADR	Boeing 737-204ADV (Line No. 318)	20633		15. 9.72	To CC-CSI 11/92. Canx 10.11.92.
G-BADS	Bell 206A JetRanger	180	EI-ASW	12. 9.72	Crashed at White Lodge, Norfolk on 13.6.73. Canx as WFU 18.9.73. Rebuilt as SE-HGH 4/77.
G-BADT	Cessna 402B Businessliner	402B-0329	N3364Q	15. 9.72	Canx as WFU 5.10.89. To N402PA 1/90.
G-BADU	Cameron O-56 HAFB	47		18. 4.72	CofA expired 29.3.78. Canx by CAA 19.5.93. (Extant .94)
G-BADV	Brochet MB.50 Pipistrelle	78	F-PBRJ	13. 9.72	Permit to Fly expired on 9.5.79 & WFU. Canx by CAA 3.4.89. (On rebuild)
G-BADW	Aerotek Pitts S-2A Special	2035		21. 9.72	CofA expired 16.9.95.
G-BADX	Aerotek Pitts S-2A Special	2036		21. 9.72	Fatal crash at Lanzarote on 26.5.78. Canx.

Regn	Type	c/n	Previous identity	Regn date	Fate or immediate subsequent identity (if known)
G-BADY	Aerotek Pitts S-2A Special	2037		21. 9.72	Destroyed in mid-air collision with Pitts S-2A G-BECM and crashed at Knott End, near Fleetwood on 29.6.84. Canx as destroyed 16.5.85.
G-BADZ	Aerotek Pitts S-2A Special	2038		21. 9.72	
G-BAEA	Aerotek Pitts S-2A Special	2039		21. 9.72	Crashed shortly after take-off from Sywell on 19.4.76. Canx.
G-BAEB	Robin DR.400/160 Knight	733		19. 9.72	
G-BAEC	Robin HR.100/210 Royal	145	EI-BDG G-BAEC	15. 9.72	
G-BAED	PA-23-250 Aztec C	27-3864	N6567Y	18. 9.72	
G-BAEE	CEA Jodel DR.1050/M1 Sicile Record	579	F-BMGN	29. 9.72	
G-BAEF	Boeing 727-46 (Line No. 254)	18879	HK-3599X G-BAEF/HK-3384X/G-BAEF/9N-ABV/G-BAEF/JA8312	28. 9.72	To HR-ALZ. Canx 19.10.92.
G-BAEG	PA-31-300 Turbo Navajo B	31-761	N7239L	27. 9.72	To G-RMAE 12/82. Canx.
G-BAEH	Hughes 269C (300C)	72-0150		27. 9.72	To F-BXQA(2) 3/78. Canx 16.3.78.
G-BAEI	Cessna 421B Golden Eagle II	421B-0259	N3375Q	4.10.72	Crashed near Bilbao, Spain on 26.8.78. Canx as destroyed 8.12.78.
G-BAEJ	American Aviation AA-5 Traveller	AA5-0200		6.10.72	To EI-BMV 7/82. Canx 22.7.82.
G-BAEK	Cameron O-65 HAFB	46		19. 9.72	To D-Primagas 5/74. Canx 8.5.74.
"G-BAEK"	Cameron O-56 HAFB	51		----	False marks. To D-Glucksreisen.
G-BAEL	Boeing 707-321 (Line No. 83)	17602	N724PA (G-AZOI)/N724PA	16.10.72	To N2276X 6/78. Canx 15.6.78.
G-BAEM	Robin DR.400/125 Petit Prince	728		25. 9.72	
G-BAEN	Robin DR.400/180 Regent	736		25. 9.72	
G-BAEO	Reims Cessna F.172M Skyhawk	0911		14. 9.72	Crashed at Barton Airport on 7.5.78. CofA expired 10.2.79. (Wreck stored at Sherburn 6/98)
G-BAEP	Reims Cessna FRA.150L Aerobat (Mod to F.150L standard)	0170		14. 9.72	
G-BAER	LeVier Cosmic Wind	106 & PFA/1571		14. 9.72	
G-BAES	Cessna 337A Super Skymaster	337A-0429	SE-CWW N5329S	26. 9.72	To G-HIVA 3/88. Canx.
G-BAET	Piper J3C-65 Cub (L-4H-PI) (Frame No. 11430)	11605	OO-AJI 43-30314	26. 9.72	
G-BAEU	Reims Cessna F.150L Commuter	0873		26. 9.72	
G-BAEV	Reims Cessna FRA.150L Aerobat	0173		27. 9.72	
G-BAEW	Reims Cessna F.172M Skyhawk II	0914	N12798	27. 9.72	Badly damaged in forced landing near Sywell on 12.11.93. Canx by CAA 22.3.94. (Stored 7/97)
G-BAEX	Reims Cessna F.172M Skyhawk II	0910		28. 9.72	To G-WACX 6/86. Canx.
G-BAEY	Reims Cessna F.172M Skyhawk II	0915		28. 9.72	
G-BAEZ	Reims Cessna FRA.150L Aerobat	0169		28. 9.72	
G-BAFA	American Aviation AA-5 Traveler	AA5-0201	N6136A	6.10.72	
G-BAFB	Mooney M.20A	1161	OY-DII OE-DOZ/D-ELER	26. 9.72	Crashed on take-off from Wantage on 30.10.74. Canx as destroyed 27.11.74. Remains derelict to Membury.
G-BAFC	Hughes 269C (300C)	72-0148		9.10.72	To OH-HIY 6/76. Canx 13.5.76.
G-BAFD	MBB Bo.105DB (Originally regd as a model Bo.105C)	S.35	D-HDAO	10.10.72	To ZS-RKL 12/98. Canx 5.11.98.
G-BAFE	BN-2A-26 Islander	311	G-51-311	17.10.72	To N92GA 11/72. Canx 17.11.72.
G-BAFF	BN-2A Mk.III Trislander	322	G-51-312	17.10.72	To DQ-FBY 1/73. Canx 1.1.73.
G-BAFG	DH.82A Tiger Moth	85995	F-BGEL French AF/EM778	13.10.72	
G-BAFH	Evans VP-1	PFA/1579		5.10.72	Permit expired 14.7.87. Canx by CAA 4.12.96.
G-BAFI	Reims Cessna F.177RG Cardinal	0066		5.10.72	Forced landed in a field near Pebbles on 22.2.95. Canx as WFU 31.8.95.
G-BAFJ	Cessna 182P Skylane	182-61335	N20977	14. 8.72	To OY-POE 9/75. Canx 1.9.75.
G-BAFK	Vickers 952 Vanguard	739	PK-MVP G-BAFK/CF-TKP	13.10.72	To F-BXOG. Canx 28.10.75.
G-BAFL	Cessna 182P Skylane	182-61469	N21180	15. 8.72	
G-BAFM	Noorduyn AT-16 Harvard IIB	14A-868	PH-SKL R.Netherlands AF B-104/FS728/43-12569	16.10.72	To HB-RCP 1/96. Canx 28.12.95.
G-BAFN	Bell 212	30550	N14845	18.10.72	To VH-NSA 10/83. Canx 15.9.83.
G-BAFO	AESL Airtourer T.6-24	B.575		19.10.72	To ZK-DKT 10/73. Canx 10.10.73.
G-BAFP	Robin DR.400/160 Knight	735		19.10.72	
G-BAFR	Wassmer Jodel D.120 Paris-Nice	72	F-BIKV F-BIKD	20.10.72	WFU due to internal fungus growth in the fuselage wood at Bembridge, IoW in 1975. Dismantled and burnt. Canx as WFU 1.4.76.
G-BAFS	PA-18-150 Super Cub	18-5338	ALAT 18-5338	3. 8.72	
G-BAFT	PA-18-150 Super Cub	18-5340	ALAT 18-5340	3. 8.72	
G-BAFU	PA-28-140 Cherokee	28-20759	PH-NLS	11.10.72	
G-BAFV	PA-18-95 Super Cub (L-18C-PI) (Frame No 18-2055)	18-2045	PH-WJK R.Netherlands AF R-40/8A-40/52-2445	24.10.72	
G-BAFW	PA-28-140 Cherokee	28-21050	PH-NLT	24.10.72	Canx by CAA 1.10.98.
G-BAFX	Robin DR.400/140 Earl	739		30.10.72	
G-BAFY	HS.748 Srs.2A/FAA	1716	G11-3	23.10.72	To (N666)/N748LL 10/73. Canx 10.10.73.
G-BAFZ	Boeing 727-46 (Line No. 226)	18877	HK-3270X G-BAFZ/HK-3201X/G-BAFZ/JA8310	30.10.72	To EI-BUP 10/87. Canx 30.10.87.
G-BAGA	Cessna 182A Skylane	182-34949	N4849D	28. 9.72	To EI-BPJ 12/84. Canx 27.11.84.
G-BAGB	SIAI-Marchetti SF.260	1-07	LN-BIV	20.10.72	
G-BAGC	Robin DR.400/140 Earl	737		13.10.72	

Regn	Type	c/n	Previous identity	Regn date	Fate or immediate subsequent identity (if known)
G-BAGD	Westland-Sikorsky S-55 Whirlwind Srs.3	WA/78	XG583	23.10.72	To VR-BES 1/74. Canx 8.1.74.
G-BAGE	Cessna T.210L Turbo-Centurion	T210-59795	SE-FNM G-BAGE/N29070	25.10.72	Engine fire on start-up at Gamston on 17.1.82 & DBF. Canx as destroyed 1.3.83. (Rear fuselage stored at Home Farm, Firbeck, near Worksop for South Yorkshire Aviation Society)
G-BAGF	Jodel D.92 Bebe	59	F-PHFC	13.11.72	(On rebuild 8/97)
G-BAGG(1)	PA-32-300 Cherokee Six E	32-7340007		30.10.72	Forced-landing at St.Michel L'Aigle on 13.5.73. Canx as destroyed 7.12.73. Rebuilt with fuselage c/n 32-7340186.
G-BAGG(2)	PA-32-300 Cherokee Six E	32-7340186		7.12.73	
G-BAGH	Cameron O-84 HAFB	53		25.10.72	To SE-ZZZ 9/73. Canx 31.8.73.
G-BAGI	Cameron O-31 HAFB	56		25.10.72	
G-BAGJ	Westland/SNIAS SA.341G Gazelle 1	WA/1039	(XW858)	26.10.72	To HB-XIL 4/79. Canx 11.4.79.
G-BAGK	Westland/SNIAS SA.341G Gazelle 1	WA/1065		26.10.72	To F-GBMC 10/78. Canx 20.2.79.
G-BAGL	Westland/SNIAS SA.341G Gazelle 1	WA/1067		26.10.72	(Stored 2/99 at Long Stratton Airfield, Norfolk)
G-BAGM	Wassmer WA.41 Super Baladou IV	164	F-BCDF F-OCOF	26.10.72	Ditched into the English Channel off Alderney on 16.9.82. Canx as destroyed 14.3.83.
G-BAGN	Reims Cessna F.177RG Cardinal II	0068		24.10.72	
G-BAGO	Cessna 421B Golden Eagle II	421B-0356	N7613Q	24.10.72	
G-BAGP	Reims Cessna FT.337P Turbo Super Skymaster (Wichita c/n 0047)	0003	F-WLIO	24.10.72	To D-ICSB 10/76. Canx 10.6.76.
G-BAGR	Robin DR.400/140 Petit Prince (Originally regd as DR.400/125)	753		30.10.72	
G-BAGS	Robin DR.400/108 2+2	760		30.10.72	
G-BAGT	Helio H.295 Super Courier	1288	CR-LJG	31.10.72	
G-BAGU	Phoenix Luton LA-5A Major	PFA/1216		6.11.72	Canx by CAA 8.8.91.
G-BAGV	Cessna U.206F Stationair	U206-01867	N9667G	31.10.72	
G-BAGW	Reims Cessna F.150J	0521	SE-FKM	1.11.72	To G-WYMP 2/82. Canx.
G-BAGX	PA-28-140 Cherokee	28-23633	N3574K	30.10.72	
G-BAGY	Cameron O-84 HAFB	54		17.10.72	(Stored 2/97)
G-BAGZ	PA-34-200-2 Seneca	34-7350007	EI-AWS G-BAGZ/N15067	2.11.72	To N474EW 9/81. Canx 22.9.81.
G-BAHA	DH.104 Dove 5	04106	CS-TAB	31.10.72	Canx as WFU on 20.2.74. Broken up at Biggin Hill in 1974.
G-BAHB	DH.104 Dove 5	04107	CS-TAC	31.10.72	To VH-CLD(2) 3/74. Canx 14.3.74.
G-BAHC	PA-23-250 Aztec C	27-3483	5Y-ADX	15.11.72	CofA expired 11.3.82 & WFU at Coventry. Used for spares at Glasgow. Canx by CAA 2.12.86.
G-BAHD	Cessna 182P Skylane	182-61501	N21228	25.10.72	
G-BAHE	PA-28-140 Cherokee C	28-26494	N5696U	30.10.72	CofA expired 8.6.95. (Stored 5/96)
G-BAHF	PA-28-140 Cherokee Fliteliner	28-7125215	N431FL	30.10.72	
G-BAHG	PA-24-260 Comanche B	24-4306	5Y-AFX N8831P	2.11.72	
G-BAHH	Wallis WA-121/Mc	K/701/X		7.11.72	Permit expired 27.5.98. (Stored 2/99 Reymerston Hall)
G-BAHI	Reims Cessna F.150H Commuter	0330	PH-EHA	6.11.72	
G-BAHJ	PA-24-250 Comanche	24-1863	PH-RED N6735P	6.11.72	
G-BAHK	Short SC.7 Skyliner 3-100-41	SH1907	G-14-79	6.11.72	To A40-SK. Canx 7.10.75.
G-BAHL	Robin DR.400/160 Chevalier	704	F-OCSR	8.11.72	
G-BAHM	Beechcraft A24R Sierra	MC-148		7.11.72	Fatal crash at Drambuie field, Drumnad Rochit on 25.5.74. Canx.
G-BAHN	Beechcraft 95-58TC Baron	TH-293		7.11.72	Fatal crash and DBF in a field at Fyfield, Hants. on 11.8.95. Canx as destroyed 17.10.95.
G-BAHO	Beechcraft C23 Sundowner	M-1456		7.11.72	
G-BAHP	Volmer VJ-22 Sportsman Amphibian	PFA/1313		9.11.72	Permit expired 18.10.93. (Noted stored in poor condition with wings removed at Aboyne in 6/99)
G-BAHR	PA-28-140 Cherokee D	28-7125617	N4227T	10.11.72	Crashed near Melton Mowbray on 8.11.81. Canx.
G-BAHS	PA-28R-200-2 Cherokee Arrow	28R-7335017	N15147	9.11.72	
G-BAHT	Reims Cessna F.172F	0160	PH-HVB	10.11.72	Crashed at Figeac, France on 9.7.76. Canx.
G-BAHU	Enstrom F-28A-UK	103	EI-BDF G-BAHU	13.11.72	To G-SERA 3/91. Canx.
G-BAHV	PA-32-300 Cherokee Six E	32-7240118	N1400T	14.11.72	To SE-FLF 10/75. Canx 16.9.75.
G-BAHW	Cessna 310Q	310Q-0671	N7950Q	16.11.72	To N3835C 3/83. Canx 14.3.83.
G-BAHX	Cessna 182P Skylane	182-61588	N21363	16.11.72	
G-BAHY	Cessna 182P Skylane	182-61644	N21460	14.11.72	To OO-AHY 11/75. Canx 26.11.75.
G-BAHZ	PA-28R-200 Cherokee Arrow II	28R-7235289	EI-AWL G-BAHZ	15.11.72	Canx by CAA 24.3.93.
G-BAIA	PA-32-300 Cherokee Six E	32-7340006		15.11.72	To G-DENI 12/95. Canx.
G-BAIB	Enstrom F-28A	097		22.11.72	To G-OABO 7/98. Canx.
G-BAIC	Reims Cessna FRA.150L Aerobat	0175		15.11.72	To 5Y-BDN 12/80. Canx 29.12.80.
G-BAID	Short SC.7 Skyvan 3-100	SH1909	G-14-81	16.11.72	To (XC-TAP)/XC-GAY 2/73. Canx 30.4.73.
G-BAIE	Short SC.7 Skyvan 3-100	SH1911	G-14-83	16.11.72	To (XC-PMX)/XC-GAZ 4/73. Canx 30.4.73.
G-BAIF	Western O-65 HAFB	019		20.11.72	Sold in Australia in 1973 & retired following canopy fire. Canx by CAA 5.12.83.
G-BAIG	PA-34-200-2 Seneca	34-7250243	OY-BSU G-BAIG/N5257T	21.11.72	
G-BAIH	PA-28R-200 Cherokee Arrow II	28R-7335011		21.11.72	
G-BAII	Reims Cessna FRA.150L Aerobat	0178		22.11.72	

Regn	Type	c/n	Previous identity	Regn date	Fate or immediate subsequent identity (if known)
G-BAIJ	Reims Cessna FRA.150L Aerobat	0185		22.11.72	Fatal crash at Raans Road Farm, Amersham on 28.6.76. Canx.
G-BAIK	Reims Cessna F.150L Commuter	0903		22.11.72	
G-BAIL	Reims Cessna FR.172J Rocket (Mod)	0370		22.11.72	Overturned on landing at Farley Farm, near Winchester on 6.3.99. Canx by CAA 6.7.99.
G-BAIM	Cessna E.310Q	310Q-0690	N8031Q	23.11.72	CofA expired 15.8.88. To Instructional Airframe at Perth. Canx as destroyed 26.2.92. Stored dismantled at Perth/ Scone in 8/98.
G-BAIN	Reims Cessna FRA.150L Aerobat	0177		23.11.72	
G-BAIO	Reims Cessna F.150L Commuter	0888		13.11.72	To G-BKAC 4/82. Canx.
G-BAIP	Reims Cessna F.150L Commuter	0898		13.11.72	
G-BAIR	Thunder Ax7-77 HAFB	003		27.11.72	Canx by CAA 26.2.90. (Inflated at Attingham Park Balloon Meet 9/93)
G-BAIS	Reims Cessna F.177RG Cardinal II	0069		13.11.72	
G-BAIT	Short SC.7 Skyliner 3A-100-40	SH1908	G-14-80	27.11.72	To LN-NPC 3/75. Canx 21.3.75.
G-BAIU	Hiller UH-12E-4 (Soloy)	2138	D-HAFA	29.11.72	CofA expired 6.6.88. Canx as WFU 25.10.90.
G-BAIV	Reims Cessna F.177RG Cardinal II	0071		14.11.72	NTU - Canx 3.5.73 as Not Imported. To F-BUMK 4/73.
G-BAIW	Reims Cessna F.172M Skyhawk	0928		14.11.72	
G-BAIX	Reims Cessna F.172M Skyhawk	0931		14.11.72	
G-BAIY	Cameron O-65 HAFB	55		29.11.72	CofA expired 30.6.81. Canx as WFU 22.1.92.
G-BAIZ	Slingsby T.61A Falke	1776		27.11.72	
G-BAJA	Reims Cessna F.177RG Cardinal II	0078		29.11.72	
G-BAJB	Reims Cessna F.177RG Cardinal II	0080		29.11.72	
G-BAJC	Evans VP-1 Srs.2	PFA/1548		30.11.72	Permit expired 22.3.99. (Stored 8/97)
G-BAJD	Evans VP-1	PFA/7001		30.11.72	Not completed. Canx 28.8.79.
G-BAJE	Cessna 177 Cardinal	177-00812	N29322	30.11.72	
G-BAJF	HS.121 Trident 2E Srs.108	2169		28.11.72	To China as 264. Canx 22.12.75.
G-BAJG	HS.121 Trident 2E Srs.108	2170		28.11.72	To China as 266 in 2/76. Canx 6.2.76.
G-BAJH	HS.121 Trident 2E Srs.108	2171		28.11.72	To China as 272 in 3/76. Canx 18.3.76.
G-BAJI	HS.121 Trident 2E Srs.108	2172		28.11.72	To China as 274 in 5/76. Canx 3.5.76.
G-BAJJ	HS.121 Trident 2E Srs.108	2173		28.11.72	To China as 276 in 6/76. Canx 1.6.76.
G-BAJK	HS.121 Trident 2E Srs.108	2174		28.11.72	To China as 278 in 7/76. Canx 28.2.83.
G-BAJL	HS.121 Trident 3B Srs.104	2327		28.11.72	To China as 268 in 9/75. Canx 22.9.75.
G-BAJM	HS.121 Trident 3B Srs.104	2328		28.11.72	To China as 270. Canx 29.10.75.
G-BAJN	American Aviation AA-5 Traveler	AA5-0259		29.11.72	
G-BAJO	American Aviation AA-5 Traveler	AA5-0260		29.11.72	
G-BAJP	BN-2A-8 Islander (Painted as G-ABJP in error)	313	"G-ABJP" G-51-313	4.12.72	To (N24JA)/XA-DAB 1/73. Canx 19.1.73.
G-BAJR	PA-28-180 Cherokee Challenger	28-7305008		1.12.72	
G-BAJS	BN-2A-3 Islander (Originally regd as a BN-2A-9)	314	(N27JA) G-BAJS	7.12.72	To "PT-EPI"/PP-EFI 5/73. Canx 18.5.73.
G-BAJT	PA-28R-200 Cherokee Arrow II	28R-7235294		28.11.72	To G-ORDN 7/89. Canx.
G-BAJU	PA-23-250 Aztec C	27-2546	N5459Y	30.11.72	To 5B-CGE 4/84. Canx 11.4.84.
G-BAJV	K & S SA.102.5 Cavalier	PFA/01-10002		8.12.72	Not completed. Canx as WFU 8.12.81.
G-BAJW	Boeing 727-46F (Line No. 236)	18878	9N-ABW G-BAJW/JA8311	12.12.72	To N190AJ. Canx 29.12.89.
G-BAJX	PA-E23-250 Aztec E	27-7304927	N14346	28.11.72	To G-OESX 4/85. Canx.
G-BAJY	Robin DR.400/180 Regent	758		4.12.72	
G-BAJZ	Robin DR.400/125 Petit Prince	759		4.12.72	
G-BAKA	Sikorsky S-61N	61-493		4.12.72	Canx 22.4.87 on sale to France. To N9119Z 9/87.
G-BAKB	Sikorsky S-61N	61-702		4.12.72	Canx 22.4.87 on sale to France. To N9118M 9/87.
G-BAKC	Sikorsky S-61N	61-703		4.12.72	Canx 22.4.87 on sale to France. To N9119S 9/87.
G-BAKD	PA-34-200-2 Seneca	34-7350013	N1378T	28.11.72	
G-BAKE	Cessna T.310Q II	T310Q-0641	N8404F	8.12.72	Canx 18.8.76 on sale to Germany. To EI-BCG 9/76.
G-BAKF	Bell 206B JetRanger II	854	N1482S	8.12.72	Struck powerline near Malmesbury on 9.1.89. Canx as WFU 20.3.89.
G-BAKG	Hughes 269C (300C)	82-0155		8.12.72	To VH-AUQ 3/90. Canx 12.12.89.
G-BAKH	PA-28-140 Cherokee F	28-7325014		12.12.72	
G-BAKI	PA-28-140 Cherokee F	28-7325015		12.12.72	Aborted take-off at Thatcham strip near Newbury on 24.8.75 and hit boundary fence. Remains dumped at Biggin Hill.
G-BAKJ	PA-30-160 Twin Comanche B	30-1232	TJ-AAI TJ-ADH/N8122Y	13.12.72	
G-BAKK	Reims Cessna F.172H	0658	4X-CEB 5B-CBK/N10658	13.12.72	CofA expired 20.4.85 & WFU at Coventry. Canx as WFU 27.1.89. Fuselage at Hinton-in-the Hedges 3/92.
G-BAKL	Fokker F-27 Friendship 200	10293	PH-FIL 9M-AOJ/PH-FIL	14.12.72	CofA expired 21.12.95. Broken up at Norwich in 12/96. Canx 11.12.96 "as destroyed".
G-BAKM	Robin DR.400/140 Earl	755		15.12.72	
G-BAKN	SNCAN Stampe SV-4C	348	F-BCOY	15.12.72	
G-BAKO	Cameron O-84 HAFB	57		18.12.72	Canx by CAA 19.5.93. (On loan to Balloon Preservation Group) (Extant 1/98)
G-BAKP	PA-E23-250 Aztec E	27-4670	N212PB (N14062)	27.12.72	Overshot on landing on wet runway at Thruxton on 1.12.84. CofA expired 31.5.87. Canx by CAA 8.5.90. To Dodson Aviation Scrapyard in the USA.

Regn	Type	c/n	Previous identity	Regn date	Fate or immediate subsequent identity (if known)
G-BAKR	SAN Jodel D.117	814	F-BIOV	27.12.72	
G-BAKS	Agusta-Bell 206B JetRanger II	8339		28.12.72	Fatal crash in a field at Cocking, West Sussex 14.11.97.
G-BAKT	Agusta-Bell 206B JetRanger II	8341		28.12.72	To G-FLYR 8/89. Canx.
G-BAKU	Agusta-Bell 206B JetRanger II	8342		28.12.72	Canx 9.2.76 on sale to UAE. To AP-AYX.
G-BAKV	PA-18-150 Super Cub	18-8993		22.12.72	
G-BAKW	Beagle B.121 Pup Srs.150	B121-175		15.12.72	
G-BAKX	Bell 206B JetRanger II	906		27.12.72	To EI-BHI 8/79. Canx 6.8.79.
G-BAKY	Slingsby T.61C Falke	1777		20.12.72	
G-BAKZ	BN-2A-21 Islander (Originally regd as BN-2A-7)	188	LN-BNI G-BAKZ/OY-DHS/G-51-188	29.12.72	To C-GUAW 5/82. Canx 13.5.82.
G-BALA	AIA Stampe SV-4C	1096	EI-BAU G-BALA/F-BKOF/French Mil	2. 1.73	To G-MCBP 12/89. Canx.
G-BALB	Air & Space 18A Gyroplane	18-75	N6170S	1. 1.73	CofA expired 16.5.74 & WFU. (Stored Biggin Hill in 1986) Canx by CAA 30.11.84. To EI-CNG 9/96.
G-BALC	Bell 206B JetRanger II	913		2. 1.73	To F-GJGV 7/90. Canx 12.6.90.
G-BALD	Cameron O-84 HAFB	58		2. 1.73	WFU after severe damage 25.6.78 and basket to G-PUFF 11/78. CofA expired 2.7.78.
G-BALE	Enstrom F-28A	119		23. 1.73	Crashed at Thruxton on 9.8.87 when a parachutist went through the rotor blades as the helicopter was hovering. Canx as destroyed 18.10.89.
G-BALF	Robin DR.400/140 Earl	772		5. 1.73	
G-BALG	Robin DR.400/180 Regent	771		5. 1.73	
G-BALH	Robin DR.400/140B Earl	766		5. 1.73	
G-BALI	Robin DR.400 2+2	764		5. 1.73	CofA expired 3.9.88. (Stored 2/97)
G-BALJ	Robin DR.400/180 Regent	767		5. 1.73	
G-BALK	SNCAN Stampe SV-4C	387	F-BBAN French Mil	3. 1.73	No UK CofA or Permit issued. Canx by CAA 4.12.96. (Possibly the bare cannibalised fuselage noted at Insch in 6/99)
G-BALL	Bede BD-5	206		5. 1.73	Not completed. Canx by CAA 28.3.85.
G-BALM	Cessna 340	340-0106	N4553L	1. 1.73	To N51388 10/92. Canx 2.9.92.
G-BALN	Cessna T.310Q	310Q-0684	N7980Q	8. 1.73	
G-BALO	BN-2A-8 Islander	316	G-51-316	3. 1.73	To 4X-AYL 5/73. Canx 29.5.73.
G-BALP	PA-39-160 Twin Comanche C/R	39-145	N8979Y	5. 1.73	To VH-HLP 2/87. Canx 17.2.87.
G-BALR	AJEP Wittman W.8 Tailwind	TW4/381 & PFA/3504		3. 1.73	Fatal crash into the side of Steeple Rock, near Ennerdale, Cumberland on 3.6.83. Canx as destroyed 29.2.84.
G-BALS(1)	K & S S.A.102.5 Cavalier	PFA/1598		3. 1.73	Not completed. Canx 27.4.77.
G-BALS(2)	Slingsby T.66 RA-45 Nipper 3	PFA/25-10052		22. 8.77	Canx by CAA 2.9.91.
G-BALT	Enstrom F-28A	123	N345AF G-BALT	8. 1.73	Damaged in forced landing at South Mimms, Herts on 20.7.95. Canx by CAA 1.7.96.
G-BALU	PA-E23-250 Aztec C	27-3122	(G-BADD) 5Y-ADL	9. 1.73	Broken up for spares at Sandown, IoW in 10/83. Canx as WFU 20.1.84.
G-BALV	BN-2A-8 Islander	315	G-51-315	9. 1.73	To N94CA 2/73. Canx.
G-BALW	PA-28R-200 Cherokee Arrow II	28R-7335007		4. 1.73	To 5H-MSU 6/90. Canx 7.3.90.
G-BALX	DH.82A Tiger Moth	82103	N6848	10. 1.73	Disappeared on a flight from Dieppe, France to Headcorn on 18.4.98. Canx by CAA 27.7.98.
G-BALY	Practavia Pilot Sprite 150	PFA/05-10009		10. 1.73	(Project part completed and stored 8/95)
G-BALZ	Bell 212	30542	EC-GCR EC-931/G-BALZ/9Y-TIL/G-BALZ/VR-BIB/N8069A/G-BALZ/ N99040/G-BALZ/EI-AWK/G-BALZ/VR-BEK/N2961W	10. 1.73	
G-BAMA	Cameron O-77 HAFB	65		11. 1.73	To OE-DZS 1/77. Canx 21.1.77.
G-BAMB	Slingsby T.61C Falke	1778		9. 1.73	
G-BAMC	Reims Cessna F.150L Commuter	0892		12. 1.73	
G-BAMD	Beechcraft 95-A55 Baron	TC-319	SE-EDC	15. 1.73	To N400BL 12/76. Canx 22.12.76.
G-BAME	Volmer Jensen VJ-22 Sportsman	VHB-1 & PFA/1309		26. 1.73	Canx by CAA 25.10.90.
G-BAMF	MBB Bo.105DB (Originally regd as a Bo.105C)	S.36	D-HDAM	10. 1.73	
G-BAMG	Avions Lobet Ganagobie	PFA/1336		11. 1.73	Canx by CAA 5.8.91. (Complete but unflown 4/97)
G-BAMH	Westland-Sikorsky S-55 Whirlwind Srs.3	WA/83	XG588	10. 1.73	To VR-BEP 10/73. Canx 31.10.73.
G-BAMI	Beechcraft 95-B55 Baron	TC-1524		19. 1.73	To G-HUMP 2/85. Canx.
G-BAMJ	Cessna 182P Skylane	182-61650	N21469	10. 1.73	
G-BAMK	Cameron D-96 Hot-Air Airship	72		11. 1.73	CofA expired 6.12.80. (To British Balloon Museum and inflated 11/90)
G-BAML	Bell 206A JetRanger	36	N7844S	5. 1.73	
G-BAMM	PA-28-235 Cherokee Dakota	28-10642	SE-EOA	16. 1.73	
G-BAMN	Cessna U.206C Super Skywagon	U206-1230	4X-ALL N71943	15. 1.73	To G-UKNO 4/84. Canx.
G-BAMO	Cessna P.206D Super Skylane	P206-0548	4X-ALP 4X-ALF/N8748Z	15. 1.73	To N90WT 4/74. Canx 24.4.74.
G-BAMP	Cessna T.210L Turbo Centurion II	210L-59725	N22221	12. 1.73	Badly damaged on landing at Marina di Campo airfield, Elba Island on 31.8.74. Canx as destroyed 8.8.75.
G-BAMR	PA-16 Clipper	16-392	F-BFMS CU-P339	12. 1.73	
G-BAMS	Robin DR.400/160 Knight	774		15. 1.73	
G-BAMT	Robin DR.400/160 Knight	775		15. 1.73	Crashed & DBR at Cudham on 8.1.78. CofA expired 15.5.79. (Wreck stored 1/92)
G-BAMU	Robin DR.400/160 Knight	778		15. 1.73	
G-BAMV	Robin DR.400/180 Regent (Originally regd as a DR.400/160 Knight)	777		15. 1.73	

Regn	Type	c/n	Previous identity	Regn date	Fate or immediate subsequent identity (if known)
G-BAMW	SAN Jodel DR.1050 Ambassadeur	278	F-BJYI	16. 1.73	Ditched in sea off Great Ormes Head, North Wales on 2.8.80. Salvaged but written off. Canx.
G-BAMX	Vickers 952 Vanguard	728	PK-MVW CF-TKE	16. 1.73	WFU at Southend on 10.7.74. Broken up for spares 8/74. Canx.
G-BAMY	PA-28R-200 Cherokee Arrow II	28R-7335015		9. 1.73	
G-BAMZ	PA-34-200-2 Seneca	34-7350035	N15209	9. 1.73	To OY-BJZ 5/82. Canx 21.5.82.
G-BANA	CEA Jodel DR.221 Dauphin	73	F-BOZR	22. 1.73	
G-BANB	Robin DR.400/180 Regent	776		22. 1.73	
G-BANC	Gardan GY-201 Minicab	A.203	F-PCZV F-BCZV	22. 1.73	
G-BAND	Cameron O-84 HAFB	52		22. 1.73	Canx as WFU 17.4.98.
G-BANE	Reims Cessna FRA.150L Aerobat	0180		22. 1.73	Destroyed in fatal crash at Ardglass, 7 miles east of Downpatrick, NI on 28.8.98. Canx as destroyed 26.11.98.
G-BANF	Phoenix Luton LA-4A Minor	PFA/838		22. 1.73	Badly damaged at Mullaghmore on 27.6.92. Permit expired 5.6.92. (Status uncertain)
G-BANG	Cameron O-84 HAFB	62		22. 1.73	Badly damaged at Wythall, West Midlands on 3.6.77; under restoration in 1988. Canx as WFU 28.4.98.
G-BANH	Cessna 188A Agwagon	188-0074	LN-KAA N9824V	22. 1.73	Crashed near Uffington on 8.6.73. Canx.
G-BANI	Cessna 188A Agwagon	188-00739	LN-BEG N9939G	22. 1.73	Crashed at Tubney Farm, near Marcham, Oxon on 13.6.77. Remains to Hardwick. Canx as destroyed 7.6.78.
G-BANJ	BN-2A-3 Islander	317	G-51-317	22. 1.73	To ZS-IZZ 4/74. Canx 8.4.74.
G-BANK	PA-34-200-2 Seneca	34-7350081	N15636	23. 1.73	WFU & parted out. Canx as WFU 31.7.99.
G-BANL	BN-2A-8 Islander	318	G-51-318	22. 1.73	To RP-C764. Canx 25.1.90.
G-BANM	BN-2A-8 Islander	356	G-51-356	22. 1.73	To XA-DEW 3/74. Canx 14.3.74.
G-BANN	BN-2A-8 Islander	357	G-51-357	22. 1.73	To N95CA 4/73. Canx 6.4.73.
G-BANO	Douglas DC-4-1009	42988	EC-ACF EC-DAQ	23. 1.73	WFU & broken up for spares at Stansted in 9/73. Canx 18.3.77.
G-BANP	Douglas DC-4-1009	42951	EC-ACD EC-DAO	23. 1.73	WFU in 5/73 at Stansted. Broken up. Sold to Laos 6.2.74. Canx.
G-BANR	SNIAS SE.313B Alouette II	1648	EI-AUI Belgian Army OL-A/South Vietnam AF 1648	24. 1.73	Restored as EI-AUI 6/74. Canx 28.6.74.
G-BANS	PA-34-200-2 Seneca	34-7350021	N15110	24. 1.73	To G-ELBC 4/91. Canx.
G-BANT	Cameron O-65 HAFB	60	F-GDZH G-BANT	24. 1.73	To F-GONT. Canx 17.5.93.
G-BANU	Jodel Wassmer D.120 Paris-Nice	247	F-BLNZ	31. 1.73	
G-BANV	Phoenix Currie Wot	PFA/3010		25. 1.73	Damaged in forced landing near Leek, Staffs on 15.9.83. Permit expired 26.4.84. (Status uncertain)
G-BANW	Scintex CP.1330 Super Emeraude	941	PH-VRF	30. 1.73	
G-BANX	Reims Cessna F.172M	0941		31. 1.73	
G-BANY	AESL Airtourer T.2 (115)	A.533		31. 1.73	DBR in forced landing near Wick, Glamorgan on 10.8.75. Canx as WFU 30.3.83. (Fuselage in open store 8/96)
G-BANZ	Reims Cessna FT.337GP Turbo Super Skymaster (Wichita c/n 0042)	0002	F-WLIN	1. 2.73	NTU - Canx 12.6.73 as Not Imported. To F-BTRP 6/73.
G-BAOA	Dassault Falcon 20C	138/440	D-CGJH D-CALL/F-WLCS	5. 2.73	NTU - Canx 5.4.73 as Not Imported. To F-BUIC 7/73.
G-BAOB	Reims Cessna F.172M	0949		2. 2.73	
G-BAOC	Socata MS.894E Rallye Minerva 220GT	12141		6. 2.73	To G-WCEI 5/85. Canx.
G-BAOD	Socata MS.880B Rallye Club	2246		6. 2.73	Forced landing near Dunkeswell, Devon on 21.7.76. Canx as WFU 25.4.83.
G-BAOE	Socata MS.880B Rallye Club	2247		6. 2.73	Fatal crash into ground at Moorseek Farm, Buckland St.Mary, near Taunton on 16.6.76. Canx as WFU 25.4.83.
G-BAOF	Socata MS.880B Rallye Club	2248		6. 2.73	Badly damaged by severe gales at Ystrad Mynach, Glamorgan on 2.1.76. (Stored Roborough) Canx.
G-BAOG	Socata MS.880B Rallye Club	2249		6. 2.73	
G-BAOH	Socata MS.880B Rallye Club	2250		6. 2.73	
G-BAOI	Socata MS.880B Rallye Club	2251		6. 2.73	To OO-MAN 10/75. Canx 29.8.75.
G-BAOJ	Socata MS.880B Rallye Club	2252		6. 2.73	
G-BAOK	Socata MS.880B Rallye Club	2253		6. 2.73	To OO-NAT 4/76. Canx 23.2.76.
G-BAOL	Socata MS.880B Rallye Club	2254		6. 2.73	Badly damaged in accident at Little Burstead, Billericay on 28.4.75. Canx as destroyed 6.6.75.
G-BAOM	Socata MS.880B Rallye Club	2255		6. 2.73	
G-BAON	Socata MS.880B Rallye Club	2256		6. 2.73	To EI-AYA 7/73. Canx 18.5.73.
G-BAOO	Cessna 421B Golden Eagle II	421B-0415	N41046	2. 2.73	To N4237L 4/81. Canx 13.4.81.
G-BAOP	Reims Cessna FRA.150L Aerobat	0190		5. 2.73	
G-BAOR	Reims Cessna F.177RG Cardinal II	0081		6. 2.73	NTU - Not Imported. To F-BVIJ 4/74. Canx.
G-BAOS	Reims Cessna F.172M Skyhawk	0946		6. 2.73	
G-BAOT	Sud MS.880B Rallye Club	2257		6. 2.73	Canx as WFU 7.9.87.
G-BAOU	American Aviation AA-5 Traveler	AA5-0298	N7298L	8. 2.73	
G-BAOV	Aviation Aviation AA-5A Cheetah (Originally AA-5 Traveler)	AA5-0299	N7299L	8. 2.73	To OY-GTE. Canx 16.10.95.
	(C/n also quoted as AA5A-0299-0197 - rebuilt as AA-5A after its accident at Bridlington on 10.4.82 using parts from G-BEFB (c/n AA5-0197) which was itself DBR on 26.3.78).				
G-BAOW	Cameron O-65 HAFB	59		6. 2.73	(On loan to Balloon Preservation Group) (Extant 1/98)
G-BAOX	Cessna 310Q	310Q-0655	N7876Q	12. 2.73	To VH-JCV 11/82. Canx 28.9.82.
G-BAOY	Cameron S-31 HAFB	61		12. 2.73	Canx by CAA 1.4.92.
G-BAOZ	Cessna 414 Chancellor	414-0381	N46833 G-BAOZ/N1527T/N1601T	12. 2.73	Crashed on landing at Yeadon on 23.3.80 & DBF. Canx as destroyed 14.4.83.

Regn	Type	c/n	Previous identity	Regn date	Fate or immediate subsequent identity (if known)
G-BAPA	Sportavia-Putzer Fournier RF-5B Sperber	51025	D-KEAI	9. 2.73	Canx as WFU 20.5.98.
G-BAPB	DHC.1 Chipmunk 22A (Fuselage no. DHH/f/1)	C1/0001	WB549	26. 2.73	
G-BAPC	Luton LA-4 Minor	MAPS.2		12. 2.73	Canx by CAA 2.9.91.
G-BAPD	Vickers 814 Viscount	340	SE-FOX G-BAPD/D-ANAD	12. 2.73	WFU & stored in 9/78. Broken up in 1/79. Parts used in rebuild of G-BMAT. Canx as WFU 2.7.81.
G-BAPE	Vickers 814 Viscount	341	4X-AVI G-BAPE/D-ANIP	12. 2.73	To N401RA 6/82. Canx 28.5.82.
G-BAPF	Vickers 814 Viscount	338	SE-FOY G-BAPF/D-ANUN	12. 2.73	CofA expired 13.6.90. Canx by CAA 17.6.92. Non-destructive training Airframe 6/95 at Moreton-in-the-Marsh.
G-BAPG	Vickers 814 Viscount	344	(SE-KBN) G-BAPG/4X-AVH/G-BAPG/D-ANIZ	12. 2.73	CofA expired 23.3.90. Stored at Southend. Broken up in 1997. Canx as WFU 17.6.92.
G-BAPH	Reims Cessna FRA.150L Aerobat	0194		8. 2.73	Damaged in collision with a hangar taxying at Bodmin on 12.7.81. Used for spares at Croydon. Canx by CAA 21.1.87. Rear fuselage 2/98 Spanhoe.
G-BAPI	Reims Cessna FRA.150L Aerobat	0195		8. 2.73	
G-BAPJ	Reims Cessna FRA.150L Aerobat	0196		8. 2.73	
G-BAPK	Reims Cessna F.150L	0911		8. 2.73	Swung off the runway on landing at Andrewsfield on 31.8.87 and overturned. Canx as WFU 8.3.88.
G-BAPL	PA-23-250 Turbo Aztec E	27-7304966	N14377	12. 2.73	
G-BAPM	Fuji FA.200-160 Aero Subaru	FA200-172		13. 2.73	Canx by CAA 6.11.98.
G-BAPN	PA-28-180 Cherokee Challenger	28-7305142		16. 2.73	Badly damaged in take-off crash at Eaglescott on 3.4.88. Canx as destroyed 12.7.94.
G-BAPO	Not allocated.				
G-BAPP	Evans VP-1 Coupe	PFA/1580		13. 2.73	
G-BAPR	Jodel D.11	5295 & PFA/914		14. 2.73	
G-BAPS	Campbell Cougar Gyroplane	CA/6000		14. 2.73	CofA expired 20.5.74. Canx by CAA 21.1.87. (On loan to International Helicopter Museum) (On display 5/97)
G-BAPT	Fuji FA.200-180 Aero Subaru	FA200-188		19. 2.73	To G-OISF 2/90. Canx.
G-BAPU	Aerotek Pitts S-2A Special	2049		19. 2.73	To SE-FTY 2/74. Canx 13.11.73.
G-BAPV	Robin DR.400/160 Chevalier	742	F-OCSR(2) N6428Y	19. 2.73	CofA expired 16.12.96. (Stored 9/97)
G-BAPW	PA-28R-180 Cherokee Arrow	28R-30697	5Y-AIR N4951J/(G-AWFD)	21. 2.73	
G-BAPX	Robin DR.400/160 Chevalier	789		21. 2.73	
G-BAPY	Robin HR.100/210 Royal	153		21. 2.73	
G-BAPZ	Piel CP-301A Emeraude	401	F-BJOR	19. 2.73	Crashed & DBF shortly after take-off on a local flight from Claxton Grange Farm, Durham on 21.4.74. Canx.
G-BARA	PA-30-160 Twin Comanche B	30-1411	5Y-AEK	21. 2.73	Crashed into Moulinet mountainous region near Nice, France on 29.5.75. Canx.
G-BARB	PA-34-200-2 Seneca	34-7350085	N15680	28. 2.73	Destroyed in fatal crash on the playing field of Sneyd School, Bloxwich on 20.1.94. Canx by CAA 20.5.94.
G-BARC	Reims Cessna FR.172J Rocket	0356	(D-EEDK)	5. 3.73	
G-BARD	Cessna 337C Super Skymaster	337-0857	SE-FBU N2557S	1. 3.73	Damaged on landing at North Cotes on 12.6.94. (Stored 12/95) Canx as WFU 7.2.96.
G-BARE	Cessna 414 Chancellor	414-0382	N1602T	5. 3.73	To SE-FZL 1/75. Canx 25.11.74.
G-BARF	Wassmer Jodel D.112	1019	F-BJPF	5. 3.73	
G-BARG	Cessna E310Q	310Q-0712	N8237Q	2. 3.73	
G-BARH	Beechcraft C23 Sundowner	M-1473		2. 3.73	
G-BARI	Beechcraft C23 Sundowner	M-1475		2. 3.73	Forced landing on approach to Baginton on 23.4.75 & DBR at Stoneleigh. Canx as destroyed on 5.8.75. (Wreck displayed in car-breakers yard 4/99 Watford)
G-BARJ	Bell 212	30563	VR-BGI G-BARJ/EI-AWN/G-BARJ/EI-AWN/G-BARJ	5. 3.73	Ditched in the Brent Field oilfield, in North Sea on 24.12.83. Canx as destroyed 19.3.84.
G-BARK	Thunder Ax7-77 HAFB	002		5. 3.73	To N711CJ 6/73. Canx 13.6.73.
G-BARL	Bell 206B JetRanger II	975		5. 3.73	To N96117 3/75. Canx 13.3.75.
G-BARM	Bell 212	30553		5. 3.73	NTU - Not Imported. To N14847/LN-OQV 4/73. Canx 19.4.73.
G-BARN	Taylor JT.2 Titch	RN-1 & PFA/60-11136		5. 3.73	Permit expired 2.10.92. (On rebuild)
G-BARO	Bell 206B JetRanger II	971	N18091	5. 3.73	To N47122 2/75. Canx 13.2.75.
G-BARP	Bell 206B JetRanger II	967	N18092	5. 3.73	
G-BARR	HS.125 Srs.600B	256019		19. 3.73	To HZ-AA1 10/84. Canx 3.10.84.
G-BARS	DHC.1 Chipmunk 22 (Fuselage no. DHB/f/445)	C1/0557	WK520	26. 2.73	
G-BART	HS.125 Srs.600B	256005	(G-BJUT) (G-BJXV)/G-BART	5. 3.73	To G-CYII 5/84. Canx.
G-BARU	PA-E23-250 Aztec E	27-7304954	N14367	6. 3.73	To OY-RPW 10/74. Canx 1.10.74.
G-BARV	Cessna 310Q (Originally regd as c/n 310Q-0753 (N1535T))	310Q-0774		7. 3.73	
G-BARW	Cessna 402B Businessliner	402B-0225	N7897Q	8. 3.73	To G-VIKI 11/82. Canx.
G-BARX	Bell 206B JetRanger II	973	N18090	8. 3.73	To F-BFDN 7/87. Canx 7.7.87.
G-BARY	Menavia Piel CP.301A Emeraude	218	F-BIJR	9. 3.73	To G-PIEL 11/88. Canx.
G-BARZ	Scheibe SF-28A Tandem Falke	5724	(D-KAUK)	8. 3.73	CofA expired 3.11.95.
G-BASA	BN-2A Mk.III-1 Trislander	349	G-51-349 VP-PAO	9. 3.73	Restored as VP-PAO 5/73. Canx 28.11.73.
G-BASB	Enstrom F-28A	124		9. 3.73	To HA-MIK 10/94. Canx 26.10.94.
G-BASC	Bell 47G-5A	25107		9. 3.73	To SX-HBD 6/79. Canx 30.5.79.
G-BASD	Beagle B.121 Pup Srs.150	B121-174	(SE-FOG) G-BASD	12. 3.73	To G-PUPP 11/93. Canx.
G-BASE	Bell 206B JetRanger II	969	N18093	8. 3.73	To G-OCBB 11/90. Canx.

Regn	Type	c/n	Previous identity	Regn date	Fate or immediate subsequent identity (if known)
G-BASF	PA-28-180 Cherokee Challenger	28-7305118		13. 3.73	To OY-ATT 9/76. Canx 1.9.76.
G-BASG	American Aviation AA-5 Traveler	AA5-0320	N5420L	12. 3.73	
G-BASH	American Aviation AA-5 Traveler	AA5-0319	EI-AWV G-BASH/N5419L	12. 3.73	
G-BASI	PA-28-140 Cherokee Cruiser F	28-7325200		13. 3.73	To G-MATZ 12/90. Canx.
G-BASJ	PA-28-180 Cherokee Challenger	28-7305136		13. 3.73	
G-BASK	PA-E23-250 Aztec E	27-7305013	N40214	13. 3.73	To OY-BJR 8/77. Canx 29.6.77.
G-BASL	PA-28-140 Cherokee F	28-7325195		13. 3.73	
G-BASM	PA-34-200-2 Seneca	34-7350120	N16272	13. 3.73	
G-BASN	Beechcraft C23 Sundowner	M-1476		13. 3.73	
G-BASO	Lake LA-4-180 Amphibian	358	N2025L	16. 3.73	
G-BASP	Beagle B.121 Pup Srs.100	B121-149	SE-FOC G-35-149	14. 3.73	
G-BASR	PA-25-235 Pawnee C	25-5082	N8644L	15. 3.73	Fatal crash into power cables near Folkingham on 8.6.82 & DBF. Canx as destroyed 13.6.83.
G-BASS	Cessna 421B Golden Eagle II	421B-0610	N1514G	12. 6.74	To N13614 10/81. Canx 16.10.81.
G-BAST	Cameron O-84 HAFB	70		15. 3.73	Canx by CAA 19.5.93. (Stored 1/98)
G-BASU	PA-31-350 Navajo Chieftain	31-7305023	N7693L	15. 3.73	Crashed on take-off from Duonreay on 12.5.87 and badly damaged. Remains later believed scrapped. Canx as destroyed 24.7.89. (Fuselage on fire dump 1/93)
G-BASV	Enstrom F-28A	113		15. 3.73	Substantially damaged in a crash at Kidlington on 27.5.82. Canx as destroyed 2.3.83.
G-BASW	BN-2A-3 Islander	275	9J-ACL "9J-ACH"/G-51-275	16. 3.73	To 5Y-AUA 3/74. Canx 22.3.74.
G-BASX	PA-34-200-2 Seneca	34-7350123	N15781	16. 3.73	
G-BASY	Jodel D.9 Bebe	RLS.1 & PFA/929		19. 3.73	To EI-BUC 1/87. Canx 8.12.86.
G-BASZ	HS.748 Srs.2A/264	1717	G-11-9	19. 3.73	To F-BUTR 5/73. Canx 29.5.73.
G-BATA	HS.125 Srs.403B	25257	G-5-19	20. 3.73	To 9M-HLG 4/84. Canx 25.4.84.
G-BATB	MBB Bo.105C	S.40	D-HDAR	9. 3.73	Canx 6.3.81 on sale to USA. To 9V-BMN 3/81.
G-BATC	MBB Bo.105DB (Originally regd as Bo.105D) (Rebuilt using new MBB pod .89; original pod to Offshore Petroleum Industry Training Board, Montrose 10/90)	S.45	D-HDAW	9. 3.73	
G-BATD	Cessna U206F Stationair	U206-02014	N60204	12. 3.73	CofA expired 13.7.79. Overturned in forced landing at Shobdon on 5.4.80. Canx as destroyed 19.6.80. (Para-trainer use 6/97)
G-BATE	PA-23-250 Aztec E	27-7305006	OY-DLD G-BATE/N40208	19. 3.73	To N555AD 4/83. Canx 8.4.83.
G-BATF	Cessna 340	340-0081	N4095L	2. 5.73	To VR-HHA 11/74. Canx 26.11.74.
G-BATG	Cameron O-77 HAFB	69		19. 3.73	To D-Humpenhaus 8/75. Canx 22.8.75.
G-BATH	Reims Cessna F.337G Super Skymaster (Wichita c/n 01465)	0056	N10631	20. 3.73	To G-NYTE 5/86. Canx.
G-BATI	Reims Cessna FR.172J Rocket	0398		20. 3.73	Fatal crash into the North Sea off Eyemouth on 16.8.77. Canx as destroyed 9.7.84.
G-BATJ	Jodel D.119 (Built by Ecole Technique Aeronautique)	287	F-PIIQ	21. 3.73	
G-BATK	BN-2A-3 Islander	325	G-51-325	21. 3.73	To (VH-ISH)/N2000J 6/73. Canx 8.6.73.
G-BATL	BN-2A-3 Islander	327	G-51-327	21. 3.73	To PP-EFJ 5/73. Canx 25.7.74.
G-BATM	PA-32-300 Cherokee Six E	32-7240040	5Y-AOV N8693N	16. 4.73	Forced landing on a golf course 2 miles from Biggin Hill on 5.8.91. Canx by CAA 6.2.92. To fire dump at Shoreham by 3/92.
G-BATN	PA-23-250 Aztec E	27-7304987	N14391	26. 3.73	
G-BATO	PA-34-200-2 Seneca	34-7350113	SX-AGK G-BATO/N15964	22. 3.73	Restored as SX-AGK 4/75. Canx 19.2.74.
G-BATP	PA-28-140 Cherokee E	28-7225399	LN-BDD	23. 3.73	Crashed at Carsphairn, Kircudbright on 28.9.75. Canx as destroyed 16.3.77.
G-BATR	PA-34-200-2 Seneca	34-7250290	9H-ABH G-BATR/LN-BDT(3)	23. 3.73	
G-BATS	Taylor JT.1 Monoplane	PFA/1448		23. 3.73	Canx by CAA 5.8.91.
G-BATT	Hughes 269C (300C)	122-0175		26. 3.73	
G-BATU	Enstrom F-28A-UK	127		26. 3.73	Badly damaged when control was lost & fell onto its side at Baginton on 8.2.89. Canx as WFU 10.1.91. Cabin section used for fund-raising near Somersham with parts from G-JDHI and G-BACH, and now wears the latters marks.
G-BATV	PA-28-180 Cherokee F	28-7105022	N5168S	26. 3.73	
G-BATW	PA-28-140 Cherokee Fliteliner	28-7225587	N742FL	26. 3.73	
G-BATX	PA-23-250 Aztec E	27-4832	N14271	27. 3.73	
G-BATY	Bell 206A JetRanger	52	N7852S	27. 3.73	To C-GXJK 10/76. Canx 27.10.76.
G-BATZ	BN-2A-8 Islander	358		27. 3.73	To N28JA 6/73. Canx 15.6.73.
G-BAUA	PA-23-250 Aztec D	27-4048	N6718Y	26. 3.73	CofA expired 27.7.92. (Open store 8/96)
G-BAUB	Bell 206B JetRanger II	303	N1403W	28. 3.73	To C-GPYT 4/76. Canx 8.4.76.
G-BAUC	PA-25-235 Pawnee C	25-5243	N8761L	26. 3.73	
G-BAUD	Robin DR.400/160 Knight	813		27. 3.73	To G-XLXL 1/92. Canx.
G-BAUE	Cessna 310Q	310Q-0695	N8048Q	26. 3.73	To N310QQ 10/97. Canx 8.10.97.
G-BAUF	Hughes 269C (300C)	102-0165		29. 3.73	Hit cables near Bishops Stortford on 29.6.79 & DBR. Canx by CAA 28.3.85.
G-BAUG	Cessna 340	340-0081	N4095L	2. 5.73	To VH-HHA 11/74. Canx.
"G-BAUG"	Cessna 310Q	310Q-0609	N7604Q	3. 5.73	Seen painted up in Force One advertisement - Really G-BAXH

Regn	Type	c/n	Previous identity	Regn date	Fate or immediate subsequent identity (if known)
G-BAUH	Dormois Jodel D.112	870	F-BILO	29. 3.73	
G-BAUI	PA-23-250 Aztec D	27-4335	LN-RTS	29. 3.73	CofA expired 5.12.88. Canx by CAA 26.1.89. (Stored 1/99 Bristol/Lulsgate)
G-BAUJ	PA-23-250 Aztec E	27-7304986	N14390	29. 3.73	CofA expired 25.7.94. (Stored 7/97 at Cranfield)
G-BAUK	Hughes 269C (300C)	23-0184		29. 3.73	CofA expired 20.9.93. (Stored 5/98 at Sywell) To HB-ZBP 5/99. Canx 20.5.99.
G-BAUL	Schweizer TSC-1A Teal	21	N2021T	10. 4.73	To LN-BNO 9/76. Canx 3.9.76.
G-BAUM	Bell 206B JetRanger II	987		2. 4.73	Crashed near Sma'Glen, Tayside on 13.7.83 & DBF. Canx as destroyed 30.5.84.
G-BAUN	Bell 206B JetRanger II (Originally 206A; later modified)	464	5N-BAY G-BAUN/5N-AOU/VR-BIA/G-BAUN/N2261W	2. 4.73	
G-BAUO	PA-E23-250 Aztec C	27-3202	SE-FLK LN-NPB	10. 4.73	WFU at Glenrothes in 10/81. Canx 2.2.82.
G-BAUP	Vickers-Armstrong 361 Spitfire LF.XVIe	CBAF.IX.4756	N8R SL721	4. 4.73	To N8WK 7/77. Canx 21.7.77.
G-BAUR	Fokker F-27 Friendship 200	10225	PH-FEP 9V-BAP/9M-AMI/(VR-RCZ)/PH-FEP	5. 4.73	WFU in 10/95. Fuselage used as cabin services training aid in 2.96 at Exeter. Canx as WFU 25.1.96.
G-BAUS	BN-2A-3 Islander	328		6. 4.73	To N800CA 5/73. Canx 3.5.73.
G-BAUT	BN-2A-21 Islander (Originally regd as a BN-2A-3)	329		6. 4.73	To VH-ISI 7/73. Canx 9.7.73.
G-BAUU	Reims Cessna F.150L	0932		5. 4.73	Fatal crash on take-off from Lessay on 16.3.75. Canx.
G-BAUV	Reims Cessna F.150L	0725	LN-BEJ	2. 4.73	Damaged prior to 7/91 and cockpit section only known still in existance at Felixkirk by 6/92. Canx by CAA 4.12.96.
G-BAUW	PA-23-250 Aztec E	27-4814	N14253	9. 4.73	
G-BAUX	Limba Lapwing MPA (MPA = Man-Powered Aircraft)	01		6. 4.73	Abandoned after initial trials. Canx by CAA 9.10.84.
G-BAUY	Reims Cessna FRA.150L Aerobat	0167	N10633	5. 4.73	
G-BAUZ	SNCAN NC.854S	118	F-BEZZ	6. 4.73	CofA expired 25.10.83. Canx as WFU 6.8.84.
G-BAVA	PA-18-150 Super Cub	18-5391	D-EFKC ALAT/18-5391	10. 4.73	Crashed on take-off from Newtownards on 20.11.77. Canx as WFU 19.4.83.
G-BAVB	Reims Cessna F.172M	0965		10. 4.73	
G-BAVC	Reims Cessna F.150L	0926		10. 4.73	Ditched 23 miles southeast of Jersey on 23.11.95. Canx as destroyed 6.2.96.
G-BAVD	Not allocated.				
G-BAVE	Beechcraft A100 King Air	B-171		10. 4.73	To N888TB 9/90. Canx 30.7.90.
G-BAVF	Beechcraft 95-58 Baron	TH-343		10. 4.73	To 5Y-HKH. Canx 23.1.90.
G-BAVG	Beechcraft E90 King Air	LW-59		10. 4.73	To N4718C 2/84. Canx 16.2.84.
G-BAVH	DHC.1 Chipmunk 22 (Fuselage no. DHB/f/738)	C1/0841	WP975	10. 4.73	CofA expired 24.3.96.
G-BAVI	Bell 206B JetRanger II	960	N83236	10. 4.73	Crashed into the English Channel on 29.5.78. Canx.
G-BAVJ	PA-31-350 Navajo Chieftain	31-7305015	N7687L	10. 4.73	To N16BL 1/81. Canx 28.1.81.
G-BAVK	Schweizer TSC-1A1 Teal	23	N41S N2023T	10. 4.73	To LN-SAU 7/78. Canx 7.7.77.
G-BAVL	PA-23-250 Aztec E	27-4671	N14063	10. 4.73	
G-BAVM	PA-31-350 Navajo Chieftain	31-7305029	N7699L	10. 4.73	To G-IFTA 11/85. Canx.
G-BAVN	Boeing-Stearman A75N-1 Kaydet (Regd with c/n "3250-2606", which is a part number)	75-5659	4X-AMT N5367N/42-17496	13. 4.73	To SE-AMT 8/84. Canx 22.10.84.
G-BAVO	Boeing-Stearman A75N-1 Kaydet (Regd with c/n "3250-1405", which is a part number. Real identity unknown)	-	4X-AIH	13. 4.73	
G-BAVP	Beechcraft A23-24 Musketeer Super III	MA-236	SE-EWZ	11. 4.73	Crashed during forced landing near Boulmer on 26.2.77. Canx 24.3.77. (Remains stored at Usworth 4/84)
G-BAVR	American Aviation AA-5 Traveler	AA5-0348		12. 4.73	
G-BAVS	American Aviation AA-5 Traveler	AA5-0349		12. 4.73	(Stored 7/93 Bournemouth) CofA expired 8.11.94. Canx by CAA 31.10.96.
G-BAVT	BN-2A-26 Islander (Originally regd as BN-2A-6)	180	EI-AUL G-51-180	13. 4.73	To VH-CPN 4/76. Canx 18.3.76.
G-BAVU	Cameron A-105 HAFB	66		11. 4.73	CofA expired 5.10.84. (Extant 9/90)
G-BAVV	Reims Cessna FT.337GP Turbo-Pressurised Super Skymaster	0004		17. 4.73	NIU - Canx 6.7.73 as Not Imported - To I-PLAS 12/73.
G-BAVW	PA-E23-250 Aztec E	27-4797	N14245	16. 4.73	To F-GDJC(2) 6/83. Canx 2.6.83.
G-BAVX	Handley Page HPR.7 Dart Herald 214	194	PP-SDN	18. 4.73	To G-DGLD 10/91. Canx.
G-BAVY	PA-E23-250 Aztec E	27-7305017	N40218	10. 4.73	To N4554A 11/83. Canx 21.11.83.
G-BAVZ	PA-23-250 Aztec E	27-7305045	N40241	18. 4.73	
G-BAWA	PA-28R-200 Cherokee Arrow II D	28R-7335130		18. 4.73	To G-OMNI 1/84. Canx.
G-BAWB	PA-E23-250 Aztec C	27-2783	N5669Y	18. 4.73	Canx as WFU 16.1.91.
G-BAWC	Not allocated.				
G-BAWD	Not allocated.				
G-BAWE	BAC 167 Strikemaster Mk.82A (Also c/n EEP/JP/3255)	PS.323	G-27-219	18. 4.73	To Muscat & Oman AF as 417 in 6/73. Canx 18.6.73.
G-BAWF	BAC 167 Strikemaster Mk.82A (Also c/n EEP/JP/3256)	PS.324	G-27-220	18. 4.73	To Muscat & Oman AF as 418 in 6/73. Canx 18.6.73.
G-BAWG	PA-28R-200 Cherokee Arrow II	28R-7335133		18. 4.73	
G-BAWH	Bell 206A JetRanger	448	N2229W	16. 4.73	To F-BXPC 11/75. Canx 10.11.75.
G-BAWI	Enstrom F-28A-UK	120		9. 4.73	Crashed on take-off from Bosworth Hall on 26.6.92. Canx by CAA 17.8.92. (Stored 10/92)

Regn	Type	c/n	Previous identity	Regn date	Fate or immediate subsequent identity (if known)
G-BAWJ	Westland-Sikorsky S-58 Wessex 60 Srs.1	WA/563	5N-AJN G-BAWJ/VR-BEA/9M-ASW/VR-BEA/G-BAWJ/PK-HBV/VR-BEA/AMDB-106	16. 4.73	To N251HL. Canx.
G-BAWK	PA-28-140 Cherokee Cruiser F	28-7325243		24. 4.73	
G-BAWL	Airborne Industries Gas Airship (Re-regd as a Santos-Dumont Gas Filled Airship on 20.7.76)	1		18. 4.73	Exported to USA. Canx by CAA 21.1.87.
G-BAWM	Wassmer Jodel D.112	584	F-BIQO	19. 4.73	Crashed on landing at Bilton Hall Lane strip, near Harrogate on 25.5.74. Canx 26.9.74.
G-BAWN	PA-30-160 Twin Comanche C	30-1948	N8790Y	24. 4.73	Canx as WFU 23.6.98.
G-BAWO	Cessna 340	340-0199	OY-DTW G-BAWO/(PH-MEE)/G-BAWO/N7741Q	24. 4.73	Crashed at Stansted on 28.11.80. Canx.
G-BAWP	Boeing 707-349C (Line No. 503)	19354	EI-ASO VH-EBZ/EI-ASO/N324F	24. 4.73	Restored as EI-ASO 5/75. Canx 16.5.75.
G-BAWR	Robin HR.100/210 Royal	156		27. 4.73	(On repair 2/99 Turweston)
G-BAWS	PA-25-235 Pawnee C	25-5371	N8910L	9. 4.73	DBF at Buscot, near Farringdon, Oxon. on 16.6.79. Canx.
G-BAWT	Socata MS.894E Rallye 220GT	12145	(D-EKHX)	1. 5.73	DBF at Biggin Hill on 27.7.80. Canx.
G-BAWU(1)	PA-E23-250 Aztec C	27-2316	9J-REL N5255Y	30. 4.73R	NTU - To G-BAWV 4/73. Canx.
G-BAWU(2)	PA-30-160 Twin Comanche B	30-1477	(G-BAWV) 9J-RFW/ZS-FAM/N8332Y	30. 4.73	(Made an emergency landing at Exeter on 2.2.99)
G-BAWV(1)	PA-30-160 Twin Comanche B	30-1477	9J-RFW ZS-FAM/N8332Y	30. 4.73R	NTU - To G-BAWU 4/73. Canx.
G-BAWV(2)	PA-E23-250 Aztec C	27-2316	(G-BAWU) 9J-REL/N5255Y	30. 4.73	CofA expired 11.10.85 & WFU at Manchester. Canx as WFU 8.12.88.
G-BAWW	Thunder Ax7-77 HAFB	004	(PH-AWW) G-BAWW	30. 4.73	CofA expired 11.5.84. Canx by CAA 2.4.92. (Extant at Attingham Park Balloon Meet 9/93)
G-BAWX	PA-28-180 Cherokee Challenger	28-7305248		2. 5.73	Substantially damaged after misjudging a landing at Sherburn-in-Elmet on 26.8.90. Canx as destroyed 26.11.90.
G-BAWY	PA-E23-250 Aztec E	27-7305049	N40244	2. 5.73	To OO-BBY 1/77. Canx 30.12.76.
G-BAWZ	Cessna 402	402-0167	N99JH G-BAWZ/5Y-ANJ/OY-AHP/N4067Q	2. 5.73	To EC-EAB 8/86. Canx 11.7.86.
G-BAXA	BN-2A-3 Islander	330		1. 5.73	To (F-BUFV)/5Y-ARZ(2) 8/73. Canx 25.7.74.
G-BAXB	BN-2A-9 Islander	332		1. 5.73	To TR-LRP 8/73. Canx 25.7.74.
G-BAXC	BN-2A-26 Islander	334		1. 5.73	To 4X-AYR 7/73. Canx 9.8.73.
G-BAXD	BN-2A Mk.III-2 Trislander	359		1. 5.73	Converted to a BN-2A Mk.III-2 using major parts from c/n 1065. To G-XTOR 4/96. Canx.
G-BAXE	Hughes 269A-1	113-0313	N8931F	2. 5.73	CofA expired 21.12.93.
G-BAXF	Cameron O-77 HAFB	74		3. 5.73	Canx by CAA 5.9.95. (Extant 2/97)
G-BAXG	HS.125 Srs.1B	25063	HB-VAN	3. 5.73	To G-ONPN 6/80. Canx.
G-BAXH	Cessna 310Q	310Q-0609	"G-BAUG" N7604Q	3. 5.73	Crashed on landing at Spa, Belgium on 21.8.83. Canx by CAA 14.11.91.
G-BAXI	PA-39 Twin Comanche C/R	39-005	N8850Y	8. 5.73	To N26545 12/81. Canx 31.12.81.
G-BAXJ	PA-32-300 Cherokee Six B	32-40763	N1362Z G-BAXJ/4X-ANY/N5224S	8. 5.73	
G-BAXK	Thunder Ax7-77 HAFB	005		9. 5.73	CofA expired 2.7.91. (Active 1/93)
G-BAXL	HS.125 Srs.3B	25069	VH-ECF	9. 5.73	To G-OBOB 7/89. Canx.
G-BAXM	Beechcraft B24R Sierra 200	MC-158		10. 5.73	To F-GCMT(2) 9/87. Canx 25.7.86.
G-BAXN	PA-34-200T Seneca II	34-7350069	N15495	10. 5.73	To EC-DVY 4/85. Canx 30.1.85.
G-BAXO	Cessna 414 Chancellor	414-0067	9J-ACI A2-ZFP/ZS-IDP/N8167Q	11. 5.73	To SE-GOT 12/75. Canx 18.12.75.
G-BAXP	PA-23-250 Aztec E	27-4608	N13990	11. 5.73	CofA expired 5.3.92. (Fuselage remains at Shoreham 9/98)
G-BAXR	Beechcraft 95-B55 Baron	TC-1574		11. 5.73	To G-SUZI 3/85. Canx.
G-BAXS	Bell 47G-5	7908	5B-CFB G-BAXS/N4098G	11. 5.73	
G-BAXT	PA-28R-200 Cherokee Arrow II	28R-7335157		14. 5.73	To G-LFSE 6/97. Canx.
G-BAXU	Reims Cessna F.150L	0959		14. 5.73	
G-BAXV	Reims Cessna F.150L	0966		14. 5.73	
G-BAXW	Reims Cessna F.150L	0973		14. 5.73	Crashed into trees at Chinnor, near Booker, Oxon on 16.9.80. Canx as destroyed 1.3.83.
G-BAXX	Reims Cessna F.150L	0960		14. 3.73	Destroyed by bomb blast at Eglinton on 21.9.78. Canx.
G-BAXY	Reims Cessna F.172M	0905	N10636	15. 5.73	
G-BAXZ	PA-28-140 Cherokee C	28-26760	PH-NLX	15. 5.73	
G-BAYA	Bell 206B JetRanger II	1035		16. 5.73	Crashed onto frozen Lake Avon, near Aviemore on 11.1.77. Remains to AIB. Canx as destroyed 9.5.77.
G-BAYB	Cameron O-77 HAFB	75		17. 5.73	To F-BUQJ 12/74. Canx 9.11.73.
G-BAYC	Cameron O-65 HAFB	68	(HB-BOU) G-BAYC	17. 5.73	(Extant 2/97) Canx as WFU 15.5.98.
G-BAYD	BN-2A-9 Islander	700		17. 5.73	To (TR-LRY)/6V-ADJ 4/74. Canx 18.2.74.
G-BAYE	BN-2A-3 Islander	699		17. 5.73	To Jamaican DF as JDFT-2 in 4/74. Canx.
G-BAYF	BN-2A-3 Islander	698		17. 5.73	To PT-KCF 5/75. Canx 12.5.75.
G-BAYG	BN-2A-21 Islander	697		17. 5.73	To PK-LAV 5/74. Canx 29.5.74.
G-BAYH	BN-2A-3 Islander	696		17. 5.73	To PT-KNE 11/74. Canx.
G-BAYI	BN-2A-6 Islander	695		17. 5.73	To PT-JSC 5/75. Canx 12.5.75.
G-BAYJ	BN-2A-9 Islander	694		17. 5.73	To 8P-PAT 12/73. Canx 8.5.75.
G-BAYK	Cessna 340	340-0156	N4588L	17. 5.73	Canx 29.12.75 on sale to Belgium. To D-INAH 7/76.
G-BAYL	SNCAN Nord 1203 Norecrin VI	161	F-BEQV	18. 5.73	Canx by CAA 14.11.91. (Fuselage only stored outside 3/98 at Chirk)
G-BAYM	Robin HR.100/210 Royal	180		18. 5.73	NTU - Canx 24.1.74 as Not Imported. To SE-FNC.
G-BAYN	Hughes 369HS (500)	13-0443S		18. 5.73	Crashed at Boxted, Essex on 29.10.75. Canx.
G-BAYO	Cessna 150L	150-74435	N19471	18. 5.73	
G-BAYP	Cessna 150L	150-74017	N18651	18. 5.73	
G-BAYR	Robin HR.100/210 Royal	164		18. 5.73	

Regn	Type	c/n	Previous identity	Regn date	Fate or immediate subsequent identity (if known)
G-BAYS	Beechcraft B19 Musketeer	MB-611	N3082W	18. 5.73	NTU - Canx 22.2.74 as Not Imported. Remained as N3082W.
G-BAYT	HS.125 Srs.600B	256012	G-BNDX G-BAYT/5N-ALX/G-BAYT/G-5-17	21. 5.73	To EC-272/EC-EOQ. Canx 17.4.89.
G-BAYU	Cessna 310Q II	310Q-0738	N5953M	21. 5.73	To G-ZIPP 6/80. Canx.
G-BAYV	SNCAN Nord 1101 Noralpha	193	F-BLTN French AF	22. 5.73	Crashed on take-off at Broomeclose Farm, Longbridge Deverill, near Warminster on 23.2.74. Remains to Ford, then Maidstone and then Hawkinge. Canx as WFU 28.4.83. (On loan to Macclesfield Historical Aviation Society)
G-BAYW	Bell 47G-2	1494	CF-KJN (VP-KOL)/CF-KJN/N2825B	23. 5.73	To N72479 2/76. Canx 13.2.76.
G-BAYX	Bell 47G-5	7874	CF-XPN N6216N	23. 5.73	Lost power while crop-spraying at Claythorpe Manor, Alford, Lincs on 7.6.86 and crashed into a field. Canx by CAA 20.3.89.
G-BAYY	Cessna 310C	35882	N1782H	24. 5.73	Donated to Carlisle airport fire section after CofA expired on 6.12.85. Canx as PWFU 20.7.94. Scrapped in 1997.
G-BAYZ	Bellanca 7GCBC Citabria	461-73		23. 5.73	
G-BAZA	HS.125 Srs.F403B (Originally regd as Srs.403B)	25272	G-5-15	30. 5.73	To N4759D 5/84. Canx 11.5.84.
G-BAZB	HS.125 Srs.400B	25252	XX505 G-5-17	30. 5.73	To N48US 12/92. Canx 14.12.92.
G-BAZC	Robin DR.400/160 Knight	824		29. 5.73	Badly damaged in crash at Crosland Moor on 21.5.88. CofA expired 24.6.88. (Stored 9/89)
G-BAZD	PA-31-310 Turbo Navajo	31-7300915	N7491L	29. 5.73	To OH-PNM 10/80. Canx 28.8.80.
G-BAZE	American American AA-5 Traveler	AA5-0380	N5480L	29. 5.73	To EI-AYD 9/73. Canx 4.9.73.
G-BAZF	American Aviation AA-5 Traveler	AA5-0381	EI-AYC G-BAZF/N5481L	29. 5.73	Fatal crash in Haldon Forest, Devon on 14.7.87 & DBF. Canx as destroyed 7.12.89.
G-BAZG	Boeing 737-204ADV (Line No. 338)	20806		30. 5.73	To HP-1195CMP 9/91. Canx 27.9.91.
G-BAZH	Boeing 737-204ADV (Line No. 341)	20807		30. 5.73	To G-SBEB 12/94. Canx.
G-BAZI	Boeing 737-204ADV (Line No. 342)	20808		30. 5.73	To G-BOSA 4/88. Canx.
G-BAZJ	Handley Page HPR.7 Dart Herald 209	183	4X-AHR G-8-1	30. 5.73	WFU at Guernsey on 31.10.84. CofA expired 24.11.84. Canx as WFU 4.1.85. Open storage in 6/97 at Guernsey. To Guernsey Airport Fire Service by 1/99.
G-BAZK	Cessna 340	340-0027	N5414M	31. 5.73	To N5414M 5/76. Canx 4.5.76.
G-BAZL	Westland/SNIAS SA.341G Gazelle Srs.1	WA/1073		16. 5.73	To F-BXPG. Canx 26.11.75.
G-BAZM	Jodel D.11	1 & PAL/1416 & PFA/915		31. 5.73	
G-BAZN	Bell 206B JetRanger II (Originally 206A; later modified)	124	9J-RIN ZS-HCJ	1. 6.73	To G-HELO 11/87. Canx.
G-BAZO	Bell 47G-2	2005	9J-RAD VP-RAD(2)/ZS-HBE/(EC-AUA)/N5187B	1. 6.73	To F-GAMD 9/76. Canx 28.7.76.
G-BAZP	Reims Cessna F.150L	0956		1. 6.73	Fatal collision with Rallye 150ST G-BEVX at Biggin Hill on 25.11.78. Canx as destroyed 1.12.78.
G-BAZR	Reims Cessna F.150L	0957		1. 6.73	Crashed into a tree at Rotherwell, near Grimsby on 6.4.78. Canx as destroyed 12.10.78.
G-BAZS	Reims Cessna F.150L	0954		1. 6.73	
G-BAZT	Reims Cessna F.172M	0996		1. 6.73	
G-BAZU	PA-28R-200 Cherokee Arrow B	28R-7135151	EI-AVH	6. 6.73	
G-BAZV	PA-E23-250 Aztec D	27-4114	N6780Y	6. 6.73	Canx 21.12.83 on sale to Germany. To 5H-AIR 4/84.
G-BAZW	BN-2A-9 Islander	333		6. 6.73	To G-350/A Ghana AF 9/73. Canx 18.9.73.
G-BAZX	BN-2A-8 Islander	335	(N91CA) G-BAZX	6. 6.73	To B-11107 4/74. Canx 2.4.74.
G-BAZY	BN-2A-9 Islander	336		6. 6.73	To ZK-MCB 10/73. Canx 18.10.73.
G-BAZZ	BN-2A-9 Islander	337		6. 6.73	To G-351/B Ghana AF 9/73. Canx 18.9.73.
G-BBAA	Cessna 340	340-0231	N7852Q	15. 6.73	To SE-GOC 11/75. Canx 17.11.75.
G-BBAB	Socata MS.894A Rallye Minerva 220	12088		6. 6.73	To TF-OSK(3) 9/81. Canx 15.9.81.
G-BBAC	Cameron O-77 HAFB	100		7. 6.73	DBF near Kingsclere on 31.7.76. Canx.
G-BBAD	Not allocated.				
G-BBAE	Lockheed L.1011-385-1-14 Tristar 100	193N-1083	C-FCXB G-BBAE/C-FCXB/G-BBAE/N64854	6. 6.73	
G-BBAF(1)	Lockheed L.1011-385-1 Tristar 50	193C-1096		6. 6.73R	NTU - To N717DA. Canx.
G-BBAF(2)	Lockheed L.1011-385-1-14 Tristar 100 (Converted to Series 100 version in 1991)	193N-1093		2. 8.74	
G-BBAG(1)	Lockheed L.1011-385-1-14 Tristar 100	193N-1101		6. 6.73R	NTU - To G-BBAH 8/74. Canx.
G-BBAG(2)	Lockheed L.1011-385-1-14 Tristar 100 (Converted to Series 100 version in 1991)	193N-1094		2. 8.74	To VR-HMW 3/93. Canx 8.3.93.
G-BBAH(1)	Lockheed L.1011-385-1 Tristar 50	193N-1103		6. 6.73R	NTU - To N62355. Canx.
G-BBAH(2)	Lockheed L.1011-385-1-14 Tristar 100 (Converted to Series 100 version in 3/91)	193N-1101	(G-BBAG)	2. 8.74	
G-BBAI(1)	Lockheed L.1011-385-1 Tristar 50	193B-1107		6. 6.73R	NTU - To N81027. Canx.

Regn	Type	c/n	Previous identity	Regn date	Fate or immediate subsequent identity (if known)
G-BBAI(2)	Lockheed L.1011-385-1-14 Tristar 100	193N-1102	C-FCXJ G-BBAI/C-FCXJ/G-BBAI	2. 8.74	
G-BBAJ(1)	Lockheed L.1011-385-1 Tristar 1	193N-1117		6. 6.73R	NTU - To JA8514 6/75. Canx.
G-BBAJ(2)	Lockheed L.1011-385-1-14 Tristar 100	193N-1106		2. 8.74	
G-BBAK	Socata MS.894A Rallye Minerva 220	12080	(D-ENMK)	6. 6.73	
G-BBAL	BN-2A-9 Islander	338		6. 6.73	To G-352/C Ghana AF 9/73. Canx 18.9.73.
G-BBAM	BN-2A-9 Islander	339		6. 6.73	To G-353/D Ghana AF 9/73. Canx 18.9.73.
G-BBAN	BN-2A-9 Islander	340		6. 6.73	To G-354/E Ghana AF 9/73. Canx 18.9.73.
G-BBAO	BN-2A-9 Islander	341		6. 6.73	To G-355/F Ghana AF 9/73. Canx 18.9.73.
G-BBAP	Bell 47G-5A	25119		6. 6.73	To N31147 9/75. Canx 18.9.75.
G-BBAR	SAN Jodel D.117	511	F-BHXJ	7. 6.73	DBF in a refuelling accident at Cherry Tree Farm, Monewden during 1986. Canx by CAA 5.8.94.
G-BBAS	HS.125 Srs.600B	256017	G-5-18	8. 6.73	To PK-PJD 11/74. Canx 7.11.74.
G-BBAT	Beechcraft C23 Sundowner	M-1484		8. 6.73	To OO-SUN 3/77. Canx 25.2.77.
G-BBAU	Enstrom F-28A	140		12. 6.73	DBR when gaught by a gust of wind while taxiing at Biggin Hill on 31.1.85. Canx as destroyed 11.4.85.
G-BBAV	PA-E23-250 Aztec C	27-3173	PH-KNV LN-NPD/SE-EPW	12. 6.73	To EI-BLW 11/81. Canx 12.11.81.
G-BBAW	Robin HR.100/210 Royal	167		12. 6.73	
G-BBAX	Robin DR.400/140 Earl	835		12. 6.73	
G-BBAY	Robin DR.400/140 Earl	841		12. 6.73	
G-BBAZ	Hiller 360 UH-12E	2165	EC-DOR G-BBAZ/N31707/ CAF112276/RCAF10276	13. 6.73	CofA expired 23.5.91. Canx by CAA 29.5.96. (Stored dismantled for eventual restoration 4/99 Gamlingay, Five Acres Farm)
G-BBBA	Hiller 360 UH-12E	2175	EC-DOS G-BBBA/N31704/ CAF112278/RCAF10278	13. 6.73	Force-landed among trees shortly after take-off from Great Driffield on 26.9.86. Canx as destroyed 7.12.87.
G-BBBB	Taylor JT.1 Monoplane	SAM/01 & PFA/1422		4. 6.73	
G-BBBC	Reims Cessna F.150L	0864	N10635	14. 6.73	
G-BBBD	PA-E23-250 Aztec E	27-7305107	N40292	14. 6.73	DBR at Shoreham on 8.12.82. Canx.
G-BBBE	American Aviation AA-5 Traveler	AA5-0391	N5491L	15. 6.73	Crashed in field adjacent to Caernarvon airfield on 4.8.79, undercarriage broken off and back broken. Canx.
G-BBBF	Not allocated.				
G-BBBG	BN-2A-8 Islander	374		15. 6.73	To (N91CA)/VP-HCD 7/73. Canx 1.8.74.
G-BBBH	BN-2A-8 Islander	375		15. 6.73	To N26JA 11/73. Canx 1.11.73.
G-BBBI	American Aviation AA-5 Traveler	AA5-0392		15. 6.73	
G-BBBJ	PA-E23-250 Aztec E	27-4556	5Y-ALY N13920	13. 6.73	To N3951H 5/83. Canx 31.5.83.
G-BBBK	PA-28-140 Cherokee C	28-22572	SE-EYF	18. 6.73	
G-BBBL	Cessna 337B Super Skymaster	337-0555	EI-AVF 5H-MNL/N5455S	19. 6.73	CofA expired 12.2.77 & stored at Hurn. Canx by CAA 21.1.87. (Stored 3/92)
G-BBBM	Bell 206B JetRanger II	1097	N18090	19. 6.73	To OO-EGM 5/96. Canx 17.4.96.
G-BBBN	PA-28-180 Cherokee Challenger	28-7305365		20. 6.73	
G-BBBO	SIPA 903	67	F-BGBQ	16. 1.74	Permit expired 5.5.98. (On restoration to fly 7/99 Liverpool)
G-BBBP	Bell 212	30577	N18090 N58027	22. 6.73	To PK-HCJ 1/81. Canx 6.1.81.
G-BBBR	Enstrom F-28A (Composite with c/n 060 N9553)	014	N4461	22. 6.73	Caught fire while spraying on 26.7.80 at West Fleetham, Northumbria. Canx.
G-BBBS	Cessna 182P Skylane	182-61436	N21131	25. 6.73	To G-BIRS 3/81. Canx.
G-BBBT	Cameron O-56 HAFB	79		25. 6.73	Canx 31.8.76 on sale to Australia.
G-BBBU	Pitts S-1D Special	EKH-1		25. 6.73	To G-OODI 12/80. Canx.
G-BBBV	Handley Page 137 Jetstream 1 (Production No. 34)	234	G-8-12	26. 6.73	To N200SE 8/74. Canx 21.8.74.
G-BBBW	Clutton-Tabenor FRED Srs.2	DLW.1 & PFA/1551		26. 6.73	
G-BBBX	Cessna 310L	310L-0134	OY-EGW N3284X	28. 6.73	
G-BBBY	PA-28-140 Cherokee Cruiser F	28-7325533		28. 6.73	
G-BBBZ	Enstrom F-28C-UK-2	138		29. 6.73	To G-BZZZ 1/82. Canx.
G-BBCA	Bell 206B JetRanger II	1101	N18091	29. 6.73	
G-BBCB	Western O-65 HAFB	018		29. 6.73	
G-BBCC	PA-23-250 Aztec D	27-4317	N6953Y	29. 6.73	
G-BBCD	Beechcraft 95-B55 Baron	TC-1607		29. 6.73	CofA expired 1.7.88. (Last regd to an owner at Rockport, Texas - present status unknown) Canx by CAA 28.7.94.
G-BBCE	Westland-Sikorsky S-58 Wessex 60 Srs.1	WA/695	PK-HBW VR-BEB/AMDB-101	3. 7.73	To 5N-AJK 7/74. Canx 27.6.74.
G-BBCF	Reims Cessna FRA.150L Aerobat	0209		3. 7.73	Damaged at Harrogate on 8.9.84. Canx as WFU 31.7.89. (Instructional Airframe at Perth - dumped by 6/98)
G-BBCG	Robin DR.400 2+2	846		4. 7.73	Damaged in hangar collapse at Rochester on 14.1.87. Canx by CAA 6.10.87.
G-BBCH	Robin DR.400 2+2	850		4. 7.73	
G-BBCI	Cessna 150H	150-69282	N50409	4. 7.73	
G-BBCJ	Cessna 150J	150-69856	N51231	4. 7.73	Damaged during a thunderstorm at Birmingham on 6.7.89. Canx as destroyed 22.8.89.
G-BBCK	Cameron O-77 HAFB	76		4. 7.73	

Regn	Type	c/n	Previous identity	Regn date	Fate or immediate subsequent identity (if known)
G-BBCL	HS.125 Srs.600B	256015	(D-CCEX) G-5-11/G-BBCL/Irish Air Corps 239/G-BBCL/ 9K-ACZ/G-BBCL/G-BJCB/G-BBCL/G-5-19	6. 7.73	To N600AV 2/85. Canx 21.2.85.
G-BBCM	PA-E23-250 Aztec E	27-4634	N14021	9. 7.73	To G-BRAV 8/88. Canx.
G-BBCN	Robin HR.100/210 Royal	168		11. 7.73	
G-BBCO	Reims Cessna F.177RG Cardinal	0088		11. 7.73	NTU - Not Imported. To D-EDXK 5/74. Canx 16.2.76.
G-BBCP	Thunder Ax6-56 HAFB	007		11. 7.73	(Extant 2/97)
G-BBCR	Moravan Zlin Z.326 Trener Master (Mod to Z.526 standard) (Note: c/n confirmed but conflicts with I-ETRM)	916	OH-TZF	12. 7.73	To G-ZLIN 6/81. Canx.
G-BBCS	Robin DR.400/140B Earl	851		12. 7.73	
G-BBCT	PA-31-350 Navajo Chieftain	31-7305068	N74925	12. 7.73	To N509SC 2/82. Canx 12.2.82.
G-BBCU	PA-E23-250 Aztec E	27-7305112	N40297	13. 7.73	To G-JTCA 12/80. Canx.
G-BBCV	Cessna A.188B AgTruck	188-01085T	N21865	16. 7.73	To SX-AFZ 6/81. Canx 5.6.81.
G-BBCW	PA-23-250 Aztec E	27-4806	N14251	17. 7.73	
G-BBCX	Wills & Moger Radio Controlled (Hot Air) Airship (Toy)	EW-1		17. 7.73	Destroyed by fire. Canx by CAA 21.1.87.
G-BBCY	Phoenix Luton LA-4A Minor	PFA/825		17. 7.73	
G-BBCZ	American Aviation AA-5 Traveler	AA5-0382	N5482L	18. 7.73	
G-BBDA	American Aviation AA-5 Traveler	AA5-0383	(EI-AYL) G-BBDA	18. 7.73	To G-NONI 8/88. Canx.
G-BBDB	PA-28-180 Cherokee Challenger	28-7305361		18. 7.73	CofA expired 7.6.85. Canx by CAA 3.4.89. (Wreck stored 4/96)
G-BBDC	PA-28-140 Cherokee Cruiser F	28-7325437		18. 7.73	
G-BBDD	PA-28-140 Cherokee Cruiser F	28-7325444	N55687	18. 7.73	To G-MIDD 1/97. Canx.
G-BBDE	PA-28R-200-2 Cherokee Arrow	28R-7335250	(EI-...) G-BBDE	18. 7.73	
G-BBDF	PA-28R-200-2 Cherokee Arrow	28R-7335255		18. 7.73	To G-BELL 7/76. Canx.
G-BBDG	BAC/Aerospatiale Concorde SST Var.100 (Originally regd with c/n 202/13523)	100-002		7. 8.73	CofA expired 1.3.82 & WFU at Filton. Canx as WFU 12/81. (Stored for spares 9/98 Filton)
G-BBDH	Reims Cessna F.172M	0990		19. 7.73	
G-BBDI	PA-18-150 Super Cub	18-5336	D-EFKA ALAT/18-5336	19. 7.73	Fatal crash when it spun in and caught fire at Portmoak on 24.8.89. Canx as destroyed 25.9.89.
G-BBDJ	Thunder Ax6-56 HAFB	006		20. 7.73	Canx by CAA 11.5.93. (With Balloon Preservation Group, Lancing 7/98)
G-BBDK	Vickers 808C Viscount	291	HB-ILR EI-AJK	25. 7.73	To G-OPFE 10/94. Canx.
G-BBDL	American Aviation AA-5 Traveler	AA5-0406		18. 7.73	
G-BBDM	American Aviation AA-5 Traveler	AA5-0407		18. 7.73	
G-BBDN	Taylor JT.1 Monoplane	PFA/1437		24. 7.73	(Under construction 10/90) Canx by CAA 4.7.91.
G-BBDO	PA-23-250 Turbo Aztec E	27-7305120	N40361	24. 7.73	
G-BBDP	Robin DR.400/160 Knight	853		25. 7.73	
G-BBDR	PA-31-300 Turbo Navajo	31-56	LN-NPG OY-BBO	26. 7.73	To OH-PNP 8/80. Canx 8.5.80.
G-BBDS	PA-31-310 Turbo Navajo	31-7300956	N7565L	26. 7.73	To G-SKKB 4/90. Canx.
G-BBDT	Cessna 150H	150-68839	N23272	26. 7.73	
G-BBDU	PA-31-310 Turbo Navajo	31-537	N6796L (9V-BBT)	30. 7.73	To G-LYDD 5/89. Canx.
G-BBDV	SIPA 903 (Originally ex F-BEYJ c/n 7 but rebuilt in 1978 from F-BEYY c/n 21, c/n amended on 9.1.79)	7/21	F-BEYY	30. 7.73	
G-BBDW	BN-2A-9 Islander	342		31. 7.73	To Ghana AF as G-356/G in 11/74. Canx 28.11.74.
G-BBDX	BN-2A-9 Islander	343		31. 7.73	To Ghana AF as G-357/H in 11/74. Canx 28.11.74.
G-BBDY	BN-2A-2 Islander	344		31. 7.73	To JA5218 11/73. Canx 25.10.73.
G-BBDZ	BN-2A-9 Islander	345		31. 7.73	To (N26JA)/YV-DAEW 12/73. Canx.
G-BBEA	Phoenix Luton LA-4A Minor	SAK-1 & PFA/843		30. 7.73	
G-BBEB	PA-28R-200-2 Cherokee Arrow	28R-7335292		31. 7.73	
G-BBEC	PA-28-180 Cherokee Challenger	28-7305478		30. 7.73	
G-BBED	Socata MS.894A Rallye Minerva 220	12097		30. 7.73	(Stored 9/95)
G-BBEE	Gates LearJet 25B	25B-135	N1103R N3803G/G-BBEE	30. 7.73	To N7600K 9/80. Canx 29.9.80.
G-BBEF	PA-28-140 Cherokee Cruiser	28-7325527		31. 7.73	
G-BBEG	Bell 206A JetRanger	442	N2221N	30. 7.73	To F-BXSU 4/76. Canx 26.4.76.
G-BBEH	PA-28R-200 Cherokee Arrow II	28R-7335297	N55837	31. 7.73	NTU - To EI-AYE 9/73. Canx 20.8.73.
G-BBEI	PA-31 Turbo Navajo	31-126	5Y-AHO N9091Y	30. 7.73	To N800MG 6/98. Canx 3.6.98.
G-BBEJ	PA-31-350 Navajo Chieftain	31-7305038	N74905	3. 8.73	To PH-KID 12/83. Canx 6.12.83.
G-BBEK	Dassault Falcon 20C	86	(HB-VDW) G-BBEK/F-BUYI/(G-BBEK)/N622R/N808F/N976F/F-WMKI	7. 8.73	To F-WRGQ 5/76. Canx.

Regn	Type	c/n	Previous identity	Regn date	Fate or immediate subsequent identity (if known)
G-BBEL	PA-28R-180 Cherokee Arrow B	28R-30877	SE-FDX	6. 8.73	
G-BBEM	Beechcraft 95-B55 Baron	TC-1616		7. 8.73	To HB-GHG 3/84. Canx 14.3.84.
G-BBEN	Bellanca 7GCBC Citabria	496-73	(D-EAUT) N36416	7. 8.73	
G-BBEO	Reims Cessna FRA.150L Aerobat	0205		3. 8.73	
G-BBEP	HS.125 Srs.600B	256030	5N-ARD G-BBEP/G-BJOY/G-BBEP	16. 8.73	To G-TOMI 4/85. Canx.
G-BBER	Bell 47G-5A	25131	N18090 N58135	8. 8.73	To SX-HAT 6/77. Canx 26.5.77.
G-BBES	Bell 206B JetRanger II	1104	N18092	8. 8.73	To LN-OSV 6/75. Canx 13.6.75.
G-BBET	Bell 206B JetRanger II	1102	N18091	8. 8.73	To I-AGUO 4/75. Canx 20.12.74.
G-BBEU	Bell 206B JetRanger II	1121	N18093	8. 8.73	To 5X-MIA 6/82. Canx 24.6.82.
G-BBEV	PA-28-140 Cherokee D	28-7125340	LN-MTM	8. 8.73	
G-BBEW	PA-23-250 Aztec E	27-7305075	EI-BYK G-BBEW/N40262	9. 8.73	CofA expired 22.7.99. Canx by CAA 16.8.99.
G-BBEX	Cessna 185A Skywagon	185-0491	EI-CMC G-BBEX/4X-ALD/N99992/N1691Z	7. 8.73	
G-BBEY	PA-23-250 Aztec E	27-7305160	(LN-FOE) G-BBEY/N40396	8. 8.73	
G-BBEZ	Short SC.7 Skyliner 3-200-34	SH1918	G-14-90	9. 8.73	To JA8793 10/73. Canx 24.10.73.
G-BBFA	Short SC.7 Skyvan 3-400-17	SH1919	G-14-91	9. 8.73	To R.Thai Police as 21919 in 11/73. Canx 19.11.73.
G-BBFB	Bell 206B JetRanger II	1129	N18094	8. 8.73	To G-CJHI 10/81. Canx.
G-BBFC	American Aviation AA-1B Trainer	AA1B-0245	(N9945L)	14. 8.73	Damaged on landing at Perranporth on 9.6.96. Canx by CAA 14.10.96.
G-BBFD	PA-28R-200-2 Cherokee Arrow B	28R-7335342		8. 8.73	
G-BBFE	Bell 206A JetRanger	29	9J-ADT G-BBFE/ZS-HCD	10. 8.73	To EC-EFE 8/87. Canx 5.8.87.
G-BBFF	PA-34-200-2 Seneca	34-7250076	N1077U	13. 8.73	Damaged on landing at Machrins Farm strip, Colonsey on 25.5.74. (To instructional airframe at Shoreham) Canx.
G-BBFG	BN-2A-8 Islander (Originally regd as BN-2A-6)	701		13. 8.73	To 9M-ATN 5/74. Canx 29.5.74.
G-BBFH	BN-2A-9 Islander (Originally regd as BN-2A-6)	702		13. 8.73	To OY-DZV 4/74. Canx 20.3.74.
G-BBFI	BN-2A-2 Islander (Originally regd as BN-2A-6)	703		13. 8.73	To P2-MKV 5/74. Canx 29.5.74.
G-BBFJ	IRMA BN-2A-8 Islander (Originally regd as BN-2A-6)	704		13. 8.73	To EI-AYN 3/74. Canx 29.4.74.
G-BBFK	BN-2A-8 Islander (Originally regd as BN-2A-6)	705		13. 8.73	To CR-APN 11/74. Canx 28.11.74.
G-BBFL	SRCM Gardan GY-201 Minicab	21	F-BHCQ	17. 8.73	Damaged in forced landing at Main Farm, Colyton, Bere Alston, Devon on 9.6.93. Permit expired 21.9.93. (On rebuild 7/98 at Dunkeswell with new fuselage)
G-BBFM	BN-2A-6 Islander	706		13. 8.73	To CR-AQE 11.74. Canx 28.11.74.
G-BBFN	BN-2A-6 Islander	707		13. 8.73	To CR-AQF 11/74. Canx 28.11.74.
G-BBFO	BN-2A-9 Islander (Originally regd as BN-2A-6)	708		13. 8.73	To TN-ACO 11/74. Canx 28.11.74.
G-BBFP	BN-2A-20 Islander (Originally regd as BN-2A-6)	709		13. 8.73	To P2-MKW 8/74. Canx 7.8.74.
G-BBFR	BN-2A-8 Islander (Originally regd as BN-2A-6)	710		13. 8.73	To F-BVTD 6/74. Canx 10.6.74.
G-BBFS	Van Den Bemden K-460 (Gas) Free Balloon	75 & VDB-16	OO-BGX	10. 8.73	Canx by CAA 19.5.93. (To British Balloon Museum, Newbury)
G-BBFT	Cessna A.188B AgTruck	188-01270T	N8257G	13. 8.73	To VH-HOP 7/85. Canx 11.7.85.
G-BBFU	PA-E23-250 Aztec E	27-7305124	N40364	13. 8.73	To G-OCFS 2/86. Canx.
G-BBFV	PA-32-260 Cherokee Six	32-778	5Y-ADF	13. 8.73	
G-BBFW	PA-E23-250 Aztec	27-219	5Y-KRB VP-KRB/N4690P	13. 8.73	CofA expired 29.11.78. (Stored at Stapleford) Canx by CAA 3.4.89.
G-BBFX	PA-34-200-2 Seneca	34-7250109	5Y-APJ N4586T/(YV-T-QTN)	13. 8.73	To OY-CEA 6/84. Canx 1.6.84.
G-BBFY	PA-31P Pressurised Navajo	31P-7300139	N331PN	15. 8.73	To N26319 12/81. Canx 16.12.81.
G-BBFZ	PA-28R-200-2 Cherokee Arrow B	28R-7335337	N9516N	15. 8.73	To OO-BFZ 3/77. Canx 9.3.77.
G-BBGA	Scheibe SF-28A Tandem Falke	5739	EI-BFD EI-122/EI-BFD/G-BBGA/D-KOEI	15. 8.73	Crashed near Enstone on 26.5.82. Canx.
G-BBGB	PA-E23-250 Aztec E	27-7305004	N40206	16. 8.73	
G-BBGC	Socata MS.893E Rallye 180GT	12215	F-BUCV	16. 8.73	
G-BBGD	Reims Cessna F.337G Super Skymaster	0060		17. 8.73	Destroyed in forced landing near West Wycombe on 13.10.76. Canx.
G-BBGE	PA-23-250 Aztec D	27-4373	N6137Y	20. 8.73	CofA expired 17.8.92. Canx by CAA 2.9.91. (Stored 9/96)
G-BBGF	Cessna 340	340-0208	N7775Q	21. 8.73	Force landed about 10 miles south of Luxor, Egypt on 5.12.86. Canx by CAA 12.9.92.
G-BBGG	American Aviation AA-5 Traveler	AA5-0429	N7129L	20. 8.73	Crashed at Sandford Hall, Oswestry on 10.5.81. Canx.
G-BBGH	American Aviation AA-5 Traveler	AA5-0430	N7130L	20. 8.73	Damaged on take-off at Usk on 29.6.91. Scrapped in 1992. Canx by CAA 13.12.96.
G-BBGI	Fuji FA.200-160 Aero Subaru	FA200-228		21. 8.73	
G-BBGJ	Cessna 180	180-31209	6O-SAE 6OS-AAF/N9110C	20. 8.73	To 5Y-BJD 2/94. Canx 7.2.94.
G-BBGK	Lake LA-4-200 Buccaneer	543	N39779	22. 8.73	To G-PARK 6/82. Canx.

Regn	Type	c/n	Previous identity	Regn date	Fate or immediate subsequent identity (if known)
G-BBGL	Oldfield Baby Great Lakes	7223-B412-B & PFA/1593		22. 8.73	
G-BBGM	PA-E23-250 Aztec D	27-4354	5Y-AKY N6997Y	22. 8.73	To 9M-ATE 2/74. Canx 6.3.74.
G-BBGN	Cameron A-375 HAFB	90		23. 8.73	Canx as WFU 22.8.89. (Cabin on display in The Science Museum)
G-BBGO	Robin HR.100/210 Royal	171		29. 8.73	Crashed on take-off at Elstree on 3.12.76. Canx as destroyed 5.12.83.
G-BBGP	Berg Homebuilt Cricket	AB-1		20. 8.73	Crashed at Denham on 3.12.73 & DBR. Canx as WFU 7.1.74.
G-BBGR	Cameron O-65 HAFB	85		20. 8.73	Envelope now porous and incapable of sustained flight. (Extant 4/93)
G-BBGS	Sikorsky S-61N Mk.II	61-471	VR-BDO N6970R	23. 8.73	Canx 22.4.87 on sale to France. To N9116R 9/87.
G-BBGT	Thunder Ax6-56 HAFB	008		24. 8.73	To EC-CPY 6/75. Canx 27.1.75.
G-BBGU	HS.125 Srs.400B	25270	G-5-13	28. 8.73	To G-BKBA 4/82. Canx.
G-BBGV	BN-2A-9 Islander	346		29. 8.73	To F-OCUC 3/74. Canx 7.11.73.
G-BBGW	Fuji FA.200-180 Aero Subaru	FA200-218		30. 8.73	Canx 16.8.76 on sale to West Germany. To N96070 8/76.
G-BBGX	Cessna 182P Skylane	182-62350	N58861	30. 8.73	
G-BBGY	HS.748 Srs.2A/248	1713	G11-8	30. 8.73	To South Korean AF as 1713 in 7/75. Canx 14.7.75.
G-BBGZ	Cambridge Hot-Air Ballooning Association HAFB (42,000 cu.ft)	CHABA.42		31. 8.73	WFU & stored in 1981. (Basket only at British Balloon Museum, Newbury)
G-BBHA	North American Rockwell Standard Turbo Commander 685	12007	N9161N	31. 8.73	To OO-JPP 11/74. Canx 28.10.74.
G-BBHB	PA-31-310 Turbo Navajo	31-252	SX-BDD N9189Y	3. 9.73	To 5Y-MAP 3/92. Canx 31.3.92.
G-BBHC	Enstrom F-28A	149		3. 9.73	CofA expired 18.9.87. Stored Shobdon. Canx as WFU 2.5.91.
G-BBHD	Enstrom F-28A	150		3. 9.73	To G-MHCE 8/96. Canx.
G-BBHE	Enstrom F-28A	153		3. 9.73	To EI-BSD 2/86. Canx 23.12.85.
G-BBHF(1)	Scottish Avn Bulldog Srs.120/124	BH120-239	G-31-17	5. 9.73	NTU - To G-ASAL 9/73. Canx 5.9.73.
G-BBHF(2)	PA-23-250 Aztec E	27-7305166	N40453	26. 9.73	
G-BBHG	Cessna 310Q II	310Q-0806	N69591	6. 9.73	Damaged on landing at Manston on 19.7.93. On rebuild 10/95 at Bournemouth. Canx as WFU 28.1.98.
G-BBHH	Reims Cessna 177RG Cardinal II	0095	5Y-ANG N8095G	7. 9.73	Ditched in sea 8 miles off Dungeness on 12.10.74. Canx as destroyed 31.10.74.
G-BBHI	Reims Cessna 177RG Cardinal II	0225	5Y-ANX N1825Q	7. 9.73	
G-BBHJ	Piper J3C-65 Cub (Frame No. 16037)	16378	OO-GEC	7. 9.73	
G-BBHK	Noorduyn AT-16-ND Harvard IIB	14-787	PH-PPS (PH-HTC)/R.Netherlands AF B-158/FH153/42-12540	7. 9.73	CofA expired 7.5.86. (On rebuild 7/99 Duxford)
G-BBHL	Sikorsky S-61N Mk.II	61-712	N4032S	7. 9.73	
G-BBHM	Sikorsky S-61N Mk.II	61-713	8Q-HUM G-BBHM/N4033S	7. 9.73	
G-BBHN	Sikorsky S-61N Mk.II	61-714		21.12.73	To 9M-AWN 10/78. Canx 16.10.78.
G-BBHO	Westland Commando Mk.1 (Line No. 84)	WA/782	G-17-1	7. 9.73	To Egyptian AF as 262 in 7/74. Canx 4.7.74.
G-BBHP	Westland Commando Mk.1 (Line No. 85)	WA/783	G-17-2	7. 9.73	To Egyptian AF as 263 in 7/74. Canx 4.7.74.
G-BBHR	Westland Commando Mk.1 (Line No. 86)	WA/784	G-17-3	7. 9.73	To Egyptian AF as 264 in 7/74. Canx 4.7.74.
G-BBHS	Westland Commando Mk.1 (Line No. 87)	WA/785	G-17-4	7. 9.73	To Egyptian AF as 265 in 7/74. Canx 4.7.74.
G-BBHT	Westland Commando Mk.1 (Line No. 88)	WA/786	G-17-5	7. 9.73	To Egyptian AF as 261 in 7/74. Canx 4.7.74.
G-BBHU	Westland/SNIAS SA.341G Gazelle Srs.1	WA/1108		7. 9.73	To G-ORGE 7/89. Canx.
G-BBHV	Westland/SNIAS SA.341G Gazelle Srs.1	WA/1096		7. 9.73	To F-GBLK 11/78. Canx 23.11.78.
G-BBHW	Westland/SNIAS SA.341G Gazelle Srs.1	WA/1098		7. 9.73	To G-IZEL 3/91. Canx.
G-BBHX	Socata MS.893E Rallye 180GT	12211		7. 9.73	Canx as destroyed 28.4.95. (Wrecked fuselage in open store 5/96 at Bidford)
G-BBHY	PA-28-180 Cherokee Challenger G	28-7305474	EI-BBS G-BBHY/N9508N	7. 9.73	
G-BBHZ	PA-31P Pressurised Navajo	31P-7300135	N131PN	7. 9.73	To 5N-AQZ 7/76. Canx 29.7.76.
G-BBIA	PA-28R-200-2 Cherokee Arrow	28R-7335287		7. 9.73	
G-BBIB	Beagle B.121 Pup Srs.150	B121-170	G-35-170	7. 9.73	To OO-WRL 3/77. Canx 9.2.77.
G-BBIC	Cessna 310Q II	310Q-0811	N69600	10. 9.73	To G-REDB 6/93. Canx.
G-BBID	PA-28-140 Cherokee F	28-7325519		10. 9.73	To N519MC 3/95. Canx 28.2.95.
G-BBIE	PA-28-140 Cherokee F	28-7325512		10. 9.73	Fatal crash into the North Sea en route to Amsterdam on 4.1.76, possibly off the coast near Clacton. Canx.
G-BBIF	PA-23-250 Aztec E	27-7305234		10. 9.73	
G-BBIG	Lovegrove Gyroplane	PCL.11		11. 9.73	Not completed. Canx as WFU 10.3.75.
G-BBIH	Enstrom F-28A-UK	026	N4875	12. 9.73	CofA expired 18.2.93.
G-BBII	Fiat G.46-3B	44	I-AEHU Italian AF MM52801	13. 9.73	Permit expired 19.7.89. (Stored 6/97)
G-BBIJ	Cessna 421B Golden Eagle II	421B-0432	N41073	13. 9.73	To G-PEAT 4/84. Canx.

Regn	Type	c/n	Previous identity	Regn date	Fate or immediate subsequent identity (if known)
G-BBIK	Bell 47G-5A	25144	5B-CCT (SX-...)/G-BBIK/N18091/N58091	13. 9.73	To SX-HBC 9/79. Canx 1.8.79.
G-BBIL	PA-28-140 Cherokee	28-22567	SE-FAR N4219J	13. 9.73	
G-BBIM	Cessna E.310Q II	310Q-0917	N69683	13. 9.73	To G-CETA 11/80. Canx.
G-BBIN	Enstrom F-28A	157	(G-BOOZ) G-BBIN	13. 9.73	CofA expired 26.9.94. (Stored 10/96 Shoreham) Canx as WFU 30.9.97.
G-BBIO	Robin HR.100/210 Royal	178		14. 9.73	
G-BBIP	Hughes 269C (300C)	63-0210		14. 9.73	To D-HGMA 5/78. Canx 19.4.78.
G-BBIR	Hughes 269C (300C)	63-0214		14. 9.73	To F-GAJK 8/76. Canx 6.8.76.
G-BBIS	Hughes 269C (300C)	73-0219		14. 9.73	To ZS-HJC 10/80. Canx 2.10.80.
G-BBIT	Hughes 269B (300B)	39-0417	N9546F	14. 9.73	CofA expired 1.12.81 & stored at Whinmoor. Canx by CAA 26.5.89.
G-BBIU	Hughes 269C (300C)	41-0112	N9680F	14. 9.73	Hit power cable at Rhosgoch Refinery, Anglesey & crashed on 25.10.79. Canx.
G-BBIV	Hughes 269C (300C)	41-0113	N9690F	14. 9.73	Extensively damaged in crash at Biggin Hill on 5.4.99. Canx as WFU 11.8.99.
G-BBIW	Hughes 269C (300C)	70-0022	N9613F	14. 9.73	To (PH-GEA)/PH-HDH 3/84. Canx 23.3.84.
G-BBIX	PA-28-140 Cherokee E	28-7225442	LN-AEN	17. 9.73	
G-BBIY	Taylor JT.1 Monoplane	PFA/1418		17. 9.73	Fatal crash at Upper Penn, Wolverhampton on 26.7.75. Canx as WFU 5.12.75.
G-BBIZ	BN-2A-9 Islander	348		17. 9.73	To (N23JA)/N84JA 11/73. Canx 1.11.73.
G-BBJA	BN-2A-3 Islander	351		17. 9.73	To PK-VIN 5/74. Canx 14.5.74.
G-BBJB	Thunder Ax7-77 HAFB	009		17. 9.73	Canx as WFU 28.4.93.
G-BBJC	BN-2A-20 Islander	352		17. 9.73	To N42JA 11/73. Canx 21.11.73.
G-BBJD	Cessna 172M	172-61374	N20537	17. 9.73	Crashed on take-off from Sywell on 30.6.78. Fuselage used as para-trainer 9/95 Badinton.
G-BBJE	SNIAS SA.318C Alouette II	2172	N8268	17. 9.73	To HB-XBP 5/78. Canx 25.5.78.
G-BBJF	Beechcraft 95-58 Baron	TH-405		17. 9.73	To G-BMLM 7/79. Canx.
G-BBJG	PA-31-350 Navajo Chieftain	31-7405401		18. 9.73	Fatal crash after take-off from Yeadon on 6.12.74. Canx.
G-BBJH	Cessna A.188B AgTruck	188B-01277T	N8268G	18. 9.73	To VH-UAY 3/82. Canx 19.3.82.
G-BBJI	Isaacs Spitfire	2 & PFA/27-10055		18. 9.73	
G-BBJJ	Scottish Avn Bulldog Srs.120/123	BH120-250		18. 9.73	To Nigerian AF as 221 in 2/74. Canx 13.2.74.
G-BBJK	Scottish Avn Bulldog Srs.120/123	BH120-251		18. 9.73	To Nigerian AF as 222 in 2/74. Canx 13.2.74.
G-BBJL	Scottish Avn Bulldog Srs.120/123	BH120-252		18. 9.73	To Nigerian AF as 223 in 2/74. Canx 13.2.74.
G-BBJM	Scottish Avn Bulldog Srs.120/123	BH120-262		18. 9.73	To Nigerian AF as 224 in 7/74. Canx 26.7.74.
G-BBJN	Scottish Avn Bulldog Srs.120/123	BH120-263		18. 9.73	To Nigerian AF as 225 in 4/74. Canx 11.4.74.
G-BBJO	Scottish Avn Bulldog Srs.120/123	BH120-264		18. 9.73	To Nigerian AF as 226 in 4/74. Canx 11.4.74.
G-BBJP	Scottish Avn Bulldog Srs.120/123	BH120-265		18. 9.73	To Nigerian AF as 227 in 5/74. Canx 20.5.74.
G-BBJR	Scottish Avn Bulldog Srs.120/123	BH120-266		18. 9.73	To Nigerian AF as 228 in 5/74. Canx 20.5.74.
G-BBJS	Sikorsky S-58ET	58-1626	LN-OSC G-BBJS/N4381S/Israeli DF/AF I-4705/BuA.150785	19. 9.73	To EC-DJN 4/80. Canx.
G-BBJT	Robin HR.200/100 Club	07	F-BUQK F-WUQK	19. 9.73	Damaged in hangar collapse at Rochester on 14.1.87. Canx as destroyed 5.3.87.
G-BBJU	Robin DR.400/140 Earl	874		19. 9.73	
G-BBJV	Reims Cessna F.177RG Cardinal	0098		20. 9.73	
G-BBJW	Reims Cessna FRA.150L Aerobat	0213		20. 9.73	To G-OISO 4/90. Canx.
G-BBJX	Reims Cessna F.150L Commuter	1017		20. 9.73	
G-BBJY	Reims Cessna F.172M Skyhawk II	1075		20. 9.73	
G-BBJZ	Reims Cessna F.172M Skyhawk II	1035		20. 9.73	
G-BBKA	Reims Cessna F.150L Commuter	1029		20. 9.73	
G-BBKB	Reims Cessna F.150L Commuter	1030		20. 9.73	CofA expired 21.7.96.
G-BBKC	Reims Cessna F.172M Skyhawk II	1049	SE-GOM G-BBKC	20. 9.73	Crashed on landing at Arnsberg, Germany on 28.5.96. Canx as WFU 17.9.96.
G-BBKD	Reims Cessna FRA.150L Aerobat	0217		20. 9.73	Crashed at Barton on 14.7.74. Wreck to Yeadon. Canx 15.10.74 as destroyed.
G-BBKE	Reims Cessna F.150L Commuter	1026		20. 9.73	
G-BBKF	Reims Cessna FRA.150L Aerobat	0222		20. 9.73	Undershot the runway on landing at Compton Abbas on 20.3.87. CofA expired 13.6.91. (Stored at Compton Abbas 6/95)
G-BBKG	Reims Cessna FR.172J Rocket	0465		20. 9.73	
G-BBKH	Reims Cessna F.172M Skyhawk II	1050		20. 9.73	To SE-GOR 12/76. Canx 3.12.76.
G-BBKI	Reims Cessna F.172M Skyhawk II	1069		20. 9.73	
G-BBKJ	Reims Cessna FT.337GP Turbo Super Skymaster (Wichita c/n P337-0078)	0008		20. 9.73	To F-GHCL 11/86. Canx 19.8.86.
G-BBKK	Cessna E.310Q	310Q-0925	N69698	20. 9.73	Canx 4.5.76 on sale to The Netherlands. To D-IOLW.
G-BBKL	Menavia Piel CP.301A Emeraude	237	F-BIMK	21. 9.73	Damaged in crash at Ketton on 14.7.91. (On rebuild Booker 7/91) Permit expired 21.1.92.
G-BBKM	Beechcraft E90 King Air	LW-83		24. 9.73	To N99855 3/76. Canx 17.3.76.
G-BBKN	Beechcraft C90 King Air	LJ-614		24. 9.73	To G-COTE 8/79. Canx.
G-BBKO	Thunder Ax7-77 HAFB	010		24. 9.73	To OO-BZZ 4/84. Canx 2.5.84.

Regn	Type	c/n	Previous identity	Regn date	Fate or immediate subsequent identity (if known)
G-BBKP	Bell 47G-5A	25148	N18092	24. 9.73	Fatal crash and burnt out at Charfield, Wotton-under-Edge on 20.3.75. Wreck to AIU. Restored on 15.11.77 for tests. WFU in 11/77.
G-BBKR	Scheibe SF-24A Motorspatz	4018	D-KECA	24. 9.73	CofA expired 30.3.79. (Stored 5/95)
G-BBKS	Reims Cessna F.150L Commuter	1021		26. 9.73	NTU - Not Imported. To 5A-DFA /74. Canx.
G-BBKT	Reims Cessna F.150L Commuter	1034		26. 9.73	NTU - Not Imported. To 5A-DFB /74. Canx.
G-BBKU	Reims Cessna FRA.150L Aerobat	0214		26. 9.73	
G-BBKV	Reims Cessna FRA.150L Aerobat (Modified in 1985 - equivalent to a F.150L)	0215		26. 9.73	Fatal crash at Skegness on 17.7.90. Canx as destroyed 7.12.90.
G-BBKW	Bell 47G-2	2445	N6770D ZK-HAQ/N6770D	26. 9.73	To F-BUXB(2) 4/76. Canx 2.4.76.
G-BBKX	PA-28-180 Cherokee Challenger	28-7305581		26. 9.73	
G-BBKY	Reims Cessna F.150L Commuter	0991		26. 9.73	
G-BBKZ	Cessna 172M	172-61495	N20694	27. 9.73	
G-BBLA	PA-28-140 Cherokee Fliteliner	28-7125384	N546FL	25. 9.73	Fatal crash 2 miles southwest of Southport Pier on 25.9.96. Canx as destroyed 22.1.97.
G-BBLB	Hiller 360 UH-12E	2157	N31701 CAF 112273/RCAF 10273	27. 9.73	Crashed & DBF at Stow Maries on 18.6.76. Canx.
G-BBLC	Hiller 360 UH-12E	2164	N31702 CAF 112275/RCAF 10275	27. 9.73	To SX-HED 5/87. Canx 13.4.87.
G-BBLD	Hiller 360 UH-12E	2176	N31703 (N31705)/CAF 112279/RCAF 10279	27. 9.73	Crashed at Ryton, near Thetford on 19.4.79. Canx.
G-BBLE	Hiller 360 UH-12E	2177	SX-HEE G-BBLE/N31705/(N31706)/CAF 112280/RCAF 10280	27. 9.73	To SX-HEE 2/88. Canx 15.9.87.
G-BBLF	Hiller 360 UH-12E	2178	N31706 (N31707)/CAF 112281/RCAF 10281	27. 9.73	Crashed during crop-spraying at Claptongate, near Spalding, Lincs on 18.7.75. Canx.
G-BBLG	Hiller 360 UH-12E	2181	N31708 CAF 112284/RCAF 10284	27. 9.73	Damaged at Hew Cuf Farm, near Peterboro on 24.6.74. Later stored at Sywell. Canx as WFU 5.12.83.
G-BBLH	Piper J3C-65 Cub (L-4B-PI) (Frame No 9838) (Regd with c/n 10549 - see G-AXDB)	10006	F-BFQY French Mil/43-1145	24. 9.73	
G-BBLI	Rockwell 500S Shrike Commander	3158	N9244N	28. 9.73	To N801AC 11/80. Canx 25.11.80.
G-BBLJ	Cessna 402B	402B-0437	N69322	28. 9.73	To 5X-LCP 5/83. Canx 23.5.83.
G-BBLK	Reims Cessna F.172M Skyhawk	1058	(PH-GDR) (PH-KDE)/G-BBLK	28. 9.73	NTU - Canx 9.4.74 as Not Imported. To PH-KDE 5/74.
G-BBLL	Cameron O-84 HAFB	84		2.10.73	Canx by CAA 19.5.93.
G-BBLM	Socata MS.880 Rallye 100S	2392		3.10.73	
G-BBLN	HS.748 Srs.2A/278	1719	CR-CAV G11-2	11.10.73	Restored as CR-CAV 11/73. Canx 21.11.73.
G-BBLO	Sikorsky S-58E/T	58-775	N8478 I-AGMI/N421A	4.10.73	Restored as N8478 2/74. Canx 7.2.74.
G-BBLP	PA-23-250 Aztec D	27-4136	N6798Y	4.10.73	CofA expired 20.7.91. Canx by CAA 13.12.96.
G-BBLR	Robin HR.100/210 Safari	177		4.10.73	NTU - Canx 2.11.73 as Not Imported. To F-BUST 12/73.
G-BBLS	American Aviation AA-5 Traveler	AA5-0440	EI-AYM G-BBLS	8.10.73	
G-BBLT	American Aviation AA-5 Traveler	AA5-0441	N8991L	8.10.73	To OO-LIZ 12/76. Canx 3.12.76.
G-BBLU	PA-34-200-2 Seneca	34-7350271	N55984	8.10.73	
G-BBLV	Cameron O-84 HAFB	83		9.10.73	To D-Raiffeisenbank 11/75. Canx 5.11.75.
G-BBLW	BN-2A-2 Islander	354		16.10.73	To JA5227 12/73. Canx 19.12.73.
G-BBLX	BN-2A-9 Islander	355		16.10.73	To N355BN 3/79. Canx 30.1.79.
G-BBLY	BN-2A-8 Islander	364		16.10.73	To CR-APQ 11/74. Canx 28.11.74.
G-BBLZ	BN-2A-8 Islander	365		16.10.73	To N80JA 1/74. Canx 19.1.74.
G-BBMA	BN-2A-8 Islander	367		16.10.73	To CR-APC 2/75. Canx 13.2.75.
G-BBMB	Robin DR.400/180 Regent	848	5Y-ASB	27. 9.73	
G-BBMC	BN-2A-8 Islander	376		16.10.73	To N88JA 1/74. Canx 19.1.74.
G-BBMD	HS.125 Srs.600B/2 (Originally regd as Srs.600B)	256024	N50GD G-BBMD	24. 9.73	To G-BSHL 12/80. Canx.
G-BBME	BAC One-Eleven Srs.401AK	066	G-16-19 G-AZMI/N5026	22. 3.74	To ZS-OAG 1/97. Canx 31.1.97.
G-BBMF	BAC One-Eleven Srs.401AK	074	VP-BDI N5032/AP-BHN/N5032/G-ATVU/N5032	8. 5.74	To 5N-EHI. Canx.
G-BBMG	BAC One-Eleven Srs.408EF	BAC.115	G-AWEJ	26. 9.73	To ZS-OAH 4/97. Canx 7.4.97.
G-BBMH	EAA Sport Biplane Model P.1	PFA/1348		11.10.73	Permit expired 29.6.87. (Status uncertain)
G-BBMI	K & W Dewoitine D.26	10853	HB-RAA Swiss AF 282	11.10.73	To N282DW 5/84. Canx 30.5.84.
G-BBMJ	PA-23-250 Aztec E	27-7305150	N40387	12.10.73	
G-BBMK	PA-31-310 Turbo Navajo	31-7300967	N7571L	15.10.73	To G-BNDD 10/86. Canx.
G-BBML	PA-31-310 Turbo Navajo	31-7401210		15.10.73	Crashed near Creil, France on 19.5.82. Canx.
G-BBMM	Cessna T.310Q II	T310Q-1000	N69825	8. 1.74	NTU - Canx 25.4.74 as Not Imported. To PH-BZL 4/74.
G-BBMN	DHC.1 Chipmunk 22 (Fuselage no. DHB/f/176)	C1/0300	WD359	12.10.73	
G-BBMO	DHC.1 Chipmunk 22 (Fuselage no. DHB/f/435)	C1/0550	WK514	12.10.73	
G-BBMP	DHC.1 Chipmunk 22 (Fuselage no. DHB/f/189)	C1/0309	WD371	12.10.73	Crashed at Felthorpe, Norfolk on 17.12.78. Sold as spares. Canx.
G-BBMR	DHC.1 Chipmunk 22 (Fuselage no. DHB/f/96)	C1/0213	WB763	12.10.73	
G-BBMS	DHC.1 Chipmunk 22 (Fuselage no. DHB/f/258)	C1/0359	WG306	12.10.73	Crashed at Dunstable on 31.5.78. Canx as destroyed 8.2.79. Remains to Southend. Rebuilt & re-regd as G-IDDY 9/79.

Regn	Type	c/n	Previous identity	Regn date	Fate or immediate subsequent identity (if known)
G-BBMT	DHC.1 Chipmunk 22 (Fuselage no. DHB/f/606)	C1/0712	WP831	12.10.73	
G-BBMU	DHC.1 Chipmunk 22 (Fuselage no. DHB/f/763)	C1/0868	WZ849	12.10.73	To N31351 3/76. Canx 5.3.76.
G-BBMV	DHC.1 Chipmunk 22 (Fuselage no. DHB/f/297)	C1/0432	WG348	12.10.73	
G-BBMW	DHC.1 Chipmunk 22 (Fuselage no. DHB/f/525)	C1/0641	WK628	12.10.73	
G-BBMX	DHC.1 Chipmunk 22 (Fuselage no. DHB/f/712)	C1/0800	WP924	12.10.73	
G-BBMY	DHC.1 Chipmunk 22 (Fuselage no. DHB/f/467)	C1/0584	WK565	12.10.73	To G-JAKE 1/80. Canx.
G-BBMZ	DHC.1 Chipmunk 22 (Fuselage no. DHB/f/450)	C1/0563	WK548	12.10.73	
G-BBNA	DHC.1 Chipmunk 22 (Fuselage no. DHB/f/359)	C1/0491	WG417	12.10.73	
G-BBNB	DHC.1 Chipmunk 22 (Fuselage no. DHH/f/32)	C1/0033	WB581	12.10.73	To ZS-LJU 12/82. Canx 9.11.82.
G-BBNC	DHC.1 Chipmunk T.10 (Fuselage no. DHB/f/571)	C1/0682	WP790	12.10.73	Canx as WFU 23.9.74. Used for spares at Rush Green. (On display 3/96 Mosquito Museum)
G-BBND	DHC.1 Chipmunk 22 (Fuselage no. DHB/f/110)	C1/0225	WD286	12.10.73	
G-BBNE	DHC.1 Chipmunk 22 (Fuselage no. DHB/f/794)	C1/0907	WZ873	12.10.73	Canx as WFU 23.9.74. To N873WZ in 1979.
G-BBNF	DHC.1 Chipmunk 22 (Fuselage no. DHB/f/556)	C1/0668	WP778	12.10.73	Crashed on landing at Chase Farm, Botley Hill, Little Burstead, Essex on 23.5.81. Canx as destroyed 5.12.83.
G-BBNG	Bell 206B JetRanger (Originally 206A; later modified)	134	VH-BHX G-BBNG/VR-BEY/G-BBNG/PK-HBO/N6268N	16.10.73	
G-BBNH	PA-34-200-2 Seneca	34-7350339	N56492	16.10.73	CofA expired 8.8.92. (Stored 10/97)
G-BBNI	PA-34-200-2 Seneca	34-7350312	N56286	16.10.73	
G-BBNJ	Reims Cessna F.150L Commuter	1038		16.10.73	
G-BBNK	PA-23-250 Aztec E	27-7305119	N40360	17.10.73	To N113RS 9/83. Canx 23.9.83.
G-BBNL	BN-2A Mk.III-1 Trislander	350	(N29JA)	19.10.73	To HK-2412 2/80. Canx 29.2.80.
G-BBNM	PA-E23-250 Aztec E	27-4619	OY-POR G-BBNM/N14001	22.10.73	To G-BLLM 1/84. Canx.
G-BBNN	PA-E23-250 Aztec D	27-4172	N6832Y	22.10.73	To G-ESKY 11/95. Canx.
G-BBNO	PA-23-250 Aztec E	27-4656	N964PA	22.10.73	CofA expired 18.1.92. (Stored 8/97)
G-BBNP	Cessna 310Q II	310Q-0903	N69613	22.10.73	NTU - Canx 17.6.74 on sale to Belgium. To D-IBMJ 6/75.
G-BBNR	Cessna 340 II	340-0305	N69452	22.10.73	To G-UNDY 10/91. Canx.
G-BBNS	Cessna 310Q II	310Q-0919	N69685	22.10.73	To EI-BMK 3/82. Canx 1.3.82.
G-BBNT	PA-31-350 Navajo Chieftain	31-7305107	N74958	22.10.73	To N1201H 11/96 / EI-CNM 12/96. Canx 28.10.96.
G-BBNU	Fuji FA.200-160 Aero Subaru	FA200-231		23.10.73	Fatal crash at Wolverton Grange, near Stratford-upon-Avon on 24.4.74. Canx.
G-BBNV	Fuji FA.200-160 Aero Subaru	FA200-232		23.10.73	
G-BBNW	Reims Cessna F.177RG Cardinal II	0102		23.10.73	NTU - Not Imported. To F-BVSN 8/74. Canx.
G-BBNX	Reims Cessna FRA.150L Aerobat (Mod.)	0219		23.10.73	
G-BBNY	Reims Cessna FRA.150L Aerobat	0223		23.10.73	Nosewheel collapsed and overturned on landing at Blackbushe on 8.6.86. CofA expired 2.8.87. Canx as destroyed 3.6.93. (Wreck in open storage 5/96)
G-BBNZ	Reims Cessna F.172M Skyhawk II	1054		23.10.73	
G-BBOA	Reims Cessna F.172M Skyhawk II	1066		23.10.73	
G-BBOB	Cessna 421B Golden Eagle II	421B-0519	(N69880)	21.11.73	Canx 10.4.89 on sale to USA.
G-BBOC	Cameron O-77 HAFB	86		24.10.73	(Active 1/95)
G-BBOD	Thunder O-5 HAFB (Toy)	013		24.10.73	(On loan to British Balloon Museum 12/93)
G-BBOE(1)	Robin HR.200/100 Club	14		. .73R	NTU - Not Imported. To F-BVCD 13.3.74. Canx.
G-BBOE(2)	Robin HR.200/100 Club	26		24.10.73	
G-BBOF	Robin DR.400/140 Major	882	(D-EFDC)	24.10.73	NTU - Not Imported. To F-BVMR/D-EFBC 7/74. Canx /74.
G-BBOG	Robin DR.400/140 Major	887		24.10.73	NTU - Not Imported. To F-BVMG 6/74. Canx /74.
G-BBOH	AJEP Pitts S-1S Special	AJEP-PS1-S-1 & PFA/1570		25.10.73	
G-BBOI	Bede BD-5B	898 & PFA/14-10092		25.10.73	Canx by CAA 2.9.91.
G-BBOJ	PA-E23-250 Aztec E	27-4698	5Y-AOK N14130	23.11.73	Ditched into Eye Estuary, off Exmouth on 3.12.80. Wreck to Cranfield & used for crash investigation work/instructional airframe. Canx.
G-BBOK	PA-E23-250 Aztec E	27-7305200	EI-BNV G-BBOK/N40482	29.10.73	To TC-GOK(2). Canx 5.10.90.
G-BBOL	PA-18-150 Super Cub	18-7561	D-EMFE N3821Z	26.10.73	
G-BBOM	PA-E23-250 Aztec E	27-7305208	N40487	29.10.73	To D2-ESB 7/84. Canx 19.7.84.
G-BBON	BN-2A-9 Islander	368		29.10.73	To N82JA 1/74. Canx 19.1.74.
G-BBOO	Thunder Ax6-56 HAFB (Originally regd with c/n 002 in error)	012		24.10.73	
G-BBOP	PA-28R-200 Cherokee Arrow II	28R-7435008		29.10.73	Sideslipped on approach to North Weald and crashed into Motorway building site on 4.7.76. Canx as destroyed 8.3.77.
G-BBOR	Bell 206B JetRanger II	1197	(SE-...) G-BBOR	30.10.73	
G-BBOS	Bell 206B JetRanger II	1207	VR-BID G-BBOS	30.10.73	To F-GEAV 4/84. Canx 12.4.84.

Regn	Type	c/n	Previous identity	Regn date	Fate or immediate subsequent identity (if known)
G-BBOT	Bell 206B JetRanger II	1209	N18093	30.10.73	To I-AGUK 5/75. Canx 20.12.74.
G-BBOU	Scottish Avn Bulldog Srs.120/123	BH120-267		30.10.73	To Nigerian AF as 229 in 6/74. Canx 5.6.74.
G-BBOV	Scottish Avn Bulldog Srs.120/123	BH120-268		30.10.73	To Nigerian AF as 230 in 6/74. Canx 5.6.74.
G-BBOW	Scottish Avn Bulldog Srs.120/123	BH120-269		30.10.73	To Nigerian AF as 231 in 6/74. Canx 5.6.74.
G-BBOX	Thunder Ax7-77 HAFB	011		24.10.73	
G-BBOY	Thunder Ax6-56A HAFB	001		24.10.73	CofA expired 5.10.83. (Based in Holland) Canx by CAA 23.6.98.
G-BBOZ	Scottish Avn Bulldog Srs.120/123	BH120-270		30.10.73	To Nigerian AF as 232 in 6/74. Canx 5.6.74.
G-BBPA	Scottish Avn Bulldog Srs.120/123	BH120-271		30.10.73	To Nigerian AF as 233 in 7/74. Canx 26.7.74.
G-BBPB	Scottish Avn Bulldog Srs.120/123	BH120-278		30.10.73	To Nigerian AF as 234 in 8/74. Canx 28.8.74.
G-BBPC	PA-31 Navajo Commuter	31-805	N7420L	30.10.73	Fatal crash on approach to Walney Island on 26.11.76. Canx as destroyed 16.5.83.
G-BBPD	Scottish Avn Bulldog Srs.120/123	BH120-280		30.10.73	To Nigerian AF as 235 in 8/74. Canx 28.8.74.
G-BBPE	Scottish Avn Bulldog Srs.120/123	BH120-281		30.10.73	To Nigerian AF as 236 in 11/74. Canx 12.11.74.
G-BBPF	Scottish Avn Bulldog Srs.120/123	BH120-282		30.10.73	To Nigerian AF as 237 in 11/74. Canx 12.11.74.
G-BBPG	Scottish Avn Bulldog Srs.120/123	BH120-283		30.10.73	To Nigerian AF as 239 in 12/74. Canx 30.12.74.
G-BBPH	Not allocated.				
G-BBPI	Scottish Avn Bulldog Srs.120/123	BH120-284		30.10.73	To Nigerian AF as 240 in 12/74. Canx 30.12.74.
G-BBPJ	Reims Cessna F.172M Skyhawk	1055		30.10.73	To OY-ENV. Canx 30.4.93.
G-BBPK	Evans VP-1	PFA/7013		30.10.73	Permit expired 8.6.90. (Stored dismantled at Lasham in 10/95)
G-BBPL	Short SC.7 Skyvan 3-100	SH1920	G-14-92	30.10.73	To Mexican AF as TP-0213/XC-UTI in 2/74. Canx 18.2.74.
G-BBPM	Enstrom F-28A-UK	165	PH-DMH G-BBPM	30.10.73	
G-BBPN	Enstrom F-28A-UK	166		30.10.73	
G-BBPO	Enstrom F-28A	176		30.10.73	
G-BBPP	PA-28-180 Cherokee Archer	28-7405007	N9559N	30.10.73	To G-WACP 4/89. Canx.
G-BBPR	Scottish Avn Bulldog Srs.120/123	BH120-279		30.10.73	To Nigerian AF as 235 in 7/74. Canx 26.7.74.
G-BBPS	SAN Jodel D.117	597	F-BHXS	30.10.73	
G-BBPT	HS.748 Srs.2A/278	1720	CR-CAW (CR-CAX)/G11-4	2.11.73	Restored as CR-CAW 12/73. Canx 4.12.73.
G-BBPU	Boeing 747-136 (Line No. 248)	20953		18. 9.74	
G-BBPV	PA-31-350 Navajo Chieftain	31-7305097	N7495L	7.11.73	Crashed at Ambarrow Farm, Sandhurst on 19.10.75. Canx.
G-BBPW	Robin HR.100/210 Royal	176		7.11.73	Damaged on coming to rest in a field west of Kemble after an abandoned take-off on 24.8.98.
G-BBPX	PA-34-200-2 Seneca	34-7250262	N1202T	7.11.73	
G-BBPY	PA-28-180 Cherokee Challenger	28-7305590		8.11.73	
G-BBPZ	PA-E23-250 Aztec D	27-4028	N6702Y	9.11.73	To N68RS 8/83. Canx 12.8.83.
G-BBRA	PA-23-250 Aztec E	27-7305197	N40479	12.11.73	
G-BBRB	DH.82A Tiger Moth	85934	OO-EVB Belgian AF T-8/ETA-8/DF198	21.11.73	(Damaged in hangar collapse at Biggin Hill on 16.1.87) (Sold for long-term rebuild - status uncertain)
G-BBRC	Fuji FA.200-180 Aero Subaru	FA200-235		8.11.73	
G-BBRD	PA-E23-250 Aztec E	27-7405242	N40512	15.11.73	DBR in bomb blast at Eglington on 21.9.78. Canx as destroyed 16.2.79.
G-BBRE	Fuji FA.200-160 Aero Subaru	FA200-236		8.11.73	To G-KARI 12/84. Canx.
G-BBRF	SCRA Potez Srs.60/48	01	F-PFOD F-BFOD	9.11.73	NTU - Canx 2.1.74 as Not Imported. To F-AZBT 1/74.
G-BBRG	Bell 47G-5A	25154	N18090	9.11.73	To 5B-CER 2/82. Canx 15.2.82.
G-BBRH	Bell 47G-5A	25155	5B-CFA G-BBRH/N18090	9.11.73	CofA expired 27.4.85. Canx as TWFU 17.9.96.
G-BBRI	Bell 47G-5A (Composite following several major rebuilds)	25158	N18092	8.11.73	
G-BBRJ	PA-E23-250 Turbo Aztec E	27-7305223	EI-BOK G-BBRJ/N40493	12.11.73	
G-BBRK(1)	Cessna 414 Chancellor	414-0505	N8092Q	21.11.73	NTU - Canx 16.1.74 as Not Imported. To G-BBYT 19.2.74.
G-BBRK(2)	DHC.1 Chipmunk 22 (Fuselage no. DHB/f/178)	C1/0302	WD361	16. 1.74	To VH-PUB 1/76. Canx 12.1.76.
G-BBRL	PA-31P-425 Pressurised Navajo	31P-7300168	N66806	12.11.73	To G-WITT 8/81. Canx.
G-BBRM	BN-2A-3 Islander	370		12.11.73	To (N83JA)/PT-JZN 2/75. Canx 10.2.76.
G-BBRN	Mitchell-Procter Kittiwake I	02 & PFA/1352	XW784	20.11.73	
G-BBRO	HS.125 Srs.600B	256042		23.11.73	To G-BKBU 4/82. Canx.
G-BBRP	BN-2A-9 Islander	371		12.11.73	Crashed on take-off from Netheravon on 20.2.82 & DBR. Scrapped in 1994. Canx.

Regn	Type	c/n	Previous identity	Regn date	Fate or immediate subsequent identity (if known)
G-BBRR	Short SC.7 Skyvan 3M-400	SH1921	G-14-93	1.11.73	To Yemen Arab Republic AF as 1153 in 4.74. Canx 11.4.74.
G-BBRS	Enstrom F-28A	258		4. 4.75	To G-LERN 2/82. Canx.
G-BBRT(1)	HS.125 Srs.600B	256036		.11.73R	NTU - Not completed, used for paint-spraying trials at Chester. Canx 11/73.
G-BBRT(2)	HS.125 Srs.600B	256029		23.11.73	To PK-PJE 1/75. Canx 17.12.74.
G-BBRU	Short SC.7 Skyvan 3M-400	SH1922	G-14-94	1.11.73	To Yemen Arab Republic AF as 1155 in 4.74. Canx 11.4.74.
G-BBRV	DHC.1 Chipmunk 22 (Fuselage no. DHB/f/164)	C1/0284	WD347	13.11.73	
G-BBRW	PA-28-140 Cherokee	28-23558	LN-KCK N3449K	13.11.73	Damaged by gales at Elstree 25.1.90. Canx as WFU 23.5.90.
G-BBRX	SIAI-Marchetti S.205-18F	342	LN-VYH OO-HAQ	13.11.73	
G-BBRY	Cessna 210 Centurion	210-57091	5Y-KRZ VP-KRZ/N7391E	15.11.73	Crashed on landing at Epsom on 2.4.78. Later used for spares at Cranfield. Canx as destroyed 5.12.83. (Open storage, unmarked 6/98 at Enstone)
G-BBRZ	American Aviation AA-5 Traveler	AA5-0471	(EI-AYV) G-BBRZ	15.11.73	
G-BBSA	American Aviation AA-5 Traveler	AA5-0472		15.11.73	
G-BBSB	Beechcraft C23 Sundowner 180	M-1516		15.11.73	
G-BBSC	Beechcraft B24R Sierra 200	MC-217		15.11.73	
G-BBSD	Beechcraft 95-58 Baron	TH-429		15.11.73	To G-GAMA 10/82. Canx.
G-BBSE	DHC.1 Chipmunk 22 (Fuselage no. DHB/f/772)	C1/0884	WZ858	15.11.73	To G-DHCI 7/89. Canx.
G-BBSF	Cessna 310Q II	310Q-0906	N69644	15.11.73	To N119RS 12/83. Canx 29.12.83.
G-BBSG	Cessna 182P Skylane	182-62473	N52234	15.11.73	To OO-MVH 2/77. Canx 7.2.77.
G-BBSH	Westland/SNIAS SA.341G Gazelle Srs.1	WA/1124		15.11.73	To HB-XFW 5/76. Canx 3.5.76.
G-BBSI	Westland/SNIAS SA.341G Gazelle Srs.1	WA/1138		15.11.73	Forced landing in playing field at Plaistow, London on 27.4.77. Canx as destroyed 31.5.77.
G-BBSJ	Westland/SNIAS SA.341G Gazelle Srs.1	WA/1141		15.11.73	To G-17-11/Qatar Police as QP-1 in 10/74. Canx 28.10.74.
G-BBSK	Westland/SNIAS SA.341G Gazelle Srs.1	WA/1156		15.11.73	To G-17-12/Qatar Police as QP-2 in 10/74. Canx 28.10.74.
G-BBSL	PA-E23-250 Aztec E	27-7405272	N40536	5.12.73	To N251SC 8/81. Canx 20.8.81.
G-BBSM	PA-32-300 Cherokee Six E	32-7440005	N11C	14.11.73	
G-BBSN	PA-E23-250 Aztec E	27-7305216	N40491	16.11.73	To AP-BBY 3/85. Canx 30.1.85.
G-BBSO	PA-28-140 Cherokee F	28-7425014		14.11.73	Crashed on take-off from Leicester on 28.5.82 & used as spares at RAE Bedford in the rebuild of G-ATJG. Canx by CAA 2.2.87.
G-BBSP	Hughes 269B	79-0429	N9552F	10.11.73	To N70WT 2/75. Canx 24.2.75.
G-BBSR	PA-E23-250 Aztec D	27-4394	N6610Y	20.11.73	To G-BMOL 6/84. Canx.
G-BBSS	DHC.1 Chipmunk 22 (Fuselage no. DHB/f/401)	C1/0520	WG470	21.11.73	
G-BBST	PA-E23-250 Aztec D	27-4403	6Y-JGO N6870Y	21.11.73	Fatal crash after mid-air collision with Beech 1900C N305BH (c/n UB-9) over Hannover, West Germany on 20.5.84. Canx as destroyed 24.8.89. (Beech 1900 repaired)
G-BBSU	Cessna 421B Golden Eagle II	421B-0605	N1509G	21.11.73	To N421RH 2/96. Canx 9.2.96.
G-BBSV	Cessna 421B Golden Eagle II	421B-0548	(N69917)	21.11.73	To G-OLDE 5/92. Canx.
G-BBSW	Pietenpol Air Camper	PFA/1506		21.11.73	
G-BBSX	Cessna 310Q II	310Q-1093		21.11.73	NTU - Not Imported. To N1242G. Canx 7/74.
G-BBSY	Bell 206A JetRanger	328	N4790R	21.11.73	Restored as N4790R 3/74. Canx 15.3.74.
G-BBSZ	Douglas DC-10-10 (Line No. 83)	46727	N1348U	22.11.73	To N917CL 5/82. Canx 14.5.82.
G-BBTA	HS.748 Srs.2A/216	1722	PK-IHR G11-6	23.11.73	Restored as PK-IHR 12/73. Canx 18.12.73.
G-BBTB	Reims Cessna FRA.150L Aerobat	0224		26.11.73	
G-BBTC	Reims Cessna FRA.150L Aerobat	0225		26.11.73	NTU - Not Imported. To OE-ATW 1/74. Canx 15.5.75.
G-BBTD	Reims Cessna F.150L	1047		26.11.73	NTU - Canx 29.3.74 as Not Imported. To OE-ATX 4/74.
G-BBTE	Reims Cessna FRA.150L Aerobat	0233		26.11.73	NTU - Canx 23.5.74 as Not Imported. To 5N-ACH 6/74.
G-BBTF	Reims Cessna F.177RG Cardinal	0105		26.11.73	NTU - Not Imported. To F-BVSQ 1/75. Canx 21.6.74.
G-BBTG	Reims Cessna F.172M Skyhawk II	1097		26.11.73	
G-BBTH	Reims Cessna F.172M Skyhawk II	1089		26.11.73	
G-BBTI	Reims Cessna F.177RG Cardinal	0114		26.11.73	NTU - Not Imported. To F-BVIN 9/74. Canx 18.6.75.
G-BBTJ	PA-23-250 Aztec E	27-7305131	N40369	27.11.73	
G-BBTK	Reims Cessna FRA.150L Aerobat	0230		27.11.73	
G-BBTL	PA-23-250 Aztec C	27-3816	N6525Y	29.11.73	CofA expired 14.8.89. (Fuselage only noted in 5/98 at Squires Gate)
G-BBTM	DHC.1 Chipmunk T.10 (Fuselage no. DHB/f/446)	C1/0558	WK521	29.11.73	To N53945 9/74. Canx.
G-BBTN	DHC.1 Chipmunk 22 (Fuselage no. DHB/f/317)	C1/0460	WG364	29.11.73	To N53944 3/75. Canx 12.3.75.
G-BBTO	DHC.1 Chipmunk 22 (Fuselage no. DHB/f/124)	C1/0239	WD299	29.11.73	To N53943 10/74. Canx 7.10.74.
G-BBTP	DHC.1 Chipmunk 22 (Fuselage no. DHH/f/89)	C1/0132	WB684	29.11.73	To N53942 3/75. Canx 12.3.75.
G-BBTR	DHC.1 Chipmunk 22 (Fuselage no. DHB/f/20)	C1/0088	WB650	29.11.73	To N53941 1/74. Canx 2.1.74.
G-BBTS	Beechcraft V35B Bonanza	D-9551	N3051W	29.11.73	
G-BBTT	Reims Cessna F.150L Commuter	1055		30.11.73	DBR at Newtownards on 9.3.75. Canx as WFU 6.1.84. (Stored 4/96)

Regn	Type	c/n	Previous identity	Regn date	Fate or immediate subsequent identity (if known)
G-BBTU	Socata ST-10 Diplomate	140	F-BTIO	18.12.73	CofA expired 14.4.88. Canx by CAA 13.9.90. (Wreck stored 3/94)
G-BBTV	Bell 206B JetRanger II	1205	N18092	18. 9.73	To HB-XKN 9/79. Canx 18.9.79.
G-BBTW	PA-31P Pressurised Navajo	31P-7300141	N7660L	3.12.73	To G-OIEA 7/89. Canx.
G-BBTX	Beechcraft C23 Sundowner 180	M-1524	5N-AGJ(2) G-BBTX	29.11.73	
G-BBTY	Beechcraft C23 Sundowner 180	M-1525		29.11.73	
G-BBTZ	Reims Cessna F.150L Commuter	1063		30.11.73	
G-BBUA	BN-2A-8 Islander	377	G-51-377 5T-TJV/F-BUTN(3)/G-BBUA	3.12.73	To D-IHER 4/85. Canx 15.10.84.
G-BBUB	BN-2A-9R Islander	378		3.12.73	To N83JA 2/74. Canx 27.2.74.
G-BBUC	BN-2A-8 Islander	379		3.12.73	To 9M-ATS 2/75. Canx 10.2.75.
G-BBUD	Sikorsky S-61N Mk.II	61-711		5.12.73	To N29111 9/95. Canx 6.10.95.
G-BBUE	American Aviation AA-5 Traveler	AA5-0479		6.12.73	
G-BBUF	American Aviation AA-5 Traveler	AA5-0480		6.12.73	
G-BBUG	PA-16-150 Clipper	16-29	F-BFMC	6.12.73	
G-BBUH	American Aviation AA-1B Traveler	AA1-0310	N6510L	7.12.73	W/o at Doncaster on 8.1.77. Canx.
G-BBUI	American Aviation AA-5 Traveler	AA5-0474	N7174L	7.12.73	Overshot and hit a gate on landing at Long Marston on 30.4.77. Canx as destroyed.
G-BBUJ	Cessna 421B Golden Eagle II	421B-0335	OY-RYD N6187Q	7.12.73	
G-BBUK	Bell 47G-2	2434	N6751D	7.12.73	To F-GANX 4/82. Canx 4.3.82.
G-BBUL	Mitchell-Procter Kittiwake 1	RB.1		7.12.73	No Permit issued - probably not completed. Canx by CAA 22.2.99.
G-BBUM	Not allocated.				
G-BBUN	Cessna 182P Skylane	182-62475	N52238	10.12.73	NTU - Not Imported. To D-EDZP 3/74. Canx 5.12.83.
G-BBUO	Cessna 150L Commuter	150-73395	N5495Q	10.12.73	Fatal crash in woods at Luscombe Hill, Dawlish on 15.1.88. Canx as destroyed 1.2.88.
G-BBUP	Beagle B.121 Pup Srs.100	B121-172	G-35-172	10.12.73	CofA expired 10.5.82 & WFU at Leicester. Canx as WFU 29.1.85.
G-BBUR	Short SC.7 Skyvan 3-100-50	SH1923	G-14-95	10.12.73	To PK-PSI 2/74. Canx 19.2.74.
G-BBUS	Short SC.7 Skyvan 3-100-50	SH1924	G-14-96	10.12.73	To PK-PSJ 3/74. Canx 13.3.74.
G-BBUT	Western O-65 HAFB	020		11.12.73	
G-BBUU	Piper J3C-75 Cub (L-4A-PI) (Regd with frame no 10354)	10529	F-BBSQ F-OAEZ/French AF/43-29238	14. 1.74	
G-BBUV	DH.106 Comet 4B	6451	G-ARCP	19.12.73	Broken up at Lasham in 10/79. Canx as WFU 23.11.78.
G-BBUW	K & S SA.102.5 Cavalier	PFA/1365		10.12.73	Not completed - construction abandoned. Unfinished airframe to The Aeroplane Collection at Warmingham Craft Centre on 5.1.89. Canx by CAA 1.6.90. Scrapped in 1995.
G-BBUX	Bell 206B JetRanger II	1231	N18091	12.12.73	To G-BRMH 9/81. Canx.
G-BBUY	Bell 206B JetRanger II	1232	N18090	12.12.73	To G-HMPH 6/88. Canx.
G-BBUZ	Reims Cessna F.177RG Cardinal	0101		12.12.73	NTU - Not Imported. To F-BVIG 4/74. Canx 18.6.75.
G-BBVA	Sikorsky S-61N Mk.II	61-718		12. 2.74	
G-BBVB	Sikorsky S-61N Mk.II	61-720		2. 4.74	To 9M-PCM 12/82. Canx 28.1.83.
G-BBVC	Slingsby T.59D Kestrel 19	1832		14.12.73	Sold in Italy in 12/73, damaged there and returned to stored at Kirkbymoorside. Became BGA.3176 in 1985. Canx by CAA 24.7.87.
G-BBVD	Not allocated.				
G-BBVE	Cessna 340	340-0304	N69451	14.12.73	To EI-CIJ 7/93. Canx 14.6.93.
G-BBVF	Scottish Aviation Twin Pioneer Srs.3	558	7978M XM961	17.12.73	Damaged in gales at Shibdon on 11.3.82. CofA expired 14.5.82. Canx 8.8.83. (On display 3/96 East Fortune)
G-BBVG	PA-23-250 Aztec C	27-2610	ET-AEB 5Y-AAT	20.12.73	CofA expire 10.9.88. Canx as WFU 10.2.89. (Stored 9/96)
G-BBVH	Vickers 807 Viscount	281	ZK-BRD	22.12.73	Nose wheel collapsed at Tangier, Morocco on 23.11.88 & DBR. Canx as WFU 7.2.89.
G-BBVI	Enstrom F-28A	182		4. 1.74	DBR at Kidlington on 19.6.78. (To Instructional Airframe at Kidlington)
G-BBVJ	Beechcraft B24R Sierra 200	MC-230		21.12.73	
G-BBVK	Beechcraft C90 King Air	LJ-631		21.12.73	To N100VN. Canx 5.3.76.
G-BBVL	Beechcraft 100 King Air	B-199	N82TC G-BBVL	21.12.73	To N600AC 9/75. Canx 5.9.75.
G-BBVM	Beechcraft 100 King Air	B-201		21.12.73	To C-GAVI 2/93. Canx 17.12.92.
G-BBVN	Douglas DC-4-1009	42922	HS-VGZ VH-TAE/JA6006/NC33683	3. 1.74	Canx 21.11.74 on sale as LN-NAC - NTU & broken up at . Southend in 5/77.
G-BBVO	Wilson-Isaacs Fury II	DBW-1 & PFA/11-10091		20.12.73	
G-BBVP	Westland-Bell 47G-3B1 (Line No. WAS/177)	WA/580	401 South Yemen AF	3. 1.74	Canx as WFU 26.3.93. (Stored 5/93)
G-BBVR	PA-31-350 Navajo Chieftain	31-7405145	N74988	2. 1.74	To N940SC 8/81. Canx 4.8.81.
G-BBVS	HS.121 Trident 2E Srs.109	2175		3. 1.74	To China as 280 11/76. Canx 8.11.76.
G-BBVT	HS.121 Trident 2E Srs.109	2176		3. 1.74	To China as 282 11/76. Canx 8.11.76.
G-BBVU	HS.121 Trident 2E Srs.109	2177		3. 1.74	To China as 284 2/77. Canx 7.2.77.
G-BBVV	HS.121 Trident 2E Srs.109	2178		3. 1.74	To China as 286 2/77. Canx 7.2.77.
G-BBVW	HS.121 Trident 2E Srs.109	2179		3. 1.74	To China as 288 4/77. Canx 1.4.77.
G-BBVX	HS.121 Trident 2E Srs.109	2180		3. 1.74	To China as 290 5/77. Canx 16.5.77.
G-BBVY	HS.121 Trident 2E Srs.109	2181		3. 1.74	To China as 292 6/77. Canx 30.6.77.
G-BBVZ	HS.121 Trident 2E Srs.109	2182		3. 1.74	To China as 294 8/77. Canx 30.8.77.
G-BBWA	HS.121 Trident 2E Srs.109	2183		3. 1.74	To China as 296 10/77. Canx 13.10.77.

Regn	Type	c/n	Previous identity	Regn date	Fate or immediate subsequent identity (if known)
G-BBWB	HS.121 Trident 2E Srs.109	2184		3. 1.74	To China as 298 11/77. Canx 7.11.77.
G-BBWC	Not allocated.				
G-BBWD	HS.121 Trident 2E Srs.109	2185		3. 1.74	To China as 263 3/78. Canx 3.11.78.
G-BBWE	HS.121 Trident 2E Srs.109	2186		3. 1.74	To China as 265 3/78. Canx 13.2.78.
G-BBWF	HS.121 Trident 2E Srs.109	2187		3. 1.74	To China as 267 4/78. Canx 17.4.78.
G-BBWG	HS.121 Trident 2E Srs.109	2188		3. 1.74	To China as 269 4/78. Canx 22.5.78.
G-BBWH	HS.121 Trident 2E Srs.109	2189		3. 1.74	To China as 271 6/78. Canx 28.2.83.
G-BBWI	DHC.1 Chipmunk 22 (Fuselage no. DHB/f/564)	C1/0676	WP785	8. 1.74	To SE-FOO 7/78. Canx 5.9.77.
G-BBWJ	DHC.1 Chipmunk 22 (Fuselage no. DHB/f/453)	C1/0566	WK551	9. 1.74	To ZS-IZW 7/74. Canx 1.7.74.
G-BBWK	DHC.1 Chipmunk 22 (Fuselage no. DHB/f/277)	C1/0374	WG317	9. 1.74	To ZS-IZU 8/74. Canx 1.7.74.
G-BBWL	DHC.1 Chipmunk 22 (Fuselage no. DHB/f/600)	C1/0706	WP810	9. 1.74	To ZS-IZV 7/74. Canx 1.7.74.
G-BBWM	PA-E23-250 Aztec E	27-7405268	N40532	9. 1.74	To G-LIZZ 7/93. Canx.
G-BBWN	DHC.1 Chipmunk 22 (Fuselage no. DHB/f/803)	C1/0913	WZ876	11. 1.74	Damaged in accident at Thorpe Salvin, ½ mile W of Netherthorpe on 25.2.96. Dismantled for spares at Tattershall. Canx as destroyed 13.3.96.
G-BBWO	BN-2A Mk.III Trislander	360		14. 1.74	To ZS-JJC 4/75. Canx 24.4.75.
"G-BBWO"	BN-2A-8 Islander	380		----	NTU - Painted in error. To G-BBWS. Canx.
G-BBWP	BN-2A Mk.III Trislander	361	(VH-BML) (N29JA)/G-BBWP	14. 1.74	To C-GOXZ 2/75. Canx 13.2.75.
G-BBWR	BN-2A Mk.III-1 Trislander	362		14. 1.74	To G-BBYO 2/74. Canx as marks WFU 27.2.74.
G-BBWS	BN-2A-8 Islander	380	"G-BBWO"	14. 1.74	To 9V-BGA 5/74. Canx 29.5.74.
G-BBWT	BN-2A-21 Islander	382		14. 1.74	To Malagasy AF as 5R-MSA/382 2/75. Canx 13.2.75.
G-BBWU	BN-2A-27 Islander	383		14. 1.74	To TF-RED 6/74. Canx 12.6.74.
G-BBWV	BN-2A-8 Islander	384		14. 1.74	To VQ-SAH 5/75. Canx 12.5.75.
G-BBWW	BN-2A-8 Islander	385		14. 1.74	To N81JA 5/75. Canx 12.5.75.
G-BBWX	BN-2A-8 Islander	386		14. 1.74	To (N86JA)/LN-VIV 5/74. Canx 10.5.74.
G-BBWY	BN-2A-7R Islander	388		14. 1.74	To N85JA 2/74. Canx 25.2.74.
G-BBWZ	American Aviation AA-1B Trainer 2	AA1B-0334		14. 1.74	
G-BBXA	Beechcraft 95-B55 Baron	TC-1672		15. 1.74	To SE-INV 2/84. Canx 13.2.84.
G-BBXB	Reims Cessna FRA.150L Aerobat	0236		16. 1.74	Badly damaged on landing at Sandtoft on 10.9.97.
G-BBXC	Reims Cessna F.150L Commuter	1078		7. 1.74	NTU - Canx 28.5.74 as Not Imported. To PH-GDR(2) 5/74.
G-BBXD	Bensen B-8M Gyroplane	JR-1		16. 1.74	Construction abandoned. Canx as WFU 27.7.76.
G-BBXE	PA-E23-250 Aztec D	27-4110	N944DS N944D	9. 1.74	To TF-IBV 5/81. Canx 1.5.81.
G-BBXF	Hughes 369HS (500HS)	103-0528S		17. 1.74	Fatal crash into a hill at Llwycoed, near Aberdare, Glamorgan on 14.6.76. Canx as destroyed 5.12.83.
G-BBXG	PA-34-200-2 Seneca	34-7450016	N56647	17. 1.74	To G-SSFC 4/94. Canx.
G-BBXH	Reims Cessna FR.172F Rocket	0113	SE-FKG	21. 1.74	
G-BBXI	Handley Page HPR.7 Dart Herald 203	184	I-TIVU	18. 1.74	Damaged in collision with airport vehicle at Hurn on 11.6.84. Broken up 7/84 for spares. Canx as PWFU 19.7.84.
G-BBXJ	Handley Page HPR.7 Dart Herald 203	196	I-TIVI	18. 1.74	Badly damaged on landing at Jersey on 24.12.74. Fuselage t[illegible] Jersey Airport Fire Service in 11/95. (Extant 12/96)
G-BBXK	PA-34-200-2 Seneca 1	34-7450056	N54366	21. 1.74	
G-BBXL	Cessna 310Q II	310Q-1076	EI-CLX G-BBXL/(N1223G)	21. 1.74	
G-BBXM	Agusta-Bell 206B JetRanger II	8378	HP-635 (N.....)/G-BBXM	24. 1.74	To D-HCAC(2) 9/77. Canx 15.8.77.
G-BBXN	Agusta-Bell 206B JetRanger II	8375	HP-634 (N.....)/G-BBXN	29. 1.74	To D-HORG 7/79. Canx 29.6.79.
G-BBXO	Enstrom F-28A-UK	181		29. 1.74	
G-BBXP	PA-34-200-2 Seneca	34-7450058	N54378	30. 1.74	To OO-XYZ. Canx 11.10.76.
G-BBXR	PA-31-350 Navajo Chieftain	31-7405140	N74984	30. 1.74	To G-FOEL 6/88. Canx.
G-BBXS	Piper J3C-90 Cub (L-4H-PI) (Regd as c/n "9865"; Frame no. 12042) (Connolly conversion)	12214	N9865F G-ALMA/44-79918	25. 1.74	
G-BBXT	Reims Cessna F.172M Skyhawk	1071		29. 1.74	Damaged in crash near Chesterfield on 10.9.88. Canx as destroyed 9.6.89.
G-BBXU	Beechcraft B24R Sierra 200	MC-238		30. 1.74	CofA expired 18.11.93. (Stored 11/95) Canx by CAA 13.12.96.
G-BBXV	PA-28-151 Cherokee Warrior	28-7415056	N9603N	31. 1.74	To G-FMAM 6/90. Canx.
G-BBXW	PA-28-151 Cherokee Warrior	28-7415050		21. 1.74	To PH-CPL. Canx 24.10.95.
G-BBXX	PA-31-350 Navajo Chieftain	31-7405402	N66869	1. 2.74	To G-NERC 4/94. Canx.
G-BBXY	Bellanca 7GCBC Citabria	614-74	(PH-...) G-BBXY/N57639	1. 2.74	
G-BBXZ	Evans VP-1	GDP-1 & PFA/1562		31. 1.74	Permit expired 8.3.96. (Stored 2/99 Swanton Morley)
G-BBYA	DH.104 Dove 6	04510	PH-FST G-5-12	1. 2.74	To SU-AZQ 2/78. Canx 13.2.78.
G-BBYB	PA-18-95 Super Cub (L-18C-PI) (Frame no. 18-1628)	18-1627	PH-TMA (D-ENCH)/ALAT 18-1627/51-15627	4. 2.74	
G-BBYC	Short SC.7 Skyliner 3-100-34	SH1925	G-14-97	4. 2.74	To PK-PSK 4/74. Canx 10.4.74.
G-BBYD	Short SC.7 Skyliner 3-100-34	SH1926	G-14-98	4. 2.74	To PK-PSL 5/74. Canx 16.5.74.
G-BBYE	Cessna 195	7550	OO-PCM LN-BDV/N9857A	8. 2.74	Canx 25.3.96 on sale to USA. To N8266R 11/98.
G-BBYF	Short SC.7 Skyliner 3-100-34	SH1927	G-14-99	4. 2.74	To (PK-DJK)/PK-PSM 10/74. Canx 30.8.74.

Regn	Type	c/n	Previous identity	Regn date	Fate or immediate subsequent identity (if known)
G-BBYG	Cessna 207 Skywagon	207-00061	G-BAAK 4X-ALQ/N91078	4. 2.74	NTU - Regd in error. Reverted to G-BAAK 2/74. Canx 4.2.74.
G-BBYH	Cessna 182P Skylane	182-62814	N52744	6. 2.74	
G-BBYI	DH.114 Heron 2D	14133	Ghana AF G-500/9G-AAA	5. 2.74	To N582PR 12/74. Canx 31.12.74.
G-BBYJ	DH.114 Heron 2D	14134	Ghana AF G-502/9G-AAB	5. 2.74	To N583PR 6/75. Canx 17.6.75.
G-BBYK	PA-E23-250 Aztec E	27-7405257	N40524	11. 2.74	To ST-ASH 12/83. Canx.
G-BBYL	Cameron O-77 HAFB	89		8. 2.74	Canx by CAA 19.5.93. (Extant 2/97)
G-BBYM	Handley Page 137 Jetstream 200 (Production No. 42)	243	G-AYWR G-8-13	13. 2.74	
G-BBYN	PA-30-160 Twin Comanche B	30-1597	OH-PAR G-BBYN/PH-ATS/N8437Y	19. 2.74	Restored as OH-PAR. Canx 17.1.79.
G-BBYO	BN-2A Mk.III-1 Trislander	362	ZS-KMH G-BBYO/G-BBWR	27. 2.74	WFU 2/92 at Guernsey. (Dismantled 1/99) (To be rebuilt using fuselage of c/n 1072/N3267J) Canx as WFU 23.2.95.
G-BBYP	PA-28-140 Cherokee F	28-7425158		19. 2.74	(Stored dismantled 1/99 Jersey)
G-BBYR	Cameron O-65 HAFB	97		14. 2.74	CofA expired 15.7.81. Canx by CAA 30.1.87. (On loan to Balloon Preservation Group 3/96) (Extant 1/98)
G-BBYS	Cessna 182P Skylane	182-61520	5Y-ATE N21256	14. 2.74	
G-BBYT	Cessna 414 Chancellor	414-0505	(G-BBRK) N8092Q	19. 2.74	To OY-BSD 1/83. Canx 30.12.82.
G-BBYU	Cameron O-56 HAFB	96		19. 2.74	WFU and stored at the Tank Museum, Bovington. Canx as WFU 9.8.89. (To British Balloon Museum & Library, Newbury)
G-BBYV	Not allocated.				
G-BBYW	PA-28-140 Cherokee F	28-7425162	N9622N	19. 2.74	To G-FIAT 7/89. Canx.
G-BBYX	BN-2A-9 Islander	387		19. 2.74	To TR-LSF 4/74. Canx 17.3.77.
G-BBYY	BN-2A-20 Islander	393		19. 2.74	To P2-CBT 5/74. Canx 13.5.74.
G-BBYZ	BN-2A-20 Islander	394		19. 2.74	To P2-MKX 9/74. Canx 10.9.74.
G-BBZA	BN-2A-26 Islander	395		19. 2.74	To ZK-MCC 1/75. Canx 10.1.75.
G-BBZB	PA-31-350 Navajo Chieftain	31-7305110	N74961	12. 2.74	To N727SC 2/81. Canx 19.2.81.
G-BBZC	BN-2A-20 Islander	396		19. 2.74	To HB-LIA 10/74. Canx 9.10.74.
G-BBZD	BN-2A-8 Islander	389		19. 2.74	To VP-LVG 8/75. Canx 6.10.75.
G-BBZE	PA-28-140 Cherokee Cruiser F	28-7425198		19. 2.74	To SX-AJU 6/82. Canx.
G-BBZF	PA-28-140 Cherokee Cruiser F	28-7425195		19. 2.74	
G-BBZG	Boeing 720-051B (Line No. 381)	18792	(OY-APU) N736US	21. 2.74	To OY-APU 12/75. Canx 5.12.75.
G-BBZH	PA-28R-200-2 Cherokee Arrow	28R-7435102		22. 2.74	
G-BBZI	PA-31-310 Turbo Navajo	31-7401211	N7590L	22. 2.74	
G-BBZJ	PA-34-200-2 Seneca	34-7450088	N40880	26. 2.74	
G-BBZK	Westland-Bell 47G-3B1 (Line No. WAS/180)	WA/581	3D-GAH ZS-HGA/G-BBZK/South Yemen AF 402	26. 2.74	CofA expired 29.8.76. (Stored Cranfield) Canx by CAA 4.4.91.
G-BBZL	Westland-Bell 47G-3B1 (Line No. WAS/184)	WA/583	404 South Yemen AF	26. 2.74	To SE-HME 6/82. Canx 2.6.82.
G-BBZM	Westland-Bell 47G-3B1 (Line No. WAS/186 or 8)	WA/584	405 South Yemen AF	26. 2.74	To HB-XFA 3/75. Canx 6.3.75.
G-BBZN	Fuji FA.200-180 Aero Subaru	FA200-230		26. 2.74	
G-BBZO	Fuji FA.200-160 Aero Subaru	FA200-238		26. 2.74	
G-BBZP	PA-31-350 Navajo Chieftain	31-7405182	N66877	1. 3.74	To N85115 11/80. Canx 26.11.80.
G-BBZR	Enstrom F-28A	177		27. 2.74	DBR at Kidlington on 6.10.76. Canx.
G-BBZS	Enstrom F-28A-UK	192		27. 2.74	Badly damaged in forced landing in a field at Clueworth Hall Farm, Tyldesley on 29.4.89. (Stored 6/93 at Goodwood) Canx as WFU 29.5.96.
G-BBZT	BN-2A-9 Islander (Originally regd as BN-2A-6)	711		27. 2.74	To YV-DAJG 8/74. Canx 8.7.74.
G-BBZU	BN-2A-9 Islander (Originally regd as BN-2A-6)	712		27. 2.74	To YV-T-MTM(3) 4/74. Canx 17.3.77.
G-BBZV	PA-28R-200 Cherokee Arrow II	28R-7435105		11. 3.74	
G-BBZW	BN-2A-27 Islander (Originally regd as BN-2A-6)	713		27. 2.74	To Indonesian Army as A-12201 in 9/74. Canx 5.9.77.
G-BBZX	BN-2A-27 Islander (Originally regd as BN-2A-6)	714		27. 2.74	To EC-CKM 10/74. Canx 30.8.74.
G-BBZY	BN-2A-27 Islander (Originally regd as BN-2A-6)	715		27. 2.74	To EC-CKL 10/74. Canx 30.8.74.
G-BBZZ	BN-2A-9 Islander (Originally regd as BN-2A-6)	716		27. 2.74	To P2-BAC 1/75. Canx 31.12.74.
G-BCAA	Scottish Avn Bulldog Srs.120/125	BH120-298		4. 3.74	To JY-ADW 8/74. Canx 29.8.74.
G-BCAB	Socata MS.894A Rallye Minerva 220	12098		4. 3.74	DBR after falling into a ditch on forced landing at Crowland on 25.2.77. Canx as destroyed 1.4.82.
G-BCAC	Socata MS.894A Rallye Minerva 220	12099		4. 3.74	Damaged on landing at Sandown, IoW on 6.5.90 and later used for static display purposes at Westpoint Enterprise Park, Trafford Park. Canx as WFU 18.1.95. Later on display .94 by Kamikazee Ken's Kitchens.

Regn	Type	c/n	Previous identity	Regn date	Fate or immediate subsequent identity (if known)
G-BCAD	Socata MS.894A Rallye Minerva 220	12101		7. 3.74	Fatal crash near the A303 road at Honiton, Devon on 18.1.87. Canx as destroyed 11.4.88.
G-BCAE	BN-2A-26 Islander (Originally regd as BN-2A-6)	717		27. 2.74	To 4X-AYE 5/75. Canx 27.5.75.
G-BCAF	BN-2A-21 Islander (Originally regd as BN-2A-6)	718		27. 2.74	To RP-C2207 5/75. Canx 21.5.75.
G-BCAG	BN-2A-26 Islander (Originally regd as BN-2A-6)	719		27. 2.74	To ZK-MCD 1/75. Canx 28.1.75.
G-BCAH	DHC.1 Chipmunk 22 (Fuselage no. DHB/f/276)	C1/0372	(EC-...) G-BCAH/WG316	6. 5.74	
G-BCAI	DHC.1 Chipmunk 22 (Fuselage no. DHB/f/399)	C1/0518	WG468	10.10.74	To ZS-JJG(2) 2/76. Canx 28.4.75.
G-BCAJ	PA-25-235 Pawnee C	25-4905	4X-APU	4. 3.74	Fatal crash 1½ miles west of Doddington, Cambridge on 14.7.77. Canx.
G-BCAK	PA-25-235 Pawnee C	25-4908	4X-APV	4. 3.74	Crashed near Enstone on 25.6.75. Canx.
G-BCAL(1)	BN-2A-27 Islander	720		27. 2.74	NTU - To G-BCHO 2/74. Canx.
G-BCAL(2)	Boeing 707-338C (Line No. 636)	19297	VH-EBX	13. 5.75	To LV-MZE 12/79. Canx 14.12.79.
G-BCAM	Thunder Ax7-77 HAFB	014		5. 3.74	To EI-BAR 2/75 (as Ax8-105). Canx 7.2.75.
G-BCAN	Thunder Ax7-77 HAFB	015		5. 3.74	(Extant 2/97)
G-BCAO	Thunder Ax6-56A HAFB (Originally regd as Ax7-77)	017		5. 3.74	To N48169 6/75. Canx 17.6.75.
G-BCAP	Cameron O-56 HAFB	92		5. 3.74	Canx as WFU 30.3.93. (On loan to Balloon Preservation Group 3/96)
G-BCAR	Thunder Ax7-77 HAFB	019		5. 3.74	Envelope to British Balloon Museum. Canx by CAA 2.4.92. (Extant 9/95)
G-BCAS	Thunder Ax7-77 HAFB	018		5. 3.74	(On loan to Balloon Preservation Group) (Extant 1/98)
G-BCAT	PA-31-310 Turbo Navajo	31-7401222	N7406L	9. 4.74	Canx by CAA 26.2.93. To N6238C 3/93.
G-BCAU	Scottish Avn Bulldog Srs.120/125	BH120-299		4. 3.74	To JY-ADX 8/74. Canx 29.8.74.
G-BCAV	Scottish Avn Bulldog Srs.120/125	BH120-300		4. 3.74	To JY-ADY 8/74. Canx 29.8.74.
G-BCAW	Scottish Avn Bulldog Srs.120/125	BH120-301		4. 3.74	To JY-ADZ 8/74. Canx 29.8.74.
G-BCAX	Scottish Avn Bulldog Srs.120/125	BH120-302		4. 3.74	To JY-AEA 8/74. Canx 29.8.74.
G-BCAY	Rockwell Commander 685	12053	(PH-NUS) G-BCAY/N57057	6. 5.74	To 9Q-CZH 2/82. Canx 3.2.82.
G-BCAZ	PA-12 Super Cruiser	12-2312	5Y-KGK VP-KGK/ZS-BYJ/ZS-BPH	12. 3.74	
G-BCBA	Boeing 720-023B (Line No. 143)	18014	P2-ANG G-BCBA/P2-ANG/G-BCBA/N7528A	10. 5.74	To 4X-BMA 10/81. Canx 23.10.81.
G-BCBB	Boeing 720-023B (Line No. 120)	18013	4R-ACS G-BCBB/C9-ARG/G-BCBB/60-SAU/G-BCBB/N7527A	9. 4.74	To 4X-BMB 10/81. Canx 26.10.81.
G-BCBC	Beechcraft 95-58 Baron	TH-483	N52RK	12. 3.74	NTU - Canx 19.7.74 as Not Imported. Remained as N52RK.
G-BCBD	Bede BD-5 (Built by A.A.A.Maitland)	E0001/600		16. 5.74	No Permit believed issued. (Status unknown) Canx by CAA 28.4.94.
G-BCBE	Bell 206B JetRanger II	1282	N18091	13. 3.74	To N65031 6/75. Canx 11.6.75.
G-BCBF	DHC.1 Chipmunk 22 (Fuselage no. DHB/f/136)	C1/0252	WD309	10.10.74	To SE-FNN 6/75. Canx 29.4.75.
G-BCBG	PA-E23-250 Aztec E	27-7305224	VP-BBN VR-BBN(2)/(VR-BDM(2))/G-BCBG/N40494	13. 3.74	
G-BCBH	Fairchild 24R-46A Argus III (UC-61K-FA)	975	(VH-AAQ) G-BCBH/ZS-AXH/HB737/43-15011	13. 3.74	
G-BCBI	Cessna 402B Businessliner	402B-0574	N1401G	14. 4.73	To G-BLTI 2/85. Canx.
G-BCBJ	PA-25-235 Pawnee C (Rebuild of 25-2380/G-ASLA/N6802Z, also quoting c/n as 25-5544, the new fuselage of G-ASLA!)	25-2380/R		18. 3.74	
G-BCBK	Cessna 421B Golden Eagle II	421B-0565	N8412F	18. 3.74	To N565B 1/99. Canx 23.12.98.
G-BCBL	Fairchild 24R-46A Argus III (UC-61K-FA)	989	OO-EKE D-EKEQ/HB-AEC/HB751/43-15025	19. 3.74	
G-BCBM	PA-23-250 Aztec C	27-3006	N5854Y	19. 3.74	
G-BCBN	Schiebe SF-27M-Ci	6401	D-KAFK	19. 3.74	Canx 29.4.85 on sale to Kenya.
G-BCBO	PA-31P Pressurised Navajo	31P-7400196	N7308L	19. 3.74	DBR in forced landing on beach near Le Touquet, France on 29.5.77. Remains to USA for rebuild. Canx by CAA 30.1.87.
G-BCBP	Socata MS.880B Rallye 100S Sport	2423		22. 3.74	CofA expired 26.8.84. Later used for spares. Canx by CAA 15.6.89.
G-BCBR	AJEP/Wittman W.8 Tailwind	TW3-380		20. 3.74	
G-BCBS	BN-2A-8 Islander	390		25. 3.74	To PT-JZJ 2/75. Canx 11.2.75.
G-BCBT	PA-28R-180 Cherokee Arrow	28R-30848	TF-ERR N7488J	25. 3.74	Canx 18.5.77 on sale to Abu Dhabi - Damaged on 25.6.77 at Tarif & stored at Southend. Canx 10.3.87 on sale to Lebanon
G-BCBU	PA-25-235 Pawnee C	25-4389	N4668Y	25. 3.74	To 5B-CCX 9/76. Canx 15.9.76.
G-BCBV	PA-25-235 Pawnee C	25-5347	N8836L	25. 3.74	To ST-AJB 9/84. Canx 22.5.84.
G-BCBW	Cessna 182P Skylane	182-62694	N52593	22. 3.74	To OO-CLP 8/95. Canx 7.8.95.
G-BCBX	Reims Cessna F.150L Commuter	1001	F-BUEO	25. 3.74	CofA expired 19.2.95. (Stored 6/97)
G-BCBY	Reims Cessna F.150L Commuter	1058	PH-TGI (G-BCBY)	25. 3.74	To EI-COP 6/97. Canx 13.6.97.
G-BCBZ	Cessna 337C Super Skymaster (Robertson STOL conversion)	337-0942	SE-FKB N2642S	28. 3.74	
G-BCCA	Cessna A.188B Agwagon	01461	N9371G	2. 4.74	To ZS-LKD 3/83. Canx 15.3.83.
G-BCCB	Pierre Robin HR.200/100 Club	29		2. 4.74	Damaged in gales at Old Sarum on 25.1.90. (Stored Old Sarum 8/90) Canx by CAA 2.3.99.
G-BCCC	Reims Cessna F.150L Commuter	1041		8. 4.74	

Regn	Type	c/n	Previous identity	Regn date	Fate or immediate subsequent identity (if known)
G-BCCD	Reims Cessna F.172M Skyhawk II	1144		8. 4.74	
G-BCCE	PA-23-250 Aztec E	27-7405282	N40544	3. 4.74	
G-BCCF	PA-28-180 Cherokee Archer	28-7405069		3. 4.74	
G-BCCG	Thunder Ax7-65 HAFB	020		4. 4.74	(Extant 1/93)
G-BCCH	Thunder Ax6-56A HAFB	024	(OO-...) G-BCCH	4. 4.74	(Balloon Preservation Group 7/98)
G-BCCI	PA-25-235 Pawnee	25-3495	N7484Z	5. 4.74	Crashed whilst crop-spraying at Seven Score Farm, near Ramsgate on 25.6.75. Canx 6.8.75 as destroyed.
G-BCCJ	American Aviation AA-5 Traveler	AA5-0546		8. 4.74	
G-BCCK	American Aviation AA-5 Traveler	AA5-0547		8. 4.74	
G-BCCL	HS.125 Srs.600B	256039		3. 4.74	To G-BKBM 4/82. Canx.
G-BCCM	Bell 47G-4A	3346	N1193W	5. 4.74	To SE-HGC 5/75. Canx 16.5.75.
G-BCCN	Robin HR.200/100 Club	30		18. 4.74	DBR in forced landing near Ecton, Northants on 9.1.77. Remains later stored at Sywell removed in 1978. Canx as destroyed 5.12.83.
G-BCCO	Robin HR.200/100 Club	32		18. 4.74	Failed to recover from spin and crashed 1 mile southeast of Sywell on 27.3.76. Canx.
G-BCCP	Robin HR.200/100 Club	35		18. 4.74	Ran off runway on landing at Sywell on 9.4.89 & overturned. Canx as WFU 25.1.90.
G-BCCR	Piel CP.301B Emeraude	PFA/712		8. 4.74	
G-BCCS	Beechcraft 95-58 Baron	TH-497		9. 4.74	NTU - Canx 19.7.74 as Not Imported. To N7365R/ZS-GLS 7/74.
G-BCCT	BN-2A Mk.III-1 Trislander	363		17. 4.74	To 9L-LAQ 5/74. Canx 21.5.74.
G-BCCU	BN-2A Mk.III-1 Trislander	366	4X-CCK G-BCCU/9L-LAR/G-BCCU/(LN-VIV)	17. 4.74	(Stored 2/99 Cumbernauld)
G-BCCV	BAC One-Eleven Srs.517FE	BAC.198	VP-LAN VP-BCQ/(G-AXLL)/G-16-12	8. 5.74	To G-BCXR 2/75. Canx.
G-BCCW	Bell 47D-1	633	LN-ORC R.Norway AF BE-B/R.Norway AF KK-O	17. 4.74	WFU 12/74 at Thruxton for spares use. Canx as WFU 30.5.78.
G-BCCX	DHC.1 Chipmunk 22 (Fuselage no. DHB/f/416)	C1/0531	WG481	17. 4.74	
G-BCCY	Robin HR.200/100 Club	37		18. 4.74	
G-BCCZ	Bell 206A JetRanger	576	N293FW	10. 4.74	Crashed into Thames near Blackfriars Bridge on 5.8.75. Canx.
G-BCDA	Boeing 727-46 (Line No. 378)	19281	JA8320	17. 4.74	To HK-3612X 12/90. Canx 26.11.90.
G-BCDB	PA-34-200-2 Seneca	34-7450110	N41346	22. 4.74	
G-BCDC	PA-18-95 Super Cub (Regd with frame no. 18-832)	18-826	4X-ANQ Israeli DF/AF / 4X-ADE/N1221A	18. 4.74	To G-PIPR 10/96. Canx.
G-BCDD	Robin HR.100/285 Tiara	503	F-WVKG	10. 5.74	NTU - Canx 31.7.74 as Not imported. To F-BVKG.
G-BCDE	Sikorsky S-58ET	58-1090	N82806 West German AF 80+25/PY+337/QA+462	23. 4.74	To ZS-HIM 6/80. Canx 2.6.80.
G-BCDF	Sikorsky S-58ET	58-1098	N82811 West German AF 80+33/PZ+463/PZ+002/QA+469/PE+209/N942	23. 4.74	To N4997E 10/78. Canx 12.10.78.
G-BCDG	Sikorsky S-58ET	58-1111	N82817 West German AF 80+46/PY+341/PH+270/PC+203/PF+209	23. 4.74	To PK-OBS 6/80. Canx 10.6.80.
G-BCDH	MBB Bo.105D	S.60	EC-DUO G-BCDH/D-HDBK	25. 4.74	To VH-HRM 1/87. Canx 26.1.87.
G-BCDI	Cessna T.310Q II	310Q-1063	N1208G	26. 4.74	To N3927J 4/83. Canx 22.4.83.
G-BCDJ	PA-28-140 Cherokee	28-24276	PH-NLV N1841J	29. 4.74	
G-BCDK(1)	Partenavia P.68B Victor	15		16. 4.74	NTU - To D-GERD 4/75. Canx 3/75.
G-BCDK(2)	Partenavia P.68B Victor	32	A6-ALN G-BCDK	4. 7.75	
G-BCDL	Cameron O-42 HAFB	115		24. 4.74	
G-BCDM	HS.748 Srs.2A/216	1735	G-11-7	25. 4.74	To PK-KHL 8/74. Canx 1.8.74.
G-BCDN	Fokker F-27 Friendship 200	10201	PH-OGA JA8615/(LV-PMR)/(LV-PTP)/PH-FDP	29. 4.74	WFU in 10/96 at Southend. Used as apprentice trainer 2/99 at Norwich. Canx as WFU 28.1.98.
G-BCDO	Fokker F-27 Friendship 200	10234	PH-OGB JA8621/PH-FEZ	29. 4.74	Damaged Amsterdam 19.7.90. Fuselage only 1/92 at Norwich. CofA expired 20.6.91. Canx 27.1.95 as PWFU. Technical College instructional airframe 10/96 Norwich.
G-BCDP	Cessna 182P Skylane	182-62704	N52606	29. 4.74	NTU - To F-BXAE 10/75. Canx 19.7.76 as Not Imported.
G-BCDR	Thunder Ax7-77 HAFB	025		1. 5.74	Canx by CAA 27.6.97.
G-BCDS	PA-23-250 Aztec E	27-7405283	N40545	2. 5.74	To 5X-BEL. Canx 6.12.85.
G-BCDT	Douglas C-54A-5-DO Skymaster	7466	HS-VGX VH-TAC/HS-VGX/VH-TAC/LV-APB/42-107447	29. 4.74	To (LN-...)/XW-PKH 11/74. Canx 21.11.74.
G-BCDU	Cessna 414 Chancellor	414-0493	N7998Q	3. 5.74	To N2694H 11/81. Canx 9.11.81.
G-BCDV	Western O-65 HAFB	022		29. 4.74	To ZS-HOA 7/77. Canx.
G-BCDW	Hughes 269C (300C)	"10309242"		3. 5.74	To ZS-HLN with c/n 103-0242 on 11/81. Canx 30.1.81.
G-BCDX	PA-E23-250 Aztec E	27-7305225	N40495 N40504	6. 5.74	To F-BVUC 7/74. Canx 6.6.74.
G-BCDY	Reims Cessna FRA.150L Aerobat	0237		7. 5.74	
G-BCDZ	HS.748 Srs.2A/227 Coastguarder (Originally regd as Srs.2A/210)	1662	HP-484	10. 6.74	To G-11-3/C-GSBF 9/84. Canx 21.9.84.
G-BCEA	Sikorsky S-61N Mk.II	61-721		7. 6.74	
G-BCEB	Sikorsky S-61N Mk.II	61-454	N4023S	2.10.74	
G-BCEC	Reims Cessna F.172M Skyhawk II	1082		7. 5.74	
G-BCED	Cessna 421B Golden Eagle II	421B-0600	N1503G	7. 5.74	Canx 24.5.76 on sale to The Netherlands. To D-IOLV.
G-BCEE	American Aviation AA-5 Traveler	AA5-0571		7. 5.74	

Regn	Type	c/n	Previous identity	Regn date	Fate or immediate subsequent identity (if known)
G-BCEF	American Aviation AA-5 Traveler	AA5-0572		7. 5.74	
G-BCEG	BN-2A Mk.III-1 Trislander	372		6. 5.74	To VH-BSP 2/75. Canx 10.2.75.
G-BCEH	BN-2A-8 Islander (Originally regd as BN-2A-26)	397		6. 5.74	To F-BVVP 8/74. Canx 20.11.74.
G-BCEI	BN-2A-20 Islander	398		6. 5.74	To (N56JA)/N90PB 7/74. Canx 25.7.74.
G-BCEJ	BN-2A-26 Islander	399		6. 5.74	To N57JA/4X-AYP 8/74. Canx 14.8.74.
G-BCEK	BN-2A-21 Islander	400		6. 5.74	To Oman AF as 301. Canx 20.11.74.
G-BCEL	BN-2A-21 Islander	401		6. 5.74	To Oman AF as 302. Canx 20.11.74.
G-BCEM	BN-2A-21 Islander	402	(N59JA)	6. 5.74	To Oman AF as 303. Canx 11.2.75.
G-BCEN	BN-2A-26 Islander (Originally regd as BN-2A-8)	403	4X-AYG SX-BFB/4X-AYG/N90JA/G-BCEN	6. 5.74	
G-BCEO	American Aviation AA-5 Traveler	AA5-0575		7. 5.74	
G-BCEP	American Aviation AA-5 Traveler	AA5-0576		7. 5.74	
G-BCER	Gardan GY-201 Minicab	8	F-BGJP	8. 5.74	
G-BCES	PA-31-350 Navajo Chieftain	31-7405418	N66916	9. 5.74	To G-OLLY 1/76. Canx.
G-BCET	Cameron O-84 HAFB (Originally regd as A-140 version)	101		9. 5.74	To F-BUVG(2) 5/75. Canx 22.5.75.
G-BCEU	Cameron O-42 HAFB	111		9. 5.74	Canx by CAA 19.5.93.
G-BCEV	Enstrom F-28A	197		9. 5.74	Crashed after lift-off from helipad at Calne, Wilts on 20.5.75. CofA expired 18.3.78. Canx as destroyed 26.9.78.
G-BCEW	Cessna 402B	402B-0588	N1475G	10. 5.74	NTU - Canx 14.7.75 as Not Imported. To D-ICOM(2) 9/75.
G-BCEX	PA-23-250 Aztec E	27-7305024	N40225	13. 5.74	
G-BCEY	DHC.1 Chipmunk 22 (Fuselage no. DHB/f/396)	C1/0515	WG465	14. 5.74	
G-BCEZ	Cameron O-84 HAFB	107		13. 5.74	(Extant 6/97)
G-BCFA	Not allocated.				
G-BCFB	Cameron O-77 HAFB	114		15. 5.74	Canx as WFU 30.4.93.
G-BCFC	Cameron O-65 HAFB	116		15. 5.74	
G-BCFD	West Ax3-15 HAFB	JW.1		16. 5.74	Canx by CAA 30.1.87. (Canopy stored for Balloon museum)
G-BCFE	Odyssey 4000 HAFB (Built by A.J.Byrne)	AJB-2		20. 5.74	Canx as WFU 19.9.85.
G-BCFF	Fuji FA.200-160 Aero Subaru	FA200-237		21. 5.74	
G-BCFG	Short SC.7 Skyvan 3M-400-19	SH1928	G-14-100	20. 5.74	To Ghana AF as G-451/B in 9/74. Canx 6.9.74.
G-BCFH	Short SC.7 Skyvan 3M-400-19	SH1929	G-14-101	20. 5.74	To Ghana AF as G-452/C in 10/74. Canx 28.10.74.
G-BCFI	Short SC.7 Skyvan 3M-400-19	SH1930	G-14-102	20. 5.74	To Ghana AF as G-450/A in 10/74. Canx 28.10.74.
G-BCFJ	Short SC.7 Skyvan 3M-400-19	SH1931	G-14-103	20. 5.74	To Ghana AF as G-453/D in 10/74. Canx 28.10.74.
G-BCFK	Short SC.7 Skyvan 3M-400-19	SH1932	G-14-104	20. 5.74	To Ghana AF as G-454/E in 12/74. Canx 6.12.74.
G-BCFL	Short SC.7 Skyvan 3M-400-19	SH1933	G-14-105	20. 5.74	To Ghana AF as G-455/F in 12/74. Canx 6.12.74.
G-BCFM	Partenavia P.68B Victor	19		22. 5.74	NTU - Canx 18.9.75 as Not Imported. To I-VICV 3/76.
G-BCFN	Cameron O-65 HAFB	109		23. 5.74	
G-BCFO	PA-18-150 Super Cub	18-5335	(D-EIOZ) ALAT 18-5335	29. 5.74	
G-BCFP	Enstrom F-28A (Incorrectly painted as G-BCWG 20-27.5.74)	196	"G-BCWG"	30. 5.74	Suffered engine failure shortly after take-off and badly damaged in subsequent forced landing near Theale, Reading on 9.9.84. Canx as WFU 10.11.86.
G-BCFR	Reims Cessna FRA.150L Aerobat	0244		30. 5.74	
G-BCFS	SAAB 91D Safir	91-433	PH-RLV	29. 5.74	To LN-MAZ 2/77. Canx 5.1.77.
G-BCFT	SAAB 91D Safir	91-435	PH-RLX	29. 5.74	To (LN-MAY)/LN-MAA 8/77. Canx 18.4.77.
G-BCFU	Thunder Ax6-56 HAFB	027		17. 5.74	To EI-BAF 7/74. Canx 5.7.74.
G-BCFV	SAAB 91D Safir	91-436	PH-RLY	29. 5.74	To N91SB 8/83. Canx 8.8.83.
G-BCFW	SAAB 91D Safir (Mod)	91-437	PH-RLZ	29. 5.74	
G-BCFX	Cessna 402B	402B-0504	N69348	29. 5.74	To F-BXOK 9/75. Canx 12.9.75.
G-BCFY	Phoenix Luton LA-4A Minor	PAL/1301 & PFA/824		29. 5.74	
G-BCFZ	Cameron A-500 HAFB	104	(PH-GAH) G-BCFZ	3. 6.74	To N4911T 3/84. Canx 12.3.84.
G-BCGA	PA-34-200-2 Seneca	34-7450166	N41975	4. 6.74	Crashed & DBR on landing at RAF Waddington on 18.12.77. CofA expired 15.7.78. (Wreck stored 4/91)
G-BCGB	Lovegrove-Bensen B.8 Gyrocopter	PCL.14		3. 6.74	
G-BCGC	DHC.1 Chipmunk 22 (Fuselage no. DHB/f/93)	C1/0776	WP903	13. 3.74	
G-BCGD	PA-28R-200 Cherokee Arrow II	28R-7435265	N9628N	4. 6.74	To EI-EDR 11/87. Canx 6.11.87.
G-BCGE	Bell 212	30630	(N59498)	6. 6.74	To N99041 1/77. Canx 1.1.77.
G-BCGF	Aerotek Pitts S-2A Special	2067	N80038	7. 6.74	To F-WVEJ/F-BVEJ 4/77. Canx 9.9.74.
G-BCGG(1)	AJEP/Wittman Tailwind	TW5-382		5. 6.74	Not completed. Canx 3.11.81.
G-BCGG(2)	CEA Jodel DR.250/160 Quadriplace	87	G-ATZL	3.11.81	
G-BCGH	SNCAN NC.854S	122	F-BAFG	10. 6.74	
G-BCGI	PA-28-140 Cherokee Cruiser F	28-7425283	N9573N	10. 6.74	
G-BCGJ	PA-28-140 Cherokee Cruiser F	28-7425286	N9574N	10. 6.74	
G-BCGK	PA-28-140 Cherokee Cruiser F	28-7425322	N9594N	10. 6.74	To G-DIAT 7/89. Canx.
G-BCGL	Jodel D.112	668	F-BIGL	24. 4.74	Damaged in accident at Platts House Farm, Kent on 22.5.93. Canx by CAA 10.1.94.

Regn	Type	c/n	Previous identity	Regn date	Fate or immediate subsequent identity (if known)
G-BCGM	Wassmer Jodel D.120 Paris-Nice	50	F-BHQM F-BHYM	15. 7.74	
G-BCGN	PA-28-140 Cherokee Cruiser F	28-7425323	N9595N	10. 6.74	
G-BCGO	PA-25-260 Pawnee	25-4551	N4782Y	12. 6.74	Ditched in sea in Sandown Bay on 15.7.79 while on oil-dispersal spraying. Recovered by helicopter and moved to beach in Whitecliff Bay. Canx as destroyed 4.9.79.
G-BCGP	Gazebo AX6-65 HAFB	1		13. 6.74	Canx as WFU 18.12.79. (Extant 2/97)
G-BCGR	Mooney M.20A	1560	PH-HRC N8382E	20. 6.74	Restored as PH-HRC 8/74. Canx 13.8.74.
G-BCGS	PA-28R-200 Cherokee Arrow II	28R-7235133	N4893T	13. 6.74	
G-BCGT	PA-28-140 Cherokee	28-24504	N6779J	17. 6.74	
G-BCGU	Handley Page 137 Jetstream 200 (Production No. 41)	241	G-AXRI	12. 6.74	To G-GLOS 2/82. Canx.
G-BCGV	Beagle B.121 Pup Srs.150	B121-176	G-35-176	17. 6.74	To HB-NAZ 6/74. Canx 26.6.74.
G-BCGW	Chittenden-Jodel D.11	CC.001 & EAA/61554 & PFA/912		14. 6.74	Permit expired 30.1.85. (Stored)
G-BCGX	Bede BD-5 A/B	4916 & PFA/14-10063		18. 6.74	No Permit issued. Canx as WFU 4.12.96.
G-BCGY	BN-2A-21 Islander (Originally regd as BN-2A-6)	721		14. 6.74	To RP-C2130 12/74. Canx 2.12.74.
G-BCGZ	BN-2A-26 Islander (Originally regd as BN-2A-6)	722		14. 6.74	To HP-709 11/74. Canx 17.11.76.
G-BCHA	BN-2A-21 Islander (Originally regd as BN-2A-6)	723		14. 6.74	To RP-C684 11/74. Canx 28.11.74.
G-BCHB	BN-2A-26 Islander (Originally regd as BN-2A-6)	724		14. 6.74	To ZK-MCE 4/75. Canx 17.4.75.
G-BCHC	BN-2A-21 Islander (Originally regd as BN-2A-6)	725		14. 6.74	To RP-C1966 4/75. Canx 30.4.75.
G-BCHD	BN-2A-21 Islander (Originally regd as BN-2A-6)	726		14. 6.74	To 5N-AOI 3/75. Canx 26.2.75.
G-BCHE	BN-2A-21 Islander (Originally regd as BN-2A-6)	727		14. 6.74	To PK-WBA 3/75. Canx 27.2.75.
G-BCHF	BN-2A-21 Islander (Originally regd as BN-2A-6)	728		14. 6.74	To "SU-AUB"/SU-AYB 1/75. Canx 17.11.76.
G-BCHG	BN-2A-21 Islander (Originally regd as BN-2A-6)	729		14. 6.74	To 7P-LAC 1/75. Canx 21.1.75.
G-BCHH	BN-2A-21 Islander (Originally regd as BN-2A-6)	730		14. 6.74	To PK-ZAA 3/75. Canx 13.3.75.
G-BCHI	Hughes 269C (300C)	93-0241		18. 6.74	To F-GALG 5/76. Canx 8.4.76.
G-BCHJ	Reims Cessna F.172H Skyhawk	0606	9H-AAA	14. 6.74	To Yemen /78. Canx 16.6.83.
G-BCHK	Reims Cessna F.172H Skyhawk	0716	9H-AAD	19. 6.74	
G-BCHL	DHC.1 Chipmunk 22A (Fuselage no. DHB/f/569)	C1/0680	WP788	20. 6.74	
G-BCHM	Westland/SNIAS SA.341G Gazelle Srs.1	WA/1168	G-17-20	14. 6.74	Badly damaged in crash Springfield Farm, Melton Mowbray on 5.7.97. (Stored 2/99 at Long Stratton Airfield, Norfolk)
G-BCHN	Westland/SNIAS SA.341G Gazelle Srs.1	WA/1184		14. 6.74	NTU - To Army Air Corps as XX440. Canx as WFU 11.3.76.
G-BCHO	BN-2A-27 Islander (Originally regd as BN-2A-6)	720	(G-BCAL)	27. 2.74	To 8R-GEE 10/74. Canx 17.11.76.
G-BCHP	Scintex CP.1310-C3 Super Emeraude	902	G-JOSI G-BCHP/F-BJVQ	24. 6.74	
G-BCHR	PA-23-250 Aztec B	27-2186	SE-LCF	5. 7.74	To HB-LBP 9/76. Canx 27.9.76.
G-BCHS	DHC.1 Chipmunk 22 (Fuselage no. DHB/f/74)	C1/0187	WB738	26. 6.74	To ZS-JJR 2/76. Canx 9.5.75.
G-BCHT	Schleicher ASK-16	16021	(BGA.1996) D-KAMY	25. 6.74	
G-BCHU(1)	SIPA 903	96	F-BGHU	. 6.74R	NTU - To G-BCML 9/74. (Was painted as G-BCHU)
G-BCHU(2)	Evans-Dawes VP-2	DVP2-7211 & PFA/7211		13. 9.74	No Permit issued. Canx by CAA 5.7.91.
G-BCHV	DHC.1 Chipmunk 22 (Fuselage no. DHB/f/595)	C1/0703	WP807	27. 6.74	CofA expired 20.6.98. Canx by CAA 29.6.99.
G-BCHW	DHC.1 Chipmunk 22 (Fuselage no. DHB/f/170)	C1/0291	WD353	27. 6.74	To N3034F 4/76. Canx 13.4.76.
G-BCHX	Scheibe SF-23A Sperling	2013	D-EGIZ	28. 6.74	Damaged on 7.8.82. Permit expired 29.6.83. (Frame stored 7/97)
G-BCHY	Westland Sea King Mk.50 (Line No. 112)	WA/789	G-17-3	26. 6.74	To R.Australian Navy as N16-112. Marks canx as WFU 4.10.74.
G-BCHZ	Westland Sea King Mk.50 (Line No. 113)	WA/790	G-17-4	26. 6.74	To R.Australian Navy as N16-113. Marks canx as WFU 4.10.74.
G-BCIA	Westland Sea King Mk.50 (Line No. 114)	WA/791	G-17-5	26. 6.74	To R.Australian Navy as N16-114. Marks canx as WFU 4.10.74.
G-BCIB(1)	Wassmer Jodel D.112	1017	F-BJPC	. .74R	NTU - To G-BCOG 2/75. Canx.
G-BCIB(2)	Short SC.7 Skyvan 3-200-37	SH1939	G-14-107	18.10.74	To JA8800 3/75. Canx 7.3.75.
G-BCIC	WSK PZL-104 Wilga 35	74210		3. 7.74	Crashed near Booker on 29.6.80. Canx.
G-BCID	PA-34-200-2 Seneca	34-7250303	N1381T	3. 7.74	
G-BCIE	PA-28-151 Cherokee Warrior (Mod)	28-7415405	N9588N	3. 7.74	Extensively damaged at Perth on 27.5.99.
G-BCIF	PA-28-140 Cherokee Cruiser F	28-7425325	N9598N	3. 7.74	Fatal crash on take-off Canterbury on 31.7.96. Canx as destroyed 13.12.96.
G-BCIG	DHC.1 Chipmunk 22 (Fuselage no. DHB/f/298)	C1/0433	WG349	2. 7.74	To N65153 8/75. Canx 4.8.75.

Regn	Type	c/n	Previous identity	Regn date	Fate or immediate subsequent identity (if known)
G-BCIH	DHC.1 Chipmunk 22 (Fuselage no. DHB/f/183)	C1/0304	WD363	3. 7.74	
G-BCII	Cessna 500 Citation I (Unit No.176)	500-0176	N176CC	11. 7.74	To G-TEFH 6/82. Canx.
G-BCIJ	American Aviation AA-5 Traveler	AA5-0603	N6143A	3. 7.74	
G-BCIK	American Aviation AA-5 Traveler	AA5-0604	N6144A	3. 7.74	
G-BCIL	American Aviation AA-1B Trainer	AA1B-0378	N6168A	5. 7.74	Ran into a fence on landing at Land's Hillock, Auchnagatt, Aberdeenshire on 14.6.86 & substantially damaged. Canx as WFU 24.11.86. (Stored 2/96)
G-BCIM	American Aviation AA-1B Trainer	AA1B-0379	N6169A	5. 7.74	Crashed at Skegness on 5.1.84. Canx as destroyed 29.2.84.
G-BCIN	Thunder Ax7-77 HAFB	030		5. 7.74	(Extant 2/97)
G-BCIO	PA-39 Twin Comanche C/R	39-15	N49JA N57RG/G-BCIO/N8860Y	9. 7.74	To G-OAJS 3/94. Canx.
G-BCIP	PA-39 Twin Comanche C/R	39-93	N8935Y	9. 7.74	To N2654E 12/81. Canx 3.12.81.
G-BCIR	PA-28-151 Cherokee Warrior	28-7415401	N9587N	9. 7.74	
G-BCIS	Beagle B.206R Srs.1	R.03/B.010	OD-AJN G-BCIS/XS767	10. 7.74	DBR on beach near Freetown, Sierra Leone on 22.12.81. Canx.
G-BCIT	Cranfield A.1 Chase Srs.1	001		10. 7.74	To G-COAI 6/98. Canx.
G-BCIU	Beagle B.206R Srs.1	R.16/B.031	XS780	11. 7.74	To N3947L 5/83. Canx 12.5.83.
G-BCIV	Beagle B.206R Srs.1	R.13/B.025	XS777	11. 7.74	DBR on landing at Halfpenny Green on 22.12.77. Used for spares at Staverton. Canx.
G-BCIW	DHC.1 Chipmunk 22 (Fuselage no. DHB/f/788) (Note : Successor G-ARMF is now painted as WZ868 "H")	C1/0899	(PH-...) G-BCIW/WZ868	8. 7.74	Damaged on landing at Hulcote Farm, Beds on 26.11.91. Canx as destroyed 18.3.92. (Wreck stored 7/98 Sandtoft, but by 9/98 was reported as rear fuselage only) Parts used in rebuild of G-ARMF.
G-BCIX	Beagle B.206R Srs.1	R.14/B.030	XS778	11. 7.74	To N24BB 8/75. Canx 22.8.75.
G-BCIY	Beagle B.206R Srs.1	R.17/B.033	XS781	11. 7.74	Canx 1.2.77 on sale to Canada. To N46880 2/77.
G-BCIZ	Beagle B.206R Srs.1	R.20/B.045	XS784	11. 7.74	To N206TB 10/75. Canx 31.10.75.
G-BCJA	Beagle B.206R Srs.1	R.07/B.016	XS771	11. 7.74	To N87590 12/74. Canx 4.12.74.
G-BCJB	Beagle B.206R Srs.1	R.08/B.017	XS772	11. 7.74	To N90810 10/74. Canx 9.10.74.
G-BCJC	Beagle B.206R Srs.1	R.15/B.034	XS779	11. 7.74	To N46882 7/75. Canx 18.7.75.
G-BCJD	Beagle B.206R Srs.1	R.18/B.036	XS782	11. 7.74	To N206BT 3/76. Canx 26.3.76.
G-BCJE	Beagle B.206R Srs.1	R.02/B.008	XS766	11. 7.74	To ZP-PJY 6/75. Canx 23.6.75.
G-BCJF	Beagle B.206R Srs.1	R.09/B.018	N181WW G-BCJF/XS773	11. 7.74	Restored as N181WW 2/97. Canx 10.1.97.
G-BCJG	Beagle B.206R Srs.1	R.12/B.024	XS776	11. 7.74	To N206QE 1/76. Canx 7.1.76.
G-BCJH	Mooney M.20F Executive 21	670126	N9549M	11. 7.74	CofA expired 30.6.91. (Stored WFU at Bourn in 4/99)
G-BCJI	PA-31-350 Navajo Chieftain	31-7405242	N54356	11. 7.74	To SE-IIH 4/81. Canx 4.3.81.
G-BCJJ	Cessna T.210L Turbo Centurion	T210-60094	N59107	16. 7.74	NTU - Canx 30.7.74 as Not Imported. To D-EMLS 7/74.
G-BCJK	PA-28-180 Cherokee Challenger	28-7405179		17. 7.74	Overshot on landing at Yeadon and struck an out-building on 11.11.76. Canx as destroyed 5.12.83.
G-BCJL	PA-28-140 Cherokee F	28-7425320		17. 7.74	To G-PETR 9/85. Canx.
G-BCJM	PA-28-140 Cherokee F	28-7425321		17. 7.74	(Nosewheel collapsed on landing at Manchester on 19.12.98)
G-BCJN	PA-28-140 Cherokee Cruiser F	28-7425350	(A9C-..) G-BCJN/N9618N	17. 7.74	
G-BCJO	PA-28R-200-2 Cherokee Arrow	28R-7435272		17. 7.74	
G-BCJP	PA-28-140 Cherokee	28-24187	N1766J	15. 8.74	
G-BCJR	PA-E23-250 Aztec E	27-7405378	N54040	23. 7.74	To G-BSOB 4/86. Canx.
G-BCJS	PA-23-250 Aztec C	27-3775	N6479Y	23. 7.74	CofA expired 25.11.87. (To local pub? at Belfast) Canx by CAA 2.12.96.
G-BCJT	Beagle B.206R Srs.1	R.04/B.011	XS768	27. 8.74	To "PZ-PJP"/ZP-PJP 2/75. Canx 16.12.74.
"G-BCJT"	BN-2A-21 Islander	474		----	NTU - Painted in error - To G-BDJT.
G-BCJU	HS.125 Srs.600B	256041	G-5-13	22. 7.74	To VR-CBD 1/82. Canx 26.1.82.
G-BCJV	BN-2A Mk.III-1 Trislander	373	(9J-LAR)	22. 7.74	To 5X-UAS 9/74. Canx 20.11.74.
G-BCJW	BN-2A Mk.III-1 Trislander	381	C-GNKW (N58JA)/G-BCJW	22. 7.74	Restored as C-GNKW 6/75. Canx.
G-BCJX	BN-2A Mk.III-2 Trislander	391		22. 7.74	To DQ-FCC 2/75. Canx 11.2.75.
G-BCJY	BN-2A-23 Islander (Originally regd as BN-2A-24S)	392		22. 7.74	To 9V-BGJ/9M-AUD 11/75. Canx 28.11.75.
G-BCJZ	PA-31-310 Turbo Navajo B	31-7401239	N61427	29. 7.74	To 5N-AEP 10/74. Canx 21.10.74.
G-BCKA	Rockwell S2R-600 Thrush Commander	1816R	N5616X	23. 7.74	To 7Q-YCS 4/78. Canx 29.3.78.
G-BCKB	Rockwell S2R-600 Thrush Commander	1819R	N5619X	23. 7.74	To F-GBED 8/83. Canx 24.5.82.
G-BCKC	Rockwell S2R-600 Thrush Commander	1822R	N5622X	23. 7.74	To ST-AKJ 9/85. Canx 20.8.85.
G-BCKD	PA-28R-200 Cherokee Arrow II	28R-7435270		19. 8.74	Fatal crash when it collided with Cessna 185 OO-PCA near Antwerp on 17.5.87. Canx as destroyed 20.4.88.
G-BCKE	Beechcraft E90 King Air	LW-126		29. 7.74	NTU - Not Imported. To RP-C201 1/75. Canx 29.1.75.
G-BCKF	K & S SA.102.5 Cavalier	71055 & PFA/1594		29. 7.74	No Permit issued. Canx by CAA 8.7.91.
G-BCKG	Hawker Sea Fury TT.20	ES.8509	D-CAFO G-9-57/WG562	30. 7.74	To (N46990)/N62143 9/74. Canx 30.9.74.
G-BCKH	Hawker Sea Fury TT.20	ES.8502	D-CAMI D-FAMI/G-9-24/VX300	30. 7.74	To N46990 5/77. Canx 25.5.77.

Regn	Type	c/n	Previous identity	Regn date	Fate or immediate subsequent identity (if known)
G-BCKI	Lake LA-4-200 Buccaneer	623	5N-AJE G-BCKI/N65722	2. 8.74	Canx on sale to Sweden 30.7.76, but believed to have sunk in a lake prior to local registration.
G-BCKJ	PA-E23-250 Aztec E	27-7405376	N54038	2. 8.74	To N5046C 5/84. Canx 10.5.84.
G-BCKK	SNCAN Stampe SV-4C	401	F-BEHZ	. .74R	NTU - Remained as F-BEHZ. Canx.
G-BCKL	Cessna 310Q II	310Q-1056	N1201G	6. 8.74	Fatal crash at Dunfinance Hill, near Perth on 4.3.76. Canx as destroyed 12.3.76.
G-BCKM	Cessna 500 Citation I (Unit No.198)	500-0198	(N198CC)	2. 8.74	To G-JETE 12/84. Canx.
G-BCKN	DHC.1 Chipmunk 22 (Fuselage no. DHB/f/602)	C1/0707	WP811	5. 8.74	
G-BCKO	PA-23-250 Aztec E	27-7405251	N40519	1. 8.74	(In Nigeria in a damaged state 1994) Canx by CAA 25.4.98. To N30LW 8/98.
G-BCKP	Phoenix Luton LA-5A Major	PFA/1213		6. 8.74	
G-BCKR	PA-28R-200 Cherokee Arrow II	28R-7435267	N9633N	6. 8.74	To OY-POW 11/76. Canx 10.11.76.
G-BCKS	Fuji FA.200-180AO Aero Subaru	FA200-250		2. 8.74	
G-BCKT	Fuji FA.200-180 Aero Subaru	FA200-251		2. 8.74	
G-BCKU	Reims Cessna FRA.150L Aerobat	0256		1. 8.74	Force landed 8 miles northeast of Birmingham on 1.1.99.
G-BCKV	Reims Cessna FRA.150L Aerobat	0251		1. 8.74	
G-BCKW	BN-2A-20 Islander	404		5. 8.74	To N81JA 9/74. Canx 24.9.74.
G-BCKX	BN-2A-9 Islander	405		5. 8.74	To YV-TAKL 10/74. Canx 11.2.75.
G-BCKY	BN-2A-21 Islander	406		5. 8.74	To N59JA 9/74. Canx 24.9.74.
G-BCKZ	BN-2A-9 Islander	407		5. 8.74	To N91JA 10/74. Canx 10.10.74.
G-BCLA	Sikorsky S-61N Mk.II	61-735		17.11.74	To 9M-ELF(2). Canx 29.10.86.
G-BCLB	Sikorsky S-61N Mk.II	61-736		5.11.74	To 9M-AVQ 7/77. Canx 25.7.77.
G-BCLC	Sikorsky S-61N Mk.II	61-737		9. 1.75	
G-BCLD	Sikorsky S-61N Mk.II	61-739		4. 2.75	
G-BCLE	BN-2A-21 Islander	408		5. 8.74	To RP-C1262 11/74. Canx.
G-BCLF	BN-2A-21 Islander	409		5. 8.74	To RP-C28 12/75. Canx 22.10.75.
G-BCLG	Bell 212	30636	EP-HBY VR-BFK/G-BCLG/9M-ATV/VR-BFK/G-BCLG/N18091	22. 8.74	To 5N-AJT 5/79. Canx 2.5.79.
G-BCLH	BN-2A-21 Islander	410		5. 8.74	To N56JA 2/75. Canx 13.2.75.
G-BCLI	American Aviation AA-5 Traveler	AA5-0643		12. 8.74	
G-BCLJ	American Aviation AA-5 Traveler	AA5-0644		12. 8.74	
G-BCLK	Rockwell 500S Strike Commander	3180	N57083	12. 8.74	To N1187G 9/81. Canx 21.9.81.
G-BCLL	PA-28-180 Cherokee C	28-2400	SE-EON	13. 8.74	
G-BCLM	CAB GY-201 Minicab 693B	A.192	F-BGSZ	14. 8.74	Crashed at Hurst Farm, near Winchfield, Hants on 11.9.83. Canx as destroyed 29.2.84.
G-BCLN	Sikorsky S-58ET (HSS-1N Seabat)	58-1539	N82828 West German AF 80+69/PY+342/QW+768/QA+481/BuA.150753	15. 8.74	To OO-AGK(2) 9/80. Canx 22.9.80.
G-BCLO	Sikorsky S-58ET (HSS-1N Seabat)	58-1658	N82844 West German AF 80+99/PY+344/PD+011/QA+461/BuA.150784	15. 8.74	To OO-AGL 9/80. Canx.
G-BCLP	Piper J3C-65 Cub	11410	(G-BCXU) F-BGXU(2)/HB-OFL/43-30119	22. 8.74	To VH-DIT 11/78. Canx 11.4.78.
G-BCLR	HS.125 Srs.400A	NA751 & 25228	N640M G-BCLR/N640M/N47BH	23. 8.74	To N120GA 12/74. Canx 30.12.74.
G-BCLS	Cessna 170B	170-20946	N8094A	23. 8.74	CofA expired 27.1.83. Canx by CAA 18.12.96. (Stored 4/99 Teesside)
G-BCLT	Socata MS.894A Rallye Minerva 220	12003	EI-BBW G-BCLT/F-BTRL	1. 8.74	
G-BCLU	SAN Jodel D.117	506	F-BHXG	28. 8.74	
G-BCLV	Bede BD-5A	4885 & PFA/14-10074		28. 8.74	Not completed and unfinished frame stored. Canx as WFU 31.7.89.
G-BCLW	American Aviation AA-1B Trainer 2	AA1B-0463		29. 8.74	
G-BCLX	American Aviation AA-1B Trainer	AA1B-0464		29. 8.74	Crashed into Loch Foyle on 17.9.75. Canx.
G-BCLY	Cessna 182P	182-62811	N52741	29. 8.74	Flew into a hill at Mitchamer Farm, near Stoughton on approach to Goodwood on 5.1.77. Canx.
G-BCLZ	Boeing 707-351B (Line No. 352)	18710	B-1828 N355US	3. 9.74	Restored as B-1828 10/75. Canx 9.10.75.
G-BCMA	Beechcraft 95-B55 Baron	TC-1805		28. 8.74	To OY-POB 1/76. Canx 19.12.75.
G-BCMB	Partenavia P.68B Victor	21		2. 9.74	CofA expired 1.9.77. Canx as WFU 4.7.83.
G-BCMC	Bell 212	30639	9Y-THL HK-4103X/G-BCMC/(EC-GHO)/EC-294/G-BCMC/EC-GCS/EC-932/G-BCMC/9Y-THL/G-BCMC/9M-ATU/V	30. 8.74	To EC-H.. Canx 4.8.99.
G-BCMD	PA-18-95 Super Cub (L-18C-PI)(Frame No. 18-2071)	18-2055	OO-SPF R.Netherlands AF R-70/52-2455	4. 9.74	
G-BCME	Thunder Ax7-77 HAFB	022		13. 9.74	To N38AC 1/75. Canx 15.1.75.
G-BCMF	Levi Go-Plane RL.6 Srs.1	EAA/3678		5. 9.74	DBR on first flight attempt at Bembridge on 16.11.74. Canx by CAA 5.12.83. (Stored 12/95 Newport, IoW)
G-BCMG	DHC.1 Chipmunk 22 (Fuselage no. DHB/f/374)	C1/0505	WG431	4. 9.74	To N431WG 1/75. Canx 16.2.76.
G-BCMH	Not allocated.				
G-BCMI	Short SC.7 Skyvan 3-100-53	SH1938	G-14-106	2. 9.74	To CR-LOD 2/75. Canx 17.2.75.
G-BCMJ	K & S SA.102.5 Cavalier (Tailwheel conv.)	MJ.1 & PFA/1546		9. 9.74	Permit expired 8.8.95. (On rebuild 7/94) Canx by CAA 2.3.99.
G-BCMK	BN-2A-21 Islander	411		9. 9.74	To JA5241 12/74. Canx 10.12.74.
G-BCML	SIPA 903	96	(G-BCHU) F-BGHU	16. 9.74	(Was painted as G-BCHU) To G-BGME 1/81. Canx.

Regn	Type	c/n	Previous identity	Regn date	Fate or immediate subsequent identity (if known)
G-BCMM	BN-2A-21 Islander	412		9. 9.74	To ZS-ORD 12/74. Canx 4.12.74.
G-BCMN	BN-2A-21 Islander	413		9. 9.74	To Oman AF as 304. Canx 10.2.75.
G-BCMO	BN-2A-21 Islander	414		9. 9.74	To Oman AF as 305. Canx 10.2.75.
G-BCMP	BN-2A-21 Islander	415		9. 9.74	To Oman AF as 306. Canx 29.1.75.
G-BCMR	Avions Pierre Robin HR.100/285 Tiara	506	F-BVYE	11. 9.74	CofA expired 18.12.82. Canx by CAA 10.10.84. To C-GMKC 2/85.
G-BCMS	BN-2A-21 Islander	416		9. 9.74	To N92JA 1/75. Canx 2.1.75.
G-BCMT	Isaacs Fury II	PFA/1522		9. 9.74	
G-BCMU	BN-2A-21 Islander	417		9. 9.74	To Oman AF as 307. Canx 17.3.77.
G-BCMV	BN-2A-21 Islander	418		9. 9.74	To Oman AF as 308. Canx 17.3.77.
G-BCMW	Beagle B.206R Srs.1	R.11/B.020	XS774	20. 8.74	To "PZ-PJO"/ZP-PJO 3/75. Canx 16.12.74.
G-BCMX	Robin HR.200/120 Club	52		11. 9.74	NTU - Not Imported. Canx 31.1.75. To F-BXEX 4/75.
G-BCMY	BN-2A-21 Islander	419		9. 9.74	To G-BPBN 7/80. Canx.
G-BCMZ	BN-2A-27 Islander	731	"G-BCNA"	9. 9.74	To EL-AHX 3/75. Canx 21.1.76.
	(Originally regd as BN-2A-6)				
G-BCNA	BN-2A-21 Islander	732		9. 9.74	To PK-ZAD 2/75. Canx.
	(Originally regd as BN-2A-6)				
"G-BCNA"	BN-2A-6 Islander	731		9. 9.74	NTU - Was painted in error - To G-BCMZ. Canx.
G-BCNB	BN-2A-27 Islander	733		9. 9.74	To EL-AHY 3/75. Canx 21.1.76.
	(Originally regd as BN-2A-6)				
G-BCNC	Gardan GY-201 Minicab	A.202	F-BICF	9. 9.74	(Stored at owner's home)
	(Built by Nouvelle Societe Cometal)				
G-BCND	BN-2A-27 Islander	734		9. 9.74	To EL-AHZ 3/75. Canx 21.1.76.
	(Originally regd as BN-2A-6)				
G-BCNE	BN-2A-27 Islander	735		9. 9.74	To YI-AHF 4/75. Canx 21.1.76.
	(Originally regd as BN-2A-6)				
G-BCNF	BN-2A-21 Islander	736		9. 9.74	To 5Y-AYE 4/75. Canx 21.1.76.
	(Originally regd as BN-2A-6)				
G-BCNG	BN-2A-27 Islander	737		9. 9.74	To YI-AHE 4/75. Canx 21.1.76.
	(Originally regd as BN-2A-6)				
G-BCNH	BN-2A-27 Islander	738		9. 9.74	To YI-AHG 6/75. Canx 21.1.76.
	(Originally regd as BN-2A-6)				
G-BCNI	BN-2A-21 Islander	739		9. 9.74	To RP-C1801 9/75. Canx.
	(Originally regd as BN-2A-6)				
G-BCNJ	BN-2A-9 Islander	740		9. 9.74	To TR-LUR 5/75. Canx 21.1.76.
	(Originally regd as BN-2A-6)				
G-BCNK	BN-2A Mk.III-1 Trislander	1001		9. 9.74	To F-OCYP/5X-UDC 5/75. Canx 20.5.75.
G-BCNL	BN-2A Mk.III-1 Trislander	1002		9. 9.74	To HK-1711X 5/75. Canx 20.5.75.
G-BCNM	BN-2A Mk.III-1 Trislander	1003		9. 9.74	To VH-BPH 1/76. Canx 11.11.75.
G-BCNN	BN-2A Mk.III-2 Trislander	1004		9. 9.74	To DQ-FCE 3/75. Canx 7.3.75.
G-BCNO	BN-2A Mk.III-1 Trislander	1005		9. 9.74	To HP-947 10/81. Canx 30.3.82.
G-BCNP	Cameron O-77 HAFB	117		16. 9.74	
G-BCNR	Thunder Ax7-77A HAFB	028		13. 9.74	Canx by CAA 19.5.93. (Extant 2/97)
G-BCNS	Cameron O-84 HAFB	127		13. 9.74	To VH-BRR 9/88. Canx 29.10.86.
	(Originally regd as O-77)				
G-BCNT	Partenavia P.68B Victor	23		17. 9.74	CofA expired 17.10.88. Canx by CAA 3.8.93. To G-UNIT 10/93.
G-BCNU	Westland Sea King Mk.45	WA/798	G-17-22	12. 9.74	To Pakistan AF as 4511. Marks WFU 3.7.75.
	(Line No. 108)				
G-BCNV	Westland Sea King Mk.45	WA/797	G-17-21	12. 9.74	To Pakistan AF as 4510. Marks WFU 3.7.75.
	(Line No. 109)				
G-BCNW	Westland Sea King Mk.45	WA/801	G-17-25	12. 9.74	To Pakistan AF as 4514. Canx 18.7.78.
	(Line No. 115)				
G-BCNX	Piper J3C-65 Cub (L-4H-PI)	"11831"	F-BEGM	17. 9.74	
	(Rebuilt in 1960/61 quoting c/n 10993. Previous French identity of 11831 and 43-30540 also still quoted. Probably Frame No.10993, c/n 11168 ex French AF/43-29877)				
G-BCNY	Fuji FA.200-180AO Aero Subaru	FA200-256		17. 9.74	Fatal crash on striking a tree on hill 2 miles north of Penboyr, Port Talbot on 8.9.75. Canx.
G-BCNZ	Fuji FA.200-160 Aero Subaru	FA200-257		16. 9.74	
G-BCOA	Cameron O-65 HAFB	125		18. 9.74	To OO-BPE 3/85. Canx 22.3.85.
G-BCOB	Piper J3C-65 Cub (L-4H-PI)	10696	F-BCPV 43-29405	19. 9.74	
	(Frame No. 10521)				
G-BCOC	Not allocated.				
G-BCOD	PA-31-350 Navajo Chieftain	31-7405483		19.11.74	To N42079 4/81. Canx 16.4.81.
G-BCOE	HS.748 Srs.2A/287	1736	9N-ACN G-BCOE	23. 9.74	To VH-IMI(2) 10/94. Canx 10.10.94.
G-BCOF	HS.748 Srs.2A/287	1737		23. 9.74	To VH-IMK(2) 1/95. Canx 29.12.94.
	(Converted to Srs.2B standard in 2/85)				
G-BCOG	Wassmer Jodel D.112	1017	(G-BCIB) F-BJPC	13. 2.75	Fatal crash in a field at Bentworth, near Alton on 26.7.98. Canx as destroyed 3.12.98.
G-BCOH	Avro 683 Lancaster Mk.10 AR	277	CF-TQC RCAF KB976	24. 9.74	Canx 23.2.93 on sale to USA, reportedly on rebuild.
	(Built by Victory Aircraft)				
G-BCOI	DHC.1 Chipmunk 22	C1/0759	WP870	24. 9.74	
	(Fuselage no. DHB/f/657)				
G-BCOJ	Cameron O-56 HAFB	124		25. 9.74	(Extant 2/97)
G-BCOK	Not allocated.				
G-BCOL	Reims Cessna F.172M Skyhawk II	1233		25. 9.74	
G-BCOM	Piper J3C-90 Cub (L-4A-PI)	10478	F-BDTP F-BFQP/OO-ADI/43-29187	27. 9.74	
	(Frame No.10303 - Officially regd as c/n 12040, the correct identity of G-BGPD. Probably exchanged fuselages in France)				
G-BCON	Cessna 310R	310R-0064		27. 9.74	Canx 29.3.76 on sale to The Netherlands. To D-IBFA.

Regn	Type	c/n	Previous identity	Regn date	Fate or immediate subsequent identity (if known)
G-BCOO	DHC.1 Chipmunk 22 (Fuselage no. DHB/f/93)	C1/0209	WB760	10.10.74	
G-BCOP	PA-28R-200-2 Cherokee Arrow	28R-7435296		8.10.74	
G-BCOR	Socata MS.880B Rallye 100ST	2544	F-OCZK	7. 1.75	
G-BCOS	DHC.1 Chipmunk 22 (Fuselage no. DHB/f/570)	C1/0681	WP789	10.10.74	Spun into sea south of Ancona, Italy on 17.8.81. Canx.
G-BCOT	Enstrom F-28C-UK (Originally regd as F-28A)	199		3.10.74	To G-JDHI 11/84. Canx.
G-BCOU	DHC.1 Chipmunk 22 (Fuselage no. DHB/f/447)	C1/0559	WK522	10.10.74	CofA expired 30.3.95. (Stored 4/95)
G-BCOV	Hawker Sea Fury TT.20	ES.3613	D-CACE G-9-62/VX302	8.10.74	To N613RD 6/85. Canx 20.6.85.
G-BCOW	Hawker Sea Fury TT.20	ES.3615	D-CACO G-9-64/VX281	8.10.74	To N8476W 7/80. Canx 1.7.80.
G-BCOX	Cox-Bede BD-5A	HJC.4523		10.10.74	
G-BCOY	DHC.1 Chipmunk 22 (Fuselage no. DHB/f/95)	C1/0212	WB762	10.10.74	
G-BCOZ	DHC.1 Chipmunk 22 (Fuselage no. DHB/f/200)	C1/0321	WD382	10.10.74	To N65265 9/75. Canx 2.9.75.
G-BCPA	Aerospatiale SA.315B Lama	2314	F-BUIY	11.10.74	To C-GCUV 4/85. Canx 18.4.85.
G-BCPB	Howes Radio-Controlled Model Free Balloon (500 cu.ft) (Toy)	RBH.1		14.10.74	Canx by CAA 20.5.93.
G-BCPC	PA-31-350 Navajo Chieftain	31-7552011	N61500	8. 1.75	To 5N-AWP 2/79. Canx 29.1.79.
G-BCPD	Gardan GY-201 Minicab	18	F-BGKN	24.10.74	
G-BCPE	Reims Cessna F.150M Commuter	1159		10.10.74	To G-PHAA 6/97. Canx.
G-BCPF	PA-23-250 Aztec D	27-4021	N6748Y	16.10.74	To CS-DBR 7/96. Canx 23.9.96.
G-BCPG	PA-28R-200 Cherokee Arrow B	28R-35705	N4985S	16.10.74	
G-BCPH	Piper J3C-65 Cub (L-4H-PI) (Frame No. 11050)	11225	F-BCZA(4) French AF/43-29934	13.12.74	
G-BCPI	PA-18-135 Super Cub	18-2544	OO-VLF OO-HME/52-6226	21.10.74	DBF at Staverton on 13.2.79. Canx as destroyed 5.12.83.
G-BCPJ	Piper J3C-65 Cub (L-4J-PI) (Frame No. 13036)	13206	F-BDTJ 45-4466	5.11.74	
G-BCPK	Reims Cessna F.172M Skyhawk II	1194	(D-ELOB)	21.10.74	
G-BCPL	American Aviation AA-5 Traveler	AA5-0663		21.10.74	Crashed at Cheltenham Racecourse, Glos. on 15.3.77. Canx.
G-BCPM	American Aviation AA-5 Traveler	AA5-0664	N6170A	21.10.74	To G-MALC 11/79. Canx.
G-BCPN	American Aviation AA-5 Traveler	AA5-0665	N6155A	21.10.74	
G-BCPO	Partenavia P.68B Victor	27		18.10.74	
G-BCPP	Partenavia P.68B Victor	28		18.10.74	NTU - Not Imported. To I-VICZ. Canx 10.3.76.
G-BCPR	Beechcraft 95-55 Baron 58	TH-573		21.10.74	NTU - Canx 21.11.74 as Not Imported. To N738D.
G-BCPS	Beechcraft B24R Sierra	MC-331		21.10.74	NTU - Canx 11.11.74 as Not Imported. To N6989R.
G-BCPT	Beechcraft C23 Sundowner	M-1619		21.10.74	NTU - Canx 3.3.75 as Not Imported. To N33UA.
G-BCPU	DHC.1 Chipmunk 22 (Fuselage no. DHB/f/736)	C1/0839	WP973	24.10.74	
G-BCPV	PA-28-140 Cherokee	28-26748	PH-VRY	30.10.74	DBR in hangar fire at Staverton on 13.2.79. Canx.
G-BCPW	Not allocated.				
G-BCPX	Andrew Szep HFC.125	AS.001 & PFA/12-10019		24.10.74	
G-BCPY	Bell 212	30655		30.10.74	To EI-BAM 11/74. Canx 15.11.74.
G-BCPZ	Rockwell 500S Shrike Commander	3200	N57274	30.10.74	To N47AC 2/83. Canx 28.2.83.
G-BCRA	Reims Cessna F.150M Commuter	1169	(D-ELOS)	29.11.74	Crashed in woods near Blackbushe on 30.7.87 due to engine failure while doing a touch-and-go landing. Canx as WFU 24.11.87.
G-BCRB	Reims Cessna F.172M Skyhawk II	1259		29.10.74	
G-BCRC	Druine D.31 Turbulent	PFA/1621		14. 2.75	Not completed. Canx as WFU 31.8.83.
G-BCRD	DH(Aust).82A Tiger Moth	1000	N17565 VH-FBR/R.Australian AF A17-565	26.11.74	To HB-UPP 8/79. Canx 24.8.79.
G-BCRE	Cameron O-77 HAFB	128		30.10.74	Canx by CAA 19.5.93. (Extant 1/98)
G-BCRF	PA-23-250 Aztec E	27-7405445	N54203 (YV-TAKY)	1.11.74	To N65SC 3/82. Canx 18.3.82.
G-BCRG	MBB Bo.105D	S.75	D-HDBZ	5.11.74	To HB-XLV 11/80. Canx 27.11.80.
G-BCRH	Alaparma B.75 Baldo	41	I-DONP MM53647	5.11.74	No UK CofA or Permit issued. Canx by CAA 2.9.91. (Stored engineless .97)
G-BCRI	Cameron O-65 HAFB	135		5.11.74	
G-BCRJ	Taylor JT.1 Monoplane	PFA/1427		5.11.74	Fatal crash 1 mile south of Andrewsfield on 17.5.98. Canx as destroyed 23.9.98.
G-BCRK	K & S SA.102.5 Cavalier	PFA/01-10049		5.11.74	
G-BCRL	PA-28-151 Cherokee Warrior	28-7415689		5.11.74	
G-BCRM	Cessna 500 Citation I (Unit No.227)	500-0227	(N227CC)	27.11.74	To N423RD 12/78. Canx 15.12.78.
G-BCRN	Reims Cessna FRA.150L Aerobat	0261		5.11.74	To EI-CTI 4/99. Canx 19.4.99.
G-BCRO	Reims Cessna FR.172J Rocket	0530		5.11.74	To EP-JBI 1/75. Canx 22.1.75.
G-BCRP	PA-E23-250 Aztec E	27-7305082	N40269	7.11.74	
G-BCRR	American Aviation AA-5B Tiger	AA5B-0006		7.11.74	

Regn	Type	c/n	Previous identity	Regn date	Fate or immediate subsequent identity (if known)
G-BCRS	Boeing 707-321 (Line No. 84)	17603	G-41-2-74 TC-JAJ/N725PA	8.11.74	To (HS-BBB)/9G-ACD 12/74. Canx 10.12.74.
G-BCRT	Reims Cessna F.150M Commuter	1164		18.11.74	
G-BCRU	Sikorsky S-58ET	58-1092	N82807 West German AF 80+27/ PF+332/QA+464	20.11.74	Crashed on landing on Platform Charlie in Forties Field (110 miles east of Peterhead) on 21.4.76, and dropped 160 feet on to adjacent barge. Remains to AIU at Farnborough. Canx as destroyed 5.12.83.
G-BCRV	Sikorsky S-58ET	58-1096	N82808 West German AF 80+31/QA+467	20.11.74	To ZS-HHY 5/79. Canx.
G-BCRW	Sikorsky S-58ET	58-1104	N82814 West German AF 80+39/PL+332/PH+264/PH+220/QA+474	20.11.74	To ZS-HVV 1/79. Canx 19.1.79.
G-BCRX	DHC.1 Chipmunk 22 (Fuselage no. DHB/f/117)	C1/0232	WD292	22.11.74	
G-BCRY	Thunder Ax7-65 HAFB	033		1.11.74	To ZK-FBH 12/74. Canx 15.1.75.
G-BCRZ	DHC.1 Chipmunk 22 (Fuselage no. DHB/f/475)	C1/0593	WK573	25.11.74	To ZS-JPT 1/76. Canx 2.10.75.
G-BCSA	DHC.1 Chipmunk 22 (Fuselage no. DHB/f/584)	C1/0691	WP799	25.11.74	
G-BCSB	DHC.1 Chipmunk 22 (Fuselage no. DHB/f/670)	C1/0770	WP899	25.11.74	(Wings noted in hangar at Bicester 16.1.99 - presumably flying with other wings!)
G-BCSC	DHC.1 Chipmunk 22 (Fuselage no. DHB/f/760)	C1/0864	WZ846	25.11.74	Canx as WFU 21.1.75. To 8439M as instructional airframe at 1404 Squadron ATC, Boundary Road, Chatham, Kent in 3/75.
G-BCSD	BN-2A-8 Islander	420		21.11.74	To N23JA 1/75. Canx 23.1.75.
G-BCSE(1)	Gates LearJet 25B	25B-188		21.11.74	To A40-AJ 10/75. Canx 30.10.75.
G-BCSE(2)	PA-31-350 Navajo Chieftain	31-7652168		8. 9.76	To G-BEVK 12/76. Canx.
G-BCSF	BN-2A-21 Islander	421		21.11.74	To RP-2131 3/75. Canx 11.3.75.
G-BCSG	BN-2A-21 Islander	422		21.11.74	To RP-C2132 2/75. Canx 19.3.75.
G-BCSH	BN-2A-27 Islander	423		21.11.74	To (N93JA)/C-GPPP 2/75. Canx 27.2.75.
G-BCSI	BN-2A-27 Islander	424		21.11.74	To OO-TOP 5/75. Canx 30.4.75.
G-BCSJ	BN-2A-21 Islander	425		21.11.74	To D-IELE 3/75. Canx 3.3.75.
G-BCSK	Beechcraft B60 Duke	P-336	N6034S	9. 1.75	NTU - Remained as N6034S. Canx 2.6.75 as Not Imported.
G-BCSL	DHC.1 Chipmunk 22 (Fuselage no. DHB/f/405)	C1/0524	WG474	26.11.74	
G-BCSM	Bellanca 8GCBC Scout	108-74		29.11.74	(Veered off runway on take-off from Sherburn-in-Elmet on 7.1.99)
G-BCSN	Scottish Avn Bulldog Srs.120/125	BH120-338		27.11.74	To JY-AEL 6/75. Canx 9.6.75.
G-BCSO	Scottish Avn Bulldog Srs.120/125	BH120-339		27.11.74	To JY-AEM 6/75. Canx 9.6.75.
G-BCSP	Scottish Avn Bulldog Srs.120/125	BH120-340		27.11.74	To JY-AEN 6/75. Canx 9.6.75.
G-BCSR	Bellanca 7ECA Citabria	1058-74		29.11.74	Lost power climbing away from Martlesham Heath on 30.8.75 & badly damaged. Stored at Southend.
G-BCSS	Socata MS.892A Rallye Commodore 150	10467	F-BLSM	18.11.74	Engine failure and overran on forced landing near Spalding on 22.11.80. Canx as PWFU 9.2.81.
G-BCST	Socata MS.893A Rallye Commodore 180	10748	F-BPQD	18.11.74	
G-BCSU	DHC.1 Chipmunk 22 (Fuselage no. DHB/f/526)	C1/0640	WK627	2.12.74	To ZS-JIT 5/75. Canx 21.4.75.
G-BCSV	Cessna 421B Golden Eagle II	421B-0875	N5416J	2.12.74	To N601SA 11/84. Canx 22.11.84.
G-BCSW	PA-E23-250 Aztec F	27-7554006	N54211	3.12.74	To D-IKLW 4/77. Canx.
G-BCSX	Thunder Ax7-77 HAFB	031		2.12.74	(Extant 9/94)
G-BCSY	Mines-Taylor JT.2 Titch	PFA/1504		5.12.74	Construction abandoned at advanced state due to CofG problems. (Stored 3/97)
G-BCSZ	PA-28R-200 Cherokee Arrow D	28R-7535006	N9584N	6.12.74	To 9H-ABK. Canx 1.6.88.
G-BCTA	PA-28-151 Cherokee Warrior	28-7515113		6.12.74	Substantially damaged 22.5.98 Sutton Road, Ripple, Kent. Canx as WFU 16.7.98.
G-BCTB	Cameron O-65 HAFB	139		6.12.74	To F-GCXD 4/81. Canx 13.11.80.
G-BCTC	Reims Cessna F.337G Super Skymaster (Wichita c/n 337-01466)	0057	D-IMMO N53822/F-WLIQ/(N1166M)	9.12.74	To 5N-AST 1/77. Canx 31.1.77.
G-BCTD	Scheibe SF-25B Falke	4651	D-KICB	10.12.74	Destroyed in collision with a T-49B Glider over Camphill on 26.8.81. Canx.
G-BCTE	MBB Bo.105D	S.83	D-HDCH	11.12.74	Restored as D-HDCH 4/76. Canx 13.4.76.
G-BCTF	PA-28-151 Cherokee Warrior (Rebuilt 89/90 using major components from G-BFXZ)	28-7515033		11.12.74	
G-BCTG	Thunder Ax6-56A HAFB	032		12.12.74	To F-BTQQ(2) 12/74. Canx 12.12.74.
G-BCTH	PA-28-140 Cherokee	28-24346	PH-VRN N6661J	12.12.74	Crashed at Old Warden on 4.11.76 & DBR. Remains at Southend. Canx.
G-BCTI	Schleicher ASK-16	16029	D-KIWA	23.12.74	
G-BCTJ	Cessna 310Q II	310Q-1072	N1219G	23.12.74	
G-BCTK	Reims Cessna FR.172J Rocket	0546		23.12.74	Overturned on landing at St.Ives, Cornwall on 25.3.85. Canx.
G-BCTL	Scottish Avn Bulldog Srs.120/125	BH.120/364		23.12.74	To Lebanese AF as L-141 9/75. Canx 30.9.75.
G-BCTM	Scottish Avn Bulldog Srs.120/125	BH.120/365		23.12.74	To Lebanese AF as L-142 9/75. Canx 30.9.75.
G-BCTN	Scottish Avn Bulldog Srs.120/125	BH.120/366		23.12.74	To Lebanese AF as L-143 9/75. Canx 30.9.75.

Regn	Type	c/n	Previous identity	Regn date	Fate or immediate subsequent identity (if known)
G-BCTO	Scottish Avn Bulldog Srs.120/125	BH.120/367		23.12.74	To Lebanese AF as L-144 10/75. Canx 30.10.75.
G-BCTP	Scottish Avn Bulldog Srs.120/125	BH.120/368		23.12.74	To Lebanese AF as L-145 10/75. Canx 30.10.75.
G-BCTR	Taylor JT.1 Titch	TR.2 & PFA/3224		13.12.74	Crashed on take-off at Brickhouse Farm, Frampton Cotterell, near Bristol on 6.7.91. Canx as destroyed 27.8.91.
G-BCTS	Scottish Avn Bulldog Srs.120/125	BH.120/369		23.12.74	To Lebanese AF as L-146 10/75. Canx 30.10.75.
G-BCTT	Evans VP-1	PFA/1543		24.12.74	
G-BCTU	Reims Cessna FRA.150M Aerobat	0268		30.12.74	
G-BCTV	Reims Cessna F.150M Commuter	1160		30.12.74	Fatal crash and burnt out near the A303 road 3 miles from Mere on 24.3.90. Canx as destroyed 12.6.90.
G-BCTW	Reims Cessna F.150M Commuter	1170		2. 1.75	Badly damaged in forced landing Strangford Lough, Northern Ireland on 12.4.89. Canx as WFU 20.6.89. Further damaged by flooding at Newtownards on 13.12.91. (Stored 2/93 Wickenby)
G-BCTX	Sikorsky S-58ET	58-1103	N82813 West German AF 80+38/PH+263/PH+219/QA+473	31.12.74	To ZS-HHZ 5/79. Canx 26.4.79.
G-BCTY	BN-2A-21 Islander	426		2. 1.75	To (9V-BGD)/Philippine Navy as 426 4/75. Canx 30.4.75.
G-BCTZ	BN-2A-8 Islander	427		2. 1.75	To N21JA 3/75. Canx 17.3.77.
G-BCUA	BN-2A-21 Islander (Originally regd as BN-2A-26)	428	(N23JA) G-BCUA	2. 1.75	To Philippine Navy as 428 in 6/75. Canx 3.6.75.
G-BCUB	Piper J3C-65 Cub (L-4J-PI) (Lippert Reed conversion) (Identity incorrect - May be c/n 13370 ex F-BFBU/45-4630, the official identity of G-BDOL. Frames possibly swopped)	13186	F-BCPC 45-4446	13.12.74	
G-BCUC	Piper J3C-65 Cub (L-4J-PI) (Frame No. 12376)	12546	F-BFMN 44-80250	1. 5.75	To EI-BEN 4/78. Canx 13.4.78.
G-BCUD	BN-2A-21 Islander	429	(I-CIRS) G-BCUD	2. 1.75	To PK-OBE 1/76. Canx 26.1.76.
G-BCUE	BN-2A-21 Islander	430		2. 1.75	To RP-2133 4/75. Canx 22.4.75.
G-BCUF	Reims Cessna F.172M Skyhawk II	1279		3. 1.75	
G-BCUG	Reims Cessna F.150M Commuter	1178		3. 1.75	Crashed in a field at North Bank farm, Skene, Aberdeen on 20.10.75. Canx as destroyed 8.12.75.
G-BCUH	Reims Cessna F.150M Commuter	1195		7. 1.75	
G-BCUI	Reims Cessna F.172M Skyhawk II	1313		7. 1.75	To PH-JAK 9/95. Canx 5.9.95.
G-BCUJ	Reims Cessna F.150M Commuter	1176		9. 1.75	
G-BCUK	Reims Cessna F.172M Skyhawk II	1311		10. 1.75	To G-WACZ 5/86. Canx.
G-BCUL	Socata MS.880B Rallye 100ST	2545	F-OCZL	27. 1.75	
G-BCUM	Stinson HW-75 Reliant Model 105	7040	F-BGQO N21189/NC21189	30.12.74	To G-BMSA 3/86. Canx.
G-BCUN	Scottish Aviation Bulldog Srs.120/122	BH120-370		9. 1.75	To Ghana AF as G-106. Canx 22.1.76.
G-BCUO	Scottish Aviation Bulldog Srs.120/122	BH120-371	G-107 Ghana AF/G-BCUO	9. 1.75	
G-BCUP	Scottish Aviation Bulldog Srs.120/122	BH120-372		9. 1.75	To Ghana AF as G-108. Canx 9.6.76.
G-BCUR	Not allocated.				
G-BCUS	Scottish Aviation Bulldog Srs.120/122	BH120-373	G-109 Ghana AF/G-BCUS	9. 1.75	
G-BCUT	Scottish Aviation Bulldog Srs.120/122	BH120-374		9. 1.75	To Ghana AF as G-110. Canx 9.6.76.
G-BCUU	Scottish Aviation Bulldog Srs.120/122	BH120-375		9. 1.75	To Ghana AF as G-111. Canx 24.6.76.
G-BCUV	Scottish Aviation Bulldog Srs.120/122	BH120-376	G-112 Ghana AF/G-BCUV	9. 1.75	
G-BCUW	Reims Cessna F.177RG Cardinal II	0119	SE-GKL	10. 1.75	To J8-VAK. Canx.
G-BCUX	HS.125 Srs.600B	256043		10. 1.75	Crashed & DBR on take-off at Dunsfold on 20.11.75. Canx.
G-BCUY	Reims Cessna FRA.150M Aerobat	0269		14. 1.75	
G-BCUZ	Beechcraft 200 Super King Air	BB-55	N9755S	17. 1.75	To G-OAKM 8/87. Canx.
G-BCVA	Cameron O-65 HAFB	147		2. 1.75	CofA expired 28.5.81. Canx by CAA 16.3.92
G-BCVB	PA-17 Vagabond	17-190	F-BFMT N4890H	22. 1.75	
G-BCVC(1)	Socata MS.880B Rallye 100ST	2546	F-OCZM	. 1.75R	NTU - To G-BCXB 2/75. Canx.
G-BCVC(2)	Socata MS.880B Rallye 100ST	2548	F-OCZO	16. 1.75	
G-BCVD	Not allocated.				
G-BCVE	Evans VP-2	V2-1015 & PFA/7210		16. 1.75	Canx as TWFU 9.6.93. (Under construction 12/97)
G-BCVF	Practavia Pilot Sprite 115	GBC.1 & PFA/1362		27. 1.75	
G-BCVG	Reims Cessna FRA.150L Aerobat	0245	(I-AFAD)	16. 1.75	
G-BCVH(1)	Reims Cessna FRA.150L Aerobat	0253	F-BVSS	. .75R	NTU - To F-ODAL. Canx.
G-BCVH(2)	Reims Cessna FRA.150L Aerobat	0258		16. 1.75	
G-BCVI	Reims Cessna FR.172J Rocket	0497		16. 1.75	To 5Y-BZA /97. Canx 11.12.96.
G-BCVJ	Reims Cessna F.172M Skyhawk II	1305		16. 1.75	
G-BCVK	BN-2A-21 Islander (Originally regd as BN-2A-6)	741		17. 1.75	To 9M-AUQ/RP-C2130 4/75. Canx 17.12.75.
G-BCVL	BN-2A-21 Islander (Originally regd as BN-2A-6)	742		17. 1.75	To PT-KRO 5/75. Canx 28.5.75.
G-BCVM	BN-2A-21 Islander (Originally regd as BN-2A-6)	743		17. 1.75	To PT-KRP 7/75. Canx 3.7.75.
G-BCVN	BN-2A-9 Islander (Originally regd as BN-2A-6)	744		17. 1.75	To 5U-AAS 7/75. Canx 8.1.76.
G-BCVO	BN-2A-21 Islander (Originally regd as BN-2A-6)	745		17. 1.75	To PK-KNF 7/75. Canx 3.7.75.

Regn	Type	c/n	Previous identity	Regn date	Fate or immediate subsequent identity (if known)
G-BCVP	BN-2A-21 Islander (Originally regd as BN-2A-6)	746		17. 1.75	To 9Q-CIN 7/75. Canx 8.1.76.
G-BCVR	BN-2A-21 Islander (Originally regd as BN-2A-6)	747		17. 1.75	To Mauritanian AF as 5T-MAS 4/76. Canx 13.4.76.
G-BCVS	BN-2A-21 Islander (Originally regd as BN-2A-6)	748		17. 1.75	To VQ-SAK 1/76. Canx 21.1.76.
G-BCVT	BN-2A-21 Islander (Originally regd as BN-2A-6)	749		17. 1.75	To PK-KNG 8/75. Canx.
G-BCVU	BN-2A-27 Islander (Originally regd as BN-2A-6)	750		17. 1.75	Canx 8.12.75 on sale to Belgium. To ST-AFU 9/75.
G-BCVV	PA-28-151 Cherokee Warrior	28-7515121		21. 1.75	Overshot on landing at Doncaster on 17.6.84 and struck earth mound at end of runway. Used for spares. Canx as destroyed 11.7.85.
G-BCVW	Sud/Socata Gardan GY-80-180 Horizon	145	D-EHST	23. 1.75	
G-BCVX	SAN Jodel DR.1050 Ambassador	132	F-BJNF	23. 1.75	Crashed on landing at Oxenhope on 22.3.87. Canx as destroyed 7.9.88. Wings to G-LAKI in 1/91.
G-BCVY	PA-34-200T Seneca II	34-7570022	N32447	28. 1.75	
G-BCVZ	Agusta-Bell 206B JetRanger II	8432		29. 1.75	To EI-BIJ 1/80. Canx 28.1.80.
G-BCWA	BAC One-Eleven Srs.518FG	BAC.205	G-AXMK VP-LAK/G-AXMK/TG-ARA/G-AXMK	22. 1.75	To (G-OBWI). Broken up for spares at Southend 3/93. Canx as WFU 30.3.93.
G-BCWB	Cessna 182P Skylane II	182-63566	N5848J	29. 1.75	
G-BCWC	Not allocated.				
G-BCWD	Sikorsky S-58ET	58-827	N47788 (N47780)/West German AF 80+14/PY+335/PB+210/PH+215	30. 1.75	To C-GBSM 1/82. Canx 28.1.82.
G-BCWE	Handley Page HPR.7 Dart Hearld 206	166	(N.....) G-BCWE/CF-EPI	30. 1.75	Canx 18.2.87 on sale to USA. To TG-ASA.
G-BCWF	Scottish Aviation Twin Pioneer Srs.3	561	XT610 G-APRS/(PI-C430)	30. 1.75	Restored as G-APRS 12/93. Canx.
G-BCWG	BAC One-Eleven Srs.518FG	BAC.204	G-AXMJ	3. 2.75	To RP-C1189 8/78. Canx 14.7.78.
"G-BCWG"	Enstrom F-28A	196		-----	(Incorrectly painted as G-BCWG 20-27.5.74) To G-BCFP.
G-BCWH	Practavia Pilot Sprite 115	PFA/1366		3. 2.75	
G-BCWI	Beavers-Bensen B.8M Gyrocopter	HB.1		3. 2.75	Crashed from 50ft while on tow by a pick-up truck at Hibaldstow Aerodrome on 29.8.79. Permit expired 1.10.81. Canx by CAA 16.12.91.
G-BCWJ	Canadair CL-44D4-6	28	N62163 VP-LAT/N602SA/CF-WYC-X	7. 2.75	Undercarriage collapsed on landing at Nairobi-Wilson, Kenya on 6.7.78 & DBR. Canx as WFU 8.11.78.
G-BCWK	Alpavia Fournier RF-3	24	F-BMDD	7. 2.75	
G-BCWL	National Steel Car Co./Westland Lysander IIIA (Composite - main airframe possibly RCAF 2403, parts from RCAF 2341, 2349, 2391)	1244	RCAF	9. 9.75	To N..... Canx 3.6.99.
G-BCWM	Agusta-Bell 206B JetRanger II	8434		10. 2.75	To G-OABY 9/91. Canx.
G-BCWN	Agusta-Bell 206B JetRanger II	8435		11. 2.75	To G-NOEL 6/80. Canx.
G-BCWO	BN-2A-21 Islander	431		13. 2.75	To LN-MAC 4/75. Canx 11.4.75.
G-BCWP	BN-2A-21 Islander	432		13. 2.75	To VH-ISL 8/75. Canx 17.7.75.
G-BCWR	BN-2A-20 Islander	433	OY-RPZ (OY-RPH)/G-BCWR	13. 2.75	Instructional Airframe still marked as OY-RPZ; broken up early 1994 at Bembridge. Canx as wfu 26.10.94; forward fuselage in use as technical mock-up & new windscreen tests
G-BCWS	BN-2A-9 Islander	434		13. 2.75	To N94JA 4/75. Canx 7.4.75.
G-BCWT	BN-2A-9 Islander	435		13. 2.75	To N58JA 4/75. Canx 10.4.75.
G-BCWU	BN-2A-27 Islander	436		13. 2.75	To J8-VAK 10/83. Canx 11.10.83.
G-BCWV	BN-2A-9 Islander	437		13. 2.75	To D-IEDA 5/75. Canx 8.5.75.
G-BCWW	Handley Page 137 Jetstream 200 (Production No. 45)	246	G-AXUN	29. 7.74	To G-CTRX 4/84. Canx.
G-BCWX	BN-2A-21 Islander	438		13. 2.75	To RP-C2134 6/75. Canx 3.6.75.
G-BCWY	BN-2A-21 Islander	439	(I-CIRS) G-BCWY	13. 2.75	To RP-C2135 7/75. Canx 18.7.75.
G-BCWZ	BN-2A-21 Islander	440		13. 2.75	To RP-C2136 6/75. Canx 16.6.75.
G-BCXA	Socata MS.880B Rallye 100ST	2547	F-OCZN	7. 2.75	To TF-OSK 10/76. Canx 11.10.76.
G-BCXB	Socata MS.880B Rallye 100ST	2546	(G-BCVC) F-OCZM	7. 2.75	
G-BCXC	Socata MS.880B Rallye 100ST	2549	F-OCZQ	7. 2.75	Canx as WFU 21.4.77. To EI-BGA 11/78.
G-BCXD	Aerotek Pitts S-2A Special	2088	N80044	19. 2.75	To D-EHEN(2) 11/81. Canx 5.10.81.
G-BCXE	Robin DR.400 2+2	1015		19. 2.75	
G-BCXF	HS.125 Srs.600B	256054	"G-BKFS" G-BCXF/9K-AED/G-BCXF/G-5-17	21. 2.75	(Incorrectly painted as G-BKFS 3-6/93) To 5N-YFS. Canx 2.7.93.
G-BCXG	Cessna 421B Golden Eagle II	421B-0845	N1954G	24. 2.75	To OY-DLN 10/75. Canx 14.10.75.
G-BCXH	PA-28-140 Cherokee F	28-7525100	N9512N	20. 2.75	Canx as destroyed 12.4.91.
G-BCXI	Schweizer-Grumman G-164A Agcat	1414		24. 2.75	Destroyed in collision with power lines at Thorton Curtis, near Humberside on 29.6.76. Canx.
G-BCXJ	Piper J3C-65 Cub (L-4J-PI) (Frame No. 12878)	13048	F-BFFH OO-SWA/44-80752	21. 2.75	
G-BCXK	Hiller UH-12E	HA3018	N118HA	24. 2.75	Restored as N118HA 7/75. Canx 7.7.75.
G-BCXL	HS.125 Srs.600B	256049	ZS-JHL G-BCXL	3. 3.75	To HZ-KA5 9/78. Canx 10.8.78.
G-BCXM	Cameron O-77 HAFB	153		26. 2.75	Destroyed in contact with trees at Chinnor, Berks on 23.1.78. Canopy left overnight but ripped beyond repair in gales. Canx.
G-BCXN	DHC.1 Chipmunk 22 (Fuselage no. DHB/f/585)	C1/0692	WP800	7. 3.75	

Regn	Type	c/n	Previous identity	Regn date	Fate or immediate subsequent identity (if known)
G-BCXO	MBB Bo.105D (This is the original pod which was replaced .92 and was rebuilt as a display piece)	S.80	D-HDCE	27. 2.75	Canx as WFU 4.3.92. (On display Lands End Theme Park 6/96 & painted as "G-CDBS")
G-BCXP	PA-E23-250 Aztec E	27-7554045	N54247	20. 2.75	To G-SATO 6/80. Canx.
G-BCXR	BAC One-Eleven Srs.517FE	BAC.198	G-BCCV VP-LAN/VP-BCQ/G-16-12	28. 2.75	To (G-ODWK). Broken up for spares at Southend 3/93. Canx as WFU 30.3.93.
G-BCXS	Rockwell Commander 690A	11209	N57208	5. 3.75	To N570WA 3/81. Canx 23.3.81.
G-BCXT	Reims Cessna F.150M	1186		28. 2.75	To G-HIVE 4/85. Canx.
G-BCXU(1)	Piper J3C-65 Cub	11410	F-BGXU(2) HB-OFL/43-30119	22. 8.74	NTU - To G-BCLP 8/74. Canx.
G-BCXU(2)	BN-2A Mk.III-2 Trislander	1006		28. 2.75	To PK-KTA 12/75. Canx 8.12.75.
G-BCXV	BN-2A Mk.III-1 Trislander	1007		28. 2.75	To HP-899 7/81. Canx 10.10.81.
G-BCXW	BN-2A Mk.III-2 Trislander	1008		28. 2.75	To DQ-FCF 6/75. Canx 7.1.76.
G-BCXX	BN-2A Mk.III-2 Trislander	1009	(N29JA)	28. 2.75	To 6Y-JJH 8/75. Canx 7.1.76.
G-BCXY	BN-2A Mk.III-2 Trislander	1010		28. 2.75	To DQ-FCG 8/75. Canx 7.1.76.
G-BCXZ	Cameron O-56 HAFB	154		4. 3.75	Canx by CAA 19.5.93. (Extant 2/97)
G-BCYA	DHC.1 Chipmunk 22 (Fuselage no. DHB/f/651)	C1/0756	WP867	7. 3.75	To SE-FNP 9/75. Canx 16.5.75.
G-BCYB	Reims Cessna F.177RG Cardinal II	0127		5. 3.75	NTU - To D-EDVH 12/75. Canx 17.12.75.
G-BCYC	BN-2A Mk.III-1 Trislander	1011	EL-AIB G-BCYC	6. 3.75	DBR in heavy landing at Dyce on 15.5.79. Fuselage in three parts on fire dump, Guernsey Airport 4/96.
G-BCYD	DHC.1 Chipmunk 22 (Fuselage no. DHB/f/608)	C1/0713	WP832	10. 3.75	To N832WP 10/75. Canx 23.10.75.
G-BCYE	DHC.1 Chipmunk 22 (Fuselage no. DHB/f/299)	C1/0437	WG350	6. 3.75	To G-BPAL 10/86. Canx.
G-BCYF	Dassault Falcon 20E	304/511	F-WRQP	4. 3.75	To G-FRAD 11/86. Canx.
G-BCYG	DHC.1 Chipmunk 22 (Fuselage no. DHB/f/526)	C1/0643	WK629	10. 3.75	To ZS-JJM 4/75. Canx 24.4.75.
G-BCYH	DAW Privateer Mk.3 Motor Glider (Regd as Cadet III; is converted Slingsby T-31B c/n 839)	2 & PFA/1568	BGA.1158 RAFGSA.264/XA297	10. 3.75	(Marked incorrectly as ex RAFGSA.246)
G-BCYI	Schleicher ASK-16	16030	"GB-CYI" D-KIWE	12. 3.75	To D-KCYI 5/94. Canx 31.8.93.
G-BCYJ	DHC.1 Chipmunk 22 (Fuselage no. DHB/f/259)	C1/0360	WG307	12. 3.75	
G-BCYK	Avro (Canada) CF-100 Canuck Mk.IV	-	18393 R.Canadian AF	18. 3.75	No CofA issued. Canx as WFU 15.9.81. (On display 7/99 Duxford)
G-BCYL	DHC.1 Chipmunk 22 (Fuselage no. DHB/f/163)	C1/0283	WD346	17. 3.75	To G-MUNK 4/86. Canx.
G-BCYM	DHC.1 Chipmunk 22 (Fuselage no. DHB/f/479)	C1/0598	WK577	13. 3.75	
G-BCYN	PA-28-180 Cherokee	28-7505135		14. 3.75	NTU - Canx 20.3.75 as Not Imported. To N1129X.
G-BCYO	PA-34-200T Seneca	34-7570086	(ST-...) G-BCYO/N33088	14. 3.75	To ST-AFT 11/75. Canx 18.11.75.
G-BCYP	Agusta-Bell 206B JetRanger II	8440		14. 3.75	To G-TPPH 12/84. Canx.
G-BCYR	Reims Cessna F.172M Skyhawk II	1288		20. 3.75	
G-BCYS	Piper J3C-65 Cub	"12990"	F-BFYH HB-ZAH/44-86094	17. 3.75	To TF-GEV 6/82. Canx 15.6.82.
G-BCYT	BN-2A-9 Islander (Originally regd as BN-2A-6)	751		18. 3.75	To 9XR-GV 9/75. Canx 8.1.76.
G-BCYU	BN-2A-21 Islander (Originally regd as BN-2A-6)	752		18. 3.75	To 9V-BGT 8/75. Canx.
G-BCYV	BN-2A-20 Islander (Originally regd as BN-2A-6)	753	P2-ISE G-BCYV	18. 3.75	To VH-TXH. Canx.
G-BCYW	BN-2A-21 Islander (Originally regd as BN-2A-6)	754		18. 3.75	To 9V-BGV 12/75. Canx 8.12.75.
G-BCYX	BN-2A-26 Islander (Originally regd as BN-2A-6)	755		18. 3.75	To VH-FCP 11/75. Canx.
G-BCYY	Westland-Bell 47G-3B1 (Line No. WAS/204)	WA/572	XV318	10. 3.75	Damaged following engine failure on take-off at Paxford on 6.6.82 & later stored at Thruxton. Canx by CAA 16.11.84.
G-BCYZ	Westland-Bell 47G-3B1 (Line No. WAS/205)	WA/573	XV319	10. 3.75	Damaged at Stownor on 6.7.83. Canx as destroyed 11.8.88.
G-BCZA	BN-2A-20 Islander (Originally regd as BN-2A-6)	756		18. 3.75	To VH-TXL 11/75. Canx 19.11.75.
G-BCZB	BN-2A-20 Islander (Originally regd as BN-2A-6)	757		18. 3.75	Canx 26.11.75 on sale to Australia. To P2-ISH 12/75.
G-BCZC	BN-2A-20 Islander (Originally regd as BN-2A-6)	758		18. 3.75	To VH-MET 1/76. Canx 8.12.75.
G-BCZD	BN-2A-21 Islander (Originally regd as BN-2A-6)	759		18. 3.75	To N11216 12/80. Canx.
G-BCZE	BN-2A-21 Islander (Originally regd as BN-2A-6)	760		18. 3.75	To LN-MAG(3) 3/76. Canx 1.4.76.
G-BCZF	PA-28-180 Cherokee Archer	28-7505090		18. 3.75	To G-WACR 12/86. Canx.
G-BCZG	Handley Page HPR.7 Dart Herald 202	159	CF-NAC	19. 3.75	To 9Q-CAH 10/83. Canx 6.10.83.
G-BCZH	DHC.1 Chipmunk 22 (Fuselage no. DHB/f/518)	C1/0635	WK622	19. 3.75	Crashed on take-off from Pentney, Norfolk on 6.9.87. (Stored 8/93)
G-BCZI	Thunder Ax7-77 HAFB	037		24. 3.75	
G-BCZJ	Westland-Bell 47G-3B1 (Line No. WAS/187)	WA/567	XV313	24. 3.75	Canx 21.11.75 on sale to USA.

Regn	Type	c/n	Previous identity	Regn date	Fate or immediate subsequent identity (if known)
G-BCZK	Westland-Bell 47G-3B1 (Line No. WAS/212)	WA/575	XV321	24. 3.75	Hit ground out of control at Baginton on 20.10.76 & severely damaged. Canx as WFU 1.12.77.
G-BCZL	Westland-Bell 47G-3B1 (Line No. WAS/219)	WA/577	XV323	24. 3.75	Crashed at Bishops Norton, Lincs on 25.7.77. Later used for spares at Baginton. Canx as WFU 5.12.83.
G-BCZM	Reims Cessna F.172M Skyhawk II	1350		3. 4.75	
G-BCZN	Reims Cessna F.150M Commuter	1149		27. 3.75	
G-BCZO	Cameron O-77 HAFB	158		27. 3.75	
G-BCZP	Cessna T.210L Turbo Centurion II	T210-60757	N1736X	3. 4.75	To G-OILS 10/80. Canx.
G-BCZR	Vickers 838 Viscount	446	(PK-RVN) G-BCZR/9G-AAU	11. 4.75	To VP-WGC 5/81. Canx 1.5.81.
G-BCZS	BN-2A-21 Islander	441		1. 4.75	To LN-MAF 5/75. Canx 19.8.77.
G-BCZT	BN-2A-21 Islander	442		1. 4.75	To N95JA 6/75. Canx 23.6.75.
G-BCZU	BN-2A-21 Islander	443		1. 4.75	To RP-2137 7/75. Canx 18.7.75.
G-BCZV	BN-2A-26 Islander	444		1. 4.75	To EI-BBA 6/75. Canx 13.6.75.
G-BCZW	BN-2A-21 Islander	445		1. 4.75	To RP-C2138 6/75. Canx 20.8.75.
G-BCZX	BN-2A-26 Islander	446		1. 4.75	To N93JA 6/75. Canx 23.6.75.
G-BCZY	BN-2A-21 Islander	447		1. 4.75	To N97JA 7/75. Canx 7.7.75.
G-BCZZ	BN-2A-21 Islander	448		1. 4.75	To RP-C2139 11/75. Canx 20.8.75.
G-BDAA	BN-2A-21 Islander	449		1. 4.75	To N96JA 7/75. Canx 7.7.75.
G-BDAB	K & S SA.102.5 Cavalier	AHB.1 & PFA/01-10008		2. 4.75	No Permit issued. Canx by CAA 4.12.90. (Not completed?)
G-BDAC	Cameron O-77 HAFB	146		2. 4.75	Canx by CAA 14.11.95. (Extant 2/97)
G-BDAD	Taylor JT.1 Monoplane	PFA/1453		2. 4.75	Damaged in start-up accident at Squires Gate on 21.7.91. Permit expired 3.4.92. (Status uncertain)
G-BDAE	BAC One-Eleven Srs.518FG	BAC.203	G-AXMI	21. 2.75	To G-OWBD 1/93. Canx.
G-BDAF	BN-2A-21 Islander	450		1. 4.75	To RP-C2140 7/75. Canx 20.8.75.
G-BDAG	Taylor JT.1 Monoplane	PFA/1430		1. 4.75	(For sale 6/97) Permit expired 2.3.98.
G-BDAH	Evans VP-1	PFA/7007		2. 4.75	(Stored 6/99 Cranfield)
G-BDAI	Reims Cessna FRA.150M Aerobat	0266		21. 4.75	
G-BDAJ	Rockwell Commander 112A	237	N1237J	10. 4.75	To G-DASH 3/87. Canx.
G-BDAK	Rockwell Commander 112A	252	N1252J	10. 4.75	
G-BDAL	Rockwell 500S Shrike Commander	3226	N57134	25. 4.75	
G-BDAM	Noorduyn AT-16-ND Harvard IIB	14-726	LN-MAA Swedish AF Fv.16047/FE992/42-12479	10. 4.75	
G-BDAN	Boeing 727-46 (Line No. 288)	19279	JA8318	15. 8.74	Fatal crash into a mountain at Los Rodeos, Tenerife, Canary Islands on 25.4.80. Canx as destroyed 28.1.81.
G-BDAO	SIPA 91	2	F-BEPT	10. 4.75	Crashed on landing at Aughrim, Co.Down on 20.6.76. (Remains stored)
G-BDAP	AJEP/Wittman TW.8 Tailwind	0387 & PFA/3507		9. 4.75	
G-BDAR	Evans VP-1 Srs.2	PFA/1537 & PFA/62-10461		10. 4.75	Permit expired 20.7.84. (Stored 6/98)
G-BDAS	BAC One-Eleven Srs.518FG	BAC.202	G-AXMH	21. 2.75	To G-OBWB 12/92. Canx.
G-BDAT	BAC One-Eleven Srs.518FG	BAC.232	G-AYOR	25. 2.75	To G-OBWA 12/92. Canx.
G-BDAU	Reims Cessna FRA.150M Aerobat	0275		10. 4.75	Fatal crash soon after take-off from Perth on 23.1.87 & caught fire. Canx as destroyed 8.3.88.
G-BDAV	PA-23-250 Aztec C	27-2763	5B-CAH N5648Y	15. 4.75	To N64NC 3/93. Canx 5.3.93.
G-BDAW	Enstrom F-28A	223		8. 4.75	To G-RONT 3/87. Canx.
G-BDAX	PA-23-250 Aztec C	27-3494	5B-CAO N6399Y	15. 4.75	Canx as WFU 13.3.92. (Stored 11/95 Barry Technical College, Cardiff)
G-BDAY	Thunder Ax5-42A Plug HAFB	042		8. 4.75	
G-BDAZ	Thunder Ax7-77A HAFB	035		15. 4.75	To EC-DDF 7/78. Canx 10.4.78.
G-BDBA	Thunder Ax7-77 HAFB (Rebuilt using new canopy with c/n 200)	043		15. 4.75	To Italy in 9/84. Canx as WFU 10.9.84.
G-BDBB	Reims Cessna F.150M Commuter	1200		15. 4.75	Fatal crash at East Haddon on 7.6.80. Canx.
G-BDBC	PA-E23-250 Aztec D	27-4546	5N-AEM N13913	15. 4.75	To 4X-AJH 9/75. Canx 29.9.75.
G-BDBD	Wittman W.8 Tailwind	133	N1198S	25. 4.75	(Roaded out 2/97)
G-BDBE	Thunder Ax7-77A HAFB (Originally regd as Ax6-56A model, type amended 14.5.75)	036		15. 4.75	Canx as WFU 23.4.82.
G-BDBF	Clutton-Tabenor FRED Srs.II (Originally regd with c/n PFA/2263/9B)	PFA/1528		15. 4.75	
G-BDBG	Thunder Ax7-77A HAFB	038		15. 4.75	To PH-ARA 1/77. Canx 16.7.75.
G-BDBH	Bellanca 7GCBC Citabria	758-74	OE-AOL	15. 4.75	
G-BDBI	Cameron O-77 HAFB	162		15. 4.75	(Extant 4/93)
G-BDBJ	Cessna 182P Skylane II	182-63646	N4644K	18. 4.75	
G-BDBK	Cameron O-56 HAFB	129		18. 4.75	To (VH-HHL(2))/JA-A0021 4/76. Canx.
G-BDBL	DHC.1 Chipmunk 22 (Fuselage no. DHB/f/517)	C1/0633	WK621	12. 5.75	To ZK-UAS 11/94. Canx 5.9.94.
G-BDBM	Cameron O-56 HAFB	164		22. 4.75	Canx as WFU 18.6.82.
G-BDBN	DHC.1 Chipmunk 22 (Fuselage no. DHB/f/362)	C1/0494	WG420	23. 4.75	To ZS-JVS 5/76. Canx 18.5.76.
G-BDBO	Not allocated.				
G-BDBP	DHC.1 Chipmunk 22 (Fuselage no. DHB/f/620)	C1/0727	WP843	23. 4.75	
G-BDBR	Agusta-Bell 206B JetRanger II	8441		23. 4.75	To G-JERY 11/88. Canx.
G-BDBS	Short SD.3-30 UTT (Airframe originally laid down as SC.7 Skyvan c/n SH.1935)	SH3001	G-14-3001	21. 4.75	WFU. CofA expired 28.9.92. Canx as WFU 1.7.93. (Stored 4/96)
G-BDBT	Short SC.7 Skyvan 3M-400	SH1944	G-14-112	21. 4.75	To Royal AF of Oman as 916 in 6/75. Canx 30.6.75.
G-BDBU	Reims Cessna F.150M	1174		30. 4.75	(Damaged by gales at Prestwick on 26.12.98)

Regn	Type	c/n	Previous identity	Regn date	Fate or immediate subsequent identity (if known)
G-BDBV	Aero Jodel D.11A	V.3	D-EGIB	23. 4.75	
G-BDBW	Heinz Zenith 100 A18	PFA/24-10045		15. 4.75	Not completed. Canx by CAA 30.1.87.
G-BDBX	Evans VP-1	V.1086 & PFA/1567		23. 4.75	Permit expired 9.6.81 & WFU. Canx by CAA 3.4.89.
G-BDBY	Cameron O-77 HAFB	156		23. 4.75	To F-WRGP/F-BRGP 6/75. Canx 16.6.75.
G-BDBZ	Westland WS-55 Whirlwind ? (HAR.10) (Regd with c/n WA.386)	WA/62	XJ398 (XD768)	23. 4.75	Not converted for civil use. Canx by CAA 28.3.85. (Instructional Airframe 1/98 Kidlington)
G-BDCA	Socata MS.892E Rallye 150ST	2616		18. 4.75	Destroyed in a crash at Bradnich, northeast of Exeter on 19.9.90. Canx by CAA 30.12.96.
G-BDCB	DHC.1 Chipmunk 22 (Fuselage no. DHB/f/611)	C1/0718	(D-E...) G-BDCB/WP835	24. 4.75	To D-ERTY(2) 8/95. Canx 7.8.95.
G-BDCC	DHC.1 Chipmunk 22 (Fuselage no. DHB/f/141)	C1/0258	WD321	25. 4.75	
G-BDCD	Piper J3C65 Cub (L-4J-PI) (Frame No. 12257)	12429	OO-AVS 44-80133	28. 4.75	
G-BDCE	Reims Cessna F.172H	0704	PH-EHB	5. 5.75	
G-BDCF	Boeing-Stearman A75-N1 (PT-17) Kaydet	75-2385	N55720	5. 5.75	Failed to recover from a spin at Barton on 17.7.77. Canx.
G-BDCG	DHC.1 Chipmunk 22 (Fuselage no. DHB/f/623)	C1/0730	WP846	5. 5.75	To N125BB 7/75. Canx 7.7.75.
G-BDCH	DHC.1 Chipmunk 22 (Fuselage no. DHB/f/774)	C1/0884	WZ860	5. 5.75	To N124VH 7/75. Canx 7.7.75.
G-BDCI	Scanor Piel CP.301C Emeraude	503	F-BIRC	25. 4.75	
G-BDCJ	American Aviation AA-1B Trainer	AA1B-0547		5. 5.75	NTU - Canx 25.6.75 as Not Imported. To N1447R.
G-BDCK	American Aviation AA-5 Traveler	AA5-0772		5. 5.75	Damaged in a forced-landing near East Lothian on 3.7.90. (Current status unknown) Canx by CAA 30.12.96.
G-BDCL	American Aviation AA-5 Traveler	AA5-0773	EI-CCI G-BDCL/EI-BGV/G-BDCL/N1373R	5. 5.75	(Stored 11/95)
G-BDCM	Reims Cessna F.177RG Cardinal II	0120	OY-BIP	6. 5.75	Canx by CAA 8.10.92. To G-LYNS 30.11.92.
G-BDCN	Boeing 707-349C (Line no. 445)	18975	G-AWTK N322F	9. 5.75	To D2-TAC 10/77. Canx 28.10.77.
G-BDCO	Beagle B.121 Pup Srs.100	B121-171	G-35-171	6. 5.75	
G-BDCP	Agusta-Bell 206B JetRanger II	8462		8. 5.75	CofA expired 12.5.77 & WFU. Canx by CAA 29.2.84.
G-BDCR	Westland Commando Mk.2A (Line No. 128)	WA/828	G-17-20	14. 5.75	To Qatar AF as QA-20 in 10/75. Marks canx as WFU 4.11.75.
G-BDCS	Cessna 421B Golden Eagle II	421B-0832	N1931G	13. 5.75	
G-BDCT	PA-25-235 Pawnee C	25-4760	CS-AIV	16. 5.75	To OY-CYP. Canx 27.6.89.
G-BDCU	Cameron O-77 HAFB	126		11. 6.75	CofA expired 20.2.86. Canx by CAA 4.8.98.
G-BDCV	Armstrong-Whitworth 660 Argosy C.1	AW.6767	XP412	9. 5.76	WFU in 1/78. Broken up for spares in 1980 at East Midlands. Canx as WFU 2.2.78.
G-BDCW	Lockheed L.1011-385-1 Tristar 200	193U-1131	(A40-TC)	16. 1.76	To A40-TW 2/76. Canx 26.2.76.
G-BDCX	Lockheed L.1011-385-1 Tristar 200	193U-1133		16. 1.76	To A40-TX 4/76. Canx 2.4.76.
G-BDCY	Lockheed L.1011-385-1 Tristar 200	193U-1138		3. 6.76	To A40-TY 6/76. Canx 21.6.76.
G-BDCZ	Lockheed L.1011-385-1 Tristar 200	193U-1140		3. 6.76	To A40-TZ 8/76. Canx 6.8.76.
G-BDDA	Sikorsky S-61N Mk.II	61-746	ZS-RBU G-BDDA/ZS-RBU/G-BDDA/N91201/G-BDDA	9. 7.75	To EI-CNL 12/96. Canx 19.12.96.
G-BDDB	Practavia Pilot Sprite	1391		20. 5.75	Fatal crash in a field at Thorpe Willoughby, near Selby on 4.12.76. Canx.
G-BDDC	DHC.1 Chipmunk 22 (Fuselage no. DHB/f/194)	C1/0315	WD376	16. 5.75	To N99140 2/77. Canx 2.2.77.
G-BDDD	DHC.1 Chipmunk 22 (Fuselage no. DHB/f/210)	C1/0326	WD387	16. 5.75	
G-BDDE	Douglas DC-8F-54 (Line No. 195)	45684	N8783R (D-ACCB)/N8783R	18. 7.75	To HI-427 11/83. Canx 4.11.83.
G-BDDF	Wassmer Jodel D.120 Paris-Nice	97	F-BIKZ	20. 5.75	
G-BDDG	Dormois Jodel D.112	855	F-BILM	20. 5.75	
G-BDDH	Fokker F-27 Friendship 200	10289	LN-DAF I-ATIB/PH-FIG	27. 5.75	To AP-BCT 7/86. Canx 26.6.86.
G-BDDI	Lake LA-4-200 Buccaneer	680	N1087L	27. 5.75	To G-BWKS 11/79. Canx.
G-BDDJ	Phoenix Luton LA-4A Minor	DDJ.1		2. 6.75	Canx by CAA 2.9.91.
G-BDDK	BN-2A-9 Islander (Originally regd as BN-2A-27)	451		27. 5.75	To N21JA 7/75. Canx 2.12.75.
G-BDDL	BN-2A-21 Islander	452		27. 5.75	To RP-C2141 7/75. Canx 20.8.75.
G-BDDM	BN-2A-8 Islander (Originally regd as BN-2A-26)	454		27. 5.75	To F-OGHA 7/75. Canx 5.11.76.
G-BDDN	BN-2A-21 Islander	455		27. 5.75	To RP-C2142 2/77. Canx.
G-BDDO	BN-2A-21 Islander	456		27. 5.75	To RP-C2143 2/77. Canx.
G-BDDP	BN-2A-21 Islander	457		27. 5.75	To N29JA 9/75. Canx.
G-BDDR	BN-2A-21 Islander	458		27. 5.75	To RP-C2144 9/75. Canx.
G-BDDS	PA-25-260 Pawnee C	25-4757	CS-AIU	22. 5.75	
G-BDDT	PA-25-235 Pawnee C (Originally regd as a Srs.260, amended on 16.2.79)	25-5324	CS-AIX N8820L	22. 5.75	
G-BDDU	BN-2A-21 Islander	459		27. 5.75	To RP-C2145 9/75. Canx.
G-BDDV	BN-2A-26 Islander	461	SX-BFH G-BDDV	27. 5.75	To (OO-PCM)/OO-MPC. Canx 28.2.86.
G-BDDW	BN-2A-21 Islander	463		27. 5.75	To RP-2169 9/75. Canx 3.12.75.

Regn	Type	c/n	Previous identity	Regn date	Fate or immediate subsequent identity (if known)
G-BDDX	Whittaker MW.2B Excalibur	001 & PFA/41-10106		28. 5.75	WFU in 1976. (On display 9/97 Flambards Village Theme Park, Helston)
G-BDDY	Consolidated-Vultee Stinson 108-3 Voyager	108-3-4267	YV-T-XTH N6267M/NC6267M	28. 5.75	Canx 18.8.78 on sale to Australia. To VH-STN(2) 9/94.
G-BDDZ	Menavia Piel CP.301A Emeraude	253	F-BIMZ	30. 5.75	Badly damaged in heavy landing at Cranwell North on 3.6.84. Permit expired 20.6.84. (On rebuild)
G-BDEA	Boeing 707-338C (Line No. 630)	19296	VH-EBW	13. 5.75	To EL-AKH 8/92. Canx 26.8.92.
G-BDEB	Socata MS.880B Rallye 100ST	2551	F-OCZR	28. 5.75	Canx by CAA 28.3.85.
G-BDEC	Socata MS.880B Rallye 100ST	2552	F-OCZS	28. 5.75	
G-BDED	Socata MS.880B Rallye 100ST	2553	F-OCZT	28. 5.75	Crashed at Papa Westray, Orkney on 4.4.81. Canx.
G-BDEE	Westland-Bell 47G-3B1 (Line No. WAS/190)	WA/568	XV314	30. 5.75	To ZS-HGB 4/76. Canx 2.4.76.
G-BDEF	PA-34-200T Seneca II	34-7570150	N33695	2. 6.75	
G-BDEG	Socata MS.880B Rallye 100ST	2554	F-OCZU	28. 5.75	To G-JENS 3/80. Canx.
G-BDEH	Wassmer Jodel D.120A Paris-Nice	239	F-BLNE	2. 6.75	
G-BDEI	Jodel D.9 Bebe	585 & PFA/936		2. 6.75	
G-BDEJ	Aero Commander 112-200	0073	EI-AVR (N1073J)	4. 6.75	To CS-ASE. Canx 25.2.88.
G-BDEK	DHC.1 Chipmunk 22 (Fuselage no. DHB/f/83)	C1/0198	WB750	17. 6.75	To N65217 7/75. Canx 2.7.75.
G-BDEL	DHC.1 Chipmunk 22 (Fuselage no. DHB/f/77)	C1/0190	WB744	17. 6.75	To N65152 7/75. Canx 2.7.75.
G-BDEM	DHC.1 Chipmunk 22 (Fuselage no. DHB/f/428)	C1/0543	WK507	17. 6.75	To VH-SSJ 2/76. Canx 24.9.75.
G-BDEN	SIAI-Marchetti SF.260 Meteor	2-61	OO-HIX	11. 6.75	To N408FD 11/92. Canx 11.11.92.
G-BDEO	Reims Cessna F.150M	1207		11. 6.75	NTU - Not Imported. To F-BXNN 12/75. Canx 5.12.83.
G-BDEP	Reims Cessna F.172M	1330	(OY-BIB)	11. 6.75	NTU - Not Imported. To F-BXZT 2/76. Canx.
G-BDER	Auster AOP.9	AUS/10/12	WZ672	24. 6.75	To N803KB 2/86. Canx 6.1.86.
G-BDES	Sikorsky S-61N Mk.II	61-747		21. 7.75	Ditched in North Sea, 3 miles southwest of the 'Claymore A' oil platform and about 19 miles from Sumburgh on 10.11.88. Canx as destroyed 23.12.88.
G-BDET	DHC.1 Chipmunk 22 (Fuselage no. DHB/f/629)	C1/0736	(PH-RTH) G-BDET/WP851	17. 6.75	
G-BDEU	DHC.1 Chipmunk 22 (Fuselage no. DHB/f/598)	C1/0704	WP808	17. 6.75	
G-BDEV	Taylor JT.1 Monoplane (Believed constructed using parts from G-AVTX)	PFA/1442		12. 6.75	Crashed on landing at Holloway Farm, Shillingstone on 11.8.96. Canx as destroyed 15.10.96.
G-BDEW	Reims Cessna FRA.150M Aerobat	0278		12. 6.75	Crashed on landing near Compton Abbas on 13.8.96. Canx as TWFU 22.10.96.
G-BDEX	Reims Cessna FRA.150M Aerobat	0279		12. 6.75	(Nosewheel collapsed on landing at Compton Abbas on 5.1.99)
G-BDEY	Piper J3C-65 Cub (L-4J-PI) (Frame No. 12366)	12538	OO-AAT OO-GAC/44-80242	17. 6.75	
	(OO-AAT was a composite aircraft comprising rebuild of c/n 11529 43-30248 OO-PAX and c/n 12538 44-80242 OO-GAC using parts of 11529 and fuselage number 12366 (ie c/n 12538))				
G-BDEZ	Piper J3C-65 Cub (L-4J-PI) (Frame No. 12211)	12383	OO-SOC OO-EPI/44-80087	17. 6.75	
	(Composite aircraft comprising rebuild of c/n 10418 43-29127 OO-SOC and c/n 12383 44-80087 OO-EPI using parts of c/n 10418 and fuselage of c/n 12383 became OO-SOC)				
G-BDFA	Not allocated.				
G-BDFB	Phoenix Currie Wot	PFA/3008		20. 6.75	
G-BDFC	Rockwell Commander 112A	0273	N1273J	17. 6.75	
G-BDFD	Agusta-Bell 206B JetRanger II	8463		18. 6.75	To F-BXPA 7/75. Canx 22.7.75.
G-BDFE	Handley Page HPR.7 Dart Herald 206	167	CF-EPC VP-BCG/CF-EPC	19. 6.75	Sold as 9Q-CAA in 3/84. Canx by CAA 4.2.87.
G-BDFF	Airborne Designs Supermarine S.5 Replica	ADB.1 & HD.001		13. 6.75	Fatal crash into the sea at Mylor, Cornwall on 23.5.87 after apparently breaking up in mid-air. Canx as WFU 15.1.92.
G-BDFG	Cameron O-65 HAFB	179		24. 6.75	
G-BDFH	Auster AOP.9 (Frame no. AUS 177 FM)	B5/10/176	XR240	24. 6.75	
G-BDFI	Reims Cessna F.150M	1201	(OH-CGD)	25. 6.75	To G-WAFC 5/95. Canx.
G-BDFJ	Reims Cessna F.150M	1182		25. 6.75	
G-BDFK	Cessna 414	0623	N69686	30. 6.75	To N91045 9/81. Canx 1.9.81.
G-BDFL	PA-28R-200 Cherokee Arrow II	28R-7535159	N33740 N9612N	27. 6.75	Crashed on landing at Newcastle on 18.2.91. Canx.
G-BDFM	Caudron C.270 Luciole	6607/32	F-BBPT French AF/F-ALVO	2. 7.75	To F-AZVO. Canx 16.4.99.
G-BDFN	PA-31-350 Navajo Chieftain	31-7405148	EI-BKI G-BDFN/5Y-ASI	7. 7.75	To SE-IKV 5/83. Canx 12.5.83.
G-BDFO	Hiller UH-12E	2290	XS703	7. 7.75	CofA expired 1.4.84 and later used for spares or stored at Chilbolton. Canx as WFU 20.11.90.
G-BDFP	Hughes 369HS (500C)	45-0728S		8. 7.75	To G-OAIM 7/82. Canx.
G-BDFR	Fuji FA.200-160 Aero Subaru	FA200-262		7. 7.75	
G-BDFS	Fuji FA.200-160 Aero Subaru	FA200-263		7. 7.75	
G-BDFT	Vickers 668 Varsity T.1	620	WJ897	8. 7.75	Destroyed in fatal crash at Marchington on 19.8.84. Canx as destroyed 1.7.85.
G-BDFU	PMPS Dragonfly MPA Mk.1	01		14. 7.75	Canx as WFU 5.12.83. (On loan to Museum of Flight/Royal Museum of Scotland) (On display 3/96)
G-BDFV	American Aviation AA-5 Traveler	AA5-0805		10. 7.75	To G-OBMW 7/79. Canx.

Regn	Type	c/n	Previous identity	Regn date	Fate or immediate subsequent identity (if known)
G-BDFW	Rockwell Commander 112A	308	N1308J	18. 6.75	
G-BDFX	Taylorcraft Auster 5	2060	F-BGXG	9. 7.75	Badly damaged on landing at Oaksey Park on 10.10.93.
			TW517		CofA expired 3.6.94. (Stored 8/98 Kemble)
G-BDFY	American Aviation AA-5 Traveler			10. 7.75	
		AA5 0806			
G-BDFZ	Reims Cessna F.150M Commuter	1184	(D-EIWB)	14. 7.75	
			(F-BXIH)		
G-BDGA	Bushby-Long Midget Mustang	PFA/1327		23. 7.75	No Permit to Fly issued. Canx by CAA 24.1.96.
G-BDGB	Barritault JB-01 Minicab	PFA/1819		23. 6.75	
G-BDGC	BN-2A Mk.III-2 Trislander	1012		7. 7.75	To 6Y-JJI 12/75. Canx 15.12.75.
G-BDGD	BN-2A Mk.III-2 Trislander	1013		7. 7.75	To (N94JA)/F-OGGS 12/75. Canx 19.11.76.
G-BDGE	BN-2A Mk.III-2 Trislander	1014		7. 7.75	To EL-AIC 12/75. Canx 7.1.76.
G-BDGF	BN-2A Mk.III-2 Trislander	1015		7. 7.75	To EL-AID 12/75. Canx 7.1.76.
G-BDGG	BN-2A Mk.III-2 Trislander	1016	C-GSAA	7. 7.75	To G-JOEY 11/81. Canx.
			G-BDGG		
G-BDGH	Thunder Ax7-77 HAFB	049		16. 7.75	(Extant 2/97)
	(Officially regd as Ax6-56)				
G-BDGI	Thunder Ax6-56A HAFB	044		16. 7.75	To TF-HOT 5/76. Canx 7.5.76.
G-BDGJ	Cameron O-56 HAFB	159		17. 7.75	Canx 29.10.86 on sale to Australia. To JA-A0020.
G-BDGK	Beechcraft D-17S Traveller	4920	HB-UIU	25. 7.75	To SE-BRY. Canx 16.5.90.
	(UC-43-BH)		SE-BRY/FZ430/43-10872		
G-BDGL	Cessna U.206 Super Skywagon		N2156F	29. 7.75	Destroyed when it crashed into woods near Wimborne on
		206-0356			8.9.85. Canx as destroyed 17.10.86.
G-BDGM	PA-28-151 Cherokee Warrior		N41307	30. 7.75	To N37975 /84. Canx.
		28-7415165			
G-BDGN	American Aviation AA-5B Tiger		N6147A	8. 8.75	Reserved as F-GKGN in 1996. Canx 31.5.96.
		AA5B-0089			
G-BDGO	Thunder Ax7-77 HAFB	048		16. 7.75	
G-BDGP(1)	CAB GY-30 Supercab	02	F-BBIP(2)	. .75R	NTU - Remained as F-BBIP(2). Canx.
G-BDGP(2)	Clay Cherub	-		. .	NTU - Preserved. Canx.
G-BDGP(3)	Cameron V-65 HAFB	658	(N.....)	2. 9.80	
			G-BDGP		
G-BDGR	DHC.1 Chipmunk 22	C1/0574	WK557	1. 8.75	To N19548 7/75. Canx.
	(Fuselage no. DHB/f/459)				
G-BDGS	Westland Commando Mk.2	WA/806	G-17-16	1. 8.75	To Egyptian AF as WA806/723. Marks canx as WFU 4.11.75.
	(Line No. 129)				
G-BDGT	Westland Commando Mk.2	WA/808	G-17-21	1. 8.75	To Egyptian AF as WA808/724. Marks canx as WFU 4.11.75.
	(Line No. 131)				
G-BDGU	Westland Commando Mk.2	WA/809	G-17-23	1. 8.75	To Egyptian AF as WA809/727. Marks canx as WFU 4.11.75.
	(Line No. 135)				
G-BDGV	Westland Commando Mk.2	WA/810	G-17-24	1. 8.75	To Egyptian AF as WA810/728. Marks canx as WFU 4.11.75.
	(Line No. 136)				
G-BDGW	Westland Commando Mk.2	WA/811	G-17-27	1. 8.75	To Egyptian AF as WA811/729. Marks canx as WFU 4.11.75.
	(Line No. 138)				
G-BDGX	Scheibe SF-25E Super Falke	4306		4. 8.75	Crashed at Husbands Bosworth on 28.12.79. Canx.
G-BDGY	PA-28-140 Cherokee	28-23613	N3536K	5. 8.75	
G-BDGZ	American Aviation AA-5B Tiger			8. 8.75	To ZS-KRO 5/80. Canx 19.5.80.
		AA5B-0090			
G-BDHA	Douglas DC-8-54F	45667	N8782R	25. 2.76	To HI-426 11/83. Canx 11.11.83.
	(Line No. 185)		(D-ACCA)/N8782R		
G-BDHB	Isaacs Fury II	PFA/1372		25. 7.75	No Permit issued. Canx by CAA 8.7.91.
G-BDHC	DHC.6-310 Twin Otter	414		10. 4.74	To N38535 8/83. Canx 11.8.83.
G-BDHD	DH.104 Riley Dove 2	04349	ZS-RML	6. 8.75	To N46870 4/77. Canx 22.4.77.
			N1516V		
G-BDHE	BN-2A-21 Islander	465		11. 8.75	To N21JA 10/75. Canx 20.10.75.
G-BDHF	BN-2A-21 Islander	467		11. 8.75	To N98JA 10/75. Canx 20.10.75.
G-BDHG	BN-2B-21 Islander	468		11. 8.75	To B-02/OTA-LB Belgium Army 5/76. Canx 19.11.76.
G-BDHH	BN-2A-21 Islander	469		11. 8.75	To RP-C850 10/75. Canx 3.12.75.
G-BDHI	BN-2A-8 Islander	470		11. 8.75	To N99JA 11/75. Canx 14.11.75.
	(Originally regd as BN-2A-26)				
G-BDHJ	Pazmany PL-1 Laminar	PFA/3604		5. 8.75	Permit expired 5.11.97. (Wings only at Bodmin 5/98)
	(Originally regd as Jones-Pazmany PL-1)				
G-BDHK	Piper J3C-65 Cub (L-4A-PI)	8969	F-PHFZ	24. 7.75	
	(Frame No. 9068)		42-38400		
	(Official c/n quoted as 261 and p.i. of 42-36414; latter is c/n 8538/N75366)				
G-BDHL	PA-E23-250 Aztec E	27-7405460	N54180	1. 8.75	Force landed in a field at Delamere on 2.8.93.
					Canx as destroyed 6.1.94.
G-BDHM	K & S SA.102.5 Cavalier			8. 8.75	No Permit to Fly issued - probably not completed.
		M.01 & PFA/01-10133			Canx by CAA 9.5.90.
G-BDHN	IRMA BN-2A-8 Islander	761		11. 8.75	To VH-TXC 1/76. Canx 29.1.76.
	(Originally regd as BN-2A-6)				
G-BDHO	IRMA BN-2A-20 Islander	762		11. 8.75	Canx 4.3.76 on sale to Australia. To P2-HAC 2/76.
	(Originally regd as BN-2A-6)				
G-BDHP	IRMA BN-2A-26 Islander	763		11. 8.75	To VH-TXF 1/76. Canx 18.2.76.
	(Originally regd as BN-2A-6)				
G-BDHR	IRMA BN-2A-9 Islander	764		11. 8.75	To TR-LWL 8/76. Canx.
	(Originally regd as BN-2A-6)				
G-BDHS	IRMA BN-2A-21 Islander	765		11. 8.75	To Mauritanian AF as 5T-MAT 4/76. Canx 3.11.76.
	(Originally regd as BN-2A-6)				
G-BDHT	IRMA BN-2A-20 Islander	766		11. 8.75	To TI-AKC 9/76. Canx 3.11.76.
	(Originally regd as BN-2A-6)				
G-BDHU	IRMA BN-2A-26 Islander	767		11. 8.75	To 9L-LAV 7/81. Canx 5.6.81.
	(Originally regd as BN-2A-6)				

Regn	Type	c/n	Previous identity	Regn date	Fate or immediate subsequent identity (if known)
G-BDHV	IRMA BN-2A-21 Islander (Originally regd as BN-2A-6)	768		11. 8.75	To VH-TXG 6/76. Canx 29.4.76.
G-BDHW	IRMA BN-2A-20 Islander (Originally regd as BN-2A-6)	769		11. 8.75	To VH-SYU 8/76. Canx 9.4.76.
G-BDHX	IRMA BN-2A-20 Islander (Originally regd as BN-2A-6)	770		11. 8.75	To TI-AKD 9/76. Canx 3.11.76.
G-BDHY	Westland-Bell 47G-3B1 (Line No. WAS/191)	WA/569	XV315	11. 8.75	To ZS-HFJ 1/76. Canx 5.2.76.
G-BDHZ	Westland-Bell 47G-3B1 (Line No. WAS/211)	WA/574	XV320	11. 8.75	To ZS-HFI 2/76. Canx 5.2.76.
G-BDIA	Westland-Bell 47G-3B1 (Line No. WAS/181)	WA/565	XV311	11. 8.75	To ZS-HGV 2/77. Canx 13.8.85.
G-BDIB	Enstrom 280C-UK-2 Shark	1017		12. 8.75	To G-LONS 8/81. Canx.
G-BDIC	DHC.1 Chipmunk 22 (Fuselage no. DHB/f/211)	C1/0328	WD388	14. 8.75	To D-EPAK 9/96. Canx 19.8.96.
G-BDID	DHC.1 Chipmunk 22 (Fuselage no. DHB/f/466)	C1/0583	WK564	15. 8.75	Spun in and burst into flames on approach to Husbands Bosworth on 22.9.87. Canx as destroyed 8.3.88.
G-BDIE	Rockwell Commander 112A	342	N1342J	14. 8.75	
G-BDIF	DH.106 Comet 4C	6463	ST-AAX (XA-NAE)	21. 8.75	WFU at Lasham 8.11.79. Broken up in 10/80. Canx.
G-BDIG	Cessna 182P Skylane II (Reims-assembled with c/n 0020)	182-63938	N9877E	26. 8.75	
G-BDIH	SAN Jodel D.117 (Regd with incorrect c/n 817)	812	F-BIOT	22. 8.75	Struck hedges in heavy landing at Rydinghurst Farm, Cranleigh on 9.12.84. Permit to Fly expired 4.7.85. (On rebuild)
G-BDII	Sikorsky S-61N Mk.II	61-750	9M-ELF G-BDII	24. 9.75	Ditched in the sea 3 miles off Handa Island on 17.10.88 and sank. Canx as destroyed 19.1.89.
G-BDIJ	Sikorsky S-61N Mk.II	61-751	9M-AYF G-BDIJ	3.10.75	
G-BDIK	Vickers 708 Viscount	37	F-BGNT	28. 8.75	WFU & stored in 10/76. Broken up in 1979 at East Midlands Airport. Canx.
G-BDIL	Bell 212	30715	N8064Z G-BDIL/N18090	26. 8.75	Crashed in the North Sea, 14 miles northeast of the Murchison Platform, off Shetland on 14.9.82. Canx as destroyed 5.12.83.
G-BDIM	DHC.1 Chipmunk 22 (Fuselage no. DHB/f/313)	C1/0459	WG363	2.12.75	Damaged 14.7.96 at Duxford when struck by debris from fatal crash of P-38J NX3145X. Canx as destroyed 14.11.97.
G-BDIN	Scottish Avn Bulldog Srs.120/125	BH120/377		20. 8.75	To JY-BAI 4/76. Canx 13.4.76.
G-BDIO	Scottish Avn Bulldog Srs.120/125	BH120/378		20. 8.75	To JY-BAH 4/76. Canx 13.4.76.
G-BDIP	Scottish Avn Bulldog Srs.120/125	BH120/378		20. 8.75	To JY-BAJ 4/76. Canx 28.4.76.
G-BDIR	Scottish Avn Bulldog Srs.120/125	BH120/380		20. 8.75	To JY-BAK 4/76. Canx 28.4.76.
G-BDIS	Scottish Avn Bulldog Srs.120/125	BH120/382		20. 8.75	To JY-BAL 4/76. Canx 28.4.76.
G-BDIT	DH.106 Comet 4	6467	XR395	1. 9.75	Broken up Blackbushe 7/84. Canx.
G-BDIU	DH.106 Comet 4	6468	XR396	1. 9.75	Broken up Bitteswell 7/81 as 8882M. Canx. (Nose section to RAF Kinloss)
G-BDIV	DH.106 Comet 4	6469	XR397	1. 9.75	CofA expired 15.3.80 & WFU. Broken up Lasham 7/85. Canx as WFU 5.3.87.
G-BDIW	DH.106 Comet 4C	6470	XR398	1. 9.75	CofA expired 8.6.81. (On display 1981 at Dusseldorf, Germany, later Flugausstellung L & P Junior Museum, Hermeskeil, Germany 4/99)
G-BDIX	DH.106 Comet 4C	6471	XR399	1. 9.75	CofA expired 11.10.81. (On display 3/96 East Fortune)
G-BDIY	Phoenix Luton LA-4A Minor	PFA/837		3. 9.75	Canx by CAA 2.9.91.
G-BDIZ	BN-2A-20 Islander (Originally regd as BN-2A-21)	464		2. 9.75	Canx 9.1.76 on sale to USA. To HP-768 10/75.
G-BDJA	BN-2A-21 Islander	466		2. 9.75	To B-01/OTA-LA Belgium Army 6/76. Canx 3.11.76.
G-BDJB	Taylor JT.1 Monoplane Srs.2	JB-JT.1-001 & PFA/1428		2. 9.75	Damaged when yawed into cornfield at Andrewsfield on 25.5.78. (On rebuild with VW1835) Canx by CAA 2.3.99.
G-BDJC	AJEP/Wittman W.8 Tailwind	387AW & PFA/3508		29. 8.75	
G-BDJD	Jodel D.112	PFA/910		3. 9.75	
G-BDJE	HS.125 Srs.600B	256052	G-5-11	2. 9.75	To G-BKBH 4/82. Canx.
G-BDJF	White-Bensen B.8MV Gyrocopter	RPW.1 & G/01-1075		4. 9.75	
G-BDJG	Phoenix Luton LA-4A Minor	PFA/828		3. 9.75	
G-BDJH	Reims Cessna F.182P Skylane (Wichita c/n 182-69346)	0022	N9885E	17. 9.75	NTU - Canx 5.4.76 as Not Imported. To F-BOFF.
G-BDJI	Westland Commando Mk.2 (Line No. 139)	WA/812	G-17-28	19. 9.75	To Egyptian AF as WA812/730. Marks canx as WFU 22.12.75.
G-BDJJ	Westland Commando Mk.2 (Line No. 141)	WA/813	G-17-30	19. 9.75	To Egyptian AF as WA813/731. Marks canx as WFU 22.12.75.
G-BDJK	Westland Commando Mk.2 (Line No. 143)	WA/814	G-17-31	19. 9.75	To Egyptian AF as WA814/732. Marks canx as WFU 22.12.75.
G-BDJL	Westland Commando Mk.2 (Line No. 144)	WA/815	G-17-33	19. 9.75	To Egyptian AF as WA815/733. Marks canx as WFU 22.12.75.
G-BDJM	Westland Commando Mk.2 (Line No. 145)	WA/816	G-17-34	19. 9.75	To Egyptian AF as WA816/734. Marks canx as WFU 22.12.75.
G-BDJN	Robin HR.200/100 Club	76		22. 9.75	
G-BDJO	DHC.1 Chipmunk 22 (Fuselage no. DHB/f/701)	C1/0795	WP919	26. 9.75	To VH-AFL 2/76. Canx 22.12.75.

Regn	Type	c/n	Previous identity	Regn date	Fate or immediate subsequent identity (if known)
G-BDJP	Piper J3C-65 Cub (Frame No. 21017)	22992	OO-SKZ PH-NCV/NC3908K	11.12.75	
G-BDJR	SNCAN NC.858S Chardonneret	2	F-BFIY	30. 9.75	Permit expired 23.5.92. (On rebuild 10/97)
G-BDJS	BN-2A-26 Islander	472		29. 9.75	To F-BVOE/EI-BBR 3/76. Canx 1.4.76.
G-BDJT	BN-2A-21 Islander	474	"G-BCJT"	29. 9.75	To N561JA 12/76. Canx 10.11.76.
G-BDJU	BN-2A-26 Islander	475		29. 9.75	To C-GIHF 2/76. Canx 17.2.76.
G-BDJV	BN-2B-21 Islander	476		29. 9.75	To B-03/OTA-LC Belgium Army 6/76. Canx 3.11.76.
G-BDJW	BN-2A-21 Islander	477		29. 9.75	To IN-126 Indian Navy 5/76. Canx 18.11.76.
G-BDJX	BN-2A-27 Islander (Originally regd as BN-2A-21)	478		29. 9.75	To 8R-GER 12/75. Canx 9.1.76.
G-BDJY	BN-2A-27 Islander	479		29. 9.75	To N4990M 9/78. Canx 5.9.78.
G-BDJZ	BN-2A-21 Islander	480		29. 9.75	To IN-127 Indian Navy 5/76. Canx 18.11.76.
G-BDKA	Morane Saulnier MS.892E Rallye 150ST	2630		30. 9.75	Fatal crash in fog 500 yards north of Cap Gris Nez, France on 21.6.76. Canx.
G-BDKB	Morane Saulnier MS.892E Rallye 150ST	2631		30. 9.75	Struck cables near Coleraine on 5.7.81 & crashed in river. (On rebuild 6/90 near Stranraer) Canx by CAA 18.2.99.
G-BDKC	Cessna A.185F Skywagon	185-02569	N1854R	30. 9.75	
G-BDKD	Enstrom F-28A	319		30. 9.75	
G-BDKE	Boeing 707-338C (Line No. 671)	19623	VH-EAC	8.10.75	Restored as VH-EAC 1/76. Canx 2.1.76.
G-BDKF	HS.125 Srs.403B	25242	VH-TOM G-5-20	2.10.75	To 3D-ABZ 12/75. Canx 16.12.75.
G-BDKG	Beechcraft 65-A80 Queen Air	LD-194	D-ILBI	14.10.75	Undercarriage collapsed on landing at Karachi, Pakistan on 8.7.79. Canx as destroyed 5.12.83.
G-BDKH	Menavia Piel CP.301A Emeraude	241	F-BIMN	15.10.75	
G-BDKI	Sikorsky S-61N Mk.II	61-755	N9118Y G-BDKI	13. 1.76	To N219AC 1/95. Canx 12.12.94.
G-BDKJ	K & S SA.102.5 Cavalier	72207 & PFA/1589		14.10.75	Damaged on landing Staverton in test flight on 14.9.97.
G-BDKK	Bede BD-5B	PFA/14-10021		14.10.75	No Permit to Fly issued. Canx by CAA 4.4.86.
G-BDKL	Hughes 369HM (500)	49-0036M	EI-ATY	20.10.75	To G-VNPP 3/83. Canx.
G-BDKM	SIPA 903	98	F-BGHX	17.11.75	
G-BDKN	BN-2A Mk.III-2 Trislander	1017		16.10.75	To PK-KTC 6/76. Canx 18.6.76.
G-BDKO	BN-2A Mk.III-2 Trislander	1018		16.10.75	To PK-KTD 8/76. Canx 10.8.76.
G-BDKP	BN-2A Mk.III-2 Trislander	1019		16.10.75	To HK-1704 5/76. Canx.
G-BDKR	BN-2A Mk.III-2 Trislander	1020		16.10.75	To N26877 7/82. Canx 5.7.82.
G-BDKS	Aerotek Pitts S-2A Special	2112		20.10.75	To G-ODAH 3/87. Canx.
G-BDKT	Cameron O-84 HAFB	167		21.10.75	To F-GCZU 9/82. Canx 19.7.82.
G-BDKU	Taylor JT.1 Monoplane (Possibly incorporates PFA/55-10301)	PFA/1456		22.10.75	
G-BDKV	PA-28R-200 Cherokee Arrow II	28R-7335297	EI-AYE (G-BBEH)/N55837	29.10.75	Ditched at Elmer Sands, near Bognor Regis on 27.3.94. Canx as destroyed 25.5.94.
G-BDKW	Rockwell Commander 112A	106	N1277J ZS-MIB/N1106J	3.11.75	
G-BDKX	BN-2A-21 Islander	481		3.11.75	To IN-128 Indian Navy 6/76. Canx 18.11.76.
G-BDKY	BN-2A-27 Islander	482		3.11.75	To 8R-GES 12/75. Canx 9.1.76.
G-BDKZ	Vickers 838 Viscount	372	(PK-RVO) G-BDKZ/9G-AAW	3.11.75	To SE-FOZ 8/76. Canx.
G-BDLA	Westland Commando Mk.2 (Line No. 146)	WA/817	G-17-35	24.10.75	To Egyptian AF as WA817/735. Canx 11.3.76.
G-BDLB	Westland Commando Mk.2 (Line No. 147)	WA/818	G-17-36	24.10.75	To Egyptian AF as WA818/736. Canx 11.3.76.
G-BDLC	Westland Commando Mk.2 (Line No. 148)	WA/819	G-17-37	24.10.75	To Egyptian AF as WA819/737. Canx 11.3.76.
G-BDLD	Westland Commando Mk.2 (Line No. 149)	WA/820	G-17-38	24.10.75	To Egyptian AF as WA820/738. Canx 11.3.76.
G-BDLE	Westland Commando Mk.2 (Line No. 150)	WA/821	G-17-39	24.10.75	To Egyptian AF as WA821/739. Canx 11.3.76.
G-BDLF	BN-2A-21 Islander	483		3.11.75	To F-OCXP 9/76. Canx 12.8.76.
G-BDLG	BN-2A-27 Islander	484		3.11.75	To 8R-GET 3/76. Canx 17.11.76.
G-BDLH	BN-2A-27 Islander	486		3.11.75	To XA-GAZ 3/76. Canx 19.11.76.
G-BDLI	BN-2A-21 Islander	488		3.11.75	To PT-KSJ 7/76. Canx 17.11.76.
G-BDLJ	BN-2A-21 Islander	489		3.11.75	To F-GAJA 7/76. Canx.
G-BDLK	BN-2A-20 Islander	490		3.11.75	To XA-GUT 7/76. Canx 24.8.77.
G-BDLL	BN-2A-27 Islander	491		3.11.75	To PT-KTP 4/76. Canx 13.4.76.
G-BDLM	Boeing 707-338C (Line No. 737)	19629	VH-EAI	8.11.75	To C-GGAB 1/82. Canx 29.12.81.
G-BDLN	BN-2A-21 Islander	492		3.11.75	To 7Q-YAZ 10/76. Canx 3.11.76.
G-BDLO	American Aviation AA-5A Cheetah	AA5A-0026	N6154A	3.11.75	
G-BDLP	Thunder Ax8-105 HAFB	058		28.10.75	To OE-DZH 5/77. Canx 20.5.77.
G-BDLR	American Aviation AA-5B Tiger	AA5B-0128		3.11.75	Destroyed when caught by crosswind on landing at Luton on 18.9.99 & collided with SD.3-30 G-SSWU.
G-BDLS	American Aviation AA-1B Trainer 2	AA1B-0564	N6153A	3.11.75	
G-BDLT	Rockwell Commander 112A	363	N1363J	4.11.75	
G-BDLU	Thunder Ax7-77 HAFB	052		5.11.75	To VH-OUR /92. Canx 6.2.76.
G-BDLV	Chilton DW.1A	DW1A/2		12.11.75	Not completed. Canx as WFU 7.9.84.
G-BDLW	Schweizer Grumman G-164A Agcat	1368	N8850H	7.11.75	To TS-ACJ 4/76. Canx 18.3.76.
G-BDLX	Scottish Aviation Twin Pioneer Srs.3	512	LN-BFO OE-BHV/(VH-...)	13.11.75	No UK CofA issued. Scrapped at Staverton in 9/80. Canx as WFU 5.12.83.
G-BDLY	K & S SA.102.5 Cavalier	PFA/01-10011		14.11.75	

Regn	Type	c/n	Previous identity	Regn date	Fate or immediate subsequent identity (if known)
G-BDLZ	Bristol 175 Britannia Srs.253F	13435	XM490	17.11.75	CofA expired 11.12.78 & WFU. Broken up in 9/79 at Luton. Canx.
G-BDMA	Short SD.3-30 Var.100 (Airframe possibly originally laid down as SC.7 Skyvan c/n SH.1936)	SH3002	G-14-3002	19.11.75	To (N335GW)/N330US 6/78. Canx 22.6.78.
G-BDMB	Robin HR.100/210 Safari	208		13.11.75	Damaged in forced landing ½ mile short of Exeter airport on 27.5.94. Canx as destroyed 23.6.94.
G-BDMC	MBB Bo.105D	S.135	D-HDEC	18.11.75	To VH-LSA. Canx 12.5.86.
G-BDMD	PA-31-350 Navajo Chieftain	31-7305119	N608HR (N74968)	18.11.75	To PH-GYN 9/82. Canx 2.9.82.
G-BDME	Robin DR.400/140B Earl	1090		25.11.75	To G-YOGI 10/86. Canx.
G-BDMF	Gulfstream G.1159 Gulfstream II	103	N801GA N855GA	17.12.75	To N833GA 5/80. Canx 20.5.80.
G-BDMG	Westland Sea King Mk.47 (Line No. 122)	WA/822	G-17-15	1.12.75	To Egyptian AF as WA822/774. Canx 18.6.76.
G-BDMH	Westland Sea King Mk.47 (Line No. 127)	WA/823	G-17-17	1.12.75	To Egyptian AF as WA823/773. Canx 11.3.76.
G-BDMI	Westland Sea King Mk.47 (Line No. 133)	WA/824	G-17-22	1.12.75	To Egyptian AF as WA824/775. Canx 18.6.76.
G-BDMJ	Westland Sea King Mk.47 (Line No. 134)	WA/825	G-17-25	1.12.75	To Egyptian AF as WA825/776. Canx 18.6.76.
G-BDMK	Westland Sea King Mk.47 (Line No. 137)	WA/826	G-17-29	1.12.75	To Egyptian AF as WA826/771. Canx 11.3.76.
G-BDML	Westland Sea King Mk.47 (Line No. 140)	WA/827	G-17-32	1.12.75	To Egyptian AF as WA827/772. Canx 11.3.76.
G-BDMM	Jodel D.11	PFA/901		5.11.75	(Stored unfinished 4/97) Canx by CAA 27.1.97.
G-BDMN	Cessna 337 Super Skymaster	337-0118	ZS-EDF N2218X	8. 1.76	To I-EMCO 12/78. Canx 15.1.79.
G-BDMO	Thunder Ax7-77A HAFB	053	(EC-...) G-BDMO	25.11.75	Canx as WFU 8.3.95. To Spain with no regn issued - WFU.
G-BDMP	PA-25-235 Pawnee	25-2057	OE-AGH 4X-API	16. 1.76	DBF in crash while crop spraying at Fenton Newmans Farm, near Drem, East Lothian on 20.6.77. Canx.
G-BDMR	IRMA BN-2A-9 Islander (Originally regd as BN-2A-6)	771		8.12.75	To TR-LWI 8/76. Canx 18.11.76.
G-BDMS	Piper J3C-65 Cub (L-4J-PI)	13049	F-BEGZ 44-80753	4.11.75	
G-BDMT	IRMA BN-2A-21 Islander (Originally regd as BN-2A-6)	772		8.12.75	To OA-4/Z2 Botswana DF 4/79. Canx 21.5.79.
G-BDMU	IRMA BN-2A-9 Islander (Originally regd as BN-2A-6)	773		8.12.75	To TR-LWO 1/77. Canx 18.7.77.
G-BDMV	IRMA BN-2A-21 Islander (Originally regd as BN-2A-6)	774		8.12.75	To ZS-JXT 8/76. Canx 2.9.76.
G-BDMW	SAN Jodel DR.100A Ambassadeur	79	F-BIVM	2.12.75	
G-BDMX	IRMA BN-2A-27 Islander (Originally regd as BN-2A-6)	775		8.12.75	To YR-BNH 10/76. Canx 25.7.77.
G-BDMY	IRMA BN-2A-27 Islander (Originally regd as BN-2A-6)	776		8.12.75	To YR-BNI 10/76. Canx 25.7.77.
G-BDMZ	IRMA BN-2A-27 Islander (Originally regd as BN-2A-6)	777		8.12.75	To YR-BNJ 10/76. Canx 25.7.77.
G-BDNA	IRMA BN-2A-27 Islander (Originally regd as BN-2A-6)	778		8.12.75	To YR-BNK 11/76. Canx 25.7.77.
G-BDNB	IRMA BN-2A-27 Islander (Originally regd as BN-2A-6)	779		8.12.75	To YR-BNE 12/76. Canx 25.8.77.
G-BDNC	Taylor JT.1 Monoplane	PFA/1454		8.12.75	
G-BDND	IRMA BN-2A-21 Islander (Originally regd as BN-2A-6)	780		8.12.75	To N99358 9/76. Canx 8.3.77.
G-BDNE	Harker Hawk	PFA/03-10004		9.12.75	Damaged in taxiing trials. (Stored Tattershall Thorpe) Canx 18.4.83.
G-BDNF	Bensen B.8M Gyroplane	WC/1		11.12.75	No Permit believed issued. Canx by CAA 20.6.91.
G-BDNG	Taylor JT.1 Monoplane	PFA/1405		12.12.75	
G-BDNH	Westland Sea King Mk.48 (Line No. 142)	WA/831	G-17-1	16.12.75	To Belgium AF as RS-01 in 7/76. Canx 6.7.76.
G-BDNI	Westland Sea King Mk.48 (Line No. 153)	WA/832	G-17-2	16.12.75	To Belgium AF as RS-02 in 7/76. Canx 6.7.76.
G-BDNJ	Westland Sea King Mk.48 (Line No. 154)	WA/833	G-17-3	16.12.75	To Belgium AF as RS-03 in 7/76. Canx 6.7.76.
G-BDNK	Westland Sea King Mk.48 (Line No. 155)	WA/834	G-17-4	16.12.75	To Belgium AF as RS-04 in 7/76. Canx 25.6.76.
G-BDNL	Westland Sea King Mk.48 (Line No. 157)	WA/835	G-17-5	16.12.75	To Belgium AF as RS-05 in 7/76. Canx 6.7.76.
G-BDNM	BN-2A-27 Islander	493		23.12.75	To PT-KTQ 4/76. Canx 13.4.76.
G-BDNN	BN-2A-27 Islander	495		23.12.75	To PT-KTR 4/76. Canx 13.4.76.
G-BDNO	Taylor JT.1 Monoplane	PFA/1431		15.12.75	Permit expired 2.5.96. (Stored 9/97 Bodmin)
G-BDNP	BN-2A-21 Islander	496		23.12.75	Force landed with engine failure 2 miles NE of Guernsey Airport & badly damaged on 18.9.81. Canx.
G-BDNR	Reims Cessna FRA.150M Aerobat	0284		18.12.75	Damaged in taxying accident at Speke on 22.1.92. Canx by CAA 14.10.96. (On rebuild 5/98 at Sibson)
G-BDNS	Saro Skeeter AOP.12 (Composite aircraft XM529/7979M boom and XM556/7870M body)	S2/5105	7979M XM529	2. 1.76	(Last reported as stored at Handforth) Canx by CAA 8.8.85.
G-BDNT	Jodel D.92 (built by J.Siry)	397	F-PINL	2. 1.76	
G-BDNU	Reims Cessna F.172M Skyhawk II	1405		2. 1.76	
G-BDNV	Cameron O-56 HAFB	193		6. 1.76	To ZS-HGJ 6/78. Canx 6.10.76.

Regn	Type	c/n	Previous identity	Regn date	Fate or immediate subsequent identity (if known)
G-BDNW	American Aviation AA-1B Trainer 2	AA1B-0588		8. 1.76	
G-BDNX	American Aviation AA-1B Trainer 2	AA1B-0590		8. 1.76	
G-BDNY	American Aviation AA-1B Trainer 2	AA1B-0595		8. 1.76	Damaged at Doncaster on 25.3.84. Canx by CAA 12.8.91.
G-BDNZ	Cameron O-77 HAFB	203		8. 1.76	Canx by CAA 19.5.93. (Extant 2/97)
G-BDOA	HS.125 Srs.600B	256056	G-5-13	9. 1.76	To G-BKCD 4/82. Canx.
G-BDOB	HS.125 Srs.600A	256061	G-5-14	12. 1.76	To N125HS 2/76. Canx 26.2.76.
G-BDOC	Sikorsky S-61N Mk.II	61-765		20. 3.76	
G-BDOD	Reims Cessna F.150M Commuter	1266		20. 1.76	
G-BDOE	Reims Cessna FR.172J Rocket	0559		20. 1.76	
G-BDOF	Cameron O-56 HAFB	190		19. 1.75	Canx as WFU 11.5.93.
G-BDOG	Scottish Aviation Bulldog Srs.200 (Being operated as a Bullfinch)	BH.200/381		18.12.75	
G-BDOH	Hiller UH-12E	2208	XS160	20. 1.76	To D-HTIM. Canx 7.5.91.
G-BDOI	Hiller UH-12E (Originally regd with c/n 2264 which became ZS-HFV - amended on 9.2.76)	2262	XS166	20. 1.76	To HA-MIJ /93. Canx 15.2.93.
G-BDOJ	BN-2A Mk.III-2 Trislander	1021		21. 1.76	To PK-KTI 5/76. Canx 9.2.77.
G-BDOK	BN-2A Mk.III-2 Trislander	1022		21. 1.76	To PK-KTH 5/76. Canx 13.10.76.
G-BDOL	Piper J3C-65 Cub (L-4J-PI) (Frame No. 13016 - see comments on G-BCUB - officially c/n 13370 and carries genuine c/n and USAAC plates for c/n 13370/45-4630)	13186	F-BCPC 45-4446	18.12.75	
G-BDOM	BN-2A Mk.III-2 Trislander	1023		21. 1.76	To N411WA 2/83. Canx 2.2.83.
G-BDON	Thunder Ax7-77A HAFB	063		17.12.75	
G-BDOO	Thunder Ax7-77 HAFB	064		17.12.75	Canx 17.10.84 on sale to Bahrein.
G-BDOP	HS.125 Srs.600A	256055	G-5-19	29.12.75	To N94B 1/76. Canx 12.1.76.
G-BDOR	Thunder Ax6-56A HAFB	056		17.12.75	Canx by CAA 2.1.92.
G-BDOS	BN-2A Mk.III-2 Trislander	1024	(4X-CCI) G-BDOS	21. 1.76	To G-OJAV 6/90. Canx.
G-BDOT	BN-2A Mk.III-2 Trislander	1025	ZK-SFF N900TA/N903GD/N3850K/VH-BPB/G-BDOT	21. 1.76	
G-BDOU	Reims Cessna FRA.150M Aerobat	0272		21. 1.76	To G-OSND 10/84. Canx.
G-BDOV	Westland Commando Mk.2B (Line No. 130)	WA/807	G-17-18	23. 1.76	To Egyptian AF as WA807/726 in 3/76. Canx 11.3.76.
G-BDOW	Reims Cessna FRA.150M Aerobat	0296		26. 1.76	
G-BDOX	Hughes 269C (300C)	16-0465		1. 4.76	To SE-HHB 12/76. Canx 30.11.76.
G-BDOY	Hughes 369HS (500)	45-0738S		12. 2.76	To G-GEEE 3/90. Canx.
G-BDOZ	Sportavia-Putzer Fournier RF-5	5109	5Y-AOZ D-KCIQ	18.12.75	Somersaulted and crashed on take-off at Fenland on 30.8.81. Aircraft extensively damaged. Canx.
G-BDPA	PA-28-151 Cherokee Warrior	28-7615033		26. 1.76	
G-BDPB	Falconar F-11-3	PEB.02 & PFA/1322	(G-AWHY)	23. 1.76	Restored as G-AWHY 8/89. Canx.
G-BDPC	Bede BD-5A	3217 & PFA/14-10028		23. 1.76	No Permit issued. Canx by CAA 5.7.91.
G-BDPD	Beechcraft 95-B55 Baron	TC-1392	5Y-ANC	12. 4.76	Restored to 5Y-ANC 11/80. Canx 6.11.80.
G-BDPE	Reims Cessna F.150M	1276		29. 1.76	NTU - Not Imported. To F-GAGI 11/76. Canx 5.12.83.
G-BDPF	Reims Cessna F.172M Skyhawk II	1436		29. 1.76	To G-BZZD 4/98. Canx.
G-BDPG	Reims Cessna F.150M	1277		2. 2.76	DBR on landing at Hurn on 5.7.80. Canx.
G-BDPH	Reims Cessna F.172M Skyhawk II	1451		2. 2.76	To G-ROUP 5/84. Canx.
G-BDPI	PA-25-235 Panwee B	25-3139	SE-EMY	2. 2.76	To ST-AJA 9/84. Canx 22.5.84.
G-BDPJ	PA-25-235 Pawnee B	25-3665	SE-EPZ	2. 2.76	Crashed at Ivychurch, Kent on 25.6.80. Reserved as PH-VBF in 8/83. (On rebuild 2/96)
G-BDPK	Cameron O-56 HAFB	191		4. 2.76	(Extant 9/95)
G-BDPL	Falconar F-11 (Originally regd with PFA c/n 33-10070)	PFA/32-10070		5. 2.76	To G-WBTS 10/90. Canx.
G-BDPM	BN-2A-26 Islander	497		5. 2.76	To HP-712 6/76. Canx 18.11.76.
G-BDPN	BN-2B-21 Islander	498		5. 2.76	To B-04/OTA-LD Belgium Army 7/76. Canx 18.11.76.
G-BDPO	BN-2A-27 Islander	499		5. 2.76	To PT-KTS 11/76. Canx 19.11.76.
G-BDPP	BN-2A-21 Islander	501		5. 2.76	To B-05/OTA-LE Belgium Army 7/76. Canx 19.11.76.
G-BDPR	BN-2A-25 Islander (At one stage was a BN-2A-41 version)	504		5. 2.76	To (N3265N)/VH-LRX 8/82 (Unofficially as a BN-2A-27LN). Canx.
G-BDPS	BN-2A-21 Islander	506		5. 2.76	To IN-129 Indian Navy 11/86. Canx 19.11.76.
G-BDPT	BN-2A-21 Islander	507		5. 2.76	To IN-130 Indian Navy 7/76. Canx 19.11.76.
G-BDPU	BN-2A-21 Islander (Originally regd as BN-2A-26)	510		5. 2.76	To B-06/OTA-LF Belgium Army 8/76. Canx 19.11.76.
G-BDPV	Boeing 747-136 (Line No. 281)	21213		9. 2.76	Canx 18.6.99 on sale to USA. Being dismantled 7/99 Roswell, NM, USA.
G-BDPW	Not allocated.				
G-BDPX	Not allocated.				
G-BDPY	Not allocated.				
G-BDPZ	Boeing 747-148 (Line No. 108)	19745	EI-ASJ HS-VGF/EI-ASJ	1. 4.76	Restored as EI-ASJ 5/81. Canx 6.5.81.
G-BDRA	Bell 47G-4	2861	N73944	6. 2.76	To SX-HAU 7/77. Canx 1.7.77.
G-BDRB	American Aviation AA-5B Tiger	AA5B-0175		6. 2.76	Crashed on take-off at Wing Farm, Warminster on 16.5.94. Canx as WFU 3.10.94.
G-BDRC	Vickers 724 Viscount	52	F-BMCG CF-TGO	9. 2.76	WFU at Exeter. Canx as WFU 9.10.84. To Fire School at Manston in 5/86.
G-BDRD	Reims Cessna FRA.150M Aerobat	0289		9. 2.76	
G-BDRE	American Aviation AA-1B Trainer	AA1B-0602		9. 2.76	Struck hedge on landing at a strip at Church Farm, near Norton Malreward on 25.3.89. Canx as destroyed 11.5.89.
G-BDRF	Taylor JT.1 Monoplane	PFA/1459		9. 2.76	Permit expired 13.5.88. Canx by CAA 9.12.96.
G-BDRG	Taylor JT.2 Titch	PFA/60-10295		19.12.78	

Regn	Type	c/n	Previous identity	Regn date	Fate or immediate subsequent identity (if known)
G-BDRH	Sikorsky S-61N Mk.II	61-470	VH-BHY	17. 2.76	Canx 22.4.87 on sale to France. To N9116Y 9/87.
			G-BDRH/9M-ARV/VR-BDN/N6969R		
G-BDRI	PA-34-200T Seneca II	34-7570303	SE-GLG	11. 2.76	To G-BSBS 10/88. Canx.
G-BDRJ	DHC.1 Chipmunk 22 (Fuselage no. DHB/f/638)	C1/0742	WP857	19. 2.76	
G-BDRK	Cameron O-65 HAFB	205		12. 2.76	(Extant 1/95)
G-BDRL	Stits SA-3A Playboy	P-689	N730GF	12. 2.76	
G-BDRM	DHC.1 Chipmunk 22 (Fuselage no. DHB/f/457)	C1/0572	WK555	16. 2.76	To N31353 3/76. Canx 15.3.76.
G-BDRN	IRMA BN-2A-21 Islander (Originally regd as BN-2A-6)	781		16. 2.76	To 9V-BJO 8/78. Canx 16.5.77.
G-BDRO	IRMA BN-2A-21 Islander (Originally regd as BN-2A-6)	782	A6-FFA	16. 2.76	To PK-ZAM 7/82. Canx 25.6.82.
			(PK-KNI)/9V-BJF/G-BDRO		
G-BDRP	IRMA BN-2A-21 Islander (Originally regd as BN-2A-6)	783		16. 2.76	To OA-2/Z1(2) Botswana DF 10/78. Canx 27.2.79.
G-BDRR	IRMA BN-2A-21 Islander (Originally regd as BN-2A-6)	784		16. 2.76	To D-IFST 4/77. Canx 5.9.77.
G-BDRS	IRMA BN-2A-26 Islander (Originally regd as BN-2A-6)	785		16. 2.76	To 9V-BJG 8/76. Canx 23.11.77.
G-BDRT	IRMA BN-2A-21 Islander (Originally regd as BN-2A-6)	786		16. 2.76	To Mauritanian AF as 5T-MAQ 11/76. Canx 25.8.77.
G-BDRU	IRMA BN-2A-21 Islander (Originally regd as BN-2A-6)	787		16. 2.76	To Mauritanian AF as 5T-MAR 11/76. Canx 25.8.77.
G-BDRV	IRMA BN-2A-26 Islander (Originally regd as BN-2A-6)	788		16. 2.76	To PH-PFS 12/77. Canx 13.12.77.
G-BDRW	IRMA BN-2A-27 Islander (Originally regd as BN-2A-6)	789		16. 2.76	To TF-ORN(3) 2/77. Canx 25.2.77.
G-BDRX	IRMA BN-2A-27 Islander (Originally regd as BN-2A-6)	790		16. 2.76	To YR-BNL 2/77. Canx 25.8.77.
G-BDRY	Hiller UH-12E	2273	XS172	18. 2.76	Badly damaged when it hit power cables at Little Steeping, near Skegness on 12.8.83. (Remains to Bourn). Canx as destroyed 28.12.84.
G-BDRZ	Reims Cessna F.150M Commuter	0293		23. 2.76	Forced landing in a field near Gerrards Cross on 25.6.78 & DBR. Canx as WFU 11.9.78.
G-BDSA	Clutton-Tabenor FRED Srs.II	LAS.1803 & PFA/29-10141	EI-BFS G-BDSA	23. 2.76	
G-BDSB	PA-28-181 Cherokee Archer II	28-7690107	N8221C	23. 2.76	
G-BDSC	Reims Cessna F.150M Commuter	1265		24. 2.76	DBR in storms at Ipswich on 16.10.87. Canx as destroyed 9.12.87.
G-BDSD	Evans VP-1	PFA/7015		26. 2.76	No Permit. Canx by CAA 5.7.91.
G-BDSE	Cameron O-77 HAFB	210		27. 2.76	
G-BDSF	Cameron O-56 HAFB	209		1. 3.76	
G-BDSG	Aerosport Woody Pusher	PFA/07-10131		23. 2.76	Not certified in UK. Believed taken to Australia in 1977. Canx by CAA 2.2.87.
G-BDSH	PA-28-140 Cherokee Cruiser F	28-7625063		1. 3.76	
G-BDSI	Cessna 180J Skywagon	180-52637	N9982N	2. 3.76	To PH-SLA 8/77. Canx 5.8.77.
G-BDSJ	Boeing 707-338C (Line No. 746)	19630	VH-EAJ	24. 3.76	To 5X-UBC 10/81. Canx 5.10.81.
G-BDSK	Cameron O-65 HAFB	166		3. 3.76	
G-BDSL	Reims Cessna F.150M Commuter	1306		5. 3.76	
G-BDSM	Slingsby/Kirby T.31 Motor Cadet III	"PFA/2464/3B" & PFA/42-10507		5. 3.76	
G-BDSN	Wassmer WA.52 Europa	54	G-BADN	8. 3.76	Destroyed in fatal crash at Breakneck Hill on 8.4.93. Canx as destroyed 27.8.93.
G-BDSO	Cameron O-31 HAFB	207		10. 3.76	Canx as WFU 22.1.92. (Extant .92)
G-BDSP	Cessna U.206F Stationair	U206-03028	N3583Q	10. 3.76	To 5Y-BHJ. Canx 15.2.91.
G-BDSR	PA-25-235 Aztec D	25-7405654	N9566P	10. 3.76	Canx 14.6.85 on sale to Kenya. To N17AP 6/85.
G-BDSS	Westland Commando Mk.2A (Line No. 151)	WA/836	G-17-6	11. 3.76	To Qatar AF as QA-22. Canx 18.6.76.
G-BDST	Westland Commando Mk.2A (Line No. 152)	WA/837	G-17-7	11. 3.76	To Qatar AF as QA-21. Canx 18.6.76.
G-BDSU	Short SD.3-30 Var.100	SH3003	G-14-3003	11. 3.76	To D-CBVK 6/77. Canx 2.6.77.
G-BDSV	Short SC.7 Skyvan 3-100	SH1947	G-14-115	11. 3.76	To YV-O-MC-8 in 6/76. Canx 8.7.76.
G-BDSW	BN-2A-21 Islander	511		16. 3.76	To N62JA 8/76. Canx 4.8.76.
G-BDSX	BN-2A-21 Islander	512		16. 3.76	To N69JA 7/76. Canx 23.7.76.
G-BDSY	BN-2A-21 Islander	513		16. 3.76	To N63JA 8/76. Canx.
G-BDSZ	BN-2A-26 Islander	514		16. 3.76	To N4564Q 11/82. Canx 3.11.82.
G-BDTA	BN-2A-26 Islander	517		16. 3.76	To (C-GUKZ)/N400JA 9/76. Canx 13.9.76.
G-BDTB	Evans VP-1 Srs.2	PFA/7009		15. 3.76	
G-BDTC	BN-2A-21 Islander (Originally regd as BN-2A-6)	791		16. 3.76	To OA-1/Z1 Botswana DF 9/77. Canx 12.77.
G-BDTD	BN-2A-21 Islander (Originally regd as BN-2A-6)	792		16. 3.76	To 7Q-YAX 4/77. Canx 1.11.77.
G-BDTE	BN-2A-21 Islander (Originally regd as BN-2A-6)	793		16. 3.76	To Mauritanian AF as 5T-MAU 6/77. Canx 5.9.77.
G-BDTF	BN-2A-27 Islander (Originally regd as BN-2A-6)	794	(9G-...) G-BDTF	16. 3.76	To 5N-ASI 2/79. Canx 9.2.79.
G-BDTG	BN-2A-21 Islander (Originally regd as BN-2A-6)	795		16. 3.76	To OA-2/Z1(1) Botswana DF 10/77. Canx 13.2.78.
G-BDTH	BN-2A-21 Islander (Originally regd as BN-2A-6)	796		16. 3.76	To JDFT-5 Jamaica DF 5/77. Canx 25.8.77.

Regn	Type	c/n	Previous identity	Regn date	Fate or immediate subsequent identity (if known)
G-BDTI	BN-2A-21 Islander (Originally regd as BN-2A-6)	797		16. 3.76	To YR-BPD 10/77. Canx 23.9.77.
G-BDTJ	BN-2A-21 Islander (Originally regd as BN-2A-6)	798		16. 3.76	To YR-BPE 10/77. Canx 9.9.77.
G-BDTK	BN-2A-21 Islander (Originally regd as BN-2A-6)	799		16. 3.76	To OA 3/Z2 Botswana DF 2/78. Canx 7.4.78.
G-BDTL	Evans VP-1	PFA/7012		17. 3.76	Permit expired 5.9.85. (Status uncertain)
G-BDTM	BN-2A-20 Islander (Originally regd as BN-2A-6)	800		16. 3.76	To VH-TWI 12/77. Canx 5.1.78.
G-BDTN	BN-2A Mk.III-2 Trislander	1026	S7-AAN VQ-SAN/G-BDTN	16. 3.76	(Stored in open with parts missing 1/99 Guernsey)
G-BDTO	BN-2A Mk.III-2 Trislander	1027	G-RBSI G-OTSB/G-BDTO/8P-ASC(2)/G-BDTO/(C-GYOX)/G-BDTO	16. 3.76	
G-BDTP	BN-2A Mk.III-2 Trislander	1028	9L-LAU G-BDTP	16. 3.76	Fatal crash near Schiphol on 14.9.86. Canx as destroyed 13.5.87.
G-BDTR	BN-2A Mk.III-2 Trislander	1029		16. 3.76	To N403JA 4/77. Canx.
G-BDTS	BN-2A Mk.III-2 Trislander	1030		16. 3.76	To VH-EGU 7/78. Canx 20.6.78.
G-BDTT	Bede BD-5	3795 & PFA/14-10084		17. 3.76	Not completed. Canx by CAA 2.2.87. (On display 4/95)
G-BDTU	Van Den Bemden Omega III (Gas) Free Balloon (20,000 cu.ft)	VDB-35 & AFB.4		16. 3.76	
G-BDTV	Mooney M.20F Executive	22-1307	N6934V	16. 3.76	
G-BDTW	Cassutt Racer IIIM	01 & PFA/34-10102		18. 3.76	
G-BDTX	Reims Cessna F.150M Commuter	1275		19. 3.76	
G-BDTY	Scottish Avn Bulldog Srs.120/127	BH120/383		19. 3.76	To Kenyan AF as 706. Canx 13.8.76.
G-BDTZ	Scottish Avn Bulldog Srs.120/127	BH120/384		19. 3.76	To Kenyan AF as 707. Canx 13.8.76.
G-BDUA	Scottish Avn Bulldog Srs.120/127	BH120/385		19. 3.76	To Kenyan AF as 708. Canx 13.8.76.
G-BDUB	Scottish Avn Bulldog Srs.120/127	BH120/386		19. 3.76	To Kenyan AF as 709. Canx 28.9.76.
G-BDUC	Scottish Avn Bulldog Srs.120/127	BH120/387		19. 3.76	To Kenyan AF as 710. Canx 28.9.76.
G-BDUD	Not allocated.				
G-BDUE	Scottish Avn Bulldog Srs.120/127	BH120/388		19. 3.76	To Kenyan AF as 711. Canx 28.9.76.
G-BDUF	Scottish Avn Bulldog Srs.120/127	BH120/389		19. 3.76	To Kenyan AF as 712 in 9/76. Canx.
G-BDUG	Scottish Avn Bulldog Srs.120/127	BH120/390		19. 3.76	To Kenyan AF as 713 in 8/76. Canx.
G-BDUH	Scottish Avn Bulldog Srs.120/127	BH120/391		19. 3.76	To Kenyan AF as 714 in 8/76. Canx.
G-BDUI	Cameron V-56 HAFB	218		19. 3.76	
G-BDUJ	PA-31-310 Turbo Navajo	31-7612040	N59814	22. 3.76	To G-NWAC 2/94. Canx.
G-BDUK	Rockwell Commander 685	12029	N9195N	23. 3.76	To N32652 8/82. Canx 20.8.82.
G-BDUL	Evans VP-1	PFA/1557		25. 3.76	
G-BDUM	Reims Cessna F.150M Commuter	1301	F-BXZB	29. 3.76	CofA expired 16.1.97. (Stored 2/99 Old Buckenham)
G-BDUN	PA-34-200T Seneca II	34-7570163	(EI-BLR) G-BDUN/SE-GIA	29. 3.76	
G-BDUO	Reims Cessna F.150M Commuter	1304		29. 3.76	
G-BDUP	Bristol 175 Britannia Srs.253F	13508	XM496	31. 3.76	To CU-T120 8/84. Canx 9.8.84.
G-BDUR	Bristol 175 Britannia Srs.253F	13513	XM519	31. 3.76	To CU-T121 8/84. Canx 14.8.84.
G-BDUS	BN-2A-21 Islander	515		30. 3.76	To N65JA 8/76. Canx 24.6.77.
G-BDUT	BN-2A-21 Islander	516		30. 3.76	To N66JA 8/76. Canx 24.6.77.
G-BDUU	BN-2A-26 Islander	518		30. 3.76	To B-11109 7/76. Canx 19.11.76.
G-BDUV	BN-2A-26 Islander	519		30. 3.76	To EI-BCE 9/76. Canx 13.9.76.
G-BDUW	BN-2A-20 Islander	520		30. 3.76	To "YV-1027P"/YV-1073P 11/76. Canx 24.6.77.
G-BDUX	Slingsby T.21B Motor Glider (Despite officially regd designation, it is based on a T.31 glider)	"1146" & PFA/42-10163		29. 3.76	Permit to Fly expired 23.2.84 & WFU at Southend. Canx as WFU 7.1.85.
G-BDUY	Robin DR.400/140B Major	1120		5. 4.76	
G-BDUZ	Cameron V-56 HAFB	213		30. 3.76	(Active 1/93)
G-BDVA	PA-17 Vagabond	17-206	CN-TVY F-BFFE	23. 4.76	
G-BDVB	PA-15 Vagabond (Modified to PA-17 standard)	15-229	F-BHHE(2) SL-AAY/F-BETG	23. 4.76	
G-BDVC	PA-17 Vagabond	17-140	F-BFBL	29. 9.76	
G-BDVD	Not allocated.				
G-BDVE	Reims Cessna F.182P Skylane (Wichita c/n 64420)	0059	N1733M	2. 4.76	To (PH-DIK)/D-EBYP(2) 1/77. Canx 17.1.77.
G-BDVF	Reims Cessna F.150M Commuter	1294		8. 4.76	NTU - Canx 30.9.77 as Not Imported. To D-EIHG.
G-BDVG	Thunder Ax6-56A HAFB	067		2. 4.76	Canx by CAA 3.4.92. (Active 9/94)
G-BDVH	HS.748 Srs.2A/301LFD	1746	5R-MJS G-BDVH/C6-BEA/G-BDVH/C6-BEA/G-BDVH	9. 4.76	To Sri Lankan AF as CR-833 in 4/86. Canx 27.4.86.
G-BDVI	DH.82A Tiger Moth	86048	CF-EIO VT-EBP/VT-ARP/EM846	9. 4.76	To N982JG /79. Canx 30.9.85.
G-BDVJ	Westland-Bell 47G-3B1 (Line No.WAS/185)	WA/566	8430M A2631\E4662/XV312/G-17-14	15. 4.76	To 5B-CGI 1/85. Canx 10.1.85.

Regn	Type	c/n	Previous identity	Regn date	Fate or immediate subsequent identity (if known)
G-BDVK	Reims Cessna F.337F Super Skymaster (Wichita c/n 337-1353)	0031	F-OCZZ F-BSIZ	15. 4.76	To EC-DBZ 8/77. Canx 17.8.77.
G-BDVL	Westland Commando Mk.2B (Line No. 126)	WA/805	G-17-14 XZ741/Egyptian AF 725/G-17-14	20. 4.76	To Egyptian AF as WA805/725 in 6/76. Canx 18.6.76.
G-BDVM	Short SC.7 Skyvan 3-100	SH1946	G-14-114	20. 4.76	Canx 23.7.76 on sale to USA. To XC-BOD.
G-BDVN	Short SC.7 Skyvan 3-100	SH1948	G-14-116	20. 4.76	To YV-O-DAC-3 in 8/76. Canx 18.8.76.
G-BDVO	Short SC.7 Skyvan 3-100	SH1949	G-14-117	20. 4.76	To YV-O-MC-9 in 8/76. Canx.
G-BDVP	Short SC.7 Skyvan 3-100	SH1950	G-14-118	20. 4.76	To XC-BOT 10/76. Canx 6.10.76.
G-BDVR	Cessna 180F	180-51219	ET-ABT N2119Z	21. 4.76	To G-BMAF 3/81. Canx.
G-BDVS	Fokker F-27 Friendship 200	10232	S2-ABK PH-FEX/PH-EXC/9M-AMM/PH-FEX	20. 4.76	18 feet nose section preserved Norfolk & Suffolk Aviation Museum. Scrapped 12/96. Canx 19.12.96 as WFU.
G-BDVT	Fokker F-27 Friendship 200	10233	S2-ABL PH-FEY/9V-BAR/9M-AMN/PH-FEY	20. 4.76	To TF-FLS(2) 9/86. Canx.
G-BDVU	Mooney M.20F Executive	22-1380		23. 4.76	
G-BDVV	BN-2A-20 Islander	521		28. 4.76	To JA5255 8/76. Canx 18.8.76.
G-BDVW	BN-2A-26 Islander	522		28. 4.76	Crashed on landing at Sanday, Orkneys on 1.6.84. Canx as destroyed 4.2.88.
G-BDVX	BN-2B-21 Islander	523		28. 4.76	To B-07/OTA-LG Belgium Army 9/76. Canx 24.8.77.
G-BDVY	BN-2A-8 Islander (Originally regd as BN-2A-27)	524		28. 4.76	To N64JA 9/76. Canx 1.9.76.
G-BDVZ	BN-2A-20 Islander	525		28. 4.76	To N111BN 5/77. Canx 25.5.77.
G-BDWA	Socata MS.892E Rallye 150ST	2695		20. 4.76	
G-BDWB	Socata MS.892E Rallye 150ST	2696		20. 4.76	To G-PIGS 6/88. Canx.
G-BDWC	Not allocated.				
G-BDWD	BN-2A-21 Islander	526		28. 4.76	To YR-BPA 9/77. Canx 5.9.77.
G-BDWE	Flaglor Sky Scooter	KF-S-66, DWE-01 & PFA/1332		12. 4.76	
G-BDWF	BN-2A-8 Islander (Originally regd as BN-2A-26)	529		28. 4.76	To N20BN 12/76. Canx 25.5.77.
G-BDWG	BN-2A-26 Islander	530	(N90255) (C-GYUF)/G-BDWG	28. 4.76	To G-LOTO 7/95. Canx.
G-BDWH	Socata MS.892E Rallye 150ST	2697		20. 4.76	
G-BDWI	PA-34-200T Seneca II	34-7670095	N7305C	27. 4.76	To PH-SUN(2) 11/84. Canx 15.10.84.
G-BDWJ	Replica Plans SE-5A	PFA/20-10034	"C1904" "F8010"	27. 4.76	
G-BDWK	Beechcraft 95-B58 Baron	TH-755	(G-BEET)	26. 4.76	To N773DC 4/95. Canx 5.4.95.
G-BDWL	PA-25-235 Pawnee B	25-3575	PH-IPO N7531Z	4. 5.76	
G-BDWM	Bonsall DB-1 Mustang Replica	DCB.1 & PFA/73-10200		3. 5.76	
G-BDWN	Sud SA.318C Alouette Astazou	1901	1901 Senegal AF/N4675/(G-ATDT)	6. 5.76	To F-GEHH 4/84. Canx 19.3.84.
G-BDWO	Howes Ax6 HAFB (Complete and extant 11.88 but never certified)	RBH.2		5. 5.76	
G-BDWP	PA-32R-300 Cherokee Lance	32R-7680176	N8784E	7. 5.76	
G-BDWR	BN-2A Mk.III-2 Trislander	1031		11. 5.76	To ZS-JYF 2/77. Canx 10.2.77.
G-BDWS	BN-2A Mk.III-2 Trislander	1032		11. 5.76	To 5Y-CMC 3/77. Canx 27.9.77.
G-BDWT	BN-2A Mk.III-2 Trislander	1033		11. 5.76	Canx 19.7.77 on sale to Malaysia. To PK-KTJ 7/77.
G-BDWU	BN-2A Mk.III-2 Trislander	1034		11. 5.76	To N414WA 12/81. Canx 6.1.82.
G-BDWV	BN-2A Mk.III-2 Trislander (Mod to three-bladed propellors by 10/93)	1035	8P-ASF G-BDWV	11. 5.76	
G-BDWW	Cameron O-77 HAFB	226		13. 5.76	DBF at Lowfold Farm, Wisborough Green, Sussex on 21.7.84. Canx as destroyed 14.8.84.
G-BDWX	Wassmer Jodel D.120A Paris-Nice	311	F-BNHT	13. 5.76	
G-BDWY	PA-28-140 Cherokee E	28-7225378	PH-NSC	14. 5.76	
G-BDWZ	Slingsby T.59J Kestrel 22 (Converted from T.59H standard in 1/79)	1867		17. 5.76	To BGA.2470/DXU in 3/79. Canx by CAA 2.2.87.
G-BDXA	Boeing 747-236B (Line No. 292)	21238	N1790B	18. 3.77	
G-BDXB	Boeing 747-236B (Line No. 302)	21239	N8280V	13. 1.77	
G-BDXC	Boeing 747-236B (Line No. 305)	21240		18. 3.77	
G-BDXD	Boeing 747-236B (Line No. 317)	21241	N8285V	4. 4.78	
G-BDXE	Boeing 747-236B (Line No. 321)	21350		23. 2.78	
G-BDXF	Boeing 747-236B (Line No. 323)	21351		23. 3.78	
G-BDXG	Boeing 747-236B (Line No. 326)	21536		16. 6.78	
G-BDXH	Boeing 747-236B (Line No. 365)	21635		23. 2.79	
G-BDXI	Boeing 747-236B (Line No. 430)	21830		21. 2.80	
G-BDXJ	Boeing 747-236B (Line No. 440)	21831	N1792B	2. 5.80	
G-BDXK(1)	Boeing 747-236F (Line No. 480)	22306		. .77R	NTU - To G-KILO 9/80. Canx.

Regn	Type	c/n	Previous identity	Regn date	Fate or immediate subsequent identity (if known)
G-BDXK(2)	Boeing 747-236B (Line No. 495)	22303		29. 4.83	
G-BDXL(1)	Boeing 747-236B (Line No. 502)	22304		. .77R	NTU - To 9M-MHI 3/82. Canx.
G-BDXL(2)	Boeing 747-236B (Line No. 506)	22305	N8280V (G-BDXM)	9. 1.84	
G-BDXM(1)	Boeing 747-236B (Line No. 506)	22305		. .77R	NTU - To N8280V/G-BDXL. Canx.
G-BDXM(2)	Boeing 747-236M (Line No. 672)	23711	N6055X	25. 2.87	
G-BDXN(1)	Boeing 747-236B (Line No. 526)	22442		. .77R	NTU - To 9M-MHJ 4/82. Canx.
G-BDXN(2)	Boeing 747-236M (Line No. 674)	23735	N6046P	17. 3.87	
G-BDXO	Boeing 747-236B (Line No. 677)	23799	N6055X	22. 4.87	
G-BDXP	Boeing 747-236M (Line No. 697)	24088	N6009F	24. 2.88	
G-BDXR	Boeing 747-236M	-		. .77R	NTU - Canx.
G-BDXS	Boeing 747-236M	-		. .77R	NTU - Canx.
G-BDXT	Boeing 747-236M	-		. .77R	NTU - Canx.
G-BDXU	Beechcraft 65-80 Queen Air	LD-135	ZS-JWD G-BDXU/"9Q-CRO"/CR-LLW/N135Q	19. 5.76	Restored as ZS-JWD 5/77. Canx 9.5.77.
G-BDXV	PA-23-250 Aztec F	27-7654089	N62614	17. 5.76	To G-BJDH 8/76. Canx.
G-BDXW	PA-28R-200 Cherokee Arrow II	28R-7635227	N9235K	17. 5.76	To G-GDOG 4/89. Canx.
G-BDXX	SNCAN NC.858S Chardonneret	110	F-BEZQ	17. 5.76	Badly damaged on landing at Newnham Farm, Binstead, IoW on 10.8.95. (On rebuild 5/96) Permit expired 3.7.96.
G-BDXY	Auster AOP.9	B5/10/187	XR269	18. 5.76	Destroyed in forced landing at Southend Hill, Cheddington on 1.9.91. Canx as destroyed 20.9.91.
G-BDXZ	Lacey-Pitts S-1S Special	2JL	N311JL	13. 5.76	Permit to Fly expired 21.5.80. Damaged and sold as spares from Chislet in 1981. Canx by CAA 2.2.87.
G-BDYA	CASA Heinkel C.2-111E	-	T8B-124 Spanish AF	21. 5.76	To N72615 8/77. Canx 2.8.77.
G-BDYB	American Aviation AA-5B Tiger	AA5B-0275		21. 5.76	To LX-OUF(3) 7/86. Canx 7.4.86.
G-BDYC	American Aviation AA-1B Trainer	AA1B-0617		21. 5.76	To EI-CCY 3/91. Canx 26.2.91.
G-BDYD	Rockwell Commander 114	14014	N1914J	21. 5.76	
G-BDYE	HS.125 Srs.1B/522	25080	3D-AAB VQ-ZIL	24. 5.76	To EI-BGW 7/79. Canx 11.6.79.
G-BDYF	Cessna 421C Golden Eagle III	421C-0055	N98468	24. 5.76	
G-BDYG	Percival P.56 Provost T.1 (Also c/n P56/56)	PAC/F/056	7696M WV493	25. 5.76	Permit expired 28.11.80. Canx by CAA 4.11.91. (On display 3/96)
G-BDYH	Cameron V-56 HAFB	233		24. 5.76	(Extant 2/97)
G-BDYI	Beechcraft 95-58 Baron	TH-207	9Q-CRR CR-LMG/ZS-INT/ZS-XAG/N9460Q	26. 5.76	Restored as N9460Q 12/76. Canx 9.12.76.
G-BDYJ	Beechcraft 95-D55 Baron	TE-631	9Q-CTN CR-LMM/ZS-EEN/ZS-FLN/N7702R	26. 5.76	NTU - Canx 24.6.76 as Not Imported. Remained as 9Q-CTN.
G-BDYK	Beechcraft 95-58 Baron	TH-634	9Q-CRP CR-LPD/N9726S	26. 5.76	Restored as N9726S 11/76. Canx 8.11.76.
G-BDYL	Beechcraft C23 Sundowner	M-1466	9Q-CTO CR-LNA/ZS-ITD/N2887B	26. 5.76	To ZS-MCD /88. Canx 8.8.88.
G-BDYM	Skysales S-31 HAFB (Toy)	1		27. 5.76	Canx by CAA 15.9.92. (Extant .92)
G-BDYN	IRMA BN-2A-21 Islander (Originally regd as BN-2A-6)	801		1. 6.76	To YR-BPF 9/77. Canx 23.9.77.
G-BDYO	IRMA BN-2A-21 Islander (Originally regd as BN-2A-6)	802		1. 6.76	To YR-BPG(1) 9/77. Canx 12.10.77.
G-BDYP	IRMA BN-2A-21 Islander (Originally regd as BN-2A-6)	803		1. 6.76	To YR-BPH(1) 10/77. Canx 12.10.77.
G-BDYR	IRMA BN-2A-27 Islander (Originally regd as BN-2A-6)	804		1. 6.76	To YR-BNN 4/78. Canx 31.3.78.
G-BDYS	IRMA BN-2A-20 Islander (Originally regd as BN-2A-6)	805		1. 6.76	Canx 3.5.77 on sale to Australia. To P2-ISK 10/77.
G-BDYT	IRMA BN-2A-20 Islander (Originally regd as BN-2A-6)	806		1. 6.76	Canx 4.5.77 on sale to Australia. To P2-ISL 10/77.
G-BDYU	IRMA BN-2A-21 Islander (Originally regd as BN-2A-6)	807		1. 6.76	To LN-MAY 7/77. Canx 8.7.77.
G-BDYV	IRMA BN-2A-27 Islander (Originally regd as BN-2A-6)	808		1. 6.76	To YR-BNM 4/78. Canx.
G-BDYW	IRMA BN-2A-21 Islander (Originally regd as BN-2A-6)	809		1. 6.76	To 5Y-BBB 10/77. Canx 7.2.78.
G-BDYX	IRMA BN-2A-21 Islander (Originally regd as BN-2A-6)	810		1. 6.76	To 5Y-BBC 10/77. Canx 16.2.78.
G-BDYY	Hiller UH-12E	2292	(EI-CDA) G-BDYY/EI-BCA/G-BDYY/XS705	24. 5.76	To SX-HCD 4/87. Canx 13.4.87.
G-BDYZ	MBB Bo.105D	S.138	D-HDEF	27. 5.76	Rebuilt with new pod S.911 in 1992. To G-BUIB 5/92. Canx as WFU 11.5.92.
G-BDZA	Scheibe SF-25E Super Falke	4320	(D-KECW)	1. 6.76	
G-BDZB	Cameron S-31 HAFB	232		27. 5.76	Canx by CAA 19.5.93.
G-BDZC	Reims Cessna F.150M Commuter	1316		1. 6.76	
G-BDZD	Reims Cessna F.172M Skyhawk II	1478		1. 6.76	

Regn	Type	c/n	Previous identity	Regn date	Fate or immediate subsequent identity (if known)
G-BDZE	Reims Cessna F.172M Skyhawk II	1483		1. 6.76	NTU - Canx 30.9.77 as Not Imported. To D-EOXY.
G-BDZF	Schweizer Grumman American G.164B Agcat	027B	N48454	2. 6.76	Crashed and overturned in a field north of Woodstock, Oxon. on 8.4.92. Canx by CAA 25.8.92. To N135VA 19.1.94.
G-BDZG	Slingsby T.59H Kestrel	1868		3. 6.76	To BGA.2481/DYG in 3/79. Canx by CAA 2.2.87.
G-BDZH	HS.125 Srs.600A	256066	G-5-15	7. 6.76	To N32RP 6/76. Canx 16.6.76.
G-BDZI	BN-2B-21 Islander	531		9. 6.76	To B-08/OTA-LH Belgium Army 10/76. Canx 24.8.77.
G-BDZJ	BN-2A-9 Islander (Originally regd as BN-2A-27)	532		9. 6.76	To N68JA 10/76. Canx 21.9.76.
G-BDZK	BN-2B-21 Islander	533		9. 6.76	To B-09/OTA-LI Belgium Army 11/76. Canx 24.8.77.
G-BDZL	BN-2A-8 Islander (Originally regd as BN-2A-26)	534		9. 6.76	To N33MN 4/77. Canx 10.5.77.
G-BDZM	BN-2A-9 Islander (Originally regd as BN-2A-27)	535		9. 6.76	To N70JA 10/76. Canx 21.9.76.
G-BDZN	BN-2A-9 Islander (Originally regd as BN-2A-27)	536		9. 6.76	To N67JA 10/76. Canx 21.9.76.
G-BDZO	BN-2A-21 Islander	537		9. 6.76	To 5Y-RAJ 1/78. Canx 10.1.78.
G-BDZP	BN-2A-27 Islander	540		9. 6.76	To S7-AAA 3/77. Canx 25.8.77.
G-BDZR	HS.125 Srs.600A	256068	G-5-20	10. 6.76	To N33RP 7/76. Canx 1.7.76.
G-BDZS	Scheibe SF-25E Super Falke	4321	(D-KECX)	8. 6.76	To F-CHCO 6/97. Canx 27.3.97.
G-BDZT	Bolkow Bo.209 Monson 160RV	127	PH-PEC D-EFJF	11. 6.76	Not rebuilt and presumed used for spares after receiving damage in gales at Teuge on 3.3.76. Stored at Heathrow. Canx as WFU 10.5.77.
G-BDZU	Cessna 421C Golden Eagle III	421C-0094	N98791	14. 6.76	
G-BDZV	Handley Page HPR.7 Dart Herald 214	191	TG-AZE F-BVFP/G-BDZV/PP-SDL	17. 6.76	
G-BDZW	PA-28-140 Cherokee Cruiser	28-7625181	N9558N	14. 6.76	Crashed in a field at Bough Spring, near Petts Wood on 19.6.88. Canx as destroyed 11.8.88.
G-BDZX	PA-28-151 Cherokee Warrior	28-7615212	N9559N	14. 6.76	
G-BDZY	Phoenix Luton LA-4A Minor	PFA/842		15. 6.76	(Under construction 11/92) No Permit issued - not completed. Canx as PWFU 26.2.99.
G-BDZZ	North American T-6G Texan	182-720	French AF 51-15033	15. 6.76	No CofA issued. To Israel & preserved as "001" at Hatzerim 12/76. Canx 20.12.76 as sold abroad.
G-BEAA	Taylor JT.1 Monoplane	H.1 & PFA/55-10249		9. 8.76	Construction abandoned. Canx as WFU 5.8.91.
G-BEAB	CEA Jodel DR.1051 Sicile	228	F-BKGH	18. 8.76	
G-BEAC	PA-28-140 Cherokee	28-21963	4X-AND	4. 6.76	CofA expired 20.11.83 & WFU at Biggin Hill.
G-BEAD	Westland WG.13 Lynx Prototype (Also c/n WG/00-01)	WA.00.001	XW835	15. 6.76	WFU on completion of trials at Yeovil. Canx 15.7.83. (Stored 8/93 RAF Dishforth)
G-BEAE	PA-25-235 Pawnee C	25-4920	PH-CLM N8505L	16. 6.76	Crashed on take-off from Havant on 8.6.83. Canx by CAA 2.2.87. To SE-KUX.
G-BEAF	Boeing 707-321C (Line No. 341) (Converted to passenger configuration 5/77, converted back in 10/77)	18591	N767PA	24. 7.76	To LV-MSG 7/78. Canx 7.7.78.
G-BEAG	PA-34-200T Seneca II	34-7670204	N9395K	18. 6.76	
G-BEAH	Auster J/2 Arrow	2366	F-BFUV F-BFVV/OO-ABS	28. 6.76	
G-BEAI	Fairchild-Hiller FH.227B Friendship	563	N7823M (ZS-JOZ)/N7823M	22. 6.76	NTU - Impounded at Luanda, Angola. To Angolan AF as T-40. Canx 29.3.82.
G-BEAJ	PA-28-180 Cherokee E	28-5603	9H-AAC N2390R	22. 6.76	To G-YULL 3/79. Canx 30.3.79.
G-BEAK	Lockheed L.1011-385-1 Tristar 50 (Mod to Srs.200)	193N-1132		10.11.75	To N110CK. Canx 21.5.96.
G-BEAL	Lockheed L.1011-385-1 Tristar 50 (Mod to Srs.200)	193N-1145		17.11.76	To SE-DPM 5/94. Canx 27.5.94.
G-BEAM	Lockheed L.1011-385-1 Tristar 50	193N-1146		17.11.76	To N112CK. Canx 15.7.96.
G-BEAN	Not allocated.				
G-BEAO	Not allocated.				
G-BEAP	Not allocated.				
G-BEAR	Viscount V-5 HAFB (Toy)	002		9. 6.81	Canx by CAA 9.12.88.
"G-BEAR"	Robinson R-22 Beta (see G-HOVR)				
G-BEAS	Not allocated.				
G-BEAT	Not allocated.				
G-BEAU	Pazmany PL-4A	01 & PFA/17-10595		6. 5.81	No Permit issued. Canx as WFU 8.7.91.
G-BEAV	Not allocated.				
G-BEAW	Not allocated.				
G-BEAX	Not allocated.				
G-BEAY	Not allocated.				
G-BEAZ	Not allocated.				
G-BEBA	HS.748 Srs.2/233LFD	1613	RP-C1032 G-BEBA/DQ-FAL/VQ-FAL	1. 7.76	To C-FKTL. Canx 7.6.89.
G-BEBB	Handley Page HPR.7 Dart Herald 214	186	PP-SDH	25. 6.76	To G-CEAS 1/86. Canx.
G-BEBC	Westland WS-55 Whirlwind HAR.10 (Line No. WAJ/30)	WA/371	8463M XP355	25. 6.76	Not converted. Canx as WFU 5.12.83. (On display 5/97 City of Norwich Aviation Museum)
G-BEBD	Westland-Bell 47G-3B1 (Line No.WAS/203)	WA/601	XT839	25. 6.76	To OE-AXO 9/76. Canx 20.9.76.
G-BEBE	American Aviation AA-5A Cheetah	AA5A-0154		28. 6.76	
G-BEBF	Auster AOP.9	B.704	(G-BITS)	3. 1.79	Thought to be a proposed rebuild from components but not completed - no Permit issued. Canx as WFU 11.1.94.

Regn	Type	c/n	Previous identity	Regn date	Fate or immediate subsequent identity (if known)
G-BEBG	WSK-PZL SZD-45A Ogar Motor Glider	B-655		29. 6.76	
G-BEBH	Reims Cessna FR.172J Rocket	0427	CS-AOW F-BRGX	30. 6.76	Restored as CS-AOW 3/82. Canx 9.11.81.
G-BEBI	Reims Cessna F.172M Skyhawk II	1461		28. 6.76	
G-BEBJ	PA-E23-250 Aztec	27-7654142	N62686	29. 6.76	Restored as N62686 11/83. Canx 22.11.83.
G-BEBK	PA-31-300 Turbo Navajo	31-751	N883MA EC-EZA/N7229L	1. 7.76	Restored as N883MA 11/82. Canx 8.11.82.
G-BEBL	Douglas DC-10-30 (Line No. 179)	46949	N54643	31. 1.77	WFU 30.11.98, stored 9/99 Manchester. For freighter conversion with marks LX-TLE reserved.
G-BEBM	Douglas DC-10-30 (Line No. 214)	46921	N54640 N8704Q	23. 2.77	Canx 19.3.99 on sale to USA. To N608GC 7/99.
G-BEBN	Cessna 177B Cardinal	177-01631	4X-CEW N34031	1. 7.76	CofA expired 6.12.96. (Stored 1/98)
G-BEBO	Turner Special TSW.2 (Originally regd as a Phoenix Currie Wot)	PFA/46-10127		30. 6.76	
G-BEBP	Boeing 707-321C (Line No. 332)	18579	N765PA	14.10.76	Crashed on approach at Lusaka, Zambia on 14.5.77. Canx.
G-BEBR	Gardan GY-201 Minicab (Officially regd with c/n PFA/1670)	PFA/1824		5. 7.76	No Permit to Fly issued. Canx by CAA 28.2.96.
G-BEBS	Andreasson BA-4B	HA/01 & PFA/38-10157		7. 7.76	
G-BEBT	Andreasson BA-4B	HA/02 & PFA/38-10158		7. 7.76	Permit expired 10.9.97. (Under construction 3/99 Breighton)
G-BEBU	Rockwell Commander 112A	272	N1272J	8. 7.76	
G-BEBV	Westland-Bell 47G-3B1 (Line No.WAN/36)	WA/345	XT186	8. 7.76	To OE-AXP 5/77. Canx 24.5.77.
G-BEBW	Westland-Bell 47G-3B1 (Line No.WAP/84)	WA/383	XT224	8. 7.76	To OE-AXU 1/77. Canx 11.1.77.
G-BEBX	Westland-Bell 47G-3B1 (Line No.WAP/133)	WA/419	XT507	8. 7.76	To OE-AXN 4/77. Canx 1.4.77.
G-BEBY	HS.780 Andover C.1	Set.14	XS607	23. 7.76	Restored to RAF as XS607 in 9/76. Canx 6.9.76.
G-BEBZ	PA-28-151 Cherokee Warrior	28-7615328	N6193J	14. 7.76	
G-BECA	Socata MS.893E Rallye 100ST	2751		14. 7.76	
G-BECB	Socata MS.893E Rallye 100ST	2783		14. 7.76	
G-BECC	Socata MS.893E Rallye 150ST	2748		14. 7.76	
G-BECD	Socata MS.893E Rallye 150ST	2812		14. 7.76	Badly damaged at Top Farm, Talow on 8.4.95 when it landed short of the runway. Canx by CAA 1.8.95.
G-BECE	Aerospace Developments AD500 Srs.B.1 Airship	1214/1		14. 7.76	Badly damaged in gales at Cardington on 9.3.79. (Parts stored for eventual museum 9/94)
G-BECF	Scheibe SF-25A Motor Falke	4555	OO-WIZ (D-KARA)	14. 7.76	Permit expired 1.3.94. (Stored 5/97)
G-BECG	Boeing 737-204ADV (Line No. 487)	21335		19. 7.76	To N102TR /97. Canx 12.12.97.
G-BECH	Boeing 737-204ADV (Line No. 489)	21336		19. 7.76	To N103TR /97. Canx 12.12.97.
G-BECI	BAC 167 Strikemaster Mk.80A	PS.355	G-27-290	27. 7.76	To R.Saudi AF as 1124 in 1976. Canx.
G-BECJ	Partenavia P.68B Victor	68		23. 7.76	To ZK-DMA(2) 2/95. Canx 10.2.95.
G-BECK	Cameron V-56 HAFB	136		27. 7.76	
G-BECL	CASA Junkers C.352L	24	T2B-212 Spanish AF	27. 7.76	To F-AZJU. Canx 19.6.90.
G-BECM	Aerotek Pitts S-2A Special	2121	N947	27. 7.76	Destroyed in mid-air collision with Pitts S-2A G-BADY and crashed at Knott End on 29.6.84. Canx by CAA 3.2.87.
G-BECN	Piper J3C-65 Cub (L-4J-PI)	12776	F-BCPS 44-80480	27. 7.76	
G-BECO	Beechcraft A36 Turbo Bonanza	E-830	N1562L	6. 7.76	To N1586L 8/93. Canx 1.9.93.
G-BECP	PA-31-310 Turbo Navajo C	31-7612078	N59892	30. 7.76	To G-BOVA 3/84. Canx.
G-BECR	Cessna 182B Skylane	182-51914	PH-KUK N2614G	30. 7.76	DBR at Bickmarsh on 2.4.78. Used for spares at Squires Gate. Canx.
G-BECS	Thunder Ax6-56A HAFB	074		4. 8.76	Canx by CAA 3.4.92.
G-BECT	CASA I-131E Jungmann	"3974"	E3B-338 Spanish AF	3. 8.76	
G-BECU	CASA I-131E Jungmann	2166	E3B-384 Spanish AF	3. 8.76	Canx as WFU 1.12.77.
G-BECV	CASA I-131 Jungmann	2033	E3B-390 Spanish AF	3. 8.76	To N333MP. Canx 22.2.77.
G-BECW	CASA I-131E Jungmann	2037	E3B-423 Spanish AF	3. 8.76	(Incorporating parts of G-BECY ex E3B-459)
G-BECX	CASA I-131 Jungmann	2032	E3B-430 Spanish AF	3. 8.76	To D-EKPH. Canx 24.8.83.
G-BECY	CASA I-131E Jungmann	-	E3B-459 Spanish AF	3. 8.76	Crashed 11.9.76 at Perpignan on its ferry flight from Spain to UK. (Parts incorporated in G-BECW ex E3B-423) Canx as WFU 28.4.77. Possibly to F-WRBB/F-PRBB with c/n R-1.
G-BECZ	Avions Mudry/CAARP CAP.10B	68	F-BXHK	26. 7.76	
G-BEDA	CASA I-131E Jungmann	2099	E3B-504 Spanish AF	3. 8.76	
G-BEDB	SNCAN Nord 1203 Norecrin II	117	F-BEOB	5. 8.76	Permit expired 11.6.80. Canx by CAA 14.11.91. (On rebuild 3/98 at Chirk)
G-BEDC	CASA I-131E Jungmann	-	E3B-525 Spanish AF	3. 8.76	Canx 15.2.77 on sale to USA.
G-BEDD	SAN Jodel D.117A	915	F-BITY	3. 8.76	
G-BEDE	Bede BD-5A	3213 & PFA/14-10059		28. 7.76	Canx by CAA 3.9.91.

Regn	Type	c/n	Previous identity	Regn date	Fate or immediate subsequent identity (if known)
G-BEDF	Boeing B-17G-105-VE Flying Fortress	8693	N17TE F-BGSR/44-85784	5. 8.76	Permit expired 5.5.98.
G-BEDG	Rockwell Commander 112A	482	N1219J	5. 8.76	
G-BEDH	Rockwell Commander 114	14074	N4744W	5. 8.76	To G-TECH 8/85. Canx.
G-BEDI	Sikorsky S-61N Mk.II	61-754	N4043S G-BEDI/N4043S	7.10.76	To C-GSBL 7/98. Canx 9.7.98.
G-BEDJ	Piper J3C-65 Cub (L-4J-PI) (Frame No. 12720)	12890	F-BDTC 44-80594	5. 8.76	Permit expired 8.10.96. (On overhaul Kemble 6/97)
G-BEDK	Hiller UH-12E	2300	XS706	5. 8.76	CofA expired 14.6.85. (Pod in open storage 1/96 Chilbolton) Canx by CAA 6.3.99.
G-BEDL	Cessna T.337D Turbo Super Skymaster	337-01178	N86406	12. 8.76	Crash landed in a field near M25 (J9 & J10) Motorway at Leatherhead Common on 3.10.98. Canx by CAA 3.6.99.
G-BEDM	BN-2A Mk.III-2 Trislander	1036		17. 8.76	To B-11112 5/79. Canx 17.4.79.
G-BEDN	BN-2A Mk.III-2 Trislander	1037		17. 8.76	To VP-VAG 7/79. Canx 16.11.79.
G-BEDO	BN-2A Mk.III-2 Trislander	1038	(N3265Q) G-BEDO	17. 8.76	To N199PC. Canx.
G-BEDP	BN-2A Mk.III-2 Trislander	1039	ZK-SFG N902TA/N1FY/N401JA/G-BEDP	17. 8.76	
G-BEDR	BN-2A Mk.III-2 Trislander	1040		17. 8.76	To N420WA 7/81. Canx 21.7.81.
G-BEDS	Thunder Ax7-77A HAFB	087		20. 8.76	Canx 2.10.84 on sale to Kuwait.
G-BEDT	HS.125 Srs.600A	256070	G-5-11	20. 8.76	To N322CC in 8/76. Canx 25.8.76.
G-BEDU	Scheibe SF-23C Sperling (Initially built as SF-23A c/n 2019)	3000	D-EMOH	23. 8.76	Fatal crash into a field soon after take-off at Mallaghboy Road, near Bellaghy, Co.Londonderry on 22.3.87. Canx by CAA 10.2.97.
G-BEDV	Vickers 668 Varsity T.1	619	WJ945	26. 7.76	Permit expired 15.10.87. Canx by CAA 15.6.89. (On display 7/99 Duxford)
G-BEDW	BN-2B-21 Islander	541		25. 8.76	To B-10/OTA-LJ Belgium Army 1/77. Canx.
G-BEDX	BN-2A-8 Islander	542		25. 8.76	To N35MN 4/77. Canx 10.5.77.
G-BEDY	BN-2A-21 Islander	543		25. 8.76	To YR-BPC 9/77. Canx 9.9.77.
G-BEDZ	BN-2A-26 Islander	544	(C-GYUG) G-BEDZ	25. 8.76	Destroyed in fatal crash at Tingwall, Shetland on 19.5.96. Canx as destroyed 14.3.97.
G-BEEA	Socata Rallye 235GT	12770	F-ODCQ	31. 8.76	To ZK-RLY 6/84. Canx 16.4.84.
G-BEEB	BN-2A-21 Islander	545		25. 8.76	To PK-TRC 9/76. Canx 6.1.78.
G-BEEC	BN-2A-8 Islander	546		25. 8.76	To N36MN 5/77. Canx 9.5.77.
G-BEED	BN-2B-21 Islander	549		25. 8.76	To B-11/OTA-LK Belgium Army 1/77. Canx 25.8.77.
G-BEEE	Thunder Ax6-56A HAFB	070		20. 8.76	Canx by CAA 19.5.93.
G-BEEF	Thunder Ax6-56A HAFB	088		20. 8.76	To VH-OXO 8/87. Canx 12.8.82.
G-BEEG	BN-2A-26 Islander	550	(C-GYUH) G-BEEG	25. 8.76	
G-BEEH	Cameron V-56 HAFB	250		24. 8.76	
G-BEEI	Cameron N-77 HAFB	249		24. 8.76	CofA expired 11.3.90. Canx by CAA 4.8.98.
G-BEEJ	Cameron O-77 HAFB	247		24. 8.76	Canx by CAA 6.3.92.
G-BEEK	Enstrom 280C-UK-2 Shark	1037		26. 8.76	To G-WSKY 7/83. Canx.
G-BEEL	Enstrom 280C-UK-2 Shark	1038		26. 8.76	To G-DUGY 8/91. Canx.
G-BEEM	HS.748 Srs.2A/288LFD	1743	CS-03 Belgian AF	31. 8.76	Restored to Belgian AF as CS-03. Canx 15.9.76.
G-BEEN	Cameron O-56 HAFB	235		29.10.76	Canx as WFU 26.6.87.
G-BEEO	Short SD.3-30 Var.100	SH3006	C-GTAM G-BEEO/G-14-3006	31. 8.76	To VP-LVR. Canx 7.12.92.
G-BEEP	Thunder Ax5-42 HAFB	086		20. 8.76	(Based in The Netherlands)(Extant 9/93)
G-BEER	Isaacs Fury II	PFA/1588		31. 8.76	
G-BEES	HS.125 Srs.600A	256071	G-5-14	27. 8.76	To (N91884)/N571DU 12/76. Canx 3.12.76.
G-BEET(1)	Beechcraft 95-B58 Baron	TH-755		. .76R	NTU - To G-BDWK 4/76. Canx.
G-BEET(2)	BAC-Sepecat Jaguar T.2	202	G-27-281	31. 8.76	To Oman AF as 204 in 6/77. Canx.
G-BEEU	PA-28-140 Cherokee F	28-7325247	PH-NSE	9. 9.76	
G-BEEV	PA-28-140 Cherokee F	28-7325229	PH-NSG	29. 9.76	Badly damaged in crash at Rayne on 16.4.91. Canx by CAA 25.6.91. (Fuselage dumped 8/94 at Andrewsfield/Braintree)
G-BEEW	Taylor JT.1 Monoplane (Modified to resemble Boeing P-26A Peashooter)	PFA/55-10189		3. 9.76	(Damaged in taxying trials early .89) (On overhaul Barton 4/95)
G-BEEX	DH.106 Comet 4C	6458	SU-ALM	10. 9.76	Not converted - Broken up Lasham 8/77. Canx 19.5.83. (Nose section to East Kirkby)
G-BEEY	DH.106 Comet 4C	6462	SU-AMV	10. 9.76	Not converted - Broken up Lasham 9/77. Canx as WFU 18.1.78
G-BEEZ	DH.106 Comet 4C	6466	SU-ANC	10. 9.76	Not converted - Broken up for spares at Lasham in 11/77. Canx as WFU 2.12.77.
G-BEFA	PA-28-151 Cherokee Warrior	28-7615416	N6978J	8. 9.76	
G-BEFB	American Aviation AA-5A Cheetah	AA5A-0197	N6146A	24. 9.76	Ran off on landing at Elstree on 26.3.78 & DBR. (Moved to Sherburn on 29.8.78) Parts possibly used in rebuild of G-BAOV in 1981. Canx as destroyed 19.7.78.
G-BEFC	American Aviation AA-5B Tiger	AA5B-0321	N6156A	24. 9.76	Fatal crash at Bell Gate Farm, Shobdon on 27.11.97. Canx 25.3.98 as destroyed.
G-BEFD	Jodel D.112	143	F-BGTK	23. 9.76	Engine failure & crashed near Yeadon on 17.9.78. Canx by CAA 24.11.86.
G-BEFE	Cameron N-77 HAFB	252		24. 9.76	CofA expired 10.5.81 & WFU. Canx by CAA 3.2.87.
G-BEFF	PA-28-140 Cherokee F	28-7325228	PH-NSF N33696	27. 9.76	
G-BEFG	PA-28-151 Cherokee Warrior	28-7715053	N4591F	27. 9.76	To JY-AFG 11/76. Canx 11.11.76.
G-BEFH	Nord 3202B	80	N2255N ALAT	16. 6.82	To F-AZGF 8/89. Canx 23.12.88.
G-BEFI	BN-2A-21 Islander	553		27. 9.76	To B-12/OTA-LL Belgium Army 2/77. Canx 25.8.77.
G-BEFJ	BN-2A-21 Islander	554		27. 9.76	To C-GYTC 1/77. Canx 5.9.77.
G-BEFK	BN-2A-26 Islander	555		27. 9.76	To N70PA 11/77. Canx 30.11.77.

Regn	Type	c/n	Previous identity	Regn date	Fate or immediate subsequent identity (if known)
G-BEFL	BN-2A-21 Islander	556		27. 9.76	To ZS-KAG 7/77. Canx 18.7.77.
G-BEFM	BN-2A-27 Islander	557		27. 9.76	To VP-LCF 5/81. Canx 27.11.80.
G-BEFN	BN-2A-8 Islander	558		27. 9.76	To N37MN 4/77. Canx 10.5.77.
G-BEFO	BN-2A Mk.III-2 Trislander	1041	5H-AZP G-BEFO/G-SARN/F-BYCJ/V2-LMB/VP-LMD/G-BEFO	27. 9.76	
G-BEFP	BN-2A Mk.III-2 Trislander	1042	(4X-CCL) G-BEFP/N30WA/JA6401/G-BEFP	27. 9.76	To 5H-AZD 1/92. Canx 8.1.92.
G-BEFR	Westward Fokker DR.1 Replica	WA/1		5.10.76	Fatal crash during a display at Stourhead House on 20.7.95. Canx as destroyed 1.11.95.
G-BEFS	Rockwell Commander 112TC	13002	N1502J	29. 9.76	To G-SAAB 12/79. Canx.
G-BEFT	Cessna 421C Golden Eagle III	421C-0133	N3898C	27. 9.76	To G-SALS 5/92. Canx.
G-BEFU	Sturgeonair MJ.7 Mustang	SAL.108 & PFA/06-10010		4.10.76	Crashed at Barton Airport, Manchester on 15.5.83. Canx.
G-BEFV	Evans VP-2	V2-2390, YA-3 & PFA/63-10203		5.10.76	(Stored incomplete 8/93) Canx by CAA 6.12.95.
G-BEFW	PA-39-160 Twin Comanche C/R	39-91	EI-AYG G-AYZP/N8933Y	6.10.76	To N89AF 11/84. Canx 14.11.84.
G-BEFX	Hiller UH-12E	2261	XS165	5.10.76	To SX-HEC 5/87. Canx 13.4.87.
G-BEFY	Hiller UH-12E	2270	XS169	5.10.76	Canx 16.4.92 on sale to Greece.
G-BEFZ	HS.125 Srs.700B	257001	VR-HIM G-BEFZ	8.10.76	To N4555E/N700SV 12/83. Canx 7.12.83.
G-BEGA	Westland-Bell 47G-3B1 (Line No. WAT/227)	WA/705	XW185	19.10.76	
G-BEGB	BN-2A-21 Islander	485	RP-C2151	19.10.76	To PK-VIS 9/78. Canx 25.8.78.
G-BEGC	BN-2A-21 Islander	494	RP-C2153	19.10.76	To VH-SQS 10/78. Canx 25.9.78.
G-BEGD	BN-2A-21 Islander	562		19.10.76	To YR-BPB 8/77. Canx 5.9.77.
G-BEGE	BN-2A-8 Islander	563		19.10.76	To N38MN 4/77. Canx 19.5.77.
G-BEGF	BN-2A-26 Islander	564		19.10.76	To N80PA 11/77. Canx 30.11.77.
G-BEGG	Scheibe SF-25E Super Falke	4326	(D-KDFB)	15.10.76	
G-BEGH	BN-2A-21 Islander	565		19.10.76	Canx 30.9.77 on sale to Singapore. To PK-ZAE 10/77.
G-BEGI	BN-2A-8 Islander	566		19.10.76	To N39MN 4/77. Canx 19.5.77.
G-BEGJ	BN-2A-26 Islander	570		19.10.76	To N402JA 4/78. Canx 6.3.78.
G-BEGK	BN-2A-6 Islander	811		19.10.76	To 9XR-GW Rwanda AF 10/77. Canx 23.11.77.
G-BEGL	BN-2A-27 Islander	812		19.10.76	To YR-BNS 12/78. Canx 22.1.79.
G-BEGM	BN-2A-21 Islander	813		19.10.76	Canx 5.1.78 on sale to Australia. To P2-COD 2/78.
G-BEGN	IRMA BN-2A-21 Islander	814		19.10.76	To S7-AAC 7/78. Canx 3.7.78.
G-BEGO	BN-2A-20 Islander	815		19.10.76	To VH-TRW 9/78. Canx 12.6.78.
G-BEGP	BN-2A-27 Islander	816		19.10.76	To YR-BNT 10/78. Canx 22.1.79.
G-BEGR	BN-2A-27 Islander	817		19.10.76	To YR-BNU 10/78. Canx 22.1.79.
G-BEGS	BN-2A-21 Islander	818		19.10.76	To 5Y-BCS 11/79. Canx 23.3.81.
G-BEGT	BN-2A-27 Islander	819		19.10.76	To XA-HIT 2/78. Canx 22.2.78.
G-BEGU	BN-2A-21 Islander	820		19.10.76	To 5Y-BCR 9/80. Canx 9.9.80.
G-BEGV	PA-23-250 Aztec F	27-7654174	N62720	15.10.76	To G-USFT 5/97. Canx.
G-BEGW	Cameron V-56 HAFB	257		18.10.76	Retired due to fabric deterioration in 12/78. Canx as WFU 19.4.82.
G-BEGX	BN-2A Mk.III-2 Trislander	1043		29.10.76	To XA-LIZ 8/81. Canx 3.4.81.
G-BEGY	BN-2A Mk.III-2 Trislander	1044	ZS-KME G-BEGY	29.10.76	To N511WA 6/85. Canx 5.6.85.
G-BEGZ	Boeing 727-193 (Line No. 377)	19620	XY-ADR N898PC	20.10.76	To VR-CBG 1/82. Canx 21.1.82.
G-BEHA	BN-2A Mk.III-2 Trislander	1045		29.10.76	To XA-KOQ 10/80. Canx 22.10.80.
G-BEHB	BN-2A Mk.III-2 Trislander	1046		29.10.76	To XA-KOP 10/80. Canx 22.10.80.
G-BEHC	BN-2A Mk.III-2 Trislander	1047	(N1348G) G-BEHC	29.10.76	To HC-BLG 3/84. Canx 9.4.84.
G-BEHD	BN-2A Mk.III-2 Trislander	1048	XA-HOI G-BEHD	29.10.76	To N905GD 7/85. Canx 8.7.85.
G-BEHE	BN-2A Mk.III-2 Trislander	1049		29.10.76	To HC-BLH 7/84. Canx 19.9.84.
G-BEHF	BN-2A Mk.III-2 Trislander	1050		29.10.76	To (N1348M)/N164LG 2/82. Canx 28.4.82.
G-BEHG	Agusta-Bell 206B JetRanger II	8530		1.11.76	To G-GGCC 2/89. Canx.
G-BEHH	PA-32R-300 Cherokee Lance	32R-7680323	N6172J	29.10.76	
G-BEHI	Cameron DS-140 Hot Air Airship	200		25.10.76	To SE-ZAA 9/79. Canx 20.9.79.
G-BEHJ	Evans VP-1	PFA/1545		26.10.76	Canx by CAA 2.9.91. (Stored .92)
G-BEHK	Agusta-Bell 47G-3B1 Soloy	1575	EI-BIY G-BEHK/XT110	29.10.76	To Z-SOL. Canx 29.6.89.
G-BEHL	Agusta-Bell 47G-3B1	1581	XT117	29.10.76	To 5B-CFT 1/84. Canx 13.12.83.
G-BEHM	Taylor JT.1 Monoplane (Mod as Wildfire PDH.001)	PFA/1420		29.10.76	(Complete .90 but CofA problems) Canx by CAA 2.9.91. (On rebuild 11/95)
G-BEHN	Westland-Bell 47G-3B1 Soloy (Line No.WAN/45)	WA/354	EI-BKG G-BEHN/XT195	29.10.76	To N8229C 8/89. Canx 9.8.89.
G-BEHO	Westland-Bell 47G-3B1 (Line No.WAP/125)	WA/413	XT501	29.10.76	Crashed at Warren Farm, near Swindon on 23.6.79. Canx.
G-BEHP	Westland-Bell 47G-3B1 (Line No.WAT/226)	WA/704	XW184	29.10.76	Destroyed in crop-spraying accident at Charisworth Farm, near Blandford Forum on 28.6.80. Canx as destroyed 24.11.86
G-BEHR	Beechcraft A200 Super King Air	BB-230		1.11.76	To F-GDLE 5/83. Canx 9.3.83.
G-BEHS	PA-25-260 Pawnee C	25-5207	OE-AFX N8755L	2.11.76	CofA expired 25.6.93. (On overhaul 2/95)
G-BEHT	PA-25-260 Pawnee C	25-5313	OE-AFY N8812L	2.11.76	To 5B-CEL 9/82. Canx 23.9.82.
G-BEHU	PA-34-200T Seneca II	34-7670265	N6175J	3.11.76	
G-BEHV	Reims Cessna F.172N Skyhawk II	1541		3.11.76	

Regn	Type	c/n	Previous identity	Regn date	Fate or immediate subsequent identity (if known)
G-BEHW	Reims Cessna F.150M Commuter	1352		3.11.76	Seriously damaged in a heavy landing just off the runway at RAF Woodvale on 8.10.95. Canx as destroyed 28.11.95.
G-BEHX	Evans VP-2	V2-2338 & PFA/7222		8.11.76	Permit expired 22.1.90. (Stored 6/97)
G-BEHY	PA-28-181 Cherokee Archer II	28-7690340	N75393	9.11.76	To A6-DUB. Canx 25.8.88.
G-BEHZ	Short SC.7 Skyvan 3-100	SH1951	G-14-119	9.11.76	To Mexican AF as TP-0215/XC-UTN 1/77. Canx.
G-BEIA	Reims Cessna FRA.150M Aerobat	0317		8.11.76	
G-BEIB	Reims Cessna F.172N Skyhawk II	1533		5.11.76	To S5-DML. Canx 19.4.96.
G-BEIC	Sikorsky S-61N Mk.II	61-222	N307Y	28.12.76	
G-BEID	Sikorsky S-61N Mk.II (Mitsubishi c/n M61-003)	61-223	N317Y JA9507/N317Y	24.11.76	Ditched in the North Sea, 17 miles off Lerwick on 13.7.88, later sank but was recovered. Canx as destroyed 23.12.88.
G-BEIE	Evans VP-2	V2-2129 & PFA/7221		15.11.76	Completed as EI-BVT instead (Regd 4/88). Canx as WFU 2.8.91.
G-BEIF	Cameron O-65 HAFB	259		17.11.76	(On loan to Balloon Preservation Group 6/97) (Extant 1/98)
G-BEIG	Reims Cessna F.150M Commuter	1361		18.11.76	
G-BEIH	PA-25-235 Pawnee D	25-7656065	N54926	16.11.76	CofA expired 24.4.86. Canx as WFU 12.11.90 & 28.1.91.
G-BEII	PA-25-235 Pawnee D	25-7656059	N54918	16.11.76	
G-BEIJ	Schweizer Grumman G.164B Agcat	116B	N48685	16.11.76	To EC-EDD. Canx 23.4.87.
G-BEIK	Beechcraft A36 Bonanza	E-987		12.11.76	To G-SNOB 11/88. Canx.
G-BEIL	Socata MS.892E Rallye 150T	2653	F-BXDL	1.12.76	
G-BEIM	PA-34-200T Seneca II	34-7670300	N6908J	1.12.76	To JY-AFK 1/77. Canx 21.1.77.
G-BEIN	HS.125 Srs.600A	256067		23.11.76	To N522X 12/76. Canx 23.12.76.
G-BEIO	HS.125 Srs.600A	256069		23.11.76	To N350MH 1/77. Canx 17.1.77.
G-BEIP	PA-28-181 Cherokee Archer II	28-7790158	N6628F	22.11.76	
G-BEIR	DHC.6-310 Twin Otter	525		24.11.76	NTU - To G-BEJP 12/76. Canx.
G-BEIS	Evans VP-1	PFA/7029		25.11.76	Permit expired 16.7.90. (Believed in open storage 2/99 Thruxton - unmarked)
G-BEIT	Schweizer Grumman G.164B Agcat	110B	N48676	26.11.76	Crashed at Northcoates, Lincs on 3.3.78. Canx.
G-BEIU	BN-2A-26 Islander	571		9.12.76	Canx 5.9.77 on sale to USA. To VP-HCT 4/77.
G-BEIV	BN-2A-8 Islander	572		9.12.76	To (N69JA)/G-51-572/N28MN 3/78. Canx 20.2.78.
G-BEIW	BN-2A-20 Islander	573		9.12.76	To YV-142CP 6/77. Canx 5.9.77.
G-BEIX	BN-2A-21 Islander	574		9.12.76	To Mauritanian AF as 5T-MAY 3/78. Canx 21.5.79.
G-BEIY	BN-2A-26 Islander	575		9.12.76	To B-11110 6/77. Canx 21.7.77.
G-BEIZ	Cessna 500 Citation I (Unit No.363)	500-0354	(N5363J)	26.11.76	To N51GA. Canx 24.1.89.
G-BEJA	Thunder Ax6-56A HAFB	098		31.12.76	Canx by CAA 27.2.90.
G-BEJB	Thunder Ax6-56A HAFB (Flies with second canopy. First one destroyed by fire at Latimer on 4.9.77)	096		31.12.76	
G-BEJC	BN-2A-21 Islander	576		9.12.76	To Mauritanian AF as 5T-MAZ 2/78. Canx 22.2.78.
G-BEJD	Avro 748 Srs.1/105	1543	LV-HHE LV-PUF	17.12.76	
G-BEJE	Avro 748 Srs.1/105	1556	LV-IDV LV-PXD	7. 2.77	WFU at Blackpool. Scrapped 5/97. Canx as WFU 16.5.97.
G-BEJF	BN-2A-21 Islander	577		9.12.76	To Mauritanian AF as 5T-MAA(2) 3/78. Canx 21.5.79.
G-BEJG	BN-2A-26 Islander	578		9.12.76	To D-IEDB 4/78. Canx 29.3.78.
G-BEJH	BN-2A-21 Islander	579		9.12.76	To YR-BPG(2) 10/78. Canx 20.10.78.
G-BEJI	BN-2A-21 Islander	580		9.12.76	To YR-BPH(2) 11/78. Canx 17.11.78.
G-BEJJ	Slingsby T.65A Vega Prototype	1885		3.12.76	WFU in 5/78. Canx as destroyed 9.4.80.
G-BEJK	Cameron S-31 HAFB	256		1.12.76	(Extant 2/97)
G-BEJL	Sikorsky S-61N Mk.II	61-224	EI-BPK G-BEJL/N4606G	30.12.76	
G-BEJM	BAC One-Eleven Srs.423ET	BAC.118	Brazil AF VC92-2111/G-16-2	8.12.76	To PK-TST 4/98. Canx 8.4.98.
G-BEJN	Rockwell Commander 690A	11165	N57091	8.12.76	To N803RA. Canx 21.5.81.
G-BEJO(1)	Saffery S.250 HAFB (Toy)	1		8.12.76	Canopy destroyed. Canx.
G-BEJO(2)	Saffery S.250 HAFB (Toy)	1		. .76R	To G-BGXU as Wallingford WMB.1 c/n 001 7/79. Canx.
G-BEJO(3)	Saffery S.700 HAFB (Toy)	1		. .76R	Canx as WFU 23.8.85.
G-BEJP	DHC.6-310 Twin Otter	525	(G-BEIR)	23.12.76	To C-GATU 6/94. Canx 13.5.94.
G-BEJR	PA-28-151 Cherokee Warrior	28-7715168	N9528N	31.12.76	To JY-AFI 1/77. Canx 24.1.77.
G-BEJS	PA-28-140 Cherokee Cruiser	28-7725047	N9515N	31.12.76	To JY-AFJ 1/77. Canx 24.1.77.
G-BEJT	PA-23-250 Aztec F	27-7754038	N62805	31.12.76	To G-YSFT 12/87. Canx.
G-BEJU	Beechcraft 65-A80 Queen Air	LD-134	ZS-OOT ZS-OCT(1)/ZS-DTL	27.12.76	NTU - Canx 27.12.76 as Not Imported. Remained as ZS-OOT.
G-BEJV	PA-34-200T Seneca II	34-7770062	N7657F	31.12.76	
G-BEJW	BAC One-Eleven Srs.423ET	BAC.154	Brazil AF VC92-2110	8.12.76	To 5N-KKK 8/93. Canx 26.7.93.
G-BEJX	Partenavia P.68B Victor	86	A6-ALO G-BELX	31.12.76	
G-BEJY	Hughes 369D (500D)	116-0011D		31.12.76	To N27385 5/82. Canx 10.5.82.
G-BEJZ	Ted Smith Aerostar 601PE	61P-0376-122	N90671	21. 2.77	Restored as N90671 10/83. Canx 20.10.83.
G-BEKA	BAC One-Eleven Srs.520FN	BAC.230	4X-BAR G-16-22/G-BEKA/PP-SDR	5. 1.77	To G-OBWC 12/92. Canx.
G-BEKB	PA-23-250 Aztec	27-323	OO-BYB D-IBYB	31.12.76	CofA expired 1.7.82 & WFU at East Midlands. Canx as PWFU 16.7.84.
G-BEKC	Avro 748 Srs.1/105	1541	LV-HHC LV-PRJ/LV-PJR	28. 2.77	Broken up in 5/92 at Ringway. Canx 21.10.92 on sale to USA - Nose section reportedly sold to Reflectone of Tampa, USA for use in the construction of an ATP simulator.
G-BEKD	Avro 748 Srs.1/105	1544	LV-HHF LV-PUM	10. 6.77	To EC-DTP 7/83. Canx 29.7.83.

Regn	Type	c/n	Previous identity	Regn date	Fate or immediate subsequent identity (if known)
G-BEKE	Avro 748 Srs.1/105	1545	LV-HHG	24. 3.77	WFU 26.7.93 at Liverpool for spares use. Broken up in 10.93
			LV-PUP		and finally scrapped in 4/95. Canx as WFU 10.9.96.
G-BEKF	Avro 748 Srs.1/105	1542	LV-HHD	24. 3.77	Crashed on take-off from Sumburgh on 31.7.79.
			LV-PUC		Canx as destroyed 14.12.79.
G-BEKG	Avro 748 Srs.1/105	1557	G-VAJK	8. 7.77	To G-DAAL 8/92. Canx
			VR CDH/G-BEKG/LV-IEE/LV-PXH		
G-BEKH	Agusta-Bell 206B JetRanger II	8531		6. 1.77	To F-GFDO 7/87. Canx 23.7.87.
G-BEKI	Sikorsky S-61N Mk.II	61-766		15. 4.77	NTU - To 9M-AVO 6/77. Canx 14.6.77.
G-BEKJ	Sikorsky S-61N Mk.II	61-768		28. 4.77	NTU - To 9M-AVP 10/77. Canx 14.6.77.
G-BEKK	Scheibe SF-25E Super Falke	4303	(PH-JAW)	11. 1.77	Crashed on take-off from Seppe, Holland on 4.8.79. Canx.
			D-KEYA		Restored as D-KEYA & rebuilt as ZS-VOX in 7/81.
G-BEKL	Bede BD-4E-150	151 & BD4E/2		11. 1.77	Permit expired 14.10.80. (On rebuild Bladon-on-Tyne 5/93)
	(Incorporates parts from G-AYKB)				
G-BEKM	Evans VP-1	PFA/7025		12. 1.77	Permit expired 23.3.95.
G-BEKN	Reims Cessna FRA.150M Aerobat	0318		12. 1.77	CofA expired 8.10.89. (Stored engineless with no nosewheel 4/99 Bourn)
G-BEKO	Reims Cessna F.182Q Skylane	0037		12. 1.77	
G-BEKP	BN-2A-21 Islander	581		13. 1.77	To EP-PBE 11/77. Canx 2.11.77.
G-BEKR	Rand Robinson KR-2			14. 1.77	Permit expired 20.8.88. (Status uncertain)
		EAA/102591 & PFA/129-11046			
G-BEKS	PA-25-235 Pawnee D	25-7656083	N82336	13. 1.77	Crashed at Green Hill, Barham, near Canterbury on 10.7.84.
					Canx as WFU 24.11.86.
G-BEKT	PA-25-235 Pawnee D	25-7656088	N82341	13. 1.77	To F-GCLG(2) 11/82. Canx 11.11.82.
G-BEKU	BN-2A-20 Islander	582		13. 1.77	Canx 9.9.77 on sale to Australia. To P2-ISD(2) 9/77.
G-BEKV	BN-2A-8 Islander	583		13. 1.77	To G-51-583/N29MN 3/78. Canx 2.3.78.
G-BEKW	BN-2A-21 Islander	584		13. 1.77	To N46958 4/77. Canx 10.6.77.
G-BEKX	BN-2A-8 Islander	585		13. 1.77	To N31MN 4/78. Canx 2.3.78.
G-BEKY	BN-2A-20 Islander	586		13. 1.77	To N407JA 3/79. Canx 9.2.79.
G-BEKZ	BN-2A-21 Islander	587		13. 1.77	To Mauritanian AF as 5T-MAV 5/77. Canx 5.9.77.
G-BELA	BN-2A-27 Islander	588		13. 1.77	To (N69JA)/N405JA 4/78. Canx 7.4.78.
G-BELB	BN-2A-21 Islander	589		13. 1.77	To S7-AAD 5/80. Canx 2.6.80.
G-BELC	BN-2A-27 Islander	590		13. 1.77	To N404JA 4/78. Canx 7.4.78.
G-BELD	IRMA BN-2A-27 Islander	821		13. 1.77	To YR-BNO 12/78. Canx 22.12.78.
	(Originally regd as BN-2A-6)				
G-BELE	IRMA BN-2A-27 Islander	822		13. 1.77	To YR-BNP 12/78. Canx 22.12.78.
	(Originally regd as BN-2A-6)				
G-BELF	IRMA BN-2A-26 Islander	823	D-IBRA	13. 1.77	
	(Originally regd as BN-2A-6)		G-BELF		
G-BELG	IRMA BN-2A-27 Islander	824		13. 1.77	To YR-BNR 12/78. Canx 22.12.78.
	(Originally regd as BN-2A-6)				
G-BELH	IRMA BN-2A-21 Islander	825		13. 1.77	To YR-BNI 11/78. Canx 17.11.78.
	(Originally regd as BN-2A-6)				
G-BELI	IRMA BN-2A-21 Islander	826		13. 1.77	To YR-BNJ 11/78. Canx 17.11.78.
	(Originally regd as BN-2A-6)				
G-BELJ	IRMA BN-2A-21 Islander	827		13. 1.77	To YR-BNK 10/78. Canx 20.10.78.
	(Originally regd as BN-2A-6)				
G-BELK	IRMA BN-2A-21 Islander	828		13. 1.77	To N50693 5/84. Canx 10.5.84.
	(Originally regd as BN-2A-6)				
G-BELL	PA-28R-200-2 Cherokee Arrow		G-BBDF	14. 7.76	Fatal crash into Taunus Mountains, near Frankfurt, West
		28R-7335255			Germany on 25.5.78. Canx.
G-BELM	IRMA BN-2A-9 Islander	829	YR-BNX(1)	13. 1.77	To TR-LXX. Canx 13.3.78.
	(Originally regd as BN-2A-6)				
G-BELN	IRMA BN-2A-6 Islander	830	YR-BNY(1)	13. 1.77	DBR in storm at Bembridge on 14.12.78. Later stored at
					Hurn. Canx as WFU 2.3.81.
G-BELO	Douglas DC-10-10	46501	N10DC	24. 1.77	To N183AT 5/83. Canx 19.5.83.
	(Line No. 2)		N101AA		
G-BELP	PA-28-151 Cherokee Warrior		N9543N	18. 1.77	
		28-7715219			
G-BELR	PA-28-140 Cherokee Cruiser		N9541N	18. 1.77	To EI-CMB 9/95. Canx 4.9.95.
		28-7725094			
G-BELS	DHC.6-310 Twin Otter	530	C-GNZT-X	20. 1.77	To ZK-MCO 12/83. Canx 12.12.83.
G-BELT	Reims Cessna F.150J	0409X		26. 1.77	
	(Mainly rebuild of G-AWUV and parts of G-ATND)				
G-BELU	Reims Cessna F.150M	1382		24. 1.77	DBR in bomb blast at Eglington on 21.9.78.
					Canx as WFU 12.3.79.
G-BELV	Cessna 404 Titan Ambassador II		(N5443G)	24. 1.77	To G-BKWA 6/83. Canx.
		404-0061			
G-BELW	Cessna 421C Golden Eagle III		(N8178G)	24. 1.77	To N8506Z 10/80. Canx 25.10.80.
		421C-0299			
G-BELX	Cameron V-56 HAFB	261		31. 1.77	
G-BELY	Short SC.7 Skyvan 3-100	SH1952	G-14-120	27. 1.77	To Mexican AF as TP-0216/XC-UTI 4/77. Canx 4.4.77.
G-BELZ	Short SC.7 Skyvan 3-100	SH1953	G-14-121	27. 1.77	To Mexican AF as TP-0217/XC-UTJ 6/77. Canx 20.6.77.
G-BEMA	Cessna 310R II	310R-0586	N87476	31. 1.77	To F-GFIF 7/85. Canx 10.6.85.
G-BEMB	Reims Cessna F.172M Skyhawk II	1487		27. 1.77	
G-BEMC	Reims Cessna F.172M Skyhawk II	1445		27. 1.77	To 5B-CEM 12/83. Canx 6.12.83.
G-BEMD	Beechcraft 95-B55 Baron	TC-2051		27. 1.77	To N155MD 9/96. Canx 4.9.96.
G-BEME	HS.125 Srs.400B	25231	5N-AQY	9. 2.77	To N125GC 10/84. Canx 19.10.84.
			G-BEME/D-CBVW		
G-BEMF	Taylor JT.1 Monoplane	PFA/1441		2. 2.77	Crashed near Hontion on 26.3.88.
					Canx as destroyed 15.12.88.
G-BEMG	IRMA BN-2A-26 Islander	831	YR-BNZ(1)	4. 2.77	To 9V-BKQ 1/79. Canx 28.3.79.
	(Originally regd as BN-2A-6)				

Regn	Type	c/n	Previous identity	Regn date	Fate or immediate subsequent identity (if known)
G-BEMH	IRMA BN-2A-20 Islander (Originally regd as BN-2A-6)	832		4. 2.77	To VH-EER 9/79. Canx 21.5.79.
G-BEMI	Thunder Ax6-56A HAFB	095		7. 2.77	Not completed. Canx 22.12.81.
G-BEMJ	IRMA BN-2A-9 Islander (Originally regd as BN-2A-6)	833		4. 2.77	Canx 11.1.79 on sale to Australia. To DQ-FCX 2/79.
G-BEMK	IRMA BN-2A-26 Islander (Originally regd as BN-2A-6)	834		4. 2.77	Canx 21.5.79 on sale to USA. To HP-813 5/79.
G-BEML	IRMA BN-2A-20 Islander (Originally regd as BN-2A-6)	835		4. 2.77	To VH-WPT 8/81. Canx 21.5.79.
G-BEMM	Slingsby Cadet III (Converted from T.31B)	1247	BGA942 RAFGSA 289/BGA942	27. 1.77	
G-BEMN	IRMA BN-2A-21 Islander (Originally regd as BN-2A-6)	836		4. 2.77	To Botswana DF as OA-5/Z3 in 2/79. Canx 21.5.79.
G-BEMO	IRMA BN-2A-21 Islander (Originally regd as BN-2A-6)	837		4. 2.77	To PK-BIG 5/79. Canx 17.5.79.
G-BEMP	IRMA BN-2B-27 Islander (Originally regd as BN-2A-6)	838		4. 2.77	To TR-LYW 2/79. Canx 8.10.79.
G-BEMR	IRMA BN-2A-26 Islander (Originally regd as BN-2A-6)	839	D-IEDC G-BEMR	4. 2.77	To V3-HFA 7/90. Canx 12.7.90.
G-BEMS	IRMA BN-2A-27 Islander (Originally regd as BN-2A-6)	840		4. 2.77	To YR-BNV 12/79. Canx 20.12.79.
G-BEMT	Bede BD-5G	206		7. 2.77	Not completed. Canx by CAA 1.11.84.
G-BEMU	Thunder Ax5-42 HAFB	097		9. 2.77	
G-BEMV	PA-28-140 Cherokee Cruiser	28-7725108	N9561N	9. 2.77	To F-GDMN 11/83. Canx 13.7.83.
G-BEMW	PA-28-181 Cherokee Archer II	28-7790243	N9566N	9. 2.77	
G-BEMX	Cessna 404 Titan Cruiser II	404-0063	(N5446G)	9. 2.77	To G-RUSH 5/82. Canx.
G-BEMY	Reims Cessna FRA.150M Aerobat	0315		9. 2.77	
G-BEMZ	Bristol 175 Britannia Srs.253F	13457	A6-HMS G-BEMZ/XL660	11. 2.77	To 9Q-CGP(2) 10/82. Canx 19.10.82.
G-BENA	Reims Cessna F.182Q Skylane	0046		11. 2.77	NTU - Not Imported. To (OO-...)/OE-DIR. Canx 20.6.77.
G-BENB	Short SD.3-30 Var.100	SH3008	D-CDLT G-BENB/(D-CDLT)/G-14-3008	16. 2.77	To G-14-3008/N330SB 6/79. Canx 29.6.79.
G-BENC	Cessna 402B	402B-0031	(N.....) G-BENC/SE-FRO/OY-AKU/N5431M	17. 2.77	To N29517 3/82. Canx 31.3.82.
G-BEND	Cameron V-56 HAFB	260		14. 2.77	
G-BENE	Cessna 402B	402B-1037	N98668	17. 2.77	To (OO-SVO)/OO-SVD. Canx 7.11.88.
G-BENF	Cessna T.210L Turbo Centurion II	210-61356	N732AE D-EIPY/N732AE	17. 2.77	Crashed at Ipswich on 29.5.81. Canx as destroyed 25.3.85. (Wreck in open storage 8/97)
G-BENG	Westland-Bell 47G-3B1 (Line No.WAS/193)	WA/593	XT831	5. 4.77	DBR in forced landing at Northfield Farm, Barnby Moor, Notts., on 9.9.80. Canx.
G-BENH	Phoenix Luton LA-5A Major	PAL/1208 & PFA/1208	(G-ARWX)	21. 2.77	Canx 2.1.86 on sale to Ireland. To EI-CGF 7/92.
G-BENI	Bell 47G-4A	7652	9L-LAN	23. 2.77	Badly damaged in crash at Lodge Farm, Kineton, Warwickshire on 19.11.79. Remains to Heliwork for spares use. Canx as destroyed 5.12.83.
G-BENJ	Rockwell Commander 112B	522	N1391J	7. 3.77	
G-BENK	Reims Cessna F.172M Skyhawk II	1509		2. 3.77	
G-BENL	PA-25-235 Pawnee D	25-7656038	N54893	1. 3.77	Crashed on take-off from Sutton Bank on 10.7.85 and badly damaged. Used for spares at Old Buckenham. Canx as WFU 17.12.90. (Stored 2/96 RAF West Raynham)
G-BENM	PA-31-325 Navajo Chieftain C	31-7712017	N62998	1. 3.77	Restored as N62998 4/81. Canx 7.4.81.
G-BENN	Cameron V-56 HAFB	278		4. 3.77	
G-BENO	Enstrom F-280C-UK Shark	1060		3. 3.77	To G-SHSS 10/89. Canx.
G-BENP	Druine D.31A Turbulent	PFA/48-10212		21. 2.77	Not completed. Canx 19.7.82.
G-BENR	Rockwell Commander 114	14002	N1902J	11. 3.77	Flew into high ground at Upper Waltham, near Chichester on 14.12.79. Canx.
G-BENS	Saffery Model HAFB (Toy)	01		11. 3.77	Canx as destroyed 18.10.88.
G-BENT	Cameron N-77 HAFB	367		9. 2.77	Canx as WFU 15.1.90.
"G-BENT"	IRMA BN-2A-6 Islander	850		----	Wreck of G-BESK painted as such after being DBR on 14.12.78.
G-BENU	BN-2A-9 Islander	591		7. 3.77	To 9Q-CMJ 6/79. Canx.
G-BENV	BN-2A-26 Islander	592		7. 3.77	Canx 5.9.77 on sale to USA. To HP-785 7/77.
G-BENW	BN-2A-21 Islander	593		7. 3.77	NTU - To RP-C2168. Canx 19.6.78.
G-BENX	BN-2A-21 Islander	594		7. 3.77	NTU - To RP-C2159. Canx 19.6.78.
G-BENY	BN-2A-20 Islander	595		7. 3.77	To 9V-BJN 1/78. Canx 8.3.78.
G-BENZ	BN-2B-21 Islander	596		7. 3.77	To N331MS 12/79. Canx 14.2.80.
G-BEOA	BN-2A-27 Islander	597		7. 3.77	To N123NP 7/79. Canx 17.7.79.
G-BEOB	BN-2A-26 Islander	598		7. 3.77	To XA-IIM 1/79. Canx 21.5.79.
G-BEOC	BN-2A-26 Islander	599		7. 3.77	To N20875 1/83. Canx 14.1.83.
G-BEOD	Cessna 180	180-32092	OO-SPZ D-EDAH/SL-AAT/N3294D	14. 3.77	Damaged on landing at Errol, Perthshire on 29.6.89. CofA expired 6.9.91. Canx by CAA 6.12.89. (Stored 3/97)
G-BEOE(1)	Reims Cessna FRA.150M Aerobat	0298	(5Y-AZY)	11. 3.77	NTU - Canx 21.3.77 as Not Imported. To D-EALP 9/78.
G-BEOE(2)	Reims Cessna FRA.150M Aerobat	0322		21. 3.77	
G-BEOF	Reims Cessna F.150M Commuter	1358		11. 3.77	NTU - Not Imported. Canx 5.12.83. To D-EGTB 2/78.
G-BEOG	Reims Cessna F.182Q Skylane II	0021		11. 3.77	Crashed into oil storage depot near Shoreham on 11.3.79. Canx.
G-BEOH	PA-28R-201T Turbo Arrow III	28R-7703038	N1905H	11. 3.77	
G-BEOI	PA-18-180 Super Cub	18-7709028	N54976	11. 3.77	

Regn	Type	c/n	Previous identity	Regn date	Fate or immediate subsequent identity (if known)
G-BEOJ	PA-31-350 Navajo Chieftain	31-7405212		14. 3.77	To N68950 5/80. Canx 27.5.80.
G-BEOK	Reims Cessna F.150M Commuter	1366		14. 3.77	
G-BEOL	Short SC.7 Skyvan 3-200	SH1954	G-14-122	16. 3.77	To JA8803(2) 8/77. Canx 1.8.77.
G-BEOM	Short SC.7 Skyvan 3-200	SH1955	G-14-123	16. 3.77	To YV-O-MC-10 in 9/77. Canx 28.9.77.
G-BEON	Sikorsky S-61N Mk.II	61-770		9. 5.77	Crashed into the sea off St.Mary's, Isles of Scilly on 16.7.83. Canx as destroyed 4.3.86.
G-BEOO	Sikorsky S-61N Mk.II	61-771		25. 7.77	To N261F 11/98. Canx 16.10.98.
G-BEOP	Cessna 401B II	402B-1058	N98707	17. 3.77	To ST-AGU 5/77. Canx 4.5.77.
G-BEOR	Cessna 210L Centurion II	210-61205	N2261S	17. 3.77	To ST-AGV 5/77. Canx 3.5.77.
G-BEOS	Bellanca 7GCBC Citabria	954-76	N88271	21. 3.77	Crashed at Aboyne on 11.10.78. Canx.
G-BEOT	PA-25-235 Pawnee D	25-7756014		29. 3.77	To SE-KKC. Canx 5.7.89.
G-BEOU	PA-31-350 Navajo Chieftain	31-7652153	N62895	28. 3.77	Restored as N62895 3/80. Canx 21.3.80.
G-BEOV	PA-28-140 Cherokee Cruiser	28-7725183	N9617N	24. 3.77	(Last known of based in Dubai). Canx as destroyed 4.10.84.
G-BEOW	PA-28-140 Cherokee Cruiser	28-7725184	(A6-...) G-BEOW/N9619N	24. 3.77	Canx 15.12.87 on sale to Sri Lanka.
G-BEOX	Lockheed 414 Hudson IIIA (A-29A-LO)	414-6464	VH-AGJ VH-SMM/R.Australian AF A16-199/FH174/41-36975	25. 3.77	Canx as WFU 22.12.81. (On display 9/97 Hendon)
G-BEOY	Reims Cessna FRA.150L Aerobat	0150	F-BTFS	30. 3.77	
G-BEOZ	Armstrong-Whitworth 650 Argosy Srs.101	AW.6660	N895U N6502R/G-1-7	28. 3.77	Canx as WFU 19.11.87. On display 10/97 East Midlands.
G-BEPA	Westland-Bell 47G-3B1 (Line No.WAP/146)	WA/424	XT512	29. 3.77	To HB-XHB 2/78. Canx 31.1.78.
G-BEPB	Pereira Osprey II	88 & PFA/70-10193		29. 3.77	
G-BEPC	SNCAN Stampe SV-4C	64	F-BFUM F-BFZM/French Mil	17.10.77	
G-BEPD	K & S SA.102.5 Cavalier	73054F & PFA/01-10062		23. 3.77	Canx by CAA 2.9.91.
G-BEPE	Short SC.5 Belfast C.1	SH1816	G-52-14 XR362/G-ASKE	30. 3.77	WFU 26.10.84. Broken up in 2/94 at Southend (started 18.2.94, gone by 25.2.94) Canx as destroyed 1.3.94.
G-BEPF	SNCAN Stampe SV-4C	424	F-BCVD	30. 3.77	(Stored 2/98 Chilbolton)
G-BEPG	BN-2A Mk.III-2 Trislander	1051		4. 4.77	To XA-JPE 1/79. Canx 21.5.79.
G-BEPH	BN-2A Mk.III-3 Trislander (Mod to three-bladed propellors by 4/94) (Originally regd as Mk.III-2, changed in 4/79 to Mk.III-3)	1052	S7-AAG G-BEPH	4. 4.77	
G-BEPI	BN-2A Mk.III-2 Trislander (Mod to three-bladed propellors by 12/93)	1053		4. 4.77	
G-BEPJ	BN-2A Mk.III-2 Trislander	1054		4. 4.77	To OE-1 Botswana DF /84. Canx 19.9.84.
G-BEPK	BN-2A Mk.III-2 Trislander	1055		4. 4.77	To OE-2 Botswana DF /84. Canx 6.12.84.
G-BEPL	Short SC.5 Belfast C.1	SH1823	XR369	31. 3.77	NTU - Not converted. Canx as WFU 11/78. Broken up at Hucknall in mid-1979.
G-BEPM	Rockwell S2R-800 Thrush Commander	5009	N4948X	29. 6.77	Canx 1.11.79 on sale to Kenya.
G-BEPN	PA-25-235 Pawnee D	25-7656022	N54877	7. 4.77	Crashed on take-off from Aldsworth, near Cirencester on 11.2.78. CofA expired 6.4.79. (Frame in store 3/96)
G-BEPO	Cameron N-77 HAFB	279		1. 4.77	(Extant 2/97 - Balloon Preservation Group?) Canx as WFU 14.5.98.
G-BEPP	Agusta-Bell 206B JetRanger II	8532	F-GAML	5. 4.77	To OH-HLK 1/87. Canx 27.1.87.
G-BEPR	PA-31-350 Navajo Chieftain	31-7752063	N27214	13. 4.77	To N37620 5/80. Canx 16.5.80.
G-BEPS	Short SC.5 Belfast C.1	SH1822	G-52-13 XR368	6. 4.77	
G-BEPT	DH.114 Heron 2	14084	(VQ-LBA) CR-SAH/(CR-GAP)/CR-SAH/CR-IAB	6. 4.77	To N586PR 3/78. Canx 28.3.78.
G-BEPU	PA-31-350 Navajo Chieftain	31-7552114	OY-BLF	5. 5.77	Restored as OY-BLF 11/80. Canx 9.10.80.
G-BEPV	Fokker S-11-1 Instructor	6274	PH-ANK(2) Dutch Navy 174/Dutch AF E-31	13. 4.77	Permit expired 15.4.93. (Frame stored 4/95)
G-BEPW	Cessna T.310R II	310R-0888	N3679G	14. 4.77	To F-GATM 9/77. Canx 7.9.77.
G-BEPX	Bristol 175 Britannia Srs.253F	13511	9Q-CAJ XM517	14. 4.77	WFU in 12/77 & used as engine test bed at Luton. Broken up in 3/80. Canx 1.7.83.
G-BEPY	Rockwell Commander 112B	524	N1399J	20. 4.77	
G-BEPZ	Cameron D-96 Hot-Air Airship	300		13. 4.77	Damaged at Warren Farm, near Hungerford on 8.1.94 & DBR during recovery. Canx as WFU 28.4.94.
G-BERA	Socata MS.892E Rallye 150ST	2821	F-ODEX	13. 4.77	
G-BERB	Socata MS.892E Rallye 150ST	2822		13. 4.77	To F-GDQY 10/84. Canx 29.10.84.
G-BERC	Socata MS.892E Rallye 150ST	2858		13. 4.77	
G-BERD	Thunder Ax6-56A HAFB	106		25. 4.77	
G-BERE	Thunder Ax6-56A HAFB	105		2. 3.77	CofA expired 13.2.79 & WFU. Canx as WFU 16.3.82
G-BERF	Bell 212	30782	VR-BIJ G-BERF/9Y-TFW/G-BERF/N9925K/N18092	28. 4.77	To 5N-AQV(2). Canx.
G-BERG	Aerospatiale SA.330J Puma	1472		28. 4.77	To VH-WOB 4/82. Canx 15.4.82.
G-BERH	Aerospatiale SA.330J Puma	1475	VH-WOE G-BERH	28. 4.77	Restored as VH-WOE 8/85. Canx 1.8.85.
G-BERI	Rockwell Commander 114	14234	N4909W	6. 5.77	
G-BERJ	Bell 47G-4A	7512	ZS-HBW	17. 4.77	Crashed at Heathcote Home Farm, near Leamington Spa on 28.6.87 while crop spraying. Canx as destroyed 26.10.90.
G-BERK	Chown Osprey Mk.6 HAFB (Toy)	AKC-99		25. 9.81	Canx as WFU 15.10.84.
G-BERL	American Aviation AA-5B Tiger	AA5B-0466	N6157A	19. 4.77	To G-OMED 10/84. Canx.

Regn	Type	c/n	Previous identity	Regn date	Fate or immediate subsequent identity (if known)
G-BERM	American Aviation AA-5A Cheetah	AA5A-0352	N6141A	19. 4.77	To G-RCPW 3/84. Canx.
G-BERN	Saffery S.330 HAFB (Toy)	4		19. 4.77	
G-BERO	Westland-Bell 47G-3B1 (Line No.WAS/210)	WA/606	XT844	19. 4.77	To HB-XHM 3/78. Canx 17.3.78.
G-BERP	HS.125 Srs.700A	NA0202 & 257003	G-5-19	25. 4.77	To N64688 5/77. Canx 27.5.77.
G-BERR	Thunder Ax7-77A HAFB	110		25. 4.77	To F-GCZC 8/82. Canx 1.6.82.
G-BERS	Thunder Ax6-56A HAFB	108		25. 4.77	To PH-YSI 6/79. Canx 30.5.79.
G-BERT	Cameron V-56 HAFB	273		19. 4.77	
G-BERU	PA-18-95 Super Cub	18-1337	D-ENLF ALAT 18-1337/51-15337	13. 7.77	NTU - Not Imported. Remained as D-ENLF. Canx 14.2.78.
G-BERV	HS.125 Srs.700A	NA0203 & 257005		25. 4.77	To N620M 6/77. Canx 15.6.77.
G-BERW	Rockwell Commander 114	14214	N4884W	6. 5.77	
G-BERX	HS.125 Srs.700A	NA0204 & 257006	G-5-18	25. 4.77	To N724B 7/77. Canx 13.7.77.
G-BERY	American Aviation AA-1B Trainer	AA1B-0193	N9693L	27.10.77	
G-BERZ	Short SC.7 Skyvan 3	SH1956		25. 4.77	To HZ-ZAL 1/78. Canx 5.1.78.
G-BESA	Beechcraft 95-58 Baron	TH-406	N25707	12. 5.77	To N98749 10/81. Canx 15.10.81.
G-BESB	IRMA BN-2A-9 Islander (Originally regd as BN-2A-6)	841	YR-BNX(2)	21. 4.77	Canx 8.11.79 on sale to Colombia. To N8536A 8/79.
G-BESC	IRMA BN-2A-20 Islander (Originally regd as BN-2A-6)	842		21. 4.77	To VH-IOA 9/81. Canx 8.1.80.
G-BESD	IRMA BN-2A-20 Islander (Originally regd as BN-2A-6)	843	YR-BNY(2)	21. 4.77	To P2-COG 9/79. Canx 27.9.79.
G-BESE	IRMA BN-2A-6 Islander	844		21. 4.77	DBR in storm at Bembridge on 14.12.78. Later stored at Hurn. Canx as WFU 2.3.81.
G-BESF	IRMA BN-2A-8 Islander (Originally regd as BN-2A-6)	845		21. 4.77	To VH-FCO 4/79. Canx 28.3.79.
G-BESG	IRMA BN-2B-26 Islander (Originally regd as BN-2A-6. Used as BN-2B development aircraft)	846		21. 4.77	To P2-BAB 5/83. Canx 25.5.83.
G-BESH	IRMA BN-2A-26 Islander (Originally regd as BN-2A-6)	847		21. 4.77	To G-HMCG 10/79. Canx.
G-BESI	IRMA BN-2A-26 Islander (Originally regd as BN-2A-6)	848		21. 4.77	To HP-870 1/80. Canx 25.2.80.
G-BESJ	IRMA BN-2A-21 Islander (Originally regd as BN-2A-6)	849		21. 4.77	To 9J-AEO 7/81. Canx 14.8.81.
G-BESK	IRMA BN-2A-6 Islander	850		21. 4.77	DBR in storm at Bembridge on 14.12.78. Wreck painted as "G-BENT". Canx.
G-BESL	PBN BN-2A-26 Islander	2001		21. 4.77	To B-11111 7/77. Canx 30.8.77.
G-BESM	PBN BN-2B-21 Islander	2002	D-IAOR N302SK/N407JA/G-BESM	21. 4.77	To 5Y-JAK 4/98. Canx 21.4.98.
G-BESN	PBN BN-2A-20 Islander	2003	N408JA G-51-2003/G-BESN	21. 4.77	To YV-337CP 7/79. Canx 18.7.79.
G-BESO	PBN BN-2A-26 Islander	2004		21. 4.77	To SX-DKB 4/94. Canx 22.4.94.
G-BESP	PBN BN-2A-26 Islander	2005		21. 4.77	To N417WA 4/81. Canx 27.4.81.
G-BESR	PBN BN-2A-26 Islander	2006		21. 4.77	To V2-LCL 12/82. Canx 19.11.82.
G-BESS	Hughes 369D (500D)	116-0029D		5. 5.77	To N4320K. Canx 9.7.91.
G-BEST	Beechcraft A200 Super King Air	BB-288		8. 6.77	To G-ORMC 1/80. Canx.
G-BESU	PBN BN-2A-27 Islander	2008		21. 4.77	To N8055X 8/79. Canx 24.8.79.
G-BESV	PBN BN-2A-26 Islander	2009		21. 4.77	To N68HA 8/79. Canx 3.9.79.
G-BESW	PBN BN-2A-26 Islander	2010		21. 4.77	To N3835Z 3/83. Canx 17.3.83.
G-BESX	PBN BN-2A-26 Islander	2007		21. 4.77	To B-11116 8/81. Canx 7.9.81.
G-BESY	BAC 167 Strikemaster Mk.80A (Officially regd as Mk.88)	PS.364	G-27-299	26. 4.77	To Saudi AF as 1133 in 7/77. Canx.
G-BESZ	BAC 167 Strikemaster Mk.80A (Officially regd as Mk.88)	PS.365	G-27-300	26. 4.77	To Saudi AF as 1134 in 7/77. Canx.
G-BETA	Rollason-Luton B.2A Beta	01 & PFA/02-10140		26. 4.77	Not completed. Canx by CAA 3.2.87.
G-BETB	BAC-Sepecat Jaguar T.2	PS.841	G-27-279	26. 4.77	To Oman AF as 203 in 6/77. Canx.
G-BETC	Cameron V-56 HAFB	253		3. 5.77	To N125CB. Canx 19.10.82.
G-BETD	Robin HR.200/100 Club	20	PH-SRL	28. 4.77	
G-BETE	Rollason Beta B.2A (Incorporates parts from PFA/1304)	PFA/02-10169		26. 4.77	(Under construction 4/97)
G-BETF	Cameron Champion 35SS HAFB (Champion Spark Plug shape)	280		17. 5.77	Canx as WFU 24.1.92. (Extant 5/94) To British Balloon Museum, Newbury.
G-BETG	Cessna 180K Skywagon	180-52873	N64146	17. 5.77	
G-BETH	Thunder Ax6-56A HAFB	113		27. 5.77	Canx as WFU 11.5.93. (Extant but unflyable 9/94) To British Balloon Museum, Newbury.
G-BETI	Pitts S-1D Special	7-0314 & PFA/09-10156		28. 4.77	
G-BETJ	Douglas DC-8-33 (Line No. 75)	45379	5Y-ASA PH-DCD	9. 5.77	CofA expired 11.11.77 & WFU. Broken up in 7/85 at Stansted. Canx.
G-BETK	Rockwell Shrike Commander 500S	3137	C9-AOD CR-AOD/N9118N	29. 4.77	Restored as N9118N 5/77. Canx 20.5.77.
G-BETL	PA-25-235 Pawnee D	25-7656016	N54874	27. 5.77	
G-BETM	PA-25-235 Pawnee D	25-7656066	N54927	5. 5.77	
G-BETN	Short SD.3-30 Var.100	SH3010	G-14-3010	5. 5.77	To N330GW 6/77. Canx 28.10.77.
G-BETO	Morane-Saulnier MS.885 Super Rallye	34	F-BKED	18. 5.77	
G-BETP	Cameron O-65 HAFB	286		3. 5.77	
G-BETR	Cessna A.188B AgTruck	188-02850T	N731EX	6. 5.77	To 5B-CEO 6/81. Canx 19.6.81.

Regn	Type	c/n	Previous identity	Regn date	Fate or immediate subsequent identity (if known)
G-BETS	Cessna A.188B AgTruck	188-01920T	SE-GGV N70431	25. 5.77	To CS-ASF. Canx 20.4.88.
G-BETT(1)	Enstrom 280C Shark	1081		. .77R	NTU - Not Imported. To N627H. Canx.
G-BETT(2)	PA-34-200-2 Seneca	34-7250011	EI-BCD PH-AVM/N1978T	20. 6.77	
G-BETU	Piper J3C-65 Cub (L-4J-PI)	12589	F-BETU 44-80293	4. 5.77	Stalled and crashed on take-off from St.Just, Lands End on 6.9.81 & extensively damaged. Canx.
G-BETV	HS.125 Srs.600B	256035	F-BKMC	10. 6.77	To G-SUFC 12/95. Canx.
G-BETW	Rand KR-2	KR2/TAW.1		26. 4.77	No Permit issued. Canx by CAA 8.7.91.
G-BETX	HS.748 Srs.2A/314LFD	1753		5. 5.77	To Tanzanian AF as JW9010 in 1/78. Canx 9.1.79.
G-BETY	HS.748 Srs.2A/314LFD	1752		5. 5.77	To Tanzanian AF as JW9009 in 1/78. Canx 9.1.79.
G-BETZ	HS.748 Srs.2A/314LFD	1751		5. 5.77	To Tanzanian AF as JW9008 in 11/77. Canx 25.11.77.
G-BEUA	PA-18-150 Super Cub	18-8212	D-ECSY N4146Z	21. 6.77	
G-BEUB	Fuji FA.200-180AO Aero Subaru	FA200-283		24. 5.77	Fatal crash while filming tall-ships race near Fowey on 30.7.79 & ditched 200 yards southwest of Cannis Rock Buoy, off Lands End, Cornwall. Wreck recovered and landed at Fowey. Canx.
G-BEUC	PA-28-181 Cherokee Archer II	28-7716162	N3507Q	17. 5.77	To G-NINA 7/88. Canx.
G-BEUD	Robin HR.100/285 Tiara	534	F-BXRC	8. 6.77	
G-BEUE	Bell 47G-2	1631	EP-HAU N6763/ALAT 1631/N2850B	17. 5.77	To F-GBLM 4/82. Canx 13.4.82.
G-BEUF	Bell 47G-2	1628	EP-HAT N6762/ALAT 1628/F-SEWO/N2847B	17. 5.77	To F-GANV 4/82. Canx 25.2.82.
G-BEUG	Bell 47G-2	1633	EP-HAV N6764/ALAT 1633/F-SEWH/N2852B	17. 5.77	To F-GANU 4/82. Canx 10.2.82.
G-BEUH	Bell 47G-2	1635	EP-HAW N6765/ALAT 1635/F-SFNU/N2854B	17. 5.77	To F-GANY 4/82. Canx 30.2.82.
G-BEUI	Piper J3C-65 Cub (L-4H-PI) (Frame No. 12002 - regd as ex 43-29245 - c/n 10536)	12174	F-BFEC(2) F-OAJF/French AF/44-79878	19. 5.77	
G-BEUJ	PA-E23-250 Aztec E	27-4753	CR-SAL CS-AGX/N14191	19. 5.77	Crashed at St.Abbs Head whilst en route Dyce to Squires Gate on 24.10.78. Canx 5.12.83.
G-BEUK	Fuji FA.200-160 Aero Subaru	FA200-284		24. 5.77	Overran the runway on take-off at Glebe Farm, Wilts., on 8.1.99 & badly damaged.
G-BEUL	Beechcraft 95-B58 Baron	TH-862		8. 6.77	To EI-CPS 5/98. Canx 21.5.98.
G-BEUM	Taylor JT.1 Monoplane	PFA/1438		8. 6.77	
G-BEUN	Cassutt Racer IIIM	PFA/34-10241		20. 2.78	
G-BEUO	BN-2A-20 Islander	503	RP-C2156	30. 5.77	To VH-IGT. Canx 25.9.78.
G-BEUP	Robin DR.400/180 Regent	1228		19. 5.77	
G-BEUR	Reims Cessna F.172M	1491	EI-BGE G-BEUR	8. 6.77	To SX-ATC 12/96. Canx 31.10.96.
G-BEUS	AIA Stampe SV-4C (Regd as Betts TB.1 c/n PFA/265-12770)	1045	F-BKFK F-DAFK/French Mil 1045	24.11.78	No CofA believed issued. To G-BVUG 10/94. Canx as WFU 24.10.95.
G-BEUT	Partenavia P.68B Victor	97		20. 5.77	Crashed into the sea off Lydd on 22.1.79. Canx. Rebuilt & re-regd as VH-IGT in 5/82.
G-BEUU	PA-18-95 Super Cub (L-18C-PI) (Frame no. possibly 18-1395 - but ought to be 18-1523)	18-1551	F-BOUU ALAT 18-1551/51-15551	27. 6.77	
G-BEUV	Thunder Ax6-56A HAFB	115		27. 5.77	Canx by CAA 20.5.93.
G-BEUW	American Aviation AA-5A Cheetah	AA5A-0374	N6158A	12. 8.77	To G-ODSF 11/84. Canx.
G-BEUX	Reims Cessna F.172N Skyhawk II	1596		30. 5.77	
G-BEUY	Cameron N-31 HAFB	283		31. 5.77	
G-BEUZ	Beechcraft 200 Super King Air	BB-309		15. 9.77	To D-ILNY(2) 8/82. Canx 7.5.82.
G-BEVA	Socata MS.892E Rallye 150ST	2859		2. 6.77	Canx by CAA 10.2.87.
G-BEVB	Socata MS.892E Rallye 150ST	2860		2. 6.77	
G-BEVC	Socata MS.892E Rallye 150ST	2861		2. 6.77	
G-BEVD	Not allocated.				
G-BEVE	Thunder Ax7-77A HAFB	118		30. 5.77	Canx 2.10.84 on sale to Kuwait.
G-BEVF	Bell 212	30700	C-GOKW	16. 6.77	Restored as C-GOKW 6/78. Canx 15.6.78.
G-BEVG	PA-34-200T Seneca II	34-7570060	VQ-SAM N32854	31. 5.77	
G-BEVH	Holland D.700 HAFB (Toy)	7723/7002		30. 5.77	Canx as WFU 27.10.88.
G-BEVI(1)	Thunder Ax6-56A HAFB	079		. .77R	NTU - To N65300 /77. Canx.
G-BEVI(2)	Thunder Ax6-56A HAFB	119		30. 5.77R	NTU - To G-GOLD 7/77. Canx.
G-BEVI(3)	Thunder Ax7-77A HAFB	125		4. 7.77	Canx as WFU 8.1.92. (Extant 2/97) To British Balloon Museum, Newbury.
G-BEVJ	Cessna U.206F Stationair	U206-02210	ZS-IWI N7462Q	13. 6.77	To I-AMAH 9/84. Canx 18.9.84.
G-BEVK	PA-31-350 Navajo Chieftain	31-7652168	G-BCSE(2)	20.12.76	To N34BL 1/84. Canx 21.1.81.
G-BEVL	Cessna 421C Golden Eagle III	421C-0223	N5476G	12. 1.77	To G-OTAD 9/85. Canx.
G-BEVM	IRMA BN-2A-26 Islander (Originally regd as BN-2A-6)	907		11.12.78	To XC-DUY 12/80. Canx 6.1.81.
G-BEVN	Boeing 707-321C (Line No. 574)	19271	(N448WA) N449PA	6. 7.77	To (N449PA)/N707HT 9/81. Canx 15.9.81.
G-BEVO	Sportavia-Putzer Fournier RF-5	5107	5N-AIX D-KAAZ	27. 6.77	Permit expired 20.8.96. (Stored 12/97)

Regn	Type	c/n	Previous identity	Regn date	Fate or immediate subsequent identity (if known)
G-BEVP	Evans VP-2	ISW/7207/1 & PFA/7207		9. 6.77	Damaged on test flight Truleigh Manor Farm, Edburton 13.6.92. Canx by CAA 24.8.94. (On rebuild 10/95)
G-BEVR	BN-2A Mk.III-2 Trislander	1056	6Y-JQE G-BEVR/XA-TEH(2)/G-BEVR	10. 6.77	(Stored dismantled 5/99 Cumbernauld as 6Y-JQE)
G-BEVS	Taylor JT.1 Monoplane	PFA/1429		8. 6.77	
G-BEVT	BN-2A Mk.III-2 Trislander (Modified to three-bladed propellors by 12/93)	1057		10. 6.77	
G-BEVU	BN-2A Mk.III-2 Trislander	1058	ZS-KMF G-BEVU	10. 6.77	To N611WA 6/85. Canx 5.6.85.
G-BEVV	BN-2A Mk.III-2 Trislander	1059	6Y-JQK G-BNZD/G-BEVV	10. 6.77	(Stored dismantled 5/99 Cumbernauld as 6Y-JQK)
G-BEVW	Socata MS.892E Rallye 150ST	2928		2. 6.77	
G-BEVX	Socata MS.892E Rallye 150ST	2930		2. 6.77	Fatal collision with Reims Cessna F.150L G-BAZP at Biggin Hill on 25.11.78. Canx.
G-BEVY	BN-2A Mk.III-2 Trislander	1060	XA-CUC(2) G-BEVY	10. 6.77	To N906GD 7/85. Canx 8.7.85.
G-BEVZ	IRMA BN-2A-21 Islander	851		10. 6.77	To EV-7911 Venezuelan Army 8/78. Canx.
G-BEWA	IRMA BN-2A-21 Islander	852		10. 6.77	To PK-VIV 11/79. Canx 9.10.79.
G-BEWB	IRMA BN-2A-27 Islander	853		10. 6.77	To YR-BNW 12/79. Canx 20.12.79.
G-BEWC	IRMA BN-2B-21 Islander	854		10. 6.77R	NTU - To G-BEWK 6/77. Canx.
G-BEWD	IRMA BN-2A-8 Islander	855		10. 6.77	To XA-JEK 10/79. Canx 16.11.79.
G-BEWE	IRMA BN-2A-26 Islander	856		10. 6.77	To JA5265 3/80. Canx 19.3.80.
G-BEWF	IRMA BN-2B-21 Islander	857		10. 6.77	To ZS-KMG 2/80. Canx 5.3.80.
G-BEWG	IRMA BN-2B-21 Islander	858		10. 6.77	To I-KUNO 2/80. Canx 6.2.80.
G-BEWH	IRMA BN-2B-26 Islander	859		10. 6.77	Canx 25.7.80 on sale to USA. To HP-843 5/80.
G-BEWI	IRMA BN-2A-21 Islander	860		10. 6.77	To PK-TAR 9/80. Canx 21.7.80.
G-BEWJ	Westland-Bell 47G-3B1 (Line No. WAP/122)	WA/412	XT500	8. 7.77	To VH-RCC 5/97. Canx 9.1.97.
G-BEWK	IRMA BN-2B-21 Islander (Originally regd as BN-2A-6)	854	(G-BEWC)	10. 6.77	To ZS-KMD 11/79. Canx 26.11.79.
G-BEWL	Sikorsky S-61N Mk.II	61-769		16. 6.77	Fatal crash and ditched in North Sea near Brent Spar oil rig on 25.7.90. Canx as destroyed 16.10.90.
G-BEWM	Sikorsky S-61N Mk.II	61-772		14. 9.77	
G-BEWN	DH(Aust).82A Tiger Moth (DHA rebuild c/n T305)	952	VH-WAL R.Australian AF A17-529	16. 6.77	
G-BEWO	Moravan Zlin Z.326T Trener Master	915	CS-ALU	23.11.77	
G-BEWP	Reims Cessna F.150M Commuter	1426		13. 6.77	Overshot the runway on landing at Aboyne on 4.10.83, overturned & badly damaged. Canx as destroyed 5.12.83. (Instructional Airframe 10/97 at Perth)
G-BEWR	Reims Cessna F.172N Skyhawk II	1613		13. 6.77	
G-BEWS	Cameron Lamp Bulb 56SS HAFB	285		15. 6.77	WFU & last known of in Australia. Canx by CAA 24.11.86.
G-BEWT	Short SD.3-30 Var.100	SH3011	G-14-3011	20. 6.77	To N331GW 6/77. Canx 28.10.77.
G-BEWU	Rockwell 500S Shrike Commander	3120	C9-AOU CR-AOU/N9172N/(D-ICKT)/N9172N	20. 6.77	NTU - Not Imported. To VP-WGQ /77. Canx.
G-BEWV	HS.125 Srs.700A	NA0205 & 257008	G-5-11	20. 6.77	NTU - To C-GYYZ 7/77. Canx 18.7.77.
G-BEWW	HS.125 Srs.600A	256001	N711AG N82BH/G-AZUF	17. 7.77	Restored as N711AG 4/84. Canx 24.4.84.
G-BEWX	PA-28R-201 Cherokee Arrow III	28R-7737070	N5723V	23. 6.77	
G-BEWY	Bell 206B JetRanger II (Originally 206A; later modified)	348	G-CULL EI-BXQ/G-BEWY/9Y-TDF	27. 6.77	
G-BEWZ	PA-32-300 Cherokee Six C	32-40887	4X-ANO N5241S	29. 6.77	Believed crashed in France sometime in 1981 or 1982. Remains stored at Le Mans, France. CofA expired 23.5.82. Canx by CAA 3.2.87.
G-BEXA	PBN BN-2A-26 Islander	2011	G-MALI G-DIVE/(ZB503)/"ZA503"/G-DIVE/G-BEXA	30. 6.77	To G-BPCB 7/88. Canx.
G-BEXB	PBN BN-2A-26 Islander	2012	N406JA G-BEXB	30. 6.77	To JA5261 3/79. Canx.
G-BEXC	PBN BN-2A-26 Islander	2013		30. 6.77	To XA-IEX 12/78. Canx 21.5.79.
G-BEXD	PBN BN-2A-27 Islander	2014		30. 6.77	Canx 25.7.80 on sale to USA. To YV-365CP 7/80.
G-BEXE	PBN BN-2A-26 Islander	2015		30. 6.77	To N8069X 10/79. Canx 22.10.79.
G-BEXF	PBN BN-2A-26 Islander	2016		30. 6.77	Canx 25.7.80 on sale to Turks & Caicos Islands. To N385KG 4/79.
G-BEXG	PBN BN-2A-26 Islander	2017		30. 6.77	To G-51-2017/N59360 5/78. Canx 11.5.78.
G-BEXH	PBN BN-2B-26 Islander	2018		30. 6.77	To 8P-RAD 11/79. Canx 13.12.79.
G-BEXI	PBN BN-2A-26 Islander	2019		30. 6.77	To VQ-TAB 11/79. Canx 25.7.80.
G-BEXJ	PBN BN-2A-26 Islander	2020		30. 6.77	To G-51-2020/(N412JA)/N60PA 7/79. Canx 30.7.79.
G-BEXK	PA-25-235 Pawnee D	25-7756004	(N82424)	14. 7.77	Crashed on 3/4.10.92. (Stored for spares 2/99 East Winch)
G-BEXL	PA-25-235 Pawnee D	25-7756005	(N82428)	14. 7.77	To SE-... Canx 9.7.87.
G-BEXM	Partenavia P.68B Victor	111		28. 6.77	Crashed and burnt out at Kings Farm, Bulphan on 26.11.79. Canx.
G-BEXN	American Aviation AA-1C Lynx	AA1C-0045	N6147A	7. 9.77	
G-BEXO	PA-23-160 Apache	23-213	OO-APH N1176P	4. 7.77	CofA expired 5.11.96. (Stored 5/97)
G-BEXP	BN-2A-8 Islander	296	F-BOAL N56JA/G-51-296	22. 7.77	To F-OGID 12/77. Canx 20.12.77.
G-BEXR	Avions Mudry/CAARP CAP.10B	76		11. 8.77	To G-CAPI(2) 3/99. Canx.
G-BEXS	Reims Cessna F.150M Commuter	1364		11. 7.77	Extensively damaged in crash near the A144 road at Holwell Park Wood, Welwyn Garden City on 25.7.90. Later stored at Leavesden. Canx as destroyed 6.10.94.

Regn	Type	c/n	Previous identity	Regn date	Fate or immediate subsequent identity (if known)
G-BEXT	Beagle B.206R Srs.1	R.02/B.008	ZP-PJY G-BCJE/XS766	11. 7.74	To N206SS 7/77. Canx 14.7.77.
G-BEXU	PA-31-350 Navajo Chieftain	31-7552001	N61464	3. 8.77	Restored as N61484 3/80. Canx 31.3.80.
G-BEXV	Cameron O-56 HAFB	291		8. 7.77	During the course of a European trip the envelope was overheated making it no longer safe to fly in 1983. Canx as destroyed 7.11.83.
G-BEXW	PA-28-181 Cherokee Archer II	28-7790521	N38122	11. 7.77	
G-BEXX	Cameron V-56 HAFB	274		29. 6.77	
G-BEXY	PA-28-140 Cherokee Cruiser	28-7725232	N9639N	11. 7.77	To EI-CIV 11/93. Canx 10.11.93.
G-BEXZ	Cameron N-56 HAFB	294		7. 7.77	
G-BEYA	Enstrom 280C Shark	1104		15. 8.77	
G-BEYB	Fairey Flycatcher Replica	WA/3		11. 7.77	(On display 6/96 RNAS Yeovilton) Canx as WFU 12.7.96.
G-BEYC	HS.125 Srs.700A	NA0206 & 257009	G-5-12	11. 7.77	To N813H 10/77. Canx 30.8.77.
G-BEYD	Handley Page HPR.7 Dart Herald 401	171	FM1020 R.Malaysian AF	13.10.77	CofA expired 27.5.83 & WFU at Southend. Broken up in 10/84. Canx as WFU 12.11.84.
G-BEYE	Handley Page HPR.7 Dart Herald 401	172	FM1021 R.Malaysian AF	5.10.77	CofA expired 15.6.83 & WFU. Scrapped at Southend in 12/84. Canx by CAA 5.3.87.
G-BEYF	Handley Page HPR.7 Dart Herald 401	175	FM1022 R.Malaysian AF	13. 7.77	WFU at Hurn 4/99 - Last flew on 8/9.4.99.
G-BEYG	Handley Page HPR.7 Dart Herald 401	178	FM1023 R.Malaysian AF	13. 7.77	To HK-2701X 11/81. Canx 10.11.81.
G-BEYH	Handley Page HPR.7 Dart Herald 401	180	FM1024 R.Malaysian AF	13. 7.77	To HK-2702X 12/81. Canx 23.12.81.
G-BEYI	Handley Page HPR.7 Dart Herald 401	181	FM1025 R.Malaysian AF	13. 7.77	NTU - Not Imported. Broken up in 1978 for spares in Malaysia.
G-BEYJ	Handley Page HPR.7 Dart Herald 401	182	FM1026 R.Malaysian AF	13. 7.77	To TG-ALE 10/84. Canx by CAA 29.1.87.
G-BEYK	Handley Page HPR.7 Dart Herald 401	187	FM1027 R.Malaysian AF	13. 7.77	WFU to fire dump in 1/97 at Southend. Scrapped in 2/98. Canx as WFU 26.2.98.
G-BEYL	PA-28-180 Cherokee Archer	28-7405098	PH-SDW	6. 9.77	
G-BEYM	Reims Cessna F.150M	1354		18. 7.77	Fatal crash when failed to recover from practising spinning at Norwich airport on 10.9.86. Canx as destroyed 26.5.89.
G-BEYN	Evans VP-2	V2-3167 & PFA/63-10271		1. 8.77	Canx by CAA 2.9.91. (Incomplete airframe stored in hangar roof 9/95 at East Fortune)
G-BEYO	PA-28-140 Cherokee Cruiser	28-7725215	N9648N	14. 7.77	
G-BEYP	Fuji FA.200-180AO Aero Subaru	FA200-285		2. 8.77	To G-KARY 3/89. Canx.
G-BEYR	Enstrom 280C Shark	1064		18. 7.77	To G-HOVA 2/82. Canx.
G-BEYS	PA-28-180 Cherokee Archer II	28-7790412	N2658Q	5. 8.77	Crashed on landing at Rochester on 20.6.81. Canx.
G-BEYT	PA-28-140 Cherokee	28-20330	D-EBWO N6280W	19. 7.77	
G-BEYU	Fuji FA.200-160 Aero Subaru	FA200-286		26. 7.77	To PH-MBW 4/82. Canx 20.4.82.
G-BEYV	Cessna T.210L Turbo Centurion II	210-61583	N732KX	19. 7.77	
G-BEYW	Taylor JT.1 Monoplane	RJS.100 & PFA/55-10279		22. 7.77	
G-BEYX	PA-31P-425 Pressurised Navajo	31P-10	ZS-NPI(3) ZS-ISK/ZS-PPN/N41750/ZS-PPN/N6808L	22. 7.77	To PH-DDH 12/81. Canx 22.12.81.
G-BEYY	PA-31-310 Turbo Navajo B	31-7300957	SE-GDA	22. 7.77	To G-OHOP 10/92. Canx.
G-BEYZ	CEA Jodel DR.1050/M1 Sicile Record	588	F-BMGV	22. 7.77	
G-BEZA	Moravan Zlin Z.226T Trener 6	0370	HA-TRL G-BEZA/D-EMUD/OK-MUA	24. 1.78	
G-BEZB	Handley Page HPR.7 Dart Herald 209	174	4X-AHS G-8-2	2. 8.77	WFU in 12/87 & stored at Hurn. Canx as WFU 8.3.88. Broken up in 1/92.
G-BEZC	American Aviation AA-5 Traveller	AA5-0493	F-BUYN (N7193L)	29. 7.77	
G-BEZD	American Aviation AA-5 Traveller	AA5-0537	F-BVJO N9537L	29. 7.77	Crashed near Elstree on 6.1.80. Canx.
G-BEZE	Rutan VariEze	PFA/74-10207		26. 7.77	Permit expired 2.6.92. (Status uncertain)
G-BEZF	American Aviation AA-5 Traveller	AA5-0538	F-BVJP N9538L	29. 7.77	
G-BEZG	American Aviation AA-5 Traveller	AA5-0561	F-BVRJ N9561L	29. 7.77	
G-BEZH	American Aviation AA-5 Traveller	AA5-0566	F-BVRK N9566L	29. 7.77	
G-BEZI	American Aviation AA-5 Traveller	AA5-0567	F-BVRL N9567L	29. 7.77	
G-BEZJ	MBB Bo.105D	S.136	D-HDED	10. 8.77	Badly damaged in crash near Strathpeffer on 5.8.89. (Stored .91) Canx as WFU 12.2.97.
G-BEZK	Reims Cessna F.172H Skyhawk	0462	D-EBUD D-ENHC/SLN-07/N20462	17. 8.77	
G-BEZL	PA-31-310 Turbo Navajo C	31-7712054	SE-GPA	1. 8.77	
G-BEZM	Reims Cessna F.182Q Skylane II	0028	G-WALK G-BEZM/F-WZDX	8. 8.77	To SX-ABI 2/95. Canx 3.2.95.

Regn	Type	c/n	Previous identity	Regn date	Fate or immediate subsequent identity (if known)
G-BEZN	Rockwell 500S Shrike Commander	3140	9Q-GTJ	8. 8.77	To (N9190N)/N500BL 11/77. Canx 9.11.77.
			CR-AQB/N9190N		
G-BEZO	Reims Cessna F.172M Skyhawk II	1392		24. 8.77	
G-BEZP	PA-32-300 Cherokee Six D	32-7740087	N38572	19. 8.77	
G-BEZR	Reims Cessna F.172M Skyhawk II	1395		24. 8.77	
G-BEZS	Reims Cessna FR.172J Rocket	0562	(I-CCAJ)	11. 8.77	Damaged in forced landing near Stapleford on 15.6.79. To Cranfield for spares or rebuild. Canx as WFU 16.3.95. (Front fuselage stored 4/99 at Bourn)
G-BEZT	Boeing 707-321C	18765	N795RN	21.10.77	To SU-BAG 7/78. Canx 12.7.78.
	(Line No. 371)		N795PA		
G-BEZU	PA-31-350 Navajo Chieftain	31-7305052	SE-GDP	12. 8.77	To G-HVRD 6/87. Canx.
G-BEZV	Reims Cessna F.172M Skyhawk II	1474	(I-CCAY)	24. 8.77	
G-BEZW	Practavia Pilot Sprite	113 & PFA/05-10252		9. 8.77	Not completed. Canx as WFU 27.1.87.
G-BEZX	Short SD.3-30 Var.100	SH3012	G-14-3012	4. 8.77	To N696HA 10/77. Canx 20.10.77.
G-BEZY	Rutan VariEze	1167 & PFA/74-10225		26. 7.77	
G-BEZZ	Jodel D.112	397	F-BHMC	12. 8.77	
	(Built by Passot Aviation)				
G-BFAA	Socata GY-80-160 Horizon	78	F-BLVY	20.10.77	CofA expired 18.11.90. (Status uncertain)
G-BFAB	Cameron N-56 HAFB	297		15. 8.77	Canx by CAA 21.4.92. (Extant 2/97 - for British Balloon Museum & Library)
G-BFAC	Reims Cessna F.177RG Cardinal	0151	N177AB	24. 8.77	Canx 31.7.97 on sale to Spain.
			G-BFAC/D-EDIS		
G-BFAD	PA-28-161 Warrior II	28-7716206	N5850V	30. 8.77	To G-OANC 4/87. Canx.
G-BFAE	PADC BN-2A-21 Islander	509	RP-C2159	15. 8.77	To RP-C2167 5/78. Canx.
G-BFAF	Aeronca 7BCM Champion	7BCM-11	N797US	15. 8.77	
	(L-16A-AE)		N2552B/47-797		
G-BFAG	Sikorsky S-58ET	58-1673	LN-OSF	25. 8.77	To (LN-OSA)/C-GAIV 3/78. Canx 1.3.78.
			West German Navy 81+06/WE+578/QE+463/BuA.150804		
G-BFAH	Phoenix Currie Wot	PFA/3017		22. 8.77	
	(Being built as Replica SE-5A and to be painted in RFC c/s) (Regd as c/n PFA/58-11376; probably confusion with PFA/101-11376, a Sopwith Pup replica by same former owner/builder)				
G-BFAI	Rockwell Commander 114	14304	N4984W	17. 8.77	
G-BFAJ	HS.125 Srs.700A	NA0207 & 257011	G-5-13	16. 8.77	To N255CT 9/77. Canx 28.9.77.
G-BFAK	GEMS MS.892A Rallye Commodore 150	10595	F-BNNJ	9. 8.77	
G-BFAL	Bell 206L Long Ranger	45077	N64689	24. 8.77	To G-TBCA 4/80. Canx.
			A6-BCL		
G-BFAM	PA-31P Pressurised Navajo	31P-39	SE-GLV	1. 9.77	To G-SASK 10/97. Canx.
			OH-PNF		
G-BFAN	HS.125 Srs.F600	25258	G-AZHS	7. 5.76	To VR-CJP 6/96. Canx 12.6.96.
			(G-AYRR)		
G-BFAO(1)	PA-32R-300 Lance	32R-7780335	D-EILI	22. 9.77	NTU - To G-FSPL 22.9.77. Canx.
			N4587Q		
G-BFAO(2)	PA-20-135 Pacer	20-674	ZS-CMH	10.10.77	
			ZS-CAH		
G-BFAP	SIAI-Marchetti S.205-20R	4-213	I-ALEN	1. 9.77	
G-BFAR	Cessna 500 Citation I	500-0368	A6-SMH	5. 9.77	To G-DANI 4/93. Canx.
	(Unit No.402)		G-BFAR/A6-SMH/G-BFAR/ZS-LPH/G-BFAR/N36912		
G-BFAS	Evans VP-1 Srs.2	PFA/7033		15. 8.77	
G-BFAT	Thunder Ax7-77 HAFB	124		9. 9.77	To C-GXCV 9/78. Canx 11.9.78.
G-BFAU(1)	Westland WG.13 Lynx UH-14A	WA/014		30. 8.77	NTU - To R.Netherlands Navy as 262. Canx.
	(Originally regd as a Westland WG.13 Lynx 01E)				
G-BFAU(2)	Westland WG.13 Lynx HAS.21	WA/029	G-17-13	15.12.77	To Brazilian Navy as N3022 in 3/78. Canx 18.7.78.
G-BFAV	Boxhall Orion HAFB (Toy)	1		30. 8.77	Canx by CAA 6.12.88.
G-BFAW	DHC.1 Chipmunk 22	C1/0733	8342M	31. 8.77	
	(Fuselage No. DHB/f/625)		WP848		
G-BFAX	DHC.1 Chipmunk 22	C1/0496	8394M	31. 8.77	
	(Fuselage No. DHB/f/364)		WG422		
G-BFAY	Hughes 369D (500D)	67-0148D		31. 1.77	To N29707. Canx 22.6.81.
G-BFAZ	LET Super Aero 45	03-007	D-GGAM	14. 9.77	NTU - Not Imported. To OY-EFC 5/81. Canx 2.7.79.
			D-EGAM/OK-K..		
G-BFBA	SAN Jodel DR.100A Ambassadeur	88	F-BIVU	12. 9.77	
G-BFBB	PA-23-250 Aztec E	27-7405294	SE-GBI	1. 9.77	
	(An Aztec wreck marked as G-BFBB for film use was stored at Halland Handling Scrapyard, Braydon, Wilts 2/96)				
G-BFBC	Taylor JT.1 Monoplane	PFA/55-10280		5. 9.77	(Under construction 2/93)
G-BFBD	Partenavia P.68B Victor	115		8. 9.77	To G-ORVR 10/95. Canx.
G-BFBE	Robin HR.200/100 Club	12	PH-SRK	9. 9.77	
G-BFBF	PA-28-140 Cherokee F	28-7325240	EI-BMG	9. 9.77	
			G-BFBF/PH-SRF		
G-BFBG	PA-28-161 Warrior II	28-7716278	N38846	7. 9.77	To G-MAYO 2/81. Canx.
G-BFBH	PA-31-325 Navajo C/R	31-7712079	N27317	23. 1.78	To G-OMEG 5/87. Canx.
G-BFBI	HS.125 Srs.700A	NA0208 & 257012	G-5-14	6. 9.77	To N125HS 10/77. Canx 14.10.77.
G-BFBJ	PA-34-200T Seneca II	34-7770342	N38796	8. 9.77	To D-GKMM 11/84. Canx 19.11.84.
G-BFBK	Agusta-Bell 47G-3B1	1549	XT138	14. 9.77	To 5B-CGH 1/85. Canx 8.1.85.
G-BFBL	PA-31-325 Navajo	31-7612074	5Y-SCL	6. 9.77	Siezed in Tanzania and sold by Insurance Company. Restored to 5Y-SCL 5/78. Canx.
			N59873		
G-BFBM	Saffery S.330 HAFB (Toy)	7		1. 9.77	
G-BFBN	PA-25-235 Pawnee D	25-7756010		7. 9.77	Crashed on take-off from Ropsley Heath Farm, Grantham on 22.3.79. Canx as WFU 9.1.84.
G-BFBO	Not allocated.				

Regn	Type	c/n	Previous identity	Regn date	Fate or immediate subsequent identity (if known)
G-BFBP	PA-25-235 Pawnee D	25-7756033		7. 9.77	Crashed near Comberton, Cambs. on 11.5.78. Canx as destroyed 21.6.78.
G-BFBR	PA-28-161 Cherokee Warrior II	28-7716277	N38845	15. 9.77	
G-BFBS	Boeing 707-351B (Line No. 348)	18693	VR-HGN N354US	2. 8.78	CofA expired 17.10.81 & WFU at Lasham. Canx as WFU 24.4.85. Broken up late 1986. (Port side was painted matt black in 1/85 for TV series "One by One" to represent BOAC freighter)
G-BFBT	Socata MS.892E Rallye 150ST	2612	F-BXDE	19. 9.77	Crashed at Llanfachraeth, near Holyhead on 25.9.78. Canx.
G-BFBU	Partenavia P.68B Victor	24	SE-FTM	25. 1.78	
G-BFBV	Brugger Colibri MB.2	PFA/43-10142		8. 9.77	Fatal crash at Frost Hill Farm, Overton on 23.8.89. Canx as destroyed 15.1.90.
G-BFBW	PA-25-235 Pawnee D	25-7756019		12. 9.77	To SE-KHF. Canx 23.1.89.
G-BFBX	PA-25-235 Pawnee D	25-7756038		20. 9.77	To LN-TAU. Canx 7.3.91.
G-BFBY	Piper J-3C-65 Cub (L-4H-PI)	10998	F-BDTG 43-29707	29. 9.77	
G-BFBZ	Boeing 707-351B (Line No. 343)	18585	VR-HGI N352US	2.12.77	CofA expired 17.10.81 & WFU at Lasham. Canx as WFU 24.4.85. Broken up 6-7/86.
G-BFCA	Lockheed L.1011-385-1 Tristar 500	193V-1157	N48354	10. 4.80	To RAF as ZD948 in 4/83. Canx 8.4.83.
G-BFCB	Lockheed L.1011-385-1 Tristar 500	193V-1159		22. 6.79	To RAF as ZD949 in 4/83. Canx 9.12.83.
G-BFCC	Lockheed L.1011-385-1 Tristar 500	193V-1164		26. 4.79	To RAF as ZD950 in 3/83. Canx 10.3.83.
G-BFCD	Lockheed L.1011-385-1 Tristar 500	193V-1165	ZD951 G-BFCD	11. 5.79	Restored to RAF as ZD951 in 10/83. Canx 9.12.83.
G-BFCE	Lockheed L.1011-385-1 Tristar 500	193V-1168	ZD952 G-BFCE	21. 7.79	Restored to RAF as ZD952 in 9/85. Canx 19.9.85.
G-BFCF	Lockheed L.1011-385-1 Tristar 500	193V-1174		29. 4.80	To RAF as ZD953 in 2/83. Canx 17.2.83.
G-BFCG	Lockheed L.1011-385-1 Tristar 500	-		. .77R	NTU - Canx.
G-BFCH	Lockheed L.1011-385-1 Tristar 500	-		. .77R	NTU - Canx.
G-BFCI	Lockheed L.1011-385-1 Tristar 500	-		. .77R	NTU - Canx.
G-BFCJ	Lockheed L.1011-385-1 Tristar 500	-		. .77R	NTU - Canx.
G-BFCK	Lockheed L.1011-385-1 Tristar 500	-		. .77R	NTU - Canx.
G-BFCL	Lockheed L.1011-385-1 Tristar 500	-		. .77R	NTU - Canx.
G-BFCM	IRMA BN-2A-26 Islander (Originally regd as BN-2A-6)	866	(G-BFCT)	16. 9.77	To B-12203 9/78. Canx 4.10.78.
G-BFCN	IRMA BN-2B-21 Islander (Originally regd as BN-2A-6)	861		16. 9.77	To JY-DCA 7/80. Canx 9.7.80.
G-BFCO	IRMA BN-2B-21 Islander (Originally regd as BN-2A-6)	862		16. 9.77	To ZS-KLK 6/80. Canx 2.6.80.
G-BFCP	IRMA BN-2A-27 Islander (Originally regd as BN-2A-6)	863		16. 9.77	To YV-364CP 1/81. Canx 21.1.81.
G-BFCR	IRMA BN-2B-27 Islander (Originally regd as BN-2A-6)	864		16. 9.77	To XC-DIB 2/80. Canx 21.1.81.
G-BFCS	IRMA BN-2A-9 Islander (Originally regd as BN-2A-6)	865		16. 9.77	Canx in 1.80 on sale to France. To 5A-DHU 12/80.
G-BFCT(1)	IRMA BN-2A-6 Islander	866		. 9.77R	NTU - To G-BFCM 9/77. Canx.
G-BFCT(2)	Cessna TU.206F Turbo Stationair II	U206-03202	(LN-TVF) N8341Q	15. 9.77	
G-BFCU	IRMA BN-2A-3 Islander (Originally regd as BN-2A-6)	867		16. 9.77	To F-BFCU(2)/F-GCMF 5/80. Canx 27.5.80.
G-BFCV	IRMA BN-2A-27 Islander (Originally regd as BN-2A-6)	868	(N410JA) G-BFCV	16. 9.77	To C-FSTJ 9/81. Canx.
G-BFCW	IRMA BN-2B-21 Islander (Originally regd as BN-2A-6)	869		16. 9.77	To TR-LZK 5/82. Canx 21.1.81.
G-BFCX	IRMA BN-2A-26 Islander (Originally regd as BN-2A-6)	870		16. 9.77	To 5B-CHG. Canx 14.4.89.
G-BFCY	Agusta-Bell 206B JetRanger II	8376	OE-DXA	22. 9.77	Damaged in forced landing at Aberdare on 3.4.84. Wreck later sold to Whinmoor. Canx by CAA 2.2.87.
G-BFCZ	Sopwith Camel F.1 Replica	WA/2		12.10.77	Permit expired 23.2.89. (On display 10/96 Brooklands Museum)
G-BFDA	PA-31-350 Navajo Chieftain	31-7305118	SE-GDR	27. 9.77	To EI-BYE 5/89. Canx 19.5.89.
G-BFDB	PA-31-350 Navajo Chieftain	31-7752159	N27239	7.10.77	To N503SC 11/81. Canx 3.11.81.
G-BFDC	DHC.1 Chipmunk 22 (Fuselage no. DHB/f/406)	C1/0525	7989M WG475	15.11.77	
G-BFDD	BN-2A Mk.III-2 Trislander	1061		19. 9.77	To B-11118 2/84. Canx 27.2.84.
G-BFDE	Sopwith Tabloid Scout Replica	168 & PFA/67-10186		22. 9.77	Permit expired 4.6.83. Canx as WFU 8.12.86. (On display 9/97 Hendon)
G-BFDF	Socata Rallye 235E	12834	F-GAKT	6.10.77	
G-BFDG	PA-28R-201T Turbo Arrow III	28R-7703365	N47381	12.10.77	To G-JEFS 4/97. Canx.
G-BFDH	Hughes 269C (300C)	87-0624		31.10.77	To I-GETA 4/79. Canx 27.3.79.
G-BFDI	PA-28-181 Cherokee Archer II	28-7790382	N2205Q	5.10.77	
G-BFDJ	Bell 212	30632	EP-HCA VR-BGP/G-BFDJ/9V-BGE/B-2309/9V-BGE	18.11.77	To 5N-AJU 5/79. Canx 10.5.79.
G-BFDK	PA-28-161 Cherokee Warrior II	28-7816010	N40061	23. 9.77	

Regn	Type	c/n	Previous identity	Regn date	Fate or immediate subsequent identity (if known)
G-BFDL	Piper J3C Cub (L-4J-PI) (Frame No. 13107)	13277	HB-OIF 45-4537	30.11.77	
G-BFDM	Wassmer Jodel D.120 Paris Nice	36	F-BHYB	29. 9.77	Canx as WFU 21.6.83.
G-BFDN	PA-31-350 Navajo Chieftain	31-7652124	N59899	3.10.77	To ZS-NWV 2/96. Canx 18.1.96.
G-BFDO	PA-28R-201T Turbo Cherokee Arrow III	28R-7703212	N38396	3.10.77	
G-BFDP(1)	PA-23-250 Aztec D	27-4295	N15RR N6938Y	. .77R	NTU - To G-DEVA 3/78. Canx.
G-BFDP(2)	Piel CP.301A Emeraude	PFA/711		17. 1.78	No Permit to Fly issued & believed not completed. Canx as WFU 8.12.86.
G-BFDR	Beechcraft B60 Duke	P-399	N4556S	11.11.77	Restored as N4556S 9/81. Canx 23.9.81.
G-BFDS	Fokker F-27 Friendship 400	10270	PH-ARO D-BARO/PH-FGM	26.10.77	Restored as PH-ARO 12/78. Canx 30.11.78.
G-BFDT	Westland WG.13 Lynx HAS.23 (Originally regd as a Westland WG.13 Lynx 01F)	WA/035		3.10.77	To Argentine Navy as 3-H-141/0734 in 10/78. Canx 2.10.78.
G-BFDU	Westland WG.13 Lynx HAS.21 (Originally regd as a Westland WG.13 Lynx 01E)	WA/025	G-17-12	3.10.77	To Brazilian Navy as N3021. Canx 2.8.78.
G-BFDV	Westland WG.13 Lynx HC.28 (Originally regd as a Westland WG.13 Lynx 02F)	WA/028	G-17-20	3.10.77	To Qatar AF as 1. Canx 6.78.
G-BFDW	HS.125 Srs.700A	NA0209 & 257014	G-5-17	3.10.77	To N46901 10/77. Canx 2.11.77.
G-BFDX	Short SD.3-30 Var.100	SH3013	G-14-3013	3.10.77	To D-CODO 12/77. Canx 20.12.77.
G-BFDY	Short SD.3-30 Var.100	SH3014	G-14-3014	3.10.77	To N794HA 3/78. Canx 10.4.78.
G-BFDZ	Taylor JT.1 Monoplane	PFA/55-10185		5.10.77	
G-BFEA	Beechcraft A200 Super King Air	BB-349	G-BRON G-BFEA	21.12.77	To N80GA 5/83. Canx 11.5.83.
G-BFEB	SAN Jodel D.150 Mascaret	34	F-BMJR(2) OO-LDY/F-BLDX	14.10.77	Damaged in forced landing at Marston Moor, Toxworth on 14.4.91. Permit expired 19.4.91. (On rebuild 5/98)
G-BFEC	PA-23-250 Aztec F	27-7754144	N63823	3.11.77	To G-TOMK 11/94. Canx.
G-BFED	PA-31-350 Navajo Chieftain	31-7752171	N27420	27.10.77	To N350SC 3/82. Canx 19.3.82.
G-BFEE	Beechcraft 95-E55 Baron	TE-921	(N7355Z) G-BFEE/ZS-WLO(1)/ ZS-EWH(3)/ZS-INX/ZS-XAB(3)/N1866W	10.10.77	Badly damaged in forced landing Berwick St.John, Wilts on 8.7.96. Canx by CAA 22.4.97.
G-BFEF	Agusta-Bell 47G-3B1	1541	XT132	11.10.77	
G-BFEG	Westland-Bell 47G-3B1 (Line No.WAN/30)	WA/439	XT180	11.10.77	Extensively damaged while crop spraying at Market Drayton, Shropshire on 9.7.79. Canx as WFU 2.12.86.
G-BFEH	SAN Jodel D.117A	828	F-BITG	5.10.77	Permit expired 30.9.94. (On overhaul 6/97)
G-BFEI	Westland-Bell 47G-3B1 (Line No.WAN/16)	WA/415	XT156	11.10.77	CofA expired 25.4.88. (Last known of at Cranfield) Canx by CAA 6.7.94.
G-BFEJ	Agusta-Bell 47G-3B1	1555	XT143	11.10.77	DBR at High Eldwick, near Bingley, Yorks on 18.4.84. Canx by CAA 28.3.85.
G-BFEK	Reims Cessna F.152 II	1442		11.10.77	
G-BFEL	Reims Cessna F.150M	1375		24.10.77	Destroyed in mid-air collision with a USAF Fairchild A-10 80-180 near Hardwick, Norfolk on 29.2.84. Canx by CAA 11.12.91.
G-BFEM	Cessna 421C Golden Eagle III	421C-0316	N8451G	11.10.77	Crashed on take-off at Lausanne, Switzerland on 11.6.82 & DBF. Canx as destroyed 5.12.83.
G-BFEN	PA-28R-201T Turbo Arrow III	28R-7703268	N38745	5.10.77	To G-SABA 8/79. Canx.
G-BFEO	Boeing 707-323C (Line No. 357)	18691	5X-UWM N7557A	14.10.77	Stored 4/86 at Davis-Monthan AFB, AZ; storage code CZ0146. Canx 14.4.86 on sale to USA.
G-BFEP	Beechcraft 65-B80 Queen Air	LD-344	F-BRNR OO-VDE	18.10.77	To G-BSSL 5/80. Canx.
G-BFER	Bell 212	30835	N18099	7.11.77	
G-BFES	Bell 212	30849	VH-MNU G-BFES/VH-MNU/G-BFES/9Y-TGV/N4985Y/G-BFES	7.11.77	To VH-NSY 2/87. Canx 9.2.87.
G-BFET	Partenavia P.68B Victor	121		7.11.77	To F-GATX 2/78. Canx 23.2.78.
G-BFEU	Aerospatiale SA.330J Puma	1478		26.10.77	To VH-WOD 4/82. Canx 15.4.82.
G-BFEV	PA-25-235 Pawnee D	25-7756060		20.10.77	
G-BFEW	PA-25-235 Pawnee D	25-7756062		20.10.77	
G-BFEX	PA-25-235 Pawnee D	25-7756042	N82525	20.10.77	To G-CMGC 11/91. Canx.
G-BFEY	PA-25-235 Pawnee D	25-7756039		20.10.77	CofA expired 19.1.87. Canx as WFU 17.7.90.
G-BFEZ	Beechcraft B60 Duke	P-285	ZS-RHS(2) N7340R	24.10.77	To G-FDGM 5/83. Canx.
G-BFFA	Beechcraft 95-B58 Baron	TH-48	ZS-SVM(2) ZS-IMA/N335T	24.10.77	To VP-WHV 11/77. Canx 4.11.77.
G-BFFB	Evans VP-2	V2-2289 & PFA/63-10159		27.10.77	Canx by CAA 2.9.91. (Stored 6/96)
G-BFFC	Reims Cessna F.152 II	1451		27.10.77	
G-BFFD	Reims Cessna F.152 II	1453		27.10.77	To G-OJRS 6/85. Canx.
G-BFFE	Reims Cessna F.152 II	1454		27.10.77	Damaged near Skegness on 13.3.97. CofA expired 19.4.98. (Stored dismantled 12/98 Edinburgh)
G-BFFF	Cessna A.188B Agtruck	02590T	N4854Q	24.10.77	Struck cables at Kilmington, Wilts. 9.6.84. Some remains sold in Australia in 7/85 and used in the rebuild of VH-DDT. Canx by CAA 12.12.86.
G-BFFG	Beechcraft 95-B55 Baron	TC-2026	SE-GRU	1.11.77	To N111FG 12/98. Canx 1.12.98.
G-BFFH	HS.125 Srs.700A	NA0216 & 257016		11.11.77	To N72505. Canx 19.12.77.
G-BFFI	PA-31-350 Navajo Chieftain	31-7752151	N27330	1.11.77	Restored as N27330 9/81. Canx 29.9.81.
G-BFFJ	Sikorsky S-61N Mk.II	61-777	N6231	17. 1.78	
G-BFFK	Sikorsky S-61N Mk.II	61-778		1. 2.78	
G-BFFL	HS.125 Srs.700A	NA0210 & 257015	G-5-18	31.10.77	To N37P 11/77. Canx 30.11.77.

Regn	Type	c/n	Previous identity	Regn date	Fate or immediate subsequent identity (if known)
G-BFFM	Cessna 421C Golden Eagle III	421C-0308	N8363G	1.11.77	Restored as N8363G 10/81. Canx 15.10.81.
G-BFFN(1)	Reims Cessna F.182Q Skyhawk II	0084	(G-BLHN)	. .77R	NTU - To G-BPPN 5/78. Canx.
G-BFFN(2)	Enstrom F-28A-UK (Composite fitted with cabin of EC-CKH c/n 188)	141	HB-XEA	4.11.77	Damaged at Shoreham on 3.11.82. Rebuilt & regd as G-WWUK on 9.3.83. Canx.
G-BFFO	Not allocated.				
G-BFFP	PA-18-180 Super Cub (Frame No. 18-8402)	18-8187	PH-OTC	9.11.77	
G-BFFR	PA-31-350 Navajo Chieftain	31-7752187	N27388	4.11.77	To PH-XPI 1/83. Canx 26.1.83.
G-BFFS	CASA C.2111D (He.111D)	-	BR2-100 Spanish AF	4.11.77	Fatal crash into mountains in Sierra de Guadarrama, near Escorial, Spain on 11.12.77. Canx 14.12.77.
G-BFFT	Cameron V-56 HAFB	360		7.11.77	
G-BFFU	HS.125 Srs.700A	NA0211 & 257017	G-5-19	11.11.77	To N62MS 12/77. Canx 9.12.77.
G-BFFV	Agusta-Bell 47G-3B1	1594	XT124	9.11.77	To 5B-CFR 1/84. Canx 5.12.83.
G-BFFW	Reims Cessna F.152 II	1447		14.11.77	
G-BFFX	Reims Cessna F.172N Skyhawk II	1648		14.11.77	To F-GBGK 8/78. Canx 23.8.78.
G-BFFY	Reims Cessna F.150M	1376		14.11.77	
G-BFFZ	Reims Cessna FR.172K Hawk XP II	0603	F-WZDU	14.11.77	Overturned on landing in a field off London Road, Chatteris on 25.2.85.
G-BFGA	Socata MS.892E Rallye 150ST	2629	F-GAFR	28.11.77	DBR in gales at Denham on 16.10.87. Canx as destroyed 7.12.87.
G-BFGB	Rockwell Commander 685	12049	N5071E	16.12.77	To N808AC 6/81. Canx 17.6.81.
G-BFGC	Reims Cessna F.150M	1423		14.11.77	Badly damaged when undercarriage hit stone wall on take-off from disused strip at Lower Argo, Fife on 1.8.80. Canx by CAA 8.12.86
G-BFGD	Reims Cessna F.172N Skyhawk II	1545	F-WZDT	14.11.77	
G-BFGE	Reims Cessna F.172N Skyhawk II	1616		14.11.77	To G-BSHR 10/84. Canx.
G-BFGF	Reims Cessna F.177RG Cardinal II	0166		14.11.77	
G-BFGG	Reims Cessna FRA.150M Aerobat	0321	F-WZDS	14.11.77	
G-BFGH	Reims Cessna F.337G Super Skymaster II (Wichita c/n 01754)	0081		14.11.77	
G-BFGI	Douglas DC-10-30 (Line No. 266)	46590		8. 1.79	To N68065 1/87. Canx 30.1.87.
G-BFGJ	Cameron D-96 Hot-Air Airship	290		11.11.77	Canx 10.8.83 on sale to Australia.
G-BFGK	SAN Jodel D.117	644	F-BIBT	27. 6.78	
G-BFGL	Reims Cessna FA.152 Aerobat	0339		14.11.77	
G-BFGM	Boeing 727-95 (Line No. 304)	19249	N1633	23.12.77	To HK-2960X 12/82. Canx 16.12.82.
G-BFGN	Boeing 727-95 (Line No. 315)	19251	N1635	30.11.77	To N29895 10/81. Canx 29.10.81.
G-BFGO	Fuji FA.200-160 Aero Subaru	FA200-219	PH-KDB	25.11.77	Damaged on CofA test taxying at Rush Green on 18.8.93. (Stored 7/96)
G-BFGP	DHC.6-310 Twin Otter	571	RP-C1217 G-BFGP	22.11.77	To C-GKBX 3/91. Canx 26.3.91.
G-BFGR	Rockwell Commander 685	12047	N57060 EC-CHL/N57060	21.11.77	To N58RG 1/83. Canx 18.1.83.
G-BFGS	Socata MS.893E Rallye 180GT	12571	F-BXYK French AF 12571 F-SCAZ/"41-AZ"	31. 8.76	
G-BFGT	Agusta-Bell 206B JetRanger II	8537		7.12.77	To SE-HIU 7/79. Canx 6.7.79.
G-BFGU	HS.125 Srs.700A	NA0212 & 257018		22.11.77	To N733H 12/77. Canx 21.12.77.
G-BFGV	HS.125 Srs.700A	NA0213 & 257019		22.11.77	NTU - To N370M 12/77. Canx 8.12.77.
G-BFGW	Reims Cessna F.150H	0370	PH-TGO	24.11.77	
G-BFGX	Reims Cessna FRA.150M Aerobat	0328	F-BUDX	28.11.77	
G-BFGY	Reims Cessna F.182P Skylane	0009	D-EJCG	28.11.77	Severely damaged when it overturned on take-off from Tempest Lelant on 4.8.87 due to nosewheel collapse. Canx as WFU 6.11.87.
G-BFGZ	Reims Cessna FRA.150M Aerobat	0329		28.11.77	
G-BFHA	Douglas C-47A-30-DK Dakota	13954/25399	T3-48 Spanish AF/N86451/43-48138	23.11.77	To N86451 in 2/78. Canx 14.2.78.
G-BFHB	Douglas C-47A-30-DK Dakota	14060/25505	T3-51 Spanish AF/N87651/43-48244	23.11.77	Canx 23.8.78 on sale to South Yemen.
G-BFHC	Douglas C-47A-15-DK Dakota	12758	T3-66 Spanish AF/EC-ACI/EC-DAU/42-108891	23.11.77	Canx 23.8.78 on sale to South Yemen.
G-BFHD	CASA C.352L	146	T2B-255 "721-8" Spanish AF	23.11.77	Canx 21.1.88 on sale to West Germany. (On display National Air & Space Museum, Dullas Airport, Washington, USA as D-ODLH)
G-BFHE	CASA C.352L	164	T2B-273 Spanish AF	23.11.77	To ZS-UYU 8/81. Canx 12.5.81.
G-BFHF	CASA C.352L	166	T2B-275 "721-15" Spanish AF	23.11.77	Sold in West Germany in 1/86. Canx as WFU 30.4.90. (On display 9/97 at Auto und Technik Museum, Sinsheim, Germany as "RJ+NP")
G-BFHG	CASA C.352L	153	T2B-262 "721-5" Spanish AF	23.11.77	To Kermit Weeks, Florida 6/93. Canx 27.9.94 on sale to USA.
G-BFHH	DH.82A Tiger Moth	85933	F-BDOH French AF/DF197	25.11.77	
G-BFHI	Piper J3C-65 Cub (L-4J-PI)	12532	F-BFBT 44-80236	25.11.77	
G-BFHJ	Reims Cessna FRA.150M Aerobat	0333		5.12.77	DBR when struck by Cessna FRA.150L G-BCRN taxying at Scone on 14.6.82. Scrapped by AST. Canx as destroyed 5.12.83.
G-BFHK	Reims Cessna F.177RG Cardinal II	0162		17. 2.78	Ditched in the English Channel 15 miles from Manston on 17.3.90. Canx as WFU 20.5.93.

Regn	Type	c/n	Previous identity	Regn date	Fate or immediate subsequent identity (if known)
G-BFHL	Reims Cessna FRA.150M Aerobat	0334		26. 1.78	Fatal crash into mountainside near Callendar, Perthshire on 17.11.81. Canx as destroyed 5.12.83.
G-BFHM	Steen Skybolt	PFA/64-10152		28.11.77	Fatal crash north by northeast of the diused RAF Worksop airfield on 7.8.89 & burnt out. Canx as destroyed 7.12.89.
G-BFHN	Scheibe SF-25E Super Falke	4334	D-KDFW	2.12.77	Struck boundary hedge on approach to Booker on 7.6.88. Canx as WFU 23.5.89. To D-KIAV(2) 10/89.
G-BFHO	PA-31-310 Turbo Navajo	31-30	EC-BNA N9022Y	21.12.77	To N4513U 8/83. Canx 1.8.83.
G-BFHP	Champion 7GCAA Citabria	114	HB-UAX	8.12.77	
G-BFHR	CEA Jodel DR.220 2+2	30	F-BOCX	1.12.77	
G-BFHS	American Aviation AA-5B Tiger	AA5B-0625		26. 1.78	To EI-BMT 6/82. Canx 22.6.82.
G-BFHT	Reims Cessna F.152 II	1441		7.12.77	
G-BFHU	Reims Cessna F.152 II	1461		7.12.77	
G-BFHV	Reims Cessna F.152 II	1470		21.12.77	
G-BFHW	Douglas DC-8F-54 (Line No. 268)	45879	N5879X OB-R-1084/YV-C-VIC	1. 3.78	Canx 18.6.80 on sale to West Germany. To HK-2380X 6/80.
G-BFHX	Evans VP-1	PFA/62-10283		2.12.77	
G-BFHY	Short SD.3-30 Var.100	SH3015	G-14-3015	9.12.77	To D-CDLA 3/78. Canx 23.3.78.
G-BFHZ	Short SC.7 Skyvan 3	SH1957		9.12.77	To HZ-ZAP 8/78. Canx 1.9.78.
G-BFIA	Short SC.7 Skyvan 3	SH1958	G-14-126	9.12.77	To 7P-AAB 11/78. Canx 11.1.79.
G-BFIB	PA-31-310 Turbo Navajo	31-684	LN-NPE OY-DVH/LN-RTJ	21.12.77	
G-BFIC	HS.125 Srs.600B	256060	HZ-MF1 G-5-12	30.12.77	To 5N-AYK 7/82. Canx 22.7.82.
G-BFID	Taylor JT.2 Titch Mk.III	PFA/60-10311		13.12.77	
G-BFIE	Reims Cessna FRA.150M Aerobat	0331		12. 1.78	
G-BFIF	Reims Cessna FR.172K Hawk XP II	0611		12. 1.78	To EI-CHJ 2/93. Canx 9.2.93.
G-BFIG	Reims Cessna FR.172K Hawk XP II	0615		12. 1.78	
G-BFIH	Douglas DC-9-15 (Line No. 35)	47048	N65358 YV-52C/YV-C-AVC/XA-DEV/TC-JAA/N8964	7. 4.78	To G-BMAA 3/80. Canx.
G-BFII	PA-23-250 Aztec E	27-4757	N14120	10. 1.78	To 9H-ABM. Canx 9.9.88.
G-BFIJ	American Aviation AA-5A Cheetah	AA5A-0486	N6160A	1. 3.78	
G-BFIK	American Aviation AA-5A Cheetah	AA5A-0488	N6140A	1. 3.78	DBR at Elstree on 8.6.83. Canx.
G-BFIL	American Aviation AA-5A Cheetah	AA5A-0505	N6141A	14. 3.78	DBR at Elstree on 30.12.82. Canx.
G-BFIM	American Aviation AA-5A Cheetah	AA5A-0506	N6142A	28. 3.78	Badly damaged in attempted go-around at Elstree on 2.1.79. Canx as destroyed 29.2.84.
G-BFIN	American Aviation AA-5A Cheetah	AA5A-0520	N6145A	22. 3.78	
G-BFIO	Slingsby T.65A Vega	1886		15.12.77	To N4312B 6/78. Canx 2.6.78.
G-BFIP	Wallbro Monoplane Replica (McCullogh/Wallis)	WA-1		16.12.77	(No external marks) (Stored 8/97)
G-BFIR	Avro 652A Anson T.21	"3634"	7881M WD413	16.12.77	To G-VROE 3/98. Canx.
G-BFIS	CAB GY-301 Supercab	01	(G-NICK) F-BFOV(2)	16.12.77	Burnt out in hangar fire at Staverton on 13.2.79. Canx.
G-BFIT	Thunder Ax6-56Z HAFB	136		20.12.77	CofA expired 3.5.91. Canx 4.8.98.
G-BFIU	Reims Cessna FR.172K Hawk XP	0591	N96098	12. 1.78	
G-BFIV	Reims Cessna F.177RG Cardinal II	0161	N96106	12. 1.78	
G-BFIW	Reims Cessna F.182Q Skylane	0027	N96094 F-WLIQ	12. 1.78	Canx as destroyed 28.11.79.
G-BFIX	Thunder Ax7-77A HAFB	133		9.12.77	(Extant 2/97)
G-BFIY	Reims Cessna F.150M	1381	OE-CMT	11. 1.78	
G-BFIZ	Reims Cessna FP.337GP Pressurised Super Skymaster	0021		10. 1.78	To I-BFIZ 12/83. Canx 7.12.83.
G-BFJA	American Aviation AA-5B Tiger	AA5B-0639		26. 1.78	Destroyed in fatal crash near Ludford, Lincs on 9.10.94. Canx as WFU 13.12.94.
G-BFJB	Bell 212	30881		8. 9.78	To VH-NSB 9/83. Canx 15.9.83.
G-BFJC	Not allocated.				
G-BFJD	Not allocated.				
G-BFJE	Not allocated.				
G-BFJF	Not allocated.				
G-BFJG	Bell 212	30878		8. 9.78	To EI-BFH 9/78. Canx 19.9.78.
G-BFJH	K & S SA.102.5 Cavalier	PFA/01-10181		6. 1.78	No Permit issued. Canx by CAA 4.12.90.
G-BFJI	Robin HR.100/250TR President	552	F-GAOT	16. 1.78	To VH-RXI(2) 12/94. Canx 28.6.94.
G-BFJJ	Evans VP-1	PFA/62-10273		30.12.77	
G-BFJK	PA-23-250 Aztec F	27-7654137	N62678	16. 1.78	
G-BFJL	PA-23-250 Aztec F	27-7654147	N62692	18. 1.78	Destroyed in the bomb explosion at Eglington on 21.9.78. Canx as destroyed 6.11.78.
G-BFJM	Reims Cessna F.152	1452		5. 1.78	Badly damaged after crashing in a field at Cullerie, 10m SW of Aberdeen on 17.5.90. Canx as destroyed 18.7.90.
G-BFJN	Westland-Bell 47G-3B1 (Line No.WAN/12)	WA/321	XT162	19. 1.78	Damaged while spraying near Spilsby on 7.7.91. Canx by CAA 21.9.92.
G-BFJO	Schweitzer Grumman G.164B-450 AgCat	318B	N6814Q	24. 2.78	To EC-EDP. Canx 3.6.87.

Regn	Type	c/n	Previous identity	Regn date	Fate or immediate subsequent identity (if known)
G-BFJP	Schweitzer Grumman G.164B-450 AgCat	319B	N6815Q	24. 2.78	To N7173Y. Canx 18.1.89.
G-BFJR	Reims Cessna F.337G Super Skymaster II (Wichita c/n 01761)	0082	N46297 (N53658)	4. 1.78	
G-BFJS	Cessna 340A II	340A-0442	N6247X	23. 1.78	To G-FBDC 9/81. Canx.
G-BFJT	Westland-Bell 47G-3B1 (Line No.WAS/207)	WA/603	XT841	3. 1.78	Canx 24.6.82 on sale to Cyprus.
G-BFJU	Westland-Bell 47G-3B1 (Line No.WAN/70)	WA/373	XT214	11. 1.78	To 5B-CEX 6/82. Canx 24.6.82.
G-BFJV	Reims Cessna F.172H	0505	PH-SKI	25. 1.78	Canx as WFU 12.7.93.
G-BFJW	Agusta-Bell 206B JetRanger II	8340	EI-BRL G-BFJW/F-BXOX/D-HMOG/(D-HNWS)	9. 3.78	Fatal crash at Ledbury on 16.12.96. Canx as destroyed 9.5.97.
G-BFJX	Aerospatiale SA.330J Puma	1481		17. 1.78	To 9M-SSC 2/80. Canx 14.2.80.
G-BFJY	Aerospatiale SA.330J Puma	1484		17. 1.78	To 9M-SSG 6/80. Canx 28.6.80.
G-BFJZ	Robin DR.400/140B Major	1290		20. 1.78	
G-BFKA	Reims Cessna F.172N Skyhawk II	1633		16. 1.78	To D-ESMP 7/95. Canx 26.1.95.
G-BFKB	Reims Cessna F.172N Skyhawk II	1601	(PH-AXO)	16. 1.78	
G-BFKC	Rand Robinson KR-2	KKC.5 & PFA/129-10809		20. 1.78	
G-BFKD	Rockwell Commander 114B	14384	N5835N	10. 5.78	To G-ROKI 7/96. Canx.
G-BFKE	Cameron V-77 HAFB	336		17. 1.78	To C-GVJI 1/79. Canx 12.1.79.
G-BFKF	Reims Cessna FA.152 Aerobat	0337		26. 1.78	
G-BFKG	Reims Cessna F.152 II	1463		26. 1.78	Blown over by jet blast from a Boeing 757 at Luton on 11.11.89. Canx as WFU 16.3.92. (Wreck stored 8/97)
G-BFKH	Reims Cessna F.152 II	1464		26. 1.78	
G-BFKI	ICA Brasov IS-28M2	05		23. 1.78	Canx 27.3.80 on sale to Romania.
G-BFKJ	PA-31-310 Turbo Navajo	31-681	N506V	2. 3.78	To G-TISH 12/85. Canx.
G-BFKK	Hunting Percival P.66 Pembroke C.1	PAC/66/76	8461M XF796	27. 1.78	To N2682U 6/81. Canx 5.6.81.
G-BFKL	Cameron N-56 HAFB	369		23. 1.78	
G-BFKM	Westland-Bell 47G-3B1 (Line No.WAS/232)	WA/710	XW190	23. 1.78	CofA expired 13.5.84. Canx as WFU 28.4.86.
G-BFKN	PA-23-250 Aztec F	27-7854011	N63890	2. 2.78	To F-GETF 8/87. Canx 28.7.87.
G-BFKO	PA-34-200T Seneca II	34-7770349	N38856	20. 1.78	Crashed in forced landing 3 miles west of Fawley Oil refinery after overshoot at Lee-on-Solent in fog on 17.11.79. Canx.
G-BFKP	Partenavia P.68B Victor	129		24. 1.78	To G-OPED 11/86. Canx.
G-BFKR	PA-24-250 Comanche	24-3551	PH-BUS D-ELPY/N8306P	3. 2.78	To N26634 12/82. Canx 6.12.82.
G-BFKS	Reims Cessna F.172L Skyhawk II	0887	F-BTFX	8. 3.78	Crashed into ground at Moore Farm, near Wycombe, shortly after take-off from Booker on 12.12.79. Canx.
G-BFKT	Reims Cessna F.172M Skyhawk II	1120	F-BVBJ	14. 3.78	To G-SKAN 7/85. Canx.
G-BFKU	PA-25-235 Pawnee D	25-7656017	N9634P	27. 2.78	Crashed in a wheat field at Turabi, Sudan on 10.10.79. Canx.
G-BFKV	PA-25-235 Pawnee D	25-7656089	N82343	28. 2.78	To SE-KLB. Canx 5.7.89.
G-BFKW	BAC/Aerospatiale Concorde SST Var.102	214 & 100-014		27. 1.78	To G-BOAG 2/81. Canx.
G-BFKX	BAC/Aerospatiale Concorde SST Var.102	216 & 100-016		27. 1.78	To G-N94AF 12/79. Canx.
G-BFKY(1)	Pitts S-1S Special	PFA/09-10015		. .78R	NTU - To G-BSIS 2/78. Canx.
G-BFKY(2)	PA-34-200 Seneca II	34-7350318	PH-NAZ N56332	22. 2.78	
G-BFKZ	Aerospatiale SA.330J Puma	1508	VH-WOF G-BFKZ	28. 2.78	To VR-BIG 3/85. Canx 29.3.85.
G-BFLA	Cessna 414 Chancellor	414-0924	OE-FLW N4714G	8. 2.78	Restored as N4714G 3/81. Canx 23.3.81.
G-BFLB	Beechcraft V35B Bonanza	D-9231	F-BSRT	25. 4.78	To ZS-LDF 7/81. Canx 10.7.81.
G-BFLC	Cessna 210L Centurion II	210-61256	N2361S	24. 2.78	Restored as N2361S. Canx 22.7.87.
G-BFLD	Boeing 707-338C (Line No. 693)	19625	VH-EAE(3)	27. 2.78	To N862BX 8/85. Canx 20.8.85.
G-BFLE	Boeing 707-338C (Line No. 546)	19293	VH-EBT	18. 4.78	To N861BX 8/85. Canx 21.8.85.
G-BFLF	HS.125 Srs.700A	NA0215 & 257023		21. 2.78	To N54555 in 3/78. Canx 13.3.78.
G-BFLG	HS.125 Srs.700A	NA0217 & 257024		21. 2.78	To N94BD 3/78. Canx 17.3.78.
G-BFLH	PA-34-200T Seneca II	34-7870065	N2126M	16. 2.78	
G-BFLI	PA-28R-201T Turbo Arrow III	28R-7803134	N2582M	16. 2.78	
G-BFLJ	PA-31-350 Navajo Chieftain	31-7752030	N63681	15. 2.78	To N37490 in 6/80. Canx 19.6.80.
G-BFLK	Reims Cessna F.152 II	1479		15. 2.78	To G-ENTW 1/93. Canx.
G-BFLL	HS.748 Srs.2A/245	1658	HK-1409	3. 3.78	To F-GODD 6/95. Canx 1.6.95.
G-BFLM	Cessna 150M Commuter	150-76352	N3017V	15. 6.78	Crashed near Bodmin on 14.1.97. Canx as WFU 12.2.97. Wreck store 5/98 at Bodmin.
G-BFLN	Cessna 150M Commuter	150-76416	N3198V	15. 6.78	Fatal crash into a disused glassworks at Knottingley, W.Yorks. on 21.3.95. Canx as destroyed 8.8.95.
G-BFLO	Reims Cessna F.172M Skyhawk II	1137	PH-DMF (EI-AYO)	13. 2.78	To G-DEMH 11/91. Canx.
G-BFLP	Amethyst Ax6-56 HAFB	001		20. 2.78	
G-BFLR	Hiller UH-12E	2025	N706WA XB-NOS/XA-TUF/XB-XIU/XC-CEC	1. 3.78	To SX-HCE 4/87. Canx 13.4.87.
G-BFLS	Westland-Bell 47G-3B1 (Line No.WAN/69)	WA/372	XT213	27. 6.78	To 5B-CFQ 12/83. Canx 13.12.83.
G-BFLT	[Was reserved by IPC Transport Press for Flight International - Canx 3/81]				

Regn	Type	c/n	Previous identity	Regn date	Fate or immediate subsequent identity (if known)
G-BFLU	Reims Cessna F.152 II	1433		15. 2.78	
G-BFLV	Reims Cessna F.172N Skyhawk II	1653		15. 2.78	To EI-CLQ 5/95. Canx 19.5.95.
G-BFLW	PA-39-160 Twin Comanche C/R	39-26	4X-ANW N8893Y	25. 5.78	To N4XZ 3/85. Canx 11.3.85.
G-BFLX(1)	Cessna 150L Commuter	150-75360	N11370	. .78R	NTU - To G-CSFC 3/78. Canx.
G-BFLX(2)	American Aviation AA-5A Cheetah	AA5A-0524	N6147A	14. 3.78	
G-BFLY(1)	Sikorsky S-61N	61-745	N4040S	. .78R	NTU - To G-BFMY 3/78. Canx.
G-BFLY(2)	Cessna 550 Citation II (Unit No.028)	550-0028	(N3246M)	14. 3.78	NTU - Not Imported. To OE-GAU. Canx.
G-BFLY(3)	Cessna 550 Citation II (Unit No.089)	550-0080	(N26624)	9. 7.79	To HB-VGR 12/79. Canx 14.12.79.
G-BFLZ	Beechcraft 95-A55 Baron	TC-220	PH-ILE HB-GOV	16. 3.78	
G-BFMA	Short SD.3-30 Var.100	SH3016	G-14-3016	15. 2.78	To D-CDLB 5/78. Canx 22.5.78.
G-BFMB	Short SD.3-30 Var.100	SH3017		15. 2.78	To PJ-DDA 7/78. Canx 31.7.78.
G-BFMC	BAC One-Eleven Srs.414EG	BAC.160	D-ANNO G-16-6	15.11.77	To 5N-GGG 8/93. Canx 27.7.93.
G-BFMD	Short SD.3-30 Var.100	SH3018	G-14-3018	15. 2.78	To PJ-DDB 8/78. Canx 1.9.78.
G-BFME	Cameron V-56 HAFB	371		17. 2.78	
G-BFMF	Cassutt Racer IIIM	PFA/34-10147		17. 2.78	Permit expired 24.5.91. (Stored 8/95) Canx by CAA 27.1.99.
G-BFMG	PA-28-161 Cherokee Warrior II	28-7716160	N3506Q	11. 5.78	
G-BFMH	Cessna 177B Cardinal	177-02034	N34836	18. 4.78	(On rebuild 1/98 Leeds-Bradford)
G-BFMI	Boeing 707-123B (Line No. 11)	17632	5B-DAK G-BFMI/N7505A	4. 3.78	Restored as 5B-DAK 2/79. Canx 16.2.79.
G-BFMJ	American Aviation AA-5B Tiger	AA5B-0725		22. 3.78	To G-ERRY 3/84. Canx.
G-BFMK	Reims Cessna FA.152 Aerobat	0344		6. 3.78	
G-BFML	American Aviation AA-5B Tiger	AA5B-0703		22. 3.78	To G-JOAN 6/80. Canx.
G-BFMM	PA-28-181 Cherokee Archer II	28-7890127	N47735	28. 2.78	
G-BFMN	PA-28R-201T Turbo Arrow III	28R-7703135	OO-DGP N5622V	23. 3.78	To G-RYAN 2/83. Canx.
G-BFMO	HS.125 Srs.700A	NA0219 & 257026		7. 3.78	To N1230A 3/78. Canx 31.3.78.
G-BFMP	HS.125 Srs.700A	NA0220 & 257027		7. 3.78	To C-GPPS 4/78. Canx.
G-BFMR	PA-20-125 Pacer	20-130	N7025K	20. 2.78	
G-BFMS	Socata MS.893 Rallye Commodore 180GT	13103		24. 2.78	Fatal crash after stalling onto the runway at Barton on 11.10.86. Remains scrapped. Canx by CAA 30.1.92.
G-BFMT	Robin HR.200/100 Club	108		1. 3.78	DBR in storms at Biggin Hill on 16.10.87. Canx as destroyed 11.12.87.
G-BFMU	American Aviation AA-5A Cheetah	AA5A-0630		23. 8.78	To G-MOGI 5/86. Canx.
"G-BFMU"	Reims Cessna F.172N Skyhawk II	1723		-----	Marks were worn on delivery although not officially issued - To G-DUVL on 16.8.78.
G-BFMV	PA-28-180 Cherokee C	28-2885	PH-ASM	24. 2.78	Struck by crashing Maule G-LOVE at Cranfield on 4.9.81. Canx as destroyed 5.12.83.
G-BFMW	Vickers 738 Viscount	67	YI-ACK	14. 3.78	CofA expired 15.6.82 & WFU. To East Midlands Airport Fire Service 27.10.83. Broken up. Canx as WFU 5.12.83.
G-BFMX	Reims Cessna F.172N Skyhawk II	1732		24. 8.78	
G-BFMY	Sikorsky S-61N Mk.II	61-745	(G-BFLY) N4040S	14. 3.78	(Used for spares 4/99 Dyce/Aberdeen)
G-BFMZ	Payne Ax6-62 HAFB	GFP.2		1. 3.78	
G-BFNA	PA-25-235 Pawnee D	25-7856014		2. 3.78	Canx 1.10.80 on sale to Zaire.
G-BFNB	PA-25-235 Pawnee D	25-7856015		2. 3.78	Canx 14.6.85 on sale to Kenya. To N18AP 6/85.
G-BFNC	Aerospatiale AS.350B Ecureuil	1009	F-WXFH	18. 4.78	To G-BWNA 11/95. Canx.
G-BFND	Agusta-Bell 206B JetRanger II	8553		30. 3.78	To G-BYSE 11/81. Canx.
G-BFNE	CASA I-131E Jungmann	1129	E3B-148 Spanish AF	17. 3.78	To G-TAFF 9/84. Canx.
G-BFNF	Aerospatiale SA.330J Puma	1514		10. 3.78	To 9M-SSD 3/80. Canx 17.3.80.
G-BFNG	Wassmer Jodel D.112	1321	F-BNHI	6. 3.78	
G-BFNH	Cameron N-77 HAFB (Originally regd with c/n 293, changed in 1979)	384		13. 3.78	Canx 6.9.89 on sale to West Germany.
G-BFNI	PA-28-161 Cherokee Warrior II	28-7816215	N9505N	8. 3.78	
G-BFNJ	PA-28-161 Cherokee Warrior II	28-7816281	N9520N	8. 3.78	
G-BFNK	PA-28-161 Cherokee Warrior II	28-7816282	N9527N	8. 3.78	
G-BFNL	IRMA BN-2A-6 Islander	871		16. 3.78	DBR in storm at Bembridge on 14.12.78. Later stored at Hurn. Canx as WFU 2.3.81.
G-BFNM	Globe GC-1B Swift	2205	N78205 NC78205	15. 6.78	(On rebuild 10/90) Canx by CAA 18.8.95.
G-BFNN	IRMA BN-2A-27 Islander (Originally regd as BN-2A-6)	872		16. 3.78	To VP-FAY 9/79. Canx 16.11.79.
G-BFNO	IRMA BN-2A-21 Islander (Originally regd as BN-2A-6)	873		16. 3.78	To Indian Navy as IN-131 in 1/81. Canx 3.2.81.
G-BFNP	Saffery S.330 HAFB (Toy)	10		16. 3.78	Canx as WFU 19.7.82.
G-BFNR	IRMA BN-2A-21 Islander (Originally regd as BN-2A-6)	874	(YV-377CP) G-BFNR	16. 3.78	To N2742N 7/82. Canx.

Regn	Type	c/n	Previous identity	Regn date	Fate or immediate subsequent identity (if known)
G-BFNS	IRMA BN-2A-21 Islander (Originally regd as BN-2A-6)	875	(YV-378CP) G-BFNS	16. 3.78	To Indian Navy as IN-132 in 1/81. Canx 16.1.81.
G-BFNT	IRMA BN-2B-26 Islander (Originally regd as BN-2A-6)	876		16. 3.78	To N425NE 7/80. Canx 8.8.80.
G-BFNU	IRMA BN-2B-21 Islander (Originally regd as BN-2A-6)	877	(YV-.....) G-BFNU	16. 3.78	WFU with damaged spar. Canx as WFU 28.1.94. Fuselage stored 5/98 at St.Just.
G-BFNV	IRMA BN-2A-26 Islander (Originally regd as BN-2A-6)	878		16. 3.78	To G-BPCD 7/88. Canx.
G-BFNW	IRMA BN-2B-27 Islander (Originally regd as BN-2A-6, amended in 8/80)	879		16. 3.78	To HP-896 3/81. Canx 23.3.81.
G-BFNX	IRMA BN-2T Turbine Islander (Originally regd as BN-2A-6)	880		16. 3.78	To N413JA 9/81. Canx 7.10.81.
G-BFNY	IRMA BN-2A-26 Islander (Originally regd as BN-2A-6)	881		16. 3.78	To XC-DUI 8/80. Canx 1.9.80.
G-BFNZ	IRMA BN-2A-26 Islander (Originally regd as BN-2A-6)	882		16. 3.78	To XC-DUL 8/80. Canx 15.7.80.
G-BFOA	IRMA BN-2A-26 Islander (Originally regd as BN-2A-6)	883		16. 3.78	To XC-DUK 9/80. Canx 29.9.80.
G-BFOB	IRMA BN-2A-26 Islander (Originally regd as BN-2A-6)	884		16. 3.78	To XC-DUN 11/80. Canx 21.10.80.
G-BFOC	IRMA BN-2A-26 Islander (Originally regd as BN-2A-6)	885		16. 3.78	To XC-DUO 8/80. Canx 1.9.80.
G-BFOD	Reims Cessna F.182Q Skylane II	0068		23. 3.78	
G-BFOE	Reims Cessna F.152 II	1475		23. 3.78	
G-BFOF	Reims Cessna F.152 II	1448		9. 3.78	
G-BFOG	Cessna 150M	150-76223	N66706	13. 3.78	
G-BFOH	Westland-Bell 47G-3B1 (Line No.WAN/65)	WA/370	XT211	13. 3.78	To 5B-CGO 4/86. Canx 15.4.86.
G-BFOI	Westland-Bell 47G-3B1 (Line No.WAP/98)	WA/518	XT811	13. 3.78	Struck ground while crop spraying at Church Hall Farm, near Paglesham on 31.7.86. Canx as destroyed 19.11.87.
G-BFOJ	American Aviation AA-1 Yankee	AA1-0395	OH-AYB (LN-KAJ)/(N6195L)	4. 4.78	
G-BFOK	Piper Aerostar 601A	61-0186-087	ZS-JEN	15. 3.78	To N7519S 3/78. Canx 31.5.78.
G-BFOL	Beechcraft 200 Super King Air	BB-387	5N-ALW (N899TB)/G-BFOL/N899TB/G-BFOL	20. 3.78	To 5N-BHL. Canx 5.11.92.
G-BFOM	PA-31-325 Turbo Navajo C	31-7512017	(F-GJHV) EI-DMI/G-BFOM/HB-LHH/N59933	17. 3.78	
G-BFON	PA-31 Turbo Navajo	31-405	SE-FHB	15. 2.78	Crashed and caught fire half a mile north of Brize Norton on 11.6.86. Remains later scrapped at Tattershall Thorpe. Canx by CAA 9.6.92.
G-BFOO	BAC 167 Strikemaster Mk.80A	PS.366	G-27-312	22. 3.78	To R.Saudi AF as 1135 in 5/78. Canx.
G-BFOP	Jodel Wassmer D.120 Paris-Nice	32	F-BHTX	23. 3.78	
G-BFOR	Thunder Ax6-56A HAFB	146		. .78R	NTU - Not built. Canx 22.12.81.
G-BFOS	Thunder Ax6-56A HAFB	147		20. 3.78	
G-BFOT	Thunder Ax6-56A HAFB	148		20. 3.78	Canx by CAA 16.12.87.
G-BFOU	Taylor JT.1 Monoplane	PFA/55-10333		17. 3.78	
G-BFOV	Reims Cessna F.172N Skyhawk II	1675		18. 5.78	
G-BFOW	Reims Cessna F.172N Skyhawk II	1643		18. 5.78	Ditched into the sea about 13 miles from Alderney on 10.2.85. (No wreckage was found) Canx as destroyed 11.7.88.
G-BFOX	DH.83 Fox Moth Replica	FM-99		13. 2.78	Project believed not commenced. Canx by CAA 2.9.91.
G-BFOY	Cessna A.188B Agtruck	02746T	N731AP	20. 3.78	Crashed at Manor Farm, Chamberlayne, Wilts on 14.6.81. Canx as destroyed 21.12.83.
G-BFOZ	Thunder Ax6-56 Plug HAFB	144		20. 3.78	Canx by CAA 16.4.92.
G-BFPA	Scheibe SF-25B Falke	46179	D-KAGM	29. 3.78	
G-BFPB	American Aviation AA-5B Tiger	AA5B-0706		7. 4.78	
G-BFPC	American Aviation AA-5B Tiger	AA5B-0751		10. 4.78	Crashed at Black Hill Farm, Ballykelly, Co.Antrim on 8.5.82. Canx as destroyed 5.12.83.
G-BFPD	American Aviation AA-5A Cheetah	AA5A-0576		18. 4.78	To G-OING 4/84. Canx.
G-BFPE	PA-28-140 Cherokee C	28-26410	OH-PCY	22. 3.78	Crashed at Clacton on-Sea on 9.6.82. CofA expired 26.5.84. (Wreck stored 4/92)
G-BFPF	Sikorsky S-61N Mk.II	61-490	ZS-HDK N4018S	21. 6.78	Restored as ZS-HDK. Canx 13.1.89.
G-BFPG	Robin HR.100/250TR Acrobin (Originally regd as HR.100/285 Tiara)	537	ZS-JSU F-ODCS	5. 4.78	To HB-EQK 4/80. Canx 15.4.80.
G-BFPH	Reims Cessna F.172K	0802	PH-VHN	23. 3.78	
G-BFPI	HS.125 Srs.700B	257025	VR-HIN G-BFPI/G-5-12	28. 3.78	To N93TC 1/84. Canx 30.1.84.
G-BFPJ	Proctor Petrel	PFA/30-10178		5. 4.78	Canx by CAA 2.9.91.
G-BFPK	Beechcraft A23-19A Musketeer Sport III	MB-322	OH-BMM	31. 3.78	To 5B-CGQ. Canx 3.4.87.
G-BFPL	Fokker D.VII Replica	0033	D-EAWM	11. 8.78	To I-.... Canx 28.7.99.
G-BFPM	Reims Cessna F.172M Skyhawk II	1384	PH-MIO	13. 4.78	Canx by CAA 9.8.99.
G-BFPN	Aerospatiale SA.330J Puma	1490		17. 4.78	To 9M-SSF 5/80. Canx 18.4.80.
G-BFPO	Rockwell Commander 112B	530	N1412J	10. 5.78	
G-BFPP	Bell 47J-2 Ranger	2851	F-BJAN TR-LKD/F-OCBU	23. 5.78	(Damaged in crash near the A64 road between Tadcaster and York on 11.7.97)
G-BFPR	PA-25-235 Pawnee D	25-7856007		4. 4.78	To I-TOZU 6/81. Canx 1.6.81.
G-BFPS	PA-25-235 Pawnee D	25-7856013		4. 4.78	
G-BFPT	Douglas C-47A-70-DL Dakota	19268	T3-65 Spanish AF/EC-ASE/42-100805	7. 4.78	Canx 8.9.78 on sale to Yemen.

Regn	Type	c/n	Previous identity	Regn date	Fate or immediate subsequent identity (if known)
G-BFPU	Douglas C-47B-15-DK Dakota	15247/26692	T3-49 Spanish AF/N86449/43-49431	7. 4.78	Burnt out at Merowe, Sudan on delivery to Alyemda on 24.9.78. Canx as destroyed 11.12.78.
G-BFPV	Douglas C-47B-50-DK Dakota	17090/34357	T3-45 Spanish AF/45-1087	7. 4.78	Canx 8.9.78 on sale to Yemen.
G-BFPW	Douglas C-47B-40-DK Dakota	16856/33604	T3-40 Spanish AF/N73855/44-77272	7. 4.78	To N3753N 4/80. Canx 21.8.80.
G-BFPX	Taylor JT-1 Monoplane	PFA/55-10263		4. 4.78	Canx by CAA 6.8.91.
G-BFPY	PA-32-260 Cherokee Six	32-1048	N5588J	11. 5.78	To G-NEAL 11/83. Canx.
G-BFPZ	Reims Cessna F.177RG Cardinal II	0079	(OO-DVE) G-BFPZ/PH-AUK/D-EGBM	3. 4.78	To N56PZ 11/97. Canx 13.8.97.
G-BFRA	Rockwell Commander 114	14292	N4972W	28. 3.78	
G-BFRB	Reims Cessna F.152 II	1501		18. 5.78	Badly damaged following collision with PA-23-250 G-BHNG on take-off from Shoreham on 19.12.81. Rebuilt & re-regd as G-SACB 3/84. Canx.
G-BFRC	American Aviation AA-5A Cheetah	AA5A-0631		15. 3.79	To G-CHTA 3/86. Canx.
G-BFRD	Bowers FlyBaby 1A	PFA/16-10300		27. 1.78	(Project near completion)
G-BFRE	American Aviation AA-5B Tiger	AA5B-0830		1. 8.78	DBR in undercarriage collapse on landing at Hull/Paull on 8.7.79. Used for spares at Elstree. Canx as destroyed 5.12.83.
G-BFRF	Taylor JT.1 Monoplane	PFA/55-10330		7. 4.78	
G-BFRG	Colt 77A HAFB	006	EI-BDJ	13. 6.78	NTU - To SE-ZYG 8/78. Canx 4.7.78.
G-BFRH	PA-28-140 Cherokee B	28-26032	OH-PCA	7. 4.78	To G-GCAT 10/81. Canx.
G-BFRI	Sikorsky S-61N Mk.II	61-809		26. 5.78	
G-BFRJ	Handley Page HPR.7 Dart Herald 209	195	4X-AHO	11. 4.78	To I-ZERC 3/84. Canx 12.3.84.
G-BFRK	Handley Page HPR.7 Dart Herald 209	197	4X-AHN	11. 4.78	To I-ZERD 12/84. Canx 21.1.85.
G-BFRL	Reims Cessna F.152 II	1490		11. 4.78	Badly damaged in heavy landing at Lulsgate on 24.8.92. (Stored 1/99 Bristol/Lulsgate) Canx by CAA 14.3.97.
G-BFRM	Cessna 550 Citation II (Unit No.027)	550-0027	N527CC N3245M	31. 1.78	
G-BFRN	Reims Cessna F.152 II	1483		11. 4.78	Crashed into a house on landing at Booker on 23.10.83. Canx as destroyed 3.8.84.
G-BFRO	Reims Cessna F.150M	1350	LN-ALM	19. 4.78	Fatal crash & DBF 6.5.97 1m W of Denny, Cumbernauld. Canx by CAA 18.8.97.
G-BFRP	Reims Cessna F.150M	1390	LN-ALN (F-GAQI)	19. 4.78	Crashed at Edale Hill, near Manchester on 23.10.83. Canx by CAA 2.2.87.
G-BFRR	Reims Cessna FRA.150M Aerobat	0326	LN-ALO	19. 4.78	
G-BFRS	Reims Cessna F.172N Skyhawk II	1555	LN-ALP	19. 4.78	
G-BFRT	Reims Cessna FR.172K Hawk XP II	0610	LN-ALQ	19. 4.78	To D-EBRT 8/90. Canx 5.7.90.
G-BFRU	Reims Cessna F.152 II	1484		17. 4.78	DBR at Shoreham on 29.5.82. Canx.
G-BFRV	Reims Cessna FA.152 Aerobat	0345		17. 4.78	
G-BFRW	Agusta-Bell 47G-3B1	1557	XT145	11. 4.78	To VH-MQU 4/82. Canx 28.4.82.
G-BFRX	PA-25-260 Pawnee D	25-7405787	SE-GDZ	23. 5.78	Damaged on landing at Sutton Bank on 27.3.94. (Spares use 1/95) Canx as destroyed 3.6.94.
G-BFRY	PA-25-260 Pawnee D	25-7405789	SE-GIB	23. 5.78	
G-BFRZ	DHC.6-310 Twin Otter	578		. .78R	NTU - To G-RBLA 4/78. Canx.
G-BFSA	Reims Cessna F.182Q Skylane II	0074	F-WZDG	17. 4.78	
G-BFSB	Reims Cessna F.152 II	1506		20. 4.78	
G-BFSC	PA-25-235 Pawnee D	25-7656068	N82302	2. 6.78	
G-BFSD	PA-25-235 Pawnee D	25-7656084	N82338	2. 6.78	
G-BFSE	Westland Commando Mk.2E (Line No. 187)	WA/866		13. 4.78	To Egyptian AF as SU-BBJ/740 12/80. Canx 16.12.80.
G-BFSF	Westland Commando Mk.2E (Line No. 188)	WA/867		13. 4.78	To Egyptian AF as SU-ARR/741 5/79. Canx 8.5.79.
G-BFSG	Westland Commando Mk.2E (Line No. 190)	WA/868		13. 4.78	To Egyptian AF as SU-ART/742 5/79. Canx 8.5.79.
G-BFSH	Westland Commando Mk.2E (Line No. 192)	WA/869		13. 4.78	To Egyptian AF as SU-ARP/744 5/79. Canx 8.5.79.
G-BFSI	HS.125 Srs.700A	NA0222 & 257030		13. 4.78	To C-GSCL 5/78. Canx 24.5.78.
G-BFSJ	Westland-Bell 47G-3B1 (Line No.WAP/146)	WA/432	XT543	31. 5.78	CofA expired 27.7.84. Canx by CAA 4.4.91.
G-BFSK	PA-23-160 Apache	23-576	OO-NVC OO-HVL/OO-PIP(2)	14. 4.78	No British CofA issued. Used as ground trainer at Kidlington 9/78. Canx as WFU 5.12.83.
G-BFSL	Cessna U206F Stationair II	U206-02471	N1107V	22. 5.78	To 5Y-BSL 6/89. Canx 11.5.89.
G-BFSM	Hughes 369D (500D)	48-0294D		. .78R	NTU - To G-GOGO 12/78. Canx.
G-BFSN	Agusta-Bell 47G-2	273	VP-YRW 9J-RIE/VP-YRW	18. 4.78	To F-BVFS 11/81. Canx 19.11.81.
G-BFSO	HS.125 Srs.700B	257028		21. 4.78	To G-5-534/N700TL. Canx 28.10.86.
G-BFSP	HS.125 Srs.700B	257031	D-CBAE G-5-701/G-BFSP/G-PRMC/G-BFSP	21. 4.78	To G-5-701/N89TJ 3/94. Canx 30.3.94.
G-BFSR	Reims Cessna F.150J	0504	OH-CBN	7. 7.78	
G-BFSS	Reims Cessna FR.172G Rocket	0167	OH-CDY	7. 7.78	
G-BFST	Partenavia P.68B Victor	30	OO-TOF	19. 4.78	To OY-CEW 6/86. Canx 30.1.86.
G-BFSU	Partenavia P.68B Victor	141		3. 5.78	To G-OROY 9/81. Canx.
G-BFSV	Aerospatiale SA.330J Puma	1526		20. 4.78	To VH-BHO 10/79. Canx 29.10.79.
G-BFSW	Short SD.3-30 Var.100	SH3019	G-14-3019	19. 4.78	To N332GW 9/78. Canx 7.9.78.
G-BFSX	Short SD.3-30 Var.100	SH3020	G-14-3020	19. 4.78	To N371HA 11/78. Canx 17.11.78.
G-BFSY	PA-28-181 Archer II	28-7890200	N9503N	19. 4.78	
G-BFSZ	PA-28-161 Warrior II	28-7816468	N9556N	19. 4.78	To G-KBPI 5/81. Canx.

Regn	Type	c/n	Previous identity	Regn date	Fate or immediate subsequent identity (if known)
G-BFTA	PA-28-161 Warrior II	28-7816553	N9577N	19. 4.78	To A6-AFC 7/85. Canx 3.7.85.
G-BFTB	PA-28R-201 Arrow III	28R-7837214	N9652C	9. 5.78	To G-HIFI 2/81. Canx.
G-BFTC	PA-28R-201T Turbo Arrow III	28R-7803197	N3868M	19. 4.78	
G-BFTD	American Aviation AA-5A Cheetah	AA5A-0507		8. 5.78	Fatal crash into high ground at Pen-yr-eryr, North Wales on 30.3.79. Canx as destroyed 5.12.83.
G-BFTE	American Aviation AA-5A Cheetah	AA5A-0658		30. 8.78	Fatal crash into a community centre at Castle Lane, Chandler's Ford on 12.9.86. Canx as destroyed 23.9.87.
G-BFTF	American Aviation AA-5B Tiger	AA5B-0879		7. 9.78	
G-BFTG	American Aviation AA-5B Tiger	AA5B-0777		15. 5.78	
G-BFTH	Reims Cessna F.172N Skyhawk II	1671		3. 5.78	
G-BFTI	IRMA BN-2A-21 Islander (Originally regd as BN-2A-6)	886		27. 4.78	To IN-133 Indian Navy 12/80. Canx 16.1.81.
G-BFTJ	IRMA BN-2A-21 Islander (Originally regd as BN-2A-6)	887		27. 4.78	To IN-134 Indian Navy 1/81. Canx 3.2.81.
G-BFTK	IRMA BN-2A-21 Islander (Originally regd as BN-2A-6)	888		27. 4.78	To IN-135 Indian Navy 1/81. Canx 4.3.81.
G-BFTL	IRMA BN-2A-21 Islander (Originally regd as BN-2A-6)	889		27. 4.78	To IN-136 Indian Navy 1/81. Canx 4.3.81.
G-BFTM	IRMA BN-2A-21 Islander (Originally regd as BN-2A-6)	890		27. 4.78	To YR-NBZ 1/81. Canx 13.1.81.
G-BFTN	Grumman G.164B-450 Agcat	204B	N6687Q	2. 5.78	To PH-APR 6/81. Canx 15.5.81.
G-BFTO	Rotorway 133 Scorpion	1131		14. 6.78	Crashed on landing at Popham on 4.4.80. Remains taken to Tattershall Thorpe. Canx as destroyed 5.12.83.
G-BFTP(1)	HS.125 Srs.700B	257020		. .78R	NTU - To (G-BFVN)/G-EFPT 6/78. Canx.
G-BFTP(2)	Short SD.3-30 Var.100	SH3021		18. 5.78	To D-CDLC 10/78. Canx 27.10.78.
G-BFTR	Bell 206L Long Ranger	45139	G-CLNT G-BFTR/N5005K	15. 5.78	To SE-HTL 1/89. Canx 5.12.88.
G-BFTS	Agusta-Bell 47G-3B1	1592	9J-AEX G-BFTS/XT126	28. 4.78	To 5B-CFW 4/84. Canx 28.12.83.
G-BFTT	Cessna 421C Golden Eagle III	421C-0462	N6789C	3. 5.78	
G-BFTU	Reims Cessna FA.152 Aerobat	0346		28. 7.78	To G-JONI 7/84. Canx.
G-BFTV	Aerospatiale SA.330J Puma	1557		5. 5.78	To 9M-SSE 3/80. Canx 24.3.80.
G-BFTW	PA-25-250 Aztec F	27-7854087	N63956	11. 5.78	To SE-IVN. Canx 4.8.86.
G-BFTX	Reims Cessna F.172N Skyhawk II	1715		2. 5.78	
G-BFTY	Cameron V-77 HAFB	420		4. 5.78	Canx as WFU 29.3.93.
G-BFTZ	Socata MS.880B Rallye Club	1269	F-BPAX	2. 6.78	CofA expired 19.9.81. Canx by CAA 14.11.91. (On loan to Newark Air Museum) (On display 2/99)
G-BFUA	HS.748 Srs.2A/230	1599	XA-SEY G-11	. .78R	NTU - Canx 6.6.78 as Not Imported. To C-GAPC.
G-BFUB	PA-32RT-300 Lance II	32R-7885052	N9509C	18. 5.78	
G-BFUC	Not allocated.				
G-BFUD	Scheibe SF-25E Super Falke	4313	D-KLDC	19. 5.78	
G-BFUE	HS.125 Srs.700A	NA0223 & 257032	G-5-14	18. 5.78	To N700BA 6/78. Canx 8.6.78.
G-BFUF	PA-30-160 Twin Comanche	30-363	F-OCZF 5R-MCA/N7361Y	19. 5.78	Canx 12.3.79 on sale to Kenya - reportedly to 5Y-III. (Dismantled & stored 9/92 at Wilson, Kenya; "Kenyan regn not issued")
G-BFUG	Cameron N-77 HAFB	394		15. 5.78	
G-BFUH	Short SD.3-30 Var.100	SH3022	G-14-3022	18. 5.78	To N372HA 1/79. Canx 11.1.79.
G-BFUI	Short SC.7 Skyvan 3	SH1959	G-14-127	18. 5.78	To Panama AF as 300 in 6/78. Canx.
G-BFUJ	Short SC.7 Skyvan 3M	SH1960	G-14-128	18. 5.78	To 7P-AAC 1/79. Canx 7.2.79.
G-BFUK	Not allocated.				
G-BFUL	Short SC.7 Skyvan 3A-100	SH1961	G-14-129	18. 5.78	To A40-SM 9/78. Canx 22.9.78.
G-BFUM	Short SC.7 Skyvan 3-100	SH1962	N6196P Botswana DF OC1\Z1/G-BFUM	18. 5.78	To 9M-PIH. Canx 27.9.93.
G-BFUN	Hughes 269C (300C)	88-0701		19. 9.78	To OE-CXC 4/82. Canx 21.4.82.
G-BFUO	PA-23-250 Aztec F	27-7854082	N63950	23. 5.78	To N106RS 9/83. Canx 12.9.83.
G-BFUP	IRMA BN-2A-26 Islander (Originally regd as BN-2A-6)	891		25. 5.78	To XC-DUR 9/80. Canx 17.9.80.
G-BFUR	IRMA BN-2A-26 Islander (Originally regd as BN-2A-6)	892		25. 5.78	To XC-DUJ 9/80. Canx 17.9.80.
G-BFUS	Cessna 404 Titan	404-0455	(N2681Y)	23.11.79	To PH-VUS 8/82. Canx 27.7.82.
G-BFUT	IRMA BN-2A-26 Islander (Originally regd as BN-2A-6)	893		25. 5.78	To XC-DUM 8/80. Canx 1.9.80.
G-BFUU	IRMA BN-2A-26 Islander (Originally regd as BN-2A-6)	894		25. 5.78	To XC-DUP 10/80. Canx 14.10.80.
G-BFUV	IRMA BN-2A-26 Islander (Originally regd as BN-2A-6)	895		25. 5.78	To XC-DUS 11/80. Canx 21.10.80.
G-BFUW	Scottish Avn Bulldog Srs.120/123	BH.120-394		9. 6.78	To Nigerian AF as 241 in 6/78. Canx 11.12.78.
G-BFUX	Scottish Avn Bulldog Srs.120/123	BH.120-395		9. 6.78	To Nigerian AF as 242 in 6/78. Canx 11.12.78.
G-BFUY	Scottish Avn Bulldog Srs.120/123	BH.120-396		9. 6.78	To Nigerian AF as 243 in 6/78. Canx 11.12.78.
G-BFUZ	Cameron V-77 HAFB	398		24. 5.78	Canx by CAA 19.5.93.
G-BFVA	Boeing 737-204ADV (Line No. 541)	21693		31. 7.78	To HP-1163CMP 8/90. Canx 1.8.90.
G-BFVB	Boeing 737-204ADV (Line No. 542)	21694	C-GNDW G-BFVB	31. 7.78	To G-SBEA 12/94. Canx.
G-BFVC	Thunder Ax7-77Z HAFB	100		9. 6.78	To HB-BAT 5/79. Canx 15.5.79.

Regn	Type	c/n	Previous identity	Regn date	Fate or immediate subsequent identity (if known)
G-BFVD	Not allocated.				
G-BFVE	Bell 212	30698	C-GOKY	23. 6.78	Restored as C-GOKY 9/80. Canx 18.9.80.
G-BFVF	PA-38-112 Tomahawk	38-78A0055	N9691N	1. 6.78	
G-BFVG	PA-28-181 Archer II	28-7890408	N31746 N9558N	1. 6.78	
G-BFVH	Airco DH.2 Replica	WA/4	"5964"	1. 6.78	Permit expired 23.7.86. (Stored/rebuild .97)
G-BFVI	HS.125 Srs.700B	257037	G-5-18	5. 6.78	To G-IFTE 5/96. Canx.
G-BFVJ	Scottish Avn Bulldog Srs.120/123	BH.120-397		9. 6.78	To Nigerian AF as 244 in 7/78. Canx 11.12.78.
G-BFVK	Scottish Avn Bulldog Srs.120/123	BH.120-398		9. 6.78	To Nigerian AF as 245 in 7/78. Canx 11.12.78.
G-BFVL	Scottish Avn Bulldog Srs.120/123	BH.120-399		9. 6.78	To Nigerian AF as 246 in 7/78. Canx 11.12.78.
G-BFVM	Westland-Bell 47G-3B1 (Line no. WAP/96)	WA/393	XT234	14. 6.78	Canx by CAA 10.11.95. (Stored 5/96)
G-BFVN	HS.125 Srs.700B	257020	(G-BFTP)	. .78R	NTU - To G-EFPT 6/78. Canx.
G-BFVO	Partenavia P.68B Victor	39	SE-FUK	29. 1.79	To F-OGVX 3/95. Canx 15.11.94.
G-BFVP	PA-23-250 Aztec F	27-7854096	N63966	6. 7.78	
G-BFVR	HS.748 Srs.2A/333	1760	G11-9	26. 6.78	To J5-GAT 12/78. Canx 12.12.78.
G-BFVS	American Aviation AA-5B Tiger	AA5B-0784	N28736	11. 8.78	
G-BFVT	Armstrong-Whitworth 650 Argosy E.1	AW.6798	XR143	29. 6.78	To N1403Z. Canx 17.7.78.
G-BFVU	Cessna 150L Commuter	150-74684	N75189	10. 8.78	
G-BFVV	Aerospatiale SA.365C1 Dauphin 2	5011	F-ODJI G-BFVV/F-WXFG	22. 6.78	
G-BFVW	Aerospatiale SA.365C3 Dauphin 2	5014	F-WXFO	22. 6.78	Canx 23.3.92 on sale to France. Still stored Marignane, France pending sale 5/96. To F-OHSB 7/97.
G-BFVX	Beechcraft C90 King Air	LJ-803		12. 6.78	To G-OLAF 11/87. Canx.
G-BFVY	Beechcraft C90 King Air	LJ-812		12. 6.78	To N627KP 5/88. Canx.
G-BFVZ	Beechcraft A200S Super King Air	BB-417		13. 7.78	To HB-GHF 7/83. Canx 12.7.83.
G-BFWA	IRMA BN-2A-21 Islander (Originally regd as BN-2A-6)	896		6. 7.78	To YR-NBY 1/81. Canx 13.1.81.
G-BFWB	PA-28-161 Warrior II	28-7816584	N31752	22. 6.78	
G-BFWC	Not allocated.				
G-BFWD	Phoenix Currie Wot	PFA/3009		22. 6.78	
G-BFWE	PA-23-250 Aztec E	27-4583	9M-AQT 9V-BDI/N13968	13. 7.78	
G-BFWF	Cessna 421B Golden Eagle II	421B-0662	ZS-JCA N1567G	10. 7.78	CofA expired 15.5.80. WFU & stored at Sibson. Canx by CAA 3.4.89. To N31KS 6/95.
G-BFWG	Rockwell Commander 112A	345	ZS-JRX N1345J	10. 7.78	To G-RDCI 5/85. Canx.
G-BFWH	Beechcraft B200 Super King Air	BB-426		13. 7.78	To N400TB 2/80. Canx 29.2.80.
G-BFWI	Beechcraft B200 Super King Air	BB-428		13. 7.78	To N51V 11/80. Canx 5.11.80.
G-BFWJ	Slingsby T.65A Vega	1887		27. 6.78	Crashed at Camphill on 5.5.79. Later became BGA.3116 in 1985. Canx.
G-BFWK	PA-28-161 Warrior II	28-7816610	N9589N	23. 6.78	Canx as WFU 26.5.98.
G-BFWL(1)	American Aviation AA-5A Cheetah	AA5A-0617	N26477	. 6.78R	NTU - To G-NASH 9/78. Canx.
G-BFWL(2)	Reims Cessna F.150L	0971	PH-KDC	4.10.78	
G-BFWM(1)	American Aviation AA-5A Cheetah	AA5A-0620	N26480	. 6.78R	NTU - To G-JUDY 8/78. Canx.
G-BFWM(2)	Hiller UH-12D	1132	N67144 58-5483	11. 7.78	No CofA issued - possibly used for spares. Canx as WFU 8.12.86.
G-BFWN	BAC One-Eleven Srs.537GF	BAC.261	5B-DAJ	6.10.78	Restored as 5B-DAJ 4/80. Canx 28.4.80.
G-BFWO	Scottish Avn Bulldog Srs.120/123	BH.120-400		3. 7.78	To Nigerian AF as 247 in 8/78. Canx 11.12.78.
G-BFWP	Scottish Avn Bulldog Srs.120/123	BH.120-401		3. 7.78	To Nigerian AF as 248 in 8/78. Canx 11.12.78.
G-BFWR	Scottish Avn Bulldog Srs.120/123	BH.120-402		3. 7.78	To Nigerian AF as 249 in 8/78. Canx 11.12.78.
G-BFWS	Scottish Avn Bulldog Srs.120/123	BH.120-403		3. 7.78	To Nigerian AF as 250 in 8/78. Canx 11.12.78.
G-BFWT	Scottish Avn Bulldog Srs.120/123	BH.120-404		3. 7.78	To Nigerian AF as 251 in 8/78. Canx 11.12.78.
G-BFWU	Scottish Avn Bulldog Srs.120/123	BH.120-405		3. 7.78	To Nigerian AF as 252 in 8/78. Canx 11.12.78.
G-BFWV	IRMA BN-2A-26 Islander (Originally regd as BN-2A-6)	897		6. 7.78	To XC-DUU 12/80. Canx 29.12.80.
G-BFWW	Robin HR.100/210 Safari	187	F-BVDY	10. 7.78	Mid-air collision with Grob G-BKNJ on 3.5.90 and crashed at Four Shires Stone, Moreton-in-Marsh. Canx by CAA 17.8.90.
G-BFWX	IRMA BN-2A-21 Islander (Originally regd as BN-2A-6)	898		6. 7.78	To YR-NBX 1/81. Canx 13.1.81.
G-BFWY	IRMA BN-2A-21 Islander (Originally regd as BN-2A-6)	899		6. 7.78	To YR-NBW 5/81. Canx 15.5.81.
G-BFWZ	IRMA BN-2A-26 Islander (Originally regd as BN-2A-6)	900		6. 7.78	To XC-DUT 1/81. Canx 15.1.81.
G-BFXA	Douglas C-53-DO Skytrooper	4890	T3-58 Spanish AF/EC-ABQ/EC-DAL/NC44884/41-20120	3. 7.78	To ST-AHK 11/78. Canx 28.11.78.

Regn	Type	c/n	Previous identity	Regn date	Fate or immediate subsequent identity (if known)
G-BFXB	Douglas R4D-1 Dakota	4225	T3-42 Spanish AF/N57V/NC95487/BuA.3135	3. 7.78	Canx 5.12.83 on sale to USA. To XA-JIH 9/79.
G-BFXC	Mooney M.20C Ranger Mk.21	2620	(EI-...) G-BFXC/9H-ABD/G-BFXC/OH-MOA/N1217X	10. 7.78	To EI-CIK 7/93. Canx 22.6.93.
G-BFXD	PA-28-161 Warrior II	28-7816583	N31750	10. 7.78	
G-BFXE	PA-28-161 Warrior II	28-7816585	N31802	10. 7.78	
G-BFXF	Andreasson BA.4B	AAB-001 & PFA/38-10351		10. 7.78	(Semi-built 3/87)
G-BFXG	Druine D.31 Turbulent	PFA/1663		10. 7.78	
G-BFXH	Reims Cessna F.152 II	1469	F-BXQJ(2)	21. 7.78	CofA expired 1.2.93. Canx by CAA 6.3.99.
G-BFXI	Reims Cessna F.172M Skyhawk II	1212	PH-ABA D-EEVC	25. 7.78	To G-ICOM 4/94. Canx.
G-BFXJ	Cessna 210 Centurion	210-57084	ZS-DLD(2) ZS-CLI/N7384E	. .78R	NTU - Not Imported. Remained as ZS-DLD(2). Canx 3/81.
G-BFXK	PA-28-140 Cherokee F	28-7325387	PH-NSK	1. 8.78	
G-BFXL	Albatros D.Va Replica (Built by Williams Flugzeugbau)	0034	D-EGKO	24. 8.78	(On display 3/96 RNAS Yeovilton) Permit expired 5.11.91. Canx as WFU 10.3.97.
G-BFXM	Jurca MJ.5 Sirocco	PFA/2205		18. 7.78	Canx by CAA 5.9.91. (Open store incomplete 2/93)
G-BFXN	PA-36-375 Pawnee Brave	36-7802023	N3831E	18. 7.78	To ZS-LPT 7/84. Canx 2.7.84.
G-BFXO	Taylor JT-1 Monoplane	PFA/55-10363		18. 7.78	No Permit issued. Canx as WFU 15.7.91.
G-BFXP	PA-31-350 Navajo Chieftain	31-7852112	N27711	17. 7.78R	NTU - To XT-ABH 10/78. Canx 1.11.78.
G-BFXR	Wassmer Jodel D.112	247	F-BFTM	27. 7.78	Permit expired 24.11.97. (Dismantled/on rebuild at Crosland Moor 5/99)
G-BFXS	Rockwell Commander 114	14271	N4949W	3. 8.78	
G-BFXT(1)	Rockwell Commander 114	14388	N5840N	. .78R	NTU - To G-PADY 12.10.78. Canx.
G-BFXT(2)	HS.125 Srs.700B	257034	G-5-14	17.10.78	To N7007X 6/88. Canx 27.6.88.
G-BFXU	American Light Aviation Co Beta Z Hot Air Airship	P-1		30. 8.78	Believed not imported from USA. No CofA issued in UK. Canx by CAA 2.2.87 & Canx as WFU 12.12.90.
G-BFXV	Air Tractor AT-302	302-127	N5228S	. .78R	NTU - Not Imported. Remained as N5228S. Canx 3/81.
G-BFXW	American Aviation AA-5B Tiger	AA5B-0940		21. 2.79	
G-BFXX	American Aviation AA-5B Tiger	AA5B-0917		3.10.78	
G-BFXY	American Aviation AA-5A Cheetah	AA5A-0672		26. 9.78	DBR when crashed on landing at White Waltham on 3.7.82. Canx by CAA 24.9.84. Rebuilt & re-regd as G-MILY 9/96.
G-BFXZ	PA-28-181 Archer II	28-7790192	N7548F	12. 9.78	Crashed on take-off from Andoversford on 11.7.84. Canx as WFU 13.7.89. Major components used in rebuild of G-BCTF in 89/90.
G-BFYA	MBB Bo.105DB	S.321	D-HJET	31.10.78	
G-BFYB	PA-28-161 Warrior II	28-7816581	N31731	27. 7.78	
G-BFYC	PA-32RT-300 Lance II	32R-7885200	N36645	31. 7.78	
G-BFYD	PA-32RT-300T Turbo Lance II	32R-7887057	N36607	31. 7.78	To D-ENER(3) 7/83. Canx 3.6.83.
G-BFYE	Robin HR.100/285 Tiara	501	F-BUQT F-WUQT	16. 8.78	Canx as WFU 15.2.90.
G-BFYF	Westland-Bell 47G-3B1 (Lino No.WAN/29)	WA/338	(PH-OFM) G-BFYF/XT179	22. 8.78	To VH-HMK 11/85. Canx 18.7.85.
G-BFYG(1)	Bell 206L Long Ranger	45140	I-VDCM	. .78R	NTU - To OE-DXC. Canx.
G-BFYG(2)	IRMA BN-2A-26 Islander (Originally regd as BN-2A-6)	906		11.12.78	To XC-DUV 11/80. Canx 26.11.80.
G-BFYH	HS.125 Srs.700A	NA0231 & 257044	G-5-17	9. 8.78	To N35D 10/78. Canx 27.10.78.
G-BFYI	Westland-Bell 47G-3B1 (Line No. WAN/17)	WA/326	XT167	24. 1.79	
G-BFYJ	Hughes 369HE (500)	109-0208E	F-BRSY	8. 8.78	To G-HSOO 11/93. Canx.
G-BFYK	Cameron V-77 HAFB	433	EI-BAY G-BFYK	16. 8.78	
G-BFYL	Evans VP-2 (Built by Wilford)	AGW.1 & PFA/63-10146		15. 8.78	
G-BFYM	PA-28-161 Warrior II	28-7816586	N31813	14. 8.78	
G-BFYN	Reims Cessna FA.152 Aerobat	0351		29. 8.78	To G-FIFE 2/95. Canx.
G-BFYO	SPAD XIII Replica (Built by Williams Flugzeugbau)	0035	D-EOWM	16.11.78	Permit expired 21.6.82. Canx as WFU 14.10.86. (On display 7/99 Duxford)
G-BFYP	Wombat Gyrocopter (Originally regd to unbuilt Philpotts/Bensen B.7 with same c/n - Wombat built .95)	AJP.1		7. 7.78	(Extant 6/96)
G-BFYR	IRMA BN-2A-26 Islander (Originally regd as BN-2A-6)	901		4. 9.78	To XC-DUW 1/81. Canx 29.1.81.
G-BFYS	IRMA BN-2A-21 Islander (Originally regd as BN-2A-6)	902		4. 9.78	To YR-NBU 5/81. Canx 15.5.81.
G-BFYT	IRMA BN-2A-21 Islander (Originally regd as BN-2A-6)	903		4. 9.78	To YR-NBV 5/81. Canx 15.5.81.
G-BFYU	Short SC.5 Belfast C.1	SH1821	G-52-15 XR367	13.11.78	Canx as WFU 27.6.92. Spares use. Stored 3/99 Southend.
G-BFYV	HS.125 Srs.700A	NA0232 & 257043	(G-5-15)	11. 9.78	To (N300LD)/N900CC 10/78. Canx 20.10.78.
G-BFYW	Slingsby T.65A Vega	1888		1. 9.78	To BGA.2592/EDA in 11/79. Canx by CAA 2.2.87.
G-BFYX	DHC.6-310 Twin Otter	611		27. 2.79	To 5N-AJQ 3/79. Canx 22.3.79.
G-BFYY	DHC.6-300 Twin Otter	607	(N984FL)	22. 1.79	To 5N-AJR 3/79. Canx 28.2.79.
G-BFYZ	Vickers 735 Viscount	69	YI-ACM	1.12.78	DBR in heavy landing at Sumburgh, Kirkwall on 25.10.79. Canx.
G-BFZA	Alpavia Fournier RF-3	5	F-BLEL	14. 9.78	(On overhaul near Thurleigh 3/90)
G-BFZB	Piper J3C-85 Cub (L-4J-PI) (Frame No.12849)	13019	D-ECEL HB-OSP/44-80723	21. 9.78	Permit expired 9.4.88. (On rebuild by P.A.Brook 9/94)

Regn	Type	c/n	Previous identity	Regn date	Fate or immediate subsequent identity (if known)
G-BFZC	Sikorsky S-61N	61-492	C-FOKM	8.12.78	Restored as C-FOKM 1/83. Canx 18.1.83.
			CF-OKM		
G-BFZD	Reims Cessna FR.182 Skylane RG II	0010		9.10.78	
G-BFZE	Aerospatiale AS.350B Ecureuil	1021		2.10.78	To ZK-HWZ 11/85. Canx 25.11.85.
G-BFZF	Boeing 707-321C (Line No. 368)	18718	N794RN	25. 9.78	To (G-CHGN)/G-BNGH 2/86. Canx.
			N794PA/N794EP/N794/N794PA		
G-BFZG	PA-28-161 Warrior II	28-7816582	N31748	18. 9.78	
G-BFZH	PA-28R-200 Cherokee Arrow	28R-35307	OY-BDB	25.10.78	
G-BFZI	HS.125 Srs.700A	NA0233 & 257047		26. 9.78	To C-GABX 11/78. Canx 17.11.78.
G-BFZJ	HS.125 Srs.700A	NA0240 & 257045		26. 9.78	To N130BA 11/78. Canx 6.11.78.
G-BFZK	Embraer EMB.110P2 Bandeirante	110-200	PT-GLS	17.11.78	To N5071N 5/84. Canx 17.5.84.
G-BFZL	Vickers 836 Viscount	435	(3D-ACM)	12. 3.79	To ZS-NNI(3) 3/98. Canx 5.3.98.
			Oman 501/VH-EQP/N40NA/A6-435/N40N/VH-TVR		
G-BFZM	Rockwell Commander 112TC-A	13191	N4661W	9.10.78	
G-BFZN(1)	Slingsby T.65A Vega	1889		. .78R	NTU - To G-VEGA 10/78. Canx.
G-BFZN(2)	Reims Cessna FA.152 Aerobat	0348		20.10.78	Forced landing in a field at Narborough, Leics on 4.10.80 and ran into a hedge. (On rebuild 2/95)
G-BFZO	American Aviation AA-5A Cheetah	AA5A-0697		1.11.78	
G-BFZP	American Aviation AA-5B Tiger	AA5B-0952		26.10.78	To G-TGER 2/86. Canx.
G-BFZR	American Aviation AA-5B Tiger	AA5B-0979		3.11.78	To EI-BJS 9/80. Canx 29.8.80.
G-BFZS	Reims Cessna F.152 II	1536		9.10.78	To G-OPAM 9/86. Canx.
G-BFZT	Reims Cessna FA.152 Aerobat	0356		4. 7.79	
G-BFZU	Reims Cessna FA.152 Aerobat	0355		29. 6.79	Damaged on landing at Shoreham on 28.12.97. CofA expired 10.9.98.
G-BFZV	Reims Cessna F.172M	1093	(EI-...)	2.11.78	
			G-BFZV/SE-FZR		
G-BFZW	Short SD.3-30 Var.100	SH3023	G-14-3023	9.10.78	To D-CDLD 1/79. Canx 25.1.79.
G-BFZX	Short SD.3-30 Var.100	SH3024	G-14-3024	9.10.78	To N724SA 1/79. Canx 11.1.79.
G-BFZY	Short SD.3-30 Var.100	SH3025	G-14-3025	9.10.78	To N373HA 6/79. Canx 1.6.79.
G-BFZZ(1)	Cessna 182K Skylane	182-57804	D-ENGO	. .78R	NTU - To G-CBIL 10/78. Canx.
			N2604Q		
G-BFZZ(2)	IRMA BN-2B-21 Islander (Originally regd as BN-2A-6)	904		24.10.78	To 5N-AVI 4/81. Canx 5.10.96.
G-BGAA	Cessna 152 II	152-81894	N67529	18. 7.78	
G-BGAB	Reims Cessna F.152 II	1531		13.10.78	
G-BGAC	PA-31-310 Turbo Navajo	31-669	OH-PNC	7. 8.78	To SI-AHI 10/79. Canx 6.10.78.
			Finnish AF PN-1/OH-PNC/SE-FPE		
G-BGAD	Reims Cessna F.152 II	1532		13.10.78	
G-BGAE	Reims Cessna F.152 II	1540		8.11.78	
G-BGAF	Reims Cessna FA.152 Aerobat	0349		13.10.78	
G-BGAG	Reims Cessna F.172N Skyhawk II	1754	"G-KING"	13.10.78	
	(Delivered in error as G-KING which was already reserved for PA-38-112 c/n 38-78A0423)				
G-BGAH	Clutton-Tabenor FRED Srs.II	PFA/29-10324		15. 2.78	Canx by CAA 2.9.91. (Still under construction 8/97)
G-BGAI	Westland-Bell 47G-3B1 (Line No.WAP/134)	WA/420	XT508	13.10.78	Burnt out in a field at Wappenham, near Towcester on 4.6.83 during crop spraying. Canx as destroyed 23.1.84.
G-BGAJ	Reims Cessna F.182Q Skylane II	0096		13.10.78	
G-BGAK	Reims Cessna F.182Q Skylane II	0097		13.10.78	Canx 20.2.97 on sale to Botswana.
G-BGAL	Saffery S.330 HAFB (Toy)	8		21. 3.78	Canx as WFU 19.7.82.
G-BGAM	Westland-Bell 47G-3B1 (Line No.WAN/10)	WA/319	XT160	13.10.78	Crashed in Loch Nevis, near Port Longaig, Inverness on 26.5.79. Canx as destroyed 15.1.80.
G-BGAN	IRMA BN-2A-27 Islander (Originally regd as a BN-2A-6)	905		24.10.78	Canx 14.8.81 on sale to USA. To HP-935/HP-998P 8/81.
G-BGAO(1)	Helio H.295 Super Courier	1467	N68861	. .78R	NTU - To G-BGIX 10/79. Canx.
G-BGAO(2)	Cessna 401A	401A-0102	LN-TVX	8. 3.79	To N4251L 4/81. Canx 30.4.81.
G-BGAP	Reims Cessna FR.182 Skylane RG II	0018		10.11.78	To G-LEAN 8/83. Canx.
G-BGAR	Reims Cessna FR.182 Skylane RG II	0020		10.11.78	NTU - Canx 15.12.78 as Not Imported. To D-EHWR 1/79.
G-BGAS	Colting Ax8-105A HAFB	001		27. 6.78	Destroyed at Flims, Switzerland on 20.9.80. Canx.
G-BGAT	Douglas DC-10-30 (Line No. 287)	46591		8. 8.79	To N13066. Canx 4.6.87.
G-BGAU	Rearwin 9000L Sportster	572D	N18548	23.10.78	No CofA or Permit believed issued. Canx by CAA 17.8.92.
			NC18548		(For rebuild - status uncertain)
G-BGAV	Rearwin 8135T Cloudster	892	N37753	23.10.78	To N377VS 9/85. Canx 3.9.85.
			NC37753		
G-BGAW	Rotorway Scorpion 133	1147		23.10.78	To G-REID 12/81. Canx.
G-BGAX	PA-28-140 Cherokee F	28-7325409	PH-NSH	20.10.78	
G-BGAY	Cameron O-77 HAFB	446		4.12.78	CofA expired 16.12.91. Canx by CAA 4.8.98.
G-BGAZ	Cameron V-77 HAFB	439		20.10.78	
G-BGBA	Robin R.2100A Club	133	F-OCBJ	2. 5.78	
G-BGBB	Lockheed L.1011-385-1 Tristar 200	193N-1178	4R-ULN	4. 3.80	To N105CK. Canx 16.12.94.
			G-BGBB/4R-ULN/G-BGBB/4R-ULN/G-BGBB		
G-BGBC	Lockheed L.1011-385-1 Tristar 200	193N-1182		16. 4.80	To N107CK. Canx 1.8.96.
G-BGBD	Evans VP-1	PFA/62-10264		24.10.78	DBR at Newtownards on 18.8.80. Canx.
G-BGBE	SAN Jodel DR.1050 Ambassadeur	260	F-BJYT	29.11.78	
G-BGBF	Druine D.31A Turbulent	PFA/1658		24.10.78	

Regn	Type	c/n	Previous identity	Regn date	Fate or immediate subsequent identity (if known)
G-BGBG	PA-28-181 Archer II	28-7990012	N39730	2.11.78	
G-BGBH	PA-23-250 Aztec F	23-7754103	N63773	25. 7.78	To G-CPPC 4/82. Canx.
G-BGBI	Reims Cessna F.150L	0688	PH-LUA	28.11.78	
G-BGBJ	HS.125 Srs.700A	NA0237 & 257052	G-5-19	31.10.78	To N737X 12/78. Canx 15.12.78.
G-BGBK	PA-38-112 Tomahawk	38-78A0433		2.11.78	CofA expired 6.9.96. Canx by CAA 30.12.96.
G-BGBL	HS.125 Srs.700A	NA0239 & 257049	G-5-17	31.10.78	To N33BK 11/78. Canx 4.12.78.
G-BGBM	SIPA 903	63	F-BGBM	22. 6.79	To G-SIPA 5/83. Canx.
G-BGBN	PA-38-112 Tomahawk	38-78A0511		29.11.78	
G-BGBO	Reims Cessna F.172N Skyhawk II	1765		10.11.78	Crashed into Mt.Ventoux, France when en route from Nice to Dijon on 7.5.83. Canx as destroyed 5.12.83.
G-BGBP	Reims Cessna F.152 II	1546		8.11.78	Badly damaged on landing at Stapleford on 18.8.92. (Fuselage & wings at Stapleford in 5/98)
G-BGBR	Reims Cessna F.172N Skyhawk II	1772		8.11.78	
G-BGBS	PA-23-250 Aztec F	27-7754140	N63819	18.12.78	To 9Q-CNZ 5/82. Canx 21.5.82.
G-BGBT	Partenavia P.68B Victor	159		10.11.78	To G-OLMA 4/85. Canx.
G-BGBU	Auster AOP.9	B5/10/131	XN435	8.11.78	No Permit to Fly issued. Canx by CAA 1.10.90. (On rebuild .92 Egham)
G-BGBV	Slingsby T.65A Vega	1890		25.10.78	To BGA.2800/EMS 2/82. Canx.
G-BGBW	PA-38-112 Tomahawk	38-78A0670		8.11.78	
G-BGBX	PA-38-112 Tomahawk	38-78A0667		12.12.78	Canx as destroyed 13.9.94.
G-BGBY	PA-38-112 Tomahawk	38-78A0711		8.11.78	
G-BGBZ	Rockwell Commander 114	14423	N5878N	9.10.78	
G-BGCA	Slingsby T.65A Vega	1891		3.11.78	To BGA.2807/EMZ 2/82. Canx by CAA 2.2.87.
G-BGCB	Slingsby T.65A Vega	1892		20.11.78	To BGA.2794/EML 12/81. Canx by CAA 11.3.97.
G-BGCC	PA-31-310 Turbo Navajo C	31-7812103	N27703	17.11.78	To G-OJPW 1/87. Canx.
G-BGCD	Cameron A-140 HAFB	448		16.11.78	To N9703N 11/86. Canx 11.5.84.
G-BGCE	Douglas C-47A-25-DL Dakota	13378	T3-2 Spanish AF/KG619/42-108953	20.11.78	To N37529 4/80. Canx 30.1.80.
G-BGCF	Douglas C-47A-90-DL Dakota	20596	T3-33 Spanish AF/N86453/43-16130	20.11.78	To N3753C 4/80. Canx 30.1.80.
G-BGCG	Douglas C-47A-85-DL Dakota	20002	N5595T G-BGCG/Spanish AF T3-27/N49V/NC50322/43-15536	20.11.78	Permit expired 8.8.80. Canx by CAA 3.4.89. (Stored 8/95)
G-BGCH	PA-38-112 Tomahawk	38-78A0569		27.11.78	CofA expired 18.1.85. Canx as WFU 24.6.86.
G-BGCI	American Aviation AA-5B Tiger	AA5B-1050		25. 1.79	To G-BIAN 6/79. Canx.
G-BGCJ	American Aviation AA-5B Tiger	AA5B-1121		28. 3.79	DBF at Doncaster on 6.9.79. Canx.
G-BGCK	American Aviation AA-5A Cheetah	AA5A-0802		25. 1.79	To G-BLSF 2/83. Canx.
G-BGCL	American Aviation AA-5A Cheetah	AA5A-0807		6. 2.79	To G-OSTU 4/95. Canx.
G-BGCM	American Aviation AA-5A Cheetah	AA5A-0835		23. 3.79	
G-BGCN	American Aviation AA-5A Cheetah	AA5A-0841		29. 3.79	To LN-HPC 9/82. Canx 23.9.82.
G-BGCO	PA-44-180 Seminole	44-7995128	N2103D	20.12.78	
G-BGCP	Gulfstream-American GA-7 Cougar	GA7-0058	N771GA	6.12.78	To (G-MALA)/G-BHBC 8/79. Canx.
G-BGCR(1)	Embraer EMB.110P1 Bandeirante	110-207	PT-GLZ	. .78R	NTU - To G-BGCS 8/79. Canx.
G-BGCR(2)	Embraer EMB.110P1 Bandeirante	110-165	PT-GLF	27. 6.79	To OY-ASL 4/81. Canx 8.4.81.
G-BGCS(1)	Embraer EMB.110P1 Bandeirante	110-211	PT-GMD	. .78R	NTU - To G-MOBL 8/79. Canx.
G-BGCS(2)	Embraer EMB.110P1 Bandeirante	110-207	(G-BGCR) PT-GLZ	31. 8.79	To C-GPDI. Canx 6.4.84.
G-BGCT	Boeing 707-123B (Line No. 140)	18054	N7526A	5.12.78	To 5B-DAO 12/79. Canx 10.12.79.
G-BGCU	Slingsby T.65A Vega	1893		28.11.78	To BGA.2611/EDV in 2/80. Canx by CAA 2.2.87.
G-BGCV	Aerospatiale AS.350B Ecureuil	1033		6.12.78	To ZK-HXB 11/85. Canx 9.10.85.
G-BGCW	Aerospatiale AS.350B Ecureuil	1040		6.12.78	To G-FERG 10/79. Canx.
G-BGCX	Taylor JT.2 Titch	PFA/3221		23.11.78	No Permit issued. Canx as PWFU 27.3.99.
G-BGCY	Taylor JT.1 Monoplane	PFA/55-10370		23.11.78	
G-BGCZ	Bell 212	30668	LZ-CAJ G-BGCZ/5N-AJS/G-BGCZ/VR-BFM/N18090	4.12.78	To AAC as ZH815 9/94. Canx to MOD 27.9.94.
G-BGDA	Boeing 737-236ADV (Line No. 599)	21790	N1285E N1275E	4.12.81	
G-BGDB	Boeing 737-236ADV (Line No. 626)	21791	N8289V	14. 2.80	To N920WA 3/98. Canx 2.3.98.
G-BGDC	Boeing 737-236ADV (Line No. 628)	21792		7. 2.80	To CC-CHR(2) 5/95. Canx 15.5.95.
G-BGDD	Boeing 737-236ADV (Line No. 635)	21793	PH-TSE G-BGDD	23. 2.80	To ZS-NNG(2) 9/95R. Canx.
G-BGDE	Boeing 737-236ADV (Line No. 643)	21794		12. 3.80	
G-BGDF	Boeing 737-236ADV (Line No. 645)	21795		20. 3.80	
G-BGDG	Boeing 737-236ADV (Line No. 648)	21796		20. 3.80	To N921PG 5/98. Canx 30.4.98.
G-BGDH	Boeing 737-236ADV (Line No. 653)	21797		14. 4.80	To PH-TSD 4/95. Canx 25.4.95.
G-BGDI	Boeing 737-236ADV (Line No. 658)	21798		30. 4.80	To N922PG 7/98. Canx 29.6.98.

Regn	Type	c/n	Previous identity	Regn date	Fate or immediate subsequent identity (if known)
G-BGDJ	Boeing 737-236ADV (Line No. 660)	21799		7. 5.80	
G-BGDK	Boeing 737-236ADV (Line No. 661)	21800	N5700N	16. 5.80	To N4361R 8/98 / N923WA. Canx 27.8.98.
G-BGDL	Boeing 737-236ADV (Line No. 669)	21801		9. 6.80	
G-BGDM	HS.125 Srs.700A	NA0218 & 257004	G-5-15	20. 6.77	To G-5-15/N37975 9/77. Canx 20.9.77.
G-BGDN	Boeing 737-236ADV (Line No. 670)	21802		11. 6.80	To CC-CHS(2) 5/95. Canx 2.6.95.
G-BGDO	Boeing 737-236ADV (Line No. 677)	21803		25. 7.80	
G-BGDP	Boeing 737-236ADV (Line No. 686)	21804	N8280V	13. 8.80	To CC-CZK 1/98. Canx 12.1.98.
G-BGDR	Boeing 737-236ADV (Line No. 697)	21805	N1786B	18. 9.80	
G-BGDS	Boeing 737-236ADV (Line No. 699)	21806		18. 9.80	
G-BGDT	Boeing 737-236ADV (Line No. 710)	21807		4.11.80	
G-BGDU	Boeing 737-236ADV (Line No. 712)	21808		13.11.80	To CC-CZL 4/98. Canx 9.4.98.
G-BGDV	Boeing 737-236	-		. .78R	NTU - Canx.
G-BGDW	Boeing 737-236	-		. .78R	NTU - Canx.
G-BGDX	Boeing 737-236	-		. .78R	NTU - Canx.
G-BGDY	Boeing 737-236	-		. .78R	NTU - Canx.
G-BGDZ	Boeing 737-236	-		. .78R	NTU - Canx.
G-BGEA	Reims Cessna F.150M	1396	OY-BJK	22. 3.79	
G-BGEB	Agusta-Bell 206A JetRanger	8222	D-HAVE	16. 1.79	DBF in fatal crash 2 miles north-east of Silverstone on 29.3.81. Canx.
G-BGEC	Cameron V-77 HAFB	461		18.12.78	To F-GCZY 11/82. Canx 4.10.82.
G-BGED	Cessna U.206F Stationair	U206-02279	LN-BGQ N1911U	12.12.78	
G-BGEE	Evans VP-1	PFA/62-10287		27.11.78	Permit expired 16.5.95. (Wings only at Priory Farm, Tibenham 8/97)
G-BGEF	Wassmer Jodel D.112	1309	F-BMYL	7.12.78	Badly damaged on landing at North Cotes on 8.10.95. (Stored 6/96 North Cotes) Canx by CAA 29.1.96.
G-BGEG	Aerospatiale SA.316B Alouette III	2236	EP-HBN	9. 3.79	NTU - Canx 4.4.79 as Not Imported. Remained as EP-HBN.
G-BGEH	Monnett Sonerai II (Single Seater)	209 & PFA/15-10254		1.12.78	
G-BGEI	Oldfield Baby Great Lakes (Used fuselage of PFA/1576 in construction)	DHG.1 & PFA/10-10016		1.12.78	
G-BGEJ	IRMA BN-2A-26 Islander (Originally regd as BN-2A-6)	908		11.12.78	To VP-HDV 5/81. Canx 5.10.81.
G-BGEK	PA-38-112 Tomahawk	38-78A0575		13.12.78	
G-BGEL	PA-38-112 Tomahawk	38-78A0714		13.12.78	To G-RVRF 11/97. Canx.
G-BGEM	Partenavia P.68B Victor	165		18.12.78	Destroyed in hangar fire at Staverton on 27.12.90. Canx by CAA 18.2.92.
G-BGEN	DHC.6-310 Twin Otter	616		14.12.78	To PK-OCK. Canx 29.12.92.
G-BGEO	PA-31-350 Navajo Chieftain	31-7405489	D-ILUT N61475	5. 1.79	Crashed near Autan, France on 18.8.87. Canx as destroyed 12.6.89.
G-BGEP	Cameron D-38 Hot-Air Airship	442		6.12.78	
G-BGER	Westland-Sikorsky S-58 Wessex 60 Srs.1	WA/503	5N-ALO G-BGER/VH-BHI(3)/G-BGER/Ghana AF G-630	11.12.78	To N252HL. Canx.
G-BGES	Phoenix Currie Wot	JR.1 & PFA/58-10291		30.11.78	Canx by CAA 12.9.91. (Stored .89)
G-BGET	PA-38-112 Tomahawk	38-78A0797		15.12.78	Forced landing in a field 1.5 miles north by northwest of Goodwood on 10.1.89. Canx as WFU 10.2.89.
G-BGEU	PA-38-112 Tomahawk	38-78A0818	N9650N	20.12.78	To EI-BJT 10/80. Canx 13.10.80.
G-BGEV	PA-38-112 Tomahawk	38-78A0794		15.12.78	Damaged in forced landing near Sleap on 29.3.86. Canx as WFU 29.6.94.
G-BGEW	SNCAN NC.854S Chardonneret	63	F-BFSJ	13.12.78	
G-BGEX	Brookland Mosquito Mk.2	JB.1		13.12.78	Permit expired 14.8.81. Canx by CAA 28.2.95. (Stored at owner's home 9/97)
G-BGEY	Short SD.3-30 Var.100	SH3026	N330L G-14-3026	14.12.78	Restored as N330L 4/79. Canx 17.4.79.
G-BGEZ	Short SD.3-30 Var.100	SH3027	G-14-3027	14.12.78	To N334GW 5/79. Canx 8.5.79.
G-BGFA	Boeing 707-430 (Line No. 162)	17721	9G-ACK D-ABOF	.12.78R	NTU - To N90498 7/81. Canx 3/81.
G-BGFB	Boeing 707-430F (Line No. 192)	18056	N9985F D-ABOG	.12.78R	NTU - To 3C-ABH 12/80. Canx 3/81.
G-BGFC	Evans VP-2	V2-1278 & PFA/63-10441		15.12.78	
G-BGFD	PA-32-300 Cherokee Six	32-7540020	D-EOSH N32186	20. 6.79	To G-OSCC 11/84. Canx.
G-BGFE	Bell 212	30558	LN-OQZ N83079	.12.78R	NTU - Not Imported. Remained as LN-OQZ. Canx 3/81.
G-BGFF	Clutton-Tabenor FRED Srs.II	PFA/29-10261		18.12.78	
G-BGFG	American Aviation AA-5A Cheetah	AA5A-0687	N6158A	25. 1.79	Badly damaged at Compton Abbas on 15.5.86 when the undercarriage collapsed on a heavy landing.
G-BGFH	Reims Cessna F.182Q Skylane II (Rebuilt with fuselage of G-EMMA .94/95; original fuselage stored Squires Gate 5/97)	0105		18. 1.79	

Regn	Type	c/n	Previous identity	Regn date	Fate or immediate subsequent identity (if known)
G-BGFI	American Aviation AA-5A Cheetah	AA5A-0733	N6142A	5. 3.79	
G-BGFJ	Jodel D.9 Bebe	PFA/1324		11.12.78	
G-BGFK	Evans VP-1	PFA/62-10343		20.12.78	Not completed. No Permit issued. (Stored; for sale 10/97) Canx by CAA 7.1.99.
G-BGFL	PA-31-350 Navajo Chieftain	31-7752047	N63728	8. 6.78	To (N83PR)/C-GGLM 6/80. Canx 25.6.80.
G-BGFM	Rollason-Luton Beta 4	BLP/R78 & PFA/02-10117		19.12.78	Not completed. Canx as destroyed 5.7.85.
G-BGFN	PA-25-235 Pawnee D	25-7856030		21.12.78	To SE-KDH. Canx 4.5.88.
G-BGFO	Not allocated.				
G-BGFP	Short SC.7 Skyvan 3A-100	SH1963	G-14-131	21.12.78	To A40-SP in 3/79. Canx 19.3.79.
G-BGFR	Short SC.7 Skyvan 3M-100	SH1964	G-14-132	21.12.78	To Botswana DF as OC2/Z2 in 6/79. Canx 22.6.79.
G-BGFS(1)	Boeing 737-2P6 (Line No. 500)	21359	A40-BG	8. 1.79	Wore marks for four days. Restored as A40-BG on 12.1.79. Canx as NTU in 1/79.
G-BGFS(2)	Westland-Bell 47G-3B1 (Regd with Line No.WAS/239, should be WAT/234)	WA/712	XW192	9. 3.79	CofA expired 21.3.85 & stored at Chilbolton. Canx as destroyed 26.5.88.
G-BGFT	PA-34-200T Seneca II	34-7870218	N9714C	17. 1.79	
G-BGFU	IRMA BN-2A-20 Islander	909		8. 1.79	To JA5270 7/81. Canx 10.7.81.
G-BGFV	IRMA BN-2A-9 Islander	910		8. 1.79	To TZ-ACS 12/81. Canx 14.12.81.
G-BGFW	IRMA BN-2A-26 Islander	911		8. 1.79	Canx 5.10.81 on sale to USA. To XC-GRO 10/81.
G-BGFX	Reims Cessna F.152 II	1555		28.12.78	CofA expired 23.6.91. (Spares use 2/95 at Biggin Hill)
G-BGFY	PA-31-350 Navajo Chieftain	31-7552035	TR-LUB N59914	5. 1.79	To N9050U 6/81. Canx 11.6.81.
G-BGFZ	Partenavia P.68B Victor	169		20. 2.79	To G-WICK 11/79. Canx.
G-BGGA	Bellanca 7GCBC Citabria 150S	1104-79		5. 2.79	
G-BGGB	Bellanca 7GCBC Citabria 150S	1105-79		7. 2.79	
G-BGGC	Bellanca 7GCBC Citabria 150S	1106-79		5. 2.79	
G-BGGD	Bellanca 8GCBC Scout	284-78		5. 2.79	
G-BGGE	PA-38-112 Tomahawk	38-79A0161		10. 1.79	
G-BGGF	PA-38-112 Tomahawk	38-79A0162		10. 1.79	CofA expired 15.10.94. (Stored 10/97 Tollerton)
G-BGGG	PA-38-112 Tomahawk	38-79A0163		10. 1.79	
G-BGGH	PA-38-112 Tomahawk	38-79A0164		10. 1.79	Fatal crash at Grimsdyke Farm, near Kidlington on 27.5.80. Canx.
G-BGGI	PA-38-112 Tomahawk	38-79A0165		10. 1.79	
G-BGGJ	PA-38-112 Tomahawk	38-79A0167	N9694N	10. 1.79	To G-OEDB 5/89. Canx.
G-BGGK	PA-38-112 Tomahawk	38-79A0168		10. 1.79	Bounced and cartwheeled on landing at Kidlington on 17.5.85. Canx as destroyed 19.7.85.
G-BGGL	PA-38-112 Tomahawk	38-79A0169		10. 1.79	
G-BGGM	PA-38-112 Tomahawk	38-79A0170		10. 1.79	
G-BGGN	PA-38-112 Tomahawk	38-79A0171		10. 1.79	
G-BGGO	Reims Cessna F.152 II	1569		8. 3.79	
G-BGGP	Reims Cessna F.152 II	1580		8. 3.79	
G-BGGR	North American AT-6A Harvard	77-4176	1608 Portuguese AF/41-217	17. 1.79	No CofA issued. Canx 20.4.79. Marks D-FOBY reserved in 4/79. Preserved at Dusseldorf 4/79.
G-BGGS	HS.125 Srs.700B	257061	G-5-19	12. 1.79	To G-OJOY 10/81. Canx.
G-BGGT	Zenith CH.200	367 & PFA/24-10430		2. 1.79	Canx as WFU 5.8.91.
G-BGGU	Wallis WA-116/RR	702		28.12.78	No Permit issued. (Extant 2/99 Reymerston Hall)
G-BGGV	Wallis WA-120 Srs.2	703		28.12.78	No Permit issued. (Not built)
G-BGGW	Wallis WA-122/RR	704		28.12.78	Permit expired 24.4.98. (Stored 2/99 Reymerston Hall)
G-BGGX	Agusta-Bell 206B JetRanger III	8563		22.12.78	To G-FLCH 5/82. Canx.
G-BGGY	Agusta-Bell 206B JetRanger III	8565		19. 1.79	Crashed at Eastnor, near Ledbury on 13.9.84. Canx as destroyed 2.12.86.
G-BGGZ	Reims Cessna F.172G	0241	D-EDHB	. .78R	NTU - To (G-BGLV)/G-OPEL 5/81. Canx.
G-BGHA	Reims Cessna F.152	1571		8. 3.79	Damaged by storms at Shoreham on 16.10.87. Canx as WFU 11.7.88.
G-BGHB	Vickers-Supermarine 379 Spitfire FR.XIVe	6S/649205	T-20 Indian AF/MV293	29.12.78	NTU - To G-SPIT 3/79. Canx.
G-BGHC	Saffery Hot Pants Firefly 1 HAFB (Toy)	13		21.12.78	Canx as destroyed 18.10.88.
G-BGHD(1)	Saffery S.200 Phoenix HAFB (Toy)	20		. .78R	NTU - To G-BHRI 3/80. Canx.
G-BGHD(2)	Saffery Helios Blister HAFB (Toy) (Polythene solar balloon)	1		21.12.78	Canx by CAA 4.2.87.
G-BGHE	Convair L-13A-CO	-	N1132V 47-346	4. 8.80	No CofA issued. (On long-term rebuild at Wichita, USA)
G-BGHF	Westland WG.30 Srs.100-60 Prototype	WA/001P		4. 1.79	CofA expired 1.8.86. Canx as WFU 29.3.89. (On display 4/98 International Helicopter Museum, Weston-super-Mare)
G-BGHG	Aerospatiale AS.350B Ecureuil	1007	F-GBBK	31. 1.79	To F-GDFM 9/81. Canx 25.8.81.
G-BGHH	Beechcraft A36 Bonanza	E-721	TR-LUX	11. 1.79	To ZS-KNU 4/80. Canx 25.2.80.
G-BGHI	Reims Cessna F.152 II	1560		15. 1.79	
G-BGHJ	Reims Cessna F.172N Skyhawk II	1777		15. 1.79	To EI-BVF 10/87. Canx 28.10.87.
G-BGHK	Reims Cessna F.152 II	1573		18. 1.79	To CS-AYG. Canx 6.8.91.
G-BGHL	Gulfstream American GA-7 Cougar	GA7-0077	N789GA	3. 4.79	To G-PLAS 6/85. Canx.
G-BGHM	Robin R.1180T Aiglon	227		19. 2.79	
G-BGHN	Agusta-Bell 47G-3B1 (Officially regd as c/n 1565 which was XT103 and crashed 10.5.67)	1564	XT102	15. 1.79	Crashed whilst spraying at Dumnagir, near Montrose on 17.6.81. Later used for spares at Baginton. Canx as destroyed 5.12.83.
G-BGHO	Agusta-Bell 47G-3B1	1568	XT105	15. 1.79	To 5B-CGJ 1/85. Canx 8.1.85.
G-BGHP	Beechcraft B76 Duchess	ME-190	N60132	16. 1.79	

Regn	Type	c/n	Previous identity	Regn date	Fate or immediate subsequent identity (if known)
G-BGHR	Beechcraft 200 Super King Air	BB-508		16. 1.79	Crashed at Tremblay, near Nantes, France on 25.9.79. Canx.
G-BGHS	Cameron N-31 HAFB	501		15. 1.79	(Extant 2/97)
G-BGHT	Falconar F-12	PFA/22-10040		17. 1.79	
G-BGHU	North American T-6G-NF Texan	182-729	1707 Portuguese AF/French AF 115042/51-15042	22. 1.79	
G-BGHV	Cameron V-77 HAFB	483		12. 1.79	
G-BGHW	Thunder Ax8-90 HAFB	175		30. 1.79	Canx by CAA 19.5.93.
G-BGHX	Chasle YC-12 Tourbillon	PFA/33-10067		22. 1.79	No Permit to Fly issued. Canx by CAA 25.2.88.
G-BGHY	Taylor JT.1 Monoplane	PFA/1455		12. 1.79	
G-BGHZ	Clutton FRED Srs.II	PFA/29-10445		12. 1.79	(Under construction 1991)
G-BGIA	Cessna 152 II	152-82172	G-SACC G-BGIA/N68187	18. 6.79	To 5B-CDR 11/84. Canx 26.9.84.
G-BGIB(1)	Cessna 152 II	152-82151	N68153	. .79R	NTU - Not Imported. To VH-MRP 9/79. Canx.
G-BGIB(2)	Cessna 152 II	152-82161	N68169	3. 7.79	
G-BGIC(1)	Cessna 172N Skyhawk 100	172-68172	N733BR	. .79R	NTU - Not Imported. Canx.
G-BGIC(2)	Cessna 172N Skyhawk 100	172-68002	N75854	25. 6.79	To SP-FTA 6/96. Canx 19.6.96.
G-BGID	Westland-Bell 47G-3B1 (Line No. WAN/31)	WA/340	XT181	28. 2.79	
G-BGIE	Embraer EMB.121A1 Xingu	121-014		16. 2.79	To PT-MBN 1/81. Canx 2.1.81.
G-BGIF	Aerospatiale AS.350B Ecureuil	1066		6. 3.79	To N26492 1/82. Canx 15.1.82.
G-BGIG	PA-38-112 Tomahawk	38-78A0773		23. 1.79	
G-BGIH	Rand KR.2	KR2 & GP.1		24. 1.79	No Permit issued. Canx by CAA 9.7.91.
G-BGII	PA-32-300 Cherokee Six	32-7840182	N20879	22. 1.79	To G-KFRA 9/97. Canx.
G-BGIJ	Cameron O-77 HAFB	133		22. 1.79	To ZS-HPV 6/88. Canx 20.11.85.
G-BGIK	Taylor JT.1 Monoplane	PFA/1415		22. 1.79	Force landed at the Rothschild Estate, Rushbrooke, Sussex on 15.6.91. Canx by CAA 2.8.91.
G-BGIL	Aerospatiale AS.350B Ecureuil	1055		14. 2.79	Crashed near Turnhouse on 13.7.82. Canx.
G-BGIM	Aerospatiale AS.350B Ecureuil	1078		14. 2.79	To G-OKAT 7/88. Canx.
G-BGIN	PA-31-350 Navajo Chieftain	31-7405433	OH-PNI	14. 8.78	Ditched into the sea off Nice, France on 6.3.80. Canx as destroyed 5.12.83.
G-BGIO	Montgomerie-Bensen B.8MR Gyrocopter	GJ.1 & G/01-1259		11. 1.79	
G-BGIP	Colt 56A HAFB	038		2. 2.79	(Extant 6/97)
G-BGIR	Boeing 707-321C (Line No. 572)	19270	N448M N448PA	. 3.79R	NTU - Remained as N448M 3/79. Canx 3/81.
G-BGIS	Boeing 707-321C (Line No. 366)	18717	N793PA	16. 3.79	To G-TRAD 1/84. Canx.
G-BGIT	Not allocated.				
G-BGIU	Reims Cessna F.172H	0620	PH-VIT	26. 2.79	
G-BGIV	Bell 47G-5	7952	8R-GDZ N2207W	31. 1.79	To N6260C 4/96. Canx 14.2.96.
G-BGIW	Bell 47G-2	1218	VP-YWM VP-WAZ/VP-YWM/ZS-HBV/VP-YWM/N5513V/52-7970	25. 1.79	No CofA issued. Canx as WFU 13.8.85.
G-BGIX	Helio H.295 Super Courier	1467	(G-BGAO) N68861	17.10.79	
G-BGIY	Reims Cessna F.172N Skyhawk II	1824		31. 1.79	
G-BGIZ	Reims Cessna F.152 II	1597		31. 1.79	Damaged at Sibson on 28.8.93. Canx as WFU 1.2.94.
G-BGJA	Reims Cessna FA.152 Aerobat	0353		31. 1.79	Crashed at Redhill on 2.8.87. Canx as WFU 9.8.89.
G-BGJB	PA-44-180 Seminole	44-7995112	N3046B	1. 2.79	To EI-CHF 2/93. Canx 19.2.93.
G-BGJC	PA-31-350 Navajo Chieftain	31-7912038	N27931	14. 3.79	Canx 14.5.79 on sale to Angola.
G-BGJD	Not allocated.				
G-BGJE	Boeing 737-236ADV (Line No. 644)	22026		21. 3.80	
G-BGJF	Boeing 737-236ADV (Line No. 654)	22027		17. 4.80	To CC-CZM 7/99. Canx 14.7.99.
G-BGJG	Boeing 737-236ADV (Line No. 656)	22028	(RA-71430) G-BGJG	29. 4.80	To YL-BAA(2) 4/94. Canx 25.3.94.
G-BGJH	Boeing 737-236ADV (Line No. 662)	22029		13. 5.80	To CC-CZN 4/99. Canx 13.4.99.
G-BGJI	Boeing 737-236ADV (Line No. 693)	22030		1.10.80	To CC-CZO 1/98. Canx 18.12.97.
G-BGJJ	Boeing 737-236ADV (Line No. 722)	22031	N8293V	18.12.80	To CC-CZP 6/98. Canx 1.6.98.
G-BGJK	Boeing 737-236ADV (Line No. 742)	22032	(YL-BAB) G-BGJK	10. 3.81	To YL-BAB 6/94. Canx 27.6.94.
G-BGJL	Boeing 737-236ADV (Line No. 743)	22033		2. 4.81	Burnt out at Manchester on 22.8.85 due to engine fire during an abandoned take-off. Canx as destroyed 12.1.89.
G-BGJM	Boeing 737-236ADV (Line No. 751)	22034	YL-LAC G-BGJM/LY-GBA/G-BGJM/(YL-LAC)/G-BGJM	8. 4.81	To YL-BAC 3/95. Canx 15.3.95.
G-BGJN	Boeing 737-236ADV	-		. .78R	NTU - Canx.
G-BGJO	Boeing 737-236ADV	-		. .78R	NTU - Canx.
G-BGJP	Boeing 737-236ADV	-		. .78R	NTU - Canx.
G-BGJR	Boeing 737-236ADV	-		. .78R	NTU - Canx.
G-BGJS	Boeing 737-236ADV	-		. .78R	NTU - Canx.
G-BGJT	Boeing 737-236ADV	-		. .78R	NTU - Canx.
G-BGJU	Cameron V-65 HAFB	499		5. 2.79	
G-BGJV	HS.748 Srs.2B/357LFD	1768	MI-GJV G-BGJV	5. 2.79	To Sri Lankan AF as 4R-HVA/CR-834. Canx 17.1.92.
G-BGJW	Gulfstream American GA-7 Cougar	GA7-0105	N737GA	8. 5.79	To G-OOGS 6/98. Canx.

Regn	Type	c/n	Previous identity	Regn date	Fate or immediate subsequent identity (if known)
G-BGJX	Airborne Industries 400	40100		6. 2.79	Destroyed in Bristol Channel, off Cardiff on 10.5.79. Canx.
G-BGJY	Clutton FRED Srs.II	-		. .79R	NTU - Canx.
G-BGJZ	Airborne Industries 400	40101		6. 2.79	Canx as WFU 22.12.81.
G-BGKA	Hunting-Percival P.56 Provost T.1	PAC/F/335	8041M XF690	5. 3.79	To G-MOOS 4/91. Canx.
G-BGKB	Socata MS.880B Rallye 110ST	3259		25. 4.79	Crashed at Maundown, Somerset on 9.6.84. Canx by CAA 4.2.87.
G-BGKC	Socata MS.880B Rallye 110ST	3262	(I-....) G-BGKC	25. 4.79	
G-BGKD	Socata MS.880B Rallye 110ST	3263		25. 4.79	Damaged in forced landing at Stone Hill, Exeter on 27.10.97. CofA expired 23.7.88.
G-BGKE	BAC One-Eleven Srs.539GL	BAC.263		30. 1.80	To MOD as ZH763. Canx to MOD 1.3.94.
G-BGKF	BAC One-Eleven Srs.539GL	BAC.264		11. 2.80	To 5N-ORO. Canx 19.7.91.
G-BGKG	BAC One-Eleven Srs.539GL	BAC.265		11. 2.80	To 5N-BIN. Canx 19.7.91.
G-BGKH	Reims Cessna A.188B Agtruck (Wichita c/n 03314T)	0030	N1979J	17. 4.79	To ST-AKP 11/85. Canx 20.11.85.
G-BGKI	Reims Cessna A.188B Agtruck (Wichita c/n 03315T)	0031	N1980J	17. 4.79	To ST-AKO 11/85. Canx 20.11.85.
G-BGKJ	MBB Bo.105D (Originally regd as a Bo.105C)	S.128	D-HDDV	20. 4.79	Ditched in sea ½ mile north of Mossbank, Shetland Isles on 25.4.89. It was towed to Toft Pier and lifted out of the water by crane and taken to Scatsa. (Demonstration airframe 7/93) Canx as WFU 29.6.94.
G-BGKK	Westland-Bell 47G-3B1	WA/707	XW187	21. 3.79	To 5B-CEW 6/82. Canx 24.6.82.
	(Line No.WAT/229. WAT/185 quoted by CAA on certification. WAS/185 related to XV312 which after 8430M became G-BDVJ and had a current CofA!)				
G-BGKL	Enstrom F-28C-UK	349		26. 2.79	To G-RANT 4/79. Canx.
G-BGKM	Aerospatiale SA.365C3 Dauphin 2	5020	F-WMHI	3. 5.79	To (F-GIIP)/F-GIPI. Canx 2.3.92.
G-BGKN	HS.125 Srs.F600B (Originally regd as Srs.600B)	256058	G-5-18	11. 5.76	To N9043U 5/81. Canx 7.5.81.
G-BGKO	Gardan GY-20 Minicab	PFA/1827		14. 2.79	
G-BGKP	MBB Bo.105C	S.212	D-HDGC	1. 8.79	DBR when lifting electricity poles at Islay on 16.2.81. Canx as destroyed 10.7.86.
G-BGKR	PA-28-161 Warrior II	28-7916220	N9561N	12. 2.79	To G-BMKR 6/84. Canx.
G-BGKS	PA-28-161 Warrior II	28-7916221	N9562N	12. 2.79	
G-BGKT	Auster AOP.9 (C/n possibly B5/10/139?)	B5/10/137	XN441	28.12.78	(On rebuild 9/97)
G-BGKU	PA-28R-201 Cherokee Arrow III	28R-7837237	N31585	8. 3.79	
G-BGKV	PA-28R-201 Cherokee Arrow III	28R-7737156	N44985	21. 5.79	
G-BGKW	Evans VP-1	PFA/62-10472		27. 3.79	Canx by CAA 5.8.91.
G-BGKX	PA-38-112 Tomahawk	38-78A0626		2. 3.79	Extensively damaged in forced landing on a small beach east of Barry Island on 2.4.85. Canx as destroyed 25.4.85.
G-BGKY	PA-38-112 Tomahawk	38-78A0737		2. 3.79	
G-BGKZ	Auster J/5F Aiglet Trainer	2776	F-BGKZ	15.12.78	Badly damaged in forced-landing nr.Nayland 30.1.93. On rebuild at Garston, Liverpool in 10/98.
G-BGLA	PA-38-112 Tomahawk	38-78A0741		9. 3.79	
G-BGLB	Bede BD.5B	3796 & PFA/14-10085		2. 3.79	Permit expired 4.8.81. Canx by CAA 21.11.91. (On display 6/94)
G-BGLC	Vickers 839 Viscount	436	3D-ACN Oman AF 502/VH-EQQ/N40NB/R.Australian AF A6-436/EP-MRS/VH-TVS	19. 3.79	To VP-WGB 11/80. Canx 30.10.80.
G-BGLD	Beechcraft B76 Duchess	ME-226		28. 2.79	Noswheel failed to lower and aircraft was damaged on landing at Manchester on 17.1.89. Canx as destroyed 9.6.89.
G-BGLE	Saffery S.330 Phoenix HAFB (Toy)	2		1. 3.79	Canx by CAA 2.12.93.
G-BGLF	Evans VP-1 Srs.2	PFA/62-10388		28. 2.79	
G-BGLG	Cessna 152 II	152-82092	N67909	11. 4.79	
G-BGLH	Cessna 152 II	152-81064	N48945	11. 4.79	Burnt out on runway 09 at Liverpool on 22.8.93. Canx as destroyed 19.10.93.
G-BGLI	Cessna 152 II	152-81522	N64997	11. 4.79	Extensively damaged in heavy landing and overturned at Rush Green on 30.6.86. Canx as WFU 20.10.86.
G-BGLJ	Bell 212	30548	(EC-GHP) EC-295/G-BGLJ/9Y-TIJ/G-BGLJ/5N-AJX/G-BGLJ/EP-HBZ/VR-BEJ/N2956W	5. 3.79	(Stored 2/99 Redhill) To EC-HCP/EC-HCZ 5/99. Canx 18.5.99.
G-BGLK	Monnett Sonerai IIL	PFA/15-10304		24. 2.78	Permit expired 31.8.89. (Stored 10/92 Linton-on-Ouse) Canx by CAA 6.3.99.
G-BGLL	Bell 212	30600	(5N-...) G-BGLL/P2-PHJ/VR-BGB/PK-HCI/VR-BGB/G-BGLL/EP-HBW/VR-BGB/9M-ATB	5. 3.79	To 5N-AQW 4/90. Canx 4.4.90.
G-BGLM	Bell 212	30631	EP-HBM VR-BFC/N18090	5. 3.79	To 5N-AJY 7/79. Canx 2.7.79.
G-BGLN	Reims Cessna FA.152 Aerobat	0354		8. 3.79	
G-BGLO	Reims Cessna F.172N Skyhawk II	1900		8. 3.79	
G-BGLP	Reims Cessna F.172N Skyhawk II	1669		8. 3.79	On delivery from Reims to Hurn on 24.7.79, force-landed at Holmsley caravan site, near Bournemouth and slid into a ditch. Canx.
G-BGLR(1)	Reims Cessna F.152 II	1674		. 4.79	NTU - Not Imported. To N8062P /79. Canx.
G-BGLR(2)	Reims Cessna F.152 II	1663		27. 4.79	To G-HFCL 10/88. Canx.
G-BGLS	Oldfield Super Baby Lakes	PFA/10-10237		11.12.78	Permit expired 18.6.88. (Status uncertain)
G-BGLT	Gulfstream G.1159 Gulfstream II	225	N17585	13. 7.79	To N55922 2/80. Canx 22.2.80.
G-BGLU	Bell 205A-1	30086	EP-HBK VR-BEO/N8120J	13. 3.79	To VR-BGU 3/79. Canx 16.3.79.

Regn	Type	c/n	Previous identity	Regn date	Fate or immediate subsequent identity (if known)
G-BGLV	Reims Cessna F.172G	0241	(G-BGGZ)	. .78R	NTU - To G-OPEL 5/81. Canx 3/81.
			D-EDHB		
G-BGLW	PA-34-200 Seneca II	34-7250132	OY-BDZ	2. 6.78	
			SE-FYS		
G-BGLX	Cameron N-56 HAFB	517		7. 3.79	Canx 20.3.98 on sale to India.
G-BGLY	Cessna 172M Skyhawk II	172-66711	N80713	. .79R	NTU - To G-BHCC 10/79. Canx 3/81.
G-BGLZ	Stits SA-3A Playboy	71-100	N9996	19. 6.79	
G-BGMA	Druine D.31 Turbulent	PFA/48-10438		27.11.78	(Not built)
G-BGMB	Taylor JT.2 Titch			18.10.78	Project abandoned. Canx by CAA 2.9.91.
		PV.1 & PFA/60-10426			
G-BGMC	DHC.6-310 Twin Otter	617		29. 3.79	To G-JEAC 3/88. Canx.
G-BGMD	DHC.6-310 Twin Otter	629		6. 7.79	To ZK-KHA(2) 8/89. Canx 18.8.89.
G-BGME	SIPA 903	96	G-BCML	1. 1.81	Permit expired 17.6.94. (Stored 1995)
			"G-BCHU"/F-BGHU		
G-BGMF	Bell 212	30670	EP-HBQ	9. 3.79	To 5N-AJQ 9/80. Canx 10.9.80.
			VR-BFN/N18091		
G-BGMG	Bell 212	30549	VH-BEL	9. 3.79	To AAC as ZH816 9/94. Canx to MOD 27.9.94.
			VR-BEL/G-BGMG/EP-HBI/VR-BEL/N14840		
G-BGMH	Bell 212	30512	9Y-THH	9. 3.79	To AAC as ZH814 9/94. Canx to MOD 3.11.94.
			G-BGMH/VR-BGL/G-BGMH/5N-AJZ/G-BGMH/EP-HBU/VR-BGL/N7099J/PK-OAK/VR-HGL/N7099J		
G-BGMI	Bell 212	30533	EP-HCB	9. 3.79	To PK-HCK 1/81. Canx 9.1.81.
			VR-BEE/N2916W		
G-BGMJ	Gardan GY-201 Minicab	12	F-BGMJ	19. 6.78	
G-BGMK	Bell 212	30868	EP-HCC	9. 3.79	To 5N-AJV 5/79. Canx 10.5.79.
			VR-BGR/N18096		
G-BGML	Bell 212	30601	EP-HBL	9. 3.79	To 5N-AJW 6/79. Canx 6.6.79.
			VR-BEX		
G-BGMM	PA-28-181 Archer II	28-7790411	N2645Q	9. 3.79	NTU - Not Imported. Canx by CAA in 3/81.
G-BGMN	HS.748 Srs.2A/347	1766	PK-OCH	9. 3.79	
			G-BGMN/9Y-TGH/G-BGMN/9Y-TFH		
G-BGMO	HS.748 Srs.2A/347	1767	ZK-MCB	9. 3.79	(Stored engineless 7/99 Liverpool)
			G-BGMO/9Y-TGI/V2-LDB/9Y-TGI/G-BGMO		
G-BGMP	Reims Cessna F.172G	0240	PH-BNV	26. 3.79	
G-BGMR	Barritault JB-01 Minicab			12. 3.79	
		PFA/56-10153			
G-BGMS	Taylor JT.2 Titch			20.10.78	
		MS.1 & PFA/60-10400			
G-BGMT	Socata MS.894E Rallye 235GT	13126		14. 9.78	
G-BGMU	Westland-Bell 47G-3B1	WA/514	XT807	14. 5.79	
	(Line No. WAP/83)				
G-BGMV	Scheibe SF-25B Falke	4648	D-KEBG	15. 5.79	
G-BGMW	Edgley EA.7 Optica	EA7/001	G-56-001	11. 5.79	Permit expired 17.7.85. Canx.
G-BGMX	Enstrom 280C-UK Shark	1173	EI-CCS	23. 5.79	To G-SHRK 1/97. Canx.
			G-SHXX/G-BGMX/EI-BHR/G-BGMX/(F-BBOS)		
G-BGMY	Partenavia P.68B Victor	182		23. 4.79	To G-OCAL 6/79. Canx.
G-BGMZ	Short SD.3-30 Var.100	SH3028		22. 3.79	To N896HA 5/79. Canx 25.5.79.
G-BGNA	Short SD.3-30 Var.100	SH3029	G-14-3029	22. 3.79	To G-BTJR 11/85. Canx.
G-BGNB	Short SD.3-30 Var.100	SH3030	N330MV	22. 3.79	To (5N-OJU)/CS-DBY 3/97. Canx 13.12.96.
			G-BGNB/G-14-3030		
G-BGNC	Short SD.3-30 Var.100	SH3031		22. 3.79	To N799SA 8/79. Canx 1.8.79.
G-BGND	Reims Cessna F.172N Skyhawk II	1576	PH-AYI	3. 3.78	
			(F-GAQA)		
G-BGNE	Short SD.3-30 Var.100	SH3032		22. 3.79	To N330SD 9/79. Canx 11.9.79.
G-BGNF	Short SD.3-30 Var.100	SH3033		22. 3.79	To N996HA 8/79. Canx 28.8.79.
G-BGNG	Short SD.3-30 Var.100	SH3034	N330FL	22. 3.79	CofA expired 12.4.96. WFU in 6/96 at Hurn. Broken up
			N331MV/G-BGNG		in 7/96. Canx as WFU 16.8.96.
G-BGNH	Short SD.3-30 Var.200	SH3035	N331L	22. 3.79	WFU. To spares in 5/92. Canx as WFU 11.11.92. Fuselage
			G-BGNH		extant 3/96 at Newcastle fire section painted all green.
G-BGNI	Short SD.3-30 Var.100	SH3036	G-14-3036	22. 3.79	To N936MA 11/79. Canx 26.11.79.
G-BGNJ	Short SD.3-30 Var.100	SH3037	G-14-3037	22. 3.79	To N50AN 11/79. Canx 3.1.80.
G-BGNK	Embraer EMB.110P2 Bandeirante		(G-YMRU)	20. 4.79	To G-DATA 8/81. Canx.
		110-201	(PT-GLT)		
G-BGNL	Hiway Super Scorpion	XX9SC		4. 4.79	Permit expired 2.8.84 & WFU at Enstone. Canx.
G-BGNM	Aerospatiale SA.365C3 Dauphin 2		EC-DOQ	27. 4.79	Canx 15.10.92 on sale to France. (Stored Marignane, France
		5023	G-BGMN/EC-DOQ/G-BGMN/EC-DOQ/		pending sale 5/96) To F-GRAU 7/99.
			G-BGMN/EC-DOQ/G-BGMN/(G-BGPU)		
G-BGNN	American Aviation AA-5A Cheetah			26. 6.79	To G-OPPL 10/85. Canx.
		AA5A-0867			
G-BGNO	American Aviation AA-5A Cheetah			26. 6.79	To G-IDEA 2/84. Canx.
		AA5A-0871			
G-BGNP	Saffery S.200 HAFB (Toy)	NHP.1		9. 3.79	Canx as WFU 31.5.85.
G-BGNR	Reims Cessna F.172N Skyhawk II	1839		10. 9.79	To G-DENR 4/97. Canx.
G-BGNS	Reims Cessna F.172N Skyhawk II	1901		23.10.79	Damaged in storms at Shoreham on 16.10.87. CofA expired
					6.1.89. Canx as WFU 11.4.88. (Wreck stored 10/92)
G-BGNT	Reims Cessna F.152 II	1644		23.10.79	
G-BGNU	Beechcraft E90 King Air	LW-304		27. 7.78	To G-SANB 4/88. Canx.
G-BGNV	Gulfstream-American GA-7 Cougar		N790GA	20. 4.79	
		GA7-0078			
G-BGNW	Boeing 737-219ADV	21131	OO-TEJ	3. 4.79	To CC-CYC 6/90. Canx 8.6.90.
	(Line No. 428)		N7362F/EI-BCC/(PH-TVM)/EI-BCC/ZK-NAQ/N8293V		
G-BGNX	PA-28RT-201T Turbo Arrow IV		N2191N	12. 3.79	To OY-BJO 1/82. Canx 23.12.81.
		28R-7931051			
G-BGNY	PA-32RT-300 Lance II	32R-7985070	N30242	3. 4.79	To G-LYNN 7/80. Canx.

Regn	Type	c/n	Previous identity	Regn date	Fate or immediate subsequent identity (if known)
G-BGNZ	Reims Cessna FRA.150L Aerobat	0234	PH-GAB D-EIQE	26. 4.79	To G-OPIC 6/95. Canx.
G-BGOA	Reims Cessna FR.182 Skylane RG	0033		10. 4.79	To 5Y-PEF 8/88. Canx 24.8.88.
G-BGOB	Not allocated.				
G-BGOC	Reims Cessna F.152 II	1589		10. 4.79	Forced landed near Cowdenbeath on 20.1.83. Used for spares. Canx by CAA 3.4.89.
G-BGOD	Colt 77A HAFB	040		4. 4.79	
G-BGOE	Beechcraft 76 Duchess	ME-240		8. 5.79	To A6-FAC. Canx 21.2.89.
G-BGOF	Reims Cessna F.152 II	1612		25. 4.79	To CS-AYH. Canx 8.10.91.
G-BGOG	PA-28-161 Warrior II	28-7916350	N9639N	8. 6.79	
G-BGOH	Reims Cessna F.182Q Skylane II	0122		11. 4.79	DBR in an arson attack at Blackpool on 7.12.89. Canx as WFU 7.12.90.
G-BGOI	Cameron O-56 HAFB	526		4. 4.79	
G-BGOJ	Reims Cessna F.150L Commuter	0931	PH-KDA	19. 4.79	To G-MABI 1/82. Canx.
G-BGOK	Cameron D-96 Airship	469		16. 3.79	To SE-ZAB 6/80. Canx 9.6.80.
G-BGOL	PA-28R-201T Turbo Arrow III	28R-7803335	N36705	11. 4.79	
G-BGOM	PA-31-310 Turbo Navajo C	31-7912030	N27864	20. 4.79	To N394AB 10/94. Canx 30.9.94.
G-BGON	Gulfstream American GA-7 Cougar	GA7-0095	N9527Z	24. 4.79	
G-BGOO	Colt Flame 56SS HAFB ("Smiling Flame" Shape)	039		27. 4.79	Canx by CAA 19.5.93. (Extant 2/97)
G-BGOP	Dassault Falcon 20F	406/557	F-WMKF	19. 4.79	
G-BGOR	North American AT-6D-NT Harvard III (Also reported as c/n 88-14880)	88-14863	1508 Portuguese AF/South African AF 7504/EX935/41-33908	28. 3.79	
G-BGOS	North American AT-6C Harvard IIA	-	1529 Portuguese AF	. .79R	NTU - Canx.
G-BGOT	North American AT-6C Harvard IIA	88-10560	1551 Portuguese AF/South African AF 7039/EX467/41-33440	28. 3.79	No CofA issued. To N37642 6/80. Canx 16.4.80.
G-BGOU	North American AT-6C Harvard IIA	88-10108	1554 Portuguese AF/ South African AF 7185/EX392/41-33365	28. 3.79	Fatal crash when dived into the ground at Broadway Farm, near Bourn on 7.9.85. Canx by CAA 4.2.87.
G-BGOV	North American AT-6C Harvard IIA	88-12044	1559 Portuguese AF/South African AF 7382/EX600/41-33573	28. 3.79	To N4434N 8/83. Canx 17.5.83.
G-BGOW	North American AT-6D Harvard III	88-14748	1661 Portuguese AF/FT971/42-44554	28. 3.79	No CofA issued. Canx 16.4.80 on sale to USA.
G-BGOX	PA-31-350 Navajo Chieftain	31-7952049	N27960	19. 4.79	To N31PR 12/96. Canx 16.12.96.
G-BGOY	PA-31-350 Navajo Chieftain	31-7952097	N35172	16. 5.79	To G-HCTL 6/89. Canx.
G-BGOZ	Westland-Bell 47G-3B1 (Line No.WAP/148)	WA/434	XT545	11. 4.79	Crashed spraying near Myton-upon-Swale, Yorks., on 18.6.81. Canx.
G-BGPA	Cessna 182Q Skylane II	182-66538	C-GYBW (N94935)	11. 7.79	
G-BGPB	CCF Harvard 4 (T-6J-CCF Texan)	CCF4-538	FAP1747 Portuguese AF/West German AF BF+050/AA+050/53-4619	4. 4.79	Damaged on landing at Little Gransden on 15.6.89. (On rebuild 7/99 Duxford)
G-BGPC	DHC.6-310 Twin Otter	635		17. 8.79	Fatal crash on hilly ground 1 mile north of Port Ellen, Islay, Argyll on 12.6.86. Remains to White Industries, Bates City, MO. Canx as destroyed 31.12.91.
G-BGPD	Piper J3C-65 Cub (L-4H-PI) (Officially regd as c/n 10478 which is ex 43-29187/00-ADI/F-BFQP. It has, however, frame no.11867 which is 44-79744/F-BDTP. Presumably the fuselages were exchanged in France - see also G-BCOM)	12040	F-BFQP F-BDTP/44-79744	18. 4.79	
G-BGPE	Thunder Ax6-56 Bolt HAFB	174		16. 7.79	To OH-KAI. Canx 25.5.88.
G-BGPF	Thunder Ax6-56Z HAFB	206		13. 7.79	Canx as WFU 21.11.89. (Extant 9/95)
G-BGPG	American Aviation AA-5B Tiger	AA5B-1226	(G-BGRW)	16. 7.79	To G-GAGA 12/88. Canx.
G-BGPH(1)	Beechcraft 200 Super King Air	BB-552		. 4.79R	NTU - To G-BGRD 23.4.79. Canx.
G-BGPH(2)	American Aviation AA-5B Tiger	AA5B-1248	(G-BGRU)	14. 8.79	
G-BGPI	Plumb BGP.1 Biplane	PFA/83-10359		26. 6.78	
G-BGPJ	PA-28-161 Warrior II	28-7916288	N9602N	24. 4.79	
G-BGPK	American Aviation AA-5B Tiger	AA5B-1258	(G-BGRV)	28. 8.79	
G-BGPL	PA-28-161 Warrior II	28-7916289	N9603N	20. 4.79	
G-BGPM	Evans VP-2	PFA/63-10335		17. 4.79	Permit expired 29.4.86. (Open storage Old Sarum 9/91 - status uncertain)
G-BGPN	PA-18-150 Super Cub	18-7909044		12. 4.79	Badly damaged in crash at Nayland in 29.1.90. CofA expired 7.3.92. (On rebuild 5/93)
G-BGPO	PA-25-235 Pawnee D	25-7856040	(N9189T)	23. 8.79	Crashed at Althorne on 4.6.83 while crop-spraying. Canx as destroyed 29.2.84.
G-BGPP	PA-25-235 Pawnee D	25-7856061	N4184E	23. 8.79	To 5N-ATH 4/88. Canx 21.1.88.
G-BGPR	HS.748 Srs.2A/351	1770		4. 4.79	To ZS-XGE 9/79. Canx 14.9.79.
G-BGPS	Aero Commander 200D	358	5N-AFT N2985T	25. 7.79	To G-SONY 11/88. Canx.
G-BGPT	Parker Teenie Two	PFA/28-10371		19. 3.79	No Permit issued. Canx by CAA 22.7.91.
G-BGPU(1)	Aerospatiale SA.365C3 Dauphin 2	5023		. .79R	NTU - To G-BGNM 4/79. Canx.
G-BGPU(2)	PA-28-140 Cherokee F	28-7325282	PH-GNT	25. 4.79	
G-BGPV	IRMA BN-2A-27 Islander (Originally regd as BN-2A-6)	912		20. 4.79	To HP-955P 5/82. Canx 11.12.81.

Regn	Type	c/n	Previous identity	Regn date	Fate or immediate subsequent identity (if known)
G-BGPW	IRMA BN-2A-26 Islander (Originally regd as BN-2A-6)	913		20. 4.79	Canx 14.12.81 on sale to USA. To HP-935 12/81.
G-BGPX	IRMA BN-2A-26 Islander (Originally regd as BN-2A-6)	914		20. 4.79	To HP-945 3/82. Canx 17.3.82.
G-BGPY	IRMA BN-2A-26 Islander (Originally regd as BN-2A-6)	915		20. 4.79	To N661J 2/82. Canx 16.2.82.
G-BGPZ	Morane-Saulnier MS.890A Rallye Commodore 145	10284	F-BLBD	3. 5.79	
G-BGRA	Taylor JT.2 Titch	PFA/60-10148		20. 4.79	Canx by CAA 26.9.91.
G-BGRB	American Aviation AA-5B Tiger	AA5B-1192		1. 6.79	DBR at Ingoldmells, Skegness on 20.9.81 and used for spares at Elstree. Canx as destroyed 5.12.83.
G-BGRC	PA-28-140 Cherokee B	28-26208	SE-FHF	12. 6.79	
G-BGRD	Beechcraft 200 Super King Air	BB-552	5Y-GRD G-BGRD/G-IPRA/G-BGRD/(G-BGPH)	23. 4.79	To N63593 10/97. Canx 17.10.97.
G-BGRE	Beechcraft 200 Super King Air	BB-568		8. 5.79	
G-BGRF	Beechcraft 95-58P Baron	TJ-224		8. 5.79	To N117RS 1/84. Canx 23.1.84.
G-BGRG	Beechcraft 76 Duchess	ME-233		8. 5.79	
G-BGRH	Robin DR.400 2+2	1411		21. 5.79	
G-BGRI	CEA Jodel DR.1051 Sicile	540	F-BLZJ	27. 4.79	
G-BGRJ	Cessna T.310R II	T310R-1594	N3421G	17. 5.79	Fatal crash into a field at Bedlestead Ridge, Warlingham, Surrey on 7.4.87. Canx as destroyed 26.6.87.
G-BGRK	PA-38-112 Tomahawk	38-79A0983		8. 5.79	
G-BGRL	PA-38-112 Tomahawk	38-79A0917		25. 4.79	
G-BGRM	PA-38-112 Tomahawk	38-79A1067		1. 8.79	
G-BGRN	PA-38-112 Tomahawk	38-79A0897		25. 4.79	
G-BGRO	Reims Cessna F.172M Skyhawk II	1129	PH-KAB(2)	4. 5.79	
G-BGRP	Robin (Type unknown)	-		. .79R	NTU - Canx 3/81.
G-BGRR	PA-38-112 Tomahawk	38-78A0336	OO-FLT	8. 5.79	Badly damaged on landing at Woodford on 22.8.97. CofA expired 7.9.97.
G-BGRS	Thunder Ax7-77Z HAFB	203		21. 5.79	
G-BGRT	Steen Skybolt	RCT.001 & PFA/64-10171		12. 9.78	
G-BGRU(1)	American Aviation AA-5B Tiger	AA5B-1248		. .79R	NTU - To G-BGPH 8/79. Canx.
G-BGRU(2)	Boeing 737-204ADV (Line No. 621)	22057		. .79R	NTU - To N8278V/G-BGYJ 10/79. Canx 3/81.
G-BGRV(1)	American Aviation AA-5B Tiger	AA5B-1258		. .79R	NTU - To G-BGPK 8/79. Canx.
G-BGRV(2)	Boeing 737-204ADV (Line No. 629)	22058		. .79R	NTU - To G-BGYK 10/79. Canx 3/81.
G-BGRW(1)	American Aviation AA-5B Tiger	AA5B-1226		. .79R	NTU - To G-BGPG 7/79. Canx.
G-BGRW(2)	Boeing 737-204ADV (Line No. 631)	22059		. .79R	NTU - To N8985V/G-BGYL 10/79. Canx 3/81.
G-BGRX	PA-38-112 Tomahawk	38-79A0609		11. 5.79	
G-BGRY	Short SC.7 Skyvan 3-100	SH1965	G-14-33	30. 4.79	To ZS-KMX 2/81. Canx 13.2.81.
G-BGRZ	BN-2A-26 Islander	116	ST-ADJ(2) G-51-46/VH-FLF	6. 6.79	To N2905C 2/82. Canx 22.2.82.
G-BGSA	Socata MS.892E Rallye 150GT	12838	F-GAKC	29. 5.79	
G-BGSB	Hunting-Percival P.56 Provost T.1 (Also c/n P56/57) (C/n officially quoted as 886391)	PAC/F/057	7992M WV494	21. 5.79	To Oman AF in 1982. Canx by CAA 11.12.87. (Preserved at Military Museum of Oman)
G-BGSC	Ayres S2R-T34 Turbo-Thrush Commander	6013	N4009H	15. 5.79	To ZS-LUZ 9/87. Canx 19.6.87.
G-BGSD	Aerotek Pitts S-2A Special	2195	N31458	19. 7.79	To F-BYAJ(2) 3/82. Canx 11.2.82.
G-BGSE	Aerotek Pitts S-2A Special	2196	N947	6. 9.79	To G-TIII 2/89. Canx.
G-BGSF	Aerotek Pitts S-2A Special	2199		25.10.79	To I-CITU 4/82. Canx.
G-BGSG	PA-44-180 Seminole	44-7995004	N36538	21. 5.79	
G-BGSH	PA-38-112 Tomahawk	38-79A0562		11. 5.79	
G-BGSI	PA-38-112 Tomahawk	38-79A0564		18. 5.79	
G-BGSJ	Piper J3C-65 Cub (L-4A-PI) (Frame No. 8917)	8781	F-BGXJ French AF/42-36657	21. 5.79	
G-BGSK	American Aviation AA-5A Cheetah	AA5A-0770		18. 6.79	To G-LSFI 2/84. Canx.
G-BGSL	American Aviation AA-5A Cheetah	AA5A-0791		18. 6.79	To G-HASL 3/84. Canx.
G-BGSM	Morane-Saulnier MS.893E Rallye 150GT	12983	F-GARY	29. 5.79	A wing was torn off when it was caught on a combine harvester trailer after landing at Overseal strip near Swadlingcote on 20.8.92. Canx as destroyed 8.10.92.
G-BGSN	Enstrom F-28C-UK-2	472-2		11. 5.79	Crashed at Marshlyn Maur, Snowdonia on 12.6.91. Canx as destroyed 12.8.91. Rebuilt & re-regd as G-OIGS 5/92.
G-BGSO	PA-31-310 Turbo Navajo	31-7912060	N3519F	27. 6.79	To G-UMMI 8/92. Canx.
G-BGSP	Slingsby T.65B Vega	1904	BGA.2458	11. 5.79	Crashed when a wing broke off in flight in Italy on 9.8.79. Canx.
G-BGSR	HS.125 Srs.700A	NA0248 & 257066	G-5-13	15. 5.79	To C-GKCI 6/79. Canx 19.6.79.
G-BGSS	PA-38-112 Tomahawk	38-79A0611		23. 5.79	Blown onto club house at Rhoose, Cardiff on 14.12.81 & DBR. Canx as WFU 3.1.84.
G-BGST	Thunder Ax7-65 Bolt HAFB	217		14. 5.79	
G-BGSU	PA-30-160 Twin Comanche B	30-1346	TR-LNH F-OCJG/N8218Y	18. 5.79	To G-DCOL 9/80. Canx.
G-BGSV	Reims Cessna F.172N Skyhawk II	1830		1. 8.79	

Regn	Type	c/n	Previous identity	Regn date	Fate or immediate subsequent identity (if known)
G-BGSW	Beechcraft F33 Bonanza	CD-1253	(EC-...) G-BGSW/OH-BDD	30. 5.79	
G-BGSX	Reims Cessna F.152 II	1603		29. 5.79	
G-BGSY	Gulfstream-American GA-7 Cougar	GA7-0096		4. 6.79	
G-BGSZ	Gulfstream American GA-7 Cougar	GA7-0091	YV-1613P N704G	4. 6.79	To G-HIRE 12/81. Canx.
G-BGTA	Bunce B.500 Firebird HAFB (Toy)	B.500/1		18. 5.79	Canx by CAA 7.12.88.
G-BGTB	Socata TB-10 Tobago	16	F-ODKE	29. 5.79	Crashed on take-off from Church Fenton on 8.6.80. Canx.
G-BGTC	Auster AOP.9	AUS/168	XP282	12.10.79	Badly damaged in crash on landing at Winderpool, near Keyworth on 2.10.96. Permit expired 9.6.97.
G-BGTD	HS.125 Srs.700B	257073	G-5-12	2. 7.79	To N7788 12/84. Canx 5.12.84.
G-BGTE	Rockwell Commander 114A	14527	N5910N	13. 6.79	To HB-NCZ 8/83. Canx 4.8.83.
G-BGTF	PA-44-180 Seminole	44-7995287	N2131Y	20. 6.79	
G-BGTG	PA-23-250 Aztec F	27-7954061	N2454M	23. 5.79	
G-BGTH	PA-23-250 Aztec F	27-7954063	N2551M	23. 5.79	To G-SALT 8/85. Canx.
G-BGTI	Piper J3C-65 Cub (L-4J-PI) (Frame No. 12770)	12940	F-BFFL 44-80644	17. 5.79	
G-BGTJ	PA-28-180 Cherokee Archer	28-7405083	OY-BIO SE-GAH	3. 7.79	
G-BGTK	Reims Cessna FR.182 Skylane RG II	0036	(D-EHZB)	23. 7.79	To G-NOCK 1/94. Canx.
G-BGTL	Gardan GY-20 Minicab	PFA/1815		28.12.78	Canx by CAA 2.9.91.
G-BGTM	Thunder Ax6-56Z HAFB	222		1. 6.79	To D-SCHWABEN 7/85. Canx 8.7.85.
G-BGTN(1)	Robin HR.100/210 Safari	188	F-BVCP	. .79R	NTU - To G-BGTP 6/79. Canx.
G-BGTN(2)	Cessna T.188C AgHusky	T188-03338T	N2033J	. .80R	NTU - To G-BHTD 4/80. Canx 3/81.
G-BGTO	Ayres S2R-500 Thrush Commander	6031	N40136	. .79R	NTU - Not Imported. Canx 3/81.
G-BGTP	Robin HR.100/210 Safari	188	(G-BGTN) F-BVCP	25. 6.79	
G-BGTR	PA-28-140 Cherokee Cruiser	28-7425005	OY-BGO	31. 5.79	To G-LSFC 9/95. Canx.
G-BGTS	PA-28-140 Cherokee F	28-7325351	OY-BGD	19. 6.79	Badly damaged taxiing at Speke on 17.6.89. Canx as WFU 13.10.89. (Stored 12/92)
G-BGTT	Cessna 310R II	310R-1641	N1AN (N2635D)	13. 7.79	
G-BGTU	BAC One-Eleven Srs.F 409AY	BAC.108	YS-01C TI-1056C	6. 1.79	To ZS-NNM. Canx 3.5.94.
G-BGTV	Boeing 737-2T5ADV (Line No. 641)	22024		2.11.79	To EI-BPV 4/85. Canx 4.4.85.
G-BGTW	Boeing 737-2T5ADV (Line No. 636)	22023		2.11.79	To PH-TVX 3/85. Canx 11.3.85.
G-BGTX	SAN Jodel D.117	698	F-BIDI	22. 6.79	
G-BGTY	Boeing 737-2Q8 (Line No. 642)	21960		2.11.79	To EI-BTW 6/88. Canx 31.5.88.
G-BGTZ	Westland-Bell 47G-3B1 (Line No. WAS/171)	WA/457	XT568	27. 6.79	To 5B-CFJ 8/83. Canx 5.8.83.
G-BGUA	PA-38-112 Tomahawk	38-79A0762		15. 6.79	Canx by CAA 23.10.95.
G-BGUB(1)	PA-32-300 Cherokee Six E	32-7940193	N2899N	. .79R	NTU - Not Imported. Canx.
G-BGUB(2)	PA-32-300 Cherokee Six E	32-7940252	N2387U	29.11.79	
G-BGUC	Not to be used.				
G-BGUD	Not to be used.				
G-BGUE	Not to be used.				
G-BGUF	Not to be used.				
G-BGUG	Not to be used.				
G-BGUH	Not to be used.				
G-BGUI	Not to be used.				
G-BGUJ	Not to be used.				
G-BGUK	Not to be used.				
G-BGUL	Not to be used.				
G-BGUM	Not to be used.				
G-BGUN	Not to be used.				
G-BGUO	Not to be used.				
G-BGUP	Not to be used.				
G-BGUR	Not to be used.				
G-BGUS	Not to be used.				
G-BGUT	Not to be used.				
G-BGUU	Not to be used.				
G-BGUV	Not to be used.				
G-BGUW	Not to be used.				
G-BGUX	Not to be used.				
G-BGUY	Cameron V-56 HAFB	441		27. 9.78	
G-BGUZ	Not allocated.				
G-BGVA	Cessna 414A Chancellor II	414A-0247	N36896	22. 6.79	To N368DV 2/91. Canx 12.2.91.
G-BGVB	CEA Robin DR.315 Petit Prince	308	F-BPOP	20. 7.79	
G-BGVC	Sportavia-Putzer Fournier RF-7	7001	D-EHAP F-WPXV	. 6.79R	NTU - To G-EHAP 6/79. Canx 3/81.
G-BGVD	Not allocated.				
G-BGVE	Scintex CP.1310-C3 Super Emeraude	931	F-BMJE	8. 6.79	
G-BGVF	Colt 77A HAFB	053		8. 6.79	Canx as WFU 17.1.90.
G-BGVG	Beechcraft 76 Duchess	ME-265		8. 6.79	To G-GBSL 3/81. Canx.
G-BGVH	Beechcraft 76 Duchess	ME-260		8. 6.79	

Regn	Type	c/n	Previous identity	Regn date	Fate or immediate subsequent identity (if known)
G-BGVI	Reims Cessna F.152 II	1611		14. 6.79	To 5B-CIB. Canx 12.4.91.
G-BGVJ	PA-28-180 Cherokee	28-830	D-ENPI N7066W	5. 9.79	To G-DEVS 3/85. Canx.
G-BGVK	PA-28-161 Warrior II	28-7816400	PH-WPT G-BGVK/N6244C	13. 6.79	
G-BGVL	PA-38-112 Tomahawk	38-78A0263	N9963T	13. 6.79	Crashed on take-off from Priory Farm, Tibenham on 16.7.93. (Spares use for G-BPHI) (Remains stored 7/95 near Shipdham) Canx as WFU 5.7.95.
G-BGVM	Wilson Cassutt Racer IIIM	WLS.1 & 282	N51WS	20. 6.79	To F-PYNM 6/90. Canx 1.8.88.
G-BGVN	PA-28RT-201 Arrow IV	28R-7918168	N2846U	22. 6.79	
G-BGVO	PA-31-310 Navajo B	31-701	F-BSGU G-AZAC/N6791L	14. 6.79	To G-NEVA 8/79. Canx.
G-BGVP	Thunder Ax6-56Z HAFB	223		9. 8.79	Canx as WFU 17.8.90.
G-BGVR	Thunder Ax6-56Z HAFB	224		9. 8.79	Canx by CAA 16.4.92.
G-BGVS	Reims Cessna F.172M	0992	PH-HVS (PH-LUK)	3. 5.79	
G-BGVT	Cessna R.182 Skylane RG II	R182-00244	N3162C	28. 6.79	
G-BGVU(1)	American Aviation AA-5B Tiger	AA5B-1080	(F-GBOO)	. .79R	NTU - To G-BGVY 8/79. Canx.
G-BGVU(2)	PA-28-180 Cherokee D	28-5359	PH-AVU	5. 7.79	Badly damaged on landing at Welshpool on 14.1.97. CofA expired 2.6.97.
G-BGVV	American Aviation AA-5A Cheetah	AA5A-0750		27. 6.79	
G-BGVW	American Aviation AA-5A Cheetah	AA5A-0774		21. 6.79	
G-BGVX	Cessna P.210N Pressurized Centurion II	P210-00319	(N4788X)	21. 6.79	To F-GGST 11/86. Canx.
G-BGVY	American Aviation AA-5B Tiger	AA5B-1080	(G-BGVU) (F-GBOO)	21. 8.79	
G-BGVZ	PA-28-181 Archer II	28-7990528	N2886A	12. 7.79	
G-BGWA(1)	Cameron V-56 HAFB	541		. 6.79R	NTU - G-SNOW 6/79. Canx.
G-BGWA(2)	Gulfstream-American GA-7 Cougar	GA7-0110	N752G	26. 7.79	To N48JJ 2/94. Canx 9.2.94.
G-BGWB	Short SC.7 Skyvan 3-100	SH1966	G-14-134	13. 6.79	To 8R-GFF 8/79. Canx 16.8.79.
G-BGWC	Robin DR.400/180 Regent	1420		26. 6.79	
G-BGWD	Robin HR.100/285 Tiara	524	F-BXRF	19. 6.79	To D-EBBV 9/87. Canx 14.7.87.
G-BGWE	Scheibe SF-28B Tandem Falke	5401	D-KDCB	20. 6.79	To C-GEVG 3/81. Canx.
G-BGWF	PA-18-150 Super Cub (Regd with frame no.18-7360)	18-7203	ST-AFJ ST-ABN	18. 6.79	To EI-CIG 6/93. Canx 11.6.93.
G-BGWG	PA-18-150 Super Cub	18-7606	ST-ABS G-ARSS	18. 6.79	To ST-AIZ 11/84. Canx 22.5.84.
G-BGWH	PA-18-150 Super Cub	18-7605	ST-ABR G-ARSR	18. 6.79	Damaged in ground loop at Clacton on 7.7.92. CofA expired 14.6.93. (Stored 9/97)
G-BGWI	Cameron V-65 HAFB (Originally regd with c/n 522)	528		21. 5.79	Canx by CAA 19.5.93.
G-BGWJ	Sikorsky S-61N Mk.II	61-819		20. 8.79	
G-BGWK	Sikorsky S-61N Mk.II	61-820	N1346C G-BGWK	10. 9.79	
G-BGWL	Sikorsky S-61N Mk.II	61-821		24.10.79	To C-GMQF 5/80. Canx 20.5.80.
G-BGWM	PA-28-181 Archer II	28-7990458	N2817Y	29. 6.79	
G-BGWN	PA-38-112 Tomahawk	38-79A0918		2. 7.79	
G-BGWO	Jodel D.112 (Valladeau built)	227	F-BHGQ	22. 6.79	
G-BGWP(1)	Douglas DC-9-14 (Line No. 6)	45712	OH-LYB N1792U/CF-TLC	. .79R	NTU - Remained as OH-LYB. Canx.
G-BGWP(2)	MBB Bo.105DBS-4 (Rebuild with new pod S.913 .93 - regn D-HIFA reserved 4/93)	S.41	F-ODMZ G-BGWP/HB-XFD/N153BB/D-HDAS	19.12.79	To G-PASA 4/89. Canx.
G-BGWR	Cessna U.206A Super Skywagon	U206-0653	G-DISC G-BGWR/PH-OTD/N4953F	6. 7.79	
G-BGWS	Enstrom F-280C Shark	1050		8.11.76	
G-BGWT	Westland-Sikorsky S-58 Wessex 60 Srs.1	WA/504	G-631 Ghana AF	23. 8.79	To N250HL 1/90. Canx 15.1.90.
G-BGWU	PA-38-112 Tomahawk	38-79A0788		2. 7.79	
G-BGWV	Aeronca 7AC Champion	7AC-4082	OO-GRI OO-TWR	23. 8.79	Extensively damaged when it crashed into bushes on approach to landing at Popham on 8.6.86. Permit expired 10.10.86. (Status uncertain)
G-BGWW	PA-23-250 Turbo Aztec E	27-4587	OO-ABH N13971	15. 6.79	
G-BGWX	Thunder Ax6-56Z HAFB	225		. .79R	NTU - Not Built. Canx 3/81.
G-BGWY	Thunder Ax6-56Z HAFB	229		23. 8.79	
G-BGWZ	Eclipse Super Eagle Hang-glider	ESE.007		29. 6.79	No CofA or Permit issued. Canx as WFU 5.12.83. (Stored 3/96 Fleet Air Arm Museum)
G-BGXA	Piper J3C-65 Cub (L-4H-PI) (Frame No. 10587 - regd with c/n 11170)	10762	F-BGXA French AF/43-29471	1. 3.78	
G-BGXB	PA-38-112 Tomahawk	38-79A1007		2. 7.79	
G-BGXC	Socata TB-10 Tobago	35		19.10.79	
G-BGXD	Socata TB-10 Tobago	39		19.10.79	
G-BGXE	Douglas DC-10-30 (Line No. 302)	47811		14.12.79	To N1852U 5/82. Canx 14.9.84.

Regn	Type	c/n	Previous identity	Regn date	Fate or immediate subsequent identity (if known)
G-BGXF	Douglas DC-10-30 (Line No. 303)	47812		19.12.79	To N1853U 5/82. Canx 31.8.84.
G-BGXG	Douglas DC-10-30 (Line No. 312)	47813		24. 3.80	To N1854U 5/82. Canx 21.9.84.
G-BGXH	Douglas DC-10-30 (Line No. 316)	47814		30. 4.80	To N5463Y 4/82. Canx 4.9.84.
G-BGXI	Douglas DC-10-30 (Line No. 325)	47815		24. 6.80	To N5464M 4/82. Canx 4.9.84.
G-BGXJ	Partenavia P.68B Victor	189		6. 9.79	
G-BGXK	Cessna 310R II	310R-1257	N6070X	7. 8.79	
G-BGXL	Bensen B.8MV Gyrocopter	HABW.1		2. 7.79	Canx by CAA 29.3.85.
G-BGXM	Rockwell Commander 690B	11374	5N-ALA N81562	3. 7.79	To OO-MRU 8/79. Canx 13.8.79.
G-BGXN	PA-38-112 Tomahawk	38-79A0898		5. 7.79	Damaged in 1991. CofA expired 24.8.91. (Wreck at Glatton, Peterborough in 6/98)
G-BGXO	PA-38-112 Tomahawk	38-79A0982		5. 7.79	
G-BGXP	Westland-Bell 47G-3B1 (Line no. WAN/41)	WA/350	XT191	20. 7.79	To G-CIGY 10/98. Canx.
G-BGXR	Robin HR.200/100 Club	53	F-BVYH	1.10.79	
G-BGXS	PA-28-236 Dakota	28-7911198	N2836Z	12. 7.79	
G-BGXT	Socata TB-10 Tobago	40		3.10.79	
G-BGXU	Wallingford WMB.1 HAFB (Toy)	001	G-BEJO(2)	10. 7.79	Canx by CAA 2.12.93.
G-BGXV	Piper J3C-65 Cub (L-4H-PI)	11599	F-BFQT OO-GAB/43-30308	20. 7.79	To G-NCUB 7/84. Canx.
G-BGXW	Thunder Ax6-56 HAFB	230		6. 8.79	To C-GHUW 8/82. Canx 30.9.81.
G-BGXX	CEA Jodel DR.1051/M1 Sicile Record	592	F-BMPA	1. 4.80	DBR at Barry Island on 2.4.85. Remains stored at Nayland. CofA expired 21.8.86. Canx by CAA 23.8.89.
G-BGXY	Sikorsky S-76A	760021	N4246S	6.11.79	Fatal crash near Peterhead on 12.3.81. Canx as destroyed 5.12.83.
G-BGXZ	Reims Cessna FA.152 Aerobat	0357		16. 7.79	To G-ZOOL 11/94. Canx.
G-BGYA	Piper Aerostar 601P	61P-0639-7963294	N8235J	1. 6.79	Restored as N8235J 12/80. Canx 8/81.
G-BGYB	Piper Aerostar 601P	61P-0653-7963302	N8249J	. 7.79R	NTU - Not Imported. Remained as N8249J. Canx 3/81.
G-BGYC	Piper Aerostar 601P	61P-0669-7963313	N6069H	26. 7.79	NTU - Not Imported. Remained as N6069H. Canx 3/81.
G-BGYD	Piper Aerostar 601P	61P-0681-7963321	N6070U	1. 8.79	NTU - Not Imported. To (N6070U)/N6081Y 8/79. Canx 3/81.
G-BGYE	Piper Aerostar 601P	61P-0693-7963330	N6072A	. .79R	NTU - Not Imported. To N3634F 10/79. Canx 3/81.
G-BGYF	Bell 206B JetRanger II	1703	N152AL	23. 7.79	Restored as N152AL 8/81. Canx 12.8.81.
G-BGYG	PA-28-161 Warrior II	28-7916431	N9528N	17. 7.79	
G-BGYH	PA-28-161 Warrior II	28-7916313	N9619N	17. 7.79	
G-BGYI	PA-31-310 Navajo	31-491	F-BYCQ F-OCPC/N6600L/(PT-BVY)	17. 8.79	To OY-AZN 1/80. Canx 13.12.79.
G-BGYJ	Boeing 737-204ADV (Line No. 621)	22057	N8278V (G-BGRU)	24.10.79	To EI-CJH 3/94. Canx 30.3.94.
G-BGYK	Boeing 737-204ADV (Line No. 629)	22058	PP-SRW G-BGYK/(G-BGRV)	24.10.79	To EI-CJG 3/94. Canx 25.3.94.
G-BGYL	Boeing 737-204ADV (Line No. 631)	22059	N8985V (G-BGRW)	24.10.79	To HP-1205CMP 4/92. Canx 16.4.92.
G-BGYM	PA-31-350 Navajo Chieftain	31-7305040	(G-BGZP) F-BTMZ/N15242	17. 8.79	To N9050N 6/81. Canx 11.6.81.
G-BGYN	PA-18-150 Super Cub	18-7709137	N62747	19. 7.79	
G-BGYO	Thunder Ax6-56Z HAFB	232		23. 7.79	To EC-DOZ 1/82. Canx 17.6.81.
G-BGYP	Gulfstream American GA-7 Cougar	GA7-0114		3. 8.79	To G-BNAB 2/84. Canx.
G-BGYR	HS.125 Srs.F600B	256045	G-5-11 EC-CQT/G-5-18	3.12.79	
G-BGYS	Embraer EMB.110P2 Bandeirante	110-231	PT-GMX	11.10.79	To N4578U 1/84. Canx 30.1.84.
G-BGYT	Embraer EMB.110P1 Bandeirante	110-234	N104VA G-BGYT/PT-SAA	11.10.79	
G-BGYU	Embraer EMB.110P2 Bandeirante	110-243	PT-SAJ	11.10.79	To N4578Q 1/84. Canx 30.1.84.
G-BGYV	Embraer EMB.110P1 Bandeirante	110-249	N105VA G-BGYV/PT-SAP	11.10.79	To G-JBAC 10/94. Canx.
G-BGYW	Hughes 269C (300C)	113-0257	BSP-6 (Bahrain State Police)	25. 9.79	Badly damaged by engine vibration at Horton, Devon on 3.6.80. Sold to Heliwork for spares use. Canx as WFU 5.12.83.
G-BGYX	Hughes 269C (300C)	113-0253	BSP-5 (Bahrain State Police)	25. 9.79	To ZS-HJG /80. Canx 27.8.80.
G-BGYY	PA-23-250 Aztec F	27-7954080	N6834A	20. 8.79	To G-BMFD 9/79. Canx.
G-BGYZ	Hughes 269C (300C)	112-0171	BPS-4 (Bahrain Public Security)	25. 9.79	To HB-XNG 3/82. Canx 16.3.82.
G-BGZA	ICA-Brasov IS-28B2	05	BGA.2056	3. 9.79	No CofA or Permit issued. (Status unknown) Canx as WFU 26.3.92.
G-BGZB	Reims Cessna F.177RG Cardinal	0072	PH-RDO	6. 8.79	Crashed in swamp on landing at Groningen, Netherlands on 2.3.81. Canx as destroyed 5.12.83.
G-BGZC	CASA 1.131 Jungmann	-	E3B-305 Spanish AF	29. 8.79	Canx by CAA 12.8.91. Believed to be the same aircraft as that now regd G-RETA.
G-BGZD	Enstrom 280C Shark	1034		27. 7.79	To G-KLAY 11/79. Canx.

Regn	Type	c/n	Previous identity	Regn date	Fate or immediate subsequent identity (if known)
G-BGZE	PA-38-112 Tomahawk	38-79A1093		26. 7.79	Damaged by storms in 10/86 at Cardiff. Canx as WFU 11.12.87.
G-BGZF	PA-38-112 Tomahawk	38-79A1015		26. 7.79	
G-BGZG	PA-38-112 Tomahawk	38-79A0995		7. 9.79	To G-OLFC 12/85. Canx.
G-BGZH	PA-38-112 Tomahawk	38-79A0996		7. 9.79	Damaged by storms at Cardiff in 10/86. CofA expired 18.11.87. Canx as WFU 11.12.87.
G-BGZI	PA-38-112 Tomahawk	38-79A0998		7. 9.79	To EI-BLT 10/81. Canx 13.10.81.
G-BGZJ	PA-38-112 Tomahawk	38-79A0999		7. 9.79	Damaged when taxied into a caravan at Cambridge on 5.8.90. (Stored 9/97 Halfpenny Green, then fuselage dumped outside 1/99 Bourne Park) Canx by CAA 25.2.97.
G-BGZK	Westland-Bell 47G-3B1 (Line No. WAP/81)	WA/382	XT223	24. 7.79	To G-XTUN 5/99. Canx.
G-BGZL	Eiri PIK.20E	20218		21. 8.79	
G-BGZM	Cessna 421C Golden Eagle III	421C-0663	N3839G	21.11.79	To G-RILL 10/80. Canx.
G-BGZN	WMB.2 Windtracker HAFB (Toy)	005		11. 1.80	Canx by CAA 8.4.98.
G-BGZO	SEEMS MS.880B Rallye Club	378	F-BKZO	24.10.79	Damaged in forced-landing East Meon, Petersfield 10.5.89. Canx by CAA 3.2.95. (Stored 12/92)
G-BGZP(1)	PA-31-350 Navajo Chieftain	31-7305040	F-BTMZ N15242	. .79R	NTU - To G-BGYM 8/79. Canx.
G-BGZP(2)	DHC.6-310 Twin Otter	682		21. 1.80	To 5Y-SKS /90. Canx 14.3.90.
G-BGZR	Meagher Model HAFB (Toy)	SCM.1001		14. 1.80	Canx by CAA 2.12.93.
G-BGZS	Keirs Heated Air Tube HAFB (Toy)	1		7. 8.79	Canx by CAA 2.12.93.
G-BGZT	Short SD.3-30 Var.100	SH3040		30. 7.79	To N937MA 2/80. Canx 29.2.80.
G-BGZU	Short SD.3-30 Var.100	SH3039		30. 7.79	To N51AN 1/80. Canx 30.1.80.
G-BGZV	Short SD.3-30 Var.100	SH3038		30. 7.79	To N332L 1/80. Canx 17.1.80.
G-BGZW	PA-38-112 Tomahawk	38-79A1068		1. 8.79	
G-BGZX	PA-32-260 Cherokee Six	32-288	9XR-MP 5Y-ADH/N3427W	6. 9.79	To G-OCTI 7/88. Canx.
G-BGZY	Wassmer Jodel D.120 Paris-Nice	118	F-BIQU	17. 8.79	
G-BGZZ	Thunder Ax6-56 Bolt HAFB	220		10. 8.79	(Extant 2/97)
G-BHAA	Cessna 152 II	152-81330	N49809	12. 2.79	
G-BHAB	Cessna 152 II	152-81664	N66707	12. 2.79	Fatal crash after colliding in mid-air with Gemini/Flash 2A G-MVCZ over Shobdon on 10.2.89. Canx as destroyed 12.5.89.
"G-BHAB"	Thunder Ax3-17-5C Sky Chariot HAFB	247		----	Incorrectly marked - To "G-BHAT"/G-BHCU 1/80. Canx.
G-BHAC	Cessna A.152 Aerobat	A152-0776	N7595B	12. 2.79	
G-BHAD	Cessna A.152 Aerobat	A152-0807	N7390L	12. 2.79	
G-BHAE	Cameron V-56 HAFB	579		14. 1.79	To OE-AZA. Canx 27.7.82.
G-BHAF	PA-38-112 Tomahawk	38-79A1092		8. 8.79	To G-RVRG 8/98. Canx.
G-BHAG(1)	Bell 212	30557	LN-OQY N83072	. .79R	NTU - Remained as LN-OQY. Canx.
G-BHAG(2)	Scheibe SF-25E Super Falke	4354	D-KDGO	15. 2.80	To OY-XTO. Canx 22.4.91.
G-BHAH	Sikorsky S-61N	61-767	C-GOKH	10.10.79	Restored as C-GOKH 3/83. Canx 9.3.83.
G-BHAI	Reims Cessna F.152 II	1625	(D-EJAY)	14. 8.79	
G-BHAJ	Robin DR.400/160 Major 80	1430		22. 8.79	
G-BHAK	PA-28RT-201 Arrow IV	28R-7918140	N29555	14. 8.79	To G-ONAB 1/83. Canx.
G-BHAL	Rango-Saffery S.200SS HAFB (Toy) (Face & pigtails shape)	NHP-2		14. 8.79	
G-BHAM	Thunder Ax6-56 Bolt HAFB	251		28. 1.80	
G-BHAN	Beechcraft 200 Super King Air	BB-597		10. 8.79	To A2-ACO 3/80. Canx 28.4.80.
G-BHAO	Beechcraft 76 Duchess	ME-304		10. 8.79	To G-OPAT 12/82. Canx.
G-BHAP	Beechcraft 65-C90 King Air	LJ-874		10. 8.79	To G-SPTS 3/80. Canx.
G-BHAR	Westland-Bell 47G-3B1 (Line No. WAN/44)	WA/353	XT194	7. 8.79	
G-BHAS	American Aviation AA-5A Cheetah	AA5A-0870	N26998	23. 8.79	To G-BHSF 1/80. Canx.
G-BHAT	Thunder Ax7-77 Bolt HAFB	250		28. 1.80	Canx as WFU 29.4.93. (Extant 9/94)
"G-BHAT"	Thunder Ax3-17-5C Sky Chariot	247	"G-BHAB"	----	False marks. To G-BHCU 9.1.80.
G-BHAU	Bristol 175 Britannia Srs.253F	13449	EI-BCI (CS-...)/EI-BCI/XL640	13. 8.79	To 9Q-CHU 3/82. Canx 18.3.82.
G-BHAV	Reims Cessna F.152 II	1633		15. 8.79	
G-BHAW	Reims Cessna F.172N Skyhawk II	1858		15. 8.79	
G-BHAX	Enstrom F-28C-2-UK	486-2	N5689N	22.10.79	
G-BHAY	PA-28RT-201 Arrow IV	28R-7918213	N2910N	17. 8.79	
G-BHAZ	Reims Cessna F.152 II	1628	(D-EHLE)	11. 9.79	To G-CHIK 10/81. Canx.
G-BHBA	Campbell Cricket CV.101	SMI/1		15. 8.79	
G-BHBB	Colting 77A HAFB	77A-012	EI-BFG	14. 9.79	Canx by CAA 19.5.93.
G-BHBC	Gulfstream-American GA-7 Cougar	GA7-0058	(G-MALA) G-BGCP/N771GA	23. 8.79	DBR in taxiing accident at Elstree on 15.8.81. Canx as WFU 21.12.83.
G-BHBD	Colting 77A HAFB	77A-015		22. 8.79	To SE-ZXS 11/82. Canx 23.11.82.
G-BHBE	Westland-Bell 47G-3B1 Soloy (Line No. WAP/136)	WA/422	XT510	29.10.79	
G-BHBF	Sikorsky S-76A II Plus	760022	N4247S	9.11.79	
G-BHBG	PA-32R-300 Cherokee Lance	32R-7780515	N408RC	18. 9.79	
G-BHBH	Cessna 550 Citation II (Unit No.148)	550-0133	N2634Y	6. 3.80	To C-GRIO 2/82. Canx 22.2.82.
G-BHBI	Mooney M.20J (201)	24-0842	N4764H	24. 9.79	
G-BHBJ	Cameron D-96 Hot-Air Airship	536		31. 1.80	To SE-ZAD 2/85. Canx 23.2.85.
G-BHBK	Viscount V-5 HAFB (Toy)	001		7. 9.79	Canx by CAA 12.12.88.

Regn	Type	c/n	Previous identity	Regn date	Fate or immediate subsequent identity (if known)
G-BHBL	Lockheed L.1011-385-1 Tristar 200	193N-1193		29. 9.80	To N104CK. Canx 7.9.94.
G-BHBM	Lockheed L.1011-385-1 Tristar 200	193N-1198		22.11.80	To N102CK. Canx 11.7.94.
G-BHBN	Lockheed L.1011-385-1 Tristar 200	193N-1204		1. 4.81	To N108CK. Canx 27.11.90.
G-BHBO	Lockheed L.1011-385-1 Tristar 200	193N-1205		13. 4.81	To N109CK. Canx 24.12.96.
G-BHBP	Lockheed L.1011-385-1 Tristar 200	293C-1211	4R-ULM G-BHBP	15. 5.81	To N106CK. Canx 31.7.95.
G-BHBR	Lockheed L.1011-385-1 Tristar 200	293C-1212		27. 5.81	To N103CK. Canx 29.7.94.
G-BHBS	PA-28RT-201T Turbo Arrow IV	28R-7931091	N3007T	21. 9.79	To N499A 6/95. Canx 19.5.95.
G-BHBT	Marquart MA-5 Charger	PFA/68-10190		3. 9.79	No Permit issued. (Stored 6/93)
G-BHBU	Westland-Bell 47G-3B1 Soloy (Line No.WAN/20)	WA/329	XT170	1.11.79	To EC-DLK 10/80. Canx.
G-BHBV	Westland-Bell 47G-3B1 Soloy (Line No.WAP/118) (Identity quoted as "XT942" and also Line No.WAS/216, which became G-BHKD)	WA/408	XT249	1.11.79	To G-SMRI 1/83. Canx.
G-BHBW	Westland-Bell 47G-3B1 Soloy (Line No.WAS/196)	WA/595	XT834	1.11.79	Substantially damaged while spraying at Back Doath, near Carmyllie on 27.4.80. (Under rebuild) Canx as destroyed 26.5.88.
G-BHBX	Agusta-Bell 47G-3B1	1551	XT139	1.11.79	No CofA issued. (Presumed used for spares by Heliwork at Thruxton) Canx as WFU 9.11.84.
G-BHBY	Westland-Bell 47G-3B1 Soloy (Line No.WAN/74)	WA/511	XT804	1.11.79	No CofA issued. (Presumed used for spares by Heliwork at Thruxton) Canx as WFU 9.11.84.
G-BHBZ	Partenavia P.68B Victor	191		10. 9.79	
G-BHCA	Fokker D.VIII Replica	HA/01 & PFA/82-10358		7. 3.80	Destroyed in fatal crash in a field near White Waltham on 21.8.81. Later stored at St.Just. Canx by CAA 4.2.87.
G-BHCB	American Aviation AA-5A Cheetah	AA5A-0863		3.10.79	To G-MELD 2/85. Canx.
G-BHCC	Cessna 172M Skyhawk II	172-66711	(G-BGLY) N80713	26.10.79	
G-BHCD	Cessna 500 Citation I	-		. .79R	NTU - Canx 3/81.
G-BHCE	SAN Jodel D.117A	381	F-BHME	1.10.79	Permit expired 27.2.85. (Status uncertain)
G-BHCF	WMB.2 Windtracker HAFB (Toy)	002		7. 9.79	Canx by CAA 2.12.93.
G-BHCG	Short SD.3-30 Var.100	SH3041	G-14-3021	12. 9.79	NTU - To N844SA 3/80. Canx 13.2.80.
G-BHCH	Short SC.7 Skyvan 3-100	SH1969	G-14-135	10. 9.79	To HZ-ZAS 12/79. Canx 3.1.80.
G-BHCI	SAN Jodel 140 Mousquetaire	40	"OO-APD" F-GAPD/LX-BUS/F-BIZJ	24. 9.79	Crashed on take-off at Challock on 14.5.83. Remains sold to Southern Sailplanes for spares use. Canx as destroyed 5.12.83.
G-BHCJ	HS.748 Srs.2A/209LFD	1663	RP-C1030 G-BHCJ/RP-C1025/PI-C1025/CF-TAZ	29.10.79	To C-FFFS. Canx 19.6.89.
G-BHCK	American Aviation AA-5A Cheetah	AA5A-0810	(F-GBON)	3.10.79	Crashed at Biggin Hill on 30.12.79. Remains removed on 18.1.80. Canx as destroyed 29.2.84.
G-BHCL	Boeing 737-2M8ADV (Line No. 659)	21955	OO-TEN	27. 9.79	Restored as OO-TEN 1/81. Canx 19.1.81.
G-BHCM	Reims Cessna F.172H	0468	SE-FBD	25. 9.79	
G-BHCN	Aerospatiale AS.350B Ecureuil	1151		26. 9.79	To G-JANY 12/78. Canx.
G-BHCO	Socata TB-10 Tobago	57		31.10.79	To G-TEDS 3/83. Canx.
G-BHCP	Reims Cessna F.152 II	1640		31.10.79	
G-BHCR	Pilatus PC-6/B1-H2 Turbo-Porter	732	HB-FFT ST-AEW/HB-FFT	19. 9.79	Crashed on take-off from Sibson on 15.2.81. Canx.
G-BHCS	Cameron N-77 HAFB	535		21. 9.79	To D-KURBIS(1) 8/82. Canx 24.8.82.
G-BHCT	PA-23-250 Aztec F	27-7954113	G-OLBC G-BHCT/N6925A	18.10.79	
G-BHCU	Thunder Ax3-17-5C Sky Chariot	247	"G-BHAT" "G-BHAB"	9. 1.80	To HB-BBS 4/80. Canx 3.4.80.
G-BHCV	Cameron A-140 HAFB	561		21. 9.79	Canx 7.7.80 on sale to Kenya.
G-BHCW	PA-22-150 Tri-Pacer	22-3006	F-BHDT	11. 2.80	(Stored 10/94) No CofA. Canx by CAA 1.4.97.
G-BHCX	Reims Cessna F.152	1642		24. 9.79	Damaged in storms at Biggin Hill on 16.10.87. Canx as destroyed 27.6.94.
G-BHCY	DHC.6-310 Twin Otter	651		13.11.79	Canx 21.12.79 on sale to USA. To 9M-SSA 12/79.
G-BHCZ	PA-38-112 Tomahawk	38-78A0321	N214MD	26. 9.79	
G-BHDA	Fitzjohn Shultz HAFB (Toy)	F.001		26. 9.79	
G-BHDB	Maule M.235C Lunar Rocket	7292C	N5636F	9.11.79	To G-ETON 1/88. Canx.
G-BHDC	Slingsby T.65A Vega	1915		1.10.79	To ZS-GOI 5/82. Canx 17.3.82.
G-BHDD	Vickers 668 Varsity T.1	-	WL626	18.10.79	(To East Midlands Aeropark and on display 4/97)
G-BHDE	Socata TB-10 Tobago	58		2. 1.80	
G-BHDF	Beechcraft 95-58P Pressurized Baron	TJ-250		27. 9.79	To 4X-DZE 7/81. Canx 28.7.81.
G-BHDG	PA-28-181 Archer II	28-7890417	N9503C	17. 4.78	Crashed into hillside near Langleyford, Northumbria on 13.2.79. Canx.
G-BHDH	Douglas DC-10-30 (Line No. 316)	47816		30. 4.80	WFU 4.99 & stored 7/99 Manchester.
G-BHDI	Douglas DC-10-30 (Line No. 327)	47831		10. 6.80	WFU & stored 2/99 Manchester, to Venice 1.7.99 for freighter conversion. Marks LX-TLD are reserved.
G-BHDJ	Douglas DC-10-30 (Line No. 337)	47840	N19B	30. 7.80	WFU 2.4.99 & stored 9/99 Manchester.
G-BHDK	Boeing TB-29A-45-BN Superfortress	11225	44-61748	27. 9.79	Canx as WFU 29.2.84. (On display 7/99 Duxford)
G-BHDL	Bell 212	30544	5N-AOE VR-BEI/G-BHDL/VR-BEI/N2997W	27. 9.79	To 9Y-TIG. Canx 27.5.93.

Regn	Type	c/n	Previous identity	Regn date	Fate or immediate subsequent identity (if known)
G-BHDM	Reims Cessna F.152 II	1684		15.10.79	
G-BHDN	Reims Cessna F.182Q Skylane II	0132		15.10.79	To G-ORAY 3/80. Canx.
G-BHDO	Reims Cessna F.182Q Skylane II	0133		15.10.79	Overturned due to nosewheel collapse on landing at Coll Ballard Strip on 7.5.89. Canx as WFU 24.7.89.
G-BHDP	Reims Cessna F.182Q Skylane II	0131		15.10.79	
G-BHDR	Reims Cessna F.152 II	1680		15.10.79	
G-BHDS	Reims Cessna F.152 II	1682		15.10.79	
G-BHDT	Socata TB-10 Tobago	59		29.11.79	To N313DT 7/99. Canx 14.7.99.
G-BHDU	Reims Cessna F.152 II	1681		15.10.79	
G-BHDV	Cameron V-77 HAFB	585		1. 2.80	
G-BHDW	Reims Cessna F.152 II	1652		15.10.79	
G-BHDX	Reims Cessna F.172N Skyhawk II	1889		5.10.79	
G-BHDY	Reims Cessna F.172N Skyhawk II	1904	(LN-HOH)	5.10.79	To G-MOGG 6/80. Canx.
G-BHDZ	Reims Cessna F.172N Skyhawk II	1911		3.12.79	
G-BHEA	Reims Cessna F.152 II	1677		3.12.79	To G-OWAK 25.2.80. Canx.
G-BHEB	Reims Cessna F.152 II	1678	(OO-HNW)	3.12.79	To G-OWAC 25.2.80. Canx.
G-BHEC	Reims Cessna F.152 II	1676		3.12.79	
G-BHED	Reims Cessna FA.152 Aerobat	0359		3.12.79	
G-BHEE	Partenavia P.68B Victor	196		16.10.79	To OY-CAF 3/81. Canx 23.2.83.
G-BHEF	Partenavia P.68B Victor	199		16.10.79	To OY-CAE 11/80. Canx 23.2.83.
G-BHEG	SAN Jodel 150 Mascaret	46	PH-ULS OO-SET	3. 7.80	
G-BHEH	Cessna 310G	310G-0016	N1720 N8916Z	14. 4.80	CofA expired 9.12.96. (On rebuild 4/98 at Shoreham)
G-BHEI	Cessna TR.182 Turbo-Skylane RG	TR182-01354	(N4608S)	3.12.79	Destroyed in mid-air collision with Mooney M.20K N1061T over Shobdon on 16.7.83. Canx as destroyed 30.5.84.
G-BHEJ	PA-32-300 Cherokee Six E	32-7940106	N2184Z	. .79R	NTU - To G-SALA 10/79. Canx 3/81.
G-BHEK	Scintex CP.1315-C3 Super Emeraude	923	F-BJMU	11.10.79	
G-BHEL	SAN Jodel D.117	735	F-BIOA	8.10.79	
G-BHEM	Bensen B.8MV Gyrocopter	EK.14 & G/01-1016		8.10.79	
G-BHEN	Reims Cessna FA.152 Aerobat	0363		3. 1.80	
G-BHEO	Reims Cessna FR.182 Skylane RG II	0049		3. 1.80	
G-BHEP	Reims Cessna F.172RG Cutlass II (Wichita c/n 172RG-0009)	0003	N4668R	26.11.79	To CS-DAG. Canx 23.3.93.
G-BHER	Socata TB-10 Tobago	60	4X-AKK G-BHER	19.10.79	
G-BHES	Socata TB-10 Tobago	61		19.10.79	To G-BLCG 3/80. Canx.
G-BHET	Socata TB-10 Tobago	62		19.10.79	To G-MRTN 7/98. Canx.
G-BHEU	Thunder Ax7-65 Srs.1 HAFB	238		16.10.79	
G-BHEV	PA-28R-200 Cherokee Arrow II	28R-7435159	PH-BOY N41244	23.10.79	
G-BHEW	Sopwith Triplane Replica (Originally c/n PFA/1539)	PPS/REP/9 & PFA/95-10485	'N5430'	11.10.79	To N5460. Canx 14.1.86.
G-BHEX	Colt 56A HAFB	056		15.10.79	
G-BHEY	Pterodactyl OR Hanglider	PF.089		22.10.79	Canx by CAA 13.6.90.
G-BHEZ	SAN Jodel 150 Mascaret	22	F-BLDO	31. 1.80	
G-BHFA	Pterodactyl OR Hanglider	PF.051		22.10.79	Canx by CAA 13.6.90.
G-BHFB	Pterodactyl OR Hanglider	PF.088		22.10.79	Canx by CAA 13.6.90.
G-BHFC	Reims Cessna F.152 II	1436		7. 4.78	
G-BHFD	DHC.6-310 Twin Otter	434	N26KA	5.11.79	To N703PV 1/85. Canx 25.1.85.
G-BHFE	PA-44-180 Seminole	44-7995324	005 Abu Dhabi DF/G-BHFE/N2383U	22.10.79	
G-BHFF	Dormois Jodel D.112	322	F-BEKJ	19.10.79	
G-BHFG	SNCAN Stampe SV-4C	45	F-BJDN French Mil	31.10.79	
G-BHFH	PA-34-200T Seneca II	34-7970482	N8075Q	23.10.79	
G-BHFI	Reims Cessna F.152 II	1685		22.10.79	
G-BHFJ	PA-28RT-201T Turbo Arrow IV	28R-7931298	N8072R	22.10.79	
G-BHFK	PA-28-151 Cherokee Warrior	28-7615088	N8325C	12.12.79	
G-BHFL	PA-28-180 Cherokee	28-7305033	N15189	12.12.79	Enigine failed on take-off from Coventry on 1.11.89 and th aircraft crash landed just outside the airfield boundary. Canx as destroyed 6.4.90.
G-BHFM	Murphy Saffery S.200 Firefly HAFB (Toy)	MM.1/19		25.10.79	Canx by CAA 4.8.98.
G-BHFN	Eiri PIK-20E Srs.1	20227		31.10.79	Canx 10.6.85 on sale to Holland.
G-BHFO	[Was an unidentified reservation - Canx by CAA in 3/81]				
G-BHFP	Eiri PIK-20E Srs.1	20230		21.11.79	Crashed on take-off from Lasham on 9.5.82. Canx as destroyed 21.6.83.
G-BHFR	Eiri PIK-20E Srs.1	20228	(D-KHJR) G-BHFR/(EI-...)/G-BHFR	8.11.79	
G-BHFS	Robin DR.400/180 Regent	1304		7. 3.78	
G-BHFT	HS.125 Srs.403B	25215	9M-SSB G-BHFT/HB-VBZ	31.10.70	To Z-VEC. Canx 1.8.89.
G-BHFU	Rango-Saffery S.330 Firefly HAFB (Toy)	NHP.3		30.10.79	Canx as WFU 31.5.85.
G-BHFV	Rango-Saffery S.200 SS Dragon HAFB (Toy)	NHP.4		30.10.79	Canx as WFU 1.10.81.

Regn	Type	c/n	Previous identity	Regn date	Fate or immediate subsequent identity (if known)
G-BHFW	Rango NA.1000 Gas Balloon (Toy)	NHP.5		30.10.79	Canx as WFU 1.10.81.
G-BHFX	Cessna 441 Conquest	441-0107	(G-CARS) (N4189G)	2.11.79	To G-PRES 1/80. Canx.
G-BHFY	Beechcraft 95-B58 Baron	TH-1111		5.11.79	To G-OSDI 7/84. Canx.
G-BHFZ	Saffery S.200 Firefly HAFB (Toy)	18		31.10.79	Canx by CAA 13.12.88.
G-BHGA	PA-31-310 Turbo Navajo	31-7912117	N3539M	12.11.79	
G-BHGB	Colt 77A HAFB	079		5. 6.80	To N2745D 8/82. Canx 23.8.82.
G-BHGC	PA-18-150 Super Cub	18-8793	PH-NKH N4447Z	3. 4.79	Crashed at Shobdon on 18.9.83. Canx.
G-BHGD	Cessna 421C Golden Eagle III	421C-0123	D-IASC OE-FLR/N3862C	13.11.79	To G-SHOE 1/81. Canx.
G-BHGE	Boeing 720-051B (Line No. 244)	18421	OY-APY (OY-APN)/N728US	12.11.79	Restored as OY-APY 7/81. Canx 2.7.81.
G-BHGF	Cameron V-56 HAFB	574		5.11.79	
G-BHGG	Reims Cessna F.172N Skyhawk II	1912		15.11.79	To G-WACL 6/89. Canx.
G-BHGH	Vickers Supermarine 509 Spitfire Trainer IX	CBAF/9590	161 Irish Air Corps/G-15-174/PV202	. .79R	NTU - To G-TRIX 7/80. Canx 3/81.
G-BHGI	Cessna 551 Citation II (Unit No.150)	551-0029	N26396	. .79R	NTU - To N168CB. Canx 3/81.
G-BHGJ	Wassmer Jodel D.120 Paris-Nice	336	F-BOYB	15. 1.80	
G-BHGK	Sikorsky S-76A II Plus	760049	N1545Y	27. 3.80	
G-BHGL	Cessna 404 Titan	404-0055	F-BYAJ F-TEDL/F-BYAJ/N5437G	27.11.79	To G-PATT 5/80. Canx.
G-BHGM	Beechcraft 76 Duchess	ME-318		19.11.79	To N800VM 2/98. Canx.
G-BHGN	Evans VP-1	PFA/62-10383		19.11.79	To G-TEDY 10/90. Canx.
G-BHGO	PA-32-260 Cherokee Six	32-7800007	PH-BGP N9656C	16.11.79	
G-BHGP	Socata TB-10 Tobago	100		17. 1.80	
G-BHGR	CEA DR.315 Petit Prince	457	F-BRZL	7.12.79	Canx as WFU 4.8.87.
G-BHGS	PA-31-350 Navajo Chieftain	31-7952245	N3543S	21. 1.80	To LN-VIN. Canx 12.12.85.
G-BHGT	Beechcraft 65-B90 King Air	LJ-446	G-AWWK	18.10.79	To G-BLNA 3/84. Canx.
G-BHGU	WMB.2 Windtracker HAFB (Toy)	004		21.11.79	Canx by CAA 6.12.88.
G-BHGV	Keirs (Hot-Air) Captive Balloon (Toy) (Rango NA.6 Type)	3		26.11.79	Canx by CAA 16.10.84.
G-BHGW	Colt 14A Cloudhopper HAFB	061		22.11.79	Canx by CAA 3.6.91 as a Colt 12A.
G-BHGX	Colt 56B HAFB	057		22.11.79	
G-BHGY	PA-28R-200 Cherokee Arrow II	28R-7435086	PH-NSL N57365	23.11.79	
G-BHGZ	Dornier-Bucker 131 Jungmann (C/n 59 also quoted)	50	HB-UUP Swiss AF A-39/HB-UTF/Swiss AF A-39	17. 9.80	Restored as HB-UUP 10/83. Canx 10.10.83.
G-BHHA	Embraer EMB.110P1 Bandeirante	110-244	PT-SAK	15. 1.80	To N59PB 10/84. Canx 27.9.84.
G-BHHB	Cameron V-77 HAFB	170		26.11.79	
G-BHHC	Reims Cessna F.172N	2016		. .79R	NTU - Not Imported. Canx 3/81.
G-BHHD	Reims Cessna F.152 II	1785		. .79R	NTU - To G-BHWS 6/80. Canx 3/81.
G-BHHE	CEA Jodel DR.1051/M1 Sicile Record	628	F-BMZC	26. 4.80	
G-BHHF	Reims Cessna F.152 II	1767		. .79R	NTU - Not Imported. To D-EBVO. Canx 3/81.
G-BHHG	Reims Cessna F.152 II	1725		4. 3.80	
G-BHHH	Thunder Ax7-65 Bolt HAFB	245		5.12.79	
G-BHHI(1)	Reims Cessna F.152 II	1777		. 3.80R	NTU - To PH-CBA(2) 3/80. Canx.
G-BHHI(2)	Reims Cessna F.152 II	1750	(PH-CBA)	10. 6.80	To G-ENTT 11/93. Canx.
G-BHHJ	Reims Cessna F.152 II	1694		3.12.79	Stalled on take-off at Leicester on 28.9.84 and came to rest inverted. The wreck was later moved to Tollerton for use in the rebuild of another Cessna F.152. Canx as WFU 14.10.85.
G-BHHK	Cameron N-77 HAFB	547		5.12.79	
G-BHHL	Westland WG.13 Lynx Mk.80	WA/142		3.12.79	To R.Netherlands Navy as S-142 in 6/80. Canx 10.6.80.
G-BHHM	Westland WG.13 Lynx Mk.80	WA/134		3.12.79	To R.Netherlands Navy as S-134 in 6/80. Canx 10.6.80.
G-BHHN	Cameron V-77 HAFB	549		29.11.79	
G-BHHO	PA-28-180 Archer	28-7505246	OO-GBJ OO-HAO/N3910X	29.11.79	Destroyed in fatal crash at Welford, Northants on 9.8.85. Canx by CAA 4.2.87.
G-BHHP	Cameron O-105 HAFB	573		. .79R	NTU - Canx 3/81.
G-BHHR	Robin DR.400/140R Regent	843	PH-SRH	30.11.79	Destroyed in fatal crash at Dalwhinnie, Inverness on 21.10.88. Canx as destroyed 26.5.89.
G-BHHS	Short SC.7 Skyvan 3-100	SH1967	G-14-1967	4.12.79	To 9M-AXM 4/80. Canx 25.3.80.
G-BHHT	Short SC.7 Skyvan 3-100	SH1970		4.12.79	To HZ-ZAT 3/80. Canx 2.3.80.
G-BHHU	Short SD.3-30 Var.400	SH3042	OY-MUC G-BHHU/N181AP/N332MV/G-BHHU/G-14-3042	4.12.79	To D-CTAG 4/99. Canx 11.3.99.
G-BHHV	Short SD.3-30 Var.100	SH3044	G-14-3044	4.12.79	To N53DD 5/80. Canx 22.4.80.
G-BHHW	Short SD.3-30 Var.100	SH3045	G-14-3045	4.12.79	To N846SA 5/80. Canx 13.5.80.
G-BHHX	Jodel D.112 (Valladeau-built)	223	F-BFAJ(2)	19. 2.80	
G-BHHY	Schweizer-Gulfstream G-164 Turbo AgCat D	2D	N6828K	17.12.79	To PH-YTO. Canx 7.1.88.
G-BHHZ	Rotorway Scorpion 133	MSI.1195		12.12.79	Permit expired 23.9.81. (Stored 12/94)
G-BHIA	Reims Cessna F.152 II	1712		3. 1.80	Damaged when it landed too far down the runway at Bantry, Ireland on 16.2.85 and came inverted on the beach beyond. Canx as WFU 23.7.92. Scrapped in 1995.
G-BHIB	Reims Cessna F.182Q Skylane II	0134		18.12.79	
G-BHIC	Reims Cessna F.182Q Skylane II	0135		18.12.79	

Regn	Type	c/n	Previous identity	Regn date	Fate or immediate subsequent identity (if known)
G-BHID	Socata TB-10 Tobago	73		2. 1.80	Fatal crash on take-off at Barnchallosch Farm, near Stoneykirk on 27.5.90 & DBF. Canx as destroyed 26.9.90.
G-BHIE	HS.125 Srs.600B	256048	HB-VDS G-5-15	11.12.79	To YU-BME 4/80. Canx 1.4.80.
G-BHIF	Colt 160A HAFB	035		12.12.79	To C-GIAI. Canx 1.4.85.
G-BHIG	Colt 31A Air Chair HAFB	060	SE-... G-BHIG	12.12.79	(Based in Sweden)
G-BHIH	Reims Cessna F.172N Skyhawk II	1945		3. 1.80	
G-BHII	Cameron V-77 HAFB	548		10.12.79	
G-BHIJ	Eiri PIK.20E Srs.1	20241		9. 1.80	
G-BHIK	Adam RA.14 Loisirs	11-bis	F-PHLK	6. 2.80	Extensively damaged in a forced landing 2 miles south of Lancaster on 17.4.85. (On rebuild)
G-BHIL	PA-28-161 Warrior II	28-8016069	N80821	17.12.79	To G-SSFT 7/86. Canx.
G-BHIM	Wassmer Jodel D.112	878	F-BIXC	27.11.79	Destroyed in fatal crash in a field at Gors Byll Farm, Llangwnadl, Pwllheli on 10.5.87. Canx by CAA 9.4.92.
G-BHIN	Reims Cessna F.152 II	1715		28. 1.80	
G-BHIO	HS.125 Srs.700B	257085	G-5-15	6. 2.80	To RP-C1714 in 12/83. Canx 5.12.83.
G-BHIP	Thunder Ax3-1 HAFB	246		5.12.79	Canx by CAA 4.12.80.
G-BHIR	PA-28R-200 Cherokee Arrow B	28R-35614	SE-FHP	21. 2.80	
G-BHIS	Thunder Ax7-65 Bolt HAFB (Originally regd with c/n 254, officially amended on 13.12.79)	240		26.11.79	(Extant 2/97)
G-BHIT	Socata TB-9 Tampico	63		7.12.79	
G-BHIU	Aerospatiale AS.350B Ecureuil	1190		14.12.79	To G-MORR 15.1.80. Canx.
G-BHIV	Aerospatiale AS.350B Ecureuil	1205		20.12.79	To G-COLN 4/84. Canx.
G-BHIW	Cessna 500 Citation I (Unit No.544)	500-0402	(N1779E)	. .79R	NTU - To XA-JFE. Canx 3/81.
G-BHIX	Cameron V-56 HAFB	589		12.12.79	To N901CB 4/83. Canx 28.4.83.
G-BHIY	Reims Cessna F.150K	0627	F-BRXR	18.12.79	
G-BHIZ	PA-31 Turbo Navajo	31-672	3X-GAV N6798L	18.12.79	Destroyed in crash at Rochester on 20.11.85. Canx as destroyed 11.12.87.
G-BHJA	Cessna A.152 Aerobat	A152-0835	N4954A	11. 3.80	Damaged in heavy landing at Bodmin on 21.7.90. (Fuselage stored 5/98 at Bodmin)
G-BHJB	Cessna A.152 Aerobat	A152-0856	N4662A	11. 3.80	
G-BHJC	Cessna A.152 Aerobat	A152-0859	N4667A	26. 2.80	Extensively damaged in fatal crash at Coedkernew, South Wales on 4.11.80. Canx.
G-BHJD	Cessna 152 II	152-83295	N48172	10. 3.80	NTU - To G-BOBI 8/80. Canx.
G-BHJE	Beechcraft 95-58P Baron	TJ-265		4. 3.80	To N588SP 3/82. Canx 26.3.82.
G-BHJF	Socata TB-10 Tobago	83		2. 1.80	
G-BHJG	Reims Cessna 172RG Cutlass	0198	N6529R	2. 1.80	To G-OIFR 6/83. Canx.
G-BHJH	Cessna 421C Golden Eagle III	421C-0810	(N2657L)	9. 1.80	To N123MM 10/81. Canx 13.10.81.
G-BHJI	Mooney M.20J (201)	24-0925	N3753H	11. 2.80	
G-BHJJ	Short SD.3-30 Var.100	SH3046		21.12.79	To N938MA 6/80. Canx 23.6.80.
G-BHJK	Maule M.5-235C Lunar Rocket	7296C	N56359	25. 2.80	
G-BHJL(1)	Short SD.3-30 Var.100	SH3043	G-14-3043	. .79R	NTU - To (G-BHJM)/SX-BGA 5/80. Canx 8.5.80.
G-BHJL(2)	[Was reserved for Sloane Aviation Ltd - Canx 3/81]				
G-BHJM	Short SD.3-30 Var.100	SH3043	(G-BHJL) G-14-3043	21.12.79	NTU - To SX-BGA 5/80. Canx 8.5.80.
G-BHJN	Sportavia Putzer Fournier RF-4D	4021	F-BORH	3. 1.80	
G-BHJO	PA-28-161 Warrior II	28-7816213	OO-FLD N9507N/N6034H	4. 1.80	
G-BHJP	Partenavia P.68C Victor	212		4. 3.80	To EI-BWH 11/87. Canx 11.12.87.
G-BHJR	Saffery S.200 HAFB (Toy)	011		28.12.79	Canx by CAA 13.12.88.
G-BHJS	Partenavia P.68B Victor	172	I-KLUB	28.12.79	
G-BHJT	Cessna 414A Chancellor II	414A-0525	N37464	23. 4.80	To G-TEAM 11/80. Canx.
G-BHJU	Robin DR.400 2+2	1288	D-ECDK	9. 1.80	
G-BHJV	Cameron Rectangular 60SS HAFB	560		2. 1.80	Canx 13.9.82 on sale to Spain.
G-BHJW	Reims Cessna F.152 II	1732		16. 1.80	Badly damaged in forced landing shortly after take-off from Leicester on 5.5.89. Canx as destroyed 7.12.89.
G-BHJX	Partenavia P.68C Victor	219		20. 3.80	To G-NEWU 8/81. Canx.
G-BHJY	Embraer EMB.110P2 Bandeirante	110-256	PT-SAW	22. 3.80	To G-BTAA 5/90. Canx.
G-BHJZ	Embraer EMB.110P2 Bandeirante	110-270	PT-SBH	31. 5.80	To G-OCSI 12/94. Canx.
G-BHKA	Evans VP-1 Srs.2	PFA/62-10496		4. 1.80	CofA Permit expired 8.10.90. (Open store 7/91) Canx as destroyed 18.3.97.
G-BHKB	Westland-Bell 47G-3B1 Soloy (Line No.WAP/87)	WA/386	XT227	9. 1.80	To D-HAAA(3) 2/87. Canx 5.11.86.
G-BHKC	Westland-Bell 47G-3B1 Soloy (Line No.WAS/208)	WA/604	XT842	17. 1.80	To 5N-ATI 4/85. Canx 8.2.85.
G-BHKD	Westland-Bell 47G-3B1 Soloy (Line No.WAS/216)	WA/610	XT848	17. 1.80	Struck building at Ledstone, near Castleford on 30.7.83. Canx as destroyed 5.12.83. Rebuilt as D-HABY(2) 3/87.
G-BHKE	Bensen B.8MS Gyrocopter	VW.1 & G/01-1009		7. 1.80	
G-BHKF	HS.125 Srs.700A	NA0254 & 257075	G-5-13	18. 1.80	NTU - To N125AM 2/80. Canx 13.2.80.
G-BHKG	Reims Cessna F.172N Skyhawk	2024		12. 6.80	To VP-FBH 2/83. Canx 30.12.82.
G-BHKH	Cameron O-65 HAFB	592		7. 1.80	
G-BHKI	Cessna 402C	402C-0259	N8860K	25. 1.80	To F-GDMZ 10/83. Canx 23.3.84.
G-BHKJ	Cessna 421C Golden Eagle III (Robertson STOL conv.)	421C-0848	(N26596)	25. 1.80	
G-BHKK	Cessna 414A Chancellor II	414A-0455	(N2734D)	25. 1.80	To G-MHGI 8/80. Canx.

Regn	Type	c/n	Previous identity	Regn date	Fate or immediate subsequent identity (if known)
G-BHKL	Colt Flying Bottle 65SS HAFB	066		17. 1.80	Canx 6.4.84 on sale to France.
G-BHKM	Colt 14A Cloudhopper HAFB (Officially regd as Colt 12A)	067		17. 1.80	(Stored in 1988 with not external marks) Canx as WFU 5.12.89.
G-BHKN	Colt 14A Cloudhopper HAFB (Officially regd as Colt 12A)	068		17. 1.80	(Stored in 1988 with not external marks) Canx as WFU 5.12.89. (Extant 2/97 Newbury)
G-BHKO	Colt 14A Cloudhopper HAFB (Officially regd as Colt 12A)	069		17. 1.80	(Stored in 1988 with not external marks) Canx as WFU 5.12.89.
G-BHKP	Colt 14A Cloudhopper HAFB (Officially regd as Colt 12A)	070		17. 1.80	(Stored in 1988 with not external marks) Canx as WFU 5.12.89.
G-BHKR	Colt 14A Cloudhopper HAFB (Officially regd as Colt 12A)	071		17. 1.80	Canx as WFU 5.12.89. (On display British Balloon Museum, Newbury)
G-BHKS	Beechcraft E90 King Air	LW-333		9. 1.80	To N90BE 12/84. Canx 4.12.84.
G-BHKT	Wassmer Jodel D.112	1265	F-BMIQ	10. 1.80	
G-BHKU	American Aviation AA-5A Cheetah	AA5A-0845	(OO-HTF)	29. 1.80	To G-PROP 2/84. Canx.
G-BHKV	American Aviation AA-5A Cheetah	AA5A-0894	N27465	31. 1.80	Badly damaged on take-off at Deanland on 11.6.94. (On rebuild off airfield 9/94) Canx by CAA 14.9.94.
G-BHKW	Westland-Bell 47G-3B1 (Line No.WAT/235)	WA/713	XW193	25. 1.80	To SX-HCC 4/87. Canx 9.3.87.
G-BHKX	Beechcraft 76 Duchess	ME-333		10. 1.80	To N2265T 2/93. Canx 18.2.93.
G-BHKY	Cessna 310R II	310R-1861	(N3156M)	13. 3.80	To N310KZ 5/97. Canx 10.4.97.
G-BHKZ	Cessna 172N Skyhawk II (Wren conversion)	172-72969	N1207F	27. 2.80	To EI-BKR 4/81. Canx 31.3.81.
G-BHLA	Cessna 421C Golden Eagle III	421C-0856	(N2660U)	17. 1.80	To G-RANY 7/85. Canx.
G-BHLB	Sikorsky S-76A	760039		21. 1.80	To C-GMQD 5/80. Canx 6.5.80.
G-BHLC	Beechcraft 200 Super King Air	BB-684	N27L N8511L/G-BHLC	4. 2.80	To G-ROWN 10/87. Canx.
G-BHLD	Beechcraft B60 Duke	P-513	N6661T	. .80R	NTU - To G-DHLD 10/80. Canx 3/81.
G-BHLE	Robin DR.400/180 Regent	1466		25. 1.80	
G-BHLF	HS.125 Srs.700B	257091		31. 1.80	To G-OCAA 4/92. Canx.
G-BHLG	Sinnett X3-4 Windrifter HAFB (Toy)	01		18. 1.80	Canx as WFU 13.5.81.
G-BHLH	Robin DR.400/180 Regent	1320	F-GBIG	11. 2.80	
G-BHLI	Rockwell 690B Turbo Commander	11546	(EI-BJU) G-BHLI/N81632	24. 1.80	To (YV-280CP)/EI-BPC 12/84. Canx 14.1.85.
G-BHLJ	Saffery-Rigg S.200 Skyliner HAFB (Toy)	IAR/01		23. 1.80	
G-BHLK	Gulfstream American GA-7 Cougar	GA7-0108	N749G	23. 1.80	CofA expired 12.5.89. (Stored at Elstree) Canx by CAA 7.3.95.
G-BHLL	Cessna 421C Golden Eagle III	421C-0882	N5874C	7. 3.80	NTU - Canx 14.4.83 as Not Imported. Remained as N5874C.
G-BHLM	Cessna 421C Golden Eagle III	421C-0871	(N5428G)	7. 3.80	To F-GJFK. Canx 4.8.88.
G-BHLN	Cessna 441 Conquest II	441-0154	(N2628Z)	12. 3.80	To G-MOXY 9/83. Canx.
G-BHLO	Cessna 441 Conquest II	441-0226	(N6854L)	23. 3.81	To N226FC. Canx 25.6.85.
G-BHLP	Cessna 441 Conquest II	441-0239	(N6856L)	16. 7.81	To N3XR. Canx 4.5.90.
G-BHLR	Aerospatiale AS.350B Ecureuil	1232		23. 1.80	To G-MAGI 7/80. Canx.
G-BHLS	PA-28-236 Dakota	28-8011061	N35650	25. 1.80	To G-LEAM 7/80. Canx.
G-BHLT	DH.82A Tiger Moth (Regd as c/n "911")	84997	ZS-DGA South African AF 2272/T6697	9. 6.80	Overturned on landing at Booker on 25.1.86 & was severely damaged. (Later dismantled and removed by road) CofA expired 26.2.90. (On rebuild 8/90)
G-BHLU	Alpavia Fournier RF-3	79	F-BMTN	14. 4.80	
G-BHLV	Coopavia-Menavia CP.301A Emeraude	217	F-BIJQ	25. 2.80	Fatal crash west of the airfield shortly after take-off from Perth/Scone on 6.9.87. Canx by CAA 14.2.92.
G-BHLW	Cessna 120	10210	N73005 NC73005	24. 3.80	
G-BHLX	American Aviation AA-5B Tiger	AA5B-0573	OY-GAR	1. 2.80	
G-BHLY	Sikorsky S-76A II Plus	760046		12. 2.80	To VH-BHL 12/98. Canx 1.12.98.
G-BHLZ	CAB GY-30 Supercab (C/n plate on aircraft gave 201)	02	F-BBIP(2) (G-BDGP)/F-BBIP(2)	18. 4.80	Destroyed in fatal crash at Dines Farm, Bethersden, Kent on 3.10.86. Canx by CAA 17.2.95.
G-BHMA	SIPA 903	61	OO-FAE(2) F-BGBK	13. 3.80	
G-BHMB	Rango NA.6 HAFB (Toy)	AL.6		28. 1.80	Canx as WFU 1.10.81.
G-BHMC	Morane-Saulnier MS.880B Rallye Club	857	F-BODR	8. 5.80	CofA expired 2.10.87. (Wreck stored at Caterham) Canx as WFU 13.7.94.
G-BHMD	Rand KR-2	"PFA/8428/7"		7. 2.80	Canx by CAA 2.9.91.
G-BHME	Wallingford WMB.2 Windtracker HAFB (Toy)	003		11. 2.80	Canx by CAA 5.8.98.
G-BHMF	Reims Cessna FA.152 Aerobat	0369		2. 6.80	DBR when it landed on top of Slingsby G-BIUZ whilst coming into land at Cranfield on 25.2.87. Rebuilt & re-regd as G-JEET 12/87. Canx.
G-BHMG	Reims Cessna FA.152 Aerobat	0368		10. 6.80	
G-BHMH	Reims Cessna FA.152 Aerobat	0367		16. 5.80	Damaged when a wing struck a tree while practising forced-landings at Hale Farm, Chiddingstone on 22.9.86. Canx as WFU 9.8.89.
G-BHMI	Reims Cessna F.172N Skyhawk II	2036	G-WADE G-BHMI	6. 8.80	
G-BHMJ	Avenger T.200-2112 HAFB (Toy)	002		29. 1.80	
G-BHMK	Avenger T.200-2112 HAFB (Toy)	003		29. 1.80	
G-BHML	Avenger T.200-2112 HAFB (Toy)	LC.1		29. 1.80	Canx by CAA 2.12.93.
G-BHMM	Avenger T.200-2112 HAFB (Toy)	MM.2		29. 1.80	Canx by CAA 4.8.98.

Regn	Type	c/n	Previous identity	Regn date	Fate or immediate subsequent identity (if known)
G-BHMN	Socata TB-10 Tobago	95		27. 2.80	Crashed & DBF on take-off from Netherthorpe on 16.9.81. Canx.
G-BHMO	Piper PA-20M Pacer	20-89	F-BDRO	16. 4.80	Extensively damaged on landing at Little Gransden on 20.8.89. CofA expired 23.11.90. Canx by CAA 1.4.97.
G-BHMP	HS.125 Srs.700A	NA0266 & 257093	G-5-11	18. 2.80	To C-GBRM 4/80. Canx 10.4.80.
G-BHMR	Stinson 108-3 Station Wagon	108-4352	F-BABO F-DABO/NC6352M	12. 2.80	(Stored 12/95)
G-BHMS	PA-34-200T Seneca II	34-7870225	N30008	6. 3.80	To N3834Z 3/83. Canx 14.3.83.
G-BHMT	Evans VP-1	PFA/62-10473		18. 2.80	
G-BHMU	Colt 21A Cloudhopper HAFB	077		11. 2.80	CofA expired 5.5.83. Canx by CAA 18.12.92.
G-BHMV	Bell 206B JetRanger II	83	VH-SJJ VH-FVR	7. 2.80	To HB-XOR 5/84. Canx 23.5.84.
G-BHMW	Fokker F-27 Friendship 200	10229	(PH-FFA)	9. 9.80	To D-BAKK 1/98. Canx. G-BHMW/F-BSIF/F-OGIF/F-BUTA/JA8618/PH-FEU
G-BHMX	Fokker F-27 Friendship 200	10259	F-BUFO JA8634/PH-FGA	17. 7.80	WFU in 7/94. Stored engineless 10/96 at Norwich. Broken up in 12/96. Canx as WFU 4.10.95.
G-BHMY	Fokker F-27 Friendship 600	10196	F-GBDK(2) (F-GBRV)/PK-PFS/JA8606/PH-FDL	6. 5.80	
G-BHMZ	Fokker F-27 Friendship 200	10244	F-GBRY PK-PFV/JA8624/PH-FFK	4. 8.80	WFU in 3/94. Stored 7/94 at Norwich. Canx as WFU 4.10.95.
G-BHNA	Reims Cessna F.152 II	1683		12. 2.80	Damaged on landing at Netherthorpe on 17.6.95. CofA expired 20.10.95. (Fuselage only stored 5/99 Netherthorpe)
G-BHNB	Cessna 210N Centurion II	210-63070	N6496N	26. 2.80	To G-MCDS 3/80. Canx.
G-BHNC	Cameron O-65 HAFB	588		7. 2.80	(Extant 2/97)
G-BHND	Cameron N-65 HAFB	582		7. 2.80	
G-BHNE	Boeing 727-2J4RE (Line No. 1417)	21676	OY-SBD	20. 3.80	To N285SC. Canx 19.11.91.
G-BHNF	Boeing 727-2J4RE (Line No. 1301)	21438	OY-SBC	8. 4.80	To N284SC. Canx 12.11.91.
G-BHNG	PA-23-250 Aztec E	27-7405432	N54125	13. 5.80	Badly damaged following collision with F.152 G-BFRB on take-off from Shoreham on 19.12.81. Canx by CAA 12.12.86. (Fuselage stored 3/97)
G-BHNH	Cessna 404 Titan II	404-0672	N6761L	15.10.80	To G-DAFS 1/84. Canx.
G-BHNI	Cessna 404 Titan Courier II	404-0644	LN-LGM SE-IFV/G-BHNI/(N5302J)	21. 7.80	To G-KIWI 1/90. Canx.
G-BHNJ	Cessna 404 Titan II	404-0656		. .80R	NTU - To N5333J. Canx 3/81.
G-BHNK	Wassmer Jodel D.120A Paris-Nice	243	F-BLNK	26. 3.80	
G-BHNL	Wassmer Jodel D.112	1206	F-BLNL	30. 1.80	
G-BHNM	PA-44-180 Seminole	44-7995327	N8077X	15. 2.80	To G-INDE 1/94. Canx.
G-BHNN	PA-32R-301 Saratoga SP	32R-8013038	N3578C	7. 2.80	To CS-AZV. Canx 15.11.91.
G-BHNO	PA-28-181 Archer II	28-8090211	N81413	7. 2.80	
G-BHNP	Eiri PIK-20E Srs.1	20253		29. 2.80	
G-BHNR	Cameron N-77 HAFB	641		8. 2.80	Canx as WFU 15.11.89.
G-BHNS	PA-28R-201 Arrow III	28R-7837026	OO-FLU N9048K	20. 1.80	Crashed at Eiriks Jokull, in Iceland on 21.6.84. Canx as destroyed 5.3.87.
G-BHNT	Reims Cessna F.172N	1949	(OY-BNL)	3. 3.80	Ditched in the sea 200 yards off Portrush on 4.3.90 and sunk. Canx as WFU 25.4.90.
G-BHNU	Reims Cessna F.172N	1977		15. 2.80	To SP-FTE 4/96. Canx 25.3.96.
G-BHNV	Westland-Bell 47G-3B1 (Line No. WAT/222)	WA/700	XW180	11. 3.80	
G-BHNW	Cessna 425 Corsair	425-0024	(N6772U)	. .80R	NTU - To G-BJET 2/81. Canx 3/81.
G-BHNX	SAN Jodel D.117	493	F-BHNX	7. 9.78	Permit expired 12.1.87. (On rebuild 4/91)
G-BHNY(1)	Cessna 425 Corsair	425-0094	N6848Y	. .80R	NTU - Not Imported. To N104HW. Canx.
G-BHNY(2)	Cessna 425 Corsair	425-0090	(N68476)	16. 7.81	To N90GA. Canx 24.7.91.
G-BHNZ	American Aviation AA-5B Tiger	AA5B-1161	(D-EGDS) N4547L	8. 4.80	To G-TYGA 2/82. Canx.
G-BHOA	Robin DR.400/160 Major 80	1478		27. 1.80	
G-BHOB	Cessna 404 Titan Courier II	404-0612	N2684S	27. 3.80	To PH-HOB(2) 8/82. Canx 21.7.82.
G-BHOC	Rockwell Commander 112A	378	N1378J	16. 4.80	Destroyed in fatal crash 3/4 of a mile south east of Leicester airfield near Little Stretton on 1.10.85. Canx as WFU 2.7.86.
G-BHOD	Electraflyer Microlite	-		. .80R	NTU - Canx 3/81.
G-BHOE	Canadair (CL-30) T-33AN Silver Star Mk.3	T33-261	G-OAHB CF-IHB/CAF 133261/RCN 21261	. .80R	NTU - To G-JETT 12/83. Canx 3/81.
G-BHOF	Sikorsky S-61N Mk.II	61-824	LN-ONK(2) G-BHOF/LN-ONK(2)/G-BHOF	27. 2.80	To G-LAWS 7/99. Canx.
G-BHOG	Sikorsky S-61N Mk.II	61-825	(LN-ONK) G-BHOG	25. 3.80	To PT-YEK 9/97. Canx 22.9.97.
G-BHOH	Sikorsky S-61N Mk.II	61-827		25. 4.80	
G-BHOI	Westland-Bell 47G-3B1 (Line No.WAN/15)	WA/324	XT165	25. 2.80	Canx 8.2.88 on sale to France.
G-BHOJ	Colt 14A Cloudhopper HAFB (Officially regd as Colt 12A)	080		27. 2.80	Canx as WFU 5.12.89. (Extant 4/95)
G-BHOK	Mooney M.20J (201)	24-0950	N3818H	13. 3.80	To EI-BKD 12/80. Canx 21.11.80.
G-BHOL	CEA Jodel DR.1050 Ambassadeur	35	F-BJQL	6. 2.80	
G-BHOM	PA-18-95 Super Cub (L-18C-PI)(Frame No 18-1272)	18-1391	OO-PIU OO-HMT/ALAT 51-15391	7. 3.80	
G-BHON	Rango NA.6 HAFB (Toy)	NHP-7		27. 2.80	Sold in Spain. Canx as WFU 18.10.88.
G-BHOO	Livesey-Purves Thunder Ax7-65 HAFB	001		26. 2.80	
G-BHOP	Thunder Ax3 Sky Chariot HAFB	262		21. 1.80	To OH-MHZ. Canx 28.2.95.
G-BHOR	PA-28-161 Warrior II	28-8016331	N82162	12. 6.80	

Regn	Type	c/n	Previous identity	Regn date	Fate or immediate subsequent identity (if known)
G-BHOS	Mooney M.20K (231)	25-0301	N231LQ	11. 3.80	To G-GTPL 7/80. Canx.
G-BHOT(1)	Thunder (Type unknown) HAFB	-		. .80R	NTU - Canx 3/81.
G-BHOT(2)	Cameron V-65 HAFB	777		15. 9.81	
G-BHOU	Cameron V-65 HAFB	657		16. 6.80	Canx by CAA 28.11.95. To Z3-OOA 4/97.
G-BHOV	Partenavia P.68C Victor	223		17. 3.80	To G-OJCT 3/83. Canx.
G-BHOW	Beechcraft 95-58PA Pressurized Baron	TJ-176	N2049E	14. 3.80	To N58BP 8/95. Canx 3.8.95.
G-BHOX	Boeing 707-123B (Line No. 31)	17640	G-TJAB 9G-ACN/N7513A	4. 3.80	To N62TA 12/80. Canx 8.12.80.
G-BHOY	Boeing 707-123B (Line No. 72)	17651	G-TJAC 9G-ACO/ST-AHG/N7524A	4. 3.80	To N61TA 11/80. Canx 21.11.80.
G-BHOZ	Socata TB-9 Tampico	84		11. 3.80	
G-BHPA	Sikorsky S-61N	61-775	"G-BNPA" PH-NZL	4. 3.80	(Painted as G-BNPA in error). Restored as PH-NZL 5/81. Canx 21.5.81.
G-BHPB	Sikorsky S-61N	61-742	PH-NZF	9. 4.80	Restored as PH-NZF 10/81. Canx 23.10.81.
G-BHPC	Mooney M.20E	1199	OY-DDS	6. 3.80	Restored as OY-DDS 2/81. Canx 18.2.81.
G-BHPD	Colt 21A HAFB	075		17. 3.80	DBF at Durban, South Africa on 5.7.80. Canx as WFU 22.12.81.
G-BHPE	PBN BN-2B-26 Islander	2021		7. 3.80	To N50PA 6/80. Canx 3.7.80.
G-BHPF	PBN BN-2B-27 Islander	2022		7. 3.80	To N17JA 6/80. Canx 9.7.80.
G-BHPG	PBN BN-2B-21 Islander	2023		7. 3.80	To N408JA 9/80. Canx 31.10.80.
G-BHPH	Short SC.7 Skyvan 3M	SH1968	G-14-136	7. 3.80	To 7Q-YMA 6/80. Canx 4.6.80.
G-BHPI	Short SC.7 Skyvan 3M	SH1971		7. 3.80	To 7Q-YMB 6/80. Canx 6.6.80.
G-BHPJ	Electraflyer Eagle Microlight	E.2137		30.10.80	Canx as WFU 30.10.80.
G-BHPK	Piper J3C-65 Cub (L-4A-PI) (Frame No 9098; official c/n is 12161/44-79865 which is F-BFYU)	8979	F-BEPK French Mil/42-38410	26. 2.80	
G-BHPL	CASA I-131E Jungmann	1058	E3B-350 Spanish AF	17. 7.80	
G-BHPM	PA-18-95 Super Cub (L-18C-PI) (Frame No. 18-1469)	18-1501	F-BOUR ALAT 51-15501	10. 4.80	(Stored 5/95)
G-BHPN	Colt 14A Cloudhopper HAFB (Originally regd as a 12A model)	081	(SE-...) G-BHPN/(SE-...)/G-BHPN	6. 3.80	(Based in Sweden)
G-BHPO	Colt 14A Cloudhopper HAFB (Originally regd as a 12A model)	082		6. 3.80	Canx by CAA 19.5.93.
G-BHPP	Embraer EMB.110P1 Bandeirante	110-278	PT-SBP	. .80R	NTU - Not Imported. To PT-SBP/XA-LES(2). Canx.
G-BHPR	Embraer EMB.110P1 Bandeirante	110-289	PT-SBY	. .80R	NTU - Not Imported. To HP-1012AC. Canx.
G-BHPS	Wassmer Jodel D.120A Paris-Nice	148	F-BIXI	11. 6.80	
G-BHPT	Piper J3C-65 Cub (Frame no 17792; original identity suspect - probably c/n 18105 and originally NC71076/N71076)	"17792"	F-BSGQ LX-AIH/N70688/NC70688	10. 4.80	
G-BHPU	Sikorsky S-61N	61-762	PH-NZI (PH-NZK)	2. 4.80	Restored as PH-NZI 2/83. Canx 8.2.83.
G-BHPV	Cessna U.206G Stationair 6 II	U206-05362	N6169U	31. 3.80	To 5H-DTD 4/86. Canx 10.3.86.
G-BHPW	Piper PA-60-601P Aerostar	61P-0765-8063380	N3634A	21. 3.80	To N97315 8/81. Canx 5.8.81.
G-BHPX	Cessna 152 II	152-82994	N46073	26. 3.80	
G-BHPY	Cessna 152 II	152-82983	N46009	26. 3.80	
G-BHPZ	Cessna 172N Skyhawk II	172-72017	N6411E	26. 3.80	
G-BHRA	Rockwell Commander 114A (Originally laid down as c/n 14436)	14505	N5891N	10. 7.79	To G-ZIPA 9/98. Canx.
G-BHRB	Reims Cessna F.152 II	1707		20. 3.80	
G-BHRC	PA-28-161 Warrior II	28-7916430	N9527N	3. 4.80	
G-BHRD	DHC.1 Chipmunk 22 (Fuselage no. DHB/f/740)	C1/0843	9M-ANA VR-SEK/WP977	27. 5.80	Damaged in forced landing near Burford on 21.1.97. Canx as destroyed 19.1.98.
G-BHRE	Saffery S.200 Persephone HAFB (Toy)	21		12. 3.80	Canx as destroyed 18.10.88.
G-BHRF	Airborne Industries AB.400 (Gas) Captive Balloon	AB.40102		3. 6.80	Canx by CAA 20.12.88.
G-BHRG	HS.748 Srs.2A/263	1676	9J-ABJ	. .80R	NTU - To 6V-AET. Canx 3/81.
G-BHRH	Reims Cessna FA.150K Aerobat	0056	PH-ECB D-ECBL/(D-EKKW)	24. 3.80	
G-BHRI	Saffery S.200 Phoenix HAFB (Toy)	20	(G-BGHD)	12. 3.80	
G-BHRJ	Sikorsky S-76A	760025	N4250S	25. 3.80	To C-GMQE /80. Canx 2.6.80.
G-BHRK(1)	Sikorsky S-76A	760056		. 3.80R	NTU - Not Imported. To N1546T. Canx.
G-BHRK(2)	Colt Saucepan 56SS HAFB	062		22. 8.80	Canx 4.7.91 on sale to USA.
G-BHRL	Thunder Ax6-56Z HAFB	270		24. 3.80	NTU - To G-BPUF 30.4.80. Canx.
G-BHRM	Reims Cessna F.152 II	1718	(F-GCHR)	8. 4.80	
G-BHRN	Reims Cessna F.152 II	1728	(F-GCHV)	8. 4.80	
G-BHRO	Rockwell Commander 112A	364	N1364J	20. 3.80	
G-BHRP	PA-44-180 Seminole	44-8095021	N81602	1. 4.80	
G-BHRR	Menavia Piel CP.301A Emeraude	270	F-BISK	28. 3.80	Permit expired 28.5.87. (Status uncertain)
G-BHRS	ICA-Brasov IS-28M2A	33		31. 3.80	Fatal crash when it spun in shortly after take-off at Woodford on 29.7.89. Canx as destroyed 9.10.89.
G-BHRT	Sikorsky S-76A	760057	N1546P	25. 4.80	To 9M-AXW 8/80. Canx 8.8.80.
G-BHRU	Saffery S.1000 Phoenix HAFB (Toy)	1		12. 3.80	Canx as WFU 10.8.87.
G-BHRV	Mooney M.20J (201)	24-0958	N3839H	2. 6.80	To CS-ASZ. Canx 26.5.89.
G-BHRW	CEA Jodel DR.221 Dauphin	93	F-BPCP	10. 7.80	
G-BHRX	Cessna 340A	340A-0115	N5478J	20. 6.80	To N2920G 3/82. Canx 9.3.82.

Regn	Type	c/n	Previous identity	Regn date	Fate or immediate subsequent identity (if known)
G-BHRY	Colt 56A HAFB	030		2. 4.80	
G-BHRZ	Colt 77B HAFB	084		8. 4.80	Canx 17.7.80 on sale to Switzerland. To SE-ZXK 6/81.
G-BHSA	Cessna 152 II	152-83693	(N4889B)	1. 5.80	
G-BHSB	Cessna 172N Skyhawk II	172-72977	(N1225F)	25. 6.80	
G-BHSC	[Was reserved for unknown type - canx 3/81 as not allotted]				
G-BHSD	Scheibe SF-25E Super Falke	4357	D-KDGG	21. 7.80	
G-BHSE	Rockwell Commander 114	14161	N4831W AN-BRL/(N4831W)	15. 5.80	
G-BHSF	American Aviation AA-5A Cheetah	AA5A-0870	G-BHAS N26998	18. 1.80	Bounced on landing at Blackbushe on 12.7.88, struck a bank and eventually collided with a lorry in a car park. Canx as WFU 9.1.89.
G-BHSG	Agusta-Bell 206A JetRanger	8056	PH-FSW	6. 5.80	To G-RIAN 9/87. Canx.
G-BHSH	Short SD.3-30 Var.100	SH3047		9. 4.80	To N939MA 6/80. Canx 9.7.80.
G-BHSI	Jodel D.9 Bebe	PFA/942		8. 4.80	Overshot on landing and crashed halfway along the runway at Headcorn on 16.5.87. Canx as destroyed 12.8.87.
G-BHSJ	Coopavia-Menavia CP.301A Emeraude	282	F-BHLQ F-OBLQ	17. 4.80	Crashed on take-off from Redhill on 18.4.83. Canx as destroyed 6.6.83.
G-BHSK	HS.125 Srs.700A	NA0270 & 257099	G-5-16	8. 4.80	To C-GDAO 6/80. Canx 5.6.80.
G-BHSL	CASA I-131E Jungmann	1117	E3B-236 Spanish AF	18. 6.80	Damaged on take off from Cranfield on 6.7.96. Permit expired 19.7.96.
G-BHSM	Agusta-Bell 206B JetRanger II	8405	EI-BHE OO-MHS/F-BVEM	6. 8.80	To D-HOCH(3) 4/90. Canx 26.3.90.
G-BHSN	Cameron N-56 HAFB	595		10. 4.80	
G-BHSO	PA-23-250 Aztec F	27-8054041	N2527Z	14. 4.80	To G-SFHR 6/82. Canx.
G-BHSP	Thunder Ax7-77Z HAFB (Originally built as D-TRIER c/n 221)	272		15. 4.80	
G-BHSR(1)	Sportavia-Putzer Fournier RF-5B Sperber	51005	D-KCIG	. .80R	NTU - To G-KCIG 6/80. Canx.
G-BHSR(2)	Cessna 404 Titan	404-0009	N3937C	. .80R	NTU - To G-BHWX 12/80. Canx.
G-BHSR(3)	PA-23-250 Aztec E	27-7305101	OY-DGZ N40286	. .80R	NTU - To G-BHXX 6/80. Canx 3/81.
G-BHSS	Pitts S-1C Special	C.1461M	N1704	19. 9.80	
G-BHST	Hughes 369D (300D)	40-0714D		12. 6.80	To OY-HES 6/94. Canx 3.5.94.
G-BHSU	HS.125 Srs.700B	257103	G-5-12	7. 5.80	To G-LTEC 4/93. Canx.
G-BHSV	HS.125 Srs.700B	257107		7. 5.80	To G-5-808/N90AR. Canx 12.7.94.
G-BHSW	HS.125 Srs.700B	257109	VR-BPT G-BHSW	7. 5.80	To VR-BPT 2/94. Canx 7.2.94.
G-BHSX	Grumman (Type unknown)	-		. .80R	NTU - Canx 3/81.
G-BHSY	CEA Jodel DR.1050 Ambassadeur	546	F-BLZO	6. 5.80	
G-BHSZ	Cessna 152 II	152-83175	N47125	26. 3.80	To G-SACF 3/85. Canx.
G-BHTA	PA-28-236 Dakota	28-8011102	N8197H	22. 4.80	
G-BHTB	Monnett Sonerai II	847		15. 4.80	NTU - Construction abandoned in favour of a Jurca Sirocco. Canx by CAA 5.10.84.
G-BHTC	CEA Jodel DR.1051/M1 Sicile Record	581	F-BMGR	1. 5.80	
G-BHTD	Cessna T.188C AgHusky	T188-03338T	(G-BGTN) N2033J	18. 4.80	Damaged in an incident at Damru Tanta, Egypt on 23.7.80. (Will probably continue to operate in the Sudan area) (Status uncertain - probably exported/destroyed)
G-BHTE	PA-23-250 Aztec E	27-7305007	N40209	13. 5.80	Restored as N40209 12/80. Canx 29.12.80.
G-BHTF	Enstron F-28C-UK	348		19. 6.80	To G-SMUJ 8/85. Canx.
G-BHTG	Thunder Ax6-56 Bolt HAFB	273		18. 4.80	
G-BHTH	North American T-6G-NT Texan	168-176	N2807G 49-3072A	20. 5.80	Damaged in fatal crash at the Enham Alamein strip, near Andover on 13.3.95. (On major rebuild 1/99 at Shoreham)
G-BHTI	K & S SA.102.5 Cavalier	PFA/01-10487		17. 4.80	Canx by CAA 2.9.91.
G-BHTJ	HS.125 Srs.700B	257097	G-BRDI G-HHOI/(G-BHTJ)	21. 4.80	To RA-02801 8/93. Canx 15.7.93.
G-BHTK	DHC.6-310 Twin Otter	708		20. 8.80	To PH-STH 9/85. Canx 27.8.85.
G-BHTL	Thunder Ax3 Skychariot HAFB	275		23. 4.80	Canx 15.10.80 on sale to Sweden.
G-BHTM	Cameron Can 80SS HAFB	563		24. 4.80	Canx by CAA 7.1.93.
G-BHTN	Rango Saffery S.300 HAFB (Toy)	NHP.8		22. 4.80	Canx as WFU 1.10.81.
G-BHTO(1)	DHC.6-310 Twin Otter	694		. .80R	NTU - To G-BHXG 7/80. Canx.
G-BHTO(2)	DHC.6-310 Twin Otter	703		. .80R	NTU - To G-MAIL 7/80. Canx 3/81.
G-BHTP	PA-31T-500 Cheyenne I	31T1-8004022	N2337V	6. 5.80	To N141GA. Canx 23.12.88.
G-BHTR	Bell 206B JetRanger III	3035	N18098	27. 6.80	To G-CORN 6/99. Canx.
G-BHTS	Wassmer Jodel D.120 Paris-Nice	19	F-BHTS	. .80R	NTU - Remained as F-BHTS. Canx.
G-BHTT	Cessna 500 Citation I (Unit No.560)	500-0404	N2614H	4. 8.80	To G-ZAPI 9/94. Canx.
G-BHTU	Morane-Saulnier MS.880B Rallye Club	286	F-BKTV	. .80R	NTU - To G-BJTV 8/81. Canx.
G-BHTV	Cessna 310R II	310R-1974	N1EU (N3206M)	21. 5.80	To G-EGLT 9/93. Canx.
G-BHTW	Reims Cessna FR.172J Rocket	0486	5Y-ATO	4. 8.80	Canx 25.9.85 on sale to Ireland. To EI-CAA 8/89.
G-BHTX	Coopavia-Menavia Piel CP.301A Emeraude	221	F-BIJU	29. 4.80	To G-BIJU 6/80. Canx.
G-BHTY	Socata MS.880B Rallye Club	1171	F-BPGY	. .80R	NTU - Canx.
G-BHTZ	American Aviation AA-5A Cheetah	AA5A-0730	N26795	17. 7.80	To G-JULY 1/82. Canx.
"G-BHTZ"	PA-18-150 Super Cub	18-8009058		----	Marks applied in error - To G-BHUF 4/80. Canx.
G-BHUA	Douglas C-47A-40-DL Dakota	9914	T3-28 Spanish AF/N44V/NC65282/42-24052	30. 4.80	Broken up for spares at Cuartro Vientos, Spain in 1981 and not delivered to the UK. Canx as WFU 5.12.83

Regn	Type	c/n	Previous identity	Regn date	Fate or immediate subsequent identity (if known)
G-BHUB	Douglas C-47A-85-DL Dakota	19975	"G-AGIV" Spanish AF T3-29/N51V/ N9985F/SE-BBH/43-15509	30. 4.80	(Used marks G-AGIV for film "Airline" in 1981) Canx as WFU 19.10.81. (On display 7/99 at Duxford)
G-BHUC	Douglas C-47B-1-DL Dakota	14319/25764	T3-20 Spanish AF/43-48503	30. 4.80	Canx 21.11.80 on sale to USA. To CP-1668 6/81.
G-BHUD	Douglas C-47A-25-DL Dakota	16028/32776	T3-46 Spanish AF/N86446/44-76444	30. 4.80	Canx 27.10.80 on sale to USA. To N2619M 11/81.
G-BHUE	SAN Jodel DR.1050 Ambassadeur	185	F-BERM(2) F-OBRM	21. 4.80	
G-BHUF	PA-18-150 Super Cub	18-8009058	"G-BHTZ"	30. 4.80	(Marks G-BHTZ were applied in error) Crashed at Dunstable on 21.8.84 & DBF. Canx as destroyed 2.12.86.
G-BHUG	Cessna 172N Skyhawk II	172-72985	N1283F	24. 6.80	
G-BHUH	Cremer PC.14 HAFB (Toy)	PAC/001		7. 5.80	Canx by CAA 8.12.88.
G-BHUI	Cessna 152 II	152-83144	N46932	27. 5.80	
G-BHUJ	Cessna 172N Skyhawk II	172-71932	N5752E	27. 5.80	
G-BHUK	Rutan Quickie	0271 & PFA/94-10494		3. 6.80	Fatal crash at Kempston, near Bedford on 22.4.81 after mid-air collision with Cessna 152 G-BHMG. Canx.
G-BHUL	Beechcraft E90 King Air	LW-83	N99855 G-BBKM	12. 5.80	Crashed ½ mile northeast of Goodwood on 22.4.85 sustaining substantial damage. Canx by CAA 4.2.87.
G-BHUM	DH.82A Tiger Moth	85453	(G-BHUZ) VT-DGA/VT-DDN/R.Indian AF/South African AF 4622/DE457	9. 6.80	
G-BHUN	PZL-104 Wilga 35	140548		12. 5.80	To ZK-PZN /91. Canx 12.9.91.
G-BHUO	Evans VP-2	PFA/63-10552		12. 5.80	
G-BHUP	Reims Cessna F.152 II	1773		2. 5.80	Damaged in forced landing in a field 1 mile west of Barton on 17.5.89. Canx by CAA 15.2.95. (Fuselage & wings at Stapleford in 5/98)
G-BHUR	Thunder Ax3 Mini Sky Chariot HAFB	277		9. 5.80	
G-BHUS	Beechcraft F90 King Air	LA-80		8. 5.80	To G-KFIT 9/81. Canx.
G-BHUT	Beechcraft F90 King Air	LA-81		8. 5.80	To G-STYR 1/81. Canx.
G-BHUU	PA-25-260 Pawnee D (Originally regd as a PA-25-235)	25-8056035		28. 5.80	
G-BHUV	PA-25-235 Pawnee D	25-8056038		8. 5.80	Damaged in crash at Warboys on 18.7.83 & believed later scrapped. Canx by CAA 11.2.91.
G-BHUW	Boeing-Stearman A75N1 (N2S-5) Kaydet	75-3475	N474 N64639/BuA.30038	16. 5.80	To D-EFTX 4/92. Canx 7.12.83.
G-BHUX	Saffery S.330 HAFB (Toy)	5		. .80R	NTU - To G-BHVE 5/80. Canx 3/81.
G-BHUY	DHC.6-310 Twin Otter	709		. .80R	NTU - Canx 17.9.80 on sale to Canada. To CC-CHV 9/80.
G-BHUZ	DH.82A Tiger Moth	85453	VT-DGA VT-DDN/R.Indian AF/South African AF 4622/DE457	. .80R	NTU - To G-BHUM 6/80. Canx 3/81.
G-BHVA	Cessna 550 Citation II (Unit No.225)	550-0200	N67989	. .80R	NTU - Not Imported. To N34SS. Canx.
G-BHVB	PA-28-161 Warrior II	28-8016260	N9638N	16. 5.80	
G-BHVC	Cessna 172RG Cutlass II	172RG-0550	N5515V	30. 5.80	To N372SA 2/99. Canx 5.2.99.
G-BHVD	Not allocated.				
G-BHVE	Saffery S.330 HAFB (Toy)	5	(G-BHUX)	15. 5.80	Canx by CAA 4.8.98.
G-BHVF	SAN Jodel D.150A Mascaret	11	F-BLDF	28.10.80	
G-BHVG	Boeing 737-2T5 (Line No. 729)	22395	N1787B	10.12.80	To C-GEPM 3/85. Canx 26.2.85.
G-BHVH	Boeing 737-2T5 (Line No. 730)	22396		27. 1.81	Canx 18.10.88 on sale to Ireland. To C-GVRE.
G-BHVI	Boeing 737-2T5 (Line No. 737)	22397	N5701E	17. 3.81	To CC-CJW 4/87. Canx 21.4.87.
G-BHVJ	Short SC.7 Skyvan 3M	SH1972	G-14-140	16. 5.80	To 7Q-YMU 6/80. Canx 26.6.80.
G-BHVK	Short SC.7 Skyvan 3M	SH1973		16. 5.80	To 7Q-YAY 9/80. Canx 23.9.80.
G-BHVL	Short SD.3-30 Var.200-023	SH3048	(G-14-3048)	16. 5.80	NTU - To SX-BGB 6/80. Canx 27.5.80.
G-BHVM	Cessna 152 II	152-81856	N67477	27. 5.80	To G-NALI 8/90. Canx.
G-BHVN	Cessna 152 II	152-83577	N4680B	9. 6.80	Fatal crash at Pebworth, northeast of Evesham on 6.6.96. Canx as destroyed 18.9.96.
G-BHVO	PA-34-200-2 Seneca	34-7250144	SE-FYY	12. 5.80	To G-FLYI 9/81. Canx.
G-BHVP	Cessna 182Q Skylane II	182-67071	N97374	15.12.80	
G-BHVR	Cessna 172N Skyhawk II	172-70196	N738SG	27. 5.80	
G-BHVS	Enstrom F-28A-UK	115	N9586	12. 6.80	Damaged in heavy landing at Shoreham on 15.10.82. Canx as destroyed 26.5.88.
G-BHVT	Boeing 727-212ADV (Line No. 1289)	21349	TI-LRR G-BHVT/TI-LRR/G-BHVT/9V-SGC/(9V-SXC)	3. 6.80	To C-FRYS. Canx 24.11.92.
G-BHVU	Cessna 414A Chancellor	414A-0317	N2686D	24. 6.80	To N53992 6/84. Canx 28.6.84.
G-BHVV	Piper J3C-65 Cub (L-4A-PI) (Frame No 9048; regd with c/n 10291/43-1430 which was F-BEGF; frames probably swopped in 1953 rebuild)	8953	F-BGXF 42-38384	27. 6.80	Permit expired 3.7.85. (Stored at Aboyne in 8/98)
G-BHVW	Thunder Ax3-17-5C Sky Chariot	279		28. 5.80	To F-GCKP 7/80. Canx 14.7.80.
G-BHVX	Beechcraft 200 Super King Air	BB-180	5N-AKR	27. 6.80	To PH-SBK 8/80. Canx 18.8.80.
G-BHVY	American Aviation AA-5B Tiger	AA5B-0845	N28835	1. 5.80	To G-ZARI 3/86. Canx.
G-BHVZ	Cessna 180 Skywagon	180-31691	F-BHMU N4739B	3. 7.80	To N36362 10/96. Canx 21.10.96.
G-BHWA(1)	Reims Cessna F.152 II	1776		. .80R	NTU - To G-BHWB 4/80. Canx.
G-BHWA(2)	Reims Cessna F.152 II	1775		28. 3.80	
G-BHWB	Reims Cessna F.152 II	1776	(G-BHWA)	14. 4.80	
G-BHWC	Not allocated.				
G-BHWD	Hughes 369D (500D)	30-0689D		21. 5.80	To VR-HHT(2) 9/82. Canx 6.9.82.

Regn	Type	c/n	Previous identity	Regn date	Fate or immediate subsequent identity (if known)
G-BHWE	Boeing 737-204ADV (Line No. 696)	22364		30. 7.80	To ZK-NAB. Canx 14.2.94.
G-BHWF	Boeing 737-204ADV (Line No. 700)	22365	N57001	23.10.80	To ZK-NAI 12/93. Canx 16.12.93.
G-BHWG	Saffery Mahatma S.200SR HAFB (Toy)	023		14. 3.80	Canx as WFU 25.3.98.
G-BHWH	Weedhopper JC-24A (Modified to JC-24C standard)	0074		23. 4.80	
G-BHWI	American Aviation AA-5B Tiger	AA5B-1104	N3752E	29. 7.80	To G-JAKK 11/82. Canx.
G-BHWJ	American Aviation AA-5A Cheetah	AA5A-0743	N28623	25. 6.80	To G-LADY 1/82. Canx.
G-BHWK	Socata MS.880B Rallye Club	870	F-BONK	27. 8.80	
G-BHWL	Socata MS.880B Rallye Club	-		. .80R	NTU - Canx 3/81.
G-BHWM	Morane Saulnier MS.880B Rallye Club	28	F-BKDO	18. 8.80	Not certified in UK & dismantled at Yew Tree Farm, Garway. Canx by CAA 4.2.87.
G-BHWN	WMB.3 Windtracker 200 HAFB (Toy)	6		2. 6.80	Canx by CAA 2.12.93.
G-BHWO	WMB.4P Windtracker II HAFB (Toy)	7		2. 6.80	Not built. Canx by CAA 4.2.87.
G-BHWP	American Aviation AA-5B Tiger	AA5B-1172	N4532L	26. 6.80	Hit fence on take-off from Tepletawn, Co.Wexford on 9.6.81. Canx as destroyed 5.12.83.
G-BHWR	American Aviation AA-5A Cheetah	AA5A-0793	N26892	25. 6.80	To G-OMOG 3/88. Canx.
G-BHWS	Reims Cessna F.152 II	1785	(G-BHHD)	16. 6.80	Badly damaged on take-off at Skaw, Isle of Whalsay, Shetlands on 15.7.94. Wreck at Perth/Scone 8/98.
G-BHWT	Short SD.3-30 Var.100	SH3049	N333MV G-BHWT	13. 6.80	Substantially damaged when it struck Viscount 806 G-APIM whilst taxiing at Southend on 11.1.88. Canx as WFU 15.12.88
G-BHWU	Short SD.3-30 Var.100	SH3050		13. 6.80	To YV-373C 8/80. Canx 15.8.80.
G-BHWV	Short SD.3-30 Var.100	SH3051		13. 6.80	To N140CN 7/80. Canx 25.7.80.
G-BHWW	Cessna U.206G Stationair 6	U206G-03573	PH-MER N7234N	5. 6.80	To 5Y-BIT 9/93. Canx 13.9.93.
G-BHWX	Cessna 404 Titan	404-0009	(G-BHSR) N3937C	1.12.80	To N2701U 11/81. Canx 20.11.81.
G-BHWY	PA-28R-200 Cherokee Arrow II	28R-7435059	N56904	17. 6.80	
G-BHWZ	PA-28-181 Archer II	28-7890299	N3379M	8. 4.80	
G-BHXA	Scottish Avn Bulldog 120/1210	BH120-407	"G-BHZR" Botswana DF OD2/G-BHXA	9. 6.80	(Stored 3/98 Liverpool)
G-BHXB	Scottish Avn Bulldog 120/1210	BH120-408	OD1 Botswana DF/G-BHXB	9. 6.80	
G-BHXC	Rockwell Commander 112TC-A	13258	N1005C	4. 6.80	To G-GRIF 10/81. Canx.
G-BHXD	Wassmer Jodel D.120 Paris-Nice	258	F-BMIA	3. 7.80	
G-BHXE	Thunder Ax3-17 Sky Chariot HAFB	280		13. 6.80	To VH-HXE 5/88. Canx 18.2.88.
G-BHXF	North American AT-6C Harvard IIA	88-10677	G-RBAC FAP 1522/South African AF 7244/EX584/41-33557	. 6.80R	NTU - To G-VALE 9/80. Canx.
G-BHXG	DHC.6-310 Twin Otter	694	(G-BHTO)	8. 7.80	To PH-STG 8/85. Canx 22.8.85.
G-BHXH	PBN BN-2B-21 Islander	2024	"G-BHXI"	16. 6.80	To N409JA 11/80. Canx 23.3.81.
G-BHXI	PBN BN-2B-26 Islander	2025		16. 6.80	To G-UERN 6/85. Canx.
"G-BHXI"	PBN BN-2B-21 Islander	2024		----	NTU - Painted in error - To G-BHXH 6/80. Canx.
G-BHXJ	Nord 1203-2 Norecrin II	103	F-BEMX	23.10.80	Stalled and crashed on take-off from Compton Abbas on 9.4.89. Canx as WFU 15.6.89.
G-BHXK	PA-28-140 Cherokee	28-21106	VR-HGB 9V-BAJ/(9M-AOM)	14. 7.80	
G-BHXL	Evans VP-2	1 & PFA/63-10520		17. 6.80	
G-BHXM	Electraflyer Eagle	1		18. 6.80	Sold to Breen Aviation for use as a static trainer. Canx as PWFU 30.9.81.
G-BHXN	Van's RV-3	EAA/105098 & PFA/99-10518		9. 6.80	Canx by CAA 2.9.91. (On rebuild 4/99 Bourn)
G-BHXO	Colt 14A Cloudhopper HAFB (Originally regd as a 12A model)	089		19. 6.80	Canx 2.7.90 on sale to Canada.
G-BHXP	Aeronca 15AC Sedan	15AC-226	EI-BJJ N1214H	. .80R	NTU - Not Imported. Remained as EI-BJJ. Canx 3/81.
G-BHXR	Thunder Ax7-65 Bolt HAFB	282		25. 6.80	Canx by CAA 2.12.86. To CX-BRQ.
G-BHXS	Wassmer Jodel D.120 Paris-Nice	133	F-BIXS	27. 8.80	
G-BHXT	Thunder Ax6-56Z HAFB	281		2. 7.80	Canx by CAA 19.5.93. (Active 2/97)
G-BHXU	Agusta-Bell 206B JetRanger III	8595		17. 7.80	Ditched in sea 14 nm N of Alderney on 29.6.95. Helicopter later sank. Canx as destroyed 28.7.95.
G-BHXV	Agusta-Bell 206B JetRanger III	8596	G-OWJM G-BHXV	17. 7.80	To G-BYBA 3/98. Canx.
G-BHXW	Agusta-Bell 206B JetRanger III	8598		17. 7.80	To G-ESAL 11/80. Canx.
G-BHXX	PA-23-250 Aztec E	27-7305101	(G-BHSR) OY-DGZ/N40286	6. 6.80	DBR when it landed short of the runway at Lydd on 11.5.86. Canx as WFU 23.9.86.
G-BHXY	Piper J3C-65 Cub (L-4H-PI) (Frame No. 11733)	11905	D-EAXY F-BFQX/44-79609	1. 7.80	
G-BHXZ	Ayres S2R-R3S Thrush Commander	R3S-006	N4016V	. .80R	NTU - To G-BJWF 2/82. Canx.
G-BHYA	Cessna R.182 Skylane RG II	R182-00532	N1717R	10. 7.80	
G-BHYB	Sikorsky S-76A	760079		29. 7.80	To C-GIMR 9/93. Canx 16.9.93.
G-BHYC	Cessna 172RG Cutlass II	172RG-0404	(N4868V)	24. 6.80	
G-BHYD	Cessna R.172K Hawk XP II	R172-2734	N736RS	11.12.80	
G-BHYE	PA-34-200T Seneca II	34-8070233	N8225U	27. 6.80	
G-BHYF	PA-34-200T Seneca II	34-8070234	N8225V	27. 6.80	
G-BHYG	PA-34-200T Seneca II	34-8070235	N8225X	30. 6.80	

Regn	Type	c/n	Previous identity	Regn date	Fate or immediate subsequent identity (if known)
G-BHYH	Aerospatiale AS.350B Ecureuil	1302		. .80R	NTU - Canx 19.12.80 as Not Imported. To F-GCVD 1/81.
G-BHYI	SNCAN Stampe SV-4A	18	F-BAAF(2) French Mil	11. 7.80	
G-BHYJ	Short SD.3-30 Var.100	SH3052	G-14-3052	27. 6.80	To N304CA 8/80. Canx 14.8.80.
G-BHYK	Short SD.3-30 Var.100	SH3053	G-14-3053	27. 6.80	To N847SA 8/80. Canx 21.8.80.
G-BHYL	Short SD.3-30 Var.100	SH3054	G-14-3054	27. 6.80	To YV-374C 9/80. Canx.
G-BHYM	Short SD.3-30 Var.100	SH3055	G-14-3055	27. 6.80	To N141CN 8/80. Canx 26.8.80.
G-BHYN	Evans VP-2	PFA/63-10571		4. 7.80	No CofA issued. Canx by CAA 1.4.97.
G-BHYO	Cameron N-77 HAFB	659		30. 6.80	
G-BHYP	Reims Cessna F.172M Skyhawk II	1108	OY-BFR	30. 6.80	
G-BHYR	Reims Cessna F.172M Skyhawk II	0922	OY-DZH SE-FZH/(OH-CFQ)	30. 6.80	
G-BHYS	PA-28-181 Archer II	28-8090319	N8218Y	30. 6.80	Badly damaged on landing in scrubland short of the runway at Biggin Hill on 7.12.85. Canx as WFU 24.6.86. (Wreck in open storage 8/97)
G-BHYT	Embraer EMB.110P2 Bandeirante	110-277	PT-SBN	30. 7.80	To C-GHOY 1/85. Canx 10.1.85.
G-BHYU	Beechcraft A200 Super King Air	BB-756		2. 7.80	To LN-KOB 7/85. Canx 11.7.85.
G-BHYV	Evans VP-1	LC.2 & PFA/1569		2. 7.80	(Flown 5/89; stored Squires Gate 8/90 - status uncertain)
G-BHYW	Agusta-Bell 206B JetRanger (Originally 206A, later modified)	8043	SE-HBM	16. 7.80	Destroyed in fatal crash in a mid-air collision with an RAF Tornado 1 mile east of Farleton, Cumbria on 23.6.93. Canx as destroyed 18.11.93.
G-BHYX	Cessna 152 II	152-81832	N67434	4. 7.80	
G-BHYY	PA-28-161 Warrior II	28-8016261	N9639N	8. 7.80	To G-ESSX 7/82. Canx.
G-BHYZ	Cameron V-77 HAFB	661		30. 6.80	To N362CB 7/81. Canx 10.7.81.
G-BHZA	Piper J3C-65 Cub (L-4H-PI) (Frame No.11883)	11876	F-BBIN 44-79580	5. 8.80	Permit expired 24.2.84. Canx by CAA 3.4.89.
G-BHZB	AIA Stampe SV-4C	1133	N17SV F-BALL(2)	. .80R	NTU - To ZS-VPM 6/86. Canx.
G-BHZC	Rockwell 690C Commander 840	11602	N840R (N5853K)	8. 9.80	To N2647C 2/82. Canx 1.2.82.
G-BHZD	PA-38-112 Tomahawk	38-80A0117	N25381	2. 4.81	To SX-ALE 8/84. Canx 26.7.84.
G-BHZE	PA-28-181 Archer II	28-7890291	OO-FLR (OO-HEM)/N3053M	4.11.80	
G-BHZF	Evans VP-2	PFA/63-10509		9. 7.80	Badly damaged on take-off near Swansea on 3.7.93. Permit expired 30.3.94.
G-BHZG	Monnett Sonerai II (PFA c/n could also be PFA/15-10198 or aircraft a combination of both!)	409 & PFA/15-10278		9. 7.80	The canopy opened and aircraft crashed into a field soon after take-off at Shoreham on 29.8.88. Canx as destroyed 15.12.88.
G-BHZH	Reims Cessna F.152 II	1786		25. 7.80	
G-BHZI	Thunder Ax3 Sky Chariot HAFB	287		17. 7.80	Canx as WFU 3.8.84.
G-BHZJ	Hughes Strato Sphere 150 HAFB (Toy)	PJH-150-02		18. 7.80	Canx by CAA 12.12.88.
G-BHZK	American Aviation AA-5B Tiger	AA5B-0743	N28670	8. 9.80	
G-BHZL	American Aviation AA-5A Cheetah	AA5A-0542	N26357	11. 9.80	Crashed into woodland at Slades Farm shortly after take-off from Elstree on 5.2.85. Canx as destroyed 26.7.85.
G-BHZM	CEA Jodel DR.1050 Ambassadeur	264	F-BJYZ	9. 9.80	CofA expired 4.7.85. Canx as WFU 12.1.89.
G-BHZN	American Aviation AA-5B Tiger	AA5B-1179	N37519	23. 7.80	To G-GAJB 4/87. Canx.
G-BHZO	American Aviation AA-5A Cheetah	AA5A-0692	N26750	21. 7.80	
G-BHZP	Scottish Avn Bulldog Srs.120/1210	BH120-409	G-31-33	23. 7.80	To Botswana DF as OD3 in 10/80. Canx 8.10.80.
G-BHZR	Scottish Avn Bulldog Srs.120/1210	BH120-410	"G-BHZS" Botswana DF OD4/G-BHZR	23. 7.80	CofA expired 7.10.80. (Stored 8/97)
G-BHZS	Scottish Avn Bulldog Srs.120/1210	BH120-411	"G-BHXA" Botswana DF OD5/G-BHZS	23. 7.80	
G-BHZT	Scottish Avn Bulldog Srs.120/1210	BH120-412	OD6 Botswana DF/G-BHZT	23. 7.80	
G-BHZU	Piper J3C-65 Cub (L-4B-PI) (Regd with Frame No 9606 which was fitted to F-BETO in 1961 rebuild replacing c/n 13164 ex 45-4424)	9775	F-BETO (F-BFKH)/43-914	17. 7.80	
G-BHZV	Wassmer Jodel D.120A Paris-Nice	278	F-BMON	23. 7.80	
G-BHZW	Auster J/2 Arrow	2370	5Y-KHD VP-KHD/VP-UAO	. .80R	NTU - To G-BJTC 2/82. Canx.
G-BHZX	Thunder Ax7-69A HAFB	288		25. 7.80	
G-BHZY	Monnett Sonerai II	648 & PFA/15-10585		29. 7.80	No Permit issued. Canx as WFU 25.7.91.
G-BHZZ	Air-Britain Manchester Eagle 8 HAFB (Toy)	MAN.1		23. 6.80	Canx as WFU 2.9.83.
G-BIAA	Socata TB-9 Tampico	141		17. 7.80	To EI-GFC 10/93. Canx 27.9.93.
G-BIAB	Socata TB-9 Tampico	142		17. 7.80	Damaged in forced-landing near Halfpenny Green on 6.8.93. Canx by CAA 10.2.94.
G-BIAC	Socata MS.894E Rallye Minerva 235GT	13323		17. 7.80	
G-BIAD	BAe 146 Srs.100	E1001		28. 7.80	NTU - To G-SSSH 3/81. Canx.
G-BIAE	BAe 146 Srs.100	E1002		28. 7.80	NTU - To G-SSHH 5/81. Canx.
G-BIAF	BAe 146 Srs.100	E1003		28. 7.80	NTU - To G-SSCH 5/81. Canx.
G-BIAG	BAe 146 Srs.100	E1004		28. 7.80	NTU - To (G-SCHH)/G-OBAF 5/81. Canx.
G-BIAH	Wassmer Jodel D.112	1218	F-BMAH	20. 8.80	
G-BIAI	WMB.2 Windtracker HAFB (Toy)	008		1. 7.80	

Regn	Type	c/n	Previous identity	Regn date	Fate or immediate subsequent identity (if known)
G-BIAJ	BAe 146 Srs.100	E1005		28. 7.80	NTU - To G-SCHH 5/81. Canx.
G-BIAK	Socata TB-10 Tobago	150		17. 7.80	
G-BIAL	Rango NA.8 Super HAFB (Toy)	AL.9		28. 7.80	
G-BIAM	Socata TB-10 Tobago	144		15. 7.80	Fatal crash near Le Touquet, France on 22.4.83.
					Canx as destroyed 5.12.83.
G-BIAN	American Aviation AA-5B Tiger		G-BGCI	12. 6.79	Crashed in the Swiss Alps on 3.8.79. Canx.
		AA5B-1050			
G-BIAO	Evans VP-2	V2-1005 & PFA/7202		28. 7.80	CofA issued 15.2.90. Canx by CAA 3.4.97.
G-BIAP	PA-16-108 Clipper	16-732	F-BBGM(2)	25. 6.80	
			F-OAGS		
G-BIAR	Rigg Skyliner II HAFB (Toy)			9. 7.80	
		AKC-59 & IAR/02			
G-BIAS	Douglas DC-8-55F	45816	N804SW	8. 2.78	Restored as N804SW 1/81. Canx 21.1.81.
	(Line No. 236)		YV-C-VIM/N804SW		
G-BIAT	Sopwith Pup Replica	EMK/001		3.12.82	Canx 9.8.89 on sale to Australia. To New Zealand marked
					as "N6160".
G-BIAU	Sopwith Pup Replica	EMK/002		4. 1.83	Permit expired 13.9.89. (On display 3/96 RNAS Yeovilton)
					Canx as WFU 10.3.97.
G-BIAV	Sikorsky S-76A	760110		27.11.80	To C-GIMN. Canx 9.9.92.
G-BIAW	Sikorsky S-76A	760111		27.11.80	To C-GIMB. Canx 2.9.92.
G-BIAX	Taylor JT.2 Titch	GFR-1 & PFA/3228		30. 7.80	(Nearing completion 9/97)
G-BIAY	American Aviation AA-5 Traveler		OY-GAD	26. 8.80	
		AA5-0423	N7123L		
G-BIAZ	Cameron AT-165 (Helium/Hot-Air Free			7. 2.78	HAFB part destroyed on mountain near Trubenbuch, Austria on
	Balloon)	400			14.1.80. Canx as destroyed 27.5.80. (Inner helium cell
	(Used for 1978 Atlantic attempt)				envelope held by British Balloon Museum, Newbury)
G-BIBA	Socata TB-9 Tampico	149		17. 7.80	
G-BIBB	Mooney M.20C Super 21	2803	OH-MOD	22. 7.80	
G-BIBC	Cessna 310R II	310R-2106	N6830X	29.10.80	To N1203W 9/96. Canx 6.9.96.
G-BIBD	Rotec Rally 2B	1175-0		7. 8.80	Canx by CAA 27.6.90.
G-BIBE	Embraer EMB.110P1 Bandeirante		N193PB	24. 9.80	To SE-IYZ 10/87. Canx 16.10.87.
		110-288	G-BIBE/PT-SBX		
G-BIBF	Smith A.12 Sport HAFB (Toy)	001		1. 8.80	Canx by CAA 13.12.88.
G-BIBG	Sikorsky S-76A II Plus	760083		18. 8.80	
G-BIBH	Not allocated.				
G-BIBI	Socata TB-10 Tobago	151		17. 7.80	To G-SONA 10/80. Canx.
G-BIBJ	Enstrom 280C-UK-2 Shark	1187		13. 8.80	
G-BIBK	Taylor JT.2 Titch	PFA/3233		12. 8.80	(Near complete 11/89) No CofA or Permit issued.
					Canx by CAA 17.3.99. To G-RKET 8/99.
G-BIBL	Taylor JT.2 Titch	PFA/3232		12. 8.80	No Permit to Fly issued. Canx by CAA 12.8.85.
	(Also allocated PFA c/n's PFA/5442 and PFA/60-10143)				
G-BIBM	American Aviation AA-5A Cheetah		N26857	4. 9.80	Crashed at East Kimber Farm, Okehampton on 13.9.84 & DBF.
		AA5A-0771			Canx by CAA 4.2.87.
G-BIBN	Reims Cessna FA.150K Aerobat	0078	F-BSHN	29.10.80	
G-BIBO	Cameron V-65 HAFB	667		7. 8.80	
G-BIBP	American Aviation AA-5A Cheetah		N26905	22. 8.80	CofA expired 10.11.92. Canx by CAA 2.4.97 as destroyed.
		AA5A-0801			
G-BIBR	American Aviation AA-5A Cheetah		N26879	. .80R	NTU - To (G-BICU)/G-BIFF 9/80. Canx.
		AA5A-0781			
G-BIBS	Cameron P-20 HAFB	671		14. 8.80	
G-BIBT	American Aviation AA-5B Tiger		N4518V	8. 9.80	
		AA5B-1047			
G-BIBU	Morris Ax7-77 HAFB	KM8G-001		18. 8.80	Canx by CAA 19.5.93.
G-BIBV	WMB.2 Windtracker HAFB (Toy)	10		18. 8.80	Canx as WFU 19.10.93.
G-BIBW	Reims Cessna F.172N Skyhawk II	1756		13.10.78	
G-BIBX	WMB.2 Windtracker HAFB (Toy)	9		18. 8.80	
G-BIBY	Beechcraft F.33A Bonanza	CE-906	N67578	26. 8.80	To N300TT 7/98. Canx 3.7.98.
G-BIBZ	Thunder Ax3 Maxi Sky Chariot HAFB			19. 8.80	Canx as WFU 13.9.94.
		290			
G-BICA	ICA-Brasov IS.28M2	09		. .80R	NTU - Canx.
	(Marks reserved for this type. C/n unconfirmed but believed to be the example which was exhibited at Farnborough as G-7-100 in 1978. G-BICA was recorded in Lloyds Casualty Reports for this type of aircraft although never registered officially)				
G-BICB	Rotec Rally 2B	1176-0		19. 8.80	No Permit issued. Canx by CAA 3.2.92.
G-BICC	Vulture Tx3 HAFB (Toy)	CC.1		31. 7.80	
G-BICD	Taylorcraft Auster 5	735	F-BFXH(2)	20. 8.80	
			MT166		
G-BICE	North American AT-6C-1NT Harvard		1545	3. 9.80	
	IIA	88-9755	Portuguese AF/South African AF 7084/EX302/41-33275		
G-BICF	Gulfstream-American GA-7 Cougar		N8500H	16. 9.80	To G-OCAB 5/86. Canx.
		GA7-0107	N29707		
G-BICG	Reims Cessna F.152 II	1796		3. 9.80	
G-BICH	WMB.2 Windtracker HAFB (Toy)	11		10. 9.80	NTU - To G-RDON 9/81. Canx.
G-BICI	Cameron R-833 HAFB	700		3. 8.81	Canx as WFU 15.11.89.
G-BICJ	Monnett Sonerai II			22. 8.80	(On rebuild .97)
		726 & PFA/15-10531			
G-BICK	HS.748 Srs.2B/FAA	1782	G-11-782	27. 8.80	To C-GHSF 4/95. Canx 3.3.95.
			CS-TAP/G-11-3/N748AV/G-BICK		
G-BICL	Cessna 425 Conquest I	425-0054	(N6776P)	. .80R	NTU - To G-NORC 3/81. Canx.
G-BICM	Colt 56A HAFB	095		1. 9.80	
G-BICN	Sequoia Falco F.8L			3. 9.80	No Permit to Fly issued. Canx as PWFU 12.4.99.
		PU-001-2 & PFA/100-10563			
G-BICO	Neale Mitefly HAFB (Toy)	NM-001		5. 9.80	Canx by CAA 2.11.88.

Regn	Type	c/n	Previous identity	Regn date	Fate or immediate subsequent identity (if known)
G-BICP	CEA Robin DR.360 Chevalier	610	F-BSPH	2.10.80	
G-BICR	Wassmer Jodel D.120A Paris-Nice	135	F-BIXR	5. 9.80	
G-BICS	Robin R.2100A Club	128	F-GBAC	4.12.80	
G-BICT	Evans VP-1	PFA/62-10455		12. 8.80	Damaged in forced landing near Evesham on 4.8.96. Permit expired 20.2.97.
G-BICU(1)	American Aviation AA-5A Cheetah	AA5A-0781	(G-BIBR) N26879	. .80R	NTU - To G-BIFF 9/80. Canx.
G-BICU(2)	Cameron V-56 HAFB	680		9. 9.80	
G-BICV	Boeing 737-2L9	21528	OY-API	31.10.80	To C6-BEX 11/83. Canx 6.11.83.
	(Line No. 517)				
G-BICW	PA-28-161 Warrior II	28-7916309	N2091U	8.10.80	
G-BICX	Maule M.5-235C Lunar Rocket	7287C	(G-MAUL) N56352	2. 2.81	
G-BICY	PA-23-160 Apache	23-1640	OO-AOL	26. 9.80	
			5N-ACL/VR-NDF/PH-ACL/N4010P		
G-BICZ	Hill Hummer	JS.1		9. 9.80	NTU - Not Imported. Canx.
G-BIDA	Socata MS.880B Rallye 100ST	3041		11. 9.80	To LN-BDU 11/87. Canx 10.9.87.
G-BIDB	BAC 167 Strikemaster Mk.89	PS.367	(SudanAF)	15. 9.80	Canx 11.8.87 as transferred to MOD. To ZG621/Ecuador AF
	(Originally regd as Mk.90)		G-BIDB/G-16-26		as T-59.
G-BIDC	Bell 212	30790	N142AL	17.10.80	To EC-DQD 2/82. Canx 25.1.82.
G-BIDD	Evans VP-1	PFA/62-10974		27.10.78	
	(Initially regd with c/n PFA/62-10167 and combined both projects)				
G-BIDE	Piel CP.301A Emeraude	PFA/50-10566		3. 9.80	This project was to have included parts of CP.301B G-ASDW but no Permit has been issued and it is believed to have been destroyed while under construction. Canx as destroyed 6.10.95.
G-BIDF	Reims Cessna F.172P Skyhawk II	2045	(PH-JPO)	18. 9.80	
G-BIDG	SAN Jodel D.150A Mascaret	08	F-BLDG	11. 9.80	
G-BIDH	Cessna 152 II	152-80546	G-DONA	12. 9.80	
			G-BIDH/N25234		
G-BIDI	PA-28R-201 Cherokee Arrow III	28R-7837135	N3759M	11.11.80	
G-BIDJ	PA-18A-150 Super Cub	18-6007	PH-MAY	22. 9.80	
	(Frame No. 18-6089)		N7798D		
G-BIDK	PA-18-150 Super Cub	"18-6591"	PH-MAI	22. 9.80	
	(L-21A-PI)		R.Netherlands AF R-211/51-15679/N7194K		
	(Composite aircraft. PH-MAI was originally c/n 18-6591 (F.No. 18-6714) ex LN-TVB/N9285D but was rebuilt 1976 using frame no. 18-503 which was c/n 18-565 and ex R.Neth AF R-211 as shown)				
G-BIDL	Osprey Mk.1G HAFB (Toy)	AKC.70		15.10.81	Canx as WFU 2.6.83.
G-BIDM	Reims Cessna F.172H	0622	SE-FMM	24. 9.80	Damaged by gales in 3/90 and stored at Ingoldmells. Canx by CAA 10.6.92.
G-BIDN	Hunting Percival P.57 Sea Prince T.1	P57/31	WF133	22. 9.80	To N57AW 10/84. Canx 13.11.84.
	(Originally regd with c/n P57/27)				
G-BIDO	Piel Claude CP.301A Emeraude	327	F-POIO	25. 3.81	Permit expired 24.6.97. (Stored 9/97)
G-BIDP	PA-28-181 Cherokee Archer II	28-7890043	N49956	13. 1.81	To D-ETDP 10/95. Canx 29.8.95.
G-BIDR	DHC.6-310 Twin Otter	725	C-GDOX	. .80R	NTU - Not Imported. To LN-WFF. Canx.
G-BIDS	Socata MS.880B Rallye Club	1277	F-BSTJ	. .80R	NTU - To EI-BMH 2/82. Canx.
	(Regn was used unofficially)				
G-BIDT	Cameron A-375 HAFB	686		29. 9.80	Ditched in Jurien Bay, Western Australia on 28.9.82 and abandoned. Canx as destroyed 22.8.89.
G-BIDU	Cameron V-77 HAFB	660		8. 1.81	
G-BIDV	Colt 17A Cloudhopper HAFB	789		29. 1.79	Canx by CAA 20.5.93. (To British Balloon Museum)
	(Second canopy - originally Colt 14A c/n 034)(Museum possibly has first canopy)				
G-BIDW	Sopwith "One and a Half" Strutter Replica	WA/5	"9382"	24. 9.80	Test Permit expired 29.12.80. Canx by CAA 4.2.87. (On display 10/95 Hendon)
G-BIDX	Dormois Jodel D.112	876	F-BIQY	19. 9.80	
G-BIDY	WMB.2 Windtracker HAFB (Toy)	13		16. 9.80	Canx by CAA 2.12.93.
G-BIDZ	Colt 21A HAFB	094		26. 9.80	Canx as WFU 9.1.90.
G-BIEA	PA-28RT-201T Turbo Arrow IV	28R-8018066	N8198V	18. 9.80	To G-TYPE 17.10.80. Canx.
G-BIEB	Agusta-Bell 47G-3B1	1577	HB-XHS XT111	26. 9.80	To 5B-CFU 1/84. Canx 13.12.83.
G-BIEC	Agusta-Bell 206B JetRanger II	8308	HB-XDP	26. 9.80	No UK CofA issued. (Derelict at Thruxton in 6/84) Canx by CAA 20.12.90.
G-BIED	Beechcraft F90 King Air	LA-100		23. 9.80	To HB-GHP 7/87. Canx 9.7.87.
G-BIEE	Beechcraft 65-C90 King Air	LJ-944		23. 9.80	To G-PTER 1/82. Canx.
G-BIEF	Cameron V-77 HAFB	679		25. 9.80	
G-BIEG	PA-32-301 Saratoga	32-8006028	N81852	9.10.80	To G-TOGA 11/82. Canx.
G-BIEH	Sikorsky S-76A (Mod)	760135		27.11.80	To VH-LAX(2). Canx 8.12.93.
G-BIEI	DHC.6-310 Twin Otter	720		10.10.80	To 9M-SSH 11/80. Canx 20.11.80.
G-BIEJ	Sikorsky S-76A II Plus	760097		21.10.80	
G-BIEK	WMB.4 Windtracker HAFB (Toy)	15		26. 9.80	Canx by CAA 19.10.93.
G-BIEL	WMB.4 Windtracker HAFB (Toy)	16		26. 9.80	Canx as WFU 18.10.88.
G-BIEM	DHC.6-310 Twin Otter	732	(8P-...) G-BIEM	26. 9.80	To C-GKBH. Canx 20.4.90.
G-BIEN	Wassmer Jodel D.120A Paris-Nice	218	F-BKNK	3. 6.81	Canx by CAA 27.8.99.
G-BIEO	Wassmer Jodel D.112	1296	F-BMOK	19. 3.82	
G-BIEP	PA-28-181 Cherokee Archer II	28-7790542	EI-BLK	20.11.80	Damaged in gales at Denham on 25.1.90.
			G-BIEP/N38342		Canx as destroyed 13.4.92.
G-BIER	Rutan LongEze	00314 & PFA/74A-10560		25. 9.80	Canx by CAA 2.9.91.

Regn	Type	c/n	Previous identity	Regn date	Fate or immediate subsequent identity (if known)
G-BIES	Maule M.5-235C Lunar Rocket	7334C	N56394	24. 7.81	
G-BIET	Cameron O-77 HAFB	674		30. 9.80	
G-BIEU	American Aviation AA-5A Cheetah	AA5A-0754	N26836	10.10.80	To G-COPY 3/82. Canx.
G-BIEV	American Aviation AA-5A Cheetah	AA5A-0803	N26906	6.10.80	Destroyed in a heavy landing at Denham on 15.11.85. Canx as destroyed 12.10.88.
G-BIEW	Cessna U.206G Stationair 6 (Reims c/n 0018)	U206-05431	(N6332U)	3. 3.80	Canx as destroyed 29.8.89.
G-BIEX	Andreasson BA-4B	PFA/38-10508		2. 1.81	Badly damaged in crash at Snape Mires on 20.4.84. Canx as destroyed 13.3.89.
G-BIEY	PA-28-151 Cherokee Warrior	28-7715213	PH-KDH OO-HCB	10.11.80	
G-BIEZ	Beechcraft F90 King Air	LA-111		8.10.80	To HB-GHO 1/87. Canx 23.1.87.
G-BIFA	Cessna 310R II	310R-1606	N36868	29. 1.81	
G-BIFB	PA-28-150 Cherokee C	28-1968	4X-AEC	6.10.80	
G-BIFC	Colt 14A HAFB	064		3.10.80	(Based in Texas, USA) Canx by CAA 3.6.91.
G-BIFD	Rockwell Commander 114	14233	SE-GSG	6. 2.81	Crashed on take-off from a strip at Wood Farm, Emberton, Bucks on 17.7.90. Canx.
G-BIFE	Cessna A.185F Skywagon II	185-04024	N6325E	27.10.80	To F-GEFO 1/87. Canx 7.1.86.
G-BIFF	American Aviation AA-5A Cheetah	AA5A-0781	(G-BICU) (G-BIBR)/N26879	1. 9.80	To G-RATE 6/84. Canx.
G-BIFG	Short SD.3-30 Var.100	SH3056	G-14-3056	2.10.80	To LV-OJG 11/80. Canx 20.11.80.
G-BIFH	Short SD.3-30 Var.100	SH3057	N488NS LV-OJH/G-BIFH/G-14-3057	2.10.80	To G-IOCS 7/96. Canx.
G-BIFI	Short SD.3-30 Var.100	SH3058	G-14-3058	2.10.80	To N848SA 11/80. Canx 14.11.80.
G-BIFJ	Short SD.3-30 Var.100	SH3059	G-14-3059	2.10.80	To N54DD 11/80. Canx 28.11.80.
G-BIFK	Short SD.3-30 Var.100	SH3060	N58MM G-BIFK/VH-KNN/G-BIFK/G-14-3060	2.10.80	To DQ-FIJ 8/95. Canx 17.8.95.
G-BIFL	Short SC.7 Skyvan 3M-300	SH1974		2.10.80	To 8R-GFK 3/81. Canx 5.12.83.
G-BIFM	SAN Jodel D.150 Mascaret	13	F-BLDH	. .80R	NTU - To G-BIFV 10/80. Canx.
G-BIFN	Bensen B.8MR Gyrocopter	KW.1 & G/01-1010		7.10.80	
G-BIFO	Evans VP-1	PFA/62-10411		29. 9.80	
G-BIFP	Colt 56C HAFB	097		14.10.80	Canx by CAA 19.5.93.
G-BIFR	Not allocated.				
G-BIFS	Beechcraft C90 King Air	LJ-636	N60JE N60JT/N1899	14.11.80	To N222BJ 4/83. Canx 12.4.83.
G-BIFT	Reims Cessna F.150L	0826	PH-CEW	9.10.80	To G-FINA 10/93. Canx.
G-BIFU	Short Skyhawk HAFB (Toy)	DKS-001		30. 9.80	Canx as WFU 4.11.88.
G-BIFV	SAN Jodel D.150 Mascaret	13	(G-BIFM) F-BLDH	16.10.80	Canx as destroyed 25.10.93.
G-BIFW	Scruggs BL.2 Wunda Balloon (Toy)	80207		14.10.80	Canx by CAA 15.12.88.
G-BIFX	Westland WG.13 Lynx Mk.86	WA/207		14.10.80	To R.Norwegian AF as 207 in 6/81. Canx 23.6.81.
G-BIFY	Reims Cessna F.150L	0829	PH-CEZ	9.10.80	
G-BIFZ	Partenavia P.68C Victor	229		24. 6.81	
G-BIGA	Short SD.3-30 Var.100	SH3061	G-14-3061	14.10.80	To (YV-375C)/VH-KNO 6/81. Canx 1.6.81.
G-BIGB	Bell 212	30853	EI-BRE G-BIGB/ZS-HHU/A2-ACJ/ZS-HHU/N16831	15.10.80	To C-GVIM. Canx 23.11.88.
G-BIGC	Cameron O-42 HAFB	688		19.12.80	To VH-HHZ 9/87. Canx 28.8.87.
G-BIGD	Cameron V-77 HAFB	676		26. 8.80	Canx by CAA 19.5.93.
G-BIGE	Foster Champion Cloudseeker Captive Balloon (Toy)	AF/CB.001		14.10.80	Canx by CAA 8.12.88.
G-BIGF	Thunder Ax7-77 Bolt HAFB	295		20.10.80	
G-BIGG	Saffery S.200 HAFB (Toy)	17		20.10.80	Canx by CAA 13.12.88.
G-BIGH	Piper J3C-65 Cub	12052	F-BFQV OO-GAS/OO-GAZ/44-79756	26. 2.81	Permit expired 10.3.87. Canx by CAA 12.8.94. To EI-CPP 3/98.
G-BIGI	Mooney M.20J (201)	24-0012	C-GMWJ N201TK	26.11.80	To 4X-ARM 7/87. Canx 12.6.87.
G-BIGJ	Reims Cessna F.172M	0936	PH-SKT	2.12.80	
G-BIGK	Taylorcraft BC-12D	8302	N96002 NC96002	29.10.80	Permit expired 19.7.99. Canx by CAA 16.8.99.
G-BIGL	Cameron O-65 HAFB	690		22.10.80	
G-BIGM	Avenger T.200-2112 HAFB (Toy)	MM.3		6.10.80	Canx by CAA 4.8.98.
G-BIGN	Nettleship Attic Srs.1 HAFB (Toy)	001		6.10.80	Canx by CAA 2.12.93.
G-BIGO	Agusta-Bell 206B JetRanger III	8608		31.12.80	To G-SPEY 4/81. Canx.
G-BIGP	Bensen B.8M Gyrocopter	RHSC.1 & G/01-1005		14.10.80	
G-BIGR	Avenger T.200-2122 HAFB (Toy)	004		6.10.80	
G-BIGS	Agusta-Bell 206B JetRanger III	8614		31.12.80	To EI-BLG 7/81. Canx 6.7.81.
G-BIGT	Colt 77A HAFB	078		28. 2.80	Badly damaged by fire at Belton Hall, near Grantham on 23.8.81. Canx by CAA 4.2.87. (Remains stored British Balloon Museum)
G-BIGU	Bensen B.8M Gyrocopter	JRM.1 & G/01-1032		5.11.80	Canx by CAA 9.8.91.
G-BIGV	American Aviation AA-5B Tiger	AA5B-1223	N4556D	27.10.80	Crashed in the Ochil Hills, 9 miles south by southwest of Perth on 26.2.81 & DBF. Canx as destroyed 5.12.83.
G-BIGW	Westland WG.13 Lynx Mk.86	WA/216		22.10.80	To R.Norwegian AF as 216 in 6/81. Canx 23.6.81.
G-BIGX	Bensen B.8M Gyrocopter	JRM.2 & G/01-1033		5.11.80	
G-BIGY	Cameron V-65 HAFB	655		4. 9.80	Canx by CAA 3.6.98.
G-BIGZ	Scheibe SF-25B Falke	46142	D-KCAI	22.12.80	

Regn	Type	c/n	Previous identity	Regn date	Fate or immediate subsequent identity (if known)
G-BIHA	Cessna 172M Skyhawk II	172-66854	N1125U	. .80R	NTU - To G-BIHI 11/80. Canx.
G-BIHB	Scruggs BL-2 Wunda Balloon (Toy)	80203		24.10.80	Canx by CAA 13.12.88.
G-BIHC	Scruggs BL-2 Wunda Balloon (Toy)	80204		24.10.80	Canx as WFU 1.11.88.
G-BIHD	Robin DR.400/160 Major 80	1510		29.10.80	
G-BIHE	Reims Cessna FA.152 Aerobat	0373		6.11.80	Force landed and overturned in a field near Sheerness on 10.3.99. Canx as destroyed 21.7.99.
G-BIHF	Replica Plans SE.5A (Plans No. 079275)	PFA/20-10548		27.10.80	
G-BIHG	PA-28-140 Cherokee	28-24376	OO-JAR N6686J	25.11.80	
G-BIHH	Sikorsky S-61N Mk.II	61-716	9M-SSK G-BIHH/OY-HBE	3.11.80	To ZS-RDV 9/93. Canx 2.9.93.
G-BIHI	Cessna 172M Skyhawk II	172-66854	(G-BIHA) N1125U	18.11.80	
G-BIHJ	Westland WG.13 Lynx Mk.88	WA/220	G-17-25	27.10.80	To West German Navy as 83+01 in 9/81. Canx 28.9.81.
G-BIHK	Westland WG.13 Lynx Mk.88	WA/223		27.10.80	To West German Navy as 83+02 in 9/81. Canx 4.2.83.
G-BIHL	Westland WG.13 Lynx Mk.88	WA/225		27.10.80	To West German Navy as 83+03 in 9/81. Canx 23.9.81.
G-BIHM	Westland WG.13 Lynx Mk.88	WA/231	G-17-27	27.10.80	To West German Navy as 83+04 in 9/81. Canx 23.9.81.
G-BIHN	Airship Industries Skyship 500	1214/02		2.11.80	Destroyed at San Francisco, CA, USA in the James Bond movie "A View To A Kill" in 1985. Canx by CAA 31.1.91.
G-BIHO	DHC.6-310 Twin Otter	738	A6-ADB G-BIHO	9. 1.81	
G-BIHP(1)	Cameron R-15 Gas/HAFB	673		. .80R	NTU - To G-CICI 11/80. Canx.
G-BIHP(2)	Van Den Bemden 1000m3 Gas Free Balloon (C/n quoted as "18" - Belgian CofR)	VDB-38	OO-VBA	19.12.80	(Believed rebuilt with 600m3 balloon c/n VDB-47)
G-BIHR	WMB.2 Windtracker HAFB (Toy)	17		4.11.80	Canx by CAA 13.12.88.
G-BIHS	North American T-6G Texan	182-29	1715 Portuguese AF/French AF 114342/51-14342	7.11.80	To N4434M 11/83. Canx 17.5.83.
G-BIHT	PA-17 Vagabond	17-41	N138N N8N/N4626H/NC4626H	9. 1.81	
G-BIHU	Saffery S.200 HAFB (Toy)	25		5.11.80	(Extant 2/97)
G-BIHV	WMB.2 Windtracker HAFB (Toy)	19		4.11.80	Canx as WFU 31.10.84.
G-BIHW	Aeronca A65TAC Defender	C.1221TA	N36683 NC36683	14.11.80	Badly damaged in crash at Shoreham on 29.6.88. (Stored 10/90 - for rebuild with basket case imported from USA .90) Canx by CAA 4.9.91.
G-BIHX	Bensen B.8MR Gyrocopter	01 & G/01-1003		12.11.80	No Permit believed issued. Canx by CAA 17.6.91.
G-BIHY	Isaacs Fury II	PFA/11-10211		17.11.80	Damaged on landing at Ronaldsway, IoM on 4.5.87. (On rebuild 3/93) Canx by CAA 3.4.97.
G-BIHZ(1)	HS.125 Srs.700B	257118		. .80R	NTU - To 5N-AVJ 1/81. Canx.
G-BIHZ(2)	BAC 167 Strikemaster Mk.89 (Originally regd as Mk.90)	PS.368	(SudanAF) G-BIHZ(2)/G-16-27	5. 2.81	Canx 5.8.87 as transferred to MOD. To ZG622/Ecuador AF as T-60.
G-BIIA	Alpavia Fournier RF-3	51	F-BMTA	14.11.80	Permit expired 16.7.87. (Status uncertain)
G-BIIB	Reims Cessna F.172M Skyhawk II	1110	PH-GBE	18.11.80	
G-BIIC	Scruggs BL-2A Wunda Balloon (Toy)	80208		20.11.80	Canx as WFU 18.10.88.
G-BIID	PA-18-95 Super Cub (L-18C-PI) (Frame No. 18-1558)	18-1606	OO-LPA OO-HMK/ALAT 18-1606/51-15606	5. 1.81	
G-BIIE	Reims Cessna F.172P Skyhawk II	2051		31.12.80	
G-BIIF	Sportavia Putzer Fournier RF-4D	4047	G-BVET F-BOXG	25.11.80	Canx by CAA 24.9.92. (Stored 8/97)
G-BIIG	Thunder Ax6-56Z HAFB	307		26.11.80	Canx by CAA 19.5.93.
G-BIIH	Scruggs BL-2T Turbo Wunda Balloon (Toy)	80210		25.11.80	Canx as WFU 1.11.88.
G-BIII	BAC One-Eleven Srs.408EF	BAC.128	G-AWKJ	15. 1.74	To RP-C1 in 7/74. Canx 8.7.74.
G-BIIJ	Reims Cessna F.152 II	1841		31.12.80	Fatal crash into the southeast face of the Tryfan Mountains in the Ogwen Valley, Snowdonia on 23.5.98. Canx as destroyed 22.9.98.
G-BIIK	Socata MS.883 Rallye 115	1552	F-BSAP	28.11.80	
G-BIIL	Thunder Ax6-56 Bolt HAFB	306		12.11.80	
G-BIIM	Scruggs BL-2A Wunda Balloon (Toy)	80211		28.11.80	Canx by CAA 12.12.88.
G-BIIN	PBN BN-2B-27 Islander (Originally regd as a BN-2B-26)	2101		1.12.80	Canx 14.12.81 on sale to USA. To TR-LZY 10/81.
G-BIIO	PBN BN-2T Turbine Islander (Originally regd as a BN-2B-26)	2102		1.12.80	To N660J 12/81. Canx by CAA 6.8.82.
G-BIIP	PBN BN-2B-27 Islander (Originally regd as a BN-2B-26)	2103	6Y-JQJ 6Y-JKJ/N411JA/G-BIIP	1.12.80	
G-BIIR	PBN BN-2B-26 Islander	2104		1.12.80	Canx 5.10.81 on sale to USA. To XA-MAO(2) 9/81.
G-BIIS	PBN BN-2B-26 Islander	2105		1.12.80	Canx 5.10.81 on sale to USA. To XA-MAP 9/81.
G-BIIT	PA-28-161 Warrior II	28-8116052	N82744	1.12.80	
G-BIIU	PA-28-181 Archer II	28-8190055	N82748	1.12.80	To G-MALA 3/81. Canx.
G-BIIV	PA-28-181 Archer II	28-7990028	N20875	19.12.80	
G-BIIW	Rango NA.10 HAFB (Toy)	NHP.10		1.12.80	Canx as WFU 18.10.88.
G-BIIX	Rango NA.12 HAFB (Toy) (Originally regd as c/n NHP-12)	NHP.11		1.12.80	
G-BIIY	PA-31-350 Navajo Chieftain	31-7952118	HZ-SCC N5FW/N3526Y	23.12.80	To ZS-KTU 1/81. Canx 6.1.81.
G-BIIZ	Great Lakes 2T-1A Sport Trainer	57	N603K NC603K	1. 4.81	

Regn	Type	c/n	Previous identity	Regn date	Fate or immediate subsequent identity (if known)
G-BIJA	Scruggs BL-2A Wundaballoon (Toy)	80209		3.12.80	Canx as destroyed 18.10.88.
G-BIJB	PA-18-150 Super Cub	18-8009001	N23923 (N2573H)	18. 8.80	
G-BIJC	Agusta-Bell 206B JetRanger II (Originally regd as a 206A JetRanger)	8226	LN-ORV	10.12.80	Canx as destroyed 12.12.90. (Based at Wilson, Nairobi)
G-BIJD	Bolkow Bo.208C Junior	636	PH-KAE (PH-DYM)/OO-SIS/(D-EGFA)	9.12.80	
G-BIJE	Piper J3C-65 Cub (L-4A-PI) (Frame no. 8504) (Originally regd with c/n 8865)	8367	F-BIGN French AF/42-15248	5. 5.81	(On rebuild 4/91)
G-BIJF	Bell 212	31163		12.12.80	Ditched near Dunlin Platform in North Sea on 12.8.81. Salvaged but badly damaged. Canx as destroyed 5.12.83.
G-BIJG	Boeing 757-236	-		. .80R	NTU - Canx.
G-BIJH	Boeing 757-236	-		. .80R	NTU - Canx.
G-BIJI	Boeing 757-236	-		. .80R	NTU - Canx.
G-BIJJ	Boeing 757-236	-		. .80R	NTU - Canx.
G-BIJK	Boeing 757-236	-		. .80R	NTU - Canx.
G-BIJL	Boeing 757-236	-		. .80R	NTU - Canx.
G-BIJM	Boeing 757-236	-		. .80R	NTU - Canx.
G-BIJN	Boeing 757-236	-		. .80R	NTU - Canx.
G-BIJO	Boeing 757-236	-		. .80R	NTU - Canx.
G-BIJP	Boeing 757-236	-		. .80R	NTU - Canx.
G-BIJR	Boeing 757-236	-		. .80R	NTU - Canx.
G-BIJS	Phoenix Luton LA-4A Minor	PAL/1348 & PFA/835		18. 5.78	Permit expired 14.11.95.
G-BIJT	American Aviation AA-5A Cheetah	AA5A-0833	N26950	16. 1.81	To G-MSTC 1/95. Canx.
G-BIJU	Coopavia-Menavia Piel CP.301A Emeraude	221	G-BHTX F-BIJU	10. 6.80	
G-BIJV	Reims Cessna F.152 II	1813		22.12.80	
G-BIJW	Reims Cessna F.152 II	1820		22.12.80	
G-BIJX	Reims Cessna F.152 II	1829		29.12.80	
G-BIJY	Reims Cessna F.172P Skyhawk	2134		. .80R	NTU - Not Imported. To F-GDDR. Canx.
G-BIJZ	Skyventurer Mk.1 HAFB (Toy)	RRS.001		8.10.80	Canx by CAA 13.12.88.
G-BIKA	Boeing 757-236 (Line No. 9)	22172	(N757B)	28. 3.83	
G-BIKB	Boeing 757-236 (Line No. 10)	22173		25. 1.83	
G BIKC	Boeing 757-236 (Line No. 11)	22174		31. 1.83	
G-BIKD	Boeing 757-236 (Line No. 13)	22175		10. 3.83	
G-BIKE	PA-28R-200 Cherokee Arrow II	28R-7335173	OY-DVT N55047	18. 4.80	
G-BIKF(1)	Boeing 757-236 (Line No. 14)	22176		. .80R	NTU - To N57008/G-BKRM 3/83. Canx.
G-BIKF(2)	Boeing 757-236 (Line No. 16)	22177	(G-BIKG)	28. 4.83	
G-BIKG(1)	Boeing 757-236 (Line No. 16)	22177		. .80R	NTU - To G-BIKF 4/83. Canx.
G-BIKG(2)	Boeing 757-236 (Line No. 23)	22178	(G-BIKH)	26. 8.83	
G-BIKH(1)	Boeing 757-236 (Line No. 23)	22178		. .80R	NTU - To G-BIKG 8/83. Canx.
G-BIKH(2)	Boeing 757-236 (Line No. 24)	22179	(G-BIKI)	18.10.83	
G-BIKI(1)	Boeing 757-236 (Line No. 24)	22179		. .80R	NTU - To G-BIKH 10/83. Canx.
G-BIKI(2)	Boeing 757-236 (Line No. 25)	22180	(G-BIKJ)	30.11.83	
G-BIKJ(1)	Boeing 757-236 (Line No. 25)	22180		. .80R	NTU - To G-BIKI 11/83. Canx.
G-BIKJ(2)	Boeing 757-236 (Line No. 29)	22181	(G-BIKK)	9. 1.84	
G-BIKK(1)	Boeing 757-236 (Line No. 29)	22181		. .80R	NTU - To G-BIKJ 1/84. Canx.
G-BIKK(2)	Boeing 757-236 (Line No. 30)	22182	(G-BIKL)	1. 2.84	
G-BIKL(1)	Boeing 757-236 (Line No. 30)	22182		. .80R	NTU - To G-BIKK 2/84. Canx.
G-BIKL(2)	Boeing 757-236 (Line No. 32)	22183	(G-BIKM)	29. 2.84	
G-BIKM(1)	Boeing 757-236 (Line No. 32)	22183		. .80R	NTU - To G-BIKL 2/84. Canx.
G-BIKM(2)	Boeing 757-236 (Line No. 33)	22184	N8293V (G-BIKN)	21. 3.84	
G-BIKN(1)	Boeing 757-236 (Line No. 33)	22184		. .80R	NTU - To N8293V/G-BIKM 3/84. Canx.
G-BIKN(2)	Boeing 757-236 (Line No. 50)	22186	(G-BIKP)	23. 1.85	
G-BIKO(1)	Boeing 757-236 (Line No. 34)	22185		. .80R	NTU - To (G-BNEP)/N8294V. Canx.

Regn	Type	c/n	Previous identity	Regn date	Fate or immediate subsequent identity (if known)
G-BIKO(2)	Boeing 757-236 (Line No. 52)	22187	(G-BIKR)	14. 2.85	
G-BIKP(1)	Boeing 757-236 (Line No. 50)	22186		. .80R	NTU - To G-BIKN 1/85. Canx.
G-BIKP(2)	Boeing 757-236 (Line No. 54)	22188	(G-BIKS)	11. 3.85	
G-BIKR(1)	Boeing 757-236 (Line No. 52)	22187		. .80R	NTU - To G-BIKO 2/85. Canx.
G-BIKR(2)	Boeing 757-236 (Line No. 58)	22189	(G-BIKT)	29. 3.85	
G-BIKS(1)	Boeing 757-236 (Line No. 54)	22188		. .80R	NTU - To G-BIKP 3/85. Canx.
G-BIKS(2)	Boeing 757-236 (Line No. 63)	22190	(G-BIKU)	31. 5.85	
G-BIKT(1)	Boeing 757-236 (Line No. 58)	22189		. .80R	NTU - To G-BIKR 3/85. Canx.
G-BIKT(2)	Boeing 757-236 (Line No. 77)	23398		1.11.85	
G-BIKU(1)	Boeing 757-236 (Line No. 63)	22190		. .80R	NTU - To G-BIKS 5/85. Canx.
G-BIKU(2)	Boeing 757-236 (Line No. 78)	23399		7.11.85	
G-BIKV	Boeing 757-236 (Line No. 81)	23400		9.12.85	
G-BIKW	Boeing 757-236 (Line No. 89)	23492		7. 3.86	
G-BIKX	Boeing 757-236 (Line No. 90)	23493		14. 3.86	
G-BIKY(1)	Boeing 757-236	23495		. .80R	NTU - Not built. Canx.
G-BIKY(2)	Boeing 757-236 (Line No. 93)	23533		28. 3.86	
G-BIKZ	Boeing 757-236 (Line No. 98)	23532		15. 5.86	
G-BILA	Dalotel-Michel DM-165L Viking	01	F-PPZE	5. 2.81	Permit to Fly expired 14.9.83. Canx as WFU 31.10.85. (On rebuild .94)
G-BILB(1)	Airbus A.300B4-203	127	F-WZED	. .80R	NTU - To G-BIMA 1/81. Canx.
G-BILB(2)	WMB-2 Windtracker HAFB (Toy)	14		22. 1.81	(Extant 2/97)
G-BILC(1)	Airbus A.300B4-203	131	F-WZEL	. .80R	NTU - To G-BIMB 2/81. Canx.
G-BILC(2)	Thunder Ax3-17/3C Sky Chariot HAFB	296		19.12.80	To EC-DOF 9/81. Canx 21.5.81.
G-BILD(1)	Airbus A.300B4-203	144	F-WZEG	. .80R	NTU - To G-BIMC 6/81. Canx.
G-BILD(2)	Piper J3C-65 Cub (L-4J-PI) (Frame No. 12443)	12613	G-KERK F-BBQD/44-80147	15.12.80	To G-OINK 3/83. Canx.
G-BILE(1)	Airbus A.300B4-203	177	F-WZMV	. .80R	NTU - To G-BIMD. Canx.
G-BILE(2)	Scruggs BL-2B HAFB (Toy)	81231		13. 3.81	
G-BILF(1)	Airbus A.300B4-203	180	F-WZMX	. .80R	NTU - To G-BIME. Canx.
G-BILF(2)	Practavia Pilot Sprite 125	PFA/05-10467		17.12.80	No Permit to Fly. Canx by CAA 12.4.99.
G-BILG(1)	Airbus A.300B4-203	190	F-WZMI	. .80R	NTU - To G-BIMF. Canx.
G-BILG(2)	Scruggs BL-2B HAFB (Toy)	81232		13. 3.81	
G-BILH(1)	Airbus A.300B4-203	229		. .80R	NTU - To G-BIMG. Canx.
G-BILH(2)	Slingsby T.65C Sport Vega	1942	BGA.2700	3. 2.81R	NTU - Remained as BGA.2700/EHN. Canx by CAA 15.10.90.
G-BILI(1)	Airbus A.300B4-203	238	F-WZMN	. .80R	NTU - To G-BIMH. Canx.
G-BILI(2)	Piper J3C-65 Cub (L-4J-PI) (Original identity unconfirmed; apparently has frame No 15044 which is c/n 15449, current as N87791)	13207	F-BDTB 45-4467	14. 1.81	
G-BILJ(1)	Airbus A.300B4-203	282	F-WZML	. .80R	NTU - To G-BIMI. Canx.
G-BILJ(2)	Reims Cessna FA.152 Aerobat	0376		31.12.80	
G-BILK(1)	Airbus A.300B4-203	305	F-WZMV	. .80R	NTU - To G-BIMJ. Canx.
G-BILK(2)	Reims Cessna FA.152 Aerobat	0372		9. 1.81	
G-BILL	PA-25-260 Pawnee D	25-7856028		3. 1.79	
G-BILM	DHC.2 Beaver	1412/1959	3B-GB Austrian AF/58-7020	. .80R	NTU - To N3930B 11/82. Canx.
G-BILN	DHC.2 Beaver	1416/1960	3B-GC Austrian AF/58-7021	. .80R	NTU - To N39302 11/82. Canx.
G-BILO	DHC.2 Beaver	1221/1795	3B-GF Austrian AF/57-2569	. .80R	NTU - To N39303 11/82. Canx.
G-BILP	Cessna 152 II	152-83741	N5094P	19. 3.81	Crashed on landing at Barton on 30.6.90. Wreck noted dumped and covered up on 30.8.90. Canx as WFU 2.11.90.
G-BILR	Cessna 152 II	152-84822	N4822P	19. 3.81	
G-BILS	Cessna 152 II	152-84857	N4954P	3. 6.81	
G-BILT	Reims Cessna F.172P Skyhawk	2057		7. 1.81	To VR-HKA 2/86. Canx 25.2.86.
G-BILU	Cessna 172RG Cutlass II	172RG-0564	N5540V	29. 1.81	
G-BILV	Reims Cessna FA.152 Aerobat	0374		9. 1.81	To G-FLIC 8/83. Canx.
G-BILW	Colt 60 HAFB (Regn not used - This is a model Colt 4.5D used in the film "The Great Muppet Caper")	301		11.12.80	Destroyed during filming in USA. Canx as destroyed 5.12.83.
G-BILX	Colt 31A HAFB	310		11.12.80	Canx as WFU 16.10.89.
G-BILY	Beechcraft 200 Super King Air	BB-828		12.12.80	To G-MCEO 4/81. Canx.
G-BILZ	Taylor JT.1 Monoplane (Regd as c/n PFA/55-10124)	PFA/55-10244		15.12.80	Badly damaged in crash on take-off from Ingoldmells on 10.6.90. Permit expired 29.2.91. (Stored 9/96 North Cotes)
G-BIMA	Airbus A.300B4-203	127	(G-BILB) F-WZED	7. 1.81	To 6Y-JMJ 2/83. Canx 18.2.83.

Regn	Type	c/n	Previous identity	Regn date	Fate or immediate subsequent identity (if known)
G-BIMB	Airbus A.300B4-203	131	(G-BILC) F-WZEL	17. 2.81	To 6Y-JMK 2/83. Canx 18.2.83.
G-BIMC	Airbus A.300B4-203	144	(G-BILD) F-WZEG	11. 6.81	To AP-BBV 6/84. Canx 28.6.84.
G-BIMD	Airbus A.300B4-203	177	(G-BILE) F-WZMV	. .80R	NTU - To VT-EHN 7/82. Canx.
G-BIME	Airbus A.300B4-203	180	(G-BILF) F-WZMX	. .80R	NTU - To VT-EHO 8/82. Canx.
G-BIMF	Airbus A.300B4-203	190	(G-BILG) F-WZMI	. .80R	NTU - To VT-EHQ 11/82. Canx.
G-BIMG	Airbus A.300B4-203	229	(G-BILH)	. .80R	NTU - Not completed, components used elsewhere. Canx.
G-BIMH	Airbus A.300B4-203	238	(G-BILI) F-WZMN	. .80R	NTU - To N210PA 6/85. Canx.
G-BIMI	Airbus A.300B4-203	282	(G-BILJ) F-WZML	. .80R	NTU - To F-WZXP/TU-TAT 9/84. Canx.
G-BIMJ	Airbus A.300B4-203	305	(G-BILK) F-WZMV	. .80R	NTU - To N209PA 6/85. Canx.
G-BIMK	Tiger T.200 Srs.1 HAFB (Toy)	7/MKB-01		22.12.80	
G-BIML	Turner Super T.40A	T/UK/001 & PFA/104-10655		9. 1.81	Did not progress beyond the planning stage and was not built. Canx as WFU 11.8.88.
G-BIMM	PA-18-150 Super Cub (L-21B-PI)(Frame No. 18-3881)	18-3868	PH-VHO R.Netherlands AF R-178/54-2468	8. 1.81	
G-BIMN	Steen Skybolt	1 & PFA/64-10329		31.12.80	
G-BIMO	SNCAN Stampe SV-4C	394	F-BADG French Mil	5. 3.81	
G-BIMP	Cessna R.172H	R172-0552	4X-CEQ Israeli DF/AF / N1771C	16. 1.81	Restored as 4X-CEQ. Canx 17.8.81.
G-BIMR	Fuji FA.200-160 Aero Subaru	FA200-295		. .80R	NTU - To G-BMLN 1/86. Canx.
G-BIMS	Fuji FA.200-180AO Aero Subaru	FA200-296		. .80R	NTU - To G-MCOX 12/81. Canx.
G-BIMT	Reims Cessna FA.152 Aerobat	0361	N8062L	9. 1.81	
G-BIMU	Sikorsky S-61N Mk.II	61-752	N8511Z VH-CRU/N4042S	9. 1.81	
G-BIMV	Sikorsky S-61N Mk.II	61-815	C-GOLH VH-IMS/C-GOLH/(VH-PTE)/N4228S	16. 2.81	Restored as C-GOLH. Canx 7.1.83.
G-BIMW	DHC.6-310 Twin Otter	740		9. 1.81	To N600LJ 8/84. Canx 7.8.84.
G-BIMX	Rutan VariEze	PFA/74-10544		6. 1.81	
G-BIMY	HS.125 Srs.700A	NA0294 & 257132		20. 1.81	Canx 8.4.81 on sale to USA. To C-FIPG 4/81.
G-BIMZ	Beechcraft 76 Duchess	ME-169	N6021K	20. 3.81	
G-BINA	Saffery S.9 HAFB (Toy)	AB-001		9.12.80	Canx by CAA 2.12.93.
G-BINB	WMB-2A Windtracker HAFB (Toy)	018		11.12.80	Canx as destroyed 21.10.93.
G-BINC	Saffery Tour de Calais HAFB (Toy)	1		15.11.80	
G-BIND	Socata Rallye 235E Gabier	13328		9. 2.81	To G-MELV 5/86. Canx.
G-BINE	Scruggs BL-2A Wundaballoon HAFB (Toy)	80213		6. 1.81	Canx by CAA 9.12.88.
G-BINF	Saffery S.200 Heatwave HAFB (Toy)	02		28. 5.81	
G-BING	Reims Cessna F.172P Skyhawk II	2084		12. 1.81	Canx by CAA 25.9.84.
G-BINH	DH.82A Tiger Moth	'OU/06/68'	VT-DOW R.Indian AF as HU-488	9. 2.81	Spun in at Ewanton Morley on 10.4.81. (On rebuild in 1982) Canx as WFU 22.11.91.
G-BINI	Scruggs BL-2C Wundaballoon HAFB (Toy)	81222		21. 1.81	Canx by CAA 8.4.98.
G-BINJ	Rango NA-12 HAFB (Toy)	MRH-15		9. 2.81	
G-BINK	Scruggs BL-2C HAFB (Toy)	81223		. .81R	NTU - Canx.
G-BINL	Scruggs BL-2B HAFB (Toy)	81216		5. 2.81	
G-BINM	Scruggs BL-2B HAFB (Toy)	81217		5. 2.81	
G-BINN	Unicorn UE-1A HAFB (Toy)	81003		20. 1.81	Canx by CAA 6.12.88.
G-BINO	Evans VP-1 (Probably also incorporates PFA/7007)	3642/9 & PFA/1547		8. 6.78	(Under construction 1/96)
G-BINP	Rango NA-9 HAFB (Toy) (First balloon WFU in 19.7.82 and replaced by new balloon)	NHP-12		12. 1.81	
G-BINR	Unicorn UE-1A HAFB (Toy)	81004		20. 1.81	
G-BINS	Unicorn UE-2A HAFB (Toy)	80002		22.12.80	
G-BINT	Unicorn UE-1A HAFB (Toy)	80001		22.12.80	
G-BINU	Saffery S.200 Heatwave HAFB (Toy)	TCBL/01		13. 1.81	
G-BINV	Saffery S.200 HAFB (Toy)	REG-1		2. 1.81	Canx as WFU 14.11.88.
G-BINW	Scruggs BL-2B HAFB (Toy)	81218		5. 2.81	
G-BINX	Scruggs BL-2B HAFB (Toy)	81219		5. 2.81	
G-BINY	Oriental Air-Bag HAFB (Toy)	OAB-001		22. 1.81	
G-BINZ	Rango NA-8 HAFB (Toy)	SBG-14		9. 2.81	Canx by CAA 2.12.93.
G-BIOA	Hughes 369D (500D)	120-0880D		9. 2.81	To OO-HFS. Canx 7.8.91.
G-BIOB	Reims Cessna F.172P Skyhawk II	2042		23. 1.81	
G-BIOC	Reims Cessna F.150L	0848	F-BUEC	3. 2.81	
G-BIOD	Short SD.3-30 Var.100	SH3062		15. 1.81	To N335GW 7/81. Canx 27.7.81.
G-BIOE	Short SD.3-30 Var.200	SH3063	N59MM G-BIOE/VH-KNP/G-BIOE/G-14-3063	15. 1.81	WFU & stored 7/97 at Newcastle. Canx as WFU 1.12.97. Broken up in 5/98 at Newcastle.
G-BIOF	Short SD.3-30 Var.100	SH3064	G-14-3064 EI-BNM/G-14-3064/N280VY/N4270A/G-BIOF/G-14-3064	15. 1.81	To (N334SB)/5N-AOX 9/85. Canx 13.9.85.
G-BIOG	Short SD.3-30 Var.100	SH3065	G-14-3065	15. 1.81	To SX-BGC 4/81. Canx 18.3.81.
G-BIOH	Short SC.7 Skyvan 3M	SH1975		15. 1.81	To 8Q-CA001 6/81. Canx 5.12.83.

Regn	Type	c/n	Previous identity	Regn date	Fate or immediate subsequent identity (if known)
G-BIOI	SAN Jodel DR.1051/M Excellence	477	F-BLJQ	21. 1.81	Never certified in UK & believed stored or used for spares at Chigwell. Canx by CAA 4.2.87.
G-BIOJ	Rockwell Commander 112TC-A	13192	N4662W	22. 1.82	
G-BIOK	Reims Cessna F.152 II	1810		2. 2.81	
G-BIOL	Colt 77A HAFB	312		26. 1.81	To D-SCHEIDEGGER. Canx 20.2.85.
G-BIOM	Reims Cessna F.152 II	1015		5. 2.81	
G-BION	Cameron V-77 HAFB	706		23. 1.81	Canx by CAA 27.10.95.
G-BIOO	Unicorn UE-2B HAFB (Toy)	81005		20. 1.81	Canx by CAA 2.12.93.
G-BIOP	Scruggs BL-2D HAFB (Toy)	81229		20. 2.81	Canx by CAA 2.12.93.
G-BIOR	Socata MS.880B Rallye Club (Composite rebuild with components from G-AZGJ)	1229	OO-SAF	3. 2.81	
G-BIOS	Scruggs BL-2B HAFB (Toy)	81220		5. 2.81	Canx as WFU 27.10.88.
G-BIOT	Bensen B.8M Gyrocopter	AJB-1 & G/01-1043		2. 2.81	Broke up in the air and crashed half a mile north of Dunkeswell on 27.11.86. Canx as destroyed 22.8.89.
G-BIOU	SAN Jodel D.117A	813	F-BIOU	9. 8.78	
G-BIOV	HS.748 Srs.2/223	1591	0111 Venezuelan Govt	. .81R	NTU - Remained as Venezuelan Govt as 0111. Canx.
G-BIOW	Slingsby T.67A	1988		26. 2.81	
G-BIOX	Potter Crompton PRO-1 HAFB (Toy)	01		9. 2.81	Canx as destroyed 2.11.93.
G-BIOY	Cremer PAC-14 Cliffords Dairies Milk Bottle HAFB (Toy)	03		10. 2.81	Canx by CAA 8.12.88.
G-BIOZ	Rotorway Exec 133	2962		4. 2.81	Fatal crash at Ridinghurst Farm, Grafham, Cranleigh, Surrey on 17.7.82 & DBF. Canx as WFU 5.12.83.
G-BIPA	American Aviation AA-5B Tiger	AA5B-0200	OY-GAM	24. 3.81	
G-BIPB	Weedhopper JC-24B	0478		11. 2.81	Canx by CAA 5.4.90.
G-BIPC	Cremer PAC-14 Hefferlump 200 HAFB (Toy)	02		9. 2.81	Canx by CAA 8.12.88.
G-BIPD	PBN BN-2A-21 Islander (Originally regd as BN-2A-27)	2026		11. 2.81	Canx 14.9.81 on sale to Singapore. To PK-VIW 10/82.
G-BIPE	PBN BN-2B-27 Islander	2031		11. 2.81	Canx 23.3.81 on sale to USA. To XC-FOE.
G-BIPF	Scruggs BL-2C HAFB (Toy)	81225		11. 2.81	Canx by CAA 13.12.88.
G-BIPG	Global Mini HAFB (Toy)	001		12. 2.81	Canx by CAA 2.11.88.
G-BIPH	Scruggs BL-2B HAFB (Toy)	81224		10. 2.81	
G-BIPI	Everett Blackbird Mk.1 Gyroplane (Possibly two airframes; original stored with R.Everett at Sproughton, Ipswich 1/91 - still present 5/97)	001		30. 4.81	Permit expired 29.4.92. (Stored at Kemble)
G-BIPJ	PA-36-375 Pawnee Brave	36-7802064	PH-ZEY	13. 2.81	To UAE Air Force as 004 in 1987. Canx by CAA 3.8.94.
G-BIPK	Saffery S.200 HAFB (Toy)	26		6. 2.81	Canx by CAA 2.12.93.
G-BIPL	American Aviation AA-5A Cheetah	AA5A-0858	N26980	18. 2.81	Crashed and burst into flames while doing touch-and-go at Denham on 3.7.86. Canx as destroyed 24.11.87.
G-BIPM	Flamboyant Ax7-65 HAFB	018		13. 5.81	Canx by CAA 8.1.93. (Based in South Africa in 1981 & in "Central Africa" in 1993)
G-BIPN	Alpavia Fournier RF-3	35	F-BMDN	26. 2.81	Permit expired 3.10.95. (Stored 4/97)
G-BIPO	Mudry/CAARP CAP-20LS/200	03	F-GAUB	5. 3.81	
G-BIPP	Beechcraft B200 Super King Air	BB-878		17. 2.81	To C-GKRL 5/83. Canx 3.5.83.
G-BIPR	Sikorsky S-76A Spirit	760154	5N-AOD G-BIPR	3. 3.81	To VH-CPH 4/87. Canx 8.4.87.
G-BIPS	Socata MS.880B Rallye 100ST	3028	F-GBCA	20. 2.81	(Damaged pre 9.92) Canx by CAA 19.10.92. (Stored 5/93)
G-BIPT	Wassmer Jodel D.112	1254	F-BMIB	11. 3.81	
G-BIPU	American Aviation AA-5B Tiger	AA5B-0900	N28941	11. 3.81	Overshot landing at Ingoldmells on 17.9.89 and ran into a dyke. Canx as destroyed 30.4.90.
G-BIPV	American Aviation AA-5B Tiger	AA5B-0981	N28266	10. 3.81	
G-BIPW	Avenger T200-2112 HAFB (Toy)	10		24. 2.81	
G-BIPX	Saffery S.9 HAFB (Toy)	JRH-001		24. 2.81	Canx by CAA 12.12.88.
G-BIPY	Montgomerie-Bensen B.8MR Gyrocopter	AJW.01 & G/01-1007		25. 2.81	
G-BIPZ	McCandless M.4 Gyroplane	Mk.4-4		27. 2.81	No CofA or Permit issued. Canx by CAA 9.8.91. (Stored 4/96)
G-BIRA	Socata TB-9 Tampico	186		6. 5.81	To EI-FLY 10/93. Canx 23.9.93.
G-BIRB	Socata MS.880B Rallye 100T	2460	F-BVAQ	30. 3.81	(To Carlisle by road for repairs but found to be too badly corroded to be worth repairing. left by road in 10/91 for a technical college in Stockton-on-Tees and became an instructional airframe) CofA expired 16.6.90. Canx by CAA 13.7.92. Stored 9/97 Yorkshire Air Museum/Hawick ATC Sqdn.
G-BIRC	PA-28-140 Cherokee Cruiser F	28-7325022	OY-BGE	31. 3.81	To G-KATS 8/83. Canx.
G-BIRD	Pitts S-1D Special	707-H & PFA/1596		3.11.77	
G-BIRE	Colt Bottle 56SS HAFB (Satzenbrau Bottle)	323		4. 3.81	(Extant 2/97)
G-BIRF	HS.748 Srs.2B/FAA	1781	G-11-15	12. 3.81	To N117CA 10/81. Canx 29.12.81.
G-BIRG	Morane-Saulnier MS.880B Rallye Club	1237	F-BPSR	13. 7.81	Damaged by gales at Biggin Hill on the night of 24/25.11.84. Canx by CAA 29.4.85.
G-BIRH	PA-18-180 Super Cub (L-21B-PI)(Frame No. 18-3857)	18-3853	PH-LET(2) R.Nethlands AF R-163/54-2453	19. 3.81	
G-BIRI	CASA I-131E Jungmann	1074	E3B-113 Spanish AF	14. 4.81	Permit expired 20.10.94. (Stored 9/96)
G-BIRJ	Reims Cessna F.172P Skyhawk	2083		10. 3.81	To VP-FBJ 2/83. Canx 16.12.83.
G-BIRK	Avenger T200-2112 HAFB (Toy)	006		10. 3.81	
G-BIRL	Avenger T200-2112 HAFB (Toy)	008		10. 3.81	
G-BIRM	Avenger T200-2112 HAFB (Toy)	007		10. 3.81	
G-BIRN	Short SD.3-30 Var.100	SH3067	G-14-3067	13. 3.81	To G-BPMA 1/89. Canx.

Regn	Type	c/n	Previous identity	Regn date	Fate or immediate subsequent identity (if known)
G-BIRO	Cessna 172P Skyhawk	172-74826	N53916	29. 4.81	Ditched in sea 3 miles southwest of Hastings on 10.12.92. Canx by CAA 13.5.93.
G-BIRP	Ridout Arena Mk.17 Skyship HAFB (Toy)	01		13. 3.81	
G-BIRR	Not allocated.				
G-BIRS	Cessna 182P Skylane	182-61436	G-BBBS N21131	10. 3.81	
G-BIRT	Robin R.1180TD Aiglon	276		25. 3.81	
G-BIRU	HS.125 Srs.700B	257136		29. 4.81	To G-5-545/OH-JET 1/87. Canx 23.1.87.
G-BIRV	Bensen B-8MV Gyrocopter	RH.1 & G/01-1013		5. 3.81	Canx by CAA 9.8.91.
G-BIRW	Morane-Saulnier MS.505 Criquet	695/28	OO-FIS F-BDQS/French AF 695	10. 4.81	Permit expired 3.6.83. Canx as WFU 15.11.88. (On display 3/96 East Fortune)
G-BIRX	Scruggs RS.500 HAFB (Toy)	81530		12. 3.81	Canx by CAA 13.12.88.
G-BIRY	Cameron V-77 HAFB	715		12. 3.81	
G-BIRZ	Zenair CH.250-100	2-454 & PFA/24-10459		10. 3.81	
G-BISA	Hase Skybag IIIT HAFB (Toy)	MH3T/01		7. 4.81	Canx as WFU 18.10.88.
G-BISB	Reims Cessna F.152 II	1816		23. 3.81	Badly damaged in forced landing at Glebe Farm, Gotham, near Nottingham on 6.11.95. Canx by CAA 25.9.96.
G-BISC	Robinson R-22	0018	N9021N	9. 6.81	Drifted sideways and overturned while landing at Kidlington on 9.10.89. Canx as WFU 29.11.89.
G-BISD	Enstrom 280C-UK-2 Shark	1215		18. 5.81	To ZS-HNI 12/84. Canx 26.6.84.
G-BISE	Enstrom 280C-UK-2 Shark	1218		13. 3.81	To G-TOYS 6/82. Canx.
G-BISF	Robinson R-22	0062		9. 4.81	To N51248 6/93. Canx 16.4.93.
G-BISG	Clutton FRED Srs.III	RAC 01-224 & PFA/29-10675		13. 3.81	Permit expired 29.10.86. (Status uncertain)
G-BISH	Cameron V-65 HAFB (Originally regd as 0-42)	707		16. 3.81	
G-BISI	Robinson R-22	0063	N9081S	9. 4.81	To VH-LQM 7/91. Canx 7.3.91.
G-BISJ	Cessna 340A II	340A-0497	OO-LFK N6328X	10. 4.81	
G-BISK	Rockwell Commander 112B	535	PH-EBE N1469J	5. 3.81	Damaged by storms at Hurn on 16.10.87. Canx as WFU 24.11.87.
G-BISL	Scruggs BL-2B HAFB (Toy)	81233		13. 3.81	
G-BISM	Scruggs BL-2C HAFB (Toy)	81234		13. 3.81	
G-BISN	Boeing-Vertol 234LR Commercial Chinook	B-829 & MJ-005	N238BV	20. 5.81	To N238CH. Canx 14.4.89.
G-BISO	Boeing-Vertol 234LR Commercial Chinook	B-816 & MJ-002	N235BV	14. 9.81	Ditched in the North Sea, 110 miles northeast of Lerwick on 2.5.84. Canx as destroyed 20.11.84. Remains departed from Aberdeen on 18.12.84 on board Mini Guppy N422AU. Rebuilt & became N235CH.
G-BISP	Boeing-Vertol 234LR Commercial Chinook	B-839 & MJ-006	N239BV	20. 5.81	To N239CH. Canx 20.6.89.
G-BISR	Boeing-Vertol 234LR Commercial Chinook	B-817 & MJ-003	N236BV	21. 6.82	To N237CH. Canx 21.2.89.
G-BISS	Scruggs BL-2C HAFB (Toy)	81235		13. 3.81	
G-BIST	Scruggs BL-2C HAFB (Toy)	81236		13. 3.81	
G-BISU	Bristol 170 Freighter 31M	13218	ZK-EPH R.New Zealand AF NZ5912/ZK-BVI/R.New Zealand AF NZ5912/G-18-194	6. 5.81	To C-FDFC 1/89. Canx 20.12.88.
G-BISV	Cameron O-65 HAFB	712		18. 3.81	Canx by CAA 19.5.93.
G-BISW	Cameron O-65 HAFB	713		18. 3.81	CofA expired 6.8.88. Canx by CAA 5.6.98.
G-BISX	Colt 56A HAFB	324		18. 3.81	
G-BISY	Scruggs BL-2C HAFB (Toy)	81237		19. 3.81	Canx as WFU 1.11.88.
G-BISZ	Sikorsky S-76A II Plus	760156		19. 3.81	
G-BITA	PA-18-150 Super Cub	18-8109037		24. 3.81	
G-BITB	Everett Gyroplane	-		. .81R	NTU - Canx.
G-BITC	Ted Smith Aerostar 601PE	61P-0515-215	N8034J	23. 8.78	To N9562F 8/81. Canx 28.7.81.
G-BITD	Socata TB-10 Tobago	192		7. 5.81	To G-HALP 8/81. Canx.
G-BITE	Socata TB-10 Tobago	193		7. 5.81	
G-BITF	Reims Cessna F.152 II	1822		27. 3.81	
G-BITG	Reims Cessna F.152 II	1824		27. 3.81	To G-ODAC 12/96. Canx.
G-BITH	Reims Cessna F.152 II	1825		27. 3.81	
G-BITI	Scruggs RS.500 HAFB (Toy)	81539		24. 3.81	Canx as WFU 18.10.88.
G-BITJ	Everett Gyroplane	-		. .81R	NTU - Canx.
G-BITK	Clutton-Tabenor FRED Srs.II	PFA/29-10369		23. 3.81	
G-BITL	Worsdell Horncastle LL-901 HAFB (Toy)	206-1		24. 3.81	Canx by CAA 2.12.93.
G-BITM	Reims Cessna F.172P Skyhawk II	2046		13. 4.81	
G-BITN	Short Albatross HAFB (Toy)	DKS-002		25. 3.81	Canx as WFU 4.11.88.
G-BITO	Wassmer Jodel D.112D	1200	F-BIUO	20. 3.81	
G-BITP	Scorpion Mk.I HAFB (Toy)	001		17. 3.81	Canx as WFU 16.7.81.
G-BITR	Sikorsky S-76A II Plus	760157	PT-HRW G-BITR	26. 3.81	
G-BITS(1)	Auster AOP.9	B.704		. 1.79R	NTU - To G-BEBF 1/79. Canx.
G-BITS(2)	Drayton B-56 HAFB (Toy)	MJB-01/81		16. 3.81	
G-BITT	Bolkow Bo.208C Junior	689	F-BRHX D-EEAL	25. 3.81	To G-BOKW 1/88. Canx.
G-BITU	Short SD.3-30 Var.100	SH3066	G-14-3066	26. 3.81	To SX-BGD 4/81. Canx 30.3.81.
G-BITV	Short SD.3-30 Var.100	SH3068	G-14-3068	26. 3.81	To G-OGIL 1/89. Canx.

Regn	Type	c/n	Previous identity	Regn date	Fate or immediate subsequent identity (if known)
G-BITW	Short SD.3-30 Var.100	SH3070	G-EASI (G-BITW)/G-14-3070	26. 3.81	Stored 7/97 at Coventry-Baginton. CofA expired 9.6.98. Canx as WFU 20.7.99. Broken up at Coventry in late 7/99.
G-BITX	Short SD.3-30 Var.100	SH3069	G-14-3069	26. 3.81	To OY-MUB. Canx 19.4.90.
G-BITY	Bell FD.31T Flying Dodo HAFB (Toy)	2604		25. 3.81	
G-BITZ	Cremer-Sandoe PACDS 14 TJP Oogeemaflip Supa HAFB (Toy)	41		25. 3.81	Canx by CAA 8.12.88.
G-BIUA	BN-2A-21 Islander	916		23. 3.81	To SAF-001 Surinam AF 2/82. Canx 5.3.82.
G-BIUB	BN-2A Islander	917		23. 3.81	NTU - Not completed. Canx 23.6.83.
G-BIUC	BN-2A Islander	918		23. 3.81	To OA-6/Z3 Botswana DF 8/81. Canx 14.8.81.
G-BIUD	BN-2A-26 Islander	919		23. 3.81	To N662J 2/82. Canx 16.2.81.
G-BIUE	BN-2A Islander	920		23. 3.81	NTU - Not Completed. Canx as WFU 12.12.86.
G-BIUF	PBN BN-2A-21 Islander (Originally regd as BN-2A-27)	2027		23. 3.81	Canx 29.10.81 on sale to Singapore. To PK-VIX 12/81.
G-BIUG	PBN BN-2A-26 Islander	2028		23. 3.81	NTU - To G-MALB 10/86. Canx.
G-BIUH	PBN BN-2A-26 Islander	2029		23. 3.81	NTU - To G-BNGA 10/86. Canx.
G-BIUI	Reims Cessna F.152 II	1863		2. 4.81	To G-TEES 9/85. Canx.
G-BIUJ	PBN BN-2T Turbine Islander	2030		23. 3.81	To G-KEMZ 9/81. Canx.
G-BIUK	Ted Smith Aerostar 601A	61-0179-086	ZS-JEV N7548S	. 3.81R	NTU - Not Imported. To N601UK 4/81. Canx.
G-BIUL	Cameron Bellows 60SS HAFB (Expansion Joint Shape)	703		27. 3.81	CofA expired 12.5.91. (Extant 2/97) Canx by CAA 26.6.98.
G-BIUM	Reims Cessna F.152 II	1807	F-WZIR	3. 4.81	
G-BIUN	Reims Cessna F.152 II	1818		3. 4.81	While on the pilot's first solo flight, the aircraft spun in on approach to Netherthorpe on 4.9.89. Canx as destroyed 9.1.90.
G-BIUO	Rockwell Commander 112A	281	OY-PRH N1281J	30. 3.81	Crashed following mid-air collision with Cirrus BGA.2138 at Longdon, near Tewkesbury, Glos. on 12.5.84. Canx as destroyed 10.1.89. Wreck on fire dump 2/98 at Bristol/ Lulsgate.
G-BIUP	SNCAN NC.854S Chardonneret	54	(G-AMPE) G-BIUP/F-BFSC	4. 6.81	
G-BIUR	Boeing 727-155C (Line No. 470)	19619	TF-FLJ(2) YA-FAW/G-BIUR/YA-FAW/N531EJ	27. 4.81	Restored as YA-FAW. Canx 28.10.82.
G-BIUS	Cessna 310R II	310R-0580	PH-ALD D-IJOS/N87649	31. 3.81	To OO-AUD 8/82. Canx 21.6.82.
G-BIUT	Scruggs BL-2C HAFB (Toy)	81228		31. 3.81	Canx by CAA 6.12.88.
G-BIUU	PA-23-250 Aztec D	27-4446	TR-LPZ 6V-ACB/N13798	4. 9.81	CofA expired 10.9.84. (Last known stored at Lydd) Canx as WFU 9.12.88.
G-BIUV	HS.748 Srs.2A/266LFD	1701	5W-FAN G-AYYH/G-11-8	11. 5.81	
G-BIUW	PA-28-161 Warrior II	28-8116128	N9506N	14. 4.81	
G-BIUX	PA-28-161 Warrior II	28-8116129	N9507N	14. 4.81	To G-KNAP 2/90. Canx.
G-BIUY	PA-28-181 Archer II	28-8190133	N8318X	3. 4.81	
G-BIUZ(1)	Slingsby T.67B	1998		6. 4.81	NTU - To structural test airframe & dismantled 1/83. Canx as WFU 11.1.83.
G-BIUZ(2)	Slingsby T.67B	2005	(G-FFLY)	31.10.83	DBR when FA.152 G-BHMF landed on top of it whilst coming into land at Cranfield on 25.2.87. Remains scrapped in 1994. Canx as destroyed 8.4.87.
G-BIVA	Robin R.2112	137	F-GBAZ	6. 5.81	
G-BIVB	Wassmer Jodel D.112	1009	(G-BIVC) F-BJII	18. 9.81	
G-BIVC(1)	Wassmer Jodel D.112	1009	F-BJII	. .81R	NTU - To G-BIVB 9/81. Canx.
G-BIVC(2)	Wassmer Jodel D.112	1219	F-BMAI	1. 6.81	
G-BIVD	Not allocated.				
G-BIVE	Monnett Sonerai 2L	1070-2L & PFA/15-10684		. .81R	NTU - Canx.
G-BIVF	Scintex CP.301-C3 Emeraude	594	F-BJVN	4.11.81	Badly damaged following ditching in Irish Sea, 1 mile north of Point of Ayr, north of IoM on 20.8.91. (Stored 4/95 Great Eversden)
G-BIVG	Thunder Ax3 Sky Chariot HAFB	339		8. 4.81	Canx as WFU 25.9.84.
G-BIVH	Thunder Ax7-77 HAFB	327		8. 4.81	To C-GTMS 12/81. Canx 18.12.81.
G-BIVI	Cremer PAC500 Hot-Air (Free) Airship (Toy)	PAC500-20566		7. 4.81	Canx by CAA 8.12.88.
G-BIVJ	Reims Cessna F.152 II	1872		21. 4.81	Landed at Ingoldmells on 9.5.85 inbound from Stapleford in poor weather conditions and on wet grass as a result of which it overshot and slid into a bank and overturned. Rebuilt & re-regd as G-OSFC 1/86. Canx.
G-BIVK	Bensen B.8M Gyrocopter	JGT-01 & G/01-1008		10. 4.81	
G-BIVL	Bensen B.8M Gyrocopter	TED-01 & G/01-1011		10. 4.81	Permit expired 29.4.87. (Extant 6/96) Canx by CAA 3.4.97.
G-BIVM	Cessna 150L	150-73717	N17374	. .81R	NTU - To (G-BJMS)/G-IDJB 10/82. Canx.
G-BIVN	Cessna A.150M Aerobat	A150-0627	N9818J	. .81R	NTU - To G-BJTB 10/82. Canx.
G-BIVO	Schweizer-Gulfstream G.164D Turbo Agcat	15D	N8311K	21. 4.81	To EC-EBD. Canx 19.11.86.
G-BIVP	Aerospatiale AS.350B Ecureuil	1465		2. 4.81	To G-SKIM 10/83. Canx.
G-BIVR	Stansted Featherlight Mk.2 HAFB (Toy)	001		15. 4.81	
G-BIVS	Stansted Featherlight Mk.2 HAFB (Toy)	002		15. 4.81	Canx by CAA 13.12.88.
G-BIVT	Saffery S.80 HAFB (Toy)	LFG-001		22. 4.81	

Regn	Type	c/n	Previous identity	Regn date	Fate or immediate subsequent identity (if known)
G-BIVU	American Aviation AA-5A Cheetah	AA5A-0772	N26859	7. 5.81	To G-CCOL 4/92. Canx.
G-BIVV	American Aviation AA-5A Cheetah	AA5A-0857	N26979	26. 5.81	
G-BIVW(1)	Pitts S-1D Special	PFA/09-10525		. .81R	NTU - To G-BKKZ 11/82. Canx.
G-BIVW(2)	Moravan Zlin Z.326 Trener-Master	932	F-BPNQ	12. 1.82	Imported as burned wreck from Carcasonne and for use as spares. (Remains stored 6/96)
G-BIVX	Saffery S.80 HAFB (Toy)	PTW.001		22. 4.81	Canx as WFU 1.11.88.
G-BIVY	Cessna 172N Skyhawk 100	172-67768	N73973	7. 5.81	To G-OSII 10/95. Canx.
G-BIVZ	Rollason-Druine D.31A Turbulent	PFA/48-10681		6. 4.81	Fatal crash at Swanton Morley on 9.8.98. Canx as destroyed 26.11.98.
G-BIWA	Stevendon Skyreacher HAFB (Toy)	102		8. 6.81	
G-BIWB	Scruggs RS.5000 HAFB (Toy)	81541		8. 6.81	
G-BIWC	Scruggs RS.5000 HAFB (Toy)	81546		26. 6.81	
G-BIWD	Scruggs RS.5000 HAFB (Toy)	81545		26. 6.81	
G-BIWE	Scruggs BL-2D HAFB (Toy)	81243		1. 7.81	Canx as WFU 8.3.88.
G-BIWF	Ridout Warren Windcatcher HAFB (Toy)	WW.013		3. 7.81	
G-BIWG	Ridout Zelenski Mk.2 HAFB (Toy) (Regd with c/n 2401)	Z.401		3. 7.81	
G-BIWH	Cremer Super Fliteliner HAFB (Toy)	15.700PC		13. 7.81	
G-BIWI	Cremer Windliner WS.1 HAFB (Toy)	15.701PC		13. 7.81	Canx by CAA 8.12.88.
	(Actually an open-ended windsock shape - not capable of any flight)				
G-BIWJ	Unicorn UE-1A HAFB (Toy)	81014		14. 7.81	(Extant 2/97)
G-BIWK	Cameron V-65 HAFB	719		22. 4.81	
G-BIWL	PA-32-301 Saratoga	32-8116056	N83684	23. 4.81	
G-BIWM	Cameron A-530 HAFB	701		28. 4.81	To F-GCXZ 9/83P. Canx 5.2.82.
G-BIWN	Wassmer Jodel D.112	1314	F-BNCN	5. 6.81	
G-BIWO	Saffery RS.500 HAFB (Toy)	81540		24. 4.81	Canx by CAA 13.12.88.
G-BIWP	Mooney M.20J (201)	24-1094	N9923S	28. 5.81	Fatal crash & DBF near Hemingbrough, N.Yorks on 29.4.99.
G-BIWR	Mooney M.20F Executive	22-1339	N6972V	1. 6.81	
G-BIWS	Cessna 182R Skylane II	182-67843	N6601N	12. 5.81	To G-ISEH 11/90. Canx.
G-BIWT	Cessna 182R Skylane II	182-67892	N6504H	1. 5.81	To N9155F 7/81. Canx 9.7.81.
G-BIWU	Cameron V-65 HAFB	717		15. 5.81	
G-BIWV	Cremer PAC 550T Uniform Hotel HAFB (Toy)	PAC 550T-11666		29. 4.81	Canx by CAA 13.12.88.
G-BIWW	American Aviation AA-5 Traveler	AA5-0263	OY-AYV	2. 6.81	
G-BIWX	CCF T-6J Texan (Harvard 4M) (Possibly c/n CCF4-409 ex.51-17227)	CCF-4...	MM53846 Italian AF/RM-22/51-17...	29. 4.81	To G-RAIX 2/98. Canx.
G-BIWY	Westland WG-30-100	901		30. 4.81	CofA expired 30.3.86 & WFU. (To Instructional Airframe) Canx as WFU 29.1.87. (Stored 12/98 Weston-super-Mare)
G-BIWZ	Zenair Zenith	-		. .81R	NTU - Canx.
G-BIXA	Socata TB-9 Tampico	205		7. 5.81	
G-BIXB	Socata TB-9 Tampico	208		7. 5.81	
G-BIXC	PBN BN-2B-21 Islander (Originally regd as BN-2B-26)	2106		1. 5.81	To G-MICV 9/81. Canx.
G-BIXD	PBN BN-2B-26 Islander	2107		1. 5.81	To N414JA 12/81. Canx 14.12.81.
G-BIXE	PBN BN-2B-21 Islander (Originally regd as BN-2B-26)	2108		1. 5.81	To SAF-002 Surinam AF 3/82. Canx 20.4.82.
G-BIXF	PBN BN-2B-26 Islander	2109		1. 5.81	To N2643X 12/81. Canx 17.12.81.
G-BIXG	PBN BN-2B-26 Islander	2110		1. 5.81	To N663J 4/82. Canx 20.4.82.
G-BIXH	Reims Cessna F.152 II	1840		30. 4.81	
G-BIXI	Cessna 172RG Cutlass II	172RG-0861	N7533B	7. 7.81	
G-BIXJ	Saffery S.40 HAFB (Toy)	TP-01		30. 4.81	Canx as WFU 29.11.93.
G-BIXK	Rand KR-2	RC.01 & PFA/129-10810		30. 4.81	Canx by CAA 2.9.91.
G-BIXL	North American P-51D-20NA Mustang	122-38675	2343 Israeli DF/AF/Swedish AF Fv.26116/44-72216	3. 7.81	
G-BIXM	Beechcraft C90 King Air	LJ-991	G-SALV G-BIXM/(YV-442CP)	13. 5.81	To N504AB 10/91. Canx 28.10.91.
G-BIXN	Boeing-Stearman A75N1 (PT-17-BW) Kaydet	75-2248	N51132 41-8689	15. 6.81	Badly damaged on take-off at Frensham Pond on 21.4.96. (Frame stored 10/97 Swanton Morley) CofA expired 3.8.96.
G-BIXO	Thunder Ax2 HAFB	308		11. 5.81	NTU - Canx 27.5.81 as not built.
G-BIXP	Vickers-Supermarine 361 Spitfire LF.IXe (C/n is firewall no.)	CBAF/IX/558	2046 Israel DF/AF/Czech AF/TE517	3. 7.81	No CofA issued. Canx as WFU 12.11.84. To G-CCIX 9.4.85.
G-BIXR	Cameron A-140 HAFB	737		13. 5.81	Canx by CAA 19.5.93.
G-BIXS	Avenger T.200-2112 HAFB (Toy)	013		13. 5.81	
G-BIXT	Cessna 182R Skylane II	182-67888	N6397H	8. 7.81	To G-RFAB 5/91. Canx.
G-BIXU	American Aviation AA-5B Tiger	AA5B-1184	N4533N	3. 7.81	To G-IRIS 12/87. Canx.
G-BIXV	Bell 212	30870	N16931	27. 5.81	
G-BIXW	Colt 0-56B HAFB	348		18. 5.81	
G-BIXX	Pearson Srs.II HAFB (Toy)	00327		8. 5.81	
G-BIXY	Piper J3C-65 Cub (L-4J-PI) (Frame No. 12447)	12617	F-BDTZ 44-80321	21. 9.81	To G-FRAN 7/86. Canx.
G-BIXZ	Grob G-109	6019	D-KGRO	14. 5.81	
G-BIYA	Short SD.3-30 Var.200	SH3071	G-14-3071	21. 5.81	To (N330AE)/N2679U 7/81. Canx 18.12.81.
G-BIYB	PA-18-150 Super Cub (L-21B-PI)(Frame No. 18-3843)	18-3841	PH-GER R.Netherlands AF R-151/5G-96/54-2441	26. 5.81	NTU - To G-BIYR 26.5.81. Canx.
G-BIYC	Aerospatiale AS.350B Ecureuil	1486		29. 5.81	To G-MAGY 10/81. Canx.

Regn	Type	c/n	Previous identity	Regn date	Fate or immediate subsequent identity (if known)
G-BIYD	Short SD.3-30 Var.200	SH3072		21. 5.81	To N2678G 12/81. Canx 18.12.81.
G-BIYE	Short SD.3-30 Var.200	SH3073		21. 5.81	To VH-KNQ 6/82. Canx 8.81.
G-BIYF	Short SD.3-30 Var.200	SH3074		21. 5.81	To N26288 12/81. Canx 18.12.81.
G-BIYG	Short SD.3-30 Var.100	SH3075	N182AP	21. 5.81	To TR-WEH/TR-LEH 10/96. Canx 21.10.96.
			N337MV/G-BIYG		
G-BIYH	Short SD.3-30 Var.100	SH3076	N183AP	21. 5.81	To C-FYXF 8/96. Canx 1.8.96.
			N338MV/G-BIYH/G-14-3076		
G-BIYI	Cameron V-65 HAFB	722		21. 5.81	
G-BIYJ	PA-18-95 Super Cub	18-1000	MM51-15303	5. 6.81	
	(L-18C-PI)		Italian AF/I-EIST/MM51-15303/51-15303		
G-BIYK	Isaacs Fury II	PFA/11-10418		20. 5.81	
G-BIYL	Reims Cessna F.172P Skyhawk	2106	D-EEBT	1. 6.81	NTU - Canx 18.9.81 as Not Imported. To F-GDDN 12/81.
G-BIYM	PA-32R-301 Saratoga SP	32R-8113065	N8385X	26. 5.81	To G-JPOT 8/94. Canx.
G-BIYN	Lewis/Pitts S-1S Special	AJT	N455T	26. 5.81	To G-UCCI 5/88. Canx.
G-BIYO	PA-31-310 Turbo Navajo	31-7912022	PH-ECG	5. 6.81	
			N27845		
G-BIYP	PA-20-125 Pacer	20-802	CN-TYP	25. 5.83	
			F-DACJ/OO-ADP		
G-BIYR	PA-18-150 Super Cub	18-3841	(G-BIYB)	26. 5.81	
	(L-21B-PI)(Frame No. 18-3843)		PH-GER/R.Netherlands AF R-151/5G-96/54-2441		
G-BIYS	Beechcraft 95-58P Pressurised Baron	TJ-188	G-UBKP	24. 6.81	To N96487 7/81. Canx 27.7.81.
G-BIYT	Colt 17A Cloudhopper HAFB	344		13. 7.81	
G-BIYU	Fokker S.11-1 Instructor	6206	(PH-HOM)	13. 5.81	
			R.Netherlands AF E-15		
G-BIYV	Cremer 14.700PC Fliteliner Srs.15			2. 6.81	Canx 27.10.88 on sale to New Zealand.
	HAFB (Toy)	C.14.700PC-007			
G-BIYW	Wassmer Jodel D.112	1209	F-BLNR	26. 5.81	
G-BIYX	PA-28-140 Cherokee Cruiser F	28-7625064	OY-BLD	19. 6.81	(On rebuild 11/96) CofA expired 19.12.96.
G-BIYY	PA-18-95 Super Cub	18-1979	MM52-2379	2. 6.81	
	(L-18C-PI)(Frame No 18-1914)		Italian AF/I-EIGA/MM52-2379/52-2379		
G-BIYZ	Cessna 182R Skylane	182-67930	N9309H	4. 6.81	Canx as WFU 15.7.81. To VH-FVG 12/81.
G-BIZA	Agusta-Bell 206B JetRanger III	8610		10. 6.81	To G-VANG 2/82. Canx.
G-BIZB	Agusta-Bell 206B JetRanger III	8611		10. 6.81	Crashed into a hill on corfu on 28.6.89 during the making of a film. Canx as destroyed 2.10.89.
G-BIZC	Agusta-Bell 206B JetRanger III	8643		10. 6.81	NTU - Canx 8.8.84 as Not Imported. To YU-HCW.
G-BIZD	Agusta-Bell 206B JetRanger III	8646		10. 6.81	NTU - Canx 8.8.84 as Not Imported. To YU-HCV.
G-BIZE	Socata TB-9 Tampico	209	9H-ABJ	15. 6.81	
			G-BIZE		
G-BIZF	Reims Cessna F.172P Skyhawk II	2070		16. 6.81	
G-BIZG	Reims Cessna F.152 II	1873		16. 6.81	
G-BIZH	Saffery S.200 HAFB (Toy)	-		. .81R	NTU - Canx.
G-BIZI	Robin DR.400/120 Dauphin 80	1543		29. 5.81	
G-BIZJ	Nord 3202B	70	N22546	. .81R	NTU - To G-BPMU 1/89. Canx.
			ALAT "AIX"		
G-BIZK	Nord 3202B-1	78	(G-BNFZ)	22.11.85	
			G-BIZK/N2255E/ALAT		
G-BIZL	Nord 3202B-1	85	N2255Y	. .81R	NTU - To G-BRVA 12/89. Canx.
			F-MAJG		
G-BIZM	Nord 3202B	91	N2256K	22.11.85	
			ALAT		
G-BIZN	Slingsby T.67A	1989		16. 6.81	(Badly damaged on take-off from Leicester on 23.7.97)
G-BIZO	PA-28R-200 Cherokee Arrow II	28R-7535339	OY-DLH	16. 6.81	
G-BIZP	Pilatus PC-6/B2-H2 Turbo-Porter	812		16. 6.81	Damaged in forced landing in playing fields at Yarwell on 18.12.83. (Wreck later removed to Sibson). Canx as destroyed 10.12.84.
G-BIZR	Socata TB-9 Tampico	210	G-BSEC	15. 6.81	
			G-BIZR		
G-BIZS	Westland WG.13 Lynx Mk.86	WA/228		9. 6.81	To R.Norwegian AF as 228 in 9/81. Canx 7.9.81.
G-BIZT	Bensen B.8M Gyrocopter	G/01-1015		10. 6.81	Permit expired 12.8.88. Canx by CAA 3.4.97. (Reportedly stored at Kilkerran 8/98)
G-BIZU	Thunder Ax6-56Z HAFB	358		15. 6.81	
G-BIZV	PA-18-95 Super Cub	18-2001	MM52-2401	12. 6.81	
	(L-18C-PI)		Italian AF/I-EIDE/MM52-2401/52-2401		
G-BIZW	Champion 7GCBC Citabria	0157	D-EGPD	16. 7.81	
G-BIZX	Beechcraft B200 Super King Air	BB-963		13.11.81	To N400GA 11/84. Canx 6.11.84.
G-BIZY	Wassmer Jodel D.112	1120	F-BKJL	13. 7.81	
G-BIZZ	Cessna 500 Citation I	500-0411	N6784Y	28. 1.82	To G-NCMT 5/87. Canx.
	(Unit No.645)				
G-BJAA	Unicorn UE-1A HAFB (Toy)	81007		2. 6.81	Canx by CAA 30.11.88.
G-BJAB	Ayres S2R-600 Thrush Commander	2513R	(PH-BOL)	17. 7.81	To N409G 1/86. Canx 20.1.86.
			G-BJAB/N4007G		
G-BJAC	Boeing-Vertol 234LR Commercial		N234BV	2. 2.81	To N234CH 2/85. Canx 12.1.85.
	Chinook	B-818/MJ-001			
G-BJAD	Clutton FRED Srs.II	CA.1 & PFA/29-10586		11. 6.81	No Permit issued, probably not completed. Canx by CAA 9.9.97.
G-BJAE	Lavadoux Starck AS.80 Holiday	04	F-PGGA	17. 6.81	Badly damaged on landing at Woburn on 17.8.91.
			F-WGGA		Permit expired 8.8.92.
G-BJAF	Piper J3C-65 Cub (L-4A-PI)	8437	D-EJAF	23. 6.81	
	(Frame No 8540)		HB-OAD/42-15318		

Regn	Type	c/n	Previous identity	Regn date	Fate or immediate subsequent identity (if known)
G-BJAG	PA-28-181 Archer II	28-7990353	PH-LDB (PH-BEG)/(OO-FLM)/N2244W	23. 6.81	
G-BJAH	Unicorn UE-1A HAFB (Toy)	81008		5. 6.81	Canx by CAA 29.11.88.
G-BJAI	Rango NA-9 HAFB	KJF-17		22. 6.81	Canx as destroyed 12.10.81.
G-BJAJ	American Aviation AA-5B Tiger	AA5B-1177	N4532V	2. 7.81	
G-BJAK	Mooney M.20C	3116	OO-CAB OO-VLB/N5814Q	8. 7.81	To N7133J 4/90. Canx 12.4.90.
G-BJAL	CASA I-131E Jungmann (Spanish AF serial conflicts with G-BUCC)	1028	E3B-114	11. 9.78	
G-BJAM	Westland-Bell 47G-3B1 (Line No. WAS/178)	WA/588	XT826	8. 7.76	To 5X-PAW. Canx 23.8.82.
G-BJAN	K & S SA.102.5 Cavalier	PFA/1554		20.12.78	No Permit to Fly issued. Canx by CAA 12.4.99.
G-BJAO	Montgomerie-Bensen B.8MR Gyrocopter (Regd with c/n GL5-01)(Built by sixth formers at Brittons Upper School and painted as G-BJOA)	GLS-01 & G/01-1001		28. 8.81	Badly damaged taxying at Kemble on 29.12.96. (Extant 6/97) Permit expired 10.12.98.
G-BJAP	DH.82A Tiger Moth (Composite rebuild)	0482 & PFA/157-12897		15. 6.81	
G-BJAR	Unicorn UE-3A HAFB (Toy)	81006		2. 6.81	Canx by CAA 20.10.98.
G-BJAS	Rango NA-9 HAFB (Toy)	TL-19		22. 6.81	
G-BJAT	Pilatus P.2-05	600-29	U-109 Swiss AF/A-109	24. 6.81	To N109PL. Canx 17.6.83.
G-BJAU	PZL-104 Wilga 35A	140542	SP-WDC(2)	8. 9.81	To ZK-PZM 5/92. Canx 12.9.91.
G-BJAV	Gardan GY-80-160 Horizon	28	OO-AJP(2) F-BLVB	8. 9.81	CofA expired 26.1.97.
G-BJAW	Cameron V-65 HAFB	745		19. 6.81	
G-BJAX	Pilatus P.2-05	600-28	U-108 Swiss AF/A-108	15. 6.81	On static display at Duxford with Permit expired 28.5.91. Scrapped & used for spares in 1994 at Tattershall Thorpe. Canx as WFU 15.4.94.
G-BJAY	Piper J3C-65 Cub (L-4H-PI) (Frame No. 11914)	12086	F-BFBN OO-EAC/44-79790	1.11.78	Permit expired 19.8.92.
G-BJAZ	Thunder Ax7-77 HAFB	359		22. 6.81	To F-GGAZ 6/87. Canx 16.2.87.
G-BJBA	Cessna 152 II	152-84310	N5394L	24. 6.81	To I-BJBA. Canx 13.5.87.
G-BJBB	Cessna 152 II	152-84252	N5086L	24. 6.81	To I-BJBB. Canx 13.5.87.
G-BJBC	Cessna TR.182 Turbo Skylane RG	R182-01390	N4703S	16. 6.81	To G-RUTH 9/81. Canx.
G-BJBD	PBN BN-2B-27 Islander	2111		25. 6.81	To N3235G. Canx 24.9.82.
G-BJBE	PBN BN-2T Turbine Islander	2112		25. 6.81	To G-HOPL 8/82. Canx.
G-BJBF	PBN BN-2B-27 Islander	2113		25. 6.81	To HK-2904 2/83. Canx 4.2.83.
G-BJBG	PBN BN-2B-27 Islander	2114		25. 6.81	To G-BLEC 10/83. Canx.
G-BJBH	PBN BN-2B-27 Islander	2115		25. 6.81	To G-51-2115/G-RAPA 5/82. Canx.
G-BJBI	Cessna 414A Chancellor	414A-0674		2. 7.81	To N140KM 6/95. Canx 27.4.95.
G-BJBJ	Boeing 737-2T5 (Line No. 847)	22632	N6868L	22. 1.82	To CN-RMX 12/87. Canx 4.12.87.
G-BJBK	PA-18-95 Super Cub (L-18C-PI)(Frame No. 18-1370)	18-1431	F-BOME ALAT/51-15431	21. 8.81	
G-BJBL	Unicorn UE-1A HAFB (Toy)	81009		30. 6.81	Canx by CAA 6.12.88.
G-BJBM	Monnett Sonerai I	MEA-117 & PFA/15-10022		2. 7.81	Permit expired 9.1.97.
G-BJBN	Ball JB980-4342 Bodybag HAFB (Toy)	001		1. 7.81	Canx by CAA 6.12.88.
G-BJBO	CEA Jodel DR.250/160 Capitaine	40	F-BNJG	24. 8.81	
G-BJBP	Beechcraft A200 Super King Air	BB-240	G-HLUB	28. 7.81	To N62360 3/93. Canx 19.3.93.
G-BJBR	Robinson R-22	0154	N9081N	15. 7.81	To F-GJHB 6/89. Canx 8.6.99.
G-BJBS	Robinson R-22 HP	0155	N9081S	15. 7.81	To VH-EWY(2) 5/95. Canx 15.11.93.
G-BJBT	Robinson R-22	0156	N9081U	15. 7.81	To G-FMUS 11/83. Canx.
G-BJBU	PA-23-250 Aztec E	27-7305194	N40476	22. 7.81	To G-WEBB 10/84. Canx.
G-BJBV	PA-28-161 Warrior II	28-8116279	N2913Y	22. 7.81	Crashed near Shoreham on 31.5.96. Canx as WFU 1.10.96.
G-BJBW	PA-28-161 Warrior II	28-8116280	N2913Z	22. 7.81	
G-BJBX	PA-28-161 Warrior II	28-8116269	N8414H	17. 7.81	
G-BJBY	PA-28-161 Warrior II	28-8116270	N8415L	20. 7.81	Badly damaged trying to take-off from Old Sarum on 23.11.97. Canx as WFU 3.3.98.
G-BJBZ	Rotorway Exec 133	01-81		17. 7.81	No Permit to Fly issued. Canx by CAA 12.4.99.
G-BJCA	PA-28-161 Warrior II	28-7916473	N2846D	30. 7.81	
G-BJCB(1)	HS.125 Srs.600A	256015	G-BBCL G-5-19	30. 8.73	Restored as G-BBCL 2/77. Canx.
G-BJCB(2)	HS.125 Srs.600B	256065	G-5-16	3. 2.77	To XA-MAH(2) 7/81. Canx 9.7.81.
G-BJCC	Unicorn UE-1A HAFB (Toy)	81010		10. 7.81	Canx by CAA 13.12.88.
G-BJCD	Bede BD-5BH	003T		21. 7.81	To N9211B 3/94. Canx 9.3.94.
G-BJCE	Reims Cessna F.172P Skyhawk	2124		20. 7.81	To PH-DKF(2) 11/86. Canx 20.10.86.
G-BJCF	Scintex CP.1310-C3 Super Emeraude	936	F-BMJH	19.11.81	
G-BJCG	Sportavia-Putzer Fournier RF-5B Sperber	5127	(D-KOCI)	23. 7.81	Canx 9.7.82 on sale to Australia. To D-KOCI(2) 7/83.
G-BJCH	B.H.M.E.D. Osset 1 HAFB (Toy)	001		27. 7.81	Canx as WFU 15.11.88.
G-BJCI	PA-18-150 Super Cub	18-6658	N9388D	10. 9.81	
G-BJCJ	PA-28-181 Archer II	28-8190280	N8415X	22. 7.81	Fatal crash at Prior Drive, Stanmore on 18.4.91. Canx as destroyed 13.5.91
G-BJCK	Bell 206B JetRanger III	3395	N18098	14. 9.81	To UAE AF as AMDB-106. Canx 1.10.81.
G-BJCL	Morane Saulnier MS.230 Parasol	1049	EI-ARG F-BGMR/French Mil.	22. 7.81	To N230MS. Canx 27.1.88.

Regn	Type	c/n	Previous identity	Regn date	Fate or immediate subsequent identity (if known)
G-BJCM	Clutton FRED Srs.II	PFA/29-10267		29. 9.78	No Permit issued. Canx by CAA 19.3.90.
G-BJCN	Cessna 337H Super Skymaster	337-01869	5N-APQ N1377L	18. 2.82	To AP-BBX 11/84. Canx 16.10.84.
G-BJCO	Socata MS.880B Rallye 100T	2505	F-BVLB	19.11.81	To EI-BMB 1/82. Canx 30.11.81.
G-BJCP	Unicorn UE-2B HAFB (Toy)	81011		10. 7.81	Canx as destroyed 19.10.93.
G-BJCR	Partenavia P.68C Victor	218	OO-EEC	24. 8.81	To PH-SOK 9/92. Canx 27.8.92.
G-BJCS	Meagher Mk.2 HAFB (Toy)	81-2001		21. 7.81	Canx as WFU 27.10.88.
G-BJCT	Boeing 737-204ADV (Line No. 858)	22638	EC-DXK G-BJCT/N1780B	8. 3.82	To ZK-NAA. Canx 9.11.93.
G-BJCU	Boeing 737-204ADV (Line No. 863)	22639	EC-DVE G-BJCU	22. 3.82	To EI-CJE 3/94. Canx 10.3.94.
G-BJCV	Boeing 737-204ADV (Line No. 867)	22640	CS-TMA G-BJCV/C-GCAU/G-BJCV/C-GXCP/G-BJCV	3. 8.82	To EI-CJC 1/94. Canx 24.1.94.
G-BJCW	PA-32R-301 Saratoga SP	32R-8113094	N2866U	6. 8.81	
G-BJCX	Reims Cessna F.152	1884		. .81R	NTU - Not Import. Canx.
G-BJCY	Slingsby T.67A	1990		4. 8.81	Fatal crash in a field at Bookham, near Leatherhead on 12.6.87. Canx as destroyed 11.4.88.
G-BJCZ	Embraer EMB-110P1 Bandeirante	110-377	PT-SEU	. .81R	NTU - To G-RVIP 2/82. Canx.
G-BJDA	Short SC.7 Skyvan 3M	SH1976		23. 7.81	To 8R-GRR. Canx 5.12.83.
G-BJDB	Short SC.7 Skyvan 3-100	SH1977		23. 7.81	To ZS-LFG 3/82. Canx 26.2.83.
G-BJDC	Short SC.7 Skyvan 3M	SH1978	G-14-1978	23. 7.81	To R.Nepal AF as RAN-23. Canx 20.7.84.
G-BJDD	Short SC.7 Skyvan 3	SH1979		23. 7.81	To HK-3011X 4/83. Canx 14.4.83.
G-BJDE	Reims Cessna F.172M	0984	OO-MSS D-EGBR	25. 8.81	
G-BJDF	Socata MS.880B Rallye 100T	3000	F-GAKP	21. 9.81	
G-BJDG	Socata TB-10 Tobago	226	F-BNGR	14. 9.81	To N99ET. Canx 27.11.87.
G-BJDH	PA-E23-250 Aztec F	27-7654089	G-BDXV N62614	2. 8.76	To G-FOTO 2/79. Canx.
G-BJDI	Reims Cessna FR.182 Skylane RG	0046	N8062H	7. 8.81	
G-BJDJ	HS.125 Srs.700B	257142	G-RCDI G-BJDJ/G-5-12	27. 7.81	
G-BJDK	Ridout European E.157 HAFB (Toy)	S.2		17. 8.81	
G-BJDL	Rango NA-9 HAFB (Toy)	DL.20		20. 7.81	Canx by CAA 12.12.88.
G-BJDM	K & S SA.102.5 Cavalier	PFA/01-10119		1.11.78	Canx by CAA 2.9.91.
G-BJDN	American Aviation AA-5A Cheetah	AA5A-0794	N26893	3. 8.81	To G-PURR 2/82. Canx.
G-BJDO	American Aviation AA-5A Cheetah	AA5A-0823	N26936	3. 8.81	
G-BJDP	Cremmer Cloud Cruiser HAFB (Toy)	15.702 PAC		7. 8.81	Canx as WFU 27.10.88.
G-BJDR	Fokker S.11-1 Instructor	7775/6202	(PH-HOR) R.Netherlands AF E-11	4.11.81	To N911J. Canx 4.10.85.
G-BJDS	Cremer British Bulldog HAFB (Toy)	AJC-12		28. 7.81	Canx by CAA 8.12.88.
G-BJDT	Socata TB-9 Tampico	227		21. 8.81	
G-BJDU	Scruggs BL-2B Srs.II HAFB (Toy)	81244		31. 7.81	Canx by CAA 29.11.88.
G-BJDV	Kingram Air Bubble HAFB (Toy)	ITS-01		4. 8.81	Canx by CAA 12.12.88.
G-BJDW	Reims Cessna F.172M Skyhawk II	1417	PH-JBE	10. 8.81	
G-BJDX	Scruggs BL-2D II HAFB (Toy)	81247		4. 8.81	Canx as WFU 18.10.88.
G-BJDY	Unicorn UE-4A HAFB (Toy)	81012		28. 7.81	Canx as WFU 19.7.82.
G-BJDZ	Unicorn UE-1A HAFB (Toy)	81013		28. 7.81	Canx by CAA 29.11.88.
G-BJEA	PBN BN-2B-21 Defender (Originally regd as a BN-2B-21 Islander)	2116		28. 7.81	To Surinam AF as SAF-003. Canx 23.8.82.
G-BJEB	PBN BN-2B-21 Defender (Originally regd as a BN-2B-21 Islander)	2117		28. 7.81	To Surinam AF as SAF-004. Canx 23.8.82.
G-BJEC	PBN BN-2T Turbine Islander (Originally regd as a BN-2B)	2118		28. 7.81	To Dubai AF as 411. Canx 14.6.83.
G-BJED	PBN BN-2T Turbine Islander (Originally regd as a BN-2B)	2119		28. 7.81	To G-MAFF 4/82. Canx.
G-BJEE	PBN BN-2T Turbine Islander (Originally regd as a BN-2B)	2120		28. 7.81	To C9-TAH 2/84. Canx 3.2.84.
G-BJEF	PBN BN-2T Turbine Islander (Originally regd as a BN-2B)	2121		28. 7.81	To C9-TAK 2/84. Canx 28.2.84.
G-BJEG	PBN BN-2T Turbine Islander (Originally regd as a BN-2B)	2122		28. 7.81	To C9-TAI 2/84. Canx 9.4.84.
G-BJEH	PBN BN-2B-21 Islander	2123		28. 7.81	To Indian Navy as IN-137. Canx 22.9.83.
G-BJEI	PA-18-95 Super Cub (L-18C-PI)(Frame No 18-1938)	18-1988	MM52-2388 Italian AF/I-EILO/MM52-2388/52-2388	27. 7.81	
G-BJEJ	PBN BN-2T Turbine Islander (Originally regd as a BN-2B)	2124		28. 7.81	To C9-TAJ 2/84. Canx 5.6.84.
G-BJEK	PBN BN-2B-27 Islander	2125		28. 7.81	To VP-FBF. Canx 4.2.83.
G-BJEL	SNCAN NC.854S Chardonneret	113	F-BEZT	7. 8.81	
G-BJEM	Cremer Flying Cube HAFB (Toy)	1		7. 8.81	Canx by CAA 8.12.88.
G-BJEN	Scruggs RS.5000 HAFB (Toy)	81548		5. 8.81	
G-BJEO	PA-34-220T Seneca III	34-8133191	PH-GEC(2) G-TOMF/G-BJEO/N8424Y	14. 8.81	Extensive damage when it swung to starboard on take-off from Birmingham on 16.5.86. Canx as WFU 4.7.94.
G-BJEP	Scruggs RS.5000 HAFB (Toy)	81552		7. 8.81	Canx as WFU 2.6.83.
G-BJER	Scruggs RS.5000 HAFB (Toy)	81553		7. 8.81	Canx as WFU 2.6.83.

Regn	Type	c/n	Previous identity	Regn date	Fate or immediate subsequent identity (if known)
G-BJES	Scruggs RS.5000 HAFB (Toy)	81551		5. 8.81	Canx by CAA 2.12.93.
G-BJET	Cessna 425 Corsair	425-0024	(G-BHNW) (N6772U)	25. 2.81	To D-IEAT. Canx 22.4.87.
G-BJEU	Scruggs BL-2D II HAFB (Toy)	81249		5. 8.81	Canx by CAA 2.12.93.
G-BJEV	Aeronca 11AC Chief	11AC-270	N85897 NC85897	12. 8.81	
G-BJEW	Cremer Cloud Clipper HAFB (Toy)	15.703 PAC		11. 8.81	Canx by CAA 13.12.88.
G-BJEX	Bolkow Bo.208C Junior	690	F-BRHY D-EEAM	27. 8.81	CofA expired 28.1.88. (Status uncertain)
G-BJEY	B.H.M.E.D. Otserp Srs.1 HAFB (Toy)	002		10. 8.81	
G-BJEZ	Cameron O-105 HAFB	763	PH-BIG G-BJEZ	10. 8.81	To F-GEAD 8/84. Canx 20.3.84.
G-BJFA	American Aviation AA-5A Cheetah	AA5A-0893	N27169	17. 8.81	To G-KILT 3/82. Canx.
G-BJFB	Eaves Dodo Mk.1A HAFB (Toy)	DD.5		27. 8.81	
G-BJFC	Ridout European E.8 HAFB (Toy)	S.1		17. 8.81	
G-BJFD	B.H.M.E.D. Temoc Srs.1 HAFB (Toy)	003		17. 8.81	Canx by CAA 8.12.88.
G-BJFE	PA-18-95 Super Cub (L-18C-PI)	18-2022	MM52-2422 Italian AF/I-EISU/MM52-2422/52-2422	17. 8.81	Permit expired 8.10.98.
G-BJFF	Enstrom F.28C-UK-2	498-2		1. 9.81	To ZS-HMO 3/84. Canx 10.2.84.
G-BJFG	Enstrom 280C-UK-2 Shark	1221	N8617N	1. 9.81	To G-KENY 3/82. Canx.
G-BJFH	Boeing 737-2S3 (Line No. 646)	22278		20. 2.80	To EI-BXY 12/88. Canx 5.12.88.
G-BJFI	Bell 47G-2A1	3173	TF-HUG 63-13673	21. 8.81	To 5B-CFV 1/84. Canx 16.12.83.
G-BJFJ	Chown Osprey Lizzieliner Mk.1A HAFB (Toy)	AKC-01		18. 8.81	Canx as WFU 10.1.83.
G-BJFK	Short SD.3-30 Var.200	SH3077	G-14-3077	18. 8.81	To 4X-CSP. Canx 12.7.91.
G-BJFL	Sikorsky S-76A II Plus	760056	N106BH N1546T/(G-BHRK)	28. 8.81	
G-BJFM	Jodel Wassmer D.120 Paris-Nice	227	F-BLFM	8.10.81	
G-BJFN	Windsor Mk IV HAFB (Toy)	101		11. 8.81	Canx as WFU 18.10.88.
G-BJFO	Windsor Mk II HAFB (Toy)	102		11. 8.81	Canx as WFU 18.10.88.
G-BJFP	Windsor Mk II HAFB (Toy)	103		11. 8.81	Canx as WFU 18.10.88.
G-BJFR	Windsor Mk IV HAFB (Toy)	201		11. 8.81	Canx by CAA 6.12.88.
G-BJFS	Windsor Mk IV HAFB (Toy)	202		11. 8.81	Canx by CAA 6.12.88.
G-BJFT	Windsor Mk IV HAFB (Toy)	203		11. 8.81	Canx by CAA 6.12.88.
G-BJFU	Windsor Mk IV HAFB (Toy)	301		11. 8.81	Canx as WFU 27.10.88.
G-BJFV	Windsor Mk V HAFB (Toy)	401		11. 8.81	Canx as WFU 18.10.88.
G-BJFW	Windsor Mk V HAFB (Toy)	402		11. 8.81	Canx as WFU 18.10.88.
G-BJFX	Windsor Mk V HAFB (Toy)	403		11. 8.81	Canx as WFU 18.10.88.
G-BJFY	Windsor Mk I HAFB (Toy)	501		11. 8.81	Canx as WFU 27.10.88.
G-BJFZ	Windsor Mk II HAFB (Toy)	502		11. 8.81	Canx as WFU 27.10.88.
G-BJGA	Windsor Mk IV HAFB (Toy)	503		11. 8.81	Canx as WFU 27.10.88.
G-BJGB	Windsor Mk I HAFB (Toy)	601		11. 8.81	Canx as WFU 8.3.88.
G-BJGC	Windsor Mk.IV HAFB (Toy)	C.101		11. 8.81	Canx by CAA 2.12.93.
G-BJGD	Windsor Mk.IV HAFB (Toy)	C.201		11. 8.81	Canx by CAA 30.6.98.
G-BJGE	Thunder Ax3 Sky Chariot HAFB	367		21. 8.81	Canx by CAA 19.5.93. (Extant 2/97)
G-BJGF	Eaves Dodo Mk.1 HAFB (Toy)	DD.1		19. 8.81	
G-BJGG	Eaves Dodo Mk.2 HAFB (Toy)	DD.2		19. 8.81	
G-BJGH	Slingsby T.67A	1991		24. 8.81	Fatal crash at Alsike, near Uppsala, Sweden on 12.7.87. Canx as destroyed 18.5.88.
G-BJGI	HS.748 Srs.2B/FAA	1789		24. 8.81	To N118CA. Canx 29.12.81.
G-BJGJ	Cessna 441 Conquest II	441-0251	(N6858L)	10. 9.81	To N711GF. Canx 6.4.82.
G-BJGK	Cameron V-77 HAFB	696		3. 9.81	
G-BJGL	Cremer Cloud Challenger HAFB (Toy)	15.704 PAC		24. 8.81	
G-BJGM	Unicorn UE-1A HAFB (Toy)	81015		21. 8.81	
G-BJGN	Scruggs RS.5000 HAFB (Toy)	81554		21. 8.81	Canx by CAA 30.11.88.
G-BJGO	Cessna 172N Skyhawk II	172-71985	N6038E	14. 9.81	
G-BJGP	Chown Osprey Lizzieliner Mk.1C HAFB (Toy)	AKC-05		21. 8.91	Canx as WFU 2.6.83.
G-BJGR	Chown Osprey Lizzieliner Mk.2A HAFB (Toy)	AKC-06		21. 8.81	Canx as WFU 2.6.83.
G-BJGS	Cremer Cloudcracker HAFB (Toy)	15.705 PAC		3. 9.81	Canx as WFU 18.10.88.
G-BJGT	Mooney M.20K	25-0572	N10485	23.12.81	To OO-DAP. Canx 2.11.90.
G-BJGU	Bell 212	31170	9V-BMG	9. 9.81	To 5N-ALS 10/81. Canx 19.10.81.
G-BJGV	Bell 212	31171	9V-BMH	9. 9.81	To 5N-ALT 4/82. Canx 19.10.81.
G-BJGW	Max Holste MH.1521M Broussard	92	F-BMMP French AF	26. 8.81	To F-GHNU 7/91. Canx 22.4.91.
G-BJGX	Sikorsky S-76A II Plus	760026	N103BH N4251S	4. 9.81	
G-BJGY	Reims Cessna F.172P Skyhawk II	2128		13.10.81	
G-BJGZ	[Was reserved in 1981 for a Toy Balloon by Cremer & Larkins for UK Skyways]				
G-BJHA	Cremer Cloud Crusader HAFB (Toy)	15.707 PAC		3. 9.81	Canx 23.3.98 as WFU.
G-BJHB	Mooney M.20J (201)	24-1190	N1145G	23.12.81	
G-BJHC	Swan Skyseeker 1 HAFB (Toy)	CS.01		2. 9.81	Canx by CAA 2.12.93.
G-BJHD	Windsor Mk.B HAFB (Toy)	B-07		9. 9.81	Canx by CAA 2.12.93.

Regn	Type	c/n	Previous identity	Regn date	Fate or immediate subsequent identity (if known)
G-BJHE	Osprey Lizzieliner Mk.1B HAFB (Toy)	AKC-02		9. 9.81	Canx by CAA 13.12.88.
G-BJHF	Osprey Lizzieliner Mk.1B HAFB (Toy)	AKC-03		9. 9.81	Canx as WFU 14.8.84.
G-BJHG	Cremer Remercynotnaluap HAFB (Toy)	15.700 PAC		3. 9.81	Canx by CAA 8.12.88
G-BJHH	Cessna 550 Citation II (Unit No.039)	550-0039	(N3273M)	15.11.78	To EI-BJL 7/80. Canx 24.7.80.
G-BJHI	Osprey Lizzieliner Mk.1B HAFB (Toy)	AKC-04		9. 9.81	Canx as WFU 10.1.83.
G-BJHJ	Osprey Lizzieliner Mk.1C HAFB (Toy)	AKC-07		9. 9.81	Canx as WFU 27.10.88.
G-BJHK	EAA Acro-Sport 1	PFA/72-10470		20. 3.80	Permit expired 15.9.96.
G-BJHL	Osprey Lizzieliner Mk.1C HAFB (Toy)	AKC-09		9. 9.81	Canx by CAA 2.12.93.
G-BJHM	Osprey Lizzieliner Mk.1B HAFB (Toy)	AKC-10		9. 9.81	Canx as WFU 18.10.88.
G-BJHN	Osprey Lizzieliner Mk.1B HAFB (Toy)	AKC-14		9. 9.81	Canx by CAA 2.12.93.
G-BJHO	Osprey Lizzieliner Mk.1C HAFB (Toy)	AKC-15		9. 9.81	Canx by CAA 2.12.93.
G-BJHP	Osprey Lizzieliner Mk.1C HAFB (Toy)	AKC.16		9. 9.81	
G-BJHR	Osprey Lizzieliner Mk.1B HAFB (Toy)	AKC-17		9. 9.81	Canx by CAA 8.12.88.
G-BJHS	Short S.25 Sandringham (Sunderland GR.3 c/n SH974 conv.)	SH.55C	(EI-BYI) G-BJHS/N158J/VH-BRF/R.New Zealand AF NZ4108/ML814	11. 9.81	To N814ML 9/93. Canx 12.8.93.
G-BJHT(1)	Colt 56D HAFB	392		. .81R	NTU - To G-BLCH 11/83. Canx.
G-BJHT(2)	Thunder Ax7-65 Bolt HAFB	368		27. 8.81	(Active 9/95)
G-BJHU	Osprey Lizzieliner Mk.1C HAFB (Toy)	AKC-18		9. 9.81	Canx by CAA 2.12.93.
G-BJHV	Voisin Scale Replica (3/4-scale replica of a 1908-type Voisin)	MPS-1		1. 9.81	No CofA or Permit issued. Canx by CAA 4.7.91. (On loan to Brooklands Museum) (On display 3/96)
G-BJHW	Osprey Lizzieliner Mk.1C HAFB (Toy)	AKC-19		9. 9.81	
G-BJHX	Osprey Lizzieliner Mk.1C HAFB (Toy)	AKC-20		9. 9.81	Canx as WFU 15.12.88.
G-BJHY	Osprey Lizzieliner Mk.1B HAFB (Toy)	AKC-21		9. 9.81	Canx by CAA 12.12.88.
G-BJHZ	Osprey Lizzieliner Mk.1B HAFB (Toy)	AKC-27		9. 9.81	Canx by CAA 8.12.88.
G-BJIA	Allport Aerostatics YUO-1A-1-DA HAFB (Toy)	01		2. 9.81	
G-BJIB	Druine D.31A Turbulent	PFA/48-10614		2. 9.81	Crashed near Eglinton on 22.9.94. Canx as destroyed 22.11.94.
G-BJIC	Eaves Dodo Mk.1A HAFB (Toy)	DD.3		4. 9.81	
G-BJID	Osprey Lizzieliner 1B HAFB (Toy)	AKC-28		4. 9.81	
G-BJIE	Witty Sphinx SP.2 HAFB (Toy)	10101		4. 9.81	Canx as WFU 1.11.88.
G-BJIF	Bensen B.8M Gyrocopter	HR-01		7. 9.81	Permit expired 13.7.82. Canx as PWFU 25.1.99.
G-BJIG	Slingsby T.67A	1992		16. 9.81	
G-BJIH	Solent Skysoarer HAFB (Toy)	KS001X		6. 9.81	Canx by CAA 6.12.88.
G-BJII	Witty Sphinx SP.2 HAFB (Toy)	10102		3. 9.81	Canx by CAA 8.12.88.
G-BJIJ	Chown Osprey Mk.1B HAFB (Toy)	08		8. 9.81	Canx as WFU 18.10.88.
G-BJIK	Chown Osprey Mk.1B HAFB (Toy)	23		9. 9.81	Canx as WFU 2.6.83.
G-BJIL	Cessna 550 Citation II (Unit No.354)	550-0328	N67988	17. 9.81	To N550MD 3/84. Canx 15.3.84.
G-BJIM	Not allotted.				
G-BJIN	Chown Osprey Mk.1B HAFB (Toy)	24		9. 9.81	Canx as WFU 2.6.83.
G-BJIO	Chown Osprey Mk.1B HAFB (Toy)	25		9. 9.81	Canx as WFU 2.6.83.
G-BJIP	Chown Osprey Mk.1B HAFB (Toy)	35		9. 9.81	Canx as WFU 15.10.84.
G-BJIR	Cessna 550 Citation II (Unit No.326)	550-0296	(D-CIFA) G-BJIR/N6888C	17. 9.81	
G-BJIS	Windsor Tiger Mk.1 HAFB (Toy)	T-101		9. 9.81	Canx as WFU 18.10.88.
G-BJIT	Bell 212	31197	N18094	30. 9.81	To 5N-ALU 10/81. Canx 19.10.81.
G-BJIU	Bell 212	31200	N18093	12.10.81	To 5N-AOF 5/88. Canx 31.5.88.
G-BJIV	PA-18-180 Super Cub	18-8262	N5972Z	17. 9.81	
G-BJIW	Watmore Holywat T.1 HAFB (Toy)	T-01		10. 9.81	Canx by CAA 12.12.88.
G-BJIX	Watmore Holywat T.1 HAFB (Toy)	R-01		10. 9.81	Canx by CAA 12.12.88.
G-BJIY	Cessna T.337D Turbo Super Skymaster (Robertson STOL Master conversion)	T337-1062	9Q-CPF PH-JWL/N86056	27. 1.82	To G-EDOT 1/90. Canx.
G-BJIZ	PA-42 Cheyenne III	42-8001055		19.10.81	To PH-JDV 6/83. Canx 31.5.83.
G-BJJA	Kingram Air Bubble HAFB (Toy)	ITS.02		9. 9.81	Canx as WFU 15.10.84.
G-BJJB	Kingram Air Bubble HAFB (Toy)	ITS.03		9. 9.81	Canx as WFU 15.10.84.
G-BJJC	Eaves Dodo Mk.1 HAFB (Toy)	DD.4		9. 9.81	Canx as WFU 15.10.84.
G-BJJD	Eaves Dodo Mk.1 HAFB (Toy)	DD.6		9. 9.81	Canx as WFU 2.6.83.
G-BJJE	Eaves Dodo Mk.3 HAFB (Toy)	DD.7		9. 9.81	
G-BJJF	Eaves Dodo Mk.4 HAFB (Toy)	DD.8		9. 9.81	Canx as WFU 27.10.88.
G-BJJG	Eaves Dodo Mk.5 HAFB (Toy)	DD.9		9. 9.81	Canx as WFU 27.10.88.
G-BJJH	Eaves Dodo Mk.4 HAFB (Toy)	DD.10		9. 9.81	Canx as WFU 10.1.83.

Regn	Type	c/n	Previous identity	Regn date	Fate or immediate subsequent identity (if known)
G-BJJI	Rooke & Hounsell SAS Sock HAFB (Toy)	RH.001		9. 9.81	Canx as WFU 18.10.88.
G-BJJJ	Rooke & Hounsell Bitterne HAFB (Toy)	RH.002		9. 9.81	Canx as WFU 18.10.88.
G-BJJK	Rooke & Hounsell Bitterne HAFB (Toy)	RH.003		9. 9.81	Canx as WFU 18.10.88.
G-BJJL	Rooke & Hounsell SAS Shoplifter HAFB (Toy)	RH.004		9. 9.81	Canx as WFU 18.10.88.
G-BJJM	Rooke & Hounsell Bitterne Mk.1 Breezebouncer HAFB (Toy)	RH.006		9. 9.81	Canx as WFU 10.1.83.
G-BJJN	Reims Cessna F.172M	1213	OY-BIH	11. 9.81	CofA expired 7.10.84. Canx as WFU 24.6.86.
G-BJJO	Bell 212	32134		16.11.81	To 5N-BHM. Canx 16.11.92.
G-BJJP	Bell 212	32135	N5736D	16.11.81	To 5N-BHN. Canx 16.11.92.
G-BJJR	Bell 212	32144	N3895P	16.11.81	Fatal crash into the North Sea near the drilling platform "Cecil Provine", 50 miles from Spurn Point on 20.11.84. Canx as destroyed 29.1.87.
G-BJJS	Witty Sphinx SP.2 HAFB (Toy)	10103		11. 9.81	Canx by CAA 29.11.88.
G-BJJT	Mabey Toyah HAFB (Toy)	MWM.01		14. 9.81	Canx by CAA 12.12.88.
G-BJJU	Witty Sphinx SP.2 HAFB (Toy)	10104		15. 9.81	Canx as WFU 18.10.88.
G-BJJV	Beechcraft B200 Super King Air	BB-1007		13.11.81	To N777GA. Canx 6.11.84.
G-BJJW	Windsor Mk.B HAFB (Toy)	B-05		9. 9.81	Canx by CAA 2.12.93.
G-BJJX	Windsor Mk.B HAFB (Toy)	B-04		9. 9.81	Canx by CAA 2.12.93.
G-BJJY	Windsor Mk.B HAFB (Toy)	B-03		9. 9.81	Canx by CAA 2.12.93.
G-BJJZ	Unicorn UE-1A HAFB (Toy)	81016		8. 9.81	Canx as WFU 10.11.88.
G-BJKA	Aerospatiale SA.365C3 Dauphin 2	5022	N3601S	16. 9.81	To F-GIIP. Canx 13.11.91.
G-BJKB	Aerospatiale SA.365C3 Dauphin 2	5026	N3601T	16. 9.81	To F-GNAI 7/98. Canx 24.6.98.
G-BJKC	Windsor Mk.B HAFB (Toy)	B-02		9. 9.81	Canx as WFU 18.10.88.
G-BJKD	Windsor Mk.B HAFB (Toy)	B-01		9. 9.81	Canx as WFU 18.10.88.
G-BJKE	Windsor Mk.A HAFB (Toy)	A-07		9. 9.81	Canx as WFU 18.10.88.
G-BJKF	Socata TB-9 Tampico	240		30. 9.81	
G-BJKG	Windsor Mk.A HAFB (Toy)	A-06		9. 9.81	Canx as WFU 18.10.88.
G-BJKH	Windsor Mk.A HAFB (Toy)	A-05		9. 9.81	Canx as WFU 18.10.88.
G-BJKI	Windsor Mk.A HAFB (Toy)	A-04		9. 9.81	Canx as WFU 18.10.88.
G-BJKJ	Windsor Mk.A HAFB (Toy)	A-03		9. 9.81	Canx as WFU 18.10.88.
G-BJKK	Windsor Mk.A HAFB (Toy)	A-02		9. 9.81	Canx as WFU 18.10.88.
G-BJKL	Windsor Mk.A HAFB (Toy)	A-01		9. 9.81	Canx as WFU 18.10.88.
G-BJKM	Windsor Mk.II HAFB (Toy)	T-401		9. 9.81	Canx as WFU 18.10.88.
G-BJKN	Windsor Mk.I HAFB (Toy)	T-101		9. 9.81	Canx as WFU 18.10.88.
G-BJKO	Windsor Mk.I HAFB (Toy)	T-04		9. 9.81	Canx as WFU 18.10.88.
G-BJKP	Windsor Mk.7 HAFB (Toy)	104		9. 9.81	Canx as WFU 18.10.88.
G-BJKR	Windsor Mk.I HAFB (Toy)	T-02		9. 9.81	Canx as WFU 18.10.88.
G-BJKS	Windsor Mk.I HAFB (Toy)	T-03		9. 9.81	Canx as WFU 18.10.88.
G-BJKT	Windsor Mk.B HAFB (Toy)	B-06		9. 9.81	Canx as WFU 18.10.88.
G-BJKU	Chown Osprey Mk.1B HAFB (Toy)	26		16. 9.81	Canx by CAA 8.12.88.
G-BJKV	Chown Osprey Mk.1F HAFB (Toy)	30		17. 9.81	Canx by CAA 8.12.88.
G-BJKW	Wills Aera II	A3JKW		1. 3.78	
G-BJKX	Reims Cessna F.152 II	1881		22. 9.81	Crashed and came to rest inverted 6 miles west of Letterkenny on 24.9.88. CofA expired 1.7.91. Canx as WFU 19.1.89. (Wreck stored 4/96 Abbeyshrule, Ireland)
G-BJKY	Reims Cessna F.152 II	1886		22. 9.81	
G-BJKZ	Chown Osprey Mk.1F HAFB (Toy)	31		17. 9.81	Canx as WFU 17.11.88.
G-BJLA	Chown Osprey Mk.1F HAFB (Toy)	33		17. 9.81	Canx by CAA 12.12.88.
G-BJLB	SNCAN NC.854S Chardonneret	58	(OO-MVM) F-BFSG	5.11.81	Crashed on landing at a farm at Goldcliff, near Newport, Gwent on 29.7.84. Permit expired 30.6.83. (Stored 8/90)
G-BJLC	Monnett Sonerai IIL	942L & PFA/15-10634		18. 9.81	
G-BJLD	Air-Britain Manchester Eagle 8 Mk.2 HAFB (Toy)	2		18. 9.81	Canx by CAA 29.11.88.
G-BJLE	Chown Osprey 1B HAFB (Toy)	32		21. 9.81	Canx as WFU 21.4.98.
G-BJLF	Unicorn UE-1C HAFB (Toy)	81018		21. 9.81	
G-BJLG	Unicorn UE-1B HAFB (Toy)	81017		21. 9.81	
G-BJLH	PA-18-95 Super Cub (L-18C-PI) (Frame No 18-1513)	18-1541	F-BOUM ALAT 51-15541	26.10.81	
G-BJLI	DH.82A Tiger Moth	DHNZ-135R	ZK-ATM NZ1455	21. 9.81	To HB-UPM. Canx 26.11.81.
G-BJLJ	Cameron D-50 Hot-Air Airship	753		22. 9.81	To N372CB 6/90. Canx 21.6.90.
G-BJLK	Short SD.3-30 Var.100	SH3078	G-14-3078	22. 9.81	WFU & stored in 1/97 at Southend. Broken up in 12/97. N5369X/G-BJLK/EI-BLP/G-BJLK/G-14-3078 Canx as WFU 28.1.98.
G-BJLL	Short SD.3-30 Var.200	SH3079	G-14-3079	22. 9.81	To N2629P. Canx 18.12.81.
G-BJLM	Short SD.3-30 Var.200	SH3080	G-14-3080	22. 9.81	To N2629Y. Canx 18.12.81.
G-BJLN	Stansted Featherlight Mk.3 HAFB (Toy)	810301		23. 9.81	Canx by CAA 29.11.88.
G-BJLO	PA-31-310 Turbo Navajo B	31-815	F-BTQG (F-BTDV)	23.10.81	
G-BJLP	Stansted Featherlight Mk.3 HAFB (Toy)	810302		23. 9.81	Canx by CAA 12.12.88.
G-BJLR	Stansted Featherlight Mk.3 HAFB (Toy)	810303		23. 9.81	Canx by CAA 8.12.88.
G-BJLS	Cessna 340A II	340A-0486	(N6315X)	4. 5.78	To G-FCHJ 7/82. Canx.

Regn	Type	c/n	Previous identity	Regn date	Fate or immediate subsequent identity (if known)
G-BJLT	Stansted Featherlight Mk.3 HAFB (Toy)	810304		23. 9.81	Canx by CAA 13.12.88.
G-BJLU	Stansted Featherlight Mk.3 HAFB (Toy)	810305		23. 9.81	Canx by CAA 2.12.93.
G-BJLV	Witty Sphinx SP.2 HAFB (Toy)	10105		23. 9.81	Canx as WFU 15.11.93.
G-BJLW	Gleave CJ.1 HAFB (Toy)	001		24. 9.81	Canx by CAA 9.12.88.
G-BJLX	Cremer Cracker HAFB (Toy)	15.711 PAC		24. 9.81	
G-BJLY	Cremer Cracker HAFB (Toy)	15.709 PAC		24. 9.81	
G-BJLZ	Cremer Cracker HAFB (Toy)	15.710 PAC		24. 9.81	Canx by CAA 29.11.88.
G-BJMA	Colt 21A Cloudhopper HAFB	352		25. 9.81	Canx 7.5.91 on sale to USA.
G-BJMB	Chown Osprey Mk.1B HAFB (Toy)	22		9. 9.81	Canx as destroyed 18.10.88.
G-BJMC	Chown Osprey Mk.4A HAFB (Toy)	40		25. 9.81	Canx as WFU 2.6.83.
G-BJMD	Chown Osprey Mk.5 HAFB (Toy)	50		9. 9.81	Canx as WFU 2.6.83.
G-BJME	Chown Osprey Mk.5 HAFB (Toy)	62		25. 9.81	Canx as WFU 2.6.83.
G-BJMF	Chown Osprey Mk.4C HAFB (Toy)	63		25. 9.81	Canx as WFU 2.6.83.
G-BJMG	Eaves European E.26C Hot-Air Airship (Toy)	S.4		25. 9.81	Canx by CAA 15.10.98.
G-BJMH	Chown Osprey Mk.3A HAFB (Toy)	37		9. 9.81	Canx as WFU 27.10.88.
G-BJMI	Eaves European E.84 HAFB (Toy)	S.3		9. 9.81	
G-BJMJ	Bensen B.8V Gyrocopter	PRS.1 & G/01-1025		28. 9.81	No Permit to Fly issued. Canx by CAA 24.1.96.
G-BJMK	Cremer Cracker HAFB (Toy)	15.716 PAC		29. 9.81	Canx as WFU 18.10.88.
G-BJML	Cessna 120	10766	N76349 NC76349	5.10.81	
G-BJMM	Cremer Cracker HAFB (Toy)	15.717 PAC		29. 9.81	Canx as WFU 18.10.88.
G-BJMN	Beechcraft 65-C90 King Air	LJ-554	N897K	5.10.81	To F-GESC 3/84. Canx 6.12.83.
G-BJMO	Taylor JT.1 Monoplane	PFA/55-10612		30. 9.81	
G-BJMP	Brugger MB.2 Colibri	PFA/43-10720		30. 9.81	Not completed. Canx by CAA 10.2.87.
G-BJMR	Cessna 310R II	310R-1624	N2631Z	16. 7.79	
G-BJMS(1)	Cessna 150L	150-73717	(G-BIVM) N17374	. .81R	NTU - To G-IDJB 10/82. Canx.
G-BJMS(2)	CCF T-6J-CCF Havard IV	CCF4-...	MM53802 Italian AF	5.10.81	To F-AZCM 9/82. Canx 4.3.82.
G-BJMT	Chown Osprey Mk.1E HAFB (Toy)	AKC-45		2.10.81	Canx by CAA 29.11.88.
G-BJMU	Ridout European E.157 HAFB (Toy)	S.6		5.10.81	Canx by CAA 2.12.93.
G-BJMV	BAC One-Eleven Srs.531FS	BAC.244	TI-LRJ TI-1096C	26.11.81	Canx as WFU 30.3.93. (Stored 1/98 Southend) (Regn G-OBWJ reserved - NTU) Scrapped in 8/98 at Southend.
G-BJMW	Thunder Ax8-105 Srs.2 HAFB	369		14.10.81	
G-BJMX	Ridout Jarre JR-3 HAFB (Toy)	81601		6.10.81	
G-BJMY	Aerospatiale AS.350B Ecureuil	1530		15.10.81	To G-JORR 1/82. Canx.
G-BJMZ	Ridout European EA-8A HAFB (Toy)	S.5		6.10.81	
G-BJNA	Ridout Arena Mk.117P HAFB (Toy)	202		6.10.81	
G-BJNB	WAR Vought F-4U Corsair Replica	PFA/118-10711		13.10.81	No Permit to Fly issued. Canx by CAA 8.11.89.
G-BJNC	Chown Osprey Mk.1E HAFB (Toy)	AKC-56		7.10.81	Canx as WFU 18.10.88.
G-BJND	Chown Osprey Mk.1E HAFB (Toy)	AKC-53		7.10.81	
G-BJNE	Chown Osprey Mk.1E HAFB (Toy)	AKC-54		7.10.81	Canx as WFU 27.10.88.
G-BJNF	Reims Cessna F.152 II	1882		21.10.81	
G-BJNG	Slingsby T.67AM Firefly (Originally regd as T.67A, then as T.67B)	1993		16.10.81	Canx as destroyed 28.7.99.
G-BJNH	Chown Osprey Mk.1E HAFB (Toy)	AKC-57		8.10.81	
G-BJNI	Chown Osprey Mk.1C HAFB (Toy)	AKC-49		9.10.81	Canx by CAA 29.11.88.
G-BJNJ	Bell 206B JetRanger III	3569		5. 2.82	To G-MFMF 6/84. Canx.
G-BJNK	Sikorsky S-76A Spirit	760164	N5443U	19.10.81	To N4493P 10/83. Canx 26.10.83.
G-BJNL	Evans VP-2	PFA/63-10719		2.11.81	Canx by CAA 2.9.91.
G-BJNM	Westland Sea King Mk.4 (Officially regd with c/n WA/210)	WA/912	ZA298	20.10.81	Restored to RN as ZA298. Canx 14.12.81.
G-BJNN	PA-38-112 Tomahawk	38-80A0064		15.10.81	
G-BJNO	American Aviation AA-5B Tiger	AA5B-1160	N4531L	12.11.81	Canx by the CAA 24.9.84.
G-BJNP	Rango NA-32 HAFB (Toy)	NHP-22		1.10.81	
G-BJNR	BAe Bulldog 120 Srs.123	BH120-418		27.10.81	To Nigerian AF as 253. Canx 14.10.82.
G-BJNS	BAe Bulldog 120 Srs.123	BH120-419		27.10.81	To Nigerian AF as 254. Canx 14.10.82.
G-BJNT	BAe Bulldog 120 Srs.123	BH120-420		27.10.81	To Nigerian AF as 255. Canx 14.10.82.
G-BJNU	BAe Bulldog 120 Srs.123	BH120-430		27.10.81	To Nigerian AF as 256. Canx 29.10.82.
G-BJNV	BAe Bulldog 120 Srs.123	BH120-431		27.10.81	To Nigerian AF as 257. Canx 29.10.82.
G-BJNW	EAA Biplane	101	N67279	19.10.81	To SE-XGN. Canx 21.10.85.
G-BJNX	Cameron O-65 HAFB	775		21.10.81	
G-BJNY	Aeronca 11CC Super Chief	11CC-264	CN-TYZ F-OAEE	28.10.81	Permit expired 9.8.90. (Stored 4/91)

Regn	Type	c/n	Previous identity	Regn date	Fate or immediate subsequent identity (if known)
G-BJNZ	PA-23-250 Aztec F	27-7954099	G-FANZ N6905A	5.10.81	
G-BJOA	PA-28-181 Archer II	28-8290048	N8453H	29.10.81	
"G-BJOA"	Montgomerie-Bensen B.8MR Gyrocopter	GLS-01 & G/01-1001		----	Painted as such - really G-BJAO.
G-BJOB	SAN Jodel D.140C Mousquetaire III	118	F-BMBD	2.11.81	
G-BJOC	Colt 240A HAFB	350		27.10.81	Canx 25.3.85 on sale to Canada.
G-BJOD	Hollmann HA-2M Sportster Gyroplane	HP81-01		26.10.81	No Permit believed issued. Canx by CAA 19.6.91. (Structurally complete 7/91)
G-BJOE	Jodel Wassmer D.120A Paris-Nice	177	F-BJIU	12.11.81	
G-BJOF	Partenavia P.68B Victor	147	EI-BKH G-PAUL	5.11.81	To G-CNIS 12/82. Canx.
G-BJOG	PBN BN-2T Turbine Islander	2033		29.10.81	NTU - This had not gained a CofA & was probably never assembled after delivery in kit form from Gosselies. Canx as WFU 29.10.86.
G-BJOH	PBN BN-2T Turbine Islander	2034		29.10.81	To G-OPBN 3/83. Canx.
G-BJOI	Isaacs Special	3		28. 4.78	No Permit believed issued. Canx by CAA 5.2.92.
G-BJOJ	PBN BN-2B-26 Islander	2126		29.10.81	To VP-FBG. Canx 4.2.83.
G-BJOK	PBN BN-2B-27 Islander	2127		29.10.81	To (9Q-CKR)/TR-LBJ 10/84. Canx 19.9.84.
G-BJOL	PBN BN-2B-26 Islander	2128	D-IFLN(1) G-BJOL	29.10.81	To J8-VAP. Canx 28.11.89.
G-BJOM	PBN BN-2B-26 Islander	2129		29.10.81	To N655J. Canx 2.6.83.
G-BJON	PBN BN-2B-26 Islander	2130		29.10.81	To VH-AEU 5/86. Canx 17.7.84.
G-BJOO	PBN BN-2B-26 Islander	2131		29.10.81	To B-12222 7/84. Canx 9.7.84.
G-BJOP	PBN BN-2B-26 Islander	2132		29.10.81	
G-BJOR	PBN BN-2B-21 Islander	2133		29.10.81	Canx 27.7.82 on sale to Singapore. To PK-VIY.
G-BJOS	PBN BN-2B-21 Islander	2134		29.10.81	To Indian Navy as IN-138 9/83. Canx 22.9.83.
G-BJOT	SAN Jodel D.117	688	F-BJCO CN-TVH/F-DABU	12.11.81	
G-BJOU	PBN BN-2B-21 Islander	2135		29.10.81	To Indian Navy as IN-139. Canx 4.10.83.
G-BJOV	Reims Cessna F.150K	0558	PH-VSD	4. 2.82	
G-BJOW	HS.125 Srs.700B	NA0313 & 257153		3.11.81	To XB-CXK 11/81. Canx 18.11.81.
G-BJOX	Not allotted.				
G-BJOY	HS.125 Srs.600B	256030	G-BBEP	27. 7.81	Restored as G-BBEP 2/82. Canx.
G-BJOZ	Scheibe SF-25B Falke	4646	D-KEBD	22.10.81	Canx 31.3.95 on sale to Ireland.
G-BJPA	Chown Osprey Mk.3A HAFB (Toy)	AKC-69		12.10.81	Canx by CAA 6.12.88.
G-BJPB	Chown Osprey Mk.4A HAFB (Toy)	AKC-42		12.10.81	Canx by CAA 2.12.93.
G-BJPC	Cremer CRMR-1 Rotorcraft Gyroplane	CRMR-810001		30.10.81	Canx by CAA 8.12.88.
G-BJPD	Chown Osprey Mk.4D HAFB (Toy)	AKC-81		12.10.81	Canx as WFU 14.11.88.
G-BJPE	Chown Osprey Mk.1E HAFB (Toy)	AKC-55		12.10.81	Canx as WFU 18.10.88.
G-BJPF	Hassell Setco Mk.SLA HAFB (Toy)	SH.01		12.10.81	Canx as WFU 10.1.83.
G-BJPG	Chown Osprey Mk.4D HAFB (Toy)	AKC-61		12.10.81	Canx as WFU 2.6.83.
G-BJPH	Chown Osprey Mk.3G HAFB (Toy)	AKC-39		12.10.81	Canx as WFU 4.8.84.
G-BJPI	Bede BD-5G	1 & PFA/14-10218		30.10.81	
G-BJPJ	Chown Osprey Mk.3A HAFB (Toy)	AKC-36		12.10.81	Canx by CAA 22.5.92.
G-BJPK	Chown Osprey Mk.1B HAFB (Toy)	AKC-44		13.10.81	Canx by CAA 29.11.88.
G-BJPL	Chown Osprey Mk.4A HAFB (Toy)	AKC-39		13.10.81	
G-BJPM	Bursell P.W.1 HAFB (Toy)	01		15.10.81	Canx by CAA 2.12.93.
G-BJPN	JK Cobra Mk.1 HAFB (Toy)	AJK.002		15.10.81	Canx by CAA 15.12.88.
G-BJPO	B & C Black Widow HAFB (Toy)	BC.02		15.10.81	Canx by CAA 7.12.88.
G-BJPP	Rango NA-8 HAFB (Toy)	SAS-24		16.10.81	
G-BJPR	Avenger T200-2112 HAFB (Toy)	014		16.10.81	
G-BJPS	Chown Osprey Mk.4B HAFB (Toy)	AKC-64		16.10.81	Canx as WFU 15.10.84.
G-BJPT	Chown Osprey Mk.3G HAFB (Toy)	AKC-79		16.10.81	
G-BJPU	Chown Osprey Mk.4B HAFB (Toy)	ADP-74		16.10.81	Canx as destroyed 18.10.88.
G-BJPV	Haigh Super Hi-Flyer HAFB (Toy)	001		16.10.81	Canx by CAA 4.8.98.
G-BJPW	Chown Osprey Mk.1C HAFB (Toy)	AKC-47		20.10.81	Canx as WFU 2.12.93.
G-BJPX	Saffery Phoenix Fuschia HAFB (Toy)	42		22.10.81	Canx as destroyed 18.10.88.
G-BJPY	Cremer Rigid Airship HAFB (Toy)	A/S-222PC		22.10.81	Canx by CAA 8.12.88.
G-BJPZ	Chown Osprey Mk.1C HAFB (Toy)	AKC-46		23.10.81	Canx by CAA 13.12.88.
G-BJRA	Chown Osprey Mk.4B HAFB (Toy)	AKC-87		23.10.81	
G-BJRB	Eaves European E.254 HAFB (Toy)	S.5		23.10.81	
G-BJRC	Eaves European E.84R HAFB (Toy)	S.7		23.10.81	

Regn	Type	c/n	Previous identity	Regn date	Fate or immediate subsequent identity (if known)
G-BJRD	Eaves European E.84R HAFB (Toy)	S.8		23.10.81	
G-BJRE	Eaves European E.3 HAFB (Toy)	S.9		23.10.81	
G-BJRF	Saffery S.80 HAFB (Toy)	MB.1		26.10.81	Canx by CAA 2.12.93.
G-BJRG	Chown Osprey Mk.4B HAFB (Toy)	AKC-95		26.10.81	
G-BJRH	Rango NA-36/Ax3 HAFB	NHP-23		4.11.81	
G-BJRI	Chown Osprey Mk.4D HAFB (Toy)	AKC-86		28.10.81	Canx by CAA 2.12.93.
G-BJRJ	Chown Osprey Mk.4D HAFB (Toy)	AKC-85		28.10.81	Canx by CAA 2.12.93.
G-BJRK	Chown Osprey Mk.1E HAFB (Toy)	AKC-41		28.10.81	Canx by CAA 2.12.93.
G-BJRL	Chown Osprey Mk.4B HAFB (Toy)	AKC-67		28.10.81	Canx by CAA 2.12.93.
G-BJRM	Cremer Cracker HAFB (Toy)	15.718 PAC		30.10.81	Canx as WFU 10.1.83.
G-BJRN	Graham 981-051/1 HAFB (Toy)	G051/1		15.10.81	Canx as WFU 14.2.85.
G-BJRO	Chown Osprey Mk.4D HAFB (Toy)	AKC-82		28.10.81	Canx by CAA 8.12.88.
G-BJRP	Cremer Cracker HAFB (Toy)	15.712 PAC		29.10.81	
G-BJRR	Cremer Cracker HAFB (Toy)	15.715 PAC		29.10.81	
G-BJRS	Cremer Cracker HAFB (Toy)	15.714 PAC		29.10.81	Canx by CAA 2.12.93.
G-BJRT	BAC One-Eleven Srs.528FL	BAC.234	D-ALFA	30.10.81	To YR-JBA 9/93. Canx 1.10.93.
G-BJRU	BAC One-Eleven Srs.528FL	BAC.238	D-ANUE	30.10.81	To YR-JBB 9/93. Canx 4.10.93.
G-BJRV	Cremer Cracker HAFB (Toy)	15.713 PAC		29.10.81	
G-BJRW	Cessna U.206G Stationair 6 II	U206-05738	(N5422X)	8. 4.80	
G-BJRX	MacNeil RMB Mk.1 HAFB (Toy)	RM-81-001		29.10.81	Canx by CAA 15.12.88.
G-BJRY	PA-28-151 Cherokee Warrior	28-7415497	N43453	18.11.81	To G-GUSS 8/95. Canx.
G-BJRZ	Partenavia P.68C Victor	231	G-OAKP G-BJRZ	10.11.81	To S5-... Canx 25.5.99.
G-BJSA	BN-2A-26 Islander	46	HB-LIC D-IBNB/I-TRAL	15.12.81	CofA expired 25.10.95. (Stored 6/97)
G-BJSB	Cessna A.185F Floatplane	185-02279	N3357S	10.11.81	Restored as N3357S. Canx 25.11.81.
G-BJSC	Chown Osprey Mk.4D HAFB (Toy)	AKC-84		12.11.81	
G-BJSD	Chown Osprey Mk.4D HAFB (Toy)	AKC-83		12.11.81	
G-BJSE	Chown Osprey Mk.4B HAFB (Toy)	AKC-51		9.11.81	Canx by CAA 2.12.93.
G-BJSF	Chown Osprey Mk.4B HAFB (Toy)	AKC-66		9.11.81	
G-BJSG	Vickers Supermarine 361 Spitfire LF.IXc	6S/735188	HS543 Indian AF/G-15-11/ML417	29. 1.81	
	(Also firewall No.6S/730116)(Was converted to VS.509 Trainer IX for Indian AF service, converted back to VS.361 LF.IXc before being civil regd)				
G-BJSH	Sindlinger HH-1 Hawker Hurricane	PFA/26-10663		5.11.81	To VH-AFW with c/n W-140 in 6/91. Canx 19.8.86.
G-BJSI	Chown Osprey Mk.1E HAFB (Toy)	AKC-43		9.11.81	
G-BJSJ	Chown Osprey Mk.1E HAFB (Toy)	AKC-52		9.11.81	Canx by CAA 8.12.88.
G-BJSK	Chown Osprey Mk.1E HAFB (Toy)	AKC-65		9.11.81	Canx by CAA 2.12.93.
G-BJSL	Flamboyant Ax7-65 HAFB	022		9.11.81	Canx by CAA 8.1.93. (Based in "Central Africa" in 1993)
G-BJSM	Allport Bursell Mil-Ed Dungleballoon Mk.1 HAFB (Toy)	MCB-01		9.11.81	Canx by CAA 7.12.88.
G-BJSN	Beechcraft 200 Super King Air	BB-1026		9.11.81R	NTU - Canx 25.6.82 as Not Imported. To YV-2251P 10/82.
G-BJSO	Boeing 737-2L9 (Line No. 620)	22071	EI-BOJ (EI-BOG)/G-BJSO/(EI-BMB)/SU-BCJ/OY-APN	3.12.81	To G-GPAB 5/84. Canx.
G-BJSP	Guido 1A-61 HAFB (Toy)	GAN01/81-2609		23.11.81	
G-BJSR	Chown Osprey Mk.4B HAFB (Toy)	AKC-93		10.11.81	Canx by CAA 2.12.93.
G-BJSS	Allport YUO-1B-1-DA Neolithic Invader Superballoon Srs.2/20 HAFB (Toy)	01-8101002		9.11.81	
G-BJST	CCF Harvard 4	CCF4-...	MM53795 SC-66	21.12.81	(On overhaul Little Gransden 11/96)
G-BJSU	Bensen B.8M Gyrocopter	G/01-1026		11.11.81	No Permit to Fly issued. Canx by CAA 24.1.96. (Stored in Garden 3/97)
G-BJSV	PA-28-161 Warrior II	28-8016229	PH-VZL (OO-HLM)/N35787	25.11.81	
G-BJSW	Thunder Ax7-65Z HAFB	378		16.11.81	
G-BJSX	Unicorn UE-1C HAFB (Toy)	82023		10.11.81	

Regn	Type	c/n	Previous identity	Regn date	Fate or immediate subsequent identity (if known)
G-BJSY	Beechcraft C90 King Air	LJ-805	ZS-KGO N2068W	19.11.81	To VR-BKW 9/90. Canx 20.9.90.
G-BJSZ	Piper J3C-65 Cub (L-4H-PI) (Regd with frame no. 11874)	12047	D-EHID (D-ECAX)/(D-EKAB)/PH-NBP/44-79751	20.11.81	Permit expired 14.6.96. (Stored 6/95)
G-BJTA	Chown Osprey Mk.4B HAFB (Toy)	ASC-119		16.11.81	Canx by CAA 2.12.93.
G-BJTB	Cessna A.150M Aerobat	A150-0627	(G-BIVN) N9818J	28.10.82	
G-BJTC	Auster J/2 Arrow	2370	(G-BHZW) 5Y-KHD/VP-KHD/VP-UAO	3. 2.82	To ZS-VAA 12/83. Canx.
G-BJTD	Thunder & Colt AS-90 Hot-Air Airship	357		20.11.81	Sold 26.8.82; probably to Canada. Canx by CAA 10.12.82.
G-BJTE	PA-38-112 Tomahawk	38-79A1076		8.12.81	To G-BJYN 3/82. Canx.
G-BJTF	Skyrider Mk.1 HAFB (Toy)	KSR-01		18.11.81	
G-BJTG	Chown Osprey Mk.4B HAFB (Toy)	ASC-111		17.11.81	Canx by CAA 2.12.93.
G-BJTH	Kestrel AC Mk.1 HAFB (Toy)	01		18.11.81	Canx by CAA 2.12.93.
G-BJTI	Woodie K2400J Mk.2 HAFB (Toy)	W007448		19.11.81	Canx by CAA 13.12.88.
G-BJTJ	Chown Osprey Mk.4B HAFB (Toy)	ASC-117		20.11.81	Canx by CAA 29.11.88.
G-BJTK	Taylor JT.1 Monoplane	PFA/1467		20.11.81	No Permit to Fly issued. Canx by CAA 24.1.96.
G-BJTL	HS.748 Srs.2B/FAA	1790	G-11-790 CS-TAQ/G-11-6/G-BJTL/G-11-6/N749AV/G-BJTL	7.12.81	To C-GHSC 5/95. Canx 14.3.95.
G-BJTM	HS.748 Srs.2B/378	1792	(N750AV) G-BJTM	7.12.81	To D-AHSE. Canx 15.5.84.
G-BJTN	Chown Osprey Mk.4B HAFB (Toy)	ASC-112		23.11.81	
G-BJTO	Piper J3C-65 Cub (L-4H-PI) (Frame no. 11352)	11527	F-BEGK OO-AAL/43-30236	1.12.81	Permit expired 5.3.86. (Stored 2/99 Fritton Decoy, Norfolk)
G-BJTP	PA-18-95 Super Cub (L-18C-PI)	18-999	MM51-15302 Italian AF/I-EICO/MM51-15302/51-15302	26.11.81	
G-BJTR	PA-18-95 Super Cub (L-18C-PI) (Frame no.18-1963 - also Italian rebuild c/n OMA.71-08)	18-1998	MM52-2398 Italian AF "EI.71"/I-EIAM/MM52-2398/52-2398	4.12.81	NTU - To G-AMEN 12/81. Canx.
G-BJTS	Chown Osprey Mk.4B HAFB (Toy)	ASC-118		20.11.81	Canx by CAA 29.11.88.
G-BJTT	Witty Spinx SP.2 HAFB (Toy)	10106		20.11.81	Canx by CAA 9.12.88.
G-BJTU	Cremer Cracker HAFB (Toy)	15.719 PAC		20.11.81	Canx by CAA 9.12.88.
G-BJTV	Morane-Saulnier MS.880B Rallye Club	286	(G-BHTU) F-BKTV	26. 8.81	No UK CofA issued (States unknown) Canx by CAA 22.11.91.
G-BJTW	Eaves European E.107 HAFB (Toy)	S.10		23.11.81	
G-BJTX	PA-31-325 Turbo Navajo	31-8012079	ZS-KKS N3636U	.11.81R	NTU - Not Imported. Canx.
G-BJTY	Chown Osprey Mk.4B HAFB (Toy)	ASC-115		23.11.81	
G-BJTZ	Chown Osprey Mk.4A HAFB (Toy)	AKC-38		27.11.81	Canx by CAA 29.11.88.
G-BJUA	Witty Sphinx SP.12 HAFB (Toy)	10108		30.11.81	Canx as WFU 18.10.88.
G-BJUB	BVS Special 01 HAFB (Toy)	VS/PW01		25.11.81	
G-BJUC	Robinson R-22 HP	0228		13. 1.82	
G-BJUD	Robin DR.400/180R Remorqueur (Rebuilt using new fuselage; original scrapped at Membury in 11/88)	870	PH-SRM	27.11.81	
G-BJUE	Chown Osprey Mk.4B HAFB (Toy)	ASC-114		23.11.81	
G-BJUF	S.H.Aerostatics Srs.2 HAFB (Toy)	02		3.11.81	Canx as destroyed 30.9.83.
G-BJUG	Socata TB-9 Tampico	248		30.12.81	Crashed on landing at Oaksey Park on 16.9.96. Canx as WFU 1.10.96
G-BJUH	Unicorn UE-1C HAFB (Toy)	81019		2.11.81	Canx as WFU 15.10.84.
G-BJUI	Chown Osprey Mk.4B HAFB (Toy)	ASC-116		23.11.81	
G-BJUJ	Short SD.3-30 Var.200	SH3081	G-14-3081	30.11.81	To N2630A. Canx 18.12.81.
G-BJUK	Short SD.3-30 Var.100	SH3082	G-14-3082 G-OCAS/G-BJUK/G-14-3082	30.11.81	CofA expired 9.4.90 & WFU at Exeter. Broken up in 6/95. Canx as WFU 2.12.96.
G-BJUL	Short SD.3-30 Var.200	SH3083		30.11.81	To SX-BGE 5/82. Canx 3.3.82.
G-BJUM	Unicorn UE-1C HAFB (Toy)	81020		2.11.81	Canx as WFU 15.10.84.
G-BJUN	Unicorn UE-1C HAFB (Toy)	81021		2.11.81	Canx as WFU 10.8.87.
G-BJUO	Unicorn UE-4B HAFB (Toy)	81022		2.11.81	DBF at Alton Towers on 12.4.82. Canx as WFU 19.7.82.
G-BJUP	Chown Osprey Mk.4B HAFB (Toy)	AKC-92		1.12.81	Canx by CAA 13.12.88.
G-BJUR	PA-38-112 Tomahawk	38-79A0915		5. 2.82	
G-BJUS	PA-38-112 Tomahawk	38-80A0065		10.12.81	CofA expired 24.4.94. (Stored 6/96)
G-BJUT	HS.125 Srs.600B	256005	(G-BJXV) G-BART	. .81R	NTU - Remained as G-BART. Canx.
G-BJUU	Chown Osprey Mk.4B HAFB (Toy)	ASC-113		23.11.81	
G-BJUV	Cameron V-20 HAFB	792		9.12.81	
G-BJUW	Chown Osprey Mk.4B HAFB (Toy)	ASC-120		8.12.81	Canx by CAA 2.12.93.
G-BJUX	Bursell HAFB (Toy)	02		8.12.81	Canx by CAA 2.12.93.
G-BJUY	Colt Ax7-77A HAFB (Special Golf Ball shape; rebuild of Colting Ax7-77A c/n 77A-003)	384	EI-BDE	15.12.81	(Based in Partille, Sweden)

Regn	Type	c/n	Previous identity	Regn date	Fate or immediate subsequent identity (if known)
G-BJUZ	B.A.T. Mk.II HAFB (Toy)	101		10.12.81	Canx by CAA 2.12.93.
G-BJVA	B.A.T. Mk.I HAFB (Toy)	1001		10.12.81	Canx by CAA 2.12.93.
G-BJVB	Cremcorn Ax1-4 HAFB (Toy)	82029		11.12.81	Canx by CAA 8.12.88.
G-BJVC(1)	Thunder Ax8-105 Srs.2 HAFB	395		. .81R	NTU - To G-BJVG 12/81. Canx.
G-BJVC(2)	Evans VP-2	PFA/63-10599		17. 2.82	Permit expired 19.6.91. (Status uncertain)
G-BJVD	Not allocated.				
G-BJVE	[Was reserved for Southernair]				
G-BJVF	Thunder Ax3 Maxi Sky Chariot HAFB (C/n duplicates that of G-SPOP)	187		15.12.81	
G-BJVG	Thunder Ax8-105 Srs.2 HAFB	395	(G-BJVC)	15.12.81	Canx 29.2.84 as not completed.
G-BJVH	Reims Cessna F.182Q Skylane	0106	D-EJMO PH-AXU(2)	21.12.81	
G-BJVI	Chown Osprey Mk.4D HAFB (Toy)	ASC-125		14.12.81	Canx as WFU 18.10.88.
G-BJVJ	Reims Cessna F.152 II	1906		6. 1.82	
G-BJVK	Grob G-109	6074		11. 3.82	CofA expired 22.5.92. (Status uncertain)
G-BJVL	Saffery Hermes HAFB (Toy)	01		16.12.81	Canx as WFU 18.10.88.
G-BJVM	Cessna 172N Skyhawk II	172-69374	N737FA	14.12.81	
G-BJVN	American Aviation AA-5A Cheetah	AA5A-0836	N26952	.12.81R	NTU - To G-BKBE 4/82. Canx.
G-BJVO	Cameron D-50 Hot Air Airship	768		22.12.81	Canx 24.7.90 on sale to USA.
G-BJVP	Cessna 550 Citation II (Unit No.375)	550-0342	N6804L	22.12.81	To N4581Y 12/83. Canx 28.12.83.
G-BJVR	PA-38-112 Tomahawk	38-79A0994		8. 1.82	To 4R-ATB 1/82. Canx 27.1.82.
G-BJVS	Menavia Piel CP.1315-C3 Super Emeraude	903	F-BJVS	5. 1.79	
G-BJVT	Reims Cessna F.152 II	1904		12. 1.82	
G-BJVU	Thunder Ax6-56 Bolt HAFB	397		31.12.81	
G-BJVV	Robin R.1180TD Aiglon	279		5.11.81	
G-BJVW	Sikorsky S-76A	760052	N104BH N1545U	15. 1.82	To 9M-AYD 12/82. Canx 3.12.82.
G-BJVX	Sikorsky S-76A II Plus	760100	N108BH N1548G	15. 1.82	
G-BJVY	Sikorsky S-76A	760024	N102BH N4249S	15. 1.82	To 9M-AYC 7/82. Canx 27.7.82.
G-BJVZ	Sikorsky S-76A II Plus	760084	N107BH N376PB	1. 2.82	To 5N-SKY. Canx 14.10.92.
G-BJWA	Short SD.3-30 Var.200	SH3084	G-14-3084	31.12.81	To SX-BGF 5/82. Canx 3.3.82.
G-BJWB	HS.125 Srs.700A	257158	G-5-14	5. 1.82	To N45KK. Canx 9.12.85.
G-BJWC	Saro Skeeter AOP.10	S2/3070	7840M XK482	30.11.82	Canx by CAA 23.2.94. (Stored 5/96 Blackpool)
G-BJWD	Zenair CH.300	PFA/113-10729		5. 1.82	Canx by CAA 2.8.91.
G-BJWE	Bell 47G-5	7960	SE-HBT	25. 2.82	To VH-JGF 7/82. Canx 27.4.82.
G-BJWF	Ayres S2R-R3S Thrush Commander	R3S-006	(G-BHXZ) N4016V	23. 2.82	To ZS-LVP 10/87. Canx 28.10.87.
G-BJWG	Beechcraft B200 Super King Air	BB-1051		8. 1.82	NTU - Canx 20.8.82 as Not Imported. To N6912T.
G-BJWH	Reims Cessna F.152 II	1919		7. 5.82	
G-BJWI	Reims Cessna F.172P Skyhawk II	2172		14. 5.82	
G-BJWJ	Cameron V-65 HAFB	802		25. 1.82	
G-BJWK(1)	Jodel Wassmer D.120A Paris-Nice	185	F-BJPK	. 1.82R	NTU - To G-BJYK 5/82. Canx.
G-BJWK(2)	Clutton FRED Srs.II	PFA/29-10767		16. 2.82	Canx as WFU 1.11.82.
G-BJWL(1)	BN-2A-8 Islander	376	4X-AYS (SX-...)/4X-AYS/N88JA/G-BBMC	. .82R	NTU - Remained as 4X-AYS. Canx.
G-BJWL(2)	BN-2A-26 Islander	166	4X-AYC G-51-166	24. 2.82	Canx 27.7.89 on sale to Lebanon. To 5B-CHD.
G-BJWM	BN-2A-26 Islander	717	4X-AYE G-BCAE	16. 2.82	To LX-AJH 9/89. Canx 5.5.89.
G-BJWN	BN-2A-26 Islander	316	4X-AYL SX-BFC/4X-AYL/G-BALO/G-51-316	9. 2.82	To ZK-FVD 12/89. Canx 14.12.89.
G-BJWO	BN-2A-26 Islander	334	4X-AYR SX-BBX/4X-AYR/G-BAXC	16. 2.82	
G-BJWP	BN-2A-26 Islander	399	4X-AYP SX-BFD/4X-AYP/SX-BFA/4X-AYP/N57JA/G-BCEJ	9. 2.82	To F-OGOV 2/90. Canx 30.11.89.
G-BJWR	DH.82A Tiger Moth (Believed major component rebuild - source not yet known)	"7712" & W-01		19. 1.82	No CofA or Permit issued. Canx as WFU 22.8.91.
G-BJWS	Aerospatiale SA.330J Puma	1517	F-GCJI	29. 1.82	Crashed and burnt out near Dyce Airport on 10.10.82. Canx as destroyed 5.12.83.
G-BJWT	Wittman W.10 Tailwind	PFA/31-10688		5. 1.82	
G-BJWU	Thunder Ax7-65Z HAFB	406		5. 1.82	To F-GBBV(2) 11/86. Canx 6.4.84.
G-BJWV	Colt 17A Cloudhopper HAFB	391		22. 1.82	
G-BJWW	Reims Cessna F.172P Skyhawk II	2148	(D-EFTV)	1. 2.82	
G-BJWX	PA-18-95 Super Cub (L-18C-PI)	18-1985	MM52-2385 Italian AF/I-EIME/MM52-2385/52-2385	23. 2.82	
G-BJWY	Sikorsky S-55 (HRS-2) Whirlwind HAR.21	55-...	A2576 WV198/BuA.130191	25. 1.82	Canx by CAA 23.2.94. (On loan to Solway Aviation Society) (On display 8/97)
G-BJWZ	PA-18-95 Super Cub (L-18C-PI) (Frame No. 18-1262)	18-1361	OO-HMO ALAT 18-1361/51-15361	18. 1.82	
G-BJXA	Slingsby T.67A	1994		8. 2.82	
G-BJXB	Slingsby T.67A	1995		8. 2.82	
G-BJXC	Aerospatiale AS.332L Super Puma	2023	F-WTNM	29. 1.82	To G-TIGB 3/82. Canx.
G-BJXD	Colt 17A Cloudhopper HAFB	383		15. 2.82	Canx as WFU 16.10.89.

Regn	Type	c/n	Previous identity	Regn date	Fate or immediate subsequent identity (if known)
G-BJXE	PA-28RT-201 Arrow IV	28R-8118003	N8460L	27. 1.82	To F-GDLZ 5/83. Canx 21.4.83.
G-BJXF	Short SD.3-30 Var.200	SH3085	G-14-3085	28. 1.82	To HS-TSA(2) 6/82. Canx 10.6.82.
G-BJXG	Short SD.3-30 Var.200	SH3086	G-14-3086	28. 1.82	To HS-TSB(2) 6/82. Canx 7.6.82.
G-BJXH	Short SD.3-30 Var.200	SH3087	G-14-3087	28. 1.82	To HS-TSC(2) 7/82. Canx 25.6.82.
G-BJXI	DH.104 Dove 6	04392	XJ347 G-AMXT/(N1561V)	. .82R	NTU - Restored as G-AMXT 4/82. Canx.
G-BJXJ	Boeing 737-219 (Line No. 846)	22657	N851L N6066Z/(ZK-NAT)	5. 3.82	To F-GLXF 6/93. Canx 20.5.93.
G-BJXK	Sportavia Putzer Fournier RF-5	5054	D-KINB	3. 2.82	
G-BJXL	Boeing 737-2T4 (Line No. 624)	22054	C-GNDG G-BJXL/C-GNDG/G-BJXL/N53AF/G-BJXL/N53AF/(N45AF)	4. 5.82	To N702ML. Canx 3.11.86.
G-BJXM	Boeing 737-2T4 (Line No. 633)	22055	N54AF G-BJXM/N54AF/(N46AF)	4. 5.82	Restored as N54AF. Canx.
G-BJXN	Boeing 747-230B (Line No. 179)	20527	(C-....) G-BJXN/N611BN/D-ABYG	15. 4.82	To N78019. Canx 31.5.90.
G-BJXO	Cessna 441 Conquest	441-0263	(N88791)	10. 2.82	To N815MC. Canx 26.6.91.
G-BJXP	Colt 56B HAFB	393		29. 3.82	(Extant 2/97)
G-BJXR	Auster AOP.9	184	XR267	2. 2.82	(On rebuild 3/96 Innsworth) Canx by CAA 12.4.99.
G-BJXS	Beechcraft F90 King Air	LA-198		9. 2.82	NTU - Canx 20.8.82 as not imported. To HK-3118X.
G-BJXT(1)	Beechcraft B200 Super King Air	BB-1072		9. 2.82	NTU - Not Imported. To Moroccan AF as CN-ANG. Canx.
G-BJXT(2)	Beechcraft B200 Super King Air	BB-1086		. .82R	NTU - Canx 20.8.82 as not imported. To D-IBVO.
G-BJXU	Thunder Ax7-77 HAFB	407		8. 2.82	Canx as destroyed 15.6.94.
G-BJXV	HS.125 Srs.600B	256005	G-BART	. .81R	NTU - To (G-BJUT)/G-BART. Canx.
G-BJXW	PA-28R-200 Cherokee Arrow II	28R-7435289	OY-CBG SE-GID/OO-HJN/N43700	10. 2.82	To G-LEEM 5/85. Canx.
G-BJXX	PA-23-250 Aztec E	27-4692	F-BTCM N14094	7. 4.82	
G-BJXY	Cameron D-50 Hot-Air Airship	818		10. 2.82	To F-GCZS 2/85. Canx 10.6.82.
G-BJXZ	Cessna 172N Skyhawk II	172-73039	PH-CAA N1949F	24. 3.82	
G-BJYA	Cessna 425 Corsair	425-0122	N6882D	15. 3.82	Restored as N6882D. Canx 7.12.83.
G-BJYB	Cessna 441 Conquest II	441-0279	N98784	2. 3.82	To LN-VIP. Canx 29.7.85.
G-BJYC	Cessna 425 Conquest I	425-0168	(N6872T)	14. 3.82	To PH-JOE. Canx 22.9.92.
G-BJYD	Reims Cessna F.152 II	1915		25. 3.82	
G-BJYE	Cessna R.182 Skylane RG II	R182-01883	N5521T	. 3.82R	NTU - To G-BJZO 9/82. Canx.
G-BJYF	Colt 56A HAFB	401		1. 3.82	
G-BJYG	PA-28-161 Warrior II	28-8216053	N8458B	4. 3.82	
G-BJYH	Aerospatiale AS.332L Super Puma	2024	F-WTNJ	8. 3.82	To G-TIGC 4/82. Canx.
G-BJYI	Aerospatiale AS.332L Super Puma	2026	F-WXFL	8. 3.82	To G-TIGD 4/82. Canx.
G-BJYJ	Aerospatiale AS.332L Super Puma	2028	F-WTNM	8. 3.82	To G-TIGE 4/82. Canx.
G-BJYK	Jodel Wassmer D.120A Paris-Nice	185	(G-BJWK) F-BJPK	11. 5.82	
G-BJYL	BAC One-Eleven Srs.515FB	BAC.208	TI-LRK G-AZPE/D-ALAS	26. 3.82	To (G-OBWH 4/93)/5N-ENO 7/95. Canx.
G-BJYM	BAC One-Eleven Srs.531FS	BAC.242	TI-LRI TI-1095C	7. 5.82	To G-OBWE 4/93. Canx.
G-BJYN	PA-38-112 Tomahawk	38-79A1076	G-BJTE	12. 3.82	
G-BJYO	PA-38-112 Tomahawk	38-79A0997		16. 4.82	Crashed at Panshanger on 31.5.84. Canx by CAA 4.2.87.
G-BJYP	PBN BN-2B-21 Islander	2136		2. 3.82	To BDF-02 Belize DF 8/83. Canx 25.8.83.
G-BJYR	PBN BN-2B-21 Islander	2137		2. 3.82	To BDF-01 Belize DF 7/83. Canx 25.8.83.
G-BJYS	PBN BN-2T Turbine Islander (Originally regd as BN-2B-26)	2138		2. 3.82	To G-IACL 9/83. Canx.
G-BJYT	PBN BN-2T Turbine Islander (Originally regd as BN-2B-26)	2139		2. 3.82	To G-WOTG 11/83. Canx.
G-BJYU	PBN BN-2T Turbine Islander (Originally regd as BN-2B-26)	2140		2. 3.82	To G-DLRA 3/84. Canx.
G-BJYV	PBN BN-2T Turbine Islander (Originally regd as BN-2B-26)	2141		2. 3.82	To 7Q-YAW 3/84. Canx 28.2.84.
G-BJYW	PBN BN-2T Turbine Islander (Originally regd as BN-2B-26)	2142		2. 3.82	To G-ORED 1/85. Canx.
G-BJYX	PBN BN-2T Turbine Islander (Originally regd as BN-2B-26)	2143		2. 3.82	To G-TEMI 7/84. Canx.
G-BJYY	PBN BN-2T Turbine Islander (Originally regd as BN-2B-26)	2144		2. 3.82	To 5T-BSA 5/84. Canx 4.5.84.
G-BJYZ	PBN BN-2T Turbine Islander (Originally regd as BN-2B-26)	2145		2. 3.82	To G-BOBC 1/86. Canx.
G-BJZA	Cameron N-65 HAFB	820		4. 3.82	
G-BJZB	Evans VP-2	PFA/63-10633		10. 3.82	
G-BJZC	Thunder Ax7-77Z HAFB	416		5. 3.82	CofA expired 17.6.94. (On loan to Balloon Preservation Group) (Extant 1/98) Canx as WFU 8.7.98.
G-BJZD	Douglas DC-10-10 (Line No. 269)	46970	G-GFAL N1002D	23. 4.82	To N581LF 11/92. Canx 1.12.92.
G-BJZE	Douglas DC-10-10 (Line No. 272)	46973	G-GSKY	31. 3.82	To N591LF 11/92. Canx 1.12.92.
G-BJZF	DH.82A Tiger Moth (Built by Norfolk Aerial Spraying Ltd from spares)	NAS-100		8. 3.82	

Regn	Type	c/n	Previous identity	Regn date	Fate or immediate subsequent identity (if known)
G-BJZG	Beechcraft 200 Super King Air	BB-133	SE-GSU N2133L	19. 3.82	To G-OAKL 9/82. Canx.
G-BJZH	Colt 77A HAFB	363		16. 3.82	Canx as WFU 27.6.90. (Believed to have operated as PP-ZZY)
G-BJZI	Embraer EMB.110P1 Bandeirante	110-412	PT-SGD	5. 5.82	To ZS-LGN 10/82. Canx 28.9.82.
G-BJZJ	Embraer EMB.110P1 Bandeirante	110-394	PT-SFL	5. 5.82	To ZS-LGM 5/82. Canx 24.5.82.
G-BJZK	Cessna T.303 Crusader	T303-00107	(N3645C)	26. 3.82	To N303MK 7/93. Canx 22.7.93.
G-BJZL	Cameron V-65 HAFB	810		19. 3.82	Canx by CAA 21.7.92.
G-BJZM	Slingsby T.67A	1996		31. 3.82	Fatal crash at Sandsfield Farm, near Brandesburton, Humberside on 29.3.87. Canx as destroyed 4.6.87.
G-BJZN	Slingsby T.67A	1997		31. 3.82	
G-BJZO	Cessna R.182 Skylane RG II	R182-01883	(G-BJYE) N5521T	9. 9.82	To G-GOZO 1/85. Canx.
G-BJZP	Thunder Ax6-56Z HAFB	417		19. 3.82	To G-BWHO 20.4.82. Canx.
G-BJZR	Colt 42A HAFB	402		18. 3.82	
G-BJZS	Bell 212	31160	C-GMXQ	31. 3.82	To C-GWRD. Canx 27.6.83.
G-BJZT	Reims Cessna FA.152 Aerobat	0379		6. 5.82	To ZK-JZT 8/96. Canx 30.4.96.
G-BJZU	Reims Cessna FA.152 Aerobat	0380		6. 5.82	To G-WACU 7/86. Canx.
G-BJZV	Boeing 737-296 (Line No. 675)	22277	C-GQBJ N57001/(C-GQBV)	4. 5.82	Restored as C-GQBJ 11/82. Canx 8.11.82.
G-BJZW	Boeing 737-296 (Line No. 759)	22516	C-GQBH	4. 5.82	Restored as C-GQBH 11/82. Canx 8.11.82.
G-BJZX	Grob G-109	6109	(D-KGRO)	3. 9.82	
G-BJZY	Bensen B.8MV Gyrocopter	DNL.21103 & G/01-1012		18. 3.82	
G-BJZZ	Hispano HA.1112-MIL Buchon (P.I. reportedly C4K-235)	235	N48157 Spanish AF C4K-172	30. 3.82	To G-HUNN 4/87. Canx.
G-BKAA	HS.125 Srs.700B	257139	(G-GAIL) G-5-18	15. 9.81	To G-MHIH 9/88. Canx.
G-BKAB	ICA Brasov IS-28M2A	23A		19. 3.82	Crashed at Rattlesden on 19.5.84. CofA expired 20.5.85. Canx as PWFU 29.3.85. (Fuselage stored 6/99 at Sandtoft)
G-BKAC	Reims Cessna F.150L Commuter	0888	G-BAIO	26. 4.82	Damaged on take-off from Retreat Farm, Little Baddow on 30.3.96. Canx as TWFU 9.7.96.
G-BKAD	Mitchell Wing U-2	MD-01		. .82R	NTU - Canx.
G-BKAE	Jodel Wassmer D.120 Paris-Nice	200	F-BKCE	5. 5.82	
G-BKAF	Clutton FRED Srs.II	PFA/29-10337		23. 3.82	
G-BKAG	Boeing 727-217ADV (Line No. 1117)	21055	(C-GRYC) G-BKAG/C-GCPA	29. 3.82	To C-GRMU 4/92. Canx 22.4.92.
G-BKAH	Scheibe SF-36A	4105	(D-KOGF)	6. 8.82	NTU - Canx 21.4.83 as Not Imported. To D-KMMG (Permit issued 11/82, regd 7/95).
G-BKAI	Aerospatiale SA.330J Puma	1586	9M-SSJ G-BKAI/C-GMNP	28. 4.82	Restored as 9M-SSJ. Canx 3.1.86.
G-BKAJ	HS.125 Srs.403B (Originally regd as Srs.400B)	25235	G-AYNR HB-VCE/G-5-18	1. 4.82	To G-5-19/N235AV. Canx 18.4.85.
G-BKAK	Beechcraft C90 King Air	LJ-619	ST-AIR G-BKAK/N166SM	15. 7.82	To N7128J 5/90. Canx 23.4.90.
G-BKAL	HS.748 Srs.2B/378	1791	(9N-ADF) G-BKAL/V2-LDK/D-AHSD/G-BKAL	5. 4.82	To ZK-MCH 5/95. Canx 22.5.95.
G-BKAM	Slingsby T.67M Firefly 160	1999		26. 4.82	
G-BKAN	Cessna 340A	340A-1528		13. 5.82	Damaged at Longleat Towers on 8.6.91. Canx as WFU 28.1.92. Remains to Dodson Aviation Scrapyard in the USA & arrived on 5.4.93. Regd as N7067W in 5/93.
G-BKAO	Wassmer Jodel D.112	249	F-BFTO	22. 3.82	
G-BKAP	Boeing 737-2L9 (Line No. 549)	21685	OY-APJ 9M-MBZ/OY-APJ	27. 4.82	Restored as OY-APJ. Canx 1.11.84.
G-BKAR	PA-38-112 Tomahawk	38-79A1091		16. 4.82	
G-BKAS	PA-38-112 Tomahawk	38-79A1075		16. 4.82	
G-BKAT	Pitts S-1C Special	KA.001 & PFA/09-10381		16. 8.78	Not built. Canx as WFU 26.7.91.
G-BKAU	BAC One-Eleven Srs.320L-AZ	BAC.107	G-AVBW	6. 4.82	To 5N-AOZ 11/83. Canx 16.11.83.
G-BKAV	BAC One-Eleven Srs.320L-AZ	BAC.109	G-AVBX	22. 4.82	To 5N-AOP 10/83. Canx 4.10.83.
G-BKAW	BAC One-Eleven Srs.320L-AZ	BAC.113	G-AVBY	22. 4.82	To 5N-AOK 11/83. Canx 16.11.83.
G-BKAX	BAC One-Eleven Srs.320L-AZ	BAC.133	G-AVYZ	22. 4.82	To 5N-AOT 10/83. Canx 4.10.83.
G-BKAY	Rockwell Commander 114	14411	SE-GSN	28. 9.81	
G-BKAZ	Cessna 152 II	152-82832	N89705	27. 4.82	
G-BKBA	HS.125 Srs.F400B (Originally regd as Srs.403B)	25270	G-BBGU G-5-13	1. 4.82	To N270AV. Canx 18.9.85.
G-BKBB	Hawker Fury I Replica	WA/6	OO-HFU OO-XFU/G-BKBB	2. 4.82	Damaged at Keiheuval, Belgium on 1.6.96 whilst as OO-HFU. (On rebuild Rotary Farm, Hatch 9/96)
G-BKBC	DHC.6-310 Twin Otter	347	VP-FAQ	27. 4.82	To LN-FKB 2/86. Canx 19.2.86.
G-BKBD	Thunder Ax3 Maxi Sky Chariot HAFB	418		5. 4.82	(Active 1/93)
G-BKBE	American Aviation AA-5A Cheetah	AA5A-0836	(G-BJVN) N26952	6. 4.82	To G-OECH 1/89. Canx.
G-BKBF	Socata MS.894A Rallye Minerva 220	11622	F-BSKZ	8. 9.82	
G-BKBG	Embraer EMB.110P1 Bandeirante	110-219	G-OBIA PT-GML	11. 5.82	To N102VN. Canx 16.12.82.
G-BKBH	HS.125 Srs.600B	256052	5N-DNL G-5-698/5N-DNL/5N-NBC/G-5-698/G-BKBH/G-5-698/G-BKBH/TR-LAU/G-BKBH/G-BDJE/G-5-11	1. 4.82	Canx by CAA 15.7.99. WFU at Southampton (noted in 8/99)
G-BKBI	Rutan Quickie Q.2	RHG.01		6. 4.82	Crashed shortly after take-off from the Badminton Fly-In on 24.4.88. Canx as destroyed 18.5.88.

Regn	Type	c/n	Previous identity	Regn date	Fate or immediate subsequent identity (if known)
G-BKBJ	Westland WG.30 Srs.100	002		7. 4.82	NTU - To G-BKGD 7/82. Canx.
G-BKBK	SNCAN Stampe SV-4A	318	OO-CLR	30. 3.82	To EI-CJR 2/94. Canx 14.2.94.
			F-BCLR		
G-BKBL	Westland WG.13 Lynx Mk.90	249	ZE388	7. 4.82	To Denmark Navy as S-249. Canx 3.3.87.
	(Regd as a Mk.87)		(Argentine Navy 3-H-143)/G-17-10/(ZE803)		
G-BKBM	HS.125 Srs.600B	256039	N410AW	1. 4.82	To EC-EAO. Canx.
			N61TF/G-BKBM/G-BCCL		
G-BKBN	Socata TB-10 Tobago	287		4. 6.82	
G-BKBO	Colt 17A Cloudhopper HAFB	342		1. 9.82	
G-BKBP	Bellanca 7GCBC Scout	465-73	N8693	1. 6.82	Badly damaged on landing at Graveley, Herts on 23.5.93. CofA expired 8.5.95. (Stored Bidford 9/95)
G-BKBR(1)	Agusta-Bell 206A JetRanger	8046	OO-CDP	. 4.82R	NTU - To G-JETR 4/82. Canx.
G-BKBR(2)	Cameron Chateau 84SS HAFB	743		11. 5.82	Canx as WFU 29.4.93. (Stored 6/93)
	(Special Shape as Forbes "Chateau de Balleroy")				
G-BKBS	Bensen B.8MV Gyrocopter	G/01-1027		14. 4.82	Permit expired 2.8.88. Canx by CAA 9.4.97.
G-BKBT	Boeing 737-2K2C	20943	(G-BLGO)	10. 6.82	Restored as PH-TVD. Canx 1.4.85.
	(Line No. 405)		PH-TVD/G-BKBT/PH-TVD		
G-BKBU	HS.125 Srs.600B	256042	G-BBRO	1. 4.82	To G-5-505/5N-AWS. Canx 21.4.83.
G-BKBV	Socata TB-10 Tobago	288	F-BNGO	4. 6.82	
G-BKBW	Socata TB-10 Tobago	289		4. 6.82	
G-BKBX	Menavia Piel CP.301A Emeraude	280	F-BMLX	. .82R	NTU - To G-BKUR 10/83. Canx.
			F-OBLY		
G-BKBY	Bell 206B JetRanger III	3588	(G-BKCF)	26. 4.82	To G-OSUE 8/87. Canx.
G-BKBZ	Colt 17A HAFB	403		23. 3.82	To N4448W. Canx 28.7.83.
G-BKCA	Cessna 404 Titan	404-0823	N6768V	15. 4.82	To ST-AWD 7/82. Canx 29.7.82.
G-BKCB	PA-28R-200 Cherokee Arrow II B		OY-POO	21. 6.82	
		28R-7435186	CS-APD/N41460		
G-BKCC	PA-28-180 Cherokee Archer		OY-BGY	13. 5.82	
		28-7405099			
G-BKCD	HS.125 Srs.600B	256056	5N-ARN	1. 4.82	To G-OMGC 1/91. Canx.
			G-BKCD/G-BDOA/G-5-13		
G-BKCE	Reims Cessna F.172P Skyhawk II	2135	N9687R	26. 4.82	
G-BKCF(1)	Bell 206B JetRanger III	3588		. 4.82R	NTU - To G-BKBY 26.4.82. Canx.
G-BKCF(2)	Rutan LongEz	ICF-01		27. 5.82	(Wings to G-IVAN, fuselage to "Scotland") No CofA issued. Canx by CAA 9.4.97.
G-BKCG	Boeing 727-17	20328	HC-BIC	30. 4.82	Restored as HC-BIC. Canx 11.7.85.
	(Line No. 806)		XA-GUU(2)/N116TA/CF-CPK		
G-BKCH	Thompson Cassutt Special			21. 4.82	
		PFA/126-10778			
G-BKCI	Brugger MB.2 Colibri			22. 4.82	
		ERN.01 & PFA/43-10692			
G-BKCJ	Oldfield Baby Great Lakes			12. 5.82	Crashed at Handsacre, Staffs on 14.9.91 after a mid-air
		PFA/10-10714			collision with Baby Great Lakes G-BKHD.
G-BKCK	CCF Harvard IV	CCF4-77	N13631	8. 3.83	To D-FAME(2) 8/97. Canx 12.8.97.
			G-BKCK/N13631/RCAF 20286		
G-BKCL	PA-30-160 Twin Comanche C	30-1982	G-AXSP	12. 1.81	
			N8824Y		
G-BKCM	Bell 206B JetRanger II	2999		27. 5.80	To EI-BVN 3/88. Canx 25.3.88.
G-BKCN	Phoenix Currie Wot			27. 4.82	
		SEOT.1 & PFA/3018			
G-BKCO	Enstrom 280C-UK Shark	1226		13. 5.82	To G-OPJT 9/83. Canx.
G-BKCP	Jodel Wassmer D.120A Paris-Nice	285	F-BMYF	. .82R	NTU - To G-BKCW 6/82. Canx.
G-BKCR	Socata TB-9 Tampico	297		6. 5.82	
G-BKCS	Cessna T.207 Turbo Super Skywagon		PH-OTG	14. 5.82	Forced landing due to engine failure at a coffee plantation
		T207-00210	N3150X/N1610U		at Foumbot, Cameroon on 31.1.86. Canx as destroyed 6.2.86.
G-BKCT	Cameron V-77 HAFB	837		10. 5.82	
G-BKCU	Sequoia F.8L Falco			5. 5.82	No Permit issued. Canx as WFU 16.2.89.
		733 & PFA/100-10793			
G-BKCV	EAA Acro Sport II			5. 5.82	
		430 & PFA/72A-10776			
G-BKCW	Jodel Wassmer D.120A Paris-Nice	285	(G-BKCP)	1. 6.82	Damaged on landing at Dundee on 13.4.97.
			F-BMYF		Permit expired 21.12.97.
G-BKCX	Mudry/CAARP CAP-10B	149		28. 7.82	
G-BKCY	PA-38-112 Tomahawk II	38-81A0027	OO-XKU	22. 5.82	CofA expired 7.11.94. (Fuselage stored 12/97 at Welshpool)
G-BKCZ	Jodel Wassmer D.120A Paris-Nice	207	F-BKCZ	23. 4.82	(On rebuild 6/92)
G-BKDA	Agusta-Bell 206B JetRanger	8337	LN-OQX	3. 6.82	To HB-XUI. Canx 25.7.89.
G-BKDB	Agusta-Bell 205A-1	4512	LN-ORU	1. 6.82	To SE-HMZ. Canx 12.10.82.
G-BKDC(1)	PA-28R-200 Cherokee Arrow II		OY-POV	. 6.82R	NTU - To G-JULI 6/82. Canx.
		28R-7435248	N43128		
G-BKDC(2)	Monnett Sonerai IIL			2. 7.82	Damaged in take-off crash at Breighton on 7.8.90.
		876 & PFA/15-10597			Permit expired 18.6.90. (Status uncertain)
G-BKDD	Bell 206B JetRanger II	1073	C-FDVB	20. 7.82	To HB-XXA 6/90. Canx 23.5.90.
			CF-DVB/N83159		
G-BKDE	Kendrick I Motorglider	1		21.12.78	Canx by CAA 2.9.91.
G-BKDF	Kendrick II Motorglider	2		21.12.78	Canx by CAA 2.9.91.
G-BKDG	PA-18-95 Super Cub	18-3365	MM52-2392	14. 5.82	To G-HELN 1/86. Canx.
	(Frame No 18-3400) (L-21B-PI)		Italian AF EI-69/EI-141/I-EIWB/MM53-7765/53-7765		
	(Regd as c/n 18-1992 but frame exchanged in Italian AF service; c/n 18-3365 was officially regd as N9837Q)				
G-BKDH	Robin DR.400/120 Dauphin 80	1582	PH-CAB	25. 5.82	
G-BKDI	Robin DR.400/120 Dauphin 80	1583	PH-CAD	25. 5.82	
G-BKDJ	Robin DR.400/120 Dauphin 80	1584	PH-CAC	25. 5.82	
G-BKDK	Thunder Ax7-77Z HAFB	428		21. 6.82	
G-BKDL	Short SD.3-30 Var.200	SH3088		21. 5.82	To HS-TSD 7/82. Canx 12.7.82.

Regn	Type	c/n	Previous identity	Regn date	Fate or immediate subsequent identity (if known)
G-BKDM	Short SD.3-30 Var.200	SH3089	G-14-3089	21. 5.82	To N330CA. Canx 25.8.82.
G-BKDN	Short SD.3-30 Var.100	SH3090	G-14-3090	21. 5.82	To G-BNTX 1/87. Canx.
G-BKDO	Short SD.3-30 Var.100	SH3091	G-14-3091	21. 5.82	To G-BNTY 1/87. Canx.
G-BKDP	Clutton FRED Srs.III	PFA/29-10650		24. 5.82	
G-BKDR	Pitts S-1S Special	PFA/09-10654		14. 6.82	Badly damaged in forced landing near Lewknor on 8.11.96. Permit expired 11.3.97. (On repair Meppershall 7/97)
G-BKDS	Colt 14A Cloudhopper HAFB	340		1. 6.82	To SE-ZBZ 3/95. Canx 9.5.84.
G-BKDT	RAF SE.5A Replica	278 & PFA/80-10325		26. 5.82	No CofA or Permit issued. Canx by CAA 11.7.91. (On display 5/97 Yorkshire Air Museum, Elvington)
G-BKDU	PA-23-250 Aztec D	27-3976	ZS-FNB N6660Y	4. 6.82	Canx 20.8.82 on sale to West Germany. To 5X-SAN.
G-BKDV	Beechcraft 65-B80 Queen Air	LD-310	ZS-NAC(4) ZS-LMR(2)/N701H/N801H/N405AE	4. 6.82	To 5H-MSK /85. Canx 30.5.84.
G-BKDW	Leonhard Stuttgart K-1260/3 - STU HAFB	0306	D-KH3	3. 6.82	Canx by CAA 7.12.88.
G-BKDX	SAN Jodel DR.1050 Ambassadeur	55	F-BITX	1. 6.82	
G-BKDY	Wassmer Jodel D.120A Paris-Nice	260	F-BMIJ	21. 6.82	Fatal crash into woods at Itchingfield near Horsham on 18.9.88. Canx as destroyed 25.10.88.
G-BKDZ	Reims Cessna F.152 II	1439	PH-VSM (PH-AXE)	1. 6.82	Fatal crash into powerlines at St.Mary Cray, Kent on 4.11.83. Canx as destroyed 29.2.84.
G-BKEA	PBN BN-2T Turbine Islander (Originally regd as BN-2B-26)	2146		8. 6.82	To G-DEMO 1/86. Canx.
G-BKEB	PBN BN-2T Turbine Islander (Originally regd as BN-2B-26)	2147		8. 6.82	To TN-AEQ. Canx 10.12.85.
G-BKEC	PBN BN-2B-21 Islander	2148		8. 6.82	To IN-140 Indian Navy. Canx 4.10.83.
G-BKED	PBN BN-2B-21 Islander	2149		8. 6.82	To IN-141 Indian Navy. Canx 30.3.84.
G-BKEE	PBN BN-2B-21 Islander	2150		8. 6.82	To IN-142 Indian Navy. Canx 18.1.84.
G-BKEF	PBN BN-2T Turbine Islander (Originally regd as BN-2B-21)	2151		8. 6.82	To 7Q-YAU 3/87. Canx 19.3.87.
G-BKEG	PBN BN-2B-26 Islander	2152		8. 6.82	To VP-LMG. Canx 26.6.86.
G-BKEH	PBN BN-2B-26 Islander	2153		8. 6.82	To EC-EBC. Canx 21.11.86.
G-BKEI	PBN BN-2B-26 Islander	2154		8. 6.82	To N667J. Canx 25.1.85.
G-BKEJ	PBN BN-2B-27 Islander	2155		8. 6.82	To N668J. Canx 25.1.85.
G-BKEK	PA-32-300 Cherokee Six	32-7540091	OY-TOP	30. 6.82	
G-BKEL	Socata TB-10 Tobago	315		. .82R	NTU - To G-BKEN 7/82. Canx.
G-BKEM	Socata TB-9 Tampico	316		6. 7.82	Crashed at Abbeville, France on 30.6.84. Canx as destroyed 3.8.94.
G-BKEN	Socata TB-10 Tobago	315	(G-BKEL)	6. 7.82	To G-POPI 4/90. Canx.
G-BKEO	Cameron House 60SS HAFB	800		11. 6.82	Canx 7.8.85 on sale to Canada.
G-BKEP	Reims Cessna F.172M Skyhawk II	1095	OY-BFJ	8. 7.82	
G-BKER	Replica Plans SE.5A	PFA/20-10641		15. 6.82	Permit expired 9.7.98.
G-BKES	Cameron Bottle 57SS HAFB (Robinsons Barley Water Bottle)	846		25. 6.82	Canx by CAA 1.5.90. (To British Balloon Museum, Newbury)
G-BKET	PA-18-95 Super Cub (L-18C-PI)	18-1990	MM52-2390 Italian AF/I-EIBI/MM52-2390/52-2390	17. 6.82	Permit expired 24.8.96. (Stored 4/97)
G-BKEU	Taylor JT.1 Monoplane	PFA/55-10553		18. 6.82	Permit expired 20.7.95.
G-BKEV	Reims Cessna F.172M Skyhawk	1443	PH-WLH OO-CNE	8. 7.82	
G-BKEW	Bell 206B JetRanger III	3010	D-HDAD	8. 7.82	
G-BKEX	Rich Prototype Glider	1		24. 6.82	
G-BKEY	Clutton FRED Srs.III	PFA/29-10208		27. 5.82	
G-BKEZ	PA-18-95 Super Cub (L-18C-PI)	18-1628	OO-SPL ALAT 51-15628	24. 6.82	To ZK-KEZ 1/98. Canx 12.9.97.
G-BKFA	Monnett Sonerai IIL	PFA/15-10524		21. 6.82	Not completed. No Permit to Fly issued. (Stored) Canx by CAA 12.4.99.
G-BKFB	Aerospatiale AS.350B Ecureuil	1613		30. 6.82	To EI-BOT 4/84. Canx 4.5.84.
G-BKFC	Reims Cessna F.152 II	1443	OO-AWB	1. 9.82	
G-BKFD	Westland WG.30 Srs.100	004	G-17-28	22. 6.82	To N5820T. Canx 6.12.82.
G-BKFE	Westland WG.30 Srs.100	005	G-17-29	22. 6.82	To N5830T. Canx 6.12.82.
G-BKFF	Westland WG.30 Srs.100	006	G-17-30	22. 6.82	To N5840T. Canx 6.12.82.
G-BKFG	Thunder Ax3 Sky Chariot HAFB	431		28. 6.82	Canx by CAA 23.1.98.
G-BKFH	Cessna T.303 Crusader	T303-00122	N4766C	29. 6.82	To G-INDC 6/83. Canx.
G-BKFI	Evans VP-1 Srs.2	PFA/62-10491		24. 6.82	
G-BKFJ	Cessna A.185F Skywagon II	A185-04285	N61981	19. 7.82	To VT-EHU 9/82. Canx 2.9.82.
G-BKFK	Isaacs Fury II	GCJ.01 & PFA/11-10038		25. 6.82	
G-BKFL	Aerosport Scamp	PFA/117-10814		17. 8.82	
G-BKFM	QAC Quickie 1	RDPC.01 & PFA/94-10570		28. 6.82	Badly damaged on landing at Pent Farm, Postling on 19.4.97. Permit expired 29.6.98.
G-BKFN	Bell 214ST Super Transport	28109	LZ-CAW G-BKFN/VH-BEE/VH-LHT/G-BKFN	16. 8.82	
G-BKFO	Not allocated.				
G-BKFP	Bell 214ST Super Transport	28110		16. 8.82	
G-BKFR	Scintex CP.301C Emeraude	519	F-BUUR F-BJFF	30. 6.82	
G-BKFS	HS.125 Srs.700B	257172	(VT-MPA) G-BKFS/G-5-765/5H-SMZ/G-5-568/5H-SMZ/G-BKFS/5H-SMZ	2. 6.82	To VT-MPA 10/93. Canx 20.10.93.
"G-BKFS"	HS.125 Srs.600B	256054	G-BCXF 9K-AED/G-BCXF/G-5-17	----	Incorrectly painted as such in 3/93 until repainted as G-BCXF in 6/93.
G-BKFT	Reims Cessna F.152 II	1908		12. 7.82	To G-WACT 6/86. Canx.
G-BKFU	Not allocated.				

Regn	Type	c/n	Previous identity	Regn date	Fate or immediate subsequent identity (if known)
G-BKFV	Rand-Robinson KR-2	FHF.01 & PFA/129-10811		8. 7.82	Fatal crash at Crofty, 3 miles north-west of Swansea on 15.6.86. Canx by CAA 23.10.92.
G-BKFW	Percival P.56 Provost T.1 (Also c/n P56/303)	PAC/F/303	XF597	21. 9.82	(Open store 7/98 Brimpton)
G-BKFX	Colt 17A Cloudhopper HAFB	414		20. 7.82	Canx 7.5.91 on sale to Australia.
G-BKFY	Beechcraft C90-1 King Air	LJ-1028		11. 8.82	To N6420H/(XB-...)/VR-CCT. Canx 3.9.91.
G-BKFZ	PA-28R-200 Cherokee Arrow II	28R-7635127	OY-BLE	17. 8.82	
G-BKGA	Socata MS.892E Rallye 150GT	13287	F-GBXJ	15. 7.82	
G-BKGB	Jodel Wassmer D.120 Paris-Nice	267	F-BMOB	21. 6.82	
G-BKGC	Maule M.6-235C Super Rocket	7413C	N56465	23. 7.82	
G-BKGD	Westland WG.30 Srs.100	002	(G-BKBJ)	15. 7.82	CofA expired 6.7.93. Canx as WFU 15.4.93. (Stored 3/93)
G-BKGE	Evans VP-2	PFA/63-10632		27. 7.82	Damaged by high winds in 1984 at Kirkmuirhill, prior its first flight. Canx as WFU 24.7.85.
G-BKGF	Saxon II	PFA/91-10436		12.12.78	No Permit to Fly issued. Canx as WFU 28.10.86.
G-BKGG	Bell 206L-1 Long Ranger	45236	I-CDVM	23. 8.82	To I-OTUS. Canx 26.8.83.
G-BKGH	Bell 205A-1	30088	5X-UWA Ugandan Police Air Wing/N8165J	14. 7.82	To C-GEAT 7/86. Canx 6.6.86.
G-BKGI	Bell 212	30524	AW-2 Ugandan Police Air Wing/5X-UWH/N7968J	14. 7.82	To VH-NSC. Canx 16.9.82.
G-BKGJ	Cameron V-31 Air Chair HAFB	863		. 7.82R	NTU - To G-BKIX 9/82. Canx.
G-BKGK	PA-31T3 Cheyenne T1040	31T-8275011		1.10.82	To N303SC. Canx 30.10.87.
G-BKGL	Beechcraft 3TM (D.18S) (Beech c/n A-764)	CA-164	CF-QPD RCAF 5193/RCAF 1564	14. 7.82	
G-BKGM	Beechcraft 3NM (D.18S) (Beech c/n A-853)	CA-203	N5063N G-BKGM/CF-SUQ/RCAF 2324	14. 7.82	
G-BKGN	Cessna U.206G Stationair 6 II	U206-06610	N9688Z	2. 8.82	To HB-CKE. Canx 31.10.86.
G-BKGO	Piper J3C-65 Cub (L-4J-PI)	12417	CN-TVO F-DACK/CN-TUK/F-BDTK/44-80121	5. 8.82	To OY-PJJ. Canx 13.5.87.
G-BKGP	Thunder Ax6-56Z HAFB	444		30. 7.82	To PH-HOR(2) 3/84. Canx 3.2.84.
G-BKGR	Cameron O-65 HAFB	864		6. 8.82	
G-BKGS	Socata MS.892A Rallye Commodore 150	11748	F-BSXS	8.10.82	To EI-BOP 3/84. Canx 8.3.84.
G-BKGT	Socata Rallye 110ST Galopin	3361		23. 7.82	
G-BKGU(1)	Boeing 737-204ADV (Line No. 946)	22966		. .82R	NTU - To G-BKHE 1/83. Canx.
G-BKGU(2)	Sikorsky S-76A	760219	N3122M	. .82R	NTU - To G-OAUS 8/82. Canx.
G-BKGV	Boeing 737-204ADV (Line No. 953)	22967		. .82R	NTU - To G-BKHF 1/83. Canx.
G-BKGW	Reims Cessna F.152 II	1878	N9071N	11. 8.82	
G-BKGX	Isaacs Fury	PFA/11-10822		2. 8.82	Canx by CAA 2.9.91.
G-BKGY	Reims Cessna F.182Q Skylane	0043	OO-CNI	30. 7.82	Destroyed in fatal crash into Mount Leinster, Ireland on 7.9.83. Canx.
G-BKGZ	Bensen B.8M Gyroplane	G/01-1038		11. 8.82	No Permit believed issued. Canx by CAAA 17.6.91.
G-BKHA	Westland-Sikorsky WS-55 Whirlwind HAR.10	WA/109	XJ763	25. 8.82	Permit to Fly expired 3.5.92. Canx as WFU 13.12.94. (Believed stored)
G-BKHB	Westland-Sikorsky WS-55 Whirlwind HAR.10	WA/33	XJ407 XD777	25. 8.82	To N7013H 7/88. Canx 15.6.88.
G-BKHC	Westland-Sikorsky WS-55 Whirlwind HAR.10	WA/348		25. 8.82	Badly damaged in crash on landing at Whatfield on 22.8.88. Canx by CAA 4.6.90.
G-BKHD	Oldfield Baby Lakes	8133-F-802B & PFA/10-10718		25. 8.82	Badly damaged in crash 10 miles north-northwest of Shrewsbury on 22.10.95. (On rebuild)
G-BKHE	Boeing 737-204ADV (Line No. 946)	22966	(G-BKGU)	26. 1.83	To EI-CJD 2/94. Canx 18.2.94.
G-BKHF	Boeing 737-204ADV (Line No. 953)	22967	(G-BKGV)	26. 1.83	To G-BTZF 4/91. Canx.
G-BKHG	Piper J3C-65 Cub (L-4H-PI)	12062	F-BCPT NC79807/44-79766	13. 9.82	
G-BKHH	Thunder Ax10-160Z HAFB	460		20. 8.82	To F-GGRE 7/90. Canx 19.2.90.
G-BKHI	BAe Jetstream Srs.3102	604	SE-IPC G-BKHI	12. 8.82	Restored as SE-IPC. Canx 22.8.90.
G-BKHJ	Cessna 182P Skylane II (Reims c/n 0040)	182-64129	PH-CAT D-EATV/N6223F	25. 8.82	
G-BKHK	HS.125 Srs.700B	257189		16. 8.82	To (G-OBSM)/G-OSAM 11/82. Canx.
G-BKHL	Thunder Ax9-140 HAFB	461		19. 8.82	Canx by CAA 19.5.93.
G-BKHM	Ben-Air Sparrowhawk VL 12/35	001		20. 8.82	Believed not completed as design and development transferred to USA. Canx by CAA 21.1.87.
G-BKHN	Enstrom 280C-UK Shark	1202	SE-HLB	. .82R	NTU - To G-BKIO 10/82. Canx.
G-BKHO	Boeing 737-2T5 (Line No. 950)	22979		16. 2.83	To HA-LEC. Canx 18.11.88.
G-BKHP	Percival P.56 Provost T.1 (Also c/n PAC/F/226)	P56/226	8060M WW397	26. 8.82	To VH-OIL(2) 7/94. Canx 12.11.93.
G-BKHR	Luton LA-4A Minor	PFA/51-10228		24. 8.82	
G-BKHS	PA-34-220T Seneca III	34-8233045	N8472H	25. 8.82	To (PH-GES)/PH-TWI 6/84. Canx 26.6.84.
G-BKHT	BAe 146 Srs.100	E1007	EC-969 G-BKHT	31. 8.82	To EC-969/EC-GEO 1/96. Canx 21.9.95.
G-BKHU	Aerospatiale AS.350B Ecureuil	1629		2. 9.82	To G-MARC 10/82. Canx.
G-BKHV	Taylor JT.2 Titch	PFA/60-10832		31. 8.82	Canx by CAA 2.9.91.
G-BKHW	Stoddard-Hamilton Glasair IIRG	357 & PFA/149-11312		27. 8.82	Canx by CAA 11.5.98.
G-BKHX	Montgomerie-Bensen B.8MR Gyroplane	G/01-1035		3. 9.82	Canx as WFU 21.10.93.

Regn	Type	c/n	Previous identity	Regn date	Fate or immediate subsequent identity (if known)
G-BKHY	Taylor JT.1 Monoplane	PFA/1416		8. 9.82	
G-BKHZ	Reims Cessna F.172P Skyhawk II	2169	D-EJOK	15.10.82	
G-BKIA	Socata TB-10 Tobago	322		25. 8.82	
G-BKIB	Socata TB-9 Tampico	323		25. 8.82	
G-BKIC	Cameron V-77 HAFB	859		12. 8.82	
G-BKID	Beechcraft C90 King Air	LJ-604	N1GV N1GC	29.10.82	Ditched into the sea 1½ miles from Kastrup Airport, Copenhagen on 26.12.83. Canx.
G-BKIE	Short SD.3-30 Var.100	SH3005	G-SLUG G-BKIE/G-METP/G-METO/ G-BKIE/C-GTAS/G-14-3005	15. 9.82	CofA expired 22.8.93. WFU & stored 1994 at Newcastle. For spares use. To CAA fire school at Teesside. (Extant 4/99 Teesside) Canx as PWFU 16.9.97.
G-BKIF	Sportavia Fournier RF-6B-100	3	F-GADR	8.10.82	To PH-KIF. Canx.
G-BKIG	HS.748 Srs.2B/400	1796		12.10.82	To MI-8203 in 12/82. Canx 25.12.82.
G-BKIH	Aerospatiale AS.355F1 Twin Squirrel	5246		17. 9.82	Destroyed in fatal crash near Swalcliffe, Oxon. 8.4.86. Canx by CAA 20.12.90.
G-BKII	Reims Cessna F.172M Skyhawk II	1370	PH-PLO (D-EGIA)	8.10.82	
	(Rebuilt after being damaged at Teuge on 5.8.81 as PH-PLO, left wing to PH-PRO, right wing to PH-JDB)				
G-BKIJ	Reims Cessna F.172M Skyhawk II	0920	PH-TGZ	15.10.82	
G-BKIK	Cameron DG-19 Helium Airship	776		23. 8.82	CofA expired 4.9.88. (On loan to Farnborough Air Sciences Trust 7/98).
G-BKIL	Not allotted.				
G-BKIM	Unicorn UE-5A HAFB (Ax7)	82028		27. 7.82	Canx by CAA 20.10.98.
G-BKIN	Alon A-2A Aircoupe	B-253	N5453F	24. 9.82	
G-BKIO	Enstrom 280C-UK Shark	1202	(G-BKHN) SE-HLB	4.10.82	To G-CTSI 15.11.82. Canx.
G-BKIP	Beechcraft C90-1 King Air	LJ-1035	N9933E	8.10.82	To G-NUIG 9/86. Canx.
G-BKIR	SAN Jodel D.117	737	F-BIOC	30. 9.82	Permit expired 28..8.92. (Stored/on slow rebuild 5/99 Birds Edge, West Yorks)
G-BKIS	Socata TB-10 Tobago	329		22. 9.82	
G-BKIT	Socata TB-9 Tampico	330		22. 9.82	
G-BKIU	Colt 17A Cloudhopper HAFB	420		29. 9.82	(Extant 2/97) Canx by CAA 15.5.98.
G-BKIV	Colt 21A Cloudhopper HAFB	447		29. 9.82	Canx by CAA 21.11.89. (Extant 2/97)
G-BKIW	PA-28-151 Cherokee Warrior II	-		. 9.82R	NTU - Canx.
G-BKIX	Cameron V-31 Air Chair HAFB	863	(G-BKGJ)	23. 9.82	CofA expired 21.9.95. Canx by CAA 4.8.98.
G-BKIY	Thunder Ax3 Sky Chariot HAFB	464		7.10.82	(On loan to Balloon Preservation Group - extant 1/98)
G-BKIZ	Cameron V-31 Air Chair HAFB	842		1. 2.83	(Active 9/93)
G-BKJA	Colt 160A HAFB	443		14.10.82	To 5Y-BDZ 3/83. Canx 3.3.83.
G-BKJB	PA-18-135 Super Cub (L-21A-PI) (Frame No. 18-522)	18-574	PH-GAI R.Netherlands AF R-204/51-15657/N1003A	1. 8.83	Damaged on landing Kingsmuir House, Anstruther, Fife on 4.8.96. (Stored 1/97)
G-BKJC	Short SD.3-60 Var.100	SH3602	G-14-3602	13.10.82	To N360MQ 11/82. Canx 11.11.82.
G-BKJD	Bell 214ST Super Transport	28114		7.12.82	To N392AL 8/97. Canx 1.8.97.
G-BKJE	Cessna 172N Skyhawk	172-73060	OY-AUE (N1972F)	22.10.82	Canx as WFU 31.3.89.
G-BKJF	Socata MS.880B Rallye 100T	2300	F-BULF	16.12.82	
G-BKJG	PBN BN-2T Turbine Islander (Originally regd as BN-2B-26)	2156		11.10.82	To G-LIPP 7/87. Canx.
G-BKJH	PBN BN-2B-21 Islander	2157	HC-BNR G-BKJH	11.10.82	To G-PASV 2/92. Canx.
G-BKJI	PBN BN-2T Turbine Islander (Originally regd as BN-2B-26)	2158		11.10.82	To 7Q-YAV 9/86. Canx.
G-BKJJ	PBN BN-2B-26 Islander	2159		11.10.82	To G-TWOB 9/85. Canx.
G-BKJK	PBN BN-2B-26 Islander	2160		11.10.82	To VP-FBD(2) 12/85. Canx 12.2.86.
G-BKJL	PBN BN-2B-21 Islander	2161		11.10.82	To TZ-ADN 9/86. Canx 14.4.87.
G-BKJM	PBN BN-2B-21 Islander	2162		11.10.82	To HC-BNS 10/87. Canx 28.7.87.
G-BKJN	PBN BN-2B-21 Islander	2163		11.10.82	To N671J. Canx 6.12.84.
G-BKJO	PBN BN-2B-26 Islander	2164		11.10.82	To VH-AEC 5/86. Canx 4.6.85.
G-BKJP	PBN BN-2B-26 Islander	2165		11.10.82	To N670J. Canx 6.12.84.
G-BKJR	Hughes 269C (300C)	44-0299	(G-BKKK) VR-HHT(1)/VR-HHM(1)/N8969F	1.11.82	Badly damaged at East Appleton, near Catterick on 13.7.84. Canx as WFU 26.5.88.
G-BKJS	Jodel Wassmer D.120A Paris-Nice	191	F-BJPS	4.10.82	
G-BKJT	Cameron O-65 HAFB	148	EI-BAN	2.11.82	Canx by CAA 19.5.93.
G-BKJU	Sikorsky S-76A	760055	N105BH G-BKJU/N105BH/N176PB	3.11.82	To C-GRJC 4/87. Canx 17.2.87.
G-BKJV	HS.125 Srs.700B	257046	4W-ACE	2.12.82	To VH-JCC. Canx 17.11.83.
G-BKJW	PA-23-250 Aztec E	27-4716	N14153	3.11.78	
G-BKJX	Aerospatiale AS.355F1 Twin Squirrel	5249		29.10.82	To G-TOFF 30.11.82. Canx.
G-BKJY	Aerospatiale AS.350B Ecureuil	1647		29.10.82	To EI-BNO(2) 3/83. Canx 4.3.83.
G-BKJZ	Grumman G.159 Gulfstream I	191	(N300XZ) N300P/N200XP	30.10.82	To VH-JPJ. Canx 18.7.88.
G-BKKA	Cessna A.188B AgTruck	188-03917T	N9988J	11.11.82	To OH-CIY. Canx 19.9.84.
G-BKKB	Cessna A.188B AgTruck	188-03919T	N9990J	13.12.82	To 5U-ABH 6/86. Canx 10.3.86.
G-BKKC	Cessna A.188B AgTruck	188-03892T	(N9963J)	. .82R	NTU - Not Imported. Canx.
G-BKKD	Cessna A.188B AgTruck	188-03899T	(N9970J)	. .82R	NTU - Not Imported. To TI-AKF. Canx.
G-BKKE	Cessna A.188B AgTruck	188-03913T	(N9984J)	. .82R	NTU - Not Imported. Canx.
G-BKKF	Cessna A.188B AgTruck	-		. .82R	NTU - Not Imported. Canx.
G-BKKG	Cessna A.188B AgTruck	-		. .82R	NTU - Not Imported. Canx.
G-BKKH	Cessna A.188B AgTruck	-		. .82R	NTU - Not Imported. Canx.
G-BKKI	Westland WG.30 Srs.100	003		1.11.82	CofA expired 28.6.85. Canx as WFU 8.1.91. (Stored 6/91)
G-BKKJ	Cessna TU.206G Turbo Stationair 6 II	U206-06043	N4890Z	30.11.82	To HB-CHU. Canx 4.5.84.
G-BKKK	[Allotted in error to Hughes 269C c/n 44-0299 - see G-BKJR]				

Regn	Type	c/n	Previous identity	Regn date	Fate or immediate subsequent identity (if known)
G-BKKL	McCulloch J.2	039	BPS-3 Bahrain Public Security/N4329G	. .82R	NTU - To N4329G/(G-BLGI)/G-ORVB 8/89. Canx.
G-BKKM	Aeronca 7DC Champion	7AC-925	EI-BJB N82296/NC82296	29.10.82	Restored as EI-BJB. Canx 17.5.90.
G-BKKN	Cessna 182R Skylane II	182-67801	N6218N	30.11.82	
G-BKKO	Cessna 182R Skylane II	182-67852	N4907H	30.11.82	
G-BKKP	Cessna 182R Skylane II	182-67968	N9600H	30.11.82	To TC-MTR 4/94. Canx 10.12.92.
G-BKKR(1)	Hughes 269C	44-0299	VR-HHT(1) VR-HHM(1)/N8969F	. .82R	NTU - To G-BKJR 11/82. Canx.
G-BKKR(2)	Rand-Robinson KR-2	DRT.01 & PFA/129-10803		26.10.82	Canx as TWFU 12.12.96.
G-BKKS	Mercury Dart Srs.1	MA 001		4.11.82	Canx as WFU 12.7.91. (Stored 4/95 - construction abandoned)
G-BKKT	Short SD.3-60 Var.100	SH3603	G-14-3603	8.11.82	To N368MQ. Canx 24.10.84.
G-BKKU	Short SD.3-60 Var.100	SH3604	G-14-3604	8.11.82	To G-RMSS 12/82. Canx.
G-BKKV	Short SD.3-60 Var.100	SH3605	G-14-3605	8.11.82	To N342MV 1/83. Canx 21.1.83.
G-BKKW	Short SD.3-60 Var.100	SH3606	G-14-3606	8.11.82	To G-DASI 2/83. Canx.
G-BKKX	Short SD.3-60 Var.100	SH3607	G-14-3607	8.11.82	To N361MQ. Canx 24.2.83.
G-BKKY	BAe Jetstream Srs.3102	606	(SE-IZA) G-BKKY/G-31-46	6.12.82	To SE-KHA. Canx 12.10.88.
G-BKKZ	Pitts S-1D Special	PFA/09-10525	(G-BIVW)	10.11.82	
G-BKLA	Socata TB-20 Trinidad	333	F-BNGX	9.11.82	To G-JDEE 5/84. Canx.
G-BKLB	Rockwell S.2R Thrush Commander	1693R	OH-ACG N5593X	.11.82R	NTU - Not Imported. Canx.
G-BKLC	Cameron V-56 HAFB	879		29.11.82	
G-BKLD	HS.748 Srs.2B/401LFD	1774	G-11-12	17.11.82	To PK-IHO 6/83. Canx 10.6.83.
G-BKLE	HS.748 Srs.2B/402	1787	G-11-22	17.11.82	To PK-IHP 5/83. Canx 10.5.83.
G-BKLF	HS.748 Srs.2B/402	1788		17.11.82	To PK-IHW 4/83. Canx 2.5.83.
G-BKLG	HS.748 Srs.2B/402	1793		17.11.82	To PK-IHT 4/83. Canx 1.5.83.
G-BKLH	HS.748 Srs.2B/402	1794		17.11.82	To PK-IHN 6/83. Canx 30.4.83.
G-BKLI	HS.748 Srs.2B/402	1795		17.11.82	To PK-IHV 4/83. Canx 4.5.83.
G-BKLJ	Westland Scout Srs.1	F.9618	5X-UUX G-17-2	6. 7.83	Not converted from 5X-UUX and believed to R.Windley as spares for G-BMIR. Canx by CAA 7.2.91. (Stored as 5X-UUX 6/93 in poor condition)
G-BKLK	Thunder Ax8-140 HAFB	473		19.11.82	To F-GEEG 3/85. Canx 8.2.84.
G-BKLL	Thunder Ax9-140 HAFB	474		19.11.82	Not completed. Canx by CAA 5.12.83.
G-BKLM	Thunder Ax9-140 HAFB	475		19.11.82	Canx by CAA 12.3.92.
G-BKLN	Thunder Ax9-140 HAFB	476		19.11.82	Canx by CAA 5.12.83 as not completed. To F-GEEF 8/84.
G-BKLO	Reims Cessna F.172M Skyhawk II	1380	PH-BET D-EFMS	22. 3.83	
G-BKLP	Reims Cessna F.172N Skyhawk II	1809	PH-BYL	22. 3.83	
G-BKLR(1)	Thunder Ax9-140 Srs.2 HAFB	479		. .82R	NTU - Not completed. Canx.
G-BKLR(2)	Cessna 210H Centurion	210-59209	D-EAJE 5Y-AJF/N6129F	. .82R	NTU - To G-BKML 12/82. Canx.
G-BKLS	Aerospatiale SA.341G Gazelle Srs.1	1455	G-TURP G-BKLS/N17MT/ N14MT/N49549	11. 1.83	Damaged in heavy landing at Stanford-le-Hope on 9.9.91. Canx as WFU 17.8.92. (On rebuild using fuselage from N341BB c/n 1421) (Original fuselage to Redhill 9/93)
G-BKLT	Aerospatiale SA.341G Gazelle Srs.1	1245	(F-GMJL) G-BKLT/N15WC/N47261	11. 1.83	To (F-GGGB)/F-GMJL. Canx 6.1.94.
G-BKLU	Aerospatiale SA.341G Gazelle Srs.1	1136	N32PA N341VH/N90957	1. 2.83	To G-GAZI 6/90. Canx.
G-BKLV	Aerospatiale SA.341G Gazelle Srs.1	1307	N341SC	1. 2.83	To G-UTZY 12/87. Canx.
G-BKLW	Aerospatiale SA.341G Gazelle Srs.1	1295	N4DQ N4QQ/N444JJ/N47316/F-WKQH	11. 1.83	To G-MANN 4/86. Canx.
G-BKLX	Colt 105A HAFB	467		25.11.82	Canx 21.3.86 on sale to Australia. To SE-ZBI.
G-BKLY	Cameron A-140 HAFB	873		16.12.82	To F-GEAN. Canx 19.4.84.
G-BKLZ	Vinten Wallis WA-116MC (Also described as Vinten VJ-22 Autogyro)	UMA-01		8.12.82	Permit expired 16.12.83. Canx as destroyed 8.6.89. (On display 4/99 at Hermeskeil Museum, near Trier, Germany as G-55-2)
G-BKMA	Mooney M.20J (201)	24-1316	N1170N	13.12.82	
G-BKMB	Mooney M.20J (201)	24-1307	N1168P	15.12.82	
G-BKMC	Mooney M.20K (231)	25-0693	N1167W	13.12.82	To HB-DGI. Canx 7.4.83.
G-BKMD	Short SC.7 Skyvan 3-100-41	SH1907	EI-BUB G-BKMD/A40-SK/G-BAHK/G-14-79	20.12.82	
G-BKME	Short SC.7 Skyvan 3-100-32	SH1885	A40-SN G-AYJN/G-14-57	14. 4.83	To N4280Y. Canx 1.8.91.
G-BKMF	Short SC.7 Skyvan 3-100-32	SH1886	A40-SO G-AYJO/G-14-58	7. 7.83	To C9-ASN 3/86. Canx.
G-BKMG	Handley Page O/400 Replica (Some components under construction .93)	TPG-1		8.12.82	Not built. Canx by CAA 4.7.91.
G-BKMH	Flamboyant Ax7-65 HAFB	024		20.12.82	Canx by CAA 8.1.93. (Based in South Africa in 1982 & in "Central Africa" in 1993)
G-BKMI	Vickers Supermarine 359 Spitfire HF.VIIIc	6S/583793	A58-671 R.Australian AF/MV154	23.12.82	
G-BKMJ	Bell 206L-2 Long Ranger (Wore marks G-CYII unofficially in 9/83 as an exhibit at Cranfield)	45724	"G-CYII" G-BKMJ/N18098	6. 1.83	To N102DD. Canx 15.6.84.
G-BKMK	PA-38-112 Tomahawk	38-80A0081	OO-GME (OO-HKD)	8. 2.83	To G-NCFE 7/99. Canx.
G-BKML	Cessna 210H Centurion	210-59209	(G-BKLR) D-EAJE/5Y-AJF/N6129F	21.12.82	Canx as WFU 19.5.86.
G-BKMM	Cessna 180K Skywagon	180-52827	N63083	11. 1.83	Destroyed in fatal crash 8 miles north of Ballymena, Co.Antrim on 3.11.94. Canx by CAA 13.3.96.

Regn	Type	c/n	Previous identity	Regn date	Fate or immediate subsequent identity (if known)
G-BKMN	BAe 146 Srs.100	E1006	EI-COF SE-DRH/G-BKMN/(G-ODAN)	10.12.82	To G-OFOA 3/98. Canx.
G-BKMO	Aerospatiale AS.350B Ecureuil	1661		11. 1.83	To G-SORR 4/83. Canx.
G-BKMP	Barnes HAFB	-		. .82R	NTU - Canx.
G-BKMR	Thunder Ax3 Maxi Sky Chariot HAFB	497		12. 1.83	(On loan to Balloon Preservation Group 10/97) Canx as WFU 23.4.98.
G-BKMS	Boeing 737-2Q8 (Line No. 748)	22453	N143AW G-BKMS/OO-RVM/TF-VLK/OO-RVM	28. 2.83	To VR-HYZ 11/89. Canx 15.11.89.
G-BKMT	PA-32R-301 Saratoga SP	32R-8213013	N8005Z	4. 2.83	
G-BKMU	Short SD.3-30 Var.100	SH3092	SE-IYO G-BKMU/G-14-3092/EI-BEH/EI-BEG/G-BKMU/G-14-3092	13.12.83	To EI-EXP 7/92. Canx 15.7.92.
G-BKMV	Short SD.3-30 Var.200	SH3093	G-14-3093	13.12.82	To (EI-BNM)/N155DD 4/83. Canx 20.4.83.
G-BKMW	Short SD.3-30 Sherpa Var.100	SH3094	G-14-3094	13.12.82	CofA expired 14.9.90. Broken up in 3/96 at Belfast City. Canx as WFU 14.11.96.
G-BKMX	Short SD.3-60 Var.100	SH3608	G-14-3608	13.12.82	
G-BKMY	Short SD.3-60 Var.100	SH3609	G-14-3609	13.12.82	NTU - To N343MV. Canx 14.3.83.
G-BKMZ	Short SD.3-60 Var.100	SH3610	G-14-3610	13.12.82	NTU - To N715NC. Canx 23.3.83.
G-BKNA	Cessna 421 Golden Eagle	421-0097	F-BUYB HB-LDZ/N4097L	28. 1.83	Fatal crash at Penbridge, Hereford on 3.8.97. CofA expired 13.8.97.
G-BKNB	Cameron V-42 HAFB	887		10. 1.83	
G-BKNC	Beechcraft 65-C90 King Air	LJ-848	OY-MBB	18. 1.83	To PH-DMJ 6/83. Canx 10.3.83.
G-BKND	Colt 56A HAFB	484		21. 1.83	Canx 5.2.97 on sale to Slovenia.
G-BKNE	PA-28-181 Warrior II	28-7816267	OO-GMB OO-HCL	19. 1.83	To G-OVER 1/88. Canx.
G-BKNF	Westland-Bell 47G-3B1 (Line No. WAP/117)	WA/407	XT248	25. 1.83	Canx 20.8.86 on sale to Australia.
G-BKNG	Boeing 727-217ADV (Line No. 1122)	21056	C-GCPB	24. 3.83	To G-NROA 4/84. Canx.
G-BKNH	Boeing 737-210 (Line No. 578)	21820	4X-BAA N491WC	5. 4.83	To PK-RIJ. Canx 31.3.93.
G-BKNI	Gardan GY-80-160D Horizon	249	F-BRJN	28. 1.83	
G-BKNJ	Grob G-109	6154		16. 2.83	Mid-air collision with Robin G-BFWW on 3.5.90 resulting in a fatal crash at Chadlington. Canx as destroyed 31.1.91.
G-BKNK	Rutan Vari-Eze	V-43	VH-EZI	20. 6.83	Restored as VH-EZI 9/92. Canx 31.1.86.
G-BKNL	Cameron D-96 Hot-Air Airship (Rebuilt with new envelope c/n 3192/G-BVHH .94)	805	(I-....) G-BKNL/N1783Q/G-BKNL	25. 1.83	
G-BKNM	PA-18-150 Super Cub (Frame No.18-5424)	18-5352	PH-MBA ALAT 18-5352	. 2.83R	NTU - To G-OTUG 2/83. Canx.
G-BKNN	Cameron Minor-E-Pakistan HAFB (Special shape as non-flying 240ft high Moslem national monument)	900		7. 2.82	Canx as WFU 29.4.93.
G-BKNO	Monnett Sonerai IIL	792 & PFA/15-10528		11. 3.83	
G-BKNP	Cameron V-77 HAFB	874		22.12.82	(Based at Kvanum, Sweden)
G-BKNR	Agusta-Bell 412	25501		1. 2.83	NTU - Not Imported. To I-VFOB. Canx 11.6.84.
G-BKNS	Agusta-Bell 412	25504		1. 2.83	NTU - Not Imported. To I-EHAC. Canx 11.6.84.
G-BKNT	Agusta-Bell 412	25505		1. 2.83	NTU - Not Imported. To I-EHAB. Canx 11.6.84.
G-BKNU	Agusta-Bell 412	25506		1. 2.83	NTU - Not Imported. To I-GONI. Canx 11.6.84.
G-BKNV	Westland WG.30 Srs.100	007		14. 2.83	To G-ELEC 6/83. Canx.
G-BKNW	Westland WG.30 Srs.100	008		14. 2.83	To G-OGAS 3/83. Canx.
G-BKNX	K & S SA.102.5 Cavalier	PFA/01-10001		21. 2.83	Canx by CAA 2.9.91.
G-BKNY	Bensen B.8MP Gyrocopter	G/01-1030		1. 3.83	No Permit issued - probably not completed. Canx by CAA 26.2.99.
G-BKNZ	Menavia Piel CP.301A Emeraude	296	F-BISZ	21. 1.83	
G-BKOA	Socata MS.893E Rallye 180GT	12432	F-BOFB F-ODAT/F-BVAT	2. 3.83	
G-BKOB	Moravan Zlin Z.326 Trener-Master	757	F-BKOB	28. 9.81	
G-BKOC	PBN BN-2B-27 Islander	2166		27. 1.83	To CC-CGE 7/85. Canx 31.7.85.
G-BKOD	PBN BN-2B-26 Islander	2167		27. 1.83	To I-LILY. Canx 26.3.86.
G-BKOE	PBN BN-2B-27 Islander (Originally regd as BN-2B-26)	2168		27. 1.83	To CC-CGG 7/85. Canx 31.7.85.
G-BKOF	PBN BN-2B-27 Islander (Originally regd as BN-2B-26)	2169		27. 1.83	To CC-CGH 7/85. Canx 31.7.85.
G-BKOG	PBN BN-2B-26 Islander (Originally regd as BN-2B-21)	2170		27. 1.83	To N672JA(2). Canx 10.7.87.
G-BKOH	PBN BN-2B-21 Islander	2171		27. 1.83	To OH-BND 6/87. Canx 3.6.87.
G-BKOI	PBN BN-2B-20 Islander	2172		27. 1.83	To JA5290 5/88. Canx 31.3.88.
G-BKOJ	PBN BN-2B-20 Islander	2173		27. 1.83	To JA5294 9/88. Canx 1.9.88.
G-BKOK	PBN BN-2B-27 Islander	2174		27. 1.83	To OY-CFV. Canx 3.7.85.
G-BKOL	PBN BN-2B-26 Islander	2175		27. 1.83	To G-OSEA 8/85. Canx.
G-BKOM	Gulfstream American GA-7 Cougar	GA7-0083	N794GA	23. 2.83	To G-CYMA 8/83. Canx.
G-BKON	Not allotted.				
G-BKOO	Barnes 7B Firefly HAFB (Was reserved as O-56 Firefly 75)	F7B-052	N3609T	25. 2.83	To HB-BGH. Canx 5.7.85.
G-BKOP	Barnes 65 Firefly HAFB	-		. .83R	NTU - Canx.
G-BKOR	Barnes 77 Firefly HAFB	F7-046		1. 7.83	Canx by CAA 15.5.98.
G-BKOS	Percival P.56 Provost T.51 (Also c/n PAC/F/157)	P56/157	178 Irish Air Corps	21. 2.83	Fatal crash near Lower Wasing Farm, Aldermaston on 19.5.91. Canx as destroyed 11.10.91.
G-BKOT	Wassmer WA.81 Piranha	813	F-GAIP	17. 2.87	(Stored 3/97)

Regn	Type	c/n	Previous identity	Regn date	Fate or immediate subsequent identity (if known)
G-BKOU	Hunting P.84 Jet Provost T.3	PAC/W/13901	(G-JETP) XN637	17. 2.83	
G-BKOV	CEA Jodel DR.220A 2+2	53	F-BOKV	21. 3.83	Badly damaged on take-off from Hucknall on 22.11.97. Canx as PWFU 21.10.98.
G-BKOW	Colt 77A HAFB	505		6. 9.84	Canx as WFU 29.4.97. (Extant 1/98)
G-BKOX	Not allotted.				
G-BKOY	Barnes 105 HAFB	-		. .83R	NTU - Canx.
G-BKOZ	Barnes 77 Firefly HAFB	-		. .83R	NTU - Canx.
G-BKPA	Hoffmann H-36 Dimona	3522		16. 6.83	
G-BKPB	Aerosport Scamp	PFA/117-10736		23. 2.83	
G-BKPC	Cessna A.185F AgCarryall	185-03809	N4599E	10. 7.80	
G-BKPD	Viking Dragonfly	302 & PFA/139-10897		11. 3.83	
G-BKPE	CEA Jodel DR.250/160 Capitaine (Rebuild)	35/75	F-BNJD	18. 3.83	
G-BKPF	Bell 206B JetRanger III	2401	EI-BFK N50005	9. 3.83	To G-NORM 18.4.83. Canx.
G-BKPG	Luscombe P3 Rattler Strike	003		7. 3.83	No Permit issued. Canx by CAA 31.7.91. (Stored 5/95 at Tatenhill)
G-BKPH	Luscombe Valiant	004		7. 3.83	No Permit issued. Canx as CAA 31.7.91.
G-BKPI	Piper J3C-65 Cub	6503	N35645 NC35645	3. 3.85	Restored as N35645. Canx 10.9.85.
G-BKPJ	Colt 77A HAFB	455		17. 3.85	Canx 18.1.84 on sale to Canada.
G-BKPK	Everett Gyroplane (Originally regd as Campbell Cricket on 19.4.83, amended to John McHugh Gyrocopter c/n JM.1 and then further amended)	005		21. 6.83	Permit expired 23.3.93. (Stored Sproughton 12/95)
G-BKPL	Socata TB-9 Tampico	80	SE-GFL	21. 3.83	To OO-RMA. Canx 21.1.85.
G-BKPM	Schempp-Hirth HS.5 Nimbus 2	84	BGA.2025	18. 3.83	Restored as BGA.2025/DDD. Canx.
G-BKPN	Cameron N-77 HAFB	923		9. 3.83	
G-BKPO	Short SD.3-60 Var.100	SH3611		15. 3.83	NTU - To G-14-3611/G-BMAJ 4/83. Canx 25.4.83.
G-BKPP	Short SD.3-60 Var.100	SH3612	G-14-3612	15. 3.83	NTU - To N362MQ. Canx 6.5.83.
G-BKPR	Short SD.3-60 Var.100	SH3613		15. 3.83	To N601A 6/83. Canx 24.6.83.
G-BKPS	American Aviation AA-5B Tiger	AA5B-0007	OO-SAS OO-HAO/(OO-WAY)/N1507R	7. 3.83	
G-BKPT	Max Holste MH.1521M Broussard	192	French AF F-RHGI	7. 4.83	To N81563 8/98. Canx 5.8.98.
G-BKPU	Max Holste MH.1521M Broussard	217	French AF F-RHMF	7. 4.83	Crashed on the east bound carriageway of the M62 Motorway on 7.6.88 while attempting to land at Barton. Stored for spares use at Barton. Canx as WFU 1.11.88.
G-BKPV	Stevex 250.1	250/1		10. 3.83	No Permit issued. Canx as WFU 27.10.95.
G-BKPW	Boeing 767-204 (Line No. 71)	22980	N5573K N8289V	15. 2.84	To VH-RML(3) 11/95. Canx 2.11.95.
G-BKPX	Jodel Wassmer D.120A Paris-Nice	240	F-BLNG	19. 1.84	
G-BKPY	SAAB 91B/2 Safir	91321	56321 R.Norwegian AF "UA-B"	23. 3.83	No CofA issued. (On display 2/99 Winthorpe as 56321)
G-BKPZ	Pitts S-1T Special	PFA/09-10852		4. 3.83	
G-BKRA	North American T-6G-NH Harvard	188-90	MM53664 Italian AF RM-9/51-15227	19. 8.83	
G-BKRB	Cessna 172N Skyhawk II (Wren conversion)	172-72969	EI-BKR G-BHKZ/N1207F	23. 3.83	CofA expired 15.5.89. Canx as WFU 20.4.88. (Wreck stored 7/95)
G-BKRC	Robin R.2160 Alpha Sport	97	F-BZAC F-WZAC	16. 3.83	To G-MATT 5/85. Canx.
G-BKRD	Cessna 320E Skyknight	320E-0101	D-IACB HB-LDN/N2201Q	24. 3.83	Crashed on take-off from Lille, France on 5.11.90. (In Open storage at Sandtoft in 2/92 minus wings) Canx as destroyed 6.4.92. (Extant 4/95)
G-BKRE	Cessna 404 Titan II	404-0813	N67662 (D-IDOS)/N67662	. 3.83R	NTU - Not Imported. To 3X-GCF. Canx.
G-BKRF	PA-18-95 Super Cub (L-18C-PI) (Frame No 18-1502)	18-1525	F-BOUI ALAT/51-15525	7.11.83	
G-BKRG	Beechcraft C-45G-BH (Regd as C-45H)	AF-222	N75WB N9072Z/51-11665	5. 5.83	(Moved from North Weald in 4/98 to Bruntingthorpe where it is likely to be used as a spares source for G-BKRN) No UK CofA issued. Canx as WFU 27.4.98.
G-BKRH	Brugger MB.2 Colibri	142 & PFA/43-10150		15. 3.83	
G-BKRI	Cameron V-77 HAFB	909		30. 3.83	
G-BKRJ	Colt 105A HAFB	458		15. 7.83	Canx as WFU 6.4.93.
G-BKRK	SNCAN Stampe SV-4C	57	French Navy	30. 3.83	
G-BKRL	Chichester-Miles Leopard	001		21. 3.83	Permit expired 14.12.91. (Stored 2/97 Cranfield) Canx as PWFU 25.1.99.
G-BKRM	Boeing 757-236 (Line No. 14)	22176	EC-321 G-BKRM/EC-EGI/EC-117/G-BKRM/N57008/(G-BIKF)	30. 3.83	To C-GANX. Canx 21.12.92.
G-BKRN	Beechcraft D.18S	CA-75	CF-DTN RCAF A675/RCAF 1500	14. 4.83	CofA expired 26.6.83. (On overhaul Bruntingthorpe 9/97)
G-BKRO	Boeing 737-2L9 (Line No. 479)	21278	EI-BMY D2-TBT/F-GCGR/D2-TBT/F-GCGR/4R-ALC/OY-APG/N1787B	20. 4.83	Restored as 4R-ALC. Canx 25.10.83.
G-BKRP	Rockwell S2R-600 Thrush Commander	1864R	OH-ACJ	13. 4.83	To 5Y-BEP 4/86. Canx 17.4.86.
G-BKRR	Cameron N-56 HAFB	918		25. 3.83	Canx as WFU 4.3.94.
G-BKRS	Cameron V-56 HAFB	908		23. 3.83	
G-BKRT	PA-34-220T Seneca III	34-8333042	N42920	24. 3.83	To CS-AZC 12/92. Canx 13.3.92.
G-BKRU	Ensign Crossley Racer	PFA/131-10797		30. 3.83	Permit expired 24.1.90. (Stored 9/90 Redhill) Canx by CAA 2.3.99.

Regn	Type	c/n	Previous identity	Regn date	Fate or immediate subsequent identity (if known)
G-BKRV	Hovey Beta Bird	PFA/135-10875		30. 3.83	CofA expired 25.6.97. Canx by CAA 18.6.98. (Stored 7/98 Crosland Moor)
G-BKRW	Cameron O-160 HAFB	915		5. 4.83	Canx by CAA 19.5.93.
G-BKRX	Cameron O-160 HAFB	916		5. 4.83	Canx by CAA 19.5.93.
G-BKRY	Thunder Ax6-56Z HAFB	501		25. 3.83	Canx 15.4.84 as not completed.
G-BKRZ	Dragon 77 HAFB	001		11. 4.83	CofA expired 5.3.94. (British Balloon Museum 2/97)
G-BKSA	Cessna 425 Conquest	425-0173	N6873Q	8. 6.83	To G-ONOR 4/84. Canx.
G-BKSB	Cessna T.310Q II	310Q-0914	VR-CEM G-BKSB/HB-LMO/OE-FYL/(N69680)	22. 4.83	
G-BKSC	Saro Skeeter AOP.12 (C/n officially S2/7076, which may be component no.)	S2/7157	XN351	23. 5.83	(On overhaul 10/96)
G-BKSD	Colt 56A HAFB	361		11. 4.83	
G-BKSE	QAC Quickie 1 (Regd with c/n PFA/94-10784)	PFA/94-10748		6. 4.83	(Status uncertain)
G-BKSF	Thunder Ax7-77 HAFB	504		8. 4.83	To N504TB. Canx 2.9.83.
G-BKSG	Hoffmann H36 Dimona	3528		21. 4.83	To JA2528 1/96. Canx 23.4.90.
G-BKSH	Colt 21A Cloudhopper HAFB	510		16. 5.83	Canx by CAA 12.5.98.
G-BKSI	Cessna P.206E Super Skylane	P206-0634	D-ECKQ N5734J	18. 4.83	To ZK-FJH 8/84. Canx.
G-BKSJ	Cameron N-108 HAFB	904		. .83R	NTU - To G-BOOZ(2) 6/83 as a N-77. Canx.
G-BKSK	QAC Quickie Q.2	PFA/94A-10765		27. 6.83	Force landed and struck hedge at Bishops Cleeve, Glos. on 8.7.86. Canx as destroyed 25.11.86.
G-BKSL	Short SD.3-60 Var.100	SH3614		25. 4.83	To N363MQ. Canx 7.6.83.
G-BKSM	Short SD.3-60 Var.100	SH3615	G-14-3615	25. 4.83	To N344MV. Canx 28.6.83.
G-BKSN	Short SD.3-60 Var.100	SH3616	G-14-3616	25. 4.83	To N345MV. Canx 2.8.83.
G-BKSO	Cessna 421C Golden Eagle III	421C-1006	N6333X	3. 5.83	To G-OOJB 3/91. Canx.
G-BKSP	Schleicher ASK-14	14028	D-KOMO	25. 5.83	
G-BKSR	Cessna 550 Citation II (Unit No.469)	550-0469	N1251V	26. 5.83	To VR-BIZ 6/93. Canx 15.6.93.
G-BKSS	SAN Jodel D.150A Mascaret	48	F-BMFC	14. 9.83	(Status uncertain)
G-BKST	Rutan VariEze	12718-001		20. 4.83	
G-BKSU	Short SD.3-30 Var.100	SH3095	G-14-3095	10. 5.83	To G-BNYA 3/87. Canx.
G-BKSV	Short SD.3-30 Var.100	SH3096	G-14-3096	10. 5.83	To N332SB. Canx 26.7.85.
G-BKSW	Bensen B.8M Gyrocopter	6655	N59353	8.11.83	Canx 22.10.84 on sale to Canada.
G-BKSX	SNCAN Stampe SV-4C	61	F-BBAF French Mil	16. 5.83	(Stored 8/90)
G-BKSY	Fouga CM.170 Magister II	61	F-ZADG French AF	7. 5.83	Canx 11.1.85 on sale to USA. To N28JV 5/92.
G-BKSZ	Cessna P.210N Pressurised Centurion	P210-00818	N4709A	19. 6.83	To N210W 2/94. Canx 7.2.94.
G-BKTA	PA-18-95 Super Cub (L-18C-PI)(Frame No 18-3246)	18-3223	OO-HBA OL-L149/53-4823	10. 5.83	
G-BKTB	Mooney M.20E Chapparal	0555	ZS-DWY	3. 6.83	NTU - Canx 13.6.83 as Not Imported.
G-BKTC	Pitts S-2E Special	PFA/09-10846		12. 5.83	Fatal crash near Wellesbourne Mountford on 8.9.85 & DBF. Canx by CAA 4.2.87.
G-BKTD	Partenavia P.68C Victor	297		21. 5.83	NTU - Canx 12.6.84 as Not Imported. To F-GEGT.
G-BKTE	Colt AS-105 Hot Air Airship	490		18. 5.83	To C-GZMG. Canx 8.3.85.
G-BKTF	BAe 125 Srs.800B	258001	"N800BA" G-5-11	17. 5.83	Wore marks N800BA but never officially issued. To G-5-522/G-UWWB 6/86. Canx.
G-BKTG	Enstrom 280C-UK Shark	1015	OY-HBP	24. 5.83	To G-FSDC 10/87. Canx.
G-BKTH	Hawker (CCF) Sea Hurricane IB	CCF/41H/4013	Z7015	24. 5.83	
G-BKTI	Beechcraft 200 Super King Air	BB-362		21.12.77	To G-SONG 3/81. Canx.
G-BKTJ	Cessna 404 Titan	404-0236	LN-VIN SE-GYL/N88721	4. 8.83	Crashed due to engine failure shortly after take-off from Birmingham/Elmdon on 27.11.85, and came to rest on allotments about 400 yards from the runway and was severely damaged. Canx by CAA 3.8.94.
G-BKTK	Hughes 369HS (500)	114-0673S	OY-HCL OO-JGR	1. 6.83	To G-STEF 11/84. Canx.
G-BKTL	Cessna 340A	340A-0987	9M-SDP	18. 7.83	To N65RS. Canx 9.8.83.
G-BKTM	PZL SZD-45A Ogar	B-656		31. 5.83	
G-BKTN	BAe Jetstream Srs.3116	612	G-31-612	7. 6.83	To HB-AEA. Canx 15.12.87.
G-BKTO	Beechcraft 58P Baron	TJ-85	ZS-JXX 7P-AAF/ZS-JXX/N1560L	. 6.83R	NTU - Not Imported. Canx.
G-BKTP	Colt AS-105 Hot-Air Airship	493		7. 6.83	To C-GIAO 4/85. Canx 11.4.85.
G-BKTR	Cameron V-77 HAFB	951		6. 6.83	
G-BKTS	Cameron O-77 HAFB	891		13. 6.83	Canx as destroyed 26.4.93.
G-BKTT	Reims Cessna F.152 II	1937		27. 7.83	To I-ECSI. Canx 15.1.92.
G-BKTU	Colt 56A HAFB	514		23. 6.83	Canx 13.9.94 on sale to the Philippines.
G-BKTV	Reims Cessna F.152 II	1450	OY-BJB	8. 8.83	
G-BKTW	Cessna 404 Titan Courier II	404-0220	G-WTVE N88682	16. 6.83	To G-LAKC 4/91. Canx.
G-BKTX	Colt 21A Cloudhopper HAFB	519		. 6.83R	NTU - To G-LLAI 7/83. Canx.
G-BKTY	Socata TB-10 Tobago	363	F-BNGZ	7. 6.83	
G-BKTZ	Slingsby T.67M Firefly 160	2004	G-SFTV	26. 8.83	
G-BKUA	Bell 206A JetRanger	387	RP-C1957 PI-C1957	9. 6.83	Canx 10.2.84 on sale to Australia.
G-BKUB	Bell 206B JetRanger	485	RP-C1797 PI-C1797	13. 6.83	To VH-JWF 9/87. Canx 20.8.86.
G-BKUC	Mudry CAARP CAP.10B	200	F-WZCF	17. 8.83	To VR-HUC /86. Canx 6.6.86.
G-BKUD	Cameron O-65 HAFB	938		27. 6.83	To VH-BKH 5/86. Canx 10.3.86.

Regn	Type	c/n	Previous identity	Regn date	Fate or immediate subsequent identity (if known)
G-BKUE	Socata TB-9 Tampico	369	F-BNGX	31. 5.83	
G-BKUF	Short SD.3-60 Var.100	SH3617		17. 6.83	To N617FB. Canx 8.7.83.
G-BKUG	Short SD.3-60 Var.100	SH3618	G-14-3618	17. 6.83	To N691A. Canx 9.8.83.
G-BKUH	Short SD.3-60 Var.100	SH3619	G-14-3619	17. 6.83	NTU - To N364MQ. Canx 14.8.83.
G-BKUI	Druine D.31 Turbulent	PFA/48-10789		28. 6.83	Canx by CAA 12.8.91.
G-BKUJ	Thunder Ax6-56 Srs.1 HAFB	520		17. 6.83	
G-BKUK	Aerospatiale AS.355F1 Twin Squirrel	5302		4. 7.83	To G-BMTC 12/83. Canx.
G-BKUL	Aerospatiale AS.355F1 Twin Squirrel	5303		4. 7.83	To G-GWHH 1/84. Canx.
G-BKUM	Aerospatiale AS.350B Ecureuil	1731		4. 7.83	To G-PLMC 8/88. Canx.
G-BKUN	Cessna 404 Titan II	404-0039	LN-MAT SE-GZC/(N5421G)	13. 7.83	To G-IFTD 9/86. Canx.
G-BKUO	Monnett Moni	0089		22. 7.83	Destroyed in fatal crash at Tibenham on 1.7.85. Canx by CAA 4.2.87.
G-BKUP	Thunder Ax7-77 Srs.1 HAFB	234	ZS-HOJ	. 7.83R	NTU - To G-BLOJ 12/84. Canx.
G-BKUR	Menavia Piel CP.301A Emeraude	280	(G-BKBX) F-BMLX/F-OBLY	19.10.83	
G-BKUS	Bensen B.8M Gyrocopter	G/01-1045		7. 7.83	
G-BKUT	Morane-Saulnier MS.880B Rallye Club	376	F-BKZT	22. 7.83	Tried to clear trees on landing at Nayes Coppice Farm, Havant, on 16.2.92 after a local flight but went off the landing strip. The front of the aircraft was extensively damaged. Canx by CAA 7.4.92.
G-BKUU	Thunder Ax7-77 Srs.1 HAFB	522		3. 8.83	
G-BKUV	Beechcraft A23-24 Musketeer Sport III	MA-260	9J-RHW N2878B	. 8.83R	NTU - Remained as 9J-RHW. Canx.
G-BKUW	BAe 125 Srs.800A	258003	G-5-20	15. 8.83	To N800BA 6/84. Canx 21.6.83.
G-BKUX	Beechcraft C90A King Air	LJ-1073		24. 8.83	To N7049U. Canx 30.11.88.
G-BKUY	BAe Jetstream Srs.3102	616	(SE-LHY) G-BKUY/G-31-616	6. 9.83	To D-CNRX 4/98. Canx 6.3.98.
G-BKUZ	Zenair CH.250	PFA/113-10888		25. 7.83	Canx by CAA 2.9.91.
G-BKVA	Socata MS.893E Rallye 180T	3274	SE-GFS F-GBXA	30. 6.83	
G-BKVB	Socata Rallye 110ST Galopin	3258	OO-PIP	22. 6.83	
G-BKVC	Socata TB-9 Tampico	372	F-BNGQ	4. 7.83	
G-BKVD	Not allotted.				
G-BKVE	Rutan VariEze	PFA/74-10236	G-EZLT	5. 7.83	
G-BKVF	Clutton FRED Srs.III	PFA/29-10791		29. 7.83	(Nearing completion 10/95)
G-BKVG	Scheibe SF-25E Super Falke	4362	(D-KNAE)	25. 8.83	
G-BKVH	Cessna 404 Titan Courier II	404-0056	G-WTVA N5438G	10. 8.83	To G-BLTH 2/85. Canx.
G-BKVI	American Aviation AA-5B Tiger	AA5B-0928	OO-NAS (OO-HRC)	. 8.83R	NTU - To G-RUBB 9/83. Canx.
G-BKVJ	Colt 21A Cloudhopper HAFB	518		10. 8.83	Canx as WFU 3.6.91.
G-BKVK	Auster AOP.9	AUS/10/2	WZ662	8. 8.83	
G-BKVL	Robin DR.400/160 Major	1625		26. 7.83	
G-BKVM	PA-18-150 Super Cub (L-21A-PI)(Frame No.18-824)	18-849	PH-KAZ R.Netherlands AF R-214/51-15684	26. 8.83	
G-BKVN	PA-23-250 Aztec F	27-8054005	N6959A	16. 8.83	To N370SA 2/99. Canx 4.2.99.
G-BKVO	Pietenpol Air Camper	PFA/47-10799		8. 8.83	
G-BKVP	Pitts S-1D Special	002 & PFA/09-10800		19. 8.83	
G-BKVR	PA-28-140 Cherokee Cruiser	28-7425338	OY-BGV	26.10.83	Canx by CAA 12.1.98. To G-MKAS 30.4.98.
G-BKVS	Bensen B.8M Gyrocopter (Built to Campbell Cricket specification)	VS-01 & G/01-1047		11. 8.83	
G-BKVT	PA-23-250 Aztec E	27-7754002	G-HARV N62760	6. 2.84	
G-BKVU	BAe Jetstream Srs.3101	604	(N93MA) G-31-615	17. 8.83	To G-31-615/N822JS 10/83. Canx 18.10.83.
G-BKVV	Beechcraft 95-B55 Baron	TC-2191	ZS-KGT N2069G	2. 8.83	CofA expired 13.9.87. (Last regd to an owner at Rockport, Texas - present status unknown) Canx 28.7.94.
G-BKVW	Airtour AH-56 HAFB	AH.003		27. 6.84	(Active 8/95)
G-BKVX	Airtour AH-56C HAFB	AH.002		27. 6.84	(Active .90)
G-BKVY	Airtour B-31 HAFB	AH.001		9. 8.83	CofA expired 17.6.97.
G-BKVZ	Boeing 767-204 (Line No. 79)	22981	N1785B	17. 1.84	To VH-RMK(3) 11/94. Canx 2.11.94.
G-BKWA	Cessna 404 Titan Ambassador II	404-0061	G-BELV (N5443G)	16. 6.83	To G-LAKD 4/91. Canx.
G-BKWB	Embraer EMB.110P2 Bandeirante	110-199	G-CHEV (PT-GLR)	18. 7.83	To G-OEAB 1/94. Canx.
G-BKWC	Not allotted.				
G-BKWD	Taylor JT.2 Titch (Originally regd as c/n 2 & PFA/60-10143; presumed absorbed both projects)	PFA/60-10232		17. 8.83	
G-BKWE	Colt 17A Cloudhopper HAFB	533		1.11.83	
G-BKWF	CEA Jodel DR.1051 Ambassadeur	245	F-BKIZ	4. 7.84	Fatal crash when it cartwheeled and burst into flames on landing at Stapleford on 29.4.86. Canx as destroyed 5.3.87.
G-BKWG	PZL-104 Wilga 35A	17820687	SP-WAC(2)	10. 8.83	
G-BKWH	Reims Cessna F.172P Skyhawk II	2196		25. 8.83	To SE-IPN. Canx 2.7.87.
G-BKWI	Aerotek Pitts S-2A Special	2268	N5303H	18. 8.83	Crashed at Bramford, near Ipswich on 10.8.96. Canx by CAA 13.12.96.
G-BKWJ	Short SD.3-60 Var.100	SH3620	G-14-3620	17. 8.83	To VH-MVX 8/83. Canx 25.8.83.

Regn	Type	c/n	Previous identity	Regn date	Fate or immediate subsequent identity (if known)
G-BKWK	Short SD.3-60 Var.300	SH3621	G-14-3621	17. 8.83	To N365MQ 9/83. Canx 17.8.83.
G-BKWL	Short SD.3-60 Var.100	SH3622	G-14-3622	17. 8.83	NTU - To N622FB. Canx 19.9.83.
G-BKWM	Short SD.3-60 Var.100	SH3623	G-14-3623	17. 8.83	To N601CA. Canx 25.10.83.
G-BKWN	Short SD.3-60 Var.100	SH3624	G-14-3624	17. 8.83	NTU - To N912SB. Canx 14.11.83.
G-BKWO	[Was reserved for a homebuild]	-		. 9.83R	NTU - Canx.
G-BKWP	Thunder AX7-77Z Srs.1 HAFB	523	(N.....) G-BKWP	8. 9.83	Canx as WFU 29.7.93.
G-BKWR	Cameron V-65 HAFB	970		26. 8.83	
G-BKWS	Embraer EMB.110P1 Bandeirante	110-261	G-CTLN PT-SBA	15. 9.83	To LN-FAP 2/85. Canx 12.2.85.
G-BKWT	Airbus A.310-203	295	F-WZEF	20. 3.84	Canx by CAA 30.6.86. To 5A-DLA.
G-BKWU	Airbus A.310-203	306	F-WZEK	20. 3.84	Canx by CAA 30.6.86. To 5A-DLB.
G-BKWV	Colt 105A HAFB	521		12. 9.83	To G-TIKI 1/84. Canx.
G-BKWW	Cameron O-77 HAFB	984		13. 9.83	
G-BKWX	Cessna 421C Golden Eagle III	421C-1222	N26610 N2708F/(N2701J)	28.10.83	To G-BUDG 1/85. Canx.
G-BKWY	Reims Cessna F.152T	1940		22. 9.83	
G-BKWZ	Noorduyn AT-6 Harvard IIB (Also quotes as built in June 1941 with c/n 76-80 and contract no. TP-7)	07-30	MM54137 Italian AF/RCAF3064	. .83R	NTU - To G-CTKL 11/83. Canx.
G-BKXA	Robin R.2160 Alpha Sport	114	F-GAOS	24.11.83	(Stored dismantled 3/99 at Cumbernauld - departed by road to France on 12.6.99)
G-BKXB	Steen Skybolt	PFA/64-10722		30. 8.83	Destroyed in fatal crash on take-off from Brunton on 17.5.87. Canx by CAA 20.6.91.
G-BKXC	Cameron V-77 HAFB	973		1. 9.83	To D-OKXC 2/94. Canx 25.1.93.
G-BKXD	Aerospatiale SA.365N Dauphin 2	6088	F-WMHD	7. 9.83	
G-BKXE	Aerospatiale SA.365N Dauphin 2	6090	F-WMHG	7. 9.83	To SE-JCK 12/95. Canx 12.10.95.
G-BKXF	PA-28R-200 Cherokee Arrow II	28R-7335351	OY-DZN N56092	10.11.83	
G-BKXG	Cessna T.303 Crusader	T303-00195	N9616C	22. 9.83	
G-BKXH	Robinson R-22	0128	SE-HOF	9. 9.83	Extensively damaged when it rolled over to starboard on take off from Stapleford 23.7.85. Canx as destroyed 7.9.88
G-BKXI	Cessna T.303 Crusader	T303-00005	N303CC (N9355T)	26. 9.83	To N20736 8/89. Canx 31.7.89.
G-BKXJ	Rutan VariEze	PFA/74-10795		29. 9.83	To G-TIMB 6/85. Canx.
G-BKXK	Aerospatiale SA.365N Dauphin 2	6096		26. 9.83	To G-PDES 3/88. Canx.
G-BKXL	Cameron Labatts Bottle 70SS HAFB	962		22. 9.83	(Based in Canada) Canx as WFU 21.10.96.
G-BKXM	Colt 17A Cloudhopper HAFB	531		3.10.83	
G-BKXN	ICA Brasov IS-28M2A	48		24.10.83	
G-BKXO	Rutan LongEz	PFA/74A-10580		24.10.83	(Stored 1/98)
G-BKXP	Auster AOP.6 (Frame no. TAY841BJ)	2830	A-14 Belgium AF/VT987	12.10.83	(On rebuild 7/91)
G-BKXR	Druine D.31A Turbulent	303	OY-AMW	1.11.83	
G-BKXS	Colt 56A HAFB	532		21.10.83	To RP-C1481 9/94. Canx 22.9.94.
G-BKXT	Cameron D-50 Hot-Air Airship	959		17.10.83	(Was based in USA). Canx as WFU 21.10.96.
G-BKXU	Cameron Dairy Queen Cone SS HAFB	963		17.10.83	To C-GHZF. Canx 21.4.88.
G-BKXV	Aerospatiale SA.365C2 Dauphin 2	5007	PH-SSL(2) F-WIPF/N90045/F-WTNU	24.10.83	Restored as PH-SSL(2) 1/85. Canx 25.1.85.
G-BKXW	North American NA.82 B-25J Mitchell	108-35186	"HD368" N9089Z/"N908"/N9089Z/44-30861	. .83R	NTU - Remained as N9089Z. Canx.
G-BKXX	Cameron V-65 HAFB	1000	(OO-...) G-BKXX	1. 9.83	
G-BKXY	Westland WG.30 Srs.100	013	N113WG G-BKXY/N113WG/G-BKXY	2.11.83	Canx as WFU 11.8.88.
G-BKXZ	BAe 146 Srs.100	E1010	PT-LEP	14.11.83	Restored as PT-LEP 12/83. Canx 5.12.83.
G-BKYA	Boeing 737-236ADV (Line No. 1047)	23159		14. 9.84	
G-BKYB	Boeing 737-236ADV (Line No. 1053)	23160		27. 9.84	
G-BKYC	Boeing 737-236ADV (Line No. 1055)	23161		8.10.84	Canx 14.10.98 on sale to USA. To OB-1711 in 10/98.
G-BKYD	Boeing 737-236ADV (Line No. 1056)	23162		25.10.84	To VR-CEF 4/95. Canx 28.4.95.
G-BKYE	Boeing 737-236ADV (Line No. 1058)	23163		1.11.84	To ZS-OLA 5/99. Canx 30.4.99.
G-BKYF	Boeing 737-236ADV (Line No. 1060)	23164		19.11.84	To N925PG 11/98. Canx 17.11.98.
G-BKYG	Boeing 737-236ADV (Line No. 1064)	23165		6.12.84	To N926PG 12/98. Canx 8.12.98.
G-BKYH	Boeing 737-236ADV (Line No. 1067)	23166		13.12.84	
G-BKYI	Boeing 737-236ADV (Line No. 1074)	23167		7. 1.85	To ZS-OLB 6/99. Canx 2.6.99.
G-BKYJ	Boeing 737-236ADV (Line No. 1077)	23168		28. 1.85	To N927PG 3/99. Canx 24.2.99.
G-BKYK	Boeing 737-236ADV (Line No. 1081)	23169		1. 2.85	
G-BKYL	Boeing 737-236ADV (Line No. 1086)	23170		22. 2.85	
G-BKYM	Boeing 737-236ADV (Line No. 1088)	23171		1. 3.85	To N930PG 8/99. Canx 27.8.99.

Regn	Type	c/n	Previous identity	Regn date	Fate or immediate subsequent identity (if known)
G-BKYN	Boeing 737-236ADV (Line No. 1091)	23172		21. 3.85	
G-BKYO	Boeing 737-236ADV (Line No. 1102)	23225		12. 4.85	
G-BKYP	Boeing 737-236ADV (Line No. 1105)	23226		24. 4.85	
G-BKYR	Boeing 737-236	-		. .83R	NTU - Canx.
G-BKYS	Boeing 737-236	-		. .83R	NTU - Canx.
G-BKYT	Boeing 737-236	-		. .83R	NTU - Canx.
G-BKYU	Boeing 737-236	-		. .83R	NTU - Canx.
G-BKYV	Boeing 737-236	-		. .83R	NTU - Canx.
G-BKYW	Boeing 737-236	-		. .83R	NTU - Canx.
G-BKYX	Boeing 737-236	-		. .83R	NTU - Canx.
G-BKYY	Boeing 737-236	-		. .83R	NTU - Canx.
G-BKYZ	Boeing 737-236	-		. .83R	NTU - Canx.
G-BKZA	Cameron N-77 HAFB	971		3.11.83	Stolen from Bath on the night of 5/6.11.86 and not recovered. Canx as destroyed 28.4.93.
G-BKZB	Cameron V-77 HAFB	995		11.11.83	
G-BKZC	Cessna A.152 Aerobat	0820	N7583L	21.11.83	CofA expired 5.5.87. (Was based in Kuwait) Canx by CAA 12.8.91.
G-BKZD	Cessna A.152 Aerobat	0826	N8132L	21.11.83	CofA expired 5.5.87. (Was based in Kuwait) Canx by CAA 22.6.89.
G-BKZE	Aerospatiale AS.332L Super Puma	2102	F-WKQE	30. 9.83	
G-BKZF	Cameron V-56 HAFB	246	F-BXUK	14.11.83	
G-BKZG	Aerospatiale AS.332L Super Puma	2106	HB-ZBT G-BKZG	30. 9.83	
G-BKZH	Aerospatiale AS.332L Super Puma	2107		30. 9.83	
G-BKZI	Bell 206B JetRanger II (P.i. either 5B-CGC or CGD - NTU) (Originally 206A later modified)	118	(5B-CG.) G-BKZI/N6238N	7.12.83	
G-BKZJ	Bensen B.8MV Gyrocopter	SHK.01 & G/01-1044		15.11.83	Canx 22.12.98 on sale to Ireland.
G-BKZK	Robinson R-22 Alpha	0368	N8434E	21.11.83	To G-EEGE 4/87. Canx.
G-BKZL	Colt AS-42 Hot Air Airship	529		29.11.83	CofA expired 2.6.86. Canx as WFU 2.7.90.
G-BKZM	Isaacs Fury II	PFA/11-10742		27. 9.83	Crashed in a field at Port Dinorwic on 14.6.90 and broke in two. (Stored 8/96)
G-BKZN	Short SD.3-60 Var.100	SH3625	G-14-3625	12.10.83	To N4489Y. Canx 28.10.83.
G-BKZO	Short SD.3-60 Var.100	SH3626	G-14-3626	12.10.83	NTU - To VH-MVW 12/83. Canx 20.12.83.
G-BKZP	Short SD.3-60 Var.100	SH3627	G-14-3627	12.10.83	To N701A. Canx 21.11.83.
G-BKZR	Short SD.3-60 Var.100	SH3628	G-OAEX G-SALU/(SE-IXO)/G-SALU/OY-MMC/G-BKZR/G-14-3628	12.10.83	To N424SA with new c/n SH3404. Canx 4.10.94.
G-BKZS	Short SD.3-60 Var.100	SH3629	G-14-3629	12.10.83	NTU - To N913SB. Canx 6.12.83.
G-BKZT	Clutton FRED Srs.II	PFA/29-10715		20.10.83	
G-BKZU	Colt 105A HAFB	534		29.11.83	To SE-ZBY. Canx 21.3.86.
G-BKZV	Bede BD-4	380	ZS-UAB	31. 8.84	
G-BKZW	Beechcraft C90 King Air	LJ-680	N185G N185DF/N1580L	8.12.83	To N7138E 5/90. Canx 23.4.90.
G-BKZX	Embraer EMB.110P1 Bandeirante	110-402	PT-SFT	28.12.83	To ZS-LGB 1/84. Canx 25.1.84.
G-BKZY	Cameron N-77 HAFB	1017		30.12.83	Canx by CAA 19.5.93.
G-BKZZ	Cessna 404 Titan	404-0637	N5285J	12.12.83	Canx 30.12.83. To D-ILOS 12/83.
G-BLAA	Sportavia-Putzer Fournier RF-5	5011	D-KIHI	3.10.83	
G-BLAB	Glaser-Dirks DG-400	4-60		28.12.83	To D-KAIR 4/84. Canx 13.3.84.
G-BLAC	Reims Cessna FA.152 Aerobat	0370		25. 3.80	(Stored 7/97)
G-BLAD	Thunder Ax7-77 Srs.1 HAFB	485		7.12.83	(Stolen from Hungerford on 5.8.92) CofA expired 15.10.92.
G-BLAE	Beechcraft 200 Super King Air	BB-239	I-ELCO N517JM/N17649	30. 1.84	To G-WWHL 4/84. Canx.
G-BLAF	Stolp SA.900 V-Star	PFA/106-10651		13. 9.83	
G-BLAG	Pitts S-1D Special	PFA/09-10195		1.12.83	
G-BLAH	Thunder Ax7-77 Srs.1 HAFB	526		3.10.83	
G-BLAI	Monnett Sonerai IIL (Regd with c/n PFA/15-10584 which conflicts with G-SYFW)	PFA/15-10583		6.12.83	(Extant 3/99 Breighton)
G-BLAJ	Pazmany PL-4A	4275/12B & PFA/17-10378		11. 1.84	To G-PAZY 11/89. Canx.
G-BLAK	CEA Jodel DR.220 2+2	5	F-BNVH	28. 9.83	To TF-LAK 4/84. Canx 3.4.84.
G-BLAL	Reims Cessna F.150K	0569	PH-KAV	13.12.78	Crashed at Bidford-on-Avon on 12.4.82. Canx.
G-BLAM	CEA Jodel DR.360 Chevalier	345	F-BRCM	6. 2.84	
G-BLAN	Aerospatiale SA.341G Gazelle Srs.1	1063	N6958 F-WTNT	16.11.83	To G-RIFF 9/87. Canx.
G-BLAO	Aerospatiale SA.341G Gazelle Srs.1	1097	N37748	16.11.83	To 4X-BHG 12/86. Canx 7.8.87.
G-BLAP	Aerospatiale SA.341G Gazelle Srs.1	1155	N62406	16.11.83	To G-SFTH 5/84. Canx.
G-BLAR	Socata MS.883 Rallye 115	1574	F-BSFR	. .83R	NTU - To G-BLWZ /85. Canx.
G-BLAS	Vickers Supermarine 361 Spitfire HF.IXe	CBAF/78883	2066 Israeli DF/AF /Israeli DF/AF 0606/MM4094/MJ730	22.11.83	To G-HFIX 8/89. Canx.
G-BLAT	SAN Jodel D.150 Mascaret	56	F-BNID	30. 1.84	
G-BLAU	Bell 47G-4	3357	N17PE N17PL/N1165W	9. 1.84	To 5B-CGK 1/85. Canx.
G-BLAV	Not allotted.				

Regn	Type	c/n	Previous identity	Regn date	Fate or immediate subsequent identity (if known)
G-BLAW	PA-28-181 Archer II	28-8190184	OO-XKV	23. 7.82	Ditched in the English Channel 3½ miles southwest of
			(PH-VSR)/N8346Y		St.Catherine's Point, IoW on 18.10.94. Canx as WFU 25.1.95.
G-BLAX	Reims Cessna FA.152 Aerobat	0385		11.10.83	
G-BLAY	Robin HR.100/200B Royal	03	F-BSJY	. .83R	NTU - Remained as F-BSJY. Canx.
			F-WSJY		
G-BLAZ	Cessna 421B Golden Eagle II		ZS-JOL	30.11.83	Canx as WFU 29.8.86. Reserved as D-IGPZ 11.12.86, Permit
		421B-0968	N87534		issued 17.12.87.
G-BLBA	Boeing 737-236	-		. .83R	NTU - Canx.
G-BLBB	Boeing 737-236	-		. .83R	NTU - Canx.
G-BLBC	Boeing 737-236	-		. .83R	NTU - Canx.
G-BLBD	Boeing 737-236	-		. .83R	NTU - Canx.
G-BLBE	Boeing 737-236	-		. .83R	NTU - Canx.
G-BLBF	Boeing 737-236	-		. .83R	NTU - Canx.
G-BLBG	Boeing 737-236	-		. .83R	NTU - Canx.
G-BLBH	Boeing 737-236	-		. .83R	NTU - Canx.
G-BLBI	Boeing 737-236	-		. .83R	NTU - Canx.
G-BLBJ	Boeing 737-236	-		. .83R	NTU - Canx.
G-BLBK	Boeing 737-236	-		. .83R	NTU - Canx.
G-BLBL	Boeing 737-236	-		. .83R	NTU - Canx.
G-BLBM	Boeing 737-236	-		. .83R	NTU - Canx.
G-BLBN	Boeing 737-236	-		. .83R	NTU - Canx.
G-BLBO	Boeing 737-236	-		. .83R	NTU - Canx.
G-BLBP	Boeing 737-236	-		. .83R	NTU - Canx.
G-BLBR	Boeing 737-236	-		. .83R	NTU - Canx.
G-BLBS	Boeing 737-236	-		. .83R	NTU - Canx.
G-BLBT	Boeing 737-236	-		. .83R	NTU - Canx.
G-BLBU	Boeing 737-236	-		. .83R	NTU - Canx.
G-BLBV	Boeing 737-236	-		. .83R	NTU - Canx.
G-BLBW	Boeing 737-236	-		. .83R	NTU - Canx.
G-BLBX	Boeing 737-236	-		. .83R	NTU - Canx.
G-BLBY	Boeing 737-236	-		. .83R	NTU - Canx.
G-BLBZ	Boeing 737-236	-		. .83R	NTU - Canx.
G-BLCA	Bell 206B JetRanger III	3443	N20982	1.12.83	
G-BLCB	BAe Jetstream Srs.3107	622	G-31-622	28.11.83	To G-31-622/VH-HSW 3/86. Canx 16.3.84.
G-BLCC	Thunder Ax7-77Z HAFB	532		7.12.83	Canx by CAA 19.5.93.
G-BLCD	PA-34-200-2 Seneca	34-7450116	PH-PLZ	28.12.83	To OO-RPW 4/84. Canx 16.4.84.
			N41409		
G-BLCE	Cessna 402C Utiliner II	402C-0008	N4648N	30.11.78	To SE-IRU 3/85. Canx 12.3.85.
G-BLCF	EAA AcroSport 2	PFA/72-10600		5.12.83	Badly damaged when crashed into a field near Swansea
					Airport on 5.8.90. Canx by CAA 9.4.97 as PWFU.
G-BLCG	Socata TB-10 Tobago	61	G-BHES	17. 3.80	
G-BLCH	Colt 56D HAFB	392	(G-BJHT)	14.11.83	
G-BLCI	EAA AcroSport P	P-10A	N6AS	29. 2.84	Badly damaged in hangar fire at Farthing Corner in late
					1996. Permit expired 16.6.97.
G-BLCJ	Cessna 441 Conquest	441-0316	N1208G	14.12.83	To G-LOVX 11/84. Canx.
G-BLCK	Vickers Supermarine 361 Spitfire		4X-FOB	22.11.83	To ZU-SPT 8/98. Canx 30.7.98.
	LF.IXe	CBAF/17-1363	Israeli DF/AF 2032/Czech AF/TE566		
G-BLCL	Cessna 441 Conquest	441-0321	N1209D	14.12.83	To N321DA 6/85. Canx 28.6.85.
G-BLCM	Socata TB-9 Tampico	194	OO-TCT	2.12.83	
			(OO-TBC)		
G-BLCN	Short SD.3-60 Var.100	SH3630	G-14-3630	8.12.83	To VH-FCU 6/84. Canx .3.84.
G-BLCO	Short SD.3-60 Var.100	SH3631	G-14-3631	8.12.83	To N914SB 12/83. Canx 13.12.83.
G-BLCP	Short SD.3-60 Var.100	SH3632	OY-MMA	8.12.83	(To be EI-regd in 7/99)
			(SE-KSU)/OY-MMA/EI-BYU/OY-MMA/G-BLCP		
G-BLCR	Short SD.3-60 Var.100	SH3633	G-14-3633	8.12.83	To G-BMAR 1/84. Canx.
G-BLCS	Short SD.3-60 Var.100	SH3634	G-14-3634	8.12.83	To N132DA 3/84. Canx 28.3.84.
G-BLCT	CEA Jodel DR.220 2+2	23	F-BOCQ	22.12.83	
G-BLCU	Scheibe SF-25B Falke	4699	D-KECC	30.12.83	
G-BLCV	Hoffmann H-36 Dimona	36113	EI-CJO	21. 3.84	
			G-BLCV		
G-BLCW	Evans VP-1	PFA/62-10835		19.12.83	
G-BLCX	Glaser-Dirks DG-400	4-71		6. 4.84	To LN-GMW. Canx 5.10.88.
G-BLCY(1)	BAe Jetstream Srs.3102	621	G-31-621	.12.83R	NTU - To G-BLDO 1/84. Canx.
G-BLCY(2)	Thunder Ax7-65Z HAFB	487		13. 1.84	
G-BLCZ	Cessna 441 Conquest	441-0332	N1210G	9. 1.84	To N441MM 4/90. Canx 12.4.90.
G-BLDA	Socata Rallye 110ST Galopin	3362	F-GDGH	5. 1.84	Destroyed by gales at Biggin Hill on 16.10.87.
					Canx as destroyed 18.5.88.
G-BLDB	Taylor JT.1 Monoplane	PFA/55-10506		28.12.83	
G-BLDC	K & S Jungster 1	PFA/44-10701		29.12.83	No Permit issued. Canx by CAA 6.3.99.
G-BLDD	WAG-Aero CUBy AcroTrainer			29.12.83	
		PFA/108-10653			
G-BLDE	Boeing 737-2E7	22876	4X-BAC	30.12.83	To PK-RII. Canx 31.3.93.
	(Line No. 922)		G-BLDE/4X-BAC/N4571A		
G-BLDF	Bell 47G-5	7802	N8558F	26. 1.84	To EC-EEZ. Canx 7.7.87.
G-BLDG	PA-25-260 Pawnee C	25-4501	SE-FLB	9. 1.84	
			LN-VYM		
G-BLDH	BAC One-Eleven Srs.492GM	BAC.262		11. 1.84	To PK-TRU 11/94. Canx 21.12.94.
G-BLDI	Douglas C-47A-75-DL Dakota	19475	K-686	18. 1.84	To N54NA 11/84. Canx 31.10.84.
			Danish AF/Norwegian AF 101012/42-101012		
G-BLDJ	PA-28-161 Warrior II	28-8216117	N9632N	18. 1.84	To G-TSFT 4/89. Canx.
G-BLDK	Robinson R-22 Alpha	0139	C-GSGU	17. 1.84	
G-BLDL	Cameron Truck 56SS HAFB	990		10. 1.84	Canx as WFU 21.10.96. (At Balloon Preservation Group 1/98)

Regn	Type	c/n	Previous identity	Regn date	Fate or immediate subsequent identity (if known)
G-BLDM	Hiller UH-12E	HA3018	N118HA G-BCXK/N118HA	13. 1.84	To HA-MID. Canx 13.9.91.
G-BLDN	Rand-Robinson KR-2	PFA/129-10913		12. 1.84	Canx as destroyed 12.11.97.
G-BLDO	BAe Jetstream Srs.3102	621	(G-BLCY) G-31-621	11. 1.84	To G-BTXL 3/87. Canx.
G-BLDP	Slingsby T.67M Firefly	2009		18. 1.84	To G-SKYC 6/97. Canx.
G-BLDR	Aerospatiale SA.365N2 Dauphin 2	6074	G-TRAF G-BLDR	24. 1.84	To PH-SSU 8/90. Canx 5.7.90.
G-BLDS	PBN BN-2B-27 Islander	2176	EC-DYF G-BLDS	13. 1.84	To FP-15 Policia National Peru. Canx 12.10.87.
G-BLDT	PBN BN-2B-21 Islander	2177		13. 1.84	To VH-INB 10/89. Canx 25.9.89.
G-BLDU	PBN BN-2B-21 Islander	2178		13. 1.84	To N117MC. Canx 18.8.88.
G-BLDV	PBN BN-2B-26 Islander	2179	D-INEY G-BLDV	13. 1.84	
G-BLDW	PBN BN-2B-27 Islander	2180	G-51-2180 EC-DYG/G-BLDW	13. 1.84	To N272BN. Canx 6.10.88.
G-BLDX	PBN BN-2B-26 Islander	2181		13. 1.84	Forced landing on Ainsdale Beach, near Southport on 21.8.87. The starboard undercarriage collapsed and its nose was damaged. The aircraft was further damaged by the rescue services in their salvage attempt and was later submerged by the incoming tide. Canx by CAA 18.1.94. Cockpit section used in constructing "G-FOXY" for children's charity events
G-BLDY	Bell 212	30866	VH-BHO(3) VR-BIC/N125BH/N16930	17. 1.84	To 5N-BHO. Canx 9.12.92.
G-BLDZ	Cameron N-77 HAFB	1005		19. 1.84	To N15WD 7/86. Canx 22.5.86.
G-BLEA	Boeing 737-2K2 (Line No. 507)	21397	(G-BLGN) PH-TVP	1. 5.84	Restored as PH-TVP 4/85. Canx 29.3.85.
G-BLEB	Colt 69A HAFB	537		20. 1.84	
G-BLEC	PBN BN-2B-27 Islander	2114	G-BJBG	28.10.83	To SX-DKA 4/93. Canx 30.3.93.
G-BLED	Short SD.3-60 Var.200	SH3635	G-14-3635	30. 1.84	To EI-BEK 2/84. Canx 6.3.84.
G-BLEE	Short SD.3-60 Var.200	SH3636	G-14-3636	30. 1.84	To EI-BEL 2/84. Canx 19.3.84.
G-BLEF	Short SD.3-60 Var.100	SH3637	G-14-3637	30. 1.84	To G-LEGS 3/84. Canx.
G-BLEG	Short SD.3-60 Var.100	SH3638	G-14-3638	30. 1.84	To G-ISLE 3/84. Canx.
G-BLEH	Short SD.3-60 Var.100	SH3639	G-14-3639	30. 1.84	To N366MQ. Canx 9.3.84.
G-BLEI	PADC BN-2A-26 Islander	3008	RP-C553	9. 3.84	To V3-HEZ 6/89. Canx 12.6.89.
G-BLEJ	PA-28-161 Warrior II	28-7816257	N2194M	8. 2.84	
G-BLEK	HS.125 Srs.700B	257213	G-5-16	20. 3.84	To N213C 6/84. Canx 8.6.84.
G-BLEL	Price Ax7-77-245 HAFB	001		23. 1.84	No CofA issued. (Extant 1/92) Canx by CAA 19.5.93.
G-BLEM	Westland WG.13 Lynx Mk.89	291	ZE408 G-17-14	7. 2.84	To Nigerian Navy as 01-F89. Canx 27.3.84.
G-BLEN	Piper J3C-90 Cub (L-4J-PI) (Frame No 12396)	12566	D-EBEN HB-OFZ/44-80270	20.12.83	To G-HEWI 7/84. Canx.
G-BLEO	Westland WG.30 Srs.100	011	N4499N G-VAJC/G-17-7	21.12.83	Restored as N4499N 2/84. Canx 14.2.84.
G-BLEP	Cameron V-65 HAFB	1022		7. 2.84	
G-BLER	Slingsby T.67M Firefly	2010		16. 2.84	To OO-VAD. Canx 28.8.87.
G-BLES	Stolp SA.750 Acroduster Too	197 & PFA/89-10428		8.12.83	
G-BLET	Thunder Ax7-77 Srs.1 HAFB	539		16. 2.84	
G-BLEU	Bensen B.80V Gyrocopter	G/01-1049		14. 2.84	Badly damaged in crash near St.Merryn on 26.4.86. Canx as destroyed on 2.4.97.
G-BLEV	Aerospatiale AS.355F1 Twin Squirrel	5311		20. 3.84	To G-ZFDB 5/89. Canx.
G-BLEW	Reims Cessna F.182Q Skylane II	0039	(F-GAQD)	21. 6.78	
G-BLEX	BAe Jetstream Srs.3102	634	G-31-634	28. 2.84	NTU - To G-31-634/G-BLKP 7/84. Canx 23.7.84.
G-BLEY	Aerospatiale SA.365N Dauphin 2	6119	F-WTNM	24. 1.84	To EI-MIP 3/96. Canx 20.3.96.
G-BLEZ	Aerospatiale SA.365N Dauphin 2	6131		24. 1.84	
G-BLFA	Not allotted.				
G-BLFB	PA-18-135 Super Cub	18-4036	(G-AOSG) OO-ALH/(OO-LVV)/Italian AF MM54-2436/I-EIVT/MM54-2436/54-2436	8. 2.84	Canx 2.4.85 on sale to Italy. To HB-PIJ.
G-BLFC	Edgley EA.7 Optica	EA.7/003	G-56-003	14. 2.84	To G-TRAK 7/87. Canx.
G-BLFD	Edgley EA.7 Optica	EA.7/004	G-56-004	14. 2.84	To G-KATY 4/85. Canx.
G-BLFE	Cameron Sphinx 72SS HAFB	1011		22. 2.84	Canx as WFU 29.4.93.
G-BLFF	Reims Cessna F.172M Skyhawk	1170	PH-SKA (D-EDJP)	7. 3.84	CofA expired 16.5.87. (Present status and location unknown) Canx as destroyed 14.7.94.
G-BLFG	Westland WG.13 Lynx Mk.89	312	G-17-15	28. 2.84	To Nigerian Navy as 02-F89. Canx 27.3.84.
G-BLFH	Westland WG.13 Lynx Mk.89	313	G-17-16	28. 2.84	To Nigerian Navy as 03-F89. Canx 27.3.84.
G-BLFI	PA-28-181 Archer II	28-8490034	N4333Z	22. 2.84	
G-BLFJ	Fokker F-27 Friendship 100	10120	G-OMAN G-SPUD/VH-TFE/PH-FAP	4. 4.84	CofA expired 28.9.95. Broken up in 12/96 at Norwich. Canx as WFU 6.1.97.
G-BLFK	Douglas C-47B-1-DL Dakota	20721	T3-34 Spanish AF/N86440/43-16255	14. 3.84	To N952CA 8/85. Canx 12.8.85.
G-BLFL	Douglas C-47B-45-DK Dakota	16954/34214	N951CA G-BLFL/Spanish AF T3-54/N73856/45-951	14. 3.84	Restored as N951CA. Canx 27.8.86.
G-BLFM	Enstrom F-28F	507	N5699X	21. 3.84	Canx 11.4.84 on sale to USA. To ZS-HNA 5/84.
G-BLFN	Aerospatiale SA.365C2 Dauphin 2	5037	PH-SSH 5N-ALI/PH-SSH/(PH-BOL)/F-WXFG	30. 3.84	Restored as PH-SSH 6/84. Canx 12.6.84.
G-BLFO	Not allocated.				
G-BLFP	Douglas DC-10-30 (Line No. 348)	48266	N3016Z	. .84R	NTU - Illegal regn - Remained as N3016Z. Canx.
G-BLFR	Douglas DC-10-30 (Line No. 94)	47863	N3878M I-DYNI	. .84R	NTU - Illegal regn - Remained as N3878M. Canx.

Regn	Type	c/n	Previous identity	Regn date	Fate or immediate subsequent identity (if known)
G-BLFS	Douglas DC-10-30 (Line No. 121)	47864	N3878F I-DYNO	. .84R	NTU - Illegal regn - Remained as N3878F. Canx.
G-BLFT	Hunting-Percival P.56 Provost T.1	PAC/F/207	7621M WV686	23. 2.84	No CofA issued. Canx by CAA 2.9.91. Believed sold to Australia .93/94.
G-BLFU	Not allotted.				
G-BLFV	Cessna 182R Skylane II	182-68214	N2849E	2. 5.84	Collided in mid-air with Reims Cessna F.152 G-WACD over Booker on 22.1.89 and crashed. Canx as destroyed 6.3.89.
G-BLFW	American Aviation AA-5 Traveler	AA5-0786	OO-GLW	22. 2.84	
G-BLFX	BAe Jetstream Srs.3101	628	N401MX G-31-628	23. 3.84	To N401MX 5/84. Canx 23.5.84.
G-BLFY	Cameron V-77 HAFB	1030		16. 3.84	
G-BLFZ	PA-31-310 Turbo Navajo C	31-7912106	PH-RWS N3538W	21. 3.84	
G-BLGA	Short SD.3-60 Var.100	SH3640	G-14-3640	24. 2.84	To N367MQ 3/84. Canx 16.3.84.
G-BLGB	Short SD.3-60 Var.100	SH3641	G-14-3641	24. 2.84	Wheels up landing at Stornoway on 9.2.98. Dismantled in 5/98 at Stornoway, then to Exeter 1/99. Canx as PWFU 19.11.98.
G-BLGC	Short SD.3-60 Var.200	SH3642	G-14-3642	24. 2.84	To EI-BEM 6/84. Canx 13.6.84.
G-BLGD	Short SD.3-60 Var.200	SH3643	G-14-3643	24. 2.84	To N631KC 4/84. Canx 24.4.84.
G-BLGE	Short SD.3-60 Var.300	SH3644	C-GLAJ N632KC/G-BLGE/G-14-3644	24. 2.84	To (SE-KGV)/C-GLAJ 7/97. Canx 11.7.97.
G-BLGF	Short SD.3-60 Var.200	SH3645	G-14-3645	24. 2.84	To N633KC. Canx 3.5.84.
G-BLGG	Short SD.3-30 Var.200	SH3097	G-14-3097	24. 2.84	To SE-INZ 6/84. Canx 5.6.84.
G-BLGH	CEA DR.300/180R Remorqueur	570	D-EAFL	10. 4.84	
G-BLGI	McCulloch J.2	039	N4329G (G-BKKL)/Bahrain Public Security BPS-3/N4329G	. .84R	NTU - To G-ORVB 8/89. Canx. (Marks were worn but not officially regd as such)
G-BLGJ	HS.748 Srs.2B/424	1800		2. 4.84	To V2-LCQ 12/84. Canx 17.12.84.
G-BLGK	Cameron Propane Bottle SS HAFB	997		2. 4.84	To C-GZVB with c/n 1640. Canx 30.5.86.
G-BLGL	Colt 21E Cloudhopper HAFB	527		. 4.84R	NTU - Canx.
G-BLGM	Cessna 425 Conquest I	425-0199	(G-CORS) (N1223A)	8. 5.84	To VR-BDR 3/94. Canx 17.3.94.
G-BLGN(1)	Boeing 737-2K2 (Line No. 507)	21397	PH-TVP	. .84R	NTU - To G-BLEA 5/84. Canx.
G-BLGN(2)	Skyhawk Gyroplane (Modified Bensen B.8 Gyroplane)	G/01-1029		2. 5.84	No Permit issued. Canx by CAA 17.7.91.
G-BLGO(1)	Boeing 737-2K2C (Line No. 405)	20943	PH-TVD G-BKBT/PH-TVD	. .84R	NTU - Restored as G-BKBT 5/84. Canx.
G-BLGO(2)	Bensen B.8MV Gyrocopter	RB-01		18. 6.84	Permit expired 15.5.87. (Stored 8/94)
G-BLGP	WAG-Aero Super CUBy	1396		. .84R	NTU - Canx. (Was reserved with a U.A.E. address)
G-BLGR	Bell 47G-4A	7501	N3236G HC-ASQ/N1186W	2. 5.84	
G-BLGS	Socata MS.893E Rallye 180T	3206		7. 7.78	
G-BLGT	PA-18-95 Super Cub (L-18C-PI) (Frame No.18-1399)	18-1445	D-EAGT D-EOCC/ALAT 51-15445	1. 6.84	
G-BLGU	Bell 47G-5	25039	OH-HAZ SE-HEG/N7098J	12. 7.84	Canx 18.7.85 on sale to Australia.
G-BLGV	Bell 206B JetRanger II	982	5B-JSB C-FDYL/CF-DYL	2. 5.84	
G-BLGW	Fokker F-27 Friendship 200	10231	PK-KFG 9V-BAQ/9M-AML/PH-FEW	20. 3.78	WFU in 5/94. Stored 7/94 at Norwich. Canx as WFU 4.10.95.
G-BLGX	Thunder Ax7-65 HAFB	551		16. 4.84	Canx by CAA 19.5.93. (Active 9/94)
G-BLGY	Grob G-109B	6269		9. 5.84	Lost power and forced landed in dense wooded area near Booker on 16.8.88. Canx as destroyed 18.10.88.
G-BLGZ	BAe 125 Srs.800A	258004	G-5-15	9. 4.84	To N800EE 6/84. Canx 7.6.84.
G-BLHA	Thunder Ax10-160 HAFB	554		12. 4.84	Canx by CAA 23.1.89. To F-GHNQ 9/89.
G-BLHB	Thunder Ax10-160 HAFB	562		12. 4.84	Canx by CAA 23.1.89.
G-BLHC	BAe Jetstream Srs.3102	637	G-31-637	17. 4.84	To G-BRGN 3/87. Canx.
G-BLHD	BAC One-Eleven Srs.492GM	BAC.260	G-16-25	7. 3.84	To HZ-KA7. Canx 21.2.91.
G-BLHE	Pitts S-1E Special	PFA/09-10885		19. 4.84	To G-OTSW 6/89. Canx.
G-BLHF	Nott/Cameron/Airship Industries ULD/2 HAFB	111		6. 3.84	Canx as WFU 4.5.93.
G-BLHG	Hoffmann H-36 Dimona	36132		18. 6.84	To G-OMRG 11/88. Canx.
G-BLHH	CEA Jodel DR.315 Petit Prince	324	F-BPRH	3. 7.84	
G-BLHI	Colt 17A Cloudhopper HAFB	506		8. 9.86	
G-BLHJ	Reims Cessna F.172P Skyhawk II	2182		26. 3.84	
G-BLHK	Colt 105A HAFB	576		19. 6.84	
G-BLHL	Coopavia-Menavia Piel CP.301A Emeraude	275	F-BLHL F-OBLM	2. 3.78	Crashed on take-off from Slinfold on 4.8.81. (Extant 5/95) (Loaned to Lincolnshire Aviation Museum, East Kirkby)
G-BLHM(1)	Bristol 149 Bolingbroke IVT	-	RCAF 10038	4. 3.82	NTU - To G-MKIV 3/82. Canx.
G-BLHM(2)	PA-18-95 Super Cub (L-18C-PI) (Frame No 18-3088)	18-3120	LX-AIM D-EOAB/Belgium AF OL-L46/53-4720	23. 7.84	
G-BLHN(1)	Reims Cessna F.182Q Skyhawk II	0084		. .77R	NTU - To (G-BFFN)/G-BPPN 5/78. Canx.
G-BLHN(2)	Robin HR.100/285 Tiara	5390	F-GABF	20. 2.78	
G-BLHO	American Aviation AA-5A Cheetah	AA5A-0741	OO-RTJ OO-HRN	21. 6.84	Canx as destroyed 25.6.90. Re-regd as G-OCAM 3/94.
G-BLHP	American Aviation AA-5A Cheetah	AA5A-0975	OO-RTH (OO-HRR)	12. 4.84	To D-ELHY(2) 1/85. Canx 16.11.84.
G-BLHR	Grumman American GA-7 Cougar	GA7-0109	OO-RTI (OO-HRC)/N751G	12. 4.84	
G-BLHS	Bellanca 7ECA Citabria 115	1342-80	OO-RTQ	12. 4.84	
G-BLHT	Varga 2150A Kachina	VAC 158-80	OO-RTW	12. 4.84	To HB-DGP 1/87. Canx 26.1.87.
G-BLHU	Varga 2150A Kachina	-		. .84R	NTU - Canx.

Regn	Type	c/n	Previous identity	Regn date	Fate or immediate subsequent identity (if known)
G-BLHV	Varga 2150A Kachina	-		. .84R	NTU - Canx.
G-BLHW	Varga 2150A Kachina	VAC 161-80		17. 7.84	
G-BLHX	Varga 2150A Kachina	-		. .84R	NTU - Canx.
G-BLHY	Varga 2150A Kachina	-		. .84R	NTU - Canx.
G-BLHZ	Varga 2150A Kachina	VAC 163-80	OO-RTZ	27. 9.84	Badly damaged in forced landing at Thong Lane, Gravesend on 19.11.84. Canx by CAA 3.6.92.
G-BLIA	DH.112 Venom FB.54 (Mk.17) (built by FFW, Essen)	900	J-1730 Swiss AF	8. 6.84	To N402DM 1/85. Canx 1.11.84.
G-BLIB	DH.112 Venom FB.54 (Mk.17) (built by FFW, Essen)	917	J-1747 Swiss AF	8. 6.84	To N5471V 8/84. Canx 31.8.84.
G-BLIC	DH.112 Venom FB.54 (Mk.17) (built by FFW, Essen)	969	N502DM (G-BLIC)/Swiss AF J-1799	13. 7.84	To ZK-VNM(2). Canx.
G-BLID	DH.112 Venom FB.50 (FB.1) (built by FFW, Essen)	815	J-1605 Swiss AF	13. 7.84	(Stored 6/97)
G-BLIE	DH.112 Venom FB.50 (FB.1) (built by FFW, Essen)	824	J-1614 Swiss AF	28. 2.85	To G-VENM 6/99. Canx.
G-BLIF	DH.112 Venom FB.50 (FB.1) (built by FFW, Essen)	826	J-1616 Swiss AF	28. 9.84	To N202DM 3/86. Canx 25.3.86.
G-BLIG	Cameron V-65 HAFB	1045		24. 4.84	CofA expired 3.8.91. Canx by CAA 4.8.98.
G-BLIH	PA-18-135 Super Cub (L-21B-PI)(Frame No 18-3827)	18-3828	(PH-KNG) (PH-KNJ)/PH-GRC)/R.Netherlands AF R-138/54-2428	12.11.84	(On rebuild)
G-BLII	PA-28-161 Warrior II	28-8216116	N9631N	13. 4.84	To A6-MAA. Canx 30.9.85.
G-BLIJ	Short SD.3-60 Var.100	SH3646	G-14-3646	24. 4.84	To N634KC. Canx 30.5.84.
G-BLIK(1)	Short SD.3-60 Var.100	SH3647	G-14-3647	. 4.84R	NTU - To (G-BLIU)/N635KC 5/84. Canx.
G-BLIK(2)	Wallis WA-116/F/S	K-218X		30. 4.84	Permit expired 24.4.98. (Stored 2/99 Reymerston Hall)
G-BLIL	Short SD.3-60 Var.100	SH3648	OY-MMB G-BLIL/G-14-3648	24. 4.84	To G-OAAS 4/90. Canx.
G-BLIM	Short SD.3-60 Var.100	SH3649	G-14-3649	24. 4.84	To N346MV. Canx 19.6.84.
G-BLIN	Short SD.3-60 Var.100	SH3650	G-14-3650	24. 4.84	To N347MV. Canx 28.6.84.
G-BLIO	Cameron R-42 Gas Free Balloon	1015		17. 4.84	CofA expired 17.5.84. Canx as destroyed 24.1.90. (At British Balloon Museum & Library, Newbury) (Extant 4/93)
G-BLIP	Cameron N-77 HAFB	1031		2. 5.84	CofA expired 26.3.94. Canx as WFU 23.6.98.
G-BLIR	Cessna 441 Conquest II	441-0337	(N1210V)	28. 8.84	To N9045C. Canx 10.4.87.
G-BLIS	DHC.6-310 Twin Otter	513	HB-LIS	15. 4.80	To 9Q-CBN 9/80. Canx.
G-BLIT	Thorp T-18CW	PFA/76-10550		24. 4.84	
G-BLIU	Short SD.3-60 Var.100	SH3647	(G-BLIK) G-14-3647	24. 4.84	To N635KC. Canx 12.6.84.
G-BLIV	Cameron O-105 HAFB	1059		17. 7.84	To OO-BWW. Canx 23.4.92.
G-BLIW	Percival P.56 Provost T.53 (Also c/n F56/125)	PAC/F/125	177 Irish Air Corps	12. 6.85	
G-BLIX	Saro Skeeter AOP.12	S2/5094	PH-HOF (PH-SRE)/XL809	3. 5.84	
G-BLIY	Socata MS.892A Rallye Commodore 150	11639	F-BSCX	9. 5.84	
G-BLIZ	PA-46-310P Malibu	46-8408062		23. 7.84	To OO-RVP. Canx 19.3.91.
G-BLJA	Short SD.3-30 UTT	SH3098	G-14-3098	9. 5.84	To R.Thailand Army as 3098 6/84. Canx 27.6.84.
G-BLJB	Short SD.3-30 UTT	SH3099	G-14-3099	9. 5.84	To R.Thailand Police as 43099 11/84. Canx 21.11.84.
G-BLJC	BAe 125 Srs.800A	258005	G-5-15 (G-5-19)/(G-5-12)	8. 5.84	To N800GG 6/84. Canx 7.6.84.
G-BLJD	Glaser-Dirks DG-400	4-85		15. 6.84	
G-BLJE	Agusta-Bell 206B JetRanger II	8242	SE-HBW	18. 5.84	To G-PEAK 3/94. Canx.
G-BLJF	Cameron O-65 HAFB	1041		14. 5.84	
G-BLJG	Cameron N-105 HAFB	1039		13. 6.84	Canx as destroyed 23.4.93.
G-BLJH	Cameron N-77 HAFB	1047		14. 5.84	CofA expired 27.6.89. (At Balloon Preservation Group 7/98)
G-BLJI	Colt 105A HAFB	561	(D-NORD/LB)	18. 5.84	Canx as WFU 13.11.98.
G-BLJJ	Cessna 305 (O-1E) Bird Dog	24509	N770BC ALAT 24509/F-MCCE	9. 1.87	No UK CofA or Permit issued. (Present status unknown) Canx by CAA 6.12.95.
G-BLJK	Evans VP-2	PFA/63-10568		17. 5.84	No Permit issued. Canx by CAA 12.7.91.
G-BLJL	Aerospatiale AS.355F1 Twin Squirrel	5312		17. 8.84	To G-CEGB 5/85. Canx.
G-BLJM	Beechcraft 95-B55 Baron	TC-1997	SE-GRT	3. 3.78	
G-BLJN	Nott-Cameron NC ULD 1 HAFB	1110		8. 1.87	NTU - To G-BNXK 9/87. Canx.
G-BLJO	Reims Cessna F.152 II	1627	OY-BNB	21. 6.84	
G-BLJP	Reims Cessna F.150L	1119	N962L	31. 5.84	To G-MABE 6/97. Canx.
G-BLJR	Short SD.3-60 Var.100	SH3651	G-14-3651	4. 6.84	To (9M-MKZ)/9M-KGN 9/84. Canx 19.9.84.
G-BLJS	Short SD.3-60 Var.100	SH3652	G-14-3652	4. 6.84	To G-14-3652/N124CA 9/84. Canx 6.9.84.
G-BLJT	Short SD.3-60 Var.100	SH3653	G-14-3653	4. 6.84	NTU - To N151CA. Canx 7.9.84.
G-BLJU	Short SD.3-60 Var.100	SH3654	G-14-3654	4. 6.84	To N369MQ 11/84. Canx 12.11.84.
G-BLJV	Short SD.3-60 Var.100	SH3655	G-14-3655	4. 6.84	To N370MQ 11/84. Canx 14.11.84.
G-BLJW	Glaser-Dirks DG.400	4-88		10. 4.84	To N488DR 6/86. Canx 30.5.86.
G-BLJX	Bensen B.8M Gyrocopter	BS.1		31. 5.84	Canx as CAA 9.8.91.
G-BLJY	Sequoia F.8L Falco	PFA/100-10985		1. 6.84	Canx by CAA 2.9.91.
G-BLJZ	PA-31P-425 Pressurised Navajo	31P-3	(PH-BAL) G-BLJZ/N4805N/HB-LGA/N6801L	13. 6.84	To 5B-CDS. Canx 19.2.86.
G-BLKA	DH.112 Venom FB.54 (FB.4) (FFW built) (Regd with c/n 431)	960	(G-VENM) Swiss AF J-1790	13. 7.84	Permit expired 14.7.95. (Stored Bruntingthorpe 3/96)
G-BLKB	Boeing 737-3T5 (Line No. 1069)	23060		3.12.84	To N753MA. Canx 4.3.93.
G-BLKC	Boeing 737-3T5 (Line No. 1080)	23061		12.12.84	To N744MA 11/92. Canx 6.11.92.
G-BLKD	Boeing 737-3T5 (Line No. 1083)	23062		3.12.84	To N733MA 4/92. Canx 1.5.92.

Regn	Type	c/n	Previous identity	Regn date	Fate or immediate subsequent identity (if known)
G-BLKE	Boeing 737-3T5 (Line No. 1092)	23063		3.12.84	To N752MA 1/93. Canx 7.1.93.
G-BLKF	Thunder Ax10-160 HAFB	563		8. 6.84	Canx by CAA 23.1.89. To F-GHNO 9/89.
G-BLKG	Thunder Ax10-160 HAFB	564		8. 6.84	Canx by CAA 23.1.89. To F-GHNP .89R.
G-BLKH	Thunder Ax10-160 HAFB	565		8. 6.84	Canx by CAA 23.1.89. To F-GHNN 9/89.
G-BLKI	Thunder Ax10-160 HAFB	566		8. 6.84	Badly damaged in France in 1984. Canx by CAA 23.1.89.
G-BLKJ	Thunder Ax7-65 HAFB	580		18. 7.84	CofA expired 3.2.96. Canx as PWFU 22.5.97. (Extant 1/98)
G-BLKK	Evans VP-1	PFA/62-10642		15. 6.84	
G-BLKL	Druine D.31 Turbulent	221	F-PIIB	21. 6.84	Permit expired 26.5.87. Canx as WFU 10.8.87.
G-BLKM	CEA Jodel DR.1051 Sicile	519	F-BLRO	26. 6.84	
G-BLKN	Beechcraft 200 Super King Air	BB-160	EI-BHG 9Q-CTK/N8493D/EI-BHG/OY-CBK/(EI-BGR)/N2160L	26. 9.84	NTU - To (G-ONPA)/G-HIGG 12/84. Canx.
G-BLKO	Hughes 369HS (500HS)	31-0300S	OO-AHL HB-XDM	22. 6.84	To G-RALI 5/85. Canx.
G-BLKP	BAe Jetstream Srs.3102	634	G-31-634 (G-BLEX)/G-31-634	9. 7.84	
G-BLKR	Westland WG.30 Srs.160	017	G-17-17	24. 6.84	To VT-EKF 9/87. Canx 14.7.87.
G-BLKS	BAe 125 Srs.800B	258010	G-5-19	. .84R	NTU - To (G-OVIP)/N84A. Canx.
G-BLKT	HS.125 Srs.600B	-		. 7.84R	NTU - Canx.
G-BLKU	Colt Flame 56SS HAFB	572		17. 7.84	Canx as WFU 1.5.92. (At British Balloon Museum & Library, Newbury)
G-BLKV	Boeing 767-204ER (Line No. 107)	23072	N6067E	7. 1.85	To ZK-NBI 6/90. Canx 31.5.90.
G-BLKW	Boeing 767-204ER (Line No. 113)	23250	N6066U	4. 3.85	To ZK-NBJ 9/90. Canx 25.9.90.
G-BLKX	PA-38-112 Tomahawk	38-79A0337	OY-BRS	2. 7.84	Destroyed in fatal crash into the back garden of a house at St.John's Road, Walthamstow, East London on 13.12.86. Canx as destroyed 29.6.92.
G-BLKY	Beechcraft B58 Baron	TH-1440		22. 8.84	
G-BLKZ	Pilatus P.2-05	600-45	U-125 Swiss AF/Swiss AF A-125	30. 7.84	
G-BLLA	Bensen B.8M Gyrocopter	G/01-1055		27. 6.84	
G-BLLB	Bensen B.8MR Gyrocopter	G/01A-1059		4. 9.84	
G-BLLC	Beechcraft 200 Super King Air	BB-438	G-LKOW (G-BLLC)/EI-BFT	2. 8.85	To F-GGPT 7/88. Canx 25.5.88.
G-BLLD	Cameron O-77 HAFB	1060		16. 7.84	
G-BLLE	Cameron Burger King 60SS HAFB	1028		28. 8.84	Canx by CAA 21.1.93. WFU in USA - no local regn.
G-BLLF	Westland WG.30 Srs.100	015	N115WG (G-BLLF)/G-17-19	22. 4.85	Canx as WFU 11.8.88.
G-BLLG	Westland WG.30 Srs.100	016		. 7.84R	NTU - To N116WG 1/91. Canx.
G-BLLH	CEA Jodel DR.220A/B 2+2	131	F-BROM	17. 7.84	
G-BLLI	Short SC.7 Skyvan 3	SH1980	G-14-1980	26. 7.84	To G-14-1980/(8P-SKY)/8P-ASG 11/84. Canx 30.11.84.
G-BLLJ	Short SD.3-30 (C-23A) Sherpa	SH3100	G-14-3100	26. 7.84	To USAF as 83-0512 in 11/84. Canx 2.11.84.
G-BLLK	Short SD.3-30 (C-23A) Sherpa	SH3101	G-14-3101	26. 7.84	To USAF as 83-0513 in 11/84. Canx 2.11.84.
G-BLLL	Short SD.3-30 UTT	SH3102	G-14-3102	26. 7.84	To R.Thailand Army as 3102 in 2/85. Canx 20.3.85.
G-BLLM	PA-23-250 Aztec E	27-4619	G-BBNM OY-POR/G-BBNM/N14001	18. 1.84	
G-BLLN	PA-18-95 Super Cub (L-18C-PI) (Frame No 18-3380)	18-3447	D-ECLN West German AF 96+23/PY+901/QZ+011/AC+508/AS+508/54-747	27. 6.84	
G-BLLO	PA-18-95 Super Cub (L-18C-PI) (Frame No 18-3058)	18-3099	D-EAUB Belgium AF OL-L25/53-4699	11. 7.84	
G-BLLP	Slingsby T.67B	2008		19. 7.84	
G-BLLR	Slingsby T.67B	2011		19. 7.84	(On overhaul 7/97)
G-BLLS	Slingsby T.67B	2013		19. 7.84	
G-BLLT	American Aviation AA-5B Tiger	AA5B-1029	OO-RTG (OO-HRS)	29. 8.84	To G-DONI 7/95. Canx.
G-BLLU	Cessna 421C Golden Eagle III	421C-0169	HB-LIF	14. 1.85	To N421CW 11/92. Canx 16.11.92.
G-BLLV	Slingsby T.67C (Originally regd as a T.67B)	2015		3. 9.84	
G-BLLW	Colt 56B HAFB	578		11. 9.84	
G-BLLX	Aerospatiale SA.315B Lama	2226	ZK-HDX	22. 8.84	To F-GFCM 10/86. Canx 1.8.86.
G-BLLY	Cessna 340A	340A-0639	N8752K	20. 7.84	To N98MM 11/92. Canx 24.11.92.
G-BLLZ	Rutan LongEz	PFA/74A-10830		16. 7.84	(On overhaul 6/95)
G-BLMA	Moravan Zlin Z.526A Trener Master (Originally regd as a Z.326)	922	F-BORS	23. 7.84	
G-BLMB	PA-18-95 Super Cub (L-18C-PI)(Frame no. 18-1521)	18-1549	D-EDRB ALAT 51-15549/51-15549	. 7.84R	NTU - To G-CLIK 7/84. Canx.
G-BLMC	Avro 698 Vulcan B.2A	-	XM575	. 8.84R	No CofA or Permit issued. (On display at East Midlands 10/97)
G-BLMD	Robinson R-22 HP	0045	N90263	13. 9.84	Badly damaged when struck power cables on take-off from near Lesmahagow, Lanark 8.4.85. Canx as destroyed 26.6.88.
G-BLME	Robinson R-22 HP	0032	N90261	16. 4.85	
G-BLMF	Cameron O-77 HAFB	1061		. 8.84R	NTU - To G-BLOG 8/84. Canx.
G-BLMG	Grob G-109B	6322		27. 9.84	
G-BLMH	BAe Jetstream Srs.3101	643	G-31-643	11. 9.84	To N157AA 4/85. Canx 29.11.84.
G-BLMI	PA-18-95 Super Cub (L-18C-PI) (Frame No.18-2086)	18-2066	D-ENWI R.Netherlands AF R-55/52-2466	5. 6.84	Permit expired 31.5.87. (Stored 8/90)
G-BLMJ	HS.125 Srs.700B	NA0346 & 257208	G-5-19 N710BR	14. 8.84	NTU - To G-BLSM 10/84. Canx.

Regn	Type	c/n	Previous identity	Regn date	Fate or immediate subsequent identity (if known)
G-BLMK	HS.125 Srs.700B	NA0347 & 257210	G-5-18 N710BQ	14. 8.84	NTU - To G-BLTP 10/84. Canx.
G-BLML	Fokker F-27 Friendship 200	10135	P2-ANC P2-TFJ/VH-TFJ/PH-FBC	20. 9.84	To G-SOFS 2/87. Canx.
G-BLMM	Fokker F-27 Friendship 600	10318	P2-ANS VH-FNS/PH-FKN	20. 9.84	To OY-CCK 10/85. Canx 17.10.85.
G-BLMN	Rutan LongEz (Regd as c/n PFA/74A-10648)	PFA/74A-10643		3. 7.84	
G-BLMO	Cameron Demistica Bottle 60SS HAFB	836		28. 8.84	Canx 29.1.90 on sale to Greece.
G-BLMP	PA-17 Vagabond	17-193	F-BFMR N4893H	15. 5.84	
G-BLMR	PA-18-150 Super Cub (L-18C-PI)(Frame No.18-2070)	18-2057	PH-NLD R.Netherlands AF R-72/52-2457	29. 5.84	(Seriously damaged in bad weather at Wellesbourne Mountford on 4.12.94)
G-BLMS	PA-18-95 Super Cub	18-1007	SX-AFE Greek Army/51-15310	21.11.84	To F-GBPD(2). Canx 19.8.86.
G-BLMT	PA-18-135 Super Cub (Frame No 18-2724)	18-2706	D-ELGH N8558C	12. 9.84	
G-BLMU	Isaacs Fury II	PFA/11-10018		24. 8.84	Stalled and crashed on take-off from Barton on 14.6.89. Canx as destroyed 7.9.89.
G-BLMV	SAN Jodel DR.1051/M Excellence	99	F-BJJC	. 8.84R	NTU - Remained as F-BJJC. Canx.
G-BLMW	Nipper T.66 RA45 Mk.IIIB	PFA/25-11020		31. 8.84	
G-BLMX	Reims Cessna FR.172H Rocket	0327	PH-RPC	5. 9.84	
G-BLMY	Grob G-109B	6313		24.10.84	Extensively damaged when undershot on landing at Booker on 11.6.86. Canx as WFU 13.5.87. Rebuilt & regd as D-KATW 6/87
G-BLMZ	Colt 105A HAFB	404		24. 9.84	
G-BLNA	Beechcraft 65-B90 King Air	LJ-446	G-BHGT G-AWWK	7. 3.84	To N7138C 5/90. Canx 23.4.90.
G-BLNB	Vickers 802C Viscount	170	G-AOHV	7. 6.84	To G-OPFI 3/94. Canx.
G-BLNC	PBN BN-2B-21 Islander	2182		3. 9.84	To TZ-APV 7/88. Canx 27.7.88.
G-BLND	PBN BN-2B-26 Islander	2183		3. 9.84	To G-LEAP 8/87. Canx.
G-BLNE	PBN BN-2T Turbine Islander AL.1 (Originally regd as BN-2B-26)	2184		3. 9.84	To AAC as ZG844. Canx on sale to MOD(PE) 12.6.89.
G-BLNF	PBN BN-2B-26 Islander	2185		3. 9.84	To D-IFBN 5/87. Canx 19.5.87.
G-BLNG	PBN BN-2B-26 Islander	2186		3. 9.84	To (D-IEDB)/D-IFOX 7/87. Canx 26.6.87.
G-BLNH	PBN BN-2B-26 Islander	2187		3. 9.84	To D-IOLA(2) 7/87. Canx 16.7.87.
G-BLNI	PBN BN-2B-26 Islander	2188		3. 9.84	To VP-FBI 10/87. Canx 23.11.87.
G-BLNJ	PBN BN-2B-26 Islander	2189		3. 9.84	
G-BLNK	PBN BN-2T Turbine Islander (Originally regd as BN-2B-26)	2190	PH-RPM G-BLNK	3. 9.84	Restored as PH-RPM 9/98. Canx 28.9.98.
G-BLNL	PBN BN-2T Turbine Islander (Originally regd as BN-2B-26)	2191	PH-RPN G-BLNL	3. 9.84	Restored as PH-RPN 5/99. Canx 12.5.99.
G-BLNM	PBN BN-2B-26 Islander	2192		3. 9.84	To TC-FBK. Canx 15.7.88.
G-BLNN	PA-38-112 Tomahawk	38-78A0508	G-CGFC	7.12.84	No CofA issued. Canx as WFU 14.12.90.
G-BLNO	Clutton FRED Srs.III	PFA/29-10559		17.10.84	
G-BLNP	Scintex CP-301C-1 Emeraude	552	F-BJFT	. .84R	NTU - To G-BLRL 11/84. Canx.
G-BLNR	PADC BN-2A-26 Islander	3009	RP-C1849	3. 9.84	To OY-CEG 8/85. Canx 13.8.85.
G-BLNS	PBN BN-2B-27 Islander	2193		3. 9.84	To B-11126. Canx 18.7.88.
G-BLNT	PBN BN-2T Turbine Islander AL.1 (Originally regd as BN-2B-26)	2194		3. 9.84	To AAC as ZG845. Canx on sale to MOD(PE) 12.6.89.
G-BLNU	PBN BN-2T Turbine Islander AL.1 (Originally regd as BN-2B-26)	2195		3. 9.84	To AAC as ZG846. Canx on sale to MOD(PE) 12.6.89.
G-BLNV	PBN BN-2T Turbine Islander AL.1 (Originally regd as BN-2B-26)	2196		3. 9.84	To AAC as ZG847. Canx on sale to MOD(PE) 12.6.89.
G-BLNW	PBN BN-2B-26 Islander	2197		3. 9.84	
G-BLNX	PBN BN-2B-26 Islander	2198		3. 9.84	To G-BPCA 1/88. Canx.
G-BLNY	PBN BN-2T Turbine Islander AL.1 (Originally regd as BN-2B-26)	2199		3. 9.84	To AAC as ZG848. Canx on sale to MOD(PE) 12.6.89.
G-BLNZ	PBN BN-2B-26 Islander	2200		3. 9.84	To VP-FBM 6/89. Canx 5.6.89.
G-BLOA	Vickers 806 Viscount	259	G-AOYJ	22. 8.84	WFU & stored in 7/93. CofA expired 31.8.93. Derelict by 1/94 at Southend. Broken up 8/96. Canx as destroyed 7.7.98.
G-BLOB	Colt 31A Air Chair HAFB	599		11. 9.84	
G-BLOC	Rand Robinson KR-2	PFA/129-10040		7. 9.84	Canx by CAA 2.9.91.
G-BLOD	Colt Ax7-77A HAFB	594		11. 9.84	Canx 25.4.86 on sale to Australia. To VH-HGE 12/92.
G-BLOE	PA-31-350 Navajo Chieftain	31-8052077	G-NITE N3559A	24. 9.84	To N2287J 5/94. Canx 18.4.94.
G-BLOF	Colt Ax7-77A HAFB	597		. 8.84R	NTU - To G-BLOK 9/84. Canx.
G-BLOG	Cameron O-77 HAFB	1061	(G-BLMF)	13. 8.84	To PH-LOG. Canx 24.6.91.
G-BLOH	Cessna 421B Golden Eagle II	421B-0368	G-NAIR G-KACT/OY-RPL/(N8055Q)	4.10.84	To G-JOES 7/85. Canx.
G-BLOI	HS.125 Srs.600B	256050	5N-ANG G-5-20	13. 9.84	To 5N-AOL 4/85. Canx 4.4.85.
G-BLOJ	Thunder Ax7-77 Srs.1 HAFB	234	(G-BKUP) ZS-HOJ	6.12.84	Canx as destroyed 23.4.93.
G-BLOK	Colt Ax7-77A HAFB	597	(G-BLOF)	11. 9.84	Canx by CAA 30.11.89. To VH-ANO 6/93.
G-BLOL	SNCAN Stampe SV-4A	554 & SS-SV-R1	G-AXRP F-BDCZ	12. 2.85	Restored as G-AXRP 9/94. (Believed stored at Hatch)
G-BLOM	DH.104 Dove	-		. 9.84R	NTU - Canx.
G-BLON	Douglas DC-3	-		. 9.84R	NTU - Canx.
G-BLOO	Sopwith Dove Replica (See notes on G-EAGA)	STR3-ST1/2		12.10.84	NTU - To G-EAGA(2) 11/89. Canx by CAA 12.7.93.

Regn	Type	c/n	Previous identity	Regn date	Fate or immediate subsequent identity (if known)
G-BLOP	Cessna 404 Titan II	404-0102	G-OEMA PH-LUN/OO-LFI/(N36999)	9.10.84	To D-ICCF. Canx 9.9.87.
G-BLOR	PA-30-160 Twin Comanche	30-59	HB-LAE N7097Y	19. 7.85	CofA expired 31.8.91. (On rebuild 10/97 at Staverton)
G-BLOS	Cessna 185A Skywagon (Also operates on floats)	185-0359	LN-BDS N4159Y	17. 9.84	
G-BLOT	Colt 56B HAFB	424		11. 9.84	
G-BLOU	Rand-Robinson KR-2	PFA/129-11118		4.12.85	No Permit to Fly issued. Canx by CAA 15.4.99.
G-BLOV	Thunder Ax5-42 Srs.1 HAFB	590		11. 9.84	Canx by CAA 11.2.91 on sale to USA - Noted active still as G-BLOV in 9/93.
G-BLOW	Focke-Wulf Piaggio FWP-149D	141	D-EEWR West German AF 91+20/YA+457/YA+010/KB+118	. 9.84R	NTU - Remained as D-EEWR. Canx.
G-BLOX	Robinson R-22	-		. 9.84R	NTU - Not Imported. Canx.
G-BLOY	Reims Cessna F.337G Super Skymaster (Wichita c/n 01791)	0084	EI-BET D-INAI/(N53697)	. .84R	NTU - To G-BLSB 11/84. Canx.
G-BLOZ	Cameron N-105 HAFB	1082		25.10.84	To SE-ZCK. Canx 21.4.87.
G-BLPA	Piper J3C-65 Cub (L-4H-PI) (Frame No.11152)	11327	OO-AJL OO-JOE/43-30036	27. 9.84	
G-BLPB	Turner TSW Hot Two Wot	TA001 & PFA/46-10606		19.10.84	
G-BLPC	BAe 125 Srs.800A	258015	G-5-17	19.10.84	To C-FTLA 1/85. Canx 4.1.85.
G-BLPD	DH.104 Devon C.2/2 (Dove 8)	04201	VP955	. .84R	NTU - To G-DVON 10/84. Canx.
G-BLPE	PA-18-95 Super Cub (L-18C-PI) (Also quoted as 18-3083)	18-3084	D-ECBE Belgium Army L-10/53-4684	28. 9.84	
G-BLPF	Reims Cessna FR.172G Rocket	0187	N4594Q D-EEFL	29. 1.85	
G-BLPG	Auster J/1N Alpha	3395	G-AZIH	21. 5.82	
G-BLPH	Reims Cessna FRA.150L Aerobat	0239	EI-BHH PH-ASH	19. 9.84	
G-BLPI	Slingsby T.67B	2016		24. 9.84	
G-BLPJ(1)	PA-31-325 Turbo Navajo C	31-7712082	5N-ASH PH-DSS/(PH-VSS)/N27323	. 9.84R	NTU - Restored as N27323. Canx.
G-BLPJ(2)	PA-23-250 Aztec C	27-3273	OY-POG LN-KAB	.10.84R	NTU - To G-BPOG 11/85. Canx.
G-BLPK	Cameron V-65 HAFB	1069		24. 9.84	CofA expired 9.8.96. Canx by CAA 19.1.99.
G-BLPL	Agusta-Bell 206B JetRanger II	8051	VR-BDY I-EVBU	27. 9.84	To 5N-AQJ /87. Canx 18.9.87.
G-BLPM	Aerospatiale AS.332L Super Puma	2122	LN-ONB G-BLPM/C-GQCB/G-BLPM	5.10.84	
G-BLPN	Socata MS.894E Rallye Minerva 220GT	12195	EI-BAB	3.10.84	NTU - Remained as EI-BAB /84. Canx.
G-BLPO	Rotorcraft	1		28. 9.84	No CofA or Permit issued. Canx as WFU 3.7.87.
G-BLPP	Cameron V-77 HAFB	432		19. 9.78	
G-BLPR	Westland WG.30 Srs.160	021		22.10.84	To VT-EKE 11/86. Canx 29.5.86.
G-BLPS	Airbus A.310-203	370	F-WZLH	. .84R	NTU - Not Imported. To TC-JCR 2/86. Canx.
G-BLPT	Rockwell Commander 690B	11484	G-LACY N81877	22. 4.81	To N2141B 2/83. Canx 16.2.83.
G-BLPU	Short SD.3-60 Var.100	SH3656	G-14-3656	3.10.84	To EI-BPD 10/84. Canx 24.10.84.
G-BLPV	Short SD.3-60 Var.100	SH3657	SE-KEX G-BLPV/G-14-3657	3.10.84	To N412SA with new c/n SH3412. Canx 12.12.94.
G-BLPW	Short SD.3-60 Var.100	SH3658	G-14-3658	3.10.84	To N371MQ 12/84. Canx 14.12.84.
G-BLPX	Short SD.3-60 Var.100	SH3659	G-14-3659	3.10.84	To N372MQ 12/84. Canx 14.12.84.
G-BLPY	Short SD.3-60 Var.100	SH3660	G-14-3660	3.10.84	To SE-KEY. Canx 8.6.88.
G-BLPZ	DH.104 Devon C.2	04270	WB534	18.10.84	To OY-BHZ. Canx 12.3.86.
G-BLRA	BAe 146 Srs.100	E1017	N117TR N462AP/CP-2249/N462AP/G-BLRA/G-5-02	3.10.84	
G-BLRB	DH.104 Dove 8	04212	VP962	22.10.84	To G-OPLC 1/91. Canx.
G-BLRC	PA-18-135 Super Cub (L-21B-PI)(Frame No.18-3790)	18-3602	OO-DKC PH-DKC/R.Netherlands AF R-112/54-2402	27.11.84	
G-BLRD	MBB Bo.209 Monsun 150FV	101	D-EBOA (OE-AHM)/D-EBOA	15.10.84	
G-BLRE	Slingsby T.67D	2012		30.11.84	Fatal crash and burned out at Cranwell Farm between Waddesdon and Aylesbury on 20.11.88. Canx as destroyed 2.12.88.
G-BLRF	Slingsby T.67C	2014		30.11.84	
G-BLRG	Slingsby T.67B	2020		30.11.84	
G-BLRH	Rutan LongEz	PFA/74A-11073		7. 2.85	No Permit to Fly issued. Canx by CAA 15.4.99.
G-BLRI(1)	PA-32R-301 Saratoga II SP	32R-8413017	N4361D	. .85R	NTU - To G-CELL 4/85. Canx.
G-BLRI(2)	Aerospatiale AS.355F1 Twin Squirrel	5325		22. 8.85	To G-NUTZ 25.10.85. Canx.
G-BLRJ	CEA Jodel DR.1051 Sicile	502	F-BLRJ	8. 2.78	
G-BLRK	PA-42-720 Cheyenne IIIA	42-5501027		31.10.84	To N9174Z. Canx 12.10.87.
G-BLRL	Scintex CP-301C-1 Emeraude	552	(G-BLNP) F-BJFT	5.11.84	
G-BLRM	Glaser-Dirks DG-400	4-107		5. 2.85	
G-BLRN	DH.104 Dove 8 (C.2/2)	04266	N531WB G-BLRN/WB531	30.10.84	
G-BLRO	Cameron V-77 HAFB	1079		.10.84R	NTU - To (G-RRSG 10/84)/G-BNIN 4/87. Canx.
G-BLRP	FMA IA-58A Pucara	017	A-517 Argentine AF	3.12.84	No Permit issued. Canx by CAA 16.11.95.
G-BLRR	Short SD.3-30 UTT	SH3105	G-14-3105	26.11.84	To R.Thailand Police as 43105. Canx 13.5.85.
G-BLRS	Cessna T.303 Crusader	T303-00306	N6312V	.11.84R	NTU - To G-PTWB 12/84. Canx.

Regn	Type	c/n	Previous identity	Regn date	Fate or immediate subsequent identity (if known)
G-BLRT	Short SD.3-60 Var.100	SH3661	SE-KRV	29.11.84	To TC-AOA 6/93. Canx 16.6.93.
			G-BLRT/G-14-3661		
G-BLRU	Short SD.3-60 Var.100	SH3667	G-14-3667	29.11.84	To B-3601 in 6/85. Canx 18.6.85.
G-BLRV	Aerospatiale SA.365N Dauphin 2	6089		28. 2.85	To N365EM. Canx 18.2.87.
G-BLRW	Cameron Elephant 77SS HAFB	1074		14.12.84	
G-BLRX	Socata TB-9 Tampico	382	(PH-BEA)	29.10.84	Damaged in gales at Stapleford on 16.10.87. (Current status unknown) Canx by CAA 12.8.94.
G-BLRY	Aerospatiale AS.332L Super Puma	2111	LN-ONA	5. 2.85	Restored as LN-ONA 4/97. Canx 9.4.97.
			G-BLRY/P2-PHP/VR-BIJ/G-BLRY/C-GQGL/G-BLRY		
G-BLRZ	Socata TB-9 Tampico	357	F-GDBR	28.11.84	Canx as destroyed 31.8.93.
G-BLSA	PA-42-720 Cheyenne IIIA	42-5501029		31.10.84	To N410LD 6/87. Canx 12.6.87.
G-BLSB	Reims Cessna F.337G Super Skymaster (Wichita c/n 01791)	0084	(G-BLOY)	15.11.84	To N337BC 3/85. Canx 25.3.85.
			EI-BET/D-INAI/(N53697)		
G-BLSC	Consolidated 28-5ACF (PBY-5A) Catalina	1997	C-FMIR	17.12.84	To VR-BPS 2/94. Canx 4.2.94.
			N608FF/CF-MIR/N10023/BuA.46633		
G-BLSD	DH.112 Venom FB.54 (built by FFW, Essen)	928	N203DM	20. 5.85	Canx as WFU 5.6.96. (Stored tailless 12/98 North Weald)
			G-BLSD/Swiss AF J-1758		
G-BLSE	DH.112 Venom FB.54 (built by FFW, Essen)	933	J-1763	20. 5.85	To N902DM 6/85. Canx 21.6.85.
			Swiss AF		
G-BLSF	American Aviation AA-5A Cheetah	AA5A-0802	G-BGCK	21. 2.83	
G-BLSG	Cessna S550 Citation II	S550-0033	(N1261K)	. .84R	NTU - To (G-BLXN 4/85)/N550ST 10/85. Canx.
G-BLSH	Cameron V-77 HAFB	1085		7.12.84	CofA expired 14.1.95. Canx 30.3.98 as WFU.
G-BLSI	Colt AS-56 Hot-Air Airship	604		17.12.84	Canx 7.6.91 on sale to New Zealand.
G-BLSJ	Thunder Ax8-90 HAFB	612		29.11.84	Canx by CAA 10.3.95.
G-BLSK	Colt 77A HAFB	617		29.11.84	
G-BLSL	Cessna 310R II	310R-1365	N3974A	26. 2.79	To SE-INH 12/83. Canx 2.12.83.
G-BLSM	HS.125 Srs.700B	NA0346 & 257208	(G-BLMJ)	18.10.84	
			G-5-19/N710BR		
G-BLSN	Colt AS-56 Hot-Air Airship	616		29.11.84	To N4446P 6/98. Canx 3.6.98.
G-BLSO	Colt AS-42 Hot-Air Airship	610		29.11.84	Canx as WFU 22.4.98. (Based in Germany)
G-BLSP	Aerospatiale AS.350B Ecureuil	1805		3. 1.85	To EI-BPM 4/85. Canx 2.4.85.
G-BLSR	Everett Gyroplane Srs.2	006		. .84R	NTU - To G-OFRB 8/85. Canx.
G-BLSS	Reims Cessna F.150J	0428	OO-CBS	11. 1.85	DBR in storms at Southend on 16.10.87. Canx as WFU 16.12.87.
G-BLST	Cessna 421C Golden Eagle III	421C-0623	N88638	29.11.78	
G-BLSU	Cameron A-210 HAFB	1095		31.12.84	
G-BLSV	PA-18-95 Super Cub (L-18C-PI) (Frame No. 18-1500)	18-1528	F-MBCH	.12.84R	NTU - To G-WGCS 12/84. Canx.
			ALAT/51-15528		
G-BLSW	Fairchild C-119G Packet	10689	3C-ABA	28.12.84	To N2700. Canx 4.10.85.
			Belgium AF CP-9/OT-CAI/51-2700		
G-BLSX	Cameron O-105 HAFB	1094		16. 1.85	
G-BLSY	Bell 222A	47027	D-HCAD	19.12.84	To D-HBTZ 3/92. Canx 16.12.91.
			N5754T		
G-BLSZ	Bell 222A	47061	D-HCHS	10.12.84	To G-DMAF 2/85. Canx.
			(D-HAAD)		
G-BLTA	Thunder AX7-77A HAFB	525		8. 6.84	
	(Originally regd as a Colt 77A Coil HAFB with same c/n)				
G-BLTB	PA-42-720 Cheyenne IIIA	42-5501030		31.10.84	To N5022M. Canx 18.11.87.
G-BLTC	Druine D.31A Turbulent	PFA/48-10964		18.12.84	
G-BLTD	Short SD.3-30 Var.100	SH3007	G-NICE	27.12.84	To G-BMTD 9/85. Canx.
			C-GTAV/G-14-3007		
G-BLTE	Reims Cessna F.182Q Skylane II	0080	OO-TWR(2)	5. 2.85	To F-GFMY 7/88. Canx 22.6.88.
			PH-AXC(2)		
G-BLTF	Robinson R-22 Alpha	0428	N8526A	10. 1.85	(Spares use 12/96)
G-BLTG	WAR Hawker Sea Fury Replica	PFA/120-10721		9. 1.85	Fatal crash at Crosland Moor on 1.9.96. Canx as destroyed 6.2.97.
G-BLTH	Cessna 404 Titan Courier II	404-0056	G-BKVH	26. 2.85	To 5Y-EAD. Canx 1.11.88.
			G-WTVA/N5438G		
G-BLTI	Cessna 402B Businessliner	402B-0574	G-BCBI	26. 2.85	Canx 11.8.87 on sale to Kenya.
			N1401G		
G-BLTJ	SNCAN Stampe SV-4A	665	F-BDNJ	18.12.84	NTU - To G-FORC 6/85. Canx.
G-BLTK	Rockwell Commander 112TC-A	13106	SE-GSD	11.12.84	
			(N4616W)		
G-BLTL	Not allocated				
G-BLTM	Robin HR.200/100 Club	96	F-GAEC	21.11.84	
G-BLTN	Thunder Ax7-65 HAFB	621		4. 1.85	
G-BLTO	Short SD.3-60 Var.100	SH3664	SE-KKZ	15. 1.85	To N426SA with new c/n SH3416. Canx 26.5.95.
			G-BLTO/EI-BSM/G-BLTO/G-14-3664		
G-BLTP	HS.125 Srs.700B	NA0347 & 257210	(G-BLMK)	18.10.84	
			G-5-18/N710BQ		
G-BLTR	Sportavia-Putzer Scheibe SF-25B Falke	4823	D-KHEC	23. 1.85	
G-BLTS	Rutan LongEz	PFA/74A-10741		14. 1.85	
G-BLTT	Slingsby T.67B	2023		16. 1.85	
G-BLTU	Slingsby T.67B	2024		16. 1.85	
G-BLTV	Slingsby T.67B	2025		16. 1.85	
G-BLTW	Slingsby T.67B	2026		16. 1.85	
G-BLTX	PA-34 Seneca	-		. 1.85R	NTU - Canx.
G-BLTY	Westland WG.30 Srs.160	019	G-17-19	14. 1.85	To VT-EKG 9/86. Canx 29.6.87.
G-BLTZ	Socata TB-10 Tobago	405	F-GDGT	28.11.84	Damaged by storm at Biggin Hill on 16.12.87. Canx as destroyed 20.1.88.

Regn	Type	c/n	Previous identity	Regn date	Fate or immediate subsequent identity (if known)
G-BLUA	Robinson R-22 HP	0091	ZS-HJW	26. 3.85	Canx by CAA 27.7.95.
G-BLUB	Grob G-109B	-		. .84R	NTU - Canx.
G-BLUC	Short SD.3-60 Var.100	SH3665	G-14-3665	24. 1.85	To N190SB 2/85. Canx 11.2.85.
G-BLUD	Short SD.3-60 Var.100	SH3666	G-14-3666	24. 1.85	To N191SB 2/85. Canx 11.2.85.
G-BLUE	Colting Ax7-77A HAFB (Regd as Colt 77A c/n 11)	77A-011		2. 5.78	(On loan to Balloon Preservation Group) (Extant 1/00)
G-BLUF	Thunder Ax10-180 HAFB	625		14. 1.85	Canx by CAA 23.1.89. To F-GHNH 1/91.
G-BLUG	Thunder Ax10-180 HAFB	626		14. 1.85	Canx by CAA 23.1.89. To F-GHNG 1/91.
G-BLUH	Thunder Ax10-180 HAFB	627		14. 1.85	Canx by CAA 23.1.89. To F-GHNI 1/91.
G-BLUI	Thunder Ax7-65 HAFB	553	(G-BMDW)	22. 2.85	
G-BLUJ	Cameron V-56 HAFB	1150		17. 4.85	CofA expired 22.9.95. Canx 4.8.98.
G-BLUK	Bond Sky Dancer (Mod)	85/1		16. 1.85	(Under construction 8/93 - wings only present 8/94) No Permit to Fly issued. Canx by CAA 15.4.99.
G-BLUL	CEA Jodel DR.1050/M1 Sicile Record	601	F-BMPJ	7. 3.85	CofA expired 24.10.91. (On overhaul 3/97)
G-BLUM	Aerospatiale SA.365N Dauphin 2	6101		21. 1.85	
G-BLUN	Aerospatiale SA.365N Dauphin 2	6114	PH-SSS G-BLUN	21. 1.85	
G-BLUO	Aerospatiale SA.365N Dauphin 2	6115		21. 1.85	To LN-OLN 6/94. Canx 6.6.94.
G-BLUP	Aerospatiale SA.365N Dauphin 2	6140		21. 1.85	To LN-OLT. Canx 5.4.94.
G-BLUR	Short SD.3-60 Var.100	SH3668	G-14-3668	24. 1.85	To N360SY 3/85. Canx 12.3.85.
G-BLUS	Lockheed L.1011-385-3 Tristar 500	293F-1235	4R-ULA	16. 4.85	Restored as 4R-ULA 4/88. Canx 14.4.88.
G-BLUT	Lockheed L.1011-385-3 Tristar 500	293F-1236	4R-ULB	1. 4.85	Restored as 4R-ULB 4/88. Canx 31.3.88.
G-BLUU	Short SD.3-60 Var.100	SH3669	G-14-3669	24. 1.85	To B-3602 in 6/85. Canx 16.12.85.
G-BLUV(1)	Airtour AH-31 HAFB	AH.004		. 1.85R	NTU - To (G-BLYV)/G-BLVA(2) 2/86. Canx.
G-BLUV(2)	Grob G-109B	6336		1. 2.85	
G-BLUW	HS.125 Srs.600B	256059	HZ-SJP HZ-DAC/G-5-19	11. 2.85	To MOD as ZF130 in 6/85. Canx 11.6.85.
G-BLUX	Slingsby T.67M Firefly 200	2027	G-7-145 G-BLUX/G-7-113	31. 1.85	
G-BLUY	Colt 69A HAFB	631		7. 3.85	Canx by CAA 19.5.93. (Extant 9/94)
G-BLUZ	DH.82B Queen Bee	1435 & SAL.150	LF858	9. 4.85	
G-BLVA(1)	Airtour AH-56 HAFB	AH.005		. .85R	NTU - To G-BLVB(2) 2/86. Canx.
G-BLVA(2)	Airtour AH-31 HAFB	AH.004	(G-BLYV) (G-BLUV)	12. 2.86	
G-BLVB(1)	Airtour AH-56 HAFB	AH.006		. .85R	NTU - To G-BLVC(2) 2/86. Canx.
G-BLVB(2)	Airtour AH-56 HAFB	AH.005	(G-BLVA)	12. 2.86	
G-BLVC(1)	Airtour AH-31 HAFB	AH.007		. .85R	NTU - To G-BLYR 12/86 as a AH-77B. Canx.
G-BLVC(2)	Airtour AH-56 HAFB	AH.006	(G-BLVB)	12. 2.86	Canx by CAA 4.8.98.
G-BLVD	Not allotted.				
G-BLVE	Boeing 747-2B4B/SCD (Line No. 262)	21097	(G-BLZX) N202AE/OD-AGH	29. 4.85	Restored as N202AE. Canx 31.5.90.
G-BLVF	Boeing 747-2B4B/SCD (Line No. 263)	21098	(G-BLZY) N203AE/OD-AGI	.10.85	Restored as N203AE. Canx 21.6.90.
G-BLVG	Embraer EMB.110P1 Bandeirante	110-364	SE-KES G-BLVG/G-RLAY/PT-SEJ	29. 1.85	To ZK-DCH. Canx 2.10.95.
G-BLVH	Boeing 757-236 (Line No. 57)	23227	(G-BNHG) (G-CJIG)/N1779B	13. 2.85	To YV-77C. Canx 17.4.90.
G-BLVI	Slingsby T.67M Firefly II	2017	(PH-KIF) G-BLVI	1. 2.85	
G-BLVJ	Colt AS-56 Hot Air Airship	624		4. 2.85	To SE-ZAE. Canx.
G-BLVK	Mudry/CAARP CAP-10B	141	JY-GSR	11. 3.85	
G-BLVL	PA-28-161 Warrior II	28-8416109	N43677	11. 2.85	
G-BLVM	PA-23-250 Aztec F	27-7854137	G-PIED N6534A	. 2.85R	NTU - To G-BLXX 3/85. Canx.
G-BLVN	Cameron N-77 HAFB	1098		4. 2.85	
G-BLVO	BAC One-Eleven Srs.203AE	041	N1547	. 2.85R	NTU - Remained as N1547. Canx.
G-BLVP	BAC One-Eleven Srs.203AE	043	N1549	. 2.85R	NTU - Remained as N1549. Canx.
G-BLVR	Honeybird	001 & PFA/141-10907		. .85R	NTU - Canx.
G-BLVS	Cessna 150M	150-76869	EI-BLS N45356	19. 2.85	
G-BLVT	Reims Cessna FR.172J Rocket	0352	PH-EDI D-EEDI	17. 4.85	To G-LOYA 8/89. Canx.
G-BLVU	Aerotek Pitts S-2A Special	2137	SE-GTX	7. 3.85	To G-HISS 3/92. Canx.
G-BLVV	Bell 206B JetRanger II	274	VR-BIH G-BLVV/PK-HBI/N4716R/(TG-H-JIF)	27. 2.85	Canx 25.3.92 on sale to Australia. To VH-BEK 10/93.
G-BLVW(1)	PA-31-310 Turbo Navajo	31-442	D-IGON (D-IHFP)/N6479L	. 2.85R	NTU - To G-IGON 3/85. Canx.
G-BLVW(2)	Reims Cessna F.172H	0422	D-ENQU	16. 5.85	
G-BLVX	Colt 105A HAFB	633		18. 2.85	To N73AF 8/86. Canx 21.3.86.
G-BLVY	Colt 21A Cloudhopper HAFB	634		18. 2.85	Canx 7.5.91 on sale to Holland.
G-BLVZ	Rockwell Commander 114B	14295	SX-AJO N4957W	20. 2.85	To G-OIBM 10/88. Canx.
G-BLWA	Short SD.3-60 Var.200	SH3662	G-14-3662	26. 2.85	NTU - To N362SA 3/85. Canx 11.3.85.
G-BLWB	Thunder Ax6-56 Srs 1 HAFB	645		22. 2.85	
G-BLWC	Aerospatiale SA.365N Dauphin 2	6099		28. 2.85	Canx 18.2.87 on sale to USA. To F-WYMD/I-COCE.
G-BLWD	PA-34-200T Seneca II	34-8070334	ZS-KKV ZS-XAT/N8253E	14. 3.85	Crashed on landing at Elstree on 15.5.99.
G-BLWE	Colt 90A HAFB	648		5. 3.85	
G-BLWF	Robin HR.100/210 Safari	183	F-BUSR	8. 3.85	

Regn	Type	c/n	Previous identity	Regn date	Fate or immediate subsequent identity (if known)
G-BLWG	Varga 2150A Kachina	VAC 155-80	OO-HTD N8360J	14. 3.85	To EI-CFK 8/91. Canx 7.6.91.
G-BLWH	Sportavia Fournier RF-6B-100	7	F-GADF	3. 4.85	
G-BLWI	Colt 69A HAFB	652		15. 3.85	NTU - To G-LCOK 27.3.85. Canx.
G-BLWJ	Short SD.3-60 Var.100	SH3670	G-14-3670	29. 3.85	To B-3603 in 6/85. Canx 16.12.85.
G-BLWK	Short SD.3-60 Var.100	SH3671	G-14-3671	29. 3.85	To B-3604 in 6/85. Canx 16.12.85.
G-BLWL	Colt 31A Cloudhopper HAFB	655		1. 4.85	Canx as WFU 16.10.89.
G-BLWM	Bristol M.1C Replica	PFA/112-10892	"C4912"	12. 3.85	Canx by CAA 12.5.88. (On display 9/97 Hendon)
G-BLWN	Short SD.3-60 Var.100	SH3672	G-14-3672	29. 3.85	To B-3605 in 7/85. Canx 19.7.85.
G-BLWO	Cameron N-77 HAFB	1136		18. 3.85	To SE-ZDS. Canx 5.4.89.
G-BLWP	PA-38-112 Tomahawk	38-78A0367	OY-BTW	7. 6.85	
G-BLWR	Currie Wot	-		. .85R	NTU - Canx.
G-BLWS	ICA-Brasov IS-28M2A	60		1. 4.85	To SX-133 11/87. Canx 6.11.87.
G-BLWT	Evans VP-1 Srs.2	PFA/62-10639		27. 3.85	
G-BLWU	Bell 206B JetRanger II	1484	ZS-PAW	26. 3.85	To G-RYOB 4/87. Canx.
G-BLWV	Reims Cessna F.152 II	1843	EI-BIN	25. 2.85	
G-BLWW	Taylor (Aerocar) Mini-Imp Model C	PFA/136-10880		1. 3.85	Permit expired 4.6.87. (Status uncertain)
G-BLWX	Cameron N-56 HAFB	1096		15. 2.85	To RP-C1483 9/94. Canx 13.9.94. (Despite sale it was extant in British marks at Ashton Court 8/95)
G-BLWY	Robin R.2160D Acrobin	176	F-GCUV SE-GXE	15. 4.85	
G-BLWZ	Socata MS.883 Rallye 115	1574	(G-BLAR) F-BSFR	. .85R	NTU - Canx.
G-BLXA	Socata TB-20 Trinidad	284	SE-IMO F-ODOH	11. 4.85	
G-BLXB	Colt 240A HAFB	665		28. 3.85	To F-GHND 7/89. Canx 22.5.89.
G-BLXC	Colt 240A HAFB	666		28. 3.85	Canx 25.10.88 on sale to USA.
G-BLXD	Slingsby T.67B	2028		1. 4.85	To ZK-WAE 5/86. Canx 21.5.86.
G-BLXE	Slingsby T.67B	2029		1. 4.85	To ZK-WAF 5/86. Canx 21.5.86.
G-BLXF	Cameron V-77 HAFB	1144		2. 4.85	
G-BLXG	Colt 21A Cloudhopper HAFB	605		2. 5.85	
G-BLXH	Alpavia Fournier RF-3	39	F-BMDQ	25. 3.85	
G-BLXI(1)	Bleriot XI Replica	EMK.010 & PFA/88-10864		. 3.85R	NTU - To BAPC.132. Canx.
G-BLXI(2)	Scintex CP.1310-C3 Super Emeraude	937	F-BMJI	1. 4.85	
G-BLXJ	Aerospatiale SA.315B Lama	2476	N403AH N47309	29. 4.85	Canx 3.8.88 on sale to USA. To F-GHCN.
G-BLXK	Agusta-Bell 205A-1	4024	1403 R.Saudi AF	2. 4.85	No UK CofA issued. Canx by CAA 20.12.90.
G-BLXL	Colt AS-105 Hot-Air Airship	628		3. 4.85	CofA lapsed 22.11.87. Canx 29.6.90 on sale to Chile.
G-BLXM	Rotorway Scorpion Executive	2		. .85R	NTU - Canx.
G-BLXN	Cessna S550 Citation S/II	S550-0033	(G-BLSG) (N1261K)	30. 4.85	NTU - Not delivered. To N550ST 10/85. Canx 23.10.85.
G-BLXO	SAN Jodel 150 Mascaret	10	F-BLDB	9. 5.85	
G-BLXP	PA-28R-200 Cherokee Arrow II	28R-7235200	N5226T	29. 7.85	
G-BLXR	Aerospatiale AS.332L Super Puma	2154		14. 5.85	
G-BLXS	Aerospatiale AS.332L Super Puma	2157		14. 5.85	To LN-OND 8/97. Canx 7.8.97.
G-BLXT	RAF SE.5A (Deconverted from Eberhart SE.5E)	-	N4488 USAAS 22-296	2.10.85	Canx by CAA 28.9.89. (To USA in 1994)
G-BLXU	Not allocated				
G-BLXV	Douglas C-47A-20-DK Dakota	12970	SE-IOK Finnish AF DO-12/OH-LCE/42-93096	19. 4.85	NTU - Not Imported. To N58NA 4/85. Canx 25.4.85.
G-BLXW	Douglas C-47A-80-DL Dakota	19560	(PH-DDZ) Finnish AF DO-6/OH-LCI/43-15094	19. 4.85	NTU - Not Imported. To N57NA 4/85. Canx 25.4.85.
G-BLXX	PA-23-250 Aztec F	27-7854137	(G-BLVM) G-PIED/N6534A	4. 3.85	
G-BLXY	Cameron V-65 HAFB	1139		9. 4.85	(Based in Tanzania in 1985)
G-BLXZ	Thunder Ax7-77 Srs.1 HAFB	651		26. 4.85	To D-MARBURG II in 10/85. Canx 15.10.85.
G-BLYA	Douglas C-53D-DO Skytrooper	11750	DO-9 Finnish AF/OH-LCG/42-68823	19. 4.85	NTU - Not Imported. To N59NA 4/85, then LN-WND 5/85. Canx 25.4.85.
G-BLYB	Beechcracft B200 Super King Air	BB-1232		23. 4.85	To N209CM 7/92. Canx 12.6.92.
G-BLYC	PA-38-112 Tomahawk	38-78A0072	D-ELID	5. 6.85	To G-LFSB 10/94. Canx.
G-BLYD	Socata TB-20 Trinidad	518		1. 5.85	
G-BLYE	Socata TB-10 Tobago	521		1. 5.85	
G-BLYF	Short SD.3-60 Var.100	SH3673	G-14-3673	14. 5.85	To B-3606 7/85. Canx 16.12.85.
G-BLYG	Short SD.3-60 Var.100	SH3674	G-14-3674	14. 5.85	To B-3607 7/85. Canx 8.12.86.
G-BLYH	Short SD.3-60 Var.200	SH3675	G-14-3675	14. 5.85	To B-3608 8/85. Canx 8.12.86.
G-BLYI	Cameron O-105 HAFB	480		30. 4.85	To N34BK 1/86. Canx 6.11.85.
G-BLYJ	Cameron V-77 HAFB	408		1. 5.85	Canx as destroyed 7.5.93.
G-BLYK	PA-34-220T Seneca III	34-8433083	N4371J	30. 5.85	
G-BLYL	HS.748 Srs.2B/424	1802	G-11-5	7. 5.85	To V2-LCS 5/85. Canx 24.5.85.
G-BLYM	Beagle B.121 Pup Srs.100	B121-145	HB-NAM (VH-EPT)/G-35-145	. 5.85R	NTU - To G-AZDG(3) 6/85. Canx.
G-BLYN	Thunder Ax8-90 HAFB	637		10. 5.85	To HB-BGD 6/85. Canx 5.6.85.
G-BLYO	PADC BN-2A-26 Islander	3011	RP-C1850	24. 6.85	To G-MALN 9/85. Canx.
G-BLYP	Robin R.3000/120	109		15. 5.85	
G-BLYR(1)	Airtour AH-31 HAFB	-		. .85R	NTU - Canx.

Regn	Type	c/n	Previous identity	Regn date	Fate or immediate subsequent identity (if known)
G-BLYR(2)	Airtour AH-77B HAFB	AH.007	(G-BLVC)	1.12.86	Stolen with its trailer from Elstree on 8.5.92 and not recovered. (Current location and status therefore unknown!) Canx by CAA 13.12.96.
G-BLYS	Robin DR.400/180 Regent	1697		2. 7.85	To D-EKVF 8/86. Canx 12.5.86.
G-BLYT(1)	Airtour AH-31 HAFB	-		. .85R	NTU - Canx.
G-BLYT(2)	Airtour AH-77 HAFB	AH.008		7. 7.87	
G-BLYU	Airtour AH-31 HAFB	-		. .85R	NTU - Canx.
G-BLYV(1)	Airtour AH-31 HAFB	AH.004	(G-BLUV)	. .85R	NTU - To G-BLVA 2/86. Canx.
G-BLYV(2)	Airtour AH-56 HAFB	-		. .85R	NTU - Canx.
G-BLYW	North American P-51D-25NA Mustang	122-40007	F-3.. Indonesian AF/N5458V/44-73543	3. 6.85	To N800DK 6/86. Canx 8.1.86.
G-BLYX	BAe 146 Srs.200	E2038		. 5.85R	NTU - To VH-JJQ 6/85. Canx.
G-BLYY	PA-28-181 Archer II	28-7890181	OO-PAV N9792K	17. 5.85	Severely damaged on landing at Crossland Moor on 31.7.99.
G-BLYZ	Edgley EA.7 Optica	EA7/005	G-56-005	13. 9.85	DBF at Old Sarum on 19.1.87. Canx as destroyed 6.2.87.
G-BLZA	Scheibe SF-25B Falke	4684	D-KBAJ	22. 5.85	
G-BLZB	Cameron N-65 HAFB	1164		21. 5.85	(On loan to Balloon Preservation Group 6/97) (Extant 1/98)
G-BLZC	Flamboyant Ax7-65 HAFB	029		14. 5.85	To ZS-... Canx 21.7.88.
G-BLZD	Robin R.1180T Aiglon	225	F-GBUZ	19. 6.85	Crashed on landing at Manston after colliding with DR.400 G-OEBA near Dover on 26.10.96. Canx by CAA 19.5.97.
G-BLZE	Reims Cessna F.152 II	1579	G-CSSC PH-AYF(2)	3. 5.85	Struck a stationary steamroller while taxiing at Redhill on 12.4.86. Canx.
G-BLZF	Thunder Ax7-77 HAFB	660		3. 6.85	
G-BLZG	Short SD.3-30 (JC-23A) Sherpa	SH3113	G-14-3113 G-14-1113	3. 6.85	To USAF as 84-0466 in 7/85. Canx 1.7.85.
G-BLZH	Reims Cessna F.152 II	1965		21. 6.85	
G-BLZI	[Was reserved for Norman (German import)]				
G-BLZJ	Aerospatiale AS.332L Super Puma	2123	LN-OMI G-BLZJ/LN-OMI/G-BLZJ/LN-OMI	13. 6.85	To G-PUMJ 12/89. Canx.
G-BLZK	PA-31-350 Navajo Chieftain	31-8052106	N35823	. 6.85R	NTU - To MOD as ZF520 6/85. Canx.
G-BLZL	Schempp-Hirth HS.6 Janus CM	20/209		. 6.85R	NTU - To G-BMBJ 9/85. Canx.
G-BLZM	Rutan LongEz	PFA/74A-10704		10. 6.85	
G-BLZN	Bell 206B JetRanger	314	ZS-HMV C-GWDH/N1408W	12. 7.85	(Overturned on its side on landing at Wycombe Air Park on 29.6.98)
G-BLZO(1)	Reims Cessna F.172P Skyhawk II	2237		. 7.85R	NTU - Not Imported. To OY-BHD 11/85, then LN-AFD on 27.2.86. Canx.
G-BLZO(2)	Reims Cessna F.172P Skyhawk II	2238		10. 7.85	Canx 1.7.86 on sale to Denmark. To LN-AFE 11/86.
G-BLZP	Reims Cessna F.152 II	1959		10. 7.85	
G-BLZR	Cameron A-140 HAFB	1067		12. 6.85	Canx by CAA 4.8.98. (Last known based in Venezuela)
G-BLZS	Cameron O-77 HAFB	479		22. 5.85	
G-BLZT	Short SD.3-60 Var.100	SH3676	G-14-3676	18. 6.85	
G-BLZU	Short SD.3-60 Var.100	SH3677	G-14-3677	18. 6.85	To C-GTAU 9/85. Canx 13.9.85.
G-BLZV	Short SD.3-60 Var.100	SH3678	G-14-3678	18. 6.85	To N342SB 11/85. Canx 6.11.85.
G-BLZW	Republic P-47D-30-RA Thunderbolt	399-55744	N47DE Peruvan AF 122/45-49205	15. 7.85	To NX47RP 3/86, then N47DE 6/86. Canx 4.11.85.
G-BLZX	Boeing 747-2B4B/SCD (Line No. 262)	21097	N202AE OD-AGH	. .85R	NTU - To G-BLVE 4/85. Canx.
G-BLZY	Boeing 747-2B4B/SCD (Line No. 263)	21098	N203AE OD-AGI	. .85R	NTU - To G-BLVF 10/85. Canx.
G-BLZZ	Mudry/Avions CAP.21	012	F-WZCJ	2. 1.86	Canx 26.7.90 on sale to Canada.
G-BMAA	Douglas DC-9-15 (Line No. 35)	47048	G-BFIH N65358/YV-52C/YV-C-AVC/XA-DEV/TC-JAA/N8964	26. 3.80	To HK-3827X 2/93. Canx 2.3.93.
G-BMAB	Douglas DC-9-15 (Line No. 54)	45738	N1057T	30.11.79	To HK-3958X 10/94. Canx 2.9.94.
G-BMAC	Douglas DC-9-15 (Line No. 56)	45739	N29259 G-BMAC/N1058T	1. 2.80	To XA-SZC 8/95. Canx 10.8.95.
G-BMAD	Cameron V-77 HAFB	1166		10. 6.85	
G-BMAE	Fokker F-27 Friendship 200	10256	PH-KFH I-ATIS/PH-FFX	9.11.82	To N275MA. Canx 22.11.88.
G-BMAF	Cessna 180F	180-51219	G-BDVR ET-ABT/N2119Z	6. 3.81	CofA expired 6.8.93. Canx by CAA 2.3.99
G-BMAG	Douglas DC-9-15 (Line No. 18)	45719	PH-DNB	1. 2.83	To XA-SXT 4/95. Canx 28.4.95.
G-BMAH	Douglas DC-9-14 (Line No. 6)	45712	OH-LYB (G-BGWP)/OH-LYB/N1792U/CF-TLC	23. 6.83	To HK-4056X 12/95 but broken up for spares in Bogota, Colombia 4/96. Canx 8.12.95.
G-BMAI	Douglas DC-9-14 (Line No. 9)	45713	OH-LYA N13614/CF-TLD	15. 9.83	To XA-SXS 4/95. Canx 28.4.95.
G-BMAJ	Short SD.3-60 Var.100	SH3611	G-14-3611 (G-BKPO)	25. 4.83	To G-WACK 4/86. Canx.
G-BMAK	Douglas DC-9-32 (Line No. 609)	47430	N503MD I-SARW/HB-IKB/5Y-BBH/5H-MOI	27. 1.84	To ZS-NRA 1/95. Canx 5.1.95.
G-BMAL	Sikorsky S-76A II Plus	760120	F-WZSA G-BMAL	27.11.80	
G-BMAM	Douglas DC-9-32 (Line No. 611)	47468	N504MD I-SARZ/HB-IKC/5Y-ALR	27. 1.84	To ZS-NRB(2) 2/95. Canx 16.2.95.
G-BMAN	BAC One-Eleven Srs.416EK	BAC.131	G-16-32 G-BMAN/G-AVOF	10. 9.82	Restored as G-AVOF 3/83. Canx.
G-BMAO	Taylor JT.1 Monoplane	PFA/1411		29. 7.85	
G-BMAP	Fokker F-27 Friendship 200	10302	S2-ABF VT-DUT/9N-AAW/VT-DUT/9N-AAS/VT-DUT/PH-FIW	29. 1.82	To N276MA. Canx 22.11.88.
G-BMAR(1)	Fokker F-27 Friendship 200	10134	N1036S P2-ANZ/P2-ANB/P2-TFI/VH-TFI/PH-FBB	. 1.82R	NTU - Remained as N1036S. Canx.

Regn	Type	c/n	Previous identity	Regn date	Fate or immediate subsequent identity (if known)
G-BMAR(2)	Short SD.3-60 Var.300	SH.3633	G-BLCR G-14-3633	12. 1.84	To C-GPCJ 5/99. Canx 4.5.99.
G-BMAS	Fokker F-27 Friendship 200	10227	F-BVTA F-OCSH/JA8616/PH-FES	1.10.81	To OY-BST 6/83. Canx.
G-BMAT	Vickers 813 Viscount	349	G-AZLT ZS-CDW/(ZS-SBW)/ZS-CDW	30. 3.81	To G-OHOT 2/89. Canx.
G-BMAU	Fokker F-27 Friendship 200	10241	5H-MRO 5H-AAP/5X-AAP/(VP-KTK)/PH-FFG	5.10.83	Crashed at Donington Park motor circuit on 18.1.87. Canx as destroyed 30.10.89.
G-BMAV	Aerospatiale AS.350B Ecureuil	1089		1. 6.79	
G-BMAW	Fokker F-27 Friendship 200	10212	5H-MRH 5H-AAC/5Y-AAC/VP-KSB/PH-FEB	6. 9.83	To N270WA. Canx 7.11.88.
G-BMAX	Clutton FRED Srs.II	PFA/29-10322		20.12.78	
G-BMAY	PA-18-135 Super Cub (L-21B-PI)(Frame No 18-3961)	18-3925	OO-LWB "EI-229"/I-EIJZ/Italian AF MM54-2525/54-2525	3. 7.85	
G-BMAZ	Boeing 707-321C (Line No. 572)	19270	TF-VLL N448M/(G-BGIR)/N448M/N448PA	7. 5.82	To N863BX 9/85. Canx 23.8.85.
G-BMBA	North American P-51D-25NA Mustang	-	MM4292 Italian AF	12. 6.85	Canx 2.8.85 on sale to USA.
G-BMBB	Reims Cessna F.150L	1136	OO-LWM PH-GAA	2. 8.85	
G-BMBC	PA-31-350 Navajo Chieftain	31-7952172	(ZF524) N3519C	9. 7.85	To RAF for spares use. Canx.
G-BMBD	Grob G-109B	6100	D-KAMS	. 7.85R	NTU - To G-DKDP 7/85. Canx.
G-BMBE	PA-46-310P Malibu	46-8508063	N6908W	26. 7.85	
G-BMBF	Nord 3202B	65	N2254X EPNER/ALAT	. .85R	NTU - Sold as spares for G-BEFH in Belgium 12/88. To F-AZMA 3/93. Canx.
G-BMBG	Colt 21A Cloudhopper HAFB	689		8. 7.85	To OE-CZH. Canx 26.8.86.
G-BMBH	Slingsby T.67M Firefly 200	2030		20. 8.85	To TC-CBA 11/85. Canx 20.11.85.
G-BMBI	PA-31-350 Navajo Chieftain	31-7752112	(ZF523) N27238	1. 8.85	To N444EM 5/93. Canx 21.5.93.
G-BMBJ	Schempp-Hirth HS.6 Janus CM	20/209	(G-BLZL)	9. 9.85	
G-BMBK	Slingsby T.67M Firefly 200	2031		20. 8.85	To TC-CBB 11/85. Canx 20.11.85.
G-BMBL	Slingsby T.67M Firefly 200	2032		20. 8.85	To TC-CBC 11/85. Canx 28.11.85.
G-BMBM	Slingsby T.67M Firefly 200	2033		20. 8.85	To TC-CBD 11/85. Canx 28.11.85.
G-BMBN	Slingsby T.67M Firefly 200	2034		20. 8.85	To TC-CBE 11/85. Canx 18.12.85.
G-BMBO	Not allotted.				
G-BMBP	Colt Whiskey Bottle SS HAFB	657		12. 8.85	Canx by CAA 8.2.90. To ZS-HYA.
G-BMBR	Issoire D77-M Motor Iris	03	BGA.2633	8. 7.85	Was never motorised - remained as BGA.2633. Canx by CAA 23.6.94.
G-BMBS	Colt 105A HAFB	704		18. 7.85	
G-BMBT	Thunder Ax8-90 HAFB	703		15. 7.85	Canx as WFU 16.4.98.
G-BMBU	Robinson R-22	0090	ZS-HJV	11. 7.85	To G-BUMF 2/86. Canx.
G-BMBV	Aerospatiale AS.332L Super Puma	2114	LN-OMC	18. 7.85	Restored as LN-OMC 9/85. Canx 2.9.85.
G-BMBW	Bensen B.8MR Gyrocopter	MV-001 & G/01-1064		27. 8.85	Permit expired 30.6.93.
G-BMBX	Robinson R-22	0067	SE-HOB	19. 7.85	Damaged when rolled over on take-off from Blackbushe on 23.4.86. Canx as destroyed 9.1.87.
G-BMBY	Beechcraft A36 Turbo Bonanza	E-2235	N72293	9. 8.85	To N109TY 4/93. Canx 20.4.93.
G-BMBZ	Scheibe SF-25E Super Falke	4322	D-KEFQ	17. 7.85	
G-BMCA	Beechcraft 200 Super King Air	BB-210	N5657N	7.10.76	To G-IBCA 12/85. Canx.
G-BMCB	Partenavia P.68B Victor	156	OO-RVT PH-RVT	20. 8.85	Fatal crash near the A453 road near East Midlands Airport on 20.10.90. Canx as destroyed 16.7.91.
G-BMCC	Thunder Ax7-77 HAFB	705		12. 7.85	
G-BMCD	Cameron V-65 HAFB	1234		26. 6.85	
G-BMCE	Bensen B.8M Gyrocopter	BAC-01		24. 7.85	No Permit issued. Canx by CAA 16.7.91.
G-BMCF	CEA Jodel DR.221 Dauphin	96	F-BPCS	. .85R	NTU - To G-BMKF 2/86. Canx.
G-BMCG	Grob G-109B	6362	(EAF-673) (Egyptian AF)	25. 7.85	
G-BMCH	Agusta-Bell 206B JetRanger III	8534	SE-HGR	24. 7.85	To D-HAFD(5) 5/93. Canx 23.12.92.
G-BMCI	Reims Cessna F.172H	0683	OO-WID	19. 8.85	
G-BMCJ	PA-31-350 Navajo Chieftain	31-8252040	N121CF N41060	11. 9.85	To G-EPED 3/95. Canx.
G-BMCK	Cameron O-77 HAFB	1180		9. 7.85	
G-BMCL	Cessna 550 Citation II (Unit No.091)	550-0082	N26627	30. 7.79	To N21DA 12/84. Canx 14.12.84.
G-BMCM	Grob G-109B	6363	(EAF-674) (Egyptian AF)	24. 7.85	To D-KWWS 10/93. Canx 29.9.93.
G-BMCN	Reims Cessna F.152 II	1471	D-ELDM	7. 8.85	
G-BMCO	Zenair Colomban MC.15 Cri-Cri (Also c/n 12-316 quoted) (Built by Zenair Canada Ltd)	S.509-316		23. 7.85	(Stored Enstone in 8/88) CofA expired 13.2.87. Canx by CAA 20.3.97.
G-BMCP	Maule M.5-235C Lunar Rocket	7315C	N5638Y	1. 5.80	To VH-MIB 3/84. Canx.
G-BMCR	Douglas C-47A-45-DL Dakota	9995	N88YA N88Y/N6K/NC6K/NC65266/42-24133	2. 8.85	Restored as N88YA 8/85. Canx 12.8.85.
G-BMCS	PA-22-135 Tri-Pacer	22-1969	5Y-KMH VP-KMH/ZS-DJI	6. 9.85	
G-BMCT	Cameron D-50 Hot Air Airship	1024		30. 7.85	Badly damaged when collided with radio mast at Seattle, Washington, USA on 7.9.86. Canx as destroyed 24.1.90.
G-BMCU	Aerospatiale AS.350B Ecureuil	1847		19. 8.85	To G-SEBI 10/85. Canx.
G-BMCV	Reims Cessna F.152 II	1963		2.10.85	

Regn	Type	c/n	Previous identity	Regn date	Fate or immediate subsequent identity (if known)
G-BMCW	Aerospatiale AS.332L Super Puma	2161	F-WYMG G-BMCW	4.10.85	
G-BMCX	Aerospatiale AS.332L Super Puma	2164		7.10.85	
G-BMCY	Aerospatiale AS.355F1 Twin Squirrel II	5327		22. 8.85	To G-RMGN 5/86. Canx.
G-BMCZ	Colt 69A HAFB	672		12. 8.85	Canx by CAA 28.2.90. To ZS-HYB.
G-BMDA	Colt 17A Cloudhopper HAFB	697		30. 7.85	To SE-ZCF 11/86. Canx 4.11.86.
G-BMDB	Replica Plans SE.5A	PFA/20-10931		12. 8.85	Badly damaged in crash at Lymington on 2.8.92. (Stored 9/96)
G-BMDC	PA-32-301 Saratoga	32-8006075	OO-PAC OO-HKK/N8242A	13. 8.85	
G-BMDD	Slingsby T.29 Motor Tutor	PFA/42-11070		8. 8.85	Permit expired 7.10.88. (Status uncertain)
G-BMDE	Pietenpol Air Camper	PFA/47-10989		12. 8.85	
G-BMDF	Boeing 737-2E7 (Line No. 917)	22875	(PK-RI.) G-BMDF/4X-BAB/N4570B	27. 3.84	To EI-CJI 7/94. Canx 7.7.94.
G-BMDG	Cameron O-105 HAFB	576	F-GCKH	12. 8.85	Canx by CAA 8.3.93. Reserved as F-GHNR in 1989.
G-BMDH	Cameron O-105 HAFB	494	F-GCKJ N292CB	12. 8.85	Canx by CAA 8.3.93.
G-BMDI	Thunder Ax8-105Z HAFB	353	F-GCZH	12. 8.85	Canx by CAA 8.3.93.
G-BMDJ	Price Ax7-77S HAFB	TPB.1 & 003		1. 8.85	(Active 9/93)
G-BMDK	PA-34-220T Seneca III	34-8133155	ZS-LOS N84209	16. 9.85	(Damaged on landing at Cardiff-Wales on 8.9.98)
G-BMDL	Cessna 402C Businessliner	402C-0269	(N1284R) G-BMDL/ZS-LPD/N1284G	7.10.85	Restored to ZS-LPD 5/87. Canx 5.5.87.
G-BMDM	Cessna 340A II	340A-1021	ZS-KRH N4620N	22.10.85	To G-LIZA 2/90. Canx.
G-BMDN	Cessna T.210N Turbo Centurion	T210-63842	ZS-LBI N6245C	4.10.85	To G-OMAD 21.10.85. Canx.
G-BMDO	ARV1 Super 2 (Built by Hornet Avn Ltd)	K.004 & PFA/152-11127		27. 8.85	
G-BMDP	Partenavia P.64B Oscar 200	08	HB-EPQ	20. 8.85	
G-BMDR	Beechcraft 95-58 Baron	TH-241	ZS-KCD A2-AAX/5Y-APF	. .85R	NTU - Not Imported. Canx.
G-BMDS	Jodel Wassmer D.120 Paris-Nice	281	F-BMOS	12. 8.85	(On overhaul Breighton 3/96)
G-BMDT	PADC BN-2A-26 Islander	3012	RP-C604	21. 8.85	Undershot on landing at Barrow-in-Furness on 14.6.86. Canx as destroyed 3.12.86.
G-BMDU	Bell 214ST Super Transport	28101	N214BE C-GSTQ/N3912B	19. 9.85	To VH-LHQ 7/90. Canx 24.7.90.
G-BMDV	Bell 47G-5	7944	RP-C1207 PI-C1207	29. 8.85	Crashed in a field 1 nm north of Cranfield on 22.5.91. Canx by CAA 4.10.91.
G-BMDW(1)	Thunder Ax7-65 HAFB	553		. .85R	NTU - To G-BLUI 2/85. Canx.
G-BMDW(2)	Dangerous Sports Club/Colt Hoppalong 1	001		30. 8.85	Canx by CAA 19.5.93.
G-BMDX	Grumman HU-16B Albatross	G-211	N29850 Spanish AF AD.1B-11/51-7161	26. 9.85	To N23ML 2/86, but re-regd N3JY 6/86 before leaving Guernsey on 17.8.86. Canx 12.6.86.
G-BMDY	Gulfstream American GA-7 Cougar	GA7-0074	OO-LCR OO-HRA	26. 8.85	To G-GOTC 6/97. Canx.
G-BMDZ	Cessna 310Q II	310Q-0121	OY-BJU SE-FRB/N76210	12.11.85	Acquired for spares use by Computaplane. Canx as WFU 22.8.88.
G-BMEA	PA-18-95 Super Cub (L-18C-PI)(Frame No 18-3206 - which if correct is c/n 18-3194 ex OL-L20/L120/53-4794. C/n 18-3204 has frame no. 18-3216)	18-3204	(D-ECZF) OL-L07/L130/53-4804	27. 8.85	
G-BMEB	Rotorway Scorpion 145	2896	VR-HJB	10.12.85	
G-BMEC	Boeing 737-2S3 (Line No. 577)	21776		11. 5.79	To EI-BPW 5/85. Canx 1.5.85.
G-BMED	Optica Industries OA-7 Optica	006	G-56-006	11. 9.85	To G-FORK 6/86. Canx.
G-BMEE	Cameron O-105 HAFB	1189		4. 9.85	(Extant 10/90)
G-BMEF	Beechcraft C90 King Air	LJ-641	N7338R (N27CG)/N7338R	12. 9.85	To N7128H 5/90. Canx 23.4.90.
G-BMEG	Socata TB-10 Tobago	530		23.10.85	
G-BMEH	Jodel 150 Special Super Mascaret (Rebuild of incomplete SAN Jodel 150 Mascaret c/n 62)	PFA/151-11047		15. 8.85	
G-BMEI	Partenavia P.68C Victor	308		8.10.85	To G-JVJA 7/86. Canx.
G-BMEJ	PA-28R-200 Cherokee Arrow	?	N21175	. .85R	NTU - Canx.
G-BMEK	Mooney M.20K (231)	25-0714	N526E G-BMEK/ZS-LOP/N1172N	7.10.85	Restored as N526E 10/98. Canx 16.10.98.
G-BMEL	PA-23-250 Aztec F	27-7854126	N63999	6.10.78	To VH-JSB 7/84. Canx.
G-BMEM	Sportavia-Putzer Fournier RF-4D	4037	CN-TZZ	9. 9.85	To D-KMEM 7/89. Canx 18.4.89.
G-BMEN	Short SD.3-60 Var.100	SH3679	G-14-3679	18. 9.85	To C-GTAX 10/85. Canx 8.10.85.
G-BMEO	Short SD.3-60 Var.200	SH3680	G-14-3680	18. 9.85	To HS-TSE 11/85. Canx 8.11.85.
G-BMEP	Short SD.3-60 Var.200	SH3681	G-14-3681	18. 9.85	To HS-TSF 11/85. Canx 25.11.85.
G-BMER	Short SD.3-60 Var.200	SH3682	G-14-3682	18. 9.85	To N373MQ 12/85. Canx 30.10.85.
G-BMES	Short SD.3-60 Var.200	SH3683	G-14-3683	18. 9.85	To N374MQ 12/85. Canx 22.11.85.
G-BMET	Taylor JT.1 Monoplane	PFA/1465		4. 9.85	
G-BMEU	Isaacs Fury II	PFA/11-10179		11. 9.85	
G-BMEV	PA-32RT-300T Turbo Lance II	32R-7887056	OO-CHB G-BMEV/ZS-KFK/N36591	30. 4.86	

Regn	Type	c/n	Previous identity	Regn date	Fate or immediate subsequent identity (if known)
G-BMEW	Lockheed 18-56 (C-60A-5-LO) Lodestar (Gulfstar conv.)	18-2444	OH-SIR OH-MAP/N283M/ N105G/N69898/42-55983	30. 9.85	Canx 15.7.86 on sale to Canada. To N283M 7/86. To Forsvarsmuseet Flysamlingn (Norwegian AF Museum) (Stored as OH-SIR 5/94 Gardermoen, Norway)
G-BMEX	Cessna A.150K Aerobat	A150-0169	N8469M	18. 9.85	
G-BMEY	PA-32R-301 Saratoga SP	32R-8213012	N8005Y ZS-LCN/N8005Y	8.10.85	To G-ROYI 10/87. Canx.
G-BMEZ	Cameron DP-70 Hot-Air Airship (Originally regd as a D-50 model)	1130		18. 9.85	To EC-FUS. Canx 20.6.91.
G-BMFA	Not allocated.				
G-BMFB	Douglas AD-4W Skyraider	7850	SE-EBK G-31-12/WV181/BuA.126867	24. 9.85	Canx 1.5.90 on sale to USA. To N4277N 5/91. (On display at Plane of Fame, Chino, USA)
G-BMFC	Douglas AD-4W Skyraider	7964	SE-EBM G-31-2/WT951/BuA.127949	16. 9.85	Canx 1.5.90 on sale to USA. To N4277L 5/91.
G-BMFD	PA-23-250 Aztec F	27-7954080	G-BGYY N6834A	6. 9.79	
G-BMFE	Cameron Truck 56SS HAFB	1186		17. 9.85	To C-GNSW 7/86. Canx 15.7.86.
G-BMFF	Optica OA.7 Optica	007	G-56-007	18. 2.86	DBF at Old Sarum on 19.1.87. Canx as destroyed 6.2.87.
G-BMFG	Dornier Do.27A-4	27-1003-342	FAP 3460 West German AF AC+955	23. 9.85	(On rebuild 5/96 Booker)
G-BMFH	Dornier Do.27A-4	27-1003-171	FAP 3497 West German AF PB+106/PB+116	23. 9.85	Fuselage stolen from Booker on 7.12.87. Canx by CAA 4.7.91.
G-BMFI	PZL-Bielsko SZD-45A Ogar	B-657		23. 9.85	
G-BMFJ	Thunder Ax7-77 HAFB	712		23.10.85	Canx 13.9.90 on sale to India. (Based in India since 12/85)
G-BMFK	PA-28-236 Dakota	28-8511014	N2407Q	26. 9.85	To SX-ANX 8/90. Canx 19.7.90.
G-BMFL	Rand Robinson KR-2	PFA/129-11049		24. 9.85	(Probably the unidentified partly built wooden fuselage noted at Willingham, Cambs in 4/99 along with possibly PFA/129-11064)
G-BMFM	BAe 146 Srs.200A	E2042	N359PS	26. 9.85	Restored as N359PS 10/85. Canx 3.10.85.
G-BMFN	QAC Quickie Tri-Q 200	EMK-017 & PFA/94A1-11062		27. 9.85	
G-BMFO	Not allocated.				
G-BMFP	PA-28-161 Warrior II	28-7916243	N3032L	1.11.85	
G-BMFR	Short SC.7 Skyvan 3	SH1904	PK-PSF G-14-76	. .85R	NTU - To OE-FDL 3/86. Canx.
G-BMFS	Short SC.7 Skyvan 3	SH1905	PK-PSG G-14-77	. .85R	NTU - Remained as PK-PSG. Canx.
G-BMFT	HS.748 Srs.2A/266	1714	VP-BFT VR-BFT/G-BMFT/5W-FAO/G11-10	18.10.85	To G-OPFW 7/98. Canx.
G-BMFU	Cameron N-90 HAFB	628		1.10.85	
G-BMFV	Cameron N-56 HAFB	629		1.10.85	Canx 9.3.87 on sale to Japan.
G-BMFW	Hughes 369E (500E)	0150E		4.10.85	To D-HULF 6/94. Canx 20.5.94.
G-BMFX	Cameron V-77 HAFB	724		. .85R	NTU - To G-BMKP 1/86. Canx.
G-BMFY	Grob G-109B	6401		8.10.85	
G-BMFZ	Reims Cessna F.152 II	1953	(G-CCPC)	3.12.85	
G-BMGA	Mooney M.20F (201)	24-1382	ZS-LKI	. .85R	NTU - Not Imported. To N5645M 10/85. Canx.
G-BMGB	PA-28R-200 Cherokee Arrow II	28R-7335099	N15814	8.11.85	
G-BMGC	Fairey Swordfish Mk.II (Built by Blackburn)	-	RCN W5856 RN W5856	23.10.85	Canx by CAA 2.9.91.
G-BMGD	Colt 17A Cloudhopper HAFB	501		21.10.85	Stolen in 1988 and not recovered. Canx by CAA 14.4.93.
G-BMGE	DHC.2 Beaver AL.1 (Regd with c/n 1734)	1468	"XP000" 7735M/XP812	14.10.85	To N5217G. Canx 15.10.85.
G-BMGF	Cessna 310R II	310R-1889	ZS-KUG N3276M	31.10.85	To G-FFOR 3/87. Canx.
G-BMGG	Cessna 152 II	152-79592	OO-ADB PH-ADB/D-EHUG/F-GBLM/N757AT	10.10.85	
G-BMGH	PA-31-325 Turbo Navajo C/R	31-7512045	ZS-LEU N8493/A2-CAT	6.12.85	Force landed at Gayton, Norfolk on 7.6.93 after the starboard engine fell off. Canx as WFU 24.1.94. (Rebuilt at Southend - noted complete late 1998)
G-BMGI	Beechcraft 95-58 Baron	TH-1268	ZS-LAX N3836D	6.12.85	Restored to ZS-LAX 2/87. Canx 10.2.87.
G-BMGJ	Beechcraft F33A Bonanza	CE-990	ZS-LFJ N1842K	. .85R	NTU - Restored to ZS-LFJ 3/86. Canx.
G-BMGK	[Was reserved for a South African import by Skyline Helicopters Ltd]				
G-BMGL	[Was reserved for a South African import by Skyline Helicopters Ltd]				
G-BMGM	[Was reserved for a South African import by Skyline Helicopters Ltd]				
G-BMGN	[Was reserved for a South African import by Skyline Helicopters Ltd]				
G-BMGO	[Was reserved for a South African import by Skyline Helicopters Ltd]				
G-BMGP	Hughes 269C (300C)	47-0585	ZS-HMK N7496F	16.10.85	To OO-HFD 1/93. Canx 21.1.93.
G-BMGR	Grob G-109B	6396		27.11.85	
G-BMGS(1)	Grumman G-21A Goose (JRF-5)	B-63	N79901 BuA.37810	. .85R	NTU - Not Imported. Canx.
G-BMGS(2)	Boeing 747-283B (Line No. 167)	20121	LN-AEO OY-KHA/(OY-KFA)	24. 4.86	To G-VOYG 2/90. Canx.
G-BMGT	Cessna 310R II	310R-1833	ZS-KSY (N2738X)	16.10.85	To G-REDD 10/96. Canx.
G-BMGU	Cessna 210M Centurion	210-62725	ZS-KRZ N6262B	9.12.85	To EI-BRY 1/86. Canx 3.1.86.
G-BMGV	Robinson R-22	0129	(EI-...) G-BMGV/OH-HAT/(SE-HOG)	22.10.85	To ZS-RHI 6/96. Canx 15.2.95.
G-BMGW	[Was reserved for a PA-31 by Greenlandair]				
G-BMGX	Short SD.3-30 UTT	SH3121		30.10.85	To Amiri Guard Air Wing as AGAW 131. Canx 5.6.86.

Regn	Type	c/n	Previous identity	Regn date	Fate or immediate subsequent identity (if known)
G-BMGY	Lake LA-4-200 Buccaneer	680	N39RG G-BWKS/G-BDDI/N1087L	1.11.85	
G-BMGZ	Aerospatiale AS.332L Super Puma	2167		23.10.85	Canx 2.7.87 as not imported. To R.Jordanian AF as 741.
G-BMHA	Rutan LongEz	PFA/74A-10973		18.10.85	
G-BMHB	PA-28-236 Dakota	28-8011143	D6-PAD N81321/N9593N	20.12.85	To OO-MHB. Canx 31.10.86.
G-BMHC	Cessna U.206G Stationair II	U206-03427	N10TB G-BMHC/N8571Q	17.11.76	
G-BMHD	Not allocated.				
G-BMHE	Cessna T.310R II	T310R-0101	ZS-JCF N69593	25.11.85	To N134SW 6/86. Canx 23.6.86.
G-BMHF	Mooney M.20J	24-1170	ZS-LER (N1141Y)	9.12.85	To ZS-LER. Canx 23.2.88.
G-BMHG	Boeing 737-2S3 (Line No. 563)	21774	N1787B	19. 3.79	Canx 1.5.85 on sale to Ireland. To (EI-BPY)/OO-TYD 11/85.
G-BMHH	Short SC.7 Skyvan 3M	SH1981	G-14-1981	5.12.85	To Amiri Guard Air Wing as AGAW-121. Canx 30.4.86.
G-BMHI	Reims Cessna F.152 II	1607	EI-BGI (EI-BGH)	7.11.85	Destroyed in mid-air collision with RAF Jaguar T.2A XX843 over Cargo, near Newtown, Powys on 29.8.91. Canx as destroyed 23.1.92.
G-BMHJ	Thunder Ax7-65 Srs.1 HAFB	743	(G-BMIL)	2. 1.86	
G-BMHK(1)	Binder CP.301S Smaragd	AB.121	D-ENSA	.11.85R	NTU - To G-DENS 20.11.85. Canx.
G-BMHK(2)	Cameron V-77 HAFB	1218		28.11.85	Canx as WFU 17.6.93.
G-BMHL	Wittman W.8 Tailwind	PFA/31-10503		28.11.85	
G-BMHM	PA-28R-201T Turbo Arrow III	28R-7803190	N3735M	20.11.85	To G-JMTT 7/86. Canx.
G-BMHN	Robinson R-22 Alpha	0500	N50022	28.10.85	To G-IBED 9/93. Canx.
G-BMHO	Colt 105A HAFB	711		30.10.85	To PH-IFR. Canx 17.11.87.
G-BMHP	PA-34-200T Seneca II	34-7870299	4X-CAW N36160	7.11.85	To F-GEOO 12/86. Canx 14.11.86.
G-BMHR	Grob G-109B	6414		15. 1.86	To EI-HCS 8/95. Canx 14.8.95.
G-BMHS	Reims Cessna F.172M	0964	PH-WAB	7. 4.86	
G-BMHT	PA-28RT-201T Turbo Arrow IV	28R-8231010	ZS-LCJ N8462Y	18.11.85	
G-BMHU	Viking Dragonfly	PFA/139-11055		30.10.85	No Permit to Fly issued. Canx by CAA 20.8.90.
G-BMHV	Short SD.3-60 Var.200	SH3684	G-14-3684	26.11.85	To N375MQ 12/85. Canx 2.12.85.
G-BMHW	Short SD.3-60 Var.200	SH3685	G-14-3685	26.11.85	To N376MQ 12/85. Canx 6.12.85.
G-BMHX	Short SD.3-60 Var.200	SH3686	G-14-3686	26.11.85	To SE-LGE 8/96. Canx 20.8.96.
G-BMHY	Short SD.3-60 Var.200	SH3687	G-14-3687	26.11.85	To G-OREX 5/91. Canx.
G-BMHZ	PA-28RT-201T Turbo Arrow IV	28R-8031001	ZS-KII N8096D	18.11.85	
G-BMIA	Thunder Ax8-90 HAFB	736		4.11.85	To N1203R 9/96. Canx 29.8.96.
G-BMIB	Bell 206B JetRanger II	2034	ZS-HGH	7.11.85	To G-LTEK 5/93. Canx.
G-BMIC	Rockwell Commander 690B	11437	N114SA (N81701)	11. 8.78	To N9171S 8/81. Canx 3.8.81.
G-BMID	Wassmer Jodel D.120 Paris-Nice	259	F-BMID	18. 8.81	
G-BMIE	Thunder Ax8-105 HAFB	722		19.11.85	To VH-OCB. Canx 25.3.86.
G-BMIF	Aerospatiale AS.350B Ecureuil	1010	LN-OTW SE-HHS/F-WZFB	8.11.85	To F-GOCH 7/96. Canx 15.5.96.
G-BMIG	Cessna 172N Skyhawk II	172-72376	ZS-KGI (N48630)	13. 5.86	
G-BMIH	HS.125 Srs.700B	257115	G-5-502 5N-AMX/G-BMIH/G-5-502/HZ-DA3	22. 1.86	
G-BMII	Dornier Do.27A-4	2102	MAAW-11 Malawi Army Air Wing/D-EGVF/Belgium AF OT-AME\D-05 /Belgium AF OL-D05/ Belgium AF D05	28. 5.86	To HC-BNK 1/88. Canx 15.6.87.
G-BMIJ	Dornier Do.27A-4	2107	MAAW-14 Malawi Army Air Wing/D-EGVO/Belgium AF OT-AMI\D-10 /Belgium AF OL-D10/ Belgium AF D10	28. 5.86	To HC-BNL 9/87. Canx 21.7.87.
G-BMIK	Dornier Do.27A-4	2108	MAAW-15 Malawi Army Air Wing/D-EGVP/Belgium AF OT-AMJ\D-11 /Belgium AF OL D11/ Belgium AF D11	28. 5.86	To HC-BPU. Canx 8.8.89.
G-BMIL(1)	Thunder Ax7-65 Srs.1 HAFB	743		. .85R	NTU - G-BMHJ 1/86. Canx.
G-BMIL(2)	Dornier Do.27A-4	522	ZS-LLU D-ECXY/Nigerian AF NAF-167/West German AF GB+371	. .85R	NTU - Restored as ZS-LLU 1/86. Canx.
G-BMIM	Rutan LongEz	8102-160	OY-CMT OY-8102	12.12.85	
G-BMIN	PA-31-350 Navajo Chieftain	31-7752145	N27315	6. 1.78	Restored as N27315 5/80. Canx 9.5.80.
G-BMIO	Stoddard-Hamilton Glasair II RG	PFA/149-11016		25.11.85	(under construction 9/93)
G-BMIP	Wassmer Jodel D.112	1264	F-BMIP	7.12.78	
G-BMIR(1)	Douglas C-47B-10-DK Dakota	14897/26342	N1350M Spanish AF T3-64/EC-ASF/43-49081	. .85R	NTU - Canx. (Was reserved for delivery flight from USA to Luftbrucke Museum, Frankfurt, via Aces High, for preservation in 3/86)
G-BMIR(2)	Westland Wasp HAS.1	F.9670	XT788	24. 1.86	No UK or Permit issued. (Stored as XT788 3/93 at Charlwood) Canx by CAA 22.12.95.
G-BMIS	Monnett Sonerai II	755 & PFA/15A-10813	VR-HIS	26. 2.87	(Status uncertain)
G-BMIT	Slingsby T.67M Firefly	2018		21.11.85	To HB-NBC 1/86. Canx 6.1.86.
G-BMIU	Enstrom F-28A	201	OO-BAM (F-BVRE)	28.11.85	Damaged in crash on landing at Baginton on 9.7.86. (Remains in open storage) Canx as WFU 8.8.90.

Regn	Type	c/n	Previous identity	Regn date	Fate or immediate subsequent identity (if known)
G-BMIV	PA-28R-201T Turbo Arrow III	28R-7703154	ZS-JZW N5816V	7. 1.86	
G-BMIW	PA-28-181 Archer II	28-8190093	ZS-KTJ N8301J	6.12.85	
G-BMIX	Socata TB-20 Trinidad	579		5.12.85	To EI-BSV 8/86. Canx 29.7.86.
G-BMIY	Oldfield Baby Great Lakes	PFA/10-10194	G-NOME	3.12.85	(Stored 6/96)
G-BMIZ	Robinson R-22 Beta	0505	N2270B	11.11.85	To OO-XCE. Canx 11.12.85.
G-BMJA	PA-32R-301 Saratoga SP	32R-8113019	ZS-KTH N8309E	23.12.85	
G-BMJB	Cessna 152 II	152-80030	N757VD	3. 2.86	
G-BMJC	Cessna 152 II	152-84989	N623AP	3. 2.86	
G-BMJD	Cessna 152 II	152-79755	N757HP	21.11.85	
G-BMJE	Boeing 707-338C (Line No. 458)	18954	60-SBN 9M-MCR/9M-ATR/VH-EBR	18.11.85	To N449J 11/85. Canx 18.11.85.
G-BMJF	PA-28R-200 Cherokee Arrow	28R-7635234	ZS-JUF N9377K	31.12.85	Restored as N9377K 6/86. Canx 23.6.86.
G-BMJG	PA-28R-200 Cherokee Arrow	28R-35046	ZS-TNS ZS-FYC/N9345N	23.12.85	Failed to gain speed on take-off at Thruxton on 11.10.98 and struck a grass bank at the end of the runway. Canx by CAA 15.4.99.
G-BMJH	Hughes 369D (500D)	50-0696D		19. 5.80	To G-KSBF 11/82. Canx.
G-BMJI	Cameron Watch 75SS HAFB	1206		28.11.85	To HB-BHA. Canx 26.2.86.
G-BMJJ	Cameron Watch 75SS HAFB	1207		28.11.85	To HB-BHB. Canx 26.2.86.
G-BMJK	Cameron Watch 75SS HAFB	1208		28.11.85	To HB-BHC. Canx 26.2.86.
G-BMJL	Rockwell Commander 114	14006	A2-JRI ZS-JRI/N1906J	8. 1.86	
G-BMJM	Evans VP-1	PFA/62-10763		21.11.85	
G-BMJN	Cameron O-65 HAFB	1212		6.12.85	
G-BMJO	PA-34-220T Seneca III	34-8533036	N6919K N9565N	5.12.85	
G-BMJP	Colt AS-56 Hot-Air Airship	751		6.12.85	Canx 17.5.91 on sale to Spain.
G-BMJR	Cessna T.337H Turbo Super Skymaster II	337-01895	G-NOVA N1259S	10. 7.84	
G-BMJS	Thunder Ax7-77 HAFB	754		3.12.85	CofA expired 7.4.96. (Extant 2/97)
G-BMJT	Beechcraft 76 Duchess	ME-376	ZS-KMI N3718W	4.12.85	
G-BMJU	HS.748 Srs.2B/FAA	1783	G-11-1 V2-LDA/C-GRXE/G-11-10/C-GRXE/N748BA/N749LL	10. 1.86	To ZS-LSO 2/86. Canx 12.2.86.
G-BMJV	Hughes 369D (500D)	11-0871D	N1110S	29. 1.86	To G-PJMD 11/89. Canx.
G-BMJW	North American AT-6D-NT Harvard III (Composite with rear fuselage of KF487)	88-15963	EZ259 South African AF 7631/EZ259/42-84182	28.11.85	No CofA issued. Canx by CAA 2.9.91. (Fuselage on rebuild 2/96)
G-BMJX	Wallis WA-116/X Srs.1	K/219/X		31.12.85	Permit expired 1.4.89. (Stored 2/99 Reymerston Hall)
G-BMJY	SPP Yakovlev C.18A	-	(France) Egypt AF 627	21. 1.86	
G-BMJZ	Cameron N-90 HAFB	1219		16.12.85	
G-BMKA	Robin R.3000/120	117		6.12.85	Damaged in gales at Lydd on 16.10.87. Canx as destroyed 31.8.88.
G-BMKB	PA-18-135 Super Cub (L-21B-PI) (Frame No.18-3818)	18-3817	OO-DKB PH-DKB/(PH-GRP)/R.Netherlands AF R-127/54-2417	11.12.85	
G-BMKC	Piper J3C-90 Cub (L-4H-PI) (Frame No.10970)	11145	F-BFBA 43-29854	2. 1.86	
G-BMKD	Beechcraft C90A King Air	LJ-1069	N223CG N67516	30.12.85	
G-BMKE	PA-28RT-201 Arrow IV	28R-7918017	ZS-LHH N2100J	3. 2.86	Extensively damaged at Willow Farm near Norwich on 10.8.93. Canx as destroyed 29.10.93.
G-BMKF	CEA Jodel DR.221 Dauphin	96	(G-BMCF) F-BPCS	3. 2.86	
G-BMKG	PA-38-112 Tomahawk II	38-82A0050	ZS-LGC N91544	3. 2.86	
G-BMKH	Colt 105A HAFB	752		30.12.85	Canx by CAA 16.5.97.
G-BMKI	Colt 21A Cloudhopper HAFB	753		30.12.85	
G-BMKJ	Cameron V-77 HAFB	1235		2. 1.86	
G-BMKK	PA-28R-200 Cherokee Arrow II	28R-7535265	ZS-JNY N9537N	16. 1.86	
G-BMKL	PA-28-181 Archer II	28-8190139	ZS-KWL N8323L	16. 1.86	To OY-CEK. Canx 10.4.87.
G-BMKM	Agusta-Bell 206B JetRanger III	8694		17. 2.86	To VR-CDG 6/93. Canx 17.6.93.
G-BMKN	Colt 31A Air Chair HAFB	762		30.12.85	Canx as WFU 3.6.91.
G-BMKO	PA-28-181 Archer II	28-7890483	N31880	7. 1.86	To G-NERI 3/93. Canx.
G-BMKP	Cameron V-77 HAFB	724	(G-BMFX)	10. 1.86	(Active 7/96)
G-BMKR	PA-28-161 Warrior II	28-7916220	G-BGKR N9561N	14. 6.84	
G-BMKS	Aerosport Scamp	PFA/117-10962		6. 1.86	Badly damaged after crashing at Crowfield on 4.5.90. Cancelled as WFU 19.7.90.
G-BMKT	Aerospatiale SA.315B Lama	2525	N9002K	14. 1.86	To I-DENY 5/86. Canx 2.5.86.
G-BMKU	Colt Apple SS HAFB	756		20. 1.86	Canx 30.6.86 on sale to Italy.
G-BMKV	Thunder Ax7-77 HAFB	772		21. 1.86	
G-BMKW	Cameron V-77 HAFB	608		29. 1.86	
G-BMKX	Cameron Elephant 77SS HAFB	1196		6. 2.86	Canx as WFU 21.10.96. Held 1/98 Balloon Preservation Group
G-BMKY	Cameron O-65 HAFB	1246		4. 3.86	
G-BMKZ	Optica OA.7 Optica	008	G-56-008	18. 2.86	DBF at Old Sarum on 19.1.87. Canx as destroyed 6.2.87.

Regn	Type	c/n	Previous identity	Regn date	Fate or immediate subsequent identity (if known)
G-BMLA	Bell UH-1H Huey	13934	VP-FBD	17. 1.86	Damaged in hangar collapse at Headcorn on 14.1.87. Canx as
			Argentine Army AE-424/77-22930		WFU 3.9.87. To VH-UHE 9/88.
G-BMLB	Jodel Wassmer D.120A Paris-Nice	295	F-BNCI	20. 1.86	
G-BMLC	Short SD.3-60 Var.200	SH3688	G-14-3688	18. 2.86	To SE-LDA 4/96. Canx 2.4.96.
G-BMLD	Short SD.3-60 Var.100	SH3689	G-14-3689	18. 2.86	To (EI-BSN)/EI-BSP 4/86. Canx 16.4.86.
G-BMLE	Short SD.3-60 Var.200	SH3690	G-14-3690	18. 2.86	To N690PC 3/86. Canx 10.3.86.
G-BMLF	Short SD.3-30 UTT	SH3122		18. 2.86	No CofA issued. Canx as WFU 22.7.91.
G-BMLG	Short SD.3-30 UTT	SH3123	G-14-3123	18. 2.86	NTU - To YV-O-GVR1. Canx 24.9.86.
G-BMLH	Mooney M.20C Ranger	690083	N9293V	24. 2.86	To G-ODJH 1/93. Canx.
G-BMLI	Beechcraft F33A Bonanza	CE-1012	ZS-LIK	28. 1.86	Restored to ZS-LIK 2/87. Canx 10.2.87.
			N6875T		
G-BMLJ	Cameron N-77 HAFB	1263		7. 3.86	(Extant 2/97)
G-BMLK	Grob G-109B	6424		24. 2.86	(Active 7/97)
G-BMLL(1)	Grob G-109B	6407	EC-DYX	. .86R	NTU - Remained as EC-DYX /86. Canx.
			D-KNEJ		
G-BMLL(2)	Grob G-109B	6420		13. 3.86	
G-BMLM	Beechcraft 95-58 Baron	TH-405	F-GEPV	2. 7.79	To N111LM 7/99. Canx 22.7.99.
			3D-ADF/ZS-LOZ/G-BMLM/G-BBJF		
G-BMLN	Fuji FA.200-160 Aero Subaru		(G-BIMR)	29. 1.86	To LN-TEZ. Canx 28.2.86.
		FA200-295			
G-BMLO	Grob G-109B	6425		24. 2.86	To G-IPSI(2) 5/86. Canx.
G-BMLP	Boeing 727-264F	20710	N728ZV	10. 7.86	To C-GRYO 9/93. Canx 10.9.93.
	(Line No. 975)		EI-BRF/N788BR/XA-CUE		
G-BMLR	Partenavia P.68C Victor	278	OY-BYS	19. 5.86	To PH-GRO. Canx 12.12.86.
			D-GOBY/(PH-GRO)		
G-BMLS	PA-28R-201 Cherokee Arrow III		N47496	11. 2.86	
		28R-7737167			
G-BMLT	Pietenpol Air Camper	PFA/47-10949		28. 1.86	
G-BMLU	Colt 90A HAFB	786		10. 4.86	
G-BMLV	Robinson R-22 Alpha	0448	4X-BBM	31. 1.86	Canx by CAA 6.11.90 - No UK CofA issued. To CC-PYI.
			N8555X		
G-BMLW	Cameron O-77 HAFB	813		6. 2.86	
	(Originally regd as V-65 with same c/n)				
G-BMLX	Reims Cessna F.150L	0700	PH-VOV	21. 3.86	
G-BMLY	Grob G-109B	6428		12. 3.86	To D-KERK 12/93. Canx 14.7.93.
G-BMLZ	Cessna 421C Golden Eagle III		G-OTAD	17.12.85	(To Canada by container 7/97)
		421C-0223	G-BEVL/N5476G		
G-BMMA	Aerospatiale AS.350B Ecureuil	1049	C-GJTB	3. 2.86	To G-PLMA 3/86. Canx.
G-BMMB	Aerospatiale AS.350B Ecureuil	1207	C-GBEW	3. 2.86	To G-PLMB 3/86. Canx.
			(N36033)		
G-BMMC	Cessna 310Q II	310Q-0041	YU-BGY	11. 2.86	
			N7541Q		
G-BMMD	Rand Robinson KR-2	PFA/129-10817		7. 2.86	
G-BMME	Hoffmann H-36 Dimona	36207		25. 3.86	Canx as destroyed 20.4.88.
G-BMMF	Clutton FRED Srs.II	PFA/29-10296		20. 2.86	
G-BMMG	Thunder Ax7-77 HAFB	595	D-TUTTA	25. 3.86	Canx as PWFU 21.10.98.
			G-BMMG/D-JUTTA		
G-BMMH	PADC BN-2A-26 Islander	3013	RP-C578	27. 3.86	To G-SBUS 10/86. Canx.
G-BMMI	Pazmany PL-4A	PFA/17-10149		6. 2.86	
G-BMMJ	Siren PIK-30	720		13. 6.86	
G-BMMK	Cessna 182P Skylane II	182-64117	OO-AVU	24. 3.86	
	(Reims-assembled c/n 0038)		N6129F		
G-BMML	PA-38-112 Tomahawk	38-80A0079	PH-TMG	2. 4.86	
			OO-HKD		
G-BMMM	Cessna 152 II	152-84793	N4652P	10. 9.86	
G-BMMN	Thunder Ax8-105 Srs.2 HAFB	783		3. 3.86	To D-OMMN /95. Canx 29.6.95.
G-BMMO	BAe 125 Srs.800A	258048	(N125BA)	26. 2.86	To C-GCIB. Canx 12.9.86.
			G-BMMO/G-5-16		
G-BMMP(1)	Boeing 737-2S3	22633		. .81R	NTU - To G-DDDV 2/81. Canx.
	(Line No. 746)				
G-BMMP(2)	Grob G-109B	6432		27. 6.86	
G-BMMR	Dornier 228-202K	8063	(D-IAOT)	1. 4.86	
	(Regd as a Srs.200)		D-CAOS		
G-BMMS	Aerospatiale SA.316B Alouette III		N4261E	11.12.86	To OE-EXT 1/87. Canx 22.1.87.
		1592	C-GXGW/N65376/9M-ASI/Malaysian AF FM-1097		
G-BMMT	PA-46-310P Malibu	46-8608019	N9230T	7. 3.86	To I-GHIO 7/86. Canx 21.7.86.
G-BMMU	Thunder Ax8-105 HAFB	719		4. 3.86	
G-BMMV	ICA-Brasov IS-28M2A	57		10. 3.86	
G-BMMW	Thunder Ax7-77 HAFB	782		10. 3.86	
G-BMMX	ICA-Brasov IS-28M2A	58		14. 4.86	
G-BMMY	Thunder Ax7-77 HAFB	716		11. 3.86	
G-BMMZ	Boeing 737-2D6ADV	20544	TZ-ADL	13. 5.86	To F-GLXH 9/92. Canx 18.9.92.
	(Line No. 290)		7T-VEC		
G-BMNA	Airbus A.300B4-2C	169	D-AHLJ	. 4.86	Restored as D-AHLJ 12/86. Canx 18.12.86.
	(Regd as a -203)		9V-STD/F-WZMP		
G-BMNB	Airbus A.300B4-203	009	D-AMAP	17.12.86	To F-GIJT 6/90. Canx 15.1.90.
			F-ODCY/(HS-VGF)/F-WLGA		
G-BMNC	Airbus A.300B4-103	012	D-AMAX	23. 3.88	To F-GIJU 11/90. Canx 8.11.90.
			F-WLGC		
G-BMND	Dornier 228-202K	8077	D-IESI	18. 4.86	To VH-NSZ. Canx 9.12.87.
	(Regd as a Srs.201)		(D-CESI)		
G-BMNE	Bell 214ST	28121	N31780	. .86R	NTU - To VH-HOQ. Canx.

Regn	Type	c/n	Previous identity	Regn date	Fate or immediate subsequent identity (if known)
G-BMNF	Beechcraft B200 Super King Air	BB-1127	N69131	7. 1.86	To 5Y-JJZ 5/98. Canx 24.6.96.
G-BMNG	Short SD.3-60 Var.200	SH3691	G-14-3691	13. 3.86	To (N691PC)/N360PC 3/86. Canx 13.3.86.
G-BMNH	Short SD.3-60 Var.200	SH3692	G-14-3692	13. 3.86	To N693PC 3/86. Canx 13.3.86.
G-BMNI	Short SD.3-60 Var.200	SH3693	G-14-3693	13. 3.86	To N695PC 4/86. Canx 18.3.86.
G-BMNJ	Short SD.3-60 Var.200	SH3694	N694PC G-BMNJ/G-14-3694	13. 3.86	To CS-TMH 9/95. Canx 15.9.95.
G-BMNK	Short SD.3-60 Var.200	SH3695	G-14-3695	13. 3.86	To (5N-AOX)/G-14-3695/(EI-BVJ)/EI-BVM 3/88. Canx 7.3.88.
G-BMNL	PA-28R-200 Cherokee Arrow II B	28R-7535040	N18MW N32280	17. 9.86	
G-BMNM	PA-28-161 Warrior II	28-8216024	N8447N	2. 4.86	To I-ACMH. Canx 25.6.87.
G-BMNN	Cessna 152 II	152-80083	N757XJ	24. 3.86	To PH-WEE 12/86. Canx 30.12.86.
G-BMNO	PA-38-112 Tomahawk II	38-81A0131	N23411	24. 3.86	Fatal crash after mid-air collision with PA-38-112 G-BOMO over Upton-on-Severn on 18.7.88. Canx as WFU 25.8.88.
G-BMNP	PA-38-112 Tomahawk II	38-81A0133	N23352	24. 3.86	(Fuselage stored 9/97 at Welshpool)
G-BMNR	BAe Jetstream Srs.3111 (Regd as a Srs.3102)	696	(G-WSOC) G-31-696	29. 5.86	To R.Saudi AF as 2102. Canx 26.6.87.
G-BMNS	BAe Jetstream Srs.3111 (Regd as a Srs.3102)	709	(G-TWSS) G-31-709	29. 5.86	To R.Saudi AF as 2101 in 1/87. Canx 26.1.87.
G-BMNT	PA-34-220T Seneca III	34-8133029	N8348T	19. 3.86	
G-BMNU	Cameron V-77 HAFB	725		7. 4.86	To N750CB. Canx 12.11.92.
G-BMNV	SNCAN Stampe SV-4C (Mod)	108	F-BBNI	14. 3.86	
G-BMNW	PA-31-350 Navajo Chieftain	31-8152139	N4088T	11. 6.86	To N31NW 8/98. Canx 13.5.98.
G-BMNX	Colt 56A HAFB	790		14. 4.86	
G-BMNY	Everett Gyroplane Srs.1	007		1.12.86	To G-ULPS 7/93. Canx.
G-BMNZ	Cessna U.206F Stationair 6	U206-02233	F-BVJT N1519U	28. 5.86	To G-BXDB 12/96. Canx.
G-BMOA	Cessna 441 Conquest	441-0362	(N1283F)	7. 4.86	To LX-ETB. Canx 23.8.88.
G-BMOB	DH.112 Venom FB.50 (FB.1) (built by FFW, Emmen)	783	J-1573 Swiss AF	. .86R	NTU - To HB-RVB. Canx.
G-BMOC	DH.112 Venom FB.50 (FB.1) (built by FFW, Emmen)	821	J-1611 Swiss AF	. .86R	NTU - To G-DHTT 10/96. Canx.
G-BMOD	DH.112 Venom FB.50 (FB.1) (built by FFW, Emmen)	749	J-1539 Swiss AF	. .86R	NTU - To G-DHUU 2/96. Canx.
G-BMOE	PA-28R-200 Cherokee Arrow II	28R-7635226	PH-PCB OO-HAS/N9221K	20. 5.86	(Force landed in a corn field near Compton Abbas 28.6.98, to Oxford for repairs)
G-BMOF	Cessna U.206G Stationair II	U206-03658	N7427N	17. 4.86	
G-BMOG	Thunder Ax7-77 HAFB	793		2. 4.86	
G-BMOH	Cameron N-77 HAFB	1270		2. 4.86	
G-BMOI	Partenavia P.68B Victor	103	I-EEVA	4. 4.86	
G-BMOJ	Cameron V-56 HAFB	1275		4. 4.86	
G-BMOK	ARV1 Super 2	011		14. 4.86	
G-BMOL	PA-23-250 Aztec D	27-4394	G-BBSR N6610Y	26. 6.84	CofA expired 26.7.87. Canx by CAA 24.5.90. (On fire dump 2/96 Elstree)
G-BMOM	ICA IS-28M2A	50		30. 6.86	(Stored 8/96)
G-BMON	Boeing 737-2K9 (Line No. 709)	22416	C-GPWC G-BMON/C-GPWC/G-BMON/N1786B	2.10.80	Restored as C-GPWC. Canx 7.12.87.
G-BMOO	Clutton FRED Srs.II	PFA/29-10770		11. 4.86	Permit expired 8.8.91. (On overhaul 7/94) Canx by CAA 22.2.99.
G-BMOP	PA-28R-201T Turbo Arrow III	28R-7703194	N38257	18. 4.86	
G-BMOR	Boeing 737-2S3 (Line No. 570)	21775	(G-BNZU) EI-BPR/(EI-BRR)/G-BMOR	24. 4.79	To F-GHXL 8/89. Canx 8.8.89.
G-BMOS	HS.125 Srs.700B	257064	HZ-OFC HZ-NAD	30. 4.86	To G-5-519/VH-JFT 7/86. Canx 5.6.86.
G-BMOT	Bensen B.8M Gyrocopter	G/01-1066		17. 4.86	
G-BMOU	Cameron V-77 HAFB	727		11. 4.86	To OO-BOU. Canx 15.9.86.
G-BMOV	Cameron O-105 HAFB	1307		11. 4.86	
G-BMOW	Grumman G.159 Gulfstream I	155	N805CC N900PA/N900PM/N24C/N22CP/N992CP/N750G	.11.86	To 9Q-CJB. Canx 22.12.92.
G-BMOX	Hovey Beta Bird	PFA/135-10976		15. 4.86	No Permit to Fly. Canx by CAA 19.4.99.
G-BMOY	Cameron A-250 HAFB	1258		24. 4.86	To 5Y-OWL 3/89. Canx 21.2.89.
G-BMOZ	Cameron O-160 HAFB	1308		23. 4.86	To F-GHOZ 5/89. Canx 5.4.89.
G-BMPA	Grumman G.159 Gulfstream I	134	N920BS N914BS/N754G	. 7.86	To (F-....)/4X-ARF. Canx 10.4.95.
G-BMPB	Reims Cessna F.172P Skyhawk	2251		18. 9.86	Canx by CAA 23.7.91. To HB-CKG 11/86.
G-BMPC	PA-28-181 Archer II	28-7790436	LN-NAT	23. 4.86	
G-BMPD	Cameron V-65 HAFB	1200		4. 6.86	
G-BMPE	Optica OA.7 Optica	009	G-56-009	14. 4.86	DBF 19.1.87 at Old Sarum. Canx as destroyed 6.2.87.
G-BMPF	Optica OA.7 Optica	010	G-56-010	14. 4.86	Canx by CAA 2.9.91. (Stored 11/95)
G-BMPG	Optica OA.7 Optica	011	G-56-011	14. 4.86	DBF 19.1.87 at Old Sarum. Canx as destroyed 6.2.87.
G-BMPH	Optica OA.7 Optica	012	G-56-012	14. 4.86	DBF 19.1.87 at Old Sarum. Canx as destroyed 6.2.87.
G-BMPI	Optica OA.7 Optica	013	G-56-013	14. 4.86	Canx as destroyed 11.7.91.
G-BMPJ	Optica OA.7 Optica	014	G-56-014	14. 4.86	DBF 19.1.87 at Old Sarum. Canx as destroyed 6.2.87.
G-BMPK	Optica OA.7 Optica	015	G-56-015	14. 4.86	DBF 19.1.87 at Old Sarum. Canx as destroyed 6.2.87.
G-BMPL	Optica OA.7 Optica	016	G-56-016	14. 4.86	(Stored 1/98 Farnborough)
G-BMPM	Optica OA.7 Optica	017	G-56-017	14. 4.86	Canx by CAA 14.10.91. (Was based in Egypt)
G-BMPN	Optica OA.7 Optica	018	G-56-018	14. 4.86	Canx by CAA 14.10.91. To VH-BMC 12/93.
G-BMPO	Cessna 182Q	182-66785	ZS-KFY (N96025)	22. 4.86	Fatal crash & DBF 5 miles northwest of Rhewl, Clwtd on 15.5.91. Canx as destroyed 8.8.91.
G-BMPP	Cameron N-77 HAFB	1303		15. 4.86	

Regn	Type	c/n	Previous identity	Regn date	Fate or immediate subsequent identity (if known)
G-BMPR	PA-28R-201 Arrow III	28R-7837175	ZS-LMF	22. 4.86	
			N417GH		
G-BMPS	Strojnik S-2A	045		18. 4.86	
	(Homebuilt motor-glider)				
G-BMPT	Colt 56A HAFB	822		23. 4.86	To G-POSH 6/86. Canx.
G-BMPU	Robinson R-22	0070	ZS-HNP	24. 4.86	To VH-LQN 6/91. Canx 7.3.91.
			LV-OOR		
G-BMPV	PA-31-325 Navajo C/R	31-8212031	N4109V	7. 5.86	To G-NAVO 7/90. Canx.
G-BMPW	Cameron N-90 HAFB	1306		. 4.86R	NTU - To G-BTCM 5/86. Canx.
G-BMPX	PA-31-350 Navajo Chieftain		N3543D	29. 5.86	To G-OGRV 6/86. Canx.
		31-7952244			
G-BMPY	DH.82A Tiger Moth	"82619"	ZS-CNR	25. 4.86	
	(C/n 82619 was not built)		SAAF		
G-BMPZ	Cessna 421C Golden Eagle III		N68WX	1. 5.86	To CN-TDF(2) 11/87. Canx 20.11.87.
		421C-0715	N2656X		
G-BMRA	Boeing 757-236	23710		2. 3.87	
	(Line No. 123)				
G-BMRB	Boeing 757-236	23975		25. 9.87	
	(Line No. 145)				
G-BMRC	Boeing 757-236	24072	(N.....)	2.12.87	
	(Line No. 160)		G-BMRC		
G-BMRD	Boeing 757-236	24073	(N.....)	2.12.87	
	(Line No. 166)		G-BMRD		
G-BMRE	Boeing 757-236	24074	(N.....)	2.12.87	
	(Line No. 168)		G-BMRE		
G-BMRF	Boeing 757-236	24101		13. 5.88	
	(Line No. 175)				
G-BMRG	Boeing 757-236	24102		31. 5.88	
	(Line No. 179)				
G-BMRH	Boeing 757-236	24266		21. 2.89	
	(Line No. 210)				
G-BMRI	Boeing 757-236	24267		17. 2.89	
	(Line No. 211)				
G-BMRJ	Boeing 757-236	24268		6. 3.89	
	(Line No. 214)				
G-BMRK	Boeing 757-236	25806		. .86R	NTU - To G-BPEI 3/94. Canx.
	(Line No. 601)				
G-BMRL	Boeing 757-236	25807		. .86R	NTU - To G-BPEJ 4/94. Canx.
	(Line No. 610)				
G-BMRM	Boeing 757-236	25808		. .86R	NTU - To G-BPEK 3/95. Canx.
	(Line No. 665)				
G-BMRN	Boeing 757-236	-		. .86R	NTU - Canx.
G-BMRO	Boeing 757-236	-		. .86R	NTU - Canx.
G-BMRP	Boeing 757-236	-		. .86R	NTU - Canx.
G-BMRR	Boeing 757-236	-		. .86R	NTU - Canx.
G-BMRS	Boeing 757-236	-		. .86R	NTU - Canx.
G-BMRT	Boeing 757-236	-		. .86R	NTU - Canx.
G-BMRU	Boeing 757-236	-		. .86R	NTU - Canx.
G-BMRV	Boeing 757-236	-		. .86R	NTU - Canx.
G-BMRW	Boeing 757-236	-		. .86R	NTU - Canx.
G-BMRX	Boeing 757-236	-		. .86R	NTU - Canx.
G-BMRY	Boeing 757-236	-		. .86R	NTU - Canx.
G-BMRZ	Boeing 757-236	-		. .86R	NTU - Canx.
G-BMSA	Stinson HW-75 Reliant Model 105		G-BCUM	26. 3.86	
		7040	F-BGQO/N21189/NC21189		
G-BMSB	Vickers Supermarine 509 Spitfire		G-ASOZ	3. 5.78	
	Trianer IX	CBAF/7122	Irish Air Corp 158/G-15-171/MJ627		
	(Regd as c/n 6S/R/749433) (Comprises fuselage of G-ASOZ and wings of IAC-159)				
G-BMSC	Evans VP-2 V2-482MSC & PFA/63-10785			25. 8.82	
G-BMSD	PA-28-181 Archer II	28-7690070	EC-CVH	2. 7.86	
			N9646N		
G-BMSE	Valentin Taifun 17E	1082	D-KHVA(17)	20. 5.86	
G-BMSF	PA-38-112 Tomahawk	38-78A0524	N4277E	9. 2.79	
G-BMSG	SAAB 32A Lansen	32028	Fv.32028	22. 7.86	(Stored 7/96 Bruntingthorpe)
			Swedish AF		
G-BMSH	Cessna 425 Corsair	425-0063	9M-AXZ	14. 5.86	To G-DCFB 7/88. Canx.
			N6844H		
G-BMSI	Cameron N-105 HAFB	1282		20. 5.86	Canx as Temp. WFU 2.4.98.
G-BMSJ	ARV1 Super 2	010		8. 5.86	To G-OPIG 10/86. Canx.
G-BMSK	Hoffmann H-36 Dimona	36208		20. 5.86	To G-LIDR 4/96. Canx.
G-BMSL	Clutton FRED Srs.III	PFA/29-11142		19. 5.86	
G-BMSM	Boeing 737-2S3	22279		20. 2.80	To EI-BRB 6/85. Canx 6.6.85.
	(Line No. 650)				
G-BMSN	Aerospatiale SA.315B Lama	2462	N47319	17. 7.86	To HB-XRE. Canx 24.9.86.
G-BMSO	Beechcraft 60 Duke	P-17	I-DUKA	. .	
			F-BRAX/HB-GDO		
G-BMSP	Hughes 369HS (500HS)	34-0574S	C-GOEA	12. 3.87	To G-NUNK 8/91. Canx.
G-BMSR(1)	Boeing 737-2S3	22660		. .82R	NTU - To N5573L/G-BRJP 2/82. Canx.
	(Line No. 849)				
G-BMSR(2)	Grumman G.159 Gulfstream I	128	N910BS	30. 7.86	Canx as TWFU 21.6.93. To F-GIIX 10/93.
			N516DM/N122Y		
G-BMSS	Cessna 310R II	310R-1532	N5265C	. .86R	NTU - Remained as N5256C. Canx.

Regn	Type	c/n	Previous identity	Regn date	Fate or immediate subsequent identity (if known)
G-BMST	Cameron N-31 HAFB	1317		4. 6.86	Canx as WFU 1.5.92. (On loan to Balloon Preservation Group 3/96) (Extant 1/98)
G-BMSU	Cessna 152 II	152-79421	N714TN	29. 8.86	
G-BMSV	PA-31-350 Navajo Chieftain	31-7852064	N27581	11. 6.86	To 5H-IAS 11/90. Canx 14.11.90.
G-BMSW	Cessna T.210M Turbo Centurion	T210-62326	N761KW	22. 5.86	Force landed at Eccles Sewage Works, near Barton on 17.6.92. Canx as destroyed 9.7.92.
G-BMSX	PA-30-160 Twin Comanche	30-881	N502TC N7802Y	1. 7.86	Restored as N502TC 5/94. Canx 27.4.94.
G-BMSY	Cameron A-140 HAFB	1105		11. 6.86	Canx as WFU 29.4.93. To RP-.... 1/95.
G-BMSZ	Cessna 152 II	152-83199	N47254	26. 8.86	To G-OWOW 5/95. Canx.
G-BMTA	Cessna 152 II	152-82864	N89776	27. 8.86	
G-BMTB	Cessna 152 II	152-80672	N25457	19. 8.86	
G-BMTC	Aerospatiale AS.355F1 Twin Squirrel	5302	G-BKUK	9.12.83	To G-BSSM 1/86. Canx.
G-BMTD	Short SD.3-30 Var.100	SH3007	G-BLTD G-NICE/C-GTAV/G-14-3007	12. 9.85	To C-GSKW. Canx 17.3.87.
G-BMTE	Boeing 737-3S3 (Line No. 1336)	23712	EC-EBZ G-BMTF	10. 2.87	To EC-355/EC-EBZ 3/87. Canx 15.12.89.
G-BMTF	Boeing 737-3S3 (Line No. 1341)	23713	EC-ECA EC-429/G-BMTF/EC-ECA/G-BMTF	12. 2.87	To N316AW. Canx 9.1.91.
G-BMTG	Boeing 737-3S3 (Line No. 1345)	23733		27. 2.87	To N314AW 11/90. Canx 21.11.90.
G-BMTH	Boeing 737-3S3 (Line No. 1359)	23734		26. 3.87	To N315AW 12/90. Canx 6.12.90.
G-BMTI	Robin R.3000/120	120		28. 7.86	Damaged in storms at Biggin Hill on 16.10.87. Canx as destroyed 18.5.88.
G-BMTJ	Cessna 152 II	152-85010	N6389P	19. 6.86	
G-BMTK	Cessna 152 II	152-85661	N94387	3. 6.86	To G-KATT 6/93. Canx.
G-BMTL	Reims Cessna F.152 II	1977		11. 9.86	
G-BMTM	Robinson R-22 HP	0242	(N9081S) ZS-HLL	29. 5.86	To EI-BUZ 6/87. Canx 2.6.87.
G-BMTN	Cameron O-77 HAFB	1305		4. 6.86	
G-BMTO	PA-38-112 Tomahawk II	38-81A0051	N25679	28.11.86	
G-BMTP	PA-38-112 Tomahawk	38-79A0034	N2392B	14. 8.86	Damaged in heavy landing Alderney 1.9.92. Canx by CAA 7.3.96. (Stored 12/96)
G-BMTR	PA-28-161 Warrior II	28-8116119	N83179	19. 6.86	
G-BMTS	Cessna 172N Skyhawk II	172-70606	N739KP	17. 7.86	
G-BMTT	PA-28-181 Archer II	28-7990242	N3002K	29. 5.86	NTU - To G-OBUS 8/86. Canx.
G-BMTU	Pitts S-1E Special	PFA/09-10801		4. 6.86	
G-BMTV	BAe Jetstream Srs.3102 (Regd as a Srs.3100)	698	G-31-698	28. 5.86	To N330PX 6/86. Canx 13.6.86.
G-BMTW	PA-31-350 Navajo Chieftain	31-8152028	N4043L	28. 5.86	To N21723 3/94. Canx 2.3.94.
G-BMTX	Cameron V-77 HAFB	733		19. 6.86	
G-BMTY	Colt 77A HAFB	721		4. 6.86	Canx by CAA 19.5.93. To N22EY.
G-BMTZ	Cessna 441 Conquest II	441-0207	N2728D	16. 6.86	To G-FRAX 9/87. Canx.
G-BMUA	Aerospatiale SA.315B Lama	2490	N49524	4. 6.86	To HB-XRF. Canx 29.8.86.
G-BMUB	Aerospatiale SA.315B Lama	2439	N47274	4. 6.86	To D-HBRA. Canx 18.3.88.
G-BMUC	Aerospatiale SA.315B Lama	2498	N49529	4. 6.86	To I-MROS. Canx 8.5.87.
G-BMUD	Cessna 182P Skylane	182-61786	OY-DVS N78847	6.11.81	
G-BMUE	Boeing 727-81 (Line No. 237)	18951	TC-AJU N55AJ/G-BMUE/D-AJAA/OO-JAA/D-AJAA/HP-620/N55AJ/N500JJ/HP-620/JA8316	20. 6.86	To N3211M. Canx 12.12.91.
G-BMUF	Cessna R.182 Skylane RG II	R182-00056	N7342W	11. 6.86	To EI-CAP 4/90. Canx 27.4.90.
G-BMUG	Rutan LongEz	PFA/74A-10987		17. 6.86	
G-BMUH	Montgomerie-Bensen B.8MR Gyrocopter	G/01-1072		5. 6.86	To G-YJET 9/96. Canx.
G-BMUI	Brugger MB.2 Colibri	PFA/43-10980		16. 7.86	To G-KARA 6/95. Canx.
G-BMUJ	Colt Drachenfisch SS HAFB	835		3. 6.86	
G-BMUK	Colt UFO SS HAFB	836		3. 6.86	(Extant 1/94)
G-BMUL	Colt Kindermond SS HAFB	837		3. 6.86	(Extant 1/94)
	(The above three are futuristic special shapes designed by Andre Heller and flown over various capital cities in Europe in 1986)				
G-BMUM	Colt 42A HAFB	821		4. 6.86	Canx 16.11.87 on sale to Finland.
G-BMUN	Cameron Harley 78SS HAFB (Harley Davidson Motorcycle shape)	1188		10. 6.86	
G-BMUO	Cessna A.152 Aerobat	A152-0788	(G-BNCI) G-BMUO/4X-ALJ/N7328L	4. 6.86	
G-BMUP	PA-31-350 Navajo Chieftain	31-8052093	5X-SAS N3581D	4. 6.86	Canx 2.6.89 on sale to Kenya. To N81882.
G-BMUR	Cameron Zero 25SS HAFB	1169		11. 6.86	Canx as WFU 21.10.96.
G-BMUS	Aerospatiale AS.355F2 Twin Squirrel	5347		1. 7.86	To G-FTWO 1/87. Canx.
G-BMUT	PA-34-200T Seneca II	34-7570320	EC-CUH N3935X	23. 1.87	
G-BMUU	Thunder Ax7-77 HAFB	827		1. 8.86	
G-BMUV	Short SD.3-60 Var.200	SH3696	G-14-3696	25. 6.86	To N711PK 7/86. Canx 30.6.86.
G-BMUW	Short SD.3-60 Var.200	SH3697	G-14-3697	25. 6.86	To N711HJ 7/86. Canx 10.7.86.
G-BMUX	Short SD.3-60 Var.200	SH3698	G-14-3698	25. 6.86	To N711MP 7/86. Canx 16.7.86.
G-BMUY	Short SD.3-60 Var.200	SH3699	G-14-3699	25. 6.86	To N377MQ 9/86. Canx 23.9.86.

Regn	Type	c/n	Previous identity	Regn date	Fate or immediate subsequent identity (if known)
G-BMUZ	PA-28-161 Warrior II	28-8016329	EC-DMA	24. 7.86	
			N9559N		
G-BMVA	Scheibe SF-25B Falke	46223	RAFGGA.512	28. 7.86	
			D-KAEN		
G-BMVB	Reims Cessna F.152 II	1974		10. 9.86	
G-BMVC	Beechcraft 95-B55A Baron	TC-2259	N66456	20. 6.86	To G-JOND 6/89. Canx.
G-BMVD	Not allotted.				
G-BMVE	PA-28RT-201 Arrow IV	28R-7918009	N3071K	24. 9.86	To G-OARC 8/99. Canx.
G-BMVF	Bell 212	30666	VH-BEY	11. 6.86	To 5N-BHE 1/96. Canx 26.1.96.
			G-BMVF/VR-BFL/N18093		
G-BMVG	QAC Quickie Q-1	PFA/94-10749		11. 6.86	
G-BMVH	Bell 206B JetRanger III	3591	N3171N	17. 6.86	To VH-UPT 10/87. Canx 10.9.87.
G-BMVI	Cameron O-105 HAFB	1326		19. 6.86	
G-BMVJ	Cessna 172N Skyhawk II	172-72232	N9347E	27. 6.86	
G-BMVK	PA-38-112 Tomahawk	38-79A0148	N404HD	14.11.86	No UK CofA issued. (Stored at Booker still as N404HD) Canx as WFU 4.7.94.
G-BMVL	PA-38-112 Tomahawk	38-79A0033	N2391B	5. 9.86	
G-BMVM	PA-38-112 Tomahawk	38-79A0025	N2359B	5. 9.86	(Active 3/98)
G-BMVN	Cessna A.185F Skywagon	A185-04329	N9308N	30. 6.86	To VT-ENN 1/87. Canx 30.12.86.
G-BMVO	Cameron N-77 HAFB	1309		23. 6.86	
G-BMVP	PA-42-1000 Cheyenne IV	42-5527035	N9534N	2. 7.86	Restored as N9295A. Canx 27.4.87.
			N9295A		
G-BMVR	Benson B.80R Gyrocopter	1074		26. 6.86	Canx as destroyed 1.2.88.
G-BMVS	Cameron Benihana 70SS HAFB	1252		27.10.86	Canx by CAA 19.5.93. (Active 10/93)
	(Also described as Chef's Hat)				
G-BMVT	Thunder Ax7-77A HAFB	102	SE-ZYY	15. 7.86	
	(Extant and flyable 11.88 but not certified)				
G-BMVU	Monnett Moni	PFA/142-10948		14. 8.86	
G-BMVV	Rutan Vari-Viggen	S.512 & PFA/65-10281		24. 8.78	No Permit to Fly issued. Canx by CAA 21.2.96.
G-BMVW	Cameron O-65 HAFB	1331		27. 6.86	
G-BMVX	Morane Saulnier MS.733 Alcyon	12	F-BHCB	8. 7.86	Destroyed in fatal crash at Parham on 1.8.94.
			French Mil F-SDBV		Canx as WFU 30.12.94.
G-BMVY	Beechcraft B200 Super King Air	BB-1257	N2678D	14. 8.86	To N841TT 8/92. Canx 13.8.92.
G-BMVZ	Cameron Cornetto 66SS HAFB	1250	I-....	9. 7.86	To OE-ZCE(1) 10/93. Canx 17.3.93.
			G-BMVZ		
G-BMWA	Hughes 269C (300C)	14-0271	N8998F	1. 7.86	
G-BMWB	Cessna 421C Golden Eagle III	421C-0699	N2655L	4. 7.86	To G-VVIP 7/92. Canx.
G-BMWC	Not allotted.				
G-BMWD	Douglas DC-9-32	47570	YU-AJF	14.10.86	Restored as YU-AJF. Canx 12.4.90.
	(Line No. 684)		G-BMWD/YU-AJF/N1343U		
G-BMWE	ARV1 Super 2	012		1. 7.86	
G-BMWF	ARV1 Super 2	013		1. 7.86	(Fuselage displayed PFA Rally 7/96)
G-BMWG	ARV1 Super 2	014		13. 8.86	Canx by CAA 13.7.94.
G-BMWH	ARV1 Super 2	015		13. 8.86	To PH-ARV 5/89. Canx 22.5.89.
G-BMWI	ARV1 Super 2	016		13. 8.86	Stalled and crashed into woods at St.Vallier de Theiy, near Cannes, France on 19.8.87. Canx as destroyed 12.10.88.
G-BMWJ	ARV1 Super 2	017		1.12.86	(Active 7/97)
G-BMWK	ARV1 Super 2	018		1.12.86	To G-ERMO 1/87. Canx.
G-BMWL	ARV1 Super 2	019		30. 3.87	NTU - To G-BNGY 6/87. Canx 9.6.87.
G-BMWM	ARV1 Super 2	020		30. 3.87	
G-BMWN	Cameron Temple 80SS HAFB	1211		9. 7.86	
G-BMWO	BN-2A-26 Islander	3014	RP-C664	16.12.86	To TC-FBI. Canx 25.3.88.
G-BMWP	PA-34-200T Seneca II	34-7670002	N3946X	18. 7.86	To N375SA 3/99. Canx 12.3.99.
G-BMWR	Rockwell Commander 112A	365	N1365J	23. 9.86	
G-BMWS	Socata TB-20 Trinidad	688		17. 9.86	To G-FIFI 1/87. Canx.
G-BMWT	PA-34-200T Seneca II	34-7870283	N31984	3. 7.86	To G-GUYS 7/87. Canx.
G-BMWU	Cameron N-42 HAFB	1346		22.12.88	
G-BMWV	Putzer Elster B	024	D-EEKB	5. 8.86	(On overhaul 9/97)
			West German AF 97+14/D-EBGI		
G-BMWW	HS.125 Srs.700B	257076	G-5-524	22. 8.86	To G-5-571/XA-LML 9/87. Canx 18.9.87.
			Malawi Army Air Wing MAAW-J1/7Q-YJI/G-5-17		
G-BMWX	Robinson R-22 Beta	0566	N24196	14. 7.86	To G-WIZY 8/97. Canx.
G-BMWY	Bell 206B JetRanger III	3239	N3903B	11. 7.86	To G-TRIK 5/88. Canx.
G-BMWZ	Aerospatiale AS.350B Ecureuil	1176	F-GGDD	22. 9.86	To HB-XTS. Canx 9.5.89.
			G-BMWZ/C-GBED		
G-BMXA	Cessna 152 II	152-80125	N757ZC	14. 7.86	
G-BMXB	Cessna 152 II	152-80996	N48840	14. 7.86	(Crashed on landing Andrewsfield 20.7.91) (On rebuild 9/97)
G-BMXC	Cessna 152 II	152-80416	N24858	14. 7.86	
G-BMXD	Fokker F-27 Friendship 500	10417	TF-FLR	6.10.86	
			HL5210/(HL5206)/PH-FOR		
G-BMXE(1)	BAe 146 Srs.200	E2058	G-5-058	. 7.86R	NTU - To G-ECAL 7/86. Canx.
			N148AC		
G-BMXE(2)	[Was reserved for an unidentified PZL in 1986/7]				
G-BMXF	Valentin Taifun 17E	1086	D-KHVA(18)	18. 8.86	To EC-EZM. Canx 21.9.90.
G-BMXG	Bell 206L-1 Long Ranger	45553	N108WE	. .86R	NTU - To G-FIMI 10/86. Canx.
			N3889C/ZS-HJP/N3889C		
G-BMXH	Robinson R-22 HP	0233	N9075D	27. 8.86	To N92236 1/96. Canx 24.10.95.
G-BMXI	Robinson R-22 HP	0218	N9074K	. 7.86R	NTU - To G-CHIL 9/86. Canx.
G-BMXJ	Reims Cessna F.150L Aerobat	0853	F-BUBA	18. 7.86	

Regn	Type	c/n	Previous identity	Regn date	Fate or immediate subsequent identity (if known)
G-BMXK	Boeing 747-211B (Line No. 368)	21517	C-GXRD	. 7.86R	NTU - To G-NIGB 3/87. Canx.
G-BMXL	PA-38-112 Tomahawk	38-80A0018	N25060	4. 9.86	
G-BMXM	Colt 180A HAFB	838	(C-....) G-BMXM	28. 7.86	Canx as WFU 13.5.91.
G-BMXN	Lake LA-4-200 Buccaneer	934	EC-DHI N2872P	30. 7.87	To OH-MXN. Canx 2.2.89.
G-BMXO	Beechcraft C90 King Air	LJ-630	N1974H N197AF/N1947H	21. 8.86	To N840SW. Canx 23.10.89.
G-BMXP	Short SD.3-60 Var.200	SH3700	G-14-3700	19. 8.86	To N378MQ 9/86. Canx 23.9.86.
G-BMXR	Short SD.3-60 Var.200	SH3701	G-14-3701	19. 8.86	To N379MQ 9/86. Canx 23.9.86.
G-BMXS	Short SD.3-60 Var.200	SH3702	G-14-3702	19. 8.86	NTU - To N380MQ 9/86. Canx 23.9.86.
G-BMXT	Short SD.3-60 Var.200	SH3703	G-14-3703	19. 8.86	NTU - To N381MQ 10/86. Canx 24.10.86.
G-BMXU	Short SD.3-60 Var.200	SH3704	G-14-3704	19. 8.86	To N382MQ 10/86. Canx 24.10.86.
G-BMXV	Cessna 401	401-0...		. .86R	NTU - Canx.
G-BMXW	DHC.6-310 Twin Otter	613	SE-GEF	22.10.86	To C-FQOL. Canx 2.9.93.
G-BMXX	Cessna 152 II	152-84953	N5469P	10. 9.86	
G-BMXY	Scheibe SF-25B	46247	D-KAVG	19. 8.86	CofA expired 12.12.89. Canx by CAA 26.10.92.
G-BMXZ	Colt 77A HAFB	847		13. 8.86	Canx 30.12.86 on sale to Zimbabwe.
G-BMYA	Colt 56A HAFB	864		13. 8.86	Canx as WFU 29.4.97.
G-BMYB	Socata TB-10 Tobago	298	EI-BOF G-HILT	. 8.86R	NTU - Restored as G-HILT 8/86. Canx.
G-BMYC	Socata TB-10 Tobago	696		1. 9.86	
G-BMYD	Beechcraft A36 Bonanza	E-2350		28.11.86	
G-BMYE	BAe 146 Srs.200	E2008	(G-OHAP) G-WAUS/G-5-146/G-WISC	15. 8.86	Reduced to spares in 5/95 at Bristol-Filton. Canx as WFU 19.5.95.
G-BMYF	Bensen B.8M Gyrocopter	PE-01		18. 8.86	
G-BMYG	Reims Cessna FA.152 Aerobat	0365	OO-JCA (OO-JCC)/PH-AXG	23.10.86	
G-BMYH	Rotorway 133 Executive	JN-01		11. 9.86	Destroyed in fatal crash in woodland at Coalport on 28.3.92. Canx as destroyed 18.9.92.
G-BMYI	American Aviation AA-5 Traveller	AA5-0568	EI-BJF F-BVRM/N9568L	1. 9.86	
G-BMYJ	Cameron V-65 HAFB	726		8. 9.86	
G-BMYK	BAe ATP	2003		18. 9.86	To G-ERIN 12/93. Canx.
G-BMYL	BAe ATP	2004		18. 9.86	To G-LOGE 10/91. Canx.
G-BMYM	BAe ATP	2002		18. 9.86	To G-MAUD 12/93. Canx.
G-BMYN	Colt 77A HAFB	873		2. 9.86	
G-BMYO	Cameron V-65 HAFB	610		3. 9.86	Canx by CAA 29.1.90.
G-BMYP	Fairey Gannet AEW.3	F.9461	8610M XL502	16. 9.86	(Stored 6/99 Sandtoft)
G-BMYR	Robinson R-22 HP	0209	ZS-HLG	19. 9.86	To G-OTED 1/96. Canx.
G-BMYS	Thunder Ax7-77Z HAFB	887		3.11.86	
G-BMYT	Boeing 727-51 (Line No. 128)	18802	TC-AJZ N802SC/(N101MU)/G-BMYT/N837N/N466US/(N406US)	8. 9.86	Stored in 9/89 at Istanbul, Turkey as TC-AJZ. Broken up in 1/92. Canx as WFU 12.12.91.
G-BMYU	Wassmer Jodel D.120 Paris-Nice	289	F-BMYU	23. 6.78	
G-BMYV	Bensen B.8M Gyrocopter	RC-001 & G/01-1041		23. 9.86	No Permit to Fly issued. Canx by CAA 21.2.96.
G-BMYW	Hughes 269C (300C)	14-0272	N8999F	22. 9.86	To G-LEMJ 8/98. Canx.
G-BMYX	HS.125 Srs.700B	257178	G-5-530 4W-ACM/G-5-14	6.11.86	To G-5-570/VH-LMP 10/87. Canx 28.8.87.
G-BMYY	Mooney M.20J	24-3010	N58117	. .86R	NTU - Remained as N58117. Canx.
G-BMYZ	Hughes 269C (300C)	113-0256	N8996F	22.10.86	To G-BWWJ 2/87. Canx.
G-BMZA	Air Command 503 Modac (Probably c/n 0389)	0589		11. 2.87	
G-BMZB	Cameron N-77 HAFB	1370		30.10.86	
G-BMZC	Cessna 421C Golden Eagle III	421C-0515	N555WV N555WW/N885WW/N885EC/N88541	7.10.86	To G-GILT 7/97. Canx.
G-BMZD	Beechcraft C90 King Air	LJ-667	N9067S	13.10.86	To N888GN 3/97. Canx 19.3.97.
G-BMZE	Socata TB-9 Tampico	708		5.12.86	
G-BMZF	WSK-Mielec LiM 2 (MiG-15bis)	1B01420	1420 Polish AF	18.12.86	Canx as WFU 23.2.90. (On display 3/96 RNAS Yeovilton)
G-BMZG	QAC Quickie Q2	PFA/94A-10919		1.10.86	
G-BMZH	Cameron A-140 HAFB	1376		11.12.86	Canx as WFU 7.4.92.
G-BMZI	Fokker F-27 Friendship 100	10106	G-IOMA D-BOBY(3)/EC-BNJ/PH-FSH/JY-ADD/PI-C530/EI-AKB/PH-FAB	21.10.86	Canx 13.5.87 on sale to West Germany. To D-BAKO 4/90.
G-BMZJ	Thunder & Colt 400A HAFB (Despite regn date this was flown as the test vehicle for the Virgin Transatlantic Ocean balloon in Spain in early 1987)	891		1. 5.91	To N42861 3/98. Canx 22.12.97.
G-BMZK	Airbus A.300B4-203	076	D-AIBD F-WZEI	21. 4.87	To EC-273/EC-EON. Canx 28.4.89.
G-BMZL	Airbus A.300B4-203	077	D-AIBF F-WZEJ	19. 5.87	To EC-274/EC-EOO. Canx 28.4.89.
G-BMZM	Rand Robinson KR-2 (Originally regd with c/n PFA/129-10071)	PFA/129-11005		14.10.86	Canx by CAA 2.9.91.
G-BMZN	Everett Gyroplane 1	008		13.11.86	
G-BMZO	Everett Gyroplane 1	009		. .86R	NTU - Canx.
G-BMZP	Everett Gyroplane 1	010		14.11.86	
G-BMZR	Everett Gyroplane 1	011		. .86R	NTU - Canx.
G-BMZS	Everett Gyroplane 1	012		13.11.86	
G-BMZT	Price Ax7-77S HAFB	002		. .86R	NTU - Canx.
G-BMZU	Boeing 727-30 (Line No. 52)	18365	HZ-TA1 N16767/D-ABIH	25.11.86	To N96B. Canx 7.10.87.

Regn	Type	c/n	Previous identity	Regn date	Fate or immediate subsequent identity (if known)
G-BMZV	Cessna 172P Skyhawk II	172-75099	N54984	10.11.86	Fatal crash 200m W of Compton Abbas 21.11.96. Canx as destroyed 27.3.97.
G-BMZW	Bensen B.8MR Gyrocopter	G/01-1021		16.10.86	
G-BMZX	Wolf W-11 Boredom Fighter	PFA/146-11042		31.10.86	
G-BMZY	Cameron Elephant 77SS HAFB	1363		20.10.86	To C-FBKZ. Canx 26.1.88.
G-BMZZ	Stephens Akro Laser Z	V.57	(HB-...) G-BMZZ/VH-AUZ	10.11.86	
G-BNAA	Vickers 806 Viscount	311	C-GWPY G-AOYH	22. 3.85	WFU & stored in 5/87 at Southend. CofA expired 22.3.88. Canx as WFU 26.2.91.
G-BNAB	Gulfstream American GA-7 Cougar	GA7-0114	G-BGYP	16. 2.84	To G-GENN 12/94. Canx.
G-BNAC	Jurca MJ-100 Spitfire	MJ100-1		7.11.86	Canx by CAA 2.9.91.
G-BNAD	Rand Robinson KR-2	PFA/129-11077		10.11.86	(Stored Ottringham, nr.Hull 7/90)
G-BNAE	PBN BN-2A-26 Islander	2032		21.10.86	To B-11123. Canx 7.7.87.
G-BNAF	PBN BN-2A-20 Islander	2035		21.10.86	To N9754N. Canx 4.12.86.
G-BNAG	Colt 105A HAFB	906		31.10.86	
G-BNAH	Colt Paper Bag SS HAFB	865	N87RT G-BNAH	12.11.86	CofA expired 14.6.96. Canx by CAA 4.8.98. (Was based in USA)
G-BNAI	Wolf W-11 Boredom Fighter	PFA/146-11083		31.10.86	
G-BNAJ	Cessna 152 II	152-82527	C-GZWF (N69173)	3.11.86	
G-BNAK	Thunder Ax8-90 HAFB	889		2.12.86	To C-GJJX 3/87. Canx 25.3.87.
G-BNAL	Fokker F-27 Friendship 600	10334	VH-FNU PH-EXC/F-BOOD/PH-FLE	28.11.86	To PT-TVA 9/95. Canx 22.9.95.
G-BNAM	Colt 8A HAFB	894		1.12.86	Canx as WFU 3.6.91.
G-BNAN	Cameron V-65 HAFB	1333		28.10.86	(Extant 2/97)
G-BNAO	Colt AS-105 Hot Air Airship	897		28.10.86	
G-BNAP	Colt 240A HAFB	898		28.10.86	Canx as destroyed 6.4.98. (Based in Germany)
G-BNAR	Taylor JT.1 Monoplane	PFA/55-10569		14.11.86	(Status uncertain)
G-BNAS	Aerospatiale AS.350B Ecureuil	1019	C-GMLT	3.11.86	To D-HMFG. Canx 19.2.88.
G-BNAT	Beechcraft C90 King Air	LJ-614	G-OMET G-COTE/G-BBKN	30. 4.86	Fatal crash near East Midlands Airport on 25.1.88. Canx as destroyed 3.10.88.
G-BNAU	Cameron V-65 HAFB	1395		13.11.86	
G-BNAV	Rutan Cozy	PFA/159-11181		17.10.86	No Permit issued. Canx by CAA 8.7.91.
G-BNAW	Cameron V-65 HAFB	1366		24.10.86	
G-BNAX	Boeing 767-205 (Line No. 81)	23057	N90549 PP-VNL/N767BE/LN-SUV/N57008	29. 5.87	To N650TW 10/87. Canx 9.10.87.
G-BNAY	Grob G-109B	6406	N920BG D-KGRO	28.11.86	To D-KRHA 5/94. Canx 12.4.94.
G-BNAZ	Socata TB-20 Trinidad	712		20.11.86	To HB-KCN. Canx 5.6.89.
G-BNBA	Short SD.3-60 Var.200	SH3705	G-14-3705	7.11.86	NTU - To SE-IXE 11/86. Canx 6.11.86.
G-BNBB	Short SD.3-60 Var.200	SH3706	G-14-3706	7.11.86	NTU - To N383MQ 11/86. Canx 7.11.86.
G-BNBC	Short SD.3-60 Var.200	SH3707	G-14-3707	7.11.86	To N385MQ 11/86. Canx 24.11.86.
G-BNBD	Short SD.3-60 Var.200	SH3708	G-14-3708	7.11.86	To G-OGCI 8/91. Canx.
G-BNBE	Short SD.3-60 Var.200	SH3709	G-14-3709	7.11.86	To N386MQ 11/86. Canx 24.11.86.
G-BNBF	Short SD.3-60 Var.200	SH3710	G-14-3710	7.11.86	To N387MQ 12/86. Canx 8.12.86.
G-BNBG	Short SD.3-60 Var.200	SH3711	G-14-3711	7.11.86	To N384MQ 12/86. Canx 8.12.86.
G-BNBH	Hughes 269C (300C)	1078		6. 8.82	To D-HEKO 7/84. Canx 3.7.84.
G-BNBI	Aerospatiale AS.355F1 Twin Squirrel	5024	ZK-HMS G-BNBI/C-GKHO	28.11.86	To G-CFLT 8/89. Canx.
G-BNBJ	Aerospatiale AS.355F1 Twin Squirrel	5077	C-GLKH	28.11.86	To G-CMMM 3/89. Canx.
G-BNBK	Aerospatiale AS.355F1 Twin Squirrel	5043	C-GBKH	28.11.86	To G-LECA 2/87. Canx.
G-BNBL	Thunder Ax7-77 HAFB	910		7. 1.87	
G-BNBM	Colt 90A HAFB	912		21.11.86	To D-ONBM 8/98. Canx 22.5.98.
G-BNBN	Lockheed P-38 Lightning Scale Replica	RCC-1		13.11.86	Canx by CAA 2.9.91.
G-BNBO	HS.125 Srs.700B	257112	G-5-536 D-CMVW	13.11.86	To G-5-553/9M-SSL 5/87. Canx 25.3.87.
G-BNBP	Colt Snowflake SS HAFB	913		21.11.86	Canx as WFU 19.7.90. (Stored 8/95)
G-BNBR	Cameron N-90 HAFB	1412		2.12.86	
G-BNBS	Enstrom F-28C	431	SE-HIL	18. 3.87	To G-SHDD 8/88. Canx.
G-BNBT	Robinson R-22 Beta	0601	N2530W	28.11.86	To F-GILS 12/89. Canx 27.11.89.
G-BNBU	Bensen B.8MV Gyrocopter	G/01-1070		1.12.86	
G-BNBV	Thunder Ax7-77 HAFB	915		2.12.86	
G-BNBW	Thunder Ax7-77 HAFB	914		11.12.86	
G-BNBX	PA-28RT-201T Turbo Arrow IV	28R-8231063	N8257H	5.12.86	To I-PGAR. Canx 23.4.87.
G-BNBY	Beechcraft 95-B55A Baron	TC-1347	G-AXXR	14. 2.83	
G-BNBZ	LET L-200D Morava	171329	D-GGDC EI-AOY/(D-GLIN)/EI-AOY/OK-SHB	16.12.86	
G-BNCA	English Electric Lightning F.2A	95113	G-27-239 8346M/XN734	10.12.86	No CofA issued. Stored at Cranfield. Canx by CAA 12.9.91.
G-BNCB	Cameron V-77 HAFB	1401		2.12.86	
G-BNCC	Thunder Ax7-77 HAFB	924		11.12.86	
G-BNCD	Socata TB-20 Trinidad	343	F-GDBY	5.12.86	To F-GFFL 5/89. Canx 28.1.88.
G-BNCE	Grumman G.159 Gulfstream I	009	N436M N436/N436M/N43M/N709G	7. 4.87	WFU in 10/91 at Aberdeen due to corrosion; stripped for spares. CofA expired 9.4.92. Canx as WFU 4.5.93. (Open store 8/96)
G-BNCF	Cameron DP-60 Hot Air Airship	1353		11.12.86	To G-INCF 9.1.87. Canx.

Regn	Type	c/n	Previous identity	Regn date	Fate or immediate subsequent identity (if known)
G-BNCG	QAC Quickie Q.2	PFA/94A-10992		27. 1.87	Badly damaged on take-off from Thruxton on 21.8.97. Canx by CAA 12.1.98.
G-BNCH	Cameron V-77 HAFB	1398		11.12.86	
G-BNCI	Cessna A.152 Aerobat	A152-0788	G-BMUO 4X-ALJ/N7328L	10. 4.87	NTU - Remained as G-BMUO. Canx 24.4.87 as regd in error.
G-BNCJ	Cameron V-77 HAFB	815		16.12.86	
G-BNCK	Cameron V-77 HAFB	1420		7. 1.87	
G-BNCL	Westland WG.13 Lynx HAS.2	WG/05-01	A2657 XX469	. .86R	(Stored 1/90) (Reportedly sold to Lancashire Fire Brigade HQ in early 1990) Canx /94.
G-BNCM	Cameron N-77 HAFB	1388		16.12.86	
G-BNCN	Glaser-Dirks DG-400	4-198		22. 1.87	
G-BNCO	PA-38-112 Tomahawk	38-79A0472	N2482F	8. 1.87	
G-BNCP	Colt AS-105 Hot Air Airship	886		9. 1.87	To ZK-ALE(2) 5/87. Canx 15.5.87.
G-BNCR	PA-28-161 Warrior II	28-8016111	(G-PDMT) ZS-LGW/N8103D	10.12.86	
G-BNCS	Cessna 180	30022	OO-SPA D-ENUX/N2822A	7. 1.87	
G-BNCT	Boeing 737-3Q8 (Line No. 1375)	23766	N1716B	24. 4.87	To N315SC. Canx 14.12.87.
G-BNCU	Thunder Ax7-77 HAFB	928		7. 1.87	
G-BNCV	Bensen B.8 Gyrocopter	LWC-01		8. 1.87	(Extant 6/96)
G-BNCW	Boeing 767-204 (Line No. 184)	23807	N6005C	4. 8.87	To VH-RMO(3) 5/96. Canx 21.5.96.
G-BNCX	Hawker Hunter T.7	41H/695454	XL621	9. 1.87	(Stored at Hurn with Permit expired 28.3.87) Canx as WFU 1.3.93. (On display Brooklands 3/99, with 'large bits' reportedly noted at Hurn 17.2.99)
G-BNCY	Fokker F-27 Friendship 500	10558	VH-FCE PH-EXH	9. 2.87	DBR at Guernsey, Channel Islands on 8.12.97. Sold for scrap in 1/98. Canx as destroyed 19.2.98.
G-BNCZ	Rutan LongEz	PFA/74A-10723		8. 1.87	(Damaged on landing Sherburn 12.2.94) (Stored 4/97)
G-BNDA	Bell 222	47031	A40-CG	9. 1.87	To G-OSEB 20.2.87. Canx.
G-BNDB	Bell 222	47041	A40-CH	9. 1.87	To G-JLBZ 24.2.87. Canx.
G-BNDC	DHC.7-102 Dash Seven	101	ZK-NEW C-GFQL	6. 3.87	To OY-CTC. Canx 26.4.88.
G-BNDD	PA-31-310 Turbo Navajo	31-7300967	G-BBMK N7571L	28.10.86	To OY-MST. Canx 18.8.92.
G-BNDE	PA-38-112 Tomahawk	38-79A0363	N2541D	13. 1.87	To EI-BUR 7/87. Canx 9.7.87.
G-BNDF	PA-38-112 Tomahawk	38-79A0186	N2439C	13. 1.87	To EI-BUS 7/87. Canx 9.7.87.
G-BNDG	Wallis WA-201/R Srs.1	K/220/X		22. 1.87	Permit expired 3.3.88. (Stored 2/99 Reymerston Hall)
G-BNDH	Colt 21A Cloudhopper HAFB	909		2.12.86	Canx as WFU 29.4.97.
G-BNDI	Short SD.3-60 Var.200	SH3712	G-OBLK G-BNDI/G-14-3712	8. 1.87	Restored as G-OBLK 4/91. Canx.
G-BNDJ	Short SD.3-60 Var.200	SH3713	G-14-3713	8. 1.87	To G-OBOH 20.1.87. Canx.
G-BNDK	Short SD.3-60 Var.200	SH3714	G-OBHD G-BNDK/G-14-3714	8. 1.87	Restored as G-OBHD 5/91. Canx.
G-BNDL	Short SD.3-60 Var.200	SH3715	G-14-3715	8. 1.87	To N711PM. Canx 3.3.87.
G-BNDM	Short SD.3-60 Var.300	SH3716	EI-CMG N360AR/G-BNDM/G-14-3716	8. 1.87	To OY-MUG 10/97. Canx 24.9.97.
G-BNDN	Cameron V-77 HAFB	1443		8. 1.87	
G-BNDO	Cessna 152 II	152-84574	N5387M	11. 2.87	
G-BNDP	Brugger MB.2 Colibri	PFA/43-10956		8. 1.87	(Stored 11/95)
G-BNDR(1)	BAe 146 Srs.200A	E2062	G-5-062	. 1.87R	NTU - To N406XV 3/87. Canx.
G-BNDR(2)	Socata TB-10 Tobago	740		12. 2.87	
G-BNDS	PA-31-350 Navajo Chieftain	31-8052038	N131PP N3550N	27. 1.87	To G-OLDA 1/97. Canx.
G-BNDT	Brugger MB.2 Colibri	PFA/43-10981		8. 1.87	
G-BNDU	Thunder Ax7-77 HAFB	895		4. 2.87	To I-RIKY. Canx 5.8.87.
G-BNDV	Cameron N-77 HAFB	1427		25. 2.87	
G-BNDW	DH.82A Tiger Moth	3942	N6638	10.12.86	(Components stored Shobdon Aircraft Maintenance 3/96)
G-BNDX	HS.125 Srs.600B	256012	G-BAYT 5N-ALX/G-BAYT/G-5-17	30. 9.83	Restored as G-BAYT 12/88. Canx.
G-BNDY(1)	Cessna 425 Conquest I	425-0234	N1262K	. .87R	NTU - Remained as N1262K. Canx.
G-BNDY(2)	Cessna 425 Conquest I	425-0236	N1262T	2. 6.87	
G-BNDZ	Cessna 441 Conquest II	441-0353	N1213R	20. 3.87	To N321AF. Canx 3.12.87.
G-BNEA	BN-2A-6 Islander	206	SE-FTA G-51-206	2. 2.78	To PH-PAR 6/80. Canx 10.6.80.
G-BNEB	PBN BN-2A-26 Islander	2037		20. 1.87	To JA5284 4/87. Canx 15.4.87.
G-BNEC	PBN BN-2A-26 Islander	2038		20. 1.87	To JA5285 5/87. Canx 30.4.87.
G-BNED	PA-22-135 Tri Pacer	22-1640	OO-JEF N3385A	26. 1.87	(Stored at W.A.Taylors .94)
G-BNEE	PA-28R-201 Arrow III	28R-7837084	N630DJ N9518N	28. 1.87	
G-BNEF	PA-31-310 Turbo Navajo B	31-7300970	N7574L	21. 4.87	To G-ISFC 3/94. Canx.
G-BNEG	Norman NAC-6 Fieldmaster 65	6001		30. 1.87	To G-NACL 4/87. Canx.
G-BNEH	BAe 125 Srs.800B	258078	G-5-713 G-BNEH/G-5-544	4. 2.87	To ZS-FSI(2) 5/92. Canx 6.5.92.
G-BNEI	PA-34-200T Seneca II	34-7870429	N3058K VQ-LBC/N9646N	12. 6.87	
G-BNEJ	PA-38-112 Tomahawk II	38-81A0055	N25690	26. 3.87	Badly damaged in gales Tatenhill 25.1.90. Canx by CAA 20.8.90.
G-BNEK	PA-38-112 Tomahawk II	38-82A0081	N9096A	28. 1.87	
G-BNEL	PA-28-161 Warrior II	28-7916314	N2246U	27. 4.87	
G-BNEM	Robinson R-22 HP	0240	N240RH C-FCVL	2. 3.87	Restored as N240RH 9/90. Canx 28.8.90.

Regn	Type	c/n	Previous identity	Regn date	Fate or immediate subsequent identity (if known)
G-BNEN	PA-34-200T Seneca II	34-8070262	N8232V	18. 2.87	
G-BNEO	Cameron V-77 HAFB	1408		9. 2.87	
G-BNEP(1)	Boeing 757-236	22185	(G-BIKO)	. .82R	NTU - To N8294V/G-BPGW 3/84. Canx.
	(Line No. 34)				
G-BNEP(2)	PA-34-220T Seneca III	34-8133090	N8386Z	19. 5.87	To VT-KCG 8/94. Canx 25.7.94.
G-BNER	PA-34-200T Seneca II	34-7870088	N2590M	27. 2.87	To EI-CMT 4/96. Canx 12.4.96.
G-BNES	Cameron V-77 HAFB	1426		19. 2.87	
G-BNET	Cameron O-84 HAFB	1368		22. 1.87	
G-BNEU	Colt 105A HAFB	944		29. 2.87	To SE-ZGF 4/95. Canx 20.5.94.
G-BNEV	Viking Dragonfly	PFA/139-10935		28.11.86	(Nearing completion 6/92)
G-BNEW	Cessna 421C Golden Eagle II	421C-1237	N2724L	2. 2.87	To N811SW. Canx 5.4.89.
G-BNEX	Cameron O-120 HAFB	1414		3. 4.87	
G-BNEY	Colt 77A HAFB	1040		27. 2.87	To I-MMAP. Canx 6.8.87.
G-BNEZ	Cessna 421C Golden Eagle III	421C-0168	N87386	16. 3.87	To G-DARR 8/92. Canx.
G-BNFA	Short SD.3-60 Var.300	SH3717	EI-BTH	17. 2.87	To G-BWMZ 7/94. Canx.
			G-14-3717/G-BNFA/G-14-3717		
G-BNFB	Short SD.3-60 Var.300	SH3718	EI-BTI	17. 2.87	To VQ-TSK. Canx 20.12.96.
			G-14-3718/G-BNFB/G-14-3718		
G-BNFC	Short SD.3-60 Var.300	SH3719	G-14-3719	17. 2.87	To G-14-3719/EI-BTJ 2/87. Canx 25.3.87.
G-BNFD	Short SD.3-60 Var.300	SH3720	EI-BTK	17. 2.87	To VH-SUM 3/95. Canx 6.4.95.
			G-14-3720/G-BNFD/G-14-3720		
G-BNFE	Short SD.3-60 Var.300	SH3721	G-14-3721	17. 2.87	To N121PC 5/87. Canx 24.6.87.
G-BNFF	Douglas DC-9-33RC	47192	PH-DNN	. .87R	NTU - To N35UA 3/87. Canx.
	(Line No. 287)		N8963U		
G-BNFG(1)	BAe 146 Srs.200	E2067		. .87R	NTU - To (N146AC)/G-5-067/G-TNTB 3/87. Canx.
G-BNFG(2)	Cameron O-77 HAFB	1416		5. 3.87	
G-BNFH	Cameron Box 75SS HAFB	1402		20. 2.87	To HB-BKN 9/87. Canx 24.9.87.
G-BNFI	Cessna 150J	150-69417	N50588	8. 1.87	
G-BNFJ	Cameron Pump 70SS HAFB	1425		20. 2.87	To C-FBKX. Canx 27.1.88.
G-BNFK	Cameron Egg 89SS HAFB	1436		20. 2.87	
	(Faberge Rosebud Egg shape)				
G-BNFL	WHE Airbuggy	1002	G-AXXN	12. 8.85	Damaged on landing at Carlisle on 2.4.88.
					Canx as WFU 6.2.97.
G-BNFM	Colt 21A Cloudhopper HAFB	668		5. 3.87	
G-BNFN	Cameron N-105 HAFB	1442		13. 3.87	
G-BNFO	Cameron V-77 HAFB	816		5. 3.87	
G-BNFP	Cameron O-84 HAFB	1474		29. 4.87	
G-BNFR	Cessna 152 II	152-82035	N67817	8. 4.87	
G-BNFS	Cessna 152 II	152-83899	N5545B	10. 4.87	
G-BNFT	Hawker Hunter T.53	41H-693833	G-9-429	27. 2.87	To N10271 5/87. Canx 16.4.87.
			R.Danish AF 35-271/R.Danish AF ET-271.		
G-BNFU	Colt 105A HAFB	983	(D-O...)	3. 3.87	Canx by CAA 10.5.95; but given export CofA.
			G-BNFU		
G-BNFV	Robin DR.400/120 Dauphin 80	1767		4. 3.87	
G-BNFW	HS.125 Srs.700B	257100	G-5-549	9. 3.87	To N858JR 5/98. Canx 11.5.98.
			D-CLVW/G-5-19		
G-BNFX	Colt 21A Cloudhopper HAFB	1032		11. 3.87	To HB-... Canx 7.5.91.
G-BNFY	Cameron N-77 HAFB	1449		11. 3.87	CofA expired 30.4.95. Canx 30.3.98 as WFU.
G-BNFZ	Nord 3202B-1	78	G-BIZK	12. 3.87	NTU - Canx 14.4.87 as regd in error. Remained as G-BIZK.
			N2255E/ALAT		
G-BNGA	PBN BN-2A-26 Islander	2029	(G-BIUH)	21.10.86	To B-11125 9/87. Canx 23.9.87.
G-BNGB	PA-34-200 Seneca	34-7250348	F-BTQT	12. 3.87	To N506DM. Canx 29.5.87.
			(F-BTMT(3))		
G-BNGC	Robinson R-22 HP	0224	N9073H	21. 4.87	Crashed at Old Warden on 20.8.90. Canx by CAA 5.11.90.
G-BNGD	Cessna 152 II	152-83284	N48120	18. 3.87	Fatal crash 21.12.97 nr Creetown. Canx as destroyed 21.5.98
G-BNGE	Auster AOP.6	1925	7704M	18. 3.87	
			TW536		
G-BNGF	DHC.7-102 Dash Seven	103	ZK-NEX	9. 4.87	Canx 29.7.88 on sale to Canada. To N773BE.
G-BNGG	BAC One-Eleven Srs.F 487GK	BAC.267	YR-BCR	. .87R	NTU - To G-TOMO 9/87. Canx.
G-BNGH	Boeing 707-321C	18718	(G-CHGN)	3. 2.86	To 5N-MAS 1/92. Canx 28.2.92.
	(Line No. 368)		G-BFZF/N794RN/N794PA/N794EP/N794/N794PA		
G-BNGI	Cameron Can 90SS HAFB	1394		23. 3.87	Canx 12.5.87 on sale to Australia! To OE-KZD.
G-BNGJ	Cameron V-77 HAFB	1487		18. 3.87	
G-BNGK	Boeing 737-2L9	22406	OY-APP	13. 5.87	To F-GEXI 12/87. Canx 6.11.87.
	(Line No. 690)		N8295V		
G-BNGL	Boeing 737-3Y0	23924		12. 4.88	To XA-SEM(2) 12/93. Canx 16.12.93.
	(Line No. 1542)				
G-BNGM	Boeing 737-3Y0	23925		12. 4.88	To XA-SEO 12/93. Canx 16.12.93.
	(Line No. 1544)				
G-BNGN	Cameron N-77 HAFB	817		3. 4.87	(Extant 2/97)
G-BNGO	Thunder Ax7-77 HAFB	971		26. 3.87	
G-BNGP	Colt 77A HAFB	1033		30. 3.87	
G-BNGR	PA-38-112 Tomahawk	38-79A0479	N2492F	26. 3.87	
G-BNGS	PA-38-112 Tomahawk	38-78A0701	N2463A	26. 3.87	Damaged in transit to UK 5/87. Fuselage stored at Carlisle-Crosby 5/98.
G-BNGT	PA-28-181 Archer II	28-8590036	N149AV	29. 4.87	
			N9559N		
G-BNGU	Cameron Golf 76SS HAFB	1396		23. 3.87	To C-GIFI. Canx 21.4.88.
G-BNGV	ARV1 Super 2	021		4. 6.87	(Badly damaged when struck by Thruster T.300 G-MVZD at Popham on 24.5.92, whilst parked)
G-BNGW	ARV1 Super 2	022		4. 6.87	(Stored 6/94)

Regn	Type	c/n	Previous identity	Regn date	Fate or immediate subsequent identity (if known)
G-BNGX	ARV1 Super 2	023		6. 7.87	(Stored 2/96)
G-BNGY	ARV1 Super 2	019	(G-BMWL)	4. 6.87	
G-BNGZ	ARV1 Super 2	024		13. 7.87	To G-OTAL 9/87. Canx.
G-BNHA	ARV1 Super 2	025		13. 7.87	To G-POOL 8/87. Canx.
G-BNHB	ARV1 Super 2	026		13. 7.87	
G-BNHC	ARV1 Super 2	027		14. 8.87	Crashed in forced landing near Perth 4.8.96. Canx 24.3.98 as destroyed.
G-BNHD	ARV1 Super 2	028		14. 8.87	CofA expired 31.3.95. Canx by CAA 10.3.98.
G-BNHE	ARV1 Super 2	029		14. 8.87	Extensively damaged by gales 25.12.97 at Liverpool.
G-BNHF	Cameron N-31 HAFB	1400		2. 2.87	To OO-... 7/95. Canx 25.7.95.
G-BNHG(1)	Boeing 757-236 (Line No. 57)	23227	(G-CJIG) N1779B	. .85R	NTU - To G-BLVH 2/85. Canx.
G-BNHG(2)	PA-38-112 Tomahawk II	38-82A0030	N91435	23. 3.87	
G-BNHH	Thunder Ax7-77 HAFB	1053		14. 5.87	CofA expired 9.4.92. Canx as WFU 4.8.98.
G-BNHI	Cameron V-77 HAFB	1249		26. 3.87	
G-BNHJ	Cessna 152 II	152-81249	N49418	4. 6.87	
G-BNHK	Cessna 152 II	152-85355	N80161	30. 3.87	
G-BNHL	Colt Beer Glass 90SS HAFB	1042		24. 3.87	Loaned to Balloon Preservation Group. (Extant 1/98) Canx as WFU 22.6.98.
G-BNHM	Thunder Ax8-105 HAFB	1044		24. 3.87	To N420TC 11/92. Canx 10.4.92.
G-BNHN	Colt Ariel Bottle SS HAFB	1045		30. 3.87	Canx as WFU 24.1.92. (Extant 4/93)
G-BNHO	Thunder Ax7-77 HAFB	1057		30. 3.87	
G-BNHP	Saffery S.330 HAFB (Toy)	9		21. 3.78	
G-BNHR	Cameron V-77 HAFB (C/n conflicts with A-210 PH-BLB)	1086		19. 5.87	Canx as WFU 23.4.98.
G-BNHS	Thunder Ax7-77 HAFB	1009		13. 4.87	Canx as destroyed 11.9.92.
G-BNHT	Alpavia Fournier RF-3	80	(D-KITX) G-BNHT/F-BMTO	13. 4.87	
G-BNHU	Thunder Ax10-180 HAFB	937		31. 3.87	Canx by CAA 23.1.89. To F-GHNL 1/91.
G-BNHV	Thunder Ax10-180 HAFB	938		31. 3.87	Canx by CAA 23.1.89. To F-GHNM 5/89.
G-BNHW	Thunder Ax10-180 HAFB	939		31. 3.87	Canx by CAA 23.1.89. To F-GHNK 1/91.
G-BNHX	Thunder Ax10-180 HAFB	940		31. 3.87	Canx by CAA 23.1.89. To F-GHNJ 12/90.
G-BNHY	AMF Sea Chevvron 2-48	CH-005		3. 4.87	Canx 26.6.90 on sale to France.
G-BNHZ	Aerospatiale SA.315B Lama	2641	N5803H	31. 3.87	To F-GEPU 6/87. Canx 24.6.87.
G-BNIA	Boeing 737-2A3 (Line No. 830)	22737	PH-TSI CX-BON/PH-TSI/CX-BON	15. 4.87	Restored as PH-TSI. Canx 30.10.87.
G-BNIB	Cameron A-105 HAFB	1508		11. 9.87	Stolen from Hednesford 4.2.91. Canx by CAA 2.4.98.
G-BNIC	BAe Jetstream Srs.3101	748	G-31-748	9. 4.87	To N161PC. Canx 22.6.87.
G-BNID	Cessna 152 II	152-84931	N5378P	24. 4.87	
G-BNIE	Cameron O-160 HAFB	1450		5. 5.87	
G-BNIF	Cameron O-56 HAFB	1464		15. 4.87	
G-BNIG	PA-28RT-201T Turbo Arrow IV	28R-8331032	N4299S	22. 4.87	To HB-PKX 7/87. Canx 10.7.87.
G-BNIH	BAC One-Eleven Srs.561RC	BAC.406	YR-BRF	17. 8.87	To (EI-BUQ)/EI-CAS(2) 6/90. Canx 1.6.90.
G-BNII	Cameron N-90 HAFB	1497		15. 4.87	
G-BNIJ	Socata TB-10 Tobago	758		27. 4.87	
G-BNIK	Robin HR.200/120 Club	43	LX-AIK LX-PAA	15. 4.87	
G-BNIL	Not allocated - Marks overlooked by CAA.				
G-BNIM	PA-38-112 Tomahawk	38-78A0148	EC-EZJ N9631T	18. 6.87	
G-BNIN	Cameron V-77 HAFB	1079	(G-RRSG) (G-BLRO)	15. 4.87	
G-BNIO	Luscombe 8AC Silvaire	2120	N45593 NC45593	15. 4.87	
G-BNIP	Luscombe 8A Silvaire	3547	N77820 NC77820	15. 4.87	Permit expired 10.2.93. (Stored 3/99 Cumbernauld)
G-BNIR	Bell 206B JetRanger II	1513	N59615	16. 4.87	To G-STOX 4/89. Canx.
G-BNIS	Bell 206B JetRanger II	1514	N35HF N135VG	22. 4.87	To G-STAK 2/89. Canx.
G-BNIT	Bell 206B JetRanger	641	N55EV N7106J	16. 4.87	DBR on striking power cables at Fordoun, Aberdeenshire on 3.6.93. Canx as destroyed 2.9.93.
G-BNIU	Cameron O-77 HAFB	1499		28. 4.87	
G-BNIV	Cessna 152 II	152-84866	N4972P	24. 4.87	
G-BNIW	Boeing-Stearman A75N1 (PT-17) Kaydet	75-1526	N49291 41-7967	22. 4.87	
G-BNIX	Embraer EMB.110P1 Bandeirante	110-217	N8536J XC-DAB/PT-GMJ	13. 4.87	To PH-FVC 2/97. Canx 10.2.97.
G-BNIY	Fokker F-27 Friendship 600	10392	9Q-CLL PH-FNP	1. 6.87	To OY-SRR. Canx 28.4.88.
G-BNIZ	Fokker F-27 Friendship 600F	10405	OY-SRA G-BNIZ/9Q-CLQ/PH-FOD	1. 6.87	
G-BNJA	WAG-Aero Wag-a-Bond	PFA/137-10886		3. 4.87	
G-BNJB	Cessna 152 II	152-84865	N4970P	27. 4.87	
G-BNJC	Cessna 152 II	152-83588	N4705B	27. 4.87	
G-BNJD	Cessna 152 II	152-82044	N67833	27. 4.87	
G-BNJE	Cessna A.152 Aerobat	A152-0805	N7386L	23. 6.87	To G-DESY 10/97. Canx.
G-BNJF	PA-32RT-300 Turbo Lance II	32R-7885098	N31539	8. 6.78	
G-BNJG	Cameron O-77 HAFB	1502		9. 5.89	
G-BNJH	Cessna 152 II	152-85401	C-GORA (N93101)	21. 7.87	

Regn	Type	c/n	Previous identity	Regn date	Fate or immediate subsequent identity (if known)
G-BNJI	BAe 146 Srs.200	E2072	EI-CTY G-BNJI/HB-IXC/N190US/N366PS/G-BNJI/G-5-072	28. 4.87	To VH-NJQ(2) 9/96. Canx 25.9.96.
G-BNJJ	Cessna 152 II	152-83625	(G-BNJN) N4767B	22. 6.87	Badly damaged when hit building at Cranfield on 18.5.88. Wreck at Spanhoe 11/90. Canx by CAA 3.2.95. (Extant 4/95)
G-BNJK	HS.748 Srs.2A/227 (Converted to MacAvia 748 Turbine Tanker water-bomber)	1594	C-GEPI HP-432	5. 5.87	Stored 6/95 at Chateauroux, France. Canx 29.2.96 by CAA.
G-BNJL	Bensen B.8 Gyrocopter	G/01-1020		30. 4.87	No Permit to Fly issued. (For sale 6/93)
G-BNJM	PA-28-161 Warrior II	28-8216078	N8015V	27. 5.87	Damaged in forced-landing at Ashdale Gill, Cumbria on 18.5.89. (Wreck stored 5/98 Biggin Hill)
G-BNJN	Cessna 152 II	152-83625	N4767B	. 5.87R	NTU - Duplicated allocation - To G-BNJJ 6/87. Canx.
G-BNJO	QAC Quickie Q2 (Constructed by M.Mellor)	2217	N17LM	6.10.87	Damaged in forced landing 1 mile east of Crowfield on 17.1.97. (Stored Netherthorpe 6/97)
G-BNJP	PA-28-161 Warrior II	28-7916191	N2212G	19. 5.87	To G-GFCE 5/90. Canx.
G-BNJR	PA-28RT-201T Turbo Arrow IV	28R-8031104	N8212U	8. 5.87	
G-BNJS	PA-32R-301T Turbo Saratoga SP	32R-8229010	N84639	28. 5.87	Destroyed when it crashed into a hill near Ambleside on 29.11.87. Canx as destroyed 29.11.87.
G-BNJT	PA-28-161 Warrior II	28-8116184	N8360T	11. 6.87	
G-BNJU	Cameron Bust 80SS HAFB	1324		13. 5.87	
G-BNJV	Cessna 152 II	152-83840	N5333B	13. 5.87	Crashed into trees and undergrowth at Stone Acre Farm, Bredhurst on 8.3.92. Canx as destroyed 31.3.92. (Stored 2/95)
G-BNJW	Rutan Cozy	PFA/159-11183		13. 5.87	No Permit to Fly believed issued. Canx by CAA 20.3.91.
G-BNJX	Cameron N-90 HAFB	1480		2. 7.87	
G-BNJY	PA-38-112 Tomahawk II	38-78A0410	N6396A	13. 5.87	Crashed into trees near Fairoaks on 8.8.90. Canx as destroyed 26.10.90.
G-BNJZ	Cassutt Racer IIIM	PFA/34-11228		14. 5.87	
G-BNKA	Robinson R-22 Beta	0647		. 5.87	NTU - To G-BNKY 8/87. Canx.
G-BNKB	Robinson R-22 Alpha	0431	N8528E	29. 5.87	While lifting off at White Waltham on 20.5.88, a skid caught a rut and the helicopter overturned. Canx as destroyed 2.12.88.
G-BNKC	Cessna 152 II	152-81036	N48894	26. 5.87	
G-BNKD	Cessna 172N Skyhawk II	172-72329	N4681D	19. 5.87	
G-BNKE	Cessna 172N Skyhawk II	172-73886	N6534J	20. 5.87	
G-BNKF	Colt AS-56 Hot-Air Airship	899		20. 5.87	
G-BNKG	Alexander/Todd Steen Skybolt	1	G-RATS G-RHFI/N443AT	11. 8.87	To G-KEST 6/91. Canx.
G-BNKH	PA-38-112 Tomahawk II	38-81A0078	N25874	14. 5.87	
G-BNKI	Cessna 152 II	152-81765	N67337	19. 5.87	
G-BNKJ	BAe 146 Srs.200	E2069	N407XV G-5-069/G-BNKJ/G-5-069	26. 5.87	To (OO-DJY)/OO-DJC. Canx 30.11.89.
G-BNKK	BAe 146 Srs.200	E2070	G-5-070	26. 5.87	To N609AW 6/87. Canx 15.6.87.
G-BNKL	Beechcraft 58PA Pressurised Baron	TJ-285	N188JB N6750V	3. 6.87	To G-ZGBE 1/94. Canx.
G-BNKM	Cessna 152 II	152-85177	N6161Q	18. 5.87	To G-OAFT 4/88. Canx.
G-BNKN	Grumman G.159 Gulfstream I	159	N809CC N200PF/N200PM/N940PM/N287AA/N751G	3. 7.87	To XA-RJB 3/92. Canx 4.3.92.
G-BNKO	Grumman G.159 Gulfstream I	154	N802CC N800PD/N800PM/N72B/N736G/N267AA	11. 9.87	To C-GNAK. Canx 22.10.91.
G-BNKP	Cessna 152 II	152-81286	N49460	18. 5.87	
G-BNKR	Cessna 152 II	152-81284	N49458	18. 5.87	
G-BNKS	Cessna 152 II	152-83186	N47202	18. 5.87	
G-BNKT	Cameron O-77 HAFB	1356		13. 2.87	
G-BNKU	Socata TB-20 Trinidad	762		28. 7.87	To G-PTRE 6/88. Canx.
G-BNKV	Cessna 152 II	152-83079	N46604	18. 5.87	
G-BNKW	PA-38-112 Tomahawk	38-78A0311	N9274T	26. 5.87	To G-OTFT 3/97. Canx.
G-BNKX	Robinson R-22	0149	N9065L	28. 5.87	(Stored 12/97) Canx as destroyed 17.12.97.
G-BNKY	Robinson R-22 Beta	0647	(G-BNKA)	27. 8.87	To G-MICH 9/87. Canx.
G-BNKZ	Hughes 369HS (500HS)	102-0421S	C-FFSO CF-FSO	26. 5.87	To SE-HTZ 2/95. Canx 29.8.90.
G-BNLA	Boeing 747-436 (Line No. 727)	23908	N60665	30. 6.89	
G-BNLB	Boeing 747-436 (Line No. 730)	23909		31. 7.89	
G-BNLC	Boeing 747-436 (Line No. 734)	23910		21. 7.89	
G-BNLD	Boeing 747-436 (Line No. 744)	23911	N6018N	5. 9.89	
G-BNLE	Boeing 747-436 (Line No. 753)	24047		14.11.89	
G-BNLF	Boeing 747-436 (Line No. 773)	24048		23. 2.90	
G-BNLG	Boeing 747-436 (Line No. 774)	24049		23. 2.90	
G-BNLH	Boeing 747-436 (Line No. 779)	24050		28. 3.90	
G-BNLI	Boeing 747-436 (Line No. 784)	24051		19. 4.90	
G-BNLJ	Boeing 747-436 (Line No. 789)	24052	N60668	23. 5.90	
G-BNLK	Boeing 747-436 (Line No. 790)	24053	N6009F	25. 5.90	

Regn	Type	c/n	Previous identity	Regn date	Fate or immediate subsequent identity (if known)
G-BNLL	Boeing 747-436 (Line No. 794)	24054		13. 6.90	
G-BNLM	Boeing 747-436 (Line No. 795)	24055	N6009F	28. 6.90	
G-BNLN	Boeing 747-436 (Line No. 802)	24056		26. 7.90	
G-BNLO	Boeing 747-436 (Line No. 817)	24057		25.10.90	
G-BNLP	Boeing 747-436 (Line No. 828)	24058		17.12.90	
G-BNLR	Boeing 747-436 (Line No. 829)	24447	N6005C	15. 1.91	
G-BNLS	Boeing 747-436 (Line No. 841)	24629		13. 3.91	
G-BNLT	Boeing 747-436 (Line No. 842)	24630		19. 3.91	
G-BNLU	Boeing 747-436 (Line No. 895)	25406		28. 1.92	
G-BNLV	Boeing 747-436 (Line No. 900)	25427		20. 2.92	
G-BNLW	Boeing 747-436 (Line No. 903)	25432		4. 3.92	
G-BNLX(1)	Boeing 747-436	25433		. .89R	NTU - Not built. Canx.
G-BNLX(2)	Boeing 747-436 (Line No. 908)	25435	(G-BNLZ)	1. 4.92	
G-BNLY(1)	Boeing 747-436 (Line No. 1058)	25434		. .89R	NTU - To G-CIVF(2) 3/95. Canx.
G-BNLY(2)	Boeing 747-436 (Line No. 1018)	25811		. .90R	NTU - To G-CIVB 2/94. Canx.
G-BNLY(3)	Boeing 747-436 (Line No. 959)	27090	N60659	10. 2.93	
G-BNLZ(1)	Boeing 747-436 (Line No. 908)	25435		. .89R	NTU - To G-BNLX(2) 4/92. Canx.
G-BNLZ(2)	Boeing 747-436 (Line No. 1022)	25812		. .90R	NTU - To G-CIVC 2/94. Canx.
G-BNLZ(3)	Boeing 747-436 (Line No. 964)	27091		4. 3.93	
G-BNMA	Cameron O-77 HAFB	830		15.12.87	
G-BNMB	PA-28-151 Cherokee Warrior	28-7615369	N6826J	6.10.87	
G-BNMC	Cessna 152 II	152-82564	N69218	29. 5.87	
G-BNMD	Cessna 152 II	152-83786	N5170B	28. 5.87	Substantially damaged after overturning in forced landing in allotments nr.Staverton on 23.7.90.
G-BNME	Cessna 152 II	152-84888	N5159P	25. 9.87	
G-BNMF	Cessna 152T	152-85563	N93858	21. 7.87	
G-BNMG	Cameron O-77 HAFB	1500		27. 5.87	
G-BNMH	Pietenpol Air Camper	NH-1-001		2. 6.87	
G-BNMI	Colt Black Knight SS HAFB	1096		1. 6.87	
G-BNMJ	PBN BN-2A-26 Islander	2039		5. 6.87	To B-12232. Canx 13.10.87.
G-BNMK	Dornier Do.27A-1	271	OE-DGO West German AF 56+04/BD+397/BA+399	14. 8.87	
G-BNML	Rand Robinson KR-2	PFA/129-11240		23. 6.87	(Stored 1/99 Shoreham)
G-BNMM	Bell 206B JetRanger II	2234	N231PM	3. 6.87	To N347BE 5/92. Canx 28.1.92.
G-BNMN	PA-28R-201 Arrow III	28R-7837044	N104PE	11. 6.87	To SE-LET 11/95. Canx 7.9.95.
G-BNMO	Cessna R.182 Skylane RG II	R182-00956	N738RK	3. 7.87	
G-BNMP	Cessna R.182 Skylane RG II	R182-01797	N4939T	3. 7.87	To ZS-NXN 5/96. Canx 16.4.96.
G-BNMR	Beechcraft 200 Super King Air	BB-780	N7Q VH-ANH(2)/N3719N	3. 6.87	To TR-LCP 7/88. Canx 27.7.88.
G-BNMS	Short SD.3-60 Var.300	SH3722	G-14-3722	18. 6.87	To N722PC 6/87. Canx 24.6.87.
G-BNMT	Short SD.3-60 Var.300	SH3723	N160DD G-BNMT/G-14-3723	18. 6.87	
G-BNMU	Short SD.3-60 Var.300	SH3724	N161DD (F-OHQP)/N161DD/G-BNMU/G-14-3724	18. 6.87	
G-BNMV	Short SD.3-60 Var.300	SH3725	G-14-3725	18. 6.87	To N162DD. Canx 18.9.87.
G-BNMW	Short SD.3-60 Var.300	SH3726	SE-LCC G-BNMW/EI-BTO/G-BNMW/G-14-3726	18. 6.87	
G-BNMX	Thunder Ax7-77 HAFB	1003		15. 6.87	
G-BNMY	Hughes 369D (500D)	70-0748D	N1091A	23. 6.87	To OE-KYW. Canx 28.7.87.
G-BNMZ	Isaacs Fury II	PFA/41-11237		11. 6.87	Not completed. Canx by CAA 24.7.91.
G-BNNA	Stolp SA.300 Starduster Too	1462	N8SD	29. 6.87	
G-BNNB	PA-34-200 Seneca	34-7350080	(N.....) G-BNNB/N15625	12. 6.87	To G-VASA 3/96. Canx.
G-BNNC	Cameron N-77 HAFB	1523		16. 6.87	CofA expired 9.10.96. Canx as WFU 2.6.98.
G-BNND	BAe 146 Srs.200A	E2074	HS-TBQ G-BNND/N146SB/N192US/N368PS/(G-BNND)/G-5-074	5. 6.87	To G-5-074/N881DV. Canx 25.1.90.
G-BNNE	Cameron N-77 HAFB	1413		15. 6.87	(Active 8/96)
G-BNNF	Aerospatiale SA.315B Lama	2591	(F-....) G-BNNF/N5770B	16. 6.87	Crashed spraying at Upper Church, Co.Tipperary, Ireland on 30.7.96. Canx as destroyed 7.10.96. To N345RA 12/96.
G-BNNG	Cessna T.337D Turbo Super Skymaster	T337-01096	G-COLD PH-NOS/N86147	23. 6.87	Damaged in wheels-up landing at Goodwood in 1985 - whilst as G-COLD. (On rebuild 3/92 at Bournemouth) Canx by CAA 14.7.92.

Regn	Type	c/n	Previous identity	Regn date	Fate or immediate subsequent identity (if known)
G-BNNH	PA-31-350 Navajo Chieftain	31-7852127	N27727	25.10.78	To N252SC 9/81. Canx 25.9.81.
G-BNNI	Boeing 727-276ADV (Line No. 1081)	20950	VH-TBK	10.12.86	
G-BNNJ	Boeing 737-3Q8 (Line No. 1506)	24068	(N881RV)	4. 1.88	To G-OCHA 3/91. Canx.
G-BNNK	Boeing 737-4Q8 (Line No. 1635)	24069		30.11.88	
G-BNNL	Boeing 737-4Q8 (Line No. 1665)	24070		26. 1.89	
G-BNNM	Colt 77A HAFB	1076		17. 6.87	To PH-RDE. Canx 18.5.88.
G-BNNN	Aerospatiale AS.355F2 Twin Squirrel	5364		12. 6.87	To G-DAFT 1/88. Canx.
G-BNNO	PA-28-161 Warrior II	28-8116099	N8307X	15. 6.87	
G-BNNP	PA-28-181 Archer II	28-8590044	N153AV	24. 6.87	Mid-air collision with DH.82A G-AOZB on 19.5.90 resulting in a fatal crash at Gatton Bottom, nr.Reigate. Canx as destroyed 19.7.90.
G-BNNR	Cessna 152 II	152-85146	N40SX N40SU/N6121Q	15. 6.87	
G-BNNS	PA-28-161 Warrior II	28-8116061	N8283C	26. 6.87	
G-BNNT	PA-28-151 Cherokee Warrior	28-7615056	N7624C	12. 6.87	
G-BNNU	PA-38-112 Tomahawk II	38-81A0037	N25650	12. 6.87	
G-BNNV	Enstrom 280C-UK Shark	1149	SE-HIY	24. 6.87	To G-GSML 6/89. Canx.
G-BNNW	Cessna P.210N Pressurised Centurion		(G-BNPW) G-BNNW/N731HZ	19. 6.87	Destroyed in fatal crash into a mountainside 30 miles north of Turin on 10.9.88, shortly after take-off from Caselle Airport. Canx as destroyed 4.1.89.
G-BNNX	PA-28R-201T Turbo Arrow III	28R-7703009	N9005F	14. 7.87	
G-BNNY	PA-28-161 Warrior II	28-8016084	N8092M	1. 9.87	
G-BNNZ	PA-28-161 Warrior II	28-8016177	N8135Y	24. 7.87	
G-BNOA	PA-38-112 Tomahawk II	31-81A0107	N23272	19. 6.87	To N737V 6/96. Canx 19.6.96.
G-BNOB	Wittman W.8 Tailwind (Constructed by D.Hammerslet)	258/DH1 & PFA/3502		13. 7.87	
G-BNOC	Embraer EMB.110P1 Bandeirante	110-223	PT-GMP	20. 9.79	To G-LOOT 1/91. Canx.
G-BNOD	PA-28-161 Warrior II	2816012	N9121N N9567N	26. 6.87	Fatal crash into hills near Glasgow on 15.9.93. Canx as destroyed 29.11.93.
G-BNOE	PA-28-161 Warrior II	2816013	N9121X N9568N	26. 6.87	
G-BNOF	PA-28-161 Warrior II	2816014	N9122B	26. 6.87	
G-BNOG	PA-28-161 Warrior II	2816015	N9122D	26. 6.87	
G-BNOH	PA-28-161 Warrior II	2816016	N9122L	26. 6.87	
G-BNOI	PA-28-161 Warrior II	2816017	N9122N	26. 6.87	
G-BNOJ	PA-28-161 Warrior II	2816018	N9122R	26. 6.87	
G-BNOK	PA-28-161 Warrior II	2816019	N9122U	26. 6.87	
G-BNOL	PA-28-161 Warrior II	2816023		26. 6.87	
G-BNOM	PA-28-161 Warrior II	2816024		26. 6.87	
G-BNON	PA-28-161 Warrior II	2816025		26. 6.87	(Extant 4/97)
G-BNOO	PA-28-161 Warrior II	2816026		26. 6.87	
G-BNOP	PA-28-161 Warrior II	2816027		26. 6.87	
G-BNOR	PA-28-161 Warrior II	2816028		26. 6.87	
G-BNOS	PA-28-161 Warrior II	2816029		26. 6.87	
G-BNOT	PA-28-161 Warrior II	2816030		26. 6.87	
G-BNOU	PA-28-161 Warrior II	2816031		26. 6.87	
G-BNOV	PA-28-161 Warrior II	2816032		26. 6.87	
G-BNOW	PA-28-161 Warrior II	2816033		26. 6.87	
G-BNOX	Cessna R.182 Skylane RG II	R182-01026	N756AW	24. 6.87	
G-BNOY	Colt 90A HAFB	1081	(D-O...) G-BNOY	19. 6.87	Canx as WFU 22.4.98.
G-BNOZ	Cessna 152 II	152-81625	EI-CCP G-BNOZ/N65570	22. 6.87	
G-BNPA	Boeing 737-3S3 (Line No. 1445)	23811	C-FGHQ G-BNPA	3. 9.87	To G-DIAR 4/91. Canx.
"G-BNPA"	Sikorsky S-61N	61-775	PH-NZL	----	NTU - Painted in error - To G-BHPA 3/80. Canx.
G-BNPB	Boeing 737-3S3 (Line No. 1517)	24059	C-FGHT G-BNPB	7. 3.88	To EC-711/EC-FGG. Canx 19.6.91.
G-BNPC	Boeing 737-3S3 (Line No. 1519)	24060		9. 3.88	To N312AW. Canx 31.7.90.
G-BNPD	PA-23-250 Aztec E	27-7405336	N101VH N40591	22.12.77	To G-RVRC 10/97. Canx.
G-BNPE	Cameron N-77 HAFB	1519	(G-BNPX)	25. 8.87	
G-BNPF	Slingsby T.31M Cadet III	826 & PFA/42-11122	XA284	3.11.87	(Wings from XE791, which became OO-ZDQ)
G-BNPG	Hunting Percival P.66 Pembroke C.1 (Also c/n K66/045)	PAC/66/082	XK884	30. 6.87	To SE-DKH. Canx 4.5.88.
G-BNPH	Hunting-Percival P.66 Pembroke C.1 (Regd with c/n "PAC66/027")	P66/41	WV740	30. 6.87	
G-BNPI	Colt 21A Cloudhopper HAFB	1038		23. 6.87	
G-BNPJ	BAe 146 Srs.200 (Converted to Srs.200QT)	E2078		14. 7.87	To G-5-078/I-TNTC 12/87. Canx 27.11.87.

Regn	Type	c/n	Previous identity	Regn date	Fate or immediate subsequent identity (if known)
G-BNPK	Cameron DP-70 Gas Airship	1456		23. 6.87	(Based in USA). Canx as WFU 21.10.96.
G-BNPL	PA-38-112 Tomahawk	38-79A0524	N2420G	28. 7.87	
G-BNPM	PA-38-112 Tomahawk	38-79A0374	N2561D	28. 7.87	
G-BNPN	PA-28-181 Archer II	28-7890059	N47379	28. 7.87	
G-BNPO	PA-28-181 Archer II	28-7890123	N47720	28. 7.87	
G-BNPP	Colt 90A HAFB	1080		6. 7.87	To D-MILKA 4/92. Canx 9.6.92.
G-BNPR	Colt 90A HAFB	1082		6. 7.87	Canx by CAA 26.3.90. To D-SUCHARD.
G-BNPS	MBB Bo.105DBS-4	S.421	N4929M D-HDMT	1. 7.87	To G-PASC 10/89. Canx.
G-BNPT	PA-38-112 Tomahawk II	38-82A0046	G-LFSD G-BNPT/N91522	16. 9.87	Restored as G-LFSD 11/96. Canx.
G-BNPU	Hunting-Percival P.66 Pembroke C.1 (Regd with c/n "K66/089")	P66/87	XL929	30. 6.87	Donated to the Chelsea College of Aeronautical & Automobile Engineering for use as an instructional airframe. Flown from Sandown to Shoreham on 7.5.88. Canx as WFU 11.8.88. (Preserved 1/99 at Shoreham)
G-BNPV	Bowers Fly Baby 1A/1B	PFA/16-11120		2. 7.87	
G-BNPW	Cessna P.210N Pressurised Centurion	P210-00471	G-BNNW N731HZ	26. 6.87	NTU - Remained as G-BNNW 6/87. Canx 2.7.87 as regd in error.
G-BNPX	Cameron N-77 HAFB	1519		9. 7.87	NTU - To G-BNPE 8/87. Canx 25.8.87 as regd in error.
G-BNPY	Cessna 152 II	152-80249	N24388	30. 6.87	
G-BNPZ	Cessna 152 II	152-85134	N6109Q	30. 6.87	
G-BNRA	Socata TB-10 Tobago	772		15. 7.87	
G-BNRB	Robin DR.400/180R	1786		7. 7.87	To OE-KSR. Canx 15.4.91.
G-BNRC	Agusta-Bell 206A JetRanger	8237	601 Oman AF	13. 7.87	To G-OBYT 1/95. Canx.
G-BNRD	Agusta-Bell 206A JetRanger	8238	602 Oman AF	13. 7.87	To G-OOPS 5/95. Canx.
G-BNRE	Agusta-Bell 206A JetRanger	8246	603 Oman AF	13. 7.87	To OE-XRF 11/96. Canx 19.12.96.
G-BNRF	Beechcraft 76 Duchess	ME-322	N6714U	. 7.87R	NTU - To G-GCCL 8/87. Canx.
G-BNRG	PA-28-161 Warrior II	28-8116217	N83810	7. 7.87	
G-BNRH	Beechcraft 95-E55 Baron	TE-1141		8. 7.87	To N554RB 8/96. Canx 22.8.96.
G-BNRI	Cessna U.206G Stationair II	U206-04024	N756ED	28. 7.87	
G-BNRJ	Cessna U.206G Stationair II	U206-03579	N7242N	8. 7.87	To OO-NRJ. Canx 31.3.88.
G-BNRK	Cessna 152 II	152-84659	N6297M	29. 7.87	
G-BNRL	Cessna 152 II	152-84250	N5084L	13. 7.87	
G-BNRM	PA-34-220T Seneca III	34-8133021	N8341U	. 7.87	NTU - Not Imported. To OO-GHM 10/87. Canx.
G-BNRN	PA-28R-201T Turbo Arrow III	28R-7803178	N321EC N3561M	20. 7.87	To G-FESL 11/88. Canx.
G-BNRO	PA-28R-200 Cherokee Arrow II	28R-7435148	N40979	9.10.87	To G-TOBE 25.11.87. Canx.
G-BNRP	PA-28-181 Archer II	28-7790528	N984BT	25.11.87	
G-BNRR	Cessna 172P Skyhawk II	172-74013	N5213K	13. 7.87	
G-BNRS	MBB Bo.105DBS-4	S.656	N14ES N4572Q/D-HDTZ	20. 7.87	To G-PASD 10/89. Canx.
G-BNRT	Boeing 737-3T5 (Line No. 1527)	23064	EC-ELV EC-213/G-BNRT	26. 2.88	To N748MA 12/92. Canx 9.12.92.
G-BNRU	Cameron V-77 HAFB	1567		27. 7.87	CofA expired 1.5.94. Canx as WFU 7.7.98.
G-BNRV	Thunder Ax7-77 HAFB	961		14. 8.87	To N2175V 3/90. Canx 31.1.90.
G-BNRW	Colt 69A HAFB	1101		27. 8.87	CofA expired 19.6.96. Canx 30.3.98 as WFU.
G-BNRX	PA-34-200T Seneca II	34-7970336	N2898A	25.11.87	
G-BNRY	Cessna 182Q Skylane II	182-65629	N735RR	20. 7.87	
G-BNRZ	Robinson R-22 Beta	0670		28. 7.87	
G-BNSA	McDonnell Douglas DC-9-83 (MD-83) (Line No. 1423)	49643	N19B	14. 1.88	To N945AS. Canx 31.1.90.
G-BNSB	McDonnell Douglas DC-9-83 (MD-83) (Line No. 1461)	49658		12. 5.88	To N946AS. Canx 31.1.90.
G-BNSC	Cessna 551 Citation II (Unit No. 559)	551-0559	(N1298H)	28. 7.87	To VR-CNB. Canx 25.2.91.
G-BNSD	Boeing 757-236 (Line No. 163)	24118	EC-EMA EC-204/G-BNSD	1. 3.88	To PH-TKY 4/92. Canx 10.4.92.
G-BNSE	Boeing 757-236 (Line No. 183)	24121	EC-EXH(2) EC-544/G-BNSE	15. 6.88	To G-BPEH 5/92. Canx.
G-BNSF	Boeing 757-236 (Line No. 187)	24122	(D-AOEB) G-BNSF/EC-ELS/EC-203/G-BNSF	27. 6.88	To EC-744/EC-FFK. Canx 5.6.91.
G-BNSG	PA-28R-201 Arrow III	28R-7837205	N9516C	30. 7.87	
G-BNSH	Sikorsky S-76A (Mod)	760112		27.11.80	To VH-LAQ(2). Canx 7.12.93.
G-BNSI	Cessna 152 II	152-84853	N4945P	6. 8.87	
G-BNSJ	Cessna 152 II	152-85289	N65576	25.11.87	To EC-ELI. Canx 16.8.88.
G-BNSK	Cessna 172N Skyhawk	172-70671	N739NJ	1. 9.87	To EC-EKD. Canx 16.8.88.
G-BNSL	PA-38-112 Tomahawk II	38-81A0086	N25956	21. 7.87	
G-BNSM	Cessna 152 II	152-85342	N68948	23. 7.87	
G-BNSN	Cessna 152 II	152-85776	N94738	21. 7.87	
G-BNSO	Slingsby T.67M Firefly II	2021		20. 8.87	
G-BNSP	Slingsby T.67M Firefly II	2044		20. 8.87	
G-BNSR	Slingsby T.67M Firefly II	2047		20. 8.87	
G-BNSS	Cessna 150M	150-76786	N45207	11. 8.87	To EI-CML 1/96. Canx 19.12.95.
G-BNST	Cessna 172N Skyhawk II	172-73661	N4670J	21. 9.87	
G-BNSU	Cessna 152 II	152-81245	N49410	2.12.87	
G-BNSV	Cessna 152 II	152-84531	N5322M	4.12.87	(Dismantled at Bourn 4/99)
G-BNSW	Cessna 152 II	152-85621	N94213	1. 9.87	

Regn	Type	c/n	Previous identity	Regn date	Fate or immediate subsequent identity (if known)
G-BNSX	Aerospatiale AS.355F2 Twin Squirrel	5367		30. 7.87	To G-DOOZ 5/88. Canx.
G-BNSY	PA-28-161 Warrior II	28-8016017	N4512M	18. 8.87	
G-BNSZ	PA-28-161 Warrior II	28-8116315	N8433B	20. 8.87	
G-BNTA	Fokker F-27 Friendship 600	10394	9Q-CLN PH-FNS	10. 9.87	To OY-SRB. Canx 1.11.88.
G-BNTB	Fokker F-27 Friendship 600	10391	9Q-CLK PH-FNP	11. 4.88	To OY-CCR 10/90. Canx 10.10.90.
G-BNTC	PA-28RT-201T Turbo Arrow IV	28R-8131081	N83428	4.11.87	
G-BNTD	PA-28-161 Cherokee Warrior II	28-7716235	N38490 N9539N	5. 8.87	
G-BNTE	FFA AS.202/18A4 Bravo	224		7. 8.87	(Extant 4/97)
G-BNTF	FFA AS.202/18A4 Bravo	225		7. 8.87	
G-BNTG	FFA AS.202/18A4 Bravo	226		7. 8.87	Fatal crash in a field near Birnie Hill Farm, 3 miles south of Maybole on 18.3.93. Canx as destroyed 2.6.93.
G-BNTH	FFA AS.202/18A4 Bravo	227		7. 8.87	
G-BNTI	FFA AS.202/18A4 Bravo	228		7. 8.87	
G-BNTJ	FFA AS.202/18A4 Bravo	229		7. 8.87	
G-BNTK	FFA AS.202/18A4 Bravo	230		7. 8.87	(Status uncertain)
G-BNTL	FFA AS.202/18A4 Bravo	231		7. 8.87	
G-BNTM	FFA AS.202/18A4 Bravo	232		7. 8.87	(Extant 4/97)
G-BNTN	FFA AS.202/18A4 Bravo	233		7. 8.87	
G-BNTO	FFA AS.202/18A4 Bravo	234		7. 8.87	(Extant 4/97)
G-BNTP	Cessna 172N Skyhawk II	172-72030	N6531E	4. 9.87	
G-BNTR	Cessna 172N Skyhawk II	172-70631	N739LQ	6. 8.87	To G-LICK 4/88. Canx.
G-BNTS	PA-28RT-201T Turbo Arrow IV	28R-8131024	N8296R	6. 8.87	
G-BNTT	Beechcraft 76 Duchess	ME-228	N54SB	8.10.87	
G-BNTU	Cessna 152 II	152-84559	N5359M	6.10.87	Force landed at Lower Leighton Farm, near Welshpool on 5.8.92. Canx as destroyed 26.8.92.
G-BNTV	Cessna 172N Skyhawk II	172-67794	N75539	4. 9.87	To G-JVMD 2/92. Canx.
G-BNTW	Cameron V-77 HAFB	1574		13. 8.87	
G-BNTX	Short SD.3-30 Var.100	SH3090	G-BKDN G-14-3090	20. 1.87	CofA expired 2.6.90. WFU & stored 10/97 at Exeter. Derelict by 12/97. Canx as WFU 23.6.98.
G-BNTY	Short SD.3-30 Var.100	SH3091	G-BKDO G-14-3091	20. 1.87	WFU & stored 1/96 at Exeter. Canx as WFU 11.6.98. CofA expired 15.5.90. (Status uncertain; presumed scrapped)
G-BNTZ	Cameron N-77 HAFB	1518		27. 8.87	
G-BNUA	BAe 146 Srs.200 (Converted to Srs.200QT)	E2086	G-5-086	18. 8.87	To G-5-086/SE-DEI. Canx 8.2.88.
G-BNUB	BAe 125 Srs.800A	258099	G-5-565	. 8.87	NTU - To N537BA 9/87. Canx.
G-BNUC	Cameron O-77 HAFB	1575		18. 8.87	(Active 9/93)
G-BNUD	Cameron A-250 HAFB	1542		12. 8.87	To (F-GFGI)/F-GGCM 9/88. Canx 24.3.88.
G-BNUE	Thunder Ax8-105Z HAFB	354	F-GCZI	7. 9.87	Canx 26.6.90 on sale to France.
G-BNUF	Thunder Ax8-105Z HAFB	382	F-GCZM	7. 9.87	Canx 26.6.90 on sale to France.
G-BNUG	Cameron O-105 HAFB	495	F-GCKX N293CB	7. 9.87	Canx by CAA 21.11.89.
G-BNUH	Cameron O-105 HAFB	575	F-GCKG	7. 9.87	Canx by CAA 21.11.89.
G-BNUI	Rutan VariEze	PFA/74-10960		12. 8.87	
G-BNUJ	Thunder Ax8-105Z HAFB	381	F-GCZL	7. 9.87	Canx 26.6.90 on sale to France.
G-BNUK	Cameron O-84 HAFB	404	F-GCKY N149CB	7. 9.87	Canx by CAA 13.12.89. To F-GHNS.
G-BNUL	Cessna 152 II	152-84486	N4852M	2.10.87	
G-BNUM	Stinson L-5C-VW Sentinel (C/n is possibly 76-3615)	76-....	N8035H N63485/44-17328	2. 9.87	NTU - To D-EONH 5/89. Canx 11.3.88.
G-BNUN	Beechcraft 58PA Baron	TJ-256	N6732Y	19. 8.87	
G-BNUO	Beechcraft 76 Duchess	ME-250	N6635Y	29. 9.87	
G-BNUP	PA-28-161 Cherokee Warrior II	28-7716097	N2282Q	19. 8.87	To EI-BXU 10/88. Canx 30.9.88.
G-BNUR	Cessna 172E	172-50703		2. 9.87	CofA expired 26.12.94. Canx as WFU 27.6.95.
G-BNUS	Cessna 152 II	152-82166	N68179	26. 8.87	
G-BNUT	Cessna 152 II	152-79458	N714VC	26. 8.87	
G-BNUU	PA-44-180T Turbo Seminole	44-8207005	N8012U	27. 8.87	To 4X-CCU 12/94. Canx 1.11.94.
G-BNUV	PA-23-250 Aztec F	27-7854038	N97BB N63894	2.10.87	
G-BNUW	Bell 206B JetRanger III	2584	N5018B (N500FB)/N5018B	27. 8.87	To G-SHZZ 4/90. Canx.
G-BNUX	Hoffmann H.36 Dimona	36236		26. 8.87	
G-BNUY	PA-38-112 Tomahawk II	38-81A0093	N26006	10. 9.87	
G-BNUZ	Robinson R-22 Beta	0680		28. 8.87	
G-BNVA	Cameron DP-70 Hot-Air Airship	1504	(HB-B..) G-BNVA	28. 8.87	To HB-BKQ. Canx 23.12.87.
G-BNVB	American Aviation AA-5A Cheetah	AA5A-0758	N26843	28. 8.87	
G-BNVC	Robinson R-22 Beta	0681		28. 8.87	To EI-XMA 10/87. Canx 19.10.87.
G-BNVD	PA-38-112 Tomahawk	38-79A0055	N2421B	16.11.87	
G-BNVE	PA-28-181 Archer II	28-8490046	N4338D	28. 8.87	
G-BNVF	Robinson R-22 Beta	0675		28. 8.87	To EC-FRD 4/93. Canx 6.1.93.
G-BNVG	ARV1 Super 2	030		29. 9.87	Canx as WFU 28.3.95.
G-BNVH	ARV1 Super 2	031		29. 9.87	Canx as WFU 28.3.95.
G-BNVI	ARV1 Super 2	032		29. 9.87	CofA expired 2.2.96. Canx by CAA 10.3.98. To N63997 7/99.

Regn	Type	c/n	Previous identity	Regn date	Fate or immediate subsequent identity (if known)
G-BNVJ	ARV1 Super 2	033		29. 9.87	To SE-KYP 6/99. (To prototype ASL Hagfors AB Opus 280) Canx 20.10.94.
G-BNVK	ARV K1 Super 2	034 & PFA/152-12424		. 9.87R	NTU - To G-BUXH 3/93. Canx.
G-BNVL	ARV1 Super 2	035		. 9.87R	NTU - Not built. Canx.
G-BNVM	ARV1 Super 2	036		. 9.87R	NTU - Not built. Canx.
G-BNVN	ARV1 Super 2	037		. 9.87R	NTU - Not built. Canx.
G-BNVO	ARV1 Super 2	038		. 9.87R	NTU - Not built. Canx.
G-BNVP	ARV1 Super 2	039		. 9.87R	NTU - Not built. Canx.
G-BNVR	ARV1 Super 2	040		. 9.87R	NTU - To SE-LCF 9/95 as ASL Opus 280 with same c/n. Canx.
G-BNVS	Cessna 152	152-81146	9M-AXP N49093	2. 9.87	To N91764. Canx 6.10.87.
G-BNVT	PA-28R-201T Turbo Cherokee Arrow III	28R-7703157	N5863V	26. 1.88	
G-BNVU	HS.125 Srs.700B	257130	G-CCAA G-DBBI	4. 9.87	To N700FR. Canx 4.3.88.
G-BNVV	Cameron DG-19 Helium Airship	1271		15. 2.88	Canx by CAA 1.2.93. (Was based in Los Angeles, USA)
G-BNVW	Dornier Do.28A-1	3023		8. 9.87	To N12828. Canx 1.10.91.
G-BNVX	Dornier Do.27A-4	2106	7P-AAX D-EGVN/Belgium AF D-09\OT-AMH /Belgium AF OL-D09/Belgium AF D-9	8. 9.87	To HC-BNK/D-EGVN 10/90. Canx 8.8.89.
G-BNVY	Cessna 500 Citation I (Unit No.098)	500-0098	PH-CTC N598CC	4. 9.87	Restored as PH-CTC. Canx 24.11.88.
G-BNVZ	Beechcraft 95-B55 Baron	TC-2042	N17720	25. 9.87	
G-BNWA	Boeing 767-336ER (Line No. 265)	24333	N6009F	19. 4.90	
G-BNWB	Boeing 767-336ER (Line No. 281)	24334	N6046P	2. 2.90	
G-BNWC	Boeing 767-336ER (Line No. 284)	24335		2. 2.90	
G-BNWD	Boeing 767-336ER (Line No. 286)	24336	N6018N	2. 2.90	
G-BNWE	Boeing 767-336ER (Line No. 288)	24337		23. 2.90	
G-BNWF	Boeing 767-336ER (Line No. 293)	24338	N1788B	22. 6.90	
G-BNWG	Boeing 767-336ER (Line No. 298)	24339		11. 7.90	
G-BNWH	Boeing 767-336ER (Line No. 335)	24340	N6005C	31.10.90	
G-BNWI	Boeing 767-336ER (Line No. 342)	24341		18.12.90	
G-BNWJ	Boeing 767-336ER (Line No. 363)	24342		24. 4.91	
G-BNWK	Boeing 767-336ER (Line No. 364)	24343		18. 4.91	
G-BNWL	Boeing 767-336ER (Line No. 365)	25203		30. 4.91	
G-BNWM	Boeing 767-336ER (Line No. 376)	25204		24. 6.91	
G-BNWN	Boeing 767-336ER (Line No. 398)	25444		30.10.91	
G-BNWO	Boeing 767-336ER (Line No. 418)	25442		2. 3.92	
G-BNWP	Boeing 767-336ER (Line No. 419)	25443		9. 3.92	
G-BNWR	Boeing 767-336ER (Line No. 421)	25732		20. 3.92	
G-BNWS	Boeing 767-336ER (Line No. 473)	25826	N6018N	19. 2.93	
G-BNWT	Boeing 767-336ER (Line No. 476)	25828		8. 2.93	
G-BNWU	Boeing 767-336ER (Line No. 483)	25829		16. 3.93	
G-BNWV	Boeing 767-336ER (Line No. 490)	27140		29. 4.93	
G-BNWW	Boeing 767-336ER (Line No. 526)	25831		3. 2.94	
G-BNWX	Boeing 767-336ER (Line No. 529)	25832		1. 3.94	
G-BNWY	Boeing 767-336ER (Line No. 608)	25834	N5005C	22. 4.96	
G-BNWZ	Boeing 767-336ER (Line No. 648)	25733		25. 2.97	
G-BNXA	BN-2A Islander	80	V2-LAC VP-LAC/N854JA/G-51-21	17. 9.87	
G-BNXB	BN-2A-26 Islander	161	V2-LAF VP-LAF/G-51-161	17. 9.87	To EC-843/EC-FIQ. Canx 4.10.91.
G-BNXC	Cessna 152 II	152-85429	N93171	24. 9.87	
G-BNXD	Cessna 172N Skyhawk II	172-72692	N6285D	25. 9.87	
G-BNXE	PA-28-161 Warrior II	28-8116034	N8262D	24. 9.87	
G-BNXF	Bell 206B Jet Ranger II	2512	N4353F N206E/N12TE	8.10.87	To HA-LFE 4/93. Canx.
G-BNXG	Cameron DP-70 Hot-Air Airship	1558		23. 9.87	Canx by CAA 18.6.93. (Last known of operating in Venezuela!) To HB-BKR.

Regn	Type	c/n	Previous identity	Regn date	Fate or immediate subsequent identity (if known)
G-BNXH	Cessna T.210N Turbo Centurion II	T210N-64592		21. 9.87	To N79MM 7/92. Canx 21.7.92.
G-BNXI	Robin DR.400/180R Remorqueur	1021	SE-FNI	13.10.87	
G-BNXJ	Robinson R-22 Beta	0699		30. 9.87	To G-OFJS 5/91. Canx.
G-BNXK	Nott/Cameron/Airship Industries ULD/3 Explorer Rozier HAFB	7 & 1110	(G-BLJN)	23. 9.87	(Hot-air envelope in Twain Harte, CA 12/97 USA/helium inner envelope stored Bristol .95)
G-BNXL	Glaser-Dirks DG-400	4-216		2.10.87	
G-BNXM	PA-18-95 Super Cub (L-21B-PI) (Italian frame rebuild No.0006)	18-4019	MM54-2619 Italian AF/EI-276/I-EIVC/MM54-2619/54-2619	23.11.87	
G-BNXN	Partenavia P.68B Victor	204	CN-TCD HB-LLV	13.11.87	To CS-AYQ. Canx 3.1.92.
G-BNXO	Colt 21A Cloudhopper HAFB	1139		22. 9.87	Canx as WFU 4.7.90.
G-BNXP	Boeing 737-3S3 (Line No. 1374)	23787	EC-ECM EC-276/G-BNXP/EC-ECM/EC-155/G-BNXP/EC-ECM	22.12.87	To "OO-CYE"/CC-CYE 11/90. Canx 5.11.90.
G-BNXR	Cameron O-84 HAFB	1515		23. 9.87	
G-BNXS	Cessna 404 Titan II (Originally regd with c/n 404-0014)	404-0414	(G-BOAJ) R.Hong Kong Aux.AF HKG-4/(N8799K)	13.11.87	To G-BWLF 10/94. Canx.
G-BNXT	PA-28-161 Cherokee Warrior II	28-7716168	N4047Q	23. 9.87	
G-BNXU	PA-28-161 Warrior II	28-7916129	N2082C	23. 9.87	
G-BNXV	PA-38-112 Tomahawk	38-79A0826	N2399N	10.12.87	
G-BNXW	Boeing 737-33A (Line No. 1444)	23827	LN-NOR G-BNXW/LN-NOR/G-BNXW/LN-NOR	2.10.87	To CS-TKD. Canx.
G-BNXX	Socata TB-20 Trinidad	664	N20GZ	15. 9.87	
G-BNXY	Cessna 172M Skyhawk II	172-66271	N9621H	24. 9.87	To G-TRIO 7/91. Canx.
G-BNXZ	Thunder Ax7-77 HAFB	1105		13.10.87	
G-BNYA	Short SD.3-30 Var.100	SH3095	G-BKSU G-14-3095	19. 3.87	To 4X-CSQ. Canx 7.4.94.
G-BNYB	PA-28-201T Turbo Dakota	28-7921040	N2856A	27. 1.88	
G-BNYC	BAe 146 Srs.200	E2089	G-5-089	6.10.87	To (F-GTNT)/G-TNTH 3/88. Canx.
G-BNYD	Bell 206B JetRanger II	1911	N3254P C-GTWM/N49712	1.10.87	
G-BNYE	Short SD.3-60 Var.300	SH3727	G-14-3727	12.10.87	To YV-O-GUR-2. Canx 1.6.88.
G-BNYF	Short SD.3-60 Var.300	SH3728	EI-BTP G-14-3728/EI-BTP/G-BNYF/G-14-3728	12.10.87	To VH-SUR 3/95. Canx 4.5.95.
G-BNYG	Short SD.3-60 Var.300	SH3729	G-14-3729	12.10.87	To N729PC. Canx 6.11.87.
G-BNYH	Short SD.3-60 Var.300	SH3730	G-14-3730	12.10.87	To N730PC. Canx 7.12.87.
G-BNYI	Short SD.3-60 Var.100	SH3731	N360CC G-BNYI/G-14-3731	12.10.87	
G-BNYJ	Cessna 421B Golden Eagle II	421B-0820	N4686Q D-IMVB/N1590G	6.10.87	To G-SVIP 3/97. Canx.
G-BNYK	PA-38-112 Tomahawk II	38-82A0059	N2376V	23.10.87	
G-BNYL	Cessna 152 II	152-80671	N25454	6.10.87	
G-BNYM	Cessna 172N Skyhawk II	172-73854	N6089J	13.11.87	
G-BNYN	Cessna 152 II	152-85433	N93185	2.10.87	
G-BNYO	Beechcraft 76 Duchess	ME-78	N2010P	28.10.87	
G-BNYP	PA-28-181 Archer II	28-8490027	N4330K	19.10.87	
G-BNYR	Cameron N-105 HAFB	1358		8.10.87	To PT-LYV 1/90. Canx 23.1.90.
G-BNYS	Boeing 767-204ER (Line No. 210)	24013	N6009F	22. 2.88	
G-BNYT	Boeing 737-2E1 (Line No. 424)	21112	EI-BDY C-GNDD/EI-BDY/CN-RML/EI-BDY/(EI-BEA)/C-GEPB/N70720/C-GEPB/N4039W/C-GEPB	3.11.87	Restored as EI-BDY. Canx 22.3.88.
G-BNYU	Faithfull Ax7-61A HAFB	001		13.10.87	Canx by CAA 4.8.98.
G-BNYV	PA-38-112 Tomahawk	38-78A0073	N9364T	13.11.87	Used as spares source 1/99 at Guernsey.
G-BNYW	Cessna 172P Skyhawk II	172-75025	N54655	12.10.87	To OO-NZB. Canx 17.2.88.
G-BNYX	Denney Kitfox Mk.1	PFA/172-11285		28.10.87	(Stored 3/96)
G-BNYY	PA-28RT-201T Turbo Arrow IV	28R-8631003	N25WA N77860/G-BNYY/N9129X/N9517N	17.11.87	To N473BS 6/97. Canx 12.6.97.
G-BNYZ	SNCAN Stampe SV-4E	200	N180SV F-BFZR/French Mil	10.12.87	
G-BNZA	Beechcraft 300LW Super King Air	FA-136		19.10.87	To N600CB. Canx 18.7.91.
G-BNZB	PA-28-161 Warrior II	28-7916521	N2900U	18.11.87	
G-BNZC	DHC.1 Chipmunk 22 (Fuselage no. DHB/f/677)	C1/0778	G-ROYS 7438M/WP905	11.11.87	
G-BNZD	BN-2A Mk.III-2 Trislander	1059	G-BEVV	22. 6.87	To 6Y-JQK 11/88. Canx 9.12.88.
G-BNZE	Fokker F-27 Friendship 500	10367	F-GPNB PH-FMO	11.12.87	To G-FEDX 25.1.88. Canx.
G-BNZF	Grob G-109B	6212	D-KGFD	20.10.87	Restored as D-KGFD 12/93. Canx 28.9.93.
G-BNZG	PA-28RT-201T Turbo Arrow IV	28R-8031132	N82376	23.11.87	
G-BNZH	Beechcraft B200 Super King Air	BB-961	N189GA ZK-RGA/N5362J/YV-476CP	28.10.87	Canx 18.9.89 on sale to Sao Tome. (Reported to S9-NAQ) Became A2-AHA in 1/91.
G-BNZI	PA-31-350 Navajo Chieftain	31-7952092	N3517T	26.11.87	To G-WROX 9/89. Canx.
G-BNZJ	Colt 21A Cloudhopper HAFB	1150		27.10.87	
G-BNZK	Thunder Ax7-77 HAFB (Initially c/n used by G-HOTI - later corrected)	1104		10.11.87	
G-BNZL	Rotorway Scorpion 133	2839		2.11.87	(Complete but stored 5/95 at Stoneacre Farm, Bredhurst)
G-BNZM	Cessna T.210N Turbo Centurion II	210-63640	N4828C	9.11.87	
G-BNZN	Cameron N-56 HAFB	1471		9.11.87	To SE-ZFA. Canx 23.1.90.

Regn	Type	c/n	Previous identity	Regn date	Fate or immediate subsequent identity (if known)
G-BNZO	Rotorway Exec 90	3535		9.11.87	
G-BNZP	Cessna 500 Citation I (Unit No.114)		N899N N999JB/(N614CC)	26.11.87	NTU - Remained as N899N. Canx 15.1.88.
G-BNZR	Clutton-Tabenor FRED Srs.II	PFA/29-10727		10.11.87	
G-BNZS	Mooney M.20K (231)	25-0631	N1154A	3.12.87	To G-DPUK 4/98. Canx.
G-BNZT	Boeing 737-2E3 (Line No. 811)	22703	EC-DYZ EI-BRZ/CC-BIN	31. 3.88	Restored as EI-BRZ. Canx 2.11.88.
G-BNZU	Boeing 737-2S3 (Line No. 570)	21775	EI-BPR (EI-BRR)/G-BMOR	. 3.88R	NTU - Restored as G-BMOR 3/88. Canx.
G-BNZV	PA-25-235 Pawnee	25-7405649	C-GSKU N9548P	22. 2.88	
G-BNZW	BAe 125 Srs.800A	NA0406 & 258105	(N551BA) G-5-577	23.11.87	To C-GKLB. Canx 8.12.87.
G-BNZX	Not allocated.				
G-BNZY	Aerospatiale SA.365N Dauphin 2	6072	PH-SSP F-WTNR	19.11.87	Restored as PH-SSP. Canx 26.1.89.
G-BNZZ	PA-28-161 Warrior II	28-8216184	N8253Z	17.11.87	
G-BOAA	BAC/Aerospatiale Concorde SST Var.102	206 & 100-006	G-N94AA G-BOAA	3. 4.74	
G-BOAB	BAC/Aerospatiale Concorde SST Var.102	208 & 100-008	G-N94AB G-BOAB	3. 4.74	
G-BOAC	BAC/Aerospatiale Concorde SST Var.102	204 & 100-004	G-N81AC G-BOAC	3. 4.74	
G-BOAD	BAC/Aerospatiale Concorde SST Var.102	210 & 100-010	G-N94AD G-BOAD	9. 5.75	
G-BOAE	BAC/Aerospatiale Concorde SST Var.102	212 & 100-012	G-N94AE G-BOAE	9. 5.75	
G-BOAF	BAC/Aerospatiale Concorde SST Var.102	216 & 100-016	G-N94AF G-BFKX	12. 6.80	
G-BOAG	BAC/Aerospatiale Concorde SST Var.102	214 & 100-014	G-BFKW	9. 2.81	
G-BOAH	PA-28-161 Warrior II	28-8416030	N43401	21. 1.88	
G-BOAI	Cessna 152 II	152-79830	C-GSJH N757LS	8. 1.88	
G-BOAJ	Cessna 404 Titan II	404-0414	HKG-4 R.Hong Kong Aux.AF/(N8799K)	.11.87R	NTU - Allocated in error. Remained as G-BNXS. Canx.
G-BOAK	PA-22-150 Tri-Pacer	22-5101	N7313D	23.11.87	(On rebuild as tail-dragger 6/93)
G-BOAL	Cameron V-65 HAFB	1600		5.11.87	
G-BOAM	Robinson R-22 Beta	0717		10.12.87	
G-BOAN	PA-30-160 Twin Comanche B	30-1069	N30PA N7970Y	4.11.87	Extensively damaged after stiking power lines at Okehampton on 15.12.94. Canx as destroyed 10.1.95.
G-BOAO	Thunder Ax7-77 HAFB	1162		2.12.87	
G-BOAP	Colt 160A HAFB	1151		24.11.87	Canx by CAA 21.11.89.
G-BOAR	SAAB J-35D Draken	-	Fv.35350 Swedish AF	19. 4.88	To N5427W. Canx 18.5.88.
G-BOAS	Air Command 503 Commander	0388 & G/04-1094		3.12.87	
G-BOAT	Cessna 310R II	310R-1236	N3749C	9. 3.78	To VH-JOB 9/83. Canx 11.8.78.
G-BOAU	Cameron V-77 HAFB	1606		10.12.87	
G-BOAV	Cameron DP-70 Hot-Air Airship	1590		24.11.87	To HB-BKP. Canx 17.12.87.
G-BOAW	DHC.7-110 Dash Seven	110	LN-TAW G-BOAW/C-GFBW	16. 3.88	To 9M-TAK 5/95. Canx 19.6.95.
G-BOAX	DHC.7-110 Dash Seven	111	C-GDNG	25. 4.88	To VP-FBQ /91. Canx 14.3.91.
G-BOAY	DHC.7-110 Dash Seven	112	C-GFBW	7. 7.88	To 9M-TAL. Canx 22.11.95.
G-BOAZ(1)	DHC.7-102 Dash Seven	113	C-GFCF	.11.87R	NTU - To C-GFCF/OE-LLU 12/88. Canx.
G-BOAZ(2)	DHC.7-102 Dash Seven	077	N8110N (G-BPSG)/OY-MBE/C-GFQL/C-GFCF	23. 5.89	To N76598/4X-AHF. Canx 1.10.93.
G-BOBA	PA-28R-201 Arrow III	28R-7837232	N31249	4. 1.88	
G-BOBB	Cameron O-120 HAFB	1609		24.11.87	
G-BOBC	PBN BN-2T Turbine Islander	2145	G-BJYZ	14. 1.86	To N54EW 12/98. Canx 9.12.98.
G-BOBD	Cameron O-160 HAFB	1594		22.12.87	
G-BOBE	Cameron O-160 HAFB	1595		22.12.87	To PH-YUP. Canx 30.11.93.
G-BOBF	Brugger MB.2 Colibri	PFA/43-11172		10.12.87	(Sold incomplete to R.Everett '97) Canx by CAA 6.3.99.
G-BOBG	Jodel D.150 (Plans No. 113)	PFA/151-11222		18.12.87	No Permit to Fly issued. Canx by CAA 29.12.95.
G-BOBH	Airtour AH-77B HAFB	009		2.12.87	
G-BOBI	Cessna 152 II	152-83295	(G-BHJD) N48172	1. 8.80	To CS-AVA. Canx 20.7.90.
G-BOBJ	PA-38-112 Tomahawk	38-80A0021	N25096 N9656N	4. 1.88	
G-BOBK	PA-38-112 Tomahawk	38-79A0503	N2352G	4. 1.88	
G-BOBL	PA-38-112 Tomahawk II	38-81A0140	N91335	4. 1.88	
G-BOBM	Beechcraft B200 Super King Air	BB-955	N999P N666EC/N18481	9.12.87	To G-WILK 12/88. Canx.
G-BOBN	Cessna 310R II	310R-1206	(N441A) G-BOBN/N5192J	20. 1.88	To C-FFCC 3/98. Canx 17.6.97.
G-BOBO	Robinson R-22 HP	0266	N712BH N100GV/N90763	7.12.87	To EI-CEF 11/91. Canx 21.10.91.
G-BOBP	Cameron A-250 HAFB	1630		4. 1.88	To 5Y-PUF. Canx 25.1.89.
G-BOBR	Cameron N-77 HAFB	1623		10.12.87	
G-BOBS	QAC Quickie Q.2	PFA/94A-10840		27. 9.82	Permit expired 22.12.92. (Damaged remains stored 4/95 at Brize Norton) Canx by CAA 18.3.99.

Regn	Type	c/n	Previous identity	Regn date	Fate or immediate subsequent identity (if known)
G-BOBT	Stolp SA.300 Starduster Too (Built by C.J.Anderson)	CJ-01	N690CM	15.12.87	
G-BOBU	Colt 90A HAFB	900		15.12.87	
G-BOBV	Reims Cessna F.150M Commuter	1415	EI-BCV	14.12.87	
G-BOBW	Air & Space 18A Gyroplane	18-65	N6145S	30.12.87	Damaged at Caldwell Hall, Stoulton, Worcs on 14.9.90. Canx as WFU 3.12.91.
G-BOBX	Grumman G.159 Gulfstream I	77	9Q-CFK N748M/N748MN/N748M/N73M/N706G/N777G	8.12.87	Stored at Birmingham with no UK CofA - acquired for spares use. Canx as WFU 25.4.89.
G-BOBY	Monnett Sonerai II	PFA/15-10223		26.10.78	Badly damaged in forced landing following loss of propeller near Barton on 31.10.82. Permit expired 8.11.82. (Stored 9/96)
G-BOBZ	PA-28-181 Archer II	28-8090257	N81671	21.12.87	
G-BOCA	PA-38-112 Tomahawk	38-79A1112	N24336	14.12.87	Damaged when struck by DH.82A G-ADIA on the ground at Goodwood on 22.9.88. Canx as destroyed 7.2.89.
G-BOCB	HS.125 Srs.1B/522	25106	G-OMCA G-DJMJ/G-AWUF/ 5N-ALY/G-AWUF/HZ-BIN	14. 9.87	CofA expired 16.10.90. WFU at Luton 1994 for spares. Canx as WFU 22.2.95. (Instructional Airframe 11/95 at Hatfield)
G-BOCC	PA-38-112 Tomahawk	38-79A0362	N2540D	14.12.87	
G-BOCD	Grob G-115	8024		10.12.87	To PH-SPH 7/96. Canx 12.7.96.
G-BOCE	Fokker F-27 Friendship 500	10384	F-BPNJ PH-FNG	14.12.87	To G-OFEC 25.1.88. Canx.
G-BOCF	Colt 77A HAFB	1178		4. 1.88	(Stored 9/95)
G-BOCG	PA-34-200T Seneca II	34-7870359	N36759	30.12.87	
G-BOCH	PA-32-300 Cherokee Six	32-7640082	N9292K	7. 1.88	To G-OCPF 9/97. Canx.
G-BOCI	Cessna 140A	15497	N5366C	17.11.87	
G-BOCJ	Cameron Watch 90SS HAFB	1592		5. 1.88	To HB-BLA 12/88. Canx 11.11.88.
G-BOCK	Sopwith Triplane Replica (Built by Northern Aeroplane Workshops)	153 & NAW-1		26. 1.88	
G-BOCL	Slingsby T.67C	2035		5. 1.88	
G-BOCM	Slingsby T.67C	2036		5. 1.88	
G-BOCN	Robinson R-22 Beta	0726	N..... G-BOCN	8. 1.88	
G-BOCO	Schweizer 269C (300C)	S.1284		17.12.87	Crashed northwest of Kidlington airfield on 11.7.89. Canx as destroyed 6.11.89. To ZK-HGG /92.
G-BOCP	PA-34-220T Seneca III	3433089		17.12.87	
G-BOCR	PA-34-220T Seneca III	3433111		26. 2.88	
G-BOCS	PA-34-220T Seneca III	3433112		26. 2.88	
G-BOCT	PA-34-220T Seneca III	3433113		26. 2.88	
G-BOCU	PA-34-220T Seneca III	3433114		26. 2.88	
G-BOCV	PA-34-220T Seneca III	3433115		26. 2.88	
G-BOCW	PA-34-220T Seneca III	3433120		25. 8.88	
G-BOCX	PA-34-220T Seneca III	3433121		29. 9.88	
G-BOCY	PA-34-220T Seneca III	3433122		29. 9.88	
G-BOCZ	PA-34-220T Seneca III	-		.12.87R	NTU - Canx.
G-BODA	PA-28-161 Warrior II	2816037	N9601N	19. 1.88	
G-BODB	PA-28-161 Warrior II	2816042		23. 2.88	
G-BODC	PA-28-161 Warrior II	2816041		23. 2.88	
G-BODD	PA-28-161 Warrior II	2816040		23. 2.88	
G-BODE	PA-28-161 Warrior II	2816039	N9603N	23. 2.88	
G-BODF	PA-28-161 Warrior II	2816038	N9602N	19. 1.88	
G-BODG	Slingsby Cadet III (Conversion of T.31B c/n 706)	PFA/42-11310	WT911	9. 6.88	(Stored incomplete 9/95) Canx by CAA 15.4.99.
G-BODH	Slingsby Cadet III (If p.i. quoted is correct, this should be built from T.8 Tutor c/n MHL/RT.13 ex G-ALNK/BGA.474)	PFA/42-10108	BGA.474	5. 1.88	
G-BODI	Stoddard-Hamilton SH-2H Glasair III (Orig. reg as SH-3R)	EMK-030 & 3088	(HB-...) G-BODI	14. 4.89	
G-BODJ	Slingsby T.67C-160	2053		21. 1.88	To G-GAFG 17.2.88. Canx.
G-BODK	Rotorway Scorpion 133	RW-133-1290		18. 1.88	Canx by CAA 20.11.95.
G-BODL	Steen Skybolt (Built by D.Doll)	1	N9RD	14. 1.88	Destroyed in fatal crash in sea near Greeb Rock, Cornwall on 25.6.94. Canx as destroyed 1.3.96.
G-BODM	PA-28-180 Cherokee Challenger	28-7305519	N56016	2. 2.88	
G-BODN	PA-28R 201 Arrow III	28R-7837210		8. 1.88	To N62PP 6/95. Canx 26.5.95.
G-BODO	Cessna 152 II	152-82404	N68923	29. 1.88	
G-BODP	PA-38-112 Tomahawk II	38-81A0010	N25616	5. 1.88	
G-BODR	PA-28-161 Warrior II	28-8116318	N8436B	5. 1.88	
G-BODS	PA-38-112 Tomahawk	38-79A0410	N2379F	3. 2.88	
G-BODT	Jodel D.18	173 & PFA/169-11290		14. 1.88	
G-BODU	Scheibe SF.25C-2000 Falke	44434	D-KIAA	19. 1.88	
G-BODV	Cameron Penta 90SS HAFB	1614		8. 1.88	To C-FDOI. Canx 22.11.88.
G-BODW	Bell 206B JetRanger II	784	N2951N N2951W	8. 1.88	Destroyed in fatal crash at Luton on 15.1.94. Canx as destroyed 5.4.94.
G-BODX	Beechcraft 76 Duchess	ME-309	N67094	26. 2.88	
G-BODY	Cessna 310R II	310R-1503	N4897A	17.12.87	
G-BODZ	Robinson R-22 Beta	0729		8. 1.88	
G-BOEA	BAe 146 Srs.100	E1095	G-5-095	25. 1.88	To A5-RGD 11/88. Canx 17.11.88.
G-BOEB	PA-38-112 Tomahawk	38-78A0784	N2377T	8. 1.88	DBR in aborted landing at Coventry on 28.9.89. Canx as WFU 14.3.90.
G-BOEC	PA-38-112 Tomahawk	38-78A0138	N9587T	8. 1.88	Canx by CAA 8.7.97. Reserved as OY-FLI on 20.5.97.
G-BOED	Cameron Sydney Opera House SS HAFB	1613		14. 1.88	Canx 21.4.94 on sale to New Zealand.

Regn	Type	c/n	Previous identity	Regn date	Fate or immediate subsequent identity (if known)
G-BOEE	PA-28-181 Cherokee Archer II	28-7690359	N6168J	20. 1.88	
G-BOEF	Short SD.3-60 Var.300	SH3732	G-14-3732	27. 1.88	To VR-BKM 8/88. Canx 15.8.88.
G-BOEG	Short SD.3-60 Var.300	SH3733	G-14-3733	27. 1.88	To N133PC. Canx 24.2.88.
G-BOEH	Robin DR.340 Major	434	F-BRVN	4. 1.88	
G-BOEI	Short SD.3-60 Var.300	SH3735	(VR-B..) G-BOEI/G-14-3735	27. 1.88	To VR-BKL 1/89. Canx 27.1.89.
G-BOEJ	Short SD.3-60 Var.300	SH3736	G-14-3736	27. 1.88	To VH-MJU 12/88. Canx 7.12.88.
G-BOEK	Cameron V-77 HAFB	1658		25. 1.88	
G-BOEL	Short SD.3-60 Var.300	SH3734	G-14-3734	27. 1.88	To N134PC. Canx 24.2.88.
G-BOEM	Aerotek Pitts S-2A Special	2255	N31525	17. 2.88	
G-BOEN	Cessna 172M Skyhawk	172-61325	N20482	12. 2.88	
G-BOEO	Aerospatiale SA.315B Lama	2590	ZS-HSK G-BOEO/N57692	22. 1.88	To F-GINN(2) 1/89. Canx 15.11.88.
G-BOEP	Bell 212	30681	VH-BEU G-BOEP/VR-BFO/N18091	21. 1.88	To 5N-BEN 12/96. Canx 20.12.96.
G-BOER	PA-28-161 Warrior II	28-8116094	N83030	21. 1.88	
G-BOES	Reims Cessna FA.152 Aerobat	0375	G-FLIP	8. 2.88	Restored as G-FLIP 12/94. Canx.
G-BOET	PA-28RT-201 Arrow IV	28R-8018020	G-IBEC G-BOET/N8116V	28. 1.88	
G-BOEU	Cameron N-90 HAFB	1605		26. 1.88	To C-FBLC. Canx 21.4.88.
G-BOEV	Robinson R-22 Beta	0749		26. 1.88	Crashed 1 mile east of Redhill on 7.9.89. Canx as destroyed 29.3.90.
G-BOEW	Robinson R-22 Beta	0750		27. 1.88	
G-BOEX	Robinson R-22 Beta	0751		27. 1.88	
G-BOEY	Robinson R-22 Beta	0752	N9081S	27. 1.88	Fatal crash nr.Redhill 16.1.97. Canx 5.6.97 as destroyed.
G-BOEZ	Robinson R-22 Beta	0753		27. 1.88	
G-BOFA	Robinson R-22	0170	N9086D	16. 2.88	To G-HBMW 7/94. Canx.
G-BOFB	Sikorsky S-76A (Mod)	760198	N9700Q PH-NZO/N5419U	28. 1.88	To VH-LAY. Canx 6.12.93.
G-BOFC	Beechcraft 76 Duchess	ME-217	N6628M	28. 1.88	
G-BOFD	Cessna U.206G Stationair 6 II	U206-04181	N756LS	27. 1.88	
G-BOFE	PA-34-200T Seneca II	34-7870381	N39493	22. 2.88	
G-BOFF	Cameron N-77 HAFB	1666		26. 1.88	
G-BOFG	Short SD.3-60 Var.300	SH3737	G-14-3737	3. 2.88	To G-OLBA 3/88. Canx.
G-BOFH	Short SD.3-60 Var.300	SH3738	G-14-3738	3. 2.88	To G-OLTN 4/88. Canx.
G-BOFI	Short SD.3-60 Var.100	SH3739	G-14-3739	3. 2.88	To G-CPTL 6/88. Canx.
G-BOFJ	Short SD.3-60 Var.300	SH3740	G-14-3740	3. 2.88	To N165DD. Canx 20.5.88.
G-BOFK	Short SD.3-60 Var.300	SH3741	G-14-3741	3. 2.88	To "G-LOGW"/G-OLGW 9/88. Canx.
G-BOFL	Cessna 152 II	152-84101	N5457H	28. 1.88	
G-BOFM	Cessna 152 II	152-84730	N6445M	28. 1.88	
G-BOFN	Beechcraft 100 King Air	B-27	5B-CGM N5377C/9M-JPA/9M-CAA/N871K	28. 1.88	To C-GWWA. Canx 26.1.89.
G-BOFO	Ultimate Aircraft 10 Dash 200	10-200-004 & PFA/180-11319	(HB-...) G-BOFO	15. 2.88	(Status uncertain)
G-BOFP	Slingsby T.67M Firefly 200	2055		9. 2.88	To TC-CBF. Canx 7.7.88.
G-BOFR	Slingsby T.67M Firefly 200	2056		9. 2.88	To TC-CBG. Canx 7.7.88.
G-BOFS	Slingsby T.67M Firefly 200	2057		9. 2.88	To TC-CBH. Canx 7.7.88.
G-BOFT	Slingsby T.67M Firefly 200	2058		9. 2.88	To TC-CBJ. Canx 22.7.88.
G-BOFU	Slingsby T.67M Firefly 200	2059		9. 2.88	To TC-CBK 7/88. Canx by CAA 20.3.91.
G-BOFV	PA-44-180 Seminole	44-7995207	N2198K	3. 2.88	To D-GANS(2) 9/93. Canx 17.8.93.
G-BOFW	Cessna A.150M Aerobat	A150-0612	N9803J	15. 2.88	
G-BOFX	Cessna A.150M Aerobat	A150-0678	N9869J	15. 2.88	
G-BOFY	PA-28-140 Cherokee Cruiser	28-7425374	N43521	3. 2.88	
G-BOFZ	PA-28-161 Warrior II	28-7816255	N2189M	10. 2.88	
G-BOGA	Cessna 500 Citation I (Unit No.220)	500-0220	N932HA N93WD/N5220J	28. 1.88	To G-OBEL 1/89. Canx.
G-BOGB	Hawker Tempest II Replica (Modified War Hawker Sea Fury Replica)	DR001 & PFA/120-11185		3. 2.88	No Permit believed issued. Canx by CAA 17.3.92.
G-BOGC	Cessna 152 II	152-84550	N5346M	8. 2.88	
G-BOGD	Cameron Dinosaur 80SS HAFB	1610		3. 2.88	To C-FDOG. Canx 22.11.88.
G-BOGE	Cessna 152 II	152-80050	N757VZ	3. 2.88	Forced landing in a field and struck a tree at Smockingham Hollow, Leics on 6.5.88. Canx as destroyed 12.10.88.
G-BOGF	PA-28RT-201T Turbo Arrow IV	28R-8031107	N8219V	. 2.88R	NTU - To G-BUND 7/88. Canx.
G-BOGG	Cessna 152 II	152-82960	N45956	15. 2.88	
G-BOGH	Cameron N-160 HAFB	1622		9. 2.88	To F-GFFM 5/89. Canx 4.5.88.
G-BOGI	Robin DR.400/180 Regent	1821		15. 2.88	
G-BOGJ	PA-28RT-201T Turbo Arrow IV	28R-8431031	N4376E N9635N	7. 3.88	To HB-PNT. Canx 3.4.90.
G-BOGK	ARV Super 2	K.006 & PFA/152-11138		10. 2.88	
G-BOGL	Thunder Ax7-77 Srs.1 HAFB	953		8. 4.88	To D-OUYO 1/96. Canx 6.12.95.
G-BOGM	PA-28RT-201T Turbo Arrow IV	28R-8031077	N8173C	10. 2.88	
G-BOGN	PA-32RT-300 Lance II	32R-7885086	N33LV N30573	10. 2.88	To G-HERO 4/88. Canx.
G-BOGO	PA-32R-301T Saratoga SP	32R-8029064	N8165W	6. 4.88	
G-BOGP	Cameron V-77 HAFB	896		30. 3.88	
G-BOGR	Colt 180A HAFB	1183		11. 5.88	CofA expired 13.3.92. Canx as WFU 28.4.97.

Regn	Type	c/n	Previous identity	Regn date	Fate or immediate subsequent identity (if known)
G-BOGS	PA-34-200T Seneca II	34-7770004	N976GM C6-BDU/N4969F	16. 2.88	Badly damaged when struck by a runaway unmanned fire vechicle at Exeter on 7.6.90. Canx as WFU 26.2.91.
G-BOGT	Colt 77A HAFB	1212		21. 3.88	Canx as WFU 9.5.97. (Extant 1/98)
G-BOGU	[Was reserved for an unidentified Piper]				
G-BOGV	Air Command 532 Elite	0399 & G/04-1102		10. 3.88	
G-BOGW	Air Command 532 Elite	AC532-UK001 & 0398		16. 2.88	
G-BOGX	Aerospatiale AS.355F2 Twin Squirrel	5370		15. 2.88	To G-BSLL 7/89. Canx.
G-BOGY	Cameron V-77 HAFB	1650		15. 2.88	
G-BOGZ	PBN BN-2A-26 Islander	2040		22. 2.88	To TC-FBL. Canx 13.6.88.
G-BOHA	PA-28-161 Warrior II	28-7816352	N3526M	16. 3.88	(Badly damaged on landing Bottesford 18.9.97)
G-BOHB	Cessna 152 II	152-79596	N757AX	10. 2.88	Badly damaged in forced landing at 2m SW of Bletchley on 12.6.90. Canx as destroyed 6.4.92.
G-BOHC	Boeing 757-236ER	24120	EC-ELA EC-516/G-BOHC/EC-ELA/EC-202/G-BOHC	29. 3.88	To G-BPEF 5/92. Canx.
G-BOHD	Colt 77A HAFB	1214		4. 3.88	(Active 8/97)
G-BOHE	Cameron O-120 HAFB	1670		8. 2.88	To D-OAOB 4/94. Canx 4.3.92.
G-BOHF	Thunder Ax8-84 HAFB	1197		8. 4.88	(Active 7/96)
G-BOHG	Air Command 532 Elite	0402 & G/04-1122		10. 3.88	
G-BOHH	Cessna 172N Skyhawk II	172-73906	N131FR N7333J	19. 2.88	
G-BOHI	Cessna 152 II	152-81241	N49406	29. 2.88	
G-BOHJ	Cessna 152 II	152-80558	N25259	29. 2.88	
G-BOHK	BAe 146 Srs.200QT	E2100	G-5-100	16. 3.88	To G-TNTJ. Canx.
G-BOHL	Cameron A-120 HAFB	1701		11. 3.88	
G-BOHM	PA-28-180 Cherokee Challenger	28-7305287	N55000	18. 2.88	
G-BOHN	PA-38-112 Tomahawk II	38-81A0151	N23593	19. 2.88	Crashed on landing Cardiff on 13.8.93. (Stored 8/94) Canx as WFU 1.11.95.
G-BOHO	PA-28-161 Warrior II	28-8016196	N747RH N9560N	25. 2.88	
G-BOHP	PA-28-161 Warrior II	28-8016050	N8079Z	25. 2.88	To G-OMPS 2/89. Canx.
G-BOHR	PA-28-151 Cherokee Warrior	28-7515245	C-GNFE	29. 2.88	
G-BOHS	PA-38-112 Tomahawk	38-79A0988	N2418P	26. 2.88	
G-BOHT	PA-38-112 Tomahawk	38-79A1079	N25304 C-GAYW/N24052	14. 4.88	
G-BOHU	PA-38-112 Tomahawk	38-80A0031	N25093	26. 2.88	
G-BOHV	Wittman W.8 Tailwind	621 & PFA/31-11151		3. 3.88	(Substantially damaged 14.3.97 at Rufforth)
G-BOHW	Van's RV-4	PFA/181-11309		16. 6.88	
G-BOHX	PA-44-180 Seminole	44-7995008	N36814	9. 3.88	
G-BOHY	HS.748 Srs.2B/378	1784	D-AHSA	11. 3.88	To 9N-ADE 10/94. Canx 26.10.94.
G-BOHZ	HS.748 Srs.2B/378	1785	D-AHSB G-11-17	11. 3.88	To (VT-WAY)/ZS-NNW(2) 12/94. Canx 15.12.94.
G-BOIA	Cessna 180K Skywagon II	180-53121	N2895K	3. 3.88	
G-BOIB	Wittman W.10 Tailwind	PFA/31-10551		3. 3.88	(Extant 8/97)
G-BOIC	PA-28R-201T Turbo Arrow III	28R-7803123	N2336M	7. 4.88	
G-BOID	Bellanca 7ECA Citabria	1092-75	N8676V	3. 3.88	
G-BOIE	Beechcraft 58P Baron	TJ-479	N6815L	18. 3.88	Restored as N6815L 8/90. Canx 3.8.90.
G-BOIF	Beechcraft 95-B55 Baron	TC-1824	N4469B YV-231P/YV-TALL	3. 3.88	Restored as N4469B 4/93. Canx 14.4.93.
G-BOIG	PA-28-161 Warrior II	28-8516027	N4390B N9519N	1. 3.88	
G-BOIH	Pitts S-1E Special	PFA/09-10970		28. 3.88	Fatal crash after take-off Meppershall 25.7.97. Canx as destroyed 18.11.97.
G-BOII	Cessna 172N Skyhawk II	172-72334	N4702D	2. 3.88	To G-RARB 6/96. Canx.
G-BOIJ	Thunder Ax7-77 Srs.1 HAFB	964		11. 3.88	
G-BOIK	Air Command 503 Commander (Erroneously regd as c/n G/04-1090)	0420 & G/04-1087		8. 3.88	
G-BOIL	Cessna 172N Skyhawk II	172-71301	N23FL N23ER/(N2494E)	2. 3.88	
G-BOIM	Cessna 150M Commuter	150-77040	N63004	30. 3.88	Crashed on take-off from Faircross Farm, near Thatcham on 17.7.96. Canx as destroyed 15.11.96.
G-BOIN	Bellanca 7ECA Citabria	1190-77	N4160Y	7. 3.88	
G-BOIO	Cessna 152 II	152-80260	N24445	7. 3.88	
G-BOIP	Cessna 152 II	152-83444	N49264	7. 3.88	Forced landing in a field and overturned at Uckington on 11.1.90. (Fuselage & wings at Stapleford in 5/98)
G-BOIR	Cessna 152 II	152-83272	N48041	7. 3.88	
G-BOIS	PA-31-300 Turbo Navajo	31-688	G-AYNB N6778L	9.11.84	To C-GCYL 5/98. Canx 6.5.98.
G-BOIT	Socata TB-10 Tobago	810		10. 3.88	
G-BOIU	Socata TB-10 Tobago	811		10. 3.88	
G-BOIV	Cessna 150M Commuter	150-78620	N704HH	30. 3.88	
G-BOIW	Cessna 152 II	152-82845	N89731	6. 4.88	
G-BOIX	Cessna 172N Skyhawk II	172-71206	C-GMMX N2253E	9. 3.88	
G-BOIY	Cessna 172N Skyhawk II	172-67738	N73901	9. 3.88	

Regn	Type	c/n	Previous identity	Regn date	Fate or immediate subsequent identity (if known)
G-BOIZ	PA-34-200T Seneca II	34-8070014	N81081	25. 2.88	
G-BOJA	Cameron O-160 HAFB	1678		11. 3.88	To C-FBAQ. Canx 22.11.88.
G-BOJB	Cameron V-77 HAFB	1615		11. 3.88	
G-BOJC	Colt 180A HAFB	1195		15. 3.88	To SU-182. Canx 7.10.88.
G-BOJD	Cameron N-77 HAFB	1653		11. 3.88	
G-BOJE	PA-28-236 Dakota	28-8211013	N84600	11. 3.88	To D-EIKW(2) 9/93. Canx 18.8.93.
G-BOJF	Air Command 532 Elite Two Seat	0425		11. 3.88	
G-BOJG	Air Command 532 Elite Two Seat	0400		11. 3.88	Destroyed in fatal crash at Bredons Norton, near Pershore on 22.6.89. Canx as destroyed 13.2.90.
G-BOJH	PA-28R-200 Cherokee Arrow II	28R-7235139	N2821T	6. 4.88	
G-BOJI	PA-28RT-201 Arrow IV	28R-7918221	N2919X	31. 3.88	
G-BOJJ(1)	Reims Cessna F.172N	1914	CS-AQW	. 3.88	NTU - Not Imported. Remained as CS-AQW. Canx.
G-BOJJ(2)	BAe 146 Srs.300	E3146	I-ATSC G-BOJJ/G-6-146	28.11.89	To EI-CLH 6/95. Canx 2.6.95.
G-BOJK	PA-34-220T Seneca III	3433020	G-BRUF N9113D	11. 3.88	
G-BOJL	GEMS MS.885 Super Rallye	122	F-BKLI	21. 3.88	(On overhaul 5/94 at Haverfordwest) Canx by CAA 18.5.99.
G-BOJM	PA-28-181 Archer II	28-8090244	N8155L	21. 3.88	
G-BOJN	Swearingen (Fairchild) SA.227AC Metro IV	AC-692B	N2707D	23. 3.88	Restored as N2707D 3/90. Canx 26.2.90.
G-BOJO	Colt 120A HAFB	1208		7. 3.88	Canx by CAA 6.8.97.
G-BOJP	BAe Jetstream Srs.3102	801	G-31-801	30. 3.88	To N414UE 5/88. Canx 13.5.88.
G-BOJR	Cessna 172P Skyhawk II	172-75574	N64539	22. 4.88	
G-BOJS	Cessna 172P Skyhawk II	172-74582	N52699	29. 3.88	
G-BOJT	Beechcraft 76 Duchess	ME-68	N2011U	11. 4.88	Went off the end of the runway at Halfpenny Green on 13.2.92. Canx as destroyed 2.3.92.
G-BOJU	Cameron N-77 HAFB	1718		21. 3.88	
G-BOJV	Bell 206B JetRanger II	2671	N79PS	6. 4.88	To ZS-HWO. Canx 18.1.90.
G-BOJW	PA-28-161 Cherokee Warrior II	28-7716038	N1668H	28. 3.88	
G-BOJX	PA-28-181 Cherokee Archer II	28-7890332	N3774M	19. 4.88	To G-SGSE 12/96. Canx.
G-BOJY	PA-28-161 Warrior II	28-7916181	N3030G	4. 5.88	To G-RSKR 4/95. Canx.
G-BOJZ	PA-28-161 Warrior II	28-7916223	N2113J	28. 3.88	
G-BOKA	PA-28-201T Turbo Dakota	28-7921076	N2860S	15. 3.88	
G-BOKB	PA-28-161 Warrior II	28-8216077	N8013Y	29. 3.88	
G-BOKC	Aerospatiale AS.365N1 Dauphin 2	6308		23. 3.88	To EC-194/EC-EKQ. Canx 26.8.88.
G-BOKD	Bell 206B JetRanger III	3654	N3171A	23. 3.88	To G-PSCI 5/88. Canx.
G-BOKE	PA-34-200T Seneca II	34-7870428	N21030	20. 4.88	To G-JLCA 9/97. Canx.
G-BOKF	Air Command 532 Elite	0404 & G/04-1101		28. 3.88	
G-BOKG	Slingsby T.31B Cadet III Motor Glider	902 & PFA/42-10611	XE789	4. 5.88	To BGA.3485/EI-139 .93. Canx by CAA 17.2.98.
G-BOKH	Whittaker MW.7 (Regd as PFA/171-11231)	PFA/171-11281	(G-MTWT)	21. 3.88	
G-BOKI	Whittaker MW.7	PFA/171-11282	(G-MTWU)	21. 3.88	Badly damaged in forced landing at Cross Hands Farm, Old Sodbury, Avon on 9.4.95. (For sale as rebuild project 7/96)
G-BOKJ	Whittaker MW.7	PFA/171-11283	(G-MTWV)	21. 3.88	
G-BOKK	PA-28-161 Warrior II	28-8116300	N8427L	6. 4.88	Damaged in forced landing Hamgreen, nr.Redditch 18.5.95. Canx as WFU 8.9.95. (On rebuild 6/96)
G-BOKL	PA-28-161 Warrior II	2816044		24. 3.88	(Extant 4/97)
G-BOKM	PA-28-161 Warrior II	2816045		24. 3.88	
G-BOKN	PA-28-161 Warrior II	2816046		24. 3.88	
G-BOKO	PA-28-161 Warrior II	2816049		24. 3.88	
G-BOKP	PA-28-161 Warrior II	2816050		24. 3.88	
G-BOKR	PA-28-161 Warrior II	2816051		24. 3.88	
G-BOKS	PA-28-161 Warrior II	2816052		24. 3.88	(Extant 4/97)
G-BOKT	PA-28-161 Warrior II	2816053		24. 3.88	
G-BOKU	PA-28-161 Warrior II	2816054		24. 3.88	
G-BOKV	Boeing 727-2H3RE	20739	PH-AHB N739BN/PH-AHB/N189CB/TS-JHO	22. 3.88	To N501DC. Canx 12.5.88.
G-BOKW	Bolkow Bo.208C Junior	689	G-BITT F-BRHX/D-EEAL	6. 1.88	Permit expired 3.11.95. Canx by CAA 19.7.96.
G-BOKX	PA-28-161 Warrior II	28-7816680	N39709	28. 3.88	
G-BOKY	Cessna 152 II	152-85298	N67409	6. 4.88	
G-BOKZ	BAe 146 Srs.200	E2102		13. 4.88	To G-5-102/EC-198/EC-ELT. Canx 11.10.88.
G-BOLA	Agusta A.109A II	7411	VR-CMP G-BOLA	5. 5.88	To VR-CLA. Canx 3.12.93.
G-BOLB	Taylorcraft BC-12-65	3165	N36211 NC36211	17. 5.88	
G-BOLC	Sportavia Fournier RF-6B-100	1	F-BVKS	28. 3.88	
G-BOLD	PA-38-112 Tomahawk	38-78A0180	N9740T	8. 7.88	(Stored 10/97)
G-BOLE	PA-38-112 Tomahawk	38-78A0475	N2506E	13. 7.88	
G-BOLF	PA-38-112 Tomahawk	38-79A0375	N583P YV-133E/YV-1696P/N9666N	13. 7.88	
G-BOLG	Bellanca 7KCAB Citabria	517-75	N8706V	25.11.88	
G-BOLH	Cessna 172P Skyhawk II	172-75015	N54631	30. 3.88	Badly damaged in forced landing 8 miles west of Shobdon on 18.6.89. Canx as destroyed 13.7.89.
G-BOLI	Cessna 172P Skyhawk II	172-75484	N63794	30. 3.88	
G-BOLJ	Grumman American GA-7 Cougar	GA7-0020	N722GA	30. 3.88	To N80LJ 10/96. Canx 14.5.96.

Regn	Type	c/n	Previous identity	Regn date	Fate or immediate subsequent identity (if known)
G-BOLK	PA-28-161 Warrior II	28-8316050	N4295C	16. 5.88	To G-LADN 7/89. Canx.
G-BOLL	Lake LA-4-200 Skimmer	295	(F-GRMX) G-BOLL/EI-ANR/N1133L	4. 5.88	
G-BOLM	Boeing 737-3T0	23942	N76361	20. 4.88	To N320AW 11/90. Canx 19.11.90.
G-BOLN	Colt 21A Cloudhopper HAFB	1226		4. 5.88	
G-BOLO	Bell 206B JetRanger II	1622	N59409	2.11.87	
G-BOLP	Colt 21A Cloudhopper HAFB	1227		4. 5.88	
G-BOLR	Colt 21A Cloudhopper HAFB	1228		3. 5.88	
G-BOLS	Clutton-Tabenor FRED Srs.II	PFA/29-10676		6. 4.88	(Flown 6/88)
G-BOLT	Rockwell Commander 114	14428	N5883N	16.10.78	
G-BOLU	Robin R.3000/120	106	F-GFAO SE-IMS	14. 4.88	
G-BOLV	Cessna 152 II	152-80492	N24983	8. 4.88	
G-BOLW	Cessna 152 II	152-80589	N25316	9. 6.88	
G-BOLX	Cessna 172N Skyhawk II	172-69099	N734TK	8. 4.88	
G-BOLY	Cessna 172N Skyhawk II	172-69004	N734PJ	31. 3.88	
G-BOLZ	Rand Robinson KR-2	PFA/129-10866		6. 4.88	
G-BOMA	BAe 146 Srs.100 Statesman	E1091	G-5-091	8. 4.88	To A6-SMK. Canx 16.12.88.
G-BOMB	Cassutt Racer IIIM	RWLB.1 & PFA/34-10386		18.12.78	(Badly damaged in crash at Weston Park, near Telford on 22.6.97)
G-BOMC	PBN BN-2T Turbine Islander	2201		31. 3.88	To G-51-2201/A40-CT. Canx 7.9.89.
G-BOMD	PBN BN-2T Turbine Islander AL.1	2202		31. 3.88	To AAC as ZG993. Canx to MOD(PE) 19.3.90.
G-BOME	PBN BN-2B-20 Islander	2203		31. 3.88	To B-3901 6/89. Canx 7.6.89.
G-BOMF	PBN BN-2B-20 Islander	2204		6. 4.88	To B-3902 7/89. Canx.
G-BOMG	PBN BN-2B-26 Islander	2205		6. 4.88	To D-IBNF 5/89. Canx 25.5.89.
G-BOMH	Aerospatiale SA.319B Alouette III	2067	ANE-301 Ecuadorian Navy	31. 3.88	Canx 20.4.88 on sale to Switzerland. To F-GHCH(2) 8/88.
G-BOMI	BAe 146 Srs.200	E2105	G-5-105	22. 4.88	To G-5-105/HA-TAB. Canx 14.11.88.
G-BOMJ	BAe 146 Srs.200	E2109		13. 4.88	To SE-DHM. Canx 9.12.88.
G-BOMK	BAe 146 Srs.200QT (Originally regd as Srs.200)	E2112	RP-C482 F-GTNU/G-5-112/(EC-231)/G-BOMK	13. 4.88	
G-BOML	Hispano HA-1112-MIL Buchon (C/n originally quoted as 170 - possibly corruption of Spanish AF serial)	151	N170BG Spanish AF C4K-107	15. 4.88	
G-BOMM	Beechcraft B200 Super King Air	BB-1089	N5NV N85CR	8. 4.88	To D-INKA 10/90. Canx 23.10.90.
G-BOMN	Cessna 150F	150-63089	N6489F	25. 4.89	
G-BOMO	PA-38-112 Tomahawk II	38-81A0161	N91324	8. 4.88	(Damaged at Welshpool on 17.5.99)
G-BOMP	PA-28-181 Cherokee Archer II	28-7790249	N8482F	8. 4.88	
G-BOMR	PA-28-151 Cherokee Warrior	28-7415234		27. 4.88	Damaged by gales at Lulsgate on 25.1.90. Canx as destroyed 9.5.90.
G-BOMS	Cessna 172N Skyhawk II	172-69448	N737JG	11. 4.88	
G-BOMT	Cessna 172N Skyhawk II	172-70396	N739AU	12. 7.88	
G-BOMU	PA-28-181 Cherokee Archer II	28-7790318	N1631H	8. 4.88	
G-BOMV	Fokker F-27 Friendship 500	10372	F-BPND PH-FMU	8. 4.88	To N708FE. Canx 21.4.88.
G-BOMW	Cameron DP-70 Hot-Air Airship	1703		12. 4.88	NTU - Canx 27.6.88.
G-BOMX	Cameron N-90 HAFB	1702		12. 4.88	NTU - To G-BOOP 11.5.88. Canx 27.6.88.
G-BOMY	PA-28-161 Warrior II	28-8216049	N8457S	28. 6.88	
G-BOMZ	PA-38-112 Tomahawk	38-78A0635	N2315A	30. 6.88	
G-BONA	Cessna 172RG Cutlass	172RG-0670	N77AG N700AG/G-BONA/N6408V	11. 5.88	To (N700WG)/N700AG 4/91. Canx 19.4.91.
G-BONB	ARV Super 2	K.009 & PFA/152-11182		13. 4.88	To G-COWS 5/88. Canx.
G-BONC	PA-28RT-201 Arrow IV	28R-7918007	C-GXYX N3069K	13. 5.88	
G-BOND	Sikorsky S-76A II Plus	760036	N4931Y	31. 1.80	
G-BONE	Pilatus P.2-06	600-62	U-142 Swiss AF/Swiss AF U-113	8. 7.81	(Stored at Hurst Green, Etchingham, East Sussex in 12/95)
G-BONF	Enstrom F-28C	398	N51661	3. 5.88	To G-WSEC 12/88. Canx.
G-BONG	Enstrom F-28A-UK	154	N9604	22. 4.88	
G-BONH	Enstrom F-28A	172	N30HW	3. 5.88	To ZK-HKD. Canx 2.12.93.
G-BONI	Fokker F.27 Friendship 500	10375	F-BPNE PH-FMX	. 4.88R	NTU - To N709FE 5/88. Canx.
G-BONJ	Colt AS-105 Hot-Air Airship	1079		19. 4.88	Canx 31.10.88 on sale to Korea.
G-BONK	Colt 180A HAFB	1167		14.12.87	
G-BONL	Bell 206B JetRanger III	2789	N2774A	4. 5.88	To F-GHRU 8/91. Canx 2.8.91.
G-BONM	Boeing 737-2A3	22738	PH-TSA CX-BOO/PH-TSA/CX-BOO	3. 5.88	Restored as PH-TSA/CX-BOO. Canx 8.11.88.
G-BONN	Aerospatiale AS.350B1 Ecureuil	2105		18. 4.88	To G-PLME 5/88. Canx.
G-BONO	Cessna 172N Skyhawk II	172-70299	C-GSMF N738WS	11. 5.88	
G-BONP	CFM Streak Shadow	SS-01P & PFA/161A-11344		4. 5.88	(Damaged by gales at Prestwick on 26.12.98)
G-BONR	Cessna 172N Skyhawk II	172-68164	C-GYGK (N733BH)	18. 4.88	
G-BONS	Cessna 172N Skyhawk II	172-68345	C-GIUF (N733KD)	18. 4.88	
G-BONT	Slingsby T.67M Firefly II	2054		3. 5.88	
G-BONU	Slingsby T.67B	2037		3. 5.88	

Regn	Type	c/n	Previous identity	Regn date	Fate or immediate subsequent identity (if known)
G-BONV	Colt 17A Cloudhopper HAFB	1238		3. 5.88	(Extant 1/98)
G-BONW	Cessna 152 II	152-80401	OY-CPL N24825	15. 4.88	
G-BONX	Robinson R-22 Beta	0781		27. 4.88	To G-KEVN 6/91. Canx.
G-BONY	Denney Kitfox Mk.1	166 & PFA/172-11351		11. 5.88	
G-BONZ	Beechcraft V35B Bonanza	D-10282	N6661D	6. 4.88	
G-BOOA	BAe 125 Srs.800B	258088	(ZK-RHP) G-5-563	26. 4.88	To G-5-563/G-BTAB 7/88. Canx.
G-BOOB	Cameron N-65 HAFB	515		12.11.79	
G-BOOC	PA-18-150 Super Cub	18-8279	SE-EPC	29. 4.88	
G-BOOD	Slingsby T.31M Motor Tutor	PFA/42-11264		4. 5.88	(At least wings are ex XE810 c/n 923)
G-BOOE	Grumman-American GA-7 Cougar	GA7-0093	N718G	7. 6.88	
G-BOOF	PA-28-181 Archer II	28-7890084	N47510	16. 6.88	
G-BOOG	PA-28RT-201T Turbo Arrow IV	28R-8331036	N4303K	6. 5.88	
G-BOOH	Jodel D.112 (Built Ets Valladeau)	481	F-BHVK	16. 5.88	
G-BOOI	Cessna 152 II	152-80751	N25590	22. 8.88	
G-BOOJ	Air Command 532 Elite II	PB206 & G/04-1098		4. 5.88	(Extant 11/96)
G-BOOK	Pitts S-1S Special (Mod)	1-0017	N8JT	25. 9.78	DBF when the diesel oil tank had leaked after landing at Spanhoe on 19.10.92. Canx as destroyed 17.11.92.
G-BOOL	Cessna 172N Skyhawk II	172-72486	C-GJSY N5271D	27. 4.88	
G-BOOM	Hawker Hunter T.7 (T.53)	41H/693749	G-9-432 R.Danish AF ET-274/R.Netherlands AF N-307	6.10.80	Canx 23.6.97 on sale to Jordan.
G-BOON	PA-32RT-300 Lance II	32R-7885253	N361DB	25. 4.88	Damaged on landing at Connemara on 10.10.97. Canx by CAA 3.3.98. Wreck at Andrewsfield 1/99.
G-BOOO	Brugger MB.2 Colibri	PFA/43-11329		19. 4.88	CofA never issued. Canx by CAA 18.3.97.
G-BOOP	Cameron N-90 HAFB	1702	(G-BOMX)	11. 5.88	Canx by CAA 31.10.95.
G-BOOR	BAe Jetstream Srs.3201	790	G-31-790	24. 5.88	To N332QA. Canx 20.10.88.
G-BOOS	Colt 240A HAFB	1229		11. 5.88	Canx by CAA 23.1.89. To F-GHNF 7/89.
G-BOOT	Colt 240A HAFB	1230		11. 5.88	Canx by CAA 23.1.89. To F-GHNE 7/89.
G-BOOU	Cameron N-77 HAFB	1720		6. 5.88	Canx by CAA 22.7.98.
G-BOOV	Aerospatiale AS.355F2 Twin Squirrel	5374		3. 5.88	
G-BOOW	Aerosport Scamp	PFA/117-10709		10. 5.88	(Damaged on test flight Earls Colne 26.11.97)
G-BOOX	Rutan LongEz	PFA/74A-10844		3. 5.88	
G-BOOY	Bell 212	30684	OY-HMA LN-OSQ	29. 4.88	To VH-NSU 6/88. Canx 31.5.88.
G-BOOZ(1)	Enstrom F-28A	157	G-BBIN	. .76R	NTU - Restored as G-BBIN 18.8.76. Canx.
G-BOOZ(2)	Cameron N-77 HAFB	904	(G-BKSJ)	21. 6.83	(Active 7/97)
G-BOPA	PA-28-181 Archer II	28-8490024	N43299	28. 4.88	
G-BOPB	Boeing 767-204ER (Line No. 243)	24239	N6009F	1.11.88	
G-BOPC	PA-28-161 Warrior II	28-8216006	N2124X	6. 5.88	
G-BOPD	Bede BD-4	632	N632DH	25. 5.88	
G-BOPE	Hiller UH-12E	5201	N4035W	6. 5.88	Crashed at Boleynagah, Whitegate, Mountshannon, Co.Clare on 2.8.90 & DBF. Canx by CAA 4.1.91.
G-BOPF	Cessna 182R Skylane II	182-68155	N9974H	6. 5.88	To OH-CTR. Canx 24.8.88.
G-BOPG	Cessna 182Q Skylane II	182-66689	N95962	6. 5.88	
G-BOPH	Cessna TR.182 Turbo Skylane RG II	R182-01031	N756BJ	11. 5.88	
G-BOPI	Aerospatiale AS.365N1 Dauphin 2	6309		17. 5.88	To G-POAV 11/88. Canx.
G-BOPJ	Boeing 737-46B	24123	N1790B	24. 4.89	To G-OBMN 11/91. Canx.
G-BOPK	Boeing 737-4Y0	24124		20. 3.89	To N689MA. Canx 8.11.91.
G-BOPL	PA-28-161 Warrior II	28-8116163	N8342J	29. 4.88	To EC-GLP 12/96. Canx 28.10.96.
G-BOPM	Brooklands Aerospace OA.7 Optica Srs.300	019		17. 5.88	To N198DP 2/98. Canx.
G-BOPN	Brooklands Aerospace OA.7 Optica Srs.301	020	9M-OPT G-BOPN	17. 5.88	To VH-OPI. Canx 19.1.99.
G-BOPO	FLS OA.7 Optica Srs.301	021	EC-FVM EC-435/G-BOPO	17. 5.88	
G-BOPP	Brooklands Aerospace OA.7 Optica Srs.301	022		17. 5.88	To EC-438 8/93. Canx 20.6.94.
G-BOPR	FLS OA.7 Optica Srs.301	023		17. 5.88	(Stored 9/95)
G-BOPS	Aerospatiale AS.355F1 Twin Squirrel	5157	I-MOST	17. 8.88	To G-SVJM 5/90. Canx.
G-BOPT	Grob G-115	8046		10. 5.88	
G-BOPU	Grob G-115	8059		10. 5.88	
G-BOPV	PA-34-200T Seneca II	34-8070265	N82323	7. 6.88	
G-BOPW	Cessna A.152 Aerobat	A152-0908	N4922A	11. 5.88	Badly damaged on landing at Sywell on 30.8.95. (Extant 5/96) CofA expired 20.6.98. Canx as destroyed 11.6.99.
G-BOPX	Cessna A.152 Aerobat	A152-0932	N761BK	11. 5.88	
G-BOPY	Putzer Elster C	011	D-EDEZ	12. 5.88	(On rebuild following accident on 31.5.84) Canx as WFU 19.3.90. To G-LUFT 3/92.
G-BOPZ	Cameron DP-70 Hot Air Airship	1703		19. 5.88	To S5-OLZ 11/95. Canx 11.7.95.
G-BORA	Colt 77A HAFB	1233		19. 5.88	Canx as WFU 17.9.98.
G-BORB	Cameron V-77 HAFB	1348		24. 8.88	

Regn	Type	c/n	Previous identity	Regn date	Fate or immediate subsequent identity (if known)
G-BORC	Colt 180A HAFB	1217		17. 6.88	To ZS-HZT 5/99. Canx 7.4.98.
G-BORD	Thunder Ax7-77 HAFB	1164		26. 5.88	
G-BORE	Colt 77A HAFB	642	D-BREAK	24. 5.88	
G-BORF	Colt AS-80 Mk.II Hot-Air Airship	1241		22.12.88	Crashed following the nose collapsing at Brooks, Alberta on 9.7.91.
G-BORG	Campbell Cricket	G/03-1085		8. 6.88	(Damaged .96)
G-BORH	PA-34-200T Seneca II	34-8070352	N8261V	7. 6.88	
G-BORI	Cessna 152 II	152-81672	N66936	8. 6.88	
G-BORJ	Cessna 152 II	152-82649	N89148	27. 5.88	
G-BORK	PA-28-161 Warrior II	28-8116095	N83036	8. 6.88	
G-BORL	PA-28-161 Warrior II	28-7816256	N2190M	28. 9.88	
G-BORM	HS.748 Srs.2B/217	1670	RP-C1043 V2-LAA/VP-LAA/9Y-TDH	29. 7.88	WFU - To Exeter fire service. Canx by CAA 18.6.92. (Extant 7/96)
G-BORN	Cameron N-77 HAFB	1777		13. 5.88	
G-BORO	Cessna 152 II	152-83767	N5130B	27. 5.88	Damaged on landing at Welshpool on 26.8.96. (Fuselage stored 9/97 at Welshpool)
G-BORP	PA-46-310P Malibu	46-8408039	N4346M	18. 5.88	To F-GMBC. Canx 2.3.93.
G-BORR	Thunder Ax8-90 HAFB	1256		13. 6.88	
G-BORS	PA-28-181 Archer II	28-8090156	N8127C	31. 5.88	
G-BORT	Colt 77A HAFB	1255		7. 6.88	
G-BORU	PA-28RT-201 Turbo Arrow II	28R-7918069	N1015S N9614N	12. 9.88	To CS-AVH. Canx 2.10.90.
G-BORV	Bell 206B JetRanger II	2202	C-GVTY N16763	8. 6.88	
G-BORW	Cessna 172P Skyhawk II	172-74301	N51357	23. 8.88	
G-BORX	Bell 206B JetRanger II	1595	C-GHYQ	9. 6.88	To OO-EAN. Canx 20.4.89.
G-BORY	Cessna 150L	150-72292	N6792G	27. 5.88	
G-BORZ	Cameron N-77 HAFB	1748		9. 6.88	To G-KEYY 6/88. Canx.
G-BOSA	Boeing 737-204	20808	G-BAZI	26. 4.88	To XA-STE 7/94. Canx 19.7.94.
G-BOSB	Thunder Ax7-77 HAFB (Regd as c/n 581; but built as c/n 1199)	1199		7. 6.88	
G-BOSC	Cessna U.206F Stationair	U206-03587	5N-ASU N7256N	8. 8.88	Canx by CAA 11.10.90. To F-GHEN 10/91.
G-BOSD	PA-34-200T Seneca II	34-7570085	N33086	7. 6.88	
G-BOSE	PA-28-181 Archer II	28-8590007	N143AV	17. 5.88	
G-BOSF	Colt 69A HAFB	1271		23. 6.88	
G-BOSG	Colt 17A Cloudhopper HAFB	1272		23. 6.88	
G-BOSH	Thunder Ax8-84 HAFB	1265		6. 6.88	Canx by CAA 19.5.93.
G-BOSI	Cessna 172M Skyhawk II	172-66712	N80714	26. 5.88	To G-OOLE 8/89. Canx.
G-BOSJ	Nord 3400	124	N9048P ALAT "MOO"	26. 5.88	(Badly damaged in crash Fenland 12.6.94) (Stored 9/97)
G-BOSK	Aerospatiale AS.355F2 Ecureuil 2	5264	D-HERP	31. 5.88	To F-WGTM(3) 3/92R. Canx 23.3.92.
G-BOSL	Boeing 737-2U4 (Line No. 652)	22161		26. 2.80	To G-ILFC 11/83. Canx.
G-BOSM	CEA Jodel DR.253B Regent	168	F-BSBH	24. 5.88	
G-BOSN	Aerospatiale AS.355F Twin Squirrel	5266	5N-AYL	22. 8.88	To 5N-... Canx 11.9.89.
G-BOSO	Cessna A.152 Aerobat	A152-0975	N761PD	25. 5.88	Overturned on landing at Fairoaks on 4.3.99.
G-BOSP	PA-28-151 Cherokee Warrior (Originally regd with c/n 28-7515037)	28-7515307	N1143X N9563N	26. 5.88	Impounded at Moorsele for drug running 9.6.96. (Stored 1/98)
G-BOSR	PA-28-140 Cherokee	28-22092	N7464R	26. 5.88	
G-BOSS	PA-34-200T Seneca II	34-7970101	N3052K	26. 2.79	To 3A-MAR 10/84. Canx 4.6.84.
G-BOST	PA-23-250 Aztec F	27-7754058	N62843	17. 8.77	Fatal crash into high ground near Cottingham, Humberside on 21.1.81. Canx.
G-BOSU	PA-28-140 Cherokee Cruiser	28-7325449	N55635	19. 7.88	
G-BOSV	Cameron V-77 HAFB	1320		17. 6.88	
G-BOSW	Bell 206B JetRanger III	3370	N2063T	29. 9.88	To G-SIZL 7/92. Canx.
G-BOSX	Bell 206B JetRanger III	3394	N20681	27. 7.88	To G-BWVE 1.9.88. Canx.
G-BOSY	Robinson R-22 Beta	0817		9. 6.88	DBF after striking power cables and crashing at Mount Tebot, Halifax on 10.3.91. Canx by CAA 2.8.91.
G-BOSZ	PA-28-161 Warrior II	28-8116120	N8318A	. 6.88R	NTU - To G-BOZI 7/88. Canx.
G-BOTA	Not allotted.				
G-BOTB	Cessna 152 II	152-85733	N94571	7. 6.88	
G-BOTC	Cessna 152 II	152-83856	(G-BOYW) N5385B	28. 9.88	To I-ECSO. Canx 15.1.92.
G-BOTD	Cameron O-105 HAFB	1611		6. 6.88	
G-BOTE	Thunder Ax8-90 HAFB	555		14. 6.88	Canx as WFU 12.12.95. (Extant 1/98)
G-BOTF	PA-28-151 Cherokee Warrior	28-7515436	C-GGIF	8. 6.88	
G-BOTG	Cessna 152 II	152-83035	N46343	9. 6.88	
G-BOTH	Cessna 182Q Skylane II	182-67558	N202PS N114SP/N5172N	9. 6.88	
G-BOTI	PA-28-151 Cherokee Warrior (Mod to PA-28-161)	28-7515251	C-GNFF	9. 6.88	
G-BOTJ	BAe Jetstream Srs.3202	795	G-OAKJ G-BOTJ/G-31-795	24. 6.88	Restored as G-OAKJ 9/89. Canx.
G-BOTK	Cameron O-105 HAFB	1765		9. 6.88	
G-BOTL	Colt 42R SS HAFB	466		23.11.82	Canx as WFU 21.11.89. (Extant 2/97)
G-BOTM	Bell 206B JetRanger III	3881	N31940	9. 6.88	
G-BOTN	PA-28-161 Warrior II	28-7916261	N2173N	9. 6.88	

Regn	Type	c/n	Previous identity	Regn date	Fate or immediate subsequent identity (if known)
G-BOTO	Bellanca 7ECA Citabria	939-73	N57398	9. 6.88	
G-BOTP	Cessna 150J	150-70736	N61017	2. 8.88	
G-BOTR	Cessna R.182 Skylane RG II	R182-00146	N2301C	. 6.88R	NTU - G-BOWO 7/88. Canx.
G-BOTS	Hughes 269C	21-1024	EI-VIP G-BOTS/N13048/(N229SC)/N1105Z	17. 6.88	Restored as EI-VIP 4/97. Canx 23.4.97.
G-BOTT	Rand-Robinson KR-2	PFA/129-11164		16. 6.88	(Project abandoned) Canx by CAA 12.4.99.
G-BOTU	Piper J3C-75 Cub	19045	N98803 NC98803	8. 7.88	
G-BOTV	PA-32RT-300 Lance II	32R-7885153	N36039	7. 6.88	
G-BOTW	Cameron V-77 HAFB	1761		14. 6.88	
G-BOTX	BAe 125 Srs.800A	NA0414 & 258121	(N559BA) G-5-593	17. 6.88	To C-FRPP. Canx 30.6.88.
G-BOTY	Cessna 150J	150-71032	N5532G	7. 6.88	Badly damaged in forced-landing Home Farm, Havering-Atte-Bower, Romford 10.9.96. Canx by CAA 8.8.97.
G-BOTZ	Bensen B.8MR Gyrocopter	G/01-1086		17. 6.88	
G-BOUA	Agusta A.109A II	7412		12. 7.88	To G-VJCB 8/88. Canx.
G-BOUB	Cameron Saucer 80SS HAFB	1641		13. 7.88	To C-GUFO. Canx 22.11.88.
G-BOUC	Cameron V-77 HAFB	1778		17. 6.88	To G-BUPI 28.7.88. Canx.
G-BOUD	PA-38-112 Tomahawk II	38-82A0017	N91365	26. 7.88	
G-BOUE	Cessna 172N Skyhawk II	172-73235	N6535F	8. 8.88	
G-BOUF	Cessna 172N Skyhawk II	172-71900	N5605E	24. 6.88	
G-BOUG	Cessna 172N Skyhawk II	172-70596	N739KD	. .88R	NTU - To G-FNLD 8/88. Canx.
G-BOUH	Cessna 172RG Cutlass	172RG-0732	N6499V	2. 8.88	Damaged on landing at Westbury-sub-Mendip on 8.1.93. To ZK-JCL. Canx 19.3.93.
G-BOUI	PA-28-236 Dakota	28-8111077	N84017	28. 6.88	To D-EVAP(2) 11/93. Canx 8.9.93.
G-BOUJ	Cessna 150M Commuter	150-76373	N3058V	25. 8.88	
G-BOUK	PA-34-200T Seneca II	34-7570124	N33476	31. 8.88	
G-BOUL	PA-34-200T Seneca II	34-7670157	N8936C	28. 6.88	
G-BOUM	PA-34-200T Seneca II	34-7670136	N8401C	3. 8.88	
G-BOUN	Rand-Robinson KR-2	PFA/129-10945		23. 6.88	
G-BOUO	Thunder Ax8-105 HAFB	867		8. 8.88	To ZS-HYJ. Canx 2.9.92.
G-BOUP	PA-28-161 Warrior II	2816059	N9139X	12. 7.88	
G-BOUR	PA-28-161 Warrior II	2816060	N9139Z	12. 7.88	
G-BOUS	PA-28RT-201 Arrow IV	28R-7918109	N32WC N9644N	23. 6.88	
G-BOUT	Zenair Colomban MC-12 Cri-Cri	12-0135	N120JN	14. 6.88	(Still operating as N120JN 7/89)
G-BOUU	Everett Autogyro	015		. .88R	(Stored 5/97)
G-BOUV	Montgomerie-Bensen B.8MR Gyrocopter	G/01-1092		23. 6.88	
G-BOUW	Robinson R-22 Beta	0824		22. 8.88	To G-OLIE 10/88. Canx.
G-BOUX	Everett Autogyro	016		. .88R	(Stored 7/94)
G-BOUY	Bell 206B JetRanger II	1376	N5450M N1PE/XC-GUW	8.11.88	To G-GOBP 2/91. Canx.
G-BOUZ	Cessna 150G	150-65606	N2606J	15. 6.88	
G-BOVA	PA-31-310 Turbo Navajo C	31-7612078	G-BECP N59892	29. 3.84	To N65TT 6/93. Canx 22.6.93.
G-BOVB	PA-15 Vagabond	15-180	N4396H NC4396H	23. 6.88	
G-BOVC	Everett Autogyro Srs.2	014		22.11.88	Permit expired 29.3.91. Canx by CAA 17.8.92. To VP-FBS /97.
G-BOVD	Not allocated.				
G-BOVE	Everett Autogyro	017		. .88R	(Stored 1/91 Sproughton, Ipswich)
G-BOVF	Everett Autogyro Srs.1	018		. .88R	NTU - To G-MICY 2/90. Canx.
G-BOVG	Reims Cessna F.172H	0627	OO-ANN D-ELTR	2. 8.88	Damaged in gales Southend in 1991 & later stored. CofA expired 14.9.91. Canx as WFU 26.9.95. (In use as an Instructional Airframe in 4/99 with 1476 Sqdn ATC, Raleigh)
G-BOVH	PA-28-161 Warrior II	28-8316091	N4311M	28. 6.88	(Badly damaged in gales Lulsgate 1.4.94) (Status uncertain)
G-BOVI	Cameron Tiger 77SS HAFB	1713		28. 6.88	Canx 22.11.88 on sale to Canada.
G-BOVJ	PA-34-220T Seneca III	34-8333058	N8202J	19.10.88	To G-WATS 2/89. Canx.
G-BOVK	PA-28-161 Warrior II	28-8516061	N69168	7. 9.88	
G-BOVL	SNCAN Stampe SV-4C	208	N20SV F-BHES/F-BBLC	28. 6.88	To G-BWEF 5/93. Canx.
G-BOVM	Scheibe SF-25E Super Falke	4323	N250BA (D-KECZ)	30. 6.88	NTU - To G-WOLD 8/88. Canx.
G-BOVN	Air Command 532 Elite Sport (Officially regd with c/n G/04-1090)	0428 & G/04-1093		13. 7.88	Destroyed in a fatal crash at Lannock Hill, near Stevenage on 1.12.90. Canx as destroyed 6.3.91.
G-BOVO	PA-28-181 Archer II	28-7990132	N2239B	13. 7.88	To G-JOYT 2/90. Canx.
G-BOVP	Air Command 532 Elite Sport	0427 & G/04-1121		13. 7.88	Fatal crash at Long Marston on 27.4.96. Canx as destroyed 1.10.96.
G-BOVR	Robinson R-22HP	0176	N9069D	28. 6.88	
G-BOVS	Cessna 150M Commuter	150-78663	N704KC	21. 7.88	
G-BOVT	Cessna 150M Commuter	150-78032	N8962U	1.12.88	
G-BOVU	Stoddard-Hamilton Glasair III	3090		16. 9.88	
G-BOVV	Cameron V-77 HAFB	1724		26. 9.88	(Owner in Australia) Canx by CAA 15.5.98.
G-BOVW	Colt 69A HAFB	1286		13. 7.88	
G-BOVX	Hughes 269C (300C)	38-0673	N58170	12. 7.88	
G-BOVY	Hughes 269C (300C)	40-0915	EI-CIL G-BOVY/N1096K	12. 7.88	Overturned on landing 17.3.99 at Redhill, substantially damaged.
G-BOVZ	Hughes 269C (300C)	99-0823	VH-TID	4. 8.88	To (OO-DMG)/OO-HFZ. Canx 28.7.92.
G-BOWA	Thunder Ax8-90 HAFB	933		25. 8.88	To RP-C.... 9/94. Canx 13.9.94.

Regn	Type	c/n	Previous identity	Regn date	Fate or immediate subsequent identity (if known)
G-BOWB	Cameron V-77 HAFB	1767		13. 7.88	
G-BOWC	Cessna 150J	150-70458	N60626	24.10.88	Force landed and overturned in a field 1½ miles west of Barton on 10.7.94. Canx as WFU 16.9.94.
G-BOWD	Reims Cessna F.337G Super Skymaster		N337BC	8. 7.88	
	(Wichita c/n 01791)	0084	G-BLSB/(G-BLOY)/EI-BET/D-INAI/(N53697)		
G-BOWE	PA-34-200T Seneca II	34-7870405	N39668	14. 7.88	
G-BOWF	Short SD.3-60 Var.300	SH3742	G-14-3742	19. 7.88	NTU - To N742CC. Canx 22.7.88.
G-BOWG	Short SD.3-60 Var.300	SH3743	G-14-3743	19. 7.88	NTU - To N743CC. Canx 26.10.88.
G-BOWH	Short SD.3-60 Var.300	SH3744	G-14-3744	19. 7.88	NTU - To N744CC. Canx 26.10.88.
G-BOWI	Short SD.3-60 Var.300	SH3745	G-14-3745	19. 7.88	NTU - To N745CC. Canx 7.11.88.
G-BOWJ	Short SD.3-60 Var.300	SH3746	G-14-3746	19. 7.88	NTU - To N746SA. Canx 7.11.88.
G-BOWK	Cameron N-90 HAFB	1764		1. 8.88	
G-BOWL	Cameron V-77 HAFB	1780		26. 7.88	
G-BOWM	Cameron V-56 HAFB	1781		26. 7.88	
G-BOWN	PA-12 Super Cruiser	12-1912	N3661N NC3661N	26. 7.88	
G-BOWO	Cessna R.182 Skylane RG II	R182-00146	(G-BOTR) N2301C	20. 7.88	
G-BOWP	Jodel Wassmer D.120A Paris-Nice	319	F-BNZM	26. 7.88	
G-BOWR	Boeing 737-3Q8	23401	OO-ILF	21.11.88	To N685SW 4/93. Canx 30.4.93.
G-BOWS	Cessna 150M	150-77424		9. 9.88	Canx 13.6.94 on sale to Mexico.
G-BOWT	Stolp SA.300 Starduster Too	126	N83749	28. 7.88	Canx 13.6.94 on sale to Mexico.
G-BOWU	Cameron O-84 HAFB	1779		1. 8.88	
G-BOWV	Cameron V-65 HAFB	1800		24. 8.88	
G-BOWW	BAe 146 Srs.300	E3120		29. 7.88	To G-5-120/N146UK. Canx 4.11.88.
G-BOWX	Mooney M.20C Ranger	2896	N78881	. 7.88R	NTU - To N202GE 12/88. Canx.
G-BOWY	PA-28RT-201T Turbo Arrow IV	28R-8131114	N404EL N83648	8. 8.88	
G-BOWZ	Bensen B.80V Gyrocopter	G/01-1060		27. 7.88	
G-BOXA	PA-28-161 Warrior II	2816075	N9149Q	1.11.88	
G-BOXB	PA-28-161 Warrior II	2816064	N9142H	12. 8.88	
G-BOXC	PA-28-161 Warrior II	2816063	N9142D	12. 8.88	(Badly damaged on take-off from Jersey on 27.1.97)
G-BOXD	BAe 146 Srs.200QT	E2113		26. 8.88	To VH-JJY 5/89. Canx 3.5.89.
G-BOXE	BAe 146 Srs.200QT	E2114		25. 8.88	To VH-JJZ 6/89. Canx 2.6.89.
G-BOXF	Cameron DP-70 Hot Air Airship	1794		26. 7.88	Canx as WFU 17.12.90.
G-BOXG	Cameron O-77 HAFB	1792		26. 8.88	(Extant 2/97)
G-BOXH	Pitts S-1S Special	MP4	N8LA	29. 7.88	
G-BOXI	HS.125 Srs.700B	257055	G-5-598 N876JC/HZ-RC2/G-5-16	19. 7.88	To F-WZIG/F-GHHG 11/90. Canx 3.7.90.
G-BOXJ	Piper J3C-90 Cub (L-4H-PI) (Frame No.12021)	12193	OO-ADJ 44-79897	1. 8.88	(Stored 10/96)
G-BOXK	Slingsby T.67C-160	2063		26. 9.88	Fatal crash at Mow Cap Castle, Staffs., on 20.10.98. Canx as destroyed 14.3.99.
G-BOXL	Slingsby T.67M Firefly 200	2066		26. 9.88	To TC-CBL. Canx 5.7.89.
G-BOXM	Slingsby T.67M Firefly 200	2067		26. 9.88	To TC-CBM. Canx 5.7.89.
G-BOXN	Robinson R-22 Beta	0844	N8000J	29. 7.88	To N81970 8/98. Canx 22.7.98.
G-BOXO	Folland Gnat T.1	FL.585	A2709 8637M/XR991	3. 8.88	To N1CL 9/89. Canx 15.8.89.
G-BOXP	Folland Gnat T.1	FL.537	A2679 XP535	3. 8.88	Regd as N8130N when purchased in 5/89, but to N1CW in 9/89 when delivered. Canx 15.8.89.
G-BOXR	Grumman-American GA-7 Cougar	GA7-0059	N772GA	19.10.88	
G-BOXS	Hughes 269C (300C)	30-0007	SE-HKB OY-HAL	1. 8.88	Struck ground and landed in a ditch 1 mile east of Sywell on 16.11.88. Canx as WFU 12.4.89.
G-BOXT	Hughes 269C (300C)	104-0367	SE-HMR PH-JOH/D-HBOL	1. 8.88	
G-BOXU	Grumman-American AA-5B Tiger	AA5B-0026	N1526R	28. 7.88	
G-BOXV	Pitts S-1S Special (Regd with c/n 7-0432)	7-0433	N27822	8. 8.88	
G-BOXW	Cassutt Racer IIIM	PFA/34-11317		11. 8.88	
G-BOXX	Robinson R-22 Beta	0815	N2640D	15. 6.88	
G-BOXY	PA-28-181 Archer II	28-7990175	N3073D	29. 7.88	
G-BOXZ	PA-28-181 Archer II	28-7990078	N22402	29. 7.88	To G-TERY 1/89. Canx.
G-BOYA	Cessna A.152 Aerobat	A152-0966	N761ML	29. 7.88	To I-.... Canx 11.4.91.
G-BOYB	Cessna A.152 Aerobat	A152-0928	N761AW	29. 7.88	
G-BOYC	Robinson R-22 Beta	0837		22. 8.88	
G-BOYD	Colt 90A HAFB	1294		9. 8.88	To G-REBI 3/89. Canx.
G-BOYE	Cessna TR.182 Turbo Skylane RG	R182-01113	N756MK	24. 8.88	To OY-SFU. Canx 20.1.93.
G-BOYF	Sikorsky S-76B	760343		15. 9.88	
G-BOYG	Cessna 421C Golden Eagle III	421C-0146	N45857	26. 9.88	To D-IDAK. Canx 23.10.91.
G-BOYH	PA-28-151 Cherokee Warrior (Mod. to PA-28-161 status)	28-7715290	N8795F	8. 8.88	
G-BOYI	PA-28-161 Warrior II	28-7816183	N9032K	8. 8.88	
G-BOYJ	BAe Jetstream 3201	800	(N32SU) G-31-800	. 8.88R	NTU - To N370MT. Canx.
G-BOYK	Montgomerie-Bensen B.8M Gyrocopter	G/01-1091		9. 9.88	Destroyed in fatal crash near the A31 road at Sturminster Marshall on 11.12.93. Canx as destroyed 29.4.94.
G-BOYL	Cessna 152 II	152-84379	N6232L	11. 8.88	
G-BOYM	Cameron O-84 HAFB	1796		25. 8.88	(Active 8/95)

Regn	Type	c/n	Previous identity	Regn date	Fate or immediate subsequent identity (if known)
G-BOYN	Boeing 737-3S3	23788	EC-ECQ EC-277/G-BOYN/EC-ECQ	24.10.88	To G-NAFH 5/91. Canx.
G-BOYO	Cameron V-20 HAFB	1843		27. 9.88	
G-BOYP	Cessna 172N Skyhawk II	172-70349	N738YU	22. 8.88	
G-BOYR	Reims Cessna FA.337G Super Skymaster (Wichita c/n 01589)	0070	PH-RPE	9. 9.88	To RA-4147 4/98. Canx 7.4.98.
G-BOYS	Cameron N-77 HAFB	1759		16. 6.88	Canx by CAA 14.5.93.
G-BOYT	PA-38-112 Tomahawk II	38-81A0043	N25663	31. 8.88	Badly damaged on landing at Welshpool on 17.9.97. Canx as WFU 5.11.97.
G-BOYU	Cessna A150L Aerobat	A150-0497	N8121L	31. 8.88	
G-BOYV	PA-28RT-201T Turbo Arrow III	28R-7703014	N1143H	1. 9.88	
G-BOYW	Cessna 152 II	152-83856	N5385B	. 8.88R	NTU - Allocated in error - To G-BOTC 9/88. Canx.
G-BOYX	Robinson R-22 Beta	0862	N90813	25. 8.88	Badly damaged when hit trees after take-off from Teesside airport on 18.7.90.
G-BOYY	Cameron A-105 HAFB	1786		22. 8.88	
G-BOYZ	Carmichael Lazer Z.200 (Mod)	10		10. 8.88	To G-VILL 6/96. Canx.
G-BOZA	Boeing 737-3L9 (Line No. 1402)	23718	PH-OZA G-BOZA/OY-MMN	24.10.88	Restored as PH-OZA 4/92. Canx 13.4.92.
G-BOZB	Boeing 737-3L9 (Line No. 1600)	24219	(PH-OZB) G-BOZB/OY-MMO/N1786B	15. 9.88	Restored as OY-MMO 5/92. Canx 6.5.92.
G-BOZC	Boeing 737-3L9 (Line No. 1602)	24220	OY-MMP N1786B	. .88R	NTU - Remained as OY-MMP. Canx.
G-BOZD	Boeing 737-3L9 (Line No. 1604)	24221	OY-MMR N1786B	. .88R	NTU - Remained as OY-MMR. Canx.
G-BOZE	Boeing 737-3L9	-		. .88R	NTU - Canx.
G-BOZF	Boeing 737-3L9	-		. .88R	NTU - Canx.
G-BOZG	Boeing 737-...	-		. .88R	NTU - Canx.
G-BOZH	Boeing 737-...	-		. .88R	NTU - Canx.
G-BOZI	PA-28-161 Warrior II	28-8116120	(G-BOSZ) N8318A	14. 7.88	
G-BOZJ	Thunder Ax8-105 Srs.2	1277		22. 8.88	To D-OOZJ. Canx 18.5.92.
G-BOZK	Aerospatiale AS.332L-1 Super Puma (Originally regd as as AS.332L, converted before being restored)	2179	F-WQED(1) LN-OMQ/G-BOZK/F-GINN	5. 8.88	
G-BOZL	Bell 206B JetRanger III	2972	(N48EA) N701BG/N70ED/N1084H	17. 8.88	To VT-ETH 10/93. Canx 12.10.93.
G-BOZM	PA-38-112 Tomahawk	38-78A0352	N6247A	25. 8.88	
G-BOZN	Cameron N-77 HAFB	1807		1. 9.88	
G-BOZO	Grumman-American AA-5B Tiger	AA5B-1282	N4536Q	12. 8.88	
G-BOZP	Beechcraft 76 Duchess	ME-99	N6010Z	26. 8.88	
G-BOZR	Cessna 152 II	152-84614	N6083M	7. 9.88	
G-BOZS	Pitts S-1C Special	221-H	N10EZ	31. 8.88	
G-BOZT	PA-28-181 Archer II	28-7790400		25. 8.88	Missing on a flight from Egginton to Belgium 29.4.95 after putting out a distress call reporting engine failure. The pilot's body was recovered from the sea on 30.4.95. Canx by CAA 25.8.95.
G-BOZU	Aero Dynamics Sparrow Hawk Mk.II	PFA/184-11371		12.12.88	
G-BOZV	Robin DR.340 Major	416	F-BRTS	9. 8.88	
G-BOZW	Bensen B.8MR Gyrocopter	G/01-1096		1. 9.88	
G-BOZX	Robinson R-22 Beta	0839		23. 8.88	To VH-AVE(4) 8/94. Canx 20.7.94.
G-BOZY	Cameron RTW-120 Airship/HAFB	1770		1. 9.88	
G-BOZZ	American Aviation AA-5B Tiger	AA5B-1155	N4530N	22. 8.88	
G-BPAA	Acro Advanced	AA-001 & PFA/200-11528		26. 8.88	
G-BPAB	Cessna 150M Commuter	150-77244	N63335	21. 9.88	
G-BPAC	PA-28-161 Cherokee Warrior II	28-7716112	N2567Q	21. 9.88	
G-BPAD	PA-34-200T Seneca II	34-7870431	N21208	23. 8.88	Destroyed in fatal crash Saddle Hill, Bowland, Lancs 15.7.92. Canx as destroyed 20.2.97.
G-BPAE	Cameron V-77 HAFB	1798		1. 9.88	
G-BPAF	PA-28-161 Cherokee Warrior II	28-7716142	N3199Q	6. 9.88	
G-BPAG	Bellanca 8KCAB Decathlon	569-79	N5026L	24.10.88	Canx 26.2.96 on sale to Belgium.
G-BPAH	Colt 69A HAFB	512		2. 6.83	
G-BPAI	Bell 47G-3B-1 (Mod)	6528	N8588F	9. 9.88	
G-BPAJ	DH.82A Tiger Moth (Possibly composite with the "real" G-AMNN)	83472	G-AOIX T7087	5.11.80	
G-BPAK	Air Command 532 Elite	0429 & G/04-1103		2. 9.88	To G-WYZZ 1/90. Canx.
G-BPAL	DHC.1 Chipmunk 22 (Fuselage no. DHB/f/299)	C1/0437	G-BCYE WG350	29.10.86	
G-BPAM	SAN Jodel D.150A Mascaret	02	F-BLDA F-WLDA	8. 6.78	To G-IEJH 2/95. Canx.
G-BPAN	Not allotted - Radio distress code.				
G-BPAO	Air Command 503 Commander	0424 & G/04-1097		8. 9.88	Permit expired 8.8.91. Canx as PWFU 23.2.99.
G-BPAP	Robinson R-22 Beta	0866		5.10.88	To D-HUFE 8/91. Canx 13.8.91.

Regn	Type	c/n	Previous identity	Regn date	Fate or immediate subsequent identity (if known)
G-BPAR	PA-31-350 Navajo Chieftain	31-7852027	N27498	8. 2.78	To G-NIKY 1/85. Canx.
G-BPAS	Socata TB-20 Trinidad	283	A2-ADR F-GDBO	9.11.88	
G-BPAT	Boeing 707-321C (Line No. 637)	19367	N457PA	28. 6.78	To 9J-AFO 6/79. Canx 28.6.79.
G-BPAU	PA-28-161 Warrior II	28-7916218	N3063H	3.11.88	
G-BPAV	Clutton FRED Srs.III	PFA/29-10274		21.11.78	(Still under construction .90)
G-BPAW	Cessna 150M Commuter	150-77923	N8348U	5. 9.88	
G-BPAX	Cessna 150M Commuter	150-77401	N63571	5. 9.88	
G-BPAY	PA-28-181 Archer II	28-8090191	N3568X	12. 9.88	
G-BPAZ	Pazmany PL-2	PFA/69-10192		22.12.78	Fatal crash near the M62/M63 motorway junction on approach to Barton on 5.6.83. Canx as destroyed 5.12.83.
G-BPBA	Bensen B.80MR Gyrocopter	G/01-1036		5. 9.88	Permit expired 17.9.90. (Extant 7/93) Canx by CAA 10.2.97.
G-BPBB	Evans VP-2	PFA/63-11261		2. 9.88	No Permit to Fly issued. Canx by CAA 20.8.90.
G-BPBC	Bell 206B JetRanger III	3364	N144TV N44TV/N2062N	2. 9.88	To VR-CWH. Canx 28.5.92.
G-BPBD	Cessna 152 II	-		. .88R	NTU - Canx.
G-BPBE	Cessna 152 II	-		. .88R	NTU - Canx.
G-BPBF	Cessna 152 II	152-79734	N757GS	. .88R	NTU - To G-HART 2/89. Canx.
G-BPBG	Cessna 152 II	152-84941	N5418P	16. 9.88	
G-BPBH	Cessna 152 II	152-82482	N69102	16. 9.88	To CS-AYK. Canx 31.7.91.
G-BPBI	Cessna 152 II	152-80368	N24772	16. 9.88	Canx as WFU 11.2.91.
G-BPBJ	Cessna 152 II	152-83639	N4793B	9. 9.88	
G-BPBK	Cessna 152 II	152-83417	N49095	9. 9.88	
G-BPBL	Cessna 152 II	152-82331	N16SU N68715	9. 9.88	To EI-CGT 12/92. Canx 4.12.92.
G-BPBM	PA-28-161 Warrior II	28-7916272	N3050N	12. 9.88	
G-BPBN	BN-2T Turbine Islander (Originally regd as a BN-2A-21)	419	G-BCMY	15. 7.80	To G-OTVS 2/83. Canx.
G-BPBO	PA-28RT-201T Turbo Arrow IV	28R-8131195	N8431H	28. 9.88	
G-BPBP	Brugger MB.2 Colibri Mk.II	PFA/43-10246		6. 2.78	
G-BPBR	PA-38-112 Tomahawk	38-80A0020	N25082	8. 9.88	(Stored 4/97)
G-BPBS	BAe 146 Srs.200QT	E2117		27. 9.88	To F-GTNT. Canx 4.5.89.
G-BPBT	BAe 146 Srs.200QC	E2119	(N415XV)	27. 9.88	To ZK-NZC(2) 1/90. Canx 24.1.90.
G-BPBU	Cameron V-77 HAFB	1844		23. 9.88	
G-BPBV	Cameron V-77 HAFB	1821		21. 9.88	(Active 5/97)
G-BPBW	Cameron O-105 HAFB	1841		14.10.88	
G-BPBX	Cameron V-77 HAFB	1804	(G-BPCU)	9.12.88	To OO-BRB. Canx 31.12.93.
G-BPBY	Cameron V-77 HAFB	1818	(G-BPCS)	9.12.88	
G-BPBZ	Thunder Ax7-77 HAFB	1258		10.10.88	
G-BPCA	PBN BN-2B-26 Islander	2198	G-BLNX	28. 1.88	
G-BPCB	PBN BN-2A-26 Islander	2011	G-BEXA G-MALI/G-DIVE/(ZB503)/"ZA503"/G-DIVE/G-BEXA	27. 7.88	To G-PASY 3/89. Canx.
G-BPCC	Bell 206B JetRanger III	2291	N16905	19. 9.88	To G-SHBB 1/89. Canx.
G-BPCD	IRMA BN-2A-26 Islander	878	G-BFNV	27. 7.88	To G-PASZ 3/89. Canx.
G-BPCE	Stolp SA.300 Starduster Too	36	N8HM	26. 9.88	Canx by CAA 1.12.89. (Stored 2/92)
G-BPCF	Piper J3C-65 Cub	4532	N140DC N28033/NC28033	12. 5.89	(Lippert Reed clipped-wing conversion; SNo.SA811SW)
G-BPCG	Colt AS-80 Mk.II Hot-Air Airship	1300		14.10.88	
G-BPCH	Beechcraft 300 Super King Air	FA-74	N72448	13.12.85	To N300TJ. Canx 10.10.88.
G-BPCI	Cessna R.172K Hawk XP II	R172-2360	N9976V	3. 1.89	
G-BPCJ	Cessna 150J	150-70797	N61096	26. 9.88	Badly damaged in gales Compton Abbas 25.1.90. Canx by CAA 4.7.90. (Instructional Airframe 3/95)
G-BPCK	PA-28-161 Warrior II	28-8016279	N8529N C-GMEI/(N9519N)	26. 9.88	
G-BPCL	Scottish Aviation Bulldog Srs.120/128	BH120/393	HKG-6 R.Hong Kong Aux.AF/G-31-19	20. 9.88	
G-BPCM	Rotorway Exec 152	E.3293	N079WP	21. 9.88	(Stored in garden 7/96)
G-BPCN	Cameron A-160 HAFB	1803		27. 9.88	CofA expired 15.10.93. Canx as destroyed 10.6.98.
G-BPCO	Short SD.3-60 Var.100	SH3604	G-RMSS G-BKKU	12. 2.88	To G-OLAH 8/91. Canx.
G-BPCP	Cessna 500 Citation I (Unit No.540)	500-0403	N1710E	21. 3.80	Crashed on landing at Jersey, Channel Islands on 1.10.80. Canx.
G-BPCR	Mooney M.20K (231)	25-0532	N98433	23. 9.88	
G-BPCS	Cameron V-77 HAFB	1818		27. 9.88	NTU - To G-BPBY 12/88. Canx 9.12.88.
G-BPCT	Bell 206L-1 Long Ranger II	45761	D-HDBB N3175G	28. 9.88	To G-LEEZ 1/92. Canx.
G-BPCU	Cameron V-77 HAFB	1804		27. 9.88	NTU - To G-BPBX 12/88. Canx 9.12.88.
G-BPCV	Montgomerie-Bensen B-8MR Gyrocopter	G/01-1088		11.10.88	
G-BPCW	Slingsby Cadet III	830 & PCW-001	XA288	6. 9.88	To EI-CJT 2/94. Canx 18.11.93.
G-BPCX	PA-28-236 Dakota	28-8211004	N8441S	25.10.88	
G-BPCY	PA-34-200T Seneca II	34-7970198	N381BB N3059Y	19. 9.88	Damaged on landing at Compton Abbas on 17.9.91. (Stored at Compton Abbas 5/95) (Scrapped 8/97) Canx as PWFU 3.2.99.
G-BPCZ	Bell 206B JetRanger III	3665	N17EA HI-405/N3172A	27. 9.88	To G-OPWL 9/89. Canx.
G-BPDA	HS.748 Srs.2A/334SCD	1756	G-GLAS 9Y-TFS/G-11-8	7.10.88	To G-ORAL 8/99. Canx.
G-BPDB	Bell 412SP	33172	N32072	. 9.88R	NTU - To G-SPBA 10/88. Canx.

Regn	Type	c/n	Previous identity	Regn date	Fate or immediate subsequent identity (if known)
G-BPDC	PA-46-310P Malibu	4608136		15. 9.88	To (N46MJ)/N46MG 7/92. Canx 9.7.92.
G-BPDD	Colt 240A HAFB	1314		30. 9.88	Canx as destroyed 7.4.98.
G-BPDE	Colt 56A HAFB	1296		26.10.88	
G-BPDF	Cameron V-77 HAFB	1806		6.10.88	
G-BPDG	Cameron V-77 HAFB	1839		21.10.88	
G-BPDH	Robinson R-22 Beta	0860		6.10.88	
G-BPDI	Cameron A-210 HAFB	1849		4.10.88	To SU-181. Canx 26.10.88.
G-BPDJ	Chris Tena Mini Coupe	275	N13877	4.10.88	(Stored 4/98 at Popham)
G-BPDK	Sorrell SNS-7 Hyperbipe	242	N85BL	6.10.88	Permit expired on 23.6.95. (On rebuild 2/99 at Barton) Canx by CAA 17.2.99.
G-BPDL	Embraer EMB.110P1 Bandeirante	110-391	N115MQ N2992C/PT-SFI	28.10.88	To G-ZAPE 11/92. Canx.
G-BPDM	CASA I-131E Jungmann	2058	E3B-369 Spanish AF	24.10.88	
G-BPDN	PA-28R-201 Cherokee Arrow	28R-7737124	N38959	7.11.88	To D-ENTS(2) 9/96. Canx 6.9.96.
G-BPDO	PA-28R-201T Turbo Cherokee Arrow III	28R-7703112	N3496Q	7.11.88	To G-DDAY 11/88. Canx.
G-BPDP	Aerospatiale AS.355F1 Twin Squirrel	5134	D-HOCH N358E/N5792M	6.10.88	NTU - To ZS-HUA. Canx 6.1.89.
G-BPDR	Schweizer 269C (300C)	S.1327		4.10.88	Crashed at Kidlington on 27.6.91. Canx as destroyed 20.8.91. To ZK-HGA(2).
G-BPDS	PA-28-161 Warrior II	28-8416021	N4328P	30. 9.88	To G-PSFT 8/96. Canx.
G-BPDT	PA-28-161 Warrior II	28-8416004	N4317Z	22.12.88	
G-BPDU	PA-28-161 Cherokee Warrior II	28-7716195	N5672V	30. 9.88	
G-BPDV	Pitts S-1S Special	27P	N330VE	15. 9.88	
G-BPDW	Eezybuild Envoy Mk.1	0001-78 & PFA/93-10447		25.10.78	Not completed. Canx by CAA 5.10.84.
G-BPDX	DHC.7-102 Dash Seven	033	N235SL OY-MBF/(PH-SDR)/N235SL/TC-JCG/N8504A	24.10.88	To G-BRYF 8/89. Canx.
G-BPDY	Westland-Bell 47G-3B1 (Line No.WAN/48)	WA/356	OY-HCO SE-HIF/XT197	10.10.88	
G-BPDZ	Cessna 340A	340A-0275	N4091G	26. 9.88	Restored as N4091G 11/93. Canx 15.11.93.
G-BPEA	Boeing 757-236ET (Line No. 218)	24370		31. 3.89	
G-BPEB	Boeing 757-236ET (Line No. 225)	24371		27. 4.89	
G-BPEC	Boeing 757-236ET (Line No. 323)	24882		6.11.90	
G-BPED	Boeing 757-236ET (Line No. 363)	25059		30. 4.91	
G-BPEE	Boeing 757-236ET (Line No. 364)	25060		3. 5.91	
G-BPEF	Boeing 757-236ET (Line No. 174)	24120	G-BOHC EC-ELA/EC-516/G-BOHC/EC-ELA/EC-202/G-BOHC	18. 5.92	
G-BPEG	Phoenix Currie Wot	PFA/58-10258		13.12.77	Not completed. Canx 30.5.84.
G-BPEH	Boeing 757-236 (Line No. 183)	24121	G-BNSE EC-EXH/EC-544/G-BNSE	1. 5.92	To TC-AHA 4/95. Canx 13.4.95.
G-BPEI	Boeing 757-236 (Line No. 601)	25806	(G-BMRK)	9. 3.94	
G-BPEJ	Boeing 757-236 (Line No. 610)	25807	(G-BMRL)	22. 4.94	
G-BPEK	Boeing 757-236 (Line No. 665)	25808	(G-BMRM)	17. 3.95	
G-BPEL	PA-28-151 Cherokee Warrior	28-7415172	C-FEYM	10.10.88	(Wreck stored 12/93)
G-BPEM	Cessna 150K	150-71707	N6207G	24.10.88	
G-BPEN	Bell 206L-1 Long Ranger II	45360	LN-OTZ SE-HNE/A6-JAQ/N1077G	.10.88R	NTU - To G-LEIS 10/88. Canx.
G-BPEO	Cessna 152 II	152-83775	C-GQVO (N5147B)	10.10.88	
G-BPEP	HS.748 Srs.2B/501	1806	G-11-1	14.10.88	To B-1771 11/88. Canx 21.11.88.
G-BPER	PA-38-112 Tomahawk II	38-82A0036	N91465	11.10.88	Damaged on landing at Welshpool on 30.8.96. (Fuselage stored 9/97 at Welshpool) Canx as destroyed 31.8.99.
G-BPES	PA-38-112 Tomahawk II	38-81A0064	N25728	2.11.88	
G-BPET	Slingsby T.67M Firefly 200	2068		19.12.88	To TC-CBN. Canx 5.7.89.
G-BPEU	Slingsby T.67M Firefly 200	2069		22.11.88	To TC-CBP. Canx 5.7.89.
G-BPEV	Slingsby T.67M Firefly 200	2075		22.11.88	To TC-CBR. Canx 5.7.89.
G-BPEW	Robinson R-22 Beta	0888		21.10.88	To G-OTOY 9/97. Canx.
G-BPEX	Boeing-Stearman A75-N1 Kaydet (PT-18-BW)	75-589	N65D N61304/40-2032	24.10.88	To F-AZGM 8/89. Canx 14.4.89.
G-BPEY	Bell 412	33041	N7034J XC-MAZ/N2199D	26.10.88	Restored as N7034J. Canx 4.8.89.
G-BPEZ	Colt 77A HAFB	1324		14.10.88	
G-BPFA	Knight Swallow GK.2	PFA/84-10374		1.11.78	No Permit to Fly issued. Canx by CAA 21.2.96.
G-BPFB	Colt 77A HAFB	1334		26.10.88	
G-BPFC	Mooney M.20C Ranger	20-1243	N3606H	21.10.88	
G-BPFD	Jodel D.112	312	F-PHJT	3.11.88	
G-BPFE	English Electric Lightning T.5	B1/95013	XS452	26.10.88	To ZU-BBD 10/96. Canx 15.7.96.
G-BPFF	Cameron DP-70 Hot-Air Airship	1831		24.10.88	
G-BPFG	Socata TB-20 Trinidad	866		3.11.88	To N34FS 4/98. Canx 14.4.98.

Regn	Type	c/n	Previous identity	Regn date	Fate or immediate subsequent identity (if known)
G-BPFH	PA-28-161 Warrior II	28-8116201	N83723	3.11.88	
G-BPFI	PA-28-181 Archer II	28-8090113	N8103G	5. 1.89	
G-BPFJ	Cameron Can 90SS HAFB (Budweiser Beer Can Shape)	1834		14.11.88	Canx as WFU 9.5.97. (Extant 1/98)
G-BPFK	Montgomerie-Bensen B.8MR Gyrocopter	SJD-1 & G/01A-1116		27.10.88	
G-BPFL	Davis DA-2A (built by A.Tribling)	051	N72RJ	27.10.88	
G-BPFM	Aeronca 7AC Champion	7AC-4751	N1193E NC1193E	13.10.88	
G-BPFN	Short SD.3-60 Var.300	SH3747	N747HH N747SA/(G-BPFN)/G-14-3747	2.11.88	
G-BPFO	Short SD.3-60 Var.300	SH3748	G-14-3748	3.11.88	NTU - To N748SA. Canx 29.11.88.
G-BPFP	Short SD.3-60 Var.300	SH3749		3.11.88	To N828BE. Canx 9.6.89.
G-BPFR	Short SD.3-60 Var.300	SH3750	B-12277 G-BPFR/G-14-3750	3.11.88	To G-BWMW 3/94. Canx.
G-BPFS	Short SD.3-60 Var.300	SH3751	G-REGN G-OCIA/G-BPFS	3.11.88	To G-BVMX 10/93. Canx.
G-BPFT	Cameron N-77 HAFB	1430		26.10.88	To RP-C1516. Canx 9.3.92.
G-BPFU	HS.748 Srs.2A/334	1757	G-EDIN 9Y-TFT/V2-LCG/VP-LCG/9Y-TFT	3.11.88	To G-OMDS 1/91. Canx.
G-BPFV	Boeing 767-204ER (Line No. 256)	24457		27. 3.89	To EC-276 4/96 / EC-GHM 8/96. Canx 9.4.96.
G-BPFW	Air Command 532 Elite	0433		27.10.88	Fatal crash at Melbourne, near Pocklington on 2.3.91. Canx by CAA 10.12.91.
G-BPFX	Colt 21A Cloudhopper HAFB	1348		7.11.88	Stored 1/98 BBAC Museum. Canx as WFU 23.12.98.
G-BPFY	Consolidated-Vultee 28-5ACF (PBY-5A) Catalina	2087	N212DM G-BPFY/N212DM/G-BPFY/C-FHNH/CF-HNH/F-ZBAV/N5555H/N2846D/Bu.64017	25.10.88	To N285RA 9/98. Canx 19.8.98.
G-BPFZ	Cessna 152 II	152-85741	N94594	27.10.88	
G-BPGA	Mooney M.20J (205SE)	24-3076		10.11.88	To EC-GGT 6/96. Canx 29.4.96.
G-BPGB	Cessna 150J	150-69722	N51042	2.11.88	(Stored Ingoldmells 10/92)
G-BPGC	Air Command 532 Elite	0440 & G/04-1108		11.10.88	Permit expired 8.8.91. (Stored in garden 5/97 at Andover)
G-BPGD	Cameron V-65 HAFB	2000		9. 9.88	
G-BPGE	Cessna U.206C Super Skywagon	U206-1013	N29017	7.11.88	
G-BPGF	Thunder Ax7-77 HAFB	1355		22.11.88	
G-BPGG	Thunder Ax6-56 HAFB	993		22.11.88	Canx 20.12.89 on sale to USA.
G-BPGH	EAA Acrosport II	422	N12JE	14.11.88	
G-BPGI	Colt 69A HAFB	1332		14.11.88	To PH-AMV. Canx 30.9.93.
G-BPGJ	Colt 31A Air Chair HAFB	1333		22.11.88	Canx by CAA 10.3.95.
G-BPGK	Aeronca 7AC Champion	7AC-7187	N4409E	7. 2.89	(Damaged in crash Llanelli 7.5.91)
G-BPGL	PA-28-180 Cherokee Archer	28-7405245	OY-TOC	2.11.88	Crashed on landing Morley airstrip, Wymondham on 1.6.96. Canx by CAA 7.10.96.
G-BPGM	Cessna 152 II	152-84932	N5380P	14.11.88	
G-BPGN	Cameron Tractor 90SS HAFB	1846		22.11.88	(Based in Canada). Canx as WFU 21.10.96.
G-BPGO	Cessna T.210N Turbo Centurion II	T210-63193	N210MP	.11.88R	NTU - Remained as N210MP. Canx.
G-BPGP	PA-28-151 Cherokee Warrior	28-7715131	N5425F	.11.88R	NTU - To G-BRGJ 7/89. Canx.
G-BPGR	BAe 125 Srs.800B	258115	G-5-599	4.11.88	To R.Saudi Arabian AF as 104. Canx 25.8.89.
G-BPGS	BAe 125 Srs.800B	258118	G-5-605 (G-5-590)	4.11.88	To R.Saudi Arabian AF as 105. Canx 25.8.89.
G-BPGT	Colt AS-80 Mk.II Hot-Air Airship	1248	(I-....) G-BPGT	14.11.88	
G-BPGU	PA-28-181 Archer II	28-8490025	N4330B	26.10.88	
G-BPGV	Robinson R-22 Beta	0887		3.11.88	
G-BPGW	Boeing 757-236 (Line No. 34)	22185	EC-EOK EC-265/G-BPGW/N8294V/(G-BNEP)/(G-BIKO)	28. 3.84	To YV-78C 11/90. Canx 2.11.90.
G-BPGX	Socata TB-9 Tampico Club	884		4.11.88	
G-BPGY	Cessna 150H	150-67325	N6525S	24. 1.89	
G-BPGZ	Cessna 150G	150-64912	N3612J	14.11.88	
G-BPHA	Air Command 532 Elite Two Seat	0406		19.12.88	Canx 26.6.90 on sale to Germany.
G-BPHB	PA-28-161 Warrior II	2816069	N9148G	14.11.88	
G-BPHC	Aerospatiale AS.355F1 Twin Squirrel	5192	N365E	2.12.88	To G-SITE 1/89. Canx.
G-BPHD	Cameron N-42 HAFB	1863		21. 2.89	(Extant 2/97)
G-BPHE	PA-28-161 Warrior II	28-7916536	N2911D	28.12.88	
G-BPHF	Agusta-Bell 206B JetRanger	8169	SE-HGS D-HARU	6. 1.89	To F-GGPI 1/90. Canx by CAA 3.5.90.
G-BPHG	Robin DR.400/180 Regent	1887		29.11.88	
G-BPHH	Cameron V-77 HAFB	1840		2.12.88	
G-BPHI	PA-38-112 Tomahawk	38-79A0002	N2535T	22.11.88	
G-BPHJ	Cameron V-77 HAFB	1881		23.11.88	
G-BPHK	Whittaker MW.7	PFA/171-11389		24.11.88	Canx by CAA 16.9.98.
G-BPHL	PA-28-161 Warrior II	28-7916315	N555PY N2247U	2.12.88	
G-BPHM	Beechcraft A36 Bonanza	E-2461	N1558W	22.12.88	To OO-MPG 2/96. Canx 9.2.96.
G-BPHN	Embraer EMB.110P1 Bandeirante	110-331	C-GYQT N4268R/N301SA/N4268R/PT-SDI	3. 1.89	To PH-FWS. Canx 25.5.89.
G-BPHO	Taylorcraft BC-12D	8497	N96197 NC96197	10. 1.89	

Regn	Type	c/n	Previous identity	Regn date	Fate or immediate subsequent identity (if known)
G-BPHP	Taylorcraft BC-12-65	2799	N33948 NC33948	12.12.88	
G-BPHR	DH(Aust).82A Tiger Moth	45	N48DH VH-BLX/R.Australian AF A17-48	3. 1.89	
G-BPHS	Cessna 152 II	152-81420	N49971	5.12.88	To G-OFRY 2/93. Canx.
G-BPHT	Cessna 152 II	152-82401	N961LP	5.12.88	
G-BPHU	Thunder Ax7-77 HAFB	1365		19.12.88	
G-BPHV	Colt Montgolfier SS HAFB	1281	F-GFLZ	9.12.88	To F-GGFK(2) 6/91. Canx 5.10.90.
G-BPHW	Cessna 140	11035	N76595 NC76595	13. 1.89	
G-BPHX	Cessna 140	12488	N2252N NC2252N	2.12.88	(Stored 2/93)
G-BPHY	Cameron Cow 110SS HAFB	1811		9.12.88	To PH-KOE 7/93. Canx 5.5.93.
G-BPHZ	Morane-Saulnier MS.505 Criquet	53/7	F-BJQC French Mil	17. 4.89	
G-BPIA	Cameron DP-90 Hot-Air Airship	1875		8.12.88	Canx 23.1.90 on sale to Brazil. (Noted still active in UK 8/90 as G-BPIA)
G-BPIB	Agusta-Bell 206B JetRanger II	8006	D-HABI SX-HAA	4. 1.89	To EC-FCP. Canx 26.3.91.
G-BPIC	Agusta-Bell 206B JetRanger III	8620	D-HEAS I-CELT	5. 6.89	To EC-... 5/93. Canx 12.5.93.
G-BPID	PA-28-161 Warrior II	28-7916325	N2137V	16. 3.89	
G-BPIE	Bell 206B JetRanger III	2533	N327WM	22.11.88	
G-BPIF	Bensen-Parsons Two-Place Gyrocopter	UK-01		19.12.88	Permit expired 28.3.96. Canx by CAA 6.3.99.
G-BPIG	Not allotted.				
G-BPIH	Rand Robinson KR-2	8023 & PFA/129-11436		19.12.88	
G-BPII	Denney Kitfox	213 & PFA/172-11496		15.12.88	
G-BPIJ	Brantly B.2B	465	N2293U	23. 3.89	
G-BPIK	PA-38-112 Tomahawk II	38-82A0028	N3947M ZP-EAP/N91423	2.12.88	(Active 9/97)
G-BPIL	Cessna 310B	35620	N620GS OO-SEF/N5420A	16.11.89	
G-BPIM	Cameron N-77 HAFB	1896		6. 1.89	
G-BPIN	Glaser-Dirks DG-400	4-242		14.12.88	
G-BPIO	Reims Cessna F.152 II	1556	PH-VSO PH-AXS	23. 1.89	
G-BPIP	Slingsby T.31 Cadet III	PFA/42-10771		14.11.88	
G-BPIR	Scheibe SF-25E Super Falke	4332	N25SF (D-KDFX)	15.12.88	
G-BPIS	Not allotted.				
G-BPIT	Robinson R-22 Beta	0907	N80011	22.12.88	
G-BPIU	PA-28-161 Warrior II	28-7916303	N3028T	28.12.88	
G-BPIV	Bristol 149 Blenheim IV (Bollingbroke IVT)(Fairchild-built)	-	"Z5722" RCAF 10201	15. 2.89	
G-BPIW	HS.748 Srs.2B/501	1807	G-11-2	25.11.88	To B-1773 2/89. Canx 9.2.89.
G-BPIX	American Aviation AA-5A Cheetah	AA5A-0811	N26916	3. 1.89	To G-GOCC 9/92. Canx.
G-BPIY	Cessna 152 II	152-84073	N5249H	19.12.88	(Badly damaged on landing Earls Colne 12.8.97)
G-BPIZ	American Aviation AA-5B Tiger	AA5B-1154	N4530L	14. 2.89	
G-BPJA	Beechcraft 58 Baron	TH-1532	N3102A	8.12.88	To F-GPJA 7/99. Canx 13.7.99.
G-BPJB	Schweizer 269C (300C)	S.1331	N75065	7.11.88	
G-BPJC	Robinson R-22 Beta	0939		28.12.88	To G-SPEE 7/94. Canx.
G-BPJD	Socata Rallye 110ST	3253	OY-CAV	22.12.88	
G-BPJE	Cameron A-105 HAFB	1864		8.11.88	
G-BPJF	PA-38-112 Tomahawk	38-78A0021	N9312T	5. 4.89	Crashed on take-off at Derby-Egginton after both wings became detached on 20.6.98. Canx by CAA 2.10.98.
G-BPJG	PA-18-150 Super Cub	18-8350	SE-EZG N4172Z	4. 1.89	
G-BPJH	PA-18-95 Super Cub (L-18C-PI)	18-1980	MM52-2380 I-EICA/Italian AF MM52-2380/52-2380	24. 5.83	
G-BPJI	Colt Jumbo 77SS HAFB	1298		.12.88R	NTU - To G-VJIM 8/89. Canx.
G-BPJJ	Colt 180A HAFB	1330		4. 1.89	To SU-185. Canx 14.4.89.
G-BPJK	Colt 77A HAFB	1362		22.12.88	
G-BPJL	Cessna 152 II	152-81296	N49473	28.12.88	
G-BPJM	Gulfstream G.1159C Gulfstream IV	1078	N17589	.12.88R	NTU - To G-DNVT 9/89. Canx.
G-BPJN	Jodel D.18	254 & PFA/169-11409		19.12.88	(Badly damaged in forced landing Pencefen Farm, near Aberystwyth on 21.7.96)
G-BPJO	PA-28-161 Cadet	2841014	N9153Z	15.12.88	
G-BPJP	PA-28-161 Cadet	2841015	N9154K	22.12.88	
G-BPJR	PA-28-161 Cadet	2841024	N9154X	17. 1.89	
G-BPJS	PA-28-161 Cadet	2841025	N9154Z	12. 1.89	Forced landing in a field near Chipping Norton, Oxon on 1.6.99.
G-BPJT	PA-28-161 Cadet	2841031	N9156X	6. 1.89	Destroyed in fatal crash on landing at Kidlington on 12.7.92. Canx as destroyed 31.10.94. (Extant 2/95)
G-BPJU	PA-28-161 Cadet	2841032	N9156Z	11. 1.89	
G-BPJV	Taylorcraft F-21	F-1005	N2004L	12. 1.89	
G-BPJW	Cessna A.150K Aerobat	A150-0127	C-FAJX CF-AJX/N8427M	4. 1.89	

Regn	Type	c/n	Previous identity	Regn date	Fate or immediate subsequent identity (if known)
G-BPJX	PA-31-350 Navajo Chieftain	31-7652017	OY-BYP LN-SAN/SE-GBD	4. 1.89	To G-BWSA 10/90. Canx.
G-BPJY	Air Command 532 Elite	0426		5. 1.89	Fatal crash on the southeast corner of Coventry airfield on 20.4.89. Canx as destroyed 13.6.89.
G-BPJZ	Cameron O-160 HAFB	1904		4. 1.89	
G-BPKA	Boeing 737-4S3 (Line No. 1700)	24163	9M-MJJ G-BPKA	14. 4.89	To G-BVNM 3/92. Canx.
G-BPKB	Boeing 737-4S3 (Line No. 1702)	24164	9M-MLA G-BPKB	14. 4.89	To G-BVNN 3/92. Canx.
G-BPKC	Boeing 737-4S3 (Line No. 1720)	24165		23. 5.89	To N690MA 3/92. Canx 3.3.92.
G-BPKD	Boeing 737-4S3 (Line No. 1722)	24166		26. 5.89	To N691MA 3/92. Canx 23.3.92.
G-BPKE	Boeing 737-4S3 (Line No. 1736)	24167	9M-MLB G-BPKE	28. 6.89	To G-BVNO 3/92. Canx.
G-BPKF	Grob G-115	8075		3. 1.89	
G-BPKG	Grob G-115	8088		28.12.88	Fatal crash at Lock Muick, near Ballater on 3.4.92. Canx as WFU 10.12.92.
G-BPKH	Robinson R-22 Beta	0640	N664AJ	15. 3.89	To VR-H.. (No marks yet known). Canx 10.3.94. Became ZK-HQY in 2/98.
G-BPKI	EAA Acrosport I	PFA/72A-11391		15. 2.89	
G-BPKJ	Colt AS-80 Mk.II Hot-Air Airship	1363		11. 1.89	Canx by CAA 10.3.95.
G-BPKK	Denney Kitfox Mk.1	264 & PFA/172-11411		19.12.88	
G-BPKL	Mooney M.20J (201)	24-1102	N1008K	12. 1.89	
G-BPKM	PA-28-161 Warrior II	28-7916341	PH-CKO N2140X/N9630N	6. 1.89	
G-BPKN	Colt AS-80 Mk.II Hot-Air Airship	1297		11. 1.89	Canx by CAA 7.1.91. (Stored 12/94)
G-BPKO	Cessna 140	8936	N89891 NC89891	12. 1.89	
G-BPKP	Hiller UH-12E-4	2315	S3-BAS (Bangladeshi Army)/S2-ABE/AP-ATV	14. 3.89	To OH-HKT. Canx 22.1.90.
G-BPKR	PA-28-151 Cherokee Warrior	28-7515446	N4341X	13. 3.89	
G-BPKS	Stolp SA.300 Staduster Too	1064		13. 3.89	Canx 24.5.93 on sale to USA.
G-BPKT	Piper J/5A Cub Cruiser	5-624	N35372 NC35372	14. 3.89	To EI-CGV 12/92. Canx 5.11.92.
G-BPKU	Bell 206A Jet Ranger	125	N26BF N6251N	26. 5.89	To OH-HKY. Canx 8.4.91.
G-BPKV	Short SD.3-60 Var.300	SH3752		18. 1.89	To D-CAAS(2) 2/91. Canx 7.12.90.
G-BPKW	Short SD.3-60 Var.300	SH3753		18. 1.89	To N753CN. Canx 20.2.89.
G-BPKX	Short SD.3-60 Var.300	SH3754		18. 1.89	To N754CN. Canx 20.2.89.
G-BPKY	Short SD.3-60 Var.300	SH3755		18. 1.89	To G-OEEC 4/89. Canx.
G-BPKZ	Short SD.3-60 Var.300	SH3756		18. 1.89	To (B-....)/N830BE. Canx 6.9.89.
G-BPLA	Boeing 737-2K2ADV (Line No. 888)	22906	PH-TVU C-FCAV/PH-TVU	8. 5.89	Restored as PH-TVU. Canx 30.4.93.
G-BPLB	Aerospatiale SA.315B Lama	2633	LN-OTE	. 1.89R	NTU - To HB-XTO. Canx.
G-BPLC	Beechcraft B200 Super King Air	BB-1215	N7225V	16.11.86	To F-GICV 4/90. Canx 29.3.90.
G-BPLD	Thunder & Colt AS-261 Hot-Air Airship	1380		25. 1.89	To F-WGGM/F-GHRI 5/91R. Canx 13.6.91.
G-BPLE	Cameron A-160 HAFB	1921		16. 1.89	To ZK-FBH 5/98. Canx 24.2.98.
G-BPLF	Cameron V-77 HAFB	1903		16. 1.89	
G-BPLG	Morane-Saulnier MS.317	6519/265	N317MS F-BFAH/French Mil	1. 3.89	No CofA or Permit issued. Canx as TWFU 27.11.91. (Stored 10/90)
G-BPLH	CEA Jodel DR.1051 Sicile	401	F-BLAE	27. 2.89	
G-BPLI	Colt 77A HAFB	792	EI-BSH	17. 3.89	(Active .90) Canx by CAA 4.8.98.
G-BPLJ	Colt 90A HAFB	1398		16. 1.89	Canx by CAA 10.3.95. (Previously based in Germany)
G-BPLK	Slingsby T.67M Firefly 260	2072		3. 2.89	To G-EFSM 7/92. Canx.
G-BPLL	Not allotted.				
G-BPLM	AIA Stampe SV-4C	1004	F-BHET French Mil/F-BDKC	8. 2.89	(On rebuild by Classic & Vintage Aircraft Services Hedge End 5/95)
G-BPLN	PBN BN-2T Turbine Islander AL.1 (Originally regd as BN-2B-26)	2206		20. 1.89	To AAC as ZG994. Canx on sale to MoD 15.3.93.
G-BPLO	PBN BN-2T Turbine Islander (Originally regd as BN-2B-26)	2207		20. 1.89	To G-CYPP 12/89. Canx.
G-BPLP	PBN BN-2B-20 Islander	2208		20. 1.89	To B-3903 10/89. Canx 12.10.89.
G-BPLR	PBN BN-2B-26 Islander	2209		20. 1.89	To JA5298 10/89. Canx 3.10.89.
G-BPLS	PBN BN-2B-20 Islander	2210		20. 1.89	To B-3904 10/89. Canx 30.10.89.
G-BPLT	Bristol M.1C Replica	AJD-1		18. 1.89	(Built for Chilean AF Museum and departed via Lyneham on Chilean AF C-130 996 on 16.3.89) Canx by CAA 22.6.89. To CC-DMA.
G-BPLU	Thunder Ax10-160 HAFB	1388		27. 1.89	To OO-BDT 8/94. Canx 22.7.94.
G-BPLV	Cameron V-77 HAFB	1822		23. 1.89	
G-BPLW	Cessna 152 II	152-85268	N6530Q	17. 1.89	DBER after crashing on take-off from Culmore, near Londonderry on 20.6.90. Canx as WFU 19.2.91.
G-BPLX	Cessna 172P Skyhawk	172-74389	N51988	20. 1.89	DBR after stalling and crashing on landing at Abbotsley, Cambs. on 20.8.90. Canx as destroyed 5.9.90.
G-BPLY	Christen Pitts S-2B Special	5149		25. 1.89	
G-BPLZ	Hughes 369HS (500HS)	91-0342S	N126CM	15. 2.89	

Regn	Type	c/n	Previous identity	Regn date	Fate or immediate subsequent identity (if known)
G-BPMA	Short SD.3-30 Var.100	SH3067	G-BIRN G-14-3067	23. 1.89	Blown over on its back by high winds while parked at Glasgow on 13.2.89 & DBR. Canx as destroyed 12.5.89. Remains to Bates City, MO, USA in 1994.
G-BPMB	Maule M.5-235C Lunar Rocket	7284C	N5635T	13. 8.79	
G-BPMC	Air Command 503 Commander	0403 & G/04-1107		16.12.88	Permit expired 2.9.91. Canx by CAA 8.3.99.
G-BPMD	Boeing-Stearman A75L3 Kaydet	75-5714	N5084N 42-17551	1. 3.89	To OO-DBM. Canx 16.2.94.
G-BPME	Cessna 152 II	152-85585	N94021	24. 1.89	
G-BPMF	PA-28-151 Cherokee Warrior	28-7515050	C-GOXL	2. 2.89	
G-BPMG	Bensen B.8MR Gyrocopter	G/01A-1115		26. 1.89	No Permit issued. Canx by CAA 18.5.92.
G-BPMH	Schempp-Hirth Nimbus 3DM (Regd as c/n 07)	7/23		20. 3.89	
G-BPMI	Colt 56A HAFB	1384		18. 1.89	Canx 17.1.95 on sale to USA.
G-BPMJ	Colt 56A HAFB	1385		18. 1.89	Was reserved as N8035E but canx in 1/95. Canx 17.1.95.
G-BPMK	Robinson R-22 Beta	0957		3. 2.89	To EI-BYB 3/89. Canx 28.2.89.
G-BPML	Cessna 172M Skyhawk II	172-67102	N1435U	17.11.89	
G-BPMM	Champion 7ECA Citabria	7ECA-498	N5132T	22. 3.89	
G-BPMN	Taylor Super Coot Model A	PFA/18-10088		18. 8.78	No Permit to Fly issued - believed not built. Canx as WFU 9.5.94.
G-BPMO	Cessna 150M	150-75897	N66177	5. 4.89	To SX-KOS 6/96. Canx 2.5.96.
G-BPMP	Douglas C-47A-50-DL Dakota	10073	N54607 (N9842A)/N54607/ Morocco AF 20669/CN-CCL/F-BEFA/42-24211	2. 2.89	Nose section in shop at Aalsmeerderbrug, The Netherlands 11/97, the remained scrapped at Coventry. Canx as WFU 18.4.95.
G-BPMR	PA-28-161 Warrior II	28-8416119	N4373S N9620N	25. 1.89	
G-BPMS	PA-38-112 Tomahawk II	38-81A0132	N23340	20. 1.89	Wing touched the runway and aircraft overturned at Glasgow on 28.3.90. Canx as destroyed 4.1.91.
G-BPMT	Aerospatiale AS.355F1 Twin Squirrel	5223	N380E	9. 2.89	To G-PLAX 5/89. Canx.
G-BPMU	Nord 3202B	70	(G-BIZJ) N22546/ALAT "AIX"	26. 1.89	(Stored 9/97)
G-BPMV	PA-28-161 Warrior II	28-8416127	N4374M N9628N	25. 1.89	
G-BPMW	QAC Quickie Q.2	PFA/94A-10970	G-OICI G-OGKN	13. 3.89	Forced landed and overturned in a field at Mallard Close, Kempshot, Basingstoke on 16.2.91.
G-BPMX	ARV1 Super 2	K.005 & PFA/152-11128		30. 1.89	
G-BPMY	Cameron N-120 HAFB	1920		3. 2.89	To Z-WSZ 5/94. Canx 9.5.94.
G-BPMZ	Slingsby T.67M Firefly 200	2078		9. 2.89	To TC-CBT. Canx 5.7.89.
G-BPNA	Cessna 150L Commuter	150-73042	N1742Q	10. 2.89	
G-BPNB	PA-38-112 Tomahawk	38-79A0315	N2438D	10. 2.89	Canx as destroyed 25.11.91.
G-BPNC	Rotorway Exec 152	3600		3. 2.89	(Damaged in forced landing Quernmore,nr.Lancaster 16.5.92)
G-BPND	Boeing 727-2D3ADV (Line No. 1082)	21021	OK-EGK N500AV/G-BPND/PH-AHZ/N500AV/HI-452/JY-ADV	18.12.87	(Stored 10/97 at Lasham)
G-BPNE	Rotorway Exec	3577		3. 2.89	DBF at Llantysolio on 3.9.89. Canx as destroyed 12.11.90.
G-BPNF	Robinson R-22 Beta	0967		1. 3.89	
G-BPNG	Bell 206B JetRanger II	1669	G-ORTC G-BPNG/N20EA/C-GHVB	16. 2.89	To G-CHGL 4/98. Canx.
G-BPNH	Piel CP.328 Super Emeraude	PFA/50-11268		. .89R	NTU - To G-BPRT 2/89. Canx.
G-BPNI	Robinson R-22 Beta	0948		6. 2.89	
G-BPNJ	HS.748 Srs.2A/263	1680	9J-ABW G-11-4	3. 2.89	To F-GHKA 4/89. Canx 29.3.89.
G-BPNK	HS.748 Srs.2A/263	1677	9J-ABK	31. 3.89	To F-GHKL(2) 7/89. Canx 26.6.89.
"G-BPNK"	HS.748 Srs.2A/256	1667	7Q-YKB	. .92R	NTU - Painted in error - To G-BURJ. Canx.
G-BPNL	QAC Quickie Q.2	PFA/94A-11014		6. 2.89	Damaged on landing Fairwood Common 30.4.95. Front fuselage and tail cone stored 1/98 Wing Farm, Longbridge Deverill.
G-BPNM	Cessna 340A	340A-0351	N989HC N999HC/(N37331)	15. 3.89	To F-GLNM 12/92. Canx 4.12.92.
G-BPNN	Montgomerie-Bensen B.8MR Gyrocopter	MV-003		3. 2.89	
G-BPNO	Moravan Zlin Z.526 Trener Master	930	F-BPNO	18. 2.86	
G-BPNP	BAe 146 Srs.100	E1002	N720BA G-BPNP/N801RW/G-5-005/N101RW/G-SSHH/N5828B/G-5-146/G-OPSA/G-SSHH/(G-BIAE)	2. 9.87	To G-BSTA 7/88. Canx.
G-BPNR	[Was reserved for Dan-Air Services Ltd]				
G-BPNS	Boeing 727-277ADV (Line No. 1030)	20550	N276WC (N276BN)/N276WC/VH-RMW	16. 1.89	To C-GRYZ 9/93. Canx 16.9.93.
G-BPNT	BAe 146 Srs.300	E3126		4. 1.89	
G-BPNU	Thunder Ax7-77 HAFB	1011		9. 2.89	
G-BPNV	PA-38-112 Tomahawk	38-79A0260	N2313D	6. 2.89	To G-SUKI 5/91. Canx.
G-BPNW	HS.748 Srs.2/217	1584	G-11-4 RP-C1042/V2-LIP/VP-LIP	7. 2.89	To structural test airframe at Woodford from 9/91. Noted stored in Maxi-Haulage Yard 8/94. Parts on fire dump at Hawarden 1/98. Canx as WFU 5.11.90.
G-BPNX	BAC One-Eleven Srs.304AX	BAC.110	G-YMRU(2) C-FQBN/CF-QBN/G-ATPH	27. 4.88	To 5N-MZE. Canx 29.5.91.
G-BPNY(1)	Boeing 737-2U4 (Line No. 652)	22161	G-ILFC G-BOSL	. .88R	NTU - To G-WGEL 7/88. Canx.
G-BPNY(2)	Boeing 727-230A (Line No. 924)	20675	N727VA D-ABMI/(D-ABYL)	30. 3.89	To N357KP 3/93. Canx 8.2.93.
G-BPNZ	Boeing 737-4Q8 (Line No. 1866)	24332		31. 5.90	To N191LF. Canx 22.5.95.

Regn	Type	c/n	Previous identity	Regn date	Fate or immediate subsequent identity (if known)
G-BPOA	Gloster Meteor T.7	-	WF877	16. 3.89	Canx as WFU 5.6.96. (Stored 5/99 at Kemble)
G-BPOB	Tallmantz Sopwith Camel F.1 Replica	TM-10	N8997	14. 3.89	
G-BPOC	Robin DR.400/180	761	F-BTZJ	22. 2.89	Fatal crash after stalling on take-off at Rochester 11.5.90. Canx as WFU 23.7.90
G-BPOD	Stolp SA.300 Starduster Too	1160	N50SD	12. 6.89	Crashed at Stanscombe Farm, Askerwell on 3.10.93. Canx by CAA 8.2.94.
G-BPOE	Colt 77A HAFB	1399		7. 2.89	Canx by CAA 14.5.98.
G-BPOF	Robinson R-22 Beta	0963		16. 2.89	To EC-FSE. Canx 26.3.93.
G-BPOG	PA-23-250 Aztec C	27-3273	(G-BLPJ) OY-POG/LN-KAB	29.11.85	To N6DA 12/85. Canx by CAA 14.2.89.
G-BPOH	Aerospatiale AS.350B1 Ecureuil	2174		7. 2.89	To G-MSDJ 3/89. Canx.
G-BPOI	Aerospatiale AS.355F2 Twin Squirrel	5409		7. 2.89	To G-GMPA 9/89. Canx.
G-BPOJ	Aerospatiale AS.365N1 Dauphin 2	6319		7. 2.89	To G-THGS 5/89. Canx.
G-BPOK	Rans S-10 Sakota	1188-036		15. 2.89	To 9H-ABV. Canx 2.3.90.
G-BPOL	Pietenpol Air Camper	PFA/47-10941		16. 2.89	
G-BPOM	PA-28-161 Warrior II	28-8416118	N4373Q N9619N	15. 2.89	
G-BPON	PA-34-200T Seneca II	34-7570040	N675ES N32644	13. 2.89	Damaged on landing at Staverton on 11.5.99.
G-BPOO	Montgomerie-Bensen B.8MR Gyrocopter	MV-002 & G/01A-1109		3. 2.89	
G-BPOP	Aircraft Designs Sheriff (Was also known as Britten SA-1 Sheriff)	3		15. 2.83	Project abandoned - only small components built. Canx by CAA 6.2.87.
G-BPOR	Bell 206B JetRanger III	3439	N90WM N21153	13. 3.89	Rolled over and badly damaged at Newtownards on 13.10.95. (Stored by Irish Helicopters Ltd 7/96) Canx 12.7.99 on sale to the USA. To N63446 7/99.
G-BPOS	Cessna 150M Commuter	150-75905	N66187	21. 2.89	
G-BPOT	PA-28-181 Cherokee Archer II	28-7790267	N8807F	7. 2.89	
G-BPOU	Luscombe 8A Silvaire	4159	N1432K NC1432K	14. 2.89	
G-BPOV	Cameron Magazine 90SS HAFB (Forbes Magazine shape)	1890		10. 3.89	
G-BPOW	PA-38-112 Tomahawk II	32-82A0077	N2592V	6. 2.89	To F-GKEJ 12/89. Canx 1.11.89.
G-BPOX	Enstrom 280C-UK Shark	1155	N51776	6. 3.89	To G-HAYN 10/96. Canx.
G-BPOY	Enstrom F-28A-UK	273	N167Q	6. 3.89	No CofA issued. (Last known of at Coventry) Canx as WFU 12.7.94.
G-BPOZ	Enstrom F-28A-UK	281	N246Q	6. 3.89	
G-BPPA	Cameron O-65 HAFB	1930		15. 2.89	
G-BPPB	PA-34-220T Seneca III	34-8133222	N83270	14. 3.89	To G-WWAS 3/95. Canx.
G-BPPC	Robinson R-22 Mariner	0987M		22. 3.89	Fatal crash on a playing field at Higginshaw Lane, Hayeside, Royton on 23.2.92. Canx as destroyed 1.6.92.
G-BPPD	PA-38-112 Tomahawk	38-79A0457	N2456F	15. 2.89	
G-BPPE	PA-38-112 Tomahawk	38-79A0189	N2445C	15. 2.89	
G-BPPF	PA-38-112 Tomahawk	38-79A0578	N2329K	15. 2.89	
G-BPPG	PA-38-112 Tomahawk	38-78A0469	N2461E	15. 2.89	Canx by CAA 27.6.95.
G-BPPH	Cameron DP-90 Gas Airship	1867		21. 1.89	To VH-XDP 8/89. Canx 8.8.89.
G-BPPI	Colt 180A HAFB	1438		21. 2.89	Canx as destroyed 2.4.98.
G-BPPJ	Cameron A-180 HAFB	1924		2. 3.89	
G-BPPK	PA-28-151 Cherokee Warrior	28-7615054	N7592C	10. 3.89	
G-BPPL	Enstrom F-28A	251	HB-XER	15. 2.89	
G-BPPM	Beechcraft B200 Super King Air	BB-1044	N7061T C-GJJT/N815CE/(N815CF)/N815CE/N62895	16. 2.89	
G-BPPN	Reims Cessna F.182Q Skyhawk II	0084	(G-BFFN) (G-BLHN)	5. 5.78	Canx by CAA 7.6.96. To SP-FPN(2) 7/96.
G-BPPO	Luscombe 8A Silvaire	2541	N3519M N71114/NC71114	15. 2.89	
G-BPPP	Cameron V-77 HAFB	1700		29. 2.88	
G-BPPR	Air Command 532 Elite	0434 & G/04-1105		22. 2.89	Permit expired 14.5.91. Canx by CAA 10.3.99.
G-BPPS	Mudry/CAARP CAP.21	9	F-GDTD	3. 5.85	
G-BPPT	PA-31-350 Navajo Chieftain	31-7405429	N54297	16. 2.89	To G-CAFZ(2) 7/91. Canx.
G-BPPU	Air Command 532 Elite	0438 & G/04-1120		22. 2.89	
G-BPPV	Piper J3C-65 Cub	16010	N88392 NC88392	21. 2.89	To EI-CUB 7/91. Canx 15.7.91.
G-BPPW	Schweizer 269C (300C)	S.1172	N3624J	22. 2.89	
G-BPPX	Schweizer 269C (300C)	S.1174	N36247	29. 3.89	To ZK-HSA. Canx 18.3.93.
G-BPPY	Hughes 269B	20-0448	N9554F	10. 3.89	
G-BPPZ	Taylorcraft BC-12D	7988	N28286 NC28286	22. 3.89	(Overturned on landing 13.4.97 at Castleton Farm, nr.Edinburgh)
G-BPRA	Aeronca 11AC Chief	11AC-1344	N9702E NC9702E	22. 3.89	
G-BPRB	Colt GA-42 Gas Airship	878		. 2.89R	NTU - To G-ISPY 7/89. Canx.
G-BPRC	Cameron Elephant 77SS HAFB	1871		21. 2.89	
G-BPRD	Pitts S-1C Special	ZZ.1	N10ZZ	21. 2.89	
G-BPRE	Aerospatiale AS.355F2 Twin Squirrel	5193	N366E	22. 2.89	To F-WYMS/LV-WHC. Canx 3.10.90.

Regn	Type	c/n	Previous identity	Regn date	Fate or immediate subsequent identity (if known)
G-BPRF	Aerospatiale AS.355F1 Twin Squirrel	5177	N363E	22. 2.89	To G-XPOL 4/91. Canx.
G-BPRG	Aerospatiale AS.355F1 Twin Squirrel	5203	G-NWPA G-NAAS/G-BPRG/N370E	21. 2.89	Restored as G-NAAS 6/94. Canx.
G-BPRH	Aerospatiale AS.355F1 Twin Squirrel	5151	N360E N5794F	22. 2.89	To G-TOPS 5/91. Canx.
G-BPRI	Aerospatiale AS.355F1 Twin Squirrel	5181	G-TVPA G-BPRI/N364E	22. 2.89	
G-BPRJ	Aerospatiale AS.355F1 Twin Squirrel	5201	N368E	22. 2.89	
G-BPRK	Aerospatiale AS.355F1 Twin Squirrel	5155	N361E	22. 2.89	NTU - Not Imported. To (F-....)/D-HEUH 6/95 (As a AS.350B2). Canx 12.10.90.
G-BPRL	Aerospatiale AS.355F1 Twin Squirrel	5154	N362E	22. 2.89	
G-BPRM	Reims Cessna F.172L Skyhawk	0825	G-AZKG	20. 4.88	
G-BPRN	PA-28-161 Warrior II	28-8116109	N83112	6. 3.89	
G-BPRO	Cessna A.150K Aerobat	A150-0221	N221AR VP-LAQ/8P-LAC/N5921J	1. 3.89	
G-BPRP	Cessna 150E	150-61269	N3569J	10. 3.89	Badly damaged by gales in 12/97 at Shoreham. (Derelict at Shoreham 8/98)
G-BPRR	Rand Robinson KR-2	PFA/129-11105		1. 3.89	
G-BPRS	Air Command 532 Elite	0432 & G/04-1112		14. 4.89	No Permit issued. Canx by CAA 3.3.99.
G-BPRT	Piel CP.328 Super Emeraude	PFA/50-11268	(G-BPNH)	21. 2.89	Destroyed on take-off Bank Top Farm, Rawtenstall 9.8.97. Canx as destroyed 7.1.98.
G-BPRU	Cameron H-20 HAFB (Originally regd as NS-20)	1900		2. 3.89	To JA-A... Canx 15.11.90.
G-BPRV	PA-28-161 Warrior II	28-8316039	N4292G	24. 2.89	Badly damaged on take-off from Welshpool on 29.3.97. Canx as destroyed 20.6.97. (Fuselage noted dumped at Dunkeswell 5/99 marked as G-..RV & an "Air Defence" sticker on nose)
G-BPRW	PA-28-181 Archer II	28-8590018	N43823	24. 2.89	To F-GIRV 8/90. Canx 24.7.90.
G-BPRX	Aeronca 11AC Chief	11AC-94	N86288 NC86288	3. 3.89	
G-BPRY	PA-28-161 Warrior II	28-8416120	N4373Y N9621N	2. 3.89	
G-BPRZ	Robinson R-22 Alpha	0455	N8556Z	6. 3.89	To ZK-HLJ(2) 10/94. Canx 26.10.94.
G-BPSA	Luscombe 8A Silvaire	3254	N71827 NC71827	3. 3.89	Damaged on take-off Tredunnock Farm, Ross-on-Wye 25.7.90. Canx by CAA 10.6.93. (Stored 10/96) Reduced to spares 1997.
G-BPSB	Air Command 532 Elite	0431		10. 3.89	No Permit issued. Canx by CAA 3.3.99.
G-BPSC	McDonnell Douglas DC-9-83 (MD-83) (Line No. 1540)	49823	N6206F	15. 3.89	Canx by CAA 6.2.90. To N83MV 2/90.
G-BPSD	McDonnell Douglas DC-9-83 (MD-83) (Line No. 1578)	49826	N13627	26. 4.89	Canx by CAA 6.2.90. To N82MV 2/90.
G-BPSE	North American AT-6D Harvard	-	42-44450	20. 4.89	Sold in the USA in 1992. Canx as WFU 5.6.96.
G-BPSF	DHC.7-102 Dash Seven	055	OY-MBD	. 3.89R	NTU - To N8102N 4/89. Canx.
G-BPSG	DHC.7-102 Dash Seven	077	OY-MBE C-GFQL/C-GFCF	. 3.89R	NTU - To N8110N 4/89. Canx.
G-BPSH	Cameron V-77 HAFB	1837		21. 2.89	
G-BPSI	Thunder Ax10-160 HAFB	1420		10. 3.89	
G-BPSJ	Thunder Ax6-56 HAFB	1479		13. 3.89	
G-BPSK	Montgomerie-Bensen B.8M Gyrocopter	G/01-1100		15. 3.89	(Active Enstone 7/95)
G-BPSL	Cessna 177 Cardinal (Fitted with Wings, Fin and Rudder from Cessna 177A N30384 c/n 177-01224)	177-01138	N659SR	3. 3.89	
G-BPSM	Cameron DP-90 Gas Airship	1899		10. 3.89	To LX-HBT. Canx 13.6.89.
G-BPSN	Boeing 757-236 (Line No. 167)	24119	EC-EHY EC-350/G-BPSN/EC-EHY/EC-157	3. 4.89	To PH-TKZ 3/92. Canx 20.3.92.
G-BPSO	Cameron N-90 HAFB (Originally regd as N-77)	1959		10. 3.89	
G-BPSP	Cameron Ship 90SS HAFB (Columbus' Santa Maria shape)	1848		10. 3.89	
G-BPSR	Cameron V-77 HAFB	1962		10. 3.89	
G-BPSS	Cameron A-120 HAFB	1947		27. 2.89	
G-BPST	Brantly B-2B	446	N2280U	. .89R	NTU - To G-OAPR 4/89. Canx.
G-BPSU	Reims Cessna F.406 Caravan II	0024	PH-PEL (F-GEUJ)/F-WZDR	. .89R	NTU - To G-THAN 6/89. Canx.
G-BPSV	Reims Cessna F.406 Caravan II	0030	PH-FWJ F-WZDT	7. 3.89	To 5Y-MMJ. Canx 30.3.94.
G-BPSW	Reims Cessna F.406 Caravan II	0032	F-WZDU	7. 3.89	To N442AB 5/93. Canx 11.5.93.
G-BPSX	Reims Cessna F.406 Caravan II	0034	F-WZDX	7. 3.89	To N443AB 5/93. Canx 11.5.93.
G-BPSY	Grob G-115A	8068	D-EAMH	10. 3.89	Canx by CAA 9.1.90. To OO-XZD.
G-BPSZ	Cameron N-180 HAFB	1911		14. 3.89	
G-BPTA	Stinson 108-2 Station Wagon	108-3429	N429C NC429C	22. 3.89	
G-BPTB	Boeing-Stearman A75N1 (PT-17) Kaydet	75-442	N55581 40-1885	22. 3.89	
G-BPTC	Taylorcraft BC-12D	9388	N94988 NC94988	18. 1.89	Permit expired 29.5.96. Canx by CAA 28.1.97.
G-BPTD	Cameron V-77 HAFB	2001		14. 3.89	
G-BPTE	PA-28-181 Cherokee Archer II	28-7690178	N8553E	9. 3.89	
G-BPTF	Cessna 152 II	152-81979	N67715	9. 3.89	
G-BPTG	Rockwell Commander 112TC	13067	N4577W	31. 3.89	

Regn	Type	c/n	Previous identity	Regn date	Fate or immediate subsequent identity (if known)
G-BPTH	Air Command 532 Elite (Built by K.Rehler)	01	N532KR	25. 4.89	No UK Permit to Fly issued. (Parts only remain .92) Canx by CAA 16.4.99.
G-BPTI	Socata TB-20 Trinidad	414	N41BM	21. 4.89	
G-BPTJ	PA-34-200T Seneca II	34-7570095	N33145	5. 4.89	To Z-PTJ. Canx 27.5.92.
G-BPTK	Cessna 150M Commuter	150-76707	N45029	. .89R	NTU - To G-BPWG 4/89. Canx.
G-BPTL	Cessna 172N Skyhawk II	172-00052	N733YJ	22. 3.89	
G-BPTM	Christen Pitts S-1T Special	1052		6. 3.89	Canx by CAA 24.11.94.
G-BPTN	Bell 206B JetRanger	334	ZK-HYI N1409W	22. 3.89	To ZK-HRL(2). Canx 4.8.89.
G-BPTO	Zenair CH.200-AA	2-563	EI-BKP	22. 3.89	Badly damaged in take-off crash from a strip at Aldersfield, Worcs. on 27.5.91.
G-BPTP	Robinson R-22	0140	N9056H	17. 3.89	
G-BPTR	Robinson R-22	0034	N9021B	28. 3.89	Struck power lines at Well Lane, Stretton, near Warrington on 23.8.92. Canx as destroyed 14.1.93.
G-BPTS	CASA I-131E Jungmann	-	E3B-153 "781-75" Spanish AF	23. 5.89	
G-BPTT	Robin DR.400/120 Dauphin 2+2	1906		14. 3.89	
G-BPTU	Cessna 152 II	152-82955	N45946	22. 3.89	
G-BPTV	Bensen B.8 Gyrocopter	G/01-1058		30. 3.89	
G-BPTW	Cameron A-160 HAFB	1968		29. 3.89	To D-OPTW 4/95. Canx 6.4.94.
G-BPTX	Cameron O-120 HAFB	1972		29. 3.89	
G-BPTY	Robinson R-22 Beta	0916		22. 3.89	To D-HIGL 3/90. Canx 23.3.90.
G-BPTZ	Robinson R-22 Beta	0958		22. 3.89	
G-BPUA	EAA P-2 Sport Biplane	SAAC-02	EI-BBF	30. 3.89	
G-BPUB	Cameron V-31 Air Chair HAFB	1114		15. 3.89	
G-BPUC	QAC Quickie Q.235	2583	N250CE	22. 3.89	
G-BPUD	Ryan PT-22-RY (ST3KR)	1265	N53189 41-15236	22. 3.89	Badly damaged in forced landing in a field at Great Ryburgh, Norfolk on 8.11.92. (Spares use 9/93) Canx as destroyed 3.3.99.
G-BPUE	Air Command 532 Elite	0441 & G/04-1136		29. 3.89	
G-BPUF	Thunder Ax6-56Z HAFB	270	(G-BHRL)	30. 4.80	
G-BPUG	Air Command 532 Elite	0401 & G/04-1157		29. 3.89	
G-BPUH	Cameron A-180 HAFB	1974		29. 3.89	CofA expired 28.7.93. Canx as WFU 10.6.98.
G-BPUI	Air Command 532 Elite	0442 & G/04-1128		31. 3.89	
G-BPUJ	Cameron N-90 HAFB	1977		17. 4.89	
G-BPUK	Robinson R-22 Beta	0947		29. 3.89	To F-GLYG 10/91. Canx 15.10.91.
G-BPUL	PA-18A-150 Super Cub (L-18C-PI)(Regd with frame no 18-2517)	18-2017	OO-LUL I-EIRU/EI-87/MM52-2417/52-2417	12. 4.89	
G-BPUM	Cessna R182 Skylane RG II	R182-00915	N738DZ	2. 5.89	
G-BPUN	Not allotted.				
G-BPUO	Colomban MC-12 (Built by D.T.Tiffany)	0062	N99DT	10. 4.89	Canx 1.10.90 on sale to USA.
G-BPUP	Whittaker MW.7	PFA/171-11473		2. 8.89	
G-BPUR	Piper J3L-65 Cub	4708	N30228 NC30228	14. 6.89	(On overhaul 2/97)
G-BPUS	Rans S-9	PFA/196-11487		7. 4.89	
G-BPUT	Aeronca 7AC Champion	7AC-3973	N85239	7. 4.89	Canx as destroyed 16.5.90.
G-BPUU	Cessna 140	13722	N4251N NC4251N	31. 3.89	
G-BPUV(1)	Beechcraft F33A Bonanza	CE-1036	N6455U	. 4.89R	NTU - To G-BRCH 6/89. Canx.
G-BPUV(2)	BAe 146 Srs.200	E2133	G-5-133	8. 6.89	NTU - To C-GRNV 9/89. Canx.
G-BPUW	Colt 90A HAFB	1436		12. 4.89	
G-BPUX	Cessna 150J Commuter	150-70619	N60851	25. 4.89	
G-BPUY	Cessna 150K Commuter	150-71427	N5927G	25. 4.89	No UK CofA issued. (Was stored at Shotteswell - present status unknown) Canx by CAA 22.12.95.
G-BPUZ	Cessna 150M Commuter	150-78318	N9369U	25. 4.89	Canx 16.3.93 on sale to Denmark. To D-ETKR 8/93.
G-BPVA	Cessna 172F Skyhawk	172-52286	N8386U	13. 4.89	
G-BPVB	Aerospatiale AS.355F1 Twin Squirrel	5300	OH-HAJ D-HEHN	4. 4.89	To G-DOLR 5/89. Canx.
G-BPVC	Cameron V-77 HAFB	1302		7. 4.89	
G-BPVD	Not allocated.				
G-BPVE	Bleriot XI 1909 Replica (Built by R.D.Henry, Texas in 1967)	1	N1197	20. 6.89	(On display Blue Max Movie Acft Museum 3/96)
G-BPVF	Aerospatiale AS.350B1 Ecureuil	2200		12. 4.89	To G-ODMC 10/89. Canx.
G-BPVG	[Was reserved for an unidentified Aeronca 11AC Chief but NTU]				
G-BPVH	Cub J3C-85 Prospector	178C	CF-DRY	7. 4.89	
G-BPVI	PA-32R-301 Saratoga SP	3213021	N91685	24. 4.89	
G-BPVJ	Cessna 152 II	152-82596	N70741	13. 4.89	
G-BPVK	Varga 2150A Kachina	VAC 85-77	N4626V	4. 5.89	
G-BPVL	PA-28-140 Cherokee Cruiser	28-7725160	N1785H	20. 4.89	To G-SCPL 5/89. Canx.
G-BPVM	Cameron V-77 HAFB	1970		4. 4.89	
G-BPVN	PA-32R-301T Saratoga SP	32R-8029073	N8178W	14. 4.89	
G-BPVO	Cassutt Racer IIIM (Built by D.Giorgi)	DG.1	N19DD	13. 4.89	
G-BPVP	Aerotek Pitts S-2B Special	5000	N5302M	13. 4.89	
G-BPVR	Colt Flying Battery SS HAFB	1335		12. 4.89	Canx as destroyed 8.5.91.
G-BPVS	Colt Baren Bear SS HAFB	1336		12. 4.89	Canx on sale to Austria 20.7.90. To OE-AZB 4/93.
G-BPVT	Thunder Ax7-65 HAFB	1475		12. 4.89	Canx by CAA 6.5.93.

Regn	Type	c/n	Previous identity	Regn date	Fate or immediate subsequent identity (if known)
G-BPVU	Thunder Ax7-77 HAFB	965		12. 4.89	
G-BPVV	Cameron V-77 HAFB	1905		19. 4.89	To OO-BKW. Canx 4.6.92.
G-BPVW	CASA I-131E Jungmann	2133	E3B-559 Spanish AF	17. 5.89	
G-BPVX	Cassutt Racer IIIM (Built by J.Clevenger)	99JC	N99JC	17. 4.89	
G-BPVY	Cessna 172D Skyhawk	172-50568	N2968U	20. 4.89	
G-BPVZ	Luscombe 8E Silvaire	5565	N2838K NC2838K	9. 5.89	
G-BPWA	PA-28-161 Warrior II	28-7816074	N47450	7. 4.89	
G-BPWB	Sikorsky S-61N Mk.II	61-822	EI-BHO G-BPWB/EI-BHO	4. 5.89	
G-BPWC	Cameron V-77 HAFB	1986		12. 4.89	
G-BPWD	Cessna 120	10026	N72839 NC72839	14. 4.89	
G-BPWE	PA-28-161 Warrior II	28-8116143	N8330P	2. 5.89	
G-BPWF	PA-28-140 Cherokee	28-23526	OY-BCN N9978W	12. 4.89	Damaged in gales at White Waltham on 25.1.90. Remains donated to 1244 ATC Sqdn at Swindon on 27.2.91. Canx as WFU 28.11.94. Scrapped in 1994.
G-BPWG	Cessna 150M Commuter	150-76707	(G-BPTK) N45029	10. 4.89	
G-BPWH	Robinson R-22 Beta	0991		17. 4.89	To G-OICV 2/93. Canx.
G-BPWI	Bell 206B JetRanger III	3087	9M-BSR VH-HXZ/ZK-HXX/XC-PFH	14. 4.89	
G-BPWJ	Beechcraft 200 Super King Air	BB-742	N56QP N562R	24. 4.89	To Burkina Faso AF as XT-MAX. Canx 19.8.91.
G-BPWK	Sportavia Fournier RF-5B Sperber	51036	N56JM (D-KEAR)	17. 4.89	
G-BPWL	PA-25-235 Pawnee	25-2304	N6690Z G-BPWL/N6690Z	14. 4.89	
G-BPWM	Cessna 150L Commuter	150-72820	N1520Q	17. 4.89	
G-BPWN	Cessna 150L Commuter	150-74325	N19308	17. 4.89	
G-BPWO	Cessna 150L Commuter	150-73727	N18010	17. 4.89	Canx 16.3.93 on sale to Denmark. To D-ETKP 8/93.
G-BPWP	Rutan LongEz (Mod)	PFA/74A-11132		17. 4.89	
G-BPWR	Cessna R172K Hawk XP II	R172-2953	N758AZ	21. 4.89	
G-BPWS	Cessna 172P Skyhawk II	172-74306	N51387	21. 4.89	
G-BPWT	Cameron DG-19 Helium Airship	1772		18. 4.89	
G-BPWU	Colt Clown SS HAFB	1369		. .89R	NTU - To G-GWIZ 4/89. Canx.
G-BPWV	Colt 56A HAFB	1444		21. 4.89	Canx by CAA 4.8.98.
G-BPWW	Focke-Wulf Piaggio FWP.149D	087	OO-FDF D-EFDF/(D-EBDF)/West German AF 90+69/SC+332/AS+496	12. 6.89	To N..... Canx 10.6.99.
G-BPWX	Montgomerie-Bensen B.8MR Gyrocopter	G/01A-1111		17. 4.89	Canx as WFU 10.1.94. To ZK-RAY 8/97.
G-BPWY	Isaacs Fury II	PFA/11-11437		21. 4.89	No Permit to Fly issued. (Sold .96) Canx by CAA 16.4.99.
G-BPWZ	PA-28-161 Warrior II	28-8316077	N4307N	21. 4.89	Badly damaged in forced landing 10.8.97 in a field at Whitehaven. Canx as PWFU 17.9.97.
G-BPXA	PA-28-181 Archer II	28-8390064	N4305T	12. 5.89	
G-BPXB	Glaser-Dirks DG-400	4-248		2. 5.89	
G-BPXC	PA-28-181 Archer II	28-8590063	N6918K	24. 4.89	Canx as WFU 6.4.90.
G-BPXD	Robin DR.400/120A Petit Prince	1354	F-GBUE	19. 4.89	To G-GBUE 5/89. Canx.
G-BPXE	Enstrom 280C Shark	1089	N379KH C-GMLH/N660H	21. 4.89	
G-BPXF	Cameron V-65 HAFB	2003		21. 4.89	(Active 8/93)
G-BPXG	Colt 42A HAFB	1445		25. 4.89	Canx by CAA 6.6.95.
G-BPXH	Colt 17A Cloudhopper HAFB	667	OO-BWG	21. 4.89	
G-BPXI	PA-23-250 Aztec F	27-7854051	PH-SYF D-IEBU/N63908	19. 5.89	To N155AK 11/93. Canx.
G-BPXJ	PA-28RT-201T Turbo Arrow IV	28R-8231023	N8061U	21. 4.89	
G-BPXK	Short SD.3-60 Var.300	SH3757		9. 5.89	To (B-....)/N831BE. Canx 6.9.89.
G-BPXL	Short SD.3-60 Var.200	SH3758		9. 5.89	To VH-MJH 9/89. Canx 12.9.89.
G-BPXM	Short SD.3-60 Var.300	SH3759		9. 5.89	To N159CC. Canx 21.8.89.
G-BPXN	Short SD.3-60 Var.300	SH3760		9. 5.89	To B-8811 10/89. Canx 24.10.89.
G-BPXO	Short SD.3-60 Var.200	SH3761		9. 5.89	To N161SB. Canx 22.11.89.
G-BPXP	Thunder Ax10-160 Srs.1 HAFB	1419		21. 4.89	To D-JUPITER 6/93. Canx 17.5.93.
G-BPXR	PBN BN-2B-20 Islander (Originally regd as a BN-2B-26)	2211		9. 5.89	To B-3905. Canx 12.2.90.
G-BPXS	PBN BN-2B-26 Islander	2212		9. 5.89	To D-ILFH(2) 1/90. Canx 18.1.90.
G-BPXT	PBN BN-2T Turbine Islander (Originally regd as a BN-2B-26)	2213		9. 5.89	To CN-TWK. Canx 22.11.90.
G-BPXU	PBN BN-2T Turbine Islander (Originally regd as a BN-2B-26)	2214		9. 5.89	To CN-TWL. Canx 22.11.90.
G-BPXV	PBN BN-2T Turbine Islander (Originally regd as a BN-2B-26)	2215		9. 5.89	To CN-TWM. Canx 22.11.90.
G-BPXW	BAe 125 Srs.800A	NA0437 & 258161	G-5-636	17. 5.89	To C-FFTM. Canx 19.7.89.
G-BPXX	PA-34-200T Seneca II	34-7970069	N923SM N9556N	21. 4.89	
G-BPXY	Aeronca 11AC Chief	11AC-S-50	N3842E	10. 4.89	
G-BPXZ	Cameron V-77 HAFB	1805		27. 4.89	CofA expired 21.9.95. Canx as PWFU 7.7.98.
G-BPYA	Rotorway Exec	3598 & M-011188		27. 4.89	Canx by CAA 20.8.93.
G-BPYB	Air Command 532 Elite	G/04-1140		23.10.89	Canx by CAA 19.5.93. To 5Y-BJZ.
G-BPYC	Cessna 310R II	310R-1813	N2644Y	27. 4.89	To VH-CIR(2) 3/97. Canx 18.2.97.
G-BPYD	BAe 125 Srs.800B	258146	G-5-629	17. 5.89	NTU - To HZ-109. Canx 25.8.89.

Regn	Type	c/n	Previous identity	Regn date	Fate or immediate subsequent identity (if known)
G-BPYE	BAe 125 Srs.800B	258148	G-5-630	17. 5.89	NTU - To HZ-110. Canx 25.8.89.
G-BPYF	Cameron A-160 HAFB	1931		9. 5.89	To F-GJAV 8/89. Canx 22.5.89.
G-BPYG	Beechcraft C23 Sundowner 180	M-2221	N6638R	3. 5.89	To G-GUCK 4/92. Canx.
G-BPYH	Robinson R-22 Beta	1005		9. 5.89	To G-DERB 6/95. Canx.
G-BPYI	Cameron O-77 HAFB	1988		9. 5.89	
G-BPYJ	Wittman W.8 Tailwind	PFA/31-11028		12. 5.89	
G-BPYK	Thunder Ax7-77 HAFB	1166		15. 5.89	
G-BPYL	Hughes 369D (500D)	100-0796D	N65AM	10. 5.89	
			G-BPYL/HB-XKT		
G-BPYM	Cameron N-90 HAFB	5532	N61113	9. 5.89	Canx as WFU 22.6.89. Restored as N61113.
	(US-built)				
G-BPYN	Piper J3C-65 Cub (L-4H-PI)	11422	F-BFYN	14. 3.79	
			HB-OFN/43-30131		
G-BPYO	PA-28-181 Archer II	2890114	(SE-KIH)	22. 5.89	
G-BPYP	Cameron O-105 HAFB	1987		4. 5.89	To 5Y-BJZ 9/94. Canx 20.9.94.
G-BPYR	PA-31-310 Turbo Navajo C	31-7812032	G-ECMA	15. 5.89	
			N27493		
G-BPYS	Cameron O-77 HAFB	2008		9. 5.89	
G-BPYT	Cameron V-77 HAFB	1984		9. 5.89	(Active 7/96)
G-BPYU	Short SD.3-30 Var.100	SH3124		11. 5.89	To C-FPQE. Canx 9.8.91.
G-BPYV	Cameron V-77 HAFB	1992		17. 5.89	
G-BPYW	Air Command 532 Elite	G/04-1114		2. 6.89	No Permit to Fly issued. Canx by CAA 12.4.99.
G-BPYX	Robinson R-22 Beta	1041		5. 6.89	To G-OMMG 2/94. Canx.
G-BPYY	Cameron A-180 HAFB	2013		11. 5.89	
G-BPYZ	Thunder Ax7-77 HAFB	1521		11. 5.89	
G-BPZA	Luscombe 8A Silvaire	4326	N1599K	18. 4.89	
			NC1599K		
G-BPZB	Cessna 120	8898	N89853	25. 5.89	
			NC89853		
G-BPZC	Luscombe 8A Silvaire	4322	N1595K	6. 6.89	Badly damaged by gales at Cranfield on 25.1.90.
			NC1595K		(Stored 10/96)
G-BPZD	SNCAN NC.858S Chardonneret	97	F-BEZD	26. 1.79	
G-BPZE	Luscombe 8E Silvaire	3904	N1177K	6. 6.89	
			NC1177K		
G-BPZF	PA-46-310P Malibu	46-8408002	N43000	5. 6.89	To N146ZF 5/95. Canx 19.4.95.
G-BPZG	PA-28R-201T Turbo Arrow III		5Y-PSI	17. 8.90	Restored as 5Y-PSI 5/94. Canx 12.5.94.
		28R-7803040	N47926		
G-BPZH	Bell 206B JetRanger II	3067	ZK-HWL	17. 5.89	To SE-HUH. Canx 2.1.90.
G-BPZI	Christen Eagle II	T.0001	N48BB	22. 5.89	
	(Built by J.Trent and R.Eicher)				
G-BPZJ	BAe Jetstream Srs.3102	649	G-31-649	31. 5.89	To VH-LJR. Canx 25.9.89.
			PH-KLC/G-31-649		
G-BPZK	Cameron O-120 HAFB	1982		7. 4.89	
G-BPZL	BAe Jetstream Srs.3201	841	N338AE	18. 5.89	To N841AE. Canx 21.6.89.
			G-31-841		
G-BPZM	PA-28RT-201 Arrow IV	28R-7918238	G-ROYW	12. 5.89	
			G-CRTI/SE-ICY		
G-BPZN	Cessna T.303 Crusader	T303-00160	G-RSUL	6. 6.90	To N65NC 4/93. Canx 5.3.93.
			(G-BPZN)/N6610C		
G-BPZO	Cameron N-90 HAFB	1998		15. 5.89	
G-BPZP	Robin DR.400/180R Remorqueur	1471	D-EFZP	4. 5.89	
G-BPZR	Piper J/2 Cub	1754	N19554	15. 5.89	To G-JTWO 10/89. Canx.
			NC19554		
G-BPZS	Colt 105A HAFB	1312		25. 5.89	
G-BPZT	Cameron N-90 HAFB	1109		25. 5.89	To S5-OAE. Canx 18.1.94.
G-BPZU	Scheibe SF-25C-2000 Falke	44471	D-KIAV	21. 7.89	
G-BPZV	Cessna T.303 Crusader	T303-00006	N9365T	5. 6.89	Ditched in sea 30 miles south by southeast of Exeter on 1.5.92. Canx as destroyed 19.6.92.
G-BPZW	Socata TB-20 Trinidad	945		1. 6.89	Canx by CAA 7.12.89.
G-BPZX	Cessna 152 II	152-85706	N94530	25. 5.89	Fatal crash after mid-air collision with RAF Tornado GR.1 ZA330/B-08 over Mattersey, Notss. on 21.1.99 & destroyed.
G-BPZY	Pitts S-1C Special	RN-1	N1159	15. 5.89	
	(Built by R.L.Neubauer)				
G-BPZZ	Thunder Ax8-105 HAFB	1441		25. 5.89	

G-BQAA to G-BQZZ - Marks not to be issued.

Regn	Type	c/n	Previous identity	Regn date	Fate or immediate subsequent identity (if known)
G-BRAA(1)	Airbus A.320-111	006	F-WWDD	. .88R	NTU - To (G-BRSA)/G-BUSB 3/88. Canx.
G-BRAA(2)	Pitts S-1C Special	101-GM	N14T	12. 5.89	(Stored Squires Gate 6/96)
	(Built by G.R.Miller)				
G-BRAB(1)	Airbus A.320-111	008	F-WWDE	. .88R	NTU - To (G-BRSB)/G-BUSC 5/88. Canx.
G-BRAB(2)	BAe 146 Srs.300	E3131	HS-TBL	23. 5.89	To EI-CLG(2) 6/95. Canx 7.6.95.
			G-BRAB/G-11-131		
G-BRAC(1)	Bristol 175 Britannia Srs.253F		EI-BDC	8. 6.78	Crashed near Logan Airport, Boston, MA, USA on 16.2.80.
		13448	XL639		Canx.
G-BRAC(2)	Airbus A.320-111	011	F-WWDF	. .88R	NTU - To (G-BRSC)/G-BUSD 7/88. Canx.
G-BRAD	Beechcraft 95-B55 Baron	TC-915	OY-ANN	19. 1.78	Extensively damaged in forced landing in a field at Guardswell Farm, 8 miles west of Dundee airport on 8.1.88. Canx as WFU 27.4.88. To Dodson Aviation Scrapyard in USA by 4/88.
			SE-EKO		
G-BRAE(1)	Airbus A.320-111	017	F-WWDG	. .88R	NTU - To (G-BRSD)/G-BUSE 12/88. Canx.
G-BRAE(2)	Colt 69A HAFB	1454		25. 5.89	Canx by CAA 29.7.98.

Regn	Type	c/n	Previous identity	Regn date	Fate or immediate subsequent identity (if known)
G-BRAF	Vickers Supermarine 394 Spitfire FR.XVIIIe (C/n also quoted as 6S/699526)	6S/663052	HS877 Indian AF/SM969	29.12.78	(Stored Hurn 11/92)
G-BRAG	Taylor JT.2 Titch	PFA/3225		15. 9.78	No Permit issued. Canx by CAA 29.7.91.
G-BRAH(1)	Airbus A.320-111	018	F-WWDH	. .88R	NTU - To (G-BRSE)/G-BUSF 5/89. Canx.
G-BRAH(2)	Cessna 310R II	310R-1225	N1909G	28. 6.89	To G-TKPZ 3/90. Canx.
G-BRAI	Airbus A.320-211	039	F-WWDM	. .88R	NTU - To (G-BRSF)/G-BUSG 5/89. Canx.
G-BRAJ(1)	Airbus A.320-211	042	F-WWDT	. .88R	NTU - To (G-BRSG)/G-BUSH 6/89. Canx.
G-BRAJ(2)	Cameron V-77 HAFB	1876		25. 5.89	(Active 1/95)
G-BRAK(1)	Airbus A.320-211	103	F-WWDB	. .88R	NTU - To (G-BRSH)/G-BUSI 3/90. Canx.
G-BRAK(2)	Cessna 172N Skyhawk II	172-73795	C-GBPN (N5438J)	23. 6.88	
G-BRAL	Grumman G.159 Gulfstream I	76	N305K N776G	30.10.80	To P4-JML 4/96. Canx 23.4.96.
G-BRAM(1)	Airbus A.320-211	109	F-WWIC	. .88R	NTU - To (G-BRSI)/G-BUSJ 8/90. Canx.
G-BRAM(2)	Mikoyan MiG-21PF	-	503/ Hungarian AF	22. 5.89	No CofA issued. (Taxiable 2/99 Hurn) Canx by CAA 16.4.99.
G-BRAN(1)	Airbus A.320-211	120	F-WWIN	. .88R	NTU - To (G-BRSJ)/G-BUSK 10/90. Canx.
G-BRAN(2)	Mikoyan MiG-21PF	-	506/ Hungarian AF	22. 5.89	To N316DM. Canx 4.1.90.
G-BRAO	Mikoyan MiG-21PF	-	1603/ Hungarian AF	22. 5.89	To N610DM Canx 14.7.89.
G-BRAP	Thermal Aircraft 104 HAFB	001		11. 5.89	
G-BRAR	Aeronca 7AC Champion	7AC-6564	N2978E NC2978E	14. 6.89	
G-BRAS	Embraer EMB.120RT Brasilia	120-071	LN-KOF G-BRAS/PT-SKO	29. 3.88	To PT-LUS 8/89. Canx 31.7.89.
G-BRAT	Wassmer Jodel D.120A Paris-Nice	165	LX-GUY LX-ZUT/LX-AIF	23. 7.79	Crashed on landing at Ostend on 13.8.83. Used for spares. Canx by CAA 6.2.87.
G-BRAU	PA-28-181 Archer II	28-7890068	N47411	25. 5.89	To G-SHED 6/89. Canx.
G-BRAV	PA-23-250 Aztec E	27-4634	G-BBCM N14021	12. 8.88	To G-RVRD 3/98. Canx.
G-BRAW	Pitts S-1C Special	52544	N24DB	24. 5.89	
G-BRAX	Payne Knight Twister 85B	203	N979	24. 5.89	(On overhaul 3/96)
G-BRAY	PA-32RT-300 Lance II	32R-7885051	D-EKWS N9507C	20. 6.84	Restored as N9507C 1/85. Canx 6.2.85.
G-BRAZ	Embraer EMB.120RT Brasilia	120-081	F-GFTC G-BRAZ/PT-SKY	12. 9.88	To PH-XLA. Canx 20.1.92.
G-BRBA	PA-28-161 Warrior II	28-7916109	N2090B	25. 5.89	
G-BRBB	PA-28-161 Warrior II	28-8116030	N8260W	28. 6.89	
G-BRBC	North American T-6G Texan (Also reported as c/n 182-155 ex.51-14469)	182-156	MM54099 RR-56/51-14470	4. 9.92	(On rebuild Audley End 9/90 - status uncertain)
G-BRBD	PA-28-151 Cherokee Warrior	28-7415315	N41702	28. 6.89	
G-BRBE	PA-28-161 Warrior II	28-7916437	N2815D	13. 6.89	
G-BRBF	Cessna 152 II	152-81993	N67748	8. 6.89	
G-BRBG	PA-28-180 Cherokee Archer	28-7505248	N3927X	12. 6.89	
G-BRBH	Cessna 150H Commuter	150-69283	N50410	13. 6.89	
G-BRBI	Cessna 172N Skyhawk II	172-69613	N737RJ	7. 7.89	
G-BRBJ	Cessna 172M Skyhawk II	172-67492	N73476	26. 5.89	
G-BRBK	Robin DR.400/180 Regent	1915		31. 5.89	
G-BRBL	Robin DR.400/180 Regent	1920		5. 7.89	
G-BRBM	Robin DR.400/180 Regent	1921		5. 7.89	
G-BRBN	Pitts S-1S Special (Built by W.L.Garner)	G.3	N81BG	14. 7.89	
G-BRBO	Cameron V-77 HAFB	1877		30. 5.89	
G-BRBP	Cessna 152 II	152-84915	N5324P	14. 6.89	
G-BRBR	Cameron V-77 HAFB	1838		30. 5.89	Canx as WFU 20.9.95.
G-BRBS	Bensen B.8M Gyrocopter	G/01-1039		30. 5.89	
G-BRBT	Trotter Ax3-20 HAFB	RMT-001		13. 6.89	
G-BRBU	Colt 17A Cloudhopper HAFB	1506		12. 6.89	
G-BRBV	Piper J/4A Cub Coupe	4-1080	N27860 NC27860	13. 6.89	
G-BRBW	PA-28-140 Cherokee Cruiser	28-7425153	N40737	3. 7.89	
G-BRBX	PA-28-181 Cherokee Archer II	28-7690185	N8674E	20. 7.89	
G-BRBY	Robinson R-22 Beta	1027		15. 6.89	
G-BRBZ	Beechcraft 400 Beechjet	RJ-60	N1560T	26. 5.89	To N89GA. Canx 18.5.95.
G-BRCA	Jodel D.112 (Valladeau built)	1203	F-BLIU	11. 7.89	
G-BRCB	Cessna 152 II	152-85903	N95490	8. 6.89	To PH-PJM. Canx 3.4.90.
G-BRCC	Cessna 152 II	152-80986	N48826	8. 6.89	Fatal crash 31.5.96 at Lydd. Canx as destroyed 19.9.96.
G-BRCD	Cessna A.152 Aerobat	A152-0796	N7377L	8. 6.89	
G-BRCE	Pitts S-1C Special	1001	N4611G	22. 6.89	
G-BRCF	Montgomerie-Bensen B.8MR Gyrocopter	G/01A-1131		12. 6.89	
G-BRCG	Grob G-109	6077	N64BG D-KGRO	15. 6.89	
G-BRCH	Beechcraft F33A Bonanza	CE-1036	(G-BPUV) N6455U	12. 6.89	Fatal crash 13.4.90 nr.Bayeux, France. Canx by CAA 17.2.95.

Regn	Type	c/n	Previous identity	Regn date	Fate or immediate subsequent identity (if known)
G-BRCI	Pitts S-1C Special (Built by Ballentyne)	4668	N351S	6. 7.89	Overturned on landing at Tatenhill 15.3.99.
G-BRCJ	Cameron NS-20 HAFB	2028		13. 6.89	
G-BRCK	Anderson EA-1 Kingfisher Amphibian	PFA/132-10798		15. 6.89	To G-BUTE 8/91. Canx.
G-BRCL	Colt Flying Hat SS HAFB	1449		13. 6.89	Canx 28.1.93. To C-FPIA 3.10.95.
G-BRCM	Cessna 172L Skyhawk	172-59960	N3860Q	19. 6.89	
G-BRCN	Cameron N-90 HAFB	1991		13. 6.89	To G-HBUG 6/89. Canx.
G-BRCO	Cameron NS-20 HAFB	2030		19. 6.89	
G-BRCP	Enstrom F-28F	761		19. 6.89	To G-SNAZ 10/94. Canx.
G-BRCR	Cameron V-77 HAFB	2009		13. 6.89	Canx by CAA 4.8.98.
G-BRCS	Colt 105A HAFB	1513		13. 6.89	Canx 28.1.93. To C-FGLM 9/93.
G-BRCT	Denney Kitfox Mk.2	396		23. 6.89	(Frame stored 4/94)
G-BRCU	Colt 105A HAFB	1517		13. 6.89	To C-FFPN. Canx 28.2.90.
G-BRCV	Aeronca 7AC Champion	7AC-282	N81661 NC81661	19. 9.89	
G-BRCW	Aeronca 11BC Chief	11AC-366	N85964 NC85964	16.10.89	
G-BRCX	Colt 105A HAFB	1456		13. 6.89	To C-FGLL. Canx 28.1.93.
G-BRCY	Colt 105A HAFB	1459		13. 6.89	To C-FFPK. Canx 28.2.90.
G-BRCZ	BAe 125 Srs.800A	NA0443 & 258163	G-5-639	23. 6.89	To C-GMOL. Canx 30.8.89.
G-BRDA	Denney Kitfox	PFA/172-11353		23. 6.89	Failed to get airborne on take-off at Cleobury Mortimer on 22.3.91 and crashed into trees at the end of the runway. Canx as WFU 7.6.91.
G-BRDB	Zenair CH.701 STOL	PFA/187-11412		11. 7.89	
G-BRDC	Thunder Ax7-77 HAFB	1547		26. 6.89	
G-BRDD	Avions Mudry CAP.10B	224		3. 8.88	
G-BRDE	Thunder Ax7-77 HAFB	1538		22. 6.89	
G-BRDF	PA-28-161 Cherokee Warrior II	28-7716085	N1139Q	26. 6.89	
G-BRDG	PA-28-161 Warrior II	28-7816047	N44934	26. 6.89	
G-BRDH	Cessna 120	9294	N72127 NC72127	7. 7.89	To G-BRUN 8/89. Canx.
G-BRDI	HS.125 Srs.700B	257097	G-HHOI (G-BHTJ)	27.11.87	Restored as G-BHTJ 8/90. Canx.
G-BRDJ	Luscombe 8A Silvaire	3411	N71984 NC71984	28. 6.89	(Badly damaged by gales Cranfield 25.1.90) (For rebuild 2/98 Chilbolton)
G-BRDK	Bell 206B JetRanger II	1865	N11LN	22. 6.89	To G-COWZ 11/89. Canx.
G-BRDL	Bell 206B JetRanger II	771	N8160J	22. 6.89	To VH-FRL(2) 6/97. Canx 17.4.97.
G-BRDM	PA-28-161 Cherokee Warrior II	28-7716004	N8464F	26. 6.89	
G-BRDN	Socata MS.880B Rallye Club	1212	OY-DTV	14. 7.89	
G-BRDO	Cessna 177B Cardinal II	177-02166	N35030	13. 7.89	
G-BRDP	Colt Jumbo SS HAFB	1526		3. 7.89	
G-BRDR	Boeing 720-051B (Line No. 361)	18688	YN-BYI SX-DBN/N735US	20. 6.89	NTU - Not Imported. To N8215Q 6/89. Canx 20.6.89.
G-BRDS	Colt Flying Coke Can SS HAFB	1472		3. 7.89	Canx by CAA 10.3.95.
G-BRDT	Cameron DP-70 Hot-Air Airship	2029		3. 7.89	
G-BRDU	Cameron DG-14 Airship	1872		22. 6.89	Canx as WFU 21.10.96.
G-BRDV	Vickers-Supermarine Spitfire Prototype Replica	HD36/001 & PFA/130-10796		3. 7.89	(Stored 4/96)
G-BRDW	PA-24-180 Comanche	24-1733	N6612P	12. 3.90	
G-BRDX	Bell 212	30785	210 Singapore AF	19. 6.89	To N8228R 8/89. Canx 3.8.89.
G-BRDY	Bell 212	30787	211 Singapore AF	19. 6.89	To N2118X. Canx 13.11.89.
G-BRDZ	Bell 212	30791	212 Singapore AF	19. 6.89	To N82283 8/89. Canx 26.7.89.
G-BREA	Bensen B.8MR Gyrocopter	G/01-1006		6. 7.89	
G-BREB	Piper J3C-65 Cub	7705	N41094 NC41094	3. 7.89	
G-BREC	Colt Flying Crisp Bag HAFB	1430		30. 6.89	Canx 7.5.91 on sale to Sweden.
G-BRED	Canadair CL-44D4-2	37	G-AZKJ N1001T/CF-PZZ-X	7. 8.80	To N106BB 11/83. Canx 14.11.83.
G-BREE	Whittaker MW.7	PFA/171-11497		22. 6.89	
G-BREF	Cessna 421C Golden Eagle III	421C-0432	(AP-...) G-BREF/N4178G	1. 6.78	To AP-BCX 11/86. Canx 21.11.86.
G-BREG	Colt 21A Cloudhopper HAFB	1508		7. 7.89	Canx 7.5.91 on sale to USA.
G-BREH	Cameron V-65 HAFB	2049		7. 7.89	
G-BREI	Christen Eagle II (Built by J.Reed)	REED-001	N428JR	13. 6.89	Crashed at Hart Ridge Farm, Ashampstead on 17.8.91. Canx as WFU 23.12.91.
G-BREJ	Schweizer 269C (300C)	S.1388		7. 7.89	Crashed at Kidlington on 2.7.91. Canx as destroyed 20.8.91. To ZK-HGJ /92.
G-BREK	Piper J3C-65 Cub	20888	N2089M	1. 8.89	No UK CofA or Permit issued. Canx by CAA 22.12.95.
G-BREL	Cameron O-77 HAFB	386		5. 4.78	
G-BREM	Air Command 532 Elite	0614 & G/04-1139		20. 7.89	(Stored 7/91)
G-BREN	Cameron Levi Jeans 65SS HAFB	436		1.11.78	To PH-BRE 9/83. Canx 17.8.82.
G-BREO	Mooney M.20K (231)	25-1150	N252BX	21. 7.89	To N252AB 12/92. Canx 23.11.92.
G-BREP	PA-28RT-201 Arrow IV	28R-7918119	N2230Z	19. 6.90	
G-BRER	Aeronca 7AC Champion	7AC-6758	N3157E NC3157E	12. 7.89	

Regn	Type	c/n	Previous identity	Regn date	Fate or immediate subsequent identity (if known)
G-BRES	Montgomerie-Bensen B.8MR Gyrocopter	G/01A-1117		20. 7.89	To G-INCH 8/91. Cañx.
G-BRET	[Unidentified reservation]	?		. .89R	NTU - Canx.
G-BREU	Montgomerie-Bensen B.8 Gyrocopter	G/01A-1137		20. 7.89	
G-BREV	BAe Jetstream Srs.3201	857	G-31-857	14. 7.89	To N857AE. Canx 14.9.89.
G-BREW	PA-31-350 Navajo Chieftain	31-7852154	N27729	15.11.78	To G-BRFA 6/89. Canx.
G-BREX	Cameron O-84 HAFB	2019		14. 7.89	
G-BREY	Taylorcraft BC-12D	7299	N43640 NC43640	14. 7.89	
G-BREZ	Cessna 172M Skyhawk II	172-66742	N80775	14. 7.89	To EI-CHS 4/93. Canx 16.4.93.
G-BRFA	PA-31-350 Navajo Chieftain	31-7852154	G-BREW N27729	30. 6.89	
G-BRFB	Rutan LongEz	PFA/74A-10646		14. 7.89	Crashed on Ireland's Eye Island east of Dublin Airport on 24.6.90.
G-BRFC	Hunting Percival P.57 Sea Prince T.1	P57/71	WP321	10. 9.80	(Stored 5/97)
G-BRFD	Bell 206B JetRanger III	3408	N2069N	21. 7.89	To G-HIER 5/91. Canx.
G-BRFE	Cameron N-77 HAFB	1835		20. 7.89	
G-BRFF	Colt 90A HAFB	1548		14. 7.89	
G-BRFG	Cessna 340A	340A-0012	N5177J	27. 9.78	To N1362C 10/81. Canx 13.10.81.
G-BRFH	Colt 90A HAFB	1543		14. 7.89	
G-BRFI	Aeronca 7DC Champion	7AC-4609	N1058E NC1058E	1. 8.89	(Damaged in heavy landing .90) (On rebuild 4/96)
G-BRFJ	Aeronca 11AC Chief	11AC-796	N9163E NC9163E	28. 7.89	
G-BRFK	Colt Pepsi Can SS HAFB	1448		14. 7.89	Canx by CAA 10.3.95. To LY-OBY /93.
G-BRFL	PA-38-112 Tomahawk	38-79A0431	N2416F	17. 8.89	
G-BRFM	PA-28-161 Warrior II	28-7916279	N2234P	17.10.89	
G-BRFN	PA-38-112 Tomahawk	38-79A0397	N2326F	23.10.89	
G-BRFO	Cameron V-77 HAFB	2025		6. 7.89	
G-BRFP	Schweizer Hughes 269C (300C)	S.1389		14. 7.89	
G-BRFR	Cameron N-105 HAFB	2042		14. 7.89	Canx as WFU 9.5.97. (Extant 1/98)
G-BRFS	Cameron N-90 HAFB	2041		14. 7.89	CofA expired 21.11.96. Canx as PWFU 20.1.99.
G-BRFT	[Unidentified reservation]	?		. .89R	NTU - Canx.
G-BRFU	Fouga CM-170R Magister	268	N219DM Israeli DF/AF / Belgium AF MT-11	7. 8.89	Canx 25.10.95 on sale to USA.
G-BRFV	Cessna T.182 Turbo Skylane 'B'	T182-68517	N9418X	3. 3.89	To D-EROM 10/93. Canx 19.11.92.
G-BRFW	Montgomerie-Bensen B.8 Two-Seat Gyrocopter	G/01-1073		20. 7.89	
G-BRFX	Pazmany PL-4A	PFA/17-10079		14. 7.89	
G-BRFY	PBN BN-2B-26 Islander	2216		25. 7.89	To VP-FBN 7/90. Canx 17.7.90.
G-BRFZ	PBN BN-2B-26 Islander	2217		25. 7.89	To F-ODUR 7/90. Canx 14.6.90.
G-BRGA	PBN BN-2B-26 Islander	2218		25. 7.89	To VP-FBO 7/90. Canx 19.7.90.
G-BRGB	PBN BN-2B-26 Islander	2219		25. 7.89	To F-ODUP 5/90. Canx 11.5.90.
G-BRGC	PBN BN-2B-26 Islander	2220		25. 7.89	To F-ODUQ 6/90. Canx 7.6.90.
G-BRGD	Cameron O-84 HAFB	2043		20. 7.89	
G-BRGE	Cameron N-90 HAFB	2047		20. 7.89	
G-BRGF	Luscombe 8E Silvaire	5475	N23FP N944BL/N2748K/NC2748K	20. 7.89	
G-BRGG	Luscombe 8A Silvaire	3795	N1068K NC1068K	20. 7.89	
G-BRGH	Clutton FRED Srs.II	FGH.001 & PFA/29-10425		26.10.78	No Permit issued. Canx by CAA 4.7.91.
G-BRGI	PA-28-180 Cherokee E	28-5827	N77VG N11VG	24. 7.89	
G-BRGJ	PA-28-151 Cherokee Warrior	28-7715131	(G-BPGP) N5425F	20. 7.89	To G-CPCH 11/93. Canx.
G-BRGK	BAe 146 Srs.300QT	E3150		27. 7.89	To SE-DIM. Canx 19.12.89.
G-BRGL	BAe Jetstream Srs.3102	720	OK-SEK G-OEDC/G-LOGU/G-BRGL/I-BLUA/G-31-720/G-BRGL/G-31-720	30. 9.86	To SE-LHV 3/97. Canx 14.3.97.
G-BRGM	BAe 146 Srs.300QT	E3151		27. 7.89	To SE-DIT. Canx 12.2.90.
G-BRGN	BAe Jetstream Srs.3102	637	G-BLHC G-31-637	20. 3.87	WFU & stored 11/96 at Prestwick.
G-BRGO	Air Command 532 Elite	0615 & G/04-1149		7. 8.89	
G-BRGP	Colt Flying Stork SS HAFB	1409		25. 7.89	Canx by CAA 10.3.95. (Active in Albuquerque, New Mexico, USA 10/96)
G-BRGR	BAe Jetstream Srs.3102	655	PH-KJD G-31-655	2. 8.89	To G-LOGR 8/91. Canx.
G-BRGS	Aerospatiale SA.341G Gazelle Srs.1	1274	F-GEQA(2) N341SG/(N341P)/N341SG/N47295	8. 8.89	To G-OCJR 6/90. Canx.
G-BRGT	PA-32-260 Cherokee Six	32-658	N3744W	7.11.89	
G-BRGU	Cameron R-60 Gas Free Balloon	2057		27. 7.89	Canx 16.1.92 on sale to Spain.
G-BRGV	PA-31-350 Navajo Chieftain	31-7852066	N27583	14. 6.78	To PH-PTD 9/84. Canx 31.9.84.
G-BRGW	Barritault JB-01 Minicab (Originally regd as an Gardan GY-201 Minicab with c/n MBW-100)	PFA/1823		13.11.78	
G-BRGX	Rotorway Exec 152	3597		3. 8.89	
G-BRGY	Colt 180A HAFB	1349		13.10.89	To F-GKGY 1/91. Canx 22.8.90.
G-BRGZ	PA-32R-301 Saratoga SP	3213026	N91787	27. 7.89	To G-HDEW 12/89. Canx.

Regn	Type	c/n	Previous identity	Regn date	Fate or immediate subsequent identity (if known)
G-BRHA	PA-32RT-300 Lance II	32R-7985076	N2093P	27. 7.89	
G-BRHB	Boeing-Stearman B75N1 (N2S-3) Kaydet		EC-AID	10. 8.89	(On rebuild in industrial estate Grays Thurrock 7/90)
		75-6508	N67955/BuA.05334		
G-BRHC	Cameron V-77 HAFB	1842		3. 8.89	
G-BRHD	PA-23-250 Turbo Aztec F	27-7754101	N63793	22. 7.77	Restored as N63793 7/82. Canx 10.7.82.
G-BRHE	Piper J3C-90 Cub (L-4B PI)	12009	EC-AIY	. .89R	NTU - To (G-BSMJ)/G-BSYO 2/91. Canx.
	(Frame No.12639)		HB-ODO/44-80513		
	(Officially regd as c/n 10244 ex 43-1383/F-BFYF which is HB-OVG)				
G-BRHF	PA-31-350 Navajo Chieftain		N7679L	28. 7.89	To G-GRAM 4/91. Canx.
		31-7305006			
	(Was regd in error with c/n 31-7352006)				
G-BRHG	Colt 90A HAFB	1568		11. 9.89	
G-BRHH	Cameron Cow 106SS HAFB	2014		3. 8.89	To C-FCOW. Canx 5.1.93.
G-BRHI	Bell 206B JetRanger III	2930	N2779W	3. 8.89	To N165JK 6/93. Canx 12.5.93.
G-BRHJ	PA-34-200T Seneca II	34-8070214	N82013	7.12.89	Damaged at Kemble on 17.5.98. Canx as destroyed 13.1.99.
G-BRHK	Thunder Colt GA-42 Gas Airship	1140		3. 8.89	To N28SQ 7/93. Canx 14.7.93.
G-BRHL	Montgomerie-Bensen B.8MR Gyrocopter			7. 8.89	
		G/01A-1123			
G-BRHM	Bensen B.8M Gyrocopter			3. 8.89	
		DPC-001 & G/01-1144			
G-BRHN	Robinson R-22 Beta	1093		4. 8.89	
G-BRHO	PA-34-200 Seneca	34-7350037	N15222	20. 9.89	
G-BRHP	Aeronca O-58B Defender	058B-8533	N58JR	2. 8.89	
	(If US Army serial is correct, type should be L-3C-AE)		N46536/43-1923		
G-BRHR	PA-38-112 Tomahawk	38-79A0969	N2377P	21. 8.89	
G-BRHS	PA-38-112 Tomahawk	38-79A0462	N2465F	4. 8.89	Crashed 28.4.97 nr.Speke. Canx 31.10.97 as WFU.
G-BRHT	PA-38-112 Tomahawk	38-79A0199	N2474C	4. 8.89	
G-BRHU	Montgomerie-Bensen B.8MR Gyrocopter			4. 8.89	
		G/01A-1133			
G-BRHV	Colt 180A HAFB	1563		8. 8.89	To D-ORHV 12/92. Canx 17.9.92.
G-BRHW	DH.82A Tiger Moth	85612	7Q-YMY	26. 7.89	(On rebuild)
			VP-YMY/ZS-DLB/South African AF 4606/DE671		
G-BRHX	Luscombe 8E Silvaire	5114	N176M	8. 8.89	
			N2387K/NC2387K		
G-BRHY	Luscombe 8E Silvaire	5138	N2411K	8. 8.89	
			NC2411K		
G-BRHZ	Stephens Akro Z	A-235	N35EJ	20.12.89	
	(Built by E.A.Johnson)(Also known as Astro 235)				
G-BRIA	Cessna 310L	310L-0010	N2210F	4. 8.89	(Stored 6/97)
G-BRIB	Cameron N-77 HAFB	2065		8. 8.89	
G-BRIC	Cameron V-65 HAFB	748		31. 7.81	To F-GEAK 8/84. Canx 30.3.84.
G-BRID	Cessna U.206A Super Skywagon		N4874F	7. 5.87	Canx as WFU 4.10.93. (Para-trainer use 1/96)
		U206-0574			
G-BRIE	Cameron N-77 HAFB	2076		8. 8.89	
G-BRIF	Boeing 767-204ER	24736	(PH-AHM)	10. 3.90	
	(Line No. 296)		G-BRIF		
G-BRIG	Boeing 767-204ER	24757	(PH-AHN)	10. 4.90	
	(Line No. 299)		G-BRIG		
G-BRIH	Taylorcraft BC-12D	7421	N43762	24. 8.89	
			NC43762		
G-BRII	Zenair CH.600 Zodiac	PFA/162-11392		18. 8.89	
G-BRIJ	Taylorcraft F-19	F-119	N3863T	23. 8.89	
G-BRIK	Slingsby Nipper T.66S RA.45 Srs.3B			26. 4.77	
		PFA/25-10174			
	(Rebuild of G-AVKH c/n S.101/1585 (Tipsy c/n 27))				
G-BRIL	Piper J/5A Cub Cruiser	5-572	N35183	2. 8.89	
			NC35183		
G-BRIM	Cameron O-160 HAFB	1856		10. 8.89	
G-BRIN	Socata TB-20 Trinidad	960		24. 8.89	To F-GNCL 3/99. Canx 15.1.99.
G-BRIO	Turner Super T-40A	PFA/104-10636		7. 8.89	
	(Regd incorrectly as PFA/104-10736)				
G-BRIP	Boeing-Stearman A75N1 (PT-17) Kaydet		N53127	. .89R	NTU - To G-BUKE 7/92. Canx.
		75-2732	41-25243		
G-BRIR	Cameron V-56 HAFB	2056		17. 8.89	
G-BRIS	Steen Skybolt	01	N870MC	30. 8.89	
	(Built by M.K.Callen)				
G-BRIT	Cessna 421C Golden Eagle III		N6713C	6. 4.78	To N5NN 4/93. Canx 2.4.93.
		421C-0446			
G-BRIU	Socata TB-10 Tobago	938		24. 8.89	To G-OFIT 9/89. Canx.
G-BRIV	Socata TB-9 Tampico Club	939		24. 8.89	
G-BRIW	Hughes 269C (300C)	112-0168	N8952F	30. 8.89	To OO-MQH 1/96. Canx 15.12.95.
G-BRIX	PA-32R-301 Saratoga SP	32R-8113030	N8319S	24. 2.81	To G-OCCA 5/89. Canx.
G-BRIY	Taylorcraft DF-65	6183	N59687	1. 2.90	
	(Built as TG-6 glider)		NC59687/42-58678		
G-BRIZ	Druine D.31 Turbulent	PFA/48-11513		8. 8.89	No Permit issued. Canx by CAA 2.3.99.
G-BRJA	Luscombe 8A Silvaire	3744	N1017K	12. 9.89	
			NC1017K		
G-BRJB	Zenair CH.600 Zodiac	6-1283		2. 8.89	(Incomplete at PFA Rally 7/95)
G-BRJC	Cessna 120	12077	N1833N	21. 8.89	
			NC1833N		
G-BRJD	Boeing 757-236	24397	EC-ESC	13. 4.89	To G-OOOS 5/91. Canx.
	(Line No. 221)		EC-349(2)/G-BRJD		

Regn	Type	c/n	Previous identity	Regn date	Fate or immediate subsequent identity (if known)
G-BRJE	Boeing 757-236 (Line No. 224)	24398	EC-EOL EC-278/G-BRJE	26. 4.89	To EC-597/EC-EOL 12/90. Canx 4.12.90.
G-BRJF	Boeing 757-236 (Line No. 271)	24772	(I-BRJF) G-BRJF/EC-EVD/EC-432/G-BRJF	26. 3.90	To I-BRJF 12/90. Canx 18.12.90.
G-BRJG	Boeing 757-236 (Line No. 272)	24771		27. 3.90	To PH-AHN. Canx 14.5.91.
G-BRJH	Boeing 757-236 (Line No. 278)	24794		20. 4.90	To EC-669/EC-FEF. Canx 11.4.91.
G-BRJI	Boeing 757-236 (Line No. 279)	24792	SX-BBZ G-BRJI/SX-BBZ/G-BRJI/EC-FMQ/EC-786/EC-EVC/EC-446/G-BRJI	30. 4.90	To SE-DUO 5/97. Canx 7.5.97.
G-BRJJ	Boeing 757-236 (Line No. 292)	24793	EC-490 G-BRJJ	20. 6.90	To G-OOOT 5/91. Canx.
G-BRJK	Luscombe 8A Silvaire	4205	N1478K NC1478K	21. 8.89	
G-BRJL	PA-15 Vagabond	15-157	N4370H NC4370H	21. 8.89	
G-BRJM	Cameron A-210 HAFB	2081		17. 8.89	To SU-... Canx 26.8.99.
G-BRJN	Pitts S-1C Special (Built by M.G.Acker)	1-MA	N6A	23. 8.89	
G-BRJO	Bell 206B JetRanger III	3594	N2295Z	18. 8.89	To G-TILT 9/91. Canx.
G-BRJP	Boeing 737-2S3 (Line No. 849)	22660	N5573L (G-BMSR)	3. 2.82	To VR-HYK 11/86. Canx 5.11.86.
G-BRJR	PA-38-112 Tomahawk	38-79A0144	N2598B	31. 8.89	
G-BRJS	BAe 146 Srs.100	E1004	G-5-04 ZD695/G-OBAF/(G-SCHH)/(G-BIAG)	23. 4.85	To (N346SS)/G-5-537/G-OJET 11/87. Canx.
G-BRJT	Cessna 150H	150-68426	N44SS N22649	31. 8.89	
G-BRJU	PA-28-151 Cherokee Warrior	28-7515026	N44762	24. 8.89	To G-JAMP 4/95. Canx.
G-BRJV	PA-28-161 Cadet	2841167	N9185G	24. 8.89	(Badly damaged 17.5.98 at Kirkbridge Airfield)
G-BRJW	Bellanca 7GCBC Citabria 150S	1200-80	OO-LPG	7. 4.82	
G-BRJX	Rand Robinson KR-2	PFA/129-11386		22. 8.89	
G-BRJY	Rand Robinson KR-2	PFA/129-11308		22. 8.89	
G-BRJZ	Cameron V-77 HAFB	2079		22. 8.89	To JA-A451 9/89. Canx 18.9.89.
G-BRKA	Luscombe 8F Silvaire	5084	N2357K NC2357K	13. 3.89	Canx as destroyed 20.4.99.
G-BRKB	Cameron N-65 HAFB	2072		7. 9.89	To ZK-RKB. Canx 11.3.93.
G-BRKC	Auster J/1 Autocrat	2749	F-BFYT	31. 8.89	(On rebuild 5/97)
G-BRKD	Piaggio P.149D	306	D-EAMS West German AF 92+10/AC+457/AS+457	15. 9.89	(Stored 1/97 Meppershall) CofA expired 5.11.92. Canx as TWFU 28.5.99.
G-BRKE	Hawker (CCF) Sea Hurricane XIIA (2B) (Built by Canadian Car and Foundary Co.)(Also parts from BW881 c/n R32007)	R30019	RCAF BW853	6.10.89	(Composite rebuild from components .90) Canx by CAA 22.12.95.
G-BRKF	Boeing 737-4S3 (Line No. 1870)	24795		11. 6.90	To G-IEAE 4/92. Canx.
G-BRKG	Boeing 737-4S3 (Line No. 1887)	24796		12. 7.90	To G-TREN 4/91. Canx.
G-BRKH	PA-28-236 Dakota	28-7911003	N21444 N2454M	30. 8.89	
G-BRKI	Robinson R-22 Beta	1088		5. 9.89	To G-OLFI 8/92. Canx.
G-BRKJ	Stoddard-Hamilton Glasair III	3059		29. 8.89	To C-GRON 23.3.95. Canx by CAA 21.3.97.
G-BRKK	Star-Lite SL-1	211 & PFA/175-11440		29. 8.89	To G-UIDA 9/91. Canx.
G-BRKL	Cameron H-34 HAFB	2075		29. 8.89	
G-BRKM	BAe ATP	2021	G-11-021 G-11-21	7. 9.89	NTU - To N852AW. Canx 29.1.90.
G-BRKN	Robinson R-22 Mariner	0578M	N2454M	5. 9.89	(Extant 4/97)
G-BRKO	Oldfield Baby Great Lakes	1	N8GL	18. 1.90	No UK Permit to Fly issued. (On overhaul 6/96) Canx by CAA 18.3.99.
G-BRKP	Colt 31A HAFB	1590		30. 8.89	(Based in Germany) Canx as PWFU 22.3.99.
G-BRKR	Cessna 182R Skylane II	182-68468	N9896E	2. 6.89	
G-BRKS	Air Command 532 Elite	GS-01 & G/04-1146		1. 9.89	Permit expired 11.3.91. Canx by CAA 10.3.99.
G-BRKT	PA-28-161 Warrior II	28-8116284	N8082Z	8. 9.89	To G-MAND 3/93. Canx.
G-BRKU	PA-28-140 Cherokee Cruiser	28-7325201	N15926	27.10.89	To G-OFTI 6/90. Canx.
G-BRKV	Cessna 421C Golden Eagle III	421C-0464	LX-ETA N6794C	5.10.89	To N464SF 4/91. Canx 12.4.91.
G-BRKW	Cameron V-77 HAFB	2093		1. 9.89	
G-BRKX	Air Command 532 Elite	0619 & G/04-1150		8. 9.89	
G-BRKY	Viking Dragonfly Mk.II	PFA/139-11117		7. 9.89	(Stored 3/97)
G-BRKZ	Air Command 532 Elite	0620 & G/04-1147		7. 9.89	To EC-... Canx 15.9.97.
G-BRLA	Piper J3C-75 Cub	18269	N98110 NC98110	29. 9.89	To OY-CUB 11/89. Canx 21.2.91.
G-BRLB	Air Command 532 Elite	0622		4. 9.89	(Extant 11/96)
G-BRLC	Thunder Ax7-77 HAFB	1594		4. 9.89	Canx by CAA 16.4.98. (Based in Brazil)
G-BRLD	Robinson R-22 Beta	1099		4. 9.89	Badly damaged in forced landing near Rayleigh on 28.3.93 (Stored 12/95 - pod at Redhill 12/96)
G-BRLE	PA-28-181 Archer II	28-8590043	OY-CGY N152AV	7. 9.89	To OO-NZF 9/94. Canx 25.7.94.

Regn	Type	c/n	Previous identity	Regn date	Fate or immediate subsequent identity (if known)
G-BRLF	Campbell Cricket	G/03-1077		6. 9.89	
G-BRLG	PA-28RT-201T Turbo Arrow IV	28R-8431027	N4379P N9600N	12. 9.89	
G-BRLH	Air Command 532 Elite	0623 & G/04-1148		12. 9.89	Permit expired 28.12.90. (Stored 4/96 Henstridge) Canx as PWFU 26.1.99.
G-BRLI	Piper J/5A Cub Cruiser	5-822	N35951 NC35951	23. 8.89	
G-BRLJ	Evans VP-2	PFA/63-10629		8. 8.89	(Nearing completion 8/90) Canx by CAA 23.10.95.
G-BRLK	Air Command 532 Elite	0618 & G/04-1155		7. 9.89	Permit expired 1.1.91. Canx by CAA 10.3.99.
G-BRLL	Cameron A-105 HAFB	2032		7. 9.89	
G-BRLM	BAe 146 Srs.100	E1144		. 9.89R	NTU - To G-11-144/G-6-144/(PK-DTA)/G-BSLP 6/90. Canx.
G-BRLN	BAe 146 Srs.100	E1152	PK-DTC G-BRLN/G-6-152	13. 9.89	To VH-NJR 2/92. Canx 17.2.92.
G-BRLO	PA-38-112 Tomahawk	38-78A0621	N2397K N9680N	26.10.89	
G-BRLP	PA-38-112 Tomahawk	38-78A0011	N9301T	4.10.89	
G-BRLR	Cessna 150G	150-64822	N4772X	4.10.89	
G-BRLS	Thunder Ax7-77 HAFB	1603		29. 9.89	
G-BRLT	Colt 77A HAFB	1588		12. 9.89	
G-BRLU	Cameron H-24 HAFB	2082		8. 9.89	Canx as WFU 21.5.97.
G-BRLV	CCF Harvard 4	CCF4-194	N90448 RCAF 20403	14. 9.89	
G-BRLW	Cessna 150M Commuter	150-78205	N9255U	26. 9.89	To 5B-CJB 1/97. Canx 21.11.96.
G-BRLX	Cameron N-77 HAFB	2095		13. 9.89	
G-BRLY	BAe ATP	2025	TC-THP G-BRLY	22. 9.89	(Stored at Woodford 5/99)
G-BRLZ	Cessna 150G	150-66980	C-GASI N30805	13. 9.89	Badly damaged in crash at Rhuallt Hill, near Prestatyn on 10.3.90. Canx as destroyed 8.11.91. (Stored - spares for G-BPMO - 4/91) (Wings at Bourn 8/92)
G-BRMA	Westland-Sikorsky WS-51 Widgeon HR.5	WA/H/050	WG719	15. 6.78	Canx as WFU 30.3.89. (On display 3/96 The International Helicopter Museum, Weston-super-Mare)
G-BRMB	Bristol 192 Belvedere HC.1	13347	7997M XG452	15. 6.78	(On display 3/96 The International Helicopter Museum, Weston-super-Mare) Canx as WFU 3.7.96.
G-BRMC	Stampe et Renard SV-4B	1160	SLN-03 Belgium AF V-18	17. 3.78	To OO-GWD. Canx 2.9.93.
G-BRMD	Cameron O-160 HAFB	2102		6.10.89	To ZS-HRE. Canx 19.7.96.
G-BRME	PA-28-181 Cherokee Archer II	28-7790105	OY-BTA	14. 9.89	
G-BRMF	Bell 206B JetRanger III	3018	5Y-KPC	27. 4.90	To G-PCOR 3/94. Canx.
G-BRMG	Vickers Supermarine 384 Seafire F.XVII (Westland-built)	FLWA.25488	A2055 SX336	19. 9.89	(On rebuild 3/96)
G-BRMH	Bell 206B JetRanger II	1231	N39AH G-BRMH/G-BBUX/N18091	22. 9.81	To OO-LMI 10/96. Canx 29.10.96.
G-BRMI	Cameron V-65 HAFB	2104		14. 9.89	
G-BRMJ	PA-38-112 Tomahawk	38-79A0784	N2316N	15. 9.89	
G-BRMK	PA-38-112 Tomahawk	38-79A0769	N2579L	15. 9.89	Fatal crash at Coventry on 31.3.91. Canx as destroyed 15.7.91.
G-BRML	PA-38-112 Tomahawk	38-79A1017	N2510P	3.10.89	
G-BRMM	Air Command 532 Elite	0624 & G/04-1159		15. 9.89	No Permit to Fly issued. Canx by CAA 16.4.99.
G-BRMN	Thunder Ax7-77 HAFB	1532		15. 9.89	Canx by CAA 30.7.98. To N515V 1/99.
G-BRMO	Robinson R-22 Beta	1125		27. 9.89	Crashed at Clements Farm, Brickendon on 2.8.91. Canx as destroyed 22.4.92.
G-BRMP	Aerospatiale SA.360C Dauphin	1010	N49513	15. 9.89	To (F-GHXQ)/F-GHXR 6/92. Canx 10.10.90.
G-BRMR	Aerospatiale SA.360C Dauphin	1023	N8479U C-GVWD	15. 9.89	Canx 10.10.90 on sale to France.
G-BRMS	PA-28RT-201 Arrow IV	28R-8118004	(N.....) G-BRMS/N82708	25. 9.89	Restored as N82708. Canx.
G-BRMT	Cameron V-31 Air Chair HAFB	2038		31. 8.89	
G-BRMU	Cameron V-77 HAFB	2109		19. 9.89	
G-BRMV	Cameron O-77 HAFB	2103		25. 9.89	
G-BRMW	Whittaker MW.7	PFA/171-11395		25. 9.89	
G-BRMX	Short SD.3-60 Var.200	SH3762		28. 9.89	To N162SB. Canx 14.12.89.
G-BRMY	Short SD.3-60 Var.200	SH3763		28. 9.89	To HB-AAM 9/90. Canx.
G-BRMZ	Short SD.3-60 Var.200	SH3764		28. 9.89	To D-CBAS 9/91. Canx 30.8.91.
G-BRNA	Short SD.3-60 Var.100	SH3765		28. 9.89	NTU - Not built. Canx by CAA 8.10.93.
G-BRNB	Short SD.3-60 Var.100	SH3766		28. 9.89	NTU - Not built. Canx by CAA 8.10.93.
G-BRNC	Cessna 150M Commuter	150-78833	N704SG	29. 9.89	
G-BRND	Cessna 152 II	152-83776	N5148B	7.11.89	
G-BRNE	Cessna 152 II	152-84248	N5082L	4.10.89	
G-BRNF	Cessna 152 II	152-83188	N47217	29. 9.89	To G-DRAG 4/90. Canx.
G-BRNG	BAe 146 Srs.200	E2077	N408XV G-5-077/N408XV	29. 9.89	To (OO-DJZ)/OO-DJD. Canx 28.12.89.
G-BRNH	Aerospatiale SA.341G Gazelle Srs.1	1413	YU-HBO	22. 9.89	To G-UZEL 11/89. Canx.
G-BRNI	Aerospatiale SA.341G Gazelle Srs.1	1301	YU-HBI	22. 9.89	To G-HTPS 11/89. Canx.
G-BRNJ	PA-38-112 Tomahawk	38-79A0415	N2395F	22. 9.89	
G-BRNK	Cessna 152 II	152-80479	N24969	22. 9.89	
G-BRNL	Cessna 172P Skyhawk II	172-75887	N5017J C-GRNU/(N65787)	22. 9.89	To TC-DBU 3/93. Canx 19.2.93.
G-BRNM	Chichester-Miles Leopard	002		17.10.89	(Extant 7/97)

Regn	Type	c/n	Previous identity	Regn date	Fate or immediate subsequent identity (if known)
G-BRNN	Cessna 152 II	152-84735	N6452M	22. 9.89	
G-BRNO	Cessna 182P Skylane II (Regd incorrectly as c/n 182-65404)	182-64504	N1959M	22. 9.89	To 5Y-... Canx 31.10.90.
G-BRNP	Rotorway Exec 152	3578		22. 9.89	
G-BRNR	Schweizer Hughes 269C (300C)	S.1405	(N424MS)	5.12.89	Badly damaged in heavy landing 19.6.97 at Kidlington. Canx as destroyed 19.9.97.
G-BRNS	Light Aero Avid Flyer	329		11.10.89	To CS-... Canx 3.11.95. Noted at Beja, Portugal on 13.9.96, still marked as G-BRNS.
G-BRNT	Robin DR.400/180 Regent	1935		3.10.89	
G-BRNU	Robin DR.400/180 Regent	1937		31.10.89	
G-BRNV	PA-28-181 Cherokee Archer II	28-7790402	N2537Q	7.12.89	
G-BRNW	Cameron V-77 HAFB	2138		2.10.89	
G-BRNX	PA-22-150 Tri-Pacer	22-2945	N2610P	3.10.89	
G-BRNY	Thunder Ax6-56A HAFB	163	OY-BON	1. 9.89	To F-GMCO 1/97. Canx 10.1.97.
G-BRNZ	PA-32-300 Cherokee Six B	32-40594	N4229R	7. 2.90	
G-BROA	Thunder Ax7-77 HAFB	1535		3.10.90	Envelope to G-BSGY. Canx as destroyed 22.3.90.
G-BROB	Cameron V-77 HAFB	2073		29. 8.89	
G-BROC	Boeing 737-46B (Line No. 1844)	24573		. .89R	NTU - To OO-SBJ 4/90. Canx.
G-BROD	HS.125 Srs.403B	25253	OY-APM G-5-18	22.11.85	To N731HS. Canx 3.12.85.
G-BROE	Cameron N-65 HAFB	2098		5.10.89	
G-BROF	Air Command 532 Elite	0625 & G/04-1154		5.10.89	No Permit to Fly issued. Canx by CAA 12.4.99.
G-BROG	Cameron V-65 HAFB	2121		6. 9.89	
G-BROH	Cameron O-90 HAFB	2120		6.10.89	
G-BROI	CFM Streak Shadow Srs.SA	K.115-SA & PFA/161-11586		16.11.89	
G-BROJ	Colt 31A HAFB	1468		6.10.89	
G-BROK	Colt 77A HAFB	1612		6.10.89	To SE-ZER. Canx 1.5.90.
G-BROL	Colt AS-80 Mk.II Hot-Air Airship	1578		6.10.89	
G-BROM	ICA-Brasov IS-28M2A	04A		5.12.77	CofA expired 18.8.87. Canx by CAA 24.2.92. (Open storage/derelict 4/95)
G-BRON	Beechcraft A200 Super King Air	BB-349	G-BFEA	9. 4.79	Restored as G-BFEA 12/82. Canx.
G-BROO	Luscombe 8F Silvaire 90	6154	N75297 HI-20(2)/N1527B/NC1527B	28. 9.89	
G-BROP	Van's RV-4	3	N19AT	25.10.89	
G-BROR	Piper J3C-65 Cub (L-4H-PI)	10885	F-BHMQ 43-29594	7.12.89	
G-BROS	Cameron O-84 HAFB	2172		6. 9.89	To D-OKIT 1/93. Canx 12.1.93.
G-BROT	Montgomerie-Bensen B.8MR Gyrocopter	G/01A-1142		7. 9.89	To G-WHIR 10/89. Canx.
G-BROU	PA-28RT-201T Turbo Arrow IV	28R-8331037	N4306K	9.11.89	To G-RUBY 1/90. Canx.
G-BROV	Colt 105A HAFB	1616		13.10.89	Canx 17.1.95 on sale to USA. To VH-BRU(2).
G-BROW	Colt 90A HAFB	1617		13.10.89	Canx 17.12.93 on sale to Zimbabwe. Wore marks "Z-TIG" unofficially in 5/95 for Harare Balloon Rally.
G-BROX	Robinson R-22 Beta	1127	N8061V	13.10.89	
G-BROY	Cameron O-90 HAFB	2173		6. 9.89	
G-BROZ	PA-18-150 Super Cub	18-6754	HB-ORC N9572D	20. 9.89	
G-BRPA	PBN BN-2B-20 Islander (Originally regd as a BN-2B-26)	2221		18.10.89	To VH-INO 6/90. Canx 12.6.90.
G-BRPB	PBN BN-2T Turbine Islander (Originally regd as a BN-2B-26)	2222		18.10.89	To G-361 Ghana AF. Canx 20.12.90.
G-BRPC	PBN BN-2T Turbine Islander (Originally regd as a BN-2B-26)	2223		18.10.89	To G-362 Ghana AF. Canx 7.3.91.
G-BRPD	PBN BN-2B-26 Islander	2224		18.10.89	To EC-750/EC-FFZ. Canx 10.6.91.
G-BRPE	Cessna 120	13326	N3068N NC3068N	11.10.89	
G-BRPF	Cessna 120	9902	N72723 NC72723	11.10.89	
G-BRPG	Cessna 120	9882	N72703 NC72703	11.10.89	
G-BRPH	Cessna 120	12137	N1893N NC1893N	11.10.89	
G-BRPI	Pitts S-1C Special	43JM	N199M	1. 3.89	To G-OWAZ 11/94. Canx.
G-BRPJ	Cameron N-90 HAFB	2071		11. 9.89	
G-BRPK	PA-28-140 Cherokee Cruiser	28-7325070	N15449	17.11.89	
G-BRPL	PA-28-140 Cherokee Cruiser	28-7325160	N15771	13.10.89	Damaged on landing 17.9.97 at Caernarfon. (On rebuild 10/97 at Caernarfon)
G-BRPM	Tipsy Nipper T.66 Srs.3B	PFA/25-11038		4. 3.85	(Still under construction in 1995)
G-BRPN	Enstrom F-28C	392	N640H	13.10.89	Canx as destroyed 2.6.93.
G-BRPO	Enstrom 280C Shark	1092	N636H	13.10.89	
G-BRPP	Brookland Hornet (Mod.)	DC-1		16.10.89	
G-BRPR	Aeronca L-3C Defender	058B-8823	N49880 43-1952	17.10.89	
G-BRPS	Cessna 177B Cardinal	177-02101	N34935	23.10.89	

Regn	Type	c/n	Previous identity	Regn date	Fate or immediate subsequent identity (if known)
G-BRPT	Rans S-10 Sakota	PFA/194-11554		18.10.89	
G-BRPU	Beechcraft 76 Duchess	ME-140	N6007Z	17.10.89	
G-BRPV	Cessna 152 II	152-85228	N6311Q	6.11.89	
G-BRPW	BAe 146 Srs.300QT	E3153		30.10.89	To G-TNTE 6/90. Canx.
G-BRPX	Taylorcraft BC-12D	6462	N39208	12.12.89	
			NC39208		
G-BRPY	PA-15 Vagabond	15-141	N4356H	23.10.89	
			NC4356H		
G-BRPZ	Luscombe 8A Silvaire	911	N22089	13.12.89	
			NC22089		
G-BRRA	Vickers Supermarine 361 Spitfire		SM-29	10.10.89	(On rebuild 7/97)
	LF.IXc	CBAF/IX/1875	R.Belgium AF/R.Netherlands AF H-59/H-119/Fokker B-1/MK912		
	(Regd with c/n CBAF/8185)				
G-BRRB	Luscombe 8E Silvaire	2611	N71184	23.10.89	
			NC71184		
G-BRRC	Scheibe SF-25B Falke	46113	D-KMAH	30.10.89	Badly damaged in a heavy landing at Marchington on 25.9.90. Canx as WFU 21.12.90.
G-BRRD	Scheibe SF-25B Falke	4811	D-KBAT	30.10.89	
G-BRRE	Colt 69A HAFB	1585		24.10.89	Canx by CAA 8.10.96.
G-BRRF	Cameron O-77 HAFB	2101		24.10.89	
G-BRRG	Glaser-Dirks DG-500M	5-E7M5		7.11.89	
G-BRRH	Ayres S2R-T34	T34-123DC		27.10.89	No UK CofA issued. To N3106S in 4/90. Canx.
G-BRRI	Ayres S2R-T34	T34-122DC		27.10.89	No UK CofA issued. To N3106P in 4/90. Canx.
G-BRRJ	PA-28RT-201T Turbo Arrow IV	28R-8431021	N4353T	27.11.89	
G-BRRK	Cessna 182Q Skylane II	182-66160	N759PW	30.10.89	
G-BRRL	PA-18-95 Super Cub	18-2050	D-EMKE	17. 9.90	(On rebuild Whitehall Farm, Benington 4/93)
	(L-18C-PI)		R.Netherlands AF R-44/52-2450		
	(Believed to comprise frame no.18-1602 which was the original frame of G-AYPO c/n 18-1615)				
G-BRRM	PA-28-161 Cadet	2841260	N9194B	25.10.89	
G-BRRN	PA-28-161 Warrior II	28-8216043	N84533	30.10.89	
G-BRRO	Cameron N-77 HAFB	2142		30.10.89	
G-BRRP	Pitts S-1S Special	7-0332	N3TD	1.11.89	To G-WAZZ 6/94. Canx.
	(Built by T.H.Decarlo)				
G-BRRR	Cameron V-77 HAFB	2070		13.10.89	
G-BRRS	Pitts S-1S Special	TM-1	N18TM	1.11.89	(Stored 5/95)
	(Built by T.D.McNamara)				
G-BRRT	CASA I-131E Jungmann	2019	E3B-415	20.11.89	To PT-ZGL /97. Canx 10.9.97.
	(Spanish AF serial conflicts with D-EGBM c/n 2062)				
G-BRRU	Colt 90A HAFB	1591		1.11.89	
G-BRRV	Colt 77A HAFB	1551		1.11.89	To OE-SZY. Canx 3.9.90.
G-BRRW	Cameron O-77 HAFB	2125		7.11.89	
G-BRRX	Hughes 369HS (500C)	111-0354S	N9083F	9.11.89	To G-SOOC 10/93. Canx.
G-BRRY	Robinson R-22 Beta	1193		14.11.89	
G-BRRZ	Robinson R-22 Beta	1129	N8050N	22.11.89	To EI-CMI 11/95. Canx 20.11.95.
G-BRSA(1)	Airbus A.320-111	006	(G-BRAA)	. .88R	NTU - To G-BUSB 3/88. Canx.
	(Originally flew wearing these marks)		F-WWDD		
G-BRSA(2)	Cameron N-56 HAFB	2113		8.11.89	
G-BRSB(1)	Airbus A.320-111	008	(G-BRAB)	. .88R	NTU - To G-BUSC 5/88. Canx.
			F-WWDE		
G-BRSB(2)	Cameron N-105 HAFB	2137		8.11.89	To OE-SZC. Canx 22.10.90.
G-BRSC(1)	Airbus A.320-111	011	(G-BRAC)	. .88R	NTU - To G-BUSD 7/88. Canx.
			F-WWDF		
G-BRSC(2)	Rans S-10 Sakota	0589-051		8.11.89	
G-BRSD(1)	Airbus A.320-111	017	(G-BRAE)	. .88R	NTU - To G-BUSE 12/88. Canx.
			F-WWDG		
G-BRSD(2)	Cameron V-77 HAFB	2174		8.11.89	
G-BRSE(1)	Airbus A.320-111	018	(G-BRAH)	. .88R	NTU - To G-BUSF 5/89. Canx.
			F-WWDH		
G-BRSE(2)	PA-28-161 Warrior II	28-8016276	N8163R	5.12.89	
G-BRSF(1)	Airbus A.320-211	039	(G-BRAI)	. .88R	NTU - To G-BUSG 5/89. Canx.
			F-WWDM		
G-BRSF(2)	Vickers Supermarine 361 Spitfire		5632	22.11.89	Canx by CAA 23.6.94. (Stored 3/96)
	HF.IXc	-	South African AF/RR232		
	(Composite including tail/parts from Mk.VIII JF629 from W.Australia and wings from ex.R.Thai AF Mk.XIV U14-6/93 / RAF RM873)				
G-BRSG(1)	Airbus A.320-211	042	(G-BRAJ)	. .88R	NTU - To G-BUSH 6/89. Canx.
			F-WWDT		
G-BRSG(2)	PA-28-161 Cadet	2841285	N92011	23.11.89	
G-BRSH(1)	Airbus A.320-211	103	(G-BRAK)	. .88R	NTU - To G-BUSI 3/90. Canx.
			F-WWDB		
G-BRSH(2)	CASA I-131E Jungmann	2156	E3B-540	29.11.89	
	(Spanish AF serial conflicts with F-AZGG)				
G-BRSI(1)	Airbus A.320-211	109	(G-BRAM)	. .88R	NTU - To G-BUSJ 8/90. Canx.
			F-WWIC		
G-BRSI(2)	PA-28-161 Cadet	2841281	N92001	16.11.89	To G-EGTR 4/98. Canx.
G-BRSJ(1)	Airbus A.320-211	120	(G-BRAN)	. .88R	NTU - To G-BUSK 10/90. Canx.
			F-WWIN		
G-BRSJ(2)	PA-38-112 Tomahawk II	38-81A0044	N25664	29.12.89	
G-BRSK	Boeing-Stearman B75N1 (N2S-3) Kaydet	75-1180	N5565N	15.11.89	(Stored 2/99 at Morley Village, Norfolk)
			BuA.3403		
G-BRSL	Cameron N-56 HAFB	468		21.12.78	

Regn	Type	c/n	Previous identity	Regn date	Fate or immediate subsequent identity (if known)
G-BRSM	Cessna 140	9619	N72454 NC72454	14.11.89	To G-GAWA 9/91. Canx.
G-BRSN	Rand Robinson KR-2	PFA/129-11178		10.11.89	
G-BRSO	CFM Streak Shadow Srs.SA	K.133-SA & PFA/161A-11601		16.11.89	
G-BRSP	Air Command 532 Elite	0626 & G/04-1158		13.11.89	
G-BRSR	PBN BN-2T Turbine Islander (Originally regd as a BN-2B-26)	2225		17.11.89	To G-360 Ghana AF. Canx 20.12.90.
G-BRSS	PBN BN-2B-20 Islander (Originally regd as a BN-2B-26)	2226		17.11.89	To OA-7 Botswana DF 10/90. Canx 8.11.90.
G-BRST	PBN BN-2B-20 Islander (Originally regd as a BN-2B-26)	2227		17.11.89	To OA-8 Botswana DF. Canx 20.12.90.
G-BRSU	PBN BN-2T Turbine Islander (Originally regd as a BN-2B-26)	2228		17.11.89	To CN-TWN. Canx 21.12.90.
G-BRSV	PBN BN-2T Turbine Islander (Originally regd as a BN-2B-26)	2229		17.11.89	To G-363 Ghana AF. Canx 11.7.91.
G-BRSW	Luscombe 8AC Silvaire	3249	N71822 NC71822	15.11.89	
G-BRSX	PA-15 Vagabond	15-117	N4334H NC4334H	27.10.89	
G-BRSY	Hatz CB-1	6	N2257J	15.11.89	
G-BRSZ	MEM RSZ-05/1 (Ax7) HAFB	1989/001	HA-716	19.12.89	NTU - Remained as HA-716. Canx by CAA 8.1.91.
G-BRTA	PA-38-112 Tomahawk	38-79A0047	N2407B	27.11.89	
G-BRTB	Bell 206B JetRanger II	1997	N9936K	22.11.89	To G-CITZ 2/99. Canx.
G-BRTC	Cessna 150G	150-65996	N3296J	1. 3.90	Blown over by gales Hurn 23.12.91 and badly damaged. (Wreck stored 8/95) Canx as PWFU 3.2.99.
G-BRTD	Cessna 152 II	152-80023	N757UW	11. 1.90	
G-BRTE	Colt 240A HAFB	1589		20.11.89	Canx 17.8.92 to Germany.
G-BRTF	Thunder Ax7-77 HAFB	1622		20.11.89	Canx 7.5.91 on sale to Brazil.
G-BRTG	BAe ATP	2019	G-11-19	20.11.89	To CS-TGL. Canx 8.12.89.
G-BRTH	Cameron A-180 HAFB (Replacement envelope c/n 3199 fitted in 1994)	2016		21.11.89	
G-BRTI	Robinson R-22 Beta	1130	EI-CDW (EI-CFJ)/G-BRTI/N8044U	23. 2.90	
G-BRTJ	Cessna 150F	150-61749	N8149S	22.11.89	
G-BRTK	Boeing-Stearman E75 (PT-13D) Kaydet	75-5949	N16716 42-17786/BuA.38728	29.11.89	(On overhaul 2/99 Swanton Morley)(Parts to PT-13D CF-EQS at Duxford)
G-BRTL	MDH Hughes 369E (500E)	0356E	(F-GHLF)	5. 1.90	
G-BRTM	PA-28-161 Warrior II	28-8416083	N4334L	12.12.89	
G-BRTN	Beechcraft 58 Baron	TH-1400	N58VF N6763U	29.11.89	
G-BRTO	Cessna 152 II	152-83092	N46716	28.11.89	Damaged at Dunkeswell 1.6.95. Canx as destroyed 19.12.95.
G-BRTP	Cessna 152 II	152-81275	N49448	28.11.89	
G-BRTR	Colt GA-42 Gas Airship	936		29.11.89	Canx by CAA 10.3.95.
G-BRTS	Bell 206B JetRanger III	2509	N755MB	22.12.89	To N96BH 4/93. Canx 12.3.93.
G-BRTT	Schweizer Hughes 269C (300C)	S.1411		29.11.89	
G-BRTU	Partenavia P-68C	307	I-VIPX	. .89R	NTU - Remained as I-VIPX. Canx.
G-BRTV	Cameron O-77 HAFB	2182		1.12.89	
G-BRTW	Glaser-Dirks DG-400	4-259		22.12.89	
G-BRTX	PA-28-151 Cherokee Warrior	28-7615085	N8307C	27.12.89	
G-BRTY	Socata TB-20 Trinidad	1009		4.12.89	To G-EWFN 1/90. Canx.
G-BRTZ	Slingsby Cadet III	PFA/42-10545		24. 1.90	
G-BRUA	Cessna 152 II	152-81212	N49267	11. 1.90	
G-BRUB	PA-28-161 Warrior II	28-8116177	N8351Y	27.12.89	
G-BRUC	BAe 146 Srs.100	E1009	TZ-ADT	19.12.89	To G-6-009/VH-NJZ 6/91. Canx 18.6.91.
G-BRUD	PA-28-181 Archer II	28-8390010	N8300S	9. 2.90	
G-BRUE	Cameron V-77 HAFB	2183		15.12.89	
G-BRUF	PA-34-220T Seneca III	3433020	N9113D	2. 2.88	To G-BOJK 11.3.88. Canx.
G-BRUG	Luscombe 8E Silvaire	4462	N1735K NC1735K	15.12.89	
G-BRUH	Colt 105A HAFB	1650		15.12.89	
G-BRUI	PA-44-180 Seminole	44-7995150	N2230E G-BRUI/N2230E	15.12.89	
G-BRUJ	Boeing-Stearman A75N1 (PT-17) Kaydet	75-4299	N55557 42-16136	6. 4.90	
G-BRUK	BAe Jetstream Srs.3102	727	I-ALKC I-BLUU/G-BRUK/G-31-727	30. 9.86	To G-SWAC 5/94. Canx.
G-BRUL	Thunder Ax8-105 Srs.2 HAFB	1646		15.12.89	To D-ORUL 6/94. Canx 15.11.93.
G-BRUM	Cessna A.152 Aerobat	A152-0870	N4693A	12. 3.86	
G-BRUN	Cessna 120	9294	G-BRDH N72127/NC72127	29. 8.89	
G-BRUO	Taylor JT.1 Monoplane	PFA/55-10859		15.12.89	
G-BRUP	Fairchild M-62A (PT-26 Cornell)	T43-7272	N46197	2. 3.90	Restored as N46197. Canx 26.4.91.
G-BRUR	Grob G-115A	8066	D-EHTA(3)	15.12.89	To D-ENFM 8/95. Canx 13.7.95.
G-BRUS	Cessna 140	11645	N77183	21.12.89	Overturned on landing at Delimarsh Farm, Hants on 26.6.94. Canx as destroyed 16.9.94.
G-BRUT	Thunder Ax8-90 HAFB	1392		30. 3.89	
G-BRUU	EAA Biplane Model P1 (Built by L.E.Lasnier)	1	N41MW N4775G	22.12.89	
G-BRUV	Cameron V-77 HAFB	2100		16. 8.89	

Regn	Type	c/n	Previous identity	Regn date	Fate or immediate subsequent identity (if known)
G-BRUW	Schweizer Hughes 269C (300C)	S.1315	N86G	9. 6.88	To G-GLEE 4/90. Canx.
G-BRUX	PA-44-180 Seminole	44-7995151	N2245E	8. 3.79	
G-BRUY	Aerospatiale AS.355F1 Twin Squirrel	5092	N330E N330P/N5788U	21.12.89	To I-ELDI 6/90. Canx 16.5.90.
G-BRUZ	MFM Raven-Europe FS-57A HAFB	E-066	F-GMFM(2) HB-BKB	1.12.89	CofA expired 15.4.93. Canx as PWFU 13.1.00. (Was based in Italy)
G-BRVA	Nord 3202B-1	85	(G-BIZL) N2255Y/F-MAJG	27.12.89	To F-AZIJ 1/96. Canx 2.3.93.
G-BRVB	Stolp SA.300 Starduster Too (Built by M.Hoover)	409	N33MH	21.12.89	
G-BRVC	Cameron N-180 HAFB	2180		15.12.89	
G-BRVD	Not allocated.				
G-BRVE	Beechcraft D-17S Traveller (UC-43-BH)	6701	N1193V NC1193V/BuA.32874/FT475/44-67724/(BuA.23689)	12. 3.90	
G-BRVF	Colt 77A HAFB	1651		19.12.89	
G-BRVG	North American SNJ-7C Texan	88-17676	N830X N4134A/BuA.90678/(42-85895)	24. 1.90	
G-BRVH	Smyth Model S Sidewinder	PFA/92-11251		19.12.89	
G-BRVI	Robinson R-22 Beta	1240		27.12.89	
G-BRVJ	Slingsby Cadet III (Modified T.31B)	701 & PFA/42-11382	(BGA.3360) WT906	24. 1.90	
G-BRVK	Cameron A-210 HAFB	2144		28.12.89	To C-.... Canx 16.6.99.
G-BRVL	Pitts S-1C Special	559H	N2NW	10. 1.90	
G-BRVM	Pilatus PC-6/B2-H4 Turbo-Porter	848	OE-ECS	.12.89R	NTU - To G-WGSC 1/90. Canx.
G-BRVN	Thunder Ax7-77 HAFB	1614		28.12.89	
G-BRVO	Aerospatiale AS.350B Ecureuil	2315		3. 1.90	
G-BRVP	Aerospatiale SA.365N1 Dauphin 2	6343		3. 1.90	To Dubai Air Wing as DU-133. Canx 14.8.90.
G-BRVR	Barnett Rotorcraft J4B-2	216-2		20. 2.90	
G-BRVS	Barnett Rotorcraft J4B-2	210-2		20. 2.90	
G-BRVT	Christen Industries Pitts S-2B Special	5189		6. 4.90	
G-BRVU	Colt 77A HAFB	1652		4. 1.90	
G-BRVV	Colt 56B HAFB	1386		8. 1.90	
G-BRVW	Denney Kitfox Mk.2	602 & PFA/172-11664		. .90R	NTU - To G-BSAZ 3/90. Canx.
G-BRVX	Cameron A-210 HAFB	2194		9. 1.90	Canx as WFU 3.6.98.
G-BRVY	Thunder Ax8-90 HAFB	1676		9. 1.90	
G-BRVZ	SAN Jodel D.117	433	F-BHNR	22.12.89	
G-BRWA	Aeronca 7AC Champion	7AC-351	N81730 NC81730	20. 3.90	
G-BRWB	North American T-6G Texan (Reported to have been originally Harvard II 41-32473, remanufactured in 1951)	182-213	Fr.Mil 51-14526	28. 3.90	
G-BRWC	Cessna 152 II	152-81918	TF-GMT N67569	19. 1.90	Damaged in crash on take-off at Sandtoft on 29.8.90 - old fuselage in open store 9/95. On rebuild using cockpit and front fuselage of G-BITG 6/96 - but see G-ODAC. Canx as PWFU 16.2.99.
G-BRWD	Robinson R-22 Beta	1231	N8064U	15. 1.90	
G-BRWE	Aerospatiale AS.332L Super Puma	2079	C-GCHI N172EH/C-GSLK	22. 2.90	To VH-BHX 9/91. Canx 8.7.91.
G-BRWF	Thunder Ax7-77 HAFB	1200		15. 1.90	
G-BRWG	Maule M.5-235C Lunar Rocket	7250C	N5632H	17. 5.79	To G-RJWW 10/87. Canx.
G-BRWH	Cameron N-77 HAFB	2186		15. 1.90	
G-BRWI	Short SD.3-60 Var.100	SH3767		2. 2.90	NTU - Not built. Canx by CAA 8.10.93.
G-BRWJ	Short SD.3-60 Var.100	SH3768		2. 2.90	NTU - Not built. Canx by CAA 8.10.93.
G-BRWK	Short SD.3-60 Var.100	SH3769		2. 2.90	NTU - Not built. Canx by CAA 8.10.93.
G-BRWL	Short SD.3-60 Var.100	SH3770		2. 2.90	NTU - Not built. Canx by CAA 8.10.93.
G-BRWM	Short SD.3-60 Var.100	SH3771		2. 2.90	NTU - Not built. Canx by CAA 8.10.93.
G-BRWN	Grumman G.159 Gulfstream I	177	N12GP OY-BEG/N4PC/N307K/N751G	13.12.85	To PK-CTE. Canx 24.2.92.
G-BRWO	PA-28-140 Cherokee Cruiser	28-7325548	N55985	11. 1.90	
G-BRWP	CFM Streak Shadow Srs.SA	K.122-SA & PFA/161A-11596		17. 1.90	
G-BRWR	Aeronca 11AC Chief	11AC-1319	N9676E	17. 1.90	
G-BRWS	PA-31-350 Navajo Chieftain	31-7752128	N27299	1. 8.77	Restored as N27299 4/81. Canx .4.81.
G-BRWT	Scheibe SF-25C-2000 Falke	44480	D-KIAY	11. 1.90	
G-BRWU	Phoenix Luton LA-4A Minor (Regd as PFA/1141)(Construction commenced by Russ Hooper; no actual PFA No. known)	PAL/1141		18. 1.90	
G-BRWV	Brugger MB.2 Colibri	PFA/43-11027		18. 1.90	
G-BRWW	Aeronca 7AC Champion	7AC-4621	N1070E NC1070E	22. 1.90	To G-OTOE 4/90. Canx.
G-BRWX	Cessna 172P Skyhawk II	172-74729	N53363	17. 1.90	
G-BRWY	Cameron H-34 HAFB	2214		17. 1.90	
G-BRWZ	Cameron Macaw 90SS HAFB	2206		29. 1.90	
G-BRXA	Cameron O-120 HAFB	2217		19. 1.90	
G-BRXB	Thunder Ax7-77 HAFB	1631		18. 1.90	
G-BRXC	PA-28-161 Warrior II	28-8416043	N4339X N9563N	19. 2.90	

Regn	Type	c/n	Previous identity	Regn date	Fate or immediate subsequent identity (if known)
G-BRXD	PA-28-181 Archer II	28-8290126	N9690N N8203E	19. 2.90	
G-BRXE	Taylorcraft BC-12D	9459	N95059 NC95059	25. 1.90	
G-BRXF	Aeronca 11AC Chief	11AC-1033	N9396E NC9396E	25. 1.90	
G-BRXG	Aeronca 7AC Champion	7AC-3910	N85178 NC85178	1. 3.90	
G-BRXH	Cessna 120	10462	N76068 NC76068	25. 1.90	
G-BRXI	BAe 146 Srs.300QT	E3154	G-6-154	31. 1.90	To G-TNTF 9/90. Canx.
G-BRXJ	Boeing 737-33A (Line No. 1462)	23830	LN-NOS N5573K	11. 4.90	Restored as LN-NOS. Canx 26.4.91.
G-BRXK	Soko P-2 Kraguj	033	30149 Yugoslav Army	1. 2.90	To G-SOKO 1/94. Canx.
G-BRXL	Aeronca 11AC Chief	11AC-1629	N3254E NC3254E	31. 1.90	
G-BRXM	Colt GA-42 Gas Airship	1152		31. 1.90	To OH-ITA. Canx 14.9.90.
G-BRXN	Montgomerie-Bensen B.8MR Gyrocopter	G/01-1160		31. 1.90	
G-BRXO	PA-34-200T Seneca II	34-7970149	N111ED N9618N	12. 4.90	
G-BRXP	SNCAN Stampe SV-4C	678	N33528 F-BGGU/French AF/(F-BDNX)	2. 2.90	(Status uncertain; departed Barton by road 4/97)
G-BRXR	HS.125 Srs.403B	25217	G-5-651 9Q-CHD/9Q-CGM/G-AXYJ/G-5-14	7. 2.90	To G-OLFR 11/90. Canx.
G-BRXS	Howard Special T-Minus (Mod Taylorcraft BC)(Built by C.Howard)	REC-1	N2278C	14. 2.90	
G-BRXT	BAe 146 Srs.200	E2115	C-GRNY G-5-115/G-11-115	16. 3.90	To SE-DRA. Canx 22.1.92.
G-BRXU	Aerospatiale AS.332L Super Puma	2092	VH-BHV(2) G-BRXU/HC-BMZ/C-GSLO	6. 3.90	
G-BRXV	Robinson R-22 Beta	1246		7. 2.90	
G-BRXW	PA-24-260 Comanche	24-4069	N8621P	16. 2.90	
G-BRXX	Colt 180A HAFB	1682		2. 2.90	To VH-BRX. Canx 17.2.94.
G-BRXY	Pietenpol Air Camper	PFA/47-11416		7. 2.90	(On repair Cranfield 7/97)
G-BRXZ	Robinson R-22 Beta	1244	EI-CEJ (EI-CEI)/G-BRXZ	7. 2.90	Canx 16.3.99 on sale to USA. To (N6060Q) 4/99 /C-GGIB 8/99.
G-BRYA	DHC.7-110 Dash Seven	062		17.11.81	
G-BRYB	DHC.7-102 Dash Seven	066	C-GRLA	17.11.81	To C-FYXT 8/96. Canx 12.8.96.
G-BRYC	DHC.7-102 Dash Seven	054	C-GFCO-X	22. 7.81	To C-FYXV 8/96. Canx 16.8.96.
G-BRYD	DHC.7-110 Dash Seven	109	C-GEWQ	24.12.87	
G-BRYE	DHC.7-102 Dash Seven	050	N8120W OE-LLT/OE-HLT	5. 5.89	To 4X-AHJ. Canx 25.5.94.
G-BRYF	DHC.7-102 Dash Seven	033	4X-AHG G-BRYF/G-BPDX/N235SL/OY-MBF/(PH-SDR)/N235SL/TC-JCG/N8504A	2. 8.89	Restored as N235SL. Canx 5.11.91.
G-BRYG	DHC.8-102A Dash Eight	237	C-GEOA	23.10.90	To PH-TTA 10/96. Canx 21.10.96.
G-BRYH	DHC.8-102A Dash Eight	241	C-GESR	15.11.90	To PH-TTB 2/98. Canx 23.2.98.
G-BRYI	DHC.8-311A Dash Eight	256	C-GEOA	26. 3.91	
G-BRYJ	DHC.8-311A Dash Eight	319	C-GEOA	27. 3.92	
G-BRYK	DHC.8-311A Dash Eight	284	N431AW C-GETI	2. 4.96	To N385DC 7/99. Canx 10.6.99.
G-BRYL	Agusta A.109A	7170	G-ROPE G-OAMH	12.10.84	To G-MEAN 4/89. Canx.
G-BRYM	DHC.8-311A Dash Eight	305	N433AW C-GDFT	25. 3.96	
G-BRYN	Socata TB-20 Trinidad (Originally regd with c/n 937 which is TB-10 N25060/N115JR)	959		22. 3.89	
G-BRYO	DHC.8-311A Dash Eight	311	N434AW C-GEVP	26. 4.96	
G-BRYP	DHC.8-311A Dash Eight	315	N435AW C-GFCF	22. 4.96	
G-BRYR	DHC.8-311A Dash Eight	336	N436AW	20. 5.96	
G-BRYS	DHC.8-311A Dash Eight	296	PH-SDG D-BKIS/C-GFQL	23. 4.97	
G-BRYT	DHC.8-311A Dash Eight	334	D-BKIR C-GFEN	11. 3.97	
G-BRYU	DHC.8-311A Dash Eight	458	C-GFEN (9M-PGA)/C-GFEN	4. 4.98	
G-BRYV	DHC.8-311A Dash Eight	462	C-GFHZ (9M-PGD)/C-GFHZ/(N350PH)	10. 4.98	
G-BRYW	DHC.8-311A Dash Eight	474	C-GDIU (9M-PG.)/C-GDIU	26. 5.98	
G-BRYX	DHC.8-311A Dash Eight	508	C-GDOE	25. 9.98	
G-BRYY	DHC.8-311A Dash Eight	519	C-FDHD	11.12.98	
G-BRYZ	DHC.8-311A Dash Eight	464	C-FCSG	16.10.98	
G-BRZA	Cameron O-77 HAFB (Originally regd with c/n 2237 - see G-BSCA)	2231		7. 2.90	
G-BRZB	Cameron A-105 HAFB	2212		7. 2.90	
G-BRZC	Cameron N-90 HAFB	2227		8. 2.90	Canx as WFU 29.4.97.
G-BRZD	HAPI Cygnet SF-2A	PFA/182-11443		8. 2.90	
G-BRZE	Thunder Ax7-77 HAFB	1633		8. 2.90	
G-BRZF	Enstrom 280C Shark	1163	N5687D	12. 3.90	To G-IDUP 5/92. Canx.

Regn	Type	c/n	Previous identity	Regn date	Fate or immediate subsequent identity (if known)
G-BRZG	Enstrom F-28A	169	N9053	8. 2.90	
G-BRZH	BN-2A-26 Islander	269	G-51-269 D-IBNA/OH-BNC/Finnish AF BN-1/OH-BNC/G-51-269	15. 2.90	To 8R-GHB 5/90. Canx 12.6.90.
G-BRZI	Cameron N-180 HAFB	2215		8. 2.90	
G-BRZJ	Robinson R-22 Beta	1217		12. 2.90	Badly damaged in crash at Newtownards on 18.5.90. Canx as WFU 31.8.90.
G-BRZK	Stinson 108-2 Station Wagon	108-2846	N9846K NC9846K	17. 4.90	
G-BRZL	Pitts S-1D Special (Built by R.C.Nelson)	01	N899RN	26. 2.90	(Stored 2/97)
G-BRZM	Bensen B.8MR Gyrocopter	G/01A-1156		13. 2.90	Fatal crash at Kilkerran on 19.4.91. Canx as WFU 16.8.91.
G-BRZN	Hughes 269B	34-0037	N9331F	14. 2.90	Canx 15.7.91 on sale to USA. To XA-RZO 7/91.
G-BRZO	Jodel D.18	PFA/169-11275		14. 2.90	
G-BRZP	PA-28-161 Warrior II	28-8616013	N9140Y	17. 4.90	
G-BRZR	PA-22-150 Tri-Pacer (Taildragger)	22-4942	N7045D	20. 6.90	To EI-UFO 2/94. Canx 6.12.93.
G-BRZS	Cessna 172P Skyhawk II	172-75004	N54585	2.10.90	
G-BRZT	Cameron V-77 HAFB	2241		21. 2.90	
G-BRZU	Colt Flying Cheese SS HAFB	1544		26. 2.90	
G-BRZV	Colt Flying Apple SS HAFB	1662		26. 2.90	
G-BRZW	Rans S-10 Sakota	0789-058 & PFA/194-11932		21. 2.90	
G-BRZX	Pitts S-1S Special (Built by M.M.Lotero)	711-H	N272H	22. 2.90	(On overhaul 9/97)
G-BRZY	Saab 91D/2 Safir	91-376	PH-RLK	23. 2.90	To G-HRLK 3/90. Canx.
G-BRZZ	CFM Streak Shadow (C/n conflicts with Renegade Spirit G-MWDM)	PFA/161A-11628		22. 2.90	
G-BSAA	HS.125 Srs.3B	25117	5N-AKT 5N-AET	1. 3.78	To G-DBAL 7/84. Canx.
G-BSAB	PA-46-350P Mirage Malibu	4622049	N9161N	1. 3.90	To I-BSAB 4/96. Canx 1.4.96.
G-BSAC	PBN BN-2B-26 Islander	2230		26. 2.90	To DQ-FHG 3/92. Canx 10.4.92.
G-BSAD	PBN BN-2T Turbine Islander (Originally regd as a BN-2B-26)	2231		26. 2.90	To TC-TKG. Canx 15.5.91.
G-BSAE	PBN BN-2T Turbine Islander (Originally regd as a BN-2B-26)	2232		26. 2.90	To CN-TWO. Canx 2.10.91.
G-BSAF	PBN BN-2T Turbine Islander (Originally regd as a BN-2B-26)	2233		26. 2.90	To CN-TWP. Canx 2.10.91.
G-BSAG	PBN BN-2B-20 Islander (Originally regd as a BN-2B-26)	2234		26. 2.90	To 9M-TAM. Canx 29.5.91.
G-BSAH	PBN BN-2T Turbine Islander CC.2 (Originally regd as a BN-2B-26)	2235		26. 2.90	To RAF as ZH536. Canx to MOD(PE) 24.12.91.
G-BSAI	Stoddard-Hamilton Glasair III	3102		31. 1.90	
G-BSAJ	CASA I-131E Jungmann	2209	E3B-209 Spanish AF	23. 1.90	
G-BSAK	Colt 21A Sky Chariot HAFB	1696		26. 2.90	
G-BSAL	Gulfstream G.1159 Gulfstream II	214	N17585	21. 7.78	To A40-HA 2/84. Canx 7.2.84.
G-BSAM	Socata MS.880B Rallye Club	831	F-BNXZ	1. 8.78	Not rebuilt due to corrosion. Broken up for spares at Fenland. Canx as destroyed 29.2.84.
G-BSAN	Gulfstream G.1159A Gulfstream III	345	N17585	10.12.82	To VR-CCN 4/90. Canx 19.4.90.
G-BSAO	Steen Skybolt (Built by B.J.Counts)	001	N303BC	26. 2.90	To EI-CIZ 12/93. Canx 22.11.93.
G-BSAP	Cameron A-120 HAFB	2249		28. 2.90	To PH-RET. Canx 11.12.92.
G-BSAR	Air Command 532 Elite	0443		20. 4.89	
G-BSAS	Cameron V-65 HAFB	2191		27. 2.90	
G-BSAT	PA-28-181 Archer II	28-8090326	N8227H	8. 2.88	Fatal crash on landing Biggin Hill 9.3.97. Canx as destroyed 5.8.97.
G-BSAU	Enstrom F-28F	765	N5FX	27. 2.90	To OO-VDK. Canx 17.3.93.
G-BSAV	Thunder Ax7-77 HAFB	1555		26. 2.90	
G-BSAW	PA-28-161 Warrior II	28-8216152	N8203C	27. 2.90	
G-BSAX	Piper J3C-65 Cub	18432	N98260 NC98260	17. 1.91	
G-BSAY	Cessna 172M Skyhawk	172-60996	N20086	23. 3.90	To D-EFEE(2) 8/93. Canx 30.4.93.
G-BSAZ	Denney Kitfox Mk.2	602 & PFA/172-11664	(G-BRVW)	5. 3.90	
G-BSBA	PA-28-161 Warrior II	28-8016041	N2574U	1. 3.90	
G-BSBB	CCF Harvard 4 (T-6J-CCF Texan)	CCF4-555	1788 Moz PLAF/FAP 1788/West German AF AA+689/53-4636	5. 3.90	To N..... 5/94. Canx 6.5.94.
G-BSBC	CCF Harvard 4 (T-6J-CCF Texan) (Possibly composite with rear fuselage of Moz PLAF/FAP 1780/AA+614/53-4622)	CCF4-548	1741 Moz PLAF/FAP 1741/West German AF BF+055/AA+055/53-4629	5. 3.90	To G-HRVD 12/92. Canx.
G-BSBD	North American T-6G Texan	182-694	1681 Moz PLAF/FAP 1681/51-15007	5. 3.90	To N..... 5/94. Canx 6.5.94.
G-BSBE	CCF Harvard 4 (T-6J-CCF Texan)	CCF4-442	1730 Moz PLAF/FAP 1730/West German AF AA+652/52-8521	5. 3.90	To G-TVIJ 12/93. Canx.
G-BSBF	CCF Harvard 4 (T-6J-CCF Texan)	CCF4-511	1736 Moz.PLAF/FAP 1736/West German AF BF+058/AA+058/52-8590	5. 3.90	To N..... 5/94. Canx 6.5.94.
G-BSBG	CCF Harvard 4 (T-6J-CCF Texan)	CCF4-483	1753 Moz.PLAF/FAP 1753/West German AF BF+053/AA+053/52-8562	5. 3.90	
G-BSBH	Short SD.3-30 Var.100 (Airframe originally laid down as SC.7 Skyvan c/n SH.1934, became prototype)	SH3000		6. 6.74	CofA expired 13.4.81. Canx as WFU 8.12.88. (To Belfast Harbour Fire Service)
G-BSBI	Cameron O-77 HAFB	2245		6. 3.90	(Extant 2/97)

Regn	Type	c/n	Previous identity	Regn date	Fate or immediate subsequent identity (if known)
G-BSBJ	Bell 206B JetRanger III	3662	N3171P N678LD	6. 3.90	To D-HEBI(2) 3/91. Canx 7.2.91.
G-BSBK	Colt 105A HAFB	1319		6. 3.90	
G-BSBL	Short SD.3-60 (Prototype) (Rebuild of SD.3-30 N844SA c/n SH3041)	SH3600		21. 5.81	NTU - To G-ROOM 5/81. Canx.
G-BSBM	Cameron N-77 HAFB	2229		8. 3.90	Stored 1/98 BBAC Museum. Canx as WFU 15.7.98.
G-BSBN	Thunder Ax7-77 HAFB	1531		6. 3.90	
G-BSBO	Marco J-5 (built by D.Austin)	009		2. 4.90	No Permit to Fly believed issued. Canx by CAA 16.5.91. To BGA.4014/HKW 6/94 with c/n 009.
G-BSBP	Jodel D.18	PFA/169-11613		15. 1.90	
G-BSBR	Cameron V-77 HAFB	2247		26. 2.90	
G-BSBS	PA-34-200T Seneca II	34-7570303	G-BDRI SE-GLG	31.10.88	To G-VVBK 1/89. Canx.
G-BSBT	Piper J3C-65 Cub	17712	N70694 NC70694	9. 3.90	
G-BSBU	Firefly 8B HAFB	F8B-322		26. 3.90	Canx by CAA 4.8.98.
G-BSBV	Rans S-10 Sakota	1089-064 & PFA/194-11769		9. 3.90	
G-BSBW	Bell 206B JetRanger III	3664	N43EA N6498V/9Y-THC	12. 3.90	
G-BSBX	Montgomerie-Bensen B.8MR Gyrocopter	G/01A-1135		12. 3.90	
G-BSBY	Cessna 150L Commuter	150-74024	N18662	22. 6.90	To F-GRDR 8/96. Canx 9.8.96.
G-BSBZ	Cessna 150M Commuter	150-77093	N63086	29. 3.90	
G-BSCA	Cameron N-90 HAFB (Originally regd with c/n 2239 - also see G-BRZA)	2237		12. 3.90	
G-BSCB	Air Command 532 Elite	0627 & G/04-1172		16. 3.90	
G-BSCC	Colt 105A HAFB	1006		15. 3.90	
G-BSCD	Hughes 269C (300C)	74-0327	PH-HSH SE-HFG	19. 3.90	To G-IBHH 8/99. Canx.
G-BSCE	Robinson R-22 Beta	1245		15. 3.90	(Badly damaged on take-off Sandtoft 31.5.97)
G-BSCF	Thunder Ax7-77 HAFB	1537		14. 3.90	
G-BSCG	Denney Kitfox Mk.2	PFA/172-11620		23. 4.90	
G-BSCH	Denney Kitfox Mk.2 (C/n was officially quoted as PFA/172-11821)	510 & PFA/172-11621		16. 3.90	
G-BSCI	Colt 77A HAFB	1683		16. 3.90	
G-BSCJ	Colt 120A HAFB	1706		15. 3.90	To I-BRIT. Canx 29.6.90.
G-BSCK	Cameron H-24 HAFB	2263		16. 3.90	
G-BSCL	Robinson R-22 Beta	1249		28. 3.90	
G-BSCM	Denney Kitfox Mk.2	638 & PFA/172-11745		28. 3.90	
G-BSCN	Socata TB-20 Trinidad	1070	D-EGTC(2) G-BSCN	27. 3.90	
G-BSCO	Thunder Ax7-77 HAFB	1635		6. 3.90	
G-BSCP	Cessna 152 II	152-83289	N48135	20. 3.90	
G-BSCR	Cessna 172M Skyhawk II	172-62182	N12693	20. 3.90	(Overran the runway on landing at Clacton on 19.6.99 and collided with a hedge)
G-BSCS	PA-28-181 Archer II	28-7890064	N47392	3. 4.90	
G-BSCT	Fouga CM-170R Magister	045	45 French AF	20. 3.90	To G-FUGA 12.4.90. Canx.
G-BSCU	Colt GA-42 Gas Airship	1299		20. 3.90	To G-ZEPY 2/92. Canx.
G-BSCV	PA-28-161 Warrior II	28-7816135	C-GQXW	22. 3.90	
G-BSCW	Taylorcraft BC-65	1798	N24461 NC24461	22. 3.90	
G-BSCX	Thunder Ax8-105 HAFB	1748		21. 3.90	
G-BSCY	PA-28-151 Cherokee Warrior (Mod to PA-28-161 status)	28-7515046	C-GOBE	22. 3.90	
G-BSCZ	Cessna 152 II	152-82199	N68226	22. 3.90	
G-BSDA	Taylorcraft BC-12D	7316	N43657 NC43657	15.11.90	
G-BSDB	Pitts S-1C Special (Built by C.R.Rogers)	01	(N1867) N77R	22. 3.90	
G-BSDC	[Was reserved for an unidentified PA-44 Seminole]				
G-BSDD	Denney Kitfox Mk.2	639 & PFA/172-11797		28. 3.90	
G-BSDE	Cameron A-105 HAFB	1495		28. 3.90	Canx as WFU 17.8.92. To D-BRAUNBAER(1).
G-BSDF	Cameron N-105 HAFB	2114		26. 3.90	To D-BRAUNBAER(2). Canx by CAA 10.6.98.
G-BSDG	Robin DR.400/180 Regent	1974		29. 3.90	
G-BSDH	Robin DR.400/180 Regent	1980		18. 4.90	
G-BSDI	Corben Junior Ace Model E (Built by Oliver and Clark)	3961	N91706	28. 3.90	
G-BSDJ	Piper J/4E Cub Coupe	4-1456	N35975 NC35975	13. 2.91	
G-BSDK	Piper J/5A Cub Cruiser	5-175	N30337 NC30337	28. 3.90	
G-BSDL	Socata TB-10 Tobago	156		7.10.80	
G-BSDM	Bell 206B JetRanger III	2570	N27EA N120KC/XA-IOF/N5012A	4. 4.90	To HB-XXI 10/90. Canx 10.10.90.
G-BSDN	PA-34-200T Seneca II	34-7970335	N2893A	2. 4.90	
G-BSDO	Cessna 152 II	152-81657	N65894	23. 5.90	
G-BSDP	Cessna 152 II	152-80268	N24468	11. 6.90	

Regn	Type	c/n	Previous identity	Regn date	Fate or immediate subsequent identity (if known)
G-BSDR	Boeing-Stearman A75N1 (PT-17) Kaydet	75-4354	N61827 42-16191	6. 4.90	To G-IIIG 3/91. Canx.
G-BSDS	Boeing-Stearman E75 (PT-13A) Kaydet	75-118	N57852 38-470	6. 4.90	
G-BSDT	Cameron O-120 HAFB	2238		30. 3.90	To C-FWDT. Canx 9.5.91.
G-BSDU	Bell 206B JetRanger III	4097	C-FHZV	5. 6.90	
G-BSDV	Colt 31A HAFB	1722		30. 3.90	
G-BSDW	Cessna 182P Skylane II	182-64688	N9125M	9. 4.90	
G-BSDX	Cameron V-77 HAFB	2050		30. 3.90	
	(Canopy fitted to G-SNOW and rebuilt with G-SNOWs original canopy c/n 541)				
G-BSDY	Beechcraft 58 Baron	TH-1557	N1557M	3. 4.90	To F-GKZT 10/98. Canx 2.9.98.
G-BSDZ	Enstrom 280FX	2051	OO-MHV (OO-JMH)/G-ODSC/G-BSDZ	3. 4.90	
G-BSEA	Thunder Ax7-77 HAFB	1524		3. 4.90	Canx by CAA 5.5.94.
G-BSEB	Cessna C34 Airmaster	322	N16403 NC16403	3. 4.90	To N16403 5/90. Canx 11.4.90. (Stored Lower Wasing Farm, Aldermaston 3/98 as NC16403)
G-BSEC	Socata TB-9 Tampico	210	G-BIZR	18.11.87	Restored as G-BIZR 3/88. Canx.
G-BSED	PA-22-160 Tri-Pacer (Taildragger conversion)	22-6377	N9404D	7. 6.90	
G-BSEE	Rans S-9	PFA/196-11635		2. 3.90	
G-BSEF	PA-28-180 Cherokee C	28-1846	N7831W	18. 4.90	
G-BSEG	Ken Brock KB-2 Gyrocopter (C/n should perhaps be G/06-1106)	G/01-1106		3. 4.90	
G-BSEH	Cameron V-77 HAFB	2167		3. 4.90	To D-OSEH 3.93. Canx 4.3.93.
G-BSEI	Cameron N-90 HAFB	2265		10. 4.90	Canx as WFU 7.2.94.
G-BSEJ	Cessna 150M Commuter	150-76261	N66767	4. 5.90	
G-BSEK	Robinson R-22	0027	N45AD N90193	10. 4.90	
G-BSEL	Slingsby T.61G Super Falke	1986		31. 3.80	
G-BSEM	Cameron Four Pack 90SS HAFB	2266		11. 4.90	Stolen with its trailer from outside a house near Bath in 1993. Canx as WFU 7.2.94.
G-BSEN	Colt 31A HAFB	1754		10. 4.90	Canx by CAA 10.3.95. (Based in USA)
G-BSEO	Beechcraft 200 Super King Air	BB-501	G-OADT G-KNCA/N518F/N571SS/SE-GHK	20. 4.90	To OK-JKB 1/92. Canx 6.1.92.
G-BSEP	Cessna 172	172-46555	N6455E	12. 4.90	
G-BSER	PA-28-160 Cherokee B	28-790	N5665W	19. 4.90	
G-BSES	Denney Kitfox	PFA/172-11587		17. 4.90	DBF in refuelling accident at Aboyne in 1992/93. (Parts only stored 3/94) Canx by CAA 6.3.99.
G-BSET	Beagle B.206R Basset CC.1	R.01/B.006	XS765	3.12.86	
G-BSEU	PA-28-181 Archer II	28-7890108	N47639	1. 5.90	
G-BSEV	Cameron O-77 HAFB	2271		20. 4.90	
G-BSEW	Sikorsky S-76A II Plus	760160	C-GHJG N5432A	19. 4.90	To 5N-DOS 1/97. Canx 20.1.97.
G-BSEX	Cameron A-180 HAFB	2254		18. 4.90	
G-BSEY	Beechcraft A36 Bonanza	E-1873	N1809F	17. 5.90	
G-BSEZ	Air Command 532 Elite	0629 & G/04-1165		18. 4.90	Permit expired 14.6.91. Canx as PWFU 29.1.99.
G-BSFA	Aero Designs Pulsar	176 & PFA/202-11754		18. 4.90	
G-BSFB	CASA I-131E Srs.2000 Jungmann (Originally regd with c/n 2052)	2053	E3B-449 Spanish AF	27. 4.90	
G-BSFC	PA-38-112 Tomahawk	38-78A0430		17.11.78	To G-LFSA 10/90. Canx.
G-BSFD	Piper J3C-65 Cub (Frame No. 15443)	16037	N88419 NC88419	25. 5.90	
G-BSFE	PA-38-112 Tomahawk II	38-82A0033	N91452	26. 4.90	
G-BSFF	Robin DR.400/180R Remorqueur	1295	D-ELMM	20. 4.90	
G-BSFG	BAe Jetstream Srs.3108	686	PH-KJF G-31-686	23. 5.90	To OY-SVF. Canx 7.8.91.
G-BSFH	BAe Jetstream Srs.3108	690	PH-KJG G-31-690	23. 5.90	To G-LOGT 8/91. Canx.
G-BSFI	SAAB-Scania SF.340A	340A-008	SE-E08	22. 6.84	To SE-ISC 2/86. Canx 7.2.86.
G-BSFJ	Thunder Ax8-105 HAFB	1762		20. 4.90	
G-BSFK	PA-28-161 Warrior II	28-8516062	N6918D	1. 5.90	
G-BSFL	PA-23-250 Turbo Aztec E	27-7305142	PH-NOA 9M-AUS/PH-NOA/N40378	14. 7.80	To EI-BXP 7/88. Canx 7.7.88.
G-BSFM	Cameron Cheese 82SS HAFB	1996		30. 4.90	To I-IORE. Canx 16.3.93.
G-BSFN	Sud SE.313B Alouette II	1500	XP967	30. 5.90	
G-BSFO	Cameron House 60SS HAFB	2202		27. 4.90	Canx by CAA 17.12.90. To JA-A501.
G-BSFP	Cessna 152T	152-85548	N93764	9. 5.90	
G-BSFR	Cessna 152 II	152-82268	N68341	9. 5.90	
G-BSFS	Sud SE.313B Alouette II (Possibly ex F-WIEM)	1582	XR378 F-WIFM	30. 5.90	
G-BSFT	PA-31-310 Turbo Navajo	31-642	G-AXYC N6737L	11. 6.79	To N23AN 3/93. Canx 5.1.93.
G-BSFU	Sud SE.313B Alouette II	1645	XR385	30. 5.90	No UK CofA issued. Canx by CAA 2.2.93. (Stored 7/97)
G-BSFV	Woods Woody Pusher (Built by P.E.Hall)	201	N16WP	30. 4.90	
G-BSFW	PA-15 Vagabond	15-273	N4484H NC4484H	26. 4.90	
G-BSFX	Denney Kitfox Mk.2	506 & PFA/172-11723		23. 4.90	

Regn	Type	c/n	Previous identity	Regn date	Fate or immediate subsequent identity (if known)
G-BSFY	Denney Kitfox Mk.2 (PFA c/n conflicts with Coyote II G-MWCH)	PFA/172-11632		16. 3.90	
G-BSFZ	PA-25-235 Pawnee D (Rebuild of c/n 25-2246 using new frame ex.N6277Z)	25-6309	G-ASFZ N6672Z	26.10.79	To SE-IXU. Canx 14.5.87.
G-BSGA	Beechcraft C90 King Air	LJ-883	N410WC N7801L	7.10.87	To N12TA. Canx 7.7.88.
G-BSGB	Gaertner Ax4 Skyranger HAFB	SR.0001		30. 3.90	(Active 2/97)
G-BSGC	PA-18-95 Super Cub (L-18C-PI)	18-3227	OO-HBC OL-L53/L-153/53-4827	22. 3.90	(On overhaul in Norfolk .96 for Portuguese owners) No UK Permit to Fly issued. Canx as WFU 15.5.99.
G-BSGD	PA-28-180 Cherokee E	28-5691	N3463R	4. 5.90	
G-BSGE	Grob G-115A	8100	(VH-...) (D-EGVV)	30. 4.90	To EI-CCN 11/90. Canx 22.10.90.
G-BSGF	Robinson R-22 Beta	1383		1. 5.90	
G-BSGG	Denney Kitfox Mk.2	PFA/172-11666		1. 5.90	
G-BSGH	Airtour AH-56B HAFB	014		1. 5.90	
G-BSGI	BAe 146 Srs.300QT	E3168	(RP-C479) G-BSGI	8. 5.90	To G-TNTL 2/92. Canx.
G-BSGJ	Monnett Sonerai II	300	N34WH	1. 5.90	
G-BSGK	PA-34-200T Seneca II	34-7870331	N36450	22. 5.90	
G-BSGL	PA-28-161 Warrior II	28-8116041	N82690	10. 5.90	
G-BSGM	Cameron V-77 HAFB	2276		10. 5.90	To YL-006 /97. Canx 19.5.97.
G-BSGN	PA-28-151 Cherokee Warrior	28-7615225	N9657K	10. 5.90	To G-PSRT 3/99. Canx.
G-BSGO	PA-32R-301 Saratoga SP	32R-8013056	N8156Z N9502N	20. 6.90	Crashed near Coventry on 26.10.90. Canx as WFU 14.12.90.
G-BSGP	Cameron N-65 HAFB	2293		1. 5.90	
G-BSGR	Boeing-Stearman E75 (PT-17) Kaydet (Also reported as c/n 75-6714 which was previously N66870/Bu.07110)	75-4721	EC-ATY N55050/42-16558	19. 6.90	(On overhaul 4/96 Brickhouse Farm, Frogland Cross) No UK CofA issued due to ID problems and regd in USA as N75864 on 3.6.94 with c/n 75-2101TC. Canx by CAA 10.3.99
G-BSGS	Rans S-10 Sakota	1289-076 & PFA/194-11724		9. 5.90	(Damaged in gales Baginton late 1.93) (Status uncertain)
G-BSGT	Cessna T.210N Turbo Centurion II (Reims c/n 0020)	210-63361	LX-ATL D-EOGB/N5308A	21. 5.90	
G-BSGU	Cessna P.206B Super Skylane	P206-0337	N4737F	15. 5.90	To Z-JBM. Canx 27.3.91.
G-BSGV	Rotorway Exec	3823		8. 5.90	Permit to Fly expired 14.7.92. Canx by CAA 7.4.95. (Stored 5/95 at Chirk)
G-BSGW	Bell 206B JetRanger III	2943	N37EA N130KC/XA-JUS	3. 5.90	To A7-HAP. Canx 5.10.90.
G-BSGX	Cameron A-120 HAFB	2319		18. 7.90	To D-GREVEN. Canx 31.10.90.
G-BSGY	Thunder Ax7-77 HAFB (Envelope ex.G-BROA c/n 1535)	1760		18. 7.90	
G-BSGZ	Colt Financial Times SS HAFB	1792		15.10.90	To G-ETFT 1/91. Canx.
G-BSHA	PA-34-200T Seneca II (C/n marked on plate as 76-70216)	34-7670216	N9707K	2. 5.90	
G-BSHB	Colt 69A HAFB	1647		8. 5.90	To SU-211 9/95. Canx 28.9.95.
G-BSHC	Colt 69A HAFB	1668		8. 5.90	
G-BSHD	Colt 69A HAFB	1736		8. 5.90	
G-BSHE	Cessna 152 II	152-81302	N49483	17. 3.89	(Badly damaged in forced landing nr.Shoreham on 6.11.92) (Stored for spares Shoreham 9/93)
G-BSHF	Robinson R-22 Beta	1382		10. 5.90	Fatal crash at Welford-on-Avon on 8.9.91. Canx as destroyed 15.1.92.
G-BSHG	Luscombe 8A Silvaire	3525	N72098 NC72098	11. 5.90	To G-NIGE 6.6.90. Canx.
G-BSHH	Luscombe 8E Silvaire	3981	N1254K NC1254K	11. 5.90	
G-BSHI	Luscombe 8DF Silvaire Trainer	1821	N39060 NC39060	11. 5.90	
G-BSHJ	Luscombe 8E Silvaire	5651	N2924K NC2924K	11. 5.90	To D-EQUS 3/95. Canx 6.10.93.
G-BSHK	Denney Kitfox Mk.2	449 & PFA/172-11752		11. 5.90	
G-BSHL	HS.125 Srs.600B/2	256024	G-BBMD N50GD/G-BBMD	5.12.80	To G-OMGA 2/91. Canx.
G-BSHM	Slingsby Cadet III (Converted T.31B) (Also quotes c/n "SSK/OW2836", which is component number for wing)	712 & PFA/42-11827	BGA.3289 WT917	21. 6.90	To PH-1121 4/99. Canx 21.10.97.
G-BSHN	Cessna 152 II	152-81605	N65541	15. 5.90	To G-MASS 3/95. Canx.
G-BSHO	Cameron V-77 HAFB	2313		16. 5.90	
G-BSHP	PA-28-161 Warrior II	28-8616002	N9107Y	31. 5.90	
G-BSHR	Reims Cessna F.172N Skyhawk II	1616	G-BFGE	23.10.84	
G-BSHS	Colt 105A HAFB	1674	(D-OCAT) G-BSHS	16. 5.90	
G-BSHT	Cameron V-77 HAFB	2321		30. 5.90	
G-BSHU	Socata TB-20 Trinidad	1096		31. 6.90	To G-KKDL 12/90. Canx.
G-BSHV	PA-18-135 Super Cub (L-18C-PI)	18-3123	OO-GDG Belgian Army L49/53-4723	5. 7.90	
G-BSHW	Hawker Tempest II (Bristol Aeroplane Co. built)	12177	HA564 Indian AF/MW376	21. 3.91	(Stored by Historic Flying Ltd at North Weald 5/96)
G-BSHX	Enstrom F-28A	155	N9605	16. 5.90	(Stored 4/96)
G-BSHY	EAA Acrosport 1	PFA/72-10928		17. 4.90	
G-BSHZ	Enstrom F-28F	427	N51702	16. 5.90	

Regn	Type	c/n	Previous identity	Regn date	Fate or immediate subsequent identity (if known)
G-BSIA	PA-28R-200 Cherokee Arrow II	28R-7435136	G-IPJC N40863	17. 5.90	Canx 23.5.90 as registered in error. Remained as G-IPJC.
G-BSIB	PA-28-161 Warrior II	28-8016304	N8182C	13. 6.90	
G-BSIC	Cameron V-77 HAFB	2322		17. 5.90	
G-BSID	Wombat Gyrocopter	CJ-001		18. 5.90	To G-WBAT 31.5.90. Canx.
G-BSIE	Enstrom 280FX Shark	2052	HA-MIN G-BSIE	17. 5.90	(Damaged at Westhoughton on 21.9.98) (On major rebuild 1/99 at Shoreham)
G-BSIF	Denney Kitfox Mk.2 (Built by C.G.Richardson)	563 & PFA/172-11889	N (?)	5. 7.90	
G-BSIG	Colt 21A Cloudhopper HAFB	1322		18. 5.90	
G-BSIH	Rutan LongEz	1200-1 & PFA/74A-11492		31. 5.90	
G-BSII	PA-34-200T Seneca II	34-8070336	N8253N	16. 5.90	
G-BSIJ	Cameron V-77 HAFB	2164		23. 5.90	
G-BSIK	Denney Kitfox Mk.1	51		5. 6.90	(Extant 5/97)
G-BSIL	Colt 120A HAFB	1784		25. 5.90	To VH-DEW 10/96. Canx 29.7.96.
G-BSIM	PA-28-181 Archer II	28-8690017	N9092Y	22. 5.90	
G-BSIN	Robinson R-22 Beta	1379	N4015H	25. 5.90	
G-BSIO	Cameron Furness House 56SS HAFB (Originally regd as Shed 80SS)	2310		25. 5.90	
G-BSIP	Cameron V-77 HAFB	2150		25. 5.90	To CC-... 1/95. Canx 9.1.95.
G-BSIR	Cessna 340	340-0217	N74PA N666HZ/N666HC	16. 5.90	To N4424X 6/98. Canx 2.6.98.
G-BSIS	Pitts S-1S Special	PFA/09-10015	(G-BFKY)	1. 2.78	Fatal crash at Rushetts Farm on 11.7.88 & destroyed. Canx as destroyed 3.11.88.
G-BSIT	Robinson R-22 Beta	0762		9. 3.88	(Badly damaged in heavy landing at Ashcroft, Cheshire on 20.4.97)
G-BSIU	Colt 90A HAFB	1774		25. 5.90	
G-BSIV	Socata TB-10 Tobago	1107		18. 6.90	To G-CTCL 7/90. Canx.
G-BSIW	BAe Jetstream Srs.3112	829	G-OEDL G-OAKK/G-BSIW/HB-AED/G-31-829/C-FCPG/G-31-829	13. 6.90	To C-GMDJ 1/97. Canx 9.1.97.
G-BSIX	Cessna 401	401-0165	G-CAFE(2) G-AWXM/N4065Q	7. 7.81	To G-ODJM 9/82. Canx.
G-BSIY	Schleicher ASK-14	14005	5Y-AID D-KOIC	4. 6.90	
G-BSIZ	PA-28-181 Archer II	28-7990377	N2162Y	25. 5.90	
G-BSJA	Cameron N-77 HAFB	1248	G-SPAR	31. 5.90	Canx by CAA 1.3.93.
G-BSJB	Bensen B.8 Gyrocopter	G/01-1080		5. 6.90	
G-BSJC	Bell 206B JetRanger III	3689	N3175S	4. 5.90	To G-BVRC 4/94. Canx.
G-BSJD	Colt 160A HAFB	1731		25. 5.90	To D-OAKF 7/98. Canx 17.10.91.
G-BSJE	Colt 120A HAFB	1732		25. 5.90	To D-POTSDAM. Canx 29.5.91.
G-BSJF	Colt 120A HAFB	1733		25. 5.90	To D-BRANDENBERG. Canx 29.5.91.
G-BSJG	Colt 120A HAFB	1734		25. 5.90	To D-OSNABRUCK/D-OSNA 5/91. Canx 29.5.91.
G-BSJH	Colt 120A HAFB	1735		25. 5.90	To D-RUGEN. Canx 29.5.91.
G-BSJI	Short SD.3-30 (C-23B) Sherpa	SH3201		8. 6.90	To US Army National Guard as 88-1861. Canx 21.11.90.
G-BSJJ	Short SD.3-30 (C-23B) Sherpa	SH3202		8. 6.90	To US Army National Guard as 88-1862. Canx 21.11.90.
G-BSJK	Short SD.3-30 (C-23B) Sherpa	SH3203		8. 6.90	To US Army National Guard as 88-1863. Canx 21.11.90.
G-BSJL	Short SD.3-30 (C-23B) Sherpa	SH3204		8. 6.90	To US Army National Guard as 88-1864. Canx 21.11.90.
G-BSJM	Short SD.3-30 (C-23B) Sherpa	SH3205		8. 6.90	To US Army National Guard as 88-1865. Canx 18.12.90.
G-BSJN	Short SD.3-30 (C-23B) Sherpa	SH3206		8. 6.90	To US Army National Guard as 88-1866. Canx 11.2.91.
G-BSJO	Short SD.3-30 (C-23B) Sherpa	SH3207		8. 6.90	To US Army National Guard as 88-1867. Canx 8.3.91.
G-BSJP	Short SD.3-30 (C-23B) Sherpa	SH3208		8. 6.90	To US Army National Guard as 88-1868. Canx 15.4.91.
G-BSJR	Short SD.3-30 (C-23B) Sherpa	SH3209		8. 6.90	To US Army National Guard as 88-1869. Canx 24.2.92.
G-BSJS	Short SD.3-30 (C-23B) Sherpa	SH3210		8. 6.90	To US Army National Guard as 88-1870. Canx 24.2.92.
G-BSJT	Cessna 152 II	152-83180	N47174	27. 6.90	To OO-SPG. Canx 19.7.91.
G-BSJU	Cessna 150M Commuter	150-76430	N3230V	14. 6.90	
G-BSJV	Cessna 172N Skyhawk II	172-71126	N2037E	14. 6.90	To N202PY 8/98. Canx 21.7.98.
G-BSJW	Everett Gyroplane Srs.2	0020		6. 6.90	(Stored Sproughton 12/95)
G-BSJX	PA-28-161 Warrior II	28-8216084	N8036N	30. 5.90	
G-BSJY	Murphy Renegade 912	0325		21. 6.90	Canx 4.12.95 on sale to France.
G-BSJZ	Cessna 150J	150-70485	N60661	7. 5.91	
G-BSKA	Cessna 150M Commuter	150-76137	N66588	31. 7.90	
G-BSKB	Cessna 150G	150-65308	N4008J	. .90R	NTU - Remained as N4008J. Canx.
G-BSKC	PA-38-112 Tomahawk	38-79A0748	OY-PJB N748RM/C-GRQI	27. 7.90	(Damaged in forced landing in a field at Moss Bank Farm, near Welwyn Garden City on 2.6.96) (Stored 9/97)
G-BSKD	Cameron V-77 HAFB	2336		4. 6.90	
G-BSKE	Cameron O-84 HAFB	1604	ZS-HYD G-BSKE	4. 6.90	
G-BSKF	Schweizer Hughes 269C (300C)	S.1335	N218MS N219MS	14. 6.90	Canx 5.10.93 on sale to Spain. To ZK-HMQ(2) 9/95.
G-BSKG	Maule MX-7-180 Star Rocket	11072C		7. 6.90	
G-BSKH	Cessna 421C Golden Eagle III	421C-0603	N88600	17. 7.90	To G-UVIP 11/98. Canx.
G-BSKI	Thunder Ax8-90 HAFB	1623		18. 5.90	
G-BSKJ	Mooney M.20J	24-0525	N201YT	27. 7.90	Destroyed in fatal crash 8 NM W of Telford on 8.1.94. Canx by CAA 29.7.94.
G-BSKK	PA-38-112 Tomahawk	38-79A0671	N2525K	11. 6.90	
G-BSKL	PA-38-112 Tomahawk	38-78A0509	N4252E	11. 6.90	
G-BSKM	Cessna 182Q Skylane II	182-66039	N559CT N759JV	11. 6.90	To G-IRPC 5/91. Canx.
G-BSKN	Grob G-109B	6527		11. 6.90	To Z-BSKN 7/94. Canx 15.7.94.
G-BSKO	Maule MXT-7-180 Star Rocket	14008C		7. 6.90	

Regn	Type	c/n	Previous identity	Regn date	Fate or immediate subsequent identity (if known)
G-BSKP	Vickers-Supermarine 379 Spitfire F.XIVe	6S/663417	SG-31 Belgian AF/RN201	27. 6.90	(On rebuild by Historic Flying Ltd 3/96)
G-BSKR	Rand Robinson KR-2	PFA/129-11068		21. 5.90	To CS-X.. 1/98. Canx.
G-BSKS	Nieuport 28C-1	6531	"N5246" US Navy	27. 6.90	Canx 1.4.93 on sale to USA.
	(Identity obscure but ex Tallmantz - and not ex N4123A)				
G-BSKT	Maule MX-7-180 Star Rocket	11070C		7. 6.90	
G-BSKU	Cameron O-84 HAFB	2330		8. 6.90	
G-BSKV	PA-28-181 Archer II	2890137	N9194X	1. 6.90	To A7-FCP 7/95. Canx 25.7.95.
G-BSKW	PA-28-181 Archer II	2890138	N91940	1. 6.90	
G-BSKX	PA-28-181 Archer II	2890139	N91947	1. 6.90	To A7-FCR 7/95. Canx 25.7.95.
G-BSKY	Douglas DC-8F-55 (Line No. 274)	45858	(CF-CPT) N789FT/CF-CPT/N1509U	17. 2.78	To HC-BJT 2/82. Canx 15.2.82.
G-BSKZ	PA-34-220T Seneca III	3433169	N9195B N9521N	1. 6.90	Ditched in Atlantic off Scotland on delivery flight 16-17.6.90. Canx as destroyed 24.7.90.
G-BSLA	Robin DR.400/180 Regent	1997		22. 6.90	
G-BSLB	Robinson R-22 Beta	1386		8. 6.90	To EI-JWM 11/92. Canx 23.10.92.
G-BSLC	Robinson R-22 Beta	1384		8. 6.90	To VH-HIP(2) 8/95. Canx 24.7.95.
G-BSLD	PA-28RT-201 Arrow IV	28R-7918231	N2943D	22. 6.90	
G-BSLE	PA-28-161 Warrior II	28-8116028	N8260L	25. 6.90	
G-BSLF	Robinson R-22 Beta	1425	OO-COK G-BSLF	12. 6.90	Crashed while hovering at Cumbernauld on 5.8.95. Canx by CAA 14.11.95.
G-BSLG	Cameron A-180 HAFB	2332		15. 6.90	
G-BSLH	CASA I-131E Jungmann Srs.2000	2222	E3B-622 Spanish AF	27. 7.90	
G-BSLI	Cameron V-77 HAFB	2115		15. 6.90	
G-BSLJ	Denney Kitfox Mk.2	364 & PFA/172-11589		15. 6.90	Badly damaged in crash on Bundoran Beach, Co.Donegal on 28.5.92. (Stored 6/97) Canx by CAA 10.3.99.
G-BSLK	PA-28-161 Warrior II	28-7916018	N20849	15. 6.90	
G-BSLL	Aerospatiale AS.355F2 Twin Squirrel	5370	G-BOGX	6. 7.89	To CC-CIM(2) 1/92. Canx 20.1.92.
G-BSLM	PA-28-160 Cherokee	28-308	N5262W	22. 6.90	
G-BSLN	Thunder Ax10-180 HAFB	1602		15. 6.90	To ZS-HYZ 3/96. Canx 25.3.96.
G-BSLO	Cameron A-180 HAFB	2162		8. 6.90	To C-GFEA 7/99. Canx 16.6.99.
G-BSLP	BAe 146 Srs.100	E1144	(PK-DTA) G-6-144/G-11-144/(G-BRLM)	20. 6.90	To PK-DTA. Canx 30.7.90.
G-BSLR	Schweizer 269C (300C)	S.1464	N69A	20. 6.90	To OO-TZZ. Canx 2.12.92.
G-BSLS	BAe 146 Srs.300	E3155	G-6-155	26. 6.90	NTU - To G-BTNU 7/90. Canx.
G-BSLT	PA-28-161 Warrior II	28-8016303	N81817	19. 6.90	
G-BSLU	PA-28-140 Cherokee	28-24733	OY-PJL OH-PJL/SE-FFA	19. 6.90	
G-BSLV	Enstrom 280FX Shark	2054	D-HHAS(2) G-BSLV	26. 6.90	
G-BSLW	Bellanca 7ECA Citabria	431-66	N9696S	16. 7.90	
G-BSLX	WAR Focke-Wulf 190 Replica	24	N698WW	19. 6.90	(Nearing completion Carlisle 2/96)
G-BSLY	Colt AS-80GD Hot-Air Airship	1641		19. 6.90	Sold to Germany as D-GEFAFLUG but with new envelope and c/n GD-001. Canx as WFU 22.4.98.
G-BSLZ	BAe 146 Srs.300QT	E3166	G-6-166	19. 6.90	To G-TNTM 2/92. Canx.
G-BSMA	Colt Flying Open Book SS HAFB	1691		21. 6.90	To C-FPIJ 24.9.93. Canx 7.1.93.
G-BSMB	Cessna U.206E Super Skywagon	U206-01659	N9459G C-GUUW/N9459G	25. 6.90	
G-BSMC	PA-32R-301T Saratoga SP	32R-8024019	N8190Y	8. 5.80	To HB-PAZ 10/81. Canx 7.10.81.
G-BSMD	SNCAN 1101 Noralpha	139	F-GDPQ F-YEEE/F-YCZK/CAN-11/French Mil	26. 6.90	(Stored 3/97)
G-BSME	Bolkow Bo.208C Junior	596	D-ECGA	25. 6.90	
G-BSMF	Avro 652A Anson C.19	-	TX183	5. 9.90	(On rebuild 12/93 Arbroath)
G-BSMG	Montgomerie-Bensen B.8M Gyrocopter	G/01-1170		22. 6.90	
G-BSMH	Colt 240A HAFB	1772		22. 6.90	Canx by CAA 4.8.98.
G-BSMI	Schweizer 269C (300C)	S.1478	PH-HWH N86C	22. 6.90	Canx as destroyed 21.10.92.
G-BSMJ	Piper J3C-90 Cub (L-4B-PI) (Frame No.12639)	12809	(G-BRHE) EC-AIY/HB-ODO/44-80513	. .90R	NTU - To G-BSYO 2/91. Canx.
	(Officially regd as c/n 10244 ex 43-1383/F-BFYF which is HB-OVG)				
G-BSMK	Cameron O-84 HAFB	2328		26. 6.90	
G-BSML	Schweizer 269C (300C)	S.1462	PH-HUH N134DM	10.10.90	
G-BSMM	Colt 31A Sky Chariot HAFB	1779		27. 6.90	
G-BSMN	CFM Streak Shadow	K.137-SA & PFA/161A-11656		26. 6.90	
G-BSMO	Denney Kitfox	PFA/172-11773		16. 7.90	
G-BSMP	PA-34-220T Seneca III	3448007	N9196W	17. 8.90	To OY-... Canx 22.2.99.
G-BSMR	BAe 146 Srs.300	E3158	G-6-158	26. 6.90	To G-6-158/G-UKRC 2/91. Canx.
G-BSMS	Cameron V-77 HAFB	2356		26. 6.90	
G-BSMT	Rans S-10 Sakota	1289-077 & PFA/194-11793		29. 6.90	
G-BSMU	Rans S-6 Coyote II	1089-090 & PFA/204-11732	(G-MWJE)	27. 6.90	
G-BSMV	PA-17 Vagabond	17-94	N4696H NC4696H	29. 6.90	
G-BSMW	Colt Flying Lager Bottle SS HAFB	1705		29. 6.90	To D-OELDE. Canx 24.12.91.
G-BSMX	Bensen B.8MR Gyrocopter	G/01-1171		3. 7.90	

Regn	Type	c/n	Previous identity	Regn date	Fate or immediate subsequent identity (if known)
G-BSMY	BAe Jetstream Srs.3201	900	G-31-900	29. 6.90	To N3142 9/90. Canx 10.9.90.
G-BSMZ	PA-28-161 Warrior II	28-8516040	N4391K N9555N	10. 7.90	To G-NSFT 8/96. Canx.
G-BSNA	Boeing 757-236 (Line No. 358)	25053		. .90R	NTU - To EC-667/EC-FEE 4/91. Canx.
G-BSNB	Boeing 757-236 (Line No. 362)	25054		. .90R	NTU - To (EC-668)/N5002K. Canx.
G-BSNC	Boeing 757-236 (Line No. 374)	25133		. .90R	NTU - To N1786B/I-AEJA. Canx.
G-BSND	Air Command 532 Elite	G/04-1180		16. 7.90	
G-BSNE	Luscombe 8E Silvaire	5757	N1130B NC1130B	2.11.90	
G-BSNF	Piper J3C-65 Cub (Lippert Reed conv.)(Frame No.3070)	3070	N23317 NC23317	17. 8.90	
G-BSNG	Cessna 172N Skyhawk II	172-70192	N738SB	19. 7.90	
G-BSNH	Robinson R-22 HP	0148	(EI-...) G-BSNH/N9065D	10. 7.90	To EI-CGU 12/92. Canx 10.12.92.
G-BSNI	Bensen B.8V Gyrocopter	G/01-1161		18. 7.90	No Permit to Fly issued. (At PFA Rally 7/96) Canx by CAA 16.4.99.
G-BSNJ	Cameron N-90 HAFB	2335		6. 7.90	
G-BSNK	Boeing-Stearman A75N1 (PT-17) Kaydet	75-1822	N38940 N55300/41-8263	. 7.90R	NTU - Remained as N38940. Canx.
G-BSNL	Bensen B.8MR Gyrocopter	G/01-1181		16. 7.90	
G-BSNM	PA-28R-200 Cherokee Arrow II	28R-7435104	N46PR G-BSNM/N46PR/N54439	18. 7.90	To G-MEAH 6/91. Canx.
G-BSNN	Rans S-10 Sakota	PFA/194-11846		31. 7.90	
G-BSNO	Denney Kitfox	PFA/172-11813		29. 6.90	Damaged on take-off from Sweethope Farm, Kalso on 9.7.97. Canx as destroyed 18.11.97.
G-BSNP	PA-28R-201T Turbo Arrow III	28R-7703236	N38537	18. 7.90	
G-BSNR	BAe 146 Srs.300	E3165	EC-FGT EC-807/G-6-165/G-BSNR/G-6-165/G-BSNR/N886DV/G-BSNR/G-6-165	13. 7.90	
G-BSNS	BAe 146 Srs.300	E3169	EC-FHU EC-839/G-6-169/G-BSNS/N887DV/G-BSNS/G-6-169	13. 7.90	
G-BSNT	Luscombe 8A Master	1679	N37018 NC37018	16. 7.90	
G-BSNU	Colt 105A HAFB	1811		23. 7.90	
G-BSNV	Boeing 737-4Q8 (Line No. 2210)	25168		5. 2.92	
G-BSNW	Boeing 737-4Q8 (Line No. 2237)	25169		12. 3.92	
G-BSNX	PA-28-181 Archer II	28-7990311	N3028S	19. 7.90	
G-BSNY	Bensen B.8M Gyrocopter	G/01-1176		16. 7.90	
G-BSNZ	Cameron O-105 HAFB	2364		16. 7.90	
G-BSOA	Bell 212	30787	N2118X G-BRDY/Singapore AF 211	11. 6.90	To 5N-AXX. Canx 14.1.91.
G-BSOB	PA-23-250 Aztec E	27-7405378	G-BCJR N54040	25. 4.86	To G-HFTG 4/87. Canx.
G-BSOC	BAe 146 Srs.300	E3161	B-1775 G-6-161	18. 7.90	Restored as B-1775. Canx 17.8.90.
G-BSOD	Not allotted.				
G-BSOE	Luscombe 8A Silvaire	4331	N1604K NC1604K	22. 8.90	No CofA issued. (Stored as N1604K 5/98 at Sturgate) Canx by CAA 16.4.99.
G-BSOF	Colt 25A Sky Chariot Mk.II HAFB	1820		27. 7.90	
G-BSOG	Cessna 172M Skyhawk II	172-63636	N1508V	16. 7.90	
G-BSOH	BAe 146 Srs.200	E2170	I-FLRX G-BSOH/PK-DTD/G-BSOH	19. 7.90	To VH-NJG 8/94. Canx 23.8.94.
G-BSOI	Aerospatiale AS.332L Super Puma	2063	C-GSLE G-BSOI/C-GSLE	21. 9.90	
G-BSOJ	Thunder Ax7-77 HAFB	1818	JA-A... G-BSOJ	31. 7.90	
G-BSOK	PA-28-161 Warrior II	28-7816191	N9749K	19. 7.90	
G-BSOL	PA-32R-301 Saratoga SP	3213007	N9130Z N9590N	22.12.87	To G-YUCS 11/89. Canx.
G-BSOM	Glaser-Dirks DG-400	4-126	LN-GMC D-KGDG	12. 7.90	
G-BSON	Green S-25 HAFB	001		7. 6.90	(Active 2/97)
G-BSOO	Cessna 172F Skyhawk	172-52431	N8531U	19. 7.90	
G-BSOP	Cameron Marshmellow 105SS HAFB	2362		23. 7.90	To OO-BSU. Canx 13.11.90.
G-BSOR	CFM Streak Shadow Srs.SA	K.131-SA & PFA/161A-11602		23.10.89	
G-BSOS	Not allotted.				
G-BSOT	PA-38-112 Tomahawk II	38-81A0053	N25682	23. 7.90	
G-BSOU	PA-38-112 Tomahawk II	38-81A0130	N23373	23. 7.90	
G-BSOV	PA-38-112 Tomahawk II	38-81A0031	N25637	20. 8.90	Damaged afyer overturning on landing at Panshanger on 7.10.95. (Stored for spares 7/97)
G-BSOW	PA-32R-300 Cherokee Lance	32R-7780215	N1998H	23. 7.90	To ZS-NRP. Canx 9.2.95.
G-BSOX	Luscombe 8AE Silvaire	2318	N45791 NC45791	7. 8.90	
G-BSOY	PA-34-220T Seneca III	3433155	OY-CEU	1. 8.90	
G-BSOZ	PA-28-161 Warrior II	28-7916080	N30220	14. 8.90	

Regn	Type	c/n	Previous identity	Regn date	Fate or immediate subsequent identity (if known)
G-BSPA	QAC Quickie Q.2 (built by C.C. & M.A.Wilde)	2227	N227T	16. 8.90	
G-BSPB	Thunder Ax8-84 HAFB	1803		24. 7.90	
G-BSPC	SAN Jodel D.140C Mousquetaire III	150	F-BMFN	2.11.81	CofA expired 31.10.85. (Stored at Headcorn) Canx by CAA 15.8.94. (On overhaul 9/97)
G-BSPD	Cameron N-65 HAFB	2331		25. 7.90	To C-FISN. Canx 25.7.90.
G-BSPE	Reims Cessna F.172P Skyhawk II	2073		31.12.80	
G-BSPF	Cessna T.303 Crusader	T303-00100	OY-SVH N3116C	31. 7.90	Canx as WFU 25.8.98.
G-BSPG	PA-34-200T Seneca II	34-8070168	N8176S	8. 8.90	
G-BSPH	HS.125 Srs.600B	256063	A6-RAK G-5-13	31.10.84	To N484W 3/85. Canx 12.3.85.
G-BSPI	PA-28-161 Warrior II	28-8116025	N8258V	26. 7.90	
G-BSPJ	Bensen B.8 Gyrocopter	G/01-1061		3. 8.90	
G-BSPK	Cessna 195A	7691	N1079D	14. 8.90	
G-BSPL	CFM Streak Shadow	K.140-SA		26. 7.90	
G-BSPM	PA-28-161 Warrior II	28-8116046	N82679	27. 7.90	
G-BSPN	PA-28R-201T Turbo Arrow III	28R-7703171	N5965V	31. 7.90	
G-BSPO	PBN BN-2B-26 Islander	2236		3. 8.90	To JA5306 9/91. Canx 14.8.91.
G-BSPP	PBN BN-2T Turbine Islander (Originally regd as a BN-2B-26)	2237		3. 8.90	To CN-TWQ. Canx 25.10.91.
G-BSPR	PBN BN-2T Turbine Islander (Originally regd as a BN-2B-26)	2238		3. 8.90	To MP-CG-02 Mauritius Coast Guard 10/92. Canx 16.10.92.
G-BSPS	PBN BN-2B-20 Islander (Originally regd as a BN-2B-26)	2239		3. 8.90	To JA5305. Canx 28.5.91.
G-BSPT	PBN BN-2B-20 Islander (Originally regd as a BN-2B-26)	2240		3. 8.90	To JA5316 5/93. Canx 28.4.93.
G-BSPU	PBN BN-2B-20 Islander (Originally regd as a BN-2B-26)	2241		3. 8.90	To D-IFLN(2) 7/91. Canx 13.6.91.
G-BSPV	CFM Streak Shadow	K.149-SA		31. 7.90	To N149LA 8/90. Canx 1.8.90.
G-BSPW	Light Aero Avid Speed Wing	PFA/189-11840		17. 7.90	
G-BSPX	Neico Lancair 320	521-320-259FB & PFA/191-11865		31. 7.90	
G-BSPY	BN-2A Islander	156	G-AXYM 5N-AIQ/G-AXYM/G-51-156	1. 6.90	
G-BSPZ	PA-28-161 Warrior II	28-8516045	N69092 N9568N	3. 8.90	Destroyed in fatal crash at Loch Freuche, 18 miles northwest of Perth on 16.10.96. Canx by CAA 1.4.97.
G-BSRA	Boeing 737-4S3 (Line No. 2061)	25116	N1789B	. .90R	NTU - To N4249R/9M-MLF. Canx.
G-BSRB	Boeing 737-4S3 (Line No. 2083)	25134		. .90R	NTU - To N1799B/9M-MLH. Canx.
G-BSRC	Cessna 150M Commuter	150-77651	N6337K	25. 7.90	To G-LFSF 7/99. Canx.
G-BSRD	Cameron N-105 HAFB	1568		3. 8.90	To D-ORSD 5/95. Canx 13.9.94.
G-BSRE	Cameron N-120 HAFB	2311		3. 8.90	To D-DRESDEN. Canx 6.11.90.
G-BSRF	CASA I-131 Jungmann	-	E3B-536 Spanish AF	3. 8.76	Crashed 18m west of Valencia during delivery from Spain on 10.9.76. Canx as destroyed 29.5.86.
G-BSRG	Robinson R-22 Beta	0797	N26607	3. 8.90	Damaged in heavy landing at Leicester on 29.1.93. Canx as destroyed 17.5.93.
G-BSRH	Pitts S-1C Special (built by L.Smith)	LS-2	N4111	7. 8.90	
G-BSRI	Neico Lancair 235	PFA/191-11467		9. 8.90	
G-BSRJ	Colt AA-1050 (Gas) Free Balloon	1782		20. 8.90	Canx by CAA 10.3.95. (Active Albuquerque 10/96)
G-BSRK	ARV1 Super 2	K.007	ZK-FSQ	8. 8.90	Damaged in forced landing near Sibson on 4.2.95. (Stored at Cambridge in 5/97)
G-BSRL	Everett Gyroplane Srs.2	0022		8. 8.90	(At Sproughton in 12/95)
G-BSRM	Aerospatiale SA.365C1 Dauphin	5057	HKG-1 R.Hong Kong Aux.AF	16. 8.90	To VH-LSL 3/91. Canx 4.3.91.
G-BSRN	Aerospatiale SA.365C1 Dauphin	5059	LN-OME(2) G-BSRN/R.Hong Kong Aux.AF HKG-2/F-WMHE	16. 8.90	To SE-JCJ 10/95. Canx 14.2.95.
G-BSRO	Aerospatiale SA.365C1 Dauphin	5060	HKG-3 R.Hong Kong Aux.AF	16. 8.90	To VH-LSR 1/91. Canx 20.12.90.
G-BSRP	Rotorway Exec (Originally regd with c/n 3647)	3824		15. 8.90	
G-BSRR	Cessna 182Q Skylane II	182-66915	N96961	25. 7.90	
G-BSRS	PA-28RT-201T Turbo Arrow IV	28R-8331039	ZS-LGJ N4307U	9. 5.85	To HB-PKV 5/87. Canx 13.5.87.
G-BSRT	Denney Kitfox Mk.2	742 & PFA/172-11873		9. 8.90	
G-BSRU	BAe 146 Srs.200	E2018	G-OSKI N603AW	9. 8.90	To G-6-018/G-HWPB 11/94. Canx.
G-BSRV	BAe 146 Srs.200	E2020	G-OSUN C-FEXN/N604AW	9. 8.90	To G-OLHB 3/94. Canx.
G-BSRW	Cameron Tiger 90SS HAFB	2290		31. 8.90	To D-TIGER. Canx 13.3.91.
G-BSRX	CFM Streak Shadow	K.148-SA & PFA/206-11870		15. 8.90	
G-BSRY	Reims Cessna F.406 Caravan II	0046	PH-ALP	22. 8.90	To OY-PED 9/95. Canx 15.9.95.
G-BSRZ	Air Command 532 Elite Two-Seat	G/05-1188		15. 8.90	
G-BSSA	Luscombe 8E Silvaire	4176	N1449K NC1449K	15. 8.90	

Regn	Type	c/n	Previous identity	Regn date	Fate or immediate subsequent identity (if known)
G-BSSB	Cessna 150L Commuter	150-74147	N19076	15. 8.90	
G-BSSC	PA-28-161 Warrior II	28-8216176	N81993 N9529N/N8234B	15. 8.90	
G-BSSD	Cameron O-105 HAFB	2382		15. 8.90	To I-VSGE. Canx 6.3.92.
G-BSSE	PA-28-140 Cherokee	28-7525192	N33440	22.10.90	(Badly damaged in take-off crash Netherthorpe 2.7.97)
G-BSSF	Denney Kitfox Mk.2	738 & PFA/172-11796		15. 8.90	
G-BSSG	BAe 146 Srs.200	E2172	G-6-172	16. 8.90	To OO-DJH. Canx 17.12.90.
G-BSSH	Bell 206L-1 Long Ranger II	45339	RP-C675	18.10.90	To N6592X. Canx 19.3.91.
G-BSSI	Rans S-6 Coyote II	0190-112 & PFA/204-11782	G-MWJA	17. 8.90	
G-BSSJ	Clutton FRED Srs.2	PFA/29-10753		23. 8.90	
G-BSSK	QAC Quickie Q.200	PFA/94A-11354		5. 9.90	
G-BSSL	Beechcraft 65-B80 Queen Air	LD-344	G-BFEP F-BRNR/OO-VDE	1. 5.80	To G-KEAB 8/88. Canx.
G-BSSM	Aerospatiale AS.355F1 Twin Squirrel	5302	G-BMTC G-BKUK	24. 1.86	To G-SASU 8/89. Canx.
G-BSSN	Air Command 532 Elite Two-Seat (Possibly c/n G/05-1187)	0631		21. 8.90	No Permit issued. Canx by CAA 10.3.99.
G-BSSO	Cameron O-90 HAFB	2255		23. 7.90	
G-BSSP	Robin DR.400/180R Remorqueur	2015		24. 9.90	
G-BSSR	PA-28-151 Cherokee Warrior	28-7615001	N1190X	29. 8.90	
G-BSSS	Cessna 421C Golden Eagle III	421C-1806	N1206P	6. 6.86	To D-ITAS 9/91. Canx 16.8.91.
G-BSST	BAC-Aerospatiale Concorde SST (Prototype)	002 & 13520		6. 5.68	WFU on 4.3.76. Canx as WFU 21.1.87. (On display at Yeovilton)
G-BSSU	Cameron N-120 HAFB	2350		21. 8.90	To D-HAMMER 10/90. Canx 26.9.90.
G-BSSV	CFM Streak Shadow	K.129-SA & PFA/206-11657		21. 8.90	
G-BSSW	PA-28-161 Warrior II	28-7816143	N47850	29. 8.90	
G-BSSX	PA-28-161 Warrior II	2816056	N9141H	11. 9.90	
G-BSSY	Polikarpov Po-2	0094	YU-CLJ	6.11.90	Canx by CAA 23.6.94. To N588NB 7/94.
G-BSSZ	Thunder Ax8-90 HAFB	1824		29. 8.90	(Stolen .91) Canx as WFU 16.4.98.
G-BSTA	BAe 146 Srs.100	E1002	G-6-002 ZS-NCA/G-BSTA/OE-BRL/G-BSTA/G-BPNP/N720BA/G-BPNP/N801RW/G-5-005/N101RW/G-SSHH/N5828B/G-5-146/G-OPSA/G-SSHH/(G-BIAE)	12. 7.88	To VH-NJV. Canx 4.9.95.
G-BSTB	Enstrom 280FX	2057		23. 8.90	To G-JOSY 10/90. Canx.
G-BSTC	Aeronca 11AC Chief	11AC-1660	N3289E NC3289E	15.10.90	(Damaged on take-off Henstridge 18.4.93) (On rebuild 12/95)
G-BSTD	Not allotted - "inappropriate sound".				
G-BSTE	Aerospatiale AS.355F2 Twin Squirrel	5453		29. 8.90	
G-BSTF	Beechcraft 300LW Super King Air	FA-101	G-UBSH(2)	30. 8.90	To HK-3654 8/91. Canx 22.1.91.
G-BSTG	Bell 206B JetRanger II	1771	G-RIKK N206BJ/N49596	7. 9.90	Damaged in arson attack at Sophia-Antipolis heliport in France on the night of 1/2.10.92. Canx as destroyed 16.2.93
G-BSTH	PA-25-235 Pawnee C	25-5009	N8599L	25. 9.90	(Port undercarriage collapsed on landing at Portmoak on 29.12.98)
G-BSTI	Piper J3C-85 Cub	19144	N6007H NC6007H	31. 8.90	
G-BSTJ	DH.82A Tiger Moth (Possibly ex R.Netherlands AF A-23 and thus c/n 86628 and PG472)	82309	OO-MEH OO-GEB/R.Netherlands AF A-13/PH-UFB/R.Netherlands AF A-13/N9192	6. 9.90	To G-DHZF 7/99. Canx.
G-BSTK	Thunder Ax8-90 HAFB	1838		17. 9.90	
G-BSTL	Rand Robinson KR-2	PFA/129-11863		6. 9.90	
G-BSTM	Cessna 172L Skyhawk	172-60143	N4243Q	25. 9.90	
G-BSTN	PA-31-350 Navajo Chieftain	31-7852069	N27589	30. 6.78	To N325SC 3/81. Canx 26.3.81.
G-BSTO	Cessna 152 II	152-82133	N68005	4. 9.90	
G-BSTP	Cessna 152 II	152-82925	N89953	4. 9.90	
G-BSTR	American Aviation AA-5 Traveler	AA5-0688	OO-ALR OO-HAN/(OO-WAZ)	8.10.90	
G-BSTS	Schleicher ASW-20L	20311	BGA.2618	10. 9.90	NTU - Remained as BGA.2618. Canx.
G-BSTT	Rans S-6 Coyote II	0190-115 & PFA/204-11880		5. 9.90	(Extensively damaged on force landing in a field at Stoke St. Milborough, near Ludlow on 3.1.93.)
G-BSTU	Cessna P.210N Pressurised Centurion II	P210-00045	N100PC (N3252P)	26.10.90	To N41KA 5/97. Canx 20.5.97.
G-BSTV	PA-32-300 Cherokee Six	32-40378	N4069R	13. 9.90	(Fuselage stored 9/94 at Popham)
G-BSTW	Luscombe 8A Silvaire	6561	N2134B NC2134B	10. 9.90	Struck cables while landing in a field at Borley Green, Southampton on 15.11.90. Canx as destroyed 8.1.91.
G-BSTX	Luscombe 8A Silvaire	3301	EI-CDZ G-BSTX/N71874/NC71874	10. 9.90	(On overhaul Armagh Field 6/97)
G-BSTY	Thunder Ax8-90 HAFB	394		12. 9.90	
G-BSTZ	PA-28-140 Cherokee Cruiser	28-7725153	N1674H	10.10.90	
G-BSUA(1)	Boeing 757-27B (Line No. 215)	24291	PH-ANK	. 9.90R	NTU - To G-OAHK 2/91. Canx.
G-BSUA(2)	Rans S-6 Coyote II	PFA/204-11910		29.10.90	
G-BSUB(1)	Boeing 757-27B (Line No. 178)	24137	PH-ANI OY-SHI/PH-ANI	. 9.90R	NTU - To G-OAHI 1/91. Canx.
G-BSUB(2)	Colt 77A HAFB	1801		30.10.90	
G-BSUC	Cameron A-120 HAFB	2361		13. 9.90	To D-HEKERMANN. Canx 31.10.90.

Regn	Type	c/n	Previous identity	Regn date	Fate or immediate subsequent identity (if known)
G-BSUD	Luscombe 8A Master	1745	N37084 NC37084	14. 9.90	
G-BSUE	Cessna U.206G Stationair 6 II	U206-04334	N756TB	6. 9.90	
G-BSUF	PA-32RT-300 Lance II	32R-7885240	N32PL ZP-PJQ/N9641N	17. 9.90	
G-BSUG	Bell 206B JetRanger III	2523	N888GC N222PF/N315GC	26. 9.90	To I-CHOP. Canx 30.11.90.
G-BSUH	Cessna 140	8092	N89088 NC89088	15.10.90	Badly damaged on take-off Gowran Grange in 6.93. Canx by CAA 28.4.95. (Stored 11/98 Abbeyshrule)
G-BSUI	Robinson R-22 Beta	1568		26.10.90	To VH-HLY 2/96. Canx 20.12.95.
G-BSUJ	Brugger MB.2 Colibri	PFA/43-10726		17. 9.90	
G-BSUK	Colt 77A HAFB	1374		21. 9.90	
G-BSUL	BAe 125 Srs.800B	258186	G-5-683 VR-BPM/G-5-683/VR-BPM/G-5-683/G-BSUL/G-5-683	17. 9.90	To G-5-683/N8186. Canx 4.5.94.
G-BSUM	Scheibe SF-27MB	6303	D-KIBE(2)	31.10.90	(Extant 4/97)
G-BSUN	Cameron N-56 HAFB	385		2. 3.78	To OO-BAX 7/80. Canx 24.4.80.
G-BSUO	Scheibe SF-25C Falke 2000	44501	D-KIOK	6.12.90	
G-BSUP	Schweizer 269C (300C)	S.1495		21. 9.90	To OO-SUP. Canx 21.10.92.
G-BSUR	Rotorway Exec 90	0002 & 5003		21. 9.90	Permit expired 1.12.93. (Stored 6/97 Sherburn-in-Elmet)
G-BSUS	Taylor JT.1 Monoplane	PFA/55-10413		28.12.78	Canx by CAA 2.9.91.
G-BSUT	Rans S-6-ESA Coyote II	0990-138 & PFA/204-11897		2.10.90	
G-BSUU	Colt 180A HAFB	1851		17. 9.90	
G-BSUV	Cameron O-77 HAFB	2407		26. 9.90	
G-BSUW	PA-34-200T Seneca II	34-7870081	N2360M	26. 9.90	
G-BSUX	Carlson Sparrow II	PFA/209-11794		5.10.90	(Stored 4/97)
G-BSUY	BAe 146 Srs.300QT	E3182		3.10.90	To G-TNTG 10/91. Canx.
G-BSUZ	Denney Kitfox Mk.3	745 & PFA/172-11875		10. 9.90	
G-BSVA	Christen A-1 Husky	1131	N9604X	2.10.90	To PH-ELT 5/96. Canx 9.5.96.
G-BSVB	PA-28-181 Archer II	2890098	N9155S	10. 9.90	
G-BSVC	Cameron A-210 HAFB	2402		1.10.90	To PH-JES 3/97. Canx 13.2.97.
G-BSVD	Not allocated.				
G-BSVE	Binder CP.301S Smargad	113	HB-SED	27. 9.90	
G-BSVF	PA-28-161 Warrior II	28-8416047	C-GVSJ N9575N	2.10.90	
G-BSVG	PA-28-161 Warrior II	28-8516013	C-GZAV	2.10.90	
G-BSVH	Piper J3C-75 Cub	15360	N87702 NC87702	2.10.90	
G-BSVI	PA-16 Clipper	16-186	N5379H	7.11.90	
G-BSVJ	Piper J3C-65 Cub	17521	N2MD N70515/NC70515	. .90R	(Extant as N2MD 7/96)
G-BSVK	Denney Kitfox Mk.2	PFA/172-11731		2.10.90	
G-BSVL	Cessna 560 Citation V	560-0077	N2745R	2.10.90	To C-GNND 12/92. Canx 15.12.92.
G-BSVM	PA-28-161 Warrior II	28-8116173	N8351N	7.11.90	
G-BSVN	Thorp T-18	107	N4881	17. 9.90	
G-BSVO	Sikorsky S-61N Mk.II	61-823	C-GROL	4.10.90	To ZS-RFU 4/95. Canx 17.3.95.
G-BSVP	PA-23-250 Aztec F	27-7754115	N63787	9. 2.78	
G-BSVR	Schweizer Hughes 269C (300C)	S.1236	OO-JWW D-HLEB	14.11.90	
G-BSVS	Robin DR.400/100 Cadet	2017		22.10.90	
G-BSVT	Embraer EMB.110P2 Bandeirante	110-153	G-BWTV PT-GLA	29.10.79	To N2932C 3/82. Canx.
G-BSVU	Stemme S-10	10-15	D-KGCS G-BSVU/D-KDLF	11.10.90	To OO-VHA. Canx 17.10.95.
G-BSVV	PA-38-112 Tomahawk	38-79A0723	N2492L	3.10.90	
G-BSVW	PA-38-112 Tomahawk	38-79A0149	N2606B	9.11.90	
G-BSVX	PA-38-112 Tomahawk	38-79A0950	N2336P	10. 1.91	
G-BSVY	PA-38-112 Tomahawk	38-79A0038	N2396B	10. 1.91	
G-BSVZ	Pietenpol Air Camper (Regd as a Pietenpol/Challis Chaffinch)(built by H.Challis)	1008	N3265	6.11.90	(Fuselage stored 5/98 Maypole Farm)
G-BSWA	Luscombe 8A Silvaire	2707	N71280 NC71280	5.10.90	Crashed and extensively damaged at Pewsey, Wiltshire on 5.7.98. Wreck stored at Wing Farm, Longbridge Deverill 10/98. Canx by CAA 2.10.98.
G-BSWB	Rans S-10 Sakota	0489-046 & PFA/194-11560		8.10.90	
G-BSWC	Boeing-Stearman E75 (PT-13D) Kaydet	75-5560	N17112 N5021V/42-17397	16.11.90	
G-BSWD	Cameron A-180 HAFB	2418		10.10.90	To C-FSWD. Canx 4.2.92.
G-BSWE	PA-18-150 Super Cub	18-8899	N9194P	23.10.90	Crashed on approach to the Farthing Corner strip, near Bedhurst on 25.9.92. Canx as WFU 18.1.93. Rebuilt & re-regd as G-HAHA in 8/94.
G-BSWF	PA-16 Clipper	16-475	N5865H	12.10.90	
G-BSWG	PA-15 Vagabond (Modified to PA-17 standard)	15-99	N4316H NC4316H	8.10.90	
G-BSWH	Cessna 152 II	152-81365	N49861	15.10.90	
G-BSWI	Rans S-10 Sakota	PFA/194-11872		16.10.90	(Badly damaged on take-off at Braehead, Forth on 26.10.93)
G-BSWJ	Cameron O-77 HAFB	2433		17.10.90	
G-BSWK	Robinson R-22 Beta	1567		26.10.90	Badly damaged in crash Hurn 13.6.97. Canx as PWFU 20.10.97.
G-BSWL	Slingsby T.61F Venture T.2	1974	EI-CCQ G-BSWL/ZA655	15.10.90	
G-BSWM	Slingsby T.61F Venture T.2	1965	ZA629	12.10.90	

Regn	Type	c/n	Previous identity	Regn date	Fate or immediate subsequent identity (if known)
G-BSWN	PBN BN-2T Turbine Islander (Originally regd as a BN-2B-26)	2242	(9J-...) G-BSWN	22.10.90	To AR-NYB/42 Pakistan Maritime Security Agency in 1/93. (Originally painted as ARNY-B in error) Canx 15.10.93.
G-BSWO	PBN BN-2B-26 Islander	2243		22.10.90	To D-ILFA(2) 7/91. Canx 8.7.91.
G-BSWP	PBN BN-2B-20 Islander (Originally regd as a BN-2B-26)	2244		22.10.90	To G-HPAA 8/91. Canx.
G-BSWR	PBN BN-2T Turbine Islander (Originally regd as a BN-2B-26)	2245		22.10.90	
G-BSWS	PBN BN-2T Turbine Islander (Originally regd as a BN-2B-26)	2246		22.10.90	To AR-NYC/46 Pakistan Maritime Security Agency 10/94. Canx 27.10.94.
G-BSWT	PBN BN-2B-26 Islander	2247	(9J-...) G-BSWT	22.10.90	To G-SSKY 5/92. Canx.
G-BSWU	PBN BN-2B-26 Islander	2248		22.10.90	To N203PR. Canx 7.10.91.
G-BSWV	Cameron N-77 HAFB	2369		22.10.90	
G-BSWW	Cameron O-105 HAFB	5507	N6069D	15.10.90	Canx as WFU 31.5.95.
G-BSWX	Cameron V-90 HAFB	2401		22.10.90	
G-BSWY	Cameron N-77 HAFB	2428		12.10.90	
G-BSWZ	Cameron A-180 HAFB	2419	C-FGWZ G-BSWZ	22.10.90	
G-BSXA	PA-28-161 Warrior II	28-8416121	N4373Z N9622N	11.12.90	
G-BSXB	PA-28-161 Warrior II	28-8416125	N4374D N9626N	4.12.90	
G-BSXC	PA-28-161 Warrior II	28-8416126	N4374F N9627N	4.12.90	
G-BSXD	Soko P-2 Kraguj	030	30146 Yugoslav Army	22.10.90	
G-BSXE	Bell 206B JetRanger II	1114	N40EA C-GMVM/N83150	19.10.90	To G-JWLS 1/99. Canx.
G-BSXF	Cameron A-180 HAFB	2400		24.10.90	To PH-WBS 6/96. Canx 7.5.96.
G-BSXG	Cessna 150K	150-71728	N6228G	29.10.90	To EI-CIN 9/93. Canx 18.8.93.
G-BSXH	Pitts S-1M Special (built by R.Merrick)	338-H	N14RM	30.10.90	To G-SWUN 4/95. Canx.
G-BSXI	Mooney M.20E Chapparal	700056	N6766V	31.10.90	
G-BSXJ	BAC One-Eleven Srs.401AK	063	N217CA C6-BDP/VP-BDP/N5023	1.11.90	Restored as N217CA 4/91. Canx 28.3.91.
G-BSXK	BAC One-Eleven Srs.401AK	089	N218CA C6-BDJ/VP-BDJ/N5043	1.11.90	To N97JF 3/91. Canx 28.3.91.
G-BSXL	BAe 146 Srs.300QT	E3186	G-6-186	15.11.90	To G-TNTK 1/92. Canx.
G-BSXM	Cameron V-77 HAFB	2446		5.11.90	
G-BSXN	Robinson R-22 Beta	1611		14.11.90	
G-BSXO	Robinson R-22 Beta	1635		14.11.90	To OO-PRE. Canx 12.7.91.
G-BSXP	Air Command 532 Elite	0633 & G/04-1195		5.11.90	
G-BSXR	Air Command 532 Elite	0203 & G/04-1192		31.10.90	No permit believed issued. Canx as WFU 16.12.97.
G-BSXS	PA-28-181 Archer II	28-7990151	N3055C	26.11.90	
G-BSXT(1)	Beechcraft B200 Super King Air	BB-1086		. .82R	NTU - To D-IBVO 12/82. Canx.
G-BSXT(2)	Piper J/5A Cub Cruiser	5-498	N33409 NC33409	8.11.90	(Stored 10/97)
G-BSXU	BAC One-Eleven Srs.407AW	093	YS-17C	1.11.90	NTU - To 5N-KBR. Canx 4.12.91.
G-BSXV	BAC One-Eleven Srs.407AW	BAC.106	YS-18C	1.11.90	NTU - To 5N-KBW. Canx 12.2.92.
G-BSXW	PA-28-161 Warrior II	28-8016130	N8119S	5.11.90	To G-JAVO 9/97. Canx.
G-BSXX	Whittaker MW.7	PFA/171-11469		16.10.90	
G-BSXY	Oldfield Baby Great Lakes	012 & PFA/10-10094	(G-JENY)	15.10.90	No Permit to Fly issued. Canx by CAA 16.4.99.
G-BSXZ	BAe 146 Srs.300	E3174	G-6-174	14.11.90	To B-1776 1/91. Canx 21.1.91.
G-BSYA	Jodel D.18	PFA/169-11316		7.11.90	
G-BSYB	Cameron N-120 HAFB	2406		7.11.90	
G-BSYC	PA-32R-300 Cherokee Lance	32R-7780159	N7745T N1435H	2. 4.91	
G-BSYD	Cameron A-180 HAFB	2426		18.10.90	
G-BSYE	Cessna 140	8216	D-ESYE (D-ETDS)/G-BSYE/N89196/NC89196	12.11.90	To D-ETJK 1/98. Canx 21.10.97.
G-BSYF	Luscombe 8A Silvaire	3455	N72028 NC72028	12.11.90	(Stored 7/95)
G-BSYG	PA-12 Super Cruiser	12-2106	N3228M NC3228M	12.11.90	
G-BSYH	Luscombe 8A Silvaire	2842	N71415 NC71415	13.11.90	
G-BSYI	Aerospatiale AS.355F1 Twin Squirrel	5197	M-MJI	14.11.90	
G-BSYJ	Cameron N-77 HAFB	2441		13.11.90	
G-BSYK	PA-38-112 Tomahawk II	38-81A0143	N23449	30. 1.91	No CofA issued. (On overhaul 2/97) Canx by CAA 10.3.99.
G-BSYL	PA-38-112 Tomahawk II	38-81A0172	N91333	23. 1.91	No CofA issued. (Stored 9/97) Canx by CAA 10.3.99.
G-BSYM	PA-38-112 Tomahawk II	38-82A0072	N2507V	30. 1.91	Damaged on 27.7.94. (Stored 3/99 Wellsbourne Mountford)
G-BSYN	BAC One-Eleven Srs.509EW	BAC.186	G-AWWZ	9. 4.90	To EI-CCW 4/91. Canx 12.4.91.
G-BSYO	Piper J3C-90 Cub (L-4B-PI) (Frame No.12639) (Officially regd as c/n 10244 ex 43-1383/F-BFYF which is HB-OVG)	12809	(G-BSMJ) (G-BRHE)/EC-AIY/HB-ODO/44-80513	19. 2.91	
G-BSYP	Bensen B.8MR Gyrocopter	G/01-1186		16.11.90	
G-BSYR	BAe 146 Srs.300	E3181	G-6-181	26.11.90	To G-6-181/HS-TBL. Canx 2.12.91.
G-BSYS	BAe 146 Srs.300	E3183	G-6-183	26.11.90	To G-6-183/G-BUHB 6/92. Canx.

Regn	Type	c/n	Previous identity	Regn date	Fate or immediate subsequent identity (if known)
G-BSYT	BAe 146 Srs.300	E3187	EC-FKF	26.11.90	To D-AHOI(2) 12/94. Canx 30.11.94.
			EC-899/G-6-187/G-BSYT/G-6-187		
G-BSYU	Robin DR.400/180 Regent	2027		26.11.90	
G-BSYV	Cessna 150M Commuter	150-78371	N9423U	16.11.90	
G-BSYW	Cessna 150M Commuter	150-78446	N9498U	16.11.90	
G-BSYX	Cessna 152 II	152-81065	N48946	16.11.90	Badly damaged in forced landing at Ince Blundell, near Formby on 5.6.94. Canx as destroyed 27.7.94. (Wreck at Ince Blundell 11/94)
G-BSYY	PA-28-161 Warrior II	2816009	N9100X	26.11.90	
G-BSYZ	PA-28-161 Warrior II	28-8516051	N6908H	22.11.90	
G-BSZA	Boeing 707-351B	18586	EL-SKD	20.11.90	To VR-BMV 3/92. Canx 29.11.91.
	(Line No. 345)		N351SR/N651TF/VR-CAO/VR-HGO/N353US		
G-BSZB	Stolp SA.300 Starduster Too	545	N5495M	3.12.90	
	(built by Mathews)				
G-BSZC	Beechcraft C-45H-BH Expeditor		N9541Z	14.12.90	
	(Originally built as	AF-258	51-11701		
	AT-7 42-2490 c/n 4166; remanufactured 4/52)				
G-BSZD	Robin DR.400/180 Regent	2029		21.11.90	
G-BSZE	Airbus A.300B4-203	192	SU-DAN	26.11.90	Restored as ZS-SDF. Canx 4.12.90.
			ZS-SDF/F-WWAN/C-GIZL/ZS-SDF/F-WZML		
G-BSZF	CEA Jodel DR.250/160 Capitaine	32	F-BNJB	29.11.90	
G-BSZG	Stolp SA.100 Starduster	101	N70P	27.11.90	
G-BSZH	Thunder Ax7-77 HAFB	1848		27.11.90	(Extant 2/97)
G-BSZI	Cessna 152 II	152-85856	N95139	17.12.90	
G-BSZJ	PA-28-181 Archer II	28-8190216	N8373Z	6.12.90	
G-BSZK	BAe Jetstream Srs.3102-09	761	I-BLUO	18.12.90	To G-LOGV 7/91. Canx.
			G-31-761		
G-BSZL	Colt 77A HAFB	1883		28.11.90	
G-BSZM	Montgomerie-Bensen B.8MR Gyrocopter	G/01-1193		30.11.90	
G-BSZN	Bucker Bu.133D-1 Jungmeister	2002	N8103	30.11.90	
	(built by Josef Bitz Flugzeugbau GmbH)		D-ECAY		
G-BSZO	Cessna 152 II	152-80221	N24334	30.11.90	
G-BSZP	Beechcraft 400 Beechjet	RJ-56	N1556W	12.11.90	To OK-UZI 12/92. Canx 18.12.93.
G-BSZR	PA-28RT-201T Turbo Arrow IV	28R-8131010	N8281B	25. 1.91	To D-ESEL 7/93. Canx 26.5.93.
G-BSZS	Robinson R-22 Beta	1235	N8058J	13.12.90	
G-BSZT	PA-28-161 Warrior II	28-8116027	N8260D	31.12.90	
G-BSZU	Cessna 150F Commuter	150-63481	N6881F	3.12.90	
G-BSZV	Cessna 150F Commuter	150-62304	N3504L	3.12.90	
G-BSZW	Cessna 152 II	152-81072	N48958	3.12.90	
G-BSZX	Cessna 150M Commuter	150-79288	(EI-...)	4.12.90	To EI-CHM 3/93. Canx 24.2.93.
			G-BSZX/N714MU		
G-BSZY	Cameron A-180 HAFB	2479		3. 1.91	
G-BSZZ	BAe 146 Srs.200	E2180	G-6-180	14.12.90	To OO-DJG. Canx 17.12.90.
G-BTAA	Embraer EMB.110P2 Bandeirante	110-256	G-BHJY	18. 5.90	To G-OEAA 1/94. Canx.
			PT-SAW		
G-BTAB	BAe 125 Srs.800B	258088	G-5-563	12. 7.88	
			G-BOOA/(ZK-RHP)/G-5-563		
G-BTAC	Douglas DC-8-54F	45768	N5768X	29. 7.77	To HK-2632X 4/81. Canx 29.4.81.
	(Line No. 240)		OB-R-1083/YV-C-VID		
G-BTAD	Macair Merlin	PFA/208-11661		6.11.90	No Permit to Fly issued. (Under construction 5/95) Canx by CAA 16.4.99.
G-BTAE	BAe 125 Srs.800B	258190	G-5-684	6.12.90	To G-5-684/PT-OHB 4/91. Canx 25.3.91.
G-BTAF	PA-28-181 Archer II	28-8490105	N137AV	11.12.90	Force landed at Hemlington, Cleveland on 23.3.94. Canx as destroyed 26.4.94. (Remains removed from Newcastle by road on 28.6.94, reported to be made into a base for a coffee table!)
G-BTAG	Cameron O-77 HAFB	2454		12.11.90	
G-BTAH	Bensen B.8M Gyrocopter	G/01-1186		13.12.90	
	(C/n officially given as G/07-1196)				
G-BTAI	BAe Jetstream Srs.3102	758	(OM-SKY)	18.12.90	To OY-MUE 9/95. Canx 13.9.95.
	(Originally regd as a Srs.3109)		G-BTAI/I-ALKD/G-BTAI/I-BLUI/G-31-758		
G-BTAJ	PA-34-200T Seneca II	34-7970440	N22MJ	19.12.90	To G-RVRB 2/97. Canx.
			N45113		
G-BTAK	EAA Acrosport 2	1-468	N440X	27.12.90	
	(built by A.P.Savage)				
G-BTAL	Reims Cessna F.152 II	1444		7. 4.78	
G-BTAM	PA-28-181 Archer II	2890093	N9153D	10. 1.91	
G-BTAN	Thunder Ax7-65Z HAFB	517		4. 5.83	
G-BTAO	Cameron A-180 HAFB	2455		17.12.90	To F-GHDN(2) 6/91. Canx 21.1.91.
G-BTAP	PA-38-112 Tomahawk	38-78A0141	N9603T	8. 1.91	
G-BTAR	PA-38-112 Tomahawk	38-79A0383	N2584D	13. 2.91	
G-BTAS	PA-38-112 Tomahawk	38-79A0545	F-GTAS	21. 2.91	
			G-BTAS/N2492G		
G-BTAT	Denney Kitfox Mk.2	689 & PFA/172-11832		6.11.90	
G-BTAU	Thunder Ax7-77 HAFB	1429		13.12.90	
G-BTAV	Colt 105A HAFB	1858		13.12.90	
G-BTAW	PA-28-161 Warrior II	28-8616031	N9259T	14.12.90	
G-BTAX	PA-31-350 Navajo Chieftain	31-7752036	N63721	3. 9.87	Canx by CAA 17.1.94. (To Canada by container 7/97)
G-BTAY	[Was reserved for engine manufacturer]				

Regn	Type	c/n	Previous identity	Regn date	Fate or immediate subsequent identity (if known)
G-BTAZ	Evans VP-2	PFA/63-11474		13.12.90	
G-BTBA	Robinson R-22 Beta	1717		18. 3.91	
G-BTBB	Thunder Ax8-105 Srs.2 HAFB	1871		23.11.90	
G-BTBC	PA-28-161 Warrior II	28-7916414	N28755	19.12.90	
G-BTBD	MBB Bo.105D	S.60	VH-LCS VH-HRM/G-BCDH/ EC-DUO/G-BCDH/D-HDBK	18.12.90	Landed on the deck of a supply ship off the west coast of Scotland on 30.8.91, and sucked up some plastic sheeting into the main rotors, distorting the airframe. To G-BUDP 3/92. Canx as WFU 6.3.92.
G-BTBE	PA-34-200T Seneca II	34-7770416	N831SR	.12.90R	NTU - Remained as N831SR. Canx.
G-BTBF	Fisher FP.202 Super Koala	SK.067 & PFA/158-11954	G-MWOZ	24.12.90	(Nearing completion 1/98 off airfield)
G-BTBG	Denney Kitfox	PFA/172-11845		18.12.90	
G-BTBH	Ryan ST3KR (PT-22-RY)	2063	N854 N50993/41-20854	18. 2.91	
G-BTBI	WAR P-47 Thunderbolt Replica (Marked as Project No. 52685A) (built by D.R.Linkous, in ½ scale)	0054	N47DL	8. 1.91	
G-BTBJ	Cessna 195B	16046	N4461C	2.10.91	
G-BTBK	Cessna 152 II	152-82677	N89218	8. 1.91	To D-ETBK 2/93. Canx 25.1.93.
G-BTBL	Montgomerie-Bensen B.8MR Merlin	G/01A-1183		21.12.90	
G-BTBM	Grumman TBM-3W2 Avenger	-	045 Dutch Navy/Dutch Navy P-102/BuA.85650	23.12.77	To N61BD 4/86. Canx 22.7.85.
G-BTBN	Denney Kitfox Mk.2	686 & PFA/172-11859		31.12.90	
G-BTBO	Cameron N-77 HAFB	2457		21.12.90	To SP-B.. 4/97. Canx 10.4.97. (Possibly to SP-BWU)
G-BTBP	Cameron N-90 HAFB	2464		21.12.90	
G-BTBR	Cameron DP-80 Hot-Air Airship	2344		21.12.90	
G-BTBS	Cameron N-180 HAFB	2440		21.12.90	Canx as WFU 2.12.98.
G-BTBT	PA-32R-301 Saratoga SP	32R-8113083	N84089	23.11.87	To N37BT 5/94. Canx 2.2.94.
G-BTBU	PA-18-150 Super Cub	18-7509010	N9665P	3. 1.91	
G-BTBV	Cessna 140	12727	N2474N NC2474N	2. 4.91	
G-BTBW	Cessna 120	14220	N2009V NC2009V	24. 1.91	
G-BTBX	Piper J3C-65 Cub	6334	N35367 NC35367	29. 1.91	
G-BTBY	PA-17 Vagabond	17-195	N4894H NC4894H	4. 1.91	
G-BTBZ	Cessna 172B Skyhawk	172-47968	ZS-CPJ N7468X	3. 1.91	To (N4277P)/N7468X 5/91. Canx 30.4.91.
G-BTCA	PA-32R-300 Cherokee Lance	32R-7780381	N5941V	10. 1.91	
G-BTCB	Air Command 582 Sport	0634 & G/04-1198		9. 1.91	(Nearing completion 5/95)
G-BTCC	Grumman F6F-5K Hellcat (Composite with centre section from F6F-3 BuA.08831 c/n A-218)	A-11286	(N10CN) N100TF/N80142/BuA.80141	31.12.90	
G-BTCD	North American P-51D-25NA Mustang	122-39608	N51JJ N6340T/RCAF 9568/44-73149	11. 1.91	
G-BTCE	Cessna 152 II (Tailwheel conversion)	152-81376	N49876	10. 1.91	
G-BTCF	CFM Streak Shadow	PFA/206-11966	(5X-...) G-BTCF	9. 1.91	To 5H-... 7/95. Canx 28.7.95.
G-BTCG	PA-23-250 Aztec C	27-3646	G-AVRX N6438Y	21. 6.82	To 5Y-BIB 4/91. Canx 16.4.91.
G-BTCH	Luscombe 8E Silvaire	6403	N1976B NC1976B	11. 2.91	
G-BTCI	PA-17 Vagabond	17-136	N4839H NC4839H	11. 1.91	
G-BTCJ	Luscombe 8AE Silvaire	1869	N41908 NC41908	16. 1.91	(For rebuild 2/98 Chilbolton)
G-BTCK	Cameron A-210 HAFB	2451		8. 1.91	
G-BTCL	Cameron A-210 HAFB	2437		8. 1.91	To ZS-HZD 8/96. Canx 27.6.96.
G-BTCM	Cameron N-90 HAFB	1306	(G-BMPW)	8. 5.86	
G-BTCN	Cameron A-300 HAFB	1827		10. 1.91	To 5N-... 6/94. Canx 29.6.94.
G-BTCO	Clutton-Tabenor FRED Srs.II	PFA/29-10558		11. 1.91	
G-BTCP	BAe 146 Srs.200	E2178	I-FLRW G-BTCP/G-6-178	24. 1.91	To VH-NJH 8/94. Canx 25.8.94.
G-BTCR	Rans S-10 Sakota	PFA/194-11877		11. 1.91	(Stored 4/96)
G-BTCS	Colt 90A HAFB	1895		11. 1.91	
G-BTCT	Aerospatiale AS.332L Super Puma	2129	1012 Panama AF	14. 1.91	
G-BTCU	WSK-PZL Antonov AN-2T	1G52-21	SP-FDS Polish AF 5221	25. 2.91	To YN-... Canx 24.9.98.
G-BTCV	Cameron V-90 HAFB	2504		17. 1.91	To G-IWON 2/92. Canx.
G-BTCW	Cameron A-180 HAFB	2458		17. 1.91	
G-BTCX	Hawker Hunter F.4	HABL-003129	7949M XF974	22. 1.91	(Stored 9/91 Hayes) To USA. Canx by CAA 10.3.99.
G-BTCY	Hawker Hunter F.4	HABL-003080	7849M XF319	22. 1.91	(Stored 11/92) To USA. Canx by CAA 10.3.99.
G-BTCZ	Cameron Chateau 84SS HAFB	2246		18. 1.91	

Regn	Type	c/n	Previous identity	Regn date	Fate or immediate subsequent identity (if known)
G-BTDA	Slingsby T.61F Venture T.2 (Regd as a Slingsby T.61G)	1870	XZ550	17. 4.91	
G-BTDB	Cameron A-180 HAFB	2353		24. 1.91	To SU-... 7/93. Canx 14.7.93.
G-BTDC	Denney Kitfox Mk.2	405 & PFA/172-11483		11. 1.91	
G-BTDD	CFM Streak Shadow	K.127-SA & PFA/161A-11622		14. 1.91	
G-BTDE	Cessna C-165 Airmaster	551	N21911 NC21911	18. 1.91	
G-BTDF	Luscombe 8AF Silvaire	2205	N45678 NC45678	17. 4.91	(Damaged in forced landing nr.Newcastle 11.4.93) (Stored 5/93) (Project for sale 1/96)
G-BTDG	Colt 105A HAFB	1850		24. 1.91	Canx by CAA 10.3.95.
G-BTDH	Hunting-Percival P.56 Provost T.1 (Also reported as P56/183)	PAC/F/183	N2416R 7925M/WV666	25. 1.91	
G-BTDI	Robinson R-22 Beta	1670		29. 1.91	
G-BTDJ	Cessna T.303 Crusader	T303-00048	I-BELT N377CB/(N377GS)/N377CB/N9839T	28. 3.91	To D-ITOL 3/93. Canx 12.1.93.
G-BTDK	Cessna 421B Golden Eagle II	421B-0654	OY-BFA N1558G	10. 8.77	To G-HASI 2/98. Canx.
G-BTDL	DHC.2 Beaver AL.1	1450	XP779	21. 1.91	To G-DHCB 6/91. Canx.
G-BTDM	DHC.2 Beaver AL.1	1648	XV268	21. 1.91	To G-BVER 8/91. Canx.
G-BTDN	Denney Kitfox Mk.2	688 & PFA/172-11826		22. 1.91	
G-BTDO	BAe 146 Srs.200QC	E2188	G-6-188	31. 1.91	To F-GLNI 10/91. Canx 3.10.91.
G-BTDP	Grumman TBM-3R Avenger	3381	N3966A BuA.53319	5. 2.91	
G-BTDR	Aero Designs Pulsar	PFA/202-11962		24. 1.91	
G-BTDS	Colt 77A HAFB	1897		29. 1.91	
G-BTDT	CASA I-131E Jungmann Srs.2000	2131	E3B-505 Spanish AF	5. 2.91	
G-BTDU	Robin DR.400/180 Regent	2047		6. 2.91	To VR-BNU 5/93. Canx 27.5.93.
G-BTDV	PA-28-161 Warrior II	28-7816355	N3548M	25. 2.91	
G-BTDW	Cessna 152 II	152-79864	N757NC	25. 2.91	
G-BTDX	PA-18-150 Super Cub	18-7809098	N62595	28. 1.91	
G-BTDY	PA-18-150 Super Cub	18-8109007	N24570	28. 1.91	DBF at Stoneacre Farm in 1993, major parts used in rebuild of G-HAHA in 1994/95.
G-BTDZ	CASA I-131E Jungmann Srs.2000	2104	E3B-524 Spanish AF	5. 2.91	
G-BTEA	Cameron N-105 HAFB	284		31. 5.77	
G-BTEB	Boeing 737-2M8 (Line No. 557)	21736	OO-TEL TC-ATU/OO-TEL/PH-RAL/OO-TEL/4X-ABL/OO-TEL	10. 3.89	To G-IBTX 11/90. Canx.
G-BTEC	Boeing 737-229 (Line No. 352)	20908	OO-SDB (OO-TEZ)/OO-SDB	27. 4.89	Restored as OO-SDB. Canx 29.3.90.
G-BTED	Boeing 737-229 (Line No. 353)	20909	OO-SDC	17. 5.89	Restored as OO-SDC. Canx 19.4.90.
G-BTEE	Cameron O-120 HAFB	2499		24. 1.91	
G-BTEF	Pitts S-1 Special (built by Brewer)	515H	N88PR	19. 2.91	
G-BTEG	Taylorcraft BC-65	2231	N27590 NC27590	31. 1.91	To EI-CES 3/92. Canx 2.1.92.
G-BTEH	Colt 77A HAFB	1864		31. 1.91	Canx by CAA 10.3.95. Noted flying in Croatia in 12.98 still marked G-BTEH. To become 9A-OA. /99.
G-BTEI	Everett Campbell Cricket Gyroplane Srs.3	023		31. 1.91	Damaged in forced landing nr.Great Orton 15.8.95. Stored 8/98 at Portmoak.
G-BTEJ	Boeing 757-208 (Line No. 368)	25085	(TF-FIJ)	23. 5.91	Restored as TF-FIJ. Canx 26.5.93.
G-BTEK	Socata TB-20 Trinidad	1240		4. 2.91	
G-BTEL	CFM Streak Shadow	K.125-SA & PFA/206-11667		31. 1.91	
G-BTEM	CFM Streak Shadow	K.166-SA		5. 2.91	To G-MWPP 14.2.91. Canx.
G-BTEN	Thunder Ax7-77 Srs.1 HAFB	1804	(D-O...) G-BTEN	21. 1.91	To D-OTEN 9/94. Canx 9.9.94.
G-BTEO	Cameron V-90 HAFB	2490		31. 1.91	CofA expired 12.6.93. To SX-... Canx by CAA 9.12.96.
G-BTEP	Cameron DP-80 Hot Air Airship	2439		31. 1.91	CofA expired 12.6.93. To SX-... Canx by CAA 9.12.96.
G-BTER	Cessna 150J	150-70519	N60713	4. 2.91	Crashed near Bembridge on 22.4.93. Canx by CAA 17.8.93. Scrapped in 1995.
G-BTES	Cessna 150H	150-68371	N22575	29. 4.91	
G-BTET	Piper J3C-65 Cub	18296	N98141 NC98141	5. 2.91	
G-BTEU	Aerospatiale AS.365N2 Dauphin 2	6392		11. 2.91	
G-BTEV	PA-38-112 Tomahawk	38-78A0025	N9315T	13. 2.91	
G-BTEW	Cessna 120	10238	CF-ELE	29. 4.91	
G-BTEX	PA-28-140 Cherokee	28-23773	CF-XXL N3907X	24. 4.91	
G-BTEY	Cameron Phone SS HAFB (Motorola Microtac Mobile Phone shape)	2505		26. 3.91	To G-PHON 12/91. Canx.
G-BTEZ	Thunder Ax8-90 Srs.1 HAFB	1945		26. 3.91	To D-OAVA 6/92. Canx 8.6.92.
G-BTFA	Denney Kitfox Mk.2	566 & PFA/172-11520		13. 2.91	(Damaged taxying North Moreton 18.6.97)
G-BTFB	Cameron DG-14 Gas Airship	2527		13. 2.91	
G-BTFC	Reims Cessna F.152 II	1668		23. 5.79	

Regn	Type	c/n	Previous identity	Regn date	Fate or immediate subsequent identity (if known)
G-BTFD	Colt AS-105 Mk.II Hot-Air Airship	1856		13. 2.91	
G-BTFE	Bensen-Parsons Two Seat Gyroplane Model 1 (Possibly Parsons Tandem Trainer)	38		13. 2.91	
G-BTFF	Cessna T.310R II	310R-0718	N1363G	25. 2.91	
G-BTFG	Boeing-Stearman A75N1 (N2S-4) Kaydet	75-3441	N4467N BuA.30010	20. 2.91	
G-BTFH	Cessna 414A Chancellor II	414A-0065	(OO-LFL) (N4674N)	1. 8.78	To G-BTSG 11/87. Canx.
G-BTFI	Colt 180A HAFB	1894		13. 2.91	Canx 24.12.91 on sale to Germany. To HB-BXZ 5/93.
G-BTFJ	PA-15 Vagabond	15-159	N4373H NC4373H	13. 2.91	
G-BTFK	Taylorcraft BC-12D	10540	N599SB N5240M	13. 2.91	
G-BTFL	Aeronca 11AC Chief	11AC-1727	N3403E NC3403E	18. 2.91	
G-BTFM	Cameron O-105 HAFB	2623		12. 8.91	
G-BTFN	Beechcraft F33C Bonanza	CJ-135	PH-BNF	27. 2.91	To N249SL 3/97. Canx 24.2.97.
G-BTFO	PA-28-161 Warrior II	28-7816580	N31728	12. 3.91	
G-BTFP	PA-38-112 Tomahawk	38-78A0340	N6201A	17. 4.91	
G-BTFR	Colt AS-105 Hot-Air Airship	632	OY-BOJ	19. 2.91	Canx as WFU 11.6.97.
G-BTFS	Cessna A.150M Aerobat	A150-0719	N20331	20. 2.91	
G-BTFT	Beechcraft 95-58 Baron	TH-979	N2036W	14. 3.91	
G-BTFU	Cameron N-90 HAFB	2391		28. 2.91	
G-BTFV	Whittaker MW.7	PFA/171-11722		8. 2.91	
G-BTFW	Montgomerie-Bensen B.8MR Gyrocopter	G/01A-1141		20. 2.91	
G-BTFX	Bell 206B JetRanger II	1648	N400MH N90219	20. 2.91	
G-BTFY	Bell 206B JetRanger II	1714	N49590	20. 2.91	
G-BTFZ	Cameron A-120 HAFB	2526		20. 2.91	To PH-UNL 3/95. Canx 6.1.95.
G-BTGA	Boeing-Stearman A75N1 (PT-17) Kaydet	75-3132	N65501 41-25625	21. 2.91	
G-BTGB	Robinson R-22 Beta	1719		18. 3.91	To G-HIPO 9/92. Canx.
G-BTGC	PA-38-112 Tomahawk	38-78A0120	N9507T	5. 3.91	To G-CWFA 8/99. Canx.
G-BTGD	Rand-Robinson KR-2	PFA/129-11150		22. 2.91	
G-BTGE	PA-28-181 Archer II	28-7890419	(PH-...) G-BTGE/N9514C	5. 3.91	To PH-BEG 11/93. Canx 8.10.93.
G-BTGF	Cessna 172P Skyhawk	172-75132	N55195	25. 2.91	To OK-MLA. Canx 3.7.91.
G-BTGG	Rans S-10 Sakota	PFA/194-11944		20. 2.91	
G-BTGH	Cessna 152 II	152-81048	N48919	2. 4.91	
G-BTGI	Rearwin 175 Skyranger	1517	N32308 NC32308	26. 2.91	
G-BTGJ	Smith DSA-1 Miniplane (built by S.J.Malovic)	NM.II	N1471	25. 3.91	(Status uncertain)
G-BTGK	PA-28-161 Warrior II	28-8416054	N4344C	28. 2.91	To G-BXAB 10/96. Canx.
G-BTGL	Light Aero Avid Speed Wing	PFA/189-11885		27. 2.91	
G-BTGM	Aeronca 7AC Champion	7AC-3665	N84943 NC84943	11. 3.91	
G-BTGN	Cessna 310R II	310R-1541	N5331C	3. 4.91	
G-BTGO	PA-28-140 Cherokee D	28-7125613	N1998T	20. 2.91	
G-BTGP	Cessna 150M Commuter	150-78921	N704WA	28. 2.91	
G-BTGR	Cessna 152 II	152-84447	N6581L	28. 2.91	
G-BTGS(1)	Smyth Sidewinder	PFA/92-10443		8. 1.79	NTU - Not built. Canx by CAA 30.9.87.
G-BTGS(2)	Stolp SA.300 Starduster Too	EAA/50553 & PFA/35-10076	G-AYMA	30. 9.87	
G-BTGT	CFM Streak Shadow	K.164-SA & PFA/206-11964	G-MWPY	1. 3.91	
G-BTGU	PA-34-220T Seneca III	34-8233106	N999PW N8160V	1. 3.91	
G-BTGV	PA-34-200T Seneca II	34-7970077	N3004H	26. 3.91	
G-BTGW	Cessna 152 II	152-79812	N757KY	5. 3.91	
G-BTGX	Cessna 152 II	152-84950	N5462P	5. 3.91	
G-BTGY	PA-28-161 Warrior II	28-8216199	N209FT N9574N	5. 3.91	
G-BTGZ	PA-28-181 Archer II	28-7890160	N47956	8. 4.91	
G-BTHA	Cessna 182P Skylane	182-63420	N2932P	22. 3.91	
G-BTHB	Bell 212	30614	74-603 Peruvian AF	6. 3.91	Canx by CAA 28.5.93.
G-BTHC	Bell 212	31194	H-31 Chilean AF	6. 3.91	To C-FBHY 3/91. Canx 6.3.91.
G-BTHD	Yakolev Yak-3U (Conversion of LET Yak C.11)	170101	(France) Egyptian AF-533	7. 3.91	(Stored 7/99 Duxford)
G-BTHE	Cessna 150L	150-75340	N11348	7. 3.91	
G-BTHF	Cameron V-90 HAFB	2543		7. 3.91	
G-BTHG	Robinson R-22 Beta	1709		8. 3.91	To EI-CFE 5/91. Canx 3.4.91.
G-BTHH	CEA Jodel DR.100A Ambassadeur	5	F-BJCH	28. 2.91	
G-BTHI	Robinson R-22 Beta	1732		26. 3.91	
G-BTHJ	Evans VP-2	PFA/63-10901		14. 3.91	(Near completion 8/92)
G-BTHK	Thunder Ax7-77 HAFB	1906		11. 3.91	

Regn	Type	c/n	Previous identity	Regn date	Fate or immediate subsequent identity (if known)
G-BTHL	PA-31-350 Navajo Chieftain	31-7952015	LN-FOA G-BTHL/N27874	23. 1.79	To ZS-MRC. Canx 5.1.90.
G-BTHM	Thunder Ax8-105 HAFB	1925		11. 3.91	
G-BTHN	Murphy Renegade 912	384 & PFA/188-12005		12. 3.91	
G-BTHO	Aerospatiale AS.350B Ecureuil	1330	N58019 N6363F/N58019	2. 4.91	To EC-727. Canx 24.4.91.
G-BTHP	Thorp T.211	101		13. 6.91	
G-BTHR	Socata TB-10 Tobago	1296		13. 3.91	
G-BTHS	PA-23-250 Aztec F	27-7754059	N62824	3.11.77	To G-WSFT 6/86. Canx.
G-BTHT	BAe 146 Srs.300QT	E3194	N599MP G-6-194/G-BTHT	28. 3.91	To VH-NJM(2) 11/95. Canx 28.11.95.
G-BTHU	Light Aero Avid Flyer	PFA/189-11427		14. 3.91	(Damaged following engine failure on second test flight Field Head Farm, Denholme 7.6.92) (On rebuild Field Head Farm, Denholme, Bradford 5/95)
G-BTHV	MBB Bo.105DBS-4	S.855	D-HMBV(4) G-BTHV/D-HFHM	20. 3.91	
G-BTHW	Beechcraft F33C Bonanza	CJ-130	PH-BNA N23787	18. 3.91	
G-BTHX	Colt 105A HAFB	1939		18. 3.91	
G-BTHY	Bell 206B JetRanger III	2290	N6606M VH-BIQ/ZK-HBQ(2)/DQ-FEN/ZK-HLU	20. 3.91	To HA-LFD. (Yet to be canx)
G-BTHZ	Cameron V-56 HAFB	486	OO-BBC	20. 3.91	(Active 9/95 - still wearing OO-BBC)
G-BTIA	BAe 146 Srs.200QC	E2148	ZS-NCB(3) G-BTIA/G-6-148/G-PRIN	27. 3.91	To G-ZAPK 4/96. Canx.
G-BTIB	Dassault Falcon 900B	109	F-WWFB	20.12.91	To Belgium AF as CD-01. Canx 23.1.95.
G-BTIC	PA-22-150 Tri-Pacer	22-6780	N9988D (N702DE)/N9988D	25. 3.91	(Badly damaged on take-off Newhouse Farm, Birds Edge, Huddersfield 24.4.93)
G-BTID	PA-28-161 Warrior II	28-8116036	N82647	25. 6.91	
G-BTIE	Socata TB-10 Tobago	187		30. 3.81	
G-BTIF	Denney Kitfox Mk.3	684 & PFA/172-11862		27. 2.91	
G-BTIG	Montgomerie-Bensen B.8MR Gyrocopter	G/01-1093		21. 3.91	
G-BTIH	PA-28-151 Cherokee Warrior	28-7615315	N6158J	20. 3.91	
G-BTII	American Aviation AA-5B Tiger	AA5B-1256	N4560S	5. 6.91	
G-BTIJ	Luscombe 8E Silvaire	5194	N2467K NC2467K	3. 4.91	
G-BTIK	Cessna 152 II	152-82993	N46068	26. 3.91	
G-BTIL	PA-38-112 Tomahawk	38-80A0004	N24730	26. 3.91	(Stored 4/96 Eaglescott)
G-BTIM	PA-28-161 Cadet	2841159	(SE-KIO) N9185D	24. 8.89	
G-BTIN	Cessna 150C	150-59905	N7805Z	26. 3.91	(Stored 3/99 Cumbernauld)
G-BTIO	SNCAN Stampe SV-4C	303	N73NS F-BCLC	28. 3.91	
G-BTIP	Denney Kitfox Mk.3	850 & PFA/172-11973		5. 3.91	Badly damaged in take-off crash at Wadswick Manor Farm, Avon on 31.5.92. Canx by CAA 16.4.99.
G-BTIR	Denney Kitfox Mk.2	PFA/172-11952		26. 3.91	
G-BTIS	Aerospatiale AS.355F1 Twin Squirrel	5261	G-TALI	10. 4.91	
G-BTIT	Not allotted.				
G-BTIU	Socata MS.892A Rallye Commodore 150	10914	F-BPQS	7. 5.91	
G-BTIV	PA-28-161 Warrior II	28-8116044	N82697	10. 5.91	
G-BTIW	CEA Jodel DR.1050/M1 Sicile Record	618	F-BMPV	28. 6.91	Extensively damaged in crash at Westbury-sub-Mendip 1.7.94. Canx as destroyed 5.9.94. (Stored 9/96 Crosland Moor)
G-BTIX	Cameron V-77 HAFB	2087		27. 3.91	
G-BTIY	Robinson R-22 Beta	1731		27. 3.91	To D-HUFI. Canx 20.11.91.
G-BTIZ	Cameron A-105 HAFB	2546		11. 3.91	
G-BTJA	Luscombe 8E Silvaire	5037	N2310K NC2310K	4. 4.91	
G-BTJB	Luscombe 8E Silvaire	6194	N1567B NC1567B	4. 4.91	
	(There has been a report that G-BTJA is, in fact, ex NC1567B, suggesting the identities of G-BTJA/BTJB were exchanged on conversion)				
G-BTJC	Luscombe 8F Silvaire	6589	N2162B	4. 4.91	
G-BTJD	Thunder Ax8-90 Srs.2 HAFB	1865		28. 3.91	
G-BTJE	Hiller UH-12E4	2520	N9731C CF-UVC/N9731C	11. 4.91	Control was lost after a duck struck the tail rotor & then struck power lines and crashed at Aber Falls, approx. 5 miles east of Bangor, North Wales on 15.3.95. (Wreck stored 2/97 Gamlingay) Canx as PWFU 19.1.99.
G-BTJF	Thunder Ax10-180 Srs.2 HAFB	1952		28. 3.91	
G-BTJG	BAe 146 Srs.300	E3163	HB-IXY G-BTJG/G-3-163/G-BTJG/EC-FIU/EC-876/G-BTJG/G-6-163/N885DV/G-6-163	12. 4.91	To D-AEWA 2/96. Canx 21.3.96.
G-BTJH	Cameron O-77 HAFB	2559		3. 4.91	
G-BTJI	Beechcraft F33C Bonanza	CJ-147	PH-BNO	3. 4.91	To N249WH 12/95. Canx 22.12.95.
G-BTJJ	PA-38-112 Tomahawk	38-79A0140	N2593B	3. 4.91	Crashed on take-off & DBR Welshpool 29.5.96. Canx as destroyed 27.11.96. Fuselage stored 3/98 at Liverpool.
G-BTJK	PA-38-112 Tomahawk	38-79A0838	N2427N	3. 4.91	(Substantially damaged on abandoned take-off at Thruxton on 22.6.96.)
G-BTJL	PA-38-112 Tomahawk	38-79A0863	N2477N	3. 4.91	

Regn	Type	c/n	Previous identity	Regn date	Fate or immediate subsequent identity (if known)
G-BTJM	Taylor JT.2 Titch	PFA/3220		9. 3.78	To G-CAPT(2) 4/89. Canx.
G-BTJN	Montgomerie-Bensen B.8MR Gyrocopter	G/01-1194		3. 4.91	
G-BTJO	Thunder Ax9-140 HAFB	1948		3. 4.91	
G-BTJP	Robinson R-22 Beta	1739		5. 4.91	To G-IJRC 10/91. Canx.
G-BTJR	Short SD.3-30 Var.100	SH3029	SE-IVX	21.11.85	To VH-LST 12/89. Canx 19.12.89.
			G-BTJR/G-BGNA/G-14-3029		
G-BTJS	Montgomerie-Bensen B.8MR Gyrocopter	G/01-1083		8. 4.91	
G-BTJT	BAe 146 Srs.300	E3128	G-6-212	26. 4.91	To G-JEAM 5/93. Canx.
			G-BTJT/HS-TBK/G-11-128		
G-BTJU	Cameron V-90 HAFB	2554		8. 4.91	
G-BTJV	PZL SZD-50-3 Puchacz	B-2025	BGA.3725	17. 4.91	(Extant unmarked 1/93)
G-BTJW	Colt 120A HAFB	1940		9. 4.91	Canx 1.6.92. To N237TC 4/93.
G-BTJX	Rans S-10 Sakota	PFA/194-12014		9. 4.91	(Nearing completion 5/97)
G-BTJY	Bell 212	30739	N211NK	15. 4.91	To C-FNMP. Canx 26.4.93.
			PT-HIA		
G-BTJZ	Taylorcraft BC-12-D1	10176	N44376	10. 4.91	To F-AZTC 4/96. Canx 9.8.95.
			NC44376		
G-BTKA	Piper J/5A Cub Cruiser	5-954	N38403	11. 4.91	(On rebuild off-strip 3/97)
			NC38403		
G-BTKB	Murphy Renegade Spirit	376 & PFA/188-11876		11. 4.91	
G-BTKC	BAe 146 Srs.200	E2184	I-FLRV	24. 4.91	To VH-NJJ 8/94. Canx 26.8.94.
			G-BTKC/G-6-184		
G-BTKD	Denney Kitfox Mk.4	853 & PFA/172-11941		15. 4.91	
	(Denney c/n erroneous and conflicts with N653CP)				
G-BTKE	Colt 90A HAFB	1655		16. 4.91	To Canx 6.4.94 on sale to USA.
G-BTKF	Thunder Ax7-77 HAFB	1881		16. 4.91	To ZS-HYN. Canx 22.10.92.
G-BTKG	Light Aero Avid Flyer	PFA/189-12037		16. 4.91	
G-BTKH	Colt GA-42 Gas Airship	1143		16. 4.91	Canx by CAA 10.3.95.
G-BTKI	North American T-6G-NF Texan	197-88		17. 4.91	(On rebuild 3/96)
	(C/n also quoted as FO-8002-088)		French AF 534592 "RA"/53-4592		
G-BTKJ	Grumman G-44 Widgeon (J4F-2)	1317	5N-AMG	14. 5.91	Restored as N67867 7/95. Canx 20.7.95.
			N67867/5N-AMD/N67867/Bu.32963		
G-BTKK	Colt 240A HAFB	1951		18. 4.91	To D-OTKK 5/93. Canx 6.4.93.
G-BTKL	MBB Bo.105DB-4	S-422	D-HDMU	2. 5.91	
			Swedish Army/D-HDMU		
G-BTKM	Cameron V-90 HAFB	2524		24. 4.91	To D-MAGNUS. Canx 28.4.92.
G-BTKN	Cameron O-120 HAFB	2579		24. 4.91	To OO-BQQ 2/98. Canx 6.1.98.
G-BTKO	Cameron A-180 HAFB	2562		24. 4.91	To D-OKPC. Canx 16.6.95.
G-BTKP	CFM Streak Shadow	PFA/206-12036		24. 4.91	
G-BTKR	Cameron O-105 HAFB	2529		24. 4.91	To D-BIELEFELD. Canx 16.1.92.
G-BTKS	Rans S-10 Sakota	PFA/194-11861		9. 7.91	(Badly damaged in forced landing at Insch on 19.8.93) (Stored 7/94)
G-BTKT	PA-28-161 Warrior II	28-8216218	N429FT	9. 5.91	Damaged in forced landing nr.Shoreham 8.8.95.
			N9606N		(Status uncertain)
G-BTKU	Cameron A-105 HAFB	2574		25. 4.91	To D-OTKU 6/96. Canx 2.4.96.
G-BTKV	PA-22-160 Tri-Pacer	22-7157	N3216Z	25. 4.91	
G-BTKW	Cameron O-105 HAFB	2566		25. 4.91	
G-BTKX	PA-28-181 Archer II	28-7890146	N47866	14. 5.91	
G-BTKY	PA-28-181 Archer II	28-7990518	N2877D	28. 6.91	To OY-RLN 5/96. Canx 28.3.96.
G-BTKZ	Cameron V-77 HAFB	2573		26. 4.91	
G-BTLA	Sikorsky S-76B	760367		22. 4.91	
G-BTLB	Wassmer WA.52 Europa	42	F-BTLB	17. 4.89	
G-BTLC	Aerospatiale AS.365N2 Dauphin 2	6406		22. 4.91	To MOD as ZJ164. Canx.
G-BTLD	BAe 146 Srs.300QT	E3198		1. 5.91	To VH-NJF 10/92. Canx 6.10.92.
G-BTLE	PA-31-350 Navajo Chieftain	31-7405428	D-IBPL	20.10.77	
			N54288		
G-BTLF	Enstrom 280 Shark	1021	N43RG	29. 4.91	To HA-MIL 11/94. Canx 9.11.94.
G-BTLG	PA-28R-200 Cherokee Arrow B	28R-35811	N5045S	29. 4.91	
G-BTLH	Socata TB-20 Trinidad	1316		29. 4.91	To G-KKES 3/92. Canx.
G-BTLI	Scheibe SF-25B Falke	46240	RAFGSA-560	2. 5.91	To D-KKPT 8/95. Canx 24.10.94.
			D-KAIF		
G-BTLJ	MDH Hughes 369E (500E)	0468E	N1610D	21. 6.91	To N500CN 5/92. Canx 21.5.92.
G-BTLK	Cessna P.210N Pressurised Centurion II	P210-00298	OY-JRD	8. 5.91	Destroyed in fatal crash near Goodwood on 16.12.91 & DBF.
			N4767K/(F-GBER)/N4767K		Canx as WFU 23.7.92.
G-BTLL	Pilatus P.3-03	323-5	A-806	18. 4.91	Permit expired. Canx by CAA 27.10.95.
			Swiss AF		(Stored 9/97 Headcorn)
G-BTLM	PA-22-160 Tri-Pacer	22-6162	N9025D	16. 5.91	
	(Univair tail-wheel conversion)				
G-BTLN	Cessna T.303 Crusader	T303-00205	N9688C	28. 5.91	To N988PK 7/93. Canx 24.6.93.
G-BTLO	Colt 120A HAFB	1863		7. 5.91	To D-OOOR 10/92. Canx 7.10.92.
G-BTLP	American Aviation AA-1C Lynx	AA1C-0109	N9732U	13. 5.91	
G-BTLR	Aerospatiale AS.365N2 Dauphin 2	6397		8. 5.91	To Dubai Air Wing/Police as DU-111. Canx 6.1.93.
G-BTLS	Aerospatiale AS.350B Ecureuil	2487		8. 5.91	To I-FLAP. Canx 31.7.91.
G-BTLT	Colt 31A HAFB	1351		8.12.88	Canx 7.5.91 on sale to USA.
G-BTLU	PBN BN-2B-26 Islander	2249		16. 5.91	To PK-HNG. Canx 14.7.92.

Regn	Type	c/n	Previous identity	Regn date	Fate or immediate subsequent identity (if known)
G-BTLV	PBN BN-2B-20 Islander (Originally regd as BN-2B-26)	2250		16. 5.91	Canx 4.9.92 on sale to Singapore. To PK-HNF.
G-BTLW	PBN BN-2B-20 Islander (Originally regd as BN-2B-26)	2251		16. 5.91	To 9M-TAC. Canx 17.6.92.
G-BTLX	PBN BN-2B-26 Islander	2252		16. 5.91	To VP-FBR 3/92. Canx 23.3.92.
G-BTLY	PBN BN-2B-26 Islander	2253		16. 5.91	To I-DEPE 5/95. Canx 3.3.94.
G-BTLZ	PBN BN-2B-20 Islander (Originally regd as BN-2B-26)	2254		16. 5.91	To Z-CAA 12/92. Canx 30.12.92.
G-BTMA	Cessna 172N Skyhawk II	172-73711	N5136J	2. 5.91	
G-BTMB	Colt 120A HAFB	1964		8. 5.91	Canx by CAA 4.5.95. To N72149 5/97.
G-BTMC	Colt 120A HAFB	1965		8. 5.91	Canx by CAA 4.5.95.
G-BTMD	Colt 120A HAFB	1975		8. 5.91	Canx 2.6.92. To N240TC 4/93.
G-BTME	Cameron O-120 HAFB	2596		13. 5.91	To D-ONKY 12/92. Canx 26.11.92.
G-BTMF	Taylorcraft BC-12D	6609	N43990 NC43990	10. 7.91	No UK CofA issued. Canx by CAA 17.4.99.
G-BTMG	BAe 125 Srs.800B	258197		14. 5.91	To G-5-696/G-OMGE 7/91. Canx.
G-BTMH	Colt 90A HAFB	1963		14. 5.91	
G-BTMI	BAe 146 Srs.300	E3193	(N883DV) G-6-193	28. 6.91	To G-BUHC 6/92. Canx.
G-BTMJ	Maule MX-7-180 Star Rocket	11073C		11. 6.91	
G-BTMK	Cessna R.172K Hawk XP II	R172-2787	N736TZ	10. 6.91	
G-BTML	Cameron Rupert Bear 90SS HAFB	2533		16. 5.91	Canx as WFU 29.4.97.
G-BTMM	Cameron N-105 HAFB	2587		30. 4.91	To OE-ZBT 5/96. Canx 2.4.96.
G-BTMN	Thunder Ax9-120 Srs.2 HAFB	2003		17. 5.91	
G-BTMO	Colt 69A HAFB	2004		20. 5.91	
G-BTMP	Everett Campbell Cricket Gyroplane Srs.2	024 & G/03-1226		20. 5.91	
G-BTMR	Cessna 172M Skyhawk II	172-64985	N64047	20. 5.91	
G-BTMS	Light Aero Avid Flyer	908 & PFA/189-12023	(CS-U..) G-BTMS	24. 4.91	
G-BTMT	Denney Kitfox Mk.1	66		10. 5.91	
G-BTMU	Thunder Ax8-105 Srs.2 HAFB	1977		20. 5.91	To D-OTMU 5/92. Canx 21.4.92.
G-BTMV	Everett Gyroplane Srs.2	025		21. 5.91	
G-BTMW	Zenair CH.701 STOL (Rotax 582)	PFA/187-11808		21. 5.91	(Stored 4/97)
G-BTMX	Denney Kitfox Mk.3	916 & PFA/172-12079		13. 5.91	
G-BTMY	Cameron Train 80SS HAFB	2561		22. 5.91	To SE-... Canx 6.7.98.
G-BTMZ	PA-38-112 Tomahawk	38-79A1128	N24529	25. 6.91	To OO-PPR 30.5.95. (Export) CofA expired on 17.6.95. Canx 26.11.98 on sale to Belgium.
G-BTNA	Robinson R-22 Beta	1800	N40820	23. 5.91	
G-BTNB	Robinson R-22 Beta	1802	N23006	30. 5.91	
G-BTNC	Aerospatiale SA.365N2 Dauphin 2	6409		21. 6.91	
G-BTND	PA-38-112 Tomahawk	38-78A0155	N9671T	23. 5.91	
G-BTNE	PA-28-161 Warrior II	28-8116212	N8379H	22. 7.91	
G-BTNF	Sud SA.318C Alouette Astazou	2254	HMR-137 Mexican Navy/XC-FUN	29. 5.91	To (F-GHUS)/JA6122. Canx 29.5.91.
G-BTNG	Aerospatiale SA.319B Alouette III	2049	HMR-132 Mexican Navy/F-WTNH	29. 5.91	Canx 29.5.91 on sale to France.
G-BTNH	PA-28-161 Warrior II	28-8216202	N253FT N9577N	28. 5.91	To G-DENH 4/97. Canx.
G-BTNI	BAe ATP	2038	TC-THU G-BTNI/G-SLAM	29. 5.91	To N238JX. Canx.
G-BTNJ	Cameron V-90 HAFB	2534		28. 5.91	Canx as WFU 3.7.97.
G-BTNK	BAe ATP	2037	N860AW G-BTNK/G-11-037/G-BTNK/G-11-037	31. 5.91	To G-CORP 3/98. Canx.
G-BTNL	Thunder Ax10-180 HAFB	2006	(OO-B..) G-BTNL	29. 5.91	
G-BTNM	Aerospatiale AS.355F2 Twin Squirrel	5480		31. 5.91	To G-DANS 4/93. Canx.
G-BTNN	Colt 21A Cloudhopper HAFB	2018		3. 6.91	(Extant 2/97)
G-BTNO	Aeronca 7AC Champion	7AC-3132	N84441 NC84441	31. 5.91	
G-BTNP	Light Aero Avid Commuter	PFA/189-11988		31. 5.91	(Damaged in forced landing Swardeston, Norfolk 25.6.92) (Stored at owner's home 8/97)
G-BTNR	Denney Kitfox Mk.3	921 & PFA/172-12035		31. 5.91	
G-BTNS	WSK PZL-104 Wilga 80	CF20890883	N71695	22. 7.91	
G-BTNT	PA-28-151 Warrior	28-7615401	N6929J	31. 5.91	
G-BTNU	BAe 146 Srs.300	E3155	(G-BSLS) G-6-155	19. 7.90	To (EI-CLG)/EI-CLJ 3/96. Canx 1.3.96.
G-BTNV	PA-28-161 Warrior II	28-7816590	N31878	20. 6.91	
G-BTNW	Rans S-6-ESA Coyote II	0391-171 & PFA/204-12077		3. 6.91	
G-BTNX	Colt 105A HAFB	2019	G-WBCV G-BTNX	3. 6.91	To SU-217. Canx 12.12.96.
G-BTNY	Fairchild M-62A (PT-19-FA) Cornell	T40-237	N33870 US Army	5. 6.91	Restored as N33870 6/95. Canx 10.5.95.
G-BTNZ	Aerospatiale AS.332L-1 Super Puma	2351	F-WYMA G-BTNZ	11. 6.91	To LN-OMX 6/96. Canx 6.6.96.
G-BTOA	Mong Sport MS-2 (built by F.H.Christian)	FHC-1	N1067Z	3. 6.91	(Stored 8/97)

Regn	Type	c/n	Previous identity	Regn date	Fate or immediate subsequent identity (if known)
G-BTOB	Colt 160A HAFB	1950		10. 6.91	To D-OTOB. Canx 17.8.92.
G-BTOC	Robinson R-22 Beta	1801	N23004	10. 6.91	
G-BTOD	PA-38-112 Tomahawk	38-78A0675	N2421A	7. 6.91	
G-BTOE	PA-28-151 Cherokee Warrior	28-7715012	N4264F	12. 6.91	To G-CPTM 7/91. Canx.
G-BTOF	Cameron V-77 HAFB	2409		11. 6.91	To G-CEJA 17.6.91. Canx.
G-BTOG	DH.82A Tiger Moth	86500	F-BGCJ French AF/NM192	5. 9.91	(On overhaul 4/94)
G-BTOH	Cameron A-105 HAFB	2592		14. 6.91	Canx by CAA 19.2.93.
G-BTOI	Cameron N-77 HAFB	2588		20. 6.91	(Extant 2/97)
G-BTOJ	Mooney M.10 Cadet	700045		21. 6.91	To N52WT 12/96. Canx 28.10.96.
G-BTOK	Socata TB-10 Tobago	1361		5. 7.91	To G-VMJM 4/92. Canx.
G-BTOL	Denney Kitfox Mk.3	919 & PFA/172-12052		26. 6.91	
G-BTOM	PA-38-112 Tomahawk	38-78A0763		15. 1.79	DBER in heavy landing at Alderney on 26.9.92. Canx as WFU 26.10.92. (Stored 10/97 at Norwich)
G-BTON	PA-28-140 Cherokee Cruiser	28-7425343	N43193	15. 7.91	
G-BTOO	Pitts S-1C Special (built by E.Lawrence)	5215-24A	N37H	12. 6.91	(On overhaul 5/92)
G-BTOP	Cameron V-77 HAFB	2484		14. 6.91	(Active 5/95)
G-BTOR	Neico Lancair 320	PFA/191-12083		19. 6.91	Partially disintegrated on landing at Wherwell on 19.6.98. Canx as destroyed 27.8.98.
G-BTOS	Cessna 140	8353	N89325 NC89325	7. 6.91	
G-BTOT	PA-15 Vagabond	15-60	N4176H NC4176H	22. 5.91	
G-BTOU	Cameron O-120 HAFB	2606		2. 7.91	CofA expired 27.1.99. Canx by CAA 28.7.99. (Regd to owner in Australia)
G-BTOV	WSK-PZL Antonov AN-2TP	1G137-58	N2AN SP-KNA/Polish AF 3758	21. 6.91	To SP-TBM 6/95. Canx 30.7.92.
G-BTOW	Socata Rallye 180T Galerien	3360	F-WNGZ	9.11.82	
G-BTOX	Aero Designs Pulsar	PFA/202-11917		27. 6.91	Canx as WFU 25.11.93.
G-BTOY	Cameron N-77 HAFB	293		12. 8.77	To OE-DZK 12/79. Canx 6.12.79.
G-BTOZ	Thunder Ax9-120 Srs.2 HAFB	2008		28. 6.91	
G-BTPA	BAe ATP	2007	EC-GYE G-BTPA/(N377AE)	19. 8.88	To EC-HGC 8/99. Canx 26.8.99.
G-BTPB	Cameron N-105 HAFB	1536		6. 7.87	
G-BTPC	BAe ATP	2010	EC-GYF G-BTPC/G-11-10/(N380AE)	1. 9.88	To EC-HGD 9/99.
G-BTPD	BAe ATP	2011	(N381AE)	1. 9.88	To EC-GYR 11/98. Canx 20.11.98.
G-BTPE	BAe ATP	2012	EC-GZH G-BTPE/(N382AE)	1. 9.88	(Stored at Woodford 8/99 still as EC-GZH)
G-BTPF	BAe ATP	2013	G-BTPF G-11-013/G-BTPF/(N383AE)	2. 9.88	To EC-HCY 5/99. Canx 17.5.99.
G-BTPG	BAe ATP	2014	(N384AE)	2. 9.88	To EC-HEH 6/99. Canx 11.6.99.
G-BTPH	BAe ATP	2015	G-11-015 G-BTPH/(N385AE)	2. 9.88	To EC-HFM 7/99. Canx 23.7.99.
G-BTPI	Not allocated. [Rejected by British Airways due to memories of Trident "Papa India" accident]				
G-BTPJ	BAe ATP	2016	(N386AE)	2. 9.88	To EC-HFR 7/99. Canx 30.7.99.
G-BTPK	BAe ATP	2041	G-11-041	3.10.91	To EC-GLC 1/97. Canx 17.1.97.
G-BTPL	BAe ATP	2042	EC-GLH G-BTPL/G-11-042	3.10.91	To EC-HES 7/99. Canx 16.7.99.
G-BTPM	BAe ATP	2043		19.11.91	To EC-GNI 4/97. Canx 7.4.97.
G-BTPN	BAe ATP	2044	G-11-044	19.11.91	To EC-GNJ 4/97. Canx 18.4.97.
G-BTPO	BAe ATP	2051	G-5-051	10. 6.92	WFU 1.12.98. Stored 5/99 Woodford.
G-BTPP	Not allotted.				
G-BTPR	Not allotted.				
G-BTPS	Not allotted.				
G-BTPT	Cameron N-77 HAFB	2575		10. 6.91	
G-BTPU	Cameron N-105 HAFB	2591		10. 6.91	Canx on sale to Germany 2.11.92. To D-OTPU 4/93.
G-BTPV	Colt 90A HAFB	1956		14. 6.91	CofA expired 1.8.97. Canx as PWFU 25.3.99.
G-BTPW	Cameron N-105 HAFB	2580		18. 6.91	To D-PROVITAL 8/92. Canx 28.7.92.
G-BTPX	Thunder Ax8-90 HAFB	1873		18. 6.91	
G-BTPY	Aeronca 11AC Chief	11AC-169	N86359 NC86359	1. 7.91	To G-IIAC 2.7.91. Canx.
G-BTPZ	Isaacs Fury II	PFA/11-11927		1. 7.91	(Extant 2/94)
G-BTRA	Denney Kitfox Mk.3	775 & PFA/172-11921		27. 6.91	Canx 22.3.94. To SE-VAC 2/96.
G-BTRB	Colt Mickey Mouse SS HAFB	1959		4. 7.91	(Based in Germany).
G-BTRC	Light Aero Avid Speed Wing	913 & PFA/189-12076		2. 7.91	
G-BTRD	Colt 240A HAFB	1982		5. 7.91	To D-OTRD. Canx 3.8.92.
G-BTRE	Reims Cessna F.172H Skyhawk	0657	N10657	3. 7.91	
G-BTRF	Aero Designs Pulsar	PFA/202-12051		4. 7.91	
G-BTRG	Aeronca 65C Super Chief	C4149	N22466 NC22466	4. 7.91	
G-BTRH	Aeronca 7AC Champion	7AC-2895	N84204 NC84204	4. 7.91	
G-BTRI	Aeronca 11CC Super Chief	11CC-246	N4540E NC4540E	4. 7.91	(Extensively damaged after hitting a tree on take-off from Lynton Cross on 11.4.96)
G-BTRJ	Boeing-Stearman B75N1 (NS2-3) Kaydet	75-6860	N5581C N68235/BuA.07256	5. 7.91	Restored as N68235 7/94. Canx 11.7.94.

Regn	Type	c/n	Previous identity	Regn date	Fate or immediate subsequent identity (if known)
G-BTRK	PA-28-161 Warrior II	28-8216206	N297FT	8. 7.91	
			N9594N		
G-BTRL	Cameron N-105 HAFB	2622		5. 7.91	
G-BTRM	Colt 120A HAFB	1994		9. 7.91	Canx 1.6.92. To N241TC 3/93.
G-BTRN	Thunder Ax9-120 Srs.2 HAFB	1983		11. 7.91	
G-BTRO	Thunder Ax8-90 HAFB	1872		11. 7.91	
G-BTRP	MDH Hughes 369E (500E)	0475E	N1607D	11. 7.91	
G-BTRR	Thunder Ax7-77 HAFB	1905		12. 7.91	
G-BTRS	PA-28-161 Warrior II	28-8116004	N8248V	12. 7.91	
G-BTRT	PA-28R-200 Cherokee Arrow II		N1189X	24. 7.91	
		28R-7535270			
G-BTRU	Robin DR.400/180 Regent	2089		12. 7.91	
G-BTRV	Boeing-Stearman B75N1 (PT-17) Kaydet		EC-AIC	12. 7.91	Was believed to be on rebuild but no UK CofA has been
		75-1572	41-8013		issued. Canx as WFU 18.4.95.
G-BTRW	Slingsby T.61F Venture T.2	1968	ZA632	5. 7.91	
G-BTRX	Cameron V-77 HAFB	1143	VH-HIH	12. 7.91	Canx as WFU 2.5.97.
G-BTRY	PA-28-161 Warrior II	28-8116190	N8363L	18. 7.91	
G-BTRZ	Jodel D.18	148 & PFA/169-11271		16. 7.91	
G-BTSA	Cessna 150K	150-71583	N6083G	10.12.91	To N4337K 8/98. Canx 13.7.98.
G-BTSB	Corben Baby Ace D	JC-1	N3599	16. 7.91	
G-BTSC	Evans VP-2	PFA/63-10342		20.10.78	(On overhaul Chilbolton 6/96)
	(Originally regd with c/n PFA/63-10343, officially amended in 1981)				
G-BTSD	Loehle 5151 Mustang	PFA/213-11867		17. 7.91	No Permit to Fly issued. Canx by CAA 20.4.99.
G-BTSE	Not allotted.				
G-BTSF	Evans VP-2	PFA/63-10355		20.10.78	Not completed. Canx 30.5.84.
G-BTSG	Cessna 414A Chancellor II	414A-0065	G-BTFH	25.11.87	To N414KB 3/93. Canx 24.2.93.
			(OO-LFL)/(N4674N)		
G-BTSH	Evans VP-2	PFA/63-10361		20.10.78	Not completed. Canx 30.5.84.
G-BTSI	BAe 125 Srs.1000B	259007		15. 7.91	To N84WA 5/98. Canx 8.5.98.
G-BTSJ	PA-28-161 Warrior II	28-7816473	N9417C	23. 7.91	
G-BTSK	Beechcraft F33C Bonanza	CJ-132	PH-BNC	1. 8.91	To N249A 6/97. Canx 29.5.97.
G-BTSL	Cameron Glass 70SS HAFB	1627		27. 1.88	
	(Tennent's Lager Glass Shape)				
G-BTSM	Cessna 180A	180-32678	P2-DEQ	9. 7.91	
			VH-DEQ/VH-DEC/N7781A		
G-BTSN	Cessna 150G	150-65106	N3806J	30. 8.91	
G-BTSO	Cessna 150M Commuter	150-78171	(F-GRSO)	30. 8.91	To EC-GLG. Canx 24.9.96.
			G-BTSO/N9221U		
G-BTSP	Piper J3C-65 Cub	7647	N41013	30. 8.91	
			NC41013		
G-BTSR	Aeronca 11AC Chief	11AC-785	N9152E	30. 8.91	
			NC9152E		
G-BTSS	Cameron Flying Shopping Trolley SS			23. 7.91	Canx as WFU 21.11.95.
	HAFB	1931			
G-BTST	Bensen B.8M Gyrocopter (Mod)	002VS		23. 7.91	(Extant 6/97)
G-BTSU	Bensen B.8MR Gyrocopter	BTG-01		24. 7.91	No Permit to Fly issued. Canx by CAA 22.3.99.
G-BTSV	Denney Kitfox Mk.3	PFA/172-11920		24. 7.91	
G-BTSW	Colt AS-80GD Hot-Air Airship	1999		24. 7.91	
	(Originally regd as AS-105GD model)				
G-BTSX	Thunder Ax7-77 HAFB	2027		24. 7.91	
G-BTSY	English Electric Lightning F.6		XR724	25. 7.91	No Permit issued. Canx as TWFU 26.5.92. (Stored 4/97)
		95207			
G-BTSZ	Cessna 177A Cardinal	177-01198	N30332	30. 7.91	
G-BTTA	Hawker Iraqi Fury FB.11		VH-HFX	25. 7.91	(At Duxford 7/99)
		37534 & ISS13	N28SF/Iraqi AF 243		
G-BTTB	Cameron V-90 HAFB	2624		22. 7.91	
G-BTTC	Cameron N-105 HAFB	2610		25. 7.91	To D-ARIEL. Canx 13.11.91.
G-BTTD	Montgomerie-Bensen B.8MR Gyrocopter			31. 7.91	
		G/01-1204			
G-BTTE	Cessna 150L	150-75558	N11602	31. 7.91	
G-BTTF	Beechcraft F33C Bonanza	CJ-133	PH-BND	31. 7.91	To G-OAHC 9/91. Canx.
G-BTTG	BAe 125 Srs.1000A	NA1001 & 259006		5. 8.91	To "N1000U"/N100U 5/92. Canx 22.4.92.
G-BTTH	Beechcraft F33C Bonanza	CJ-134	PH-BNE	6. 8.91	To N249WL 9/97. Canx 17.9.97.
			N24138		
G-BTTI	Thunder Ax8-90 HAFB	1997		7. 8.91	(Status uncertain; stolen, complete with trailer,
					from Putney 26.10.91) Canx as WFU 16.4.98.
G-BTTJ	Thunder Ax9-120 Srs.2 HAFB	1981		8. 8.91	Canx as WFU 7.4.98.
G-BTTK	Thunder Ax8-105 HAFB	2036		9. 8.91	
G-BTTL	Cameron V-90 HAFB	2649		12. 8.91	
G-BTTM	Denney Kitfox Mk.3			. .91R	NTU - To G-BTWB 8/91. Canx.
		920 & PFA/172-12278			
G-BTTN	Vicker-Supermarine 349 Spitfire		BL628	13. 8.91	To VH-FVB 6/95. Canx 12.4.95.
	F.Vb	CBAF/1660			
G-BTTO	BAe ATP	2033	EC-GJU	16. 8.91	(Stored at Woodford 9/99 marked as EC-GJU)
			G-BTTO/G-OEDE/G-BTTO/TC-THV/G-BTTO/S2-ACZ/G-11-033		
G-BTTP	BAe 146 Srs.300	E3203	G-6-203	20. 8.91	
G-BTTR	Aerotek Pitts S-2A Special	2208	N38MP	16. 8.91	
G-BTTS	Colt 77A HAFB	1861		16. 8.91	
G-BTTT	Not allotted - Radio code.				
G-BTTU	Cameron V-90 HAFB	2646		22. 8.91	To D-OTTU 12/94. Canx 15.8.94.
G-BTTV	Schweizer 269C (300C)	S.1551	N86G	27. 8.91	To F-GRCA 4/96. Canx 16.2.96.
G-BTTW	Thunder Ax7-77 HAFB	2016		27. 8.91	
G-BTTX	BAe 125 Srs.1000A	NA1000 & 259005		19. 8.91	To G-5-735/N1AB 3/92. Canx 11.3.92.

Regn	Type	c/n	Previous identity	Regn date	Fate or immediate subsequent identity (if known)
G-BTTY	Denney Kitfox Mk.2	PFA/172-11823		29. 7.91	
G-BTTZ	Slingsby T.61F Venture T.2	1961	ZA625	30. 7.91	
G-BTUA	Slingsby T.61F Venture T.2	1985	ZA666	20. 8.91	
G-BTUB	LET Yakovlev C.11	172623	(France)	29. 8.91	
	(Also quotes identity of 039)		Egyptian AF 543		
G-BTUC	Embraer EMB-312 Tucano	312-007	G-14-007	19. 6.88	CofA lapsed 11.9.93. (Stored Belfast Harbour)
			PP-ZTC		Canx as WFU 20.12.96.
G-BTUD	CFM Image	IM-01 & PFA/222-12012	G-MWPV	21. 8.91	Permit expired 21.1.95. Canx as PWFU 5.2.99.
G-BTUE	BAe ATP	2039	TC-THT	5. 9.91	To G-OEDH 8/94. Canx.
			G-11-039/G-BTUE/G-11-039		
G-BTUF	HS.125 Srs.F403B	25248	G-5-707	17. 9.91	To G-SHOP 10/92. Canx.
			G-BTUF/G-5-707/D-CFCF		
G-BTUG	Socata MS.893E Rallye 180T	3208		10. 7.78	
G-BTUH	Cameron N-65 HAFB	1452		28. 8.91	(Originally the "attached" balloon to G-WASH c/n 1451)
G-BTUI	Cameron O-105 HAFB	2615		28. 8.91	To D-EIMERMACHER. Canx 27.11.91.
G-BTUJ	Thunder Ax9-120 HAFB	2022		30. 8.91	
G-BTUK	Aerotek Pitts S-2A Special	2260	N5300J	2. 9.91	
G-BTUL	Aerotek Pitts S-2A Special	2200	N900RS	2. 9.91	
			N31467		
G-BTUM	Piper J3C-85 Cub	19516	N6335H	6. 9.91	
	(Frame No. 19536)		NC6335H		
G-BTUN	Colt Flying Drinks Can SS HAFB	1955		9. 9.91	To PT-Z.. 4/98. Canx 17.4.98.
	(Skol Lager Can)				
G-BTUO	Cameron RX-100 Gas Free Balloon	2656		6. 9.91	To N41445 10/91. Canx 16.3.92 on sale as PH-VOY!
G-BTUP	Robinson R-22 Beta	1933		10. 9.91	To OE-XYY. Canx 28.1.92.
G-BTUR	PA-18-95 Super Cub (L-18C-PI)	18-3205	OO-LVM	11. 9.91	
			OL-L08/L-131/53-4805		
G-BTUS	Whittaker MW.7	PFA/171-11999		5. 9.91	(Extensively damaged on crash 6 miles NE of Collingham on 18.7.93)
G-BTUT	PA-34-200T Seneca II	34-8070112	(N.....)	8. 1.91	To N448M 1/96. Canx 1.12.95.
			G-BTUT/N8144M/N9642N		
G-BTUU	Cameron O-120 HAFB	2669		16. 9.91	
G-BTUV	Aeronca 65TAC Defender	C.1661TA	N36816	12. 9.91	(On rebuild 1/99 Guernsey)
			NC36816		
G-BTUW	PA-28-151 Cherokee Warrior	28-7415066	N54458	12. 9.91	
G-BTUX	Aerospatiale SA.365N2 Dauphin 2	6424		12. 9.91	
G-BTUY	BAe 146 Srs.300	E3202	G-6-202	17. 9.91	To B-1781. Canx 16.1.95.
G-BTUZ	American General AG-5B Tiger	10075	N11939	3.10.91	
G-BTVA	Thunder Ax7-77 HAFB	2009		16. 9.91	
G-BTVB	Everett Gyroplane Srs.3	026		24. 9.91	
G-BTVC	Denney Kitfox Mk.2	PFA/172-11784		23. 9.91	
G-BTVD	Not allocated.				
G-BTVE	Hawker Demon I	-	2292M	18. 9.91	(Frame noted at PFA Rally at Cranfield on 4.7.99)
	(Composite of ex Irish front and K8203 rear)(Boulton Paul - built)		K8203		
G-BTVF	Rotorway Executive 90	5058		13. 9.91	No Permit or CofA issued.
G-BTVG	Cessna 140	12350	N2114N	30. 8.91	
			NC2114N		
G-BTVH	Colt 77A HAFB	1027	G-ZADT	24. 9.91	
			G-ZBCA		
G-BTVI	PBN BN-2B-26 Islander	2255		9. 9.91	To B-68801. Canx 8.7.92.
G-BTVJ	PBN BN-2B-26 Islander	2256		9. 9.91	To TL-ABU 6/93. Canx 6.7.93.
G-BTVK	PBN BN-2B-20 Islander	2257		9. 9.91	To OA-9 Botswana DF 3/93. Canx 2.6.93.
	(Originally regd as a BN-2B-26 model)				
G-BTVL	PBN BN-2B-20 Islander	2258		9. 9.91	To OA-10 Botswana DF 3/93. Canx 2.6.93.
	(Originally regd as a BN-2B-26 model)				
G-BTVM	PBN BN-2T Turbine Islander	2259		9. 9.91	To CN-TWR 11/93. Canx 24.11.93.
	(Originally regd as a BN-2B-26 model)				
G-BTVN	PBN BN-2B-20 Islander	2260		9. 9.91	To G-NESU 5/95. Canx.
	(Originally regd as a BN-2B-26 model)				
G-BTVO	BAe 146 Srs.300	E3205	G-6-205	18. 9.91	To B-1777 11/92. Canx 16.11.92.
G-BTVP	Phoenix Currie Wot	PFA/3020		26. 7.91	To G-CWBM 3/94. Canx.
G-BTVR	PA-28-140 Cherokee Cruiser	28-7625012	N4328X	16. 9.91	
G-BTVS	Aerospatiale AS.355F1 Twin Squirrel	5249	G-STVE	25. 7.90	To G-OHCP 3/94. Canx.
			G-TOFF/G-BKJX		
G-BTVT	BAe 146 Srs.200	E2200	(I-FLRZ)	14.11.91	To D-ACFA 10/92. Canx 15.10.92.
			G-BTVT/G-6-200		
G-BTVU	Robinson R-22 Beta	1937		26. 9.91	
G-BTVV	Reims Cessna FA.337G Super Skymaster	0058	PH-RPD	25. 9.91	
	(Wichita c/n 01476)		N1876M		
G-BTVW	Cessna 152 II	152-79631	N757CK	23. 9.91	
G-BTVX	Cessna 152 II	152-83375	N48786	23. 9.91	
G-BTVY	Cessna 402B	402B-1364	N402R	26. 9.91	Restored as N402R 7/93. Canx 9.6.93.
			N888EE/(N4609A)		
G-BTVZ	Cameron A-140 HAFB	2680		30. 9.91	To D-OFUN(1). Canx 24.11.92.
G-BTWA	Bell 206B JetRanger II	1540	D-HJFF	30.10.78	To SX-HBV 8/85. Canx 25.6.85.
G-BTWB	Denney Kitfox Mk.3	920 & PFA/172-12278	(G-BTTM)	21. 8.91	No Permit issued. Canx by CAA 14.3.99.
G-BTWC	Slingsby T.61F Venture T.2	1975	ZA656	23. 9.91	

Regn	Type	c/n	Previous identity	Regn date	Fate or immediate subsequent identity (if known)
G-BTWD	Slingsby T.61F Venture T.2	1976	ZA657	23. 9.91	
G-BTWE	Slingsby T.61F Venture T.2	1980	ZA661	23. 9.91	
G-BTWF	DHC.1 Chipmunk 22	C1/0564	WK549	30. 9.91	(On rebuild 1996)
	(Fuselage no. DHB/f/451)				
G-BTWG	Thunder Ax10-160 Srs.2 HAFB	2062		1.10.91	To D-OTWG 9/94. Canx 23.8.94.
G-BTWH	Thunder Ax7-77 HAFB	1976		1.10.91	To OO-BTN. Canx 14.6.94.
G-BTWI	EAA Acrosport I	230	N10JW	2.10.91	
G-BTWJ	Cameron V-77 HAFB	2670		3.10.91	
G-BTWK	Colt 210A HAFB	2077		4.10.91	Canx 25.3.96 on sale to Egypt.
G-BTWL	Wag-Aero CUBy Acro Sport Trainer	PFA/108-10893		3.10.91	
G-BTWM	Cameron V-77 HAFB	2163		4.10.91	
G-BTWN	Maule MXT-7-180 Star Rocket	14025C		7.10.91	
G-BTWO	Not allotted.				
G-BTWP	Robinson R-22 Beta	1950		8.10.91	To G-HRHE 1/97. Canx.
G-BTWR	Bell P-63A-7BE Kingcobra	33-397	N52113	7.10.91	
	(C/n officially 33-37		NX52113/42-69097		
	which equates to 42-68897 & also has been quoted as c/n 296A-5-3)				
G-BTWS	Thunder Ax7-77 HAFB	1971		9.10.91	CofA expired 8.3.96. Canx as PWFU 22.3.99.
					(Was based in Germany)
G-BTWT	DHC.6-320 Twin Otter	516		25.11.76	To PH-STI(2) 9/85. Canx 13.9.85.
G-BTWU	PA-22-135 Tri-Pacer	22-2135	N3320B	10.10.91	(Partially dismantled at Haverfordwest 5/99)
G-BTWV	Cameron O-90 HAFB	2675		10.10.91	
G-BTWW	Agusta-Bell 206B JetRanger III	8567	EI-BJV	26. 7.78	To G-BYBC 3/98. Canx.
			G-BTWW		
G-BTWX	Socata TB-9 Tampico	1401		14.10.91	
G-BTWY	Aero Designs Pulsar	PFA/202-12040		15.10.91	
G-BTWZ	Rans S-10 Sakota	PFA/194-12117		15.10.91	(Under construction 3/97)
G-BTXA	Aerospatiale AS.350B2 Ecureuil	2559		16.10.91	To G-RICC on 30.10.91. Canx.
G-BTXB	Colt 77A HAFB	2072		16.10.91	
G-BTXC(1)	Kolb Twinstar Mk.2	PFA/205-11645		16.10.91	NTU - To G-MWWM 17.10.91. Canx.
	(C/n conflicts with G-GPST)				
G-BTXC(2)	Team Minimax	294 & PFA/186-11648	G-MWFC	21.10.91	Restored as G-MWFC 7/96. Canx.
G-BTXD(1)	Rans S-6-ESD Coyote II	PFA/204-11849		16.10.91	NTU - To G-MWWL 17.10/91. Canx.
G-BTXD(2)	Rans S-6-ESA Coyote II	PFA/204-12104		22.10.91	
G-BTXE	Vickers Supermarine 394 Spitfire		N6 IAF	23.10.91	To N280TP 2/93. Canx 2.12.92.
	FR.XVIIIe	6S/676372-165	Indian AF HS654/TP280		
G-BTXF	Cameron V-90 HAFB	2692		2.10.91	
G-BTXG	BAe Jetstream Srs.3102	719	OK-REJ	23.10.91	To SE-FVP 6/97. Canx 3.6.97.
	(Originally regd as Srs.3100)		G-BTXG/OY-EEC/G-BTXG/N418MX/G-31-719		
G-BTXH	Colt AS-56 Hot-Air Airship	2078		23.10.91	
G-BTXI	Noorduyn AT-16-ND Harvard IIB	14-429	Fv.16105	25.10.91	
			Swedish AF/RCAF FE695/FE695/42-892		
G-BTXJ	Robinson R-22 Beta	1882		25.10.91	To G-LIPE 1/92. Canx.
G-BTXK	Thunder Ax7-65 HAFB	1910	ZS-HYP	28.10.91	
			G-BTXK		
G-BTXL	BAe Jetstream Srs.3102	621	(D-C...)	20. 3.87	To LN-FAJ 10/93. Canx 21.10.93.
			G-BTXL/G-BLDO/(G-BLCY)/G-31-621		
G-BTXM	Colt 21A Cloudhopper HAFB	2082		29.10.91	
G-BTXN	BAe 146 Srs.300	E3129	HS-TBM	20.11.91	To G-JEAL 4/93. Canx.
			G-5-129		
G-BTXO	BAe 146 Srs.100	E1104	CP-2247	29.11.91	To VH-NJE(2) 5/96. Canx 19.6.96.
			G-BTXO/HS-TBO/G-5-104		
G-BTXP	Cameron RX-100 HAFB	2666		30.10.91	To EC-937 11/91. Canx 5.11.91.
G-BTXR	Cassutt Racer	M.14372	N68PM	30.10.91	To G-NARO 4/98. Canx.
	(built by P.Musso)(Also known as Musso Racer Original)				
G-BTXS	Cameron O-120 HAFB	2141		16.10.91	
G-BTXT	Maule MXT-7-180 Star Rocket	14027C		7.10.91	
G-BTXU	Cameron A-210 HAFB	2702		30.10.91	Canx by CAA 6.9.93. To ZK-FAR.
G-BTXV	Cameron A-210 HAFB	2703		30.10.91	
G-BTXW	Cameron V-77 HAFB	2717		31.10.91	
G-BTXX	Bellanca 8KCAB Decathlon	595-80	OY-CYC	1.10.91	
			SE-IEP/N5063G		
G-BTXY	Aerospatiale AS.365N2 Dauphin 2	6422	F-GHYE	4.11.91	Canx 21.2.92 on sale to Singapore. To 9M-SAS.
			F-WYMA		
G-BTXZ	Zenair CH.250	PFA/113-12170		24.10.91	
G-BTYA	Bell 212	30615	VH-BEE	31.10.91	To 9Y-TIF. Canx 5.6.92.
			VR-BEZ/EP-HBX/VR-BEZ/N18090		
G-BTYB	Cessna 150L	150-73791	N18108	4.11.91	To TC-... Canx 29.9.92. Noted at Ilker Carter Airfield,
					Northern Cyprus 4/96, still as G-BTYB.
G-BTYC	Cessna 150L	150-75767	N66002	4.11.91	
G-BTYD	Cameron N-90 HAFB	2690		4.11.91	CofA lapsed 23.1.96. Canx as PWFU 18.7.96.
G-BTYE	Cameron A-180 HAFB	2704		5.11.91	
G-BTYF	Thunder Ax10-180 Srs.2 HAFB	2086		7.11.91	
G-BTYG	BAe Jetstream Srs.3101	711	N415MX	8.11.91	To OY-SVJ 3/92. Canx 26.3.92.
			G-31-711		
G-BTYH	Pottier P.80S	PFA/160-11121		11.11.91	
G-BTYI	PA-28-181 Archer II	28-8190078	N8287T	15.11.91	
G-BTYJ	Schleicher ASH-25	25130		15.11.91	NTU - Became BGA.3800/HAZ. Canx by CAA 25.7.94.
G-BTYK	Cessna 310R II	310R-0138	N200VC	21.11.91	
			N5018J		

Regn	Type	c/n	Previous identity	Regn date	Fate or immediate subsequent identity (if known)
G-BTYL	Hawker Hunter T.7	41H-693688	XL595	29.11.91	Fatal crash at Broomhead Moor, near Bolsterstone, S.Yorks. on 11.6.93. Canx as destroyed 6.12.93.
G-BTYM	PA-28-161 Warrior II	28-7916435	N29500	26.11.91	To N295BC. Canx 16.12.91.
G-BTYN	BAe 125 Srs.1000A	NA1002 & 259009	G-5-716	5.11.91	To N229U 5/92. Canx 22.4.92.
G-BTYO	BAe 125 Srs.1000A	NA1003 & 259011	G-5-717	5.11.91	To N14GD 6/92. Canx 18.6.92.
G-BTYP	BAe 125 Srs.1000A	NA1004 & 259013	G-5-711	5.11.91	To N125BA 6/92. Canx 18.6.92.
G-BTYR	BAe 125 Srs.1000A	NA1005 & 259014	G-5-712	5.11.91	To N680BA 6/92. Canx 18.6.92.
G-BTYS	BAe 125 Srs.1000A	259015	G-5-718	5.11.91	To N1000E. Canx 3.2.92.
G-BTYT	Cessna 152 II	152-80455	N24931	25.11.91	
G-BTYU	BAe Jetstream Srs.3202	945	G-31-945	2.12.91	To HL5214 1/92. Canx 9.1.92.
G-BTYV	Fokker Dr.I Replica (Buily by J.B.Shively)	01JS	N152JS	27.11.91	To F-AZJG 6/93. Canx 1.4.93.
G-BTYW	Cessna 120	11725	N77283 NC77283	27.11.91	
G-BTYX	Cessna 140	11004	N76568 NC76568	27.11.91	
G-BTYY	Curtiss Robin C-2	475	N348K NC348K	8.10.91	
G-BTYZ	Colt 210A HAFB	2083		17.10.91	
G-BTZA	Beechcraft F33A Bonanza	CE-957	PH-BNT D-EBKX	22.11.91	
G-BTZB	Yakovlev Yak-50	801810	DOSAAF 77	27.11.91	
G-BTZC	Colt 90A HAFB	1876		5.12.91	To D-OTZC 7/93. Canx 24.3.93.
G-BTZD	Yakovlev Yak.1 Srs.1 (C/n is identity stamped on engine bearers) (Salvaged from lake in N.Russia mid .91 after forced landing c.42)	8188	1342 (Soviet AF)	10.12.91	(Stored by Historic Flying Ltd off-site 3/96)
G-BTZE	LET Yakovlev C.11	171312	(France) Egypt AF/OK-JIK	11. 2.92	(On display in Blue Max Movie Aircraft Museum 3/96)
G-BTZF	Boeing 737-204ADV (Line No. 953)	22967	G-BKHF (G-BKGV)	29. 4.91	To EI-CJF 3/94. Canx 24.3.94.
G-BTZG	BAe ATP	2046		11.12.91	To (PK-MAA)/PK-MTV. Canx 24.2.92.
G-BTZH	BAe ATP	2047		11.12.91	To (PK-MAC)/PK-MTW. Canx 30.3.92.
G-BTZI	BAe ATP	2048		11.12.91	To (PK-MAD)/PK-MTX. Canx 29.4.92.
G-BTZJ	BAe ATP	2049	PK-MTY (PK-MAE)/G-BTZJ	11.12.91	
G-BTZK	BAe ATP	2050	(PK-MAF) G-BTZK	11.12.91	To PK-MTZ. Canx 6.7.92.
G-BTZL	Oldfield Baby Lakes (Built by H.R.Swack)	8506-M-28B	N2288B	12.12.91	(Stored 3/97 Fullers Hill Farm, Little Gransden)
G-BTZM	Boeing-Stearman N2S-5 Kaydet (PT-13D-BW)	75-5540	N4738V BuA.61418/42-17377	10. 1.92	To F-AZIC 10/97. Canx 17.2.92.
G-BTZN	BAe 146 Srs.300	E3149	N146PZ ZP-CCY/N146PZ/G-BTZN/HS-TBN/G-11-149	10. 1.92	To EI-CLY 4/97. Canx 16.4.97.
G-BTZO	Socata TB-20 Trinidad	1409		18.12.91	
G-BTZP	Socata TB-9 Tampico Club	1421		18.12.91	
G-BTZR	Colt 77B HAFB	2087		18.12.91	
G-BTZS	Colt 77B HAFB	2088		18.12.91	
G-BTZT	BAe Jetstream Srs.3101	715	N416MX G-31-715	23.12.91	To G-IJYS 10/92. Canx.
G-BTZU	Cameron Concept 60 HAFB	2734		20.12.91	
G-BTZV	Cameron V-77 HAFB	2410		20.12.91	
G-BTZW	Piper J3C-65 Cub	16317	N88689 NC88689	7.11.91	To G-CUBY 3/95. Canx.
G-BTZX	Piper J3C-65 Cub	18871	N98648 NC98648	27. 2.92	
G-BTZY	Colt 56A HAFB	2084		17.10.91	
G-BTZZ	CFM Streak Shadow	K.169-SA & PFA/206-12155		23.12.91	
G-BUAA	Corben Baby Ace D (Built by D.E.Hale)	561	N516DH	19.11.91	
G-BUAB	Aeronca 11AC Chief	11AC-1759	N3458E NC3458E	17. 1.92	
G-BUAC	Slingsby Cadet III (Original identity unknown, allegedly wholly home-built)	PFA/42-12059	(ex)	17. 1.92	(Stored 1/99 at Brunton, Northumberland)
G-BUAD	Colt AS-105 Mk.II Hot-Air Airship	2069		23.12.91	Canx by CAA 10.3.95. To HB-BVI 12/95.
G-BUAE	Thunder Ax8-105 Srs.2 HAFB	2032		9. 9.91	To D-OUAE 1/95. Canx 6.1.95.
G-BUAF	Cameron N-77 HAFB (Rebuilt from 5N-ATT)	2746		2. 1.92	
G-BUAG	Jodel D.18	PFA/169-11651		3. 1.92	
G-BUAH	Rotorway Exec 90	5059		3. 1.92	To G-SFOX 10/93. Canx.
G-BUAI	Everett Gyroplane Srs.3	030		6. 1.92	
G-BUAJ	Cameron N-90 HAFB	2735		7. 1.92	
G-BUAK	Thunder Ax8-105 Srs.2 HAFB	2080		8. 1.92	To D-OUAK. Canx 18.4.96.
G-BUAL	Colt 105A HAFB	2070		10. 1.92	To D-OSEX 4/94. Canx 15.11.93.
G-BUAM	Cameron V-77 HAFB	2470		10. 1.92	
G-BUAN	Cessna 172N Skyhawk II	172-70290	N738WH	23.12.91	
G-BUAO	Luscombe 8A Silvaire	4089	N1362K NC1362K	15. 1.92	
G-BUAP	Robin DR.400/180 Regent	2106		15. 1.92	To G-MRSL 4/92. Canx.
G-BUAR	Vickers-Supermarine 358 Seafire LF.IIIc (Westland built)	-	Aeronavale PP972/PP972	21. 1.92	(On rebuild 5/97)

Regn	Type	c/n	Previous identity	Regn date	Fate or immediate subsequent identity (if known)
G-BUAS	Thunder Ax10-180 Srs.II HAFB	2140		22. 1.92	Canx as destroyed 18.10.93. To ZS-HYY 9/95.
G-BUAT	Thunder Ax9-120 HAFB	2093		24. 1.92	
G-BUAU	Cameron A-180 HAFB	2744		17. 1.92	(Active 8/96)
G-BUAV	Cameron O-105 HAFB	2767		27. 1.92	Canx by CAA 15.5.98.
G-BUAW	Pitts S-1C Special	1921-77	N29DH	27. 1.92	Badly damaged on landing at Norwich on 16.4.95. (On rebuild 2/99 Swanton Morley)
G-BUAX	Rans S-10 Sakota	PFA/194-11848		28. 1.92	
G-BUAY	Cameron A-210 HAFB	2751		28. 1.92	
G-BUAZ	Beechcraft F33C Bonanza	CJ-137	PH-BNH	28. 1.92	To G-COLA 31.3.92. Canx.
G-BUBA	PA-18S-150 Super Cub Floatplane	18-7909047	N6BL N83522	17. 1.92	
G-BUBB	Light Aero Avid Flyer	PFA/189-12201		3. 2.92	Canx by CAA 13.8.98.
G-BUBC	QAC Quickie Tri-Q 200	PFA/94-11909		3. 2.92	
G-BUBD	PBN BN-2T Turbine Islander (Originally regd as a BN-2B-26)	2261		14. 2.92	To CN-TWS 12/93. Canx 16.12.93.
G-BUBE	PBN BN-2T Turbine Islander (Originally regd as a BN-2B-26)	2262		14. 2.92	To CN-TWT 12/93. Canx 16.12.93.
G-BUBF	PBN BN-2B-26 Islander	2263		14. 2.92	To LV-WFR 1/94. Canx 4.1.94.
G-BUBG	PBN BN-2T Turbine Islander (Originally regd as a BN-2B-26)	2264		14. 2.92	To G-JSPC 12/94. Canx.
G-BUBH	PBN BN-2B-20 Islander (Originally regd as a BN-2B-26)	2265		14. 2.92	To OA-11/Z12 Botswana DF. Canx 7.2.94.
G-BUBI	PBN BN-2T Turbine Islander (Originally regd as a BN-2B-26)	2266		14. 2.92	To CN-TWU 10/93. Canx 6.10.93.
G-BUBJ	PBN BN-2B-20 Islander (Originally regd as a BN-2B-26)	2267		14. 2.92	To JA5318 6/94. Canx 10.6.94.
G-BUBK	PBN BN-2B-20 Islander (Originally regd as a BN-2B-26)	2268		14. 2.92	To JA5319 6/95. Canx 14.6.95.
G-BUBL	Thunder Ax8-105 HAFB	1147		10.12.87	To British Balloon Museum, Newbury in 1993. Canx as WFU 16.6.98.
G-BUBM	PBN BN-2B-20 Islander (Originally regd as a BN-2B-26)	2269		14. 2.92	To JA5320 12/94. Canx 6.12.94.
G-BUBN	PBN BN-2B-26 Islander	2270	(B-....) G-BUBN	14. 2.92	
G-BUBO	PBN BN-2B-26 Islander	2271	(B-....) G-BUBO	14. 2.92	To D-ILFB 3/96. Canx 12.2.96.
G-BUBP	PBN BN-2B-20 Islander (Originally regd as a BN-2B-26)	2272		14. 2.92	To JA5321 8/95. Canx 10.8.95.
G-BUBR	Cameron A-250 HAFB	2779		5. 2.92	
G-BUBS	Lindstrand LBL-77B HAFB (New envelope wef 9.95?)	144		10.10.94	
G-BUBT	Stoddard-Hamilton IIS RG Glasair	2026 & PFA/149-11633		6. 2.92	
G-BUBU	PA-34-220T Seneca III	34-8233060	N8043B	9. 7.87	
G-BUBV	Thunder Ax8-105 Srs.2 HAFB	2132		10. 2.92	To D-OOOS 8/92. Canx 14.8.92.
G-BUBW	Robinson R-22 Beta	2048		7. 2.92	
G-BUBX	Cameron O-120 HAFB	2784		10. 2.92	To VH-CBM(3) 8/95. Canx 2.5.95.
G-BUBY	Thunder Ax8-105 Srs.2 HAFB	2115		3. 2.92	
G-BUBZ	PA-22-150 Tri-Pacer (Mod) (Tailwheel conversion)	22-6716	N9826D	10. 4.92	To VH-FOX. Canx 18.6.93.
G-BUCA	Cessna A.150K Aerobat	A150-0220	N5920J	14. 6.89	
G-BUCB	Cameron H-34 HAFB	2777		11. 2.92	
G-BUCC	CASA I-131E Jungmann (Spanish serial conflicts with G-BJAL) (Originally regd with c/n 1631 and previous identity of E3B-564 which conflicted with D-EHDT(3) c/n 2181)	1109	G-BUEM G-BUCC/Spanish AF E3B-114	11. 9.78	
G-BUCD	Colt 120A HAFB	2130		6. 2.92	To D-OKSB 2/93. Canx 22.2.93.
G-BUCE	Colt 120A HAFB	2137		6. 2.92	To D-OUCE. Canx 17.12.92.
G-BUCF	Grumman F8F-1B Bearcat	D.779	122095 R.Thailand AF/BuA.122095	18. 2.92	To N2209 8/93. Canx 12.11.92.
G-BUCG	Schleicher ASW-20L (Mod)	20396	BGA.3140 I-FEEL	19. 2.92	
G-BUCH	Stinson V-77 (AT-19) Reliant	77-381	N9570H FB531(RN)	21. 2.92	
G-BUCI	Auster AOP.9	B5/10/150	XP242	10. 2.92	
G-BUCJ	DHC.2 Beaver AL.1	1442	XP772	23. 3.92	(Stored wingless 7/99 Duxford)
G-BUCK	CASA I-131E Jungmann Srs.1000 (Originally regd with c/n 1713)	1113	E3B-322 Spanish AF	11. 9.78	
G-BUCL	Robinson R-22 Beta	1993		18. 2.92	To G-EIBM 3/94. Canx.
G-BUCM	Hawker Sea Fury FB.11	-	VX653	26. 2.92	(On rebuild 7/99 Duxford)
G-BUCN	Colt Whisky Bottle 10SS HAFB	2125		26. 2.92	To G-WHFO 3/92. Canx.
G-BUCO	Pietenpol Air Camper	PFA/47-11829		10. 2.92	
G-BUCP	BAe 125 Srs.800B	258212	G-5-710	21. 2.92	To G-5-710/D-CSRI 7/94. Canx 22.6.94.
G-BUCR	BAe 125 Srs.800B	258050	HZ-OFC G-5-503	28. 2.92	To G-5-503/I-OSLO. Canx 29.7.92.
G-BUCS	Cessna 150F	150-62368	N3568L	25. 8.89	
G-BUCT	Cessna 150L	150-75326	N11320	14. 6.89	
G-BUCU	Short SD.3-30 (C-23B) Sherpa	SH3211	G-14-3211	28. 2.92	To USAF as 90-7011 2/92. Canx 2.2.93.
G-BUCV	Short SD.3-30 (C-23B) Sherpa	SH3212	G-14-3212	28. 2.92	To USAF as 90-7012 2/92. Canx 2.2.93.
G-BUCW	Short SD.3-30 (C-23B) Sherpa	SH3213	G-14-3213	28. 2.92	To USAF as 90-7013 2/92. Canx 2.2.93.
G-BUCX	Short SD.3-30 (C-23B) Sherpa	SH3214	G-14-3214	28. 2.92	To USAF as 90-7014 2/92. Canx 11.9.92.
G-BUCY	Short SD.3-30 (C-23B) Sherpa	SH3215	G-14-3215	28. 2.92	To USAF as 90-7015 2/92. Canx 11.9.92.
G-BUCZ	Short SD.3-30 (C-23B) Sherpa	SH3216	G-14-3216	28. 2.92	To USAF as 90-7016 2/92. Canx 11.9.92.
G-BUDA	Slingsby T.61F Venture T.2	1963	ZA627	18. 2.92	

Regn	Type	c/n	Previous identity	Regn date	Fate or immediate subsequent identity (if known)
G-BUDB	Slingsby T.61F Venture T.2	1964	ZA628	18. 2.92	
G-BUDC	Slingsby T.61F Venture T.2	1971	ZA652	18. 2.92	
G-BUDD	Team Minimax 91A	PFA/186-12211	G-MWZM	25. 2.92	Restored as G-MWZM 11/95. Canx.
G-BUDE	PA-22-135 Tri-Pacer	22-980	N1144C	9. 4.92	
	(Tailwheel conversion)				
G-BUDF	Rand Robinson KR-2	PFA/129-11155		20. 2.92	
G-BUDG	Cessna 421C Golden Eagle III		G-BKWX	10. 1.85	To D-IDDD. Canx 14.3.90.
		421C-1222	N26610/N2708F/(N2701J)		
G-BUDH	Light-Aero Avid Aerobat			28. 2.92	Crashed 2.1.98 at Ingoe, Northumberland.
		PFA/189-12018			Canx 31.3.98 as destroyed.
G-BUDI	Aero Designs Pulsar	PFA/202-12185		25. 2.92	
G-BUDJ	BAe Jetstream Srs.3202	960	G-31-960	2. 3.92	To (HS-ASD)/HS-DCA. Canx 19.8.92.
G-BUDK	Thunder Ax7-77 HAFB	2076		2. 3.92	
G-BUDL	Taylorcraft Auster III	458	PH-POL	5. 3.92	(On rebuild 3/97)
	(Regd with frame no. TAY 5810)		8A-2/R.Netherlands AF R-17/NX534		
G-BUDM	Colt Flying Hand SS HAFB	2122		5. 3.92	To PT-Z.. 4/98. Canx 17.4.98.
G-BUDN	Cameron Shoe 90SS HAFB	2761		6. 3.92	
	(Converse Allstar Trainers shape)				
G-BUDO	PZL-110 Koliber 150	03900045	(D-EIVT)	12. 3.92	
	(C/n also quoted as 039200045)				
G-BUDP	MBB Bo.105DBS-4	S.60/850	G-BTBD	23. 3.92	To G-DNLB 4/92. Canx.
	(Rebuilt with new pod S.850)		VH-LCS/VH-HRM/G-BCDH/EC-DUO/G-BCDH/D-HDBK		
G-BUDR	Denney Kitfox Mk.3			16. 3.92	
		1086 & PFA/172-12107			
G-BUDS	Rand Robinson KR-2	PFA/129-10937		31.12.85	
G-BUDT	Slingsby T.61F Venture T.2	1883	XZ563	30. 3.92	
G-BUDU	Cameron V-77 HAFB	2447		16. 3.92	
G-BUDV	Cameron A-210 HAFB	2815		16. 3.92	To VH-UDV 12/97. Canx 14.11.97.
G-BUDW	Brugger MB.2 Colibri	PFA/43-10644	G-GODS	19. 3.92	
G-BUDX	Boeing 757-236	25592		13. 5.92	To (N592KA)/SE-DSK. Canx 10.5.95.
	(Line No. 453)				
G-BUDY	Colt 17A Cloudhopper HAFB	413		28. 6.82	(Was based in France) Canx by CAA 19.5.93.
G-BUDZ	Boeing 757-236	25593	C-FNXY	25. 6.92	To (N593KA)/SE-DSL. Canx 10.5.95.
	(Line No. 466)		G-BUDZ		
G-BUEA	ATR-42-300	268	F-WWEW	30. 4.92	
G-BUEB(1)	ATR-42-300	296	F-WWLV	. .92R	NTU - To VR-BNH. Canx.
G-BUEB(2)	ATR-42-300	304	F-WWLE	29. 6.92	To F-.... Canx 30.7.99.
G-BUEC	Van's RV-6	21015 & PFA/181C-11884		17. 3.92	
G-BUED	Slingsby T.61F Venture T.2	1979	ZA660	12. 3.92	
G-BUEE	Cameron A-210 HAFB	2803		20. 3.92	
G-BUEF	Cessna 152 II	152-80862	N25928	17. 3.92	
G-BUEG	Cessna 152 II	152-80347	N24736	17. 3.92	
G-BUEH	Aerospatiale AS.355F1 Twin Squirrel		N27UG	17. 3.92	To 5N-BAL. Canx 22.5.92.
		5102	(N281CC)/N27UG/N5784X		
G-BUEI	Thunder Ax8-105 HAFB	2172		23. 3.92	
G-BUEJ	Colt 77B Bullitt HAFB	2166		23. 3.92	To C-FZIN 8/97. Canx 31.10.96.
G-BUEK	Slingsby T.61F Venture T.2	1879	XZ559	30. 3.92	
G-BUEL	Colt Bottle II SS HAFB	2141		26. 3.92	Canx by CAA 30.7.98.
	(Korbel California Champagne Bottle Shape)				
G-BUEM	CASA I-131E Jungmann	1109	G-BUCC	30. 6.88	Restored as G-BUCC 9/91. Canx.
	(Spanish serial conflicts with G-BJAL)		E3B-114 Spanish AF		
G-BUEN	VPM M-14 Scout	VPM14-UK-101		19. 3.92	
G-BUEO	Maule MX-7-180 Star Rocket	11082C		24. 3.92	(Badly damaged on take-off in France 21.8.95)
G-BUEP	Maule MXT-7-180 Star Rocket	14023C		24. 3.92	
G-BUER	Robinson R-22 Beta	1998		25. 3.92	To CS-HDL 7/95. Canx 16.6.95.
G-BUES	Cameron N-77 HAFB	2828		26. 3.92	
G-BUET	Colt Flying Drinks Can SS HAFB	2162		30. 3.92	Stored 1/98 BBAC Museum. Canx as WFU 29.4.97.
	(Budweiser Can Shape)				
G-BUEU	Colt 21A Cloudhopper HAFB	2163		30. 3.92	Stored 1/98 BBAC Museum. Canx as WFU 29.4.97.
	(Budweiser Can Shape)				
G-BUEV	Cameron O-77 HAFB	2810	EI-CFW	31. 3.92	
			G-BUEV		
G-BUEW	Rans S-6 Coyote II		G-MWYF	1. 4.92	To EI-... Canx 7.3.96.
		D-190111 & PFA/204-12021	(EI-CEL)		
G-BUEX	Schweizer Hughes 269C (300C)	S.1412	G-HFLR	14. 4.92	
G-BUEY	Thunder Ax10-180 Srs.2 HAFB	2167		2. 4.92	To ZS-HYM 9/92. Canx 2.9.92.
G-BUEZ	Hawker Hunter F.6A	S4U-3275	8736M	3. 4.92	(Stored 7/99 Duxford)
	(AWA-built)		XF375		
G-BUFA	Cameron R-77 Gas Balloon	2712		19. 3.92	(Stored .96)
G-BUFB	Cameron R-77 Gas Balloon	2745		19. 3.92	Canx as destroyed 23.3.93.
G-BUFC	Cameron R-77 Gas Balloon	2823		19. 3.92	(Stored .96)
G-BUFD	Cameron R-77 Gas Balloon	2824		19. 3.92	Canx as destroyed 23.3.93.
G-BUFE	Cameron R-77 Gas Balloon	2825		19. 3.92	(Stored .96)
G-BUFF	Wassmer Jodel D.112	1302	F-BMYD	9. 8.78	No CofA or Permit issued. Canx as CAA 29.8.91.
G-BUFG	Slingsby T.61F Venture T.2	1977	ZA658	3. 4.92	
G-BUFH	PA-28-161 Warrior II	28-8416076	N43520	15. 4.92	
G-BUFI	BAe 146 RJ70	E1229		29. 7.92	To TC-THI. Canx 4.7.96.
G-BUFJ	Cameron V-90 HAFB	2809		7. 4.92	
G-BUFK	Cassutt Racer IIIM	PFA/34-11069		7. 4.92	(Nearing completion 5/95 - for sale 7/96)
G-BUFL	BAe Jetstream Srs.3102	638	OH-JAC	8. 4.92	To SE-LHP 4/97. Canx 3.4.97.
			G-BUFL/N408MX/G-31-638		
G-BUFM	BAe Jetstream Srs.3102	640	G-LAKH	8. 4.92	To G-OAKA 7/96. Canx.
			G-BUFM/N410MX/G-31-640		

Regn	Type	c/n	Previous identity	Regn date	Fate or immediate subsequent identity (if known)
G-BUFN	Slingsby T.61F Venture T.2	1967	ZA631	8. 4.92	
G-BUFO	Cameron UFO 70SS HAFB	1929		10. 3.89	
	(Orig. regd as a Wedgwood SS)(Flying Saucer shape for Richard Branson's April Fool joke)				
G-BUFP	Slingsby T.61F Venture T.2	1982	ZA663	8. 4.92	
G-BUFR	Slingsby T.61F Venture T.2	1880	XZ560	9. 4.92	
G-BUFS	Thunder Ax9-120 Srs.2 HAFB	2017		9. 4.92	To D-ONBY 9/92. Canx 10.9.92.
G-BUFT	Cameron O-120 HAFB	2814		9. 4.92	
G-BUFU	Colt 105A HAFB	2161		14. 4.92	Canx by CAA 12.9.95. (Previously based overseas - Germany?)
G-BUFV	Light Aero Avid Speed Wing Mk.4	PFA/189-12192		15. 4.92	
G-BUFW	Aerospatiale AS.355F1 Twin Squirrel	5112	N57904	21. 4.92	To 5N-BAL. Canx 29.5.92.
G-BUFX	Cameron N-90 HAFB	2835		22. 4.92	
G-BUFY	PA-28-161 Warrior II	28-8016211	N130CT N8TS/N3571K	14. 4.92	
G-BUFZ	Colt 77B HAFB	2139		22. 4.92	Canx 9.12.92 on sale to Australia. To ZK-ROE.
G-BUGA	Not to be used.				
G-BUGB	Stolp SA.750 Acroduster Too	PFA/89-11942		22. 4.92	(Nearing completion 9/97)
G-BUGC	Jurca MJ.5 Sirocco (Regd as PFA/59-2207)	PFA/2207	(G-BWDJ)	14. 4.92	(Nearing completion 7/95)
G-BUGD	Cameron V-77 HAFB	2195		23. 4.92	(Expected to go to France in 1999)
G-BUGE	Bellanca 7GCAA Citabria	339-77	N4165Y	23. 4.92	
G-BUGF	Cameron A-120 HAFB	2846		23. 4.92	To OO-BBG 10/96. Canx 17.9.96.
G-BUGG	Cessna 150F	150-62479	N8379G	24. 3.92	
G-BUGH	Rans S-10 Sakota	0790-110 & PFA/194-11899		24. 4.92	
G-BUGI	Evans VP-2 Volksplane	PFA/7201		16. 4.92	(Nearing completion Dunkeswell 9/95)
G-BUGJ	Robin DR.400/180 Regent	2137		28. 4.92	
G-BUGK	Thunder Ax9-120 Srs.2 HAFB	2177		28. 4.92	To D-OBCG 9/92. Canx 5.8.92.
G-BUGL	Slingsby T.61F Venture T.2	1966	ZA630	29. 4.92	
G-BUGM	CFM Streak Shadow	K.176-SA & PFA/206-12069		29. 4.92	
G-BUGN	Colt 210A HAFB	2193		1. 5.92	
G-BUGO	Colt 56B HAFB	2143		18. 5.92	
G-BUGP	Cameron V-77 HAFB	2278	OO-BEE	10. 3.92	
G-BUGR	Not to be used.				
G-BUGS	Cameron V-77 HAFB	2482		14. 4.92	
G-BUGT	Slingsby T.61F Venture T.2	1871	XZ551	22. 4.92	
G-BUGU	Not to be used.				
G-BUGV	Slingsby T.61F Venture T.2	1884	XZ564	28. 4.92	
G-BUGW	Slingsby T.61F Venture T.2	1962	ZA626	22. 4.92	
G-BUGX	Socata MS.880B Rallye Club	2957	OO-FLO	24. 4.92	
G-BUGY	Cameron V-90 HAFB	2800		9. 4.92	
G-BUGZ	Slingsby T.61F Venture T.2	1981	ZA662	22. 4.92	
G-BUHA	Slingsby T.61F Venture T.2	1970	ZA634	29. 4.92	
G-BUHB	BAe 146 Srs.300	E3183	G-6-183 G-BSYS/G-6-183	18. 6.92	To D-AEWB 8/96. Canx 14.8.96.
G-BUHC	BAe 146 Srs.300	E3193	G-BTMI (N883DV)/G-6-193	30. 6.92	
G-BUHD	BAe 146 Srs.300	-		. .92R	NTU - Canx.
G-BUHE	BAe 146 Srs.300	-		. .92R	NTU - Canx.
G-BUHF	BAe 146 Srs.300	-		. .92R	NTU - Canx.
G-BUHG	BAe 146 Srs.300	-		. .92R	NTU - Canx.
G-BUHH	Not allotted.				
G-BUHI	Boeing 737-3Q8 (Line No. 2418)	26284		. .92R	NTU - To N571LF 12/92. Canx.
G-BUHJ	Boeing 737-4Q8 (Line No. 2447)	25164		19. 3.93	
G-BUHK	Boeing 737-4Q8 (Line No. 2486)	26289		14. 6.93	
G-BUHL	Boeing 737-4S3 (Line No. 2083)	25134	9M-MLH N1799B/(G-BSRB)	22. 3.93	
G-BUHM	Cameron V-77 HAFB	2481		7. 5.92	
G-BUHN	Cameron N-90 HAFB	2760		7. 5.92	To OE-ZCB(1). Canx 11.4.94.
G-BUHO	Cessna 140	14402	N2173V	1. 5.92	(Damaged in gales Stapleford 2/96) (On rebuild 6/96 at Squires Gate)
G-BUHP	Ailes De K Flyair 1100	01219935		7. 5.92	
G-BUHR	Slingsby T.61F Venture T.2	1874	XZ554	8. 5.92	
G-BUHS	Stoddard-Hamilton Glasair I TD (built by F.L.Binder)	149	C-GYMB	8. 5.92	
G-BUHT	Cameron A-210 HAFB	2852		22. 5.92	Canx as WFU 2.12.98.
G-BUHU	Cameron N-105 HAFB	2785		13. 5.92	
G-BUHV	BAe 146 Srs.300	E3207	G-6-207	26. 5.92	To B-2711 11/92. Canx 27.11.92.
G-BUHW	BAe 146 Srs.300	E3217	G-6-217	26. 5.92	To VH-NJN 10/94. Canx 27.10.94.
G-BUHX	Robinson R-22 Beta	2012		15. 5.92	To G-SANS 10/97. Canx.
G-BUHY	Cameron A-210 HAFB	2858		14. 5.92	
G-BUHZ	Cessna 120	14950	N3676V	1. 5.92	
G-BUIA	Colt 77B HAFB	2200		20. 5.92	To PP-Z.. 6/95. Canx 2.6.95.
G-BUIB	MBB Bo.105DBS-4 (Original acft remanufactured with new pod S-911 .92)	S-138/911	G-BDYZ D-HDEF	21. 5.92	
G-BUIC	Denney Kitfox Mk.2	PFA/172-11802		1. 5.92	

Regn	Type	c/n	Previous identity	Regn date	Fate or immediate subsequent identity (if known)
G-BUID	BAe 125 Srs.800B	258208	TC-ANC G-5-700/G-BUID	27. 5.92	To TC-ANC 10/93. Canx 1.11.93.
G-BUIE	Cameron N-90 HAFB	2863		22. 5.92	
G-BUIF	PA-28-161 Warrior II	28-7916406	N28375	29. 5.92	
G-BUIG	Campbell Cricket	G/03-1173		27. 5.92	
G-BUIH	Slingsby T.61F Venture T.2	1070	XZ558	29. 5.92	
G-BUII	Cameron A-180 HAFB	2872		29. 5.92	Reserved as ZS-HZH in 1997. Canx 11.6.97.
G-BUIJ	PA-28-161 Warrior II	28-8116210	N83784	3. 6.92	
G-BUIK	PA-28-161 Warrior II	28-7916469	N2845P	2. 6.92	
G-BUIL	CFM Streak Shadow	K.182-SA & PFA/206-12121		8. 5.92	
G-BUIM	BAe 125 Srs.800B	258068	G-5-738 HZ-SJP/G-5-539	8. 6.92	To N68GP. Canx 25.2.93.
G-BUIN	Thunder Ax7-77 HAFB	1882		5. 6.92	
G-BUIO	BAe Jetstream Srs.3202	835	C-GZRT G-31-835	1. 9.92	To OH-JAB. Canx 19.2.93.
G-BUIP	Denney Kitfox Mk.2	710 & PFA/172-11874		8. 6.92	
G-BUIR	Light Aero Avid Speed Wing Mk.4	PFA/189-12213		9. 6.92	(Damaged in forced landing at Heapham, nr.Gainsborough 26.1.97) (On rebuild off-airfield 7/97)
G-BUIS	Rotorway Exec 90	5075		5. 5.92	To TC-... 11/93. Canx 30.11.93.
G-BUIT	Denney Kitfox Mk.3	PFA/172-11924		10. 6.92	Stalled and crashed on its maiden flight from Rochester Airport 18.1.93. The aircraft struck the ground in a near vertical attitude, seriously injuring both on board. Canx as destroyed 5.5.93.
G-BUIU	Cameron V-90 HAFB	2641		11. 6.92	
G-BUIV	SNCA SE.3130 Alouette II	1185	XN132 F-WIPG	11. 6.92	To (PH-THC)/PH-NSW 5/93. Canx 12.5.93.
G-BUIW	Robinson R-22 Beta	2049		10. 6.92	Fatal crash near Amport on 9.3.98. Canx as destroyed 17.6.99.
G-BUIX	BAe 125 Srs.1000B	259024	G-5-737	10. 6.92	To (C-....)/N5ES. Canx 4.10.95.
G-BUIY	BAe 125 Srs.800A	258025	G-5-742 3D-AVL	21. 7.92	To N7C 3/94. Canx 15.3.94.
G-BUIZ	Cameron N-90 HAFB	2850		12. 6.92	
G-BUJA	Slingsby T.61F Venture T.2	1972	ZA653	22. 5.92	
G-BUJB	Slingsby T.61F Venture T.2	1978	ZA659	21. 5.92	
G-BUJC	Partenavia P.68C Victor	284	OO-TJJ	12. 6.92	To TF-VEN 5/94. Canx 20.5.94.
G-BUJD	Robinson R-22 Beta	2146	N23376	19. 6.92	To HB-XZL. Canx 22.3.93.
G-BUJE	Cessna 177B Cardinal	177-01920	N34646	10. 6.92	
G-BUJF	Eurocopter AS.355N Twin Squirrel	5525	F-WYMF	16. 6.92	To G-METD 4/93. Canx.
G-BUJG	Eurocopter AS.350B2 Ecureuil	2668	G-HEAR G-BUJG	16. 6.92	To G-WKRD 3/99. Canx.
G-BUJH	Colt 77B HAFB	2207		23. 6.92	
G-BUJI	Slingsby T.61F Venture T.2	1882	XZ562	22. 5.92	
G-BUJJ	Light Aero Avid Speed Wing (built by M.Cox)	213	N614JD	20.10.92	
G-BUJK	Montgomerie-Bensen B.8MR Merlin	G/01-1211		25. 6.92	
G-BUJL	Aero Designs Pulsar	PFA/202-11892		16. 6.92	
G-BUJM	Cessna 120	11784	N77343 NC77343	19. 6.92	
G-BUJN	Cessna 172N Skyhawk II	172-72713	N6315D	19. 6.92	Damaged in gales at Wellesbourne Mountford on 18.1.95. (On repair 9/97 at Earls Colne/Braintree)
G-BUJO	PA-28-161 Cherokee Warrior II	28-7716077	N1014Q	19. 6.92	
G-BUJP	PA-28-161 Warrior II	28-7916047	N21624	19. 6.92	
G-BUJR	Cameron A-180 HAFB	2821		22. 6.92	
G-BUJS	Colt 17A Cloudhopper HAFB	2222		22. 6.92	Canx by CAA 10.3.95.
G-BUJT	BAe Jetstream Srs.3101	699	N414MX G-31-699	8. 7.92	Stored as N414MX 11/96 at Prestwick. Used for spares. Canx as PWFU 22.7.97.
G-BUJU	Cessna 150H	150-67285	N6485S	30. 6.92	
G-BUJV	Light Aero Avid Mk.4 Speed Wing	PFA/189-12250		3. 7.92	(Badly damaged on landing at Caernarfon on 13.8.93)
G-BUJW	Thunder Ax8-90 Srs.2 HAFB	2208		6. 7.92	
G-BUJX	Slingsby T-61F Venture T.2	1873	XZ553	7. 7.92	
G-BUJY	DH.82A Tiger Moth (Identity unconfirmed since VT-DPE reported still at Shipdham 4/94)	"OU/04/1967"	VT-DPE Indian AF HU-858	1. 7.92	(On rebuild 3/94)
G-BUJZ	Rotorway Exec 90	5119		9. 7.92	(Badly damaged on take-off at Eggesford on 23.10.93)
G-BUKA	Swearingen (Fairchild) SA.227AC Metro IV	AC-706B	ZK-NSQ N27185/G-BUKA/N27185	24. 8.88	
G-BUKB	Rans S-10 Sakota	PFA/194-12078		13. 7.92	
G-BUKC	Cameron A-180 HAFB	2870		3. 7.92	
G-BUKD	Robinson R-22 Beta	2147	N23381	8. 7.92	To G-SUMT 9/92. Canx.
G-BUKE	Boeing-Stearman A75N1 (PT-17) Kaydet	75-2732	(G-BRIP) N53127/41-25243	17. 7.92	
G-BUKF	Denney Kitfox Mk.4	PFA/172A-12247		2. 6.92	
G-BUKG	Robinson R-22 Beta	1780		14. 7.92	To N1118N 6/96. Canx 20.5.96.
G-BUKH	Druine D.31 Turbulent	PFA/48-11419		14. 8.92	
G-BUKI	Thunder Ax7-77 HAFB	2239		8. 7.92	
G-BUKJ	BAe ATP	2052	EC-GLD G-OEDF/G-BUKJ/TC-THZ/G-BUKJ	5. 8.92	To EC-HCO 5/99. Canx 8.5.99.

Regn	Type	c/n	Previous identity	Regn date	Fate or immediate subsequent identity (if known)
G-BUKK	Bucker Bu.133D Jungmeister (Dornier-built)	27	N44DD HB-MKG/Swiss AF U-80	15.11.89	
G-BUKL	Brantly B-2B	2006	N2550U	13. 7.92	Restored as N2550U 5/96. Canx 30.3.95.
G-BUKM	Pilatus P.3-05	505-54	A-867 Swiss AF	18. 6.92	To HB-RCD. Canx 9.11.93.
G-BUKN	PA-15 Vagabond	15-215	N4427H NC4427H	15. 7.92	
G-BUKO	Cessna 120	13089	N2828N NC2828N	15. 7.92	(Damaged on take-off Manor Farm,Bishopstone 28.12.97)
G-BUKP	Denney Kitfox Mk.2 (Rotax 582)	PFA/172-12301		22. 7.92	
G-BUKR	Socata MS.880B Rallye 100T	2923	LN-BIY	27. 7.92	
G-BUKS	Colt 77B HAFB	2241		6. 7.92	
G-BUKT	Luscombe 8E Silvaire	2197	N45670 NC45670	30. 7.92	
G-BUKU	Luscombe 8E Silvaire	4720	N1993K NC1993K	30. 7.92	
G-BUKV	Colt AS-105 Mk.II Hot-Air Airship	2212	(ZS-...) G-BUKV	3. 8.92	To ZS-HYO. Canx 4.6.93.
G-BUKW	BAe 125 Srs.1000B	259021	G-5-736	3. 8.92	To XA-GRB(2) 11/92. Canx 24.11.92.
G-BUKX	PA-28-161 Warrior II	28-7816674	N231PA	5. 8.92	
G-BUKY	CCF T-6J Harvard 4	CCF4-464	FAP1766 Portuguese AF/West German AF BF+063/AA+063/52-8543	13. 7.92	
G-BUKZ	Evans VP-2 Volksplane	PFA/63-10761		5. 8.92	(Extant 5/97)
G-BULA	Cameron Raindrop 77SS HAFB	2895		7. 8.92	To C-FULA 8/94. Canx 29.6.94.
G-BULB	Thunder Ax7-77 HAFB	1968		3. 7.92	
G-BULC	Light Aero Avid Flyer Mk.4	PFA/189-12202		6. 7.92	
G-BULD	Cameron N-105 HAFB	2136		6. 8.92	
G-BULE	Price TPB.2 HAFB	004		10. 8.92	
G-BULF	Colt 77A HAFB	2043		10. 8.92	
G-BULG	Van's RV-4 (built by L.Johnson)	JRV4-1	C-FELJ	28. 7.92	
G-BULH	Cessna 172N Skyhawk II	172-69869	N738CJ	2. 7.92	
G-BULI	BAe 125 Srs.1000B	259016	G-5-732 (D-BJET)	10. 8.92	To (5N-...)/G-5-732/N291H 6/94. Canx 6.1.93.
G-BULJ	CFM Streak Shadow	K.191-SA & PFA/206-12199		10. 8.92	
G-BULK	Thunder Ax9-120 Srs.2 HAFB	2237		3. 7.92	
G-BULL	Scottish Avn Bulldog Srs.120/128	BH120/392	HKG-5 R.Hong Kong Aux.AF/G-31-18	20. 9.88	
G-BULM	Aero Designs Pulsar	PFA/202-12010		11. 8.92	
G-BULN	Colt 210A HAFB	2265		13. 8.92	
G-BULO	Luscombe 8A Silvaire	4216	N1489K NC1489K	13. 8.92	
G-BULP	Thunder Ax9-120 Srs.2 HAFB	2266		14. 8.92	To D-OULP 6/96. Canx 14.5.96.
G-BULR	PA-28-140 Cherokee B	28-25230	HB-OHP N7320F	8. 7.92	
G-BULS	Cameron A-210 HAFB	2891		21. 8.92	To JY-RUN 9/94. Canx 1.9.94.
G-BULT	Campbell Cricket	G/03-1213		20. 8.92	
G-BULU	Short S.312 Tucano T.1	S.146 & T.117		20. 8.92	Probably NTU - To RAF as ZF485 21.9.92. Canx by CAA 23.2.94
G-BULV	Aeronca 11AC Chief	11AC-1773	N3493E NC3493E	21. 8.92	To G-RONC 1/93. Canx.
G-BULW	Rans S-10 Sakota	PFA/194-11663		18. 8.92	To PH-RNS 98R. Canx 17.4.98.
G-BULX	Robinson R-22 Beta	2169		1. 9.92	To HB-XHQ 10/94. Canx 20.10.94.
G-BULY	Light Aero Avid Flyer	PFA/189-12309		12. 8.92	
G-BULZ	Denney Kitfox Mk.2	PFA/172-11546		31. 7.92	
G-BUMA	Not to be issued.				
G-BUMB	Not to be issued.				
G-BUMC	Not to be issued.				
G-BUMD	Not to be issued.				
G-BUME	Not to be issued.				
G-BUMF	Robinson R-22	0090	G-BMBU ZS-HJV	10. 2.86	Rolled over on take-off from a field at Stokenchurch on 24.7.88 & extensively damaged. Canx as destroyed 5.11.90.
G-BUMG	Not to be issued.				
G-BUMH	Not to be issued.				
G-BUMI	Not to be issued.				
G-BUMJ	Not to be issued.				
G-BUMK	Not to be issued.				
G-BUML	Not to be issued.				
G-BUMM	Not to be issued.				
G-BUMN	Not to be issued.				
G-BUMO	Not to be issued.				
G-BUMP	PA-28-181 Cherokee Archer II (Rebuild of PH-MVA which was w/o at Harfsen on 30.7.78)	28-7790437	PH-MVA OO-HCH/N3105Q	17. 1.79	
G-BUMR	Not to be issued.				
G-BUMS	Not to be issued.				
G-BUMT	Not to be issued.				
G-BUMU	Not to be issued.				
G-BUMV	Not to be issued.				
G-BUMW	Not to be issued.				

Regn	Type	c/n	Previous identity	Regn date	Fate or immediate subsequent identity (if known)
G-BUMX	Not to be issued.				
G-BUMY	Not to be issued.				
G-BUMZ	Not to be issued.				
G-BUNA	SNCAN Stampe SV-4C	222	N10SV F-BCBG	8. 1.81	To OY-EFF 10/82. Canx 10.11.82.
G-BUNB	Slingsby T.61F Venture T.2	1969	7A633	25. 8.92	
G-BUNC	PZL-104 Wilga 35A	129444	SP-TWP	2. 9.92	
G-BUND	PA-28RT-201T Turbo Arrow IV	28R-8031107	(G-BOGF) N8219V	18. 7.88	
G-BUNE	Colt Flying Drinks Can SS HAFB (Pepsi Cola can shape)	2245		26. 8.92	(Was based in USA) Canx as destroyed 11.6.98.
G-BUNF	Colt Flying Drinks Can SS HAFB (Pepsi Cola can shape)	2263		26. 8.92	Canx by CAA 4.8.98.
G-BUNG	Cameron N-77 HAFB	2905		2. 9.92	
G-BUNH	PA-28RT-201T Turbo Arrow IV	28R-8031166	N8255H	26. 8.92	
G-BUNI	Cameron Bunny 90SS HAFB (Cadburys Caramel Bunny shape)	2897		23. 9.92	
G-BUNJ	K & S SA.102.5 Cavalier	PFA/01-10058		10. 9.92	(Stored 4/99 at Great Massingham Village)
G-BUNK	Cessna 404 Titan	404-0813	3X-GCF (G-BKRE)/N67662/(D-IDOS)/N67662	15. 9.92	To N404MG 9/92. Canx 15.9.92.
G-BUNL	HS.125 Srs.700B	257007	D-CADA G-5-721/D-CADA/HB-VFA	10. 9.92	To RA-02800 5/93. Canx 5.4.93.
G-BUNM	Denney Kitfox Mk.3	PFA/172-12111		15. 9.92	
G-BUNN	Whittaker MW-6S Fatboy Flyer Srs.A	PFA/164-11929		12. 8.92	To G-MZDI 8/96. Canx.
G-BUNO	Neico Lancair 320	PFA/191-12332		11. 9.92	
G-BUNP	Thunder Ax8-90 Srs.2 HAFB	2287		21. 9.92	To G-GEMS 11/92. Canx.
G-BUNR	PA-34-200T Senaca II	34-7870177	EI-CFI N9245C	21. 9.92	To G-OACG 3/94. Canx.
G-BUNS	Reims Cessna F.150K	0648	F-BSIL	28. 8.92	(Stored 3/97)
G-BUNT	AIA Stampe SV-4C	1139	G-AYCK F-BANE	30. 9.91	Restored as G-AYCK 3/94. Canx.
G-BUNU	Bell 206L-3 Long Ranger	51011	G-GWIN N2266T	21. 9.92	To N27EA 1/93. Canx 19.1.93.
G-BUNV	Thunder Ax7-77 HAFB	1967		23. 9.92	
G-BUNW	BAe 125 Srs.1000B	259029	G-5-751	25. 9.92	To EK-B021/EZ-B021. Canx 12.2.93.
G-BUNX	Cameron V-77 HAFB	2483		29. 9.92	To C-FUNX 12/96. Canx 29.11.96.
G-BUNY	Beechcraft 95-B55 Baron	TC-2097	N513TC N18428	18.12.87	To TC-... Canx 20.9.91.
G-BUNZ	Thunder Ax10-180 Srs.2 HAFB	2271		7. 9.92	
G-BUOA	Whittaker MW-6S Srs.A Fatboy Flyer	PFA/164-11959		25. 9.92	
G-BUOB	CFM Streak Shadow	K.186-SA & PFA/206-12156		29. 9.92	
G-BUOC	Cameron A-210 HAFB	2924		5.10.92	
G-BUOD	Replica Plans SE.5A	PFA/20-10474		5.10.92	
G-BUOE	Cameron V-90 HAFB	2938		6.10.92	
G-BUOF	Druine D.62B Condor	PFA/49-11236		6.10.92	
G-BUOG	Colt 90A HAFB	2224		6.10.92	To D-OUOG 5/94. Canx 22.4.94.
G-BUOH	Herbert Jet Hawk Ducted Fan Trainer	PFA/244-12352		6.10.92	No Permit to Fly issued. Canx by CAA 3.8.95.
G-BUOI	PA-20-135 Pacer	20-571	OY-ALS D-EHEN/N7750K	18. 9.92	
G-BUOJ	Cessna 172N Skyhawk II	172-71701	N5064E	8.10.92	
G-BUOK	Rans S-6-116 Coyote II (Originally regd as S-6-ESA)	0692-314 & PFA/204A-12317		9.10.92	
G-BUOL	Denney Kitfox Mk.3	PFA/172-12142		12.10.92	
G-BUOM	DHC.6-210 Twin Otter	200	G-DOSH N66200	13.10.92	To N123FX 2/93. Canx 22.1.93.
G-BUON	Light Aero Avid Aerobat	PFA/189-12160		13.10.92	
G-BUOO	QAC Quickie Tri-Q 200 (built by L.D.Fulper)	01	N10RX	17. 5.93	(Badly damaged on landing Cranfield 4.7.97)
G-BUOP	Dorrington Skycycle D2 Airship	D2-218		15.10.92	
G-BUOR	CASA I-131E Jungmann Srs.2000	2134	N89542 EC-336/Spaniah AF E3B-508	21.10.92	
G-BUOS	Vickers-Supermarine 394 Spitfire FR.XVIIIe (Regd with c/n 6S/676224)	6S/672224	HS687 Indian AF/SM845	19.10.92	(On rebuild 9/96)
G-BUOT	Colt 77A HAFB	2252		20.10.92	To VH-AOW 10/96. Canx 12.9.96.
G-BUOU	Colt 90A HAFB	2295		20.10.92	Canx 4.12.95 on sale to Spain.
G-BUOV	Colt 105A HAFB	1992		21.10.92	To VT-ETF 3/93. Canx 28.10.92.
G-BUOW	Aero Designs Pulsar XP	PFA/202-12206		22.10.92	
G-BUOX	Cameron V-77 HAFB	2925		23.10.92	
G-BUOY	Aerospatiale SA.315B Alouette III	2468	N4138N D-HAFA/N3602C/C-GUON/N47293	26.10.92	Crashed at Tambobamba, Peru on 31.12.94. Canx as destroyed 17.2.95.
G-BUOZ	Thunder Ax10-180 HAFB	1962		29.10.92	Canx 12.5.95 on sale to Greece.

Regn	Type	c/n	Previous identity	Regn date	Fate or immediate subsequent identity (if known)
G-BUPA	Rutan LongEz (built by D.Moore)	750	N72SD	22. 9.92	
G-BUPB	Stolp SA.300 Starduster Too (built by R.Harte in 1979)	RH.100	N8035E	3.11.92	
G-BUPC	Rollason Beta B2	PFA/02-12369		29.10.92	
G-BUPD	Cameron N-90 HAFB	2866		3.11.92	To OO-BSG 3/93. Canx 11.2.93.
G-BUPE	Cameron N-90 HAFB	2922		3.11.92	To OO-BOJ. Canx 8.2.93.
G-BUPF	Bensen B.8MR Gyrocopter	G/01-1209		5.11.92	
G-BUPG	Cessna 180J Skywagon	180-52490	N52086	15.10.92	(Extant 5/98)
G-BUPH	Colt 25A Sky Chariot HAFB	2023		10.11.92	Canx by CAA 4.8.98.
G-BUPI	Cameron V-77 HAFB	1778	G-BOUC	28. 7.88	
G-BUPJ	Sportavia-Putzer Fournier RF-4D	4119	N7752	10.11.92	(On overhaul 6/95)
G-BUPK	Aerospatiale AS.350B Ecureuil	2076	JA9740	17.11.92	To EI-CGQ 1/93. Canx 15.1.93.
G-BUPL	BAe 125 Srs.1000B	259030	G-5-753	19.11.92	To G-DCCI 12/92. Canx.
G-BUPM	VPM M-16 Tandem Trainer	VPM16-UK-102		16.10.92	
G-BUPN	PA-46-350P Malibu Mirage	4622086	N91884	18.11.92	To N90D 7/99. Canx 26.7.99.
G-BUPO	Moravan Zlin Z.526F Trener Master	1267	YR-OAZ YR-ZAO	23.11.92	
G-BUPP	Cameron V-42 HAFB	2789		21. 7.92	(Stored 2/97)
G-BUPR	Jodel D.18	PFA/169-11289		23.11.92	
G-BUPS	ATR-42-300	109	DQ-FEP F-WWEF	16.12.92	
G-BUPT	Cameron O-105 HAFB	2960		25.11.92	
G-BUPU	Thunder Ax7-77 HAFB	2305		25.11.92	
G-BUPV	Great Lakes 2T-1A Sport Trainer	126	N865K NC865K	26.11.92	(On rebuild)
G-BUPW	Denney Kitfox Mk.3	PFA/172-12281		22.10.92	
G-BUPX	Robin DR.400/180 Regent	2176		26.11.92	To G-CONB 4/93. Canx.
G-BUPY	Commander Aircraft 114B	14554	N6008X	25. 9.92	To 9M-... 4/93. Canx 29.4.93.
G-BUPZ	Colt AS-105 Mk.II Hot-Air Airship	2313		27.11.92	To HB-... Canx 18.2.93.
G-BURA	Thunder Ax8-105 Srs.2 HAFB	2298		14. 1.93	To PH-CMP 3/99. Canx 29.7.98.
G-BURB	Denney Kitfox Mk.3	PFA/172-12144		9.12.92	The pilot lost control after a heavy landing at Wellesbourne Mountford on 6.5.95 and the aircraft was badly damaged when it cartwheeled. Canx as destroyed 20.12.95.
G-BURC	Not allotted.				
G-BURD	Reims Cessna F.172N Skyhawk II	1677	D-EMCP PH-AXI	26. 4.78	
G-BURE	Jodel D.9 Bebe	PFA/944		30.11.92	(Nearing completion 12/95)
G-BURF	Rand Robinson KR-2	PFA/129-11345		30.11.92	(For sale complete 10/97)
G-BURG	Colt 77A HAFB	2042		12. 1.93	
G-BURH	Cessna 150E	150-61225	EI-AOO G-BURH/EI-AOO/N2125J	2.12.92	
G-BURI	Enstrom F-28C	433	N51743	11.12.92	
G-BURJ	HS.748 Srs.2A/256	1667	"G-BPNK" 7Q-YKB	14.12.92	To 9N-ACP. Canx 12.5.93.
G-BURK	Luscombe 8A Master	1474	N28713 NC28713	19.10.92	To G-DAIR 10/97. Canx.
G-BURL	Colt 105A HAFB	2297		18.11.92	
G-BURM	English Electric Canberra TT.18 (built by Handley Page)	-	WJ680	11.12.92	
G-BURN	Cameron O-120 HAFB	2793		18. 2.92	
G-BURO	PZL-104 Wilga 35A	CF14800561	SP-TWR	3.12.92	Crashed at Aston Down on 4.9.94. Canx as WFU 28.11.94.
G-BURP	Rotorway Exec 90	5116		8.10.92	
G-BURR	Auster AOP.9	-	7851M WZ706	28. 9.92	No Permit issued. (On overhaul 3/97 Middle Wallop) Canx by CAA 18.3.99.
G-BURS	Sikorsky S-76A II Plus	760040	(HP-...) G-BURS/G-OHTL	4. 5.89	
G-BURT	PA-28-161 Warrior II	28-7716105	N2459Q	10. 6.81	
G-BURU	BAe Jetstream Srs.3206	974	(F-OHFT) G-31-974	14. 1.93	To F-GMVH 5/93. Canx 5.5.93.
G-BURV	BAe 125 Srs.800B	258213	D-CWBW G-5-709	22.12.92	To N10857. Canx 12.3.96.
G-BURW	Light Aero Avid Speed Wing	PFA/189-12086		31.12.92	Crashed on take-off Sparwood Farm, Plaistow .96. Canx by CAA 22.10.96.
G-BURX	Cameron N-105 HAFB	2959		8. 1.93	To G-NPNP 1/93. Canx.
G-BURY	Cessna 152 II	152-81724	N67285	19.11.92	To G-DACF 6/97. Canx.
G-BURZ	Hawker Nimrod II	41H-59890	K3661	22.12.91	(On rebuild by Aero Vintage Ltd from components 8/95)
G-BUSA	Aerospatiale AS.355F1 Twin Squirrel	5104		21. 9.81	To G-PAMI 11/85. Canx.
G-BUSB	Airbus A.320-211 (Not fitted with winglets)	0006	(G-BRSA) (G-BRAA)/F-WWDD	30. 3.88	(Originally flown as G-BRSA)
G-BUSC	Airbus A.320-211 (Not fitted with winglets)	0008	(G-BRSB) (G-BRAB)/F-WWDE	26. 5.88	
G-BUSD	Airbus A.320-211 (Not fitted with winglets)	0011	(G-BRSC) (G-BRAC)/F-WWDF	21. 7.88	
G-BUSE	Airbus A.320-211 (Not fitted with winglets)	0017	(G-BRSD) (G-BRAE)/F-WWDG	1.12.88	
G-BUSF	Airbus A.320-211 (Not fitted with winglets)	0018	(G-BRSE) (G-BRAH)/F-WWDH	26. 5.89	

Regn	Type	c/n	Previous identity	Regn date	Fate or immediate subsequent identity (if known)
G-BUSG	Airbus A.320-211 (Fitted with winglets)	0039	(G-BRSF) (G-BRAI)/F-WWDM	30. 5.89	
G-BUSH	Airbus A.320-211 (Fitted with winglets)	0042	(G-BRSG) (G-BRAJ)/F-WWDT	19. 6.89	
G-BUSI	Airbus A.320-211 (Fitted with winglets)	0103	(G-BRSH) (G-BRAK)/F-WWDB	23. 3.90	
G-BUSJ	Airbus A.320-211 (Fitted with winglets)	0109	(G-BRSI) (G-BRAM)/F-WWIC	6. 8.90	
G-BUSK	Airbus A.320-211 (Fitted with winglets)	0120	(G-BRSJ) (G-BRAN)/F-WWIN	12.10.90	
G-BUSL	Boeing 737-33A (Line No. 1739)	24096	PP-SNW	24.12.92	To VT-JAC 4/93. Canx 13.5.93.
G-BUSM	Boeing 737-33A (Line No. 1741)	24097	PP-SNZ (PP-SNX)	24.12.92	To VT-JAD 4/93. Canx 25.5.93.
G-BUSN	Rotorway Exec 90	5141		6. 1.93	
G-BUSO	Cameron Pylon 80SS HAFB (Electric Plyon shape)	2958		8. 1.93	To G-PYLN 18.1.93. Canx.
G-BUSP	Cameron Cart SS HAFB	2952		8. 1.93	To C-FRTP 3/94. Canx 8.3.94.
G-BUSR	Aero Designs Pulsar	PFA/202-12356		15.12.92	
G-BUSS	Cameron Bus 90SS HAFB	1685		11. 3.88	
G-BUST	Neico Lancair IV	LIV-114A		23.10.92	
G-BUSU	Colt 42A HAFB	2323		12. 1.93	Canx by CAA 10.3.95. To VH-JLB 3/98.
G-BUSV	Colt 105A HAFB	2324		12. 1.93	
G-BUSW	Rockwell Commander 114	14079	N4749W	18. 1.93	
G-BUSX	Gates LearJet 35A	35A-662	G-NEVL	12. 1.93	To N35UK. Canx 27.5.93.
G-BUSY	Thunder Ax6-56A HAFB	111		20. 6.77	CofA expired 27.4.86. (Extant 2/97)
G-BUSZ	Light-Aero Avid Speedwing Mk.4	PFA/189-12280		20. 1.93	
G-BUTA	CASA I-131E Jungmann Srs.2000 (Correct c/n not known)	1101/A	E3B-336 Spanish AF	20. 1.93	(Stored 7/98 at Breighton)
G-BUTB	CFM Streak Shadow	K.190 & PFA/206-12243		20. 1.93	
G-BUTC	Cyclone Ax3	B.1122981 & PFA/245-12365	G-MYHO	11. 1.93	
G-BUTD	Van's RV-6	PFA/181-12152		21. 1.93	
G-BUTE	Anderson EA-1 Kingfisher Amphibian	PFA/132-10798	G-BRCK	15. 8.91	
G-BUTF	Aeronca 11AC Chief	11AC-1578	N3231E NC3231E	21. 1.93	(Stored 1/98)
G-BUTG	Zenair CH-601HD Zodiac	PFA/162-12225		22. 1.93	
G-BUTH	CEA Jodel DR.220 2+2	6	F-BNVK	10. 2.93	
G-BUTI	Firefly 7-15 HAFB	F7-789	N25933	13. 1.93	To N2571K 10/94. Canx 24.10.94.
G-BUTJ	Cameron O-77 HAFB	2991		25. 1.93	
G-BUTK	Murphy Rebel	PFA/232-12091		25. 1.93	
G-BUTL	PA-24-250 Comanche	24-2352	G-ARLB	4. 4.84	
G-BUTM	Rans S-6-116 Coyote II	PFA/204A-12414		22. 1.93	
G-BUTN	MBB Bo.105DBS-4 (Rebuilt with new pod S-912 .93)	S.34/912	G-AZTI EI-BTE/G-AZTI/EC-DRY/G-AZTI/D-HDAN	29. 1.93	To G-NAAA 4/99. Canx.
G-BUTO	Pitts S-1C Special (built by B.J.Sherrill)	362H	N9S	1. 2.93	Spun in and destroyed in crash Wychenor, near Burton-on-Trent on 8.4.97. Canx by CAA 17.4.97 as destroyed.
G-BUTP	Bede BD-5G	008801		5. 2.93	No Permit to Fly issued. (Was based in Germany) Canx by CAA 25.3.99.
G-BUTR	Aerospatiale AS.365N2 Dauphin 2	6450	F-WYMM	3. 2.93	To ZS-RDL 7/93. Canx 9.7.93.
G-BUTS	Lindstrand AS-300 Hot-Air Airship	008		5. 2.93	Canx 18.5.93 on sale to France.
G-BUTT	Reims Cessna FA.150K Aerobat	0029	G-AXSJ	18. 8.86	
G-BUTU	FLS OA-7 Optica 301	024		29. 1.93	(Stored incomplete 8/95) Canx as PWFU 23.5.97.
G-BUTV	FLS OA-7 Optica 301	025		29. 1.93	(Stored incomplete 8/95) Canx as PWFU 23.5.97.
G-BUTW	BAe Jetstream Srs.3206	975	(F-OHFU) G-31-975	23. 2.93	To F-GMVI 5/93. Canx 4.5.93.
G-BUTX	Bucker 133C Jungmeister (C/n may be 1010 - or may be CASA built I-133L)(Bucker Flugzeugbau-built)	-	E1-4 Spanish AF ES.1-4/35-4	3. 2.93	(Stored 7/98 at Breighton)
G-BUTY	Brugger MB.2 Colibri	PFA/43-12387		30.11.92	
G-BUTZ	PA-28-180 Cherokee C	28-3107	G-DARL 4R-ARL/4R-ONE/SE-EYD	23. 4.93	To ZK-ROE. Canx.
G-BUUA	Slingsby T.67M Firefly II	2111		17. 3.93	
G-BUUB	Slingsby T.67M Firefly II	2112		17. 3.93	
G-BUUC	Slingsby T.67M Firefly II	2113		17. 3.93	
G-BUUD	Slingsby T.67M Firefly II	2114		17. 3.93	
G-BUUE	Slingsby T.67M Firefly II	2115		17. 3.93	
G-BUUF	Slingsby T.67M Firefly II	2116		17. 3.93	
G-BUUG	Slingsby T.67M Firefly II	2117		17. 3.93	
G-BUUH	Slingsby T.67M Firefly II	2118		17. 3.93	Abandoned after control was lost in a spin and crashed near the A1, 5 miles south of Retford on 12.7.95. Canx as destroyed 18.10.95.
G-BUUI	Slingsby T.67M Firefly II	2119		17. 3.93	
G-BUUJ	Slingsby T.67M Firefly II	2120		17. 3.93	
G-BUUK	Slingsby T.67M Firefly II	2121		17. 3.93	
G-BUUL	Slingsby T.67M Firefly II	2122		17. 3.93	

Regn	Type	c/n	Previous identity	Regn date	Fate or immediate subsequent identity (if known)
G-BUUM	PA-28RT-201 Arrow IV	28R-7918090	N2145X	14. 1.93	
G-BUUN	Lindstrand LBL-105A HAFB	015		9. 2.93	
G-BUUO	Cameron N-90 HAFB	2994		9. 2.93	
G-BUUP	BAe ATP	2008	CS-TGA G-11-8/(N378AE)	18. 2.93	To G-MANU 8/97. Canx.
G-BUUR	BAe ATP	2024	CS-TGC G-BUUR/CS-TGC/G-11-024	18. 2.93	To G-OEDJ 9/94. Canx.
G-BUUS	Skyraider Gyrocopter	P.01		9. 2.93	Permit expired 11.5.95. (At PFA Rally 7/96) Canx by CAA 7.5.99.
G-BUUT	Interavia 70TA HAFB	04509-92		21. 1.93	
G-BUUU	Cameron Bottle 77SS HAFB (Bells Whisky Bottle shape)	2980		11. 2.93	
G-BUUV	Lindstrand LBL-77A HAFB	014		11. 2.93	Canx 9.6.97 as destroyed.
G-BUUW	BAe 125 Srs.800A	258227	G-5-769	17. 2.93	To Japanese SDF as 39-3042 11/93. Canx 19.1.94.
G-BUUX	PA-28-180 Cherokee D	28-5128	OY-BCW	17. 2.93	
G-BUUY	BAe 125 Srs.1000B	259031	G-5-754	17. 2.93	To G-5-754/G-HJCB 10/93. Canx.
G-BUUZ	BAe Jetstream Srs.3206	976	(F-OHFV) G-31-976	10. 3.93	To F-GMVJ 5/93. Canx 6.5.93.
G-BUVA	PA-22-135 Tri-Pacer	22-1301	N8626C	12. 2.93	
G-BUVB	Colt 77A HAFB	2041		22. 2.93	
G-BUVC	BAe Jetstream Srs.3202	970	F-GLPY (F-OHFS)/G-BUVC/G-31-970	10. 3.93	To F-GMVP(2) 9/94. Canx 12.9.94.
G-BUVD	BAe Jetstream Srs.3202	977	(F-OHFR) (F-OHFW)/G-31-977	10. 3.93	To F-GMVK 4/93. Canx 31.3.93.
G-BUVE	Colt 77B HAFB	2376		8. 3.93	
G-BUVF	DHC.2 Beaver 1 (Regd with US Army "c/n" 1623)	965	S-9 R.Netherlands AF/55-4585	5. 3.93	Reserved as PH-DHC on 24.2.99.
G-BUVG	Cameron N-56 HAFB	3012		8. 3.93	(Extant 2/97)
G-BUVH	Cameron Dragon SS HAFB	3016		8. 3.93	To C-GBGF 5/98. Canx 21.10.96.
G-BUVI	Colt 210A HAFB	2375		8. 3.93	To PH-UVI 6/96. Canx 18.6.96.
G-BUVJ	Robinson R-22 Beta	0902		8. 3.93	To N220WP 6/93. Canx 31.3.93.
G-BUVK	Cameron A-210 HAFB	2996		8. 3.93	Canx as WFU 2.12.98.
G-BUVL	Fisher Super Koala	PFA/228-11399		3. 3.93	
G-BUVM	CEA Jodel DR.250/160 Capitaine	54	OO-NJR F-BNJR	11. 3.93	(Stored 7/95)
G-BUVN	CASA I-131E Jungmann 2000	2092	EC-333 Spanish AF E3B-487	12. 3.93	
G-BUVO	Reims Cessna F.182P	0022	G-WTFA PH-VDH/D-EJCL	10. 3.93	
G-BUVP	CASA I-131E Jungmann 2000 (Regd with c/n 2155)	2139	EC-338 Spanish AF E3B-539	12. 3.93	
G-BUVR	Christen A-1 Husky	1162		12. 3.93	
G-BUVS	Colt 77A HAFB	2381		12. 3.93	
G-BUVT	Colt 77A HAFB	2382		12. 3.93	
G-BUVU	Cameron A-160 HAFB	3025		16. 3.93	To OO-BNY. Canx 15.6.93.
G-BUVV	Cameron N-90 HAFB	3040		19. 3.93	To OO-BPA. Canx 23.6.93.
G-BUVW	Cameron N-90 HAFB	3020		19. 3.93	
G-BUVX	CFM Streak Shadow	PFA/206-12410		22. 3.93	
G-BUVY	Aviat Pitts S-2B Special	5218	N6073U	23. 3.93	To G-SIIB 24.3.93. Canx.
G-BUVZ	Thunder Ax10-180 Srs.2 HAFB	2380		24. 3.93	
G-BUWA	Vickers-Supermarine 349 Spitfire F.Vc (Westland-built)	WASP/20/288	C-FDUY 7555M/5378M/AR614	19. 3.93	(On display 11/97)
G-BUWB	Cameron O-90 HAFB	3049		25. 3.93	To OO-BYW 7/93. Canx 28.6.93.
G-BUWC	BAe 125 Srs.800B	258240	G-5-772	25. 3.93	To G-SHEA 6/93. Canx.
G-BUWD	BAe 125 Srs.800B	258243	G-5-778	25. 3.93	To G-SHEB 5/93. Canx.
G-BUWE	Replica Plans SE.5A	PFA/20-11816		25. 3.93	
G-BUWF	Cameron N-105 HAFB	3036		26. 3.93	
G-BUWG	American Aircraft Falcon XP	600241		26. 3.93	No Permit to Fly believed issued. Canx by CAA 5.5.94. (Possibly to Spain)
G-BUWH	Parsons Two-Place Gyroplane	G/08-1215		1. 4.93	
G-BUWI	Lindstrand LBL-77A HAFB	023		5. 4.93	
G-BUWJ	Pitts S-1C Special (built by J.T.Griffins)	2002	N110R	25. 3.93	
G-BUWK	Rans S-6-116 Coyote II	PFA/204A-12448		7. 4.93	
G-BUWL	Piper J/4A Cub Coupe	4-1047	N27828 NC27828	8. 4.93	(On rebuild at Oaksey Park) No CofA issued. Canx by CAA 8.5.99.
G-BUWM	BAe ATP	2009	CS-TGB G-BUWM/CS-TGB/G-11-9/(N379AE)	19. 4.93	(Stored Woodford 8/97)
G-BUWN	Lindstrand LBL-180A HAFB	025		19. 4.93	Canx 24.2.99 on sale to USA. Reserved as N49CD 2/99.
G-BUWO	Lindstrand LBL-240A HAFB	026		19. 4.93	Canx 24.2.99 on sale to USA. Reserved as N62CD 2/99.
G-BUWP	BAe ATP	2053	G-11-053	30. 3.93	(Stored at Woodford 5/99)
G-BUWR	CFM Streak Shadow	K.177-SA & PFA/206-12068		26. 4.93	
G-BUWS	Denney Kitfox Mk.2	PFA/172-11831		26. 4.93	
G-BUWT	Rand Robinson KR-2	PFA/129-10952		5. 4.93	
G-BUWU	Cameron V-77 HAFB	3053		27. 4.93	
G-BUWV	CFM Streak Shadow	PFA/206-12338		27. 4.93	No CofA or Permit issued. Canx by CAA 25.8.98.
G-BUWW	Cameron O-105 HAFB	3023		1. 4.93	
G-BUWX	BAe 125 Srs.1000B	259034	G-5-761	27. 4.93	To N290H. Canx 16.6.95.
G-BUWY	Cameron V-77 HAFB	2961		27. 4.93	
G-BUWZ	Robin HR.200/120B	254		22. 4.93	

Regn	Type	c/n	Previous identity	Regn date	Fate or immediate subsequent identity (if known)
G-BUXA	Colt 210A HAFB	2400		28. 4.93	
G-BUXB	Sikorsky S-76A	760086	(F-GSJG)	11. 6.93	
			G-BUXB/VR-CCZ/N399BB/N39RP		
G-BUXC	CFM Streak Shadow	PFA/206-12177		20. 4.93	
G-BUXD	Maule MXT-7-160 Star Rocket	17001C	N9231R	4. 5.93	
G-BUXE	Cameron A-250 HAFB	3071		4. 5.93	To ZS-HZM 2/98. Canx 19.3.98.
G-BUXF	Cameron O-120 HAFB	3100		24. 2.93	To LV-WJL 12/94. Canx 11.10.94.
	(Originally regd as A-180 model)				
G-BUXG	Glaser-Dirks DG-400	4-129	D-KEHJ	6. 5.93	To D-KLGR 10/98. Canx 26.5.98.
G-BUXH	ARV K1 Super 2	034 & PFA/152-12424	(G-BNVK)	16. 3.93	To G-ORIX 9/93. Canx.
G-BUXI	Steen Skybolt	PFA/64-10755		16. 3.93	
G-BUXJ	Slingsby T.61F Venture T.2	1878	XZ558	6. 5.93	
G-BUXK	Pietenpol Air Camper	PFA/47-11901		12. 5.93	
G-BUXL	Taylor JT.1 Monoplane	PFA/55-11819		12. 5.93	
G-BUXM	QAC Quickie Tri-Q	2343	N4435Y	23. 2.93	(Stored 10/97)
	(built by F.Stowe)				
G-BUXN	Beechcraft C23 Sundowner	M-1752	N9256S	13. 5.93	
G-BUXO	Pober P-9 Pixie	PFA/105-10647		17. 5.93	
G-BUXP	American Aircraft Falcon XPS	PFA/250-12439		16. 3.93	
G-BUXR	Cameron A-250 HAFB	3056		13. 5.93	
G-BUXS	MBB Bo.105DBS-4	S-41/913	G-PASA	19. 5.93	
	(Rebuild with new pod S-913 .93 - regn D-HIFA reserved 4/93)		G-BGWP/F-ODMZ/G-BGWP/HB-XFD/N153BB/D-HDAS		
G-BUXT	Dornier 228-202K	8065	D-CBOL	24. 5.93	
			TC-FBM/D-CBOL		
G-BUXU	Beechcraft D.17S (GB-2) Traveler	4823	N9113H	20. 5.93	
			BuA.33024		
G-BUXV	PA-22-160 Tri-Pacer	22-6685	N9769D	20. 5.93	
	(Super Pacer tailwheel conversion)				
G-BUXW	Thunder Ax8-90 Srs.2 HAFB	2405		25. 5.93	
G-BUXX	PA-17 Vagabond	17-28	N4611H	31. 3.93	
			NC4611H		
G-BUXY	PA-25-235 Pawnee	25-2705	C-GZCR	18. 3.93	
			N6959Z		
G-BUXZ	Yakovlev Yak-3U	1701231	NX11SN	. .93R	NTU - To G-BWOE 3/96. Canx.
	(converted from LET Yak C.11)		(France)/Egyptian AF		
G-BUYA	Lindstrand LBL-77A HAFB	034		27. 5.93	To SE-ZHR 1/99. Canx 2.10.98.
G-BUYB	Aero Designs Pulsar	PFA/202-12193		28. 5.93	
G-BUYC	Cameron Concept 80 HAFB	3095		28. 5.93	
G-BUYD	Thunder Ax8-90 HAFB	2422		28. 5.93	
G-BUYE	Aeronca 7AC Champion	7AC-4327	N85584	30. 4.93	
			NC85584		
G-BUYF	American Aircraft Falcon XP	600179	N512AA	13. 5.93	
	(built by R.W.Harris)				
G-BUYG	Colt Flying Gin Bottle 12SS HAFB			28. 5.93	
	(Gordon's Gin Bottle shape)	2331			
	(Originally regd as Thunder Ax8-90 Flying Gin Bottle SS HAFB with same c/n)				
G-BUYH	Cameron A-210 HAFB	3045		28. 5.93	
G-BUYI	Thunder Ax7-77 HAFB	1266		20. 6.88	
G-BUYJ	Lindstrand LBL-105A HAFB	039		1. 6.93	
G-BUYK	Denney Kitfox Mk.4	PFA/172A-12214		1. 6.93	
G-BUYL	Rotary Air Force RAF 2000	H2-92-361	C-FPFN	2. 6.93	
	(built by D.Lafleur)				
G-BUYM	Thunder Ax8-105 HAFB	2419		3. 6.93	
G-BUYN	Cameron O-84 HAFB	1214	OE-KZG	4. 6.93	(Extant in Thailand 2/97)
G-BUYO	Colt 77A HAFB	2398		4. 6.93	
G-BUYP	Lindstrand Salami SS HAFB	033		7. 6.93	To OO-BMB 7/94. Canx 15.6.94.
G-BUYR	Mooney M.20C Mark 21	2650	N1369W	7. 6.93	
G-BUYS	Robin DR.400/180 Regent	2197		21. 6.93	
G-BUYT	Ken Brock KB-2 Gyrocopter	JH-1 & G/06-1214		7. 6.93	
G-BUYU	Bowers Fly Baby 1A	PFA/16-12222		7. 6.93	
G-BUYV	Cameron N Ele 90SS HAFB	3086		8. 6.93	To G-WBMG 7/93. Canx.
G-BUYW	BAe ATP	2061	HL5227	11. 6.93	To OY-SVI 2/98. Canx.
			G-BUYW/G-11-061		
G-BUYX	Aerospatiale AS.350B-2 Ecureuil	2732	F-WYMO	9. 6.93	To VR-BBB 9/93. Canx 24.9.93.
G-BUYY	PA-28-180 Cherokee B	28-1028	C-FXDP	18. 3.93	
			CF-XDP/N7214W		
G-BUYZ	Cameron O-120 HAFB	3103		11. 6.93	To OO-BBQ. Canx 21.9.93.
G-BUZA	Denney Kitfox Mk.3	1178 & PFA/172-12547		10. 6.93	(Extant 1/97)
G-BUZB	Aero Designs Pulsar XP	PFA/202-12312		14. 6.93	
G-BUZC	Everett Gyroplane Srs.3A	034		14. 7.93	(Badly damaged on take-off 7.94) (Stored Sproughton 12/95)
G-BUZD	Aerospatiale AS.332L Super Puma	2069	C-GSLJ	11. 2.93	
			PT-HRN/C-GSLJ/HC-BNB/C-GSLJ/N189EH/C-GSLJ		
G-BUZE	Light Aero Avid Speed Wing	PFA/189-12047		16. 6.93	
G-BUZF	Colt 77B HAFB	1993		16. 6.93	
G-BUZG	Zenair CH.601HD Zodiac	PFA/162-12457		17. 6.93	

Regn	Type	c/n	Previous identity	Regn date	Fate or immediate subsequent identity (if known)
G-BUZH	Star-Lite SL-1 (built by H.M.Cottle)	119	N4HC	17. 6.93	(On overhaul 6/97)
G-BUZI	Aerospatiale AS.355F1 Twin Squirrel	5079	N57894	3. 1.89	To F-GJFU 7/97. Canx 30.6.97.
G-BUZJ	Lindstrand LBL-105A HAFB	038		17. 6.93	Canx as WFU 11.8.97.
G-BUZK	Cameron V-77 HAFB	2962		17. 6.93	
G-BUZL	VPM M-16 Tandem Trainer	VPM16-UK-105		18. 6.93	
G-BUZM	Light Aero Avid Mk.3 Speed Wing	PFA/189-12179		30. 4.93	
G-BUZN	Cessna 172H	172-56056	N2856L	24. 6.93	
G-BUZO	Pietenpol Air Camper	PFA/47-12408		28. 6.93	
G-BUZP	Bell 206L-3 Long Ranger	51189	EC-FOC N302MC	28. 6.93	To N7069F 7/93. Canx 1.7.93.
G-BUZR	Lindstrand LBL-77A HAFB	044		29. 6.93	
G-BUZS	Colt Flying Pig SS HAFB	2415		2. 7.93	
G-BUZT	Kolb Twinstar Mk.3	PFA/205-12367		1. 7.93	
G-BUZU	Vickers-Supermarine 379 Spitfire FR.XIV	-	Indian AF NH799	1. 7.93	To ZK-XIV. Canx 4.3.94.
G-BUZV	Ken Brock KB-2 Gyrocopter	G/06-1152		1. 7.93	
G-BUZW	Robinson R-22 Beta	1512	OH-HJA (N151NH)	30. 6.93	To OO-JIM. Canx 2.8.93.
G-BUZX	BAe 125 Srs.800B	258067	D-CEVW G-5-525	24. 6.93	To G-5-807/N801MM 7/94. Canx 24.6.94.
G-BUZY	Cameron A-250 HAFB	2936		29. 4.93	
G-BUZZ	Agusta-Bell 206B JetRanger II	8178	F-GAMS HB-XGI/OE-DXF	13. 4.78	
G-BVAA	Light Aero Avid Speed Wing Mk.4	PFA/189-12166		10. 6.93	
G-BVAB	Zenair CH.601HDS Zodiac	PFA/162-12475		26. 5.93	
G-BVAC	Zenair CH.601HD Zodiac	PFA/162-12504		1. 6.93	
G-BVAD	Cameron Concept 80SS HAFB	3091		2. 7.93	To JA-A753. Canx 17.9.93.
G-BVAE	BAe 146 RJ85	E2239		23. 7.93	To G-6-239/PK-PJJ. Canx 1.12.93.
G-BVAF	Piper J3C-85 Cub	4645	OO-UBU N28199/NC28199	14. 6.93	
G-BVAG	Lindstrand LBL-90A HAFB	022		7. 7.93	
G-BVAH	Denney Kitfox Mk.3	PFA/172-12031		22.10.91	
G-BVAI	PZL-110 Koliber 150	03900040	OY-CYJ	7. 7.93	
G-BVAJ	Rotorway Exec 90	5118		7. 7.93	No Permit to Fly issued. (Extant Chirk 5/94) Canx by CAA 22.3.99.
G-BVAK	Slingsby T.67M Firefly 260	2109		8. 7.93	To N7020D 1/94 (then USAF as T-3A with serial 92-0625). Canx 21.1.94.
G-BVAL	Slingsby T.67M Firefly 260	2110		8. 7.93	To N3154Z 1/94 (then USAF as T-3A with serial 92-0626). Canx 21.1.94.
G-BVAM	Evans VP-1	PFA/62-12132		7. 7.93	
G-BVAN	Socata MS.892E Rallye 150GT	12376	F-BVAN	21.11.88	
G-BVAO	Colt 25A Sky Chariot HAFB	2024		9. 7.93	
G-BVAP	Thunder Ax10-180 Srs.2 HAFB	2421		9. 7.93	To LN-CBW 8/96. Canx 16.7.96.
G-BVAR	Lindstrand LBL-105A HAFB	035		9. 7.93	(Operated by L.Madou and based in Belgium, this balloon was reportedly destroyed at Zell-am-See, Austria 16.1.94 after being caught in turbulence!) To OO-BLQ 7/94. Canx 15.6.94.
G-BVAS	BAe 125 Srs.800B	258076	D-CGVW G-5-535	9. 7.93	To RA-02807 5/95. Canx 8.3.95.
G-BVAT	Murphy Renegade F30	PFA/188-11965		25. 6.93	Canx 30.6.97 on sale to France.
G-BVAU	Cameron A-210 HAFB	3107		14. 7.93	To ZS-HZJ 1/98. Canx 12.12.97.
G-BVAV	Team Minimax 91	PFA/186-11841		19. 7.93	To G-MYKZ 26.7.93. Canx.
G-BVAW	Staaken Z-1 Flitzer	PFA/223-12058		12. 7.93	
G-BVAX	Colt 77A HAFB	1213		30. 3.88	
G-BVAY	Rutan VariEze (built by R.N.Sanders)	RS.8673/345	N5MS	3. 9.93	
G-BVAZ	Montgomerie-Bensen B.8MR Gyrocopter	G/01-1190		12. 7.93	(Extant 11/96) No CofA or Permit issued. Canx by CAA 24.8.98.
G-BVBA	Colt 69A HAFB	2424		20. 7.93	Canx by CAA 10.3.95.
G-BVBB	Lindstrand LBL-120A HAFB	048		26. 7.93	To D-OVBB 7/94. Canx 13.7.94.
G-BVBC	Cessna 172K	172-58536	N84587	21. 7.93	To EC-GFG 2/96. Canx 30.11.95.
G-BVBD	Vertical Avn Technologies S-52-3 (Converted Sikorsky S-52)	52-014	N4643S BuA.125521	21. 7.93	(Stored 10/95)
G-BVBE	Hunting-Percival P.84 Jet Provost T.3A	PAC/W/9269	XN461 XM461	21. 7.93	To F-AZMI 3/97. Canx 19.3.97.
	(The airframes for XM461 and XN461 seem to have been accidentally exchanged during RAF service. N6204H is quoted as ex XM461, but has FNo. PAC/W/10140, which was XN461. Now regd with c/n PAC/W/9212 which is c/n of G-TORE!)				
G-BVBF	PA-28-151 Cherokee Warrior	28-7515206	N31JM N32633	22. 7.93	No UK CofA issued. Canx by CAA 18.3.99.
G-BVBG	PA-32R-300 Cherokee Lance	32R-7680151	N19BP	22. 7.93	
G-BVBH	BAe 125 Srs.800B	258073	D-CFVW G-5-532	22. 7.93	To G-5-532/N802MM 7/94. Canx 24.6.94.
G-BVBI	DH.114 Heron 2	14130	XM296	22. 7.93	To N82D 8/96. Canx 29.8.96.
G-BVBJ	Colt Flying Coffee Jar 1 SS HAFB (Maxwell House Jar)	2427		27. 7.93	Stored 1/98 BBAC Museum. Canx as WFU 29.4.97.

Regn	Type	c/n	Previous identity	Regn date	Fate or immediate subsequent identity (if known)
G-BVBK	Colt Flying Coffee Jar 2 SS HAFB (Maxwell House Jar)	2428		27. 7.93	Stored 1/98 BBAC Museum. Canx as WFU 29.4.97.
G-BVBL	PA-38-112 Tomahawk II	38-82A0004	N91339	2. 8.93	
G-BVBM	Lindstrand LBL-180A HAFB	041		2. 8.93	To D-OBVB 7/97. Canx 17.6.97.
G-BVBN	Cameron A-210 HAFB	2904		2. 8.93	
G-BVBO	Vertical Avn Technologies S-52-3 (Converted Sikorsky S-52)	52-046	N9329R Bu.128616	4. 8.93	(Stored 10/95)
G-BVBP	Avro 683 Lancaster B.X (built by Victory Aircraft, Canada)	-	RCAF KB994 KB994	4. 8.93	(Open storage 5/96)
G-BVBR	Light Aero Avid Speed Wing	PFA/189-12085		3. 8.93	
G-BVBS	Cameron N-77 HAFB	3128		4. 8.93	
G-BVBT	DHC.1 Chipmunk 22 (Fuselage no. DHB/f/432)	C1/0547	WK511	4. 8.93	
G-BVBU	Cameron V-77 HAFB	3076		5. 8.93	(Marks OO-BYS are allotted)
G-BVBV	Light Aero Avid Speed Wing	PFA/189-12187		4. 8.93	
G-BVBW	Lindstrand LBL-120A HAFB	047		5. 8.93	To D-OVBW 7/94. Canx 13.7.94.
G-BVBX	Cameron N-90M HAFB	3102		10. 8.93	Canx as TWFU 10.2.97.
G-BVBY	Boeing 737-436	25844	TC-ALS G-BVBY/(G-DOCY)	2. 9.93	To OO-LTQ. Canx 28.4.94.
G-BVBZ	Boeing 737-436	25858	(G-DOCZ)	1.10.93	To EC-657/EC-FXJ 8/94. Canx 10.5.94.
G-BVCA	Cameron N-105 HAFB	3129		11. 8.93	
G-BVCB	Rans S-10 Sakota	PFA/194-11882		11. 8.93	
G-BVCC	Monnett Sonerai 2LT	PFA/15-10547		12. 8.93	
G-BVCD	BAe 146 Srs.200QT	E2211	G-6-211	19. 8.93	To F-GOMA 6/94. Canx 18.4.94.
G-BVCE	BAe 146 Srs.300	E3209	G-6-209	5.11.93	To B-1778 5/94. Canx 9.5.94.
G-BVCF	Lindstrand Flying M SS HAFB	050		16. 8.93	Canx by CAA 31.7.98.
G-BVCG	Van's RV-6	PFA/181-11783		17. 8.93	
G-BVCH	Thunder Ax10-180 Srs.II HAFB	2423		18. 8.93	To F-GMGL. Canx 23.11.93.
G-BVCI	Robinson R-22 Beta	2176		18. 8.93	To OH-H.. Canx 25.8.99.
G-BVCJ	Agusta A.109A II	7265	G-CLRL G-EJCB	23. 8.93	
G-BVCK	Lindstrand LBL-105A HAFB	049		23. 8.93	Canx by CAA 26.2.97. To N7219Y 4/97.
G-BVCL	Rans S-6-116 Coyote II	PFA/204A-12551		25. 8.93	
G-BVCM	Cessna 525 Citation Jet	525-0022	N1329N	2. 5.94	
G-BVCN	Colt 56A HAFB	2445		25. 8.93	
G-BVCO	Clutton-Tabenor FRED Srs.2	PFA/29-10947		25. 8.93	
G-BVCP	Piper CP.1 Metisse (Very modified Tipsy Nipper)	PFA/253-12512		24. 6.93	(At PFA Rally 7/97)
G-BVCR	Kolb Twinstar Mk.3	PFA/205-12391		26. 8.93	NTU - To G-MYLP 9/93. Canx.
G-BVCS	Aeronca 7BCN Champion	7AC-1346	N69BD N82702/NC82702	1. 9.93	
G-BVCT	Denney Kitfox Mk.4-1200	1761 & PFA/172A-12456		27. 8.93	
G-BVCU	BAe 125 Srs.800B	258226	G-5-755	6. 9.93	To D-CSRB. Canx 13.12.93.
G-BVCV	Fairchild M-62A (PT-19A) Cornell	T42-3418	CX-BCU Uruguay AF 621/42-33752	2. 8.93	Fatal crashed shortly after take-off from Woburn Abbey on 15.8.98. Canx as destroyed 3.2.99.
G-BVCW	Sikorsky S-76A (Mod)	760093	D-HOSA(2)	15. 9.93	Restored as D-HOSA(2) 2/95. Canx 23.12.94.
G-BVCX	Sikorsky S-76A II Plus	760183	N951L N5450M	21. 9.93	To OY-HIW. Canx 24.6.99.
G-BVCY	Cameron H-24 HAFB	3136		3. 9.93	
G-BVCZ	Colt 240A HAFB	2480		3. 9.93	
G-BVDA	Lindstrand LBL-240A HAFB	053		3. 9.93	Canx by CAA 31.7.98. To N240PB 12/98.
G-BVDB	Thunder Ax7-77 HAFB	2364	G-ORDY G-BVDB	6. 9.93	
G-BVDC	Van's RV-3	PFA/99-12218		12. 7.93	
G-BVDD	Colt 69A HAFB	2170		6. 9.93	
G-BVDE	Taylor JT-1 Monoplane	PFA/55-11278		6. 9.93	
G-BVDF	Cameron Doll 105SS HAFB	3112		7. 9.93	
G-BVDG	VPM M-15 Gyrocopter	VPM15-UK-103		7. 9.93	To 5Y-VPM 10/95. Canx 24.10.95.
G-BVDH	PA-28RT-201 Arrow IV	28R-7918030	N2176L	13. 9.93	
G-BVDI	Van's RV-4	2058	N55GJ	13. 9.93	
G-BVDJ	Campbell Cricket	G/03-1189		13. 9.93	
G-BVDK	BAe Jetstream Srs.3100	636	N407MX G-31-636	29. 9.93	To N636JX. Canx 21.4.94.
G-BVDL	BAe 125 Srs.1000B	259025	(5N-...) G-5-759	15. 9.93	To G-5-759/N292H 5/94. Canx 17.5.94.
G-BVDM	Cameron Concept 60 HAFB	3141		15. 9.93	
G-BVDN	PA-34-220T Seneca III	34-8133185	G-IGHA G-IPUT/N8424D	16. 9.93	
G-BVDO	Lindstrand LBL-105A HAFB	055		16. 9.93	
G-BVDP	Sequoia F.8L Falco	PFA/100-10879		17. 9.93	
G-BVDR	Cameron O-77 HAFB	2452		21. 9.93	
G-BVDS	Lindstrand LBL-69A HAFB	102		23. 9.93	
G-BVDT	CFM Streak Shadow	PFA/206-12462		23. 9.93	
G-BVDU	Cameron N-77 HAFB	3139		24. 9.93	To JA-A... 10/94. Canx 24.10.94.
G-BVDV	Cameron A-120 HAFB	3140		24. 9.93	To VH-OUR 3/95. Canx 23.11.94.
G-BVDW	Thunder Ax8-90 HAFB	2507		30. 9.93	
G-BVDX	Cameron V-90 HAFB	3159	OO-BMY G-BVDX	30. 9.93	

Regn	Type	c/n	Previous identity	Regn date	Fate or immediate subsequent identity (if known)
G-BVDY	Cameron Concept 60 HAFB	3167		30. 9.93	
G-BVDZ	Taylorcraft BC-12D	9043	N96743 NC96743	21. 1.94	
G-BVEA	Nostalgair N.3 Pup	01-GB & PFA/212-11837	G-MWEA	7. 6.93	
G-BVEB	PA-32R-301 Saratoga SP	3213055	N9224X	15. 9.93	
G-BVEC	ATR-42-300	356	F-WWEW	30. 4.93	
G-BVED	ATR-42-300	315	F-WWEN	4.11.93	
G-BVEE	Not allocated.				
G-BVEF	ATR-42-300	331	F-GKNF F-WWLP	24. 3.94	
G-BVEG	Hunting-Percival P.84 Jet Provost T.3A	PAC/W/13893	XN629	19. 8.93	To G-KNOT 6/99. Canx.
G-BVEH	Wassmer Jodel D.112	1294	F-BMOH	29.10.93	
G-BVEI	Colt 90A HAFB	2496		5.10.93	To D-OUDO(2) 1/97. Canx 20.1.97.
G-BVEJ	Cameron V-90 HAFB	3169		5.10.93	
G-BVEK	Cameron Concept 80 HAFB	3133		5.10.93	
G-BVEL	Evans VP-1 Srs.2	PFA/62-11983		6.10.93	No Permit to Fly issued. Canx by CAA 22.3.99.
G-BVEM	Lindstrand LBL-77A HAFB	005		6.10.93	Canx 7.11.94 on sale to Japan.
G-BVEN	Cameron Concept 80 HAFB	3164		6.10.93	
G-BVEO	BAe ATP	2059	G-11-059	12.10.93	Canx as WFU 30.7.97. To G-11-059, then G-OBWN 12/98.
G-BVEP	Luscombe 8A Master	1468	N28707 NC28707	8.10.93	No UK CofA issued. (Stored 10/97 Oaksey Park)
G-BVER	DHC.2 Beaver 1	1648	G-BTDM XV268	13. 8.91	(Status uncertain)
G-BVES	Cessna 340A II	340A-0077	N1378G	8. 9.93	
G-BVET	Sportavia Putzer Fournier RF-4D	4047	F-BOXG	31.10.79	To G-BIIF 11/80. Canx.
G-BVEU	Cameron O-105 HAFB	3145		12.10.93	
G-BVEV	PA-34-200 Seneca	34-7250316	N1428T HB-LLN/D-GHSG/N1428T	8.10.93	
G-BVEW	Lindstrand LBL-150A HAFB	057		14.10.93	
G-BVEX	Lindstrand LBL-105A HAFB	056		18.10.93	Reserved as D-OVEX 6.5.97. Canx 3.12.97.
G-BVEY	Denney Kitfox Mk.4/1200	PFA/172A-12527		14.10.93	
G-BVEZ	Hunting-Percival P.84 Jet Provost T.3A	PAC/W/9287	XM479	13.10.93	
G-BVFA	Rans S-10 Sakota	PFA/194-12298		7. 9.93	
G-BVFB	Cameron N-31 HAFB	3175		20.10.93	
G-BVFC	BAe 125 Srs.800B	258130	G-TPHK G-FDSL/G-5-620	26.10.93	To G-ETOM 10/95. Canx.
G-BVFD	PA-38-112 Tomahawk	38-79A0764	N2551L	25.10.93	To (PH-MGF)/"PH-MEG"/PH-MEC 10/96. Canx 8.11.95.
G-BVFE	BAe 125 Srs.800A	258242		25.10.93	To G-5-793/Japanese SDF as 49-3043. Canx 16.2.95.
G-BVFF	Cameron V-77 HAFB	3161		26.10.93	(Extant 2/97)
G-BVFG	PBN BN-2T Turbine Islander	2273		8.11.93	To CN-TWV 11/94. Canx 13.12.94.
G-BVFH	PBN BN-2T Turbine Islander	2274		8.11.93	To CN-TWW 11/94. Canx 13.12.94.
G-BVFI	PBN BN-2T Turbine Islander	2275		8.11.93	To CN-TWX 11/94. Canx 13.12.94.
G-BVFJ	PBN BN-2T Turbine Islander	2276		8.11.93	To A2-MOA 1/95. Canx 20.3.95.
G-BVFK	PBN BN-2T Turbine Islander	2277		8.11.93	To G-JSAT 2/98. Canx.
G-BVFL	Lindstrand LBL-21A HAFB	061		27.10.93	Canx by CAA 29.10.97.
G-BVFM	Rans S-6-116 Coyote II (Tricycle u/c)	0793-522 & PFA/204A-12579		2.11.93	
G-BVFN	Pitts S-1E Special	JAS.7	N41JS	1.11.93	
G-BVFO	Light Aero Avid Speed Wing	PFA/189-12053		9. 9.93	Force landed in a field near Shepton Mallet on 11.6.95.
G-BVFP	Cameron V-90 HAFB	3179		2.11.93	
G-BVFR	CFM Streak Shadow	K.237-SA & PFA/206-12567		3.11.93	
G-BVFS	Slingsby T.31M Cadet III	PFA/42-11387	(ex)	3.11.93	(Extant 3/94)
G-BVFT	Maule M.5-235C Lunar Rocket	7183C	N6180M	5.11.93	
G-BVFU	Cameron Sphere 105SS HAFB	3137		18.11.93	
G-BVFV	BAe 146 Srs.200A	E2073	EI-JET G-BVFV/HB-IXD/N191US/N367PS/G-5-073	3.12.93	To VH-NJU(2) 9/96. Canx 20.9.96.
G-BVFW	Nanchang CJ-6A (Yak-18)	1032011	Chinese AFPLA	9.11.93	To VH-CXS(2) 11/96. Canx 30.9.96.
G-BVFX	Nanchang CJ-6A (Yak-18)	1532008	Chinese AFPLA	9.11.93	
G-BVFY	Colt 210A HAFB	2493		30. 9.93	To DQ-BVF 11/98. Canx 18.11.98.
G-BVFZ	Maule M.5-180C Lunar Rocket	8082C	N5664D	21. 2.94	
G-BVGA	Bell 206B JetRanger III	2922	N54AJ VH-SBC	11.11.93	
G-BVGB	Thunder Ax8-105 Srs.2 HAFB	2408		11.11.93	
G-BVGC	Cessna 411A	411A-0274	EI-BCT G-AVEK/N3274R	16.11.93	No UK CofA issued since return from Irish registry. (On overhaul 6/96 at Leicester) Canx as PWFU 10.2.99.
G-BVGD	Aerotechnik L-13SEH Vivat	930513		15.11.93	To OK-.... Canx 5.5.98.
G-BVGE	Westland WS-55 Whirlwind HAR.10	WA/100	8732M XJ729	18.11.93	
G-BVGF	Europa Avn Europa	PFA/247-12565		18.11.93	
G-BVGG	Lindstrand LBL-69A HAFB	011		30.11.93	
G-BVGH	Hawker Hunter T.7 (Regd with c/n HABL-004328)	HABL/003360	XL573	26.11.93	

Regn	Type	c/n	Previous identity	Regn date	Fate or immediate subsequent identity (if known)
G-BVGI	Pereira Osprey 2	PFA/70-10536		29.11.93	(Stored 5/97)
G-BVGJ	Cameron Concept 80 HAFB	3099		7.12.93	
	(Originally regd as C-90 model)				
G-BVGK	Lindstrand Flying Newspaper SS HAFB	059		3.12.93	To SE-ZHC 2/98. Canx 15.12.97.
G-BVGL	Sikorsky S-76A	760121	EC-GOI G-BVGL/XC-FEO/N5400C/N1548B	1.12.93	To N517AL 8/97. Canx 6.8.97.
G-BVGM	Sikorsky S-76A	760134	EC-GOJ G-BVGM/XC-FEM/N1548D	1.12.93	To N518AL 8/97. Canx 6.8.97.
G-BVGN	Sikorsky S-76A	760138	XC-FEL N1548Y	1.12.93	To VH-HUD 12/93. Canx 9.12.93.
G-BVGO	Denney Kitfox Mk.4/1200	PFA/172A-12362		15.11.93	
G-BVGP	Dornier Bucker Bu.133C Jungmeister	42	F-AZFQ N15696/HB-MIE/D-EIII/HB-MIE/Swiss AF U-95	3.12.93	
G-BVGR	RAF BE.2E (RAF 1e)	-	37 R Norwegian AF/133/A1325	8.12.93	(For Historic Aircraft Collection, Jersey) (On rebuild 8/95)
G-BVGS	Robinson R-22 Beta	2389	N2363S	9.12.93	
G-BVGT	Crofton Auster J/1A Special			19.11.93	
	(Rebuild of previously unregd Auster J/1 Autocrat frame; ex Beagles 60s and later used as engine test rig)	PFA/00-220			
G-BVGU	Cameron N-90 HAFB	3189		9.12.93	To OE-ZKW(2) 11/95. Canx 4.10.95.
G-BVGV	Colt 21A Cloudhopper HAFB	2534		17.12.93	To OE-ZRB 9/95. Canx 4.9.95.
G-BVGW	Luscombe 8A Silvaire	4823	N2096K NC2096K	18.11.93	
G-BVGX	Thunder Ax8-90 Srs.2 HAFB	2490		16.12.93	
G-BVGY	Luscombe 8E Silvaire	4754	N2027K NC2027K	18.11.93	
G-BVGZ	Fokker DR.1 Triplane Replica	VHB-10 & PFA/238-12654		20.12.93	
	(built by V.H.Bellamy)				
G-BVHA	Boeing 737-436	25859	(G-GBTA)	1.11.93	To G-GBTA 2/94. Canx.
G-BVHB	Boeing 737-436	25860	OO-LTS G-BVHB/(G-GBTB)	3.12.93	Restored as OO-LTS. Canx 31.3.94.
G-BVHC	Grob G-115D-2 Heron	82005	D-EARG	14.12.93	
G-BVHD	Grob G-115D-2 Heron	82006	D-EARJ	14.12.93	
G-BVHE	Grob G-115D-2 Heron	82008	D-EARQ	14.12.93	
G-BVHF	Grob G-115D-2 Heron	82011	D-EARV	14.12.93	
G-BVHG	Grob G-115D-2 Heron	82012	D-EARX	14.12.93	
G-BVHH	Cameron D-96 Hot-Air Airship	3192		20.12.93	Envelope to G-BKNL .94. Canx as WFU 8.2.94.
G-BVHI	Rans S-10 Sakota	PFA/194-12608		20.12.93	
G-BVHJ	Cameron A-180 HAFB	3155		20.12.93	
G-BVHK	Cameron V-77 HAFB	3209		23.12.93	
G-BVHL	Nicollier HN.700 Menestrel II	PFA/217-12614		24.12.93	No Permit issued. Canx by CAA 8.5.99.
G-BVHM	PA-38-112 Tomahawk	38-79A0313	G-DCAN N9713N	14.11.91	
	(Officially regd with c/n 38-79A0312)				
G-BVHN	Lindstrand LBL-G144 Gas-Filled Balloon	076		24.12.93	No UK CofA issued. Canx as WFU 3.6.99.
G-BVHO	Cameron V-90 HAFB	3158		29.12.93	
G-BVHP	Colt 42A HAFB	2533		31.12.93	
G-BVHR	Cameron V-90 HAFB	3174		5. 1.94	
G-BVHS	Murphy Rebel	PFA/232-12180		5. 1.94	
G-BVHT	Light Aero Avid Mk.4 Speed Wing	PFA/189-12226		28.10.93	
G-BVHU	Colt Flying Bottle 13SS HAFB	2499		6. 1.94	
G-BVHV	Cameron N-105 HAFB	3215		6. 1.94	
G-BVHW	BAe 125 Srs.800B	258079	G-GJCB G-5-542	19. 1.94	To SE-DRV 6/95. Canx 3.4.95.
G-BVHX	PBN BN-2T-4R MSSA	4003		21. 1.94	Stored 1/99 Bembridge.
G-BVHY	PBN BN-2T-4R MSSA	4004		21. 1.94	Stored 1/99 Bembridge.
G-BVHZ	PBN BN-2T-4S Defender 4000	4005		21. 1.94	To G-SURV 4/94. Canx.
G-BVIA	Rand Robinson KR-2	PFA/129-11004		14. 1.94	
G-BVIB	Bell 206L-3 Long Ranger	51348	SE-HUF C-FHZY	17. 1.94	To N80EA 1/94. Canx 10.2.94.
G-BVIC	English Electric Canberra B.2/B.6	71105	XH568	25.10.93	Stored 9/97 Bruntingthorpe.
	(Note - c/n relates to nose section only - which was ex WG788 from 1970 rebuild; XH568 was c/n 71399)				
G-BVID	Lindstrand LBL Lozenge SS HAFB	064		17. 1.94	
G-BVIE	PA-18-95 Super Cub (L-18C-PI)	18-1549	G-CLIK (G-BLMB)/D-EDRB/ALAT 51-15549/51-15549	26. 1.94	
	(Frame no. 18-1521)				
G-BVIF	Montgomerie-Bensen B.8MR Gyrocopter	G/01A-1228		26. 1.94	
G-BVIG	Cameron A-250 HAFB	3213		26. 1.94	
G-BVIH	PA-28-161 Warrior II	28-7916191	G-GFCE G-BNJP/N2212G	26.10.93	
G-BVII	Cameron N-90 HAFB	3212		26. 1.94	To OO-BVD. Canx 29.4.94.
G-BVIJ	Cameron O-90 HAFB	3231		26. 1.94	To OO-BKB. Canx 29.4.94.
G-BVIK	Maule MXT-7-180 Star Rocket	14056C		31. 1.94	
G-BVIL	Maule MXT-7-180 Star Rocket	14059C		31. 1.94	
G-BVIM	Cameron N-77 HAFB	2222		2. 2.94	
G-BVIN	Rans S-6-ESA Coyote II	PFA/204-12533		25.10.93	

Regn	Type	c/n	Previous identity	Regn date	Fate or immediate subsequent identity (if known)
G-BVIO	Colt Flying Drinks Can SS HAFB (Budweiser Can shape)	2538		4. 2.94	
G-BVIP	Piper Aerostar 601P	61P-0572-7963249	(N8086J)	18.10.78	To N37860 7/80. Canx 4.4.79.
G-BVIR	Lindstrand LBL-69A HAFB	079		2. 2.94	
G-BVIS	Brugger MB.2 Colibri	PFA/43-10666		2. 2.94	(Under construction 5/95)
G-BVIT	Campbell Cricket	G/03-1229		4. 2.94	
G-BVIU	Cameron A-180 HAFB (Originally regd with c/n 3241 which became JA-A760)	3243		7. 2.94	To OO-BBH. Canx 13.5.94.
G-BVIV	Light Aero Avid Speed Wing	PFA/189-12034		25.10.93	
G-BVIW	PA-18-150 Super Cub	18-8277	SE-EPD	4. 2.94	
G-BVIX	Lindstrand LBL-180A HAFB	082		8. 2.94	
G-BVIY	Cameron A-105 HAFB	2862	PH-OCE	11. 2.94	Restored as PH-OCE 6/98. Canx 17.4.98.
G-BVIZ	Europa Avn Europa	52 & PFA/247-12601		24. 1.94	
G-BVJA	Fokker F.100-650	11489	PH-EZE	22. 4.94	
G-BVJB	Fokker F.100-650	11488	PH-EZD	7. 7.94	
G-BVJC	Fokker F.100-650	11497	PH-EZJ	2.12.94	
G-BVJD	Fokker F.100-650	11503	PH-EZO	14.12.94	
G-BVJE	Aerospatiale AS.350B1 Ecureuil	1991	SE-HRS	3. 2.94	
G-BVJF	Montgomerie-Bensen B.8MR Gyrocopter	G/01-1082		18. 2.94	
G-BVJG	Cyclone Ax3/K	C.3123187 & PFA/245-12663	(G-MYOP)	15. 2.94	
G-BVJH	Aero Designs Pulsar	PFA/202-12196		22. 2.94	(Stored 3/99 Brunei)
G-BVJI	BAe 125 Srs.800B	258258	(N953H) G-BVJI/G-5-798	25. 2.94	To N54SB 11/97. Canx 10.11.97.
G-BVJJ	Cameron DP-90 Hot-Air Airship	3216		25. 2.94	
G-BVJK	Glaser-Dirks DG-800A	8-24-A21		30. 3.94	
G-BVJL	Colt 240A HAFB	2561		1. 3.94	To C-GDQP 8/98. Canx 3.7.98.
G-BVJM	VPM M-16 Tandem Trainer	VPM16-UK-106		1. 3.94	To G-POSA 8/96. Canx.
G-BVJN	Europa Avn Europa	66 & PFA/247-12666		2. 3.94	
G-BVJO	Cameron R-77 Gas Free Balloon	3228		8. 3.94	
G-BVJP	ATR-42-320	371	F-WWLN	7. 4.94	
G-BVJR	IAV-Bacau Yakovlev YAK-52	9411711	48 Romanian AF	9. 3.94	To LY-ANE 5/94. Canx 4.5.94.
G-BVJS	Colt Piggy Bank SS HAFB	2487		9. 3.94	CofA expired 3.6.99. Canx as destroyed 29.7.99. (Was last regd to an owner in Hamburg, Germany)
G-BVJT	Reims Cessna F.406 Caravan II	0073		2. 2.94	
G-BVJU	Evans VP-1	PFA/62-10691		10. 3.94	
G-BVJV	Airbus A.320-231	437	N437RX G-BVJV/C-FWOQ/G-BVJV/N437RX/F-WWDM	19. 4.94	To G-EPFR 11/97. Canx.
G-BVJW	Airbus A.320-231	467	C-FWOR G-BVJW/C-FWOR/G-BVJW/F-WWBC	11. 5.94	To N467RX 11/97. Canx 13.11.97.
G-BVJX	Marquart MA.5 Charger	PFA/68-11239		12. 1.94	
G-BVJY	HS.125 Srs.700B	257054	RA-02802 G-BVJY/RA-02802/G-BVJY/C6-BET	24. 3.94	To G-NCFR 4/97. Canx.
G-BVJZ	PA-28-161 Warrior II	28-7816248	N2088M	22. 3.94	
G-BVKA	Boeing 737-59D	24694	SE-DNA (SE-DLA)	15. 2.94	
G-BVKB	Boeing 737-59D	27268	SE-DNM	24. 3.94	
G-BVKC	Boeing 737-59D	24695	SE-DNB (SE-DLB)	5. 5.94	
G-BVKD	Boeing 737-59D	26421	SE-DNK	25.11.94	
G-BVKE	Team Minimax 88	PFA/186-11993		25. 1.94	To A6-... Canx 25.9.98.
G-BVKF	Europa Avn Europa	50 & PFA/247-12638		11. 3.94	
G-BVKG	Colt Flying Hot Dog SS HAFB	2571		15. 3.94	
G-BVKH	Thunder Ax8-90 HAFB	2574		15. 3.94	
G-BVKI	Cameron N-90 HAFB	3249		17. 3.94	To OO-BGH 6/94. Canx 20.6.94.
G-BVKJ	Bensen B.8M Gyrocopter	G/01-1221		17. 3.94	
G-BVKK	Slingsby T.61F Venture T.2	1984	ZA665	22. 2.94	
G-BVKL	Cameron A-180 HAFB	3255		17. 3.94	
G-BVKM	Rutan VariEze	1933	N7137G	5. 4.94	
G-BVKN	Sikorsky S-76A (Mod)	760090	VH-BHQ(2) G-BVKN/R.Jordian AF 726	4. 3.94	Restored as VH-BHQ(2) 2/99. Canx 8.2.99.
G-BVKO	Sikorsky S-76A (Mod)	760107	731 R.Jordanian AF	4. 3.94	To VH-BHM(2) 9/94. Canx 12.8.94.
G-BVKP	Sikorsky S-76A (Mod)	760114	ABLE-1 R.Jordanian AF 733	4. 3.94	To I-HBBS 12/97. Canx 17.12.97.
G-BVKR	Sikorsky S-76A Plus	760115	734 R.Jordanian AF	4. 3.94	
G-BVKS	Sikorsky S-76A (Mod)	760118	ABLE-2 R.Jordanian AF 735	4. 3.94	To VH-BHI(6) 5/95. Canx 11.5.95.
G-BVKT	BAe Jetstream Srs.4100	41018	N140MA G-BVKT/G-4-018	23. 3.94	To G-MAJB 6/94. Canx.
G-BVKU	Slingsby T.61F Venture T.2	1877	XZ557	22. 3.94	
G-BVKV	Cameron N-90 HAFB	3236		24. 3.94	
G-BVKW	Lindstrand LBL-240A HAFB	093		25. 3.94	To OE-... Canx 8.6.99.
G-BVKX	Colt 14A Cloudhopper HAFB	2580		28. 3.94	

Regn	Type	c/n	Previous identity	Regn date	Fate or immediate subsequent identity (if known)
G-BVKY	Colt 69A HAFB	2581		28. 3.94	To HB-QCK 6/96. Canx 24.5.96.
G-BVKZ	Thunder Ax9-120 HAFB	2547		23. 3.94	
G-BVLA	NEICO Lancair 320	PFA/191-11751		29. 3.94	
G-BVLB	Cameron Flying Beer Can 77SS HAFB	3239		28. 3.94	To SE-ZGY 5/97. Canx 8.4.97.
G-BVLC	Cameron N-42 HAFB	3256		28. 3.94	(Extant 2/97)
G-BVLD	Campbell Cricket	G/01A-1163		29. 3.94	
G-BVLE	McCandless M.4 Gyrocopter	G/10-1232		29. 3.94	(Near completion 4/96)
G-BVLF	CFM Starstreak Shadow SS-D	K.250-SSD		4. 3.94	(At PFA Rally 7/96)
G-BVLG	Aerospatiale AS.355F1 Twin Squirrel	5011	N57745	31. 3.94	
G-BVLH	Europa Avn Europa	PFA/247-12491		30. 3.94	
G-BVLI	Cameron V-77 HAFB	5568	N9544G	30. 3.94	
G-BVLJ	BAe 146 Srs.100	E1160	EI-CJP	7. 4.94	To VH-JSF(2) 11/95. Canx 28.11.95.
			G-BVLJ/A2-ABF/G-6-160		
G-BVLK	Rearwin 8125 Cloudster	803	N25403	6. 4.94	(On rebuild 2/96)
			NC25403		
G-BVLL	Lindstrand LBL-210A HAFB	101		9. 3.94	
G-BVLM	DH.115 Vampire T.55	976	ZH563	6. 4.94	To JY-... /97. Canx 23.6.97.
	(Built by FFW, Emmen)		Swiss AF U-1216		
G-BVLN	Aero Designs Pulsar XP	PFA/202-12530		6. 4.94	
G-BVLO	BAe 125 Srs.1000B	259027	5H-BLM	6. 4.94	To "N333RL"/N333RU. Canx 19.7.95.
			G-5-746		
G-BVLP	PA-38-112 Tomahawk II	38-82A0002	N91355	8. 4.94	
G-BVLR	Van's RV-4	PFA/181-12306		13. 4.94	
G-BVLS	Thunder Ax8-90 Srs.2 HAFB	2577		13. 4.94	
G-BVLT	Bellanca 7GCBC Citabria	1103-79	SE-GHV	6. 4.94	
G-BVLU	Druine D.31 Turbulent	PFA/1604		18. 4.94	(Extant 9/96)
G-BVLV	Europa Avn Europa	39 & PFA/247-12585		10. 3.94	
G-BVLW	Light Aero Avid Hauler Mk.4	PFA/189-12577		24. 3.94	
G-BVLX	Slingsby T.61F Venture T.2	1973	ZA654	19. 4.94	
G-BVLY	Robinson R-22 Beta	2184	SP-GSA(2)	7. 4.94	To LN-OTV(2) 2/96. Canx 15.2.96.
G-BVLZ	Lindstrand LBL-120A HAFB	063		4. 3.94	
G-BVMA	Beechcraft 200 Super King Air	BB-797	G-VPLC	22. 7.93	
			N84B		
G-BVMB	Hawker Hunter T.7A	41H/695347	XL613	26. 4.94	(Stored 3/96 Hurn)
	(Regd as a T.7 with c/n 41H/695334)				
G-BVMC	Robinson R-44 Astro	0060		15. 4.94	
G-BVMD	Luscombe 8E Silvaire	5265	9Q-CGB	15. 4.94	
			KAT-?/VP-YRB/ZS-BWC/NC2538K		
G-BVME	Aerospatiale AS.365N2 Dauphin 2	6301	F-WIPI(2)	20. 4.94	To F-.... Canx 16.10.95.
			F-WKAY/F-WYML		
G-BVMF	Cameron V-77 HAFB	3195		22. 4.94	
G-BVMG	Bensen B.80V Gyrocopter	G/01-1056		25. 4.94	
G-BVMH	Wag-Aero Sport Trainer	PFA/108-12647		28. 4.94	
G-BVMI	PA-18-150 Super Cub	18-4649	N1136Z	6. 4.94	
	(Frame No.18-4613; initially/		D-EIAC/(PH-WDP)/D-EIAC/D-EKAF/N10F		
	currently regd with c/n 18-8482 and ex.OH-PIN/N4262Z but rebuilt from N1136Z/D-EIAC after crash on landing at Popham on 15.8.95. Original airframe rebuilt as G-CUBP)				
G-BVMJ	Cameron Eagle 90SS HAFB	3262		28. 4.94	
G-BVMK	Robinson R-44 Astro	0064		29. 4.94	To G-LATK 7/94. Canx.
G-BVML	Lindstrand LBL-210A HAFB	094		29. 4.94	
G-BVMM	Robin HR.200/100 Club	41	F-BVMM	18. 8.80	
G-BVMN	Ken Brock KB-2 Gyrocopter	G/06-1218		29. 4.94	
G-BVMO	Rockwell Commander 685	12038	5N-AMH	5. 5.94	To N61983 10/97. Canx 30.9.97.
			D-IGAG		
G-BVMP	BAe 146 Srs.200	E2210	G-6-210	20. 5.94	To I-FLRE 7/94. Canx 18.7.94.
G-BVMR	Cameron V-90 HAFB	3269		28. 3.94	
G-BVMS	BAe 146 Srs.200	E2227	G-6-227	21. 6.94	To I-FLRO 1/95. Canx 11.10.94.
G-BVMT	BAe 146 Srs.200	E2220	G-6-220	29. 6.94	To I-FLRI 9/94. Canx 4.10.94.
G-BVMU	Aerostar Yakovlev Yak-52	9411809	YR-013	11. 5.94	
	(C/n should be 9211809 - date on tail plate reads 30-10-92)				
G-BVMV	Lindstrand LBL-150A HAFB	104		12. 5.94	Canx by CAA 26.2.97. To N994AF 6/97.
G-BVMW	Lindstrand LBL-77A HAFB	106		12. 5.94	Canx by CAA 26.2.97. To N72198 4/97.
G-BVMX	Short SD.3-60 Var.100	SH3751	G-BPFS	25.10.93	
			G-REGN/G-OCIA/G-BPFS		
G-BVMY	Short SD.3-60 Var.100	SH3755	G-OEEC	26.11.93	To SE-LHY 12/97. Canx 27.11.97.
			G-BPKY		
G-BVMZ	Robin HR.100/210 Safari	198	F-BVMZ	20. 3.85	
G-BVNA	Aces High Cuby II	LC2F-931052605 & PFA/257-12584	G-MYMA	27. 4.94	
G-BVNB	PBN BN-2B-26 Islander	2278		19. 5.94	To HC-BUZ 1/96. Canx 19.12.95.
G-BVNC	PBN BN-2B-20 Islander	2279		19. 5.94	To VH-ZZT 3/95. Canx 4.5.95.
	(Originally regd as a BN-2B-26)				
G-BVND	PBN BN-2B-20 Islander	2280		19. 5.94	To VH-ZZU 3/95. Canx 10.5.95.
	(Originally regd as a BN-2B-26)				
G-BVNE	PBN BN-2B-20 Islander	2281		19. 5.94	To VH-ZZV 7/95. Canx 26.6.95.
	(Originally regd as a BN-2B-26)				

Regn	Type	c/n	Previous identity	Regn date	Fate or immediate subsequent identity (if known)
G-BVNF	PBN BN-2B-20 Islander (Originally regd as a BN-2B-26)	2282		19. 5.94	To VH-ZZW 8/95. Canx 24.7.95.
G-BVNG	DH.60G-III Moth Major	?	EC-AFK Spanish AF EE1-81/30-81	17. 5.94	(On rebuild Shoreham 2/96)
G-BVNH	Agusta A.109C	7643	G-LAXO	13. 6.94	
G-BVNI	Taylor JT.2 Titch	PFA/60-11107		20. 5.94	(Extant 5/96)
G-BVNJ	HS.780MF Andover C.1 (Also c/n 1575)	Set.4	XS597	19. 5.94	To 3D-ATS 11/94. Canx 21.11.94.
G-BVNK	HS.780MF Andover C.1	Set.21	XS637	19. 5.94	To 9Q-CJJ 4/95. Canx 19.4.95.
G-BVNL	Rockwell Commander 114	14118	I-ECCE N4789W	13. 5.94	
G-BVNM	Boeing 737-4S3	24163	G-BPKA 9M-MJJ/G-BPKA	31. 3.92	
G-BVNN	Boeing 737-4S3	24164	G-BPKB 9M-MLA/G-BPKB	18. 3.92	
G-BVNO	Boeing 737-4S3	24167	G-BPKE 9M-MLB/G-BPKE	18. 3.92	
G-BVNP	Robinson R-44 Astro	0067		27. 5.94	To D-HLGM 8/94. Canx 27.7.94.
G-BVNR	Cameron N-105 HAFB	3288		24. 5.94	
G-BVNS	PA-28-181 Cherokee Archer II	28-7690358	N6163J	13. 4.94	(Damaged by gales at Prestwick on 26.12.98)
G-BVNT	Thunder Ax9-120 Srs.2 HAFB	2520		24. 5.94	To D-OVNT. Canx 9.4.96.
G-BVNU	FLS Sprint Club	004		25. 5.94	
G-BVNV	Colt 210A HAFB	2457		8. 9.94	To N204TC 4/96. Canx 5.3.96.
G-BVNW	Aerospatiale AS.355N Twin Squirrel	5557	(D-HWPC)	1. 6.94	To VR-BQM 9/94. Canx 30.9.94.
G-BVNX	Sikorsky S-76A Plus	760213	F-GHIN N26PP/N76RP/N76GY/N31210	9. 5.94	To C-GIMX 10/96. Canx 10.10.96.
G-BVNY	Rans S-7 Courier	PFA/218-11951		24. 5.94	
G-BVNZ	Lindstrand LBL-77A HAFB	087		1. 6.94	To VH-SPB(3) 6/95. Canx 31.5.95.
G-BVOA	PA-28-181 Archer II	28-7990145	N2132C	31. 5.94	
G-BVOB	Fokker F-27 Friendship 500	10366	PH-FMN PT-LZM/F-BPNA/PH-FMN	5. 7.94	
G-BVOC	Cameron V-90 HAFB	3291		8. 6.94	
G-BVOD	Montgomerie-Parsons Two-Place Gyroplane	G/08-1238		8. 6.94	
G-BVOE	Hawker Sea Fury FB.11	41H-609972	N232J N54M/CF-OYF/RCN TG114	13. 6.93	Restored as N232J 1/95. Canx 27.1.95.
G-BVOF	Cameron N-77 HAFB	3295		14. 6.94	Canx by CAA 21.9.94; possibly to Greece.
G-BVOG	Cameron RN-9 HAFB	3285		14. 6.94	
G-BVOH	Campbell Cricket	G/03-1220		14. 6.94	(Badly damaged in crash nr.Carlisle Airport 14.8.97)
G-BVOI	Rans S-6-116 Coyote II	PFA/204A-12712		14. 6.94	
G-BVOJ	Lindstrand LBL-31A HAFB	124		20. 6.94	Canx as WFU 29.4.97.
G-BVOK	Aerostar Yakovlev Yak-52	9111505	RA-9111505/DOSAAF 55	14. 6.94	
G-BVOL	Douglas C-47B-40-DL Dakota	9836	ZS-NJE(2) SAAF 6867/FD938/42-23974	14. 6.94	Spares for PH-PBA then to use as museum exhibit at Aviodome Museum. Canx to Holland 16.5.96.
G-BVOM	Fokker F-27 Friendship 500	10381	PH-FND PT-LZN/F-BPNH/PH-FND	5. 7.94	To EC-GYL 12/98. Canx 8.1.99.
G-BVON	Lindstrand LBL-105A HAFB	001	N532LB G-BVON	16. 6.94	
G-BVOO	Lindstrand LBL-105A HAFB	123		16. 6.94	
G-BVOP	Cameron N-90 HAFB	3317		21. 6.94	
G-BVOR	CFM Streak Shadow	K.238-SA & PFA/206-12695		31. 3.94	
G-BVOS	Europa Avn Europa	PFA/247-12562		11. 4.94	
G-BVOT	Glaser-Dirks DG-800A	8-34-A26		21. 6.94	To JA..... Canx 12.11.98.
G-BVOU	HS.748 Srs.2A/270	1721	CS-TAH G-11-6	21. 6.94	
G-BVOV	HS.748 Srs.2A/372	1777	CS-TAO G-11-4	21. 6.94	
G-BVOW	Europa Avn Europa	84 & PFA/247-12679		27. 6.94	
G-BVOX	Taylorcraft F-22	2208	N221UK	20. 5.94	(Stored 10/96)
G-BVOY	Rotorway Exec 90	5238		17. 6.94	
G-BVOZ	Colt 56A HAFB	2595		21. 6.94	
G-BVPA	Thunder Ax8-105 Srs.2 HAFB	2600		24. 6.94	
G-BVPB	Robinson R-44 Astro	0073		28. 6.94	To G-OMEL 9/96. Canx.
G-BVPC	DHC.1 Chipmunk 22A (Fuselage no. DHB/f/476)	C1/0595	WK574	23. 5.94	To VH-DHU(3) 4/99. Canx 12.12.94.
G-BVPD	CASA I-131E Jungmann	2086	F-AZNG E3B-482	12. 7.94	
G-BVPE	BAe 146 Srs.300	E3213	(N889DV) G-6-213	25. 7.94	To VH-NJL(2) 10/94. Canx 20.10.94.
G-BVPF	Lindstrand LBL-69A HAFB	127		30. 6.94	Canx by CAA 26.2.97. To N522LB 6/97.
G-BVPG	Lindstrand LBL-180A HAFB	128		30. 6.94	Canx by CAA 26.2.97. To PH-JNJ 11/97.
G-BVPH	Bensen-Parsons Two-Place Gyroplane	G/08-1234		30. 6.94	
G-BVPI	Evans VP-1	PFA/1578		7.12.78	Badly damaged in crash at Old Sarum on 17.4.88. (Stored at Old Sarum 5/89) Canx by CAA 18.3.99.
G-BVPJ	Lindstrand LBL-90A HAFB	122		1. 7.94	Canx as WFU 19.12.95. To G-UNGE 12/96.
G-BVPK	Cameron O-90 HAFB	3313		1. 7.94	

Regn	Type	c/n	Previous identity	Regn date	Fate or immediate subsequent identity (if known)
G-BVPL	Zenair CH.601HD Zodiac	PFA/162-12693		4. 7.94	
G-BVPM	Evans VP-2 Coupe	V2-1016 & PFA/7205		6.11.78	Permit expired 31.4.94. (Stored at owner's house 7/95)
G-BVPN	Piper J3C-65 Cub (Regd as c/n 5298; but has frame no 7002 which was N38207, probably used in rebuild of N31073 in early 70s)	6917	G-TAFY N31073/N38207/N38307/NC38307	6. 7.94	
G-BVPO	DH.100 Vampire FB.6 (built by FFW, Emmen)	615	HB-RVO Swiss AF J-1106	11. 7.94	Canx 23.6.97 on sale to Jordan.
G-BVPP	Folland Gnat T.1	FL.536	"XR993" 8620M/XP534	22. 4.94	
G-BVPR	Robinson R-22 Beta	1612	G-KNIT	17. 6.94	
G-BVPS	Jodel D.112	PFA/917		6. 7.94	
G-BVPT	Dornier 228-202K	8165	D-CALK D-CBDV	29. 7.94	Canx 26.6.98 on sale to Germany.
G-BVPU	Cameron A-140 HAFB	3296		12. 7.94	
G-BVPV	Lindstrand LBL-77B HAFB	119		13. 7.94	
G-BVPW	Rans S-6-116 Coyote II	PFA/204A-12737		12. 7.94	
G-BVPX	Lovegrove Tyro Gyro Mk.II	G/011-1237		13. 7.94	Canx by CAA 29.7.99.
G-BVPY	CFM Streak Shadow	PFA/206-12375		14. 6.94	
G-BVPZ	Lindstrand LBL-210A HAFB	121		18. 7.94	Canx by CAA 26.2.97. To N234TZ 6/97.
G-BVRA	Europa Avn Europa	PFA/247-12635		25. 7.94	
G-BVRB	Douglas C-47B-25-DK Dakota	15813/32561	F-GDXP French Navy F-TEFJ/F-RAOD/F-RAXP/F-RAMP/KN307/44-76229	27. 7.94	To F-GNFD 5/95. Canx 9.5.95.
G-BVRC	Bell 206 JetRanger III	3689	G-BSJC N3175S	27. 4.94	To G-SPYI 5/96. Canx.
G-BVRD	VPM M-16 Tandem Trainer	VPM16-UK-108		27. 7.94	(Badly damaged on test flight Cranfield 12.1.95)
G-BVRE	Van's RV-6A	PFA/181-12677		1. 8.94	
G-BVRF	BAe 125 Srs.800A	258247	G-5-813	1. 8.94	To Japanese SDF as 52-3002 in 1/95. Canx 26.5.95.
G-BVRG	BAe 125 Srs.800A	258250	G-5-815	1. 8.94	To Japanese SDF as 52-3003 in 12/94. Canx 20.12.94.
G-BVRH	Taylorcraft BL-65	1657	N24322 NC24322	15. 7.94	
G-BVRI	Thunder Ax6-56 HAFB	2622		2. 8.94	
G-BVRJ	BAe 146 RJ70	E1254		9. 8.94	To (9H-ABW)/9H-ACM. Canx 20.9.94.
G-BVRK	Rans S-6-ESA Coyote II	1193-566	G-MYPK	14. 7.94	
G-BVRL	Lindstrand LBL-21A HAFB	130		3. 8.94	
G-BVRM	Cameron A-210 HAFB	3134		4. 8.94	
G-BVRN	Fokker F-27 Friendship 500	10427	PH-FPB (G-BVRN)/PH-FPB/HL5211/(HL5207)/PH-FPB	7. 3.95	(To become EC-... /99)
G-BVRO	Lindstrand LBL-240A HAFB	095		9. 8.94	To JY-RUM 9/94. Canx 27.9.94.
G-BVRP	Lindstrand LBL-9A HAFB	108		9. 8.94	
G-BVRR	Lindstrand LBL-77A HAFB	133		9. 8.94	
G-BVRS	Beechcraft B90 King Air	LJ-481	G-KJET G-AXFE	29.12.93	
G-BVRT	Embraer EMB.110P1 Bandeirante	110-304	SE-KYE G-LATC/PT-SCL	30. 8.94	Officially canx 1.5.96 to Trinidad and Tobago. To J8-VAZ 5/96.
G-BVRU	Lindstrand LBL-105A HAFB	131		15. 8.94	
G-BVRV	Van's RV-4 (built by T.C.Hahn)	793	N144TH	23. 6.94	
G-BVRW	BAe 125 Srs.800XP	258266	G-5-811	16. 8.94	To (N293H)/N800XP. Canx 16.8.95.
G-BVRX	Sikorsky S-76A II Plus	760165	C-FTGD N20FB/N299FB/N544WL/N54439	17. 2.95	Restored as C-FTGD 7/95. Canx 7.7.95.
G-BVRY	Cyclone Ax3K	C.3013085 & PFA/245-12471		18. 8.94	
G-BVRZ	PA-18-95 Super Cub (Regd with frame no. 18-3381)	18-3442	SE-ITP LN-LJG/D-EDCM/96+19/QW+901/QZ+001/AC+507/AS+506/54-752	22.11.94	
G-BVSA	BAe 146 Srs.300	E3159	I-ATSD G-6-159/G-5-159	2. 9.94	To EI-CLI 4/95. Canx 18.4.95.
G-BVSB	Team Minimax 91A	PFA/186-12241		1. 7.94	
G-BVSC	Bell 206B JetRanger III	3103	N8092Q G-BVSC/F-GGDP/N212TV	22. 8.94	CofA expired 7.4.95. (W/o at Jedrzejowice on 9.7.95 whilst N8092Q, restored on 27.12.95) Canx as WFU 28.10.96.
G-BVSD	Sud SE.3130 Alouette II	1897	V-54 Swiss AF	8. 9.94	
G-BVSE	Eurocopter AS.355N Twin Squirrel	5574		24. 8.94	To G-SEPB 2/95. Canx.
G-BVSF	Aero Designs Pulsar	PFA/202-12071		1. 7.94	
G-BVSG	PBN BN-2B-20 Islander	2283		3.10.94	To VH-ZZX 9/95. Canx 10.8.95.
G-BVSH	PBN BN-2B-20 Islander	2284		3.10.94	To VH-ZZY. Canx 30.8.95.
G-BVSI	PBN BN-2B-20 Islander (Originally regd as BN-2B-26)	2285		31. 1.95	To JA5322 11/95. Canx 28.11.95.
G-BVSJ	PBN BN-2T Turbine Islander (Originally regd as BN-2B-26)	2286		31. 1.95	
G-BVSK	PBN BN-2T Turbine Islander	2287		31. 1.95	To F-OIAR 12/96. Canx 4.12.96.
G-BVSL	PBN BN-2T Turbine Islander	2288		31. 1.95	
G-BVSM	Rotary Air Force RAF 2000	EW-42		24. 8.94	
G-BVSN	Light Aero Avid Speed Wing	PFA/189-12088		24. 8.94	
G-BVSO	Cameron A-120 HAFB	3339		25. 8.94	
G-BVSP	Hunting P.84 Jet Provost T.3A	PAC/W/6327	XM370	31. 8.94	
G-BVSR	Colt 210A HAFB	2470		8. 9.94	

Regn	Type	c/n	Previous identity	Regn date	Fate or immediate subsequent identity (if known)
G-BVSS	Jodel 150 Mascaret	PFA/151-11878		22. 8.94	
G-BVST	Jodel 150 Mascaret	130 & PFA/235-12198		11. 8.94	
G-BVSU	Lindstrand LBL-105A HAFB	138		1. 9.94	To N199DB 7/95. Canx 5.6.95.
G-BVSV	Cameron C-80 HAFB	3194		5. 9.94	
G-BVSW	Cameron C-80 HAFB	3210		5. 9.94	
G-BVSX	Team Minimax 91A	PFA/186-12463		9. 9.94	
G-BVSY	Thunder Ax9-120 HAFB	2631		16. 8.94	
G-BVSZ	Pitts S-1E(S) Special	PFA/09-11235		9. 9.94	
G-BVTA	Tri-R Kis	PFA/239-12450		26. 8.94	(Extant 10/97)
G-BVTB	BAC P.84 Jet Provost T.5A	EEP/JP/977	XW313	7. 9.94	To N313RH 6/95. Canx 12.6.95.
G-BVTC	BAC P.84 Jet Provost T.5A	EEP/JP/997	XW333	7. 9.94	
G-BVTD	CFM Streak Shadow	K.159-SA & PFA/206-11972		14. 9.94	
G-BVTE	Fokker F.28-0070	11538	PH-EZX	13. 4.95	
G-BVTF	Fokker F.28-0070	11539	PH-EZZ PH-EZA	24. 5.95	
G-BVTG	Fokker F.28-0070	11551	PH-EZK	1. 9.95	
G-BVTH	Fokker F.28-0070	11577	PH-EZG	. .94R	NTU - Not delivered - To PH-KZF. Canx.
G-BVTI	Colt 140A HAFB	2637		21. 9.94	To D-OWIS 11/95. Canx 27.10.95.
G-BVTJ	ATR-72-202	342	F-WWEV F-GKOI/F-WWLX	7.12.94	
G-BVTK	ATR-72-202	357	F-WWEW F-GKOJ	21.10.94	
G-BVTL	Colt 31A Air Chair HAFB	2572		5. 7.94	
G-BVTM	Reims Cessna F.152 II	1827	G-WACS D-EFGZ	31. 8.94	
G-BVTN	Cameron N-90 HAFB	3361		16. 9.94	
G-BVTO	PA-28-151 Cherokee Warrior	28-7415253	G-SEWL D-EDOS/N9550N	19. 9.94	
G-BVTP	HS.125 Srs.400A	25255	XW788	15. 9.94	To (N255TS)/N4QB 11/94. Canx 3.11.94.
G-BVTR	HS.125 Srs.400A	25264	XW789	15. 9.94	To N264TS 11/94. Canx 3.11.94.
G-BVTS	HS.125 Srs.400A	25266	XW790	15. 9.94	To (N266TS)/N135CK 1/95. Canx 15.12.94.
G-BVTT	HS.125 Srs.400A	25268	XW791	15. 9.94	To (N268TS)/N41953. Canx 3.11.94.
G-BVTU	Lindstrand LBL-105A HAFB	147		19. 9.94	Canx by CAA 26.2.97. To HB-QDT 7/97.
G-BVTV	Rotorway Exec 90	5243		16. 9.94	
G-BVTW	Aero Designs Pulsar	PFA/202-12172		14. 9.94	
G-BVTX	DHC.1 Chipmunk 22A (Fuselage no. DHB/f/599)	C1/0705	WP809	2. 8.94	
G-BVTY	Dornier 228-202K	8162	D-CUBI D-CBDZ(3)/PH-FXA/D-CATY(2)/D-CBDS(2)	28. 9.94	To (D-IASD)/D-CBDM(6) /96. Canx 23.1.96.
G-BVTZ	Dornier 228-202K	8157	D-CTCB D-CBDV(4)/TC-FBM/D-CIRC/(TC-FBM)/D-CBDF(2)	28. 9.94	To D-CBDQ(7) 10/96. Canx 8.11.96.
G-BVUA	Cameron O-105 HAFB	3369		27. 9.94	
G-BVUB	Cessna U.206G Stationair 6 II	U206-05944	OY-NUB LN-NFC/N6552X	22. 9.94	To N206GD 6/96. Canx 11.4.96.
G-BVUC	Colt 56A HAFB	2608	G-639	30. 9.94	
G-BVUD	Cameron A-250 HAFB	3370		30. 9.94	
G-BVUE	Cameron C-80 HAFB	3374		30. 9.94	
G-BVUF	Thunder Ax10-180 Srs.2 HAFB (Also has Cameron c/n 3508)	2642		3.10.94	
G-BVUG	AIA Stampe SV.4C (Regd as Betts TB.1 c/n PFA/265-12770)	1045	G-BEUS F-BKFK/F-DAFK/French Mil 1045	3.10.94	(On rebuild 3/97 at Spanhoe Lodge)
G-BVUH	Thunder Ax6-65B HAFB	243	JA-A0075	3.10.94	
G-BVUI	Lindstrand LBL-25A Cloudhopper HAFB	148		5.10.94	
G-BVUJ	Ken Brock KB-2 Gyrocopter	G/06-1244		10.10.94	
G-BVUK	Cameron V-77 HAFB	3372		11.10.94	
G-BVUL	PA-34-200T Seneca	34-7570128	OY-PEA N33531	11.10.94	To I-BVUL 5/97. Canx 2.12.96.
G-BVUM	Rans S-6-116 Coyote II	PFA/204A-12685		11.10.94	
G-BVUN	Van's RV-4	3363UK & PFA/181-12488		11.10.94	
G-BVUO	Cameron R-150 Gas Free Balloon	3365		13.10.94	
G-BVUP	Schleicher ASW-24E	24828	D-KEWI(2)	14.10.94	
G-BVUR	Aerospatiale AS.365N2 Dauphin 2	6477	F-WYMJ (JA6740)	19.10.94	To JA6740 3/95. Canx 6.1.95.
G-BVUS	Lindstrand LBL-90A HAFB	143		20.10.94	To N442GF 6/95. Canx 31.5.95.
G-BVUT	Evans VP-1 Srs.2	PFA/62-12092		24.10.94	Crashed & destroyed on take-off from Pepperbox strip, Wilts. on 13.3.99.
G-BVUU	Cameron C-80 HAFB	3383		11.10.94	
G-BVUV	Europa Avn Europa	PFA/247-12762		23. 9.94	
G-BVUW	BAe 146 Srs.100	E1035	B-584L B-2704/G-5-035	26. 1.95	To J8-VBC 4/95. Canx 7.4.95.
G-BVUX	BAe 146 Srs.100	E1068	J8-VBA G-BVUX/B-585L/B-2705/G-5-068	22.11.94	To N861MC 10/97. Canx 22.10.97.
G-BVUY	BAe 146 Srs.100	E1071	B-2706 G-5-071	25.11.94	To J8-VBB 2/95. Canx 17.2.95.
G-BVUZ	Cessna 120	11334	Z-YGH VP-YGH/VP-NAM/VP-YGH	20. 9.94	

Regn	Type	c/n	Previous identity	Regn date	Fate or immediate subsequent identity (if known)
G-BVVA	Aerostar Yakovlev Yak-52 (Has c/n plate 889109 and marked as ex.LY-AMV, which was based in France .95)	877610	LY-ANN DOSAAF 52 (yellow)	24.10.94	
G-BVVB	Carlson Sparrow II	PFA/209-11809		26. 9.94	
G-BVVC	Hawker Hunter F.6A (Armstrong-Whitworth-built)	S4/U/3362	8685M XF516	28.10.94	(Stored 3/96)
G-BVVD	Not allocated.				
G-BVVE	Wassmer Jodel D.112	1070	F-BKAJ	28.10.94	
G-BVVF	Nanchang CJ-6A (Yak 18)	2232028	Chinese PLAF	10.10.94	
G-BVVG	Nanchang CJ-6A (Yak 18)	2751219	Chinese PLAF	10.10.94	(Delivered to new owners in France 26.5.99)
G-BVVH	Europa Avn Europa	PFA/247-12505		31.10.94	
G-BVVI	Hawker Audax I (Avro-built)	-	2015M K5600	3.11.94	(On rebuild 8/95)
G-BVVJ	Cameron N-77 HAFB	3388		3.11.94	To OH-OHO 11/98. Canx 12.10.98.
G-BVVK	DHC.6-310 Twin Otter	666	LN-BEZ	21.12.94	
G-BVVL	EAA Acrosport 2	PFA/72A-10887		11.11.94	
G-BVVM	Zenair CH.601HD Zodiac	PFA/162-12539		3.10.94	
G-BVVN	Brugger MB.2 Colibri	PFA/43-10979		12.10.94	
G-BVVO	Yakovlev Yak-50	853007	LY-AMO DOSAAF	3.11.94	To LY-AHC 3/98. Canx 26.2.98.
G-BVVP	Europa Avn Europa	88 & PFA/247-12697		20. 9.94	
G-BVVR	Stits SA-3A Playboy	P-736	N4620S	14.11.94	
G-BVVS	Van's RV-4	PFA/181-12324		15.11.94	
G-BVVT	Colt 240A HAFB	2682		17.11.94	
G-BVVU	Lindstrand Four SS HAFB	155		18.11.94	To HB-QAP. Canx 9.3.95.
G-BVVV	Bell 206L-1 LongRanger II	45548	D-HUGO OE-KXT/C-GLMM	30. 9.94	To G-NEUF 11/98. Canx.
G-BVVW	IAV-Bacau Yakovlev Yak-52 (C/n plate shows c/n 833519)	844605	RA-01361 DOSAAF 15/DOSAAF 95	16.11.94	
G-BVVX	Yakovlev Yak-18A	?	307 Russian AF	11.11.94	(On rebuild 10/96)
G-BVVY	Air Command 532 Elite	G/04-1104	G-CORK	22.11.94	
G-BVVZ	Corby CJ-1 Starlet	PFA/134-12293		9.11.94	
G-BVWA	Socata MS.880B Rallye 100T	2747	F-GACD	29.11.94	
G-BVWB	Thunder Ax8-90 Srs.2 HAFB	3000		2.12.94	
G-BVWC	English Electric Canberra B.2 (Mod) (C/n relates to nose section which was originally fitted to XH568) (Avro-built)	71399	WK163	2.12.94	
G-BVWD	BAe 146 RJ85	E2253	G-6-253	8.12.94	To D-AVRB 12/94. Canx 8.12.94.
G-BVWE	Cameron C-80 HAFB	3414		6.12.94	
G-BVWF	BAC P.84 Jet Provost T.5	PAC/W/23907	XS230	7.12.94	To G-VIVM 3/96. Canx.
G-BVWG	Hawker Hunter T.8C (Regd with c/n 41H-695320)	41H-693836	XL598	8.12.94	To ZU-ATH. Canx 12.6.95.
G-BVWH	Cameron Light Bulb N-90SS HAFB	3404		8.12.94	(Active 8/96)
G-BVWI	Cameron Light Bulb 65SS HAFB	3405		8.12.94	
G-BVWJ	Lindstrand LBL-240A HAFB	165		15.12.94	To N353LB 1/95. Canx 19.1.95.
G-BVWK	Air & Space 18-A Gyroplane	18-14	SE-HID N6108S	19.12.94	(Stored 4/97)
G-BVWL	Air & Space 18-A Gyroplane	18-63	SE-HIE N90588/N6152S	19.12.94	(Stored 4/97)
G-BVWM	Europa Avn Europa	PFA/247-12620		14.12.94	
G-BVWN	Hawker Hunter T.7	41H-693751	XL600	23.12.94	To G-VETA 7/96. Canx.
G-BVWO	Lindstrand LBL-90A HAFB	173		28.12.94	To N173AF 6/97. Canx by CAA 24.3.97.
G-BVWP	DHC.1 Chipmunk 22 (Fuselage no. DHB/f/637)	C1/0741	WP856	19.12.94	
G-BVWR	Bell 206B JetRanger	276	C-GNXQ N4714R	20.12.94	To G-OBAY 7/98. Canx.
G-BVWS	Bell 206B JetRanger II	1788	C-GGXX N49610	20.12.94	To OO-KBM 12/95. Canx 19.12.95.
G-BVWT	Bell 206B JetRanger II	2043	C-GUXC N9965K	20.12.94	To OO-LER. Canx 5.12.95.
G-BVWU	English Electric Canberra T.17 (Handley Page-built)	HP/H1/174B	WJ607	22.12.94	To ZU-AUE 9/95. Canx 6.6.95.
G-BVWV	Hawker Hunter F.6A (Officially regd with c/n 41H-674112)	41H-679991	8829M XE653	22.12.94	To ZU-AUJ 9/95. Canx 30.8.95.
G-BVWW	Lindstrand LBL-90A HAFB	169		28.12.94	
G-BVWX	VPM M-16 Tandem Trainer	VPM16-UK-111		3. 1.95	
G-BVWY	Porterfield CP.65	720	N27223 NC27223	23.11.94	
G-BVWZ	PA-32-301 Saratoga	3206055	I-TASP N9184N	3. 1.95	
G-BVXA	Cameron N-105 HAFB	3441		4. 1.95	
G-BVXB	Cameron V-77 HAFB	3442		4. 1.95	
G-BVXC	English Electric Canberra B(I).8 (Regd as a B.6 version)	6649	WT333	9. 1.95	(Stored 9/97)
G-BVXD	Cameron O-84 HAFB	3432		5. 1.95	
G-BVXE	Steen Skybolt	PFA/64-11123	G-LISA	5. 1.95	

Regn	Type	c/n	Previous identity	Regn date	Fate or immediate subsequent identity (if known)
G-BVXF	Cameron O-120 HAFB	3400		21. 9.94	(Basket noted on display at Los Cerillos, Chile 12.3.96)
G-BVXG	Lindstrand LBL-90A HAFB	110		5. 1.95	
G-BVXH	Lindstrand LBL-77A HAFB	167		5. 1.95	To N515LB 3/97. Canx 10.2.97.
G-BVXI	Klemm Kl.35D	1981	D-EFEG SE-BHT/Swedish AF Fv.5052	5. 1.95	(On rebuild after crash on 7.4.62)
G-BVXJ	CASA Bucker Bu.133 Jungmeister	-	E.1-9 Spanish AF/ES.1-9/35-9	11. 1.95	
G-BVXK	Aerostar Yakovlev Yak-52	9111306	RA-44508 DOSAAF 26	12. 1.95	
G-BVXL	Avions Mudry CAP.231EX	02	F-GKKF F-WGZC	5. 1.95	NTU - To F-GKKI 2/95. Canx 5.1.95.
G-BVXM	Aerospatiale AS.350B Ecureuil	2013	I-AUDI I-CIOC	10. 1.95	
G-BVXN	Mil Mi-17	520M15	RA-25389 CCCP-25389	12. 1.95	To 9L-LBD. Canx 13.3.95.
G-BVXO	Mil Mi-17	520M16	RA-25390 CCCP-25390	12. 1.95	To 9L-LBE. Canx 13.3.95.
G-BVXP	Cameron N-105 HAFB	1311	VH-URU(2)	13. 1.95	(Active 10/96)
G-BVXR	DH.104 Devon C.2	04436	XA880	13. 1.95	(Stored 5/99 at Kemble)
G-BVXS	Taylorcraft BC-12D	9284	N96984 NC96984	27. 1.95	
G-BVXT	BAC P.84 Jet Provost T.5A	EEP/JP/953	XW289	18. 1.95	To G-JPVA 2/95. Canx.
G-BVXU	Zenair CH.601HD Zodiac	PFA/162-12740		19. 1.95	To G-OMWE 3/97. Canx.
G-BVXV	Not allotted.				
G-BVXW	Short SC.7 Skyvan 3A-100	SH1889	LX-DEF Argentine Coast Guard PA-52/G-14-61	15.11.95	
G-BVXX	PBN BN-2B-20 Islander (Originally regd as BN-2B-26)	2289		31. 1.95	To 6Y-JNS 6/96. Canx 5.6.96.
G-BVXY	PBN BN-2B-20 Islander (Originally regd as BN-2B-26)	2290		31. 1.95	To D-IFKU 6/96. Canx 5.6.96.
G-BVXZ	Lindstrand LBL-210A HAFB	068		30. 1.95	To CS-B.. Canx 25.11.98.
G-BVYA	Airbus A.320-231	354	F-WQAY (N301SA)/F-WWDZ	7. 4.95	
G-BVYB	Airbus A.320-231	357	F-WQAZ (N302SA)/F-WWBH	20. 4.95	
G-BVYC	Airbus A.320-231	411	F-WQBA (N303SA)/F-WWDX	26. 4.95	
G-BVYD	PBN BN-2B-20 Islander (Originally regd as BN-2B-26)	2291		13. 2.95	To JA5323 7/96. Canx 22.7.96.
G-BVYE	PBN BN-2B-20 Islander (Originally regd as BN-2B-26)	2292		13. 2.95	Stress damaged during second flight in Romania 28.8.96, beyond economical repair. (Stored in Romania in 8/96) Canx as PWFU 27.11.98.
G-BVYF	PA-31-350 Navajo Chieftain	31-7952102	G-SAVE N3518T	8. 2.95	
G-BVYG	Robin DR.300/120 Petit Prince	611	F-BSQB F-BSPI	9. 1.95	
G-BVYH	Hawker Hunter GA.11 (Officially regd with c/n 41H-004048)	HABL-003037	XE707	31. 1.95	To N707XE (with c/n 41H/004048). Canx 6.6.95.
G-BVYI	Hawker Hunter T.8C (Officially regd with c/n 41H-695942)	HABL/R/003050	XF289	31. 1.95	To N289XF (with c/n 41H/695942). Canx 6.6.95.
G-BVYJ	Cameron Fire Extinguisher 90SS HAFB	3398		2. 2.95	
G-BVYK	Team Minimax 91A	PFA/186-12598		13. 2.95	
G-BVYL	Colt 56A HAFB	3537		14. 2.95	To G-DANG 1/98. Canx.
G-BVYM	Robin DR.300/140 Major	656	F-BTBL	9.12.94	
G-BVYN	Agusta-Bell 412	25502	I-INGO	3. 2.95	To VR-BQC 4/95. Canx 13.4.95.
G-BVYO	Robin R.2160	288		11. 1.95	
G-BVYP	PA-25-235 Pawnee B	25-3481	N7475D OY-CLT	13. 2.95	
G-BVYR	Cameron A-250 HAFB	3411		2. 2.95	
G-BVYS	BAe 146 RJ100	E3259	G-6-259	24. 2.95	To HB-IXT 1/96. Canx 13.11.95.
G-BVYT	QAC Quickie Q.2	2443	N3797S	18. 1.95	
G-BVYU	Cameron A-140 HAFB	3544		17. 2.95	
G-BVYV	BAe 125 Srs.800	258268		20. 2.95	To Japanese SDF as 62-3004. Canx 13.10.95. (Was officially canx on export to the USA)
G-BVYW	BAe 125 Srs.800XP	258277		20. 2.95	To N97SH. Canx 15.11.95.
G-BVYX	Light-Aero Avid Speed Wing Mk.4	PFA/189-12370		16. 2.95	
G-BVYY	Pietenpol Air Camper	PFA/47-12559		20. 2.95	
G-BVYZ	Stemme S-10V	14-011	D-KGDD	6. 3.95	
G-BVZA	Lindstrand LBL-77A HAFB	182		20. 2.95	Canx by CAA 26.2.97. To N514LA 4/97.
G-BVZB	Lindstrand LBL-31A Air Chair HAFB	187		20. 2.95	Canx by CAA 26.2.97. (Based Littleton, Colorado, USA)
G-BVZC	BAe Jetstream 4102	41047	G-4-047	23. 2.95	To OY-SVW 5/95. Canx 3.5.95.
G-BVZD	Tri-R Kis	PFA/239-12416		21. 2.95	
G-BVZE	Boeing 737-59D	26422	SE-DNL	7. 3.95	
G-BVZF	Boeing 737-59D	25038	SE-DND (SE-DNC)	3. 4.95	
G-BVZG	Boeing 737-5Q8	25160	SE-DNF	12. 4.95	
G-BVZH	Boeing 737-5Q8	25166	SE-DNG	25. 4.95	
G-BVZI	Boeing 737-5Q8	25167	SE-DNH	15. 5.95	

Regn	Type	c/n	Previous identity	Regn date	Fate or immediate subsequent identity (if known)
G-BVZJ	Rand-Robinson KR-2	PFA/129-11049		21. 2.95	
G-BVZK	BAe 125 Srs.800XP	258278		22. 2.95	To N872AT. Canx 4.12.95.
G-BVZL	BAe 125 Srs.800XP	258279		22. 2.95	To N817H/4X-CZM 12/95. Canx 14.12.95.
G-BVZM	Cessna 210M Centurion II	210-61674	OO-CNJ N732PV	28. 2.95	
G-BVZN	Cameron C-80 HAFB	3546		28. 2.95	
G-BVZO	Rans S-6-116 Coyote II	0494-606 & PFA/204A-12710		1. 3.95	
G-BVZP	Rotorway Exec 90	5174		7. 2.95	No Permit to Fly issued. Canx by CAA 29.2.96.
G-BVZR	Zenair CH.601HD Zodiac	PFA/162-12417		2. 3.95	
G-BVZS	HS.780MF Andover CC.2 (Srs.2/206)	1564	XS792	8. 3.95	To 5Y-IAK 4/95. Canx 10.4.95.
G-BVZT	Lindstrand LBL-90A HAFB	183		9. 3.95	
G-BVZU	Airbus A.320-231	280	EC-GKM G-BVZU/N280RX/TC-GAB/N280RX/N638AW/N280RX/F-WWDV	5. 4.95	Restored as N280RX 10/97. Canx 31.10.97.
G-BVZV	Rans S-6-116 Coyote II	PFA/204A-12832		16. 2.95	
G-BVZW	Fokker F-27 Friendship 500	10425	9Q-CBU PH-FOZ/VH-EWS/F-BYAF/OY-APA/(OY-DKR)/PH-FOZ	13. 4.95	To (PH-TLP)/PH-FOZ 12/98. Canx 1.12.98.
G-BVZX	Cameron H-34 HAFB	3564		15. 3.95	
G-BVZY	Mooney M.20R Ovation	29-0045		13. 3.95	
G-BVZZ	DHC.1 Chipmunk 22 (Fuselage no. DHB/f/577)	C1/0687	WP795	5. 1.95	
G-BWAA	Cameron N-133 HAFB	3471		9. 3.95	
G-BWAB	Jodel D.140 Mousquetaire	PFA/251-12469		25. 1.95	
G-BWAC	Waco YKS-7	4693	N50RA N2896D/NC50	19. 8.92	
G-BWAD	Rotary Air Force RAF 2000	147 & G/13-1254		27. 2.95	
G-BWAE	Rotary Air Force RAF 2000	G/13-1252		27. 2.95	(Damaged on landing at Kemble on 30.7.96)
G-BWAF	Hawker Hunter F.6A (Armstrong-Whitworth built)	S4/U/3393	8831M XG160	24. 2.95	(Stored as XG160 "U" 9/97 Hurn)
G-BWAG	Cameron O-120 HAFB	3478		3. 2.95	
G-BWAH	Montgomerie-Bensen B.8MR Gyrocopter	G/01-1208		16. 3.95	
G-BWAI	CFM Streak Shadow	PFA/206-12556		21. 3.95	
G-BWAJ	Cameron V-77 HAFB	3579		22. 3.95	
G-BWAK	Robinson R-22 Beta	2507	N83311	22. 3.95	
G-BWAL	PA-31-350 Navajo Chieftain	31-7652093	SU-BBY G-BWAL/A6-ABA/N59861	1.11.77	To TF-JMG 4/84. Canx 25.4.84.
G-BWAM	Cameron C-60 HAFB	3453		23. 3.95	To HB-QET 5/98. Canx 1.5.98.
G-BWAN	Cameron N-77 HAFB	3499		24. 3.95	
G-BWAO	Cameron C-80 HAFB	3436		24. 3.95	
G-BWAP	Clutton-Tabenor FRED Srs.3	PFA/29-10959		24. 3.95	
G-BWAR	Denney Kitfox Mk.3	PFA/172-12432		16. 3.95	
G-BWAS	PA-31-350 Navajo Chieftain	31-8152160	N4091W	21. 4.88	To N9247L 9/95. Canx 1.9.95.
G-BWAT	Pietenpol Air Camper	PFA/47-11594		15. 3.95	
G-BWAU	Cameron V-90 HAFB	3569		27. 3.95	
G-BWAV	Schweizer Hughes 269C (300C)	S.1204	SE-JAY LN-OTS/OY-HDW/N41S	28. 2.95	
G-BWAW	Lindstrand LBL-77A HAFB	207		28. 3.95	
G-BWAX	Cameron A-210 HAFB	3352		30. 3.95	To D-OUCH 4/95. Canx 31.3.95.
G-BWAY	Beechcraft A36 Bonanza	E-2429	N3113F	16. 6.88	To N36VU 9/94. Canx 30.6.94.
G-BWAZ	Eurocopter AS.350B2 Ecureuil	2621	OO-AKK OO-XKK/F-WYML	25. 4.95	To F-GPFE 6/97. Canx 10.6.97.
G-BWBA	Cameron V-65 HAFB	3456		27. 2.95	
G-BWBB	Lindstrand LBL-14A HAFB	222		3. 4.95	
G-BWBC	Cameron N-90AS HAFB	3574		12. 6.95	
G-BWBD	Lindstrand LBL-90A HAFB	231		3. 4.95	Canx by CAA 26.2.97. To N952CL 4/97.
G-BWBE	Colt Flying Ice Cream Cone SS HAFB	3560		3. 4.95	
G-BWBF	Colt Flying Ice Cream Cone SS HAFB	3561		3. 4.95	
G-BWBG	Cvjetkovic CA-65 Skyfly	PFA/1566		6. 4.95	(Extant 7/97)
G-BWBH	Thunder Fork Lift Truck 90SS HAFB	3472		6. 4.95	
G-BWBI	Taylorcraft F-22A	2207	N22UK	3. 4.95	
G-BWBJ	Colt 21A HAFB	3532		6. 4.95	
G-BWBK	Lindstrand LBL-77B HAFB	180		6. 4.95	Canx by CAA 26.2.97.
G-BWBL	Lindstrand LBL-90A HAFB	233		6. 4.95	To N4030A 4/97. Canx by CAA 26.2.97.
G-BWBM	Lindstrand LBL-90A HAFB	239		6. 4.95	To N721LB 3/97. Canx by CAA 10.2.97.
G-BWBN	Cameron V-90 HAFB	3583		7. 4.95	To OY-COU. Canx 20.4.99.
G-BWBO	Lindstrand LBL-77A HAFB	157		10. 4.95	
G-BWBP	Bell 212	30687	EC-GCT EC-891/G-BWBP/9Y-TFA/VR-BFP	11. 4.95	Restored as 9Y-TFA 10/97. Canx 9.10.97.
G-BWBR	Cameron A-180 HAFB	3344		11. 4.95	To F-GLIC 5/97. Canx by CAA 5.3.97.
G-BWBS	BAC P.84 Jet Provost T.5A	EEP/JP/1053	XW431	13. 4.95	Fatal crash into North Sea 8 nm SW of Clacton on 24.12.98.
G-BWBT	Lindstrand LBL-90A HAFB	184		3. 4.95	

Regn	Type	c/n	Previous identity	Regn date	Fate or immediate subsequent identity (if known)
G-BWBU	Aerospatiale AS.365N2 Dauphin 2	6485	F-WQDP	18. 4.95	To 9M-YTL. Canx 31.8.95.
G-BWBV	Colt Piggy Bank SS HAFB	3535		19. 4.95	
G-BWBW	Cameron A-180 HAFB	2614		20. 6.91	Canx as destroyed 15.6.95.
G-BWBX	Bell 206B JetRanger III	3128	D-HOLY N20WW/N57521	13. 4.95	To OY-HHT 8/95. Canx 7.8.95.
G-BWBY	Schleicher ASH-26E	26076		30. 8.95	
G-BWBZ	ARV1 Super 2	PFA/152-12802		10. 3.95	
G-BWCA	CFM Streak Shadow	PFA/206-11985		19. 4.95	
G-BWCB	BAe 125 Srs.1000B	259032	F-WQAU ZS-NHL/G-5-760	20. 4.95	To VR-CXX 6/95. Canx 15.6.95.
G-BWCC	Van Den Bemden 460m3 (Gas) Free Balloon (C/n is probably corruption of Dutch CofR 622)	"022"	PH-BOX	5. 4.95	
G-BWCD	Cameron A-120 HAFB	2399	G-OCBC	7. 4.95	To D-OWCD 4/96. Canx 12.3.96.
G-BWCE	Campbell Cricket	G/03-1235		24. 4.95	
G-BWCF	Yakovlev Yak-52	852904	LY-ANQ DOSAAF	25. 4.95	To ZK-YAC 3/96. Canx 21.12.95.
G-BWCG	Lindstrand LBL-42A HAFB	223		25. 4.95	
G-BWCH	Lindstrand AS-250 Hot-Air Airship (Originally regd as LBL-9S HAFB)	247		25. 4.95	Canx by CAA 26.2.97.
G-BWCI	Light Aero Avid Hauler Mk.4	PFA/189-12299		19. 8.92	(Badly damaged 16.5.98 2m W of Fenland Airfield)
G-BWCJ	Lindstrand LBL-14M HAFB	248		25. 4.95	Canx by CAA 26.2.97.
G-BWCK	Everett Gyroplane Srs.3	036		26. 4.95	(At Sproughton 5/97)
G-BWCL	Lindstrand LBL-180A HAFB	150		27. 4.95	
G-BWCM	Lindstrand LBL-77A HAFB	246		16. 5.95	To N513LB 2/97. Canx 10.2.97.
G-BWCN	Dornier Do.28D-2 Skyservant	4335	5N-AYE D-ILID/9V-BKL/D-ILID	28. 4.95	
G-BWCO	Dornier Do.28D-2 Skyservant	4337	EI-CJU (N5TK)/5N-AOH/D-ILIF	19. 6.95	
G-BWCP	Airbus A.320-212	189	N483GX F-WWDC	18. 4.95	To C-GRYY. Canx 12.12.95.
G-BWCR	HS.125 Srs.700B (Not officially registered as G-JETG but marks were applied on the aircraft in 1995/6)	257070	"G-JETG" G-BWCR/G-5-604/HB-VGG/G-5-604/HB-VGG	1. 5.95	To G-DEZC 5/96. Canx.
G-BWCS	BAC P.84 Jet Provost T.5	EEP/JP/957	XW293	28. 4.95	
G-BWCT	Tipsy T.66 Nipper Srs.1	11	"OO-NIC" PH-MEC/D-EMEC/OO-NIC	27. 4.95	
G-BWCU	Bell 206L-1 Long Ranger	45232	N2758A C-FPET/N2758A/JA9234/N27545/JA9234	31. 5.95	To G-OCRP 12/97. Canx.
G-BWCV	Europa Avn Europa	PFA/247-12591		4. 5.95	(Badly damaged on take-off Coxwold, Thirsk 31.10.97)
G-BWCW	Barnett Rotorcraft J4B	G/14-1256		5. 5.95	
G-BWCX	Lindstrand LBL-90A HAFB	241		9. 5.95	Canx by CAA 18.8.97.
G-BWCY	Murphy Rebel	PFA/232-12135		15. 5.95	
G-BWCZ	Revolution Helicopters Mini-500	0010		1. 5.95	
G-BWDA	ATR-72-202	444	F-WWEQ	29. 6.95	
G-BWDB	ATR-72-202	449	F-WWEE	14. 6.95	
G-BWDC	BAe 125 Srs.800XP	258280		11. 5.95	To N351SP. Canx 27.11.95.
G-BWDD	BAe 125 Srs.800XP	258281		11. 5.95	To N914H/VH-ELJ(3) 11/95. Canx 11.12.95.
G-BWDE	PA-31P Pressurised Navajo	31P-7400193	G-HWKN HB-LIR/D-IAIR/N7304L	12. 5.95	CofA expired 18.12.96. (Stored 10/97)
G-BWDF	WSK PZL-104 Wilga 35A	21950955		17. 5.95	
G-BWDG	Lindstrand LBL-240A HAFB	262		16. 5.95	To N519LB 3/97. Canx 21.2.97.
G-BWDH	Cameron N-105 HAFB	3549		22. 5.95	
G-BWDI	Cessna 340	340-0232	N16HB N7853Q	22. 5.95	Canx 24.11.97 on sale to USA. To N60099 2/99.
G-BWDJ	Jurca MJ.5 Sirocco (Regd as PFA/59-2207)	PFA/2207		3.12.87	NTU - To G-BUGC 4/92. Canx.
G-BWDK	Lindstrand LBL-60A HAFB	210		24. 5.95	To OY-COE 8/96. Canx 2.8.96.
G-BWDL	Cameron Concept-90 HAFB	3552		26. 5.95	To C-FWDU 5/97. Canx 28.1.97.
G-BWDM	Lindstrand LBL-120A HAFB	263		26. 5.95	
G-BWDN	CFM Streak Shadow SA	PFA/206-12838		1. 6.95	To 9V-... Canx 11.11.98.
G-BWDO	Sikorsky S-76B	760356	VR-CPN N9HM	2. 6.95	
G-BWDP	Europa Avn Europa	62 & PFA/247-12637		7. 6.95	
G-BWDR	Hunting-Percival P.84 Jet Provost T.3A	PAC/W/6603	XM376	6. 6.95	
G-BWDS	Hunting-Percival P.84 Jet Provost T.3A (C/n probably incomplete - possibly PAC/W/9231)	PAC/W/932	XM424	6. 6.95	
G-BWDT	PA-34-220T Seneca III	34-8233045	PH-TWI (PH-GES)/G-BKHS/N8472H	21. 9.88	
G-BWDU	Cameron V-90 HAFB	3143		19. 6.95	
G-BWDV	Schweizer 269C (300C)	S.1712	N86G	16. 6.95	
G-BWDW	BAe 125 Srs.800XP	258282	G-5-827	12. 6.95	To N916H. Canx 18.12.95.
G-BWDX	Europa Avn Europa	PFA/247-12603		13. 6.95	
G-BWDY	Sky 65-24 HAFB	001		13. 6.95	
G-BWDZ	Sky 105-24 HAFB	002		13. 6.95	
G-BWEA	Lindstrand LBL-120A HAFB	252		14. 6.95	

Regn	Type	c/n	Previous identity	Regn date	Fate or immediate subsequent identity (if known)
G-BWEB	BAC P.84 Jet Provost T.5A	EEP/JP/1044	XW422	19. 6.95	
G-BWEC	Cassutt-Colson Variant	PFA/34-10444		20.12.78	Permit expired 11.9.91. (On overhaul 5/96)
G-BWED	Thunder Ax7-77 HAFB	3575		20. 6.95	
G-BWEE	Cameron V-42 HAFB	3480		8. 3.95	
G-BWEF	SNCAN Stampe SV-4C	208	G-BOVL N20SV/F-BHES/F-BBLC	13. 6.93	Crashed on landing 27.3.99 Redhill.
G-BWEG	Europa Avn Europa	PFA/247-12600		4. 4.95	
G-BWEH	HOAC DV-20 Katana	20123		19. 6.95	
G-BWEI	Cessna 172N Skyhawk II	172-67663	N73767	20. 6.95	
G-BWEJ	Bell 206B JetRanger	1184	F-OGUM F-GHUX/N59462	22. 6.95	To EC-GEF 11/95. Canx 21.8.95.
G-BWEK	Aero Commander 685	12040	CS-APB N9132N	22. 6.95	To N9143C. Canx 23.10.95.
G-BWEL	Sky 200-24 HAFB	003		27. 6.95	
G-BWEM	Vickers-Supermarine 358 Seafire L.III (Westland-built)	-	157 Irish Air Corps/RX168	28. 6.95	(On rebuild by Hull Aero 1/99 Bourne Park)
G-BWEN	Macair Merlin GT	050194 & PFA/208A-12859		20. 6.95	(Extant 7/98)
G-BWEO	Lindstrand LBL-14M HAFB (Originally regd as a AM400 version with same c/n)	285		23. 6.95	
G-BWEP	Lindstrand LBL-77M HAFB (Originally regd as a AM2200 version with same c/n)	286		23. 6.95	
G-BWER	Lindstrand LBL-14M HAFB (Originally regd as a AM400 version with same c/n)	287		23. 6.95	
G-BWES	BAC One-Eleven Srs.488GH	BAC.259	PK-TAL G-BWES/5N-UDE/LX-MAM/HZ-MAM	26. 6.95	Restored as PK-TAL. Canx 23.2.96.
G-BWET	PA-28-161 Cherokee Warrior II	28-7716074	SX-ALX D-EFFQ/N9612N	27. 6.95	To G-ISDB 2/96. Canx.
G-BWEU	Reims Cessna F.152 II	1894	EI-BNC N9097Y	15. 6.95	
G-BWEV	Cessna 152 II	152-83182	EI-BVU N47184	28. 6.95	
G-BWEW	Cameron N-105 HAFB	3637		30. 6.95	
G-BWEX	Dornier 228-202K	8085	CS-AZZ PH-FXB/CS-AZZ/D-CALU/D-CBDQ/F-GGAV/D-CALU	10. 7.95	Canx 1.2.99 on sale to Germany. To N402VA 2/99.
G-BWEY	Bensen B.8 Gyrocopter	G/01-1197		3. 7.95	
G-BWEZ	Piper J3C-85 Cub	6021	N29050 NC29050	3. 7.95	
G-BWFA	Cameron A-120 HAFB	3622		3. 7.95	To ZK-FAY. Canx 2.10.95.
G-BWFB	DH.104 Dove 7A (C.2)	04088	VP959	12. 7.95	To N959VP 12/97. Canx 1.12.97.
G-BWFC	Boeing-Vertol 234LR Commercial Chinook	B-236/MJ-004	N237BV	5. 5.81	Fatal crash into sea on approach to Sumburgh on 6.11.86 inbound from the Brent oilfield. Canx as destroyed 18.5.88.
G-BWFD	HOAC DV-20 Katana	20127		5. 7.95	
G-BWFE	HOAC DV-20 Katana	20129		5. 7.95	
G-BWFF	Enstrom 480	5007		13. 7.95	To G-OZAR 31.7.95. Canx.
G-BWFG	Robin HR.200/120B	293		20. 7.95	
G-BWFH	Europa Avn Europa	PFA/247-12842		14. 7.95	(Complete & noted at Shoreham on 24.4.99)
G-BWFI	HOAC DV-20 Katana	20128		17. 7.95	
G-BWFJ	Evans VP-1	PFA/62-10349		1. 9.78	Permit expired 27.1.93. (Stored Old Sarum 5/94)
G-BWFK	Lindstrand LBL-77A HAFB	289		17. 7.95	
G-BWFL	Cessna 500 Citation I (Unit No.264)	500-0264	F-GLJA N205FM/N5264J	19. 7.95	To G-OEJA 8/96. Canx.
G-BWFM	Yakovlev Yak-50	781208	NX5224R DDR-WQX/DM-WQX	19. 7.95	(At 7/99 Duxford)
G-BWFN	HAPI Cygnet SF-2A	PFA/182-11335		19. 7.95	
G-BWFO	Colomban MC-15 Cri-Cri	PFA/133-11253		19. 7.95	
G-BWFP	IDA Yakovlev Yak-52 (C/n plate shows c/n 855606 (ex.DOSAAF 61 (blue)) - possibly composite)	855503	RA-44501 DOSAAF 43	20. 7.95	
G-BWFR	Hawker Hunter F.58 (Officially regd with c/n 41H-694935)	41H-697398	J-4031 Swiss AF	24. 7.95	(Stored 9/98 Scampton)
G-BWFS	Hawker Hunter F.58 (Officially regd with c/n 41H-698741)	41H-697425	J-4058 Swiss AF	24. 7.95	(Stored 9/98 Scampton)
G-BWFT	Hawker Hunter T.8M (Officially regd with c/n 41H-695332)	41H-694512	XL602	24. 7.95	
G-BWFU	LET Yakovlev Yak C-11	170103	OK-...	26. 7.95	To G-DYAK 10/98. Canx.
G-BWFV	HOAC DV-20 Katana	20132		26. 7.95	
G-BWFW	HOAC DV-20 Katana	20133		26. 7.95	Badly damaged in forced landing nr.Sedburgh, Cumbria 15.9.96. Canx as destroyed 30.1.97.
G-BWFX	Europa Avn Europa	38 & PFA/247-12586		26. 7.95	
G-BWFY	Aerospatiale AS.350B1 Ecureuil	1963	N518R	31. 7.95	
G-BWFZ	Murphy Rebel	PFA/232-12536	G-SAVS	19. 7.95	
G-BWGA	Lindstrand LBL-105A HAFB	295		2. 8.95	CofA expired 24.3.97. Canx as WFU 14.5.99.
G-BWGB	BAe 125 Srs.800XP	258283	G-5-828	10. 8.95	To N918H. Canx 12.2.96.
G-BWGC	BAe 125 Srs.800XP	258284	G-5-830	10. 8.95	To N919H. Canx 11.1.96.
G-BWGD	BAe 125 Srs.800XP	258285	G-5-831	10. 8.95	To N808H. Canx 25.9.95.
G-BWGE	BAe 125 Srs.800XP	258286	G-5-832	10. 8.95	To N807H. Canx 25.9.95.
G-BWGF	BAC P.84 Jet Provost T.5A	EEP/JP/989	XW325	10. 8.95	

Regn	Type	c/n	Previous identity	Regn date	Fate or immediate subsequent identity (if known)
G-BWGG	Max Holste MH.1521C-1 Broussard	20	F-GGKG	10. 7.95	(Stored 3/97)
			F-WGKG/French military		
G-BWGH	Europa Avn Europa	PFA/247-12589		23. 8.95	(Extant 9/97)
G-BWGI	VPM M-16 Tandem Trainer			10. 8.95	To G-YFLY 10/96. Canx.
		VPM16-UK-114			
G-BWGJ	Chilton DW.1A	PFA/225-12615		11. 8.95	(Complete 8/97)
G-BWGK	Hawker Hunter GA.11	HABL-003032	XE689	15. 8.95	
	(Regd with c/n HABL-004042)				
G-BWGL	Hawker Hunter T.8C	HABL-003086	XF357	15. 8.95	(On rebuild 6/99 at Hurn)
	(Regd with c/n 41H-695946)				
G-BWGM	Hawker Hunter T.8C	HABL-003007	XE665	15. 8.95	
	(Regd with c/n 41H-695940)				
G-BWGN	Hawker Hunter T.8C	41H-670689	WT722	15. 8.95	
	(Regd with c/n 41H-695943)				
G-BWGO	Slingsby T.67M Firefly 200	2048	SE-LBC	15. 8.95	
			LN-TFC/G-7-123		
G-BWGP	Cameron C-80 HAFB	3631		17. 8.95	
G-BWGR	North American TB-25N-NC Mitchell		NL9494Z	18. 8.95	(Stored 10/97)
	(Regd with c/n 108-35250)	108-34200	44-30925		
G-BWGS	BAC P.84 Jet Provost T.5A		XW310	18. 8.95	
		EEP/JP/974			
G-BWGT	Hunting-Percival P.84 Jet Provost		8991M	21. 8.95	
	T.4	PAC/W/21624	XR679		
	(Also reported as c/n PAC/W/19992)				
G-BWGU	Cessna 150F	150-62962	EI-CDU	18. 8.95	(Stored 1/97)
			N8862G		
G-BWGV	Eurocopter AS.355N Twin Squirrel			21. 8.95	To G-SEPC 11/95. Canx.
		5596			
G-BWGW	BAe Jetstream Srs.4122	41060	G-4-060	21. 8.95	To R.Thailand Army as 41060. Canx 8.12.95.
G-BWGX	Cameron N-42 HAFB	3633		21. 8.95	
G-BWGY	HOAC DV-20 Katana	20134		22. 8.95	
G-BWGZ	HOAC DV-20 Katana	20135		22. 8.95	
G-BWHA	Hawker Hurricane IIB	41H/G5/21232	Z5053	23. 8.95	(On rebuild 8/95) (Sold to R.A.Roberts, Billingshurst .96?)
	(Regd with c/n 41H-G3121232)		(Soviet AF)/Z5053		(Reported as on rebuild by Peter Watts at Dursley, Glos
	(Gloster-built)				2/96 for H.Taylor; painted as Z5252 "GO-B")
G-BWHB	Cameron O-65 HAFB	2759		23. 8.95	
G-BWHC	Cameron N-77 HAFB	3647		25. 8.95	
G-BWHD	Lindstrand LBL-31A HAFB	292		29. 8.95	
G-BWHE	Enstrom 480	5008		29. 8.95	To OO-VLW 9/95. Canx 12.9.95.
G-BWHF	PA-31-325 Navajo C/R	31-7612076	F-GECA	7. 9.85	
			D-IBIS/N59862		
G-BWHG	Cameron N-65 HAFB	3619		7. 9.95	
G-BWHH	PA-18-135 (L-21B-PI) Super Cub		PH-KNA	9. 8.95	
	(Frame No.18-3789)	18-3605	R.Netherlands Army R-115/54-2405		
G-BWHI	DHC.1 Chipmunk 22A	C1-0637	WK624	8. 9.95	(Stored 11/97 Duxford)
	(Fuselage no. DHB/f/520)				
G-BWHJ	CFM Starstreak Shadow SA-II			12. 9.95	
		K.269 & PFA/206-12907			
G-BWHK	Rans S-6-116 Coyote II (Rotax 582)			15. 9.95	
	(Tricycle u/c)	PFA/204A-12908			
G-BWHL	Enstrom 480	5009		15. 9.95	To D-HMLY 11/95. Canx 10.11.95.
G-BWHM	Sky 140-24 HAFB	006		18. 9.95	
G-BWHN	Aerospatiale AS.332L Super Puma		C-GSLC	24.10.95	To OY-HDT 7/99. Canx. 22.6.99.
		2017	HC-HQJ/C-GSLC/HC-BNC/C-GSLC		
G-BWHO	Thunder Ax6-56Z HAFB	417	G-BJZP	20. 4.82	To VH-SUS 5/86. Canx 10.3.86.
G-BWHP	CASA I-131E Jungmann	2109	E3B-513	18. 8.95	
			Spanish AF		
G-BWHR	Tipsy T.66 Nipper Srs.1		(OO-KAM)	19. 9.95	(Composite homebuild of original Fairey built c/n 29 & 71)
		PFA/25-12843	OO-69		
G-BWHS	Rotary Air Force RAF.2000	G/13-1253		25. 9.95	
G-BWHT	Everett Campbell Cricket	046		27. 9.95	No Permit to Fly believed issued. Canx by CAA 5.11.97.
G-BWHU	Westland Scout AH.1	F.9517	XR595	27. 9.95	
G-BWHV	Denney Kitfox Mk.2	PFA/172-11857		28. 9.95	
G-BWHW	Cameron A-180 HAFB	3634		29. 9.95	
G-BWHX	Mil Mi-8	99257043	RA-27008	2.10.95	To 3D-... 2/97. Canx 25.2.97.
			CCCP-27008		
G-BWHY	Robinson R-22	0098	N90366	24. 3.87	
G-BWHZ	Mil Mi-8	99250993	RA-27009	2.10.95	To 3D-... 2/97. Canx 25.2.97.
			CCCP-27009		
G-BWIA	Rans S-10 Sakota	PFA/194-12044		15. 9.95	(Under construction 3/97)
G-BWIB	Scottish Avn Bulldog Srs.120/122		G-103	10.10.95	
		BH120/227	Ghana AF		
G-BWIC	BAe Jetstream Srs.4100	41036	VH-AFR	16.10.95	To N436JX. Canx 30.10.95.
			G-4-036		
G-BWID	Druine D.31 Turbulent	201	F-PHFR	16.10.95	
G-BWIE	Hawker Hunter T.7A	41H-695448	9223M	17.10.95	To SE-DXH. Canx 1.6.98.
	(Regd with c/n 41H-695336)		XL616		
G-BWIF	Robinson R-44 Astro	0209		17.10.95	To EC-GGI 4/96. Canx 8.2.96.
G-BWIG	Wigglesworth G-17S Scale Replica			7. 8.81	Canx as WFU 5.8.91.
		KW-1			
	(Possibly a homebuilt based on the Beechcraft Staggerwing)				
G-BWIH	BAe Jetstream Srs.4107	41034	VH-SMH	24.10.95	To N434JX. Canx 2.11.95.
			G-4-034		

Regn	Type	c/n	Previous identity	Regn date	Fate or immediate subsequent identity (if known)
G-BWII	Cessna 150G	150-65308	N4008J	22. 9.95	
			(G-BSKB)/N4008J		
G-BWIJ	Europa Avn Europa	PFA/247-12513		19.10.95	
G-BWIK	DH.82A Tiger Moth	86417	7015M	20.10.95	(On rebuild)
			NL985		
G-BWIL	Rans S-10 Sakota		G-WIEN	4.10.95	
		1089-065 & PFA/194-11770			
G-BWIM	Sikorsky S-76A II Plus	760221	CC-ECH	20.10.95	To N717AL 5/97. Canx 29.4.97.
G-BWIN	Douglas DC-10-30	46936	N831LA	29.11.95	Restored as N831LA 6/96. Canx 3.5.96.
	(Line No. 147)		N417DG/XA-DUG		
G-BWIO	HOAC DV-20 Katana	20147		24.10.95	To OE-... Canx 29.7.99.
G-BWIP	Cameron N-90 HAFB	3668		20.10.95	
G-BWIR	Dornier 328-110	3023	D-CDXF(2)	18.10.95	
			N328DA/D-CDHH		
G-BWIS	Mooney M-20M TLS	27-0205		28. 9.95	To D-ELVY(3) 12/97. Canx 17.11.97.
G-BWIT	QAC Quickie 1	484	N4482Z	21. 9.95	(Substantially damaged in crash nr.Baginton 12.10.97)
G-BWIU	Hawker Hunter F.58	41H-691770	J-4021	26.10.95	(Stored 9/98 Scampton)
	(Also reported as c/n 41H/694926)		Swiss AF		
G-BWIV	Europa Avn Europa			27.10.95	
		210 & PFA/247-12871			
G-BWIW	Sky 180-24 HAFB	008		1.11.95	
G-BWIX	Sky 120-24 HAFB	009		31.10.95	
G-BWIY	Lindstrand LBL-105A HAFB	322		3.11.95	To N..... Canx 25.5.99.
G-BWIZ	Quickie Tri-Q 200	PFA/94-12330		21. 8.95	Permit expired 23.6.98. Canx by CAA 8.5.99.
G-BWJA(1)	Boeing 737-3Q8	24299	EC-FER	.11.95R	NTU - Remained as EC-FER. Canx.
	(Line No. 1598)		EC-594/EC-ELJ/EC-189		
G-BWJA(2)	Boeing 737-3Y0	24462	EC-FJR	2. 4.96	To G-EZYC(2) 5/97. Canx.
	(Line No. 1691)		EC-897/G-TEAA/EI-BZQ/(N116AW)/EI-BZQ/EC-ENS/EC-244/N5573K		
G-BWJB	Thunder Ax8-105 HAFB	197		15. 6.79	
G-BWJC	Cameron N-65 HAFB	3754		3.11.95	
G-BWJD	Cameron R-200 Gas Free Balloon	3724		3.11.95	(Steve Fossett/Round World Attempt 1/96)
					W/o in India 20.1.97. Canx 24.3.98 as WFU.
G-BWJE	Sky 105-24 HAFB	010		3.11.95	
G-BWJF	BAe Jetstream Srs.4101	41038	VH-IMR	10.11.95	To N438JX. Canx 11.1.96.
			G-4-038		
G-BWJG	Mooney M.20J (201MSE)	24-3319	N1083P	7.11.95	
G-BWJH	Europa Avn Europa	PFA/247-12643		10.11.95	
G-BWJI	Cameron V-90 HAFB	3727		13.11.95	
G-BWJJ	Cameron N-105 HAFB	3142		13.11.95	To D-O... Canx 23.12.98.
G-BWJK	Rotorway Exec 152	CWT-1	G-OKIT	24.10.95	
G-BWJL	Cameron N-120 HAFB	3416		13.11.95	
G-BWJM	Bristol M.1C Replica	NAW-2		23.11.95	
	(built by Northern Aeroplane Workshops)				
G-BWJN	Montgomerie-Bensen B.8MR Gyrocopter			16.11.95	
		G/01-1262			
G-BWJO	PBN BN-2B-20 Islander	2294		23.11.95	To VH-CSS 3/99. Canx 23.2.99.
	(Originally regd as BN-2T)				
G-BWJP	Cessna 172C Skyhawk	172-49424	N1824Y	21.11.95	
G-BWJR	Sky 120-24 HAFB	007		22.11.95	
G-BWJS	Colt 120A HAFB	3746	(OO-B..)	22.11.95	Canx to Belgium 21.10.96. To PH-KRE 1/97.
			G-BWJS		
G-BWJT	Yakovlev Yak-50	812003	RA-01385	23.11.95	
			DOSAAF 50		
G-BWJU	DHC.1 Chipmunk 22	C1/0654	WK639	23.11.95	To N6540C 4/97. Canx 3.3.97.
	(Fuselage no. DHB/f/545)				
G-BWJV	Not allocated				
G-BWJW	Westland Scout AH.1	F.9705	XV130	29.11.95	
	(Nacelle No. F8 6144)				
G-BWJX	HS.125 Srs.700B	257062	G-5-708	7.12.95	NTU - To RA-02809 1/96. Canx 12.1.96.
			N7062B/G-5-708/HB-VGF/G-5-708/HB-VGF/G-5-16		
G-BWJY	DHC.1 Chipmunk 22	C1/0519	WG469	5.12.95	
	(Fuselage no. DHB/f/400)				
G-BWJZ	DHC.1 Chipmunk 22	C1/0653	WK638	23.11.95	
	(Fuselage no. DHB/f/544)				
G-BWKA	Hawker Hunter F.58	41H-697442	J-4075	12.10.95	To JY-... /97. Canx 23.6.97.
			Swiss AF		
G-BWKB	Hawker Hunter F.58	41H-697448	J-4081	12.10.95	
			Swiss AF		
G-BWKC	Hawker Hunter F.58	41H-697394	J-4025	12.10.95	(Coded RJAF '712/E' 2/99 Hurn)
			Swiss AF		
G-BWKD	Cameron O-120 HAFB	3773		8.12.95	
G-BWKE	Cameron AS-105GD Hot Air Airship			8.12.95	
		3685			
G-BWKF	Cameron N-105 HAFB	3736		8.12.95	
G-BWKG	Europa Avn Europa	PFA/247-12451		28.11.95	
G-BWKH	BAC One-Eleven Srs.527FK	BAC.226	RP-C1181	. .95R	NTU - To VR-BEB. Canx.
G-BWKI	Fokker F.28-0070	11578	PH-EZI	. .95R	NTU - Not delivered - To PH-KZG 11/96. Canx.
G-BWKJ	Rans S-7 Courier	PFA/218-12918		14.12.95	
G-BWKK	Auster AOP.9	AUS.166 & B5/10/165	XP279	30. 7.79	
G-BWKL	HS.125 Srs.700B	257118	5N-AVJ	15.12.95	To VP-BBH 6/98. Canx 12.6.98.
			(G-BIHZ)		
G-BWKM	Eurocopter MBB BK.117C-1	7510	D-HECO	20.12.95	Restored as D-HECO(2) 2/96. Canx 13.2.96.
			D-HMBJ		

Regn	Type	c/n	Previous identity	Regn date	Fate or immediate subsequent identity (if known)
G-BWKN	Airbus A.320-212	190	N484GX F-WWDD	17. 1.96	To G-UKLJ 3/96. Canx.
G-BWKO	Airbus A.320-212	343	N485GX F-WWDH	17. 1.96	To G-UKLK 4/96. Canx.
G-BWKP	Sky 105-24 HAFB	011		18.12.95	To G-DONG 2/97. Canx.
G-BWKR	Sky 90-24 HAFB	014		18.12.95	
G-BWKS	Lake LA-4-200 Buccaneer	680	G-BDDI N1087L	9.11.79	To N39RG 9/84. Canx 19.9.84.
G-BWKT	Stephens Akro Lazer	PFA/123-11421		19.12.95	(Under construction 8/97)
G-BWKU	Cameron A-250 HAFB	3730		21.12.95	
G-BWKV	Cameron V-77 HAFB	3780		27.12.95	
G-BWKW	Thunder Ax8-90 HAFB	3770		28.12.95	
G-BWKX	Cameron A-250 HAFB	3731		2. 1.96	
G-BWKY	BAe 146 RJ85	E2277	G-6-277	24. 1.96	To D-AVRJ 2/96. Canx 21.2.96.
G-BWKZ	Lindstrand LBL-77A HAFB	340		21.12.95	
G-BWLA	Lindstrand LBL-69A HAFB	339		3. 1.96	
G-BWLB	Lindstrand Drewer Bottle SS HAFB	316		3. 1.96	Canx by CAA 26.2.97. To PP-... /97.
G-BWLC	MDH Hughes 369E (500E)	0454E	HB-XIJ SE-JAM	3. 1.96	To G-LOGO 10/96. Canx.
G-BWLD	Cameron O-120 HAFB	3774		16. 1.96	
G-BWLE	Bell 212	31225	N4247M SU-CAA	5. 1.96	(On rebuild 9/98 at Redhill)
G-BWLF	Cessna 404 Titan II	404-0414	G-BNXS (G-BOAJ)/G-BNXS/R.Hong Kong Aux.AF HKG-4/(N8799K)	26.10.94	
G-BWLG	BAe 146 Srs.200QC	E2176	VH-NJQ G-PRCS	19. 1.96	To F-GMMP 4/96. Canx 4.4.96.
G-BWLH	Lindstrand HS-110 Hot Air Airship	331		10. 1.96	
G-BWLI	Aerospatiale AS.350B2 Ecureuil	2382	G-IINA N9088A	15. 1.96	To HB-XJC 3/96. Canx 13.3.96.
G-BWLJ	Taylorcraft DCO-65 (Originally regd with c/n 0-4331)	04331	C-GUSA (ex)	16. 1.96	
G-BWLK	Lindstrand LBL-69A HAFB	338		17. 1.96	Canx by CAA 26.2.97. To N7216Z 4/97.
G-BWLL	Murphy Rebel	PFA/232-12499		22. 1.96	
G-BWLM	Sky 65-24 HAFB	015		24. 1.96	
G-BWLN	Cameron O-84 HAFB	3737		24. 1.96	
G-BWLO	Bell 206B JetRanger	488	N2290W	22. 1.96	
G-BWLP	HOAC DV-20 Katana	20141	OE-UDV	6. 2.96	
G-BWLR	Max Holste MH.1521C1 Broussard	185	F-GGKJ F-WGKJ/French AF F-RACE	25. 1.96	
G-BWLS	HOAC DV-20 Katana	20142	OE-UHK	6. 2.96	
G-BWLT	HOAC DV-20 Katana	20149		6. 2.96	
G-BWLU	Sky 90-24 HAFB	005		29. 1.96	To D-OQQQ 7/96. Canx 16.5.96.
G-BWLV	HOAC DV-20 Katana	20151		6. 2.96	
G-BWLW	Light Aero Avid Speed Wing Mk.4	PFA/189-12763		26. 1.96	
G-BWLX	Westland Scout AH.1 (Regd with c/n F.86058) (Nacelle No. probably F8 6148)	F.9709	XV134	29.12.95	
G-BWLY	Rotorway Exec 90	5142		11. 1.93	(Stored 3/98 Chirk)
G-BWLZ	Wombat Gyrocopter	G/09-1255		28.12.95	Canx as destroyed 2.10.97. (Stored 3/98 at Chirk)
G-BWMA	Colt 105A HAFB	1853		31.10.90	
G-BWMB	Jodel D.119 (Original F-BGMA c/n 77 became F-PHQH and was rebuilt as a Larrieu JL.2; this is presumed to be a rebuild using some components of c/n 77 plus newly built c/n 1492)	77-1492	F-BGMA	17. 2.78	Badly damaged in forced landing near Edge Hill, 7 miles NW of Banbury, Oxon on 7.12.80. Canx as destroyed 12.2.81.
G-BWMC	Cessna 182P Skylane II	182-63117	N5462J G-BWMC/OO-RGM/(OO-RAN)/F-BVOU/N7333N	30. 1.96	
G-BWMD	Enstrom 480	5013		5. 2.96	Reserved as F-GOTA in 1996.
G-BWME	Lindstrand LBL-150A HAFB	332		6. 2.96	Canx by CAA 26.2.97.
G-BWMF	Gloster Meteor T.7	G5/356460	7917M WA591	15.12.95	(On rebuild 3/96)
G-BWMG	Aerospatiale AS.332L Super Puma	2046	OY-HMG	1. 2.96	
G-BWMH	Lindstrand LBL-77B HAFB	152		7. 2.96	
G-BWMI	PA-28RT-201T Turbo Arrow IV	28R-8031131	F-GCTG N9571N	31. 1.96	
G-BWMJ	Nieuport Scout 17/23 Replica (Reportedly built in 1981; previous identity?) (Originally regd as a Nieuport 17/2B Replica)	PFA/121-12351		8. 2.96	
G-BWMK	DH.82A Tiger Moth	84483	T8191	9. 2.96	(Fuselage stored 5/99 at Welshpool)
G-BWML	Cameron A-275 HAFB	3725		12. 2.96	
G-BWMM	Lindstrand LBL-31A HAFB	352		12. 2.96	Canx by CAA 26.2.97. To N352JN 7/97.
G-BWMN	Rans S-7 Courier	PFA/218-12446		14. 2.96	
G-BWMO	Oldfield Baby Great Lakes (built by J.List)	JAL.3	G-CIII N11JL	14. 2.96	
G-BWMP	Gulfstream 695A Turbo Commander 1000	96034	ZS-KZS (N9554S)	4.10.85	To N508AB 4/93. Canx 19.4.93.
G-BWMR	Robinson R-22 Beta	2056		18. 6.92	To EC-GDT 11/95. Canx 13.4.95.
G-BWMS	DH.82A Tiger Moth	82712	OO-EVJ T-29/R4771	14. 2.96	
G-BWMT	Lindstrand LBL-69A HAFB	315		16. 2.96	To PH-LBL 4/96. Canx 2.4.96.
G-BWMU	Cameron Monster Truck 105SS HAFB	3607		20. 2.96	

Regn	Type	c/n	Previous identity	Regn date	Fate or immediate subsequent identity (if known)
G-BWMV	Colt AS-105 Mk.II Hot Air Airship	3775		22. 2.96	
G-BWMW	Short SD.3-60 Var.100	SH3750	G-BPFR B-12277/G-BPFR/G-14-3750	21. 3.94	To 5Y-BKP 6/95. Canx 6.6.95.
G-BWMX	DHC.1 Chipmunk 22 (Fuselage no. DHB/f/346)	C1/0481	WG407	19. 2.96	
G-BWMY	Cameron Bradford and Bingley 90SS HAFB	3808		23. 2.96	
G-BWMZ	Short SD.3-60 Var.100	SH3717	G-BNFA EI-BFH/G-14-3717/G-BNFA/G-14-3717	8. 7.94	To 5Y-BKW 12/95. Canx 13.12.95.
G-BWNA	Aerospatiale AS.350B Ecureuil	1009	G-BFNC F-WXFH	29.11.95	To F-GLYR 4/96. Canx 15.4.96.
G-BWNB	Cessna 152 II	152-80051	N757WA	23. 8.96	
G-BWNC	Cessna 152 II	152-84415	N6487L	23. 8.96	
G-BWND	Cessna 152 II	152-85905	N95493	23. 8.96	
G-BWNE	PBN BN-2B-20 Islander	2295		28. 2.96	To Botswana Defence Force as OA12 in 5/98. Canx 30.9.98.
G-BWNF	PBN BN-2T Turbine Islander (Originally regd as a BN-2B-20 version)	2296		28. 2.96	
G-BWNG	PBN BN-2B-20 Islander	2297		28. 2.96	(For Australia)
G-BWNH	Cameron A-375 HAFB	3553		28. 2.96	
G-BWNI	PA-24-180 Comanche	24-136	N5123P	15. 2.96	
G-BWNJ	Hughes 269C	86-0528	N42LW N27RD/N7458F	29. 2.96	
G-BWNK	DHC.1 Chipmunk 22 (Fuselage no. DHB/f/214)	C1/0317	WD390	4. 3.96	
G-BWNL	Europa Avn Europa	PFA/247-12675		27. 2.96	(Extant 4/97) (Damaged in crash Fishburn 14.12.97)
G-BWNM	PA-28R-180 Cherokee Arrow	28R-30435	N934BD	5. 3.96	
G-BWNN	Rand-Robinson KR-2	PFA/129-11342		5. 3.96	
G-BWNO	Cameron O-90 HAFB	3716		5. 3.96	
G-BWNP	Cameron Club 90SS HAFB (Club Orange Soft Drink Can shape)	1717	EI-BVQ	6. 3.96	
G-BWNR	PA-38-112 Tomahawk	38-78A0449	N2361E	6. 3.96	
G-BWNS	Cameron O-90 HAFB	3842		6. 3.96	
G-BWNT	DHC.1 Chipmunk 22 (Fuselage no. DHB/f/672)	C1/0772	WP901	7. 3.96	
G-BWNU	PA-38-112 Tomahawk	38-78A0334	N9294T	8. 3.96	
G-BWNV	PA-38-112 Tomahawk	38-79A1019	N2538P	8. 3.96	
G-BWNW	Lindstrand LBL-25A Cloudhopper HAFB	363		8. 3.96	Canx by CAA 26.2.97. To N40287 12/97.
G-BWNX	Thunder Ax10-180 Srs.2 HAFB	2352	G-OWBC	2. 1.96	
G-BWNY	Aeromot AMT-200 Super Ximango	200-055		11. 6.96	
G-BWNZ	Agusta A.109C	7654		3. 4.96	
G-BWOA	Sky 105-24 HAFB	027		13. 3.96	
G-BWOB	Luscombe 8F Silvaire	6179	N1552B NC1552B	14. 3.96	
G-BWOC	PA-31-350 Navajo Chieftain	31-8152115	N40898	12.10.87	To G-MOHS 4/96. Canx.
G-BWOD	IAV Yakovlev Yak-52	833810	LY-ALY DOSAAF 139	14. 3.96	
G-BWOE	Yakovlev Yak-3U (converted from LET Yak C.11)	1701231	(G-BUXZ) NX11SN/(France)/Egyptian AF	14. 3.96	(Nearing completion 7/99 Duxford)
G-BWOF	BAC P.84 Jet Provost T.5	EEP/JP/955	XW291	18. 3.96	
G-BWOG	Not allotted				
G-BWOH	PA-28-161 Cadet	2841061	D-ENXG N9142S	18. 3.96	
G-BWOI	PA-28-161 Cadet	2841307	D-EJTM N9264N/N9208P	18. 3.96	
G-BWOJ	PA-28-161 Cadet	2841331	D-ESTM N92242/(N123ND)/N92242	18. 3.96	
G-BWOK	Lindstrand LBL-105G HAFB (Originally regd as a LBL-GB-1000 HAFB)	370		19. 3.96	
G-BWOL	Hawker Sea Fury FB.11	ES.3617 & 61631	D-CACY(2) G-9-66/WG599	18. 3.96	(Stored as D-CACY 7/99 Duxford)
G-BWOM	Cessna 550 Citation II (Unit No.671)	550-0671	N671EA 9M-TAA/(N6761L)	22. 3.96	
G-BWON	Europa Avn Europa	PFA/247-12720		29. 1.96	
G-BWOO	Lindstrand HS-110 Hot-Air Airship	362		21. 3.96	To OO-BDP 2/98. Canx 12.12.97.
G-BWOP	Not allotted				
G-BWOR	PA-18-135 (L-18C) Super Cub	18-2547	OO-WIS OO-HMF/ALAT/52-6229	21. 3.96	
G-BWOS	Bell 212	35074	PNC-189 (Colombian Police)/C-FTIP	22. 3.96	(On rebuild ex.crash 10.12.94)
G-BWOT	Hunting P.84 Jet Provost T.3A (Also reported as c/n PAC/W/949267)	PAC/W/10138	XN459	25. 3.96	
G-BWOU	Hawker Hunter F.58A (Regd with c/n 41H-003067) (C/n equates to XF306/7776M/G-9-402, which became J-4133; possibly composite)	HABL-003067	J-4105 Swiss AF/G-9-315/A2565/XF303	26. 3.96	(Stored at Scampton)
G-BWOV	Enstrom F-28A	222	N690BR G-BWOV/F-BVRG	26. 3.96	
G-BWOW	Cameron N-105 HAFB	3805		31. 1.96	

Regn	Type	c/n	Previous identity	Regn date	Fate or immediate subsequent identity (if known)
G-BWOX	DHC.1 Chipmunk 22 (Fuselage no. DHB/f/621)	C1/0728	WP844	27. 3.96	
G-BWOY	Sky 31-24 HAFB	029		28. 3.96	
G-BWOZ	CFM Streak Shadow SA	K.154SA & PFA/206-12988		1. 4.96	
G-BWPA	Cameron A-340 HAFB	3714		29. 3.96	
G-BWPB	Cameron V-77 HAFB	3866		1. 4.96	
G-BWPC	Cameron V-77 HAFB	3867		1. 4.96	
G-BWPD	Cameron V-90 HAFB	3868		1. 4.96	Canx 23.12.98 on sale to Mexico.
G-BWPE	Murphy Renegade Spirit UK	PFA/188-12791		2. 4.96	
G-BWPF	Sky 120-24 HAFB	028		3. 4.96	
G-BWPG	Robin HR.200/120B	299		15. 4.96	Fatal crash 29.10.97 off Cromarty Gap, Nigg Bay. Canx as destroyed 26.1.98.
G-BWPH	PA-28-181 Cherokee Archer II	28-7790311	N1408H	4. 4.96	
G-BWPI	Sky 120-24 HAFB	018		9. 4.96	
G-BWPJ	Steen Skybolt	PFA/64-12854		9. 4.96	
G-BWPK	PBN BN-2T-4R MSSA	4006		24. 4.96	To G-SJCH 9/99 as a BN-2T-4S.
G-BWPL	Airtour AH-56 HAFB	011	G-OAFC	19. 3.96	(Extant 2/97)
G-BWPM	PBN BN-2T-4R MSSA	4007		24. 4.96	
G-BWPN	PBN BN-2T-4S Defender 4000	4008		24. 4.96	To Irish Air Corps as IAC 254. Canx 14.8.97.
G-BWPO	PBN BN-2T-4S Defender 4000	4009		24. 4.96	To 9M-TPS 11/97. Canx 24.11.97.
G-BWPP	Sky 105-24 HAFB	031		9. 4.96	
G-BWPR	PBN BN-2T-4S Defender 4000	4010		24. 4.96	
G-BWPS	CFM Streak Shadow SA	PFA/206-12954		9. 2.96	
G-BWPT	Cameron N-90 HAFB	3838		5. 3.96	
G-BWPU	PBN BN-2T-4S Defender 4000	4011	(9M-TPD) G-BWPU	24. 4.96	
G-BWPV	PBN BN-2T-4S Defender 4000	4012		24. 4.96	
G-BWPW	PBN BN-2T-4S Defender 4000	4013		24. 4.96	
G-BWPX	PBN BN-2T-4S Defender 4000	4014		24. 4.96	
G-BWPY	HOAC DV-20 Katana	20158	OE-UDV	10. 6.96	
G-BWPZ	Cameron N-105 HAFB	3889		19. 4.96	
G-BWRA	Sopwith LC-1T Triplane Replica	PFA/21-10035	G-PENY	19. 4.96	
G-BWRB	DHC.6-310 Twin Otter	691		7. 5.80	To N230BV 12/89. Canx 9.11.89.
G-BWRC	Light Aero Avid Hauler Mk.4	PFA/189-12979		22. 2.96	
G-BWRD	Klemm Kl.35D (Also reported as being original Luftwaffe aircraft, sold to Austria post-war)	1642	D-EFTG(2) D-EHUX/SE-AIP/Swedish AF Fv.5081/SE-AIP	12. 4.96	(On display 2/99 Sandown) Canx as WFU 16.7.98.
G-BWRE	SNCAN Stampe SV-4C	396	D-EJKA(2) F-BDOT/French Mil	12. 4.96	(On display 2/99 Sandown) Canx as WFU 16.7.98.
G-BWRF	Morane-Saulnier MS.505 Criquet	73	D-EFTY(2) F-BAUV/French AF	12. 4.96	To D-EGTY(2) 7/98P. Canx 2.6.98.
G-BWRG	Benes-Mraz M.1D Sokol	304	D-EGWP(2) (D-EFTB)/HB-TBG/OK-DIX	12. 4.96	(On display 2/97 Sandown) Canx as WFU 16.7.98.
G-BWRH	Bleriot XI Replica (built B.Murray)	001	D-EFTE N25WM	12. 4.96	(On display 2/99 Sandown) Canx as WFU 16.7.98.
G-BWRI	Mignet Henri HM-19C Pou-du-Ciel	01	HB-SPG	12. 4.96	(On display 2/97 Sandown as HB-SPG) Canx as WFU 16.7.98.
G-BWRJ	Koch Fokker Dr.1 Replica (built by J.Koch)	003	D-EFTN	12. 4.96	(On display 2/99 Sandown) Canx as WFU 16.7.98.
G-BWRK	Lindstrand Man SS HAFB	356		22. 4.96	Canx by CAA 26.2.97. (Based in Canada)
G-BWRL	Sky 77-24 HAFB	023		22. 4.96	To LV-WTC 8/97. Canx 30.1.97.
G-BWRM	Colt 105A HAFB	3734		23. 4.96	
G-BWRN	BAe 125 Srs.800B	258237	D-CCVW G-5-775	22. 4.96	To 9M-DRL 7/96. Canx 26.7.96.
G-BWRO	Europa Avn Europa	PFA/247-12849		22. 4.96	
G-BWRP	Beechcraft 58 Baron	TH-1737	VR-BVB N3217H	23. 4.96	
G-BWRR	Cessna 182Q Skylane II	182-66660	N95861	29. 3.94	
G-BWRS	SNCAN Stampe SV-4C	437	(N.....) F-BCVQ	24. 4.96	
G-BWRT	Cameron Concept-60 HAFB	3078	EI-BYP	22.10.96	
G-BWRU	Lindstrand Audi Saloon Car SS HAFB	369		23. 4.96	Canx as PWFU 17.4.99.
G-BWRV	Lindstrand LBL-90A HAFB	371		23. 4.96	
G-BWRW	Sky 220-24 HAFB	032		23. 4.96	
G-BWRX	DHC.1 Chipmunk 22 (Fuselage no. DHB/f/671)	C1/0771	WP900	24. 4.96	To F-AZJL 10/96. Canx 1.10.96.
G-BWRY	Cameron N-105 HAFB	3817		24. 4.96	
G-BWRZ	Lindstrand LBL-105A HAFB	383		26. 4.96	
G-BWSA	PA-31-350 Navajo Chieftain	31-7652017	G-BPJX OY-BYP/LN-SAN/SE-GBD	16.10.90	To EI-CEC 10/91. Canx 17.10.91.
G-BWSB	Lindstrand LBL-105A HAFB	384		26. 4.96	
G-BWSC	PA-38-112 Tomahawk II	38-81A0125	N23203	29. 4.96	
G-BWSD	Campbell Cricket	G/03-1216		3. 5.96	
G-BWSE	Cameron N-90 HAFB	3907		9. 5.96	To G-SAMI 8/96. Canx.
G-BWSF	Sky 180-24 HAFB	022		10. 5.96	
G-BWSG	BAC P.84 Jet Provost T.5	EEP/JP/988	XW324	13. 5.96	
G-BWSH	Hunting P.84 Jet Provost T.3A	PAC/W/10159	XN498	13. 5.96	

Regn	Type	c/n	Previous identity	Regn date	Fate or immediate subsequent identity (if known)
G-BWSI	K & S SA.102.5 Cavalier	PFA/01-10624		18. 4.84	
G-BWSJ	Denney Kitfox Mk.3	PFA/172-12204		15. 5.96	
G-BWSK	Enstrom 280FX	2016	ZK-HIR JA7724	16. 5.96	
G-BWSL	Sky 77-24 HAFB	004		16. 6.96	
G-BWSM	Cameron Maple Leaf 95SS HAFB	3849		16. 5.96	To C-GCXZ 5/98. Canx 19.5.98.
G-BWSN	Denney Kitfox Mk.3	PFA/172-12141		16. 5.96	
G-BWSO	Cameron Apple Sainsbury 90SS HAFB	3915		17. 5.96	
G-BWSP	Cameron Carrots Sainsbury 80SS HAFB	3914		17. 5.96	
G-BWSR	Cameron A-210 HAFB	3700		1. 5.96	
G-BWSS	Sky 200-24 HAFB	020		17. 5.96	To N701SB 5/97. Canx 3.4.97.
G-BWST	Sky 200-24 HAFB	036		20. 5.96	
G-BWSU	Cameron N-105 HAFB	3848		20. 5.96	
G-BWSV	IAV-Bacau Yakovlev Yak-52	877601	DOSAAF 43	20. 5.96	
G-BWSW	IAV-Bacau Yakovlev Yak-52	866807	DOSAAF 88	20. 5.96	Canx as destroyed 26.2.99.
G-BWSX	PA-28-236 Dakota II	28-7911130	C-FLMJ N2169V	28. 5.96	
G-BWSY	BAe 125 Srs.800B	258201	G-OCCI (D-C...)/G-5-699	28. 5.96	
G-BWSZ	Montgomerie-Bensen B.8MR Gyrocopter	G/01-1268		14. 5.96	
G-BWTA	HOAC DV-20 Katana	20159	OE-UDV	10. 6.96	
G-BWTB	Lindstrand LBL-105A HAFB	374		29. 5.96	
G-BWTC	Moravan Zlin Z.242L	0697		2. 8.96	
G-BWTD	Moravan Zlin Z.242L	0698		2. 8.96	
G-BWTE	Cameron O-140 HAFB	3885		30. 5.96	
G-BWTF	Lindstrand Bear SS HAFB	375		3. 6.96	
G-BWTG	DHC.1 Chipmunk 22 (Fuselage no. DHB/f/31)	C1/0119	WB671	4. 6.96	
G-BWTH	Robinson R-22 Beta	1767	HB-XYD N4052R	5. 6.96	
G-BWTI	Cameron A-250 HAFB	3863		6. 6.96	To ZK-FAR(2) 7/96. Canx 25.6.96.
G-BWTJ	Cameron V-77 HAFB	3917		7. 6.96	
G-BWTK	Rotary Air Force RAF 2000 GTX-SE	G/13-1264		7. 6.96	
G-BWTL	ATR-72-202	441	F-WWLG	7.12.95	
G-BWTM	ATR-72-202	470	F-WWED	8. 3.96	
G-BWTN	Lindstrand LBL-90A HAFB	357		12. 6.96	
G-BWTO	DHC.1 Chipmunk 22 (Fuselage no. DHB/f/754)	C1/0852	WP984	5. 6.96	
G-BWTP	Montgomerie-Parsons Two-Place Gyroplane	G/08-1276		12. 6.96	To G-UNIV 8/99. Canx.
G-BWTR	Slingsby T.61F Venture T.2	1881	XZ561	12. 6.96	
G-BWTS	Aero L-39ZO Albatros	731002	28+02 German AF/East German AF 140	13. 6.96	To ES-YLL /97. Canx 15.12.97.
G-BWTT	Aero L-39ZO Albatros	731013	28+10 German AF/East German AF 150	13. 6.96	To N298RD 1/98. Canx 26.1.98.
G-BWTU	Lindstrand LBL-77A HAFB	376		17. 6.96	
G-BWTV	Embraer EMB.110P2 Bandeirante	110-153	PT-GLA	12. 1.78	To G-BSVT 10/79. Canx.
G-BWTW	Mooney M.20C	20-1188	EI-CHI N6955V	5. 6.96	
G-BWTX	PA-42-720 Cheyenne III	42-8001041	N4089A	9.10.87	To N669CA 5/95. Canx 2.5.95.
G-BWTY	Air Command 532 Elite Two-Seat	G/05-1274		14. 6.96	No Permit issued. (Extant 1/97) Canx as WFU 3.6.97.
G-BWTZ	BAe Jetstream Srs.4100	41094	G-4-094	24. 6.96	To R.Thailand Army as 41094 in 11/96. Canx 27.11.96.
G-BWUA	Campbell Cricket	G/03-1248		17. 6.96	
G-BWUB	PA-18S-135 Super Cub (Regd with c/n 18-3786) (L-21C) (Floatplane)	18-3986	N786CS G-BWUB/SX-AHB/EI-263/I-FIUO/MM54-2586/54-2586	13. 6.96	
G-BWUC	PA-18S-135 Super Cub (Regd with frame no. 18-3719)(L-21C)	18-3569	SX-ASM EI-181/I-EIYB/MM54-2369/54-2369	13. 6.96	To N719CS 6/97. Canx 23.5.97. (Noted on rebuild in 3/99 at Cumbernauld marked as G-BWUC)
G-BWUD	Lavochkin La-9	828	Chinese AF	14. 6.96	(Stored dismantled 7/99 Duxford)
G-BWUE	Hispano HA-1112-M1L (Also reported as c/n 172 - c/n 223 should be C4K-155)	223	N9938 G-AWHK/Spanish AF C4K-102	14. 6.96	(On rebuild at Breighton in 7/98)
G-BWUF	WSK SBLim-5 (MiG-17)	1C1211	1211 Polish AF	14. 6.96	(On overhaul 7/99 Duxford)
G-BWUG	Piper J/5C (AE-1) Cub Cruiser	5-1477	(ZK-USN) N62073/NC62073/BuA.30274	21. 6.96	(On overhaul 8/97)
G-BWUH	PA-28-181 Archer III	2843048	N9272E	30. 8.96	
G-BWUI	BAe Jetstream Srs.4102	41037	HL5226 G-4-037	24. 7.96	To VH-CCW 2/98. Canx 24.2.98.
G-BWUJ	Rotorway Exec	6153		2. 7.96	
G-BWUK	Sky 160-24 HAFB	043		2. 7.96	
G-BWUL	Noorduyn AT-16 Harvard IIB	14A-1415	N16NA G-BWUL/FT375/43-13116	4. 7.96	
G-BWUM	Sky 105-24 HAFB	038		5. 7.96	
G-BWUN	DHC.1 Chipmunk 22 (Fuselage no. DHB/f/137)	C1/0253	WD310	5. 7.96	

Regn	Type	c/n	Previous identity	Regn date	Fate or immediate subsequent identity (if known)
G-BWUO	PA-18-95 Super Cub (L-18C-PI)	18-1629	OO-MEU OO-HNG/ALAT/51-15629	9. 7.96	To N7238X 4/97. Canx 25.4.97.
G-BWUP	Europa Avn Europa	PFA/247-12703		3. 7.96	(Under construction Kemble 1/97)
G-BWUR	Thunder Ax10-210 Srs.2 HAFB	3910		11. 7.96	
G-BWUS	Sky 65-24 HAFB	040		16. 7.96	
G-BWUT	DHC.1 Chipmunk 22 (Fuselage no. DHB/f/808)	C1/0918	WZ879	4. 6.96	
G-BWUU	Cameron N-90 HAFB	3954		17. 7.96	
G-BWUV	DHC.1 Chipmunk 22A (Fuselage no. DHB/f/546)	C1/0655	WK640	18. 7.96	(On overhaul 5/97)
G-BWUW	BAC P.84 Jet Provost T.5A	EEP/JP/1045	XW423	18. 7.96	(Stored 3/97)
G-BWUX	Lindstrand LBL-210A HAFB	391		23. 7.96	Canx by CAA 26.2.97.
G-BWUY	Thunder Ax10-180 HAFB	3646		23. 7.96	
G-BWUZ	Campbell Cricket	G/03-1267		24. 6.96	
G-BWVA	BAe 125 Srs.800B	258235	D-CBVW(3) G-5-774	18. 7.96	To OY-RAA 1/97. Canx 8.10.96.
G-BWVB	Pietenpol Air Camper	PFA/47-11777		24. 7.96	
G-BWVC	Jodel D.18	PFA/169-11331		29. 7.96	
G-BWVD	Cameron R-210 Gas Free Balloon	3901		8. 8.96	W/o at Sultan Pur, India on 20.1.97. Canx 24.3.98 as WFU.
G-BWVE	Bell 206B JetRanger III	3394	G-BOSX N20681	1. 9.88	
G-BWVF	Pietenpol Air Camper	PFA/47-11936		5. 8.96	
G-BWVG	Robin HR.200/120B	308		16. 7.96	
G-BWVH	Robinson R-44 Astro	0072	SX-HDE (D-HBBT)	10. 9.96	
G-BWVI	Stern ST.80 Balade	PFA/166-11190		7. 8.96	
G-BWVJ	Cameron R-450 Gas Free Balloon	3759		8. 8.96	(For Round The World attempt from Chateau d'Oex, Switzerland) w/o 12.1.97 off S.France. Canx as destroyed 25.2.97.
G-BWVK	Cameron Calling Card 110SS HAFB	3947		12. 8.96	To C-GETN 4/99. Canx 31.3.99.
G-BWVL	Cessna 150M	150-77229	N50NA N63286	13. 8.96	
G-BWVM	Colt AA-1050 Gas Free Balloon	3806		14. 8.96	
G-BWVN	Whittaker MW.7	PFA/171-11839		19. 8.96	
G-BWVO	PA-32-300 Cherokee Six	32-7340123	OO-JPC N55520	21. 8.96	To G-IFFR 4/97. Canx.
G-BWVP	Sky 160-24 HAFB	044		21. 8.96	
G-BWVR	Aerostar Yakovlev Yak-52	878202	LY-AKQ DOSAAF 134	27. 8.96	
G-BWVS	Europa Avn Europa	PFA/247-12686		28. 8.96	
G-BWVT	DH(Aust).82A Tiger Moth	1039	N1350 VH-SNZ/RAAF A17-604/VH-AIN/R.Australian AF A17-604	27. 8.96	
G-BWVU	Cameron O-90 HAFB	3204		28. 8.96	
G-BWVV	Jodel D.18	PFA/169-12699		29. 8.96	
G-BWVW	Not allocated.				
G-BWVX	Aerostar Yakovlev Yak-52	866811	LY-AOJ DOSAAF 92 (yellow)	16. 9.96	
G-BWVY	DHC.1 Chipmunk 22A (Fuselage no. DHB/f/665)	C1/0766	WP896	3. 9.96	(Stored 2/97)
G-BWVZ	DHC.1 Chipmunk 22A (Fuselage no. DHB/f/492)	C1/0614	WK590	16. 7.96	
G-BWWA	Ultravia Pelican Club GS	PFA/165-12242		6. 9.96	
G-BWWB	Europa Avn Europa	PFA/247-12670		9. 9.96	
G-BWWC	DH.104 Dove 7	04498	XM223	14. 6.96	(Stored 3/99 Cumbernauld)
G-BWWD	Cameron N-105 HAFB	3972		10. 9.96	To 5N-... 10/96. Canx 21.10.96.
G-BWWE	Lindstrand LBL-90A HAFB	410		11. 9.96	
G-BWWF	Cessna 185A Skywagon	185-0240	9J-MCK 5Y-BBG/ET-ACI/N4040Y	13. 9.96	To N4893K 4/97. Canx 18.3.97.
G-BWWG	Socata MS.894A Rallye 235E Gabier	13121	EI-BIF HB-EYT/N344RA	23.10.96	
G-BWWH	Yakovlev Yak-50	853010	LY-ABL(2) LY-XNI/DOSAAF	16. 9.96	
G-BWWI	Aerospatiale AS.332L Super Puma	2040	OY-HMF (G-TIGT)	11. 9.96	
G-BWWJ	Hughes 269C (300C)	113-0256	G-BMYZ N8996F	25. 2.87	
G-BWWK	Hawker Nimrod I	41H-43617	S1581	13. 9.96	(On rebuild .97)
G-BWWL	Colt Flying Egg SS HAFB	1813	JA-A0513	19. 9.96	
G-BWWM	Diamond DA-20-A1 Katana	10143		2. 7.96	To G-RIBS 7/97. Canx.
G-BWWN	Isaacs Fury II	PFA/11-10957		23. 9.96	
G-BWWO	Cameron A-250 HAFB	3935		23. 9.96	To G-SCRU 30.9.96. Canx.
G-BWWP	Rans S-6-116 Coyote II	PFA/204A-12648		2.10.96	
G-BWWR	Robinson R-44 Astro	0284		2.10.96	To OO-EGJ 5/98. Canx 30.4.98.
G-BWWS	Rotary Air Force RAF 2000 GTX-SE	G/13-1277		7.10.96	
G-BWWT	Dornier 328-110	3022	D-CDXO VT-VIG/D-CDHG	12.11.96	
G-BWWU	PA-22-150 Tri-Pacer	22-5002	N7139D	9.10.96	

Regn	Type	c/n	Previous identity	Regn date	Fate or immediate subsequent identity (if known)
G-BWWV	Bell 206B JetRanger III	2988	N206WR N1086Y	10.10.96	To N108HM 6/97. Canx 25.6.97.
G-BWWW	BAe Jetstream Srs.3102	614	G-31-614	18. 7.83	
G-BWWX	Yakovlev Yak-50	853003	LY-AOI DOSAAF	11.10.96	
G-BWWY	Lindstrand LBL-105A HAFB	411		14.10.96	
G-BWWZ	Denney Kitfox Mk.3	PFA/172-13054		15.10.96	
G-BWXA	Slingsby T.67M Firefly 260	2236		19. 3.96	
G-BWXB	Slingsby T.67M Firefly 260	2237		19. 3.96	
G-BWXC	Slingsby T.67M Firefly 260	2238		19. 3.96	
G-BWXD	Slingsby T.67M Firefly 260	2239		19. 3.96	
G-BWXE	Slingsby T.67M Firefly 260	2240		19. 3.96	
G-BWXF	Slingsby T.67M Firefly 260	2241		19. 3.96	
G-BWXG	Slingsby T.67M Firefly 260	2242		19. 3.96	
G-BWXH	Slingsby T.67M Firefly 260	2243		19. 3.96	
G-BWXI	Slingsby T.67M Firefly 260	2244		19. 3.96	
G-BWXJ	Slingsby T.67M Firefly 260	2245		19. 3.96	
G-BWXK	Slingsby T.67M Firefly 260	2246		19. 3.96	
G-BWXL	Slingsby T.67M Firefly 260	2247		19. 3.96	
G-BWXM	Slingsby T.67M Firefly 260	2248		19. 3.96	
G-BWXN	Slingsby T.67M Firefly 260	2249		19. 3.96	
G-BWXO	Slingsby T.67M Firefly 260	2250		19. 3.96	
G-BWXP	Slingsby T.67M Firefly 260	2251		19. 3.96	
G-BWXR	Slingsby T.67M Firefly 260	2252		19. 3.96	
G-BWXS	Slingsby T.67M Firefly 260	2253		19. 3.96	
G-BWXT	Slingsby T.67M Firefly 260	2254		19. 3.96	
G-BWXU	Slingsby T.67M Firefly 260	2255		19. 3.96	
G-BWXV	Slingsby T.67M Firefly 260	2256		19. 3.96	
G-BWXW	Slingsby T.67M Firefly 260	2257		19. 3.96	
G-BWXX	Slingsby T.67M Firefly 260	2258		19. 3.96	
G-BWXY	Slingsby T.67M Firefly 260	2259		19. 3.96	
G-BWXZ	Slingsby T.67M Firefly 260	2260		19. 3.96	
G-BWYA	Eurocopter AS.350B2 Ecureuil	2915		25. 6.96	To G-WHST 8/96. Canx.
G-BWYB	PA-28-160 Cherokee	28-263	N6374A G-BWYB/6Y-JLO/6Y-JCH/VP-JCH	16. 9.96	
G-BWYC	Cameron N-90 HAFB	3994		17.10.96	
G-BWYD	Europa Avn Europa	PFA/247-12621		28. 8.96	
G-BWYE	Cessna 310R II	310R-1654	F-GBPE (N26369)	6. 9.96	
G-BWYF	Sky 90-24 HAFB	041		21.10.96	To N211SB 4/97. Canx 19.3.97.
G-BWYG	Cessna 310R II	310R-1580	F-GBMY (N1820E)	28.10.96	
G-BWYH	Cessna 310R II	310R-1640	F-GBPC N2634Y	28.10.96	(Damaged by gales at Edinburgh on 26.12.98 when Cessna 404 G-ILGW was blown into it)
G-BWYI	Denney Kitfox Mk.3	PFA/172-12143		30.10.96	
G-BWYJ	Bell 206L-1 LongRanger	45552	D-HOBD D-HGAD	31.10.96	To G-OHHI 4/98. Canx.
G-BWYK	Yakovlev Yak-52	812004	RA-01386 DOSAAF 51	9. 8.96	
G-BWYL	Cameron A-200 HAFB	3996		30. 9.96	
G-BWYM	HOAC DV-20 Katana	20067	D-EWAU	27. 1.97	
G-BWYN	Cameron O-77 HAFB	1162	G-ODER	13.11.96	
G-BWYO	Sequoia Falco F.8L	PFA/100-10920		7.11.96	(Under construction 10/97)
G-BWYP	Sky 56-24 HAFB	053		8.11.96	
G-BWYR	Rans S-6-116 Coyote II	PFA/204A-13058		8.11.96	
G-BWYS	Cameron O-120 HAFB	3997		30. 9.96	
G-BWYT	BAe ATP	2063	HL5228 G-11-063	18.11.96	To OY-SVU 11/97. Canx 19.11.97.
G-BWYU	Sky 120-24 HAFB	052		13.11.96	
G-BWYV	Lindstrand LBL-210A HAFB	347		21.11.96	CofA expired 16.12.97. Canx as WFU 10.8.98.
G-BWYW	PBN BN-2B-20 Islander	2293		2.12.96	(For Japan)
G-BWYX	PBN BN-2B-20 Islander	2298		2.12.96	
G-BWYY	PBN BN-2B-20 Islander	2299		2.12.96	(For Australia)
G-BWYZ	PBN BN-2B-20 Islander	2300		2.12.96	(For Australia)
G-BWZA	Europa Avn Europa	PFA/247-12626		1.11.96	
G-BWZB	Agusta-Bell 206B JetRanger III	8591	F-GCFS	22.11.96	To CS-HDV 9/97. Canx 12.5.97.
G-BWZC	Aerospatiale AS.355F1 Twin Squirrel	5185	G-MOBZ N107KF/N5799R	15.11.96	To G-OGRK 3/99. Canx.
G-BWZD	Light Aero Avid Flyer Mk.4	PFA/189-12453		29.11.96	
G-BWZE	Hunting Percival P.84 Jet Provost T.3A (Regd with c/n PAC/EEP/684 - see XN510/G-BXBI)	PAC/W/6605	XM378	29.11.96	
G-BWZF	PBN BN-2B-20 Islander	2301		12.12.96	(For Japan)
G-BWZG	Robin R.2160	311	F-WZZZ	6.11.96	
G-BWZH	Bell 206B JetRanger III	4406	N53114	9.12.96	To G-TUSK 1/97. Canx.
G-BWZI	Agusta A.109A II	7269	OH-HAD N109AK	29.11.96	
G-BWZJ	Cameron A-250 HAFB	4021		2.12.96	
G-BWZK	Cameron A-210 HAFB	4020		2.12.96	
G-BWZL	Fokker F.27-050	20280	V8-RB1 PH-LXU	5.12.96	Restored as PH-LXU 7/97. Canx 17.7.97.

Regn	Type	c/n	Previous identity	Regn date	Fate or immediate subsequent identity (if known)
G-BWZM	Fokker F.27-050	20282	V8-RB2 PH-MXE	6.12.96	Restored as PH-MXE 7/97. Canx 17.7.97.
G-BWZN	Beechcraft F33A Bonanza	CE-542	EC-CLP Spanish AF E.24B-39	5.12.96	To N2HJ 4/97. Canx 27.1.97.
G-BWZO	Cameron Spaceship 110SS HAFB	4041		6.12.96	To PH-UVO 8/98. Canx 24.6.98.
G-BWZP	Cameron Home Special 105SS HAFB	4051		6.12.96	
G-BWZR	Bell 412EP	36144	ZJ234 G-BWZR/C-FZLM	6.12.96	Restored to MOD as Griffin HT.1 ZJ234 8/97. Canx 22.8.97.
G-BWZS	Eurocopter AS.350BB Ecureuil	2945	ZJ243 G-BWZS/F-WQDV(3)	10.12.96	Restored to MOD as Squirrel HT.2 ZJ243 8/97. Canx 22.8.97.
G-BWZT	Europa Avn Europa	PFA/247-12727		9.12.96	
G-BWZU	Lindstrand LBL-90B HAFB	418		12.12.96	
G-BWZV	Robinson R-22 Beta	0985	G-LIAN	11.12.96	To G-UNYT 11/97. Canx.
G-BWZW	Bell 206B JetRanger	12	G-CTEK N7812S	26.11.96	
G-BWZX	Aerospatiale AS.332L Super Puma	2120	F-WQDX(3) G-BWZX/F-WQDX(3)/5V-MCD/5V-TAH/LN-OLE	12.12.96	
G-BWZY	Hughes 269A	95-0378	G-FSDT N269CH/N1336D/64-18066	4.12.96	
G-BWZZ	Hunting Percival P.84 Jet Provost T.3A	PAC/W/9278	XM470	5. 9.96	
G-BXAA	Bell 206B JetRanger	83	F-GKYR HB-XOR/G-BHMV/VH-SJJ/VH-FVR	3. 4.96	To G-OPNI 24.4.96. Canx.
G-BXAB	PA-28-161 Warrior II	28-8416054	G-BTGK N4344C	7.10.96	
G-BXAC	Rotary Air Force RAF 2000 GTX-SE	G/13-1279		21.11.96	
G-BXAD	Cameron Thunder Ax11-225 Srs.2 HAFB	4052		18.12.96	
G-BXAE	Sikorsky S-61N Mk.II	61-776	LN-OQO	16. 1.97	To EI-MES 3/97. Canx 27.3.97.
G-BXAF	Pitts S-1D Special	PFA/09-12258		6.12.96	
G-BXAG	Eurocopter AS.350BB Ecureuil	2951	ZJ255 G-BXAG	20.12.96	Restored to MOD as Squirrel HT.1 ZJ255 8/97. Canx 22.8.97.
G-BXAH	Piel CP.301A Emeraude (Built by Fliegerclub Eichstatt EV)	AB.422	D-EBAH(2)	29.10.96	
G-BXAI	Cameron Colt 120A HAFB	4056		20.12.96	
G-BXAJ	Lindstrand LBL-14A HAFB	425		23.12.96	
G-BXAK	IAV-Bacau Yakovlev Yak-52	811508	LY-ASC DOSAAF	23.12.96	
G-BXAL	Cameron Bertie Bassett 90SS HAFB	4034		13. 1.97	
G-BXAM	Cameron N-90 HAFB	4035		13. 1.97	
G-BXAN	Scheibe SF-25C Falke 1700	44299	D-KDGQ	13. 1.97	
G-BXAO	Pearce Jabiru SK	PFA/274-13066		14. 1.97	(Extensively damaged in forced landing 3.5.98 at Ledicot, near Shobdon due to engine failure)
G-BXAP	Cameron Hard Hat 90SS HAFB	4045		16. 1.97	
G-BXAR	BAe 146 RJ100	E3298	G-6-298	27. 3.97	
G-BXAS	BAe 146 RJ100	E3301	G-6-301	23. 4.97	
G-BXAT	Airbus A.320-211	436	F-GJVY (PH-GCL)/F-WWDE	12. 5.97	To F-GJVU 10/97. Canx 24.10.97.
G-BXAU	Pitts S-1 Special (Built by G.Goodrich)	GHG.9	N9GG	22. 1.97	
G-BXAV	Aerostar Yakovlev Yak-52	9111608	RA-01325 DOSAAF 73	24. 1.97	
G-BXAW	Airbus A.321-211	666	D-ASSY D-AVZM	7. 4.97	To 6Y-JMD 1/99. Canx 13.1.99.
G-BXAX	Cameron N-77 HAFB	2010		25. 5.89	
G-BXAY	Bell 206B JetRanger III	3946	N85EA N521RC/N3210D	24. 1.97	
G-BXAZ	PA-31 Turbo Navajo	31-245	G-AXAZ N9184Y	5. 7.85	To OY-BHF 6/86. Canx 5.6.86.
G-BXBA	Cameron A-210 HAFB	4072		10. 1.97	
G-BXBB	PA-20-150 Pacer	20-959	EC-AOZ N1133C	24. 1.97	
G-BXBC	Anderson EA-1 Kingfisher Amphibian	PFA/132-11302		28. 1.97	
G-BXBD	CASA I-131 Jungmann (Identity uncertain as another "E3B-317" is on display Musee de Jean Tinguely, Basel, Switzerland)	1052	E3B-317	28. 1.97	
G-BXBE	Bell 412EP	36145	ZJ236 G-BXBE/C-FZLN	28. 1.97	Restored to MOD as Griffin HT.1 ZJ236 8/97. Canx 22.8.97.
G-BXBF	Bell 412EP	36151	ZJ235 G-BXBF/C-FZNF	28. 1.97	Restored to MOD as Griffin HT.1 ZJ235 8/97. Canx 22.8.97.
G-BXBG	Cameron A-275 HAFB	4023		28. 1.97	
G-BXBH	Hunting Percival P.84 Jet Provost T.3A	PAC/W/9241	XM365	29. 1.97	
G-BXBI	Hunting Percival P.84 Jet Provost T.3A (Regd with c/n EEP/JP/684)	PAC/W/11799	XN510	29. 1.97	
G-BXBJ	Hunting Percival P.84 Jet Provost T.3A (Regd with c/n PAC/W/94/9278 - see XM470/G-BWZZ)	PAC/W/10149	XN470	29. 1.97	

Regn	Type	c/n	Previous identity	Regn date	Fate or immediate subsequent identity (if known)
G-BXBK	Avions Mudry/CAARP CAP.10B	17	N170RC French AF "307-SO"	30. 1.97	
G-BXBL	Lindstrand LBL-240A HAFB	317		31. 1.97	
G-BXBM	Cameron O-105 HAFB	3990		31. 1.97	
G-BXBN	Rans S-6-116 Coyote II	PFA/204A-13062		31. 1.97	
G-BXBO	DH.82A Tiger Moth (DHA rebuild c/n T.259)	82360	(D-EAJO) VH-ALC/N9259	3. 2.97	No UK CofA issued. Canx by CAA 19.4.99. (Was based in Germany 1997/98)
G-BXBP	Denney Kitfox Mk.2	PFA/172-12149		3. 2.97	
G-BXBR	Cameron A-120 HAFB	1983	SE-ŻDY	4. 2.97	
G-BXBS	Cameron V-90 HAFB	4096		6. 2.97	
G-BXBT	Aerospatiale AS.355F1 Twin Squirrel	5262	G-TMMC G-JLCO	11. 2.97	Damaged in heavy landing at Kidlington on 11.5.99.
G-BXBU	Avions Mudry/CAARP CAP.10B	103	N173RC French AF	11. 2.97	
G-BXBV	ATR-42-310	245	TS-LBA (EI-BYQ)/F-WWET	14. 5.97	
G-BXBW	HOAC DV-20 Katana	20148	D-ESHM	25. 2.97	
G-BXBX	PA-31-350 Navajo Chieftain	31-7405207	OY-ASC HB-LEN/N66928	13.12.77	To N350SC 3/81. Canx 6.3.81.
G-BXBY	Cameron A-105 HAFB	4077		13. 2.97	
G-BXBZ	WSK PZL-104 Wilga 80 (C/n quoted officially as CF21930941)	CF21910941	EC-GDA ZK-PZQ	13. 2.97	
G-BXCA	Hapi Cygnet SF-2A	PFA/182-12921		22. 1.97	
G-BXCB	Agusta A.109A II	7347	F-GJSH G-ISEB/G-IADT/G-HBCA	17. 2.97	
G-BXCC	PA-28-201T Turbo Dakota	28-7921068	N2855A (D-EKBM)/N2855A	19. 2.97	
G-BXCD	Team Minimax 91A	PFA/186-12393		18. 2.97	
G-BXCE	Eurocopter AS.350BB Ecureuil	2971	ZJ256 G-BXCE	19. 2.97	Restored to MOD as Squirrel HT.1 ZJ256 8/97. Canx 22.8.97.
G-BXCF	Sky 200-24 HAFB	048		19. 2.97	To N213SB 4/97. Canx 19.3.97.
G-BXCG	CEA Jodel DR.250/160 Capitaine	60 & PFA/299-13146	D-EHGG	22. 5.97	
G-BXCH	Europa Avn Europa	PFA/247-12980		19. 2.97	
G-BXCI	Eurocopter AS.350B2 Ecureuil	2967		21. 2.97	To VH-WOK(2) 6/97. Canx 16.7.97.
G-BXCJ	Campbell Cricket Replica	G/03-1177		24. 2.97	
G-BXCK	Cameron Douglas-Lurpak Butterman 110SS HAFB	4076		25. 2.97	
G-BXCL	Montgomerie Bensen B.8MR Gyrocopter	G/01-1287		26. 2.97	
G-BXCM	Lindstrand LBL-150A HAFB	443		26. 2.97	
G-BXCN	Sky 105-24 HAFB	047		27. 2.97	
G-BXCO	Colt 120A HAFB	4086		3. 3.97	
G-BXCP	DHC.1 Chipmunk 22 (Fuselage no. DHB/f/641)	C1/0744	WP859	27. 2.97	
G-BXCR	DHC.1 Chipmunk 22 (Fuselage no. DHB/f/704)	C1/0796	WP920	3. 3.97	
G-BXCS	Cameron N-90 HAFB	4122		4. 3.97	
G-BXCT	DHC.1 Chipmunk 22 (Fuselage no. DHB/f/49)	C1/0145	WB697	3. 3.97	
G-BXCU	Rans S-6-116 Coyote II	PFA/204A-13105		6. 3.97	
G-BXCV	DHC.1 Chipmunk 22 (Fuselage no. DHB/f/719)	C1/0807	WP929	3. 3.97	
G-BXCW	Denney Kitfox Mk.3	PFA/172-12619		6. 3.97	
G-BXCX	Robinson R-22 Beta	0885	G-MFHL	17. 1.97	
G-BXCY	American Aviation AA-5A Cheetah	AA5A-0646	N26686	31. 1.97	
G-BXCZ	American Aviation AA-5A Cheetah	AA5A-0876	N27152	31. 1.97	
G-BXDA	DHC.1 Chipmunk 22 (Fuselage no. DHB/f/643)	C1/0747	WP860	7. 3.97	
G-BXDB	Cessna U.206F Stationair 6	U206-02233	G-BMNZ F-BVJT/N1519U	18.12.96	
G-BXDC	Montgomerie-Bensen B.8MR Gyrocopter	G/01-1219		5. 2.97	
G-BXDD	Rotary Air Force RAF 2000 GTX-SE	G/13-1284		9. 1.97	
G-BXDE	Rotary Air Force RAF 2000 GTX-SE	G/13-1280		14. 1.97	
G-BXDF	Beechcraft 95-B55 Baron	TC-2011	SE-IXG OY-ASB	7. 3.97	
G-BXDG	DHC.1 Chipmunk 22 (Fuselage no. DHB/f/527)	C1/0644	WK630	7. 3.97	
G-BXDH	DHC.1 Chipmunk 22 (Fuselage no. DHB/f/153)	C1/0270	WD331	10. 3.97	
G-BXDI	DHC.1 Chipmunk 22 (Fuselage no. DHB/f/191)	C1/0312	WD373	10. 3.97	
G-BXDJ	Eurocopter AS.350BB Ecureuil	2973	ZJ257 G-BXDJ	14. 3.97	Restored to MOD as Squirrel HT.1 ZJ257 8/97. Canx 22.8.97.
G-BXDK	Bell 412EP	36095	N2291Q XA-SYM/N2291Q	17. 3.97	To MOD as Griffin HT.1 ZJ242 12/97. Canx 1.12.97.

Regn	Type	c/n	Previous identity	Regn date	Fate or immediate subsequent identity (if known)
G-BXDL	Hunting Percival P.84 Jet Provost T.3A	PAC/W/9286	8983M XM478	18. 3.97	
G-BXDM	DHC.1 Chipmunk 22 (Fuselage no. DHB/f/617)	C1/0723	WP840	28. 2.97	
G-BXDN	DHC.1 Chipmunk 22 (Fuselage no. DHB/f/496)	C1/0618	WK609	18. 3.97	
G-BXDO	Rutan Cozy	PFA/159-12032		21. 3.97	
G-BXDP	DHC.1 Chipmunk 22 (Fuselage no. DHB/f/548)	C1/0659	WK642	27. 2.97	
G-BXDR	Lindstrand LBL-77A HAFB	441		25. 3.97	
G-BXDS	Bell 206B JetRanger III	2734	OY-HDK N661PS	1. 4.97	To G-OVBJ 2/98. Canx.
G-BXDT	Robin HR.200/120B	315		25. 3.97	
G-BXDU	Aero Designs Pulsar	PFA/202-11991		25. 3.97	
G-BXDV	Sky 105-24 HAFB	049		26. 3.97	
G-BXDW	Sky 120-24 HAFB	059		26. 3.97	
G-BXDX	Lindstrand LBL-77M HAFB	452		26. 3.97	
G-BXDY	Europa Avn Europa	PFA/247-12914		27. 3.97	
G-BXDZ	Lindstrand LBL-105A HAFB	437		4. 4.97	
G-BXEA	Rotary Air Force RAF 2000 GTX-SE	G/13-1270		2. 4.97	
G-BXEB	Rotary Air Force RAF 2000 GTX-SE	G/13-1285		2. 4.97	
G-BXEC	DHC.1 Chipmunk 22 (Fuselage no. DHB/f/534)	C1/0647	WK633	3. 4.97	
G-BXED	Bell 222U	47527	CS-HDI N3188L	7. 4.97	To N72442 4/97. Canx 11.4.97.
G-BXEE	Enstrom 280C Shark	1117	OH-HAN N336AT	9. 4.97	
G-BXEF	Europa Avn Europa	PFA/247-12790		7. 4.97	
G-BXEG	ATR-42-320	329	ZS-NKY F-WQAB/F-GKNE/F-WWLO	12. 4.95	
G-BXEH	ATR-42-320	306	VR-BOQ (F-OGQV)/F-WWEF	1. 3.96	To PT-MFT 7/98. Canx 22.7.98.
G-BXEI	North American EF-82E-NA Twin Mustang	144-38142	NACA.133 46-256	7. 4.97	To N142AM 5/98. Canx 8.5.98.
G-BXEJ	VPM M-16 Tandem Trainer	D-9302	D-MIFF	8. 4.97	
G-BXEK	Cameron Koala A-315 SS HAFB	4071		11. 4.97	To VH-HOW 6/97. Canx 23.5.97.
G-BXEL	MDH MD-500N	LN-059	N5207E TC-HIC/N5207E	10. 4.97	
G-BXEM	Campbell Cricket Mk.4	G/03-1282	(EI-...) G-BXEM	11. 4.97	
G-BXEN	Cameron N-105 HAFB	4090		11. 4.97	
G-BXEO	Eurocopter AS.350BB Ecureuil	2975	ZJ258 G-BXEO	11. 4.97	Restored to MOD as Squirrel HT.1 ZJ258 8/97. Canx 22.8.97.
G-BXEP	Lindstrand LBL-14M HAFB	460		14. 4.97	
G-BXER	PA-46-350P Malibu Mirage	4636110		21. 7.97	
G-BXES	Hunting Percival P.66 Pembroke C.1 (Regd with c/n PAC/W/3032)	P66/101	N4234C 9042M/XL954	14. 4.97	
G-BXET	PA-38-112 Tomahawk	38-80A0028	N25089	14. 4.97	(On re-assembly at Welshpool on 2.5.99 still faintly marked as N25089)
G-BXEU	BAe 146 RJ100	E3308	G-6-308	14. 4.97	To OO-DWA 25.6.97. Canx 24.6.97.
G-BXEV	Eurocopter AS.355N Twin Squirrel	5633	F-WQDC(5)	16. 4.97	To Irish Army Air Corps as IAC 255 in 8/97. Canx 22.8.97.
G-BXEW	Robinson R-22 Beta	2677		15. 4.97	To G-CNDY 5/97. Canx.
G-BXEX	PA-28-181 Cherokee Archer II	28-7790463	N3562Q	16. 4.97	
G-BXEY	Colt AS-105GD Hot-Air Airship	3936		15. 4.97	
G-BXEZ	Cessna 182P Skylane II (Reims assembled with c/n 0054)	182-64344	OH-CHJ N1479M	16. 4.97	
G-BXFA	Glaser-Dirks DG-800B	8-104-B38	D-KOCP	14. 4.97	To D-KOCP 7/98. Canx 21.7.98.
G-BXFB	Pitts S-1 Special (Built by B.J.Dziuba)	9543	N77ZZ	16. 4.97	
G-BXFC	Jodel D.18	PFA/169-11322		17. 4.97	
G-BXFD	Enstrom 280C Shark	1084	N88MD N632H	18. 4.97	
G-BXFE	Mudry/CAARP CAP.10B	135	N175RC French AF	18. 4.97	
G-BXFF	Bell 412EP	36156	ZJ237 G-BXFF/C-FZVV	22. 4.97	Restored to MOD as Griffin HT.1 ZJ237 8/97. Canx 22.8.97.
G-BXFG	Europa Avn Europa	PFA/247-12500		21. 4.97	
G-BXFH	Bell 412EP	36125	C-FZXD N6282C	23. 4.97	To MOD as Griffin HT.1 ZJ238 9/97. Canx 10.9.97.
G-BXFI	Hawker Hunter T.7	41H-670815	WV372	24. 4.97	
G-BXFJ	Eurocopter AS.350BB Ecureuil	2982	ZJ259 G-BXFJ	24. 4.97	Restored to MOD as Squirrel HT.1 ZJ259 8/97. Canx 22.8.97.
G-BXFK	CFM Streak Shadow	PFA/206-12329		24. 4.97	
G-BXFL	Thunder Ax10-210 Srs.2 HAFB	4099		25. 4.97	To C-GAIG 9/97. Canx 27.8.97.
G-BXFM	Cameron R-500 Orbiter 2 Gas Balloon	4129		25. 4.97	To HB-QBV 12/97. Canx 9.10.97.
G-BXFN	Cameron Colt 77A HAFB	4145		25. 4.97	
G-BXFO	Sky 105-24 HAFB	087		25. 4.97	Canx 10.9.97 on sale to Poland. To SP-BVO 4/98.

Regn	Type	c/n	Previous identity	Regn date	Fate or immediate subsequent identity (if known)
G-BXFP	BAC.167 Strikemaster Mk.87 (Regd as c/n "602")	PS.165	OJ5 Botswana DF/Kenyan AF 602/G-27-192	29. 4.97	(Flies marked as "NZ6361" - The real NZ6361 c/n EEP/JP/3233 is regd VH-ZEP)
G-BXFR	BAC.167 Strikemaster Mk.87 (Regd as c/n "604")	PS.167	OJ9 Botswana DF/Kenyan AF 604/G-27-194	29. 4.97	To N604GV. Canx 5.8.99.
G-BXFS	BAC.167 Strikemaster Mk.87 (Regd as c/n "605")	PS.168	OJ10 Botswana DF/Kenyan AF 605/G-27-195	29. 4.97	
G-BXFT	BAC.167 Strikemaster Mk.83 (Regd as c/n "802")	PS.159	OJ2 Botswana DF/ZG806/Kuwait AF 111/G-27-152	29. 4.97	To N4242T 7/98. Canx 19.6.97.
G-BXFU	BAC.167 Strikemaster Mk.83 (Regd as c/n "805")	PS.158	OJ1 Botswana DF/ZG805/Kuwait AF 110/G-27-151	29. 4.97	
G-BXFV	BAC.167 Strikemaster Mk.83 (Regd as c/n "806")	PS.162	OJ7 Botswana DF/ZG809/Kuwait AF 114/G-27-155	29. 4.97	
G-BXFW	BAC.167 Strikemaster Mk.83 (Regd as c/n "808")	PS.161	OJ6 Botswana DF/ZG808/Kuwait AF 113/G-27-154	29. 4.97	To ZU-PER 3/98 with c/n "APS.161". Canx 20.2.98.
G-BXFX	BAC.167 Strikemaster Mk.83 (Regd as c/n "809")	PS.173	OJ8 Botswana DF/ZG811/Kuwait AF 119/G-27-188	29. 4.97	
G-BXFY	Cameron Bierkrug 90SS HAFB	4133		29. 4.97	Marks D-OIBP reserved in 1998.
G-BXFZ	Sky 65-24 HAFB	065		22. 4.97	
G-BXGA	Eurocopter AS.350B2 Ecureuil	2493	OO-RCH OO-XCH/F-WZFX	30. 4.97	
G-BXGB	Eurocopter AS.350BB Ecureuil	2985	ZJ260 G-BXGB	30. 4.97	Restored to MOD as Squirrel HT.1 ZJ260 8/97. Canx 22.8.97.
G-BXGC	Cameron N-105 HAFB	4137		6. 5.97	
G-BXGD	Sky 90-24 HAFB	067		6. 5.97	
G-BXGE	Cessna 152 II	152-82700	N89283	8. 5.97	Damaged in forced landing 2 miles E of Bala on 4.8.97. (Fuselage stored 9/97 at Welshpool)
G-BXGF	Not allocated.				
G-BXGG	Europa Avn Europa	PFA/247-12803		29. 4.97	
G-BXGH	Diamond DA-20-A1 Katana	10151		20. 5.97	
G-BXGI	DAI/Hoffmann HK-36TTC Super Dimona	36543	OE-UHK	7. 5.97	
G-BXGJ	Eurocopter AS.350BB Ecureuil	2986	ZJ261 G-BXGJ	12. 5.97	Restored to MOD as Squirrel HT.1 ZJ261 8/97. Canx 22.8.97.
G-BXGK	Lindstrand LBL-203M HAFB	468		12. 5.97	
G-BXGL	DHC.1 Chipmunk 22 (Fuselage no. DHB/f/814)	C1/0924	WZ884	12. 5.97	
G-BXGM	DHC.1 Chipmunk 22 (Fuselage no. DHB/f/718)	C1/0806	WP928	9. 5.97	
G-BXGN	Cameron Waving Flag 90SS HAFB	4134		13. 5.97	To C-GCYD 5/98. Canx 19.5.98.
G-BXGO	DHC.1 Chipmunk 22 (Fuselage no. DHH/f/103)	C1/0097	WB654	13. 5.97	
G-BXGP	DHC.1 Chipmunk 22 (Fuselage no. DHB/f/817)	C1/0927	WZ882	12. 5.97	
G-BXGR	Sikorsky S-76C	760377	I-PRLT N62375/JA6692	14. 5.97	To VP-CHC 15.5.97. Canx 15.5.97.
G-BXGS	Rotary Air Force RAF 2000 GTX-SE	G/13-1290		14. 5.97	
G-BXGT	Iniziative Industriali Italian Sky Arrow 650TC	PFA/298-13085		7. 5.97	
G-BXGU	Scottish Avn Bulldog Srs.120/122	BH120/229	G-105 Ghana AF	15. 5.97	To G-GRRR 10/98. Canx.
G-BXGV	Cessna 172R Skyhawk II	172-80240	N9300F	7. 1.98	
G-BXGW	Robin HR.200/120B	317		16. 5.97	
G-BXGX	DHC.1 Chipmunk 22 (Fuselage no. DHB/f/488)	C1/0609	WK586	19. 5.97	
G-BXGY	Cameron V-65 HAFB	4125		18. 4.97	
G-BXGZ	Stemme S-10V	14-023	D-KSTE EC-GGD/D-KGDF(2)	18. 8.97	
G-BXHA	DHC.1 Chipmunk 22 (Fuselage no. DHB/f/713)	C1/0801	WP925	20. 5.97	
G-BXHB	Eurocopter AS.350BB Ecureuil	2993	ZJ262 G-BXHB	20. 5.97	Restored to MOD as Squirrel HT.1 ZJ262 8/97. Canx 22.8.97.
G-BXHC	Bell 412EP	36162	C-GAFF	22. 5.97	To MOD as Griffin HT.1 ZJ239 8/97. Canx 5.8.97.
G-BXHD	Beechcraft 76 Duchess	ME-284	OY-ARM N223JC	22. 5.97	
G-BXHE	Lindstrand LBL-105A HAFB	459		23. 5.97	
G-BXHF	DHC.1 Chipmunk 22 (Fuselage no. DHB/f/721)	C1/0808	WP930	28. 5.97	
G-BXHG	Cessna 172M Skyhawk II	172-64993	N64057	28. 5.97	To N172AM 2/98. Canx 27.2.98.
G-BXHH	American Aviation AA-5A Cheetah	AA5A-0105	N9705U	3. 6.97	
G-BXHI	Hughes 269C (300C)	77-0616	G-GBHH TF-HRH/TF-HHO/N45CD/N9250F/(N51CC)	18. 6.97	
G-BXHJ	Hapi Cygnet SF-2A	PFA/182-12159		29. 5.97	
G-BXHK	Eurocopter AS.350BB Ecureuil	2991	ZJ263 G-BXHK	29. 5.97	Restored to MOD as Squirrel HT.1 ZJ263 8/97. Canx 22.8.97.
G-BXHL	Sky 77-24 HAFB	055		29. 5.97	
G-BXHM	Lindstrand LBL-25A Cloudhopper HAFB	466		30. 5.97	
G-BXHN	Lindstrand Budweiser Can SS HAFB	465		30. 5.97	
G-BXHO	Lindstrand Telewest Sphere SS HAFB	474		30. 5.97	

Regn	Type	c/n	Previous identity	Regn date	Fate or immediate subsequent identity (if known)
G-BXHP	Lindstrand LBL-105A HAFB	458		30. 5.97	
G-BXHR	Stemme S-10V	14-030		23. 7.97	
G-BXHS	DHC.1 Chipmunk 22	C1/0395	WG323	2. 6.97	To C-GBRW 12/97. Canx 21.11.97.
	(Fuselage no. DHB/f/283)				
G-BXHT	Bushby-Long Midget Mustang			3. 6.97	
		PFA/168-13077			
G-BXHU	Campbell Cricket Mk.6	G/16-1292		3. 6.97	
G-BXHV	Agusta A.109C	7613	9M-SJ1	5. 6.97	To N43453 5/98. Canx 8.5.98.
G-BXHW	Eurocopter AS.350BB Ecureuil	2992	ZJ264	5. 6.97	Restored to MOD as Squirrel HT.1 ZJ264 8/97. Canx 22.8.97.
			G-BXHW		
G-BXHX	Eurocopter AS.350BB Ecureuil	2995		5. 6.97	To MOD as Squirrel HT.1 ZJ265 8/97. Canx 5.8.97.
G-BXHY	Europa Avn Europa	PFA/247-12514		6. 6.97	
G-BXHZ	Vickers-Supermarine 361 Spitfire		SAAF	9. 6.97	
	HF.IX	CBAF.10164	SM520		
G-BXIA	DHC.1 Chipmunk 22	C1/0056	WB615	9. 6.97	
	(Fuselage no. DHH/f/64)				
G-BXIB	Bell 206L-3 Long Ranger	51300	EC-EQQ	9. 6.97	
G-BXIC	Cameron A-275 HAFB	4162		9. 6.97	
G-BXID	IAV-Bacau Yakovlev Yak-52	888802	LY-ALG	10. 6.97	
			DOSAAF 74 (yellow)		
G-BXIE	Cameron Colt 77B HAFB	4181		11. 6.97	
G-BXIF	PA-28-181 Cherokee Archer II		PH-SWM	12. 6.97	
		28-7690404	OO-HAY/N6827J		
G-BXIG	Zenair CH.701 STOL	PFA/187-12065		16. 6.97	
G-BXIH	Sky 200-24 HAFB	076		16. 6.97	
G-BXII	Europa Avn Europa	PFA/247-12812		30. 4.97	
G-BXIJ	Europa Avn Europa	PFA/247-12698		16. 6.97	
G-BXIK	Bell 212	31191	SE-HVB	18. 6.97	To VT-DAM 11/98. Canx 26.11.98.
			C-FRUV/SE-HVB/OY-HME/N2052U		
G-BXIL	Eurocopter AS.350BB Ecureuil	2994		20. 6.97	To MOD as Squirrel HT.1 ZJ266 8/97. Canx 11.8.97.
G-BXIM	DHC.1 Chipmunk 22	C1/0548	WK512	13. 5.97	
	(Fuselage no. DHB/f/433)				
G-BXIN	PA-28R-200 Cherokee Arrow II		D-EDVL	20. 6.97	To G-EDVL 30.6.97. Canx.
		28R-7235245	N1243T		
G-BXIO	SAN Jodel DR.1050M Excellance	493	F-BNIO	16. 5.97	
G-BXIP	Eurocopter AS.350BB Ecureuil	2996		26. 6.97	To MOD as Squirrel HT.1 ZJ267 8/97. Canx 18.8.97.
G-BXIR	Bell 412EP	36163	C-GAIE	24. 6.97	To MOD as Griffin HT.1 ZJ240 10/97. Canx 13.10.97.
G-BXIS	Bell 412EP	36164	C-GAIG	24. 6.97	To MOD as Griffin HT.1 ZJ241 11/97. Canx 6.11.97.
G-BXIT	Zebedee V-31 HAFB	Z1/3999		8. 5.97	
G-BXIU	Cameron R-270 Gas Balloon	4118		24. 6.97	Force-landed at Krasnodar, Russia 5.1.98 during attempted round-the-world balloon flight. Canx 24.3.98 as WFU.
G-BXIV	Agusta A.109A	7135	F-GERU	13. 6.97	
			HB-XOK/D-HFZF		
G-BXIW	Sky 105-24 HAFB	073		24. 6.97	
G-BXIX	VPM M-16 Tandem Trainer	G/12-1292		13. 6.97	
G-BXIY	Blake Bluetit	01	BAPC.37	26. 6.97	(Pre-war composite from Spartans G-AAGN/G-AAJB & Avro 504K) (On rebuild 3/96, noted 4/98 at Popham)
G-BXIZ	Lindstrand LBL-31A HAFB	476		3. 7.97	
G-BXJA	Cessna 402B	402B-0356	N5753M	17. 7.97	
			XA-RFK/N5753M		
G-BXJB	IAV-Bacau Yakovlev Yak-52	877403	LY-ABR	30. 6.97	
			DOSAAF 15 (yellow)		
G-BXJC	Cameron A-210 HAFB	4191		2. 7.97	
G-BXJD	PA-28-180 Cherokee C	28-4215	OY-BBZ	27. 6.97	
G-BXJE	Eurocopter AS.350BB Ecureuil	2997		4. 7.97	To MOD as Squirrel HT.1 ZJ268 8/97. Canx 15.8.97.
G-BXJF	Hughes 369HS (500HS)	55-0745S	N99KS	7. 7.97	To G-CSPJ 24.7.97. Canx.
			N9KS		
G-BXJG	Lindstrand LBL-105B HAFB	478		11. 7.97	
G-BXJH	Cameron N-42 HAFB	4194		15. 7.97	
G-BXJI	Tri-R Kis	PFA/239-12573		2. 7.97	(Under construction 3/99 at Cumbernauld)
G-BXJJ	PA-28-161 Cadet	2841200	G-GFCC	26. 6.97	
			N9189N		
G-BXJK	Aerospatiale SA.341G Gazelle Srs.1		F-GEHC	30. 6.97	
		1417	N341AT/N49536		
G-BXJL	Cameron Real Fruit 90SS HAFB	4172		15. 7.97	
G-BXJM	Cessna 152 II	152-82380	OO-HOQ	15. 7.97	Crashed on landing at Redhill on 19.3.99.
			F-GHOQ/N68797		
G-BXJN	Eurocopter AS.350BB Ecureuil	2999		16. 7.97	To MOD as Squirrel HT.1 ZJ269 8/97. Canx 27.8.97.
G-BXJO	Cameron O-90 HAFB	4190		16. 7.97	
G-BXJP	Cameron C-80 HAFB	4171		17. 7.97	
G-BXJR	Eurocopter AS.350BB Ecureuil	3000		18. 7.97	To MOD as Squirrel HT.1 ZJ270 9/97. Canx 4.9.97.
G-BXJS	Schempp-Hirth Janus CM	35/265	OH-819	7. 7.97	
G-BXJT	Sky 90-24 HAFB	072		18. 7.97	
G-BXJU	Sky 90-24 HAFB	077		18. 7.97	
G-BXJV	Dimona DA-20-A1 Katana	10152		23. 7.97	
G-BXJW	Dimona DA-20-A1 Katana	10211	(OE-...)	23. 7.97	
			N811CH		
G-BXJX	PA-28-161 Warrior II	2816076	HB-POM	7. 8.97	To G-GRRC 3/98. Canx.
			D-EJTB/N9149X		
G-BXJY	Van's RV-6	PFA/181-12447		23. 7.97	
G-BXJZ	Cameron C-60 HAFB	4168		23. 7.97	
G-BXKA	Airbus A.320-214	714	N714AW	24.11.97	
			G-BXKA/F-WWIX		

Regn	Type	c/n	Previous identity	Regn date	Fate or immediate subsequent identity (if known)
G-BXKB	Airbus A.320-214	716	N716AW	10.12.97	
			G-BXKB/F-WWIZ		
G-BXKC	Airbus A.320-214	730	F-WWBQ	15.12.97	
G-BXKD	Airbus A.320-214	735	F-WWBV	17.12.97	
G-BXKE	Eurocopter AS.350BB Ecureuil	3003		25. 7.97	To MOD as Squirrel HT.1 ZJ271 9/97. Canx 11.9.97.
G-BXKF	Hawker Hunter T.7	HABL-003314	8676M	28. 7.97	
	(Regd with c/n 41H-003315,		XL577		
	c/n HABL-003315 belongs to XL576/8835M which became N576NL)				
G-BXKG	Cameron R-420 HAFB	4142		30. 7.97	Canx 4.9.97 on sale to USA.
G-BXKH	Cameron Colt Sparkasse Box 90SS HAFB	4161		4. 8.97	
G-BXKI	Robinson R-44 Astro	0220	OY-HEK	15. 8.97	
G-BXKJ	Cameron A-275 HAFB	4215		4. 8.97	
G-BXKK	Cameron Golf Ball 105SS HAFB	4054		4. 8.97	
G-BXKL	Bell 206B JetRanger III	3006	N5735Y	8.10.97	
G-BXKM	Rotary Air Force RAF 2000 GTX-SE	G/13-1291		5. 8.97	
G-BXKN	Eurocopter AS.350BB Ecureuil	3005		5. 8.97	To MOD as Squirrel HT.1 ZJ272 9/97. Canx 18.9.97.
G-BXKO	Sky 65-24 HAFB	083		11. 8.97	
G-BXKP	Eurocopter AS.350BB Ecureuil	3006		11. 8.97	To MOD as Squirrel HT.1 ZJ273 9/97. Canx 25.9.97.
G-BXKR	Eurocopter AS.350BB Ecureuil	3008		11. 8.97	To MOD as Squirrel HT.1 ZJ274 10/97. Canx 3.10.97.
G-BXKS	PA-31-350 Navajo Chieftain	31-7752105	N350RC	12. 8.97	To G-OAMT 1/98. Canx.
			EC-EBN/N27230		
G-BXKT	Aerospatiale AS.350B Ecureuil	1490	F-GKRT	3. 9.97	To G-NUTY 7/98. Canx.
			N333FH/N5797V		
G-BXKU	Cameron Colt AS-120 Mk.II Hot Air Airship	4165		15. 8.97	
G-BXKV	Enstrom 280FX	2077	D-HHML	15. 8.97	To G-PBYY 15.8.97. Canx.
G-BXKW	Slingsby T.67M Firefly 200	2061	VR-HZS	15. 8.97	
			HKG-13/G-7-129		
G-BXKX	Taylorcraft Auster 5	803	D-EMXA	19. 8.97	
			HB-EOK/MS938		
G-BXKY	Cameron DP-90 Hot Air Airship	4198		19. 8.97	
G-BXKZ	Cameron O-77 HAFB	4220		19. 8.97	Reserved as PT-WPX on 14.11.97. Canx 16.12.97.
G-BXLA	Robinson R-22 Beta	1368	SE-HVX	12. 8.97	
			N4014G		
G-BXLB	Eurocopter AS.350BB Ecureuil	3013		20. 8.97	To MOD as Squirrel HT.1 ZJ275 10/97. Canx 3.10.97.
G-BXLC	Sky 120-24 HAFB	085	(F-GLUI)	20. 8.97	
G-BXLD	Cameron Colt 120A HAFB	4188		26. 8.97	To D-O... Canx 31.8.99.
G-BXLE	Eurocopter AS.350BB Ecureuil	3014		27. 8.97	To MOD as Squirrel HT.1 ZJ276 10/97. Canx 13.10.97.
G-BXLF	Lindstrand LBL-90A HAFB	487		3. 9.97	
G-BXLG	Cameron C-80 HAFB	4250		5. 3.98	
G-BXLH	Eurocopter AS.350BB Ecureuil	3017		5. 9.97	To MOD as Squirrel HT.1 ZJ277 10/97. Canx 13.10.97.
G-BXLI	Bell 206B JetRanger III	4041	N206JR	8. 9.97	
			G-JODY		
G-BXLJ	Cessna 172M Skyhawk	172-67065	N1394U	8. 9.97	Fatal crash into the Berywn Mountains, Mid-Wales on 12.2.99 & destroyed. Canx as destroyed 26.2.99.
G-BXLK	Europa Avn Europa	PFA/247-12613		11. 9.97	
G-BXLL	Eurocopter AS.365N2 Dauphin 2	6528		11. 9.97	To JA98YH 2/98. Canx 21.1.98.
G-BXLM	BAe Jetstream Srs.3102	645	N645JD	16. 9.97	To SE-LGC 5/99. Canx 10.5.99.
			G-BXLM/PH-KJA/G-31-645		
G-BXLN	Sportavia-Putzer Fournier RF-4D	4022	F-BORK	15. 9.97	
G-BXLO	Hunting Percival P.84 Jet Provost T.4	PAC/W/19986	9032M	14. 8.97	
			XR673		
G-BXLP	Sky 90-24 HAFB	084		18. 9.97	
G-BXLR	PZL-110 Koliber 160A	04980077	SP-WGF(2)	10. 6.98	
	(Regd with c/n 04970077)				
G-BXLS	PZL-110 Koliber 160A	04980078	SP-WGG	23. 6.98	
	(Regd with c/n 04970078)				
G-BXLT	Socata TB-200 Tobago XL	1457	F-GRBB	28. 4.97	
			EC-FNX/EC-234/F-GLFP		
G-BXLU	Eurocopter AS.355N Twin Squirrel	5641		19. 9.97	To VP-BPB 5/98. Canx 28.5.98.
G-BXLV	Enstrom F-28F	733	1711	11. 9.97	
			Thai Government/KASET		
G-BXLW	Enstrom F-28F	734	1712	11. 9.97	
			Thai Government/KASET		
G-BXLX	Enstrom F-28F	735	1713	11. 9.97	
			Thai Government/KASET		
G-BXLY	PA-28-151 Cherokee Warrior	28-7715220	G-WATZ	19. 9.97	
			N7641F		
G-BXLZ	Europa Avn Europa	PFA/247-12815		24. 6.97	
G-BXMA	Beechcraft 200 Super King Air	BB-726	N622JA	31. 7.97	
			N522JA/N222JD		
G-BXMB	Eurocopter AS.350BB Ecureuil	3019		15. 9.97	To MOD as Squirrel HT.1 ZJ278 10/97. Canx 17.10.97.
G-BXMC	Eurocopter AS.350BB Ecureuil	3021		15. 9.97	To MOD as Squirrel HT.1 ZJ279 10/97. Canx 30.10.97.
G-BXMD	Eurocopter AS.350BB Ecureuil	3026		19. 9.97	To MOD as Squirrel HT.1 ZJ280 11/97. Canx 3.11.97.
G-BXME	Eurocopter AS.350BB Ecureuil	3028		19. 9.97	To MOD as Squirrel HT.2 ZJ244 11/97. Canx 11.11.97.
G-BXMF	Cassutt Racer IIIM	PFA/34-13003		19. 9.97	
G-BXMG	Rotary Air Force RAF 2000 GTX	H2-92-3-59	PH-TEN	18. 8.97	

Regn	Type	c/n	Previous identity	Regn date	Fate or immediate subsequent identity (if known)
G-BXMH	Beechcraft 76 Duchess	ME-168	F-GDMO	19. 9.97	
			N6021Y		
G-BXMI	Eurocopter AS.350BB Ecureuil	3022		25. 9.97	To MOD as Squirrel HT.2 ZJ245 11/97. Canx 13.11.97.
G-BXMJ	Eurocopter AS.350BB Ecureuil	3031		25. 9.97	To MOD as Squirrel HT.2 ZJ246 11/97. Canx 21.11.97.
G-BXMK	Lindstrand LBL-240A HAFB	324		25. 9.97	To PH-GPJ 3/98. Canx 22.12.97.
G-BXML	Mooney M.20A	1594	OY-AIZ	26. 9.97	
G-BXMM	Cameron A-180 HAFB	4252		28.10.97	
G-BXMN	DH.82A Tiger Moth	86243	N82RD	2.10.97	Forced landing at Springwood, near Blackburn on 25.5.99.
			N8353/ZS-IGJ/CR-AGL/Portuguese AF/NL772		
G-BXMO	English Electric Canberra B.6	71417	WT327	8.10.97	To N30UP 3/98 with c/n "6663". Canx 16.12.97.
	(Regd with c/n "R3/EA3/6663" - which belongs to nose of WK163)				
G-BXMP	Bell 206LT Long Ranger 4 (Mod)	52062	(N58968)	9.10.97	To EC-H.. Canx 26.4.99.
			G-OCOP/N58968		
G-BXMR	Robinson R-22 Beta	1932	N923FM	9.10.97	
			N2306E		
G-BXMS	Robinson R-22 Beta	2740		30. 9.97	To G-WURL 13.10.97. Canx.
G-BXMT	Robinson R-22 Beta	2739		1.10.97	To G-SBUT 5/98. Canx.
G-BXMU	WSK PZL-104 Wilga 80	20890880	EC-GMH	9.10.97	(Engineless 5/99 Netherthorpe)
			ZK-PZP/SP-FWP		
G-BXMV	Scheibe SF-25C Falke 1700	44223	D-KDFV(2)	7. 8.97	
G-BXMW	Cameron A-275 HAFB	4247		19. 2.98	
G-BXMX	Phoenix Currie Wot	PFA/58-13055		23. 9.97	
G-BXMY	Hughes 269C (300C)	74-0328	N9599F	20.10.97	
G-BXMZ	Diamond DA-20-A1 Katana	10236		4.12.97	
G-BXNA	Light Aero Avid Flyer	118	(N5531J)	10.10.97	
G-BXNB	Eurocopter AS.350BB Ecureuil	3035	F-WQDL(5)	13.10.97	To MOD as Squirrel HT.2 ZJ247 11/97. Canx 27.11.97.
G-BXNC	Europa Avn Europa	PFA/247-12970		13.10.97	
G-BXND	Cameron Thomas the Tank Engine 110SS HAFB	4254		2. 2.98	
G-BXNE	Eurocopter AS.350BB Ecureuil	3037		15.10.97	To MOD as Squirrel HT.2 ZJ248 12/97. Canx 4.12.97.
G-BXNF	Fokker F.100-650	11316	TU-TIV	15.10.97	To VH-FWH 5/99. Canx 14.5.99.
			PH-RRG/G-FIOO/PH-EZW		
G-BXNG	Beechcraft 58 Baron	TH-874	N18747	13.10.97	
G-BXNH	PA-28-161 Warrior II	28-7816314	N2828M	22.10.97	
G-BXNI	Eurocopter AS.350B2 Ecureuil	1216	F-WQDU(4)	24.10.97	To PT-YJC 1/98. Canx 27.11.97.
			C-GNML		
G-BXNJ	Eurocopter AS.350BB Ecureuil	3040		24.10.97	To MOD as Squirrel HT.2 ZJ249 12/97. Canx 11.12.97.
G-BXNK	Pierre Robin DR.400/180 Regent	2367		21.10.97	To G-DUDZ 12/97. Canx.
G-BXNL	Cameron A-120 HAFB	4241		3. 3.98	
G-BXNM	Cameron A-210 HAFB	4245		12.12.97	
G-BXNN	DHC.1 Chipmunk 22	C1/0849	WP983	4. 8.97	
	(Fuselage no. DHB/f/752)				
G-BXNO	Yakovlev Yak-50	822305	LY-ASD	13.10.97	
			DOSAAF 82		
G-BXNP	Airbus A.321-211	775	D-AVZF	26. 2.98	To 6Y-JME 2/99. Canx 25.2.99.
G-BXNR	Colt Bibendum 110SS HAFB	4221		4.12.97	Canx 22.12.97 on sale to France. To F-GOLB 7/98.
G-BXNS	Bell 206B JetRanger III	2385	N16822	3.11.97	
G-BXNT	Bell 206B JetRanger III	2398	N94CA	11.11.97	
			N123AL		
G-BXNU	Pearce Jabiru SK	PFA/274-13218		31.10.97	
G-BXNV	Cameron Colt AS-105 GD Hot-Air Airship	4231		19. 2.98	
G-BXNW	SNCAN Stampe SV-4C	141	F-BBPB	24.11.78	To G-GMAX 6/87. Canx.
G-BXNX	Lindstrand LBL-210A HAFB	318		3.11.97	
G-BXNY	Eurocopter AS.350BB Ecureuil	3047		4.11.97	To MOD as Squirrel HT.2 ZJ251 12/97. Canx 22.12.97.
G-BXNZ	Hawker Hunter F.58	41H-697433	J-4066	7.11.97	
	(Regd with c/n 41H-28364)		Swiss AF		
G-BXOA	Robinson R-22 Beta	1614	N41132	10.11.97	
			JA7832		
G-BXOB	Europa Avn Europa	PFA/247-12892		6.11.97	
G-BXOC	Evans VP-2	PFA/63-10305		29. 9.97	
G-BXOD	English Electric Canberra B.6	71398	XH567	11.11.97	To N40UP 3/98. Canx 16.3.98.
G-BXOE	Westland Scout AH.1	F.9761	XW798	12.11.97	To G-ONEB 1/98. Canx.
	(Officially regd with c/n F8-10213)				
G-BXOF	Diamond DA-20-A1 Katana	10256		4.12.97	
G-BXOG	Eurocopter AS.350BB Ecureuil	3042		14.11.97	To MOD as Squirrel HT.2 ZJ250 1/98. Canx 15.1.98.
G-BXOH	Cessna 172R Skyhawk II	172-80143	N9989F	17.11.97	To G-CURR 5/98. Canx.
G-BXOI	Cessna 172R Skyhawk II	172-80145	N9990F	17.11.97	
G-BXOJ	PA-28-161 Warrior III	2842010	N9265G	15.12.97	
G-BXOK	Eurocopter AS.350BB Ecureuil	3049		21.11.97	To MOD as Squirrel HT.2 ZJ252 1/98. Canx 16.1.98.
G-BXOL	Boeing 757-23A	24528	SE-DSM	26.11.97	To PH-AHP 4/99. Canx 9.4.99.
	(Line No. 250)		OO-ILI		
G-BXOM	Isaacs Spitfire	PFA/27-12768		25.11.97	
G-BXON	Auster AOP.9	AUS/10/60	WZ729	1.12.97	
G-BXOO	American Aviation AA-5A Cheetah	AA5A-0674	N26721	10.12.97	
G-BXOP	Boeing 767-3S1ER	25221	N770TA	10. 2.98	To PH-AAM 23.3.99/SE-DZF 24.3.99. Canx 23.3.99.
	(Line No. 384)		(N688EV)/B-16688/(YS-...)		
G-BXOR	Robin HR.200/120B	321		1.12.97	
G-BXOS	Cameron A-200 HAFB	4286		19. 2.98	
G-BXOT	Cameron C-70 HAFB	4200		21.10.97	
G-BXOU	CEA Jodel DR.360 Chevalier	312	F-BPOU	6.10.97	
G-BXOV	Cameron Colt 105A HAFB	4227		12.12.97	

Regn	Type	c/n	Previous identity	Regn date	Fate or immediate subsequent identity (if known)
G-BXOW	Cameron Colt 105A HAFB	4228		9. 1.98	
G-BXOX	American Aviation AA-5A Cheetah	AA5A-0694	F-GBDS	27. 2.98	
G-BXOY	QAC Quickie Q.200	PFA/94-12183		17.11.97	
G-BXOZ	PA-28-181 Cherokee Archer II	28-7790173	N6927F	14.10.97	
G-BXPA	Eurocopter AS.365N2 Dauphin 2	6534		3.12.97	To JA61NH 3/98. Canx 6.3.98.
G-BXPB	Diamond DA-20-A1 Katana	10257		4.12.97	
G-BXPC	Diamond DA-20-A1 Katana	10258		4.12.97	
G-BXPD	Diamond DA-20-A1 Katana	10259		4.12.97	
G-BXPE	Diamond DA-20-A1 Katana	10263		4.12.97	
G-BXPF	Venture Thorp T.211	105	N6524Y	8.12.97	Damaged at Kirkbride on 31.12.98. (Stored at Barton 2/99)
G-BXPG	Eurocopter AS.350BB Ecureuil	3052		4.12.97	To MOD as Squirrel HT.2 ZJ253 1/98. Canx 23.1.98.
G-BXPH	Sky 220-24 HAFB	096		4.12.97	Reserved as D-OAIX 22.6.98.
G-BXPI	Van's RV-4	PFA/181-12426		2. 1.98	
G-BXPJ	Eurocopter AS.350BB Ecureuil	3055		8.12.97	To MOD as Squirrel HT.2 ZJ254 2/98. Canx 2.2.98.
G-BXPK	Cameron A-250 HAFB	4226		2. 2.98	
G-BXPL	PA-28-140 Cherokee	28-24560	N7224J	10.12.97	Forced landing in a field short of the runway at Bournemouth on 22.7.99.
G-BXPM	Beechcraft 58 Baron	TH-1677	N207ZM	10.10.97	
G-BXPN	Bell 206B JetRanger III	4160	N18EA D-HOBA/(D-HOBE)	10.12.97	To G-ONYX 1/98. Canx.
G-BXPO	Venture Thorp T.211	104	N6524Q	10.12.97	
G-BXPP	Sky 90-24 HAFB	092		17.12.97	
G-BXPR	Cameron Colt Can 110SS HAFB	4218		2. 2.98	
G-BXPS	PA-23-250 Aztec C	27-3498	G-AYLY N6258Y	10.12.90	
G-BXPT	Ultramagic H-77 HAFB	77-160		22.12.97	
G-BXPU	HS.125 Srs.F3B/RA	25171	(N171AV) G-BXPU/G-AXPU/G-IBIS/G-AXPU/HB-VBT/G-5-19	18. 3.83	To G-OPOL 6/86. Canx.
G-BXPV	PA-34-220T Seneca IV	3448035	A7-FCH N9198X	24.12.97	
G-BXPW	PA-34-220T Seneca IV	3448034	A7-FCG N9171R	9. 2.98	
G-BXPX	Agusta A.109A II	7390	(N.....) G-BXPX/I-DVRE	12.12.97	To 8P-... Canx 19.4.99.
G-BXPY	Robinson R-44 Astro	0154	OY-HFV	22.12.97	
G-BXPZ	DHC.8-311A Dash Eight	422	N377DC OE-LTE/C-GLOT	6. 3.98	
G-BXRA	Avions Mudry/CAARP CAP.10B	03	03 French AF/F-TFVR	12.12.97	
G-BXRB	Avions Mudry/CAARP CAP.10B	100	100 French AF	12.12.97	
G-BXRC	Avions Mudry/CAARP CAP.10B	134	134 French AF	12.12.97	
G-BXRD	Enstrom 280FX Shark	2012	PH-JVM N213M	22.12.97	
G-BXRE	Fokker F.28-4000 Fellowship	11187	N102EW 9G-ADA/PH-EXW	5. 1.98	
G-BXRF	Scintex CP.1310-C3 Super Emeraude	935	OO-NSF F-BMJG	9. 1.98	
G-BXRG	PA-28-181 Archer II	28-7990036	PH-LEC N21173	29. 1.98	
G-BXRH	Cessna 185A Skywagon	185-0413	HB-CRX N1613Z	10.12.97	
G-BXRI	Cessna T.303 Crusader	T303-00133	HB-LNI (N5143C)	27. 1.98	
G-BXRJ	PA-28-181 Archer II	28-8290108	HB-PGO	16. 1.98	To G-DENK 2/98. Canx.
G-BXRK	Robinson R-22 Beta	1341	N341MB	20. 1.98	
G-BXRL	Westland Scout AH.1 (C/n officially quoted as F8-4347 which would be the rear bulkhead build no., the pod no. is probably F8-4267)(Canx by CAA 19.11.98 & restored 4.6.99 with c/n quoted as F.9639 which belongs to XT633 (G.I. at Arborfield)	F.9636	XT630	20. 1.98	DBR after striking trees on landing at Hambleton Hall, Leics. on 15.7.98.
G-BXRM	Cameron A-210 HAFB	4237		23. 4.98	
G-BXRN	Reims Cessna F.152 II	1440	G-RICH OO-FTC	27. 1.98	
G-BXRO	Cessna U.206G Stationair II	U206-04217	OH-ULK N756NE	9. 2.98	
G-BXRP	Schweizer 269C (300C)	S.1334	OH-HSP N7506U	27. 1.98	
G-BXRR	Westland Scout AH.1	F.9740	XW612	28. 1.98	
G-BXRS	Westland Scout AH.1	F.9741	XW613	28. 1.98	
G-BXRT	Robin DR.400/180 Regent	2382		23. 2.98	
G-BXRU	Airbus A.300B4-2C	031	N63661 HL7238/F-WZEQ/F-WUAY/F-WLGC	3. 2.98	To EL-LIC 3/98 /F-OHLE 5/98. Canx 27.5.98.
G-BXRV	Van's RV-4	PFA/181-12482		12. 1.98	
G-BXRW	Airbus A.320-231	308	EC-GNB N308RX/LZ-ABC/F-WWDL	30. 3.98	To EC-GUR 5/98. Canx 8.5.98.
G-BXRX	Airbus A.320-231	314	EC-GLT N314RX/LZ-ABD/F-WWDO	. 1.98R	NTU - Remained as EC-GLT /98. Canx.
G-BXRY	Bell 206B JetRanger	208	N4054G	19. 3.98	
G-BXRZ	Rans S-6-116 Coyote II	PFA/204A-13195		3. 2.98	

Regn	Type	c/n	Previous identity	Regn date	Fate or immediate subsequent identity (if known)
G-BXSA	Cameron PM-80 HAFB	4297		11. 3.98	
G-BXSB	Cameron PM-80 HAFB	4298		11. 3.98	
G-BXSC	Cameron C-80 HAFB	4251		12.12.97	
G-BXSD	Cessna 172R Skyhawk II	172-80310	N431ES	12. 3.98	
G-BXSE	Cessna 172R Skyhawk II	172-80352	N9321F	19. 5.98	
G-BXSF	Cessna 172R Skyhawk II	172-80419	N9967F	15. 5.98	
G-BXSG	Robinson R-22 Beta	2789		3. 2.98	
G-BXSH	Glaser-Dirks DG-800B	8-121B50		5. 2.98	
G-BXSI	Pearce Jabiru SK	PFA/274-13204		5. 2.98	
G-BXSJ	Cameron C-80 HAFB	4330		24. 3.98	
G-BXSK	Beechcraft 76 Duchess	ME-192	EI-CMX N60450	12. 2.98	
G-BXSL	Westland Scout AH.1	F.9762	XW799	17. 2.98	
G-BXSM	Cessna 172R Skyhawk II	172-80320	N432ES	10. 3.98	
G-BXSN	Sikorsky S-61N Mk.II	61-721	EI-BLY C-GPOH/VH-IMQ/VH-PTF/N611EH	17. 2.98	
G-BXSO	Lindstrand LBL-105A HAFB	114	HB-BBJ	18. 2.98	
G-BXSP	Grob G-109B	6335	D-KNEA	25. 3.98	
G-BXSR	Reims Cessna F.172N	2003	PH-SPY D-EITH	6. 2.98	
G-BXSS	Eurocopter AS.365N3 Dauphin 2	6537	F-WQDI(6)	20. 2.98	To JA6OTH 9/98. Canx 1.9.98.
G-BXST	PA-25-235 Pawnee C	25-4952	PH-BAT N8532L	9. 2.98	
G-BXSU	Team Minimax 91A	PFA/186-12357	G-MYGL	20. 2.98	
G-BXSV	Not allocated.				
G-BXSW	Cameron Mountie 120SS HAFB	4299		20. 2.98	
G-BXSX	Cameron V-77 HAFB	4329		6. 4.98	
G-BXSY	Robinson R-22 Beta	2778		27. 1.98	
G-BXSZ	Meridian Ultralights Maverick	PFA/259-12955		24. 2.98	To G-MZLE 27.2.98. Canx.
G-BXTA	Airbus A.320-214	764	F-WWDF	29. 4.98	To G-VTAN 4/99. Canx.
G-BXTB	Cessna 152 II	152-82516	OH-CMS N69151	25. 2.98	
G-BXTC	Taylor JT.1 Monoplane	PFA/55-13142		25. 2.98	
G-BXTD	Europa Avn Europa	PFA/247-12772		26. 2.98	
G-BXTE	Cameron A-275 HAFB	4028		30. 3.98	
G-BXTF	Cameron N-105 HAFB	4304		2. 4.98	
G-BXTG	Cameron N-42 HAFB	4305		2. 4.98	
G-BXTH	Westland Gazelle HT.3	WA/1120	XW866	13. 3.98	
G-BXTI	Pitts S-1S Special (Used c/n NT-1/4591-C in South Africa)	NP-1	ZS-VZX	9. 3.98	
G-BXTJ	Cameron N-77 HAFB	4332		6. 4.98	
G-BXTK	Dornier Do.28D-2	4080	D-IDBB German AF 58+05	15. 5.98	
G-BXTL	Schweizer Hughes 269C-1	0075		13. 3.98	
G-BXTM	Schweizer Hughes 269C-1	0076		13. 3.98	Badly damaged after rolling onto its side on landing at Kidlington on 4.1.99.
G-BXTN	ATR-72-202	483	F-WWEV	24.10.97	
G-BXTO	Hindustan HAL-26 Pushpak	PK-128	9V-BAI VT-DWM	12. 2.98	
G-BXTP	Diamond DA-20-A1 Katana	10306	N636DA	10. 3.98	
G-BXTR	Diamond DA-20-A1 Katana	10307	N607DA	10. 3.98	
G-BXTS	Diamond DA-20-A1 Katana	10308	N638DA	10. 3.98	
G-BXTT	American Aviation AA-5B Cheetah	AA5B-0749	F-GBDH	27. 2.98	
G-BXTU	Robinson R-22 Beta	2790		3. 3.98	
G-BXTV	Bug (Homebuilt single-seat helicopter)	BUG.2		12. 3.98	
G-BXTW	PA-28-181 Archer III	2843137	N41279	26. 2.98	
G-BXTX	PA-28-161 Warrior II	28-8516008	PH-LEH N130AV/N43682	11. 3.98	
G-BXTY	PA-28-161 Cadet	2841179	PH-LED	11. 3.98	
G-BXTZ	PA-28-161 Cadet	2841181	PH-LEE	11. 3.98	
G-BXUA	Campbell Cricket Mk.5	G/03-1272		12. 3.98	
G-BXUB	Lindstrand Syrup Bottle SS HAFB	508		30. 4.98	
G-BXUC	Robinson R-22 Beta	0908	OY-HFB	17. 3.98	
G-BXUD	Agusta A.109E Power	11014		5. 5.98	To G-POWR 7/98. Canx.
G-BXUE	Sky 240-24 HAFB	098		30. 4.98	
G-BXUF	Agusta-Bell 206B JetRanger III	8633	EC-DUS OE-DXE	12. 5.98	
G-BXUG	Lindstrand Baby Bel SS HAFB	512		14. 5.98	
G-BXUH	Lindstrand LBL-31A HAFB	513		2. 6.98	
G-BXUI	Glaser-Dirks DG-800B	8-105B39	BGA.4382 D-KKLC	12. 5.98	
G-BXUJ	Robinson R-22B2 Beta	2775		27. 3.98	To EI-CPO 9/98. Canx 7.9.98.
G-BXUK	Robinson R-44 Astro	0093	D-HIFF	19. 6.95	Extensively damaged after hitting trees on landing at Cliffpark Hall, Rushden Spencer on 11.8.96.
G-BXUL	Vought (Goodyear) FG-1D Corsair (Also quoted as ex BuA.88439; regd as c/n P32823)	3205	N55JP "NZ5611"/R.New Zealand Navy NZ5648/BuA.88391	25. 3.98	
G-BXUM	Europa Avn Europa	PFA/247-12611		19. 3.98	
G-BXUN	Robinson R-44 Clipper	0435		31. 3.98	To CS-HEH 4/98. Canx 15.4.98.
G-BXUO	Lindstrand LBL-105A HAFB	520		27. 3.98	

Regn	Type	c/n	Previous identity	Regn date	Fate or immediate subsequent identity (if known)
G-BXUP	Schweizer 269C (300C)	S.1317	SE-HTB	30. 3.98	
G-BXUR	MDHC Hughes 369E (500E)	0204E	HA-MSC	2. 4.98	To G-OTDB 4/98. Canx.
G-BXUS	Sky 65-24 HAFB	111		6. 4.98	
G-BXUT	PA-34-200 Seneca	34-7250315	N1427T	11. 5.98	
			HB-LMK/N1427T		
G-BXUU	Cameron V-65 HAFB	4362		23. 4.98	
G-BXUV	PA-31-50 Navajo Chieftain		PH-OTH	14. 4.98	Restored as PH-OTH 6/99. Canx 1.6.99.
		31-7552075	N59979		
G-BXUW	Cameron Colt 90A HAFB	4317		23. 4.98	
G-BXUX	Fountain MF Cherry BX-2			14. 4.98	
		PFA/179-12571			
G-BXUY	Cessna 310Q	310Q-0231	N137SA	16. 4.98	
			D-IHMT/N7731Q		
G-BXUZ	Cessna 152 II	152-82810	N89638	14. 4.98	(Fuselage at Stapleford in 8/98)
G-BXVA	Socata TB-200 Tobago XL	1325	F-GJXL	15. 4.98	
			F-WJXL		
G-BXVB	Cessna 152 II	152-82584	N69250	15. 4.98	
G-BXVC	PA-28RT-201T Turbo Arrow IV		D-ELIV(3)	20. 4.98	
		28R-7931113	N2152V		
G-BXVD	CFM Streak Shadow SA	PFA/206-13304		1. 4.98	
G-BXVE	Lindstrand LBL-330A HAFB	492		6. 5.98	
G-BXVF	Thunder Ax11-250 Srs.2 HAFB	4371		22. 5.98	
G-BXVG	Sky 77-24 HAFB	99		28. 5.98	
G-BXVH	Sky 25-16 HAFB	120		23. 4.98	
G-BXVI	Vickers Supermarine 361 Spitfire		6944M	27.12.84	(On rebuild 4/89 - status uncertain)
	LF.XVIe	CBAF/IX/4644	"RF114"/RW386		
G-BXVJ	Cameron O-120 HAFB	2201	PH-VVJ	12. 3.98	
			G-IMAX		
G-BXVK	Robin HR.200/120B	326		1. 7.98	
G-BXVL	Sky 180-24 HAFB	113		16. 6.98	
G-BXVM	Van's RV-6A	PFA/181-13103		26. 2.98	
G-BXVN	Sky 105-24 HAFB	115		17. 8.98	
G-BXVO	Van's RV-6A	PFA/181-12575		28. 4.98	(Almost complete at Sleap in 5/99)
G-BXVP	Sky 31-24 HAFB	056		28. 4.98	
G-BXVR	Sky 90-24 HAFB	061		20. 7.98	
G-BXVS	Brugger MB.2 Colibri	PFA/43-11948		5. 5.98	
G-BXVT	Cameron O-77 HAFB	1444	PH-MKB	30. 7.98	
G-BXVU	PA-28-161 Warrior II	28-7816063	N47372	5. 5.98	
G-BXVV	Cameron V-90 HAFB	4369		5. 5.98	
G-BXVW	Colt Piggy Bank SS HAFB	4366		2. 7.98	
G-BXVX	Rutan Cozy	PFA/159-12680		6. 5.98	
G-BXVY	Cessna 152 II	152-79808	N757KU	11. 5.98	
G-BXVZ	WSK-PZL Mielec TS-11 Iskra	3H16-25	SP-DOF	27. 3.98	
			Polish AF?/SP-DOF		
G-BXWA	Beechcraft 76 Duchess	ME-232	OY-CYM	8. 4.98	
			(SE-IUY)/D-GBTD		
G-BXWB	Pierre Robin HR.100/200B Royale	08	HB-EMT	29. 4.98	
G-BXWC	Cessna 152 II	152-83640	N4794B	11. 5.98	
G-BXWD	Agusta A.109A-II	7266	N565RJ	14. 5.98	
			I-URIA/D-HEMZ/N109BD		
G-BXWE	Fokker F.100-650	11327	PH-CFE	6. 7.98	
			F-GJAO/PH-CFE/PH-EZL/(G-FIOX)/PH-EZL		
G-BXWF	Fokker F.100-650	11328	PH-CFF	13. 7.98	
			F-GKLX/PH-CFF/PH-EZM/(G-FIOY)/PH-EZM		
G-BXWG	Sky 120-24 HAFB	114		28. 5.98	
G-BXWH	Denney Kitfox 4-1200 Sportster			4. 3.98	
		PFA/172A-12343			
G-BXWI	Cameron N-120 HAFB	4395		12. 6.98	
G-BXWJ	Robinson R-22 Beta	1685	N4060W	19. 5.98	
G-BXWK	Rans S-6-ESA Coyote II			19. 5.98	
		PFA/204-13317			
G-BXWL	Sky 90-24 HAFB	117		20. 7.98	
G-BXWM	BAe Jetstream Srs.4124	41102	G-4-102	22. 5.98	To B-HRS 2/99. Canx 22.2.99.
G-BXWN	BAe Jetstream Srs.4124	41104	G-4-104	22. 5.98	To B-HRT 2/99. Canx 22.2.99.
G-BXWO	PA-28-181 Archer II	28-8190311	D-ENHA(2)	22. 5.98	
			N8431C		
G-BXWP	PA-32-300 Cherokee Six	32-7340088	N8143D	26. 5.98	Restored as N8143D 6/98. Canx.
			OE-DRR/N16452		
G-BXWR	CFM Streak Shadow	PFA/206-13205	G-MZMI	22. 5.98	
G-BXWS	Scheibe SF-25E Super Falke	4304	F-CHCG	26. 5.98	
			D-KEYB		
G-BXWT	Van's RV-6	PFA/181-12639		19. 7.96	
G-BXWU	FLS Sprint 160	003	G-70-503	5. 6.98	(Not yet completed 12/98 North Weald)
G-BXWV	FLS Sprint 160	005	G-70-505	5. 6.98	(Not yet completed 12/98 North Weald)
G-BXWW	Robinson R-22 Beta	0847	EI-CCT	2. 6.98	To N82222 8/98. Canx 23.7.98.
			(EI-KMA)/G-STOI		
G-BXWX	Sky 25-16 HAFB	082		29. 5.98	
G-BXWY	Cameron A-105 HAFB	4410		12. 6.98	
G-BXWZ	Cameron A-210 HAFB	4083		9. 6.98	
G-BXXA	ATR-72-202	301	F-WQGJ	27. 4.98	
			F-OHAG/F-WWLY		
G-BXXB	Enstrom 280FX	2006	ZK-HHN	1. 6.98	To G-MHCK 5.6.98. Canx.
			JA7702		

Regn	Type	c/n	Previous identity	Regn date	Fate or immediate subsequent identity (if known)
G-BXXC	Scheibe SF-25C Falke 1700	44151	D-KEFA(2)	3. 6.98	
G-BXXD	Cessna 172R Skyhawk II	172-80068	N9739F	15. 6.98	
G-BXXE	Rand KR-2	PFA/129-10927		8. 6.98	
G-BXXF	Cameron A-210 HAFB	4300		2. 4.98	
G-BXXG	Cameron N-105 HAFB	3662		19. 6.98	
G-BXXH	Hatz CB-1	PFA/143-12445		9. 6.98	
G-BXXI	Grob G-109B	6400	F-CAQR F-WAQR	9. 6.98	
G-BXXJ	Colt Flying Yacht SS HAFB	1797	JA-A015	10. 6.98	
G-BXXK	Reims Cessna F.172N	1806	D-EOPP	15. 6.98	
G-BXXL	Cameron N-105 HAFB	4408		16. 7.98	
G-BXXM	Robinson R-44 Astro	0448		16. 6.98	To CS-H.. Canx 20.8.98.
G-BXXN	Robinson R-22 Beta	0720	N720HH	16. 6.98	
G-BXXO	Lindstrand LBL-90B HAFB	534		6. 7.98	
G-BXXP	Sky 77-24 HAFB	124		20. 7.98	
G-BXXR	AV-8 Gyroplane	G/15-1263		29. 6.98	
G-BXXS	Sky 105-24 HAFB	116		30. 7.98	
G-BXXT	Beechcraft 76 Duchess	ME-212	N212BE F-GBOZ	17. 7.98	
G-BXXU	Colt 31A HAFB	4427		21. 8.98	
G-BXXV	Eurocopter EC-135T-1	0049		2. 7.98	
G-BXXW	Enstrom F-28F	771	JA7823	2. 7.98	To N330SA. Canx 23.7.98.
G-BXXX	Not allocated.				
G-BXXY	PA-34-220T Seneca III	34-8333061	PH-TLN N4295X	3. 7.98	
G-BXXZ	CFM Starstreak Shadow SA-II	PFA/206-13171		19. 5.98	
G-BXYA	Aero CSS-13 Aeroklubowy (Licence built Polikarpov PO-2)	0365	SP-ACP(3) (SP-FCN)/SP-ACN(3)/PLW-...	3. 7.98	To N..... Canx 13.11.98.
G-BXYB	PA-31-300 Turbo Navajo	31-641	G-AXYB 5N-AEQ/G-AXYB/N6736L	23. 1.80	To G-IMBE 11/80. Canx.
G-BXYC	Schweizer 269C	S.1716	D-HFDZ(2)	8. 7.98	
G-BXYD	Eurocopter EC-120B	1006		7. 7.98	
G-BXYE	Scintex CP.301-C1 Emeraude	559	F-BTEO F-PTEO/F-WTEO/F-BJFV	8. 7.98	
G-BXYF	Colt AS-105 GD Airship	4433		7. 8.98	
G-BXYG	Cessna 310D	39089	HB-LSF F-GEJT/3A-MCA/F-BBOT/F-OBOT/(N6789T)	14. 8.98	
G-BXYH	Cameron N-105 HAFB	4441		7. 8.98	
G-BXYI	Cameron H-34 HAFB	4442		7. 8.98	
G-BXYJ	SAN Jodel DR.1050 Ambassadeur	143	F-BJNA	28. 7.98	
G-BXYK	Robinson R-22 Beta	1579	N4037B	27. 7.98	
G-BXYL	Cameron A-275 HAFB	4450		22. 7.98	
G-BXYM	PA-28-235 Cherokee B	28-10858	SE-FAM	18. 8.98	
G-BXYN	Van's RV-6	PFA/181-13265		29. 7.98	
G-BXYO	PA-28RT-201 Arrow IV	28R-8018046	PH-SDD N8164M	18. 8.98	
G-BXYP	PA-28RT-201 Arrow IV	28R-8018050	PH-SBO N8168H	18. 8.98	
G-BXYR	PA-28RT-201 Arrow IV	28R-8018101	PH-SDA N8251B	3. 8.98	
G-BXYS	PA-28RT-201 Arrow IV	28R-7918145	PH-SBS N29561	3. 8.98	
G-BXYT	PA-28RT-201 Arrow IV	28R-7918198	PH-SBN (PH-SBM)/OO-HLA/N2878W	3. 8.98	
G-BXYU	Reims Cessna F.152 II	1804	OH-CKD SE-IFY	31. 7.98	
G-BXYV	ATR-72-202	322	B-22708 F-WWEQ	12.10.98	
G-BXYW	Robinson R-22 Beta	1528	HA-MIU N528SH	4. 8.98	To G-OSMS 2/99. Canx.
G-BXYX	Van's RV-6 (Built by M.T.Hathaway)	22293	N2399C	31. 7.98	
G-BXYY	Reims Cessna FR.172E Rocket	0016	OY-AHO F-WLIP	20. 4.98	
G-BXYZ	Rockwell 690C Commander 840	11620	(G-NATZ) N5872K	7.10.80	To HK-3680 12/91. Canx 10.12.91.
G-BXZA	PA-38-112 Tomahawk	38-79A0864	N2480N	6. 8.98	
G-BXZB	Nanchang CJ-6A	2632019	Chinese PLAF	18. 9.98	
G-BXZC	Not allocated.				
G-BXZD	Westland Gazelle HT.2	WA/1174	XW895	25. 8.98	
G-BXZE	Westland Gazelle HT.3	WA/1228	XW910	25. 8.98	
G-BXZF	Lindstrand LBL-90A HAFB	575		8. 1.99	
G-BXZG	Cameron A-210 HAFB	4424		21. 8.98	
G-BXZH	Cameron A-210 HAFB	4423		21. 8.98	
G-BXZI	Lindstrand LBL-90A HAFB	543		14. 8.98	
G-BXZJ	Sky 70-16 HAFB	131		14. 8.98	
G-BXZK	Boeing MD-900 Explorer	900-00057	G-76-057 N9238T	27. 8.98	
G-BXZL	Bell 47G-5	7801	ZS-HDT Z-WNR/Z-WKC/VP-WKC/ZS-HDT/(ZS-HST)/N8544F	18. 8.98	To N7801R 1/99. Canx 18.1.99.
G-BXZM	Cessna 182S Skylane II	182-80310	N2683L	8.10.98	

Regn	Type	c/n	Previous identity	Regn date	Fate or immediate subsequent identity (if known)
G-BXZN	ATI CH1	00002	N8186E	25. 8.98	
	(A single seat helicopter powered by two tipjets)				
G-BXZO	Pietenpol Air Camper	PFA/47-12818		10. 7.98	
G-BXZP	Pilatus P.3-05	462-11	HB-RCM	25. 8.98	Restored as HB-RCM 2/99. Canx 19.1.99.
			Swiss AF A-824		
G-BXZR	Cameron R 650 Gas Free Balloon	4380		10. 9.98	To HB-BRA 11/98. Canx 26.11.98.
G-BXZS	Sikorsky S-76A (Mod)	760287	N190AL	14. 9.98	
			N190AE/N153AE/N7265A		
G-BXZT	Socata MS.880B Rallye Club	1733	OO-EDG	2. 9.98	
			D-EBDG/F-BSVL		
G-BXZU	Micro Aviation B.22S Bantam	98-015	ZK-JJL	21. 9.98	
G-BXZV	CFM Streak Shadow SA	PFA/206-13357		18. 9.98	
G-BXZW	Fokker F.27-050	20154	OY-MMV	18. 9.98	Restored as OY-MMV 7/99. Canx 8.7.99.
			PH-EXO		
G-BXZX	Bell 206B JetRanger III	2288	N27EA	28. 8.98	
			N286CA/N93AT/N16873		
G-BXZY	CFM Streak Shadow Srs.DD	296-DD		21. 9.98	
G-BXZZ	Sky 160-24 HAFB	109		14. 7.98	
G-BYAA	Boeing 767-204ER	25058	PH-AHM	23. 4.91	
	(Line No.362)		G-BYAA/N60659		
G-BYAB	Boeing 767-204ER	25139	PH-AHN	11. 6.91	
	(Line No.373)		G-BYAB		
G-BYAC	Boeing 757-204ER	26962		10. 4.92	To TC-ARA 4/97. Canx 11.4.97.
	(Line No.440)				
G-BYAD	Boeing 757-204ER	26963		6. 5.92	
	(Line No.450)				
G-BYAE	Boeing 757-204ER	26964		12. 5.92	
	(Line No.452)				
G-BYAF	Boeing 757-204ER	26266		13. 1.93	
	(Line No.514)				
G-BYAG	Boeing 757-204ER	26965		22. 1.93	Skidded off runway on landing at Gerona, Spain on 14.9.99 & DBR.
	(Line No.517)				
G-BYAH	Boeing 757-204ER	26966		5. 2.93	
	(Line No.520)				
G-BYAI	Boeing 757-204	26967		1. 3.93	
	(Line No.522)				
G-BYAJ	Boeing 757-204	25623		4. 3.93	
	(Line No.528)				
G-BYAK	Boeing 757-204	26267		6. 4.93	
	(Line No.538)				
G-BYAL	Boeing 757-204	25626		13. 5.93	
	(Line No.549)				
G-BYAM	Boeing 757-2T7	23895	G-DRJC	15. 3.93	To N513NA 8/99. Canx 16.8.99.
	(Line No.132)				
G-BYAN	Boeing 757-204	27219		26. 1.94	
	(Line No.596)				
G-BYAO	Boeing 757-204	27235		3. 2.94	
	(Line No.598)				
G-BYAP	Boeing 757-204	27236		15. 2.94	
	(Line No.600)				
G-BYAR	Boeing 757-204	27237		1. 3.94	
	(Line No.602) (Originally reportedly reserved with c/n 27227 - a c/n not used)				
G-BYAS	Boeing 757-204	27238		9. 3.94	
	(Line No.604) (Originally reportedly reserved with c/n 27228 - a c/n not used)				
G-BYAT	Boeing 757-204	27208		21. 3.94	
	(Line No.606)				
G-BYAU	Boeing 757-204	27220		18. 5.94	
	(Line No.618)				
G-BYAV	Taylor JT.1 Monoplane	PFA/55-11010		27. 8.98	
G-BYAW	Boeing 757-204	27234		3. 4.95	
	(Line No.663)				
G-BYAX	Boeing 757-204	28834		24. 2.99	
	(Line No.850)				
G-BYAY	Boeing 757-204	28836	N1786B	13. 4.99	
	(Line No.861)				
G-BYAZ	CFM Streak Shadow	PFA/206-12656		1. 9.98	
G-BYBA	Agusta-Bell 206B JetRanger III	8596	G-BHXV	31. 3.98	
			G-OWJM/G-BHXV		
G-BYBB	PA-32RT-300 Lance II	32R-7885144	N31957	25. 1.90	To G-WOZA 5/91. Canx.
G-BYBC	Agusta-Bell 206B JetRanger III	8567	G-BTWW	31. 3.98	
			EI-BJV/G-BTWW		
G-BYBD	Reims Cessna F.172H Skyhawk	0487	G-OBHX	6. 7.98	
			G-AWMU		
G-BYBE	Wassmer Jodel D.120A Paris-Nice	269	OO-FDP	24. 7.98	
G-BYBF	Robin R.2160i Acrobin	329		1.10.98	
G-BYBG	PA-28-181 Archer III	2843157	N47BK	21. 9.98	To G-LACD 11/98. Canx.
G-BYBH	PA-34-200T Seneca II	34-8070078	N4023K	. .98R	[Not officially allocated as at 31.8.99]
			N3567B		
G-BYBI	Bell 206B JetRanger III	3668	ZS-RGP	19.10.98	
			N5757M		
G-BYBJ	Medway Hybred 44XLR	MR156/135		22. 1.99	
G-BYBK	Murphy Rebel	260R	N95LD	19. 8.98	
	(Built by L. Dyer)				

Regn	Type	c/n	Previous identity	Regn date	Fate or immediate subsequent identity (if known)
G-BYBL	Gardan GY-80-160D Horizon	127	F-BMUY	25. 9.98	
G-BYBM	Pearce Jabiru SK	PFA/274-13377		18. 9.98	
G-BYBN	Cameron N-77 HAFB	3082		30. 9.98	
G-BYBO	Medway Hybred 44XLR Eclipser	155/134E		14. 9.98	
G-BYBP	Cessna A.185F Skywagon	A185-03804	(G-WEWE) OO-DCD/(OO-PCN)/F-GDCD/F-ODIA/N4593E	15.10.98	
G-BYBR	Rans S.6-116 Coyote II	PFA/204A-13081		10. 7.98	
G-BYBS	Sky 80-16 HAFB	136		27.10.98	
G-BYBT	Fokker F.27-050	20153	OY-MMU PH-EXN	13.10.98	Restored as OY-MMU 7/99. Canx 7.7.99.
G-BYBU	Murphy Renegade Spirit UK	PFA/188-13229		12.10.98	
G-BYBV	Mainair Rapier	1183-1198-7 & W986		20.10.98	
G-BYBW	Team Minimax	PFA/186-12120		19.10.98	
G-BYBX	Slingsby T.67M Firefly 260	2261		21.10.98	
G-BYBY	Thorp T-18C Tiger (built by K.Knowles)	492	N77KK	17. 7.98	
G-BYBZ	Pearce Jabiru SK	PFA/274-13290		7. 9.98	
G-BYCA	PA-28-140 Cherokee D	28-7125223	PH-VRZ N11C	24. 9.98	
G-BYCB	Sky 21-16 HAFB	142		28.10.98	
G-BYCC	Pearce Jabiru SK	PFA/274-13225		24. 7.98	
G-BYCD	Cessna 140 (Mod)	140-13744	N4273N NC4273N	28. 9.98	
G-BYCE	Robinson R-44 Astro	0520		12.10.98	
G-BYCF	Robinson R-22 B2 Beta	2866		12.10.98	
G-BYCG	Agusta-Bell 47G-3B1	1513	EC-EGO Spanish AF HE.7B-22/751-12 / Z.7B-22	12.10.98	Canx by CAA 9.2.99.
G-BYCH	Agusta-Bell 47G-4A	2519	EC-BMB Italian AF MM80504	12.10.98	Canx by CAA 9.2.99.
G-BYCI	Agusta-Bell 47G-4A	2530	EC-BSC	12.10.98	Canx by CAA 9.2.99.
G-BYCJ	CFM Streak Shadow Srs.DD	PFA/161-13258		14.10.98	
G-BYCK	Robinson R-22 Beta	1478	N101EJ	20.10.98	To G-XTEC 23.10.98. Canx.
G-BYCL	X'Air	BMAA/HB/088		15.10.98	
G-BYCM	Rans S.6-ES Coyote II	PFA/204-13315		15. 9.98	
G-BYCN	Rans S.6-ES Coyote II	PFA/204-13314		15. 9.98	
G-BYCO	Rans S.6-ES Coyote II	PFA/204-13318		17. 9.98	
G-BYCP	Beechcraft B200 Super King Air	BB-966	F-GDCS	15.10.98	
G-BYCR	Stoddard-Hamilton Glastar	PFA/295-13241		28.10.98	Not completed. To G-LEZZ 4.11.98. Canx.
G-BYCS	CEA Jodel DR.1051 Sicile	201	F-BJUJ	28.10.98	
G-BYCT	Aero L-29A Delfin	395142	ES-YLH Estonian AF/Soviet AF	29.10.98	
G-BYCU	Robinson R-22 Beta	1094	G-OCGJ	3.11.98	
G-BYCV	Meridian Ultralights Maverick	PFA/259-12955		24. 9.98	
G-BYCW	Mainair Blade	1185-1198-7 & W988		5.11.98	
G-BYCX	Westland Wasp HAS.1B (Reg with c/n "W1A-B-Z3") (Fuselage no. WA-B-23)	F.9754	ZK-HOX South African AF 92	9.11.98	
G-BYCY	Iniziative Industriali Italian Sky Arrow 650T	PFA/298-13332		10.11.98	
G-BYCZ	Pearce Jabiru SK	PFA/274-13388		16.10.98	
G-BYDA	Douglas DC-10-30 (Line No. 260)	46990	OY-CNO XA-SYE/F-GGMZ/C-GFHX/9V-SDA	25. 3.99	
G-BYDB	Grob G-115C	8025	D-EUGB VH-JVL/D-EFCG(2)	26. 3.99	
G-BYDC	Socata TB-10 Tobago	146	F-GCOL	11.11.98	To G-IGGL 3/99. Canx.
G-BYDD	Mooney M.20J	24-0847	D-EIWM	19.10.98	
G-BYDE	Vickers-Supermarine 361 Spitfire IX	CBAF/IX/....	Soviet AF PT879	11.11.98	
G-BYDF	Sikorsky S-76A	760364	JA6615	9. 1.98	
G-BYDG	Beechcraft C-24R Sierra	MC-627	OY-AZL	9.11.98	
G-BYDH	Airbus A.300B4-203F	210	F-OHPO F-WHPK/SX-BAZ/N213PA/F-WZMK	14. 1.99	(Stored at Filton 4/99 as F-WHPK)
G-BYDI	Cameron A-210 HAFB	4495		4. 2.99	
G-BYDJ	Colt 120A HAFB	3527		17.11.98	
G-BYDK	Stampe SV-4C	55	F-BCXY(2)	20.11.98	
G-BYDL	Hawker Hurricane IIB (Gloster built)	-	Soviet AF Z5207	17.11.98	
G-BYDM	Cyclone Pegasus Quantum 15	7488		18.11.98	
G-BYDN	Fokker F.100-650	11329	N130ML SE-DUF/PH-CFE/PH-EZV/(G-FIOZ)/PH-EZV	4. 6.99	
G-BYDO	Fokker F.100-650	11323	N131ML SE-DUB/PH-CFA/(PH-LNP)/PH-EZC/(G-FIOT)/PH-EZC	17. 3.99	
G-BYDP	Fokker F.100-650	11321	(F-WQJA) N132ML/SE-DUA/PH-RRC/(G-FIOS)/PH-EZA	18. 2.99	
G-BYDR	North American B-25D-30NC Mitchell Mk.II	100-20644	N88972 CF-OGQ/RCAF KL161/43-3318	22. 3.99	(At Duxford 7/99)

Regn	Type	c/n	Previous identity	Regn date	Fate or immediate subsequent identity (if known)
G-BYDS	Messerschmitt Bf.109E-3	1342	Luftwaffe	24.11.98	(On rebuild in UK 11/98)
	(Recovered from a beach at Wissant, France in 1988)				
G-BYDT	Cameron N-90 HAFB	4499		28. 1.99	
G-BYDU	Cameron Cart SS HAFB	4500		28. 1.99	
G-BYDV	Van's RV-6	PFA/181-13264		3.11.98	
G-BYDW	Rotary Air Force 2000 GTX-SE	G/13-1302		1.12.98	
G-BYDX	American General AG-5B Tiger	10051	N374SA	6. 1.99	
			G-BYDX/F-GKBH/N1191Y		
G-BYDY	Beechcraft 58 Baron	TH-1852	C-GBWF	10.11.98	
G-BYDZ	Cyclone Pegasus Quantum 15	7493		22.12.98	
G-BYEA	Cessna 172P Skyhawk	172-75464	PH-ILL	7.10.98	
			(PH-JLL)/N63661		
G-BYEB	Cessna 172P Skyhawk	172-74634	PH-ILM	7.10.98	
			(PH-JLM)/N52917		
G-BYEC	Glaser-Dirks DG-800B	8-102B36	D-KSDG	13.11.98	
G-BYED	BAC P.84 Jet Provost T.5A	EEP/JP/966	N166A	23.11.98	
			XW302		
G-BYEE	Mooney M.20K (231)	25-0282	N231JZ	20. 7.88	
G-BYEF	Lockheed L.188CF Electra	2086	EI-CHX	14.12.98	
			SE-IVR/N853U/PH-LLC		
G-BYEG	Cessna 182S Skylane II	182-80404	N23697	3. 3.99	
G-BYEH	CEA Jodel DR.250/160 Capitaine	15	OO-SOL	6.10.98	
			F-BMZL		
G-BYEI	Cameron Chick 90SS HAFB	4519		1. 4.99	
G-BYEJ	Scheibe SF-28A Tandem Falke	5713	OE-9070	18.12.98	
			(D-KDAM)		
G-BYEK	Stoddard-Hamilton Glastar	PFA/295-13087		14. 9.98	
G-BYEL	Van's RV-6	PFA/181-12560		7. 1.99	
G-BYEM	Cessna R182 Skylane RG	R182-00822	N494	8. 1.99	
			D-EVLI/N737FT		
G-BYEN	Cessna 172P Skyhawk	172-74163	PH-ILU	6.10.98	
			(PH-JLU)/N97003		
G-BYEO	Zenair CH.601HDS Zodiac	PFA/162-13345		11. 1.99	
G-BYEP	Lindstrand LBL-90B HAFB	560		20.11.98	
G-BYER	Cameron C-80 HAFB	4513		19.11.98	
G-BYES	Cessna 172P Skyhawk II	172-74514	PH-ILN(2)	7.10.98	
			(PH-JLN)/N172TP/N52424		
G-BYET	Cessna 172P Skyhawk II	172-75122	PH-ILP(3)	7.10.98	
			(PH-JLP)/N55158		
G-BYEU	Cyclone Pegasus Quantum 15	7495		28. 1.99	
G-BYEV	Cessna 172R Skyhawk II	172-80663	N2377J	9. 2.99	To G-LAVE 10.3.99. Canx.
			N41297		
G-BYEW	Cyclone Pegasus Quantum 15	7499		15. 1.99	
G-BYEX	Sky 120-24 HAFB	135		21. 1.99	
G-BYEY	Lindstrand LBL-21 Silver Dream HAFB	577		15. 1.99	
G-BYEZ	Dyn'Aero MCR-01	PFA/301-13185		25.11.98	
G-BYFA	Reims Cessna F.152 II	1968	G-WACA	19.11.98	
G-BYFB	Cameron N-105 HAFB	4532		15. 1.99	
G-BYFC	Pearce Jabiru SK	PFA/274-13344		5. 2.99	
G-BYFD	Grob G-115A	8100	EI-CCN	30. 4.99	
			G-BSGE/(VH-...)/(D-EGVV)		
G-BYFE	Cyclone Pegasus Quantum 15	7496		21. 6.99	
G-BYFF	Cyclone Pegasus Quantum 15	7500		1. 2.99	
G-BYFG	Europa Avn Europa XS	PFA/247-13407		22. 1.99	
G-BYFH	Bede BD-5B	665		22. 1.99	
G-BYFI	CFM Starstreak Shadow SA	PFA/206-13300		11. 2.99	
G-BYFJ	Cameron N-105 HAFB	4545		4. 3.99	
G-BYFK	Cameron Printer 105SS HAFB	4522		4. 3.99	
G-BYFL	Hoffmann HK-36TTS Super Dimona	36623		5. 2.99	
G-BYFM	CEA Jodel DR.1050/M1 Sicile Record	PFA/304-13237		26. 2.99	
G-BYFN	Thruster T.600N	9029-T600N-030		8. 2.99	
G-BYFO	HS.125 Srs.700B	257040	HB-VMD	11. 2.99	To G-OWDB 18.2.99. Canx.
			VP-BPE/VR-BPE/N47TJ/EC-ETI/EC-375/G-OWEB/HZ-RC1		
G-BYFP	PA-28-181 Archer II	2843238	N4137N	5. 7.99	
			G-BYFP/N41270		
G-BYFR	PA-32R-301 Saratoga II HP	3246133		13. 4.99	
G-BYFS	Airbus A.320-231	230	(D-AFRO)	27. 3.99	To D-AFRO(2) 4/99. Canx 14.4.99.
			A40-MA/N230RX/SX-BSJ/N230RX/F-WWDI		
G-BYFT	Pietenpol Air Camper	PFA/47-13057		22.12.98	
G-BYFU	Lindstrand LBL-105B HAFB	594		9. 3.99	
G-BYFV	Team Minimax 91	PFA/186-13431		5. 2.99	
G-BYFW	Cameron Rugby 90SS HAFB	4533		4. 3.99	
G-BYFX	Colt 77A HAFB	4547		4. 3.99	
G-BYFY	Mudry CAP.10B	263	F-GKKD	9. 3.99	
G-BYFZ	Cessna TU.206G Turbo Stationair II	U206-05128	EC-ESG	8. 3.99	To N206TG 3/99. Canx 9.3.99.
			N4855U		

Regn	Type	c/n	Previous identity	Regn date	Fate or immediate subsequent identity (if known)
G-BYGA	Boeing 747-436 (Line No. 1190)	28855		15.12.98	
G-BYGB	Boeing 747-436 (Line No. 1194)	28856		17. 1.99	
G-BYGC	Boeing 747-436 (Line No. 1195)	25823		19. 1.99	
G-BYGD	Boeing 747-436 (Line No. 1196)	28857		26. 1.99	
G-BYGE	Boeing 747-436 (Line No. 1198)	28858		5. 2.99	
G-BYGF	Boeing 747-436 (Line No. 1200)	25824		17. 2.99	
G-BYGG	Boeing 747-436 (Line No. 1212)	28859		29. 4.99	
G-BYGH	Boeing 747-436	28860		. .98R	NTU - Not built. Canx in 5/99.
G-BYGI	Boeing 747-436	-		. .98R	NTU - Canx in 5/99.
G-BYGJ	Boeing 747-436	-		. .98R	NTU - Canx in 5/99.
G-BYGK	Boeing 747-436	-		. .98R	NTU - Canx in 5/99.
G-BYGL	Boeing 747-436	-		. .98R	NTU - Canx in 5/99.
G-BYGM	Boeing 747-436	-		. .98R	NTU - Canx in 5/99.
G-BYGN	Boeing 747-436	-		. .98R	NTU - Canx in 5/99.
G-BYGO	Boeing 747-436	-		. .98R	NTU - Canx in 5/99.
G-BYGP	Boeing 747-436	-		. .98R	NTU - Canx in 5/99.
G-BYGR	Boeing 747-436	-		. .98R	NTU - Canx 25.8.98.
G-BYGS	Boeing 747-436	-		. .98R	NTU - Canx 25.8.98.
G-BYGT	Boeing 747-436	-		. .98R	NTU - Canx 25.8.98.
G-BYGU	Boeing 747-436	-		. .98R	NTU - Canx 25.8.98.
G-BYGV	Boeing 747-436	-		. .98R	NTU - Canx 25.8.98.
G-BYGW	Boeing 747-436	-		. .98R	NTU - Canx 15.4.98.
G-BYGX	Boeing 747-436	-		. .98R	NTU - Canx 15.4.98.
G-BYGY	Boeing 747-436	-		. .98R	NTU - Canx 15.4.98.
G-BYGZ	Boeing 747-436	-		. .98R	NTU - Canx 15.4.98.
G-BYHA	ATR-42-320	190	HS-TRK F-WWEF	15.12.98	To I-RIMS 6/99. Canx 26.7.99.
G-BYHB	ATR-42-320	206	HS-TRL F-WWEU	15.12.98	To I-RIML 6/99. Canx 23.8.99.
G-BYHC	Cameron Z-90 HAFB	4555		16. 3.99	
G-BYHD	Robinson R-22 Beta	1455	N900AB	22. 3.99	
G-BYHE	Robinson R-22 Beta	2023	N82128 LV-VAB	14. 1.99	
G-BYHF	Dornier 328-110	3050	N350AD D-CAOT(7)/(D-CDXR)	18. 3.99	
G-BYHG	Dornier 328-110	3098	D-CDAE D-CDXZ(3)	7. 4.99	
G-BYHH	PA-28-161 Warrior III	2842050	N4126Z	15. 6.99	
G-BYHI	PA-28-161 Warrior II	28-8116084	SE-IDP	4. 1.99	
G-BYHJ	[Not officially allocated as at 31.8.99]				
G-BYHK	PA-28-181 Archer II	2843240	N4128V G-BYHK/N9519N	20. 5.99	
G-BYHL	DHC.1 Chipmunk 22 (Regd with fuselage no. DHB/f/260 as c/n)	C1/0361	WG308	15. 3.99	
G-BYHM	BAe 125 Srs.800B	258233	VP-BTM VR-BTM/(VR-BQH)/F-WQCD/D-CAVW/G-5-770	12. 2.99	
G-BYHN	Mainair Blade	1191-0399-7 & W994		9. 4.99	
G-BYHO	Mainair Blade	1197-0599-7 & W1000		16. 3.99	
G-BYHP	CEA DR.253B Regent	161	OO-CSK	29. 3.99	
G-BYHR	Cyclone Pegasus Quantum 15	7518		6. 4.99	
G-BYHS	Mainair Blade	1187-0299-7 & W990		11. 3.99	
G-BYHT	Robin DR.400/180R Remorqueur	811	HB-EUU	9. 4.99	
G-BYHU	Cameron N-105 HAFB	4567		30. 4.99	
G-BYHV	X'Air	BMAA/HB/090		25. 3.99	
G-BYHW	Cameron A-160 HAFB	2848	D-OWEH	25. 3.99	
G-BYHX	Cameron AS-250 HAFB	4565		16. 4.99	
G-BYHY	Cameron V-77 HAFB	4493		22. 3.99	
G-BYHZ	Sky 160-24 HAFB	140		13. 5.99	
G-BYIA	Pearce Jabiru SK	PFA/274-13436		10. 2.99	
G-BYIB	Rans S.6-ES Coyote II	PFA/204-13387		26. 3.99	
G-BYIC	Cessna TU.206G Turbo Stationair 6 Floatplane	TU206-05476	OY-NUA N113RS/N3RS/N6398U	27. 4.99	
G-BYID(1)	Pierre Robin HR.200/120B	334		9. 4.99R	NTU - To G-NSOF 6/99. Canx.
G-BYID(2)	Rans S.6-ES Coyote II	PFA/204-13348		11. 5.99	
G-BYIE	Robinson R-22 Beta	2933		22. 4.99	
G-BYIF	Pearce Jabiru XL	PFA/274A-13364		26. 3.99	(Struck trees on landing at Stowting, near Ashford, Kent on 24.7.99)
G-BYIG	Murphy Renegade Spirit UK	PFA/188-12519		26. 2.99	
G-BYIH	[Not officially allocated as at 31.8.99]				
G-BYII	Team Minimax	PFA/186-11820		22. 1.99	
G-BYIJ	CASA I-131E Jungmann Srs.2000	2110	E3B-514 Spanish AF	16. 7.90	
G-BYIK	Europa Avn Europa	PFA/247-12771		2. 2.99	
G-BYIL	Cameron N-105 HAFB	4591		29. 4.99	
G-BYIM	Pearce Jabiru UL	PFA/274A-13397		22.12.98	

Regn	Type	c/n	Previous identity	Regn date	Fate or immediate subsequent identity (if known)
G-BYIN	Rotary Air Force RAF 2000	G/13-1305		19. 1.99	
G-BYIO	Colt 105A HAFB	4601		30. 4.99	
G-BYIP	Aerotek Pitts S-2A Special	2244	N109WA TC-ECN	23. 2.99	
G-BYIR	Aerotek Pitts S-1S Special	1-0063	N103WA TC-ECP	23. 2.99	
G-BYIS	Cyclone Pegasus Quantum 15	7508		25. 2.99	
G-BYIT	Pierre Robin DR.400/500	0010		27. 1.99	
G-BYIU	Cameron V-90 HAFB	4552		6. 4.99	
G-BYIV	Cameron PM-80 HAFB	4595		14. 5.99	
G-BYIW	Cameron PM-80 HAFB	4596		14. 5.99	
G-BYIX	Cameron PM-80 HAFB	4597		14. 5.99	
G-BYIY	Lindstrand LBL-105B HAFB	601		26. 3.99	
G-BYIZ	Cyclone Pegasus Quantum 15	7504		8. 2.99	
G-BYJA	Rotary Air Force RAF 2000 GTX SE	G/13-1297		6. 4.99	
G-BYJB	Mainair Blade	1192-0499-7 & W995		6. 4.99	
G-BYJC	Cameron N-90 HAFB	4562		30. 4.99	
G-BYJD	Pearce Jabiru UL	PFA/274-13376		16. 4.99	
G-BYJE	Team Minimax 91	PFA/186-12327		6. 4.99	
G-BYJF	Thorp T.211	107	N2545C	20. 5.99	
G-BYJG	Lindstrand LBL-77A HAFB	600		16. 4.99	
G-BYJH	Grob G.109B	6512	D-KFRI	19. 5.99	
G-BYJI	Europa Avn Europa	004 & PFA/247-13010	G-ODTI	19. 4.99	
G-BYJJ	Cameron C-80 HAFB	4436	(SX-MAX)	20. 4.99	
G-BYJK	Cyclone Pegasus Quantum 15	7524		7. 5.99	
G-BYJL	Aero Designs Pulsar	PFA/202-13311		20. 4.99	
G-BYJM	Cyclone Pegasus Quantum 15	7523		25. 5.99	
G-BYJN	Lindstrand LBL-105A HAFB	605		30. 4.99	
G-BYJO	Rans S.6-ES Coyote II	PFA/204-13338		4. 3.99	
G-BYJP	Aerotek Pitts S-1S Special	1-0064	N105WA TC-ECR	16. 3.99	
G-BYJR	Lindstrand LBL-77B HAFB	608		30. 4.99	
G-BYJS	Socata TB-20 Trinidad	1875	F-OIGE	15. 1.99	
G-BYJT	Zenair CH.601HD Zodiac	PFA/162-13130		4. 5.99	
G-BYJU	X'Air	396		6. 5.99	
G-BYJV	Cameron A-210 HAFB	4612		4. 6.99	
G-BYJW	Cameron Sphere 105SS HAFB	4585		15. 6.99	
G-BYJX	Cameron C-70 HAFB	4580		30. 4.99	
G-BYJY	Lindstrand Pharmarcist SS HAFB	581		19. 4.99	
G-BYJZ	Lindstrand LBL-105A HAFB	609		27. 5.99	
G-BYKA	Lindstrand LBL-69A HAFB	612		7. 5.99	
G-BYKB	Rockwell Commander 114	14121	SE-GSM N4801W	18. 5.99	
G-BYKC	Mainair Blade	1196-0599-7 & W999		7. 5.99	
G-BYKD	Mainair Blade	1198-0599-7 & W1001		7. 5.99	
G-BYKE	Rans S.6-ESA Coyote II	PFA/204-13327		22. 1.99	
G-BYKF	Enstrom F-28F	725	JA7684	19. 5.99	
G-BYKG	Pietenpol Air Camper	PFA/47-12827		17. 3.99	
G-BYKH	Aerospatiale AS.355F2 Twin Squirrel	5169	SX-HNP VR-CCM/N57967	27. 7.99	To G-EMHH 3.8.99. Canx.
G-BYKI	Cameron N-105 HAFB	4635		4. 6.99	
G-BYKJ	Westland Scout AH.1 (Officially regd with c/n F8-6043 - 'pod' build no.)	F.9696	XV121	6. 8.99	
G-BYKK	Robinson R-44 Astro	0572		4. 3.99	
G-BYKL	PA-28-181 Archer II	28-8090162	HB-PFB N8129Y	15. 7.99	
G-BYKM	PA-34-220T Seneca III	34-8133177	HB-LMV	22. 6.99	
G-BYKN	PA-28-161 Warrior II	28-7916307	HB-PDO N2838C/N9613N	22. 6.99	
G-BYKO	PA-28-161 Warrior II	28-8516063	HB-PKA F-GECN/N6920C	22. 6.99	
G-BYKP	PA-28RT-201T Turbo Arrow IV	28R-7931029	HB-PDB N3010G	22. 6.99	
G-BYKR	PA-28-161 Warrior II	2816061	HB-PLM	22. 6.99	
G-BYKS	Leopoldoff L.6 Colibri	129	N10LC F-BGIT/F-WGIT	19. 4.99	
G-BYKT	Cyclone Pegasus Quantum 15	7529		28. 5.99	
G-BYKU	BFC Quad City Challenger II	PFA/177A-13252		25. 5.99	
G-BYKV	Avro 504K Replica	0015		27. 5.99	
G-BYKW	Lindstrand LBL-77B HAFB	620		22. 6.99	
G-BYKX	Cameron N-90 HAFB	4657		10. 8.99	
G-BYKY	Pearce Jabiru SK	PFA/274-13385		6. 5.99	
G-BYKZ	Sky 140-24 HAFB	147		25. 2.99	
G-BYLA	Clutton-Tabenor Fred Srs.III	PFA/29-10775		11. 5.99	
G-BYLB	DH.82A Tiger Moth	83286	T5595	24. 5.99	
G-BYLC	Cyclone Pegasus Quantum 15	7528		25. 6.99	
G-BYLD	Pietenpol Air Camper	PFA/47-13392		27. 4.99	

Regn	Type	c/n	Previous identity	Regn date	Fate or immediate subsequent identity (if known)
G-BYLE	PA-38-112 Tomahawk II	38-82A0031	N91437	18. 6.99	
G-BYLF	Zenair CH.601HDS	PFA/162-13179		3. 6.99	
G-BYLG	Pierre Robin HR.200/120B	336		20. 7.99	
G-BYLH	Pierre Robin HR.200/120B	335		9. 7.99	
G-BYLI	Nova Vertex 22	14319		9. 4.99	
	(Austrian built Hang-Glider)				
G-BYLJ	Letov LK-2M Sluka	PFA/263-13464		9. 6.99	
G-BYLK	Mainair Blade	1201-0699-7 & W1004		9. 6.99	
G-BYLL	Sequoia Falco F.8L	PFA/100-10843		6.12.85	
G-BYLM	PA-46-350P Malibu Mirage	4636217		30. 7.99	
G-BYLN	X'Air	BMAA/HB/096		7. 7.99	
G-BYLO	Tipsy Nipper T.66 Srs.1	04	OO-NIA	27. 4.99	
G-BYLP	Rand-Robinson KR-2	PFA/129-11431		19. 4.99	
G-BYLR	Cessna 404 Titan	404-0046	OH-CDC	14. 6.99	
			SE-GZH/N5428G		
G-BYLS	Bede BD-4	PFA/37-11288		13.12.90	
G-BYLT	X'Air	BMAA/HB/005		8. 6.99	
G-BYLU	Cameron A-140 HAFB	4566		22. 6.99	
G-BYLV	Thunder Ax8-105 Srs.2 HAFB	4061		6. 7.99	
G-BYLW	Lindstrand LBL-77A HAFB	615		11. 6.99	
G-BYLX	Lindstrand LBL-105A HAFB	614		11. 6.99	
G-BYLY	Cameron V-77 HAFB	3375	G-ULIA(2)	16. 7.97	
G-BYLZ	Rutan Cozy	PFA/159-12464		21. 5.99	
G-BYMA	BAe Jetstream Srs.3202	840	(G-OESU)	28. 7.99	
			OH-JAE/N840JX/C-GSCS/G-31-840/N332QK/G-31-840		
G-BYMB	Diamond DA-20-C1 Katana	C0051		9. 7.99	
G-BYMC	PA-38-112 Tomahawk II	38-82A0034	N91457	18. 6.99	
G-BYMD	PA-38-112 Tomahawk II	38-82A0009	N91342	18. 6.99	
G-BYME	Sud Gardan GY-80-180 Horizon	207	F-BPAA	24. 5.99	
G-BYMF	Cyclone Pegasus Quantum 15	7540		9. 7.99	
G-BYMG	Cameron A-210 HAFB	4631		17. 9.99	
G-BYMH	Cessna 152 II	152-84980	N6127P	15. 7.99	
G-BYMI	Cyclone Pegasus Quantum 15	7533		9. 7.99	
G-BYMJ	Cessna 152 II	152-85564	N93865	16. 7.99	
G-BYMK	Dornier 328-110	3062	LN-ASK	6. 6.99	
			D-CDXE(2)		
G-BYML	Dornier 328-110	3069	D-CDUL	27. 7.99	
			LN-ASL/D-CDXT(2)		
G-BYMM	Raj Hamsa X'Air	417 & BMAA/HB/093		29. 4.99	Stolen from Chilbolton Airfield on 15.9.99.
G-BYMN	Rans S.6-ESA Coyote II	PFA/204-13477		16. 6.99	
G-BYMO	Campbell Cricket	G/03-1266		16. 7.99	
G-BYMP	Campbell Cricket Mk.1	G/03-1265		16. 6.99	
G-BYMR	X'Air	BMAA/HB/094		18. 6.99	
G-BYMS	Agusta A.109E Power	11053		3. 8.99	
G-BYMT	Cyclone Pegasus Quantum 15	7549		16. 7.99	
G-BYMU	Rans S.6-ES Coyote II	PFA/204-13424		25. 6.99	
G-BYMV	Rans S.6-ES Coyote II	PFA/204-13444		25. 6.99	
G-BYMW	Boland 52-12	001		25. 6.99	
	(built by C.Jones, and is engineless - a balloon prehaps!)				
G-BYMX	Cameron A-105 HAFB	4629		16. 7.99	
G-BYMY	Cameron N-90 HAFB	4653		19. 7.99	
G-BYMZ	[Not officially allocated as at 31.8.99]				
G-BYNA	Reims Cessna F.172H Skyhawk	0626	OO-VDW	15. 1.99	
			PH-VDW/(G-AWTH)/F-WLIT		
G-BYNB	Boeing 737-804	30466		. 7.99R	
G-BYNC	Boeing 737-804	28321		. 7.99R	(delivery due 4/00)
G-BYND	Cyclone Pegasus Quantum 15	7546		16. 7.99	
G-BYNE	Pilatus PC-6/B2-H4 Turbo Porter	631	HB-FLW	10. 8.99	
			C-FRAV/N631SA/N62128/HS-.../N62148/XW-PFC/XW-PDK/HB-FCR		
G-BYNF	[Not officially allocated as at 31.8.99]				
G-BYNG	Cessna T.303 Crusader	T303-00306	G-PTWB	3.11.88	Restored as G-PTWB 7/99. Canx.
			(G-BLRS)/N6312V		
G-BYNH	Rotorway Exec 162F	6323		5. 7.99	
G-BYNI	Rotorway Exec 90	5216		16. 7.99	
G-BYNJ	Cameron N-77 HAFB	4661		26. 7.99	
G-BYNK	Pierre Robin HR.200/160	338		28. 7.99	
G-BYNL	Pearce Jabiru SK	PFA/274-13328		20. 7.99	
G-BYNM	Mainair Blade	1204-0799-7 & W1007		20. 7.99	
G-BYNN	Cameron V-90 HAFB	4643		16. 7.99	
G-BYNO	Cyclone Pegasus Quantum 15	7556		5. 8.99	
G-BYNP	Rans S.6-ES Coyote II	PFA/204-13414		22. 7.99	
G-BYNR	Pearce Jabiru UL	0129	EI-MAT	23. 7.99	
G-BYNS	Pearce Jabiru SK	PFA/274-13235		23. 7.99	
G-BYNT	X'Air	BMAA/HB/107		20. 7.99	
G-BYNU	Cameron/Thunder Ax7-77 HAFB	3520		29. 7.99	
G-BYNV	Sky 105-24 HAFB	165		11. 8.99	
G-BYNW	Cameron H-34 HAFB	4666		27. 7.99	
G-BYNX	Cameron RX-105 HAFB	4656		26. 7.99	
G-BYNY	Beechcraft 76 Duchess	ME-247	N247ME	4. 8.99	
			OE-FES/N6635H		
G-BYNZ	Westland Scout AH.1	F.9736	XW281	6. 8.99	
	(Officially regd with c/n F8-9047 - 'pod' build no.)				

Regn	Type	c/n	Previous identity	Regn date	Fate or immediate subsequent identity (if known)
G-BYOA	Slingsby T.67M Firefly 260	2262		8. 6.99	
G-BYOB	Slingsby T.67M Firefly 260	2263		8. 6.99	
G-BYOC	[Not officially allocated as at 31.8.99]				
G-BYOD	[Not officially allocated as at 31.8.99]				
G-BYOE	[Not officially allocated as at 31.8.99]				
G-BYOF	Robin R.2160i Acrobin	337		29. 7.99	
G-BYOG	Cyclone Pegasus Quantum 15	7555		15. 9.99	
G-BYOH	X'Air	BMAA/HB/101		23. 7.99	
G-BYOI	Sky 80-16 HAFB	163		5. 8.99	
G-BYOJ	X'Air	BMAA/HB/108		23. 7.99	
G-BYOK	Cameron V-90 HAFB	3726		9. 8.99	
G-BYOL	Cessna 340A II	340A-0439	N6242X	30. 5.89	To N93DR 5/93. Canx 6.5.93.
G-BYOM	Sikorsky S-76C (Mod)	760464	G-IJCB	25. 8.99	
G-BYON	Mainair Blade	1199-0599-7 & W1002		4. 8.99	
G-BYOO	CFM Streak Shadow	PFA/206-12806		6. 8.99	
G-BYOP	Robinson R-22 Beta	1682	N4072S	17. 8.99	
G-BYOR	X'Air	BMAA/HB/117		11. 8.99	
G-BYOS	Mainair Blade	1209-0899-7 & W1012		6. 8.99	
G-BYOT	Rans S.6-ES Coyote II	PFA/204-13363		29. 7.99	
G-BYOU	Rans S.6-ES Coyote II	PFA/204-13460		1. 6.99	
G-BYOV	Cyclone Pegasus Quantum 15	7554		17. 8.99	
G-BYOW	Mainair Blade	1207-0899-7 & W1010		9. 8.99	
G-BYOX	Cameron Z-90 HAFB	4672		31. 8.99	
G-BYOY	[Not officially allocated as at 31.8.99]				
G-BYOZ	Mainair Rapier	1208-0899-7 & W1011		12. 8.99	
G-BYPA	Aerospatiale AS.355F2 Twin Squirrel		G-NWPI	20. 8.99	
		5348	F-GMAO		
G-BYPB	Cyclone Pegasus Quantum 15	7566		3. 9.99	
G-BYPC	Lindstrand LBL-AS2 HAFB	634		17. 8.99	
G-BYPD	[Not officially allocated as at 31.8.99]				
G-BYPE	Sud Gardan GY-80-160D Horizon	180	F-BNYD	10. 8.99	
G-BYPF	Thruster T.600N	9089-T600N-034		17. 8.99	
G-BYPG	Thruster T.600N	9089-T600N-035		17. 8.99	
G-BYPH	Thruster T.600N	9089-T600N-036		17. 8.99	
G-BYPI	Thruster T.600N	9089-T600N-037		17. 8.99	
G-BYPJ	Cyclone Pegasus Quantum 15	7565		17. 9.99	
G-BYPK	Europa Avn Europa	PFA/247-13502		20. 8.99	
G-BYPL	Cyclone Pegasus Quantum 15	7558		9. 9.99	
G-BYPM	Europa Avn Europa XS	PFA/247-13418		16.12.98	
G-BYPN	Socata MS.880B Rallye Club	2043	F-BTPN	23. 7.99	
G-BYPO	Raj Hamsa X'Air	BMAA/HB/111		25. 8.99	
G-BYPP	[Not officially allocated as at 31.8.99]				
G-BYPR	Zenair CH.601HD Zodiac			25. 8.99	
		PFA/162-12816			
G-BYPS	Cameron Carrots 80SS HAFB	2258		20. 3.90	To G-HUCH 3/91. Canx.
G-BYPT	Rans S.6-ES Coyote II	PFA/204-13508		27. 8.99	
G-BYPU	[Not officially allocated as at 31.8.99]				
G-BYPV	Cameron Colt 120A HAFB	4628		31. 8.99	
G-BYPW	Raj Hamsa X'Air	BMAA/HB/113		1. 9.99	
G-BYPX	[Not officially allocated as at 31.8.99]				
G-BYPY	Ryan ST3-KR	1001	F-AZEV	. 9.99R	
			N18926		
G-BYPZ	Rans S.6-116 Coyote II			14. 7.99	
		PFA/204A-13448			
G-BYRA	BAe Jetstream Srs.3101	845	OH-JAG	. 9.99R	
			N845JX/N845AE/N374MT/G-31-845		
G-BYRB					
G-BYRC					
G-BYRD	Mooney M.20K (231)	25-0507	N97310	2. 3.81	Fuselage broken in two on overshoot on landing at East Winch on 30.8.93. Canx as WFU 9.12.93.
G-BYRE	Rans S-10 Sakota	PFA/194-11729		23. 7.91	No Permit to Fly issued. Canx by CAA 8.5.99.
G-BYRF					
G-BYRG	Rans S.6-ES Coyote II	PFA/204-13518		9. 9.99	
G-BYRH					
G-BYRI					
G-BYRJ					
G-BYRK	Cameron V-42 HAFB	4662		14. 7.99	
G-BYRL					
G-BYRM					
G-BYRN	PA-31-350 Navajo Chieftain		G-YLAN	22. 5.90	To N100RN 9/95. Canx 7.9.95.
		31-8152080	N40790		
G-BYRO	Mainair Blade	1210-0899-7 & W1013		20. 8.99	
G-BYRP	Mainair Blade	1075-1295-7 & W877		15. 9.99	
G-BYRR	Mainair Blade	1211-0999-7 & W1015		17. 8.99	
G-BYRS	Rans S.6-ES Coyote II	PFA/204-13425		17. 9.99	
G-BYRT	Beechcraft F33A Bonanza	CE-971	ZS-LFB	1. 9.99	
			N18384		
G-BYRU					
G-BYRV	Raj Hamsa X'Air	BMAA/HB/106		10. 9.99	
G-BYRW					
G-BYRX					
G-BYRY					
G-BYRZ					

Regn	Type	c/n	Previous identity	Regn date	Fate or immediate subsequent identity (if known)
G-BYSA	Europa Avn Europa XS	PFA/247-13199		23. 8.99	
G-BYSB					
G-BYSC					
G-BYSD					
G-BYSE	Agusta-Bell 206B JetRanger II	8553	G-BFND	3.11.81	
G-BYSF					
G-BYSG					
G-BYSH					
G-BYSI					
G-BYSJ					
G-BYSK					
G-BYSL	Cameron O-56 HAFB	1269		10. 4.86	
G-BYSM					
G-BYSN					
G-BYSO					
G-BYSP					
G-BYSR					
G-BYSS					
G-BYST					
G-BYSU					
G-BYSV					
G-BYSW					
G-BYSX					
G-BYSY					
G-BYSZ					
G-BYTA	Kolb Twinstar Mk.3	PFA/205-13240		2. 9.99	
G-BYTB					
G-BYTC					
G-BYTD					
G-BYTE	Robinson R-22 Beta	1250		18. 4.90	
G-BYTF					
G-BYTG					
G-BYTH					
G-BYTI					
G-BYTJ					
G-BYTK					
G-BYTL					
G-BYTM					
G-BYTN					
G-BYTO	ATR-72-212	472	G-OILA F-WWEJ	. 8.99R	
G-BYTP	ATR-72-212	473	G-OILB F-WWEG	30. 4.99	
G-BYTR					
G-BYTS					
G-BYTT					
G-BYTU					
G-BYTV					
G-BYTW					
G-BYTX					
G-BYTY					
G-BYTZ					
G-BYUA	Grob G-115E Tutor	82086/E	D-EUKB	22. 7.99	
G-BYUB	Grob G-115E Tutor	82087/E		22. 7.99	
G-BYUC	Grob G-115E Tutor	82088/E		22. 7.99	
G-BYUD	Grob G-115E Tutor	82089/E		22. 7.99	
G-BYUE	Grob G-115E Tutor	82090/E		12. 8.99	
G-BYUF	Grob G-115E Tutor	82091/E		12. 8.99	
G-BYUG	Grob G-115E Tutor	82.../E		. 7.99R	
G-BYUH	Grob G-115E Tutor	82.../E		. 7.99R	
G-BYUI	Grob G-115E Tutor	82.../E		. 7.99R	
G-BYUJ	Grob G-115E Tutor	82.../E		. 7.99R	
G-BYUK	Grob G-115E Tutor	82.../E		. 7.99R	
G-BYUL	Grob G-115E Tutor	82.../E		. 7.99R	
G-BYUM	Grob G-115E Tutor	82.../E		. 7.99R	
G-BYUN	Grob G-115E Tutor	82.../E		. 7.99R	
G-BYUO	Grob G-115E Tutor	82.../E		. 7.99R	
G-BYUP	Grob G-115E Tutor	82.../E		. 7.99R	
G-BYUR	Grob G-115E Tutor	82.../E		. 7.99R	
G-BYUS	Grob G-115E Tutor	82.../E		. 7.99R	
G-BYUT	Grob G-115E Tutor	82.../E		. 7.99R	
G-BYUU	Grob G-115E Tutor	82.../E		. 7.99R	
G-BYUV	Grob G-115E Tutor	82.../E		. 7.99R	
G-BYUW	Grob G-115E Tutor	82.../E		. 7.99R	
G-BYUX	Grob G-115E Tutor	82.../E		. 7.99R	
G-BYUY	Grob G-115E Tutor	82.../E		. 7.99R	
G-BYUZ	Grob G-115E Tutor	82.../E		. 7.99R	
G-BYVA	Grob G-115E Tutor	82.../E		. 7.99R	
G-BYVB	Grob G-115E Tutor	82.../E		. 7.99R	
G-BYVC	Grob G-115E Tutor	82.../E		. 7.99R	
G-BYVD	Grob G-115E Tutor	82.../E		. 7.99R	
G-BYVE	Grob G-115E Tutor	82.../E		. 7.99R	
G-BYVF	Grob G-115E Tutor	82.../E		. 7.99R	

Regn	Type	c/n	Previous identity	Regn date	Fate or immediate subsequent identity (if known)
G-BYVG	Grob G-115E Tutor	82.../E		. 7.99R	
G-BYVH	Grob G-115E Tutor	82.../E		. 7.99R	
G-BYVI	Grob G-115E Tutor	82.../E		. 7.99R	
G-BYVJ	Grob G-115E Tutor	82.../E		. 7.99R	
G-BYVK	Grob G-115E Tutor	82.../E		. 7.99R	
G-BYVL	Grob G-115E Tutor	82.../E		. 7.99R	
G-BYVM	Grob G-115E Tutor	82.../E		. 7.99R	
G-BYVN	Grob G-115E Tutor	82.../E		. 7.99R	
G-BYVO	Grob G-115E Tutor	82.../E		. 7.99R	
G-BYVP	Grob G-115E Tutor	82.../E		. 7.99R	
G-BYVR	Grob G-115E Tutor	82.../E		. 7.99R	
G-BYVS	Grob G-115E Tutor	82.../E		. 7.99R	
G-BYVT	Grob G-115E Tutor	82.../E		. 7.99R	
G-BYVU	Grob G-115E Tutor	82.../E		. 7.99R	
G-BYVV	Grob G-115E Tutor	82.../E		. 7.99R	
G-BYVW	Grob G-115E Tutor	82.../E		. 7.99R	
G-BYVX	Grob G-115E Tutor	82.../E		. 7.99R	
G-BYVY	Grob G-115E Tutor	82.../E		. 7.99R	
G-BYVZ	Grob G-115E Tutor	82.../E		. 7.99R	
G-BYWA	Grob G-115E Tutor	82.../E		. 7.99R	
G-BYWB	Grob G-115E Tutor	82.../E		. 7.99R	
G-BYWC	Grob G-115E Tutor	82.../E		. 7.99R	
G-BYWD	Grob G-115E Tutor	82.../E		. 7.99R	
G-BYWE	Grob G-115E Tutor	82.../E		. 7.99R	
G-BYWF	Grob G-115E Tutor	82.../E		. 7.99R	
G-BYWG	Grob G-115E Tutor	82.../E		. 7.99R	
G-BYWH	Grob G-115E Tutor	82.../E		. 7.99R	
G-BYWI	Grob G-115E Tutor	82.../E		. 7.99R	
G-BYWJ	Grob G-115E Tutor	82.../E		. 7.99R	
G-BYWK	Grob G-115E Tutor	82.../E		. 7.99R	
G-BYWL	Grob G-115E Tutor	82.../E		. 7.99R	
G-BYWM	Grob G-115E Tutor	82.../E		. 7.99R	
G-BYWN	Grob G-115E Tutor	82.../E		. 7.99R	
G-BYWO	Grob G-115E Tutor	82.../E		. 7.99R	
G-BYWP	Grob G-115E Tutor	82.../E		. 7.99R	
G-BYWR	Grob G-115E Tutor	82.../E		. 7.99R	
G-BYWS	Grob G-115E Tutor	82.../E		. 7.99R	
G-BYWT	Grob G-115E Tutor	82.../E		. 7.99R	
G-BYWU	Grob G-115E Tutor	82.../E		. 7.99R	
G-BYWV	Grob G-115E Tutor	82.../E		. 7.99R	
G-BYWW	Grob G-115E Tutor	82.../E		. 7.99R	
G-BYWX	Grob G-115E Tutor	82.../E		. 7.99R	
G-BYWY	Grob G-115E Tutor	82.../E		. 7.99R	
G-BYWZ	Grob G-115E Tutor	82.../E		. 7.99R	
G-BYXA	Grob G-115E Tutor	82.../E		. 7.99R	
G-BYXB	Grob G-115E Tutor	82.../E		. 7.99R	
G-BYXC	Grob G-115E Tutor	82.../E		. 7.99R	
G-BYXD	Grob G-115E Tutor	82.../E		. 7.99R	
G-BYXE	Grob G-115E Tutor	82.../E		. 7.99R	
G-BYXF	Grob G-115E Tutor	82.../E		. 7.99R	
G-BYXG	Grob G-115E Tutor	82.../E		. 7.99R	
G-BYXH	Grob G-115E Tutor	82.../E		. 7.99R	
G-BYXI	Grob G-115E Tutor	82.../E		. 7.99R	
G-BYXJ	Grob G-115E Tutor	82.../E		. 7.99R	
G-BYXK	Grob G-115E Tutor	82.../E		. 7.99R	
G-BYXL	Grob G-115E Tutor	82.../E		. 7.99R	
G-BYXM	Grob G-115E Tutor	82.../E		. 7.99R	
G-BYXN					
G-BYXO					
G-BYXP					
G-BYXR					
G-BYXS					
G-BYXT					
G-BYXU	PA-28-161 Cherokee Warrior II	28-7716097	EI-BXU G-BNUP/N2282Q	8. 1.99	
G-BYXV					
G-BYXW					
G-BYXX					
G-BYXY					
G-BYXZ					
G-BYYA					
G-BYYB					
G-BYYC					
G-BYYD					
G-BYYE					
G-BYYF					
G-BYYG					
G-BYYH					
G-BYYI					
G-BYYJ					
G-BYYK					
G-BYYL					
G-BYYM					

Regn	Type	c/n	Previous identity	Regn date	Fate or immediate subsequent identity (if known)
G-BYYN					
G-BYYO					
G-BYYP					
G-BYYR					
G-BYYS					
G-BYYT					
G-BYYU					
G-BYYV					
G-BYYW					
G-BYYX					
G-BYYY					
G-BYYZ					
G-BYZA					
G-BYZB					
G-BYZC					
G-BYZD					
G-BYZE					
G-BYZF					
G-BYZG					
G-BYZH					
G-BYZI					
G-BYZJ					
G-BYZK					
G-BYZL					
G-BYZM					
G-BYZN					
G-BYZO					
G-BYZP					
G-BYZR					
G-BYZS					
G-BYZT					
G-BYZU					
G-BYZV					
G-BYZW					
G-BYZX					
G-BYZY					
G-BYZZ					
G-BZAA					
G-BZAB					
G-BZAC	Sikorsky S-76A Spirit	760018	N4244S	9.11.79	To C-GIMA 10/92. Canx 9.9.92.
G-BZAD					
G-BZAE					
G-BZAF					
G-BZAG					
G-BZAH					
G-BZAI					
G-BZAJ					
G-BZAK					
G-BZAL					
G-BZAM					
G-BZAN					
G-BZAO					
G-BZAP					
G-BZAR					
G-BZAS					
G-BZAT	BAe 146 RJ100	E3320	G-6-320	18.11.97	
G-BZAU	BAe 146 RJ100	E3328		25. 4.98	
G-BZAV	BAe 146 RJ100	E3331		19. 5.98	
G-BZAW	BAe 146 RJ100	E3354		11. 6.99	
G-BZAX	BAe 146 RJ100	E3356	G-6-356	9. 7.99	
G-BZAY					
G-BZAZ					
G-BZBA					
G-BZBB					
G-BZBC					
G-BZBD					
G-BZBE					
G-BZBF					
G-BZBG					
G-BZBH	Thunder Ax7-65 Bolt HAFB	173		28.11.78	
G-BZBI					
G-BZBJ					
G-BZBK					
G-BZBL					
G-BZBM					
G-BZBN					
G-BZBO					
"G-BZBO"	Boeing 747-148 (Line No. 108)	19745	EI-ASJ G-BDPZ/EI-ASJ/HS-VGF/EI-ASJ	----	Not officially registered but painted as such for filming purposes from 30.10.84 until 2.11.84. Reverted to EI-ASJ.
G-BZBP					
G-BZBR					
G-BZBS					

Regn	Type	c/n	Previous identity	Regn date	Fate or immediate subsequent identity (if known)
G-BZBT					
G-BZBU					
G-BZBV					
G-BZBW					
G-BZBX					
G-BZBY	Colt 56SS HAFB ("Buzby" shape)	047		1. 5.79	Canx as WFU 12.1.90.
G-BZBZ					
G-BZCA					
G-BZCB					
G-BZCC					
G-BZCD					
G-BZCE					
G-BZCF					
G-BZCG					
G-BZCH					
G-BZCI					
G-BZCJ					
G-BZCK					
G-BZCL					
G-BZCM					
G-BZCN					
G-BZCO					
G-BZCP					
G-BZCR					
G-BZCS					
G-BZCT					
G-BZCU					
G-BZCV					
G-BZCW					
G-BZCX					
G-BZCY					
G-BZCZ					
G-BZDA					
G-BZDB					
G-BZDC					
G-BZDD					
G-BZDE					
G-BZDF					
G-BZDG					
G-BZDH					
G-BZDI					
G-BZDJ					
G-BZDK					
G-BZDL					
G-BZDM					
G-BZDN					
G-BZDO					
G-BZDP					
G-BZDR					
G-BZDS					
G-BZDT					
G-BZDU					
G-BZDV					
G-BZDW					
G-BZDX					
G-BZDY					
G-BZDZ					
G-BZEA					
G-BZEB					
G-BZEC					
G-BZED					
G-BZEE					
G-BZEF					
G-BZEG					
G-BZEH					
G-BZEI					
G-BZEJ					
G-BZEK					
G-BZEL					
G-BZEM					
G-BZEN					
G-BZEO					
G-BZEP					
G-BZER					
G-BZES					
G-BZET					
G-BZEU					
G-BZEV					
G-BZEW					
G-BZEX					
G-BZEY					
G-BZEZ					

Regn	Type	c/n	Previous identity	Regn date	Fate or immediate subsequent identity (if known)
G-BZFA					
G-BZFB					
G-BZFC					
G-BZFD					
G-BZFE	PA-23-250 Aztec E	27-4577	G-AZFE EI-BPA/G-AZFE/N13962	6.10.87	To G-VHFA 6/89. Canx.
G-BZFF					
G-BZFG					
G-BZFH					
G-BZFI					
G-BZFJ					
G-BZFK					
G-BZFL	Cessna 401	401-0166	G-AWSF N4066Q	12. 1.81	To G-ROAR 3/82. Canx.
G-BZFM					
G-BZFN					
G-BZFO					
G-BZFP					
G-BZFR					
G-BZFS					
G-BZFT					
G-BZFU					
G-BZFV					
G-BZFW					
G-BZFX					
G-BZFY					
G-BZFZ					
G-BZGA					
G-BZGB					
G-BZGC	Aerospatiale AS.355F1 Twin Squirrel	5077	G-CCAO G-SETA/G-NEAS/G-CMMM/G-BNBJ/C-GLKH	26. 3.99	
G-BZGD					
G-BZGE	Medway Hybred 44XLR Eclipser	159/139E		6. 5.99	
G-BZGF					
G-BZGG					
G-BZGH	Reims Cessna F.172N Skyhawk II	1789	EI-BGH (EI-BGI)	1.12.98	
G-BZGI					
G-BZGJ					
G-BZGK					
G-BZGL					
G-BZGM					
G-BZGN					
G-BZGO					
G-BZGP					
G-BZGR					
G-BZGS					
G-BZGT					
G-BZGU					
G-BZGV					
G-BZGW					
G-BZGX					
G-BZGY					
G-BZGZ					
G-BZHA	Boeing 767-336ER (Line No. 702)	29230	N60668	22. 5.98	
G-BZHB	Boeing 767-336ER (Line No. 704)	29231		30. 5.98	
G-BZHC	Boeing 767-336ER (Line No. 708)	29232		29. 6.98	
G-BZHD					
G-BZHE					
G-BZHF					
G-BZHG					
G-BZHH					
G-BZHI					
G-BZHJ					
G-BZHK					
G-BZHL					
G-BZHM					
G-BZHN					
G-BZHO					
G-BZHP					
G-BZHR					
G-BZHS					
G-BZHT					
G-BZHU					
G-BZHV					
G-BZHW					
G-BZHX					
G-BZHY					
G-BZHZ					

Regn	Type	c/n	Previous identity	Regn date	Fate or immediate subsequent identity (if known)
G-BZIA					
G-BZIB					
G-BZIC					
G-BZID					
G-BZIE					
G-BZIF					
G-BZIG					
G-BZIH					
G-BZII					
G-BZIJ					
G-BZIK					
G-BZIL					
G-BZIM					
G-BZIN					
G-BZIO					
G-BZIP					
G-BZIR					
G-BZIS					
G-BZIT					
G-BZIU					
G-BZIV					
G-BZIW					
G-BZIX					
G-BZIY					
G-BZIZ					
G-BZJA					
G-BZJB					
G-BZJC					
G-BZJD					
G-BZJE					
G-BZJF					
G-BZJG					
G-BZJH					
G-BZJI					
G-BZJJ					
G-BZJK					
G-BZJL					
G-BZJM					
G-BZJN					
G-BZJO					
G-BZJP					
G-BZJR					
G-BZJS					
G-BZJT					
G-BZJU					
G-BZJV					
G-BZJW					
G-BZJX					
G-BZJY					
G-BZJZ					
G-BZKA					
G-BZKB					
G-BZKC					
G-BZKD					
G-BZKE					
G-BZKF					
G-BZKG					
G-BZKH					
G-BZKI					
G-BZKJ					
G-BZKK	Cameron V-56 HAFB	396		2. 8.78	
G-BZKL					
G-BZKM					
G-BZKN					
G-BZKO					
G-BZKP					
G-BZKR					
G-BZKS					
G-BZKT					
G-BZKU					
G-BZKV					
G-BZKW					
G-BZKX					
G-BZKY					
G-BZKZ					
G-BZLA					
G-BZLB					
G-BZLC					
G-BZLD					
G-BZLE					
G-BZLF					
G-BZLG					
G-BZLH					

Regn	Type	c/n	Previous identity	Regn date	Fate or immediate subsequent identity (if known)
G-BZLI					
G-BZLJ					
G-BZLK					
G-BZLL					
G-BZLM					
G-BZLN					
G-BZLO					
G-BZLP					
G-BZLR					
G-BZLS					
G-BZLT					
G-BZLU					
G-BZLV					
G-BZLW					
G-BZLX					
G-BZLY					
G-BZLZ					
G-BZMA					
G-BZMB					
G-BZMC					
G-BZMD					
G-BZME					
G-BZMF					
G-BZMG					
G-BZMH					
G-BZMI					
G-BZMJ					
G-BZMK					
G-BZML					
G-BZMM					
G-BZMN					
G-BZMO					
G-BZMP					
G-BZMR					
G-BZMS					
G-BZMT					
G-BZMU					
G-BZMV					
G-BZMW					
G-BZMX					
G-BZMY					
G-BZMZ					
G-BZNA					
G-BZNB					
G-BZNC					
G-BZND					
G-BZNE					
G-BZNF					
G-BZNG					
G-BZNH					
G-BZNI					
G-BZNJ					
G-BZNK					
G-BZNL					
G-BZNM					
G-BZNN					
G-BZNO					
G-BZNP					
G-BZNR					
G-BZNS					
G-BZNT					
G-BZNU					
G-BZNV					
G-BZNW					
G-BZNX					
G-BZNY					
G-BZNZ					
G-BZOA					
G-BZOB					
G-BZOC					
G-BZOD					
G-BZOE					
G-BZOF					
G-BZOG					
G-BZOH					
G-BZOI					
G-BZOJ					
G-BZOK					
G-BZOL					
G-BZOM					
G-BZON					
G-BZOO					
G-BZOP					

Regn	Type	c/n	Previous identity	Regn date	Fate or immediate subsequent identity (if known)
G-BZOR					
G-BZOS					
G-BZOT					
G-BZOU					
G-BZOV					
G-BZOW					
G-BZOX					
G-BZOY					
G-BZOZ					
G-BZPA					
G-BZPB					
G-BZPC					
G-BZPD					
G-BZPE					
G-BZPF					
G-BZPG					
G-BZPH					
G-BZPI					
G-BZPJ					
G-BZPK					
G-BZPL					
G-BZPM					
G-BZPN					
G-BZPO					
G-BZPP					
G-BZPR					
G-BZPS					
G-BZPT					
G-BZPU					
G-BZPV					
G-BZPW					
G-BZPX					
G-BZPY					
G-BZPZ					
G-BZRA					
G-BZRB					
G-BZRC					
G-BZRD					
G-BZRE					
G-BZRF					
G-BZRG					
G-BZRH					
G-BZRI					
G-BZRJ					
G-BZRK					
G-BZRL					
G-BZRM					
G-BZRN					
G-BZRO					
G-BZRP					
G-BZRR					
G-BZRS					
G-BZRT					
G-BZRU					
G-BZRV					
G-BZRW					
G-BZRX					
G-BZRY					
G-BZRZ					
G-BZSA					
G-BZSB					
G-BZSC					
G-BZSD					
G-BZSE					
G-BZSF					
G-BZSG					
G-BZSH					
G-BZSI					
G-BZSJ					
G-BZSK					
G-BZSL					
G-BZSM					
G-BZSN					
G-BZSO					
G-BZSP					
G-BZSR					
G-BZSS					
G-BZST					
G-BZSU					
G-BZSV					
G-BZSW					
G-BZSX					
G-BZSY					

Regn	Type	c/n	Previous identity	Regn date	Fate or immediate subsequent identity (if known)
G-BZSZ					
G-BZTA					
G-BZTB					
G-BZTC					
G-BZTD					
G-BZTE					
G-BZTF					
G-BZTG					
G-BZTH					
G-BZTI					
G-BZTJ					
G-BZTK					
G-BZTL					
G-BZTM					
G-BZTN					
G-BZTO					
G-BZTP					
G-BZTR					
G-BZTS					
G-BZTT					
G-BZTU					
G-BZTV					
G-BZTW					
G-BZTX					
G-BZTY					
G-BZTZ					
G-BZUA					
G-BZUB					
G-BZUC					
G-BZUD					
G-BZUE					
G-BZUF					
G-BZUG					
G-BZUH					
G-BZUI					
G-BZUJ					
G-BZUK					
G-BZUL					
G-BZUM					
G-BZUN					
G-BZUO					
G-BZUP					
G-BZUR					
G-BZUS					
G-BZUT					
G-BZUU					
G-BZUV					
G-BZUW					
G-BZUX					
G-BZUY					
G-BZUZ					
G-BZVA					
G-BZVB					
G-BZVC					
G-BZVD					
G-BZVE					
G-BZVF					
G-BZVG					
G-BZVH					
G-BZVI					
G-BZVJ					
G-BZVK					
G-BZVL					
G-BZVM					
G-BZVN					
G-BZVO					
G-BZVP					
G-BZVR					
G-BZVS					
G-BZVT					
G-BZVU					
G-BZVV					
G-BZVW					
G-BZVX					
G-BZVY					
G-BZVZ					
G-BZWA					
G-BZWB					
G-BZWC					
G-BZWD					
G-BZWE					
G-BZWF					
G-BZWG					

Regn	Type	c/n	Previous identity	Regn date	Fate or immediate subsequent identity (if known)
G-BZWH					
G-BZWI					
G-BZWJ					
G-BZWK					
G-BZWL					
G-BZWM					
G-BZWN					
G-BZWO					
G-BZWP					
G-BZWR					
G-BZWS					
G-BZWT					
G-BZWU					
G-BZWV					
G-BZWW	BAe ATP	2005	(N375AE) G-BZWW	22. 1.88	To G-OATP(2) 12/88. Canx.
G-BZWX					
G-BZWY					
G-BZWZ					
G-BZXA					
G-BZXB					
G-BZXC					
G-BZXD					
G-BZXE					
G-BZXF					
G-BZXG					
G-BZXH					
G-BZXI					
G-BZXJ					
G-BZXK					
G-BZXL					
G-BZXM					
G-BZXN					
G-BZXO					
G-BZXP					
G-BZXR					
G-BZXS					
G-BZXT					
G-BZXU					
G-BZXV					
G-BZXW					
G-BZXX					
G-BZXY					
G-BZXZ					
G-BZYA					
G-BZYB					
G-BZYC					
G-BZYD					
G-BZYE					
G-BZYF					
G-BZYG					
G-BZYH					
G-BZYI					
G-BZYJ					
G-BZYK					
G-BZYL					
G-BZYM					
G-BZYN					
G-BZYO					
G-BZYP					
G-BZYR					
G-BZYS					
G-BZYT					
G-BZYU					
G-BZYV					
G-BZYW					
G-BZYX					
G-BZYY					
G-BZYZ					
G-BZZA					
G-BZZB					
G-BZZC					
G-BZZD	Reims Cessna F.172M Skyhawk II	1436	G-BDPF	14. 4.98	
G-BZZE					
G-BZZF					
G-BZZG					
G-BZZH					
G-BZZI					
G-BZZJ					
G-BZZK					
G-BZZL					
G-BZZM					
G-BZZN					

Regn	Type	c/n	Previous identity	Regn date	Fate or immediate subsequent identity (if known)
G-BZZO					
G-BZZP					
G-BZZR					
G-BZZS					
G-BZZT					
G-BZZU					
G-BZZV					
G-BZZW					
G-BZZX					
G-BZZY					
G-BZZZ	Enstrom F-28C-UK-2	138	G-BBBZ	12. 1.82	To G-OSWA 5/95. Canx.

NOTES

NOTES

NOTES

NOTES

SECTION 5 - UK OUT-OF-SEQUENCE REGISTRATIONS

With the exception of G-BSST (5/68) and G-VSTO (6/71) the out-of-sequence registration allocations did not start until 1974.

Regn	Type	c/n	Previous identity	Regn date	Fate or immediate subsequent identity (if known)
G-C					G-C
G-CAAA	The series from G-CAAA to G-CAXP was used by Canada from 1920 until 1928.				
G-CAFE(2)	Cessna 401	401-0165	G-AWXM	30. 7.79	To G-BSIX 7/81. Canx.
			N4065Q		
G-CAFZ(2)	PA-31-350 Navajo Chieftain		G-BPPT	24. 7.91	To G-PZIZ 10/98. Canx.
		31-7405429	N54297		
G-CAHA(2)	PA-34-200T Seneca II	34-7770010	N23PL	7. 7.98	
			SE-GPY/(D-IICC)/SE-GPY		
G-CAIN(2)	CFM Shadow Srs.CD	062	G-MTKU	26. 1.99	
G-CALL(2)	PA-23-250 Aztec F	27-7754061	N62826	21.12.77	
G-CALV(2)	PA-30-160 Twin Comanche C	30-1917	G-AZFO	23. 1.89	To N320MR 9/97. Canx 24.9.97.
	(Mod. to PA-39 C/R Status)		N8761Y		
G-CAMB(2)	Aerospatiale AS.355F2 Twin Squirrel		N813LP	17.12.96	
		5416			
G-CAMM(2)	Hawker Cygnet Replica	PFA/77-10245	(G-ERDB)	30. 5.91	
G-CAMP(2)	Cameron N-105 HAFB	4546		24. 3.99	
G-CAMR(2)	BFC Quad City Challenger II			26. 3.99	
		PFA/177-12569			
G-CAPI(2)	Avions Mudry/CAARP CAP.10B	76	G-BEXR	16. 3.99	
G-CAPT(2)	Taylor JT.2 Titch	PFA/3220	G-BTJM	14. 4.89	Destroyed in fatal crash in Vosges Mountains, France on 22.6.93. Canx as destroyed 5.10.94.
G-CAPX(2)	Avions Mudry CAP-10B	280		21. 9.98	
G-CARS(2)	Cessna 441 Conquest	441-0107	(N4189G)	. .79R	NTU - To G-BHFX 11/79. Canx.
"G-CARS"	Pitts S-2A Special	-	"G-RKSF"	----	(Stored 2/90 Sywell)
	(Non-flying replica - alias BAPC.134)				
G-CAXF(2)	Cameron O-77 HAFB	1274		19. 3.86	To VT-AKY 3/97. Canx 20.1.97.
G-CAYN	Dornier Do.228-200	8108	D-IABE	9. 8.88	To SE-LHD 6/96. Canx 5.6.96.
			D-CBDO(2)/G-MLNR/D-IOHI/D-COHI		
G-CBAC	Short SD.3-60 Var.200	SH3675	B-3608	20.10.95	(Stored at Baiyun, Guangzhou, China 10/96)
			G-BLYH/G-14-3675		
G-CBAL	PA-28-161 Warrior II	28-8116087	LN-MAD	25. 3.94	
			N83007		
G-CBBI	HS.125 Srs.700B	257013		11. 7.77	To N219JA 9/81. Canx 15.9.81.
G-CBCL	Stoddard-Hamilton Glastar			5. 9.97	
		PFA/295-13089			
G-CBEA	BAe Jetstream Srs.3102-01	609	(SE-LGH)	29. 3.83	To N609BA 5/98. Canx 22.5.98.
			G-CBEA/G-31-49/(N331BF)		
G-CBHH	Agusta-Bell 206B JetRanger	8192	F-GALU	22. 3.96	To G-GUST 8/96. Canx.
			G-AYBE		
G-CBIA	BAC One-Eleven Srs.416EK	BAC.166	G-16-24	28. 6.79	To 5N-AYW 10/89. Canx 13.10.89.
			PK-PJC/9V-BEF/G-AWXJ/HB-ITK/G-AWXJ		
G-CBIL(1)	Cessna 182G Skylane	182-55135	EI-ATF	. 5.78R	NTU - Restored as G-ASRR 6/78. Canx.
			G-ASRR/N3735U		
G-CBIL(2)	Cessna 182K Skylane	182-57804	(G-BFZZ)	9.10.78	
			D-ENGO/N2604Q		
G-CBJB	Sikorsky S-76A II Plus	760101	N288SP	23.11.89	To G-CHCD 1/98. Canx.
			C-GIMN/YV-326C		
G-CBKT	Cameron O-77 HAFB	1754		7. 6.88	
G-CBNB	Eurocopter EC-120B	1040		8. 6.99	
G-CBOR	Reims Cessna F.172N Skyhawk II	1656	PH-BOR	28. 5.87	
			PH-AXG(1)		
G-CBRA	Eurocopter AS.365N2 Dauphin 2	6414	I-GRDN	10. 5.94	To I-DDVE 6/98. Canx 9.6.98.
			F-WYMJ		
G-CBRI	Eurocopter EC-120B	1027		6. 5.99	To G-IGPW 7/99. Canx.
G-CCAA	HS.125 Srs.700B	257130	G-DBBI	17.12.82	To G-BNVU 9/87. Canx.
G-CCAO	Aerospatiale AS.355F1 Twin Squirrel		G-SETA	25. 1.96	To G-BZGC 3/99. Canx.
		5077	G-NEAS/G-CMMM/G-BNBJ/C-GLKH		
G-CCAR	Cameron N-77 HAFB	464		5.12.78	
	(Rebuilt 8/80 after w/o at Newton Abbot 13.7.80 using new envelope c/n 670; c.89 with c/n 2108 and in .92 with c/n 2658 !)				
G-CCAT	American Aviation AA-5A Cheetah		G-OAJH	16. 1.92	
		AA5A-0893	G-KILT/G-BJFA/N27169		
G-CCAU	Eurocopter EC-135T-1	0040	G-79-01	30. 6.98	
G-CCCB	Beechcraft 350 Super King Air	FL-73	N8270R	. .92R	NTU - In static display at Farnborough 9/92 as such. Remained as N8270R. Canx.
G-CCCC	Cessna 172H	172-55822	SE-ELU	9. 2.79	
			N2622L		
G-CCCL	Cessna 500 Citation I	500-0354	N51GA	5. 7.89	To G-TJHI 1/92. Canx.
	(Unit No.363)		G-BEIZ/(N5363J)		
G-CCCP	IAV Bacau Yakovlev Yak-52	899404	LY-AKV	30.11.93	
			DOSAAF 16 (Yellow)		
G-CCDI	Cameron N-77 HAFB	1775		4. 1.89	To G-CTGR 8/97. Canx.
G-CCIX	Vickers-Supermarine 361 Spitfire		G-BIXP	9. 4.85	Canx as TWFU 6.1.93. (Stored pending rebuild by PPS 3/96)
	LF.IXe	CBAF/IX/558	Israeli DF/AF 2046/Czech AF/TE517		(C/n is firewall no.)

Regn	Type	c/n	Previous identity	Regn date	Fate or immediate subsequent identity (if known)
G-CCLY	Bell 206B JetRanger III	3594	G-TILT G-BRJO/N2295Z	26. 4.95	
G-CCOA	Scottish Avn Bulldog Srs.120/122	BH120-375	G-111 Ghana AF/G-BCUU	4. 9.96	
G-CCOL	American Aviation AA-5A Cheetah	AA5A-0772	G-BIVU N26859	24. 4.92	
G-CCON	Beechcraft F33C Bonanza	CJ-145	PH-BNM	16. 9.91	To G-CGON 7/98. Canx.
G-CCOZ	Monnett Sonerai II	0197 & PFA/15-10107		31. 5.78	
G-CCPC	Reims Cessna F.152 II	1953		. .85R	NTU - To G-BMFZ 12/85. Canx.
G-CCSC	Cameron N-77 HAFB	4282		16. 1.98	
G-CCUB	Piper J3C-65 Cub	2362A	N33528 NC33528	2. 4.81	(On rebuild 5/98 Cumbernauld)
G-CCVV	Vickers-Supermarine 379 Spitfire FR.XIVe	6S/649186	"42" Indian AF/MV262	18. 5.88	Canx as TWFU 6.1.93. (On rebuild by PPS 3/96)
G-CDAH	Aerocar Sooper Coot A (Originally regd as Taylor Super Coot A)	E.E.1 & PFA/18-10039		30. 1.78	(Possibly some conection with G-COOT) Canx by CAA 6.9.91.
G-CDAN	Vickers-Supermarine 361 Spitfire LF.XVIe	CBAF/10895	TB863	30.11.82	(C/n is firewall no.) To ZK-XVI 1/89. Canx 16.1.89.
G-CDAV	PA-34-220T Seneca V	3449033	N9284Q	27.11.97	
G-CDBI	PA-23-250 Aztec E	23-7305193	N40475	16. 6.78	To G-PUMP 7/82. Canx.
G-CDBL	Clutton FRED Srs.2	123		13.10.78	Not completed. Canx as WFU 3.3.80.
G-CDBS	MBB Bo.105DBS-4 (See also G-BCXO)	S.738	D-HDRZ VH-MBK/N970MB/D-HDRZ	29. 9.89	
"G-CDBS"	MBB Bo.105D	S.80	G-BCXO D-HDCE	----	Painted as such in 1996 - see G-BCXO.
G-CDEE	Aviat Inc Pitts S-2B Special	5251	N171JH	12. 5.93	To PH-PEP 4/96 (as a Christen Pitts S-2B). Canx 21.3.96.
G-CDET	Culver LCA Cadet	129	N29261 NC29261	10.11.86	
G-CDEZ	Cessna Citation	-		. 6.96R	NTU - Canx.
G-CDGA	Taylor JT.1 Monoplane	6020/1 & PFA/55-10382		28.12.78	
G-CDGL	Saffery S.330 HAFB (Toy)	12		15.12.78	Canx by CAA 31.1.94.
G-CDHW	Boeing 707-3L6C (Line No. 900)	21096	9M-TMS N48055	28.10.77	To A6-HRM 2/79. Canx 2.2.79.
G-CDON	PA-28-161 Warrior II	28-8216185	N8254D	24. 5.88	
G-CDOS	Beechcraft 58 Baron	TH-1531	N3089G	14.10.88	To F-GKGB(2) 2/92. Canx 5.2.92.
G-CDRU	CASA I-131E Jungmann	2321	EC-DRU Spanish AF E3B-530	19. 1.90	
G-CEAA	Airbus A.300B2-1C	062	F-WQGQ F-BUAI	2. 7.98	(Stored enginless 3/99 at Bournemouth)
G-CEAB	Airbus A.300B2-1C	027	F-WQGS F-BUAH/F-WLGC/F-WLGB	. 2.98R	(Stored enginless 3/99 at Bournemouth)
G-CEAC	Boeing 737-229 (Line No. 360)	20911	OO-SDE C-GNDX/OO-SDE/C-GNDX/OO-SDE	11. 6.99	
G-CEAD	Boeing 737-229 (Line No. 358)	20910	OO-SDD EC-EEG/OO-SDC	. 9.99	
G-CEA.	Boeing 737-229 (Line No. 421)	21137	OO-SDM	.11.98R	(for delivery 10/99)
G-CEA.	Boeing 737-229C (Line No. 576)	21738	OO-SDR	.11.98R	
G-CEA.	Boeing 737-229 (Line No. 351)	20907	OO-SDA LX-LGN/OO-SDA	.10.98R	
G-CEA.	Boeing 737-229 (Line No. 365)	20912	OO-SDF	.10.98R	
G-CEA.	Boeing 737-229C (Line No. 401)	20915	OO-SDJ	.10.98R	
G-CEA.	Boeing 737-229C (Line No. 403)	20916	OO-SDK	.10.98R	
G-CEA.	Boeing 737-229 (Line No. 418)	21135	OO-SDG	.10.98R	
G-CEAL	Short SD.3-60 Var.200	SH3761	N161CN N161SB/G-BPXO	11. 9.95	
G-CEA.	Boeing 737-229 (Line No. 420)	21136	OO-SDL	.10.98R	
G-CEA.	Boeing 737-229C (Line No. 437)	21139	OO-SDP	.10.98R	
G-CEA.	Boeing 737-229 (Line No. 431)	21176	OO-SDN 9M-MBP/OO-SDN/N8277V	.10.98R	
G-CEAP	Lockheed L.1011-385-1 Tristar 200	193N-1145	SE-DPM G-BEAL	21. 5.96	To G-IOIT 5/98. Canx.
G-CEA.	Boeing 737-229 (Line No. 433)	21177	OO-SDO	.10.98R	
G-CEAS	Handley Page HPR.7 Dart Herald 214	186	G-BEBB PP-SDH	31. 1.86	Canx as WFU 23.6.97. (Stored engineless 7/97 Hurn)
G-CEGA	PA-34-200T Seneca II	34-8070367	N8272B	20.11.80	
G-CEGB	Aerospatiale AS.355F1 Twin Squirrel	5312	G-BLJL	20. 5.85	To G-WIRE 1/90. Canx.
G-CEGR	Beechcraft 200 Super King Air	BB-351	N68CP N351FW/N6666C/N6666K	23. 7.97	
G-CEJA	Cameron V-77 HAFB	2469	G-BTOF	17. 6.91	

Regn	Type	c/n	Previous identity	Regn date	Fate or immediate subsequent identity (if known)
G-CELL	PA-32R-301 Saratoga II SP	32R-8413017	(G-BLRI) N4361D	16. 4.85	To G-REAH 8/94. Canx.
G-CELT(1)	Embraer EMB.110P2 Bandeirante	110-162		. .78R	NTU - Built as a EMB-111A(N) for Chilean Navy as 265. Canx 31.3.78.
G-CELT(2)	Embraer EMB.110P2 Bandeirante	110-161		16. 4.78	To N4942S 4/84. Canx 9.4.84.
G-CENT	Cessna T.210L Turbo Centurion II	210-61146	A6-AMM N2185S	20. 2.79	To G-RADE 9/82. Canx.
G-CERT	Mooney M.20K (252TSE)	25-1134		5.10.87	
G-CETA	Cessna 310Q II	310Q-0917	G-BBIM N69683	10.11.80	To G-TVMM 3/88. Canx.
G-CETC	Aeronca 15AC Sedan	15AC-429	HB-ETC	7.10.83	To EI-ETC 10/93. Canx 21.9.93.
G-CEXA	Fokker F-27 Friendship 500RF	10503	N703A PH-EXK	19. 1.96	
G-CEXB	Fokker F-27 Friendship 500RF	10550	N743A PH-EXF	15.11.95	
G-CEXC	Airbus A.300B4-103F	124	N407U N407UA/N220EA/F-GBNO	18. 7.97	
G-CEXD	Fokker F-27 Friendship 600	10351	PH-KFE HB-AAX/PH-FLX	18. 2.97	
G-CEXE	Fokker F-27 Friendship 500	10654	SU-GAF PH-EXJ	2. 4.97	
G-CEXF	Fokker F-27 Friendship 500	10660	SU-GAE PH-EXC	2. 4.97	
G-CEXH	Airbus A.300B4-203F	117	D-ASAZ N14966/N966C/F-OGTB/9V-STA/F-WZER	30. 3.98	
G-CEXI	Airbus A.300B4-203F	121	D-ASAA N15967/N967C/F-OGTC/9V-STB/F-WZEK	3. 9.98	
G-CEXP	Handley Page HPR.7 Dart Herald 209	195	I-ZERC G-BFRJ/4X-AHO	29.10.87	WFU at Gatwick on 8.3.96. Canx by CAA 22.3.96. On display on Terminal Building 4/96 at Gatwick.
G-CEXS	Lockheed L.188CF Electra	1091	N5539 N171PS/N971HA/N171PS	14. 4.92	
G-CEZY	Thunder Ax9-140 Srs.2 HAFB	427		15. 7.82	To F-GGRA(3) 7/90. Canx 19.2.90.
G-CFBI	Colt 56A HAFB	570		11. 7.84	
G-CFIN	Dornier Do.228-200	8096	D-IOHA (D-COHA)	5.12.86	To D-CBDN(2) 11/87. Canx 30.11.87.
G-CFLT	Aerospatiale AS.355F1 Twin Squirrel	5024	G-BNBI ZK-HMS/G-BNBI/C-GKHO	22. 8.89	Destroyed in fatal crash near Middlewich, Cheshire on 22.10.96. Canx as destroyed 6.2.97.
G-CFLY	Cessna 172F Skyhawk	172-52635	PH-SNO N8731U	25. 8.78	Canx by CAA 5.6.95. (Stored 6/96 Blackpool)
G-CFME	Socata TB.10 Tobago	1795	F-GNHU	15. 4.98	
G-CGCG	Robinson R-22 Beta	2050		5. 3.92	Crashed on take-off from Newtownards on 17.4.93. Canx as WFU 8.7.93.
G-CGFC	PA-38-112 Tomahawk	38-78A0508		18. 9.78	Canx as destroyed 23.6.83. Re-regd as G-BLNN 12/84 for a proposed rebuild.
G-CGHM	PA-28-140 Cherokee Cruiser	28-7425143	PH-NSM	25. 4.79	
G-CGOD	Cameron N-77 HAFB	2647		5. 9.91	
G-CGON	Beechcraft F33C Bonanza	CJ-145	G-CCON PH-BNM	13. 7.98	
G-CHAA	Cameron O-90 HAFB	2471		24.10.91	
G-CHAL	Robinson R-22 Beta	1087		2. 8.89	To G-OHLL 12/97. Canx.
G-CHAM	Cameron Pot 90SS HAFB (Chambourcy Pot shape)	2912		29. 9.92	
G-CHAP	Robinson R-44 Astro	0326		9. 4.97	
G-CHAR	Grob G-109B	6435		21. 5.86	
G-CHAS	PA-28-181 Archer II	28-8090325	N82228	18. 3.91	
G-CHAT	Bell 206B JetRanger II	1748	G-KFDF N90306	9. 8.90	To N36AJ 6/91. Canx 21.6.91.
G-CHAV	Europa Avn Europa	PFA/247-12769		28.12.94	
G-CHAZ	Rans S-6-ESA Coyote II	1291-250 & PFA/204-12436		7.10.93	NTU - To G-MYMP 11/93. Canx.
G-CHCA	Aerospatiale AS.332L-1 Super Puma	2007	F-WQDZ(3) C-GSEM/HC-B../C-GSEM/HC-BPE/C-GSEM/HK-3197X/C-GSEM/N332CH/OE-GXB	13. 1.98	To OY-HEO 6/99. Canx 24.6.99.
G-CHCB	Aerospatiale AS.332L-1 Super Puma	2015	(F-....) C-GQYX/HC-BRH/C-GQYX/HC-BOZ/C-GQYX/P2-PHY/C-GQYX/N5789M	29. 6.98	To OY-HHA. Canx 24.6.99.
G-CHCC	Aerospatiale AS.332L-1 Super Puma	2087	(F-....) N25AN/N77GY/N58023	27. 8.98	
G-CHCD	Sikorsky S-76A II Plus	760101	G-CBJB N288SP/C-GIMN/YV-326C	16. 1.98	
G-CHDI	Cessna 414A Chancellor II	414A-1212	N12464	15. 4.86	To D-ILLL(2) 9/88. Canx 27.7.88.
G-CHEB	Europa Avn Europa	PFA/247-12967		16. 9.96	
G-CHEM	PA-34-200T Seneca II	34-8170032	N8292Y	26. 8.87	
G-CHES	PBN BN-2A-26 Islander	2011	G-PASY G-BPCB/G-BEXA/G-MALI/G-DIVE/(ZB503)/"ZA503"/G-DIVE/G-BEXA	19. 4.94	
G-CHET	Europa Avn Europa	PFA/247-13277		12. 2.98	
G-CHEV	Embraer EMB.110P2 Bandeirante	110-199	(PT-GLR)	11.12.78	To G-BKWB 7/83. Canx.
G-CHGL	Bell 206B JetRanger II	1669	G-BPNG G-ORTC/G-BPNG/N20EA/C-GHVB	29. 4.98	
G-CHGN	Boeing 707-321C (Line No. 368)	18718	G-BFZF N794RN/N794PA/N794EP/N794/N794PA	. 2.86R	NTU - To G-BNGH 2/86. Canx.

Regn	Type	c/n	Previous identity	Regn date	Fate or immediate subsequent identity (if known)
G-CHIC	Hughes 269C (300C)	98-0718		28.11.78	Fatal crash 1m north of Betws-y-Coed, Wales on 13.11.79. Canx as destroyed 14.1.80.
G-CHIK	Reims Cessna F.152 II	1628	G-BHAZ (D-EHLE)	19.10.81	
G-CHIL	Robinson R-22 HP	0218	(G-BMXI) N9074K	12. 9.86	To G-RALD 1/96. Canx.
G-CHIP	PA-28-181 Archer II	28-8290095	N81337	22. 2.82	
G-CHIS	Robinson R-22 Beta	1740		5. 4.91	
G-CHKL	Cameron Kookaburra 120SS HAFB	3733		8.11.95	
G-CHLA	Aerospatiale AS.355F1 Twin Squirrel	5175	N818RL C-FLXH/N818RL/N818R/N5798U	23. 9.94	To G-WEKR 2/96. Canx.
G-CHLT	Stemme S-10	10-30	D-KGCD	3. 7.91	
G-CHMP	Bellanca 7ACA Champ (This aircraft was flying as G-CHMP prior to 10/90)	62-72	N68556	21.12.92	
G-CHNL	Fokker F-27 Friendship 600	10508	OY-SRZ N61AN/OB-R-1042/PH-EXA	20. 3.95	Fatal crash 1 mile from Guernsey airport on 12.1.99. Canx as destroyed 28.5.99.
G-CHNX	Lockheed L.188AF Electra	1068	EI-CHO (G-CHNX)/N5535	1.11.94	
G-CHOC	Bell 206B JetRanger II	1125	D-HMAC	5. 9.77	To ZS-HJH 11/80. Canx 6.11.80.
G-CHOK	Cameron V-77 HAFB	1752		25. 5.88	
G-CHOP	Westland-Bell 47G-3B1 (Line No. WAN/79)	WA/380	XT221	19.12.78	
G-CHPY	DHC.1 Chipmunk 22 (Fuselage no. DHH/f/78)	C1/0093	WB652	7. 3.97	
G-CHRO	Thunder & Colt Flying Book SS HAFB	1370		19.12.88	Canx 28.4.92 on sale in France.
G-CHRP	Colt Flying Book SS HAFB	1387		14. 4.89	CofA expired 1.2.94. Canx as WFU 10.6.98.
G-CHRR	Colt Flying Book SS HAFB (The above are similar flying copies of the Longman Chronicle of the 20th Century books)	1395		14. 4.89	CofA expired 24.5.90. (Was based USA) Canx as WFU 29.5.98.
G-CHSR	BAe 146 Srs.200	E2088	G-5-088	20. 1.88	To G-MANS 5/94. Canx.
G-CHSU	Eurocopter EC-135T-1	0079		4. 2.99	
G-CHTA	American Aviation AA-5A Cheetah	AA5A-0631	G-BFRC	3. 3.86	
G-CHTT	Varga 2150A Kachina	VAC 162-80		7. 9.84	Badly damaged in forced-landing 2m north of Hatherleigh, Devon on 27.4.86. Canx by CAA 9.8.94. Fuselage at Southend 1/98. (Spares use for G-BPVK 3/99)
G-CHUB	Colt Cylinder Two N-51 HAFB (Fire Extinguisher shape)	1720		11. 4.90	
G-CHUG	Europa Avn Europa	PFA/247-12960		29. 7.96	
G-CHUK	Cameron O-77 HAFB	2773		6. 3.92	
G-CHYL	Robinson R-22 Beta	1197		28.11.89	
G-CHZN	Robinson R-22 Beta	0884	G-GHZM G-FENI	9. 4.99	
G-CIAO	Iniziative Industriali Italian Sky Arrow 1450-L	PFA/298-13095		23. 7.97	
G-CIAS	PBN BN-2B-21 Islander	2162	HC-BNS G-BKJM	1. 5.91	
G-CICI	Cameron R-15 Gas/HAFB	673	(N.....) G-CICI/(G-BIHP)	11.11.80	
G-CIFR	PA-28-181 Cherokee Archer II	28-7790208	PH-MIT OO-HBB/N7654F	18. 6.97	
G-CIGY	Westland-Bell 47G-3B1 (Line no. WAN/41)	WA/350	G-BGXP XT191	26.10.98	
G-CIII	Oldfield Baby Great Lakes (Built by J.List)	JAL.3	N11JL	20. 7.89	To G-BWMO 2/96. Canx.
G-CINE	Bell 206L-1 Long Ranger	45402	LN-OSE	27. 2.84	To C-FLRU 10/91. Canx 11.9.91.
G-CINY	Stoddard-Hamilton Glasair IIRG	PFA/149-13011		7. 6.96	To G-OPNH 10/98. Canx.
G-CIPI	AJEP Wittman W.8 Tailwind	AJEP/2 & PFA/1363	G-AYDU	22. 7.87	
G-CITA	Bellanca 7KCAB Citabria	543-75	N14091 G-CITA/N53785/SE-KUI/N53785	2. 2.96	CofA expired 21.3.99. Canx by CAA 24.8.99.
G-CITB	Boeing 747-2D3BF/SCD (Line No. 514)	22579	JA8192 G-CITB/JY-AFS	10. 9.87	Restored as JA8192 11/90. Canx 14.11.90.
G-CITI	Cessna 501 Citation I/SP (Unit No.463)	501-0084	VP-CDM VR-CDM/G-CITI/N3160M/(N11JC)/(N463CJ)/N3160M	21. 9.87	
G-CITY	PA-31-350 Navajo Chieftain	31-7852136	N27741	12. 9.78	
G-CITZ	Bell 206B JetRanger II	1997	G-BRTB N9936K	19. 2.99	
G-CIVA	Boeing 747-436 (Line No. 967)	27092		19. 3.93	
G-CIVB	Boeing 747-436 (Line No. 1018)	25811	(G-BNLY)	15. 2.94	
G-CIVC	Boeing 747-436 (Line No. 1022)	25812	(G-BNLZ)	26. 2.94	
G-CIVD	Boeing 747-436 (Line No. 1048)	27349		14.12.94	
G-CIVE	Boeing 747-436 (Line No. 1050)	27350		20.12.94	
G-CIVF(1)	Boeing 747-436 (Line No. 1079)	25814		. .93R	NTU - To G-CIVI 5/96. Canx.

Regn	Type	c/n	Previous identity	Regn date	Fate or immediate subsequent identity (if known)
G-CIVF(2)	Boeing 747-436 (Line No. 1058)	25434	(G-BNLY)	29. 3.95	
G-CIVG(1)	Boeing 747-436	25815		. .93R	NTU - Not built. Canx.
G-CIVG(2)	Boeing 747-436 (Line No. 1059)	25813	N6009F	20. 4.95	
G-CIVH	Boeing 747-436 (Line No. 1078)	25809		23. 1.96	
G-CIVI	Boeing 747-436 (Line No. 1079)	25814	(G-CIVF)	2. 5.96	
G-CIVJ	Boeing 747-436 (Line No. 1102)	25817		11. 2.97	
G-CIVK	Boeing 747-436 (Line No. 1104)	25818		28. 2.97	
G-CIVL	Boeing 747-436 (Line No. 1108)	27478		28. 3.97	
G-CIVM	Boeing 747-436 (Line No. 1116)	28700		5. 6.97	
G-CIVN(1)	Boeing 747-436 (Line No. 1149)	25821		. .93R	NTU - To G-CIVT 3/98. Canx.
G-CIVN(2)	Boeing 747-436 (Line No. 1129)	28848		29. 9.97	
G-CIVO(1)	Boeing 747-436 (Line No. 1154)	25810		. .93R	NTU - To G-CIVU 4/98. Canx.
G-CIVO(2)	Boeing 747-436 (Line No. 1135)	28849	N6046P	5.12.97	
G-CIVP(1)	Boeing 747-436 (Line No. 1156)	25819		. .93R	NTU - To N6009F/G-CIVV 5/98. Canx.
G-CIVP(2)	Boeing 747-436 (Line No. 1144)	28850		17. 2.98	
G-CIVR(1)	Boeing 747-436 (Line No. 1157)	25822		. .93R	NTU - To G-CIVW 5/98. Canx.
G-CIVR(2)	Boeing 747-436 (Line No. 1146)	25820		2. 3.98	
G-CIVS	Boeing 747-436 (Line No. 1148)	28851		13. 3.98	
G-CIVT	Boeing 747-436 (Line No. 1149)	25821	(G-CIVN)	20. 3.98	
G-CIVU	Boeing 747-436 (Line No. 1154)	25810	(G-CIVO)	24. 4.98	
G-CIVV	Boeing 747-436 (Line No. 1156)	25819	N6009F (G-CIVP)	22. 5.98	
G-CIVW	Boeing 747-436 (Line No. 1157)	25822	(G-CIVR)	15. 5.98	
G-CIVX	Boeing 747-436 (Line No. 1172)	28852		3. 9.98	
G-CIVY	Boeing 747-436 (Line No. 1178)	28853		29. 9.98	
G-CIVZ	Boeing 747-436 (Line No. 1190)	28854		31.10.98	
G-CJAN	PA-28-181 Arrow II	28-7790326	OO-FLI OO-HCD/N1662H	14.12.78	To ZK-FHQ 2/84. Canx 23.1.84.
G-CJBC	PA-28-180 Cherokee D	28-5470	OY-BDE	28.11.80	
G-CJCB	Bell 206L-3 Long Ranger III	51002	G-LIII N1084D	18. 4.83	To VH-LHP 4/90. Canx 19.4.90.
G-CJCI	Pilatus P.2-06	600-63	U-143 Swiss AF	30. 7.84	
G-CJDH	Pitts S-1S Special (built by J.S.Stevens, USA)	101	N47142	27. 5.81	Badly damaged in forced landing at Drove Lane Farm, near Yapton, Sussex on 9.11.84. Canx as destroyed 22.3.89.
G-CJET	Gates LearJet 35A	35A-365	G-SEBE G-ZIPS/(N45645)/G-ZONE	30. 6.87	To G-GJET 3/95. Canx.
G-CJHH	Cessna 550 Citation II (Unit No.147)	550-0132	N2633Y	6. 3.80	To N13627 10/81. Canx 15.10.81.
G-CJII	Bell 206B JetRanger II	1129	G-BBFB N18094	22.10.81	To G-CORC 12/89. Canx.
G-CJIG	Boeing 757-236 (Line No. 57)	23227	N1779B	. .85R	NTU - To (G-BNHG)/G-BLVH 2/85. Canx.
G-CJIM	Taylor JT.1 Monoplane	PFA/1419		28.12.78	No Permit to Fly issued. (Still under construction 7/95) Canx by CAA 24.3.99.
G-CJUD	Denney Kitfox Mk.3	847 & PFA/172-11939		17. 1.91	
G-CJWS	PA-34-200T Seneca II	34-7970109	N2078N	11.11.88	Undercarriage collapsed on landing at Guernsey on 1.11.92. Canx 15.2.93 on sale to USA. To Dodson Aviation Scrapyard, Ottawa, KS, USA.
G-CKCK	Enstrom 280FX Shark	2071	OO-PVL	5. 5.95	Badly damaged on take-off from Eastwood End Farm, Adlington, Cheshire on 29.10.95. CofA expired 14.5.98.
G-CKEN	Wombat Autogyro	CJ-002		1. 6.90	No permit issued. (Not constructed) Canx by CAA 9.12.96.
G-CLAC	PA-28-161 Warrior II	28-8116241	N8369U	18. 5.87	
G-CLAG	Lindstrand LBL-90A HAFB	582		26. 1.99	(Based in Germany)
G-CLAN	PA-31-350 Navajo Chieftain	31-7852052	N27549	22. 3.78	To PH-PTC 5/84. Canx 18.4.84.
G-CLAS	Short SD.3-60 Var.200	SH3635	EI-BEK G-BLED/G-14-3635	28. 7.93	

Regn	Type	c/n	Previous identity	Regn date	Fate or immediate subsequent identity (if known)
G-CLAW	Embraer EMB.110P1 Bandeirante	110-278	N790RA XA-LES(2)/PT-SBP/(G-BHPP)/PT-SBP	26. 7.88	To G-SWAG 1/91. Canx.
G-CLAX	Jurca MJ.5 Sirocco Type F.2 Srs.39	PFA/2204	G-AWKB	22. 4.99	
G-CLEA	PA-28-161 Warrior II	28-7916081	N30296	28. 8.80	
G-CLEF	Beechcraft 95-B58P Baron	TJ-114	C-GXQP	11.11.77	To N2407X 2/83. Canx 9.2.83.
G-CLEO	Zenair CH.601HD Zodiac	PFA/162-13500		9. 8.99	
G-CLEM	Bolkow Bo.208A-2 Junior	561	G-ASWE D-EFHE	22. 9.81	
G-CLHX	BAe 146 RJ85	E2270	G-6-270	23.10.95	To D-AVRI 12/95. Canx 6.12.95.
G-CLIC	Cameron N-105 HAFB (New envelope c/n 3395 c 4/95)	2557		18. 4.91	
G-CLIK	PA-18-95 Super Cub (L-18C-PI) (Frame no. 18-1521)	18-1549	(G-BLMB) D-EDRB/ALAT 51-15549/51-15549	31. 7.84	To G-BVIE 1/94. Canx.
G-CLIP	Eurocopter AS.355N Twin Squirrel	5580		25.11.94	
G-CLIV	PA-28R-201T Turbo Arrow III	28R-7703086	N3011Q	19.12.90	To G-OOTC 1/94. Canx.
G-CLKE	Robinson R-44 Astro	0185	G-HREH D-HREH	22. 9.98	
G-CLNT	Bell 206L Long Ranger	45139	G-BFTR N5005K	31. 3.87	Restored as G-BFTR 4/88. Canx.
G-CLOE	Sky 90-24 HAFB	019		11. 3.96	
G-CLOS	PA-34-200 Seneca II	34-7870361	HB-LKE N36783	17. 6.86	
G-CLRK	Sky 77-24 HAFB	101		3. 3.98	
G-CLRL	Agusta A.109A II	7265	G-EJCB	22. 8.89	To G-BVCJ 8/93. Canx.
G-CLUB	Reims Cessna FRA.150N Aerobat	0347	OO-AWZ(2) F-WZAZ/(F-WZDZ)	10. 2.83	
G-CLUE	PA-34-200T Seneca II	34-7970502	N8089Z	15. 9.92	
G-CLUT	Clutton Special	EC.3		7.11.78	Canx 5.12.83 on sale to USA.
G-CLUX	Reims Cessna F.172N Skyhawk II	1996	PH-AYG(3)	1. 5.80	
G-CLYV	Robinson R-22 Beta	1677		12. 2.91	Ditched in Killary Harbour, Co.Galway on 15.8.96. Canx as destroyed 30.9.97.
G-CMAC	Cessna 340A II	340A-0722	G-JIMS G-PETE/N2667N	18. 4.94	To N15FH 9/95. Canx 1.11.95.
G-CMAL	Auster 5 Alpha	3404	G-APAF	9. 7.86	Restored as G-APAF 9/88. Canx.
G-CMCM	Robinson R-22 Beta	1491		12. 9.90	To G-EXOR 11/91. Canx.
G-CMDR	Rockwell Commander 114	14005	N115CP N115PL/N1905J	23. 3.90	To N6095Z 4/97. Canx 3.4.97.
G-CMGC	PA-25-235 Pawnee D	25-7756042	G-BFEX N82525	19.11.91	
G-CMMM	Aerospatiale AS.355F1 Twin Squirrel	5077	G-BNBJ C-GLKH	31. 3.89	To G-NEAS 8/89. Canx.
G-CMMP	Boeing 737-3L9 (Line No. 1602)	24220	OY-MMP (G-BOZC)/OY-MMP/N1786B	30.11.88	Restored as OY-MMP 11/91. Canx 15.11.91.
G-CMMR	Boeing 737-3L9 (Line No. 1604)	24221	OY-MMR (G-BOZD)/OY-MMR/N1786B	1. 2.90	Restored as OY-MMR 11/91. Canx 3.12.91.
G-CNDY	Robinson R-22 Beta	2677	G-BXEW	15. 5.97	
G-CNET	Aerospatiale AS.355F1 Twin Squirrel	5120	G-MCAH	14. 1.86	To G-PAPA 2/87. Canx.
G-CNIS	Partenavia P.68B Victor	147	G-BJOF EI-BKH/G-PAUL	13.12.82	To OY-TLC 12/94. Canx 24.11.94.
G-CNMF	BAe 146 Srs.200	E2079	G-5-079 G-CNMF/G-5-079	20.11.87	To G-MIMA 3/93. Canx.
G-CNSI	Beechcraft 200 Super King Air	BB-641	G-OSKA	3. 4.80	To G-CUKL 6/83. Canx.
G-COAI	Cranfield A.1 Chase Srs.1	001	G-BCIT	1. 6.98	
G-COAL	Bell 206B JetRanger III	2901		12. 2.80	To G-OAMG 2/86. Canx.
G-COBA	Ted Smith Aerostar 600A	60-0470-155	N9827Q	25. 1.78	To N78TS 11/78. Canx 25.10.78.
G-COCO	Reims Cessna F.172M Skyhawk II	1373	PH-SMO OO-ADI	27.10.80	
G-CODE	Bell 206B JetRanger III	3850	N222DM N84TC	27. 8.96	
G-COES	McDonnell Douglas DC-9-83 (MD-83) (Line No. 1784)	49937	N30010	21. 2.91	To EI-CMM 2/96. Canx 31.1.96.
G-COEZ	Airbus A.320-231	179	OY-CNH F-WWIS	10. 2.97	
G-COIN	Bell 206B JetRanger II	897	EI-AWA	11. 3.85	
G-COKE	Cameron O-65 HAFB	1475		24. 6.87	(Was based in Hong Kong) Canx by CAA 4.6.98.
G-COLA	Beechcraft F33C Bonanza	CJ-137	G-BUAZ PH-BNH	31. 3.92	
G-COLB	Boeing 737-3Q8 (Line No. 2383)	26283	N373TA	28. 5.98	
G-COLC	Boeing 737-3Q8 (Line No. 2424)	26286	N374TA	26. 5.98	
G-COLD	Cessna T.337D Turbo Super Skymaster	T337-01096	PH-NOS N86147	6. 5.82	Damaged in wheels-up landing at Goodwood in 1985. Re-regd & on rebuild as G-BNNG 6/87. Canx.
G-COLE	Boeing 737-3Q8 (Line No. 2139)	24962	PP-VOX	13.11.98	
G-COLL	Enstrom 280C-UK-2 Shark	1223	N86179	17. 8.81	
G-COLN	Aerospatiale AS.350B Ecureuil	1205	G-BHIV	17. 4.84	To G-UNIC 9/88. Canx.

Regn	Type	c/n	Previous identity	Regn date	Fate or immediate subsequent identity (if known)
G-COLR	Colt 69A HAFB	780		8. 4.86	Canx as WFU 21.5.93. (Stored 1/98)
G-COLT	Ted Smith Aerostar 601P	61P-0336-098	N90693	7. 7.78	To C-GBVB 4/80. Canx 12.3.80.
G-COMB	PA-30-160 Twin Comanche B	30-1362	G-AVBL N8236Y	14. 9.84	
G-COMM	PA-23-250 Aztec C	27-3500	G-AZMG 5Y-APA/(5Y-AMA)/5X-UVF/5Y-AFS	2. 1.81	CofA expired 25.4.96. Canx as PWFU 15.9.97.
G-COMP	Cameron N-90 HAFB	1564		24. 9.87	
G-CONB	Robin DR.400/180 Regent	2176	G-BUPX	14. 4.93	(Stored 3/97)
G-CONC	Cameron N-90 HAFB	2139		13.11.89	
G-CONE	BAe Jetstream Srs.3103	603	G-31-42	12.11.82	To G-31-42/D-CONE(2) 9/83. Canx 6.9.83.
G-CONI	Lockheed L.749A-79 Constellation (Freighter)	2553	N7777G (N173X)/N7777G/TI-1045P/PH-LDT/PH-TET/(NC.....)	12. 5.82	Canx as WFU 13.6.84. (On display at Wroughton as N7777G)
G-CONL	Socata TB-10 Tobago	173	F-GCOR	22.12.98	
G-COOK	Cameron N-77 HAFB	1457		18. 2.87	Canx by CAA 26.9.91.
G-COOL	Cameron O-31 HAFB	491		19. 9.78	Canx 9.7.87 on sale in China.
	(Initially stitched as G-FIZZ in error before delivery with c/n 440 which was destroyed at Northam, Australia on 12.10.78; rebuilt in 11/79 with c/n 491)				
G-COOP	Cameron N-31 HAFB	382		2. 3.78	CofA expired 13.5.87. (To Balloon Preservation Group 7/98)
G-COOT	Taylor Coot A (Possibly ex.G-CDAH)	EE-1A		16. 9.81	
G-COPE	Enstrom 280C-UK-2 Shark	1057	D-HORO	27. 5.81	Badly damaged at Brewers Oak Farm, Shropshire on 7.5.90. Canx as destroyed 20.8.90. (Wreck stored 11/90)
G-COPS	Piper J3C-65 Cub (L-4H-PI) (Regd as c/n 36-817, which is USAAC contract no.; Frame no. 11739)	11911	F-BFYC French AF/44-79615	17. 7.79	
G-COPT	Aerospatiale AS.350B Ecureuil	2168	9M-FSA 9V-BOR	25. 2.98	
G-COPY	American Aviation AA-5A Cheetah	AA5A-0754	G-BIEU N26836	8. 3.82	Damaged when ran away at Dunkirk, near Canterbury on 4.7.97 (the accident was initially reported as being at Biggin Hill - its homebase). Canx as PWFU 18.2.99.
G-CORB	Socata TB-20 Trinidad	1178	F-GKUX	12. 4.99	
G-CORC	Bell 206B JetRanger II	1129	G-CJHI G-BBFB/N18094	18.12.89	
G-CORD	Slingsby Nipper T.66 RA.45 Srs.3 (Rebuild from S.105/1565)	S.129/1676	G-AVTB (9J-...)	21. 3.88	
G-CORK	Air Command 532 Elite	G/04-1104		7.11.88	To G-BVVY 11/94. Canx.
G-CORN	Bell 206B JetRanger III	3035	G-BHTR N18098	4. 6.99	
G-CORP	BAe ATP	2037	G-BTNK N860AW/G-BTNK/G-11-037/G-BTNK/G-11-037	2. 3.98	
G-CORR	Aerospatiale AS.355F1 Twin Squirrel	5260		25. 1.83	To G-MUFF 8/87. Canx.
G-CORS	Cessna 425 Conquest I	425-0199	(N1223A)	. .83R	NTU - To G-BLGM 5/84. Canx.
G-CORT	Agusta-Bell 206B JetRanger III	8739		21. 6.96	
G-COSY	Lindstrand LBL-56A HAFB	017		18. 2.93	
G-COTE	Beechcraft C90 King Air	LJ-614	G-BBKN	22. 8.79	To G-OMET 11/79. Canx.
G-COTT	Cameron Flying Cottage 60SS HAFB (First flown 15.2.81 as G-HOUS which was already allocated)	687	"G-HOUS"	13. 2.81	
G-COUP	Ercoupe 415C	1903	N99280 NC99280	27. 5.93	
G-COUR	Agusta-Bell 206B JetRanger II	8046	G-FSDG G-ROOT/G-JETR/(G-BKBR)/OO-CDP	9.10.95	To OE-XLM 5/98. Canx 8.5.98.
G-COVE	Pearce Jabiru UL	PFA/274A-13409		23. 7.99	
G-COWE	Beechcraft C90A King Air	LJ-1116	N76RU N76RJ	25. 5.88	To N25AE 12/94. Canx 30.11.94.
G-COWI	Cessna 414A Chancellor II	414A-0455	G-MLCS G-MHGI/G-BHKK/(N2734D)	12. 2.87	To N901AA 6/92. Canx 25.6.92.
G-COWS	ARV Super 2	K.009 & PFA/152-11182	G-BONB	27. 5.88	
G-COWZ	Bell 206B JetRanger II	1865	G-BRDK N11LN	14.11.89	Force-landed 6nm east of Loch Ness on 8.5.92. Canx as WFU 22.6.92. Fuselage noted at Rand, South Africa on 14.3.96 for rebuild and still present as such 10.2.98.
G-COYS	Colt 42A HAFB	1868		1.11.90	Canx by CAA 10.3.95.
G-COZI	Rutan Cozy III	PFA/159-12162		19. 7.93	
G-COZY	Ruton Cozy	PFA/159-11116		13.11.85	Canx by CAA 2.9.91.
G-CPAC	PA-28R-200 Cherokee Arrow II	28R-7635284	PH-SMW OO-HAU/N75220	27. 5.81	To G-DMCS 5/84. Canx.
G-CPCD	CEA Jodel DR.221 Dauphin	81	F-BPCD	11.12.90	
G-CPCH	PA-28-151 Cherokee Warrior	28-7715131	G-BRGJ (G-BPGP)/N5425F	11.11.93	
G-CPEL	Boeing 757-236 (Line No. 224)	24398	N602DF EC-EOL/EC-597/G-BRJE/EC-EOL/EC-278/G-BRJE	24. 8.92	
G-CPEM	Boeing 757-236 (Line No. 747)	28665		28. 3.97	
G-CPEN	Boeing 757-236 (Line No. 751)	28666		23. 4.97	
G-CPEO	Boeing 757-236 (Line No. 762)	28667		11. 7.97	
G-CPEP	Boeing 757-2Y0 (Line No. 400)	25268	C-GTSU EI-CLP/N400KL/XA-TAE	16. 4.97	
G-CPER	Boeing 757-236 (Line No. 784)	29113		29.12.97	

Regn	Type	c/n	Previous identity	Regn date	Fate or immediate subsequent identity (if known)
G-CPES	Boeing 757-236 (Line No. 793)	29114		17. 3.98	
G-CPET	Boeing 757-236 (Line No. 798)	29115		12. 5.98	
G-CPEU	Boeing 757-236 (Line No. 864)	29941		1. 5.99	
G-CPEV(1)	Boeing 757-236 (Line No. 867)	29942		. .98R	NTU - To N544NA 14.5.99. Canx.
G-CPEV(2)	Boeing 757-236 (Line No. 871)	29943	N1795B (G-CPEW)	11. 6.99	
G-CPEW	Boeing 757-236 (Line No. 871)	29943		. .98R	NTU - To N1795B/G-CPEV(2) 6/99. Canx.
G-CPEX	Boeing 757-236 (Line No. 872)	29944		. .98R	NTU - To N545NA 24.5.99. Canx.
G-CPEY	Boeing 757-236 (Line No. 873)	29945		. .98R	NTU - To N546NA 6/99. Canx.
G-CPEZ	Boeing 757-236 (Line No. 877)	29946	N1795B	. .98R	NTU - To N547NA 6/99. Canx.
G-CPFC	Reims Cessna F.152 II	1430		1.12.77	
G-CPLI	Robinson R-22 Beta	1710		8. 3.91	Badly damaged in crash at Headcorn on 29.9.92. (On rebuilt 1/93 at Redhill) Canx as WFU 29.5.96.
G-CPMK	DHC.1 Chipmunk 22 (Fuselage no. DHB/f/761)	C1/0866	WZ847	28. 6.96	
G-CPMS	Socata TB.20 Trinidad	1607	F-GNHA	7. 4.98	
G-CPOL	Aerospatiale AS.355F1 Twin Squirrel	5007	N5775T C-GJJB/N5775T	30.11.95	
G-CPPC	PA-23-250 Aztec F	23-7754103	G-BGBH N63773	19. 4.82	To G-XSFT 6/86. Canx.
G-CPSF	Cameron N-90 HAFB	3747	G-OISK	21. 4.99	
G-CPTL	Short SD.3-60 Var.100	SH3739	G-BOFI G-14-3739	23. 6.88	To G-ZAPG 3/93. Canx.
G-CPTM	PA-28-151 Cherokee Warrior	28-7715012	G-BTOE N4264F	9. 7.91	
G-CPTS	Agusta-Bell 206B JetRanger II	8556		1. 6.78	
G-CRAK	Cameron N-77 HAFB	2291		7. 6.90	
G-CRAN	Robin R.1180TD Aiglon 2	269		19. 5.80	Fatal crash at Staden Industrial Estate, Buxton on 15.6.96. Canx as destroyed 10.10.96.
G-CRAY	Robinson R-22 Beta	0919		12. 1.89	
G-CRDA	Cessna 421C Golden Eagle III	421C-0653	N37367	20. 6.79	To N44431 3/81. Canx 5.3.81.
G-CRES	Denney Kitfox Mk.2	PFA/172-11574		7. 6.90	
G-CRIC	Colomban MC.15 Cri-Cri (First UK Cri-Cri to be built from scratch, ff 10.9.88 at Blackpool)	PFA/133-10915		22. 7.83	
G-CRIL	Rockwell Commander 112B	521	N1388J	22. 6.79	
G-CRIS	Taylor JT.1 Monoplane	PFA/55-10318		5. 6.79	
G-CRML	Cessna 414A Chancellor III	414A-1209	N1246D	18. 6.92	
G-CROC	Thunder Ax9-140 HAFB	1556		4. 7.89	To N2174G 3/90. Canx 31.1.90.
G-CROL	Maule MXT-7-180 Star Rocket	14032C	N9232F	24.11.93	
G-CROS	BAe 146 RJ85 (Originally regd with c/n R2226)	E2226		14.12.92	To HB-IXF 4/93. Canx 23.4.93.
G-CROY	Europa Avn Europa	PFA/247-12896		7. 2.97	
G-CRPH	Airbus A.320-231	424	F-WQBB F-WWIV	10. 4.95	
G-CRPS	Bell 206B JetRanger II	1967	A6-BCC	22. 9.97	
G-CRTI	PA-28RT-201 Arrow IV	28R-7918238	SE-ICY	9. 6.82	To G-ROYW 12/86. Canx.
G-CRUM	Westland Scout AH.1 (Pod no. F8-6151 confirmed)	F.9712	XV137	17. 3.98	
G-CRUS	Cessna T.303 Crusader	T303-00313	N6498V	27. 2.90	
G-CRUZ	Cessna T.303 Crusader	T303-00004	N9336T	7.12.90	
G-CRZY	Thunder Ax8-105 HAFB	058	OE-DZH G-BDLP	3. 8.82	Canx by CAA 1.3.93.
G-CSBM	Reims Cessna F.150M	1359	PH-AYC	24. 5.78	
G-CSCS	Reims Cessna F.172N Skyhawk II	1707	PH-MEM (PH-WEB)/N9899A	28.11.86	
G-CSDJ	Pearce Jabiru UL	PFA/274A-13337		23. 3.99	
G-CSFC	Cessna 150L Commuter	150-75360	(G-BFLX) N11370	21. 3.78	
G-CSFT	PA-23-250 Aztec D	27-4521	G-AYKU N13885	20. 9.84	CofA expired 3.12.94. Canx as WFU 5.6.96. (Fuselage dumped outside 12/98 at North Weald)
G-CSJH	BAe 146 Srs.200	E2094	(N410XV) G-5-094	20. 1.88	To SE-DRD 9/93. Canx 10.9.93.
G-CSKY	Agusta-Bell 206B JetRanger III	8588	G-TALY	16. 6.83	To G-JOKE 1/85. Canx.
G-CSNA	Cessna 421C Golden Eagle III	421C-0677	(D-IOSS) N26522	11. 6.79	
G-CSPJ	Hughes 369HS (500HS)	55-0745S	G-BXJF N99KS/N9KS	24. 7.97	
G-CSSC	Reims Cessna F.152 II	1579	PH-AYF(2)	16. 5.79	To G-BLZE 5/85. Canx.
G-CSVS	Boeing 757-236ER (Line No. 449)	25620	G-IEAC	19.10.93	To TF-GRL 4/98. Canx 30.4.98.
G-CSWL	Bell 206L-1 Long Ranger	45565	G-SIRI G-CSWL/F-GDAD	6. 5.97	

Regn	Type	c/n	Previous identity	Regn date	Fate or immediate subsequent identity (if known)
G-CSZA	Vickers 807D Viscount	282	(N140RA)	16. 2.78	WFU & stored 5/80. Broken up 9/82. Canx 4.10.82.
			G-CSZA/VP-LAU/VP-LKA/ZK-BRE		
G-CSZB	Vickers 807D Viscount	248	(N141RA)	12. 5.78	WFU in 1996. CofA expired 24.1.97. Stored 1/98 at Southend.
			G-CSZB/VQ-GAB(2)/ZK-NAI/SP-LVC/G-AOXU		Canx as WFU 19.8.98.
G-CSZC	Vickers 807 Viscount	428	(VP-LAU)	. .78R	NTU - Remained as ZK-BWO. Canx.
			ZK-BWO/(ZK-BRG)		
G-CTCL	Socata TB-10 Tobago	1107	G-BSIV	16. 7.90	
G-CTEK	Bell 206B JetRanger	12	N7812S	10. 2.95	To G-BWZW 11/96. Canx.
G-CTEL	Cameron N-90 HAFB	3933		27. 8.96	
G-CTGR	Cameron N-77 HAFB	1775	G-CCDI	28. 8.97	
G-CTHS	PA-31-350 Navajo Chieftain	31-7952100	N3518D	14. 5.79	Fatal crash at St.Agreve, 40km west of Valence, France on 24.9.80. Canx as destroyed 29.2.84.
G-CTIX	Vickers Supermarine 509 Spitfire Trainer IX	-	N462JC	9. 4.85	
			G-CTIX/Israeli DF/AF 2067/0607/Italian AF MM4100/PT462		
G-CTKL	Noorduyn AT-6 Harvard IIB	07-30	(G-BKWZ)	22.11.83	
	(Also quoted as built in June 1941 with c/n 76-80 and contract no. TP-7)		Italian AF MM54137/RCAF3064		
G-CTLN	Embraer EMB.110P1 Bandeirante	110-261	PT-SBA	17. 4.80	To G-BKWS 9/83. Canx.
G-CTOY	Denney Kitfox Mk.3	1176 & PFA/172-12150		14.10.91	Permit expired 10.5.93. (Stored Earls Colne 5/94)
G-CTPW	Bell 206B JetRanger III	4374	(N9145B)	30.11.95	
G-CTRN	Enstrom F-28C-UK	453		11. 4.79	To G-MHCJ 3/98. Canx.
G-CTRX	Handley Page 137 Jetstream 200 (Production No. 45)	246	G-BCWW G-AXUN	19. 4.84	CofA expired 29.5.91. (Stored 1/94 Guernsey) Canx by CAA 25.9.95; fuselage to Eindhoven, The Netherlands in 5/97 for spares use. Nose is expected to be displayed, rest scrapped
G-CTSI	Enstrom 280C-UK Shark	1202	G-BKIO	15.11.82	To G-WRFM 4/89. Canx.
			(G-BKHN)/SE-HLB		
G-CTWW	PA-34-200T Seneca II	34-7970191	G-ROYZ	21. 7.93	(Damaged in wheels-up landing at Rufforth on 14.5.99)
			G-GALE/N3052X		
G-CUBB	PA-18-180 Super Cub	18-3111	PH-WAM	5.12.78	
	(L-18C-PI)(Frame No. 18-3009)		Belgian AF OL-L37/53-4711		
G-CUBI	PA-18-135 Super Cub	18-3181	PH-GAV	26. 2.79	CofA expired 4.11.94. Canx by CAA 29.1.99.
	(L-18C-PI) (Official c/n is 18-559, which relates to PH-GAV prior to its 1970 rebuild when it incorporated frame no. 18-3170 from PH-VCV)		PH-VCV/R.Netherlands AF R-83/Belgian AF L-107/53-4781		
G-CUBJ	PA-18-150 Super Cub	18-2036	PH-MBF	15.12.82	
	(L-18C-PI) (Frame No.18-2035) (Regd with c/n 18-5395 (see G-SUPA) which relates to PH-MBF prior to its 1972 rebuild.)		PH-NLF/R.Netherlands AF R-43/8A-43/52-2436		
G-CUBP	PA-18-150 Super Cub	18-8482	G-BVMI	8. 8.96	
	(Frame No.18-8725; regd with c/n 18-8823, the "official" identity of N1136Z/(PH-WDP)/D-EIAC but which was itself rebuilt 1984/85 with frame no.18-4613 from D-EKAF. This latter frame was fitted to G-BVMI following its accident 15.8.95 and G-BVMIs repaired frame became G-CUBP)		OH-PIN/N4262Z		
G-CUBY	Piper J3C-65 Cub	16317	G-BTZW	2. 3.95	
	(Rebuilt with new fuselage 96/97)		N88689/NC88689		
G-CUCU	Colt 180A HAFB	3869		22. 4.96	
G-CUGA	Gulfstream American GA-7 Cougar	GA7-0051	N764GA	13.11.87	To N51EH 10/95. Canx 3.10.95.
			N10ZA/N764SA		
G-CUKL	Beechcraft 200 Super King Air	BB-641	G-CNSI	21. 6.83	To (F-GGLH)/F-GGVV 5/89. Canx 5.4.89.
			G-OSKA		
G-CULL	Bell 206B JetRanger II	348	EI-BXQ	5. 5.89	Restored as G-BEWY 4/93. Canx.
			G-BEWY/9Y-TDF		
G-CULT	Cameron D-38 Hot-Air Airship	693		15.12.80	To N27376 5/82. Canx 10.5.82.
G-CUPN	PA-46-350P Malibu Mirage	4636144		11. 2.98	
G-CURE	Colt 77A HAFB	1424		3. 7.89	Canx as WFU 29.4.97. Donated to BBAC Museum 13.11.97.
	(Standard shape plus Alka Seltzer tablet blisters)				
G-CURR	Cessna 172R Skyhawk II	172-80143	G-BXOH	27. 5.98	
			N9989F		
G-CUTY	Europa Avn Europa	PFA/247-12910		20. 8.96	
G-CVAN	Reims Cessna F.406 Caravan II	0019	F-WZDR	4. 1.88	To D2-ECQ 12/90. Canx 12.12.90.
G-CVBF	Cameron A-210 HAFB	3588		2. 6.95	
G-CVIL	Piper J3C-65 (L-4H-PI) Cub	12005	OO-VIL	23. 8.96	
	(Frame No.11832)		OO-VVV/44-79709		
G-CVIX	Hawker Siddeley 110 Sea Vixen D.3	10125	XP924	26. 2.96	(Stored 1/97 Swansea/Fairwood Common)
	(Regd as FAW.2 with c/n 10132 - which was XP958 w/o 14.7.66 in the Strait of Johore)				
G-CVOK	PA-32-300 Cherokee Six	32-7940217	OE-DOH	22. 6.89	To G-ILTS 3/90. Canx.
			N2941C		
G-CVPM	VPM M-16 Tandem Trainer	VPM16-UK-110		26. 3.98	
G-CVYD	Airbus A.320-231	393	B-HYO	24. 2.98	
			VR-HYO/F-WWIR		
G-CVYE	Airbus A.320-231	394	B-HYP	23. 3.98	
			VR-HYP/F-WWBB		
G-CVYG	Airbus A.320-231	443	B-HYT	10.11.98	
			VR-HYT/F-WWBV		
G-CWAG	Sequoia Falco F.8L	PFA/100-10895		11. 5.92	
G-CWBM	Phoenix Currie Wot	PFA/3020	G-BTVP	28. 3.94	
G-CWCW	Cameron R-900 HAFB	4386		9.11.98	
G-CWFA	PA-38-112 Tomahawk	38-78A0120	G-BTGC	17. 8.99	
			N9507T		
G-CWIZ	Aerospatiale AS.350B Ecureuil	1847	CS-HDF	18.10.95	
			G-DJEM/G-ZBAC/G-SEBI/G-BMCU		

Regn	Type	c/n	Previous identity	Regn date	Fate or immediate subsequent identity (if known)
G-CWOT	Phoenix Currie Wot	PFA/3019		31. 1.78	
	(Used parts from G-AXWY)				
G-CXCX	Cameron N-90 HAFB	1242		14. 3.86	
	(Replacement envelope c/n 3332)				
G-CXMF	Gulfstream G.1159 Gulfstream II	204	N17588	21. 7.78	To N806CC 5/84. Canx 16.5.84.
G-CYAA	The series from G-CYAA to G-CYHD was allocated to Canadian military aircraft use from 6/20 until 1931.				
G-CYGI(2)	Hapi Cygnet SF-2A	PFA/182-12084		17.12.93	No Permit to Fly issued. Canx by CAA 8.5.99.
G-CYII	HS.125 Srs.600B	256005	G-BART	24. 5.84	To EC-EAC 7/86. Canx 24.7.86.
			(G-BJUT)/(G-BJXV)/G-BART		
"G-CYII"	Bell 206L-2 Long Ranger	45724	G-BKMJ	----	Marks G-CYII used unofficially in 9/83 as an exhibit at
			N18098		Cranfield. Returned to G-BKMJ.
G-CYLS	Cessna T.303 Crusader	T303-00005	N20736	20.12.90	
			G-BKXI/N303CC/(N9355T)		
G-CYMA	Gulfstream American GA-7 Cougar		G-BKOM	15. 8.83	
		GA7-0083	N794GA		
G-CYPP	PBN BN-2T Turbine Islander	2207	G-BPLO	1.12.89	To 5B-CPA 6/90. Canx 14.6.90.
G-CYUR	The series from G-CYUR to G-CYZZ was allocated to Canadian military aircraft from 6/20 until 1931.				
G-CZAR	Cessna 560 Citation V	560-0046	(N26656)	29.11.89	
G-CZCZ	Avions Mudry/CAARP CAP.10B	54	OE-AYY	28. 7.94	
			F-WZCG/HB-SAK/F-BUDT		

G-D

G-D

Regn	Type	c/n	Previous identity	Regn date	Fate or immediate subsequent identity (if known)
G-DAAH	PA-28RT-201T Turbo Arrow IV		N3026U	27. 4.79	
		28R-7931104			
G-DAAL	Avro 748 Srs.1A/105	1557	G-BEKG	11. 8.92	CofA expired 16.9.96. WFU in 12/96. Broken up in 1/97 at
			G-VAJK/VR-CBH/		Blackpool for spares use. Canx as PWFU 18.3.97.
			G-BEKG/LV-IEE/LV-PXH		
G-DAAM	Robinson R-22 Beta	2043		3. 6.92	
G-DACA	Hunting Percival P.57 Sea Prince		WF118	6. 5.80	Permit expired 17.7.81. (Stored 6/97 Charlwood)
	T.1	P57/12			
G-DACC	Cessna 401B	401B-0112	N77GR	1. 9.86	
			N4488A/G-AYOU/N7972Q		
G-DACF	Cessna 152 II	152-81724	G-BURY	13. 6.97	
			N67285		
G-DACR	Airbus A.320-212	349	G-OEXC	27. 2.96	To OY-CNR 1/97. Canx 27.1.97.
			F-WWBU		
G-DACS	Short SD.3-30 Var.200	SH3089	C-GLAL	6. 7.98	
			N330CA/G-BKDM/G-14-3089		
G-DADS	Hughes 369HS (500)	22-0369S	N888SS	11. 6.90	
			N9101F		
G-DADY	Lindstrand LBL-77A HAFB	146		15. 9.94	To N353TT 5/97. Canx by CAA 26.2.97.
G-DAFL	Thunder Ax8-90 HAFB	2503		13. 8.93	To F-GNCS 9/94. Canx 9.8.94.
G-DAFS	Cessna 404 Titan II	404-0672	G-BHNH	24. 1.84	Ditched in the sea between Jura and Colonsay on 31.5.90.
			N6761L		Canx as destroyed 26.7.90.
G-DAFT	Aerospatiale AS.355F2 Twin Squirrel		G-BNNN	15. 1.88	To G-HARO 8/96. Canx.
		5364			
G-DAFY	Beechcraft 58 Baron	TH-1591	N5684C	6.10.93	
G-DAIO	McDonnell Douglas DC-9-83 (MD-83)			. .87R	NTU - To G-PATB 4/87. Canx.
	(Line No. 1356)	49400			
G-DAIR	Luscombe 8A Master	1474	G-BURK	3.10.97	
			N28713/NC28713		
G-DAJB	Boeing 757-2T7ER	23770		26. 2.87	
	(Line No. 125)				
G-DAJC	Boeing 767-31KER	27206		15. 4.94	
	(Line No. 533)				
G-DAJW	K & S Jungster I	PFA/1517		20.11.78	Canx by CAA 2.9.91.
G-DAKK	Douglas C-47A-35-DL Dakota	9798	(G-OFON)	26. 7.94	
			F-GEOM/French Navy 36/OK-WZB/OK-WDU/42-23936		
G-DAKO	PA-28-236 Dakota	28-7911187	PH-ARW	29. 7.99	
			(PH-MFB)/D-EECG/PH-ARW/OO-HCX/N29718		
G-DAKS	Douglas C-47A-75-DL Dakota	19347	"G-AGHY"	14. 9.79	Used marks G-AGHY for filming "Airline" in 1981.
			G-DAKS/TS423/42-100884		To N147DC 12.3.98. Canx 5.3.98.
G-DALE	Bell 206L-1 LongRanger II	45452	G-HBUS	16. 5.89	To N720B 1/90. Canx 2.1.90.
G-DAMI	Robinson R-22 Beta	1483		15. 8.90	To OE-XIW 12/93. Canx 15.12.93.
G-DAMY	Europa Avn Europa			21.10.94	
		105 & PFA/247-12781			
G-DAND	Socata TB-10 Tobago	72		5.12.79	
G-DANE	PA-28R-200 Cherokee Arrow B		OY-RPD	9. 2.89	Fatal crash on the South Downs Way at North Stoke, near
		28R-35745	SE-FHX		Houghton on 8.7.89. Canx as destroyed 17.10.89.
G-DANG	Colt 56A HAFB	3537	G-BVYL	19. 1.98	To N..... Canx 16.3.99.
G-DANI	Cessna 500 Citation I	500-0368	G-BFAR	29. 4.93	To N104AB 4/96. Canx 10.4.96.
	(Unit No.402)		A6-SMH/G-BFAR/A6-SMH/G-BFAR/ZS-LPH/G-BFAR/N36912		
G-DANN	SNCAN Stampe SV-4B	1200	OO-SVV	3. 2.81	Restored as OO-SVV 9/95. Canx 21.9.95.
			Belgium AF V-58		
G-DANS	Aerospatiale AS.355F2 Twin Squirrel		G-BTNM	28. 4.93	To G-OFIN 6/99. Canx.
		5480			

Regn	Type	c/n	Previous identity	Regn date	Fate or immediate subsequent identity (if known)
G-DANT	Rockwell Commander 114	14298	N4978W	9. 7.96	
G-DANZ	Eurocopter AS.355N Twin Squirrel	5658		14. 9.98	
G-DAPH	Cessna 180K Skywagon II	180-53016	N2620K	29. 1.92	
G-DARA	PA-34-220T Seneca III	34-8333060	PH-TCT N83JR/N4297J/N9632N	8.11.88	
G-DARE	PA-34-200T Seneca II	34-7870356	G-WOTS G-SEVL/N36742	22.11.91	To G-SENX 5/95. Canx.
G-DARL	PA-28-180 Cherokee C	28-3107	4R-ARL 4R-ONE/SE-EYD	3. 7.90	To G-BUTZ 4/93. Canx.
G-DARR	Cessna 421C Golden Eagle III	421C-0168	G-BNEZ N87386	13. 8.92	To G-KWLI 11/98. Canx.
G-DART	Rollason-Luton Beta 2	PFA/1364		11.10.78	No permit issued. Canx by CAA 4.7.91.
G-DASH	Rockwell Commander 112A	237	G-BDAJ N1237J	31. 3.87	
G-DASI	Short SD.3-60 Var.100	SH3606	G-BKKW G-14-3606	14. 2.83	
G-DASL	SNIAS SA.315B Lama	2537		20. 4.79	To F-GCLB 4/80. Canx 28.2.80.
G-DASU	Cameron V-77 HAFB	2300		6. 4.90	
G-DATA	Embraer EMB.110P2 Bandeirante	110-201	N110PJ G-DATA/G-BGNK/(G-YMRU)/(PT-GLT)	18. 8.81	To G-EIIO 2/88. Canx.
G-DATS	Cessna 310R II	310R-1294	(N6128X)	18. 5.78	To G-RIST 4/81. Canx.
G-DAVE	Jodel D.112 (Valladeau built)	667	F-BICH	16. 8.78	
G-DAVI	Cessna TU.206G Turbo Stationair 6	T206-04544	(N9429M)	19. 9.79	Crashed at Bellamy Farm, Piddletrenthide on 22.5.82. Canx as destroyed 5.12.83.
G-DAVO	American Aviation AA-5B Tiger	AA5B-1226	G-GAGA G-BGPG/(G-BGRW)	5. 1.96	
G-DAVT	Schleicher ASH-26E	26090		24. 4.96	
G-DAVY	Evans VP-2	PFA/63-10399		2.11.78	Canx by CAA 2.9.91.
G-DAWN	Cessna T.210M Turbo Centurion II (Wichita c/n 61910)	0005	(N732ZS)	22. 5.78	To (PH-MDA)/PH-DOC 7/82. Canx 5.7.82.
G-DAYI	Europa Avn Europa	PFA/247-13027		19. 8.96	
G-DAYS	Europa Avn Europa	PFA/247-12810		9. 5.95	
G-DAYY	Lindstrand Fruit Bottle SS HAFB	089		13. 4.94	Canx by CAA 26.2.97.
G-DBAA	Beechcraft B200 Super King Air	BB-1367	G-OBAA N5657N	2. 9.97	To N367AJ 26.9.97. Canx 24.9.97.
G-DBAC	Embraer EMB.110P1 Bandeirante	110-311	HB-LQE N303JA/(N119ME)/N303JA/PT-SCR	30. 9.94	To 8P-TIA 8/95. Canx 1.9.95.
G-DBAF	BAC One-Eleven Srs.201AC	BAC.011	EI-BWK N104EX/G-ASJG	17. 7.90	To EL-ALD 3/96. Canx 5.3.96.
G-DBAL	HS.125 Srs.3B	25117	G-BSAA 5N-AKT/5N-AET	20. 7.84	Canx as WFU 16.4.93. On fire dump at Southampton 11/95.
G-DBAR	Beechcraft 200 Super King Air	BB-819	N56GA	29. 4.87	To N425P 2/94. Canx 18.2.94.
G-DBBI	HS.125 Srs.700B	257130		27. 1.81	To G-CCAA 12/82. Canx.
G-DBHH	Agusta-Bell 206B JetRanger	8111	G-AWVO VH-BHI(5)/PK-HCA/G-AWVO/9Y-TDN/PK-HBG/G-AWVO	24. 5.96	Being broken up for spares at Redhill 11/96.
G-DBII	Cessna 560 Citation V	560-0032	N1229M	29.11.89	To N96MT 11/93. Canx 23.11.93.
G-DBMS	Cessna U.206G Stationair 6	U206-03910	N7373C	12. 2.90	To N206MG 12/92. Canx 9.12.92.
G-DBMW	Bell 206B-4 JetRanger IV	4401		8. 3.96	
G-DBOW	HS.125 Srs.600A	256032	(N14BR) N4BR/N38BH	3. 1.78	To C-GLBD 8/80. Canx 13.8.80.
G-DBYE	Mooney M.20M	27-0098	N91462	24. 3.98	
G-DCAC	McDonnell Douglas DC-9-83 (MD-83) (Line No. 1773)	49935	N3004C	19.11.90	To HB-IKM 1/96. Canx 25.3.96.
G-DCAN	PA-38-112 Tomahawk (Officially regd with c/n 38-79A0312)	38-79A0313	N9713N	15. 2.79	To G-BVHM 11/91. Canx.
G-DCAT	Schweizer-Gulfstream G.164D Turbo Agcat	12D	N8312K	21. 4.81	Struck cables and crashed while crop spraying near South Park Farm, Cridling, near Pontefract on 3.7.85. Canx by CAA 15.1.92. Reportedly to USA, but the frame was noted at Mavis Enderby in 6/96.
G-DCAV	PA-32R-301 Saratoga II HP	3246075	N92864	8. 5.97	
G-DCCC	BAe 125 Srs.800B	258002	VH-NJM G-DCCC/VH-III/(VH-CCC)/G-DCCC/(G-5-16)	4. 5.83	To (N800RY)/N1169D 12/96. Canx 5.12.96.
G-DCCH	MBB Bo.105DBS-4 (Originally regd as a Bo.105D)	S.770	D-HDYF	19. 9.86	
G-DCCI	BAe 125 Srs.1000B	259030	G-BUPL G-5-753	14.12.92	To N530QS 4/96. Canx 12.4.96.
G-DCDB	Bell 407	53137	N7238A	. 5.97R	NTU - Remained as N7238A. Canx.
G-DCEA	PA-34-200T Seneca II	34-8070079	N3567D	13. 2.91	
G-DCFB	Cessna 425 Corsair	425-0063	G-BMSH 9M-AXZ/N6844H	20. 7.88	To N79MM 9/92. Canx 14.9.92.
G-DCFR	Cessna 550 Citation II (Unit No. 418)	550-0419	G-WYLX VH-JVS/G-JETD/N1217N	21.11.95	To G-FJET 7/97. Canx.
G-DCIO	Douglas DC-10-30 (Line No. 354)	48277		27. 1.81	WFU on 28.3.99. (Stored 9/99 Manchester)
G-DCKK	Reims Cessna F.172N Skyhawk II	1589	PH-GRT PH-AXA	19. 5.80	
G-DCOL	PA-30-160 Twin Comanche B	30-1346	G-BGSU TR-LNH/F-OCJG/N8218Y	10. 9.80	To N3WZ 8/83. Canx 30.8.83.

Regn	Type	c/n	Previous identity	Regn date	Fate or immediate subsequent identity (if known)
G-DCOX	PA-31-310 Turbo Navajo	31-7812081	G-DIDI N27MT/N27644	27. 1.89	To N7069D 7/93. Canx 23.7.93.
G-DCPA	Eurocopter MBB BK.117C-1C	7511	D-HECU XA-THH/D-HXXL/G-LFBA/D-HECU(3)/D-HMBF(3)	16.12.97	
G-DCSW	PA-32R-301 Saratoga II SP	3213027	N9179G	25.10.90	To N848T 1/98. Canx 5.1.98.
G-DCXL	SAN Jodel D.140C Mousquetaire III	101	F-BKSM	27. 5.88	
G-DDAY	PA-28R-201T Turbo Cherokee Arrow III	28R-7703112	G-BPDO N3496Q	24.11.88	
G-DDCD	DH.104 Dove 8	04528	G-ARUM	17. 1.84	To G-OEWA 6/98. Canx.
G-DDDV	Boeing 737-2S3 (Line No. 746)	22633	(G-BMMP)	16. 2.81	To A40-BL 11/89. Canx 15.11.89.
G-DDMV	North American T-6G-NF Texan	168-313	N3240N Haitian AF 3209/49-3209	30. 4.90	
G-DDSC	Europa Avn Europa XS	PFA/247-13291		14. 4.98	
G-DEAL	Robinson R-22 Beta	0867	N7166H	30. 9.88	Destroyed in a crash at Bledlow Great Wood, near Chinnor, Bucks on 28.3.90. Canx as destroyed 9.8.90.
G-DEAN	Solar Wings Pegasus XL-Q	SE-TE-0117 & SW-WQ-0123	G-MVJV	30.11.98	
G-DEBA	BAe 146 Srs.200	E2028	N171US N351PS	1. 5.96	
G-DEBB	Beechcraft 35-B33 Debonair	CD-602	N9713Y	19. 6.91	Wheels-up landing at Canterbury on 12.7.94. Dismantled at Hurn in 9/94. Canx by CAA 19.10.94. To N338S in 7/95.
G-DEBC	BAe 146 Srs.200	E2024	N166US N348PS	23. 5.96	
G-DEBD	BAe 146 Srs.200	E2034	N174US N354PS	23. 5.96	
G-DEBE	BAe 146 Srs.200	E2022	N163US N346PS	5. 8.96	
G-DEBF	BAe 146 Srs.200	E2023	N165US N347PS	25. 9.96	
G-DEBG	BAe 146 Srs.200	E2040	N178US N357PS	1. 4.97	
G-DEBH	BAe 146 Srs.200	E2045	N185US N362PS	27. 8.97	
G-DEBI	Beechcraft A36 Bonanza	E-674	TR-LUH	1. 6.78	To ZS-LEY 12/81. Canx 6.10.81.
G-DEBJ	BAe 146 Srs.100	E1004	VH-NJA PK-MTA/G-OJET/G-5-537/(N346SS)/G-BRJS/G-5-04/ZD695/G-OBAF/(G-SSCH)/(G-BIAG)	6. 8.98	
G-DEBK	BAe 146 Srs.200	E2012	C-FHAV N601AW	19. 2.99	
G-DEBL	BAe 146 Srs.200	E2014	C-FHAX N602AW	2.12.98	
G-DEBM	BAe 146 Srs.200	E2016	C-FHAZ N605AW	8. 1.99	
G-DEBN	BAe 146 Srs.100	E1015	EC-GEP EC-971/N568BA/XA-RST/N461AP/G-5-01	15.12.98	
G-DEBS	Colt AA-150 Gas Free Balloon	465		18.11.82	Canx as WFU 16.10.89.
G-DEBY	Beechcraft 35-A33 Debonair	CD-214	G-ASHR EI-ALI	17. 6.86	Ditched in sea shortly after take-off from Frejus, France on 29.7.86. Canx as destroyed 23.2.95.
G-DEBZ	Boeing 737-3S3 (Line No. 1517)	24059	RP-C4006 EC-FGG/EC-711/G-BNPB/C-FGHT/G-BNPB	10. 5.99	
G-DEDE	Cessna 421C Golden Eagle III (RAM conversion)	421C-0261	N6148G	20. 1.87	To 5Y-TRI /91. Canx 21.10.91.
G-DEER	Robinson R-22 Beta	2827		17. 7.98	
G-DEJL	Robinson R-22 Beta	2001		31. 3.92	Substantially damaged in crash at The Estate, South Elkington on 19.4.99. Canx as WFU 22.7.99.
G-DELB	Robinson R-22 Beta	0799	N26461	18. 5.88	DBR at Sherburn-in-Elmet on 27.12.94. Canx by CAA 20.4.95.
G-DELF	Aero L-29A Delfin	194555	ES-YLM Soviet AF 12 (red)	28. 8.97	
G-DELI	Thunder Ax7-77 HAFB	160		12. 7.78	Canx 7.4.98 as destroyed.
G-DELL	Robinson R-22 Beta	1069	N80466	19. 7.89	To G-TGRS 11/97. Canx.
G-DELS	Robin DR.400/180 Regent	1981	F-GJZA	22.10.90	Fatal crash at Tockington Park Farm, Bristol on 22.7.96. Canx as destroyed 14.11.96.
G-DELT	Robinson R-22 Beta	0898		11.11.88	
G-DELY	Cessna TU.206G Turbo Stationair II	TU206-06058	LN-HOP N4956Z	28. 9.89	To N206KM 12/92. Canx 14.12.92.
G-DEMH	Reims Cessna F.172M Skyhawk II (Mod)	1137	G-BFLO PH-DMF/(EI-AYO)	18.11.91	
G-DEMO	PBN BN-2T Turbine Islander	2146	G-BKEA	14. 1.86	To G-05/OT-GLA Belgium Gendarmerie National 10/93. Canx 29.10.93.
G-DENA	Reims Cessna F.150G	0204	G-AVEO EI-BOI/G-AVEO	14.12.95	
G-DENB	Reims Cessna F.150G	0136	G-ATZZ	14.12.95	
G-DENC	Reims Cessna F.150G	0107	G-AVAP	14.12.95	
G-DEND	Reims Cessna F.150M	1201	G-WAFC G-BDFI/(OH-CGD)	6. 6.97	
G-DENE	PA-28-140 Cherokee	28-21710	G-ATOS	5. 2.98	
G-DENH	PA-28-161 Warrior II	28-8216202	G-BTNH N253FT/N9577N	14. 4.97	
G-DENI	PA-32-300 Cherokee Six	32-7340006	G-BAIA	7.12.95	
G-DENK	PA-28-181 Archer II	28-8290108	G-BXRJ HB-PGO	5. 2.98	
G-DENN	Bell 206B-4 JetRanger IV	4409	N75486	10. 6.96	

Regn	Type	c/n	Previous identity	Regn date	Fate or immediate subsequent identity (if known)
G-DENR	Reims Cessna F.172N Skyhawk II	1839	G-BGNR	30. 4.97	
G-DENS	Binder CP.301S Smaragd	AB.121	(G-BMHK) D-ENSA	20.11.85	
G-DENT	Cameron N-145 HAFB	4135		8. 4.97	
G-DENW	PA-44-180 Seminole	44-7995052	N21439	25.10.88	To G-SEMI 2/99. Canx.
G-DENZ	PA-44-180 Seminole	44-7995327	G-INDE G-BHNM/N0077X	3. 7.97	
G-DERR	Robinson R-22 Beta	1005	G-BPYH	28. 6.95	
G-DERV	Cameron Truck 56SS HAFB	1719		21. 3.88	
G-DESI	Aero Designs Pulsar XP	PFA/202-12147		14.11.91	
G-DESS	Mooney M.20J (201)	24-1272	N11598	20.10.87	
G-DEST	Mooney M.20J (201)	24-3429		6.11.98	
G-DESY	Cessna A.152 Aerobat	A152-0805	G-BNJE N7386L	20.10.97	
G-DEVA	PA-23-250 Aztec D	27-4295	(G-BFDP) N15RR/N6938Y	20. 3.78	To N5461U 1/84. Canx 9.1.84.
G-DEVN	DH.104 Devon C.2/2	04269	WB533	26.10.84	Permit expired 4.2.85. Canx by CAA 16.11.90. (On display .92 Shoreham)
G-DEVR	McDonnell Douglas DC-9-83 (MD-83) (Line No. 1793)	49941	G-JSMC N3002A	24. 3.94	To N881RA 4/96. Canx 18.4.96.
G-DEVS	PA-28-180 Cherokee	28-830	G-BGVJ D-ENPI/N7066W	5. 3.85	
G-DEXI	Cessna 340A II	340A-0422	N6216X	11. 6.87	To G-NAIL 8/90. Canx.
G-DEXP	ARV1 Super 2	003 & PFA/152-11154		24. 4.85	
G-DEXY	Beechcraft E90 King Air	LW-136	N750DC N30CW/N84GA/N328TB/TR-LTT	6. 4.89	
G-DEZC	HS.125 Srs.700B	257070	G-BWCR "G-JETG"/G-BWCR/G-5-604/HB-VGG/G-5-604/HB-VGG	28. 5.96	
G-DFIN	Aerospatiale SA.365N Dauphin 2	6028	F-WTNO G-DFIN	22. 4.82	To I-AGFN 2/87. Canx 12.2.87.
G-DFLT	Reims Cessna F.406 Caravan II	0036	F-WZDZ	22. 5.89	To G-MAFA 6/98. Canx.
G-DFLY	PA-38-112 Tomahawk	38-79A0450		15. 2.79	
G-DFTS	Reims Cessna FA.152 Aerobat	0340		4.11.77	To G-RLFI 1/90. Canx.
G-DFUB	Boeing 737-2K9 (Line No. 702)	22415		24. 9.80	To CS-TET. Canx 4.1.88.
G-DGDG	Glaser-Dirks DG-400/17	4-27		25. 3.83	
G-DGDP	Boeing 737-2T7 (Line No. 856)	22762	C-FPWE G-DGDP/C-FPWE/G-DGDP/C-FPWE/G-DGDP	22. 2.82	To C-FCPN. Canx.
G-DGIV	Glaser-Dirks DG-800B	8-145B69		27.11.98	
G-DGLD	Handley Page HPR.7 Dart Herald 214	194	G-BAVX PP-SDN	30.10.91	WFU at Exeter by 3/94. CofA expired 15.4.96. Dumped by 2/96. Canx as WFU 19.6.96. Broken up in 6/96.
G-DGWW	Rand Robinson KR-2	PFA/129-11044		7. 3.91	
G-DHAV	DH.115 Vampire T.11 (T.55) (Regd with nacelle no. DHP.48913) (Also reported as FFW built with c/n 994?)	15682	U-1234 Swiss AF/XH308	13.10.95	
G-DHCB	DHC.2 Beaver 1 Floatplane	1450	G-BTDL XP779	20. 6.91	
G-DHCC	DHC.1 Chipmunk 22 (Fuselage no. DHB/f/281)	C1/0393	WG321	28. 5.97	
G-DHCI	DHC.1 Chipmunk 22 (Fuselage no. DHB/f/772)	C1/0884	G-BBSE WZ858	12. 7.89	
G-DHDV	DH.104 Dove 8	04205	VP981	26.10.98	
"G-DHEA"	HS.125 Srs 3B/RA	25144	G-OHEA G-AVRG/G-5-12	25.11.86	Noted on dump Cranfield 6/99 marked as such - Is really the WFU G-OHEA.
G-DHGS	Robinson R-22 Beta	2592		19. 4.96	
G-DHLB	Cameron N-90 HAFB	3261		20. 4.94	
G-DHLD	Beechcraft B60 Duke	P-513	(G-BHLD) N6661T	29.10.80	To N807RA 5/82. Canx 28.5.82.
G-DHLI	Colt World 90SS HAFB	2603		2. 6.94	Canx as PWFU 9.4.99.
G-DHLZ	Colt 31A Air Chair HAFB	2604		2. 6.94	Canx as PWFU 9.4.99.
"G-DHMM"	DH.94 Moth Minor	940..		----	False marks applied in early-1939 for a photograph.
G-DHSS	DH.112 Venom FB.50 (FB.1R) (built by FFW, Emmen)	836	J-1626 Swiss AF	26. 3.99	
G-DHSW	Boeing 737-3Y0 (Line No. 1206)	23495	C-FPWD G-DHSW/C-FPWD/G-DHSW/C-FPWD/G-DHSW	14. 2.86	To EC-635 4/94, then EC-FVT 7/94. Canx 22.4.94.
G-DHTM	DH.82A Tiger Moth Replica (On rebuild from original unidentified components)	PFA/157-11095		6. 1.86	
G-DHTT	DH.112 Venom FB.50 (FB.1) (built by FFW, Emmen)	821	(G-BMOC) Swiss AF J-1611	17.10.96	
G-DHUU	DH.112 Venom FB.50 (FB.1) (built by FFW, Emmen)	749	(G-BMOD) Swiss AF J-1539	26. 2.96	
G-DHVV	DH.115 Vampire T.55 (Also quoted as c/n 974)(Built by FFW)	55092	U-1214 Swiss AF	5. 9.91	
G-DHWW	DH.115 Vampire T.55 (built by FFW, Emmen)	979	U-1219 Swiss AF	5. 9.91	
G-DHXX	DH.100 Vampire FB.6 (built by FFW, Emmen)	682	J-1173 Swiss AF	5. 9.91	
G-DHYY	DH.115 Vampire T.11	15112	WZ553	17. 3.95	(Stored 3/96)
G-DHZF	DH.82A Tiger Moth	82309	G-BSTJ OO-MEH/OO-GEB/R.Netherlands AF A-13/PH-UFB/R.Netherlands AF A-13/N9192	7. 7.99	

Regn	Type	c/n	Previous identity	Regn date	Fate or immediate subsequent identity (if known)
G-DHZZ	DH.115 Vampire T.55 (built by FFW, Emmen)	990	U-1230 Swiss AF	5. 9.91	
G-DIAL	Cameron N-90 HAFB	1851		7.11.88	
G-DIAN	Extra EA.230	14	D-ELBK(2)	10.12.87	To LV-X159 8/92. Canx 8.6.92.
G-DIAR	Boeing 737-3S3 (Line No. 1445)	23811	G-BNPA C-FGHQ/G-BNPA	24. 4.91	To N841LF 9/91. Canx 3.10.91.
G-DIAT	PA-28-140 Cherokee Cruiser F	28-7425322	G-BCGK N9594N	19. 7.89	
G-DICE	Enstrom F-28F	787	D-HANA	8.11.96	
G-DICK	Thunder Ax6-56Z HAFB	159		6. 7.78	
G-DIDI	PA-31-310 Turbo Navajo	31-7812081	N27MT N27644	14. 7.86	To G-DCOX 1/89. Canx.
G-DIET	Lindstrand Drinks Can SS HAFB (Diet Pepsi Can)	220		1. 5.95	
G-DIGI	PA-32-300 Cherokee Six	32-7940224	D-EIES N2947M	13.10.98	
G-DIKY	Murphy Rebel	PFA/232-13182		13. 2.98	
G-DIMB	Boeing 767-31KER (Line No. 657)	28865		28. 4.97	
G-DIME	Rockwell Commander 114	14123	N49829 C-GIHP	9. 3.88	
G-DINA	American Aviation AA-5B Tiger	AA5B-1218	N4555Y	27. 2.81	
G-DING	Colt 77A HAFB	1862		28. 6.91	
G-DINO	Cyclone Pegasus Quantum 15	7225	G-MGMT	15.12.98	
G-DINT	Bristol 156 Beaufighter 1F	STAN B1 184604	3858M X7688	17. 6.91	(On rebuild from various ex Australian components 7/97)
G-DIPI	Cameron Tub 80SS HAFB	1745		6. 5.88	
G-DIPS	Taylor JT.1 Monoplane	PFA/55-10320		19.12.78	No Permit to Fly issued. (Project stored .90) Not completed. Canx by CAA 31.3.99.
G-DIPZ	Colt 17A Cloudhopper HAFB	1245		3. 5.88	To OO-BRV. Canx 13.5.93.
G-DIRE	Robinson R-22 Beta	1663		29. 1.91	
G-DIRK	Glaser-Dirks DG-400	4-124	D-KEKT	18. 9.86	
G-DIRT	Thunder Ax7-77Z HAFB	345		23. 4.81	Permit expired 8.6.84. Canx by CAA 12.1.99.
G-DISC	Cessna U.206A Super Skywagon	U206-0653	G-BGWR PH-OTD/N4953F	16. 3.84	Restored as G-BGWR 1/96. Canx.
G-DISK	PA-24-250 Comanche (Officially regd with c/n 24-1197)	24-1190	G-APZG EI-AKW	9. 8.89	
G-DISO	SAN Jodel 150A Mascaret	24	9Q-CPK OO-APK(2)/F-BLDT	16.12.86	
G-DIVA	Cessna R.172K Hawk XP II	3071	N758FX	10. 2.86	
G-DIVE	PBN BN-2A-26 Islander	2011	(ZB503) "ZA503"/G-DIVE/G-BEXA	13. 6.79	To G-MALI 7/85. Canx.
G-DIWY	PA-32-300 Cherokee Six B	32-40731	OY-DLW D-EHMW/N8931N	26.11.91	
G-DIXI	PA-31-350 Navajo Chieftain	31-8152014	N40717	24. 4.86	To OY-SKY 10/92. Canx 15.9.92.
G-DIXY	PA-28-181 Archer III	2843195	N41284	10.12.98	
G-DIZO	Wassmer Jodel D.120A Paris-Nice	326	G-EMKM F-BOBG	30. 5.91	
G-DIZY	PA-28R-201T Turbo Arrow III	28R-7703401	N47570	13.10.88	
G-DIZZ	Hughes 369HE (500E)	89-0105E	N9029F	19. 2.97	
G-DJAE	Cessna 500 Citation I (Unit No.339)	500-0339	G-JEAN N300EC/N707US/G-JEAN/(N5339J)	3.11.98	
G-DJAR	Airbus A.320-231	164	OY-CNE (D-ACSL)/OY-CNE/F-WWIE	18. 3.97	
G-DJBB	Cessna 500 Citation I (Unit No.365)	500-0355	N36846	8. 2.77	To D-IAEV 10/78. Canx 4.10.78. (Later converted to Cessna 501 Citation II with c/n 501-0267)
G-DJBE	Cessna 550 Citation II (Unit No.171)	550-0154	(N8777N)	6. 6.80	To G-EJET 1/90. Canx.
G-DJBI	Cessna 550 Citation II (Unit No.030)	550-0030	(N3249M)	25. 8.78	To G-FERY 7/80. Canx.
G-DJCR	Varga 2150A Kachina	VAC 155-80	EI-CFK G-BLWG/OO-HTD/N8360J	11. 4.96	(Fuselage only noted in 8/98 at Perth-Scone)
G-DJEA	Cessna 421C Golden Eagle III	421C-0654	TC-AAA N37379/(N24BS)/N37379	16. 4.98	
G-DJEM	Aerospatiale AS.350B Ecureuil	1847	G-ZBAC G-SEBI/G-BMCU	15. 6.89	To CS-HDF. Canx 11.5.94.
G-DJHB	Beechcraft A23-19 Musketeer Sport III	MB-200	G-AZZE LN-TVH	6. 8.82	
G-DJHH	Cessna 550 Citation II (Unit No.290)	550-0262	N6862C	19. 5.81	To G-TIFF 4/86. Canx.
G-DJIM	DHCA.1 (This allocation is reliably reported not to be an aircraft at all - it is quoted as a manhole cover, the registration being taken to highlight the ridiculous practices regarding registrations at the time)	DHCA.1		28.12.78	No Permit to Fly issued. Canx by CAA 24.3.99.
G-DJJA	PA-28-181 Archer II	28-8490014	N4326D	14. 9.87	
G-DJLW	HS.125 Srs.3B/RA	25140	G-AVVB G-5-17/(G-5-16)	19. 1.89	
G-DJMJ	HS.125 Srs.1B/522	25106	G-AWUF 5N-ALY/G-AWUF/HZ-BIN	6. 1.84	To G-OMCA 9/87. Canx.
G-DJMS	PA-28-181 Arrow II	28-8090238	N8155H	6. 5.80	Crashed 4½ miles north of Port Erwin, IoM on 30.10.82. Canx as destroyed 5.12.83.

Regn	Type	c/n	Previous identity	Regn date	Fate or immediate subsequent identity (if known)
G-DJNH	Denney Kitfox Mk.3	772 & PFA/172-11896		20. 9.90	
G-DJOS	BAC One-Eleven Srs.531FS	BAC.237	G-AYWB VR-CAB/TI-LRL/TI-LRF/TI-1084C/G-AYWB	25. 4.90	To EI-CCU 12/90. Canx 17.12.90.
G-DKDP	Grob G-109B	6100	(G-BMBD) D-KAMS	9. 7.85	
G-DKGF	Viking Dragonfly Mk.1	PFA/139-10898		16.10.86	(Fuselage stored at Enstone 6/98)
G-DLCB	Europa Avn Europa	46 & PFA/247-12652		16.11.95	
G-DLDL	Robinson R-22 Beta	1971		2. 1.92	
G-DLFN	Aero L-29 Delfin	294872	ES-YLE Estonian AF/Soviet AF	28. 5.98	
G-DLOM	Socata TB-20 Trinidad	1102	N2823Y	13.12.90	
G-DLRA	PBN BN-2T Turbine Islander (Mod)	2140	ZG989 G-DLRA/G-BJYU	9. 3.84	Restored to MOD as ZG989 12/91. Canx to MOD(PE) 10.12.91.
G-DLTA	Slingsby T.67M Firefly 160	2002	G-SFTX	18. 8.88	To G-OPUB 10/96. Canx.
G-DLTI	Robinson R-22 Beta	0606	N2540J	9. 3.87	To EC-562/EC-FVN /94. Canx 7.3.94.
G-DLTR	PA-28-180 Cherokee E	28-5803	G-AYAV	15. 3.96	
G-DMAC	Pearce Jabiru UL	PFA/274-13321		15.10.98	
G-DMAF	Bell 222A	47061	G-BLSZ D-HCHS/(D-HAAD)	19. 2.85	To SE-HTN. Canx 21.12.88.
G-DMAN	HS.125 Srs.600B	256033	F-BUYP	16.12.77	To HZ-YA1. Canx 11.6.84.
G-DMCA	Douglas DC-10-30 (Line No. 348)	48266	N3016Z (G-BLFP)/N3016Z	12. 3.96	
G-DMCD	Robinson R-22 Beta	1201	G-OOLI G-DMCD	14.11.89	
G-DMCH	Hiller 360 UH-12E	5155		28. 4.81	Crashed & DBF at Whicham Valley, Cumbria on 21.8.93. Canx by CAA 24.11.93.
G-DMCS	PA-28R-200 Cherokee Arrow II	28R-7635284	G-CPAC PH-SMW/OO-HAU/N75220	29. 5.84	
G-DMWW	CFM Streak Shadow Srs.DD	304-DD		12.10.98	
G-DNCN	Agusta-Bell 206A JetRanger	8185	9H-AAJ 8185 Libyan Arab Republic AF/5A-BAM	21.11.97	
G-DNCS	PA-28R-201T Turbo Arrow III	28R-7803024	N47841	3. 1.89	(Stored 12/97)
G-DNLB	MBB Bo.105DBS-4 (Rebuilt with new pod S.850 .92)	S.60/850	G-BUDP G-BTBD/VH-LCS/VH-HRM/G-BCDH/EC-DUO/G-BCDH/D-HDBK	10. 4.92	
G-DNLD	Cameron Donald 97SS HAFB (Donald Duck head shape)	1554		3.11.87	(Extant 10/90 - N2045D allotted) Canx by CAA 17.4.98. (Based Disney World, USA)
G-DNVT	Gulfstream G.1159C Gulfstream IV	1078	(G-BPJM) N17589	29. 9.89	
G-DOBN	Cessna 402B II	402B-1243	N24PL N4604G	25. 4.96	
G-DOCA	Boeing 737-436 (Line No. 2131)	25267		21.10.91	
G-DOCB	Boeing 737-436 (Line No. 2144)	25304		16.10.91	
G-DOCC	Boeing 737-436 (Line No. 2147)	25305		24.10.91	
G-DOCD	Boeing 737-436 (Line No. 2156)	25349		6.11.91	
G-DOCE	Boeing 737-436 (Line No. 2167)	25350		20.11.91	
G-DOCF	Boeing 737-436 (Line No. 2178)	25407		9.12.91	
G-DOCG	Boeing 737-436 (Line No. 2183)	25408		16.12.91	
G-DOCH	Boeing 737-436 (Line No. 2185)	25428		19.12.91	
G-DOCI	Boeing 737-436 (Line No. 2188)	25839		8. 1.92	
G-DOCJ	Boeing 737-436 (Line No. 2197)	25840		15. 1.92	
G-DOCK	Boeing 737-436 (Line No. 2222)	25841		25. 2.92	
G-DOCL	Boeing 737-436 (Line No. 2228)	25842		2. 3.92	
G-DOCM	Boeing 737-436 (Line No. 2244)	25843		19. 3.92	
G-DOCN	Boeing 737-436 (Line No. 2379)	25848		21.10.92	
G-DOCO	Boeing 737-436 (Line No. 2381)	25849		26.10.92	
G-DOCP	Boeing 737-436 (Line No. 2386)	25850		2.11.92	
G-DOCR	Boeing 737-436 (Line No. 2387)	25851		6.11.92	
G-DOCS	Boeing 737-436 (Line No. 2390)	25852		1.12.92	
G-DOCT	Boeing 737-436 (Line No. 2409)	25853		22.12.92	
G-DOCU	Boeing 737-436 (Line No. 2417)	25854		18. 1.93	

Regn	Type	c/n	Previous identity	Regn date	Fate or immediate subsequent identity (if known)
G-DOCV	Boeing 737-436 (Line No. 2420)	25855		25. 1.93	
G-DOCW	Boeing 737-436 (Line No. 2422)	25856		2. 2.93	
G-DOCX	Boeing 737-436 (Line No. 2451)	25857		29. 3.93	
G-DOCY	Boeing 737-436 (Line No. 2514)	25844	OO-LTQ G-BVBY/TC-ALS/G-BVBY/(G-DOCY)	17.10.96	
G-DOCZ	Boeing 737-436 (Line No. 2522)	25858	EC-FXJ EC-657/G-BVBZ/(G-DOCZ)	12.12.94	
G-DODB	Robinson R-22 Beta	0911	N8005R	3. 5.96	
G-DODD	Reims Cessna F.172P Skyhawk II	2175		5.10.82	
G-DODI	PA-46-350P Malibu Mirage	4636019		26.10.95	
G-DODO	Grob G-115A	8008	D-ENFT	9.11.89	To G-TAYI 9/90. Canx.
G-DODR	Robinson R-22 Beta	1325	N80721	5. 6.96	
G-DODS	PA-46-310P Malibu	4608010	N9100N	11.12.86	To N146DS 1/95. Canx 2.2.95.
G-DODY	PA-46-350P Malibu Mirage	4622188		10. 3.95	To (D-ERUU)/D-ERBU 1/96. Canx 14.12.95.
G-DOEA	American Aviation AA-5A Cheetah	AA5A-0895	G-RJMI N27170	30. 4.96	
G-DOFY	Bell 206B JetRanger III	3637	N2283F	26. 8.87	
G-DOGS	Cessna R.182 Skylane RG II	R182-00070	N7309X	30. 5.80	To 9J-DOG. Canx 11.9.98.
G-DOGZ	Horizon 1	PFA/241-13129		10. 8.98	
G-DOLL	Thunder Ax6-56Z HAFB	355		11. 5.81	To OO-BHF 10/84. Canx 11.9.84.
G-DOLR	Aerospatiale AS.355F1 Twin Squirrel	5300	G-BPVB OH-HAJ/D-HEHN	12. 5.89	To G-ECOS 9/92. Canx.
G-DOLY	Cessna T.303 Crusader	T303-00107	N303MK G-BJZK/(N3645C)	20. 7.94	
G-DONA	Cessna 152 II	152-80546	G-BIDH N25234	28. 3.89	Restored as G-BIDH 4/92. Canx.
G-DONG	Sky 105-24 HAFB	011	G-BWKP	5. 2.97	
G-DONI	American Aviation AA-5B Tiger	AA5B-1029	G-BLLT OO-RTG/(OO-HRS)	20. 7.95	
G-DONS	PA-28RT-201T Turbo Arrow IV	28R-8131077	N8336L	22. 4.88	
G-DONZ	Europa Avn Europa	PFA/247-12545		1. 6.94	
G-DOOK	Beechcraft 60 Duke	P-94	D-ICAV G-AXEN	24.10.85	To SE-KKY. Canx 1.6.89.
G-DOOR	Socata MS.893E Rallye 180GT	13086	EI-BHD F-GBCF	24.11.88	To G-OACI 5/98. Canx.
G-DOOZ	Aerospatiale AS.355F2 Twin Squirrel	5367	G-BNSX	13. 5.88	
G-DORB	Bell 206B JetRanger III	3955	SE-HTI TC-HBN	15. 8.90	
G-DORE	Partenavia P.68C Victor	217	OY-CAD	16.11.82	To G-TELE 2/87. Canx.
G-DORK	Embraer EMB.110P1 Bandeirante	110-369	N698RA PT-SEN	15. 8.90	To G-OCSZ 4/95. Canx.
G-DORN	EKW C-3605	332	HB-RBJ Swiss AF C-552	15. 5.98	(On final stages of rebuild 12/98 North Weald)
G-DOSH	DHC.6-210 Twin Otter	200	N66200	13.12.89	To G-BUOM 10/92. Canx.
G-DOUG	Agusta-Bell 206B JetRanger III	8557		9. 8.78	To G-MKAN 1/80. Canx.
G-DOVE	Cessna 182Q Skylane II	182-66724	N96446	26. 6.80	
G-DOWN	Colt 31A Air Chair HAFB	1570		3. 8.89	
G-DPPA	Bell 206B JetRanger III	4090	C-FHPA	1. 3.90	To N62AJ 5/92. Canx 8.5.92.
G-DPPH	Agusta A.109E Power	11053		. 9.99	
G-DPPS	Eurocopter AS.355N Twin Squirrel	5502	F-WYMM	20. 3.92	To G-NMHS 3/98. Canx.
G-DPST	Phillips ST-2 Speedtwin	PFA/207-12674		10. 5.96	
G-DPUK	Mooney M.20K (231)	25-0631	G-BNZS N1154A	2. 4.98	
G-DRAC	Cameron Dracula Skull SS HAFB	2655		14.11.91	
G-DRAG	Cessna 152 II (Tailwheel conversion)	152-83188	G-REME G-DRAG/G-BRNF/N47217	27. 4.90	
G-DRAI	Robinson R-22 Beta	0918	N8008V	2. 2.89	To N2018Y 7/99. Canx 30.6.99.
G-DRAM	Reims Cessna FR.172F Rocket (Floatplane)	0102	OH-CNS	18. 9.98	
G-DRAR	Hughes 369E (500E)	0486E	N101LH N1608Z	15. 9.95	
G-DRAW	Colt 77A HAFB	1830		31. 8.90	
G-DRAY	Taylor JT.1 Monoplane	PFA/1452		13. 7.78	
G-DRBG	Cessna 172M Skyhawk II	172-65263	G-MUIL N64486	18. 1.95	
G-DREX	Cameron Saturn 110SS HAFB	4217		28.10.97	
G-DRGN	Cameron N-105 HAFB	2024		13. 6.91	
G-DRGS	Cessna 182S Skylane II	182-80375	N2389X	17.11.98	
G-DRHL	Eurocopter AS.350B2 Ecureuil	3032		12. 1.98	
G-DRJC	Boeing 757-2T7 (Line No. 132)	23895		9. 4.87	To G-BYAM 3/93. Canx.
G-DRMM	Europa Avn Europa	PFA/247-13201		27. 7.98	
G-DRNT	Sikorsky S-76A II Plus	760201	N93WW N3WQ/N3WL/N3121G	5. 4.90	

(Note: A static "G-DRNT" was in use at Petak Offshore Industry Training Centre, Norwich 10/97)

Regn	Type	c/n	Previous identity	Regn date	Fate or immediate subsequent identity (if known)
G-DROP(1)	Cessna TU.206G Turbo Stationair 6 II	U206-04568	N9783M	. .79R	NTU - To G-SKYE 8/79. Canx.
G-DROP(2)	Cessna U.206C Super Skywagon	U206-1230	G-UKNO G-BAMN/4X-ALL/N71943	7. 8.87	
G-DRSV	Robin DR.315X Petit Prince (Regd with c/n PFA/210-11765 because of major rebuild work)	624	F-ZWRS	7. 6.90	
G-DRUM	Thruster TST Mk.1	8068-TST-081	G-MVBR	12. 1.99	
G-DRVE	Airbus A.320-212	221	F-GLGI ZS-NZS/F-WWIK	15. 5.96	To OY-CNB 3/97. Canx 18.3.97.
G-DRYI	Cameron N-77 HAFB	2046		7. 8.89	
G-DRYS	Cameron N-90 HAFB	3377		1.12.95	
G-DRZF	CEA DR.360 Chevalier	451	F-BRZF	4. 9.91	
G-DSAM	Aerospatiale AS.350B Ecureuil	1730	D-HHGG	1. 9.87	To CS-HCY. Canx 4.8.93.
"G-DSEL"	Europa Avn Europa	-		----	False marks worn at PFA Rally at Cranfield 4.7.99.
G-DSGC	PA-25-260 Pawnee C	25-4890	OY-BDA	3. 5.95	
G-DSGN	Robinson R-22 Beta	0738		20. 1.88	To G-OTHL 11/94. Canx.
G-DSID	PA-34-220T Seneca IV	3447001		21. 7.95	
G-DTCP	PA-32R-300 Cherokee Lance	32R-7780255	G-TEEM N2604Q	26. 1.93	
G-DTOO	PA-38-112 Tomahawk	38-79A0312		15. 2.79	Badly damaged whilst taxying at Seething on 9.7.94. Canx as WFU 31.1.95. (Fuselage dumped 3/99 at Panshanger)
G-DUCH	Beechcraft 76 Duchess	ME-382	N38033	2. 2.87	To N7WZ 10/96. Canx 7.10.96.
G-DUCK	Grumman G.44 Widgeon	1218	N3103Q N58337/42-38217/NC28679	15.11.88	(On rebuild .92 Ipswich) Moved to France in 10/92 and expected to be completed as a SCAN 30! Canx 24.3.93 on sale to France.
G-DUDE	Van's RV-8	PFA/303-13246		16. 7.99	
G-DUDS	CASA I-131E Jungmann Srs.2000	2108	D-EHDS Spanish AF E3B-512	27. 6.90	
G-DUDZ	Pierre Robin DR.400/180 Regent	2367	G-BXNK	3.12.97	
G-DUET	Wood Duet (This may be a modified Brugger MB.2 Colibri c/n PFA/43-10468)	D.001		19.12.78	
G-DUGI	Lindstrand LBL-90A HAFB	562		16. 8.99	
G-DUGY	Enstrom 280C-UK-2 Shark	1038	G-BEEL	16. 8.91	To G-HRVY 4/95. Canx.
G-DUKE	Beechcraft B60 Duke	P-367	N6779S	22. 3.78	Restored as N6779S 2/82. Canx 10.2.82.
G-DUNC	Cessna 182S Skylane II	182-80195	N9305F	27. 5.98	
G-DUNG	Sky 65-24 HAFB	125		20. 7.98	
G-DUNN	Zenair CH.250 Mono Z (Originally regd as Zenair CH.200)	AD-1 & PFA/24-10450		5.10.78	(Under construction .88)
G-DURO	Europa Avn Europa	PFA/247-12554		15.11.93	
G-DURX	Colt 77A HAFB (Originally regd as Thunder 77A)	1522		25. 5.89	
G-DUSK	DH.115 Vampire T.11	15596	XE856	1. 2.99	
G-DUST	Stolp SA.300 Starduster Too (Constructed by J.O.Perritt)	JP-2	N233JP	28. 4.88	Badly damaged in collision with Luscombe Silvaire G-AKTM 16.7.89 after landing at Badminton.
G-DUVL	Reims Cessna F.172N Skyhawk II (Previous identity was carried when delivered although not officially issued)	1723	"G-BFMU"	16. 8.78	
G-DVBF	Lindstrand LBL-210A HAFB	188		6. 3.95	
G-DVON	DH.104 Devon C.2/2 (Dove 8)	04201	(G-BLPD) VP955	26.10.84	(Stored 5/98 Little Staughton, wings at Kemble 5/99)
G-DWHH	Boeing 737-2T7 (Line No. 850)	22761	C-FPWD G-DWHH/C-FPWD/G-DWHH/C-FPWD/G-DWHH	22. 2.82	To C-FCPM. Canx 28.10.86.
G-DWIA	Chilton DW.1A Replica	PFA/225-12256		25. 1.93	
G-DWIB	Chilton DW.1B Replica	PFA/225-12374		22.12.93	
G-DWMI	Bell 206L-1 Long Ranger	45193	N18092	15. 2.79	To D-HHSW 1/92. Canx 28.1.92.
G-DWPH	UltraMagic M-77 HAFB	77/109		17. 3.95	
G-DXRG	Camaron Agfa 105SS HAFB	1801		22. 8.88	CofA expired 25.6.94. (Last known based in Germany) Canx as WFU 9.12.96.
G-DYAK	LET Yakovlev Yak C-11	170103	G-BWFU OK-...	27.10.98	(Nearing completion 4/99 at Gransden)
G-DYNE	Cessna 414 Chancellor	414-0070	N8170Q	4. 8.87	
G-DYNG	Colt 105A HAFB	1721	G-HSHS	9. 2.98	
G-DYOU	PA-38-112 Tomahawk	38-78A0436		19.10.78	Badly damaged on landing at Booker on 23.7.92. Canx as WFU 24.5.95. (Stored 6/97)
G-DZEL	Europa Avn Europa	PFA/247-12569		25. 9.95	To G-MKPU 12/97. Canx.

G-E

See also Section Three for G-EAAA to G-EBZZ allocations

Regn	Type	c/n	Previous identity	Regn date	Fate or immediate subsequent identity (if known)
G-ECAB	Curtiss JN-4D	1917	N2525 (ex.US Army)	28. 5.99	
G-ECAL	BAe 146 Srs.200	E2058	(G-BMXE) G-5-058/N148AC	31. 7.86	Restored as G-5-058/N148AC. Canx 24.9.86.
G-ECAS	Boeing 737-36N (Line No. 2835)	28554		16.12.96	
G-ECAV	Beechcraft 200 Super King Air	BB-561	N36GA N963JC	17. 4.86	
G-ECAW	Bell 206L-4 Long Ranger	52124	9M-BCM N8159Z	20. 8.99	
G-ECBH	Reims Cessna F.150K	0577	D-ECBH	16. 5.85	

Regn	Type	c/n	Previous identity	Regn date	Fate or immediate subsequent identity (if known)
G-ECCO	Gulfstream American GA-7 Cougar	GA7-0103	OO-RTB OO-HRJ/N734G	15. 5.80	Crashed into the sea ½ mile south of Wheelers Bay, Ventnor, IoW on 24.2.85. Canx as destroyed 21.1.87.
G-ECDX	DH.71 Tiger Moth Replica (built by Ron Souch)	SP.7		1.11.94	(Nearing completion 8/97)
G-ECGC	Reims Cessna F.172N Skyhawk II	1850		10.10.79	
G-ECGO	Bolkow Bo.208C Junior	599	D-ECGO	24. 8.89	(Damaged by gales at Prestwick on 26.12.98)
G-ECHO	Enstrom 280C-UK-2 Shark	1017	G-LONS G-BDIB	28. 5.82	
G-ECJM	PA-28R-201T Turbo Arrow III	28R-7803178	G-FESL G-BNRN/N321EC/N3561M	25. 9.90	
G-ECKE	Avro 504K Replica (AJD Engineering Ltd built)(Originally regd with c/n 0012)	0014		6.10.93	
G-ECKO	Colt 180A HAFB	1761		23. 7.90	Canx by CAA 16.8.95.
G-ECLI	Schweizer 269C (300C)	S.1784	N69A	16. 7.99	
G-ECMA	PA-31-310 Turbo Navajo C	31-7812032	N27493	3. 2.78	To G-BPYR 5/89. Canx.
G-ECOS	Aerospatiale AS.355F1 Twin Squirrel	5300	G-DOLR G-BPVB/OH-HAJ/D-HEHN	24. 9.92	
G-ECOX	Grega GN.1 Air Camper (Originally regd as an Pietenpol Air Camper GN.1)	WLAW.1 & PFA/47-10356		5.12.78	(Under construction 12/93)
G-EDCA(1) G-EDCA(2)	See Section Three.				
G-EDDI	Robinson R-22 Beta	1844		3. 7.91	To OO-LJR 6/95. Canx 15.6.95.
G-EDDY	PA-28RT-201 Arrow IV	28R-7918263	N8079E	21. 1.80	To F-GFLG 8/87. Canx 3.6.87.
G-EDEN	Socata TB-10 Tobago	66		8. 1.80	
G-EDFS	Pietenpol Air Camper	PFA/47-13206		24. 3.98	
G-EDGE	Jodel D.150 Mascaret	111 & PFA/151-11223		14. 9.88	
G-EDGI	PA-28-161 Warrior II	28-7916565	D-EBGI(2) N2941R	19. 1.99	
G-EDHE	PA-24-180 Comanche	24-3239	N51867 G-ASFH/EI-AMM	25. 3.81	To G-MOTO 3/87. Canx.
G-EDIE	Robinson R-44 Astro	0179		6. 6.95	To G-ZONK 7/97. Canx.
G-EDIF	Evans VP-2	PFA/63-10262		8. 9.78	NTU - To G-VPII 10/88. Canx by CAA 31.7.91.
G-EDIN	HS.748 Srs.2A/334	1757	9Y-TFT V2-LCG/VP-LCG/9Y-TFT	.11.86	To G-BPFU 11/88. Canx.
G-EDIT	Beechcraft B95 Travel Air	TD-417	G-AXUX OE-FAD/D-GINU	25. 3.87	To N881TX 8/94. Canx 2.8.94.
G-EDMC	Cyclone Pegasus Quantum 15	7513		11. 3.99	
G-EDNA	PA-38-112 Tomahawk	38-78A0364	OY-BRG	4. 9.84	
G-EDOT	Cessna T.337D Turbo Super Skymaster (Robertson STOL Master conversion)	T337-1062	G-BJIY 9Q-CPF/PH-JWL/N86056	17. 1.90	To G-RGEN 5/96. Canx.
G-EDRV	Van's RV-6A	PFA/181A-13451		20. 8.99	
G-EDRY	Cessna T.303 Crusader	T303-00280	N4817V	9. 3.87	
G-EDVL	PA-28R-200 Cherokee Arrow II	28R-7235245	G-BXIN D-EDVL/N1243T	30. 6.97	
G-EEAC	PA-31-310 Turbo Navajo B	31-761	G-SKKA G-FOAL/G-RMAE/G-BAEG/N7239L	5. 5.94	
G-EEEE	Slingsby T.31 Motor Glider	1500 PFA/42-10381		15. 9.78	No Permit issued. Canx as WFU 29.12.95.
G-EEGE	Robinson R-22 Alpha	0368	G-BKZK N8434E	9. 4.87	Crashed and overturned on landing at Sandtoft on 4.9.92. Canx as destroyed 13.1.93.
G-EEGL	Christen Eagle II (built by Aircraft Engineering Services)	AES/01/0353	5Y-EGL	14.12.90	
G-EELS	Cessna 208B Caravan I	208B-0619		3. 3.97	
G-EEMV	Hawker Sea Fury FB.11	41H-636335	N588 VH-BOU/WH588 (RAN)/WH588	10.12.97	
G-EENA	PA-32R-301 Saratoga SP	32R-8013011	C-GBBU	3.10.97	
G-EENI	Europa Avn Europa	PFA/247-12831		28. 7.98	
G-EENY	Gulfstream American GA-7 Cougar	GA7-0094	N721G	21. 6.79	
G-EESA	Europa Avn Europa	PFA/247-12535	G-HIIL	9. 4.96	
G-EESE	Cessna U.206G Stationair 6 II	U206-03883	OO-DMA N7344C	28. 2.85	Damaged on landing at Magilligan, Co.Londonderry on 31.12.88. Canx as destroyed 17.7.90. (Wreck stored 6/97)
G-EEUP	SNCAN Stampe SV-4C	451	F-BCXQ	1. 9.78	
G-EEVS	Agusta A.109A II	7393	G-OTSL	5. 8.91	To G-SLNE 7/96. Canx.
G-EEZE	Rutan LongEz (Originally regd as VariEze c/n 1567, possibly new kit)	11 & PFA/74-10308		13.12.77	No Permit to Fly issued. Canx by CAA 8.5.99.
G-EFIR	PA-28-181 Archer II	28-8090275	D-EFIR(3) N8179R	5. 5.99	
G-EFIS	Westland WG.30 Srs.100	014	G-17-18	24. 6.84	To N114WG 11/84. Canx 27.11.84.
G-EFPT	HS.125 Srs.700B	257020	(G-BFVN) (G-BFTP)	15. 6.78	To VR-BHE. Canx.
G-EFRY	Light Aero Avid Aerobat	PFA/189-12096		22. 3.93	
G-EFSM	Slingsby T.67M Firefly 260	2072	G-BPLK	16. 7.92	
G-EFTE	Bolkow Bo.207	218	D-EFTE	4. 1.90	
G-EGAL	Christen Eagle II	0042-86	SE-XMU	11. 3.96	
G-EGAP	Sequoia F.8L Falco	PFA/100-11256		29. 7.87	No Permit to Fly issued. Canx by CAA 3.4.96.
G-EGEE	Cessna 310Q	310Q-0040	G-AZVY SE-FKV/N7540Q	14.11.83	

Regn	Type	c/n	Previous identity	Regn date	Fate or immediate subsequent identity (if known)
G-EGEL	Christen Eagle II (built by MLP Aviation Ltd)	S.308		4. 2.91	
G-EGGG	Lindstrand LBL-90A HAFB (Humpty Dumpty shape)	269		14. 6.95	Canx by CAA 26.2.97. To N912HD 5/97.
G-EGGS	Robin DR.400/180 Regent	1443		15.11.79	
G-EGHB	Ercoupe 415D	1876	N3414G N99253/NC99253	1. 9.95	
G-EGHH	Hawker Hunter F.58	41H-697450	J-4083 Swiss AF	4. 7.95	(Under restoration 6/99 at Hurn)
G-EGHR	Socata TB-20 Trinidad	795	F-GGIQ	19.12.97	
G-EGJA	Socata TB-20 Trinidad	1101	N2807D	13.12.90	
G-EGLD	PA-28-161 Cadet	2841283	N92007	23.11.89	
G-EGLE	Christen Eagle II (Airmore Aviation built)	F.0053		30. 3.81	
G-EGLT	Cessna 310R II	310R-1874	G-BHTV N1EU/(N3206M)	9. 9.93	
G-EGNR	PA-38-112 Tomahawk	38-79A0233	OY-VIG SE-KNI/N2570C	6.10.97	
G-EGTR	PA-28-161 Cadet	2841281	G-BRSI(2) N92001	25. 4.98	
G-EGUL	Christen Eagle II	Argence 0001	G-FRYS N66EA	19. 1.93	
G-EGUY	Sky 220-24 HAFB	103		24. 4.98	
G-EGVL	Cameron A-250 HAFB	3303		20. 5.94	Canx as WFU 17.8.98.
G-EHAP	Sportavia-Putzer Fournier RF-7	7001	(G-BGVC) D-EHAP/F-WPXV	26. 6.79	To G-LTRF 12/97. Canx.
G-EHBJ	CASA I-131E Jungmann Srs.2000	2150	E3B-550 Spanish AF	19. 7.90	
G-EHIL	EH Industries EH-101 (Airframe No. PP3)	50003		9. 7.87	To MoD as ZH647 in 1993. Canx as PWFU 28.4.99.
G-EHJM	PA-31P-425 Pressurised Navajo	31P-7530002	N54934 OE-FHT/N54934	10. 7.96	To SX-BFU 8/98. Canx 21.4.98.
G-EHMJ	Beechcraft S35 Bonanza	D-7879	D-EHMJ	12. 1.99	
G-EHMM	Robin DR.400/180R Remorqueur	867	D-EHMM	10.12.84	
G-EHUP	Aerospatiale SA.341G Gazelle Srs.1	1407	F-GIJR N869GT/N869/N49523	3.10.97	
G-EIBM	Robinson R-22 Beta	1993	G-BUCL	25. 3.94	
G-EIIO	Embraer EMB.110P2 Bandeirante	110-201	G-DATA N110PJ/G-DATA/G-BGNK/(G-YMRU)/(PT-GLT)	19. 2.88	To VH-OZF 4/90. Canx 29.3.90.
G-EIIR	Cameron N-77 HAFB	358		16.11.77	
G-EIKY	Europa Avn Europa	PFA/247-12634		27. 9.94	
G-EIST	Robinson R-22 Beta	0852	N9081H	21. 9.88	To G-KAYT 6/94. Canx.
G-EITE	Luscombe 8AF Silvaire	3407	N71980	27. 7.88	Bounced on landing at Castle Bytham, Lincs. 23.9.95 after a flight from Temple Bruer. Engine power was applied but then lost and the aircraft force landed in a field. The port undercarriage then collapsed and the aircraft rolled over. Canx as WFU 11.12.95.
G-EIWT	Reims Cessna FR.182 Skylane RG II	0052	D-EIWT OO-BLI/F-GCYU	28. 1.86	
G-EJCB	Agusta A.109A-II	7265		2. 1.85	To G-CLRL 8/89. Canx.
G-EJET	Cessna 550 Citation II (Unit No.171)	550-0154	G-DJBE (N8777N)	11. 1.90	To G-JETJ 2/93. Canx.
G-EJGO	Zlin Z.226 Trener 6HE Special	0199	D-EJGO OK-MHB	7. 8.85	
G-EJMG	Reims Cessna F.150H	0301	D-EJMG(2)	27. 4.98	
G-EJOC	Aerospatiale AS.350B Ecureuil	1465	G-GEDS G-HMAN/G-SKIM/G-BIVP	21.12.94	
G-EKKL	PA-28-161 Warrior II	28-8416087	D-EKKL(2) N43588	24. 3.99	
G-EKOE	Robin DR.400/180R Remorquer	1484	D-EKOE	18. 1.85	Engine fire on start-up & burnt out at Dunstable on 7.5.87. Canx as destroyed 14.8.87.
G-EKOS	Reims Cessna FR.182 Skylane RG II	0017	D-EKOS	15. 7.98	
G-EKPT	BAC One-Eleven Srs.523FJ	BAC.211	G-AXLN VR-CAL/TG-AYA/PP-SDU/G-AXLN	30. 4.90	To EI-CCX 12/90. Canx 17.12.90.
G-ELAN	Boeing-Stearman B75N1 (N2S-3) Kaydet	75-7598	N68994 BuA.07994	25. 1.89	Canx 13.2.92 on sale to USA.
G-ELBC	PA-34-200-2 Seneca	34-7350021	G-BANS N15110	4. 4.91	
G-ELDG	McDonnell Douglas DC-9-32 (Line No. 648)	47484	OE-LDG	18. 4.90	To N949VV. Canx 7.5.96.
G-ELDH	McDonnell Douglas DC-9-32 (Line No. 667)	47555	OE-LDH	11. 5.90	To N964VV. Canx 9.2.96.
G-ELDI	McDonnell Douglas DC-9-32 (Line No. 672)	47559	OE-LDI	5. 5.90	To N948VV. Canx 13.3.96.
G-ELEC	Westland WG.30 Srs.200	007	G-BKNV	17. 6.83	Stored at Yeovil. Permit expired 28.6.95. Canx as WFU 27.2.98.
G-ELEN	Pierre Robin DR.400/180	2363		16. 9.97	
G-ELFI	Robinson R-22 Beta	1126	N80513	2.10.89	
G-ELIT	Bell 206L Long Ranger	45091	SE-HTK N2652	28. 7.99	
G-ELIZ	Denney Kitfox Mk.2	717 & PFA/172-11835		19. 7.90	(Damaged on take-off from Brighstone, IoW on 10.5.93)

Regn	Type	c/n	Previous identity	Regn date	Fate or immediate subsequent identity (if known)
G-ELKA	Christen Eagle II (built by D.James)	0001	N121DJ	18.10.94	
G-ELKS	Light Aero Avid Speed Wing Mk.4	PFA/189-13109		6. 1.98	
G-ELLA	PA-32R-301 Saratoga II HP	3246050	N9279Q G-ELLA	13. 8.96	
G-ELLE	Cameron N-90 HAFB	4498		11. 1.99	
G-ELLI	Bell 206B JetRanger III	4231	D-HMOF	24. 6.97	
G-ELLY	North American AT-6D Harvard III	88-14661	FAP1504 South African AF 7441/EX894/41-33867	17. 1.79	Fatal crash near Rabat, Malta on 22.6.82. Canx as destroyed 29.2.84.
G-ELMH	North American AT-6D-NT Harvard III	88-16336	FAP1662 Portuguese AF/EZ341/42-84555	22. 7.92	
G-ELOT	Cessna 550 Citation II (Unit No.601)	550-0601	(N1303M)	21.11.88	To G-OCDB 8/92. Canx.
G-ELRA	BAe 125 Srs.1000B	259003	G-5-702	8. 1.90	To N503QS /97. Canx 24.6.97.
G-ELSA	Europa Avn Europa	002 & PFA/247-12758		13. 6.94	To (N9114W)/N512SA 1/96. Canx 27.11.95.
G-ELZN	PA-28-161 Warrior II	28-8416078	D-ELZN N9579N	20. 7.99	
G-ELZY	PA-28-161 Warrior II	28-8616027	D-ELZY(2) N9095Z/(N163AV)/N9641N	13. 4.99	
G-EMAK	PA-28R-201 Cherokee Arrow III	28R-7737082	D-EMAK N38180	30. 8.85	(Stored 12/97)
G-EMAN	Aerospatiale AS.355F1 Twin Squirrel	5175	G-WEKR G-CHLA/N818RL/C-FLXH/N818RL/N818R/N5798U	29. 4.96	To G-REEM 3/98. Canx.
G-EMAS	Eurocopter EC-135T-1	0107		6. 7.99	
G-EMAU	Eurocopter AS.355N Twin Squirrel	5561		22.12.93	Destroyed in fatal accident at Welford, Northants., on 10.10.98. Canx as WFU 23.12.98.
G-EMAX	PA-31-350 Navajo Chieftain	31-7952029	N276CT SE-KKP/Swedish Navy 54202/SE-KKP/LN-PAI	8.12.98	
G-EMAZ	PA-28-181 Archer II	28-8290088	N8073W G-EMAZ/N8073W	26. 4.90	
G-EMBA	Embraer ERJ-145EU (Regd as a EMB-145EU)	145-016	PT-SYM	17. 7.97	
G-EMBB	Embraer ERJ-145EU (Regd as a EMB-145EU)	145-021	PT-SYR	27. 8.97	
G-EMBC	Embraer ERJ-145EU (Regd as a EMB-145EU)	145-024	PT-SYU	1.10.97	
G-EMBD	Embraer ERJ-145EU (Regd as a EMB-145EU)	145-039	PT-SZE	7. 1.98	
G-EMBE	Embraer ERJ-145EU (Regd as a EMB-145EU)	145-042	PT-SZH	3. 2.98	
G-EMBF	Embraer ERJ-145EU (Regd as a EMB-145EU)	145-088	PT-SB.	10.11.98	
G-EMBG	Embraer ERJ-145EU (Regd as a EMB-145EU)	145-094	PT-SBQ	18.11.98	
G-EMBH	Embraer ERJ-145EU (Regd as a EMB-145EU)	145-107	PT-S..	20. 1.99	
G-EMBI	Embraer ERJ-145EU (Regd as a EMB-145EU)	145-126	PT-S..	23. 4.99	
G-EMBJ	Embraer ERJ-145EU (Regd as a EMB-145EU)	145-134	PT-S..	24. 5.99	
G-EMBK	Embraer ERJ-145EU (Regd as a EMB-145EU)	145-167	PT-S..	26. 8.99	
G-EMBL	Embraer ERJ-145EU (Regd as a EMB-145EU)	145-177	PT-S..	. 9.99	
G-EMBM	Embraer ERJ-145EU	145-...		. .97R	(delivery due 11/99)
G-EMBN	Embraer ERJ-145EU	145-...		. .98R	(delivery due 1/00)
G-EMBO	Embraer ERJ-145EU	145-...		. .98R	(delivery due 3/00)
G-EMER	PA-34-200-2 Seneca	34-7350002	N3081T	29. 7.91	
"G-EMFC"	PA-28 Cherokee	?		. 8.89	Noted at East Midlands painted white/yellow with black registration for publicity purposes.
G-EMHH	Aerospatiale AS.355F2 Twin Squirrel	5169	G-BYKH SX-HNP/VR-CCM/N57967	3. 8.99	
G-EMIN	Europa Avn Europa	PFA/247-12673		1. 3.94	
G-EMJA	CASA I-131E Jungmann Srs.2000	013 & PFA/242-12340	(Sp.AF)	2. 9.94	(Composite from Spanish spares imported in .91)
G-EMKM	Wassmer Jodel D.120A Paris-Nice	326	F-BOBG	25. 1.80	To G-DIZO 5/91. Canx.
G-EMLY	Cyclone Pegasus Quantum 15	7531		30. 6.99	
G-EMMA	Reims Cessna F.182Q Skylane II	0099		4. 1.79	Landed short of its strip at Holme Court, near Biggleswade 29.12.92 and overturned, due to engine failure on final approach. Fuselage used in rebuild of G-BGFH .94/95. Canx as WFU 10.3.93.
G-EMMS	PA-38-112 Tomahawk	38-78A0526	OO-TKT N4414E	14. 9.79	
G-EMMY	Rutan VariEze	577 & PFA/74-10222		21. 8.78	
G-EMNI	Phillips ST.1 Speedtwin Mk.2	006 & PFA/207-12880		25. 5.95	
G-EMRD	HS.748 Srs.2B/378	1797	G-HDBD G-11-747/CS-TAR/G-11-1/D-AHSF/G-11-2	11.10.96	To ZS-PLO 6/99. Canx 15.6.99.
G-EMSI	Europa Avn Europa	PFA/247-12817		24. 1.95	
G-EMSY	DH.82A Tiger Moth	83666	G-ASPZ D-EDUM/E-6/T7356	27. 6.91	(On rebuild 3/98 at Chilbolton with parts from OO-MOT)

Regn	Type	c/n	Previous identity	Regn date	Fate or immediate subsequent identity (if known)
G-ENAM	Cessna 340A	340A-1814	N1232G	23. 4.86	To D-IBEL(2) 5/93. Canx 20.4.93.
G-ENCE	Partenavia P.68B Victor	141	G-OROY G-BFSU	1. 6.84	
G-ENIE	Nipper T.66 Srs.IIIB	PFA/25-10214		17. 3.78	
G-ENII	Reims Cessna F.172M Skyhawk II	1352	PH-WAG (D-EDQM)	18. 1.79	
G-ENIS	BAe Jetstream Srs.3102	655	G-LOGR G-BRGR/PH-KJD/G-31-655	31. 8.94	To SP-FTG 10/95. Canx 10.10.95.
G-ENIU	PA-24-260 Comanche B	24-4657	G-AVJU N9199P	23. 7.87	To G-KSVB 11/91. Canx.
G-ENNA	PA-28-161 Warrior II	28-7916060	N22065	1. 5.90	To G-ESFT 5/97. Canx.
G-ENNY	Cameron V-77 HAFB	1399		1.12.86	
G-ENOA	Reims Cessna F.172F	0138	G-ASZW	2. 9.81	
G-ENRI	Lindstrand LBL-105A HAFB	294		4. 8.95	
G-ENRY	Cameron N-105 HAFB	2096		26. 9.89	
G-ENSI	Beechcraft F33A Bonanza	CE-699	D-ENSI	17. 3.78	
G-ENTT	Reims Cessna F.152 II	1750	G-BHHI (PH-CBA)	9.11.93	
G-ENTW	Reims Cessna F.152 II	1479	G-BFLK	21. 1.93	
G-ENUS	Cameron N-90 HAFB	1914		18. 1.89	
G-EOCO	Boeing 707-338C (Line No. 550)	19294	N707HW B-2426/N707HW/OB-T-1264/N707HW/9Q-CDA/N707MB/P2-ANH/VH-EBU/P2-ANH/VH-EBU	6.10.89	Canx 2.9.92 on sale to USA. To USAF as 93-0597 17.5.92.
G-EOFF	Taylor JT.2 Titch	PFA/60-10319		6. 7.78	Canx as TWFU 1.12.95.
G-EOFS	Europa Avn Europa	PFA/247-13033		22. 7.98	
G-EOHL	Cessna 182L Skylane	182-59279	D-EOHL N70505	4. 3.99	
G-EOMA	Airbus A.330-243X	265	F-WWKU	26. 4.99	
G-EORG	PA-38-112 Tomahawk	38-78A0427		18. 9.78	(Rebuilt with new fuselage; old one stored 2/95)
G-EORJ	Europa Avn Europa	PFA/247-13139		23. 7.99	
G-EORR	Aerospatiale AS.350B Ecureuil	1040	G-FERG G-BGCW	6. 7.81	To G-OBAC 2/83. Canx.
G-EPAR	Robinson R-22 Beta	2781		26. 2.98	
G-EPDI	Cameron N-77 HAFB	370		25. 1.78	
G-EPED	PA-31-350 Navajo Chieftain	31-8252040	G-BMCJ N121CF/N41060	22. 3.95	
G-EPFR	Airbus A.320-231	437	C-FTDF G-EPFR/G-BVJV/N437RX/G-BVJV/C-FWDQ/G-BVJV/N437RX/F-WWDM	18.11.97	Marks D-AFRO reserved on 5.11.98.
G-EPJM	PA-28-181 Archer III	2843166	N41268	10. 9.98	
G-EPOL	Aerospatiale AS.355F1 Twin Squirrel	5302	G-SASU G-BSSM/G-BMTC/G-BKUK	13. 1.98	
G-EPOX	Aero Designs Pulsar XP	PFA/202-12355		27. 4.94	
G-EPTR	PA-28R-200 Cherokee Arrow II	28R-7235090	D-EPTR OH-PTR/(SE-KVF)/N4558T	26. 5.98	
G-ERBL	Robinson R-22 Beta	2711		26. 6.97	
G-ERCO	Ercoupe 415D	3210	N2585H NC2585H	7. 4.93	
G-ERDB	Hawker Cygnet Replica	PFA/77-10245		2.10.78	Not completed. Canx by CAA 6.2.87. To G-CAMM(2) 5/91.
G-ERDS	DH.82A Tiger Moth	85028	ZS-BCU South African AF 2267/T6741	27. 7.94	
G-ERIC	Rockwell Commander 112TC	13010	SE-GSA	26. 9.78	
G-ERIK	Cameron N-77 HAFB	1753		18. 5.88	
G-ERIN	BAe ATP	2003	G-BMYK	14.12.93	To G-MANL 10/94. Canx.
G-ERIS	Hughes 369D (500D) (Mod to 500E standard)	11-0871D	G-PJMD G-BMJV/N1110S	1. 3.96	
G-ERIX	Boeing-Stearman E75 (PT-13D) Kaydet	75-5093	N5055V 42-16930	9. 3.88	
G-ERMO	ARV Super 2	018	G-BMWK	7. 1.87	
G-ERMS	Thunder AS-33 Hot Air Airship (Now regd as Ax3 Sky Chariot)	A.1		28.11.78	
G-ERMV	Avro 748 Srs.1A/101	1537	G-FBMV G-ARMW/V2-LVO/G-ARMW/VP-LIT/G-ARMW	16. 3.92	To 9N-ACH. Canx 4.9.92.
G-ERNI	PA-28-181 Archer II	28-8090146	G-OSSY N81215	9.10.91	
G-EROS	Cameron H-34 HAFB	2296		6. 4.90	
G-ERRY	American Aviation AA-5B Tiger	AA5B-0725	G-BFMJ	20. 3.84	
G-ERTY	DH.82A Tiger Moth	82814	(D-E...) G-ERTY/D-EFYZ(1)/LX-JON/G-ANDC/R4897	1. 7.81	To D-EXMM 5/97. Canx 2.5.97.
"G-ERTY"	Avro 652A Anson I	-	LT135	----	False marks worn by an instructional airframe used by Air Service Training Ltd at Hamble in 1949/early 1950s.
"G-ERTY"	DH.82A Tiger Moth	83820	G-AKXW T7441	----	False marks worn by an instructional airframe used by the Airwork engineering school at Perth in 9/61.
G-ESAL	Agusta-Bell 206B JetRanger III	8598	G-BHXW	5.11.80	To D-HMSF 12/83. Canx 8.12.83.
G-ESFT	PA-28-161 Warrior II	28-7916060	G-ENNA N22065	16. 5.97	
G-ESKU	PA-23-250 Aztec C	27-3823	G-AWIY N6599Y	11. 4.96	
G-ESKY	PA-23-250 Aztec D	27-4172	G-BBNN N6832Y	24.11.95	
G-ESSO	Reims Cessna F.172F	0137	G-EWUD G-ATBK	30. 8.90	Restored as G-EWUD 12.9.90. Canx.

Regn	Type	c/n	Previous identity	Regn date	Fate or immediate subsequent identity (if known)
G-ESTA	Cessna 550 Citation II (Unit No.143)	550-0127	G-GAUL N550TJ/(N29TG)/N29TC/N2631N	24. 6.98	
G-ESTE	American Aviation AA-5A Cheetah	AA5A-0780	G-GHNC N26877	28. 4.87	
G-ESUS	Rotorway Exec 162F	6169		7.10.96	
G-ETBY	PA-32-260 Cherokee Six (Rebuild using spare frame no.32-858S)	32-211	G-AWCY (N3365W)	13. 7.89	
G-ETCD	Colt 77A HAFB	1095		17. 7.87	Canx by CAA 4.8.98.
G-ETDA	PA-28-161 Warrior II	28-8116256	N84051	9. 3.88	
G-ETDB	PA-38-112 Tomahawk	38-81A0032		6. 5.88	Crashed at Vauville, France on 30.6.90. Canx as destroyed 1.11.96.
G-ETDC	Cessna 172P Skyhawk II	172-74690	N53133	4. 5.88	
G-ETFT	Colt Financial Times SS HAFB	1792	G-BSGZ	11. 1.91	
G-ETHY	Cessna 208 Caravan	208-00293		19.10.98	To N1295M 12/98. Canx 10.11.98.
G-ETIN	Robinson R-22 Beta	0853	N9081D	7. 9.88	
G-ETME	Nord 1002	274	N108J F-BFRV/French AF 274	. .99R	(At Duxford 7/99)
G-ETOM	BAe 125 Srs.800B	258130	G-BVFC G-TPHK/G-FDSL/G-5-620	31.10.95	To D-CPAS 4/98. Canx 17.3.98.
G-ETON	Maule M.5-235C Lunar Rocket	7292C	G-BHDB N5636F	5. 1.88	Destroyed in a barn fire near Hickstead, Sussex in mid-90. Canx as destroyed 26.9.90.
G-ETUP	Reims Cessna F.150L	1106	PH-HLG	19. 1.79	Crashed at Fareham Creek on 13.11.83. Canx.
G-EUOA	Airbus A.320-...	1...	F-W...	.11.98R	
G-EUOB	Airbus A.320-...	1...	F-W...	.11.98R	
G-EUOC	Airbus A.320-...	1...	F-W...	.11.98R	
G-EUOD	Airbus A.320-...	1...	F-W...	.11.98R	
G-EUOE	Airbus A.320-...	1...	F-W...	.11.98R	
G-EUOF	Airbus A.320-...	1...	F-W...	.11.98R	
G-EUOG	Airbus A.320-...	1...	F-W...	.11.98R	
G-EUOH	Airbus A.320-...	1...	F-W...	.11.98R	
G-EUOI	Airbus A.320-...	1...	F-W...	.11.98R	
G-EUOJ	Airbus A.320-...	1...	F-W...	.11.98R	
G-EUOK	Airbus A.320-...	1...	F-W...	.11.98R	
G-EUOL	Airbus A.320-...	1...	F-W...	.11.98R	
G-EUOM	Airbus A.320-...	1...	F-W...	.11.98R	
G-EUON	Airbus A.320-...	1...	F-W...	.11.98R	
G-EUOO	Airbus A.320-...	1...	F-W...	.11.98R	
G-EUOP	Airbus A.320-...	1...	F-W...	.11.98R	
G-EUOR	Airbus A.320-...	1...	F-W...	.11.98R	
G-EUOS	Airbus A.320-...	1...	F-W...	.11.98R	
G-EUOT	Airbus A.320-...	1...	F-W...	.11.98R	
G-EUOU	Airbus A.320-...	1...	F-W...	.11.98R	
G-EUOV	Airbus A.320-...	1...	F-W...	.11.98R	
G-EUOW	Airbus A.320-...	1...	F-W...	.11.98R	
G-EUOX	Airbus A.320-...	1...	F-W...	.11.98R	
G-EUOY	Airbus A.320-...	1...	F-W...	.11.98R	
G-EUOZ	Airbus A.320-...	1...	F-W...	.11.98R	
G-EUPA	Airbus A.319-131	1082	D-AVYK	.11.98R	(delivery due 9/99)
G-EUPB	Airbus A.319-131	1115	D-AV..	.11.98R	(delivery due 10/99)
G-EUPC	Airbus A.319-131	1118	D-AV..	.11.98R	(delivery due 10/99)
G-EUPD	Airbus A.319-131	1...	D-AV..	.11.98R	
G-EUPE	Airbus A.319-131	1...	D-AV..	.11.98R	
G-EUPF	Airbus A.319-131	1...	D-AV..	.11.98R	
G-EUPG	Airbus A.319-131	1...	D-AV..	.11.98R	
G-EUPH	Airbus A.319-131	1...	D-AV..	.11.98R	
G-EUPI	Airbus A.319-131	1...	D-AV..	.11.98R	
G-EUPJ	Airbus A.319-131	1...	D-AV..	.11.98R	
G-EUPK	Airbus A.319-131	1...	D-AV..	.11.98R	
G-EUPL	Airbus A.319-131	1...	D-AV..	.11.98R	
G-EUPM	Airbus A.319-131	1...	D-AV..	.11.98R	
G-EUPN	Airbus A.319-131	1...	D-AV..	.11.98R	
G-EUPO	Airbus A.319-131	1...	D-AV..	.11.98R	
G-EUPP	Airbus A.319-131	1...	D-AV..	.11.98R	
G-EUPR	Airbus A.319-131	1...	D-AV..	.11.98R	
G-EUPS	Airbus A.319-131	1...	D-AV..	.11.98R	
G-EUPT	Airbus A.319-131	1...	D-AV..	.11.98R	
G-EUPU	Airbus A.319-131	1...	D-AV..	.11.98R	
G-EUPV	Airbus A.319-131	1...	D-AV..	.11.98R	
G-EUPW	Airbus A.319-131	1...	D-AV..	.11.98R	
G-EUPX	Airbus A.319-131	1...	D-AV..	.11.98R	
G-EUPY	Airbus A.319-131	1...	D-AV..	.11.98R	
G-EUPZ	Airbus A.319-131	1...	D-AV..	.11.98R	
G-EURA	Agusta-Bell 47J-2 Ranger	2061	G-ASNV	21. 7.83	
G-EURO	Cessna 310R II	310R-0579	N87468	13. 6.78	To G-TVKE 4/82. Canx.
G-EURP	Boeing 737-35B (Line No. 1624)	24237	N5573B (D-AGED)	21.10.88	To D-AGEG 11/90. Canx 6.11.90.
G-EURR	Boeing 737-3L9 (Line No. 1365)	23717	OY-MMM	19. 3.90	To D-AGEH 3/91. Canx 5.3.91.
G-EUXS	Europa Avn Europa	PFA/247-12923		20. 3.97	Canx 14.4.98 on sale to USA.
G-EVAN	Taylor JT.2 Titch	PFA/3231		14.12.78	No Permit to Fly issued. Construction suspended. Canx as PWFU 24.3.99.
G-EVER	Robinson R-22 Beta	1109		25. 8.89	To N63992 7/99. Canx 30.6.99.
G-EVES	Dassault Falcon 900B	165	F-WWFD	13.11.97	

Regn	Type	c/n	Previous identity	Regn date	Fate or immediate subsequent identity (if known)
G-EVET	Cameron Concept 80 HAFB	3703		30.10.95	
G-EVNS	Cessna 441 Conquest II	441-0264	(F-ODJP) N8879S	17.11.83	To F-ODUJ 12/87. Canx 2.12.87.
G-EVNT	Lindstrand LBL-180A HAFB	071		13.12.93	
G-EWAN	Protech PT-2C Sassy	PFA/249-12425		23. 6.93	
G-EWBJ	Socata TB-10 Tobago	101		24. 3.80	To SX-BSI 9/93. Canx 29.9.93.
G-EWCL	Sikorsky S-76A	760058	N38PP N38RP	5.10.90	To N519AL 2/98. Canx 7.1.98.
G-EWFN	Socata TB-20 Trinidad	1009	G-BRTY	22. 1.90	
G-EWIZ	Pitts S-2SE Special	S.18	VH-EHQ	12.11.82	
G-EWUD	Reims Cessna F.172F	0137	G-ESSO G-EWUD/G-ATBK	26. 5.87	Forced landed in Dee Estuary, near West Kirby on 14.8.92 and badly damaged by incoming tide with one wing torn off. (Stored 2/93) Canx by CAA 29.4.94.
G-EXEA	Extra EA.300/L	082		9. 3.99	
G-EXEC	PA-34-200-2 Seneca	34-7450072	(G-EXXC) OY-BGU	11. 5.78	
G-EXEL	Embraer EMB.120RT Brasilia	120-116	PT-SNI	8. 3.89	To VH-XFX. Canx 11.6.93.
G-EXEX	Cessna 404 Titan II	404-0037	SE-GZF (N5418G)	3. 5.79	
G-EXIT	Socata MS.894E Rallye 235GT	12979	F-GARX	22. 9.78	
G-EXLR	BAe 125 Srs.800B (Converted to Srs.1000B, also c/n 259001)	258151		8. 1.90	To Wichita, KS by sea 10/95 and scrapped 1/96. Canx 25.6.97.
G-EXOR	Robinson R-22 Beta	1491	G-CMCM	20.11.91	To G-PBES 3/95. Canx.
G-EXPL	American Champion 7GCBC Citabria	1220-96		9. 5.96	
G-EXPM	BAC One-Eleven Srs.217EA	BAC.124	A12-124 R.Australian AF	5. 3.90	To 5N-TOM. Canx 6.12.91.
G-EXPR	Colt 90A HAFB	1064		17. 8.87	
G-EXPS	Short SD.3-60 Var.100	SH3661	TC-AOA G-BLRT/SE-KRV/G-BLRT/G-14-3661	11. 5.99	
G-EXTR	Extra EA.260	004	D-EDID	10. 8.92	
G-EXXC	PA-34-200-2 Seneca	34-7450072	OY-BGU	. .78R	NTU - To G-EXEC 5/78. Canx.
G-EYAS	Denney Kitfox Mk.2	PFA/172-11858		3. 3.93	
G-EYCO	Robin DR.400/180 Regent	1949		12. 3.90	
G-EYEI	Bell 206A JetRanger	597	N2258W	17. 7.87	Crashed into a building at Eastwood Toll, Glasgow on 24.1.90. Canx as destroyed 14.3.90.
G-EYES	Cessna 402C Utiliner II	402C-0008	SE-IRU G-BLCE/N4648N	16. 7.90	
G-EYET	Robinson R-44 Astro	0052	G-JPAD	30.11.98	
G-EYNL	MBB Bo.105DBS-5	S.382	LN-OTJ D-HDLR/EC-DSO/D-HDLR	19. 8.96	
G-EYRE	Bell 206L-1 Long Ranger II	45229	G-STVI N60MA/N5091K	12.11.90	
G-EZEE	Rutan 33 VariEze	1737	F-PYKJ F-WYKJ	12. 9.83	Crashed & caught fire on landing at Hungary Hall Farm, near RAF Wyton on 24.10.94. Canx as destroyed 31.1.95.
G-EZLT	Rutan VariEze	PFA/74-10236		13.12.78	To G-BKVE 7/83. Canx.
G-EZOS	Rutan VariEze	002 & PFA/74-10221		10. 7.78	
G-EZYA	Boeing 737-3Y0 (Line No. 1233)	23498	G-MONG C-GPWG/G-MONG/C-GPWG/G-MONG	30. 5.96	To "N308SW"/N308SA 3/99. Canx 29.3.99.
G-EZYB	Boeing 737-3M8 (Line No. 1614)	24020	N797BB I-TEAA/OO-LTA/(OO-BTA)	17.10.96	
G-EZYC(1)	Boeing 737-375 (Line No. 1395)	23708	4L-AAA PT-TEC/(C-GZPW)	. 2.97R	NTU - To D-AGEX 2/97. Canx.
G-EZYC(2)	Boeing 737-3Y0 (Line No. 1691)	24462	G-BWJA EC-FJR/EC-897/G-TEAA/EI-BZQ/(N116WA)/EI-BZQ/EC-ENS/EC-244/N5573K	28. 5.97	
G-EZYD	Boeing 737-3M8 (Line No. 1662)	24022	N798BB I-TEAE/OO-LTC/(OO-BTC)	5. 2.97	
G-EZYE	Boeing 737-3Q8 (Line No. 1506)	24068	SE-DTA G-OCHA/G-BNNJ/(N881DV)	4. 6.97	To N317WN 4/99. Canx 1.4.99.
G-EZYF	Boeing 737-375 (Line No. 1395)	23708	D-AGEX (G-EZYC)/4L-AAA/PT-TEC/(C-GZPW)	3.11.97	
G-EZYG	Boeing 737-33V (Line No. 3062)	29331	N1768B	19. 8.98	
G-EZYH	Boeing 737-33V (Line No. 3072)	29332	N1787B	17. 9.98	
G-EZYI	Boeing 737-33V (Line No. 3084)	29333	N1787B	24.11.98	
G-EZYJ	Boeing 737-33V (Line No. 3089)	29334	N1786B	18.12.98	
G-EZYK	Boeing 737-33V (Line No. 3094)	29335	N1786B	31. 1.99	
G-EZYL	Boeing 737-33V (Line No. 3102)	29336	N1787B	12. 3.99	
G-EZYM	Boeing 737-33V (Line No. 3113)	29337		23. 6.99	
G-EZYN	Boeing 737-33V (Line No. 3114)	29338		8. 7.99	To HB-III 7/99. Canx 26.7.99.
G-EZYO	Boeing 737-33V (Line No. 3119)	29339		23. 8.99	
G-EZYP	Boeing 737-33V (Line No. 3...)	29340		17. 9.99	
G-EZYR	Boeing 737-33V (Line No. 3...)	29341		. .98R	

Regn	Type	c/n	Previous identity	Regn date	Fate or immediate subsequent identity (if known)
G-EZYR	Boeing 737-33V (Line No. 3...)	29341		. .98R	
G-EZYS	Boeing 737-33V (Line No. 3...)	29342		. .98R	

G-F G-F

Regn	Type	c/n	Previous identity	Regn date	Fate or immediate subsequent identity (if known)
G-FAAA	The series from G-FAAA to G-FAAZ was used for Lighter-than-air Aircraft from 1920 until 1928.				
G-FAAA	Short Balloon	-		. .20	Canx in 1/30.
G-FAAB	Spencer & Sons Balloon	-		. .20	Canx in 1/30.
G-FAAC	Spencer & Sons Balloon	-		. .20	Canx in 1/30.
G-FAAD	Spencer & Sons Balloon	-		. .20	Canx in 1/30.
G-FAAE	RF Dagnall Balloon	SB.7		. .20	Canx.
G-FAAF	Beardmore R.36 Airship	-		. .20	Broken up in 1927. Canx in 12/22.
G-FAAG	Armstrong-Whitworth R.33 Airship	-		14. 1.21	WFU 23.11.26. Dismantled in 5/28. (On display is a section of the control gandola at RAF Hendon) Canx.
G-FAAH	Short Balloon	-		. 8.21	Canx in 9/24.
G-FAAI	Short Balloon	-		. .21	Canx in 1/27.
G-FAAJ	Short Balloon	-		. .21	Canx in 1/33.
G-FAAK	Spencer & Sons Kite Balloon	-		. 8.24	Canx in 4/25.
G-FAAL	Goodyear R Kite Balloon (Probably ex US Navy)	-		. 2.25	Canx in 1/26.
G-FAAM	Spencer & Sons Balloon	-		. 5.25	Canx in 1/27.
G-FAAN	Short Balloon	-		. 7.25	Canx in 1/30.
G-FAAO	Spencer & Sons Balloon	-		. 7.25	Canx (date not known).
G-FAAP	Short B.40 Balloon	-		.11.25	Canx (date not known).
G-FAAQ	NBRC Balloon	-		. 4.26	Canx in 1/30.
G-FAAR	NBRC Balloon	-		. .26	Canx in 1/33.
G-FAAS	Spencer & Sons Balloon	-		. 6.26	Canx (date not known).
G-FAAT	Commercial Airships Ltd KSR.1 Airship	-		. 9.26	Construction abandoned. Canx (date not known).
G-FAAU	Spencer & Sons Parachute Balloon	-		. 3.27	Canx (date not known).
G-FAAV	Airship Guarantee Co R.100 Airship	-		. 5.30	Scrapped in 1931. Canx in 11/31.
G-FAAW	Royal Airship Works R.101 Airship	-		. .30	Fatal crash & DBF near Beauvais, France on 5.10.30, on a flight to India. Canx.
G-FAAX	ADC AD.1 Airship	AD.1		. .29	Dismantled in 6/31 after an accident. Canx in 12/31.
G-FAAY	Not allocated.				
G-FAAZ	Not allocated.				
G-FABB	Cameron V-77 HAFB	822	LX-FAB	13.12.89	
G-FABI	Robinson R-44 Astro	0325		25. 4.97	
G-FABM	Beechcraft 95-B55A Baron	TC-2259	G-JOND G-BMVC/N66456	22. 2.91	
G-FABS	Thunder Ax9-120 Srs.2 HAFB	2399		8. 6.93	Canx by CAA 29.5.96.
G-FACA	Cessna 172P Skyhawk II	172-76633	N9843L	1. 8.86	To A6-FAA. Canx 8.2.88.
G-FACB	Cessna 172P Skyhawk II	172-75432	N658NS	10. 9.86	To A6-FAB. Canx 8.2.88.
G-FADS	PA-23-250 Aztec F	23-7954110	N6914A	6.12.79	To N33KB 6/83. Canx 14.6.83.
G-FAGN	Robinson R-22 Beta	0615	(EI-...) G-FAGN/(N2566W)	28.11.86	
G-FAIR	Socata TB-10 Tobago	241		13.10.81	(Stored 7/95) Canx by CAA 2.10.98.
G-FALC	Aeromere F.8L Falco Srs.3	224	G-AROT	19. 2.81	
G-FALK	Sequoia F.8L Falco Srs.4	IC-01 & PFA/100-10762		1. 2.82	Canx by CAA 2.9.91.
G-FALL	Cessna 182L Skylane	182-58955	OY-AHS N4230S	18. 9.79	To EI-CDP 5/91. Canx 1.9.88.
G-FAME	CFM Starstreak Shadow SA-II	K.273SA & PFA/206-12973		23. 5.96	
G-FAMH	Zenair CH.701 STOL	PFA/187-13301		26. 6.98	
G-FAMY	Maule M.5-180C	8089C	N5668B	24. 1.91	
G-FANC	Temco Fairchild 24R-46 Argus	R46-347	N77647 NC77647	16.10.89	
G-FANG	American Aviation AA-5A Cheetah	AA5A-0851	N26972	15. 2.82	Crashed on landing Elstree 17.7.96 & DBER after colliding with a wing of a parked DC-3. Canx as destroyed 11.11.96.
G-FANL	Cessna R.172K Hawk XP II	R172-2873	N736XQ	7. 6.79	
G-FANN	HS.125 Srs.600B	256019	HZ-AA1 G-BARR	13. 2.89	Stored at Dunsfold, no UK CofA issued. Canx as WFU 29.3.93. (On fire dump 6/96 Dunsfold - still painted as HZ-AA1)
G-FANS	BN-2A-3 Islander (Ducted-fan conversion)	251	5Y-AMU G-51-251	13. 4.77	To G-HGPC 11/83. Canx.
G-FANZ	PA-23-250 Aztec F	23-7954099	N6905A	19.11.79	To G-BJNZ 10/81. Canx.
G-FARM	Socata MS.894E Rallye 235GT	12832	F-GARF	10.10.78	
G-FARO	Star-Lite SL-1	PFA/175-11359		19. 6.89	
G-FARR	SAN Jodel 150 Mascaret	58	F-BNIN	21. 7.81	
G-FASL	BAe 125 Srs.800B	258149		17. 5.89	To N155T 3/93. Canx 23.3.93.
G-FAST	Reims Cessna F.337G Super Skymaster (Wichita c/n 01768)	0083	(PH-DUW) (PH-IDE)/G-FAST/(PH-AXT)/(N53669)	25.11.77	To N137SW, then C-GRBR. Canx 30.12.97.
G-FATB	Commander Aircraft 114B	14624	N6037Y	3. 7.96	
G-FAVI	Beechcraft E90 King Air	LW-59	G-OOAG N4718C/G-BAVG	6. 7.89	To VR-CGK. Canx 20.7.92.
G-FAYE	Reims Cessna F.150M	1252	PH-VSK	24. 1.80	

Regn	Type	c/n	Previous identity	Regn date	Fate or immediate subsequent identity (if known)
G-FBDC	Cessna 340A II	340A-0442	G-BFJS N6247X	8. 9.81	Damaged on landing at Somerford on 4.5.87. Canx as WFU 16.6.87.
G-FBHH	Hughes 369HS (500)	33-0461S	N2186K PK-AVH/PK-PDO	1. 8.96	To G-OZAP 2/99. Canx.
G-FBIX	DH.100 Vampire FB.9	22100	7705M WL505	24. 7.91	(On rebuild 2/96 Bruntingthorpe)
G-FBMB	Canadair CL.601-2B16 Challenger 3A	5041	C-FCTZ C-GLWT	18. 6.90	To C-FTIE 9/94. Canx 23.9.94.
G-FBMV	Avro 748 Srs.1A/101	1537	G-ARMW V2-LVO/G-ARMW/VP-LII/G-ARMW	19. 3.91	To G-ARMW 1/92. Canx.
G-FBMW	Cameron N-90 HAFB	3019		23. 4.93	
G-FBPI	ANEC IV Missel Thrush	PFA/312-13417		19. 1.99	
G-FBRN	PA-28-181 Archer II	28-8290166	D-EBRN N82628	3. 8.98	
G-FBWH	PA-28R-180 Cherokee Arrow	28R-30368	SE-FCV	23. 8.78	
G-FCAL	Cessna 441 Conquest II	441-0293	C-FMHD N88723	19. 3.96	
G-FCAS	PA-25-250 Aztec F	25-7854086	N63962	21. 6.78	To N509GC 2/85. Canx 20.2.85.
G-FCHJ	Cessna 340A II	340A-0486	G-BJLS (N6315X)	7. 7.82	To G-OPLB 7/95. Canx.
G-FCLA	Boeing 757-28A (Line No. 738)	27621	N1789B	26. 2.97	
G-FCLB	Boeing 757-28A (Line No. 749)	28164	N751NA G-FCLB	25. 3.97	
G-FCLC	Boeing 757-28A (Line No. 756)	28166		9. 5.97	
G-FCLD	Boeing 757-25FET (Line No. 752)	28718		25. 4.97	
G-FCLE	Boeing 757-28A (Line No. 805)	28171		24. 5.98	
G-FCLF	Boeing 757-28A (Line No. 858)	28835	N1787B	24. 3.99	
G-FCLG	Boeing 757-28A (Line No. 208)	24367	N701LF EI-CLM/N381LF/N240LA/C-GTSK/C-GNXI/C-GAWB	18.12.98	
G-FCLH	Boeing 757-28A (Line No. 676)	26274	N751LF EI-CLU/N161LF	17. 2.99	
G-FCLI	Boeing 757-28A (Line No. 672)	26275	N651LF (N161LF)/EI-CLV/N151LF	17. 3.99	
G-FCLJ	Boeing 757-2Y0 (Line No. 555)	26160	N160GE EI-CJX/N3519M/N1786B/(B-2830)	26. 4.99	
G-FCLK	Boeing 757-2Y0 (Line No. 557)	26161	N161GE EI-CJY/N3521N	6. 4.99	
G-FCSP	Robin DR.400/180 Regent	2022		24.10.90	
G-FDAV	Westland SA.341G Gazelle 1	WA/1108	G-RIFA G-ORGE/G-BBHU	17. 5.93	
G-FDGM	Beechcraft B60 Duke	P-285	G-BFEZ ZS-RHS(2)/N7340R	13. 5.83	To N160GM 12/94. Canx 18.11.94.
G-FDSL	BAe 125 Srs.800B	258130	G-5-620	11. 1.89	To G-TPHK 2/90. Canx.
G-FEAD	Fokker F-27 Friendship 600	10387	PH-FNK SE-IRG/VH-TQP/PH-FNK	6. 2.90	To N741FE 5/92. Canx 5.5.92.
G-FEAE	Fokker F-27 Friendship 600	10349	PH-FLV SE-ITH/I-ATIC/PH-FLV	12. 2.90	To N742FE 5/92. Canx 6.5.92.
G-FEBE	Cessna 340A II	340A-0345	N405LS (N37320)	12. 7.88	
G-FEBZ	Fokker F-27 Friendship 500	10371	F-BPNC PH-FMT	29. 2.88	To N707FE 4/88. Canx 13.4.88.
G-FEDL	Hughes 369D (500D)	90-0785D	N54808 N1096G	8.11.88	To ZS-RCD 3/92. Canx 5.2.92.
G-FEDX	Fokker F-27 Friendship 500	10367	G-BNZE F-BPNB/PH-FMO	25. 1.88	To N705FE 3/88. Canx 15.3.88.
G-FEFE	Scheibe SF-25B Falke	46126	EI-BVZ D-KADB	11. 4.94	
G-FELL	Europa Avn Europa	PFA/247-13208		17. 3.98	
G-FELT	Cameron N-77 HAFB	1174		19. 7.85	
G-FENI	Robinson R-22 Beta	0884		10.11.88	To G-GHZM 8/95. Canx.
G-FERG	Aerospatiale AS.350B Ecureuil	1040	G-BGCW	5.10.79	To G-EORR 7/81. Canx.
G-FERM	Cessna 425 Corsair	425-0063	N89HB G-FERM/N82HB/OE-FGE/(D-IACE)/OE-FGE/N79MM/G-DCFB/G-BMSH/9M-AXZ/N6844H	19. 7.96	To N425TY 5/97. Canx 19.5.97.
G-FERY	Cessna 550 Citation II (Unit No.030)	550-0030	G-DJBI (N3249M)	2. 7.80	To G-MSLY 9/88. Canx.
G-FESC	Cessna 180H	180-52227	N9727G	5. 6.97	Restored as N9727G 7/97. Canx 24.6.97.
G-FESL	PA-28R-201T Turbo Arrow III	28R-7803178	G-BNRN N321EC/N3561M	8.11.88	To G-ECJM 9/90. Canx.
G-FEZZ	Agusta-Bell 206B JetRanger II	8317	SU-YAD YU-HAT	16. 9.98	
G-FFAB	Cameron N-105 HAFB	4067		20. 2.97	
G-FFBR	Thunder Ax8-105 HAFB	1280		28. 6.88	(Reported as PP-ZTP) Canx by CAA 16.4.98. (Based Brazil)
G-FFEN	Reims Cessna F.150M Skyhawk	1204	PH-VGL	25. 8.78	
G-FFHI	Aerospatiale AS.355F1 Twin Squirrel	5303	G-GWHH G-BKUL	27. 1.94	To RAF as ZJ140 (on 3-year contract). Canx 29.3.96.
G-FFLT	HS.125 Srs.600B	256057	HZ-KA2 G-5-17	24. 2.86	To VR-BNW 6/94. Canx 4.5.94.
G-FFLY(1)	Slingsby T.67B	2005		28. 6.83	NTU - To G-BIUZ(2) 10/83. Canx.

Regn	Type	c/n	Previous identity	Regn date	Fate or immediate subsequent identity (if known)
G-FFLY(2)	Slingsby T.67M Firefly	2007		26.10.83	Crashed at Cranfield on 5.5.86. Canx as destroyed 30.5.86.
G-FFOR	Cessna 310R II	310R-1889	G-BMGF ZS-KUG/N3276M	31. 3.87	
G-FFOX	Hawker Hunter T.7B (Composite, probably originally T.8C	41H-670792	'WV318' WV322/9096M)	10. 1.96	
G-FFRA	Dassault Falcon 20DC	132	N902FR (N23FR)/(N149FE)/N2FE/N560L/N4348F/F-WMKG	28. 5.92	
G-FFRI	Aerospatiale AS.355F1 Twin Squirrel	5120	G-GLOW G-PAPA/G-CNET/G-MCAH	15. 4.93	
G-FFTI	Socata TB-20 Trinidad	1065		23. 2.90	
G-FFTN	Bell 206B JetRanger II	812	ZK-HWV N33AL	23.12.86	Extensively damaged at Badvoon Forest in the Scottish Highlands on 29.6.92. Canx by CAA 27.1.93.
G-FFUN	Solar Wings Pegasus Quantum 15	6655	G-MYMD	9. 6.99	
G-FFWD	Cessna 310R II	310R-0579	G-TVKE G-EURO/N87468	20. 2.90	
G-FGID	Vought FG-1D Corsair (Goodyear built)	3111	N8297 N9154Z/BuA.88297	1.11.91	
G-FHAS	Scheibe SF-25E Super Falke	4359	(D-KOOG)	14. 5.81	
G-FIAT	PA-28-140 Cherokee F	28-7425162	G-BBYW N9622N	19. 7.89	
G-FIBS	Aerospatiale AS.350BA Ecureuil	2074	JA9732	14. 6.94	
G-FIFE	Reims Cessna FA.152 Aerobat	0351	G-BFYN	15. 2.95	
G-FIFI	Socata TB-20 Trinidad	688	G-BMWS	16. 1.87	
G-FIGA	Cessna 152 II	152-84644	N6243M	3. 6.87	
G-FIGB	Cessna 152 II	152-85925	N95561	16.11.87	
G-FIHL	Cessna 421C Golden Eagle III	421C-0128	N3876C	9. 5.79	Restored as N3876C 2/81. Canx 27.2.81.
G-FIJF	Lockheed L.188CF Electra	1144	N668Q N668F/N24AF/N138US	. .92R	NTU - To EI-CET 7/92. Canx.
G-FIJJ	Reims Cessna F.177RG Cardinal (Wichita c/n 00194)	0031	G-AZFP	29. 4.99	
G-FIJR	Lockheed L.188PF Electra	1138	(EI-HCF) G-FIJR/C-FIJR/CF-IJR/N134US	12. 9.91	
G-FIJV	Lockheed L.188CF Electra	1129	EI-HCE G-FIJV/C-FIJV/CF-IJV/N7143C	29. 8.91	
G-FILE	PA-34-200T Seneca II	34-8070108	N8140Z	23. 7.87	
G-FILL	PA-31-310 Navajo C	31-7912069	OO-EJM N3521C	28. 6.96	
G-FILM	SNIAS SE.318B Alouette II	1648	EI-AUI G-BANR/EI-AUI/ OL-A Belgian Army/1648 South Vietnam AF	14. 5.80	Struck cables and crashed at Grobnik, Yugoslavia on 23.5.82. Canx as destroyed 8.6.82.
G-FILO	Robin DR.400/180 Regent	2063		16. 4.91	
G-FIMI	Bell 206L-1 Long Ranger	45553	EC-FHS EC-809/G-FIMI/(G-BMXG)/N108WE/N3889C/ZS-HJP/N3889C	10.10.86	To N28EA 1/93. Canx 10.12.92.
G-FINA	Reims Cessna F.150L	0826	G-BIFT PH-CEW	12.10.93	
G-FIND	Reims Cessna F.406 Caravan II	0045	PH-ALV F-WZDT	16. 8.90	To 5Y-LAN 6/94. Canx 1.6.94.
G-FINE	Piper PA-60-601P Aerostar	61P-0585-7963258	N8078J	31. 1.79	To N97317 8/81. Canx 11.8.81.
G-FINN	Cameron Reindeer 90SS HAFB	1654		12. 4.88	Canx as WFU 31.7.96.
G-FINS	Agusta-Bell 206B JetRanger II	8507	G-FSCL D-HASE/SE-HGI/ OY-HCR/SE-HGI/HB-XFI	3.12.87	Extensively damaged after striking power cables on landing at Ingleby, Lincs on 23.4.99. Canx as destroyed 11.8.99.
G-FIOA	Fokker F.100-650	11330	PH-EZB	. .90R	NTU - Remained as PH-EZB. Canx in 1991.
G-FIOB	Fokker F.100-620	11274	PH-ZCK PH-EZB/(PH-KLK)	. .90R	NTU - Remained as PH-ZCK. Canx in 1991.
G-FIOC	Fokker F.100-620	11275	PH-ZCL PH-EZV/(PH-KLL)	. .90R	NTU - Remained as PH-ZCL. Canx in 1991.
G-FIOD	Fokker F.100-620	11277	PH-ZCM PH-EZW/(PH-KLN)	. .90R	NTU - Remained as PH-ZCM. Canx in 1991.
G-FIOE	Fokker F.100-620	11279	PH-ZCN PH-EZX/(PH-KLO)	. .90R	NTU - Remained as PH-ZCN. Canx in 1991.
G-FIOO	Fokker F.100-650	11316	PH-EZW	15. 2.91	To PH-RRG 6/91. Canx 10.6.91.
G-FIOR	Fokker F.100-650	11318	TU-TIS PH-RRH/G-FIOR/PH-EZB	15. 2.91	To VH-FWI 1/99. Canx 20.1.99.
G-FIOS	Fokker F.100-650	11321	PH-EZA	15. 2.91	To PH-RRC 6/91. Canx 10.6.91.
G-FIOT	Fokker F.100-650	11323	PH-EZC	. .90R	NTU - Remained as PH-EZC. Canx in 1991.
G-FIOU	Fokker F.100-650	11324	PH-EZG	. .90R	NTU - Remained as PH-EZG. Canx in 1991.
G-FIOV	Fokker F.100-650	11325	PH-EZI	. .90R	NTU - Remained as PH-EZI. Canx in 1991.
G-FIOW	Fokker F.100-650	11326	PH-EZJ	. .90R	NTU - Remained as PH-EZJ. Canx in 1991.
G-FIOX	Fokker F.100-650	11327	PH-EZL	. .90R	NTU - Remained as PH-EZL. Canx in 1991.
G-FIOY	Fokker F.100-650	11328	PH-EZM	. .90R	NTU - Remained as PH-EZM. Canx in 1991.
G-FIOZ	Fokker F.100-650	11329	PH-EZV	. .90R	NTU - Remained as PH-EZV. Canx in 1991.
G-FIRE	Vickers-Supermarine 379 Spitfire FR.XIVc	6S/648206	SG128 Belgium AF/G-15-1../NH904	21. 3.79	To N8118J 2/89. Canx 13.2.89.
G-FIRS	Robinson R-22 Beta	2807		15. 4.98	
G-FISH	Cessna 310R II	310R-1845	N2740Y	8. 5.81	Damaged on landing Little Ness, nr.Shrewsbury on 11.11.95. (Stored dismantled 12/98 at Edinburgh)
G-FISK	Pazmany PL-4A	PFA/17-10129		14.12.88	(Stored 6/99 at Little Snoring, Norfolk - wings removed)
G-FISS	Robinson R-22 Beta	1774	N40833	15. 5.91	Crashed on heavy landing at Redhill on 31.3.96. Canx as WFU 15.8.96. (Cabin only noted 10/96 Redhill)

Regn	Type	c/n	Previous identity	Regn date	Fate or immediate subsequent identity (if known)
G-FIST	Fiesler Fi.156C-3 Storch	156-5802	D-EDEC I-FAGG/MM12822	23.11.83	Rebuild to flying condition abandoned, but no UK CofA issued. Canx 24.4.95 on sale to Italy. (On display .95 at Italian AF Museum, Vigna di Valle, Italy).
G-FITZ	Cessna 335	335-0044	G-RIND N2710L	20. 4.95	
G-FIVE	DH.125 Srs.1/521	25004	G-ASEC	18. 6.79	WFU by 6/83. Broken up at Luton in 1985, used for spares - wings to c/n 25008/G-ASSI. Canx as WFU 14.5.85.
G-FIZU	Lockheed L.188CF Electra	2014	EI-CHY G-FIZU/SE-IZU/(N857ST)/N857U/PH-LLG	6. 4.93	
G-FIZZ	PA-28-161 Warrior II	28-7816301	N2721M	1.12.78	
"G-FIZZ"	Cameron O-31 HAFB	440		----	Initially stitched with this regn in error before delivery - corrected to G-COOL.
G-FJCE	Thruster T.600T	9120-T600T-032		25.11.98	
G-FJET	Cessna 550 Citation II (Unit No.418)	550-0419	G-DCFR G-WYLX/VH-JVS/G-JETD/N1217N	7. 7.97	
G-FJGC	PA-31-350 Navajo Chieftain	31-7752110	N27235	23. 3.78	Restored as N27235 4/80. Canx.
G-FJKI	Cessna 404 Titan Courier II	404-0226	G-VWGB (N88692)	24.11.82	To TL-ABJ 1/88. Canx 2.12.87.
G-FJMS	Partenavia P.68B Victor	113	G-SVHA OY-AJH	7. 9.92	
G-FKKM	PA-28RT-201T Turbo Arrow IV	28R-8031103	ZS-KKM N82115	22. 1.87	To N987DC 1/95. Canx 16.1.95.
G-FKNH	PA-15 Vagabond	15-291	CF-KNH N4517H/NC4517H	19. 3.97	
G-FLAG	Colt 77A HAFB	2000		20. 9.90	
G-FLAK	Beechcraft 95-E55 Baron	TE-1128	N4771M	26. 9.89	
G-FLAT	Schweizer 269C (300C)	S.1398		28. 9.89	To G-JMDI 9/91. Canx.
G-FLAV	PA-28-161 Warrior II	28-8016283	N8171X	7. 4.94	
G-FLCA	Fleet 80 Canuck	068	CS-ACQ CF-DQP	18. 7.90	(On rebuild 3/96 - wings on rebuild at Old Buckenham /91, fuselage under restoration at Chilbolton 7/91, then Baxterley/Nuneaton /94)
G-FLCH	Agusta-Bell 206B JetRanger III	8563	G-BGGX	27. 5.82	To G-NATO 8/88. Canx.
G-FLCO	Sequoia F.8L Falco	719 & PFA/100-10781		14. 6.82	No Permit to Fly issued. Canx by CAA 21.2.96.
G-FLCT	Hallam Fleche	PFA/309-13389		21.10.98	
G-FLEA	Socata TB-10 Tobago	235	PH-TTP G-FLEA	31. 7.81	
G-FLEN	PA-28-161 Warrior II	28-8516034	N6910Y N9541N	6. 4.88	Fatal crash into sea off Boscombe Pier on 6.11.97. Canx as destroyed 6.2.98.
G-FLEW	Lindstrand LBL-90A HAFB	586		21. 1.99	
G-FLIC	Reims Cessna FA.152 Aerobat	0374	G-BILV	16. 8.83	To G-MPBH 12/88. Canx.
G-FLII	Grumman American GA-7 Cougar	GA7-0003	G-GRAC C-GRAC/(N1367R)/N730GA	18.12.91	
G-FLIK	Pitts S-1S Special	PFA/09-10513		7. 1.81	
G-FLIP	Reims Cessna FA.152 Aerobat	0375	G-BOES G-FLIP	29.12.80	
G-FLIT	Rotorway Executive 162F	6324		22.12.98	
G-FLIX	Cessna E.310P II	310P-0221	G-AZFL N5921M	11. 3.81	Substantially damaged after hitting a drainage ditch on landing at Newbury Racecourse on 4.12.90. (To Staverton by road 13.12.90, left by road 7.2.91 - To Dodson Aviation Scrapyard in the USA) Canx by CAA 14.1.91.
G-FLIZ	Staaken Z-21 Flitzer	006 & PFA/223-13115		24. 3.97	(Painted as D-694)
G-FLMS	Colt 600A HAFB	1261		10. 5.88	Canx as destroyed 8.5.91.
G-FLOA	Cameron O-120 HAFB	4006		4.10.96	
G-FLOR	Europa Avn Europa	PFA/247-12793		11.11.98	
G-FLOX	Europa Avn Europa	PFA/247-12732		28. 6.95	
G-FLPI	Rockwell Commander 112A	205	SE-FLP (N1205J)	16. 3.79	
G-FLRU	BAC One-Eleven Srs.518FG	BAC.201	G-AXMG 5B-DAF/G-AXMG	4. 5.90	To (EI-CCV)/EI-CDO 5/91. Canx 2.5.91.
G-FLSI	FLS Aerospace Sprint 160	001		20. 8.93	(Stored 5/98 North Weald)
G-FLTA	BAe 146 Srs.200	E2048	N189US N365PS	25. 2.98	
G-FLTI	Beechcraft F90 King Air	LA-59	N7P	16. 3.90	
G-FLTY	Embraer EMB.110P1 Bandeirante	110-215	G-ZUSS G-REGA/N711NH/PT-GMH	28. 8.92	
G-FLTZ	Beechcraft 95-58 Baron	TH-1154	G-PSVS N5824T/YV-266P	21. 9.93	
G-FLUF	Lindstrand Bunny SS HAFB	002		7. 4.93	(Not built)
G-FLUG	Gyroflug SC-01B-160 Speed Canard	S.43	D-EEGX	9. 3.89	To VH-ZXZ 7/97. Canx 9.7.97.
G-FLUT	Stitts SA-6B Flut-R-Bug	PFA/211-11772		24.10.90	No Permit to Fly issued. Canx as WFU 5.9.95.
G-FLVU	Cessna 501 Citation I (Unit No.580)	501-0178	N83ND N4246A/LV-PML/N67799	11. 6.98	
G-FLYA	Mooney M.20J (201SE)	24-3124		8. 6.89	
G-FLYE	Cameron A-210 HAFB	4216		12.12.97	
G-FLYI	PA-34-200-2 Seneca	34-7250144	G-BHVO SE-FYY	1. 9.81	Damaged in an accident at Elstree on 21.11.91. Canx by CAA 10.6.97. (On rebuild 1/98 at Southend with parts from OO-JPJ)

Regn	Type	c/n	Previous identity	Regn date	Fate or immediate subsequent identity (if known)
G-FLYP	Beagle B.206 Srs.2	B.058	N40CJ N97JH/G-AVHO/VQ-LAY/G-AVHO	15.10.98	
G-FLYR	Agusta-Bell 206B JetRanger II	8341	G-BAKT	9. 8.89	Fatal crash & DBF at Glamis Castle, Perthshire on 13.7.97. Canx as destroyed 22.12.97.
G-FLYS	Robinson R-44 Astro	0347		5. 6.97	
G-FLYT	Europa Avn Europa (Tailwheel)	57 & PFA/247-12653		15. 5.95	
G-FLYU	Robinson R-22 Beta	2589		9. 4.96	Badly damaged at Hestercombe House, Taunton on 28.11.97. Canx as WFU 5.1.98.
G-FLYV	Slingsby T.67M Firefly 200	2052		23. 3.88	Fatal crash near boundary of Old Warden airfield on 4.5.96. Canx as destroyed 17.9.96.
G-FLYZ	Robinson R-44 Astro	0490		7. 7.98	
G-FMAL	Agusta-Bell 206A JetRanger	8056	G-RIAN G-BHSG/PH-FSW	3. 4.89	To G-SOOR 2/94. Canx.
G-FMAM	PA-28-151 Cherokee Warrior	28-7415056	G-BBXV N9603N	7. 6.90	
G-FMFC	Embraer EMB.110P2 Bandeirante	110-156		24. 2.78	To N4764A 3/84. Canx 1.3.84.
G-FMSG	Reims Cessna FA.150K Aerobat	0081	G-POTS G-AYUY	4. 1.95	
G-FMUS	Robinson R-22	0156	(EI-...) G-FMUS/G-BJBT/N9081U	11.11.83	To ZS-RFV 3/95. Canx 7.3.95.
G-FNLD	Cessna 172N Skyhawk II	172-70596	(G-BOUG) N739KD	3. 8.88	
G-FNLY	Reims Cessna F.172M Skyhawk II	0910	G-WACX G-BAEX	20. 3.89	
G-FNWY	Lockheed L.188A Electra	1036	C-FNWY N83MR/XA-FAM/N5524	3. 4.91	To N3209A 12/91. Canx 3.12.91.
G-FOAL	PA-31-300 Turbo Navajo B	31-761	G-RMAE G-BAEG/N7239L	15. 6.88	To G-SKKA 10/89. Canx.
G-FOAM	Socata MS.892A Rallye Commodore 150	10737	G-AVPL	17. 6.82	To EI-BUJ 2/87. Canx 3.2.87.
G-FOCK	WAR Focke-Wulf Fw.190A Replica	PFA/81-10396		31.10.78	Not built. Canx by CAA 5.7.91.
G-FODI	Robinson R-44 Astro	0513		21. 9.98	
G-FOEL	PA-31-350 Navajo Chieftain	31-7405140	G-BBXR N74984	27. 6.88	To 4X-CCJ 10/94. Canx 6.10.94.
G-FOGG	Cameron N-90 HAFB	1365		21.11.86	
G-FOGY	Robinson R-22 Beta	1020	N62991 F-GGAI	5. 7.99	
G-FOIL	PA-31-310 Turbo Navajo	31-651	D-IHFD N6744L	29. 6.79	To G-OWER 4/84. Canx.
G-FOKW	Focke-Wulf Fw.190A-5 (Crashed near Leningrad 19.7.43)	0151227	"A"(White) DG+HO/(Luftwaffe)	6. 3.96	(On rebuild 2/99 at Martham Village, Norfolk)
G-FOLD	Light Aero Avid Speed Wing	PFA/189-12041		30.10.92	
G-FOLI	Robinson R-22 Beta	2813		25. 4.98	
G-FOLY	Aerotek Pitts S-2A Special (Mod)	2213	N31477	26. 7.89	
G-FONE	Colt Cityman SS HAFB	993		27. 1.87	Canx 9.3.87 on sale to Finland.
G-FOOD	Beechcraft B200 Super King Air	BB-947	N1847V	31. 1.84	To N500WF 12/96. Canx 11.12.96.
G-FOOR	Bell 47G-4A (Mod)	7604	N6242N	28. 6.89	NTU - Restored as N6242N 8/89. Canx 21.7.89.
G-FOPP	Neico Lancair 320	PFA/191-12319		14. 8.92	(Shell noted at PFA Rally, Cranfield 7/96)
G-FORC	SNCAN Stampe SV-4A	665	(G-BLTJ) F-BDNJ	6. 6.85	
G-FORD	SNCAN Stampe SV-4B	129	F-BBNS	7. 2.78	Destroyed whilst on approach to a strip at East Titherly, near Romsey on 16.7.96. (Stored 2/98 Chilbolton)
G-FORE	Bell 47G-4A (Mod)	7661	N1415W	16. 3.90	To G-OIBC 5/93. Canx.
G-FORK	Optica Industries OA-7 Optica	006	G-BMED G-56-006	5. 6.86	DBF at Old Sarum on 19.1.87. Canx as destroyed 30.1.87.
G-FORM	Lindstrand Newspaper SS HAFB	115		6. 7.94	Canx by CAA 3.8.98.
G-FORT	Boeing B-17G-95-DL Flying Fortress	8627	F-BEEC ZS-EEC/F-BEEC/44-85718	11. 4.84	To N900RW. Canx 2.7.87.
G-FORZ	Pitts S-1S Special	PFA/09-13393		3.11.98	
G-FOTO	PA-E23-250 Aztec F	27-7654089	G-BJDH G-BDXV/N62614	27. 2.79	
G-FOUR	HS.125 Srs.3B	25131	F-BPMC G-AVRE/G-5-11	7. 8.78	To I-RASO 3/83. Canx.
G-FOUX	American Aviation AA-5A Cheetah	AA5A-0818	N8488H	5. 2.81	To G-ODAM 11/88. Canx.
G-FOWL	Colt 90A HAFB	1198		11. 3.88	
G-FOWS	Cameron N-105 HAFB	3995		11.12.96	
G-FOXA	PA-28-161 Cadet	2841240	N9192B	17.11.89	
G-FOXC	Denney Kitfox Mk.3	773 & PFA/172-11900		8. 1.91	
G-FOXD	Denney Kitfox	PFA/172-11018		22.11.89	
G-FOXE	Denney Kitfox Mk.2	740 & PFA/172-11994		1. 8.90	Struck water and sank in lake at Stewartby Country Park, Beds. on 3.7.94.
G-FOXG	Denney Kitfox Mk.2	452 & PFA/172-11886		15. 8.90	
G-FOXI	Denney Kitfox Mk.2	PFA/172-11508		21. 9.89	

Regn	Type	c/n	Previous identity	Regn date	Fate or immediate subsequent identity (if known)
G-FOXM	Bell 206B JetRanger II	1514	G-STAK G-BNIS/N35HF/N135VG	5. 2.93	
G-FOXS	Denney Kitfox Mk.2	465 & PFA/172-11571		15. 8.90	
G-FOXX	Denney Kitfox	PFA/172-11509		1.11.89	No Permit to Fly issued. Canx by CAA 8.5.99.
G-FOXY	Reims Cessna F.172M Skyhawk II	0994	PH-VDK	19. 1.79	Fatal crash into a TV aerial mast on Mont Lambert, St.Martin-les-Boulogne, France on 15.4.83. Canx as destroyed 12.12.83.
"G-FOXY"	PBN BN-2B-26 Islander	-		----	Cockpit section of G-BLDX (c/n 2181) used in the construction of this small mock-up for children's charity events.
G-FOXZ	Denney Kitfox	PFA/172-11834		4.12.90	
G-FOYL	PA-23-250 Aztec C	27-3355	G-AVNK N6142Y	28. 8.79	To N525D 6/85. Canx 10.6.85.
G-FPCL	Gulfstream American GA-7 Cougar	GA7-0038	OO-VER. OO-HTE/N748GA	25. 6.91	Canx 24.11.98 on sale to USA. To N38GE 2/99.
G-FPEL	Schweizer 269C (300C)	S.1362		22. 2.89	To F-GNCD. Canx 5.10.93.
G-FPLA	Beechcraft B200 Super King Air	BB-944	N31WL HB-GHZ/HL5260/N1824V	3.12.97	
G-FPLB	Beechcraft B200 Super King Air	BB-1048	N739MG N223MD/9Y-TGY	3.12.97	
G-FPLC	Cessna 441 Conquest II	441-0207	G-FRAX G-BMTZ/N27280	14. 1.98	
G-FRAA	Dassault Falcon 20F	385	N118R N139F/F-WJMJ	26. 1.87	To N120WH 5/95. Canx 9.5.95.
G-FRAB	Dassault Falcon 20F	356	N27RX N27R/N4468F/F-WMKG	26. 1.87	To F-GPAE/N111F 7/94. Canx 28.6.94.
G-FRAC	Dassault Falcon 20F	254	(N910FR) C-FYPB/CF-YPB/N4423F/F-WNGO	19.12.86	To F-GPAB 4/95. Canx 13.4.95.
G-FRAD	Dassault Falcon 20E	304/511	G-BCYF F-WRQP	26.11.86	
G-FRAE	Dassault Falcon 20E	280/503	N910FR I-EDIS/F-WPXK	23. 9.87	
G-FRAF	Dassault Falcon 20E	295/500	N911FR I-EDIM/F-WRQQ	1. 9.87	
G-FRAG	PA-32-300 Cherokee Six	32-7940284	N3566L	21. 1.80	
G-FRAH	Dassault Falcon 20DC	223	G-60-01 N900FR/(N904FR)/N22FE/N4407F/F-WPUX	31. 5.90	
G-FRAI	Dassault Falcon 20DC	270	N901FR (N907FR)/N37FE/N4435F/F-WPUZ	17.10.90	
G-FRAJ	Dassault Falcon 20DC	20	N903FR (N25FR)/N5FE/(N146FE)/N5FE/N367GA/N367G/N842F/F-WMKJ	30. 4.91	
G-FRAK	Dassault Falcon 20DC	213	N905FR N32FE/N4390F/F-WJMM	9.10.91	(Expected to become N213FC in 1999)
G-FRAL	Dassault Falcon 20DC	151	N904FR (N24FR)/N3FE/(N148FE)/N3FE/N810PA/N810F/N4360F/F-WMKI	17. 3.93	
G-FRAM	Dassault Falcon 20DC	224	N907FR N23FE/N4408F/F-WPUY	13. 5.93	
G-FRAN	Piper J3C-65 Cub (L-4J-PI) (Frame No. 12447)	12617	G-BIXY F-BDTZ/44-80321	14. 7.86	
G-FRAO	Dassault Falcon 20DC	214	N906FR N33FE/N4400F/F-WNGO	23.10.92	
G-FRAP	Dassault Falcon 20DC	207	N908FR N27FE/N4395F/F-WMKF	12. 7.93	
G-FRAR	Dassault Falcon 20DC	209	N909FR N28FE/N4396F/F-WLCX	2.12.93	
G-FRAS	Dassault Falcon 20C	82/418	CAF 117501 CAF 20501/F-WJMM	31. 7.90	
G-FRAT	Dassault Falcon 20C	87/424	CAF 117502 CAF 20502/F-WJMJ	31. 7.90	
G-FRAU	Dassault Falcon 20C	97/422	CAF 117504 CAF 20504/F-WJMJ	31. 7.90	
G-FRAV	Dassault Falcon 20C	103/423	CAF 117505 CAF 20505/F-WJKH	31. 7.90	To F-GPAA 4/93. Canx 1.4.93.
G-FRAW	Dassault Falcon 20C	114/420	CAF 117507 CAF 20507/F-WJMM	31. 7.90	
G-FRAX	Cessna 441 Conquest II	441-0207	G-BMTZ N2728D	4. 9.87	To G-FPLC 1/98. Canx.
G-FRAY	Cassutt Racer IIIM (Mod)	PFA/34-11211		24.10.90	
G-FRAZ	Cessna 441 Conquest II	441-0035	SE-GYC (N36965)	14. 9.87	
G-FRBA	Dassault Falcon 20C	178/459	OH-FFA F-WPXF	16. 7.96	
G-FRBY	Beechcraft 95-E55 Baron	TE-868	N78PS N77PS	23. 9.94	
G-FRCE	Folland Gnat T.1	FL.598	8604M XS104	28.11.89	(Stored 3/96)
G-FRED	Clutton FRED Srs.II	PFA/29-10339		18. 5.78	Canx by CAA 2.9.91. (Incomplete and stored 4/96 Priory Farm, Tibbenham)
G-FREE	Aerotek Pitts S-2A Special	2188	LN-NAC	20. 3.85	To D-EDEE(2) 11/86. Canx 12.9.86.
G-FRGN	PA-28-236 Dakota	2811046	N9244N	8. 2.96	

Regn	Type	c/n	Previous identity	Regn date	Fate or immediate subsequent identity (if known)
G-FRGY	Hughes 369HS (500)	33-0456S	N500MW N9136F	11. 1.89	Fatal crash & burnt out at Faugh, near Carlisle on 6.12.89. Canx as destroyed 14.12.89.
G-FRJB	Britten SA-1 Sheriff	0001		18. 5.81	Not completed. Unfinished airframe on display without marks 4/96 at East Midlands Aeropark. Canx by CAA 6.2.87.
G-FROG	Hughes 369HS (500)	110-0270S	OO-KAR	15. 4.81	To G-WELD 11/81. Canx.
G-FROZ	Cessna 421C Golden Eagle III	421C-1012	LN-VIR N6792D	4. 7.85	To D-IJJJ 8/92. Canx 15.7.92.
G-FRST	PA-44-180T Turbo Seminole	44-8207020	N8236B N9615N	5.11.82	
G-FRYI	Beechcraft 200 Super King Air	BB-210	G-OAVX G-IBCA/G-BMCA/N5657N	15. 3.96	
G-FRYS	Christen Eagle II	Argence 0001	N66EA	19. 9.88	To G-EGUL 1/93. Canx.
G-FSCL	Agusta-Bell 206B JetRanger II	8507	D-HASE SE-HGI/OY-HCR/SE-HGI/HB-XFI	23. 1.85	To G-FINS 12/87. Canx.
G-FSDA	Agusta-Bell 206B JetRanger II	8052	G-AWJW	21. 1.83	To G-SHRR 2/90. Canx.
G-FSDC	Enstrom 280C-UK Shark	1015	G-BKTG OY-HBP	7.10.87	To G-VETS 9/95. Canx.
G-FSDG	Agusta-Bell 206B JetRanger II	8046	G-ROOT G-JETR/(G-BKBR)/OO-CDP	2. 4.85	To G-COUR 10/95. Canx.
G-FSDH	Hughes 269A	66-0602	(OO-...) N602CH/66-18319	2. 8.88	To OO-ERG. Canx 5.4.94.
G-FSDT	Hughes 269A	95-0378	N269DH N1336D/64-18066	22. 8.88	To G-BWZY 12/96. Canx.
G-FSFT	PA-44-180 Seminole	44-7995190	EI-CCO N2135G	12.10.98	
G-FSII	Gregory Free Spirit Mk.II	004		26. 2.91	No Permit to Fly issued. Canx by CAA 27.3.99.
G-FSIX	English Electric Lightning F.6	95116	XP693	31.12.92	To ZU-BEY 2/97. Canx 13.2.97.
G-FSPL	PA-32R-300 Lance	32R-7780335	(G-BFAO) D-EILI/N4587Q	22. 9.77	To ZK-SPL 6/97. Canx 25.6.97.
G-FTAX	Cessna 421C Golden Eagle III	421C-0308	N8363G G-BFFM/N8363G	23. 8.84	
G-FTFT	Colt Financial Times 90SS HAFB	1163		14. 1.88	To British Balloon Museum in 2/97. Canx as WFU 13.5.98.
G-FTIL	Robin DR.400/180 Remorquer	1825		10. 3.88	(Badly damaged at Biggin Hill on 27.7.90)
G-FTIM	Robin DR.400/100 Cadet	1829		6. 5.88	
G-FTIN	Robin DR.400/100 Cadet	1830		6. 5.88	
G-FTIO	Robin DR.400/100 Cadet	1831		6. 5.88	To G-ZACH 10/92. Canx.
G-FTTA	PA-31-350 Navajo Chieftain	31-7852051	N27535	19.12.78	To SE-ILY 10/83. Canx 19.10.83.
G-FTUO	Van's RV-4	926	C-FTUQ	23.12.97	
G-FTWO	Aerospatiale AS.355F2 Twin Squirrel	5347	G-OJOR G-FTWO/G-BMUS	27. 1.87	
G-FUEL	Robin DR.400/180 Regent	1537		15. 5.81	
G-FUGA	Fouga CM-170R Magister	045	G-BSCT French AF 45	12. 4.90	To F-.... Canx 20.4.99.
G-FUJI	Fuji FA.200-180 Aero Subaru	FA200-156	D-EMMI	14. 9.79	Damaged on landing in a field at Newton, Powys on 5.5.92. Canx as WFU 1.3.94. (Stored 7/95)
G-FULL	PA-28R-200 Cherokee Arrow II	28R-7435248	G-HWAY G-JULI/(G-BKDC)/OY-POV/N43128	26.11.84	
G-FUND	Thunder Ax7-65Z HAFB	376		3.11.81	
G-FUNK	Yakovlev Yak-50	852908	RA-852908	27. 3.98	
G-FUNN	Plumb BGP-1 Biplane	PFA/83-12744		16.10.95	
G-FURY	Hawker Sea Fury FB.XI	224	WJ244	5. 7.78	Crashed near Waddington following engine failure on 2.8.81. Permit expired 12.6.82. Canx as destroyed 6.2.89.
G-FUSI	Robinson R-22 Beta	2506	N83306	16. 3.95	
G-FUZY	Cameron N-77 HAFB	1751		6. 5.88	
G-FUZZ	PA-18-95 Super Cub (Frame No. 18-1086) (L-18C-PI)	18-1016	(OO-HMY) ALAT-FMBIT/51-15319	11. 9.80	
G-FVBF	Lindstrand LBL-210A HAFB	311		6.12.95	
G-FVEE	Monnett Sonerai I	PFA/15-10041		19.12.78	No Permit issued. Canx by CAA 22.7.91.
G-FWPW	PA-28-236 Dakota	2811018	N9145L	10.10.88	
G-FWRP	Cessna 421C Golden Eagle III	421C-0418	N3919C	9.12.82	
G-FXII	Vickers-Supermarine 366 Spitfire F.XII	6S/197707	EN224	4.12.89	(On rebuild from components 3/96)
G-FXIV	Vickers-Supermarine 379 Spitfire FR.XIVc	-	T44 HS... Indian AF/MV370	11. 4.80	Canx as WFU 5.2.85. (On display Luftfahrtmuseum, Laatzen-Hannover, Germany 9/96 as MV370)

G-FYAA The series from G-FYAA to G-FYNZ is used for unmanned toy balloons from 1.1.82 onwards.

Regn	Type	c/n	Previous identity	Regn date	Fate or immediate subsequent identity (if known)
G-FYAA	Osprey Mk.4D HAFB (Toy)	ASC-139		4. 1.82	Canx by CAA 13.12.88.
G-FYAB	Osprey Mk.4B HAFB (Toy)	ASC-107		4. 1.82	Canx by CAA 13.12.88.
G-FYAC	Portswood Mk.XVI HAFB (Toy)	ASK-163		4. 1.82	Canx by CAA 9.12.88.
G-FYAD	Portswood Mk.XVI HAFB (Toy)	ASK-164		4. 1.82	Canx by CAA 9.12.88.
G-FYAE	Portswood Mk.XVI HAFB (Toy)	ASK-165		4. 1.82	Canx by CAA 9.12.88.
G-FYAF	Portswood Mk.XVI HAFB (Toy)	ASK-166		4. 1.82	Canx by CAA 9.12.88.
G-FYAG	Portswood Mk.XVI HAFB (Toy)	ASK-167		4. 1.82	Canx by CAA 12.12.88.
G-FYAH	Portswood Mk.XVI HAFB (Toy)	ASK-168		4. 1.82	Canx by CAA 9.12.88.
G-FYAI	Portswood Mk.XVI HAFB (Toy)	ASK-169		4. 1.82	Canx by CAA 9.12.88.
G-FYAJ	Kelsey Skyrocket HAFB (Toy)	PJK-001		4. 1.82	Canx as WFU 27.10.88.
G-FYAK	European E.21 HAFB (Toy)	S.12		4. 1.82	Canx by CAA 2.12.93.
G-FYAL	Osprey Mk.4E2 HAFB (Toy)	ASC-239		5. 1.82	Canx by CAA 9.12.88.
G-FYAM	Osprey Mk.4E2 HAFB (Toy)	ASC-246		5. 1.82	Canx by CAA 29.11.88.

Regn	Type	c/n	Previous identity	Regn date	Fate or immediate subsequent identity (if known)
G-FYAN	Williams Westwind HAFB (Toy)	MDW-1		6. 1.82	
G-FYAO	Williams Westwind HAFB (Toy)	MDW-001		6. 1.82	
G-FYAP	Williams Westwind Two HAFB (Toy)	MDW-003		6. 1.82	Canx by CAA 8.12.88.
G-FYAR	Williams Westwind Two HAFB (Toy)	MDW-004		6. 1.82	Canx.
G-FYAS	Osprey Mk.4H2 HAFB (Toy)	ASC-240		6. 1.82	Canx by CAA 29.11.88.
G-FYAT	Osprey Mk.4D HAFB (Toy)	ASC-209		6. 1.82	Canx by CAA 2.12.93.
G-FYAU	Williams Westwind Two HAFB (Toy)	MDW-002		6. 1.82	
G-FYAV	Osprey Mk.4E2 HAFB (Toy)	ASC-247		12. 1.82	
G-FYAW	Portswood Mk.XVI HAFB (Toy)	ASK-157		20. 1.82	Canx as WFU 18.10.88.
G-FYAX	Osprey Mk.4B HAFB (Toy)	AKC-90		15. 1.82	Canx by CAA 8.12.88.
G-FYAY	Osprey Mk.1E HAFB (Toy)	ASC-137		15. 1.82	Canx by CAA 29.11.88.
G-FYAZ	Osprey Mk.4D2 HAFB (Toy)	ASC-241		15. 1.82	Canx as WFU 31.3.98.
G-FYBA	Portswood Mk.XVI HAFB (Toy)	ASK-152		15. 1.82	Canx by CAA 2.12.93.
G-FYBB	Portswood Mk.XVI HAFB (Toy)	ASK-151		15. 1.82	Canx as WFU 15.10.84.
G-FYBC	Portswood Mk.XVI HAFB (Toy)	ASK-154		15. 1.82	Canx as WFU 15.10.84.
G-FYBD	Osprey Mk.1E HAFB (Toy)	ASC-136		20. 1.82	
G-FYBE	Osprey Mk.4D HAFB (Toy)	ASC-128		20. 1.82	
G-FYBF	Setco Osprey Mk.5 HAFB (Toy)	ASC-218/SH-13		20. 1.82	
G-FYBG	Osprey Mk.4G2 HAFB (Toy)	ASC-204		20. 1.82	
G-FYBH	Osprey Mk.4G HAFB (Toy)	ASC-214		20. 1.82	
G-FYBI	Osprey Mk.4H HAFB (Toy)	ASC-234		20. 1.82	
G-FYBJ	Osprey Mk.3B HAFB (Toy)	ACM-121		22. 1.82	Canx as WFU 26.4.85.
G-FYBK	Osprey Mk.4G2 HAFB (Toy)	ASC-228		25. 1.82	Canx as WFU 14.7.88.
G-FYBL	Osprey Mk.4D HAFB (Toy)	ASC-210		25. 1.82	Canx as destroyed 8.10.87.
G-FYBM	Osprey Mk.4G HAFB (Toy)	ASC-212		28. 1.82	Canx by CAA 6.12.88.
G-FYBN	Osprey Mk.4G2 HAFB (Toy)	ASC-227		28. 1.82	Canx by CAA 29.11.88.
G-FYBO	Osprey Mk.4B HAFB (Toy)	AKC-94		29. 1.82	Canx as WFU 27.10.88.
G-FYBP	European E.84PW HAFB (Toy)	S.20		29. 1.82	
G-FYBR	Osprey Mk.4G2 HAFB (Toy)	ASC-203		29. 1.82	
G-FYBS	Portswood Mk.XIV HAFB (Toy)	ASK-160		29. 1.82	Canx as WFU 26.4.85.
G-FYBT	Portswood Mk.XVI HAFB (Toy)	ASK-172		29. 1.82	Canx by CAA 12.12.88.
G-FYBU	Portswood Mk.XVI HAFB (Toy)	ASK-170		29. 1.82	Canx as WFU 31.3.98.
G-FYBV	Osprey Mk.4D2 HAFB (Toy)	ASC-245		1. 2.82	Canx by CAA 9.12.88.
G-FYBW	Osprey Mk.4D HAFB (Toy)	ASC-126		2. 2.82	Canx as WFU 1.11.88.
G-FYBX	Portswood Mk.XVI HAFB (Toy)	ASK-161		1. 2.82	Canx as WFU 21.4.98.
G-FYBY	Osprey Mk.4D HAFB (Toy)	ACK-101		1. 2.82	Canx by CAA 30.11.88.
G-FYBZ	Osprey Mk.1E HAFB (Toy)	ASC-135		3. 2.82	Canx as WFU 18.10.88.
G-FYCA	Osprey Mk.4D HAFB (Toy)	ASC-123		3. 2.82	Canx as WFU 31.3.89.
G-FYCB	Osprey Mk.4B HAFB (Toy)	ASC-129		3. 2.82	Canx as WFU 18.10.88.
G-FYCC	Osprey Mk.4G2 HAFB (Toy)	ASC-205		8. 2.82	Canx by CAA 4.8.98.
G-FYCD	BHMED Gulfstream Three (Toy)	350		8. 2.82	Canx as destroyed 23.12.88.
G-FYCE	Portswood Mk.XVI HAFB (Toy)	ASK-180		8. 2.82	Canx as WFU 18.10.88.
G-FYCF	Portswood Mk.XVI HAFB (Toy)	ASK-179		8. 2.82	Canx as WFU 7.12.89.
G-FYCG	Portswood Mk.XVI HAFB (Toy)	ASK-178		8. 2.82	Canx as WFU 7.12.89.
G-FYCH	Joste Swan Mk.I HAFB (Toy)	RSJ.001		8. 2.82	Canx 31.7.89 on sale to Australia.
G-FYCI	Portswood Mk.XVI HAFB (Toy)	ASK-173		8. 2.82	Canx as destroyed 8.10.88.
G-FYCJ	Osprey Mk.4H2 HAFB (Toy)	ASC-238		8. 2.82	Canx as WFU 14.7.88.
G-FYCK	Lovell Supaliner Mk.1 HAFB (Toy)	GPL.001		9. 2.82	Canx by CAA 13.12.88.
G-FYCL	Osprey Mk.4G HAFB (Toy)	ASC-213		9. 2.82	
G-FYCM	Osprey Mk.7 HAFB (Toy)	ACK-100		15. 2.82	Canx as WFU 14.8.84.
G-FYCN	Osprey Mk.4B HAFB (Toy)	ASC-127		15. 2.82	Canx by CAA 2.12.93.
G-FYCO	Osprey Mk.4B HAFB (Toy)	ASC-130		15. 2.82	Canx by CAA 2.12.93.
G-FYCP	Osprey Mk.1E HAFB (Toy)	ASC-138		15. 2.82	Canx by CAA 2.12.93.
G-FYCR	Osprey Mk.4D HAFB (Toy)	ASC-122		15. 2.82	Canx by CAA 2.12.93.
G-FYCS	Portswood Mk.XVI HAFB (Toy)	ASK-271		16. 2.82	Canx by CAA 13.12.88.
G-FYCT	Osprey Mk.4D HAFB (Toy)	ASK-277		18. 2.82	Canx by CAA 2.12.93.
G-FYCU	Osprey Mk.4D HAFB (Toy)	ASK-251		18. 2.82	Canx by CAA 2.12.93.
G-FYCV	Osprey Mk.4D HAFB (Toy)	ASK-276		19. 2.82	
G-FYCW	Osprey Mk.4D HAFB (Toy)	ASK-280		22. 2.82	Canx by CAA 2.12.93.
G-FYCX	Sumner Jefferson Mk.IV HAFB (Toy)	JRS.001		22. 2.82	Canx by CAA 13.12.88.
G-FYCY	Osprey Mk.4G HAFB (Toy)	ASC-211		22. 2.82	Canx as WFU 4.2.85.
G-FYCZ	Osprey Mk.4D2 HAFB (Toy)	ASC-244		24. 2.82	
G-FYDA	Saffrey SB.1000 Firefly Atom HAFB (Toy)	43		2. 3.82	Canx as destroyed 18.10.88.
G-FYDB	European E.84EL Euroliner HAFB (Toy)	S.23		17. 3.82	Canx as WFU 27.10.88.
G-FYDC	European EDH.1 HAFB (Toy)	S.24		17. 3.82	
G-FYDD	Osprey Mk.4D HAFB (Toy)	ASK-269		19. 3.82	Canx by CAA 2.12.93.
G-FYDE	Osprey Mk.4D HAFB (Toy)	ASK-268		19. 3.82	Canx by CAA 13.12.88.
G-FYDF	Osprey Mk.4D HAFB (Toy)	ASK-278		22. 3.82	
G-FYDG	Osprey Mk.4D HAFB (Toy)	ASK-270		29. 3.82	Canx as WFU 8.11.88.
G-FYDH	Saffrey Premier Voyage HAFB (Toy)	44		29. 4.82	Canx as TWFU 21.8.87.
G-FYDI	Williams Westwind Two HAFB (Toy)	MDW-005		29. 3.82	Canx as WFU 8.11.88.
G-FYDJ	Osprey Mk.4D HAFB (Toy)	ASK-300		2. 4.82	Canx as WFU 15.10.84.

Regn	Type	c/n	Previous identity	Regn date	Fate or immediate subsequent identity (if known)
G-FYDK	Williams Westwind Two HAFB SD (Toy)	MDW-008		29. 3.82	Canx as destroyed 9.11.93.
G-FYDL	Not allotted.				
G-FYDM	Williams Westwind Four HAFB (Toy)	MDW-007		29. 3.82	Canx as destroyed 9.11.93.
G-FYDN	European 8C HAFB (Toy)	DD34/S.22		5. 4.82	
G-FYDO	Osprey Mk.4D HAFB (Toy)	ASK-262		15. 4.82	
G-FYDP	Williams Westwind Three HAFB (Toy)	MDW-006		29. 3.82	
G-FYDR	European 118 HAFB (Toy)	DD33/S.21		5. 4.82	Canx by CAA 13.12.88.
G-FYDS	Osprey Mk.4D HAFB (Toy)	ASK-261		15. 4.82	
G-FYDT	Viking Warrior Mk.1 HAFB (Toy)	DT-001		16. 4.82	Canx as WFU 18.10.88.
G-FYDU	Osprey Mk.4D HAFB (Toy)	ASK-267		23. 4.82	Canx as WFU 18.10.88.
G-FYDV	Osprey Mk.4D HAFB (Toy)	ASK-266		19. 4.82	Canx by CAA 12.12.88.
G-FYDW	Osprey Mk.4B HAFB (Toy)	ASK-282		27. 4.82	
G-FYDX	Osprey Mk.4B HAFB (Toy)	ASK-290		7. 5.82	Canx as WFU 18.10.88.
G-FYDY	Osprey Mk.4B HAFB (Toy)	ASK-297		17. 5.82	Canx by CAA 8.12.88.
G-FYDZ	Portswood Mk.XVI HAFB (Toy)	ASK-273		17. 5.82	Canx by CAA 7.12.88.
G-FYEA	Osprey Mk.4B HAFB (Toy)	ASK-296		17. 5.82	Canx by CAA 7.12.88.
G-FYEB	Rango Rega Srs.II (Gas Airship) (Toy)	NHP-31		18. 5.82	
G-FYEC	Osprey Mk.4B HAFB (Toy)	ASK-298		17. 5.82	Canx by CAA 13.12.88.
G-FYED	Osprey Mk.1C HAFB (Toy)	ASK-292		19. 8.82	Canx by CAA 13.12.88.
G-FYEE	Osprey Mk.4B HAFB (Toy)	ASK-299		17. 5.82	Canx by CAA 13.12.88.
G-FYEF	Portswood Mk.XVI HAFB (Toy)	ASK-272		17. 5.82	Canx by CAA 13.12.88.
G-FYEG	Osprey Mk.1C HAFB (Toy)	ASK-295		21. 5.82	Canx by CAA 2.12.93.
G-FYEH	European EJ.1 HAFB (Toy)	S.18		27. 5.82	Canx as WFU 4.2.85.
G-FYEI	Portswood Mk.XVI HAFB (Toy)	ASK-274		27. 5.82	Canx by CAA 4.8.98.
G-FYEJ	Rango NA-24 (Gas FB) (Toy) (Half-scale Chartres Balloon Replica)	NHP-30		27. 5.82	
G-FYEK	Unicorn UE-1C HAFB (Toy)	82024		2. 7.82	
G-FYEL	European E.84Z HAFB (Toy)	S.25		24. 6.82	
G-FYEM	Rango NA-8 HAFB (Toy)	RGS-32	(G-FYEU)	2. 8.82	
G-FYEN	Not allotted.				
G-FYEO	Scallan Eagle Mk.1A HAFB (Toy)	001		20. 7.82	
G-FYEP	Boing 746-200A HAFB (Toy)	NAKL-01		18. 5.82	Canx as WFU 18.10.88.
G-FYER	Osprey Mk.4B HAFB (Toy)	ASK-289		29. 7.82	Canx by CAA 13.12.88.
G-FYES	Osprey Mk.2SJM HAFB (Toy)	ASK-181		29. 7.82	Canx by CAA 13.12.88.
G-FYET	Markmike Mk.2 HAFB (Toy)	02		13. 7.82	Canx by CAA 12.12.88.
G-FYEU	Rango NA-8 HAFB (Toy)	RGS-32		2. 8.82	NTU - To G-FYEM sameday. Canx.
G-FYEV	Osprey Mk.1C HAFB (Toy)	ASK-294		10. 8.82	
G-FYEW	Saturn Mk.2A HAFB (Toy)	MJS-02		20. 8.82	Canx by CAA 29.11.88.
G-FYEX	Not allotted.				
G-FYEY	Largess Binbagbubble HAFB (Toy)	MLB.001A-001		10. 9.82	Canx by CAA 13.12.88.
G-FYEZ	Scallan Firefly Mk.1 HAFB (Toy)	MNS-748		22. 9.82	
G-FYFA	European E.84LD HAFB (Toy)	S.26		12.10.82	
G-FYFB	Osprey Mk.1E HAFB (Toy)	ASK-291		28.10.82	Canx as destroyed 18.10.88.
G-FYFC	European E.84NZ HAFB (Toy)	DD39/S.27		10.11.82	Canx 1.11.88 on sale to New Zealand.
G-FYFD	Osprey Mk.2CM HAFB (Toy)	ASC-187		22.11.82	Canx by CAA 7.12.88.
G-FYFE	Osprey Mk.2GB HAFB (Toy)	ASC-190		25.11.82	Canx by CAA 29.11.88.
G-FYFF	Osprey Mk.2SW HAFB (Toy)	ASC-191		25.11.82	Canx by CAA 13.12.88.
G-FYFG	European E.84DE HAFB (Toy)	S.28		26.11.82	
G-FYFH	European E.84DS HAFB (Toy)	S.30		26.11.82	
G-FYFI	European E.84PS HAFB (Toy)	S.29		1.12.82	
G-FYFJ	Williams Westwind Two HAFB (Toy)	MDW-010		14.12.82	
G-FYFK	Williams Westwind Two HAFB (Toy)	MDW-011		14.12.82	Canx by CAA 2.12.93.
G-FYFL	Osprey Mk.2CL HAFB (Toy)	ATC-185		14.12.82	Canx by CAA 12.12.88.
G-FYFM	Trojan Mk.IV HAFB (Toy)	004		7. 1.83	Canx by CAA 13.12.88.
G-FYFN	Osprey Saturn 2 DC3 HAFB (Toy)	ATC-250/MJS-11		17. 2.83	
G-FYFO	Not allotted.				
G-FYFP	Not allotted.				
G-FYFR	Not allotted.				
G-FYFS	Rango NA-55 HAFB (Toy)	NHP-35		1. 9.83	Canx by CAA 12.12.88.
G-FYFT	Rango NA-32BC HAFB (Toy)	NHP-37		12. 3.84	
G-FYFU	Rango NA-39 Gas FB (Toy)	NHP-39		14. 5.84	Canx as WFU 18.10.88.
G-FYFV	Saffery Grand Edinburgh Fire Balloon HAFB (Toy)	01		25. 7.84	Canx as WFU 1.6.98.
G-FYFW	Rango NA-55 (Radio Controlled Balloon) (Toy)	NHP-40		8.10.84	
G-FYFX	Rango NA-42 HAFB (Toy)	NHP-42		28. 2.85	Canx as WFU 18.10.88.
G-FYFY	Rango NA-55 (Radio Controlled Balloon) (Toy)	AL-43		28. 2.85	
G-FYFZ	Booth C-141D HAFB (Toy)	NM-29/002		18.10.85	Canx by CAA 30.8.90.
G-FYGA	Rango NA-50 (Radio Controlled Balloon) (Toy)	NHP-47		7. 1.86	

Regn	Type	c/n	Previous identity	Regn date	Fate or immediate subsequent identity (if known)
G-FYGB	Rango NA-105 (Radio Controlled Balloon) (Toy)	NHP-45		7. 1.86	
G-FYGC	Rango NA-42B HAFB (Toy)	LW-52		17.10.86	Canx by CAA 2.12.93.
G-FYGD	Not allocated.				
G-FYGE	Rango NA-42B HAFB (Toy)	NHP-53		7. 1.87	Canx by CAA 8.12.88.
G-FYGF	Busby Buz-B20 HAFB (Toy)	DSD-001		8. 7.87	
G-FYGG	Busby Buz-B20 HAFB (Toy)	DSD-002		4.11.87	Canx by CAA 4.1.96.
G-FYGH	Busby Buz-B20W HAFB (Toy)	DSD-01N		8. 6.89	Canx by CAA 18.10.95.
G-FYGI	Rango NA-55 (Radio Controlled Balloon) (Toy)	NHP-54		26. 6.90	
G-FYGJ	Wells Airspeed-300 HAFB (Toy)	001		8.10.91	
G-FYGK	Rango NA-42 POC HAFB (Toy)	NHP-55		31.10.91	
G-FYGL	Noble Glowball HAFB (Toy)	GB-01		18. 9.92	Canx by CAA 4.8.98.
G-FYGM	Saffery/Smith Princess HAFB (Toy)	551		24.11.97	
G-FYNB	Booth C-141C HAFB (Toy)	NM-29/001		23. 6.83	Canx by CAA 30.8.90.
G-FYNC	Rango NA-555 (Radio Controlled Balloon) (Toy)	NHP-50		4. 8.86	Canx by CAA 12.12.88.
G-FYYA	General Avia F.22A Pinguino	018		13. 8.98	
G-FZZI	Cameron H-34 HAFB	2105		30.10.89	
G-FZZY	Colt 69A HAFB	779		19. 2.86	Canx as WFU 29.4.97. To BBAC Museum 13.11.97.
G-FZZZ	Colt 56A HAFB	507		23. 2.83	Canx as WFU 29.4.97.

G-G

Regn	Type	c/n	Previous identity	Regn date	Fate or immediate subsequent identity (if known)
G-GAAA	The series from G-GAAA to G-GAAE was used by five gliders only in 1937 to allow them to participate in competitions at Wasserkuppe in Germany during 7/37.				
G-GAAA	Slingsby (Buxton) Hjordis	215C	BGA.301 BGA.242	21. 5.37	To South Africa as ZS-23. Canx.
G-GAAB	Slingsby T.9 King Kite	262A	BGA.302	21. 5.37	Crashed on 26.6.46. Canx.
G-GAAC	Slingsby T.9 King Kite	264A	BGA.303	21. 5.37	Crashed at the Wasserkuppe, Germany on 4.7.37. Canx.
G-GAAD	Slingsby T.9 King Kite	263A	BGA.304	21. 5.37	To RAF as VD207. Canx.
G-GAAE	Slingsby T.4 Falcon III (Regd with c/n 265A)	258A	(BGA.305) BGA.297	21. 5.37	Restored as BGA.297. Canx.
G-GABD	Gulfstream American GA-7 Cougar	GA7-0043	D-GABD	13. 4.82	
G-GACA	Hunting Percival P.57 Sea Prince T.1	P57/58	WP308	2. 9.80	(Stored 6/97 - still coded "CU/572")
G-GAEL	BAe 125 Srs.800B	258007	G-5-20	17.11.83	To G-5-554/C-GKRL. Canx 1.4.87.
G-GAFG	Slingsby T.67C-160	2053	G-BODJ	17. 2.88	Crashed and burned out on take-off from Denham on 30.6.89. Canx as destroyed 26.7.89.
G-GAFX	Boeing 747-245F (Line No. 266)	20827	N641FE VP-BXP/N641FE/(N632FE)/N812FT/N702SW	28. 8.99	
G-GAGA	American Aviation AA-5B Tiger	AA5B-1226	G-BGPG (G-BGRW)	2.12.88	To G-DAVO 1/96. Canx.
G-GAII	Hawker Hunter GA.11 (Regd with c/n 41H-004038)	HABL-003028	XE685	7.12.94	
G-GAIL(1)	HS.125 Srs.700B	257139	G-5-18	. .81R	NTU - To G-BKAA 9/81. Canx.
G-GAIL(2)	Cessna 550 Citation II (Unit No.397)	550-0353	(N12149)	19. 3.82	To N3251H 10/82. Canx 26.10.82.
G-GAIR	Ted Smith Aerostar 601P	61P-0275-060	N90488	1. 9.86	To G-PAMS 7/89. Canx.
G-GAIW	Cameron A-140 HAFB	4131		21. 5.97	
G-GAJB	American Aviaton AA-5B Tiger	AA5B-1179	G-BHZN N37519	6. 4.87	
G-GALA	PA-28-180 Cherokee E	28-5794	G-AYAP	31. 7.89	
G-GALE	PA-34-200T Seneca II	34-7970191	N3052X	29. 5.79	To G-ROYZ 5/92. Canx.
G-GAMA	Beechcraft 95-58 Baron	TH-429	G-BBSD	13.10.82	To G-WWIZ 10/96. Canx.
G-GAMC	Cessna T.303 Crusader	T303-00098	(F-GDFN) N2693C	25. 2.83	
G-GANE	Sequoia F.8L Falco	906 & PFA/100-11100		25. 9.85	
G-GANJ	Sportavia-Putzer Fournier RF-6B-100	38	F-GANJ	16. 8.84	(Stored 5/95)
G-GARY	Cessna TR.182 Turbo Skylane RG	R182-00937	N738KV	15. 3.91	Canx 15.4.93 on sale to Denmark. To D-ETKS 6/93.
G-GASA	Hughes 369HS (500)	13-0440S	G-TATI HB-XEE	4. 4.84	While moving an underslung load on 13.4.88 the load struck the tail rotor near the A9 road at Cuaich. Canx as destroyed 27.10.88.
G-GASB	Hughes 369HS (500)	11-0275S	D-HFSF HB-XCW	9. 4.84	Caught fire on take-off from a football pitch at South Heighton, Sussex on 15.8.87 due to engine failure. (Wreck later to Shoreham) Canx as destroyed 14.8.91.
G-GASC	Hughes 369HS (500)	110-0270S	G-WELD G-FROG/OO-KAR	11. 7.85	
G-GASM	Enstrom 480	5023		19. 6.97	To N8629A 8/97. Canx 7.8.97.
G-GASP	PA-28-181 Cherokee Archer II	28-7790013	N4328F	15.10.90	
G-GASS	Thunder Ax7-77 HAFB	1746		19. 4.90	

Regn	Type	c/n	Previous identity	Regn date	Fate or immediate subsequent identity (if known)
G-GATI	Beechcraft 200 Super King Air	BB-400	G-ONEA N3035C/N3030C	8. 6.94	To N164AB 6/96. Canx 14.6.96.
G-GAUL	Cessna 550 Citation II (Unit No.143)	550-0127	N550TJ (N29TG)/N29TC/N2631N	26. 7.89	To G-ESTA 6/98. Canx.
G-GAWA	Cessna 140	9619	G-BRSM N72454/NC72454	17. 9.91	(Badly damaged on take-off from Baginton on 8.3.97)
G-GAYE	Cessna 421C Golden Eagle III	421C-0676	N26520	16. 1.80	To N9397E. Canx 11.9.81.
G-GAYL	Gates LearJet 35A	35A-429	G-ZING	23. 8.82	To G-ZENO 5/96. Canx.
G-GAZA	Aerospatiale SA.341G Gazelle Srs.1	1187	G-RALE G-SFTG/N87712	19. 6.92	
G-GAZE	Robinson R-22 Alpha	0427	N8522K	12. 7.84	To EC-FAI. Canx 12.12.90.
G-GAZI	Aerospatiale SA.341G Gazelle Srs.1	1136	G-BKLU N32PA/N341VH/N90957	29. 6.90	
G-GAZZ	Aerospatiale SA.341G Gazelle Srs.1	1271	F-GFHD YV-242CP/HB-XGA/F-WMHC	14. 3.90	
G-GBAC	DHC.6-310 Twin Otter	764	(VQ-TAN) G-GBAC/A6-ADC/G-OILY/N30BV/N25RM	10.10.94	To 70-ADH 12/94. Canx 6.12.94.
G-GBAO	Robin R.1180TD Aiglon (Rebuild of R.1180 prototype F-WVKU c/n 01)	277	F-GBAO(2)	9. 9.81	
G-GBCA	Agusta A.109A-II	7272		27. 1.84	Crashed on take-off from Glyndebourne on 7.6.85. Canx as WFU 3.9.85.
G-GBFF	Reims Cessna F.172N	1565	F-GBFF	16. 6.99	
G-GBHH	Hughes 269C	77-0616	TF-HRH TF-HHO/N45CD/N9250F/(N51CC)	23. 9.96	To G-BXHI 6/97. Canx.
G-GBHI	Socata TB-10 Tobago	19	F-GBHI	12.11.97	
G-GBLP	Reims Cessna F.172M Skyhawk II	1042	G-GWEN G-GBLP/N14496	9.11.84	
G-GBLR	Reims Cessna F.150L	1109	N961L (D-EDJE)	30. 4.85	(Badly damaged on landing at Sywell on 15.1.96) (Stored 5/96)
G-GBSC	Beechcraft E90 King Air	LW-242		25. 4.77	To N555GA 12/81. Canx 3.12.81.
G-GBSL	Beechcraft 76 Duchess	ME-265	G-BGVG	27. 3.81	
G-GBTA	Boeing 737-436 (Line No. 2532)	25859	G-BVHA (G-GBTA)	7. 2.94	
G-GBTB	Boeing 737-436 (Line No. 2545)	25860	OO-LTS G-BVHB/OO-LTS/G-BVHB/(G-GBTB)	23.10.96	
G-GBUE	Robin DR.400/120A Petit Prince	1354	G-BPXD F-GBUE	11. 5.89	
G-GBXS	Europa Avn Europa XS	0005		1. 4.98	
G-GCAL	Douglas DC-10-10 (Line No. 2)	46501	N183AT G-BELO/N10DC/N101AA	2. 4.86	To N220AU. Canx 27.11.91.
G-GCAT	PA-28-140 Cherokee B	28-26032	G-BFRH OH-PCA	22.10.81	
G-GCCL	Beechcraft 76 Duchess	ME-322	(G-BNRF) N6714U	5. 8.87	
G-GCJL	BAe Jetstream Srs.4100	41001		5. 2.91	
G-GCKI	Mooney M.20K (231)	25-0401	N4062H	15. 8.80	
G-GCNZ	Cessna 150M Commuter	150-75933	C-GCNZ	8.11.88	Canx as destroyed 8.6.99. (Possibly resulting from an arson incident at Elstree!)
G-GCUB	PA-18-150 Super Cub	18-7922	SE-GCO Swedish Army 51249	11. 2.99	
G-GDAM	PA-18-135 Super Cub (L-21B-PI) (Frame No. 18-3648)	18-3535	PH-PVW (PH-DKE)/R-107/54-2335	30. 6.81	CofA expired 11.8.91. (Stored .96) Canx by CAA 18.3.99.
G-GDAY	Robinson R-22 Beta	0676		10. 8.87	(Extensively damaged in crash at Blackpool on 24.4.99)
G-GDER	Robin R.1180TD Aiglon	280	F-GDER	15. 5.97	
G-GDEZ	BAe 125 Srs.1000B	259026	N9026 G-5-743/ZS-ACT/ZS-CCT/G-5-743	30.10.95	
G-GDGR	Socata TB-20 Trinidad	378	F-GDGR	23. 7.97	
G-GDOG	PA-28R-200 Cherokee Arrow II	28R-7635227	G-BDXW N9235K	17. 4.89	
G-GDTU	Avions Mudry CAP.10B	193	F-GDTU (N.....)/F-GDTK/F-WZCI	27. 5.99	
G-GDXK	Cameron A-140 HAFB	4467		22. 9.98	
G-GEAR	Reims Cessna FR.182Q Skylane RG	0004		21. 6.78	
G-GEDI	Dassault Falcon 2000	49	VP-BEF (PH-EFB)/F-WWMD	23. 7.98	
G-GEDS	Aerospatiale AS.350B Ecureuil	1465	G-HMAN G-SKIM/G-BIVP	14. 4.89	To G-EJOC 12/94. Canx.
G-GEEE	Hughes 369HS (500)	45-0738S	G-BDOY	2. 3.90	
G-GEEP	Robin R.1180TD Aiglon	266		9. 4.80	
G-GEES	Cameron N-77 HAFB	357		8.11.77	
G-GEEZ	Cameron N-77 HAFB	1159		3. 5.85	
G-GEHP	PA-28RT-201 Arrow IV	28R-8218014	F-GEHP N82023	24. 4.98	
G-GEIL	BAe 125 Srs.800B	258021	G-5-15	31. 1.85	To VR-CEJ 12/93. Canx 6.12.93.
G-GEMS	Thunder Ax8-90 Srs.2 HAFB	2287	G-BUNP	6.11.92	
G-GENE	Cessna 501 Citation I (Unit No.573)	501-0170	N501HP (N6778Y)	8.12.81	To G-MTLE 5/86. Canx.
G-GENN	Gulfstream American GA-7 Cougar	GA7-0114	G-BNAB G-BGYP	2.12.94	
G-GEOF	Pereira Osprey 2	PFA/70-10384		7. 9.78	
G-GEUP	Cameron N-77 HAFB	880		8.12.82	

Regn	Type	c/n	Previous identity	Regn date	Fate or immediate subsequent identity (if known)
G-GFAB	Cameron N-105 HAFB	2048		4. 8.89	
G-GFAL	Douglas DC-10-10 (Line No. 269)	46970	N1002D	19. 5.78	To G-BJZD 4/82. Canx.
G-GFCA	PA-28-161 Cadet	2841100	N9174X	24. 4.89	
G-GFCB	PA-28-161 Cadet	2841101	N9175F	24. 4.89	
G-GFCC	PA-28-161 Cadet	2841200	N9189N	24.10.89	To G-BXJJ 6/97. Canx.
G-GFCD	PA-34-220T Seneca III	34-8133073	G-KIDS N83745	31. 5.90	
G-GFCE	PA-28-161 Warrior II	28-7916191	G-BNJP N2212G	29. 5.90	To G-BVIH 10/93. Canx.
G-GFCF	PA-28-161 Cadet	2841259	G-RHBH N9193Z	28. 6.90	
G-GFEY	PA-34-200T Seneca II	34-7870343	D-GFEY D-IFEY/N36599	13. 5.98	
G-GFKY	Zenair CH.250 (built by D.Koch)	34	C-GFKY	23. 4.93	
G-GFLY	Reims Cessna F.150L	0822	PH-CES	28. 8.80	
G-GFRY	Bell 206L-3 Long Ranger III	51067	N600EA N4378D/JA9364	1. 9.92	To N16EA 10/97. Canx 26.9.97.
G-GFTA	PA-28-161 Warrior III	2842047	N4132L	1. 4.99	
G-GFTB	PA-28-161 Warrior III	2842048	N4120V	7. 5.99	
G-GGAE	HS.125 Srs.3B/RA	25157	VR-BGD D-CAMB	18. 1.78	To G-JSAX 7/83. Canx.
G-GGCC	Agusta-Bell 206B JetRanger II	8530	G-BEHG	3. 2.89	To G-XXII 11/93. Canx.
G-GGGG	Thunder Ax7-77 HAFB	162		2. 8.78	
G-GGLE	PA-22-108 Colt (Mod) (Taildragger conversion) (Incorporates parts from G-AROM c/n 22-8805)	22-8914	N5234Z	13. 5.93	
G-GGOW	Colt 77A HAFB	1542		19. 6.89	
G-GGTT	Agusta-Bell 47G-4A	2538	F-GGTT I-ANDO	21. 8.97	
G-GHCL	Bell 206B JetRanger II	925	G-SHVV N72GM/N83106	8. 7.92	
G-GHIA	Cameron N-120 HAFB	2442		13.11.90	
G-GHIN	Thunder Ax7-77 HAFB	1802		16. 7.90	
G-GHKX	PA-28-161 Warrior II	28-8416005	F-GHKX N4318X	10. 6.99	
G-GHNC	American Aviation AA-5A Cheetah	AA5A-0780	N26877	22. 8.80	To G-ESTE 4/87. Canx.
G-GHRW	PA-28RT-201 Arrow IV	28R-7918140	G-ONAB G-BHAK/N29555	8.12.83	
G-GHSI	PA-44-180T Turbo Seminole	44-8107026	SX-ATA N8278Z	2.12.94	(Damaged late .94)
G-GHZJ	Socata TB-9 Tampico	941	F-GHZJ	4. 3.98	
G-GHZM	Robinson R-22 Beta	0884	G-FENI	1. 8.95	To G-CHZN 4/99. Canx.
G-GIGI	Socata MS.893A Rallye Commodore 180	11637	G-AYVX F-BSFJ	28. 9.81	
G-GIII	Gulfstream G.1159A Gulfstream III	345	5X-UOI G-GIII/VR-CCN/G-BSAN/N17585	31. 1.92	To 5X-UOI 12/93. Canx 21.12.93.
G-GILL	Cessna 402C Businessliner II	402C-0006	N4643N	10. 7.79	Restored as N4643N 9/84. Canx 5.7.84.
G-GILT	Cessna 421C Golden Eagle III	421C-0515	G-BMZC N555WV/N555WW/N885WW/N885EC/N88541	3. 7.97	
G-GILY	Robinson R-22 Beta	0688		21. 9.87	Destroyed in forced landing at Micklefield Green Farm, Sarratt, Herts on 5.11.89. Canx by CAA 10.7.96.
G-GINA	Aerospatiale AS.350B Ecureuil	1016		21. 3.78	To N130FH 5/91. Canx 9.5.91.
G-GINZ	Hughes 269C (300C)	129-0869	F-GINZ SE-HMX/PH-HAN/C-GFKF/N1091N	31.10.97	To G-ZBHH 8/99. Canx.
G-GIRL	Cessna 421C Golden Eagle III	421C-0276	HB-LIM (N6637G)	18.11.77	To N2668B 2/82. Canx.
G-GIRO	Schweizer 269C (300C)	S.1328	N41S	16. 9.88	
G-GIRY	American General AG-5B Tiger	10146	F-GIRY	5. 2.99	
G-GJAN	Cessna 340A II	340A-0422	G-NAIL G-DEXI/N6216X	14.11.94	To N34TM. Canx 12.9.95.
G-GJCB	BAe 125 Srs.800B	258079	G-5-542	2.12.86	To G-BVHW 1/94. Canx.
G-GJCD	Robinson R-22 Beta	0966		22. 2.89	
G-GJET	Gates LearJet 35A	35A-365	G-CJET G-SEBE/G-ZIPS/(N4564S)/G-ZONE	9. 3.95	
G-GJKK	Mooney M.20K (252TSE)	25-1227	F-GJKK	26.11.93	
G-GKAT	Enstrom 280C Shark	1200	F-GKAT N5694Y	26. 8.97	
G-GKFC	Tiger Cub RL5A-LW Sherwood Ranger	PFA/237-12947	G-MYZI	24.11.98	
G-GKNB	Beechcraft 200 Super King Air	BB-705		12. 3.80	To D-IBAB 5/87. Canx 14.7.87.
G-GLAD	Gloster Gladiator II	-	"N2276" N5903	5. 1.95	(On rebuild 7/99 Duxford)
G-GLAM	BAe Jetstream Srs.3102-09	839	G-OEDG G-GLAM/G-IBLX/G-31-839	8. 2.91	To ZK-JSA 5/97. Canx 15.5.97.
G-GLAS	HS.748 Srs.2A/334SCD	1756	9Y-TFS G-11-8	.11.86	To G-BPDA 10/88. Canx.
G-GLAW	Cameron N-90 HAFB	1808		10.10.88	
G-GLBL	Lindstrand AM.32000 HAFB	444		3.10.96	
G-GLED	Cessna 150M Commuter	150-76673	C-GLED	6. 1.89	

Regn	Type	c/n	Previous identity	Regn date	Fate or immediate subsequent identity (if known)
G-GLEE	Schweizer Hughes 269C (300C)	S.1315	G-BRUW N86G	12. 4.90	To G-OGOB 10/90. Canx.
G-GLEN	Bell 212	30913	LN-OQS G-GLEN	13. 3.79	Canx 6.7.89 on sale to Australia. To P2-PAV /89.
G-GLOR	Cessna 425 Corsair	425-0174	N6873R	10. 3.82	To N384MA 11/93. Canx 25.10.93.
G-GLOS	Handley Page 137 Jetstream 200 (Production No. 41)	241	G-BCGU G-AXRI	10. 2.82	To OO-IBL 7/95. Canx 18.7.95.
G-GLOW	Aerospatiale AS.355F1 Twin Squirrel	5120	G-PAPA G-CNET/G-MCAH	16.11.89	To G-FFRI 4/93. Canx.
G-GLTT	PA-31-350 Navajo Chieftain	31-8452004	N27JV N606SM	19. 9.97	
G-GLUE	Cameron N-65 HAFB	390		17. 3.81	
G-GLUG	PA-31-350 Navajo Chieftain	31-8052077	N2287J G-BLOE/G-NITE/N3559A	1. 9.94	
G-GLYN	Boeing 747-211B (Line No. 326)	21516	C-GXRA N1785B	.10.86	To N207AE. Canx 28.2.91.
G-GMAX	SNCAN Stampe SV-4C	141	G-BXNW F-BBPB	19. 6.87	Damaged in crash at Booker on 3.6.91. (On rebuild 5/96)
G-GMJM	McDonnell Douglas DC-9-83 (MD-83) (Line No. 1915)	49951	N13627	15.11.91	To HB-IKN 1/96. Canx 30.1.96.
G-GMPA	Aerospatiale AS.355F2 Twin Squirrel	5409	G-BPOI	26. 9.89	
G-GMSI	Socata TB-9 Tampico	145		18. 9.80	
G-GNAT	Folland Gnat T.1	FL.595	8638M XS101	14. 4.82	
G-GNSY	Handley Page HPR.7 Dart Herald 209	197	I-ZERD G-BFRK/4X-AHN	30. 6.87	Canx by CAA 8.4.97 as PWFU.
G-GNTA	SAAB-Scania SF.340A (QC) Cityliner	340A-049	HB-AHK SE-E49	5. 4.91	
G-GNTB	SAAB-Scania SF.340A (QC) Cityliner	340A-082	HB-AHL SE-E82	30. 9.91	
G-GNTC	SAAB-Scania SF.340A (QC) Cityliner	340A-020	HB-AHE OK-RGS/HB-AHE/SE-E20	25. 9.92	
G-GNTD	SAAB-Scania SF.340A (QC) Cityliner	340A-100	SE-ISK SE-E01	30.12.92	
G-GNTE	SAAB-Scania SF.340A (QC) Cityliner	340A-133	SE-ISM SE-F33	22. 1.93	
G-GNTF	SAAB-Scania SF.340A (QC) Cityliner	340A-113	HB-AHO SE-F13	27.10.94	
G-GNTG	SAAB-Scania SF.340A (QC) Cityliner	340A-126	HB-AHR SE-F26	18.11.94	
G-GNTH	SAAB-Scania SF.340B Cityliner	340B-169	N588MA SE-F69	23. 1.97	
G-GNTI	SAAB-Scania SF.340B Cityliner	340B-172	N589MA SE-F72	30. 1.97	
G-GNTJ	SAAB-Scania SF.340B Cityliner	340B-192	N591MA SE-F92	26. 2.97	
G-GNTZ	BAe 146 Srs.200	E2036	HB-IXB N175US/N355PS	26.11.94	
G-GOAL	Lindstrand LBL-105A HAFB	420		18.11.96	Canx as WFU 17.12.98.
G-GOBP	Bell 206B JetRanger II	1376	G-BOUY N5450M/N1PE/XC-GUW	5. 2.91	To G-OBRU 4/94. Canx.
G-GOBT	Colt 77A HAFB	1815		13. 2.91	
G-GOCC	American Aviation AA-5A Cheetah	AA5A-0811	G-BPIX N26916	2. 9.92	
G-GOCX	Cameron N-90 HAFB	2619		7. 8.91	
G-GODS	Brugger MB.2 Colibri (Initially regd as PFA/43-10407; new project no. issued .80 and still under construction 7/89 - but now see G-BUDW)	PFA/43-10644		19. 1.79	Canx by CAA 2.9.91.
G-GOFX	Enstrom 280FX	2035		25. 5.89	To ZS-HWR. Canx 15.2.90.
G-GOGO	Hughes 369D (500D)	48-0294D	(G-BFSM)	19.12.78	To (PH-...)/SE-JBU. Canx 7.4.94.
G-GOGW	Cameron N-90 HAFB	3304		31. 8.94	
G-GOKT	Douglas DC-10-30 (Line No. 338)	47838	RP-C2114 (RP-C2004)	1. 5.96	
G-GOLD	Thunder Ax6-56A HAFB	119	(G-BEVI)	4. 7.77	(Canopy on display at Hallett's Panorama, Greenwich 1/89) Canx by CAA 13.4.93.
G-GOLF	Socata TB-10 Tobago	250		21.12.81	
G-GOLO	Robinson R-22 Beta	1124		10.10.89	Forced landed at Wayker Farm, Winkfield on 17.1.92. Canx as destroyed 16.4.92.
G-GOMM	PA-32R-300 Lance	32-7780030	N6571F	16. 5.80	Force landed and crashed through a fence at Eyehurst Farm, Kingswood, Surrey 15.8.95. (Fuselage stored 4/99 Stansted)
G-GONE	DH.112 Venom FB.50 (FB.1) (built by FFW, Essen)	752	J-1542 Swiss AF	17. 9.84	(Under restoration 6/99 at Hurn)
G-GOOD	Socata TB-20 Trinidad	1657	F-GNHJ	4.11.94	
G-GOOS	Reims Cessna F.182Q Skylane II	0145		27. 3.80	To G-LEGG 6/96. Canx.
G-GORE	CFM Streak Shadow (PFA c/n conflicts with Minimax G-MWFD)	K.138-SA & PFA/206-11646		12. 4.90	
G-GOSH	Cessna 404 Titan Ambassador II	404-0404	N8771K	24. 4.79	Canx 8.7.82 on sale to The Netherlands. To D-IFFG.
G-GOSS	CEA Jodel DR.221 Dauphin 2	125	F-BPRA	4.12.80	
G-GOTC	Gulfstream American GA-7 Cougar	GA7-0074	G-BMDY OO-LCR/OO-HRA	25. 6.97	
G-GOTO	PA-32R-301T Saratoga II TC	3257026	N92965	8. 1.98	

Regn	Type	c/n	Previous identity	Regn date	Fate or immediate subsequent identity (if known)
G-GOZO	Cessna R.182 Skylane RG II	R182-01883	G-BJZO (G-BJYE)/N5521T	9. 1.85	
G-GPAA	Boeing 737-2T4ADV (Line No. 707)	22368	N52AF EI-BOM/N52AF/(EI-BOM)/N52AF	14. 5.84	Restored as EI-BOM 11/84. Canx 8.11.84.
G-GPAB	Boeing 737-2L9 (Line No. 620)	22071	G-BJSO EI-BOJ/(EI-BOG)/G-BJSO/(EI-BMB)/SU-BCJ/OY-APN	22. 5.84	Restored as EI-BOJ 11/84. Canx 8.11.84.
G-GPMW	PA-28R-201T Turbo Arrow IV	28R-8031041	N3676V	3. 7.89	
G-GPST	Phillips ST.1 Speedtwin (PFA c/n conflicts with Kolb Twinstar G-MWWM)	1 & PFA/207-11645		21. 6.90	
G-GRAC	Grumman American GA-7 Cougar	GA7-0003	C-GRAC (N1367R)/N730GA	12. 8.86	To G-FLII 12/91. Canx.
G-GRAM	PA-31-350 Navajo Chieftain	31-7305006	G-BRHF N7679L	14. 3.91	(Fitted with one wing from PA-31 G-LYDD) To G-PMAX 7/99. Canx.
G-GRAY	Cessna 172N Skyhawk II	172-72375	N4859D	3.12.79	(Badly damaged ditching in Firth of Forth, near Mussleburgh on 2.4.93) (Stored 4/97)
G-GREG	CEA Jodel DR.220 2+2	47	F-BOKR	3.10.84	CofA expired 19.2.91. (Fuselage only for sale by R.Voice in 1992) Canx by CAA 1.4.97.
G-GREN	Cessna T.310R II	310R-1282	N426CB N6015X	24. 7.90	
G-GRID	Aerospatiale AS.355F1 Twin Squirrel	5012	TG-BOS	28. 3.89	
G-GRIF	Rockwell Commander 112TC-A	13258	G-BHXC N1005C	2.10.81	
G-GRIN	Van's RV-6	PFA/181-12409		8. 1.98	
G-GRIP	Colt Bibendum 110SS HAFB	4224		5. 1.98	
G-GROB	Grob G-109	6139		30. 9.82	Canx as destroyed 12.6.91.
G-GROL	Maule MXT-7-180 Star Rocket	14091C		16. 6.98	
G-GROW	Cameron N-77 HAFB	705		13. 2.81	CofA expired 4.5.84. Canx as WFU 7.4.93.
G-GRRC	PA-28-161 Warrior II	2816076	G-BXJX HB-POM/D-EJTB/N9149X	9. 3.98	
G-GRRR	Scottish Avn Bulldog Srs.120/122	BH120/229	G-BXGU Ghana AF G-105	19.10.98	(On rebuild 1/99 Bourne Park)
G-GRUB	PA-28-180 Cherokee E	28-5800	G-AYAS	4. 3.86	Overran runway and struck a fence on landing at St.Merrion on 2.12.90 & DBR. Canx by CAA 10.1.91.
G-GRYZ	Beechcraft F.33A Bonanza	CE-1668	F-GRYZ D-ESNE/N80011/(OY-GEN)/N80011	. 6.99R	
G-GSAM	BAe 125 Srs.800B	258133	G-5-611	10.10.88	To G-5-642/N800FK. Canx 4.9.89.
G-GSEB	Dassault Falcon 900B	161	VP-CTT F-GSAA/F-WWFF	14. 4.98	To PH-ILC 6/99. Canx 3.6.99.
G-GSFC	Robinson R-22 Beta	0569	N2425J	3. 7.86	
G-GSFT	PA-44-180 Seminole	44-7995202	EI-BYZ N2193K	12.10.98	
G-GSKY	Douglas DC-10-10 (Line No. 272)	46973		19. 5.78	To G-BJZE 3/82. Canx.
G-GSML	Enstrom 280C-UK Shark	1149	G-BNNV SE-HIY	14. 6.89	To G-MHCF 9/96. Canx.
G-GSMP	Eiri PIK-20E Srs.1	20236		14.12.79	To N32668 8/82. Canx.
G-GSTC	Europa Avn Europa	?		. 7.99R	(Noted at PFA Rally, Cranfield on 4.7.99)
G-GTAX	PA-31-350 Navajo Chieftain	31-7405442	G-OIAS OY-CBF/D-IGSA/N54322	11. 3.88	
G-GTHM	PA-38-112 Tomahawk II	38-81A0171	C-GTHM	17.11.86	
G-GTPL	Mooney M.20K (231)	25-0301	G-BHOS N231LQ	15. 7.80	
G-GUAY	Enstrom 480	5036		1.12.98	
G-GUCK	Beechcraft C23 Sundowner 180	M-2221	G-BPYG N6638R	9. 4.92	
G-GUFO	Cameron Saucer 80SS HAFB	1641	C-GUFO G-BOUB	10. 6.98	
G-GUGI	Eurocopter EC-135T-1	0065		9.10.98	
G-GULF	Lindstrand LBL-105A HAFB	320		3.11.95	
G-GULL	SMAN Petrel Amphibian	PFA/269-12833	29-DX F-JBSG/G-GULL	6. 3.95	
G-GUNN	Reims Cessna F.172H	0500	G-AWGC	22.10.81	Badly damaged in gales at Stornoway on 10.11.82. Canx by CAA 4.2.87.
G-GUNS	Cameron V-77 HAFB	2221		9. 5.90	
G-GURL	Cameron A-210 HAFB	2387		3. 9.90	Canx as WFU 2.12.98.
G-GUSS	PA-28-151 Cherokee Warrior	28-7415497	G-BJRY N43453	16. 8.95	
G-GUST	Agusta-Bell 206B JetRanger II	8192	G-CBHH F-GALU/G-AYBE	30. 8.96	
G-GUYI	PA-28-181 Archer II	28-7890334	N3815M	23.11.87	Crashed 60 miles southwest of Goose Bay, Canada on 22.11.87 whilst on delivery. Canx by CAA 20.1.88.
G-GUYS	PA-34-200T Seneca II	34-7870283	G-BMWT N31984	14. 7.87	
G-GVBF	Lindstrand LBL-180A HAFB	250	PH-VBF G-GVBF	19. 5.95	
G-GVIP	Agusta A.109E Power	11024		1. 7.98	
G-GWEA	PA-31-350 Navajo Chieftain	31-8152164	N551PH (N551PX)/N2728F/N4092L	10.10.86	To G-VAUK 8/88. Canx.
G-GWEN	Reims Cessna F.172M Skyhawk II	1042	G-GBLP N14496	8. 2.88	Restored as G-GBLP 5/96. Canx.

Regn	Type	c/n	Previous identity	Regn date	Fate or immediate subsequent identity (if known)
G-GWHH	Aerospatiale AS.355F Twin Squirrel	5303	G-BKUL	17. 1.84	To G-FFHI 1/94. Canx.
G-GWIL	Aerospatiale AS.350B Ecureuil	1790		20. 7.84	To G-IIPM 12/96. Canx.
G-GWIN	Bell 206L-3 Long Ranger	51011	N2266T	31. 8.89	To G-BUNU 9/92. Canx.
G-GWIT	Cameron O-84 HAFB	1465		16. 7.87	To D-OLBI 5/95. Canx 10.5.95.
G-GWIZ	Colt Clown SS HAFB	1369	(G-BPWU)	25. 4.89	
G-GWYN	Reims Cessna F.172M Skyhawk II	1217	PH-TWN	5. 3.81	
G-GYAV	Cessna 172N Skyhawk II	172-71362	C-GYAV	26. 8.87	
G-GYBO	Gardan GY-80-160 Horizon	228	OY-DTN SE-FGL/OY-DTN	4. 8.98	
G-GYMM	PA-28R-200 Cherokee Arrow D	28R-7135049	G-AYWW N11C	22. 2.90	
G-GYRO	Campbell Cricket	G/03-1046		26. 2.82	
	(Originally regd as Bensen B.8 Gyrocopter with c/n 01 & G/01-1046; amended in 1990)				
G-GZDO	Cessna 172N Skyhawk II	172-71826	C-GZDO (N5299E)	11.10.88	

G-H G-H

Regn	Type	c/n	Previous identity	Regn date	Fate or immediate subsequent identity (if known)
G-HACK	PA-18-150 Super Cub	18-7168	SE-CSA	20.11.97	
G-HADA	Enstrom 480	5017		17. 9.96	
G-HADI	Gulfstream G.1159 Gulfstream II	235	N17581	26. 7.79	To N5519C. Canx 12.12.85.
G-HAEC	Commonwealth CAC-18 (P-51D) Mustang Mk.23	CACM-192-1517	VR-HIU (RP-C651)/PI-C651/VH-FCB/VH-PCB/R.Australian AF A68-192	1. 5.85	
	(Composite rebuilt 74/76 using major components from Philippine AF P-51D 44-72917)				
G-HAGS	Benson B.8 Gyrocopter	G/01-1052		31.10.86	Canx as CAA 9.8.91.
G-HAGT	Airbus A.320-212	294	F-WWID	2. 4.92	To G-HBAP 2/96. Canx.
G-HAHA	PA-18-150 Super Cub	18-8899	G-BSWE N9194P	22. 8.94	(Rebuilt 94/95 using major parts from G-BTDY) To G-WLAC 6/98. Canx.
G-HAIG	Rutan LongEz	1983-L & PFA/74A-11149		20. 5.86	
G-HAJJ	Glaser-Dirks DG-400	4-225		15. 2.88	
G-HALC	PA-28R-200 Cherokee Arrow II	28R-7335042	N91253 C-FFQQ/CF-FQQ	26.11.90	
G-HALE	Robinson R-44 Astro	0492		6. 8.98	
G-HALJ	Cessna 140	8336	N89308 NC89308	30. 4.96	
G-HALK	HS.125 Srs.600B	256033	G-PJWB N330G/HZ-YA1/G-DMAN/F-BUYP	10. 4.87	To N6033. Canx 2.6.89.
G-HALL	PA-22-160 Tri-Pacer	22-7423	G-ARAH	8.11.79	
G-HALO	Elisport CH-7 Angel	A.031	I-2858	12.11.93	(Stored 6/97)
G-HALP	Socata TB-10 Tobago	192	G-BITD	19. 8.81	
G-HAMA	Beechcraft 200 Super King Air	BB-30	N244JB N211JB/N3090C/N3030C/N200CA	16.11.84	
G-HAMI	Fuji FA.200-180 Aero Subaru	FA200-188	G-OISF G-BAPT	31. 1.92	
G-HAMP	Bellanca 7ACA Champ	30-72	N9173L	8. 8.88	
G-HAND	Cameron Startac 105SS HAFB	3895		19. 8.96	
G-HANK	Reims Cessna FR.172H Rocket	0245	G-AYTH	14.12.82	CofA expired 14.12.82 (Last known of at St.Just)
	(Regd as a FR.172E, plate on a/c proclaimed it to be a FR.172H - 1st in UK)				Canx as destroyed 6.12.88.
G-HANS	Robin DR.400 2+2	1384		2. 3.79	
G-HAPR	Bristol 171 Sycamore HR.14	13387	8010M XG547	15. 6.78	(On display 3/96 Weston-super-Mare)
G-HAPY	DHC.1 Chipmunk 22A (Fuselage no. DHB/f/589)	C1/0697	WP803	3. 7.96	
G-HARE	Cameron N-77 HAFB	1467		12. 3.87	
G-HARF	Gulfstream G.1159C Gulfstream IV	1117	N1761J	9.10.91	
G-HARH	Sikorsky S-76B	760391	N7600U	30. 9.91	
G-HARI	X'Air	BMAA/HB/099		11. 6.99	
G-HARO	Aerospatiale AS.355F2 Twin Squirrel	5364	G-DAFT G-BNNN	21. 8.96	
G-HART	Cessna 152 II (Tailwheel conversion)	152-79734	(G-BPBF) N757GS	2. 2.89	
G-HARV	PA-23-250 Aztec E	23-7754002	N62760	20.12.78	To G-BKVT 2/84. Canx.
G-HARY	Alon A-2 Aircoupe	A.188	G-ATWP	15. 3.93	
G-HASI	Cessna 421B Golden Eagle II	421B-0654	G-BTDK OY-BFA/N1558G	17. 2.98	
G-HASL	American Aviation AA-5A Cheetah	AA5A-0791	G-BGSL	13. 3.84	Badly damaged in crash ½ mile from Staverton on 25.6.86 when on approach. Canx by CAA 10.1.91.
G-HAST	Cessna 421B Golden Eagle II	421B-0828	N29855 HP-.../YV-999P/YV-T-ALZ/(N1927G)	10. 4.86	Fatal crash in woods at Bedlars Green, about half a mile from Stansted on 20.10.87 shortly after take-off & DBF. Canx as destroyed 26.5.88.
G-HATZ	Hatz CB-1 (Built by R.F.Dangelo)	17	N54623	11. 5.89	
G-HAUG	Sikorsky S-76B	760358	G-HPLC	26. 9.94	Fatal accident at Jenkinstown Wood, Ravensdale, Co.Louth, Ireland on 12.12.96. Canx by CAA as destroyed 31.10.97.
G-HAUL	Westland WG.30-300	020	(G-17-22)	3. 7.86	Permit expired 27.10.86. Canx as WFU 22.4.92. (On display 4/98)
G-HAUS	Hughes 369HM (500)	52-0214M	G-KBOT G-RAMM/EI-AVN/N9037F	20. 7.99	

Regn	Type	c/n	Previous identity	Regn date	Fate or immediate subsequent identity (if known)
G-HAVA	Westland SA.341G Gazelle 1	WA/1141	CS-HCZ F-WYMW/F-GKMU/Qatar Police QP-1/G-BBSJ/G-17-11	16. 4.97	Badly damaged when struck a hangar door at Gamston 28.7.97. Canx as destroyed 28.7.97.
G-HAWK	Hawker Siddeley HS.1182 Hawk T.50	41H/4020010	ZA101 (XX155)	30. 6.75	Restored to MOD as ZA101. Canx to MOD(PE) 13.3.90.
G-HAYN	Enstrom 280C-UK Shark	1155	G-BPOX N51776	2.10.96	To G-MHCG 3/97. Canx.
G-HAZE	Thunder Ax8-90 HAFB	989		3. 8.88	
G-HBAC	Aerospatiale AS.355F1 Twin Squirrel	5324	G-HJET F-GEOX/F-WYMC/OY-HDL	15. 5.89	To G-XCEL 5/95. Canx.
G-HBAP	Airbus A.320-212	294	G-HAGT F-WWID	2. 2.96	To OY-CNP 2/97. Canx 18.2.97.
G-HBBC	DH.104 Dove 8	04211	G-ALFM VP961/G-ALFM/VP961	24. 1.96	
G-HBCA	Agusta A.109A II	7347		7.11.85	To G-IADT 1/89. Canx.
G-HBCO	PA-31-325 Navajo C/R	31-8112012	N4038M	13. 3.87	To 9M-BAE. Canx 16.6.92.
G-HBMW	Robinson R-22	0170	G-BOFA N9068D	7. 7.94	
G-HBUG	Cameron N-90 HAFB	1991	G-BRCN	21. 6.89	
G-HBUS	Bell 206L-1 LongRanger II	45452		25.11.80	To G-DALE 5/89. Canx.
G-HCFR	BAe 125 Srs.800B	258240	HB-VLT G-SHEA/G-BUWC/G-5-772	23. 7.98	
G-HCHU	Cessna TU.206G Turbo Stationair 6 II	U206-06043	HB-CHU G-BKKJ/N4890Z	26. 3.85	To EC-EGD. Canx 30.7.87.
G-HCRP	McDonnell Douglas DC-9-83 (MD-83) (Line No. 1778)	49936	N3001D	19.11.90	To TC-INB 3/95. Canx 30.3.95.
G-HCSL	PA-34-220T Seneca III	34-8133237	N84375	9. 5.91	
G-HCTL	PA-31-350 Navajo Chieftain	31-7952097	G-BGOY N35172	19. 6.89	To N17KA 12/98. Canx 25.11.98.
G-HDBA	HS.748 Srs.2B/426	1798	A6-GRM(2) G-HDBA	13.11.84	To 9N-ACW. Canx 9.2.94.
G-HDBB	HS.748 Srs.2B/426	1799	A6-ABM(2) G-HDBB	13.11.84	To 9N-ACX. Canx 9.3.94.
G-HDBC	HS.748 Srs.2B/378	1786	D-AHSC G-11-18	24. 6.88	To (VT-GOA)/ZS-NWW 10/95. Canx 6.10.95.
G-HDBD	HS.748 Srs.2B/378	1797	G-11-747 CS-TAR/G-11-1/D-AHSF/G-11-2	26. 2.90	Canx by CAA 21.2.96. To G-EMRD 10/96.
G-HDDP	Eurocopter EC-135T-1	0055		29. 6.98	To G-HDPP 3.7.98. Canx.
G-HDEW	PA-32R-301 Saratoga SP	3213026	G-BRGZ N91787	4.12.89	
G-HDIX	Enstrom 280FX	2076	N506DH D-HDIX	19. 2.98	
G-HDOG	Thunder Colt Flying Hot Dog SS HAFB	2407		6. 8.93	To N7215H 4/97. Canx 3.4.97.
G-HDPP	Eurocopter EC-135T-1	0055	G-HDDP	3. 7.98	
G-HEAD	Colt 56SS Flying Head HAFB (Compac Computerised Head shape)	304	SE-ZHE G-HEAD	18. 8.81	
G-HEAR	Eurocopter AS.350B2 Ecureuil	2668	G-BUJG	31. 7.92	Restored as G-BUJG 1.9.92. Canx.
G-HEAT	Bell 206B JetRanger III	2745		26. 6.79	To N2964N 3/82. Canx 10.3.82.
G-HEBE	Bell 206B JetRanger III	3745	CS-HDN N3179A	5. 2.97	
G-HELE	Bell 206B JetRanger III	3789	G-OJFR N18095	21. 2.91	
G-HELI	Saro Skeeter AOP.12 (Composite of cabin 7870M/XM556 and boom 7979M/XM529)	S2/5110	Composite	15. 6.78	Canx 22.3.95 on sale to Germany. (On display Luftwaffen Museum, Germany)
G-HELN	PA-18-95 Super Cub (Frame No 18-3400) (L-21B-PI) (Regd as c/n 18-1992 but frame exchanged in Italian AF service; c/n 18-3365 was officially regd as N9837Q)	18-3365	G-BKDG MM52-2392/EI-69/EI-141/I-EIWB/MM53-7765/53-7765	10. 1.86	
G-HELO	Bell 206B JetRanger II	124	G-BAZN 9J-RIN/ZS-HCJ	9.11.87	To D-HAFA(4) 5/93. Canx 27.8.92.
G-HELP	Colt 17A Cloudhopper HAFB	902		16. 2.87	CofA expired 7.8.95. Canx as PWFU 25.3.99.
G-HELV	DH.115 Vampire T.55 (built by FFW, Essen)	975	U-1215 Swiss AF	17. 9.91	
G-HELX	Cameron N-31 HAFB	1191		20. 9.85	Canx as WFU 5.5.92.
G-HELY	Agusta A.109A	7174		3. 8.79	To N109MJ 10/92. Canx 23.10.92.
G-HEMS	Aerospatiale SA.365N Dauphin 2	6009	F-WYMJ G-HEMS/N365AM/N365AH	22. 8.88	
G-HENK	Cameron V-77 HAFB	423		9. 6.78	To PH-HBS 7/79. Canx 26.7.79.
G-HENS	Cameron N-65 HAFB	740		8. 7.81	Canx by CAA 8.4.93. (Extant but stored 5/97)
G-HENY	Cameron V-77 HAFB	2486		9. 1.91	
G-HERA	Robinson R-22 Beta	1426		26. 6.90	Overturned onto its port side on landing at Blackpool on 24.2.99 & extensively damaged. Canx as destroyed 15.6.99.
G-HERB	PA-28R-201 Arrow III	28R-7837118	ZS-LAG N3504M	5. 6.86	
G-HERO	PA-32RT-300 Lance II	32R-7885086	G-BOGN N33LV/N30573	26. 4.88	(Open storage at Dieppe, France in 7/98)
G-HERS(1)	Jodel D.18	255 & PFA/169-11410		.12.88R	NTU - Canx. (Displayed as such partly completed at Cranfield in 7/89)
G-HERS(2)	Cessna 750 Citation X	750-0075	N5196U	1. 7.99	
G-HETH	Robinson R-22 Beta	1194		14.11.89	Fatal crash & DBF in a field at Codmore Wood, near Latimer, Bucks. on 29.5.92. Canx as destroyed 17.8.92.
G-HEVY	Boeing 707-324C (Line No. 537)	19350	N17327 G-HEVY/(N112BV)/PP-VLO/N17327	23. 1.90	To EL-LAT 2/96. Canx 28.2.96.

Regn	Type	c/n	Previous identity	Regn date	Fate or immediate subsequent identity (if known)
G-HEWI	Piper J3C-90 Cub (L-4J-PI) (Frame No 12396)	12566	G-BLEN D-EBEN/HB-OFZ/44-80270	20. 7.84	
G-HEWS	Hughes 369D (500D)	51-1003D		13. 5.81	Badly damaged in forced landing near Banchory on 5.12.87. Canx as destroyed 26.5.88. (Wreck stored 3/90 Sywell)
G-HEWT	Hughes 369D (500D)	50-0702D	N80BF N1095D	14. 4.87	To D-HSUR. Canx 24.10.91.
G-HEYY	Cameron Bear 72SS HAFB (Hofmeister Lager Bear "George")(Originally regd as a N-65)	1244		21. 1.86	
G-HFBM	Curtiss Robin C-2	352	LV-FBM NC9279	24. 4.90	
G-HFCA	Cessna A150L Aerobat (Texas Taildragger conv)	A150-0381	N6081J	30. 8.91	
G-HFCB	Reims Cessna F.150L	0798	G-AZVR	10. 2.87	
G-HFCI	Reims Cessna F.150L	0823	PH-CET	11. 9.80	
G-HFCL	Reims Cessna F.152 II	1663	G-BGLR(2)	11.10.88	
G-HFCT	Reims Cessna F.152 II (Originally regd with c/n 1681)	1861		27. 1.81	
G-HFGP	Beechcraft 200 Super King Air	BB-749	N41TV N100H/(N100HD)/N100H	9.11.87	To N200AB. Canx 19.2.90.
G-HFIX	Vickers-Supermarine 361 Spitfire HF.IXe	CBAF/7243	G-BLAS Israeli DF/AF 2066/06-06/Italian AF MM4094/MJ730	22. 8.89	(Also quoted as c/n CBAF.78883)
G-HFLA	Schweizer 269C (300C)	S.1428		8.12.89	
G-HFLR	Schweizer 269C (300C)	S.1412		30.10.89	To G-BUEX 4/92. Canx.
G-HFTG	PA-23-250 Aztec E	27-7405378	G-BSOB G-BCJR/N54040	30. 4.87	
G-HGAS	Cameron N-77 HAFB	1969		4. 5.89	
G-HGGS	Embraer EMB.110P1 Bandeirante	110-294	PT-SCC	15.11.79	Fatal crash into a hill 6 miles south-east of Dalcross, Scotland on 19.11.84. (The wreck was not found until 21.11.84) Canx as destroyed 22.2.85.
G-HGPC	PBN BN-2A-27 Islander	251	G-FANS 5Y-AMU/G-51-251	17.11.83	To 8R-GGU. Canx 3.4.89.
G-HGPI	Socata TB-20 Trinidad	851		4. 8.88	
G-HHNT	Hawker Hunter T.7	41H-695449	8837M XL617	7. 7.89	To N617NL 2/90. Canx 12.12.89.
G-HHOI	HS.125 Srs.700B	257097	(G-BHTJ)	6. 6.80	To G-BRDI 11/87. Canx.
G-HHUN	Hawker Hunter F.4	HABL-003020	XE677	30.10.89	Fatal crash near Duxford on 5.6.98. Canx as destroyed 2.10.98.
G-HIAH	Revolution Helicopters Mini-500	0052		4. 3.96	No Permit believed issued. Canx by CAA 10.3.99.
G-HIBM	Cameron N-145 HAFB	3197		8. 2.94	
G-HIEL	Robinson R-22 Beta	1120		28. 9.89	
G-HIER	Bell 206B JetRanger III	3408	G-BRFD N2069N	20. 5.91	To EI-HER 7/94. Canx 27.6.94.
G-HIFI	PA-28R-201 Arrow III	28R-7837214	G-BFTB N9652C	16. 2.81	To F-GEOQ 6/87. Canx 24.4.87.
G-HIGG	Beechcraft 200 Super King Air	BB-160	(G-ONPA) (G-BLKN)/EI-BHG/9Q-CTK/N8493D/EI-BHG/OY-CBK/(EI-BGR)/N2160L	7.12.84	To N65171 9/90. Canx 29.8.90.
G-HIGH	Reims Cessna FT.337GP Pressurised Turbo Super Skymaster (Wichita c/n 0060)	0007	OO-KAL	13.12.77	To I-HIGH 4/84. Canx 16.4.84.
G-HIGS	Cessna 404 Titan II	404-0048	G-ODAS D-ICIK/LN-MAR/(SE-GZD)/(N5430G)	28. 6.84	To G-ZAPB 6/89. Canx.
G-HIHI	PA-32R-301 Saratoga SP (Regd with c/n 32R-13012)	3213012		11. 5.88	To SX-ARK 3/99. Canx 17.3.99.
G-HIHO	Boeing 747-123 (Line No. 87)	20108	(LX-NCV) N14939/N9669	19. 6.87	To VH-EEI. Canx 10.3.88.
G-HIII	Extra EA.300	057	D-ETYD	10. 1.95	
G-HIIL	Europa Avn Europa	PFA/247-12535		8. 9.94	To G-EESA 4/96. Canx.
G-HILL	Cessna U.206F Stationair 6 II	U206-01706	PH-ADN D-EEXY/N9506G	31. 3.80	To EI-BNK 12/82. Canx.
G-HILO	Rockwell Commander 114	14224	N4894W	6. 2.98	
G-HILR	Hiller UH-12E-3/Soloy	5025	N525HA	28. 3.78	To D-HOSI 6/92. Canx 16.12.91.
G-HILS	Reims Cessna F.172H Skyhawk	0522	G-AWCH	20.12.88	
G-HILT	Socata TB-10 Tobago	298	(G-BMYB) EI-BOF/G-HILT	13. 5.82	
G-HIND	Maule MT-7-235 Star Rocket	18037C		26. 3.98	
G-HINT	Cameron N-90 HAFB	1845		11.10.88	Canx by CAA 9.4.98.
G-HIPE	Sorrell SNS-7 Hyperbipe (built by R.Stephen)	209	N18RS	6. 4.93	
G-HIPO	Robinson R-22 Beta	1719	G-BTGB	11. 9.92	
G-HIRE	Gulfstream American GA-7 Cougar	GA7-0091	G-BGSZ YV-1613P/N704G	10.12.81	
G-HISS	Aerotek Pitts S-2A Special	2137	G-BLVU SE-GTX	17. 3.92	(Stored 11/97)
G-HIUP	Cameron A-250 HAFB	4464		16. 4.99	
G-HIVA	Cessna 337A Super Skymaster	337A-0429	G-BAES SE-CWW/N5329S	28. 3.88	
G-HIVE	Reims Cessna F.150M	1186	G-BCXT	19. 4.85	
G-HJCB	BAe 125 Srs.1000B	259031	G-5-754 G-BUUY/G-5-754	15.10.93	To N301PH 12/97. Canx 18.11.97.
G-HJET	Aerospatiale AS.355F1 Twin Squirrel	5324	F-GEOX F-WYMC/OY-HDL	16.11.87	To G-HBAC 5/89. Canx.

Regn	Type	c/n	Previous identity	Regn date	Fate or immediate subsequent identity (if known)
G-HJSS	AIA Stampe SV-4C	1101	G-AZNF	7. 9.92	
			F-BGJM/French Mil		
G-HKHM	Hughes 369D (500D)	71-1019D	B-HHM	8. 4.99	
			VR-HHM(3)/N50605		
G-HKIT	BAC One Eleven Srs.521FH	BAC.196	(VP-BEC)	17. 6.97	
			VR-BEC/LV-JNT/G-16-10		
G-HLAA	Airbus A.300B4-203F	047	EI TLN	0.10.97	
			G-HLAA/N740SC/F-BVGJ/F-WUAX		
G-HLAB	Airbus A.300B4-203F	045	N743SC	20. 2.98	
			F-BVGI/F-WNDA		
G-HLAC	Airbus A.300B4-203F	074	N829SC	23.11.98	
			F-BVGL		
G-HLCF	CFM Starstreak Shadow SA-II	PFA/206-12796		10. 5.96	
G-HLEN	Aerospatiale AS.350B Ecureuil	1836	G-LOLY	22. 4.93	
			JA9897/N5805T/HP-.../N5805T		
G-HLFT	Short SC.5 Belfast C.1 (Mod to Mk.2)	SH.1819	XR365	11. 9.81	
G-HLIX	Cameron Helix Oilcan 61SS HAFB (Originally regd as 80SS)	1192		20. 9.85	Canx as WFU 29.4.97. Stored 1/98 BBAC Museum.
G-HLUB	Beechcraft A200 Super King Air	BB-240		21. 2.77	To G-BJBP 7/81. Canx.
G-HMAN	Aerospatiale AS.350B Ecureuil	1465	G-SKIM	7. 3.86	To G-GEDS 4/89. Canx.
			G-BIVP		
G-HMBB	MBB BK.117B-2 (Originally regd as BK-117B-1C)	7184	D-HIMA	4. 6.91	To D-HBRE 6/97. Canx 25.6.96.
			(N5405K)/D-HIMA		
G-HMBJ	Commander Aircraft 114B	14636	N6036F	30. 6.97	
G-HMCG	IRMA BN-2A-26 Islander	847	G-BESH	5.10.79	To N29884 4/82. Canx 16.4.82.
G-HMED	PA-28-161 Warrior III	2842020	LX-III	21. 7.97	
G-HMES	PA-28-161 Warrior II	28-8216070	OY-CSN	21. 4.89	
			N8471N		
G-HMJB	PA-34-220T Seneca III	34-8133040	N8356R	12. 7.89	
G-HMMM	Cameron N-65 HAFB	1378		21.10.86	To RP-C1484 ? 9/94. Canx 13.9.94.
G-HMPH	Bell 206B JetRanger II	1232	G-BBUY	20. 6.88	
			N18090		
G-HMPT	Agusta-Bell 206B JetRanger II	8168	D-HARO	7.11.91	
G-HNRY	Cessna 650 Citation VI	650-0219	N219CC	23.10.92	
			N6829Z		
G-HNTR	Hawker Hunter T.7	HABL-003311	8834M	7. 7.89	No CofA issued. Canx as WFU 11.10.91.
			XL572		(On display 9/97)
G-HOBO	Denney Kitfox Mk.4	PFA/172A-12140		10. 9.92	
G-HOCK	PA-28-180 Cherokee D	28-4395	G-AVSH	15. 5.86	
G-HODG	Robinson R-22 Beta	1481		31. 7.90	To G-OGOC 6/91. Canx.
G-HOFC	Europa Avn Europa	119 & PFA/247-12736		25. 9.95	
G-HOFM	Cameron N-56 HAFB	1245		21. 1.86	(Extant 7/95)
G-HOGS	Cameron Pig 90SS HAFB	4121		7. 4.97	
G-HOHO	Colt Santa Claus SS HAFB	1671		21.12.89	
G-HOLL	Cessna 500 Citation I (Unit No.088)	500-0088	(OO-FAY)	1.10.87	Restored as PH-CTA /90. Canx 30.1.90.
			PH-CTA/N588CC		
G-HOLS	Warner Special	PFA/96-10493		26. 7.79	Not completed & used for spares. Canx by CAA 24.9.85.
	(Proposed rebuild of Auster 5 G-AMSZ with a Bonner engine)				
G-HOLT	Taylor JT.1 Monoplane	PFA/55-10394		23.10.78	Canx by CAA 2.9.91.
G-HOLY	Socata ST-10 Diplomate	108	F-BSCZ	31. 1.90	
G-HOME	Colt 77A HAFB	032		26. 2.79	
G-HONE	Hawker Hunter F.58	XE-64 & 41H-697443	J-4076	23. 8.95	To SE-DXE 11/96. Canx 17.6.96.
	(Originally regd with c/n 41H-700384)		Swiss AF		
G-HONG	Slingsby T.67M Firefly 200	2060	VR-HZR	24. 3.94	
			"VR-HZM"/HKG-12/G-7-128		
G-HONK	Cameron O-105 HAFB	1813		30. 9.88	
G-HONY	Lilliput Type 1 Srs.A HAFB	L-01		31. 7.98	
G-HOOK	Hughes 369D (500D)	70-0708D		4. 8.80	To D-HASH(2) 7/85. Canx 24.7.85.
G-HOOP	PA 46-350P Malibu Mirage	4636027		10. 1.96	To N71DH 9/97. Canx 10.9.97.
G-HOOV	Cameron N-56 HAFB	388		2. 3.78	Retired in 1981 and Basket/burner used by G-NUTS.
G-HOPE	Beechcraft F33A Bonanza	CE-805	N2024Z	27. 2.79	
G-HOPI	Cameron N-42 HAFB	2724		5.12.91	
G-HOPL	PBN BN-2T Turbine Islander	2112	G-BJBE	2. 8.82	To 9M-BSS 4/83. Canx.
G-HOPP	SAAB-Scania SF.340A	340A-008	SE-ISC	28.11.86	Restored as SE-ISC. Canx 28.10.88.
			G-BSFI/SE-E08		
G-HOPS	Thunder Ax8-90 Srs.1 HAFB	1220		11. 3.88	
G-HOPY	Van's RV-6A	PFA/181-12742		4.12.95	
G-HORN	Cameron V-77 HAFB	570		29.11.79	
G-HORS	Cameron Flying Dala Horse SS HAFB	2954		20. 1.93	(Based in Sweden) Canx by CAA 9.12.96.
G-HOSE	Cessna 152 II	152-81900	N67538	18. 7.78	To G-SACA 2/84. Canx.
G-HOSI	Colt 77A HAFB	1879		30.10.90	On landing after a flight at San Giustino, near Florence, Italy on 13.7.91, the balloon envelope collapsed quickly onto the basket and burner, which was still alight. The envelope caught fire and was burnt out, together with the basket. Canx as destroyed 6.2.92.
G-HOSK	PA-32R-301 Saratoga II SP	32R-8013132	PH-WET	25. 3.82	To G-TRIP 12/85. Canx.
			OO-HKN/N8261X		

Regn	Type	c/n	Previous identity	Regn date	Fate or immediate subsequent identity (if known)
G-HOSP	Cessna 441 Conquest II	441-0078	G-AUTO (N88842)	6.10.89	To N441FC 11/90. Canx 14.11.90.
G-HOST	Cameron N-77 HAFB	434		4. 9.78	
G-HOTI	Colt 77A HAFB	750		13. 7.87	
	(Initially regd as c/n 1104 - conflicts with G-BNZK)				
G-HOTL	Cessna 551 Citation II (Unit No.051)	551-0095	N66LB N1AP/N3296M	6. 4.88	To N999WA. Canx 9.3.89.
G-HOTS	Thunder Colt AS-80B Hot-Air Airship	320		6. 2.81	CofA expired 11.3.85. (Was based in Brazil) Canx by CAA 16.12.91.
G-HOTT	Cameron O-120 HAFB	2581		30. 4.91	
G-HOTZ	Colt 77B HAFB	2218		16. 6.92	
G-HOUL	Clutton FRED Srs.II	PFA/29-10434		15.12.78	Canx by CAA 5.8.91.
G-HOUS	Colt 31A Air Chair HAFB	099		7.10.80	
"G-HOUS"	Cameron Flying Cottage 60SS HAFB (First flown 15.2.81 with these marks which were already allocated)	687		----	Marks corrected to G-COTT 2/81.
G-HOVA	Enstrom 280C Shark	1064	G-BEYR	22. 2.82	To SE-HOY. Canx 21.11.88.
G-HOVR	Robinson R-22 Beta	0800	N2647M	6. 5.88	Badly damaged when starboard skid struck the ground during hovering practice at Cranfield on 9.1.89. Canx by CAA 10.1.91. Rebuilt for static use, painted as "G-BEAR" and extant 5/91.
G-HOWE	Thunder Ax7-77 HAFB	1340		10. 4.89	
G-HPAA	PBN BN-2B-20 Islander	2244	G-BSWP	14. 8.91	
G-HPLC	Sikorsky S-76B	760358		16.11.89	To G-HAUG 9/94. Canx.
G-HPSE	Commander Aircraft 114B	14638	N6038V	26. 8.97	
G-HPUX	Hawker Hunter T.7	41H-693455	8807M XL587	12. 3.99	(On display 7/99 Duxford)
G-HPVC	Partenavia P.68 Victor	13	OH-PVB	25. 4.83	To G-MOET 5/93. Canx.
G-HPWH	Agusta A.109E Power	11051	G-HWPH	9. 8.99	
G-HRAY	Agusta-Bell 206B JetRanger III	8610	G-VANG G-BIZA	9. 4.86	To G-OMDR 12/97. Canx.
G-HREH	Robinson R-44 Astro	0185	D-HREH	10. 9.97	To G-CLKE 9/98. Canx.
G-HRHE	Robinson R-22 Beta	1950	G-BTWP	24. 1.97	
G-HRHI	Beagle B.206R Basset Srs.1	R.06/B.014	XS770	6. 7.89	
G-HRHS	Robinson R-44 Astro	0323		15. 4.97	
G-HRIO	Robin HR.100/210 Safari	149	F-BTZR	22. 1.87	
G-HRIS	Cessna P.210N Pressurised Centurion II	P210-00388	N4972K	17. 6.85	To PH-MRD 7/98. Canx 9.6.98.
G-HRLK	Saab 91D/2 Safir	91-376	G-BRZY PH-RLK	6. 3.90	
G-HRLM	Brugger MB.2 Colibri	PFA/43-10118		28.12.78	
G-HRNT	Cessna 182S Skylane II	182-80395	N2369H	29. 1.99	
G-HROI	Rockwell Commander 112A	326	N1326J	19. 6.89	
G-HRON	DH.114 Heron 2B	14102	XR442 G-AORH	4. 4.91	(Stored 6/97)
G-HRVD	CCF Harvard 4 (T-6J-CCF Texan)	CCF4-548	G-BSBC Moz PLAF 1741/FAP 1741/W.German AF BF+055/AA+055/53-4629	8.12.92	(On rebuild 12/95)
	(Possibly composite with rear fuselage of Moz PLAF/FAP 1780/AA+614/53-4622)				
G-HRVY	Enstrom 280C-UK-2 Shark	1038	G-DUGY G-BEEL	27. 4.95	To G-OITV 4/96. Canx.
G-HRZN	Colt 77A HAFB	536		14.12.83	
G-HSAA	Hughes 369HS	109-0203S	SE-HFO LN-OQN/D-HNNN/LN-OQI	17. 5.94	Extensively damaged in forced landed near Old Stratford on 10.7.94. Canx 23.2.95. To N80998 1/96.
G-HSDW	Bell 206B JetRanger II	1789	ZS-HFC	16.12.85	
G-HSHS	Colt 105A HAFB	1721		5.11.90	To G-DYNG 2/98. Canx.
G-HSKY	Hughes 369HM (500)	49-0036M	G-VNPP G-BDKL/EI-ATY	23. 1.84	Badly damaged in mid-air collision with WB-47G-4A G-AXKO and forced landed at Park Farm, Tudeley, near Tonbridge on 5.2.86. (Wreck taken to Booker) Canx by CAA 15.8.88.
G-HSON	Cessna 441 Conquest II	441-0294	(N88743)	18. 2.82	To G-OFHJ 10/86. Canx.
G-HSOO	Hughes 369HE (500)	109-0208E	G-BFYJ F-BRSY	3.11.93	
G-HSTH	Lindstrand HS-110 HAFB	546		20. 8.98	
G-HTAX	PA-31-350 Navajo Chieftain	31-7405435	N54305	7. 6.88	To Canada by container in 7/97.
G-HTPS	Aerospatiale SA.341G Gazelle Srs.1	1301	G-BRNI YU-HBI	16.11.89	
G-HTRF	Robinson R-22 Beta	0988		6. 3.89	To D-HHAI(2) 5/94. Canx 18.2.94.
G-HTVI	Cameron N-90 HAFB	1375	G-PRIT	29.10.96	
G-HTWO	Hawker Hunter F.58 (Originally regd with c/n 41H-698283)	XE-75 & 41H-697454	J-4087 Swiss AF	23. 8.95	To SE-DXF 11/96. Canx 17.6.96.
G-HUBB	Partenavia P.68B Victor	194	OY-BJH SE-GXL	27. 5.83	
G-HUCH	Cameron Carrots 80SS HAFB	2258	G-BYPS	13. 3.91	
G-HUEY	Bell UH-1H-BF Iroquois (Incorrectly quoted as ex 73-21872)	13560	AE-413 (Argentine Army)/73-22077	23. 7.85	
G-HUFF	Cessna 182P Skylane II (Reims-assembled with c/n 0033)	182-64076	PH-CAS N6059F	31.10.78	
G-HUGE	Boeing 747-2D3B (Line No. 297)	21252	JY-AFB	29. 3.85	To N512DC 10/90. Canx 8.11.90.
G-HUGG	Gates LearJet 35A	35A-432	VR-CAD N330BC/N4445Y/F-GDCN	9. 4.96	

Regn	Type	c/n	Previous identity	Regn date	Fate or immediate subsequent identity (if known)
G-HUGH	PA-32RT-300T Turbo Lance II	32R-7887197	G-IFLY N21200	11. 2.80	Fatal crash into Ottershaw Park, adjacent to Fairoaks on 25.4.85. Canx as destroyed 21.1.87.
G-HUGO	Colt 260A HAFB	2559		20. 1.94	
G-HUKT	PA-28-181 Archer II	28-8190138	N8321P	13. 9.85	To PH-PLG. Canx 14.7.87.
G-HULL	Reims Cessna F.150M	1255	PH-TGR	19. 1.79	
G-HUMF	Robinson R-22 Beta	0534	N23743	18. 2.86	
G-HUMP	Beechcraft 95-B55 Baron	TC-1524	G-BAMI	6. 2.85	To N31309. Canx 29.10.91.
G-HUMT	Bell 206B JetRanger II	1148	ZS-HDY	7.11.86	To (F-GKLS)/F-GNFP 6/93R. Canx 16.6.93.
G-HUNI	Bellanca 7GCBC Scout	541-73	OO-IME D-EIME	21.10.96	
G-HUNK	Lindstrand LBL-77A HAFB	551		9. 9.98	
G-HUNN	Hispano HA.1112-M1L Buchon	235	G-BJZZ N48157/Spanish AF C4K-172	29. 4.87	To N109GU. Canx 9.10.91.
G-HUNT	Hawker Hunter F.51	41H-680277	G-9-440 Danish AF E-418	5. 7.78	To N50972 1/88. Canx 10.12.87.
G-HUNY	Reims Cessna F.150G	0157	G-AVGL	27. 6.83	
G-HURI	Hawker (CCF) Hurricane XIIA (IIB)	72036	RCAF 5711	9. 6.83	
	(Composite - probably includes parts from c/n 44019/RCAF 5424, RCAF 5625 and RCAF 5547)				
G-HURN	Robinson R-22 Beta	1441		18. 7.90	
G-HURR	Hawker (CCF) Hurricane XII (IIB)	52024	RCAF 5589	30. 7.90	
G-HURY	Hawker Hurricane IV (RAF identity unlikely; KZ321 was w/o 23.5.43)	-	(Israel) Yugoslav AF/KZ321	31. 3.89	(On rebuild 7/99 with wings at Duxford & fuselage off-site)
G-HUSH	Hughes 269C (300C)	89-0826		28. 2.80	To CS-HAV 4/82. Canx 26.3.82.
G-HUTT	Denney Kitfox Mk.2	509 & PFA/172-11634		24. 1.90	
G-HUWS	Hughes 269C (300C)	63-0211	N8983F	24. 7.89	Overturned on landing at Henbury Manor on 22.7.90. (Stored 10/90 Shoreham) Canx by CAA 23.12.91.
G-HVAN	RL-5A LW Sherwood Ranger	PFA/237-13074		10.12.98	
G-HVBF	Lindstrand LBL-210A HAFB	372		23. 5.96	
G-HVDM	Vickers-Supermarine 361 Spitfire LF.IXc	CBAF.IX.1732	8633M R.Netherlands AF 3W-17/H-25/MK732	18. 1.91	Reserved as PH-OUQ on 24.2.99.
G-HVIP	Hawker Hunter T.68	HABL-003215	J-4208 Swiss AF/G-9-415/Swedish AF Fv.34080/G-9-56	7. 7.95	
G-HVRD	PA-31-350 Navajo Chieftain	31-7305052	G-BEZU SE-GDP	11. 6.87	
G-HVRS	Robinson R-22 Beta	1225		22.12.89	
G-HWAY	PA-28R-200 Cherokee Arrow II	28R-7435248	G-JULI (G-BKDC)/OY-POV/N43128	20. 7.83	To G-FULL 11/84. Canx.
G-HWBK	Agusta A.109A	7173		17.11.80	To F-GRMK 9/94. Canx 24.8.94.
G-HWKN	PA-31P Pressurised Navajo	31P-7400193	HB-LIR D-IAIR/N7304L	21. 1.88	To G-BWDE 5/95. Canx.
G-HWKR	Colt 90A HAFB	1610		4.12.89	
G-HWPB	BAe 146 Srs.200	E2018	G-6-018 G-BSRU/G-OSKI/N603AW	30.11.94	To G-JEAR 11/95. Canx.
G-HWPH	Agusta A.109E Power	11051		24. 6.99	To G-HPWH 8/99. Canx.
G-HYDE	Agusta-Bell 206B JetRanger III	8593		6. 5.80	To HB-XBA 8/84. Canx 1.8.84.
G-HYGA	BAe 125 Srs.800B	258034	G-5-12	26.11.85	To G-5-595/N85DW 5/94. Canx 25.5.94.
G-HYHY	PA-46-350P Malibu Mirage	4636131		13. 8.97	
G-HYLT	PA-32R-301 Saratoga SP	32R-8213001	N84588	23. 4.86	
G-HYPO	Colt 180A HAFB	1569		26. 7.89	To D-OYPQ 3/93. Canx 25.1.93.
G-HYST	Enstrom 280FX Shark	2082		9. 7.98	

G-I

Regn	Type	c/n	Previous identity	Regn date	Fate or immediate subsequent identity (if known)
G-IAAA	The series from G-IAAA to G-IAAZ was allocated to India from 1919 until 1928.				
G-IABC	Tri-R Kis	PFA/239-12655		3. 2.94	Fatal crash in English Channel off Calais on 29.7.96. Canx as destroyed 30.4.97.
G-IACL	PBN BN-2T Turbine Islander	2138	G-BJYS	21. 9.83	To G-IAHL 11/83. Canx.
G-IADT	Agusta A.109A II	7347	G-HBCA	12. 1.89	To G-ISEB 10/89. Canx.
G-IAFT	Cessna 152 II	152-85123	EI-BVW N6093Q	20. 6.95	
G-IAHL	PBN BN-2T Turbine Islander	2138	G-IACL G-BJYS	24.11.83	To 9M-LYG 6/85. Canx 24.6.85.
G-IAIN	Cessna P.210N Pressurized Centurion II	210-00042	N3623P	30. 5.80	To N116RS 11/83. Canx 25.11.83.
G-IAMP	Cameron H-34 HAFB	2541		11. 3.91	
G-IANG	Bell 206L Long Ranger	45132	SE-HSV PH-HMH/N16845	22. 1.98	
G-IANJ	Reims Cessna F.150K	0548	G-AXVW	19. 5.98	
G-IANS	Rockwell Commander 690B	11465	N81767 EI-BFL/N81767	16.10.79	To HB-GHE 3/83. Canx 28.3.83.
G-IANT	Cessna 404 Titan Ambassador II	404-0214	N88674	22. 5.78	To PH-ANT(2) 6/82. Canx 30.6.82.
G-IASI	Beechcraft 95-B58 Baron	TH-1258	N38332 N2585J	24. 6.81	To ST-AIK 5/82. Canx.

Regn	Type	c/n	Previous identity	Regn date	Fate or immediate subsequent identity (if known)
G-IASL	Beechcraft 60 Duke	P-21	G-SING D-IDTA/SE-EXT	18. 4.97	
G-IBAC	Beechcraft 95-B58 Baron	TH-1141	N584CY N36642	23. 7.86	Restored as N584CY 1/93. Canx 29.12.92.
G-IBAK	Cessna 421C Golden Eagle III	421C-1099	N68681	11. 6.86	To PH-VDR. Canx 14.4.92.
G-IBBC	Cameron Sphere 105SS HAFB	4082		2. 4.97	
G-IBBO	PA-28-181 Archer II	28-7790107	D-EPCA N5389F	17.12.98	
G-IBBS	Europa Avn Europa	PFA/247-12745		8. 9.94	
G-IBCA	Beechcraft 200 Super King Air	BB-210	G-BMCA N5657N	3.12.85	To G-OAVX 9/88. Canx.
G-IBEC	PA-28RT-201 Arrow IV	28R-8018020	G-BOET N8116V	27.12.89	Restored as G-BOET 2/90. Canx.
G-IBED	Robinson R-22 Alpha	0500	G-BMHN N50022	7. 9.93	Stored at Botany Bay Village, Lancs in 5/99 still marked as G-BMHN on port side.
G-IBET	Cameron Can 70SS HAFB	1625		25. 1.88	
G-IBFC	BFC Challenger II	PFA/177B-13369		9.11.98	
G-IBFW	PA-28R-201 Arrow III	28R-7837235	N31534	22. 1.79	
G-IBHH	Hughes 269C (300C)	74-0327	G-BSCD PH-HSH/SE-HFG	20. 8.99	
G-IBIS	HS.125 Srs.3B-RA	25171	G-AXPU HB-VBT/G-5-19	16. 7.80	Restored as G-AXPU 8/82. Canx.
G-IBLL	Rockwell 690D Turbo Commander 900	15015	N5874N	5. 1.84	To G-NTMN 9/86. Canx.
G-IBLW	BAe Jetstream Srs.3102-09	838	OO-EDA G-OEDD/G-WENT/G-IBLW/G-31-838	6.10.88	To ZK-JSH 5/97. Canx 28.5.97.
G-IBLX	BAe Jetstream Srs.3102-09	839	G-31-839	6.10.88	To G-GLAM 2/91. Canx.
G-IBRO	Reims Cessna F.152 II	1957	EI-BRO	11.10.95	
G-IBTW	Boeing 737-2Q8 (Line No. 642)	21960	EI-BTW G-BGTY	11. 4.89	To CC-CLD 3/90. Canx 30.3.90.
G-IBTX	Boeing 737-2M8 (Line No. 557)	21736	G-BTEB OO-TEL/TC-ATU/OO-TEL/PH-RAL/OO-TEL/4X-ABL/OO-TEL	16.11.90	To F-GLXG 4/93. Canx 30.3.93.
G-IBTY	Boeing 737-2E3 (Line No. 811)	22703	EI-BRZ G-BNZT/EC-DYZ/EI-BRZ/CC-BIN	14.12.88	To VT-EWB 5/92. Canx 1.6.92.
G-IBTZ	Boeing 737-2U4ADV (Line No. 761)	22576	EI-BTZ N134AW/G-OSLA	13.12.88	To VT-EWC 5/92. Canx 1.6.92.
G-ICAB	Robinson R-44 Astro	0086		28.11.94	
G-ICAS	Aviat Pitts S-2B Special	5344	N511P	19. 6.97	
G-ICAT	Cessna 421C Golden Eagle III	421C-0617	(EI-...) G-ICAT/EI-CAT/G-OPEE/N421PB/N8507Z/G-OSSH/N88627	8. 8.90	Restored as EI-CAT. Canx 12.12.90.
G-ICCL	Robinson R-22 Beta	1608	G-ORZZ	25.11.93	
G-ICED	Cessna 501 Citation I (Unit No.638)	501-0230	N5RL N653F/N2616G/(N2617B)	26. 8.87	To N505CC 11/93. Canx 2.11.93.
G-ICES	Thunder Ax6-56 Srs.SP-1 HAFB (Ice Cream special shape)	283		3. 7.80	
G-ICEY	Lindstrand LBL-77A HAFB	043		11. 8.93	
G-ICFR	BAe 125 Srs.800B	258050	N9LR G-5-503/I-OSLO/G-5-503/G-BUCR/HZ-OFC/G-5-503	23.11.94	
G-ICKY	Lindstrand LBL-77A HAFB	029		19. 5.93	
G-ICOI	Lindstrand LBL-105A HAFB	564		3.11.98	
G-ICOM	Reims Cessna F.172M Skyhawk II	1212	G-BFXI PH-ABA/D-EEVC	25. 4.94	
G-ICOZ	Lindstrand LBL-105A HAFB	565		3.11.98	
G-ICRU	Bell 206A JetRanger	97	(C-GXVE) N7845S	23. 1.80	Crashed at Crosby on 23.5.84. Canx as WFU 20.6.86.
G-ICSG	Aerospatiale AS.355F1 Twin Squirrel	5104	G-PAMI G-BUSA	6. 4.93	
G-ICUB	Piper J3C-65 Cub (Frame No.8999; official identity of c/n 13255 is incorrect - probably rebuilt 1945)	8912	F-BEGT NC79805/45-4515/42-36788	20. 8.81	To EI-BSX 3/86. Canx 19.3.86.
G-IDAY	Skyfox CA-25N Gazelle	CA25N-028	VH-RCR	29. 4.96	
G-IDDI	Cameron N-77 HAFB	2383		21. 8.90	
G-IDDY	DHC.1 Chipmunk (Mod) (Fuselage no. DHB/f/258)(Also known as the Hendon Air Mighty Munk)	HA/MM/4-81 & NB.130 & C1/0359	G-BBMS WG306	26. 9.79	
G-IDEA	American Aviation AA-5A Cheetah	AA5A-0871	G-BGNO	7. 2.84	
G-IDII	DR.107 One Design	PFA/264-12953		16. 6.99	
G-IDJB	Cessna 150L	150-73717	(G-BJMS) (G-BIVM)/N17374	28.10.82	Force landed and overturned in a field at Claxton Grange Farm on 13.12.90. Canx by CAA 21.10.91.
G-IDUP	Enstrom 280C Shark	1163	G-BRZF N5687D	11. 5.92	
G-IDWR	Hughes 369HS (500HS)	69-0101S	G-AXEJ	26. 5.81	
G-IEAA	Boeing 737-33A (Line No. 1763)	24098		18. 9.89	To XA-SLY. Canx 16.12.93.
G-IEAB	Boeing 757-23A (Line No. 259)	24636		1. 2.90	To G-LCRC 10/93. Canx.
G-IEAC	Boeing 757-236ER (Line No. 449)	25620		28. 4.92	To G-CSVS 10/93. Canx.
G-IEAD	Boeing 757-236 (Line No. 272)	24771	P4-AAA PH-AHN/G-BRJG	9. 4.92	To TF-FIK. Canx 29.12.93.

Regn	Type	c/n	Previous identity	Regn date	Fate or immediate subsequent identity (if known)
G-IEAE	Boeing 737-4S3 (Line No. 1870)	24795	G-BRKF	30. 4.92	To N686MA. Canx 6.5.94.
G-IEAF	Airbus A.320-231	362	F-WWIN	27. 1.93	To G-YJBM 9/93. Canx.
G-IEAG	Airbus A.320-231	363	F-WWBX	19. 3.93	To G-SUEE 9/93. Canx.
G-IECL	HS.125 Srs.700A	NA0201 & 257002	VR-BNB N886GB/N700NY/N40GT/N40WB/N700HS/G-5-20	23. 8.93	To N701TS. Canx 9.9.96.
G-IEJH	SAN Jodel D.150A Mascaret	02	G-BPAM F-BLDA/F-WLDA	28. 2.95	
G-IEPF	Robinson R-22 Beta	0565	N2419X	1. 7.86	To F-GMLZ. Canx 1.3.94.
G-IESA	Cessna 421C Golden Eagle III	421C-0263	N421RN N33TS/N6232G	19. 6.87	Restored as N421RN. Canx 10.7.91.
G-IESH	DH.82A Tiger Moth	83738	G-ANPE F-BHAT/G-ANPE/T7397	4. 6.82	Restored as G-ANPE 2/89. Canx.
G-IEYE	Robin DR.400/180 Regent	2123		29. 1.92	
G-IFAB	Reims Cessna F.182Q Skylane	0127	OO-ELM (OO-HNU)	6. 1.98	
G-IFFR	PA-32-300 Cherokee Six	32-7340123	G-BWVO OO-JPC/N55520	1. 4.97	
G-IFIT	PA-31-350 Navajo Chieftain	31-8052078	G-NABI G-MARG/N3580C	31.12.85	
G-IFLI	American Aviation AA-5A Cheetah	AA5A-0831	N26948	7. 7.82	
G-IFLP	PA-34-200T Seneca II	34-8070029	N81WS N81149	4. 1.88	
G-IFLY	PA-32RT-300T Turbo Lance II	32R-7887197	N21200	10. 1.79	To G-HUGH 2/80. Canx.
G-IFOX	Robinson R-22 Beta	1938		3.10.91	Damaged in crash at Snowdonia on 3.8.97. Rebuilt & re-regd as G-LEDA 11/98. Canx.
G-IFTA	PA-31-350 Navajo Chieftain	31-7305029	G-BAVM N7699L	6.11.85	To N5BU 11/93. Canx 11.11.93.
G-IFTB	Beechcraft B200C Super King Air	BL-37	N351BC N500GP	29.12.93	To 5Y-TWC 2/97. Canx 10.2.97.
G-IFTC	HS.125 Srs F3B/RA	25171	G-OPOL G-BXPU/(N171AV)/G-BXPU/G-AXPU/G-IBIS/G-AXPU/HB-VBT/G-5-19	21. 7.94	
G-IFTD	Cessna 404 Titan II	404-0039	G-BKUN LN-MAT/SE-GZC/(N5421G)	17. 9.86	To 5Y-TMR. Canx 6.1.93.
G-IFTE	HS.125 Srs.700B	257037	G-BFVI G-5-18	16. 5.96	
G-IFTS	Robinson R-44 Astro	0366		16. 9.97	
G-IGAR	PA-31-310 Turbo Navajo C	31-7812004	D-IGAR N27378	8. 8.84	To G-ONAV 1/93. Canx.
G-IGEL	Cameron N-90 HAFB	2726		7. 4.92	
G-IGGL	Socata TB-10 Tobago	146	G-BYDC F-GCOL	26. 3.99	
G-IGHA	PA-34-220T Seneca III	34-8133185	G-IPUT N8424D	28. 8.91	To G-BVDN 9/93. Canx.
G-IGHH	Enstrom 480	5034		1.12.98	
G-IGLA	Colt 240A HAFB	2228		3. 7.92	
G-IGLE	Cameron V-90 HAFB	2609		11. 6.91	
G-IGOA	Boeing 737-3Y0 (Line No. 1853)	24678	EI-BZK	16. 7.98	
G-IGOC	Boeing 737-3Y0 (Line No. 1811)	24546	EI-BZH G-IGOC/EI-BZH	1. 5.98	
G-IGOE	Boeing 737-3Y0 (Line No. 1813)	24547	EI-BZI	19. 5.98	
G-IGOF	Boeing 737-3Q8 (Line No. 1846)	24698	PK-GWF	2. 4.98	
G-IGOG	Boeing 737-3Y0 (Line No. 1580)	23927	F-GLLE PT-TEK	3. 9.98	
G-IGOH	Boeing 737-3Y0 (Line No. 1562)	23926	F-GLLD PT-TEJ	6.11.98	
G-IGOI	Boeing 737-33A (Line No. 1669)	24092	G-OBMD	30.12.98	
G-IGOJ	Boeing 737-36N (Line No. 3082)	28872	N1795B	11.11.98	
G-IGOK	Boeing 737-36N (Line No. 3107)	28594	N1786B	24. 4.99	
G-IGOL	Boeing 737-36N (Line No. 3112)	28596	N1015X	26. 6.99	
G-IGOM	Boeing 737-36N (Line No. 3115)	28599		13. 7.99	
G-IGON	PA-31-310 Turbo Navajo	31-442	(G-BLVW) D-IGON/(D-IHFP)/N6479L	26. 3.85	To N3181D 12/91. Canx 4.11.91.
G-IGOP	Boeing 737-36N (Line No. 3118)	28602		12. 8.99	
G-IGOR	Boeing 737-36N (Line No. 3...)	28606		. .98R	(delivery due 10/99)
G-IGPW	Eurocopter EC-120B	1027	G-CBRI	31. 7.99	
G-IHDH	PA-28R-201 Arrow IV	28R-7918098	G-MRJV PH-WEL/N2090Y	13. 4.83	Restored to N2090Y 9/84. Canx.
G-IHSA	Robinson R-22 Beta	0959		16. 2.89	To ZS-RJJ 10/97. Canx 8.10.97.
G-IHSB	Robinson R-22 Beta	0982		16. 3.89	
G-IHSC	Robinson R-22 Beta	0983		16. 3.89	To OE-XHM. Canx 5.8.91.

Regn	Type	c/n	Previous identity	Regn date	Fate or immediate subsequent identity (if known)
G-IIAC	Aeronca 11AC Chief	11AC-169	G-BTPY N86359/NC86359	2. 7.91	
G-IIAN	Aero Designs Pulsar	PFA/202-12123		10. 9.91	
G-IIBD	PA-44-180T Turbo Seminole	44-8107017	(D-G...) G-IIBD/N180AP/N82554	31. 5.91	To (N338D)/N344D 3/95. Canx 22.2.95.
G-IIFR	Robinson R-22 Beta	2841		2. 9.98	
G-IIIA	Swearingen SA.226T(B) Merlin IIIB	T-342	N1008S	20. 6.80	To 9Q-CQP 4/84. Canx 25.4.84.
G-IIIB	Swearingen SA.226T(B) Merlin IIIB	T-302	N5497M	16. 5.79	To 9Q-COI 1/83. Canx 24.1.83.
G-IIIG	Boeing-Stearman A75N1 (PT-17) Kaydet	75-4354	G-BSDR N61827/42-16191	25. 3.91	
G-IIIH	BAC One Eleven Srs.518FG	BAC.200	(VP-BED) VR-BED/LV-MEX/(G-AXMF)/PT-TYV/G-AXMF	17. 6.97	
G-IIII	Christen Pitts S-2B Special	5010	N5330G	6. 1.89	
G-IIIL	Pitts S-1T Special	008	OH-XPT G-IIIL/N15JE	15. 2.89	
"G-IIIM"	Hunting Percival P.66 Pembroke C.1	PAC/66/06	8108M WV703	----	(Stored at Tattershall Thorpe as marked but never officially regd as such) Broken up in 1988.
G-IIIR	Pitts S-1S Special (built by Mr. Milam)	604	N27M	21. 1.93	
G-IIIT	Aerotek Pitts S-2A Special	2222	N7YT	16. 1.89	
G-IIIV	Pitts Super Stinker 11-260	PFA/273-13005		4. 2.97	
G-IIIX	Pitts S-1S Special	AJT	G-LBAT G-UCCI/G-BIYN/N455T	22. 5.89	
G-IINA	Aerospatiale AS.350B2 Ecureuil	2382	N9088A	11.12.90	To G-BWLI 1/96. Canx.
G-IIPM	Aerospatiale AS.350B Ecureuil	1790	G-GWIL	18.12.96	
G-IIRB	Bell 206B JetRanger III	3958	N903CA	22.11.89	To G-PENT 7/99. Canx.
G-IIRG	Stoddard-Hamilton Glasair IIS RG	PFA/149-11937		29. 6.93	
G-IIRR	Gulfstream G.1159 Gulfstream II	210	HB-IEY	11. 7.86	Canx 16.3.90 on sale to Bermuda. To (HK-.....)/8P-LAD.
G-IITI	Extra EA.300	018	D-EFRR	12. 5.92	
G-IIXX	Montgomerie-Parsons Two Place Gyrocopter	G/08-1225		13.10.93	
G-IIZI	Extra EA.300	037	JY-RNB D-ETXA	12.12.96	
G-IJAC	Light Aero Avid Speed Wing Mk.4	PFA/189-12095		31.12.92	
G-IJCB	Sikorsky S-76C (Mod)	760464		16.12.96	To G-BYOM 8/99. Canx.
G-IJET	HS.125 Srs.700B	257212	N81CN N81CH/G-RACL/G-5-12	9. 7.87	To G-5-659/OH-BAP 4/90. Canx 11.4.90.
G-IJJB	Beechcraft B200 Super King Air	BB-1257	N841TF N841TT/G-BMVY/N2678D	9. 5.95	To N606AJ 2/97. Canx 11.2.97.
G-IJMC	VPM M-16 Tandem Trainer	VPM16-UK-106	G-POSA G-BVJM	10. 6.98	
G-IJOE	PA-28RT-201T Turbo Arrow IV	28R-8031178	N8265X N9599N	14. 8.90	
G-IJRC	Robinson R-22 Beta	1739	G-BTJP	23.10.91	Canx as destroyed 10.6.98.
G-IJYS	BAe Jetstream Srs.3102	715	G-BTZT N416MX/G-31-715	5.10.92	
G-IKAP	Cessna T.303 Crusader	T303-00182	N63SA D-IKAP(2)/N9518C	4. 3.99	
G-IKBP	PA-28-161 Warrior II	28-8216132	N81762	16. 7.90	
G-IKIS	Cessna 210M Centurion II (Reims-assembled with c/n 0002)	210-61754	N732TD	15. 5.78	(Based in Zambia in 1978)
G-IKPS	PA-31-310 Navajo C	31-7912098	D-IKPS (N444BK)/D-IKPS/N3539G	9. 8.96	
G-ILEA	PA-31-310 Navajo C	31-7812117	D-ILEA N27775	7. 7.97	
G-ILEE	Colt 56A Duo Chariot HAFB	2624		29. 7.94	
G-ILEG	Robin HR.100/200B Royal	113	G-AZHK	10. 4.86	Restored as G-AZHK 8/89. Canx.
G-ILES	Cameron O-90 HAFB	2360		29. 6.90	
"G-ILES"	DH.82A Tiger Moth	-		----	Noted at the Airwork engineering school at Perth in 9/61 and 9/67 marked as such.
G-ILFC	Boeing 737-2U4 (Line No. 652)	22161	G-BOSL	1.11.83	To (G-BPNY)/G-WGEL 7/88. Canx.
G-ILGW	Cessna 404 Titan II	404-0690	D-ILGW N404MW/N25DC/N616R/(N6763Y)	21. 1.98	Fatal crash and burned out in a field at Linwood, near Paisley, 3.5 miles west of Glasgow soon after take-off on 3.9.99.
G-ILLE	Boeing-Stearman E75 (PT-13D) Kaydet	75-5028	N68979 42-16865/BuA.60906	7. 3.90	
G-ILLI	Reims Cessna FR.182 Skylane RG II	0043	(HB-CCU) N1660C	17. 5.80	To HB-CHB 6/83. Canx 27.6.83.
G-ILLS	HS.125 Srs.3B	25133	G-AVRF	23. 8.89	To VT-EQZ 1/90. Canx 22.12.89.
G-ILLY	PA-28-181 Archer II	28-7690193	SE-GND	21. 2.80	
G-ILSE	Corby CJ-1 Starlet	PFA/134-10818		9. 1.84	(Nearing completion 9/97)
G-ILTS	PA-32-300 Cherokee Six	32-7940217	G-CVOK OE-DOH/N2941C	28. 3.90	(Damaged when struck fence on take-off from Gorey, Ireland on 12.11.96)
G-ILYS	Robinson R-22 Beta	1142		5.10.89	
G-IMAG	Colt 77A HAFB (Second envelope c/n 2254; first DBF 6.92)	1718		9. 3.90	
G-IMAN	Colt 31A Sky Chariot HAFB	2605		23. 6.94	

Regn	Type	c/n	Previous identity	Regn date	Fate or immediate subsequent identity (if known)
G-IMAX	Cameron O-120 HAFB	2201		8. 1.90	To PH-VVJ 9/92. Canx 8.7.92.
G-IMBE	PA-31-300 Turbo Navajo	31-641	D2-ERA G-IMBE/G-BXYB/G-AXYB/5N-AEQ/G-AXYB/N6736L	10.11.80	CofA expired 5.10.84. Canx by CAA 17.4.89.
G-IMBY	Pietenpol Air Camper	PFA/47-12402		22.12.93	
G-IMGL	Beechcraft B200 Super King Air	BB-1564	VP-CMA N205JT	9. 8.99	
G-IMLH	Bell 206B JetRanger III	3640	N18096	28. 7.83	To D-HSBA 4/93. Canx 1.3.93.
G-IMLI	Cessna 310Q	310Q-0491	G-AZYK N4182Q	3. 4.86	
G-IMOK	Hoffmann HK-36R Super Dimona	36317	I-NELI OE-9352	31. 7.97	
G-IMPW	PA-32R-301 Saratoga SP	32R-8013085	N8186A	20.11.87	To G-OPSL 1/99. Canx.
G-IMPX	Rockwell Commander 112B	512	N1304J	25.10.90	
G-IMPY	Light Aero Avid Flyer C	PFA/189-11439		10. 4.89	
G-INAS	Aerospatiale AS.350B Ecureuil	-		. .81R	NTU - Canx.
G-INAV	Aviation Composites Mercury	AC.001		23. 2.87	(Probably completed as G-YURO)
G-INCA	Glaser-Dirks DG-400	4-199		22. 1.87	
G-INCF	Cameron DP-60 Hot Air Airship	1353	G-BNCF	9. 1.87	To LX-UFO. Canx 14.10.87.
G-INCH	Montgomerie-Bensen B.8MR Gyrocopter	G/01A-1117	G-BRES	20. 8.91	
G-INDC	Cessna T.303 Crusader	T303-00122	G-BKFH N4766C	28. 6.83	
G-INDE	PA-44-180 Seminole	44-7995327	G-BHNM N8077X	24. 1.94	To G-DENZ 7/97. Canx.
G-INDY	Robinson R-44 Astro	0071		11. 7.94	
G-INGA	Thunder Ax8-84 HAFB	2149		16. 6.92	
G-INGB	Robinson R-22 Beta	0788		6. 5.88	Canx by CAA 20.6.98. To G-ZAPY 8.7.98.
G-INGE	Thruster T.600N	9039-T600N-033		23. 2.99	
G-INGR	Reims Cessna F.150J	0492	G-AWXU	1. 8.96	
G-INMO	PA-31-310 Turbo Navajo	31-8112021	N4074Q	2. 3.81	To 4X-AKV. Canx 1.12.92.
G-INNI	Wassmer Jodel D.112	540	F-BHPU	30. 8.94	
G-INNS	Robinson R-44 Astro	0057		24. 3.94	To TC-HIT 8/97. Canx 24.7.97.
G-INNY	Replica Plans SE.5A	PFA/20-10439		18.12.78	
G-INOW	ARV Monnett Moni	223 & PFA/142-10953		30. 3.84	Permit expired 20.8.88. (Stored 8/97)
G-INSR	Cameron N-90 HAFB	4320		23. 4.98	
G-INTC	Robinson R-22 Beta	1243		31. 1.90	Substantially damaged after rolling onto its side on landing at Halfpenny Green on 5.1.99. Canx as destroyed 11.2.99.
G-INVU	Agusta-Bell 206B JetRanger II	8530	G-XXII G-GGCC/G-BEHG	1. 3.95	
G-IOCO	Beechcraft 95-B58 Baron	TH-1783		6. 6.96	
G-IOCS	Short SD.3-30 Var.100	SH3057	G-BIFH N488NS/LV-OJH/G-BIFH/G-14-3057	25. 7.96	CofA expired 10.10.98. WFU at Southend 12/98. DBF on 14.5.99 at Southend.
G-IOII	Lockheed L.1011-385-1-15 Tristar 100	193T-1118	N556WP VR-HHK/N64854	18. 8.97	Stored 10/98 at Stansted. Canx by CAA 1.10.98. For sale 7/99.
G-IOIO	Bell 206B JetRanger III	4359	N47EA	11. 4.96	
G-IOIT	Lockheed L.1011-385-1 Tristar 200	193N-1145	G-CEAP SE-DPM/G-BEAL	6. 5.98	Stored 3/98 at Stansted. Canx by CAA 1.10.98. For sale 7/99.
G-IOMA	Fokker F-27 Friendship 100	10106	D-BOBY(3) EC-BNJ/PH-FSH/JY-ADD/PI-C530/EI-AKB/PH-FAB	20. 9.82	To G-BMZI 10/86. Canx.
G-IOOI	Robin DR.400/160 Major 80	1700		31. 5.85	
G-IOOO	Rockwell 695A Commander 1000	96033	(N9953S)	25. 1.82	To HK-3366X 5/88. Canx 12.5.88.
G-IOPT	Cessna 182P Skylane	182-61731	N182EE D-ECVM/N21585	9. 6.98	
G-IOSI	CEA Jodel DR.1051 Sicile	526	F-BLRS	6.10.80	
G-IOWE	Europa Avn Europa XS	PFA/247-13303		30. 7.99	
G-IPEC	SIAI-Marchetti S.205-18F	225	G-AVEG (OO-HAN)	30. 5.84	To VH-AZY(3) 9/94. Canx 18.7.94.
G-IPJC	PA-28R-200 Cherokee Arrow II	28R-7435136	(G-BSIA) G-IPJC/N40863	27. 4.90	Disappeared from radar on a flight from Stapleford to Glasgow on 13.2.92 and the wreck was subsequently discovered at Skiddaw, near Keswick. Canx as destroyed 8.5.92.
G-IPPM	K & S SA.102.5 Cavalier	PFA/01-10423		27.11.78	Canx by CAA 2.9.91.
G-IPRA	Beechcraft 200 Super King Air	BB-552	G-BGRD (G-BGPH)	27.11.79	Restored as G-BGRD 8/92. Canx.
G-IPSI(1)	Rutan VariEze	1512 & PFA/74-10284		. .78R	NTU - To G-IPSY 6/78. Canx.
G-IPSI(2)	Grob G-109B	6425	G-BMLO	29. 5.86	
G-IPSY	Rutan VariEze	1512 & PFA/74-10284	(G-IPSI)	19. 6.78	
G-IPUP	Beagle B.121 Pup Srs.150	B121-036	HB-NAC G-35-036	17. 7.95	
G-IPUT	PA-34-220T Seneca III	34-8133185	N8424D	5. 1.90	To G-IGHA 8/91. Canx.
G-IRAF	Rotary Air Force RAF 2000 GTX-SE	G/13-1278		17. 6.96	
G-IRAN	Cessna 152 II	152-83907	OH-CKM C-GBJY/(N6150B)	19. 8.97	
G-IRIS	American Aviation AA-5B Tiger	AA5B-1184	G-BIXU N4533N	14.12.87	
G-IRLO	Socata MS.893E Rallye 150GT	13227	F-GBSA	15. 4.82	DBR at Ipswich on 24.5.82. Canx.
G-IRLS	Reims Cessna FR.172J Rocket	0477	PH-KOK	1. 5.80	Badly damaged on landing at Kilrush, Ireland on 6.4.97. Canx by CAA 23.7.97.

Regn	Type	c/n	Previous identity	Regn date	Fate or immediate subsequent identity (if known)
G-IRLY	Colt 90A HAFB	1620		28.12.89	
G-IROY	Rotorway Exec 152	3525		24. 2.98	
G-IRPC	Cessna 182Q Skylane II	182-66039	G-BSKM N559CT/N759JV	15. 5.91	
G-ISCA	PA-28RT-201 Arrow IV	28R-8118012	N8288Y N9608N	12. 2.91	
G-ISDB	PA-28-161 Cherokee Warrior II	28-7716074	G-BWET SX-ALX/D-EFFQ/N9612N	19. 2.96	
G-ISDN	Boeing-Stearman A75N1 (N2S-3) Kaydet	75-1263	N4197X XB-WOV/BuA.3486	6. 2.95	
G-ISEB	Agusta A.109A II	7347	G-IADT G-HBCA	31.10.89	To F-GJSH 12/94. Canx 17.11.94.
G-ISEE	BAe 146 RJ85 (LF 507) (Originally regd as Srs.200) (CAT III Development Aircraft)	E2208	(N.....) G-ISEE/G-6-208	7. 2.91	To G-6-208/N501XJ 4/97. Canx 28.4.97.
G-ISEH	Cessna 182R Skylane II	182-67843	G-BIWS N6601N	9.11.90	
G-ISFC	PA-31-310 Turbo Navajo B	31-7300970	G-BNEF N7574L	23. 3.94	
G-ISIS	DH.82A Tiger Moth	86251	G-AODR NL779	20.12.83	(Crashed at Nympsfield on 18.9.61 as G-AODR) (On rebuild)
G-ISKY	Bell 206B JetRanger III	3654	G-PSCI G-BOKD/N3171A	5. 4.95	
G-ISLA	BN-2A-26 Islander	206	PH-PAR G-BNEA/SE-FTA/G-51-206	7. 5.97	
G-ISLE	Short SD.3-60 Var.100	SH3638	G-BLEG G-14-3638	7. 3.84	To CS-TMN 12/98. Canx 23.12.98.
G-ISMO	Robinson R-22 Beta	0870	OH-HOR G-ISMO/N8214T	14.10.88	
G-ISPL	Robinson R-22 Mariner	1771M	SE-JAL	3. 2.99	
G-ISPY	Colt GA-42 Gas Airship (Originally regd with c/n P78)	878	(G-BPRB)	3. 7.89	To G-ZEPI 4/92. Canx.
G-ISTT	Thunder Ax8-84 HAFB	1787		12. 6.90	
G-ITAL	Cameron N-77 HAFB	3363		11.10.94	To ZK-FAL. Canx 3.12.98.
G-ITDA	PA-32R-301 Saratoga SP	32R-8113020	N8310D	27.11.90	To G-MALL 8/93. Canx.
G-ITII	Aerotek Pitts S-2A Special	2223	I-VLAT	5. 7.95	
G-ITON	Maule MX-7-235 Star Rocket	10050C	N5670R	11. 9.96	
G-ITPS	Pilatus PC-6/B2-H4 Turbo Porter	862		9. 3.89	To (F-GPGA)/D-FAXI 8/94. Canx 24.8.94.
G-ITTU	PA-23-250 Aztec F	27-7554006	D-IKLW G-BCSW/N54211	19.11.84	Restored as N54211 10/97. Canx 11.9.97.
G-ITUP	Hughes 369D (500D)	50-0696D	G-KSBF G-BMJH	10. 6.88	To EI-BYV 2/90. Canx 15.2.90.
G-IUAN	Cessna 525 CitationJet	525-0324	N5163C (N428PC)	30. 6.99	
G-IVAC	Airtour AH-77B HAFB	012		28.11.89	
G-IVAN	Shaw Twin-Eze (Originally regd as an Rutan VariEze)	39 & PFA/74-10502	(Fitted with wings from G-BKCF)	11. 9.78	
G-IVAR	Yakovlev Yak-50	791504	D-EIVI (N5219K)/DDR-WQT/DM-WQT	24. 2.89	
G-IVEL	Sportavia-Putzer Fournier RF-4D	4029	G-AVNY	29. 6.95	
G-IVET	Europa Avn Europa	PFA/247-12511		23. 5.97	
G-IVIV	Robinson R-44 Astro	0016	(N803EH)	2. 8.93	
G-IVOR	Aeronca 11AC Chief	11AC-1035	EI-BKB G-IVOR/EI-BKB/N9397E	18. 6.82	
G-IWON	Cameron V-90 HAFB	2504	G-BTCV	17. 2.92	
G-IWPL	Reims Cessna F.172M Skyhawk	1058	PH-KDE G-BBLK/(PH-GDR)/(PH-KDE)/G-BBLK	4. 1.79	To VP-FBP 8/90. Canx 9.8.90.
G-IXCC	Vickers-Supermarine 361 Spitfire LF.IXe	-	(Fokker) PL344	18. 5.88	(On display in Blue Max Movie Acft Museum 8/95)
G-IYAK	SPP Yakovlev Yak C.11	171103	(France) Egyptian AF/OK-JIM	12. 1.94	(On rebuild 5/96)
G-IYOB	Aerospatiale SA.341G Gazelle Srs.1	1145	G-WELA G-SFTD/G-RIFC/G-SFTD/N641HM/N341BB/F-WKQH	7. 9.92	To G-PYOB 8/95. Canx.
G-IZEL	Westland SA.341G Gazelle 1	WA/1098	G-BBHW	14. 3.91	To G-WDEV 9/98. Canx.
G-IZIT	Rans S-6-116 Coyote II	PFA/204A-12965		7. 3.96	(Crashed on landing at Southend on 6.9.98)
G-IZMO	Thunder Ax8-90 HAFB	863		8.10.86	To SE-ZGZ 7/96. Canx 9.5.96.
G-IZZS	Cessna 172S Skyhawk II	172S-8152	N952SP	1. 7.99	

G-J

Regn	Type	c/n	Previous identity	Regn date	Fate or immediate subsequent identity (if known)
G-JACK	Cessna 421C Golden Eagle III	421C-1411	N421GQ N125RS/N12028	29. 4.97	
G-JACO	Pearce Jabiru UL	PFA/274A-13371		14. 4.99	
G-JACS	PA-28-181 Archer III	2843078	N9278J	15. 4.97	
G-JACT	Partenavia P.68C Victor	366	G-NVIA	12. 8.87	To SE-LKI 7/98. Canx 20.7.98.
G-JADE	Beechcraft 95-B58 Baron	TH-1191		10. 7.80	To 5Y-TAM 10/92. Canx 5.10.92.
G-JADJ	PA-28-181 Archer II (Originally built as c/n 2890240)	2843009	N49TP N92552	27. 7.99	
G-JAFC	Cameron N-77 HAFB	1077		24. 9.84	To OO-AFC. Canx 10.8.87.

Regn	Type	c/n	Previous identity	Regn date	Fate or immediate subsequent identity (if known)
G-JAFE	DHC.2 Beaver 1	1601	9J-AFE	15.10.90	To C-FOQW. Canx 3.7.92.
			N54832/Zambian AF 403		
G-JAHL	Bell 206B JetRanger III	3565	N666ST	2. 1.98	
G-JAJV	Partenavia P.68C Victor	253	OO-TJG	3. 1.84	To G-OLES 6/90. Canx.
			(OO-XJG)		
G-JAKE	DHC.1 Chipmunk 22	C1/0584	G-BBMY	21. 1.80	
	(Fuselage no. DHB/f/467)		WK666		
G-JAKI	Mooney M.20R Ovation	29-0030		7. 2.95	
G-JAKK	American Aviation AA-5B Tiger		G-BHWI	11.11.82	To G-NGBI 3/85. Canx.
		AA5B-1104	N3752E		
G-JAKO	Cessna TU.206G Turbo Stationair 6 II		N9778M	26. 7.79	To 7P-AAM 4/84. Canx 16.3.84.
		TU206-04565			
G-JAKS	PA-28-160 Cherokee	28-339	G-ARVS	2. 7.99	
G-JAKY	PA-31-325 Turbo Navajo C/R		D-IDIS	21. 3.79	To N325MG 12/92. Canx 30.12.92.
		31-7712047			
G-JALC	Boeing 757-225	22194	N504EA	6. 3.95	
	(Line No. 5)				
G-JAMC	Bell 222	47050		22. 1.81	To G-METC 3/83. Canx.
G-JAMD	BAe Jetstream Srs.4100	41004	G-JXLI	3. 4.92	To G-JMAC 6/92. Canx.
G-JAMI	Bell 206L Long Ranger	46605	N18090	6. 3.78	To SE-HMO 3/83. Canx 15.3.83.
G-JAMP	PA-28-151 Cherokee Warrior		G-BRJU	3. 4.95	
		28-7515026	N44762		
G-JAMS	Cameron O-31 HAFB	424		27. 6.78	NTU - Not built. Canx as WFU 6.11.78. Later built as A-105 version & regd as HB-BAI.
G-JANA	PA-28-181 Archer II	28-7990483	N2838X	12. 2.87	
G-JANB	Colt Flying Bottle SS HAFB	1643		16. 2.90	
	(J & B Whisky Bottle shape)				
G-JANE	Cessna 340A II	340A-0435	N6237X	8. 8.78	To N340SM 3/93. Canx 19.3.93.
G-JANI	Robinson R-44 Astro	0110	D-HIMM(2)	21. 7.95	
G-JANK	PA-E23-250 Aztec C	27-2754	EI-BOO	24. 4.95	
			G-ATCY/N5640Y		
G-JANM	Airbus A.320-212	301	G-KMAM	1.12.95	To OY-CNM 11/96. Canx 22.11.96.
			F-WWIX		
G-JANN	PA-34-220T Seneca III	3433133	N9154W	23. 6.89	
G-JANO	PA-28RT-201 Arrow IV	28R-7918091	SE-IZR	14. 5.98	
			N2146X		
G-JANS	Reims Cessna FR.172J Rocket	0414	PH-GJO	11. 8.78	
			D-EGJO		
G-JANT	PA-28-181 Archer II	28-8390075	N4297J	23. 2.87	
	(Originally built as c/n 28-8290117 N81992/YV-2234P; not delivered and remanufactured)				
G-JANY	Aerospatiale AS.350B Ecureuil	1151	G-BHCN	13.12.78	To Abu Dhabi AF as 107 in 11/81. Canx 11.11.81.
G-JARA	Robinson R-22 Beta	1837		11. 6.91	
G-JASE	PA-28-161 Warrior II	28-8216056	N8461R	13. 2.91	
G-JASM	Robinson R-22 Alpha	0447	N8555P	18.10.84	Crashed at Thruxton on 23.2.92. Canx as destroyed 29.5.92.
G-JASP	PA-23-250 Turbo Aztec E	27-7405402	C-GREG	29. 5.80	To OK-EKU 3/97. Canx 13.3.97.
			N9669N		
G-JATP	BAe ATP	2055	G-11-055	30. 3.93	To G-LOGG 9/93. Canx.
G-JAVA	American Aviation AA-5A Cheetah		N26705	7. 8.89	To G-OCML 9/91. Canx.
		AA5A-0662			
G-JAVO	PA-28-161 Warrior II	28-8016130	G-BSXW	17. 9.97	
			N8119S		
G-JAWS	Enstrom 280C Shark	1174	N5690Q	30. 8.79	To ZS-HNH 12/84. Canx 26.6.84.
G-JAWZ	Pitts S-1S Special	PFA/09-12846		6.11.95	
G-JAYI	Auster J/1 Autocrat	2030	OY-ALU	5. 2.93	
			D-EGYK/OO-ABF		
G-JAYV	BAe 146 RJ85	E2269		28. 4.95	To D-AVRF 7/95. Canx 30.6.95.
G-JAZZ	American Aviation AA-5A Cheetah		N26932	30. 3.82	
		AA5A-0819			
G-JBAC	Embraer EMB.110P1 Bandeirante		G-BGYV	20.10.94	To VP-B.. Canx 8.7.99.
		110-249	N105VA/G-BGYV/PT-SAP		
G-JBAE	BAe Jetstream Srs.3101-01	602	G-31-39	12. 6.82	To N92MA 1/83. Canx 26.1.83.
G-JBCA	Cessna S550 Citation II	S550-0146	(N1296B)	7. 8.87	To N1296B. Canx 28.9.87.
G-JBDB	Agusta-Bell 206B JetRanger II	8238	G-OOPS	11. 4.96	
			G-BNRD/Oman AF 602		
G-JBDH	Robin DR.400/180 Regent	1901		17. 3.89	
G-JBET	Beechcraft F33A Bonanza	CE-1273	N15574	25. 8.88	To OO-DMC 4/96. Canx 29.3.96.
G-JBJB	Colt 69A HAFB	1274		26. 7.88	
G-JBPR	Wittman W.10 Tailwind	PFA/31-11490		25. 5.89	(Under construction 10/94)
G-JBRN	Cessna 182S Skylane II	182-80029	N432V	11. 6.99	
			G-RITZ/N9872F		
G-JBUS	Clutton FRED Srs.II	PFA/29-10396		29. 6.78	Canx by CAA 2.9.91.
G-JBWI	Robinson R-22 Beta	1040		19. 6.89	To G-TYPO 8/99. Canx.
G-JCAS	PA-28-181 Archer II	28-8690036	N9093N	12. 6.89	
			(N170AV)/N9648N		
G-JCBA	Sikorsky S-76B	760352	N95UT	. 9.99	
			N95LT/N120PP/N120PM		
G-JCBG	Dassault Falcon 900EX	44	F-WWFG	23. 7.99	
			G-JCBG/F-WWFG		
G-JCBI	Dassault Falcon 2000	27	F-WWMM	13.11.96	
G-JCBJ	Sikorsky S-76C	760502		9. 7.99	
G-JCFR	Cessna 550 Citation II	550-0282	G-JETC	14. 7.95	
	(Unit No.315)		N68644		

Regn	Type	c/n	Previous identity	Regn date	Fate or immediate subsequent identity (if known)
G-JCGR	Cessna T.207A Turbo Super Skywagon	T207-00110	OE-KAD D-ECKJ(3)/OO-VLP/PH-KRB/D-ELSA(2)/HB-CUL/N91191	16. 8.95	To HL.... Canx 26.10.98.
G-JCJC	Colt Flying Jeans SS HAFB	1747		8. 6.90	To SE-ZHS 12/98. Canx 5.10.98.
G-JCKT	Stemme S-10VT	11-004	D-KSTE(6)	8. 4.98	
G-JCMW	Rand-Robinson KR-2	PFA/129-11064		3. 2.99	
G-JCTI	Partenavia P.68B Victor	109	G-OJOE SE-GUI	28.10.81	To G-JVMR 4/83. Canx.
G-JCUB	PA-18-135 Super Cub (L-21B-PI)(Frame No. 18-3630)	18-3531	PH-VCH R.Netherlands AF R-103/54-2331	21. 1.82	
G-JCWW	Fokker F.28-4000 Fellowship	11135	PH-ZBT PH-EXR	3. 6.79	To F-GDFD 5/81. Canx 26.5.81.
G-JDEE	Socata TB-20 Trinidad	333	G-BKLA F-BNGX	1. 5.84	
G-JDEL	Jodel D.150 Mascaret	112 & PFA/151-11276	G-JDLI	19. 9.95	
G-JDFW	Airbus A.320-212	299	G-SCSR F-WWIQ	20.11.95	To OY-CNW 12/96. Canx 20.12.96.
G-JDHI	Enstrom F-28C-UK	199	G-BCOT	5.11.84	CofA expired 31.10.88. Canx by CAA 2.8.94. Parts used for fund-raising near Somersham with parts from G-BATU and G-BACH, and now wears the latters marks.
G-JDIX	Mooney M.20B Mark 21	1866	G-ARTB	28.11.85	
G-JDLI	Jodel D.150 Mascaret	112 & PFA/151-11276		21. 2.91	To G-JDEL 9/95. Canx.
G-JDST	PA-31-350 Navajo Chieftain	31-7952161	N35229	16. 8.79	To LN-TEL 11/84. Canx 8.11.84.
G-JDTI	Cessna 421C Golden Eagle III	421C-1226	N42E	11. 8.87	
G-JEAA	Fokker F-27 Friendship 500F	10664	N239MA PH-EXG	31. 3.88	To VT-UPD 7/95. Canx 21.7.95.
G-JEAB	Fokker F-27 Friendship 500F	10667	N240MA (N240N)/PH-EXI	27. 4.88	To VT-UPC 4/95. Canx 3.4.95.
G-JEAC	DHC.6-310 Twin Otter	617	G-BGMC	4. 3.88	To OY-SLA. Canx 25.1.90.
G-JEAD	Fokker F-27 Friendship 500RF	10627	VH-EWU PH-EXL	14.11.90	
G-JEAE	Fokker F-27 Friendship 500	10633	VH-EWV PH-FSO/PH-EXC	2. 1.91	
G-JEAF	Fokker F-27 Friendship 500	10637	OY-SRD G-JEAF/VH-EWW/PH-EXE	2. 1.91	
G-JEAG	Fokker F-27 Friendship 500	10639	D-ADAP(2) G-JEAG/VH-EWX/PH-EXG	14.11.90	
G-JEAH	Fokker F-27 Friendship 500	10669	VH-EWY PH-EXL	21. 1.91	
G-JEAI	Fokker F-27 Friendship 500	10672	VH-EWZ PH-EXS	18.12.90	
G-JEAJ	BAe 146 Srs.200	E2099	G-OLCA G-5-099	20. 9.93	
G-JEAK	BAe 146 Srs.200	E2103	G-OLCB (N412XV)/G-5-103	18. 3.93	
G-JEAL	BAe 146 Srs.300	E3129	G-BTXN HS-TBM/G-5-129	1. 4.93	To EI-CTM 3/99. Canx 23.3.99.
G-JEAM	BAe 146 Srs.300	E3128	G-BTJT G-6-212/G-BTJT/HS-TBK/G-11-128	24. 5.93	
G-JEAN	Cessna 500 Citation I (Unit No.339)	500-0339	N300EC N707US/G-JEAN/(N5339J)	24. 9.76	To G-DJAE 11/98. Canx.
G-JEAO	BAe 146 Srs.100	E1010	G-UKPC C-GNVX/N802RW/(N102RW)/G-5-512/PT-LEP/G-BKXZ/PT-LEP	19. 9.94	
G-JEAP	Fokker F-27 Friendship 500	10459	9Q-CBI(2) OY-APF/9Q-CBI(2)/PH-RUA/VH-EWR/F-BYAH/OY-APF/PH-EXD/(TN-ABZ)	13. 4.95	
G-JEAR	BAe 146 Srs.200	E2018	G-HWPB G-6-018/G-BSRU/G-OSKI/N603AW	14.11.95	
G-JEAS	BAe 146 Srs.200	E2020	G-OLHB G-BSRV/G-OSUN/C-FEXN/N604AW	13. 2.96	
G-JEAT	BAe 146 Srs.100	E1071	N171TR J8-VBB/G-BVUY/B-2706/G-5-071	11.10.96	
G-JEAU	BAe 146 Srs.100	E1035	N135TR J8-VBC/G-BVUW/B-584L/B-2704/G-5-035	30.12.96	
G-JEAV	BAe 146 Srs.200	E2064	N764BA CC-CEN/N414XV/G-5-064/N404XV	17. 6.97	
G-JEAW	BAe 146 Srs.200	E2059	N759BA CC-CEJ/N401XV/G-5-059/N401XV/G-5-059	21. 7.97	
G-JEAX	BAe 146 Srs.200	E2136	N136JV C-FHAP/N136TR/(N719TA)/N882DV/G-5-136	16. 2.98	
G-JEBA	BAe 146 Srs.300	E3181	HS-TBL G-6-181/G-BSYR/G-6-181	16. 6.98	
G-JEBB	BAe 146 Srs.300	E3185	HS-TBK G-6-185	26. 6.98	
G-JEBC	BAe 146 Srs.300	E3189	HS-TBO G-6-189	4. 6.98	
G-JEBD	BAe 146 Srs.300	E3191	HS-TBJ G-6-191	14. 7.98	
G-JEBE	BAe 146 Srs.300	E3206	HS-TBM G-6-206	28. 5.98	

Regn	Type	c/n	Previous identity	Regn date	Fate or immediate subsequent identity (if known)
G-JEDA	DHC.8-311 Dash Eight (Regd as Bombardier/DHC)	309	N394DC OE-LLW/C-GFHZ	23. 6.99	
G-JEDB	DHC.8-311 Dash Eight (Regd as Bombardier/DHC)	323	(N395DC) OE-LLX/C-GFEN	29. 7.99	
G-JEDH	Robin DR.400/180 Regent	2343		3. 2.97	
G-JEEN	Cessna 550 Citation II (Unit No.029)	550-0029	(N3247M)	11.10.78	To N502AL 7/79. Canx 17.7.79
G-JEET	Reims Cessna FA.152 Aerobat	0369	G-BHMF	10.12.87	
G-JEFF	PA-38-112 Tomahawk	38-79A0763		8. 3.79	(Stored WFU 1/99 Guernsey)
G-JEFS	PA-28R-201T Turbo Arrow III	28R-7703365	G-BFDG N47381	14. 4.97	
G-JEKP	Agusta-Bell 206B JetRanger III	8598	D-HMSF G-ESAL/G-BHXW	13. 2.97	
G-JELY	PA-18A-150 Super Cub (Frame No.18-6206)	18-6117	PH-MAV N8182D	2. 4.84	To D-EBNS. Canx 20.6.88.
G-JENA	Mooney M.20J (201)	24-1304	N1168D	5. 7.82	
G-JENI	Cessna R.182 Skylane RG II	R182-00267	N3284C	17. 9.87	
G-JENN	American Aviation AA-5B Tiger	AA5B-1187	N4533T	7.12.81	
G-JENS	Socata MS.880B Rallye 100ST	2554	G-BDEG F-OCZU	24. 3.80	Failed to gain height on take-off from Garway on 15.6.92. Canx by CAA 9.10.92.
G-JENY	Oldfield Baby Great Lakes	012 & PFA/10-10094		13.12.78	NTU - To G-BSXY 10/90. Canx by CAA 21.2.96.
G-JERS	Robinson R-22 Beta	1610		21.12.90	
G-JERY	Agusta-Bell 206B JetRanger II	8441	G-BDBR	16.11.88	To F-GKLS(2) 2/93. Canx 14.1.93.
G-JESS	PA-28R-201T Turbo Arrow III	28R-7803334	G-REIS N36689	18. 9.95	
G-JEST	PA-22-160 Tri-Pacer (Converted to taildragger in 1/89)	22-7620	G-ARGY	13. 4.87	Failed to get airborne and cartwheeled on take-off from Flecknoe on 4.10.91. Canx by CAA 4.10.91. Restored as G-ARGY 1/92.
G-JETA	Cessna 550 Citation II (Unit No.101)	550-0094	(N26630)	3. 9.79	To G-RDBS 5/99. Canx.
G-JETB	Cessna 550 Citation II (Unit No.319)	550-0288	(G-OXEH) G-JETB/G-MAMA/G-JETB/N4564P/G-JETB/N6865C	28. 5.81	DBR in overshot on landing on 26.5.93 at Eastleigh, Southampton. Canx by CAA 10.8.94
G-JETC	Cessna 550 Citation II (Unit No.315)	550-0282	N68644	28. 5.81	To G-JCFR 7/95. Canx.
G-JETD	Cessna 550 Citation II (Unit No.418)	550-0419	N1217N	3. 8.82	To VH-JVS. Canx 2.12.88.
G-JETE	Cessna 500 Citation I (Unit No.198)	500-0198	G-BCKM (N198CC)	10.12.84	To N9UJ. Canx 18.2.93.
G-JETG	Gates LearJet 35A	35A-324	G-JETN G-JJSG	5. 3.98	
"G-JETG"	HS.125 Srs.700B	257070	G-BWCR G-5-604/HB-VGG/G-5-604/HB-VGG	----	Not officially registered as such but marks were painted on the aircraft in 1995/6. Remained as G-BWCR.
G-JETH	Armstrong-Whitworth Sea Hawk FGA.6 (Composite with WM983/A2511)	AW.6385	"XE364" XE489	10. 8.83	(On display 6/97)
G-JETI	BAe 125 Srs.800B	258056	G-5-509	9. 7.86	
G-JETJ	Cessna 550 Citation II (Unit No.171)	550-0154	G-EJET G-DJBE/(N8777N)	9. 2.93	
G-JETK	BAe 125 Srs.800B	258133	N800FK G-5-642/G-GSAM/G-5-611	4.12.91	Restored as N800FK. Canx 21.6.93.
G-JETL	Gates LearJet 35A	35A-656	N3810G	26. 2.90	To N335SB 12/92. Canx 23.12.92.
G-JETM	Gloster Meteor T.7	-	VZ638	10. 8.83	(On display 6/97 Southend)
G-JETN	Gates LearJet 35A	35A-324	G-JJSG	20. 8.92	To G-JETG 3/98. Canx.
G-JETP(1)	Hunting P.84 Jet Provost T.3	PAC/W/13901	XN637	. .83R	NTU - To G-BKOU 2/83. Canx.
G-JETP(2)	Hunting P.84 Jet Provost T.52A (T.4)	PAC/W/17635	(5B-...) G-JETP/Singapore AF 355/ S.Yemen AF 107/G-27-92 (or -94)/XP666	13.12.83	(Possibly ex.105, not 107?) Permit to Fly expired 10.12.93. (Was stored at Paphos, Cyprus) Canx by CAA 18.3.99.
G-JETR	Agusta-Bell 206A JetRanger	8046	(G-BKBR) OO-CDP	26. 4.82	To G-ROOT 8/82. Canx.
G-JETS	Beagle A.61 Terrier 2 (Conversion of Auster AOP.6 c/n 2274)	B.622	G-ASOM G-35-11/VF505	19. 4.83	Restored as G-ASOM 8/91. Canx.
G-JETT	Canadair CL-30 (T-33AN) Silver Star Mk.3	T33-261	(G-BHOE) G-OAHB/CF-IHB/CAF 133261/RCN 21261	4. 6.82	To N33VC 7/85. Canx 2.7.85.
G-JETU	Aerospatiale AS.355F2 Twin Squirrel	5450	VR-CET JA6623	18. 4.96	
G-JETX	Bell 206B JetRanger III	3208	N3898L	9. 2.88	
G-JETZ	MDH Hughes 369E (500E)	0450E	VR-HJI	26. 3.97	
G-JFCX	BAe 125 Srs.800B	258215	G-5-727	26. 7.91	To Japanese ASDF as 29-3041. Canx 9.12.92.
G-JFHL	PA-28-161 Warrior II	28-7916317	N2249U	26. 7.89	To G-VICC 3/92. Canx.
G-JFOX	Denney Kitfox Mk.2	711 & PFA/172-11825	G-LANG	9. 8.94	To 9M-... Canx 26.3.99.
G-JFRS	Cessna 550 Citation II (Unit No.569)	550-0569	N1299P	6. 4.88	To G-OSNB 7/90. Canx.
G-JFWI	Reims Cessna F.172N Skyhawk II	1622	PH-DPA PH-AXY	1. 9.80	
G-JGAL	Beechcraft E90 King Air	LW-327	N6671M	30. 4.87	To N788SW 4/96. Canx 29.3.96.
G-JGCL	Cessna 414A Chancellor II	414A-0479	N2737F	4. 6.80	To N414CA 2/93. Canx 24.2.93.
G-JGFF	Agusta-Bell 206B JetRanger II	8594		11. 6.80	Forced landing and turned on its side at Trillgate Farm, Bullcross, near Stroud on 17.7.86. Canx as WFU 23.11.89.

Regn	Type	c/n	Previous identity	Regn date	Fate or immediate subsequent identity (if known)
G-JGMN	CASA I-131E Jungmann (Carries c/n plate 2104 in rear cockpit)	2011	E3B-407 Spanish AF	17. 4.91	
G-JGSI	Cyclone Pegasus Quantum 15	7515		19. 4.99	
G-JHAN	Beechcraft B200 Super King Air	BB-1324	N1541T	12. 4.90	To N7087N 8/93. Canx 6.8.93.
G-JHAS	Schweizer 269C (300C)	S.1493		14. 9.90	
G-JHEW	Robinson R-22 Beta	0672	N23677	20. 7.87	
G-JHLN	HS.748 Srs.2A/310LFD	1750	CS-TAU 5N-ARJ/G-11-2/TJ-CCE/TJ-AAO/TJ-XAH	26. 7.90	To C-GTAD. Canx 16.4.92.
G-JHSX	BAe 125 Srs.800A	258245		29. 1.93	To Japanese SDF as 52-3001 in 1/95. Canx 12.7.95.
G-JIII	Stolp SA.300 Starduster Too (built by C.S.Johnson)	2-3-12	N9043	27. 5.93	(On re-assembly Cumbernauld 2/99)
G-JILL	Rockwell Alpine Commander 112TC/A	13304	OO-HPB G-JILL/N8070R/HB-NCW/(N4667W)	25. 7.80	
G-JIMB	Beagle B.121 Pup Srs.100	B121-033	G-AWWF G-35-033	7. 4.94	
G-JIMI	Hughes 369D (500D)	120-0856D	N1109T	26.11.90	To CS-HCE. Canx 16.12.91.
G-JIMS	Cessna 340A II	340A-0722	G-PETE N2667N	24. 2.81	To G-CMAC 4/94. Canx.
G-JIMW	Agusta-Bell 206B JetRanger II	8440	G-UNIK G-TPPH/G-BCYP	4. 1.96	
G-JIMY	PA-28-140 Cherokee D	28-7125139	G-AYUG	5. 5.81	To G-OMAT 8/87. Canx.
G-JJAN	PA-28-181 Archer II	2890007	N9105Z	28. 3.88	
G-JJCB	BAe 125 Srs.800B	258022	G-5-16	7. 1.85	To G-5-569/HZ-KSA. Canx 18.9.87.
G-JJSG	Gates LearJet 35A	35A-324		12. 8.80	To G-JETN 8/92. Canx.
G-JLBI	Bell 206L-1 Long Ranger	45189	D-HBBZ N5021L/(D-HNRA)	3.12.81	To G-RASS 7/87. Canx.
G-JLBZ	Bell 222	47041	G-BNDB A40-CH	24. 2.87	To G-VERT 2/90. Canx.
G-JLCA	PA-34-200T Seneca II	34-7870428	G-BOKE N21030	3. 9.97	
G-JLCO	Aerospatiale AS.355F1 Twin Squirrel	5262		6. 5.83	To G-TMMC 12/87. Canx.
G-JLCY	Agusta A.109A II	7307	(D-H...) G-JLCY/N109AB	3. 1.89	To D-HFMW(2) 3/91. Canx 19.3.91.
G-JLEE	Agusta-Bell 206B JetRanger III	8588	G-JOKE G-CSKY/G-TALY	10. 2.88	
G-JLHS	Beechcraft A36 Bonanza	E-2571	N8046U	30.11.90	
G-JLMW	Cameron V-77 HAFB	1768		23. 6.88	
G-JLRW	Beechcraft 76 Duchess	ME-165	N60206	4.11.87	
G-JLTB	Varga 2150A Kachina	VAC156-80	OO-RTV N8373J	16. 8.84	Badly damaged in forced landing at Dundry Lane, Winford, near Lulsgate on 11.12.84. (Wreck moved to Elstree & used for spares). Canx as WFU 26.5.88.
G-JLXI	BAe Jetstream 61 (ATP)	2064		3. 3.94	WFU in 1996 Prestwick. Scrapped 4/97. Canx as WFU 12.6.97.
G-JMAC	BAe Jetstream Srs.4100	41004	G-JAMD G-JXLI	12. 6.92	(Stored 3/99 Woodford)
G-JMAT	Schweizer 269C (300C)	S.1558		21. 4.92	To G-PLPC 4/97. Canx.
G-JMCA	PA-31-350 Navajo Chieftain	31-7852167	N27815	14.11.78	To LN-NAF 11/81. Canx 27.10.81.
G-JMCC	Beechcraft 95-B58 Baron	TH-1046	N6061U	18. 3.80	To 5H-KAJ. Canx 16.2.88.
G-JMDD	Cessna 340A II	340A-0313	N4143G	1. 2.88	Damaged at Marshfield on 12.6.93. Canx as WFU 16.9.93.
G-JMDI	Schweizer 269C (300C)	S.1398	G-FLAT	24. 9.91	
G-JMFW	Taylor JT.1 Monoplane III	001		28.11.78	Canx by CAA 2.9.91.
G-JMHB	Robin DR.400/140B Petit Prince	1449	F-GCIC	5. 4.89	To G-OEBA 1/93. Canx.
G-JMSO	Mitsubishi MU.300 Diamond 1A	A062SA	N349DM	26. 3.84	To N362MD 2/85. Canx 20.2.85.
G-JMTS	Robin DR.400/180 Regent	2045		29.11.90	
G-JMTT	PA-28R-201T Turbo Arrow III	28R-7803190	G-BMHM N3735M	8. 7.86	
G-JMVB	Agusta-Bell 206B JetRanger III	8560	G-OIML	29.10.82	To EI-BXX 11/88. Canx 14.11.88.
G-JMWT	Socata TB-10 Tobago	11	F-GBHF	31.12.80	To G-OFLG 12/91. Canx.
G-JNEE	Cameron R-420 Gas Balloon	4232		21.10.97	
G-JNNB	Colt 90A HAFB	2063		20.12.91	
G-JOAN	American Aviation AA-5B Tiger	AA5B-0703	G-BFML	25. 6.80	To G-MURF 10/87. Canx.
G-JOCK	Beechcraft A36 Bonanza	E-2782	G-OVVB N82469	26. 3.97	To N936AA 4/99. Canx 1.4.99.
G-JOCO	Agusta-Bell 206B JetRanger III	8719	D-HOJO	8.11.89	Badly damaged in take-off crash at Micklefield, near Leeds on 11.12.89. Canx as destroyed 13.3.91.
G-JODL	SAN Jodel DR.1050/M Excellence	99	F-BJJC (G-BLMV)/F-BJJC	28. 4.86	(Overshot on landing at Wharf Farm, Market Bosworth on 10.10.98)
G-JODY	Bell 206B JetRanger III	4041		17. 4.89	To N206JR 4/97. Canx 4.4.97.
G-JOEL	Bensen B.8M Gyrocopter (C/n possibly incorrect - Bensen is PFA G/11-....)	G/03-1300		6. 7.99	
G-JOES	Cessna 421B Golden Eagle II	421B-0368	G-BLOH G-NAIR/G-KACT/OY-RPL/(N8055Q)	4. 7.85	To PH-SYG. Canx 25.7.88.
G-JOEY	BN-2A Mk.III-2 Trislander (Mod to 3-bladed propellors in 7/93)	1016	G-BDGG C-GSAA/G-BDGG	27.11.81	
G-JOHN	PA-28R-201T Turbo Arrow III	28R-7803042	N47935	1.12.77	To N233JD. Canx 6.12.85.
G-JOIN	Cameron V-65 HAFB	1257		8. 5.86	
G-JOJO	Cameron A-210 HAFB	2674		20. 9.91	Crashed on take-off at Micklefield on 11.12.89. Canx.
G-JOKE	Agusta-Bell 206B JetRanger III	8588	G-CSKY G-TALY	7. 1.85	To G-JLEE 2/88. Canx.

Regn	Type	c/n	Previous identity	Regn date	Fate or immediate subsequent identity (if known)
G-JOLY	Cessna 120	13872	OO-ACE	3. 9.81	
G-JONB	Robinson R-22 Beta	2593		29. 4.96	
G-JOND	Beechcraft 95-B55A Baron	TC-2259	G-BMVC	20. 6.89	To G-FABM 2/91. Canx.
			N66456		
G-JONE	Cessna 172M Skyhawk II	172-64490	N9724V	2.12.80	
G-JONH	Robinson R-22 Beta	2170		3. 6.93	
G-JONI	Reims Cessna FA.152 Aerobat	0346	G-BFTU	6. 7.84	
G-JONN	Bell 206L-1 Long Ranger	45492	N81871	7. 2.90	To N7063E 7/93. Canx 26.5.93.
			CC-CKP/CC-PQE/N3172K/(N31TD)/N3172K		
G-JONO	Colt 77A HAFB	1086		22. 6.87	
G-JONP	Revolution Helicopters Mini-500	0053		13. 3.96	No Permit issued. Canx by CAA 19.8.97.
G-JONS	PA-31-350 Navajo Chieftain	31-7952187	N35333	3.10.79	To (N380MG)/N999JT 1/93. Canx 6.1.93.
G-JONY	Cyclone Ax2000 HKS	7503		12. 3.99	
G-JONZ	Cessna 172P Skyhawk II	172-76233	N97835	28. 9.89	
G-JOON	Cessna 182D Skylane	182-53067	(N.....)	9. 6.81	
			G-JOON/OO-ACD/N9967T		
G-JORR	Aerospatiale AS.350B Ecureuil	1530	G-BJMY	22. 1.82	To EC-ERD 11/89. Canx 21.7.89.
G-JOSE	Cessna U.206G Stationair 6 II	U206-05223	N5342U	31.12.79	Canx 18.2.86 on sale to Tanzania. To N777TG. Then to 5H-TGT 6/86.
G-JOSH	Cameron N-105 HAFB	1319		13. 8.86	Canx by CAA 10.7.96.
G-JOSI	Scintex CP.1310-C3 Super Emeraude	902	G-BCHP	24.11.80	Restored as G-BCHP 1/83. Canx.
			F-BJVQ		
G-JOSS	Aerospatiale AS.350B Ecureuil	1205	F-WQJY	31. 8.99	
			3A-.../G-WILX/G-RAHM/G-UNIC/G-COLN/G-BHIV		
G-JOST	Europa Avn Europa	PFA/247-12916		17. 6.98	
G-JOSY	Enstrom 280FX	2057	G-BSTB	11.10.90	DBF at Loxwood, West Sussex on 9.2.92. Canx as destroyed 4.2.94.
G-JOYC	Beechcraft F33A Bonanza	CE-1496	C-FIIG	21.12.90	To N33UB 6/94. Canx 15.6.94.
G-JOYS	Beechcraft 58 Baron	TH-1556	N1556U	4. 8.94	Destroyed in fatal crash approx 1nm southeast of Kulusuk Airport, Greenland on 26.7.99.
G-JOYT	PA-28-181 Archer II	28-7990132	G-BOVO	13. 2.90	
			N2239B		
G-JOYZ	PA-28-181 Archer III	2843018	N9262R	19. 1.96	
G-JPAD	Robinson R-44 Astro	0052		10. 3.94	To G-EYET 11/98. Canx.
G-JPMA	Pearce Jabiru UL	PFA/274A-13399		24. 5.99	
G-JPOT	PA-32R-301 Saratoga SP	32R-8113065	G-BIYM	1. 8.94	
			N8385X		
G-JPRO	BAC P.84 Jet Provost T.5A	EEP/JP/1055	XW433	10. 8.95	
G-JPTV	BAC P.84 Jet Provost T.5A	EEP/JP/1005	XW355	2. 5.96	
G-JPVA	BAC P.84 Jet Provost T.5A	EEP/JP/953	G-BVXT	22. 2.95	
			XW289		
G-JRBH	Robinson R-22 Beta	2852		11. 8.98	
G-JRBI	Aerospatiale AS.350B Ecureuil	1647	EI-BNO(2)	22. 3.84	To EI-BYT 9/89. Canx 6.9.89.
			G-BKJY		
G-JRCM	Hawker Fury I Replica	RM/2		5. 3.79	Construction abandoned. Canx as WFU 24.2.86.
G-JRCT	Cessna 550 Citation II (Unit No.098)	550-0088	N2663N	19. 9.79	To N222TG 9/83. Canx 21.9.83.
G-JRMM	Rockwell Commander 690B	11530	N81734	31.10.79	To G-TVSA 4/86. Canx.
G-JRSL	Agusta A.109E Power	11036		9.11.98	
G-JRSY	Fokker F-27 Friendship 200	10324	F-GCMR	23. 9.83	To N266MA 3/84. Canx 30.3.84.
			OO-PSF/I-ATIL/PH-FKU		
G-JSAK	Robinson R-22 Beta	2959		30. 6.99	
G-JSAT	PBN BN-2T Turbine Islander	2277	G-BVFK	5. 2.98	
G-JSAX	HS.125 Srs.3B/RA	25157	G-GGAE	26. 7.83	WFU at Eastleigh 12/82. (Noted minus outer wings & rudder at Eastleigh on 15.4.86) Canx as WFU 10.1.86.
			VR-BGD/D-CAMB		
G-JSBA	BAe Jetstream Srs.3102-01	608	(N331BE)	29. 3.83	To N331BJ 3/85. Canx 4.3.85.
			G-JSBA/G-31-48		
G-JSCL	Rans S-10 Sakota	1289-075 & PFA/194-11781		12. 4.90	Damaged in crash at Fmlyns Field, Rhuallt on 16.7.91. (Stored 9/96) Canx as WFU 16.12.97.
G-JSGM	Cessna P.210N Pressurised Centurion II	210-00408	N7549K	20.11.80	DBR at Scone, near Perth on 27.1.83. Canx.
G-JSJX	Airbus A.321-211	808	(EC-...)	3. 4.98	
			D-AVZP		
G-JSMC	McDonnell Douglas DC-9-83 (MD-83) (Line No. 1793)	49941	N3002A	12.12.90	To G-DEVR 3/94. Canx.
G-JSON	Cameron N-105 HAFB	2933		21. 5.92	
G-JSPC	PBN BN-2T Turbine Islander	2264	G-BUBG	21.12.94	
G-JSSD	Handley Page 137 Jetstream 1 (Production No. 28)	227	N510F	14. 6.79	CofA expired 9.10.90. WFU at Prestwick. Canx by CAA 4.1.96.
			N510E/N12227/G-AXJZ		On display 8/96 at East Fortune.
	(Converted to BAe.3100 Prototype and first flew as such on 28.3.80)				
G-JTCA	PA-23-250 Aztec E	27-7305112	G-BBCU	29.12.80	
			N40297		
G-JTIE	Cessna 421C Golden Eagle III	421C-0437	G-RBBE	24. 8.82	To G-MARR 11/86. Canx.
			N6678C		
G-JTPC	Aeromot AMT-200 Super Ximango	200-067		28. 5.97	
G-JTWF	Boeing 737-3Y0 (Line No. 2876)	28558		. .96R	NTU - To G-OJTW 4/97. Canx.

Regn	Type	c/n	Previous identity	Regn date	Fate or immediate subsequent identity (if known)
G-JTWO	Piper J/2 Cub	1754	G-BPZR N19554/NC19554	23.10.89	
G-JTYE	Aeronca 7AC Champion (Mod to 7BCM standard)	7AC-4185	N85445 NC85445	26. 9.91	
G-JUDE	Robin DR.400/180 Regent	1869		14.10.88	
G-JUDI	North American AT-6D-NT Harvard III (Also regd with c/n "EX915-326165")	88-14722	FAP 1502 South African AF 7439/EX915/41-33888	17.11.78	
G-JUDY	American Aviation AA-5A Cheetah	AA5A-0620	(G-BFWM) N26480	31. 8.78	
G-JUIN	Cessna T.303 Crusader	T303-00014	OO-PEN N9401T	29. 2.88	
G-JULI	PA-28R-200 Cherokee Arrow II	28R-7435248	(G-BKDC) OY-POV/N43128	30. 6.82	To G-HWAY 7/83. Canx.
G-JULS	Stemme S-10V	14-028	D-KGDC(3)	12. 6.97	
G-JULU	Cameron V-90 HAFB	3611		7. 7.95	
G-JULY	American Aviation AA-5A Cheetah	AA5A-0730	G-BHTZ N26795	26. 1.82	Forced landed in a field near Bramley on 21.10.87. (Stored 10/89) Canx as destroyed 27.1.88.
G-JULZ	Europa Avn Europa	PFA/247-13045		8.10.96	
G-JUMP	Agusta-Bell 206B JetRanger III	8564		26. 7.78	To EI-BMP 4/82. Canx 28.4.82.
G-JUNE	PA-28-161 Warrior II	28-7716058	N1900H	9. 2.79	Ditched into the sea off Kulusuk, Greenland on 12.1.84. Canx.
G-JUNG	CASA I-131E Jungmann Srs.1000	1121	(N.....) G-JUNG/Spanish AF E3B-143	23.11.88	
G-JURE	Socata TB-10 Tobago	597	N106U	6.11.92	
G-JURG	Rockwell Commander 114A GT (Laid-down as c/n 14449)	14516	N4752W	19. 9.79	
G-JVAJ	PA-31T1 Cheyenne I	31T-8104053	N23ES N2468Y	4.10.88	To N454CA 11/93. Canx 22.11.93.
G-JVBF	Lindstrand LBL-210A HAFB	265		5. 6.95	
G-JVJA	Partenavia P.68C Victor	308	G-BMEI	21. 7.86	To ZK-SMB 12/94. Canx 26.10.94.
G-JVMD	Cessna 172N Skyhawk II	172-67794	G-BNTV N75539	7. 2.92	
G-JVMR	Partenavia P.68B Victor	109	G-JCTI G-OJOE/SE-GUI	5. 4.83	To TF-VEY 10/95. Canx 31.10.95.
G-JWBB	CEA Jodel DR.1051 Sicile	534	G-LAKI F-BLZD	17. 8.92	
G-JWBI	Agusta-Bell 206B JetRanger II	8435	G-RODS G-NOEL/G-BCWN	3. 4.96	
G-JWDG	American Aviation AA-5A Cheetah	AA5A-0662	G-OCML G-JAVA/N26705	9.10.91	
G-JWDS	Reims Cessna F.150G	0216	G-AVNB	15.12.88	
G-JWFT	Robinson R-22 Beta	0989		16. 3.89	
G-JWIV	CEA Jodel DR.1051 Sicile	431	F-BLMD	6. 9.78	Badly damaged in forced landing at Hobbynoor Cross, Coldridge, Devon on 23.9.95.
G-JWLS	Bell 206B JetRanger II	1114	G-BSXE N40EA/C-GMVM/N83150	8. 1.99	
G-JWSD	Robinson R-22 Beta	0840		8. 8.88	To OO-JDA. Canx 5.5.93.
G-JXLI	BAe Jetstream Srs.4100	41004		5. 2.91	To G-JAMD 4/92. Canx.

G-K G-K

Regn	Type	c/n	Previous identity	Regn date	Fate or immediate subsequent identity (if known)
G-KACT	Cessna 421B Golden Eagle II	421B-0368	OY-RPL (N8055Q)	20. 6.78	To G-NAIR 7/82. Canx.
G-KADY	Rutan LongEz	PFA/74A-11094		3. 9.85	(60% complete by .87)
G-KAFC	Cessna 152 II	152-84394	N6443L	24. 8.81	Damaged in storms at Biggin Hill on 16.10.87. Canx as destroyed 12.10.88. (Spares Use 12/95)
G-KAFE	Cameron N-65 HAFB	1505		18. 5.87	
G-KAIR	PA-28-181 Archer II	28-7990176	N3075D	28.12.78	
G-KAMM	Hawker Hurricane XIIA (Canadian Car and Foundary Co. built)	CCF/R32007	BW881	23. 2.95	(On rebuild 3/95) (On rebuild from components)
G-KAMP	PA-18-135 (L-18C) Super Cub	18-3451	D-EDPM Luftwaffe 96+27/NL+104/AC+502/AS+501/54-751	9. 5.97	
G-KAOM	Scheibe SF-25C Falke	4417	D-KAOM	3. 2.98	
G-KAPW	Percival P.56 Provost T.1	PAC/F/311	XF603	22. 9.97	
G-KARA	Brugger MB.2 Colibri	PFA/43-10980	G-BMUI	1. 6.95	
G-KARI	Fuji FA.200-160 Aero Subaru	FA200-236	G-BBRE	19.12.84	
G-KART	PA-28-161 Warrior II	28-8016088	N8097B	10. 7.91	
G-KARY	Fuji FA.200-180AO Aero Subaru	FA200-285	G-BEYP	28. 3.89	
G-KASH	American Aviation AA-5 Traveler	AA5-0083	G-AZUG	15. 9.83	To OO-AET 8/85. Canx 22.8.85.
G-KASS	HS.125 Srs.F3B	25127	G-5-623 G-AVPE	16. 3.89	To N125GK 8/93. Canx 10.6.93.
G-KATA	HOAC DV-20 Katana	20021	OE-UDV	4. 2.94	
G-KATE	Westland WG.30 Srs.100	010		7. 7.83	CofA expired 16.9.88. Canx as WFU 3.6.92. (Stored 10/93 Penzance)
G-KATH	Cessna P.210N Pressurised Centurion II	210-00130	(N4898P)	27.11.78	To G-PIIX 6/95. Canx.
G-KATI	Rans S-7 Courier	PFA/218-12917		5. 3.96	

Regn	Type	c/n	Previous identity	Regn date	Fate or immediate subsequent identity (if known)
G-KATS	PA-28-140 Cherokee Cruiser F	28-7325022	G-BIRC OY-BGE	26. 8.83	
G-KATT	Cessna 152 II	152-85661	G-BMTK N94387	10. 6.93	
G-KATY	Edgeley EA.7 Optica	EA.7/004	G-BLFD G-56-004	2. 4.85	Fatal crash into woodland & DBF near Ringwood on 15.5.85. Canx as destroyed 22.1.87.
G-KAUR	Colt 315A HAFB	2636		1. 3.94	
G-KAWA	Denney Kitfox Mk.2	PFA/172-11822		11. 3.91	Badly damaged in forced landing at Wavendon, Bucks on 30.6.95.
G-KAWW	Westland Wasp HAS.1	F.9663	3908 R.New Zealand Navy/G-17-6/XT781	29. 3.99	
G-KAXF	Hawker Hunter F.6A (Armstrong-Whitworth-built)	S4/U/3361	8830M XF515	20.12.95	
G-KAXL	Westland Scout AH.1 (Regd with c/n F8-7976) (Nacelle No. F8-6154)	F.9715	XV140	16.11.95	
G-KAYE	Glaser-Dirks DG-400	4-160		3. 3.86	To N400YE 4/87. Canx 12.3.87.
G-KAYT	Robinson R-22 Beta	0852	G-EIST N9081H	14. 6.94	Force landed and overturned onto its side in a field at Keynham, Leics. on 31.8.94. Canx as destroyed 18.1.95.
G-KBAC	Short SD.3-60 Var.100	SH3758	VH-MJH G-BPXL	2. 1.98	
G-KBCA	Beechcraft 200 Super King Air	BB-501	N518F N571SS/SE-GHK	10. 7.87	To G-OADT 1/89. Canx.
G-KBKB	Thunder Ax8-90 Srs.2 HAFB	2089		30.10.91	
G-KBOT	Hughes 369HM (500M)	52-0214M	G-RAMM EI-AVN/N9037F	30. 7.98	To G-HAUS 7/99. Canx.
G-KBPI	PA-28-161 Warrior II	28-7816468	G-BFSZ N9556N	21. 5.81	
G-KCAS	Beechcraft 95-B55 Baron	TC-1572	(G-KCEA) N2840W	4. 2.87	To N55BN 3/93. Canx 22.2.93.
G-KCAV	Cessna 414A Chancellor II	414A-0019	N6577C	26. 1.78	Restored as N6577C 7/81. Canx 23.7.81.
G-KCEA	Beechcraft 95-B55 Baron	TC-1572	N2840W	27. 1.87R	NTU - To G-KCAS 4.2.87. Canx by CAA 4.2.87.
G-KCIG	Sportavia-Putzer Fournier RF-5B Sperber	51005	(G-BHSR) D-KCIG	19. 6.80	
G-KDET	PA-28-161 Cadet	2841158	(SE-KIR) N91842	8. 8.89	
G-KDEY	Scheibe SF-25E Super Falke	4325	D-KDEY	8. 1.99	
G-KDFF	Scheibe SF-25E Super Falke	4330	D-KDFF	25. 4.83	
G-KDIX	Jodel D.9	PFA/54-10293		23.11.78	
G-KDLN	LET Zlin Z.37A-2 Cmelak	19-05	OK-DLN	14. 8.95	
G-KEAA	Beechcraft 65-70 Queen Air	LB-35	G-REXP G-AYPC	3. 8.88	CofA expired 6.11.89 & WFU at Elstree. To N70AA 9/95. Canx 14.9.95.
G-KEAB	Beechcraft 65-B80 Queen Air	LD-344	G-BSSL G-BFEP/F-BRNR/OO-VDE	3. 8.88	CofA expired 27.9.87. Canx as WFU 24.5.91. (Stored 1/99 Shoreham)
G-KEAC	Beechcraft 65-A80 Queen Air	LD-176	G-REXY G-AVNG/D-ILBO	3. 8.88	(Stored 11/96 Biggin Hill)
G-KEAN	PA-28-140 Cherokee B	28-25128	G-AWTM N11C	17.12.85	To G-TEWS 5/88. Canx.
G-KEEN	Stolp SA.300 Starduster Too	800	PH-HAB (PH-PET)/G-KEEN/N800RE	19. 7.78	
G-KEES	PA-28-180 Cherokee Archer	28-7505025	OO-AJV OO-HAC/N32102	29. 5.97	(Under repair 2/99 at Morley St.Botolph, Norfolk)
G-KELL	Van's RV-6	PFA/181-12845		16. 5.95	
G-KEMC	Grob G-109B	6024	D-KEMC	19.10.84	
G-KEMI	PA-28-181 Archer III	2943180	N41493	28.10.98	
G-KEMZ	PBN BN-2T Turbine Islander	2030	G-BIUJ	17. 9.81	To 9Q-CLW 11/81. Canx 17.11.81.
G-KENB	Air Command 503 Commander	G/04-1153		7.11.89	
G-KENI	Rotorway Exec 152	3599		14. 3.89	(Stored 8/93)
G-KENM	Luscombe 8EF Silvaire	2908	N21NK N71481/NC71481	9. 1.91	
G-KENN	Robinson R-22 Beta	0715		10.12.87	Damaged when main rotor struck the tail boom near Sandtoft 31.10.94; rebuilt to static condition. Canx as WFU 31.1.95 (On display above disco floor 8/95)
G-KENS	PA-32-300 Cherokee Six	32-7940069	N2209U	16. 3.79	Crashed at Bodmin on 16.9.79 & DBR. Canx as destroyed 5.12.83.
G-KENT	Cessna 414A Chancellor	414A-0229	N8828K	9. 5.79	To G-LOVO 6/81. Canx.
G-KENY	Enstrom 280C-UK-2 Shark	1221	G-BJFG N8617N	1. 3.82	To G-OMCP 7/86. Canx.
G-KERC	SNCAN NC.854S Chardonneret	55	F-BFSD	6. 2.80	Stalled and crashed at High Cross, Herts. on 23.10.93. Canx by CAA 16.2.94.
G-KERK	Piper J3C-65 Cub (L-4J-PI) (Frame No. 12443)	12613	F-BBQD 44-80147	8. 5.80	To G-BILD 12/80. Canx.
G-KERR	Reims Cessna FR.172K Hawk XP II	0625	PH-AXB(2)	20.12.78	Canx 6.10.89 on sale to Turkey.
G-KERY	PA-28-180 Cherokee C	28-3049	G-ATWO N9021J	5.10.83	
G-KEST	Alexander/Todd Steen Skybolt	1	G-BNKG G-RATS/G-RHFI/N443AT	11. 6.91	
G-KEVB	PA-28-181 Archer III	2843098	N9289E (G-KEVB)/N9289E	29. 8.97	
G-KEVN	Robinson R-22 Beta	0781	G-BONX	5. 6.91	
G-KEVS	Scintex CP.1310C-3 Super Emeraude	934	OO-PLS	. 2.95R	Reportedly !
G-KEYB	Cameron O-84 HAFB	1897		12.12.88	Not built. Canx by CAA 4.2.98.

Regn	Type	c/n	Previous identity	Regn date	Fate or immediate subsequent identity (if known)
G-KEYS	PA-23-250 Aztec F	27-7854052	N63909	6.10.78	
G-KEYY	Cameron N-77 HAFB	1748	G-BORZ	14. 6.88	
G-KFAN	Scheibe SF-25B Falke	AB46301	D-KFAN	14. 5.96	
G-KFDF	Bell 206B JetRanger II	1748	N90306	30. 3.88	To G-CHAT 8/90. Canx.
G-KFIT	Beechcraft F90 King Air	LA-80	G-BHUS	11. 9.81	To N614RG 5/94. Canx 17.5.94.
G-KFOX	Denney Kitfox Mk.2			11.10.88	
		298 & PFA/172-11447			
G-KFRA	PA-32-300 Cherokee Six	32-7840182	G-BGII	9. 9.97	
			N20879		
G-KFZI	Williams KFZ-1 Tigerfalck			2. 2.89	
		PFA/153-11054			
	(Originally laid-down as Kestrel Sport c/n PFA/1530)				
G-KGAO	Scheibe SF-25C Falke 1700	44386	D-KGAO	30. 7.99	
G-KGMT	Aerospatiale AS.355F1 Twin Squirrel		G-PASE	7. 8.98	
		5042	N57818		
G-KHOM	Aeromot AMT-200 Super Ximango			5. 5.98	
		200-091			
G-KHRE	Socata MS.893E Rallye 150SV		F-GAYR	25. 3.82	
	Garnement	2931			
G-KIAM	Grob G-109B	6321		1.10.84	To D-KHWH 11/93. Canx 29.9.93.
G-KIDS	PA-34-220T Seneca III	34-8133073	N83745	23. 4.81	To G-GFCD 5/90. Canx.
G-KILO	Boeing 747-236F	22306	(G-BDXK)	30. 9.80	To VR-HVY 4/82. Canx.
	(Line No. 480)				
G-KILT	American Aviation AA-5A Cheetah		G-BJFA	17. 3.82	To G-OAJH 4/86. Canx.
		AA5A-0893	N27159		
G-KILY	Robinson R-22 Alpha	0483	N8561M	13.10.88	To G-VMSL 2/98. Canx.
G-KIMB	Robin DR.300/140 Major	470/01	F-BPXX	23. 3.90	
			F-WPXX		
G-KIMM	Europa Avn Europa XS	PFA/247-13404		20. 7.99	
G-KINE	American Aviation AA-5A Cheetah		N27173	20. 7.82	(Damaged when nose undercarriage collapsed taxiing at
		AA5A-0896			Elstree on 20.12.85)
G-KING	PA-38-112 Tomahawk	38-78A0423		21.11.78	To SL-DBH. Canx 19.6.92.
"G-KING"	Reims Cessna F.172N	1754		.10.78	NTU - To G-BGAG 10/78. Canx.
	(Delivered in error as G-KING which was already reserved for a PA-38)				
G-KINK	Cessna 340	340-0045	G-PLEV	1.11.89	Extensively damaged after stiking power lines on approach
			D-ICED/(N5791M)		to Halfpenny Green on 30.5.96. Canx as destroyed 22.5.97.
G-KIRK	Piper J3C-65 Cub	10536	F-BBQC	28. 2.79	(Damaged on landing at Brent Knoll, Somerset on 26.12.97)
	(Regd with frame c/n 12490)		F-OAJF/French AF/43-29245		
G-KISS	Rand Robinson KR-2	PFA/129-10899		2. 8.83	(Under construction .90)
G-KITE	PA-28-181 Archer II	28-8490053	N4338X	12. 4.88	
G-KITF	Denney Kitfox Mk.1	156	N156BH	10. 5.89	
	(Built by J.B.Hartline)				
G-KITI	Pitts S-2E Special	002	N36BM	21. 6.90	
	(Built by R.Jones as Jones Turkey Two)				
G-KITS	Europa Avn Europa Tri-Gear			13. 6.94	
		003 & PFA/247-12844			
G-KITT	Curtiss TP-40M Kittyhawk	27490	F-AZPJ	4. 3.98	
	(c/n officially quoted as 31423.		N1009N(2)/N1233N/RCAF 840/43-5802		
	This was P-40N 43-23484/RCAF 877/N1009N(1), scrapped in 1965 and whose identity was adopted by RCAF 840)				
G-KITY	Denney Kitfox Mk.2			18. 8.89	
		456 & PFA/172-11565			
G-KIWI	Cessna 404 Titan Courier II		G-BHNI	25. 1.90	
		404-0644	LN-LGM/SE-IFV/G-BHNI/(N5302J)		
G-KJET	Beechcraft 65-B90 King Air	LJ-481	G-AXFE	4. 5.88	To G-BVRS 12/93. Canx.
G-KKDL	Socata TB-20 Trinidad	1096	G-BSHU	3.12.90	
G-KKES	Socata TB-20 Trinidad	1316	G-BTLH	2. 3.92	
G-KKJV	Zlin Z.37A-2 Cmelak	24-18	OK-KJV	30. 7.93	DBR in gales at Dunkeswell in 11.93. Canx as WFU. (Wreck at
					Dunkeswell)
G-KKUH	Boeing 737-3Q8	24300		31. 1.89	To SE-DLA 10/90. Canx 25.10.90.
	(Line No. 1666)				
G-KLAY	Enstrom 280C Shark	1034	G-BGZD	5.11.79	To F-GKHG. Canx 31.12.96.
G-KLEE	Bell 206B JetRanger III	3370	G-SIZL	11.10.95	
			G-BOSW/N2063T		
G-KLIK	Air Command 532 Elite (Mod)			21. 4.89	Canx by CAA 13.7.99.
		G/04-1113			
G-KMAC	Bell 206B JetRanger III	2494	N16998	16. 7.86	To VT-ETM 11/93. Canx 17.11.93.
G-KMAM	Airbus A.320-212	301	F-WWIX	22. 4.92	To G-JANM 12/95. Canx.
G-KMCD	Beechcraft B200 Super King Air		V5-BDL	29. 2.96	To OY-LKH 4/98. Canx 23.3.98.
		BB-1325	N15587		
G-KNAP	PA-28-161 Warrior II	28-8116129	G-BIUX	15. 2.90	
			N9507N		
G-KNDY	Bell 206B JetRanger III	4100	SE-HUG	21.10.91	To N144H 1/94. Canx 18.1.94.
G-KNIT	Robinson R-22 Beta	1612		14.12.90	To G-BVPR 6/94. Canx.
G-KNOB	Lindstrand LBL-180A HAFB	065		20.12.93	
G-KNOT	Hunting-Percival P.84 Jet Provost		G-BVEG	9. 6.99	
	T.3A	PAC/W/13893	XN629		
G-KNOW	PA-32-300 Cherokee Six	32-7840111	N9694C	21. 9.88	
G-KODA	Cameron O-77 HAFB	1448		26. 3.87	
G-KOFM	Glaser-Dirks DG-600/18M	6-66M16	D-KOFM	13. 7.99	
G-KOKL	Hoffmann H-36 Dimona	36276	D-KOKL	4. 3.98	
G-KOLB	Kolb Twinstar Mk.3A	PFA/205-12228		30. 6.93	
G-KOLI	PZL-110 Koliber 150	03900038		23. 7.90	
	(Licence-built Socata Rallye)				

Regn	Type	c/n	Previous identity	Regn date	Fate or immediate subsequent identity (if known)
G-KOLL	Glaser-Dirks DG-400	4-1	D-KOLL	14. 4.93	Restored as D-KOLL 1/94. Canx 15.11.93.
G-KOLY	Enstrom F-28A-UK (Composite fitted with cabin of EC-CKH c/n 188)	141	G-WWUK G-BFFN/HB-XEA	30. 3.89	Crashed at East Bach Farm on 19.4.93. Canx as TWFU 13.7.93.
G-KONG	Slingsby T.67M Firefly 200	2041	VR-HZP HKG-10/G-7-119	24. 3.94	
G-KOOL	DH.104 Devon C.2/2	04220	VP967	12. 1.82	Not coverted for civil use & donated to East Surrey Technical College on 3.8.85. Canx by CAA 24.6.87. (Instructional Airframe 4/93)
G-KORN	Cameron Berentzen Bottle 70SS HAFB	1655		10. 5.88	(On loan to the Balloon Preservation Group)
G-KOTA	PA-28-236 Dakota	28-8011044	N8130R	23.12.88	
G-KPAO	Robinson R-44 Astro	0382	G-SSSS	19.11.98	
G-KRAY	Robinson R-22 HP	0266	EI-CEF G-BOBO/N712BH/N100GV/N90763	25. 5.95	
G-KRES	Stoddard-Hamilton Glasair IIS RG	PFA/149-12984		12. 6.96	
G-KRII	Rand-Robinson KR-2	PFA/129-10934		4. 8.89	
G-KRIS	Maule M.5-235C Lunar Rocket	7357C	N56420	21. 4.81	
G-KROO	BAC One-Eleven Srs.217EA	BAC.125	A12-125 R.Australian AF	5. 3.90	To 5N-SDP. Canx 24.1.92.
G-KSBF	Hughes 369D (500D)	50-0696D	G-BMJH	18.11.82	To G-ITUP 6/88. Canx.
G-KSIR	Stoddard-Hamilton Glasair IIS RG	2151 & PFA/149-12137		15. 4.94	
G-KSVB	PA-24-260 Comanche B	24-4657	G-ENIU G-AVJU/N9199P	8.11.91	
G-KTEE	Cameron V-77 HAFB	2177		28.12.89	
G-KTKT	Sky 260-24 HAFB	110		19. 5.98	
G-KUKU	Pfalzkuku (3/4-scale Spitfire)	PFA/66-10180		4. 1.79	No Permit to Fly issued. Canx by CAA 1.6.95. (Noted active at Avranches, France in 1989)
G-KUTU	QAC Quickie Q.2	PFA/94A-10758		8. 3.82	Bounced on landing at Cranfield on 18.5.85 & badly damaged. (Stored 7/98 at Booker)
G-KVBF	Cameron A-340HL HAFB	4313		6. 4.98	
G-KWAX	Cessna 182E Skylane	182-53808	N9902 YV-T-PTS/(N2808Y)	18. 5.78	
G-KWIK	Partenavia P.68B Victor	152		27. 9.78	
G-KWIP	Europa Avn Europa	27 & PFA/247-12557		26. 9.95	
G-KWKI	QAC Quickie Q.200	PFA/94-12158		22.10.91	
G-KWLI	Cessna 421C Golden Eagle III	421C-0168	G-DARR G-BNEZ/N87386	13.11.98	
G-KYAK	LET Yakovlev C.11	171101	F-AZQI G-KYAK/F-AZHQ/G-KYAK/Israeli AF/DF / Egyptian AF 590/Czech AF 1701	21.12.78	
G-KYBF	Cameron A-340HL HAFB	4313		6. 4.98	
G-KYIN	Cessna 421C Golden Eagle III	421C-0612	G-OAKS N88620	28. 3.89	To N421AX 3/96. Canx 24.3.96.
G-KYNG	Aviamilano F.8L Falco 1	105	I-KYNG HB-UOH/I-STRI	6. 8.97	

G-L

G-L

Regn	Type	c/n	Previous identity	Regn date	Fate or immediate subsequent identity (if known)
G-LABS	Europa Avn Europa	PFA/247-12595		1. 3.94	
G-LACA	PA-28-161 Warrior II	28-7816036	N44883	22. 6.90	
G-LACB	PA-28-161 Warrior II	28-8216035	N8450A	12. 6.90	
G-LACD	PA-28-181 Archer III	2843157	G-BYBG N47BK	11.11.98	
G-LACE	Europa Avn Europa	PFA/247-12962		15. 4.96	
G-LACR	Denney Kitfox	PFA/172-11945		4.12.90	
G-LACY	Rockwell Commander 690B	11484	N81877	5. 3.79	To G-BLPT 4/81. Canx.
G-LADA	PA-32-300 Cherokee Six D	32-7140008	G-AYWK N8616N	28. 1.80	To G-MCAR 11/83. Canx.
G-LADD	Enstrom 480	5037		20. 5.99	
G-LADE	PA-32-300 Cherokee Six D	32-7940030	N3008L	21.11.80	
G-LADI	PA-30-160 Twin Comanche	30-334	G-ASOO	8. 4.94	
G-LADN	PA-28-161 Warrior II	28-8316050	G-BOLK N4295C	31. 7.89	To OO-NZG 6/95. Canx 19.6.95.
G-LADS	Rockwell Commander 114	14314	N4994W (N114XT)/N4994W	6.12.90	
G-LADY	American Aviation AA-5A Cheetah	AA5A-0743	G-BHWJ N28623	26. 1.82	DBR at Sandown, IoW on 10.9.82. Canx.
G-LAGR	Cameron N-90 HAFB	1628		25. 1.88	
G-LAIN	Robinson R-22 Beta	1992		7. 2.92	
G-LAIR	Stoddard-Hamilton Glasair IIS	2106		12. 9.91	(Under construction 2/99 at Roughton, Norfolk)
G-LAKC	Cessna 404 Titan Courier II	404-0220	G-BKTW G-WTVE/N88682	30. 4.91	To N103FA 3/94. Canx 18.3.94.
G-LAKD	Cessna 404 Titan Ambassador II	404-0061	G-BKWA G-BELV/(N5443G)	30. 4.91	To 5Y-BIY. Canx 28.1.94.
G-LAKE	Lake LA-250 Renegade	70	(EI-PJM) G-LAKE/N8415B	12. 7.88	
G-LAKH	BAe Jetstream Srs.3102	640	G-BUFM N410MX/G-31-640	6. 8.92	Restored as G-BUFM 7/94. Canx.

Regn	Type	c/n	Previous identity	Regn date	Fate or immediate subsequent identity (if known)
G-LAKI	CEA Jodel DR.1051 Sicile	534	F-BLZD	12.11.79	To G-JWBB 8/92. Canx.
G-LAKJ	BAe Jetstream Srs.3103	626	D-CONU(2) G-31-626	21. 7.93	To OY-SVP 6/94. Canx.
G-LAMA	Aerospatiale SA.315B Lama	2348	SE-HET	17. 3.98	
G-LAMB	Beechcraft C90 King Air	LJ-887	N10XH N444DC/N66864	18. 5.87	To D-IIWN 3/91. Canx 30.1.91.
G-LAMM	Europa Avn Europa	PFA/247-12941		20.11.95	
G-LAMS	Reims Cessna F.152 II	1431	N54558	23. 6.88	
G-LANA	Socata TB-10 Tobago	109	EI-BIH	15. 7.81	To G-SERL 5/92. Canx.
G-LANC	Avro 683 Lancaster B.X (Built by Victory Aircraft, Canada)	-	 RCAF KB889	31. 1.85	Canx by CAA 2.9.91. (On display 7/99 Duxford)
G-LAND	Robinson R-22 Beta	0639		28. 4.87	
G-LANE	Reims Cessna F.172N Skyhawk II	1853		27. 6.79	
G-LANG	Denney Kitfox Mk.2	711 & PFA/172-11825		14. 9.90	To G-JFOX 8/94. Canx.
G-LAPN	Light Aero Avid Aerobat	PFA/189-12146		4. 3.93	
G-LARA	Robin DR.400/180 Regent	2050		14. 2.91	
G-LARE	PA-39 Twin Comanche C/R	39-16	N8861Y	20. 2.91	
G-LARK	Helton Lark 95	9517	N5017J	3.12.85	
G-LASH	Monnett Sonerai II	PFA/15-10424		21.11.78	Canx by CAA 2.9.91.
G-LASR	Stoddard-Hamilton SH.2 Glasair II	2027		8. 1.90	
G-LASS	Rutan VariEze	PFA/74-10209		20. 9.78	
G-LAST	Cessna 340 II	340-0305	G-UNDY G-BBNR/N69452	2. 9.96	
G-LATC	Embraer EMB.110P1 Bandeirante	110-304	PT-SCL	12.11.80	To SE-KYE 11/92. Canx 26.11.92.
G-LATK	Robinson R-44 Astro	0064	G-BVMK	18. 7.94	
G-LAVE	Cessna 172R Skyhawk II	172-80663	G-BYEV N2377J/N41297	10. 3.99	
G-LAWS	Sikorsky S-61N Mk.II	61-824	G-BHOF LN-ONK(2)/G-BHOF/LN-ONK(2)/G-BHOF	7. 7.99	
G-LAXO(1)	Agusta A.109C	7649		. .90R	NTU - Not Imported. To JA6695. Canx.
G-LAXO(2)	Agusta A.109C	7643		3. 1.91	To G-BVNH 6/94. Canx.
G-LAXY	Everett Gyroplane Srs.3	035 & G/03-1233		17. 2.94	
G-LAZA	Lazer Z.200	PFA/123-12682		15. 6.95	
G-LAZE	SAN Jodel DR.1050 Ambassadeur	172	F-BJNU	17. 8.79	CofA expired 10.10.82. (Stored at Tollerton) Canx as WFU 14.2.89.
G-LAZL	PA-28-161 Warrior II	28-8116216	D-EAZL N9536N	9. 6.99	
G-LAZR	Cameron O-77 HAFB	2240		6. 3.90	
G-LAZY	Lindstrand LBL Armchair SS HAFB	129		18. 7.94	
G-LAZZ	Stoddard-Hamilton Glastar	PFA/295-13059		31.10.96	
G-LBAT	Pitts S-1S Special	AJT	G-UCCI G-BIYN/N455T	1. 9.88	To G-IIIX 5/89. Canx.
G-LBCS	Colt 31A HAFB	1891		10. 1.91	
G-LBLB	Lindstrand LBL-105A HAFB	254		24.10.95	Canx 3.12.97 on sale to Germany.
G-LBLI	Lindstrand LBL-69A HAFB	010		4.11.92	
G-LBLZ	Lindstrand LBL-105A HAFB	012		27. 1.93	To N7219R 4/97. Canx 2.4.97.
G-LBMM	PA-28-161 Warrior II	28-7816440	N6940C	28.11.89	
G-LBNK	Cameron N-105 HAFB	3559		20. 3.95	
G-LBRC	PA-28RT-201 Arrow IV	28R-7918051	N2245P	20. 7.88	
G-LCCO	PA-31-325 Turbo Navajo C/R	31-7812082	N27690	16. 8.78	Fatal crash near Earl Stonham, Stowmarket on 20.8.80. Canx as destroyed 5.12.83.
G-LCGL	Comper CLA.7 Swift Replica	PFA/103-11089		1. 7.92	
G-LCIO	Colt 240A HAFB	1381		23. 1.89	Seriously damaged on landing after the first overflight of Mount Everest by a hot air balloon on 21.10.91. Canx as WFU 25.5.94. (Stored 12/94)
G-LCOK	Colt 69A HAFB	652	(G-BLWI)	27. 3.85	Canx as WFU 14.7.93.
G-LCON	Eurocopter AS.355N Twin Squirrel	5572		28. 6.94	
G-LCRC	Boeing 757-23A (Line No. 259)	24636	G-IEAB	27.10.93	
G-LDYS	Thunder Ax6-56Z HAFB (Regd as Colt 56A)	347		18. 5.81	
G-LEAF	Reims Cessna F.406 Caravan II	0018	EI-CKY PH-ALN/OO-TIW/F-WZDX	7. 3.96	
G-LEAM	PA-28-236 Dakota	28-8011061	G-BHLS N35650	1. 7.80	
G-LEAN	Reims Cessna FR.182 Skylane RG II	0018	G-BGAP	17. 8.83	Overturned on take-off from Glen Ormiston Farm, near Peebles on 8.11.92. Canx as WFU 2.2.93. Wreckage on fire dump at Edinburgh 10/94.
G-LEAP	PBN BN-2T Turbine Islander	2183	G-BLND	19. 8.87	
G-LEAR	Gates LearJet 35A	35A-265	G-ZEST N1462B	20. 8.79	
G-LEAS	Sky 90-24 HAFB	158		4. 5.99	
G-LEAU	Cameron N-31 HAFB	761		5. 8.81	
G-LECA	Aerospatiale AS.355F1 Twin Squirrel	5043	G-BNBK C-GBKH	6. 2.87	

Regn	Type	c/n	Previous identity	Regn date	Fate or immediate subsequent identity (if known)
G-LEDA	Robinson R-22 Beta	1938	G-IFOX	12.11.98	
G-LEDN	Short SD.3-30 Var.100	SH3064	5N-AOX (N334SB)/G-BIOF/G-14-3064/EI-BNM/G-14-3064/N280VY/N4270A/G-BIOF/G-14-3064	12. 1.89	
G-LEED	Denney Kitfox Mk.2	450 & PFA/172-11577		24. 4.91	
G-LEEM	PA-28R-200 Cherokee Arrow II	28R-7435289	G-BJXW OY-CBG/SE-GID/OO-HJN/N43700	28. 5.85	Badly damaged in crash in a housing development 1 mile northeast of Newtownards 14.5.91. Canx as WFU 20.11.91. (Wreck stored 1/93)
G-LEES	Glaser-Dirks DG-400	4-238		4.10.88	
G-LEEZ	Bell 206L-1 Long Ranger II	45761	G-BPCT D-HDBB/N3175G	22. 1.92	
G-LEGG	Reims Cessna F.182Q Skylane II	0145	G-GOOS	26. 6.96	
G-LEGO	Cameron O-77 HAFB	1975		14. 4.89	
G-LEGS	Short SD.3-60 Var.100	SH3637	G-BLEF G-14-3637	7. 3.84	
G-LEIC	Reims Cessna FA.152 Aerobat	0416		16. 9.86	
G-LEIS	Bell 206L-1 Long Ranger II	45360	(G-BPEN) LN-OTZ/SE-HNE/A6-JAQ/N1077G	27.10.88	To G-OSIB 4/91. Canx.
G-LEMJ	Hughes 269C (300C)	14-0272	G-BMYW N8999F	27. 8.98	
G-LEND	Cameron N-77 HAFB	2012		25. 5.89	
G-LENI	Aerospatiale AS.355F1 Twin Squirrel	5311	G-ZFDB G-BLEV	9. 8.95	
G-LENN	Cameron V-56 HAFB	1833		29. 9.88	
G-LENS	Thunder Ax7-77Z HAFB	168		3.11.78	Canx as TWFU 21.12.95.
G-LEON	PA-31-350 Navajo Chieftain	31-7852111	N27746	28. 7.78	To N5432X 4/94. Canx 13.4.94.
G-LEOS	Robin DR.400/120 Dauphin 2+2	1884		29.11.88	
G-LEPF	Fairchild F.24R-46A Argus III	952	HB-EPF N1041G/HB714/43-14988	31. 7.87	
G-LEPI	Colt 160A HAFB	831		8. 5.86	Canx by CAA 10.3.95.
G-LERN	Enstrom F-28A	258	G-BBRS	26. 2.82	To OO-PRW 4/82. Canx 13.4.82.
G-LESJ	Denney Kitfox Mk.3	PFA/172-12001		4.10.94	
G-LEVI	Aeronca 7AC Champion	7AC-4001	N85266 NC85266	17. 4.90	
G-LEXI	Cameron N-77 HAFB	438		26.10.78	
G-LEZE	Rutan LongEz	PFA/74A-10702		31. 3.82	
G-LEZJ	Denney Kitfox 4-1200 Speedster	PFA/172B-12529		7. 3.96	
G-LEZZ	Stoddard-Hamilton Glastar	PFA/295-13241	G-BYCR	4.11.98	
G-LFBA	Eurocopter MBB BK.117C-1C	7511	D-HECU(3) D-HMBF(3)	28. 7.95	To D-HXXL 5/97. Canx 16.4.97.
G-LFCA	Reims Cessna F.152 II	1697		10.12.79	To G-TAYS 10/91. Canx.
G-LFIX	Vickers-Supermarine 509 Spitfire Trainer IX (C/n is firewall plate no.)	CBAF/8463	162 Irish Air Corp/G-15-175/ML407	1. 2.80	
G-LFJB	Boeing 737-71Q (or -81Q) (Line No. ...)	29051	N8254G	. 6.99R	
G-LFSA	PA-38-112 Tomahawk	38-78A0430	G-BSFC	22.10.90	
G-LFSB	PA-38-112 Tomahawk	38-78A0072	G-BLYC D-ELID	20.10.94	
G-LFSC	PA-28-140 Cherokee Cruiser	28-7425005	G-BGTR OY-BGO	4. 9.95	
G-LFSD	PA-38-112 Tomahawk II	38-82A0046	G-BNPT G-LFSD/G-BNPT/N91522	21.10.96	
G-LFSE	PA-28R-200 Cherokee Arrow II	28R-7335157	G-BAXT	9. 6.97	
G-LFSF	Cessna 150M Commuter	150-77651	G-BSRC N6337K	9. 7.99	
G-LFSI	PA-28-140 Cherokee C	28-26850	G-AYKV	14. 7.89	
G-LFVB	Vickers Supermarine 349 Spitfire LF.Vb	CBAF/2403	8070M 5377M/EP120	9. 5.94	
G-LGAS	Lindstrand LBL-210S HAFB	326		19. 2.96	Canx 19.6.97 on sale to Egypt.
G-LGIO	Colt 240A HAFB	2028		12. 8.91	Canx by CAA 10.3.95.
G-LGNA	SAAB-Scania 340B	340B-199	N592MA SE-F99	11. 6.99	
G-LGNB	SAAB-Scania 340B	340B-216	N595MA SE-G16	8. 7.99	
G-LGRM	Bell 206B JetRanger II	1376	G-OBRU G-GOBP/G-BOUY/N5450M/N1PE/XC-GUW	7. 1.99	
G-LHPL	Aerospatiale AS.350B Ecureuil	2189	N612LH 9M-BAZ/ZK-HJW/JA9808	11. 5.99	
G-LIAM	Aerotek Pitts S-2A	2230	N8AB	11. 5.92	Fatal crash on the bank of the River Chess at Latimer Park Trout Farm, near Chesham on 17.11.92. Canx by CAA 27.4.93.
G-LIAN	Robinson R-22 Beta	0985		16. 3.89	To G-BWZV 12/96. Canx.
G-LIBB	Cameron V-77 HAFB	2463		21. 6.91	
G-LIBS	Hughes 369HS (500C)	43-0469S	N9147F	20. 8.85	
G-LICK	Cessna 172N Skyhawk II	172-70631	G-BNTR N739LQ	19. 4.88	To N172AG 7/99. Canx 23.7.99.
G-LIDA	Hoffman HK.36R Super Dimona	36355		15. 4.92	
G-LIDD	DH.104 Dove 8A	04525	G-ARSN Irish Air Corps 201/EI-ARV/G-ARSN	15. 6.83	To VH-OBI 10/87. Canx 30.10.87.

Regn	Type	c/n	Previous identity	Regn date	Fate or immediate subsequent identity (if known)
G-LIDE	PA-31-350 Navajo Chieftain	31-7852156	N27800	26.10.78	
G-LIDR	Hoffmann H-36 Dimona	36208	G-BMSK	1. 4.96	
G-LIDS	Robinson R-22 Beta	2808		21. 4.98	
G-LIFE	Thunder Ax7-56Z HAFB	135		11. 1.78	
G-LIFT	Bell 47G-2	2588	N6783D CF-UAI/N6783D	13. 9.78	To F-GBEG(2) 8/83. Canx 19.5.83.
G-LIGG	Reims Cessna F.182Q Skylane	0089	G-THAM PH-AXE(2)	2. 8.88	Fatal crash into high ground at Findon, West Sussex on 20.11.94. Canx as destroyed 24.2.95.
G-LIII	Bell 206L Long Ranger III	51002	N1084D	29.12.82	To G-CJCB 4/83. Canx.
G-LILI	Cessna 425 Conquest I	425-0054	G-YOTT N345GA/G-NORC/(G-BICL)/(N6776P)	13. 1.93	To N425SM 12/98. Canx 7.12.98.
G-LILY	Bell 206B JetRanger III	4107	G-NTBI C-FIJD	14. 3.95	
G-LIMA	Rockwell Commander 114	14415	N5870N	17.10.78	
G-LIME	Schempp-Hirth Janus CM	24/220		17. 4.86	Had engine failure on approach to Aboyne on 26.10.88 and struck several parked cars. Canx as destroyed 17.2.89. Rebuilt in West Germany & re-regd as D-KKMM in 4/90.
G-LINC	Hughes 369HS (500C)	43-0467S	C-FDUZ CF-DUZ	14. 5.87	
G-LIND	Agusta-Bell 206B JetRanger III	8721	G-OONS	20. 6.94	Restored to G-OONS 10/95. Canx.
G-LINE	Eurocopter AS.355N Twin Squirrel	5566		22. 3.94	
G-LING	Thunder Ax7-65 Srs.1 HAFB	446		2. 9.82	To F-GINP 2/91. Canx 13.2.90.
G-LINK	Sikorsky S-61N Mk.II	61-806		9. 3.78	To PT-HTT. Canx 19.6.87.
G-LINT	Pitts S-1S Special	EMK.104 & PFA/09-10628		4. 2.81	Destroyed in fatal crash half a mile north of Elstree on 15.3.86. (Wreck later removed to RAE Farnborough for investigation) Canx by CAA 30.6.87.
G-LIOA	Lockheed 10A Electra	1037	N5171N NC243/NC14959	6. 5.83	(On display 9/93)
G-LION	PA-18-135 Super Cub (L-21B-PI) (Frame No. 18-3841)	18-3857	PH-KLB (PH-DKG)/R.Netherlands AF R-167/54-2457	29. 9.80	
G-LIOT	Cameron O-77 HAFB	2378		7. 8.90	
G-LIPE	Robinson R-22 Beta	1882	G-BTXJ	23. 1.92	
G-LIPP	PBN BN-2T Turbine Islander (Converted back to a BN-2B-26 in 1998)	2156	G-BKJG	10. 7.87	To 9H-ADF (Armed Forces of Malta). Canx 23.9.98.
G-LISA	Steen Skybolt	PFA/64-11123		11. 9.86	To G-BVXE 1/95. Canx.
G-LISE	Robin DR.400/500 (Originally reg with c/n 2379)	0001		27. 7.98	
G-LITE	Rockwell Commander 112A	291	OY-RPP N1291J	13. 6.80	
G-LITZ	Pitts S-1E Special	PFA/09-11131		3. 3.92	
G-LIVA	Enstrom 480	5010	N900SA G-PBTT/JA6169	27. 8.98	
G-LIVE	Grob G-109B	6397		8.10.85	To D-KEVE 4/87. Canx 15.4.87.
G-LIVH	Piper J3C-65 (L-4H-PI) Cub (Regd with frame no.11354)	11529	OO-JAN OO-AAT/OO-PAX/43-30238	31. 3.94	
G-LIVR	Enstrom 480	5038		14. 7.99	
G-LIZA	Cessna 340A II	340A-1021	G-BMDM ZS-KRH/N4620N	15. 2.90	
G-LIZI	PA-28-160 Cherokee	28-52	G-ARRP	26. 1.89	
G-LIZY	Westland Lysander III (C/n also quoted as "Y1351")	"504/39"	RCAF 1558 V9300	20. 6.86	Canx as WFU 18.4.89. (On display 7/99 Duxford)
G-LIZZ	PA-E23-250 Aztec E	27-7405268	G-BBWM N40532	26. 7.93	
G-LJCC	Murphy Rebel	PFA/232-13355		8. 7.98	
G-LJET	Gates LearJet 35A	35A-643	(N35NK) G-LJET/N39418	2.12.88	
G-LKOW	Beechcraft 200 Super King Air	BB-438	(G-BLLC) EI-BFT	19. 7.84	To G-BLLC 8/85. Canx.
G-LLAI	Colt 21A Cloudhopper HAFB	519	(G-BKTX)	18. 7.83	Canx by CAA 16.7.90.
G-LLTT	PA-32R-301 Saratoga II HP	3246060	N9283P	31. 1.97	
G-LLYD	Cameron N-31 HAFB	3558		20. 3.95	
G-LNYS	Reims Cessna F.177RG Cardinal II	0120	G-BDCM OY-BIP	30.11.92	
G-LOAF	Schempp-Hirth Janus CM	36/269	OH-830	10. 3.93	To F-C... Canx 29.7.99.
G-LOAG	Cameron N-77 HAFB	359		10.11.77	CofA expired 6.4.84. Canx as destroyed 31.3.93. (Stored 12/94)
G-LOAN	Cameron N-77 HAFB	1434		9. 1.87	
G-LOAT	Rutan Cozy	PFA/159-13213		28. 5.98	
G-LOBE	Thunder Ax6-56Z HAFB	170		28.11.78	Stolen in Italy. Canx 13.2.80.
G-LOBI	Thunder Ax7-77Z HAFB	425		18. 6.82	To HB-BDV 10/83 (as Ax8-105Z version). Canx.
G-LOBO	Cameron O-120 HAFB	3389		3. 1.95	
G-LOCH	Piper J3C-90 Cub (L-4J-PI) (Frame No.12517)	12687	HB-OCH 44-80391	10.12.84	
G-LOCK(1)	Agusta-Bell 206B JetRanger II	8592		. .79R	NTU - Not Imported. To F-GCMP 6/80. Canx.
G-LOCK(2)	Agusta-Bell 206B JetRanger II	8587		25.10.79	To G-TPTR 8/81. Canx.
G-LOFA	Lockheed L.188CF Electra	2002	N359Q F-OGST/N359Q/ N359AC/TI-LRM/N359AC/HC-AVX/N359AC/VH-ECA	10. 2.94	WFU & engineless 6/98 at Coventry due to problems with airframe found on checks; stripped for spares. Canx as WFU 29.7.98.
G-LOFB	Lockheed L.188CF Electra	1131	N667F N133AJ/CF-IJW/N131US	28. 6.94	

Regn	Type	c/n	Previous identity	Regn date	Fate or immediate subsequent identity (if known)
G-LOFC	Lockheed L.188CF Electra	1100	N665F	15. 6.95	
			N289AC/N6123A		
G-LOFD	Lockheed L.188CF Electra	1143	LN-FOG	12. 6.97	
			LN-MOD/N9745C/CF-IJC/N9745C		
G-LOFE	Lockheed L.188CF Electra	1144	EI-CET	5. 1.99	
			(G-FIJF)/N668Q/N668F/N24AF/N128US		
G-LOFM	Maule MX-7-180A Star Rocket	20027C	N3111U	19. 7.95	
G-LOFT	Cessna 500 Citation I	500-0331	LN-NAT	12. 1.95	
	(Unit No.331)		EC-FUM/EC-500/LN-NAT/N40AC/N96RE/N86RE/N331CC/(N5331J)		
G-LOGA	BAe ATP	2040		19. 8.91	To G-MANF 9/94. Canx.
G-LOGB	BAe ATP	2045	G-11-045	11.12.91	To G-MANE 6/94. Canx.
G-LOGC	BAe ATP	2017	G-OLCC	15. 4.92	To G-MANH 11/94. Canx.
G-LOGD	BAe ATP	2018	(G-MANG)	27. 4.92	To G-MANG 8/94. Canx.
			G-LOGD/G-OLCD		
G-LOGE	BAe ATP	2004	G-BMYL	25.10.91	To G-MANJ 9/94. Canx.
G-LOGF	BAe ATP	2054	G-11-054	31. 8.93	To G-MANC 11/94. Canx.
G-LOGG	BAe ATP	2055	G-JATP	8. 9.93	To G-MANB 9/94. Canx.
			G-11-055		
G-LOGH	BAe ATP	2056	G-11-056	31. 8.93	To G-MANA 2/94. Canx.
G-LOGI	McDonnell Douglas DC-9-83 (MD-83)			. .86R	NTU - To N6202S/G-PATA 4/87. Canx.
	(Line No. 1332)	49398			
G-LOGJ	BAe Jetstream Srs.4100	41005		19.10.92	To G-MAJC 9/94. Canx.
G-LOGK	BAe Jetstream Srs.4100	41007		19.10.92	To G-MAJE 9/94. Canx.
G-LOGL	BAe Jetstream Srs.4100	41009		19.10.92	To G-MAJG 8/94. Canx.
G-LOGO	MDH Hughes 369E (500E)	0454E	G-BWLC	4.10.96	
			HB-XIJ/SE-JAM		
G-LOGP	BAe Jetstream Srs.3102	649	VH-LJR	19. 7.91	To G-SWAD 8/94. Canx.
			G-BPZJ/G-31-649/PH-KJC/G-31-649		
G-LOGR	BAe Jetstream Srs.3102	655	G-BRGR	30. 8.91	To G-ENIS 8/94. Canx.
			PH-KJD/G-31-655		
G-LOGS	Robinson R-22 Beta	1486		11. 9.90	Canx 27.4.98 on sale to Spain.
G-LOGT	BAe Jetstream Srs.3108	690	G-BSFH	29. 8.91	Restored as PH-KJG 10/93. Canx 27.9.93.
			PH-KJG/G-31-690		
G-LOGU	BAe Jetstream Srs.3102	720	G-BRGL	18. 7.91	To G-OEDC 3/94. Canx.
			I-BLUA/G-31-720/G-BRGL/G-31-720		
G-LOGV	BAe Jetstream Srs.3102	761	G-OEDA	8. 7.91	To ZK-JSI 8/97. Canx 5.8.97.
			G-LOGV/G-BSZK/I-BLUO/G-31-761		
"G-LOGW"	Short SD.3-60 Var.300	SH3741	G-BOFK	----	Painted in error - To G-OLGW 9/88.
			G-14-3741		
G-LOKO	Cameron Locomotive 105SS HAFB	3680		19. 9.95	To HB-QBN 3/96. Canx 23.2.96.
G-LOLL	Cameron V-77 HAFB	2964		4.12.92	
G-LOLO	Robinson R-22 Beta	1662	G-NIKI	27. 1.95	Crashed and rolled over at Bournemouth on 22.5.98. Canx by CAA 9.10.98.
G-LOLY	Aerospatiale AS.350B Ecureuil	1836	JA9897	16. 9.92	To G-HLEN 4/93. Canx.
			N5805T/HP-.../N5805T		
G-LOND	Vickers 806 Viscount	257	G-AOYI	8. 2.85	CofA expired 20.6.88. Stored at Southend. Canx by CAA
			G-LOND/G-AOYI/(G-AOYH)		1.6.92. Broken up at Southend in 2/93.
G-LONG	Bell 206L-1 Long Ranger II	45227		2. 5.79	To N43027 1/98. Canx 19.12.97.
G-LONS	Enstrom 280C-UK-2 Shark	1017	G-BDIB	10. 8.81	Damaged on 19.1.82. Rebuilt & re-regd as G-ECHO 5/82. Canx.
G-LOOK	Reims Cessna F.172M Skyhawk	1234	PH-MIG	4. 5.79	Extensively damaged in landing accident at RAF Laarbruch, West Germany on 11.8.85. Canx as WFU 8.1.86. (Starboard mainplane stored at Fenland 9/98)
G-LOOP	Pitts S-1C Special	850	5Y-AOX	11. 5.78	
G-LOOT	Embraer EMB.110P1 Bandeirante		G-BNOC	17. 1.91	CofA expired in 10/90. Canx as WFU. (Open store 9/99
		110-223	PT-GMP		at Southend)
G-LORA	Cameron A-250 HAFB	3828		22. 2.96	
G-LORC	PA-28-161 Cadet	2841339	D-ESTC	12. 1.99	
			N9184W/(SE-KMP)/(N620FT)		
G-LORD	PA-34-200T Seneca II	34-7970347	N2908W	6. 5.88	
G-LORI	HS.125 Srs.403B	25246	G-AYOJ	19. 7.83	Canx by CAA 21.4.93. (Open storage 3/95 in Nigeria)
			(G-5-16)/9Q-COH/G-AYOJ		
G-LORN	Avions Mudry CAP-10B	282		4. 3.99	
G-LORR	PA-28-181 Archer III	2843037		19. 4.96	
G-LORT	Light Aero Avid Mk.4 Speed Wing			12. 2.92	
		1124 & PFA/189-12219			
G-LORY	Thunder Ax4-31Z HAFB	171		28.11.78	
G-LOSM	Gloster Meteor NF.11	S4/U/2342	WM167	8. 6.84	
	(Armstrong-Whitworth built)				
G-LOSS	Cameron N-77 HAFB	1369		23. 9.86	
G-LOST	Denney Kitfox Mk.3 Floatplane			10. 8.95	
		PFA/172-12055			
G-LOTI	Bleriot Type XI Replica			21.12.78	(On display 3/97)
		PFA/88-10410			
G-LOTO	BN-2A-26 Islander	530	G-BDWG	27. 7.95	
			(N90255)/(C-GYUF)/G-BDWG		
G-LOUI	Extra EA.300	015	D-EGRN	14. 4.92	To OO-WWW 8/96. Canx 21.8.96.
			G-OHER/D-EGRN		
G-LOUN	Eurocopter AS.355N Twin Squirrel			24. 1.97	
		5627			
G-LOUP	Partenavia P.68B Victor	182	G-OCAL	21. 2.89	Extensively damaged on failing to get airbourne on take-off
			G-BGMY		at Bodmin on 7.2.93. Canx as WFU 29.9.93.
G-LOVA	BAe Jetstream Srs.3102	640	G-OAKA	28. 5.98	
			G-BUFM/G-LAKH/G-BUFM/N410MX/G-31/640		

Regn	Type	c/n	Previous identity	Regn date	Fate or immediate subsequent identity (if known)
G-LOVB	BAe Jetstream Srs.3102	622	VH-HSW G-31-622/G-BLCB/G-31-622	12. 8.99	
G-LOVE	Maule M.5-235C Lunar Rocket	7365C	N56438	2. 9.81	Fatal crash on landing & struck PA-28-180 G-BFMV at Cranfield on 4.9.81. Canx.
G-LOVO	Cessna 414A Chancellor	414A-0229	G-KENT N8828K	24. 6.81	To G-WITE 8/85. Canx.
G-LOVX	Cessna 441 Conquest	441-0316	G-BLCJ N1208G	22.11.84	To N405MA. Canx 23.2.90.
G-LOWA	Colt 77A HAFB	1451		14. 4.89	
G-LOWE	Monnett Sonerai I	367 & PFA/15-10344		16.11.78	Canx as TWFU 16.9.97.
G-LOWS	Sky 77-24 HAFB	025		19. 3.96	
G-LOYA	Reims Cessna FR.172J Rocket	0352	G-BLVT PH-EDI/D-EEDI	4. 8.89	
G-LOYD	Aerospatiale SA.341G Gazelle Srs.1 (Rebuilt .90 using major components of N6957 c/n 1060, old fuselage dumped at Sywell 3/91)	1289	G-SFTC N47298	19. 6.85	
G-LPAD	Lindstrand LBL-105A HAFB	632		5. 8.99	
G-LPGI	Cameron A-210 HAFB	4196		13. 8.97	
G-LPGO	Cameron V-77 HAFB	1862		11. 1.89	To VH-LPO. Canx 28.5.93.
G-LRBJ	BAe 125 Srs.1000B	259004		7. 2.91	To G-5-779/VR-CPT. Canx 26.5.93.
G-LRBW	Lindstrand HS-110 Hot Air Airship	253		2. 8.95	Canx by CAA 26.2.97.
G-LRII	Bell 206L-1 Long Ranger II	45249		18. 5.79	To N165BH. Canx 30.4.91.
G-LSFC	PA-28-140 Cherokee Cruiser	28-7425005	G-BGTR OY-BGO	4. 9.95	
G-LSFI	American Aviation AA-5A Cheetah	AA5A-0770	G-BGSK	13. 2.84	
G-LSHI	Colt 77A HAFB	1264		20. 7.88	
G-LSKW	Cessna 182P Skylane	182-61095	OO-PWW N7455Q	11. 1.99	Restored as OO-PWW 5/99. Canx 31.3.99.
G-LSLH	Schweizer Hughes 269C (300C)	S.1486		15. 8.90	Dropped to the ground and overturned on its side while hovering at Kidlington on 27.3.95. Canx as destroyed 28.6.95. To ZK-HXH 11/96.
G-LSMI	Reims Cessna F.152 II	1710		1. 2.80	
G-LSTR	Kendal/Stoddard-Hamilton Glastar	PFA/295-13095		20. 4.98	
G-LTEC	HS.125 Srs.700B	257103	G-BHSU G-5-12	21. 4.93	To VR-BOJ 12/94. Canx 7.12.94.
G-LTEK	Bell 206B JetRanger II	2034	G-BMIB ZS-HGH	28. 5.93	To G-OSMD 2/99. Canx.
G-LTFB	PA-28-140 Cherokee	28-23343	G-AVLU	28. 2.97	
G-LTFC	PA-28-140 Cherokee B	28-26259	G-AXTI	8. 6.94	
G-LTNG	English Electric Lightning T.5	B1/95011	8503M XS451	8.11.89	To ZU-BEX 2/97. Canx 13.2.97.
G-LTRF	Sportavia-Putzer Fournier RF-7	7001	G-EHAP (G-BGVC)/D-EHAP/F-WPXV	10.12.97	
G-LTSB	Cameron LTSB 90SS HAFB	4483		15. 1.99	
G-LUAR	Socata TB-10 Tobago	307		13. 5.82	To G-PATN 3/97. Canx.
G-LUBE	Cameron N-77 HAFB	1127		25. 2.85	
G-LUCA	Thunder Ax7-77Z HAFB	707		31. 7.85	Canx by CAA 4.8.98.
G-LUCE	Cameron A-210 HAFB	2269		8. 5.90	To ZS-HZF 1/97. Canx 8.10.96.
G-LUCK	Reims Cessna F.150M	1238	PH-LEO (D-EHRA)	13.12.79	
G-LUCS	Colt 90A HAFB	1579		9. 8.89	To D-OAAH 8/93. Canx 5.8.93.
G-LUCY	PA-30-160 Twin Comanche B	30-1197	G-AVCP N8082Y	9.11.81	To VH-UOY 4/85. Canx 22.3.85.
G-LUED	Aero Designs Pulsar	PFA/202-12122		9. 3.92	
G-LUFF	Rotorway Exec 90	6191		24. 4.97	
G-LUFT	Putzer Elster C	011	G-BOPY D-EDEZ	31. 3.92	(Stored as D-EDEZ 9/96 at North Cotes/Cleethorpes)
G-LUGG	Colt 21A Cloudhopper HAFB	1446		12. 4.89	Canx 15.4.94 on sale to Czech Republic.
G-LUKE	Rutan LongEz	PFA/74A-10978		4. 7.84	
G-LUKY	Robinson R-44 Astro	0357		10. 7.97	
G-LULU	Grob G-109	6137		6. 9.82	
G-LUMA	Pearce Jabiru SK XL	PFA/274-13458		11. 5.99	
G-LUNA	PA-32RT-300T Turbo Lance II	32R-7987108	N2246Q	19. 3.79	
G-LUSC	Luscombe 8E Silvaire	3975	D-EFYR LN-PAT/(NC1248K)	1.11.84	(On rebuild 9/97)
G-LUSI	Temco Luscombe 8F Silvaire	6770	N838B	3.10.89	
G-LUST	Luscombe 8E Silvaire	6492	N2065B NC2065B	9.11.89	
G-LUXE	BAe 146 Srs.300 (Prototype Srs.300)	E3001	G-5-300 G-SSSH/(G-BIAD)	9. 4.87	
G-LYDA	Hoffmann H-36 Dimona	3515	OE-9213	5. 4.94	
G-LYDD	PA-31-310 Turbo Navajo	31-537	G-BBDU N6796L/(9V-BBT)	8. 5.89	Damaged when wing 'exploded' taxying for take-off on ferry-flight at Lydd on 17.7.91. (Fuselage stored 6/96) One wing used by PA-31-350 G-GRAM. Canx as WFU 30.3.93.
G-LYDE	Eiri PIK-20E	20217	(LN-...) G-LYDE	1. 8.79	To LN-GME 11/86. Canx 4.11.86.
G-LYND	PA-25-235 Pawnee (Rebuild of 25-2246 using new frame)	25-6309	SE-IXU G-BSFZ/G-ASFZ/N6672Z	8. 9.93	

Regn	Type	c/n	Previous identity	Regn date	Fate or immediate subsequent identity (if known)
G-LYNE	North American P-51D-20-NA Mustang	122-31887	41 Israeli DF/AF /N22B/44-72028	5.12.95	(On rebuild 12/95)
G-LYNK	CFM Streak Shadow Srs.DD	303-DD		12.10.98	
G-LYNN	PA-32RT-300 Lance II	32R-7985070	G-BGNY N30242	16. 7.80	To G-NROY 11/93. Canx.
G-LYNX	Westland WG.13 Lynx 800	WA/102	(ZA500) G-LYNX/ZB500	6.11.78	On display at International Helicopter Museum since 3/96 with serial ZB500. Canx as WFU 27.2.98.
G-LYON	Douglas DC-10-30 (Line No. 305)	47818	N537MD S2-ADB/N115WA/N519MD/PP-VMS/9V-SDG	11. 3.98	
G-LYPG	Pearce Jabiru UL	PFA/274A-13466		6. 7.99	
G-LYTE	Thunder Ax7-77 HAFB	1113		29. 9.87	

G-M

Regn	Type	c/n	Previous identity	Regn date	Fate or immediate subsequent identity (if known)
G-MAAC	Advanced Airship Corporation ANR-1	01		16. 1.89	(Sold incomplete 12/93)
G-MAAG	PA-30-160 Twin Comanche	30-279	G-ASOB	4. 4.85	To PH-COM 11/86. Canx 30.12.86.
G-MAAH	BAC One-Eleven Srs.488GH	BAC.259	PK-TAL G-BWES/PK-TAL/G-BWES/5N-UDE/LX-MAM/HZ-MAM	6.10.98	To VP-CDA 8/99. Canx 18.8.99.
G-MABE	Reims Cessna F.150L	1119	G-BLJP N962L	20. 6.97	
G-MABI	Reims Cessna F.150L	0931	G-BGOJ PH-KDA	22. 1.82	Made a forced landing ½ mile east of Staverton on 28.12.95. Canx as WFU 7.3.96.
G-MACD	Agusta-Bell 47G-3B1	1546	XT135	31.10.77	To HB-XHT 6/78. Canx 15.6.78.
G-MACH	SIAI-Marchetti SF.260	1-14	F-BUVY(2) OO-AHR(2)/OO-HAZ/(OO-RAB)/I-SJAD	29.10.80	
G-MACK	PA-28R-200 Cherokee Arrow II	28R-7635449	N5213F	18. 8.78	
G-MACS	Cassutt Racer IIIM (built by W.E. Hook)	200	N3790A	17. 3.94	Veered off the runway after landing at Breighton 3.3.95 & struck a hangar and severely damaged. Canx by CAA 18.7.95.
G-MACX	BAe Jetstream Srs.3102	641	OY-SVZ SE-IPD/G-REGB/SE-IPD/G-31-641	1. 6.95	Restored as OY-SVZ 8/95. Canx 3.7.95.
G-MADD	Robinson R-22 Beta	1633	G-MEAT	18. 1.93	To OH-HWB 5/97. Canx 13.5.97.
G-MADI	Cessna 310R II	310R-0544	N87396 G-MADI/N87396	10. 9.76	To G-TEDD 12/88. Canx.
G-MADM	Cameron O-105 HAFB	2595	G-SMAX	14. 4.92	To D-OILY 10/92. Canx 9.10.92.
G-MAFA	Reims Cessna F.406 Caravan II	0036	G-DFLT F-WZDZ	2. 6.98	
G-MAFB	Reims Cessna F.406 Caravan II	0080	F-WWSR	27. 5.98	
G-MAFE	Dornier 228-202K	8009	G-OALF G-MLDO/PH-SDO/D-IDON/D-CATI/SX-BHB/D-IDON/(PH-HAL)/D-IDON	21.12.92	
G-MAFF	PBN BN-2T Turbine Islander	2119	G-BJED	20. 4.82	
G-MAFI	Dornier 228-200	8115	D-CAAE	16. 2.87	
G-MAFS	Dornier 228-200	8084	D-ILAB (D-CLAB)	29. 8.86	To VP-FBK 1/87. Canx 30.1.87.
G-MAGC	Cameron Grand Illusion SS HAFB	4000		19. 1.95	
G-MAGG	Pitts S-1SE Special	PFA/09-10873		17. 3.83	
G-MAGI	Aerospatiale AS.350B Ecureuil	1232	G-BHLR	14. 7.80	To C-GTAM 10/84. Canx 10.10.84.
G-MAGL	Sky 77-24 HAFB	164		14. 7.99	
G-MAGS	Cessna 340A II	340A-0905	N2701D	7. 2.80	To G-XGBE 9/91. Canx.
G-MAGY	Aerospatiale AS.350B Ecureuil	1486	G-BIYC	8.10.81	To G-PROM 10/96. Canx.
G-MAHO	Aerospatiale AS.350B Ecureuil	1547		5. 2.82	Collided with a ship and crashed into the Humber Estuary on 14.3.83. Canx as destroyed 5.12.83.
G-MAIK	PA-34-220T Seneca V	3448078	N73BS	17.11.97	
G-MAIL	DHC.6-310 Twin Otter	703	(G-BHTO)	25. 7.80	To F-ODGL 12/82. Canx.
G-MAIN	Mainair Blade	1202-0689-7 & W1005		16. 6.99	
G-MAIR	PA-34-200T Seneca II	34-7970140	N3029R	15. 2.89	
G-MAJA	BAe Jetstream Srs.4100	41032	G-4-032	22. 4.94	
G-MAJB	BAe Jetstream Srs.4100	41018	G-BVKT N140MA/G-BVKT/G-4-018	1. 6.94	
G-MAJC	BAe Jetstream Srs.4100	41005	G-LOGJ	12. 9.94	
G-MAJD	BAe Jetstream Srs.4100	41006	G-WAWR	27. 3.95	
G-MAJE	BAe Jetstream Srs.4100	41007	G-LOGK	12. 9.94	
G-MAJF	BAe Jetstream Srs.4100	41008	G-WAWL	6. 2.95	
G-MAJG	BAe Jetstream Srs.4100	41009	G-LOGL	16. 8.94	
G-MAJH	BAe Jetstream Srs.4100	41010	G-WAYR	4. 4.95	
G-MAJI	BAe Jetstream Srs.4100	41011	G-WAND	20. 3.95	
G-MAJJ	BAe Jetstream Srs.4100	41024	G-WAFT G-4-024	27. 2.95	
G-MAJK	BAe Jetstream Srs.4100	41070	G-4-070	27. 7.95	
G-MAJL	BAe Jetstream Srs.4100	41087	G-4-087	1. 4.96	
G-MAJM	BAe Jetstream Srs.4100	41096	G-4-096	23. 9.96	
G-MAJR	DHC.1 Chipmunk 22 (Fuselage no. DHB/f/591)	C1/0699	WP805	25. 9.96	
G-MAJS	Airbus A.300B4-605R	604	(G-MONT) F-WWAX	26. 4.91	
G-MALA(1)	Gulfstream-American GA-7 Cougar	GA7-0058	G-BGCP N771GA	. .79R	Marks were painted on aircraft, but became G-BHBC on 23.8.79 instead.
G-MALA(2)	PA-28-181 Archer II	28-8190055	G-BIIU N82748	6. 3.81	
G-MALB	PBN BN-2A-26 Islander	2028	(G-BIUG)	21.10.86	To C-FCVK. Canx 23.9.88.

Regn	Type	c/n	Previous identity	Regn date	Fate or immediate subsequent identity (if known)
G-MALC	American Aviation AA-5 Traveler	AA5-0664	G-BCPM N6170A	19.11.79	
G-MALE	Airbus A.320-212	422	F-WWIP	. .94R	NTU - To G-OZBA 3/94. Canx.
G-MALI	PBN BN-2A-26 Islander	2011	G-DIVE (ZB503)/"ZA503"/G-DIVE/G-BEXA	15. 7.85	Restored as G-BEXA. Canx.
G-MALK	Reims Cessna F.172N Skyhawk II	1886	PH-SVS PH-AXF(3)	1. 7.81	Badly damaged in forced landing near Lochgilphead, Strathclyde on 23.7.97. Canx as destroyed 23.12.97. (Stored dismantled 12/98 at Edinburgh)
G-MALL	PA-32R-301 Saratoga SP	32R-8113020	G-ITDA N8310D	26. 8.93	To N200LL 9/94. Canx 29.7.94.
G-MALN	PADC BN-2A-26 Islander	3011	G-BLYO RP-C1850	9. 9.85	To J8-VAN 10/87. Canx 9.10.87.
G-MALS	Mooney M.20K (231)	25-0573	N1061T	16. 8.84	
G-MALT	Colt Flying Hop SS HAFB	1447		14. 4.89	
G-MAMA	Cessna 550 Citation II (Unit No.319)	550-0288	G-JETB N4564P/G-JETB/N6865C	13.11.88	Restored as G-JETB 10/89. Canx.
G-MAMC	Rotorway Exec 90	5057		24. 5.94	Substantially damaged when it overturned on landing at Cumbernauld on 22.9.98. (On rebuild 6/99)
G-MAMD	Beechcraft B200 Super King Air	BB-1549	N1069S	16. 7.99	
G-MAMO	Cameron V-77 HAFB	1616		17.11.87	
G-MANA	BAe ATP	2056	G-LOGH G-11-056	21. 2.94	
G-MANB	BAe ATP	2055	G-LOGG G-JATP/G-11-055	14. 9.94	
G-MANC	BAe ATP	2054	G-LOGF G-11-054	7.11.94	
G-MAND	PA-28-161 Warrior II	28-8116284	G-BRKT N8082Z	8. 3.93	
G-MANE	BAe ATP	2045	G-LOGB G-11-045	7. 6.94	
G-MANF	BAe ATP	2040	G-LOGA	19. 9.94	
G-MANG	BAe ATP	2018	G-LOGD (G-MANG)/G-LOGD/G-OLCD	22. 8.94	
G-MANH	BAe ATP	2017	G-LOGC G-OLCC	16.11.94	
G-MANI	Cameron V-90 HAFB	3038		8. 3.93	
G-MANJ	BAe ATP	2004	G-LOGE G-BMYL	6. 9.94	
G-MANK	BAe ATP	2002	G-MAUD G-BMYM	. .94R	NTU - Remained as G-MAUD. Canx.
G-MANL	BAe ATP	2003	G-ERIN G-BMYK	3.10.94	
G-MANM	BAe ATP	2005	G-OATP(2) G-BZWW/(N375AE)/G-BZWW	17.10.94	
G-MANN	Aerospatiale SA.341G Gazelle Srs.1	1295	G-BKLW N4DQ/N4QQ/N444JJ/N47316/F-WKQH	14. 4.86	
G-MANO	BAe ATP	2006	OK-TFN G-MANO/G-UIET/G-11-6/G-5-376/(N376AE)	28.11.94	
G-MANP	BAe ATP	2023	OK-VFO G-MANP/G-PEEL	28.10.94	
G-MANS	BAe 146 Srs.200	E2088	G-CHSR G-5-088	5. 5.94	
G-MANT	Cessna 210L Centurion II	210-60970	G-MAXY N5505V	22. 5.85	Struck a hedge in forced landing and crashed near Kidlington on 16.2.92. Canx by CAA 3.4.92. (On display on seafront crazy golf site 4/99 Great Yarmouth)
G-MANU	BAe ATP	2008	G-BUUP CS-TGA/G-11-8/(N378AE)	20. 8.97	
G-MANW	Tri-R Kis	PFA/239-12628		12. 9.96	
G-MANX	Clutton-Tabenor FRED Srs.II	PW.2 & PFA/29-10327		31. 5.78	(Crashed near Ronaldsway following engine failure on 30.10.81) (On rebuild Wellesbourne Mountford 7/90)
G-MAPP	Cessna 402B	402B-0583	D-INRH N1445G	16. 4.99	
G-MAPR	Beechcraft A36 Bonanza	E-2713	N55916	17. 9.92	
G-MAPS	Sky Flying Map SS HAFB	105		20. 7.98	
G-MARA	Airbus A.321-231	983	D-AVZB	31. 3.99	
G-MARC	Aerospatiale AS.350B Ecureuil	1629	G-BKHU	29.10.82	To HB-XOQ. Canx 11.4.94.
G-MARE	Schweizer 269C (300C)	S.1320		12. 8.88	
G-MARG	PA-31-350 Navajo Chieftain	31-8052078	N3580C	17. 6.81	To G-NABI 6/84. Canx.
G-MARI	PA-32R-301 Saratoga SP	32R-8313029	N8248H	6. 4.88	To G-MOVI 2/89. Canx.
G-MARK	Reims Cessna F.337H Super Skymaster (Wichita c/n 01822)	337-0085A		20. 1.78	To AP-BBT 2/84. Canx 30.1.84.
G-MARR	Cessna 421C Golden Eagle III	421C-0437	G-JTIE G-RBBE/N6678C	25.11.86	To A6-... (Reportedly as A6-MAR). Canx 11.8.94. (Noted at Dubai on 9.4.95 still marked as G-MARR)
G-MARS	Beechcraft 400 Beechjet	RJ-36	N3236Q G-RSRS/N3236Q/G-RSRS/N3236Q	25. 7.89	To I-RDSF 9/92. Canx 12.8.92.
G-MART	Cessna 208B Caravan I	208B-0584		15.11.96	To OY-PBF 4/97. Canx 15.4.97.
G-MARY	Cassutt Racer Special 1 (See G-TRUC)	2		14. 3.80	(Under construction 4/91) Canx by CAA 2.9.91.
G-MASA	Air & Space 18-A Gyrocopter	18-12	G-MELI N6106S	16. 5.91	Canx 18.4.94 on sale to Ireland.
G-MASC	SAN Jodel 150A Mascaret	37	F-BLDZ	1. 2.91	

Regn	Type	c/n	Previous identity	Regn date	Fate or immediate subsequent identity (if known)
G-MASF	PA-28-181 Cherokee Archer II	28-7790191	OY-EPT LN-NAP	24. 6.97	
G-MASH	Westland-Bell 47G-4A	WA/725	G-AXKU G-17-10	3.11.89	
G-MASK	Aerospatiale AS.355F1 Twin Squirrel	5326	G-PASK (F-GIVX)/I-DEDA	9. 5.96	Fatal crash in a field at Burnham, near Rochester, Kent on 26.7.98. Canx as destroyed 2.12.98.
G-MASL	Mooney M.20J (201)	24-3100	N1012U	20. 6.89	To CS-DBA. Canx 21.12.93.
G-MASS	Cessna 152 II	152-81605	G-BSHN N65541	6. 3.95	
G-MAST	PA-28R-180 Cherokee Arrow D	28R-30411	G-AZGM N4550J	23. 9.80	Crashed at Roughtally's Wood, near North Weald on 14.7.81. Canx by CAA 6.2.87. (Wreck in open store 12/93 Southend)
G-MASX	Masquito M.80	03		19. 6.98	
G-MASY	Masquito M.80	02		19. 6.98	
G-MASZ	Masquito M.58	01		29. 4.97	
G-MATE(1)	Moravan Zlin Z.50LS	0055		. .90R	NTU - To OK-TRO 9/91. Canx.
G-MATE(2)	Moravan Zlin Z.50LS	0068		26.10.90	
G-MATI	Stolp SA.200 Starduster Too (Constructed by R.B.Huntington)	1	N523H	13.10.87	Canx 19.10.95 on sale to USA.
G-MATP	BAe ATP	2001	(G-OATP)	15. 1.86	To G-PLXI 8/94. Canx.
G-MATS	Colt GA-42 Gas Airship	738	JA1009 G-MATS	11. 6.87	Restored as JA1009 /94. Canx.
G-MATT	Robin R.2160 Alpha Sport	97	G-BKRC F-BZAC/F-WZAC	7. 5.85	
G-MATZ	PA-28-140 Cherokee Cruiser E	28-7325200	G-BASI	11.12.90	
G-MAUD	BAe ATP	2002	(G-MANK) G-MAUD/G-BMYM	14.12.93	
G-MAUK	Colt 77A HAFB	901		16. 2.87	
G-MAUL(1)	Maule M.5-235C Lunar Rocket	7287C	N56352	. .80R	NTU - To G-BICX 2/81. Canx.
G-MAUL(2)	Maule M.5-235C Lunar Rocket	7316C	N56386	1. 5.80	Overturned in forced landing at Heilly, France on 30.3.81. Remains used for spares at Staverton. Canx as destroyed 21.12.83.
G-MAVE	Europa Avn Europa	PFA/247-24388		23. 9.94	Canx as destroyed 27.11.98.
G-MAVI	Robinson R-22 Beta	0960		7. 2.89	
G-MAWL	Maule M.4-210C Rocket	1065C	D-EEAO N2011U	29. 5.81	
G-MAXI	PA-34-200T Seneca II	34-7670150	N8658C	11. 2.81	
G-MAXW	Short SD.3-60 Var.100	SH3660	SE-KEY G-BLPY/G-14-3660	2. 8.91	To N413SA with new c/n SH3413. Canx 9.12.94.
G-MAXX	Lindstrand LBL Battery SS HAFB	621		16. 7.99	
G-MAXY	Cessna 210L Centurion II	210-60970	N5505V	17. 7.80	To G-MANT 5/85. Canx.
G-MAYA	Aero L-29 Delfin	394912	ES-YLO Estonian AF 64/Soviet AF 64 (red)	16. 6.98	
G-MAYO	PA-28-161 Warrior II	28-7716278	G-BFBG N38846	20. 2.81	
"G-MAZY"	DH.82A Tiger Moth (Composite ex Newark components and G-AMBB/T6801, although also reported as ex DE561, which was lost at sea in 1942)	-		-	(Rebuilt for static display and on loan to Newark Air Museum 2/99)
G-MBAA	Hiway Skytrike Mk.II/Excalibur	01		23. 4.81	
G-MBAB	Hovey WD-II Whing Ding II	MA.59 & PFA/116-10706		26. 5.81	
G-MBAC	MEA Pterodactyl Srs.2	DG-1		2. 6.81	Fatal crash at Rudgwick, near Horsham, Sussex on 29.7.81. Canx as destroyed 2.8.84.
G-MBAD	Weedhopper JC-24A	0382		3. 6.81	
G-MBAE	Ultraflight Lazair	A42-109 & PFA/110-10659		9. 6.81	Canx by CAA 13.6.90.
G-MBAF(1)	R.J. Swift 3	1		23. 6.81	Canx by CAA 24.6.87 - catching up.
G-MBAF(2)	Southdown Puma Sprint 440	P.455		. 6.81	To G-MVAF 6/87. Canx.
G-MBAG	Wheeler (Skycraft) Scout	BJ-1		15. 6.81	Canx by CAA 13.6.90.
G-MBAH	Harker D.H. Microlight	HA-4		18. 6.81	Not completed. Canx as destroyed 12.10.88.
G-MBAI	Ultrasports Tripacer 250/Solar Wings Typhoon	T1180-53		25. 6.81	Canx by CAA 13.6.90.
G-MBAJ	Chargus T.250/Hiway Demon	CG.1		26. 6.81	Canx by CAA 1.9.93.
G-MBAK	Eurowing Spirit	JP.1		26. 6.81	Canx by CAA 13.6.90.
G-MBAL	Ultrasports Tripacer 250/Hiway Demon	HD.51		29. 6.81	
G-MBAM	Wheeler (Skycraft) Scout II	0384W		3. 7.81	Canx by CAA 6.9.94.
G-MBAN	American Aerolights Eagle	2788		6. 7.81	Canx as WFU 11.7.88.
G-MBAO	Rotec Rally 2B	RM-1		16. 7.81	Crashed at Popham on 13.3.83. Canx by CAA 1.8.83.
G-MBAP	Rotec Rally 2B	PL-1		16. 7.81	Canx by CAA 10.1.91. (Stored 1/91)
G-MBAR	Wheeler (Skycraft) Scout	389W		8. 7.81	
G-MBAS	Ultrasports Tripacer 250/Solar Wings Typhoon	T181-63		8. 7.81	Canx as WFU 10.2.88.
G-MBAT	Hiway Skytrike/Super Scorpion	250/8		9. 7.81	Canx as WFU 9.5.86.
G-MBAU	Hiway Skytrike/Super Scorpion	160/7		9. 7.81	Canx as WFU 12.2.97.
G-MBAV	Weedhopper JC-24	UK.1		10. 7.81	Canx by CAA 13.6.90.
G-MBAW	Pterodactyl Ptraveler	017		14. 7.81	DBR on 23.10.83. Canx.
G-MBAX	Hiway Skytrike 250	25-P7		15. 7.81	Canx by CAA 13.6.90.
G-MBAY	Wheeler (Skycraft) Scout	341		21. 7.81	Canx by CAA 13.5.86.
G-MBAZ	Rotac Rally 2B	WSS-1		23. 7.81	Canx.
G-MBBA	Ultraflight Lazair III	259		3. 8.81	Canx 8.2.93 on sale to Canada.
G-MBBB	Wheeler (Skycraft) Scout II	0388W		3. 8.81	

Regn	Type	c/n	Previous identity	Regn date	Fate or immediate subsequent identity (if known)
G-MBBC	Chargus T.250/Southdown Lightning	T.250/09		10. 8.81	Canx as WFU 18.10.88.
G-MBBD	Pterodactyl Ptraveler	RJP-01		10. 8.81	Canx by CAA 13.6.90.
G-MBBE	Striplin Sky Ranger	325		12. 8.81	Canx by CAA 13.6.90.
G-MBBF	Chargus Titan 38/TS440	T.01		13. 8.81	Canx by CAA 13.6.90.
G-MBBG	Weedhopper JC-24B	FB-1		26. 8.81	Canx as TWFU 17.12.91.
G-MBBH	Mainair Tri-Flyer/Flexiform Sealander 160	FS-1		3. 9.81	Canx by CAA 9.6.93.
G-MBBI	Ultraflight Mirage Mk.II	M81000		8. 9.81	Canx 27.4.92 on sale to Ireland.
G-MBBJ(1)	Windsor Motorglider	WHG.001		. .81R	NTU - Canx.
G-MBBJ(2)	Hiway Demon (C/n is engine no)	80-00029		15. 2.82	Canx by CAA 1.2.95.
G-MBBK	Ultraflight Mirage	MGS-1		10. 9.81	Sold on 16.6.83 & dismantled for spares. Canx as PWFU 10.8.83.
G-MBBL	Southdown Lightning 170	L170P/308		11. 9.81	Canx by CAA 13.6.90.
G-MBBM	Eipper Quicksilver MX	10960		11. 9.81	
G-MBBN	American Aerolights Eagle (C/n duplicates G-MJCX)	2759		11. 9.81	Canx by CAA 6.9.94.
G-MBBO	Rotec Rally 2B	AJD-1		11. 9.81	Canx by CAA 13.6.90.
G-MBBP	Chotia Weedhopper	GLM-1		14. 9.81	Canx as WFU 27.9.89.
G-MBBR	Weedhopper JC-24B	UK7-JW001		14. 9.81	Canx by CAA 23.4.90.
G-MBBS	Chargus T.250/Vortex	209		15. 9.81	Canx by CAA 13.6.90.
G-MBBT	Ultrasports Tripacer 330 Srs.1/ Solar Wings Typhoon	81-92		16. 9.81	Canx as WFU 20.4.88.
G-MBBU	Southdown Puma DS 440 (Originally regd as Southdown Savage 195)	S.195/365		17. 9.81	Canx by CAA 24.1.95. To France as 38-AQ as Aerosport Puma.
G-MBBV	Rotec Rally 2B	BA-10T		17. 9.81	Canx as destroyed 3.4.90.
G-MBBW	Hiway Skytrike 160/Flexiform Hilander (Originally regd with c/n FS-1 - until 31.1.84)	FS-3		18. 9.81	Crashed into trees on take-off at Penrallt Eifid, Dyfed on 1.5.94. Canx as WFU 21.7.94.
G-MBBX	Chargus T.250/Flexiform Sealander (Originally regd as Chargus Skytrike/Flexiform Sealander with same c/n)	SAG-1		18. 9.81	Canx by CAA 6.9.94.
G-MBBY	Ultrasports Tripacer/Flexiform Solo Sealander	JEH-1		22. 9.81	
G-MBBZ	Volmer VJ-24W	7		23. 9.81	Canx as WFU 29.11.95. (Stored 10/97 at Old Sarum)
G-MBCA	Chargus T.250/Cyclone	P.1		24. 9.81	Canx as WFU 22.2.94.
G-MBCB	Southdown Lightning	PGH.1		25. 9.81	Canx as WFU 7.9.87.
G-MBCC	Mainair Tri-Flyer/Flexiform Sealander	002-781		25. 9.81	Canx by CAA 14.6.83. Trike unit to G-MJZH in 5/83. Wing sold in Lancashire.
G-MBCD	La Mouette Atlas	OLA-1081		28. 9.81	Canx by CAA 6.9.94.
G-MBCE	American Aerolights Eagle Rainbow	E.3990		29. 9.81	Canx by CAA 24.1.95.
G-MBCF	Pterodactyl Ascender/Fledgling (Also quoted as Ptraveler)	772		30. 9.81	Canx as destroyed 5.1.95.
G-MBCG	Ultrasports Tripacer T.250/Solar Wings Typhoon	T481-121P		30. 9.81	Canx by CAA 6.9.94.
G-MBCH	Hiway Skytrike II	RC-1		30. 9.81	Canx 4.7.84 on sale to Denmank.
G-MBCI	Hiway Skytrike II/Solar Wings Typhoon	T481-119P		30. 9.81	
G-MBCJ	Mainair Tri-Flyer/Solar Wings Typhoon S	JRN-1		30. 9.81	
G-MBCK	Eipper Quicksilver MX	GWR-10962		30. 9.81	
G-MBCL	Hiway Skytrike 160/Solar Wings Typhoon (C/n probably T1181-307)(Originally regd as Mainair Sports Tri-Flyer/Hiway Demon with c/n 001-581 & LD17D; Wing changed in 1982, Trike unit changed in 1983)	2332 & T1181-07		30. 9.81	
G-MBCM	Hiway Skystrike/Demon 175	LR-17D		1.10.81	Canx by CAA 9.2.93.
G-MBCN	Hiway Skystrike/Super Scorpion	MJH-181		1.10.81	Canx as WFU 1.10.93.
G-MBCO	UAS Storm Buggy/Flexiform Sealander	PB-1		2.10.81	Canx by CAA 20.7.83.
G-MBCP	Mainair Tri-Flyer 250/Flexiform Sealander	PB-2 & 043-231281		2.10.81	Canx by CAA 13.6.90.
G-MBCR	Ultraflight Mirage	100		5.10.81	Canx by CAA 6.9.94.
G-MBCS	American Aerolights Eagle	2708		5.10.81	Canx as WFU 3.4.90.
G-MBCT	American Aerolights Eagle	3200		5.10.81	Canx as WFU 3.4.90.
G-MBCU	American Aerolights Eagle Amphibian	3181		5.10.81	
G-MBCV	Hiway Skytrike/Southdown Lightning	L195/126		5.10.81	Canx by CAA 23.6.93.
G-MBCW	Hiway Skytrike/Demon 175	CFSE-1		6.10.81	Canx as WFU 3.9.91.
G-MBCX	Hornet 250/Airwave Nimrod 165	H090 & 0090 LJH		12.10.81	
G-MBCY	American Aerolights Eagle	2967		12.10.81	Canx by CAA 13.6.90.
G-MBCZ	Hiway Skytrike 160/Chargus Vortex	312		12.10.81	Canx by CAA 20.1.92.
G-MBDA	Rotec Rally 2B	BA-045		12.10.81	Canx as destroyed 3.4.90.
G-MBDB	Solar Wings Typhoon	DJS-1		12.10.81	Canx by CAA 13.6.90.
G-MBDC	Hornet/Skyhook Cutlass	H0140		13.10.81	Canx by CAA 13.10.93.
G-MBDD	Hiway Skytrike/Demon 175 (Regd with c/n MM175D)(Originally regd as a Skyhook/La Mouette Atlas c/n JCRL-1, then with c/n 260A-139823) (Reported as Mainair Tri-Flyer in sale advert .97)	MM-17D		14.10.81	Canx by CAA 6.10.97.

Regn	Type	c/n	Previous identity	Regn date	Fate or immediate subsequent identity (if known)
G-MBDE	Sharp & Sons Tartan/Flexiform Solo Striker	FS-2		15.10.81	
	(Originally regd as Flexiform Powerwing Skytrike with c/n FS-1 - Trike/Wing & c/n changed in 12/82) (Now regd as Ultrasports Tripacer)				
G-MBDF	Rotec Rally 2B	BTJ-02		15.10.81	Canx as WFU 7.1.92.
G-MBDG	Eurowing Goldwing	F.20		19.10.81	
G-MBDH	Mainair Tri-Flyer/Hiway Demon (C/n conflicts with G-MBDK)	007-881		19.10.81	Canx by CAA 5.12.95.
G-MBDI	Flexiform Sealander	KB-1		2.11.81	No Permit believed issued. Canx by CAA 17.2.99.
G-MBDJ	Mainair Tri-Flyer/Flexiform Sealander	LHP-1		19.10.81	
G-MBDK	Mainair Tri-Flyer/Solar Wings Typhoon	007-17881		19.10.81	Canx by CAA 13.6.90.
	(Originally regd as with c/n DJA-1)(C/n conflicts with G-MBDH)				
G-MBDL	Striplin (AES) Lone Ranger	109		21.10.81	Canx by CAA 13.6.90. (Stored in poor condition 4/96 Sunderland)
G-MBDM	Southdown Sigma	SST/001		26.10.81	
G-MBDN	Hornet/La Mouette Atlas (Originally regd with c/n H0010)	H030		30.10.81	Canx by CAA 27.10.93.
G-MBDO	UAS Storm Buggy/Flexiform Sealander	C167 & DM823S		26.10.81	Canx by CAA 18.6.91.
	(Originally regd as Ultrasports Tripacer with c/n 80-00280)				
G-MBDP	Hiway Skytrike 250/Flexiform Sealander	ANB-01		18.11.81	Canx by CAA 13.6.90.
G-MBDR	UAS Storm Buggy/Solar Wings Typhoon I	007 & T781-201L		4.11.81	Canx by CAA 6.9.94.
	(Wing c/n conflicts with G-MMPK which was probably a different aircraft)				
G-MBDS	Mitchell Wing B-10	P753		29.10.81	Converted to a Hang-Glider. Canx as WFU 28.3.83.
G-MBDT	American Aerolights Eagle	E2928		3.11.81	Canx as WFU 14.2.89.
G-MBDU	Chargus Titan 38/TS440	C08		28.10.81	Canx by CAA 5.12.95.
G-MBDV	Pterodactyl Ptraveller (Incorporates wing from G-MBHY 8/82)	DJT-1		28.10.81	Canx as WFU 19.10.87.
G-MBDW	Ultrasports Tripacer Srs.A	HU-1		21.10.81	Canx by CAA 6.9.94.
G-MBDX	Electraflyer Eagle	AL-1		30.10.81	Canx by CAA 6.9.94.
G-MBDY	Weedhopper 2	GNM-01		17. 2.82	Canx by CAA 13.6.90.
G-MBDZ	Eipper Quicksilver MX	MR-11027		2.11.81	
G-MBEA	Hornet/Airwave Nimrod	H130		3.11.81	Canx as WFU 31.1.89.
G-MBEB	Hiway Skytrike 250 Mk.II/Super Scorpion	RM-1		3.11.81	The Trike unit was sold to the Royal School of Military Engineering Hang Gliding Club in 1982 - it is unclear if there was a wing! Canx by CAA 18.10.93.
G-MBEC	Hiway Super Scorpion Mk.II	CSW-1		4.11.81	Canx by CAA 13.6.90.
G-MBED	Chargus Titan 38/TS440	HBA-1		5.11.81	Canx by CAA 22.7.87.
G-MBEE	Hiway Skytrike 160/Super Scorpion 1IC	67		5.11.81	Canx by CAA 24.1.95.
G-MBEF	Eipper Quicksilver MX	PL-1		6.11.81	Canx by CAA 13.6.90.
G-MBEG	Eipper Quicksilver MX	PL-2 & 10682		6.11.81	Canx by CAA 23.1.90.
G-MBEH	Electraflyer Eagle	PL-3		6.11.81	Canx as WFU 9.8.84.
G-MBEI	Electraflyer Eagle	PL-4		6.11.81	Canx as WFU 9.8.84.
G-MBEJ	Electraflyer Eagle	PL-5		6.11.81	Canx by CAA 3.2.92.
G-MBEK	Electraflyer Eagle	PL-6		6.11.81	Canx as WFU 9.8.84.
G-MBEL	Electraflyer Eagle	PL-7		6.11.81	Canx as WFU 14.9.89.
G-MBEM	Electraflyer Eagle	PL-8		6.11.81	Canx as WFU 9.8.84.
G-MBEN	Eipper Quicksilver MXI	PL-9 & 5395		6.11.81	Canx as WFU 14.1.92.
G-MBEO	Flexiform Sealander	HWW-01		9.11.81	Canx by CAA 17.5.90.
G-MBEP	American Aerolights Eagle 215B	2877		9.11.81	Canx as WFU 16.5.96. (On display 3/98 Caernarfon)
G-MBER	Skyhook TR1	TR1/1		10.11.81	Canx as WFU 13.10.88.
G-MBES	Skyhook TR2/Cutlass	TR2/18		10.11.81	Exemption expired 28.2.87. Canx by CAA 10.2.87.
G-MBET	MEA Mistral Trainer	MEA.103		10.11.81	
G-MBEU	Chargus T.250/Hiway Demon	T.250-06		10.11.81	
G-MBEV	Chargus Titan 38	LUFC-01		11.11.81	
G-MBEW	UAS Storm Buggy/Chargus Cyclone (Regd as Solar Buggy)	NW-01		11.11.81	Canx by CAA 13.6.90.
G-MBEX	Hiway Skytrike T.160/Demon	PJ-1		11.11.81	WFU (reason unknown) on 16.11.82. Canx as WFU 6.1.83.
G-MBEY	Hiway Skytrike 160/Super Scorpion C Mk.1	AE.1		11.11.81	Skytrike sold in Jersey 15.4.83, the Super Scorpion Wing sold to Midland Microlight Aircraft for use as a Hang-Glider. Canx by CAA 17.6.83.
G-MBEZ	Pterodactyl Ptraveller II	PAS-01		12.11.81	Canx by CAA 13.6.90.
G-MBFA	Hiway Skytrike 250/Super Scorpion	IGSC-01	(G-MBWJ) G-MBFA	12.11.81	Canx by CAA 26.2.93.
G-MBFB	Skyhook Powertrike	T3 10/81		12.11.81	Crashed on take off from Broxton, Cheshire on 24.7.82. Canx by CAA 4.11.82.
G-MBFC	Hiway Skytrike/Birdman Cherokee	CH220171679		18.11.81	WFU (reason unknown) on 2.7.83. Canx as WFU 6.7.83.
G-MBFD	Gemini Hummingbird	64		13.11.81	Canx by CAA 13.6.90.
G-MBFE	American Aerolights Eagle Rainbow (C/n duplicates G-MBNM)	3392		23.11.81	Canx by CAA 26.9.90.
G-MBFF	Southern Aerosports Scorpion	HR.01		16.11.81	Type refused certification. Canx as WFU 22.10.86.
G-MBFG	Skyhook TR1/Sabre	TR1/2		16.11.81	Canx as WFU 14.9.93.
G-MBFH	Hiway Skytrike	RMB.1		16.11.81	Canx by CAA 13.6.90.
G-MBFI	Hiway Skytrike II/Solar Wings Typhoon	BJR.1		16.11.81	Canx by CAA 4.6.90.
G-MBFJ	Chargus T.250/Solar Wings Typhoon	AWK.1		16.11.81	Canx by CAA 16.9.93.

Regn	Type	c/n	Previous identity	Regn date	Fate or immediate subsequent identity (if known)
G-MBFK	Hiway Skytrike/Demon 175	LR17D		16.11.81	
G-MBFL	Hiway Skytrike/Demon	27/2U17D		16.11.81	Canx by CAA 13.6.90.
G-MBFM	Hiway Skytrike	GPK.1		16.11.81	Canx by CAA 3.2.92.
G-MBFN	Hiway Skytrike II/Demon	RET-01		17.11.81	Canx as WFU 18.4.90.
	(Originally regd as Hornet/Hiway Demon - Wing exchanged in 10/82)				
G-MBFO	Eipper Quicksilver MX	MLD-01		17.11.81	
G-MBFP	Southern Aerosports Scorpion	A0004		17.11.81	Canx as WFU 4.12.86.
G-MBFR	American Aerolights Eagle	WGB-01		17.11.81	Canx by CAA 13.6.90.
G-MBFS	American Aerolights Eagle	RF-01		19.11.81	Canx as WFU 24.5.90.
G-MBFT	Southdown Sigma 12 Meter	21		19.11.81	Canx by CAA 13.6.90.
G-MBFU	Ultrasports Tripacer/Hiway Demon	THJP-01		23.11.81	Canx by CAA 30.1.96.
G-MBFV	Hiway Skytrike/Airwave Comet	RW-01		23.11.81	Canx as WFU 18.4.90.
G-MBFW	Hiway Skytrike	BB-01		24.11.81	Canx by CAA 27.5.85.
G-MBFX	Hiway Skytrike 250/Solar Wings Typhoon	NW-01 & T281-78L		24.11.81	Canx by CAA 20.5.97.
G-MBFY	Ultraflight Mirage II	115		24.11.81	
G-MBFZ	MSS Eurowing Goldwing	MSS-01		25.11.81	
G-MBGA	Mainair Tri-Flyer/Flexiform Solo Sealander	001		25.11.81	
	(Originally regd as Mainair Tri-Flyer/Solar Wings Typhoon with same c/n)				
G-MBGB	American Aerolights Eagle	JCM-01		25.11.81	Canx as PWFU 2.3.99.
G-MBGC	Not allotted.				
G-MBGD	Pterodactyl Oshkosh 430D Replica	CW-01		26.11.81	Canx by CAA 13.6.90.
G-MBGE	Hiway Skytrike I/Super Scorpion	SS2-38832		26.11.81	Canx by CAA 13.6.90.
G-MBGF	Twamley Trike/Birdman Cherokee	RWT-01		26.11.81	
G-MBGG	Solar Wings Pegasus/Charger Forger	T783-866L		27.11.81	Canx as WFU 30.5.90.
	(Originally regd as Chargus/Titan 38 with c/n AGD-01)				
G-MBGH	Chargus T.250	AGD-02		27.11.81	Canx by CAA 23.4.90.
G-MBGI	Chargus Titan 38	AGD-03		27.11.81	Canx by CAA 23.4.90.
G-MBGJ	Hiway Skytrike Mk.II/Demon	25T5 & PFL-01		27.11.81	Canx by CAA 26.2.88.
G-MBGK	Electraflyer Eagle	RJO-01		30.11.81	Canx by CAA 31.3.89.
G-MBGL	Flexiform Sealander	HF-1		1.12.81	Canx as WFU 25.10.88.
G-MBGM	Eipper Quicksilver MX	RG.10989		1.12.81	Canx by CAA 13.6.90.
G-MBGN	Weedhopper Model A	0061		1.12.81	Canx by CAA 13.6.90.
G-MBGO	American Aerolights Eagle	4444		25.11.81	Canx by CAA 13.6.90.
	(Originally regd with c/n IMW-01)				
G-MBGP	Hiway Skytrike/Solar Wings Typhoon	T481-141L		1.12.81	
G-MBGR	Eurowing Goldwing	EW-24 & SWA01		2.11.81	Canx by CAA 15.9.93.
	(Originally regd as Catto Goldwing Canard with same c/n)				
G-MBGS	Rotec Rally 2B	PCB-1		2.12.81	
G-MBGT	American Aerolights Eagle	3799		2.12.81	Canx by CAA 9.6.93.
G-MBGU	Chargus Trike/Solar Wings Typhoon	IDBH-1		2.12.81	Crashed & DBR on 17.4.83. Canx as WFU 22.7.83.
G-MBGV	Skyhook TR1/Cutlass	TR1/6		3.12.81	Canx by CAA 6.9.94.
G-MBGW	Hiway Skytrike/Super Scorpion	GWRC-1 & 23		3.12.81	Canx as WFU 22.11.95. (Stored 10/95)
G-MBGX	Southdown Lightning DS	RBDB-1		7.12.81	
G-MBGY	Hiway Skytrike/Demon	WH-1		7.12.81	No Permit issued. Canx by CAA 10.2.87.
G-MBGZ	American Aerolights Eagle	3420		7.12.81	Canx by CAA 13.6.90.
G-MBHA	Sheffield Trident/Flexiform Sealander	8112		9.12.81	Canx by CAA 1.7.93.
	(Trike also reported as Mainair Tri-Flyer)				
G-MBHB	Centrair Moto Delta G-11	002		29.12.81	Canx by CAA 13.6.90.
G-MBHC	Chargus T.250/Southdown Lightning	T.250/011		9.12.81	Canx by CAA 6.9.94.
G-MBHD	Chargus T.250/Hiway Vulcan	DK-1		17.12.81	Canx by CAA 6.9.93.
G-MBHE	American Aerolights Eagle	4210		18.12.81	
G-MBHF	Pterodactyl Ptraveler	DBG-01		22.12.81	Canx by CAA 13.6.90.
G-MBHG	UAS Solar Storm Buggy	6172333		18.12.81	Canx 15.2.83 on sale to Ireland.
G-MBHH	Hiway Skytrike Mk.II/Flexiform Sealander	GJN-01		22.12.81	Canx by CAA 5.12.95.
G-MBHI	Ultrasports Tripacer 250/La Mouette Atlas 18	PTA-1		29.12.81	Canx by CAA 13.6.90.
G-MBHJ	Hornet 250/Skyhook Cutlass C	GH-1		30.12.81	Canx by CAA 24.1.95. (Stored 12/97)
	(Originally regd as Cutlass B with same c/n)				
G-MBHK	Mainair Tri-Flyer 250/Flexiform Solo Striker	EB-1 & 036-241181		30.12.81	
G-MBHL	Skyhook Skytrike	S-187		30.12.81	Canx by CAA 13.6.90.
G-MBHM	Weedhopper	JH-01		30.12.81	Canx by CAA 13.6.90.
G-MBHN	Weedhopper	SH-01		30.12.81	Canx by CAA 13.6.90.
G-MBHO	Skyhook Super Sabre	AB-01		31.12.81	Canx by CAA 13.6.90.
G-MBHP	American Aerolights Eagle II	2986		31.12.81	Canx by CAA 3.2.92.
G-MBHR	Hiway Skytrike/Flexiform Wing	YPO-01		31.12.81	Canx by CAA 13.6.90.
G-MBHS	Flexiform Skytrike	MVR/JH-01		4. 1.82	Sold on 5.12.82. Canx by CAA 12.4.83.

Regn	Type	c/n	Previous identity	Regn date	Fate or immediate subsequent identity (if known)
G-MBHT	Chargus T.250/Southdown Lightning (Originally regd as Southdown Emu with same c/n)	T.250/007		5. 1.82	Canx by CAA 15.12.89.
G-MBHU	Hiway Skytrike/Flexiform Hilander	RMS-01		5. 1.82	Canx by CAA 5.3.93.
G-MBHV	Pterodactyl Ptraveller	HP-01		6. 1.82	Canx as WFU 18.10.88.
G-MBHW	American Aerolights Eagle	MECF-01		5. 1.82	Canx by CAA 24.1.95.
G-MBHX	Pterodactyl Ptraveler	WFT-01		5. 1.82	Canx as WFU 10.6.97.
G-MBHY	Pterodactyl Ptraveler	TCNC-01		6. 1.82	Dived into ground at Long Marston Aerodrome on 15.5.82 and destroyed - sold to a new owner at Aldershot for spares. Canx as WFU 23.7.82. Wing to G-MBDV in 8/82.
G-MBHZ	Pterodactyl Ptraveler	TD-01		6. 1.82	
G-MBIA	Hiway Skytrike/Flexiform Sealander	6172349/336		6. 1.82	
G-MBIB	Mainair Tri-Flyer 250/Flexiform Sealander	030-241181 & 6320		6. 1.82	Crashed at Holker Hall, Cumbria on 12.4.82. Canx by CAA 13.6.90.
G-MBIC	Maxair (Hill) Hummer 250TX	2X-2514F & BW-01		7. 1.82	Canx by CAA 6.9.94.
G-MBID	American Aerolights Eagle	LFL-01	(G-MBVN) G-MBID	7. 1.82	Canx by CAA 9.6.93.
G-MBIE	Mainair Tri-Flyer 250/Flexiform Striker	020-151081 & FML-01		8. 1.82	Canx by CAA 13.6.90.
G-MBIF	American Aerolights Eagle	FML-02		8. 1.82	Canx by CAA 13.6.90.
G-MBIG	American Aerolights Eagle	3018		6. 1.82	Canx by CAA 13.6.90.
G-MBIH	Hiway Skytrike/Flexiform	FR.S0010		11. 1.82	Canx by CAA 13.6.90.
G-MBII	Hiway Skytrike	21Y6		11. 1.82	Canx as WFU 13.9.93.
G-MBIJ	Hiway Skytrike/Solar Wings Typhoon	DJ-01		11. 1.82	Canx by CAA 26.8.83 - the units having been sold separately (and anonymously) in 8/83.
G-MBIK	Wheeler (Skycraft) Scout	DKM-01 & 387W		11. 1.82	Canx by CAA 18.4.90.
G-MBIL	Southern Aerosports Scorpion 1	A0013		11. 1.82	Canx by CAA 22.7.87.
G-MBIM	American Aerolights Sea Eagle	3205		12. 1.82	Canx as WFU 4.6.90.
G-MBIN	Wheeler (Skycraft) Sea Scout	364		12. 1.82	Canx by CAA 13.6.90.
G-MBIO	American Aerolights Eagle 215B	E.4007-Z		12. 1.82	
G-MBIP	Gemini Hummingbird	069		20. 1.82	Canx by CAA 13.6.90.
G-MBIR	Gemini Hummingbird	070		20. 1.82	Canx by CAA 13.6.90.
G-MBIS	American Aerolights Eagle	3182		18. 1.82	Canx by CAA 13.6.90.
G-MBIT	Hiway Skytrike 250/Demon	2501		18. 1.82	
G-MBIU	Wills Trike/Hiway Super Scorpion	MEW-01		18. 1.82	Canx by CAA 5.12.95.
G-MBIV	Hiway Skytrike/Flexiform Sealander (Originally regd as Flexform Trike 440)	EJPTO-01		18. 1.82	Canx by CAA 7.7.92.
G-MBIW	Hiway Skytrike/Mainair Sports Tri-Flyer	019-137081		19. 1.82	Sold on 17.4.82. Canx by CAA 20.8.82.
G-MBIX	Ultrasports Tripacer/Southdown Puma DS (Lightning)	81-00087		19. 1.82	Canx as destroyed 19.7.89.
G-MBIY	Ultrasports Tripacer/Southdown Puma 1 (Lightning Phase II)	81-00067 & 330 & L170-439		19. 1.82	
G-MBIZ	Mainair Tri-Flyer/Hiway Vulcan	039-251181 & SD9V		20. 1.82	
G-MBJA	Eurowing Goldwing	EW-34		20. 1.82	
G-MBJB	Hiway Skytrike Mk.II	2557		20. 1.82	Canx 1.11.88 on sale to Ireland.
G-MBJC	American Aerolights Eagle	3351		21. 1.82	Canx by CAA 13.6.90.
G-MBJD	American Aerolights Eagle 215B	4169		21. 1.82	
G-MBJE	Ultrasports Tripacer 250/Airwave Nimrod (Originally assembled with Chargus Vortex 120 wing but exchanged in 3/82)	MEG-01		22. 1.82	Canx by CAA 2.9.88.
G-MBJF	Hiway Skytrike Mk.II/Vulcan (C/n is engine no)	80-00099		22. 1.82	
G-MBJG	Chargus T.250/Airwave Nimrod	UP CMT165045		25. 1.82	
G-MBJH	Chargus Titan	07		25. 1.82	Canx as WFU 18.10.88.
G-MBJI	Southern Aerosports Scorpion	002		25. 1.82	Type refused certification. Canx as destroyed 22.10.86.
G-MBJJ	Ultrasports Mirage Mk.II	125		5. 1.82	Canx by CAA 13.6.90.
G-MBJK	American Aerolights Eagle	2742		16. 1.82	
G-MBJL	Hornet/Airwave Nimrod	JSRM-01		26. 1.82	
G-MBJM	Striplin Lone Ranger	LR-81-00138		26. 1.82	
G-MBJN	American Aerolights Eagle	MEC-01		26. 1.82	
G-MBJO	Birdman Cherokee Mk.I	CHL-5100680		28. 1.82	No Permit believed issued. Canx by CAA 15.3.99.
G-MBJP	Southdown Trike/Hiway Demon (Originally regd as Hiway Skytrike/Demon with same c/n)	LAS-01		28. 1.82	Canx by CAA 21.3.90.
G-MBJR	American Aerolights Eagle	3528		28. 1.82	Canx by Caa 14.7.88.
G-MBJS	Hiway Skytrike/Solar Wings Typhoon SII (Originally regd as Mainair Tri-Flyer 250 with c/n TWH-01, then with c/n 041-28981 which is out-of-sequence and may be 014-28981)(Later rebuild with Trike from G-MWXE)	26X7 & T383-731L		28. 1.82	Canx by CAA 24.1.95. (Extant 10/97)
G-MBJT	Hiway Skytrike 250 Mk.II	25P1		29. 1.82	Canx as WFU 20.1.88.
G-MBJU	American Aerolights Eagle (Originally regd with c/n 3300)	E.2942		16. 2.82	Permit expired 10.8.93. Canx by CAA 17.4.97.

Regn	Type	c/n	Previous identity	Regn date	Fate or immediate subsequent identity (if known)
G-MBJV	Rotec Rally 2B	CJGW-01		1. 2.82	Canx by CAA 13.6.90.
G-MBJW	Hiway Demon Mk.II	VB-19D		1. 2.82	Canx by CAA 13.6.90.
G-MBJX	Hiway Super Scorpion	MM-01		2. 2.82	Canx by CAA 13.6.90.
G-MBJY	Rotec Rally 2B	CRVH-01		2. 2.82	Canx by CAA 13.6.90.
G-MBJZ	Eurowing Catto CP.16	022		2. 2.82	Canx by CAA 5.12.84.
G-MBKA	MEA Mistral Trainer	001		4. 2.82	Canx by CAA 24.1.95.
G-MBKB	MEA Pterodactyl Ptraveler	47		3. 2.82	Canx by CAA 13.6.90. (Stored 8/92)
G-MBKC	Southdown Lightning Phase I	DAI-01		3. 2.82	Canx by CAA 23.3.99.
G-MBKD	UAS Solar Buggy 340/Chargus Vortex 120P (Originally regd as Chargus T.250 with same c/n - Trike changed in 3/84)	TK-01		3. 2.82	Canx by CAA 6.10.93.
G-MBKE	Eurowing Catto CP-16	RST-01		3. 2.82	Canx by CAA 13.6.90.
G-MBKF	Striplin Sky Ranger	PRB-01		4. 2.82	Canx as WFU 26.7.90.
G-MBKG	Batchelor-Hunt Skytrike	BHM-01		4. 2.82	Canx by CAA 24.1.95.
G-MBKH	Milward Trike/Southdown Lightning DS (Originally regd as Southdown Skytrike with same c/n)	PHM-01		5. 2.82	Canx by CAA 24.1.95.
G-MBKI	Solar Wings Typhoon	STJ-01		8. 2.82	Canx by CAA 13.6.90.
G-MBKJ	Chargus Titan 38/TS440	16CH/80-00075		5. 2.82	Canx by CAA 13.6.90.
G-MBKK	Pterodactyl Ascender	TBD-01		10. 2.82	Canx by CAA 13.6.90.
G-MBKL	Hiway Skytrike/Demon	DCB-01		8. 2.82	Canx as WFU 27.10.88.
G-MBKM	Not allocated.				
G-MBKN	Chargus Titan 38/TS440	14/80-00041		11. 2.82	Canx as WFU 30.5.90.
G-MBKO	Chargus Titan 38/TS440	13/80-00047		11. 2.82	Canx as WFU 30.5.90.
G-MBKP	Hiway Skytrike 160	RAD-01		9. 2.82	Canx as WFU 17.5.90.
G-MBKR	Hiway Skytrike 250 (C/n is corruption of engine type)	EC25PS04		9. 2.82	Canx by CAA 13.6.90.
G-MBKS	Hiway Skytrike 160 Srs.1	21X7		10. 2.82	Canx by CAA 3.8.94.
G-MBKT	Mitchell Wing B-10	TB-01		10. 2.82	Canx as WFU 16.6.87.
G-MBKU	Hiway Skytrike/Demon	25M2		10. 2.82	Canx by CAA 25.11.94.
G-MBKV	Eurowing Goldwing	EW-26		10. 2.82	Canx by CAA 24.1.95.
G-MBKW	MEA Pterodactyl Ptraveler	PT-105		10. 2.82	Canx by CAA 14.5.98.
G-MBKX	Mainair Tri-Flyer/Flexiform Sealander	NGSL-1		11. 2.82	Canx by CAA (date?). Trike used in the construction of G-MJDO.
G-MBKY	American Aerolights Eagle 215B (C/n is probably engine no., originally regd with c/n BF-01)	ZFE-15288		12. 2.82	
G-MBKZ	Hiway Skytrike/Super Scorpion (C/n is corruption of engine type)	EC25P8-04		12. 2.82	
G-MBLA	Hiway Skytrike/Flexiform (Originally regd as Flexiform Trike/Sealander with same c/n)	0012		12. 2.82	Canx by CAA 5.12.95.
G-MBLB	Eipper Quicksilver MX	SMCL-01		12. 2.82	Canx as WFU 16.6.87.
G-MBLC	Mainair Sports Tri-Flyer	DR-01		12. 2.82	Canx 11.10.83 on sale to West Germany.
G-MBLD	Flexiform Trike/Flexiform Dual Striker	3FF-001		15. 2.82	Canx by CAA 24.1.95.
G-MBLE	Hiway Skytrike Mk.II/Demon	2592		16. 2.82	Canx by CAA 18.4.90.
G-MBLF	Ultrasports Tripacer/Hiway Demon 195	80-00348		17. 2.82	Canx by CAA 13.6.90.
G-MBLG	Chargus Titan 38	15/80-00069		17. 2.82	Canx by CAA 13.6.90.
G-MBLH	Mainair Tri-Flyer 330/Airwave Nimrod (Initially used Hornet trike, with c/n H180)	110		17. 2.82	Canx by CAA 24.1.95.
G-MBLI	Southern Aerosports Scorpion	FSE-01		18. 2.82	Wing failure & crashed at Kitchenham Farm, near Battle, Sussex on 7.8.82. Canx by CAA 22.7.87.
G-MBLJ	Eipper Quicksilver MX	FSE-02		18. 2.82	Canx by CAA 3.2.92.
G-MBLK	Ultrasports Tripacer/Southdown Puma (Lightning DS)	DS-390		18. 2.82	Canx as WFU 23.6.97.
G-MBLL	American Aerolights Eagle	JDB-01		18. 2.82	Canx by CAA 13.6.90.
G-MBLM	Hiway Skytrike 250/Southdown Sigma	25R7		18. 2.82	
G-MBLN	Pterodactyl Ptraveler 430D	HCM-01		19. 2.82	
G-MBLO	Mainair Tri-Flyer/Flexiform Sealander 160 (Originally regd as Hiway Skytrike)	10676		22. 2.82	No Permit believed issued. Canx by CAA 10.2.99.
G-MBLP	MEA Pterodactyl	RNG-01		22. 2.82	Canx by CAA 13.6.90.
G-MBLR	Ultrasports Tripacer/Solar Wings Typhoon	KND-01 & 80-00228		22. 2.82	Canx by CAA 23.6.97.
G-MBLS	MEA Mistral Trainer	001		23. 2.82	Canx by CAA 6.9.94.
G-MBLT	Chargus Titan 38/TS440	IKA-01		23. 2.82	Canx by CAA 13.6.90.
G-MBLU	Ultrasports Tripacer/Southdown Lightning L195	L195/191		26. 2.82	
G-MBLV	Medway Hybred/Solar Wings Storm	449		26. 2.82	Canx by CAA 26.5.92.
G-MBLW	Southern Aerosports Scorpion	36		26. 2.82	Type refused certification. Canx as WFU 4.11.86.
G-MBLX	Eurowing Goldwing	82-004		1. 3.82	Canx by CAA 13.6.90.
G-MBLY	Flexiform Dual Striker	2415921		1. 3.82	Canx by CAA 20.8.90.
G-MBLZ	Southern Aerosports Scorpion	OA-1		1. 3.82	Canx by CAA 22.7.87.
G-MBMA	Eipper Quicksilver MX	MM-01		21. 1.82	Canx by CAA 13.6.90.
G-MBMB	Southern Aerosports Scorpion	OA-2		1. 3.82	Crashed on take-off on first flight from Pendeford, near Wolverhampton on 27.3.82. Canx by CAA 22.7.87.
G-MBMC	Waspair HM.81 Tomcat	FDB-01		2. 3.82	Canx by CAA 13.6.90.
G-MBMD	Eurowing Catto CP-16	CP 250		2. 3.82	Canx by CAA 13.6.90.

Regn	Type	c/n	Previous identity	Regn date	Fate or immediate subsequent identity (if known)
G-MBME	American Aerolights Eagle Z-Drive	E3597		3. 3.82	Canx by CAA 3.2.92.
G-MBMF	Rotec Rally 2B	JGW-01		3. 3.82	Canx by CAA 13.6.90.
G-MBMG	Rotec Rally 2B	RJP-01		3. 3.82	
G-MBMH	American Aerolights Eagle	3125		3. 3.82	Canx as WFU 23.4.90.
G-MBMI	Chargus T.440	T440/3		1. 3.82	Canx by CAA 13.6.90
G-MBMJ	Mainair Tri-Flyer 250	PAG-01		4. 3.82	Canx by CAA 2.9.88.
G-MBMK	Weedhopper Srs.B	484		4. 3.82	Canx by CAA 17.5.90.
G-MBML	American Aerolights Eagle	4152		4. 3.82	Canx by CAA 13.6.90.
G-MBMM	Scheibe SF-25C Falke	4412	D-KAEU	. .82R	NTU - Allocated in error. To G-MFMM 4/82. Canx.
G-MBMN	Hiway Skytrike/Skyhook Silhouette	ADFC-01		5. 3.82	Canx by CAA 13.6.90.
G-MBMO	Hiway Skytrike/Flexiform Striker 160	21V9		5. 3.82	Canx by CAA 28.11.94.
G-MBMP	Mitchell Wing B-10	101		5. 3.82	Canx as WFU 8.6.90.
G-MBMR	Ultrasports Tripacer/Solar Wings Typhoon	LM-01		5. 3.82	Canx by CAA 2.9.88.
G-MBMS	Hornet/Skyhook Sabre	RLS-01 & H.150		5. 3.82	Canx by CAA 27.1.88.
	(Originally regd as Hornet/Airwave with same c/n - type officially amended in 6/84 but in fact had that wing at Cranfield 7/83)				
G-MBMT	Mainair Tri-Flyer/Southdown Lightning 195	TRY-01		8. 3.82	Canx by CAA 23.8.99.
G-MBMU	Eurowing Goldwing	EW-38		12. 3.82	Canx by CAA 1.3.93.
G-MBMV	Chargus Titan 38/TS440	RNP-01		8. 3.82	Crashed at Botoloph Claydon on 8.1.83. Canx as destroyed 19.7.89.
G-MBMW	Nuttall Trike/Solar Wings Typhoon	088-05882 & T481-131		8. 3.82	Canx by CAA 2.6.97.
	(Originally regd as Mainair Tri-Flyer with c/n ATRN-01, then c/n 088-05882; the latter trike to G-MJGZ)				
G-MBMX(1)	Eipper Quicksilver MX	DJNB-01		9. 3.82	DBF in 8/82 when parked near a tractor which caught fire. Canx as destroyed 31.8.82.
G-MBMX(2)	Eipper Quicksilver MX	DJNB-02		. .82	Canx by CAA 13.6.90.
G-MBMY	Pterodactyl Pfledgling	GC-01		10. 3.82	Canx by CAA 13.6.90.
G-MBMZ	Ultrasports Tripacer/Flexiform Sealander	US/46 & FF/419		12. 3.82	Canx by CAA 23.6.97.
	(Originally regd with c/n 0-B-01)				
G-MBNA	American Aerolights Eagle	3503		12. 3.82	Canx by CAA 26.1.89.
G-MBNB	Southern Lightning L175	L175/030		15. 3.82	Owner believed to have emigrated to Spain in 4/83 and subsequently deceased. Canx by CAA 31.7.84.
G-MBNC	Southdown Puma	P.002 & L195/343		15. 3.82	Canx by CAA 2.4.90.
G-MBND	Skyhook TR2	TR2/22		15. 3.82	Canx by CAA 13.6.90.
G-MBNE	Southern Aerosports Scorpion Mk.2	0060		15. 3.82	Crashed on take-off from Fenland on 14.6.82 (also quoted as crashed on 16.7.82).
G-MBNF	American Aerolights Eagle	DR-01		15. 3.82	Canx by CAA 6.9.94.
G-MBNG	Hiway Skytrike 250/Demon 175	25L2 & HU17D		15. 3.82	Canx by CAA 23.6.97.
	(Regd with c/n 80-00259 - engine no)				
G-MBNH	Southern Aerosports Scorpion	4		23. 3.82	Canx by CAA 22.7.87. (Stored 7/92)
	(C/n also quoted as 990063)				
G-MBNI	Ultrasports Tripacer/Solar Wings Typhoon	BS-01		16. 3.82	Dismantled with the Trike now forming part of G-MMLG and the wing being used as a Hang-Glider. Canx by CAA 29.3.84.
G-MBNJ	Eipper Quicksilver MX	CJL-3444/12145		26. 4.82	Canx by CAA 3.2.92.
G-MBNK	American Aerolights Eagle	E.2398MJ		17. 3.82	
G-MBNL	Hiway Skytrike C.2	2145		17. 3.82	Canx as WFU 9.12.91.
G-MBNM	American Aerolights Eagle	3392(II)		17. 3.82	Canx by CAA 13.6.90.
	(C/n duplicates G-MBFE though different aircraft - this one is confirmed correct and c/n amended from 3392)				
G-MBNN	Scoble Mk.I Gazelle P.160	SG.001		17. 3.82	Canx by CAA 13.6.90.
	(Originally regd as SMD Gazelle P.160 with same c/n)				
G-MBNO	Not allotted.				
G-MBNP	Eurowing Catto CP-16	MHCB.01		19. 3.82	Canx by CAA 13.6.90.
G-MBNR	Hornet/Flexiform Striker	DTK.01		23. 3.82	Canx as destroyed 16.12.85.
G-MBNS	Chargus Titan 38	0038		3.12.82	Canx by CAA 13.6.90.
	(Originally reserved for c/n 90-00040 - which may be a corrupt engine number)				
G-MBNT	American Aerolights Eagle	MDO-01		24. 3.82	(Stored 9/95)
G-MBNU	Hiway Skytrike/Flexiform Hilander	DWIW-01		23. 3.82	Canx as WFU 26.9.88.
G-MBNV	Sheffield Trident	816		24. 3.82	
G-MBNW	Meagher Flex-wing	JTM-01		24. 3.82	Canx by CAA 13.6.90.
G-MBNX	Hiway Skytrike 250/Solar Wings Storm	FK-01		24. 3.82	Canx as WFU 4.3.88.
G-MBNY	Steer Terror/Manta Pfledge II	MJS.II		24. 3.82	
G-MBNZ	Hiway Skytrike/Demon	EBJP/01		24. 3.82	Canx by CAA 6.9.94.
G-MBOA	Hiway 160 Skytrike/Flexiform Hilander	FS.1		24. 3.82	Canx as WFU 22.8.94.
G-MBOB	American Aerolights Eagle	NJO-01		26. 3.82	Canx by CAA 30.10.90.
G-MBOC	Ultrasports Tripacer 250/Southdown Lightning Mk.I	532A		26. 3.82	Canx as TWFU 16.12.87.
G-MBOD	American Aerolights Eagle	3082		26. 3.82	Canx by CAA 27.1.98.
G-MBOE	Southdown Puma/Solar Wings	MDH-01		26. 3.82	Canx by CAA 3.2.92.
G-MBOF	Pakes Jackdaw	LGP-01		26. 3.82	
G-MBOG	Mainair Tri-Flyer 330/Flexiform Sealander	055-27282 & DER-01		22. 4.82	Canx by CAA 13.6.90.

Regn	Type	c/n	Previous identity	Regn date	Fate or immediate subsequent identity (if known)
G-MBOH	MEA Mistral Trainer	008		29. 3.82	
G-MBOI	Ultralight Mirage II	CT06095		29. 3.82	Canx by CAA 13.6.90.
	(Originally regd with c/n ARR-01)				
G-MBOJ	Pterodactyl Pfledgling	SPD-01		30. 3.82	Destroyed in crash at Cholmondeley, Cheshire on 6.8.89. Canx as destroyed 18.12.89.
G-MBOK	Brooks Pulsar (Chargus Cyclone)	153/042/6		1. 4.82	
	(Originally regd as Dunstable Microlight/Solar Typhonn S4 with same c/n)				
G-MBOL	Pterodactyl Pterodactyl 360SAX	RN-01		1. 4.82	Canx by CAA 13.6.90.
G-MBOM	Hiway Skytrike/Flexiform Hilander	21U4		1. 4.82	Canx by CAA 1.9.94.
	(Orig. regd with c/n JFB-01)				
G-MBON	Eurowing Goldwing	EW-33 & SWA-02		1. 4.82	
G-MBOO	Not allotted.				
G-MBOP	Hiway Skytrike/Demon 175	ER 17D		1. 4.82	Canx as WFU 18.10.88.
G-MBOR	Chotia Weedhopper 460B	DJW-01		5. 4.82	Canx by CAA 8.7.93.
G-MBOS	Hiway Super Scorpion	CH-01		5. 4.82	Canx by CAA 13.6.90.
G-MBOT	Hiway Skytrike 250/Demon	25M3		2. 4.82	Canx by CAA 6.1.92.
G-MBOU	Wheeler (Skycraft) Scout Mk III/3/R	432R/3		2. 4.82	Camx by CAA 10.3.99.
	(Same c/n as G-MBUD)				
	(Offically regd as c/n 43ZR3)				
G-MBOV	Hornet/Southdown Lightning 170	L170/170		2. 4.82	Canx by CAA 24.1.95.
G-MBOW	Solar Wings Typhoon	JM-01		2. 4.82	Canx by CAA 14.6.90.
G-MBOX	American Aerolights Eagle	JSP-01		6. 4.82	Canx by CAA 12.4.94.
G-MBOY	American Aerolights Eagle	-		. .82R	NTU - Canx.
	(Possibly duplicated allocation)				
G-MBOZ	Eipper Quicksilver MX	10992		16. 4.82	Crashed through hedge and overturned on take-off from Flixton on 17.7.82. Canx by CAA 13.6.90.
	(C/n is engine no.)				
G-MBPA	Weedhopper Srs.2	CHS-01		21. 4.82	Canx as destroyed 3.2.92.
G-MBPB(1)	Whittaker MW.4	001		. .82R	NTU - To G-MBTH 4/82. Canx.
G-MBPB(2)	Pterodactyl Ptraveller	PEB-01		7. 4.82	Canx by CAA 13.6.90.
G-MBPC	American Aerolights Eagle Amphibian	E.3129		6. 4.82	Canx by CAA 6.9.94.
	(Orig. regd with c/n RSM-01)				
G-MBPD	American Aerolights Eagle	RGH-01		6. 4.82	Canx by CAA 3.2.92.
G-MBPE	Ultrasports Trike/Flexiform Sealander	LAH-01		7. 4.82	Canx by CAA 16.6.93.
G-MBPF	Southern Aerosports Scorpion	D.0006		13. 4.82	Type refused certification. Canx as WFU 4.11.86.
G-MBPG	Mainair Tri-Flyer/Solar Wings Typhoon	189-1983 & T381-105		13. 4.82	(Stored 8/97)
	(Originally regd as Hunt Skytrike with c/n JAH.6)				
G-MBPH	Southern Aerosports Scorpion	-		. .82R	NTU - Canx.
G-MBPI	MEA Mistral Trainer	500		13. 4.82	Canx by CAA 13.6.90.
G-MBPJ	Centrair Moto-Delta G.11	001		14. 5.82	
G-MBPK	[Was reserved for British Air Ferries Ltd]			. .82R	NTU - Canx.
G-MBPL	Hiway Skytrike/Demon	RWS-01		15. 4.82	Canx by CAA 30.9.93.
G-MBPM	Eurowing Goldwing	EW-21		14. 4.82	
G-MBPN	American Aerolights Eagle	3895		16. 4.82	Canx by CAA 17.1.92.
G-MBPO	Seymour Volnik Arrow	001		16. 4.82	Canx by CAA 3.8.94.
G-MBPP	American Aerolights Eagle	E2364		19. 4.82	Canx by CAA 16.12.91.
G-MBPR	American Aerolights Eagle	3112		19. 4.82	Canx by CAA 13.6.90.
	(C/n also issued to G-MBSO 5/82 - possibly in error)				
G-MBPS	Willgress Gryphon/Willpower	1/1004		19. 4.82	Canx by CAA 6.9.94.
G-MBPT	Hiway Skytrike 250/Demon	KMS-01		21. 4.82	Canx by CAA 13.6.90.
G-MBPU	Hiway Skytrike 250/Demon	DSS-01		21. 4.82	Canx by CAA 5.7.99.
G-MBPV	Not allotted.				
G-MBPW	Weedhopper JC-24	1306		8. 2.82	Canx by CAA 24.3.99.
G-MBPX	Eurowing Goldwing SP	EW-42		21. 4.82	
G-MBPY	Ultrasports Tripacer/Solar Wings Typhoon	RKP-01		21. 4.82	
	(Originally regd as Wasp Gryphon with same c/n)				
G-MBPZ	Mainair Tri-Flyer 250/Flexiform Striker	CRH-01 & 047-241281		23. 8.82	Canx by CAA 24.1.95. (Stored 3/94)
G-MBRA	Eurowing Catto CP-16	JB-01		20. 4.82	Canx as destroyed 3.4.90.
G-MBRB	Electraflyer Eagle Mk.I	E.2229		9.12.81	
G-MBRC	Wheeler (Skycraft) Scout Mk.III 3/A	0438 R/3		20. 4.82	Canx by CAA 13.6.90.
G-MBRD	American Aerolights Eagle 215B	E.2635		20. 4.82	
G-MBRE	Wheeler (Skycraft) Scout	73962		21. 4.82	
G-MBRF	Weedhopper 460	460/1361		21. 4.82	Canx by CAA 6.9.94.
G-MBRG	Not allotted.				
G-MBRH	Ultraflight Mirage Mk.II	RALH-01		20. 4.82	
G-MBRI	Not allotted.				
G-MBRJ	Not allotted.				
G-MBRK	Huntair Pathfinder	RMK-1		22. 4.82	Canx by CAA 9.6.93.
G-MBRL	Flexiform Striker	?		. .82R	NTU - Canx.
G-MBRM	Hiway Skytrike/Demon	YX-19D		20. 4.82	Canx by CAA 18.1.93.
G-MBRN	Hiway Skytrike/Demon 175	WZ-17D		22. 4.82	Canx by CAA 13.6.90.
G-MBRO(1)	Hiway Skytrike 160/Birdman Cherokee 200	CH 200119399 & SM160-15046		22. 4.82	NTU - Canx.
G-MBRO(2)	Utrasports Trpacer 330/Airwave Magic Nimrod 165	AMN/165/408/25/8/82		. 8.82	Canx by CAA 24.1.95.

Regn	Type	c/n	Previous identity	Regn date	Fate or immediate subsequent identity (if known)
G-MBRP	American Aerolights Eagle	E.2583		23. 4.82	Canx as WFU 3.4.90.
G-MBRR	Not allotted.				
G-MBRS	American Aerolights Eagle 215B	RWC.1		23. 4.82	(Stored 6/90)
G-MBRT	Airwave Comet/Trike UP CMT 165 (Trike unit unidentified)	110A		21. 4.82	Sold in Ireland on 23.10.82. Canx by CAA 11.3.83.
G-MBRU	Skyhook TR2/Cutlass CD (Originally regd with c/n BASO-01)	TR2/34		23. 4.82	Canx by CAA 13.6.90.
G-MBRV	Eurowing Goldwing	EW-41		22. 4.82	Canx by CAA 3.2.92.
G-MBRW	Not allotted.				
G-MBRX	Not allotted.				
G-MBRY	Not allotted.				
G-MBRZ	Hiway Skytrike 250/Vulcan	ACS-01		22. 4.82	Canx by CAA 6.9.94. (Stored 2/99 at Melton Constable, Norfolk)
G-MBSA	Ultraflight Mirage Mk.II	229		19. 4.82	Canx by CAA 5.12.95.
G-MBSB	Ultraflight Mirage Mk.II (C/n duplicates PH-1B8)	230		19. 4.82	Canx by CAA 13.6.90.
G-MBSC	Ultraflight Mirage Mk.II	231		19. 4.82	Canx by CAA 6.9.94.
G-MBSD(1)	Ultraflight Mirage Mk.II	232		. .82R	NTU - Canx.
G-MBSD(2)	Southdown Puma (Lightning DS)	301	(G-MBSP)	19. 4.82	Used for spares by Breen Aviation in 1982. Canx by CAA 8.7.93.
G-MBSE	Ultraflight Mirage Mk.II	233		19. 4.82	Canx 19.10.82 on sale to France.
G-MBSF	Ultraflight Mirage Mk.II	234		19. 4.82	No Permit believed issued. Canx as PWFU 16.2.99.
G-MBSG	Ultraflight Mirage Mk.II	235		19. 4.82	No Permit believed issued. Canx by CAA 12.2.99.
G-MBSH	American Aerolights Eagle	4584		9. 6.82	Canx by CAA 13.6.90.
G-MBSI	American Aerolights Eagle	4586		8. 7.82	Canx by CAA 13.6.90.
G-MBSJ	American Aerolights Eagle	5001		8. 6.82	Canx by CAA 14.11.91.
G-MBSK	American Aerolights Eagle 215B	5002		14. 6.82	Canx by CAA 6.6.96.
G-MBSL	American Aerolights Eagle	4276		20. 4.82	Canx by CAA 13.6.90.
G-MBSM	American Aerolights Eagle	5008		4. 6.82	Used for spares. Canx by CAA 13.6.90.
G-MBSN	American Aerolights Eagle	5004		9. 6.82	Canx by CAA 13.6.90.
G-MBSO	American Aerolights Eagle (C/n duplicates G-MBPR - possibly in error)	3112		25. 5.82	Used for spares. Canx as WFU 7.8.84.
G-MBSP(1)	Ultrasports Puma/Lightning DS	301		. .82R	NTU - To G-MBSD 4/82. Canx.
G-MBSP(2)	Ultraflight Mirage II	97		25. 5.82	Used for spares in 1982. Canx by CAA 11.7.84.
G-MBSR	Ultrasports Puma (Lightning DS)	302		14. 6.82	Canx by CAA 24.1.95.
G-MBSS	Ultrasports Puma DS (Lightning DS)	303		8. 9.82	Canx by CAA 17.8.92.
G-MBST(1)	[Was reserved for Breen Aviation]	-		. .82R	NTU - Canx.
G-MBST(2)	Mainair Gemini/Southdown Puma Sprint (Originally regd with c/n BB-01)(See G-MJXA & G-MMTM)	141-29383		10. 4.84	
G-MBSU	Ultraflight Mirage II	237		23. 7.82	Canx by CAA 13.6.90.
G-MBSV	Ultraflight Mirage II	238		14. 5.82	Canx by CAA 4.8.94.
G-MBSW	Ultraflight Mirage II	239		22. 6.82	Canx by CAA 16.9.93.
G-MBSX	Ultraflight Mirage II	240		14. 6.82	
G-MBSY	Ultraflight Mirage II	241		14. 6.82	Stalled & crashed at Enstone on 8.7.82. Canx by CAA 13.6.90.
G-MBSZ	Ultraflight Mirage II	242		14. 6.82	Canx by CAA 6.9.94.
G-MBTA	UAS Solar Buggy	No.5 Mk.2		22. 4.82	Canx by CAA 3.2.92.
G-MBTB	Mainair Tri-Flyer 250/Solar Wings Typhoon S4 (Originally regd as Davis Tri-Flyer "S" with c/n 016-29981)	FS-01 & 016-29981 & T582-466L		22. 4.82	Canx by CAA 5.12.95.
G-MBTC	Weedhopper JC-24B	ANM-01		11. 5.82	(Stored 8/97)
G-MBTD	Solar Wings 250/Birdman Cherokee	KJB-01		26. 4.82	Canx by CAA 13.6.90.
G-MBTE	Hornet/Hiway Demon (Regd with former Hornet Trike c/n)(Originally regd as Hornet Dual/Single Trainer Trike with c/n 1 DUAL)	H050		26. 4.82	(Damaged mid .94)
G-MBTF	Mainair Tri-Flyer Dual/Southdown Sprint (Originally regd as Tri-Flyer Skytrike with c/n MSL-01, then as a Gemini with present c/n)	168-30683		26. 4.82	
G-MBTG	Mainair Gemini/Southdown Sprint (Originally regd as Mainair Tri-Flyer Dual)	064-19482 & P.431		26. 4.82	
G-MBTH	Whittaker MW.4	001	(G-MBPB)	6. 4.82	(Stored in trailer 8/97)
G-MBTI	Hovey WD-II Whing-Ding	ACRS-2		27. 4.82	Canx by CAA 3.2.92.
G-MBTJ	Ultrasports Tripacer/Solar Wings Typhoon	CSRS-01		2. 4.82	
G-MBTK	Mainair Tri-Flyer/Chargus Vortex 120P	042-231281		28. 4.82	Canx as WFU 19.9.86.
G-MBTL	Hiway Super Scorpion	CSB-01		27. 4.82	Canx by CAA 13.6.90.
G-MBTM	Rotec Rally 2B	012T		. .82R	NTU - Canx.
G-MBTN	Mitchell Wing B-10	257		28. 4.82	Canx by CAA 13.6.90.
G-MBTO	Mainair Tri-Flyer 277/Flexiform Striker (Originally regd with Hiway Demon wing)	WHS-01 & 029-211181		28. 4.82	Canx by CAA 23.2.93.
G-MBTP	Hiway Skytrike/Demon	SEH-01		28. 4.82	Canx as WFU 7.6.90.
G-MBTR	Skyhook	RS-01		28. 4.82	Canx by CAA 13.6.90.
G-MBTS	Hovey WD-II Whing-Ding (C/n is probably owner's PFA membership no)	PFA 8484/7		4. 2.82	Canx by CAA 6.9.94. (Stored in north hangar 10/96 at Shoreham)
G-MBTT	Ultrasports Tripacer/Solar Wings Typhoon (C/n is engine no)	82-00256		28. 4.82	Canx by CAA 4.5.84. The Wing was sold as a Hang-Glider in 4/84 and the Trike unit became G-MMOH.

Regn	Type	c/n	Previous identity	Regn date	Fate or immediate subsequent identity (if known)
G-MBTU	Lovegrove Cloudhopper Mk.II	PCL.19		27. 4.82	Canx as WFU 16.11.88.
G-MBTV	Waspair HM.81 Tomcat	089		30. 4.82	Canx as destroyed 24.5.90.
G-MBTW	Raven Vector 600	1188		10. 5.82	
G-MBTX	Hornet Microlight (C/n also quoted as 00210 - engine no.)	H.011		11. 5.82	Canx as WFU 14.5.86.
G-MBTY	American Aerolights Eagle	3207		11. 5.82	Canx as WFU 27.4.90. (Stored 2/96)
G-MBTZ	Huntair Pathfinder 1	005 & LWB-01		28. 4.82	Canx by CAA 6.9.94.
G-MBUA	Hiway Demon	RJN-01		30. 4.82	
G-MBUB	Hiway Skytrike 250/Vulcan (Originally regd as Horne Sigma Skytrike/Southdown Sigma with c/n LGH-01 - re-regd 17.5.84)	25M2/2		29. 4.82	Canx by CAA 27.5.93.
G-MBUC	Huntair Pathfinder	004		29. 4.82	Canx by CAA 12.12.82. Sold in 8/82 and taken to Chiredzi, Zimbabwe in 11/82 - noted operating at Charles Prince, Zimbabwe in 1986.
G-MBUD	Wheeler (Skycraft) Scout Mk.III/R/3 (Modified to Super Scout) (Same c/n as G-MBOU)	0432/R/3		12. 5.82	Canx by CAA 6.9.94.
G-MBUE	MBA Tiger Cub 440 (Originally regd as Micro-Bipe with c/n 001)	MBA-001		29. 4.82	Canx by CAA 6.9.94. (On display 3/96)
G-MBUF	Huntair Pathfinder	007		29. 4.82	Canx 31.1.83 on sale to France.
G-MBUG	Southdown Aerosports Scorpion Twin	FH-01		4. 5.82	Canx by CAA 4.11.86.
G-MBUH	Hiway Skytrike 330/Demon 175	RC-01/A		4. 5.82	Canx as WFU 9.8.93.
G-MBUI	Wheeler (Skycraft) Scout Mk.I	GCM-01		7. 5.82	Canx as WFU 10.7.85.
G-MBUJ	Rotec Rally 2B	1/26482		25. 5.82	Canx by CAA 13.6.90.
G-MBUK	Mainair Tri-Flyer/Solar Wings Typhoon (Originally regd as Ultrasports Tripacer with c/n JDB-01)	063-31382 & T582-473		30. 4.82	Canx by CAA 26.6.98.
G-MBUL	American Aerolights Eagle	3595		4. 5.82	Canx by CAA 6.9.94.
G-MBUM	Not allotted.				
G-MBUN	Southern Aerosports Scorpion	006		18. 5.82	Destroyed in fatal crash at Headcorn, Kent on 23.8.82. Canx by CAA 23.10.86.
G-MBUO	Southern Aerosports Scorpion	0011		1. 6.82	Canx by CAA 22.7.87.
G-MBUP	Hiway Skytrike/Solar Wings Storm	5293		4. 2.82	Canx as TWFU 5.12.89.
G-MBUR	Rotec Rally 2B	DJSM-01		12. 5.82	Donated to RAF Museum, Hendon on 28.10.83. Canx as WFU 16.11.83.
G-MBUS	MEA Mistral Trainer	FGJ-01		7. 5.82	Canx as destroyed 25.10.88.
G-MBUT	UAS Storm Buggy/Flexiform Striker	DM823S		7. 5.82	Canx by CAA 20.12.94.
G-MBUU	Mainair Tri-Flyer/Southdown Puma MS (Lightning DS) (Officially regd with c/n 053-2181 - above seen stamped on aircraft)	053-2182		7. 5.82	Canx as WFU 2.9.88.
G-MBUV	Huntair Pathfinder 1	025 & SM8291		10. 5.82	Canx as WFU 9.8.89.
G-MBUW	Hornet Trike/Skyhook Sabre (Trike may have been a Skyhook TR2)	H160		10. 5.82	Canx as WFU 17.5.90.
G-MBUX	Pterodactyl Ptraveller	JJH-01		10. 5.82	Canx by CAA 4.6.90.
G-MBUY	American Aerolights Eagle	3156		4. 5.82	Canx by CAA 13.6.90.
G-MBUZ	Wheeler (Skycraft) Scout II	0366		4. 5.82	
G-MBVA	Volmer VJ-23E	01		5. 5.82	Canx as WFU 4.8.94.
G-MBVB	Ultralight Mirage Mk.II	114		5. 5.82	Canx 15.10.84 on sale to Zimbabwe.
G-MBVC	American Aerolights Eagle	4006		5. 5.82	Canx as WFU 24.11.94.
G-MBVD	Not to be allotted.				
G-MBVE	Hiway Skytrike 160 (Valmet)	TJD-01		6. 5.82	Canx by CAA 13.6.90.
G-MBVF	Hornet Microlight	PDH-01		6. 5.82	Canx by CAA 13.6.90.
G-MBVG	American Aerolights Eagle	3083		6. 5.82	Canx by CAA 13.6.90.
G-MBVH	Mainair Tri-Flyer/Flexiform Striker	065-6482		12. 5.82	Canx as WFU 5.1.95.
G-MBVI	Hiway Skytrike 250/Super Scorpion	CYSSC 2		12. 5.82	Canx by CAA 13.6.90.
G-MBVJ	Skyhook TR1/Sabre C	TR1/33		24. 5.82	Canx by CAA 24.1.95.
G-MBVK	Ultraflight Mirage Mk.II	236		13. 5.82	Canx by CAA 19.8.94. (Stored Stapleford 1/95)
G-MBVL	Southern Aerosports Scorpion	008		13. 5.82	Canx by CAA 22.7.87.
G-MBVM	Ultraflight Mirage Mk.II	NG-01		15. 4.82	Canx as WFU 6.4.90.
G-MBVN(1)	American Aerolights Eagle	LFL-01	G-MBID	. .82R	NTU - Remained as G-MBID. Canx 24.6.82.
G-MBVN(2)	American Aerolights Eagle	DAC-01		10. 5.82	
G-MBVO	Hovey WD-III Whing-Ding (Originally to be built as a WD-II)	001		14. 5.82	Canx by CAA 13.6.90.
G-MBVP	Mainair Tri-Flyer 330/Flexiform Striker	061-19382 & PMW-01		14. 5.82	Canx by CAA 23.12.94.
G-MBVR	Rotec Rally 2B	JFB-001		14. 5.82	Canx by CAA 24.1.95.
G-MBVS	Hiway Skytrike 250/Super Scorpion	25 T3		14. 5.82	Canx by CAA 17.3.99.
G-MBVT	American Aerolights Eagle	3784		14. 5.82	Canx by CAA 9.6.93.
G-MBVU	Mainair Tri-Flyer 250/Flexiform Sealander (Originally regd as a Flexiform Striker)	RS.5		14. 5.82	Canx by CAA 24.1.95.
G-MBVV	Hiway Skytrike Mk.II/Demon 175	IS-01		14. 5.82	
G-MBVW	Skyhook TR2/Cutlass	TR2/23		14. 5.82	Dived into ground at North Connel Aerodrome, Oban on 30.4.83 & badly damaged.
G-MBVX	Tigair Power Fledge	P-0006		17. 5.82	Canx by CAA 13.6.90.

Regn	Type	c/n	Previous identity	Regn date	Fate or immediate subsequent identity (if known)
G-MBVY	Eipper Quicksilver MX II	3316		17. 5.82	Canx by CAA 10.5.96.
G-MBVZ	Hornet Trike 250/Solar Wings Storm	H.210		18. 5.82	Canx as WFU 9.5.90.
G-MBWA	American Aerolights Eagle	PS-01		18. 5.82	Canx by CAA 3.2.92.
G-MBWB	Hiway Skytrike	CKB-01		18. 5.82	Canx by CAA 20.1.88.
G-MBWC	Not allotted.				
G-MBWD	Rotec Rally 2B	AC-01		18. 5.82	Canx by CAA 6.9.94.
G-MBWE	American Aerolights Eagle	2937		18. 5.82	Canx by CAA 24.3.99.
G-MBWF	Mainair Tri-Flyer 330/Flexiform Striker	GAA-01 & 682-01		19. 5.82	
G-MBWG	Huntair Pathfinder 1	006		19. 5.82	
G-MBWH	Jordan Duet 1 (Originally regd as Designability Duet 1)	D82001		20. 5.82	
G-MBWI	Lafayette Hi-Nuski Mk.1	30680		8. 6.82	Canx by CAA 13.6.90. (Stored 3/96)
G-MBWJ	Hiway Skytrike 250/Super Scorpion	PCL-20	G-MBFA	19. 5.82R	NTU - Remained as G-MBFA. Canx by CAA 23.6.82.
G-MBWK	Mainair Tri-Flyer	GW-01		19. 5.82	Canx by CAA 13.6.90.
G-MBWL	Huntair Pathfinder Mk.1	MLP-01		20. 5.82	Canx 6.1.93 on sale to Ireland.
G-MBWM	American Aerolights Eagle	4197		20. 5.82	Canx by CAA 16.12.91.
G-MBWN	American Aerolights Eagle	4463		20. 5.82	Canx by CAA 16.12.91.
G-MBWO	Hiway Skytrike 250 Mk.II/Demon 175	DI-17D		20. 5.82	Canx by CAA 24.1.95.
G-MBWP	Ultrasports Tripacer 330/Flexiform Striker	EC-01		20. 5.82	Canx by CAA 20.8.93.
G-MBWR	Mainair Tri-Flyer 330/Skyhook Sabre (Originally regd as Hornet 260 with c/n H290 - changed in 6/84)	KBW-01 & 058-12382		20. 5.82	Canx by CAA 8.10.93.
G-MBWS	Turley Vector 600	1016		20. 5.82	Canx by CAA 4.11.82.
G-MBWT	Huntair Pathfinder	004		21. 5.82	DBR in crash at Eaglescott on 11.6.84. Canx by CAA 24.8.94.
G-MBWU	Hiway Skytrike/Demon 175	DK-17D		21. 5.82	Canx by CAA 6.9.94.
G-MBWV	Chargus Titan	090		21. 5.82	Fatal crash near the M3 motorway soon after take-off from Popham on 23.10.82. Canx as destroyed 26.10.82. Components were later used by G-MJKZ.
G-MBWW	Southern Aerosports Scorpion Pacer Srs.1	001EP		28. 5.82	Canx by CAA 22.7.87.
G-MBWX	Southern Aerosports Scorpion Dual Seat Trainer	002		28. 5.82	Type refused certification. Canx by CAA 23.10.86.
G-MBWY	American Aerolights Eagle	CCCW-1		24. 5.82	No Permit believed issued. Canx by CAA 15.3.99.
G-MBWZ	American Aerolights Eagle (Originally regd as Breen Eagle with same c/n)	2671		24. 5.82	Canx by CAA 13.6.90.
G-MBXA	Southern Aerosports Scorpion	OAL.1		24. 5.82	Canx as destroyed 4.11.86.
G-MBXB	Southdown Puma DS	L195/397 & PFL-01		24. 5.82	Canx by CAA 24.1.95.
G-MBXC	Eurowing Goldwing	EW-24		24. 5.82	WFU in 1986. Canx by CAA 13.6.90.
G-MBXD	Huntair Pathfinder	010		24. 5.82	Canx by CAA 13.6.90.
G-MBXE	Hiway Skytrike/Demon 175	GS-1		25. 5.82	Canx by CAA 23.6.97.
G-MBXF	Hiway Skytrike 250/Super Scorpion	JGR-1		25. 5.82	Canx by CAA 24.1.95.
G-MBXG	Mainair Tri-Flyer 330	052-20182		25. 5.82	Canx as WFU 29.11.88.
G-MBXH	Southdown Puma 440 (Lightning SS) (Also c/n quoted as L195/374)	L195/394		25. 5.82	Canx by CAA 25.10.91.
G-MBXI	Hiway Skytrike 250/Demon	25W4		4. 2.82	Canx as WFU 9.12.94.
G-MBXJ	Hiway Skytrike 250/Demon 175 (Originally regd with c/n DM-17D/EC25PS40; amended 21.5.84)	DM-17D		25. 5.82	Canx by CAA 24.3.99.
G-MBXK	Southdown Puma (Lightning DS) (Originally recorded in CAA records with c/n KND-02 in error)	KND-01		1. 6.82	Canx by CAA 2.9.88.
G-MBXL	Eipper Quicksilver MX II	3624		26. 5.82	Canx by CAA 13.6.90.
G-MBXM	American Aerolights Eagle (Has same c/n as G-MMAV)	2664		26. 5.82	Canx as destroyed 26.6.90.
G-MBXN	Ultrasports Tripacer 250/Southdown Lightning L.170	L170/293		26. 5.82	Canx by CAA 13.6.90.
G-MBXO	Sheffield Trident Microlight	003		27. 5.82	Canx by CAA 2.1.92.
G-MBXP	Hornet/Hiway Skytrike (Originally regd with c/n E-1 E25PS-40)	H150/E025PS-40		27. 5.82	Canx by CAA 24.1.95.
G-MBXR	Lancashire Micro Trike 330/Skyhook Sabre (Orig. regd as Hiway Skytrike 250. The wing was sold on its own and attached to the Lancashire Micro-Trike 30.6.83. The Hiway Trike was sold separately and anonymously with a c/n of EC 25 PS 04 quoted - this is the engine type)	AG-01		28. 5.82	Canx by CAA 16.12.87.
G-MBXS	Electraflyer Floater	F1482		28. 5.82	Wing used as a hang-glider, and trike unit to spares in about 12/82. Canx as WFU 27.2.84.
G-MBXT	Eipper Quicksilver MX II (C/n also now quoted as 3660 and engine no. 13427)	3383		4. 6.82	Canx by CAA 22.6.89.
G-MBXU	Rotec Rally 2B	015-S		1. 6.82	Canx as destroyed 9.5.85.
G-MBXV	Gemini Hummingbird	102		4. 6.82	Fatal crash at Bulwardine Farm, Claverley on 11.7.82. Canx by CAA 16.12.87.
G-MBXW	Hiway Skytrike II/Demon 175 (Also quoted as Nikite 250 trike)	DS17D		3. 6.82	Canx by CAA 14.5.97.
G-MBXX	Ultraflight Mirage II	111		21. 1.82	(Stored St.Just 5/94)
G-MBXY	Hornet Microlight	H0100		3. 6.82	Canx by CAA 13.6.90.
G-MBXZ	Skyhook TR2/Cutlass	TR2/26		3. 6.82	Canx as WFU 2.9.88.
G-MBYA	Southern Aerosports Scorpion	IMS-01		10. 6.82	Type refused certification. Canx by CAA 14.11.86.

Regn	Type	c/n	Previous identity	Regn date	Fate or immediate subsequent identity (if known)
G-MBYB	Southern Aerosports Scorpion	-		. .82R	NTU - Canx.
G-MBYC	Southern Aerosports Scorpion	-		. .82R	NTU - Canx.
G-MBYD	American Aerolights Eagle 215B	3510		3. 6.82	
G-MBYE	Eipper Quicksilver MX	12003		3. 6.82	Canx by CAA 16.12.91.
G-MBYF	Skyhook TR2/Cutlass	TR2/27		2. 6.82	Canx by CAA 8.10.93.
G-MBYG	[Was reserved for an unknown type in 1982 for J.D.M.Wilson of Onchan, IOM - who unfortunately died before completion of the project]				
G-MBYH	Maxair Hummer	001		4. 6.82	Canx by CAA 19.5.97.
G-MBYI	Ultraflight Lazair IIIE (Originally regd with c/n A522)	A464/001		4. 6.82	Crashed on take-off from Long Marston on 28.8.82.
G-MBYJ	Hiway Skytrike Mk.II 250/Super Scorpion C Mk.II	MTOSC2 & 25V1		4. 6.82	Canx by CAA 24.1.95.
G-MBYK	Huntair Pathfinder 1	012		4. 6.82	
G-MBYL	Huntair Pathfinder 1	009		4. 6.82	
G-MBYM	Eipper Quicksilver MX	JW-01		4. 6.82	Permit expired 21.9.96. (Stored 2/99 at Heywood Diss)
G-MBYN	Livesey Super-Fly	DML-01		7. 6.82	Canx as WFU 17.5.90.
G-MBYO	American Aerolights Eagle	4467		8. 6.82	Canx by CAA 24.3.99.
G-MBYP	Hornet 440/Skyhook Cutlass	H300		8. 6.82	Canx by CAA 13.6.90.
G-MBYR	American Aerolights Eagle	3310		25. 6.82	Canx by CAA 24.3.99.
G-MBYS	Ultraflight Mirage Mk.II	243		14. 6.82	Used for spares in 1983. Canx by CAA 22.5.97.
G-MBYT	Ultraflight Mirage Mk.II	98		14. 6.82	Canx by CAA 5.12.95. (Stored 8/95 in Ireland)
G-MBYU	American Aerolights Eagle	5003		20. 7.82	Canx by CAA 6.9.94.
G-MBYV	Mainair Tri-Flyer 330/Hiway Demon	056-27282 & ITF-01		9. 6.82	Canx by CAA 13.6.90.
G-MBYW	Levi Magpie	RL-10		9. 6.82	Canx as WFU 17.5.90.
G-MBYX	American Aerolights Eagle	E 2904		9. 6.82	Canx by CAA 24.3.99.
G-MBYY	Southern Aerosports Scorpion	DJL-01		10. 6.82	Canx by CAA 22.7.87.
G-MBYZ	American Aerolights Eagle	3975		10. 6.82	Canx as WFU 4.4.85.
G-MBZA	Ultrasports Tripacer/Hiway Demon 175 (Regd as Mainair Tri-Flyer 330)	MAR-01 & 100873		10. 6.82	Permit expired 8.1.95. Canx by CAA 29.6.95.
G-MBZB	Hiway Skytrike/Demon 175	KK17D		10. 6.82	Canx as WFU 31.8.94.
G-MBZC	Mainair Tri-Flyer/Solar Wings Typhoon	058-12382		10. 6.82	PWFU 27.3.84. Canx as WFU 30.3.84.
G-MBZD	Hiway Skytrike 160 Srs.1 (Valmet)	GGW-01		10. 6.82	Canx as WFU 25.10.88.
G-MBZE	Ultrasports Tripacer/Southdown Puma (Lightning)	PAL-01		11. 6.82	Trike unit sold for spares in 1983, and wing sold in 7/83. Canx by CAA 3.8.84.
G-MBZF	American Aerolights Eagle	4183		11. 6.82	Canx by CAA 3.2.92.
G-MBZG	Southern Aerosports (Twinflight) Scorpion 2-seater	0016		18. 6.82	Canx by CAA 22.7.87.
G-MBZH	Eurowing Goldwing	EW-50		14. 6.82	
G-MBZI	Eurowing Goldwing	EW-51		14. 6.82	Canx by CAA 15.9.93.
G-MBZJ	Southdown Puma (Lightning)	L170-415		14. 6.82	
G-MBZK	Ultrasports Tri-Pacer 250/Solar Wings Typhoon	AAL-01		14. 6.82	
G-MBZL	Weedhopper	ARP-01		14. 6.82	Canx by CAA 23.6.97.
G-MBZM	UAS Storm Buggy/Flexiform Sealander	JL824ER		14. 6.82	Canx by CAA 3.2.92.
G-MBZN	Ultrasports/Southdown Puma (Lightning DS)	80-00131 & DJC-01		14. 6.82	
G-MBZO	Mainair Tri-Flyer/Flexiform Medium Striker	GRH-01 & 021-101081		15. 6.82	
G-MBZP	Skyhook TR2/Cutlass	T3-12/82		15. 6.82	Canx by CAA 9.2.89.
G-MBZR	Eipper Quicksilver MX II	RG-01		15. 6.82	Canx as CAA 3.4.90.
G-MBZS	Southdown Puma	L195-423		15. 6.82	Canx by CAA 13.6.90.
G-MBZT	Skyhook Skytrike/Solar Wings Typhoon	SH-01		16. 6.82	Canx as destroyed 17.11.92.
G-MBZU	Skyhook Sabre C	GNBK-1		16. 6.82	Canx by CAA 6.9.94.
G-MBZV	American Aerolights Eagle 215B	4227-Z		16. 6.82	Canx as TWFU 27.10.97.
G-MBZW	American Aerolights Eagle	E.3104		16. 6.82	Canx as WFU 18.4.90.
G-MBZX	American Aerolights Eagle	MJJ-01		16. 6.82	Canx by CAA 13.6.90.
G-MBZY	Waspair HM.81 Tomcat	ACW-01		16. 6.82	Canx by CAA 13.6.90.
G-MBZZ	Southern Aerosports Scorpion	PJH-01		12. 2.82	Canx by CAA 22.7.87.
G-MCAH	Aerospatiale AS.355F1 Twin Squirrel	5120		1.12.81	To G-CNET 1/86. Canx.
G-MCAL	Aerospatiale AS.355F2 Twin Squirrel	5346		16. 5.86	To G-POON 9/86. Canx.
G-MCAR	PA-32-300 Cherokee Six D	32-7140008	G-LADA G-AYWK/N8616N	11.11.83	
G-MCBP	AIA Stampe SV-4C	1096	G-BALA EI-BAU/G-BALA/F-BKOF/French Mil	13.12.89	Crashed in a field at Woodhatch, near Reigate on 14.8.93. Canx as destroyed 15.11.93.
G-MCDS	Cessna 210N Centurion II	210-63070	G-BHNB N6496N	28. 3.80	To EI-BUF 12/86. Canx 18.12.86.
G-MCEA	Boeing 757-225 (Line No. 20)	22200	N510EA	6. 2.95	
G-MCEO	Beechcraft 200 Super King Air	BB-828	(N828AB) G-SWFT/G-SIBE/G-MCEO/G-BILY	14. 4.81	To G-OLDZ 6/96. Canx.
G-MCJL	Cyclone Pegasus Quantum 15	7497		16. 3.99	
G-MCKE	Boeing 757-28AER (Line No. 213)	24368		3. 3.89	To N521AT. Canx 25.11.96.
G-MCMS	Aero Designs Pulsar	PFA/202-11982		3. 2.93	

Regn	Type	c/n	Previous identity	Regn date	Fate or immediate subsequent identity (if known)
G-MCOX	Fuji FA.200-180AO Aero Subaru	FA200-296	(G-BIMS)	29.12.81	
G-MCPI	Bell 206B JetRanger III	3191	G-ONTB N3896C	4. 4.90	
G-MCPL	PA-28-161 Warrior II	28-8116013	N8255E	23. 8.89	Fatal crash at Friardykes Dod, Dunbar Common, Lothian on 20.11.90. Canx as destroyed 24.5.91
G-MDAC	PA-28-181 Archer II	28-8290154	N8242T	6.11.87	
G-MDAS	PA-31-310 Turbo Navajo B	31-7401239	5N-AEP G-BCJZ/N61427	28. 3.80	To G-OSFT 1/93. Canx.
G-MDBD	Airbus A.330-243	266	F-WWKG	24. 6.99	
G-MDEW	Lindstrand LBL Drinks Can SS HAFB (Mountain Dew Can Shape)	099		4. 3.94	
G-MDII	McDonnell Douglas MD-11 (Line No. 453)	48411		. .90R	NTU - To N514MD 7/90. Canx.
G-MDJI	Beechcraft B200 Super King Air	BB-1162	N71CS (N71CE)/N71CS/(N71C)/N557D	25. 2.87	Fatal crash into Ottleychevin Hill on 19.10.87. Canx as destroyed 8.3.88.
G-MDKD	Robinson R-22 Beta	1247		18. 4.90	
G-MDRB	PA-31-350 Navajo Chieftain	31-7752062	N63749	11.11.77	To PH-NTB 11/83. Canx 17.10.83.
G-MDTV	Cameron N-105 HAFB	1919		17. 4.89	To N45845 8/96. Canx 12.7.96.
G-MEAD	Enstrom 280C-UK Shark	1056	N581H	26. 2.86	To SE-HOO. Canx 9.10.87.
G-MEAH	PA-28R-200 Cherokee Arrow II	28R-7435104	G-BSNM N46PR/G-BSNM/N46PR/N54439	14. 6.91	
G-MEAN	Agusta A.109A	7170	G-BRYL G-ROPE/G-OAMH	20. 4.89	To G-USTA 12/96. Canx.
G-MEAT	Robinson R-22 Beta	1633		24.12.90	To G-MADD 1/93. Canx.
G-MEBC	Cessna 310I	310I-0052	G-ROGA G-ASVV/N8052M	17. 6.83	Damaged in landing accident at Goodwood on 31.3.94. Canx as WFU 7.12.94.
G-MEDA	Airbus A.320-231	480	N480RX F-WWDU	12.10.94	(Reserved as N480RX)
G-MEDB	Airbus A.320-231	376	3B-RGY F-WWIK/(F-OHMB)/(XA-SGB)/F-WWIK	19. 3.97	
G-MEDC	Beechcraft 95-58 Baron	TH-1309	N18322	21. 8.89	To N58KK 12/92. Canx 1.12.92.
G-MEDD	Airbus A.320-231	386	3B-RGZ F-WWBI/(F-OHMC)/(XA-SGC)/F-WWBI	19. 3.97	
G-MEDI	Beechcraft C90 King Air	LJ-747	EC-DDS ECT-014/N23756	10. 9.76	To G-OFBL 7/83. Canx.
G-MEGA	PA-28R-201T Turbo Arrow III	28R-7803303	N999JG	13. 2.86	
G-MELD	American Aviation AA-5A Cheetah	AA5A-0863	G-BHCB	18. 2.85	
G-MELI	Air & Space 18-A Gyrocopter	18-12	N6106S	27.10.89	No CofA believed issued. Canx by CAA 10.1.91. To G-MASA 5/91.
G-MELT	Reims Cessna F.172H Skyhawk	0580	G-AWTI	23. 9.83	
G-MELV	Socata Rallye 235E Gabier	13328	G-BIND	21. 5.86	
G-MEME	PA-28R-201 Arrow III	2837051	N9219N	17. 8.90	
G-MENI	Aerospatiale AS.355F2 Twin Squirrel	5283	N355LH VH-HSG/F-WZKJ	29. 1.97	Crashed at Long Marston, North Yorkshire 12.8.97 after collision with Katana OE-AMH. Canx as destroyed 17.11.97.
G-MEOW	CFM Streak Shadow	PFA/206-12025		23. 4.93	
G-MERC	Colt 56A HAFB	842		11. 6.86	
G-MERE	Lindstrand LBL-77A HAFB	092		7. 4.94	
G-MERF	Grob G-115A	8091	EI-CAB (D-EGVV)	24. 7.95	
G-MERG	Mooney M.20J	24-3078	N5277Z	18.11.91	To N205RG 5/95. Canx 18.5.95.
G-MERI	PA-28-181 Archer II	28-8090267	N8175J	17. 7.80	
G-MERL	PA-28RT-201 Arrow IV	28R-7918036	N2116N	27. 6.86	
G-MERV	PA-28-161 Cherokee Warrior II	28-7716101	N2364Q	29. 5.90	To EC-GFH 2/96. Canx 4.7.95.
G-META	Bell 222	47028	N5733H	1. 8.80	To CS-HDS 12/96. Canx 23.12.96.
G-METB	Bell 222	47055		13. 2.81	To CS-HDU 12/96. Canx 23.12.96.
G-METC	Bell 222	47050	G-JAMC	9. 3.83	To CS-HDT 12/96. Canx 23.12.96.
G-METD	Eurocopter AS.355N Twin Squirrel	5525	G-BUJF F-WYMF	6. 4.93	To G-SEPA 7/96. Canx.
G-METE	Gloster Meteor F(TT).8	G5/361641	VZ467	5.11.91	(Stored 8/97)
G-METO	Short SD.3-30 Var.100	SH3005	G-BKIE C-GTAS/G-14-3005	7. 9.84	To G-METP 9/85. Canx.
G-METP	Short SD.3-30 Var.100	SH3005	G-METO G-BKIE/C-GTAS/G-14-3005	12. 9.85	Restored as G-BKIE. Canx.
G-METR	Cessna 414A Chancellor II	414A-0062	OY-CGC N4670N	15. 8.91	To Z-WTF 3/95. Canx 3.2.95.
G-MEUP	Cameron A-120 HAFB	2117		5.10.89	
G-MEXP	Sgian Dubh (Built by H.Lorimer)	?		. 7.99R	
G-MEYO	Enstrom 280FX	2059	SX-HCN	13. 1.95	
G-MFAL	Rockwell 690D Commander 900	15033	N49GA (N5925N)	28. 9.89	To VR-BMZ 5/92. Canx.
G-MFEU	HS.125 Srs.600B	256062	G-5-15	31. 1.77	To G-TMAS 12/84. Canx.
G-MFHI	Europa Avn Europa	PFA/247-12841		14.11.97	
G-MFHL	Robinson R-22 Beta	0885		4.10.88	To G-BXCX 1/97. Canx.
G-MFHT	Robinson R-22 Beta	2601	N8334H	20. 6.96	
G-MFLI	Cameron V-90 HAFB	2650		14. 8.91	
G-MFMF	Bell 206B JetRanger III	3569	G-BJNJ	4. 6.84	

Regn	Type	c/n	Previous identity	Regn date	Fate or immediate subsequent identity (if known)
G-MFMM	Scheibe SF-25C Falke	4412	(G-MBMM) D-KAEU	20. 4.82	
G-MGAA	BFC Quad City Challenger II	CH2-..97-1568 & PFA/177A-13124		18. 8.97	
G-MGAG	Aviasud Mistral	BMAA/HB/009 & 870545		20. 6.89	
G-MGAN	Robinson R-44 Astro	0588		10. 5.99	
G-MGCA	Pearce Jabiru UL	PFA/274-13228		8. 5.98	
G-MGCB	Cyclone Pegasus XL-Q (Trike ex G-MWUT)	SW-TE-0344 & 7267		16.10.96	
G-MGCK	Whittaker MW.6 Merlin	PFA/164-11262		30. 3.93	
G-MGDB	CFM Shadow Srs.DD	300-DD		19.12.97	To G-ODVB 11/98. Canx.
G-MGDL	Cyclone Pegasus Quantum 15	7400		17. 2.98	
G-MGDM	Cyclone Pegasus Quantum 15	7406		19. 3.98	
G-MGEC	Rans S-6-ESD Coyote II XL	PFA/204-13209		13.10.97	
G-MGEF	Cyclone Pegasus Quantum 15	7261		18. 9.96	
G-MGFK	Cyclone Pegasus Quantum 15	7396		2. 2.98	
G-MGFO	Cyclone Pegasus Quantum 15	7410		24. 3.98	Canx by CAA 10.5.99.
G-MGGG	Cyclone Pegasus Quantum 15 Super Sport	7377		3.11.97	
G-MGGT	CFM Streak Shadow Srs.M	K.252 & PFA/206-12723		3. 6.94	
G-MGGV	Cyclone Pegasus Quantum 15	7484		12.10.98	
G-MGMC	Cyclone Pegasus Quantum 15	7430		28. 4.98	
G-MGMT	Cyclone Pegasus Quantum 15	7225		28. 5.96	To G-DINO 12/98. Canx.
G-MGND	Rans S-6-ESD Coyote II XL	PFA/204-13152		27. 6.97	
G-MGOD	Medway Raven X	MRB110/106		6. 7.93	
G-MGOM	Medway Hybred 44XLR (Reported as being a Medway Raven)	MR125/103		22.11.91	
G-MGOO	Murphy Renegade Spirit UK	301 & PFA/188-11580		14.11.89	
G-MGPD	Solar Wings Pegasus XL-R	6905		9. 1.95	
G-MGPH	CFM Streak Shadow SA-M	PFA/206-13166	G-RSPH	27.11.97	
G-MGRH	Quad City Challenger II	CH2-1189-0482		20. 2.90	
G-MGRW	Cyclone Ax3/S	BMAA/HB/024 & C.3093155/S		8.11.93	
G-MGTG	Cyclone Pegasus Quantum 15	7369	G-MZIO	19.12.97	
G-MGTR	Hunt Wing/Experience	BMAA/HB/067		24. 7.97	
G-MGTW	CFM Shadow Srs.DD	287-DD		23. 1.98	
G-MGUN	Cyclone Ax2000	7284		18.12.96	
G-MGUX	Hunt Wing/Experience	BMAA/HB/064		24. 7.97	
G-MGUY	CFM Shadow Srs.CD	078		23.11.87	
G-MGWH	Thruster T.300	9013-T300-507		8.12.92	
G-MHBD	Cameron O-105 HAFB	1021		23. 2.84	Canx as WFU 17.4.98.
G-MHCA	Enstrom F-28C-UK	348	G-SHWW G-SMUJ/G-BHTF	10. 5.90	
G-MHCB	Enstrom 280C Shark	1031	N892PT	11.10.95	
G-MHCC	Bell 206B JetRanger II	1363	N3196N C-GOKD	26. 7.89	Ditched in sea and sank 33 miles from Blackpool on 20.3.92. Canx as WFU 21.5.92.
G-MHCD	Enstrom 280C-UK Shark	1112	G-SHGG N627H	12. 7.96	
G-MHCE	Enstrom F-28A	150	G-BBHD	22. 8.96	
G-MHCF	Enstrom 280C-UK Shark	1149	G-GSML G-BNNV/SE-HIY	19. 9.96	
G-MHCG	Enstrom 280C-UK Shark	1155	G-HAYN G-BPOX/N51776	7. 3.97	
G-MHCH	Enstrom 280C Shark	1043	N557H	19. 5.97	
G-MHCI	Enstrom 280C Shark	1152	N100WZ	20. 5.97	
G-MHCJ	Enstrom F-28C-UK	453	G-CTRN	30. 3.98	
G-MHCK	Enstrom 280FX	2006	G-BXXB ZK-HHN/JA7702	5. 6.98	
G-MHCL	Enstrom 280C Shark	1144	N51740	30. 6.98	
G-MHGI	Cessna 414A Chancellor II	414A-0455	G-BHKK (N2734D)	5. 8.80	To G-MLCS 9/82. Canx.
G-MHIH	HS.125 Srs.700B	257139	G-BKAA (G-GAIL)/G-5-18	19. 9.88	To RA-02803 2/94. Canx 11.1.94.
G-MHSL	MBB Bo.105DBS-4	S.819	D-HFCC	27. 2.90	To G-PASG 12/92. Canx.
G-MICH	Robinson R-22 Beta	0647	G-BNKY	3. 9.87	
G-MICK	Reims Cessna F.172N Skyhawk II	1592	PH-JRA PH-AXB	9. 1.80	
G-MICV	PBN BN-2B-21 Islander	2106	G-BIXC	9. 9.81	To (5B-CFP)/5B-ICV 5/82. Canx 14.5.82.
G-MICY	Everett Autogyro Srs.1	018	(G-BOVF)	26. 2.90	
G-MICZ	PA-46-310P Malibu	46-8508096	N2494X	3. 7.95	
G-MIDA	Airbus A.321-231	806	D-AVZQ	31. 3.98	
G-MIDB	Airbus A.321-231	968	(G-MIDE)	. .98R	NTU - To G-MIDH 3/99. Canx.
G-MIDC	Airbus A.321-231	835	D-AVZZ	12. 6.98	
G-MIDD	PA-28-140 Cherokee Cruiser F	28-7325444	G-BBDD N55687	20. 1.97	
G-MIDE(1)	Airbus A.321-231	968		. .98R	NTU - To (G-MIDB)/G-MIDH 3/99. Canx.

Regn	Type	c/n	Previous identity	Regn date	Fate or immediate subsequent identity (if known)
G-MIDE(2)	Airbus A.321-231	864	D-AVZB	14. 8.98	
G-MIDF	Airbus A.321-231	810	D-AVZS	24. 4.98	
G-MIDG	Bushby-Long MM-1 Midget Mustang	385	N11DE	14. 3.90	
	(Built by T.L.Owens)				
G-MIDH	Airbus A.321-231	968	(G-MIDB)	22. 3.99	
			(G-MIDE)/D-AVZX		
	(Noted painted with marks G-MIDE under the wing prior to delivery)				
G-MIDI	Airbus A.321-231	974	D-AVZA	26. 3.99	
G-MIDJ	Airbus A.321-231	1045	D-AVZO	16. 7.99	
G-MIDK	Airbus A.321-231	1207	D-AVZ.	. .98R	(delivery due in 2/00)
G-MIDL	Airbus A.321-231	1...	D-AVZ.	. .98R	(delivery due in 2/01)
G-MIDM	Airbus A.321-231	1...	D-AVZ.	. .98R	(delivery due in 3/01)
G-MIDR	Airbus A.320-232	1...	F-WW..	. .98R	(delivery due in 2/02)
G-MIDS	Airbus A.320-232	1...	F-WW..	. .98R	(delivery due in 3/01)
G-MIDT	Airbus A.320-232	1...	F-WW..	. .98R	(delivery due in 3/01)
G-MIDU	Airbus A.320-232	1...	F-WW..	. .98R	(delivery due in 2/01)
G-MIDV	Airbus A.320-232	1...	F-WW..	. .98R	(delivery due in 11/00)
G-MIDW	Airbus A.320-232	1...	F-WW..	. .98R	(delivery due in 3/00)
G-MIDX	Airbus A.320-232	1...	F-WW..	. .98R	(delivery due in 3/00)
G-MIDY	Airbus A.320-232	1014	F-WWDQ	28. 6.99	
G-MIDZ	Airbus A.320-232	934	F-WWII	19. 1.99	
G-MIFF	Robin DR.400/180 Regent	2076		31. 5.91	
G-MIGI	Colt 105A HAFB	1775		28. 6.90	To D-OVIV 1/93. Canx 13.1.93.
G-MIII	Extra EA.300/L	013	D-EXFI	5. 9.95	
G-MIKE	Brookland Hornet	MG.1		15. 5.78	
	(Originally regd as an Gyroflight Hornet)				
G-MIKI	Rans S-6-ESA Coyote II			28. 2.97	
		PFA/204-13094			
G-MIKY	Cameron Mickey Mouse 90SS HAFB	1323		11. 7.86	Canx by CAA 19.5.93.
G-MILA	Reims Cessna F.172N Skyhawk II	1686	D-EGHC(2)	9. 6.98	
			PH-AYJ		
G-MILB	Cessna 340A II	340A-1022	HB-LLH	20. 9.84	To F-GEDD 2/86. Canx 25.10.85.
			N4621N		
G-MILE	Cameron N-77 HAFB	2411		26. 9.90	
G-MILI	Bell 206B JetRanger III	2275	C-GGAR	5.10.94	
			5H-MPV		
G-MILK	Socata TB-10 Tobago	82		10. 1.80	To G-MOOR 7/91. Canx.
G-MILL	PA-32-301T Turbo Saratoga		N8431Z	26. 7.88	Ditched in the Atlantic off Libreville, Gabon on 5.6.90.
		32-8124026	N9530N		Canx by CAA 12.8.93.
G-MILN	Cessna 182Q Skylane	182-65770	N735XQ	9. 7.99	
G-MILY	American Aviation AA-5A Cheetah		G-BFXY	2. 9.96	
		AA5A-0672			
G-MIMA	BAe 146 Srs.200	E2079	G-CNMF	3. 3.93	
			G-5-079/G-CNMF/G-5-079		
G-MIME	Europa Avn Europa	PFA/247-12850		26. 9.97	(Fuselage only noted 10/98 at Lasham)
G-MIMI	Socata TB-20 Trinidad	582	N20DN	27. 7.89	Destroyed in fatal crash in a field at Roves Farm, Sevenhampton, 4 miles north of Swindon on 21.3.93. Canx by CAA 3.8.93.
G-MIND	Cessna 404 Titan II	404-0004	G-SKKC	27. 4.93	
			G-OHUB/SE-GMX/(N3932C)		
G-MINE	Cessna 550 Citation II	550-0343	(N1214D)	2. 3.82	To N721US 3/83. Canx 17.3.83.
	(Unit No.391)				
G-MINI	Phoenix Currie Wot	PFA/58-10294		4. 8.78	No UK Permit issued. Canx as WFU 6.8.99.
G-MINS	Nicollier HN.700 Menestrel II			23.10.92	
		PFA/217-12354			
G-MINT	Pitts S-1S Special	PFA/09-10292		7. 2.83	
G-MINX	Bell 47G-4A (Mod)	7604	N6242N	16. 3.90	
			(G-FOOR)/N6242N		
G-MIOO	Miles M.100 Student 2	100/1008	G-APLK	26.10.84	Badly damaged in forced landing at Duxford on 24.8.85.
			G-MIOO/G-APLK/		Permit expired 6.5.86. (To Museum of Berkshire Aviation
			XS941/G-APLK/G-35-4		Trust) (Stored for rebuild 4/97)
G-MISH	Cessna 182R Skylane II	182-67888	G-RFAB	16. 6.95	
			G-BIXT/N6397H		
G-MISR	Robinson R-22 Beta	1738		9. 4.91	To PH-AJK 3/93. Canx 17.2.93.
G-MISS	Taylor JT.2 Titch	PFA/3234		18.12.78	
G-MIST	Cessna T.210K Turbo Centurion		G-AYGM	8.12.80	DBER after crashing into a ditch on take-off from Bretton
		T210-59338	N9438M		Hall Farm airstrip, near Chester racecourse on 10.7.92. Canx as TWFU 16.12.92. To Dodson Aviation Scrapyard 2/93.
G-MITR	Maule MXT-7-180	14021C		11. 6.91	To VH-AOJ 9/93. Canx 22.9.93.
G-MITS	Cameron N-77 HAFB	1115		20. 2.85	
	(Rebuilt with new envelope c/n 3217 .94)				
G-MITZ	Cameron N-77 HAFB	1638		17. 3.88	
G-MIWS	Cessna 310R II	310R-1585	G-ODNP	1. 2.96	
			N19TP/N2DD/N1836E		
G-MJAA	Ultrasports Tripacer 330/Flexiform			17. 6.82	Canx by CAA 5.12.95.
	Striker (C/n is engine no)	82-00258			
G-MJAB	Ultrasports Skytrike	564		17. 6.82	Canx by CAA 2.9.88.
G-MJAC	American Aerolights Eagle III	3075		17. 6.82	Canx as WFU 9.4.90.
G-MJAD	Eipper Quicksilver MX	3034		17. 6.82	Canx by CAA 22.11.91.
G-MJAE	American Aerolights Eagle	1021		12. 7.82	
	(C/n is probably engine no)				
G-MJAF	Southdown Puma 440 (Lightning DS)			17. 6.82	Canx by CAA 16.4.98.
		BHA-01			

Regn	Type	c/n	Previous identity	Regn date	Fate or immediate subsequent identity (if known)
G-MJAG	Skyhook TR1/Sabre C	TR1/24		18. 6.82	Canx by CAA 23.2.93.
G-MJAH	American Aerolights Eagle 1A	BW.01		18. 6.82	Canx by CAA 15.8.85.
G-MJAI	American Aerolights Eagle	LFL-02		22. 6.82	Canx as WFU 28.5.93.
G-MJAJ	Eurowing Goldwing	EW-36		18. 6.82	
G-MJAK	Hiway Demon	FCP-01		18. 6.82	Canx by CAA 13.6.90.
G-MJAL	Wheeler (Skycraft) Scout Mk.III/3/R	0433 R/3		18. 6.82	
G-MJAM	Eipper Quicksilver MX	JCL-01		18. 6.82	
G-MJAN	Hiway Skytrike/Flexiform Hilander	RPFD-01 & 21U9		21. 6.82	
G-MJAO	Hiway Skytrike/Super Scorpion 2	KHSSC 2		21. 6.82	Canx by CAA 9.6.93.
G-MJAP	Hiway Skytrike/Vulcan 160	21W3		22. 6.82	
G-MJAR	Chargus Titan	QA-01		22. 6.82	Canx by CAA 2.9.93.
G-MJAS	Southern Aerosports Scorpion	-		. .82R	NTU - Canx.
G-MJAT	Hiway Skytrike/Demon	21Y9		22. 6.82	Canx by CAA 6.4.90.
G-MJAU	Hiway Skytrike 250/Super Scorpion	APC-01		23. 6.82	Canx by CAA 13.6.90.
G-MJAV	Hiway Skytrike/Demon 175	817003		23. 6.82	(Stored 7/96)
	(Originally regd with c/n 81-00042)				
G-MJAW	Nicholls 250/Solar Wings Typhoon	MRN-01		23. 6.82	Canx by CAA 13.6.90.
G-MJAX	American Aerolights Eagle	3877		23. 6.82	Canx by CAA 9.12.91.
G-MJAY	Eurowing Goldwing	EW-58		23. 6.82	
G-MJAZ	Aerodyne (Raven) Vector 610	1251	PH-1J1 G-MJAZ	23. 6.82	(Stored 1/97)
G-MJBA	Aerodyne (Raven) Vector 610	1252		23. 6.82	Canx by CAA 13.6.90.
G-MJBB	Aerodyne (Raven) Vector 610	1253		23. 6.82	Canx by CAA 13.6.90.
G-MJBC	Aerodyne (Raven) Vector 610	1254		23. 6.82	Canx by CAA 13.6.90.
G-MJBD	Aerodyne (Raven) Vector 610	1255		23. 6.82	Canx by CAA 13.6.90.
G-MJBE	Wheeler (Skycraft) Scout X	001		23. 6.82	Canx by CAA 13.6.90.
	(Built by Newall Aircraft and Tool Co.Ltd)				
G-MJBF	Ultrasports Tripacer 330/Southdown Puma (Lightning 195)	DJG-01		23. 6.82	Canx by CAA 6.9.94.
	(Also quotes engine no. 81-00091 as c/n)				
G-MJBG	Mainair Tri-Flyer 330/Solar Wings Typhoon	062-27382 & T681-187L		24. 6.82	Canx by CAA 13.6.90.
	(C/n was quoted as "EC34PM" - engine type)(Also quotes power unit 82-00124)				
G-MJBH	American Aerolights Eagle	3095		24. 6.82	Canx as WFU 19.12.94.
G-MJBI	Eipper Quicksilver MX	3075		24. 6.82	
	(Originally regd with c/n ASR-01)				
G-MJBJ	Hiway Skytrike	-		. .82R	NTU - Canx.
G-MJBK	Swallow AeroPlane Swallow B	582007-2		18.11.83	Canx by CAA 23.6.97.
G-MJBL	American Aerolights Eagle	2892		25. 6.82	
G-MJBM	Eurowing Catto CP-16	AHM-01		28. 6.82	Canx by CAA 13.6.90.
G-MJBN	American Aerolights Rainbow Eagle	3132		28. 6.82	Canx by CAA 6.9.94. (Open store 7/95)
G-MJBO	Bell Microlight Type A	GB-01		28. 6.82	Canx as WFU 18.4.90.
G-MJBP	Eurowing Catto CP-16	IW-01		28. 6.82	Canx by CAA 13.6.90.
G-MJBR	Eipper Quicksilver Model B	JD-01		29. 6.82	Canx as WFU 19.9.86.
G-MJBS	UAS Storm Buggy	JL814S		29. 6.82	
G-MJBT	Eipper Quicksilver MX II	DJ/NBII & 3662		30. 6.82	Canx by CAA 24.1.95. (Stored 8/95)
G-MJBU	Microwave	ARFF-01		30. 6.82	Fatal crash in a field near Outwards Farm, Camber, Sussex on 19.9.82. Canx as destroyed 10.5.85.
	(Homebuilt by A.R.F.Fountain)				
G-MJBV	American Aerolights Eagle 215B	RSP-001		1. 7.82	
G-MJBW	American Aerolights Eagle	JDP-01		1. 7.82	Canx by CAA 13.6.90.
G-MJBX	Pterodactyl Ptraveler	BJE-01		1. 7.82	Canx by CAA 24.3.99.
G-MJBY	Rotec Rally 2B	RPW-01		1. 7.82	Canx by CAA 13.6.90.
G-MJBZ	Huntair Pathfinder 1	PK-17		2. 7.82	
G-MJCA	Skyhook Sabre	33		2. 7.82	Canx by CAA 6.9.94.
G-MJCB	Hornet Microlight 330	H.320		2. 7.82	Canx by CAA 3.2.92.
G-MJCC	Southdown Puma	700		2. 7.82	Canx by CAA 24.1.95.
	(Flew with Skyhook wing mid-84)				
G-MJCD	Tetley Trike/Southdown Sigma	BT-01		2. 7.82	Canx by CAA 2.9.88.
G-MJCE	Southdown Panther Sprint X	RGC-01		5. 7.82	
	(Originally regd as Ultrasports Tripacer/Southdown Puma Sprint with same c/n)				
G-MJCF	Hill (Maxair) Hummer	SMC-01		5. 7.82	Canx by CAA 24.1.95.
G-MJCG	Southern Flyer Mk.1	001		5. 7.82	Canx by CAA 6.9.94.
G-MJCH	Ultraflight Mirage Mk.II	SMC-02		5. 7.82	Canx 19.4.93 on sale to Ireland.
G-MJCI	Kruchek Firefly 440/Flexiform Dual Striker	HK-01		5. 7.82	Canx by CAA 23.2.93.
G-MJCJ	Hiway Spectrum	2157		5. 7.82	Canx by CAA 26.1.89.
G-MJCK	Southern Aerosports Scorpion	A0014		5. 7.82	Canx by CAA 22.7.87.
G-MJCL	Eipper Quicksilver MX II	RFW-01		5. 7.82	(On overhaul 9/96)
G-MJCM	Southern Flyer Mk.1	004		5. 7.82	Canx by CAA 13.6.90.
G-MJCN	Southern Flyer Mk.1	005		5. 7.82	
G-MJCO	Striplin Lone Ranger	SAC160/JW002		6. 7.82	Canx by CAA 13.6.90.
G-MJCP	Huntair Pathfinder 440	RCW-01		. 7.82	Canx by CAA 7.9.93.
G-MJCR	American Aerolights Eagle	RFH-01		7. 7.82	Canx by CAA 13.6.90.
G-MJCS	Pterodactyl EF.5	DE.150		7. 7.82	Canx by CAA 13.6.90.

Regn	Type	c/n	Previous identity	Regn date	Fate or immediate subsequent identity (if known)
G-MJCT	Hiway Skytrike/Demon	CA-01		7. 7.82	Canx by CAA 27.8.91.
G-MJCU	Tarjani/Solar Wings Typhoon S5	SCG-01		7. 7.82	
G-MJCV	Southern Flyer Mk.1	GNH-01		7. 7.82	Canx as WFU 23.8.89.
G-MJCW	Hiway Skytrike/Super Scorpion	MGS-01		7. 7.82	
G-MJCX	American Aerolights Eagle 215B (Same c/n as G-MBBN)	2759		7. 7.82	
G-MJCY	Eurowing Goldwing	EW-48		7. 7.82	Canx by CAA 6.9.94.
G-MJCZ	Southern Aerosports Scorpion 2-Seat	CB-01		8. 7.82	Canx by CAA 22.7.87.
G-MJDA	Hornet Executive 330/Skyhook Sabre C	H340		12. 7.82	Permit expired 28.2.87. Canx as WFU 13.8.99.
G-MJDB	Hiway Skytrike/Birdman Cherokee (Originally regd as Solar Wings Typhoon)	JKC-01		8. 7.82	Canx by CAA 24.1.95.
G-MJDC	Mainair Gemini 440/Flexiform Dual Striker (Original trike Mainair TriFlyer c/n 080-18682 was replaced in 6/84, becoming G-MNBY in 5/85)	ACD-01 & 201-201083-2		8. 7.82	Canx by CAA 13.6.90.
G-MJDD	Not allotted in error.				
G-MJDE	Huntair Pathfinder 1	020		9. 7.82	
G-MJDF	Ultrasports Tripacer 250/Flexiform Striker	SA 1010		9. 7.82	Canx by CAA 13.6.90.
G-MJDG	Hornet 250/Flexiform Medium Striker (Originally Hornet Supertrike/Skyhook with c/n H280, with the wing being replaced in 3/84 and dismantled for spares)	H230		9. 7.82	Canx by CAA 26.11.97.
G-MJDH	Huntair Pathfinder 1	015		9. 7.82	
G-MJDI	Southern Flyer Mk.1	SDH-01		9. 7.82	Canx by CAA 6.9.94.
G-MJDJ	Hiway Skytrike/Demon	VW17D		9. 7.82	
G-MJDK	American Aerolights Eagle	3072		14. 7.82	Canx by CAA 3.2.92.
G-MJDL	American Aerolights Eagle	MTE-01		12. 7.82	Canx as WFU 27.10.88.
G-MJDM	Wheeler (Skycraft) Scout Mk.III 3/A	297A		12. 7.82	Canx by CAA 13.6.90.
G-MJDN	Skyhook Single Seat	GM-01		12. 7.82	Badly damaged on forced landing near Doncaster Airport on 25.4.83. Canx by CAA 13.6.90.
G-MJDO	Mainair Tri-Flyer/Southdown Puma (Lightning DS) (Was fitted with Trike from G-MBKX, which then went to G-MMIR)	NGS-01 & CSB-01		20. 7.82	Canx 23.3.95 on sale to Portugal.
G-MJDP	Eurowing Goldwing	GW-001		12. 7.82	
G-MJDR	Hiway Skytrike/Demon	PJB-01		14. 7.82	
G-MJDS	Eipper Quicksilver MX II (Quoted c/n is engine number)	11303		21. 7.82	Canx as WFU 16.8.82. Used for spares.
G-MJDT	Eipper Quicksilver MX II (Also quotes engine no. 12017 as c/n)	3661		15. 7.82	Canx as WFU 10.6.85.
G-MJDU	Eipper Quicksilver MX II	14002		15. 7.82	
G-MJDV	Skyhook TR1	TR1/25		15. 7.82	Canx as WFU 4.6.90.
G-MJDW	Eipper Quicksilver MX II	RI-01		15. 7.82	
G-MJDX	Ultrasports Tripacer/Moyes Mega II	PHD-01		16. 7.82	Canx by CAA 27.10.93.
G-MJDY	Ultrasports Tripacer 250/Solar Wings Medium Storm	RH-001		14. 7.82	Canx by CAA 24.1.95.
G-MJDZ	Goodwin Enterprise Lynx/Chargus Cyclone 180 (The original Cyclone wing was sold attached to a new power unit and trike 25.8.83 and given c/n GMD-02. The original trike went elsewhere)	GMD-01		19. 7.82	Canx as destroyed 21.7.87.
G-MJEA	Flexiform Striker	SJO-01		19. 7.82	Canx by CAA 13.6.90.
G-MJEB(1)	American Aerolights Eagle	-		. .82R	NTU - Canx.
G-MJEB(2)	Southdown Puma Sprint	1231/0041		18. 4.85	
G-MJEC	Mainair Tripacer/Southdown Lightning (Originally regd as Southdown Puma 1 (Lightning Phase II) with same c/n)	L170/449		20. 7.82	Canx as WFU 16.11.95.
G-MJED	Eipper Quicksilver MX	RH-01		20. 7.82	Canx by CAA 13.6.90.
G-MJEE	Mainair Tri-Flyer 250/Solar Wings Typhoon	038-251181		20. 7.82	
G-MJEF	Gryphon Sailwings Gryphon 180	0455		20. 7.82	Canx as WFU 26.7.89.
G-MJEG	Eurowing Goldwing	GJS-01		20. 7.82	
G-MJEH	Rotec Rally 2B	018T		20. 7.82	Canx by CAA 17.3.99.
G-MJEI	American Aerolights Eagle	3381		21. 7.82	Canx by CAA 26.7.90.
G-MJEJ	American Aerolights Eagle	3674		21. 7.82	Canx by CAA 9.9.85.
G-MJEK	Hiway Skytrike 330/Demon	AE 17D		16. 7.82	Canx by CAA 14.9.93.
G-MJEL	GMD-01 Trike/Airwave Nimrod (Originally regd as Stratos Prototype 3 Axis Srs.1 with c/n 001.ST; type amended in 10/83)	GMD-01 & 001.ST		4. 8.82	Canx by CAA 2.9.88.
G-MJEM	Griffin 440/Flexiform Dual Striker (Originally regd as Garland Skytrike with c/n 0010/330)	RGG-01		21. 7.82	Canx as WFU 10.11.88.
G-MJEN	Eurowing Catto CP-16	CP.036		22. 7.82	Canx by CAA 13.6.90.
G-MJEO	American Aerolights Eagle 215B	4562		26. 7.82	(Extant 8/95)
G-MJEP	Pterodactyl Ptraveller	MEA.14		23. 7.82	Canx by CAA 24.1.95.
G-MJER	Ultrasports Tripacer/Flexiform Solo Striker	DSD-01		23. 7.82	
G-MJES	Stratos Prototype 3 Axis Srs.1	003.ST		4. 8.82	Canx by CAA 13.6.90.

Regn	Type	c/n	Previous identity	Regn date	Fate or immediate subsequent identity (if known)
G-MJET	Stratos Prototype 3 Axis Srs.1	002.ST		4. 8.82	Canx by CAA 14.9.87.
G-MJEU	Hiway Skystrike	PB-01		26. 7.82	Canx by CAA 13.6.90.
G-MJEV	SMD Scoble Gazelle/Flexiform Striker	SMA 101		26. 7.82	Canx by CAA 13.6.90.
G-MJEW	Eagle Electra Flyer	RCW-01		26. 7.82	Canx by CAA 13.10.87.
G-MJEX	Eipper Quicksilver MX II	13894		27. 7.82	Canx by CAA 14.11.91.
G-MJEY	Southdown Puma (Lightning DS) (Probably Mainair Tri-Flyer)	PMC-01		27. 7.82	
G-MJEZ	Raven Vector 600	PAS-01		27. 7.82	Canx as WFU 18.5.90.
G-MJFA	Hiway Tri-Flyer/Hiway Super Scorpion	GWW-01		27. 7.82	Converted to a Hang-Glider. The Hiway Tri-Flyer trike unit was sold 29.1.83 and used in building G-MNFA in 12/83 with same c/n. Canx as WFU 23.2.83.
G-MJFB	Ultrasports Tripacer 330/Flexiform Striker	AJK-01		27. 7.82	
G-MJFC	Southern Aerosports Scorpion Dual	ISB-01		27. 7.82	Canx as WFU 8.8.83.
G-MJFD	Ultrasport Tripacer/Moyes Mega II	RNOK-01		27. 7.82	Canx as WFU 18.5.88.
G-MJFE	Hiway Super Scorpion	NF-01		29. 7.82	Canx by CAA 13.6.90.
G-MJFF	Huntair Pathfinder 1	016		10. 8.82	Damaged in crash following collision with tree at Henley-in-Arden, Warwickshire on 29.8.83. Canx by CAA 24.1.95.
G-MJFG	Eurowing Goldwing	014		28. 7.82	Canx as destroyed 5.12.91.
G-MJFH	Eipper Quicksilver MX (Originally regd with c/n 11866 - engine no.)	3077		28. 7.82	(Stored 1/94) Canx by CAA 23.6.97.
G-MJFI	Ultrasports Tripacer 330/Flexiform Striker	MRP-01		28. 7.82	Canx as destroyed 21.1.98.
G-MJFJ	Hiway Skytrike 250/Demon 175	DH17D		28. 7.82	Canx by CAA 10.1.94.
G-MJFK	Mainair Tri-Flyer/Flexiform Dual Sealander	JH-01		28. 7.82	
G-MJFL	Mainair Tri-Flyer 440/Flexiform Dual Sealander	JH-02 & 086-26782		28. 7.82	Canx as WFU 20.12.94.
G-MJFM	Huntair Pathfinder 1	ML-01		2. 9.82	
G-MJFN	Huntair Pathfinder 1	026		26. 8.82	Canx by CAA 13.6.90.
G-MJFO	Not allotted.				
G-MJFP	American Aerolights Eagle 215B	5010		2. 8.82	
G-MJFR	American Aerolights Eagle	5014		5. 8.82	Canx as WFU 27.4.90.
G-MJFS	American Aerolights Eagle 215B	5015		17. 8.82	Canx by CAA 23.6.97.
G-MJFT	American Aerolights Eagle	5009		13. 8.82	Canx by CAA 13.6.90.
G-MJFU	Not allotted.				
G-MJFV	Ultrasports Tripacer/Southdown Puma 1 (Lightning 170)	401		30. 7.82	Canx by CAA 15.3.93.
G-MJFW	Southdown Puma 2	305		3. 8.82	Canx by CAA 13.6.90.
G-MJFX	Skyhook TR1/Sabre	TR1/38		2. 8.82	
G-MJFY(1)	Hornet 250/Solar Wings Storm (Originally regd as Hornet 250/Skyhook Sabre with c/n H.270; amended in 2/84)	H.270/SLE 80126		29. 7.82R	NTU - Canx 21.6.84 as "regd in error". To G-MNFY 6/84.
G-MJFY(2)	Skyhook TR1 Mk.2/Sabre	014056922		. 6.84	Canx by CAA 13.6.90.
G-MJFZ	Hiway Skytrike/Demon	JAL-01		29. 7.82	Canx by CAA 13.6.90.
G-MJGA	Hiway Skytrike 160/Moonraker 78	JHW-01		29. 7.82	Canx by CAA 13.6.90.
G-MJGB	American Aerolights Eagle	NPD-01		29. 7.82	Canx by CAA 4.6.90.
G-MJGC	Hornet Microlight	H.260		30. 7.82	Canx by CAA 24.1.95.
G-MJGD	Huntair Pathfinder (Also quotes engine no. 82-00240)	024		31. 7.82	Canx by CAA 16.9.93.
G-MJGE	Eipper Quicksilver MX II	DB-01		30. 7.82	Canx by CAA 23.6.97.
G-MJGF	Poisestar Aeolus Mk.I	1		2. 9.82	Canx by CAA 13.6.90.
G-MJGG	Skyhook TR1/Cutlass 195	AS-26		2. 8.82	Canx by CAA 23.6.97.
G-MJGH	Hiway Skytrike/Flexiform Sealander	PN-01		2. 8.82	Canx by CAA 13.6.90.
G-MJGI	Eipper Quicksilver MX II	JRW1021/JMH14888		3. 8.82	Canx by CAA 3.2.92.
G-MJGJ	American Aerolights Eagle	3175		3. 8.82	Canx by CAA 13.6.90.
G-MJGK	Eurowing Goldwing	040		3. 8.82	Canx by CAA 13.6.90.
G-MJGL	Chargus Titan 38	17		4. 8.82	Owner believed to have emigrated to Spain in 4/83 and subsequently deceased. Canx by CAA 31.7.84. Also canx (again) as WFU 6.9.93.
G-MJGM	Hiway Skytrike/Demon 195	FU 19D		5. 8.82	Canx by CAA 6.9.94.
G-MJGN	Greenslade Mono-trike/Hiway Wing	001		5. 8.82	Canx as WFU 24.1.85.
G-MJGO	Barnes Avon Trike 330/Wasp Gryphon	2510		5. 6.82	
G-MJGP	Hiway Skytrike/Demon	001		5. 8.82	Canx as destroyed 15.9.89.
G-MJGR	Hiway Skytrike/Demon	HLC-01		5. 8.82	Canx as WFU 18.12.91.
G-MJGS	American Aerolights Eagle	PDG-01		14. 8.82	Canx by CAA 13.6.90.
G-MJGT	Skyhook Cutlass	TS-1		5. 8.82	Canx by CAA 2.9.88.
G-MJGU	Pterodactyl Mk.I	JDL-01		20. 8.82	Canx by CAA 13.6.90.
G-MJGV	Eipper Quicksilver MX II	11403		17. 8.82	(Stored 7/90) Canx as WFU 20.5.93.
G-MJGW	Hiway Skytrike/Solar Wings Typhoon	T581-156		6. 8.82	Canx by CAA 2.9.88.
G-MJGX	Southdown Puma 250 (Also described as "Hiway Skyrider")	BB.TDJ-1		2. 2.83	(Stored 8/93) Canx by CAA 6.4.94.
G-MJGY	Ultrasports Puma 440	700/02		6. 8.82	Sold in Ireland in 6/83.

Regn	Type	c/n	Previous identity	Regn date	Fate or immediate subsequent identity (if known)
G-MJGZ	Mainair Tri-Flyer 330/Flexiform Striker (Trike ex.G-MBMW)	JFB-01 & 088-05882		6. 8.82	Canx by CAA 13.6.90.
G-MJHA	Hiway Skytrike 250 Mk.II/Demon 175	MO 17D		9. 8.82	Canx by CAA 24.1.95. (Stored 8/93)
G-MJHB	AES Sky Ranger	SR.100		9. 8.82	Canx by CAA 13.6.90. (Fuselage stored 3/97)
G-MJHC	Ultrasports Tripacer 330/Southdown Lightning Mk.II	82-00044		9. 8.82	
G-MJHD	Campbell-Jones Ladybird	001		27. 8.82	Canx by CAA 13.6.90.
G-MJHE	Hiway Skytrike 250/Demon	25 V2		10. 8.82	Canx as WFU 8.12.94.
G-MJHF	Skyhook Trike	RAW-01		10. 8.82	Canx by CAA 3.2.92.
G-MJHG	Huntair Pathfinder 330	AN-01		11. 8.82	Canx by CAA 13.6.90.
G-MJHH	Soleair Dactyl (Pterodactyl)	CNG-01		11. 8.82	Canx by CAA 13.6.90.
G-MJHI	Soleair Dactyl (Pterodactyl)	SBG-01		11. 8.82	Canx by CAA 13.6.90.
G-MJHJ	Wickington GWW.1 Redwing	001		11. 8.82	Canx as WFU 3.4.90.
G-MJHK	Ultrasports Tripacer 330/Hiway Demon 195	BR-01		11. 8.82	Canx by CAA 4.12.90.
G-MJHL	Mainair Tri-Flyer Mk.II/Skyhook Sailwing	D-075J		11. 8.82	Canx as WFU 12.4.90.
G-MJHM	Ultrasports Tripacer/Hiway Demon 175 (Regd with c/n ME-170)	ME17D		11. 8.82	
G-MJHN	American Aerolights Eagle	3867		11. 8.82	Canx as WFU 15.8.85.
G-MJHO	Shilling Bumble Bee Srs.1	1		26. 8.82	Canx by CAA 6.9.94.
G-MJHP	American Aerolights Eagle	4219		23. 8.82	Canx by CAA 24.1.95.
G-MJHR	GS Trike/Southdown Lightning DS	GNS-01		12. 8.82	
G-MJHS	American Aerolights Eagle	2938		17. 8.82	Canx by CAA 13.6.90.
G-MJHT	Eurowing Goldwing	EW-71		13. 8.82	Canx by CAA 13.6.90.
G-MJHU	Eipper Quicksilver MX	10692		13. 8.82	(Stored 9/96)
G-MJHV	Hiway Skytrike 250/Demon	AG-17		13. 8.82	
G-MJHW	Southdown Puma I	PCC-01		18.10.82	Canx by CAA 22.7.87.
G-MJHX	Eipper Quicksilver MX II (Originally regd with c/n GJP-01)	1033		13. 8.82	(Stored 9/97)
G-MJHY	American Aerolights Eagle	JTHM-01		13. 8.82	Canx by CAA 13.6.90.
G-MJHZ	Ultrasports Tripacer 330/Southdown Lightning 170 (Puma DS) (Originally regd with c/n L17D/267)	L170/267		13. 8.82	
G-MJIA	Ultrasports Tripacer/Flexiform Solo Striker (Originally regd as Mainair Tri-Flyer/Flexiform Striker with c/n BW.1, then c/n SE-007 by 9/83)	SE.007		13. 8.82	
G-MJIB	Hornet 250/Skyhook Sabre Flexwing	H.350		13. 8.82	(Based in France) Canx by CAA 25.3.99.
G-MJIC	Ultrasports Tripacer/Flexiform Solo Striker (Originally regd as Ultrasports Puma 330 with same c/n)	82-00043		13. 8.82	
G-MJID	Southdown Puma DS	L431		13. 8.82	Canx by CAA 24.1.95.
G-MJIE	Hornet 330/Solar Wings Medium Typhoon (Originally regd as Perrills/Typhoon with c/n CJD.001; the trike was sold seperately in early 1984)	H.490 & T281-83L		13. 8.82	Canx by CAA 23.6.97.
G-MJIF	Mainair Tri-Flyer/Flexiform Striker (C/n is engine type) "E-1 EC25PS-04"			16. 8.82	
G-MJIG	Hiway Skytrike/Demon 175	KP17D		16. 8.82	Canx by CAA 24.1.95.
G-MJIH	Ultrasports Tripacer/Hiway Super Scorpion	ARC-01		16. 8.82	Canx by CAA 8.10.93.
G-MJII	American Aerolights Eagle	3193		16. 8.82	Canx by CAA 13.6.90.
G-MJIJ	Ultrasports Tripacer 250/Solar Wings Typhoon	DT166		17. 8.82	Canx as WFU 2.5.84.
G-MJIK	Southdown Lightning	JFC-01		17. 8.82	Canx by CAA 14.11.91.
G-MJIL	Bremner Mitchell Wing B-10 Special	P.1059		17. 8.82	Canx by CAA 6.9.94.
G-MJIM	Skyhook Cutlass	PR-01		18. 8.82	Canx by CAA 13.6.90.
G-MJIN	Hiway Skytrike	PWH-01		18. 8.82	Canx by CAA 24.10.88.
G-MJIO	American Aerolights Eagle	2626		18. 8.82	Canx as PWFU 25.3.99.
G-MJIP	Wheeler Scout Mk.III/3/A	440R/3		18. 8.82	Canx by CAA 13.6.90.
G-MJIR	Eipper Quicksilver MX II (Originally regd with c/n JT-01 - rebuilt after crashing 14.8.83 using parts & c/n from Quicksilver PH-1J5 in 1985)	1392		18. 8.82	(Stored 8/96)
G-MJIS	American Aerolights Eagle	4008		19. 8.82	Canx by CAA 7.9.94.
G-MJIT	Hiway Skytrike/Super Scorpion	FMDH-01		19. 8.82	Canx as WFU 5.12.91.
G-MJIU	Eipper Quicksilver MX	3030		19. 8.82	Canx by CAA 24.1.95.
G-MJIV	Pterodactyl	GEF-01		20. 8.82	Canx by CAA 7.9.94.
G-MJIW	Southdown Lightning DS/Mainair Dual Trike	ARH-01		23. 8.82	Owner believed to have emigrated to Spain in 4/83 and subsequently deceased. Canx by CAA 31.7.84.
G-MJIX	Mainair Tri-Flyer/Flexiform Hilander	SWAG-01		23. 8.82	Canx as destroyed 16.8.89.
G-MJIY	Flexiform Striker/Solar Wings Panther (Originally regd as Flexiform Voyager then as Ultrasports Tripacer/Flexiform Striker with same c/n)	002 CSRS		23. 8.82	
G-MJIZ	Ultrasports Tripacer/Southdown Lightning	JS-189		23. 8.82	
G-MJJA	Huntair Pathfinder 1 (Originally regd with c/n 032)	031		23. 8.82	
G-MJJB	Eipper Quicksilver MX	3526		23. 8.82	

Regn	Type	c/n	Previous identity	Regn date	Fate or immediate subsequent identity (if known)
G-MJJC	Eipper Quicksilver MX II	AB22554-14826		24. 8.82	Badly damaged in crash at Harden Road, Keighley on 16.4.83. Canx by CAA 13.6.90.
G-MJJD	Birdman Cherokee 200	BJS-01		24. 8.82	Canx as WFU 12.10.93.
G-MJJE	Douglas Type 1	RD-1		24. 8.82	Canx by CAA 13.6.90.
G-MJJF	Ultrasports Tripacer/Solar Wings Medium Typhoon (Originally regd as Sealey Microlight)	JGS-01 & 116-108		25. 8.82	
G-MJJG	Southdown Lightning	L170/460		13. 9.82	Canx as destroyed 9.4.84.
G-MJJH	Southdown Puma	L195/481		13. 9.82	Canx as destroyed 9.11.83.
G-MJJI	MacKinder Skyrider	01		25. 8.82	Canx by CAA 15.6.90.
G-MJJJ	Hiway Skytrike Mk.II 250/Moyes Delta Maxi (Originally regd as a Knight Microlight)	RJB-01		25. 8.82	Canx by CAA 2.9.88.
G-MJJK	Eipper Quicksilver MX II	3397		25. 8.82	
G-MJJL	Solar Wing Storm	SML80202		25. 8.82	Canx by CAA 24.1.95.
G-MJJM	Birdman Cherokee Mk.I	CHM 5451279		25. 8.82	Canx as WFU 23.8.89.
G-MJJN	Southdown Puma (Lightning DS)	JEL-01		25. 8.82	Canx by CAA 23.6.97.
G-MJJO	Mainair Tri-Flyer/Flexiform Dual Striker (Mainair c/n probably 073-31582)	JDH-01		26. 8.82	
G-MJJP	American Aerolights Eagle	4156		26. 8.82	Canx by CAA 13.6.90.
G-MJJR	Huntair Pathfinder 330 Type "A" (Originally regd as Pathfinder Mk.1)	008		8. 9.82	Destroyed in fatal crash near Chirk on 21.4.90. Canx as destroyed 10.5.90.
G-MJJS	Swallow AeroPlane Swallow B	782037-2		13. 9.82	Canx by CAA 7.9.94.
G-MJJT	Huntair Pathfinder	039		27. 8.82	Badly damaged when hit fence at Shobdon following engine failure on 4.6.83. Canx by CAA 13.6.90.
G-MJJU	Chargus T.250/Hiway Demon	MRS-01		31. 8.82	Canx by CAA 1.9.93.
G-MJJV	Wheeler (Skycraft) Scout	0369		31. 8.82	Canx by CAA 3.8.94.
G-MJJW	Chargus Kilmarnock (Originally regd as Chargus Titan 38)	JSP-01		31. 8.82	Canx by CAA 13.6.90.
G-MJJX	Hiway Skytrike/Demon 175	OA 17D		1. 9.82	Canx by CAA 19.2.93.
G-MJJY	Tirith Firebird (Status unknown - company in liquidation 11.12.86)	01-0001		10. 9.82	Canx as WFU 30.7.93.
G-MJJZ	Hiway Skytrike 250/Demon 175	DN17D		1. 9.82	Canx by CAA 1.9.93.
G-MJKA	Skyhook TR1 Mk.II/Sabre	260A-138823		1. 9.82	Canx by CAA 24.1.95.
G-MJKB	Striplin Sky Ranger (Also quoted as c/n SRI-6-I)	ST 161		2. 9.82	
G-MJKC	Mainair Tri-Flyer 330/Flexiform Striker	095-21882 & GJL-01		2. 9.82	Canx by CAA 24.1.95.
G-MJKD	Southdown Puma	-		. .82R	NTU - Canx.
G-MJKE	Mainair Tri-Flyer 330/Hiway Demon 175	097-27882		2. 9.82	Canx as WFU 23.7.93.
G-MJKF	Hiway Demon	WGR-01		2. 9.82	
G-MJKG	John Ivor Skytrike	RC-02		6. 9.82	Canx by CAA 1.3.85.
G-MJKH	Eipper Quicksilver MX II (Originally reserved with c/n 3844)(Also quotes former engine no.11881 as c/n)	1020		28. 1.83	(Stored 1/98)
G-MJKI	Eipper Quicksilver MX/Lakeland Special	4408		28. 1.83	Canx by CAA 11.8.97.
G-MJKJ	Eipper Quicksilver MX/Redwing	4446		28. 1.83	Canx by CAA 28.7.87.
G-MJKK	Huntair Pathfinder	038		6. 9.82	Canx 31.1.83 on sale to France.
G-MJKL	Southdown Puma	AT.1		6. 9.82	Canx by CAA 13.6.90.
G-MJKM	Chargus Titan 38/TS440	JEB 001		6. 9.82	Canx by CAA 13.6.90.
G-MJKN	Ultrasports Tripacer/Hiway Demon	JEB 002		6. 9.82	Canx by CAA 13.6.90.
G-MJKO	Farnell 250 Trike/Goldmarque Gyr 188 (Originally regd as Goldmark 250 Skytrike with c/n WEB-01)	90039P		7. 9.82	
G-MJKP	Hiway Skystrike/Super Scorpion	PEB-01		7. 9.82	Canx as WFU 9.12.94.
G-MJKR	Rotec Rally 2B	HBCG-01		7. 9.82	Canx by CAA 7.9.94.
G-MJKS	Mainair Tri-Flyer 250/Demon 175	JSAW-01		7. 9.82	Canx as WFU 16.5.94.
G-MJKT	SMD Gazelle 160/Hiway Super Scorpion	P2-160		7. 9.82	Canx by CAA 13.6.90.
G-MJKU	Mainair Tri-Flyer/Hiway Demon 175 (Also quotes ENo.81-00520)	RDM-01		7. 9.82	Canx by CAA 7.9.94.
G-MJKV	Hornet/Skyhook Cutlass CD	H 370		7. 9.82	Canx by CAA 13.8.93.
G-MJKW	Hill (Maxair) Hummer TX (C/n duplicates G-MJMR)	DR-01		7. 9.82	Canx by CAA 13.6.90.
G-MJKX	Skyrider Airsports Phantom (Originally regd with c/n QCH-01)	PH.82005		14. 9.82	
G-MJKY	Mainair Tri-Flyer 250/Flexiform Hilander (Originally regd as Hiway Skytrike)	DM.2 & 032-241181		8. 9.82	(Wing to G-MMUG) Canx by CAA 24.1.95.
G-MJKZ	Mainair/Flexiform (Fitted with some components from G-MBWV)	096 25882		8. 9.82	Canx as WFU 10.10.83. Was used by Flexiform Skysails for destruct load testing in 10/83.
G-MJLA	Southdown Puma 2 (Lightning DS)	306		14. 9.82	Canx by CAA 23.6.97.
G-MJLB	Southdown Puma 2	307		21. 9.82	
G-MJLC	American Aerolights Double Eagle	701		23. 9.82	Canx as destroyed 20.6.89.

Regn	Type	c/n	Previous identity	Regn date	Fate or immediate subsequent identity (if known)
G-MJLD	Wheeler (Skycraft) Scout Mk.III/3/A	0437 R/3		8. 9.82	Canx by CAA 7.9.94.
G-MJLE	Lightwing Rooster 2 Type 5	JL 5		9. 9.82	Canx by CAA 13.6.90.
G-MJLF	SMD Gazelle/Flexiform Medium Striker (Originally regd as Southern Microlight Trike with same c/n)	AS-01		9. 9.82	Canx by CAA 7.9.94.
G-MJLG	Hiway Skytrike Mk.II	PC.1		9. 9.82	Canx by CAA 13.6.90.
G-MJLH	American Aerolights Double Eagle 430B	200118		9. 9.82	Canx by CAA 14.11.91.
G-MJLI	Hiway Skytrike 250/Demon	AKC-01		9. 9.82	Canx by CAA 17.2.93.
G-MJLJ	Flexiform Sealander	QA-01		10. 9.82	Canx by CAA 7.9.94.
G-MJLK	Dragonfly 250-II	D.105		10. 9.82	Canx as WFU 18.4.90. (Stored completely dismantled 6/96)
G-MJLL	Hiway Skytrike/Demon	DH-01		17. 9.82	Canx by CAA 19.1.90.
G-MJLM	Mainair Tri-Flyer 250/Fuga	AP-01 & 044-231281		17. 9.82	Canx by CAA 24.1.95.
G-MJLN	SMD Gazelle/Flexiform Striker	SMA 3		14. 9.82	Canx by CAA 13.6.90.
G-MJLO	Hiway Skytrike/Goldmarque Gyr (Originally regd with c/n RK-01)	HW-63		14. 9.82	Canx by CAA 17.9.93.
G-MJLP	Nib II Vertigo	1		15. 9.82	Canx by CAA 15.7.85. To G-MNDR 7/85.
G-MJLR	Skyhook SK.1	TMJT-01		15. 9.82	Canx by CAA 20.1.92.
G-MJLS	Rotec Rally 2B	2782		24. 9.82	Canx by CAA 4.2.92.
G-MJLT	American Aerolights Eagle	2908		17. 9.82	Canx by CAA 10.8.94.
G-MJLU	Flexiform Trike 440/Skyhook Cutlass CD Dual	BAG-01		20. 9.82	Canx by CAA 19.7.96.
G-MJLV	Eipper Quicksilver	WWG-01		20. 9.82	Canx as WFU 6.4.90.
G-MJLW	Chargus Cyclone (Prone Trike)	165001		20. 9.82	Canx as WFU 18.4.90.
G-MJLX	Rotec Rally 2B	JH-01		21. 9.82	Canx as WFU 23.4.90.
G-MJLY	American Aerolights Eagle	AMR-01		30. 9.82	No Permit believed issued. Canx by CAA 15.3.99.
G-MJLZ	Hiway Skytrike 330/Demon 175	MX 17D		22. 9.82	Canx by CAA 13.6.90.
G-MJMA	Hiway Skytrike/Demon	JCC-01		22. 9.82	
G-MJMB	Weedhopper	846		23. 9.82	Canx by CAA 7.9.94.
G-MJMC	Huntair Pathfinder	047		8.10.82	Canx by CAA 13.6.90.
G-MJMD	Hiway Skytrike/Demon 175	OE17D		27. 9.82	
G-MJME	Ultrasports Tripacer/Moyes Mega II	WIA		27. 9.82	Canx as WFU 29.1.88.
G-MJMF	Weedhopper Type B	GB.6		. .82R	NTU - To G-MJML 9/82. Canx.
G-MJMG	Weedhopper Type C (Regn originally applied to a Weedhopper B, but this was not flown and was stored at Reddish)	SR-01		27. 9.82	Canx by CAA 13.6.90.
G-MJMH	American Aerolights Eagle (C/n quoted as 23978 by CAA on cancellation)	Z.3978		27. 9.82	Canx as destroyed 5.4.90.
G-MJMI	Skyhook Sabre	260A-138824		27. 9.82	Canx as WFU 24.5.90. (Stored 8/92)
G-MJMJ	Wheeler (Skycraft) Scout III 3/A	0439 R/3		27. 9.82	Canx by CAA 13.6.90.
G-MJMK	Ultrasports Tripacer/Southdown Lightning (Incorrectly entered in register as c/n HSBW-01)	MSBW-01		28. 9.82	Canx by CAA 25.11.88.
G-MJML	Weedhopper Type B	GB.6	(G-MJMF)	28. 9.82	Canx by CAA 13.6.90.
G-MJMM	Chargus T.250/Vortex	327		28. 9.82	Canx by CAA 7.10.94.
G-MJMN	Mainair Tri-Flyer 330/Flexiform Striker	087-04882		29. 9.82	(Stored 12/97)
G-MJMO	Lancashire Micro-Trike 330/Flexiform Medium Striker	820501		29. 9.82	Canx by CAA 13.6.90.
G-MJMP	Eipper Quicksilver MX II	1023		30. 9.82	Canx by CAA 26.8.94.
G-MJMR	Mainair Tri-Flyer 250/Solar Wings Typhoon	DR-01 & 048-5182		30. 9.82	(Stored 12/97)
G-MJMS	Hiway Skytrike/Demon	EEW-01		30. 9.82	
G-MJMT	Hiway Skytrike/Demon 175	RL 17D		30. 9.82	
G-MJMU	Hiway Skytrike 250/Demon 175 (C/n is dubious - see also G-MJOI and duplicates PH-1B2)	817003		1.10.82	
G-MJMV	Hiway Vulcan 2	RR-2		4.10.82	Canx as WFU 11.4.90.
G-MJMW	Eipper Quicksilver MX	RJD 1029 & 14816		4.10.82	Canx as WFU 24.8.94.
G-MJMX	Mainair Tri-Flyer Dual 440/Flexiform Striker (Originally regd as Ultrasports Tripacer)	179-5883 & RM-01		4.10.82	
G-MJMY	Kold Flyer Srs.1	268		4.10.82	Badly damaged in forced landing at Crookshall, near High Wycombe on 30.6.83. Canx as WFU 23.8.84.
G-MJMZ	Robertson Ultralight B1-RD	6692		7.10.82	Canx by CAA 13.6.90.
G-MJNA	Mainair Tri-Flyer 440	MTB-01 & 089-13882		5.10.82	Canx by CAA 13.6.90.
G-MJNB	Hiway Skytrike/Solar Wings Typhoon	2332		5.10.82	Canx as WFU 14.1.92.
G-MJNC	Hiway Skytrike/Demon 175	TG17D		5.10.82	Canx by CAA 13.6.90.
G-MJND	Mainair Tri-Flyer/Solar Wings Typhoon	GP-01		8.10.82	Canx 30.4.86 on sale to Italy.
G-MJNE	Hornet Supreme Dual-Seat/Skyhook Cutlass	H410		8.10.82	Canx by CAA 14.10.85.
G-MJNF	Harmsworth Trike/Solar Wings Storm	CCH-01		12.10.82	Canx as WFU 29.5.85.
G-MJNG	Eipper Quicksilver MX	RBP-01		12.10.82	Canx by CAA 13.6.90.
G-MJNH	Skyhook Cutlass	260A-156824		13.10.82	Canx by CAA 25.3.99.

Regn	Type	c/n	Previous identity	Regn date	Fate or immediate subsequent identity (if known)
G-MJNI	Hornet/Skyhook Sabre	666		13.10.82	Canx by CAA 20.6.90.
G-MJNJ	Gregory Trike/Solar Wings Typhoon	MRG-01		14.10.82	Canx by CAA 13.6.90.
G-MJNK	Hiway Skytrike/Demon 175	EA17D		14.10.82	
G-MJNL	American Aerolights Eagle	5016		22.11.82	Canx by CAA 9.2.93.
G-MJNM	American Aerolights Double Eagle 430B	702		25.11.82	
G-MJNN	Ultraflight Mirage II	104		12.10.82	
G-MJNO	American Aerolights Double Eagle Amphibian	703		24.11.82	
G-MJNP	American Aerolights Eagle	4153		14.10.82	Canx by CAA 24.1.95. (Stored 2/99 at Melton Constable, Norfolk)
G-MJNR	UAS Solar Buggy/Skyhook Cutlass CD	DJS-01		15.10.82	Canx by CAA 22.7.87.
G-MJNS	Swallow AeroPlane Swallow B	782039-2		9. 7.86	(Stored 7/93)
G-MJNT	Hiway Skytrike/Demon 175	RO17D		18.10.82	
G-MJNU	Skyhook TR1/Cutlass	TR1/17		19.10.82	
G-MJNV	Eipper Quicksilver MX	10537		19.10.82	Canx as destroyed 25.3.99.
G-MJNW	Skyhook TR1/Silhouette	TR1/4		21.10.82	Canx by CAA 13.6.90.
G-MJNX	Eipper Quicksilver MX	RH-01		22.10.82	Canx by CAA 13.6.90.
G-MJNY	Skyhook TR1/Sabre	TR1/35		3.11.82	
G-MJNZ	Skyhook TR1/Sabre	TR1/36		3.11.82	Canx as WFU 5.4.90.
G-MJOA	Chargus T.250/Vortex	235		25.10.82	Canx as destroyed 24.8.94.
G-MJOB	Skyhook TR2/Cutlass CD	TR2/39		25.10.82	Canx by CAA 13.6.90.
G-MJOC	Huntair Pathfinder	048		25.10.82	
G-MJOD	Rotec Rally 2B	AK-01		28.10.82	Canx by CAA 17.3.99.
G-MJOE	Eurowing Goldwing	EW-55		29.10.82	
G-MJOF	Eipper Quicksilver MX	SMW-01		1.11.82	Canx by CAA 13.6.90.
G-MJOG	American Aerolights Eagle	3810		1.11.82	Canx by CAA 18.10.88.
G-MJOH	Mainair Tri-Flyer 330/Flexiform Striker (Originally regd with Mainair trike c/n 291082)	103-241082 & RJB-014		1.11.82	Canx 12.10.88 on sale to Zimbabwe.
G-MJOI	Ultrasports Tripacer/Hiway Demon (See comments on G-MJMU)	817003		1.11.82	Canx as WFU 1.11.89.
G-MJOJ	Flexiform Dual Skytrike	DH-1		1.11.82	Canx by CAA 2.9.88.
G-MJOK	Mainair Tri-Flyer 250	054-28181		2.11.82	Canx by CAA 7.9.94.
G-MJOL	Hornet/Skyhook Cutlass	KWEB-01		2.11.82	Canx by CAA 24.8.94.
G-MJOM	Southdown Puma Spirit DS (Lightning 195)	82-00104 & 487		2.11.82	Canx by CAA 18.4.89.
G-MJON	Southdown Puma 40F	488		3.11.82	Canx by CAA 13.6.90.
G-MJOO	Southdown Puma 40F/Lightning	489		3.11.82	Canx as WFU 17.11.95.
G-MJOP	Southdown Puma 40F	490		3.11.82	Canx by CAA 13.6.90.
G-MJOR	Soleair Phoenix	BG-84-04/1		3.11.82	Canx by CAA 5.12.95.
G-MJOS	Ultrasports Tripacer/Southdown Lightning 170	DSPL-01		5.11.82	Canx by CAA 5.12.95.
G-MJOT	Ultrasports Tripacer/Airwave Nimrod (Also quotes Trike c/n 18-00074 - probably corrupted engine no.)	A/M/N/1857120		5.11.82	Canx by CAA 13.6.90.
G-MJOU	Hiway Skytrike II/Demon 175 (Probably shares trike with G-MMBS)	HP-01		8.11.82	(Stored 9/96)
G-MJOV	Ultrasports Tripacer/Solar Wings Typhoon	T581-146		8.11.82	Canx by CAA 24.1.95.
G-MJOW	Eipper Quicksilver MX	NH.16607 & NH.4602		8.11.82	Canx by CAA 25.10.88.
G-MJOX	Mainair Tri-Flyer 330/Solar Wings Typhoon	LJ-01 & 076-20582		13. 1.83	Canx by CAA 13.6.90.
G-MJOY	Eurowing Catto CP-16	JPBC-01		8.11.82	Canx by CAA 13.6.90.
G-MJOZ	Southdown Puma	-		. .82R	NTU - Canx.
G-MJPA	Rotec Rally 2B	AT-01		5. 1.83	
G-MJPB	Manuel Ladybird	WLM-14		9.11.82	Canx by CAA 13.6.90. (On loan to Brooklands Museum) (Stored 3/96)
G-MJPC	American Aerolights Double Eagle 430B	PHH-01		9.11.82	No Permit believed issued. (Stored 9/96 Hougham, Lincs) Canx as PWFU 17.2.99.
G-MJPD	Hiway Skytrike/Demon 175	HF17D		9.11.82	Canx by CAA 23.6.97.
G-MJPE	Hiway Skytrike/Demon 175 (Also reported as Mainair Tri-Flyer)	OG17D		10.11.82	
G-MJPF	American Aerolights Double Eagle 430-R	704		19.11.82	Canx by CAA 13.6.90.
G-MJPG	American Aerolights Double Eagle 430-R	705		16.11.82	Canx by CAA 2.8.94.
G-MJPH	Huntair Pathfinder	042		29.11.82	Canx as WFU 4.6.90.
G-MJPI	Flexiform Dual Striker (C/n is engine no.)	80-00018		25.11.82	Canx by CAA 27.1.88.
G-MJPJ	Flexiform Dual 440/Sealander	MBEP-01		15.11.82	Canx by CAA 1.6.93.
G-MJPK	Hiway Hornet/Vulcan	EBJP-02		11.11.82	Canx by CAA 13.6.90.
G-MJPL	Hiway Skytrike/Birdman Cherokee	PAL-01		18.11.82	Canx as destroyed 9.4.90.
G-MJPM	Huntair Pathfinder Mk.I	058		18.11.82	Canx by CAA 13.6.90.
G-MJPN	Mitchell Wing B-10	P 103		19.11.82	Canx as WFU 8.3.88.
G-MJPO	Eurowing Goldwing	018		16.11.82	

Regn	Type	c/n	Previous identity	Regn date	Fate or immediate subsequent identity (if known)
G-MJPP	Hiway Skytrike/Solar Wings Typhoon (Originally regd as Super Scorpion)	KLM-01		28.11.82	
G-MJPR	Hiway Skytrike 250/Birdman Cherokee	GMJ-01		23.11.82	Canx as WFU 18.5.90.
G-MJPS	American Aerolights Double Eagle 430-R	706		18.11.82	Canx by CAA 7.9.94
G-MJPT	Dragon Srs.150	006		28.11.82	Canx as WFU 3.1.89.
G-MJPU(1)	Southdown Puma	-		. .82R	NTU - Canx.
G-MJPU(2)	Ultrasports 440/Solar Wings Panther XL (Originally regd as Typhoon DS with same c/n - wing later fitted to G-MMHZ)	KND-01 & T1283-948X		8. 2.83	
G-MJPV	Eipper Quicksilver MX	JBW-01		30.11.82	
G-MJPW	Mainair Tri-Flyer/Airwave Merlin	AG.EXP1		30.11.82	Canx by CAA 13.6.90.
G-MJPX	Hiway Skytrike 250/Demon	RT-01		30.11.82	Canx by CAA 13.6.90.
G-MJPY	American Aerolights Eagle	3265		2.12.82	Canx as WFU 6.4.90.
G-MJPZ	American Aerolights Eagle	3000		6.12.82	Canx as WFU 18.4.90.
G-MJRA	Mainair Tri-Flyer 250/Hiway Demon	PRJM-01		21.12.82	Canx by CAA 24.1.95.
G-MJRB	Eurowing Goldwing	JSP-01		7.12.82	Canx as WFU 1.9.93.
G-MJRC	Eipper Quicksilver MX	3157		7.12.82	Canx as WFU 6.4.90.
G-MJRD	Hiway Skytrike/Super Scorpion C (Originally regd as Gaze Microlight)	GB-0001		8.12.82	Canx by CAA 23.6.97.
G-MJRE	Hornet Trike/Hiway Demon	JGB-003		15.12.82	Canx 23.6.87 on sale to USA.
G-MJRF	Ultrasports Tripacer/Hiway Super Scorpion	GJS-01		15.12.82	Canx by CAA 8.5.84.
G-MJRG	Ultrasports/Southdown Puma DS (Originally regd as Solar Wings Panther Dual 440; later fitted with Wing from G-MMCS)	128		19. 1.83	Canx by CAA 5.12.95.
G-MJRH	Hiway Skytrike	GP-1		20.12.82	Canx by CAA 24.1.95.
G-MJRI	American Aerolights Eagle	2912		31.12.82	Canx as WFU 3.8.94.
G-MJRJ	Hiway/Skytrike/Demon 175	MT-01		21.12.82	Canx by CAA 13.6.90.
G-MJRK	Mainair Tri-Flyer 330/Flexiform Striker	119-161282 & BJB-01		14. 1.83	Canx by CAA 4.2.92.
G-MJRL	Eurowing Goldwing	EW-79 & SWA-5K		30.12.82	
G-MJRM	Dragon Srs.150	0017		11. 1.83	Canx by CAA 13.6.90.
G-MJRN	Mainair 330 Tri-Flyer/Flexiform Striker	MJS-01		30.12.82	Canx by CAA 4.2.92.
G-MJRO	Eurowing Goldwing	EW-77 & SWA-04		31.12.82	
G-MJRP	Mainair Tri-Flyer 330/Hiway Demon 175 (Fitted with engine from G-MJVN)	118-161282 & OF17D		4. 1.83	
G-MJRR	(Striplin) Sky Ranger Srs.1 (Home designed by J.R.Reece)	JR-3		26. 4.82	
G-MJRS	Eurowing Goldwing	EW-80 & SWA-6K		5. 1.83	(Damaged mid 1996)
G-MJRT	Southdown Puma (Lightning DS) (Formerly used Tri-Flyer 440 c/n 109-261182)	TJF-01		5. 1.83	
G-MJRU	MBA Sopwith Tiger Cub 440	SO.86		6. 1.83	
G-MJRV	Eurowing Goldwing	BMAA/HB/084 & EW-69		7. 1.83	
G-MJRW	Southdown Puma I	82-00083		10. 1.83	Canx as WFU 16.9.83.
G-MJRX	Southdown Puma II	80-00078		10. 1.83	Canx by CAA 2.9.88.
G-MJRY	MBA Super Tiger Cub 440	SO.94		10. 1.83	Canx by CAA 13.6.90.
G-MJRZ	MBA Super Tiger Cub 440	SO.119		10. 1.83	Canx by CAA 13.6.90.
G-MJSA	Mainair Tri-Flyer Dual 440/Flexiform Striker	MKWH-01 & 116-151282		12. 1.83	Canx as destroyed 24.11.94.
G-MJSB	Eurowing Catto CP-16	EWCP-34		10. 2.83	Canx by CAA 13.6.90.
G-MJSC	American Aerolights Eagle	004		13. 1.83	Canx by CAA 13.6.90.
G-MJSD	Rotec Rally 2B Srs.1	AT-01		19. 1.83	Canx by CAA 13.6.90.
G-MJSE	Skyrider Airsports Phantom	SF-101		24. 1.83	
G-MJSF	Skyrider Airsports Phantom	SF-105	SE-... G-MJSF	24. 1.83	
G-MJSG	Mainair Tri-Flyer/Solar Wings Typhoon	121-19183		24. 1.83	Canx 19.11.84 on sale to Australia.
G-MJSH	American Aerolights Eagle	2265		24. 1.83	Canx by CAA 13.6.90.
G-MJSI	Huntair Pathfinder II	100		24. 1.83	Canx by CAA 13.6.90.
G-MJSJ	Mainair Trike/Flexiform Striker	HTV-01		31. 1.83	Destroyed on 31.8.83. Canx as destroyed 19.9.83.
G-MJSK	TC Trike/Skyhook Sabre	TC.1		31. 1.83	Canx by CAA 13.6.90.
G-MJSL	Dragon Srs.200	0018		24. 2.83	
G-MJSM	Weedhopper B	JRB-01		1. 2.83	Canx by CAA 13.6.90.
G-MJSN	Flexiform Sealander	DGH-01		1. 2.83	Canx as WFU 14.3.85.
G-MJSO	Hiway Skytrike II/Demon 175	SA17D		1. 2.83	
G-MJSP	Romain MBA Super Tiger Cub Special 440 (Nosewheel conversion)	SO.54		7. 2.83	
G-MJSR	Lancashire Micro-Trike Duet 440/Flexiform Striker (Originally regd as Flexiform Micro-Trike II with c/n P12011282)	PK.011282 & 440PM/LM/1083		10. 1.83	Canx by CAA 16.10.90.
G-MJSS	American Aerolights Eagle	GF-100		4. 2.83	Exemption expired 31.8.85. Canx by CAA 10.2.87.
G-MJST	MEA Pterodactyl Ptraveler	GCS-01		2.12.81	

Regn	Type	c/n	Previous identity	Regn date	Fate or immediate subsequent identity (if known)
G-MJSU	MBA Tiger Cub 440 (Regd with c/n SO.175)	SO.75/1		2. 2.83	Canx by CAA 23.6.93. (Stored 9/97)
G-MJSV	MBA Tiger Cub 440 (Officially regd with c/n SO.287)	SO.87/2		2. 2.83	Canx by CAA 9.11.89. (Stored 5/95)
G-MJSW	Eipper Quicksilver MX II (Also quotes engine no. 15871 as c/n)	1058		3. 2.83	Fatal crash at Swansea on 30.5.83.
G-MJSX	Simplicity Microlight	NS-01		7. 2.83	Canx by CAA 13.6.90.
G-MJSY	Eurowing Goldwing	EW-63		8. 2.83	
G-MJSZ	Harker DH Wasp	HA.5		10. 2.83	
G-MJTA	Mainair Tri-Flyer/Flexiform Dual Striker	SA.2010		11. 2.83	Canx as destroyed 16.11.90.
G-MJTB	Eipper Quicksilver MX	RFGK-01		16. 2.83	Canx by CAA 13.6.90.
G-MJTC	Ultrasports Tripacer/Solar Wings Typhoon	T1282-677		14. 2.83	Canx by CAA 20.5.97.
G-MJTD	Gardner T-M Scout (Thomas-Morse S4 Scout 2/3rd scale replica; painted in US Army Signal Corps c/s with serial 41386) (Possibly c/n PFA/111-10664)	83/001		14. 2.83	
G-MJTE	Skyrider Airsports Phantom	SF-106		15. 2.83	
G-MJTF	Armstrong Trike/Gryphon Wing	ATA-01		15. 2.83	Canx as WFU 9.8.94.
G-MJTG	AES Sky Ranger	SR.101		15. 2.83	Canx by CAA 13.6.90.
G-MJTH	SMD Gazelle/Flexiform Dual Striker	010		18. 2.83	Canx by CAA 24.2.95.
G-MJTI	Huntair Pathfinder II	101		21. 2.83	Canx by CAA 19.9.94.
G-MJTJ	Weedhopper	MJB-01		21. 2.83	Canx by CAA 13.6.90.
G-MJTK	American Aerolights Eagle	NRM-01		21. 2.83	Canx by CAA 16.7.90.
G-MJTL	Aerostructure Pipistrelle P2C	018 & SAL/P2C/001		9. 3.83	Canx as WFU 29.7.96.
G-MJTM	Aerostructure Pipistrelle P2B	019 & SAL/P2B/002		21. 2.83	
G-MJTN	Eipper Quicksilver MX	DAHC-01		22. 2.83	Canx by CAA 8.7.94.
G-MJTO	Jordan Duet Srs.1	D 101		19. 7.83	
G-MJTP	Mainair Tri-Flyer 440/Flexiform Sealander (Possibly Dual Striker)	AJDH-01 & 139-7383		25. 2.83	
G-MJTR	Southdown Puma DS Mk.1	H362		9. 3.83	
G-MJTS	Skyhook TR1	TR1/41		28. 2.83	Canx 13.2.84 on sale to Portugal.
G-MJTT	Dragon Srs.150	D150/001		7. 3.83	Canx 27.3.84 on sale to France.
G-MJTU	Mainair Tri-Flyer 250/Skyhook Cutlass 185	077-10682		28. 2.83	Canx by CAA 15.10.93.
G-MJTV	Chargus Titan 38 (Also c/n T86 quoted - possibly a corruption of its official c/n)	T38/16		28. 2.83	Canx as WFU 27.10.88.
G-MJTW	Eurowing Catto CP-16 (Also described as Eurowing Floater)	EWT-004		28. 2.83	Canx by CAA 15.10.92.
G-MJTX	Skyrider Airsports Phantom	SF-110		1. 3.83	
G-MJTY	Huntair Pathfinder Mk.1	CHS-01		2. 3.83	No Permit to Fly issued. Canx by CAA 2.4.96.
G-MJTZ	Skyrider Airsports Phantom (Also quotes ENo. 82-00119)	MBS-01		29. 4.83	
G-MJUA	MBA Super Tiger Cub (C/n probably SO.121)	MW-01 & MBA 80121		7. 3.83	Canx as destroyed 11.6.90.
G-MJUB	MBA Tiger Cub 440 (C/n probably SO.43)	FO.43		7. 3.83	Canx by CAA 7.9.94.
G-MJUC	MBA Tiger Cub 440	RRH-01 & PFA/140-10908		7. 3.83	(Stored Kirkbride 5/96)
G-MJUD	Southdown Puma 440 (C/n is engine no.)	80-00071		8. 3.83	Canx by CAA 13.6.90.
G-MJUE	Southdown Puma/Lightning II (Also described as Southdown Wildcat II Trike with Lightning II wing)	82-00435 & P.109		8. 3.83	
G-MJUF	MBA Super Tiger Cub 440	MCT-01		8. 3.83	Canx by CAA 27.4.90. (Stored on trailer 6/96)
G-MJUG	Huntair Pathfinder II	HL-01		9. 3.83	Fatal crash at Rimont, Southern France on 21.7.83. Canx as destroyed 9.8.83.
G-MJUH	MBA Tiger Cub 440	JEJ-01		9. 3.83	Canx as WFU 2.7.96.
G-MJUI	Sharp & Sons Tartan/Flexiform Striker	BB-01		10. 3.83	Canx as WFU 26.8.94.
G-MJUJ	Eipper Quicksilver MX II	1025		10. 3.83	
G-MJUK	Eipper Quicksilver MX II	1040		10. 3.83	Canx by CAA 24.1.95.
G-MJUL	Southdown Puma Sprint	F 512S		28. 3.83	Canx by CAA 9.7.96.
G-MJUM	Hiway Skytrike 250/Flexiform Striker (C/n is engine no)	82-00493		28. 3.83	
G-MJUN	Hiway Skytrike/Demon 175	0B 17D		21. 3.83	Canx by CAA 13.6.90.
G-MJUO	Eipper Quicksilver MX II	104C		22. 3.83	Canx by CAA 24.1.95.
G-MJUP	Weedhopper B	775		22. 3.83	Canx by CAA 7.9.94.
G-MJUR	Skyrider Airsports Phantom	SF-108		5. 4.83	
G-MJUS	MBA Tiger Cub 440	SO.140 & PFA/140-10903		23. 3.83	Canx as destroyed 2.12.87.
G-MJUT	Eurowing Goldwing	DLE-01		23. 3.83	
G-MJUU	Eurowing Goldwing	EW-70		28. 3.83	
G-MJUV	Huntair Pathfinder Mk.1	045		18. 5.83	
G-MJUW	MBA Tiger Cub 440	SO.69		29. 3.83	
G-MJUX	Skyrider Airsports Phantom	RFF-01		29. 2.84	
G-MJUY	Eurowing Goldwing	EW-82		6. 4.83	Canx by CAA 24.1.95. (Stored, complete 9/96)
G-MJUZ	Dragon Srs.150	015		30. 3.83	(Stored 9/96)

Regn	Type	c/n	Previous identity	Regn date	Fate or immediate subsequent identity (if known)
G-MJVA	Skyrider Airsports Phantom	-		. .83R	NTU - Canx.
G-MJVB	Skyhook TR 2	TR2/42		14. 4.83	Canx as WFU 13.10.88.
G-MJVC	Hiway Skytrike/Demon	JM.1		12. 4.83	Canx by CAA 24.1.95.
G-MJVD	Not allotted.				
G-MJVE	Medway Hybred Skytrike 44XL/Solar Wings Typhoon XL II	4.4.83/1		19. 4.83	
G-MJVF	CFM Shadow Srs.CD	002		12. 4.83	
G-MJVG	Hiway Skytrike	RH-01		13. 4.83	Canx by CAA 2.9.88.
G-MJVH	American Aerolights Eagle	2383		13. 4.83	Canx by CAA 13.6.90.
G-MJVI	Lightwing Rooster 1 Srs.4	4		8. 4.83	Canx by CAA 13.6.90.
G-MJVJ	Hornet Invader/Flexiform Striker	099-10982 & RFPO 10		14. 4.83	Suffered engine failure after take-off & badly damaged in crash at Oaker Bank field, Killinghall, near Harrogate on 17.5.85. Canx by CAA 28.2.92.
G-MJVK	Mainair Tri-Flyer 250/Silhouette	070-24582		14. 4.83	Dismantled with Trike to G-MMDJ in 6/83. Canx by CAA 6.3.84.
G-MJVL	Flexiform Striker	HP-01		14. 4.83	Canx by CAA 23.6.97.
G-MJVM	Dragon Srs.150	-		. .83R	NTU - Canx.
G-MJVN	Southdown Puma/Flexiform Striker	82-00030-PR1		18. 4.83	WFU and engine to G-MJRP.
G-MJVO	American Aerolights Eagle	3027		26. 4.83	Canx by CAA 27.5.85.
G-MJVP	Eipper Quicksilver MX II	1149		19. 4.83	
G-MJVR	Ultrasports Panther/Flexiform Dual Striker (Originally regd as a Tripacer)	LAH		20. 4.83	Canx by CAA 28.11.95.
G-MJVS	Watering Trike/Hiway Super Scorpion	RW-01		25. 4.83	Canx by CAA 13.6.90.
G-MJVT	Eipper Quicksilver MX	10961		20. 4.83	
G-MJVU	Eipper Quicksilver MX II	1118		3. 4.84	
G-MJVV	Hornet Supreme Dual/Skyhook Cutlass	H 390		27. 4.83	Canx by CAA 5.12.95.
G-MJVW	Ultrasports Tripacer/Airwave Nimrod	TPM.1		27. 4.83	Canx as WFU 26.2.88.
G-MJVX	Skyrider Airsports Phantom	JAG-01 & SF-102		27. 4.83	Canx by CAA 13.6.90.
G-MJVY	Dragon Srs.150	D.150/013		4. 5.83	
G-MJVZ	Ultrasports Tri-Pacer/Hiway Demon (C/n is engine no)	81-00601		15. 6.82	Canx as TWFU 25.3.92.
G-MJWA	Mainair Tri-Flyer/Birdman Cherokee	JACT-01		12. 3.84	Canx by CAA 22.6.89.
G-MJWB	Eurowing Goldwing	EW-59		24. 5.83	(For sale 7/96)
G-MJWC	Skyhook HS.525A/Paraglide Fabric Self-Inflating Wing	201		5. 7.83	Canx as WFU 18.5.90.
G-MJWD	Mainair Tri-Flyer Dual 440/Solar Wings Typhoon XL	075-27582 & T483-845XL		3. 5.83	Canx by CAA 9.5.97.
G-MJWE	Ultrasports Tripacer 250/Hiway Demon	RWD-01		4. 5.83	Canx by CAA 14.9.93.
G-MJWF	MBA Tiger Cub 440	BRH-001		4. 5.83	
G-MJWG	MBA Tiger Cub 440	BMAA/HB/001 & DHC-001 & PFA/140-10961		4. 5.83	
G-MJWH	Chargus T.250/Vortex	?		. .83R	(Wing on display 4/96)
	(Regn reserved in 1983 for a Chargus T.250 plus engine for F.Embleton, fitted to a 1974 Vortex hang glider. It was abandoned and only the wing is on display)				
G-MJWI	Twamley Trike/Flexiform Striker	RWT-01		8. 7.83	Canx by CAA 27.3.99.
G-MJWJ	MBA Tiger Cub 440	013/191		9. 5.83	
G-MJWK	Huntair Pathfinder 1	JWK-01		1.10.82	
G-MJWL	Chargus T.250 Vortex 120	CP.101V		6. 4.84	Canx as WFU 30.5.90.
G-MJWM	Chargus T.250 Vortex 120	CP.102V		6. 4.84	Canx as WFU 30.5.90.
G-MJWN	Hornet 330/Flexiform Striker	H430		10. 5.83	
	(Also c/n is quoted as 4430 - possibly a corruption of above)				
G-MJWO	Hiway Skytrike 250/Super Scorpion	25U10		10. 5.83	Canx as WFU 19.1.95.
G-MJWP	MBA Tiger Cub	SO.192		10. 5.83	Canx 22.10.84 on sale to USA.
G-MJWR	MBA Tiger Cub 440	S.30		10. 5.83	Canx as WFU 25.3.92.
G-MJWS	Eurowing Goldwing	EW-22		16. 5.83	(Stored 4/94) Canx by CAA 23.6.97.
G-MJWT	American Aerolights Eagle	2880		10. 5.83	Canx as WFU 18.4.90.
G-MJWU	Maxiair Hummer TX	DD-01		11. 5.83	Canx as WFU 24.8.94.
G-MJWV	Mainair Tri-Flyer/Southdown Puma MS	169-6683		11. 5.83	Canx by CAA 5.12.95.
	(Originally regd as Mainair Gemini 440/Southdown Lightning DS with c/n 163-15683 & WB-01)				
G-MJWW	MBA Super Tiger Cub 440 (Possibly c/n PFA/140-10904)	MU-001		11. 5.83	
G-MJWX	Lancashire Microtrike/Flexiform Dual Striker	2/4402PM/PGK/583		11. 5.83	Canx by CAA 24.1.95.
G-MJWY	Hiway Skytrike 250/Flexiform Striker	FS.4		11. 5.83	Canx by CAA 24.1.95.
G-MJWZ	Ultrasports/Solar Wings Panther XL-S	T583-781XL		9. 9.85	
	(Despite regn date, aircraft was at Biggin Hill as such in 5/83)				
G-MJXA	Mainair 440 Two-Seater Tri-Flyer/ Flexiform Striker	141-29383		13. 5.83	Canx by CAA 5.12.95.
	(Originally regd with trike Lancashire Micro-Trike Dual c/n CH-01; replacement trike ex.G-MBST(2) - later to G-MMTM)				

Regn	Type	c/n	Previous identity	Regn date	Fate or immediate subsequent identity (if known)
G-MJXB	Eurowing Goldwing	EW-49		16. 5.83	Canx by CAA 7.12.95.
G-MJXC	Mitchell Wing B-10	P 1061		16. 5.83	Fatal crash on beach near Fluke Hall, Pilling, Lancs on 15.2.84. Canx as WFU 28.6.84.
G-MJXD	MBA Tiger Cub 440	011/061		16. 5.83	
G-MJXE	Mainair Tri-Flyer 330/Hiway Demon 175	102-131082 & HS-001		17. 5.83	
G-MJXF	MBA Tiger Cub 440	EJH-01		1. 6.83	Canx by CAA 5.9.94.
G-MJXG	Flexiform Striker	155		18. 5.83	Canx by CAA 13.6.90.
G-MJXH	Mitchell Wing B-10	B 1115		18. 5.83	Canx by CAA 13.6.90.
G-MJXI	Flexiform Striker	MIM 35		19. 5.83	Canx by CAA 13.6.90.
G-MJXJ	MBA Tiger Cub 440	SO.100		20. 5.83	Canx as PWFU 6.3.99.
G-MJXK	Skyrider Aerosports Phantom	MGS-01		26. 5.83	Canx as WFU 7.11.83.
G-MJXL	MBA Super Tiger Cub	SO.29		23. 5.83	Canx by CAA 13.6.90.
G-MJXM	Hiway Skytrike	21-W		. .83R	NTU - Canx.
G-MJXN	American Aerolights Eagle	PL/9		24. 5.83	Canx as WFU 26.7.90.
G-MJXO	Middleton CM5	5		24. 5.83	Canx as WFU 26.7.90.
G-MJXP	Dragon D.150	-		. .83R	NTU - Canx.
G-MJXR	Huntair Pathfinder II	133		1. 6.83	Canx as WFU 11.10.85.
G-MJXS	Huntair Pathfinder II	134		25. 5.83	(Stored 6/96)
G-MJXT	Phoenix Falcon I	0001		22. 6.83	Canx by CAA 4.7.96.
G-MJXU	MBA Tiger Cub 440	SO.166		17. 6.83	Canx by CAA 24.5.90.
G-MJXV	Hornet Invader 440/Flexiform Striker	AJD-01 & RP.011		31. 5.83	Canx by CAA 20.8.93.
G-MJXW	Southdown Sigma	CJT-01		31. 5.83	Canx by CAA 13.6.90.
G-MJXX	Lancashire Micro-Trike/Flexiform Dual Striker (Possibly now Mainair Tri-Flyer Dual)	AAL-01		16. 6.83	(For sale 1/97)
G-MJXY	Hiway Skytrike 330/Demon 175	KQ17D		31. 5.83	
G-MJXZ	Chargus T.250/Hiway Demon	RPF-01		31. 5.83	Canx by CAA 23.6.97.
G-MJYA	Huntair Pathfinder	-		. .83R	NTU - Canx.
G-MJYB	Eurowing Goldwing	030		31. 5.83	Canx by CAA 24.4.90.
G-MJYC	Ultrasports/Solar Wings Panther XL Dual 440	JM-01		1.10.85	
G-MJYD	MBA Tiger Cub 440	SO.179		1. 6.83	Canx by CAA 13.1.94.
G-MJYE	Popplewell Trike/Southdown Lightning	GP-02		1. 6.83	Canx as destroyed 4.10.90.
G-MJYF	Mainair Gemini/Flash	305-585-3 & W45		18. 4.85	
G-MJYG	Skyhook Orion Canard	SKC.1		. 6.83	Canx as WFU 9.1.86.
G-MJYH	Skyhook 3-Axis Experimental Prototype	SKM.1		3. 6.83	Canx as destroyed 9.1.86.
G-MJYI	Mainair Tri-Flyer	MJJ-01		3. 6.83	Canx by CAA 24.1.95.
G-MJYJ	MBA Tiger Cub (Regd as c/n OS.177)	SO.177		6. 6.83	Canx by CAA 23.6.93.
G-MJYK	Noble Hardman Snowbird	SB/001		6. 6.83	Canx as destroyed 9.5.84.
G-MJYL	Mono-Pole Trike/Airwave Nimrod 165	UP-CMT-165-271-AN		13. 6.83	Canx 9.9.93 on sale to Zambia.
G-MJYM	Southdown Puma Sprint Special	-		. .83R	NTU - Canx.
G-MJYN	Mainair Tri-Flyer 440/Southdown Puma Sprint MS (Also quoted as Gemini 440)(Trike c/n duplicates G-MMUF)	165-13683		7. 6.83	Canx by CAA 13.6.90.
G-MJYO	Mainair Tri-Flyer 330/Flexiform Dual Striker	166-13683		7. 6.83	Canx by CAA 13.6.90.
G-MJYP	Mainair Gemini 440/Flexiform Dual Striker (Also quotes c/n 8300059 - probably engine no.)	167-13683		7. 6.83	
G-MJYR	Catto CP-16	-		. .83R	NTU - Canx.
G-MJYS	American Aerolights Eagle	-		. .83R	NTU - Canx. (Possibly re-regd G-MMAV)
G-MJYT	Southdown Puma Sprint	-		. .83R	NTU - Canx.
G-MJYU	Mainair Tri-Flyer/Solar Wings Solar XL	170-16583		8. 6.83	Trike to G-MMMB. Canx 14.5.84 on sale to USA.
G-MJYV	Mainair Tri-Flyer 330/Flexiform Rapier 1 + 1	175-19783		23.11.83	
G-MJYW	Lancashire Micro-Trike Dual 330/Wasp Gryphon III (See G-MMPL)	2/330PM/PGK/6.83/K		28. 6.83	
G-MJYX	Mainair Tri-Flyer 330/Hiway Demon	108-251182		9. 6.83	Canx by CAA 26.5.89.
G-MJYY	Hiway Skytrike 330/Demon 175	ZD17D		9. 6.83	
G-MJYZ	Lancashire Micro-Trike/Flexiform Striker	1/330PM/PGK/683		10. 6.83	Canx by CAA 9.6.93.
G-MJZA	MBA Tiger Cub	SO.45		10. 6.83	Canx by CAA 3.8.94.
G-MJZB	Lancashire Micro-Trike/Flexiform Dual Striker	PC.141		13. 6.83	Canx by CAA 19.5.97.
G-MJZC	MBA Tiger Cub 440	SO.169		14. 6.83	
G-MJZD(1)	[Was reserved for an unidentified MBA Tiger Cub in 1983 for Sunderland Microlight Centre]				
G-MJZD(2)	Mainair Gemini/Flash	311-585-3 & W50		18. 4.85	
G-MJZE	MBA Tiger Cub 440	SO.168		14. 6.83	Canx by CAA 29.6.93.
G-MJZF	Cruiser 175/La Mouette Atlas 16	01		14. 6.83	Canx by CAA 7.9.94.
G-MJZG	Mainair Tri-Flyer 440/Flexiform Striker	164-12683		14. 6.83	Canx by CAA 24.1.95.

Regn	Type	c/n	Previous identity	Regn date	Fate or immediate subsequent identity (if known)
G-MJZH	Mainair Tri-Flyer 250/Southdown Lightning 195 (Trike unit formerly G-MBCC)	BFC-01 & 002-781		27. 6.83	
G-MJZI	Eurowing Goldwing	EW-84JS		15. 6.83	Canx by CAA 6.9.93.
G-MJZJ	Hiway Skytrike/Skyhook Cutlass	GDHS-01		15. 6.83	Canx by CAA 26.9.90.
G-MJZK(1)	Southdown Puma Sprint	!		. 6.83R	To Ministry of Defence (PE). (At Popham 8/83) Canx.
G-MJZK(2)	Southdown Puma Sprint	1111/0081		3. 3.86	
G-MJZL	Eipper Quicksilver MX II	EEW-01		15. 6.83	
G-MJZM	MBA Tiger Cub 440	SO.35		16. 6.83	Canx as WFU 30.5.90.
G-MJZN	Pterodactyl	CJB-01		17. 6.83	Canx by CAA 13.6.90.
G-MJZO	Lancashire Micro-Trike/Flexiform Solo Striker	1/330PM/LM/683/2		24. 6.83	
G-MJZP	MBA Tiger Cub 440	HCB-01		21. 6.83	Canx as WFU 12.6.97.
G-MJZR	Eurowing Zephyr Z	EWZ-201		13. 6.83	Canx by CAA 13.6.90.
G-MJZS	MMT Scorpion	1		27. 6.83	Canx as WFU 2.11.88.
G-MJZT	Mainair Tri-Flyer/Flexiform Striker	JDR-01		21. 6.83	Canx by CAA 16.2.93.
G-MJZU	Mainair Tri-Flyer/Flexiform Dual Striker	JDR-02		21. 6.83	
G-MJZV	Livesey Micro 5	DL-2		21. 6.83	Canx as WFU 17.5.90.
G-MJZW	Eipper Quicksilver MX (Also engine no.14814)	1037		21. 6.83	Canx by CAA 5.2.92.
G-MJZX	Maxair Hummer TX	TX/16		21. 6.83	
G-MJZY	Goldmarque Shadow/Nikite Trike	0001		21. 6.83	Canx as WFU 10.12.84.
G-MJZZ	Hornet 440 Supreme Dual/Skyhook Cutlass	H 440		24. 6.83	Canx by CAA 23.9.93.
G-MKAK	Colt 77A HAFB	2039		15. 8.91	
G-MKAN	Agusta-Bell 206B JetRanger III	8557	G-DOUG	24. 1.80	To G-TKHM 1/81. Canx.
G-MKAS	PA-28-140 Cherokee Cruiser	28-7425338	G-BKVR OY-BGV	30. 4.98	
G-MKAY	Cessna 172N Skyhawk II	172-71214	N2268E	27.10.81	Badly damaged on landing at Netherlea Farm, near Pennistone, Yorks on 9.11.91. Canx by CAA 7.1.92.
G-MKEE	EAA Acro Sport	PFA/72-10197		20.12.78	No Permit issued. Canx by CAA 4.7.91.
G-MKIV	Bristol 149 Bolingbroke IVT	-	(G-BLHM) RCAF 10038	26. 3.82	Badly damaged in crash onto the golf course near Denham airfield on 21.6.87. Canx as destroyed 1.11.88. (On restoration to static display 7/99 at Duxford)
G-MKIX	Vickers-Supermarine 361 Spitfire LF.IXe (Firewall No. CBAF.8563)	CBAF/IX/2200	"EN398" N238V/OO-ARE/Belgium AF SM-36/Fokker B-8/R.Netherlands AF H-60/ R.Netherlands AF H-103/NH238	12.12.83	Permit expired 22.5.93. (Believed stored .96)
G-MKOA	HS.125 Srs.F403B	25227	G-AYFM	14. 6.82	To 5N-AMY 2/83. Canx 3.2.83.
G-MKPU	Europa Avn Europa	PFA/247-12569	G-DZEL	22.12.97	
G-MKVB	Vickers-Supermarine 349 Spitfire LF.Vb	CBAF/2461	5718M BM597	2. 5.89	
G-MKVC	Vickers-Supermarine 349 Spitfire F.Vc (Westland-built)	WWA/2822	A58-106 R.Australian AF/EE606	18. 5.88	Fatal crash and burned out near the 'White Lion' public house in Holfords Lane, Hartley Wintney on 1.7.89. Canx as destroyed 30.1.90.
G-MKVI	DH.100 Vampire FB.6 (built by FFW, Essen)	676	J-1167 Swiss AF	2. 6.92	(Stored 3/97)
G-MKXI	Vickers-Supermarine 365 Spitfire PR.XI	6S/504719	R.Netherlands AF/PL965	13.11.89	(Damaged near Ashford, Kent on 2.8.98)
G-MLAS	Cessna 182E	182-53826	OO-HPE D-EGPE/N2826Y	2. 5.79	Crashed on 14.12.80. CofA expired 2.10.82. Canx by CAA 4.2.87. (Cabin in use as para-trainer 5/98 at St.Merryn)
G-MLBU	PA-46-310P Malibu	46-8408057	N984BS N9607N	22. 1.86	To N146BU 4/93. Canx 13.4.93.
G-MLBY	Cessna 340A III	1045	ZS-KOZ N6823M	4. 6.84	To N70107. Canx 23.6.88.
G-MLCS	Cessna 414A Chancellor II	414A-0455	G-MHGI G-BHKK/(N2734D)	20. 9.82	To G-COWI 2/87. Canx.
G-MLDO	Dornier 228-202K	8009	PH-SDO D-IDON/D-CATI/SX-BHB/D-IDON/(PH-HAL)/D-IDON	2. 3.87	To G-OALF 8/88. Canx.
G-MLEE	Cessna 650 Citation III	650-0151	N1326G	29. 2.88	To N91D 3/90. Canx 19.3.90.
G-MLFF	PA-23-250 Aztec E	27-7305194	G-WEBB G-BJBU/N40476	31. 1.90	
G-MLGL	Colt 21A Cloudhopper HAFB	522		3. 4.84	Canx by CAA 19.5.93.
G-MLJL	Airbus A.330-243	254	F-WWKT	15. 6.99	
G-MLNR	Dornier 228-201	8108	D-IOHI D-COHI	27. 1.87	To D-CBDO(2). Canx 4.12.87.
G-MLTI	Dassault Falcon 900B	164	F-WWFC	13. 6.97	
G-MLTY	Aerospatiale AS.365N2 Dauphin 2	6431	N365EL JA6673	4. 6.99	
G-MLUA	PA-28-140 Cherokee C	28-26928	G-AYJT N11C	2.12.91	To EI-CGP 11/92. Canx 23.11.92.
G-MLWI	Thunder Ax7-77 HAFB	1000		3. 9.86	
G-MMAA	Dragon Srs.200	001		14. 7.82	Lost power and crashed on take-off from Rhoose on 6.9.82. Canx as destroyed 27.3.84.
G-MMAB	Dragon Srs.200	002		14. 7.82	Canx 27.3.84 on sale to France.
G-MMAC	Dragon Srs.200	003	OY-... G-MMAC	14. 7.82	
G-MMAD	Dragon Srs.200	004		7. 9.82	Canx 27.3.84 on sale to Japan.
G-MMAE	Dragon Srs 200 (Same c/n G-MMRS)	005		7. 9.82	

Regn	Type	c/n	Previous identity	Regn date	Fate or immediate subsequent identity (if known)
G-MMAF	Dragon Srs.150	D.150-003		18. 5.83	Force landed on rocky beach near Rhoose and badly damaged on 19.6.83. Canx as destroyed 30.5.84. Also canx (again) by CAA 7.9.94.
G-MMAG	MBA Tiger Cub 440	SO.47		22. 6.83	
G-MMAH	Eipper Quicksilver MX II (Also ENo.14805)	TM.1016		23. 6.83	Canx by CAA 26.10.95.
G-MMAI	Dragon Srs.150	0032		1. 7.83	
G-MMAJ	Mainair Tri-Flyer 440/Southdown Puma Sprint X (Originally regd as Mainair Gemini with same c/n)	MLS.01 & 193-14983		12.10.83	
G-MMAK	MBA Tiger Cub 440	SO.155		20. 9.83	
G-MMAL	Mainair Tri-Flyer/Flexiform Dual Striker	DHM-01		20. 9.83	(On rebuild 10/97)
G-MMAM	MBA Tiger Cub 440	SO.197		23. 9.83	
G-MMAN	Mainair Tri-Flyer 330/Flexiform Solo Striker	192-6983		27. 9.83	
G-MMAO	Southdown Puma Sprint X	HS.549		28.12.83	(Stored 8/97)
G-MMAP	Maxair Hummer TX	250TX-17		29. 9.83	
G-MMAR	Mainair Gemini/Southdown Puma Sprint MS	195-11083-2		23. 9.83	
G-MMAS	Mainair Tri-Flyer 440/Southdown Spirit	194-21983		23. 9.83	Canx by CAA 7.9.94.
G-MMAT	Mainair Tri-Flyer/Southdown Puma Spirit MS	205-21183		23. 9.83	Canx as WFU 21.1.86.
G-MMAU	Mainair Tri-Flyer/Flexiform Rapier 1+1	203-301083		23. 9.83	Canx by CAA 23.6.97.
G-MMAV	American Aerolights Eagle (Same c/n as G-MBXM)	AV.01 & 2664		8. 6.83	Canx by CAA 13.6.90.
G-MMAW	Mainair 330/Flexiform Rapier 1+1 (Solo Striker)	131-10283		18. 7.83	
G-MMAX	Hiway Skytrike/Flexiform Dual Striker	0011		5. 9.83	
G-MMAY	Patterson WW2 Trike/Airwave Magic Nimrod	WW 2		23. 8.83	Canx as WFU 12.6.90.
G-MMAZ	Southdown Puma Sprint X	MAPB-01		5. 8.83	
G-MMBA	Hiway Skytrike 250/Super Scorpion (Originally regd with a Robin trike)	RE 6S CII		29. 6.83	Canx by CAA 24.1.95.
G-MMBB	American Aerolights Eagle	MAL-01		2.11.82	Canx by CAA 7.9.94. (Stored 2/99 North Walsham Airfield, Norfolk)
G-MMBC	Medway Hybred 330/Hiway Super Scorpion (See G-MMHZ)	27683/2		27. 6.83	Canx by CAA 6.10.93.
G-MMBD	Spectrum 330	003		4. 8.83	Canx as WFU 28.1.87.
G-MMBE	MBA Tiger Cub 440	SO.74		30. 6.83	Canx by CAA 4.2.92.
G-MMBF	American Aerolights Eagle	NVM-01		30. 6.83	Canx by CAA 7.9.94.
G-MMBG	Hiway Skytrike/Chargus Cyclone (Also ENo. 10680)	21V5		30. 6.83	Canx as WFU 23.4.90.
G-MMBH	MBA Super Tiger Cub 440	SO.37		30. 6.83	Canx as WFU 22.12.93.
G-MMBI	American Aerolights Eagle	-		. .83R	NTU - Canx. (Probably duplicated in G-MMBK)
G-MMBJ	Hiway Skytrike 250/Solar Wings Typhoon	RFB-01		5. 7.83	
G-MMBK	American Aerolights Eagle	2480		1. 7.83	Canx by CAA 23.1.95.
G-MMBL	Ultrasports/Southdown Puma Lightning DS	80-00083		4. 7.83	
G-MMBM	Soarmaster 125 Trike/La Mouette Azure	78273/81		4. 7.83	Canx by CAA 13.6.90.
G-MMBN	Eurowing Goldwing	EW-89		28. 6.83	(Stored 8/93)
G-MMBO	Not allotted.				
G-MMBP	Hiway Skytrike/Super Scorpion 2	21W6		11. 8.82	Canx by CAA 22.6.83. Wing sold and then used as a Hang-Glider, Trike to G-MNPR.
G-MMBR	Hiway Skytrike III/Demon 175	SSMT-01		28. 6.83	Canx by CAA 13.6.90.
G-MMBS	Hiway Skytrike 330/Flexiform Striker (Possibly shares trike with G-MJOU)	JTRC-01		6. 7.83	(Stored 9/96)
G-MMBT	MBA Tiger Cub 440 (Probably either c/n PFA/140-10924 & PFA/140-10990)	SO.131 & TA.01		19. 7.83	(Stored at owners home 1/91)
G-MMBU	Eipper Quicksilver MX II	CAL-222		8. 7.83	(Damaged late .97)
G-MMBV	Huntair Pathfinder	044		8. 7.83	
G-MMBW	MBA Tiger Cub 440	SO.134 & TA.05		19. 7.83	Canx as destroyed 5.9.94.
G-MMBX	MBA Tiger Cub 440	SO.151 & TA.08		19. 7.83	Canx as WFU 19.4.93.
G-MMBY	Ultrasports Tripacer 440/Solar Wings Typhoon XL (Panther)	T483-759XL		20. 7.83	
G-MMBZ	Solar Wings Typhoon P (C/n probably T981-217)	T981-52.17		20. 7.83	
G-MMCA	Hiway Skytrike/Solar Wings Storm	21W8		14. 7.83	Canx by CAA 13.6.90.
G-MMCB	Huntair Pathfinder II	136		13. 7.83	Canx as WFU 23.11.88. (On display at The Science Museum)
G-MMCC	American Aerolights Eagle	MAL-02		2.11.82	Canx by CAA 13.6.90.
G-MMCD	Mainair Tri-Flyer 440/Southdown Lightning DS	505 & 140-18383		12. 7.83	Canx as WFU 10.7.89.
G-MMCE	MBA Tiger Cub 440	SO.72		10. 8.83	Canx as WFU 6.4.92.

Regn	Type	c/n	Previous identity	Regn date	Fate or immediate subsequent identity (if known)
G-MMCF	Ultrasports/Solar Wings Panther 330 (C/n also quoted as T1082-175)	T1081-275		22.11.83	Canx by CAA 8.8.89.
G-MMCG	Eipper Quicksilver MX I	10990		14. 7.83	Permit expired 7.7.98. Canx by CAA 23.7.99.
G-MMCH	Ultrasports Tripacer 330/Southdown Lightning Phase II	82-00263		13. 7.83	Destroyed in fatal crash at Martin airfield, near Metheringham, Lincs on 18.6.86. Canx by CAA 13.6.90.
G-MMCI	Southdown Puma Sprint X (Orig. regd as Mk.I)	DMP-01 & P.421		28. 9.83	
G-MMCJ	Flexiform Dual Striker	JJ-165		13. 2.87	
G-MMCK	Stewkie Aer-O-Ship LTA (The LTA stands for Lighter Than Air - the wing is helium filled giving a net lift of some 90lbs)	ST.001/LTA		20. 7.83	Canx by CAA 13.6.90.
G-MMCL	Stewkie Aer-O-Ship HAA Amphibian	ST.002/HAA		20. 7.83	Canx by CAA 15.6.90.
G-MMCM	Mainair Tri-Flyer/Southdown Puma Sprint	CM-2		28. 6.83	
G-MMCN	Hiway Skytrike 250/Solar Wings Storm	SMB.8069		19. 7.83	Canx as WFU 9.1.95.
G-MMCO	Hornet Invader/Southdown Sprint	RP.015		27. 7.83	Canx by CAA 23.6.97.
G-MMCP	Ultrasports Tripacer 330/Southdown Lightning Phase II	JDH-01		21. 7.83	Canx by CAA 10.1.91.
G-MMCR	Eipper Quicksilver MX (The c/n is the zip code and telephone number of Eipper!)	CA92069/(714)744-1514		22. 7.83	Canx by CAA 23.1.95.
G-MMCS	Southdown Puma Sprint	?		. .83R	NTU - Wing attached to the trike regd G-MJRG.
G-MMCT	Hiway Skytrike 330/Demon	RGG-01		26. 7.83	Canx by CAA 13.6.90.
G-MMCU	Dragon Srs.150	D150/051		3. 8.83	Canx 27.3.84 on sale to Turkey.
G-MMCV	Hiway Skytrike II/Solar Wings Typhoon III	T583-783		27. 7.83	
G-MMCW	Southdown Puma Sprint 440	572 & 1121/0124		16. 9.83	
G-MMCX	MBA Super Tiger Cub 440	MU.002		8. 8.83	
G-MMCY	SMD Gazelle 440/Flexiform Striker	SSA961/SG141383		10. 8.83	Canx by CAA 20.8.93.
G-MMCZ	Mainair Tri-Flyer/Flexiform Dual Striker (Mainair Trike c/n 180-.....)	TE-01		10. 8.83	
G-MMDA	Mitchell Wing B-10	01		4. 8.83	Canx by CAA 25.6.90.
G-MMDB	Hornet/La Mouette Atlas 18	DB-01		22. 3.83	Canx by CAA 18.4.95.
G-MMDC	Eipper Quicksilver MX II	1503-3450110		24.10.83	Canx by CAA 4.2.92.
G-MMDD	Huntair Pathfinder	023		2.11.82	Canx by CAA 7.9.94.
G-MMDE	Mainair Tri-Flyer 250/Solar Wings Typhoon S	DES-1 & 025-211081-6		12. 8.83	Canx as WFU 18.8.94.
G-MMDF	Southdown Wild Cat Mk.II/Lightning Phase II	007		24. 8.83	
G-MMDG	Eurowing Goldwing	001		15. 8.83	Canx by CAA 6.10.93.
G-MMDH	Manta Fledge 2B	837		15. 8.83	Canx by CAA 23.1.95.
G-MMDI	Hiway Skytrike Mk.I/Super Scorpion	JB05SC2		24. 8.83	Canx as WFU 21.9.93.
G-MMDJ	Mainair Tri-Flyer 250/Solar Wings Typhoon (The trike is from G-MJVK, hence duplicate c/n)	070-24582		9. 9.83	Canx by CAA 23.6.97.
G-MMDK	Mainair Tri-Flyer/Flexiform Striker (Also quoted as Airwave Merlin)	181-16883		7. 9.83	
G-MMDL	Dragon Srs.150	D150/0061		30. 8.83	Canx by CAA 13.6.90.
G-MMDM	MBA Tiger Cub 440	DM-01		27. 7.83	Canx by CAA 13.6.90.
G-MMDN	Mainair Tri-Flyer/Flexiform Dual Striker (Initially had Hornet Invader trike and still regd with Hornet c/n)	RP.012		30. 9.83	
G-MMDO	Hornet Invader Dual/Southdown Sprint	RP.014		2.11.83	Canx as WFU 1.2.93.
G-MMDP	Mainair Gemini/Southdown Sprint X (C/n conflicts with G-MMPD; probably fitted with new Gemini trike) (Originally regd as Tri-Flyer 440/Southdown Sprint with c/n RED-01)	183-22883		20. 9.83	
G-MMDR	Huntair Pathfinder II	137		30. 8.83	
G-MMDS(1)	Ultrasports/Solar Wings Panther 440	?		. .83R	NTU - Crashed at Costessey Showground, near Norwich on 10.9.83 prior to formal registration.
G-MMDS(2)	Ultrasports/Solar Wings Panther XLS 440	KND-02		13. 7.84	
G-MMDT	Mainair Tri-Flyer Dual 440/Flexiform Striker	178-20583		1. 9.83	Canx by CAA 28.2.95. (Stored 8/95)
G-MMDU	MBA Tiger Cub 440	SO.49		5. 9.83	(Stored dismantled Chirk 3/98) Canx by CAA 23.6.97.
G-MMDV	Ultrasports/Solar Wings Panther	TME-01 & 83-00170		5. 9.83	Canx by CAA 27.5.93.
G-MMDW	Pterodactyl Pfledgling	RCW-01		6. 9.83	Canx by CAA 2.2.93.
G-MMDX	Lloyd Trident/Solar Wings Typhoon	EJL-01		7. 9.83	(Status uncertain)
G-MMDY	Southdown Puma Sprint	S.064		7. 9.83	
G-MMDZ	Mainair Tri-Flyer Dual/Flexiform Dual Striker	0036/2		7. 9.83	Canx as destroyed 21.1.93.

Regn	Type	c/n	Previous identity	Regn date	Fate or immediate subsequent identity (if known)
G-MMEA	MBA Tiger Cub 440	BAL-01		7. 9.83	Canx by CAA 13.6.90.
G-MMEB	Hiway Skytrike/Super Scorpion	AAR-10		8. 9.83	Canx by CAA 23.1.95.
G-MMEC	Southdown Puma DS	AEW-01		9. 9.83	Canx as WFU 6.4.90.
G-MMED	Poisestar Aeolus Mk.I	002		7.12.83	Canx by CAA 13.6.90.
G-MMEE	American Aerolights Eagle	2850		13.10.83	Canx by CAA 4.2.92.
G-MMEF	Hiway Skytrike/Super Scorpion	SM160B 10664		13. 9.83	
G-MMEG	Eipper Quicksilver MX	DJND-02		14. 9.83	(Stored .94) Canx by CAA 23.6.97.
G-MMEH	Ultrasports/Solar Wings Panther 250	S.86111		1. 9.83	Ditched in the sea off Lydd on 6.6.84. Canx by CAA 13.6.90.
G-MMEI	Hiway Skytrike/Demon	3644C		21. 9.83	
G-MMEJ	Mainair Tri-Flyer/Flexiform Striker	215-41183 & FF/LAI/83/JDR/03		15. 9.83	
G-MMEK	Medway Hybred 44XL/Solar Wings Typhoon XL II	12983/6		16. 9.83	
G-MMEL	Medway Hybred 44XL/Solar Wings Typhoon XL II	10983/4		16. 9.83	Canx by CAA 2.7.96.
G-MMEM	Medway Hybred 44XL/Solar Wings Typhoon XL II	12983/5		16. 9.83	Canx by CAA 18.10.93.
G-MMEN	Medway Hybred 44XL/Solar Wings Typhoon XL II	10983/3		16. 9.83	Canx as destroyed 15.6.87.
G-MMEO	Ultrasports Tripacer/Southdown Lightning Phase II	135		21. 9.83	
	(Originally regd as a Southdown Puma II, restored 15.1.92 as Lightning Phase II with same c/n)				
G-MMEP	MBA Tiger Cub 440	BMAA/HB/036 & PMY-01		22. 9.83	Canx by CAA 4.2.92.
G-MMER	[Was reserved for Long Marston Aviation]			. .83R	NTU - Canx.
G-MMES	Southdown Puma Sprint	SS.582		21.12.83	DBR 1.7.84. Canx by CAA 27.3.99.
G-MMET	Skyhook TR1 Pixie Mk.II/Sabre	TR1/11		11.10.83	Canx as WFU 3.8.94.
G-MMEU	MBA Tiger Cub 440	PFA/104-10923 & SO.53		4.10.83	Canx as WFU 21.12.94.
G-MMEV	American Aerolights Eagle	JGJ-01		5.10.83	Canx by CAA 13.6.90.
G-MMEW	MBA Tiger Cub 440	SO.63		17.10.83	Canx by CAA 8.8.89.
G-MMEX	Solar Wings Sprint	PWR-01		19.10.83	Canx by CAA 23.6.97.
G-MMEY	MBA Tiger Cub 440	SO.206		21.10.83	
G-MMEZ	Mainair Gemini 440/Southdown Sprint	326-785-3 & P.456		1. 4.85	Canx by CAA 25.7.96. Trike to G-MMZK /97.
	(Initially flown as Southdown Puma Sprint prior to 3/84 - presumed same wing)				
G-MMFA	Not allotted.				
G-MMFB	Mainair Tri-Flyer 440/Flexiform Dual Striker	FF/LAI/83/JDR/10		20. 9.83	Canx by CAA 23.1.95.
G-MMFC	Mainair Gemini/Flexiform Striker	KR235-484-2 & FF/LAI/83/JDR/11		20. 9.83	Permit expired 29.12.94. Canx by CAA 25.8.98.
	(Originally regd as a Tri-Flyer/Striker)				
G-MMFD	Mainair Tri-Flyer 440/Flexiform Dual Striker	210-31083-2 & FF/LAI/83/JDR/12		20. 9.83	
G-MMFE	Mainair Tri-Flyer 440/Flexiform Dual Striker	FF/LAI/83/JDR/13		20. 9.83	
G-MMFF	Mainair Tri-Flyer 440/Flexiform Dual Striker	FF/LAI/83/JDR/14		20. 9.83	Canx as destroyed 12.4.90.
G-MMFG	Mainair Tri-Flyer 440/Flexiform Dual Striker	FF/LAI/83/JDR/15		20. 9.83	
G-MMFH	Mainair Tri-Flyer 440/Flexiform Striker	FF/LAI/83/JDR/16		20. 9.83	Canx by CAA 13.6.90.
G-MMFI	Mainair Tri-Flyer 440/Flexiform Striker	FF/LAI/83/JDR/17		20. 9.83	Canx by CAA 4.6.93.
G-MMFJ	Hiway Skytrike 330/Flexiform Striker	FF/LAI/83/JDR/18		20. 9.83	Canx as WFU 22.11.95.
	(Originally regd as Mainair Tri-Flyer 440)				
G-MMFK	Mainair Gemini 440/Flexiform Striker	234-284-2 & FF/LAI/83/JDR/19		20. 9.83	
	(Originally regd as Mainair Tri-Flyer 440, then as a Lancashire Micro Duet II using c/n PM/440/PGK/2/12/83)				
G-MMFL	Ultrasports Tripacer 330/Flexiform Sealander	JGM-01		25.10.83	
	(Originally regd as Flexiform Striker with c/n "EC34PM")				
G-MMFM	Piranha Srs.200/Solar Wings Typhoon (Also c/n GAB-831)	GAB-01		25.10.83	Canx by CAA 23.6.97.
G-MMFN	MBA Tiger Cub 440	SO.113		31.10.83	
G-MMFO	Not allotted.				
G-MMFP	MBA Tiger Cub 440	SO.3/88		31.10.83	Canx by CAA 4.5.90.
G-MMFR	MBA Tiger Cub 440	SO.4/82		31.10.83	Canx by CAA 4.5.90.
G-MMFS	MBA Tiger Cub 440	SO.64		1.11.83	
G-MMFT	MBA Tiger Cub 440	SO.56		2.11.83	
G-MMFU	Not allotted.				
G-MMFV	Mainair Tri-Flyer 440/Flexiform Dual Striker	83-00130 & 212-271083		8.12.83	
G-MMFW	Chapel Trike/Skyhook Cutlass	1 AO		18.11.83	Canx by CAA 8.10.93.
G-MMFX	MBA Tiger Cub 440	SO.101		8.11.83	Canx by CAA 7.9.94.
G-MMFY	Sims Trike/Flexiform Dual Striker	AZT001CS		14.12.83	Canx by CAA 2.7.96.

Regn	Type	c/n	Previous identity	Regn date	Fate or immediate subsequent identity (if known)
G-MMFZ	Striplin (AES) Sky Ranger	HAW-01		18.11.83	
G-MMGA	Bass Gosling	NO.002		14.11.83	Canx by CAA 12.5.89.
G-MMGB	Southdown Puma Sprint/Breen Special	543		8. 6.83	Canx 2.8.84 on sale to Iceland.
G-MMGC	Southdown Puma Sprint	-		. .83R	NTU - Canx.
G-MMGD	Southdown Puma Sprint	-		. .83R	NTU - Canx.
G-MMGE	Hiway Skytrike/Super Scorpion	NRD-01		17.11.83	Canx by CAA 1.2.93.
G-MMGF	MBA Tiger Cub 440	SO.124		18.11.83	
G-MMGG	Southdown Puma	JDP-01		21.11.83	Canx by CAA 13.6.90.
G-MMGH	Mainair Tri-Flyer/Flexiform Dual Striker	JDR-06		21.11.83	Canx by CAA 13.6.90.
G-MMGI	Mainair Tri-Flyer/Flexiform Dual Striker	JDR-05		21.11.83	Canx by CAA 13.6.90.
G-MMGJ	MBA Tiger Cub 440	JL-01 & SO.216		22.11.83	Canx by CAA 13.6.90.
G-MMGK	Hiway Skytrike/Skyhook Silhouette	NES-01		22.11.83	Canx by CAA 13.6.90.
G-MMGL	MBA Tiger Cub 440	BMAA/HB/050 & SO.148		23.11.83	(Stored Rufforth 8/95)
G-MMGM	Southdown Puma Sprint	?		. .83R	NTU - Fatal crash in Spain. Canx.
G-MMGN	Southdown Puma Sprint	-		. .83R	NTU - Canx.
G-MMGO	MBA Tiger Cub 440	SO.102		23.11.83	Canx by CAA 7.9.94.
G-MMGP	Southdown Puma Sprint X	RGC-01		24.11.83	
G-MMGR	Mainair Tri-Flyer/Flexiform Dual Striker	LAI/DS/09		15.12.83	Canx by CAA 9.6.93.
G-MMGS	Ultrasports/Solar Wings Panther Dual	T1283-939XL		28.12.83	
G-MMGT	Hunt Avon Skytrike/Hunt Wing	JAH-7		28.11.83	
	(Originally regd as Hunt Trike 440/Solar Wings Typhoon 180XL)				
G-MMGU	SMD Gazelle 440/Flexiform Sealander	30-4883		1.12.83	
G-MMGV	Whittaker MW.5 Sorcerer Srs.A	001		2.12.83	
G-MMGW	Whittaker MW.5 Sorcerer Srs.B	002		2.12.83	Canx by CAA 13.6.90.
G-MMGX	Southdown Puma DS	RC.1		7.12.83	Canx by CAA 14.11.91.
G-MMGY	Dean Piranha 1000	BMW-1000-83		5.12.83	Canx by CAA 7.9.94.
G-MMGZ	Mitchell U2 Super Wing	PU 514		6.12.83	Canx as WFU 25.10.88.
G-MMHA	Skyhook TR1 Pixie/Zeus	TR1/44		9.12.83	Canx by CAA 23.1.95.
G-MMHB	Skyhook TR1 Pixie/Apollo	TR1/45		9.12.83	Canx by CAA 23.6.97.
G-MMHC	American Aerolights Eagle	LD.1		6.12.83	Canx by CAA 13.6.90.
G-MMHD	Hornet/Hiway Demon 175	H.161		7.12.83	Canx by CAA 23.1.95.
G-MMHE	Mainair Gemini 440/Southdown Sprint MS	229-184-2		8.12.83	Canx by CAA 30.10.98.
	(Replacement trike - previously regd with Gemini c/n 188-31883-2 which then became G-MMLZ)				
G-MMHF	Southdown Puma Sprint	EBDA-01		8.12.83	
G-MMHG	Hiway Skytrike 250/Solar Wings Storm	DRB-01		13.12.83	Canx by CAA 22.9.93.
G-MMHH	Ultrasports/Solar Wings Panther Dual 440	DRB-02		13.12.83	Canx by CAA 13.6.90.
G-MMHI	MBA Tiger Cub 440	SO.138		15.12.83	Canx by CAA 13.6.90.
G-MMHJ	Hiway Skytrike/Flexiform Hilander	AB-1		16.12.83	Canx by CAA 7.9.94.
G-MMHK	Hiway Skytrike/Super Scorpion	KSC.83		19.12.83	
G-MMHL	Hiway Skytrike/Super Scorpion	KSC.84		19.12.83	
G-MMHM	Hiway Skytrike/Goldmarque Gyr	G.188		19.12.83	Canx as WFU 27.6.85.
G-MMHN	MBA Tiger Cub 440	SO.136		19.12.83	
G-MMHO	MBA Tiger Cub 440	SO.137		19.12.83	Canx by CAA 13.6.90.
G-MMHP	Hiway Hiro Skytrike/Demon 175			19.12.83	
	(Regd with c/n OL175)	PCC-01 & OL17D			
G-MMHR	Mainair Gemini/Southdown Sprint DS	213-271083-2 & P.427		29.12.83	
	(Originally regd as Mainair Tri-Flyer)				
G-MMHS	SMD Gazelle/Flexiform Dual Striker	104-11283		21.12.83	
	(Originally regd as SMD Viper with same c/n)				
G-MMHT	SMD Gazelle 440/Flexiform Striker	102-8883		21.12.83	Canx by CAA 5.12.95.
G-MMHU	Hiway Skytrike/Flexiform Striker	PFDS.1		21.12.83	Canx as destroyed 10.5.90.
	(Originally regd as Super Scorpion)				
G-MMHV	Chargus T.225/Vortex 120	PDL-001		14.12.83	Canx by CAA 13.6.90.
G-MMHW	Chargus T.225/Vortex 120	PDL-002		14.12.83	Canx by CAA 13.6.90.
G-MMHX	Hornet Invader 440/Southdown Sprint	RP.016		21.12.83	Canx by CAA 13.10.88.
G-MMHY	Hornet Invader 440/Flexiform Dual Striker	RP.017		21.12.83	
G-MMHZ	Ultrasports/Solar Wings Panther XL-S	TP2-0001 & T1283-948XL		3. 1.84	
	(Originally regd as Typhoon XL with same c/n)(Formerly used Medway Hybred 330 c/n 27683/2 which duplicated G-MMBC - also now quoted as Solar Wings Pegasus)(Wing ex G-MJPU)				
G-MMIA	Westwind Phoenix XP-3	XP3-001		19. 1.84	Canx by CAA 13.6.90.
G-MMIB	MEA Mistral Trainer	DH-01		3. 2.84	Canx by CAA 5.12.95.

Regn	Type	c/n	Previous identity	Regn date	Fate or immediate subsequent identity (if known)
G-MMIC	Luscombe Vitality	V.001		1. 6.82	Canx by CAA 13.6.90.
G-MMID	Flexiform Dual Striker	063		3. 1.84	Canx as WFU 14.11.95.
G-MMIE	MBA Tiger Cub 440	G7-7		3. 1.84	
G-MMIF	Coulson Trike 330/Wasp Gryphon	FC.15		3. 1.84	Canx as WFU 27.1.88.
G-MMIG	MBA Tiger Cub 440	G12-9RB		3. 1.84	Canx as destroyed 23.4.90.
G-MMIH	MBA Tiger Cub 440	SO.130		25. 4.84	
G-MMII	Southdown Puma Sprint 440	P.500		26. 1.84	
G-MMIJ	Ultrasports Tripacer/Airwave Nimrod 165	ZX-00165		1.11.83	
G-MMIK	Eipper Quicksilver MX II	1042		6. 1.84	Canx as WFU 4.5.90.
G-MMIL	Eipper Quicksilver MX II (C/n conflicts with G-MMNA)	1046		6. 1.84	
G-MMIM	MBA Tiger Cub 440	BMAA/HB/060 & SO.28		11. 1.84	
G-MMIN	Luscombe Vitality	V.002		14. 6.82	Canx by CAA 13.6.90.
G-MMIO	Huntair Pathfinder II	159		16. 1.84	Canx by CAA 7.9.94. (Stored 6/96)
G-MMIP	Hiway Skytrike 250/Vulcan	CGD-01		18. 1.84	Canx by CAA 1.10.91.
G-MMIR	Mainair Gemini/Southdown Sprint	051-20182		25. 1.84	
	(Originally regd as Tri-Flyer 440/Puma Sprint MS with c/n GCH-01)(Regd with original Trike c/n 051-20182 (ex G-MBKX, later G-MJDO)(Stored Long Marston 1/98); now rebuilt with Trike 314-585-3, ex G-MMZK; Wing ex G-MMTI)				
G-MMIS	Hiway Hiro Skytrike/Demon	MPW-01		1. 2.84	Canx by CAA 7.9.94.
G-MMIT	Hiway Skytrike 250/Demon 330	TC-01		1. 2.84	Canx by CAA 13.6.90.
G-MMIU	Southdown Puma Sprint	P.503		7. 2.84	Canx by CAA 13.6.90.
G-MMIV	Mainair Gemini/Southdown Puma Sprint	EC-02 & 231-184-2		3. 2.84	Canx by CAA 21.1.98.
G-MMIW	Southdown Puma Sprint	590		9. 2.84	
G-MMIX	MBA Tiger Cub 440	MBCB-01		14. 2.84	(Extant 1/98)
G-MMIY	Eurowing Goldwing	-		. .84R	NTU - Canx.
G-MMIZ	Southdown Lightning II	CB-01		24. 2.84	Canx by CAA 23.1.95.
G-MMJA	Mitchell Wing B-10	JA-01		2. 9.83	Canx by CAA 13.6.90.
G-MMJB	American Aerolights Eagle	JB-01		21. 3.83	Canx as destroyed 6.2.86. (Wing displayed at Long Marston in 8/95)
G-MMJC	Lancashire Micro-Trike 440/Southdown Sprint	2/440PM/LM/883		4. 8.83	Canx by CAA 8.9.94.
G-MMJD	Southdown Puma Sprint	SP/1001		28. 6.83	
G-MMJE	Southdown Puma Sprint	P.525		18. 9.84	Canx by CAA 29.1.93.
G-MMJF	Ultrasports/Solar Wings Panther Dual XL-S	T284-988XL		27. 2.84	
G-MMJG	Mainair Tri-Flyer/Flexiform Dual Striker	185-1983		31. 9.83	
G-MMJH	Southdown Puma Sprint	JH-03		28.10.83	Canx by CAA 18.10.93.
G-MMJI	Southdown Puma Sprint	P.529		10. 5.84	Canx as destroyed 6.8.91.
G-MMJJ	Solar Wings Typhoon	-		. .84R	NTU - Canx.
G-MMJK	Hiway Skytrike/Demon	MAB-01		6. 3.84	Canx by CAA 23.1.95.
G-MMJL	UAS Storm Buggy 440/Flexiform 1+1 Sealander	0537		27. 4.83	Canx by CAA 7.9.94.
G-MMJM	Southdown Puma Sprint 440	PD.500 & 1111/0001		27. 2.84	
G-MMJN	Eipper Quicksilver MX II	14891		5. 3.84	Canx by CAA 27.1.93.
G-MMJO	MBA Tiger Cub 440	SO.90/5		12. 3.84	Canx by CAA 7.9.94.
G-MMJP	Southdown Lightning II	SO.03/83		27. 2.84	Canx by CAA 13.6.90.
G-MMJR	MBA Tiger Cub 440	SO.180		26.10.83	Canx by CAA 13.6.90.
G-MMJS	MBA Tiger Cub 440	WAM.1		8. 1.87	Canx by CAA 7.9.94. (Stored 1/93)
G-MMJT	Mainair Gemini/Southdown Sprint X	JBT-01		20.12.83	
	(Originally regd as Tri-Flyer 440 Dual/Southdown Puma Sprint MS with same c/n)				
G-MMJU	Mainair Tri-Flyer/Hiway Demon	DW-01		5. 3.84	Canx by CAA 30.10.89.
G-MMJV	MBA Tiger Cub 440	SO.195 & PFA/140-10902		5. 3.84	
G-MMJW	Mainair Tri-Flyer 440/Southdown Puma Sprint	207-71083		5.10.83	Canx by CAA 4.7.96.
G-MMJX(1)	Southdown Puma Sprint	?		. .83R	NTU - Canx.
G-MMJX(2)	Teman Mono-Fly	01		6. 3.84	
G-MMJY	MBA Tiger Cub 440	SO.67		7. 3.84	Canx by CAA 13.6.90.
G-MMJZ	Skyhook TR1 Pixie/Zeus	TR1/47		27. 3.84	Canx by CAA 23.6.97.
G-MMKA	Ultrasports/Solar Wings Panther Dual XL	T284-986XL		8. 3.84	
G-MMKB	Ultraflight Mirage II	BKP-01		8. 3.84	Canx by CAA 23.1.95.
G-MMKC	Mainair Gemini 440/Southdown Sprint MS	201-201083-2		12.10.83	Canx by CAA 5.12.95.
G-MMKD	Southdown Puma Sprint	P.514		27. 2.84	
	(Fitted with skis for Venezuelan expedition in 1984)				
G-MMKE	Birdman Chinook WT-11	01817		2. 4.84	
G-MMKF	Ultrasports/Solar Wings Panther Dual XL	T284-987XL		7. 3.84	Canx by CAA 23.1.95.
G-MMKG	Medway Hybred 44XL/Solar Wings Typhoon XL2	22284/7		9. 3.84	(Reported 8/96 with wing previously marked G-MNYX)
G-MMKH	Medway Hybred 44XL/Solar Wings Typhoon XL	22284/8		9. 3.84	
G-MMKI	Ultrasports/Solar Wings Panther 330	LA-01		12. 3.84	Canx by CAA 4.2.92.

Regn	Type	c/n	Previous identity	Regn date	Fate or immediate subsequent identity (if known)
G-MMKJ	Ultrasports/Solar Wings Panther 330	LA-02		12. 3.84	Crashed on landing 27.5.97. Canx as PWFU 23.7.97.
G-MMKK	Mainair Gemini/Flash	240-384-2		12. 3.84	Canx by CAA 30.6.92.
G-MMKL	Mainair Gemini/Flash	238-384-2 & W11		12. 3.84	Damaged in forced landing at Armaside Farm, Lorton, Cumbria on 12.8.86.
G-MMKM	Mainair Gemini/Flexiform Dual Striker	221-184-?		12. 3.84	
	(Originally regd as Tri-Flyer with c/n 210-121283-2 - To G-MMXH)(Regd/stamped with c/n 221-0184-0002)				
G-MMKN	Mitchell Wing B-10	LD-01		13. 3.84	Canx as destroyed 4.6.90.
G-MMKO	Southdown Puma Sprint	P.513		15. 2.84	Canx 14.6.95 on sale to Portugal. (Was based at Lagos, The Algarve)
	(Fitted with floats for Venezuelan expedition in 1984)				
G-MMKP	MBA Tiger Cub 440	SO.203		13. 3.84	
G-MMKR	Mainair Tri-Flyer 440/Southdown Lightning DS	209-171083		14. 3.84	
	(Originally regd with c/n CM-01)				
G-MMKS	Nikite 260/Southdown Lightning 195	373 & 002		15. 3.84	Canx by CAA 23.1.95.
	(Originally regd with 375 & 002 - changed in 1986)				
G-MMKT	MBA Tiger Cub 440	SO.85		7.11.83	Canx by CAA 7.9.94.
G-MMKU	Mainair Gemini/Southdown Puma Sprint MS	232-284-2 & P.519		19. 3.84	
G-MMKV	Southdown Puma Sprint	P.521		24. 4.84	
G-MMKW	Mainair Tri-Flyer 250/Solar Wings Storm	RJM-01		22. 3.84	Canx by CAA 2.12.86.
G-MMKX(1)	Ultrasports Phantom	?		. .83R	NTU - Crashed into Loch Ness on 9.7.83 prior to being regd.
G-MMKX(2)	Skyrider Airsports Phantom 330	PH-107R		18. 3.85	
G-MMKY	Jordon Duet Srs.1	CHS-01		19. 3.84	Canx by CAA 1.9.95.
G-MMKZ	Southdown Puma 440/Lightning DS	P.449		19. 3.84	Canx by CAA 6.3.91.
G-MMLA	American Aerolights Eagle 430B	19791		19. 3.84	Canx as destroyed 11.7.89.
G-MMLB	MBA Super Tiger Cub 440	SO.57		19. 3.84	
G-MMLC	Scaled Composites 97M	0001	N97ML	30. 8.83	Canx 26.9.88 on sale to USA.
G-MMLD	Moran Trike/Solar Wings Typhoon S	NPM-01 & T283-699		20. 3.84	Canx by CAA 7.9.94.
G-MMLE	Eurowing Goldwing SP	EW-81		21. 3.84	
G-MMLF	MBA Tiger Cub 440	SO.115		23. 3.84	
G-MMLG	Mainair Gemini/Solar Wings Pegasus XL-R	BS-02		29. 3.84	Canx 24.6.94 on sale to Ireland.
	(Built with Trike from G-MBNI)(Initially regd as Ultrasports Tripacer 330/Solar Wings Typhoon S4 XL)				
G-MMLH	Hiway Skytrike Mk.II 330/Demon	PMH-01 & DJL-01		28. 3.84	
G-MMLI	Mainair Tri-Flyer 250/Solar Wings Typhoon S	RPAT-01 & T484-423L		26. 3.84	Canx by CAA 7.9.94.
	(Initially regd as Hiway Skytrike Mk.II 250)				
G-MMLJ	Hiway Skytrike/Flexiform Sealander	-		. .84R	NTU - Canx.
G-MMLK	MBA Tiger Cub 440	SO.112		26. 3.84	Canx by CAA 23.6.97.
G-MMLL	Midland Ultralights Sirocco 377GB	MU-01		30. 3.84	Landed in trees at Weston-under-Lizard, Staffs on 16.8.86 and badly damaged during recovery. Canx by CAA 18.10.93.
G-MMLM	MBA Tiger Cub 440	SO.172		26. 3.84	
G-MMLN	Skyhook TR1 Pixie/Zeus	TR1/48		13. 4.84	Canx by CAA 23.1.95.
G-MMLO	Skyhook TR1 Pixie/Zeus	TR1/49		9. 4.84	Canx as WFU 25.11.94.
G-MMLP	Mainair Gemini 440/Southdown Sprint	ACT-01 & 242-20484-2		3. 4.84	
G-MMLR	Ultrasports/Solar Wings Panther 330	LA-02		1. 6.84	Canx by CAA 13.6.90.
G-MMLS	Skyhook Pixie/Flexiform Medium Striker	AP-01 & NP70ZN2		29. 3.84	Canx 3.1.85 on sale to Israel.
G-MMLT	Ultrasports/Solar Wings Panther 440	83-00176 & T384-1022XL		29. 3.84	To 4X-HAR 10/85. Canx 5.2.85.
G-MMLU	Southdown Puma 330	-		. .84R	NTU - Canx.
G-MMLV	Southdown Puma 330 (Lightning)	P3-84-4-164		29.11.84	
	(C/n quoted as NOP 3-84-164)				
G-MMLW	Southdown Puma 250	-		. .84R	NTU - Canx.
G-MMLX	Ultrasports/Solar Wings Panther XL-S	T584-1063XL		3. 7.84	
G-MMLY	Soarmaster Powered Hang Glider	-		. .84R	NTU - Canx.
G-MMLZ	Mainair Gemini 440/Southdown Sprint	188-31883 & P.428		30. 3.84	Canx by CAA 23.9.93.
	(Originally regd with Mainair Tri-Flyer with c/n IR-01; then with trike unit ex.G-MMHE)				
G-MMMA	Lancashire Micro-Trike 440/Flexiform Dual Striker	1/440PM/LM/1283/2		3. 1.84	Canx by CAA 13.6.90.
G-MMMB	Mainair Tri-Flyer/Southdown Sprint	CR-01/170 & 170-16583		5. 4.84	
	(Trike unit ex G-MJYU)(Also quoted as c/n CM-01/170)				
G-MMMC	Southdown Puma SS	MEH-01		15.11.83	Canx by CAA 13.6.90.
G-MMMD	Mainair Gemini/Southdown Sprint	224-184-2 & P.504		30.12.83	
	(Originally regd as Flexiform Dual Striker with c/n SSO-01)(Sprint c/n possibly "SIW 0553")				
G-MMME	American Aerolights Eagle	LD.2		11. 1.84	Canx by CAA 13.6.90.
G-MMMF	American Aerolights Eagle	BA 2002		11. 5.84	Canx by CAA 13.6.90.

Regn	Type	c/n	Previous identity	Regn date	Fate or immediate subsequent identity (if known)
G-MMMG	Eipper Quicksilver MXL (Originally regd with c/n 3476357)	1383		5. 6.84	
G-MMMH	Hadland Willow/Flexiform Striker	MJH 383		9.12.83	
G-MMMI	Ultrasports Tripacer/Southdown Lightning DS Phase II (Originally regd with unit as Sign Wing Crusader I with same c/n)	SW-01		30. 3.84	
G-MMMJ	Hornet Invader/Southdown Sprint	RRW-01 & RP.019		2. 4.84	Canx by CAA 13.10.88.
G-MMMK	Hornet Invader/Flexiform Striker	RP.020		2. 4.84	Canx by CAA 25.10.88.
G-MMML	Dragon Srs.150	D150/002	OY-... G-MMML	28. 6.83	
G-MMMM	Southern Aerosports Scorpion	CGH-01		20. 5.82	Fatal crash at Buckland, near Reigate, Surrey on 27.6.82. Canx as destroyed 17.8.84.
G-MMMN	Ultrasports/Solar Wings Panther Dual XL-S	83-00238 & PXL 843-150		4. 4.84	
G-MMMO	Mainair Tri-Flyer/Solar Wings Typhoon	BRU-01		29. 3.84	Canx as destroyed 12.4.90.
G-MMMP	Mainair Gemini/Flexiform Dual Striker	-		. .83R	NTU - Canx.
G-MMMR	Ultrasports Tripacer 330/Flexiform Striker	MAR-01		14. 3.84	
G-MMMS	MBA Tiger Cub 440	PFA/140-10943 & SO.196		3.10.83	Canx by CAA 23.6.97.
G-MMMT	Hornet/Southdown Sigma	H060		29. 3.84	Canx by CAA 7.9.94.
G-MMMU	Hornet 440/Skyhook Cutlass Dual CD	RRW-03 & H480		29. 3.84	Canx by CAA 23.1.95.
G-MMMV	Hornet/Skyhook Cutlass Dual Trainer	H470 & 83-00475		29. 3.84	To EI-CKO 8/94. Canx 23.2.94.
G-MMMW	Hornet Invader/Flexiform Dual Striker	KMS-01 & RP.018		29. 3.84	
G-MMMX	Hornet 250/Airwave Nimrod	H070		29. 3.84	Canx by CAA 14.8.95.
G-MMMY	Hornet/Airwave Nimrod	H080		29. 3.84	Canx by CAA 13.6.90.
G-MMMZ	Mainair Tri-Flyer/Southdown Puma Sprint MS	JSP-02 & 186-30883		2. 4.84	Canx by CAA 13.6.90.
G-MMNA	Eipper Quicksilver MX II (C/n conflicts with G-MMIL)	1046		30. 3.84	Permit expired 2.11.93. Canx by CAA 28.1.99.
G-MMNB	Eipper Quicksilver MX	4286		30. 3.84	
G-MMNC	Eipper Quicksilver MX Duster	4276		30. 3.84	
G-MMND	Eipper Quicksilver MX II Q2	1038		30. 3.84	(Status uncertain)
G-MMNE	Eipper Quicksilver MX II Q2	1039	EC-AJ8 G-MMNE	30. 3.84	Canx by CAA 23.1.95.
G-MMNF	Hornet Dual	H500		2. 4.84	Canx by CAA 2.1.92.
G-MMNG	Simpson Hedge Tiger/Solar Wings Typhoon XL	RS-01 & 006/5/85		6. 9.85	NTU - To G-MNSG. Canx as TWFU 25.8.88.
G-MMNH	Dragon Srs.150	D150/42		27. 7.83	
G-MMNI	Galley Trike/Solar Wings Typhoon S	SG-01 & T482-405		3. 4.84	Canx as WFU 18.10.88.
G-MMNJ	Hiway Skytrike/Super Scorpion	107567		4. 4.84	Canx by CAA 13.6.90.
G-MMNK	Solar Wings Typhoon S4	975093		4. 4.84	Canx by CAA 13.6.90.
G-MMNL	Solar Wings Typhoon S4	975086		4. 4.84	Canx by CAA 13.6.90.
G-MMNM	Hornet 330/Skyhook Sabre	H310		9. 4.84	
G-MMNN	Sherry Buzzard	1		6. 4.84	
G-MMNO	American Aerolights Eagle	PJP-01		6. 4.84	Canx by CAA 13.6.90.
G-MMNP	Ultrasports/Solar Wings Panther 250	RR-01		6. 4.84	Canx by CAA 7.9.94.
G-MMNR	Wright Dove	01/AW		16. 4.84	Canx by CAA 13.6.90.
G-MMNS	Mitchell Super Wing U-2	PFA/114-10690		11. 4.84	
G-MMNT	Flexiform Solo Striker	SSL-1		16. 4.84	
G-MMNU	Ultrasports/Solar Wings Panther	RJS-01		16. 4.84	Canx by CAA 23.1.95.
G-MMNV	Weedhopper	NLR-01		17. 4.84	Canx as WFU 4.6.90.
G-MMNW	Mainair Tri-Flyer/Hiway Demon 175	TJ-01		2. 8.84	
G-MMNX	Ultrasports/Solar Wings Panther XL	PXL 844-153		8. 5.84	
G-MMNY	Skyhook TR1/Zeus	TR1/15		30. 4.84	Canx by CAA 13.6.90.
G-MMNZ	Hiway Skytrike/Demon	-		. .84R	NTU - Canx.
G-MMOA	MBA Tiger Cub 440	-		. .84R	NTU - Canx.
G-MMOB	Mainair Gemini/Southdown Sprint	EM-01 & 244-584-2		11. 5.84	
G-MMOC	Huntair Pathfinder Mk.II	161		2. 5.84	Canx as WFU 6.4.90.
G-MMOD	MBA Tiger Cub 440	SO.207		3. 5.84	Canx by CAA 29.7.96.
G-MMOE	Mitchell Wing B-10	P.1117		3. 5.84	Canx by CAA 13.6.90.
G-MMOF	MBA Tiger Cub 440	SO.76		14. 6.83	
G-MMOG	Huntair Pathfinder Mk.I	011		9. 5.84	Canx 26.7.95 on sale to Ireland.
G-MMOH	Solar Wings Pegasus XL-R (New Trike fitted, replacing one formerly on G-MBTT (Ultrasports Tripacer 330))	SW-TB-1450 & T484-1054XL		4. 5.84	(Extant 4/96)
G-MMOI	MBA Tiger Cub 440	SO.92		8. 5.84	Canx by CAA 13.7.93.

Regn	Type	c/n	Previous identity	Regn date	Fate or immediate subsequent identity (if known)
G-MMOJ	Airwave Comet	-		. .84R	NTU - Canx.
G-MMOK	Ultrasports/Solar Wings Panther XL-S	T584-1066XL		9. 5.84	
G-MMOL	Wheeler (Skycraft) Scout R3	409 R/3		9. 5.84	Canx by CAA 3.8.94.
G-MMOM	Mainair Gemini/Flexiform Striker	DH-02 & 235-484-2		11. 5.84	Trike to G-MMUT. Canx as WFU 28.3.88.
G-MMON	Microflight Monarch	001		19.11.82	Canx as WFU 27.10.88.
G-MMOO	Hornet 330/Southdown Storm	H350 & SLC8088		5. 6.84	Canx by CAA 14.5.97.
G-MMOP	Ultrasports/Solar Wings Panther Dual 440	PXL 844-165		14. 5.84	Canx as WFU 28.3.88.
G-MMOR	American Aerolights Eagle	534	PH-1G4	10. 5.84	Canx by CAA 13.6.90.
G-MMOS	Eipper Quicksilver MX QII	1090	PH-1G9	22. 5.84	Restored as PH-1G9. Canx 24.9.87.
G-MMOT	Mainair Tri-Flyer/Solar Wings Typhoon XL	T583-798XL		14. 5.84	Canx 28.6.88 on sale to Kenya.
G-MMOU	American Aerolights Eagle	TC-01		14. 5.84	Canx by CAA 13.6.90.
G-MMOV	Hiway Skytrike/Demon	TPD-01		17. 5.84	Canx by CAA 13.6.90.
G-MMOW	Mainair Gemini/Flash	246-684-3		21. 5.84	
G-MMOX	Mainair Gemini/Flash	248-784-3 & W05		21. 5.84	Canx by CAA 7.8.96.
G-MMOY	Mainair Gemini/Southdown Sprint	247-784-2		21. 5.84	Canx by CAA 3.11.88.
G-MMOZ	Mainair Tri-Flyer 440/Flexiform Striker	206-121183		21. 5.84	Canx as WFU 21.1.86.
G-MMPA	Mainair Tri-Flyer Merlin/Flexiform Striker	208-151183		21. 5.84	Canx as WFU 21.1.86.
G-MMPB	Hiway Skystrike Mk.I/Solar Wings Typhoon S	PTFB.1		3. 1.84	Canx by CAA 13.6.90.
G-MMPC	Skyhook TR1/Sabre	JSG-01		2. 7.84	Canx by CAA 13.6.90.
G-MMPD	Mainair Tri-Flyer/Southdown Sigma (See G-MMDP)	ARJD-01 & 183-22883		21. 5.84	Canx by CAA 27.9.93.
G-MMPE	Eurowing Goldwing	MA.0040		21. 5.84	Canx by CAA 3.5.95.
G-MMPF	Eurowing Goldwing	MA.0041		21. 5.84	Canx by CAA 13.6.90.
G-MMPG	Ultrasports Tripacer/Southdown Puma Sprint (Lightning II)	NEA-01		8. 6.84	
G-MMPH	Southdown Puma Sprint	P.545		20. 6.84	
G-MMPI	Pterodactyl Ptraveler	108		23. 5.84	Canx as WFU 24.8.94.
G-MMPJ	Mainair Gemini/Southdown Sprint	264-884-2 & P.567		10. 8.84	Canx by CAA 24.4.92.
	(Originally regd as a Tri-Flyer 440 with c/n MSB-01)				
G-MMPK	UAS Solar Buggy/Solar Wings Typhoon I	T781-201L		9.12.83	Canx by CAA 13.6.90.
	(C/n conflight with G-MBDR which was probably a different aircraft)				
	(Originally regd with wing Wasp Gryphon c/n BL-LBDB-PW)				
G-MMPL	Lancashire Micro-Trike 440/Flexiform Dual Striker (See G-MJYW)	PDL-02 & 2/330PM/PGK/683/K		5.12.83	
G-MMPM	Southdown Puma 330	82-00297		9.11.82	Canx by CAA 13.6.90.
G-MMPN	Chargus T250/Southdown Lightning Phase II	SMP-01		7. 6.84	Canx by CAA 2.9.88.
G-MMPO	Mainair Gemini/Flash	325-785-3 & W65		18. 4.85	
G-MMPP	ParaPlane	1254		19. 3.84	Canx by CAA 13.6.90.
G-MMPR	Dragon Srs.150	0011		18. 4.83	Canx by CAA 8.10.93. (Extant - active? - 8/95)
G-MMPS	American Aerolights Eagle	2879		4. 6.84	Canx by CAA 13.6.90.
G-MMPT	SMD Gazelle/Flexiform Dual Striker	ECP-01		5. 6.84	
G-MMPU	Ultrasports Tripacer/Solar Wings Typhoon S4	RJH-01		5. 6.84	
	(Originally regd as Hiway Super Scorpion II with same c/n)				
G-MMPV	MBA Tiger Cub 440	SO.153		5. 6.84	Fatal crash on first flight at Wingmore, Kent on 19.6.89. Canx by CAA 7.9.94.
G-MMPW	Hornet 330/Airwave Nimrod	H-450		28.12.83	Canx by CAA 27.1.93.
G-MMPX	Ultrasports/Solar Wings Panther XL-S	T584-1079XL		12. 6.84	Canx as WFU 4.11.91.
G-MMPY	Solar Wings Typhoon	AWR-01		2. 7.84	Canx by CAA 13.6.90.
G-MMPZ	Teman Mono-Fly	JWH-01		2. 7.84	
G-MMRA	Mainair Tri-Flyer 250/Solar Wings Medium Storm	SMK80200P		3. 7.84	Canx as WFU 23.11.94.
G-MMRB	Hiway Skytrike 250/Super Scorpion	HI06SS		5. 4.84	Canx by CAA 13.6.90.
G-MMRC	Goodwin Lynx/Southdown Sailwings Lightning Phase IIP	GMD-03		12.12.83	Canx by CAA 24.1.95.
G-MMRD	Hornet Supreme 440/Skyhook Cutlass CD	H460		28.12.83	Canx by CAA 5.12.95.
G-MMRE	Maxair Hummer	RD-01		5. 4.84	Canx by CAA 12.11.90.
G-MMRF	MBA Tiger Cub 440	MUL-G04-RB6 & SO.97		5.10.83	Crashed on take-off from Lytham St.Annes on 6.11.83. Canx by CAA 28.6.94.
G-MMRG	Eipper Quicksilver MX	10831		19. 6.84	Canx by CAA 13.6.90.
G-MMRH	Hiway Skytrike/Demon	JSM-01 & 25R1		20. 6.84	
G-MMRI	Hornet Executive 250/Skyhook Sabre	AGL-01 & H170		21. 6.84	Canx by CAA 13.10.93.

Regn	Type	c/n	Previous identity	Regn date	Fate or immediate subsequent identity (if known)
G-MMRJ	Ultrasports/Solar Wings Panther XL-S	PXL846-167 & T684-1098XL		21. 6.84	Canx by CAA 20.2.91. (Stored 5/93)
G-MMRK	Ultrasports/Solar Wings Panther XL-S	PXL846-175 & T684-1107XL		9. 7.84	
G-MMRL	Ultrasports/Solar Wings Panther XL-S	PXL846-174 & T684-1102XL		17. 7.84	
G-MMRM	Mainair Tri-Flyer	-		. .84R	NTU - Canx.
G-MMRN	Southdown Puma Sprint 440	P.544		16. 7.84	
G-MMRO	Mainair Gemini/Southdown Sprint	PP-01 & 258-784-2 & P.557		17.10.84	(Stored 8/97)
G-MMRP	Mainair Gemini/Southdown Sprint	259-884-2 & P.561		7. 2.85	
G-MMRR	Ultrasports/Solar Wings Panther 250 (Canx as Tripacer 250/Lightning 195)	1851 & L195/269		5. 7.84	Canx by CAA 16.12.91.
G-MMRS	Dragon Srs.150 (Same c/n as G-MMAE)	005		8. 4.83	Crashed near Cardiff on 3.4.83 following accidental parachute deployment. Canx by CAA 13.6.90.
G-MMRT	Southdown Raven X (Originally regd to Puma Sprint c/n T.513 & P.532; amended 8.86 but allegedly reverted back in 1987)	2232/0175		11. 7.84	(Damaged mid 96)
G-MMRU	Tirith Firebird FB-2	01-0002		13. 7.84	Canx as WFU 30.7.93.
G-MMRV	MBA Tiger Cub 440	SO.65		26. 3.84	Canx by CAA 21.5.97. (Was based Pennington, NJ, USA)
G-MMRW	Mainair Gemini 440/Flexiform Dual Striker	LAI/DS/25 & 216-71283-2		5. 1.84	
G-MMRX	Willmott J.W.1	2002		16. 7.84	(See G-MMUD) Canx as WFU 29.7.96.
G-MMRY	Chargus T.250/Hiway Vulcan	EDG-01		17. 7.84	
G-MMRZ	Ultrasports/Solar Wings Panther XL-S	PXL847-168 & T684-1099XL		16. 7.84	
G-MMSA	Ultrasports/Solar Wings Panther XL-S (C/n probably T784-1142XL)	PXL847-189 & T184-1142XL		9. 8.84	
G-MMSB	Huntair Pathfinder Mk.II	115		6. 5.83	Canx as WFU 6.4.90.
G-MMSC	Mainair Gemini/Southdown Puma Spirit 440	P.574		10.10.84	Canx 28.1.87 on sale to Portugal.
G-MMSD	Chargus Titan	-		. .84R	NTU - Canx.
G-MMSE	Eipper Quicksilver MX	10021		23. 7.84	
G-MMSF	Mainair Gemini/Southdown Spirit	-		. .84R	Destroyed when approach misjudged on practice forced landing adjacent to Kirkbride aerodrome on 9.8.84.
G-MMSG	Ultrasports/Solar Wings Panther XL-S (Now regd with c/n 8841/65XC; c/n conflicts with G-MMTT) (Originally regd as Hedge Tiger/Solar Wings Typhoon XL with c/ns RS-01 & 006/5/85)	T884-1165XL	(G-MMNG)	6. 9.85	
G-MMSH	Ultrasports/Solar Wings Panther XL-S	PXL984-192 & T884-1163XL		28. 5.85	
G-MMSI	ParaPlane	JBN.524		27. 7.84	Canx 1.5.90 on sale to USA.
G-MMSJ	ParaPlane	JBN.523		27. 7.84	Canx 1.5.90 on sale to USA.
G-MMSK	Ultrasports Tripacer 250/Hiway Super Scorpion	-		. .84R	NTU - Canx.
G-MMSL	Ultrasports/Solar Wings Panther XL-S	PXLS847-200		2. 8.84	Canx by CAA 13.6.90.
G-MMSM	Mainair Gemini/Flash	334-885-3 & W71		18. 4.85	Canx by CAA 7.8.96.
G-MMSN	Mainair Gemini/Southdown Sprint (Originally regd with c/n PM-01 & using Tri-Flyer unit c/n 098-30882; changed in 8/85)	162-15683 & P.558		23. 8.84	Canx by CAA 7.8.96.
G-MMSO	Mainair Gemini/Southdown Sprint (Originally regd as Mainair Tri-Flyer 440)	256-784-2 & P.539		14. 1.86	
G-MMSP	Mainair Gemini/Flash	265-984-2		17. 8.84	
G-MMSR	MBA Tiger Cub 440	SO.135		9.12.83	Canx by CAA 25.1.94.
G-MMSS	Ultrasports Tripacer/Southdown Lightning (Originally regd as Solar Wings Panther 330 with same c/n)	SRS HJ2426		27. 3.84	Canx by CAA 11.12.98.
G-MMST	Southdown Puma Sprint	1221/0003		7. 1.85	Canx by Caa 14.7.88.
G-MMSU	American Aerolights Eagle B	3005		7. 8.84	Canx 20.8.92 on sale to USA.
G-MMSV	Southdown Puma Sprint	1221/0004		21. 5.86	
G-MMSW	MBA Tiger Cub 440	SO.68		8. 8.84	
G-MMSX	Ultrasports/Southdown Puma Sprint (Originally regd with wing Solar Wings Panther c/n MJL-01)	83-00568		. .85	Sold in South Africa 7/85. Canx by CAA 13.6.90.
G-MMSY	Ultrasports/Solar Wings Panther	BD.3		29. 8.84	Canx as WFU 16.11.88.
G-MMSZ	Medway Half Pint/Aerial Arts 130SX	2/21385		27. 3.85	
G-MMTA	Ultrasports/Solar Wings Panther XL-S	PXL884-194 & T884-1164XL		25.10.84	
G-MMTB	Mainair Gemini/Southdown Sprint	?		. .84R	(Extant 1/94)
G-MMTC	Ultrasports/Solar Wings Pegasus Dual XL-R	T684-1101XL		28. 9.84	
G-MMTD	Mainair Tri-Flyer 330/Hiway Demon 175	EIA-01		16. 8.84	
G-MMTE	Mainair Gemini/Southdown Puma Sprint	P.559		20. 8.84	Canx as WFU 20.9.93.
G-MMTF	Southdown Puma Sprint	1121/0048		18. 4.85	Canx 7.10.93 on sale to Portugal.

Regn	Type	c/n	Previous identity	Regn date	Fate or immediate subsequent identity (if known)
G-MMTG	Mainair Gemini/Southdown Sprint	267-984-2 & P.577		21. 8.84	(For sale 10/97)
	(Originally regd as Mainair Tri-Flyer with c/n RPWJ-01; type amended on 12.10.84)				
G-MMTH	Southdown Puma Sprint	P.538		4. 9.84	
G-MMTI	Southdown Puma Sprint	1221/0005		13. 9.84	
	(C/n conflicts with ZS-VLZ (regd 7/85))(See comments on G-MMIR - possibly fitted with new wing)				
G-MMTJ	Southdown Puma Sprint	1221/0006		17. 1.85	
G-MMTK	Medway Hybred 44XL/Solar Wings Typhoon XL	12784/9		30. 8.84	
G-MMTL	Mainair Gemini/Southdown Sprint	268-1084-2 & P.576		3.10.84	
G-MMTM	Mainair Gemini/Southdown Sprint	141-29383 & P.575		12. 7.85	Canx by Caa 11.7.88.
	(Initially regd as Mainair Tri-Flyer with c/n 269-1084-2 & P.58)(Fitted with trike ex.G-MJXA/G-MBST(2))				
G-MMTN	Hiway Skytrike/Super Scorpion	2158		4. 9.84	Canx as WFU 23.4.90.
G-MMTO	Mainair Tri-Flyer/Southdown Sprint	236-384-2 & P.498		6. 9.84	
	(Originally regd with c/n REDB-01)				
G-MMTP	Eurowing Goldwing	008		13. 9.84	Canx by CAA 13.6.90.
G-MMTR	Ultrasports/Solar Wings Pegasus XL-R	KND-03		27. 9.84	
G-MMTS	Ultrasports/Solar Wings Panther XL	T784-1157XL		18. 9.84	
G-MMTT	Ultrasports/Solar Wings Panther XL-S	T684-1165XL		12.12.84	
	(C/n possibly T884-1165XL; but this conflicts with G-MMSG)				
G-MMTU	Flylite Super Scout	S/S03/02		26. 9.84	Canx by CAA 13.6.90.
G-MMTV	American Aerolights Eagle 215B Seaplane	SGP-1		25. 9.84	
G-MMTW	American Aerolights Eagle	KRG-01		26. 9.84	Canx by CAA 13.6.90.
G-MMTX	Mainair Gemini/Southdown Sprint	275-1284-2 & P.590		25. 3.85	
	(Originally regd with c/n P.577)				
G-MMTY	Fisher FP202U	2140		28. 9.84	
G-MMTZ	Eurowing Goldwing	SWA-7 & EW-60		28. 9.84	
G-MMUA	Southdown Puma Sprint	1221/0007		21.12.84	
G-MMUB	Ultrasports Tripacer 250/Hiway Demon	REDB-01		28. 9.84	Canx by CAA 14.9.93.
	(Same c/n as originally used by G-MMTO)				
G-MMUC	Mainair Gemini/Southdown Sprint	253-784-2 & P.560		28. 9.84	Canx by CAA 12.8.92.
G-MMUD	Willmott Junior Cub	2002		28. 9.84	(See G-MMRX) Canx as WFU 23.4.90.
G-MMUE	Mainair Gemini/Flash	273-1284-2 & W10		16.10.84	
G-MMUF	Mainair Gemini/Flash	165-13683 & W09		10.10.84	Canx as destroyed 27.8.92.
	(Originally regd with trike c/n 1284-1)(Trike c/n duplicates G-MJYN)(Also quoted as being Solar Wings Pegasus Flash)				
G-MMUG	Mainair Tri-Flyer 250/Solar Wings Typhoon S4	032-221181 & T884-1178S		6. 9.82	Canx by CAA 21.10.96.
	(Originally regd with c/n GB-1)(Wing confirmed as ex G-MJKY)				
G-MMUH	Mainair Tri-Flyer/Southdown Sprint	270-1084-2 & P.579		8.11.84	
G-MMUI	Solar Wings Typhoon XL-S	-		. .84R	NTU - Canx.
G-MMUJ	Southdown Puma Sprint/Cougar	1121/0009		6.12.84	Canx as PWFU 6.3.99.
G-MMUK	Ultrasports Tripacer II/Solar Wings Typhoon S4	BRK-01 & T782-532		15.10.84	
	(Initially Mainair Tri-Flyer 250 but replaced by new homebuild trike)				
G-MMUL	Ward Elf	E-47		16.10.84	Canx by CAA 12.4.89.
G-MMUM	MBA Tiger Cub 440	NCB-01 & SO.019		8. 3.83	
G-MMUN	Ultrasports/Solar Wings Panther Dual XL	T1084-1231XL		23.10.84	
G-MMUO	Mainair Gemini/Flash	272-1084-2 & W08		29.10.84	
G-MMUP	Airwave Nimrod 140	PPC.11		10.11.83	Canx by CAA 13.6.90.
G-MMUR	Hiway Skytrike 250/Solar Wings Storm	SL.180180		28.12.84	
G-MMUS	Mainair Gemini/Flash	284-185-3 & W24		29. 1.85	
G-MMUT	Mainair Gemini/Flash	235-484-2 & W04		5.10.84	
	(Originally regd as Mainair Tri-Flyer 440 with c/n 262-884-2; replaced by trike ex.G-MMOM)				
G-MMUU	ParaPlane PM-1	1574		31.10.84	Canx as WFU 16.4.87.
G-MMUV	Southdown Puma Sprint	1121/0010		7.11.84	
G-MMUW	Mainair Gemini/Flash	260-784-2 & W13		17. 1.85	
	(Originally regd with trike c/n 1284-1)				
G-MMUX	Mainair Gemini/Southdown Sprint	285-185-3 & P.587		28.12.84	
G-MMUY	Mainair Gemini/Flash	291-285-3 & W27		4. 2.85	Canx 2.5.91 on sale to Spain.
G-MMUZ	American Aerolights Eagle	4394		31.12.84	Canx by CAA 13.6.90.

Regn	Type	c/n	Previous identity	Regn date	Fate or immediate subsequent identity (if known)
G-MMVA	Southdown Puma Sprint	1121/0011 & P.588		7.11.84	
G-MMVB	Skyhook Pixie/Hiway Super Scorpion	SSC-001		8.10.84	Canx by CAA 13.6.90.
G-MMVC	Ultrasports/Solar Wings Panther XL-S	T684-1106XL		13.11.84	
G-MMVD	Not to be allotted.				
G-MMVE	[Was reserved for A.K.Voase]				
G-MMVF	Ultrasports/Solar Wings Panther XL	PXL884-178		13.11.84	Canx by CAA 13.6.90.
G-MMVG	MBA Tiger Cub 440	SO.139		14.11.84	No Permit believed issued. Canx by CAA 15.3.99.
G-MMVH	Southdown Raven X	2122/0015		10. 1.85	
G-MMVI	Southdown Puma Sprint	1121/0012		28.11.84	
G-MMVJ	Southdown Puma Sprint	1121/0013		5. 6.85	Canx by CAA 7.8.96.
G-MMVK	Sigh-Wing ParaPlane	SW.2		3.12.84	Canx by CAA 13.6.90.
G-MMVL	Ultrasports/Solar Wings Panther XL-S	T1084-1248XL		6. 9.85	Canx by CAA 24.4.92.
G-MMVM	Whiteley Orion 1/Chargus Cyclone	PNW-01		7. 1.85	Canx by CAA 17.11.87.
G-MMVN	Flight Research Nomad 425F/Solar Wings Typhoon	DCD-01		19.11.87	Permit expired 2.5.96. Canx as PWFU 10.11.97.
G-MMVO	Southdown Puma Sprint	1232/0017		20. 3.85	
G-MMVP	Mainair Gemini/Flash	276-1284-2 & W12		17.12.84	
G-MMVR	Hiway Skytrike Mk.1/Solar Wings Storm	SMC.8091		7.12.84	Canx by CAA.
G-MMVS	Skyhook Pixie/Zeus	TR1/52		28. 2.85	
G-MMVT	Mainair Gemini/Flash	277-1284-2 & W14		28.12.84	Canx by CAA 8.10.93.
G-MMVU	Mainair Gemini/Flash	278-1284-2 & W16		28.12.84	Canx by CAA 30.10.91.
G-MMVV	Not allotted.				
G-MMVW	Skyhook Pixie/Zeus	TR1/51		6. 2.85	Canx by CAA 7.9.94.
G-MMVX	Southdown Puma Sprint (Possibly Mainair Gemini Trike)	41183 & P.452		29.11.83	
G-MMVY	American Aerolights Eagle 215B	E1579466		31.12.84	Canx by CAA 24.1.95.
G-MMVZ	Southdown Puma Sprint	1121/0016		15. 1.85	
G-MMWA	Mainair Gemini/Flash	271-1184-1 & W07		22.11.84	
G-MMWB	Huntair Pathfinder II	LWB.3		28. 6.84	Canx by CAA 27.3.99.
G-MMWC	Eipper Quicksilver MXII	1041		22.10.84	
G-MMWD	Southdown Puma Sprint	P.598		31.12.84	Canx 25.7.86 on sale to Zimbabwe.
G-MMWE	Hiway Skytrike 250/Spectrum	REDB-02		2. 1.85	Canx as WFU 3.4.90.
G-MMWF	Hiway Skytrike 250/Super Scorpion	-		. .84R	NTU - Canx.
G-MMWG	Mainair Tri-Flyer/Flexiform Solo Striker (Originally regd as Greenslade Mono-Trike)	FF/LAI/83/JDR/11		17.12.84	
G-MMWH	Southdown Puma Sprint (Originally regd with c/n MWH-01)	P.548		21. 6.84	
G-MMWI	Southdown Puma (Lightning 190)	CAC-01		3. 1.85	
G-MMWJ	Pterodactyl Ptraveler	WFX-33		5. 3.85	
G-MMWK	Robinson Trike/Hiway Demon	JAR-01		8. 1.85	Canx by CAA 28.9.94.
G-MMWL	Eurowing Goldwing	SWA-09 & EW-91		9. 4.85	
G-MMWM	[Was reserved for Ultrasports]				
G-MMWN	Mainair Tri-Flyer/Flexiform Striker (Possibly Ultrasports Tripacer)	1283.NH		21.11.84	
G-MMWO	Ultrasports/Solar Wings Panther XL-S	T1184-1281XL		22. 1.85	
G-MMWP	American Aerolights Eagle 215B	3788		22.10.84	Canx by CAA 24.1.95.
G-MMWR	[Was reserved for Mainair]				
G-MMWS	Mainair Tripacer/Flexiform Striker	983.SH		21.11.84	
G-MMWT	CFM Shadow Srs.C	B.009		27. 3.85	
G-MMWU	Ultrasports Tripacer 250/Hiway Super Scorpion	JD.207		3. 1.85	Canx by CAA 13.6.90.
G-MMWV	Flight Research Nomad 425F/Solar Wings Typhoon S4	NF.19		10. 6.85	Canx by CAA 13.6.90.
G-MMWW	Mainair Gemini/Flexiform Dual Striker	LAI/DS/26 & 217-71283-2		19.12.83	Fatal crash following in-flight failure, Boothstown, Manchester on 14.3.84. Canx by CAA 4.2.92.
G-MMWX	Southdown Puma Sprint	1121/0047		10. 4.85	
G-MMWY	Skyhook Pixie/Silhouette	NMC-01		9. 1.85	Canx by CAA 7.9.94.
G-MMWZ	Southdown Puma Sprint	1121/0030		19. 2.85	
G-MMXA	Mainair Gemini/Flash (Originally regd with trike c/n 1284-1)	245-684-2 & W15		28.12.84	Canx by CAA 29.11.90.
G-MMXB	Not allotted.				
G-MMXC	Mainair Gemini/Flash (Trike reported as c/n 292 in 9/96 - see G-MMXL)	279-1284-2 & W17		28.12.84	

Regn	Type	c/n	Previous identity	Regn date	Fate or immediate subsequent identity (if known)
G-MMXD	Mainair Gemini/Flash	282-185-3 & W20		28.12.84	
G-MMXE	Mainair Gemini/Flash	280-1284-2 & W18		28.12.84	Canx by CAA 30.6.93.
G-MMXF	Mainair Gemini/Flash	281-1284-2 & W19		28.12.84	Canx as destroyed 10.1.90.
G-MMXG	Mainair Gemini/Flash	288-485-1 & W32		17. 1.85	
G-MMXH	Mainair Gemini/Flash (Trike ex.G-MMKM)	210-121283-2 & W25		4. 2.85	
G-MMXI	Horizon Prototype	001		4. 2.85	Canx by CAA 19.7.93.
G-MMXJ	Mainair Gemini/Flash	289-185-3 & W22		17. 1.85	
G-MMXK	Mainair Gemini/Flash	274-485-2 & W35		17. 1.85	
G-MMXL	Mainair Gemini/Flash	292-385-3 & W36		17. 1.85	
G-MMXM	Mainair Gemini/Flash	287-185-3 & W26		16. 1.85	Canx by CAA 24.5.96.
G-MMXN	Southdown Puma Sprint	1121/0021		24. 1.85	
G-MMXO	Southdown Puma Sprint	1121/0018		23. 1.85	
G-MMXP	Southdown Puma Sprint	1121/0014		19. 7.85	Canx by CAA 12.4.89.
G-MMXR	Southdown Puma DS	RPF.242		25. 1.85	Canx by CAA 18.12.95.
G-MMXS	Southdown Puma Sprint	1121/0019		28. 1.85	
G-MMXT	Mainair Gemini/Flash	302-485-3 & W41		29. 1.85	
G-MMXU	Mainair Gemini/Flash	254-784-2 & W21		29. 1.85	
G-MMXV	Mainair Gemini/Flash	298-385-3 & W37		29. 1.85	
G-MMXW	Mainair Gemini/Southdown Sprint	286-185-3 & P.597		23. 1.85	
G-MMXX	Mainair Gemini/Flexiform Dual Striker	LAI-83-JDR26		17.12.84	Badly damaged in crash at Fordingbridge Junior School, near Ringwood, Hants on 28.9.85. Canx by CAA 27.1.93.
G-MMXY	Not allotted.				
G-MMXZ	Eipper Quicksilver MXII	1946		22.11.84	Canx as WFU 23.2.95.
G-MMYA	Solar Wings Pegasus XL-P/Se	XL-P Proto & T784-1151XL		30. 1.85	
G-MMYB	Solar Wings Pegasus XL Tug	XLT Proto		30. 1.85	Canx by CAA 6.12.88.
G-MMYC	Waspair Gryphon/Cheetah	OR/W/Y/OR/BL		28. 1.85	Canx as WFU 13.12.88.
G-MMYD	CFM Shadow Srs.B	004		28. 1.85	Canx 22.2.85 on sale to Holland.
G-MMYE	Southdown Puma Sprint	1111/0020		. .85R	NTU - Canx.
G-MMYF	Southdown Puma Sprint	1121/0026		28. 3.85	
G-MMYG	Southdown Puma Sprint	1121/0027		. .85R	NTU - Canx.
G-MMYH	Southdown Puma Sprint	1121/0028		. .85R	NTU - Canx.
G-MMYI	Southdown Puma Sprint	1121/0036		6. 3.85	
G-MMYJ	Southdown Puma Sprint	1121/0031		18. 2.85	
G-MMYK	Southdown Puma Sprint	1121/0032		18. 2.85	Canx by CAA 7.8.96.
G-MMYL	Cyclone 70/Aerial Arts 130SX	CH.01		8. 3.85	
G-MNYM	Mainair Gemini/Flash	-		. .85R	NTU - Canx.
G-MMYN	Ultrasports/Solar Wings Panther XL-R	T784-1158XL		27. 2.85	
G-MMYO	Southdown Puma Sprint	1121/0037		11. 4.85	
G-MMYP	Not allotted.				
G-MMYR	Eipper Quicksilver MXII	3345		27. 2.85	
G-MMYS	Southdown Puma Sprint	1121/0038		26. 3.85	Canx by CAA 20.8.93.
G-MMYT	Southdown Puma Sprint	1121/0046		15. 4.85	
G-MMYU	Southdown Puma Sprint (Originally regd with c/n DGH-01 - amended on 13.8.85)	1231/0045		11. 6.85	
G-MMYV	Mainair Tri-Flyer/Flexiform Striker	JW 2		22. 3.85	
G-MMYW	Hiway Skytrike 440 Dual/Demon 115	TJW-01		1. 5.85	Damaged in an accident on 12.10.86. Canx by CAA 13.6.88.
G-MMYX	Mitchell Wing U-2	PFA/114-11041		14. 2.85	Canx as destroyed 3.6.91.
G-MMYY	Southdown Puma Sprint	1231/0042		18. 7.85	
G-MMYZ	Southdown Puma Sprint	1231/0034		28. 2.85	Damaged in gales at Roddidge in 1.98
G-MMZA	Mainair Gemini/Flash (Wing c/n may be W06)	266-984-3 & W60		4. 3.85	
G-MMZB	Mainair Gemini/Flash	319-685-3 & W58		4. 3.85	
G-MMZC	Mainair Gemini/Flash	301-485-3 & W40		4. 3.85	Canx as CAA 31.7.96.
G-MMZD	Mainair Gemini/Flash	309-585-3 & W49		4. 3.85	
G-MMZE	Mainair Gemini/Flash	300-485-3 & W39		4. 3.85	
G-MMZF	Mainair Gemini/Flash	299-485-3 & W38		4. 3.85	
G-MMZG	Ultrasports/Solar Wings Panther XL-S	SW-WA-1022		12. 8.85	

Regn	Type	c/n	Previous identity	Regn date	Fate or immediate subsequent identity (if known)
G-MMZH	Ultrasports Tripacer/Solar Wings Typhoon	T982-59		9. 2.87	Canx by CAA 7.9.94.
G-MMZI	Medway Half Pint Srs.1/Aerial Arts 130SX	57		6. 3.85	
G-MMZJ	Mainair Gemini/Flash	312-585-3 & W51		18. 3.85	
G-MMZK	Mainair Gemini/Flash	326-785-3 & W53		18. 3.85	
	(Trike ex G-MMEZ; originally regd with trike c/n 314-585-3; to G-MMIR)				
G-MMZL	Mainair Gemini/Flash	317-685-3 & W56		18. 3.85	Trike to G-MNMI. Canx by CAA 8.12.92.
G-MMZM	Mainair Gemini/Flash	304-585-3 & W44		18. 3.85	
G-MMZN	Mainair Gemini/Flash	283-185-3 & W23		18. 3.85	
G-MMZO	Microflight Spectrum	004		15. 3.85	Canx as WFU 10.3.87.
G-MMZP	Ultrasports/Solar Wings Panther XL	HP-01		14. 3.85	
G-MMZR	Southdown Puma Sprint	1121/0039		4. 7.85	
G-MMZS	Eipper Quicksilver MX I	4343		18. 3.85	Canx as WFU 16.2.93.
G-MMZT	Ultrasports Tripacer/Chargus Cyclone	JB-01		11. 4.85	Canx as WFU 8.6.90.
G-MMZU	Southdown Puma DS	006		12. 4.85	No Permit believed issued. Canx by CAA 17.2.99.
G-MMZV	Mainair Gemini/Flash	313-585-3 & W52		18. 4.85	
G-MMZW	Southdown Puma Sprint	1121/0043		28. 3.85	
G-MMZX	Southdown Puma Sprint	1231/0051		17. 4.85	
G-MMZY	Ultrasports Tripacer 330/Flexiform Striker	KMS-02		20. 3.85	Canx by CAA 5.1.93.
G-MMZZ	Maxair Hummer	0010		8. 4.82	
G-MNAA	Striplin Sky Ranger	81-0018SR		9. 5.84	Canx as WFU 8.1.92.
G-MNAB	Ultrasports/Solar Wings Panther XL	T784-1127XL		16. 7.84	Fatal crash into sea off Inverbervie, near Stirling on 27.10.84. (Wreckage not recovered). Canx as destroyed 25.1.88.
G-MNAC	Mainair Gemini/Flash	335-885-3 & W72		18. 4.85	Canx by CAA 30.9.93.
G-MNAD	Mainair Gemini/Flash	340-885-3 & W76		18. 4.85	Canx by CAA 6.8.96.
G-MNAE	Mainair Gemini/Flash	343-885-3 & W77		18. 4.85	
G-MNAF	Ultrasports/Solar Wings Panther XL-S	SW-WA-1001		24. 4.85	Canx by CAA 21.1.99.
G-MNAG	Hiway Skytrike Srs.1/Flexiform Hilander	38		16. 4.85	Canx by CAA 24.1.95.
G-MNAH	Ultrasports/Solar Wings Panther XL-S	SW-WA-1002		24. 4.85	
G-MNAI	Ultrasports/Solar Wings Panther XL-S	SW-WA-1003		15. 5.85	
G-MNAJ	Ultrasports/Solar Wings Panther XL-S	SW-TA-1004 & SW-WA-1004		17. 5.85	
G-MNAK	Ultrasports/Solar Wings Panther XL-S	SW-WA-1005		15. 5.85	
G-MNAL	MBA Tiger Cub 440	SO.32		20.12.83	Canx by CAA 23.6.97.
G-MNAM	Ultrasports/Solar Wings Panther XL-S	SW-WA-1006		17. 5.85	
G-MNAN	Solar Wings Pegasus XL-R	SW-TB-0001 & SW-WA-1007		2. 7.85	
G-MNAO	Solar Wings Pegasus XL-R	SW-TB-0002 & SW-WA-1008		2. 6.85	
G-MNAP ?	Mainair Tri-Flyer 440/Flexiform Dual Striker	106-161182		9. 1.84	Canx 5.2.85 on sale to Israel.
G-MNAP	Solar Wings Pegasus XL-R	SW-WA-1009		. .85R	NTU - Canx.
G-MNAR	Solar Wings Pegasus XL-R	SW-WA-1011		6. 8.85	
G-MNAS	Solar Wings Pegasus XL-R	SW-WA-1010		1.11.85	(Burnt wreck noted at Shobdon in 4/87) Canx as destroyed 9.2.89.
G-MNAT	Solar Wings Pegasus XL-R	SW-WA-1012		. .85R	NTU - Canx.
G-MNAU	Solar Wings Pegasus XL-R	SW-WA-1013		30. 9.85	
G-MNAV	Southdown Puma Sprint	1121/0033		28. 2.85	
G-MNAW	Solar Wings Pegasus XL-R	SW-TB-1010 & SW-WA-1014		16. 8.85	
	(Trike c/n believed correct but also reported on LN-YCO with Flash Wing W686)				
G-MNAX	Solar Wings Pegasus XL-R	SW-WA-1015		16. 8.85	
G-MNAY	Solar Wings Pegasus XL-R	SW-TB-1015 & SW-WA-1016		6. 8.85	
G-MNAZ	Solar Wings Pegasus XL-R	SW-TB-1016 & SW-WA-1017		6. 8.85	
G-MNBA	Solar Wings Pegasus XL-R	SW-TB-1024 & SW-WA-1018		6. 9.85	
G-MNBB	Solar Wings Pegasus XL-R	SW-TB-1020 & SW-WA-1019		20. 9.85	
G-MNBC	Solar Wings Pegasus XL-R	SW-TB-1026 & SW-WA-1020		11.10.85	

Regn	Type	c/n	Previous identity	Regn date	Fate or immediate subsequent identity (if known)
G-MNBD	Mainair Gemini/Flash	341-585-3 & W42		6. 1.86	(Damaged late .96)
	(Officially regd 6.1.86 despite permit to fly issued 6.6.85)				
G-MNBE	Southdown Puma Sprint	1121/0050		17. 5.85	
G-MNBF	Mainair Gemini/Flash	306-585-3 & W46		2. 5.85	
G-MNBG	Mainair Gemini/Flash	347-585-3 & W66		9. 5.85	
G-MNBH	Southdown Puma Sprint	1231/0056		20. 5.85	
G-MNBI	Ultrasports/Solar Wings Panther XL-S	PXL884-178 & T884-1161XL		3. 5.85	
	(C/n conflicted with G-MMVF)				
G-MNBJ	Skyhook TR1 Pixie	HLC-01		7. 5.85	Canx by CAA 20.8.93.
G-MNBK	Hiway Skytrike/Demon	HW-34		10. 5.85	Canx by CAA 7.9.94.
G-MNBL	American Aerolights Z Eagle 215B	BA-1001		9. 1.84	
G-MNBM	Southdown Puma Sprint	1231/0058		25. 6.85	
G-MNBN	Mainair Gemini/Flash	303-485-3 & W43		11. 6.85	
G-MNBO	Not allotted.				
G-MNBP	Mainair Gemini/Flash	338-885-3 & W75		15. 5.85	
G-MNBR	Mainair Gemini/Flash	345-985-3 & W79		15. 5.85	
G-MNBS	Mainair Gemini/Flash	308-585-3 & W48		15. 5.85	
G-MNBT	Mainair Gemini/Flash	322-685-3 & W62		15. 5.85	
G-MNBU	Mainair Gemini/Flash	337-885-3 & W74		15. 5.85	
G-MNBV	Mainair Gemini/Flash	333-685-3 & W70		15. 5.85	
G-MNBW	Mainair Gemini/Flash	332-685-3 & W69		15. 5.85	
G-MNBX	Chargus T.250	-		. .85R	NTU - Canx.
G-MNBY	Mainair Gemini/Southdown Sprint	080-18682 & PH637		29. 5.85	Canx as destroyed 10.10.94.
	(Trike originally on G-MJDC)				
G-MNBZ	Medway Half Pint/Aerial Arts 130SX	3/21585 & 130SX-100		5. 5.86	(Wing to G-MNDE) To G-MNVL 9/86. Canx as WFU 16.5.90.
G-MNCA	Hunt Avon/Hiway Demon 175	DA-01		28. 5.85	
	(Originally regd as Adams Trike)				
G-MNCB	Mainair Gemini/Flash	307-585-3 & W47		30. 5.85	To EI-CKT 9/94. Canx 7.7.94.
G-MNCC	Mainair Gemini/Solar Wings Typhoon	PMB-01		24. 5.85	Canx by CAA 13.6.90.
G-MNCD	Harmsworth Tie-Trike/Solar Wings Typhoon	CCH-01		29. 5.85	Canx by CAA 30.12.94.
G-MNCE	Skyhook Pixie/Hiway Super Scorpion	CRI-51		28. 5.85	Canx by CAA 13.6.90.
G-MNCF	Mainair Gemini/Flash	321-685-3 & W61		3. 6.85	
G-MNCG	Mainair Gemini/Flash	320-685-3 & W59		3. 6.85	
G-MNCH	Lancashire Micro-Trike/Hiway Demon	CFH-01		1. 6.84	Canx by CAA 23.6.97.
G-MNCI	Southdown Puma Sprint	1231/0059		7. 6.85	
G-MNCJ	Mainair Gemini/Flash	351-785-3 & W83		3. 6.85	
G-MNCK	Southdown Puma Sprint	1231/0055		11. 7.85	Damaged in gales at Roddidge in 1.98.
G-MNCL	Southdown Puma Sprint	1121/0060		3. 6.85	
G-MNCM	CFM Shadow Srs.C	006		31. 5.85	
G-MNCN	Hiway Skytrike 250/Vulcan	NJC-01		12. 6.85	Canx by CAA 13.6.90.
G-MNCO	Eipper Quicksilver MX II	1045		3. 6.85	
G-MNCP	Southdown Puma Sprint	1231/0071		24. 6.85	
G-MNCR	Hiway Skytrike II 330/Flexiform Striker	SS.7284		22. 2.84	Canx as WFU 4.8.94.
G-MNCS	Skyrider Airsports Phantom	PH.00098		2. 1.86	
	(Originally regd with c/n EAM-01)				
G-MNCT	Skyhook Pixie/Solar Wings Typhoon	-		. .85R	NTU - Canx.
G-MNCU	Medway Hybred/Solar Wings Typhoon 44XL	26485/10		13. 6.85	
G-MNCV	Medway Hybred/Solar Wings Typhoon 44XL	26485/11		13. 6.85	
	(Originally regd with c/n VEJS-01)(Reported as Pegasus XL-R Wing SW-WA-1030 when restored on 1.7.97)				
G-MNCW	Hornet Dual Trainer/Southdown Raven	HRWA 0050 & 2000/0099		26. 6.85	Canx as WFU 29.7.96.
G-MNCX	Mainair Gemini/Flash	323-785-3 & W63		1. 7.85	Canx by CAA 7.8.96.
G-MNCY	Skyhook Pixie	TR1/58		20. 6.85	Canx by CAA 13.6.90.
G-MNCZ	Solar Wings Pegasus XL-T	SW-WB-0001		2. 7.85	Canx as WFU 6.5.87.
G-MNDA	Thruster TST Mk.1	8504		10. 6.85	Canx by CAA 27.1.88. To EI-BYA 2/89.
G-MNDB	Southdown Puma Sprint	P.523		22. 3.84	Canx by CAA 4.7.96.

Regn	Type	c/n	Previous identity	Regn date	Fate or immediate subsequent identity (if known)
G-MNDC	Mainair Gemini/Flash	336-885-3 & W73		12. 6.85	
G-MNDD	Mainair Scorcher	358-885-1 & W85		12. 6.85	
G-MNDE	Medway Half Pint/Aerial Arts 130SX (Wing ex G-MNBZ)	3/8685		19. 6.85	
G-MNDF	Mainair Gemini/Flash	327-785-3 & W67		25. 6.85	
G-MNDG	Southdown Puma Sprint	1121/0057		18. 7.85	
G-MNDH	Hiway Skytrike/Demon 175	NH2852-1		18. 6.85	Canx by CAA 20.3.89.
G-MNDI	MBA Tiger Cub 440	TA06 & SO.150		20. 6.85	Canx by CAA 22.11.95.
G-MNDJ	Ultrasports Tripacer	-		. .85R	NTU - Canx.
G-MNDK	Mainair Tri-Flyer 440/Southdown Puma Sprint DS	209-171083		11.10.83	Canx by CAA 13.6.90.
G-MNDL	Southdown Puma Sport	1231/0072		24. 6.85	Canx as WFU 10.4.86.
G-MNDM	Mainair Gemini/Flash	324-785-3 & W64		11. 7.85	
G-MNDN	Southdown Puma Sprint	1231/0061		28. 6.85	Fatal crash at Chaddesdon, Derby on 17.8.85. Canx as destroyed 26.7.90.
G-MNDO	Solar Wings Pegasus/Flash	SW-WF-0001		2. 7.85	
G-MNDP	Southdown Puma Sprint	1121/0063		28. 6.85	
G-MNDR	NIB II Vertigo/Solar Wings Storm	SJS-01	G-MJLP	15. 7.85	Canx as WFU 12.4.90.
G-MNDS	Ultrasports/Solar Wings Panther	-		. .85R	NTU - Canx.
G-MNDT	Ultrasports/Solar Wings Panther	-		. .85R	NTU - Canx.
G-MNDU	Midland Ultralights Sirocco 377GB	MU-011		22. 7.85	
G-MNDV	Midland Ultralights Sirocco 377GB	MU-012		1. 4.86	(Stored Tarn Farm, Cockerham 5/93)
G-MNDW	Midland Ultralights Sirocco 377GB	MU-014		30. 7.85	
G-MNDX	Not allotted.				
G-MNDY	Southdown Puma Sprint (Originally regd with c/n T.504)	DY-01 & P.536		2. 5.84	
G-MNDZ	Southdown Puma Sprint	1121/0062		28. 6.85	
G-MNEA	Southdown Airwolf	2232/0067		3. 6.85	Canx by CAA 13.6.90.
G-MNEB	Southdown Airwolf	2232/0068		3. 6.85	Canx by CAA 13.6.90.
G-MNEC	Southdown Airwolf	2232/0069		3. 6.85	Canx by CAA 13.6.90.
G-MNED	Skyhook Pixie/Zeus	TR1/59		25. 7.85	Canx by CAA 13.6.90.
G-MNEE	Not allotted.				
G-MNEF	Mainair Gemini/Flash	344-885-3 & W78		8. 7.85	
G-MNEG	Mainair Gemini/Flash	360-885-3 & W92		8. 7.85	
G-MNEH	Mainair Gemini/Flash	361-885-3 & W90		8. 7.85	
G-MNEI	Medway Hybred/Solar Wings Typhoon 44XL	8785/12 & SW-WA-1035		9. 7.85	(Stored 8/96)
G-MNEJ	Mainair Gemini/Flash	318-685-3 & W57		11. 7.85	Fatal crash after becoming overstressed and broke-up in mid-air whilst local flying at Middleton Sand, near Morecambe, Lancs on 22.10.85. Canx as destroyed 29.8.86.
G-MNEK	Medway Half Pint/Aerial Arts 130SX	4/8785		12. 7.85	
G-MNEL	Medway Half Pint/Aerial Arts 130SX	5/8785		12. 7.85	
G-MNEM	Solar Wings Pegasus XL-R (Originally regd with c/n CS-01)	SW-TB-1007 & SW-WA-1034		16. 7.85	
G-MNEN	Southdown Puma Sprint	1231/0075		18. 7.85	Canx by CAA 4.7.96.
G-MNEO	Southdown Raven	2232/0174		14. 8.85	Canx by CAA 7.8.96.
G-MNEP	Aerostructure Pipistrelle P2B	007		23. 7.85	Canx by CAA 3.2.93.
G-MNER	CFM Shadow Srs.CD	008		15. 7.85	
G-MNES	CFM Shadow Srs.B	010		15. 7.85	To France as 92-CU. Canx 5.12.85.
G-MNET	Mainair Gemini/Flash	349-885-3 & W81		23. 7.85	
G-MNEU	Not allotted.				
G-MNEV	Mainair Gemini/Flash	362-1085-3 & W108		23. 7.85	
G-MNEW	Mainair Tri-Flyer/Southdown Lightning	MAR-01		8. 7.85	Canx by CAA 24.1.95.
G-MNEX	Mainair Gemini/Flash	357-785-1 & W84		23. 7.85	
G-MNEY	Mainair Gemini/Flash	365-1085-3 & W94		23. 7.85	
G-MNEZ	Skyhook TR1 Mk.2/Flexiform Sealander	HL-01		12. 8.85	Canx as WFU 26.8.94.
G-MNFA	Mainair Tri-Flyer/Solar Wings Thypoon (Trike ex G-MJFA)	DRJ-01 & GWW-01		29.12.83	
G-MNFB	Southdown Puma Sprint	1231/0077		22. 7.85	
G-MNFC	Midland Ultralights Sirocco 377GB	MU-015		16.10.85	Fatal crash when the tailplane broke off shortly after take-off from a strip 2 miles SSE of Bromyard 28.4.95 and the aircraft dived into the ground. Canx as WFU 19.7.95.

Regn	Type	c/n	Previous identity	Regn date	Fate or immediate subsequent identity (if known)
G-MNFD	Southdown Raven	2232/0090		4. 2.86	Canx by CAA 13.6.90.
G-MNFE	Mainair Gemini/Flash	350-885-3 & W82		29. 7.85	
G-MNFF	Mainair Gemini/Flash	371-1185-3 & W110		29. 7.85	
G-MNFG	Southdown Puma Sprint	1231/0078		31. 7.85	
G-MNFH	Mainair Gemini/Flash	364-1085-3 & W93		6. 8.85	(Stored 9/97)
G-MNFI	Medway Half Pint/Aerial Arts 130SX	6/25785		2. 8.85	Canx by CAA 23.6.97.
G-MNFJ	Mainair Gemini/Flash	346-985-3 & W80		20. 9.85	
G-MNFK	Mainair Gemini/Flash 2	359-885-3 & W91		12. 8.85	
G-MNFL	AMF Microflight Chevvron	CH.002		19. 8.85	
G-MNFM	Mainair Gemini/Flash	366-1085-3 & W98		10.10.85	
G-MNFN	Mainair Gemini/Flash	367-1085-3 & W99		6.11.85	
G-MNFO	Not allotted.				
G-MNFP	Mainair Gemini/Flash	368-1085-3 & W100		23.10.85	
G-MNFR	Mainair Tri-Flyer/Solar Wings Medium Typhoon	T981-272		15. 8.85	Canx by CAA 23.6.98.
G-MNFS	Ikarus Sherpa Dopplesitzer	8403/1064		7. 8.85	Canx as WFU 23.4.90.
G-MNFT	Mainair Gemini/Flash	363-1085-3 & W107		12. 8.85	Canx as destroyed 31.8.94.
G-MNFU	Not allotted.				
G-MNFV	Ultrasports Tripacer 250/La Mouette Atlas 18	LM-18-731		12. 8.85	Canx by CAA 23.6.97.
G-MNFW	Medway Hybred 44XL	10885/13		15. 8.85	
G-MNFX	Southdown Puma Sprint	1231/0079		14. 8.85	
G-MNFY	Hornet 250/Solar Wings Storm	H.270 & SLE 80126	G-MJFY(1)	21. 6.84	Canx by CAA 19.7.93.
G-MNFZ	Southdown Puma Sprint	T.597 & 1231/0080		22. 8.85	
G-MNGA	Aerial Arts Chaser 110SX	110SX/138		13. 9.85	Canx by CAA 2.2.93.
G-MNGB	Mainair Gemini/Flash	218-81183-2 & W01		14.12.83	
G-MNGC	CFM Shadow Srs.B	005		19. 8.85	Canx by CAA 13.6.90.
G-MNGD	Ultrasports Tripacer/Solar Wings Medium Typhoon	012 & T681-171		13. 8.85	
	(Originally regd a Quest Air Skystrike with c/n PRD-01)				
G-MNGE	Solar Wings Pegasus/Photon (Medway trike; JPX engine)	SW-WP-0001		21. 8.85	Canx as WFU 16.11.88.
G-MNGF	Solar Wings Pegasus/Flash	SW-TB-1022 & SW-WF-0003		21. 8.85	
G-MNGG	Solar Wings Pegasus XL-R	T784-1159XL		21. 8.85	
G-MNGH	Skyhook TR1 Pixie/Zeus	TR1/61		24. 9.85	
G-MNGI	Chargus Vortex 120	28		. .85R	NTU - Canx.
G-MNGJ	Skyhook TR1 Pixie/Zipper	TR1/60		13. 1.86	Canx by CAA 20.11.95. To G-59-6. DBF at Mainair's factory, Rochdale on 22.11.98.
G-MNGK	Mainair Gemini/Flash	374-1085-3 & W112		5. 9.85	
G-MNGL	Mainair Gemini/Flash	376-1085-3 & W114		5. 9.85	(Stored 10/95)
G-MNGM	Mainair Gemini/Flash	394-1285-3 & W109		5. 9.85	
	(Original trike unit 377-1085-3 & W109, fitted with Rotax 447 SNo 3499167 stolen from Popham 15/16.3.86; now fitted with 394-1285-3 - see G-MNJU)				
G-MNGN	Mainair Gemini/Flash	378-1185-3 & W115		5. 9.85	
G-MNGO	Hiway Skytrike/Solar Wings Storm	21U8		5. 9.85	Canx by CAA 20.3.89. (Stored at Husbands Bosworth in 4/98)
G-MNGP	Gryphon	-		. .85R	NTU - Canx.
	(Reportedly at a microlight rally near Lisbon in 10/86)				
G-MNGR	Southdown Puma Sprint	1231/0086		18. 9.85	
G-MNGS	Ultrasports Tripacer/Southdown Puma (Lightning 195)	GJS-02		8. 5.84	
	(Tripacer trike unit from G-MJRF)				
G-MNGT	Mainair Gemini/Flash	372-1085-3 & W106		30. 9.85	
	(Reported 4/96 as Huntwing 462LC)				
G-MNGU	Mainair Gemini/Flash	373-1085-3 & W111		30. 9.85	
G-MNGV	Not allotted.				
G-MNGW	Mainair Gemini/Flash	386-1185-3 & W121		30. 9.85	
G-MNGX	Southdown Puma Sprint	1231/0088		26. 9.85	
G-MNGY	Hiway Skytrike 160/Skyhook Cutlass	AJW-01		1.10.85	Canx by CAA 7.9.94.

Regn	Type	c/n	Previous identity	Regn date	Fate or immediate subsequent identity (if known)
G-MNGZ	Mainair Gemini/Flash	385-1085-3 & W120		10.10.85	
G-MNHA	Noble Hardman Snowbird	SB-002		13. 8.84	Canx by CAA 13.6.90.
G-MNHB	Solar Wings Pegasus XL-R/Se	SW-WA-1045		1.11.85	
G-MNHC	Solar Wings Pegasus XL-R	SW-TB-1032 & SW-WA-1046		31.10.85	
G-MNHD	Solar Wings Pegasus XL-R	SW-TB-1033 & SW-WA-1047		5.11.85	
G-MNHE	Solar Wings Pegasus XL-R	SW-TB-1036 & SW-WA-1048		11.12.85	
G-MNHF	Solar Wings Pegasus XL-R	SW-TB-1038 & SW-WA-1049		29.11.85	
G-MNHG	Solar Wings Pegasus XL-R	SW-WA-1050		29.11.85	Canx by CAA 6.9.93.
G-MNHH	Solar Wings Pegasus XL-S	SW-WA-1051		22. 1.86	
G-MNHI	Solar Wings Pegasus XL-R	SW-TB-1042 & SW-WA-1052		8. 1.86	
G-MNHJ	Solar Wings Pegasus XL-R	SW-WA-1053		11. 3.86	
G-MNHK	Solar Wings Pegasus XL-R	SW-WA-1054		9. 7.86	
G-MNHL	Solar Wings Pegasus XL-R	SW-WA-1055		9. 7.86	
G-MNHM	Solar Wings Pegasus XL-R	SW-TB-1078 & SW-WA-1056		11. 7.86	
G-MNHN	Solar Wings Pegasus XL-R	SW-WA-1057		11. 8.86	
G-MNHO	Solar Wings Pegasus XL-R	SW-WA-1058		. .85R	NTU - Canx. (Presumed sold abroad).
G-MNHP	Solar Wings Pegasus XL-R	SW-WA-1059		11. 8.86	(Damaged when struck power cables nr.Bristol 18.11.95)
G-MNHR	Solar Wings Pegasus XL-R	SW-TB-1081 & SW-WA-1060		7. 8.86	
G-MNHS	Solar Wings Pegasus XL-R	SW-TB-1082 & SW-WA-1061		21. 8.86	
G-MNHT	Solar Wings Pegasus XL-R	SW-WA-1062		4. 8.86	
G-MNHU	Solar Wings Pegasus XL-R	SW-WA-1063		4. 8.86	
G-MNHV	Solar Wings Pegasus XL-R	SW-TB-1095 & SW-WA-1064		18. 8.86	
G-MNHW	Medway Half Pint	7/30885		9. 9.85	Canx by CAA 9.6.93.
G-MNHX	Jackson Trident 250/Solar Wings Typhoon S4	002		24. 9.85	Canx as WFU 15.12.92.
G-MNHY	Mainair Tri-Flyer 440/Flexiform Striker	KW-01		12. 9.85	Canx by CAA 13.6.90.
G-MNHZ	Mainair Gemini/Flash	310-585-3 & W118		15.10.85	
G-MNIA	Mainair Gemini/Flash	370-1185-3 & W105		10.10.85	
G-MNIB	American Aerolights Eagle 215B	CRC-01		29. 1.86	Canx by CAA 7.9.94.
G-MNIC	MBA Tiger Cub 440	SO.170		26. 3.84	Canx by CAA 13.6.90.
G-MNID	Mainair Gemini/Flash	369-1185-3 & W104		7. 2.86	(Stolen from Rufforth 10/11-97; engine no.3706877)
G-MNIE	Mainair Gemini/Flash	388-1185-3 & W123		21.11.85	
G-MNIF	Mainair Gemini/Flash	403-286-4 & W147		7. 1.86	
G-MNIG	Mainair Gemini/Flash	391-1285-3 & W139		9. 1.86	
G-MNIH	Mainair Gemini/Flash	379-1185-3 & W116		10.12.85	
G-MNII	Mainair Gemini/Flash	390-1285-3 & W128		6.11.85	(Trike reported at St.Michaels-on-Wyre 9/96?)
G-MNIJ	Ultrasports Tripacer 250/Hiway Super Scorpion Mk.2	BDJ-01		29. 5.84	Shortly after take-off this was seen to enter a spiral dive and crashed at Winterbourne Kingston, Dorset on 30.5.85. Canx as destroyed 4.2.86.
G-MNIK	Solar Wings Pegasus/Photon	SW-TP-0002 & SW-WP-0002		29.10.85	(Stored for possible rebuild 4/96)
G-MNIL	Southdown Puma Sprint	1231/0094		4.11.85	
G-MNIM	Maxair Hummer	PJB-01		29.10.85	
G-MNIN	Designability (Jordan) Duet	018		7.11.85	Canx by CAA 25.9.95.
G-MNIO	Mainair Gemini/Flash (Yellow Flash wing stolen from Popham 15/16.3.86)	394-1285-3 & W135		6.11.85	Canx as WFU 24.7.89.
G-MNIP	Mainair Gemini/Flash	393-1285-3 & W134		6.11.85	
G-MNIR	Skyhook Pixie/Aerial Arts 130SX	130SX/156		7.11.85	Canx by CAA 13.9.94.
G-MNIS	CFM Shadow Srs.C	014		11.11.85	
G-MNIT	Aerial Arts Alpha Mk.II/130SX (Originally regd as Hiway Skytrike II with same c/n)	130SX/176		27. 2.86	
G-MNIU	Solar Wings Pegasus Photon	SW-WP-0003		27.11.85	(Damaged & stored 3/90)
G-MNIV	Hiway Skytrike/Solar Wings Typhoon	HW-16		25. 2.86	Canx by CAA 3.8.94.
G-MNIW	Mainair Tri-Flyer 250/Airwave Nimrod 165	050/19181	EI-BOB	29.11.85	

Regn	Type	c/n	Previous identity	Regn date	Fate or immediate subsequent identity (if known)
G-MNIX	Mainair Gemini/Flash	395-1285-3 & W136		29.11.85	
G-MNIY	Skyhook TR1 Pixie/Zipper	TR1/62		5.12.85	Canx by CAA 20.11.95. DBF whilst stored at Mainair's factory, Rochdale on 22.11.98.
G-MNIZ	Mainair Gemini/Flash	392-1285-3 & W130		26. 2.86	
G-MNJA	Hiway Skytrike 250/Southdown Lightning	PJH-01		9.12.85	Canx by CAA 22.12.95.
G-MNJB	Southdown Raven X	2232/0098		10.12.85	
G-MNJC	MBA Tiger Cub 440	SO.215		8. 6.84	
G-MNJD	Mainair Gemini/Southdown Puma Sprint MS	JBB-01 & 243-484-2 & P.537		2. 4.84	(Stored 5/97)
	(Originally regd with c/n 243-10484-2 - amended in 1984)				
G-MNJE	Mainair Gemini/Southdown Puma Sprint	329-385-3 & 1231/0084		18. 9.85	Canx as destroyed 8.6.95.
G-MNJF	Dragon Srs.150	0068	(OY)9-17	2. 1.86	
G-MNJG	Mainair Gemini/Southdown Puma Sprint MS	SA.2030 & 251-684-2 & P.593		29. 9.83	
	(Originally regd as Tri-Flyer)				
G-MNJH	Solar Wings Pegasus/Flash	SW-TB-1023 & SW-WF-0004		22.10.85	
G-MNJI	Solar Wings Pegasus/Flash	SW-TB-1025 & SW-WF-0005		21.10.85	To SE-YXI 8/99. Canx 2.9.97.
G-MNJJ	Solar Wings Pegasus/Flash	SW-TB-1029 & SW-WF-0006		22.10.85	
G-MNJK	Solar Wings Pegasus/Flash	SW-TB-1027 & SW-WF-0007		21.10.85	
G-MNJL	Solar Wings Pegasus/Flash	SW-WF-0008		21.10.85	
G-MNJM	Solar Wings Pegasus/Flash	SW-WF-0009		28.11.85	Canx 16.4.87 on sale to USA.
G-MNJN	Solar Wings Pegasus/Flash	SW-WF-0010		19.11.85	
G-MNJO	Solar Wings Pegasus/Flash	SW-TB-1035 & SW-WF-0011		19.11.85	
G-MNJP	Solar Wings Pegasus/Flash	SW-TB-1040 & SW-WF-0012		30.12.85	(Stored 10/97) Canx as WFU 31.7.98.
	(Mainair wing c/n W127-1185-1 - see G-MNZA)				
G-MNJR	Solar Wings Pegasus/Flash	SW-WF-0013		30.12.85	
G-MNJS	Southdown Puma Sprint	1231/0085		18. 9.85	
G-MNJT	Southdown Raven X	2232/0087		20. 9.85	
G-MNJU	Mainair Gemini/Flash	384-1185-3 & W119		20. 9.85	
G-MNJV	Medway Half Pint/Aerial Arts 130SX (Regd as c/n 9/19985)	8/19985		10.10.85	
G-MNJW	Mitchell Wing B-10	JDW-01		26. 1.84	
G-MNJX	Medway Hybred 44XL	15885/14		9.12.85	
G-MNJY	Medway Half Pint/Aerial Arts 130SX	9/191185		10. 1.86	Canx by CAA 26.9.95.
G-MNJZ	Aerial Arts Alpha/130SX	130SX/170		17. 1.86	Canx as WFU 21.11.95.
G-MNKA	Solar Wings Pegasus/Photon	SW-WP-0004		15. 1.86	Canx 26.4.94 on sale to Ireland.
G-MNKB	Solar Wings Pegasus/Photon	SW-WP-0005		14. 1.86	
G-MNKC	Solar Wings Pegasus/Photon	SW-TP-0006 & SW-WP-0006		14. 1.86	
G-MNKD	Solar Wings Pegasus/Photon	SW-WP-0007		14. 1.86	
G-MNKE	Solar Wings Pegasus/Photon	SW-WP-0008		14. 1.86	
G-MNKF	Solar Wings Pegasus/Photon	SW-WP-0009		28. 1.86	Canx as WFU 16.11.88.
G-MNKG	Solar Wings Pegasus/Photon	SW-TP-0010 & SW-WP-0010		28. 1.86	(Trike stored 9/97)
G-MNKH	Solar Wings Pegasus/Photon	SW-TP-0011 & SW-WP-0011		28. 1.86	
G-MNKI	Solar Wings Pegasus/Photon	SW-WP-0012	(EI-...) G-MNKI	28. 1.86	
G-MNKJ	Solar Wings Pegasus/Photon	SW-WP-0013		28. 1.86	Canx by CAA 4.7.96.
G-MNKK	Solar Wings Pegasus/Photon	SW-WP-0014		28. 1.86	
G-MNKL	Mainair Gemini/Flash	397-1285-3 & W143		6. 1.86	
G-MNKM	MBA Tiger Cub 440	SO.213		30.12.85	
G-MNKN	Wheeler (Skycraft) Scout Mk.III/3/R	410		6. 1.86	Canx as WFU 19.2.99.
G-MNKO	Solar Wings Pegasus XL-Q	SW-TB-1158 & SW-WX-0001		2. 1.86	
G-MNKP	Solar Wings Pegasus/Flash	SW-TB-1043 & SW-WF-0014		9. 1.86	

Regn	Type	c/n	Previous identity	Regn date	Fate or immediate subsequent identity (if known)
G-MNKR	Solar Wings Pegasus/Flash	SW-TB-1045 & SW-WF-0015		14. 1.86	
G-MNKS	Solar Wings Pegasus/Flash	SW-TB-1044 & SW-WF-0016		9. 1.86	
G-MNKT	Brooks Trike/Solar Wings Typhon S4	CRS-01		15. 1.86	Canx by CAA 16.8.94.
G-MNKU	Southdown Puma Sprint	1231/0100		29. 1.86	
G-MNKV	Solar Wings Pegasus/Flash	SW-TB-1047 & SW-WF-0017		15. 1.86	
G-MNKW	Solar Wings Pegasus/Flash	SW-WF-0018		28. 1.86	
G-MNKX	Solar Wings Pegasus/Flash	SW-WF-0019		28. 2.86	
G-MNKY	Southdown Raven X	2232/0101		4. 2.86	Canx by CAA 7.8.96.
G-MNKZ	Southdown Raven X	2232/0102		4. 2.86	
G-MNLA	Ultrasports Tripacer/Solar Wings Typhoon	T582-1087		15. 1.86	Canx by CAA 13.6.90.
G-MNLB	Southdown Raven X	2232/0117		11. 4.86	
G-MNLC	Southdown Raven X	2232/0103		6. 2.86	Canx by CAA 7.8.96.
G-MNLD	Solar Wings Pegasus/Photon	SW-WP-0015		28. 1.86	Canx as WFU 16.11.88.
G-MNLE	Southdown Raven X	2232/0128		30. 4.86	
G-MNLF	Ultrasports Tripacer/Southdown Puma	KB-01		1. 4.86	Canx by CAA 15.6.90.
G-MNLG	Edwards Trike/Southdown Lightning	DJE-01		24. 1.86	Canx by CAA 13.6.90.
G-MNLH	Romain Cobra Biplane	001		23. 1.86	
G-MNLI	Mainair Gemini/Flash 2	407-286-4 & W152		28. 1.86	
G-MNLJ	Mainair Gemini/Flash	399-186-4 & W144		. .86R	NTU - Canx.
G-MNLK	Southdown Raven X	2232/0108		4. 2.86	
G-MNLL	Southdown Raven X	2232/0109		4. 2.86	
G-MNLM	Southdown Raven X	2232/0110		6. 2.86	
G-MNLN	Southdown Raven X	2232/0111		6. 2.86	
G-MNLO	Southdown Raven X	2232/0112		6. 2.86	Badly damaged in fatal crash on take-off from Upottery, near Honiton, Devon on 6.4.86.
G-MNLP	Southdown Raven X	2232/0113		6. 2.86	Canx by CAA 9.2.93.
G-MNLR	Farrell Trike/Solar Wings Typhoon	BJF-01		1. 5.84	Canx as destroyed 24.5.90.
G-MNLS	Southdown Raven X	2232/0114		6. 2.86	Canx by CAA 7.8.96.
G-MNLT	Southdown Raven X	2232/0115		6. 2.86	
G-MNLU	Southdown Raven X	2232/0116		6. 2.86	
G-MNLV	Southdown Raven X	2232/0118		6. 2.86	
G-MNLW	Medway Half Pint/Aerial Arts 130SX	10/31186		10. 2.86	
G-MNLX	Mainair Gemini/Flash 2	413-386-4 & W165		6. 2.86	
G-MNLY	Mainair Gemini/Flash	406-386-4 & W151		14. 2.86	
G-MNLZ	Southdown Raven X	2232/0123		6. 2.86	
G-MNMA	Solar Wings Pegasus/Flash	SW-WF-0021		24. 3.86	Landed short & overturned at Church Farm, Biddenham, Beds on 28.6.86 & badly damaged. Canx by CAA 7.8.96.
G-MNMB	Solar Wings Pegasus/Flash	SW-WF-0022		14. 3.86	Canx as TWFU 2.5.95.
G-MNMC	Mainair Gemini/Southdown Puma Sprint MS (Originally regd with c/n MLC-01/KR/226184-2, then with c/n 226-184-2 - which is a corruption on the original c/n)	222-284-2 & P.524		20. 3.84	
G-MNMD	Southdown Raven X (Originally regd with c/n 2232/0121)	2000/0121		10. 2.86	
G-MNME	Hiway Skytrike/Demon	WTP-01 & 3535009		12. 2.86	
G-MNMF	Maxair Hummer TX	0020		25. 5.84	Canx by CAA 7.9.94.
G-MNMG	Mainair Gemini/Flash 2	419-386-4 & W177		11. 2.86	
G-MNMH	Mainair Gemini/Flash 2	417-486-4 & W168		11. 2.86	
G-MNMI	Mainair Gemini/Flash 2 (Original trike replaced with c/n 317-685-3 ex G-MMZL)	420-586-4 & W178		11. 2.86	
G-MNMJ	Mainair Gemini/Flash 2	387-1185-3 & W122		11. 2.86	
G-MNMK	Solar Wings Pegasus XL-R	SW-WA-1038		19. 8.85	
G-MNML	Southdown Puma Sprint (Originally regd with c/n DAC-01)	1111/0065		4. 8.83	
G-MNMM	Aerotech MW.5(K) Sorcerer (Regd with c/n SK-0001-01) (Originally regd with c/n SR101-R4008-01)	5K-0001-02		11. 2.86	
G-MNMN	Medway Hybred 44XLR	8286/16		7. 3.86	
G-MNMO	Mainair Gemini/Flash 2	398-186-4 & W141		27. 2.86	
G-MNMP	Pritchard Experimental Mk.I	001		24. 2.84	Canx by CAA 13.6.90.

Regn	Type	c/n	Previous identity	Regn date	Fate or immediate subsequent identity (if known)
G-MNMR	Ultrasports Tripacer 250/Solar Wings Typhoon 180	1347316		17. 2.86	Canx as WFU 28.11.94.
G-MNMS	Wheeler Scout	0010		25. 5.84	Canx by CAA 27.3.99.
G-MNMT	Southdown Raven X	2232/0126		19. 2.86	Canx by CAA 22.3.89.
G-MNMU	Southdown Raven X	2232/0127		17. 2.86	
G-MNMV	Mainair Gemini/Flash	375-1085-3 & W113		3. 3.86	
G-MNMW	Whittaker MW.6-1-1 Merlin	PFA/164-11144		16. 4.86	
G-MNMX	Sigh-Wing Paraplane	SW.3		17. 2.86	Canx as WFU 3.4.90.
G-MNMY	Aerial Arts 110SX/Cyclone 70	CH-02		6. 3.86	
G-MNMZ	Southdown Raven	2232/0106		. .86R	NTU - Canx.
G-MNNA	Southdown Raven X	2232/0129		4. 3.86	
G-MNNB	Southdown Raven	2122/0130		4. 3.86	
G-MNNC	Southdown Raven X	2232/0131		4. 3.86	
G-MNND	Solar Wings Pegasus/Flash 2	SW-WF-0100		27. 2.86	
G-MNNE	Mainair Gemini/Flash 2	410-386-4 & W154		27. 2.86	
G-MNNF	Mainair Gemini/Flash 2	402-286-4 & W148		28. 2.86	(Stored 1/98)
G-MNNG	Squires Lightfly/Solar Wings Pegasus Photon (Originally regd with Airwave Magic 4 wing & c/n S70 Mk1)	SW-WP-0019		25. 2.86	
G-MNNH	Medway SX130 Export	20286/11		25. 4.86	Canx as destroyed 4.6.90.
G-MNNI	Mainair Gemini/Flash 2 (Wing also quoted as c/n W173)	427-486-4 & W170		28. 2.86	
G-MNNJ	Mainair Gemini/Flash 2	405-286-4 & W150		28. 2.86	Canx as destroyed 17.8.98.
G-MNNK	Mainair Gemini/Flash 2	428-486-4 & W185		28. 2.86	(Trike stolen from Fradley on 1.1.93)
G-MNNL	Mainair Gemini/Flash 2	429-486-4 & W186		28. 2.86	
G-MNNM	Mainair Scorcher Solo	424-486-1 & W182	(G-MNPE)	20. 3.86	
G-MNNN	Southdown Raven X	2232/0132		4. 3.86	
G-MNNO	Southdown Raven X	2232/0133		26. 3.86	
G-MNNP	Mainair Gemini/Flash 2	409-386-4 & W155		5. 3.86	
G-MNNR	Mainair Gemini/Flash 2 (Wing originally quoted as c/n W157)	430-586-4 & W188		6. 3.86	
G-MNNS	Eurowing Goldwing	EW-74		8. 4.86	Canx by CAA 7.4.99.
G-MNNT	Medway Hybred 44XLR	1185/15		7. 3.86	Canx as WFU 5.7.96.
G-MNNU	Mainair Gemini/Flash 2 (See comments under G-MTBK)	408-386-4 & W153		19. 3.86	
G-MNNV	Mainair Gemini/Flash 2	431-586-4 & W187		10. 3.86	
G-MNNW	Southdown Raven X	2232/0134		23. 4.86	Canx as destroyed 27.7.87.
G-MNNX	Not allotted.				
G-MNNY	Solar Wings Pegasus/Flash	SW-TB-1059 & SW-WF-0023		14. 3.86	
G-MNNZ	Solar Wings Pegasus/Flash 2	SW-TB-1060 & SW-WF-0101		24. 4.86	
G-MNOA to G-MNOZ	This batch was not allocated due to clerical oversight.				
G-MNPA	Solar Wings Pegasus/Flash 2	SW-WF-0102		18. 4.86	
G-MNPB	Solar Wings Pegasus/Flash 2	SW-WF-0103		18. 4.86	Badly damaged on landing at Wombleton on 12.8.86. (Extant 8/97)
G-MNPC	Mainair Gemini/Flash 2	423-586-4 & W181		17. 3.86	
G-MNPD	Midland Ultralights 130SX/Firefly	130SX/240		28. 4.86	Canx by CAA 24.1.95.
G-MNPE	Mainair Scorcher Solo	424-486-1 & W182		. .86R	NTU - To G-MNNM 3/86. Canx.
G-MNPF	Mainair Gemini/Flash 2	404-286-4 & W149		24. 3.86	Canx by CAA 21.6.93.
G-MNPG	Mainair Gemini/Flash 2	437-686-4 & W204		20. 3.86	
G-MNPH	Lancashire Micro-Trike 440/Flexiform Dual Striker	1/440PM/LM/1283/1		3. 1.84	Canx as WFU 13.5.86.
G-MNPI	Southdown Pipistrelle 2C (Mod)	SAL-P2C-003		17. 3.86	(Damaged in 1994)
G-MNPJ	Southdown Pipistrelle 2C	SAL-P2C-004		17. 3.86	Canx as WFU 9.4.90.
G-MNPK	Southdown Pipistrelle 2C	SAL-P2C-005		17. 3.86	Canx as WFU 9.4.90.
G-MNPL	Ultrasports Panther 330/Solar Wings Typhoon S	T184-965P		3. 7.84	Canx by CAA 24.10.88.
G-MNPM	Southdown Pipistrelle 2C	SAL-P2C-006		17. 3.86	Canx as WFU 9.4.90.

Regn	Type	c/n	Previous identity	Regn date	Fate or immediate subsequent identity (if known)
G-MNPN	Southdown Pipistrelle 2C	SAL-P2C-007		17. 3.86	Canx as WFU 9.4.90.
G-MNPO	Romain Cobra Biplane	002		18. 3.86	Canx by CAA 13.6.90.
G-MNPP	Romain Cobra Biplane	003		18. 3.86	Canx by CAA 7.9.94.
G-MNPR	Hiway Skytrike 160/Demon 175 (Trike ex.G-MMBP)	21W6 & WB-01		22. 6.83	Canx by CAA 29.12.94.
G-MNPS	Skyhook TR1 Pixie/Zeus C	TR1-65		25. 3.86	Canx as WFU 3.4.90.
G-MNPT	Skyhook TR1 Pixie/Zeus C	TR1-66		25. 3.86	Canx as WFU 13.10.88.
G-MNPU	Skyhook TR1 Pixie/Zeus C	TR1-67		25. 3.86	Canx as WFU 3.4.90.
G-MNPV	Mainair Scorcher Solo	432-586-1 & W189		24. 3.86	
G-MNPW	AMF Chevron	CH-001		14. 5.84	Canx as WFU 19.12.85.
G-MNPX	Mainair Gemini/Flash 2	412-486-4 & W164		24. 3.86	Canx by CAA 19.7.99.
G-MNPY	Mainair Scorcher Solo	452-886-1 & W229		25. 3.86	
G-MNPZ	Mainair Scorcher Solo	449-886-1 & W226		25. 3.86	(Rotax 503/3-blade prop test acft)
G-MNRA	CFM Shadow Srs.B	015		20. 3.86	Canx 25.4.86 on sale to Australia. To 25-0251.
G-MNRB	Southdown Puma/Raven	2000/0105		25. 3.86	Canx by CAA 13.6.90.
G-MNRC	Skyhook TR1/Sabre C	TR1-21		26. 3.86	Canx as WFU 13.10.88.
G-MNRD	Ultraflight Lazair IIIE	81		17. 6.83	
G-MNRE	Mainair Scorcher Solo	453-886-1 & W230		25. 3.86	
G-MNRF	Mainair Scorcher Solo	461-986-1 & W238		25. 3.86	
G-MNRG	Mainair Scorcher Solo	462-986-1 & W239		25. 3.86	
G-MNRH	Mainair Scorcher Solo	463-986-1 & W240		25. 3.86	Canx by CAA 3.11.88.
G-MNRI	Hornet Dual Trainer/Southdown Raven (Replacement Trike HRWA-0082 now fitted)	HRWA 0051 & 2000/0119		26. 3.86	
G-MNRJ	Hornet Dual Trainer/Southdown Raven	HRWA 0052 & 2000/0120		26. 3.86	
G-MNRK	Hornet Dual Trainer/Southdown Raven	HRWA 0053 & 2000/0183		26. 3.86	
G-MNRL	Hornet Dual Trainer/Southdown Raven	HRWA 0054 & 2000/0184		26. 3.86	
G-MNRM	Hornet Dual Trainer/Southdown Raven	HRWA 0055 & 2000/0214		26. 3.86	
G-MNRN	Hornet Dual Trainer/Southdown Raven	HRWA 0056 & 2000/0...		26. 3.86	Canx by CAA 13.10.88.
G-MNRO	Southdown Raven	2232/0092		2. 4.86	Canx by CAA 13.6.90.
G-MNRP	Southdown Raven X	2232/0135		7. 4.86	
G-MNRR	Southdown Raven X	2232/0136		30. 4.86	Canx by CAA 7.8.96.
G-MNRS	Southdown Raven X	2232/0137		7. 4.86	
G-MNRT	Midland Ultralights Sirocco 377GB	MU-016		1. 4.86	
G-MNRU	Midland Ultralights Sirocco 377GB	MU-017		1. 4.86	Canx by CAA 18.10.93.
G-MNRV	American Aerolights Eagle	E.2681		27. 3.86	Canx by CAA 13.6.90.
G-MNRW	Mainair Gemini/Flash 2	411-486-4 & W156		7. 4.86	
G-MNRX	Mainair Gemini/Flash 2	434-686-4 & W220		8. 4.86	
G-MNRY	Mainair Gemini/Flash 2	418-486-4 & W169		7. 4.86	
G-MNRZ	Mainair Scorcher Solo	426-586-1 & W184		4. 4.86	
G-MNSA	Mainair Gemini/Flash 2	442-786-4 & W219		18. 4.86	
G-MNSB	Southdown Puma Sprint	539 & 1121/0066		15. 6.83	
G-MNSC	Flexiform Hi-Line/TC3	TC-001		29. 4.86	Canx by CAA 13.6.90.
G-MNSD	Ultrasports Tripacer/Solar Wings Typhoon S4 (Originally regd as Sheffield Trident/Solar Wings Typhoon with c/n STT-652)	T182-341L		23. 4.86	
G-MNSE	Mainair Gemini/Flash 2	444-886-4 & W224		4. 4.86	
G-MNSF	Hornet Dual Trainer/Southdown Raven	HRWA 0057		27. 3.86	Canx by CAA 13.10.88.
G-MNSG	Hornet Dual Trainer/Southdown Raven	HRWA 0058		27. 3.86	Canx by CAA 13.6.90.
G-MNSH	Solar Wings Pegasus Flash 2	SW-WF-0104		14. 4.86	
G-MNSI	Mainair Gemini/Flash 2	445-786-4 & W213		9. 4.86	
G-MNSJ	Mainair Gemini/Flash 2	443-886-4 & W223		11. 4.86	
G-MNSK	Hiway Skystrike/Demon (C/n is Engine no.)	80-00043		7. 4.86	Canx by CAA 24.1.95.
G-MNSL	Southdown Raven X	2232/0145		17. 4.86	

Regn	Type	c/n	Previous identity	Regn date	Fate or immediate subsequent identity (if known)
G-MNSM	Hornet/Hiway Demon	H050		10. 4.86	Canx by CAA 23.11.88.
G-MNSN	Solar Wings Pegasus Flash 2	SW-TB-1066 & SW-WF-0105		25. 4.86	
G-MNSO	Solar Wings Pegasus Flash 2	SW-WF-0106		20. 6.86	Canx as WFU 24.8.92.
G-MNSP	Aerial Arts 130SX/Seajay	130SX/258		28. 4.86	Canx by CAA 17.5.93.
G-MNSR	Mainair Gemini/Flash 2	399-486-4 & W144		17. 4.86	
G-MNSS	American Aerolights Eagle 215B	4131		24. 4.86	
G-MNST	Raven Vector 600	1039		17. 4.86	Canx by CAA 7.9.94.
G-MNSU	Aerial Arts 130SX	130SX/259		24. 4.86	Canx by CAA 25.6.90.
G-MNSV	CFM Shadow Srs.B	012		24. 4.86	
G-MNSW	Southdown Raven X	2232/0147		23. 4.86	
G-MNSX	Southdown Raven X	2232/0148		30. 4.86	
G-MNSY	Southdown Raven X	2232/0149		30. 4.86	
G-MNSZ	Noble Hardman Snowbird	SB-003		19. 5.86	Canx by CAA 1.9.93.
G-MNTA	Chris 1-1	001		. .86R	NTU - Canx.
G-MNTB	Trapeze/Solar Wings Typhoon S4	T284/004		28. 4.86	Canx by CAA 5.12.95.
G-MNTC	Southdown Raven X	2232/0150		30. 4.86	
G-MNTD	Aerial Arts Chaser/110SX (C/n conflicts with G-MTSF)	110SX/255		24. 4.86	
G-MNTE	Southdown Raven X	2232/0151		30. 4.86	
G-MNTF	Southdown Raven X	2232/0152		30. 4.86	
G-MNTG	Southdown Raven X	2232/0153		30. 4.86	(Stored 5/97)
G-MNTH	Mainair Gemini/Flash 2	446-886-4 & W171		8. 5.86	Canx by CAA 29.7.94.
G-MNTI	Mainair Gemini/Flash 2	447-886-4 & W231		8. 5.86	
G-MNTJ	American Aerolights Eagle	DSJB-01		23. 6.86	Canx by CAA 13.6.90.
G-MNTK	CFM Shadow Srs.CD	024		8. 5.86	
G-MNTL	Arbee/Wasp Gryphon (C/n is engine no.)	STIHL 8592857/003		4. 6.86	Canx by CAA 7.9.94.
G-MNTM	Southdown Raven X	2232/0154		19. 5.86	
G-MNTN	Southdown Raven X	2232/0155		2. 6.86	
G-MNTO	Southdown Raven X	2232/0156		5. 6.86	
G-MNTP	CFM Shadow Srs.B	K.022		19. 5.86	
G-MNTR	Not allotted.				
G-MNTS	Mainair Gemini/Flash 2	450-886-4 & W227		3. 4.86	
G-MNTT	Medway Half Pint/Aerial Arts 130SX	12/1486		7. 4.86	(Extant 6/95)
G-MNTU	Mainair Gemini/Flash 2	460-886-4 & W233		9. 7.86	
G-MNTV	Mainair Gemini/Flash 2	455-886-4 & W241		2. 9.86	
G-MNTW	Mainair Gemini/Flash 2	456-886-5 & W242		11. 9.86	
G-MNTX	Mainair Gemini/Flash 2	415-486-4 & W166		20. 5.86	
G-MNTY	Southdown Raven X	2232/0157		29. 5.86	
G-MNTZ	Mainair Gemini/Flash 2	457-886-4 & W243		3. 6.86	
G-MNUA	Mainair Gemini/Flash 2	458-886-4 & W235		29. 5.86	
G-MNUB	Mainair Gemini/Flash 2	459-986-4 & W236		3. 6.86	
G-MNUC	Solar Wings Pegasus Flash 2	SW-WF-0116		11. 6.86	Canx as WFU 5.7.96.
G-MNUD	Solar Wings Pegasus Flash 2	SW-TE-0003 & SW-WF-0110		10. 6.86	
G-MNUE	Solar Wings Pegasus Flash 2	SW-WF-0108		10. 6.86	
G-MNUF	Mainair Gemini/Flash 2	472-786-4 & W252		13. 6.86	(Stored 12/97)
G-MNUG	Mainair Gemini/Flash 2	465-986-4 & W245		13. 6.86	
G-MNUH	Southdown Raven X	2232/0158		17. 6.86	
G-MNUI	Mainair Tri-Flyer/Skyhook Cutlass	MH-01		21. 5.86	
G-MNUJ	Solar Wings Pegasus Photon	SW-TP-0018 & SW-WP-0018		11. 6.86	(Stored 9/97 Eshott) Canx by CAA 27.3.99.
G-MNUK	Midland Ultralights SX130/Firefly	SX130/314 & MU-F012		9. 7.86	Canx by CAA 24.1.95.
G-MNUL	Midland Ultralights SX130/Firefly	SX130/315 & MU-F013		9. 7.86	Canx by CAA 12.9.94.
G-MNUM	Mainair Gemini/Southdown Puma Sprint MS (Originally regd with c/n 222-284-2)	AS-02 & 226-184-2 & P.508		12. 3.84	
G-MNUN	Southdown Raven X	2232/0159		. .86R	NTU - Canx.
G-MNUO	Mainair Gemini/Flash 2	421-586-4 & W179		9. 7.86	

Regn	Type	c/n	Previous identity	Regn date	Fate or immediate subsequent identity (if known)
G-MNUP	Mainair Gemini/Flash 2 (Regd as c/n 469-686-4)	469-886-4 & W249		11. 6.86	Canx as WFU 24.11.97.
G-MNUR	Mainair Gemini/Flash 2	470-986-4 & W250		14. 8.86	
G-MNUS	Mainair Gemini/Flash 2	464-986-4 & W244		11. 6.86	Canx by CAA 12.8.97.
G-MNUT	Southdown Raven X	2232/0160		10. 6.86	(Stored 7/95)
G-MNUU	Southdown Raven X	2232/0162		26. 6.86	
G-MNUV	Southdown Raven X	2232/0161		15. 6.86	Canx by CAA 7.8.96.
G-MNUW	Southdown Raven X	2232/0163		17. 6.86	
G-MNUX	Solar Wings Pegasus XL-R	SW-WA-1076		24. 6.86	
G-MNUY	Mainair Gemini/Flash 2	422-586-4 & W180		23. 6.86	
G-MNUZ	Mainair Gemini/Flash 2	473-786-4 & W253		17. 6.86	Canx by CAA 6.6.95.
G-MNVA	Solar Wings Pegasus XL-R	SW-WA-1075		17. 6.86	Crashed into mountains in .92. Canx as WFU 22.3.93.
G-MNVB	Solar Wings Pegasus XL-R	SW-TB-1073 & SW-WA-1077		7. 7.86	
G-MNVC	Solar Wings Pegasus XL-R	SW-TB-1074 & SW-WA-1078		7. 7.86	
G-MNVD	Not to be allotted.				
G-MNVE	Solar Wings Pegasus XL-R	SW-WA-1079		19. 6.86	
G-MNVF	Solar Wings Pegasus Flash 2	SW-WF-0112		26. 6.86	(Damaged mid .96) Canx as WFU 17.6.98.
G-MNVG	Solar Wings Pegasus Flash 2	SW-WF-0109		11. 6.86	
G-MNVH	Solar Wings Pegasus Flash 2	SW-TE-0001 & SW-WF-0122		23. 6.86	
G-MNVI	CFM Shadow Srs.C	026		17. 6.86	
G-MNVJ	CFM Shadow Srs.BD	028		17. 6.86	
G-MNVK	CFM Shadow Srs.CD	029		17. 6.86	
G-MNVL	Medway Half Pint/Aerial Arts 130SX	3/21585 & 130SX-100	G-MNBZ	22. 9.86	Canx by CAA 23.6.97.
G-MNVM	Southdown Raven X	2232/0164		17. 6.86	(Was based at Harare, Zimbabwe) Canx by CAA 7.8.96.
G-MNVN	Southdown Raven	2132/0165		27. 6.86	
G-MNVO	Hovey Whing-Ding II	CW-01		14. 8.86	
G-MNVP	Southdown Raven X	2232/0166		23. 6.86	(Damaged late .96)
G-MNVR	Mainair Gemini/Flash 2	471-986-4 & W251		27. 6.86	
G-MNVS	Mainair Gemini/Flash 2	476-986-4 & W257		9. 7.86	
G-MNVT	Mainair Gemini/Flash 2	477-786-4 & W258		27. 6.86	(Stored Hinton-in-the-Hedges 4/90)
G-MNVU	Mainair Gemini/Flash 2	468-986-4 & W248		26. 6.86	
G-MNVV	Mainair Gemini/Flash 2	467-986-4 & W247		26. 6.86	(Stored 12/97)
G-MNVW	Mainair Gemini/Flash 2	466-986-4 & W246		26. 6.86	
G-MNVX	Solar Wings Pegasus Flash 2	SW-WF-0107		27. 6.86	Canx 19.5.89 on sale to Spain.
G-MNVY	Solar Wings Pegasus Photon	SW-WP-0020		27. 6.86	Canx by CAA 24.1.95. (On rebuild 3/97)
G-MNVZ	Solar Wings Pegasus Photon	SW-WP-0021		27. 6.86	
G-MNWA	Southdown Raven X	2232/0167		26. 6.86	
G-MNWB	Thruster TST	086-118-UK-001		25. 6.86	
G-MNWC	Mainair Gemini/Flash 2	416-486-4 & W167		27. 6.86	Permit expired 7.10.95. Canx by CAA 20.10.97.
G-MNWD	Mainair Gemini/Flash 2	474-986-4 & W254		27. 6.86	
G-MNWE	Southdown Raven X	2232/0168		. .86R	NTU - Canx.
G-MNWF	Southdown Raven X	2232/0169		9. 7.86	Canx by CAA 18.2.92.
G-MNWG	Southdown Raven X	2232/0170		4. 8.86	
G-MNWH	Aerial Arts Alpha/130SX	130SX/319		9. 7.86	Canx 13.1.97 on sale to Greece.
G-MNWI	Mainair Gemini/Flash 2	478-986-4 & W264		9. 7.86	
G-MNWJ	Mainair Gemini/Flash 2	489-1086-4 & W283		9. 7.86	Canx 30.8.96 on sale to Iceland.
G-MNWK	CFM Shadow Srs.C	030		9. 7.86	
G-MNWL	Arbiter Svs Trike/Aerial Arts 130SX	130SX/333		23. 7.86	
G-MNWM	CFM Shadow Srs.B	K.016		9. 7.86	Canx as WFU 8.10.93.
G-MNWN	Mainair Gemini/Flash 2	475-986-4 & W256		15. 7.86	Canx by CAA 3.8.94. To Australia as T2-2745.
G-MNWO	Mainair Gemini/Flash 2	490-1086-4 & W287		15. 7.86	
G-MNWP	Solar Wings Pegasus/Flash 2	SW-TB-1083 & SW-WF-0113		4. 8.86	
G-MNWR	Medway Hybred 44XLR	23686/17		4. 8.86	
G-MNWS	Buchair Trike/Airwave Magic III	AWB-001		12. 8.86	Canx as destroyed 18.10.88.

Regn	Type	c/n	Previous identity	Regn date	Fate or immediate subsequent identity (if known)
G-MNWT	Southdown Raven	2122/0171		23. 7.86	Canx by CAA 7.8.96.
G-MNWU	Solar Wings Pegasus/Flash 2LC	SW-TE-0006 & SW-WF-0111		4. 8.86	
G-MNWV	Solar Wings Pegasus/Flash 2	SW-TB-1090 & SW-WF-0121		4. 8.86	
G-MNWW	Solar Wings Pegasus XL-R/Se	SW-TE-0008 & SW-WA-1005		8.10.86	(Active 3/97)
G-MNWX	Solar Wings Pegasus XL-R	SW-TB-1093 & SW-WA-1086		4. 8.86	
G-MNWY	CFM Shadow Srs.CD	K.021 & PFA/161-11130		28. 7.86	
G-MNWZ	Mainair Gemini/Flash 2	436-686-4 & W203		19. 8.86	
G-MNXA	Southdown Raven X	2232/0180		5. 8.86	
G-MNXB	Mainair Tri-Flyer/Solar Wings Photon	SW-WP-0022		29. 7.86	
G-MNXC	Aerial Arts Chaser/110SX	110SX/335		4. 8.86	
G-MNXD	Southdown Raven	2132/0173		13. 8.86	
G-MNXE	Southdown Raven X	2232/0202		7. 8.86	
G-MNXF	Southdown Raven	2132/0176		2. 9.86	
G-MNXG	Southdown Raven X	2232/0181		3. 9.86	
G-MNXH	Hometrike/La Mouette Azure	DSB-01		19. 8.86	Canx as WFU 25.4.90.
G-MNXI	Southdown Raven X	2232/0179		19. 8.86	
G-MNXJ	Medway Half Pint	14/7886		3. 9.86	Canx as CAA 17.1.95.
G-MNXK	Medway Half Pint	15/7886		3. 9.86	Canx by CAA 9.6.93.
G-MNXL	Medway Half Pint	16/7886		2. 9.86	Canx as destroyed 10.1.89.
G-MNXM	Medway Hybred 44XLR	30786/20		3. 9.86	Canx by CAA 6.12.93.
G-MNXN	Medway Hybred 44XLR	28786/18		3. 9.86	(Stored 7/97)
G-MNXO	Medway Hybred 44XLR	29786/19		3. 9.86	
G-MNXP	Solar Wings Pegasus Flash 2	SW-TB-1094 & SW-WF-0117		16. 9.86	
G-MNXR	Mainair Gemini/Flash 2	479-986-4 & W265		19. 8.86	
G-MNXS	Mainair Gemini/Flash 2	480-986-4 & W267		8. 9.86	Canx 27.10.88 on sale to Portugal.
G-MNXT	Mainair Gemini/Flash 2	481-986-4 & W268		19. 8.86	
G-MNXU	Mainair Gemini/Flash 2	482-1086-4 & W272		18. 8.86	
G-MNXV	Not allotted [Dupicated G-MNWZ]				
G-MNXW	Mainair Gemini/Flash 2	435-686-4 & W202		18. 8.86	Canx as destroyed 1.7.92.
G-MNXX	CFM Shadow Srs.CD	K.027		13. 8.86	
G-MNXY	Whittaker MW.5 Sorcerer	PFA/163-11140		13. 8.86	Canx as destroyed 25.9.96.
G-MNXZ	Whittaker MW.5 Sorcerer	PFA/163-11156		13. 8.86	
G-MNYA	Solar Wings Pegasus Flash 2	SW-TB-1098 & SW-WF-0119		3. 9.86	
G-MNYB	Solar Wings Pegasus XL-R	SW-TB-1096 & SW-WA-1089		8. 9.86	
G-MNYC	Solar Wings Pegasus XL-R	SW-TB-1097 & SW-WA-1090		3. 9.86	
G-MNYD	Aerial Arts Chaser/110SX	110SX/320		19. 8.86	
G-MNYE	Aerial Arts Chaser/110SX	110SX/321		19. 8.86	
G-MNYF	Aerial Arts Chaser/110SX	110SX/322		19. 8.86	
G-MNYG	Southdown Raven	2122/0172		19. 8.86	
G-MNYH	Southdown Puma Spirit	1121/0205		11. 9.86	Canx as destroyed 30.7.96.
G-MNYI	Southdown Raven X	2232/0211		3. 9.86	
G-MNYJ	Mainair Gemini/Flash 2	485-1086-4 & W275		8. 9.86	
G-MNYK	Mainair Gemini/Flash 2	494-1086-4 & W296		11. 9.86	
G-MNYL	Southdown Raven X	2232/0195		2. 9.86	
G-MNYM	Southdown Raven X	2232/0196		2. 9.86	
G-MNYN	Southdown Raven X	2232/0197		2. 9.86	Canx 25.10.89 on sale to Zimbabwe.
G-MNYO	Southdown Raven X	2232/0198		2. 9.86	Canx 15.6.87 on sale to West Germany.
G-MNYP	Southdown Raven X	2232/0207		3. 9.86	
G-MNYR	La Mouette Cosmos	C.4416		. .86R	NTU - Canx.
G-MNYS	Southdown Raven X	2232/0208		8. 9.86	
G-MNYT	Solar Wings Pegasus XL-R	SW-TB-1099 & SW-WA-1091		11. 9.86	(Damaged mid.97) (Stored 1/98)
G-MNYU	Solar Wings Pegasus XL-R/Se	SW-TB-1100 & SW-WA-1092		16. 9.86	
G-MNYV	Solar Wings Pegasus XL-R/Se	SW-TB-1101 & SW-WA-1093		11. 9.86	
G-MNYW	Solar Wings Pegasus XL-R	SW-WA-1094		11. 9.86	
G-MNYX	Solar Wings Pegasus XL-R/LC (See comments on G-MMKG)	SW-TE-0009 & SW-WA-1095		19. 9.86	
G-MNYY	Solar Wings Pegasus Flash 2	SW-WF-0123		8. 9.86	Canx by CAA 6.10.93. (Wing to LN-YDI).

Regn	Type	c/n	Previous identity	Regn date	Fate or immediate subsequent identity (if known)
G-MNYZ	Solar Wings Pegasus Flash 2	SW-WF-0114		11. 9.86	
G-MNZA	Solar Wings Pegasus Flash 2 (Mainair Alpha c/n W127-1185-1 - see G-MNJP)	SW-TB-1103 & SW-WF-0120		3.10.86	(Active 10/97)
G-MNZB	Mainair Gemini/Flash 2	483-1086-4 & W273		8. 9.86	
G-MNZC	Mainair Gemini/Flash 2	484-1086-4 & W274		16. 9.86	
G-MNZD	Mainair Gemini/Flash 2	493-1086-4 & W295		8. 9.86	(Stored 9/96)
G-MNZE	Mainair Gemini/Flash 2 (Wing regd as W279 - see G-MTEK)	495-1086-4 & W297		8. 9.86	
G-MNZF	Mainair Gemini/Flash 2	496-1186-4 & W291		8. 9.86	
G-MNZG	Aerial Arts 110SX/Chaser	110SX/377		18. 9.86	Canx by CAA 23.6.97.
G-MNZH	AMF Chevvron 2-32	CH.003		23. 9.86	Canx as WFU 1.10.93. To PH-1W9.
G-MNZI	Prone Power Mk.2/Solar Wings Typhoon	PP-01		22. 9.86	
G-MNZJ	CFM Shadow Srs.BD	033		19. 9.86	
G-MNZK	Solar Wings Pegasus XL-R/Se	SW-WA-1096		24. 9.86	
G-MNZL	Solar Wings Pegasus XL-R	SW-TB-1106 & SW-WA-1097		1.10.86	(Stored 6/96)
G-MNZM	Solar Wings Pegasus XL-R	SW-WA-1100		30.10.86	Canx by CAA 6.12.88.
G-MNZN	Solar Wings Pegasus Flash 2	SW-WF-0124		23. 9.86	Canx by CAA 28.2.92.
G-MNZO	Solar Wings Pegasus Flash 2	SW-TE-0012 & SW-WF-0125		30. 9.86	
G-MNZP	CFM Shadow Srs.BD	K.039 & PFA/161-11206		19. 9.86	
G-MNZR	CFM Shadow Srs.BD	040		19. 9.86	
G-MNZS	Aerial Arts 130SX/Alpha	130SX/376		23. 9.86	
G-MNZT	Hornet Dual Trainer/Southdown Raven	HRWA 0059 & 2000/0224		21.10.86	To 9H-ABI. Canx 15.12.87.
G-MNZU	Eurowing Goldwing	EW-88		24. 9.86	
G-MNZV	Southdown Raven X	2232/0219		27.10.86	CofA lapsed 15.12.95. Canx as destroyed 25.11.96. To G-RAVE 12/98.
G-MNZW	Southdown Raven X	2232/0220		17.10.86	Canx by CAA 15.3.99 (- with c/n 1121/0220 !).
G-MNZX	Southdown Raven X	2232/0221		10.10.86	Canx by CAA 7.8.96.
G-MNZY	Mainair Tri-Flyer 330/Airwave Nimrod	078-14682		17.10.86	
G-MNZZ	CFM Shadow Srs.CD	036		19. 9.86	
G-MOAC	Beechcraft F33A Bonanza	CE-1349	N1563N	25. 5.89	
G-MOAK	Schempp-Hirth Nimbus 3DM	19/46		23. 5.91	
G-MOAT	Beechcraft 200 Super King Air	BB-462	N27CD N27C/N2063T	14. 5.87	To N220TT 3/94. Canx 9.3.94.
G-MOBI	Aerospatiale AS.355F1 Twin Squirrel	5260	G-MUFF G-CORR	11.11.93	
G-MOBL	Embraer EMB.110P1 Bandeirante	110-211	(G-BGCS) PT-GMD	2. 8.79	To G-OFLT 12/90. Canx.
G-MOBZ	Aerospatiale AS.355F1 Twin Squirrel	5185	N107KF N5799R	11. 9.96	To G-BWZC 11/96. Canx.
G-MOET	Partenavia P.68 Victor	13	G-HPVC OH-PVB	11. 5.93	Canx 11.11.96 on sale to Morocco. To F-WQHL 12/96P / F-OHCT 8/97.
G-MOFB	Cameron O-120 HAFB	4275		13. 1.98	
G-MOFF	Cameron O-77 HAFB	2040		27. 7.89	
G-MOFZ	Cameron O-90 HAFB	3350		7. 9.94	
G-MOGG	Reims Cessna F.172N	1904	G-BHDY (LN-HOH)	9. 6.80	To D-ERBF 12/95. Canx 1.11.95.
G-MOGI	American Aviation AA-5A Cheetah	AA5A-0630	G-BFMU	1. 5.86	
G-MOGY	Robinson R-22 Beta	0899		23.11.88	
G-MOHR	Cameron Sarotti 105SS HAFB	1894		22.12.88	Canx as WFU 24.1.92.
G-MOHS	PA-31-350 Navajo Chieftain	31-8152115	G-BWOC N40898	29. 4.96	
G-MOKE	Cameron V-77 HAFB	3686		4.10.95	
G-MOLE	Taylor JT.2 Titch	PFA/60-10725		20. 1.87	(Under construction at Standalone Farm, Meppershall 10/90)
G-MOLI	Cameron A-250 HAFB	3429		26. 1.95	
G-MOLL	PA-32-301T Turbo Saratoga	32-8024040	N82535	25. 3.91	
G-MOLY	PA-23-160 Apache	23-1686	EI-BAW G-APFV/EI-ALK	7. 6.79	
G-MONA	Socata MS.880B Rallye Club	1218	G-AWJK	5. 4.79	To EI-CIA 4/93. Canx 21.4.93.
G-MONB	Boeing 757-2T7ER (Line No. 15)	22780		7. 3.83	
G-MONC	Boeing 757-2T7ER (Line No. 18)	22781	PH-AHO G-MONC/D-ABNY/G-MONC/EC-211/G-MONC	15. 4.83	
G-MOND	Boeing 757-2T7 (Line No. 19)	22960	D-ABNZ G-MOND	28. 4.83	
G-MONE	Boeing 757-2T7ER (Line No. 56)	23293		27. 2.85	

Regn	Type	c/n	Previous identity	Regn date	Fate or immediate subsequent identity (if known)
G-MONF	Boeing 737-3Y0	23497	C-FPWE	23. 4.86	To N665WN 11/94. Canx 14.11.94.
	(Line No. 1227)		G-MONF/C-FPWE/G-MONF/C-FPWE/G-MONF		
G-MONG	Boeing 737-3Y0	23498	C-GPWG	23. 4.86	To G-EZYA 5/96. Canx.
	(Line No. 1233)		G-MONG/C-GPWG/G-MONG		
G-MONH	Boeing 737-3Y0	23685		19. 2.87	To F-GIXJ 4/95. Canx 27.4.95.
	(Line No. 1357)				
G-MONI	Monnett Moni	PFA/142-10925		12. 1.84	
G-MONJ	Boeing 757-2T7ER	24104		26. 2.88	
	(Line No. 170)				
G-MONK	Boeing 757-2T7ER	24105		26. 2.88	
	(Line No. 172)				
G-MONL	Boeing 737-3Y0	24255		24.10.88	To XA-RJP. Canx 20.12.91.
	(Line No. 1625)				
G-MONM	Boeing 737-3Y0	24256		4.11.88	To EC-542/EC-FVJ 1/94. Canx 26.1.94.
	(Line No. 1629)				
G-MONN	Boeing 737-33A	24029		4.10.88	To VH-CZX 11/93. Canx 22.11.93.
	(Line No. 1601)				
G-MONO	Taylor JT.1 Monoplane			18. 8.78	Canx by CAA 2.9.91.
		FDH.1 & PFA/1424			
G-MONP	Boeing 737-33A	24028		14.10.88	To F-GIXK 3/95. Canx 30.3.95.
	(Line No. 1599)				
G-MONR	Airbus A.300B4-605R	540	VH-YMJ	15. 3.90	
			G-MONR/F-WWAT		
G-MONS	Airbus A.300B4-605R	556	VH-YMK	17. 4.90	
			G-MONS/F-WWAY		
G-MONT(1)	Airbus A.300B4-605R	604	F-WWAX	. .90R	NTU - To G-MAJS 4/91. Canx.
G-MONT(2)	Boeing 737-33A	24026	F-GFUC	26.10.90	To F-GHVM 5/91. Canx 15.5.91.
	(Line No. 1595)				
G-MONU(1)	Airbus A.300B4-605R	605	F-WWAY	. .90R	NTU - To G-OJMR 5/91. Canx.
G-MONU(2)	Boeing 737-33A	24025	F-GFUB	26.10.90	To F-GHVO 4/92. Canx 29.4.92.
	(Line No. 1556)				
G-MONV	Boeing 737-33A	25033		5. 4.91	To OY-MBN 4/96. Canx 12.4.96.
	(Line No. 2025)				
G-MONW	Airbus A.320-212	391	F-WWDO	24. 2.93	
G-MONX	Airbus A.320-212	392	F-WWDR	19. 3.93	
G-MONY	Airbus A.320-212	279	C-GVNY	11. 1.93	Restored as C-FLSF 5/99. Canx 20.5.99.
			G-MONY/C-GVNY/G-MONY/C-GVNY/G-MONY/C-FLSF/F-WWDU		
G-MONZ	Airbus A.320-212	446	C-FTDI	28.10.93	
			G-MONZ/F-WWDJ		
G-MOON	Mooney M.20K (252TSE)	25-1143	N252BT	22. 6.88	
G-MOOR	Socata TB-10 Tobago	82	G-MILK	23. 7.91	
G-MOOS	Hunting-Percival P.56 Provost T.1		G-BGKA	5. 4.91	
		PAC/F/335	8041M/XF690		
G-MORE	Schleicher ASH-26E	26026	BGA.4075	16.11.95	To D-KHFP 3/99. Canx 8.1.99.
G-MORL	Maule MX-7-180	11069C		1. 5.90	To F-GICZ 10/92. Canx 28.5.92.
G-MORR	Aerospatiale AS.350B Ecureuil	1190	G-BHIU	15. 1.80	To G-NOEI 1/84. Canx.
G-MOSI	DH.98 Mosquito TT.35	-	N98DH	10.11.81	Permit expired 17.12.84. Sold to USAF Museum in 2/85 and
			N9797/G-ASKA/RS709		flown to USA. Canx by CAA 21.1.87. (On display
					Wright Patterson AFB, Ohio, USA)
G-MOSS	Beechcraft 95-D55 Baron	TE-548	G-AWAD	12. 6.95	
G-MOSY	Cameron O-84 HAFB	2315	EI-CAO	17. 4.96	
G-MOTA	Bell 206B JetRanger III	4494	N81521	20.10.98	
G-MOTE	Cessna 402B	402B-1046	SE-GMG	18. 4.86	To EI-BUK 10/86. Canx 24.10.86.
			(N98683)		
G-MOTH	DH.82A Tiger Moth	85340	7035M	31. 1.78	
	(Rebuilt to DH.82 standard)		DE306		
G-MOTI	Robin DR.400/500	0006		23.11.98	
G-MOTO	PA-24-180 Comanche	24-3239	G-EDHE	24. 3.87	
			N51867/G-ASFH/EI-AMM		
G-MOTT	Light Aero Avid Speed Wing			29. 5.92	
		PFA/189-11738			
G-MOUL	Maule M.6-235C Super Rocket	7518C		1. 5.90	
G-MOUR	Folland Gnat T.1	FL.596	8624M	16. 5.90	
			XS102		
G-MOUS	Cameron Mickey 90SS HAFB	1553		15.10.87	Canx by CAA 26.2.98.
G-MOVE	PA-60-601P Aerostar		OO-PKB	5. 1.79	
		61P-0593-7963263	G-MOVE/(N8144J)		
G-MOVI	PA-32R-301 Saratoga SP	32R-8313029	G-MARI	6. 2.89	
			N8248H		
G-MOXY	Cessna 441 Conquest II	441-0154	G-BHLN	16. 9.83	Fatal crash into trees on approach to Blackbushe on
			(N2628Z)		26.4.87. Canx as destroyed 28.6.89.
G-MOZY	DH.98 Mosquito Scale Replica	AE.1		13.11.78	Canx by CAA 2.9.91.
	(3/5ths scale replica, 2 x 120hp Lycomings)				
G-MOZZ	Avions Mudry CAP.10B	256		30.10.90	
G-MPBH	Reims Cessna FA.152 Aerobat	0374	G-FLIC	8.12.88	
			G-BILV		
G-MPBI	Cessna 310R II	310R-0584	F-GEBB	21. 7.97	
			HB-LMD/N87473		
G-MPCD	Airbus A.320-212	379	C-FTDU	14. 3.94	
			G-MPCD/C-FTDU/G-MPCD/C-FTDU/G-MPCD/C-FTDU/G-MPCD/F-WWDY		
G-MPCU	Cessna 402B	402B-0823	SE-IRL	16. 2.88	To N98AR 6/95. Canx 12.5.95.
			OO-TAT/(OO-SEL)/N3946C		

Regn	Type	c/n	Previous identity	Regn date	Fate or immediate subsequent identity (if known)
G-MPWA	Wassmer WA.54 Atlantic	144	F-GBIS F-OBUS(2)	4.12.79	NTU - Not imported. To F-GCJU 7/80. Canx 27.2.80.
G-MPWH	Rotorway Exec	01 & 3579		22. 6.90	
G-MPWI	Robin HR.100/210 Safari	163	F-GBTY F-ODFA/F-BUPD	3. 3.80	
G-MPWT	PA-34-220T Seneca III (Originally built as c/n 34-8233163)	34-8333068	N4294X N9539N/N8218K	26. 9.88	
G-MRAJ	MDH Hughes 369E (500E)	0010E	N51946	19. 3.98	
G-MRCI	Sequoia Falco F.8L (Originally regd with c/n CG.3) (built by C.W.Gutzman)	CG-B	N11ST	23.10.92	To N241TE 3/97 as a Gutzman Falco F.8. Canx 15.4.96.
G-MRED	Elmwood CA-05 Christavia Mk.1	PFA/185-12935		20. 8.96	
G-MRFB	HS.125 Srs.3B	25132	G-AZVS OY-DKP	14. 8.85	To G-OCBA 5/89. Canx.
G-MRJV	PA-28R-201 Arrow IV	28R-7918098	PH-WEL N2090Y	24. 2.82	To G-IHDH 4/83. Canx.
G-MRKT	Lindstrand LBL-90A HAFB	037		7. 6.93	
G-MRLN	Sky 240-24 HAFB	161		4. 8.99	
G-MRMR	PA-31-350 Navajo Chieftain	31-7952092	OH-PRE(2) G-WROX/G-BNZI/N3517T	21. 8.97	
G-MROC	Cyclone Pegasus Quantum 15	7498		22. 1.99	
G-MRPP	PA-34-220T Seneca III	34-8233134	N8202P	8. 5.90	To 5B-CJI 7/99. Canx 7.7.99.
G-MRRV	Avro 748 Srs.1A/106	1549	G-ARRW EI-BSE/G-ARRW	28. 2.92	To 9N-ACM. Canx 10.11.92.
G-MRSL	Robin DR.400/180 Regent	2106	G-BUAP	14. 4.92	To F-GOVD 1/96. Canx 18.12.95.
G-MRSN	Robinson R-22 Beta	1654		21. 1.91	
G-MRST	PA-28RT-201 Arrow IV	28R-7918068	9H-AAU 5B-CEC/N3019U	27.11.86	
G-MRTC	Cessna 550 Citation II (Unit No.597)	550-0597	G-SSOZ N13027	13. 4.93	To N24EP. Canx 24.10.96.
G-MRTI	Cameron Eagle 110SS HAFB	3394		23. 1.95	W/o on first flight in Australia in 1995. Canx as destroyed 3.12.97.
G-MRTN	Socata TB-10 Tobago	62	G-BHET	9. 7.98	
G-MRTY	Cameron N-77 HAFB	1008		24. 4.84	
G-MSAL	Morane-Saulnier MS.733 Alcyon	143	F-BLXV French Mil F-TFVF/F-TEBL	16. 6.93	(Stored 10/97)
G-MSDJ	Aerospatiale AS.350B1 Ecureuil	2174	G-BPOH	28. 3.89	
G-MSDS	Cessna 404 Titan Ambassador II	404-0239	N88725	5. 1.79	Canx 23.10.86 on sale to USA. To D-IEBB.
G-MSES	Cessna 150L	150-72747	N1447Q	9.11.95	To EI-CMV 5/96. Canx 13.5.96.
G-MSFC	PA-38-112 Tomahawk II	38-81A0067	N25735	11. 5.90	
G-MSFT	PA-28-161 Warrior II	28-8416093	G-MUMS N118AV	2. 4.97	
G-MSFY	HS.125 Srs.700B	257200	G-5-14	10. 5.83	Canx by CAA 29.6.89. To VR-BMD 7/89.
G-MSIX	Glaser Dirks DG-800B	8-156B80		21. 4.99	
G-MSKA	Boeing 737-5L9 (Line No. 1919)	24859	OY-MAC (OY-MMZ)	18.10.96	
G-MSKB	Boeing 737-5L9 (Line No. 1961)	24928	OY-MAD (OY-MMO)	12.11.96	
G-MSKC	Boeing 737-5L9 (Line No. 2038)	25066	OY-MAE	3.12.96	
G-MSKD	Boeing 737-5L9 (Line No. 1816)	24778	HL7230 OY-MAA/(OY-MMW)	14. 1.98	
G-MSKE	Boeing 737-5L9 (Line No. 2788)	28084	OY-APB	4. 1.99	
G-MSKJ	BAe Jetstream Srs.4100	41034	N434JX G-BWIH/VH-SMH/G-4-034	4. 7.96	
G-MSKK	Canadair RJ200ER Regional Jet (CL.600-2B19)	7226	C-GCBS C-FMKZ	25. 5.98	
G-MSKL	Canadair RJ200ER Regional Jet (CL.600-2B19)	7247	C-FMML	1. 7.98	
G-MSKM	Canadair RJ200ER Regional Jet (CL.600-2B19)	7248	C-FMMN	28. 7.98	
G-MSKN	Canadair RJ200ER Regional Jet (CL.600-2B19)	7283		14. 1.99	
G-MSKO	Canadair RJ200ER Regional Jet (CL.600-2B19)	7299	C-FMOS	19. 3.99	
G-MSKP	Canadair RJ200ER Regional Jet (CL.600-2B19)	7329	C-FMOS	22. 7.99	
G-MSKR	Canadair RJ200ER Regional Jet (CL.600-2B19)	73..		. 9.99	
G-MSLY	Cessna 550 Citation II (Unit No.030)	550-0030	G-FERY G-DJBI/(N3249M)	20. 9.88	To N64CC. Canx 11.1.89.
G-MSMS	Eurocopter AS.350B2 Ecureuil	3119		21. 8.98	
G-MSOO	Revolution Helicopters Mini-500	0016		16.10.95	(For sale complete 10/97)
G-MSSA	PBN BN-2T-4R MSSA Islander	2143		21. 8.91	To N360TL 1/93. Canx 15.12.92.
G-MSTC	American Aviation AA-5A Cheetah	AA5A-0833	G-BIJT N26950	30. 1.95	
G-MSTG	North American P-51D-25-NT Mustang	124-48271	NZ2427 45-11518	2. 9.97	
G-MTAA	Solar Wings Pegasus XL-R	SW-TB-1108 & SW-WA-1102		15.10.86	

Regn	Type	c/n	Previous identity	Regn date	Fate or immediate subsequent identity (if known)
G-MTAB	Mainair Gemini/Flash 2	492-1086-4 & W290		8.10.86	(Stored 1/98)
G-MTAC	Mainair Gemini/Flash 2	486-1086-4 & W278		15.10.86	
G-MTAD	Mainair Gemini Skyflash	503-1186-4 & W306		15.10.86	Canx as WFU 2.7.96.
G-MTAE	Mainair Gemini/Flash 2	500-1186-4 & W302		15.10.86	
G-MTAF	Mainair Gemini/Flash 2	499-1186-4 & W301		15.10.86	
G-MTAG	Mainair Gemini/Flash 2	487-1086-4 & W281		15.10.86	
G-MTAH	Mainair Gemini/Flash 2	488-1086-4 & W282		16.10.86	
G-MTAI	Solar Wings Pegasus XL-R	SW-TB-1109 & SW-WA-1103		14.10.86	(Extant 4/97)
G-MTAJ	Solar Wings Pegasus XL-R	SW-WA-1104		16.10.86	
G-MTAK	Solar Wings Pegasus XL-R	SW-WA-1105		21.10.86	Canx by CAA 23.12.92.
G-MTAL	Solar Wings Pegasus Photon	SW-WP-0023		15.10.86	
G-MTAM	Solar Wings Pegasus Flash 2	SW-WF-0126		21.10.86	To A2-UAJ 9/91. Canx 5.9.91.
G-MTAN	Bragg Dual Seat/Aeronautica Costa Blanca	A-03135274		13.10.86	Canx by CAA 4.4.91.
G-MTAO	Solar Wings Pegasus XL-R	SW-TB-1107 & SW-WA-1107		21.10.86	
G-MTAP	Southdown Raven X	2232/0225		15.10.86	
G-MTAR	Mainair Gemini/Flash 2	504-1286-4 & W307		16.10.86	Canx by CAA 16.2.93.
G-MTAS	Whittaker MW.5B Sorcerer	PFA/163-11166		14.10.86	
G-MTAT	Solar Wings Pegasus XL-R	SW-TB-1113 & SW-WA-1108		28.10.86	
G-MTAU	Solar Wings Pegasus XL-R	SW-WA-1109		21.10.86	Canx 2.8.93 on sale to Italy.
G-MTAV	Solar Wings Pegasus XL-R	SW-TB-1115 & SW-WA-1110		21.10.86	(Stored Hougham, Lincs 9/96)
G-MTAW	Solar Wings Pegasus XL-R	SW-WA-1111		21.10.86	
G-MTAX	Solar Wings Pegasus XL-R	SW-TB-1117 & SW-WA-1112		27.10.86	
G-MTAY	Solar Wings Pegasus XL-R	SW-TB-1118 & SW-WA-1113		27.10.86	
G-MTAZ	Solar Wings Pegasus XL-R	SW-TB-1119 & SW-WA-1114		28.10.86	
G-MTBA	Solar Wings Pegasus XL-R	SW-WA-1115		27.10.86	(Stored 5/97)
G-MTBB	Southdown Raven X	2232/0226		16.10.86	
G-MTBC	Mainair Gemini/Flash 2	501-1186-4 & W303		16.10.86	(Trike stored 5/96) Canx by CAA 7.8.96.
G-MTBD	Mainair Gemini/Flash 2 (Wing regd as W229)	498-1186-4 & W299		16.10.86	
G-MTBE	CFM Shadow Srs.CD	K.035		16.10.86	
G-MTBF	Ultraflight Mirage Mk.II	101		17.10.86	Canx 27.4.92 on sale to Ireland.
G-MTBG	Mainair Gemini/Flash 2	506-1286-4 & W309		27.10.86	
G-MTBH	Mainair Gemini/Flash 2	524-187-5 & W327		28.10.86	
G-MTBI	Mainair Gemini/Flash 2	508-1286-4 & W311		27.10.86	
G-MTBJ	Mainair Gemini/Flash 2	509-1286-4 & W312		27.10.86	
G-MTBK	Southdown Raven X (Wing reportedly ex.G-MNNU)	2232/0230		28.10.86	
G-MTBL	Solar Wings Pegasus XL-R	SW-TB-1121 & SW-WA-1117		6.11.86	
G-MTBM	Mainair Tri-Flyer 250/Airwave Nimrod	042-231281		8. 1.87	Canx as destroyed 6.6.95.
G-MTBN	Southdown Raven X	2232/0227		28.10.86	
G-MTBO	Southdown Raven X	2232/0233		28.10.86	
G-MTBP	Aerotech MW.5B Sorcerer	SR102-R440B-02		28.10.86	(Stored 5/96)
G-MTBR	Aerotech MW.5B Sorcerer	SR102-R440B-03		20. 1.87	
G-MTBS	Aerotech MW.5B Sorcerer	SR102-R440B-04		27.10.86	
G-MTBT	Aerotech MW.5B Sorcerer (Wings possibly from G-MWGI)	BMAA/HB/027 & SR102-R440B-05		10. 4.87	Canx by CAA 7.8.96. (Stored 7/96)
G-MTBU	Solar Wings Pegasus XL-R	SW-WA-1118		13.11.86	Canx as WFU 5.6.95.
G-MTBV	Solar Wings Pegasus XL-R	SW-WA-1119		6.11.86	
G-MTBW	Mainair Gemini/Flash 2	520-187-5 & W322		6.11.86	Fatal crash at Old Airfield, Aldridge on 15.4.97. Canx by CAA 23.2.98.
G-MTBX	Mainair Gemini/Flash 2	510-1286-4 & W313		6.11.86	

Regn	Type	c/n	Previous identity	Regn date	Fate or immediate subsequent identity (if known)
G-MTBY	Mainair Gemini/Flash 2	507-1286-4 & W310		6.11.86	
G-MTBZ	Southdown Raven X (Regd with c/n 0232/0232)	2232/0232		10.11.86	
G-MTCA	CFM Shadow Srs.C	K.011		6.11.86	(Damaged mid .97)
G-MTCB	Noble Hardman Snowbird III	SB-004		21.11.86	Canx 19.1.87 on sale to Malaysia.
G-MTCC	Mainair Gemini/Flash 2	497-1186-4 & W298		13.11.86	
G-MTCD	Southdown Raven X	2232/0236		21.11.86	Canx as WFU 6.4.98.
G-MTCE	Mainair Gemini/Flash 2	511-1286-4 & W314		2.12.86	
G-MTCF	Hiway Skytrike/Farnell Flexwing	01		17.11.86	Canx as destroyed 10.5.90.
G-MTCG	Solar Wings Pegasus XL-R/Se	SW-TB-1125 & SW-WA-1123		16.12.86	(Stored 9/97)
G-MTCH	Solar Wings Pegasus XL-R	SW-TB-1126 & SW-WA-1124		28.11.86	
G-MTCI	Aerial Arts Chaser S	429		3.12.86	Canx as destroyed 12.10.88.
G-MTCJ	Aerial Arts Avenger	430		3.12.86	Canx by CAA 7.8.96.
G-MTCK	Solar Wings Pegasus Flash 2	SW-WF-0127		11.12.86	
G-MTCL	Southdown Raven X	2232/0238		. .86R	NTU - Canx.
G-MTCM	Southdown Raven X	2232/0239		11.12.86	
G-MTCN	Solar Wings Pegasus XL-R	SW-WA-1126		16.12.86	Canx by CAA 14.6.93.
G-MTCO	Solar Wings Pegasus XL-R	SW-TB-1129 & SW-WA-1127		7. 1.87	
G-MTCP	Aerial Arts Chaser/110SX	110SX/476		16.12.86	
G-MTCR	Solar Wings Pegasus XL-R	SW-WA-1128		16.12.86	
G-MTCS	CFM Shadow Srs.BD	046		16.12.86	Canx as destroyed 20.4.88.
G-MTCT	CFM Shadow Srs.CD	042		16.12.86	
G-MTCU	Mainair Gemini/Flash 2A	451-1286-4 & W228		5. 1.87	
G-MTCV	Microflight Spectrum	005		7. 1.87	Canx as WFU 2.6.94.
G-MTCW	Mainair Gemini/Flash 2	502-1186-4 & W304		5. 1.87	
G-MTCX	Solar Wings Pegasus XL-R	SW-TB-1131 & SW-WA-1129		9. 1.87	
G-MTCY	Southdown Raven X	2232/0256		5. 1.87	Canx by CAA 10.9.93.
G-MTCZ	Ultrasports Tripacer 250/Solar Wings Storm	80-00138		22. 1.87	Canx as WFU 3.8.94. (C/n also quoted as 20-00138)
G-MTDA	Hornet Dual Trainer/Southdown Raven	HRWA 0060 & 2000/0245		5. 1.87	
G-MTDB	Owen Pola Mk.1	POLA/X001/001		19.12.86	No Permit believed issued. Canx by CAA 16.2.99.
G-MTDC	Owen Pola Mk.1	POLA/X001/002		19.12.86	No Permit believed issued. Canx by CAA 16.2.99.
G-MTDD	Aerial Arts Chaser/110SX (Originally regd as c/n 110SX/437)	110SX/137		26. 1.87	
G-MTDE	Aerial Arts Chaser/110SX	110SX/438		5. 1.87	(Damaged late .95)
G-MTDF	Mainair Gemini/Flash 2	515-287-5 & W319		5. 1.87	
G-MTDG	Solar Wings Pegasus XL-R/Se	SW-WA-1130		20. 1.87	(Stored 9/97)
G-MTDH	Solar Wings Pegasus XL-R	SW-TB-1133 & SW-WA-1131		22. 1.87	
G-MTDI	Solar Wings Pegasus XL-R/Se	SW-TB-1134 & SW-WA-1132		22. 1.87	(Stored 9/97)
G-MTDJ	Medway Hybred 44XL	1587/23		20. 1.87	
G-MTDK	Aerotech MW.5B Sorcerer	SR102-R440B-06		22. 1.87	
G-MTDL	Solar Wings Pegasus XL-R/Se	SW-WA-1133		22. 1.87	Canx as WFU 21.4.97.
G-MTDM	Mainair Gemini/Flash 2	514-187-5 & W318		20. 1.87	DBR in crash at the Haywood strip, near Callow, 3 miles SW of Hereford on 25.1.92. Canx as WFU 12.11.93.
G-MTDN	Ultraflight Lazair IIIE	A465/002		22. 1.87	
G-MTDO	Eipper Quicksilver MXII	1124		27. 2.87	
G-MTDP	Solar Wings Pegasus XL-R	SW-TB-1136 & SW-WA-1134		22. 1.87	
G-MTDR	Mainair Gemini/Flash 2	516-287-5 & W276		26. 1.87	
G-MTDS	Solar Wings Pegasus Photon	SW-WP-0024		29. 1.87	(Stored 5/97)
G-MTDT	Solar Wings Pegasus XL-R	SW-TB-1137 & SW-WA-1135		2. 2.87	
G-MTDU	CFM Shadow Srs.CD	K.037		26. 1.87	
G-MTDV	Solar Wings Pegasus XL-R	SW-WA-1136		3. 2.87	
G-MTDW	Mainair Gemini/Flash 2	517-387-5 & W212		2. 2.87	
G-MTDX	CFM Shadow Srs.CD	K.043		10. 2.87	
G-MTDY	Mainair Gemini/Flash 2	513-187-5 & W317		11. 2.87	
G-MTDZ	Eipper Quicksilver MXII	2075		13. 2.87	Canx by CAA 3.8.94.
G-MTEA	Solar Wings Pegasus XL-R	SW-WA-1138		16. 2.87	Canx by CAA 15.2.94.
G-MTEB	Solar Wings Pegasus XL-R	SW-WA-1139		9. 2.87	
G-MTEC	Solar Wings Pegasus XL-R	SW-TB-1142 & SW-WA-1140		9. 2.87	(Stored 6/97)

Regn	Type	c/n	Previous identity	Regn date	Fate or immediate subsequent identity (if known)
G-MTED	Solar Wings Pegasus XL-R	SW-WA-1141		9. 2.87	
G-MTEE	Solar Wings Pegasus XL-R	SW-TB-1144 & SW-WA-1142		13. 2.87	
	(C/n plate incorrectly shows SW-WA-1144 & SW-WA-1142)(New wing? - see G-MTLG)				
G-MTEF	Solar Wings Pegasus XL-R	SW-WA-1143		13. 2.87	Canx as WFU 2.8.96.
G-MTEG	Mainair Gemini/Flash 2	519-387-5 & W261		13. 2.87	Canx by CAA 4.1.93.
G-MTEH	Mainair Gemini/Flash 2	521-387-5 & W262		13. 2.87	
G-MTEI	Mainair Gemini/Flash 2	440-287-5 & W269		18. 2.87	Canx to RAE (Military) 15.10.87.
G-MTEJ	Mainair Gemini/Flash 2	522-387-5 & W277		18. 2.87	
G-MTEK	Mainair Gemini/Flash 2	523-387-5 & W279		3. 3.87	
G-MTEL	Mainair Gemini/Flash 2	525-487-5 & W280		18. 2.87	Canx by CAA 7.8.96.
G-MTEM	Mainair Gemini/Flash 2	526-487-5 & W284		25. 2.87	Canx by CAA 4.7.96.
G-MTEN	Mainair Gemini/Flash 2	527-487-5 & W285		25. 2.87	
G-MTEO	Midlands Ultralights Sirocco 377GB	MU-019		27. 2.87	Canx by CAA 19.7.95. (Stored 8/96)
G-MTEP	Midlands Ultralights Sirocco 377GB	MU-018		25. 2.87	Canx as destroyed 15.10.87.
G-MTER	Solar Wings Pegasus XL-R/Se	SW-TB-1146 & SW-WA-1144		19. 2.87	
G-MTES	Solar Wings Pegasus XL-R	SW-TB-1147 & SW-WA-1145		19. 2.87	
G-MTET	Solar Wings Pegasus XL-R	SW-WA-1146		19. 2.87	
G-MTEU	Solar Wings Pegasus XL-R/Se	SW-WA-1147		19. 2.87	
G-MTEV	Solar Wings Pegasus XL-R	SW-WA-1148		19. 2.87	Canx as destroyed 27.7.98.
G-MTEW	Solar Wings Pegasus XL-R/Se	SW-TB-1151 & SW-WA-1149		19. 2.87	
G-MTEX	Solar Wings Pegasus XL-R	SW-TB-1152 & SW-WA-1150		19. 2.87	
G-MTEY	Mainair Gemini/Flash 2	518-387-5 & W217		20. 2.87	
G-MTEZ	Ultraflight Lazair IIIE	A950/004		23. 2.87	Canx by CAA 7.9.94.
G-MTFA	Solar Wings Pegasus XL-R	SW-TE-0014 & SW-WA-1156		24. 2.87	
G-MTFB	Solar Wings Pegasus XL-R	SW-WA-1157		24. 2.87	
G-MTFC	Medway Hybred 44XLR	22087/24		23. 3.87	
G-MTFD	Hodgson Trike/Hiway Demon	MAH-01		27. 2.87	Canx as WFU 9.4.90.
G-MTFE	Solar Wings Pegasus XL-R	SW-TB-1157 & SW-WA-1155		6. 3.87	
G-MTFF	Mainair Gemini/Flash 2	528-487-5 & W286		12. 3.87	
G-MTFG	AMF Chevvron 2-32C	CH.004		9. 3.87	
G-MTFH	Aerotech MW.5B Sorcerer	SR102-R440B-07		5. 3.87	To EI-CTL 5/99. Canx 19.4.99.
G-MTFI	Mainair Gemini/Flash 2	531-487-5 & W289		12. 3.87	
G-MTFJ	Mainair Gemini/Flash 2	532-487-5 & W320		12. 3.87	
G-MTFK	Moult Trike/Flexiform Striker	DIM-01		23. 3.87	Canx by CAA 13.6.90. (Stored 7/97)
G-MTFL	Ultraflight Lazair IIIE	A466/003		12. 3.87	
G-MTFM	Solar Wings Pegasus XL-R	SW-WA-1158		13. 3.87	
G-MTFN	Whittaker MW.5 Sorcerer	PFA/163-11207		13. 3.87	
G-MTFO	Solar Wings Pegasus XL-R/Se	SW-TB 1159 & SW-WA-1159		18. 3.87	
G-MTFP	Solar Wings Pegasus XL-R	SW-TB-1160 & SW-WA-1160		18. 3.87	
G-MTFR	Solar Wings Pegasus XL-R/Se	SW-TB-1161 & SW-WA-1161		18. 3.87	
G-MTFS	Solar Wings Pegasus XL-R	SW-WA-1162		18. 3.87	Canx as WFU 15.9.92.
G-MTFT	Solar Wings Pegasus XL-R	SW-WA-1163		18. 3.87	
G-MTFU	CFM Shadow Srs.BD	K.034		18. 3.87	
G-MTFV	Not allotted.				
G-MTFW	Mainair Gemini/Flash 2	533-487-5 & W292		18. 3.87	Canx by CAA 5.11.90.
G-MTFX	Mainair Gemini/Flash 2	534-487-5 & W321		26. 3.87	(Badly damaged on landing near Sandtoft on 28.7.96)
G-MTFY	CFM Streak Shadow (Probably simply a Shadow Srs.BD)	050		24. 3.87	To EI-CMF 9/95. Canx 18.9.95.
G-MTFZ	CFM Shadow Srs.CD	053		24. 3.87	
G-MTGA	Mainair Gemini/Flash 2	535-587-5 & W293		26. 3.87	
G-MTGB	Thruster TST Mk.1	837-TST-011		10. 4.87	
G-MTGC	Thruster TST Mk.1	837-TST-012		10. 4.87	

Regn	Type	c/n	Previous identity	Regn date	Fate or immediate subsequent identity (if known)
G-MTGD	Thruster TST Mk.1	837-TST-013		10. 4.87	
G-MTGE	Thruster TST Mk.1	837-TST-014		10. 4.87	
G-MTGF	Thruster TST Mk.1	837-TST-015		10. 4.87	
G-MTGG	Solar Wings Pegasus Photon	SW-WP-10025		10. 4.87	Canx as WFU 16.11.88.
G-MTGH	Mainair Gemini/Flash 2	536-587-5 & W294		31. 3.87	
G-MTGI	Solar Wings Pegasus XL-R	SW-WA-1164		1. 4.87	Canx as destroyed 13.1.95.
G-MTGJ	Solar Wings Pegasus XL-R	SW-TB-1165 & SW-WA-1165		1. 4.87	
G-MTGK	Solar Wings Pegasus XL-R	SW-WA-1166		1. 4.87	
G-MTGL	Solar Wings Pegasus XL-R	SW-WA-1167		1. 4.87	
G-MTGM	Solar Wings Pegasus XL-R	SW-WA-1168		1. 4.87	
G-MTGN	CFM Shadow Srs.BD	K.041		31. 3.87	
G-MTGO	Mainair Gemini/Flash 2	550-587-5 & W336		10. 4.87	
G-MTGP	Thruster TST Mk.1	847-TST-016		10. 4.87	(Damaged early .97)
G-MTGR	Thruster TST Mk.1	847-TST-017		10. 4.87	
G-MTGS	Thruster TST Mk.1	847-TST-018		10. 4.87	
G-MTGT	Thruster TST Mk.1	847-TST-019		10. 4.87	
G-MTGU	Thruster TST Mk.1	847-TST-020		10. 4.87	
G-MTGV	CFM Shadow Srs.CD	052		8. 4.87	
G-MTGW	CFM Shadow Srs.CD	054	I-.... G-MTGW	8. 4.87	
G-MTGX	Hornet Dual Trainer/Southdown Raven	HRWA 0061 & 2000/0270		13. 4.87	
G-MTGY	Quester/Southdown Lightning	0003/1		8. 4.87	Canx as destroyed 15.3.90.
G-MTGZ	Solar Wings Pegasus Photon	SW-WP-10026		28. 4.87	Canx as WFU 16.11.88.
G-MTHA	Solar Wings Pegasus Photon	SW-WP-10027		10. 4.87	Canx as WFU 16.11.88.
G-MTHB	Aerotech MW.5B Sorcerer	SR102-R440B-08		10. 4.87	
G-MTHC	Southdown Raven X	2232/0257		15. 4.87	
G-MTHD	Ultrasports Tripacer/Hiway Demon 195	JMS-01		13. 4.87	
G-MTHE	Solar Wings Pegasus XL-Q	SW-WX-0002		28. 4.87	Canx as WFU 27.10.88.
G-MTHF	Solar Wings Pegasus XL-R	SW-WA-1170		13. 4.87	To 9J-YCK 2/96. Canx 1.6.94.
G-MTHG	Solar Wings Pegasus XL-R	SW-WA-1171		13. 4.87	
G-MTHH	Solar Wings Pegasus XL-R	SW-WA-1172		13. 4.87	
G-MTHI	Solar Wings Pegasus XL-R	SW-TB-1172 & SW-WA-1173		13. 4.87	
G-MTHJ	Solar Wings Pegasus XL-R	SW-TB-1173 & SW-WA-1174		13. 4.87	
G-MTHK	Solar Wings Pegasus XL-R	SW-WA-1175	(EI-BUU) G-MTHK	13. 4.87	Canx by CAA 15.12.93.
G-MTHL	Solar Wings Pegasus XL-R	SW-TB-1175 & SW-WA-1176		13. 4.87	To SE-VBH 3/96. Canx 15.12.95.
G-MTHM	Solar Wings Pegasus XL-R	SW-WA-1177		13. 4.87	Canx 1.7.96 on sale to Greece.
G-MTHN	Solar Wings Pegasus XL-R	SW-WA-1178		13. 4.87	
G-MTHO	Solar Wings Pegasus XL-R	SW-WA-1179		13. 4.87	
G-MTHP	Solar Wings Pegasus XL-R	SW-TE-0019 & SW-WA-1180		13. 4.87	To SE-YRZ. Canx 4.12.95.
G-MTHR	CFM Shadow Srs.BD	055		22. 4.87	To Z-MAG. Canx 16.11.87.
G-MTHS	CFM Shadow Srs.CD	059		22. 4.87	Permit expired 17.5.97. Canx by CAA 11.6.99.
G-MTHT	CFM Shadow Srs.CD	058		22. 4.87	
G-MTHU	Hornet Dual Trainer/Southdown Raven	HRWA 0062 & 2000/0269		30. 4.87	
G-MTHV	CFM Shadow Srs.BD	K.049		7. 5.87	
G-MTHW	Mainair Gemini/Flash 2	540-587-5 & W325		14. 5.87	
G-MTHX	Mainair Gemini/Flash 2	542-587-5 & W330		14. 5.87	Canx by CAA 4.7.96.
G-MTHY	Mainair Gemini/Flash 2A	543-687-5 & W331		14. 5.87	Permit expired 27.6.94. (Active 7/96)
G-MTHZ	Mainair Gemini/Flash 2A	541-587-5 & W329		14. 5.87	
G-MTIA	Mainair Gemini/Flash 2A	544-687-5 & W332		14. 5.87	
G-MTIB	Mainair Gemini/Flash 2A	545-687-5 & W333		14. 5.87	
G-MTIC	Mainair Gemini/Flash 2A	546-587-5 & W334		14. 5.87	
G-MTID	Southdown Raven X	2232/0276		18. 5.87	
G-MTIE	Solar Wings Pegasus XL-R	SW-WA-1183		18. 5.87	
G-MTIF	Solar Wings Pegasus XL-R	SW-TB-1181 & SW-WA-1184		18. 5.87	Canx 29.4.98 on sale to Turkey.
G-MTIG	Solar Wings Pegasus XL-R	SW-WA-1185		18. 5.87	Canx by CAA 7.8.96.
G-MTIH	Solar Wings Pegasus XL-R	SW-WA-1186		18. 5.87	(Damaged mid .97)
G-MTII	Solar Wings Pegasus XL-R	SW-WA-1187		18. 5.87	(Damaged mid .95)
G-MTIJ	Solar Wings Pegasus XL-R/Se	SW-TB-1185 & SW-WA-1188		18. 5.87	
G-MTIK	Southdown Raven X	2232/0272		19. 5.87	

Regn	Type	c/n	Previous identity	Regn date	Fate or immediate subsequent identity (if known)
G-MTIL	Mainair Gemini/Flash 2A	549-687-5 & W338		21. 5.87	
	(Originally regd with c/n 549-687-5 & W388)				
G-MTIM	Mainair Gemini/Flash 2A	553-687-5 & W341		21. 5.87	
G-MTIN	Mainair Gemini/Flash 2A	547-687-5 & W335		1. 6.87	
G-MTIO	Solar Wings Pegasus XL-R	SW-WA-1190		26. 5.87	
G-MTIP	Solar Wings Pegasus XL-R	SW-TB-1188 & SW-WA-1191		26. 5.87	
G-MTIR	Solar Wings Pegasus XL-R/Se	SW-WA-1192		26. 5.87	
	(Original wing apparently fitted to G-MTZI in Portugal)				
G-MTIS	Solar Wings Pegasus XL-R	SW-WA-1193		26. 5.87	
G-MTIT	Not allotted.				
G-MTIU	Solar Wings Pegasus XL-R	SW-TB-1191 & SW-WA-1194		26. 5.87	
G-MTIV	Solar Wings Pegasus XL-R	SW-TB-1192 & SW-WA-1195		26. 5.87	
G-MTIW	Solar Wings Pegasus XL-R	SW-TB-1193 & SW-WA-1196		26. 5.87	
G-MTIX	Solar Wings Pegasus XL-R	SW-WA-1197		26. 5.87	
G-MTIY	Solar Wings Pegasus XL-R	SW-WA-1198		26. 5.87	
G-MTIZ	Solar Wings Pegasus XL-R	SW-TB-1196 & SW-WA-1199		26. 5.87	
G-MTJA	Mainair Gemini/Flash 2A	551-687-5 & W339		15. 6.87	
G-MTJB	Mainair Gemini/Flash 2A	554-687-5 & W343		2. 6.87	
G-MTJC	Mainair Gemini/Flash 2A	555-687-5 & W344		1. 6.87	
G-MTJD	Mainair Gemini/Flash 2A	552-687-5 & W340		5. 6.87	
G-MTJE	Mainair Gemini/Flash 2A	556-687-5 & W345		24. 6.87	
G-MTJF	Mainair Gemini/Flash 2A	557-687-5 & W346		15. 6.87	Canx by CAA 7.8.96. (Stored 7/96)
G-MTJG	Medway Hybred 44XLR	22587/25		16. 6.87	
G-MTJH	Solar Wings Pegasus/Flash	SW-TB-1050 & W342-687-3		17. 6.87	
	(Trike previously fitted to G-MMUF)				
G-MTJI	Southdown Raven X	2232/0260		23. 6.87	
G-MTJJ	Solar Wings Pegasus XL-Q	SW-TB-1198	(VH-...) G-MTJJ	17. 6.87	To Australia as T2-2507. Canx 9.1.90.
G-MTJK	Mainair Gemini/Flash 2A	559-787-5 & W348		17. 6.87	
G-MTJL	Mainair Gemini/Flash 2A	548-687-5 & W337		17. 6.87	
G-MTJM	Mainair Gemini/Flash 2A	560-787-5 & W349		24. 6.87	
G-MTJN	Midland Ultralights Sirocco 377GB (Mod)	MU-020		23. 6.87	
G-MTJO	Mainair Gemin/Flash 2	539-587-5 & W326		16. 7.87	Canx 15.5.89 on sale to Spain.
G-MTJP	Medway Hybred 44XLR	25687/27		6. 7.87	
G-MTJR	Solar Wings Pegasus XL-R	SW-WA-1209		15. 7.87	(Damaged late .97)
G-MTJS	Solar Wings Pegasus XL-Q	SW-TE-0022 & SW-WX-0013		6. 7.87	
G-MTJT	Mainair Gemini/Flash 2A	558-787-5 & W347		16. 7.87	Canx by CAA 2.8.89.
G-MTJU	MBA Tiger Cub	SO.204		9. 7.87	Canx by CAA 13.6.90.
G-MTJV	Mainair Gemini/Flash 2A	562-787-5 & W351		16. 7.87	
G-MTJW	Mainair Gemini/Flash 2A	563-787-5 & W352		16. 7.87	
G-MTJX	Hornet Dual Trainer/Southdown Raven	HRWA 0063 & 2000/0279		5. 8.87	
G-MTJY	Mainair Gemini/Flash 2A	564-887-5 & W353		15. 7.87	(Damaged mid .94) (Stored 9/95)
G-MTJZ	Mainair Gemini/Flash 2A	561-787-5 & W350		16. 7.87	
G-MTKA	Thruster TST Mk.1	867-TST-021		21. 7.87	
G-MTKB	Thruster TST Mk.1	867-TST-022		21. 7.87	
G-MTKC	Thruster TST Mk.1	867-TST-023		21. 7.87	Canx 7.9.87 on sale to Norway.
G-MTKD	Thruster TST Mk.1	867-TST-024		21. 7.87	(Damaged mid .96)
G-MTKE	Thruster TST Mk.1	867-TST-025		21. 7.87	
G-MTKF	Solar Wings Pegasus XL-R	SW-WA-1200	(VH-...) G-MTKF	13. 7.87	To Australia as T2-2506. Canx 9.1.90.
G-MTKG	Solar Wings Pegasus XL-R/Se	SW-TB-1199 & SW-WA-1201		13. 7.87	
G-MTKH	Solar Wings Pegasus XL-R	SW-TB-1200 & SW-WA-1202		13. 7.87	

Regn	Type	c/n	Previous identity	Regn date	Fate or immediate subsequent identity (if known)
G-MTKI	Solar Wings Pegasus XL-R (Also reported as c/n SW-TB-1204)	SW-TB-1201 & SW-WA-1203		13. 7.87	
G-MTKJ	Solar Wings Pegasus XL-R/Se	SW-TB-1202 & SW-WA-1204		13. 7.87	
G-MTKK	Solar Wings Pegasus XL-R	SW-WA-1205		13. 7.87	Canx by CAA 7.8.96.
G-MTKL	Southdown Raven X	2232/0278		. .87R	NTU - To G-MTMO 9/87. Canx.
G-MTKM	Gardner T-M Scout S2	87/003		12. 8.87	
G-MTKN	Mainair Gemini/Flash 2A	566-887-5 & W355		15. 7.87	
G-MTKO	Mainair Gemini/Flash 2A	567-787-5 & W356		13. 7.87	
G-MTKP	Solar Wings Pegasus XL-R	SW-WA-1207		13. 7.87	(Damaged mid .95)
G-MTKR	CFM Shadow Srs.BD	067	9H-ABL G-MTKR	20. 7.87	
G-MTKS	CFM Shadow Srs.BD	066		20. 7.87	Canx by CAA 21.7.93.
G-MTKT	CFM Shadow Srs.BD	063		20. 7.87	To EI-CHR 5/93. Canx 30.10.87.
G-MTKU	CFM Shadow Srs.CD	062		20. 7.87	To G-CAIN(2) 1/99. Canx.
G-MTKV	Mainair Gemini/Flash 2A	565-887-5 & W354		26. 8.87	
G-MTKW	Mainair Gemini/Flash 2A	569-887-5 & W358		13. 7.87	
G-MTKX	Mainair Gemini/Flash 2A	568-887-5 & W357		13. 7.87	
G-MTKY	Mainair Gemini/Flash 2A	570-887-5 & W359		28. 7.87	To G-OLJT 9/98. Canx.
G-MTKZ	Mainair Gemini/Flash 2A	571-887-5 & W360		31. 7.87	
G-MTLA	Mainair Gemini/Flash 2A	572-887-5 & W361		31. 7.87	Destroyed in fatal crash at Rhuallt, nr St.Asaph when the wings folded up on test flight on 17.7.96. Canx as destroyed 30.4.97.
G-MTLB	Mainair Gemini/Flash 2A	573-887-5 & W362		31. 7.87	
G-MTLC	Mainair Gemini/Flash 2A	574-887-5 & W363		31. 7.87	
G-MTLD	Mainair Gemini/Flash 2A	575-887-5 & W364		31. 7.87	
G-MTLE	Cessna 501 Citation I (Unit No.573)	501-0170	G-GENE N501HP/(N6778Y)	7. 5.86	To N170EA 1/94. Canx 13.1.94.
G-MTLF	Solar Wings Pegasus XL-R	SW-WA-1210		31. 7.87	Fatal crash near Pennistone, Yorks on 8.2.89. Canx as destroyed 11.9.89.
G-MTLG	Solar Wings Pegasus XL-R (Fitted with wing ex G-MTEE; thus is SW-WA-1142)	SW-TB-1207 & SW-WA-1211		31. 7.87	(Extant 6/97)
G-MTLH	Solar Wings Pegasus XL-R	SW-TB-1208 & SW-WA-1212		31. 7.87	(Trike stored 4/96)
G-MTLI	Solar Wings Pegasus XL-R	SW-WA-1213		31. 7.87	
G-MTLJ	Solar Wings Pegasus XL-R/Se	SW-TB-1210 & SW-WA-1214		31. 7.87	
G-MTLK	Southdown Raven X	2232/0299		12. 8.87	Canx by CAA 16.3.92.
G-MTLL	Mainair Gemini/Flash 2A	578-987-5 & W367		14. 8.87	(Stored 3/93)
G-MTLM	Thruster TST Mk.1	887-TST-027		5. 8.87	(Noted wingless & engineless at Old Sarum in 6/98)
G-MTLN	Thruster TST Mk.1	887-TST-028		5. 8.87	
G-MTLO	Thruster TST Mk.1	887-TST-029		5. 8.87	
G-MTLP	Thruster TST Mk.1	887-TST-030		5. 8.87	Canx as destroyed 11.10.96.
G-MTLR	Thruster TST Mk.1	887-TST-031		5. 8.87	
G-MTLS	Solar Wings Pegasus XL-R	SW-WA-1215		12. 8.87	Canx by CAA 18.3.92.
G-MTLT	Solar Wings Pegasus XL-R	SW-WA-1216		12. 8.87	
G-MTLU	Solar Wings Pegasus XL-R/Se	SW-TB-1213 & SW-WA-1217		12. 8.87	
G-MTLV	Solar Wings Pegasus XL-R	SW-TB-1214 & SW-WA-1218		12. 8.87	Canx as CAA 24.8.89.
G-MTLW	Solar Wings Pegasus XL-R	SW-TB-1215 & SW-WA-1219		12. 8.87	
G-MTLX	Medway Hybred 44XLR	20687/26		14. 8.87	
G-MTLY	Solar Wings Pegasus XL-R	SW-WA-1220		12. 8.87	
G-MTLZ	Whittaker MW.5 Sorcerer	PFA/163-11241		13. 8.87	
G-MTMA	Mainair Gemini/Flash 2A	579-987-5 & W368		14. 8.87	
G-MTMB	Mainair Gemini/Flash 2A	580-987-5 & W369		14. 8.87	Canx by CAA 1.12.98.
G-MTMC	Mainair Gemini/Flash 2A	581-987-5 & W370		14. 8.87	
G-MTMD	Whittaker MW.6 Merlin	PFA/164-11225		12. 8.87	
G-MTME	Solar Wings Pegasus XL-R	SW-WA-1221		18. 8.87	
G-MTMF	Solar Wings Pegasus XL-R	SW-WA-1222		18. 8.87	
G-MTMG	Solar Wings Pegasus XL-R	SW-WA-1223		18. 8.87	
G-MTMH	Solar Wings Pegasus XL-R	SW-WA-1224		18. 8.87	
G-MTMI	Solar Wings Pegasus XL-R/Se	SW-TB-1220 & SW-WA-1225		18. 8.87	
G-MTMJ	Maxair Hummer	MJM-01		18. 8.87	Canx as PWFU 10.3.99.

Regn	Type	c/n	Previous identity	Regn date	Fate or immediate subsequent identity (if known)
G-MTMK	Southdown Raven X	2000/0289		2. 9.87	
G-MTML	Mainair Gemini/Flash 2A	582-1087-5 & W371		27. 8.87	
G-MTMM	CFM Shadow Srs.BD	057		3. 9.87	Canx by CAA 7.8.96.
G-MTMN	CFM Shadow Srs.BD	075		4. 9.87R	NTU - To G-MTNA 4.9.87. Canx 30.10.87.
G-MTMO	Southdown Raven X	2232/0278	(G-MTKL)	11. 9.87	
G-MTMP	Hornet Dual Trainer/Southdown Raven	HRWA 0064 & 2000/0288		28. 8.87	(Extant 7/97)
G-MTMR	Hornet Dual Trainer/Southdown Raven	HRWA 0065 & 2000/0297		28. 8.87	
G-MTMS	Hornet Dual Trainer/Southdown Raven	HRWA 0066 & 2000/0311		11. 9.87	Canx by CAA 9.1.91.
G-MTMT	Mainair Gemini/Flash 2A	583-1087-5 & W372		3. 9.87	
G-MTMU	Mainair Gemini/Flash 2A	584-1087-5 & W373		3. 9.87	Trike stolen from Blackburn in 2/94. Canx by CAA 2.7.96.
G-MTMV	Mainair Gemini/Flash 2A	585-1087-5 & W374		3. 9.87	
G-MTMW	Mainair Gemini/Flash 2A	587-1087-5 & W376		9. 9.87	
G-MTMX	CFM Shadow Srs.CD	070		4. 9.87	
G-MTMY	CFM Shadow Srs.CD	071		4. 9.87	
G-MTMZ	CFM Shadow Srs.BD	074		4. 9.87	
G-MTNA	CFM Shadow Srs.BD	075	(G-MTMN)	4. 9.87	To Australia as 25-0254. Canx 5.5.89.
G-MTNB	Southdown Raven X	2232/0305		9. 9.87	
G-MTNC	Mainair Gemini/Flash 2A	588-1087-5 & W377		15. 9.87	
G-MTND	Medway Hybred 44XLR	25887/29		18. 9.87	Canx by CAA 18.10.95.
G-MTNE	Medway Hybred 44XLR	7987/32		12.10.87	
	(Presumed fitted with new trike since original to G-MVDC .88)				
G-MTNF	Medway Hybred 44XLR	1987/31		12.10.87	
G-MTNG	Mainair Gemini/Flash 2A	590-1087-5 & W379		21. 9.87	
G-MTNH	Mainair Gemini/Flash 2A	589-1087-5 & W378		17. 9.87	
G-MTNI	Mainair Gemini/Flash 2A	595-1187-5 & W384		18. 9.87	
G-MTNJ	Mainair Gemini/Flash 2A	593-1187-5 & W382		17. 9.87	
G-MTNK	Weedhopper JC-24B	1936		28. 9.87	
G-MTNL	Mainair Gemini/Flash 2A	591-1187-5 & W380		21. 9.87	
G-MTNM	Mainair Gemini/Flash 2A	592-1187-5 & W381		22. 9.87	
G-MTNN	Mainair Gemini/Flash 2A	596-1187-5 & W385		23. 9.87	Canx 16.11.93 on sale to Italy.
G-MTNO	Solar Wings Pegasus XL-Q	SW-TB-1252 & SW-WQ-0001		23. 9.87	
G-MTNP	Solar Wings Pegasus XL-Q	SW-TB-1253 & SW-WQ-0002		23. 9.87	
G-MTNR	Thruster TST Mk.1	897-TST-032		1.10.87	
G-MTNS	Thruster TST Mk.1	897-TST-033		1.10.87	
G-MTNT	Thruster TST Mk.1	897-TST-034		1.10.87	
G-MTNU	Thruster TST Mk.1	897-TST-035		1.10.87	
G-MTNV	Thruster TST Mk.1	897-TST-036		1.10.87	
G-MTNW	Thruster TST Mk.1	897-TST-037		1.10.87	
G-MTNX	Mainair Gemini/Flash 2A	606-1187-5 & W393		29. 9.87	(Damaged late .97)
G-MTNY	Mainair Gemini/Flash 2A	594-1187-5 & W383		2.10.87	
G-MTNZ	Solar Wings Pegasus XL-Q	SW-WQ-0003		2.10.87	Canx as PWFU 2.9.96.
G-MTOA	Solar Wings Pegasus XL-R	SW-TB-1221 & SW-WA-1226		15. 9.87	
G-MTOB	Solar Wings Pegasus XL-R	SW-TB-1222 & SW-WA-1227		15. 9.87	
G-MTOC	Solar Wings Pegasus XL-R	SW-TB-1223 & SW-WA-1228		15. 9.87	
G-MTOD	Solar Wings Pegasus XL-R	SW-WA-1229		15. 9.87	
G-MTOE	Solar Wings Pegasus XL-R	SW-WA-1230		15. 9.87	
G-MTOF	Solar Wings Pegasus XL-R/Se	SW-TB-1226 & SW-WA-1231		15. 9.87	
G-MTOG	Solar Wings Pegasus XL-R	SW-WA-1232		22. 9.87	
G-MTOH	Solar Wings Pegasus XL-R	SW-TB-1228 & SW-WA-1233		22. 9.87	
G-MTOI	Solar Wings Pegasus XL-R	SW-TB-1229 & SW-WA-1234		22. 9.87	
G-MTOJ	Solar Wings Pegasus XL-R/Se	SW-WA-1235		22. 9.87	
G-MTOK	Solar Wings Pegasus XL-R	SW-WA-1236		2.10.87	
G-MTOL	Solar Wings Pegasus XL-R	SW-WA-1237		2.10.87	
G-MTOM	Solar Wings Pegasus XL-R/Se	SW-TB-1233 & SW-WA-1238		2.10.87	

Regn	Type	c/n	Previous identity	Regn date	Fate or immediate subsequent identity (if known)
G-MTON	Solar Wings Pegasus XL-R	SW-TB-1234 & SW-WA-1239		2.10.87	
G-MTOO	Solar Wings Pegasus XL-R	SW-TB-1235 & SW-WA-1240		2.10.87	
G-MTOP	Solar Wings Pegasus XL-R/Se	SW-WA-1241		2.10.87	
G-MTOR	Solar Wings Pegasus XL-R	SW-TB-1237 & SW-WA-1242		9.10.87	
G-MTOS	Solar Wings Pegasus XL-R	SW-TB-1238 & SW-WA-1243		9.10.87	
G-MTOT	Solar Wings Pegasus XL-R	SW-WA-1244		9.10.87	
G-MTOU	Solar Wings Pegasus XL-R/Se	SW-TB-1240 & SW-WA-1245		9.10.87	
G-MTOV	Solar Wings Pegasus XL-R	SW-TB-1241 & SW-WA-1246		19.10.87	Canx as WFU 9.12.93.
G-MTOW	Solar Wings Pegasus XL-R	SW-WA-1247		19.10.87	
G-MTOX	Solar Wings Pegasus XL-R	SW-TB-1243 & SW-WA-1248		19.10.87	
G-MTOY	Solar Wings Pegasus XL-R	SW-WA-1249		19.10.87	
G-MTOZ	Solar Wings Pegasus XL-R	SW-TB-1245 & SW-WA-1250		19.10.87	
G-MTPA	Mainair Gemini/Flash 2A	598-1187-5 & W394		13.10.87	
G-MTPB	Mainair Gemini/Flash 2A	599-1187-5 & W387		15.10.87	
G-MTPC	Southdown Raven X	2232/0309		15.10.87	
G-MTPD	Solar Wings Pegasus XL-Q	SW-WQ-0006		4.11.87	Canx as destroyed 9.4.90.
G-MTPE	Solar Wings Pegasus XL-R	SW-TB-1258 & SW-WA-1260		21.10.87	
G-MTPF	Solar Wings Pegasus XL-R	SW-TB-1259 & SW-WA-1261		21.10.87	
G-MTPG	Solar Wings Pegasus XL-R	SW-WA-1262		21.10.87	
G-MTPH	Solar Wings Pegasus XL-R	SW-TB-1261 & SW-WA-1263		30.10.87	
G-MTPI	Solar Wings Pegasus XL-R/Se	SW-TB-1262 & SW-WA-1264		30.10.87	
G-MTPJ	Solar Wings Pegasus XL-R	SW-TB-1263 & SW-WA-1265		30.10.87	
G-MTPK	Solar Wings Pegasus XL-R	SW-WA-1266		30.10.87	
G-MTPL	Solar Wings Pegasus XL-R	SW-TB-1265 & SW-WA-1267		30.10.87	
G-MTPM	Solar Wings Pegasus XL-R	SW-TB-1266 & SW-WA-1268		30.10.87	
G-MTPN	Solar Wings Pegasus XL-Q	SW-TB-1267 & SW-WQ-0004		21.10.87	Canx by CAA 2.12.98.
G-MTPO	Solar Wings Pegasus XL-Q	SW-TE-0032 & SW-WQ-0005		21.10.87	
G-MTPP	Solar Wings Pegasus XL-R	SW-WA-1259		21.10.87	
G-MTPR	Solar Wings Pegasus XL-R	SW-WA-1257		21.10.87	
G-MTPS	Solar Wings Pegasus XL-Q	SW-WX-0011		23.10.87	
G-MTPT	Thruster TST Mk.1	8107-TST-038		23.10.87	
G-MTPU	Thruster TST Mk.1	8107-TST-039		23.10.87	
G-MTPV	Thruster TST Mk.1	8107-TST-040		23.10.87	
G-MTPW	Thruster TST Mk.1	8107-TST-041		23.10.87	
G-MTPX	Thruster TST Mk.1	8107-TST-042		23.10.87	
G-MTPY	Thruster TST Mk.1	8107-TST-043		23.10.87	
G-MTPZ	Solar Wings Pegasus XL-R	SW-WA-1274		10.11.87	Canx by CAA 7.8.96.
G-MTRA	Mainair Gemini/Flash 2A	605-1187-5 & W395		28.10.87	
G-MTRB	Mainair Gemini/Flash 2A	600-1187-5 & W388		27.10.87	
G-MTRC	Midland Ultralights Sirocco 377GB	MU-021		2.11.87	
G-MTRD	Midland Ultralights Sirocco 377GB	MU-022		2.11.87	Canx as TWFU 1.3.96.
G-MTRE	Whittaker MW.6 Merlin	PFA/164-11168		27.10.87	
G-MTRF	Mainair Gemini/Flash 2A	601-1187-5 & W389		30.10.87	
G-MTRG	Mainair Gemini/Flash 2A	613-1287-5 & W402		2.11.87	Canx by CAA 7.8.96.
G-MTRH	Mainair Tri-Flyer/Hiway Demon	HW175D		27.10.87	Canx by CAA 7.9.94.
G-MTRI	Hiway Demon	SDP-01		2.11.87	Canx by CAA 8.6.90.
G-MTRJ	AMF Chevvron 2-32C	CH.006		30.10.87	
G-MTRK	Hornet Dual Trainer/Southdown Raven	HRWA 0067 & 2000/0324		4.11.87	
G-MTRL	Hornet Dual Trainer/Southdown Raven	HRWA 0068 & 2000/0326		4.11.87	
G-MTRM	Solar Wings Pegasus XL-R	SW-TE-0030 & SW-WA-1276		10.11.87	
G-MTRN	Solar Wings Pegasus XL-R	SW-WA-1269		2.12.87	
G-MTRO	Solar Wings Pegasus XL-R/Se	SW-TB-1271 & SW-WA-1270		2.12.87	

Regn	Type	c/n	Previous identity	Regn date	Fate or immediate subsequent identity (if known)
G-MTRP	Solar Wings Pegasus XL-R	SW-WA-1271		3.12.87	Canx by CAA 5.3.91.
G-MTRR	Solar Wings Pegasus XL-R	SW-WA-1272		3.12.87	
G-MTRS	Solar Wings Pegasus XL-R	SW-WA-1273		2.12.87	
G-MTRT	Southdown Raven X	2232/0325		12.11.87	
G-MTRU	Solar Wings Pegasus XL-Q	SW-WQ-0009		10.11.87	
G-MTRV	Solar Wings Pegasus XL-Q	SW-TB-1276 & SW WX 0010		10.11.87	
G-MTRW	Southdown Raven X	2232/0328		12.11.87	
G-MTRX	Whittaker MW.5 Sorcerer	PFA/163-11202		11.11.87	(Stored 8/96)
G-MTRY	Noble Hardman Snowbird Mk.IV	SB-005		24.11.87	
G-MTRZ	Mainair Gemini/Flash 2A	611-1287-5 & W400		17.11.87	
G-MTSA	Mainair Gemini/Flash 2A	607-1187-5 & W396		16.11.87	Canx as destroyed 10.2.95.
G-MTSB	Mainair Gemini/Flash 2A	608-1187-5 & W397		16.11.87	
G-MTSC	Mainair Gemini/Flash 2A	618-1188-5 & W407		17.11.87	
G-MTSD	Southdown Raven X	2232/0312		24.11.87	
G-MTSE	Mainair Tri-Flyer/Flexiform Striker	9800-000		23.11.87	Canx by CAA 29.3.85.
G-MTSF	Aerial Arts Chaser/110SX (C/n conflicts with G-MNTD)	110SX/255		23.11.87	Canx by CAA 7.9.94.
G-MTSG	CFM Shadow Srs.BD	079		24.11.87	
G-MTSH	Thruster TST Mk.1	8117-TST-044		3.12.87	
G-MTSI	Thruster TST Mk.1	8117-TST-045		3.12.87	
G-MTSJ	Thruster TST Mk.1	8117-TST-046		3.12.87	
G-MTSK	Thruster TST Mk.1	8117-TST-047		3.12.87	
G-MTSL	Thruster TST Mk.1	8117-TST-048		3.12.87	
G-MTSM	Thruster TST Mk.1	8117-TST-049		3.12.87	
G-MTSN	Solar Wings Pegasus XL-R (Also reported as trike c/n SW-TB-1272)	SW-TB-1278 & SW-WA-1280		14.12.87	
G-MTSO	Solar Wings Pegasus XL-R/Se	SW-WA-1281		14.12.87	
G-MTSP	Solar Wings Pegasus XL-R	SW-WA-1282		14.12.87	
G-MTSR	Solar Wings Pegasus XL-R	SW-TB-1281 & SW-WA-1283		14.12.87	
G-MTSS	Solar Wings Pegasus XL-R	SW-WA-1284		14.12.87	
G-MTST(1)	Thruster TST Mk.1	8127-TST-007		3.12.87	NTU - Not built. Canx by CAA 12.12.88.
G-MTST(2)	Thruster TST Mk.1	8128-TST-111		12.12.88	
G-MTSU	Solar Wings Pegasus XL-R	SW-WA-1285		4. 1.88	
G-MTSV	Solar Wings Pegasus XL-R	SW-WA-1286		4. 1.88	
G-MTSW	Solar Wings Pegasus XL-R	SW-WA-1287		4. 1.88	To Australia as T2-2541. Canx 12.6.89.
G-MTSX	Solar Wings Pegasus XL-R	SW-TB-1282 & SW-WA-1288		4. 1.88	(Extant 1/98)
G-MTSY	Solar Wings Pegasus XL-R/Se	SW-TB-1283 & SW-WA-1289		14. 1.88	
G-MTSZ	Solar Wings Pegasus XL-R/Se	SW-TB-1284 & SW-WA-1290		14. 1.88	
G-MTTA	Solar Wings Pegasus XL-R	SW-TE-0035 & SW-WA-1291		14. 1.88	
G-MTTB	Solar Wings Pegasus XL-R	SW-WA-1292		14. 1.88	
G-MTTC	Solar Wings Pegasus XL-R	SW-WA-1293		15. 1.88	Canx by CAA 7.8.96.
G-MTTD	Solar Wings Pegasus XL-Q	SW-TB-1286 & SW-WQ-0011		15. 1.88	
G-MTTE	Solar Wings Pegasus XL-Q	SW-TB-1287 & SW-WQ-0012		15. 1.88	
G-MTTF	Whittaker MW.6 Merlin	PFA/164-11273		14.12.87	
G-MTTG	Tri-Pacer 250/Excalibur	SCG-01		15.12.87	Canx as WFU 25.3.94.
G-MTTH	CFM Shadow Srs.BD	K.061		15.12.87	
G-MTTI	Mainair Gemini/Flash 2A	620-188-5 & W409		14.12.87	
G-MTTJ	CFM Shadow Srs.BD	025		14.12.87	Canx 12.4.88 on sale to France.
G-MTTK	Southdown Puma (Lightning DS)	DO-8477		15.12.87	
G-MTTL	Tri-Pacer 330/Excalibur	EXS-872		23. 3.88	Canx by CAA 20.11.95.
G-MTTM	Mainair Gemini/Flash 2A	609-1287-5 & W398		5. 1.88	
G-MTTN	Skyrider Airsports Phantom	PH.00100		22. 1.88	
G-MTTO	Mainair Gemini/Flash 2A	610-188-5 & W399		4. 1.88	Fatal crash at Aldford, 6 miles south of Chester on 27.6.92. Canx by CAA 30.10.92.
G-MTTP	Mainair Gemini/Flash 2A	612-188-5 & W401		18. 1.88	
G-MTTR	Mainair Gemini/Flash 2A	614-188-5 & W403		27. 1.88	
G-MTTS	Mainair Gemini/Flash 2A	621-188-5 & W410		4. 1.88	
G-MTTT	Not allotted.				
G-MTTU	Solar Wings Pegasus XL-R	SW-TB-1332 & SW-WA-1294		25. 2.88	

Regn	Type	c/n	Previous identity	Regn date	Fate or immediate subsequent identity (if known)
G-MTTV	Solar Wings Pegasus XL-Q	SW-TE-0036 & SW-WQ-0010		28. 1.88	To 00-984 10/90. Canx 11.9.90.
G-MTTW	Mainair Gemini/Flash 2A	622-188-5 & W411		15. 1.88	
G-MTTX	Solar Wings Pegasus XL-Q	SW-TB-1293 & SW-WQ-0013		15. 2.88	
G-MTTY	Solar Wings Pegasus XL-Q	SW-WQ-0014		21. 1.88	Canx by CAA 7.8.96.
G-MTTZ	Solar Wings Pegasus XL-Q	SW-WQ-0015		21. 1.88	
G-MTUA	Solar Wings Pegasus XL-R/Se	SW-TB-1294 & SW-WA-1295		15. 1.88	
G-MTUB	Thruster TST Mk.1	8018-TST-050		15. 1.88	
G-MTUC	Thruster TST Mk.1	8018-TST-051		15. 1.88	
G-MTUD	Thruster TST Mk.1	8018-TST-052		15. 1.88	
G-MTUE	Thruster TST Mk.1	8018-TST-053		15. 1.88	
G-MTUF	Thruster TST Mk.1	8018-TST-054		15. 1.88	
G-MTUG	Thruster TST Mk.1	8018-TST-055		15. 1.88	
G-MTUH	Solar Wings Pegasus XL-RS	SW-WX-0014		15. 1.88	Canx by CAA 28.2.92.
G-MTUI	Solar Wings Pegasus XL-R/Se	SW-WA-1296		21. 1.88	
G-MTUJ	Solar Wings Pegasus XL-R	SW-WA-1297		21. 1.88	
G-MTUK	Solar Wings Pegasus XL-R	SW-WA-1298		21. 1.88	
G-MTUL	Solar Wings Pegasus XL-R/Se	SW-TB-1299 & SW-WA-1299		21. 1.88	
G-MTUM	Solar Wings Pegasus XL-R	SW-WA-1300		21. 1.88	Canx 9.1.90 on sale to Spain.
G-MTUN	Solar Wings Pegasus XL-Q (Fitted with Wing from G-MVUK?)	SW-TB-1301 & SW-WQ-0016		20. 1.88	(Stored 1/98)
G-MTUO	Solar Wings Pegasus XL-Q/Lc	SW-TB-1302 & SW-WQ-0017		20. 1.88	To SE-YRX. Canx 26.10.95.
G-MTUP	Solar Wings Pegasus XL-Q	SW-TB-1303 & SW-WQ-0018		20. 1.88	
G-MTUR	Solar Wings Pegasus XL-Q	SW-TB-1304 & SW-WQ-0019		20. 1.88	
G-MTUS	Solar Wings Pegasus XL-Q	SW-TB-1305 & SW-WQ-0020		20. 1.88	
G-MTUT	Solar Wings Pegasus XL-Q	SW-TE-0040 & SW-WQ-0021		21. 1.88	
G-MTUU	Mainair Gemini/Flash 2A	623-288-5 & W412		10. 2.88	
G-MTUV	Mainair Gemini/Flash 2A	624-288-5 & W413		28. 1.88	
G-MTUW	Mainair Gemini/Flash 2A	625-188-2 & W414		26. 1.88	Fatal crash at Meltham, Yorks on 7.5.89 after in-flight structural failure. Canx as destroyed 1.6.89.
G-MTUX	Medway Hybred 44XLR	241287/33		2. 2.88	
G-MTUY	Solar Wings Pegasus XL-Q	SW-TE-0041 & SW-WQ-0022		28. 1.88	
G-MTUZ	Hornet Dual Trainer/Southdown Raven	HRWA 0069 & 2000/0329		28. 1.88	Canx by CAA 24.1.95.
G-MTVA	Solar Wings Pegasus XL-R	SW-WA-1301		28. 1.88	Canx by CAA 9.1.90.
G-MTVB	Solar Wings Pegasus XL-R	SW-TB-1307 & SW-WA-1302		28. 1.88	
G-MTVC	Solar Wings Pegasus XL-R	SW-TB-1308 & SW-WA-1303		28. 1.88	
G-MTVD	Not allotted.				
G-MTVE	Solar Wings Pegasus XL-R	SW-WA-1304		28. 1.88	Canx by CAA 26.6.89.
G-MTVF	Solar Wings Pegasus XL-R	SW-WA-1305		28. 1.88	Canx by CAA 9.1.90.
G-MTVG	Mainair Gemini/Flash 2A	628-388-6 & W417		12. 2.88	
G-MTVH	Mainair Gemini/Flash 2A	626-288-6 & W415		17. 2.88	
G-MTVI	Mainair Gemini/Flash 2A	629-388-6 & W416		12. 2.88	
G-MTVJ	Mainair Gemini/Flash 2A	627-388-6 & W418		12. 2.88	
G-MTVK	Solar Wings Pegasus XL-R	SW-WA-1306		15. 2.88	
G-MTVL	Solar Wings Pegasus XL-R/Se	SW-WA-1307		15. 2.88	
G-MTVM	Solar Wings Pegasus XL-R	SW-WA-1308		15. 2.88	
G-MTVN	Solar Wings Pegasus XL-R	SW-WA-1309		15. 2.88	
G-MTVO	Solar Wings Pegasus XL-R	SW-TB-1315 & SW-WA-1310		15. 2.88	(Stored 1/98)
G-MTVP	Thruster TST Mk.1 (C/n plate marked incorrectly as 8208-TST-056)	8028-TST-056		10. 2.88	
G-MTVR	Thruster TST Mk.1	8028-TST-057		10. 2.88	
G-MTVS	Thruster TST Mk.1	8028-TST-058		10. 2.88	
G-MTVT	Thruster TST Mk.1	8028-TST-059		10. 2.88	
G-MTVU	Thruster TST Mk.1	8028-TST-060		10. 2.88	Fatal crash at Sandown, IoW on 27.6.93. Canx by CAA 27.9.93.
G-MTVV	Thruster TST Mk.1	8028-TST-061		10. 2.88	
G-MTVW	Southdown Lightning	BD-01		15. 2.88	Canx by CAA 13.6.90.
G-MTVX	Solar Wings Pegasus XL-Q	SW-TE-0042 & SW-WQ-0025		3. 3.88	

Regn	Type	c/n	Previous identity	Regn date	Fate or immediate subsequent identity (if known)
G-MTVY	Solar Wings Pegasus XL-Q	SW-WQ-0026		3. 3.88	Canx by CAA 7.8.96.
G-MTVZ	Powerchute Raider	80104		3. 3.88	
G-MTWA	Solar Wings Pegasus XL-R	SW-WA-1311		25. 2.88	
G-MTWB	Solar Wings Pegasus XL-R	SW-TB-1342 & SW-WA-1312		25. 2.88	
G-MTWC	Solar Wings Pegasus XL-R	SW-TB-1321 & SW-WA-1313		25. 2.88	
G-MTWD	Solar Wings Pegasus XL-R	SW-TB-1320 & SW-WA-1314		25. 2.88	
G-MTWE	Solar Wings Pegasus XL-R	SW-WA-1315		25. 2.88	
G-MTWF	Mainair Gemini/Flash 2A	630-388-6 & W419		25. 2.88	
G-MTWG	Mainair Gemini/Flash 2A	631-288-6 & W420		25. 2.88	
G-MTWH	CFM Shadow Srs.CD	K.064		25. 2.88	
G-MTWI	Aviasud Mistral	001		. .88R	NTU - Canx.
G-MTWJ	Aviasud Mistral	002		. .88R	NTU - Canx.
G-MTWK	CFM Shadow Srs.CD	073		25. 2.88	
G-MTWL	CFM Shadow Srs.BD	076		25. 2.88	
G-MTWM	CFM Shadow Srs.CD	080		25. 2.88	
G-MTWN	CFM Shadow Srs.CD	081		25. 2.88	
G-MTWO	Weedhopper JC-24B	AJG.003		25. 2.88	Canx by CAA 7.9.94.
G-MTWP	CFM Shadow Srs.BD (See comments under G-MZBN)	K.069		29. 2.88	
G-MTWR	Mainair Gemini/Flash 2A	632-388-6 & W421		3. 3.88	
G-MTWS	Mainair Gemini/Flash 2A	633-388-6 & W422		3. 3.88	
G-MTWT	Whittaker MW.7	PFA/171-11281		3. 3.88	NTU - To G-BOKH 21.3.88. Canx.
G-MTWU	Whittaker MW.7	PFA/171-11282		3. 3.88	NTU - To G-BOKI 21.3.88. Canx.
G-MTWV	Whittaker MW.7	PFA/171-11283		3. 3.88	NTU - To G-BOKJ 21.3.88. Canx.
G-MTWW	Ultrasports Tripacer/Solar Wings Typhoon (Regd with c/n 7781199)	T781-199		3. 3.88	Canx as destroyed 11.6.97.
G-MTWX	Mainair Gemini/Flash 2A	634-488-6 & W423		11. 3.88	
G-MTWY	Thruster TST Mk.1	8038-TST-062		15. 3.88	
G-MTWZ	Thruster TST Mk.1	8038-TST-063		15. 3.88	
G-MTXA	Thruster TST Mk.1	8038-TST-064		15. 3.88	
G-MTXB	Thruster TST Mk.1	8038-TST-065		15. 3.88	
G-MTXC	Thruster TST Mk.1	8038-TST-066		15. 3.88	
G-MTXD	Thruster TST Mk.1	8038-TST-067		15. 3.88	
G-MTXE	Hornet Dual Trainer/Southdown Raven	HRWA 0070 & 2000/0347		11. 3.88	
G-MTXF	Hornet Dual Trainer/Southdown Raven	HRWA 0071 & 2000/0343		11. 3.88	Canx 19.1.90 on sale to Pakistan.
G-MTXG	Solar Wings Pegasus XL-Q	SW-WQ-0029		11. 3.88	Canx by CAA 7.8.96.
G-MTXH	Solar Wings Pegasus XL-Q	SW-WQ-0030		11. 3.88	
G-MTXI	Solar Wings Pegasus XL-Q	SW-TB-1329 & SW-WQ-0031		11. 3.88	
G-MTXJ	Solar Wings Pegasus XL-Q	SW-TB-1330 & SW-WQ-0032		11. 3.88	
G-MTXK	Solar Wings Pegasus XL-Q	SW-WQ-0033		11. 3.88	
G-MTXL	Noble Hardman Snowbird Mk.IV	SB-006		4. 5.88	
G-MTXM	Mainair Gemini/Flash 2A	636-488-6 & W425		10. 5.88	
G-MTXN	MBA Tiger Cub 440	SO.24		23. 3.88	Canx as WFU 4.6.90.
G-MTXO	Whittaker MW.6 Merlin	PFA/164-11326		11. 3.88	
G-MTXP	Mainair Gemini/Flash 2A	637-488-6 & W426		23. 3.88	
G-MTXR	CFM Shadow Srs.CD	K.038		23. 3.88	
G-MTXS	Mainair Gemini/Flash 2A	638-488-6 & W427		23. 3.88	(Damaged late .97)
G-MTXT	MBA Tiger Cub 440	SO.25		23. 3.88	Canx as WFU 18.11.94.
G-MTXU	Noble Hardman Snowbird Mk.IV	SB-007		3. 5.88	Canx as destroyed 27.6.96.
G-MTXV	Noble Hardman Snowbird Mk.IV	SB-008		3. 5.88	To OO-B71. Canx 15.11.93.
G-MTXW	Noble Hardman Snowbird Mk.IV	SB-009		3. 5.88	Canx by CAA 8.1.90.
G-MTXX	Hornet Dual Trainer/Southdown Raven (Originally regd with c/n HRWA 0072 & 2000/0355)	HRWA 0072 & 2000/0333		30. 3.88	Canx 19.1.90 on sale to Pakistan.
G-MTXY	Hornet Dual Trainer/Southdown Raven	HRWA 0073 & 2000/0354		30. 3.88	
G-MTXZ	Mainair Gemini/Flash 2A	641-588-6 & W430		10. 5.88	
G-MTYA	Solar Wings Pegasus XL-Q	SW-TE-0047 & SW-WQ-0037		29. 3.88	
G-MTYB	Solar Wings Pegasus XL-Q	SW-TE-0048 & SW-WQ-0038		29. 3.88	Canx 18.4.89 on sale to Turkey.
G-MTYC	Solar Wings Pegasus XL-Q	SW-WQ-0039		30. 3.88	
G-MTYD	Solar Wings Pegasus XL-Q	SW-TE-0050 & SW-WQ-0040		29. 3.88	
G-MTYE	Solar Wings Pegasus XL-Q	SW-WQ-0041		29. 3.88	
G-MTYF	Solar Wings Pegasus XL-Q	SW-WQ-0042		29. 3.88	

Regn	Type	c/n	Previous identity	Regn date	Fate or immediate subsequent identity (if known)
G-MTYG	Solar Wings Pegasus XL-Q	SW-WQ-0043		29. 3.88	Canx as destroyed 24.1.92.
G-MTYH	Solar Wings Pegasus XL-Q	SW-TE-0054 & SW-WQ-0044		30. 3.88	
G-MTYI	Solar Wings Pegasus XL-Q	SW-WQ-0045		30. 3.88	
G-MTYJ	Solar Wings Pegasus XL-Q	SW-WQ-0046		30. 3.88	To Australia as 32-0537. Canx 21.11.89.
G-MTYK	Solar Wings Pegasus XL-Q	SW-WQ-0047		30. 3.88	Canx as destroyed 11.8.94.
G-MTYL	Solar Wings Pegasus XL-Q (Also c/n 6412)	SW-TE-0058 & SW-WQ-0048		30. 3.88	
G-MTYM	Solar Wings Pegasus XL-Q	SW-WQ-0049		30. 3.88	
G-MTYN	Solar Wings Pegasus XL-Q	SW-TE-0060 & SW-WQ-0050		30. 3.88	(Stored 6/97)
G-MTYO	Solar Wings Pegasus XL-Q	SW-WQ-0051		30. 3.88	Canx by CAA 7.8.96.
G-MTYP	Solar Wings Pegasus XL-Q	SW-WQ-0052		30. 3.88	(Stored 9/97)
G-MTYR	Solar Wings Pegasus XL-Q	SW-WQ-0053		30. 3.88	(Stored 6/97)
G-MTYS	Solar Wings Pegasus XL-Q	SW-TE-0064 & SW-WQ-0054		30. 3.88	(Stored 4/97)
G-MTYT	Solar Wings Pegasus XL-Q	SW-TE-0065 & SW-WQ-0055		30. 3.88	
G-MTYU	Solar Wings Pegasus XL-Q	SW-WQ-0056		30. 3.88	
G-MTYV	Southdown Raven X	2232/0341		8. 4.88	
G-MTYW	Southdown Raven X	2232/0344		8. 4.88	
G-MTYX	Southdown Raven X	2232/0345		8. 4.88	
G-MTYY	Solar Wings Pegasus XL-R	SW-WA-1326		6. 5.88	
G-MTYZ	Mainair Gemini/Flash 2A	647-688-6 & W437		10. 5.88	Fatal crash at Balne, near Selby on 24.4.89 after in-flight structural failure. Canx as destroyed 30.8.89.
G-MTZA	Thruster TST Mk.1	8048-TST-068		13. 4.88	
G-MTZB	Thruster TST Mk.1	8048-TST-069		13. 4.88	
G-MTZC	Thruster TST Mk.1	8048-TST-070		13. 4.88	
G-MTZD	Thruster TST Mk.1	8048-TST-071		13. 4.88	
G-MTZE	Thruster TST Mk.1	8048-TST-072		13. 4.88	
G-MTZF	Thruster TST Mk.1	8048-TST-073		13. 4.88	
G-MTZG	Mainair Gemini/Flash 2A	642-588-6 & W431		10. 5.88	
G-MTZH	Mainair Gemini/Flash 2A	643-588-6 & W433		9. 6.88	
G-MTZI	Solar Wings Pegasus XL-R (Extant 3/95 in Portugal - fitted with wing ex G-MTIR)	SW-WA-1327		6. 5.88	
G-MTZJ	Solar Wings Pegasus XL-R	SW-TB-1335 & SW-WA-1328		6. 5.88	
G-MTZK	Solar Wings Pegasus XL-R	SW-TB-1336 & SW-WA-1329		6. 5.88	
G-MTZL	Mainair Gemini/Flash 2A	645-588-6 & W435		10. 5.88	
G-MTZM	Mainair Gemini/Flash 2A	646-588-6 & W436		3. 5.88	
G-MTZN	Mainair Gemini/Flash 2A	648-688-6 & W438		10. 5.88	Ditched in the English Channel off Calais on 25.7.92. Canx as WFU 4.9.92.
G-MTZO	Mainair Gemini/Flash 2A	649-688-6 & W439		6. 5.88	
G-MTZP	Solar Wings Pegasus XL-Q	SW-WQ-0059		6. 5.88	
G-MTZR	Solar Wings Pegasus XL-Q	SW-TB-1338 & SW-WQ-0060		6. 5.88	
G-MTZS	Solar Wings Pegasus XL-Q	SW-WQ-0061		6. 5.88	
G-MTZT	Solar Wings Pegasus XL-Q	SW-WQ-0062		6. 5.88	
G-MTZU	Solar Wings Pegasus XL-Q	SW-TB-1341 & SW-WQ-0063		6. 5.88	CofA lapsed 4.9.92. Canx as destroyed 12.5.94.
G-MTZV	Mainair Gemini/Flash 2A	650-688-6 & W440		6. 5.88	
G-MTZW	Mainair Gemini/Flash 2A	651-688-6 & W441		25. 5.88	
G-MTZX	Mainair Gemini/Flash 2A	652-688-6 & W442		23. 6.88	
G-MTZY	Mainair Gemini/Flash 2A	653-688-6 & W443		24. 5.88	
G-MTZZ	Mainair Gemini/Flash 2A	654-688-6 & W444		14. 6.88	
G-MUFF	Aerospatiale AS.355F1 Twin Squirrel	5260	G-CORR	19. 8.87	To G-MOBI 11/93. Canx.
G-MUFY	Robinson R-22 Beta	1248	D-HICH	13.12.96	
G-MUIL	Cessna 172M Skyhawk II	172-65263	N64486	5. 6.91	To G-DRBG 1/95. Canx.
G-MUIR	Cameron V-65 HAFB	2037		23. 6.89	
G-MULL	Douglas DC-10-30 (Line No. 291)	47888	YA-LAS	21. 3.85	WFU on 1.4.99. Stored 9/99 Manchester.
G-MUMS	PA-28-161 Warrior II	28-8416093	N118AV	16. 8.91	To G-MSFT 4/97. Canx.
G-MUNE	Mooney M.20K (231)	25-0712	N1172J	20. 4.88	Fatal crash at Manor Farm, North Baddesley on 23.7.88 & DBF. Canx as destroyed 20.3.89.
G-MUNI	Mooney M.20J (201SE)	24-3118		12. 5.89	
G-MUNK	DHC.1 Chipmunk 22 (Fuselage no. DHB/f/163)	C1/0283	G-BCYL WD346	15. 4.86	Ditched in sea 2 miles southeast of Harwich, Essex on 26.9.86 and sank. Canx as destroyed 29.6.87.
G-MURF	American Aviation AA-5B Tiger	AA5B-0703	G-JOAN G-BFML	22.10.87	To PH-EAL. Canx 18.1.93.

Regn	Type	c/n	Previous identity	Regn date	Fate or immediate subsequent identity (if known)
G-MURI	Gates LearJet 35A	35A-646	N712JB N717JB/N646EA/XA-UMA/N3812G	19. 2.98	
G-MURR	Whittaker MW.6 Merlin	PFA/164-12501		6. 4.99	
G-MURY	Robinson R-44 Astro	0201		19. 7.95	
G-MUSI	Robinson R-22 Beta	0754		11. 3.88	To D-HRRR 7/91. Canx 4.6.91.
G-MUSO	Rutan LongEz	PFA/74A-10590		11. 6.83	
G-MUSS	Robinson R-22 Beta	0806		12. 5.88	To G-UPCC 6/89. Canx.
G-MUST	Commonwealth CAC-18 (P-51D) Mustang Mk.22	1524	VH-BOZ R.Australian AF A68-199	20.12.79	Export licence refused by Australian authorities in 1980 and at the Fighter World Museum, RAAF Williamtown since 1992. Canx by CAA 3.3.97.
G-MUTE	Colt 31A Air Chair HAFB	2099		2.12.91	
G-MUVG	Cessna 421C Golden Eagle III	421C-1064	N421DD	24. 1.97	
G-MUZO	Europa Avn Europa	PFA/247-12623		11. 1.94	
G-MVAA	Mainair Gemini/Flash 2A	655-688-6 & W445		8. 6.88	
G-MVAB	Mainair Gemini/Flash 2A	656-688-6 & W446		10. 5.88	
G-MVAC	CFM Shadow Srs.CD	K.077		12. 5.88	
G-MVAD	Mainair Gemini/Flash 2A	657-688-6 & W447		10. 5.88	
G-MVAE	Not allotted.				
G-MVAF	Southdown Puma Sprint 440	P.455	G-MBAF	24. 6.87	
G-MVAG	Thruster TST Mk.1	8058-TST-074		18. 5.88	
G-MVAH	Thruster TST Mk.1	8058-TST-075		18. 5.88	
G-MVAI	Thruster TST Mk.1	8058-TST-076		18. 5.88	
G-MVAJ	Thruster TST Mk.1	8058-TST-077		18. 5.88	
G-MVAK	Thruster TST Mk.1	8058-TST-078		18. 5.88	
G-MVAL	Thruster TST Mk.1	8058-TST-079		18. 5.88	
G-MVAM	CFM Shadow Srs.CD	082		18. 5.88	
G-MVAN	CFM Shadow Srs.CD	K.048 & PFA/161-11219		18. 5.88	
G-MVAO	Mainair Gemini/Flash 2A	658-688-6 & W448		24. 5.88	
G-MVAP	Mainair Gemini/Flash 2A	659-688-6 & W449		24. 5.88	
G-MVAR	Solar Wings Pegasus XL-R	SW-WA-1331		24. 5.88	
G-MVAS	Solar Wings Pegasus XL-R	SW-WA-1332		24. 5.88	
G-MVAT	Solar Wings Pegasus XL-R	SW-WA-1333		24. 5.88	
G-MVAU	Solar Wings Pegasus XL-R	SW-TB-1346 & SW-WA-1334		24. 5.88	
G-MVAV	Solar Wings Pegasus XL-R	SW-TB-1347 & SW-WA-1335		24. 5.88	
G-MVAW	Solar Wings Pegasus XL-Q	SW-TB-1348 & SW-WQ-0064		24. 5.88	
G-MVAX	Solar Wings Pegasus XL-Q	SW-TB-1349 & SW-WQ-0065		24. 5.88	
G-MVAY	Solar Wings Pegasus XL-Q	SW-WQ-0066		24. 5.88	
G-MVAZ	Solar Wings Pegasus XL-Q	SW-WQ-0067		24. 5.88	
G-MVBA	Solar Wings Pegasus XL-Q	SW-WQ-0068		24. 5.88	
G-MVBB	CFM Shadow Srs.BD	K.051		24. 5.88	
G-MVBC	Mainair Tri-Flyer/Aerial Arts 130SX	130SX-616		24. 5.88	
G-MVBD	Mainair Gemini/Flash 2A	660-688-6 & W450		8. 6.88	
G-MVBE	Mainair Scorcher	661-688-6 & W451		28. 7.88	
G-MVBF	Mainair Gemini/Flash 2A	662-688-6 & W452		14. 6.88	
G-MVBG	Mainair Gemini/Flash 2A	663-688-6 & W453		25. 5.88	
G-MVBH	Mainair Gemini/Flash 2A	664-688-6 & W454		25. 5.88	
G-MVBI	Mainair Gemini/Flash 2A	665-788-6 & W455		7. 6.88	
G-MVBJ	Solar Wings Pegasus XL-R	SW-WA-1338		7. 6.88	
G-MVBK	Mainair Gemini/Flash 2A	666-788-6 & W456		7. 6.88	
G-MVBL	Mainair Gemini/Flash 2A	669-788-6 & W459		7. 6.88	
G-MVBM	Mainair Gemini/Flash 2A	667-788-6 & W457		7. 6.88	
G-MVBN	Mainair Gemini/Flash 2A	668-788-6 & W458		8. 6.88	
G-MVBO	Mainair Gemini/Flash 2A	671-788-6 & W461		8. 6.88	
G-MVBP	Thruster TST Mk.1	8068-TST-080		14. 6.88	
G-MVBR	Thruster TST Mk.1	8068-TST-081		14. 6.88	Canx by CAA 5.11.98. To G-DRUM 12.1.99.
G-MVBS	Thruster TST Mk.1 (Regd as c/n 8060-TST-082)	8068-TST-082		14. 6.88	(Extant 8/97)
G-MVBT	Thruster TST Mk.1	8068-TST-083		14. 6.88	
G-MVBU	Thruster TST Mk.1	8068-TST-084		14. 6.88	(Stored 9/97)
G-MVBV	Thruster TST Mk.1	8068-TST-085		14. 6.88	Canx 8.6.89 on sale to France.

Regn	Type	c/n	Previous identity	Regn date	Fate or immediate subsequent identity (if known)
G-MVBW	CFM Shadow Srs.BD	083		14. 6.88	To VT-UME 4/92. Canx 30.8.91.
G-MVBX	Solar Wings Pegasus XL-R	SW-TB-1356 & SW-WA-1343		17. 6.88	To OO-A01. Canx 21.2.91.
G-MVBY	Solar Wings Pegasus XL-R	SW-WA-1344		17. 6.88	
G-MVBZ	Solar Wings Pegasus XL-R	SW-TB-1358 & SW-WA-1345		17. 6.88	Canx by CAA 6.9.89.
G-MVCA	Solar Wings Pegasus XL-R	SW-WA-1346		17. 6.88	
G-MVCB	Solar Wings Pegasus XL-R	SW-TB-1360 & SW-WA-1347		17. 6.88	
G-MVCC	CFM Shadow Srs.CD	K.045		17. 6.88	
G-MVCD	Medway Hybred 44XLR (Marked as a Raven)	MR001/34		14. 6.88	
G-MVCE	Mainair Gemini/Flash 2A	672-788-6 & W462		23. 6.88	
G-MVCF	Mainair Gemini/Flash 2A	673-788-6 & W463		14. 7.88	
G-MVCG	Skyhook Cutlass	JDG-01		23. 6.88	Despite this regn being canx by CAA 13.6.90, it was reported as being badly damaged in collision with a tree on a circuit at Stirling on 16.6.96.
G-MVCH	Noble Hardman Snowbird Mk.IV	SB-010		11.10.88	Canx as destroyed 17.7.96.
G-MVCI	Noble Hardman Snowbird Mk.IV	SB-011		11.10.88	
G-MVCJ	Noble Hardman Snowbird Mk.IV	SB-012		11.10.88	
G-MVCK	Cosmos Trike/La Mouette Profil 19	SDA-01		19. 7.88	
G-MVCL	Solar Wings Pegasus XL-Q	SW-WQ-0075		27. 6.88	(Damaged late .97)
G-MVCM	Solar Wings Pegasus XL-Q	SW-TE-0070 & SW-WQ-0076		27. 6.88	
G-MVCN	Solar Wings Pegasus XL-Q	SW-WQ-0077		27. 6.88	
G-MVCO	Solar Wings Pegasus XL-Q	SW-TE-0072 & SW-WQ-0078		27. 6.88	
G-MVCP	Solar Wings Pegasus XL-Q	SW-TE-0073 & SW-WQ-0079		27. 6.88	
G-MVCR	Solar Wings Pegasus XL-Q	SW-WQ-0080		27. 6.88	
G-MVCS	Solar Wings Pegasus XL-Q	SW-TE-0075 & SW-WQ-0081		27. 6.88	
G-MVCT	Solar Wings Pegasus XL-Q	SW-TE-0076 & SW-WQ-0082		27. 6.88	
G-MVCU	Solar Wings Pegasus XL-Q	SW-WQ-0083		27. 6.88	Fatal crash after breaking up in mid-air and crashing at Sunken Island, West Mersea, Essex on 4.5.92. Canx by CAA 23.7.92.
G-MVCV	Solar Wings Pegasus XL-Q	SW-WQ-0084		27. 6.88	
G-MVCW	CFM Shadow Srs.BD	084		28. 6.88	
G-MVCX	Chargus Vortex	TF-01		28. 6.88	Canx as destroyed 17.5.90.
G-MVCY	Mainair Gemini/Flash 2A	674-788-6 & W464		14. 7.88	
G-MVCZ	Mainair Gemini/Flash 2A	675-788-6 & W465		26. 8.88	Collided in mid-air with Cessna 152 G-BHAB over Shobdon on 10.2.89. Canx by CAA 7.8.96.
G-MVDA	Mainair Gemini/Flash 2A	676-788-6 & W466		13. 7.88	
G-MVDB	Medway Hybred 44XLR	MR005/36		28. 7.88	
G-MVDC	Medway Hybred 44XL (Fitted with trike from G-MTNE)	MR009/37		13. 7.88	
G-MVDD	Thruster TST Mk.1	8078-TST-086		12. 7.88	
G-MVDE	Thruster TST Mk.1	8078-TST-087		12. 7.88	
G-MVDF	Thruster TST Mk.1	8078-TST-088		12. 7.88	
G-MVDG	Thruster TST Mk.1	8078-TST-089		12. 7.88	
G-MVDH	Thruster TST Mk.1	8078-TST-090		12. 7.88	
G-MVDI	Thruster TST Mk.1	8078-TST-091		12. 7.88	To EI-CKI 6/94. Canx 14.4.94.
G-MVDJ	Medway Hybred 44XLR	MR010/38		20. 7.88	
G-MVDK	Aerial Arts Chaser S	CH.702		5. 8.88	
G-MVDL	Aerial Arts Chaser S	CH.701		11. 8.88	
G-MVDM	Aerial Arts Chaser S	CH.703		11. 8.88	To G-MZTS 3/96. Canx.
G-MVDN	Aerial Arts Chaser S	CH.704		11. 8.88	
G-MVDO	Aerial Arts Chaser S	CH.705		11. 8.88	Canx by CAA 4.12.95.
G-MVDP	Aerial Arts Chaser S	CH.706		11. 8.88	
G-MVDR	Aerial Arts Chaser S	CH.708		11. 8.88	
G-MVDS	Hiway Skytrike/Demon 175	PB-01		30. 6.88	Canx by CAA 24.1.95.
G-MVDT	Mainair Gemini/Flash 2A	670-788-6 & W460		20. 7.88	
G-MVDU	Solar Wings Pegasus XL-R	SW-WA-1348		13. 7.88	
G-MVDV	Solar Wings Pegasus XL-R	SW-WA-1349		13. 7.88	
G-MVDW	Solar Wings Pegasus XL-R	SW-WA-1350		13. 7.88	
G-MVDX	Solar Wings Pegasus XL-R	SW-WA-1351		13. 7.88	
G-MVDY	Solar Wings Pegasus XL-R	SW-WA-1352		13. 7.88	
G-MVDZ	Solar Wings Pegasus XL-R	SW-WA-1353		12. 7.88	
G-MVEA	Solar Wings Pegasus XL-R	SW-TB-1367 & SW-WA-1354		20. 7.88	
G-MVEB	Solar Wings Pegasus XL-R	SW-WA-1355		22. 7.88	Canx by CAA 7.8.96.
G-MVEC	Solar Wings Pegasus XL-R	SW-TB-1369 & SW-WA-1356		20. 7.88	
G-MVED	Solar Wings Pegasus XL-R/Se	SW-TB-1370 & SW-WA-1357		20. 7.88	
G-MVEE	Medway Hybred 44XLR	MR004/35		22. 7.88	

Regn	Type	c/n	Previous identity	Regn date	Fate or immediate subsequent identity (if known)
G-MVEF	Solar Wings Pegasus XL-R	SW-WA-1358		19. 7.88	
G-MVEG	Solar Wings Pegasus XL-R	SW-TE-0080 & SW-WA-1359		19. 7.88	
G-MVEH	Mainair Gemini/Flash 2A	677-788-6 & W468		26. 8.88	
G-MVEI	CFM Shadow Srs.CD	085		26. 7.88	
G-MVEJ	Mainair Gemini/Flash 2A	678-888-6 & W469		27. 7.88	
G-MVEK	Mainair Gemini/Flash 2A	679-888-6 & W470		27. 7.88	
G-MVEL	Mainair Gemini/Flash 2A	680-888-6 & W471		27. 7.88	
G-MVEM	Mainair Gemini/Flash 2A	681-888-6 & W432		27. 7.88	To ZS-WMH. Canx 19.6.90.
G-MVEN	CFM Shadow Srs.CD	K.047		26. 7.88	
G-MVEO	Mainair Gemini/Flash 2A	682-888-6 & W472		28. 7.88	
G-MVEP	Mainair Gemini/Flash 2A	683-888-6 & W473		15. 9.88	Fatal crash on 27.10.97 in a field at Reeves Lane, Roydon, Essex. Canx as destroyed 10.2.98.
G-MVER	Mainair Gemini/Flash 2A	684-888-6 & W474		28. 7.88	
G-MVES	Mainair Gemini/Flash 2A	685-888-6 & W475		5. 8.88	
G-MVET	Mainair Gemini/Flash 2A	686-888-6 & W476		19. 8.88	
G-MVEU	Hornet Dual Trainer/Southdown Raven	HRWA 0074 & MHR-100		7. 9.88	To Australia as T2-2535. Canx 9.1.90.
G-MVEV	Mainair Gemini/Flash 2A	687-888-6 & W477		5. 8.88	
G-MVEW	Mainair Gemini/Flash 2A	688-988-6 & W478		16. 9.88	
G-MVEX	Solar Wings Pegasus XL-Q	SW-WQ-0088		5. 8.88	
G-MVEY	Solar Wings Pegasus XL-Q	SW-WQ-0089		9. 8.88	Canx by CAA 28.6.96.
G-MVEZ	Solar Wings Pegasus XL-Q	SW-TE-0084 & SW-WQ-0090		9. 8.88	
G-MVFA	Solar Wings Pegasus XL-Q	SW-TE-0085 & SW-WQ-0091		9. 8.88	
G-MVFB	Solar Wings Pegasus XL-Q	SW-TE-0086 & SW-WQ-0092		9. 8.88	
G-MVFC	Solar Wings Pegasus XL-Q	SW-WQ-0093		9. 8.88	
G-MVFD	Solar Wings Pegasus XL-Q	SW-TE-0088 & SW-WQ-0094		9. 8.88	
G-MVFE	Solar Wings Pegasus XL-Q	SW-WQ-0095		9. 8.88	
G-MVFF	Solar Wings Pegasus XL-Q	SW-TE-0090 & SW-WQ-0096		9. 8.88	
G-MVFG	Solar Wings Pegasus XL-Q	SW-TE-0091 & SW-WQ-0097		9. 8.88	
G-MVFH	CFM Shadow Srs.CD	086		9. 8.88	
G-MVFI	Solar Wings Pegasus XL	APW-01		9. 8.88	Canx by CAA 13.6.90.
G-MVFJ	Thruster TST Mk.1	8088-TST-092		11. 8.88	
G-MVFK	Thruster TST Mk.1	8088-TST-093		11. 8.88	
G-MVFL	Thruster TST Mk.1	8088-TST-094		11. 8.88	
G-MVFM	Thruster TST Mk.1	8088-TST-095		11. 8.88	
G-MVFN	Thruster TST Mk.1	8088-TST-096		11. 8.88	
G-MVFO	Thruster TST Mk.1	8088-TST-097		11. 8.88	
G-MVFP	Solar Wings Pegasus XL-R	SW-TB-1371 & SW-WA-1365		9. 8.88	
G-MVFR	Solar Wings Pegasus XL-R	SW-TB-1372 & SW-WA-1366		9. 8.88	
G-MVFS	Solar Wings Pegasus XL-R/Se	SW-TB-1373 & SW-WA-1367		9. 8.88	
G-MVFT	Solar Wings Pegasus XL-R	SW-WA-1368		9. 8.88	
G-MVFU	Solar Wings Pegasus XL-R	SW-WA-1369		9. 8.88	Canx by CAA 7.8.96.
G-MVFV	Solar Wings Pegasus XL-R	SW-WA-1370		9. 8.88	
G-MVFW	Solar Wings Pegasus XL-R	SW-WA-1371		9. 8.88	
G-MVFX	Solar Wings Pegasus XL-R	SW-WA-1372		9. 8.88	
G-MVFY	Solar Wings Pegasus XL-R	SW-WA-1373		9. 8.88	
G-MVFZ	Solar Wings Pegasus XL-R	SW-TB-1380 & SW-WA-1374		9. 8.88	
G-MVGA	Aerial Arts Chaser S	CH.707		11. 8.88	
G-MVGB	Medway Hybred 44XLR	MR011/39		1. 9.88	
G-MVGC	AMF Chevvron 2-32C	010		2. 9.88	
G-MVGD	AMF Chevvron 2-32	011		5. 9.88	
G-MVGE	AMF Chevvron 2-32C	012		26. 9.88	
G-MVGF	Aerial Arts Chaser S	CH.720		2. 9.88	
G-MVGG	Aerial Arts Chaser S	CH.721		2. 9.88	
G-MVGH	Aerial Arts Chaser S	CH.722		2. 9.88	
G-MVGI	Aerial Arts Chaser S	CH.723		1. 9.88	
G-MVGJ	Aerial Arts Chaser S	CH.724		2. 9.88	
G-MVGK	Aerial Arts Chaser S	CH.726		2. 9.88	(Stored 5/97)
G-MVGL	Medway Hybred 44XLR	MR012/40		1. 9.88	
G-MVGM	Mainair Gemini/Flash 2A	691-988-6 & W481		25. 8.88	

Regn	Type	c/n	Previous identity	Regn date	Fate or immediate subsequent identity (if known)
G-MVGN	Solar Wings Pegasus XL-R/Se	SW-TB-1381 & SW-WA-1377		23. 8.88	
G-MVGO	Solar Wings Pegasus XL-R	SW-TB-1382 & SW-WA-1378		23. 8.88	
G-MVGP	Solar Wings Pegasus XL-R	SW-WA-1379	(EC-...) G-MVGP	23. 8.88	
G-MVGR	Solar Wings Pegasus XL-R/Se	SW-WA-1380		23. 8.88	
G-MVGS	Solar Wings Pegasus XL-R	SW-TB-1385 & SW-WA-1381		23. 8.88	
G-MVGT	Solar Wings Pegasus XL-Q	SW-TE-0092 & SW-WQ-0099		23. 8.88	
G-MVGU	Solar Wings Pegasus XL-Q	SW-WQ-0100		23. 8.88	
G-MVGV	Solar Wings Pegasus XL-Q	SW-TE-0094 & SW-WQ-0101		23. 8.88	
G-MVGW	Solar Wings Pegasus XL-Q	SW-WQ-0102		23. 8.88	
G-MVGX	Solar Wings Pegasus XL-Q	SW-WQ-0103		23. 8.88	Canx as WFU 31.8.93.
G-MVGY	Medway Hybred 44XLR	MR015/41		31. 8.88	
G-MVGZ	Ultraflight Lazair IIIE	A.338	(ex ?)	21.10.88	
G-MVHA	Aerial Arts Chaser S-1000	CH.729		24. 8.88	
G-MVHB	Powerchute Raider	80105		26. 8.88	
G-MVHC	Powerchute Raider	80106		26. 8.88	
G-MVHD	CFM Shadow Srs.CD	088		8. 9.88	
G-MVHE	Mainair Gemini/Flash 2A	692-988-6 & W482		4.10.88	
G-MVHF	Mainair Gemini/Flash 2A	693-988-6 & W483		4.10.88	
G-MVHG	Mainair Gemini/Flash 2A	694-988-6 & W484		14.10.88	
G-MVHH	Mainair Gemini/Flash 2A	607-1187-5 & W485		24.10.88	
	(Originally Trike No 695, replaced by 607 ex G-MTSA .95)				
G-MVHI	Thruster TST Mk.1	8098-TST-100		26. 9.88	
G-MVHJ	Thruster TST Mk.1	8098-TST-101		26. 9.88	
G-MVHK	Thruster TST Mk.1	8098-TST-102		27. 9.88	
G-MVHL	Thruster TST Mk.1	8098-TST-103		27. 9.88	
G-MVHM	Whittaker MW.5 Sorcerer (Mod)	PFA/163-11314		8. 9.88	
G-MVHN	Aerial Arts Chaser S	CH.728		9. 9.88	
G-MVHO	Solar Wings Pegasus XL-Q	SW-WQ-0104		23. 9.88	
G-MVHP	Solar Wings Pegasus XL-Q	SW-WQ-0105		23. 9.88	
G-MVHR	Solar Wings Pegasus XL-Q	SW-TE-0099 & SW-WQ-0106		23. 9.88	
G-MVHS	Solar Wings Pegasus XL-Q	SW-WQ-0107		23. 9.88	
G-MVHT	Solar Wings Pegasus XL-Q	SW-WQ-0108		23. 9.88	
G-MVHU	Solar Wings Pegasus XL-Q	SW-TE-0182 & SW-WQ-0109		23. 9.88	
G-MVHV	Solar Wings Pegasus XL-Q	SW-WQ-0110		23. 9.88	
G-MVHW	Solar Wings Pegasus XL-Q	SW-TE-0101 & SW-WQ-0111		23. 9.88	
G-MVHX	Solar Wings Pegasus XL-Q	SW-TE-0105 & SW-WQ-0112		23. 9.88	
G-MVHY	Solar Wings Pegasus XL-Q	SW-TE-0106 & SW-WQ-0113		23. 9.88	
G-MVHZ	Hornet Dual Trainer/Southdown Raven	HRWA 0076 & MHR-101		26. 9.88	
G-MVIA	Solar Wings Pegasus XL-R	SW-WA-1375		4.10.88	
G-MVIB	Mainair Gemini/Flash 2A	700-1088-4 & W490		14.10.88	
G-MVIC	Mainair Gemini/Flash 2A	699-1188-4 & W489		4.10.88	
G-MVID	Aerial Arts Chaser S	CH.731		14.10.88	Canx by CAA 7.8.96.
G-MVIE	Aerial Arts Chaser S	CH.732		14.10.88	
G-MVIF	Medway Hybred 44XLR	MR020/43		4.10.88	
G-MVIG	CFM Shadow Srs.B	K.044		5.10.88	(Damaged in 1993) (Stored 8/93)
G-MVIH	Mainair Gemini/Flash 2A	697-1088-6 & W487		14.10.88	
G-MVII	Hornet Dual Trainer/Southdown Raven	HRWA 0077 & MHR-104		14.10.88	NTU - Not Built. Canx by CAA 3.10.89.
G-MVIJ	Hornet Dual Trainer/Southdown Raven	HRWA 0078 & MHR-105		14.10.88	NTU - Not built. Canx by CAA 12.4.90.
G-MVIK	Hornet Dual Trainer/Southdown Raven	HRWA 0079 & MHR-106		14.10.88	NTU - Not built. Canx by CAA 12.4.90.
G-MVIL	Noble Hardman Snowbird Mk.IV	SB-014		6. 2.89	
G-MVIM	Noble Hardman Snowbird Mk.IV	SB-015		6. 2.89	(Stored 6/96)
G-MVIN	Noble Hardman Snowbird Mk.IV	SB-016		6. 2.89	
G-MVIO	Noble Hardman Snowbird Mk.IV	SB-017		12. 4.89	
G-MVIP	AMF Chevvron 2-32	008		11. 5.88	
G-MVIR	Thruster TST Mk.1	8108-TST-104		21.10.88	
	(C/n plate marked as 8118-TST-104)				
G-MVIS	Thruster TST Mk.1	8108-TST-105		21.10.88	(Damaged mid .95)
G-MVIT	Thruster TST Mk.1	8108-TST-106		21.10.88	Canx 16.5.90 on sale to Canada.
G-MVIU	Thruster TST Mk.1	8108-TST-107		21.10.88	

Regn	Type	c/n	Previous identity	Regn date	Fate or immediate subsequent identity (if known)
G-MVIV	Thruster TST Mk.1	8108-TST-108		21.10.88	
G-MVIW	Thruster TST Mk.1	8108-TST-109		21.10.88	Canx by CAA 23.3.99.
G-MVIX	Mainair Gemini/Flash 2A	702-1088-6 & W492		14.10.88	(Damaged mid .96)
G-MVIY	Mainair Gemini/Flash 2A	701-1088-6 & W491		14.10.88	
G-MVIZ	Mainair Gemini/Flash 2A	703-1088-6 & W493		14.10.88	
G-MVJA	Mainair Gemini/Flash 2A	696-988-6 & W486		5.12.88	
G-MVJB	Mainair Gemini/Flash 2A	704-1088-6 & W494		24.10.88	Permit expired 29.7.97. (Stored 2/99 at North Walsham Airfield, Norfolk)
G-MVJC	Mainair Gemini/Flash 2A	705-1088-6 & W495		24.10.88	
G-MVJD	Solar Wings Pegasus XL-R	SW-TE-0109 & SW-WA-1386		24.10.88	
G-MVJE	Mainair Gemini/Flash 2A	706-1188-6 & W496		21.10.88	
G-MVJF	Aerial Arts Chaser S	CH.743		21.11.88	
G-MVJG	Aerial Arts Chaser S	CH.749		22.11.88	
G-MVJH	Aerial Arts Chaser S	CH.751		14.11.88	
G-MVJI	Aerial Arts Chaser S	CH.752		17.11.88	
G-MVJJ	Aerial Arts Chaser S	CH.753		14.11.88	
G-MVJK	Aerial Arts Chaser S	CH.754		14.11.88	
G-MVJL	Mainair Gemini/Flash 2A	698-1188-6 & W488		21.10.88	(Extant 1/98)
G-MVJM	Microflight Spectrum	007		21.10.88	
G-MVJN	Solar Wings Pegasus XL-Q	SW-TE-0110 & SW-WQ-0116		26.10.88	(Stored 6/96)
G-MVJO	Solar Wings Pegasus XL-Q	SW-WQ-0117		26.10.88	
G-MVJP	Solar Wings Pegasus XL-Q	SW-WQ-0118		26.10.88	
G-MVJR	Solar Wings Pegasus XL-Q	SW-WQ-0119		26.10.88	
G-MVJS	Solar Wings Pegasus XL-Q	SW-WQ-0120		26.10.88	Canx by CAA 12.5.89.
G-MVJT	Solar Wings Pegasus XL-Q	SW-TE-0115 & SW-WQ-0121		26.10.88	
G-MVJU	Solar Wings Pegasus XL-Q	SW-TE-0116 & SW-WQ-0122		26.10.88	
G-MVJV	Solar Wings Pegasus XL-Q	SW-TE-0117 & SW-WQ-0123		26.10.88	To G-DEAN 11/98. Canx.
G-MVJW	Solar Wings Pegasus XL-Q	SE-TE-0118 & SW-WQ-0124		26.10.88	
G-MVJX	Solar Wings Pegasus XL-Q	SW-WQ-0125		26.10.88	Canx as destroyed 17.10.96. (Wing stored 9/97)
G-MVJY	Hornet Dual Trainer/Southdown Raven	HRWA 0080 & MHR-112		26.10.88	NTU - Not built. Canx by CAA 12.4.90.
G-MVJZ	Ultrasports Tripacer/Birdman Cherokee	CHM 5071079		27.10.88	Canx by CAA 12.5.89.
G-MVKA	Medway Hybred 44XLR	MR021/44		7.11.88	Canx as WFU 13.8.97.
G-MVKB	Medway Hybred 44XLR	MR023/45		11.11.88	
G-MVKC	Mainair Gemini/Flash 2A	709-1188-6 & W499		16.11.88	
G-MVKD	Solar Wings Pegasus XL-R	SW-WA-1390		14.11.88	Canx 8.11.89 on sale to Australia.
G-MVKE	Solar Wings Pegasus XL-R	SW-WA-1391		14.11.88	(Stored 6/96)
G-MVKF	Solar Wings Pegasus XL-R	SW-WA-1392		14.11.88	
G-MVKG	Solar Wings Pegasus XL-R	SW-TB-1390 & SW-WA-1393		14.11.88	
G-MVKH	Solar Wings Pegasus XL-R	SW-TB-1391 & SW-WA-1394		14.11.88	
G-MVKI	Solar Wings Pegasus XL-R	SW-WA-1395		14.11.88	Canx by CAA 7.8.96.
G-MVKJ	Solar Wings Pegasus XL-R	SW-TB-1393 & SW-WA-1396		14.11.88	
G-MVKK	Solar Wings Pegasus XL-R	SW-WA-1397		14.11.88	
G-MVKL	Solar Wings Pegasus XL-R	SW-WA-1398		14.11.88	
G-MVKM	Solar Wings Pegasus XL-R	SW-TE-0136 & SW-WA-1399		14.11.88	
G-MVKN	Solar Wings Pegasus XL-Q	SW-TE-0120 & SW-WQ-0126		14.11.88	
G-MVKO	Solar Wings Pegasus XL-Q	SW-TE-0121 & SW-WQ-0127		14.11.88	
G-MVKP	Solar Wings Pegasus XL-Q	SW-TE-0122 & SW-WQ-0128		14.11.88	
G-MVKR	Solar Wings Pegasus XL-Q	SW-WQ-0129		14.11.88	Canx by CAA 29.11.94.
G-MVKS	Solar Wings Pegasus XL-Q	SW-TE-0124 & SW-WQ-0130		14.11.88	(Stored 8/95)
G-MVKT	Solar Wings Pegasus XL-Q	SW-WQ-0131		14.11.88	
G-MVKU	Solar Wings Pegasus XL-Q	SW-TE-0126 & SW-WQ-0132		14.11.88	
G-MVKV	Solar Wings Pegasus XL-Q (Originally regd with c/n SW-WQ-0133)	SW-WQ-0152		14.11.88	
G-MVKW	Solar Wings Pegasus XL-Q	SW-WQ-0134		14.11.88	
G-MVKX	Solar Wings Pegasus XL-Q	SW-TE-0129 & SW-WQ-0135		14.11.88	
G-MVKY	Aerial Arts Chaser S	CH.755		5.12.88	
G-MVKZ	Aerial Arts Chaser S	CH.756		5.12.88	

Regn	Type	c/n	Previous identity	Regn date	Fate or immediate subsequent identity (if known)
G-MVLA	Aerial Arts Chaser S	CH.762		12.12.88	
G-MVLB	Aerial Arts Chaser S	CH.763		5.12.88	
G-MVLC	Aerial Arts Chaser S	CH.764		22.11.88	
G-MVLD	Aerial Arts Chaser S	CH.765		22.11.88	
G-MVLE	Aerial Arts Chaser S	CH.766		5.12.88	
G-MVLF	Aerial Arts Chaser S	CH.767		11. 1.89	
G-MVLG	Aerial Arts Chaser S	CH.768		14.11.88	
G-MVLH	Aerial Arts Chaser S	CH.769		22.11.88	
G-MVLI	Aerial Arts Chaser S	CH.770		. .88R	NTU - Canx.
G-MVLJ	CFM Shadow Srs.CD	092		11.11.88	
G-MVLK	Hornet Dual Trainer/Southdown Raven	HRWB 0050 & MHR-102		16.11.88	NTU - Not built. Canx by CAA 12.4.90.
G-MVLL	Mainair Gemini/Flash 2A	708-1188-6 & W498		23.11.88	
G-MVLM	Solar Wings Pegasus Bandit	SW-WX-0015		23.11.88	Canx as WFU 29.3.94. (Trike stored for rebuild 4/96)
G-MVLN	CFM Shadow Srs.BD	093		22.11.88	To HA-YABD. Canx 27.4.89.
G-MVLO	CFM Shadow Srs.BD	094		22.11.88	To HA-YABE. Canx 27.4.89.
G-MVLP	CFM Shadow Srs.B	095		22.11.88	
G-MVLR	Mainair Gemini/Flash 2A	713-1288-6 & W503		30.11.88	
G-MVLS	Aerial Arts Chaser S	CH.773		21. 2.89	
G-MVLT	Aerial Arts Chaser S	CH.774		5.12.88	
G-MVLU	Aerial Arts Chaser S	CH.775		5.12.88	
G-MVLV	Aerial Arts Chaser S	CH.776		27. 4.89	Crashed in sea off Hayling Island on 19.7.89. Canx as destroyed 25.9.89.
G-MVLW	Aerial Arts Chaser S	CH.778		28.12.88	
G-MVLX	Solar Wings Pegasus XL-Q	SW-TE-0133 & SW-WQ-0114		30.11.88	
G-MVLY	Solar Wings Pegasus XL-Q	SW-WQ-0142		5.12.88	
G-MVLZ	Solar Wings Pegasus XL-Q	SW-WQ-0143		5.12.88	Canx by CAA 17.8.95.
G-MVMA	Solar Wings Pegasus XL-Q	SW-TE-0139 & SW-WQ-0144		5.12.88	
G-MVMB	Solar Wings Pegasus XL-Q	SW-WQ-0145		5.12.88	
G-MVMC	Solar Wings Pegasus XL-Q	SW-TE-0141 & SW-WQ-0146		5.12.88	
G-MVMD	Powerchute Raider	80924		15.12.88	
G-MVME	Thruster TST Mk.1	8128-TST-110		12.12.88	
G-MVMF	Thruster TST Mk.1	8128-TST-111		. .88R	NTU - Canx.
G-MVMG	Thruster TST Mk.1	8128-TST-112		12.12.88	(Damaged mid .96)
G-MVMH	Thruster TST Mk.1	8128-TST-113		12.12.88	Canx as destroyed 7.11.89.
G-MVMI	Thruster TST Mk.1	8128-TST-114		12.12.88	
G-MVMJ	Thruster TST Mk.1	8128-TST-115		12.12.88	To G-MYWZ 2/93. Canx.
G-MVMK	Medway Hybred 44XLR	MR022/46		12.12.88	
G-MVML	Aerial Arts Chaser S	CH.781		28.12.88	
G-MVMM	Aerial Arts Chaser S	CH.797		21. 2.89	
G-MVMN	Mainair Gemini/Flash 2A	714-1288-6 & W506		18. 1.89	Canx as destroyed 4.8.99.
G-MVMO	Mainair Gemini/Flash 2A	715-1288-6 & W507		12.12.88	
G-MVMP	Eipper Quicksilver MX II	1380		28.12.88	Canx by CAA 7.9.94.
G-MVMR	Mainair Gemini/Flash 2A	717-1288-6 & W509		9. 1.89	
G-MVMS	Mainair Razor	707-1088-1 & W497		27.10.88	Fatal crash at Newhey, near Rochdale on 7.6.89 after in-flight structural failure. Canx as destroyed 6.9.89.
G-MVMT	Mainair Gemini/Flash 2A	718-189-6 & W510		22.12.88	
G-MVMU	Mainair Gemini/Flash 2A	719-189-6 & W511		22.12.88	
G-MVMV	Mainair Gemini/Flash 2A	720-189-6 & W512		22.12.88	
G-MVMW	Mainair Gemini/Flash 2A	710-1188-6 & W500		11.11.88	
G-MVMX	Mainair Gemini/Flash 2A (Trike stamped incorrectly as W512)	721-189-6 & W513		23.12.88	
G-MVMY	Mainair Gemini/Flash 2A	722-189-6 & W514		22.12.88	
G-MVMZ	Mainair Gemini/Flash 2A	723-189-6 & W515		22.12.88	
G-MVNA	Powerchute Raider	81230		12. 7.89	
G-MVNB	Powerchute Raider	81231		12. 7.89	
G-MVNC	Powerchute Raider	81232		12. 7.89	
G-MVND	Powerchute Raider	81233		12. 7.89	Canx by CAA 7.8.96.
G-MVNE	Powerchute Raider	90219		12. 7.89	
G-MVNF	Powerchute Raider	81235		12. 7.89	Canx as WFU 12.7.96.
G-MVNG	Powerchute Raider	90621		12. 7.89	Canx 23.11.92 on sale to Australia.
G-MVNH	Powerchute Raider	90220		12. 7.89	Canx 16.5.90 on sale to Australia.
G-MVNI	Powerchute Raider	90625		12. 7.89	
G-MVNJ	Powerchute Raider	81239		12. 7.89	Canx by CAA 7.8.96.
G-MVNK	Powerchute Raider	90623		12. 7.89	
G-MVNL	Powerchute Raider	90624		12. 7.89	

Regn	Type	c/n	Previous identity	Regn date	Fate or immediate subsequent identity (if known)
G-MVNM	Mainair Gemini/Flash 2A	725-189-6 & W517		6. 1.89	
G-MVNN	Aerotech MW.5(K) Sorcerer	BMAA/HB/022 & 5K-0003-02		28. 3.90	
G-MVNO	Aerotech MW.5(K) Sorcerer	5K-0004-02		4. 5.89	
G-MVNP	Aerotech MW.5(K) Sorcerer	5K-0005-02		13. 7.89	
G-MVNR	Aerotech MW.5(K) Sorcerer	5K-0006-02		4. 5.89	
G-MVNS	Aerotech MW.5(K) Sorcerer	5K-0007-02		19. 7.89	
G-MVNT	Aerotech MW.5(K) Sorcerer	5K-0008-02		28. 3.90	
G-MVNU	Aerotech MW.5(K) Sorcerer	5K-0009-02		4. 5.89	
G-MVNV	Aerotech MW.5(K) Sorcerer	5K-0010-02		. .89R	NTU - Canx.
G-MVNW	Mainair Gemini/Flash 2A	726-189-6 & W518		25. 1.89	
G-MVNX	Mainair Gemini/Flash 2A	727-289-6 & W519		10. 1.89	
G-MVNY	Mainair Gemini/Flash 2A	724-189-6 & W516		11. 1.89	
G-MVNZ	Mainair Gemini/Flash 2A	728-289-6 & W520		11. 1.89	
G-MVOA	Aerial Arts Chaser S (Also reported as Aerial Arts Alligator with c/n AL.780)	CH.780		16. 1.89	(Stored 2/99 Eshott)
G-MVOB	Mainair Gemini/Flash 2A	729-289-6 & W521		16. 1.89	
G-MVOC	Eurowing Goldwing	0012		16. 1.89	NTU - Canx 31.1.89.
G-MVOD	Aerial Arts Chaser/110SX	110SX/653		16. 1.89	
G-MVOE	Solar Wings Pegasus XL-R	SW-WA-1401		23. 1.89	
G-MVOF	Mainair Gemini/Flash 2A	730-289-6 & W522		31. 1.89	
G-MVOG	Huntair Pathfinder Mk.1	KRG-02		26. 1.89	Canx by CAA 7.9.94.
G-MVOH	CFM Shadow Srs.CD	K.090		23. 1.89	
G-MVOI	Noble Hardman Snowbird Mk.IV	SB-018		6. 2.89	
G-MVOJ	Noble Hardman Snowbird Mk.IV	SB-019		26. 7.89	
G-MVOK	Noble Hardman Snowbird Mk.IV	SB-020		7.11.89	Canx by CAA 9.2.93.
G-MVOL	Noble Hardman Snowbird Mk.IV	SB-021		29. 8.89	(Noted hangared with wings removed at Pembrey in 3/99)
G-MVOM	Medway Htbred 44XLR	MR035/51		31. 1.89	Canx as WFU 28.9.93.
G-MVON	Mainair Gemini/Flash 2A	731-289-6 & W523		30. 1.89	
G-MVOO	AMF Chevvron 2-32C	014		10. 1.89	
G-MVOP	Aerial Arts Chaser S	CH.787		21. 2.89	
G-MVOR	Mainair Gemini/Flash 2A	732-289-6 & W524	(EC-...) G-MVOR	6. 2.89	
G-MVOS	Southdown Puma/Raven	PJB-02		6. 2.89	
G-MVOT	Thruster TST Mk.1	8029-TST-116		17. 2.89	
G-MVOU	Thruster TST Mk.1	8029-TST-117		17. 2.89	
G-MVOV	Thruster TST Mk.1	8029-TST-118		17. 2.89	
G-MVOW	Thruster TST Mk.1	8029-TST-119		17. 2.89	
G-MVOX	Thruster TST Mk.1	8029-TST-120		17. 2.89	
G-MVOY	Thruster TST Mk.1	8029-TST-121		17. 2.89	Damaged mid 1996. Permit expired 25.6.97. Wreck stored 2/99 at Kimberley Airfield, Norfolk.
G-MVOZ	Mainair Gemini/Flash 2A	734-289-6 & W526	EI-... G-MVOZ	7. 2.89	(Possibly EI-BXN(2) from 25.9.89 until 1.4.93) Canx 24.2.94 on sale to Italy.
G-MVPA	Mainair Gemini/Flash 2A	735-289-7 & W527		29. 3.89	
G-MVPB	Mainair Gemini/Flash 2A	736-389-7 & W528		29. 3.89	
G-MVPC	Mainair Gemini/Flash 2A (Has c/n stamp 740-389-7 & W532 - see G-MVPI)	737-389-7 & W529		7. 2.89	
G-MVPD	Mainair Gemini/Flash 2A	738-389-7 & W530		7. 2.89	
G-MVPE	Mainair Gemini/Flash 2A	739-389-7 & W531		7. 2.89	
G-MVPF	Medway Hybred 44XLR	MR036/52		27. 2.89	
G-MVPG	Medway Hybred 44XLR	MR026/53		15. 2.89	
G-MVPH	Whittaker MW.6S Fatboy Flyer	PFA/164-11404		7. 2.89	
G-MVPI	Mainair Gemini/Flash 2A (See comments on G-MVPC)	740-389-7 & W532		9. 2.89	
G-MVPJ	Rans S-5 Coyote	88-083 & PFA/193-11470		15. 2.89	
G-MVPK	CFM Shadow Srs.BD	K.091		15. 2.89	
G-MVPL	Medway Hybred 44XLR	MR034/50		1. 3.89	
G-MVPM	Whittaker MW.6 Merlin	PFA/164-11272		21. 2.89	
G-MVPN	Whittaker MW.6 Merlin	PFA/164-11280		21. 2.89	

Regn	Type	c/n	Previous identity	Regn date	Fate or immediate subsequent identity (if known)
G-MVPO	Mainair Gemini/Flash 2A	741-389-7 & W533		3. 3.89	
G-MVPP	Hornet ZA	ZA001		10. 3.89	Fatal crash near Marlbough on 9.6.89. Canx as destroyed 2.10.89.
G-MVPR	Solar Wings Pegasus XL-Q	SW-TE-0149 & SW-WQ-0163		14. 3.89	
G-MVPS	Solar Wings Pegasus XL-Q	SW-WQ-0140		14. 3.89	
G-MVPT	Solar Wings Pegasus XL-Q	SW-WQ-0141		29. 3.89	
G-MVPU	Solar Wings Pegasus XL-Q	SW-TE-0150 & SW-WQ-0164		29. 3.89	
G-MVPV	Solar Wings Pegasus XL-Q	SW-WQ-0187		28. 3.89	Canx as destroyed 27.10.95.
G-MVPW	Solar Wings Pegasus XL-R	SW-WA-1411		28. 3.89	
G-MVPX	Solar Wings Pegasus XL-Q	SW-WQ-0158		28. 3.89	
G-MVPY	Solar Wings Pegasus XL-Q	SW-WQ-0188		28. 3.89	
G-MVPZ	Rans S-4 Coyote (Originally regd as Rans S-5)	88-084 & PFA/193-11494		31. 3.89	Crashed into tree at Rushmead Farm, South Wraxall, Wilts on 17.8.97. Canx by CAA 2.3.98.
G-MVRA	Mainair Gemini/Flash 2A	743-489-7 & W535		10. 4.89	
G-MVRB	Mainair Gemini/Flash 2A	747-489-7 & W539		29. 3.89	
G-MVRC	Mainair Gemini/Flash 2A	748-489-7 & W540		29. 3.89	
G-MVRD	Mainair Gemini/Flash 2A	749-489-7 & W541		9. 5.89	
G-MVRE	CFM Shadow Srs.CD	K.087		10. 4.89	
G-MVRF	Rotec Rally 2B	AIE-01		28. 4.89	
G-MVRG	Aerial Arts Chaser S	CH.798		14. 4.89	
G-MVRH	Solar Wings Pegasus XL-Q	SW-TE-0160 & SW-WQ-0177		10. 4.89	
G-MVRI	Solar Wings Pegasus XL-Q	SW-TE-0145 & SW-WQ-0159		10. 4.89	
G-MVRJ	Solar Wings Pegasus XL-Q	SW-WQ-0154		10. 4.89	
G-MVRK	Solar Wings Pegasus XL-Q	SW-WQ-0153		10. 4.89	CofA lapsed 1.3.97. Canx as destroyed 25.6.97.
G-MVRL	Aerial Arts Chaser S	CH.801		18. 4.89	
G-MVRM	Mainair Gemini/Flash 2A	752-489-7 & W545		12. 4.89	
G-MVRN	Rans S-4 Coyote	88-085 & PFA/193-11503		10. 4.89	
G-MVRO	CFM Shadow Srs.BD	K.105		3. 4.89	
G-MVRP	CFM Shadow Srs.CD	097		7. 4.89	
G-MVRR	CFM Shadow Srs.CD	098		7. 4.89	
G-MVRS	CFM Shadow Srs.BD	099		7. 4.89	Canx as destroyed 5.7.90.
G-MVRT	CFM Shadow Srs.BD (Originally regd with c/n 100)	104		7. 4.89	
G-MVRU	Solar Wings Pegasus XL-Q	SW-TE-0166 & SW-WQ-0183		12. 4.89	
G-MVRV	Powerchute Kestrel	90210		28. 4.89	
G-MVRW	Solar Wings Pegasus XL-Q	SW-TE-0161 & SW-WQ-0178		12. 4.89	
G-MVRX	Solar Wings Pegasus XL-Q	SW-WQ-0165		12. 4.89	
G-MVRY	Medway Hybred 44XLR	MR049/56		12. 4.89	
G-MVRZ	Medway Hybred 44XLR	MR043/57		9. 5.89	
G-MVSA	Solar Wings Pegasus XL-Q/Lc	SW-TE-0183 & SW-WQ-0192		18. 4.89	To SE-YRY. Canx 27.11.95.
G-MVSB	Solar Wings Pegasus XL-Q	SW-TE-0184 & SW-WQ-0193		18. 4.89	
G-MVSC	Solar Wings Pegasus XL-Q	SW-WQ-0194		18. 4.89	Canx by CAA 7.8.96.
G-MVSD	Solar Wings Pegasus XL-Q	SW-TE-0186 & SW-WQ-0195		18. 4.89	
G-MVSE	Solar Wings Pegasus XL-Q	SW-WQ-0196		18. 4.89	
G-MVSF	Murphy Renegade Spirit UK	PFA/188-11423		21. 4.89	To PH-1Z5. Canx 12.6.90.
G-MVSG	Aerial Arts Chaser S	CH.804		24. 4.89	
G-MVSH	AMF Chevvron 2-32C	016		. .89R	NTU - To G-MVVV 5/89. Canx.
G-MVSI	Medway Hybred 44XLR	MR040/58		18. 4.89	(Stored 1/98)
G-MVSJ	Aviasud Mistral	BMAA/HB/013 & 072		18. 4.89	
G-MVSK	Aerial Arts Chaser S	CH.806		27. 4.89	
G-MVSL	Aerial Arts Chaser S	CH.807		15. 5.89	
G-MVSM	Midland Ultralights Sirocco 377GB	MU-023		21. 4.89	
G-MVSN	Mainair Gemini/Flash 2A	754-589-7 & W547		28. 4.89	
G-MVSO	Mainair Gemini/Flash 2A	755-589-7 & W548		27. 4.89	
G-MVSP	Mainair Gemini/Flash 2A	756-589-7 & W549		27. 4.89	
G-MVSR	Medway Hybred 44XLR	MR038/59		15. 5.89	
G-MVSS	Hornet RS-ZA	HRWB-0056 & ZA104		9. 5.89	Canx 15.5.89 on sale to USA.
G-MVST	Mainair Gemini/Flash 2A	750-589-7 & W543		12. 6.89	
G-MVSU	Microflight Spectrum	008		4. 5.89	

Regn	Type	c/n	Previous identity	Regn date	Fate or immediate subsequent identity (if known)
G-MVSV	Mainair Gemini/Flash 2A	757-589-7 & W550		11. 5.89	
G-MVSW	Solar Wings Pegasus XL-Q	SW-TE-0189 & SW-WQ-0198		17. 5.89	
G-MVSX	Solar Wings Pegasus XL-Q	SW-WQ-0199		11. 5.89	
G-MVSY	Solar Wings Pegasus XL-Q	SW-WQ-0200		11. 5.89	
G-MVSZ	Solar Wings Pegasus XL-Q	SW-WQ-0201		11. 5.89	
G-MVTA	Solar Wings Pegasus XL-Q	SW-WQ-0202		11. 5.89	
G-MVTB	Mainair Gemini/Flash 2A	758-689-7 & W551		. 5.89R	NTU - To Australia as 32-0503. Canx.
G-MVTC	Mainair Gemini/Flash 2A	759-689-7 & W552		30. 5.89	
G-MVTD	Whittaker MW.6 Merlin	PFA/164-11367		11. 5.89	
G-MVTE	Whittaker MW.6 Merlin	PFA/164-11372		17. 5.89	
G-MVTF	Aerial Arts Chaser S	CH.808		30. 5.89	
G-MVTG	Solar Wings Pegasus XL-Q	SW-WQ-0204		25. 5.89	
G-MVTH	Solar Wings Pegasus XL-Q	SW-WQ-0205		25. 5.89	Canx by CAA 8.4.91.
G-MVTI	Solar Wings Pegasus XL-Q	SW-WQ-0206		25. 5.89	
G-MVTJ	Solar Wings Pegasus XL-Q	SW-TE-0197 & SW-WQ-0207		25. 5.89	
G-MVTK	Solar Wings Pegasus XL-Q	SW-TE-0198 & SW-WQ-0208		25. 5.89	
G-MVTL	Aerial Arts Chaser S	CH.809		13. 6.89	
G-MVTM	Aerial Arts Chaser S	CH.810		13. 6.89	
G-MVTN	Not allotted by CAA in error.				
G-MVTO	Not allotted by CAA in error.				
G-MVTP	Not allotted by CAA in error.				
G-MVTR	Not allotted by CAA in error.				
G-MVTS	Not allotted by CAA in error.				
G-MVTT	Not allotted by CAA in error.				
G-MVTU	Not allotted by CAA in error.				
G-MVTV	Not allotted by CAA in error.				
G-MVTW	Not allotted by CAA in error.				
G-MVTX	Not allotted by CAA in error.				
G-MVTY	Not allotted by CAA in error.				
G-MVTZ	Not allotted by CAA in error.				
G-MVUA	Mainair Gemini/Flash 2A	760-689-7 & W553		14. 6.89	
G-MVUB	Thruster T.300	089-T300-373		13. 6.89	
G-MVUC	Medway Hybred 44XLR	MR046/60		13. 6.89	
G-MVUD	Medway Hybred 44XLR	MR037/55		19. 6.89	
G-MVUE	Solar Wings Pegasus XL-Q	SW-WQ-0212		13. 6.89	Canx as TWFU 10.2.92.
G-MVUF	Solar Wings Pegasus XL-Q	SW-TE-0203 & SW-WQ-0213		13. 6.89	
G-MVUG	Solar Wings Pegasus XL-Q	SW-TE-0204 & SW-WQ-0214		13. 6.89	
G-MVUH	Solar Wings Pegasus XL-Q	SW-TE-0205 & SW-WQ-0215		13. 6.89	
G-MVUI	Solar Wings Pegasus XL-Q	SW-TE-0206 & SW-WQ-0216		13. 6.89	
	(Wing incorrectly marked as c/n SW-TE-0216)				
G-MVUJ	Solar Wings Pegasus XL-Q	SW-WQ-0217		13. 6.89	
G-MVUK	Solar Wings Pegasus XL-Q	SW-TE-0208 & SW-WQ-0218		13. 6.89	Canx by CAA 8.9.97.
G-MVUL	Solar Wings Pegasus XL-Q	SW-WQ-0219		13. 6.89	
G-MVUM	Solar Wings Pegasus XL-Q	SW-WQ-0220		13. 6.89	
G-MVUN	Solar Wings Pegasus XL-Q	SW-WQ-0221		13. 6.89	
G-MVUO	AMF Chevvron 2-32C	015		14. 6.89	
G-MVUP	Aviasud Mistral	BMAA/HB/003 & 1087-48	83-CQ	10. 8.89	
G-MVUR	Hornet RS-ZA	HRWA-0050 & ZA107		3. 7.89	
	(Originally regd as c/n HRWA-0076; HRWA-0050 was G-MVLK)				
G-MVUS	Aerial Arts Chaser S	CH.813		3. 7.89	
G-MVUT	Aerial Arts Chaser S	CH.814		4. 7.89	
G-MVUU	Hornet R-ZA	HRWB-0061 & ZA110		13. 7.89	
G-MVUV	Powerchute Raider	-		. .89R	NTU - Canx.
G-MVUW	Powerchute Raider	-		. .89R	NTU - Canx.
G-MVUX	Powerchute Raider	-		. .89R	NTU - Canx.
G-MVUY	Powerchute Raider	-		. .89R	NTU - Canx.
G-MVUZ	Powerchute Raider	-		. .89R	NTU - Canx.
G-MVVA	Powerchute Raider	-		. .89R	NTU - Canx.
G-MVVB	Powerchute Raider	-		. .89R	NTU - Canx.
G-MVVC	Powerchute Raider	-		. .89R	NTU - Canx.
G-MVVD	Powerchute Raider	-		. .89R	NTU - Canx.
G-MVVE	Powerchute Raider	-		. .89R	NTU - Canx.
G-MVVF	Medway Hybred 44XLR	MR054/61		11. 7.89	
G-MVVG	Medway Hybred 44XLR	MR045/62		12. 7.89	
G-MVVH	Medway Hybred 44XLR	MR047/63		11. 7.89	
G-MVVI	Medway Hybred 44XLR	MR050/64		12. 7.89	
G-MVVJ	Medway Hybred 44XLR	MR056/65		12. 7.89	Canx by CAA 30.9.98.
G-MVVK	Solar Wings Pegasus XL-R	SW-TB-1414 & SW-WA-1423		11. 7.89	(Damaged mid .97)
G-MVVL	Solar Wings Pegasus XL-R	SW-WA-1424		11. 7.89	Canx as WFU 3.12.90.

Regn	Type	c/n	Previous identity	Regn date	Fate or immediate subsequent identity (if known)
G-MVVM	Solar Wings Pegasus XL-R	SW-TB-1416 & SW-WA-1425		12. 7.89	
G-MVVN	Solar Wings Pegasus XL-Q	SW-TE-0214 & SW-WQ-0226		11. 7.89	
G-MVVO	Solar Wings Pegasus XL-Q	SW-TE-0215 & SW-WQ-0227		11. 7.89	
G-MVVP	Solar Wings Pegasus XL-Q	SW-TE-0216 & SW-WQ-0228		11. 7.89	(Damaged late .97)
G-MVVR	Medway Hybred 44XLR	MR058/66		20. 7.89	
G-MVVS	Southdown Puma Sprint	1127/0037		29. 9.89	Canx by CAA 7.9.94.
G-MVVT	CFM Shadow Srs.CD	K.101 & PFA/161-11569		26. 7.89	
G-MVVU	Aerial Arts Chaser S	CH.816		19. 7.89	
G-MVVV	AMF Chevvron 2-32C	016	PH-1W9 G-MVVV/(G-MVSH)	11. 5.89	
G-MVVW	Aerial Arts Chaser S	CH.817		26. 7.89	
G-MVVX	Powerchute Raider	90626		25. 7.89	Canx 23.11.92 on sale to South Africa.
G-MVVY	Powerchute Raider	90627		25. 7.89	Canx 23.11.92 on sale to Australia. To 32-0526.
G-MVVZ	Powerchute Raider	90628		25. 7.89	
G-MVWA	Powerchute Raider	90629		25. 7.89	Canx by CAA 7.8.96.
G-MVWB	Powerchute Raider	90630		25. 7.89	
G-MVWC	Powerchute Raider	90631		25. 7.89	Canx 22.10.90 on sale to Japan.
G-MVWD	Powerchute Raider	90732	9H-ACH G-MVWD	25. 7.89	
G-MVWE	Powerchute Raider	90733		25. 7.89	Canx by CAA 12.1.93.
G-MVWF	Powerchute Raider	90734		25. 7.89	
G-MVWG	Powerchute Raider	90735		25. 7.89	Canx 23.11.92 on sale to Australia.
G-MVWH	Powerchute Raider	90736		25. 7.89	
G-MVWI	Powerchute Raider	90737		25. 7.89	
G-MVWJ	Powerchute Raider	90738		25. 7.89	Canx by CAA 19.12.94.
G-MVWK	Powerchute Raider	90739		25. 7.89	Canx by CAA 19.12.94.
G-MVWL	Powerchute Raider	90740		25. 7.89	Canx by CAA 19.12.94.
G-MVWM	Powerchute Raider	90741		25. 7.89	Canx by CAA 19.12.94.
G-MVWN	Thruster T.300	089-T300-374		26. 7.89	
G-MVWO	Thruster T.300	089-T300-375		26. 7.89	Canx as destroyed 5.9.94.
G-MVWP	Thruster T.300	089-T300-376		26. 7.89	
G-MVWR	Thruster T.300	089-T300-377		26. 7.89	
G-MVWS	Thruster T.300	089-T300-378		26. 7.89	
G-MVWT	CFM Shadow Srs.BD	117		20. 7.89	Canx 25.1.90 on sale to Phillipines. (Extant in UK marks 11/95)
G-MVWU	Medway Hybred 44XLR	MR057/68		24. 7.89	Canx as destroyed 16.9.98.
G-MVWV	Medway Hybred 44XLR	BMAA/HB/005 & MR060/69		24. 7.89	
G-MVWW	Aviasud Mistral 532	0389-81		25. 7.89	
G-MVWX	Microflight Spectrum	009		24. 7.89	
G-MVWY	Aerial Arts Chaser S	CH.819		. .89R	NTU - Canx.
G-MVWZ	Aviasud Mistral	BMAA/HB/008 & 1288-70		2. 8.89	
G-MVXA	Whittaker MW.6 Merlin	PFA/164-11337		17. 8.89	
G-MVXB	Mainair Gemini/Flash 2A	762-789-7 & W555		3. 8.89	
G-MVXC	Mainair Gemini/Flash 2A	763-889-7 & W556		4. 8.89	
G-MVXD	Medway Hybred 44XLR	MR061/70		3. 8.89	
G-MVXE	Medway Hybred 44XLR	MR063/71		23. 8.89	
G-MVXF	Weedhopper JC-31A	RAS-01		28. 7.89	Canx by CAA 27.3.99.
G-MVXG	Aerial Arts Chaser S	CH.820		5. 9.89	
G-MVXH	Microflight Spectrum	010		2. 8.89	
G-MVXI	Medway Hybred 44XLR	MR064/72		9. 8.89	
G-MVXJ	Medway Hybred 44XLR	MR065/73		25. 8.89	
G-MVXK	Medway Hybred 44XLR	MR066/74		10. 8.89	Canx by CAA 7.8.96. To Australia as T2-2535.
G-MVXL	Thruster TST Mk.1	8089-TST-122		18. 8.89	
G-MVXM	Medway Hybred 44XLR (Reported as a Medway Raven)	MR055/75		17. 8.89	
G-MVXN	Aviasud Mistral	BMAA/HB/002 & 65		18. 8.89	
G-MVXO	Aerial Arts Chaser S	CH.821		17. 8.89	CofA lapsed 13.2.92. Canx as destroyed 1.6.94.
G-MVXP	Aerial Arts Chaser S	CH.822		17. 8.89	
G-MVXR	Mainair Gemini/Flash 2A	764-889-7 & W557		22. 8.89	
G-MVXS	Mainair Gemini/Flash 2A	766-889-7 & W559		22. 8.89	
G-MVXT	Mainair Gemini/Flash 2A	767-889-7 & W560		22. 8.89	Canx by CAA 4.7.96.
G-MVXU	Aviasud Mistral	BMAA/HB/006 & 93		29. 8.89	(Stored 8/95) Canx by CAA 23.4.98.
G-MVXV	Aviasud Mistral	BMAA/HB/004 & 92		22. 8.89	
G-MVXW	Rans S-4 Coyote	89-098 & PFA/193-11545		22. 8.89	
G-MVXX	AMF Chevvron 2-32	018		27. 7.89	
G-MVXY	AMF Paracat 1-24	001		25. 8.89	Canx as destroyed 3.8.94.
G-MVXZ	Team Minimax 91	PFA/186-11429		4. 9.89	
G-MVYA	Aerial Arts Chaser S.508	CH.823		5. 9.89	Canx as WFU 18.8.94.
G-MVYB	Solar Wings Pegasus XL-Q	SW-TE-0223 & SW-WQ-0238		8. 9.89	

Regn	Type	c/n	Previous identity	Regn date	Fate or immediate subsequent identity (if known)
G-MVYC	Solar Wings Pegasus XL-Q	SW-WQ-0239		8. 9.89	
G-MVYD	Solar Wings Pegasus XL-Q	SW-TE-0225 & SW-WQ-0240		8. 9.89	
G-MVYE	Thruster TST Mk.1	8089-TST-123		13. 9.89	
G-MVYF	Hornet R-ZA	HRWB-0066 & ZA112		22. 9.89	Canx by CAA 8.1.91.
G-MVYG	Hornet R-ZA	HRWB-0067 & ZA119		22. 9.89	
G-MVYH	Hornet R-ZA	HRWB-0072 & ZA125		22. 9.89	(Damaged early .97)
G-MVYI	Hornet R-ZA	HRWB-0074 & ZA122		22. 9.89	
	(A trike unit with c/n HRWB-0074 amended to HRWB-0081 was seen Popham 4/96)				
G-MVYJ	Hornet R-ZA	HRWB-0075 & ZA111		22. 9.89	
	(Trike unit shows deleted c/n HRWB-0070)				
G-MVYK	Hornet R-ZA	HRWB-0076 & ZA117		22. 9.89	
G-MVYL	Hornet R-ZA	HRWB-0077 & ZA115		22. 9.89	
G-MVYM	Hornet R-ZA	HRWB-0078 & ZA130		22. 9.89	
G-MVYN	Hornet R-ZA	HRWB-0079 & ZA136		22. 9.89	
G-MVYO	Hornet R-ZA	HRWB-0080 & ZA134		22. 9.89	
	(C/n ZA134 was same as G-MWEY)				
G-MVYP	Medway Hybred 44XLR	MR071/77		19. 9.89	
G-MVYR	Medway Hybred 44XLR	MR068/76		19. 9.89	
G-MVYS	Mainair Gemini/Flash 2A	770-989-7 & W563		19. 9.89	
G-MVYT	Noble Hardman Snowbird Mk.IV	SB-022		26. 9.89	
G-MVYU	Noble Hardman Snowbird Mk.IV	SB-023		7.11.89	
G-MVYV	Noble Hardman Snowbird Mk.IV	SB-024		21. 8.90	
G-MVYW	Noble Hardman Snowbird Mk.IV	SB-025		22.10.90	
G-MVYX	Noble Hardman Snowbird Mk.IV	SB-026		25.11.91	
G-MVYY	Aerial Arts Chaser S	CH.824		26. 9.89	
G-MVYZ	CFM Shadow Srs.BD	121		25. 9.89	
G-MVZA	Thruster T.300	089-T300-379		26. 9.89	
G-MVZB	Thruster T.300	089-T300-380		26. 9.89	
G-MVZC	Thruster T.300	089-T300-381		26. 9.89	
G-MVZD	Thruster T.300	089-T300-382		26. 9.89	
G-MVZE	Thruster T.300	089-T300-383		26. 9.89	
G-MVZF	Thruster T.300	089-T300-384		26. 9.89	Canx by CAA 7.8.96.
G-MVZG	Thruster T.300	089-T300-385		26. 9.89	
G-MVZH	Thruster T.300	089-T300-386		26. 9.89	To RP-C1521 .94.
G-MVZI	Thruster T.300	089-T300-387		26. 9.89	
G-MVZJ	Solar Wings Pegasus XL-Q	SW-WQ-0241		26. 8.89	
G-MVZK	Quad City Challenger II UK	PFA/177-11498		28. 9.89	Crashed near Northcotes on 11.9.93.
G-MVZL	Solar Wings Pegasus XL-Q	SW-TE-0227 & SW-WQ-0242		4.10.89	
G-MVZM	Aerial Arts Chaser S	CH.825		2.11.89	
G-MVZN	Aerial Arts Chaser S	CH.826		2.11.89	Canx as WFU 26.7.93.
G-MVZO	Medway Hybred 44XLR	MR072/78		25.10.89	
G-MVZP	Murphy Renegade Spirit UK	256 & PFA/188-11630		17.10.89	(Stored 6/96)
G-MVZR	Avidsud Mistral	BMAA/HB/011 & 90		9.10.89	(Stored 9/96)
G-MVZS	Mainair Gemini/Flash 2A	771-1089-7 & W564		17.10.89	
G-MVZT	Solar Wings Pegasus XL-Q	SW-TE-0228 & SW-WQ-0243		6.10.89	
G-MVZU	Solar Wings Pegasus XL-Q	SW-TE-0229 & SW-WQ-0244		6.10.89	
G-MVZV	Solar Wings Pegasus XL-Q	SW-TE-0230 & SW-WQ-0245		6.10.89	
G-MVZW	Hornet R-ZA	HRWB-0063 & ZA142		27.10.89	
G-MVZX	Murphy Renegade Spirit UK	PFA/188-11590		18.10.89	
G-MVZY	Aerial Arts Chaser S	CH.827		2.11.89	(Damaged mid .95)
G-MVZZ	AMF Chevvron 2-32	019		27. 7.89	
G-MWAA	Medway Hybred 44XLR	30987/30		23.10.89	Canx as WFU 18.1.95.
G-MWAB	Mainair Gemini/Flash 2A	772-1089-7 & W565		24.10.89	
G-MWAC	Solar Wings Pegasus XL-Q	SW-TE-0236 & SW-WQ-0260		25.10.89	
G-MWAD	Solar Wings Pegasus XL-Q	SW-WQ-0261		25.10.89	
G-MWAE	CFM Shadow Srs.CD	130		24.10.89	
G-MWAF	Solar Wings Pegasus XL-R	SW-TB-1422 & SW-WA-1441		30.10.89	
G-MWAG	Solar Wings Pegasus XL-R	SW-WA-1442		30.10.89	
G-MWAH	Hornet RS-ZA	HRWB-0052 & ZA137		1.11.89	
G-MWAI	Solar Wings Pegasus XL-R	SW-WA-1443		1.11.89	
G-MWAJ	Murphy Renegade Spirit UK	217 & PFA/188-11438		1.11.89	
G-MWAK	Solar Wings Pegasus XL-Q	SW-TE-0239 & SW-WQ-0262		2.11.89	To ZS-WZT. Canx 12.2.92.
G-MWAL	Solar Wings Pegasus XL-Q	SW-TE-0240 & SW-WQ-0263		2.11.89	
G-MWAM	Thruster T.300	089-T300-388		14.11.89	
G-MWAN	Thruster T.300	089-T300-389		14.11.89	
G-MWAO	Thruster T.300	089-T300-390		14.11.89	Canx by CAA 7.8.96.
G-MWAP	Thruster T.300	089-T300-391		14.11.89	

Regn	Type	c/n	Previous identity	Regn date	Fate or immediate subsequent identity (if known)
G-MWAR	Thruster T.300	089-T300-392		14.11.89	
G-MWAS	Thruster T.300	089-T300-393		14.11.89	(Damaged mid .94)
G-MWAT	Solar Wings Pegasus XL-Q	SW-WQ-0265		13.11.89	(For sale 11/97)
G-MWAU	Mainair Gemini/Flash 2A	773-1189-7 & W566		7.12.89	
G-MWAV	Solar Wings Pegasus XL-R	SW-WA-1444		13.11.89	
G-MWAW	Whittaker MW.6 Merlin	PFA/164-11460		10.11.89	
G-MWAX	Hornet RS-ZA	HRWB-0054 & ZA106		14.11.89	To Australia as T2-2514. Canx 8.3.90.
G-MWAY	Hornet RS-ZA	HRWB-0055 & ZA113		14.11.89	To Australia as T2-2538. Canx 8.3.90.
G-MWAZ	Hornet RS-ZA	HRWB-0057 & ZA108		14.11.89	To Australia as T2-2537. Canx 8.3.90.
G-MWBA	Hornet RS-ZA	HRWB-0059 & ZA116		14.11.89	To Australia as T2-2597. Canx 8.3.90.
G-MWBB	Hornet RS-ZA	HRWB-0060 & ZA114		14.11.89	To Australia as T2-2513. Canx 8.3.90.
G-MWBC	Hornet RS-ZA	HRWB-0062 & ZA123		14.11.89	To Australia as T2-2568. Canx 8.3.90.
G-MWBD	Hornet RS-ZA	HRWB-0064 & ZA138		14.11.89	To Australia as T2-2545. Canx 8.3.90.
G-MWBE	Hornet RS-ZA	HRWB-0065 & ZA139		14.11.89	To Australia as T2-2598. Canx 8.3.90.
G-MWBF	Hornet RS-ZA	HRWB-0068 & ZA109		14.11.89	To Australia as T2-2577. Canx 8.3.90.
G-MWBG	Hornet RS-ZA	HRWB-0070 & ZA140		14.11.89	To Australia as T2-2510. Canx 8.3.90.
G-MWBH	Hornet RS-ZA	HRWB-0071 & ZA120		14.11.89	
G-MWBI	Medway Hybred 44XLR	MR073/79		21.11.89	
G-MWBJ	Medway Puma Sprint	MS003/1		21.11.89	
G-MWBK	Solar Wings Pegasus XL-Q	SW-TE-0248 & SW-WQ-0271		16.11.89	
G-MWBL	Solar Wings Pegasus XL-R/Se	SW-TB-1424 & SW-WA-1446		16.11.89	
G-MWBM	Hornet R-ZA	HRWB-0082 & ZA141		29.11.89	
G-MWBN	Hornet R-ZA	HRWB-0103 & ZA155		21.11.89	
	(Trike regd as HRWB-0081, but frame restamped as 0103; wing originally ZA143)				
G-MWBO	Rans S-4 Coyote	89-097 & PFA/193-11503		29.11.89	
G-MWBP	Hornet R-ZA	HRWB-0083 & ZA144		29.11.89	(Damaged mid .95)
G-MWBR	Hornet RS-ZA	HRWB-0084 & ZA145		29.11.89	
G-MWBS	Hornet R-ZA	HRWB-0085 & ZA146		29.11.89	
G-MWBT	Hornet R-ZA	HRWB-0086 & ZA147		29.11.89	Canx by CAA 8.1.91.
G-MWBU	Hornet R-ZA	HRWB-0087 & ZA148		29.11.89	
G-MWBV	Hornet R-ZA	HRWB-0088 & ZA149		29.11.89	Canx as WFU 12.9.95.
G-MWBW	Hornet R-ZA	HRWB-0089 & ZA150		29.11.89	
G-MWBX	Hornet R-ZA	HRWB-0090 & ZA151		29.11.89	
G-MWBY	Hornet R-ZA	HRWB-0091 & ZA152		29.11.89	
G-MWBZ	Hornet R-ZA	HRWB-0092 & ZA153		29.11.89	
	(Trike unit originally marked as HRWB-0096; then HRWB-0104 - both overstamped)				
G-MWCA	Hornet R-ZA	HRWB-0093 & ZA154		29.11.89	
G-MWCB	Solar Wings Pegasus XL-Q	SW-WQ-0273		1.12.89	
G-MWCC	Solar Wings Pegasus XL-R/Se	SW-TB-1387 & SW-WA-1447		1.12.89	
G-MWCD	Aerial Arts Chaser S	CH.831		. .89R	NTU - To (G-MWEB)/G-MWXX 12/91. Canx.
G-MWCE	Mainair Gemini/Flash 2A	775-1289-7 & W568		19.12.89	
G-MWCF	Solar Wings Pegasus XL-Q	SW-WQ-0276		13.12.89	
G-MWCG	Microflight Spectrum	011		15.12.89	
G-MWCH	Rans S-6-ESD Coyote II	0989-067 & PFA/204-11632		15.12.89	
	(PFA c/n conflicts with Kitfox G-BSFY)				
G-MWCI	Powerchute Kestrel	91245		3. 1.90	
G-MWCJ	Powerchute Kestrel	91246		3. 1.90	
G-MWCK	Powerchute Kestrel	91247/3787874/120503		3. 1.90	
G-MWCL	Powerchute Kestrel	91248		3. 1.90	Permit expired 5.4.99. Canx by CAA 23.7.99.
G-MWCM	Powerchute Kestrel	91249		3. 1.90	Canx by CAA 22.7.96.
G-MWCN	Powerchute Kestrel	91250		3. 1.90	
G-MWCO	Powerchute Kestrel	91251		3. 1.90	
G-MWCP	Powerchute Kestrel	91252		3. 1.90	
G-MWCR	Southdown Puma Sprint	1121/0070 & P.516		24. 2.84	
G-MWCS	Powerchute Kestrel	91253		3. 1.90	
G-MWCT	Powerchute Kestrel	91254		3. 1.90	Canx 23.11.92 on sale to Australia.
G-MWCU	Solar Wings Pegasus XL-R	SW-WA-1449		27.12.89	
G-MWCV	Solar Wings Pegasus XL-Q	SW-TE-0256 & SW-WQ-0278		27.12.89	
G-MWCW	Mainair Gemini/Flash 2A	776-0190-7 & W569		29.12.89	
G-MWCX	Medway Hybred 44XLR	MR076/80		8. 1.90	
G-MWCY	Medway Hybred 44XLR	MR077/81		15. 1.90	
G-MWCZ	Medway Hybred 44XLR	MR078/82		10. 1.90	
G-MWDA	Jakeway Powered Parachute	0001		2. 1.90	Canx by CAA 7.9.94.
G-MWDB	CFM Shadow Srs.CD	100		3. 7.89	
G-MWDC	Solar Wings Pegasus XL-R/Se	SW-TE-0255 & SW-WA-1450		5. 1.90	
G-MWDD	Solar Wings Pegasus XL-Q	SW-WQ-0280		15. 1.90	
G-MWDE	Hornet RS-ZA	HRWB-0094 & ZA126		10. 1.90	Canx by CAA 13.11.90.
G-MWDF	Hornet RS-ZA	HRWB-0095 & ZA155		10. 1.90	Canx by CAA 31.3.92. (Stored 4/96)
G-MWDG	Hornet RS-ZA	HRWB-0096 & ZA156		10. 1.90	Canx by CAA 31.3.92.
G-MWDH	Hornet RS-ZA	HRWB-0097 & ZA157		10. 1.90	Canx by CAA 31.3.92.
G-MWDI	Hornet RS-ZA	HRWB-0098 & ZA158		10. 1.90	

Regn	Type	c/n	Previous identity	Regn date	Fate or immediate subsequent identity (if known)
G-MWDJ	Mainair Gemini/Flash 2A	777-0190-7 & W570		17. 1.90	
G-MWDK	Solar Wings Pegasus XL-Q	SW-WQ-0281		17. 1.90	
G-MWDL	Solar Wings Pegasus XL-Q	SW-TE-0260 & SW-WQ-0282		17. 1.90	
G-MWDM	Murphy Renegade Spirit UK (PFA c/n conflicts with Streak Shadow G-BRZZ)	319 & PFA/100A-11028		18. 1.90	
G-MWDN	CFM Shadow Srs.BD	K.102		17. 1.90	
G-MWDO	Spencer Avn Club	SA-C-901-M		18. 1.90	Canx by CAA 7.9.94.
G-MWDP	Thruster TST Mk.1	8129-TST-124		30. 1.90	
G-MWDR	Thruster T.300	089-T300-394		30. 1.90	Canx by CAA 8.4.91.
G-MWDS	Thruster T.300	089-T300-395		30. 1.90	Canx by CAA 5.11.90.
G-MWDT	Thruster T.300	090-T300-396		30. 1.90	Canx by CAA 8.4.91.
G-MWDU	Thruster T.300	090-T300-397		30. 1.90	Canx by CAA 8.4.91.
G-MWDV	Thruster T.300	090-T300-398		30. 1.90	Canx by CAA 8.4.91.
G-MWDW	Thruster T.300	090-T300-399		30. 1.90	Canx by CAA 8.4.91.
G-MWDX	Thruster T.300	090-T300-400		30. 1.90	Canx by CAA 8.4.91.
G-MWDY	Thruster T.300	090-T300-401		30. 1.90	Canx by CAA 8.4.91.
G-MWDZ	Eipper Quicksilver MXL Sport II	022		29. 1.90	
G-MWEA	Nostalgair N.3 Pup	01-GB & PFA/212-11837		23. 1.90	To G-BVEA 6/93. Canx.
G-MWEB	Aerial Arts Chaser S	CH.831	(G-MWCD)	. .90R	NTU - To G-MWXX 12/91. Canx.
G-MWEC	Aerial Arts Chaser S	CH.832		. .90R	NTU - To G-MWXY 12/91. Canx.
G-MWED	Aerial Arts Chaser S	CH.833		. .90R	NTU - Canx.
G-MWEE	Solar Wings Pegasus XL-Q	SW-WQ-0147		12.12.88	Canx by CAA 17.11.97.
G-MWEF	Solar Wings Pegasus XL-Q	SE-TE-0261 & SW-WQ-0283		30. 1.90	(Stored 9/97)
G-MWEG	Solar Wings Pegasus XL-Q	SW-WQ-0284		30. 1.90	
G-MWEH	Solar Wings Pegasus XL-Q	SW-WQ-0286		7. 2.90	
G-MWEI	Mainair Gemini/Flash 2A	779-0290-7 & W572		7. 2.90	Fatal crash after stiking trees near Cleobury Mortimer on 1.11.90. Canx by CAA 7.8.96.
G-MWEJ	Rans S-5 Coyote	89-094 & PFA/193-11625		7. 2.90	Fatal crash at a golf course near Garstang, Lancs. on 25.7.90. Canx by CAA 31.10.90.
G-MWEK	Whittaker MW.5 Sorcerer	PFA/163-11284		20. 2.90	
G-MWEL	Mainair Gemini/Flash 2A	780-0290-7 & W573		13. 2.90	
G-MWEM	Medway Hybred 44XLR	MR079/83		21. 2.90	Canx as destroyed 5.7.96.
G-MWEN	CFM Shadow Srs.CD	K.113		20. 2.90	
G-MWEO	Whittaker MW.5 Sorcerer	PFA/163-11263		21. 2.90	
G-MWEP	Rans S-4 Coyote	89-096 & PFA/193-11616		21. 2.90	
G-MWER	Solar Wings Pegasus XL-Q	SW-TE-0265 & SW-WQ-0287		1. 3.90	
G-MWES	Rans S-4 Coyote	89-099 & PFA/193-11737		1. 2.90	
G-MWET	Hornet RS-ZA	HRWB-0099 & ZA159		21. 2.90	Canx by CAA 7.8.96.
G-MWEU	Hornet RS-ZA	HRWB-0100 & ZA160		21. 2.90	Canx by CAA 8.1.91.
G-MWEV	Hornet RS-ZA	HRWB-0101 & ZA161		21. 2.90	(Stolen in 4/95 - engine no.3799219)
G-MWEW	Hornet RS-ZA	HRWB-0102 & ZA162		21. 2.90	Canx by CAA 8.1.91.
G-MWEX	Hornet RS-ZA	HRWB-0103 & ZA163		21. 2.90	Canx by CAA 8.1.91.
G-MWEY	Hornet RS-ZA (Originally regd as RS-ZA with c/n ZA134 same as G-MVYO)	HRWB-0104 & ZA135		21. 2.90	
G-MWEZ	CFM Shadow Srs.CD	136		22. 2.90	
G-MWFA	Solar Wings Pegasus XL-R	SW-WA-1454		27. 2.90	
G-MWFB	CFM Shadow Srs.CD	K.119		1. 3.90	
G-MWFC	Team Minimax	294 & PFA/186-11648	G-BTXC G-MWFC	1. 3.90	
G-MWFD	Team Minimax (PFA c/n conflicts with Shadow G-GORE)	293 & PFA/186-11646		1. 3.90	
G-MWFE	Southdown Lightning 195	RMM-L-U-195		8. 3.90	Canx by CAA 18.8.94.
G-MWFF	Rans S-4 Coyote	89-106		10. 1.90	
G-MWFG	Powerchute Kestrel	00358		20. 3.90	
G-MWFH	Powerchute Kestrel	00359		20. 3.90	Canx by CAA 26.2.96.
G-MWFI	Powerchute Kestrel	00360		20. 3.90	
G-MWFJ	Powerchute Kestrel	00361		20. 3.90	To ZU-AEX 2/93. Canx 27.11.92.
G-MWFK	Powerchute Kestrel	00362		20. 3.90	Canx 13.2.97 on sale to Ireland.
G-MWFL	Powerchute Kestrel	00363		20. 3.90	
G-MWFM	Powerchute Kestrel	00364		20. 3.90	Canx 16.5.90 on sale to Australia.
G-MWFN	Powerchute Kestrel	00365		20. 3.90	
G-MWFO	Solar Wings Pegasus XL-R	SW-WA-1455		8. 3.90	Canx by CAA 17.4.97.
G-MWFP	Solar Wings Pegasus XL-R	SW-TB-1406 & SW-WA-1456		12. 3.90	
G-MWFR	Solar Wings Pegasus Quasar	SW-WQ-0264		12. 3.90	To N66601 with c/n SW-TQ-0001 3/91. Canx 27.2.91.
G-MWFS	Solar Wings Pegasus XL-Q	SW-TE-0267 & SW-WQ-0289		14. 3.90	
G-MWFT	MBA Tiger Cub 440	WFT-02		24.11.83	
G-MWFU	Quad City Challenger II UK	PFA/177-11654		16. 3.90	

Regn	Type	c/n	Previous identity	Regn date	Fate or immediate subsequent identity (if known)
G-MWFV	Quad City Challenger II UK	PFA/177-11655		16. 3.90	
G-MWFW	Rans S-4 Coyote	PFA/193-11662		16. 3.90	
G-MWFX	Quad City Challenger II UK	CH2-1189-UK-0485 & PFA/177-11706		20. 3.90	
G-MWFY	Quad City Challenger II UK	PFA/177-11668		20. 3.90	
G-MWFZ	Quad City Challenger II UK	CH2-0190-UK-0506 & PFA/177-11707		20. 3.90	
G-MWGA	Rans S-5 Coyote	89-092 & PFA/193-11810		20. 3.90	
G-MWGB	Medway Hybred 44XLR	MR080/84		26. 3.90	CofA lapsed 2.2.93. Canx as destroyed 1.6.94.
G-MWGC	Medway Hybred 44XLR	MR087/85		26. 3.90	
G-MWGD	Medway Hybred 44XLR (Fitted with new wing after original stolen 12/94)	MR088/86		26. 3.90	
G-MWGE	Medway Hybred 44XLR	MR089/87		26. 3.90	Badly damaged on landing at Popham on 29.2.96. Canx by CAA 10.9.98.
G-MWGF	Murphy Renegade Spirit UK	220 & PFA/188-11771		21. 3.90	
G-MWGG	Mainair Gemini/Flash 2A	785-0390-7 & W578		26. 3.90	
G-MWGH	Aerotech MW.5(K) Sorcerer	5K-0011-02		. .90R	NTU - To EI-CAN 6/90. Canx.
G-MWGI	Aerotech MW.5B Sorcerer	5K-0012-02		28. 3.90	WFU & spares to G-MTBT, incl wing.
G-MWGJ	Aerotech MW.5(K) Sorcerer	5K-0014-02		6. 9.90	
G-MWGK	Aerotech MW.5(K) Sorcerer	5K-0015-02	G-MWLV	19. 9.90	
G-MWGL	Solar Wings Pegasus XL-Q	SW-WQ-0293		28. 3.90	
G-MWGM	Solar Wings Pegasus XL-Q	SW-WQ-0294		28. 3.90	
G-MWGN	Rans S-4 Coyote	89-113 & PFA/193-11709		26. 3.90	
G-MWGO	Aerial Arts 110SX/Chaser	110SX/566		28. 3.90	
G-MWGP	Murphy Renegade Spirit UK	257 & PFA/188-11701		29. 3.90	Canx by CAA 30.6.92. To G-MZIZ 10/92.
G-MWGR	Solar Wings Pegasus XL-Q	SW-TE-0272 & SW-WQ-0296		6. 4.90	
G-MWGS	Powerchute Kestrel	00366		26. 4.90	Canx 4.1.91 on sale to Spain.
G-MWGT	Powerchute Kestrel	00367		26. 4.90	
G-MWGU	Powerchute Kestrel	00368	(9H-...) G-MWGU	26. 4.90	
G-MWGV	Powerchute Kestrel	00369		26. 4.90	
G-MWGW	Powerchute Kestrel	00370		26. 4.90	
G-MWGX	Powerchute Kestrel	00371		26. 4.90	Canx 5.10.90 on sale to Portugal.
G-MWGY	Powerchute Kestrel	00372		26. 4.90	
G-MWGZ	Powerchute Kestrel	00373		26. 4.90	
G-MWHA	Powerchute Kestrel	00374		26. 4.90	Canx 5.10.90 on sale to Portugal.
G-MWHB	Powerchute Kestrel	00375		26. 4.90	Canx 23.10.90 on sale to Japan.
G-MWHC	Solar Wings Pegasus XL-Q	SW-TE-0274 & SW-WQ-0304		24. 4.90	
G-MWHD	Microflight Spectrum	012		18. 4.90	
G-MWHE	Microflight Spectrum	014		18. 4.90	Canx by CAA 11.12.98.
G-MWHF	Solar Wings Pegasus XL-Q	SW-TE-0275 & SW-WQ-0305		24. 4.90	
G-MWHG	Solar Wings Pegasus XL-Q	SW-TE-0276 & SW-WQ-0306		24. 4.90	
G-MWHH	Team Minimax	326 & PFA/186-11814		23. 4.90	
G-MWHI	Mainair Gemini/Flash 2A	784-0390-5 & W577		26. 4.90	
G-MWHJ	Solar Wings Pegasus XL-Q	SW-TE-0277 & SW-WQ-0307		27. 4.90	
G-MWHK	Murphy Renegade Spirit UK	PFA/188-11562		26. 4.90	Canx 27.3.96 on sale to Belgium. To France as 59-TF.
G-MWHL	Solar Wings Pegasus XL-Q	SW-WQ-0308		1. 5.90	
G-MWHM	Whittaker MW.6S Fatboy Flyer	PFA/164-11463		18. 5.90	
G-MWHN	Solar Wings Pegasus Quasar	SW-WQQ-0311		4. 5.90	Canx 12.11.90 on sale to USA.
G-MWHO	Mainair Gemini/Flash 2A	778-0190-5 & W571		10. 5.90	
G-MWHP	Rans S-6-ESD Coyote II	1089-093 & PFA/204-11768		8. 5.90	
G-MWHR	Mainair Gemini/Flash 2A	787-0590-7 & W580		16. 5.90	
G-MWHS	AMF Chevvron 2-32C	021		18. 5.90	
G-MWHT	Solar Wings Pegasus Quasar TC	SW-TQ-0005 & SW-WQQ-0314		15. 5.90	
G-MWHU	Solar Wings Pegasus Quasar	SW-WQQ-0315		15. 5.90	
G-MWHV	Solar Wings Pegasus Quasar	SW-WQQ-0316		15. 5.90	
G-MWHW	Solar Wings Pegasus XL-Q	SW-WQ-0317		15. 5.90	

Regn	Type	c/n	Previous identity	Regn date	Fate or immediate subsequent identity (if known)
G-MWHX	Solar Wings Pegasus XL-Q	SW-TE-0280 & SW-WQ-0318		15. 5.90	
G-MWHY	Mainair Gemini/Flash 2A	788-0590-7 & W581		16. 5.90	(Damaged mid .97) Permit expired 28.11.97. Canx by CAA 25.8.99.
G-MWHZ	Trion J.1	BMAA/HB/018 & J-001		18. 5.90	Damaged on taxi trials at Needham, Norfolk in 1990. (Stored 9/97) Canx by CAA 9.7.98
G-MWIA	Mainair Gemini/Flash 2A	789-0690-7 & W582		21. 5.90	
G-MWIB	Aviasud Mistral	BMAA/HB/010 & 094		16. 5.90	
G-MWIC	Whittaker MW.5C Sorcerer	PFA/163-11224		20. 2.90	
G-MWID	Solar Wings Pegasus XL-Q	SW-TE-0281 & SW-WQ-0324		30. 5.90	Permit expired 16.7.96.
G-MWIE	Solar Wings Pegasus XL-Q	SW-TE-0282 & SW-WQ-0325		30. 5.90	
G-MWIF	Rans S-6-ESD Coyote II	1089-095 & PFA/204-11749		30. 5.90	
G-MWIG	Mainair Gemini/Flash 2A	790-0690-7 & W583		4. 6.90	
G-MWIH	Mainair Gemini/Flash 2A	791-0690-5 & W584		4. 6.90	
G-MWII	Medway Hybred 44XLR	MR031/47		7. 6.90	Canx by CAA 7.9.94.
G-MWIJ	Medway Hybred 44XLR	MR092/88		7. 6.90	Canx by CAA 7.8.96.
G-MWIK	Medway Hybred 44XLR	MR094/89		7. 6.90	
G-MWIL	Medway Hybred 44XLR	MR096/90		8. 6.90	
G-MWIM	Solar Wings Pegasus Quasar TC	SW-TQ-0008 & SW-WQQ-0326		11. 6.90	
G-MWIN	Mainair Gemini/Flash 2A	793-0690-7 & W586		12. 6.90	
G-MWIO	Rans S-4 Coyote	90-117 & PFA/193-11774		11. 6.90	
G-MWIP	Whittaker MW.6 Merlin	PFA/164-11360		7. 6.90	
G-MWIR	Solar Wings Pegasus XL-Q	SW-TE-0283 & SW-WQ-0330		8. 6.90	
G-MWIS	Solar Wings Pegasus XL-Q	SW-WQ-0331		8. 6.90	
G-MWIT	Solar Wings Pegasus XL-Q	SW-TE-0285 & SW-WQ-0332		8. 6.90	
G-MWIU	Solar Wings Pegasus Quasar TC	SW-TQ-0010 & SW-WQQ-0333		8. 6.90	
G-MWIV	Mainair Gemini/Flash 2A (Was also allotted marks G-MWJB - in error)	792-0690-5 & W585		15. 6.90	
G-MWIW	Solar Wings Pegasus Quasar	SW-TQ-0011 & SW-WQQ-0334		18. 6.90	
G-MWIX	Solar Wings Pegasus Quasar TC	SW-TQ-0012 & SW-WQQ-0335		18. 6.90	
G-MWIY	Solar Wings Pegasus Quasar	SW-TQ-0014 & SW-WQQ-0336		22. 6.90	
G-MWIZ	CFM Shadow Srs.CD	096		22.11.88	
G-MWJA	Rans S-6 Coyote II	0190-112 & PFA/204-11782		14. 6.90	To G-BSSI 8/90. Canx.
G-MWJB	Mainair Gemini/Flash 2A	792-0690-5 & W585		. .90R	NTU - Already registered as G-MWIV. Canx.
G-MWJC	Solar Wings Pagasus Quasar	SW-WQQ-0337		18. 6.90	Canx 12.2.93 on sale to Ireland but w/o in fatal accident at Newbridge, Co.Galway before an EI- regn was acquired.
G-MWJD	Solar Wings Pegasus Quasar	SW-TQ-0016 & SW-WQQ-0339		22. 6.90	
G-MWJE	Rans S-6 Coyote II	1089-090 & PFA/204-11732		22. 6.90	NTU - To G-BSMU 27.6.90. Canx.
G-MWJF	CFM Shadow Srs.BD	K.123		26. 6.90	(Damaged mid .96) (Wings stored 8/97)
G-MWJG	Solar Wings Pegasus XL-R	SW-TB-1415 & SW-WA-1472		26. 6.90	
G-MWJH	Solar Wings Pegasus Quasar	SW-WQQ-0340		29. 6.90	
G-MWJI	Solar Wings Pegasus Quasar	SW-WQQ-0341		29. 6.90	
G-MWJJ	Solar Wings Pegasus Quasar	SW-TQ-0019 & SW-WQQ-0342		29. 6.90	
G-MWJK	Solar Wings Pegasus Quasar	SW-WQQ-0343		29. 6.90	
G-MWJL	AMF Chevvron 2-32	023		16. 7.90	
G-MWJM	AMF Chevvron 2-32C	024		31. 7.90	
G-MWJN	Solar Wings Pegasus XL-Q	SW-TE-0288 & SW-WQ-0344		29. 6.90	
G-MWJO	Solar Wings Pegasus XL-Q	SW-TE-0289 & SW-WQ-0345		29. 6.90	
G-MWJP	Medway Hybred 44XLR	MR097/91		29. 6.90	
G-MWJR	Medway Hybred 44XLR	MR098/92		28. 6.90	
G-MWJS	Solar Wings Pegasus Quasar TC	SW-WQQ-0349		6. 7.90	
G-MWJT	Solar Wings Pegasus Quasar TC	SW-TQ-0022 & SW-WQQ-0350		16. 7.90	

Regn	Type	c/n	Previous identity	Regn date	Fate or immediate subsequent identity (if known)
G-MWJU	Solar Wings Pegasus Quasar	SW-TQ-0023 & SW-WQQ-0351		6. 7.90	
G-MWJV	Solar Wings Pegasus Quasar	SW-TQ-0024 & SW-WQQ-0352		6. 7.90	
G-MWJW	Whittaker MW.5 Sorcerer	JDW-02 & PFA/163-11186		11. 5.90	
G-MWJX	Medway Puma Sprint	MS009/3		17. 7.90	
G-MWJY	Mainair Gemini/Flash 2A	797-0790-7 & W590		16. 7.90	
G-MWJZ	CFM Shadow Srs.CD	K.132		19. 7.90	
G-MWKA	Murphy Renegade Spirit UK (Also incorporates project PFA/188-11690)	PFA/188-11864		26. 7.90	
G-MWKB	Hornet R-ZA	HRWB-0105 & ZA164		30. 7.90	Canx by CAA 8.1.91.
G-MWKC	Hornet R-ZA	HRWB-0106 & ZA165		30. 7.90	Canx by CAA 8.1.91.
G-MWKD	Hornet R-ZA	HRWB-0107 & ZA166		30. 7.90	Canx by CAA 8.1.91.
G-MWKE	Hornet RS-ZA (Trike c/n overstamped on HRWB-0107)	HRWB-0108 & ZA167		30. 7.90	
G-MWKF	Hornet R-ZA (Trike unit originally stamped as HRWB-0099)	HRWB-0109 & ZA168		30. 7.90	Canx by CAA 8.1.91. (Trike stored 5/97)
G-MWKG	Hornet RS-ZA	HRWB-0110 & ZA169		30. 7.90	Canx by CAA 8.1.91.
G-MWKH	Hornet RS-ZA	HRWB-0111 & ZA170		30. 7.90	Canx by CAA 8.1.91.
G-MWKI	Hornet RS-ZA	HRWB-0112 & ZA171		30. 7.90	Canx by CAA 8.1.91.
G-MWKJ	Hornet RS-ZA	HRWB-0113 & ZA172		30. 7.90	Canx by CAA 8.1.91.
G-MWKK	Hornet RS-ZA	HRWB-0114 & ZA173		30. 7.90	Canx by CAA 8.1.91.
G-MWKL	Hornet RS-ZA	HRWB-0115 & ZA174		30. 7.90	Canx by CAA 8.1.91.
G-MWKM	Hornet RS-ZA	HRWB-0116 & ZA175		30. 7.90	Canx by CAA 8.1.91.
G-MWKN	Hornet RS-ZA	HRWB-0117 & ZA176		30. 7.90	Canx by CAA 8.1.91.
G-MWKO	Solar Wings Pegasus XL-Q	SW-WQ-0357		31. 7.90	
G-MWKP	Solar Wings Pegasus XL-Q	SW-TE-0291 & SW-WQ-0358		31. 7.90	
G-MWKR	Hornet R-ZA	HRWB-0118 & ZA177		21. 8.90	Canx by CAA 8.1.91.
G-MWKS	Hornet R-ZA	HRWB-0119 & ZA178		21. 8.90	Canx by CAA 8.1.91.
G-MWKT	Hornet R-ZA	HRWB-0120 & ZA179		21. 8.90	Canx by CAA 8.1.91.
G-MWKU	Hornet R-ZA	HRWB-0121 & ZA180		21. 8.90	Canx by CAA 8.1.91.
G-MWKV	Hornet R-ZA	HRWB-0122 & ZA181		21. 8.90	Canx by CAA 8.1.91.
G-MWKW	Microflight Spectrum	015		3. 8.90	
G-MWKX	Microflight Spectrum	016		3. 8.90	Dismantled in the bushes at Eshott 2/99.
G-MWKY	Solar Wings Pegasus XL-Q	SW-TE-0292 & SW-WQ-0362		3. 8.90	
G-MWKZ	Solar Wings Pegasus XL-Q	SW-TE-0293 & SW-WQ-0363		3. 8.90	
G-MWLA	Rans S-4 Coyote	89-114 & PFA/193-11787		3. 8.90	
G-MWLB	Medway Hybred 44XLR	MR104/93		15. 8.90	
G-MWLC	Medway Hybred 44XLR	MR086/94		15. 8.90	Rebuilt as G-MWRM in 1991. Canx by CAA 3.12.98.
G-MWLD	CFM Shadow Srs.CD	106		9. 5.89	
G-MWLE	Solar Wings Pegasus XL-R	SW-TB-1425 & SW-WA-1474		9. 8.90	
G-MWLF	Solar Wings Pegasus XL-R	SW-WA-1475		9. 8.90	
G-MWLG	Solar Wings Pegasus XL-R	SW-TB-1427 & SW-WA-1476		9. 8.90	
G-MWLH	Solar Wings Pegasus Quasar	SW-WQQ-0364		9. 8.90	(Badly damaged in crash 8.3.97)
G-MWLI	Solar Wings Pegasus XL-Q (Trike c/n duplicates G-MWVM)	SW-TQ-0031 & SW-WQQ-0365	G-65-8 G-MWLI	9. 8.90	(Damaged mid .96) Permit expired 31.7.96.
G-MWLJ	Solar Wings Pegasus Quasar	SW-WQQ-0366		9. 8.90	
G-MWLK	Solar Wings Pegasus Quasar TC	SW-TQ-0033 & SW-WQQ-0367		9. 8.90	
G-MWLL	Solar Wings Pegasus XL-Q	SW-TE-0287 & SW-WQ-0338		16. 8.90	
G-MWLM	Solar Wings Pegasus XL-Q	SW-WQ-0322		17. 8.90	
G-MWLN	Whittaker MW.6S Fatboy Flyer	PFA/164-11844		16. 8.90	
G-MWLO	Whittaker MW.6 Merlin	PFA/164-11373		21. 8.90	
G-MWLP	Mainair Gemini/Flash 2A	801-0990-5 & W594		24. 8.90	
G-MWLR	Mainair Gemini/Flash 2A	802-0990-7 & W595		29. 8.90	Stolen from Croxteth Park, Liverpool on 10.9.92. Canx by CAA 23.3.93.
G-MWLS	Medway Hybred 44XLR	MR081/95		29. 8.90	
G-MWLT	Mainair Gemini/Flash 2A	804-0990-7 & W597		31. 8.90	
G-MWLU	Solar Wings Pegasus XL-R/Se	SW-TE-0304 & SW-WA-1478		6. 9.90	Permit expired 14.10.91. (Stored 9/97)
G-MWLV	Aerotech MW.5(K) Sorcerer	5K-0015-02		6. 9.90	To G-MWGK 19.9.90. Canx.
G-MWLW	Team Minimax	PFA/186-11717		14. 9.90	(Damaged on take-off at Deanland on 4.6.93)
G-MWLX	Mainair Gemini/Flash 2A	805-0990-7 & W598		5.10.90	
G-MWLY	Rans S-4 Coyote	PFA/193-11691		20. 9.90	

Regn	Type	c/n	Previous identity	Regn date	Fate or immediate subsequent identity (if known)
G-MWLZ	Rans S-4 Coyote	90-116 & PFA/193-11887		8.10.90	
G-MWMA	Powerchute Kestrel	00398		7.11.90	
G-MWMB	Powerchute Kestrel	00399		7.11.90	
G-MWMC	Powerchute Kestrel	00400		7.11.90	
G-MWMD	Powerchute Kestrel	00401		7.11.90	
G-MWME	Powerchute Kestrel	00402		7.11.90	Canx by CAA 19.12.94. To Australia as 32-0584.
G-MWMF	Powerchute Kestrel	00403		7.11.90	Permit expired 27.6.95. Canx by CAA 14.11.97.
G-MWMG	Powerchute Kestrel	00404		7.11.90	
G-MWMH	Powerchute Kestrel	00405		7.11.90	
G-MWMI	Solar Wings Pegasus Quasar	SW-TQ-0043 & SW-WQQ-0383		21. 9.90	
G-MWMJ	Solar Wings Pegasus Quasar	SW-TQ-0044 & SW-WQQ-0384		21. 9.90	
G-MWMK	Solar Wings Pegasus Quasar	SW-WQQ-0385		21. 9.90	
G-MWML	Solar Wings Pegasus Quasar	SW-TQ-0046 & SW-WQQ-0386		21. 9.90	
G-MWMM	Mainair Gemini/Flash 2A	800-0890-7 & W593		24. 8.90	
G-MWMN	Solar Wings Pegasus XL-Q	SW-TE-0297 & SW-WQ-0387		25.10.90	
G-MWMO	Solar Wings Pegasus XL-Q	SW-TE-0298 & SW-WQ-0388		2.10.90	
G-MWMP	Solar Wings Pegasus XL-Q	SW-WQ-0389		2.10.90	
G-MWMR	Solar Wings Pegasus XL-R	SW-WA-1483		2.10.90	
G-MWMS	Mainair Gemini/Flash 2A	807-1090-5 & W600		3.10.90	
G-MWMT	Mainair Gemini/Flash 2A	808-1090-7 & W601		3.10.90	
G-MWMU	CFM Shadow Srs.CD	150		2.10.90	
G-MWMV	Solar Wings Pegasus XL-R	SW-TE-0307 & SW-WA-1484		5.10.90	
G-MWMW	Murphy Renegade Spirit UK	254 & PFA/188-11544		21. 8.89	
G-MWMX	Mainair Gemini/Flash 2A	810-1090-7 & W603		17.10.90	
G-MWMY	Mainair Gemini/Flash 2A	809-1090-7 & W602		17.10.90	
G-MWMZ	Solar Wings Pegasus XL-Q	SW-WQ-0393		8.10.90	
G-MWNA	Solar Wings Pegasus XL-Q	SW-WQ-0394		8.10.90	
G-MWNB	Solar Wings Pegasus XL-Q	SW-TE-0303 & SW-WQ-0395		8.10.90	
G-MWNC	Solar Wings Pegasus XL-Q	SW-WQ-0396		8.10.90	
G-MWND	Tiger Cub RL5A Sherwood Ranger	001 & PFA/237-12229		9.10.90	
G-MWNE	Mainair Gemini/Flash 2A	803-1090-7 & W596		17.10.90	
G-MWNF	Murphy Renegade Spirit UK	PFA/188-11853		15.10.90	
G-MWNG	Solar Wings Pegasus XL-Q	SW-TE-0305 & SW-WQ-0399		17.10.90	
G-MWNH	Powerchute Mk.III	01		30. 1.91	Canx by CAA 19.12.94.
G-MWNI	Aerotech MW.5(K) Sorcerer	5K-0017-02		. .90R	NTU - To G-MYAN 3/92. Canx.
G-MWNJ	Aerotech MW.5(K) Sorcerer	5K-0018-02		. .90R	NTU - Canx.
G-MWNK	Solar Wings Pegasus Quasar TC	SW-WQQ-0403		1.11.90	
G-MWNL	Solar Wings Pegasus Quasar	SW-TQ-0055 & SW-WQQ-0404		1.11.90	
G-MWNM	Solar Wings Pegasus Quasar	SW-WQQ-0405		1.11.90	
G-MWNN	Solar Wings Pegasus Quasar	SW-WQQ-0406		1.11.90	Canx by CAA 28.2.92.
G-MWNO	AMF Chevvron 2-32	025		12.11.90	
G-MWNP	AMF Chevvron 2-32C	026		31.10.90	
G-MWNR	Murphy Renegade Spirit UK	PFA/188-11926		12.11.90	
G-MWNS	Mainair Gemini/Flash 2A	811-1190-7 & W604		6.11.90	
G-MWNT	Mainair Gemini/Flash 2A	812-1190-7 & W605		6.11.90	
G-MWNU	Mainair Gemini/Flash 2A	813-1190-5 & W606		6.11.90	
G-MWNV	Powerchute Kestrel	00406		12.11.90	
G-MWNW	Powerchute Kestrel	00407		12.11.90	Canx 17.2.97 on sale to Morocco.
G-MWNX	Powerchute Kestrel	00408		12.11.90	
G-MWNY	Powerchute Kestrel	00409		12.11.90	
G-MWNZ	Powerchute Kestrel	00410		12.11.90	
G-MWOA	Powerchute Kestrel	00411/3856712/140219		12.11.90	Canx 20.12.94 on sale to Kenya.
G-MWOB	Powerchute Kestrel	00412		12.11.90	To EI-CGW 1/93. Canx.

Regn	Type	c/n	Previous identity	Regn date	Fate or immediate subsequent identity (if known)
G-MWOC	Powerchute Kestrel	00413		12.11.90	(Damaged late .94)
G-MWOD	Powerchute Kestrel	00414		12.11.90	
G-MWOE	Powerchute Kestrel	00415		12.11.90	
G-MWOF	Microflight Spectrum	018		13.11.90	Canx by CAA 4.6.96. (On rebuild 6/97)
G-MWOG	Not allotted.				
G-MWOH	Solar Wings Pegasus XL-R/Se	SW-WA-1485		28.11.90	
G-MWOI	Solar Wings Pegasus XL-R	SW-TB-1430 & SW-WA-1486		29.11.90	
G-MWOJ	Mainair Gemini/Flash 2A	814-1290-7 & W608		6.12.90	
G-MWOK	Mainair Gemini/Flash 2A	815-1290-7 & W609		6.12.90	
G-MWOL	Mainair Gemini/Flash 2A	816-1290-7 & W610		6.12.90	
G-MWOM	Solar Wings Pegasus Quasar TC	SW-WQQ-0412		1. 3.91	
G-MWON	CFM Shadow Srs.CD	K.128		18.12.90	
G-MWOO	Murphy Renegade Spirit UK	318 & PFA/188-11811		14. 9.90	
G-MWOP	Solar Wings Pegasus Quasar TC	SW-TQC-0059 & SW-WQQ-0410		31.12.90	
G-MWOR	Solar Wings Pegasus XL-Q	SW-WQ-0411		21.12.90	
G-MWOS	Cosmos Chronos 14	B.462		2. 1.91	Canx 21.3.95 on sale to South Africa.
G-MWOT	Icarus Covert Insertion and Recovery Vehicle	0001		25.10.90	Canx by CAA 29.7.96.
G-MWOU	Medway Hybred 44XLR	MR109/96		20.11.90	Canx as WFU 26.3.96.
G-MWOV	Whittaker MW.6 Merlin	PFA/164-11301		9. 1.91	
G-MWOW	CFM Shadow Srs.B	K.007	83-AG	16. 9.85	(Stored at Davidstow Moor 10/95)
G-MWOX	Solar Wings Pegasus XL-Q	SW-WQ-0413		7. 1.91	
G-MWOY	Solar Wings Pegasus XL-Q	SW-TE-0310 & SW-WQ-0414		7. 1.91	
G-MWOZ	Fisher FP.202 Super Koala	SK.067 & PFA/158-11954		3.12.90	To G-BTBF 24.12.90. Canx.
G-MWPA	Mainair Gemini/Flash 2A	817-0191-7 & W611		9. 1.91	
G-MWPB	Mainair Gemini/Flash 2A	823-0191-7 & W617		3. 1.91	
G-MWPC	Mainair Gemini/Flash 2A	826-0191-7 & W620		3. 1.91	
G-MWPD	Mainair Gemini/Flash 2A	824-0191-7 & W618		9. 1.91	
G-MWPE	Solar Wings Pegasus XL-Q (Trike ex G-MVGX)	SW-TE-0096 & SW-WQ-0416		9. 1.91	
G-MWPF	Mainair Gemini/Flash 2A	825-0191-7 & W619		11. 1.91	
G-MWPG	Microflight Spectrum	019		9. 1.91	
G-MWPH	Microflight Spectrum	020		9. 1.91	
G-MWPI	Microflight Spectrum TI	021		9. 1.91	(Damaged early .97)
G-MWPJ	Solar Wings Pegasus XL-Q	SW-TE-0312 & SW-WQ-0418		17. 1.91	
G-MWPK	Solar Wings Pegasus XL-Q	SW-TE-0313 & SW-WQ-0419		17. 1.91	
G-MWPL	MBA Tiger Cub 440	SO.144		21. 2.84	Canx as destroyed 12.10.88.
G-MWPM	Medway Flaven	F.001		22. 1.91	Canx by CAA 7.9.94.
G-MWPN	CFM Shadow Srs.CD	K.147		22. 1.91	
G-MWPO	Mainair Gemini/Flash 2A	827-0191-7 & W621		29. 1.91	
G-MWPP	CFM Streak Shadow Srs.M	K.166-SA & PFA/206-11992	G-BTEM	14. 2.91	
G-MWPR	Whittaker MW.6 Merlin	PFA/164-11260		16.10.90	
G-MWPS	Murphy Renegade Spirit UK	PFA/188-11931		18. 2.91	
G-MWPT	Hunt Avon/Hunt Wing	BMAA/HB/015 & JAH-8	EI-CKF G-MWPT	18. 2.91	Destroyed in accident (details?)
G-MWPU	Solar Wings Pegasus Quasar TC	SW-WQQ-0426		20. 2.91	
G-MWPV	CFM Image	IM-01 & PFA/222-12012		21. 2.91	To G-BTUD 8/91. Canx.
G-MWPW	AMF Chevvron 2-32C	027		26.11.90	
G-MWPX	Solar Wings Pegasus XL-R	SW-WA-1488		27. 2.91	
G-MWPY	CFM Streak Shadow Srs.SA	K.164-SA & PFA/206-11964		26. 2.91	To G-BTGT 1.3.91. Canx.
G-MWPZ	Murphy Renegade Spirit UK	PFA/188-11631		18. 3.91	
G-MWRA	Mainair Gemini/Flash 2A	818-0191-7 & W612		5. 2.91	Canx 27.5.99 on sale to Cyprus.
G-MWRB	Mainair Gemini/Flash 2A	819-0191-7 & W613		5. 2.91	
G-MWRC	Mainair Gemini/Flash 2A	820-0191-7 & W614		5. 2.91	
G-MWRD	Mainair Gemini/Flash 2A	821-0191-7 & W615		5. 2.91	

Regn	Type	c/n	Previous identity	Regn date	Fate or immediate subsequent identity (if known)
G-MWRE	Mainair Gemini/Flash 2A	822-0191-7 & W616		5. 2.91	
G-MWRF	Mainair Gemini/Flash 2A	829-0191-7 & W623		4. 2.91	
G-MWRG	Mainair Gemini/Flash 2A	830-0191-7 & W624		5. 2.91	
G-MWRH	Mainair Gemini/Flash 2A	831-0191-7 & W625		5. 2.91	
G-MWRI	Mainair Gemini/Flash 2A	828-0191-7 & W622		1. 3.91	
G-MWRJ	Mainair Gemini/Flash 2A	832-0291-7 & W626		28. 2.91	
G-MWRK	Rans S-6 Coyote II	0191-154 & PFA/204-11930		13. 2.91	
G-MWRL	CFM Shadow Srs.CD	K.152		13. 2.91	
G-MWRM	Medway Hybred 44XLR	MR086/94/91/S	G-MWLC (rebuilt)	26. 2.91	
G-MWRN	Solar Wings Pegasus XL-R	SW-TE-0316 & SW-WA-1489		5. 3.91	
G-MWRO	Solar Wings Pegasus XL-R	SW-WA-1490		5. 3.91	
G-MWRP	Solar Wings Pegasus XL-R	SW-TE-0318 & SW-WA-1491		1. 3.91	
G-MWRR	Mainair Gemini/Flash 2A	834-0391-7 & W628		7. 3.91	
G-MWRS	Ultravia Super Pelican	E001-201		9. 5.84	
G-MWRT	Solar Wings Pegasus XL-R	SW-TB-1431 & SW-WA-1492		15. 3.91	
G-MWRU	Solar Wings Pegasus XL-R	SW-WA-1493		15. 3.91	
G-MWRV	Solar Wings Pegasus XL-R	SW-TB-1433 & SW-WA-1494		15. 3.91	
G-MWRW	Solar Wings Pegasus XL-Q	SW-TE-0320 & SW-WQ-0431		25. 3.91	
G-MWRX	Solar Wings Pegasus XL-Q	SW-WQ-0432		25. 3.91	
G-MWRY	CFM Shadow Srs.CD (Originally c/n quoted as K.158)	K.162		26. 3.91	
G-MWRZ	AMF Chevvron 2-32C	028		10. 4.91	
G-MWSA	Team Minimax	PFA/186-11855		8. 4.91	
G-MWSB	Mainair Gemini/Flash 2A	837-0591-7 & W631		30. 4.91	
G-MWSC	Rans S-6-ESD Coyote II	PFA/204-12019		13. 5.91	
G-MWSD	Solar Wings Pegasus XL-Q	SW-TE-0319 & SW-WQ-0430		6. 3.91	
G-MWSE	Solar Wings Pegasus XL-R	SW-TE-0323 & SW-WA-1496		10. 4.91	
G-MWSF	Solar Wings Pegasus XL-R	SW-TE-0324 & SW-WA-1497		10. 4.91	
G-MWSG	Solar Wings Pegasus XL-R	SW-TE-0325 & SW-WA-1498		10. 4.91	
G-MWSH	Solar Wings Pegasus Quasar TC	SW-TQC-0064 & SW-WQQ-0435		30. 4.91	
G-MWSI	Solar Wings Pegasus Quasar TC	SW-TQC-0065 & SW-WQQ-0436		23. 5.91	
G-MWSJ	Solar Wings Pegasus XL-Q	SW-WQ-0437		12. 4.91	
G-MWSK	Solar Wings Pegasus XL-Q	SW-WQ-0438		12. 4.91	
G-MWSL	Mainair Gemini/Flash 2A	835-0491-7 & W629		16. 4.91	
G-MWSM	Mainair Gemini/Flash 2A	836-0491-7 & W630		16. 4.91	
G-MWSN	Solar Wings Pegasus Quasar TC	SW-WQQ-0443		30. 4.91	Canx as WFU 9.7.96.
G-MWSO	Solar Wings Pegasus XL-R	SW-TE-0329 & SW-WA-1503		25. 4.91	
G-MWSP	Solar Wings Pegasus XL-R	SW-TE-0330 & SW-WA-1504		25. 4.91	
G-MWSR	Solar Wings Pegasus XL-R	SW-TE-0331 & SW-WA-1505		25. 4.91	
G-MWSS	Medway Hybred 44XLR	MR117/97		7. 5.91	
G-MWST	Medway Hybred 44XLR	MR118/98		8. 5.91	(Damaged mid .97)
G-MWSU	Medway Hybred 44XLR	MR119/99		1. 5.92	
G-MWSV	Solar Wings Pegasus Quasar TC	SW-WQQ-0447		14. 5.91	Canx by CAA 28.2.92.
G-MWSW	Whittaker MW.6 Merlin	PFA/164-11328		15. 2.91	
G-MWSX	Aerotech MW.5 Sorcerer	PFA/163-11549		3. 5.91	
G-MWSY	Aerotech MW.5 Sorcerer	PFA/163-11218		3. 5.91	
G-MWSZ	CFM Shadow Srs.CD	K.158		4. 4.91	
G-MWTA	Solar Wings Pegasus XL-Q	SW-WQ-0444		8. 5.91	
G-MWTB	Solar Wings Pegasus XL-Q	SW-TE-0333 & SW-WQ-0445		8. 5.91	
G-MWTC	Solar Wings Pegasus XL-Q	SW-WQ-0446		13. 5.91	
G-MWTD	Microflight Spectrum	022		13. 5.91	

Regn	Type	c/n	Previous identity	Regn date	Fate or immediate subsequent identity (if known)
G-MWTE	Microflight Spectrum	023		13. 5.91	
G-MWTF	Mainair Gemini/Southdown Sprint (Originally regd with c/n 249-682-2)	249-684-2 & GDCB-01		30. 7.84	
G-MWTG	Mainair Gemini/Flash 2A	838-0591-7 & W632		16. 5.91	
G-MWTH	Mainair Gemini/Flash 2A	839-0591-7 & W633		21. 5.91	
G-MWTI	Solar Wings Pegasus XL-Q	SW-WQ-0274		23. 5.91	
G-MWTJ	CFM Shadow Srs.CD	K.167		16. 5.91	
G-MWTK	Solar Wings Pegasus XL-R/Se	SW-TE-0335 & SW-WA-1507		28. 5.91	
G-MWTL	Solar Wings Pegasus XL-R	SW-TE-0336 & SW-WA-1508		28. 5.91	
G-MWTM	Solar Wings Pegasus XL-R	SW-WA-1509		28. 5.91	
G-MWTN	CFM Shadow Srs.CD	K.153		23. 5.91	
G-MWTO	Mainair Gemini/Flash 2A	840-0591-7 & W634		28. 5.91	
G-MWTP	CFM Shadow Srs.CD	K.107		23. 5.91	
G-MWTR	Mainair Gemini/Flash 2A	842-0591-7 & W636		31. 5.91	
G-MWTS	Whittaker MW.6S Fatboy Flyer	PFA/164-12015		31. 5.91	
G-MWTT	Rans S-6-ESD Coyote II	20391-175 & PFA/204-12016		30. 4.91	
G-MWTU	Solar Wings Pegasus XL-R	SW-WA-1501		21. 6.91	
G-MWTV	Solar Wings Pegasus XL-R	SW-WA-1506		21. 6.91	To EI-CGJ 4/93. Canx 19.3.93.
G-MWTW	Whittaker MW.6S Fatboy Flyer	PFA/164-11493		3. 6.91	To EI-CJZ 3/94. Canx 13.9.93.
G-MWTX	Medway Hybred 44XLR	MR120/100		20. 6.91	Canx as WFU 7.3.96.
G-MWTY	Mainair Gemini/Flash 2A	843-0691-7 & W637		12. 6.91	
G-MWTZ	Mainair Gemini/Flash 2A	844-0691-7 & W638		12. 6.91	
G-MWUA	CFM Shadow Srs.CD	K.161		10. 6.91	
G-MWUB	Solar Wings Pegasus XL-R	SW-WA-1510		12. 6.91	
G-MWUC	Solar Wings Pegasus XL-R	SW-WA-1511		12. 6.91	
G-MWUD	Solar Wings Pegasus XL-R	SW-WA-1512		12. 6.91	
G-MWUE	Solar Wings Pegasus XL-R	SW-WA-1513	EI-CGL G-MWUE	13. 6.91	
G-MWUF	Solar Wings Pegasus XL-R	SW-TB-1439 & SW-WA-1514		13. 6.91	
G-MWUG	Solar Wings Pegasus XL-R	SW-TB-1440 & SW-WA-1515		14. 6.91	
G-MWUH	Murphy Renegade Spirit UK (Built in Canada/Saudi Arabia)	343		12. 6.91	Permit expired 2.10.95. (Stored 4/97)
G-MWUI	AMF Chevvron 2-32C	029		2. 7.91	
G-MWUJ	Medway Hybred 44XLR	MR122/101		27. 6.91	
G-MWUK	Rans S-6-ESD Coyote II	PFA/204-12090		1. 7.91	
G-MWUL	Rans S-6-ESD Coyote II	0391-172 & PFA/204-12054		10. 6.91	
G-MWUM	Rans S-6-ESD Coyote II	PFA/204-11997		10. 6.91	Canx 29.7.94 on sale to Germany.
G-MWUN	Rans S-6-ESD Coyote II (Rebuilt with new airframe after w/o 13.10.94)	PFA/204-12075		10. 6.91	
G-MWUO	Solar Wings Pegasus XL-Q	SW-TE-0296 & SW-WQ-0379		26. 6.91	
G-MWUP	Solar Wings Pegasus XL-R	SW-WA-1517		21. 6.91	
G-MWUR	Solar Wings Pegasus XL-R	SW-TE-0342 & SW-WA-1518		21. 6.91	
G-MWUS	Solar Wings Pegasus XL-R	SW-TE-0343 & SW-WA-1519		21. 6.91	
G-MWUT	Solar Wings Pegasus XL-R	SW-TE-0344 & SW-WA-1520		21. 6.91	Crashed on landing at Brunton on 6.9.96. Trike to G-MGCB 10/96. Canx as destroyed 21.10.96.
G-MWUU	Solar Wings Pegasus XL-R	SW-TE-0346 & SW-WA-1521		28. 6.91	
G-MWUV	Solar Wings Pegasus XL-R	SW-TE-0347 & SW-WA-1522		28. 6.91	
G-MWUW	Solar Wings Pegasus XL-R	SW-TE-0348 & SW-WA-1523		28. 6.91	Canx by CAA 16.2.98.
G-MWUX	Solar Wings Pegasus XL-Q	SW-WQ-0454		28. 6.91	
G-MWUY	Solar Wings Pegasus XL-Q	SW-TE-0345 & SW-WQ-0455		28. 6.91	
G-MWUZ	Solar Wings Pegasus XL-Q	SW-TE-0350 & SW-WQ-0456		28. 6.91	
G-MWVA	Solar Wings Pegasus XL-Q	SW-TE-0351 & SW-WQ-0457		28. 6.91	
G-MWVB	Solar Wings Pegasus XL-R	SW-TB-1434 & SW-WA-1500		17. 7.91	To EI-CKU 10/94. Canx 19.3.93.
G-MWVC	Solar Wings Pegasus XL-R	SW-WA-1502		17. 7.91	To EI-CGM 11/92. Canx 7.5.92.
G-MWVD	Not to be allotted.				

Regn	Type	c/n	Previous identity	Regn date	Fate or immediate subsequent identity (if known)
G-MWVE	Solar Wings Pegasus XL-R	SW-TB-1441 & SW-WA-1524		18. 7.91	
G-MWVF	Solar Wings Pegasus XL-R/Se	SW-TB-1442 & SW-WA-1525		18. 7.91	
G-MWVG	CFM Shadow Srs.CD	151		5. 8.91	
G-MWVH	CFM Shadow Srs.CD	181		5. 8.91	
G-MWVI	Whittaker MW.6 Merlin	PFA/164-11132		1. 9.89	Canx by CAA 3.3.99.
G-MWVJ	Mainair Mercury	791-0690-5 & W596		9. 8.91	(Believed to be composite of G-MWIH (trike) and G-MWNE (wing) for trials purposes only) Canx as WFU 2.7.96.
G-MWVK	Mainair Mercury	849-0891-5 & W643		13. 8.91	
G-MWVL	Rans S-6 ESD Coyote II (Originally built with frame c/n 0491-186)(Tricycle u/c)	0892-341 & PFA/204-12118		13. 8.91	
G-MWVM	Solar Wings Pegasus Quasar IITC (Trike c/n duplicates G-MWLI)	SW-TQ-0031 & SW-WX-0020	G-65-8	2. 9.91	
G-MWVN	Mainair Gemini/Flash 2A	850-0891-7 & W644		19. 8.91	
G-MWVO	Mainair Gemini/Flash 2A	852-0891-7 & W646		27. 8.91	
G-MWVP	Murphy Renegade Spirit UK	PFA/188-11735		22. 8.91	Damaged on landing at Redlands, near Swindon on 3.7.93. Permit expired 29.4.94.
G-MWVR	Mainair Gemini/Flash 2A	855-0991-7 & W650		30. 8.91	
G-MWVS	Mainair Gemini/Flash 2A	856-0991-7 & W651		30. 8.91	
G-MWVT	Mainair Gemini/Flash 2A	860-1091-7 & W655		2. 9.91	
G-MWVU	Medway Hybred 44XLR	MR123/102		18. 9.91	
G-MWVV	Solar Wings Pegasus XL-Q	SW-WQ-0463		16. 8.91	Canx as WFU 27.4.95.
G-MWVW	Mainair Gemini/Flash 2A	853-0891-7 & W647		9. 9.91	
G-MWVX	Quad City Challenger II UK	PFA/177-12057		14. 8.91	Canx by CAA 9.7.96.
G-MWVY	Mainair Gemini/Flash 2A	854-0991-7 & W649		4. 9.91	
G-MWVZ	Mainair Gemini/Flash 2A	863-1091-7 & W658		4. 9.91	
G-MWWA	Solar Wings Pegasus Quasar IITC	SW-TQC-0073 & SW-WQT-0467		17. 9.91	
G-MWWB	Mainair Gemini/Flash 2A	864-1091-7 & W659		18. 9.91	
G-MWWC	Mainair Gemini/Flash 2A	868-1191-7 & W663		23. 9.91	
G-MWWD	Murphy Renegade Spirit UK	344 & PFA/188-11719		23. 9.91	Extensively damaged when it veered to starboard and crashed on landing at Snetterton on 15.6.92.
G-MWWE	Team Minimax	PFA/186-11925		1.10.91	
G-MWWF	Kolb Twinstar Mk.3	PFA/205-12110	G-59-1	4.10.91	Fatal crash at Stradbroke, Suffolk on 21.7.94. Canx by CAA 29.11.94.
G-MWWG	Solar Wings Pegasus XL-Q	SW-WQ-0468		3.10.91	
G-MWWH	Solar Wings Pegasus XL-Q	SW-TE-0356 & SW-WQ-0469		3.10.91	
G-MWWI	Mainair Gemini/Flash 2A	870-1291-7 & W665		11.10.91	
G-MWWJ	Mainair Gemini/Flash 2A	865-1191-7 & W660		22.10.91	
G-MWWK	Mainair Gemini/Flash 2A	866-1191-7 & W661		22.10.91	
G-MWWL	Rans S-6-ESD Coyote II (Regd with c/n PFA/204-11840)	PFA/204-11849	(G-BTXD)	17.10.91	
G-MWWM	Kolb Twinstar Mk.2 (C/n conflicts with G-GPST) (Originally regd with the PFA as a 'Phillips Twin' with c/n PFA/207-11645)	PFA/205-11645	(G-BTXC)	17.10.91	
G-MWWN	Mainair Gemini/Flash 2A	872-1291-7 & W667		22.10.91	
G-MWWO	Solar Wings Pegasus XL-R/Se	SW-TB-1443 & SW-WA-1528		22.10.91	(Stored 9/97)
G-MWWP	Rans S-4 Coyote	PFA/193-12073		21.10.91	(On repair 1/99 Strathaven)
G-MWWR	Microflight Spectrum	024		23.10.91	
G-MWWS	Thruster T.300	089-T300-370	EI-BYW	4.11.91	(Stored 3/97)
G-MWWT	Thruster Super T.300	9012-ST300-503		25.10.91	
G-MWWU	Air Creation Fun 18 GT Bis	001		25.10.91	Canx as WFU 1.10.93.
G-MWWV	Solar Wings Pegasus XL-Q	SW-WQ-0470		30.10.91	
G-MWWW	Whittaker MW.6S Fatboy Flyer	PFA/164-11540		2. 9.91	Canx as destroyed 11.10.96.
G-MWWX	Microflight Spectrum	025		25.10.91	Badly damaged in crash near East Fortune on 13.4.97. (Noted minus tail at Eshott 12.2.99)
G-MWWY	Microflight Spectrum	026		25.10.91	Fatal crash on take-off from Netherthorpe on 12.8.97. Canx as destroyed 29.12.97.
G-MWWZ	Cyclone Chaser S	CH.829		29.10.91	
G-MWXA	Mainair Gemini/Flash 2A	873-0192-7 & W668		30.10.91	
G-MWXB	Mainair Gemini/Flash 2A	869-1191-7 & W664		6.11.91	

Regn	Type	c/n	Previous identity	Regn date	Fate or immediate subsequent identity (if known)
G-MWXC	Mainair Gemini/Flash 2A	874-0192-7 & W669		6.11.91	
G-MWXD	Mainair Gemini/Flash 2A	876-0192-7 & W671		6.11.91	
G-MWXE	Hiway Skytrike 330/Flexiform Solo Striker	26X7 & BPB-01		4.11.91	Canx as WFU 8.12.93. (Stored 3/97 - see G-MBJS)
G-MWXF	Mainair Mercury	867-1191-5 & W662		12.11.91	
G-MWXG	Solar Wings Pegasus Quasar IITC	SW-TQC-0074 & SW-WQT-0471		7.11.91	
G-MWXH	Solar Wings Pegasus Quasar IITC	SW-TQC-0075 & SW-WQT-0472		7.11.91	
G-MWXI	Solar Wings Pegasus Quasar IITC	SW-WQT-0473		7.11.91	
G-MWXJ	Mainair Mercury	861-1091-5 & W656		15.11.91	
G-MWXK	Mainair Mercury	862-1191-5 & W657		15.11.91	(Extant 5/97)
G-MWXL	Mainair Gemini/Flash 2A	859-1091-7 & W654		12.12.91	
G-MWXM	Solar Wings Pegasus XL-R	SW-WA-1529		15.11.91	To EI-CGN 11/92. Canx 7.5.92.
G-MWXN	Mainair Gemini/Flash 2A	878-0192-7 & W673		20.11.91	
G-MWXO	Mainair Gemini/Flash 2A	880-0192-7 & W675		25.11.91	
G-MWXP	Solar Wings Pegasus XL-Q	SW-TE-0359 & SW-WQ-0475		26.11.91	
G-MWXR	Solar Wings Pegasus XL-Q	SW-WQ-0476		26.11.91	
G-MWXS	Mainair Gemini/Flash 2A	883-0292-7 & W678		4.12.91	
G-MWXT	AMF Chevvron 2-32C	054		5.12.91	Canx 15.6.92 on sale to Japan.
G-MWXU	Mainair Gemini/Flash 2A	882-0192-7 & W677		9.12.91	
G-MWXV	Mainair Gemini/Flash 2A	879-1291-7 & W674		9.12.91	(Stored 4/97)
G-MWXW	Cyclone Chaser S	CH.830		9.12.91	
G-MWXX	Cyclone Chaser S	CH.831	(G-MWEB) (G-MWCD)	9.12.91	
G-MWXY	Cyclone Chaser S	CH.832	(G-MWEC)	19.12.91	
G-MWXZ	Cyclone Chaser S	CH.836		31.12.91	
G-MWYA	Mainair Gemini/Flash 2A	886-0292-7 & W681		3. 1.92	
G-MWYB	Solar Wings Pegasus XL-Q	SW-TE-0364 & SW-WQ-0485		15. 1.92	
G-MWYC	Solar Wings Pegasus XL-Q	SW-TE-0365 & SW-WQ-0486		15. 1.92	
G-MWYD	CFM Shadow Srs.C	K.179		8. 1.92	
G-MWYE	Rans S-6-ESD Coyote II	0591-189 & PFA/204-12223		10. 1.92	
G-MWYF	Rans S-6 Coyote II	D-190111 & PFA/204-12021	(EI-CEL)	14. 1.92	To G-BUEW 4/92. Canx.
G-MWYG	Mainair Gemini/Flash 2A	884-0292-7 & W679		15. 1.92	
G-MWYH	Mainair Gemini/Flash 2A	887-0292-7 & W682		15. 1.92	
G-MWYI	Solar Wings Pegasus Quasar IITC	SW-TQC-0083 & SW-WQT-0488		30. 1.92	
G-MWYJ	Solar Wings Pegasus Quasar IITC	SW-TQC-0084 & SW-WQT-0489		24. 1.92	
G-MWYK	Mainair Gemini/Flash 2A	891-0392-7 & W686		17. 1.92	To SE-VBK 8/96. Canx 16.8.95.
G-MWYL	Mainair Gemini/Flash 2A	877-0192-7 & W672		17. 1.92	
G-MWYM	Cyclone Chaser S 1000	CH.838		21. 1.92	
G-MWYN	Rans S-6-ESD Coyote II	0491-185 & PFA/204-12168		22. 1.92	
G-MWYO	CGS Hawk II Arrow	H-11-063-R503	N215HK	24. 1.92	Canx 9.2.93 on sale to France.
G-MWYP	CGS Hawk I Arrow	H-T-468-R447	N216HK	24. 1.92	Canx 9.2.93 on sale to France.
G-MWYR	CGS AG-Hawk	H-T-469-R447-AG	N217HK	24. 1.92	Canx 9.2.93 on sale to France.
G-MWYS	CGS Hawk I Arrow	BMAA/HB/020 & H-T-470-R447		17. 2.93	
G-MWYT	Mainair Gemini/Flash 2A	881-0392-7 & W676		3. 2.92	
G-MWYU	Solar Wings Pegasus XL-Q	SW-WQ-0491		30. 1.92	
G-MWYV	Mainair Gemini/Flash 2A	896-0392-7 & W691		3. 2.92	
G-MWYW	Mainair Gemini/Flash 2A	898-0492-7 & W693		3. 2.92	To SE-YPP. Canx 9.3.93.
G-MWYX	Mainair Gemini/Flash 2A	897-0492-7 & W692		13. 2.92	To SE-VBB 5/96. Canx 30.11.95.
G-MWYY	Solar Wings Pegasus XL-Q	SW-TE-0365 & SW-WQ-0492		17. 2.92	(Stored 8/97)
G-MWYZ	Solar Wings Pegasus XL-Q	SW-WQ-0474		20.11.91	
G-MWZA	Mainair Mercury	888-0292-5 & W683		7. 2.92	
G-MWZB	AMF Chevvron 2-32C	033		10. 2.92	

Regn	Type	c/n	Previous identity	Regn date	Fate or immediate subsequent identity (if known)
G-MWZC	Mainair Gemini/Flash 2A	899-0492-7 & W694		7. 2.92	
G-MWZD	Solar Wings Pegasus Quasar IITC	SW-TQC-0086 & SW-WQT-0494		2. 3.92	
G-MWZE	Solar Wings Pegasus Quasar IITC	SW-TQC-0087 & SW-WQT-0495		17. 2.92	
G-MWZF	Solar Wings Pegasus Quasar IITC (Trike c/n duplicates G-MYEK)	SW-TQD-0108 & SW-WQT-0496		17. 2.92	
G-MWZG	Mainair Gemini/Flash 2A	889-0392-7 & W684		7. 2.92	
G-MWZH	Solar Wings Pegasus XL-R	SW-WA-1532		17. 2.92	
G-MWZI	Solar Wings Pegasus XL-R	SW-TE-0367 & SW-WA-1533		17. 2.92	
G-MWZJ	Solar Wings Pegasus XL-R/Se	SW-TE-0368 & SW-WA-1534		17. 2.92	
G-MWZK	Solar Wings Pegasus XL-Q	SW-TE-0369 & SW-WQ-0497		17. 2.92	Canx 16.8.95 on sale to Sweden.
G-MWZL	Mainair Gemini/Flash 2A	900-0492-7 & W695		17. 2.92	
G-MWZM	Team Minimax 91	PFA/186-12211	G-BUDD G-MWZM	18. 2.92	
G-MWZN	Mainair Gemini/Flash 2A	902-0492-7 & W697		25. 2.92	
G-MWZO	Solar Wings Pegasus Quasar IITC	SW-WQT-0498		26. 2.92	
G-MWZP	Solar Wings Pegasus Quasar IITC	SW-TQC-0090 & SW-WQT-0499		26. 2.92	
G-MWZR	Solar Wings Pegasus Quasar IITC	SW-WQT-0500		26. 2.92	
G-MWZS	Solar Wings Pegasus Quasar IITC	SW-WQT-0501	EI-CIP G-MWZS	26. 2.92	
G-MWZT	Solar Wings Pegasus XL-R	SW-TE-0370 & SW-WA-1535		26. 2.92	
G-MWZU	Solar Wings Pegasus XL-R	SW-WA-1536		26. 2.92	
G-MWZV	Solar Wings Pegasus XL-R	SW-WA-1537		26. 2.92	
G-MWZW	Solar Wings Pegasus XL-R	SW-TE-0373 & SW-WA-1538		26. 2.92	
G-MWZX	Solar Wings Pegasus XL-R	SW-TE-0374 & SW-WA-1539		26. 2.92	
G-MWZY	Solar Wings Pegasus XL-R	SW-TE-0375 & SW-WA-1540		26. 2.92	
G-MWZZ	Solar Wings Pegasus XL-R	SW-TE-0376 & SW-WA-1541		26. 2.92	
G-MXIV	Vickers Supermarine 379 Spitfire FR.XIVc	6S/583887	T3 Indian AF/NH749	11. 4.80	To NX749DP 5/85. Canx 15.5.85.
G-MXIX	Vickers Supermarine 390 Spitfire PR.XIX	6S/594677	PS853 7548M/PS853	23. 2.95	To G-RRGN 12/96. Canx.
G-MXVI	Vickers Supermarine 361 Spitfire LF.XVIe	CBAF/IX/4394	6850M TE184	17. 2.89	
G-MYAA	CFM Shadow Srs.CD	K.139		11. 4.90	To G-PSUE 4/99. Canx.
G-MYAB	Solar Wings Pegasus XL-R/Se	SW-TE-0377 & SW-WA-1542		26. 2.92	
G-MYAC	Solar Wings Pegasus XL-Q	SW-TE-0378 & SW-WQ-0502		26. 2.92	
G-MYAD	Solar Wings Pegasus XL-Q	SW-TE-0379 & SW-WQ-0503		26. 2.92	
G-MYAE	Solar Wings Pegasus XL-Q	SW-TE-0380 & SW-WQ-0504		26. 2.92	
G-MYAF	Solar Wings Pegasus XL-Q	SW-WQ-0505		26. 2.92	
G-MYAG	Quad City Challenger II	PFA/177-12167		25. 2.92	
G-MYAH	Whittaker MW.5 Sorcerer	PFA/163-11233		2. 3.92	
G-MYAI	Mainair Mercury	892-0392-5 & W687		11. 3.92	
G-MYAJ	Rans S-6-ESD Coyote II	PFA/204-12227		3. 3.92	
G-MYAK	Solar Wings Pegasus Quasar IITC	SW-WQT-0506	D-.... G-MYAK	5. 3.92	
G-MYAL	Rotec Rally 2B	DJC-01		5. 3.92	Canx by CAA 29.3.99.
G-MYAM	Murphy Renegade Spirit UK	PFA/188-11907		6. 3.92	
G-MYAN	Aerotech MW.5(K) Sorcerer (Modified to floatplane with Full Lotus floats)	5K-0017-02	(G-MWNI)	24. 3.92	
G-MYAO	Mainair Gemini/Flash 2A	894-0392-7 & W689		11. 3.92	
G-MYAP	Thruster T.300	9022-T300-501		12. 3.92	
G-MYAR	Thruster T.300	9022-T300-502		12. 3.92	
G-MYAS	Mainair Gemini/Flash 2A	895-0392-7 & W690		11. 3.92	
G-MYAT	Team Minimax	PFA/186-12017		6. 3.92	

Regn	Type	c/n	Previous identity	Regn date	Fate or immediate subsequent identity (if known)
G-MYAU	Mainair Gemini/Flash 2A	890-0392-7 & W685		25. 3.92	
G-MYAV	Mainair Mercury	893-0392-5 & W688		23. 3.92	
G-MYAW	Team Minimax 91	PFA/186-12164		11. 3.92	
G-MYAX	Mainair Gemini/Flash 2A	905-0592-7 & W704		13. 3.92	Canx as WFU 27.2.95.
G-MYAY	Microflight Spectrum	027		13. 3.92	
G-MYAZ	Murphy Renegade Spirit UK	PFA/188-12027		16. 3.92	
G-MYBA	Rans S-6-ESD Coyote II	PFA/204-12210		12. 3.92	
G-MYBB	Maxair Drifter	BMAA/HB/014 & MD.001		10. 4.92	
G-MYBC	CFM Shadow Srs.CD	BMAA/HB/047 & K.195 & PFA/206-12221 (PFA c/n erroneously indicates type is Streak Shadow)		18. 3.92	
G-MYBD	Solar Wings Pegasus Quasar IITC	SW-WQT-0511		26. 3.92	
G-MYBE	Solar Wings Pegasus Quasar IITC	SW-WQT-0512		26. 3.92	
G-MYBF	Solar Wings Pegasus XL-Q	SW-TE-0384 & SW-WQ-0513		26. 3.92	
G-MYBG	Solar Wings Pegasus XL-Q	SW-TE-0385 & SW-WQ-0514		26. 3.92	
G-MYBH	Eipper Quicksilver GT500	0173		25. 3.92	Canx as WFU 18.3.99.
G-MYBI	Rans S-6-ESD Coyote II	PFA/204-12186		26. 3.92	
G-MYBJ	Mainair Gemini/Flash 2A	908-0593-7 & W706		2. 4.92	
G-MYBK	Solar Wings Pegasus Quasar II TC	SW-WQT-0516		6. 4.92	To Australia as T2-2566. Canx 4.9.92.
G-MYBL	CFM Shadow Srs.CD	K.194		2. 4.92	
G-MYBM	Team Minimax 91	PFA/186-12212		3. 4.92	
G-MYBN	Hiway Skytrike Mk.II/Demon 175	BRL-01		14. 4.92	
G-MYBO	Solar Wings Pegasus XL-R	SW-WA-1545		16. 4.92	
G-MYBP	Solar Wings Pegasus XL-R/Se	SW-TB-1446 & SW-WA-1546		16. 4.92	
G-MYBR	Solar Wings Pegasus XL-Q	SW-TE-0386 & SW-WQ-0517		16. 4.92	
G-MYBS	Solar Wings Pegasus XL-Q	SW-WQ-0518		16. 4.92	
G-MYBT	Solar Wings Pegasus Quasar IITC	SW-WQT-0519		16. 4.92	
G-MYBU	Cyclone Chaser S	CH.837		28. 4.92	
G-MYBV	Solar Wings Pegasus XL-Q	SW-TE-0393 & SW-WQ-0522		5. 5.92	
G-MYBW	Solar Wings Pegasus XL-Q	SW-WQ-0523		5. 5.92	
G-MYBX	Solar Wings Pegasus XL-Q	SW-WQ-0524	(F-....) G-MYBX	5. 5.92	
G-MYBY	Solar Wings Pegasus XL-Q	SW-TE-0396 & SW-WQ-0525		5. 5.92	
G-MYBZ	Solar Wings Pegasus XL-Q	SW-TE-0397 & SW-WQ-0526		5. 5.92	
G-MYCA	Whittaker MW.6 Merlin	PFA/164-11821		14. 5.92	
G-MYCB	Cyclone Chaser S	CH.839		18. 5.92	
G-MYCC	Murphy Renegade Spirit	222 & PFA/188-11597		23. 5.89	Crashed following engine failure in the Algarve, Portugal in summer .92. CofA lapsed 10.6.92. Canx as destroyed 19.10.94.
G-MYCD	CFM Shadow Srs.CD	K.146		19. 7.90	To SE-YUO 7/99. Canx 17.9.98.
G-MYCE	Solar Wings Pegasus Quasar IITC	SW-TQC-0098 & SW-WQT-0527		14. 5.92	
G-MYCF	Solar Wings Pegasus Quasar IITC	SW-TQC-0099 & SW-WQT-0528		14. 5.92	
G-MYCG	Solar Wings Pegasus Quasar IITC	SW-WQT-0529		14. 5.92	
G-MYCH	Solar Wings Pegasus XL-R	SW-WA-1551		15. 5.92	Canx 3.8.95 on sale to Portugal.
G-MYCI	Solar Wings Pegasus XL-R	SW-WA-1552		15. 5.92	To 9J-YCI 3/96. Canx 24.3.93.
G-MYCJ	Mainair Mercury	906-0592-5 & W704 (Wing c/n unconfirmed; duplicated G-MYAX)		19. 5.92	
G-MYCK	Mainair Gemini/Flash 2A	909-0592-7 & W707		19. 5.92	
G-MYCL	Mainair Mercury	910-0592-5 & W708		19. 5.92	
G-MYCM	CFM Shadow Srs.CD	196		20. 5.92	
G-MYCN	Mainair Mercury	901-0492-5 & W696		22. 5.92	
G-MYCO	Murphy Renegade Spirit UK	PFA/188-12020		28. 5.92	
G-MYCP	Whittaker MW.6 Merlin	PFA/164-11505		2. 6.92	
G-MYCR	Mainair Gemini/Flash 2A	875-0192-7 & W670		10. 6.92	
G-MYCS	Mainair Gemini/Flash 2A	911-0592-7 & W710		12. 6.92	
G-MYCT	Team Minimax 91	PFA/186-12163		30. 3.92	

Regn	Type	c/n	Previous identity	Regn date	Fate or immediate subsequent identity (if known)
G-MYCU	Whittaker MW.6 Merlin (Mod) (PFA c/n conflicts with Streak Shadow G-ORAF)	PFA/164-11627		9. 6.92	
G-MYCV	Mainair Mercury	913-0792-5 & W712		12. 6.92	
G-MYCW	Powerchute Kestrel	00420		15. 6.92	
G-MYCX	Powerchute Kestrel	00421		15. 6.92	
G-MYCY	Powerchute Kestrel	00422/3986510/140456		15. 6.92	
G-MYCZ	Powerchute Kestrel	00423		15. 6.92	
G-MYDA	Powerchute Kestrel	00424		15. 6.92	
G-MYDB	Powerchute Kestrel	00425		15. 6.92	
G-MYDC	Mainair Mercury	916-0792-5 & W715		23. 6.92	
G-MYDD	CFM Shadow Srs.CD	K.197		22. 6.92	Canx by CAA 23.1.97.
G-MYDE	CFM Shadow Srs.CD	K.187		24. 6.92	
G-MYDF	Team Minimax 91	PFA/186-12129		24. 6.92	
G-MYDG	Solar Wings Pegasus XL-R	SW-WA-1555		26. 6.92	To ZU-AEH. Canx 26.10.92.
G-MYDH	Solar Wings Pegasus XL-R	SW-WA-1556		26. 6.92	To 9J-YDH. Canx 24.3.93.
G-MYDI	Solar Wings Pegasus XL-R	SW-WA-1557		26. 6.92	
G-MYDJ	Solar Wings Pegasus XL-R	SW-WA-1558		1. 7.92	
G-MYDK	Rans S-6-ESD Coyote II	0392-276 & PFA/204-12239		21. 4.92	
G-MYDL	Aerotech MW.5(K) Sorcerer	PFA/163-12106		26. 6.92	
G-MYDM	Whittaker MW.6S Fatboy Flyer	PFA/164-12105		26. 6.92	
G-MYDN	Quad City Challenger II UK	CH2-1091-UK-0736 & PFA/177-12245		30. 6.92	
G-MYDO	Rans S-5 Coyote	89-110 & PFA/193-12274		6. 7.92	
G-MYDP	Kolb Twinstar Mk.3	PFA/205-12231		15. 7.92	
G-MYDR	Thruster T.300	9072-T300-505		21. 7.92	
G-MYDS	Quad City Challenger II UK	CH2-1289-UK-0500 & PFA/177-11716		6. 3.90	
G-MYDT	Thruster T.300	9072-T300-506		21. 7.92	
G-MYDU	Thruster T.300	9072-T300-504		21. 7.92	
G-MYDV	Mainair Gemini/Flash 2A	917-0892-7 & W716		29. 7.92	
G-MYDW	Whittaker MW.6 Merlin	PFA/164-12184		27. 7.92	
G-MYDX	Rans S-6-ESD Coyote II	PFA/204-12238		27. 7.92	
G-MYDY	Not allotted.				
G-MYDZ	Mignet HM-1000 Balerit	66		3. 8.92	
G-MYEA	Solar Wings Pegasus XL-Q	SW-TE-0404 & SW-WQ-0537		28. 7.92	
G-MYEB	Solar Wings Pegasus XL-Q	SW-WQ-0538		28. 7.92	Canx as WFU 6.4.95.
G-MYEC	Solar Wings Pegasus XL-Q	SW-TE-0406 & SW-WQ-0539		28. 7.92	
G-MYED	Solar Wings Pegasus XL-R (Trike may be SW-TE-0403)	SW-TE-0405 & SW-WA-1559		28. 7.92	
G-MYEE	Thruster TST Mk.1 (Regd with c/n 087-TST-206) (Possibly ex ZK-FRW; imported 12/90)	8089-TST-206		11. 8.92	(Noted as a wreck at Thruster UK's factory on 16.7.98) Canx as destroyed 16.10.98.
G-MYEF	Whittaker MW.6 Merlin	PFA/164-11327		28. 5.92	Canx by CAA 6.3.99.
G-MYEG	Solar Wings Pegasus XL-R	SW-TB-1447 & SW-WA-1560		4. 8.92	
G-MYEH	Solar Wings Pegasus XL-R	SW-WA-1561		4. 8.92	
G-MYEI	Cyclone Chaser S	CH.841		18. 8.92	
G-MYEJ	Cyclone Chaser S	CH.842		18. 8.92	
G-MYEK	Solar Wings Pegasus Quasar IITC (See also comments on G-MWZF)	SW-TQD-0108 & SW-WQT-0540		7. 8.92	
G-MYEL	Solar Wings Pegasus Quasar IITC	SW-WQT-0541		7. 8.92	Canx as WFU 2.3.93.
G-MYEM	Solar Wings Pegasus Quasar IITC	SW-TQD-0101 & SW-WQT-0542		7. 8.92	
G-MYEN	Solar Wings Pegasus Quasar IITC	SW-TQD-0105 & SW-WQT-0543		7. 8.92	
G-MYEO	Solar Wings Pegasus Quasar IITC	SW-TQD-0106 & SW-WQT-0544		7. 8.92	
G-MYEP	CFM Shadow Srs.CD	K.205		13. 8.92	
G-MYER	Cyclone Ax2000	B.1052901 & CA.001	G-69-3 59-GD	19. 8.92	
G-MYES	Rans S-6-ESD Coyote II	0392-283 & PFA/204-12254		3. 7.92	
G-MYET	Whittaker MW.6 Merlin	PFA/164-12318		19. 8.92	
G-MYEU	Mainair Gemini/Flash 2A	918-0892-7 & W718		1. 9.92	
G-MYEV	Whittaker MW.6 Merlin	PFA/164-11250		25. 8.92	
G-MYEW	Powerchute Kestrel	00417		28. 8.92	Canx by CAA 10.8.95.
G-MYEX	Powerchute Kestrel	00426		28. 8.92	
G-MYEY	Powerchute Kestrel	00427		28. 8.92	Canx by CAA 19.12.94.
G-MYEZ	Powerchute Kestrel	00428		28. 8.92	Canx by CAA 19.12.94.
G-MYFA	Powerchute Kestrel	00429		28. 8.92	

Regn	Type	c/n	Previous identity	Regn date	Fate or immediate subsequent identity (if known)
G-MYFB	Powerchute Kestrel	00430		28. 8.92	To ZU-AEY 2/93. Canx 2.2.93.
G-MYFC	Powerchute Kestrel	00431		28. 8.92	Canx 19.12.94 on sale to Turkey.
G-MYFD	Powerchute Kestrel	00432		28. 8.92	Canx by CAA 19.12.94.
G-MYFE	Rans S-6-ESD Coyote II	PFA/204-12232		1. 9.92	
G-MYFF	Not allotted.				
G-MYFG	Hunt Avon Skytrike/Hunt Wing	BMAA/HB/017 & 92040006		4. 9.92	Canx by CAA 16.7.98.
G-MYFH	Quad City Challenger II UK	CH2-0292-0798 & PFA/177-12282		9. 9.92	
G-MYFI	Cyclone Ax3	C.3093159 & CA.002		9. 9.92	
G-MYFJ	Solar Wings Pegasus Quasar IITC	SW-WQT-0552		11. 9.92	
G-MYFK	Solar Wings Pegasus Quasar IITC	SW-TQD-0113 & SW-WQT-0553		11. 9.92	
G-MYFL	Solar Wings Pegasus Quasar IITC	SW-TQD-0103 & SW-WQT-0541/A		11. 9.92	
	(Originally regd as c/n SW-WQT-0554; replacement wing fitted to trike G-MYEL after its wing was stolen on 1.1.93)				
G-MYFM	Murphy Renegade Spirit UK	PFA/188-12249		9. 9.92	
G-MYFN	Rans S-5 Coyote	89-112 & PFA/193-12273		16. 9.92	
G-MYFO	Cyclone Chaser S	CH.843		22. 9.92	
G-MYFP	Mainair Gemini/Flash 2A	920-0992-7 & W719		2.10.92	
G-MYFR	Mainair Gemini/Flash 2A	921-0992-7 & W720		30. 9.92	
G-MYFS	Solar Wings Pegasus XL-R	SW-TB-1453 & SW-WA-1564		30. 9.92	(Damaged mid .95)
G-MYFT	Mainair Scorcher	922-0992-3 & W234		30. 9.92	
G-MYFU	Mainair Gemini/Flash 2A	924-1092-7 & W722		7.10.92	
G-MYFV	Cyclone Ax3	C.2083050		6.10.92	
G-MYFW	Cyclone Ax3	C.2083051		13.10.92	
G-MYFX	Solar Wings Pegasus XL-Q	SW-WQ-0378	(ex)	25. 6.93	
G-MYFY	Cyclone Ax3	C.2083047		1.10.92	
G-MYFZ	Cyclone Ax3	C.2083048		20.10.92	
G-MYGA	Solar Wings Pegasus XL-R	SW-WA-1565		19.10.92	Canx as WFU 6.4.95.
G-MYGB	Solar Wings Pegasus XL-R	SW-WA-1566		19.10.92	Canx as WFU 6.4.95.
G-MYGC	Solar Wings Pegasus XL-R	SW-WA-1567		19.10.92	Canx as WFU 6.4.95.
G-MYGD	Cyclone Ax3	C.2083049		21.10.92	
G-MYGE	Whittaker MW.6 Merlin	PFA/164-11650		20.10.92	
G-MYGF	Team Minimax 91	PFA/186-12175		22.10.92	
G-MYGG	Mainair Mercury	927-1192-7 & W724		18.11.92	Fatal crash near Sandtoft on 31.8.95. Canx by CAA 5.1.96.
G-MYGH	Rans S-6-ESD Coyote II	0692-318 & PFA/204-12335		30.10.92	
G-MYGI	Cyclone Chaser S	CH.844		2.11.92	
G-MYGJ	Mainair Mercury	923-0992-7 & W721		5.10.92	
G-MYGK	Cyclone Chaser S	CH.846		3.11.92	
G-MYGL	Team Minimax 91	PFA/186-12357		29.10.92	To G-BXSU 2/98. Canx.
G-MYGM	Quad City Challenger II UK	CH2-0391-UK-0662 & PFA/177-12261		6.11.92	
G-MYGN	AMF Super Chevvron 2-32C	034		29.12.92	
G-MYGO	CFM Shadow Srs.CD	K.114		28. 7.92	
G-MYGP	Rans S-6-ESD Coyote II	0992-349 & PFA/204-12368		10.11.92	
G-MYGR	Rans S-6-ESD Coyote II	PFA/204-12378		16.11.92	
G-MYGS	Aerotech MW.5(K) Sorcerer	BMAA/HB/016 & 5K-0002-02		28. 3.90	Fatal crash after hitting HT cables at Wyke Champflower, Somerset on 4.8.96. Canx as destroyed 20.12.96.
G-MYGT	Solar Wings Pegasus XL-R	SW-WA-1569		13.11.92	
G-MYGU	Solar Wings Pegasus XL-R	SW-TE-0414 & SW-WA-1570		13.11.92	
G-MYGV	Solar Wings Pegasus XL-R	SW-TE-0415 & SW-WA-1571		13.11.92	
G-MYGW	Solar Wings Pegasus XL-Q	SW-WQ-0556		16.11.92	Canx as WFU 6.4.95.
G-MYGX	Solar Wings Pegasus XL-Q	SW-WQ-0557		16.11.92	Canx as WFU 6.4.95.
G-MYGY	Solar Wings Pegasus XL-Q	SW-WQ-0558		16.11.92	Canx as WFU 6.4.95.
G-MYGZ	Mainair Gemini/Flash 2A	928-1192-7 & W726		18.11.92	
G-MYHA	Solar Wings Pegasus XL-R	SW-WA-1572		20.11.92	Canx as WFU 6.4.95.
G-MYHB	Solar Wings Pegasus XL-R	SW-WA-1573		20.11.92	Canx as WFU 6.4.95.
G-MYHC	Solar Wings Pegasus XL-R	SW-WA-1574		20.11.92	Canx as WFU 6.4.95.
G-MYHD	Solar Wings Pegasus XL-R	SW-WA-1575		20.11.92	Canx as WFU 6.4.95.
G-MYHE	Solar Wings Pegasus XL-R	SW-WA-1576		20.11.92	Canx as WFU 6.4.95. (Noted stored at Popham 1.5.99)
G-MYHF	Mainair Gemini/Flash 2A	929-1092-7 & W727		25.11.92	
G-MYHG	Cyclone Ax3	C.2103070		27.11.92	(On repair in 1/99 at Strathaven)
G-MYHH	Cyclone Ax3	C.2103069 & CA.006		30.11.92	
G-MYHI	Rans S-6-ESD Coyote II	PFA/204-12279		8.12.92	

Regn	Type	c/n	Previous identity	Regn date	Fate or immediate subsequent identity (if known)
G-MYHJ	Cyclone Ax3 (Reported 9/94 with c/n C.3093157 - see G-MYME)	C.2103073		11.12.92	
G-MYHK	Rans S-6-ESD Coyote II	0692-311 & PFA/204-12349		3.12.92	
G-MYHL	Mainair Gemini/Flash 2A	932-0193-7 & W730		21.12.92	
G-MYHM	Cyclone Ax3	C.2103068 & CA.007		18.12.92	
G-MYHN	Mainair Gemini/Flash 2A	933-0193-7 & W731		29.12.92	
G-MYHO	Cyclone Ax3	B.1122981 & PFA/245-12365		8. 1.93	To G-BUTC 11.1.93. Canx.
G-MYHP	Rans S-6-ESD Coyote II	0892-313 & PFA/204-12406		8. 1.93	
G-MYHR	Cyclone Ax3	C.2103071		15. 1.93	
G-MYHS	Powerchute Kestrel	00433		26. 1.93	
G-MYHT	Powerchute Kestrel	00434		26. 1.93	Canx by CAA 19.12.94.
G-MYHU	Powerchute Kestrel	00435		26. 1.93	Canx by CAA 19.12.94.
G-MYHV	Powerchute Kestrel	00436		26. 1.93	Canx by CAA 19.12.94.
G-MYHW	Powerchute Kestrel	00437		26. 1.93	Canx by CAA 19.12.94.
G-MYHX	Mainair Gemini/Flash 2A	930-1292-7 & W728		2.12.92	
G-MYHY	Powerchute Kestrel	00438		26. 1.93	Canx by CAA 19.12.94. (Noted at Popham 2.5.98)
G-MYHZ	Powerchute Kestrel	00439		26. 1.93	Canx by CAA 19.12.94.
G-MYIA	Quad City Challenger II UK	PFA/177-12400		21. 1.93	
G-MYIB	Powerchute Kestrel	00440		26. 1.93	Canx by CAA 19.12.94.
G-MYIC	Powerchute Kestrel	00441		26. 1.93	Canx by CAA 19.12.94.
G-MYID	Powerchute Kestrel	00442		26. 1.93	Canx by CAA 19.12.94.
G-MYIE	Whittaker MW.6S Fatboy Flyer	PFA/164-11800		26. 1.93	
G-MYIF	CFM Shadow Srs CD	217		2. 2.93	
G-MYIG	Murphy Renegade Spirit	PFA/188-11725		2. 2.93	Canx as TWFU 26.7.94. To G-TBMW 10/98.
G-MYIH	Mainair Gemini/Flash 2A	937-0293-7 & W734		9. 3.93	
G-MYII	Team Minimax 91	PFA/186-12119		10.11.92	
G-MYIJ	Cyclone Ax3	C.2103072		8. 2.93	
G-MYIK	Kolb Twinstar Mk.3	PFA/205-12220		13. 1.93	
G-MYIL	Cyclone Chaser S	CH.849		3. 3.93	
G-MYIM	Solar Wings Pegasus Quasar IITC	SW-WQT-0579	(EI-...) G-MYIM	22. 2.93	
G-MYIN	Solar Wings Pegasus Quasar IITC	SW-TQD-0123 & SW-WQT-0580		22. 2.93	
G-MYIO	Solar Wings Pegasus Quasar IITC	SW-TQD-0124 & SW-WQT-0581		22. 2.93	
G-MYIP	CFM Shadow Srs.CD	K.198		16. 3.93	
G-MYIR	Rans S-6-ESD Coyote II	0892-344 & PFA/204-12458		17. 3.93	
G-MYIS	Rans S-6-ESD Coyote II	PFA/204-12382		31.12.92	
G-MYIT	Cyclone Chaser S	CH.850		19. 3.93	
G-MYIU	Cyclone Ax3	C.3013084		22. 3.93	
G-MYIV	Mainair Gemini/Flash 2A	938-0393-7 & W735		30. 3.93	
G-MYIW	Mainair Mercury	939-0493-7 & W736		2. 4.93	Permit expired 4.2.96. Canx by CAA 20.2.97.
G-MYIX	Quad City Challenger II UK	CH2-0191-UK-0615 & PFA/177-12260		5. 1.93	
G-MYIY	Mainair Gemini/Flash 2A	942-0493-7 & W737		1. 4.93	
G-MYIZ	Team Minimax 91	PFA/186-12347		31. 3.93	
G-MYJA	Not allotted.				
G-MYJB	Mainair Gemini/Flash 2A	943-0593-7 & W738		7. 4.93	
G-MYJC	Mainair Gemini/Flash 2A	944-0593-7 & W739		7. 4.93	
G-MYJD	Rans S-6-ESD Coyote II	0792-324 & PFA/204-12360		23. 4.93	
G-MYJE	CFM Shadow Srs.CD	185		26. 9.91	To G-TEHL 11/98. Canx.
G-MYJF	Thruster T.300	9013-T300-509		14. 4.93	
G-MYJG	Thruster Super T.300	9043-ST300-510		14. 4.93	
G-MYJH	Thruster T.300	9013-T300-508		14. 4.93	
G-MYJI	Solar Wings Pegasus Quasar IITC	SW-WQT-0590		27. 4.93	Canx 4.4.95 on sale to France.
G-MYJJ	Solar Wings Pegasus Quasar IITC	SW-TQD-0131 & SW-WQT-0591		27. 4.93	
G-MYJK	Solar Wings Pegasus Quasar IITC	SW-WQT-0592		27. 4.93	
G-MYJL	Rans S-6-ESD Coyote II	PFA/204-12476		28. 4.93	
G-MYJM	Mainair Gemini/Flash 2A	945-0593-7 & W740		29. 4.93	
G-MYJN	Mainair Mercury	946-0593-7 & W741		29. 4.93	
G-MYJO	Cyclone Chaser S	CH.851		30. 4.93	

Regn	Type	c/n	Previous identity	Regn date	Fate or immediate subsequent identity (if known)
G-MYJP	Murphy Renegade Spirit UK	357 & PFA/188-12045		3. 4.91	
G-MYJR	Mainair Mercury	947-0593-7 & W742		12. 5.93	
G-MYJS	Solar Wings Pegasus Quasar IITC	6581		19. 5.93	
G-MYJT	Solar Wings Pegasus Quasar IITC	6582		19. 5.93	
G-MYJU	Solar Wings Pegasus Quasar IITC	6573		19. 5.93	
G-MYJV	Solar Wings Pegasus Quasar IITC	6564		19. 5.93	Canx 29.9.93 on sale to Spain.
G-MYJW	Cyclone Chaser S	CH.856		19. 5.93	
G-MYJX	Whittaker MW.8	001 & PFA/243-12345		24. 5.93	
G-MYJY	Rans S-6-ESD Coyote II	0692-317 & PFA/204-12346		24. 5.93	
G-MYJZ	Whittaker MW.5D Sorcerer	PFA/163-12385		22. 4.93	
G-MYKA	Cyclone Ax3	C.3013086		25. 5.93	
G-MYKB	Kolb Twinstar Mk.3	PFA/205-12398		31. 3.93	
G-MYKC	Mainair Gemini/Flash 2A	948-0593-7 & W743		26. 5.93	
G-MYKD	Cyclone Chaser S	CH.857		26. 5.93	
G-MYKE	CFM Shadow Srs.BD	K.031		14. 1.88	
G-MYKF	Cyclone Ax3	C.3013083		8. 6.93	
G-MYKG	Mainair Gemini/Flash 2A	950-0693-7 & W745		21. 6.93	
G-MYKH	Mainair Gemini/Flash 2A	951-0693-7 & W746		21. 6.93	
G-MYKI	Mainair Mercury	953-0693-7 & W748		21. 6.93	
G-MYKJ	Team Minimax	PFA/186-12215		10. 6.93	
G-MYKL	Medway Raven X	MRB116/104		6. 7.93	
G-MYKM	Medway Raven X	MRB106/105		6. 7.93	
G-MYKN	Rans S-6-ESD Coyote II	PFA/204-12361		23. 6.93	
G-MYKO	Whittaker MW.6S Fatboy Flyer	PFA/164-11919		25. 6.93	
G-MYKP	Solar Wings Pegasus Quasar IITC	6627		28. 7.93	
G-MYKR	Solar Wings Pegasus Quasar IITC	6635		7. 7.93	
G-MYKS	Solar Wings Pegasus Quasar IITC	6636		7. 7.93	
G-MYKT	Cyclone Ax3	C.3013082		5. 7.93	
G-MYKU	Medway Raven X	MRB117/107		9. 7.93	
G-MYKV	Mainair Gemini/Flash 2A	954-0793-7 & W749		13. 7.93	
G-MYKW	Mainair Mercury	960-0893-7 & W755		9. 7.93	
G-MYKX	Mainair Mercury	961-0893-7 & W756		3. 9.93	Canx by CAA 27.3.99.
G-MYKY	Mainair Mercury	962-0893-7 & W757		6. 8.93	
G-MYKZ	Team Minimax 91	PFA/186-11841	G-BVAV	26. 7.93	(Extensively damaged in force landing at Ginge Farm, Wantage on 14.7.96)
G-MYLA	Rans S-6-ESD Coyote II	PFA/204-12543		30. 7.93	
G-MYLB	Team Minimax 91	PFA/186-12419		2. 8.93	
G-MYLC	Solar Wings Pegasus Quantum 15	6634		9. 8.93	
G-MYLD	Rans S-6-ESD Coyote II	PFA/204-12394		1. 3.93	
G-MYLE	Solar Wings Pegasus Quantum 15	6609		9. 8.93	
G-MYLF	Rans S-6-ESD Coyote II	0493-483 & PFA/204-12544		4. 8.93	(Tricycle u/c)
G-MYLG	Mainair Gemini/Flash 2A	959-0893-7 & W754		6. 8.93	
G-MYLH	Solar Wings Pegasus Quantum 15	6632		27. 8.93	
G-MYLI	Solar Wings Pegasus Quantum 15	6645		11. 8.93	(Damaged late .97)
G-MYLJ	Cyclone Chaser S	CH.858		24. 8.93	
G-MYLK	Solar Wings Pegasus Quantum 15	6602		27. 8.93	
G-MYLL	Solar Wings Pegasus Quantum 15	6650		31. 8.93	
G-MYLM	Solar Wings Pegasus Quantum 15	6651	(EC-...) G-MYLM	31. 8.93	
G-MYLN	Kolb Twinstar Mk.3	PFA/205-12430		3. 9.93	
G-MYLO	Rans S-6-ESD Coyote II	PFA/204-12334		9. 9.93	
G-MYLP	Kolb Twinstar Mk.3	PFA/205-12391	(G-BVCR)	9. 9.93	
G-MYLR	Mainair Gemini/Flash 2A	964-0993-7 & W759		17. 9.93	
G-MYLS	Mainair Mercury	966-0993-7 & W761		5.10.93	
G-MYLT	Mainair Blade	967-1093-7 & W762		23. 9.93	
G-MYLU	Hunt Wing/Experience	92040001		27. 9.93	Canx by CAA 28.10.97.
G-MYLV	CFM Shadow Srs.CD	220		24. 9.93	
G-MYLW	Rans S-6-ESD Coyote II	1292-401 & PFA/204-12560		4. 8.93	
G-MYLX	Medway Raven X	MRB113/109		6.10.93	
G-MYLY	Medway Raven X	MRB001/108		23. 9.93	

Regn	Type	c/n	Previous identity	Regn date	Fate or immediate subsequent identity (if known)
G-MYLZ	Solar Wings Pegasus Quantum 15	6672		6.10.93	
G-MYMA	Aces High Cuby II	LC2F-931052605 & PFA/257-12584		6. 8.93	To G-BVNA 4/94. Canx.
G-MYMB	Solar Wings Pegasus Quantum 15	6674		6.10.93	
G-MYMC	Solar Wings Pegasus Quantum 15	6675		6.10.93	
G-MYMD	Solar Wings Pegasus Quantum 15	6655		8.10.93	To G-FFUN 6/99. Canx.
G-MYME	Cyclone Ax3 (See comments under G-MYHJ)	C.3093157		13.10.93	
G-MYMF	Cyclone Ax3	C.3093158		18.10.93	
G-MYMG	Team Minimax 91	PFA/186-12336		18.10.93	Canx by CAA 18.3.99.
G-MYMH	Rans S-6-ESD Coyote II	0793-520 & PFA/204-12576		20.10.93	(Tricycle u/c)
G-MYMI	Kolb Twinstar Mk.3	PFA/205-12537		21.10.93	
G-MYMJ	Medway Raven X	MRB004/110		28.10.93	
G-MYMK	Mainair Gemini/Flash 2A	968-1193-7 & W763		29.10.93	
G-MYML	Mainair Mercury	969-1193-7 & W765		29.10.93	
G-MYMM	Air Creation Fun 18S GT bis	93/001		30. 9.93	
G-MYMN	Whittaker MW.6 Merlin	PFA/164-12124		29.10.93	
G-MYMO	Mainair Gemini/Flash 2A	955-0793-7 & W750		24. 6.93	
G-MYMP	Rans S-6-ESD Coyote II	1291-250 & PFA/204-12436	(G-CHAZ)	5.11.93	
G-MYMR	Rans S-6-ESD Coyote II	PFA/204-12580		17.11.93	
G-MYMS	Rans S-6-ESD Coyote II	0893-526 & PFA/204-12581		17.11.93	
G-MYMT	Mainair Mercury	970-1193-7 & W766		19.11.93	
G-MYMU	Kolb Twinstar Mk.3	PFA/205-12427		19.11.93	Crashed on take-off at Yew Tree Farm, Whitmore, Keele, Staffs on 16.6.96. Canx as destroyed 28.11.96.
G-MYMV	Mainair Gemini/Flash 2A	971-1193-7 & W767		26.11.93	
G-MYMW	Cyclone Ax3	C.3093156		23.11.93	
G-MYMX	Solar Wings Pegasus Quantum 15	6705		1.12.93	
G-MYMY	Cyclone Chaser S	CH.860		7. 9.93	
G-MYMZ	Cyclone Ax3	C.3093154		7.12.93	
G-MYNA	CFM Shadow Srs.C	K.023		10. 2.88	
G-MYNB	Solar Wings Pegasus Quantum 15	6719		14.12.93	
G-MYNC	Mainair Mercury	973-1293-7 & W769		17.12.93	
G-MYND	Mainair Gemini/Flash 2A	841-0591-7 & W635		28. 5.91	
G-MYNE	Rans S-6-ESD Coyote II	PFA/204-12497		25. 6.93	
G-MYNF	Mainair Mercury	974-1293-7 & W770		17. 1.94	
G-MYNG	CFM Streak Shadow Srs.SA-M	K.224		13. 5.93	Canx 13.7.94 on sale to Taiwan.
G-MYNH	Rans S-6-ESD Coyote II	0493-487 & PFA/204-12616		30.12.93	(Tailwheel u/c)
G-MYNI	Team Minimax 91	PFA/186-12314		22. 2.93	
G-MYNJ	Mainair Mercury	972-1293-7 & W768		14. 1.94	
G-MYNK	Solar Wings Pegasus Quantum 15	6614		17.11.93	Canx by CAA 25.8.99.
G-MYNL	Solar Wings Pegasus Quantum 15	6648		17.11.93	
G-MYNM	Solar Wings Pegasus Quantum 15	6723		17.11.93	To PH-2S8 5/95. Canx 17.2.95.
G-MYNN	Solar Wings Pegasus Quantum 15	6679		17.11.93	
G-MYNO	Solar Wings Pegasus Quantum 15	6724		10. 1.94	
G-MYNP	Solar Wings Pegasus Quantum 15	6688		17.11.93	
G-MYNR	Solar Wings Pegasus Quantum 15	6692		17.11.93	
G-MYNS	Solar Wings Pegasus Quantum 15	6694		17.11.93	
G-MYNT	Solar Wings Pegasus Quantum 15	6693		17.11.93	
G-MYNU	Solar Wings Pegasus Quasar IITC	6695		5. 1.94	
G-MYNV	Solar Wings Pegasus Quantum 15	6725		10. 1.94	
G-MYNW	Cyclone Chaser S	CH.855		6. 1.94	
G-MYNX	CFM Streak Shadow SA-M	K.193-SA-M & PFA/206-12268		15. 6.92	
G-MYNY	Kolb Twinstar Mk.3	PFA/205-12478		22.11.93	
G-MYNZ	Solar Wings Pegasus Quantum 15	6709		18. 1.94	
G-MYOA	Rans S-6-ESD Coyote II	PFA/204-12578		23.11.93	
G-MYOB	Mainair Mercury	976-1293-7 & W772		8.12.93	
G-MYOC	Not allotted.				
G-MYOD	Solar Wings Pegasus Quasar IITC	6662		25. 1.94	Permit expired 13.2.95. Canx by CAA 23.2.96. (Was based at Vieux-Ferrette, France) Possibly to France as W30-GE.
G-MYOE	Solar Wings Pegasus Quantum 15	6668		31. 1.94	
G-MYOF	Mainair Mercury	975-1293-7 & W771		3.12.93	
G-MYOG	Kolb Twinstar Mk.3	PFA/205-12449		19. 1.94	
G-MYOH	CFM Shadow Srs.CD	K.201		27. 1.94	
G-MYOI	Rans S-6-ESD Coyote II	PFA/204-12503		3. 2.94	
G-MYOJ	Thruster T.300N	9035-T300-511		7. 2.94	NTU - To G-MYWD 4/95. Canx by CAA 18.4.95.
G-MYOK	Thruster T.300T	9035-T300-512		7. 2.94	NTU - To G-MYWE 4/95. Canx by CAA 18.4.95.
G-MYOL	Air Creation Fun 18S GT bis	94/001		7. 2.94	
G-MYOM	Mainair Gemini/Flash 2A	981-0294-7 & W777		14. 2.94	

Regn	Type	c/n	Previous identity	Regn date	Fate or immediate subsequent identity (if known)
G-MYON	CFM Shadow Srs.CD	240		12. 1.94	
G-MYOO	Kolb Twinstar Mk.3M	PFA/205-12200		11. 5.92	
G-MYOP	Cyclone Ax3/K	C.3123187 & PFA/245-12663		11. 2.94	NTU - To G-BVJG 15.2.94. Canx.
G-MYOR	Kolb Twinstar Mk.3	PFA/205-12602		16. 2.94	
G-MYOS	CFM Shadow Srs.CD	246		18. 2.94	
G-MYOT	Rans S-6-ESD Coyote II	PFA/204-12668		21. 2.94	
G-MYOU	Solar Wings Pegasus Quantum 15	6726		29. 3.94	
G-MYOV	Mainair Mercury	979-0294-7 & W775		1. 3.94	
G-MYOW	Mainair Gemini/Flash 2A	983-0294-7 & W779		16. 3.94	
G-MYOX	Mainair Mercury	984-0294-7 & W780		23. 2.94	
G-MYOY	Cyclone Ax3	C.3123191		23. 2.94	
G-MYOZ	BFC Quad City Challenger II UK	CH2-1093-1045 & PFA/177A-12640		24. 2.94	
G-MYPA	Rans S-6-ESD Coyote II	0893-527 & PFA/204-12678		24. 2.94	
G-MYPB	Cyclone Chaser S	CH.862		25. 2.94	Canx by CAA 3.12.97.
G-MYPC	Kolb Twinstar Mk.3	PFA/205-12437		2. 3.94	
G-MYPD	Mainair Mercury	982-0294-7 & W778		11. 3.94	
G-MYPE	Mainair Gemini/Flash 2A	985-0394-7 & W781		11. 3.94	
G-MYPF	Solar Wings Pegasus Quasar IITC	SW-WQT-0564		5. 4.94	
G-MYPG	Solar Wings Pegasus XL-Q	SW-WQ-0176		29. 3.89	
G-MYPH	Solar Wings Pegasus Quantum 15	6764		29. 3.94	
G-MYPI	Solar Wings Pegasus Quantum 15	6767		29. 3.94	
G-MYPJ	Rans S-6-ESD Coyote II	1293-569 & PFA/204-12692		18. 3.94	Badly damaged by fire 11.1.98 at RAF Boulmer.
G-MYPK	Rans S-6-ESA Coyote II	1193-566		18. 3.94	To G-BVRK 7/94. Canx.
G-MYPL	CFM Shadow Srs.CD	BMAA/HB/080 & K.213		14. 2.94	
G-MYPM	Cyclone Ax3	C.3123188		23. 3.94	
G-MYPN	Solar Wings Pegasus Quantum 15	6727		12. 4.94	
G-MYPO	Hunt Wing/Experience (Also allocated c/n BMAA/HB/026)	BMAA/HB/019 & 9409011		28. 3.94	
G-MYPP	Whittaker MW.6S Fatboy Flyer	PFA/164-12413		11. 4.94	
G-MYPR	Cyclone Ax3	C.3123190		13. 4.94	
G-MYPS	Whittaker MW.6 Merlin	PFA/164-11585		19. 4.94	
G-MYPT	CFM Shadow Srs.CD	K.212		22. 4.94	
G-MYPU	Airwave Microchute UQ/Rave Motor	27 BMAA/HB/023 & PSP.101746		22. 4.94	Permit expired 20.6.96. Canx by CAA 20.7.99.
G-MYPV	Mainair Mercury	986-0394-7 & W782		18. 3.94	
G-MYPW	Mainair Gemini/Flash 2A	991-0494-7 & W787		3. 5.94	
G-MYPX	Solar Wings Pegasus Quantum 15	6785		28. 4.94	
G-MYPY	Solar Wings Pegasus Quantum 15	6786		12. 5.94	
G-MYPZ	BFC Quad City Challenger II UK (Regd incorrectly as CH2-0194-UK-1046)	CH2-1093-UK-1046 & PFA/177A-12689		2. 3.94	
G-MYRA	Kolb Twinstar Mk.3	PFA/205-12434		29. 3.94	
G-MYRB	Whittaker MW.5 Sorcerer	PFA/163-11543		14. 4.94	
G-MYRC	Mainair Blade	988-0594-7 & W784		1. 6.94	
G-MYRD	Mainair Blade	989-0594-7 & W785		20. 5.94	
G-MYRE	Cyclone Chaser S	CH.863		10. 5.94	
G-MYRF	Solar Wings Pegasus Quantum 15	6795		13. 5.94	
G-MYRG	Team Minimax	PFA/186-11891		17. 5.94	
G-MYRH	BFC Quad City Challenger II UK	CH2-1093-1044 & PFA/177A-12690		10. 3.94	
G-MYRI	Medway Hybred 44XLR	MR180/841		23. 5.94	
G-MYRJ	BFC Quad City Challenger II UK	CH2-1093-1042 & PFA/177A-12658		28. 3.94	
G-MYRK	Murphy Renegade Spirit UK	215 & PFA/188-11425		3.10.89	
G-MYRL	Team Minimax 91	PFA/186-11967		17. 5.94	
G-MYRM	Solar Wings Pegasus Quantum 15	6800		26. 5.94	
G-MYRN	Solar Wings Pegasus Quantum 15	6801		26. 5.94	
G-MYRO	Cyclone Ax3	C.4043211		6. 6.94	
G-MYRP	Letov LK-2M Sluka	0209 & PFA/263-12725		6. 6.94	
G-MYRR	Letov LK-2M Sluka (Regd with c/n 05)	0205		10. 6.94	
G-MYRS	Solar Wings Pegasus Quantum 15	6803		13. 6.94	
G-MYRT	Solar Wings Pagasus Quantum 15	6732		1. 3.94	
G-MYRU	Cyclone Ax3	C.4043210		7. 6.94	
G-MYRV	Cyclone Ax3	C.4043209		8. 6.94	
G-MYRW	Mainair Mercury	999-0694-7 & W795		17. 6.94	
G-MYRX	Mainair Gemini/Flash 2A	995-0694-7 & W792		22. 6.94	

Regn	Type	c/n	Previous identity	Regn date	Fate or immediate subsequent identity (if known)
G-MYRY	Solar Wings Pegasus Quantum 15	6813		15. 6.94	
G-MYRZ	Solar Wings Pegasus Quantum 15	6812		15. 6.94	
G-MYSA	Cyclone Chaser S	CH.864		15. 6.94	
G-MYSB	Solar Wings Pagasus Quantum 15	6809		22. 6.94	
G-MYSC	Solar Wings Pegasus Quantum 15	6811		22. 6.94	
G-MYSD	BFC Quad City Challenger II	CH2-1093-1043 & PFA/177A-12600		23. 6.94	
G-MYSE	Mainair Mercury	997-0694-7 & W794		30. 6.94	Canx 20.12.95 on sale to Italy.
G-MYSF	Robinson Powered Paraglider	001		30. 6.94	Canx as WFU 27.3.96.
G-MYSG	Mainair Mercury	993-0694-7 & W790		12. 7.94	
G-MYSH	Mainair Blade	994-0694-7 & W791		12. 7.94	To EC-CE9 5/96. Canx.
G-MYSI	HM.14/93	PFA/255-12700		18. 7.94	
G-MYSJ	Mainair Gemini/Flash 2A	1001-0894-7 & W797		2. 8.94	
G-MYSK	Team Minimax 91	PFA/186-12203		25. 7.94	
G-MYSL	Aviasud Mistral	BMAA/HB/007 & 66	83-DE	27. 2.92	
G-MYSM	CFM Shadow Srs.CD	BMAA/HB/049 & K.243		22. 3.94	
G-MYSN	Whittaker MW.6S Fatboy Flyer	PFA/164-12285		27. 7.94	
G-MYSO	Cyclone Ax3	C.4043215		1. 8.94	
G-MYSP	Rans S-6-ESD Coyote II	0392-284 & PFA/204-12265		26. 5.92	
G-MYSR	Solar Wings Pegasus Quantum 15	6837		22. 8.94	
G-MYSS	Murphy Maverick/A	82M & PFA/259-12610		12. 8.94	To C-GYSS 2/96 with c/n 082M. Canx 14.8.95.
G-MYST	Aviasud Mistral	BMAA/HB/012 & 0489-83 & GB.01		11. 7.89	
G-MYSU	Rans S-6-ESD Coyote II	PFA/204-12753		5. 8.94	
G-MYSV	Aerial Arts Chaser S	CH.812	(ex)	24. 8.94	
G-MYSW	Solar Wings Pegasus Quantum 15	6834		13. 7.94	
G-MYSX	Solar Wings Pegasus Quantum 15	6832		13. 7.94	
G-MYSY	Solar Wings Pegasus Quantum 15	6864		15. 8.94	
G-MYSZ	Mainair Mercury (C/n confirmed but see comments under G-MYYY)	1006-0894-7 & W802		2. 9.94	
G-MYTA	Team Minimax 91	PFA/186-12461		20. 5.94	
G-MYTB	Mainair Mercury	1004-0894-7 & W800		19. 7.94	
G-MYTC	Solar Wings Pegasus XL-Q	SW-WQ-0246	(ex)	28. 9.94	
G-MYTD	Mainair Blade	1002-0894-7 & W798		18. 8.94	
G-MYTE	Rans S-6-ESD Coyote II	PFA/204-12718		22. 7.94	
G-MYTF	Mainair Blade	1007-0994-7 & W803		26. 9.94	Canx as WFU 20.10.95.
G-MYTG	Mainair Blade	1008-0994-7 & W804		16. 9.94	
G-MYTH	CFM Shadow Srs.CD	089		7.11.88	
G-MYTI	Solar Wings Pegasus Quantum 15	6874		6.10.94	
G-MYTJ	Solar Wings Pegasus Quantum 15	6877		29. 9.94	
G-MYTK	Mainair Mercury	1009-1094-7 & W805		29. 9.94	
G-MYTL	Mainair Blade	1010-1094-7 & W807		4.10.94	
G-MYTM	Cyclone Ax3	C.3123189		13. 4.94	
G-MYTN	Solar Wings Pegasus Quantum 15	6878		30. 9.94	
G-MYTO	Quad City Challenger II UK	PFA/177-12583		22. 7.94	
G-MYTP	CGS Arrow Flight Hawk II	H-CGS-489-P & PFA/266-12801	N215	6.10.94	
G-MYTR	Solar Wings Pegasus Quasar IITC	6880		11.10.94	
G-MYTS	Hunt Wing/Avon	BMAA/HB/032 & 92009014		12.10.94	Canx by CAA 30.9.98.
G-MYTT	Quad City Challenger II	PFA/177-12761		11.10.94	
G-MYTU	Mainair Blade	1011-1094-7 & W808		21.10.94	
G-MYTV	Hunt Wing/Avon	BMAA/HB/029 & 92040010		13.10.94	
G-MYTW	Mainair Blade	1012-1194-7 & W809		4.11.94	
G-MYTX	Mainair Mercury	1003-0894-7 & W799		23. 9.94	
G-MYTY	CFM Streak Shadow Srs.M (Possibly c/n K.242)	PFA/206-12607		11. 7.94	
G-MYTZ	Air Creation Fun 18S GT bis	94/003		7.11.94	
G-MYUA	Air Creation Fun 18S GT bis	94/002		8.11.94	
G-MYUB	Mainair Mercury	1014-1194-7 & W812		14.12.94	
G-MYUC	Mainair Blade	1015-1294-7 & W813		16.11.94	
G-MYUD	Mainair Mercury	1016-1294-7 & W814		24.11.94	
G-MYUE	Mainair Mercury	1017-1294-7 & W815		22.11.94	
G-MYUF	Murphy Renegade Spirit	PFA/188-12795		16.11.94	
G-MYUG	Hunt Wing/Avon Skytrike	BMAA/HB/038 & 9409034		21.11.94	Canx as PWFU 6.5.99.
G-MYUH	Solar Wings Pegasus XL-Q	6810		28.11.94	
G-MYUI	Cyclone Ax3 (Frame stamped with c/n 0102822; possibly rebuilt)	C.4043213		13.12.94	

Regn	Type	c/n	Previous identity	Regn date	Fate or immediate subsequent identity (if known)
G-MYUJ	Meridian Ultralights Maverick (Carries identity '69' - c/n ?)	402 & PFA/259-12750		30.12.94	To G-ONFL 11/98. Canx.
G-MYUK	Mainair Mercury	1020-0195-7 & W818		12.12.94	
G-MYUL	Quad City Challenger II UK	PFA/177-12687		10. 1.95	
G-MYUM	Mainair Blade	1018-1294-7 & W816		24.11.94	
G-MYUN	Mainair Blade	1019-0195-7 & W817		5.12.94	
G-MYUO	Cyclone Pegasus Quantum 15	6911		23. 1.95	(Damaged late .97)
G-MYUP	Letov LK-2M Sluka (Also c/n UK.2)	829409x24 & PFA/263-12785		20.12.94	
G-MYUR	Hunt Wing/Avon	BMAA/HB/034		24. 1.95	
G-MYUS	CFM Shadow Srs.CD	257		26. 1.95	
G-MYUT	Hunt Wing/Experience	BMAA/HB/042 & 9409039		26. 1.95	Canx by CAA 23.6.98.
G-MYUU	Cyclone Pegasus Quantum 15	6917		30. 1.95	
G-MYUV	Cyclone Pegasus Quantum 15	6918		6. 2.95	
G-MYUW	Mainair Mercury	1024-0295-7 & W822		7. 2.95	
G-MYUX	Airwave Microchute UQ/Rave Motor 24	PSP.101892		9. 2.95	Canx as WFU 28.9.95.
G-MYUY	Airwave Microchute UQ/Reggae Motor 30	PSP.104006		9. 2.95	
G-MYUZ	Rans S-6-ESD Coyote II	1293-568 & PFA/204-12741		5. 1.95	
G-MYVA	Kolb Twinstar Mk.3	PFA/205-12756		13. 2.95	
G-MYVB	Mainair Blade	1021-0195-7 & W819		15.12.94	
G-MYVC	Cyclone Pegasus Quantum 15	6904		13. 2.95	
G-MYVD	Not to be allotted.				
G-MYVE	Mainair Blade	1027-0295-7 & W825		8. 2.95	
G-MYVF	Solar Wings Pegasus Quantum 15	6952		15. 2.95	To France as 44-RH. Canx 17.11.95.
G-MYVG	Letov LK-2M Sluka	PFA/263-12786 & 829409x26		15. 2.95	
G-MYVH	Mainair Blade	1028-0295-7 & W826		21. 2.95	
G-MYVI	Air Creation Fun 18S GT bis	94/004		17. 2.95	
G-MYVJ	Cyclone Pegasus Quantum 15	6974		24. 2.95	
G-MYVK	Cyclone Pegasus Quantum 15	6970		27. 2.95	
G-MYVL	Mainair Mercury	1030-0395-7 & W828		1. 3.95	
G-MYVM	Cyclone Pegasus Quantum 15	6893		9. 3.95	
G-MYVN	Cyclone Ax3	C.4043212		16. 3.95	
G-MYVO	Mainair Blade	1013-1194-7 & W811		8.11.94	
G-MYVP	Rans S-6-ESD Coyote II	PFA/204-12828		27. 3.95	
G-MYVR	Cyclone Pegasus Quantum 15	6980		21. 3.95	
G-MYVS	Mainair Mercury	1037-0495-7 & W835		12. 4.95	
G-MYVT	Letov LK-2M Sluka	PFA/263-12835 & 829409x25		17. 3.95	
G-MYVU	Medway Budget Raven	MRB126/108		3. 4.95	Canx by CAA 25.10.95.
G-MYVV	Medway Hybred 44XLR	MR127/109		3. 4.95	
G-MYVW	Medway Raven X	MRB128/110		15. 5.95	
G-MYVX	Medway Hybred 44XLR	MR129/111		3. 4.95	
G-MYVY	Mainair Blade	1033-0495-7 & W831		29. 3.95	
G-MYVZ	Mainair Blade	1034-0495-7 & W832		31. 3.95	
G-MYWA	Mainair Mercury	1035-0495-7 & W833		30. 3.95	
G-MYWB	Edel Corniche/Scorpion	004 & BMAA/HB/071		31. 3.95	Canx by CAA 7.8.98.
G-MYWC	Hunt Wing/Avon	BMAA/HB/043 & 9409038		3. 4.95	
G-MYWD	Thruster T.600N	9035-T600-511	(G-MYOJ)	18. 4.95	
G-MYWE	Thruster T.600T	9035-T600-512	(G-MYOK)	18. 4.95	
G-MYWF	CFM Shadow Srs.CD	BMAA/HB/068 & K.248		18. 4.95	
G-MYWG	Cyclone Pegasus Quantum 15	6998		20. 4.95	
G-MYWH	Hunt Wing/Experience	BMAA/HB/037 & 9409025		20.12.94	
G-MYWI	Cyclone Pegasus Quantum 15	7006		1. 5.95	
G-MYWJ	Cyclone Pegasus Quantum 15	6919		24. 1.95	
G-MYWK	Cyclone Pegasus Quantum 15	7011		1. 5.95	
G-MYWL	Cyclone Pegasus Quantum 15	6995		2. 5.95	
G-MYWM	CFM Shadow Srs.CD	BMAA/HB/056 & K.227		9. 5.95	
G-MYWN	Cyclone Chaser S	CH.865		9. 5.95	
G-MYWO	Cyclone Pegasus Quantum 15	6932		9. 5.95	
G-MYWP	Kolb Twinstar Mk.3	PFA/205-12561		7. 3.95	
G-MYWR	Cyclone Pegasus Quantum 15	7002		10. 5.95	
G-MYWS	Cyclone Chaser S	6946 & CH.866		17. 5.95	
G-MYWT	Cyclone Pegasus Quantum 15	6997		19. 5.95	
G-MYWU	Cyclone Pegasus Quantum 15	7024		25. 5.95	
G-MYWV	Rans S-4C Coyote	093-212 & PFA/193-12826		30. 5.95	
G-MYWW	Cyclone Pegasus Quantum 15	7021		30. 5.95	
G-MYWX	Cyclone Pegasus Quantum 15	7019		6. 6.95	
G-MYWY	Cyclone Pegasus Quantum 15	6982		20. 3.95	
G-MYWZ	Thruster TST Mk.1	8128-TST-115	G-MVMJ	22. 2.93	

Regn	Type	c/n	Previous identity	Regn date	Fate or immediate subsequent identity (if known)
G-MYXA	Team Minimax 91	PFA/186-12266		13. 6.95	
G-MYXB	Rans S-6-ESD Coyote II			20. 6.95	
		PFA/204-12787			
G-MYXC	BFC Quad City Challenger II UK			16. 5.95	
		CH2-0294-UK-1099			
G-MYXD	Cyclone Pegasus Quasar IITC	7029		21. 6.95	
G-MYXE	Cyclone Pegasus Quantum 15	7061		23. 6.95	
G-MYXF	Air Creation Fun 18S GT bis	94/005		23. 6.95	
G-MYXG	Rans S-6-ESD Coyote II			29. 6.95	
		PFA/204-12879			
G-MYXH	Cyclone Ax3	7028		3. 7.95	
G-MYXI	Cook Aries 1	BMAA/HB/048		4. 7.95	
G-MYXJ	Mainair Blade	1048-0795-7 & W846		17. 7.95	
G-MYXK	BFC Quad City Challenger II			11. 7.95	
		CH2-1194-1254 & PFA/177A-12877			
G-MYXL	Mignet HM-1000 Balerit	112		11. 7.95	
G-MYXM	Mainair Blade	1047-0795-7 & W845		19. 7.95	
G-MYXN	Mainair Blade	1046-0795-7 & W844		27. 7.95	
G-MYXO	Letov LK-2M Sluka			27. 7.95	
		8295s001 & PFA/263-12873			
G-MYXP	Rans S-6-ESD Coyote II			31. 7.95	
		PFA/204-12886			
G-MYXR	Murphy Renegade Spirit UK			2. 8.95	
		PFA/188-12755			
G-MYXS	Kolb Twinstar Mk.3	PFA/205-12528		4. 5.94	
G-MYXT	Cyclone Pegasus Quantum 15	7073		4. 8.95	
G-MYXU	Thruster T.300 (Mod)	9024-T300-513		16. 8.95	
G-MYXV	Quad City Challenger II UK			19. 7.95	
		CH2-1194-UK-1243			
G-MYXW	Cyclone Pegasus Quantum 15	7090		24. 8.95	
G-MYXX	Cyclone Pegasus Quantum 15	7081		25. 8.95	
G-MYXY	CFM Shadow Srs.CD			29. 8.95	
		BMAA/HB/059 & K.245			
G-MYXZ	Cyclone Pegasus Quantum 15	7023		21. 6.95	
G-MYYA	Mainair Blade	1052-0995-7 & W850		1. 9.95	
G-MYYB	Cyclone Pegasus Quantum 15	7079		4. 9.95	
G-MYYC	Cyclone Pegasus Quantum 15	7094		12. 9.95	
G-MYYD	Cyclone Chaser S	CH.7099		15. 9.95	
G-MYYE	Hunt Wing/Hunt Avon	BMAA/HB/041		21. 9.95	
G-MYYF	Quad City Challenger II UK			27. 9.95	
		PFA/177-12811			
G-MYYG	Mainair Blade	1054-0995-7 & W852		4.10.95	
G-MYYH	Mainair Blade	1056-1095-7 & W854		3.10.95	
G-MYYI	Cyclone Pegasus Quantum 15	7101		28. 9.95	
G-MYYJ	Hunt Wing/Hunt Avon	BMAA/HB/033		29. 9.95	
G-MYYK	Cyclone Pegasus Quantum 15	7100		2.10.95	
G-MYYL	Cyclone Ax3	7110		4.10.95	
G-MYYM	Trekking Microchute/Motor 27			17.10.95	
		TH10124M			
G-MYYN	Cyclone Pegasus Quantum 15	7022		3.10.95	
G-MYYO	Medway Raven X	MRB134/114		5.10.95	
G-MYYP	AMF Chevvron 2-45CS	036		31.10.95	
G-MYYR	Team Minimax 91	PFA/186-12724		31.10.95	Extensively damaged at Cranfield on 5.7.98.
G-MYYS	Team Minimax	PFA/186-11989		7.11.95	
G-MYYT	Hunt Wing/Experience	BMAA/HB/065		14.11.95	
G-MYYU	Mainair Mercury	1062-1295-7 & W862		17.11.95	
G-MYYV	Rans S-6-ESD Coyote IIXL			17.11.95	
		0896-1026XL & PFA/204-12943			
G-MYYW	Mainair Blade	1051-0895-7 & W849		8. 8.95	
G-MYYX	Cyclone Pegasus Quantum 15	7126		17.11.95	
G-MYYY	Mainair Blade	1031-0495-7 & W829		15. 3.95	
	(Incorrectly stamped with wing c/n W802 - see G-MYSZ)				
G-MYYZ	Medway Raven X	MRB135/116		10. 1.96	
G-MYZA	Whitaker MW.6 Merlin (Mod)			17. 7.95	
		PFA/164-11396			
G-MYZB	Cyclone Pegasus Quantum 15	7124		22.11.95	
G-MYZC	Cyclone Ax3	7125		5.12.95	
G-MYZD	Cyclone Pegasus Quantum 15	7135		5.12.95	Canx as WFU 12.1.96.
G-MYZE	Team Minimax 91	PFA/186-12570		28. 9.95	
G-MYZF	Cyclone Ax3	7133		11.12.95	
G-MYZG	Cyclone Ax3	7137		11. 1.96	
G-MYZH	Chargus Titan 38	JPA-1		16. 1.96	
G-MYZI	Tiger Cub RL5A-LW Sherwood Ranger			17. 1.96	To G-GKFC 11/98. Canx.
		PFA/237-12947			
G-MYZJ	Cyclone Pegasus Quantum 15	7150		24. 1.96	
G-MYZK	Cyclone Pegasus Quantum 15	7157		5. 2.96	
G-MYZL	Cyclone Pegasus Quantum 15	7158		5. 2.96	
G-MYZM	Cyclone Pegasus Quantum 15	7159		5. 2.96	
G-MYZN	Whittaker MW.6S-LW Fatboy Flyer			31. 1.96	
		PFA/164-12431			
G-MYZO	Medway Raven X	MRB136/115		12. 2.96	
G-MYZP	CFM Shadow Srs.DD			7. 2.96	
		249 & PFA/161-12914			

Regn	Type	c/n	Previous identity	Regn date	Fate or immediate subsequent identity (if known)
G-MYZR	Rans S-6-ESD Coyote II XL	PFA/204-12958		9. 2.96	
G-MYZS	Airwave Rave/Vega 1	BMAA/HB/054 & 001		16. 2.96	
G-MYZT	Airwave Rave/Vega 2	002		16. 2.96	
G-MYZU	Airwave Rave/Scorpion	005		16. 2.96	
G-MYZV	Rans S-6-ESD Coyote II XL	PFA/204-12946		26. 2.96	
G-MYZW	Cyclone Chaser S	7165		27. 2.96	
G-MYZX	Cyclone Chaser S	7172		28. 2.96	
G-MYZY	Cyclone Pegasus Quantum 15	7156		8. 2.96	
G-MYZZ	Cyclone Pegasus Quantum 15	7178		1. 3.96	To ZU-BCG 1/97. Canx 21.8.96.
G-MZAA	Mainair Blade	1059-1195-7 & W857		24.10.95	
G-MZAB	Mainair Blade	1043-0695-7 & W841		26. 5.95	
G-MZAC	BFC Quad City Challenger II	CH2-0294-1100 & PFA/177A-12716		21. 7.95	
G-MZAD	Mainair Blade	1061-1295-7 & W861		29.11.95	
G-MZAE	Mainair Blade	1063-1295-7 & W863		4.12.95	
G-MZAF	Mainair Blade	1045-0795-7 & W843		1.12.95	
G-MZAG	Mainair Blade	1042-0695-7 & W840		26. 5.95	
G-MZAH	Rans S-6-ESD Coyote II	0393-470 & PFA/204-12553		3. 9.93	
G-MZAI	Mainair Blade	1065-0196-7 & W867		4.12.95	
G-MZAJ	Mainair Blade	1067-0196-7 & W869		20.12.95	
G-MZAK	Mainair Mercury	1070-0296-7 & W872		15. 1.96	
G-MZAL	Mainair Blade	1076-0396-7 & W878		21. 2.96	
G-MZAM	Mainair Blade	1044-0695-7 & W842		31. 5.95	
G-MZAN	Cyclone Pegasus Quantum 15	7188		7. 3.96	
G-MZAO	Mainair Blade	1069-0296-7 & W871		15. 3.96	
G-MZAP	Mainair Blade	1036-0495-7 & W834		31. 3.95	
G-MZAR	Mainair Blade	1072-0296-7 & W874		13. 2.96	
G-MZAS	Mainair Blade	1049-0895-7 & W847		15. 8.95	
G-MZAT	Mainair Blade	1060-1195-7 & W860		29.11.95	
G-MZAU	Mainair Blade	1064-0196-7 & W864		29.11.95	Canx as destroyed 8.5.99.
G-MZAV	Mainair Blade	1078-0396-7 & W881		11. 3.96	
G-MZAW	Cyclone Pegasus Quantum 15	7160		14. 2.96	
G-MZAX	Cyclone Pegasus Quantum 15	7152		11. 3.96	
G-MZAY	Mainair Blade	1077-0396-7 & W880		15. 3.96	
G-MZAZ	Mainair Blade	1040-0595-7 & W838		26. 5.95	
G-MZBA	Mainair Blade	1068-0296-7 & W870		15. 3.96	
G-MZBB	Cyclone Pegasus Quantum 15	7139		13. 3.96	
G-MZBC	Cyclone Pegasus Quantum 15	7077		15. 8.95	
G-MZBD	Rans S-6-ESD Coyote II XL	0795-850XL & PFA/204-12957		15. 3.96	
G-MZBE	CFM Streak Shadow SA-M	PFA/206-12905		18. 3.96	
G-MZBF	Letov LK-2M Sluka	PFA/263-12881		18. 3.96	
G-MZBG	Whittaker MW.6S Fatboy Flyer	PFA/164-12891		20. 3.96	
G-MZBH	Rans S-6-ESD Coyote II	PFA/204-12244		21. 3.96	
G-MZBI	Cyclone Pegasus Quantum 15	7189		21. 3.96	
G-MZBJ	Cyclone Chaser S	7142		25. 3.96	CofA lapsed 22.3.97. Canx as destroyed 10.6.97.
G-MZBK	Letov LK-2M Sluka	8295s002 & PFA/263-12872		26. 3.96	
G-MZBL	Mainair Blade	1080-0496-7 & W883		1. 4.96	
G-MZBM	Cyclone Pegasus Quantum 15	7196		12. 4.96	
G-MZBN	CFM Shadow Srs.CD (C/n conflicts with G-MTWP - possibly that aircraft rebuilt)	BMAA/HB/073 & 069		22. 4.96	
G-MZBO	Cyclone Pegasus Quantum 15	7218		3. 5.96	
G-MZBP	Airwave Microchute UQ/Motor 27 (Also allocated c/n BMAA/HB/075)	BMAA/HB/028		29. 3.96	
G-MZBR	Southdown Raven	2232/0082		24. 5.96	
G-MZBS	CFM Shadow Srs.D	PFA/161-13008		14. 5.96	
G-MZBT	Cyclone Pegasus Quantum 15	7224		22. 5.96	
G-MZBU	Rans S-6-ESD Coyote II XL	PFA/204-12992		30. 5.96	
G-MZBV	Rans S-6-ESD Coyote II XL	0396-950XL & PFA/204-13009		30. 5.96	
G-MZBW	Quad City Challenger II UK	PFA/177-12971		19. 2.96	
G-MZBX	Whittaker MW.6S-LW Fatboy Flyer	PFA/164-12563		16. 5.96	
G-MZBY	Cyclone Pegasus Quantum 15 (Reported as c/n 7224 - see G-MZBT)	7227		30. 5.96	
G-MZBZ	Quad City Challenger II UK	PFA/177-12928		11. 3.96	
G-MZCA	Rans S-6-ESD Coyote II XL	0396-953XL & PFA/204-12997		31. 5.96	
G-MZCB	Cyclone Chaser S	7220		4. 6.96	
G-MZCC	Mainair Blade	1086-0696-7 & W889		7. 6.96	
G-MZCD	Mainair Blade	1087-0696-7 & W890		10. 6.96	

Regn	Type	c/n	Previous identity	Regn date	Fate or immediate subsequent identity (if known)
G-MZCE	Mainair Blade	1088-0696-7 & W891		17. 6.96	
G-MZCF	Mainair Blade	1089-0696-7 & W892		30. 8.96	
G-MZCG	Mainair Blade	1090-0696-7 & W893		17. 6.96	
G-MZCH	Whittaker MW.6S Fatboy Flyer	PFA/164-12131		7. 6.96	
G-MZCI	Cyclone Pegasus Quantum 15	7231		10. 6.96	
G-MZCJ	Cyclone Pegasus Quantum 15	7233		14. 6.96	
G-MZCK	AMF Chevvron 2-32C	038		11. 7.96	
G-MZCL	Ultrasports Tripacer/Moyes Mega II	JAJ-01		21. 6.96	
G-MZCM	Cyclone Pegasus Quantum 15	7219		3. 5.96	
G-MZCN	Mainair Blade	1079-0396-7 & W882		27. 6.96	
G-MZCO	Mainair Mercury	1091-0796-7 & W894		26. 6.96	
G-MZCP	Solar Wings Pegasus XL-Q	SW-TE-0434 & SW-WQ-0576		11. 2.93	
G-MZCR	Cyclone Pegasus Quantum 15	7234		28. 6.96	
G-MZCS	Team Minimax 91	PFA/186-12646		20.12.95	
G-MZCT	CFM Shadow Srs.CD	277		11. 7.96	
G-MZCU	Mainair Blade	1082-0496-7 & W885		1. 5.96	
G-MZCV	Cyclone Pegasus Quantum 15	7235		11. 7.96	
G-MZCW	Cyclone Pegasus Quantum 15	7239		11. 7.96	Canx as TWFU 31.7.96.
G-MZCX	Hunt Wing/Avon Skytrike	BMAA/HB/072 & 9510055		17. 7.96	
G-MZCY	Cyclone Pegasus Quantum 15	7236		19. 7.96	
G-MZCZ	Hunt Wing/Experience	BMAA/HB/039 & 9409024		24. 7.96	
G-MZDA	Rans S-6-ESD Coyote II XL	PFA/204-13019		29. 7.96	
G-MZDB	Cyclone Pegasus Quantum 15	7237		31. 7.96	Canx by CAA 15.11.96.
G-MZDC	Cyclone Pegasus Quantum 15	7246		2. 8.96	
G-MZDD	Cyclone Pegasus Quantum 15	7114	G-69-23	11. 7.96	
G-MZDE	Cyclone Pegasus Quantum 15	7238		12. 7.96	
G-MZDF	Mainair Blade	1093-0896-7 & W896		15. 8.96	
G-MZDG	Rans S-6-ESD Coyote II XL	PFA/204-13030		7. 8.96	
G-MZDH	Cyclone Pegasus Quantum 15	7248		12. 8.96	
G-MZDI	Whittaker MW.6S Fatboy Flyer Srs.A	PFA/164-11929	G-BUNN	15. 8.96	
G-MZDJ	Medway Raven X	MRB138/119		19. 8.96	
G-MZDK	Mainair Blade (C/n reported as 1084-0696-7)	1084-0596-7 & W887		9. 5.96	
G-MZDL	Whittaker MW.6S Fatboy Flyer	PFA/164-12412		19. 8.96	
G-MZDM	Rans S-6-ESD Coyote II XL	0396-954XL & PFA/204-13022		2. 9.96	
G-MZDN	Cyclone Pegasus Quantum 15	7255		5. 9.96	
G-MZDO	Cyclone Ax3	7252		11. 9.96	
G-MZDP	AMF Chevvron 2-32C	020		3. 4.90	(Damaged in mid 1995) Permit expired 16.3.96.
G-MZDR	Rans S-6-ESD Coyote II XL	PFA/204-13012		8. 8.96	
G-MZDS	Cyclone Ax3	7253		16. 9.96	
G-MZDT	Mainair Blade	1096-0996-7 & W899		19. 9.96	
G-MZDU	Cyclone Pegasus Quantum 15	7260		19. 9.96	
G-MZDV	Cyclone Pegasus Quantum 15	7199		9. 4.96	
G-MZDW	Trekking Microchute UQ/Motor 27	BMAA/HB/078		23. 9.96	
G-MZDX	Letov LK-2M Sluka	PFA/263-12882		30. 9.96	
G-MZDY	Cyclone Pegasus Quantum 15	7263		2.10.96	
G-MZDZ	Hunt Avon/Wing	BMAA/HB/045 & 9501042		23.10.96	
G-MZEA	BFC Quad City Challenger II	CH2-0294-1101 & PFA/177A-12728		22. 4.96	
G-MZEB	Mainair Blade	1074-0396-7 & W876		22. 7.96	
G-MZEC	Cyclone Pegasus Quantum 15	7278		24.10.96	
G-MZED	Mainair Blade	1092-0796-7 & W895		3. 7.96	
G-MZEE	Cyclone Pegasus Quantum 15	7245		9. 8.96	
G-MZEF	Mainair Blade	1094-0896-7 & W897		12. 8.96	DBF at Mainair's factory, Rochdale on 22.11.98. Canx as destroyed 19.2.99.
G-MZEG	Mainair Blade	1095-0896-7 & W898		8. 8.96	
G-MZEH	Cyclone Pegasus Quantum 15	7259		19. 9.96	
G-MZEI	Whittaker MW.5D Sorcerer	PFA/163-12011		28.10.96	
G-MZEJ	Mainair Blade	1097-0996-7 & W900		8.10.96	
G-MZEK	Mainair Mercury	1098-1096-7 & W901		14.10.96	
G-MZEL	Cyclone Ax3	7250		30.10.96	
G-MZEM	Cyclone Pegasus Quantum 15	7277		8.11.96	
G-MZEN	Rans S-6-ESD Coyote II (Tricycle u/c)	PFA/204-12823		9. 7.96	
G-MZEO	Rans S-6-ESD Coyote II XL	PFA/204-13046		19.11.96	
G-MZEP	Mainair Rapier	1103-1296-7 & W906		13.12.96	
G-MZER	Cyclone Ax2000	7251		4.12.96	

Regn	Type	c/n	Previous identity	Regn date	Fate or immediate subsequent identity (if known)
G-MZES	Letov LK-2M Sluka			5.12.96	
		8296K10 & PFA/263-13064			
G-MZET	Cyclone Pegasus Quantum 15	7288		9.12.96	
G-MZEU	Rans S-6-ESD Coyote II XL			23.12.96	
		PFA/204-13023			
G-MZEV	Mainair Rapier	1101-1296-7 & W904		7. 1.97	
G-MZEW	Mainair Blade	1105-0197-7 & W908		13. 1.97	
G-MZEX	Cyclone Pegasus Quantum 15	7292		19.11.96	
G-MZEY	Micro Aviation B.22S Bantam	96-002	ZK-TII	7. 1.97	
G-MZEZ	Cyclone Pegasus Quantum 15	7285		8.11.96	
G-MZFA	Cyclone Ax2000	7301		17.12.96	
G-MZFB	Mainair Blade	1108-0197-7 & W911		7. 1.97	
G-MZFC	Letov LK-2M Sluka	PFA/263-13063		7. 1.97	
G-MZFD	Mainair Rapier	1109-0197-7 & W912		24. 1.97	
G-MZFE	Hunt Avon/Wing			16. 1.97	
		BMAA/HB/061 & 9507049			
G-MZFF	Hunt Avon/Wing	BMAA/HB/074 & 960458		22. 1.97	
G-MZFG	Cyclone Pegasus Quantum 15	7305		21. 1.97	
G-MZFH	AMF Chevvron 2-32C	039		27. 3.97	
G-MZFI	Lorimer Iolaire	BMAA/HB/035		30. 1.97	
G-MZFJ	Cyclone Ax2000	7281		10. 2.97	Canx by CAA 5.2.99. To G-OAJB 16.2.99.
G-MZFK	Whittaker MW.6 Merlin	PFA/164-11626		10. 2.97	
G-MZFL	Rans S-6-ESD Coyote II XL			12. 2.97	
		0696-999XL & PFA/204-13041			
G-MZFM	Cyclone Pegasus Quantum 15	7310		21. 2.97	
G-MZFN	Rans S-6-ESD Coyote II			26. 2.97	
		PFA/204-12977			
G-MZFO	Thruster T.600N	9037-T600N-001		4. 3.97	
G-MZFP	Thruster T.600T	9047-T600T-002		4. 3.97	(Crashed during crosswind take-off at Priory Farm, Tibbenham on 25.6.99)
G-MZFR	Thruster T.600N	9047-T600N-003		4. 3.97	
G-MZFS	Mainair Blade	1110-0297-7 & W913		8. 1.97	
	(Regd with Trike c/n 1010-0297-7)				
G-MZFT	Cyclone Pegasus Quantum 15	7264		2.10.96	
G-MZFU	Thruster T.600N	9047-T600N-004		4. 3.97	
G-MZFV	Cyclone Pegasus Quantum 15	7324		13. 3.97	
G-MZFW	Mainair Rapier	1111-0297-7 & W914		17. 1.97	DBF at Mainair's factory, Rochdale on 22.11.98.
G-MZFX	Cyclone Ax2000	7322		14. 3.97	
G-MZFY	Rans S-6-ESD Coyote II XL			17. 3.97	
		PFA/204-13043			
G-MZFZ	Mainair Blade	1119-0497-7 & W922		2. 4.97	
G-MZGA	Cyclone Ax2000	7303		17.12.96	
G-MZGB	Cyclone Ax2000	7302		28. 1.97	
G-MZGC	Cyclone Ax2000	7304		20.12.96	
G-MZGD	Rans S-6 Coyote	PFA/193-13096		1. 4.97	
G-MZGE	Medway Hybred 44XLR	MR143/125		8. 4.97	
G-MZGF	Letov LK-2M Sluka	PFA/263-13073		8. 4.97	
G-MZGG	Cyclone Pegasus Quantum 15	7327		10. 4.97	
G-MZGH	Hunt Avon/Hunt Wing	BMAA/HB/070		20.12.96	
G-MZGI	Mainair Blade	1117-0397-7 & W920		11. 4.97	
G-MZGJ	Kolb Twinstar Mk.3	PFA/205-12421		16. 4.97	
G-MZGK	Cyclone Pegasus Quantum 15	7331		30. 4.97	
G-MZGL	Mainair Rapier	1104-0197-7 & W907		18.12.96	
G-MZGM	Cyclone Ax2000	7334		1. 5.97	
G-MZGN	Cyclone Pegasus Quantum 15	7332		2. 5.97	
G-MZGO	Cyclone Pegasus Quantum 15	7320		20. 3.97	
G-MZGP	Cyclone Ax2000	7333		7. 5.97	
G-MZGR	Team Minimax	PFA/186-12323		8. 5.97	
G-MZGS	CFM Shadow Srs.DD	PFA/161-13050		8. 5.97	
G-MZGT	RH7B Tiger Light	PFA/230-13013		10. 3.97	
	(Five eights scale Tiger Moth)				
G-MZGU	Arrowflight Hawk II (UK)			8. 5.97	
		PFA/266-13075			
G-MZGV	Cyclone Pegasus Quantum 15	7339		12. 6.97	
G-MZGW	Mainair Blade	1112-0297-7 & W915		19. 2.97	
G-MZGX	Thruster T.600N	9057-T600N-005		28. 4.97	
G-MZGY	Thruster T.600N	9057-T600N-006		28. 4.97	
G-MZGZ	Thruster T.600N	9057-T600N-007		28. 4.97	
G-MZHA	Thruster T.600T	9057-T600T-008		28. 4.97	
G-MZHB	Mainair Blade	1114-0297-7 & W917		19. 2.97	
G-MZHC	Thruster T.600T	9067-T600T-009		13. 5.97	
G-MZHD	Thruster T.600T	9067-T600T-010		13. 5.97	
G-MZHE	Thruster T.600N	9067-T600N-011		13. 5.97	
G-MZHF	Thruster T.600N	9067-T600N-012		13. 5.97	
G-MZHG	Whittaker MW.6T	PFA/164-11420		16. 6.97	
G-MZHH	Cyclone Pegasus Quantum Super		G-69-37	17. 6.97	Canx 13.1.98 on sale to France.
	Sport 15	7325			
G-MZHI	Cyclone Pegasus Quantum 15	7337		27. 5.97	
G-MZHJ	Mainair Rapier	1123-0697-7 & W926		17. 6.97	
G-MZHK	Cyclone Pegasus Quantum Super			24. 6.97	
	Sport 15	7352			
G-MZHL	Mainair Rapier	1126-0797-7 & W929		30. 6.97	
G-MZHM	Team Himax 1700R	PFA/272-12912		8. 1.97	

Regn	Type	c/n	Previous identity	Regn date	Fate or immediate subsequent identity (if known)
G-MZHN	Cyclone Pegasus Quantum 15	7351		27. 6.97	
G-MZHO	Quad City Challenger II	PFA/177-12936		15. 7.97	
G-MZHP	Cyclone Pegasus Quantum 15	7353		15. 7.97	
G-MZHR	Cyclone Ax2000	7307		7. 3.97	
G-MZHS	Thruster T.600T	9077-T600T-013		4. 7.97	
G-MZHT	Whittaker MW.6 Merlin	PFA/164-11244		12. 6.97	
G-MZHU	Thruster T.600T	9077-T600T-019		4. 7.97	
G-MZHV	Thruster T.600T	9077-T600T-018		4. 7.97	
G-MZHW	Thruster T.600N	9077-T600N-017		4. 7.97	
G-MZHX	Thruster T.600N	9077-T600N-016		4. 7.97	
G-MZHY	Thruster T.600N	9077-T600N-015		4. 7.97	
G-MZHZ	Thruster T.600N	9077-T600N-014		4. 7.97	
G-MZIA	Team Himax 1700R	PFA/272-13020		25. 4.97	
G-MZIB	Cyclone Pegasus Quantum 15	7354		15. 7.97	
G-MZIC	Cyclone Pegasus Quantum 15	7348		24. 6.97	
G-MZID	Whittaker MW.6 Merlin	PFA/164-11383		15. 7.97	
G-MZIE	Cyclone Pegasus Quantum 15	7359		6. 8.97	
G-MZIF	Cyclone Pegasus Quantum 15	7355		16. 7.97	
G-MZIG	Mainair Blade	1107-0197-7 & W910		13. 2.97	Canx 5.3.99 on sale to France.
G-MZIH	Mainair Blade	1128-0797-7 & W931		16. 7.97	
G-MZII	Team Minimax 88	PFA/186-11842		19. 3.97	
G-MZIJ	Cyclone Pegasus Quantum 15	7362		14. 8.97	
G-MZIK	Cyclone Pegasus Quantum 15	7368		8. 9.97	
G-MZIL	Mainair Rapier	1132-0897-7 & W935		1. 9.97	
G-MZIM	Mainair Rapier	1124-0697-7 & W927		9. 6.97	
G-MZIN	Whittaker MW.6 Merlin	PFA/164-12820		9. 9.97	(Crashed at Newnham on 28.3.99)
G-MZIO	Cyclone Pegasus Quantum 15	7369		26. 9.97	To G-MGTG 12/97. Canx.
G-MZIP	Murphy Renegade Spirit UK	216 & PFA/188-11426		4. 7.89	
G-MZIR	Mainair Blade	1134-0997-7 & W937		18. 9.97	
G-MZIS	Mainair Blade	1115-0397-7 & W918		17. 2.97	
G-MZIT	Mainair Blade	1129-0897-7 & W932		16. 7.97	
G-MZIU	Cyclone Pegasus Quantum 15	7371		15.10.97	
G-MZIV	Cyclone Ax2000	7372		21.10.97	
G-MZIW	Mainair Blade	1127-0797-7 & W930		16. 7.97	
G-MZIX	Mignet HM-1000 Balerit	130		23. 9.97	
G-MZIY	Rans S-6-ESD Coyote II XL	1096-1050XL & PFA/204-13184		29. 9.97	
G-MZIZ	Murphy Renegade Spirit UK	257 & PFA/188-11701	G-MWGP	21.10.92	
G-MZJA	Mainair Blade	1135-0997-7 & W938		30. 9.97	
G-MZJB	Aviasud Mistral	047	(ex)	30. 9.97	
G-MZJC	Micro Aviation B.22S Bantam	97-011	ZK-JIK	14.10.97	
G-MZJD	Mainair Blade	1130-0897-7 & W933		7. 8.97	
G-MZJE	Mainair Rapier	1136-1097-7 & W939		17.10.97	
G-MZJF	Cyclone Ax2000	7378		2.12.97	
G-MZJG	Cyclone Pegasus Quantum 15	7335		2. 5.97	
G-MZJH	Cyclone Pegasus Quantum 15	7350		25. 6.97	
G-MZJI	Rans S-6-ESD Coyote II XL	1096-1046XL & PFA/204-13221		3.11.97	
G-MZJJ	Meridian Ultralights Maverick	PFA/259-13016		5.11.97	
G-MZJK	Mainair Blade	1100-1196-7 & W903		19.11.96	
G-MZJL	Cyclone Ax2000	7363		11. 8.97	
G-MZJM	Rans S-6-ESD Coyote II XL (Tricycle u/c)	PFA/204-13215		19.11.97	
G-MZJN	Cyclone Pegasus Quantum 15	7376		11.11.97	
G-MZJO	Cyclone Pegasus Quantum 15	7338		17. 6.97	
G-MZJP	Whittaker MW.6S Fatboy Flyer	PFA/164-13049		21.10.97	
G-MZJR	Cyclone Ax2000	7385		11.11.97	
G-MZJS	Meridian Ultralights Maverick	PFA/259-13017		12.12.97	(Under construction 3/98 at Chirk)
G-MZJT	Cyclone Pegasus Quantum 15	7399		23.12.97	
G-MZJU	Cyclone Pegasus Quantum 15	7382		23.12.97	
G-MZJV	Mainair Blade	1141-0198-7 & W944		7. 1.98	
G-MZJW	Cyclone Pegasus Quantum 15	7390		27. 1.98	
G-MZJX	Mainair Blade	1139-0198-7 & W942		9. 1.98	
G-MZJY	Cyclone Pegasus Quantum 15	7394		23.12.97	
G-MZJZ	Mainair Blade	1121-0597-7 & W924		23. 6.97	
G-MZKA	Cyclone Pegasus Quantum 15	7380		1.12.97	
G-MZKB	Kolb Twinstar Mk.3	PFA/205-13160		18. 7.97	Canx by CAA 17.4.99.
G-MZKC	Cyclone Ax2000	7398		22. 1.98	
G-MZKD	Cyclone Pegasus Quantum 15	7404		19. 3.98	
G-MZKE	Rans S-6-ESD Coyote II XL	PFA/204-13248		19. 1.98	
G-MZKF	Cyclone Pegasus Quantum 15	7407		21. 1.98	
G-MZKG	Mainair Blade	1145-0198-7 & W948		23. 1.98	
G-MZKH	CFM Shadow Srs.DD	292-DD		23. 1.98	
G-MZKI	Mainair Rapier	1147-0298-7 & W950		12. 2.98	
G-MZKJ	Mainair Blade	1039-0595-7 & W837		19. 5.95	
G-MZKK	Mainair Blade	1140-0198-7 & W943		12. 2.98	

Regn	Type	c/n	Previous identity	Regn date	Fate or immediate subsequent identity (if known)
G-MZKL	Cyclone Pegasus Quantum 15	7360		18. 8.97	
G-MZKM	Mainair Blade	1133-0897-7 & W936		15. 8.97	
G-MZKN	Mainair Rapier	1138-1297-7 & W941		12.12.97	
G-MZKO	Mainair Blade	1131-0897-7 & W934		5. 8.97	
G-MZKP	Thruster T.600N	9038-T600N-020		27. 1.98	
G-MZKR	Thruster T.600N	9038-T600N-021		27. 1.98	
G-MZKS	Thruster T.600N	9038-T600N-022		27. 1.98	
G-MZKT	Thruster T.600T	9038-T600T-023		27. 1.98	
G-MZKU	Thruster T.600T	9038-T600T-024		27. 1.98	
G-MZKV	Mainair Blade	1144-0198-7 & W947		28. 1.98	
G-MZKW	Quad City Challenger II	PFA/177-12518		22. 3.94	
G-MZKX	Cyclone Pegasus Quantum 15	7395		15. 1.98	
G-MZKY	Cyclone Pegasus Quantum 15	7403		16. 1.98	
G-MZKZ	Mainair Blade	1137-0298-7 & W940		18. 2.98	
G-MZLA	Cyclone Pegasus Quantum 15	7415		27. 2.98	
G-MZLB	Hunt Wing/Experience	BMAA/HB/058		25. 2.98	
G-MZLC	Mainair Blade	1146-0298-7 & W949		26. 2.98	
G-MZLD	Cyclone Pegasus Quantum 15	7416		24. 3.98	
G-MZLE	Meridian Ultralights Maverick	PFA/259-12955	G-BXSZ	27. 2.98	
G-MZLF	Cyclone Pegasus Quantum 15	7417		30. 3.98	
G-MZLG	Rans S-6-ESD Coyote II XL	PFA/204-13192		3. 3.98	
G-MZLH	Cyclone Pegasus Quantum 15	7426		1. 4.98	
G-MZLI	Mignet HM-1000 Balerit	133		5. 3.98	
G-MZLJ	Cyclone Pegasus Quantum 15	7421		20. 3.98	
G-MZLK	Hunt Avon Skytrike/Solar Wings Typhoon	T285-1471		9. 3.98	
G-MZLL	Rans S-6-ESD Coyote II	PFA/204-13067		22. 9.97	
G-MZLM	Cyclone Ax2000	7425		22. 4.98	
G-MZLN	Cyclone Pegasus Quantum 15	7431		14. 4.98	
G-MZLO	CFM Shadow Srs.D	K.298-D		1. 4.98	
G-MZLP	CFM Shadow Srs.D	K.299-D		1. 4.98	
G-MZLR	Cyclone Pegasus XL-Q	7441		28. 5.98	
G-MZLS	Cyclone Ax2000	7428		6. 7.98	
G-MZLT	Cyclone Pegasus Quantum 15	7438		24. 4.98	
G-MZLU	Cyclone Ax2000	7439		28. 7.98	
G-MZLV	Cyclone Pegasus Quantum 15	7437		29. 4.98	
G-MZLW	Cyclone Pegasus Quantum 15	7440		28. 4.98	
G-MZLX	Micro Aviation B.22S Bantam	97-013	ZK-JIV	9.12.97	
G-MZLY	Letov LK-2M Sluka	PFA/263-13065		20. 4.98	
G-MZLZ	Mainair Blade	1154-0498-7 & W957		21. 4.98	
G-MZMA	Solar Wings Pegasus Quasar IITC	6611		1. 9.93	
G-MZMB	Mainair Blade	1149-0398-7 & W952		5. 3.98	
G-MZMC	Cyclone Pegasus Quantum 15	7206		10. 5.96	
G-MZMD	Mainair Blade	1148-0398-7 & W951		5. 3.98	
G-MZME	Medway Hybred 44XLR Eclipser	151/129E		28. 4.98	
G-MZMF	Cyclone Pegasus Quantum 15 Super Sport (HKS)	7387		30. 4.98	
G-MZMG	Cyclone Pagasus Quantum 15	7446		27. 5.98	
G-MZMH	Cyclone Pegasus Quantum 15	7402		27. 1.98	
G-MZMI	CFM Streak Shadow	PFA/206-13205		30. 4.98	To G-BXWR 22.5.98. Canx.
G-MZMJ	Mainair Blade	1155-0598-7 & W958		8. 5.98	
G-MZMK	AMF Chevvron 2-32C	040		19. 5.98	
G-MZML	Mainair Blade	1158-0698-7 & W961		19. 5.98	
G-MZMM	Mainair Blade	1162-0698-7 & W965		19. 5.98	
G-MZMN	Cyclone Pegasus Quantum 15	7445		21. 5.98	
G-MZMO	Team Minimax 91	PFA/186-12951		20. 5.98	
G-MZMP	Mainair Blade	1160-0698-7 & W963		20. 5.98	
G-MZMR	Rans S-6-ESA Coyote II	PFA/204-13315		21. 5.98	
G-MZMS	Rans S-6-ES Coyote II	PFA/204-13294		26. 5.98	
G-MZMT	Cyclone Pegasus Quantum 15	7449		18. 6.98	
G-MZMU	Rans S-6-ESD Coyote II	PFA/204-13242		5. 6.98	
G-MZMV	Mainair Blade	1152-0496-7 & W955		30. 3.98	
G-MZMW	Mignet HM-1000 Balerit	125		2.10.96	
G-MZMX	Cyclone Ax2000	7451		8. 9.98	
G-MZMY	Mainair Blade	1153-0498-7 & W956		16. 3.98	
G-MZMZ	Mainair Blade	1081-0496-7 & W884		22. 4.96	
G-MZNA	Quad City Challenger II UK	CH2-0894-UK-1193	EI-CLE	19. 3.98	
G-MZNB	Cyclone Pegasus Quantum 15	7456		17. 7.98	
G-MZNC	Mainair Blade	1161-0698-7 & W964		22. 6.98	
G-MZND	Mainair Rapier	1170-0898-7 & W973		24. 6.98	
G-MZNE	Whittaker MW.6-2 Fatboy Flyer	PFA/164-13120		26. 6.98	
G-MZNF	Tiger Cub RL5A-LW Sherwood Ranger	PFA/237-12964		29. 6.98	To G-PUSY 6/99. Canx.

Regn	Type	c/n	Previous identity	Regn date	Fate or immediate subsequent identity (if known)
G-MZNG	Cyclone Pegasus Quantum 15	7457		11. 8.98	
G-MZNH	CFM Shadow Srs.DD	K.297-DD		30. 6.98	
G-MZNI	Mainair Blade	1163-0698-7 & W966		3. 7.98	
G-MZNJ	Mainair Blade	1168-0798-7 & W971		6. 7.98	
G-MZNK	Mainair Blade	1164-0798-7 & W967		6. 7.98	
G-MZNL	Mainair Blade	1165-0798-7 & W968		6. 7.98	
G-MZNM	Team Minimax 91	PFA/186-12304		10. 7.98	
G-MZNN	Team Minimax 91	PFA/186-13125		10. 7.98	
G-MZNO	Mainair Blade	1167-0798-7 & W970		9. 6.98	
G-MZNP	Cyclone Pegasus Quantum 15 Super Sport (HKS)	7466		22. 7.98	
G-MZNR	Cyclone Pegasus Quantum 15	7465		17. 8.98	
G-MZNS	Cyclone Pegasus Quantum 15	7473		31. 7.98	
G-MZNT	Cyclone Pegasus Quantum 15	7470		25. 9.98	
G-MZNU	Mainair Rapier	1174-0898-7 & W977		5. 8.98	
G-MZNV	Rans S-6-ESD Coyote II	PFA/204-12884		7. 8.98	
G-MZNW	Thruster T.600N HKS	9098-T600N-025		10. 8.98	
G-MZNX	Thruster T.600N	9098-T600N-026		10. 8.98	
G-MZNY	Thruster T.600N	9098-T600N-027		10. 8.98	
G-MZNZ	Letov LK-2M Sluka	PFA/263-13274		21. 4.98	
G-MZOA	Thruster T.600T	9108-T600T-028		10. 8.98	
G-MZOB	Thruster T.600T	9098-T600T-029		10. 8.98	
G-MZOC	Mainair Blade	1172-0898-7 & W975		10. 8.98	
G-MZOD	Cyclone Pegasus Quantum 15	7435		28. 4.98	
G-MZOE	Cyclone Ax2000	7472		17. 9.98	
G-MZOF	Mainair Blade	1122-0697-7 & W925		5. 6.97	
G-MZOG	Cyclone Pegasus Quantum 15	7471		12.10.98	
G-MZOH	Whittaker MW.5D Sorcerer	PFA/163-13060		14. 8.98	
G-MZOI	Letov LK-2M Sluka	PFA/263-13238		17. 8.98	
G-MZOJ	Cyclone Pegasus Quantum 15	7478		9.11.98	
G-MZOK	Whittaker MW.6 Merlin	PFA/164-11568		24. 8.97	
G-MZOL	Tiger Cub RL5B-LWS Sherwood Ranger	PFA/237-12887		26. 8.98	To G-WZOL 1/99. Canx.
G-MZOM	CFM Shadow Srs.DD	K.302-DD		8. 9.98	
G-MZON	Mainair Rapier	1180-1098-7 & W983		11. 9.98	
G-MZOO	Murphy Renegade Spirit UK	0221		30. 5.90	Canx 11.7.96 on sale to Germany.
G-MZOP	Mainair Blade	1178-0998-7 & W981		11. 9.98	
G-MZOR	Mainair Blade	1173-0898-7 & W976		21. 9.98	
G-MZOS	Cyclone Pegasus Quantum 15	7458		6.10.98	
G-MZOT	Letov LK-2M Sluka	PFA/263-13346		21. 9.98	
G-MZOV	Cyclone Pegasus Quantom 15	7512		9. 3.99	
G-MZOW	Cyclone Pegasus Quantom 15	7502		9. 3.99	(Being rigged at Insch in 6/99)
G-MZOX	Letov LK-2M Sluka	PFA/263-13415		15. 2.99	
G-MZOY	Team Minimax 91	PFA/186-12526		29. 3.99	
G-MZOZ	Rans S-6-ESD Coyote II XL	PFA/204-13168		20. 5.98	
G-MZPB	Mignet HM-1000 Balerit	124		4.10.96	
G-MZPD	Solar Wings Pegasus Quantum 15	7013		9. 5.95	
G-MZPH	Mainair Blade	1177-0998-7 & W980		26. 8.98	
G-MZPJ	Team Minimax 91	PFA/186-12277		23.11.92	
G-MZPW	Solar Wings Pegasus Quasar IITC	6892		26.10.94	
G-MZRC	Cyclone Pegasus Quantum 15	7482		25.11.98	
G-MZRH	Cyclone Pegasus Quantum 15	7269		11.10.96	
G-MZRM	Cyclone Pegasus Quantum 15	7455		10. 7.98	
G-MZRS	CFM Shadow Srs.CD	141		4. 4.90	
G-MZSC	Cyclone Pegasus Quantum 15	7370		3.10.97	
G-MZSD	Mainair Blade	1179-0998-7 & W978		21. 8.98	
G-MZSM	Mainair Blade	1000-0794-7 & W796		15. 7.94	
G-MZTA	Mignet HM-1000 Balerit	120		14. 5.96	
G-MZTS	Aerial Arts Chaser S	CH.703	G-MVDM	19. 3.96	
G-MZUB	Rans S-6 ESD Coyote II XL	PFA/204-13244		30. 4.98	
G-MZZT	Kolb Twinstar Mk.3 (Mod)	PFA/205-12596		1. 5.98	
G-MZZY	Mainair Blade	1050-0895-7 & W848		13.11.95	
G-MZZZ	Whittaker MW.6S Fatboy Flyer	PFA/164-11908		21.12.90	(Project for sale 8/97) Canx by CAA 29.3.99.

G-N

Regn	Type	c/n	Previous identity	Regn date	Fate or immediate subsequent identity (if known)
G-NAAA	MBB Bo.105DBS-4	S.34/912	G-BUTN G-AZTI/EI-BTE/G-AZTI/EC-DRY/G-AZTI/D-HDAN	6. 4.99	
G-NAAB	MBB Bo.105DBS-4	S.416	D-HDMO D-HSTP/D-HDMO	23. 3.99	
G-NAAS	Aerospatiale AS.355F1 Twin Squirrel	5203	G-BPRG G-NWPA/G-NAAS/G-BPRG/N370E	23. 3.90	

Regn	Type	c/n	Previous identity	Regn date	Fate or immediate subsequent identity (if known)
G-NAAT	Folland Gnat T.1	FL.507	XM697	27.11.89	Believed to be suitable only for rebuild to static display standard and currently stored at Bournemouth. Canx as WFU 10.4.95. (Open storage 1/97 - painted as XM697)
G-NABI	PA-31-350 Navajo Chieftain	31-8052078	G-MARG N3580C	8. 6.84	To G-IFIT 12/85. Canx.
G-NABS	Robinson R-22 Beta	1564		29.10.90	Crashed on approach to Cumbernauld on 30.6.91. Canx by CAA 5.9.91. To N5115C 11/92.
G-NACA	Norman NAC-2 Freelance 180	2001		23.11.87	(Stored 5/98 Coventry)
G-NACI	Norman NAC-1 Freelance 180	NAC.001	G-AXFB	20. 6.84	(Stored 5/98 Coventry)
G-NACL	Norman NAC-6 Firemaster 65 (Note - fitted with rudder/marks of G-NACM 2/96)	6001	G-BNEG	23. 4.87	Permit expired 5.12.90. (Stored 5/98 Coventry)
G-NACM	Norman NAC-6 Fieldmaster 34	6002	Z-NACM G-NACM	10. 6.87	Canx 19.8.98 on sale to Turkey.
G-NACN	Norman NAC-6 Firemaster 65 (Originally regd as a Fieldmaster)	6003	Z-NACN G-NACN	3. 9.87	To TC-ZBD. Canx 19.8.98.
G-NACO	Norman NAC-6 Firemaster 65 (Originally regd as a Fieldmaster)	6004		2.12.87	CofA expired 27.8.92. (Stored 5/98 Coventry)
G-NACP	Norman NAC-6 Fieldmaster 34	6005		2.12.87	CofA expired 6.9.93. (Stored 5/98 Coventry)
G-NADS	Team Minimax 91	PFA/186-12995		8. 2.99	
G-NAFH	Boeing 737-3S3 (Line No. 1393)	23788	G-BOYN EC-ECQ/EC-277/G-BOYN/EC-ECQ	15. 5.91	To N851LF. Canx 3.10.91.
G-NAIL	Cessna 340A II	340A-0422	G-DEXI N6216X	2. 8.90	To G-GJAN 11/94. Canx.
G-NAIR	Cessna 421B Golden Eagle II	421B-0368	G-KACT OY-RPL/(N8055Q)	5. 7.82	To G-BLOH 10/84. Canx.
G-NALI	Cessna 152 II	152-81856	G-BHVM N67477	30. 8.90	To G-OBEN 8/93. Canx.
G-NANA	VPM M-16 Tandem Trainer	G/12-1249		29.11.94	
G-NARO	Cassutt Racer (Also known as Musso Racer Original)	M.14372	G-BTXR N68PM	14. 4.98	
G-NASA	Lockheed T-33A-5-LO	580-6350	G-TJET R.Danish AF DT-566/51-8566	3. 6.91	(Stored Bruntingthorpe 3/96) Reportedly crated & exported to USA in 11/96. (Not canx yet!)
G-NASH	American Aviation AA-5A Cheetah	AA5A-0617	(G-BFWL) N26477	13. 9.78	
G-NATO	Agusta-Bell 206B JetRanger III	8563	G-FLCH G-BGGX	24. 8.88	To OO-VWE. Canx 25.5.90.
G-NATS	Rockwell Commander 690B	11541	N81689	15. 6.79	To N321MC 4/81. Canx 6.4.81.
G-NATT	Rockwell Commander 114A	14538	N5921N	14. 1.80	
G-NATX	Cameron O-65 HAFB	1681		3. 3.88	
G-NATY	Folland Gnat T.1	FL.548	8642M XR537	19. 6.90	(On rebuild 2/99 at Hurn) No Permit to Fly issued.
G-NATZ	Rockwell 690C Commander 840	11620	N5872K	. .80R	NTU - To G-BXYZ 10/80. Canx.
G-NAVO	PA-31-325 Navajo C/R	31-8212031	G-BMPV N4109V	6. 7.90	
G-NAVY	DH.104 Sea Devon C.20 (Dove 6)	04406	XJ348 G-AMXX	6. 1.82	Canx as WFU 2.7.91. (On display 4/99 at Hermeskeil Museum, near Trier, Germany as XJ348)
G-NAZO	PA-31-310 Turbo Navajo B	31-776	SE-INR EI-BOL/G-AZIM/N7250L	27.10.88	To 5Y-BKB 4/94. Canx 11.4.94.
G-NBAC	Embraer EMB.110P1 Bandeirante	110-252	G-POST (N110PL)/G-POST/PT-SAS	10.10.94	WFU & used for spares 2/95 at Griffin-Spalding, GA, USA. Canx as WFU 25.7.95.
G-NBDD	Robin DR.400 2+2 Tricycle	1103	F-BXVN	26. 9.88	
G-NBSI	Cameron N-77 HAFB	427		3. 8.78	Canx as WFU 14.6.93.
G-NCFC	PA-38-112 Tomahawk II	38-81A0107	N737V G-BNOA/N23272	14. 1.97	
G-NCFE	PA-38-112 Tomahawk II	38-80A0081	G-BKMK OO-GME/(OO-HKD)/N9676N	1. 7.99	
G-NCFR	HS.125 Srs.700B	257054	G-BVJY RA-02802/G-BVJY/RA-02802/G-BVJY/C6-BET	28. 4.97	
G-NCMT	Cessna 500 Citation I (Unit No.645)	500-0411	G-BIZZ N6784Y	26. 5.87	To SE-DLZ. Canx 20.3.89.
G-NCUB	Piper J3C-65 Cub (L-4H-PI)	11599	G-BGXV F-BFQT/OO-GAB/43-30308	6. 7.84	
G-NDGC	Grob G-109	6150		7. 4.83	
G-NDNI	Norman NDN-1 Firecracker	001		30. 3.77	(Stored 5/98 Coventry)
G-NDOL	Europa Avn Europa	44 & PFA/247-12594		30.11.93	
G-NDRW	Colt AS-80 Mk.II Hot-Air Airship	2085		2.12.91	
G-NEAL	PA-32-260 Cherokee Six	32-1048	G-BFPY N5588J	7.11.83	
G-NEAS	Aerospatiale AS.355F1 Twin Squirrel	5077	G-CMMM G-BNBJ/C-GLKH	17. 8.89	To G-SETA 12/89. Canx.
G-NEAT	Europa Avn Europa	65 & PFA/247-12642		28. 6.94	
G-NEEL	Rotorway Exec 90	0001 & 5002		7. 8.90	
G-NEEP	Bell 206B JetRanger II	2142	N777FW N3CR	5.10.88	To G-ODIG 6/93. Canx.
G-NEGS	Thunder Ax7-77 HAFB	1059		18. 3.87	
G-NEIL	Thunder Ax3 Maxi Sky Chariot HAFB	379		2.12.81	
G-NELL	Rockwell Commander 112A	373	OY-DLJ N1373J	14.11.80	To (OO-CWR)/OO-RES. Canx 20.9.89.

Regn	Type	c/n	Previous identity	Regn date	Fate or immediate subsequent identity (if known)
G-NEPB	Cameron N-77 HAFB (Type and c/n were quoted for marks G-OKYA when regd on 4.3.87 - since corrected)	1264		7. 3.86	
G-NERC	PA-31-350 Navajo Chieftain	31-7405402	G-BBXX N66869	26. 4.94	
G-NERI	PA-28-181 Archer II	28-7890483	G-BMKO N31880	19. 3.93	Crashed on approach 1 mile east of Lulsgate on 6.8.98. Canx as destroyed 24.11.98. (Remains stored 1/99 Bristol/ Lulsgate)
G-NESI	Van's RV-6	PFA/181-13381		24.11.98	
G-NESS	Rockwell Commander 685	12022	N57022	7.12.78	To N1525 9/81. Canx 21.9.81.
G-NESU	PBN BN-2B-20 Islander	2260	G-BTVN	30. 5.95	
G-NESV	Eurocopter EC-135T-1	0067		4. 2.99	
G-NETY	PA-18-150 Super Cub	1809108	N4159K	8. 9.95	
G-NEUF	Bell 206L-1 LongRanger II	45548	G-BVVV D-HUGO/OE-KXT/C-GLMM	20.11.98	
G-NEUS	Brugger MB.2 Colibri	PFA/43-10392		2.11.78	No Permit issued. Canx by CAA 16.7.91.
G-NEVA	PA-31-310 Navajo B	31-701	G-BGVO F-BSGU/G-AZAC/N6791L	9. 8.79	To N290WS 8/83. Canx 1.8.83.
G-NEVL	Gates LearJet 35A	35A-662		2.10.90	To G-BUSX 1/93. Canx.
G-NEVS	Aero Designs Pulsar XP	PFA/202-12283		12.11.93	
G-NEWR	PA-31-350 Navajo Chieftain	31-7952129	N35251	23. 8.79	
G-NEWS	Bell 206B JetRanger III	2547	N18098	29.11.78	
G-NEWT	Beechcraft A35 Bonanza (Mod. to C35 engine status)	D-1168	G-APVW EI-BIL/G-APVW/N9866F/4X-ACL/ IDF/AF 0604/ZS-BTE	28. 2.90	
G-NEWU	Partenavia P.68C Victor	219	G-BHJX	12. 8.81	To G-SITU 8/84. Canx.
G-NEWZ	Bell 206B JetRanger III	4475	C-GBVZ	28. 1.98	
G-NEXT	Aerospatiale AS.355F1 Twin Squirrel	5115	G-WDKR G-NEXT/I-NEXT/G-NEXT/G-OMAV	21.10.87	To MOD as ZJ635 10/99.
G-NFLC	Handley Page 137 Jetstream 1 (Production No. 22)	222	G-AXUI G-8-9	12.12.95	
G-NGBI	American Aviation AA-5B Tiger	AA5B-1104	G-JAKK G-BHWI/N3752E	5. 3.85	Overshot landing at Thurrock on 12.7.90, crossed over a road and came to rest in a hedge. Canx as WFU 7.11.96.
G-NGRM	Spezio DAL-1 Tuholer (built by R.Mitchell)	134	N6RM	14. 8.90	
G-NHRH	PA-28-140 Cherokee	28-22807	OY-BIC SE-EZP	19. 5.82	
G-NHVH	Maule M.5-235C Lunar Rocket	7276C	N5634N	4. 7.80	
G-NIAL	Aerospatiale AS.350B Ecureuil	1745		29. 2.84	To G-PLMD 5/88. Canx.
G-NICE	Short SD.3-30 Var.100	SH3007	C-GTAV G-14-3007	26. 1.82	To G-BLTD 12/84. Canx.
G-NICH	Robinson R-22 Beta	0937		4. 1.89	
G-NICK(1)	CAB GY-301 Supercab	1	F-BFOV(2)	. .77R	NTU - To G-BFIS 12/77. Canx.
G-NICK(2)	PA-18-95 Super Cub (Frame No. 18-2085) (L-18C-PI)	18-2065	PH-CWA R.Netherlands AF R-79/8A-79/52-2465	17.10.79	Permit expired 26.6.85. Canx by CAA 3.4.89. (On rebuild 2/96)
G-NICO	Robinson R-22 Beta	1224		22.12.89	To G-WADS 4/96. Canx.
G-NIFR	Beechcraft 76 Duchess	ME-408	N1808A	16.12.88	To G-TRAN 3/93. Canx.
G-NIGB	Boeing 747-211B (Line No. 368)	21517	N208AE G-NIGB/(G-BMXK)/C-GXRD	18. 3.87	Restored as N208AE 2/91. Canx 11.2.91.
G-NIGE	Luscombe 8E Silvaire	3525	G-BSHG N72098/NC72098	6. 6.90	
G-NIGL	Europa Avn Europa	PFA/247-12775		6. 7.95	
G-NIGS	Thunder Ax7-65 HAFB	1663		30. 1.90	
G-NIII	BAC One-Eleven Srs.408EF	BAC.128	5N-AYV G-NIII/RP-C1/G-BIII/G-AWKJ	15. 4.85	Restored as 5N-AYV. Canx.
G-NIKD	Cameron O-120 HAFB	2480		17.12.90	To ZK-FAD. Canx 19.10.93.
G-NIKE	PA-28-181 Archer II	28-8390086	N4315N	4. 7.89	
G-NIKI	Robinson R-22 Beta	1662		30. 1.91	To G-LOLO 1/95. Canx.
G-NIKY	PA-31-350 Navajo Chieftain	31-7852027	G-BPAR N27498	21. 1.85	Restored as N27498 11/93. Canx 4.11.93.
G-NILE	Colt 77A HAFB	77A-016		14. 9.79	To OO-BLE 4/88. Canx 17.2.88.
G-NIMO	Colt 105A HAFB	2210		5. 6.92	To PH-GWJ. Canx 5.2.93.
G-NINA	PA-28-161 Cherokee Warrior II	28-7716162	G-BEUC N3507Q	29. 7.88	
G-NINB	PA-28-180 Cherokee Challenger G	28-7305234	SE-KHR OY-DLR/CS-AHY/N11C	16. 7.99	
G-NINE	Murphy Renegade 912	448 & PFA/188-12191		16. 6.93	
G-NIOS	PA-32R-301 Saratoga SP	32R-8513004	N4381Z N105DX/N4381Z	28. 9.90	
G-NIPA	Slingsby Nipper T.66 RA.45 Srs.3	S.120/1627	G-AWDD	7. 6.96	Permit expired 3.11.93. (On rebuild 2/99 at Lopham Airfield, Norfolk)
G-NIPU	Beechcraft 58PA Baron	TJ-74	N1PU N313A/N1PU/N1PT/N1899L	7. 6.88	To G-PAPU 7/89. Canx.
G-NIPY	Hughes 369HS (500HS)	124-0676S	OH-HMD SE-JAK/N65BL/N9232F	26.11.97	
G-NISR	Rockwell 690A Turbo Commander	11243	HB-GFS	10. 7.85	
G-NITA	PA-28-180 Cherokee C (Used spare frame no. 28-3807S)	28-2909	G-AVVG N7517W	16. 1.84	
G-NITE	PA-31-350 Navajo Chieftain	31-8052077	N3559A	2. 7.80	To G-BLOE 9/84. Canx.
G-NIUK	Douglas DC-10-30 (Line No. 158)	46932	9Q-CLT	27. 8.85	To N609GC 7/99. Canx 8.7.99.

Regn	Type	c/n	Previous identity	Regn date	Fate or immediate subsequent identity (if known)
G-NIUS	Reims Cessna F.172N Skyhawk II	1651		14. 3.78	To EI-BSC 12/85. Canx 9.12.85.
G-NJAG	Cessna 207 Skywagon	207-00093	D-EMDN (N91152)	2. 8.78	
G-NJAP	Cessna T.207A Skywagon	T207-00642	N1349W	6.10.83	To I-TOAD 9/84. Canx 18.9.84.
G-NJIA	BAe 146 Srs.300	E3161	B-1775 G-BSOC/B-1775/G-6-161	. 8.99	
G-NJIB	BAe 146 Srs.300	E3174	B-1776 G-BSXZ/G-6-174	. 6.99R	
G-NJIC	BAe 146 Srs.300	E3202	B-1781 G-BTUY/G-6-202	. 6.99R	
G-NJID	BAe 146 Srs.300	E3205	B-1777 G-BTVO/G-6-205	. 6.99R	
G-NJIE	BAe 146 Srs.300	E3209	B-1778 G-BVCE/G-6-209	. 6.99R	
G-NJML	PA-34-220T Seneca III	34-8333057	N8202Z	10. 4.91	Fatal crash at Bolt Farm, Canewdon on 6.3.97. Canx as destroyed 16.7.97.
G-NJSH	Robinson R-22 Beta	0780		19. 4.88	
G-NLEE	Cessna 182Q Skylane II	182-65934	G-TLTD N759EL	1.12.93	
G-NMAN	PA-31-310 Turbo Navajo	31-376	G-AXDD N9284Y	20. 7.81	To N125RS 1/84. Canx.
G-NMHS	Eurocopter AS.355N Twin Squirrel	5502	G-DPPS F-WYMM	26. 3.98	
G-NNAC	PA-18-135 Super Cub (L-21B-PI)(Frame No 18-3820)	18-3820	PH-PSW R.Netherlands AF R-130/54-2420	19. 5.81	
G-NOBI	Spezio DAL-1 Tuholer Sport (Built by N.E.Stidman) (Originally regd as a Spezio Sport HES-1)	162	N1603	28.11.90	(Stored 8/97)
G-NOBY	Rand Robinson KR-2	PFA/129-10894		29. 4.83	No CofA or Permit issued. Canx by CAA 2.9.91.
G-NOCK	Reims Cessna FR.182 Skylane RG II	0036	G-BGTK (D-EHZB)	18. 1.94	(Damaged at Top Farm, near Royston on 9.6.98)
G-NODE	American Aviation AA-5B Tiger	AA5B-1182	N4533L	22. 5.81	
G-NODY	American General AG-5B Tiger	10076	N1194C	3.10.91	
G-NOEI	Aerospatiale AS.350B Ecureuil	1190	G-MORR G-BHIU	16. 1.84	Destroyed in crash at Silverstone on 8.10.85. Canx as destroyed 22.1.87.
G-NOEL	Agusta-Bell 206B JetRanger II	8435	G-BCWN	19. 6.80	To G-RODS 6/84. Canx.
G-NOHB	PA-34-220T Seneca III	34-8133270	N220HB N9604N	7. 5.92	To N711JH 5/93. Canx 24.5.93.
G-NOIR	Bell 222	47031	G-OJLC G-OSEB/G-BNDA/A40-CG	9. 8.91	
G-NOME	Oldfield Baby Great Lakes	PFA/10-10194		25. 9.78	To G-BMIY 12/85. Canx.
G-NONI	American Aviation AA-5 Traveler	AA5-0383	G-BBDA (EI-AYL)/G-BBDA	1. 8.88	
G-NOOR	Commander Aircraft 114B	14656		6. 2.98	
G-NORC	Cessna 425 Conquest I	425-0054	(G-BICL) (N6776P)	25. 3.81	To N345GA 5/84. Canx 4.5.84.
G-NORD	SNCAC NC.854 Chardonneret	7	F-BFIS	20.10.78	(On rebuild)
G-NORM	Bell 206B JetRanger III	2401	G-BKPF EI-BFK/N50005	18. 4.83	Crashed at Brook Close Farm, Parwich, Derbyshire on 13.5.84. Canx as destroyed 26.11.84.
G-NORS	Cessna 425 Conquest I	425-0224	N1226S	13. 1.87	To D-IPAS 10/91. Canx 23.10.91.
G-NORX	Cessna 421C Golden Eagle III	421C-0647	EI-BLH G-NORX/N88600	28. 3.79	To G-OFRH 9/84. Canx.
G-NOSE	Cessna 402B	402B-0823	N98AR G-MPCU/SE-IRL/OO-TAT/(OO-SEL)/N3946C	23. 4.96	
G-NOTA	MDH MD.520N	LN-022	VR-CPD N520QP/N52113	14. 9.93	To OY-HEP 3/95. Canx 15.3.95.
G-NOTE	PA-28-181 Archer III	2843082	D-ESPI N9282N	19. 9.97	
G-NOTT	Nott ULD/2 HAFB	06		11. 6.86	
G-NOTY	Westland Scout AH.1 (Pod no. F8-4261, rear bulkhead build no. F8-4341)	F.9630	XT624	5.11.97	
G-NOVA	Cessna T.337H Turbo Super Skymaster II	337-01895	N1259S	8. 1.80	To G-BMJR 7/84. Canx.
G-NOVO	Colt AS-56 Hot-Air Airship	1067		20. 5.87	
G-NPKJ	Van's RV-6	PFA/181-13138		12. 2.98	
G-NPNP	Cameron N-105 HAFB	2959	G-BURX	18. 1.93	
G-NPWR	Cameron RX-100 HAFB (Designation unconfirmed)	2849		13. 7.92	To BBAC Museum 13.11.97. Canx as WFU 15.7.98.
G-NRDC	Norman NDN-6 Fieldmaster	004		8. 6.81	Permit to Fly expired 17.10.87. Canx by CAA 3.2.95. (Stored 8/97 at Sandown, IoW)
G-NROA	Boeing 727-217ADV (Line No. 1122)	21056	G-BKNG C-GCPB	12. 4.84	To C-GRYR 10/92. Canx 26.10.92.
G-NROY	PA-32RT-300 Lance II	32R-7985070	G-LYNN G-BGNY/N30242	26.11.93	
G-NSEW	Robinson R-44 Astro	0615		6. 7.99	
G-NSFT	PA-28-161 Warrior II	28-8516040	G-BSMZ N4391K/N9555N	20. 8.96	Damaged in forced landing near Cashmoor Inn, Dorset on 21.3.97. (Wreck stored 10/97) Canx as destroyed 28.1.98.
G-NSGI	Cessna 421C Golden Eagle III	421C-0844	N421EL XA-RAE/N421EB/(N21MW)/N421EB/N2659Z	13. 1.92	To N9AY 8/96. Canx 25.7.96.
G-NSHR	Robinson R-22 Beta	2809		8. 5.98	
G-NSOF	Pierre Robin HR.200/120B	334	(G-BYID)	4. 6.99	

Regn	Type	c/n	Previous identity	Regn date	Fate or immediate subsequent identity (if known)
G-NSTG	Reims Cessna F.150F	0058	G-ATNI	16. 8.89	
	(Wichita c/n 63499)(Taildragger conv.)		(G-ATOG)		
G-NTBI	Bell 206B JetRanger III	4107	C-FIJD	14. 6.90	To G-LILY 3/95. Canx.
G-NTEE	Robinson R-44 Astro	0024		14.12.93	
G-NTMN	Rockwell 690D Turbo Commander 900	15015	G-IBLL	3. 9.86	To N27MW. Canx 22.12.88.
			N5874N		
G-NTOO	Aerospatiale AS.365N2 Dauphin 2	0372		19.10.90	Canx 1.11.96 on sale to MoD. To MOD as ZJ165.
G-NTWO	Aerospatiale AS.365N2 Dauphin 2	6358		11. 9.90	To LN-ODB 3/99. Canx 9.3.99.
G-NUIG	Beechcraft C90-1 King Air	LJ-1035	G-BKIP	3. 9.86	To F-GLJD 4/95. Canx 7.4.95.
			N9933E		
G-NUIT	Beechcraft 99	U-70	C-GESP	19. 9.83	To D-IEXB 6/84. Canx 6.6.84.
			N8013R/N1191C		
G-NUNK	Hughes 369HS (500HS)	34-0574S	G-BMSP	13. 8.91	To N5197Y 1/93. Canx 2.9.92.
			C-GOEA		
G-NUNN	PA-24-180 Comanche	24-1344	G-AWKW	11. 3.85	To 5B-CGD(2). Canx 19.12.86.
			N6239P		
G-NUTS	Cameron Mr Peanut 35SS HAFB	711		18. 2.81	Canx as WFU 8.1.90.
G-NUTY	Aerospatiale AS.350B Ecureuil	1490	G-BXKT	20. 7.98	
			F-GXRT/N333FH/N5797V		
G-NUTZ	Aerospatiale AS.355F1 Twin Squirrel	5325	G-BLRI(2)	25.10.85	Canx 29.3.96 on sale to MoD. To RAF as ZJ139.
G-NVBF	Lindstrand LBL-210A HAFB	249		19. 5.95	
G-NVIA	Partenavia P.68C Victor	366		10. 7.87	To G-JACT 8/87. Canx.
G-NVSA	DHC.8-311A Dash Eight	451	(YR-GPN)	20.11.98	
			C-GDNG		
G-NVSB	DHC.8-311A Dash Eight	517	C-GHRI	14. 1.99	
G-NVSC	DHC.8-311A Dash Eight	5..		. .98R	(For delivery in 1999)
G-NWAC	PA-31-310 Turbo Navajo	31-7612040	G-BDUJ	18. 2.94	
			N59814		
G-NWNW	Cameron V-90 HAFB	2818		2. 4.92	Canx by CAA 4.8.98.
G-NWPA	Aerospatiale AS.355F1 Twin Squirrel	5203	G-NAAS	11. 9.92	Restored as G-BPRG 4/94. Canx.
			G-BPRG/N370E		
G-NWPB	Thunder Ax7-77Z HAFB	278		13. 5.80	Canx by CAA 27.4.90.
G-NWPI	Aerospatiale AS.355F2 Twin Squirrel	5348	F-GMAO	9. 2.94	To G-BYPA 8/99. Canx.
G-NWPR	Cameron N-77 HAFB	1181		15. 8.85	Canx by CAA 21.8.98.
	(Rebuilt with new envelope c/n 1667)				
G-NWPS	Eurocopter EC-135T-1	0063		15.10.98	
G-NYTE	Reims Cessna F.337G Super Skymaster		G-BATH	12. 5.86	
	(Wichita c/n 01465)	0056	N10631		
G-NZAA	The series from G-NZAA to G-NZAZ was allocated to New Zealand from 1921 until 1929.				
G-NZEA	The series from G-NZEA to G-NZEF was allocated to New Zealand from 1928 until 1929.				
G-NZGL	Cameron O-105 HAFB	1361		3. 9.86	
G-NZSS	Boeing-Stearman E75 (N2S-5) Kaydet	75-8611	N4325	31. 1.89	
			BuA.43517/42-109578		

G-O G-O

Regn	Type	c/n	Previous identity	Regn date	Fate or immediate subsequent identity (if known)
G-OAAA	PA-28-161 Warrior II	2816107	N9142N	8. 9.93	
G-OAAC	Airtour AH-77B HAFB	010		13. 9.88	
G-OAAL	PA-38-112 Tomahawk	38-78A0623	N4471E	25.10.88	
G-OAAS	Short SD.3-60 Var.100	SH3648	G-BLIL	19. 4.90	To SE-KCI 6/98. Canx 26.6.98.
			OY-MMB/G-BLIL/G-14-3648		
G-OABA	Boeing 737-33A	24097	VT-JAD	15. 5.98	
	(Line No. 1741)		G-BUSM/PP-SNZ/(PP-SNX)		
G-OABB	SAN Jodel D.150 Mascaret	01	F-BJST	21. 1.97	
			F-WJST		
G-OABC	Colt 69A HAFB	1159		17.11.87	
G-OADD	Boeing 737-3L9	24570	9V-TRC	20. 4.99	
	(Line No. 1800)		OY-MME		
G-OABE	Boeing 737-4Y0	24545	EC-ETB	29. 4.98	To PT-TDE 11/98. Canx 2.11.98.
	(Line No. 1805)		EC-401/C-FVND		
G-OABF	Boeing 737-4Y0	24688	EC-FZT	19. 6.98	To EC-GYK 10/98. Canx 14.10.98.
	(Line No. 1876)		EC-738/9M-MJI/(G-OOAB)		
G-OABG	Hughes 369E (500E)	0039E		16. 3.84	Destroyed in fatal crash 5 miles north of Alton Towers on 19.10.96. Canx as destroyed 30.1.97.
G-OABI	Cessna 421C Golden Eagle III	421C-0664		8. 5.79	To N421G 10/92. Canx 1.10.92.
G-OABL	Boeing 737-33A	24096	VT-JAC	6. 5.98	
	(Line No. 1739)		G-BUSL/PP-SNW		
G-OABO	Enstrom F-28A	097	G-BAIB	10. 7.98	
G-OABR	American General AG-5B Tiger	10124	C-GZLA	15. 4.98	
			N256ER		
G-OABY	Agusta-Bell 206B JetRanger II	8434	G-BCWM	13. 9.91	To OE-XDD 3/93. Canx 25.3.93.
G-OACE	Valentin Taifun 17E	1017	D-KCBA	22. 1.87	(Open storage at Enstone in 6/98 minus starboard wing).
G-OACG	PA-34-200T Seneca II	34-7870177	G-BUNR	10. 3.94	
			EI-CFI/N9245C		

Regn	Type	c/n	Previous identity	Regn date	Fate or immediate subsequent identity (if known)
G-OACI	Socata MS.893E Rallye 180GT	13086	G-DOOR EI-BHD/F-GBCF	5. 5.98	
G-OACP	OGMA DHC.1 Chipmunk 20 (Portuguese-built)	OGMA-35	(CS-DAO) Portuguese AF 1345	20. 8.96	
G-OACS	Bell 206B JetRanger III	3786	G-OCAP N18096	4. 2.86	Restored as G-OCAP. Canx.
G-OADE	Reims Cessna F.177RG Cardinal	0049	G-AZKH (PH-LTH)/G-AZKH	20. 5.82	Damaged in forced landing near Reading on 27.4.86. (Wreck to Coventry by road on 2.5.86) Rebuilt & re-regd as G-TOTO in 8/89. Canx.
G-OADS	Cessna 401	401-0165	G-OROG G-ZEUS/G-ODJM/G-BSIX/G-CAFE(2)/G-AWXM/N4065Q	4. 4.86	To 5Y-BGW 4/90. Canx 17.4.90.
G-OADT	Beechcraft 200 Super King Air	BB-501	G-KBCA N518F/N571SS/SE-GHK	26. 1.89	To G-BSEO 4/90. Canx.
G-OADY	Beechcraft 76 Duchess	ME-56	N5022M	27.10.86	
G-OAEL	American Aviation AA-5A Cheetah	AA5A-0663	N26706	14. 6.89	To G-OPWK 5/92. Canx.
G-OAER	Lindstrand LBL-105A HAFB	359		4. 3.96	
G-OAEX	Short SD.3-60 Var.100	SH3628	G-SALU (SE-IXO)/G-SALU/OY-MMC/G-BKZR/G-14-3628	9. 3.89	Restored as G-BKZR 8/91. Canx.
G-OAFB	Beechcraft B200 Super King Air	BB-1235	N7247R	1. 4.86	To D-IZZZ 5/92. Canx 28.2.92.
G-OAFC	Airtour AH-56 HAFB	011		15. 6.89	Canx as WFU 17.1.96. To G-BWPL 19.3.96.
G-OAFT	Cessna 152 II	152-85177	G-BNKM N6161Q	19. 4.88	
G-OAFY	Aerospatiale SA.341G Gazelle Srs.1	1155	G-SFTH G-BLAP/N62406	26. 5.89	To G-PAGS 3/96. Canx.
G-OAHB	Canadair (CL-30) T-33AN Silver Star Mk.3	T33-261	CF-IHB CAF 133261/RCN 21261	9. 5.74	Canx as WFU 15.9.81. To (G-BHOE)/G-JETT 6/82.
G-OAHC	Beechcraft F33C Bonanza	CJ-133	G-BTTF PH-BND	2. 9.91	
G-OAHF	Boeing 757-27B (Line No. 169)	24136	OY-SHF PH-AHF	12. 4.91	To 4X-EBF 5/96. Canx 14.5.96.
G-OAHI	Boeing 757-27B (Line No. 178)	24137	(G-BSUB) PH-AHI/OY-SHI/PH-ANI	23. 1.91	Restored as PH-AHI. Canx 21.1.92.
G-OAHK	Boeing 757-27B (Line No. 215)	24291	(G-BSUA) PH-AHK	8. 2.91	To N250LA 12/93. Canx 29.11.93.
G-OAIM	Hughes 369HS (500C)	45-0728S	G-BDFP	16. 7.82	Fatal crash in forced landing at Felstead, 7m N of Chelmsford on 31.8.90. Canx by CAA 8.11.90.
G-OAIR	Embraer EMB.110P1 Bandeirante	110-222	PT-GMO	15. 9.79	To N4582Q 12/83. Canx 16.12.83.
G-OAJB	Cyclone Ax2000	7281	G-MZFJ	16. 2.99	
G-OAJF	BAe 146 Srs.300	E3118	HB-IXZ G-6-118/G-OAJF	7. 6.88	To D-AQUA 4/96. Canx 22.4.96.
G-OAJH	American Aviation AA-5A Cheetah	AA5A-0893	G-KILT G-BJFA/N27169	4. 4.86	To G-CCAT 1/92. Canx.
G-OAJS	PA-39 Twin Comanche C/R	39-15	G-BCIO N49JA/N57RG/G-BCIO/N8860Y	9. 3.94	
G-OAKA	BAe Jetstream Srs.3102	640	G-BUFM G-LAKH/G-BUFM/N410MX/G-31-640	12. 7.96	To G-LOVA 5/98. Canx.
G-OAKC	PA-31-350 Navajo Chieftain	31-7952247	G-WSSC EI-BRC/G-WSSC/N3543W	27. 4.89	To N2245P 4/94. Canx 28.3.94.
G-OAKI	BAe Jetstream Srs.3102	718	N417MX G-31-718	5. 5.92	To SX-BSR 6/99. Canx 3.6.99.
G-OAKJ	BAe Jetstream Srs.3202	795	G-BOTJ G-OAKJ/G-BOTJ/G-31-795	20. 7.89	
G-OAKK	BAe Jetstream Srs.3112	829	G-BSIW HB-AED/G-31-829/C-FCPG/G-31-829	7. 9.93	To G-OEDL 9/94. Canx.
G-OAKL	Beechcraft 200 Super King Air	BB-133	G-BJZG SE-GSU/N2133L	6. 9.82	To N113RL 12/95. Canx 14.12.95.
G-OAKM	Beechcraft 200 Super King Air	BB-55	G-BCUZ N9755S	11. 8.87	To N200BC 1/93. Canx 22.1.93.
G-OAKP	Partenavia P.68C Victor	231	G-BJRZ	1. 9.93	Restored as G-BJRZ 2.9.93. Canx.
G-OAKS	Cessna 421C Golden Eagle III	421C-0612	N88620	4. 4.79	To G-KYIN 3/89. Canx.
G-OAKZ	Beechcraft C90A King Air	LJ-1170	N3085Y	27.10.88	To G-SVSS 6/92. Canx.
G-OALA	Airbus A.320-231	247	EI-TLH N247RX/F-WWDK	30. 5.95	Restored as EI-TLH 11/96. Canx 5.11.96.
G-OALD	Socata TB-20 Trinidad	490	N54TB F-GBLL	17. 3.88	
G-OALF	Dornier 228-202K	8009	G-MLDO PH-SDO/D-IDON/D-CATI/SX-BHB/D-IDON/(PH-HAL)/D-IDON	18. 8.88	To G-MAFE 12/92. Canx.
G-OALS	Colt Football SS HAFB	2174		29. 5.92	To PH-LEV 6/95. Canx 14.6.95.
G-OAMG	Bell 206B JetRanger III	2901	G-COAL	25. 2.86	
G-OAMH	Agusta A.109A	7170		16. 1.80	To G-ROPE 5/84. Canx.
G-OAML	Cameron AML-105 HAFB	3881		4.12.96	
G-OAMP	Reims Cessna F.177RG Cardinal (Wichita c/n 00098)	0006	G-AYPF	30.11.93	
G-OAMS	Boeing 737-37Q (Line No. 2961)	28548		9.12.97	
G-OAMT	PA-31-350 Navajo Chieftain	31-7752105	G-BXKS N350RC/EC-EBN/N27230	23. 1.98	
G-OAMY	Cessna 152 II	152-84639	N6214M	5. 8.85	

Regn	Type	c/n	Previous identity	Regn date	Fate or immediate subsequent identity (if known)
G-OANC	PA-28-161 Warrior II	28-7716206	G-BFAD N5850V	29. 4.87	Overshot runway on landing at Old Warden on 12.4.99.
G-OANI	PA-28-161 Warrior II	28-8416091	N43570	8. 1.91	Damaged on landing at Upton Farm, Dover on 16.6.96. (Wreck at Kidlington 9/96)
G-OANN	Zenair CH.601HDS Zodiac	PFA/162-12932		2. 2.96	
G-OANT	PA-23-250 Aztec F	27-7654188	G-TRFM N62738	1. 3.89	To N250KK 12/93. Canx 15.12.93.
G-OAPA	Pilatus PC-6/B2-H2 Turbo-Porter	815		5. 4.82	To HB-FKF. Canx 2.2.88.
G-OAPB	Colt Bottle 14SS HAFB	4406		9.11.98	
G-OAPE	Cessna T.303 Crusader	T303-00245	N303MF D-INKA/N9960C/N303HW/N9960C	3. 2.99	
G-OAPR	Brantly B-2B	446	(G-BPST) N2280U	21. 4.89	
G-OAPW	Glaser-Dirks DG-400	4-268		17. 4.90	
G-OARA	PA-28R-201 Arrow	2837002	N802ND N9622N	28.10.98	
G-OARC	PA-28RT-201 Arrow IV	28R-7918009	G-BMVE N3071K	17. 8.99	
G-OARG	Cameron C-80 HAFB	3379		20.10.94	
G-OART	PA-23-250 Aztec D	27-4293	G-AXKD N6936Y	26.11.93	
G-OARV	ARV1 Super 2 (Rebuilt using Kit No.008 following accident 24.5.86)	001 & PFA/152-11060		18. 6.84	
G-OASH	Robinson R-22 Beta	0761	N2627Z	13. 6.88	
G-OASP	Aerospatiale AS.355F2 Twin Squirrel	5479	F-GJAJ F-WYMH	3. 8.95	
G-OAST	Cessna TR.182 Turbo Skylane RG II	01115	(N756MM)	4. 9.79	To F-GDLM 5/83. Canx 25.4.83.
G-OATC	PA-31-310 Turbo Navajo C	31-7812103	G-OJPW G-BGCC/N27703	6. 8.90	Restored as N27703 11/92, then to N36SG 3/93. Canx 5.11.92.
G-OATD	Short SD.3-30 Var.100	SH3096	G-14-3096 N332SB/G-BKSV/G-14-3096	23. 2.89	Badly damaged by terrorist bomb at Belfast Harbour on 27.11.89. Fuselage in open store 12/94 at Belfast. Canx as destroyed 10.4.90.
G-OATP(1)	BAe ATP	2001		. .86R	NTU - To G-MATP 1/86. Canx.
G-OATP(2)	BAe ATP	2005	G-BZWW (N375AE)/G-BZWW	20.12.88	To G-MANM 10/94. Canx.
G-OATS	PA-38-112 Tomahawk	38-78A0007	N9659N	14. 3.78	
G-OATV	Cameron V-77 HAFB	2149		14. 2.90	
G-OAUS	Sikorsky S-76A	760219	(G-BKGU) N3122M	11. 8.82	
G-OAVW	BN-2A Mk.III-1 Trislander	319	G-AZLJ G-51-319	3. 2.86	To G-OREG 1/87. Canx.
G-OAVX	Beechcraft 200 Super King Air	BB-210	G-IBCA G-BMCA/N5657N	1. 9.88	To G-FRYI 3/96. Canx.
G-OAWA	Cessna 421C Golden Eagle III	421C-0608	N88611	3. 5.79	To N421DR 8/80. Canx.
G-OAWS	Cameron 77A HAFB	4340		23. 4.98	
G-OAWY	Cessna 340A II	340A-0743	N2671F	13.10.88	To N98LL 2/93. Canx 18.2.93.
G-OBAA	Beechcraft B200 Super King Air	BB-1367	N5657N	15. 5.90	To G-DBAA 9/97. Canx.
G-OBAC	Aerospatiale AS.350B Ecureuil	1040	G-EORR G-FERG/G-BGCW	25. 2.83	To ZK-HYS 3/87. Canx 29.1.87.
G-OBAE	HS.125 Srs.700B	257094		31. 1.80	To HB-VEK 8/83. Canx 23.8.83.
G-OBAF	BAe 146 Srs.100	E1004	(G-SCHH) (G-BIAG)	28. 5.81	To RAF as ZD695 in 9/83. Canx 3.5.83.
G-OBAL	Mooney M.20J (201LM)	24-1601	N56569	27.11.86	
G-OBAM	Bell 206B JetRanger III	4511	N6379U	25. 5.99	
G-OBAN	SAN Jodel D.140B Mousquetaire II	80	G-ATSU F-BKSA	20. 2.92	
G-OBAT	Reims Cessna F.152 II	1771	G-OENT G-OBAT/(D-EMIN)	25. 7.80	DBER when crashed on take-off from Sladbury's Farm Strip, Holland-on-Sea on 11.12.92. Canx by CAA 8.3.99.
G-OBAY	Bell 206B JetRanger	276	G-BVWR C-GNXQ/N4714R	27. 7.98	
G-OBBC	Colt 90A HAFB	1358		11. 5.89	
G-OBBO	Cessna 182S Skylane II	182-80534	N7274Z	8. 6.99	
G-OBCA	Cessna 421C Golden Eagle III	421C-0471	N6812C	22. 5.78	To G-SAIR 4/86. Canx.
G-OBDA	Diamond DA-20-A1 Katana	10260		2. 7.98	
G-OBEA	BAe Jetstream Srs.3102-01	607	(N.....) G-OBEA/G-31-47	29. 3.83	To N607BA 7/98. Canx 16.7.98.
G-OBED	PA-34-200T Seneca II	34-7870345	N36579	17. 1.86	To 5H-JET 6/95. Canx 13.6.95.
G-OBEL	Cessna 500 Citation I (Unit No.220)	500-0220	G-BOGA N932HA/N93WD/N5220J	31. 1.89	To (N619EA)/G-ORHE 3/96. Canx.
G-OBEN	Cessna 152 II	152-81856	G-NALI G-BHVM/N67477	16. 8.93	
G-OBEV	Europa Avn Europa	PFA/247-12813		3. 2.98	
G-OBEY	PA-23-250 Aztec C	27-2569	G-BAAJ SE-EIU	11. 5.79	
G-OBFC	PA-28-161 Warrior II	2816118	N9252X	15. 7.96	
G-OBFS	PA-28-161 Warrior III	2842039	N41274	4.12.98	
G-OBGC	Socata TB-20 Trinidad	1898		13. 5.99	

Regn	Type	c/n	Previous identity	Regn date	Fate or immediate subsequent identity (if known)
G-OBHD	Short SD.3-60 Var.200	SH3714	G-BNDK G-OBHD/G-BNDK/G-14-3714	20. 1.87	
G-OBHH	Bell 206B JetRanger	405	G-WLLY G-RODY/G-ROGR/G-AXMM/N1469W	27. 3.96	Restored as G-WLLY 6/97. Canx.
G-OBHX	Reims Cessna F.172H Skyhawk	0487	G-AWMU	20. 8.86	To G-BYBD 7/98. Canx.
G-OBIA	Embraer EMB.110P1 Bandeirante	110-219	PT-GML	3. 9.79	To G-BKBG 5/82. Canx.
G-OBIB	Colt 120A HAFB	4229		9. 1.98	
G-OBIG	Aerospatiale AS.355F1 Twin Squirrel	5157	G-SVJM G-BOPS/I-MOST	28. 8.96	
G-OBIL	Robinson R-22 Beta	0792		10. 5.88	
G-OBIO	Robinson R-22 Beta	1402	N7724M	29. 6.98	
G-OBIP	Robinson R-22 Beta	1195		28.12.89	To EI-TKI 8/91. Canx 12.8.91.
G-OBJH	Colt 77A HAFB	2569		11. 3.94	
G-OBLC	Beechcraft 76 Duchess	ME-249	N6635R	3. 6.87	
G-OBLD	Agusta-Bell 206B JetRanger III	8716		15.12.88	To G-OMEC 1/90. Canx.
G-OBLE	CASA I.131 Jungmann	2141	E3B-541 Spanish AF	31. 3.80	To SE-AMD 11/84. Canx 5.11.84.
G-OBLK	Short SD.3-60 Var.200	SH3712	G-BNDI G-OBLK/G-BNDI/G-14-3712	20. 1.87	
G-OBLN	DH.115 Vampire T.11 (Regd with nacelle no. DHP.48700)	15664	XE956	14. 9.95	(On rebuild 2/96)
G-OBLT	BAe 125 Srs.800B	258164	OK-2 Botswana DF/OK-1/G-5-654	15. 7.92	To R.Saudi AF as 130 in 12/94. Canx 27.2.95.
G-OBMA	Boeing 737-33A (Line No. 1471)	23831		23.10.87	To VH-CZV 11/93. Canx 15.11.93.
G-OBMB	Boeing 737-33A (Line No. 1473)	23832		23.10.87	To VH-CZW 12/93. Canx 16.12.93.
G-OBMC	Boeing 737-33A (Line No. 1654)	24030		9. 1.89	To XA-SGJ 1/94. Canx 31.1.94.
G-OBMD	Boeing 737-33A (Line No. 1669)	24092		10. 2.89	To G-IGOI 12/98. Canx.
G-OBME	Boeing 737-33A (Line No. 1603)	23867		14.10.88	Destroyed in crash at Kegworth, near East Midlands Airport on 8.1.89. Canx as destroyed 11.4.89.
G-OBMF	Boeing 737-4Y0 (Line No. 1616)	23868		14.10.88	
G-OBMG	Boeing 737-4Y0 (Line No. 1647)	23870	(TC-...) N1791B	31. 3.89	To OK-TVR 3/99. Canx 29.3.99.
G-OBMH	Boeing 737-33A (Line No. 1831)	24460		19. 3.90	
G-OBMI	Boeing 737-33A (Line No. 1833)	24461		. .89R	NTU - To G-OBMJ 3/90. Canx.
G-OBMJ	Boeing 737-33A (Line No. 1833)	24461	(G-OBMI)	22. 3.90	
G-OBMK	Boeing 737-4S3 (Line No. 2255)	25596		6. 4.92	To G-OGBA 4/97. Canx.
G-OBML	Boeing 737-3Q8 (Line No. 1666)	24300	SE-DLA G-KKUH	20.11.91	To B-2980 5/97. Canx 12.5.97.
G-OBMM	Boeing 737-4Y0 (Line No. 2176)	25177		4.12.91	
G-OBMN	Boeing 737-46B (Line No. 1663)	24123	G-BOPJ N1790B	5.11.91	To EC-GRX 1/98. Canx 19.12.97.
G-OBMO	Boeing 737-4Q8 (Line No. 2239)	26280		13. 3.92	
G-OBMP	Boeing 737-3Q8 (Line No. 2193)	24963		8. 1.92	
G-OBMR	Boeing 737-5Y0 (Line No. 2220)	25185	XA-RJS	7. 5.96	
G-OBMS	Reims Cessna F.172N Skyhawk II	1584	OO-BWA (PH-AXC)/(OO-HWA)/D-EBYX	16. 4.84	(Stored at Sherburn in 6/98)
G-OBMW	American Aviation AA-5 Traveler	AA5-0805	G-BDFV	4. 7.79	
G-OBMX	Boeing 737-59D (Line No. 2028)	25065	SE-DNE (SE-DND)	23. 9.93	
G-OBMY	Boeing 737-59D (Line No. 2186)	26419	SE-DNI	30. 9.93	To OY-SEG 9/98. Canx 29.9.98.
G-OBMZ	Boeing 737-53A (Line No. 1868)	24754	SE-DNC	22. 9.93	
G-OBNF	Cessna 310K	310K-0109	F-BNFI N7009L	20. 7.94	
G-OBOB	HS.125 Srs.3B	25069	G-BAXL VH-ECF	25. 7.89	Crashed 3 miles west of Columbia, MO, USA on 31.1.90. Remains to White Industries, Bates City, MO, USA. Canx as destroyed 12.4.90.
G-OBOH	Short SD.3-60 Var.200	SH3713	G-BNDJ G-14-3713	20. 1.87	To EI-CPR 2/99. Canx 1.2.99.
G-OBOY	Aviat Pitts S-2B Special	5310		10. 7.95	To N104FU 4/99. Canx 16.3.99.
G-OBOZ	Boeing 757-23APF (Line No. 340)	24971	N5002K	29. 8.91	To N573CA 9/92. Canx 8.9.92.
G-OBPG	Brantly B.2B	483	G-AWIO	7.10.87	Restored as G-AWIO 6/92. Canx.
G-OBPL	Embraer EMB.110P2 Bandeirante	110-199	PH-FVB G-OEAB/G-BKWB/G-CHEV/(PT-GLR)	27.11.98	
G-OBRU	Bell 206B JetRanger II	1376	G-GOBP G-BOUY/N5450M/N1PE/XC-GUW	28. 4.94	To G-LGRM 1/99. Canx.

Regn	Type	c/n	Previous identity	Regn date	Fate or immediate subsequent identity (if known)
G-OBRY	Cameron N-180 HAFB	3010		1. 3.93	
G-OBSF	American Aviation AA-5A Cheetah	AA5A-0374	G-ODSF G-BEUW/N6158A	21. 9.88	Damaged on landing at Blackbushe on 8.2.97. Repaired & re-regd as G-ODAE 11/97. Canx.
G-OBSM	HS.125 Srs.700B	257189	G-BKHK	.11.82R	NTU - To G-OSAM 11/82. Canx.
G-OBSV	Partenavia P.68B Observer	329-20/OB		20. 6.85	To EC-GHS 8/96. Canx 9.5.96.
G-OBTS	Cameron C-80 HAFB	3589		18. 4.95	
G-OBTW	Bell 206B JetRanger	779	N2VG N196PB/N196P/N2946W	20. 5.96	Fatal crash at Little Hadham, Herts on 18.3.97. Canx as destroyed 28.7.97.
G-OBUD	Colt 69A HAFB	698		26. 6.85	Canx as WFU 29.4.97.
G-OBUS	PA-28-181 Archer II	28-7990242	(G-BMTT) N3002K	4. 8.86	Struck a bank & crashed on the motor racing circuit at Goodwood on 18.4.89. CofA expired 14.8.89. Canx as destroyed 30.8.89. (Instructional Airframe 8/97)
G-OBUY	Colt 69A HAFB	2031		7. 8.91	
G-OBWA	BAC One-Eleven Srs.518FG	BAC.232	G-BDAT G-AYOR	1.12.92	
G-OBWB	BAC One-Eleven Srs.518FG	BAC.202	G-BDAS G-AXMH	8.12.92	
G-OBWC	BAC One-Eleven Srs.520FN	BAC.230	G-BEKA 4X-BAR/G-16-22/G-BEKA/PP-SDR	8.12.92	(Stored 4/99 Southend)
G-OBWD	BAC One-Eleven Srs.518FG	BAC.203	G-BDAE G-AXMI	14. 1.93	
G-OBWE	BAC One-Eleven Srs.531FS	BAC.242	G-BJYM TI-LRI/TI-1095C	7. 4.93	
G-OBWF	BAC One-Eleven Srs.509EW	BAC.210	G-AXYD	7. 4.93	(Still painted as G-AXYD and officially sold to Nigeria 13.4.95) (Stored 1/98 at Southend; scrapped in 12/98)
G-OBWG	BAC One-Eleven Srs.509EW	BAC.184	G-AWWX	7. 4.93	(Still painted as G-AWWX and officially sold to Nigeria 13.4.95) (Stored 1/98 at Southend; scrapped in 9/98)
G-OBWH	BAC One-Eleven Srs.515FB	BAC.208	G-BJYL TI-LRK/G-AZPE/D-ALAS	7. 4.93	NTU - To 5N-ENO 7/95. Canx 13.4.95.
G-OBWI	BAC One-Eleven Srs.518FG	BAC.205	G-BCWA G-AXMK/VP-LAK/G-AXMK/TG-ARA/G-AXMK	. .93R	NTU - Marks not worn. Broken up at Southend 3/93. Canx.
G-OBWJ	BAC One-Eleven Srs.531FS	BAC.244	G-BJMV TI-LRJ/TI-1096C	. .93R	NTU - Marks not worn. Scrapped at Southend in 8/98.
G-OBWK	BAC One-Eleven Srs.517FE	BAC.198	G-BCXR G-BCCV/VP-LAN/VP-BCQ/(G-AXLL)/G-16-12	. .93R	NTU - Marks not worn. Broken up at Southend 3/93. Canx.
G-OBWL	BAe ATP	2057	G-11-057 (G-OBWL)/G-11-057	26. 9.97	
G-OBWM	BAe ATP	2058	G-11-058	22.12.97	
G-OBWN	BAe ATP	2059	G-11-059 G-BVEO/G-11-059	22.12.98	
G-OBWO	BAe ATP	2060	(EI-COS) G-11-060	16. 6.98	
G-OBYA	Boeing 767-304ER (Line No. 610)	28039	D-AGYA G-OBYA	15. 5.96	
G-OBYB	Boeing 767-304ER (Line No. 613)	28040		17. 5.96	
G-OBYC	Boeing 767-304ER (Line No. 614)	28041	D-AGYC G-OBYC	21. 5.96	
G-OBYD	Boeing 767-304ER (Line No. 649)	28042		4. 3.97	
G-OBYE	Boeing 767-304ER (Line No. 691)	28979		26. 2.98	To D-AGYE 10/98. Canx 30.10.98.
G-OBYF	Boeing 767-304ER (Line No. 705)	28208		8. 6.98	To D-AGYF 6/98. Canx 9.6.98.
G-OBYG	Boeing 767-304ER (Line No. 733)	29137		13. 1.99	(Marks D-AGYG reserved since 8.9.98)
G-OBYH	Boeing 767-304ER (Line No. 737)	28883		4. 2.99	To D-AGYH 3/99. Canx 22.3.99.
G-OBYT	Agusta-Bell 206A JetRanger	8237	G-BNRC Oman AF 601	30. 1.95	
G-OCAA	HS.125 Srs.700B	257091	G-BHLF	22. 4.92	
G-OCAB	Gulfstream American GA-7 Cougar	GA7-0107	G-BICF N8500H/N29707	14. 5.86	To G-VJAI 12/87. Canx.
G-OCAD	Sequoia F.8L Falco	PFA/100-12114		8. 6.92	(Damaged in crash on take-off from Tatenhill on 10.8.97)
G-OCAL	Partenavia P.68B Victor	182	G-BGMY	19. 6.79	To G-LOUP 2/89. Canx.
G-OCAM	American Aviation AA-5A Cheetah	AA5A-0741	G-BLHO OO-RTJ/OO-HRN	24. 3.94	
G-OCAN	Cessna 340A	340A-0990	D-ICIC (N3970C)	17. 3.89	To VR-CHR. Canx 27.3.92.
G-OCAP	Bell 206B JetRanger III	3786	G-OACS G-OCAP/N18096	12. 1.84	To EC-FHX. Canx 26.6.91.
G-OCAR	Colt 77A HAFB (Originally regd as a Thunder 77A with same c/n)	1099		6. 8.87	
G-OCAS	Short SD.3-30 Var.100	SH3082	G-BJUK G-14-3082	3. 6.82	Restored as G-14-3082/G-BJUK 12/84. Canx.
G-OCAT	Eiri PIK-20E	20226	(D-KGAT) G-OCAT	19.11.79	
G-OCAW	Lindstrand Bananas SS HAFB	388		22. 5.96	
G-OCAZ	American Aviation AA-5B Tiger	AA5B-0466	G-OMED G-BERL/N6157A	9. 5.94	Fatal collision with ASK.13 BGA.4221 near Westcott on 5.5.96. Canx as destroyed 8.10.96.
G-OCBA	HS.125 Srs.3B	25132	EI-WDC G-OCBA/G-MRFB/G-AZVS/OY-DKP	2. 5.89	Restored as EI-WDC 10/94. Canx 4.10.94.

Regn	Type	c/n	Previous identity	Regn date	Fate or immediate subsequent identity (if known)
G-OCBB	Bell 206B JetRanger II	969	G-BASE N18093	16.11.90	
G-OCBC	Cameron A-120 HAFB	2399		22.11.90	To G-BWCD 4/95. Canx.
G-OCBS	Lindstrand LBL-210A HAFB	602		21. 7.99	
G-OCCA	PA-32R-301 Saratoga SP	32R-8113030	G-BRIX N8319S	12. 5.89	To N422LB 7/99. Canx 20.7.99.
G-OCCB	Robinson R-44 Astro	0159	G-STMM	25. 4.96	To G-THEL 9/98. Canx.
G-OCCC	BAe 125 Srs.800B	258013	G-5-14	13. 9.84	To N334 3/94. Canx 28.3.94.
G-OCCI	BAe 125 Srs.800B	258201	(D-C...) G-5-699	6.12.91	Canx as TWFU 24.3.95. To G-BWSY 5/96.
G-OCDB	Cessna 550 Citation II (Unit No.601)	550-0601	G-ELOT (N1303M)	20. 8.92	
G-OCDS	Aviamilano F.8L Falco Srs.II	114	G-VEGL OO-MEN/I-VEGL	6. 9.85	
G-OCEA	Short SD.3-60 Var.200	SH3762	N162CN N162SB/G-BRMX	26.10.95	(Stored 6/96 at Biggin Hill)
G-OCFR	Gates LearJet 35A	35A-614	G-VIPS G-SOVN/HB-VJC/G-PJET/N3815G	15. 6.92	
G-OCFS	PA-23-250 Aztec E	27-7305124	G-BBFU N40364	25. 2.86	To G-TRCO 2/90. Canx.
G-OCGJ	Robinson R-22 Beta	1094		8. 8.89	To G-BYCU 11/98. Canx.
G-OCHA	Boeing 737-3Q8 (Line No. 1506)	24068	G-BNNJ (N881BV)	21. 3.94	To SE-DTA 12/94. Canx 6.12.94.
G-OCHD	Beechcraft 300LW Super King Air	FA-95	N7259B	16. 3.87	To N125RP 7/90. Canx 2.7.90.
G-OCHL	Bell 206B JetRanger III	3235	N3903N	11. 5.88	To 5N-BAP 12/93. Canx 23.12.93.
G-OCIA	Short SD.3-60 Var.300	SH3751	G-BPFS	22. 2.89	To G-REGN 10/89. Canx.
G-OCIN	Cessna 150K	150-71728	EI-CIN G-BSXG/N6228G	6. 4.99	
G-OCJK	Schweizer Hughes 269C (300C)	S.1294	N69A	10.12.87	
G-OCJR	Aerospatiale SA.341G Gazelle Srs.1	1274	G-BRGS F-GEQA(2)/N341SG/(N341P)/N341SG/N47295	27. 6.90	To G-OGAZ 1/94. Canx.
G-OCJS	Cameron V-90 HAFB	2805		24. 4.92	
G-OCJW	Cessna 182R Skylane II	182-68316	G-SJGM N357WC	18. 4.97	
G-OCLH	BAe 146 RJ85	E2268	G-6-268	1. 9.95	To D-AVRH 10/95. Canx 10.10.95.
G-OCME	BN-2A Mk.III-1 Trislander	262	G-AYWI G-51-262	14. 5.86	Badly damaged in forced landing in a field near Hale, Cheshire on 9.2.87. Canx as destroyed 22.3.89. (Stored in scrapyard 1/93)
G-OCML	American Aviation AA-5A Cheetah	AA5A-0662	G-JAVA N26705	9. 9.91	To G-JWDG 9.10.91. Canx.
G-OCND	Cameron O-77 HAFB	1020		6. 2.84	Canx by CAA 19.5.95.
G-OCNW	BAC One-Eleven Srs.201AC	012	EI-BWL N105EX/G-ASJH	26.10.90	Broken up at Southend 8.95 and later taken to St. Leonards near Hurn. Then used in a simulated air crash scene (marked as 'I-ZACF') for the new ITV drama series 'Call Red'. This featured the work of a helicopter air ambulance team and the episode concerned was shown on TV on 15.1.96. Canx by CAA 8.12.95.
G-OCOP	Bell 206LT Long Ranger 4 (Mod)	52062	N58968	29. 7.94	Reserved as N58968 in 5/97, re-regd as G-BXMP 10/97. Canx.
G-OCPA	Eiri PIK-20E Srs.1	20213		12. 6.79	DBR at Lasham on 15.7.79. Canx. To OH-605.
G-OCPC	Reims Cessna FA.152 Aerobat	0343		20. 1.78	
G-OCPF	PA-32-300 Cherokee Six	32-7640082	G-BOCH N9292K	22. 9.97	
G-OCPI	Cessna 500 Citation I (Unit No.093)	500-0093	G-OXEC N611SW/OO-FBY/PH-CTB/N593CC	23. 7.91	To N62BR /97. Canx 10.9.97.
G-OCPL	American Aviation AA-5A Cheetah	AA5A-0352	G-RCPW G-BERM/N6141A	12. 7.89	Badly damaged when struck by PA-28 G-ATTU as it landed at Elstree on 27.6.92. (Stored 1/93) Canx as WFU 5.3.97.
G-OCPS	Colt 120A HAFB	2047		27. 5.92	
G-OCRI	Colomban MC-15 Cri-Cri	524 & PFA/133-12288		24. 6.92	
G-OCRP	Bell 206L-1 Long Ranger	45232	G-BWCU N2758A/C-FPET/N2758A/JA9234/N27545/JA9234	18.12.97	Canx 29.1.99 on sale to Antigua. To V4-AAB.
G-OCSB	Cessna 525 Citation Jet	525-0177	N1280A (RP-C717)/N1280A/N5163C	28. 1.98	
G-OCSI	Embraer EMB.110P2 Bandeirante	110-270	G-BHJZ PT-SBH	29.12.94	Stored 3/98 engineless at Bembridge.
G-OCST	Agusta-Bell 206B JetRanger III	8694	(N38AH) VR-CDG/G-BMKM	14.12.94	
G-OCSZ	Embraer EMB.110P1 Bandeirante	110-369	G-DORK N698RA/PT-SEN	18. 4.95	WFU at Southend & scrapped in 4/98.
G-OCTA	BN-2A Mk.III-2 Trislander (Mod to three-bladed propellors by 10/93)	1008	VR-CAA (G-OLPL)/VR-CAA/DQ-FCF/G-BCXW	14. 7.87	
G-OCTI	PA-32-260 Cherokee Six	32-288	G-BGZX 9XR-MP/5Y-ADH/N3427W	26. 7.88	
G-OCTU	PA-28-161 Cadet	2841280	N91997	16.11.89	
G-OCUB	Piper J3C-90 Cub (L-4J-PI) (Frame No. 13078) (Official c/n of 13215 is 45-4475/PH-UCW - which was rebuilt as the "new" PH-UCH in Dutch service)	13248	OO-JOZ PH-NKC/PH-UCH/45-4508	21. 4.81	
G-OCWC	American Aviation AA-5A Cheetah	AA5A-0878	G-WULL N27153	28. 5.86	To G-PING 12/95. Canx.
G-OCWT	Aerospatiale AS.350B2 Ecureuil	2664	SE-HRU	28. 8.92	To N513TS 6/97. Canx 26.6.97.

Regn	Type	c/n	Previous identity	Regn date	Fate or immediate subsequent identity (if known)
G-ODAC	Reims Cessna F.152 II	1824	G-BITG	19.12.96	(Crashed at Kildonan, Isle of Arran on 26.5.90) (On rebuild 7/97)
G-ODAD	Colt 77A HAFB	2001		20. 2.91	
G-ODAE	American Aviation AA-5A Cheetah	AA5A-0374	G-OBSF G-ODSF/G-BEUW/N6158A	17.11.97	Damaged on landing at Blackbushe on 8.2.97. Wreck at Elstree 5.7.98. Canx as WFU 14.9.98.
G-ODAH	Aerotek Pitts S-2A Special	2112	G-BDKS	23. 3.87	To F-GIIZ. Canx 18.8.93.
G-ODAM	American Aviation AA-5A Cheetah	AA5A-0818	G-FOUX N8488H	16.11.88	
G-ODAN	BAe 146 Srs.100	E1006		31. 8.82	NTU - To G-BKMN 12/82. Canx.
G-ODAS	Cessna 404 Titan II	404-0048	D-ICIK LN-MAR/(SE-GZD)/(N5430G)	24.11.82	To G-HIGS 6/84. Canx.
G-ODAT	Aero L-29 Delfin	194227	ES-YLV Estonian AF/Soviet AF	28. 7.99	
G-ODAY	Cameron N-56 HAFB	551		16. 7.79	Canx by CAA 18.12.92.
G-ODBN	Lindstrand Flowers SS HAFB	389		22. 5.96	
G-ODCS	Robinson R-22 Beta	2828		19. 5.98	
G-ODDY	Lindstrand LBL-105A HAFB	042		15. 7.93	
G-ODEB	Cameron A-250 HAFB	4328		23. 4.98	
G-ODEL	Falconar F-11-3	PFA/32-10219		14. 8.78	(Badly damaged on landing at Little Gransden on 4.9.88) (On rebuild)
G-ODEN	PA-28-161 Cadet	2841282	N92004	22.11.89	
G-ODER	Cameron O-77 HAFB	1162		7. 5.85	To G-BWYN 11/96. Canx.
G-ODGS	Pierce Jabiru UL	PFA/274A-13472		2. 8.99	
G-ODHL	Cameron N-77 HAFB	1538		22. 2.88	
G-ODIG	Bell 206B JetRanger II	2142	G-NEEP N777FW/N3CR	11. 6.93	
G-ODIL	Bell 206B JetRanger	1486	N59596	5. 8.88	Badly damaged in crash at Kinder Scout on 24.10.97. Canx 6.2.98 on sale to USA.
G-ODIN	Avions Mudry/CAARP CAP-10B	192	F-GDTH	16.12.93	
G-ODIR	PA-23-250 Aztec D	27-4099	G-AZGB N878SH/N10F	30. 8.89	To G-OPME 3/94. Canx.
G-ODIS	Cameron Cabin SS HAFB	2820		7. 5.92	To SE-ZHO 4/97. Canx by CAA 9.12.96.
G-ODIY	Colt 69A HAFB	1786		12. 6.90	
G-ODJG	Europa Avn Europa	PFA/247-12889		3. 5.96	
G-ODJH	Mooney M.20C Ranger	690083	G-BMLH N9293V	19. 1.93	
G-ODJM	Cessna 401	401-0165	G-BSIX G-CAFE(2)/G-AWXM/N4065Q	30. 9.82	To G-ZEUS 6/84. Canx.
G-ODJP	Robinson R-22	0024	N9018Z	26. 8.87	Crashed at Hall Villa Lane, Doncaster on 26.10.93. Canx by CAA 19.1.94.
G-ODLG(1)	DH.114 Heron 2	14091	XR443 G-ARKV/VR-NCE	. 4.90R	NTU - To G-ORSJ 4/90. Canx.
G-ODLG(2)	DH.114 Heron 2	14072	(VH-NJP) G-ODLG/(G-ORSJ)/XR445/G-ARKU/VR-NAQ	20. 4.90	To VH-NJP 9/93. Canx 8.9.93.
G-ODLY	Cessna 310J	310J-0077	G-TUBY G-ASZZ/N3077L	21. 3.88	
G-ODMC	Aerospatiale AS.350B1 Ecureuil	2200	G-BPVF	17.10.89	
G-ODMM	PA-31-350 Navajo Chieftain	31-8152050	N4076A	18.11.87	To N14TT 2/93. Canx 15.2.93.
G-ODNP	Cessna 310R II	310R-1585	N19TP N2DD/N1836E	25. 5.90	To G-MIWS 2/96. Canx.
G-ODOC	Robinson R-44 Astro	0372		27. 8.97	
G-ODOG	PA-28R-200 Cherokee Arrow D II	28R-7235197	EI-BPB G-BAAR/N11C	2. 8.96	
G-ODON	American Aviation AA-5B Tiger	AA5B-0972	N28256	27. 8.81	To VH-DSY 9/88. Canx 19.8.88.
G-ODOT	Robinson R-22 Beta	2779		23. 1.98	
G-ODSC	Enstrom 280FX	2051	G-BSDZ	31. 5.90	To (OO-JMH)/OO-MHV. Canx 12.6.92.
G-ODSF	American Aviation AA-5A Cheetah	AA5A-0374	G-BEUW N6158A	6.11.84	To G-OBSF 9/88. Canx.
G-ODSK	Boeing 737-37Q (Line No. 2904)	28537		23. 7.97	
G-ODTI	Europa Avn Europa	004 & PFA/247-13010		26. 2.96	To G-BYJI 4/99. Canx.
G-ODTW	Europa Avn Europa	PFA/247-12890		7. 9.95	
G-ODUS	Boeing 737-36Q (Line No. 2880)	28659	D-ADBX	17. 3.98	
G-ODVB	CFM Shadow Srs.DD	300-DD	G-MGDB	3.11.98	
G-OEAA	Embraer EMB.110P2 Bandeirante	110-256	G-BTAA G-BHJY/PT-SAW	6. 1.94	Fatal crash near the A61 road shortly after take-off from Leeds-Bradford Airport 24.5.95. Canx as destroyed 16.6.95.
G-OEAB	Embraer EMB.110P2 Bandeirante	110-199	G-BKWB G-CHEV/(PT-GLR)	6. 1.94	To PH-FVB 8/96. Canx 9.8.96.
G-OEAC	Mooney M.20J (201)	24-1636	N57656	16. 6.88	
G-OEAT	Robinson R-22 Beta	0650	G-RACH	8. 1.98	
G-OEBA	Robin DR.400/140B Petit Prince	1449	G-JMHB F-GCIC	27. 1.93	Fatal collision with R1180T G-BLZD & crashed near Dover on 26.10.96. Canx as destroyed 14.3.97.
G-OECH	American Aviation AA-5A Cheetah	AA5A-0836	G-BKBE (G-BJVN)/N26952	24. 1.89	
G-OEDA	BAe Jetstream Srs.3102	761	G-LOGV G-BSZK/I-BLUO/G-31-761	14. 3.94	Restored as G-LOGV 3/96. Canx.
G-OEDB	PA-38-112 Tomahawk	38-79A0167	G-BGGJ N9694N	9. 5.89	

Regn	Type	c/n	Previous identity	Regn date	Fate or immediate subsequent identity (if known)
G-OEDC	BAe Jetstream Srs.3102	720	G-LOGU	14. 3.94	To OK-SEK 6/95. Canx 9.6.95.
			G-BRGL/I-BLUA/G-31-720/G-BRGL/G-31-720		
G-OEDD	BAe Jetstream Srs.3102-09	838	G-WENT	30. 3.94	To OO-EDA 7/94. Canx 13.7.94.
			G-IBLW/G-31-838		
G-OEDE	BAe ATP	2033	G-BTTO	28. 6.94	Restored as G-BTTO 4/95. Canx.
			TC-THV/G-BTTO/S2-ACZ/G-11-033		
G-OEDF	BAe ATP	2052	G-BUKJ	30. 6.94	To EC-GLD 3/97. Canx 28.2.97.
			TC-THZ/G-BUKJ		
G-OEDG	BAe Jetstream Srs.3102-09	839	G-GLAM	1. 6.94	Restored as G-GLAM 2/96. Canx.
			G-IBLX/G-31-839		
G-OEDH	BAe ATP	2039	(G-OGVA)	4. 8.94	To EC-GKI 11/96. Canx 11.11.96.
			G-OEDH/G-BTUE/TC-THT/G-11-039/G-BTUE/G-11-039		
G-OEDI	BAe ATP	2038	N238JX	15. 8.94	To EC-GKJ 11/96. Canx 22.11.96.
			G-BTNI/TC-THU/G-BTNI/(G-SLAM)		
G-OEDJ	BAe ATP	2024	G-BUUR	1. 9.94	To EC-GUX 6/98. Canx 1.6.98.
			CS-TGC/G-BUUR/CS-TGC/G-11-024		
G-OEDL	BAe Jetstream Srs.3112	829	G-OAKK	28. 9.94	Restored as G-BSIW 6/96. Canx.
			G-BSIW/HB-AED/G-31-829/C-FCPG/G-31-829		
G-OEDP	Cameron N-77 HAFB	2189		28.12.89	
G-OEEC	Short SD.3-60 Var.300	SH3755	G-BPKY	18. 4.89	To G-BVMY 11/93. Canx.
G-OEGG	Cameron Egg 65SS HAFB (Cadbury's Creme Egg shape)	2140		4.12.89	
G-OEGL	Christen Eagle II (built by J.Hayward)	001	N46JH	12. 1.98	(Struck a tree on landing at Swanborough Farm, Popham on 18.6.99)
G-OEJA	Cessna 500 Citation I (Unit No.264)	500-0264	G-BWFL	2. 8.96	
			F-GLJA/N205FM/N5264J		
G-OEMA	Cessna 404 Titan II	404-0102	PH-LUN	14.12.82	To G-BLOP 10/84. Canx.
			OO-LFI/(N36999)		
G-OEMH	Westland-Bell 47G-4A	WA/716	G-AXKK	17. 6.93	Crashed to the ground while hovering on a local flight from
			G-17-1		Leicester on 19.4.95. Canx as WFU 24.11.95.
G-OEMS	Beechcraft 200 Super King Air	BB-406	N222PA	2.12.86	To F-GHOC 8/89. Canx 25.5.89.
G-OENT	Reims Cessna F.152 II	1771	G-OBAT	11.12.92	Restored as G-OBAT 22.12.92. Canx.
			(D-EMIN)		
G-OEPF	Hughes 369E (500E)	0009E	G-OMJH	12. 7.84	To G-SUTT 9/84. Canx.
G-OERR	Lindstrand LBL-60A HAFB	469		30. 6.97	
G-OERS	Cessna 172N Skyhawk II	172-68856	G-SSRS	24. 5.94	
			N734HA		
G-OERX	Cameron O-65 HAFB	4004		23. 1.96	
G-OEST	BAe Jetstream Srs.3202	836	OH-JAD	18. 6.99	
			N836JX/C-FGLH/G-31-836/N332QJ/G-31-836		
G-OESU	BAe Jetstream Srs.3202	840	OH-JAE	. 6.99R	NTU - To G-BYMA 7/99. Canx.
			N840JX/C-GSCS/G-31-840/N332QK/G-31-840		
G-OESX	PA-23-250 Aztec E	27-7304927	G-BAJX	15. 4.85	Crashed in the sea off Chioggio, Venice, 12.8 miles south
			N14346		of Porto Levante on 21.11.91. Wreckage was not recovered until 28.12.91. Canx by CAA 18.2.92.
G-OEWA	DH.104 Dove 8	04528	G-DDCD	10. 6.98	Stored at Staverton in 5/98 for eventual restoration.
			G-ARUM		
G-OEXC	Airbus A.320-212	349	F-WWBU	6.11.92	To G-DACR 2/96. Canx.
G-OEYE	Rans S-10 Sakota	PFA/194-11955		25. 4.91	(Stored minus propellor 5/99 Crosland Moor)
G-OEZE	Rutan VariEze	PFA/74-10290		29.11.78	No Permit issued. Canx by CAA 9.7.91.
G-OEZY	Europa Avn Europa	42 & PFA/247-12590		8. 8.95	
G-OFAB	Bell 206B JetRanger III	2949	N22AB	3. 2.88	To SE-HVE 1/90. Canx 31.1.90.
			N5743X		
G-OFAR	Cessna 402C Utiliner	402C-0015	(N4656A)	13.12.78	To TT-BAC(3) 10/84. Canx 17.10.84.
G-OFAS	Robinson R-22 Beta	0559		17. 6.86	
G-OFBJ	Thunder Ax7-77A HAFB	2050		2. 9.91	
G-OFBL	Beechcraft C90 King Air	LJ-747	G-MEDI	4. 7.83	To N529JH /89. Canx 11.4.89.
			EC-DDS/ECT-014/N23756		
G-OFCM	Reims Cessna F.172L Skyhawk	0839	G-AZUN	21.10.81	
			(OO-FCB)		
G-OFEC	Fokker F-27 Friendship 500	10384	G-BOCE	25. 1.88	To N706FE 4/88. Canx 7.4.88.
			F-BPNJ/PH-FNG		
G-OFED	Enstrom F-280C-UK-2 Shark	1195		22. 1.81	To G-OPOP 1/84. Canx.
G-OFEK	Cessna TU.206E Turbo Stationair	01615	(4X-...)	12. 6.89	To 4X-CAZ. Canx 27.6.90.
			G-OFEK/N9415G		
G-OFER	PA-18-150 Super Cub	18-7709058	N83509	29.12.89	
G-OFFA	Pietenpol AirCamper	PFA/47-13181		3.11.98	
G-OFHJ	Cessna 441 Conquest II	441-0294	G-HSON	3.10.86	To N294VB 4/99. Canx 30.3.99.
			(N88724)		
G-OFHL	Aerospatiale AS.350B Ecureuil	1805	EI-BPM	25. 6.93	
			G-BLSP		
G-OFHS	Hughes 369E (500E)	0018E		25.10.83	To N189MD. Canx 20.6.86.
G-OFIL	Robinson R-44 Astro	0555		15. 1.99	
G-OFIN	Aerospatiale AS.355F2 Twin Squirrel	5480	G-DANS	18. 6.99	
			G-BTNM		
G-OFIT	Socata TB-10 Tobago	938	G-BRIU	11. 9.89	
G-OFIZ	Cameron Can 80SS HAFB	2106		30.10.89	Canx as TWFU 10.2.97.
G-OFJC	Eiri PIK-20E	20291	OH-641	19. 3.93	
G-OFJS	Robinson R-22 Beta	0699	G-BNXJ	28. 5.91	
G-OFLG	Socata TB-10 Tobago	11	G-JMWT	11.12.91	
			F-GBHF		

Regn	Type	c/n	Previous identity	Regn date	Fate or immediate subsequent identity (if known)
G-OFLI	Colt 105A HAFB	991		20. 1.87	
G-OFLT	Embraer EMB.110P1 Bandeirante	110-211	G-MOBL (G-BGCS)/PT-GMD	11.12.90	
G-OFLY	Cessna T.210M Turbo Centurion II	210-61600	(D-EBYM) N732LQ	13.10.79	
	(Although delivered on 22.5.78 as G-OFLY it had not been officially regd and went to Doncaster for storage 25.5.78)				
G-OFMB	Rand Robinson KR-2 (built by M.A.Shepard)	7808	N5337X	29. 4.97	
G-OFOA	BAe 146 Srs.100	E1006	G-BKMN EI-COF/SE-DRH/G-BKMN/(G-ODAN)	3. 3.98	
G-OFON	Douglas C-47A-35-DL Dakota	9798	F-GEOM French Navy 36/OK-WZB/OK-WDU/42-23936	. 7.94R	NTU - To G-DAKK 7/94. Canx.
G-OFOR	Thunder Ax3 Maxi Sky Chariot HAFB	596		5.10.84	
G-OFOX	Denney Kitfox	PFA/172-11523		1.11.89	
G-OFRA	Boeing 737-36Q (Line No. 3023)	29327		5. 5.98	
G-OFRB	Everett Gyroplane Srs.2	006	(G-BLSR)	7. 8.85	Permit expired 17.6.92. Canx by CAA 9.6.99.
G-OFRH	Cessna 421C Golden Eagle III	421C-0647	G-NORX EI-BLH/G-NORX/N88600	14. 9.84	Canx 7.1.94 on sale to Indonesia.
G-OFRL	Cessna 414A Chancellor	414A-0220	(N5685C)	6. 3.79	Crashed on take-off from Hurn on 15.5.84. Canx as WFU 9.8.85. (Wreck stored)
G-OFRT	Lockheed L.188CF Electra	1075	N347HA N423MA/N23AF/N64405/SE-FGC/N5537	29.10.91	
G-OFRY	Cessna 152 II	152-81420	G-BPHS N49971	8. 2.93	
G-OFTI	PA-28-140 Cherokee Cruiser	28-7325201	G-BRKU N15926	11. 6.90	
G-OFUN	Valentin Taifun 17E	1063	D-KHVA(5)	26. 9.85	To D-KEUN 8/94. Canx 12.3.93.
G-OGAN	Europa Avn Europa	PFA/247-12734		28. 7.94	
G-OGAR	PZL SZD-45A Ogar	B-601	SP-0004	29. 1.90	
G-OGAS	Westland WG.30 Srs.100	008	G-17-1 G-OGAS/G-BKNW	23. 3.83	CofA expired 19.5.88. Canx as WFU 3.6.92. (Open storage 9/97 Penzance)
G-OGAT	Beechcraft 200 Super King Air	BB-655	N89GA F-GCGX	6. 8.93	To N655BA 4/97. Canx 1.5.97.
G-OGAV	Lindstrand LBL-240A HAFB	074		4. 2.94	
G-OGAZ	Aerospatiale SA.341G Gazelle Srs.1	1274	G-OCJR G-BRGS/F-GEQA(2)/N341SG/(N341P)/N341SG/N47295	12. 1.94	
G-OGBA	Boeing 737-4S3 (Line No. 2255)	25596	G-OBMK	4. 4.97	
G-OGBB	Boeing 737-34S (Line No. 2983)	29108		27. 1.98	
G-OGBC	Boeing 737-34S (Line No. 3001)	29109	N1787B	26. 2.98	
G-OGBD	Boeing 737-3L9 (Line No. 2688)	27833	OY-MAR D-ADBJ/OY-MAR	16. 3.98	
G-OGBE	Boeing 737-3L9 (Line No. 2692)	27834	OY-MAS	24.11.98	
G-OGCA	PA-28-161 Warrior II	28-8016262	N8154L	16. 8.90	
G-OGCI	Short SD.3-60 Var.200	SH3708	G-BNBD G-14-3708	5. 8.91	To N435SA with new c/n SH3415. Canx 5.5.95.
G-OGDN	Beechcraft A200 Super King Air	BB-669		5.12.79	To N80GA 10/89. Canx 24.10.89.
G-OGEE	Christen Pitts S-2B Special	5200	OH-SKY	1. 6.95	
G-OGEM	PA-28-181 Archer II	28-8190226	N83816	10. 3.88	
G-OGET	PA-39-160 Twin Comanche C/R	39-87	G-AYXY N8930Y	14. 3.83	
G-OGGS	Thunder Ax8-84 HAFB	1595		1. 9.89	
G-OGHH	Enstrom 480	5015		14. 2.96	
G-OGHL	Aerospatiale AS.355F1 Twin Squirrel	5164	N5796S	18. 4.97	
G-OGIL	Short SD.3-30 Var.100	SH3068	G-BITV G-14-3068	23. 1.89	Collided with a parked van, hangar doors and SD.3-30 G-BIFH while taxying at Newcastle on 1.7.92. WFU in 10/92. Canx as WFU 12.11.92. On display 4/96 North East Aircraft Museum, Sunderland.
G-OGJS	Rutan Puffer Cozy	PFA/159-11169		27. 1.89	
G-OGKN	QAC Quickie Q.2	PFA/94A-10790		1.12.82	To G-OICI 1/85. Canx.
G-OGOA	Aerospatiale AS.350B Ecureuil	1745	G-PLMD G-NIAL	16. 1.90	
G-OGOB	Schweizer Hughes 269C (300C)	S.1315	G-GLEE G-BRUW/N86G	2.10.90	
G-OGOC	Robinson R-22 Beta	1481	G-HODG	27. 6.91	Rolled over onto its side while hovering at Halfpenny Green on 19.8.98. Canx as destroyed 25.11.98.
G-OGOG	Robinson R-22 Beta	1475	G-TILL	2. 7.97	
G-OGOJ	American Aviation AA-5A Cheetah	AA5A-0877	N3772B	21. 8.81	Fatal crash and caught fire about ½ mile from the airfield boundary at Le Touquet, France on 17.9.85. Canx as destroyed 14.10.85.
G-OGOS	Everett Gyroplane	004	7Q-YES G-OGOS	30. 7.84	(Badly damaged in crash at St.Merryn on 1.10.89 - possibly rebuilt) (Stored Sproughton 12/95)
G-OGRK	Aerospatiale AS.355F1 Twin Squirrel	5185	G-BWZC G-MOBZ/N107KF/N5799R	26. 3.99	
G-OGRV	PA-31-350 Navajo Chieftain	31-7952244	G-BMPX N3543D	11. 6.86	To G-VIPP 8/93. Canx.

Regn	Type	c/n	Previous identity	Regn date	Fate or immediate subsequent identity (if known)
G-OGTS	Air Command 532 Elite	0432 & G/04-1125		19.12.88	
G-OGVA	BAe ATP	2039	G-OEDH G-BTUE/TC-THT/G-11-039/G-BTUE/G-11-039	. .95R	NTU - Remained as G-OEDH. Canx.
G-OHAJ	Boeing 737-36Q (Line No. 3035)	29141		2. 6.98	
G-OHAL	Pietenpol Air Camper	PFA/47-12840		25.11.96	
G-OHAP(1)	BAe 146 Srs.200	E2008	G-WAUS G-5-146/G-WISC	. .86R	NTU - To G-BMYE 8/86. Canx.
G-OHAP(2)	BAe 146 Srs.200A	E2061	N403XV G-5-061	15. 8.86	To G-5-061/N403XV 9/86. Canx 9.9.86.
G-OHBD	Beechcraft B200 Super King Air	BB-864	G-UBHL	11. 6.87	To N150GA. Canx 1.9.88.
G-OHCA	Short SC.5 Belfast C.1	SH.1817	XR363	11. 9.81	Stored unconverted at Southend. Scrapped in 2/94. (Remains gone by 25.2.94) Canx as destroyed 1.3.94.
G-OHCP	Aerospatiale AS.355F1 Twin Squirrel	5249	G-BTVS G-STVE/G-TOFF/G-BKJX	14. 3.94	
G-OHDC	Colt Film Cassette SS HAFB (Agfa Film shape)	2633		8. 8.94	
G-OHEA	HS.125 Srs 3B/RA	25144	G-AVRG G-5-12	25.11.86	WFU & broken up at Cranfield by end-1994. Canx as WFU 23.6.94. (Remains on dump Cranfield 6/99 marked as G-DHEA)
G-OHER	Extra EA.300	015	D-EGRN	11. 9.90	To D-EGRN/G-LOUI 4/92. Canx 28.5.91.
G-OHHI	Bell 206L-1 Long Ranger	45552	G-BWYJ D-HOBD/D-HGAD	30. 4.98	
G-OHHL	Robinson R-22 Beta	1433		4. 6.90	To EI-MAC 4/97. Canx 11.4.97.
G-OHIG	Embraer EMB.110P1 Bandeirante	110-235	G-OPPP XC-DAI/PT-SAB	29. 3.95	Broken up at Southend in 7/98. Fuselage in grounds of Valley Nurseries, Beech, near Alton 4/99.
G-OHIM	Extra EA.300	003	D-EBTS G-OHIM/D-EBTS	5. 9.90	To D-EMIM(2) 12/93. Canx 22.9.93.
G-OHKS	Cyclone Pegasus Quantum 15	7505		24. 3.99	
G-OHLA	Cessna 501 Citation I (Unit No.514)	501-0249	N133DM ZS-LOW/N4263X/RP-C237/N2650M	15. 9.88	To I-DIDY. Canx 3.11.89.
G-OHLL	Robinson R-22 Beta	1087	G-CHAL	2.12.97	
G-OHMS	Aerospatiale AS.355F1 Twin Squirrel	5194	N367E	15. 6.90	
G-OHNA	Mainair Blade	1189-0199-7 & W992		6.11.98	
G-OHOG	PA-28-140 Cherokee	28-22762	G-AVFY	23. 5.91	Badly damaged in crash at Sandown, IoW on 21.7.96. Canx by CAA 16.4.97
G-OHOP	PA-31-310 Turbo Navajo B	31-7300957	G-BEYY SE-GDA	6.10.92	To N325TB 11/98. Canx 27.10.98.
G-OHOT	Vickers 813 Viscount	349	G-BMAT G-AZLT/ZS-CDW/(ZS-SBW)/ZS-CDW	10. 2.89	Destroyed in fatal crash at Stow-by-Chartley, near Uttoxeter on 25.2.94. Canx as destroyed 7.7.94
G-OHSA	Cameron N-77 HAFB	4269		2. 2.98	
G-OHTL	Sikorsky S-76A Spirit	760040		31. 1.80	To G-BURS 5/89. Canx.
G-OHUB	Cessna 404 Titan II	404-0004	SE-GMX (N3932C)	28. 2.84	To G-SKKC 6/90. Canx.
G-OIAN	Morane Saulnier MS.880B Rallye Club	5116	PH-MSB	17. 5.82	No UK CofA issued. Canx by CAA 2.9.91.
G-OIAS	PA-31-350 Navajo Chieftain	31-7405442	OY-CBF D-IGSA/N54322	12. 8.83	To G-GTAX 3/88. Canx.
G-OIBC	Bell 47G-4A (Mod)	7661	G-FORE N1415W	25. 5.93	To D-HIPO(2) 11/96. Canx 24.10.95.
G-OIBM	Rockwell Commander 114B	14295	G-BLVZ SX-AJO/N4957W	14.10.88	
G-OIBO	PA-28-180 Cherokee C	28-3794	G-AVAZ	21. 1.87	
G-OICE	Cessna 525 Citation Jet	525-0028	N1330S	5.10.93	
G-OICI	QAC Quickie Q.2	PFA/94A-10790	G-OGKN	4. 1.85	To G-BPMW 3/89. Canx.
G-OICO	Lindstrand LBL-42A HAFB	566		3.11.98	
G-OICS	Bell 206B JetRanger III	3165	N678TM	18. 1.89	To G-WGAL 3/93. Canx.
G-OICV	Robinson R-22 Beta	0991	G-BPWH	11. 2.93	Substantially damaged when it overturned while hovering at Blackpool on 18.7.99.
G-OIDW	Reims Cessna F.150G	0188	N70163 D-EGTW	24. 4.90	
G-OIEA	PA-31P Pressurised Navajo	31P-7300141	G-BBTW N7660L	13. 7.89	
G-OIFM	Cameron Dude 90SS HAFB (Radio One FM DJ's head/headphones)	2841		18. 6.92	
G-OIFR	Reims Cessna 172RG Cutlass	0198	G-BHJG N6529R	17. 6.83	To D-EMHH(2) 9/89. Canx 1.9.89.
G-OIGS	Enstrom F-28C-UK-2	472-2	G-BGSN	27. 5.92	Crashed in a field at Molton Cote Farm, Ebberston on 3.5.97. Canx by CAA 8.9.97.
G-OIII	BAe 146 RJ100A	E3221		16. 4.92	To N504MM. Canx 19.12.94.
G-OILA	ATR-72-212	472	F-WWEJ	28. 3.96	
G-OILB	ATR-72-212	473	F-WWEG	30. 5.96	To G-BYTP 4/99. Canx.
G-OILS	Cessna T.210L Turbo Centurion II	210-60757	G-BCZP N1736X	8.10.80	(Crashed Botley, Southampton 29.1.82 and now kept by Gary Numan's Swimming Pool)
G-OILX	Aerospatiale AS.355F1 Twin Squirrel II	5327	G-RMGN G-BMCY	27. 1.93	To MOD as ZH141 in 2/99. Canx 25.2.99.
G-OILY	DHC.6-310 Twin Otter	764	N30BV N25RM	7. 5.91	To A6-ADC. Canx 4.11.92.
G-OIMC	Cessna 152 II	152-85506	N93521	15. 5.87	
G-OIML	Agusta-Bell 206B JetRanger III	8560		13.11.78	To G-JMVB 10/82. Canx.

Regn	Type	c/n	Previous identity	Regn date	Fate or immediate subsequent identity (if known)
G-OING	American Aviation AA-5A Cheetah	AA5A-0576	G-BFPD	25. 4.84	Badly damaged in crash following engine failure on take-off from Denham on 11.9.85 and landed straight ahead into a bunker on Denham Golf Course. Canx as WFU 3.12.87.
G-OINK	Piper J3C-65 Cub (L-4J-PI) (Frame No. 12443)	12613	G-BILD G-KERK/F-BBQD/44-80317	22. 3.83	
G-OIOI	EH Industries EH-101	50008/PP8		23.11.88	To RAF as ZJ116. Canx to MOD 1.4.96.
G-OIOM	Bell 206L-3 Long Ranger III	51154	N32WT	27. 2.87	To EI-CHL 2/88. Canx 15.2.88.
G-OIOO	PA-23-250 Aztec C	27-3619	G-AVLV N6352Y	7. 8.81	Dismantled at Glasgow in 10/83. CofA expired 10.2.84. Departed Glasgow by road in 10/83 to Dodson Aviation Scrapyard in the USA. Canx by CAA 4.2.87.
G-OIOW	Hughes 369D (500D)	49-0488D	C-GQCH	3. 2.89	To ZS-RCN 4/92. Canx 16.4.92.
G-OIOZ	Thunder Ax9-120 Srs.2 HAFB	4434		17.11.98	
G-OISF	Fuji FA.200-180 Aero Subaru	FA200-188	G-BAPT	27. 2.90	To G-HAMI 1/92. Canx.
G-OISK	Cameron N-90 HAFB	3747		23. 1.96	To G-CPSF 4/99. Canx.
G-OISO	Reims Cessna FRA.150L Aerobat (Mod. to FA.150 standard)	0213	G-BBJW	3. 4.90	
G-OITA	Boeing 767-33AER (Line No. 560)	27376	VH-ITA(2) N276AW/N1794B	24. 7.95	To I-DEIB 2/97. Canx 21.2.97.
G-OITB	Boeing 767-33AER (Line No. 561)	27377	VH-ITB N361AW/N6009F	21. 7.95	To I-DEIC 3/97. Canx 25.3.97.
G-OITC	Boeing 767-33AER (Line No. 584)	27468	(VH-ITH)	28. 6.95	To I-DEID 11/96. Canx 8.11.96.
G-OITD	Cessna 310F	310-0148	G-AROK N5848X	30. 9.85	Used as spares at Denham for rebuild of Cessna 310G G-ASYV which has become G-XITD. Canx as WFU 23.10.87. Remains scrapped at Denham 21.11.89.
G-OITF	Boeing 767-33AER (Line No. 578)	27908	N6055X	7. 8.95	To I-DEIF 11/96. Canx 20.11.96.
G-OITG	Boeing 767-33AER (Line No. 603)	27918		26. 2.96	To I-DEIG 4/97. Canx 4.4.97.
G-OITL	Boeing 767-33AER (Line No. 611)	28147		30. 4.96	To I-DEIL 4/97. Canx 30.4.97.
G-OITN	Aerospatiale AS.355F1 Twin Squirrel	5088	N400HH N5788B	3.10.89	
G-OITV	Enstrom 280C-UK-2 Shark	1038	G-HRVY G-DUGY/G-BEEL	9. 4.96	
G-OJAB	Pearce Jabiru SK	PFA/274-13031		19. 9.96	
G-OJAC	Mooney M.20J (201)	24-1490	N5767E	20. 8.90	
G-OJAE	Hughes 269C (300C)	90-0966	N1101W	12. 2.90	
G-OJAK	Robinson R-22 Beta	1233	N8067U	31. 1.90	To TC-HKS 4/91. Canx 3.4.91.
G-OJAV	BN-2A Mk.III-2 Trislander	1024	G-BDOS (4X-CCI)/G-BDOS	6. 6.90	
G-OJAY	Embraer EMB.110P1 Bandeirante	110-379	N62DA PT-SEW	24. 5.91	To ZK-NDC. Canx 3.10.95.
G-OJBA	Beechcraft B200 Super King Air	BB-1226	N501EB N200HB/N7234U	6. 8.90	To N16GA 8/93. Canx 11.8.93.
G-OJBB	Enstrom 280FX	2084		14. 6.99	
G-OJBM	Cameron N-90 HAFB	2899		28. 9.92	
G-OJBW	Lindstrand J & B Bottle SS HAFB	436		26. 8.97	
G-OJCB	Agusta-Bell 206B JetRanger II	8554		7. 4.78	
G-OJCM	Rotorway Exec 90	5117		4. 8.92	Substantially damaged when overturned while carrying out engine run-ups on the ground at Whitchurch, Shropshire on 25.9.95. (Stored 3/96) Canx by CAA 21.8.96.
G-OJCT	Partenavia P.68C Victor	223	G-BHOV	7. 3.83	To C9-ATK 7/88. Canx 29.7.88.
G-OJCW	PA-32RT-300 Lance II	32R-7985062	N3016K	9. 1.80	
G-OJDA	EAA Acrosport 2	PFA/72-11067		1. 4.98	(Under construction 9/98 at Fenland)
G-OJDC	Thunder Ax7-77 HAFB	875		9. 1.89	
G-OJEA	DHC.6-310 Twin Otter	699		12. 5.80	To ET-AIL 2/85. Canx 21.2.85.
G-OJEE	Bede BD-4	L35644-27A & PFA/37-10484		10. 8.78	No Permit issued. Canx by CAA 8.7.91.
G-OJEG	Airbus A.321-231	1015	D-AVZN	14. 5.99	
G-OJEM	HS.748 Srs.2B/378	1791	ZK-MCH G-BKAL/(9N-ADF)/ G-BKAL/V2-LDK/D-AHSD/G-BKAL	22. 3.96	Damaged in forced landing due to an engine fire 31.3.98 at Stansted. Broken up in 6/98. Canx as WFU 27.7.98.
G-OJEN	Cameron V-77 HAFB	3302		26. 5.94	
G-OJET	BAe 146 Srs.100	E1004	G-5-537 (N346SS)/G-BRJS/G-5-04/ZD695/G-OBAF/(G-SSCH)/(G-BIAG)	13.11.87	To PK-MTA. Canx 9.12.96.
G-OJFC	Beechcraft A36 Bonanza	E-2945	N3216P	22.11.95	To ZS-CMC(2) 8/97. Canx 18.8.97.
G-OJFR	Bell 206B JetRanger III	3789	N18095	19. 4.85	To G-HELE 2/91. Canx.
G-OJGA	Beechcraft B200 Super King Air	BB-1172	N200LM N67219	8. 7.88	To VH-FDG. Canx 22.4.92.
G-OJGT	Maule M.5-235C Lunar Rocket	7285C	LN-AEL (LN-BEK)/N5635V	30. 6.98	
G-OJHB	Colt Flying Ice Cream Cone SS HAFB	2591		23. 6.94	
G-OJHL	Europa Avn Europa	PFA/247-13039		12. 5.97	
G-OJIL	PA-31-350 Navajo Chieftain	31-7625175	OY-BTP	28. 5.97	
G-OJIM	PA-28R-201T Turbo Arrow III	28R-7703200	N38299	4. 8.86	
G-OJJB	Mooney M.20K (252TSE)	25-1161		12. 8.88	
G-OJJF	Druine D.31 Turbulent	378 & 31	OO-30	6. 1.97	
G-OJLC	Bell 222	47031	G-OSEB G-BNDA/A40-CG	1. 3.91	To G-NOIR 8/91. Canx.

Regn	Type	c/n	Previous identity	Regn date	Fate or immediate subsequent identity (if known)
G-OJMA	Cessna 421B Golden Eagle II	421B-0648	OY-BIG (N1552G)	20.10.78	To N127AC 9/81. Canx 11.9.81.
G-OJMR	Airbus A.300B4-605R	605	(G-MONU) F-WWAY	3. 5.91	
G-OJNB	Lindstrand LBL-21A HAFB	085		14. 2.94	
G-OJOE	Partenavia P.68B Victor	109	SE-GUI	2. 2.79	To G-JCTI 10/81. Canx.
G-OJON	Taylor JT.2 Titch III	PFA/3208		6.10.78	(Nearing completion 9/97)
G-OJOR	Aerospatiale AS.355F2 Twin Squirrel	5347	G-FTWO G-BMUS	11. 6.87	Restored as G-FTWO 10/89. Canx.
G-OJOY	HS.125 Srs.700B	257061	G-BGGS G-5-19	19.10.81	To N700SS 12/83. Canx 6.12.83.
G-OJPB	HS.125 Srs.F600	25258	VP-CJP VR-CJP/G-BFAN/G-AZHS/(G-AYRR)	25. 9.97	
G-OJPI	Robinson R-22 Beta	0834		20. 7.88	Fatal crash into hillside at Allt Llwyd, near the Talybont reservoir in the Brecon Beacons on 20.11.93. Canx as destroyed 23.2.94.
G-OJPW	PA-31-310 Turbo Navajo C	31-7812103	G-BGCC N27703	19. 1.87	To G-OATC 8/90. Canx.
G-OJRH	Robinson R-44 Astro	0321		11. 4.97	
G-OJRS	Reims Cessna F.152 II	1453	G-BFFD	21. 6.85	Burnt out on runway at Cranfield on 16.1.88 due to engine fire. Canx by CAA 16.5.91.
G-OJSW	Boeing 737-8Q8 (Line No. 160)	28218		11.12.98	
G-OJSY	Short SD.3-60 Var.100	SH3603	N368MQ G-BKKT	26. 3.86	
G-OJTA	Stemme S-10V	14-018	D-KGDA(2)	18. 9.95	
G-OJTW	Boeing 737-36N (Line No. 2876)	28558	(G-JTWF)	26. 4.97	
G-OJUG	PA-31-350 Navajo Chieftain	31-7752190	G-SCOT N27361	4. 5.90	To N711WE 11/92. Canx 11.11.92.
G-OJVA	Van's RV-6	PFA/181-12292		6. 9.96	
G-OJVC	Auster J/1N Alpha	1977	G-AHCL	14. 6.83	Restored as G-AHCL 9/92. Canx.
G-OJVH	Reims Cessna F.150H	0356	G-AWJZ	27. 3.81	
G-OJVI	Robinson R-22 Beta	0818	(G-OJVJ)	13. 7.88	To N60661 9/98. Canx 5.8.98.
G-OJVJ	Robinson R-22 Beta	0818		23. 6.88	NTU - To G-OJVI 13.7.88. Canx.
G-OJWE	Cameron A-210 HAFB	4081		20. 2.97	(Badly damaged after struck powerlines at North Ferriby, near Hull on 20.7.97)
G-OJWS	PA-28-161 Warrior II	28-7816415	N6377C	13. 7.88	
G-OKAG	PA-28R-180 Cherokee Arrow	28R-30075	N3764T	15. 4.88	
G-OKAT	Aerospatiale AS.350B Ecureuil	1078	G-BGIM	1. 7.88	To SE-JDD 7/95. Canx 17.7.95.
G-OKAY	Pitts S-1E Special (Built by W.Henlin)	12358	N35WH	27. 5.80	
G-OKBT	Colt 25A Sky Chariot Mk.II HAFB	2301		10.11.92	
G-OKCC	Cameron N-90 HAFB	1741		6. 5.88	
G-OKDN	Boeing 737-8Q8 (Line No. 77)	28226		27. 7.98	
G-OKED	Cessna 150L	150-74250	N19223	29. 1.93	
G-OKEN	PA-28R-201T Turbo Arrow III	28R-7703390	N47518	20.10.87	
G-OKES	Robinson R-44 Astro	0053		16. 3.94	
G-OKEV	Europa Avn Europa	PFA/247-13091		11. 6.97	
G-OKEY	Robinson R-22 Beta	2004		14. 1.92	
G-OKIS	Tri-R Kis	PFA/239-12248		15. 6.92	(Stored 8/97)
G-OKIT	Rotorway Exec 152	CWT-1		7. 7.87	To G-BWJK 10/95. Canx.
G-OKLE	Sikorsky S-76B	760381	PH-NZW	7. 7.94	Restored as PH-NZW 10/96. Canx 23.10.96.
G-OKMA	Tri-R Kis	PFA/239-12808		22.11.95	
G-OKPW	Tri-R Kis	PFA/239-12359		17. 8.93	
G-OKSP	Cessna 500 Citation I (Unit No.392)	500-0364	N40DA N20WP/(N221JB)/N221AC/HB-VFF/N36892	26. 8.86	To G-ORJB 7/92. Canx.
G-OKYA	Cameron V-77 HAFB (Initially regd as N-77 with c/n 1264, which became G-NEPB on 7.3.86) (Replacement envelope c/n 3331)	1259		4. 3.87	
G-OKYM	PA-28-140 Cherokee	28-23303	G-AVLS N11C	10. 5.88	
G-OLAF	Beechcraft C90 King Air	LJ-803	G-BFVX	2.11.87	To N9TN 5/95. Canx 1.5.95.
G-OLAH	Short SD.3-60 Var.100	SH3604	G-BPCO G-RMSS/G-BKKU	14. 8.91	
G-OLAN	McDonnell Douglas MD-11 (Line No. 454)	48412		. .90R	NTU - To N892DL 12/90. Canx.
G-OLAU	Robinson R-22 Beta	1119		5. 9.89	
G-OLAW	Lindstrand LBL-25A Cloudhopper HAFB	170		9.12.94	
G-OLBA	Short SD.3-60 Var.300	SH3737	G-BOFG G-14-3737	18. 3.88	To D-CCAS 2/93. Canx 5.2.93.
G-OLBC	PA-23-250 Aztec F	27-7954113	G-BHCT N6925A	20. 3.89	Restored as G-BHCT 4/93. Canx.
G-OLBL	Lindstrand LBL-90A HAFB	419		24. 2.97	
G-OLCA	BAe 146 Srs.200	E2099	G-5-099	24. 5.88	To G-JEAJ 9/93. Canx.
G-OLCB	BAe 146 Srs.200	E2103	(N412XV) G-5-103	24. 5.88	To G-JEAK 3/93. Canx.
G-OLCC	BAe ATP	2017		5.12.88	To G-LOGC 4/92. Canx.
G-OLCD	BAe ATP	2018		5.12.88	To G-LOGD 4/92. Canx.

Regn	Type	c/n	Previous identity	Regn date	Fate or immediate subsequent identity (if known)
G-OLDA	PA-31-350 Navajo Chieftain	31-8052038	G-BNDS N131PP/N3550N	27. 1.97	To G-PLAC 12/98. Canx.
G-OLDB	PA-31-350 Navajo Chieftain	31-8152014	OY-SKY G-DIXI/N40717	29. 5.97	
G-OLDD	BAe 125 Srs.800B	258106	N888SS (N107CF)/PK-RGM/PK-WSJ/G-5-580	11. 3.99	
G-OLDE	Cessna 421B Golden Eagle II	421B-0548	G-BBSV (N69917)	11. 5.92	To CS-DCB 12/97. Canx 5.12.97.
G-OLDI	Ayres S2R-T15 Turbo Thrush Commander 500	T15-020DC	N4026D	6.11.81	To VH-WBE 12/84. Canx 6.12.84.
G-OLDN	Bell 206L Long Ranger	45077	G-TBCA G-BFAL/N64689/A6-BCL	2.10.84	
G-OLDS	Colt AS-105 Hot Air Airship	494		7. 2.83	Canx as WFU 16.10.89.
G-OLDV	Colt 90A HAFB	2592		5. 5.94	CofA expired 10.11.98. Canx as WFU 29.6.99.
G-OLDY	Phoenix Luton LA-5 Major	PFA/1206		28.12.78	No Permit to Fly issued. Canx by CAA 15.2.96. (Offered for sale when nearly completed)
G-OLDZ	Beechcraft 200 Super King Air	BB-828	G-MCEO (N828AB)/G-SWFT/G-SIBE/G-MCEO/G-BILY	28. 6.96	To N62GA. Canx 3.8.99.
G-OLEE	Reims Cessna F.152 II	1797		11. 9.80	
G-OLEN	Cessna 425 Corsair	425-0106	(N6850M)	6. 8.81	To N425GA 1/84. Canx 16.1.84.
G-OLEO	Thunder Ax10-210 Srs.2 HAFB	3974		9. 1.97	
G-OLES	Partenavia P.68C Victor	253	G-JAJV OO-TJG/(OO-XJG)	13. 6.90	To PH-EMC 5/93. Canx 10.3.93.
G-OLFC	PA-38-112 Tomahawk	38-79A0995	G-BGZG	6.12.85	
G-OLFI	Robinson R-22 Beta	1088	G-BRKI	3. 8.92	Crashed into lake at Kirtons Farm Country Club, near Reading on 29.5.93. Canx as WFU 12.8.93.
G-OLFR	HS.125 Srs.403B	25217	G-BRXR G-5-651/9Q-CHD/9Q-CGM/G-AXYJ/G-5-14	2.11.90	To 5N-AES 11/93. Canx 9.11.93.
G-OLFS	Socata MS.880B Rallye Club	1850	G-AYYZ	25. 4.88	To EI-CFV 5/92. Canx 28.4.92.
G-OLFT	Rockwell Commander 114	14274	G-WJMN N4954W	28. 3.85	
G-OLGA	CFM Starstreak Shadow SA-II	PFA/206-13164		15.10.97	
G-OLGW	Short SD.3-60 Var.300	SH3741	"G-LOGW" G-BOFK/G-14-3741	1. 9.88	To G-ZAPD 8/92. Canx.
G-OLHB	BAe 146 Srs.200	E2020	G-BSRV G-OSUN/C-FEXN/N604AW	24. 3.94	To G-JEAS 2/96. Canx.
G-OLIE	Robinson R-22 Beta	0824	G-BOUW	7.10.88	To OO-TVI. Canx 31.12.91.
G-OLIN	PA-30-160 Twin Comanche B	30-1716	OY-DLC G-AWMB/N8569Y	22.12.81	Crashed on take-off from Stapleford on 16.8.87. Canx as destroyed 11.4.88. (Stored .92)
G-OLIZ	Robinson R-22 Beta	0779		29. 9.88	
G-OLJT	Mainair Gemini/Flash 2A	570-887-5 & W359	G-MTKY	16. 9.98	
G-OLLE	Cameron O-84 HAFB	1520		15. 4.87	
G-OLLI	Cameron O-31 HAFB (Special Shape - Golly)	196		11. 5.76	
G-OLLY	PA-31-350 Navajo Chieftain	31-7405418	G-BCES N66916	27. 1.76	
G-OLMA	Partenavia P.68B Victor	159	G-BGBT	15. 4.85	
G-OLOW	Robinson R-44 Astro	0100		3.10.94	
G-OLPG	Colt 77A HAFB	2568		11. 3.94	
G-OLPL	BN-2A Mk.III-2 Trislander	1008	VR-CAA DQ-FCF/G-BCXW	. .87R	NTU - Remained as VR-CAA /87, then to G-OCTA 7/87. Canx.
G-OLRT	Robinson R-22 Beta	1378	N4014R	21. 5.90	
G-OLSC	Cessna 182A Skylane	182-34078	G-ATNU EI-ANC/N6078B	19. 8.87	Bounced on landing and nosewheel collapsed at Knettishall on 6.6.93. (Painted as "G-ATCX" for film use - fuselage stored 5/98 St.Merryn) Canx by CAA 3.4.97.
G-OLSF	PA-28-161 Cadet	2841284	G-OTYJ G-OLSF/N9200B	23.11.89	
G-OLTN	Short SD.3-60 Var.100	SH3738	G-BOFH G-14-3738	5. 4.88	To G-ZAPF 2/93. Canx.
G-OLUM	Robinson R-22 Beta	1044		19. 6.89	To EI-WCC 10/93. Canx 12.10.93.
G-OLVR	Clutton FRED Srs.II	PFA/29-10321		17.11.78	
G-OLXX	BAe 146 RJ70A	E1228	VH-NJT(2) G-OLXX/G-6-228	28. 1.94	Restored as VH-NJT(2) 12/95. Canx 8.12.95.
G-OLYD	Beechcraft 58 Baron	TH-1427	N7255H ZS-LYC/N7255H	12. 9.97	
G-OLYN	Sky 260-24 HAFB	088		24. 4.98	
G-OMAC	Reims Cessna FR.172E Rocket	0022	PH-HAI (PH-KRC)/D-EDDC	3. 7.84	
G-OMAD	Cessna T.210N Turbo Centurion	T210-63842	N106GC N6245C/G-OMAD/G-BMDN/ZS-LBI/N6245C	21.10.85	To PH-MRL 1/95. Canx 17.1.95.
G-OMAF	Dornier 228-200	8112	D-CAAD	16. 2.87	
G-OMAK	Airbus A.319-132 CJ	913	F-WWIF G-OMAK/D-AYVL	7. 1.99	Restored as F-WWIF 6/99. Canx 9.6.99.
G-OMAN	Fokker F-27 Friendship 100	10120	G-SPUD VH-TFE/PH-FAP	29. 9.82	To G-BLFJ 4/84. Canx.
G-OMAP	Rockwell Commander 685	12036	F-GIRX F-OCGX/F-ZBBU/N6525V	4.11.94	
G-OMAR	PA-34-220T Seneca III	34-8233142	N82033	17. 6.88	
G-OMAT	PA-28-140 Cherokee D	28-7125139	G-JIMY G-AYUG	27. 8.87	

Regn	Type	c/n	Previous identity	Regn date	Fate or immediate subsequent identity (if known)
G-OMAV	Aerospatiale AS.355F1 Twin Squirrel	5115		1.12.81	To G-NEXT 10/87. Canx.
G-OMAX	Brantly B.2B	473	G-AVJN	7. 8.87	
G-OMCA	HS.125 Srs.1B/522	25106	G-DJMJ G-AWUF/5N-ALY/G-AWUF/HZ-BIN	10. 9.87	To G-BOCB 14.9.87. Canx.
G-OMCL	Cessna 550 Citation II (Unit No.412)	550-0413	N12160	23. 7.82	To N213VP 3/93/OY-PDN. Canx 8.1.93.
G-OMCP	Enstrom 280C-UK-2 Shark	1221	G-KENY G-BJFG/N8617N	15. 7.86	To G-SHUU 10/89. Canx.
G-OMDD	Cameron Ax8-90 Srs.2 HAFB	4345		2. 4.98	
G-OMDG	Hoffmann H-36 Dimona	3510	OE-9215	19.11.98	
G-OMDH	MDH Hughes 369E (500E)	0293E		14.11.88	
G-OMDR	Agusta-Bell 206B JetRanger III	8610	G-HRAY G-VANG/G-BIZA	8.12.97	
G-OMDS	HS.748 Srs.2A/334	1757	G-BPFU G-EDIN/9Y-TFT/V2-LCG/VP-LCG/9Y-TFT	23. 1.91	To Sri Lankan AF as 4R-HVB/CR-835. Canx 7.1.92.
G-OMEC	Agusta-Bell 206B JetRanger III	8716	G-OBLD	16. 1.90	
G-OMED	American Aviation AA-5B Tiger	AA5B-0466	G-BERL N6157A	22.10.84	To G-OCAZ 5/94. Canx.
G-OMEG	PA-31-325 Navajo C/R	31-7712079	G-BFBH N27317	26. 5.87	To ZS-MSM. Canx 1.12.89.
G-OMEL	Robinson R-44 Astro	0073	G-BVPB	30. 9.96	
G-OMET	Beechcraft C90 King Air	LJ-614	G-COTE G-BBKN	21.11.79	To G-BNAT 4/86. Canx.
G-OMGA	HS.125 Srs.600B/2	256024	G-BSHL G-BBMD/N50GD/G-BBMD	26. 2.91	To YR-DVA. Canx 19.5.94.
G-OMGB	HS.125 Srs.600B	256039	EC-EAO EC-183/EC-EAO/G-BKBM/N410AW/ N61TF/G-BKBM/G-BCCL	9.10.90	WFU at Luton 1.10.94. To Houston, TX, USA for spares recovery. Canx as WFU 11.11.94.
G-OMGC	HS.125 Srs.600B	256056	G-BKCD 5N-ARN/G-BKCD/G-BDOA/G-5-13	17. 1.91	WFU at Luton 8.9.94. To Houston, TX, USA for spares recovery. Canx as WFU 11.11.94.
G-OMGD	HS.125 Srs.700B	257184	9K-AGA YI-AKG/9K-AGA/G-5-12	28.12.94	
G-OMGE	BAe 125 Srs.800B	258197	G-5-696 G-BTMG	1. 7.91	
G-OMGG	BAe 125 Srs.800B	258058	N125JW G-5-637/N125JW/VH-NMR/ZK-EUI/(ZK-EUR)/G-5-510	21.11.94	
G-OMHC	PA-28RT-201 Arrow IV	28R-7918105	N3072Y	10. 2.81	
G-OMHI	Mills MH-1 (Home-built light helicopter)	MH.001		8.10.97	
G-OMIA	Socata MS.893A Rallye Commodore 180	12074	D-ENME(3) F-BUGE/(D-ENMH)	21. 7.98	
G-OMID	HS.125 Srs.700B	257214	G-UKCA HZ-SJP/G-5-17	6. 8.92	To VR-BCF 2/93. Canx 12.2.93.
G-OMIG	WSK SBLim-2A (MiG-15UTI) (Built by Aero Vodochody as S.103/MiG 15bis; later rebuilt in Poland)	622047	6247 (Polish AF)	10.11.92	
G-OMIK	Europa Avn Europa	PFA/247-12991		12. 1.98	
G-OMIL	Beechcraft 95-B58 Baron	TH-1019	N40CG	28. 5.91	To N7958D 11/93. Canx 29.10.93.
G-OMJB	Bell 206B JetRanger II	2051	N315JP N712WG/N712WC/N9989K	20. 4.89	
G-OMJD	Robinson R-22 Beta	0832		28. 7.88	To EI-BYS 9/89. Canx 21.9.89.
G-OMJH	Hughes 369E (500E)	0009E		4. 8.83	To G-OEPF 7/84. Canx.
G-OMJT	Rutan LongEz	968 & PFA/74A-10703		14.10.92	
G-OMKF	Aero Designs Pulsar	PFA/202-11866		15. 1.91	
G-OMMC	Mooney M.20J	24-3023		16. 4.87	To N162TK 8/95. Canx 14.8.95.
G-OMMG	Robinson R-22 Beta	1041	G-BPYX	25. 2.94	
G-OMMM	Colt 90A HAFB	2328		20. 1.93	
G-OMNH	Beechcraft 200 Super King Air	BB-108	N108BM RP-C1979/TR-LWC	19. 8.98	
G-OMNI	PA-28R-200 Cherokee Arrow II D	28R-7335130	G-BAWA	3. 1.84	
G-OMOB	Robinson R-22 Beta	0816		16. 6.88	Canx as destroyed 17.9.92.
G-OMOG	American Aviation AA-5A Cheetah	AA5A-0793	G-BHWR N26892	4. 3.88	
G-OMPS	PA-28-161 Warrior II	28-8016050	G-BOHP N8079Z	14. 2.89	Overshot the runway on landing at Tours (St.Symphorien) airport, France 20.8.92. Canx as WFU 15.9.92. Wrecked fuselage dumped outside 5/97 Montpellier-Mediterrannee Airport.
G-OMRB	Cameron V-77 HAFB	2184		29. 8.90	
G-OMRG	Hoffmann H-36 Dimona	36132	G-BLHG	15.11.88	
G-OMSG	Robinson R-22 Beta	2738		8.10.97	
G-OMUC	Boeing 737-36Q (Line No. 3047)	29405		29. 6.98	
G-OMUM	Rockwell Commander 114	14067	PH-JJJ (PH-MMM)/N4737W	24. 1.97	
G-OMWE	Zenair CH.601HD Zodiac	PFA/162-12740	G-BVXU	21. 3.97	
G-OMXS	Lindstrand LBL-105A HAFB	172		7.12.94	
G-ONAB	PA-28RT-201 Arrow IV	28R-7918140	G-BHAK N29555	11. 1.83	To G-GHRW 12/83. Canx.
G-ONAD	Cessna 421C Golden Eagle III	421C-0709	N4467Q XA-IUK/N26556	20. 5.87	To CS-ASL. Canx 21.10.88.

Regn	Type	c/n	Previous identity	Regn date	Fate or immediate subsequent identity (if known)
G-ONAF	Naval Aircraft Factory N3N-3	-	N45192 BuA.4406	31. 1.89	
G-ONAV	PA-31-310 Turbo Navajo C	31-7812004	G-IGAR D-IGAR/N27378	29. 1.93	
G-ONCA	Beechcraft 200 Super King Air	BB-676	N1326B 9Y-TGR	25. 5.88	To N676DP. Canx 27.3.89.
G-ONCB	Lindstrand LBL-31A HAFB	393		4. 6.96	
G-ONCL	Colt 77A HAFB	1637		4. 4.90	
G-ONEA	Beechcraft 200 Super King Air	BB-400	N3035C N3030C	2.11.88	To G-GATI 6/94. Canx.
G-ONEB	Westland Scout AH.1	F.9761	G-BXOE XW798	21. 1.98	
G-ONET	PA-28-180 Cherokee E	28-5802	G-AYAU	3. 6.98	
G-ONEX	Beechcraft 200 Super King Air	BB-379	G-VRES	16. 2.93	To 5Y-DDE 6/94. Canx 21.6.94.
G-ONFL	Meridian Ultralights Maverick	402 & PFA/259-12750	G-MYUJ	27.11.98	
G-ONGC	Robin DR.400/180R Remorqueur	1385	EI-CKA SE-GHM	11.11.98	
G-ONHH	Forney F.1A Aircoupe	5725	G-ARHA N3030G	13.12.89	
G-ONIX	Cameron C-80 HAFB	4411		12. 8.98	
G-ONKA	Aeronca K	K283	N19780 NC19780	21.10.91	
G-ONMT	Robinson R-22 Beta	2963		20. 7.99	
G-ONON	Rotary Air Force RAF 2000 GTX-SE	G/13-1313		13. 8.99	
G-ONOR	Cessna 425 Conquest	425-0173	G-BKSA N6873Q	25. 4.84	To N30WF 4/94. Canx 26.4.94.
G-ONOW	Bell 206A JetRanger	605	G-AYMX	8. 8.88	
G-ONPA(1)	Beechcraft 200 Super King Air	BB-160	(G-BLKN) EI-BHG/9Q-CTK/N8493D/EI-BHG/OY-CBK/(EI-BGR)/N2160L	. .84R	NTU - To G-HIGG 12/84. Canx.
G-ONPA(2)	PA-31-350 Navajo Chieftain	31-7952110	N89PA N35225	6. 5.98	
G-ONPI	Thunder Ax10-160 HAFB	1819		15. 8.90	Envelope destroyed while trying to disentangle it from the branches of trees it was blown into at Northend Farm, Chiddingford, Surrey on 1.4.95. Canx by CAA 8.6.95.
G-ONPN	HS.125 Srs.1B	25063	G-BAXG HB-VAN	20. 6.80	Sold as 5N-ASZ in 7/85. Canx by CAA 6.2.87.
G-ONPP	Hughes 369HS (500)	13-0442S	OY-HCP D-HGER	22. 3.83	To G-ROMA 1/84. Canx.
G-ONTA	Hughes 369D (500D)	1146D		3.12.82	To CS-HCI. Canx 8.5.92.
G-ONTB	Bell 206B JetRanger III	3191	N3896C	15. 1.88	To G-MCPI 4/90. Canx.
G-ONTV	Agusta-Bell 206B JetRanger III	8733	D-HUNT TC-HKJ/(D-HSAV)/I-GPFP/I-PIEF	1. 4.98	
G-ONUN	Van's RV-6A	PFA/181-12976		20. 2.96	
G-ONYX	Bell 206B JetRanger III	4160	G-BXPN N18EA/D-HOBA/(D-HOBE)	22. 1.98	
G-ONZO	Cameron O-77 HAFB	1089		13.11.84	
G-OOAA(1)	Boeing 737-4Y0 (Line No. 1861)	24686		. 7.89R	NTU - To 9M-MJH 5/90. Canx.
G-OOAA(2)	Airbus A.320-231	291	(N.....) F-WWBZ	11. 4.92	
G-OOAB(1)	Boeing 737-4Y0 (Line No. 1876)	24688		. 7.89R	NTU - To 9M-MJI 6/90. Canx.
G-OOAB(2)	Airbus A.320-231	292	(N.....) F-WWDN	24. 4.92	
G-OOAC	Airbus A.320-231	327	F-WWDQ	15. 9.92	
G-OOAD	Airbus A.320-231	336	F-WWIG	24. 9.92	
G-OOAE	Airbus A.321-112	852	(G-UNIF) D-AVZG	14. 7.98	
G-OOAF	Airbus A.321-211	677	G-UNID G-UKLO/D-AVZO	4.12.98	
G-OOAG	Beechcraft E90 King Air	LW-59	N4718C G-BAVG	7. 4.86	To G-FAVI 7/89. Canx.
G-OOAH	Airbus A.321-211	781	G-UNIE D-AVZK	4. 1.99	
G-OOAI	Airbus A.321-211	1006	(G-UNIG) D-AVZJ	30. 4.99	
G-OOAJ	Airbus A.321-211	1017	(G-UNIH) D-AVZM	12. 5.99	
G-OOAL	Boeing 767-38AER (Line No. 741)	29617		29. 3.99	
G-OOAM	Boeing 767-38AER (Line No. ...)	?		. .99R	(delivery due 1999)
G-OOAN	Boeing 767-39HER (Line No. 484)	26256	G-UKLH	26. 1.99	
G-OOAO	Boeing 767-39HER (Line No. 488)	26257	G-UKLI	11. 1.99	
G-OODE	SNCAN Stampe SV-4C	500	G-AZNN F-BDGI	9. 5.77	
G-OODI	Pitts S-1D Special	EKH.1	G-BBBU	23.12.80	

Regn	Type	c/n	Previous identity	Regn date	Fate or immediate subsequent identity (if known)
G-OODO	Stephens Akro Srs.2 (Modified Akro known as Pace Spirit)	RGDW-1 & PFA/123-10732		3. 9.81	Destroyed in crash at Rendham, near Saxmundham on 12.5.84. Canx as destroyed 27.2.87.
G-OODS	Extra EA.230	SAS.01		22. 4.85	(Probably completed as G-PMNL) Canx by CAA 11.7.91.
G-OODW	PA-28-181 Archer II	28-8490031	N4332C	14. 7.87	
G-OODY	PA-28R-200 Arrow B II	28R-7635418	N4601F	27. 9.78	To ZK-FHP 1/84. Canx 23.1.84.
G-OOER	Lindstrand LBL-25A Cloudhopper HAFB	125		15. 8.94	
G-OOFI	Cameron N-77 HAFB	1314		17. 6.86	To OO-BHJ 2/96. Canx 15.12.95.
G-OOFY	Rollason-Luton Beta B.2	PFA/02-10372		11. 9.78	No Permit issued. Canx by CAA 11.7.91.
G-OOGA	Gulfstream American GA-7 Cougar (Note : YV-1334P also quoted as c/n 0111, but G-OOGA confirmed correct)	GA7-0111	SE-IEA N758G	3. 2.86	
G-OOGI	Gulfstream American GA-7 Cougar	GA7-0077	G-PLAS G-BGHL/N789GA	16. 1.95	
G-OOGO	Grumman-American GA-7 Cougar	GA7-0049	N762GA	12.11.97	
G-OOGS	Gulfstream American GA-7 Cougar	GA7-0105	G-BGJW N737GA	19. 6.98	
G-OOJB	Cessna 421C Golden Eagle III	421C-1006	G-BKSO N6333X	13. 3.91	
G-OOJC	Bensen B.8MR Gyrocopter	G/01-1303		4.12.98	
G-OOLE	Cessna 172M Skyhawk II	172-66712	G-BOSI N80714	25. 8.89	
G-OOLI	Robinson R-22 Beta	1201	G-DMCD	9. 7.91	Restored as G-DMCD 3/96. Canx.
G-OOLY	Everett Gyroplane	003		4. 6.84	Stored at Milden in 7/85. Permit expired 31.7.85. Canx as WFU 12.5.89.
G-OONE	Mooney M.20J (205SE)	24-3039		31. 7.87	
G-OONI	Thunder Ax7-77 HAFB	1534		9. 3.90	
G-OONS	Agusta-Bell 206B JetRanger III	8721	G-LIND G-OONS	13. 2.90	Damaged in a heavy landing 1½ miles S of Enniskillen on 21.10.96. Canx on sale to Ireland 10.4.97.
G-OONY	PA-28-161 Warrior II	28-8316015	N83071	26. 7.89	
G-OOOA	Boeing 757-28A (Line No. 127)	23767	C-FOOA G-OOOA/C-FOOA/G-OOOA/C-FOOA/G-OOOA	6. 3.87	
G-OOOB	Boeing 757-28A (Line No. 130)	23822	C-FOOB G-OOOB/C-FOOB/G-OOOB/C-FOOB/G-OOOB/C-FOOB/G-OOOB/C-FOOB/G-OOOB/C-FOOB/G-OOOB/C-FOOB/G-OOOB/C-FOOB/G-OOOB/C-FOOB/G-OOOB	19. 2.87	To be C-FRYH 12/98.
G-OOOC	Boeing 757-28A (Line No. 162)	24017	C-FRYL G-OOOC/C-FXOC/G-OOOC/C-FXOC/G-OOOC/C-FXOC/G-OOOC/C-FXOC/G-OOOC/C-FXOC/G-OOOC/C-FXOC/G-OOOC	19. 1.88	
G-OOOD	Boeing 757-28A (Line No. 180)	24235	C-FXOD (G-OOOD)/C-FXOD/G-OOOD/C-FXOD/G-OOOD/(C-FXOD)/G-OOOD/(C-....)/G-OOOD	25. 2.88	To C-GRYU 12/98. Canx 17.12.98.
G-OOOG	Boeing 757-23A (Line No. 219)	24292	C-FOOG G-OOOG/C-FOOG/G-OOOG/C-FOOG/G-OOOG/C-FOOG/G-OOOG/C-FOOG/G-OOOG	29. 3.89	To become C-GRYY in 12/98.
G-OOOH	Boeing 757-23A (Line No. 220)	24293		6. 4.89	To N989AN 6/94. Canx 16.6.94.
G-OOOI	Boeing 757-23A (Line No. 209)	24289	N510SK EC-EMV/EC-247	19.10.89	
G-OOOJ	Boeing 757-23A (Line No. 212)	24290	N510FP EC-EMU/EC-248	19.10.89	
G-OOOM	Boeing 757-225 (Line No. 114)	22612	N523EA	20. 4.90	To SE-DUN 11/96. Canx 1.11.96.
G-OOOO	Mooney M.20J (205)	24-3046	N205EE	25. 1.88	
G-OOOS	Boeing 757-236 (Line No. 221)	24397	G-BRJD EC-ESC/EC-349/G-BRJD	14. 5.91	
G-OOOT	Boeing 757-236 (Line No. 292)	24793	G-BRJJ EC-490/G-BRJJ	16. 5.91	To SE-DUP 12/97. Canx 9.12.97.
G-OOOU	Boeing 757-2Y0 (Line No. 388)	25240		30. 8.91	
G-OOOV	Boeing 757-225 (Line No. 74)	22211	N521EA	12. 2.92	
G-OOOW	Boeing 757-225 (Line No. 75)	22611	N522EA	20. 1.92	
G-OOOX	Boeing 757-2Y0 (Line No. 526)	26158		24. 2.93	
G-OOOY	Boeing 757-28AET (Line No. 802)	28203		21. 5.98	
G-OOPS	Agusta-Bell 206B JetRanger II	8238	G-BNRD Oman AF 602	9. 5.95	To G-JBDB 4/96. Canx.
G-OOSE	Rutan VariEze	1536 & PFA/74-10326		7.12.78	(Under construction 8/91)
G-OOSP	HS.125 Srs.400B	25178	5N-BUA G-AWXO	24. 6.96	To 5N-WMA 8/96. Canx 1.10.96.
G-OOSY	DH.82A Tiger Moth (Composite rebuild)	85831	F-BGFI French AF/DE971	6. 9.94	(On rebuild 9/94)
G-OOTC	PA-28R-201T Turbo Arrow III	28R-7703086	G-CLIV N3011Q	18. 1.94	
G-OOUT	Colt Flying Shuttlecock SS HAFB	1938		16. 5.91	
G-OOXP	Aero Designs Pulsar XP	PFA/202-11915		25.10.90	
G-OPAC	Robinson R-22 Beta	1008		11. 5.89	Crashed at North Church Farm, Berkhampsted on 14.8.94. Canx as destroyed 23.11.94.

Regn	Type	c/n	Previous identity	Regn date	Fate or immediate subsequent identity (if known)
G-OPAG	PA-34-200 Seneca	34-7250348	N506DM G-BNGB/F-BTQT/(F-BTMT(3))	16.10.90	
G-OPAL	Robinson R-22 Beta	0535	N23750	11. 2.86	
G-OPAM	Reims Cessna F.152 II (Texas Taildragger conversion)	1536	G-BFZS	5. 9.86	
G-OPAS	Vickers 806 Viscount	263	G-AOYN	5.10.94	WFU in 6/96 at Southend. Broken up. Canx 28.7.97 as destroyed.
G-OPAT	Beechcraft 76 Duchess	ME-304	G-BHAO	6.12.82	
G-OPAZ	Pazmany PL-2	PFA/69-10673		20. 3.98	
G-OPBH	Aero Designs Pulsar	PFA/202-12246		28. 4.92	Canx as TWFU 12.12.94.
G-OPBN	PBN BN-2T Turbine Islander (AEW Defender trials aircraft)	2034	G-BJOH	28. 3.83	To G-SRAY 4/86. Canx.
G-OPDM	Enstrom 280FX Shark	2021	N8627Q PH-GBL/N650PG	7. 1.98	
G-OPDS	Denney Kitfox Mk.4	PFA/172A-12259		8. 1.93	
G-OPED	Partenavia P.68B Victor	129	G-BFKP	6.11.86	To ZK-ZSP. Canx 23.6.95.
G-OPEE	Cessna 421C Golden Eagle III	421C-0617	N421PB N8507Z/G-OSSH/N88627	30. 4.87	To EI-CAT 12/90. Canx 20.7.90.
G-OPEL	Reims Cessna F.172G	0241	(G-BGLV) (G-BGGZ)/D-EDHB	26. 5.81	Blown over by high winds at Stapleford on 13.5.84 & DBR. (Sold for spares use & to Glasgow by road in early 8/84) Canx as destroyed 25.7.84. (Wreck stored)
G-OPEP	PA-28RT-201T Turbo Arrow IV	28R-7931070	OY-PEP N2217Q	3.12.97	
G-OPFC	BAe 125 Srs.1000B	258159		8. 1.90	To N10855. Canx 19.1.96.
G-OPFE	Vickers 808C Viscount	291	G-BBDK HB-ILR/EI-AJK	27.10.94	Badly damaged on wheels-up landing at Belfast on 24.3.96. Canx as WFU 10.5.96.
G-OPFI	Vickers 802C Viscount	170	G-BLNB G-AOHV	1. 3.94	To 3D-PFI 9/99. Canx 25.8.99.
G-OPFT	Cessna 172R Skyhawk II	172-80316	N9491F	11. 3.98	
G-OPFW	HS.748 Srs.2A/266	1714	G-BMFT VP-BFT/VR-BFT/G-BMFT/5W-FAO/G11-10	1. 7.98	
G-OPHA	Robinson R-44 Astro	0359		17. 7.97	To CS-HDW 12/97. Canx 29.12.97.
G-OPHT	Schleicher ASH-26E	26105		6. 2.97	
G-OPIB	English Electric Lightning F.6	95238	XR773	31.12.92	To ZU-BEW 2/97. Canx 13.2.97.
G-OPIC	Reims Cessna FRA.150L Aerobat	0234	G-BGNZ PH-GAB/D-EIQE	20. 6.95	
G-OPIG	ARV1 Super 2	010	G-BMSJ	31.10.86	Force landed at Bere Regis on 8.4.92. Canx as WFU 3.2.93. To G-XARV 11/95.
G-OPIK	Eiri PIK-20E Srs.1	20233	PH-651	27. 1.82	
G-OPIP	Pearce Jabiru XL	0253		14. 4.99	No UK Permit to Fly issued. Canx by CAA 28.6.99.
G-OPIT	CFM Streak Shadow Srs.SA	K.126-SA & PFA/161A-11624		22.11.89	
G-OPIX	Cessna 180K Skywagon II	180-53170	N186MA N13270	26. 9.90	To ZK-SCB 11/94. Canx 7.11.94.
G-OPJC	Cessna 152 II	152-82280	N68354	7. 6.88	
G-OPJD	PA-28RT-201T Turbo Arrow IV	28R-8231028	N8097V	2.10.89	
G-OPJH	Rollason Druine D.62B Condor	RAE/619	G-AVDW	15. 4.97	(Unmarked at Old Sarum in 6/98)
G-OPJK	Europa Avn Europa	17 & PFA/247-12487		29. 4.93	
G-OPJT	Enstrom 280C-UK Shark	1226	G-BKCO	29. 9.83	To G-OTHE 9/87. Canx.
G-OPKF	Cameron Bowler Hat 90SS HAFB	2314		12. 6.90	Canx as PWFU 29.4.97.
G-OPLB	Cessna 340A II	340A-0486	G-FCHJ G-BJLS/(N6315X)	11. 7.95	
G-OPLC	DH.104 Dove 8	04212	G-BLRB VP962	10. 1.91	
G-OPMB	Cessna P.210N Pressurized Centurion II	P210-00215	N4553K	2. 2.88	To (EI-CAS)/EI-CAX 7/90. Canx 19.6.90.
G-OPME	PA-23-250 Aztec D	27-4099	G-ODIR G-AZGB/N878SH/N10F	31. 3.94	
G-OPMT	Lindstrand LBL-105A HAFB	052		30. 9.93	
G-OPNH	Stoddard-Hamilton Glasair IIRG	PFA/149-13011	G-CINY	14.10.98	
G-OPNI	Bell 206B JetRanger	83	G-BXAA F-GKYR/HB-XOR/G-BHMV/VH-SJJ/VH-FVR	24. 4.96	Crashed in sea off Charmouth, near Lyme Regis on 5.4.99.
G-OPOL	HS.125 Srs.F3B/RA	25171	G-BXPU (N171AV)/G-BXPU/G-AXPU/G-IBIS/G-AXPU/HB-VBT/G-5-19	17. 6.86	To G-IFTC 7/94. Canx.
G-OPOP	Enstrom 280C-UK-2 Shark	1195	G-OFED	23. 1.84	To F-OIAD. Canx 21.11.95.
G-OPPL	American Aviation AA-5A Cheetah	AA5A-0867	G-BGNN	11.10.85	
G-OPPP	Embraer EMB.110P1 Bandeirante	110-235	XC-DAI PT-SAB	3. 1.91	To G-OHIG 3/95. Canx.
G-OPPS	Avions Mudry CAP.231 (Originally regd as CAP.230)	11	F-GGYN F-WZCI/G-OPPS	12. 3.90	To G-PELG 4/99. Canx.
G-OPRA	PA-31 Turbo Navajo	31-109	G-VICK G-AWED/N9076Y	26. 2.92	To N107G.
G-OPRO	MDH Hughes 369E (500E)	0360E	N1607L	9. 3.90	DBR when it crashed in a field near Lydd on 6.6.92. Canx as destroyed 7.6.93. To ZK-HOL 8/96.
G-OPSA	BAe 146 Srs.100	E1002	G-SSHH (G-BIAE)	20. 1.84	To G-5-146/N5828B 10/84. Canx 28.9.84.

Regn	Type	c/n	Previous identity	Regn date	Fate or immediate subsequent identity (if known)
G-OPSF	PA-38-112 Tomahawk	38-79A0998	EI-BLT G-BGZI	13.10.82	
G-OPSL	PA-32R-301 Saratoga SP	32R-8013085	G-IMPW N8186A	4. 1.99	
G-OPST	Cessna 182R Skylane II	182-67932	N9317H	16. 6.88	
G-OPTS	Robinson R-22 Beta	2712		16. 7.97	
G-OPUB	Slingsby T.67M Firefly 160	2002	G-DLTA G-SFTX	18.10.96	
G-OPUP	Beagle B.121 Pup Srs.150	B121-062	G-AXEU (5N-AJC)/G-35-062	31.10.84	
G-OPUS	Pearce Jabiru SK	PFA/274-13343		16. 7.98	
G-OPWH	Dassault Falcon 900B	151	F-WWFK	31.10.95	
G-OPWK	American Aviation AA-5A Cheetah	AA5A-0663	G-OAEL N26706	26. 5.92	
G-OPWL	Bell 206B JetRanger III	3665	G-BPCZ N17EA/HI-405/N3172A	27. 9.89	To D-HRFB 4/92. Canx 8.4.92.
G-OPWS	Mooney M.20K (231)	25-0663	N1162W	12. 4.91	
G-OPYE	Cessna 172S Skyhawk II	172S-8059	N653SP	19. 2.99	
G-ORAC	Cameron Van 110SS HAFB	4577		22. 6.99	
G-ORAF	CFM Streak Shadow (PFA c/n conflicts with MW.6 G-MYCU)	K.134-SA & PFA/161A-11627		18. 5.90	
"N-ORAK"	BAe ATP	2071		----	Fuselage marked as such 6/96 with fire service at Woodford.
G-ORAL	HS.748 Srs.2A/334SCD	1756	G-BPDA G-GLAS/9Y-TFS/G-11-8	13. 8.99	
G-ORAR	PA-28-181 Archer III	2890224	N9255G	6. 6.95	
G-ORAV	Cessna 337D Super Skymaster	337-1088	G-AXGJ N86127	4. 6.80	To OY-BHR. Canx 6.2.86.
G-ORAY	Reims Cessna F.182Q Skylane II	0132	G-BHDN	26. 3.80	To F-.... 3/98. Canx.
G-ORBY	Sukhoi Su-26MX	5201	CCCP-5201	26. 3.92	To N19PC 11/97. Canx 22.10.97.
G-ORCE	Cessna 550 Citation II (Unit No.391)	550-0343	A6-SMS N56FB/N20GT/N721US/G-MINE/(N1214D)	13. 4.88	To N789TT 12/93. Canx 22.12.93.
G-ORCL	Cessna 421C Golden Eagle III	421C-1223	N27089	8. 5.87	To N200DC 7/99. Canx 15.7.99.
G-ORDN	PA-28R-200 Cherokee Arrow II	28R-7235294	G-BAJT	21. 7.89	Badly damaged on landing at Stapleford on 27.5.96. Canx by CAA 18.4.97. (Wreck in open store 2/99 Stapleford)
G-ORDO	PA-30-160 Twin Comanche B	30-1648	N8485Y	19. 4.91	
G-ORDY	Thunder Ax7-77 HAFB	2364	G-BVDB	9. 7.97	Restored as G-BVDB 10/98. Canx.
G-ORED	PBN BN-2T Turbine Islander	2142	G-BJYW	10. 1.85	
G-OREG	BN-2A Mk.III-1 Trislander	319	SX-CBN G-OREG/G-OAVW/G-AZLJ/G-51-319	29. 1.87	Restored as G-AZLJ 9/96. Canx.
G-OREV	Revolution Helicopters Mini 500	0112		8. 8.96	
G-OREX	Short SD.3-60 Var.200	SH3687	G-BMHY G-14-3687	30. 5.91	To N428SA with new c/n SH3414. Canx 25.1.95.
G-OREY	Cameron O-90 HAFB	2813		10. 3.92	To F-GOBY 5/99. Canx 30.3.98.
G-ORFC	Jurca MJ.5 Sirocco	PFA/2210		16. 5.85	
G-ORFE	Cameron Golf 76SS HAFB	2474		2. 7.91	Canx 2.12.98 on sale to USA.
G-ORFH	ATR-42-310	346	F-WWEI	29.12.93	
G-ORGE	Westland SA.341G Gazelle Srs.1	WA/1108	G-BBHU	22. 7.87	To G-RIFA 6/90. Canx.
G-ORGI	Hawker Hurricane IIB (Canadian Car and Foundary Co. - built)	-	RCAF 5481	20.11.89	To N678DP 2/92. Canx 31.1.92.
G-ORHE	Cessna 500 Citation I (Unit No.220)	500-0220	(N619EA) G-OBEL/G-BOGA/N932HA/N93WD/N5220J	25. 3.96	
G-ORIG	Glaser-Dirks DG-800A	8-39-A29		5. 4.94	
G-ORIX	ARV K1 Super 2	034 & PFA/152-12424	G-BUXH (G-BNVK)	16. 9.93	
G-ORJB	Cessna 500 Citation I (Unit No.392)	500-0364	G-OKSP N40DA/N20WP/(N221JB)/N221AC/HB-VFF/N36892	2. 7.92	
G-ORJS	Bell 206L-3 Long Ranger	51414	C-FJIW G-ORJS	19.12.90	To 9M-BBC. Canx 24.2.93.
G-ORJW	Laverda F.8L Falco Srs.4	403	(PH-...) G-ORJW/D-ELDV/D-ELDY	2.12.85	
G-ORMA	Aerospatiale AS.355F1 Twin Squirrel	5192	G-SITE G-BPHC/N365E	9.11.98	
G-ORMB	Robinson R-22 Beta	1607		14.12.90	
G-ORMC	Beechcraft A200 Super King Air	BB-288	G-BEST	9. 1.80	To SE-IRP 2/85. Canx 28.1.85.
G-ORME	Bell 206B JetRanger III	3000	N5733X	5.10.88	To F-GHRS 8/91. Canx 2.8.91.
G-ORMG	Cessna 172R Skyhawk II	172-80344	N9518F	25. 9.98	
G-ORMP	Cessna 414A Chancellor II	414A-0019	N6577C G-KCAV/N6577C	14. 6.90	To N6161Z 12/92. Canx 24.11.92.
G-OROB	Robinson R-22 Beta	0965	G-TBFC N80287	11. 6.90	(Spares use 9/97)
G-OROD	PA-18-150 Super Cub	18-7856	SE-CRD	27. 6.89	
G-OROG	Cessna 401	401-0165	G-ZEUS G-ODJM/G-BSIX/G-CAFE(2)/G-AWXM/N4065Q	29. 1.85	To G-OADS 4/86. Canx.
G-OROM	Eurocopter AS.355N Twin Squirrel	5619		21.11.96	Fatal crash 28.1.98 nr.M40 Motorway, nr Souldern, Oxon. Canx as destroyed 13.5.98.
G-ORON	Colt 77A HAFB	1149		8. 3.88	
G-OROY	Partenavia P.68B Victor	141	G-BFSU	21. 9.81	To G-ENCE 6/84. Canx.
G-OROZ	Aerospatiale AS.350B2 Ecureuil	2617		26. 2.92	

Regn	Type	c/n	Previous identity	Regn date	Fate or immediate subsequent identity (if known)
G-ORPR	Cameron O-77 HAFB	2341		26. 6.90	
G-ORSJ(1)	DH.114 Heron 2	14072	XR445 G-ARKU/VR-NAQ	. 4.90R	NTU - To G-ODLG 4/90. Canx.
G-ORSJ(2)	DH.114 Heron 2	14091	(G-ODLG) XR443/G-ARKV/VR-NCE	20. 4.90	On fire dump at Booker 3/95. Scrapped 6/96. Canx as WFU 23.8.93.
G-ORSP	Beechcraft A36 Bonanza	E-2723	N56037	26.10.92	
G-ORTC	Bell 206B JetRanger II	1669	G-BPNG N20EA/C-GHVB	18.12.89	Restored as G-BPNG 1/91. Canx.
G-ORTM	Glaser-Dirks DG-400	4-209		6. 3.87	
G-ORTW	Lindstrand AM.25000 HAFB (Presumably Richard Branson's "Round the World" Balloon)	304		15. 8.95	
G-ORVB	McCulloch J.2	039	(G-BLGI) N4329G/(G-BKKL)/Bahrain Public Security BPS-3/N4329G	2. 8.89	
G-ORVR	Partenavia P.68B Victor	115	G-BFBD	2.10.95	
G-ORZZ	Robinson R-22 Beta	1608		13.12.90	To G-ICCL 11/93. Canx.
G-OSAB	Enstrom 280FX Shark	2024	N86259	15. 3.89	To G-SOPP 10/97. Canx.
G-OSAL	Cessna 421C Golden Eagle III	421C-0218	OY-BEC SE-GZI/N5471G	13. 7.83	
G-OSAM	HS.125 Srs.700B	257189	(G-OBSM) G-BKHK	23.11.82	To N700BA 12/84. Canx 28.12.84.
G-OSAS	BAe 146 Srs.200	E2204	G-6-204	16. 4.92	To G-6-204/I-FLRA 4/94. Canx 10.3.94.
G-OSCA	Cessna 500 Citation I (Unit No.270)	500-0270	G-SWET N4238X/N68CB/N72BC/N712N/N712J/N5270J	31. 1.96	
G-OSCB	Colt 90A HAFB	2267		1.10.92	Canx by CAA 4.8.98.
G-OSCC	PA-32-300 Cherokee Six	32-7540020	G-BGFD D-EOSH/N32186	27.11.84	
G-OSCH	Cessna 421C Golden Eagle III	421C-0706	G-SALI N26552	13. 9.95	
G-OSCO	Team Minimax	PFA/186-12878		24.12.96	
G-OSDI	Beechcraft 95-B58 Baron	TH-1111	G-BHFY	27. 7.84	
G-OSEA	PBN BN-2B-26 Islander	2175	G-BKOL	27. 8.85	
G-OSEB	Bell 222	47031	G-BNDA A40-CG	20. 2.87	To G-OJLC 3/91. Canx.
G-OSEE	Robinson R-22 Beta	0917		11. 1.89	
G-OSFA	Hoffmann HK-36TC Super Dimona	36.649		15. 6.99	
G-OSFC	Reims Cessna F.152 II	1872	G-BIVJ	31. 1.86	
G-OSFT	PA-31-310 Turbo Navajo B	31-7401239	G-MDAS 5N-AEP/G-BCJZ/N61427	22. 1.93	To N31NB 4/97. Canx 8.4.97.
G-OSGB	PA-31-350 Navajo Chieftain	31-7952155	G-YSKY N3529D	25. 1.99	
G-OSHA	Hughes 269C (300C)	118-0735	N95KS N58272	6. 8.90	No UK CofA issued. Canx by CAA 16.5.91.
G-OSHB	Hughes 269B	78-0375	N9534F N12SC/N9534F	7. 8.90	No UK CofA issued. Canx by CAA 16.5.91.
G-OSHC	Hughes 269C (300C)	64-0323	N8989F	6.12.90	To OO-DLM 8/94. Canx 18.8.94.
G-OSHD	Hughes 269B	16-0235	N9457F	20. 2.91	To CS-HDD. Canx 11.2.94.
G-OSHE	Hughes 269C (300C)	128-0743	N58204	23. 5.91	To EC-FNQ. Canx 24.3.92.
G-OSHH	Cessna 404 Titan	404-0410	N8729K	8. 1.79	To ST-AIT 11/82. Canx 16.12.82.
G-OSHL	Robinson R-22 Beta	1000		19. 4.89	
G-OSIB	Bell 206L-1 Long Ranger	45360	G-LEIS (G-BPEN)/LN-OTZ/SE-HNE/A6-JAQ/N1077G	23. 4.91	Severely damaged in forced landing at Righton Farm, 5 miles east of Oxford on 28.8.93. Canx as WFU 20.10.93.
G-OSII	Cessna 172N Skyhawk 100	172-67768	G-BIVY N73973	17.10.95	
G-OSIP	Robinson R-22 Beta	2916		9. 2.99	
G-OSIS	Pitts S-1S Special	PFA/09-12043		19. 9.94	(Under construction 5/98 at Sywell)
G-OSIX	PA-32-260 Cherokee Six	32-499	G-AZMO SE-EYN	5. 8.86	
G-OSKA	Beechcraft 200 Super King Air	BB-641		22.11.79	To G-CNSI 4/80. Canx.
G-OSKI	BAe 146 Srs.200	E2018	N603AW	7. 8.89	To G-BSRU 8/90. Canx.
G-OSKP	Enstrom 480	5002	F-GSOT G-OSKP/N480EN	6. 6.94	
G-OSKY	Cessna 172M Skyhawk II	172-67389	A6-KCB N73343	27. 2.79	
G-OSLA	Boeing 737-2U4ADV (Line No. 761)	22576		24. 3.81	To N134AW 11/83. Canx 2.11.83.
G-OSLO	Schweizer 269C (300C)	S.1360	N7507L	15. 3.89	
G-OSMC	Cessna 550 Citation II (Unit No.135)	550-0122	C-FCEL N70GM/N135CC/N2746E	6. 7.89	To HB-VKH. Canx 21.3.91.
G-OSMD	Bell 206B JetRanger II	2034	G-LTEK G-BMIB/ZS-HGH	12. 2.99	
G-OSMR	Lake LA-4-200 Buccaneer	650	EI-BNB N1057L	13. 3.96	
G-OSMS	Robinson R-22 Beta	1528	G-BXYW HA-MIU/N528SH	22. 2.99	
G-OSMT	Europa Avn Europa	PFA/247-12705		15. 6.94	
G-OSNB	Cessna 550 Citation II (Unit No.569)	550-0569	G-JFRS N1299P	2. 7.90	To 5Y-TWE /97. Canx 24.11.97.
G-OSND	Reims Cessna FRA.150M Aerobat	0272	G-BDOU	16.10.84	
G-OSNI	PA-23-250 Aztec C	27-3852	G-AWER N6556Y	2. 7.98	

Regn	Type	c/n	Previous identity	Regn date	Fate or immediate subsequent identity (if known)
G-OSOE	HS.748 Srs.2A/275	1697	G-AYYG	17.11.97	
			ZK-MCF/C-GRCU/ZK-MCF/G-AYYG/ZK-MCF/G-AYYG/ZK-MCF/G-AYYG/G-11-9		
G-OSOO	MDH Hughes 369E (500E)	0298E		10. 5.89	
G-OSOW	PA-28-140 Cherokee	28-23780	G-AVWH	13. 6.94	
G-OSPI	Robinson R-22 Beta	0793		9. 6.88	To EI-CFX 6/92. Canx 10.6.92.
G-OSPL	Cessna P.210N Pressurized Centurion II	P210-00639	N5101W	9. 2.83	To F-GCJR(2) 12/84. Canx 12.11.84.
G-OSPS	PA-18-95 Super Cub (L-18C-PI) (Frame no. 18-1527)	18-1555	OO-SPS (G-AWRH)/OO-HMI/ALAT 51-15555	9. 7.92	
G-OSPT	PA-31-350 Chieftain	31-7405209	N54362	17. 4.79	To N42076 3/81. Canx 18.3.81.
G-OSRF	Cessna 421C Golden Eagle III	421C-0692	N90503 G-OSRF/N2654X	14. 9.79	To N421EE 12/92. Canx 23.12.92.
G-OSSH	Cessna 421C Golden Eagle III	421C-0617	N88627	11. 1.79	To N8507Z 10/80. Canx 23.10.80.
G-OSST	Colt 77A HAFB	737		28.10.85	
G-OSSY	PA-28-181 Archer II	28-8090146	N81215	19. 8.85	To G-ERNI 10/91. Canx.
G-OSTA	Auster J/1 Autocrat	1957	G-AXUJ PH-OTO	22. 7.99	
G-OSTC	American Aviation AA-5A Cheetah	AA5A-0848	N26967	22. 4.91	
G-OSTU	American Aviation AA-5A Cheetah	AA5A-0807	G-BGCL	18. 4.95	
G-OSTY	Reims Cessna F.150G	0129	G-AVCU	21. 3.97	
G-OSUE	Bell 206B JetRanger III	3588	G-BKBY (G-BKCF)	14. 8.87	Destroyed in fatal crash near Crowthorpe on 14.8.92. Canx as WFU 26.11.92.
G-OSUN	BAe 146 Srs.200	E2020	C-FEXN N604AW	23. 8.89	To G-BSRV 8/90. Canx.
G-OSUP	Lindstrand LBL-90A HAFB	098		17. 3.94	
G-OSUS	Mooney M.20K (231)	25-0429	OY-SUS (N3597H)	7.11.94	
G-OSVO	Cameron Hopper Servo 30SS HAFB	3077		30. 4.93	
G-OSVY	Sky 31-24 HAFB	104		28. 5.98	
G-OSWA	Enstrom F-28C-UK-2	138	G-BZZZ G-BBBZ	26. 5.95	Canx 11.8.97 on sale to Hungary.
G-OTAC	Robinson R-22 Beta	2737		8.10.97	
G-OTAD	Cessna 421C Golden Eagle III	421C-0223	G-BEVL N5476G	25. 9.85	To G-BMLZ 12/85. Canx.
G-OTAF	Aero L-39ZO Albatros	232337	N40VC	9. 2.95	
			N159JC/(N4321X)/Chad AF TT-ROB/Libyan Arab AF 2337		
G-OTAL	ARV1 Super 2	024	G-BNGZ	10. 9.87	
G-OTAM	Cessna 172M Skyhawk II	172-64098	N29060	13. 2.89	
G-OTAN	PA-18-135 (L-21B-PI) Super Cub (Frame No.18-3850)	18-3845	OO-TAN (OO-DPD)/R.Netherlands AF R-155/54-2445	28.10.96	
G-OTAX	PA-31-350 Navajo Chieftain	31-7952019	N27877	1. 9.87	Restored as N27877 3/91. Canx 20.3.91.
G-OTBY	PA-32-300 Cherokee Six	32-7940219	N2932G	14. 2.91	
G-OTCH	CFM Streak Shadow	K.207 & PFA/206-12401		28.10.93	
G-OTDB	MDHC Hughes 369E (500E)	0204E	G-BXUR HA-MSC	7. 4.98	
G-OTED	Robinson R-22 HP	0209	G-BMYR ZS-HLG	17. 1.96	
G-OTEL	Thunder Ax8-90 HAFB	1790		13. 6.90	
G-OTFT	PA-38-112 Tomahawk	38-78A0311	G-BNKW N9274T	14. 3.97	
G-OTGT	Cessna 560 Citation V	560-0517	N5145V	22. 6.99	
G-OTHE	Enstrom 280C-UK Shark	1226	G-OPJT G-BKCO	22. 9.87	
G-OTHL	Robinson R-22 Beta	0738	G-DSGN	28.11.94	
G-OTIM	Bensen B.8MV Gyrocopter	G/01-1084		5. 6.90	
G-OTKI	Cessna 550 Citation II (Unit No. 265)	550-0230	(N6804N)	. .81R	NTU - To N3254G. Canx.
G-OTMC	Beechcraft 400 BeechJet	RJ-50	N1550Y	23.10.89	To N56GA 10/92. Canx 1.10.92.
G-OTNT(1)	BAe 146 Srs.200QT	E2056	N146QT N146FT/G-5-056	. .87R	NTU - To G-5-056/G-TNTA 4/87. Canx.
G-OTNT(2)	Cameron Cider Bottle 120SS HAFB	3067		9. 7.93	
G-OTOE	Aeronca 7AC Champion	7AC-4621	G-BRWW N1070E/NC1070E	2. 4.90	Badly damaged on landing at Coombe Farm, Spreyton on 31.5.95.
G-OTOM	Reims Cessna FR.172J Rocket	0424	D-EGJG	4. 5.79	To 5H-VDA 11/81. Canx 16.11.81.
G-OTOO	Stolp SA.300 Starduster Too	PFA/35-13352		26. 8.98	
G-OTOW	Cessna 175BX Skylark (Modified to 172 standard)	175-56997	G-AROC N8297T	22. 9.82	Restored as G-AROC 2/98. Canx.
G-OTOY	Robinson R-22 Beta	0888	G-BPEW	5. 9.97	
G-OTRG	Cessna TR.182 Turbo-Skylane RG II	R182-00766	(N736SU)	14. 3.79	
G-OTRV	Van's RV-6	PFA/181-13302		27. 5.98	
G-OTSB	BN-2A Mk.III-2 Trislander (Mod to three-bladed propellors by 12/93)	1027	G-BDTO 8P-ASC/G-BDTO/(C-GYOX)/G-BDTO	7. 1.86	To G-RBSI 2/96. Canx.
G-OTSL	Agusta A.109A II	7393		10.11.87	To G-EEVS 8/91. Canx.

Regn	Type	c/n	Previous identity	Regn date	Fate or immediate subsequent identity (if known)
G-OTSP	Aerospatiale AS.355F1 Twin Squirrel	5177	G-XPOL G-BPRF/N363E	31. 3.98	
G-OTSW	Pitts S-1E Special	PFA/09-10885	G-BLHE	15. 6.89	Canx as TWFU 12.1.96. To G-YOYO 5/96.
G-OTTA	Colt 1.5 MCB HAFB	468		5. 8.83	Canx as WFU 21.11.89.
G-OTTI	Cameron OTTI 34SS HAFB	3490		23. 3.95	
G-OTTO	Cameron Katalog 82SS HAFB	2843		15. 6.92	
G-OTUG	PA-18-150 Super Cub (Frame No 18-5121)	18-5352	(G-BKNM) PH-MBA/ALAT 18-5352	17. 2.83	
G-OTUP	Lindstrand LBL-180A HAFB	111		28. 3.94	
G-OTUX	PA-28R-201T Turbo Arrow III	28R-7703293	SE-GPZ	24. 3.81	To F-GEON 7/87. Canx 26.5.87.
G-OTVS	BN-2T Turbine Islander	419	G-BPBN G-BCMY	14. 2.83	Damaged at Headcorn on 11.3.89. CofA expired 18.5.90. (Open store 3/96 at Headcorn) Canx by CAA 8.4.94.
G-OTWO	Rutan Defiant	114		24. 6.87	(Stored Lydd 11/97)
G-OTYA	Robinson R-22 Beta	0984	OH-HKK G-STMI	15. 5.97	Canx as WFU 9.12.98.
G-OTYJ	PA-28-161 Cadet	2841284	G-OLSF N92008	8. 4.91	Restored as G-OLSF 2/98. Canx.
G-OUAE	Cameron Wimi Airbus 90SS HAFB	2280		14. 6.90	Canx 8.8.94 on sale to the UAE.
G-OULD	Gould Mk.1 HAFB (84,000 cu.ft)	CAG.1		22. 7.81	Canx by CAA 9.3.98.
G-OUPP	Bell 206B JetRanger III	3600	N206SH N2261L	5. 1.87	To F-GFDY 2/88. Canx 14.1.88.
G-OURO	Europa Avn Europa (Tri-gear)	16 & PFA/247-12522		13.12.93	(ff 21.6.96)
G-OUSA	Colt 105A HAFB	1049		12. 3.87	Canx by CAA 3.3.97. (Based in Texas, USA)
G-OUTA	Boeing 737-33A (Line No. 1436)	23635	N6069P N3282Y	25. 1.88	To F-GFUA 6/88. Canx 22.6.88.
G-OUVI	Cameron O-105 HAFB	1766		4. 5.89	
G-OUZO	Airbus A.320-231	449	EI-VIR N449RX/SX-BSV/(G-VSEE)/N449RX/F-WWIG	8.11.95	
G-OVAA	Colt Jumbo SS HAFB (Conventional HAFB with nose/wings/tail of Virgin 747)	1426		11. 5.89	
G-OVAN	Short SC.7 Skyvan 3-100-34	SH1892	PK-PSD G-AYZA/G-14-64	26. 3.86	DBR on landing Ampuria Brava, Spain on 28.1.94. Canx as destroyed 17.6.94.
G-OVAX	Colt AS-80 Mk II Hot-Air Airship	1501		3. 7.89	
G-OVBF	Cameron A-250 HAFB	3494		1. 3.95	
G-OVBJ	Bell 206B JetRanger III	2734	G-BXDS OY-HDK/N661PS	19. 2.98	
G-OVER	PA-28-181 Warrior II	28-7816267	G-BKNE OO-GMB/OO-HCL	14. 1.88	Fatal crash west of the A429 road near Detling on 16.6.88. Canx as destroyed 17.5.89.
G-OVET	Cameron O-56 HAFB	3939		25. 6.96	
G-OVFM	Cessna 120	14720	N2119V NC2119V	29. 4.88	
G-OVFR	Reims Cessna F.172N Skyhawk II	1892		23. 5.79	
G-OVID	Light Aero Avid Flyer (built by J.Pelafigue)	NMFC.11760	N879UP	31. 5.91	(Stored 1/97)
G-OVIP(1)	BAe 125 Srs.800B	258010	(G-BLKS) G-5-19	. .84R	NTU - To N84A. Canx.
G-OVIP(2)	Gulfstream G.1159 Gulfstream II	91	N219GA VH-ASM/G-AYMI/N17586	2. 3.85	To VR-BRM. Canx 13.2.89.
G-OVMC	Reims Cessna F.152 II	1667		29. 5.79	(Stored 6/97)
G-OVNE	Cessna 401A	401A-0036	N401XX (N171SF)/N71SF/N6236Q	11. 3.88	CofA lapsed 8.10.92. Canx by CAA 8.2.94.
G-OVNR	Robinson R-22 Beta	1634		24.12.90	
G-OVVB	Beechcraft A36 Bonanza	E-2782	N82469	13. 9.93	To G-JOCK 3/97. Canx.
G-OWAC	Reims Cessna F.152 II	1678	G-BHEB (OO-HNW)	25. 2.80	
G-OWAK	Reims Cessna F.152 II	1677	G-BHEA	25. 2.80	
G-OWAL	PA-34-220T Seneca III	3448030	D-GAPN(2) N9163K	7. 7.98	
G-OWAR	PA-28-161 Warrior II	28-8616054	TF-OBO N9521N	18. 2.88	
G-OWAZ	Pitts S-1C Special	43JM	G-BRPI N199M	22.11.94	(Extensively damaged on landing 8.3.97 at Sleap)
G-OWBC	Thunder Ax10-180 Srs.2 HAFB	2352		9. 6.93	To G-BWNX 1/96. Canx.
G-OWCG	Bell 222	47041	G-VERT G-JLBZ/G-BNDB/A40-CH	12. 8.94	
G-OWDB	HS.125 Srs.700B	257040	G-BYFO HB-VMD/VP-BPE/VR-BPE/N47TJ/EC-ETI/EC-375/G-OWEB/HZ-RC1	18. 2.99	
G-OWEB	HS.125 Srs.700B	257040	HZ-RC1	3. 9.87	To EC-375/EC-ETI 3/90. Canx 20.12.89.
G-OWEL	Colt 105A HAFB	1773		18. 5.90	
G-OWEN	K & S Jungster 1	PFA/44-10124		13.11.78	
G-OWER	PA-31-310 Turbo Navajo	31-651	(HB-...) G-OWER/G-FOIL/D-IHFD/N6744L	9. 4.84	To VR-BJM 12/86. Canx 10.12.86.
G-OWET	Thurston TSC-1A2 Teal	037	C-FNOR (N1342W)	28. 9.94	
G-OWGC	Slingsby T.61F Venture T.2	1875	XZ555	14. 8.91	
G-OWIN	IRMA BN-2A-8 Islander	653	EI-AWM G-AYXE	22. 3.83	
G-OWIZ	Luscombe 8A Silvaire	3071	N71644 NC71644	18.10.89	

Regn	Type	c/n	Previous identity	Regn date	Fate or immediate subsequent identity (if known)
G-OWJM	Agusta-Bell 206B JetRanger III	8596	G-BHXV	20. 3.81	Restored as G-BHXV 1/85. Canx.
G-OWLC	PA-31-300 Turbo Navajo	31-679	G-AYFZ N6771L	13. 6.91	
G-OWLD	BAe 146 Srs.200	E2031	N173US N353PS	16. 7.96	To EI-CNQ 7/97. Canx 2.7.97.
G-OWND	Robinson R-44 Astro	0644		26. 8.99	
G-OWNR	Beechcraft B200 Super King Air	BB-929	N848J	20. 8.87	To N81AJ 11/93. Canx 26.11.93.
G-OWOW	Cessna 152 II	152-83199	G-BMSZ N47254	10. 5.95	
G-OWVA	PA-28-140 Cherokee Cruiser	28-7625038	N4459X	12. 6.87	To G-RVRA 1/97. Canx.
G-OWWF	Colt 2500A HAFB	1500		25. 9.89	Flown on Trans-Pacific flight and badly damaged on landing on a frozen lake in North West Territories, Canada 17.1.91. Canx as destroyed 10.3.97.
G-OWWW	Europa Avn Europa	PFA/247-12683		9. 6.94	
G-OWYN	Aviamilano F.14 Nibbio	208	HB-EVZ I-SERE	2. 2.87	
G-OXBY	Cameron N-90 HAFB	1993	PH-DUM	9. 6.94	
G-OXEC	Cessna 500 Citation I (Unit No.093)	500-0093	N611SW OO-FBY/PH-CTB/N593CC	22. 5.89	To G-OCPI 7/91. Canx.
G-OXEH	Cessna 550 Citation II (Unit No.319)	550-0288	G-JETB G-MAMA/G-JETB/N4564P/G-JETB/N6865C	. .93R	NTU - Remained as G-JETB. Canx.
G-OXKB	Cameron Jaguar XK8 Sports Car 110SS HAFB	3941		9. 7.96	
G-OXLI	BAe Jetstream Srs.4100	41003		5. 2.91	WFU & stored in 11/96 at Prestwick. Canx as WFU 31.7.97.
G-OXRG	Colt Film Can SS HAFB (Agfacolor Film Cassette shape)	2138		17. 1.92	Canx as WFU 29.4.97.
G-OXTC	PA-23-250 Aztec D	27-4344	G-AZOD N697RC/N6976Y	31. 5.89	
G-OXVI	Vickers Supermarine 361 Spitfire LF.XVIe	CBAF/IX/4262	7246M TD248	22. 8.89	
G-OYAK	SPP Yakovlev Yak C.11 (C/n also quoted as 1701139 and 690120)	171205	705 Egyptian AF/OK-KIH	25. 2.88	
G-OYES	Mainair Blade	1186-1198-7 & W989		12.11.98	
G-OZAP	Hughes 369HS (500HS)	33-0461S	G-FBHH N2186K/PK-AVH/PK-PDO	19. 2.99	To N846D. Canx 12.8.99.
G-OZAR	Enstrom 480	5007	G-BWFF	31. 7.95	
G-OZBA	Airbus A.320-212	422	(G-MALE) F-WWIP	25. 3.94	To 6Y-JMB(2) 5/99. Canx 7.5.99.
G-OZBB	Airbus A.320-212	389	C-FTDW G-OZBB/C-FTDW/G-OZBB/C-FTDW/G-OZBB/C-FTDW/G-OZBB/F-WWDI	21. 3.94	
G-OZBC	Airbus A.321-231	633	D-ASSE D-AVZJ/F-WWIJ	24. 4.97	
G-OZEE	Light Aero Avid Speed Wing Mk.4	PFA/189-12308		18. 4.94	
G-OZLN	Moravan Zlin Z.242L	0651	OK-XNA (SE-KMM)	2.10.92	
"G-OZOE"	Westland WG.30	?		----	Noted at Lydd 11.12.98 with false marks.
G-OZOI	Cessna R.182 Skylane RG II	R182-01950	G-ROBK	31. 5.85	
G-OZRH	BAe 146 Srs.200	E2047	N188US N364PS	29. 1.96	
G-OZUP	Colt 77A HAFB	1157		10.11.87	Canx by CAA 4.8.98.
G-OZZI	Pearce Jabiru SK	PFA/274-13176		15. 8.97	

G-P

Regn	Type	c/n	Previous identity	Regn date	Fate or immediate subsequent identity (if known)
G-PACE	Robin R.1180T Aiglon	218		16.10.78	
G-PACK	Cessna 152 II	150-81575	N65477	23. 1.89	To CS-AYR. Canx 16.12.91.
G-PACL	Robinson R-22 Beta	1893	N2314S	17.12.91	
G-PACY	Rutan Vari-Viggin	0001 & PFA/65-10449		18.12.78	No Permit issued. Canx by CAA 8.7.91.
G-PADI	Cameron V-77 HAFB	1809		18. 8.88	
G-PADS	Commander Aircraft 114B	14637	N60987	15. 1.98	
G-PADY	Rockwell Commander 114	14388	(G-BFXT) N5840N	12.10.78	To I-PADI 4/86. Canx 17.4.86.
G-PAGE	Reims Cessna F.150L	0824	PH-CEU	5. 6.80	To CS-AVI 8/93. Canx 19.2.90.
G-PAGS	Aerospatiale SA.341G Gazelle Srs.1	1155	G-OAFY G-SFTH/G-BLAP/N62406	11. 3.96	
G-PAIZ	PA-12 Super Cruiser	12-2018	N3215M	11. 4.94	
G-PALL	PA-46-350P Malibu Mirage	4636091	G-RMST	4. 3.99	
G-PALM	PA-34-200T Seneca II	34-7570039	SE-LAN N32625	23. 6.92	Restored as N32625 3/93. Canx 31.3.93.
G-PALS	Enstrom 280C-UK-2 Shark	1191	N5688M	17. 7.80	Failed to gain lift on take-off from Shoreham on 14.10.89 and rolled over on its side in a field 2 miles north-west of Hartfield.
G-PAMI	Aerospatiale AS.355F1 Twin Squirrel	5104	G-BUSA	26.11.85	To G-ICSG 4/93. Canx.

Regn	Type	c/n	Previous identity	Regn date	Fate or immediate subsequent identity (if known)
G-PAMS	Ted Smith Aerostar 601P	61P-0275-060	G-GAIR N90488	27. 7.89	
G-PAPA	Aerospatiale AS.355F1 Twin Squirrel	5120	G-CNET G-MCAH	2. 2.87	To G-GLOW 11/89. Canx.
G-PAPS	PA-32R-301T Turbo Saratoga SP	32R-8529005	F-GELX N4385D	8. 7.97	
G-PAPU	Beechcraft 58PA Baron	TJ-74	G-NIPU N1PU/N313A/N1PU/N1PT/N1899L	6. 7.89	To F-.... Canx 15.7.99.
G-PARA	Cessna 207 Skywagon	207-00153	D-EIKA (N1553U)	31. 1.79	To A6-DAT. Canx 11.3.98.
G-PARI	Reims Cessna F.172RG Cutlass II (Wichita c/n 0010)	0004	N4685R	19.11.79	
G-PARK	Lake LA-4-200 Buccaneer	543	G-BBGK N39779	14. 6.82	To EI-BUH 5/87. Canx 21.5.87.
G-PARR	Colt Bottle 90SS HAFB (Old Parr Whisky bottle shape)	1953		15. 3.91	Canx as TWFU 10.2.97.
G-PARS	Evans VP-2	V2-1932 & PFA/63-10170		7. 9.78	Canx by CAA 2.9.91.
G-PART	Partenavia P.68B Victor	62	OY-CEY D-GATE/PH-EEO/(N718R)	19.12.84	To F-GMPT 3/95. Canx 22.2.95.
G-PASA	MBB Bo.105DBS-4 (Rebuild with new pod S-913 .93 - regn D-HIFA reserved 4/93)	S.41	G-BGWP F-ODMZ/G-BGWP/HB-XFD/N153BB/D-HDAS	3. 4.89	Canx as WFU 20.4.93. To G-BUXS 5/93.
G-PASB	MBB Bo.105D	S.135	VH-LSA G-BDMC/D-HDEC	2. 3.89	(Original pod from 1994 rebuild - see G-WMAA) Canx as WFU 9.8.94. (On rebuild 3/96)(Gutted airframe display 4/98)
G-PASC	MBB Bo.105DBS-4	S.421	G-BNPS N4929M/D-HDMT	27.10.89	
G-PASD	MBB Bo.105DBS-4	S.656	G-BNRS N14ES/N4572Q/D-HDTZ	27.10.89	
G-PASE	Aerospatiale AS.355F1 Twin Squirrel	5042	N57818	18. 7.90	To G-KGMT 8/98. Canx.
G-PASF	Aerospatiale AS.355F1 Twin Squirrel	5033	G-SCHU N915EG/N5777H	7. 3.91	
G-PASG	MBB Bo.105DBS-4	S.819	G-MHSL D-HFCC	7.12.92	
G-PASH	Aerospatiale AS.355F1 Twin Squirrel	5040	F-GHLI LX-HUG/F-GHLI/N356E	17. 5.96	
G-PASK	Aerospatiale AS.355F1 Twin Squirrel	5326	(F-GIVX) I-DEDA	25. 1.96	To G-MASK 5/96. Canx.
G-PASS	Boeing MDH MD-900 Explorer (Built in MD-902 configuration)	900-00056	N9234P	12.10.98	
G-PASU	IRMA BN-2T Turbine Islander	2144	5T-BSA G-BJYY	27. 5.93	
G-PASV	IRMA BN-2B-21 Islander	2157	G-BKJH HC-BNR/G-BKJH	26. 2.92	
G-PASW	BN-2A Islander	150	G-AXXJ OO-ARI(3)/G-AXXI/G-51-150	22. 5.90	To 4X-CAH. Canx 19.7.91.
G-PASX	MBB Bo.105DBS-4	S.814	D-HDZX	20.12.89	
G-PASY	PBN BN-2A-26 Islander	2011	G-BPCB G-BEXA/G-MALI/G-DIVE/(ZB503)/"ZA503"/G-DIVE/G-BEXA	6. 3.89	To G-CHES 4/94. Canx.
G-PASZ	IRMA BN-2A-26 Islander	878	G-BPCD G-BFNV	6. 3.89	To 5B-CHV. Canx 5.7.91.
G-PATA	McDonnell Douglas DC-9-83 (MD-83) (Line No. 1332)	49398	N6202S (G-LOGI)	24. 4.87	To EI-CBE 3/90. Canx 23.3.90.
G-PATB	McDonnell Douglas DC-9-83 (MD-83) (Line No. 1356)	49400	(G-DAIO)	29. 4.87	To 9Y-THY. Canx 14.2.90.
G-PATC	McDonnell Douglas DC-9-83 (MD-83) (Line No. 1429)	49662	N1005W (N940MC)	26. 4.88	To F-GHEC 12/88. Canx 9.12.88.
G-PATD	McDonnell Douglas DC-9-83 (MD-83) (Line No. 1437)	49663	F-GHEH G-PATD/N30008/(N941MC)	5. 5.88	To EC-438/EC-EUF 4/90. Canx 5.4.90.
G-PATE	Boeing 737-33A (Line No. 1727)	24093		8. 6.89	To PP-VOR 5/90. Canx 11.5.90.
G-PATF	Europa Avn Europa	PFA/247-12757		5. 1.99	
G-PATG	Cameron O-90 HAFB	3856		13. 3.96	
G-PATN	Socata TB-10 Tobago	307	G-LUAR	25. 3.97	
G-PATP	Lindstrand LBL-77A HAFB	471		8. 7.97	
G-PATS	Europa Avn Europa	PFA/247-12888		19. 7.95	
G-PATT	Cessna 404 Titan	404-0055	G-BHGL F-BYAJ/F-TEDL/F-BYAJ/N5437G	12. 5.80	To 5Y-SNM 11/89. Canx 27.10.89.
G-PATW	Bell 206B JetRanger III	2503	LN-OPN N712HH	20.10.89	Fatal crash after hitting power lines shortly after take-off from Kip Hall, Stanley, Co.Durham on 14.7.90. Canx as destroyed 19.11.90.
G-PATY	Colt Flying Sausage SS HAFB	569		18. 5.84	Canx by CAA 19.5.95.
G-PATZ	Europa Avn Europa	PFA/247-12625		2. 6.98	
G-PAUL	Partenavia P.68B Victor	147		29. 6.78	To EI-BKH 1/81. Canx.
G-PAVL	Robin R.3000/120	170	F-GOVH	22.11.96	
G-PAWL	PA-28-140 Cherokee	28-24456	G-AWEU	8. 9.82	Canx by CAA 2.5.97. (Stored 12/97)
G-PAWS	American Aviation AA-5A Cheetah	AA5A-0806	N2623Q	8. 2.82	
G-PAXO	Robinson R-22	0166	N9067Y	12.11.86	Cartwheeled on take-off from Booker on 29.4.87. Canx as destroyed 23.10.87.
G-PAXX	PA-20-135 Pacer	20-1107	(G-ARCE) F-BLLA/CN-TDJ/F-DADR	20. 5.83	

Regn	Type	c/n	Previous identity	Regn date	Fate or immediate subsequent identity (if known)
G-PAZY	Pazmany PL-4A	4275/12B & PFA/17-10378	G-BLAJ	20.11.89	
G-PBAC	Embraer EMB.110P1 Bandeirante	110-212	F-GCLA F-OGME/F-GCLA/PT-GME	27. 6.96	To G-TABS 8/98. Canx.
G-PBBT	Cameron N-56 HAFB	1535		23. 6.87	
G-PBEL	CFM Shadow Srs.DD	305-DD		27.10.98	
G-PBES	Robinson R-22 Beta	1491	G-EXOR G-CMCM	17. 3.95	
G-PBHF	Robinson R-22 Beta	0889	N8005Y	12. 9.88	To VH-AVL(3) 8/94. Canx 14.6.94.
G-PBTT	Enstrom 480	5010	JA6169	30. 6.98	To N900SA. Canx 23.7.98.
G-PBUS	Pearce Jabiru SK	PFA/274-13269		18. 8.98	
G-PBWH	BAe 125 Srs.800B	258182	G-5-676	22. 8.90	To N128RS 10/95. Canx 18.9.95.
G-PBYY	Enstrom 280FX	2077	G-BXKV D-HHML	15. 8.97	
G-PCAF	Pietenpol Air Camper	PFA/47-12433		1. 6.94	
G-PCDP	Moravan Zlin Z.526F Trener Master	1163	SP-CDP	24.10.94	
G-PCOM	PA-30-160 Twin Comanche B	30-1053	HB-LDD N7957Y	15.10.97	
G-PCOR	Bell 206B JetRanger III	3018	G-BRMF 5Y-KPC	15. 3.94	To VR-HJJ 7/96. Canx 22.7.96.
G-PCUB	PA-18-135 Super Cub (L-21B-PI) (Frame No 18-3893) (Regd incorrectly as c/n 18-3674)	18-3874	(PH-KER) R.Netherlands AF R-184/54-2474	16. 2.81	Canx by CAA 10.3.99.
G-PDCC	Aerospatiale AS.350B Ecureuil	1395	G-PORR F-WZFF	17. 8.84	To SE-HRR. Canx.
G-PDES	Aerospatiale SA.365N Dauphin 2	6096	G-BKXK	25. 3.88	To F-WYMX. Canx 23.11.90.
G-PDGG	Aeromere F.8L Falco Srs.3	208	OO-TOS I-BLIZ	6. 1.98	
G-PDHJ	Cessna T.182R Turbo Skylane II	T182-68092	N6888H	3. 1.85	
G-PDMH	Cessna 340A II	340A-0461	N6282N G-RITA/N6282N	20. 4.98	
G-PDMT	PA-28-161 Warrior II	28-8016111	ZS-LGW N8103D	4.11.86	NTU - To G-BNCR 12/86. Canx 10.12.86.
G-PDOC	PA-44-180 Seminole	44-7995090	G-PVAF N2242A	17.12.85	
G-PDOG	Cessna 305C Bird Dog (L-19E)	24550	F-GKGP French Mil	25. 9.98	
G-PDON	WMB.2 Windtracker HAFB (Toy)	12		11. 9.80	Canx as WFU 17.1.96.
G-PDSI	Cessna 172N Skyhawk II	172-70420	N739BU	4. 1.88	
G-PDWI	Revolution Helicopters Mini-500	0248		14. 2.97	
"G-PDWO"	DHC.1 Chipmunk 22 (Fuselage no. DHB/f/40)	C1/0134	G-AORP WB686	----	Noted painted as such at Perth in 9/67 (until 1974/5).
G-PEAK	Agusta-Bell 206B JetRanger II	8242	G-BLJE SE-HBW	7. 3.94	
G-PEAL	Aerotek Pitts S-2A Special	2048	N81LF N48KA	11. 5.88	Badly damaged in forced landing near the A456 road at Budleigh, near Kidderminster 28.6.91. (Stored 9/97)
G-PEAT	Cessna 421B Golden Eagle II	421B-0432	G-BBIJ N41073	5. 4.84	
G-PEEL	BAe ATP	2023		6.10.89	To G-MANP 10/94. Canx.
G-PEET	Cessna 401A	401A-0099	LX-NTA N3299Q	8. 1.80	To 5Y-BIE. Canx 25.1.93.
G-PEGG	Colt 90A HAFB	1550		28. 6.89	
G-PEGI	PA-34-200T Seneca II	34-7970339	N2907A	27.11.89	
G-PEKT	Socata TB-20 Trinidad	532	N24AS	28. 7.89	
G-PELE	Cameron Pele 80SS HAFB	1582		5. 1.88	Canx by CAA 12.8.96.
G-PELG	Avions Mudry CAP 231	11	G-OPPS F-GGYN/F-WZCI/G-OPPS	6. 4.99	
G-PELI	Pelican Club GS	PFA/165-11214		30. 5.90	To SE-YTO. Canx 13.9.94.
G-PENI	Hughes 369D (500D)	110-0832D	N1108V	26. 2.81	To N2734X 5/82. Canx.
G-PENN	American Aviation AA-5B Tiger	AA5B-0996	(I-TIGR) N3756L	4. 7.80	
G-PENT	Bell 206B JetRanger III	3958	G-IIRB N903CA	12. 7.99	
G-PENY	Sopwith LC-1T Triplane Replica	PFA/21-10035		15. 1.79	To G-BWRA 4/96. Canx.
G-PEPD	PA-31-350 Navajo Chieftain	31-7852164	N27813 C-GHPN/N9017K	16.11.78	To N9745S 7/81. Canx 31.7.81.
G-PERL	Robinson R-22 Beta	0861	N90815	27. 9.88	To G-WIZA 11/94. Canx.
G-PERR	Cameron Bottle 60SS HAFB	699		28. 1.81	Canx as WFU 24.1.92. (Stored 9/93 at British Balloon Museum)
G-PERS	Colt Persil Box SS HAFB	1134		12.10.87	Canx as WFU 22.6.92.
G-PERZ	Bell 206B JetRanger III	4411	N6272T	7. 1.97	
G-PEST	Hawker Tempest II (Bristol-built)(Regd with c/n "1181")	12202	HA604 Indian AF/MW401	9.10.89	(On rebuild 11/96)
G-PETE	Cessna 340A II	340A-0722	N2667N	11. 6.79	To G-JIMS 2/81. Canx.
G-PETR	PA-28-140 Cherokee F	28-7425320	G-BCJL	23. 9.85	
G-PFAA	EAA Model P2 Biplane	PEB/03 & PFA/1338		19. 9.78	
G-PFAB(1)	Clutton FRED Srs.II	PEB/04		19. 9.78	No Permit to Fly issued. Canx as WFU 6.12.85.
G-PFAB(2)	Colomban MC-15 Cri-Cri	376		6.12.85	Canx by CAA 25.2.88 as not built.

Regn	Type	c/n	Previous identity	Regn date	Fate or immediate subsequent identity (if known)
G-PFAB(3)	Colomban MC-15 Cri-Cri	001	F-PYPU	25. 2.88	To G-SHOG 10/96. Canx.
G-PFAC	Clutton FRED Srs.II	PFA/29-10309		19. 9.78	Badly damaged in crash at Dunkeswell on 10.12.88. Canx by CAA 3.4.97.
G-PFAD	Wittman W.8 Tailwind	PFA/31-10259		19. 9.78	Permit expired 21.4.87. (Stored 8/93) Canx by CAA 3.4.97.
G-PFAE	Taylor JT.1 Monoplane	PFA/1426		19. 9.78	Not completed. Canx by CAA 2.9.91.
G-PFAF	Clutton FRED Srs.II	PFA/29-10310		30.10.78	
G-PFAG	Evans VP-1	PFA/7022		13.11.78	
G-PFAH	Evans VP-1	PFA/7004		23.11.78	
G-PFAI	Clutton EC.2 Easy Too	PFA/1361		20.11.78	Canx as WFU 8.8.91.
G-PFAK	Kendal Mayfly	PFA/90-10431		27.11.78	WFU in 7/82 as unsuitable for flight. Canx as WFU 1.8.83. Engine to G-BKCI.
G-PFAL	Clutton FRED Srs.II	PFA/29-10243		7.12.78	(Stored 4/96)
G-PFAM	Clutton FRED Srs.II	WR.1		7.12.78	Canx by CAA 2.8.91.
G-PFAN	Avro 558 Replica	PFA/1369		11.12.78	Canx by CAA 2.9.91.
G-PFAO	Evans VP-1	PFA/7008		12.12.78	
G-PFAP	Phoenix Currie Wot (Built as an SE-5A replica)	PFA/58-10315		12.12.78	
G-PFAR	Isaacs Fury II	PFA/11-10220		18.12.78	
G-PFAS	Garden GY-20 Minicab	PFA/1814		14.12.78	No Permit believed issued. Canx by CAA 16.1.91.
G-PFAT	Monnett Sonerai II	PFA/15-10312		26.10.78	(Stored Newcastle 5/93)
G-PFAU(1)	Evans VP-2	PFA/63-10440		18.12.78	Not completed. Canx 26.10.83.
G-PFAU(2)	Rand KR-2	PFA/129-10909		26.10.83	Canx as WFU 19.8.91.
G-PFAV	Druine D.31 Turbulent	PFA/48-10367		18.12.78	Canx by CAA 2.9.91.
G-PFAW	Evans VP-1	PFA/62-10183		18.12.78	
G-PFAX	Clutton FRED Srs.II	PFA/29-10417		19.12.78	Canx by CAA 2.9.91.
G-PFAY	EAA Biplane	PFA/1525		18.12.78	(Project never commenced)
G-PFAZ	Evans VP-1	V-2465 & PFA/62-10696		19.12.78	Extensively damaged after striking a school building at Pelton Fell & crashed 16.9.90. Canx as destroyed 16.11.90.
G-PFBT	Vickers 806 Viscount	265	G-AOYP	22. 3.94	
G-PFML	Robinson R-44 Astro	0082		9. 9.94	
G-PGAC	MCR-01	PFA/301-13186		27. 1.99	(Nearing completion 4/99 Cambridge)
G-PHAA	Reims Cessna F.150M Commuter	1159	G-BCPE	19. 6.97	
G-PHEL	Robinson R-22 Beta	1669	G-RUMP N2405T	15. 8.96	
G-PHIL	Brookland Hornet (Originally regd as Gyroflight Hornet with c/n 16)	17		7. 7.78	(Stored 5/90)
G-PHON	Cameron Phone SS HAFB (Motorola Microtac Mobile Phone shape)	2505	G-BTEY	13.12.91	
G-PHOT	Thunder & Colt Film Cassette SS HAFB	4507		3. 2.99	
G-PHSI	Colt 90A HAFB	2181		12. 5.92	
G-PHTG	Socata TB-10 Tobago	1008		15.11.89	
G-PHYL	Denney Kitfox Mk.4	PFA/172A-12189		14. 9.98	
G-PIAF	Thunder Ax7-65 HAFB	1885		19.11.90	
G-PICS	Cessna 182F Skylane	182-54832	G-ASHO N3432U	25. 6.81	Destroyed in fatal crash at Thirlmere, near Keswick on 17.1.94. Canx as WFU 13.7.94.
G-PICT	Colt 180A HAFB	1723		22. 3.90	
G-PIDS	Boeing 757-225 (Line No. 6)	22195	N505EA	9. 1.95	
G-PIED	PA-23-250 Aztec F	27-7854137	N6534A	17. 4.79	To (G-BLVM)/G-BLXX 3/85. Canx.
G-PIEL	Menavia Piel CP.301A Emeraude	218	G-BARY F-BIJR	17.11.88	
G-PIES	Thunder Ax7-77Z HAFB	263		13. 2.80	Canx by CAA 23.8.89. (Extant 2/97)
G-PIET	Pietenpol Air Camper	PFA/47-12267		1. 4.93	
G-PIGG	Lindstrand Flying Pig SS HAFB	473		18. 8.97	
G-PIGN	Bolmet Paloma Mk.1	R-334		7. 1.81	No Permit issued - Probably not built. Canx as WFU 5.12.88.
G-PIGS	Socata MS.892E Rallye 150ST	2696	G-BDWB	13. 6.88	
G-PIGY	Short SC.7 Skyvan 3A-100	SH1943	LX-JUL 5T-MAM/(G-14-111)	21.12.95	
G-PIIX	Cessna P.210N Pressurised Centurion II	P210-00130	G-KATH (N4898P)	12. 6.95	
G-PIKE	Robinson R-22 Mariner	1718M		18. 3.91	
G-PIKK	PA-28-140 Cherokee	28-22932	G-AVLA N11C/(N9509W)	19. 8.88	
G-PIKN	Extra Walter EA.230	008	N230JA	25.10.88	To G-TAFO 10/91. Canx.
G-PILE	Rotorway Exec 90	5143		27. 7.93	
G-PILL	Light-Aero Avid Flyer Mk.4	PFA/189-12333		12. 8.97	
G-PINE	Thunder Ax8-90 HAFB	1546		30. 5.89	
G-PING	Aviation Aviation AA-5A Cheetah	AA5A-0878	G-OCWC G-WULL/N27153	6.12.95	(Substantially damaged on landing at Elstree on 23.6.96)
G-PINK	Cameron N-77 HAFB	399		22. 6.78	To PH-INK 8/82. Canx 17.2.82.
G-PINT	Cameron Barrel 60SS HAFB (Wells Brewery Beer Barrel shape)	794		4. 1.82	
G-PINX	Lindstrand Pink Panther SS HAFB	032		23. 4.93	
G-PIPA	PA-28-181 Archer III	2890215		14.12.94	
G-PIPE	Cameron N-56 SS HAFB (Standard N-56 balloon with extension to resemble pipe stem)	562		13. 5.80	Canx by CAA 13.3.92.
G-PIPR	PA-18-95 Super Cub (Regd with frame no. 18-832)	18-826	G-BCDC 4X-ANQ/Israeli DF/AF / 4X-ADE/N1221A	11.10.96	(On rebuild)
G-PIPS	Van's RV-4	PFA/181-11836		3. 8.90	
G-PIPY	Cameron Scottish Piper 105SS HAFB	3815		30. 1.96	

Regn	Type	c/n	Previous identity	Regn date	Fate or immediate subsequent identity (if known)
G-PISA	Thunder Ax7-77 Plug HAFB	184		18.12.78	Not completed - To G-SPOP 29.12.78 with c/n 187. Canx as destroyed 11.3.85.
G-PITS	Pitts S-2AE Special	PFA/09-11001		4. 7.85	(Stored dismantled 3/98 at Abbeyshrule)
G-PITT	Aerotek Pitts S-2A Special	2247	N540BB N31513	14. 6.89	Fatal crash at Inch airfield on 2.12.89. Canx as destroyed 22.2.90.
G-PITZ	Pitts S-2A Special	100ER	N183ER	2.10.87	
G-PIXI	Cyclone Pegasus Quantum 19	7557		27. 8.99	
G-PIXS	Cessna 336 Skymaster	336-0130	N86648	9. 9.88	(Stored at Lydd 11/97)
G-PIZZ	Lindstrand LBL-105A HAFB	629		27. 7.99	
G-PJAY	Cessna 340A	340A-0989	N98DA N3967C	25. 8.89	To 5B-CHN 2/90. Canx 20.2.90.
G-PJCB	Agusta A.109A	7437		25. 5.89	Fatal crash after it struck cables near the A5030 road at Rochester, Staffs. on 27.6.90. Canx as WFU 5.11.91.
G-PJET	Gates LearJet 35A	35A-614	N3815G	10.12.87	To HB-VJC 10/88. Canx 30.9.88.
G-PJMD	Hughes 369D (500D) (Mod to 500E standard)	11-0871D	G-BMJV N1110S	1.11.89	To G-ERIS 3/96. Canx.
G-PJMT	Lancair 320	PFA/191-12348		8. 5.98	
G-PJRT	BAe Jetstream 4100	41002		5. 2.91	CofA expired 1.5.94 & WFU. Stored in 11/96 at Prestwick. Canx as PWFU 27.3.99.
G-PJTM	Reims Cessna FR.172K Hawk XP II	0611	EI-CHJ G-BFIF	13.10.98	
G-PJWB	HS.125 Srs.600B	256033	N330G HA-YA1/G-DMAN/F-BUYP	3. 2.87	To G-HALK 4/87. Canx.
G-PKBD	Douglas DC-9-32 (Line No. 772)	47666	PJ-SNB	5. 8.88	To N941VV. Canx 28.4.95.
G-PKBE	Douglas DC-9-32 (Line No. 593)	47523	HB-IDP	18.10.88	To N940VV. Canx 25.5.95.
G-PKBM	Douglas DC-9-32 (Line No. 761)	47648	PJ-SNA	14. 1.87	To N942VV. Canx 26.6.95.
G-PKPK	Schweizer Hughes 269C (300C)	S.1454	EI-CAR N69A	3. 8.93	
G-PLAC	PA-31-350 Navajo Chieftain	31-8052038	G-OLDA G-BNDS/N131PP/N3550N	23.12.98	
G-PLAN	Reims Cessna F.150L Commuter	1066	PH-SPR	11. 8.78	
G-PLAS	Gulfstream American GA-7 Cougar	GA7-0077	G-BGHL N789GA	12. 6.85	To G-OOGI 1/95. Canx.
G-PLAT	Beechcraft 200 Super King Air	BB-487	N8PY VH-PIL/N198SC/PT-OYR/N40QN/VH-NIC/N40QN/N400N/N243KA	27. 4.99	
G-PLAX	Aerospatiale AS.355F1 Twin Squirrel	5223	G-BPMT N380E	2. 5.89	To OO-HSB 2/97. Canx 29.1.97.
G-PLAY	Robin R.2100A Club	170	F-ODIT	1. 8.79	
G-PLEE	Cessna 182Q Skylane II	182-66570	N95538	4.12.87	
G-PLEV	Cessna 340	340-0045	D-ICED (N5791M)	21.10.81	To G-KINK 11/89. Canx.
G-PLGI	HS.125 Srs.700B	257034	N510HS N7007X/(XA-...)/N7007X/G-BFXT(2)/G-5-14	26. 7.95	To N402GJ 4/99. Canx 22.4.99.
G-PLIV	Pazmany PL-4	PFA/17-10155		19.12.78	(Project for sale 90% complete 10/97)
G-PLMA	Aerospatiale AS.350B Ecureuil	1049	G-BMMA C-GJTB	26. 3.86	Fatal crash near the A38 road at Lochgilphead on 5.5.95. Canx as destroyed 14.9.95.
G-PLMB	Aerospatiale AS.350B Ecureuil	1207	G-BMMB C-GBEW/(N36033)	26. 3.86	
G-PLMC	Aerospatiale AS.350B Ecureuil	1731	G-BKUM	23. 8.88	
G-PLMD	Aerospatiale AS.350B Ecureuil	1745	G-NIAL	10. 5.88	To G-OGOA 1/90. Canx.
G-PLME	Aerospatiale AS.350B1 Ecureuil	2105	G-BONN	6. 5.88	DBR in forced landing near Douglas, Strathclyde on 9.9.93. Canx as destroyed 27.10.93. To D-HUBW 9/95 as AS.350B2.
G-PLMF	Aerospatiale AS.350B1 Ecureuil	1962	SE-JAG N777WN	21. 8.92	To CC-CXX 6/98. Canx 17.6.98.
G-PLMG	Aerospatiale AS.350B2 Ecureuil	2513	OY-HEF	27.10.93	Fatal crash near Ballahulish on 7.12.94. Canx as destroyed 8.3.95.
G-PLMH	Eurocopter AS.350B2 Ecureuil	2156	F-WQDJ G-PLMH/HB-XTE/F-WQPK/HB-XTE	9. 1.95	
G-PLMI	Aerospatiale SA.365C1 Dauphin 2	5001	F-GFYH(2) F-WZAE	19. 6.95	
G-PLOW	Hughes 269B	67-0317	G-AVUM	13. 9.83	(Cockpit section only stored at Bruntingthorpe in 8/97)
G-PLPC	Schweizer Hughes 269C (300C)	S.1558	G-JMAT	14. 4.97	
G-PLUG	Colt 105A HAFB	1958		17. 4.91	Canx by CAA 23.7.96.
G-PLUM	Bell 206L Long Ranger	45058	LN-OQK	31. 8.83	To SE-HRD. Canx 27.3.86.
G-PLUS	PA-34-200T Seneca II	34-8070111	N81406	25. 3.80	
G-PLXI	BAe ATP (Development acft with PW 127D engines)	2001	G-MATP (G-OATP)	26. 8.94	(Stored 10/97)
G-PLYD	Socata TB-20 Trinidad	994		4.12.89	To F-GLIE 11/98. Canx 29.10.98.
G-PLYM	FLS Aerospace Sprint 160	002		7. 3.94	To G-SCLX 7/94. Canx.
G-PMAM	Cameron V-65 HAFB	1155		29. 5.85	(Extant 2/97)
G-PMAX	PA-31-350 Navajo Chieftain	31-7305006	G-GRAM G-BRHF/N7679L	7. 7.99	
G-PMCN	Monnet Sonerai II	PFA/15-10409		1.11.78	Canx by CAA 2.8.91.
G-PMNF	Vickers-Supermarine 361 Spitfire HF.IX	CBAF/10372	South African AF/TA805	29. 4.96	(On rebuild by S.W.Atkins .95)
G-PMNL	Extra EA.230	007 & PFA/123-11007		22. 1.86	Canx 1.4.93 on sale to Switzerland. To N230PW 4/93.
G-PNAV	PA-31P-425 Preesurized Navajo	31P-7530012	N234TB	3. 9.87	To HA-ACJ 8/94. Canx 7.9.94.
G-PNEU	Colt Bibendum 110SS HAFB	4223		5. 1.98	

Regn	Type	c/n	Previous identity	Regn date	Fate or immediate subsequent identity (if known)
G-PNNY	Cessna 500 Citation I (Unit No.165)	500-0165	N19MQ N19M	27.11.89	To VR-CSP 5/92. Canx 13.5.92.
G-PNUT	Cameron Mr.Peanut 35SS HAFB	643	N400AB G-PNUT	4. 2.80	(Stored)
G-POAH	Sikorsky S-76B	760399		30. 3.92	
G-POAV	Aerospatiale AS.365N1 Dauphin 2	6309	G-BOPI	9.11.88	To N111EP 6/92. Canx.
"G-PODP"	Westland-Sikorsky S-55 Whirlwind Srs.3	WA/117	5N-ABP VR-NDL/G-AODP	----	Was incorrectly painted as "G-PODP" at Yeovil in 2/63 after repaint & minor overhaul. Corrected to G-AODP.
G-POKE	Pitts S-1E Special (Built by S.Vaughn)	345H	N40SV	27. 5.81	Destroyed in fatal crash into sea ½ mile east of Bognor Pier on 2.7.85. Canx by CAA 4.2.87.
G-POLE	Rutan LongEz	PFA/74A-11037		18.10.84	No Permit believed issued. Canx by CAA 6.10.92.
G-POLO	PA-31-350 Navajo Chieftain	31-7852143	N27750	9.10.78	To EI-JTC 11/93. Canx 15.9.93.
G-POLT	Robinson R-44 Astro	0370		24. 9.97	
G-POLY	Cameron N-77 HAFB	428		13. 7.78	
G-POND	Oldfield Baby Great Lakes (built by G.E.Davis)	01	N87ED	2.10.90	
G-PONY	Colt 31A Air Chair HAFB	434		23. 8.82	Canx by CAA 19.5.95.
G-POOH	Piper J3C-65 Cub (Frame No. 7015)	6932	F-BEGY NC38324	17.10.79	
G-POOL	ARV1 Super 2	025	G-BNHA	28. 8.87	(Stored at Chilbolton in 6/97)
G-POON	Aerospatiale AS.355F2 Twin Squirrel	5346	G-MCAL	17. 9.86	To ZS-HSW 5/88. Canx 11.5.88.
G-POOP	MCR-01	PFA/301-13190		5.11.97	
G-POPA	Beechcraft A36 Bonanza	E-2177	N7007F N7204R	20. 5.92	
G-POPE	Eiri PIK-20E Srs.1	20257		5. 3.80	
G-POPI	Socata TB-10 Tobago	315	G-BKEN (G-BKEL)	20. 4.90	
G-POPP	Colt 105A HAFB	1776		1. 3.91	CofA expired 21.11.96. Canx as PWFU 5.2.99.
G-POPS	PA-34-220T Seneca III	34-8133150	N8407H	11. 6.90	
G-POPW	Cessna 182S Skylane II	182-80204	N9451L	10. 7.98	
G-PORK	American Aviation AA-5B Tiger	AA5B-0625	EI-BMT G-BFHS	28. 2.84	Crashed on take-off from Eaglescott on 13.7.99.
G-PORR	Aerospatiale AS.350B Ecureuil	1395	F-WZFF	29.12.80	To G-PDCC 8/84. Canx.
G-PORT	Bell 206B JetRanger III	2784	N37AH N39TV/N397TV/N2774R	23. 8.89	
G-POSA	VPM M-16 Tandem Trainer	VPM16-UK-106	G-BVJM	12. 8.96	To G-IJMC 6/98. Canx.
G-POSH	Colt 56A HAFB	822	G-BMPT	10. 6.86	
G-POSN	BAe 125 Srs.800B	258120	G-5-606	28.10.88	To HB-VLI 8/95. Canx 5.5.95.
G-POST	Embraer EMB.110P1 Bandeirante	110-252	(N110PL) G-POST/PT-SAS	26. 2.80	To G-NBAC 10/94. Canx.
G-POTS	Reims Cessna FA.150K Aerobat	0081	G-AYUY	11.11.91	To G-FMSG 1/95. Canx.
G-POTT	Robinson R-44 Astro	0383		21.11.97	
G-POWA	PA-24-400 Comanche	26-104	VH-BSH VH-GWR/N8885P	19. 9.79	To N400WG. Canx 19.9.86.
G-POWE	Robinson R-44 Astro	0261		27. 6.96	Fatal crash 20.4.98 in woods nr Market Harborough. Canx as destroyed 10.8.98.
G-POWL	Cessna 182R Skylane II	182-67813	N9070G D-EOMF/N6265N	11.11.82	
G-POWR	Agusta A.109E Power	11014	G-BXUD	20. 7.98	
G-POZO	Socata TB-20 Trinidad	1258	I-POZO	7. 5.93	To I-ROZO 6/94. Canx 23.5.94.
G-PPAH	Enstrom 480	5032		9. 3.98	
G-PPHJ	Reims Cessna F.172P Skyhawk II	2048	F-GCYN	3. 3.81	Fatal crash into hillside near Cowdenbeath, Fife on 23.10.81. Canx as destroyed 5.12.83.
G-PPLH	Robinson R-22 Beta	1007		11. 5.89	
G-PPLI	Pazmany PL-1	PFA/61-10238		28.12.78	No Permit to Fly issued. Project abandoned. Canx by CAA 21.2.96.
G-PPPE	Colt 77A HAFB	1878		29.10.90	Canx by CAA 10.3.95.
G-PPPP	Denney Kitfox Mk.3	771 & PFA/172-11830		9. 1.91	
G-PRAG	Brugger MB.2 Colibri	PFA/43-10362		29.11.78	
G-PRCS	BAe 146 Srs.200QC	E2176		18. 7.90	To VH-NJQ 7/91. Canx 18.7.91.
G-PREM	Robinson R-22 Beta	1059	N8045T	5. 7.89	Landed on a barn at Cold Ash, near Newbury on 18.10.89. Canx as destroyed 28.11.89.
G-PRES	Cessna 441 Conquest	441-0107	G-BHFX (G-CARS)/(N4189G)	31. 1.80	To N455SC 9/83. Canx 23.9.83.
G-PRET	Robinson R-44 Astro	0381		8.10.97	
G-PRII	Hawker Hunter PR.11	41H-670690	N723WT A2616/WT723	14. 7.99	
G-PRIM	PA-38-112 Tomahawk	38-78A0669	N2398A	28. 1.87	
G-PRIN	BAe 146 Srs.200	E2148		7. 9.89	To G-6-148/G-BTIA 3/91. Canx.
G-PRIT	Cameron N-90 HAFB	1375		6.11.86	To G-HTVI 10/96. Canx.
G-PRIX	Cessna 414A Chancellor	414A-0049	N6649C	9. 6.78	To N24138 1/83. Canx 24.1.83.
G-PRMC	HS.125 Srs.700B	257031	G-BFSP	16. 4.85	Restored as G-BFSP 1/91. Canx.
G-PRNT	Cameron V-90 HAFB	2819		23. 3.92	
G-PROC	Boeing 737-3Q8 (Line No. 1128)	23256	N871L	27. 5.86	To N397P. Canx 3.11.86.
G-PROD	Eurocopter AS.350B2 Ecureuil	2825		7. 2.95	
G-PROK	Boeing 737-3Q8 (Line No. 1249)	23506	N781L	10. 6.87	To EC-117/EC-EGQ 12/87. Canx 22.12.87.

Regn	Type	c/n	Previous identity	Regn date	Fate or immediate subsequent identity (if known)
G-PROM	Aerospatiale AS.350B Ecureuil	1486	G-MAGY G-BIYC	11.10.96	
G-PROP	American Aviation AA-5A Cheetah	AA5A-0845	G-BHKU (OO-HTF)	16. 2.84	
G-PROV	Hunting P.84 Jet Provost T.52A (T.4)	PAC/W/23905	352 Singapore AF/South Yemen AF 104/G-27-7/XS228	13.12.83	
G-PRSI	Cyclone Pagasus Quantum 15	7492		17.12.98	
G-PRTT	Cameron N-31 HAFB	1374		6.11.86	
G-PRUE	Cameron O-84 HAFB	1510		18. 6.87	CofA expired 13.4.96. Canx by CAA 9.6.98.
G-PRXI	Vickers-Supermarine 365 Spitfire PR.XI	6S/583723	PL983 G-15-109/N74138/NC74138/PL983	6. 6.83	(C/n also quoted as 6S/501431) (Believed stored .96)
G-PSCI	Bell 206B JetRanger III	3654	G-BOKD N3171A	17. 5.88	To G-ISKY 4/95. Canx.
G-PSFT	PA-28-161 Warrior II	28-8416021	G-BPDS N4328P	1. 8.96	
G-PSIC	North American P-51C-10-NA Mustang (Composite with major components of P-51D Israeli DF/AF 13)	103-26778	NL51PR 43-25147	16. 4.98	(At Chino, USA on rebuild 7/99)
G-PSID	North American P-51D-20-NA Mustang	122-31514	N166G N3350/N335J/N6171C/44-63788	27. 7.81	To F-AZFI 5/88. Canx 19.2.88.
G-PSON	Colt Cylinder One SS HAFB (Panasonic Battery Shape)	1780	PH-SON	14. 3.95	
G-PSPS	Thunder & Colt AS.80 Hot-Air Airship	314	(4X-BLO) G-PSPS	10. 4.81	Canx by CAA 11.3.86. To N142RW.
G-PSRT	PA-28-151 Cherokee Warrior	28-7615225	G-BSGN N9657K	18. 3.99	
G-PSST	Hawker Hunter F.58A	HABL-003115	J-4104 Swiss AF/G-9-317/A2568 (RN Instructional Airframe)/XF947	12. 2.97	(Stored 6/99 at Hurn)
G-PSUE	CFM Shadow Srs.CD	K.139	G-MYAA	1. 4.99	
G-PSVS	Beechcraft 95-58 Baron	TH-1154	N5824T YV-266P	14. 8.84	To G-FLTZ 9/93. Canx.
G-PTAG	Europa Avn Europa	PFA/247-13121		14.12.98	
G-PTER	Beechcraft 65-C90 King Air	LJ-944	(N135JA) G-PTER/G-BIEE	22. 1.82	To HB-GHT 8/87. Canx 25.8.87.
G-PTRE	Socata TB-20 Trinidad	762	G-BNKU	14. 6.88	
G-PTWB	Cessna T.303 Crusader	T303-00306	G-BYNG G-PTWB/(G-BLRS)/N6312V	6.12.84	
G-PTWO	Pilatus P.2-05	600-30	U-110 Swiss AF/Swiss AF A-110	26. 2.81	
G-PTYE	Europa Avn Europa	1 & PFA/247-12496		22. 1.96	
G-PUBS	Colt Beer Glass 56SS HAFB	037		7. 6.79	Canx by CAA 1.12.95. (Extant 2/97)
G-PUDD	Robinson R-22 Beta	0863		14. 9.88	Fatal crash at Martin, near Fordingbridge on 8.6.94. Canx as destroyed 21.11.94.
G-PUDL	PA-18-150 Super Cub	18-7292	SE-CSE	24. 2.98	
G-PUDS	Europa Avn Europa	PFA/247-12999		9.10.97	
G-PUFF	Thunder Ax7-77 Bolt HAFB (Comprises burner of G-BALD and new Thunder canopy and new basket)	165/58	Composite	17.11.78	
G-PUFN	Cessna 340A II	340A-0114	N532KG N532KC/N5477J	4.12.96	
G-PULL	PA-18-150 Super Cub (Frame No.18-5429)	18-5356	PH-MBB ALAT 18-5356	17. 2.83	Badly damaged in fatal crash after stalling on take-off from Eaglescott on 13.6.86. Canx as WFU 25.11.87. (Stored 8/90 Tattershall Thorpe)
G-PULP	Colt Orangina Bottle SS HAFB	1247		11. 8.88	To OO-BUE. Canx 26.10.90.
G-PULS	Aero Designs Pulsar	PULS-0001-01 & PFA/202-11581		7. 7.89	Fatal crash at Deenethorpe on 9.7.95. Canx as WFU 25.10.95.
G-PUMA	Aerospatiale AS.332L Super Puma	2038	F-WMHB	31. 1.83	
G-PUMB	Aerospatiale AS.332L Super Puma	2075		31. 1.83	
G-PUMD	Aerospatiale AS.332L Super Puma	2077	F-WXFD	31. 1.83	
G-PUME	Aerospatiale AS.332L Super Puma	2091		3. 8.83	
G-PUMG(1)	Aerospatiale AS.332L Super Puma	2095	F-WMHF	3. 8.83R	NTU - Not Imported. To N5803C 9/84. Canx.
G-PUMG(2)	Aerospatiale AS.332L Super Puma	2018	F-ODOS	4. 4.85	
G-PUMH	Aerospatiale AS.332L Super Puma	2101		3. 8.83	
G-PUMI	Aerospatiale AS.332L Super Puma	2170		27. 1.86	
G-PUMJ	Aerospatiale AS.332L Super Puma	2123	G-BLZJ LN-OMI/G-BLZJ/LN-OMI/G-BLZJ/LN-OMI	22.12.89	Restored as LN-OMI 6/96. Canx 16.5.96.
G-PUMK	Aerospatiale AS.332L Super Puma	2067	LN-OMF(3) G-PUMK/LN-OMF(3)/F-WXFP	23. 3.90	
G-PUML	Aerospatiale AS.332L Super Puma	2073	LN-ODA G-PUML/LN-OMG	20. 7.90	
G-PUMM	Eurocopter AS.332L-2 Super Puma	2477		29. 7.98	
G-PUMN	Eurocopter AS.332L-2 Super Puma	2484	LN-OHF	16. 7.99	
G-PUMO	Eurocopter AS.332L-2 Super Puma	2467		30. 9.98	

Regn	Type	c/n	Previous identity	Regn date	Fate or immediate subsequent identity (if known)
G-PUMP	PA-23-250 Aztec E	23-7305193	G-CDBI N40475	23. 7.82	Fatal crash at Waseley Country Pary, near Birmingham on 27.2.83. Canx as destroyed 29.2.84.
G-PUNK	Thunder Ax8-105 HAFB	1719		28. 3.90	
G-PUPP	Beagle B.121 Pup Srs.150	B121-174	G-BASD (SE-FOG)/G-BASD	23.11.93	
G-PURE	Cameron Can 70SS HAFB (Guinness Can)	1913		18. 1.89	Canx as WFU 29.4.97.
G-PURR	American Aviation AA-5A Cheetah	AA5A-0794	G-BJDN N26893	22. 2.82	
G-PURS	Rotorway Exec 152	3827		19. 1.90	
G-PUSH	Rutan LongEz	PFA/74A-10740		11. 7.83	
G-PUSI	Cessna T.303 Crusader	T303-00273	N3479V	26. 7.88	
G-PUSS	Cameron N-77 HAFB	1577		6.10.87	(Extant 2/97)
G-PUSY	Tiger Cub RL-5A-LW Sherwood Ranger	PFA/237-12964	G-MZNF	25. 6.99	
G-PUTT	Cameron Golfball 76SS HAFB	2060	LX-KIK	8. 8.95	(Extant 2/97)
G-PVAF	PA-44-180 Seminole	44-7995090	N2242A	18.12.78	To G-PDOC 12/85. Canx.
G-PVAM	Port Victoria PV.7 Grain Kitten Replica	AJM AJM.II-N539		14.12.78	No Permit issued. Canx by CAA 8.7.91.
G-PVBF	Lindstrand LBL-260S HAFB	504		7. 4.98	
G-PVCU	Cameron N-77 HAFB	4376		22. 5.98	
G-PVET	DHC.1 Chipmunk 22 (Fuselage no. DHH/f/18)	C1/0017	WB565	23. 5.97	
G-PWBE	DH.82A Tiger Moth (Built from spares by Lawrence Engineering Services pre-1959)	LES.1	VH-KRW	23. 7.99	
G-PWEL	Robinson R-22 Beta	2982		. 9.99	
G-PYCO	Dassault Falcon 2000	78	F-WWMJ	21. 4.99	
G-PYLN	Cameron Pylon 80SS HAFB (Electricity Pylon shape)	2958	G-BUSO	18. 1.93	
G-PYOB	Aerospatiale SA.341G Gazelle Srs.1	1145	G-IYOB G-WELA/G-SFTD/ G-RIFC/G-SFTD/N641HM/N341BB/F-WKQH	8. 8.95	(Rotor struck ground on landing at Boones Farm, High Garrett, Braintree on 30.6.99)
G-PYRO	Cameron N-65 HAFB	567		8. 1.80	
G-PZAZ	PA-31-350 Navajo Chieftain	31-7405214	G-VTAX (G-UTAX)/N54266	18. 1.95	
G-PZIZ	PA-31-350 Navajo Chieftain	31-7405429	G-CAFZ(2) G-BPPT/N54297	30.10.98	
"G-QZDE"	Westland WG.30 (Mod)	-		----	A none flying mock-up of a 'Coastguard' helicopter based on a WG.30 airframe with bits added, at Lydd on 5.12.98. Use by the BBC for a film called 'Silent Witness'.

G-R G-R

Regn	Type	c/n	Previous identity	Regn date	Fate or immediate subsequent identity (if known)
G-RAAD	Mooney M.20L PFM	26-0035	N160MP	22. 8.88	Canx 3.2.98 on sale to Aruba.
G-RAAR	BAe 125 Srs.800B	258210	G-5-705	16. 8.91	To HB-VMI 7/98. Canx 27.7.98.
G-RACA	Hunting Percival P.57 Sea Prince T.1	P57/49	WM735	2. 9.80	Permit expired 4.11.80. Canx by CAA 28.11.95. (Open storage 8/96 - for removal to Carlisle)
G-RACE	Piper Aerostar 601P	61P-0569-7963247	N8083J	18.10.78	To N3839H 5/83. Canx 16.5.83.
G-RACH	Robinson R-22 Beta	0650		18. 6.87	To G-OEAT 1/98. Canx.
G-RACL	HS.125 Srs.700B	257212	G-5-12	16. 3.84	To N81CH. Canx 7.8.86.
G-RACO	PA-28R-200 Cherokee Arrow II	28R-7535300	N1498X	12. 9.91	
G-RADA	Soko P-2 Kraguj	024	30140 Yugoslav AF	25. 9.96	
G-RADE	Cessna T.210L Turbo Centurion II	210-61146	G-CENT A6-AMM/N2185S	3. 9.82	To 5Y-BHT. Canx 25.7.91.
G-RADI	PA-28-181 Archer II	28-8690002	N2582X N9608N	6. 5.98	
G-RAEM	Rutan LongEz	557 & PFA/74A-10638		15. 3.82	
G-RAES	Boeing 777-236ER (Line No. 76)	27491	(G-ZZZN)	10. 6.97	
G-RAFA	Grob G-115A	8081	D-EGVV	2. 3.89	
G-RAFB	Grob G-115A	8079	D-EGVV	2. 3.89	
G-RAFC	Robin R.2112 Alpha	192		19. 5.80	
G-RAFE	Thunder Ax7-77 Bolt HAFB	176		18.12.78	
G-RAFF	Gates LearJet 35A	35A-504	N8568B N10871	12. 6.84	
G-RAFG	Slingsby T.67C	2076		2.11.89	
G-RAFI	Hunting-Percival P.84 Jet Provost T.4	PAC/W/17641	8458M XP672	18.12.92	
G-RAFT	Rutan LongEz	PFA/74A-10734		9. 8.82	(Stored 10/97)
G-RAFW	Mooney M.20E Chapparal Mk.21	805	G-ATHW N5881Q	14.11.84	
G-RAGG	Maule M.5-235C Lunar Rocket	7260C	N5632M	8. 9.95	
G-RAGS	Pietenpol Air Camper	PFA/47-11551		8. 6.94	
G-RAHL	Beechcraft 400A Beechjet	RK-61	N82378	7. 4.93	To N461CW. Canx 7.8.98.
G-RAHM	Aerospatiale AS.350B Ecureuil	1205	G-UNIC G-COLN/G-BHIV	18.12.89	To G-WILX 5/90. Canx.
G-RAID	Douglas AD-4NA Skyraider (SFERMA c/n 42)	7722	F-AZED TR-KMM/French AF 42 F-UIDK/F-TGZD/F-T.FQ/F-T.QV/BuA.126922	7. 6.93	

Regn	Type	c/n	Previous identity	Regn date	Fate or immediate subsequent identity (if known)
G-RAIL	Colt 105A HAFB	1434		31. 3.89	
G-RAIN(1)	PA-31 Turbo Navajo	31-514	SE-FHM	. 7.78R	NTU - To USA 12/78. Although not officially issued these marks were applied before departing Stateside on 15.12.78.
G-RAIN(2)	Maule M.5-235C Lunar Rocket	7262C	N5632J	26. 7.79	
G-RAIX	CCF T-6J Texan (Harvard 4M)	CCF-4...	G-BIWX	16. 2.98	
	(Possibly c/n CCF4-409 ex.51-17227)		MM53846/RM-22/51-17...		
G-RAJS	General Avia F.22C	023		22. 4.99	
G-RALD	Robinson R-22 HP	0218	G-CHIL	25. 1.96	
			(G-BMXI)/N9074K		
G-RALE	Aerospatiale SA.341G Gazelle Srs.1		G-SFTG	3. 1.86	Canx by CAA 6.9.88. To G-GAZA 6/92.
		1187	N87712		
G-RALI	Hughes 369HS (500HS)	31-0300S	G-BLKO	30. 5.85	Canx by CAA 8.8.91.
			OO-AHL/HB-XDM		
G-RALY	Robinson R-22	0066	SE-HOA	30. 8.84	Badly damaged on landing at Crosby on 27.9.85. Canx as destroyed 25.8.88.
G-RAMI	Bell 206B JetRanger III	2955	N1080N	18.10.90	
G-RAMM	Hughes 369HM (500M)	52-0214M	EI-AVN	15. 7.93	To G-KBOT 7/98. Canx.
			N9037F		
G-RAMP	Piper J3C-65 Cub	6658	N35941	5. 7.90	
			NC35941		
	(Type as regd but always regd in USA as J3L-65)				
G-RAMS	PA-32R-301 Saratoga SP	32R-8013134	N8271Z	17.10.80	
G-RAMY	Bell 206B JetRanger	1401	N59554	22. 9.95	
G-RANA	Cameron Cheese 82SS HAFB	1996	I-IORE	4.10.95	
			G-BSFM		
G-RAND	Rand Robinson KR-2	RLW-01		19.10.78	No Permit to Fly issued. Canx as PWFU 19.4.99.
G-RANG	Cameron A-340 HAFB	4024		3.10.96	To ZK-F.. Canx 12.7.99.
G-RANS	Rans S-10 Sakota	PFA/194-11537		17. 8.89	
G-RANT	Enstrom F-28C-UK	349	G-BGKL	4. 4.79	Extensively damaged on landing at Marine Hotel Golf Course, North Berwick on 11.11.80. Canx as WFU 26.5.88.
G-RANY	Cessna 421C Golden Eagle III		G-BHLA	22. 7.85	To D-IVVV 6/92. Canx 8.5.92.
		421C-0856	(N2660U)		
G-RANZ	Rans S-10 Sakota	PFA/194-11536		2.11.89	(Open store 9/97)
G-RAPA	PBN BN-2T-4R Defender 4000	2115	N360WT	11. 5.82	(Stored 4/97)
	(Also c/n 4001)		G-RAPA/G-51-2115/G-BJBH		
	(Originally regd as BN-2B-27, then BN-2T Turbine Islander in 1983)				
G-RAPE	Colt 300A HAFB	808		7. 4.88	Canx 26.2.98 on sale to Canada.
G-RAPH	Cameron O-77 HAFB	1673		21. 3.88	
G-RAPP	Cameron H-34 HAFB	2380		16. 8.90	(Quoted as not built and yet was certified !)
G-RARB	Cessna 172N Skyhawk II	172-72334	G-BOII	4. 6.96	
			N4702D		
G-RARE	Thunder Ax5-42 SS HAFB	266		20. 2.80	
	(Special shape in form of J & B Rare Whisky Bottle)				
G-RASC	Evans VP-2	V2-1178 & PFA/63-10422		14.12.78	Crashed on take-off from Bagby on 9.7.95. Canx as TWFU 19.9.95. (Stored 4/97)
G-RASS	Bell 206L-1 Long Ranger	45189	G-JLBI	30. 7.87	To F-GLGD 1/92. Canx 10.1.92.
			D-HBBZ/N5012L/(D-HNRA)		
G-RATE	American Aviation AA-5A Cheetah		G-BIFF	11. 6.84	
		AA5A-0781	(G-BICU)/(G-BIBR)/N26879		
G-RATS	Alexander/Todd Steen Skybolt	1	G-RHFI	15. 5.85	To G-BNKG 8/87. Canx.
			N443AT		
G-RATZ	Europa Avn Europa	PFA/247-12582		16. 6.95	
G-RAVE	Southdown Raven X	2232/0219	G-MNZV	22.12.98	
G-RAVI	Colt 300A HAFB	2098		2. 1.92	Canx 3.9.97 on sale to Turkey.
G-RAVL	Handley Page 137 Jetstream 200	208	G-AWVK	2.12.86	
	(Production No. 7)		N1035S/G-AWVK		
G-RAVY	Cessna 500 Citation I	500-0109	N44SA	23.11.88	To I-AMCU 4/90. Canx 7.3.90.
	(Unit No.109)				
G-RAYA	Denney Kitfox Mk.4	PFA/172A-12403		14.12.92	
G-RAYE	PA-32-260 Cherokee Six	32-460	G-ATTY	30. 5.96	
			N11C		
G-RAYS	Zenair CH.250 Zodiac			26.10.78	(Under construction 4/97 at Yearby/Middlesborough)
		RED.001 & PFA/24-10460			
G-RAZA	Aerospatiale AS.365N2 Dauphin 2		3A-MGS	21. 5.99	To N585RH. Canx 5.8.99.
		6476	N373QC		
G-RBAC	North American AT-6C Harvard IIA		FAP1522	25. 1.79	To (G-BHXF)/G-VALE 9/80. Canx.
		88-10677	South African AF 7244/EX584/41-33557		
G-RBBB	Europa Avn Europa	PFA/247-12664		6. 5.94	(Ground-looped at Carisle on 7.7.98)
G-RBBE	Cessna 421C Golden Eagle III		N6678C	3. 8.78	To G-JTIE 8/82. Canx.
		421C-0437			
G-RBIN	Robin DR.400 2+2	1225	D-EEVT	25.10.78	Crashed on the M2 Motorway near Rochester on 21.5.93. Canx by CAA 7.9.93.
G-RBLA	DHC.6-310 Twin Otter	578	(PH-DDF)	17. 4.78	To LN-FKA. Canx 22.11.84.
			G-RBLA/(G-BFRZ)		
G-RBMV	Cameron O-31 HAFB	4658		20. 7.99	
G-RBOS	Colt AS-105 Hot-Air Airship	390		9. 2.82	(Stored 9/93 for Science Museum) Canx by CAA 3.4.97.
G-RBOW	Thunder Ax7-65 HAFB	1439		24. 4.89	
G-RBSI	BN-2A Mk.III-2 Trislander	1027	G-OTSB	27. 2.96	Restored as G-BDTO 3/98. Canx.
	(Three-bladed propellors)		G-BDTO/8P-ASC/G-BDTO/(C-GYOX)/G-BDTO		
G-RBUT	Hughes 369HS	61-0328S	C-FTXZ	27.11.90	To G-SWEL 7/96. Canx.
			CF-TXZ		
G-RCAF	North American AT-6C Harvard IIA		FAP1560	6. 3.79	To N42BA 7/80. Canx 16.4.80.
		88-9723	South African AF 7168/EX287/41-33260		

Regn	Type	c/n	Previous identity	Regn date	Fate or immediate subsequent identity (if known)
G-RCCL	Beechcraft 65-C90 King Air	LJ-824		1. 9.78	To N2687W 12/82. Canx 20.12.82.
G-RCDI	HS.125 Srs.700B	257142	G-BJDJ G-5-12	24.12.92	Restored as G-BJDJ 1/97. Canx.
G-RCED	Rockwell Commander 114	14241	VR-CED N4917W	19. 6.92	
G-RCEJ	BAe 125 Srs.800B	258021	VR-CEJ G-GEIL/G-5-15	15. 6.95	
G-RCGI	Robinson R-22 Beta	0897		14.12.88	To CS-HBM 4/90. Canx 1.3.90.
G-RCHA	PA-28-181 Archer III	2843094	N9269S	30. 7.97	
"G-RCHA"	DH.82A Tiger Moth	-		----	False marks worn by an instructional airframe used by Air Service Training Ltd at Ansty in 1949.
G-RCMC	Murphy Renegade Spirit	485 & PFA/188-12483		1. 2.93	
G-RCMF	Cameron V-77 HAFB	1618		23.11.87	
G-RCML	Sky 77-24 HAFB	148		9. 3.99	
G-RCPW	American Aviation AA-5A Cheetah	AA5A-0352	G-BERM N6141A	20. 3.84	To G-OCPL 7/89. Canx.
G-RCYI	PA-28-161 Cadet	2841166	N9185F	5.10.89	To OO-TVI. Canx 10.12.91.
"G-RCYR"	DH.89A Dragon Rapide	6879	EC-AGP G-AMAI/NR803	----	Exhibited with these false marks at Frankfurt prior to sale to J.Koch in 1990 as D-ILIT.
G-RDBS	Cessna 550 Citation II (Unit No.101)	550-0094	G-JETA (N26630)	7. 5.99	
G-RDCI	Rockwell Commander 112A	345	G-BFWG ZS-JRX/N1345J	15. 5.85	
G-RDON	WMB.2 Windtracker HAFB (Toy)	11	G-BICH	23. 9.81	Canx as WFU 17.1.96.
G-RDVE	Airbus A.320-231	163	OY-CND F-WWDU	26. 2.97	
G-READ	Colt 77A HAFB	1158	EI-BYI G-READ	16.11.87	(Still flying as EI-BYI 9/97)
G-REAH	PA-32R-301 Saratoga II SP	32R-8413017	G-CELL (G-BLRI)/N4361D	15. 8.94	
G-REAP	Pitts S-1S Special	PFA/09-11557		7. 2.90	
G-REAS	Van's RV-6A	PFA/181-12188		16. 8.94	
G-REAT	Grumman-American GA-7 Cougar	GA7-0033	N29699	6.10.78	
G-REBE	Bensen B.8MR Gyrocopter	G/01-1202		19. 7.91	To N94AW 11/94. Canx 27.9.94.
G-REBI	Colt 90A HAFB	1294	G-BOYD	13. 3.89	Canx by CAA 6.4.98.
G-REBK	Beechcraft B200 Super King Air	BB-1202	D-IHAP N44VM/N7207M	22. 5.97	
G-REBL	Hughes 269B	67-0318	N9493F	25. 7.89	(Stored 3/97)
G-RECK	PA-28-140 Cherokee B	28-25656	G-AXJW N11C	17. 3.88	
G-RECO	Jurca MJ-5L2 Sirocco	96	F-PYYD F-WYYD	30. 9.91	(Stored Shoreham 6/93)
G-REDB	Cessna 310Q	310Q-0811	G-BBIC N69600	17. 6.93	
G-REDD	Cessna 310R II	310R-1833	G-BMGT ZS-KSY/(N2738X)	2.10.96	
G-REDX	Experimental Aviation Berkut	PFA/252-12481		27. 1.95	(Under construction 2/99 Little Ellingham, Norfolk)
G-REEC	Sequoia Falco F.8L (built by B.Eriksen)	654	LN-LCA	2. 7.96	
G-REEK	American Aviation AA-5A Cheetah	AA5A-0429	N7129L	12. 9.77	
G-REEM	Aerospatiale AS.355F1 Twin Squirrel	5175	G-EMAN G-WEKR/G-CHLA/N818RL/C-FLXH/N818RL/N818R/N5798U	9. 3.98	
G-REEN	Cessna 340	340-0063	G-AZYR N5893M	2. 2.84	
G-REES	SAN Jodel D.140C Mousquetaire III	156	F-BMFR	23. 4.80	
G-REFI	Enstrom 280C-UK Shark	1090	N638H	2. 5.89	Destroyed by fire at Dublin on 22.9.95. Canx by CAA 21.11.96. (Stored for rebuild 1/97)
G-REGA	Embraer EMB.110P1 Bandeirante	110-215	N711NH PT-GMH	26. 2.89	To G-ZUSS 3/91. Canx.
G-REGB	BAe Jetstream Srs.3102	641	SE-IPD G-31-641	12. 1.89	Restored as SE-IPD. Canx 6.10.89.
G-REGG	Robin DR.400/140 Major	856	PH-SRI	6.12.78	Burnt out in hangar fire at Panshanger on 24.7.80. Canx as destroyed 29.2.84.
G-REGN	Short SD.3-60 Var.300	SH3751	G-OCIA G-BPFS	31.10.89	Restored as G-BPFS 5/90. Canx.
G-REGS	Thunder Ax7-77 HAFB	1812		4. 7.90	Canx as CAA 4.8.98.
G-REID	Rotorway Scorpion 133	1147	G-BGAW	7.12.81	Permit expired 18.3.91. Canx by CAA 19.4.99.
G-REIS	PA-28R-201T Turbo Arrow III	28R-7803334	N36689	15. 8.78	To G-JESS 9/95. Canx.
G-REKL	Percival Mew Gull Replica	-		. .81R	NTU - Canx.
G-REME	Cessna 152 II (Tailwheel conversion)	152-83188	G-DRAG G-BRNF/N47217	19. 6.92	Restored as G-DRAG 4/93. Canx.
G-RENE	Murphy Renegade	PFA/188-12030		6.11.91	
G-RENO	Socata TB-10 Tobago	249		10.12.81	
G-RENT	Robinson R-22 Beta	0758	N2635M	17. 3.88	(Badly damaged in crash Newtownards 30.9.92)
G-REPM	PA-38-112 Tomahawk	38-79A0354	N2528D	8. 1.87	(Stored 6/96)
G-REST	Beechcraft P35 Bonanza	D-7171	G-ASFJ	14.12.82	

Regn	Type	c/n	Previous identity	Regn date	Fate or immediate subsequent identity (if known)
G-RETA	CASA I-131E Jungmann Srs.2000 (Possibly ex.G-BGZC)	2197	E3B-305 Spanish AF	24. 3.80	
"G-RETA"	Airspeed AS.40 Oxford 1	-	DF472	----	False marks worn by an instructional airframe used by Air Service Training Ltd at Hamble in 1949, then Perth in 2/60.
G-REVS	Bell 206B JetRanger	239	G-AWOL N4085G	21. 6.90	Extensively damaged when the tail rotor struck tree while landing at the Hambleton Hall Hotel, 17 miles east of Leicester on 17.9.94. Canx as destroyed 15.2.95.
G-REXP	Beechcraft 65-70 Queen Air	LB-35	G-AYPC	23. 9.85	To G-KEAA 8/88. Canx.
G-REXS	PA-28-181 Archer II	28-8090102	N8093Y	14. 1.80	
G-REXY	Beechcraft 65-A80 Queen Air	LD-176	G-AVNG D-ILBO	14. 1.85	To G-KEAC 8/88. Canx.
G-REZE	Rutan VariEze	PFA/74-11086		28. 9.89	Destroyed when crashed into trees on landing at Bembridge on 19.11.95.
G-RFAB	Cessna 182R Skylane II	182-67888	G-BIXT N6397H	8. 5.91	To G-MISH 6/95. Canx.
G-RFDS	Agusta A.109A II	7411	N1YU VP-CLA/VR-CLA/G-BOLA/VR-CMP/G-BOLA	24. 5.99	
G-RFIL	Colt 77A HAFB	1496		25. 5.89	
G-RFIO	Aeromot AMT-200 Super Ximango (Licence-built Fourner RF-10)	200-048		6. 3.95	
G-RFSB	Sportavia Fournier RF-5B Sperber	51045	N55HC	2.12.88	
G-RGEN	Cessna T.337D Turbo Super Skymaster (Robertson STOL Master conversion)	T337-1062	G-EDOT G-BJIY/9Q-CPF/PH-JWL/N86056	24. 5.96	
G-RGER	Bell 206B JetRanger III	3945	N75EA JA9452/N32018	5. 9.94	To G-TOYZ 11/96. Canx.
G-RGII	Cessna 172RG Cutlass	172RG-0979	N9702B HP-983/N9702B	25.10.90	To CS-AZD. Canx 10.8.92.
G-RGUS	Fairchild F.24R-46A Argus III (UC-61K-FA)	1145	(PH-...) G-RGUS/ZS-UJZ/ZS-BAY/KK527/44-83184	16. 9.86	
G-RHBH	PA-28-161 Cadet	2841259	N9193Z	20.11.89	To G-GFCF 6/90. Canx.
G-RHCB	Schweizer 269C-1	0036	N201WL (F-GILQ)/N41S	20. 3.98	
G-RHCC	PA-31-350 Navajo Chieftain	31-8152013	N888TT N40710	17. 8.87	To N81TT 5/93. Canx 27.4.93.
G-RHCN	Reims Cessna FR.182 Skylane RG II	0054		16. 5.80	To N34SJ 8/94. Canx 21.7.94.
G-RHFI	Alexander/Todd (Steen) Skybolt	1	N443AT	31.12.80	To G-RATS 5/85. Canx.
G-RHHT	PA-32RT-300 Lance II	32R-7885190	N36476	3. 7.78	
G-RHYS	Rotorway Exec 90	5140		8.11.93	
G-RIAN	Agusta-Bell 206A JetRanger	8056	G-SOOR G-FMAL/G-RIAN/G-BHSG/PH-FSW	16. 9.87	
G-RIAT	Robinson R-22 Beta	2684		27. 5.97	
G-RIBS	Diamond DA-20-A1 Katana	10143	G-BWWM	7. 7.97	
G-RIBV	Cessna 560 Citation V Ultra	560-0506	N50820	17. 3.99	
G-RICC	Aerospatiale AS.350B2 Ecureuil	2559	G-BTXA	30.10.91	
G-RICE	Robinson R-22 Beta	2509	N93MK	14. 3.97	
G-RICH	Reims Cessna F.152 II	1440	OO-FTC	6. 9.85	To G-BXRN 1/98. Canx.
G-RICK	Beechcraft 95-B55 Baron	TC-1472	G-BAAG	23. 5.84	
G-RICO	American General AG-5B Tiger	10162	N130U	14. 5.99	
G-RICS	Europa Avn Europa	PFA/247-12747		19. 3.96	(Under construction Kemble 1/97)
G-RIDE	Stephens Akro	111	N81AC N55NM	10. 8.78	(Stored 3/95)
G-RIDS	Neico Lancair 235	PFA/191A-11626		21. 8.91	Crashed into trees on take-off at Brunton on 10.7.96. Canx as destroyed 25.11.96.
G-RIFA	Westland SA.341G Gazelle 1	WA/1108	G-ORGE G-BBHU	13. 6.90	To G-FDAV 5/93. Canx.
G-RIFB	Hughes 269C	116-0562	N7428F	17. 5.90	
G-RIFC	Aerospatiale SA.341G Gazelle Srs.1	1145	G-SFTD N641HM/N341BB/F-WKQH	14. 6.91	Restored as G-SFTD 8/92. Canx.
G-RIFF	Aerospatiale SA.341G Gazelle Srs.1	1063	G-BLAN N6958/F-WTNT	17. 9.87	Made heavy landing at Hall Lane Farm, Runcorn on 7.3.90. Remains dumped 5/90 at Barton. Canx as WFU 25.7.90.
G-RIFN	Avion Mudry CAP.10B	276		6. 6.96	
G-RIGB	Thunder Ax7-77 HAFB	1201		16. 3.88	
G-RIGH	PA-32R-301 Saratoga II HP	3246123	N41272	23.12.98	
G-RIGS	PA-60-601P Aerostar	61P-0621-7963281	N8220J	18. 5.79	
G-RIKK	Bell 206B JetRanger II	1771	N206BJ N49596	19. 6.89	To G-BSTG 9/90. Canx.
G-RILL	Cessna 421C Golden Eagle III	421C-0663	G-BGZM N3839G	29.10.80	To VR-CLL. Canx 29.3.94.
G-RILY	Monnett Sonerai IIL	PFA/15-10353		20.12.78	Permit expired 5.10.89. (Stored 4/95 Nayland) Canx by CAA 26.3.97.
G-RIMM	Westland Wasp HAS.1 (Also c/n F8 2896)	F.9605	NZ3907 R.New Zealand Navy/XT435	11. 3.99	
G-RIND	Cessna 335	335-0044	N2710L	1. 9.80	Extensively damaged after verring off the runway and struck a fence on take-off at Rochester on 15.12.94. Rebuilt & re-regd as G-FITZ 4/95. Canx.
G-RING	Reims Cessna FR.182 Skylane RG	0025	D-EFGP	4. 1.84	Badly damaged in forced landing east of the A34 road west of Chipping Farm and 2 miles northwest of Kidlington on 23.2.91. Canx as destroyed 5.11.91.

Regn	Type	c/n	Previous identity	Regn date	Fate or immediate subsequent identity (if known)
G-RINO	Thunder Ax7-77 HAFB	975		24. 6.87	
G-RINS	Rans S-6ESD Coyote II	PFA/204-13361		15. 3.99	
G-RINT	CFM Streak Shadow	K.199-SA & PFA/206-12251		7.12.93	
G-RIOO	Beechcraft B200 Super King Air	BB-1244	N251DL N72357	16.11.88	To F-GSFA 1/92. Canx 12.12.91.
G-RIPS	Cameron Action Man/Parachutist 110SS HAFB	4092		29. 4.97	
G-RISE	Cameron V-77 HAFB	2395		21. 9.90	
G-RIST	Cessna 310R II	310R-1294	G-DATS (N6128X)	28. 4.81	
G-RITA	Cessna 340A II	340A-0461	N6282N	31.10.88	Restored as N6282N 8/92. Canx 13.8.92.
G-RITZ	Cessna 182S Skylane II	182-80029	N9872F	12. 2.98	To N432V 5/99. Canx 22.3.99.
G-RIVR	Thruster TST.600F (Fitted with Full Lotus floats)	9029-T600F-0031		. 5.99R	(Noted at Popham 1/2.5.99 & at PFA Rally at Cranfield 4.7.99)
G-RIVT	Van's RV-6	PFA/181-12743		31. 7.95	
G-RIZE	Cameron O-90 HAFB	3163		13.12.93	
G-RIZI	Cameron N-90 HAFB	3080		12. 5.93	
G-RIZZ	PA-28-161 Warrior II	28-7816494	D-EMFW N9563N	11. 2.99	
G-RJAH	Boeing-Stearman D75N1 (PT-27BW) Kaydet	75-4041	N75957 RCAF FJ991/42-15852	6. 4.90	
G-RJCP	Rockwell Commander 114B	14606	N6001M	3. 7.96	
G-RJER	McDonnell Douglas DC-9-83 (MD-83) (Line No. 1906)	49949		1.10.91	To N882RA. Canx 3.5.96.
G-RJET	BAe 146 Srs.100	E1199	N170RJ G-RJET	30. 1.91	To A5-RGE 12/92. Canx 18.12.92.
G-RJGR	Boeing 757-225 (Line No. 8)	22197	N701MG N507EA	22.11.94	
G-RJMI	American Aviation AA-5A Cheetah	AA5A-0895	N27170	3. 6.82	To G-DOEA 4/96. Canx.
G-RJMS	PA-28R-201 Arrow III	28R-7837059	N6223H	19. 1.88	
G-RJRI	HS.125 Srs.700B	257130	N700FR G-5-588/N700FR/G-BNVU/G-CCAA/G-DBBI	20. 9.88	To RP-C235 6/90. Canx 7.6.90.
G-RJWW	Maule M.5-235C Lunar Rocket	7250C	G-BRWG N5632H	6.10.87	
G-RJXA	Embraer ERJ-145EP (Regd as EMB-145EP)	145-136	PT-S..	18. 6.99	
G-RJXB	Embraer ERJ-145EP (Regd as EMB-145EP)	145-142	PT-S..	23. 6.99	
G-RJXC	Embraer ERJ-145EP	145-153	PT-SEE	15. 7.99	
G-RKET	Taylor JT.2 Titch	PFA/3233	G-BIBK	25. 8.99	
G-RKSF	Pitts S-2A Special	2192	N947	10. 7.79	To OY-BSP. Canx 1.6.83.
"G-RKSF"	Pitts S-2A Special (Non-flying replica - alias BAPC.134)	-		----	See "G-CARS".
G-RLAY	Embraer EMB.110P1 Bandeirante	110-364	PT-SEJ	9.10.81	To G-BLVG 1/85. Canx.
G-RLFI	Reims Cessna FA.152 Aerobat	0340	G-DFTS	17. 1.90	
G-RLMC	Cessna 421C Golden Eagle III	421C-0118	PH-SBI D-IMAZ/I-CCNN/N3849C	9. 3.88	
G-RMAC	Europa Avn Europa	PFA/247-12717		3. 7.97	
G-RMAE	PA-31-300 Turbo Navajo B	31-761	G-BAEG N7239L	1.12.82	To G-FOAL 6/88. Canx.
G-RMAM	Musselwhite MAM.1	MAM/01		2.10.78	Canx by CAA 2.9.91.
G-RMAN	Aero Designs Pulsar	PFA/202-13071		6. 6.97	
G-RMCT	Short SD.3-60 Var.100	SH3656	EI-BPD G-BLPU/G-14-3656	27.11.92	
G-RMGN	Aerospatiale AS.355F1 Twin Squirrel II	5327	G-BMCY	15. 5.86	To G-OILX 1/93. Canx.
G-RMGW	Denney Kitfox Mk.3	PFA/172-11918		12. 1.93	To SE-YSS 7/95. Canx 18.11.94.
G-RMIT	Van's RV-4	PFA/181-12207		4. 9.96	(Under construction 1/99 at Shoreham)
G-RMKM	Rockwell Commander 112TC	13082	OY-PRN N4592W	21. 8.78	Ditched in sea off Floddaymore, 6.8 miles east of Benbecula Aerodrome on 3.10.81. Canx as destroyed 29.2.84.
G-RMSS	Short SD.3-60 Var.100	SH3604	G-BKKU G-14-3604	15.12.82	To G-BPCO 2/88. Canx.
G-RMST	PA-46-350P Malibu Mirage	4636091		21. 1.97	To G-PALL 3/99. Canx.
G-RMUG	Cameron Nescafe Mug 90SS HAFB	3450		3. 5.95	
G-RNAS	DH.104 Sea Devon C.20 (Dove 6)	04473	XK896	16.11.82	CofA expired 3.7.84. Canx by CAA 17.4.97. To Filton as spares source for G-HBBC 10/98.
G-RNAV	PA-31-350 Navajo Chieftain	31-7852128	N27728	28.11.78	To N4261A/RAF as ZF522 6/85. Canx.
G-RNBW	Bell 206B JetRanger II	2270	F-GQFH F-WQFH/HB-XUF/F-GFBP/N900JJ/N16UC	9. 1.98	
G-RNCO	Rockwell Commander 690C	11664	N110RS N5916K	10. 8.84	To N7057A. Canx 24.1.89.
G-RNEE	Cameron R-420 Gas Free Balloon	4426		15. 9.98	
G-RNGR	Agusta-Bell 206B JetRanger III	8718		2. 6.89	To OO-DOU. Canx 26.7.93.
G-RNIE	Cameron Ball 70SS HAFB	2333		3. 8.90	
G-RNLD	Agusta A.109C	7633	I-ANAG	21. 6.96	
G-RNLI	Vickers-Supermarine 236 Walrus 1	S2/5591	W2718	13.12.90	(On rebuild 6/95)
G-RNMO	Short SD.3-30 Var.100	SH3023	D-CDLD G-BFZW/G-14-3023	13.12.85	To G-ZAPC 11/90. Canx.

Regn	Type	c/n	Previous identity	Regn date	Fate or immediate subsequent identity (if known)
G-RNRM	Cessna A.185F Skywagon	A185-02541	N1826R	20. 1.87	
G-RNSY	Fokker F-27 Friendship 200	10228	F-GCMA 6V-AEG/F-BUFU/JA8617/PH-FET	30.11.83	To N267MA. Canx 13.5.84.
G-RNTV	PA-30-160 Twin Comanche C	30-1856	G-AXDL N8707Y	15. 9.87	To OY-CLW. Canx 23.4.93.
G-ROAM	Schempp-Hirth Nimbus 4DM	22/31		24. 9.96	
G-ROAN	Boeing-Stearman B.75N-1 (N2S-3) Kaydet	75-7394	N4685N BuA.07790	16. 2.79	Badly damaged when overturned in high winds at Krk, Yugoslavia on 21.10.83. Wreck to Tattershall Thorpe, then battered fuselage frame at Wickenby on 30.4.88. Canx as WFU 18.1.89. To N768WM.
G-ROAR	Cessna 401	401-0166	G-BZFL G-AWSF/N4066Q	8. 3.82	
G-ROBB	Grob G.109B	6318		1.10.84	Damaged in accident at Sandtoft on 31.10.94. Canx by CAA 10.1.95.
G-ROBD	Europa Avn Europa	PFA/247-12671		23. 2.94	
G-ROBE	Grob G.109B	6277		16. 5.84	Canx as destroyed 26.9.89.
G-ROBI	Grob G.109B	6229		19.12.83	Canx by CAA 18.10.93. To USA and noted at Houston, TX in 11/98 still in UK marks. To N80217 in 2/99.
G-ROBK	Cessna R.182 Skylane RG II	R182-01950		26. 5.83	To G-OZOI 5/85. Canx.
G-ROBN	Robin R.1180T Aiglon (Officially regd with c/n 122)	220		16. 8.78	
G-ROBO	Robinson R-22 Beta	0701	N2615E	5.11.87	To OH-HJK 4/95. Canx 4.4.95.
G-ROBS	Robinson R-22 Beta	0860		18. 1.90	Crashed at Southend on 17.5.93. Canx as WFU 24.8.93.
G-ROBT	Hawker Hurricane I (Gloster built; on rebuild by Hawker Restorations Ltd from remains salvaged .88 from wreck site at Dunkirk Beach)	-	P2902	19. 9.94	(Parts on rebuild Chessington .96)
"G-ROBT"	Blackburn C.A.3 Biplane	-		----	Canx.
G-ROBY	Colt 17A Cloudhopper HAFB	483		7. 2.83	
G-ROCH	Cessna T.303 Crusader	T303-00129	N4962C	29. 3.90	
G-ROCK	Thunder Ax7-77 HAFB	781		25. 2.86	
G-ROCR	Schweizer Hughes 269C (300C)	S.1336	N219MS	14. 6.90	
G-RODD	Cessna 310R II	310R-0544	G-TEDD G-MADI/N87396/G-MADI/N87396	2.10.89	
G-RODG	Pearce Jabiru XL	PFA/274A-13379		14. 4.99	
G-RODI	Isaacs Fury	CM.1 & PFA/11-10130		22.12.78	(Force landed near Fordingbridge on 5.10.94) (Stored 3/97)
G-RODS	Agusta-Bell 206B JetRanger II	8435	G-NOEL G-BCWN	12. 6.84	To G-JWBI 4/96. Canx.
G-RODY	Bell 206B JetRanger	405	G-ROGR G-AXMM/N1469W	14.11.91	To G-WLLY 3/93. Canx.
G-ROGA	Cessna 310I	310I-0052	G-ASVV N8052M	13. 4.83	To G-MEBC 6/83. Canx.
G-ROGG	Robinson R-22 Beta	1487		31. 8.90	
G-ROGR	Bell 206B JetRanger	405	G-AXMM N1469W	12. 1.82	Badly damaged in crash at St.Helens on 27.7.91. Rebuilt & re-regd as G-RODY 11/91. Canx.
G-ROGY	Cameron Concept 60 HAFB	3055		11. 5.93	
G-ROIN	Aerospatiale AS.350BA Ecureuil	2344	F-GMAR N516AJ	5. 6.98	
G-ROKI	Rockwell Commander 114B	14384	G-BFKD N5835N	16. 7.96	Fatal crash at Mesmont, near Sombernon, France on 29.5.98. Canx as destroyed 2.10.98.
G-ROLA	PA-34-200T Seneca II	34-7670066	N4537X G-ROLA/N4537X	4.12.85	
G-ROLF	PA-32R-301 Saratoga SP	32R-8113018	N83052	7. 1.81	
G-ROLL	Aerotek Pitts S-2A Special	2175	N31444	20. 2.80	
G-ROLO	Robinson R-22 Beta	1226		24. 1.90	
G-ROMA	Hughes 369HS (500HS)	13-0442S	G-ROPI G-ROMA/G-ONPP/OY-HCP/D-HGER	16. 1.84	(Damaged early .93) (To March Helicopters for spares; pod in store 6/96)
G-ROME	Iniziative Industriali Italian Sky Arrow 650TC	C.011		26. 5.99	
G-ROMS	Lindstrand LBL-105G HAFB	401		13. 9.96	
G-ROMW	Cyclone Pegasus Ax2000	7486		4. 2.99	
G-RONA	Europa Avn Europa	PFA/247-12588		17. 1.95	
G-RONC	Aeronca 11AC Chief	11AC-1773	G-BULV N3493E/NC3493E	21. 1.93	Permit expired 11.7.96. Canx by CAA 15.10.96. To SE-XPV 6/97.
G-RONG	PA-28R-200 Cherokee Arrow II	28R-7335148	N16451	14. 6.90	
G-RONI	Cameron V-77 HAFB	2349		27. 7.90	
G-RONN	Robinson R-44 Astro	0267	N770SC G-RONN/D-HIRR	8. 1.98	
G-RONS	Robin DR.400/180 Regent	2088		17. 7.91	
G-RONT	Enstrom F-28A	223	G-BDAW	31. 3.87	To OO-NMT 4/95. Canx 5.4.95.
G-RONW	Clutton FRED Srs.II	PFA/29-10121		18.12.78	
G-ROOF	Brantly B.2B	474	G-AXSR N2237U	10.12.85	Restored as G-AXSR 4/93. Canx.
G-ROOK	Reims Cessna F.172P Skyhawk II	2081	PH-TGY G-ROOK	12. 1.81	
G-ROOM	Short SD.3-60 (Prototype) (Rebuild of SD.3-30 N844SA c/n SH.3041)	SH3600	(G-BSBL)	29. 5.81	Destroyed by IRA bomb at Belfast Harbour airport on 27.11.89. To spares in 1990. Canx as destroyed 24.5.90.
G-ROOT	Agusta-Bell 206A JetRanger	8046	G-JETR (G-BKBR)/OO-CDP	3. 8.82	To G-FSDG 4/85. Canx.
G-ROOV	Europa Avn Europa XS	PFA/247-13204		16. 7.98	
G-ROPA	Europa Avn Europa	PFA/247-12396		27.11.92	No Permit to Fly issued. Canx by CAA 9.4.99.

Regn	Type	c/n	Previous identity	Regn date	Fate or immediate subsequent identity (if known)
G-ROPE	Agusta A.109A	7170	G-OAMH	15. 5.84	To G-BRYL 10/84. Canx.
G-ROPI	Hughes 369HS (500HS)	13-0442S	G-ROMA G-ONPP/OY-HGP/D-HGER	17. 4.85	Restored as G-ROMA 4/89. Canx.
G-RORI	Folland Gnat T.1	FL.549	8621M XR538	18.10.93	
G-RORO	Cessna 337B Super Skymaster	337-0554	G-AVIX N5454S	8. 1.80	(Overran the runway and collided with a hedge on landing at Castle Rock, Northern Ireland on 25.6.99)
G-RORY	Focke-Wulf Piaggio FWP.149D (Piaggio c/n 338)	014	G-TOWN D-EFFY/West German AF 90+06/BB+394	2. 8.88	
G-ROSE	Evans VP-1	PFA/7031		22. 1.79	
G-ROSI	Thunder Ax7-77 HAFB	1284		29. 6.88	
G-ROSS	Practavia Pilot Sprite (Regd with plans no. 132)	PFA/05-10404		28. 2.80	
G-ROSY	Robinson R-22 Beta	2042		22. 1.92	To ZK-HGR 7/96. Canx 31.5.96.
G-ROTA	Bensen B.8 Gyroplane	001 & G/01-1067		4. 2.85	No Permit believed issued. Canx by CAA 18.6.91.
G-ROTI	Luscombe 8A Silvaire	2117	N45590 NC45590	18. 4.89	
G-ROTO	Rotorway Exec 90	5076		7.11.91	Fatal crash in a field near the A11 road at Six Mile Bottom, 8km E of Cambridge on 1.8.98. Canx as destroyed 12.11.98.
G-ROTR	Brantly B.2B	403	N2192U	9.12.91	
G-ROTS	CFM Streak Shadow Srs.SA	K.120-SA & PFA/161A-11603		21.12.89	
G-ROUP	Reims Cessna F.172M Skyhawk II	1451	G-BDPH	23. 5.84	
G-ROUS	PA-34-200T Seneca II	34-7870187	N9412C	26. 4.78	
G-ROUT	Robinson R-22 Beta	1241	N8068U	23. 1.90	
G-ROVE	PA-18-135 Super Cub (L-21B-PI)(Frame No.18-3853)	18-3846	PH-VLO (PH-DKF)/R.Netherlands AF R-156/54-2446	6. 5.82	
G-ROVI	Aviamilano F.8L Falco Srs.2	117	I-ROVI	11.10.88	Fatal crashed at Stangford Lough on 9.9.89. Canx as destroyed 19.12.89.
G-ROVY	Robinson R-22 Beta	2957		9. 7.99	
G-ROWE	Reims Cessna F.182P Skylane II	0007	OO-CNG	18.12.95	
G-ROWI	Europa Avn Europa XS	PFA/247-13482		16. 6.99	
G-ROWL	American Aviation AA-5B Tiger	AA5B-0595	(N28410)	26.10.77	
G-ROWN	Beechcraft 200 Super King Air	BB-684	G-BHLC N27L/N8511L/G-BHLC	13.10.87	
G-ROWS	PA-28-151 Warrior	28-7715296	N8949F	15. 9.78	
G-ROYI	PA-32R-301 Saratoga SP	32R-8213012	G-BMEY N8005Y/ZS-LCN/N8005Y	13.10.87	To SE-KZT. Canx 25.10.91.
G-ROYL	Taylor JT.1 Monoplane	RLW.02		29.12.78	No Permit issued. Canx by CAA 11.7.91.
G-ROYS	DHC.1 Chipmunk 22 (Fuselage no. DHB/f/677)	C1/0778	7438M WP905	1. 8.78	To G-BNZC 11/87. Canx.
G-ROYW	PA-28RT-201 Arrow IV	28R-7918238	G-CRTI SE-ICY	2.12.86	To G-BPZM 5/89. Canx.
G-ROYY	Robinson R-22 Beta	0886		6.10.88	To EI-CGK 11/92. Canx 12.11.92.
G-ROYZ	PA-34-200T Seneca II	34-7970191	G-GALE N3052X	12. 5.92	To G-CTWW 7/93. Canx.
G-ROZI	Robinson R-44 Astro	0252		26. 3.96	
G-ROZY	Cameron R-36 Gas Free Balloon	1141		20. 5.85	
G-RPAH	Rutan VariEze	BH.1		9. 3.79	Canx by CAA 2.9.91.
G-RPEZ	Rutan LongEz	PFA/74A-10746		3. 4.84	(Stored uncomplete 1/94)
G-RRGN	Vickers Supermarine 390 Spitfire PR.XIX	6S/594677	G-MXIX PS853/7548M/PS853	23.12.96	
G-RRJE	Airbus A.320-212	222	F-GLGJ ZS-NZT/F-WWIL	15. 5.96	To OY-CNC 3/97. Canx 5.3.97.
G-RRRR	DAW Privateer Motor Glider 1200	PFA/42-10387		15. 9.78	No Permit to Fly issued. Canx by CAA 5.1.96.
G-RRSG(1)	Cameron V-77 HAFB	1079	(G-BLRO)	31.10.84	NTU - Canx by CAA 24.9.86 as not built. To G-BNIN 4/87.
G-RRSG(2)	Thunder Ax7-77 HAFB	874		24. 9.86	
G-RRTM	Sikorsky S-70C (RTM.322 development aircraft)	70-583	N31248	6. 1.86	To N60FH 12/95. Canx 25.10.95.
G-RSCJ	Cessna 525 CitationJet	525-0298	N.....	15. 1.99	
G-RSFT	PA-28-161 Warrior II	28-8616038	G-WARI N9276Y	15.12.95	
G-RSKR	PA-28-161 Warrior II	28-7916181	G-BOJY N3030G	27. 4.95	
G-RSMA	Bell 206B JetRanger III	2584	G-SHZZ G-BNUW/N5018B/(N500FB)/N5018B	22. 5.95	To F-GOPY 6/98. Canx 30.3.98.
G-RSPH	CFM Streak Shadow SA-M	PFA/206-13166		18. 7.97	To G-MGPH 11/97. Canx.
G-RSRS	Beechcraft 400 BeechJet	RJ-36	N3236Q G-RSRS/N3236Q	19. 8.88	Restored as N3236Q. Canx 7.6.89.
G-RSSF	Denney Kitfox Mk.2	PFA/172-12125		9.10.92	
G-RSUL	Cessna T.303 Crusader	T303-00160	(G-BPZN) N6610C	16. 4.87	To G-BPZN 6/90. Canx.
G-RSVP	Robinson R-22 Beta	2788		5. 2.98	
G-RSWO	Cessna 172R Skyhawk II	172-80206	N9401F	25. 2.98	
G-RSWW	Robinson R-22 Beta	1775	N40815	16. 5.91	
G-RTBI	Thunder Ax6-56 HAFB	2584		19. 4.94	

Regn	Type	c/n	Previous identity	Regn date	Fate or immediate subsequent identity (if known)
G-RTHL	Leivers Special	ROB-1		27. 2.80	No Permit issued. Canx by CAA 9.7.91.
G-RTWI	Cameron R-550 HAFB	4384		3. 6.98	
G-RTWW	Robinson R-44 Astro	0438		20. 3.98	
G-RUBB	American Aviation AA-5B Tiger	AA5B-0928	(G-BKVI) OO-NAS/(OO-HRC)	20. 9.83	
G-RUBI	Thunder Ax7-77 HAFB	1051		27. 2.87	
G-RUBY	PA-28RT-201T Turbo Arrow IV	28R-8331037	G-BROU N4306K	5. 1.90	
G-RUDD	Cameron V-65 HAFB	844		19. 5.82	
G-RUDI	QAC Quickie Q.2	PFA/94A-11209		3. 9.91	No Permit to Fly issued. Canx by CAA 8.4.99.
G-RUFF	Mainair Blade	1203-0799-7 & W1006		18. 6.99	
G-RUGB	Cameron Egg 89SS HAFB (Rugby Ball shape)	1936		9. 2.89	Canx by CAA 14.7.98.
G-RUGS	Campbell Cricket Mk.4	G/03-1307		11. 2.99	
G-RUIA	Reims Cessna F.172N Skyhawk II	1856	PH-AXA(3)	4.10.79	
G-RUMM	Grumman F8F-2P Bearcat	D.1088	NX700HL NX700H/N1YY/N4995V/BuA.121714	20. 3.98	
G-RUMN	American American AA-1A Trainer	AA1A-0086	N87599 D-EAFB/(N9386L)	30. 5.80	
G-RUMP	Robinson R-22 Beta	1669	N2405T	29.11.90	To G-PHEL 8/96. Canx.
G-RUMT	Grumman F7F-3P Tigercat	C.167	NX7235C BuA.80425	6. 4.98	
G-RUMW	Grumman FM-2 Wildcat	5765	N4845V BuA.86711	15. 4.98	
G-RUNG	SAAB-Scania SF.340A	340A-086	F-GGBV SE-E86	3. 6.97	
G-RUNT	Cassutt Racer IIIM	161149 & PFA/34-10860		12. 4.83	
G-RUSA	Cyclone Pegasus Quantum 15	7517		7. 4.99	
G-RUSH	Cessna 404 Titan Courier II	404-0063	G-BEMX (N5446G)	25. 5.82	To 5Y-SAC 4/90. Canx 24.4.90.
G-RUSO	Robinson R-22 Beta	1387		25. 5.90	
G-RUSS	Cessna 172N Skyhawk 100	172-68563	N733UR	30. 6.80	CofA expired 19.9.86. Canx by CAA 6.10.92. (Stored 6/95 Southend)
G-RUTH	Cessna TR.182 Turbo Skylane RG	R182-01390	G-BJBC N4703S	4. 9.81	To HB-CHG. Canx 9.8.83.
G-RVAN	Van's RV-6	PFA/181-12657		25. 4.97	
G-RVAW	Van's RV-6	PFA/181-13234		24.11.97	
G-RVCL	Van's RV-6	PFA/181A-13439		18. 2.99	
G-RVDJ	Van's RV-6	PFA/181-12938		8. 2.99	
G-RVEE	Van's RV-6	PFA/181-12262		16. 2.93	
G-RVET	Van's RV-6	PFA/181-12852		9. 3.98	
G-RVGA	Van's RV-6A	PFA/181-13079		11. 5.98	
G-RVIA	Van's RV-6A	PFA/181-12289		13. 8.97	
G-RVIB	Van's RV-6	PFA/181-13220		22. 6.99	
G-RVIN	Van's RV-6	PFA/181-13236		28.11.97	
G-RVIP	Embraer EMB.110P1 Bandeirante	110-377	(G-BJCZ) PT-SEU	12. 2.82	To C-GHOV. Canx 10.1.85.
G-RVIT	Van's RV-6	PFA/181-12422		1. 5.95	
G-RVIV	Van's RV-4	PFA/181-12366		31.12.97	
G-RVMJ	Van's RV-4	PFA/181-13433		16. 2.99	
G-RVRA	PA-28-140 Cherokee Cruiser	28-7625038	G-OWVA N4459X	14. 1.97	
G-RVRB	PA-34-200T Seneca II	34-7970440	G-BTAJ N22MJ/N45113	24. 2.97	
G-RVRC	PA-23-250 Aztec E	27-7405336	G-BNPD N101VH/N40591	14.10.97	
G-RVRD	PA-23-250 Aztec E	27-4634	G-BRAV G-BBCM/N14021	16. 3.98	
G-RVRF	PA-38-112 Tomahawk	38-78A0714	G-BGEL	21.11.97	
G-RVRG	PA-38-112 Tomahawk	38-79A1092	G-BHAF	3. 8.98	
G-RVRV	Van's RV-4	PFA/181-13024		29. 9.98	
G-RVSA	Van's RV-6	PFA/181-12574		19. 5.99	
G-RVSX	Van's RV-6	PFA/181-13090		18. 9.97	
G-RVVI	Van's RV-6	PFA/181-12418		26. 1.93	
G-RWHC	Cameron A-180 HAFB	2700		16. 4.92	
G-RWIN	Rearwin 175 Skyranger	1522	N32391 NC32391	12. 9.90	
G-RWSS	Denney Kitfox Mk.2	PFA/172-12008		16. 4.91	
G-RWWW	Westland WS-55 Whirlwind HCC.12	WA/418	8727M XR486	21. 6.90	(Stored 9/97)
G-RXUK	Lindstrand LBL-105A HAFB	232		29. 3.95	
G-RYAL	Pearce Jabiru UL	PFA/274A-13365		6. 7.99	
G-RYAN	PA-28R-201T Turbo Arrow III	28R-7703135	G-BFMN OO-DGP/N5622V	7. 2.83	To F-GJHD 3/90. Canx 1.2.90.
"G-RYCR"	DH.82A Tiger Moth	86618	F-BGEE PG732	----	On display at Frankfurt wearing these false marks.
G-RYOB	Bell 206B JetRanger II	1484	G-BLWU ZS-PAW	16. 4.87	To G-UEST 9/89. Canx.
G-RZZB	Robinson R-22 Beta	1881		16. 9.91	To OH-HMZ 11/95. Canx 20.10.95.

Regn	Type	c/n	Previous identity	Regn date	Fate or immediate subsequent identity (if known)
G-S					G-S
G-SAAB	Rockwell Commander 112TC	13002	G-BEFS N1502J	5.12.79	
G-SAAM	Cessna T.182R Turbo Skylane II	T182-68200	G-TAGL G-SAAM/N2399E	23. 5.84	
G-SAAS	Ayres S2R-T34 Turbo-Thrush Commander	6009	N4010S	16. 2.79	To ZS-LUW 9/87. Canx 19.6.87.
G-SABA	PA-28R-201T Turbo Arrow III	28R-7703268	G-BFEN N38745	22. 8.79	
G-SABR	North American F-86A-5NA Sabre (Regd with c/n 151-083)	151-43547	N178 N68388/48-178	6.11.91	
G-SACA	Cessna 152 II	152-81900	G-HOSE N67538	16. 2.84	To CS-AZB. Canx 26.5.92.
G-SACB	Reims Cessna F.152 II	1501	G-BFRB	7. 3.84	
G-SACC	Cessna 152 II	152-82172	G-BGIA N68187	7. 3.84	Restored as G-BGIA 3.5.84. Canx.
G-SACD	Reims Cessna F.172H	0385	G-AVCD	13. 6.83	
G-SACE	Reims Cessna F.150L	0743	G-AZLK	7. 3.84	Damaged on take-off from Blythe Bridge on 19.4.92 and crashed into a field. Canx as WFU 25.3.97.
G-SACF	Cessna 152 II	152-83175	G-BHSZ N47125	21. 3.85	Badly damaged on landing at Egginton on 21.3.97. Canx by CAA 11.8.97.
G-SACH	Stoddard-Hamilton Glastar	PFA/295-13088		27. 8.99	
G-SACI	PA-28-161 Warrior II	28-8216123	N81535	26. 7.89	
G-SACK	Robin R.2160	316		2. 5.97	
G-SACO	PA-28-161 Warrior II	28-8416085	N4358Z	1. 6.89	
G-SACR	PA-28-161 Cadet	2841046	N91618	6. 2.89	
G-SACS	PA-28-161 Cadet	2841047	N91619	6. 2.89	
G-SACT	PA-28-161 Cadet	2841048	N9162D	6. 2.89	
G-SACU	PA-28-161 Cadet	2841049	N9162X	6. 2.89	(Damaged on landing at Sherburn-in-Elmet on 29.4.96)
G-SACV	PA-28-161 Cadet	2841241	N9192E	9.11.89	Fatal crash on High Cross Moor, 4 miles southeast of Lancaster on 20.5.91. Canx as destroyed 7.8.91.
G-SACZ	PA-28-161 Warrior II	28-7916258	N2098N	26. 7.89	
G-SADE	Reims Cessna F.150L	0752	G-AZJW	28. 5.91	
G-SAEW	Aerospatiale AS.355F2 Twin Squirrel	5435	N244BB N244BH	20.12.96	
G-SAFE	Cameron N-77 HAFB	511		14. 2.79	
G-SAFR	Saab 91D Safir	91-382	PH-RLR	10.10.95	(On rebuild on industrial estate in Rugby 7/96)
G-SAGA	Grob G-109B	6364	OE-9254	28. 6.90	
G-SAGE	Luscombe 8A Silvaire	2581	G-AKTL N71154/NC71154	15. 8.90	
G-SAHI	FLS Sprint 160 (Originally regd as Trago Mills SAH-1)	001		21.10.80	(Stored 4/98 North Weald)
G-SAIL	Boeing 707-323C (Line No. 356)	18690	N7556A	29. 9.78	Canx 21.4.86 on sale to USA. (N7556A allocated 25.6.86 but NTU & canx same day) Stored at Davis-Monthan AFB, AZ for spares use 10/92; storage code CZ0147.
G-SAIR	Cessna 421C Golden Eagle III	421C-0471	G-OBCA N6812C	1. 4.86	
G-SAIX	Cameron N-77 HAFB	626	N386CB	14. 1.99	
G-SALA	PA-32-300 Cherokee Six E	32-7940106	(G-BHEJ) N2184Z	17.10.79	
G-SALI	Cessna 421C Golden Eagle III	421C-0706	N26552	12. 1.88	To G-OSCH 9/95. Canx.
G-SALL	Reims Cessna F.150L	0682	PH-LTY D-ECPH	19. 1.79	
G-SALS	Cessna 421C Golden Eagle III	421C-0133	G-BEFT N3898C	15. 5.92	To N421CC 12/93. Canx 20.12.93.
G-SALT	PA-23-250 Aztec F	27-7954063	G-BGTH N2551M	7. 8.85	To G-ZSFT 4/89. Canx.
G-SALU	Short SD.3-60 Var.100	SH3628	(SE-IXO) G-SALU/OY-MMC/G-BKZR/G-14-3628	10.10.85	To G-OAEX 3/89. Canx.
G-SALV	Beechcraft C90 King Air	LJ-991	G-BIXM (YV-442CP)	25.10.84	Restored as G-BIXM 12/89. Canx.
G-SALY	Hawker Sea Fury FB.XI	41H-696792	WJ288	12. 7.83	To N15S 1/91. Canx 2.1.91.
G-SAMA	PA-31-350 Navajo Chieftain	31-7952035	N27897	16.12.87	To N135PB 9/93. Canx 21.9.93.
G-SAMG	Grob G-109B	6278		16. 5.84	
G-SAMI	Cameron N-90 HAFB	3907	G-BWSE	21. 8.96	
G-SAMM	Cessna 340A II (RAM-conversion)	340A-0742	N37TJ N2671A	7. 3.88	
G-SAMS	Socata MS.880B Rallye Club	873	F-BONP	28.11.78	Canx as WFU 2.11.94.
G-SAMY	Europa Avn Europa	PFA/247-12901		17. 8.95	
G-SAMZ	Cessna 150D	150-60536	G-ASSO N4536U	19. 4.84	
G-SANB	Beechcraft E90 King Air	LW-304	(N113SB) G-SANB/G-BGNU	15. 4.88	To F-GMRN 5/99. Canx 8.1.99.
G-SAND	Schweizer 269C (300C)	S.1399		17. 8.89	
G-SANS	Robinson R-22 Beta	2012	G-BUHX	31.10.97	
G-SARA	PA-28-181 Archer II	28-7990039	N21270	6. 4.81	
G-SARH	PA-28-161 Warrior II	28-8216173	N8232Q	18. 2.91	

Regn	Type	c/n	Previous identity	Regn date	Fate or immediate subsequent identity (if known)
G-SARK	BAC 167 Strikemaster Mk.84 (Officially regd with c/n EEP/JP/1931)	PS.148	N2146S Singapore AF 311/G-27-140	13. 1.95	(Stored 8/97)
G-SARN	BN-2A Mk.III-2 Trislander	1041	F-BYCJ V2-LMB/VP-LMB/G-BEFO	3. 8.88	Restored as G-BEFO 1/91. Canx.
G-SARO	Saro Skeeter AOP.12	S2/5097	XL812	17. 7.78	
G-SASK	PA-31P Pressurised Navajo	31P-39	G-BFAM SE-GLV/OH-PNF	30.10.97	
G-SASU	Aerospatiale AS.355F1 Twin Squirrel	5302	G-BSSM G-BMTC/G-BKUK	25. 8.89	To G-EPOL 1/98. Canx.
G-SATC	Reims Cessna F.150L	0883	PH-ECT D-ECTS	23.10.79	Crashed near Giruan, Ayr on 26.7.80. Canx as destroyed 5.12.83.
G-SATI	Cameron Sphere 105SS HAFB	1901		16.12.88	(Based in Germany) Canx by CAA 9.12.96.
G-SATL	Cameron Sphere 105SS HAFB	2696		5.12.91	
G-SATO	PA-23-250 Aztec E	27-7554045	G-BCXP N54257	5. 6.80	To EI-EEC 2/92. Canx 30.1.92.
G-SAUF	Colt 90A HAFB (Built as, or has new envelope, c/n 2492)	1497		25. 5.89	
G-SAVE	PA-31-350 Navajo Chieftain	31-7952102	N3518T	14. 5.79	To G-BVYF 2/95. Canx.
G-SAVS	Murphy Rebel	PFA/232-12536		27. 7.93	To G-BWFZ 7/95. Canx.
G-SAWI	PA-32RT-300T Turbo lance	32R-7887069	OY-CJJ N36719	23. 6.99	
G-SAXO	Cameron N-105 HAFB	3864		1. 4.96	
G-SBAC	Short SD.3-60 Var.200	SH3636	EI-BEL G-BLEE/G-14-3636	5. 2.92	To N408SA with new c/n SH3408. Canx 15.9.95.
G-SBAE	Reims Cessna F.172P	2200	D-EOCD(3)	3. 6.98	
G-SBAS	Beechcraft B200 Super King Air	BB-1007	SE-IVZ N777GA/G-BJJV	16.11.90	
G-SBEA	Boeing 737-204ADV (Line No. 542)	21694	G-BFVB C-GNDW/G-BFVB	15.12.94	To N109TR. Canx 3.11.98.
G-SBEB	Boeing 737-204ADV (Line No. 341)	20807	G-BAZH	15.12.94	To N107TR. Canx 3.11.98.
G-SBEC	Cessna 501 Citation I (Unit No.661)	501-0255	N707WF N501MR/N661TW/N661TV	13. 6.88	To N400LX. Canx 14.12.89.
G-SBLT	Steen Skybolt	MH-01		14. 4.92	
G-SBMO	Robin R.2160i Acrobin	116	EI-BMO SE-GSZ	12. 2.99	
G-SBRV	Vickers BRV Special	BRV.001		22.11.78	No Permit issued. Canx as WFU 9.12.86.
G-SBUS	PADC BN-2A-26 Islander	3013	G-BMMH RP-C578	31.10.86	
G-SBUT	Robinson R-22 Beta	2739	G-BXMT	18. 5.98	
G-SCAH	Cameron V-77 HAFB	788		18. 1.82	
G-SCAN	Vinten Wallis WA-116 Srs.100	001		5. 7.82	Permit expired 10.7.91. (Stored 2/99 Reymerston Hall)
G-SCAT	Reims Cessna F.150F (Taildragger) (Wichita c/n 63455)	0054	G-ATRN (G-ATMN)	15. 9.86	
G-SCBI	Socata TB-20 Trinidad	1908	F-OIGV	10. 8.99	
G-SCCC	BAe 125 Srs.1000B	259037	G-5-771	22. 3.93	To G-SHEC 12/95. Canx.
G-SCFO	Cameron O-77 HAFB	1131		3. 5.85	(Extant 1/98)
G-SCHH(1)	BAe 146 Srs.100	E1004	(G-BIAG)	3. 5.81	NTU - To G-OBAF 28.5.81. Canx.
G-SCHH(2)	BAe 146 Srs.100	E1005	G-5-02 ZD696/G-SCHH/ZD696/G-SCHH/(ZK-SHH)/G-SCHH/(G-BIAJ)	30. 7.82	To G-5-005/VH-NJY 7/91. Canx 25.7.91.
G-SCHU	Aerospatiale AS.355F1 Twin Squirrel	5033	N915EG N5777H	15. 9.89	To G-PASF 3/91. Canx.
G-SCLX	FLS Aerospace Sprint 160	002	G-PLYM	14. 7.94	
G-SCOT	PA-31-350 Navajo Chieftain	31-7752190	N27361	8.11.77	To G-OJUG 5/90. Canx.
G-SCOW	Aerospatiale AS.355F2 Twin Squirrel	5346	ZS-HSW G-POON/G-MCAL	19. 5.99	
G-SCOX	Enstrom F-28F	771	N330SA G-BXXW/JA7823	3. 9.98	
G-SCPL	PA-28-140 Cherokee Cruiser	28-7725160	G-BPVL N1785H	4. 5.89	
G-SCRU	Cameron A-250 HAFB	3935	G-BWWO	30. 9.96	
G-SCSR	Airbus A.320-212	299	F-WWIQ	14. 4.92	To G-JDFW 11/95. Canx.
G-SCTA	Westland Scout AH.1 (Regd with c/n F.86048) (Nacelle No. F8 6140)	F.9701	XV126	18.12.95	
G-SCTT	Handley Page HPR.7 Dart Herald 210	173	F-BLOY(2) F-OCLY/HB-AAK/G-ASPJ/(HB-AAI)	30. 8.88	WFU & stored engineless in 2/97. Canx as PWFU 8.4.97.
G-SCUB	PA-18-135 Super Cub (L-21B-PI)(Frame No. 18-3849)	18-3847	PH-GAX R.Netherlands AF R-157/54-2447	13.12.78	
G-SCUD	Montgomerie-Bensen B.8MR Gyrocopter	G/01-1294		18. 8.97	
G-SCUH	Boeing 737-3Q8 (Line No. 1107)	23254		2. 5.85	To N780MA. Canx 5.7.93.
G-SCUL	Rutan Cozy	PFA/159-13212		28. 5.98	
G-SDEV	DH.104 Sea Devon C.20 (Dove 6)	04472	XK895	29. 3.90	CofA expired 21.7.96. (Stored 5/99 at Kemble)
G-SDLW	Cameron O-105 HAFB	2460		11. 3.91	
G-SEAB	Republic RC-3 Seabee	413	N6210K NC6210K	6. 5.88	(Fuselage stored 6/98 at Tollerton)
G-SEAH	Hawker Sea Hawk FB.5 (Armstrong-Whitworth built)	6032	A2503 WM994	5. 4.83	To N994WM 8/95. Canx 23.11.94.

Regn	Type	c/n	Previous identity	Regn date	Fate or immediate subsequent identity (if known)
G-SEAI	Cessna U.206G Stationair II Seaplane	U206-04059	N756FQ	20. 3.92	(Damaged by gales at Prestwick on 26.12.98)
G-SEAN	Bell 206L-3 Long Ranger	51278	N7061H	8. 6.89	To D-HASA(4) 8/91. Canx 26.7.91.
G-SEAR	Pazmany PL-4A	PFA/17-10234		22.12.78	Lost power soon after take-off at Shobdon on 12.7.87 & crashed in a field. Canx as destroyed 1.2.88.
G-SEAS	PA-31-310 Navajo	31-7912017	OY-CED LN-DCC/N27040	11. 9.89	Extensively damaged in fatal crash near Guildford on 15.8.93. Canx as destroyed 11.11.93.
G-SEAT	Colt 42A HAFB	817		28. 5.86	
G-SEBB	Brugger Colibri MB.2	PFA/7503		21.11.86	Canx by CAA 2.9.91.
G-SEBE	Gates LearJet 35A	35A-365	G-ZIPS (N45645)/G-ZONE	2. 9.85	To G-CJET 6/87. Canx.
G-SEBI	Aerospatiale AS.350B Ecureuil	1847	G-BMCU	1.10.85	To G-ZBAC 5/87. Canx.
G-SEED	Piper J3C-90 Cub (L-4H-PI) (Frame No 10932; Official identity c/n 12499 & 44-80203, probably rebuilt 1945)	11098	EI-BAP F-BFBZ/44-80203/43-29807	28. 1.80	
G-SEEK	Cessna T.210N Turbo-Centurion II	210-64579	N9721Y	14.10.83	
G-SEGA	Cameron Sonic 90SS HAFB (Sonic The Hedgehog shape)	2896		16. 9.92	
G-SEGO	Robinson R-22 Beta	0871	N9081N	12.10.88	
G-SEJW	PA-28-161 Cherokee Warrior II	28-7816469	N9557N	19. 4.78	
G-SELL	Robin DR.400/180 Regent	1153	D-EEMT	7. 3.85	
G-SELY	Agusta-Bell 206B JetRanger III	8740		26. 7.96	
G-SEMI	PA-44-180 Seminole	44-7995052	G-DENW N21439	23. 2.99	
G-SENA	Rutan LongEz (Built by R.Bazin)	1325	F-PZSQ F-WZSQ	11.11.96	
G-SEND	Colt 90A HAFB	2100		2.12.91	
G-SENX	PA-34-200T Seneca II	34-7870356	G-DARE G-WOTS/G-SEVL/N36742	15. 5.95	
G-SEPA	Eurocopter AS.355N Twin Squirrel	5525	G-METD G-BUJF/F-WYMF	25. 7.96	
G-SEPB	Eurocopter AS.355N Twin Squirrel	5574	G-BVSE	1. 2.95	
G-SEPC	Eurocopter AS.355N Twin Squirrel	5596	G-BWGV	29.11.95	
G-SEPT	Cameron N-105 HAFB	1880		22.11.88	
G-SERA	Enstrom F-28A-UK	103	G-BAHU EI-BDF/G-BAHU	14. 3.91	
G-SERL	Socata TB-10 Tobago	109	G-LANA EI-BIH	28. 5.92	
G-SETA	Aerospatiale AS.355F1 Twin Squirrel	5077	G-NEAS G-CMMM/G-BNBJ/C-GLKH	13.12.89	To G-CCAO 1/96. Canx.
G-SEUK	Cameron TV 80SS HAFB (Samsung Computer Shape)	3810		12. 4.96	
G-SEVA	Replica Plans SE.5A	PFA/20-10955		19. 6.85	
G-SEVE	Cessna 172N Skyhawk II	172-69970	N738GR	10. 1.90	
G-SEVL	PA-34-200T Seneca II	34-7870356	N36742	10. 3.89	To G-WOTS 8/89. Canx.
G-SEWL	PA-28-151 Cherokee Warrior	28-7415253	D-EDOS N9550N	25. 8.81	To G-BVTO 9/94. Canx.
G-SEXI	Cessna 172M Skyhawk II	172-63806	N1964V	21. 4.92	
G-SEXY	American American AA-1 Yankee (Regd incorrectly as c/n 0042)	AA1-0442	G-AYLM	30. 6.81	Badly damaged in forced landing at Burscough, Lancs on 11.2.94. CofA expired 17.3.95. (Fuselage used as a travelling exhibit in 1998)
G-SFBH	Boeing 737-46N (Line No. 2886)	28723		28. 5.97	
G-SFHR	PA-23-250 Aztec F	27-8054041	G-BHSO N2527Z	24. 6.82	
G-SFOX	Rotorway Exec 90	5059	G-BUAH	11.10.93	(Stored Hawarden 7/97)
G-SFPA	Reims Cessna F.406 Caravan II	0064		11.11.91	
G-SFPB	Reims Cessna F.406 Caravan II	0065		11.11.91	
G-SFRY	Thunder Ax7-77 HAFB	1667		23. 1.90	
G-SFTA	Westland SA.341G Gazelle 1	WA/1039	"G-BAGJ" G-SFTA/HB-XIL/G-BAGJ/(XW858)	10. 9.82	Crashed near Alston, Cumbria on 7.3.84. Rebuilt to static condition and painted in Army c/s. Canx as WFU 21.5.86. (On display 4/96)
G-SFTB	Aerospatiale SA.341G Gazelle Srs.1	1275	N47297	17.11.82	Crashed into Tanklin Tarn, near Carlisle on 9.11.83. Canx.
G-SFTC	Aerospatiale SA.341G Gazelle Srs.1	1289	N47298	17.11.82	To G-LOYD 6/85. Canx.
G-SFTD	Aerospatiale SA.341G Gazelle Srs.1	1145	G-RIFC G-SFTD/N641HM/N341BB/F-WKQH	18.10.82	To G-WELA 9/92. Canx.
G-SFTE	Aerospatiale SA.341G Gazelle Srs.1	1109	N9985F	8.12.82	DBF at Old Sarum on 17.1.87. Canx as destroyed 2.5.90.
G-SFTF	Aerospatiale SA.341G Gazelle Srs.1	1262	C-GTDE N369PL/N4727B/F-WXFN	18.10.82	To F-GDXX 2/87. Canx 10.2.87.
G-SFTG	Aerospatiale SA.341G Gazelle Srs.1	1187	N87712	21.12.82	To G-RALE 1/86. Canx.
G-SFTH	Aerospatiale SA.341G Gazelle Srs.1	1155	G-BLAP N62406	23. 5.84	To G-OAFY 5/89. Canx.
G-SFTR	Norman NDN-1T Turbo Firecracker	005		29. 7.83	To N2157C 10/89. Canx 31.10.89.

Regn	Type	c/n	Previous identity	Regn date	Fate or immediate subsequent identity (if known)
G-SFTS	Norman NDN-1T Turbo Firecracker	006		29. 7.83	Canx 7.5.92 on sale to USA. To N50FK 8/93.
G-SFTT	Norman NDN-1T Turbo Firecracker	007		29. 7.83	To N70878 9/93. Canx.
G-SFTV	Slingsby T.67M Firefly 160	2004		7. 2.83	To G-BKTZ 8/83. Canx.
G-SFTW	Slingsby T.67M Firefly 160	2003		14. 3.83	To HB-NBB 11/84. Canx 5.11.84.
G-SFTX	Slingsby T.67M Firefly 160	2002		7. 2.83	To G-DLTA 8/88. Canx.
G-SFTY	Slingsby T.67M Firefly 160	2001		7. 2.83	Crashed at Torquhan, Scotland on 30.1.84. Canx as destroyed 30.10.84.
G-SFTZ	Slingsby T.67M Firefly 160	2000		7. 2.83	
G-SGAS	Colt 77A HAFB	2073		31.10.91	
G-SGSE	PA-28-181 Cherokee Archer II	28-7890332	G-BOJX N3774M	2.12.96	
G-SHAA	Enstrom 280-UK Shark	1011	N280Q	8. 7.88	
G-SHAH	Reims Cessna F.152 II	1839	OH-IHA SE-IHA	7. 2.97	
G-SHAM	Beechcraft C90 King Air (Mod)	LJ-819	N2063A	12. 4.99	
G-SHAW	PA-30-160 Twin Comanche B	30-1221	LN-BWS	21. 3.78	
G-SHBB	Bell 206B JetRanger III	2291	G-BPCC N16905	11. 1.89	Crashed at Bottom Barn Farm, Cudham on 18.12.89 shortly after take-off from Biggin Hill. Canx as destroyed 12.2.90.
G-SHCB	Schweizer 269C-1	0038	N41S	28. 6.96	
G-SHCC	Bell 206B JetRanger II	1172	N280C	14.11.88	(Stored dismantled 12/98 Leeds/Bradford)
G-SHDD	Enstrom F-28C	431	G-BNBS SE-HIL	23. 8.88	To OE-XAM 10/93. Canx 7.9.93.
G-SHEA	BAe 125 Srs.800B	258240	G-BUWC G-5-772	18. 6.93	To HB-VLT 3/97. Canx 10.2.97.
G-SHEB	BAe 125 Srs.800B	258243	G-BUWD G-5-778	24. 5.93	To VH-XMO 3/96. Canx 28.2.96.
G-SHEC	BAe 125 Srs.1000A	259037	G-SCCC G-5-771	19.12.95	To XA-TGK 1/99. Canx 12.1.99.
G-SHED	PA-28-181 Archer II	28-7890068	G-BRAU N47411	12. 6.89	
G-SHEL	Cameron O-56 HAFB	298		20.12.77	Canx by CAA 4.8.98. (Was based in Hong Kong)
G-SHFF	Enstrom F-28C-UK	369	N604H	6. 1.89	Badly damaged when caught by a gust of wind while hovering to land at Barton on 10.2.90. Wreck stored 6/90 at Barton. Canx as destroyed 14.5.90.
G-SHFL	Cameron N-77 HAFB	2196		7. 2.90	CofA expired 24.4.94. (Was based in Hong Kong) Canx by CAA 4.6.98.
G-SHGG	Enstrom 280C-UK Shark	1112	N627H	16. 1.89	To G-MHCD 7/96. Canx.
G-SHIM	CFM Streak Shadow	K.228-SA & PFA/206-12501		19. 5.93	
G-SHIP	PA-23-250 Aztec F	27-7654015	N62490	18. 1.77	Crashed on landing at Keystone on 4.12.83. Canx as WFU 13.2.89. (Display piece in "paint-ball" at Woodland 11/92)
G-SHIV	Gulfstream-American GA-7 Cougar	GA7-0092	N713G	22.11.84	
G-SHJJ	Bell 206B JetRanger II	2757	N220PJ N27676	22.12.88	To D-HHFS(2) 4/89. Canx 7.4.89.
G-SHKK	Hughes 269A	111-0299	N8716F	17. 5.89	Exported to New Zealand as spares source late in 1992. Canx by CAA 12.8.94.
G-SHLL	Hughes 269A	76-0625	N269QD 66-18342	22. 5.89	Canx as WFU 8.11.90.
G-SHNN	Enstrom 280C Shark	1119	N51685	22. 5.89	
G-SHOE	Cessna 421C Golden Eagle III	421C-0123	G-BHGD D-IASC/ OE-FLR/N3862C	15. 1.81	Undershot approach and stalled on landing at Deauville, France on 8.11.85. (Returned to Kidlington for intended rebuild) Canx as WFU 29.7.86. Fuselage on fire dump 9/96 at Southampton.
G-SHOG	Colomban MC-15 Cri-Cri	001	G-PFAB(3) F-PYPU	3.10.96	
G-SHOK	Cessna 421C Golden Eagle III	421C-0466	N6800C	7. 6.79	To N29794 2/82. Canx.
G-SHOO	Hughes 269A (TH-55A)	56-0542	N5378S 64-18206	24. 7.89	Sold & used for spares in New Zealand in 1992. Canx by CAA 7.11.94.
G-SHOP	HS.125 Srs.F403B	25248	(N792A) G-5-707/G-SHOP/G-BTUF/G-5-707/G-BTUF/G-5-707/D-CFCF	20.10.92	To N792A. Canx 8.8.96.
G-SHOT	Cameron V-77 HAFB	972		14.12.83	
G-SHOW	Morane-Saulnier MS.733 Alcyon	125	F-BMQJ French AF 125-MZ/ 125-VZ/F-TFVZ	1.10.80	Permit expired 24.5.83. Sold to a US buyer at the Duxford auction in 4/83 but never delivered. Canx by CAA 4.12.84. (Stored at Booker until roaded out 8/96)
G-SHPP	Hughes 269A (TH-55A)	36-0481	N80559 64-18169	24. 7.89	
G-SHRK	Enstrom 280C-UK Shark	1173	N373SA G-SHRK/G-BGMX/EI-CCS/G-SHXX/G-BGMX/EI-BHR/G-BGMX/(F-GBOS)	6. 1.97	
G-SHRL	Jodel D.18	PFA/169-12217		18. 9.92	
G-SHRR	Agusta-Bell 206B JetRanger II	8052	G-FSDA G-AWJW	15. 2.90	Fatal crash at Nether Kellett, near the Carnforth junction on the M6 motorway on 11.8.97. Canx as destroyed 20.10.97.
G-SHSH	Europa Avn Europa	PFA/247-12722		7. 4.98	
G-SHSP	Cessna 172S Skyhawk II	172S-8079	N9552Q	25. 3.99	
G-SHSS	Enstrom 280C-UK Shark	1060	N6892X G-SHSS/EI-CHG/G-SHSS/(EI-...)/G-SHSS/G-BENO	11.10.89	
G-SHST	Colt 180A HAFB	1329		10.10.88	To D-OHST. Canx 8.6.92.
G-SHUG	PA-28R-201T Turbo Cherokee Arrow III	28R-7703048	N1026Q	17. 5.88	

Regn	Type	c/n	Previous identity	Regn date	Fate or immediate subsequent identity (if known)
G-SHUU	Enstrom 280C-UK-2 Shark	1221	G-OMCP G-KENY/G-BJFG/N8617N	16.10.89	
G-SHVV	Bell 206B JetRanger II	925	N72GM N83106	15.11.89	To G-GHCL 7/92. Canx.
G-SHWW	Enstrom F-28C-UK	348	G-SMUJ G-BHTF	26. 1.90	To G-MHCA 5/90. Canx.
G-SHXX	Enstrom 280C-UK Shark	1173	G-DCMX EI-BHR/G-BGMX/(F-GBOS)	22. 2.90	To EI-CCS 11/90. Canx 16.11.90.
G-SHZZ	Bell 206B JetRanger III	2584	G-BNUW N5018B/(N500FB)/N5018B	24. 4.90	To G-RSMA 5/95. Canx.
G-SIAL	Hawker Hunter F.58 (Officially regd with c/n 41H-699856)	41H-697457	J-4090 Swiss AF	2.10.95	(On overhaul 7/99 Duxford)
G-SIAN	Cameron V-77 HAFB	2667		17. 9.91	Canx by CAA 4.8.97.
G-SIBC	Cessna T.337G Pressurised Super Skymaster	P337-0200	I-SIBC N92N	31. 5.94	To N1ZM 1/96. Canx 27.12.95.
G-SIBE	Beechcraft 200 Super King Air	BB-828	G-MCEO G-BILY	25. 4.84	To G-SWFT 5/86. Canx.
G-SIGN	PA-39-160 Twin Comanche C/R	39-8	OY-TOO N8853Y	9. 2.78	
G-SIIB	Aviat Pitts S-2B Special	5218	G-BUVY N6073U	24. 3.93	
G-SIII	Extra EA.300	058	D-ETYE	10. 1.95	
G-SILK	Piper Aerostar 601P	61P-0607-7963272	N8207J	18. 4.79	To N60AC/N606AC 7/86. Canx 11.7.86.
G-SILS	Pietenpol Air Camper	PFA/47-13331		29. 6.98	
G-SILV	Cessna 340A	340A-1008	D-IHOS (N4272C)	10.10.80	Canx 8.1.87 on sale to France. To TR-LCL 3/87.
G-SIME	Auster J/1N Alpha	2019	G-AHHP	9. 1.81	Restored as G-AHHP 11/85. Canx.
G-SIMI	Cameron A-315 HAFB	3391		10. 3.95	
G-SIMN	Robinson R-22 Beta	2769		10.12.97	
G-SING	Beechcraft 60 Duke	P-21	D-IDTA SE-EXT	12. 7.85	To G-IASL 4/97. Canx.
G-SION	PA-38-112 Tomahawk II	38-81A0146	N23661	30. 1.91	
G-SIPA	SIPA 903	63	G-BGBM F-BGBM	31. 5.83	Damaged in forced landing near RAF Swinderby on 20.3.88. (Stored 7/99 "on the Wirral")
G-SIRI	Bell 206L-1 Long Ranger	45565	G-CSWL F-GDAD	5. 5.98	Restored as G-CSWL 20.5.98. Canx.
G-SIRR	North American P-51D-25NA Mustang (Adopted identity of c/n 122-40548 ex.44-74008/RCAF 9274/N8676E/N76AF/(N151MC) in 1982/84 rebuild)	122-39798	N51RR (N151MC)/TNI-AU F-3../44-73339	3. 2.97	
G-SITE	Aerospatiale AS.355F1 Twin Squirrel	5192	G-BPHC N365E	26. 1.89	To G-ORMA 11/98. Canx.
G-SITU	Partenavia P.68C Victor	219	G-NEWU G-BHJX	1. 8.84	To G-WTBC 2/91. Canx.
G-SIVA	MDC Hughes 369E (500E)	0372E	G-TBIX	21. 1.94	
G-SIVB	MDHC MD.600N	RN023	N9223Y (N958SD)	24. 4.98	To N511VA 10/98. Canx 2.10.98.
G-SIXA	Douglas DC-6A/B (Line No. 803)	45326	OY-DRM CF-CZS/G-ARXZ/CF-CZS	22. 5.79	WFU at Manston. Canx 29.4.85 on sale to USA. Broken up in 4/85.
G-SIXB	Douglas DC-6B (Line No. 853)	45329	OY-DRC LN-SUT/SE-BDG/CF-CZV	9. 3.79	To 3D-ASA 12/79. Canx.
G-SIXC	Douglas DC-6A/B (Line No. 1032)	45550	N93459 N90645/B-1006/XW-PFZ/B-1006	20. 3.87	
G-SIXD	PA-32-300 Cherokee Six D	32-7140007	HB-OMH N8615N	25. 3.98	
G-SIXI	PA-34-220T Seneca V	3449091	N61HB	. 1.99R	
G-SIXX	Colt 77A HAFB	1327		21.10.88	
G-SIXY	Van's RV-6	PFA/181-13368		9. 3.99	
G-SIZE	Lindstrand LBL-310A HAFB	028		9. 6.93	
G-SIZL	Bell 206B JetRanger III	3370	G-BOSW N2063T	16. 7.92	To G-KLEE 10/95. Canx.
G-SJAB	PA-39-160 Twin Comanche C/R	39-85	(N.....) G-AYWZ/N8928Y	14. 9.81	
G-SJAD	Dornier 228-200	8058	VH-NSC D-IERA/(D-CERA(2))	20. 1.87	To D-IHKB. Canx 9.11.87.
G-SJCH	PBN BN-2T-4S Defender 4000	4006	G-BWPK	. 9.99	
G-SJDI	Robinson R-44 Astro	0626		16. 7.99	
G-SJGM	Cessna 182R Skylane II	182-68316	N357WC	8. 2.88	To G-OCJW 4/97. Canx.
G-SJMC	Boeing 767-31KER (Line No. 528)	27205	N6038E	16. 3.94	
G-SKAN	Reims Cessna F.172M Skyhawk II	1120	G-BFKT F-BVBJ	8. 7.85	
G-SKIE	Steen Skybolt	AACA/357	ZK-DEN	29. 8.97	
G-SKIL	Cameron N-77 HAFB	2264		19. 3.90	
G-SKIM	Aerospatiale AS.350B Ecureuil	1465	G-BIVP	10.10.83	To G-HMAN 3/86. Canx.
G-SKIP	Cameron N-77 HAFB	801		20. 1.80	Canx as WFU 26.5.93.
G-SKIS	Tri-R Kis	PFA/239-12630		3. 2.94	
G-SKKA	PA-31-300 Turbo Navajo B	31-761	G-FOAL G-RMAE/G-BAEG/N7239L	24.10.89	To G-EEAC 5/94. Canx.
G-SKKB	PA-31-310 Turbo Navajo B	31-7300956	G-BBDS N7565L	18. 4.90	To N97RJ 9/97. Canx 4.9.97.
G-SKKC	Cessna 404 Titan II	404-0004	G-OHUB SE-GMX/(N3932C)	11. 6.90	To G-MIND 4/93. Canx.

Regn	Type	c/n	Previous identity	Regn date	Fate or immediate subsequent identity (if known)
G-SKSA	Airship Industries Skyship 500	1214/03		11. 1.82	Canx by CAA 22.4.96. (Last known of in the USA under conversion to a heavy lift version)
G-SKSB	Airship Industries Skyship 500	1214/04		10. 3.83	To N502LP. Canx 28.8.91.
G-SKSC	Airship Industries Skyship 600-01	1215/01		10. 3.83	To RAF as ZH762. Canx to MOD 3.12.93.
G-SKSD	Airship Industries Skyship 600-08	1215/02		10. 3.83	To VH-HAA 6/87. Canx 8.5.87.
G-SKSE(1)	Airship Industries Skyship 600	1215/03		10. 3.83	NTU - To G-SKSG 3/84. Canx.
G-SKSE(2)	Airship Industries Skyship 500	1214/05		10. 3.83	To JA1003 7/84. Canx 12.7.84.
G-SKSF	Airship Industries Skyship 600	1215/04	N601SK G-SKSF	10. 3.83	To N4304K as a Westinghouse Airship Inc Sentinel 1000 with c/n S1000-01. Canx 25.1.91.
G-SKSG	Airship Industries Skyship 600	1215/03	(C-....) G-SKSG/(G-SKSE)	23. 3.84	Canx as destroyed 17.1.96. (Was based at Toronto, Canada)
G-SKSH	Airship Industries Skyship 500	1214/06		23. 3.84	To N601LP. Canx 26.2.90.
G-SKSI	Airship Industries Skyship 500HL	1214/07		. .84R	NTU - To N503LP 12/98. Canx.
G-SKSJ	Airship Industries Skyship 600	1215/05		16. 7.84	To N600LP with c/n SK600-05. Canx 31.8.89.
G-SKSK	Airship Industries Skyship 600	1215/06		. .87R	NTU - To VH-HAN 6/87. Canx.
G-SKSL	Airship Industries Skyship 600	1215/07		20. 5.87	To N602SK. Canx 19.5.89.
G-SKSM	Airship Industries Skyship 600	1215/08		20. 5.87	Canx 9.9.88 on sale to Korea.
G-SKSN	Airship Industries Skyship 600	1215/09		19.12.88	To JA1006 3/89. Canx 3.3.89.
G-SKYA	Fairchild-Hiller FH.227B Friendship	536	N7815M	18. 1.79	To PT-LBV. Canx 16.6.81.
G-SKYB	Fairchild-Hiller FH.227B Friendship	539	N7817M	19. 4.79	To PT-LBG. Canx 17.10.80.
G-SKYC(1)	Fairchild-Hiller FH.227B Friendship	542	N7819M	. .79R	NTU - Restored as N7819M. Canx.
G-SKYC(2)	Slingsby T.67M Firefly	2009	G-BLDP	13. 6.97	
G-SKYD	Christen Pitts S-2B Special	5057	N5331N	15.10.92	(Damaged in ground loop on landing at Duxford on 21.6.96)
G-SKYE	Cessna TU.206G Turbo Stationair 6 II	U206-04568	(G-DROP) N9783M	1. 8.79	
G-SKYG	Iniziative Industriali Italian Sky Arrow 650TC	C.008		15.12.98	
G-SKYH	Cessna 172N Skyhawk 100	172-68098	A6-GRM N76034	20. 2.79	Crashed on landing at Connaught, Ireland on 21.7.91. Canx by CAA 6.2.92. (Stored 4/96)
G-SKYI	Air Command 532 Elite	0430		1. 9.88	(Marked as G-SKY1)
G-SKYL	Cessna 182S Skylane II	182-80176	N4104D	19. 6.98	
G-SKYM	Reims Cessna F.337E Super Skymaster (Wichita c/n 01291)	0019	G-AYHW	4. 9.80	Canx as WFU 5.12.83.
G-SKYP	Cameron A-120 HAFB	2547		27. 3.91	To SU-... 5/98. Canx 20.5.98.
G-SKYR	Cameron A-180 HAFB	2826		31. 3.92	
G-SKYS	Cameron O-84 HAFB	1354		16. 9.86	Canx by CAA 19.5.95.
G-SKYT	Iniziative Industriali Italian Sky Arrow 650TC	C.004		6. 9.96	
G-SKYX	Cameron A-210 HAFB	4613		22. 6.99	
G-SKYY	Cameron A-250 HAFB	3402		9. 3.95	
G-SKYZ	PA-34-200T Seneca II	34-7870260	N31712	20. 1.95	
G-SLAC	Cameron N-77 HAFB	2295		7. 6.90	
G-SLAM	BAe ATP	2038		24. 4.91	NTU - To G-BTNI 5/91. Canx.
G-SLCE	Cameron C-80 HAFB	4022		24. 2.97	
G-SLCI	Thunder Ax8-90 HAFB	1624		31.10.89	To F-GSLC 5/99. Canx 18.9.98.
G-SLEA	Avions Mudry/CAARP CAP.10B	124		19.12.80	
G-SLII	Cameron O-90 HAFB	2388		20. 9.90	
G-SLIK	Taylor JT.2 Titch	F.1/13 & PFA/60-10380		7. 9.78	Canx by CAA 5.8.91.
G-SLIM	Colt 56A HAFB	629		11. 2.85	Canx as WFU 29.4.97.
G-SLNE	Agusta A.109A II	7393	G-EEVS G-OTSL	23. 7.96	
G-SLOT	Cessna 340A II	340A-1505	N68698	3. 6.87	To N68698 7/92. Canx 26.5.92.
G-SLTN	Socata TB-20 Trinidad	763	HB-KBR	6. 8.99	
G-SLUG	Short SD.3-30 Var.100	SH3005	G-BKIE G-METP/G-METO/G-BKIE/C-GTAS/G-14-3005	2. 7.91	Restored as G-BKIE 9/92. Canx.
G-SLYN	PA-28-161 Cherokee Warrior II	28-8116204	N161WA N8373K	12. 4.89	
G-SMAF	Sikorsky S-76A	760149	N130TL N5425U	6. 9.88	
G-SMAN	Airbus A.330-243X	261	F-WWKR	26. 3.99	
G-SMAX	Cameron O-105 HAFB	2595		22. 5.91	Canx by CAA 25.9.91. To G-MADM 4/92.
G-SMCI	Bell 206B JetRanger III	3763	N3183H	27.10.88	To F-GKAB 3/90. Canx 10.1.90.
G-SMDB	Boeing 737-36N (Line No. 2862)	28557		15. 3.97	
G-SMDH	Europa Avn Europa XS	PFA/247-13367		8.10.98	
G-SMDJ	Aerospatiale AS.350B2 Ecureuil	3187		21. 4.99	
G-SMHK	Cameron D-38 Hot-Air Airship	697		5. 1.81	Canx as WFU 14.7.93. (Was based in Hong Kong)

Regn	Type	c/n	Previous identity	Regn date	Fate or immediate subsequent identity (if known)
G-SMIF	Robinson R-22 Beta	0772	N2639Z	22. 3.88	Crashed on landing at Prescott Hill, 5 miles northeast of Staverton on 10.9.88. Canx as destroyed 7.3.89.
G-SMIG	Cameron O-65 HAFB	922		6. 6.83	
G-SMIT	Messerschmitt Bf.109G-6/U-2	163824	N109MS G-SMIT/Luftwaffe 163824	10.12.79	(On display in Treloar Warfare Technology Centre, Australia .96) Canx by CAA 3.3.97.
G-SMJJ	Cessna 414A Chancellor II	414A-0425	N2694H	24. 3.81	
G-SMRI	Westland-Bell 47G-3B1 Soloy (Line No.WAP/118)	WA/408	G-DHDV	11. 1.83	Canx 11.7.86 on sale to West Germany.
G-SMTC	Colt Flying Hut SS HAFB	1828		7. 1.91	
G-SMTH	PA-28-140 Cherokee C	28-26916	G-AYJS	28. 9.90	
G-SMUJ	Enstrom F-28C-UK	348	G-BHTF	28. 8.85	To G-SHWW 1/90. Canx.
G-SNAK	Lindstrand LBL-105A HAFB	404		23. 9.96	
G-SNAP	Cameron V-77 HAFB	1217		29.11.85	
G-SNAX	Colt 69A HAFB	1680		6. 3.90	
G-SNAZ	Enstrom F-28F	761	G-BRCP	31.10.94	
G-SNDY	Piper J3C-65 Cub	3751	N25797 NC25797	1. 3.90	
G-SNEV	CFM Streak Shadow SA	PFA/206-13042		17. 9.96	
G-SNIP	Reims Cessna F.172H Skyhawk	0687	G-AXSI	12.12.80	Restored as G-AXSI 1/89. Canx.
G-SNOB	Beechcraft A36 Bonanza	E-987	G-BEIK	3.11.88	Undershot and crashed on landing at White Waltham on 1.8.92. Canx by CAA 12.10.92. To N25UP 10/93.
G-SNOW	Cameron V-77 HAFB (Originally regd as a V-56)(Fitted with replacement envelope .89 - c/n 2050 which was the original G-BSDX)	541	(G-BGWA)	21. 6.79	
G-SOAR	Eiri PIK-20E	20214		21. 6.79	
G-SOAS	Piper PA-61P Aerostar 601P	61P-0800-8063411	EC-DKQ N6081U	1.11.89	To 4X-CBB 12/94. Canx 20.12.94.
G-SOEI	HS.748 Srs.2A/242	1689	ZK-DES	25. 2.98	
G-SOFA	Cameron N-65 HAFB	968		30. 8.83	
G-SOFE	Cessna 441 Conquest	441-0109	N26226	14.11.86	Restored as N26226. Canx 5.3.90.
G-SOFI	PA-60-601P Aerostar (Machen Superstar II conversion c/n 002)	61P-0658-7963306	N222LL N8144J	10. 3.86	To N601P 4/94. Canx 17.3.94.
G-SOFS	Fokker F-27 Friendship 200	10135	G-BLML P2-ANC/P2-TFJ/VH-TFJ/PH-FBC	27. 2.87	Broken up 12/91 at Southend. Canx as WFU 3.12.91.
G-SOFT	Thunder Ax7-77 HAFB	1339		5.12.88	
G-SOFY	PA-46-310P Malibu	46-8408022	N901LE N4336P	3. 7.85	To HB-PKP 2/87. Canx 12.2.87.
G-SOHI	Agusta A.109E Power	11045		23. 4.99	
G-SOKO	Soko P-2 Kraguj	033	G-BRXK Yugoslav Army 30149	6. 1.94	Canx by CAA 6.2.98. (Stored 4/99 Liverpool)
G-SOLA	Star-Lite SL-1	203TG & PFA/175-11311		9. 6.88	(Stored at Hedge End 6/93)
G-SOLD	Robinson R-22 Alpha	0471	N8559X	16. 5.85	
G-SOLH	Bell 47G-5	2639	G-AZMB CF-NJW	5. 3.97	
G-SOLO	Anvil-Pitts S-2S Special	AA/1/1980		30. 5.80	
G-SOLY	Westland-Bell 47G-3B1 Soloy (Line No. WAP/82)	WA/513	XT806	9. 4.79	Canx 25.2.85 on sale to Nigeria.
G-SONA	Socata TB-10 Tobago	151	G-BIBI	24.10.80	(Stored 8/94)
G-SONG	Beechcraft A200 Super King Air	BB-362	G-BKTI	31. 3.81	To N4562P. Canx 3.1.84.
G-SONY	Aero Commander 200D	358	G-BGPS 5Y-AFT/N2985T	24.11.88	
G-SOOC	Hughes 369HS (500C)	111-0354S	G-BRRX N9083F	6.10.93	
G-SOOD	Hughes 369D (500D)	1142D		30. 7.82	To ZS-HML 12/82. Canx 13.12.82.
G-SOOE	Hughes 369E (500E)	0227E		27. 4.87	
G-SOOK	Sukhoi SU-26M	04-01	RA-0401 DOSAAF 30	23. 3.95	
G-SOOM	Glaser-Dirks DG-500M	5E42-M20		14. 5.92	
G-SOOO	PA-30-160 Twin Comanche C	30-1879	G-AXMY N8726Y	29.12.81	To N4552W, but ditched into sea off Iceland on 11.3.83 on its ferry flight to USA. Canx.
G-SOOR	Agusta-Bell 206A JetRanger	8056	G-FMAL G-RIAN/G-BHSG/PH-FSW	22. 2.94	Restored as G-RIAN 3/97. Canx.
G-SOOS	Colt 21A Cloudhopper HAFB	1263		7. 6.88	
G-SOOT	PA-28-180 Cherokee C	28-4033	G-AVNM N11C	19. 8.88	
G-SOPP	Enstrom 280FX Shark	2024	G-OSAB N86259	23.10.97	
G-SORR	Aerospatiale AS.350B Ecureuil	1661	G-BKMO	19. 4.83	To ZK-HND 3/86. Canx 11.11.85.
G-SORT	Cameron N-90 HAFB	2878		13. 7.92	
G-SOUL	Cessna 310R II	310R-0140	N5020J	27. 6.88	
G-SOUP	Cameron C-80 HAFB	3387		24.10.94	(Not built)
G-SOVN	Gates LearJet 35A	35A-614	HB-VJC G-PJET/N3815G	16. 3.89	To G-VIPS 5/90. Canx.
G-SPAM	Light Aero Avid Aerobat	829 & PFA/189-12074		9. 5.91	
G-SPAR	Cameron N-77 HAFB (Originally regd with c/n 1287)	1248		4. 3.86	To G-BSJA 5/90. Canx.
G-SPBA	Bell 412SP	33172	(G-BPDB) N32072	24.10.88	To 9M-SSP /90. Canx 24.1.90.
G-SPEE	Robinson R-22 Beta	0939	G-BPJC	20. 7.94	
G-SPEL	Sky 220-24 HAFB	045		26. 7.96	

Regn	Type	c/n	Previous identity	Regn date	Fate or immediate subsequent identity (if known)
G-SPEY	Agusta-Bell 206B JetRanger III	8608	G-BIGO	1. 4.81	
G-SPFX	Rutan Cozy	PFA/159-13113		30. 4.97	
G-SPIN	Aerotek Pitts S-2A Special	2110	N5CQ	13. 3.80	
G-SPIT	Vickers-Supermarine 379 Spitfire FR.XIVe	6S/649205	(G-BGHB) Indian AF T-20/MV293	2. 3.79	
G-SPOG	San Jodel DR.1050 Ambassadeur	155	G-AXVS F-BJNL	25. 9.95	(On rebuild .95)
G-SPOL	MBB Bo.105DBS-4	S.392	VR-BGV D-HDLH	23. 3.90	
G-SPOP	Thunder Ax7-77 HAFB (Originally construction strated as G-PISA c/n 184)(C/n same as G-BJVF)	187		29.12.78	Not completed. Canx 22.12.81.
G-SPOR	Beechcraft B200 Super King Air	BB-1557	N57TL N57TS	3. 9.99	
G-SPOT	Partenavia P.68B Observer	15	D-GERD G-BCDK(1)	11. 6.81	Crashed into the sea on the approach to Vagar airfield, Faroe Islands on 6.7.87. Canx as destroyed 16.1.89.
G-SPRT	Cameron R-450 HAFB	4350		23. 4.98	Canx as destroyed 6.10.98.
G-SPTS	Beechcraft C90 King Air	LJ-874	G-BHAP	10. 3.80	To N44486. Canx 7.9.83.
G-SPUD	Fokker F-27 Friendship 100	10120	VH-TFE PH-FAP	31. 1.79	To G-OMAN 9/82. Canx.
G-SPUR	Cessna 550 Citation II (Unit No.714)	550-0714	N593EM N12035	27.10.98	
G-SPYI	Bell 206B JetRanger III	3689	G-BVRC G-BSJC/N3175S	9. 5.96	
G-SRAY	PBN BN-2T Turbine Islander CC.2 (AEW Defender Trials Acft)	2034	G-OPBN ZF573/G-OPBN/G-BJOH	29. 4.86	To MOD as ZF573. Canx 12.6.86.
G-SRES	Beechcraft 300 Super King Air	FA-39		1. 3.85	To HK-3463X 8/89. Canx 29.8.89.
G-SRJG	Boeing 757-236 (Line No. 236)	24771	TF-FIK G-IEAD/P4-AAA/PH-AHN/G-BRJG	10. 5.94	To TC-AJA 4/95. Canx 7.4.95.
G-SROE	Westland Scout AH.1	F.9508	XP907	26.10.95	
G-SRVO	Cameron N-90 HAFB	3551		10. 4.95	
G-SSBS	Colting 77A HAFB	77A-010		2. 5.78	Canx by CAA 4.8.98.
G-SSCH	BAe 146 Srs.100	E1003	(G-BIAF)	29. 5.81	To G-5-14/N246SS. Canx 6.3.86.
G-SSCL	MDHC Hughes 369E (500E)	0491E	N684F	25. 4.98	
G-SSFC	PA-34-200 Seneca	34-7450016	G-BBXG N56647	28. 4.94	
G-SSFS	HS.748 Srs.2A/378	1792	D-AHSE G-BJTM/(N750AV)/G-BJTM	6. 3.92	To C-FQVE. Canx 20.10.93.
G-SSFT	PA-28-161 Warrior II	28-8016069	G-BHIL N80821	16. 7.86	
G-SSGS	Europa Avn Europa	082		25. 1.94	
G-SSHH	BAe 146 Srs.100A	E1002	N5828B G-5-146/G-OPSA/G-SSHH/(G-BIAE)	29. 5.81	To N101RW. Canx 9.5.86.
G-SSIX	Rans S-6-116 Coyote II	PFA/204A-12749		5. 9.94	(Extensively damaged in forced landing 4.6.98 at Parc Coed Machen Farm, nr.Cardiff-Wales Airport)
G-SSJT	Cessna 210L Centurion	210-60105	N59122	22. 1.90	Restored as N59122 5/93. Canx 26.5.93.
G-SSKY	PBN BN-2B-26 Islander	2247	G-BSWT	11. 5.92	
G-SSOZ	Cessna 550 Citation II (Unit No.597)	550-0597	N13027	7. 2.89	To G-MRTC 4/93. Canx.
G-SSRS	Cessna 172N Skyhawk II	172-68856	N734HA	1. 5.90	To G-OERS 5/94. Canx.
G-SSSC	Sikorsky S-76C	760408		26.10.93	
G-SSSD	Sikorsky S-76C	760415		26.10.93	
G-SSSE	Sikorsky S-76C	760417		23.11.93	
G-SSSH	BAe 146 Srs.100 (Modified to Srs.300 development aircraft with new c/n E3001)	E1001	(G-BIAD)	23. 3.81	Canx as WFU 9.4.87. To G-5-300/G-LUXE 4/87.
G-SSSS	Robinson R-44 Astro	0382		31.10.97	To G-KPAO 11/98. Canx.
"G-SST"	BAC/Aerospatiale Concorde Replica	-		----	On display outside Hermeskeil Musum, Trier, Germany. (Also marked "F-WTSA")(Extant 4/99)
G-SSTI	Cameron N-105 HAFB	3238		30. 3.94	
G-SSWT	Short SD.3-30 Var.100	SH3095	4X-CSQ G-BNYA/G-BKSU/G-14-3095	2. 6.98	Damaged when main undercarriage collapsed after landing at Luton on 13.2.99.
G-SSWU	Short SD.3-30 Var.100	SH3076	C-FYXF G-BIYH/N183AP/N338MV/G-BIYH/G-14-3076	24. 2.99	(Damaged, whilst parked, when AA-5B G-BDLR collided with it at Luton on 18.9.99)
G-SSWV	Sportavia-Putzer Fournier RF-5B Sperber	51032	N55WV	31. 5.90	
G-STAG	Cameron O-65 HAFB	796		1. 2.82	Canx as WFU 11.5.93.
G-STAK	Bell 206B JetRanger II	1514	G-BNIS N35HF/N135VG	9. 2.89	To G-FOXM 2/93. Canx.
G-STAN	Fokker F-27 Friendship 200	10131	VH-CAV PH-FAY	30. 4.79	WFU in 5/95 at Norwich. CofA expired 2.4.96. Broken up in 12/96. Canx as WFU 20.12.96.
G-STAP	Reims Cessna FA.152 Aerobat	0362	EI-BIE	10. 6.87	To 5B-CIC. Canx 16.4.91.
G-STAR	Ted Smith Aerostar 601P	61P-0484-196	N8018J	14. 4.78	To N9743Y. Canx 13.8.81.
G-STAT	Cessna U.206F Stationair 6 II	U206-03485	A6-MAM N8732Q	20. 2.79	Damaged on landing at Hibaldstow on 30.5.98. (Noted abandoned 6/99 at Hibaldstow)
G-STAV	Cameron O-84 HAFB	2913		29. 9.92	
G-STEF	Hughes 369HS (500)	114-0673S	G-BKTK OY-HCL/OO-JGR	7.11.84	
G-STEM	Stemme S-10V	14-027		2. 7.97	
G-STEN	Stemme S-10	10-32	D-KGCH	9. 1.92	
G-STEP	Schweizer Hughes 269C	S.1494		1.10.90	
G-STER	Bell 206B JetRanger III	4116	OO-EGA	23. 3.94	
G-STEV	CEA Jodel DR.221 Dauphin	61	F-BOZD	9. 3.82	
G-STEW	PA-28-181 Archer II	28-8090008	OY-BRU	15. 8.83	To ZS-LON 12/83. Canx 23.11.83.

Regn	Type	c/n	Previous identity	Regn date	Fate or immediate subsequent identity (if known)
G-STIO	Socata ST-10 Diplomate	125	OH-SAB	7. 6.78	To EI-BUG 2/87. Canx 8.1.87.
G-STMI	Robinson R-22 Beta	0984		16. 3.89	To OH-HKK 7/96. Canx 26.6.96.
G-STMM	Robinson R-44 Astro	0159		5. 4.95	To G-OCCB 4/96. Canx.
G-STMP	SNCAN Stampe SV-4A	241	F-BCKB	11. 3.83	(On overhaul Ivybridge 5/93)
G-STNO	Socata TB-20 Trinidad	1815	F-OHUY F-WWRG	15. 7.97	
G-STOI	Robinson R-22 Mariner	0847M		7. 9.88	To (EI-KMA)/EI-CCT 12/90. Canx 29.10.90.
G-STOL	Socata MS.894A Rallye Minerva 220	11824	F-BSXR	20. 1.78	Damaged by storm at Southend on 16.10.87. Canx as destroyed 17.11.87.
G-STOW	Cameron Wine Box 90SS HAFB	4420		2.10.98	
G-STOX	Bell 206B JetRanger II	1513	G-BNIR N59615	27. 4.89	
G-STOY	Robinson R-22 Beta	0700		10.11.87	
G-STPI	Cameron A-250 HAFB	4102		26. 2.97	
G-STRK	CFM Streak Shadow	K.143-SA & PFA/161A-11762		4. 4.90	
G-STRM	Cameron N-90 HAFB	3568		3. 7.95	
G-STST	Bell 206B JetRanger III	3755		13. 4.84	DBF in fatal crash near Colwyn Bay on 22.5.94. Canx as destroyed 12.8.94
G-STUA	Aerotek Pitts S-2A Special (Mod)	2164	N13GT	6. 3.91	
G-STUB	Christen Pitts S-2B Special	5163	N260Y	5. 5.94	
G-STUD	DHC.6-310 Twin Otter	545	N302EH N64791/N302EH	10.10.79	DBR 20.4.83 at Flotta, Scotland.
G-STVE	Aerospatiale AS.355F1 Twin Squirrel	5249	G-TOFF G-BKJX	8. 4.88	To G-BTVS 7/90. Canx.
G-STVI	Bell 206L-1 Long Ranger II	45229	N60MA N5091K	15. 4.88	To G-EYRE 11/90. Canx.
G-STVN	Handley Page HPR.7 Dart Herald 210	188	F-BOIZ F-OCLZ/HB-AAL	30. 8.88	Canx as PWFU 8.4.97.
G-STWO	ARV1 Super 2	002 & PFA/152-11048		24. 4.85	
G-STYL	Pitts S-1S Special (Built by G.E.Smith)	GJSN-1P	N665JG	26. 1.88	Permit expired 6.6.94. (Stored 4/96 Crosland Moor)
G-STYR	Beechcraft F90 King Air	LA-81	G-BHUT	2. 1.81	To N42636. Canx.
G-SUEE	Airbus A.320-231	363	G-IEAG F-WWBX	23. 9.93	
G-SUES	North American AT-6D Harvard III	88-14552	FAP1506 South African AF7424/EX881/41-33854	18. 1.79	To (LN-LFW)/LN-WNH 7/86. Canx 10.2.84.
G-SUEZ	Agusta-Bell 206B JetRanger II	8319	SU-YAE YU-HAZ	16. 9.98	
G-SUFC	HS.125 Srs.600B	256035	G-BETV F-BKMC	7.12.95	To VP-BCN 4/98. Canx 9.4.98.
G-SUIT	Cessna 210N Centurion II	210-64576	N9698Y	17.11.92	
G-SUKI	PA-38-112 Tomahawk	38-79A0260	G-BPNV N2313D	22. 5.91	
G-SULL	PA-32R-301 Saratoga SP	32R-8113002	N82818	19. 6.86	Crashed on take-off from Crowfield on 1.2.95. Canx as WFU 17.5.95. To Home Office Fire & Emergency Training Centre.
G-SULY	Monnett Moni	PFA/142-11208		15. 7.87	No Permit to Fly issued. Canx by CAA 4.5.99.
G-SUMT	Robinson R-22 Beta	2147	G-BUKD N23381	24. 9.92	
G-SUNI	Bell 206B JetRanger III	4062		22. 9.89	To N50GH 12/92. Canx 16.12.92.
G-SUNY	Robinson R-44 Astro	0540		8.12.98	
G-SUPA	PA-18-150 Super Cub (Regd with Frame No. 18-5512)	18-5395	PH-BAJ PH-MBF/ALAT 18-5395	13.12.78	
G-SUPR	BAe Jetstream Srs.3202	956	G-31-956	4.11.91	DBR in fatal crash at Prestwick on 6.10.92. Canx as destroyed 21.1.93.
G-SURE	BAC One-Eleven Srs.416EK	BAC.129	G-AVOE	13. 4.82	Restored as G-AVOE 5/83. Canx.
G-SURF	North American T-6G Texan	182-750	FAP1710 French AF 115063/51-15063	28. 3.79	No CofA issued. Canx 16.4.80 on sale in USA.
G-SURG	PA-30-160 Twin Comanche B	30-1424	G-VIST G-AVHZ/N8287Y	18. 6.90	
G-SURV	PBN BN-2T-4S Defender 4000	4005	G-BVHZ	14. 4.94	
G-SUSI	Cameron V-77 HAFB	1133		22. 7.85	
G-SUSY	North American P-51D-25NA Mustang	122-39232	N12066 Nicaraguan AF GN-120/44-72773	23. 7.87	
G-SUTN	Iniziative Industriali Italian Sky Arrow 650TC	C.007		27. 8.98	
G-SUTT	Hughes 369E (500E)	0009E	G-OEPF G-OMJH	12. 9.84	To N33MM. Canx 11.10.91.
G-SUZE	PA-31-310 Turbo Navajo	31-700	G-AYUF EI-BAE/G-AYUF/N6790L	14.10.82	To N3835K. Canx 14.3.83.
G-SUZI	Beechcraft 95-B55 Baron	TC-1574	G-BAXR	11. 3.85	
G-SUZN	PA-28-161 Warrior II	28-8016187	N3573C N9540N	16. 1.91	
G-SUZY	Taylor JT.1 Monoplane	PFA/55-10395		1.12.78	(Damaged on landing at Totnes 20.4.95) (On rebuild 5/97)
G-SVBF	Cameron A-180 HAFB	3587		2. 6.95	
G-SVEA	PA-28-161 Warrior II	28-7916082	N30299	16.12.98	
G-SVHA	Partenavia P.68B Victor	113	OY-AJH	17.12.80	To G-FJMS 9/92. Canx.
G-SVIP	Cessna 421B Golden Eagle II	421B-0820	G-BNYJ N4686Q/D-IMVB/N1590G	12. 3.97	
G-SVIV	SNCAN Stampe SV-4C	475	N65214 F-BDBL	7. 8.90	

Regn	Type	c/n	Previous identity	Regn date	Fate or immediate subsequent identity (if known)
G-SVJM	Aerospatiale AS.355F1 Twin Squirrel	5157	G-BOPS I-MOST	24. 5.90	To G-OBIG 8/96. Canx.
G-SVLB	HS.125 Srs.700B	257112	9M-SSL (D-CLUB)/9M-SSL/G-5-553/G-BNBO/G-5-536/D-CMVW	31. 3.95	To RA-02850 3/98. Canx 30.3.98.
G-SVSS	Beechcraft C90A King Air	LJ-1170	G-OAKZ N3085Y	6. 6.92	To N4131S 9/94. Canx 20.9.94.
G-SWAC	BAe Jetstream Srs.3102	727	G-BRUK I-ALKC/I-BLUU/G-BRUK/G-31-727	11. 5.94	To C-FAGM/C-GKGM 12/96. Canx 15.11.96.
G-SWAD	BAe Jetstream Srs.3102	649	G-LOGP VH-LJR/G-BPZJ/G-31-649/PH-KJC/G-31-649	22. 8.94	To SP-FTH(2) 1/96. Canx 26.1.96.
G-SWAG	Embraer EMB.110P1 Bandeirante	110-278	G-CLAW N790RA/XA-LES/PT-SBP/(G-BHPP)/PT-SBP	17. 1.91	Restored as N790RA. Canx 8.6.93.
G-SWAN	Rockwell Commander 690B	11517	N690EX	7. 8.79	To N9054F. Canx 16.8.81.
G-SWEB	Cameron N-90 HAFB	2413		1.10.90	(Sold; Active 10/97)
G-SWEL	Hughes 369HS	61-0328S	G-RBUT C-FTXZ/CF-TXZ	18. 7.96	
G-SWET	Cessna 500 Citation I (Unit No.270)	500-0270	N4238X N68CB/N72BC/N712N/N712J/N5270J	10. 2.92	To G-OSCA 1/96. Canx.
G-SWFT	Beechcraft 200 Super King Air	BB-828	G-SIBE G-MCEO/G-BILY	29. 5.86	To (N828AB)/Restored as G-MCEO 5/96. Canx.
G-SWIF	Vickers-Supermarine 552 Swift F.7	VA.9597	XF114	1. 6.90	(Stored 9/99 Scampton)
G-SWIM	Aerocar Super Coot (Mod) (Officially regd, and canx, as Taylor Coot Amphibian (Modified) with same PFA c/n)	PFA/18-11486		21. 8.90	No Permit to Fly issued. Canx by CAA 14.4.99.
G-SWIS	DH.100 Vampire FB.6 (FFW, Essen built)	658	J-1149 Swiss AF	21. 5.91	No CofA issued. Canx by CAA 3.4.97 as PWFU. (Stored 9/97)
G-SWIV	Lindstrand LBL-240A HAFB	019		10. 3.93	To PH-REX 12/97. Canx 31.10.97.
G-SWJW	Airbus A.300B4-203	302	OH-LAB F-WZMY	19. 5.98	
G-SWOT	Phoenix Currie Super Wot	PFA/3011		10. 9.80	
G-SWPR	Cameron N-56 HAFB	829		16. 3.82	
G-SWSH	Revolution Helicopters Mini-500	0049		10.10.95	
G-SWUN	Pitts S-1M Special (Mod)	338-H	G-BSXH N14RM	18. 4.95	(Stored 3/97)
G-SXVI	Vickers Supermarine 361 Spitfire LF.XVIe	-	7001M 6709M/TE356	25. 2.87	To N356V. Canx 15.1.90.
G-SYCO	Europa Avn Europa	PFA/247-12540		27.11.95	
G-SYFW	WAR Focke-Wulf 190 Replica	269 & PFA/81-10584		28. 2.83	(Stored dismantled 1/99 Guernsey)
G-SYKS	Cessna 550 Citation II (Unit No.599)	550-0599		7.11.88	To N599FW. Canx 27.10.89.
G-SYPA	Aerospatiale AS.355F2 Twin Squirrel	5193	LV-WHC F-WYMS/G-BPRE/N366E	25. 9.96	

G-T

Regn	Type	c/n	Previous identity	Regn date	Fate or immediate subsequent identity (if known)
G-TAAL	Cessna 172R Skyhawk II	172-80733	N9535G	11. 8.99	
G-TABS	Embraer EMB.110P1 Bandeirante	110-212	G-PBAC F-GCLA/F-OGME/F-GCLA/PT-GME	18. 8.98	
G-TACA	Hunting Percival P.57 Sea Prince T.1	P57/53	WM739	6. 5.80	Left Staverton by road on 14.4.89 for the Midas Metal Scrapyard at Gloucester. Canx as WFU 12.5.89.
G-TACE	HS.125 Srs.403B	25223	G-AYIZ F-BSSL/PJ-SLB/G-AYIZ/G-5-15	23. 1.81	Canx as WFU 9.1.90. (Open store 10/95)
G-TACK	Grob G-109B	6279		30. 5.84	
G-TAFF	CASA I-131E Jungmann	1129	G-BFNE Spanish AF E3B-148	7. 9.84	
G-TAFI	Dornier Bucker Bu.133C Jungmeister	24	N2210 HB-MIF/Swiss AF U-77	27. 1.93	
G-TAFO	Extra Walter EA.230	008	G-PIKN N230JA	10.10.91	To (N13LS)/(N230JA)/N3570 11/92. Canx 11.11.92.
G-TAFY	Piper J3C-65 Cub (Regd as c/n 5298; but has frame no 7002 which was N38207, probably used in rebuild of N31073 in early 70s)	6917	N31073 N38207/N38307/NC38307	10. 3.88	To G-BVPN 7/94. Canx.
G-TAGL	Cessna T.182R Turbo Skylane II	182-68200	G-SAAM N2399E	9. 9.85	Restored as G-SAAM 7/86. Canx.
G-TAGS	PA-28-161 Cherokee Warrior II	28-8416026	N4329D	6. 5.88	
G-TAIL	Cessna 150J	150-70152	N60220	21. 4.89	(Damaged in gales Southend 3/4.1.98)
G-TAIR	PA-34-200T Seneca II	34-7970055	N3059H	17.11.87	
G-TALI	Aerospatiale AS.355F1 Twin Squirrel	5261		21. 3.83	To G-BTIS 4/91. Canx.
G-TALK	Colt 105A HAFB	992		27. 1.87	To OH-FUN 4/87. Canx 9.3.87.
G-TALL	BAe Jetstream Srs.3100	601	G-31-601	16.11.81	To (N.....)/G-31-601/G-WMCC 9/83. Canx 5.9.83.
G-TALY	Agusta-Bell 206B JetRanger III	8588		12. 3.79	To G-CSKY 6/83. Canx.
G-TAMY	Cessna 421B Golden Eagle II	421B-0512	SE-FNS N2BH/N69865	14.11.77	
G-TAND	Robinson R-44 Astro	0478		12. 6.98	
G-TANI	Gulfstream American GA-7 Cougar	GA7-0107	G-VJAI G-OCAB/G-BICF/N8500H/N29707	18. 5.95	

Regn	Type	c/n	Previous identity	Regn date	Fate or immediate subsequent identity (if known)
G-TANK	Cameron N-90 HAFB	3625		20. 6.95	
G-TANS	Socata TB-20 Trinidad	1870	F-GRBX	25. 9.98	
G-TAPE	PA-23-250 Aztec D	27-4054	G-AWVW	7.10.83	
			OY-RPF/G-AWVW/N6799Y		
G-TARA	Christen Eagle II	FT/99/BL85 & PFA/138-10890		19. 3.85	To G-ZAPP 9/89. Canx.
	(C/n also quoted as FT/99/84)				
G-TARN	Pietenpol Air Camper	PFA/47-13349		3. 8.98	
G-TARO	BAC One-Eleven Srs.525FT	BAC.272	YR-BCO	28. 3.84	Restored as YR-BCO 12/85. Canx 24.12.85.
G-TART	PA-28-236 Dakota	28-7911261	N2945C	18.12.90	
G-TARV	ARV1 Super 2	PFA/152-12627		1. 6.94	
G-TASH	Cessna 172N Skyhawk (Mod)	172-70531	PH-KOS	4.11.98	
			N739GL		
G-TASK	Cessna 404 Titan II	404-0829	PH-MPC	10. 3.93	
			SE-IHL/N6806Q		
G-TATE	Cameron A-180 HAFB	3144		16. 9.93	Reserved as F-GOTE in 1997. Canx 15.5.97.
G-TATI	Hughes 369HS (500)	13-0444S	HB-XEE	14. 2.83	To G-GASA 4/84. Canx.
G-TATT	Gardan GY-20 Minicab	PFA/56-10347		30.11.78	
G-TATY	Robinson R-44 Astro	0627		27. 7.99	
G-TAXI	PA-23-250 Aztec E	27-7305085	N40270	6. 4.78	(Stored 8/97)
G-TAXY	PA-31 Turbo Navajo	31-104	LN-PAD	7. 8.78	CofA expired 17.3.83 & WFU at Luton. Donated to Luton Fire
			LN-NPB/SE-EZK		Service. Canx by CAA 19.6.89.
G-TAYI	Grob G-115A	8008	(D-ENFT)	12. 9.90	
			G-TAYI/G-DODO/D-ENFT		
G-TAYS	Reims Cessna F.152 II	1697	G-LFCA	28.10.91	
G-TBAC	Short SD.3-60 Var.200	SH3695	EI-BVM	1.10.92	To N419SA with new c/n SH3402. Canx 30.6.94.
			(EI-BVJ)/G-14-3695/5N-AOX/G-BMNK/G-14-3695		
G-TBAG	Murphy Renegade II	PFA/188-11912		11.12.90	
G-TBCA	Bell 206L Long Ranger	45077	G-BFAL	9. 4.80	To G-OLDN 10/84. Canx.
			N64689/A6-BCL		
G-TBFC	Robinson R-22 Beta	0965	N80287	17. 4.89	To G-OROB 6/90. Canx.
G-TBGL	Agusta A.109A II	7412	G-VJCB	6. 1.99	
			G-BOUA		
G-TBIC	BAe 146 Srs.200	E2025	N167US	15. 1.97	
			N349PS		
G-TBIO	Socata TB-10 Tobago	340	F-BNGZ	10. 2.83	
G-TBIX	MDC Hughes 369E (500E)	0372E		2. 2.90	To G-SIVA 1/94. Canx.
G-TBMW	Murphy Renegade Spirit	PFA/188-11725	G-MYIG	20.10.98	
G-TBRD	Canadair CL-30 (T-33AN) Silver Star Mk.3	T33-261	N33VC	18.12.96	(On display 7/99 Duxford)
			G-JETT/(G-BHOE)/G-OAHB/CF-IHB/CAF 133261/RCN 21261		
G-TBSL	Colt 90A HAFB	1443		10. 4.89	To D-OKTO. Canx 7.4.92.
G-TBXX	Socata TB-20 Trinidad	276		16. 3.82	
G-TBZI	Socata TB-21 Trinidad TC	871	N21HR	25. 7.96	
G-TBZO	Socata TB-20 Trinidad	444		8. 8.84	
G-TCAN	Colt 69A HAFB	1996		19. 7.91	
G-TCAP	BAe 125 Srs.800B	258115	G-5-599	24. 4.96	
			R.Saudi AF 104/G-5-665/R.Saudi AF 104/G-BPGR/G-5-599		
G-TCAR	Robin HR.100/210D Safari	147	F-BTZE	3.10.84	Fatal crash after striking some electricity cables on landing approach to Stapleford on 26.12.94 and crashed 1½ miles north of the aerodrome. Canx by CAA 22.5.95.
G-TCAT	Schweizer-Gulfstream G.164D Turbo AgCat	07D	N8161K	17.12.79	To EC-EBE. Canx 9.12.86.
G-TCDI	DH.125 Srs.F403B	25248	N792A	10.10.96	
			G-SHOP/(N792A)/G-5-707/G-SHOP/G-BTUF/G-5-707/D-CFCF		
G-TCMP	Robinson R-22 Beta	0890		3.11.88	
G-TCOM	PA-30-160 Twin Comanche B	30-1967	N555JC	29. 1.96	
			N8810Y		
G-TCSL	Rockwell Commander 112A	322	N506CA	17. 9.92	Damaged on take off from Spanhoe on 5.12.94. Canx as destroyed 2.3.95. (On display 12/95)
G-TCTC	PA-28RT-201T Turbo Cherokee Arrow IV	2831001	N9130B	1.12.89	
	(Originally built as N9524N c/n 28R-8631006)				
G-TCUB	Piper J3C-65 Cub (NE-2)	13970	N9039Q	31. 7.87	
	(Frame No 13805)		N67666/NC67666/BuA.29684/45-55204		
G-TDAA	Cessna U.206G Stationair 6	U206-05581	N5135K	12. 8.80	Canx 8.7.85 on sale to France. To TR-LBT 10/85.
G-TDAD	Socata TB-20 Trinidad	1197		7.11.90	Fatal crash near the summit of the 1,839 ft Glas Bheinn mountain on the Isle of Jura 22.8.92. Canx by CAA 9.11.92.
G-TDFS	IMCO Callair A-9	1200	G-AVZA	8.10.86	
			SE-EUA/N26D		
G-TDTW	CCF Hawker Hurricane	-	RCAF 5450	. . R	(On rebuild 6/96) (Composite rebuild)
G-TEAA	Boeing 737-3Y0	24462	EI-BZQ	4. 4.90	To EC-897/EC-FJR. Canx 2.12.91.
	(Line No. 1691)		(N116AW)/EI-BZQ/EC-ENS/EC-244/N5573K		
G-TEAB	Boeing 737-3Y0	23923	(N117AW)	7. 3.90	To EI-CEE 10/91. Canx 25.10.91.
	(Line No. 1540)		EI-EZP/LN-AEQ/EI-BZP/EC-EIA/EC-152		
G-TEAC	North American AT-6C Harvard IIA	88-9696	FAP1523	18. 1.79	Fatal crash near Woodham Walter, Essex on 4.3.95.
			SAAF7333/EX688/41-33253		Canx as destroyed 20.7.95.
G-TEAD	Boeing 737-33A	23636	N509DC	. .90R	NTU - Remained as N509DC. Canx.
	(Line No. 1438)		EC-EHJ/EC-135/N1789B/N3283G		
G-TEAL	Thurston TSC-1A1 Teal	15	C-GDQD	8.12.92	Damaged in gales at Crosland Moor in 3/93. (On rebuild 5/99 Crosland Moor)

Regn	Type	c/n	Previous identity	Regn date	Fate or immediate subsequent identity (if known)
G-TEAM	Cessna 414A Chancellor II	414A-0525	G-BHJT N37464	24.11.80	To N118RS 1/84. Canx 31.1.84.
G-TECC	Aeronca 7AC Champion	7AC-5269	N1704E NC1704E	26. 6.91	
G-TECH	Rockwell Commander 114	14074	G-BEDH N4744W	8. 8.85	
G-TECK	Cameron V-77 HAFB	625		21. 3.86	
G-TECN	Enstrom 480	5021		27. 5.97	Substantially damaged at Killochries Fold on 21.3.98. Canx as destroyed 21.10.98.
G-TEDD	Cessna 310R II	310R-0544	G-MADI N87396/G-MADI/N87396	19.12.88	To G-RODD 10/89. Canx.
G-TEDF	Cameron N-90 HAFB	2634		8. 8.91	
G-TEDS	Socata TB-10 Tobago	57	G-BHCO	29. 3.83	
G-TEDY	Evans VP-1	PFA/62-10383	G-BHGN	4.10.90	
G-TEDZ	Nipper T.66 RA.45 Srs.3B (Fairey c/n 30)	PFA/25-11051		27. 2.96	
G-TEEM	PA-32R-300 Cherokee Lance	32R-7780255	N2604Q	27. 3.92	To G-DTCP 1/93. Canx.
G-TEES	Reims Cessna F.152 II	1863	G-BIUI	5. 9.85	Damaged at Sherburn-in-Elmet on 25.3.91. Canx as destroyed 3.5.91. To ZK-JCP 8/93 (for rebuild).
G-TEEZ	Cameron N-90 HAFB	4005		27.11.96	
G-TEFC	PA-28-140 Cherokee F	28-7325088	OY-PRC N15530	18. 6.80	
G-TEFH	Cessna 500 Citation I (Unit No.176)	500-0176	G-BCII N176CC	17. 6.82	To N150TT 4/94. Canx 24.3.94.
G-TEHL	CFM Streak Shadow Srs.M	185	G-MYJE	20.11.98	
G-TELE	Partenavia P.68C Victor	217	G-DORE OY-CAD	26. 2.87	To I-CITT 5/90. Canx 1.8.90.
G-TELL	Cessna 421C Golden Eagle III	421C-0811	N2657N	21. 2.89	Restored as N2657N 5/94. Canx 31.5.94.
G-TELY	Agusta A.109A II	7326	N1HQ N200SH	10. 3.89	
G-TEMI	PBN BN-2T Turbine Islander (CASTOR development project)	2143	G-BJYX	6. 7.84	To G-MSSA 8/91. Canx.
G-TEMP	PA-28-180 Cherokee E	28-5806	G-AYBK N11C	15. 5.89	
G-TEMT	Hawker Tempest II	420	HA586 (R.Indian AF)/MW763	9.10.89	(On rebuild 11/96)
G-TENT	Auster J/1N Alpha	2058	G-AKJU TW513	1. 2.90	
G-TERI	Beechcraft F33A Bonanza	CE-1466	N5664X	31.10.90	To N33VW 6/93. Canx 11.6.93.
G-TERN	Europa Avn Europa	PFA/247-12780		18. 7.97	
G-TERY	PA-28-181 Archer II	28-7990078	G-BOXZ N22402	13. 1.89	
G-TESS	Quickie Quickie	479 & PFA/94-10608		28. 5.82	No Permit issued. Canx by CAA 29.12.95.
G-TEST	PA-34-200-2 Seneca	34-7450116	OO-RPW G-BLCD/PH-PLZ/N41409	28. 7.89	
G-TEWS	PA-28-140 Cherokee B	28-25128	G-KEAN G-AWTM/N11C	23. 5.88	
G-TFCI	Reims Cessna FA.152 Aerobat	0358		25.10.79	
G-TFOX	Denney Kitfox Mk.2	PFA/172-11817		3. 6.91	
G-TFRB	Air Command 532 Elite Sport	0628 & G/04-1167		26. 4.90	
G-TFUN	Valentin Taifun 17E	1011	D-KIHP	28.12.83	(Noted 31.5.98 at Squires Gate with wings dismantled)
G-TGAS	Cameron O-160 HAFB	1315		12. 8.87	
G-TGER	American Aviation AA-5B Tiger	AA5B-0952	G-BFZP	20. 2.86	
G-TGRS	Robinson R-22 Beta	1069	G-DELL N80466	5.11.97	
G-THAM	Reims Cessna F.182Q Skylane	0089	PH-AXE(2)	13.11.78	To G-LIGG 8/88. Canx.
G-THAN	Reims Cessna F.406 Caravan II	0024	(G-BPSU) PH-PEL/(F-GEUJ)/F-WZDR	12. 6.89	Restored as PH-PEL. Canx 14.10.92.
G-THCL	Cessna 550 Citation II (Unit No.563)	550-0563	N1298P	15.10.87	
G-THEA	Boeing-Stearman E75 (N2S-5) Kaydet (Original identity and c/n not confirmed correct - if USN serial is correct, c/n would be 75-7743)	75-5736A	(EI-RYR) G-THEA/N1733B/BuA.38122	18. 3.81	
G-THEL	Robinson R-44 Astro	0159	G-OCCB G-STMM	2. 9.98	
G-THEO	Team Minimax 91	PFA/186-13099		9. 2.99	
G-THGS	Aerospatiale AS.365N1 Dauphin 2	6319	G-BPOJ	15. 5.89	To LN-OPQ. Canx 6.9.93.
G-THLS	MBB Bo.105DBS-4 (Rebuilt with new pod S.859 .92)	S.80/859	G-BCXO D-HDCE	20. 2.92	
G-THOM	Thunder Ax6-56 HAFB	366		14. 7.81	
G-THOR	Thunder Ax8-105 HAFB (Replacement canopy for c/n 026/SE-ZZO)	150		15. 6.78	CofA expired 14.12.81. (Based in Holland) Canx by CAA 23.6.98.
G-THOS	Thunder Ax7-77 HAFB	769		20. 2.86	
G-THOT	Pearce Jabiru SK	PFA/274-13159		16. 9.97	
G-THRE	Cessna 182S Skylane II	182-80454	N2391A	6. 5.99	
G-THSL	PA-28R-201 Arrow II	28R-7837278	N36396	11. 9.78	

Regn	Type	c/n	Previous identity	Regn date	Fate or immediate subsequent identity (if known)
G-THUN	Republic P-47D-40RA Thunderbolt (Composite rebuild from wreck of original N47DD plus an unidentified P-47N fuselage)	399-55731	N47DD Peruvian AF 119/Peruvian AF 545/45-49192	18. 6.99	
G-THUR	Beechcraft 200 Super King Air	BB-782	5Y-BIW G-THUR/N21MU/N4491Z/YV-397CP	13.12.89	Restored as 5Y-BIW. Canx by CAA 11.4.97.
G-THZL	Socata TB-20 Trinidad	534	F-GJDR N65TD	9. 5.96	
G-TIBC	Cameron A-180 HAFB	2107		12.10.89	To OH-JTI 2/95. Canx 22.2.95.
G-TICK	Cameron V-77 HAFB	1593		28.10.87	Canx as WFU 24.6.98.
G-TICL	Airbus A.320-231	169	OY-CNG F-WWIH	10.12.96	
G-TIDE	North American AT-6A Harvard	78-6698	FAP1620 41-16320	28. 3.79	To N3762J 5/80. Canx 16.4.80.
G-TIDS	SAN Jodel D.150 Mascaret	44	OO-GAN	15. 4.86	
G-TIFF	Cessna 550 Citation II (Unit No.290)	551-0262	G-DJHH N6862C	16. 4.86	To N7028U. Canx 4.8.88.
G-TIGA	DH.82A Tiger Moth	83547	G-AOEG T7120	5. 6.85	
G-TIGB	Aerospatiale AS.332L Super Puma	2023	G-BJXC F-WTNM	31. 3.82	
G-TIGC	Aerospatiale AS.332L Super Puma	2024	G-BJYH F-WTNJ	14. 4.82	
G-TIGD	Aerospatiale AS.332L Super Puma	2026	G-BJYI F-WXFL	15. 4.82	Crashed at Dyce on 4.7.83. Canx as destroyed 5.12.83.
G-TIGE	Aerospatiale AS.332L Super Puma	2028	G-BJYJ F-WTNM	15. 4.82	
G-TIGF	Aerospatiale AS.332L Super Puma	2030	F-WKQJ	15. 4.82	
G-TIGG	Aerospatiale AS.332L Super Puma	2032	F-WXFT	15. 4.82	
G-TIGH	Aerospatiale AS.332L Super Puma	2034	F-WXFL	15. 4.82	Fatal crash in North Sea 100 miles northeast of Shetland on 14.3.92. Canx as destroyed 3.8.92. (Escape trainer use 12/95)
G-TIGI	Aerospatiale AS.332L Super Puma	2036	F-WTNP	15. 4.82	
G-TIGJ	Aerospatiale AS.332L Super Puma	2042	VH-BHT(2) G-TIGJ	15. 4.82	
G-TIGK	Aerospatiale AS.332L Super Puma	2044		15. 4.82	Struck by lightning and ditched in North Sea 19.1.95, 15 miles NE of the 'Piper Bravo' oil production platform and about 140 miles NE of Aberdeen. Canx as destroyed 20.6.95. Remains stored 10/97 at Redhill.
G-TIGL	Aerospatiale AS.332L Super Puma	2050		15. 4.82	
G-TIGM	Aerospatiale AS.332L Super Puma	2045		15. 4.82	
G-TIGN	Aerospatiale AS.332L Super Puma	2056		18. 2.83	Flew into hillside in low visibility while on a flight from Shenzhan, China on 22.5.89. Canx as destroyed 18.9.89.
G-TIGO	Aerospatiale AS.332L Super Puma	2061	F-WMHH	18. 2.83	
G-TIGP	Aerospatiale AS.332L Super Puma	2064		11. 3.83	
G-TIGR	Aerospatiale AS.332L Super Puma	2071	F-WTNW	11. 3.83	
G-TIGS	Aerospatiale AS.332L Super Puma	2086		6. 5.83	
G-TIGT(1)	Aerospatiale AS.332L Super Puma	2040		17. 6.82	NTU - Not Imported. To OY-HMF. Canx 9.8.82.
G-TIGT(2)	Aerospatiale AS.332L Super Puma	2078		6. 5.83	
G-TIGU	Aerospatiale AS.332L Super Puma	2096		12. 1.84	To VH-BHK 8/99. Canx 16.8.99.
G-TIGV	Aerospatiale AS.332L Super Puma	2099	LN-ONC G-TIGV/LN-ONC/G-TIGV/LN-OPC/G-TIGV	12. 1.84	
G-TIGW	Aerospatiale AS.332L Super Puma	2059		23. 2.84	To VH-BHH 3/99. Canx 26.2.99.
G-TIGX	Aerospatiale AS.332L Super Puma	2060		23. 2.84	To C-GQLS 10/84. Canx 12.10.84.
G-TIGY	Aerospatiale AS.332L Super Puma	2089		8. 8.84	To C-GQCO 12/84. Canx 12.12.84.
G-TIGZ	Aerospatiale AS.332L Super Puma	2115	C-GQKK G-TIGZ	8. 8.84	
G-TIII	Aerotek Pitts S-2A Special	2196	G-BGSE N947	27. 2.89	
G-TIKI	Colt 105A HAFB	521	G-BKWV	16. 1.84	Canx by CAA 6.8.90. (To Australia ?)
G-TIKO	Hatz CB-1	PFA/143-13396		9. 7.99	
G-TILE	Robinson R-22 Beta	1100		4. 8.89	
G-TILI	Bell 206B JetRanger III	2061	F-GHFN N7037A/XC-BOQ(2)	6. 3.96	
G-TILL	Robinson R-22 Beta	1475		23. 7.90	To G-OGOG 7/97. Canx.
G-TILT	Bell 206B JetRanger III	3594	G-BRJO N2295Z	25. 9.91	To G-CCLY 4/95. Canx.
G-TIMB	Rutan VariEze	PFA/74-10795	G-BKXJ	11. 6.85	

Regn	Type	c/n	Previous identity	Regn date	Fate or immediate subsequent identity (if known)
G-TIME	Ted Smith Aerostar 601P	61P-0541-230	(N8058J)	21. 7.78	
G-TIMJ	Rand Robinson KR-2	PFA/129-11112		25.11.85	(Nearing completion 8/93) No Permit to Fly issued. Canx by CAA 4.5.99.
G-TIMK	PA-28-181 Archer II	28-8090214	OO-TRT PH-EAS/OO-HLN/N8142H	25. 8.81	
G-TIMM	Folland Gnat T.1	FL.519	8618M XP504	19. 2.92	
G-TIMP	Aeronca 7BCM Champion	7AC-3392	N84681 NC84681	14. 8.92	
G-TIMS	Falconar F-12A	PFA/22-12134		1.10.91	
G-TIMW	PA-28-140 Cherokee C	28-26404	G-AXSH	22. 3.85	Struck the ground in a field ½ mile north of Netherthorpe airfield on 25.3.90. Canx by CAA 3.9.90. (Stored at Sywell in 3/91)
G-TINA	Socata TB-10 Tobago	67		30.10.79	
G-TINE	Aeronca 7AC Champion	7AC-1024	OY-ALA D-EBGF/N82391/NC82391	28. 4.97	To N9120U 7/97. Canx 24.6.97.
G-TING	Cameron O-120 HAFB	4007		4.10.96	
G-TINI	Reims Cessna F.406 Caravan II	0015	PH-FWE EC-FOH/EC-177/PH-FWE/F-WZDX	25.11.97	To OY-PBG. Canx 14.9.98.
G-TINS	Cameron N-90 HAFB	1626		27. 1.88	
G-TINY	Moravan Zlin Z.526F Trener Master	1257	OK-CMD G-TINY/YR-ZAD	20. 4.94	
G-TIPS	Tipsy Nipper T.66 Srs.5 (Rebuild of Fairey c/n 50)	PFA/25-12696	OO-VAL 9Q-CYJ/9O-CYJ/(OO-CYJ)/(OO-CCD)	27. 3.95	
G-TIRE	Colt Flying Tyre SS HAFB	623		22. 1.85	Canx 2.7.90 on sale to Canada.
G-TISH	PA-31-310 Turbo Navajo	31-681	G-BFKJ N506V	3.12.85	To 5B-CGU. Canx 15.11.91.
G-TJAA	Boeing 707-139B (Line No. 108)	17903	9G-ACJ S2-AAL/N778PA/N778/N778PA/TC-JBE/N778PA/N74613/N778PA/N74613/(CU-...)	4. 4.79	Restored as N778PA 9/80. Canx 6.8.80.
G-TJAB	Boeing 707-123B (Line No. 31)	17640	9G-ACN N7513A	17. 7.79	To G-BHOX 3/80. Canx.
G-TJAC	Boeing 707-123B (Line No. 72)	17651	9G-ACO ST-AHG/N7524A	3. 7.79	To G-BHOY 3/80. Canx.
G-TJAY	PA-22-135 Tri-Pacer	22-730	N730TJ N2353A	11. 5.93	
G-TJCB	HS.125 Srs.700B	257127		18. 8.80	To OY-MPA. Canx 7.11.85.
G-TJET	Lockheed T-33A-5-LO	580-6350	DT-566 R.Danish AF/51-8566	8. 1.82	To G-NASA 6/91. Canx.
G-TJHI	Cessna 500 Citation I (Unit No.363)	500-0354	G-CCCL N51GA/G-BEIZ/(N5363J)	17. 1.92	
G-TJPM	BAe 146 Srs.300QT	E3150	SE-DIM G-BRGK	4. 7.94	
G-TKAY	Europa Avn Europa	PFA/247-12804		2. 6.99	
G-TKGR	Lindstrand Racing Car SS HAFB	380		28. 8.96	
G-TKHM	Agusta-Bell 206B JetRanger III	8557	G-MKAN G-DOUG	7. 1.81	To HB-XPW. Canx 31.10.86.
G-TKIS	Tri-R Kis (Tailwheel version)	029 & PFA/239-12358		23.12.93	
G-TKPZ	Cessna 310R II	310R-1225	G-BRAH(2) N1909G	19. 3.90	
G-TKYO	Boeing 747-212B (Line No. 449)	21939	9V-SQN	31. 3.89	To N616FF 12/94. Canx 15.12.94.
G-TLDK	PA-22-150 Tri-Pacer	22-4726	N6072D	27. 1.97	
G-TLME	Robinson R-44 Astro	0062		13. 4.94	
G-TLOL	Cessna 421C Golden Eagle III	421C-0838	(N2659K)	4. 3.80	To G-TREC 7/96. Canx.
G-TLTD	Cessna 182Q Skylane II	182-65934	N759EL	27. 6.90	To G-NLEE 12/93. Canx.
G-TMAS	HS.125 Srs.600B	256062	EC-ERX EC-319/G-TMAS/G-MFEU/G-5-15	17.12.84	To 5N-MAY 12/93. Canx 6.12.93.
G-TMCC	Cameron N-90 HAFB	4327		30. 3.98	
G-TMDP	Airbus A.320-231	168	OY-CNF (D-ADSL)/OY-CNF/F-WWIF	19.11.96	
G-TMJH	Hughes 369E (500E)	0033E		16. 3.84	To D-HGTJ 4/91. Canx 20.3.91.
G-TMKI	Percival P.56 Provost T.1	PAC/F/268	WW453	1. 7.92	(Stored 7/96)
G-TMMC	Aerospatiale AS.355F1 Twin Squirrel	5262	G-JLCO	14.12.87	To G-BXBT 2/97. Canx.
G-TNTA	BAe 146 Srs.200QT	E2056	G-5-056 (G-OTNT)/N146QT/N146FT/G-5-056	9. 4.87	To EC-HDH 5/99. Canx 24.5.99.
G-TNTB	BAe 146 Srs.200QT	E2067	G-5-067 (N145AC)/(G-BNFG)	3. 3.87	
G-TNTD	BAe 146 Srs.200QT	E2109	RP-C481 G-TNTD/SE-DHM/G-BOMJ	29.12.89	
G-TNTE	BAe 146 Srs.300QT	E3153	G-BRPW	8. 6.90	
G-TNTF	BAe 146 Srs.300QT	E3154	G-BRXI G-6-154	13. 9.90	To EC-712/EC-FFY. Canx 11.6.91.
G-TNTG	BAe 146 Srs.300QT	E3182	G-BSUY	21.10.91	
G-TNTH	BAe 146 Srs.200QT	E2089	(F-GTNT) G-BNYC/G-5-089	16. 3.88	To EC-281/EC-EPA. Canx 2.6.89.
G-TNTI	Airbus A.300B4-203F	155	N72987 TC-ALR/N72987/(N987C)/N224EA/F-GBNS	. 8.99	
G-TNTJ	BAe 146 Srs.200QT	E2100	G-BOHK G-5-100	30. 9.88	To D-ANTJ 10/89. Canx 13.10.89.

Regn	Type	c/n	Previous identity	Regn date	Fate or immediate subsequent identity (if known)
G-TNTK	BAe 146 Srs.300QT	E3186	G-BSXL G-6-186	30. 1.92	
G-TNTL	BAe 146 Srs.300QT	E3168	RP-C479 G-TNTL/G-BSGI/(RP-C479)/G-BSGI	7. 2.92	
G-TNTM	BAe 146 Srs.300QT	E3166	RP-C480 G-TNTM/G-BSLZ/G-6-166	28. 2.92	
G-TNTN	Thunder Ax6-56 HAFB	1991		25. 4.91	
G-TNTO	BAe 146 Srs.200QT	E2117	F-GTNT G-BPBS	31. 8.93	To EC-615/EC-FVY 8/94. Canx 28.4.94.
G-TNTP	BAe 146 Srs.200QT	E2105	HA-TAB G-5-105/G-BOMI/G-5-105	1.10.93	To EC-719/EC-FZE 10/94. Canx 13.10.94.
G-TNTR	BAe 146 Srs.300QT	E3151	SE-DIT G-BRGM	4. 7.94	
G-TOAD	SAN Jodel D.140B Mousquetaire	27	F-BIZG	27. 9.88	
G-TOAK	Socata TB-20 Trinidad	468	N83AV	5.12.89	
G-TOBA	Socata TB-10 Tobago	625	N600N	4. 4.91	
G-TOBE	PA-28R-200 Cherokee Arrow II	28R-7435148	G-BNRO N40979	25.11.87	Badly damaged in forced landing between Frittenden and Cranbrook, Kent on 6.3.92. Canx as WFU 6.5.92. (Stored 8/96)
G-TOBI	Reims Cessna F.172K	0792	G-AYVB	5. 1.84	
G-TOBY	Cessna 172B Skyhawk	172-47852	G-ARCM N6952X	8. 4.81	Damaged in gales at Sandown, IoW 15.10.83. Canx by CAA 27.2.90. Instructional Airframe 1/99 at Shoreham. (Wings removed by 24.4.99)
G-TODD	ICA IS-28M2A	59		18. 4.86	
G-TODE	Ruschmeyer R.90-230RG	016	D-EEAX(2)	20. 6.94	
G-TOFF	Aerospatiale AS.355F1 Twin Squirrel	5249	G-BKJX	30.11.82	To G-STVE 4/88. Canx.
G-TOFT	Colt 90A HAFB	1693		8. 3.90	
G-TOGA	PA-32-301 Saratoga	32-8006028	G-BIEG N81852	15.11.82	Badly damaged in forced landing at Belmont, Lancs on 29.8.93. Canx as WFU 24.9.93. (Wreck stored 9/95 - but roaded out late .95)
G-TOGO	Van's RV-6	PFA/181A-13447		6. 4.99	
G-TOMA	Curtiss P-40C Tomahawk	194	N80FR Soviet AF 53/41-13390	30.11.98	To N2689 as a Curtiss Wright P-40B in 4/99. Canx 31.3.99.
G-TOMF	PA-34-220T Seneca III	34-8133191	G-BJEO N8424Y	11. 8.82	To PH-GEC(2) 9/84. Canx 19.9.84.
G-TOMG	Hunting P.84 Jet Provost T.4	PAC/W/19987	9030M XR674	31. 8.94	Fatal crash and burned out in a field at Woolaston, near Lydney, Glos. on 1.8.99.
G-TOMI	HS.125 Srs.600B	256030	G-BBEP 5N-ARD/G-BBEP/G-BJOY/G-BBEP	23. 4.85	To N217A. Canx 5.11.96.
G-TOMK	PA-23-250 Aztec F	27-7754144	G-BFEC N63823	9.11.94	To G-VSFT 4/96. Canx.
G-TOMO	BAC One-Eleven Srs.F 487GK	BAC.267	(G-BNGG) YR-BCR	17. 9.87	Restored as YR-BCR. Canx 9.7.92.
G-TOMS	PA-38-112 Tomahawk	38-79A0453		22. 1.79	
G-TOMY	Mitsubishi MU.300 Diamond 1A	A090SA	N312DM	9. 2.88	To N300LG. Canx 3.3.95.
G-TONE	Pazmany PL-4	PFA/17-10695		24. 6.87	No Permit issued. Canx by CAA 29.12.95.
G-TONI	Cessna 421C Golden Eagle III	421C-0219	D-IMMH HZ-ZMA/N5472G	26. 7.78	To N421VA 5/94. Canx 19.4.94.
G-TONW	McDonnell Douglas DC-9-83 (MD-83) (Line No. 1934)	49952	N9012J	3.12.91	To B-28023. Canx 11.12.95.
G-TONY	Beechcraft B60 Duke	P-259	ZS-NHG(2) ZS-ITJ(2)/N3140W	27. 7.77	Restored as ZS-NHG(2) 5/80. Canx 19.5.80.
G-TOOL	Thunder Ax8-105 HAFB	1670		29. 3.90	
G-TOON	Cessna 152 II	152-81989	N67742	18. 8.78	Crashed into the sea off Worthing on 10.10.78. Canx.
G-TOPC	Aerospatiale AS.355F1 Twin Squirrel	5313	I-LGOG 3A-MCS/D-HOSY/OE-BXV/D-HOSY	29. 7.97	
G-TOPF	HS.125 Srs.403B	25238	G-AYER 9K-ACR/G-AYER	11. 7.84	To N125GC 4/86. Canx 23.8.85.
G-TOPS	Aerospatiale AS.355F2 Twin Squirrel	5151	G-BPRH N360E/N5794F	7. 5.91	
G-TORE	Hunting-Percival P.84 Jet Provost T.3A (Officially regd with c/n K84-03/6523/4)	PAC/W/9212	XM405	14. 6.91	(Stored 7/96) (See comments under G-BVBE)
G-TOSH	Robinson R-22 Beta	0933	N2629S LV-RBD/N8012T	14. 3.97	
G-TOTO	Reims Cessna F.177RG Cardinal	0049	G-OADE G-AZKH/(PH-LTH)/G-AZKH	29. 8.89	
G-TOTY	Robinson R-22 Beta	1046	N8023F	26. 6.89	To ZK-HWA. Canx 13.10.93.
G-TOUR	Robin R.2112	187		9.10.79	
G-TOWN	Focke-Wulf Piaggio FWP.149D (Piaggio c/n 338)	014	D-EFFY West German AF 90+06/BB+394	6. 8.85	To G-RORY 8/88. Canx.
G-TOWS	PA-25-260 Pawnee C (Mod 4 blade Hoffman prop.)	25-4853	PH-VBT D-EAVI/N4370Y	17. 7.91	
G-TOYS	Enstrom 280C-UK-2 Shark	1218	G-BISE	17. 6.82	(Stored 4/96)
G-TOYZ	Bell 206B JetRanger III	3949	G-RGER N75EA/JA9452/N32018	21.11.96	
G-TPHK	BAe 125 Srs.800B	258130	G-FDSL G-5-620	28. 2.90	To G-BVFC 10/93. Canx.
G-TPII	Colt 21A Cloudhopper HAFB	1251		6. 5.88	To (PH-HAS)/PH-BKB /92. Canx 13.11.91.
G-TPPH	Agusta-Bell 206B JetRanger II	8440	G-BCYP	13.12.84	To G-UNIK 12/88. Canx.
G-TPSL	Cessna 182S Skylane II	182-80398	N23700	11.12.98	

Regn	Type	c/n	Previous identity	Regn date	Fate or immediate subsequent identity (if known)
G-TPTR	Agusta-Bell 206B JetRanger II	8587	G-LOCK(2)	25. 8.81	Crashed while filming a vehicle at the Motor Industry Research Association test track near Bracknall on 13.3.89. (For spares use 7/90 Thruxton) Canx as destroyed 9.10.89.
G-TPTS	Robinson R-44 Astro	0457		24. 4.98	
G-TPTT	Airbus A.320-212	348	F-GLGE F-WWBT	29. 2.96	To OO-AEY 6/99. Canx 4.6.99.
G-TRAC	Robinson R-44 Astro	0598		10. 5.99	
G-TRAD	Boeing 707-321C (Line No. 366)	18717	G-BGIS N793PA	20. 1.84	Canx 24.4.86 on sale to USA. To HK-3232X 4/86.
G-TRAF	Aerospatiale SA.365N2 Dauphin 2	6074	G-BLDR	3.10.84	Restored as G-BLDR 7/89. Canx.
G-TRAK	Edgley OA.7 Optica (Mod) (Originally regd as an Optica Industries OA.7 Optica)	EA.7/003	G-BLFC G-56-003	10. 7.87	To N130DP 2/98. Canx 21.1.98.
G-TRAM	Cyclone Pegasus Quantum 15	7552		29. 7.99	
G-TRAN	Beechcraft 76 Duchess	ME-408	G-NIFR N1808A	15. 3.93	
G-TRAV	Cameron A-210 HAFB	3181		6.12.93	
G-TRCO	PA-23-250 Aztec E	27-7305124	G-OCFS G-BBFU/N40364	16. 2.90	To PH-JFG 2/91. Canx 28.1.91.
G-TREC	Cessna 421C Golden Eagle III	421C-0838	G-TLOL (N2659K)	2. 7.96	
G-TRED	Cameron Colt Bibendum 110SS HAFB	4222		12.12.97	
G-TREE	Bell 206B JetRanger III	2826	N2779U	15. 6.87	
G-TREK	Jodel D.18	182 & PFA/169-11265		1. 5.92	
G-TREN	Boeing 737-4S3 (Line No. 1887)	24796	G-BRKG	3. 4.91	
G-TREV	Saffery S.330 HAFB (Toy) (Officially regd with c/n 10)	11		11.10.78	Canx by CAA 23.11.88.
G-TRFM	PA-23-250 Aztec F	27-7654188	N62738	4. 2.86	To G-OANT 3/89. Canx.
G-TRIB	Lindstrand HS-110 Hot-Air Airship	174		23. 1.95	To N..... Canx 14.6.99.
G-TRIC	DHC.1 Chipmunk 22A (Fuselage no. DHB/f/13)	C1/0080	G-AOSZ WB635	18.12.89	
G-TRIK	Bell 206B JetRanger III	3239	G-BMWY N3903B	25. 5.88	To N80PL 2/93. Canx 11.2.93.
G-TRIM	Monnett Moni (Regd with the plans number as part of c/n)	00258T & PFA/142-11012		16. 2.84	
G-TRIN	Socata TB-20 Trinidad	1131		25. 6.90	
G-TRIO	Cessna 172M Skyhawk II	172-66271	G-BNXY N9621H	30. 7.91	
G-TRIP	PA-32R-301 Saratoga II SP	32R-8013132	G-HOSK PH-WET/OO-HKN/N8261X	10.12.85	
G-TRIV	Colt Trivial Pursuit 77SS HAFB	1250		11. 5.88	To (PH-BKB)/PH-HAS /92. Canx 13.11.91.
G-TRIX	Vickers-Supermarine 509 Spitfire Trainer IX	CBAF/9590	(G-BHGH) Irish Air Corp 161/G-15-174/PV202	2. 7.80	Damaged on landing at Goodwood on 15.9.96. (On repair Earls Colne 5/97)
G-TROP	Cessna T.310R II	T310R-1381	N4250C	31.12.86	
G-TROT	PA-31-350 Navajo Chieftain	31-7952098	N35176	7. 6.79	To LN-FAM 12/81. Canx 8.12.81.
G-TROY	North American T-28 Fennec (Regd as a T-28A)	142 & 174-545	F-AZFV French AF 142/51-7692	21. 4.99	
G-TRUC	Cassutt Speed One (Possibly same aircraft as initially regd G-MARY, which was still under construction at Wickenby in 5/89)	PFA/34-11400		20. 6.89	No Permit to Fly issued. Canx by CAA 4.5.99.
G-TRUE	MDH Hughes 369E (300E)	0490E	N6TK ZK-HFP	12. 9.94	
G-TRUK	Stoddard-Hamilton Glasair IIRG	575R & PFA/149-11015		23. 7.84	
G-TRUX	Colt 77A HAFB	1860		13.11.90	
G-TSAM	BAe 125 Srs.800B	258028	G-5-12	31. 1.85	
G-TSAR	Beechcraft 58 Baron	TH-1698	N81287	9. 2.94	
G-TSFT	PA-28-161 Warrior II	28-8216117	G-BLDJ N9632N	5. 4.89	
G-TSGJ	PA-28-181 Archer II	28-8090109	N8097W	12. 9.88	
G-TSIX	North American AT-6C-1NT Harvard IIA	88-9725	1535 Portuguese AF/South African AF 7183/EX289/41-33262	19. 3.79	
G-TSKY	Beagle B.121 Pup Srs.150	B121-010	OE-CFM HB-NAA/G-AWDY/HB-NAA/G-AWDY	6. 4.98	
G-TSMI	Rockwell Commander 114	14249	OO-TSM	8. 6.93	
G-TTAM	Taylor JT.2 Titch	PFA/3229		14.12.78	No Permit to Fly issued. Canx by CAA 28.4.99.
G-TTDD	Zenair CH.701 STOL	PFA/187-13106		1. 9.97	
G-TTEL	PA-23-250 Aztec D	27-4110	TF-JSG TF-IBV/G-BBXE/N944DS	30. 9.88	Starboard engine caught fire 15 miles northwest of Le Touquet, France on 21.6.91. CofA expired 19.10.91. Canx as TWFU 3.10.91.
G-TTHC	Robinson R-22 Beta	1196		21.12.89	
G-TTIM	Cassutt Racer IIIM	PFA/34-13116		10. 7.98	
G-TTMC	Airbus A.300B4-203	299	OH-LAA (LX-LGP)/F-WZMX	25. 4.98	
G-TTOY	CFM Streak Shadow SA	PFA/206-12805		15. 4.96	
G-TTPT	McDonnell Douglas DC-9-83 (MD-83) (Line No. 1788)	49940	N30016	1. 3.91	To TC-IND 3/96. Canx 3.4.96.
G-TTWO	Colt 56A HAFB	087		14. 5.80	Canx as WFU 14.11.95.
G-TUBE	Hughes H.369E (500E)	0322E		2. 5.89	To D-HXXX 9/91. Canx 20.8.91.

Regn	Type	c/n	Previous identity	Regn date	Fate or immediate subsequent identity (if known)
G-TUBS	Beechcraft 65-80 Queen Air	LD-116	G-ASKM	7. 3.85	(Stored 7/97) Canx as destroyed 10.2.98.
G-TUBY	Cessna 310J	310J-0077	G-ASZZ N3077L	6. 6.83	To G-ODLY 3/88. Canx.
G-TUDR	Cameron V-77 HAFB	1135		20. 5.85	
G-TUGG	PA-18-180 (Mod) Super Cub (Frame No.18-8497)	18-8274	PH-MAH N5451Y	10. 1.83	
G-TUGY	Robin DR.400/180 Regent	2052	D-EPAR	27. 4.90	
G-TUKE	Robin DR.400/180 Major 80	1542		2. 6.81	Extensively damaged when it crashed on the runway on take-off at Rochester on 30.7.95.
G-TUNE	Robinson R-22 Beta	0818	N60661 G-OJVI/(G-OJVJ)	12. 1.98	
G-TURB	Druine D.31 Turbulent	PFA/1660		11. 6.81	No Permit to Fly issued. Canx by CAA 21.2.96.
G-TURF	Reims Cessna F.406 Caravan II	0020	PH-FWF (EI-CND)/PH-FWF/F-WZDS	17.10.96	
G-TURK	Cameron Sultan 80SS HAFB	1711		12. 4.88	
G-TURN	Steen Skybolt	003 & PFA/64-11349		14. 7.88	
G-TURP	Aerospatiale SA.341G Gazelle Srs.1	1455	G-BKLS N17MT/N14MT/N49549	21. 1.88	Made heavy landing soon after take-off from Green Acre Farm, Stanford-le-Hope on 9.9.91. Repaired & restored as G-BKLS 11/91. Canx.
G-TUSK	Bell 206B JetRanger III	4406	G-BWZH N53114	13. 1.97	
G-TVAA	Agusta A.109E Power	11052		. 9.99	
G-TVBF	Lindstrand LBL-310A HAFB	439		2. 4.97	
G-TVII	Hawker Hunter T.7 (T.70)	41H-693834	XX467 R.Jordanian AF 836/R.Saudi AF 70-617/G-9-214/XL605	8.12.97	
G-TVIJ	CCF Harvard 4 (T-6J-CCF Texan)	CCF4-442	G-BSBE Moz PLAF 1730/FAP 1730/AA+652/52-8521	10.12.93	
G-TVKE	Cessna 310R II	310R-0579	G-EURO N87468	20. 4.82	To G-FFWD 2/90. Canx.
G-TVMM	Cessna 310Q II	310Q-0917	G-CETA G-BBIM/N69683	3. 3.88	CofA expired 6.8.95. Canx as WFU 4.2.97.
G-TVPA	Aerospatiale AS.355F1 Twin Squirrel	5181	G-BPRI N364E	18. 5.93	Restored as G-BPRI 4/99. Canx.
G-TVSA	Rockwell Commander 690B	11530	G-JRMM N81734	14. 4.86	To N489GA. Canx 13.1.89.
G-TVSI	Campbell Cricket	CA/340	G-AYHH	8. 4.82	
G-TVTV	Cameron TV 90SS HAFB	2357		14. 9.90	
G-TWEL	PA-28-181 Archer II	28-8090290	N81963	12. 6.80	
G-TWEY	Colt 69A HAFB	700		24. 7.85	
G-TWIG	Reims Cessna F.406 Caravan II	0014	PH-FWD F-WZDS	21.10.98	
G-TWIN	PA-44-180 Seminole	44-7995072	N30267	6.11.78	
G-TWIZ	Rockwell Commander 114	14375	SE-GSP N5808N	9. 5.90	
G-TWOB	PBN BN-2B-26 Islander	2159	G-BKJJ	6. 9.85	To 9M-TAD 2/92. Canx 30.3.92.
G-TWSS	BAe Jetstream Srs.3111	709	G-31-709	. .86R	NTU - To G-BMNS 5/86. Canx.
G-TWTD	CCF Hawker Sea Hurricane X (Canadian Car and Foundry - built)	CCF/41H/8020	(Russia) AE977	6. 5.94	(On rebuild 7/96)
G-TXSE	Rotary Air Force RAF 2000 GTX-SE	G/13-1271		1. 3.96	
G-TYGA	American Aviation AA-5B Tiger	AA5B-1161	G-BHNZ (D-EGDS)/N4547L	22. 2.82	
G-TYME	Rockwell Commander 690B	11512	(N3754C) YV-252CP/N81872	31.10.83	To N400DS. Canx 13.2.90.
G-TYNE	Socata TB-20 Trindad	1523	F-GRBM F-WWRW/CS-AZH/F-OHDE	6.11.97	
G-TYPE	PA-28RT-201T Turbo Arrow IV	28R-8018066	G-BIEA N8198V	17.10.80	Crashed near Fox Coverts Farm on 10.8.82. Canx.
G-TYPO	Robinson R-22 Beta	1040	G-JBWI	9. 8.99	
G-TYRE	Reims Cessna F.172M Skyhawk II	1222	OY-BIA	16. 2.79	
G-TZAR	PA-46-350P Malibu Mirage	4622052	N9168Q	23. 7.90	To N350PM. Canx 26.11.91.
G-TZII	Thorp T.211B	PFA/305-13285		2. 6.99	

G-U G-U

G-UAAA The series from G-UAAA to G-UABD was allocated to South Africa from 1927 until 1/29.

Regn	Type	c/n	Previous identity	Regn date	Fate or immediate subsequent identity (if known)
G-UAPA	Robin DR.400/140B Major	2213	F-GMXC	11. 1.95	
G-UAPO	Ruschmeyer R.90-230RG	019	D-EECT(2)	2. 3.95	
G-UARD	Sequoia F.8L Falco	872 & PFA/100-11057		20. 2.85	No CofA or Permit issued. Canx by CAA 2.9.91.
G-UBAC	Short SD.3-60 Var.100	SH3689	SE-KXU G-UBAC/EI-BSP/(EI-BSN)/G-BMLD/G-14-3689	8. 4.93	To N6368X 10/97. Canx 28.1.98.
G-UBBE	Cameron Clown SS HAFB	2857		13. 8.92	To SE-ZGU 2/97. Canx 9.12.96.
G-UBHL	Beechcraft B200 Super King Air	BB-864		11.11.80	To G-OHBD 6/87. Canx.
G-UBKP	Beechcraft 95-58P Pressurised Baron	TJ-188		10.11.78	To G-BIYS 6/81. Canx.
G-UBSH(1)	Beechcraft 2000 Starship	?		. .84R	NTU - Canx.

Regn	Type	c/n	Previous identity	Regn date	Fate or immediate subsequent identity (if known)
G-UBSH(2)	Beechcraft 300LW Super King Air	FA-101		9. 4.86	To G-BSTF 8/90. Canx.
G-UCCC	Cameron Sign 90SS HAFB	3918		5. 7.96	
G-UCCI	Pitts S-1S Special	AJT	G-BIYN N455T	25. 5.88	To G-LBAT 9/88. Canx.
G-UCPA	Eiri PIK-20E	20265		28. 5.80	To VH-GUX 1/83. Canx 21.2.83.
G-UDAY	Robinson R-22 Beta	1101		4. 8.89	
G-UERN	PBN BN-2B-26 Islander	2025	G-BHXI	17. 6.85	To J3-GAF 6/93. Canx 23.6.93.
G-UESS	Cessna 500 Citation I (Unit No.326)	500-0326	N45LC EP-PAQ/N5326J	18. 6.80	Ditched into the sea in the area of the Shiant Islands on approach to Stornoway on 8.12.83. Canx as destroyed 29.2.84
G-UEST	Bell 206B JetRanger II	1484	G-RYOB G-BLWU/ZS-PAW	8. 9.89	
G-UESY	Robinson R-22 Beta	2801		13. 3.98	
G-UFLY	Reims Cessna F.150H	0264	G-AVVY	29. 9.89	
G-UIDA	Star-Lite SL-1	211 & PFA/175-11440	G-BRKK	23. 9.91	Permit expired 11.3.99. Canx by CAA 1.6.99. (Was regd to a US-based owner).
G-UIDE	Wassmer Jodel D.120 Paris-Nice	262	F-BMIY	27. 5.80	
G-UIET	BAe ATP	2006	G-11-6 G-5-376/(N376AE)	26. 8.88	To G-MANO 11/94. Canx.
G-UILD	Grob G-109B	6419		28. 1.86	
G-UILE	Neico Lancair 320	PFA/191-12538		17. 1.94	
G-UINN	Stolp SA.300 Starduster Too	HB.1980-1	EI-CDQ C-GTLJ	16. 3.98	
G-UJAB	Pearce Jabiru UL	PFA/274A-13373		27. 1.99	
G-UKAC	BAe 146 Srs.300	E3142	G-5-142	25.10.89	
G-UKAG	BAe 146 Srs.300	E3162	G-6-162	28.11.90	
G-UKCA	HS.125 Srs.700B	257214	HZ-SJP G-5-17	1. 9.87	To G-OMID 8/92. Canx.
G-UKFA	Fokker F.100-620	11246	N602RP C-FICY/PH-EZB	1. 7.92	
G-UKFB	Fokker F.100-620	11247	N602TR C-FICW/PH-EZC	1. 7.92	
G-UKFC	Fokker F.100-620	11263	N602DG C-FICL/PH-EZF	1. 7.92	
G-UKFD	Fokker F.100-620	11259	C-FICP PH-EZJ	22. 7.92	
G-UKFE	Fokker F.100-620	11260	C-FICQ PH-EZK	22. 7.92	
G-UKFF	Fokker F.100-620	11274	PH-ZCK (G-FIOB)/PH-ZCK/PH-EZB/(PH-KLK)	9.11.93	
G-UKFG	Fokker F.100-620	11275	PH-ZCL (G-FIOC)/PH-ZCL/PH-EZV/(PH-KLL)	19.11.93	
G-UKFH	Fokker F.100-620	11277	PH-ZCM (G-FIOD)/PH-ZCM/PH-EZW/(PH-KLN)	29. 9.93	
G-UKFI	Fokker F.100-620	11279	PH-ZCN (G-FIOE)/PH-ZCN/PH-EZX/(PH-KLO)	12.10.93	
G-UKFJ	Fokker F.100-620	11248	F-GIOV C-FICB/PH-INC/PH-EZD	30. 1.96	
G-UKFK	Fokker F.100-620	11249	F-GIOX C-FICO/PH-INA/PH-EZE	19. 2.96	
G-UKFL	Fokker F.100-620	11268	PH-KLC F-GIDT/F-OGQI/F-GIDT/F-OGQI/PH-KLC	14. 8.97	
G-UKFM	Fokker F.100-620	11269	PH-KLD F-GIDQ/F-OGQL/(F-GIDQ)/PH-KLD	27.10.98	
G-UKFN	Fokker F.100-620	11270	PH-KLE F-GIDP/PH-KLE	16. 6.97	
G-UKFO	Fokker F.100-620	11271	PH-KLG F-GIDO/F-OGQM/(F-GIDO)/PH-KLG	20.10.97	
G-UKFP	Fokker F.100-620	11272	PH-KLH F-GIDN/F-OGQA/F-GIDN/F-OGQA/PH-KLH	27.10.98	
G-UKFR	Fokker F.100-620	11273	PH-KLI F-GIDM/F-OGQB/PH-KLI	21. 3.97	
G-UKHP	BAe 146 Srs.300	E3123	G-5-123	26.10.88	
G-UKID	BAe 146 Srs.300	E3157	G-6-157	28. 2.90	
G-UKJF	BAe 146 Srs.100	E1011	C-GNVY N803RW/(N103RW)/G-5-513/PT-LEQ	17.10.89	To D-AWDL 7/98. Canx 2.7.98.
G-UKLA	Boeing 737-4Y0 (Line No. 1582)	23865	VT-MGE G-UKLA/9M-MLC/G-UKLA	14.10.88	To PH-BPA 6/97. Canx 27.6.97.
G-UKLB	Boeing 737-4Y0 (Line No. 1723)	24344	VT-MGF G-UKLB/9M-MLI/G-UKLB/9M-MJL/G-UKLB/C-GATJ/C-FVNC/G-UKLB	25. 5.89	To PH-BPB 9/97. Canx 5.9.97.
G-UKLC	Boeing 737-42C (Line No. 1871)	24231		15. 6.90	To PH-BPD 2/97. Canx 3.2.97.
G-UKLD	Boeing 737-42C (Line No. 2060)	24232		7. 6.91	To PH-BPE 2/97. Canx 17.2.97.
G-UKLE	Boeing 737-4Y0 (Line No. 1747)	24468	VT-MGG G-UKLE	19. 7.89	To PH-BPC 11/97. Canx 20.11.97.
G-UKLF	Boeing 737-42C (Line No. 2062)	24813		11. 6.91	To PH-BPF 3/97. Canx 20.3.97.
G-UKLG	Boeing 737-42C (Line No. 2270)	24814		23. 4.92	To PH-BPG 4/97. Canx 11.4.97.
G-UKLH	Boeing 767-39HER (Line No. 484)	26256		1. 4.93	To G-OOAN 1/99. Canx.

Regn	Type	c/n	Previous identity	Regn date	Fate or immediate subsequent identity (if known)
G-UKLI	Boeing 767-39HER	26257		13. 4.93	To G-OOAO 1/99. Canx.
	(Line No. 488)				
G-UKLJ	Airbus A.320-212	190	G-BWKN	18. 3.96	To (SE-DVH)/PH-DVR 2/98. Canx 16.2.98.
			N484GX/F-WWDD		
G-UKLK	Airbus A.320-212	343	G-BWKO	11. 4.96	To F-OHFT 11/98. Canx 6.11.98.
			N485GX/F-WWDH		
G-UKLL	Airbus A.320-212	189	G-CRYY	17. 4.96	To F-OHFR(2) 5/99. Canx 4.5.99.
			G-BWCP/N483GX/F-WWDC		
G-UKLM	Sikorsky S-76B	760336	PH-NZV	17. 3.93	Restored as PH-NZV 7/98. Canx 27.7.98.
G-UKLN	BAe 146 Srs.200	E2069	OO-DJC	7. 5.91	Restored as OO-DJC 10/94. Canx 14.10.94.
			(OO-DJY)/G-BNKJ/N407XV/G-5-069/G-BNKJ/G-5-069		
G-UKLO	Airbus A.321-211	677	D-AVZO	7. 5.97	To G-UNID 1/98. Canx.
G-UKLS	Sikorsky S-76B	760325	PH-NZS	26. 1.96	Restored as PH-NZS 2/98. Canx 24.2.98.
G-UKLT	Sikorsky S-76B	760326	PH-NZT	22. 2.96	Restored as PH-NZT 7/98. Canx 15.7.98.
G-UKLU	Sikorsky S-76B	760329	PH-NZU	28.12.95	Restored as PH-NZU 7/98. Canx 15.7.98.
G-UKNO	Cessna U.206C Super Skywagon	U206-1230	G-BAMN	19. 4.84	To G-DROP 8/87. Canx.
			4X-ALL/N71943		
G-UKNZ	Colt Flying Kiwi SS HAFB	1525		25. 5.89	To ZK-PIP. Canx 21.1.93.
G-UKOZ	Pearce Jabiru SK	PFA/274-13310		16. 6.99	
G-UKPC	BAe 146 Srs.100	E1010	C-GNVX	3. 4.89	To G-JEAO 9/94. Canx.
			N802RW/(N102RW)/G-5-512/PT-LEP/G-BKXZ/PT-LEP		
G-UKRB	Colt 105A HAFB	1769		10.12.90	
G-UKRC	BAe 146 Srs.300	E3158	G-6-158	14. 2.91	
			G-BSMR/G-6-158		
G-UKRH	BAe 146 Srs.200	E2077	OO-DJD	7. 5.91	Restored as OO-DJD. Canx 30.11.95.
			(OO-DJZ)/G-BRNG/N408XV/G-5-077/N408XV		
G-UKSC	BAe 146 Srs.300	E3125	G-5-125	26.10.88	
G-UKTA	Fokker F.27-050	20246	PH-KXF	22. 2.95	
G-UKTB	Fokker F.27-050	20247	PH-KXG	21. 3.95	
G-UKTC	Fokker F.27-050	20249	PH-KXH	25. 1.95	
G-UKTD	Fokker F.27-050	20256	PH-KXT	20. 1.95	
G-UKTE	Fokker F.27-050	20270	PH-LXJ	14. 2.95	
G-UKTF	Fokker F.27-050	20271	PH-LXK	31. 1.95	
G-UKTG	Fokker F.27-050	20276	PH-LXP	28. 2.95	
G-UKTH	Fokker F.27-050	20277	PH-LXR	28. 3.95	
G-UKTI	Fokker F.27-050	20279	PH-LXT	17. 3.95	
G-UKTJ	ATR-72-202	509	F-WW..	19.12.97	
G-UKTK	ATR-72-202	519	F-WWLQ	30. 1.98	
G-UKTL	ATR-72-202	523	F-WWLD	10. 3.98	(Substantially damaged 14.5.98 at Norwich when it was struck by Boeing 737-3Y0 EC-FKJ c/n 23749)
G-UKTM	ATR-72-202	508	F-WWLU	23. 4.98	
G-UKTN	ATR-72-202	496	F-WWLT	4. 6.98	
G-UKUK	Head Ax8-105 HAFB	248	N8303U	1. 9.97	
G-ULAB	Robinson R-22 Beta	2444	N8311Z	18. 8.94	
G-ULAS	DHC.1 Chipmunk 22	C1/0554	WK517	14. 6.96	
	(Fuselage no. DHB/f/442)				
G-ULIA(1)	Cameron V-77 HAFB	2860		20. 5.92	Stolen 8/94 Bristol Balloon Fiesta and later impounded for smuggling. Actioned 27.3.99 & purchased by original owner. Restored to original marks with new basket and burner - in theory as G-ULIA(3) in 4/99.
G-ULIA(2)	Cameron V-77 HAFB	3375		1. 2.95	Canx as PWFU 21.7.97 but became G-BYLY on 16.7.97.
	(Regd with c/n of G-ULIA(1) - corrected when re-regd as G-BYLY)				
G-ULIA(3)	Cameron V-77 HAFB	2860	G-ULIA(1)	30. 4.99	
	(See comment for G-ULIA(1))				
G-ULLS	Lindstrand LBL-90A HAFB	434		18. 2.97	
G-ULPS	Everett Gyroplane Srs.1	007	G-BMNY	13. 7.93	
G-ULTR	Cameron A-105 HAFB	4100		24. 2.97	
G-UMBO	Colt Jumbo SS HAFB	747		2. 4.86	
	(Special shape with nose/tail/wings of Virgin 747)				
	(Built as c/n 816 & regd as a Thunder Ax7-77A, but c/n & type amended later)				
	(Replacement envelope c/n 1645 fitted in 1990)				
G-UMMI	PA-31-325 Turbo Navajo	31-7912060	G-BGSO	11. 8.92	
			N3519F		
G-UMST	Denney Kitfox 4-1200 Speedster	PFA/172B-12392		25. 5.94	Fatal crash on take-off at Newmill Farm, Dolphinton, Lanarkshire on 5.5.95. Canx as destroyed 26.9.95.
G-UNDY	Cessna 340 II	340-0305	G-BBNR	30.10.91	To G-LAST 9/96. Canx.
			N69452		
G-UNGE	Lindstrand LBL-90A HAFB	122	G-BVPJ	6.12.96	
G-UNIA	Airbus A.330-223	320	F-WW..	. .98R	NTU - To become G-OOA_ 2/00. Canx.
G-UNIB	Airbus A.330-223	330	F-WW..	. .98R	NTU - To become G-OOA_ 3/00. Canx.
G-UNIC	Aerospatiale AS.350B Ecureuil	1205	G-COLN	9. 9.88	To G-RAHM 12/89. Canx.
			G-BHIV		
G-UNID	Airbus A.321-211	677	G-UKLO	15. 1.98	To G-OOAF 12/98. Canx.
			D-AVZO		
G-UNIE	Airbus A.321-211	781	D-AVZK	3. 3.98	To G-OOAH 1/99. Canx.
G-UNIF	Airbus A.321-211	852	D-AVZG	. .98R	NTU - To G-OOAE 7/98. Canx.
G-UNIG	Airbus A.321-211	1006	D-AVZJ	. .98R	NTU - To G-OOAI 4/99. Canx.
G-UNIH	Airbus A.321-211	1017	D-AVZM	. .98R	NTU - To G-OOAJ 5/99. Canx.
G-UNII	Airbus A.3..	?		. .98R	
G-UNIJ	Airbus A.3..	?		. .98R	
G-UNIK	Agusta-Bell 206B JetRanger II	8440	G-TPPH	2.12.88	To G-JIMW 1/96. Canx.
			G-BCYP		

Regn	Type	c/n	Previous identity	Regn date	Fate or immediate subsequent identity (if known)
G-UNIP	Cameron Oil Container SS HAFB (Unipart Sureflow Oil Can)	2532		15. 3.91	
G-UNIT	Partenavia P.68B Victor	23	G-BCNT	21.10.93	
G-UNIV	Montgomerie-Parsons Two-Place Gyroplane (Mod.)	G/08-1276	G-BWTP	3. 8.99	
G-UNNY	BAC 167 Strikemaster Mk.87 (Regd with c/n "601") (Also c/n EEP/JP/2872)	PS.164	G-AYHR Botswana DF OJ4/Kenyan AF 601/G-27-191/G-AYHR/G-27-191	19. 3.98	
G-UNRL	Lindstrand RR-21 HAFB	260		25. 5.95	
G-UNST	Beechcraft F33C Bonanza	CJ-141	PH-BNL	3. 7.91	Destroyed in fatal crash in a field at the rear of Shadoxhurst Garage, near Ashford, Kent on 20.7.93. Canx as WFU 4.8.93.
G-UNYT	Robinson R-22 Beta	0985	G-BWZV G-LIAN	17.11.97	
G-UORO	Europa Avn Europa	PFA/247-12522		13.12.93	
G-UPCC	Robinson R-22 Beta	0806	G-MUSS	29. 6.89	Badly damaged on landing 5.6.94 at Speke. Canx by CAA 29.10.97.
G-UPDN	Cameron V-65 HAFB	1221		11.12.85	Canx by CAA 6.4.93.
G-UPHL	Cameron Concept 80SS HAFB	3002		23. 2.93	
G-UPMW	Robinson R-22 Beta	1982		31.12.91	
G-UPPP	Colt 77A HAFB	852		4. 8.86	
G-UPPY	Cameron DP-80 Hot-Air Airship	2274		29. 3.90	
G-UPUP	Cameron V-77 HAFB	1828		21. 7.89	
G-UPVC	Agusta A.109A	7187		23.12.80	To N109MF 3/82. Canx 9.3.82.
G-UROP	Beechcraft 95-B55 Baron	TC-2452	N64311	17. 9.90	
G-URRR	Air Command 582 Sport	0630 & G/04-1200		13. 6.90	
G-URUH	Robinson R-44 Astro	0354		3. 7.97	
G-USAF(1)	North American T-28B Trojan	200-343	AMARC 5T082 BuA.138272	. .82R	NTU - Not Imported. To C-FPTR 9/93.
G-USAF(2)	North American T-28C Trojan	226-166	BuA.140589	28. 6.82	Exported to Canada 23.1.91. Canx by CAA 2.9.91. To C-FPTR 3/92.
G-USAM	Cameron Uncle Sam SS HAFB (Uncle Sam head shape)	1120		20. 5.85	
G-USFT	PA-23-250 Aztec F	27-7654174	G-BEGV N62720	8. 5.97	
G-USGB	Colt 105A HAFB	1130		26. 8.87	
G-USIL	Thunder Ax7-77 HAFB	1587		22. 8.89	
G-USMC	Cameron Chestie 90SS HAFB (US Marine Corps Bulldog shape)	1251		24. 4.86	
G-USSR	Cameron Doll 90SS HAFB (Russian Doll shape)	2273		29. 3.90	
G-USSY	PA-28-181 Archer II	28-8290011	N8439R	7.11.88	
G-USTA	Agusta A.109A	7170	G-MEAN G-BRYL/G-ROPE/G-OAMH	3.12.96	Extensively damaged in heavy landing at Bedlam Street, Hurstpierpoint on 27.3.99. (Wreck stored at Biggin Hill) Canx as WFU 5.8.99.
G-USTB	Agusta A.109A	7163	D-HEEG (D-HEEF)/VR-CKN/HB-XKM	9. 6.97	
G-USTE	Robinson R-44 Astro	0315		11. 3.97	
G-USTI	Cameron H-34 HAFB	2468		6.12.90	Canx as WFU 31.7.96.
G-USTO	Beechcraft A24R Sierra	MC-91	G-USTO (OO-LCC)/G-USTO/G-AYPA	20.10.83	To OO-MAD 7/86. Canx 24.7.86.
G-USTV	Messerschmitt Bf.109G-2/Trop (built by Erla Maschinenwerk GmbH)	10639	8478M RN228/Luftwaffe	26.10.90	Badly damaged on landing near Duxford on 12.10.97. Canx as PWFU 24.9.98. (On display IoW Museum)
G-USTY	Clutton FRED Srs.III	PFA/29-10390		11.10.78	Badly damaged in forced landing at Ollerton on 14.7.96. (On rebuild 6/97)
G-USUK	Colt 2500A HAFB	1100		1. 6.87	Canx as WFU 21.8.90. (Gondola on display 7/99 Duxford - remainder stored)
G-UTAX	PA-31-350 Navajo Chieftain	31-7405214	N54266	24. 9.87	NTU - To G-VTAX 8.10.87. Canx 8.10.87.
G-UTIL	Lockspeiser Lord Development Aircraft LDA-01	LDA.01 & PFA/1346	G-AVOR	12. 8.86	DBF at Old Sarum on 16.1.87. Canx as destroyed 5.3.87.
G-UTSI	Rand-Robinson KR-2	KBG-01		2.10.89	(Nearing completion 8/97)
G-UTSY	PA-28R-201 Cherokee Arrow III	28R-7737052	N3346Q	29. 8.86	
G-UTZY	Aerospatiale SA.341G Gazelle Srs.1	1307	G-BKLV N341SC	21.12.87	
G-UVIP	Cessna 421C Golden Eagle III	421C-0603	G-BSKH N88600	23.11.98	
G-UWWB	BAe 125 Srs.800B	258001	G-5-522 G-BKTF/"N800BA"/G-5-11	18. 6.86	To G-5-557/ZK-TCB 6/87. Canx 2.6.87.
G-UZEL	Aerospatiale SA.341G Gazelle Srs.1	1413	G-BRNH YU-HBO	21.11.89	
G-UZLE	Colt 77A HAFB	2021		1. 8.91	

G-V G-V

Regn	Type	c/n	Previous identity	Regn date	Fate or immediate subsequent identity (if known)
G-VAEL	Airbus A.340-311	015	F-WWJG (N3402N)	15.12.93	
G-VAGA	PA-15 Vagabond	15-248	N4458H NC4458H	14.11.80	(Badly damaged at Roundabout Airstrip, Horsebridge, near Hailsham on 15.5.98)

Regn	Type	c/n	Previous identity	Regn date	Fate or immediate subsequent identity (if known)
G-VAIR	Airbus A.340-313X	164	F-WWJA	21. 4.97	
G-VAJC	Westland WG.30 Srs.100	011	G-17-7	7. 7.83	To N4499N 10/83. Canx 11.10.83.
G-VAJK	Avro 748 Srs.1A/105	1557	VR-CBH G-BEKG/LV-IEE/LV-PXH	29. 2.84	Restored as G-BEKG 7/86. Canx.
G-VAJT	Socata MS.894E Rallye Minerva 220GT	12195	EI-BAB (S9-NAF)/EI-BAB/(G-BLPN)/EI-BAB	25. 7.89	
G-VALE	North American AT-6C Harvard IIA	88-10677	(G-BHXF) G-RBAC/FAP 1522/South African AF 7244/EX584/41-33557	17. 9.80	To N3GCA 11/85. Canx 12.11.85.
G-VALS	Pietenpol Air Camper	PFA/47-13157		30. 7.97	
G-VAMP	Thunder Ax6-56 Bolt HAFB	185		18.12.78	Canx 4.1.85 on sale to Australia. To VH-JUR 7/87.
"G-VAMP"	DH.115 Vampire T.11	-	XK623	----	(Unofficial marks worn)(On display 4/93 at Caernarfon)
G-VANG	Agusta-Bell 206B JetRanger III	8610	G-BIZA	24. 2.82	To G-HRAY 4/86. Canx.
G-VANS	Van's RV-4 (built by T.Saylor)	355	N16TS	7. 9.92	
G-VANZ	Van's RV-6A	PFA/181-12531		15. 7.93	
G-VARG	Varga 2150A Kachina	VAC 157-80	OO-RTY N80716	14. 5.84	
G-VASA	PA-34-200 Seneca	34-7350080	G-BNNB (N.....)/G-BNNB/N15625	29. 3.96	
G-VAST	Boeing 747-41R (Line No. 1117)	28757		17. 6.97	
G-VAUK	PA-31-350 Navajo Chieftain	31-8152164	G-GWEA N551PH/(N551PX)/N2728F/N4092L	22. 8.88	To N900MM 1/93. Canx 29.1.93.
G-VAUN	Cessna 340 II	340-0538	D-IOWS N5148J	25.11.77	
G-VBAC	Short SD.3-60 Var.300	SH3736	VH-MJU G-BOEJ/G-14-3736	15. 9.97	
G-VBEE	Boeing 747-219B (Line No. 527)	22723	ZK-NZW	5. 4.99	
G-VBIG	Boeing 747-4Q8 (Line No. 1081)	26255		10. 6.96	
G-VBUS	Airbus A.340-311	013	F-WWJE (N3401A)	26.11.93	
G-VCAT	Boeing 747-267B (Line No. 566)	22872	B-HIE VR-BIE	16.10.98	
G-VCED	Airbus A.320-231	193	OY-CNI F-WWIX	21. 1.97	
G-VCIO	EAA Acrosport 2	PFA/72-12388		9.10.97	
G-VCJH	Robinson R-22 Beta	1569		26.10.90	Substantially damaged when it overturned while taking off from Booker on 13.7.99.
G-VCML	Beechcraft 58 Baron	TH-1346	N2289R	31.10.97	
G-VCSI	Rotorway Exec	3660		25.10.90	(Stored 5/94) No CofA issued. Canx by CAA 3.4.97.
G-VDIR	Cessna T.310R II	310R-0211	N5091J	31. 1.91	
G-VEGA	Slingsby T.65A Vega	1889	(G-BFZN)	20.10.78	To BGA.2729 2/81. Canx 12.3.81.
G-VEGL	Aviamilano F.8L Falco Srs.II	114	OO-MEN I-VEGL	4. 2.83	To G-OCDS 9/85. Canx.
G-VELA	SIAI-Marchetti S.205-22R (Marked as S.208A Waco Vela)	4-149	N949W	30.10.89	
G-VELD	Airbus A.340-313X	214	F-WWJY	16. 3.98	
G-VELT	Cessna 340A	340A-0687	HB-LLZ N5462G	6.11.84	To EC-DYT 4/86. Canx 13.3.86.
G-VENI	DH.112 Venom FB.50 (FB.1) (FFW built)	733	J-1523 Swiss AF	8. 6.84	
G-VENM(1)	DH.112 Venom FB.54 (FB.4) (FFW built) (Regd with c/n 431)	960	J-1790 Swiss AF	. .84R	NTU - To G-BLKA 7/84. Canx.
G-VENM(2)	DH.112 Venom FB.50 (FB.1) (FFW built)	824	G-BLIE Swiss AF J-1614	16. 6.99	
G-VERA	Gardan GY-201 Minicab	PFA/56-12236		7. 6.94	
G-VERT	Bell 222	47041	G-JLBZ G-BNDB/A40-CH	22. 2.90	To G-OWCG 8/94. Canx.
G-VETA	Hawker Hunter T.7	41H-693751	G-BVWN XL600	2. 7.96	
G-VETS	Enstrom 280C-UK Shark	1015	G-FSDC G-BKTG/OY-HBP	11. 9.95	
G-VEZE	Rutan VariEze	PFA/74-10285		2. 9.77	
G-VFAB	Boeing 747-4Q8 (Line No. 1028)	24958		28. 4.94	
G-VFAR	Airbus A.340-313X	225	(G-VPOW) F-WWJW	12. 6.98	
G-VFLY	Airbus A.340-311	058	F-WWJE	24.10.94	
G-VFSI	Robinson R-22 Beta	1785	N4081L	19.12.96	
G-VGIN	Boeing 747-243B (Line No. 134)	19732	N747BL B-2440/N358AS/(N611PE)/N358AS/I-DEMU	30. 1.86	
G-VHFA	PA-23-250 Aztec E	27-4577	G-BZFE G-AZFE/EI-BPA/G-AZFE/N13962	27. 6.89	To N250TB 10/98. Canx 18.9.98.
G-VHOL	Airbus A.340-311	002	F-WWAS	30. 5.97	
G-VHOT	Boeing 747-4Q8 (Line No. 1043)	26326		12.10.94	
G-VIBA	Cameron DP-80 Hot Air Airship	1729		28. 5.91	
G-VIBE	Boeing 747-219B (Line No. 568)	22791	ZK-NZZ 9M-MHH/ZK-NZZ/N6018N	. 9.99	
G-VICC	PA-28-161 Warrior II	28-7916317	G-JFHL N2249U	3. 3.92	

Regn	Type	c/n	Previous identity	Regn date	Fate or immediate subsequent identity (if known)
G-VICE	MDH Hughes 369E (500E)	0365E	D-HLIS	16. 5.95	Reserved as N82722 in 7/95.
G-VICI	DH.112 Venom FB.50 (FB.1) (FFW built)	783	HB-RVB (G-BMOB)/Swiss AF J-1573	6. 2.95	
G-VICK	PA-31 Turbo Navajo	31-109	G-AWED N9076Y	10.11.83	To G-OPRA 2/92. Canx.
G-VICM	Beechcraft F33C Bonanza	CJ-136	PH-BNG	3. 7.91	
G-VICS	Commander Aircraft 114B	14655	N655V	3. 2.98	
G-VIDI	DH.112 Venom FB.50 (FB.1) (FFW built)	811	J-1601 Swiss AF	8. 6.84	Extensively damaged after crashing back onto the runway on take-off at Chester on 7.7.96. Canx by CAA 2.1.97. Scrapped
G-VIEW	Vinten Wallis WA-116L Srs.100	002		5. 7.82	Permit expired 6.10.85. (Stored 2/99 Reymerston Hall)
G-VIGN	Boeing 747-243B	?		. .85R	NTU - Canx.
G-VIIA	Boeing 777-236ER (Line No. 41)	27483	N5022E (G-ZZZF)	3. 7.97	
G-VIIB	Boeing 777-236ER (Line No. 49)	27484	N5023Q (G-ZZZG)	23. 5.97	
G-VIIC	Boeing 777-236ER (Line No. 53)	27485	N5061R (G-ZZZH)	6. 2.97	(Also reported as ex N5013R)
G-VIID	Boeing 777-236ER (Line No. 56)	27486	(G-ZZZI)	18. 2.97	
G-VIIE	Boeing 777-236ER (Line No. 58)	27487	(G-ZZZJ)	27. 2.97	
G-VIIF	Boeing 777-236ER (Line No. 61)	27488	(G-ZZZK)	19. 3.97	
G-VIIG	Boeing 777-236ER (Line No. 65)	27489	(G-ZZZL)	9. 4.97	
G-VIIH	Boeing 777-236ER (Line No. 70)	27490	(G-ZZZM)	7. 5.97	
G-VIII	Vickers-Supermarine 359 Spitfire LF.VIII	6S/479770	I-SPIT Indian AF T17/MT719	27. 4.89	To N719MT 8/93. Canx 9.7.93.
G-VIIJ	Boeing 777-236ER (Line No. 111)	27492	(G-ZZZP)	29.12.97	
G-VIIK	Boeing 777-236ER (Line No. 117)	28840		3. 2.98	
G-VIIL	Boeing 777-236ER (Line No. 127)	27493		13. 3.98	
G-VIIM	Boeing 777-236ER (Line No. 130)	28841		26. 3.98	
G-VIIN	Boeing 777-236ER (Line No. 157)	29319		21. 8.98	
G-VIIO	Boeing 777-236ER (Line No. 182)	29320		26. 1.99	
G-VIIP	Boeing 777-236ER (Line No. 193)	29321		9. 2.99	
G-VIIR	Boeing 777-236ER (Line No. 203)	29322		18. 3.99	
G-VIIS	Boeing 777-236ER (Line No. 206)	29323		1. 4.99	
G-VIIT	Boeing 777-236ER (Line No. 217)	29962		26. 5.99	
G-VIIU	Boeing 777-236ER (Line No. 221)	29963		28. 5.99	
G-VIIV	Boeing 777-236ER (Line No. 228)	29964		29. 6.99	
G-VIIW	Boeing 777-236ER (Line No. 233)	29965		30. 7.99	
G-VIIX	Boeing 777-236ER (Line No. 236)	29966		11. 8.99	
G-VIIY	Boeing 777-236ER (Line No. 251)	29967		. 4.98R	(delivery due 22.10.99)
G-VIKE	Bellanca 17-30A Super Viking 300A	79-30911	N302CB	8. 7.80	
G-VIKI	Cessna 402B Businessliner	402B-0225	G-BARW N7897Q	8.11.82	To ZS-LOX 3/84. Canx 24.1.84.
G-VIKY	Cameron A-120 HAFB	3068		27. 4.93	
G-VILL	Carmichael Lazer Z.200 (Mod)	10	G-BOYZ	10. 6.96	
G-VINO	Sky 90-24 HAFB	102		25. 2.98	
G-VIPI	BAe 125 Srs.800B	258222	G-5-745	27. 7.92	
G-VIPP	PA-31-350 Navajo Chieftain	31-7952244	G-OGRV G-BMPX/N3543D	6. 8.93	
G-VIPS	Gates LearJet 35A	35A-614	G-SOVN HB-VJC/G-PJET/N3815G	3. 5.90	To G-OCFR 6/92. Canx.
G-VIPY	PA-31-350 Navajo Chieftain	31-7852143	EI-JTC G-POLO/N27750	10.10.97	
G-VIRG	Boeing 747-287B (Line No. 274)	21189	N354AS LV-LZD/N1791B	14. 6.84	
G-VISA	Cessna A.152 Aerobat	A152-0801	N7382L	21. 3.90	To OO-VCO. Canx 19.2.93.
G-VIST	PA-30-160 Twin Comanche B	30-1424	G-AVHZ N8287Y	17. 6.83	To G-SURG 6/90. Canx.
G-VITE	Robin R.1180T Aiglon	219		16.10.78	
G-VIVA	Thunder Ax6-56 Bolt HAFB (Officially regd as Ax7-65 Bolt)	190		28.11.78	
G-VIVI	Taylor JT.2 Titch	PFA/60-12405		4.11.96	

Regn	Type	c/n	Previous identity	Regn date	Fate or immediate subsequent identity (if known)
G-VIVM	BAC P.84 Jet Provost T.5	PAC/W/23907	G-BVWF XS230	25. 3.96	
G-VIXN	DH.110 Sea Vixen FAW.2 (TT) (Is infact as D.3 version)	10145	8828M XS587	5. 8.85	
G-VIZZ	Sportavia Putzer RS.180 Sportsman	6018	D-EFBK	25.10.79	
G-VJAB	Pearce Jabiru UL	PFA/274-13322		25. 6.98	
G-VJAI	Gulfstream American GA-7 Cougar	GA7-0107	G-OCAB G-BICF/N8500H/N29707	10.12.87	To G-TANI 5/95. Canx.
G-VJAY	HS.125 Srs.F400B	25254	G-5-624 G-AYLG/3D-AVL/G-AYLG	28. 3.89	To VT-UBG 9/93. Canx 20.8.93.
G-VJCB	Agusta A.109A II	7412	G-BOUA	22. 8.88	To G-TBGL 1/99. Canx.
G-VJCT	Partenavia P.68C Victor	327		10. 5.85	To ZK-FUZ. Canx 8.9.95.
G-VJET	Avro 698 Vulcan B.2	-	XL426	7. 7.87	(On display 8/97 at Southend)
G-VJFK	Boeing 747-238B (Line No. 238)	20842	VH-EBH	4. 2.91	
G-VJIM	Colt Jumbo 77SS HAFB	1298	(G-BPJI)	7. 8.89	
G-VKRS	Cessna S550 Citation II	S550-0133	(N1294K)	16. 4.87	To N7074K 11/88. Canx 1.11.88.
G-VLAD	Yakovlev Yak-50	791502	D-EIVR N51980/DDR-WQR/DM-WQR	14.11.88	
G-VLAX	Boeing 747-238B (Line No. 241)	20921	VH-EBI	1. 5.91	
G-VLCN	Avro 698 Vulcan B.2	-	XH558	6. 2.95	(On display 9/97)
G-VMAX	Mooney M.20K	25-0504	ZS-KYP N9716G	12. 2.86	
G-VMDE(1)	Cessna P.210N Pressurised Centurion II	P210-00051	N3742P	5. 5.78	NTU - Not Imported. To LV-PAG/LV-MOR 5/78. Canx 6/78.
G-VMDE(2)	Cessna P.210N Pressurised Centurion II	P210-00088	(N4717P)	20. 7.78	
G-VMED	Airbus A.320-214	978	F-WWDC	16. 4.99	
G-VMIA	Boeing 747-123 (Line No. 87)	20108	EI-CAI VH-EEI/G-HIHO/(LX-NCV)/N14939/N9669	23. 3.90	
G-VMJM	Socata TB-10 Tobago	1361	G-BTOK	21. 4.92	
G-VMPR	DH.115 Vampire T.11	15621	8196M XE920	13. 3.95	
G-VMSL	Robinson R-22 Beta	0483	G-KILY N8561M	5. 2.98	
G-VNOM	DH.112 Venom FB.50 (FB.1R) (built by FFW, Essen)	842	J-1632 Swiss AF	13. 7.84	No UK CofA issued. Canx by CAA 25.3.91.
G-VNPP	Hughes 369HM (500)	49-0036M	G-BDKL EI-ATY	30. 3.83	To G-HSKY 1/84. Canx.
G-VOAR	PA-28-181 Archer III	2843011	N9256Q	3.11.95	
G-VODA	Cameron N-77 HAFB	2208		8. 2.90	
G-VOID	PA-28RT-201T Turbo Arrow IV	28R-8118049	ZS-KTM N83232	17. 8.87	
G-VOLH	Airbus A.321-211	823	(EC-...) D-AVZX	15. 5.98	
G-VOLT	Cameron N-77 HAFB	2157		8.11.89	
G-VOTE	Ultramagic M-77 HAFB	77-164		10. 3.99	
G-VOYG	Boeing 747-283B (Line No. 167)	20121	G-BMGS LN-AEO/OY-KHA/(OY-KFA)	2. 2.90	Flown from Gatwick to RAF Kemble on 7.11.98 & WFU. To be stripped for spares and scrapped. Canx as PWFU 11.2.99.
G-VPII	Evans VP-2	PFA/63-10262	(G-EDIF)	4.10.88	(Wings stored 2/92 Rayne Hall Farm)
G-VPLC	Beechcraft 200 Super King Air	BB-797	N84B	14.11.86	To G-BVMA 7/93. Canx.
G-VPOW	Airbus A.340-313X	225	F-WWJW	. .98R	NTU - To G-VFAR 6/98. Canx.
G-VPSJ	Europa Avn Europa	PFA/247-12520		29. 7.93	
G-VPTO	Evans VP-2	PFA/7216		22.12.78	No Permit issued. Canx by CAA 2.9.91.
G-VPUF	Boeing 747-219B (Line No. 563)	22725	ZK-NZY N6005C	. .98R	(delivery due 10/00)
G-VRES	Beechcraft 200 Super King Air	BB-379		26. 1.78	To G-ONEX 2/93. Canx.
G-VRGN	Boeing 747-212B (Line No. 419)	21937	9V-SQL	31. 7.89	To N618FF. Canx 1.3.95.
G-VROE	Avro 652A Anson C.21	"3634"	" -AIWX" G-VROE/G-BFIR/7881M/WD413	3. 3.98	
G-VRST	PA-46-350P Malibu Mirage	4636189		7.12.98	
G-VRUM	Boeing 747-267B (Line No. 582)	23048	B-HIF VR-HIF/N6066U	2.11.98	
G-VRVI	Cameron O-90 HAFB	2522		27. 2.91	
G-VSBC	Beechcraft B200 Super King Air	BB-1290	N3185C JA8859/N3185C	17. 6.93	
G-VSEA	Airbus A.340-311	003	F-WWDA	7. 7.97	
G-VSEE	Airbus A.320-231	449	N449RX F-WWIG	. .94R	NTU - To SX-BSV 1/94. Canx.
G-VSEL	Beechcraft A200 Super King Air	BB-362	N200TK N4562P/G-SONG/G-BKTI	21.11.84	To N506AB. Canx 22.1.92.
G-VSFT	PA-23-250 Aztec F	27-7754144	G-TOMK G-BFEC/N63823	23. 4.96	
G-VSKY	Airbus A.340-311	016	F-WWJH (N3403G)	21. 1.94	
G-VSOP	Cameron Bottle 60SS HAFB	835		19. 5.82	Canx by CAA 1.3.93.

Regn	Type	c/n	Previous identity	Regn date	Fate or immediate subsequent identity (if known)
G-VSSS	Boeing 747-219B (Line No. 528)	22724	ZK-NZX 9M-MHG/ZK-NZX	. .98R	(delivery due 1/01)
G-VSTO	Hawker Siddeley Harrier GR.1	B3/41H/727246	XV742	7. 6.71	Restored to RAF as XV742 8/71. Canx 5.8.71.
G-VSUN	Airbus A.340-313	114	F-WWJI (F-GLZJ)	30. 4.96	
G-VTAN	Airbus A.320-214	764	G-BXTA F-WWDF	29. 4.99	
G-VTAX	PA-31-350 Navajo Chieftain	31-7405214	(G-UTAX) N54266	8.10.87	To G-PZAZ 1/95. Canx.
G-VTEN	Vinten-Wallis WA.117 Venom	UMA-01 & 003		22. 4.85	Permit expired 3.12.85. Canx as WFU 12.6.89. (Stored 2/99 Reymerston Hall)
G-VTII	DH.115 Vampire T.11 (Fuselage no. DHP40273)	15127	WZ507	9. 1.80	
G-VTOL	Hawker Siddeley Harrier T.52 (Originally regd as a T.2, changed to T.52 on 15.4.71)	B3/41H/735795	ZA250 G-VTOL/(XW273)	27. 7.70	CofA expired 2.11.86. Canx by CAA 3.90. (On loan to Brooklands Museum 3/99)
G-VTOP	Boeing 747-4Q8 (Line No. 1100)	28194		28. 1.97	
G-VULC	Avro 698 Vulcan B.2A	-	N655AV G-VULC/XM655	27. 2.84	(On display 6/96)
G-VVBF	Colt 315A HAFB	4058		3. 3.97	
G-VVBK	PA-34-200T Seneca II	34-7570303	G-BSBS G-BDRI/SE-GLG	26. 1.89	
G-VVIP	Cessna 421C Golden Eagle III	421C-0699	G-BMWB N2655L	7. 7.92	
G-VWGB	Cessna 404 Titan Courier II	404-0226	(N88692)	4. 5.78	To G-FJKI 11/82. Canx.
G-VWSE	Cessna 404 Titan II	404-0458	(N2682F)	19. 2.80	To ST-AIW 5/83. Canx 4.5.83.
G-VXLG	Boeing 747-41R (Line No. 1177)	29406		30. 9.98	
G-VYGR	Colt 120A HAFB	2479		24. 9.93	
G-VZZZ	Boeing 747-219B (Line No. 523)	22722	ZK-NZV	7. 7.99	

G-W

Regn	Type	c/n	Previous identity	Regn date	Fate or immediate subsequent identity (if known)
G-WAAC	Cameron N-56 HAFB	492		14. 2.79	
G-WACA	Reims Cessna F.152 II	1968		16. 9.86	Damaged on landing at Wycombe Air Park on 21.11.94. Canx as WFU 25.1.95. To G-BYFA 11/98.
G-WACB	Reims Cessna F.152 II	1972		16. 9.86	
G-WACC	Reims Cessna F.152 II	1976		16. 9.86	Canx as WFU 14.3.89.
G-WACD	Reims Cessna F.152 II	1979		16. 9.86	Collided in mid-air with Cessna 182R G-BLFV over Booker on 22.1.89 and crashed. Canx as destroyed 29.3.89.
G-WACE	Reims Cessna F.152 II	1978		16. 9.86	
G-WACF	Cessna 152 II	152-84852	N628GH (LV-PMB)/N628GH	20. 1.87	
G-WACG	Cessna 152 II	152-85536	ZS-KXY (N93699)	4.11.86	
G-WACH	Reims Cessna FA.152 Aerobat	0425		18. 6.87	
G-WACI	Beechcraft 76 Duchess	ME-289	N6703Y	26. 7.88	
G-WACJ	Beechcraft 76 Duchess	ME-278	N6700Y	3. 1.89	
G-WACK	Short SD.3-60 Var.100	SH3611	G-BMAJ G-14-3611/(G-BKPO)	21. 4.86	To C-GPCE 4/99. Canx 16.3.99.
G-WACL	Reims Cessna F.172N Skyhawk II	1912	G-BHGG	19. 6.89	
G-WACO	Waco UPF-7	5400	N29903 NC29903	28. 1.87	Veered off runway on landing at Speke on 15.4.89 & crashed through the old perimeter fence. CofA expired 13.5.90. (On rebuild 4/97)
G-WACP	PA-28-180 Cherokee Archer	28-7405007	G-BBPP N9559N	5. 4.89	
G-WACR	PA-28-180 Cherokee Archer	28-7505090	G-BCZF N9517N	18.12.86	
G-WACS	Reims Cessna F.152 II	1827	D-EFGZ	28. 5.86	To G-BVTM 8/94. Canx.
G-WACT	Reims Cessna F.152 II	1908	G-BKFT	24. 6.86	
G-WACU	Reims Cessna FA.152 Aerobat	0380	G-BJZU	10. 7.86	
G-WACV	Cessna 182N Skylane II	182-60466	G-AZEA N8926G	5. 8.86	Fatal crash at Gussetts Wood, Hambledon on 6.12.92. Canx as destroyed 30.3.93.
G-WACW	Cessna 172P Skyhawk II	172-74057	N5307K	16. 5.88	
G-WACX	Reims Cessna F.172M Skyhawk II	0910	G-BAEX	23. 6.86	To G-FNLY 3/89. Canx.
G-WACY	Reims Cessna F.172P Skyhawk II	2217	F-GDOZ	3.10.86	
G-WACZ	Reims Cessna F.172M Skyhawk II	1311	G-BCUK	19. 5.86	
G-WADE	Reims Cessna F.172N Skyhawk II	2036	G-BHMI	17. 1.84	Restored as G-BHMI 6/86. Canx.
G-WADI	PA-46-350P Malibu Mirage	4636205		8. 5.99	
G-WADS	Robinson R-22 Beta	1224	G-NICO	25. 4.96	
G-WAFC	Reims Cessna F.150M	1201	G-BDFI (OH-CGD)	10. 5.95	To G-DEND 6/97. Canx.
G-WAFT	BAe Jetstream Srs.4100	41024	G-4-024	30. 9.93	To G-MAJJ 2/95. Canx.
G-WAGG	Robinson R-22 Beta	2960		7. 7.99	
G-WAGI	Robinson R-22 Beta	0828	N26584	13. 7.88	To OH-HPO 11/98. Canx 20.10.98.
G-WAGY	Reims Cessna F.172N Skyhawk II	2008		8. 4.80	To EC-EQG. Canx 3.8.89.

Regn	Type	c/n	Previous identity	Regn date	Fate or immediate subsequent identity (if known)
G-WAIR	PA-32-301 Saratoga	32-8506010	N2607X	14. 1.91	
			N9577N		
G-WAIT	Cameron V-77 HAFB	2390		20.11.90	
G-WAKO	Waco UPF-7	5870	N39737	3. 7.91	Restored as N39737 1/93. Canx 22.9.92.
			NC39737		
G-WALK	Reims Cessna F.182Q Skylane II	0028	G-BEZM	14. 4.86	Restored as G-BEZM 8/89. Canx.
			F-WZDX		
G-WALL	Beechcraft 95-58PA Pressurised Baron	TJ-34	N6042S	10. 9.86	To N87RR 8/93. Canx 5.8.93.
G-WALS	Cessna A.152 Aerobat	A152-0843	N4614A	27. 9.88	Badly damaged in storms at Shoreham in 1/99.
G-WALT	Cameron Flying Castle SS HAFB (Disneyland Castle)	2556		22. 5.91	Canx as WFU 12.5.97.
G-WAND	BAe Jetstream Srs.4100	41011		25. 3.93	To G-MAJI 3/95. Canx.
G-WARA	PA-28-161 Warrior III	2842021	N9289N	3. 9.97	
			(G-WARA)/N9289N		
G-WARB	PA-28-161 Warrior III	2842034	N41286	4. 9.98	
G-WARC	PA-28-161 Warrior III	2842035	N41244	11. 9.98	
G-WARD	Taylor JT.1 Monoplane	WB.VI & PFA/1407		1.12.80	
G-WARE	PA-28-161 Warrior II	28-8416080	N4357L	21. 7.89	
G-WARF	Cessna 182S Skylane II	182-80546	N7089F	10. 6.99	
G-WARI	PA-28-161 Warrior II	28-8616038	N9276Y	9.12.88	To G-RSFT 12/95. Canx.
G-WARK	Schweizer Hughes 269C (300C)	S.1354		13.11.89	
G-WARM	Bell 206L-1 Long Ranger	45347	N18098	16. 4.80	To N5393X 4/84. Canx 2.4.84.
G-WARO	PA-28-161 Warrior III	2842015	N92946	24.10.97	
			(G-WARO)/N92946		
G-WARP	Cessna 182F Skylane	182-54633	G-ASHB	6. 6.95	
			"G-ASHA"/N3233U		
G-WARR	PA-28-161 Warrior II	28-7916321	N3074U	15. 9.88	
G-WARS	PA-28-161 Warrior III	2842022	N9281X	7.11.97	
			(G-WARS)/N9281X		
G-WARU	PA-28-161 Warrior III	2842023	N92880	6.11.97	
			(G-WARU)/N92880		
G-WARV	PA-28-161 Warrior III	2842036	N41247	9.10.98	
G-WARW	PA-28-161 Warrior III	2842037	N41254	17.11.98	
G-WARX	PA-28-161 Warrior III	2842038	N4126D	15.12.98	
G-WARY	PA-28-161 Warrior III	2842024	N9287X	13.11.97	
			(G-WARY)/N9287X		
G-WARZ	PA-28-161 Warrior III	2842025	N92844	26.11.97	
			(G-WARZ)/N92944		
G-WASH	Cameron N-850 HAFB	1451		3. 3.87	(For sale 7/96)
G-WASP	Brantly B-2B	445	G-ASXE	7. 2.77	
"G-WASR"	Westland/Saro P.531 (Executive-style interior mock-up)	-		----	Noted on the Westland stand at the 22nd SBAC Show, Farnborough on 4-10.9.61. Not built.
G-WATH	Thunder Colt 77A HAFB	2054		16. 9.91	CofA expired 4.3.94. Canx.5.12.96. To N76TS 1/98.
G-WATS	PA-34-220T Seneca III	34-8333058	G-BOVJ	3. 2.89	(Extensively damaged when struck by PA-28-161 G-BJCA at Wellesbourne Mountford on 21.5.96)
			N8202J		
G-WATT	Cameron Cooling Tower SS HAFB	2158		8.11.89	
G-WATZ	PA-28-151 Cherokee Warrior	28-7715220	N7641F	22. 6.89	To G-BXLY 9/97. Canx.
G-WAUS	BAe 146 Srs.200	E2008	G-5-146	21. 8.84	To (G-OHAP)/G-BMYE 8/86. Canx.
			G-WISC		
G-WAVE(1)	Sportavia-Putzer Fournier RF-9	011		18.10.84	NTU - Not imported. Canx by CAA 21.6.85.
G-WAVE(2)	Grob G-109B	6381		1. 8.85	Ditched in sea off St.Mary's, Isle of Scilly on 26.7.86 - salvaged and to AIB Farnborough.
G-WAWL	BAe Jetstream Srs.4100	41008		19.10.92	To G-MAJF 2/95. Canx.
G-WAWR	BAe Jetstream Srs.4100	41006		19.10.92	To G-MAJD 3/95. Canx.
G-WAYR	BAe Jetstream Srs.4100	41010		19.10.92	To G-MAJH 4/95. Canx.
G-WAZZ	Pitts S-1S Special (Built by T.H.Decarlo)	7-0332	G-BRRP	17. 6.94	
			N3TD		
G-WBAT	Wombat Gyrocopter	CJ-001	G-BSID	31. 5.90	Permit expired 4.3.97. Canx by CAA 12.7.99.
G-WBCV	Colt 105A HAFB	2019	G-BTNX	16. 6.94	Restored as G-BTNX 12/95. Canx.
G-WBMG	Cameron N Ele 90SS HAFB	3086	G-BUYV	5. 7.93	
G-WBPR	BAe 125 Srs.800B	258085	G-5-551	29. 9.87	
G-WBTS	Falconair F-11W-200	PFA/32-10070	G-BDPL	22.10.90	Damaged in gales at Hook on 16.10.87. (On rebuild 5/99 White Waltham)
G-WCAT	Colt Flying Mitt SS HAFB	1744		30. 5.90	Balloon Preservation Group "Washcat" (Extant 1/98)
G-WCEI	Socata MS.894E Rallye Minerva 220GT	12141	G-BAOC	28. 5.85	
G-WDEB	Thunder Ax7-77 HAFB	1606		26. 9.89	
G-WDEV	Westland SA.341G Gazelle 1	WA/1098	G-IZEL	30. 9.98	
			G-BBHW		
G-WDKR	Aerospatiale AS.355F1 Twin Squirrel	5115	G-NEXT	24. 7.95	Restored as G-NEXT 8.9.95. Canx.
			I-NEXT/G-NEXT/G-OMAV		
G-WEAC	BN-2A Mk.III-2 Trislander	1042	5H-AZD	16.12.94	
			G-BEFP/(4X-CCL)/G-BEFP/N30WA/JA6401/G-BEFP		
G-WEBB	PA-23-250 Aztec E	27-7305194	G-BJBU	22.10.84	To G-MLFF 1/90. Canx.
			N40476		
G-WEEZ	Mooney M.20J (205)	24-3176		13. 8.90	Canx by CAA 19.8.94.
G-WEKR	Aerospatiale AS.355F1 Twin Squirrel	5175	G-CHLA	27. 2.96	To G-EMAN 4/96. Canx.
			N818RL/C-FLXH/N818RL/N818R/N5798U		
G-WELA	Aerospatiale SA.341G Gazelle Srs.1	1145	G-SFTD	7. 9.92	To G-IYOB 9/92. Canx.
			G-RIFC/G-SFTD/N641HM/N341BB/F-WKQH		

Regn	Type	c/n	Previous identity	Regn date	Fate or immediate subsequent identity (if known)
G-WELD	Hughes 369HS (500)	110-0270S	G-FROG OO-KAR	26.11.81	To G-GASC 7/85. Canx.
G-WELI	Cameron N-77 HAFB	1078		26. 9.84	
G-WELL	Beechcraft E90 King Air	LW-198	N202CC (N7PB)/N202CC	18. 7.85	
G-WELS	Cameron N-65 HAFB	1297		7. 4.86	
G-WEND	PA-28RT-201 Arrow IV	28R-8118026	PH-SYL N8296L	8.11.82	
G-WENT	BAe Jetstream Srs.3102-09	838	G-IBLW G-31-838	15. 1.91	To G-OEDD 3/94. Canx.
G-WERY	Socata TB-20 Trinidad	305		2. 4.82	
G-WEST	Agusta A.109A	7213		21. 1.81	
G-WESX	CFM Streak Shadow	K.116-SA & PFA/161A-11561		2. 2.90	
G-WETI	Cameron N-31 HAFB	449		27.11.78	(Extant 2/97)
G-WEWE	Cessna A.185F Skywagon	A185-03804	OO-DCD (OO-PCN)/F-GDCD/F-ODIA/N4593E	.10.98R	NTU - To G-BYBP 10/98. Canx.
G-WFEP	ATR-42-310	149	N4210G F-WWEV	9. 2.98	
G-WFFW	PA-28-161 Warrior II	28-8116161	N8342A	26.10.93	
G-WFOX	Robinson R-22 Beta	2826		2. 6.98	(Struck ground with tail rotor at Tatenhill on 7.7.99 during start-up)
G-WFRD	Bell 206L-4 Long Ranger	52007	D-HSHH	1.11.95	Badly damaged on landing 15.11.97 Sandon, nr.Chelmsford. Canx as destroyed 23.4.98. (Reserved as N5BQ in 4/98) (Damaged fuselage at Stapleford in 5/98)
G-WGAL	Bell 206B JetRanger III	3165	G-OICS N678TM	22. 3.93	
G-WGCL	Rockwell Commander 685	12043	CS-AQO N57028	7.11.95	
G-WGCS	PA-18-95 Super Cub (L-18C-PI) (Frame No. 18-1500)	18-1528	(G-BLSV) ALAT F-MBCH/51-15528	21.12.84	
G-WGEL	Boeing 737-2U4 (Line No. 652)	22161	(G-BPNY) G-ILFC/G-BOSL	3. 7.88	To VT-SIB 11/93. Canx 19.11.93.
G-WGHB	Canadair (CL-30) T-33AN Silver Star Mk.3	T33-640	CF-EHB RCAF 21640	9. 5.74	
G-WGSC	Pilatus PC-6/B2-H4 Turbo-Porter	848	(G-BRVM) OE-ECS	2. 1.90	
G-WHAT	Colt 77A HAFB	1911		15. 3.91	
G-WHAZ	Agusta-Bell 206A JetRanger	8112	OH-HRE G-WHAZ/OH-HRE	26. 6.97	
G-WHDP	Cessna 182S Skylane II	182-80178	N178TC	12. 5.98	
G-WHEE	Cyclone Pegasus Quantum 15	7510		26. 3.99	
G-WHFO	Colt Whisky Bottle 10SS HAFB	2125	G-BUCN	19. 3.92	To ZU-HZW 2/97. Canx 21.10.96.
G-WHIM	Colt 77A HAFB	1476		10. 4.89	
G-WHIR	Montgomerie-Bensen B.8MR Gyrocopter	G/01A-1142	G-BROT	9.10.89	Fatal crash on the Island of Coll, Stornoway (date?). Canx as WFU 7.12.98.
G-WHIT	Westland-Bell 47G-3B1 (Line No. WAS/198)	WA/571	A2638 E4672/XV317	14.10.80	To OY-HDH 2/84. Canx 7.2.84.
G-WHIZ	Pitts S-1 Special	353-H		18. 5.77	No Permit issued. Canx by CAA 26.3.97. Probably taken to Australia by owned.
"G-WHIZ"	Vickers 701 Viscount	17	G-AMOE	----	Half of fuselage mated to G-AOHJ. (Was preserved in 4/77 at Lampton Pleasure Park) Broken up in 3/93.
"G-WHIZ"	Vickers 732 Viscount	75	G-ANRS SU-AKY/G-ANRS/OD-ACH/G-ANRS/OD-ACH/G-ANRS	----	Used as a gift shop at Rhoose-Cardiff carried these marks unofficially. Scrapped in 2/96.
G-WHOG	CFM Streak Shadow	K.253-SA & PFA/206-12776		21. 9.94	
G-WHOW	Thunder Ax7-65 HAFB	1972		29. 4.91	To N836TC 3/95. Canx 17.1.95.
G-WHRL	Schweizer 269C (300C)	S.1453	EC-GGX CS-HDG/G-WHRL/N41S	19. 4.90	
G-WHST	Eurocopter AS.350B2 Ecureuil	2915	G-BWYA	9. 8.96	
G-WHYZ	Hughes 369HS (500)	125-0785S	5B-CGZ N9265F	28. 9.88	To EC-EVZ 7/90. Canx 28.2.90.
G-WIBB	Jodel D.18	PFA/169-11640		18. 6.96	
G-WIBS	CASA I-131E Jungmann Srs.2000	2005	E3B-401 Spanish AF	25. 3.99	
G-WICH	Clutton FRED Srs.2	PFA/29-10331		3. 1.79	No Permit issued. (Based in Perth, Australia) Canx by CAA 2.9.91.
G-WICK	Partenavia P.68B Victor	169	G-BGFZ	27.11.79	To F-GNHI. Canx 20.1.94.
G-WIDE	Short SD.3-60 Var.100	SH3601		17. 1.84	To N360SA 10/82. Canx 29.10.82.
G-WIEN	Rans S-10 Sakota	1089-065 & PFA/194-11770		30. 3.90	No Permit to Fly issued. Canx by CAA 6.9.95. To G-BWIL 10/95.
G-WIGL	Robinson R-22 Beta	2713		30. 6.97	DBR 21.11.97 at Wellesbourne Mountford. Canx 23.3.98 as WFU
G-WILD	Aerotek Pitts S-1T Special	1017	ZS-LMM	6.12.85	
G-WILG	WSK PZL-104 Wilga 35	62153	G-AZYJ SP-WEA(2)	15. 4.97	
G-WILI	PA-32R-301 Saratoga SP (Originally regd with c/n 32R-8613004 in error - this belongs to N9289Y)	3213004	N9128N N9582N	21.11.88	To OO-RAG 6/95. Canx 30.5.95.
G-WILK	Beechcraft B200 Super King Air	BB-955	G-BOBM N999P/N666EC/N18481	19.12.88	To N933RT 3/92. Canx 20.3.92.
G-WILL	Agusta-Bell 206B JetRanger III	8576		23. 5.79	To HB-XOD 2/83. Canx 2.2.83.
G-WILO	Bell 206B JetRanger III	3053	ZS-HIV	19. 9.86	To N345BB 10/91. Canx 19.9.91.

Regn	Type	c/n	Previous identity	Regn date	Fate or immediate subsequent identity (if known)
G-WILS	PA-28RT-201T Turbo Arrow IV	28R-8431005	PH-DPD N4330W	16. 1.96	
G-WILX	Aerospatiale AS.350B Ecureuil	1205	G-RAHM G-UNIC/G-COLN/G-BHIV	18. 5.90	Canx 29.10.90 on sale to Monaco. To F-WQJY.
G-WILY	Rutan LongEz	1200 & PFA/74A-10724		8. 6.83	(Stored off airfield 4/97)
G-WIMP	Colt 56A HAFB	755		13. 2.86	
G-WIND	Boeing 707-323C (Line No. 354)	18689	N7555A (OD-AGK)/N7555A	11. 8.78	To J6-SLF 3/82. Canx 17.3.82.
G-WINE	Thunder Ax7-77Z HAFB	472		25.11.82	
G-WING	Cessna 404 Titan	404-0442	(N2680H)	10.10.79	Overshot on landing at Yeadon on 4.2.80 & w/o. Canx by CAA 4.2.87.
G-WINK	American Aviation AA-5B Tiger	AA5B-0327	N74658	14.12.90	
G-WINS	PA-32-300 Cherokee Six	32-7640065	N8476C	24. 4.91	
G-WIRE	Aerospatiale AS.355F1 Twin Squirrel	5312	G-CEGB G-BLJL	22. 1.90	
G-WIRL	Robinson R-22 Beta	0671		27. 7.87	
G-WISC	BAe 146 Srs.200	E2008		3. 3.82	To G-5-146/G-WAUS 8/84. Canx.
G-WISH	Lindstrand Cake SS HAFB (Birthday Cake shape)	006		14.12.92	
G-WISK	Schweizer Hughes 269C (300C)	S.1463	N41S	8. 5.90	To SE-JBB. Canx 7.12.92.
G-WISP	Robinson R-44 Astro	0566		16. 3.99	
G-WISS	BAe ATP	2020	(N851AW) G-WISS/G-11-20	12. 6.89	NTU - To G-11-20/N851AW 1/90. Canx 3.1.90.
G-WITE	Cessna 414A Chancellor	414A-0229	G-LOVO G-KENT/N8828K	27. 8.85	To OO-CJP 2/92. Canx 12.2.92.
G-WITT	PA-31P-425 Pressurized Navajo	31P-7300168	(LN-BGZ) G-WITT/G-BBRL/N66806	10. 8.81	To ZK-ZNZ 8/84. Canx 22.8.84.
G-WIXI	Avions Mudry CAP.10B	279		27. 1.98	
G-WIXY	Avions Mudry/CAARP CAP.10B	77	F-BXHQ	27. 3.81	To F-GEOR 6/87. Canx 21.5.87.
G-WIZA	Robinson R-22 Beta	0861	G-PERL N90815	16.11.94	
G-WIZB	Grob G-115A	8104	EI-CAD (D-EGVV)	2. 9.98	
G-WIZD	Lindstrand LBL-180A HAFB	066		12.11.93	
G-WIZO	PA-34-220T Seneca III	34-8133171	N8413U	16.12.86	
G-WIZR	Robinson R-22 Beta	2799		9. 3.98	
G-WIZY	Robinson R-22 Beta	0566	G-BMWX N24196	26. 8.97	
G-WIZZ	Agusta-Bell 206B JetRanger II	8540		7.12.77	
G-WJAN	Boeing 757-21K (Line No. 746)	28674		18. 3.97	
G-WJMN	Rockwell Commander 114	14274	N4954W	29. 8.79	To G-OLFT 3/85. Canx.
G-WJPN	Beechcraft 65-A80 Queen Air (A80-8800 conv.)	LD-228	N197MC	14. 7.97	To EC-G.. Canx 13.11.98.
G-WKRD	Eurocopter AS.350B2 Ecureuil	2668	G-BUJG G-HEAR/G-BUJG	16. 3.99	
G-WLAC	PA-18-150 Super Cub	18-8899	G-HAHA G-BSWE/N9194P	2. 6.98	
G-WLAD	BAC One-Eleven Srs.304AX	BAC.112	C-FQBO CF-QBO/G-ATPI	1.11.84	To 5N-OVE. Canx 9.5.91.
G-WLCY	BAe 146 Srs.200	E2030	N172US N352PS	26. 3.96	To G-ZAPL 5/97. Canx.
G-WLGA	WSK PZL-104 Wilga 80 (Originally regd with c/n CF21930932)	CF21910932	EC-FYY F-GMLR	8.11.96	
G-WLLY	Bell 206B JetRanger	405	G-OBHH G-WLLY/G-RODY/G-ROGR/G-AXMM/N1469W	24. 3.93	
G-WMAA	MBB Bo.105DBS-4 (Rebuilt using new airframe S.914 .94)	S.135/914	G-PASB VH-LSA/G-BDMC/D-HDEC	8. 9.94	
G-WMAN	Aerospatiale SA.341G Gazelle 1	1277	ZS-HUR N4491R/YV-54CP	4. 8.99	
G-WMCC	BAe Jetstream Srs.3102-01	601	G-31-601 (N.....)/G-TALL/G-31-601	22. 9.83	Stored engineless in 8/96. Canx 26.11.97 on sale to USA, but parted out at Birmingham, UK.
G-WMCN	Robinson R-44 Astro	0320		9. 4.97	Canx as destroyed 18.2.99.
G-WMPA	Aerospatiale AS.355F2 Twin Squirrel	5401		7. 2.89	
G-WMTM	American Aviation AA-5B Tiger	AA5B-1035	N4517V	8. 1.91	
G-WNGS	Cameron N-105 HAFB	4385		15. 7.98	
G-WOLD	Scheibe SF-25E Super Falke	4323	(G-BOVM) N250BA/(D-KECZ)	24. 8.88	To F-CHSC. Canx 20.2.92.
G-WOLF	PA-28-140 Cruiser	28-7425439	OY-TOD	20. 3.80	
G-WOLL	Grumman G.164A AgCat	797	G-AYTM N6555	3. 2.81	To EC-ECP 5/87. Canx 19.3.87.
G-WOOD	Beechcraft 95-B55A Baron	TC-1283	SE-GRC G-AYID/SE-EXK	17. 9.79	
G-WOOF	Enstrom 480	5027		3. 3.98	
G-WOOL	Colt 77A HAFB	2044		23. 2.93	
G-WORK	Thunder Ax10-180 Srs.2 HAFB	2396		12. 5.93	To DQ-PBF 11/97. Canx 3.11.97.
G-WOSP	Bell 206B JetRanger III	2545	N18096	29.11.78	To EC-938/EC-GCN 8/95. Canx 5.5.95.
G-WOTG	PBN BN-2T Turbine Islander	2139	(ZF444) G-WOTG/G-BJYT	10.11.83	

Regn	Type	c/n	Previous identity	Regn date	Fate or immediate subsequent identity (if known)
G-WOTS	PA-34-200T Seneca II	34-7870356	G-SEVL N36742	1. 8.89	To G-DARE 11/91. Canx.
G-WOZA	PA-32RT-300 Lance II	32R-7885144	G-BYBB N31957	23. 5.91	To D-EVIO(2) 7/99. Canx 13.7.99.
G-WPAS	Boeing MD-900 Explorer	900-00053	N92237	1. 7.98	
G-WPLC	Beechcraft 200 Super King Air	BB-803	N3825S N380TT/N3825S	11. 4.89	To 5Y-TWA 11/92. Canx 5.11.92.
G-WPUI	Cessna P.172D	P172-57173	G-AXPI 9M-AMR/N11B/(N8573X)	24. 6.80	To EI-BRS 9/85. Canx 19.8.85.
G-WRAY	PA-32RT-300T Turbo Lance II	32R-7887046	OY-BRD (OY-BRO)	5. 9.79	To G-WROY 1/83. Canx.
G-WRCF	Beechcraft 200 Super King Air	BB-472	N4489A YV-247CP	15. 1.88	To N305JS 1/98. Canx 19.1.98.
G-WREN	Aerotek Pitts S-2A Special	2229	N947	28. 1.81	
G-WRFM	Enstrom 280C-UK Shark	1202	G-CTSI G-BKIO/(G-BKHN)/SE-HLB	21. 4.89	
G-WRIT	Colt 77A HAFB (Originally regd as a Thunder Ax7-77 HAFB)	1328		15. 9.88	
G-WRLD	Cameron R-15 Gas Balloon	2365		31. 7.90	Canx by CAA 10.4.95. (Was given export CofA)
G-WRMN	Glaser-Dirks DG-400	4-155		27. 1.86	To SX-ABH 2/95. Canx 20.2.95.
G-WROX	PA-31-350 Navajo Chieftain	31-7952092	G-BNZI N3517T	21. 9.89	To OH-PRE(2). Canx 28.5.93.
G-WROY	PA-32RT-300T Turbo Lance II	32R-7887046	G-WRAY OY-BRD/(OY-BRO)	26. 1.83	To HB-PKU 5/87. Canx 24.4.87.
G-WRWR	Robinson R-22 Beta	2964		20. 7.99	
G-WSEC	Enstrom F-28C	398	G-BONF N51661	19.12.88	
G-WSFT	PA-23-250 Aztec F	27-7754059	G-BTHS N62824	18. 6.86	Undercarriage collapsed on landing at Morlaix, France on 2.5.99.
G-WSJE	Beechcraft 200 Super King Air	BB-484	N84KA	30.10.86	Fatal crash at Mac's Garage, Leslie Road, Rayleigh on 12.9.87 shortly after take-off from Southend & DBF. Canx as destroyed 12.10.88.
G-WSKY	Enstrom 280C-UK-2 Shark	1037	G-BEEK	25. 7.83	
G-WSOC	BAe Jetstream Srs.3111	696	G-31-696	. .86R	NTU - To G-BMNR 5/86. Canx.
G-WSSC	PA-31-350 Navajo Chieftain	31-7952247	EI-BRC G-WSSC/N3543W	29.11.79	To G-OAKC 4/89. Canx.
G-WSSL	PA-31-350 Navajo Chieftain	31-7852140	N27734	20.10.78	Restored as N27734 7/93. Canx 17.6.93.
G-WTBC	Partenavia P.68C Victor	219	G-SITU G-NEWU/G-BHJX	20. 2.91	To TF-FTP 8/95. Canx 1.8.95.
G-WTFA	Reims Cessna F.182P	0022	PH-VDH D-EJCL	6.10.86	Crashed in Briere Marsh, Montoir de Bretagne, France on 30.5.88. Canx by CAA 26.2.93. Rebuilt & re-regd as G-BUVO in 3/93.
G-WTMK	Robin DR.400/180 Regent	1996		22. 6.90	DBF after running off the runway and hitting the landing lights on landing at Le Touquet on 7.10.90. Canx as destroyed 7.11.90.
G-WTVA	Cessna 404 Titan Courier II	404-0056	N5438G	1. 3.78	To G-BKVH 8/83. Canx.
G-WTVB	Cessna 404 Titan Courier II	404-0088	N8784G	8. 3.78	To 5Y-EAB 9/88. Canx 8.9.88.
G-WTVC	Cessna 404 Titan Courier II	404-0050	N5432G	15. 2.78	Restored as N5432G 5/85. Canx 30.5.85.
G-WTVE	Cessna 404 Titan Courier II	404-0220	N88682	11. 5.78	To G-BKTW 6/83. Canx.
G-WTVF	Cessna 402B Businessliner	402B-1324	N6361X	30. 7.79	To 5H-TZZ 8/81. Canx 4.8.81.
G-WUFF	Europa Avn Europa	PFA/247-12942		19. 1.99	
G-WULF	WAR Focke-Wulf FW.190 Replica	204 & PFA/81-10328		24. 2.78	
G-WULL	American Aviation AA-5A Cheetah	AA5A-0878	N27153	12. 5.82	Overshot on landing at Elstree on 4.1.86 and hit trees about 100 yards from the south-east end of the runway. Rebuilt & re-regd as G-OCWC 5/86. Canx.
G-WURL	Robinson R-22 Beta	2740	G-BXMS	13.10.97	
G-WVBF	Lindstrand LBL-210A HAFB	312		6.12.95	
G-WWAL	PA-28R-180 Cherokee Arrow B	28R-30461	G-AZSH N4612J	23.10.98	
G-WWAS	PA-34-220T Seneca III	34-8133222	G-BPPB N83270	2. 3.95	
G-WWHL	Beechcraft 200 Super King Air	BB-239	G-BLAE I-ELCO/N517JM/N17649	9. 4.84	Restored as N517JM 9/88. Canx 4.8.88.
G-WWII	Vickers-Supermarine 379 Spitfire F.XIVe	6S/663452	Indian AF SM832	9. 7.79	To F-AZSJ 2/98. Canx 6.2.98.
G-WWIZ	Beechcraft 95-58 Baron	TH-429	G-GAMA G-BBSD	18.10.96	
G-WWJC	Fokker F.28-4000 Fellowship	11133	PH-ZBU PH-EXO	10.10.79	To F-GDFC 5/81. Canx 23.5.81.
G-WWUK	Enstrom F-28A-UK (Composite fitted with cabin of EC-CKH c/n 188)	141	G-BFFN HB-XEA	9. 3.83	To G-KOLY 3/89. Canx.
G-WWWG	Europa Avn Europa	40 & PFA/247-12597		31. 7.95	
G-WWWW	Aerospatiale AS.355F1 Twin Squirrel	5355		9. 2.87	To F-GKBD 5/90. Canx 12.4.90.
G-WYAT	CFM Streak Shadow SA	PFA/206-12993		9. 6.97	

Regn	Type	c/n	Previous identity	Regn date	Fate or immediate subsequent identity (if known)
G-WYCH	Cameron Witch 90SS HAFB (Witch on broomstick plus cat!)	1330		30. 9.86	
G-WYLX	Cessna 550 Citation II (Unit No.418)	550-0419	VH-JVS G-JETD/N1217N	23.12.91	To G-DCFR 11/95. Canx.
G-WYMP	Reims Cessna F.150J	0521	G-BAGW SE-FKM	26. 2.82	
G-WYMR	Robinson R-44 Astro	0439		15. 4.98	
G-WYND	Wittman W.8 Tailwind	PFA/31-12407		2. 8.99	
G-WYNN	Rand Robinson KR-2 (Originally regd as c/n PFA/129-11093; probably composite of both projects)	PFA/129-11141		28. 8.85	
G-WYNS	Aero Designs Pulsar XP	PFA/202-11976		22. 2.91	
G-WYNT	Cameron N-56 HAFB	1038		3. 4.84	
G-WYPA	MBB Bo.105DBS/4	S.815	D-HDZY	27.10.89	
G-WYRL	Robinson R-22 Alpha	0452	N8556D	25. 1.85	To EI-BVR 4/88. Canx 28.4.88.
G-WYTE	Bell 47G-2A-1	3294	TF-MUN 64-15426	8.12.83	Canx 6.10.94 on sale to USA, was not in fact regd there and was exported to Costa Rica. To TI-AVR 12/94.
G-WYZZ	Air Command 532 Elite	0429 & G/04-1103	G-BPAK	22. 1.90	Permit to Fly expired 27.3.90. Canx by CAA 22.3.99.
G-WZOL	Tiger Cub RL5B-LWS Sherwood Ranger	PFA/237-12887	G-MZOL	20. 1.99	
G-WZZZ	Colt AS-42 Hot Air Airship (Rebuilt 84/85 using new AS-56 envelope c/n 607)	459		10.12.82	

G-X

G-X

Regn	Type	c/n	Previous identity	Regn date	Fate or immediate subsequent identity (if known)
G-XAIR	BAe 146 RJ85	E2235		7. 5.93	To G-6-235/HB-IXK 6/93. Canx 25.6.93.
G-XALP	Schweizer 269C (300C)	S.1314		27. 6.88	
G-XANT	Cameron N-105 HAFB	3003		4. 3.93	
G-XARJ	BAe 146 RJ85	E2233	G-6-233	8. 6.93	To G-6-233/HB-IXH 6/93. Canx 23.6.93.
G-XARV	ARV1 Super 2	010	G-OPIG G-BMSJ	8.11.95	
G-XBHX	Boeing 737-36N (Line No. 3031)	28572		21. 5.98	
G-XCEL	Aerospatiale AS.355F1 Twin Squirrel	5324	G-HBAC G-HJET/F-GEOX/F-WYMC/OY-HDL	16. 5.95	
G-XCUB	PA-18-150 Super Cub	18-8109036		1. 5.81	
G-XENA	PA-28-161 Cherokee Warrior II	28-7716158	N3486Q	29. 6.98	
G-XGBE	Cessna 340A II	340A-0905	G-MAGS N2701D	2. 9.91	Force landed in a field at Sheepy Magna, Leics. on 7.9.93. Canx by CAA 22.3.94.
G-XIAN	BAe 146 Srs.100-21	E1019	G-5-019 G-5-523/G-5-019	22. 8.86	To B-2701 9/86. Canx 8.9.86.
G-XIIX	Robinson R-22 Beta	0736		8. 2.88	
G-XING	Embraer EMB-121A Xingu	121-030	PT-MAW	30. 7.80	To G-XTWO 4/82. Canx.
G-XITD	Cessna 310G (Includes parts from G-OITD)	310G-0048	G-ASYV HB-LBY/N8948Z	15.10.87	Damaged in wheels-up landing at Leavesden on 14.7.88. Canx as WFU 10.1.89. (Instructional Airframe 1/92 Arbury College, Cambridge)
G-XLTG	Cessna 182S Skylane	182-80234	N9571L	17. 7.98	
G-XLXL	Robin DR.400/160 Knight	813	G-BAUD	3. 1.92	
G-XMAF	Gulfstream G.1159A Gulfstream III	407	N17603	16. 8.84	To N407GA 12/91. Canx 12.12.91.
G-XMAN	Boeing 737-36N (Line No. 3041)	28573		18. 6.98	
G-XMAS	PA-32RT-300 Lance II	32-7885130	N31793	23. 5.79	To D-EBRB 6/82. Canx 15.6.82.
G-XPBI	Letov LK-2M Sluka	PFA/263-13341		4.12.98	
G-XPOL	Aerospatiale AS.355F1 Twin Squirrel	5177	G-BPRF N363E	3. 4.91	To G-OTSP 3/98. Canx.
G-XPTS	Robinson R-44 Astro	0433		11. 3.98	
G-XPXP	Aero Designs Pulsar XP	218 & PFA/202-11958		30. 3.92	
G-XRAY	Rand Robinson KR-2	PFA/129-11227		30. 4.87	
G-XRMC	BAe 125 Srs.800B	258180	G-5-675	3. 7.90	
G-XSDJ	Europa Avn Europa XS	PFA/247-13378		3. 2.99	
G-XSFT	PA-23-250 Aztec F	27-7754103	G-CPPC G-BGBH/N63773	18. 6.86	
G-XSKY	Cameron N-77 HAFB	2508		26. 3.91	
G-XTEC	Robinson R-22 Beta	1478	G-BYCK N101EJ	23.10.98	
G-XTEK	Robinson R-44 Astro	0647		11. 8.99	
G-XTOR	BN-2A Mk.III-2 Trislander (New fuselage c/n 1065/N3266G (NTU) fitted 2/96)	359	G-BAXD	1. 4.96	
G-XTRA	Extra EA.230	012A	D-EDLF	21. 1.87	
G-XTRS	Extra EA.300/L	047	D-EXJH	8.10.98	
G-XTUN	Westland Bell 47G-3B1 (Line No. WAP/81)	WA/382	G-BGZK XT223	11. 5.99	
G-XTWO	Embraer EMB-121A Xingu	121-030	G-XING PT-MAW	1. 4.82	Canx 7.6.88 on sale to Brazil. To French Navy as 30.
G-XUSA	Cessna A.150K Aerobat	A150-00050	N8350M	9.10.86	Fatal crash in a field at Maldon, Essex on 25.9.87. (Badly damaged remains to the AIU at Farnborough for investigation) Canx as destroyed 25.10.88.

Regn	Type	c/n	Previous identity	Regn date	Fate or immediate subsequent identity (if known)
G-XVIA	Vickers-Supermarine 361 Spitfire LF.XVIe (Regd with c/n CBAF/11581)	CBAF.IX.4640	8075M RW382/"RW729"/7245M/RW382	2. 7.91	To N382RW. Canx 17.3.95.
G-XVIB	Vickers-Supermarine 361 Spitfire LF.XVIe	CBAF.IX.4610	N476TE G-XVIB/8071M/7451M/TE476	3. 7.89	Restored as N476TE 1/96. Canx 21.9.95.
G-XVIE	Vickers-Supermarine 361 Spitfire LF.XVIe	CBAF.IX.3807	8073M 7281M/7257M/TB252	3. 7.92	(Stored 7/97)
G-XWWF	Lindstrand LBL-56A HAFB	595		25. 2.99	
G-XXEA	Sikorsky S-76C	760492		21.12.98	
G-XXII	Agusta-Bell 206B JetRanger II	8530	G-GGCC G-BEHG	25.11.93	To G-INVU 3/95. Canx.
G-XXIV	Agusta-Bell 206B JetRanger III	8717		27. 4.89	
G-XXVI	Sukhoi SU-26M	0410	CCCP-0401	2. 4.93	
G-Y					G-Y
G-YABU	Gulfstream Commander 695A	96083	N90GA	11. 7.85	To N901AS 9/87. Canx 23.9.87.
G-YAKA	Yakovlev Yak-50	822303	LY-ANJ DOSAAF 80	10.11.94	
G-YAKI	Aerostar Yakovlev Yak-52	866904	LY-ANM DOSAAF 100 (yellow)	20. 9.94	
G-YAKL	Yakovlev Yak-50	832606	"RA-2606" RA-01334/(ex)	5. 4.94	To N50MY 3/97. Canx 5.7.96.
G-YAKM	Yakovlev Yak-55M	920506	RA-01333 DOSAAF 40	. .94R	Marks reportedly reserved.
G-YAKO	Yakovlev Yak-52	822203	RA-01493	8. 5.99	
G-YAKS	IAV Bacau Yakovlev Yak-52	9311708		16.12.93	
G-YAKX	IDA Bacau Yakovlev Yak-52	9111307	RA-9111307/DOSAAF 27	13. 3.96	
G-YAKY	Aerostar Yakovlev Yak-52	844109	LY-AKX DOSAAF 24 (red)	26. 2.96	
G-YANK	PA-28-181 Archer II	28-8090163	N81314	19. 3.93	
G-YAWW	PA-28R-201T Turbo Arrow IV	28R-8031024	N2929Y	15.11.90	
G-YBAA	Reims Cessna FR.172J Rocket	0579	5Y-BAA	15.11.84	
G-YCUB	PA-18-150 Super Cub	1809077	N4993X N4157T	23. 8.96	
G-YEAR	Revolution Helicopters Mini-500	0050		6.10.95	
G-YELL	Murphy Rebel	PFA/232-12381		1. 5.95	
G-YEOM	PA-31-350 Navajo Chieftain	31-8352022	N41108	3. 1.89	
G-YEWS	Rotorway Exec 152	DGP-1 & 3850		22. 6.89	Permit expired 17.6.93. (Stored 8/95 - for sale 10/97) Canx by CAA 22.3.99.
G-YFLY	VPM M-16 Tandem Trainer	VPM16-UK-114	G-BWGI	14.10.96	
G-YIII	Reims Cessna F.150L	0827	PH-CEX	5. 6.80	
G-YIIK	Robinson R-44 Astro	0640		9. 8.99	
G-YJBM	Airbus A.320-231	362	G-IEAF F-WWIN	28. 9.93	
G-YJET	Montgomerie-Bensen B.8MR Gyrocopter	G/01-1072	G-BMUH	25. 9.96	
G-YKEN	Robinson R-22 Beta	2875		22.10.98	
G-YKIV	Reims Cessna F.150L	0825	PH-CEV	5. 6.80	Fatal crash into the sea off Flamborough Head on 8.6.83. Canx as destroyed 5.12.83.
G-YKSZ	IAV Bacau Yakovlev Yak-52	9311709		16.12.93	
G-YLAN	PA-31-350 Navajo Chieftain	31-8152080	N40790	29. 4.88	To G-BYRN 5/90. Canx.
G-YLYB	Cameron N-105 HAFB	4482		15. 1.98	
G-YMBO	Robinson R-22 Mariner	2054M	OY-HFR	21. 8.95	
G-YMMA	Boeing 777-236ER (Line No. 242)	30302	N5017Q	. 8.98R	(delivery due 6.1.00)
G-YMMB	Boeing 777-236ER (Line No. 265)	30303		. 8.98R	(delivery due 12.1.00)
G-YMMC	Boeing 777-236ER (Line No. 268)	30304		. 8.98R	(delivery due 1.2.00)
G-YMMD	Boeing 777-236ER (Line No. 269)	30305		. 8.98R	(delivery due 8.2.00)
G-YMME	Boeing 777-236ER (Line No. 275)	30306		. 8.98R	(delivery due 3/00)
G-YMMF	Boeing 777-236ER (Line No. 281)	30307		. 8.98R	(delivery due 5/00)
G-YMMG	Boeing 777-236ER (Line No. ...)	?		. 8.98R	
G-YMMH	Boeing 777-236ER (Line No. ...)	?		. 8.98R	
G-YMMI	Boeing 777-236ER (Line No. ...)	?		. 8.98R	
G-YMMJ	Boeing 777-236ER (Line No. ...)	?		. 8.98R	

Regn	Type	c/n	Previous identity	Regn date	Fate or immediate subsequent identity (if known)
G-YMMK	Boeing 777-236ER (Line No. ...)	?		. 8.98R	
G-YMML	Boeing 777-236ER (Line No. ...)	?		. 8.98R	
G-YMMM	Boeing 777-236ER (Line No. ...)	?		. 8.98R	
G-YMMN	Boeing 777-236ER (Line No. ...)	?		. 8.98R	
G-YMMO	Boeing 777-236ER (Line No. ...)	?		. 8.98R	
G-YMMP	Boeing 777-236ER (Line No. ...)	?		. 8.98R	(delivery due in 2002)
G-YMRU(1)	Embraer EMB.110P2 Bandeirante	110-201	(PT-GLT)	. .79R	NTU - To G-BGNK 4/79. Canx.
G-YMRU(2)	BAC One-Eleven Srs.304AX	BAC.110	C-FQBN CF-QBN/G-ATPH	.17. 3.84	To G-BPNX 4/88. Canx.
G-YMYM	Lindstrand Ice Cream Cone SS HAFB	007		7. 7.93	
G-YNOT	Rollason Druine D.62B Condor	RAE/649	G-AYFH	10.11.83	
G-YOGI	Robin DR.400/140B Major	1090	G-BDME	1.10.86	
G-YORK	Reims Cessna F.172M Skyhawk II	1354	PH-LUY F-WLIT	14.12.78	
G-YOTT	Cessna 425 Conquest I	425-0054	N345GA G-NORC/(G-BICL)/(N6776P)	5. 7.88	To G-LILI 1/93. Canx.
G-YOYO	Pitts S-1E Special	PFA/09-10885	G-OTSW G-BLHE	22. 5.96	
G-YPSY	Andreasson BA.4B (Regd in error as c/n PFA/32-10352)	PFA/38-10352		7. 6.78	(Badly damaged on take-off and overturned at Bagby on 31.8.93)
G-YRAT	VPM M-16 Tandem Trainer	VPM16-UK-104		16.11.92	Badly damaged in forced landing 1½ miles SW of Kemble on 23.2.96. (Stored 6/97) Canx by CAA 18.6.96.
G-YRIL	Luscombe 8E Silvaire	5945	N1318B NC1318B	3. 2.92	
G-YROB	Air Command 532 Elite	AC.503 & G/04-1110		7. 2.89	Fatal crash at Beaumont-cum-Moze, Clacton on 24.12.90. Wreck to AIU at Farnborough 5/91. Canx by CAA 26.3.97.
G-YROI	Air Command 532 Elite	0002	N532CG	3. 9.87	
G-YROS	Montgomerie-Bensen B.8M Gyrocopter	G/01-1004		29. 1.81	
G-YROY	Montgomerie-Bensen B.8MR Gyrocopter	G/01A-1145		12. 9.89	
G-YSFT	PA-23-250 Aztec F	27-7754038	G-BEJT N62805	1.12.87	
G-YSKY	PA-31-350 Navajo Chieftain	31-7952155	N3529D	19. 1.88	To G-OSGB 1/99. Canx.
G-YSTT	PA-32R-301 Saratoga II HP	3246056	N848T	4. 8.97	
G-YTWO	Reims Cessna F.172M Skyhawk II	1396	PH-CIA	8. 6.79	Badly damaged on landing at Cromer on 12.10.97. (Stored at Sherburn in 6/98)
G-YUCS	PA-32R-301 Saratoga SP	3213007	G-BSOL N9130Z/N9590N	1.11.89	To HB-PEJ 5/95. Canx 11.5.95.
G-YUGO	HS.125 Srs.1B/R522	25094	G-ATWH HZ-BO1/G-ATWH	25. 8.88	Canx as WFU 29.3.93. (Open store 9/97)
G-YULL	PA-28-180 Cherokee E	28-5603	G-BEAJ 9H-AAC/N2390R	30. 3.79	
G-YUMM	Cameron N-90 HAFB	2723		12.12.91	
G-YUPI	Cameron N-90 HAFB	1602		12. 1.88	
G-YURO	Europa Avn Europa	001 & PFA/220-11981		6. 4.92	Permit expired 9.6.95. Canx as WFU 22.4.98. To Yorkshire Air Museum and on display 11/97.
G-YVBF	Lindstrand LBL-317S HAFB	505		2. 4.98	
G-YVET	Cameron V-90 HAFB	3182		11.10.93	

G-Z G-Z

Regn	Type	c/n	Previous identity	Regn date	Fate or immediate subsequent identity (if known)
G-ZAAR	Cessna 414 Chancellor	414-0909	N4641G	4. 5.78	To N1036M 12/79. Canx 20.12.79.
G-ZABC	Sky 90-24 HAFB	062		10. 4.97	
G-ZACH	Robin DR.400/100 Cadet	1831	G-FTIO	20.10.92	
G-ZADT	Colt 77A HAFB	1027	G-ZBCA	1. 9.89	To G-BTVH 9/91. Canx.
G-ZAIR	Zenair CH.601HD Zodiac	PFA/162-12194		21. 2.92	
G-ZAND	Robinson R-22 Beta	1679		11. 2.91	To OH-HRU 4/96. Canx 20.3.96.
G-ZAPA	Cessna 404 Titan II	404-0012	SE-GMH Swedish AF Fv.87003/SE-GMH/(N3943C)	10. 4.89	To N41059 5/92. Canx 20.5.92.
G-ZAPB	Cessna 404 Titan II	404-0048	G-HIGS G-ODAS/D-ICIK/LN-MAR/(SE-GZD)/(N5430G)	2. 6.89	To N8OBS 11/92. Canx 27.10.92.
G-ZAPC	Short SD.3-30 Var.100	SH3023	G-RNMO D-CDLD/G-BFZW/G-14-3023	26.11.90	Damaged in heavy landing at Speke on 3.1.97. Canx as destroyed 14.2.97.
G-ZAPD	Short SD.3-60 Var.300	SH3741	G-OLGW "G-LOGW"/G-BOFK/G-14-3741	6. 8.92	
G-ZAPE	Embraer EMB.110P1 Bandeirante	110-391	G-BPDL N115MQ/N2992C/PT-SFI	3.11.92	Fatal crash at Ponsonby Fell, 3m E of Sellafield, Cumbria on 13.1.93. Canx as destroyed 6.9.93.
G-ZAPF	Short SD.3-60 Var.100	SH3738	G-OLTN G-BOFH/G-14-3738	3. 2.93	To 4X-CSL 5/95. Canx 3.5.95.

Regn	Type	c/n	Previous identity	Regn date	Fate or immediate subsequent identity (if known)
G-ZAPG	Short SD.3-60 Var.100	SH3739	G-CPTL G-BOFI/G-14-3739	3. 3.93	To EI-COR 8/97. Canx 26.8.97.
G-ZAPH	Reims Cessna F.406 Caravan II	0049	N6589E	. .93R	NTU - Remained as N6589E. Canx.
G-ZAPI	Cessna 500 Citation I (Unit No.560)	500-0404	G-BHTT N2614H	13. 9.94	
G-ZAPJ(1)	ATR-42-512	457	F-WWET	. .95R	NTU - To F-GPYA 3/96. Canx.
G-ZAPJ(2)	ATR-42-312	113	EI-CIQ DQ-FEQ/F-WWEJ	17. 5.96	
G-ZAPK	BAe 146 Srs.200QC	E2148	G-BTIA ZS-NCB/G-BTIA/G-6-148/G-PRIN	25. 4.96	
G-ZAPL	BAe 146 Srs.200	E2030	G-WLCY N172US/N352PS	9. 5.97	
G-ZAPM	Boeing 737-33A (Line No. 2608)	27285	DQ-FJD N102AN/CS-TKG	2. 6.99	
G-ZAPP	Christen Eagle II	PFA/138-10890	G-TARA	11. 9.89	Fatal crash at Pleshey, Essex on 9.2.90 & extensively DBF. Canx as destroyed 14.5.90.
G-ZAPY	Robinson R-22 Beta	0788	G-INGB	8. 7.98	
G-ZARA	Nord 3400	37	37 ALAT "MAB"	18. 5.90	No Permit or CofA issued. Last known of on rebuild at Sibsey. Canx by CAA 30.6.97.
G-ZARI	American Aviation AA-5B Tiger	AA5B-0845	G-BHVY N28835	7. 3.86	
G-ZARV	ARV1 Super 2	PFA/152-13035		26. 2.97	
G-ZAZA	PA-18-95 Super Cub (L-18C-PI)	18-2041	D-ENAS R.Netherlands AF R-66/52-2441	1. 5.84	
G-ZBAC	Aerospatiale AS.350B Ecureuil	1847	G-SEBI G-BMCU	18. 5.87	To G-DJEM 6/89. Canx.
G-ZBCA	Colt 77A HAFB	1027		23. 2.87	To G-ZADT 9/89. Canx.
G-ZBHH	Hughes 269C (300C)	129-0869	G-GINZ F-GINZ/SE-HMX/PH-HAN/C-GFKF/N1091N	20. 8.99	
G-ZBRA	Thunder Ax10-160 HAFB	1530		4. 4.91	
G-ZEAL	Gates LearJet 35A	35A-275	N10872	26.11.79	To (N43PE)/N43FE 3/83. Canx 1.3.83.
G-ZEBO	Thunder Ax8-105 Srs.2 HAFB	2197	(N.....) G-ZEBO	22. 5.92	
G-ZEBR	Colt 210A HAFB	2272		10. 9.92	
G-ZEIN	Slingsby T.67M Firefly 260	2234		19. 7.95	
G-ZEIZ	Gates LearJet 36A	36A-047		16. 2.81	To N2972Q 12/82. Canx 6.12.82.
G-ZELL	Aerospatiale SA.341G Gazelle Srs.1	1280	F-GEQB(2) N49494	27. 4.90	To SX-HDK 11/95. Canx 30.11.95.
G-ZENO	Gates LearJet 35A	35A-429	G-GAYL G-ZING	16. 5.96	
G-ZEPI	Colt GA-42 Gas Airship	878	G-ISPY (G-BPRB)	9. 4.92	
G-ZEPP	Cameron D-96 Hot-Air Airship	361	(PH-ZEP) G-ZEPP	22. 6.78	To PH-ZEP 8/82. Canx 13.8.82.
G-ZEPY	Colt GA-42 Gas Airship	1299	G-BSCU	6. 2.92	
G-ZERO	American Aviation AA-5B Tiger	AA5B-0051	OO-PEC	3. 9.80	
G-ZEST	Gates LearJet 35A	35A-265	N1462B	18. 5.79	To G-LEAR 8/79. Canx.
G-ZEUS	Cessna 401	401-0165	G-ODJM G-BSIX/G-CAFE(2)/G-AWXM/N4065Q	8. 6.84	To G-OROG 1/85. Canx.
G-ZFDB	Aerospatiale AS.355F1 Twin Squirrel	5311	G-BLEV	2. 5.89	To G-LENI 8/95. Canx.
G-ZGBE	Beechcraft 58PA Pressurized Baron	TJ-275	G-BNKL N188JB/N6750V	27. 1.94	To N275EB 6/98. Canx 9.6.98.
G-ZIGG	Robinson R-22 Beta	1423		30. 5.90	Crashed at New Common Farm, Market Weston, Suffolk on 21.4.96. Canx by CAA 17.10.96.
G-ZIGI	Robin DR.400/180 Regent	2107		19.11.91	
G-ZING	Gates LearJet 35A	35A-429		9. 9.81	To G-GAYL 8/82. Canx.
G-ZIPA	Rockwell Commander 114A	14505	G-BHRA N5891N	3. 9.98	
G-ZIPI	Robin DR.400/180 Regent	1557		22. 2.82	
G-ZIPP	Cessna E310Q II	310Q-0738	G-BAYU N5953M	30. 6.80	Damaged on landing at Rotterdam on 26.1.94. Canx as destroyed 2.6.94. (Was reserved as PH-KOM /94 but found to be unrepairable and transported by road to Beek for spares).
G-ZIPS	Gates LearJet 35A	35A-365	(N4564S) G-ZONE	20.12.83	To G-SEBE 9/85. Canx.
G-ZIPY	Wittman W.8 Tailwind	PFA/31-11339		29. 5.91	
G-ZLIN	Moravan Zlin Z.326 Trener Master (Mod to Z.526 standard) (Note: c/n confirmed but conflicts with I-ETRM)	916	G-BBCR OH-TZF	30. 6.81	
G-ZLOJ	Beechcraft A36 Bonanza	E-1677	ZS-LOJ N6748J	11. 9.98	
G-ZLYN	Moravan Zlin Z.526F Trener Master	1255	OK-CMC YR-ZAB	4. 8.95	
G-ZONE	Gates LearJet 35A	35A-365		4. 2.81	To (N4564S)/G-ZIPS 12/83. Canx.
G-ZONK	Robinson R-44 Astro	0179	G-EDIE	16. 7.97	
G-ZOOI	Lindstrand LBL-105A HAFB	390		22. 5.96	
G-ZOOL	Reims Cessna FA.152 Aerobat	0357	G-BGXZ	11.11.94	
G-ZOOM	Gates LearJet 35A	35A-236		18. 7.79	To N8537B 1/81. Canx 20.1.81.
G-ZORO	Europa Avn Europa	PFA/247-12672		20. 6.95	
G-ZSFT	PA-23-250 Aztec F	27-7954063	G-SALT G-BGTH/N2551M	5. 4.89	

Regn	Type	c/n	Previous identity	Regn date	Fate or immediate subsequent identity (if known)
G-ZSOL	Moravan Zlin Z.50L	0025	EC-DLZ	11. 9.81	To N50ZA 2/97. Canx 22.1.97.
G-ZTED	Europa Avn Europa	PFA/247-12492		30. 4.96	
G-ZULU	PA-28-161 Warrior II	28-8316043	N4292X	25. 2.88	
G-ZUMP	Cameron N-77 HAFB (Rebuilt with new canopy c/n 1107 in 1985)	377		18. 1.78	(To British Balloon Museum .93) Canx as WFU 8.4.98.
G-ZUMY	Task Silhouette	25		30.12.93	No Permit to Fly issued. Canx by CAA 4.5.99
G-ZUSS	Embraer EMB.110P1 Bandeirante	110-215	G-REGA N711NH/PT-GMH	8. 3.91	To G-FLTY 8/92. Canx.
G-ZVBF	Cameron A-400 HAFB	4280		21. 1.98	
G-ZZAG	Cameron Z-77 HAFB	4588		6. 4.99	
G-ZZIM	Stephens Akro Type Z (Mod) (Carmichael Laser 200 version)	EMK.015 & WAS.008-85		14.11.83	Fatal crash into the railway embankment alongside the London-Peterborough railway line near Tempsford after striking overhead electric cables on 23.4.88. Canx as destroyed 7.9.88.
G-ZZIP	Mooney M.20J (205)	24-3167	N1086N	14. 6.91	
G-ZZZA	Boeing 777-236 (Line No. 6)	27105	N77779	20. 5.96	
G-ZZZB	Boeing 777-236 (Line No. 10)	27106	N77771	28. 3.97	
G-ZZZC	Boeing 777-236 (Line No. 15)	27107	N5014K	13.11.95	
G-ZZZD	Boeing 777-236 (Line No. 17)	27108		28.12.95	
G-ZZZE	Boeing 777-236 (Line No. 19)	27109		12. 1.96	
G-ZZZF	Boeing 777-236ER (Line No. 41)	27483	N5022E	. .95R	NTU - To G-VIIA 7/97. Canx.
G-ZZZG	Boeing 777-236ER (Line No. 49)	27484	N5023Q	. .95R	NTU - To G-VIIB 5/97. Canx.
G-ZZZH	Boeing 777-236ER (Line No. 53)	27485	N5061R	. .95R	NTU - To G-VIIC 2/97. Canx.
G-ZZZI	Boeing 777-236ER (Line No. 56)	27486		. .95R	NTU - To G-VIID 2/97. Canx.
G-ZZZJ	Boeing 777-236ER (Line No. 58)	27487		. .95R	NTU - To G-VIIE 2/97. Canx.
G-ZZZK	Boeing 777-236ER (Line No. 61)	27488		. .95R	NTU - To G-VIIF 3/97. Canx.
G-ZZZL	Boeing 777-236ER (Line No. 65)	27489		. .95R	NTU - To G-VIIG 4/97. Canx.
G-ZZZM	Boeing 777-236ER (Line No. 70)	27490		. .95R	NTU - To G-VIIH 5/97. Canx.
G-ZZZN	Boeing 777-236ER (Line No. 76)	27491		. .95R	NTU - To G-RAES 6/97. Canx.
G-ZZZP	Boeing 777-236ER (Line No. 111)	27492		. .95R	NTU - To G-VIIJ 12/97. Canx.
G-ZZZZ	Wakelin Point Maker Mk.1 Model Free Balloon (It is believed that this may not exist - it being registered initially to protest at the desecration of the British Register both in respect of out-of-sequence allocations and the registration of toy balloons)	MJW.1		4. 9.78	Canx by CAA 4.2.87.

SECTION 6 - UNITED KINGDOM ALPHANUMERIC REGISTER

The registration block from G-N94AA onwards was used for six British registered Concorde aircraft when British Airways entered into an agreement with US carriers Braniff Airlines for the latter to fly Concordes to Washington-Dallas as an extension of the former's London-Washington route, registration of the aircraft proved to be a problem. Under American law aircraft operated by a US carrier may not carry a foreign registration so the solution was to adopt a 'alphanumeric' registration system. Services were commenced on 12.1.79 by G-N94AE. The agreement was terminated by Braniff in 5.80. In theory aircraft went onto the American register at Washington and was 'restored' to the British register upon their return from Dallas.

Regn	Type	c/n	Previous identity	Regn date	Fate or immediate subsequent identity (if known)
G-N94AA	BAC/Aerospatiale Concorde 102	100-006	G-BOAA	12. 1.79	Restored as G-BOAA 7/80. Canx 28.7.80.
G-N94AB	BAC/Aerospatiale Concorde 102	100-008	G-BOAB	12. 1.79	Restored as G-BOAB 9/80. Canx 17.9.80.
G-N81AC	BAC/Aerospatiale Concorde 102	100-004	G-BOAC	5. 1.79	Restored as G-BOAC 8/80. Canx 11.8.80.
G-N94AD	BAC/Aerospatiale Concorde 102	100-010	G-BOAD	9. 1.79	Restored as G-BOAD 6/80. Canx 19.6.80.
G-N94AE	BAC/Aerospatiale Concorde 102	100-012	G-BOAE	5. 1.79	Restored as G-BOAE 7/80. Canx 1.7.80.
G-N94AF	BAC/Aerospatiale Concorde 102	100-016	G-BFKX	14.12.79	To G-BOAF 6/80. Canx 12.6.80.

SECTION 7 - REGISTRATIONS USED BY SOME COUNTRIES WHICH FORMERLY COMPRISED THE BRITISH EMPIRE

By the terms of the International Convention for Air Navigation, signed on 13.10.19, all aircraft of member countries were to be registered with allotted markings consisting of a nationality mark (an initial letter identifying the country), followed by a hyphen and the registration marks (a combination of four letters identifying each individual machine). In the original allocation of nationality marks, the British Empire, as a whole, was granted the letter G, with division of the four-letter registration block between Great Britain and the Dominions. Great Britain selected the initial registration mark E for heavier-than-air, and the mark F for lighter-than-air machines, followed by the marks AAA to ZZZ (eg; G-EAAA), whilst the Dominions adopted two initial marks relating to each Country (AU for Australia, CA for Canada, IA for India, NZ for New Zealand and UA for Union of South Africa), to be complemented by the marks AA to ZZ (eg; G-AUAA).

In the case of aircraft in a non-airworthy state the nationality-prefix letter (eg; "G-") was to be ommitted. In an airworthy state the normal form of registration applied; and in the instance where the machine was both in an airworthy state and proposed to be used for commercial purposes, the normal form of the registration would be applied but underlined with a black bar. How often this exact ruling was enforced is not known.

AUSTRALIA

THE 1915 REGISTER OF CIVIL AIRCRAFT

Registration of Aircraft in Australia was introduced in 1915 via Statutory Rule No.31 of 1915 and this was then quickly replaced by Statutory Rule No.113 of 1915. Certificates of Registration were to be issued by the various State Commandants and Headquarters were to be notified of those issued. The notification requirement was soon ignored, apparently starting around the time of the departure of Lt. Col. E.H. Reynolds overseas in early 1916. His replacement displayed neither the interest or drive required on the subject to ensure the notification of registrations to Headquarters. As a result this matter was permitted to fall into decline by c.1918.

The notes that appear below relate only to those machines which are known to have been registered. The majority of registrations are for machines in Victoria as this material has been retained in Australian Archives. Documents on the subject for other states appear to have been destroyed.

Judging from the active role played by the various Intelligence Sections in the Ministry Districts it would appear reasonable to expect most, if not all, of the aeroplanes that were operable were registered. Support for such a view can be seen in the request from the Military Commandant in Sydney for 50 copies of the Application for Registration form in April 1915.

Type	Regn date	Remarks or fate (if known)
Biplane (Built by V.B.Sylander)	. 4.15	Fate unknown.
Kalgoorlie Aeroplane Syndicate Biplane	. 5.15	Fate unknown.
Fraser et al Monoplane (Built by Messrs Fraser, Layton and Reynolds)	. 7.15	Fate unknown.
Queensland Volunteer Flying Civilians Biplane (Re-construction of a Caudron G.II)	31. 7.15	Fate unknown.
Bleriot XI Monoplane (Built in 1914, imported into Australia in same year)	18. 2.16	To Mascot, Sydney for repairs in 1918 - repairs not carried out and stored. (On display at Powerhouse Museum, Ultimo, Sydney since 1934)
O.T. Ltd Balloon	. 2.16	Fate unknown.
O.T. Ltd Biplane	. 4.16	Fate unknown.
Biplane (Built by L.J.R. Jones)	. 5.16	Fate unknown.
Scout Biplane (Built by H.C.Miller)	8. 6.16	Fate unknown, but engine and possibly other components to Biplane built by B.G.Watson.
Avro-type Biplane	4.10.16	Canx as per letter dated 1.12.16.
Biplane (Built by B.G.Watson)	.10.16	Wings collapsed whilst performing loops and crashed into the sea 40 yards off-shore from Point Cook on 28.3.17. Engine, propeller and assorted parts of the airframe to the Industrial and Technological Museum of Victoria late in 1919.
Balloon (Built by Taylor in England in 1913)	. 5.18	Removed from register in Victoria to New South Wales on 31.8.18.
Balloon (Built by Taylor at Sydney in 4/18)	. 5.18	DBF in Victoria on 29.7.18.

THE SECOND REGISTER OF CIVIL AIRCRAFT

In Australia markings, G-AU.., were not adopted until the Air Navigation Act 1921 was granted assent and the Air Navigation Regulations were introduced in 1921.

The Civil Aviation Branch (of the Department of Defence) retained the initial block of registrations, G-AUAA to G-AUAZ, for their own use, and therefore the Register commenced with the issuance of the marks G-AUBA. The idea of consequential issuance of registrations was retained, but immediately a number of odd variations were included.

All of the first group of registrations, within the range G-AUBA to G-AUCW plus G-AUJJ and G-AUKH, were validated for a 12 month period and back-dated from 28.6.21, no matter when the paper-work was completed. As more machines were registered in the ensuing months, this practice continued, until 5.11.21 when CofR No.51 was issued against registration G-AUDN. Certificate No.52 onwards then received shorter validation periods, apparently in an attempt to align all renewal dates, and this procedure continued until the issuance of Certificate No.61, at which point it was abandoned. From then onward, new and renewed certificates were validated on a 12 monthly basis from specific dates. We have elected to use the actual date on which the early Certificates were issued in the "Registration date" column below.

Registration marks G-AUBI and G-AUBN have been listed as "Original allocation untraced"; these may have been intended for the Shaw-Ross 504K (w/o at Port Melbourne, Vic on 22.5.21), the A.A. & E. Co. 504K-Dyak c/n AAEC/D.4 (eventually as G-AUEO), the third Sopwith Gnu, or other as yet unidentified aircraft.

"Double-letter" combinations; eg; G-AUAA, G-AUBB, G-AUCC et seq were not to be used. Whilst the exact reasoning for this foible has yet to be clearly established. The clear fact that this directive was ignored in certain instances from day one of the operation of course renders the whole proposal ineffectual. As well, at the insistance of several operators, an argument was accepted that there was no real need to paint a complete new set of registration letters on the imported machines which already carried civil registrations - with the relatively high costs involved, it would be easier to simply replace the second and third letter combinations as already marked on the machine, with the Australian-required "AU". To confuse a little more, where it was considered appropriate, the operator's initials could be (and were) made available as registration letters if they were within a reasonable range of the letter-group then being allocated.

These latter exemptions can be seen clearly in any listing of the allocated registration letters. It can be seen that by accepting the "part repaint" idea, the proposal that double letters not be used was in fact negated in the very first group of registrations allotted (eg; G-AUJJ). Other examples of such "part repaint" policy include G-AUKH, G-AUPZ and G-AUCQ. The issuance of G-AUCA as the "personalised" markings for the Civil Aviation Branch's own first aircraft is, in turn, the first such example on the Australian register.

The International Commission for Air Navigation Convention allocated Australia the prefixes of 'VH-', 'VI-', VJ-, 'VK-', 'VL-' and 'VM-', which would be distinctive for each State, as from 1.1.29.

All Australian registered machines would change to the VH- prefix and that the compromise would be accepted whereby the extent 'last three' letters would be retained. This was to placate the many owners and operators who advised the Civil Aviation Branch of their thoughts on the cost of a new paint job - and is of course the reason why the Australian Civil Aircraft Register started at VH-U.. Australia was the only member of the Empire were this practice was adopted, the others, including Canada with a much larger register, all recommenced their registers from the individual letters AAA.

Regn	Type	c/n	Previous identity	Regn date	Fate or immediate subsequent identity (if known)
G-AU					G-AU
G-AUAA to G-AUTU - Allocated to Australia from 6/21.					
G-AUAA	DH.37 (Certificate of Registration No. 98)	105		1. 7.24	Re-regd as VH-UAA by 31.8.30. Canx.
G-AUAB	DH.50A (Certificate of Registration No. 99)	106		31. 7.24	Re-regd as VH-UAB by 31.8.30. Canx.
G-AUAC	DH.53 Humming Bird (Certificate of Registration No. 100)	103		31. 7.24	Re-regd as VH-UAC by 31.8.30. Canx.
G-AUAD	DH.53 Humming Bird (Certificate of Registration No. 101)	104		31. 7.24	Re-regd as VH-UAD by 2/31. Canx.
G-AUAE	DH.60 Moth (Cirrus I) (Certificate of Registration No. 127)(To Cirrus II 3/29, to Gipsy I 28.8.29)	192		5.11.25	Re-regd as VH-UAE by 31.8.30. Canx.
"G-AUAE"	DH.60 Moth	-		----	Static exhibit only, mounted on floats based at Wangarratta, Victoria, Australia. Constructed from residue parts left over from the rebuild of the real VH-UAE.
G-AUAF	DH.60 Moth (Cirrus I) (Certificate of Registration No. 135)	243		12. 8.26	Crashed & DBR into partially-constructed reservoir on Essendon Aerodrome, Victoria on 6.8.27. Canx 6.8.27.
G-AUAG	DH.60 Moth (Cirrus I) (Certificate of Registration No. 136)	244		12. 7.26	Re-regd as VH-UAG by 31.8.30. Canx.
G-AUAH	DH.60 Moth (Cirrus I) (Certificate of Registration No. 137)(To Cirrus II by 8/29)	245		12. 8.26	Damaged in forced-landing during an ANZAC Parade at Maroubra Junction, New South Wales on 22.3.30. Canx 24.3.30. Rebuilt & re-regd as VH-UAH on 20.9.30.
G-AUAI	Not allotted.				
G-AUAJ	DH.60 Moth (Cirrus I) (Certificate of Registration No. 138)(To Cirrus II in late 1928)	241		12. 7.26	Re-regd as VH-UAJ by 31.8.30. Canx.
G-AUAK	DH.60 Moth (Cirrus I) (Certificate of Registration No. 139)(To Cirrus II in 1929)	242		12. 7.26	To avoid a collision on take-off, pilot stalled the aircraft and nose-dived 40 ft. to the ground at Mascot Aerodrome, New South Wales on 4.2.30. Canx 23.4.30. Rebuilt & regd as VH-UAK by 31.8.30.
G-AUAL	DH.60 Moth (Cirrus I) (Certificate of Registration No. 140)(To Cirrus II on 16.5.27, then Gipsy I by 1/30)	246		12. 8.26	Re-regd as VH-UAL by 31.8.30. Canx.
G-AUAM	DH.60 Moth (Cirrus II) (Certificate of Registration No. 181)	364		26.11.27	Re-regd as VH-UAM on 28.5.29. Fatal crash after stalling at Parafield, South Australia on 14.7.29. Canx 12.11.29.
G-AUAN	Not allotted.				
G-AUAO	Not allotted.				
G-AUAP	DH.60 Moth (Cirrus II) (Certificate of Registration No. 182)	365		26.11.27	Crashed during low aerobatics at Parafield, South Australia on 11.3.28. Canx 4.4.28.
G-AUAQ	Not allotted.				
G-AUAR	DH.60 Moth (Cirrus II) (Certificate of Registration No. 199)	366		12. 4.28	Re-regd as VU-UAR by 31.10.29. Canx.
G-AUAS	DH.60 Moth (Cirrus II) (Certificate of Registration No. 176)(To Cirrus I in 1/29)	367		27. 8.27	Re-regd as VH-UAS by 31.10.29. Canx.
G-AUAT	DH.60 Moth (Cirrus II) (Certificate of Registration No. 218)	368		28. 8.28	Re-regd as VH-UAT by 31.8.30. Canx.
G-AUAU	Not allotted.				
G-AUAV	DH.60 Moth (Cirrus II)	369		10. 7.29	Marks probably never carried. Re-regd as VH-UAV (CofR No.302) by 31.8.30. Canx.
G-AUAW	DH.60G Gipsy Moth	1072		. 2.29R	NTU - To VH-UAW (CofR No. 294) on 24.5.29. Canx.
G-AUAX	Not allotted.				
G-AUAY	DH.50A (Certificate of Registration No. 190)	137		1. 3.28	Re-regd as VH-UAY by 31.8.30. Canx.
G-AUAZ	Not allotted.				

Regn	Type	c/n	Previous identity	Regn date	Fate or immediate subsequent identity (if known)
G-AUBA	Avro 504K (Certificate of Registration No. 1) (Re-conditioned using wings of G-AUBJ)(Certificate of Registration No. 152 issued 14.2.27)	-	H2030	12. 7.21	Crashed at Kempsey, New South Wales on 18.5.27. Canx 18.4.28.
G-AUBB	Not allotted.				
G-AUBC	Farman S.11 Shorthorn (Certificate of Registration No. 2)	1505	CFS-.. B....	12. 7.21	Crashed whilst en route Melbourne-Tamworth between 24.2.26 and 9.3.26. Canx 27.6.26. (On display unmarked at Rockcliffe, Canada)
G-AUBD	RAF B.E.2e (Certificate of Registration No. 3)	-	C7198	12. 7.21	CofR expired 27.6.22. Canx.
G-AUBE	Avro 504K (Certificate of Registration No. 4)	AAEC/4	(G-EAIY)	12. 7.21	Canx 27.6.23.
G-AUBF	RAF B.E.2e (Certificate of Registration No. 5)	2312	C6986	12. 7.21	CofA expired 4.12.26. Canx as WFU 4.12.26.
G-AUBG	Avro 504-Dyak (Certificate of Registration No. 6, then Certificate of Registration No. 147 issued 30.6.27)	AAEC/D.1		12. 7.21	Re-regd as VH-UBG on 23.9.29. Canx.
G-AUBH	Airco DH.6 (Certificate of Registration No. 47)	3204	B2802	31. 8.21	Canx 27.6.22. Struck a fence on take-off from the beach at Cronulla, New South Wales on 31.12.22.
G-AUBI	Original allocation untraced.				
G-AUBJ	Avro 504-Dyak (Certificate of Registration No. 7, then Certificate of Registration No. 96 issued 3.12.23, then Certificate of Registration No. 115 issued 1.12.24, then Certificate of Registration No. 130 issued 30.6.26)	AAEC/D.5		12. 7.21	CofR expired 15.2.28. Canx 20.2.28.
G-AUBK	Avro 504K (Certificate of Registration No. 8)	-		12. 7.21	Crashed near Ipswich, Queensland on 9.2.27. Canx in 2/27.
G-AUBL	Avro 504K (Certificate of Registration No. 9, the Certificate of Registration No. 74 issued 1.12.22, then Certificate of Registration No. 85 issued 15.9.23, then Certificate of Registration No. 94 issued 10.4.24, then Certificate of Registration No. 112 issued 11.11.24)	-	D6396	12. 7.21	Crashed during Light Aeroplane Trials at Richmond, New South Wales on 4.12.24. Canx 15.1.25. Sold as "incompletely repaired" on 16.1.27.
G-AUBM	Avro 504K (H2486 was hit while stationary by H9718 at Abu Sueir on 31.10.27, the quoted p.i. must be in error)	-	'H2486'	. .21R	NTU - Fatal crash at racecourse, near Gloucester, New South Wales on 11.6.21 before any CofR was issued.
G-AUBN	Original allocation untraced.				
G-AUBO	Airco DH.6 (Certificate of Registration No. 10, then Certificate of Registration No. 118 issued 2.3.25, then Certificate of Registration No. 146 issued 15.11.26)	-	C7444	12. 7.21	Crashed on take-off from beach at Maroochydore, Queensland on 27.1.27. Canx 24.1.28.
G-AUBP	Avro 504K (Certificate of Registration No. 39)	-		9. 8.21	CofA expired 27.6.23. Canx 27.6.23. Purchased in 10/23 for spares and used in construction of G-AUEP.
G-AUBQ	Avro 504K	-	H1915	. .21R	NTU - Struck rough ground taking off near Cowra, New South Wales on 18.7.21, before a CofR was issued.
G-AUBR	Avro 504K (Certificate of Registration No. 43)	-	H1909	18. 8.21	Crashed at Yabree Station, near Wagga Wagga, New South Wales on 19.9.21. Canx in 9/21.
G-AUBS	Avro 504-Dyak (Certificate of Registration No. 11)	AAEC/D.6		12. 7.21	CofR expired & Canx 27.6.22.
G-AUBT	Boulton & Paul P.9 (Certificate of Registration No. 12, then Certificate of Registration No.72 issued 4.11.22)	P.9-3		12. 7.21	Hit car on take-off from Serviceton, Victoria on 8.11.22 and crashed. Canx 20.1.23.
G-AUBU	Airco DH.6	-		. .21R	NTU - Damaged prior to registration at Neutral Bay, New South Wales, and possibly DBER.
G-AUBV	Farman Sport (Certificate of Registration No. 13)	8		12. 7.21	Canx 27.6.31. Destroyed in hangar fire at Port Melbourne, Victoria on 7.8.31.
"G-AUBV"	Avro 504 Replica			----	On display at Powerhouse Museum, Sydney, New South Wales.
G-AUBW	Airco DH.6 (Certificate of Registration No. 14)	-	CFS C9374	12. 7.21	Canx 27.6.31. Destroyed in hangar fire at Port Melbourne, Victoria on 7.8.31.
G-AUBX	Sopwith Gnu (Certificate of Registration No. 15)	2976/5	G-EAHQ K-169	12. 7.21	Crashed at Culgoa, Victoria on 30.8.21. Canx 11.3.22.
G-AUBY	Sopwith Gnu (Certificate of Registration No. 16)	2976/6	G-EAIL	12. 7.21	Re-regd as VH-UBY by 31.8.30. Canx.
G-AUBZ	Airco DH.4 (Certificate of Registration No. 30, then Certificate of Registration No. 70 issued 9.10.22)	-	F2682	15. 7.21	Re-regd as VH-UBZ by 27.2.30. Canx.
G-AUCA	Bristol 28 Coupe Tourer (Certificate of Registration No. 46)	6117		31. 8.21	Crashed at Bourke, New South Wales on 16.3.23. Canx. Rebuilt as G-AUDX using spare airframe c/n 6113.
G-AUCB	Avro 504K (Certificate of Registration No. 17)	AAEC/1	(G-EAIV)	12. 7.21	CofA expired. Canx 27.6.23.
G-AUCC	Not allotted.				
G-AUCD	Avro 504K (Certificate of Registration No. 18)	AAEC/5		12. 7.21	CofA expired. Canx 27.6.23.
G-AUCE	Avro 504K (Certificate of Registration No. 19)	AAEC/6		12. 7.21	CofA expired. Canx 27.6.23.
G-AUCF	Armstrong Whitworth F.K.8 (Certificate of Registration No. 20, then Certificate of Registration No. 68 issued 19.9.22)	-	H4561	12. 7.21	Stalled & crashed at Jericho, Queensland on 25.2.23. Canx 19.4.23.
G-AUCG	Avro 504K (Certificate of Registration No. 23)	-		12. 7.21	Marks never worn. Struck off Register on 24.9.21. Crashed near Minlaton, South Australia on 10.1.22. Regn canx on 17.2.22 as no application for re-regn had been made.
G-AUCH	Bristol Monoplane M.1c (Certificate of Registration No. 22)	2819	C5001	12. 7.21	CofR expired 27.6.22. Canx. 98hp Gipsy Mk.I engine installed and rebuilt as VH-UQI on 15.10.31.
G-AUCI	Avro 504K	-	H1973	. 5.21R	NTU - Sold in 1921. No CofR issued. To G-AUEN on 22.5.24.
G-AUCJ	Avro 504K (Certificate of Registration No. 21)	-	E3432	12. 7.21	Crashed on landing at Belmont Common, Victoria on 25.12.22. Later sold. Canx 5.7.29.
G-AUCK	Sopwith Pup (Certificate of Registration No. 24)	-	C476	12. 7.21	Re-regd as VH-UCK after 11.7.31. Canx.
G-AUCL	Avro 504J (Certificate of Registration No. 58)	-		7.12.21	Re-reged as VH-UCL by 6/31. Canx.

Regn	Type	c/n	Previous identity	Regn date	Fate or immediate subsequent identity (if known)
G-AUCM	Airco DH.4 (Certificate of Registration No. 31, then Certificate of Registration No. 67 issued 19.9.22)	-	F2691	15. 7.21	Canx 15.7.30.
G-AUCN	Avro 504K (Certificate of Registration No. 25)	-		12. 7.21	Fatal crash near Mildura, Victoria on 10.1.22. Canx in 2/22.
G-AUCO	RAF B.E.2e	-		. .21R	NTU - Overturned in forced landing near Branxton, New South Wales in 7/21. No CofR issued. Rebuilt and registered as G-AUDV on 16.11.22.
G-AUCP	Boulton & Paul P.9 (Certificate of Registration No. 32, then Certificate of Registration No. 82 issued 9.5.23, then Certificate of Registration No. 93 issued 7.2.24, then Certificate of Registration No. 129 issued 30.6.26)	P.9-7		15. 7.21	Crashed at Willaura, Victoria on 16.12.27. Canx 9.1.28.
G-AUCQ	Avro 534 Baby (Certificate of Registration No. 28, then Certificate of Registration No. 114 issued 18.12.24, then Certificate of Registration No. 126 issued 14.10.25)	534/1	G-EACQ K-131	12. 7.21	Re-regd as VH-UCQ in 10/30. (On display Queensland Cultural Centre, Brisbane, Australia marked as G-EACQ) Canx.
G-AUCR	Avro 547 Triplane (Certificate of Registration No. 33)	547/1	G-EAQX	15. 7.21	No CofA issued; WFU & broken up. CofR expired & Canx 27.6.22.
G-AUCS	Armstrong Whitworth F.K.8 (Certificate of Registration No. 34, then Certificate of Registration No. 71 issued 23.10.22, then Certificate of Registration No. 84 issued 12.9.23)	-		15. 7.21	CofR expired 30.8.24. Canx 19.12.24. Dismantled.
G-AUCT	Boulton & Paul P.9 (Certificate of Registration No. 35)	P.9-5		15. 7.21	CofR expired & WFU. Canx 27.6.22 "Rebuilt as monoplane".
G-AUCU	Curtiss Seagull (Certificate of Registration No. 36, then Certificate of Registration No. 86 issued 27.8.23)	MF419/29		15. 7.21	Canx 31.7.25.
G-AUCV	Curtiss Seagull (Certificate of Registration No. 37, then Certificate of Registration No. 83 issued 27.8.23, then Certificate of Registration No. 125 issued 21.9.25)	MF419/28		15. 7.21	Crashed on bank of Brisbane River at New Farm, Queensland on 17.1.26. Canx 20.9.26.
G-AUCW	Farman S.11 Shorthorn (Certificate of Registration No. 29, then Certificate of Registration No. 59 issued 22.12.21)	1326	CFS-.. B....	15. 7.21	Re-regd as VH-UCW on 12.12.31. Canx.
G-AUCX	RAF F.E.2b (Certificate of Registration No. 38)	-	CFS-14 A774	2. 8.21	Crashed at Boulder, Western Australia on 7.2.22. Canx 17.2.22.
G-AUCY	Avro 504K (Certificate of Registration No. 42, then Certificate of Registration No. 75 issued 14.12.22, then Certificate of Registration No.78 issued 23.3.23)	-	H7499	15. 8.21	Crashed during forced landing near Burra, South Australia on 3.11.25. Canx 22.12.25.
G-AUCZ	Avro 504-Dyak (Certificate of Registration No. 40, then Certificate of Registration No. 132 issued 30.6.26)	AAEC/D.7		9. 8.21	Nose-dived into ground from 100ft at Smeaton, Victoria on 9.6.30 & DBR. Canx.
G-AUDA	Avro 504K (Certificate of Registration No. 41)	-	J5512	15. 8.21	Damaged in forced landing at Stanwell, Queensland on 29.5.24. Canx 28.6.24. Burnt during rebuild 29.11.24.
G-AUDB	Boulton & Paul P.9 (Certificate of Registration No. 44)	P.9-4		31. 8.21	Crashed at Briagolong, Victoria on 5.11.21 & DBF. Canx.
G-AUDC	Farman Sport (Certificate of Registration No. 45)	25		31. 8.21	Crashed at Cowes, Victoria on 9.2.23. CofA No.35 withdrawn 21.2.23. Canx 21.2.23.
G-AUDD	Not allotted.				
G-AUDE	Armstrong Whitworth F.K.8 (Certificate of Registration No. 48, then Certificate of Registration No. 69 issued 19.9.22)	69	F4231	8. 9.21	Damaged in forced landing near Blackall, Queensland on 13.9.23. Dismantled and later burnt as 'useless' on 28.11.23. Canx 13.3.24.
G-AUDF	Bristol 28 Coupe Tourer (Certificate of Registration No. 52)	6108	G-EAXK	7.12.21	DBF at Onslow, Western Australia on 27.1.25. Canx.
G-AUDG	Bristol 28 Coupe Tourer (Certificate of Registration No. 53)	6111		7.12.21	DBF at Wauchope, New South Wales on 17.12.28. Canx.
G-AUDH	Bristol 28 Coupe Tourer (Certificate of Registration No. 54) (Some existing metal parts and new woodwork of G-AUDH used to rebuild aircraft with registration of G-AUDZ in 1924)	6115		7.12.21	Crashed at Port Hedland, Western Australia on 15.7.24. Canx.
G-AUDI	Bristol 28 Coupe Tourer (Certificate of Registration No. 55)	6116		7.12.21	Crashed near Murchison River, Western Australia on 5.12.21. Parts used to rebuild G-AUDX. Canx.
G-AUDJ	Bristol 28 Coupe Tourer (Certificate of Registration No. 56)	6118		7.12.21	Crash landed near Pine Creek, Northern Territory on 11.9.28. Canx 27.11.28.
G-AUDK	Bristol 28 Coupe Tourer (Certificate of Registration No. 57)	6119		7.12.21	Crashed on landing at Lae, New Guinea on 15.2.28. Canx 13.8.28. Remains sold.
G-AUDL	Farman Sport (Certificate of Registration No. 49)	24		8.10.21	Canx 27.6.31. DBF at Port Melbourne, Victoria on 7.8.31.
G-AUDM	Avro 504-Dyak (Certificate of Registration No. 50, then Certificate of Registration No. 116 issued 1.12.24)	AAEC/D.8		19.10.21	Canx 30.1.26.
G-AUDN	Sopwith Dove (Certificate of Registration No. 51)	3004/3	G-EAJI	5.11.21	Re-regd as VH-UDN by 23.4.30. Canx.
G-AUDO	Airco DH.6 (Mod) (Certificate of Registration No. 60, then Certificate of Registration No. 166 issued 22.6.27)	-	C1972	12. 1.22	Canx 30.9.28.
G-AUDP	Sopwith Dove	3004/6	G-EAKT	. .21R	NTU - Crashed prior to being registered. Canx.
G-AUDQ	Avro 504K (Certificate of Registration No. 61)	-	G-EAEC E3501	10. 4.22	Crashed at Jerrawa near Yass, New South Wales on 21.5.23. Canx 27.6.23.
G-AUDR	Avro 504-Dyak (Certificate of Registration No. 63, then Certificate of Registration No. 92 issued 11.1.24, then Certificate of Registration No. 122 issued 12.6.25)	AAEC/D.9		18. 7.22	Wrecked by gale at Moora Valley (between 12 & 17.6.25). Canx 17.6.26.
G-AUDS	Airco DH.6 (Mod) (Certificate of Registration No. 64)	-	B3858	27. 7.22	No CofA issued. Crashed into Orange Show Ground arena, New South Wales and DBF on 29.4.25. Canx.
G-AUDT	AAEC B1 Commercial 4-6 Seater (Certificate of Registration No. 65)	B.1		9. 8.22	No CofA issued. Canx 7.8.23.
G-AUDU	Sopwith Wallaby (Certificate of Registration No. 66, then Certificate of Registration No. 88 issued 1.11.23)	3109	G-EAKS	31. 8.22	Destroyed in forced landing 13 miles west of Bowning, New South Wales on 13.10.28. Canx 10.12.28.
G-AUDV	RAF B.E.2e (Certificate of Registration No. 73, then Certificate of Registration No. 119 issued 17.3.25)	61	(G-AUCO)	16.11.22	Re-regd as VH-UDV on 11.11.30. Canx.

Regn	Type	c/n	Previous identity	Regn date	Fate or immediate subsequent identity (if known)
G-AUDW	Airco DH.6 (Certificate of Registration No. 76)	3202		22. 2.23	Crashed at Perth aerodrome, Western Australia on 19.11.25. Canx in 11/25.
G-AUDX	Bristol 28 Coupe Tourer (Built using components from G-AUCA & G-AUDI) (Certificate of Registration No. 77)	6113		5. 3.23	Sold on 16.6.30. Crashed in Queensland (details?). Canx 20.9.30.
G-AUDY	Not allotted.				
G-AUDZ	Bristol 28 Coupe Tourer (Certificate of Registration No. 113) (Some existing metal parts and new woodwork of G-AUDH used in construction of this aircraft)	6115		12.11.24	Canx in 2/31.
G-AUEA	Airco DH.6 (Mod) (Certificate of Registration No.79)(Built from spares by C.D.Pratt)	"2"	C7625	5. 4.23	Re-regd as VH-UEA on 14.10.29. Canx.
G-AUEB	Bristol Fighter F.2b (Certificate of Registration No. 80)	4965	H1248	12. 4.23	Crashed at Wau, Papau New Guinea on 17.4.28. Canx 11.9.28.
G-AUEC	Avro 504K (Certificate of Registration No. 81, then Certificate of Registration No. 95 issued 12.5.24)	-	H1960	28. 6.23	Crashed at Euroa, Victoria in mid-1924 (details?). Canx 11.5.25.
G-AUED	DH.9C (Certificate of Registration No. 89)	86		21.11.23	Fatal crash at Tambo, Queensland on 24.3.27. Canx.
G-AUEE	Not allotted.				
G-AUEF	DH.9C (Certificate of Registration No. 90)	87		21.11.23	Damaged at Cloncurry, Queensland during take-off on 24.9.26. Canx.
G-AUEG	Airco DH.9 (Certificate of Registration No. 102)	-	A6-5	8. 8.24	Restored to R.Australian AF as A6-5 on 18.12.24. Canx.
G-AUEH	Airco DH.9 (Certificate of Registration No. 109)	-	A6-4	2. 9.24	Restored to R.Australian AF as A6-4 on 18.12.24. Canx.
G-AUEI	DH.50A (Certificate of Registration No. 110)	129		5.11.24	Re-regd as VH-UEI by 31.8.30. Canx.
G-AUEJ	DH.50A (Certificate of Registration No. 111)	130		5.11.24	Force-landed at Methul, New South Wales and DBF on 9.6.32. Canx 20.6.32.
G-AUEK	DH.50A (Certificate of Registration No. 117)	131		17.12.24	Re-regd as VH-UEK by 31.8.30. Canx.
G-AUEL	DH.50A (Certificate of Registration No. 107)	127		28.10.24	Re-regd as VH-UEL by 31.8.30. Canx.
G-AUEM	DH.50A (Certificate of Registration No. 108)	128		28.10.24	Re-regd as VH-UEM on 9.12.29. Canx.
G-AUEN	Avro 504K (Certificate of Registration No. 97)	-	(G-AUCI) H1973	22. 5.24	DBF after fatal hand-swinging accident at Maylands, Western Australia on 22.10.26. Canx 27.10.26.
G-AUEO	Avro 504-Dyak (Certificate of Registration No. 224)	AAEC/D.4		2.10.28	Canx 18.3.30. Crashed at Tweed Heads on last flight 7.2.32. Sold 11.11.37.
G-AUEP	Avro 504K (Constructed from G-AUBP plus spares) (Certificate of Registration No. 103)	-		7.10.24	Crashed at Lae, New Guinea on 6.6.28. Later caught fire and destroyed. Canx 7.6.28.
G-AUEQ	ANEC II (Certificate of Registration No. 104)	3		16.10.24	Marks not applied. Damaged by flood water at Maylands Aerodrome, Western Australia on 5.1.27. Repaired & re-regd as VH-UEQ in 12/30. Canx.
G-AUER	DH.50A (Certificate of Registration No. 105)	116	G-EBIW	15.10.24	Re-regd as VH-UER by 31.8.30. Canx.
G-AUES	Blanch Experimental (Certificate of Registration No. 106)	1		. . R	NTU. Canx.
G-AUET	ANEC II (Certificate of Registration No. 120)	1		5. 5.25	Canx 4.5.26.
G-AUEU	Airco DH.9C (Certificate of Registration No. 121)	-		14. 5.25	DBR by gale after landing at Point Pirie, South Australia on 16.2.28. Canx 17.3.28.
G-AUEV	Curtiss JN-4D (Certificate of Registration No. 124)	273	10074 US Army Air Corps	17. 7.25	Re-regd as VH-UEV in 12/30. Canx.
G-AUEW	Avro 504K (Certificate of Registration No. 128, then Certificate of Registration No. 144)	-		20.11.25	Crashed into sea near the mouth of the Buang River after take-off from Lae, New Guinea on 18.12.27. Canx 15.10.29.
G-AUEX(1)	DH.50	73	G-EBFN	17. 3.26R	NTU - To G-AUEY 13.4.26. Canx.
G-AUEX(2)	Curtiss JN-4D (Certificate of Registration No. 133)	273		26. 6.26	Crashed at Glenory, Victoria on 1.12.26. Canx 23.2.27.
G-AUEY	DH.50 (Certificate of Registration No. 131)	73	(G-AUEX) G-EBFN	13. 4.26	Re-regd as VH-UEY by 24.8.30. Canx.
G-AUEZ	ANEC III (Certificate of Registration No. 141)	1		16. 8.26	Re-regd as VH-UEZ by 31.8.30. Canx.
G-AUFA	DH.50A (Certificate of Registration No. 142)	1		17. 8.26	Re-regd as VH-UFA by 20.1.30. Canx.
G-AUFB	Airco DH.9C (Certificate of Registration No. 143)	853	G-EBKV H9337	24. 9.26	Crashed 8 miles north of Wau in the Bulolo River, New Guinea on 3.3.28. Canx 8.6.28.
G-AUFC	ANEC III (Lasco Lascowl) (Certificate of Registration No. 164)	2		21. 5.25	Crashed on landing at Hay, New South Wales on 27.12.27. CofA suspended on 9.1.28. Reduced to spares in 5/29. Canx 22.5.29.
G-AUFD	DH.50A (Certificate of Registration No. 148)	1		1.12.26	Crashed on take-off from Geraldton, Western Australia on 11.5.29. Canx 23.12.29.
G-AUFE	DH.50A (Certificate of Registration No. 150)	2		22.12.26	Re-regd as VH-UFE by 24.8.30. Canx.
G-AUFF	Not allotted.				
G-AUFG	Curtiss Ireland Comet (Certificate of Registration No. 149)	-		22.12.26	Crashed at St.Peters, New South Wales on 24.8.28. Canx 29.8.28.
G-AUFH	Curtiss Ireland Comet (Certificate of Registration No. 155)	0-38		1. 3.27	Re-regd as VH-UFH by 31.8.30. Canx.

Regn	Type	c/n	Previous identity	Regn date	Fate or immediate subsequent identity (if known)
G-AUFI	DH.60 Moth (Cirrus I) (Certificate of Registration No. 154)	277		15. 2.27	Fatal crash after striking an electric power standard and fell back to a roadway in flames at East Perth, Western Australia on 18.7.27. Canx in 7/27.
G-AUFJ	DH.60 Moth (Cirrus I) (Certificate of Registration No. 151)(To Cirrus II pre-3/29)	278		22.12.26	Re-regd as VH-UFJ by 28.1.30 when it crashed at Miles, Queensland & was DBR. Canx 19.8.30.
G-AUFK	DH.60 Moth (Cirrus I) (Certificate of Registration No. 162)(To Cirrus II by 4/29)	279		13. 4.27	Re-regd as VH-UFK by 31.8.30. Canx.
G-AUFL	DH.60 Moth (Cirrus II) (Certificate of Registration No. 157)	352		21. 3.27	Re-regd as VH-UFL by 22.1.30. Canx.
G-AUFM	DH.9C (Certificate of Registration No. 153)	-		12. 2.27	Crashed at Camooweal, Queensland on 13.1.28. Canx 4.1.29. Dismantled for spares.
G-AUFN	DH.50A (Certificate of Registration No. 169)	3		8. 7.27	Re-regd as VH-UFN by 31.8.30. Canx.
G-AUFO	Wackett Widgeon	-		. .	NTU - Aircraft transferred to R.Australian AF. Canx.
G-AUFP	Avro 504K (Certificate of Registration No. 91, then Certificate of Registration No. 145 issued 22.10.26)	PL.6110	G-EAFP E3363	18.12.23	Crashed at Wallacedale, Victoria on 3.1.27. Canx in 1.27.
G-AUFQ	Curtiss Ireland Meteor (Certificate of Registration No. 163)	M.8		5. 5.27	Re-regd as VH-UFQ by 31.8.30. Canx.
G-AUFR	DH.60 Moth (Cirrus II) (Certificate of Registration No. 158)	351		21. 3.27	Re-regd as VH-UFR by 22.1.30. Canx.
G-AUFS	Airco DH.9 (Certificate of Registration No. 159)	-	H9340	31. 3.27	Re-regd as VH-UFS by 31.12.30 Canx.
G-AUFT	DH.60 Moth (Cirrus II) (Certificate of Registration No. 161)	363		11. 4.27	Re-regd as VH-UFT by 31.8.30. Canx.
G-AUFU	DH.60 Moth (Cirrus I) (Certificate of Registration No. 160)	275		8. 4.27	Re-regd as VH-UFU on 21.8.29. Canx.
G-AUFV	DH.60 Moth (Cirrus II) (To D.H., South Melbourne as components - construction completed using locally made upper mainplane and tail unit) (Certificate of Registration No. 165)	1A		1. 6.27	Re-regd as VH-UFV by 31.12.32. Canx.
G-AUFW	DH.50A (Certificate of Registration No. 168)	2		11. 6.27	Re-regd as VH-UFW by 20.1.30 Canx.
G-AUFX	Farman Sport (Certificate of Registration No. 167)	7085		29. 6.27	Re-regd as VH-UFX by 31.8.30. Canx.
G-AUFY	Avro 594 Avian II (Certificate of Registration No. 186)	R3/AV/126		27. 1.28	Re-regd as VH-UFY by 31.8.30. Canx.
G-AUFZ	Avro 594 Avian II (Certificate of Registration No. 187)	R3/AV/127		27. 1.28	Re-regd as VH-UFZ by 31.8.30. Canx.
G-AUGA	Avro 594 Avian II (Certificate of Registration No. 183)	R3/AV/123		3. 1.28	Re-regd as VH-UGA by 31.8.30. Canx.
G-AUGB	Curtiss JN-4D (Certificate of Registration No. 171)	2885		3. 8.27	Re-regd as VH-UGB by 31.8.30. Canx.
G-AUGC	Not allotted.				
G-AUGD	DH.50A (Certificate of Registration No. 172)	3		9. 8.27	Re-regd as VH-UGD by 20.1.30. Canx.
G-AUGE	DH.60 Moth (Cirrus II) (Certificate of Registration No. 173)	2		11. 8.27	Re-regd as VH-UGE by 31.8.30. Canx.
G-AUGF	ANEC III (Lasco Lascowl) (Certificate of Registration No. 175)	3		15. 8.27	Re-regd as VH-UGF by 31.8.30. Canx.
G-AUGG	Not allotted.				
G-AUGH	DH.60 Moth (Cirrus II) (Certificate of Registration No. 174)	354		12. 8.27	Re-regd as VH-UGH by 31.8.30. Canx.
G-AUGI	Westland Widgeon III (Certificate of Registration No. 179)	WA.1681		26. 9.27	Re-regd as VH-UGI on 6.1.33. Canx.
G-AUGJ	DH.60X Moth (Cirrus II) (Certificate of Registration No. 177)	408		7. 9.27	Re-regd as VH-UGJ by 31.8.30. Canx.
G-AUGK	Alexander Eaglerock (Certificate of Registration No. 188)	298		21. 2.28	Re-regd as VH-UGK by 31.8.30. Canx.
G-AUGL	DH.60X Moth (Cirrus III) (Certificate of Registration No. 180)	407		3.10.27	Crashed after take-off from Coonabarabran, New South Wales and DBF on 22.8.28. Canx 30.8.28.
G-AUGM	DH.60X Moth (Cirrus III) (Certificate of Registration No. 201)	453		20. 4.28	Re-regd as VH-UGM in 1/30. Canx.
G-AUGN	DH.60X Moth (Cirrus II) (Certificate of Registration No. 184)	411		26. 1.28	Re-regd as VH-UGN by 4/31. Canx.
G-AUGO	DH.60X Moth (Cirrus III) (Certificate of Registration No. 178)	424		13. 9.27	Re-regd as VH-UGO on 15.1.30. Canx.
G-AUGP	Avro 504K (Certificate of Registration No. 189)	-		27. 2.28	Stalled at 40ft after take-off from Melbourne, Victoria on 21.3.30. Canx 28.5.30.
G-AUGQ	Not allotted.				
G-AUGR	Ryan B.1 Brougham (Certificate of Registration No. 192)	-		12. 3.28	Landed in sea on approach to Lae, New Guinea on 23.4.28. Canx 26.3.29.
G-AUGS	DH.60X Moth (Cirrus III) (Certificate of Registration No. 214)	604		9. 8.28	Re-regd as VH-UGS by 31.8.30. Canx.
G-AUGT	DH.60X Moth (Cirrus II) (Certificate of Registration No. 215)	605		13. 8.28	Re-regd as VH-UGT pre-8.32. Canx.
G-AUGU	DH.60X Moth (Cirrus III) (Certificate of Registration No. 216)	606		23. 8.28	Accident at Encounter Bay, South Australia on 29.3.29. Canx 21.6.29. To VH-UGU on 8.6.33. Canx.
G-AUGV	DH.60G Gipsy Moth (Certificate of Registration No. 268)	833		21. 6.29	Re-regd as VH-UGV by 31.8.30. Canx.
G-AUGW	DH.60G Gipsy Moth (Certificate of Registration No. 295)	834		6. 6.29	Re-regd as VH-UGW by 31.8.30. Canx.
G-AUGX	DH.60X Moth (Cirrus III) (Certificate of Registration No. 193)	425		15. 3.28	Re-regd as VH-UGX on 28.1.30. Canx.

Regn	Type	c/n	Previous identity	Regn date	Fate or immediate subsequent identity (if known)
G-AUGY	Travelair 2000 (Certificate of Registration No. 194)	287	NC3669	20. 3.28	Re-regd as VH-UGY on 7.4.30. Canx.
G-AUGZ	Junkers W.34b (Certificate of Registration No. 195)	2601	D-1294	20. 3.28	Re-regd as VH-UGZ pre-3/30. Canx.
G-AUHA	DH.60X Moth (Cirrus II) (Certificate of Registration No. 197)	427		30. 3.28	Crashed at Marulan, New South Wales on 11.2.29. Canx 20.2.29. Rebuilt as DH.60G c/n 7 & re-regd as VH-ULH (CofR No. 306) on 30.7.29.
G-AUHB	DH.60X Moth (Cirrus III) (Certificate of Registration No. 198)	412		30. 3.28	Re-regd as VH-UHB by 31.8.30. Canx.
G-AUHC	Avro 594 Avian III (Certificate of Registration No. 196)	R3/CN/413		28. 3.28	Re-regd as VH-UHC by 31.8.30. Canx.
G-AUHD	DH.60X Moth (Cirrus III) (Certificate of Registration No. 217)	464		23. 8.28	Crashed at Hillston, New South Wales on 14.10.28. Canx 23.10.28.
G-AUHE	DH.50A (Certificate of Registration No. 204)	4		10. 5.28	Re-regd as VH-UHE by 20.1.30. Canx.
G-AUHF	DH.60X Moth (Cirrus III) (Certificate of Registration No. 200)	406		19. 4.28	Fatal crash into sea after stalling at low altitude off Gerrigong Beach, New South Wales on 16.11.29. Canx 16.12.29
G-AUHG	DH.60X Moth (Cirrus III) (Certificate of Registration No. 202)	465		8. 5.28	Crashed at Port Melbourne, Victoria on 12.1.29. Rebuilt & re-regd as VH-UHG on 29.4.29. Canx.
G-AUHH	Not allotted.				
G-AUHI	DH.50J (Certificate of Registration No. 203)	5		10. 5.28	Crashed at Golden Grove, South Australia and DBF on 4.9.28. Canx 11.9.28.
G-AUHJ	DH.60X Moth (Cirrus III) (Certificate of Registration No. 205)	466		25. 5.28	Crashed at Bulolo, Wau, New Guinea on 7.10.30 (still marked as G-AUHJ). Canx 7.9.31.
G-AUHK	Avro 594 Avian III (Certificate of Registration No. 213)	R3/CN/120		7. 8.28	Re-regd as VH-UHK by 31.8.30. Canx.
G-AUHL	Farman Sport (Certificate of Registration No. 207)	30		15. 6.28	Re-regd as VH-UHL on 2.5.29. Canx.
G-AUHM	Farman Sport (Certificate of Registration No. 208)	31		15. 6.28	Re-regd as VH-UHM by 31.8.30. Canx.
G-AUHN	DH.60G Gipsy Moth (Certificate of Registration No. 239)	875		28.12.28	Fatal crash from 2500 ft. at Brighton-le-Sands, New South Wales on 8.8.30. Canx 20.11.31.
G-AUHO	DH.60G Gipsy Moth (Certificate of Registration No. 240)	876		28.12.28	Crashed on landing at Goulburn, New South Wales and DBF on 28.5.29. Canx 5.6.29.
G-AUHP	DH.60G Gipsy Moth (Certificate of Registration No. 321)	877		30. 8.29	Re-regd as VH-UHP by 31.3.30. Canx.
G-AUHQ	DH.60G Gipsy Moth (Certificate of Registration No. 246)	878		21. 1.29	Re-regd as VH-UHQ by 3/32. Canx.
G-AUHR	DH.60G Gipsy Moth	879		.11.28R	NTU - To VH-UHR on 16.8.30 (CofR No.396). Canx.
G-AUHS	DH.60G Gipsy Moth (Certificate of Registration No. 271)	880		4. 3.29	Re-regd as VH-UHS by 31.3.30. Canx.
G-AUHT	Airco DH.9 (Certificate of Registration No. 209)	-		28. 7.28	Re-regd as VH-UHT by 17.4.30. Canx.
G-AUHU	Westland Widgeon III (Certificate of Registration No. 211)	WA.1695	G-EBUB	30. 7.28	Re-regd as VH-UHU by 7.4.30. Canx.
G-AUHV	American Eagle (Certificate of Registration No. 212)	238		1. 8.28	Re-regd as VH-UHV on 27.5.29. Canx.
G-AUHW	DH.61 Giant Moth (Certificate of Registration No. 230)	330		19.11.28	Re-regd as VH-UHW by 31.8.30. Canx.
G-AUHX	Avro 594 Avian III (Certificate of Registration No. 220)	R3/CN/235	G-EBXZ	31. 7.28	Re-regd as VH-UHX by 31.8.30. Canx.
G-AUHY	Avro 594 Avian IIIA (Certificate of Registration No. 228)	R3/CN/164		1.11.28	Re-regd as VH-UHY by 31.8.30. Canx.
G-AUHZ	Avro 594 Avian IIIA (Certificate of Registration No. 219)	R3/CN/144		3. 9.28	Re-regd as VH-UHZ on 13.3.33. Canx.
G-AUIA	DH.60G Gipsy Moth (Certificate of Registration No. 259)	835		5. 2.29	Re-regd as VH-UIA on 15.5.29. Canx.
G-AUIB	DH.60G Gipsy Moth (Certificate of Registration No. 296)	848		19. 6.29	Re-regd as VH-UIB by 31.8.30. Canx.
G-AUIC	DH.60G Gipsy Moth (Certificate of Registration No. 247)	849		22. 1.29	Re-regd as VH-UIC on 16.12.29. Canx.
G-AUID	DH.60G Gipsy Moth (Certificate of Registration No. 231)	819		27.11.28	Re-regd as VH-UID by 31.12.32. Canx.
G-AUIE	DH.60G Gipsy Moth (Certificate of Registration No. 248)	820		22. 1.29	Re-regd as VH-UIE in 3/30. Canx.
G-AUIF	DH.60G Gipsy Moth (Certificate of Registration No. 233)	821		10.12.28	Re-regd as VH-UIF by 31.8.30. Canx.
G-AUIG	DH.60G Gipsy Moth (Certificate of Registration No. 234)	822		10.12.28	Re-regd as VH-UIG by 31.8.30. Canx.
G-AUIH	DH.60G Gipsy Moth (Certificate of Registration No. 244)	823		16. 1.29	Re-regd as VH-UIH by 31.8.30. Canx.
G-AUII	Not allotted.				
G-AUIJ	DH.60G Gipsy Moth (Certificate of Registration No. 238)	824		10. 1.29	Re-regd as VH-UIJ by 31.8.30. Canx.
G-AUIK	Avro 594 Avian IIIA (Certificate of Registration No. 221)	R3/CN/145		13. 9.28	Re-regd as VH-UIK pre-9/30. Canx.
G-AUIL	Avro 594 Avian IIIA (Certificate of Registration No. 222)	R3/CN/146		13. 9.28	Re-regd as VH-UIL on 29.3.32. Canx.
G-AUIM	DH.51B Floatplane (Certificate of Registration No. 170)(Originally regd as DH.51A, converted in 1929)	100	G-EBIM	28. 7.27	Re-regd as VH-UIM by 31.8.30. Canx.
G-AUIN	Westland Widgeon III (Certificate of Registration No. 223)	WA.1697	G-EBUD	26. 9.28	Crashed at Grenfell, New South Wales on 30.11.29. Canx 16.12.29.

Regn	Type	c/n	Previous identity	Regn date	Fate or immediate subsequent identity (if known)
G-AUIO	DH.60G Gipsy Moth (Certificate of Registration No. 249)	891		22. 1.29	Re-regd as VH-UIO by 31.12.32. Canx.
G-AUIP	DH.60G Gipsy Moth (Certificate of Registration No. 255)	892		25. 1.29	Re-regd as VH-UIP by 18.11.29. Canx.
G-AUIQ	DH.60G Gipsy Moth (Certificate of Registration No. 270)	893		28. 2.29	Re-regd as VH-UIQ by 31.8.30. Canx.
G-AUIR	DH.60G Gipsy Moth (Certificate of Registration No. 263)	894		13. 2.29	Re-regd as VH-UIR by 31.12.32. Canx.
G-AUIS	DH.60G Gipsy Moth (Certificate of Registration No. 254)	895		24. 1.29	Crashed on take-off in cross-wind and DBF at Urunga, New South Wales on 26.12.29. Canx 31.12.29. Engine used in construction of DH.60M Moth VH-UII in 1930/31.
G-AUIT	Simmonds Spartan (Certificate of Registration No. 269)	3	ZK-AAP	25. 2.29	Re-regd as VH-UIT by 31.8.30. Canx.
G-AUIU	Avro 594 Avian IIIA (Certificate of Registration No. 245)	R3/CN/192		17. 1.29	Re-regd as VH-UIU on 29.1.30. Canx.
G-AUIV	Avro 594 Avian IIIA (Certificate of Registration No. 235)	R3/CN/193		14.12.28	Re-regd as VH-UIV by 31.8.30. Canx.
G-AUIW	Not allotted.				
G-AUIX	Ryan B.1 Brougham (Certificate of Registration No. 225)	148	N6963	10.10.28	Crashed on take-off at Athens, Greece on 26.11.28, on flight from Australia to England. Canx 31.12.28.
G-AUIY	Westland Widgeon III (Certificate of Registration No. 227)	WA.1773		30.10.28	Crashed after take-off at Wagga Wagga, New South Wales on 24.12.28. Canx 31.7.29.
G-AUIZ	Ryan B.1 Brougham (Certificate of Registration No. 226)	92	N4938	15.10.28	Re-regd as VH-UIZ by 31.8.30. Canx.
G-AUJA	Airco DH.9C (Certificate of Registration No. 229)	-	G-EBXR H9276	8.11.28	Forced landing in sea off Salamaua, New Guinea on 2.11.29. Canx 12.12.29.
G-AUJB	DH.61 Giant Moth (Certificate of Registration No. 283)	334	"G-AUJD"	3. 5.29	Re-regd as VH-UJB on 16.7.29. Canx.
G-AUJC	DH.61 Giant Moth (Certificate of Registration No. 284)	333		3. 5.29	Re-regd as VH-UJC by 31.8.30. Canx.
G-AUJD	Junkers W.34b (Certificate of Registration No. 232)	2604		4.12.28	Badly damaged when undercarriage collapsed on landing at Wampit, New Guinea on 17.1.31. Canx 3.12.31.
"G-AUJD"	DH.61 Giant Moth	334		----	Incorrect marks carried on flights made between 17.4.29 and 22.4.29, then corrected marks G-AUJB applied.
G-AUJE	Curtiss Robin (Certificate of Registration No. 241)	AB.34		31.12.28	Re-regd as VH-UJE by 31.8.30. Canx.
G-AUJF	Avro 594 Avian IIIA (Certificate of Registration No. 236)	R3/CN/184		14.12.28	Re-regd as VH-UJF by 31.8.30. Canx.
G-AUJG	Avro 594 Avian IIIA (Certificate of Registration No. 237)(Fitted with Mk.IV undercarriage and wings in 1929)	R3/CN/185		17.12.28	Re-regd as VH-UJG by 31.8.30. Canx.
G-AUJH	DH.60G Gipsy Moth (Certificate of Registration No. 265)	982		13. 2.29	Re-regd as VH-UJH on 18.9.30. Canx.
G-AUJI	DH.60G Gipsy Moth (Certificate of Registration No. 272)	983		4. 3.29	Re-regd as VH-UJI by 31.8.30. Canx.
G-AUJJ	Sopwith Dove (Certificate of Registration No. 26)	3004/4	G-EAJJ	12. 7.21	Scrapped in 6/25. Canx 27.6.25.
G-AUJK	DH.60G Gipsy Moth (Certificate of Registration No. 273)	984		21. 3.29	Re-regd as VH-UJK by 31.8.30. Canx.
G-AUJL	DH.60G Gipsy Moth	985		. 1.29R	NTU - To VH-UJL (CofR No.274) on 2.4.29. Canx.
G-AUJM	DH.60G Gipsy Moth (Certificate of Registration No. 285)	986		3. 5.29	Re-regd as VH-UJM on 7.5.29. Canx.
G-AUJN	DH.60G Gipsy Moth (Certificate of Registration No. 317)	987		. 1.29R	Re-regd as VH-UJN (CofR No. 317) on 26.8.29. Canx.
G-AUJO	DH.66 Hercules (Certificate of Registration No. 293)	344		28. 5.29	Re-regd as VH-UJO on 22.2.33. Canx.
G-AUJP	DH.66 Hercules (Certificate of Registration No. 291)	345		27. 5.29	Re-regd as VH-UJP on 6.1.31. Canx.
G-AUJQ	DH.66 Hercules (Certificate of Registration No. 292)	346		27. 5.29	To G-ABMT 6/31. Canx 26.5.31.
G-AUJR	DH.66 Hercules (Certificate of Registration No. 297)	347		21. 6.29	To G-ABCP 7/30. Canx 19.6.30.
G-AUJS	DH.50A (Certificate of Registration No. 242)	6		4. 1.29	Re-regd as VH-UJS by 20.1.30. Canx.
G-AUJT	Atlantic-Fokker IV/F.XI Universal (Certificate of Registration No. 243)	436	NC8046	16. 1.29	Re-regd as VH-UJT by 17.4.30. Canx.
G-AUJU	DH.60G Gipsy Moth (Certificate of Registration No. 260)	836		7. 2.29	Re-regd as VH-UJU by 31.8.30. Canx.
G-AUJV	DH.60G Gipsy Moth (Certificate of Registration No. 256)	846		25. 1.29	Re-regd as VH-UJV by 31.8.30. Canx.
G-AUJW	DH.60G Gipsy Moth (Certificate of Registration No. 258)	837		25. 1.29	Re-regd as VH-UJW by 20.11.29. Canx.
G-AUJX	DH.60G Gipsy Moth (Certificate of Registration No. 257)	838		25. 1.29	Re-regd as VH-UJX by 17.4.30. Canx.
G-AUJY	Avro 594 Avian IIIA (Certificate of Registration No. 251)	R3/CN/155	G-EBYR	24. 1.29	Re-regd as VH-UJY on 28.8.29. Canx.
G-AUJZ	Avro 594 Avian IV (Certificate of Registration No. 252)	R3/CN/202		24. 1.29	Re-regd as VH-UJZ by 31.10.29. Canx.
G-AUKA(1)	Avro 594 Avian IV	R3/CN/201		24. 1.29	NTU - To G-AUKD on 24.1.29. Canx.
G-AUKA(2)	Westland Widgeon III	WA.1775		. 4.29R	Force landed between Alice Springs and Wyndham, in Tanami Desert, Northern Territory on 10.4.29. No CofR issued. Canx. Remains found on 30.8.78 and are now in the Central Australian Museum, Alice Springs, Northern Territory.

Regn	Type	c/n	Previous identity	Regn date	Fate or immediate subsequent identity (if known)
"G-AUKA"	Westland Widgeon III	-		----	Really VH-UHU c/n WA.1695.
G-AUKB	Wackett Widgeon II	-	"G-AEKB"	. .25	Launched 7.7.25 carrying the markings G-AEKB, said to stand for E.K.Bowden, Minister of Defence at the time. Regn NTU. Transferred to RAAF.
G-AUKC	DH.60M Moth	711		. 3.29R	NTU - To VH-UKC on 9.5.29 (CofR No.286). Canx.
G-AUKD	Avro 594 Avian IV (Certificate of Registration No. 253)	R3/CN/201	(G-AUKA)	24. 1.29	Re-regd as VH-UKD on 31.7.30. Canx.
G-AUKE	Westland Widgeon III (Certificate of Registration No. 266)	WA.1777		19. 2.29	Re-regd as VH-UKE by 31.8.30. Canx.
G-AUKF	DH.60H Gipsy Moth (Certificate of Registration No. 277)	974		. 1.29R	NTU - To VH-UKF (CofR No. 277) on 4.4.29. Canx.
G-AUKG	DH.60G Gipsy Moth (Certificate of Registration No. 250)	897		20. 2.29	Re-regd as VH-UKG in 2/30. Canx.
G-AUKH	Sopwith Dove (Certificate of Registration No. 27)	3004/5	G-EAKH	12. 7.21	Last flown on 18.6.25. Scrapped in 6/28. Canx 19.6.28.
G-AUKI	Airco DH.9C (Certificate of Registration No. 262)	-		13. 2.29	Re-regd as VH-UKI on 9.7.29. Crashed at Port Moresby, New Guinea on 13.7.29. Canx 16.12.29.
	Note: This aircraft has absolutely no connection whatsoever with G-EAQM/F1278, which flew marked only as "P.D." and arrived in Australia in 8/20, then stored until purchased by Australian War Museum in 1923, and is currently on display at Australian War Memorial Canberra, Australia.				
G-AUKJ	DH.60G Gipsy Moth	975		. 1.29R	NTU - To VH-UKJ (CofR No. 276) on 4.4.29. Canx.
G-AUKK	Not allotted.				
G-AUKL	DH.60G Gipsy Moth (Certificate of Registration No. 275)	973		2. 4.29	Re-regd as VH-UKL by 5/31. Canx.
G-AUKM	Not allotted.				
G-AUKN	DH.60G Gipsy Moth	972		. 1.29R	NTU - To VH-UKN (CofR No. 279) on 9.4.29. Canx.
G-AUKO to G-AUKT	Not allotted. Not allotted.				
G-AUKU	DH.60G Gipsy Moth	1065		. 2.29R	NTU - To VH-UKU (CofR No. 290) on 22.5.29. Canx.
G-AUKV	DH.60G Gipsy Moth	1066		. 2.29R	NTU - To VH-UKV (CofR No. 301) on 5.7.29. Canx.
G-AUKW	Not allotted.				
G-AUKX	DH.60G Gipsy Moth	1073		. 2.29R	NTU - To VH-UKX (CofR No. 298) on 24.6.29. Canx.
G-AUKY	Not allotted.				
G-AUKZ	Not allotted.				
G-AULA	DH.60G Gipsy Moth (Certificate of Registration No. 261)	847		8. 2.29	Re-regd as VH-ULA by 31.8.30. Canx.
G-AULB	Not allotted.				
G-AULC	DH.60G Gipsy Moth (Certificate of Registration No. 267)	898		20. 2.29	Re-regd as VH-ULC by 31.8.30. Canx.
G-AULD to G-AULI	Not allotted. Not allotted.				
G-AULJ	DH.60G Gipsy Moth	1074		. 2.29R	(Noted at Archerfield, Queensland on 24.2.30 and 17.3.30 marked as G-AULJ) Re-regd as VH-ULJ (CofR No.307) on 3.8.29. Canx.
G-AULK	Not allotted.				
G-AULL	DH.60M Moth	712		. 2.29R	NTU - To VH-ULL on 30.8.29 (CofR No.320). (Crashed at Modbury, South Australia on 26.11.29; remains noted at Parafield, South Australia on 23.2.30 marked as G-AULL) Canx 22.12.30.
G-AULM to G-AULP	Not allotted. Not allotted.				
G-AULQ	DH.60G Gipsy Moth	976		. 1.29R	NTU - To VH-ULQ (CofR No. 311) on 13.8.29. Canx.
G-AULR	DH.60G Gipsy Moth	977		. 1.29R	NTU - To VH-ULR (CofR No. 313) on 16.8.29. Canx.
G-AULS to G-AUMD	Not allotted. Not allotted.				
G-AUME	DH.60 Moth (Cirrus II) (Certificate of Registration No. 185)	193	G-EBME	26. 1.28	Fatal crash ¼ mile west of Essendon Airfield, Victoria on 26.12.28. Canx 31.12.28.
G-AUMF to G-AUMU	Not allotted. Not allotted.				
G-AUMV	DH.60G Gipsy Moth (Certificate of Registration No. 264)	896		13. 2.29	Re-regd as VH-UMV by 31.12.32. Canx.
G-AUMW to G-AUNA	Not allotted. Not allotted.				
G-AUNB	DH.60M Moth	1408		. .29R	NTU - To VH-UNB on 22.12.29 (CofR No.349). (Noted at Archerfield, Queensland on 24.2.30 marked as G-AUNB) Canx.
G-AUNC to G-AUNI	Not allotted. Not allotted.				
G-AUNJ	Avro 618 Ten (Certificate of Registration No. 358)	371		8. 2.30	Re-regd as VH-UNJ by 17.3.30. Canx.
G-AUNK	Avro 619 Five (Certificate of Registration No. 360)	370		10. 2.30	Re-regd as VH-UNK by 17.3.30. Canx.
G-AUNL to G-AUNY	Not allotted. Not allotted.				
G-AUNZ	Ryan B.1 Brougham	47		. .28R	NTU - Disappeared on flight from RAAF Base Richmond, New South Wales to New Zealand on 10.1.28. Canx.

Regn	Type	c/n	Previous identity	Regn date	Fate or immediate subsequent identity (if known)
G-AUOA to G-AUPO	Not allotted.				
G-AUPP	DH.60 Moth (Cirrus II) (Certificate of Registration No. 156)	355	G-EBPP	14. 3.27	Re-regd as VH-UPP on 31.10.29. Canx.
G-AUPQ to G-AUPY	Not allotted.				
G-AUPZ	Short Shrimp Seaplane (Certificate of Registration No. 62)	S.540	G-EAPZ	19. 6.22	Crashed in Rose Bay, New South Wales on 20.1.23 & DBR. Canx 28.1.23.
G-AUQA to G-AUSR	Not allotted.				
G-AUSS	Sopwith Antelope (Certificate of Registration No. 87 - Covering letter issued with CofR mentions No.81 which was issued to G-AUEC)	3398	G-EASS	19. 4.23	Re-regd as VH-USS by 31.8.30. Canx.
G-AUST	Not allotted.				
G-AUSU	Fokker F.VIIa/3m (Certificate of Registration No. 210)	4954	N1985	4. 7.28	Re-regd as VH-USU on 11.6.29. Canx.
G-AUSV to G-AUTK	Not allotted.				
G-AUTL	DH.61 Giant Moth (Certificate of Registration No. 191)	325	G-EBTL	6. 3.28	Re-regd as VH-UTL by 17.4.30. Canx.
G-AUTM to G-AUTT	Not allotted.				
G-AUTU	Avro 594 Avian III (Certificate of Registration No. 206)	R3/AV/125	G-EBTU	30. 5.28	Re-regd as VH-UTU by 31.8.30. Canx.

CANADA

The G-CA.. register served until 31.12.28, with the marks G-CAWI being the last in this series of registration marks to be issued. On the following day Canada adopted the nationality marks CF, followed by a hyphen and three registration marks running from AAA to ZZZ. Those aircraft which had been registered previously with G-CA.. markings continued to display them until they were retired from service. The last aircraft to fly with these marks was the DH.60G Moth G-CAPA, which was exported to the United States in 10.55 to fly for Warner Bros. registered as N1510V.

A seperate series was created in Canada, with the initial marks CY, for aircraft operated on Canadian Government Air Operations by the Royal Canadian Air Force (eg; G CYAA). The issue of these quasi-military markings continued until 1931, by which time they were being displayed in abbreviated form - ie; the last two letters only. Aircraft still wearing these marks were absorbed into the then-existent RCAF numerical series in 1939. Registrations were issued from G-CYAA until G-CYHE was reached in 1926, with further aircraft being issued registration marks working backwards from G-CYZZ (in 1927) until G-CYUR (in 1931), the batch from G-CYHE to G-CYUQ were not allotted as the RCAF were using a numercial series for registration marks on aircraft in their use by this time.

US aircraft did not conform either to the licencing requirements of the International Convention for Air Navigation (of 1919) or to those of the Canadian Air Regulations. The problem of American aircraft wishing to fly in Canada arose at the start of the 1920 flying season, since in the previous year they had been permitted to operate freely in this country. The problem was resolved with US aircraft, that could pass inspection, would be allowed to fly in Canada following the normal procedures, but that the allotted Canadian registration marks must be preceded by the US nationality mark, N (eg; N-CACM). The Air Regulations were amended, on 21.7.20, to allow this temporary concession whilst the US Government drafted its own legislation. In the event, over six years were to pass before the United States started licencing aircraft.

Regn	Type	c/n	Previous identity	Regn date	Fate or immediate subsequent identity (if known)

G-CA G-CA

G-CAAA to G-CAXP - Allocated to Canada from 4/20 until 1/29.

G-CAAA Curtiss JN-4 - C-210 20. 4.20 Fatal crash at Shaunavon, Sask. on 30.6.26.
(Certificate of Registration No. 1, (Royal Air Force Canada)
then Certificate of Registration No. 236 issued 18.10.23, then Certificate of Registration No. 256 issued 22.5.24)
G-CAAB Curtiss JN-4 - C-1457 22. 4.20 Fatal crash at Saskatoon, Sask. on 3.5.20.
(Certificate of Registration No. 2) (Royal Air Force Canada)
G-CAAC Curtiss HS-2L 2901-H-2 A-1876 2. 6.20 DBR on take-off from lake north of Fauquier, Ont. on 2.9.22. (On display 1997 Rockcliffe, Canada)
(Certificate of Registration No. 25) (US Navy)
G-CAAD Curtiss HS-2L - A-1878 30. 9.20 DBR on take-off from Tadoussac, Que. on 4.8.22.
(Certificate of Registration No. 94) (US Navy)
G-CAAE Avro 504K - G-EABO 16. 7.20 Crashed at St.Louis, PQ on 22.5.22. CofA expired 31.7.24. Canx.
(Certificate of Registration No. 48) D6202
G-CAAF Curtiss JN-4 AB.2 27. 4.20 Crashed near Minoru Park Racecourse, Vancouver, BC. on 24.5.20.
(Certificate of Registration No. 3) (Royal Air Force Canada)
G-CAAG Curtiss JN-4 - C-206 27. 4.20 CofA expired 30.4.24. Canx.
(Certificate of Registration No. 4, (Royal Air Force Canada)
then Certificate of Registration No. 186 issued 24.8.21)
G-CAAH Curtiss JN-4 - 3. 5.20 Crashed on landing at Bowness Park, Calgary, Alta. on 12.6.21.
(Certificate of Registration No. 5) (US Army Air Service)
G-CAAI Curtiss JN-4 - C-1347 7. 5.20 CofA expired 30.4.24. Canx.
(Certificate of Registration No. 6) (Royal Air Force Canada)
G-CAAJ Curtiss JN-4 19 8. 5.20 CofA expired 13.8.24. Dismantled & stored at Shaunavon, Sask. in 1924. Canx.
(Certificate of Registration No. 10,
then Certificate of Registration No. 233 issued 13.8.23)
G-CAAK Curtiss JN-4 - C-122 10. 5.20 DBR in force landing at Calgary, Alta. on 28.6.23.
(Certificate of Registration No. 7, (Royal Air Force Canada)
then Certificate of Registration No. 223 issued 22.5.23)
G-CAAL Curtiss JN-4 11 12. 5.20 Crashed near Swift Current, Sask. on 7.10.30.
(Certificate of Registration No. 8, then Certificate of Registration No. 318 issued 11.8.27, then Certificate of Registration No. 496 issued 13.8.28)
G-CAAM Curtiss JN-4 - C-590 14. 5.20 Crashed at Regina, Sask. on 27.9.23.
(Certificate of Registration No. 11, (Royal Air Force Canada)
then Certificate of Registration No. 227 issued 4.6.23)
G-CAAN Curtiss JN-4 - C-197 18. 5.20 DBR in severe windstorm at Winnipeg(?), Man. on 7.2.21.
(Certificate of Registration No. 16) (Royal Air Force Canada)
G-CAAO Curtiss JN-4 - C-282 18. 5.20 CofA expired 30.4.24. Stored at Winnipeg. Canx.
(Certificate of Registration No. 15) (Royal Air Force Canada)
G-CAAP Curtiss JN-4 - C-291 19. 5.20 DBF at Winnipeg, Man. in 7/21.
(Certificate of Registration No. 17) (Royal Air Force Canada)
G-CAAQ Avro 504K - H2292 20. 5.20 Crashed on take-off from Winnipeg, Man. on 13.8.27. Fuselage used to build G-CASY in 1928/29.
(Certificate of Registration No. 19,
then Certificate of Registration No. 262 issued 5.9.24, then Certificate of Registration No. 269 issued 8.7.25)
G-CAAR Avro 504K - D9076 20. 5.20 Crashed on landing at Fort Frances, Ont. on 26.8.20.
(Certificate of Registration No. 20)
G-CAAS Curtiss JN-4 - C-437 26. 5.20 CofA expired 30.4.24. Canx.
(Although G-CADI has the same p.i. (Royal Air Force Canada)
it is unlikely that they are the same aircraft unless the fuselage was used to build G-CADI later in 1920)
(Certificate of Registration No. 40)
G-CAAT Curtiss JN-4 - C-628 27. 5.20 Canx 1.1.25. Possibly scrapped.
(Certificate of Registration No. 23, (Royal Air Force Canada)
then Certificate of Registration No. 237 issued 24.10.23)
G-CAAU Curtiss JN-4 - C-1350 4. 6.20 Crashed at St.Laurent, Montreal, Que. on 24.8.21.
(Certificate of Registration No. 26) (Royal Air Force Canada)

Regn	Type	c/n	Previous identity	Regn date	Fate or immediate subsequent identity (if known)
G-CAAV	Curtiss JN-4 (Certificate of Registration No. 31)	-	C-118 (Royal Air Force Canada)	8. 6.20	CofA expired 1.4.24. Scrapped. Canx.
G-CAAW	Curtiss JN-4 (Certificate of Registration No. 32)	-	C-290 (Royal Air Force Canada)	8. 6.20	CofA expired 1.4.24. Scrapped. Canx.
G-CAAX	Martinsyde Type A Mk.1 (Certificate of Registration No. 55)	15/216/1		21. 7.20	Crashed at Lake Onatchiway, Que. on 18.8.20.
G-CAAY	Sopwith Dove (C/n also quoted as 33937) (Certificate of Registration No. 42)	2714	G-EACM K-122	23. 6.20	DBR at Sault Ste Marie, Ont. in 1921. Canx.
G-CAAZ	Curtiss HS-2L (Certificate of Registration No. 53)	-	A-2119 (US Navy)	21. 7.20	DBF in hangar fire at Burlington, Ont. on 12.9.21.
G-CABA	Curtiss JN-4 (Certificate of Registration No. 9)	AB.1	(Royal Air Force Canada)	12. 5.20	DBR after hitting a car on landing at Chénéville, Que. on 3.8.21.
G-CABB	Curtiss JN-4 (Certificate of Registration No. 12) then Certificate of Registration No. 234 issued 11.9.23)	-	(Royal Air Force Canada)	17. 5.20	CofA expired 30.4.24. Canx.
G-CABC	Curtiss JN-4 (Certificate of Registration No. 13)	AB.3	(Royal Air Force Canada)	17. 5.20	CofA expired 30.4.24. Canx.
G-CABD	Avro 504K (Certificate of Registration No. 14)	AB.4	D8842	17. 5.20	CofA expired 31.7.24. Canx.
G-CABE	Curtiss JN-4 (Possibly c/n AB.5) (Certificate of Registration No. 18)	-	C-162 (Royal Air Force Canada)	19. 5.20	CofA expired 30.4.24. Canx.
G-CABF	Curtiss F Boat (Possibly c/n AB.6)	-		. .20R	DBR at Toronto, Ont on 5.7.20 during test flight before CofR was issued.
G-CABG	Curtiss JN-4 (Certificate of Registration No. 21)	AB.7	(Royal Air Force Canada)	22. 5.20	CofA expired 20.10.21. Canx.
G-CABH	Curtiss JN-4 (Possibly c/n AB.8)(Certificate of Registration No. 27)	-		24. 5.20	CofA expired 1.4.24. Canx.
G-CABI	Curtiss JN-4 (Possibly also c/n AB.9)(Certificate of Registration No. 22, then Certificate of Registration No. 178 issued 2.6.21)	5002		25. 5.20	DBR in forced landing near Peterborough, Ont. on 16.9.22.
G-CABJ	Curtiss JN-4 (Certificate of Registration No. 24, then Certificate of Registration No. 290 issued 17.9.26)	AB.10	C-187 (Royal Air Force Canada)	28. 5.20	CofA expired 31.7.27. Canx.
G-CABK	Curtiss JN-4 (Possibly c/n AB.11) (Certificate of Registration No. 28)	-	C-122 (Royal Air Force Canada)	31. 5.20	DBF in hangar fire at Burlington, Ont. on 12.9.21.
G-CABL	Curtiss JN-4 (Possibly c/n AB.12) (Certificate of Registration No. 29)	-	C-109 (Royal Air Force Canada)	31. 5.20	DBF in hangar fire at Burlington, Ont. on 12.9.21.
G-CABM	Aeromarine 40L (Certificate of Registration No. 30)	AB.13		7. 6.20	Fatal crash at Tiptonville, Tenn., USA on 9.1.21.
G-CABN	Curtiss JN-4 (Possibly c/n AB.14) (Certificate of Registration No. 33)	-	C-1353 (Royal Air Force Canada)	16. 6.20	DBR in 7/20 (details unknown). Canx.
G-CABO	Curtiss JN-4 (Possibly c/n AB.15) (Certificate of Registration No. 34)	-	C-144 (Royal Air Force Canada)	13. 6.20	DBR on 10.8.20 (details unknown). Canx.
G-CABP	Avro 504K (Certificate of Registration No. 35)	AB.16	(ex.RAF)	17. 6.20	Damaged at Edmonton, Alta. on 3.1.21. Canx.
G-CABQ	Curtiss JN-4 (Possibly c/n AB.17) (Certificate of Registration No. 41, then Certificate of Registration No. 185 issued 5.9.21)	-	C-1303 (Royal Air Force Canada)	21. 6.20	CofR lapsed on 1.8.24. To CF-ALE on 20.3.30. Canx.
G-CABR	Curtiss JN-4 (Possibly c/n AB.18) (Certificate of Registration No. 44, then Certificate of Registration No. 204 issued 26.6.22)	-	C-1022 (Royal Air Force Canada)	26. 6.20	Crashed into a flagpole on take-off from Boissevain, Man. on 2.8.22.
G-CABS	Avro 548 (Possibly c/n AB.19)	-	B8997	. .20	Forced landing at Charles, Man on 16.7.20 - Rebuilt & re-regd as G-CACI on 15.6.21. Canx.
G-CABT	Curtiss JN-4 (Possibly also c/n AB.20) (Certificate of Registration No. 45, then Certificate of Registration No. 196 issued 25.4.22)	5005		2. 7.20	DBF on landing near Edgerton, Alta. in 10/22. Canx.
G-CABU	Curtiss JN-4 (Possibly c/n AB.21) (Certificate of Registration No. 47)	-	C-1293 (Royal Air Force Canada)	7. 7.20	DBR when force landed on sea near Nalan Island, BC. on 20.9.20.
G-CABV	Avro 504K (Possibly c/n AB.22)(Certificate of Registration No. 52)	-	9738	19. 7.20	CofA expired 31.7.24. Canx. Wings possibly used on G-CAAQ.
G-CABW	Curtiss JN-4 (Possibly c/n AB.23) (Certificate of Registration No. 51)	-	C-148 (Royal Air Force Canada)	15. 7.20	CofR lapsed 30.4.24. Canx.
G-CABX	Curtiss JN-4 (Certificate of Registration No. 87)	AB.24	(Royal Air Force Canada)	28. 8.20	CofR lapsed 31.7.24. To G-CATE on 13.7.28. Canx.
G-CABY	Curtiss JN-4 (Possibly also c/n AB.25)(Certificate of Registration No. 58)	5004		22. 7.20	CofA expired 29.12.21. (May have been w/o in 7/20). Canx.
G-CABZ	Curtiss JN-4 (Possibly also c/n AB.26) (Certificate of Registration No. 83)	1837		10. 8.20	Stripped by vandals whilst stored in field at Yorkton, Sask. during winter of 1923/24. Canx.
G-CACA(1)	Standard J-1 (Possibly c/n AB.27)(Curtiss built) (Certificate of Registration No. 85)	-	AS.22455 (US Army Air Service)	20. 8.20	DBR in windstorm at Winnipeg(?), Man. on 15.7.22. Canx.
G-CACA(2)	Standard J-1 (Maker listed as Fisher Body Co.)	-		11. 7.24	Crashed on take-off from a field 13 miles east of Estevan, Sask. on 1.10.24.

Regn	Type	c/n	Previous identity	Regn date	Fate or immediate subsequent identity (if known)
G-CACB	Curtiss JN-4D	8708		23. 8.20	Canx 20.1.21. (Was operated in USA).
	(Possibly also c/n AB.28)		(US Army Air Service)		
	(Certificate of Registration No. 88)				
G-CACC	Curtiss JN-4	AB.29		26. 8.20	CofR lapsed & Canx 30.4.24.
	(Certificate of Registration No. 86)		(Royal Air Force Canada)		
G-CACD	Avro 548	1160		5.10.20	CofR lapsed 31.7.24. Canx.
	(Certificate of Registration No. 93)				
G-CACE	Nieuport 81.E2	1714		22. 6.21	DBF at Armour Heights (Toronto), Ont. on 31.8.21.
	(Certificate of Registration No. 81)				
G-CACF	Curtiss JN-4	5014		20. 4.21	DBF on 9.7.21 (details unknown). Canx.
	(Certificate of Registration No. 156)				
G-CACG	Norman-Thompson NT.2B	-	G-EAQO	9. 6.21	CofR lapsed 31.8.26. Canx.
	(Certificate of Registration No. 80,		N2290		
	then Certificate of Registration No. 249 issued 21.5.24)				
G-CACH	Standard J-1	-	N-CACH	17. 3.23	CofR lapsed 1.5.24. To USA. Canx.
	(Certificate of Registration No. 217,		US Army Air Service AS.4887		
	then Certificate of Registration No. 239 issued 9.1.24)				
G-CACI	Avro 548	-	G-CABS	15. 6.21	W/o (details?). Canx 16.11.23.
	(Certificate of Registration No. 82)		D8997		
G-CACJ	Curtiss JN-4	-	C-574	23. 5.22	Crashed on landing at Esquimalt Harbour, BC. on 24.2.23.
	(Certificate of Registration No. 199)		(Royal Air Force Canada)		
G-CACK	Curtiss JN-4	945	C-945	1. 6.21	Canx 30.4.24.
	(Certificate of Registration No. 173)		(Royal Air Force Canada)		
G-CACL	Standard J-1	-	41315	21. 2.23	CofR lapsed 1.5.23. Canx.
	(Certificate of Registration No. 218)		(US Army Air Service)		
N-CACM	Curtiss HS-2L	-	A-4248	11. 8.21	Canx 1.5.22. To USA.
	(Certificate of Registration No. 183)		(US Navy)		
G-CACN	Avro 548	1161		27. 6.21	Crashed on take-off from Ardmore, Alta. on 6.7.21. Canx.
	(Certificate of Registration No. 174)				
G-CACO	Curtiss JN-4	-		12. 7.21	DBR in forced landing at Victoria, BC. on 19.3.22. Canx.
	(Certificate of Registration No. 177,		(Royal Air Force Canada)		
	then Certificate of Registration No. 195 issued 28.1.22)				
G-CACP	Curtiss JN-4	5018		26.10.21	DBR in accident on 25.8.25. (details?). Canx.
	(Certificate of Registration No. 192, then Certificate of Registration No. 205 issued 20.6.22, then Certificate of Registration No. 272 issued 11.7.25)				
G-CACQ	Curtiss JN-4	-	C-426	31. 5.22	Abandoned at Melfort, Sask. at end of 1922 flying season.
	(Certificate of Registration No. 200)		(Royal Air Force Canada)		CofA expired 1.8.24. Canx.
G-CACR	Curtiss JN-4	61		26. 6.22	CofR lapsed 13.9.23. Canx.
	(Certificate of Registration No. 203)				
G-CACS	Curtiss HS-2L	583		26. 6.23	DBR in hard landing on a lake 30 miles north of Sept Iles,
	(Certificate of Registration No. 230,		(US Navy)		Que. on 16.7.26, sank after drifting to centre of lake.
	then Certificate of Registration No. 267 issued 26.6.25)				
G-CACT	Curtiss HS-2L	-	A-2260	16. 5.23	DBF after fuel tanks exploded when wing fabric ignited
	(Certificate of Registration No. 220,		(US Navy)		after engine backfired at Haileybury, Ont. on 22.10.25.
	then Certificate of Registration No. 265 issued 9.5.25)				
G-CACU	Curtiss HS-2L	-	A-2267	11. 5.23	Canx 16.6.24.
	(Certificate of Registration No. 221)		(US Navy)		
G-CACV	Curtiss HS-2L	-	A-2266	26. 5.23	Crashed while attemping to aviod a bridge at Biscotasing,
	(Certificate of Registration No. 224)		(US Navy)		Ont. on 17.7.23. Canx.
G-CACW	Curtiss HS-2L	-	A-2276	1. 6.23	Canx 16.6.24.
	(Certificate of Registration No. 225)		(US Navy)		
G-CACX	Curtiss HS-2L	-	A-2272	8. 6.23	WFU & possibly burned. Canx 10.8.25.
	(Certificate of Registration No. 226)		(US Navy)		
G-CACY	Curtiss HS-2L	-	A-2275	23. 6.23	CofA expired 16.6.24. Canx.
	(Certificate of Registration No. 228)		(US Navy)		
G-CACZ	Curtiss HS-2L	-		3. 7.23	Canx 16.6.24.
	(Certificate of Registration No. 231)		(US Navy)		
G-CADA	Curtiss JN-4	5006		25. 6.20	To G-CADN on 12.10.20. Canx 5.1.21.
	(Certificate of Registration No. 43)				
G-CADB	Curtiss HS-2L	-	A-1727	12. 7.20	DBR after landing in trees on forced landing near Brooklin,
	(Certificate of Registration No. 46)		(US Navy)		Ont. on 10.9.20. Canx.
G-CADC	Curtiss JN-4	-	C-249	23. 7.20	Canx 1.10.26.
	(Certificate of Registration No. 59,		(Royal Air Force Canada)		
	then Certificate of Registration No. 284 issued 26.6.26)				
G-CADD	Curtiss JN-4	-	C-434	13. 7.20	Canx 30.4.24.
	(Certificate of Registration No. 49)		(Royal Air Force Canada)		
G-CADE	Curtiss JN-4	-	C-120	12. 7.20	Flew into trees on take-off from Magog, Que. on 1.7.21.
	(Certificate of Registration No. 50)		(Royal Air Force Canada)		Canx 30.4.24.
G-CADF	Curtiss JN-4	-	C-123	21. 7.20	Canx 30.4.24.
	(Certificate of Registration No. 56,		(Royal Air Force Canada)		
	then Certificate of Registration No. 206 issued 9.7.22)				
G-CADG	Martinsyde Type A Mk.1	15/2		21. 7.20	DBR after striking a buoy on take-off and floats torn off
	(Certificate of Registration No. 57)				at Chicoutimi, Que. on 30.5.21. Canx.
G-CADH	Curtiss JN-4	5010		21. 7.20	Reportedly damaged during a take-off from Hoey, Sask.
	(Originally regd with c/n 5013)				in 7/23. CofA expired 15.8.23. Canx.
	(Certificate of Registration No. 54, then Certificate of Registration No. 181 issued 5.8.21, then Certificate of Registration No. 222 issued 18.5.22)				
G-CADI(1)	Curtiss JN-4	-	C-437	25. 8.20	Crashed in spin after controls jammed at Shawville, Que.
	(Certificate of Registration No. 84)		(Royal Air Force Canada)		on 22.9.20 & DBR. Canx.
	(C-437 had been flown at Ottawa in 1919, but had been damaged in a windstorm - rebuilt with new wings - bears same RAFC serial as G-CAAS)				
G-CADI(2)	Curtiss MF Seagull	270-17		2. 7.24	Dismantled. Canx 23.11.26.
	(Certificate of Registration No. 257, then Certificate of Registration No. 271 issued 27.7.25)				

Regn	Type	c/n	Previous identity	Regn date	Fate or immediate subsequent identity (if known)
G-CADJ	Curtiss JN-4 (Certificate of Registration No. 90)	-	(Royal Air Force Canada)	1. 9.20	Flew into hydro wires after engine failed during take-off at Quebec, Que. on 6.10.21. Canx.
G-CADK	Curtiss JN-4 (Regn modified to GC-ADK at one stage)(Certificate of Registration No. 89, then Certificate of Registration No. 209 issued 29.6.22, then Certificate of Registration No. 477 issued 19.6.28)	5012		4. 9.20	CofA expired 30.9.28. Canx.
G-CADL	Curtiss MF 1920 Seagull (Certificate of Registration No. 91)	736-1		30. 9.20	Crashed after loss of control when aircraft hit 'bump' and went into a spin at Grand Piles, Que. on 4.5.21. Canx.
G-CADM	Curtiss HS-2L (Certificate of Registration No. 129)	-	A-1721 (US Navy)	25.10.20	CofA expired 31.7.24. Canx.
G-CADN	Curtiss JN-4 (Certificate of Registration No. 95, then Certificate of Registration No. 232 issued 10.8.23)	5006	G-CADA	12.10.20	Canx 8.9.27.
G-CADO	Curtiss JN-4 (Certificate of Registration No. 130)	5015		29.10.20	DBF on 9.7.21. (Details?). Canx.
G-CADP	Junkers-Larsen JL-6 (Certificate of Registration No. 151, then Certificate of Registration No. 197 issued 17.5.22)	561		27. 1.21	Flown illegally in northern BC. in 1929, seized by RCMP on 23.9.29 and disabled - scrapped in 1930. Canx.
G-CADQ	Junkers-Larsen JL-6 (Certificate of Registration No. 152)	558		27. 1.21	DBR at Simpson on 21.8.21. CofA expired 31.7.24. Scrapped. Canx.
N-CADR	Boeing CL-4S (Seaplane) (Regd with c/n A.700, but this is a mix-up between the US Navy serial A-700 and the orig. Boeing designation C-700). (Certificate of Registration No. 137)	60		26.11.20	Crashed in 1921 (details?). Canx 12.8.22.
N-CADS	Boeing B-1 (Certificate of Registration No. 138)	86		26.11.20	Badly damaged when flew too low and hit water resulting in the hull bottom being torn open on a flight from Victoria to Seattle on 29.3.23. Canx. Rebuilt & reregd as N-ABNA.
N-CADT	Junkers-Larsen JL-6 (Certificate of Registration No. 153)	566		21. 2.21	Canx 11.11.21. Returned to US.
G-CADU	Curtiss HS-2L (Certificate of Registration No. 201)	-	A-2261 (US Navy)	27. 5.22	Canx 10.8.25 as w/o (due to unknown details).
G-CADV	Loening M-23 Air Yacht (Certificate of Registration No. 216)	1	N-ABCF	26. 8.22	DBR when fire extinguisher fell and jammed rudder bar on take-off resulting in hitting water and hull collapsing at Lac a la Tortue, Que. on 2.6.23. Canx.
G-CADW	Curtiss JN-4 (Regd as Curtiss Canuck) (Certificate of Registration No. 214)	5020		15. 9.22	DBR on stalling at low altitude after take-off near Hudson, Ont. on 26.3.26. Canx.
G-CADX	Was allotted to C.B.Coombs on 31.8.27 - NTU.				
G-CADY	Curtiss HS-2L (Certificate of Registration No. 229)	-	A-2115 (US Navy)	15. 6.23	Canx 16.6.24.
G-CADZ	Curtiss HS-2L	-		11. 6.23R	NTU. Canx.
G-CAEA	Martinsyde Type A Mk.II (Certificate of Registration No. 208, then Certificate of Registration No. 219 issued 7.5.22)	216-1		12. 6.21	Fatal crash after stalling in turn after take-off from river near Chicoutimi, Que. on 11.7.23. Canx.
G-CAEB	Vickers Type 69 Viking Amphibian Mk.IV (Certificate of Registration No. 216, then Certificate of Registration No. 1187 issued 8.8.32)	18		5. 6.22	DBF after catching fire in air and burned to water-line after landing on river at Fraser Arm, near Vancouver, BC. on 16.9.32. (Had been rebuilt by Canadian Boeing at Vancouver just prior to its final accident) Canx.
G-CAEC	Curtiss JN-2 (Probably a Curtiss JN-4D with USAAS serial 3505)	3505		. .21R	No CofR issued. DBR when sideslipped into ground during crosswind landing at Hampstead, Que. on 22.6.21.
N-CAED	Dayton-Wright FP.2 Forest Patrol (Certificate of Registration No. 207)	1		1. 6.22	Badly damaged when float bracing wire failed during take-off from Michipicoten Harbour, Ont. on 28.9.22, whilst performing experimental work.
G-CAEE	Curtiss HS-2L	-		11. 6.23R	NTU. Canx.
G-CAEF	Curtiss Seagull (Certificate of Registration No. 235)	883-3		1. 8.23	Canx.
G-CAEG	Curtiss Expermental (Built from hull and empennage of Curtiss Seagull with wings from unknown type - called Seagull erroneously) (Certificate of Registration No. 268)	538		17. 6.25	W/o on 12.6.29. Canx 17.6.29.
G-CAEH	Thomas-Morse S-4C Scout (Certificate of Registration No. 238, then Certificate of Registration No. 273 issued 18.1.26)	543	38925 (US Army Air Service)	21.11.23	DBR in forced landing at Beechville, Ont. on 27.7.27. Later rebuilt and re-regd CF-AMM. Canx.
G-CAEI	Curtiss JN-4 (Certificate of Registration No. 261)	-		24. 8.24	Badly damaged after entering into a flat spin at 1200ft at Hamilton, Ont. on 26.8.27. (Probably rebuilt as G-CAJF).
G-CAEJ	Curtiss JN-4 (Certificate of Registration No. 255)	5021		31. 5.24	DBF at Woodstock, NB. on 3.12.26. Canx 31.8.27.
G-CAEK	Huff-Daland HD-19 Petrel 5 (Certificate of Registration No. 251)	3		22. 5.24	CofR canx 18.8.28.
G-CAEL	Norman Thompson NT.2B (Certificate of Registration No. 250)	-	(Royal Naval Air Service)	13. 6.24	Scrapped in 9/29. Canx 14.3.30.
G-CAEM	Norman Thompson NT.2B	-	N2573 (Royal Naval Air Service)	. 6.24R	No CofR issued. Scrapped in 9/29. Canx.
G-CAEN	Standard J-1	-		19. 5.24	Abandoned at Marcelin, Sask. in 7/26. (Sold to party at Lethbridge, Alta. in early 1927). CofA expired 30.11.26. Canx 30.3.35.
G-CAEO	Standard J-1	-	2383 (US Army Air Service)	15. 6.24	DBR when aircraft nosed-over on take-off from Pincher Creek, Alta. on 13.8.24. Canx 15.6.25.
G-CAEP	Curtiss JN-4A (Certificate of Registration No. 264)	-		7. 2.25	DBR when waves broke it up after float damaged in forced landing at Vancouver, BC. on 10.5.25. Canx.
G-CAEQ	Curtiss JN-4 (Assembled from spares by A.D.Goodwin)	-	(G-CAFJ) G-CAEQ	11. 7.24	WFU. CofA expired 23.2.30. Canx.
G-CAER	Was allotted to J.E.Palmer, Lethbridge, Alta - NTU.				
G-CAES	Standard J-1	-		. .24R	NTU - Canx.
G-CAET	Westland Limousine III	WAC.8	G-EARV	.12.24R	Condemned on inspection at Lac a la Tortue, Que. due to wood rot & scrapped. No CofR issued.

Regn	Type	c/n	Previous identity	Regn date	Fate or immediate subsequent identity (if known)
G-CAEU	Airco DH.9C (Certificate of Registration No. 263)	-	G-EBDF H5652	13. 1.25	DBR on forced landing in trees due to downdraft in Kekeko Hills on 24.1.25. Canx.
G-CAEV	Fokker C.II	174		1. 4.25	Badly damaged when struck a fence during landing at Hamilton, Ont. on 13.5.28. Canx 21.11.28 as not rebuilt.
G-CAEW	Aeromarine 40-F	-	A-5063 (US Navy)	13. 6.25	Badly damaged when overturned in windstorm at Hamilton, Ont. on 16.7.25. Canx. Engine used to power G-CAFS.
G-CAEX	Curtiss JN-4 (Originally regd with c/n 561, then c/n 2056 quoted in 8/27) (Certificate of Registration No. 270, then Certificate of Registration No. 274 issued 21.1.26, then Certificate of Registration No. 354 issued 26.4.28)	5061		30. 6.25	Canx 18.1.29 as not airworthy.
G-CAEY	Curtiss HS-2L (Certificate of Registration No. 266)	-		2. 6.25	CofR lapsed 28.2.31. Canx.
G-CAEZ	Was allotted to J.V.Elliot, Hamilton, Ont. - NTU.				
G-CAFA	Was allotted to Brock & Weymouth, Montreal, Que. for an Aeromarine - NTU.				
G-CAFB	Curtiss Lark (Regd with c/n L79-1-1)	5		30. 3.26	Badly damaged near Hudson, Ont. on 12.9.27. (Canadian Vickers works number CV-77 allotted to rebuild but believed not done due to cost). Canx.
G-CAFC	Canadian Vickers Vedette	-		25. 5.26R	NTU. No CofR issued. Canx.
G-CAFD	Aeromarine All Metal	AMC No.1		25. 5.26	Dismantled. Canx 28.2.30.
G-CAFE	Was allotted to Pacific Airways Ltd, Vancouver, BC. for a Curtiss HS-2L - marks objected to - to G-CAFH in 6/26.				
G-CAFF	Canadian Vickers Vedette II (Certificate of Registration No. 279)	CV-31		8. 5.26	Badly damaged at Round Lake, Ont. on 3.8.27. Canx.
G-CAFG	Canadian Vickers Vanessa	CV-36		15. 4.26	To RCAF as G-CYZJ 26.4.27. Canx.
G-CAFH	Curtiss HS-2L (Certificate of Registration No. 281)	-	(G-CAFE) US Navy A-1274	14. 6.26	Canx 25.9.28.
G-CAFI	Curtiss HS-3L (Originally regd as HS-2L, converted in 6/29)(Regd with c/n CV-152, but this was a Vickers Vedette Va) (Certificate of Registration No. 291, then Certificate of Registration No. 655 issued 13.6.29, then Certificate of Registration No. 724 issued 17.8.29)	185	A-1258 (US Navy)	10. 5.26	Shipped to Bermuda in 1930. Canx.
G-CAFJ	Curtiss JN-4	-	G-CAEQ	20. 5.26R	NTU - Reverted as G-CAEQ. Canx.
G-CAFK	Boeing C-672 (Model 5) (Regd as a Boeing B-1 with c/n 672)	32	A-672 (US Navy)	1. 6.25	Damaged 25.5.26 (details?). Canx 2.7.29.
G-CAFL	Canadian Vickers Vedette	-		25. 5.26R	NTU. No CofR issued. Canx.
G-CAFM	Thomas-Morse S-4C Scout (Certificate of Registration No. 285)	-		8. 7.26	Canx.
G-CAFN	Schreck FBA.17 HE.2 (Certificate of Registration No. 288)	23		1. 7.26	CofR lapsed 1.7.27. Canx.
G-CAFO	Schreck FBA.17 HE.2 (Certificate of Registration No. 287)	40		1. 7.26	CofR lapsed 26.6.33. Canx.
G-CAFP	Curtiss HS-2L (Certificate of Registration No. 282)	-		6. 7.26	Stalled & crashed at Stacker Lake, Que. on 11.10.27. Canx.
"G-CAFP"	Schreck FBA.17 HE.2	-		----	Marks were applied illegally, probably by Quebec Government, and operated by the Compagnie Aerienne Franco-Canadienne in Quebec.
G-CAFQ	Curtiss HS-2L (Certificate of Registration No. 283)	212		6. 7.26	DBR in gale after forced landing at Kogaska, Que. on 4.6.27. Canx.
G-CAFR	Curtiss JN-4 (Certificate of Registration No. 286)	5062		14. 7.26	DBR & crashed after stalling and went into spin below 500ft at London, Ont. on 6.8.26. Canx.
G-CAFS	Curtiss JN-4 (Regd as a Curtiss Canuck) (Certificate of Registration No. 289, then Certificate of Registration No. 335 issued 7.12.37)	5063		14. 8.26	DBR after hitting tree during crosswind take-off from St.Thomas, Ont. on 22.5.28. Rebuild requested on 24.6.28 with Allison wing - NTU. Canx.
G-CAFT	Standard J-1 (Records list a 'Robertson body with Brewster wings')(Certificate of Registration No. 400)	400		15. 9.26	Condemned & canx 20.9.28.
G-CAFU	Atlantic Aircraft/Fokker Universal (Rebuilt by Canadian Vickers as c/n CV-55 in 1927) (Certificate of Registration No. 343, then Certificate of Registration No. 1006 issued 22.6.31, then Certificate of Registration No. 1036 issued 27.8.31, then Certificate of Registration No. 1225 issued 24.12.32, then Certificate of Registration No. 1426 issued 14.6.34, then Certificate of Registration No. 1636 issued 7.11.35)	404		6.10.26	Stalled in turn after take-off from Charlie Lake, Fort St.John, BC. on 17.12.39 & DBR. Canx.
G-CAFV	Curtiss JN-4 (Certificate of Registration No. 293, then Certificate of Registration No. 334 issued 29.12.27)	5064		16.12.26	Sold prior to 11.9.29. Canx 14.3.30.
G-CAFW	Stinson SB-1 Detroiter (Certificate of Registration No. 292)	70		11.12.26	Scrapped at Pointe aux Trembles, Que. on 11.9.29. Canx 28.2.30.
G-CAFX	Curtiss JN-4 (Regd as a Curtiss Canuck)(Certificate of Registration No. 313)	5065		29. 5.27	Damaged on 22.9.27. Canx 29.10.28. Scrapped during 9/29.
G-CAFY	Curtiss JN-4 (Regd as a Curtiss Canuck) (Certificate of Registration No. 314)	5066		21. 5.27	DBF in workshop fire at Hamilton, Ont. on 18.8.29. Canx 14.3.30.
G-CAFZ	Not allotted - was probably reserved for J.V.Elliot Air Service.				
G-CAGA	Canadian Vickers Vedette II (Certificate of Registration No. 296)	CV-53		17. 5.27	To RCAF as G-CYGA on 2.8.27. Canx.
G-CAGB	Canadian Vickers Vedette II (Certificate of Registration No. 297)	CV-54		26. 5.27	Fatal crash when hull ruptured on landing at Lac la Peche, Que. on 9.6.27. Canx.
G-CAGC	Fairchild FC-2 (Certificate of Registration No. 306)	4		14. 7.27	DBR when overturned whilst taxying in rough water at Senneterre, Que. on 12.8.30. Canx.
G-CAGD	Fokker Universal (Certificate of Registration No. 319, then Certificate of Registration No. 1097 issued 17.12.31, then Certificate of Registration No. 1204 issued 22.9.32)	406		22. 2.27	DBR when stalled in turn avoiding high-tension lines during take-off from Edmonton, Alta. on 30.11.32. Canx.
G-CAGE	Fokker Universal (Certificate of Registration No. 320)	407		23. 3.27	DBR when stalled in turn on landing approach after test flight from The Pas, Manitoba on 5.1.28. Canx.

Regn	Type	c/n	Previous identity	Regn date	Fate or immediate subsequent identity (if known)
G-CAGF	Stinson SB-1 Detroiter (Certificate of Registration No. 294)	103	NC3707	6. 4.27	Restored as NC3707 in 6/27. Canx. To G-CANI on 30.4.28.
G-CAGG to G-CAGS	Not allotted.				
G-CAGT	Curtiss HS-2L (Possibly ex.RCAF G-CYGU, sold 10.4.28)(Certificate of Registration No. 413)	-		31. 5.28	Laid up on shore at Roberval since 1929. Canx 14.3.30.
G-CAGU to G-CAHD	Not allotted.				
G-CAHE	Atlantic Aircraft/Fokker Universal (Certificate of Registration No. 299, then Certificate of Registration No. 939 issued 17.10.30, then Certificate of Registration No. 1165 issued 28.6.32, then Certificate of Registration No. 1361 issued 29.11.33, then Certificate of Registration No. 1510 issued 11.12.34, then Certificate of Registration No. 2075 issued 24.7.37, then Certificate of Registration No. 2292 issued 25.7.38)	408		8. 7.27	CofR lapsed 25.7.38. (Temporary Permit to Fly issued in 7/40 - fate?).
G-CAHF	Atlantic Aircraft/Fokker Universal (CofR No. 300)	409		8. 7.27	Inspected at North Sydney, NS. but was ruled to be not airworthy on 27.8.30. Canx.
G-CAHG	Atlantic Aircraft/Fokker Universal (CofR No. 301)	410		8. 7.27	Forced landed on ice off Labrador coast due to fuel shortage whilst on patrol and abandoned on 17.2.28. Canx.
G-CAHH	Atlantic Aircraft/Fokker Universal (CofR No. 302)	411		8. 7.27	Not airworthy on inspection at Sydney, NS. on 27.8.30. Canx
G-CAHI	Atlantic Aircraft/Fokker Universal (CofR No. 303)	412		8. 7.27	Not airworthy on inspection at Sydney, NS. on 27.8.30. Canx
G-CAHJ	Atlantic Aircraft/Fokker Universal (Certificate of Registration No. 304, then Certificate of Registration No. 1169 issued 28.6.32, then Certificate of Registration No. 1362 issued 4.12.33, then Certificate of Registration No. 1511 issued 11.12.34, then Certificate of Registration No. 2005 issued 4.6.37, then Certificate of Registration No. 2270 issued 6.7.38)	414		8. 7.27	Dismantled. CofA expired 6.1.39. Canx.
G-CAHK	DH.60X Moth Seaplane (First Moth to be regd in Canada) (Certificate of Registration No. 305)	377		8. 7.27	Capsized at moorings in gale during the night of 26.8.27 at Wakeham Bay, Que. & DBR. Canx.
G-CAHL	Fairchild FC-2 Seaplane (Certificate of Registration No. 307)	5		3. 8.27	To Jamaica in 1930, possibly as VP-JAC. Canx.
G-CAHM	Was allotted to E.L.Janney for Martin Commercial aircraft - NTU.				
G-CAHN	Was allotted to E.L.Janney for Martin Commercial aircraft - NTU.				
G-CAHO	Curtiss JN-4C	-		. .27R	(May have been the remains of G-CABI which were stored near Gore's Landing, Ont after an accident at Peterborough in 1922 - listed as JN-4C in register) Canx.
G-CAHP	Curtiss JN-4D (Certificate of Registration No. 298)	-		9. 6.27	WFU in 1928 - fate unknown. Canx 28.2.31.
G-CAHQ	Curtiss HS-2L (Certificate of Registration No. 295)	-		18. 5.27	Canx 14.3.30.
G-CAHR	Ryan B-1 Brougham (Certificate of Registration No. 351)	32	NC3113 N1577	22. 3.28	Struck tree during landing at Whitehorse, YT. on 5.5.28 & DBR. Canx.
G-CAHS	DH.60X Moth Seaplane (Certificate of Registration No. 315)	409		22. 8.27	Student pilot lost control on solo flight and crashed into English Bay, Vancouver, BC. on 19.3.28 & DBR. Canx.
G-CAHT	Standard J-1 (Certificate of Registration No. 321, then Certificate of Registration No. 781 issued 6.11.29)	-		13. 8.27	Forced landing due to engine failure at Long Branch, Ont. on 10.8.30 & DBR. Canx.
G-CAHU	Standard J-1 (Certificate of Registration No. 316, then Certificate of Registration No. 430 issued 13.6.28, then Certificate of Registration No. 1197 issued 20.8.32)	-		22. 8.27	Forced landing 8 miles east of Nanton, Alta. on 22.10.32 & DBR. Canx.
G-CAHV	Waco 9 (Used c/n 257 whilst in US as N2470) (Certificate of Registration No. 312)	A-786	N2470	10. 8.27	(Accident at London, Ont. on 5.11.27) Canx post 1933 - ultimate fate unknown.
G-CAHW	Was allotted to Vernon Morrison, London, Ont. - NTU.				
G-CAHX	Lincoln Sport (Homebuilt)	-		. .27R	No CofR issued - NTU. (On display 5/99 Reynolds Alberta Museum) Canx.
G-CAHY	Standard J-1 (Certificate of Registration No. 322)	-		27. 8.27	Canx 22.6.28.
G-CAHZ	Standard J-1 (Certificate of Registration No. 317)	-		3. 9.27	Wheels caught fence on landing approach and nosed over at Peterborough, Ont. in 1927 & badly damaged. Canx.
G-CAIA	Was allotted to Canadian Air Services Co., Peterborough, Ont for Standard J-1 aircraft - NTU as possibly used as spares for G-CAHY & G-CAHZ.				
G-CAIB	Was allotted to Canadian Air Services Co., Peterborough, Ont for Standard J-1 aircraft - NTU as possibly used as spares for G-CAHY & G-CAHZ.				
G-CAIC	Was allotted to Canadian Air Services Co., Peterborough, Ont for Standard J-1 aircraft - NTU as possibly used as spares for G-CAHY & G-CAHZ.				
G-CAID	Fairchild FC-2 (Regd as a Fairchild Cabin Monoplane)(Certificate of Registration No. 324)	16		24. 9.27	DBR at Regina, Sask. on 23.9.30 (details?). Canx.
G-CAIE	Fairchild FC-2 (Regd as a Fairchild Cabin Monoplane) (Certificate of Registration No. 325)	17		3.10.27	Forced landing due to engine failure near Sioux Lookout, Ont. on 24.12.27 & DBR. Canx.
G-CAIF	Hess Blue Bird	-		. .27R	NTU. Canx.
G-CAIG	DH.60X Moth Seaplane (Certificate of Registration No. 331)	434		14.12.27	Fatal crash when it stalled during approach at St.Charles airport, Winnipeg, Man. on 16.6.28. Canx.
G-CAIH	Fairchild FC-2 (Certificate of Registration No. 333, then Certificate of Registration No. 1056 issued 15.10.31, then Certificate of Registration No. 1143 issued 2.6.32, then Certificate of Registration No. 1236 issued 14.1.33)	18		28.10.27	Canx 18.1.34. Rebuilt & re-regd as CF-AUX.

Regn	Type	c/n	Previous identity	Regn date	Fate or immediate subsequent identity (if known)
G-CAII	Waco 9 (Certificate of Registration No. 323, then Certificate of Registration No. 1230 issued 3.1.33, then Certificate of Registration No. 1508 issued 15.12.34, then Certificate of Registration No. 1640 issued 4.12.35, then Certificate of Registration No. 1905 issued 18.3.37)	51		8. 9.27	Dismantled. CofA expired 18.4.38. Canx.
G-CAIJ	Curtiss JN-4 (Certificate of Registration No. 326)	5067		9.10.27	DBR when stalled in turn during practice flight at Montreal, Que. on 15.6.28. Canx.
G-CAIK	Was allotted to Gen. Sutton - NTU.				
G-CAIL	DH.60 Moth (Cirrus I) (Certificate of Registration No. 328)	273		11.10.27	DBF east of Lac la Rouge, Sask. on 6.3.29. Canx.
G-CAIM	Not allotted.				
G-CAIN	Not allotted.				
G-CAIO	Laird Swallow	-		. .27R	Destroyed in fire at International Airways repair shop at Hamilton, Ont. on 18.8.29. Canx.
G-CAIP	Fairchild FC-2W1 (Regd as a Fairchild Cabin Monoplane - Wasp engine) (Certificate of Registration No. 332)	48		21.12.27	DBF when aircraft caught fire while engine being heated at St.Felicien, Que. on 5.4.29. Canx.
G-CAIQ	Fairchild FC-2W3 (Regd as a Fairchild Cabin Monoplane - Wasp engine)(Certificate of Registration No. 336) (DoT records gave c/n 28, but US Dept of Commerce Export Certificate gave c/n 49)	49		9. 1.28	DBR in forced landing at Chibougamou, Que. on 9.1.29. Canx.
G-CAIR	Driggs Dart II (Certificate of Registration No. 329)	7		13.12.27	DBR at Victoria, BC in 10.28. Canx.
G-CAIS	Alexander Combination Wing Eaglerock (CofR No. 330)	354		13.12.27	DBR after colliding with DH.60 Moth G-CAKH during landing at Lulu Island, BC. on 9.3.30. Canx 3.5.31.
G-CAIT	Swallow Land Plane (Certificate of Registration No. 338)	805	NC2033	15. 2.28	Aircraft declared unairworthy after sale on 2.7.29 and not flown. Canx 27.12.30.
G-CAIU	Fairchild FC-2 (Converted to Model 51 in 5/31) (Rebuilt with wings from G-CANB after being DBF at Senneteere on 12.12.37) (Certificate of Registration No. 368, then Certificate of Registration No. 985 issued 4.5.31, then Certificate of Registration No. 1665 issued 9.3.36, then Certificate of Registration No. 2128 issued 18.10.37)	107		18. 5.28	CofA expired 1.6.41. Canx.
G-CAIV	Atlantic Aircraft/Fokker Universal (CofR No. 346)	425		23. 1.28	Badly damaged at Peace River, Alta. during take-off on rough ice on 15.12.31. Canx.
G-CAIW	Fairchild FC-2W2 (Rebuilt as a Model 71C with new c/n 25 in 3/34) (Certificate of Registration No. 423, then Certificate of Registration No. 1372 issued 5.3.34)	112		6. 6.28	CofA expired 23.11.37. Reduced to parts and used in construction of CF-BKP. Canx.
G-CAIX	Atlantic Aircraft/Fokker Universal (CofR No. 347)	427		10. 2.28	DBR in forced landing due to lack of fuel and ran into a barn at Elk Lake, Ont. on 12.3.31. Canx.
G-CAIY	Atlantic Aircraft/Fokker Universal (CofR No. 341)	428		23. 2.28	DBF when it caught fire while warming engine at Reindeer Lake, Man. on 6.3.28. Canx.
G-CAIZ	Atlantic Aircraft/Fokker Universal (CofR No. 342, then Certificate of Registration No. 2018 issued 29.6.37)	429		23. 2.28	CofA expired 11.12.40. Canx.
G-CAJA	Curtiss JN-4 (Regd as Modified Curtiss Canuck) (Certificate of Registration No. 339, then Certificate of Registration No. 1032 issued 20.8.31)	-		15. 2.28	CofA expired 25.12.33. Canx.
G-CAJB	Waco 10 (Certificate of Registration No. 337)	1279		1. 2.28	Fatal crash when aircraft hit water low flying at Presqu'Ile, Ont. on 5.8.30. Canx.
G-CAJC	Stinson SB-1 Detroiter (Certificate of Registration No. 340)	104	N3708	2. 2.28	Canx 12.5.31. Reduced to spares and remains burnt.
G-CAJD	Atlantic Aircraft/Fokker Universal (CofR No. 353)	430		11. 4.28	Went through ice on landing at Charron Lake, Man. on 10.12.31 & DBR. Canx.
G-CAJE	Waco 125 (Originally regd as a Waco 10)(Certificate of Registration No. 345)	1275	NC4202	14. 3.28	CofA expired 8.4.33. Stored at Weston, Ont in 5/34. Canx.
G-CAJF	Curtiss JN-4 (Regd as a Curtiss Canuck) (Possibly rebuild of G-CAEI)(Certificate of Registration No. 344)	-		12. 3.28	CofA expired in 6/31. Stored. Destroyed in fire at Beattle Milling Co. mill at Campbellford, Ont. on 14.1.51. Canx.
G-CAJG	Standard J-1	-		. .28R	NTU - Canx.
G-CAJH	Atlantic Aircraft/Fokker Universal (CofR No. 373)	403	NC3013	22. 5.28	DBR when overturned in severe storm at Goldpines, Ont. on 14.8.28 - dismantled. Canx.
G-CAJI	Dornier Do.J Wal	77		23. 4.28	Whilst on transatlantic flight from Pisa, Italy to Halifax, NS. via the Azores, it force landed 500 miles from Horta, in Atlantic Ocean, due to fire in aft engine housing on 1.8.28, aircraft salvaged by freighter Valprato four days later, taken to Canadian Vickers in Montreal for repair but scrapped due to excessive cost. Canx.
G-CAJJ	Fairchild FC-2 (Certificate of Registration No. 349)	60	NC4081	2. 4.28	DBF when aircraft caught fire while engine being heated at Amos, Que. on 5.2.35. Canx.
G-CAJK	Ryan M-2 (Re-engined with Wright J-4B in 8/31) (Certificate of Registration No. 348, then Certificate of Registration No. 801 issued 3.1.30, then Certificate of Registration No. 1035 issued 31.8.31)	22	NC2769	16. 3.28	Forced landing on ice floe in St.Lawrence River on 29.2.32, drifted to sea and lost near Les Mechins, Que. Canx.
G-CAJL	Curtiss JN-4C (The type, maker and c/n are suspect. The Hi-lift wing was sold as a Parasol monoplane conversion of a JN-4) (Certificate of Registration No. 374, then Certificate of Registration No. 531 issued 17.11.28, then Certificate of Registration No. 931 issued 12.6.30)	2850		22. 5.28	DBR 2 miles northwest of Montreal, Que. in 9/31 (details?). Canx.
G-CAJM	Was allotted to Eastern Canada Airways - NTU.				
G-CAJN	Schreck FBA.17 HT.4 (Certificate of Registration No. 415)	75		19. 6.28	CofA expired 23.5.31. Canx.
G-CAJO	Schreck FBA.17 HT.4 (Certificate of Registration No. 457)	80/1207		24. 7.28	CofA expired 9.5.31. Canx.
G-CAJP	Schreck FBA.17 HMT.2 (Certificate of Registration No. 416)	49	F-AIFJ	19. 6.28	CofA expired 16.5.31. Canx.

Regn	Type	c/n	Previous identity	Regn date	Fate or immediate subsequent identity (if known)
G-CAJQ	Schreck FBA.17 HT.4 (Certificate of Registration No. 417)	76		19. 6.28	CofA expired 31.5.32. Canx.
G-CAJR	Schreck FBA.17 HT.4 (Certificate of Registration No. 418)	77		19. 6.28	CofA expired 5.6.31. Canx.
G-CAJS	Schreck FBA.17 HB.2 (Certificate of Registration No. 434)	2	F-AGAS	30. 6.28	CofA expired 16.5.31. Canx.
G-CAJT	DH.61 Giant Moth (Certificate of Registration No. 471)	328		8. 8.28	Hit rise after take-off from field 5 miles east of Calgary, Alta. on 23.10.28 & DBF. Canx.
G-CAJU	DH.60X Moth (Re-engined with DH Gipsy II in 8/33)(Certificate of Registration No. 352)	560		27. 4.28	CofR lapsed 5.1.42. Dismantled. Canx.
G-CAJV	DH.60X Moth (Certificate of Registration No. 406)	554		13. 6.28	DBF after stalling and spinning in at North Wallace, NS. on 7.8.32. Canx.
G-CAJW	DH.60X Moth (Certificate of Registration No. 355)	535		27. 4.28	Crashed on take-off from Sturgeon River, Ont. on 1.10.28 & DBR. Canx. Re-regd CF-OAA 5.3.29 after rebuild with metal fuselage (with new c/n 761).
G-CAJX	Was allotted to de Havilland in 1928 - NTU.				
G-CAJY	DH.60X Moth (Re-engined with ADC Cirrus III in 1934) (Certificate of Registration No. 438, then Certificate of Registration No. 1467 issued 17.8.34, then Certificate of Registration No. 2094 issued 30.9.37)	619		4. 7.28	W/o on 30.9.38. CofR lapsed 7.10.38. Canx.
G-CAJZ	DH.60X Moth (Certificate of Registration No. 439, then Certificate of Registration No. 1110 issued 1.4.32, then Certificate of Registration No. 1233 issued 29.12.32, then Certificate of Registration No. 1252 issued 2.3.33, then Certificate of Registration No. 1358 issued 14.12.33)	620		4. 7.28	Fatal crash when landing on 'glassy' water in poor visibility at Lake Winnipeg, Man. on 17.8.34 & DBR. Canx.
G-CAKA	DH.60X Moth (Certificate of Registration No. 435)	448		4. 7.28	Stalled at 50ft in turn after engine cut on approach at Victoria, BC. on 10.3.29 & DBR. Canx.
G-CAKB	DH.60X Moth (Certificate of Registration No. 549)	449		25. 5.28	Stalled at low altitude at Sanford, Man. on 24.9.33. Canx.
G-CAKC	DH.60X Moth (Certificate of Registration No. 409)	454		14. 6.28	Forced landing in field due to engine failure 1 mile south of Alberton, Ont. on 21.12.35 & DBR. Canx.
G-CAKD	DH.60X Moth (Certificate of Registration No. 550, then Certificate of Registration No. 2116 issued 26.10.37, then Certificate of Registration No. 2760 issued 27.1.41)	455		12. 5.28	Canx 6.2.41. (Owner to RCAF - fate?).
G-CAKE	DH.60X Moth (Certificate of Registration No. 443)	458		9. 7.28	DBR during attempted landing 2 miles west of Brockville, Ont. on 14.8.38. Canx.
G-CAKF	DH.60X Moth (Certificate of Registration No. 444)	459		9. 7.28	DBR in USA on 28.4.32 (details?). Canx.
G-CAKG	DH.60X Moth (Certificate of Registration No. 410)	462		14. 6.28	Fatal crash when wing struts collapsed in air during tight loop near Saskatoon, Sask. on 8.10.29 & DBR. Canx.
G-CAKH(1)	DH.60X Moth (Certificate of Registration No. 403)	463		12. 6.28	To RCAF as G-CYXI on 15.8.28, but crashed just prior to delivery. Canx.
G-CAKH(2)	DH.60X Moth (Certificate of Registration No. 403)	530	G-CYXI	. 7.28	Grounded on inspection 25.4.31 & WFU. Scrapped in 9/37. Canx.
G-CAKI	DH.60X Moth (Certificate of Registration No. 384)	472		30. 5.28	DBR in hangar fire at Moose Jaw, Sask. on 7.10.28. Canx.
G-CAKJ	DH.60X Moth (Certificate of Registration No. 404)	473		12. 6.28	Stalled during aborted landing at Edmonton, Alta. on 20.8.35 & DBR. Canx.
G-CAKK	DH.60X Moth (Certificate of Registration No. 379)	562		25. 5.28	Crashed in unknown circumstances at Oshawa, Ont. on 31.8.29 & DBR. Canx.
G-CAKL	DH.60X Moth (Certificate of Registration No. 380)	563		25. 5.28	DBR when stalled in turn and spun in at Jordan Station, Ont. on 26.12.28. Canx.
G-CAKM	DH.60X Moth (Certificate of Registration No. 385)	564		18. 6.28	DBR due to unknown circumstances on 24.10.28. Canx.
G-CAKN	DH.60X Moth (Certificate of Registration No. 381)	565		25. 5.28	Fatal crash when it stalled in steep climbing turn after take-off from Granby, Que. on 29.8.28 & DBR. Canx.
G-CAKO	DH.60X Moth (Certificate of Registration No. 375)	567		25. 5.28	W/o in Saskatoon by Dept of National Defence on 23.12.36 - stored. Attempted rebuild at Clark's Crossing, Sask. in 1937 not completed. Canx.
G-CAKP	DH.60X Moth (Fitted with Coupé canopy in 1/33) (Certificate of Registration No. 376)	568		25. 5.28	Overturned during landing at Regina, Sask. on 11.2.36 & DBR. Reduced to spares. Canx.
G-CAKQ	DH.60X Moth (Certificate of Registration No. 377)	569		25. 5.28	Was in damaged condition due to unknown circumstances on CCA inspection in 2/33. Donated to Calgary Institute of Technology and Art as instructional airframe 29.5.33. Canx.
G-CAKR	DH.60X Moth (Certificate of Registration No. 378)	570		25. 5.28	Crashed after passenger closed throttle to simulate forced landing at 100ft after take-off from Toronto, Ont. on 14.1.34 & DBR. Canx.
G-CAKS	DH.60X Moth (Certificate of Registration No. 386)	571		1. 6.28	Hit ground during diving finish in race at Toronto, Ont. on 1.9.32 & DBR. Canx.
G-CAKT	DH.60X Moth (Fitted with Coupé canopy in 1/33)(Certificate of Registration No. 387)	572		1. 6.28	DBR in practice landing at Regina, Sask. on 4.9.33. Canx.
G-CAKU	DH.60X Moth (Certificate of Registration No. 395)	573		12. 6.28	Stalled in tight turn & crashed at Winnipeg, Man. on 22.8.29. Canx.
G-CAKV	DH.60X Moth (Rebuilt with wings from G-CAKT in 1933) (Certificate of Registration No. 396)	574		12. 6.28	Severely damaged in 1936 (details?). Repair requested on 24.7.36 with parts from G-CAKP but refused by authorities - scrapped. Canx.
G-CAKW	DH.60X Moth (Certificate of Registration No. 397)	575		12. 6.28	Fatal crash at Vancouver, BC. on 22.7.29. Canx.
G-CAKX	DH.60X Moth (Certificate of Registration No. 411)	582		29. 6.28	Overturned during landing on 'glassy' water at Halifax, NS. on 10.8.29 & DBR. Canx.
G-CAKY	DH.60X Moth (Certificate of Registration No. 398)	577		12. 6.28	Stalled during precautionary landing in a field due to approaching darkness near Clinton, Ont. on 16.12.31. Canx.

Regn	Type	c/n	Previous identity	Regn date	Fate or immediate subsequent identity (if known)
G-CAKZ	DH.60X Moth (Certificate of Registration No. 399)	578		25. 6.28	DBF in hangar fire at Ottawa, Ont. on 29.11.28. Canx.
G-CALA	DH.60X Moth (Certificate of Registration No. 392)	579		. 6.28	Fatal crash following structural failure in air during loop at Calgary, Alta. on 19.5.29 & DBR. Canx.
G-CALB	DH.60X Moth (Certificate of Registration No. 393)	580		12. 6.28	Went into spin at 100ft at Edmonton, Alta. on 25.3.29 & DBR. Canx.
G-CALC	DH.60X Moth (Certificate of Registration No. 394)	581		12. 6.28	Overturned during landing at London, Ont. on 20.4.30 & DBR. Engine to G-CAKY. Canx.
G-CALD	DH.60X Moth (Certificate of Registration No. 412)	576		14. 6.28	Engine cut on take-off and capsized in forced landing near Green Bank, NS. on 4.7.29. Severely damaged during salvage.
G-CALE	DH.60G Gipsy Moth (Certificate of Registration No. 569, then Certificate of Registration No. 618 issued 28.4.31, then Certificate of Registration No. 1464 issued 19.1.32, then Certificate of Registration No. 1966 issued 17.5.37)	843		22.11.28	Collided with CF-CEH and locked wings then fell into harbour at Halifax, NS. on 19.1.38 & DBR. Canx.
G-CALF	Was reserved for Dept. of National Defence in 1928, but not allotted.				
to					
G-CAMZ	Was reserved for Dept. of National Defence in 1928, but not allotted.				
G-CANA	DH.60X Moth (Certificate of Registration No. 408, then Certificate of Registration No. 552 issued 1.2.29)	595		14. 6.29	Stalled in turn at Century airport, Toronto, Ont. on 6.4.32 & DBR. Canx.
G-CANB	Fairchild FC-2 (Re-fuselaged with airframe from G-CAVS in 5/34) (Certificate of Registration No. 356, then Certificate of Registration No. 1004 issued 13.6.31, then Certificate of Registration No. 1389 issued 7.5.34, then Certificate of Registration No. 1659 issued 5.3.36, then Certificate of Registration No. 1693 issued 21.5.36)	62	NC4082	5. 5.28	Went through ice at Fish Lake, Que. on 20.12.37 resulting in ice splitting fuselage tubing. Scrapped. Wings used in rebuild of G-CAIU 12/37. Canx.
G-CANC	Fairchild FC-2 (Certificate of Registration No. 357)	26	NC3616	5. 5.28	Nosed over during forced landing at St.Sylvere, Que. on 29.4.30 & DBR. Canx.
G-CAND	Canadian Vickers Vedette I (Rebuilt with wings from G-CANE in 8/34, the converted to Mk.V after rebuild with wings from CF-OAB and P&W Wasp Junior engine by 7/41)(Certificate of Registration No. 401, then Certificate of Registration No. 1573 issued 14.6.35, then Certificate of Registration No. 2830 issued 3.7.41)	CV-74		12. 6.28	CofA expired 11.5.44. Canx.
G-CANE	Canadian Vickers Vedette I (Converted to Mk.II with J-4 engine in 1930, then back to Mk.I with J-5 engine in 8/32) (Certificate of Registration No. 402, then Certificate of Registration No. 1188 issued 24.8.32)	CV-75		12. 6.28	Hull in poor condition. CofA expired 23.8.33. Wings used in rebuild of G-CAND in 8/34. Canx.
G-CANF	Fairchild FC-2 (Converted to Model 51 with Wright J-6 engine in 12/30)(Certificate of Registration No. 367)	98		18. 5.28	CofR lapsed 17.11.33 & WFU. Canx.
G-CANG	Swallow Land Plane (Certificate of Registration No. 369)	916	NC4354	18. 5.28	Fatal crash after loss of control during intentional spin at Toronto, Ont. on 24.6.28 & DBR. Canx.
G-CANH	Swallow Land Plane (Certificate of Registration No. 370)	917	NC4807	18. 5.28	Grounded in 8/30 as not airworthy. CofA expired 28.2.31. Canx.
G-CANI	Stinson SB-1 Detroiter (Certificate of Registration No. 358, then Certificate of Registration No. 1111 issued 25.2.32)	103	NC3707 G-CAGF/NC3707	30. 4.28	DBR when engine failed during take-off from field at Cochrane, Alta. on 19.7.34. Canx.
G-CANJ	Standard J-1 (Certificate of Registration No. 382, then Certificate of Registration No. 621 issued 21.5.29)	-	N3416	26. 5.28	Destroyed in wind strom on 28.11.29. Canx 29.11.29.
G-CANK	Fairchild FC-2	-		. .28R	NTU. Canx.
G-CANL	Avro 594 Avian III (Certificate of Registration No. 425)	R3/CN/127		27. 6.28	Crashed when wheels caught in telephone wires during landing approach at Winnipeg, Man. on 16.2.30 & DBR. Canx.
G-CANM	Avro 594 Avian III (Re-engined with ADC Cirrus III/C in 1/30) (Certificate of Registration No. 426, then Certificate of Registration No. 1650 issued 28.12.35)	R3/CN/128		27. 6.28	Canx post-11/36.
G-CANN	Avro 594 Avian III (Certificate of Registration No. 427)	R3/CN/129		27. 6.28	DBR in hangar fire at Winnipeg, Man. on 4.3.31. Canx.
G-CANO	Avro 594 Avian III (Certificate of Registration No. 428)	R3/CN/130		27. 6.28	DBF while stacked down in farmer's field at Yorkton, Sask. on 20.8.31. Canx.
G-CANP	Avro 594 Avian III (Certificate of Registration No. 454)	R3/CN/131		20. 7.28	Capsized during landing on Sinclair Lake, near Gogama, Ont. on 2.6.30 & DBR. Canx.
G-CANQ	Avro 594 Avian III (To 3-Seater with ADC Cirrus III engine in 6/32) (Fitted with Coupé canopy in 1/33) (Certificate of Registration No. 455, then Certificate of Registration No. 1063 issued 29.9.31, then Certificate of Registration No. 1322 issued 28.7.33, then Certificate of Registration No. 2101 issued 13.10.37)	R3/CN/132		20. 7.28	Severely damaged when groundlooped during take-off from Holden, Alta. on 21.9.38. Offered to RCAF in wrecked condition on 17.11.39. Canx.
G-CANR	Standard J-1 (C/n quoted is from US register; the Canadian register lists manufacturer as Lincoln Standard) (Certificate of Registration No. 383)	1965	NC684	12. 5.28	Canx 2.7.30.
G-CANS	DH.60X Moth (Certificate of Registration No. 389)	555		2. 6.28	Stalled in steep turn and spun in from 1500ft at Vancouver, BC. on 28.6.29 & DBF. Canx.
G-CANT	Standard J-1 (Clipped wing) (Certificate of Registration No. 480)	116		16. 8.28	Canx 10.5.29. Dismantled.
G-CANU	Swallow Land Plane (Re-engined with OXX-6 in 5/29) (Certificate of Registration No. 371)	929		18. 5.28	DBR after hitting fence on take-off from Metcalfe, Ont. on 17.9.32. Canx.
G-CANV	Swallow Land Plane (Certificate of Registration No. 372)	930		18. 5.28	Stalled in turn after take-off from field while barn-storming and hit frozon surface of Ottawa River at Rockland, Ont. on 28.2.29 & DBR. Canx.
G-CANW	Not allotted.				
G-CANX	Not allotted.				
G-CANY	Curtiss JN-4 (Listed as modified Canuck)(Certificate of Registration No. 504)	-		6. 8.28	Canx 14.3.30.
G-CANZ	Canadian Vickers HS-3L (Certificate of Registration No. 391)	CV-108	A-1152 (US Navy)	12. 6.28	Reportedly lost at sea (details?). Canx 28.2.30.

Regn	Type	c/n	Previous identity	Regn date	Fate or immediate subsequent identity (if known)
G-CAOA	Curtiss HS-2L (Certificate of Registration No. 248)	487		16. 5.24	WFU in 1932 due to normal wear and tear. Canx 15.5.33.
G-CAOB	Curtiss HS-2L (Certificate of Registration No. 253)	-		25. 5.24	Forced landing in Lake Superior off Gros Cap, Ont. due to water in fuel, aircraft sank after drifting out into lake on 8.10.26 & DBR. Canx.
G-CAOC	Curtiss HS-2L (Certificate of Registration No. 252)	-	A-2027 (US Navy)	22. 5.24	Hit severe 'bump' during landing resulting in loss of control and landed in trees at Savanne Lake, Ont. on 16.8.24 & DBR. Canx.
G-CAOD	Curtiss HS-2L (Certificate of Registration No. 254)	589		29. 5.24	DBR while landing in fog near Michipicoten Harbour, Ont. on 12.6.25. Canx.
G-CAOE	Curtiss HS-2L (Certificate of Registration No. 242)	-	A-2014 (US Navy)	29. 4.24	Landed at fire site, hit rock during take-off and sank at Snake Lake, Ont. on 2.8.26. Canx.
G-CAOF	Curtiss HS-2L (Certificate of Registration No. 241)	490		23. 4.24	DBF at Goose Island, Lac Seul, Ont. on 27.6.29. Canx.
G-CAOG	Curtiss HS-2L (Certificate of Registration No. 239)	522		15. 4.24	WFU due to normal wear and tear in 12.29. Canx 30.4.32.
G-CAOH(1)	Curtiss HS-2L (Certificate of Registration No. 240)	479		15. 4.24	Severely damaged when it hit obstruction and hull damaged during take-off at Toronto, Ont. on 27.4.24. Rebuilt with new hull from USA in 7/24 & became G-CAOH(2).
G-CAOH(2)	Curtiss HS-2L (Certificate of Registration No. 259)	-	A-2019 (US Navy)	31. 7.24	Fatal crashed when stalled in turn at too low an altitude at Sault Ste Marie, Mich. on 19.10.27. Canx.
G-CAOI	Curtiss HS-2L (Certificate of Registration No. 244)	-	A-2015 (US Navy)	2. 5.24	WFU due to normal wear and tear in 12.29. Canx 30.4.32.
G-CAOJ	Curtiss HS-2L (Certificate of Registration No. 245)	-		9. 5.24	DBR during storm at Fort Frances, Ont. in 8/31. Canx 30.4.32.
G-CAOK	Curtiss HS-2L (Certificate of Registration No. 247)	523		16. 5.24	WFU due to normal wear and tear in 12.32. Canx 15.5.33.
G-CAOL	Curtiss HS-2L (Certificate of Registration No. 246)	-	A-2070 (US Navy)	9. 5.24	WFU due to normal wear and tear in 9.27. Canx 31.3.28.
G-CAOM	Curtiss HS-2L (Certificate of Registration No. 243)	571		29. 4.24	DBR in forced landing due to unknown circumstances at Shebandowan Lake, Ont. on 14.8.27. Canx.
G-CAON	Curtiss HS-2L (Certificate of Registration No. 260)	-	A-1367 (US Navy)	6. 9.24	WFU due to normal wear and tear in 12.29. Canx 30.4.32.
G-CAOO	Loening 23L Air Yacht	3		6.11.24	Became airborne whilst taxying at high speed climbing to 200ft and dived into water at Ramsay Lake, Ont. on 21.7.26 & DBR. Canx.
G-CAOP	Curtiss HS-2L (Certificate of Registration No. 275)	-	A-1143 (US Navy)	31. 1.26	DBR during landing on 'glassy' water at Fort Frances, Ont. in 10/30. Canx.
G-CAOQ	Curtiss HS-2L (Certificate of Registration No. 276)	9514		31. 1.26	WFU due to normal wear and tear in 1932. Canx 15.5.33.
G-CAOR	Curtiss HS-2L (Certificate of Registration No. 277)	-	A-1949 (US Navy)	31. 1.26	DBR after hitting deadhead during take-off run at Fort Frances, Ont. in 7/30. Canx 30.4.32.
G-CAOS	Curtiss HS-2L (Certificate of Registration No. 278)	-	A-1250 (US Navy)	31. 1.26	Forced landing due to engine failure at Long Lac, Ont. in 10.27 & DBR. Canx 31.3.28.
G-CAOT	Loening 23L Air Yacht	-		31. 1.26	Hit water hard during landing to refuel at Ramsay Lake, Ont. in 7/27. Canx 12.9.27.
G-CAOU	DH.60X Moth (Converted to DH.60M c/n 756 with DH Gipsy I engine on 7.3.29) (Re-engined with DH Gipsy II on 29.5.34) (Certificate of Registration No. 308, then Certificate of Registration No. 7211 issued 9.6.48)	400		20. 7.27	Severely damaged after hitting stake in water while landing at ferry dock, Wolf Island, Ont. on 24.9.48. Sold in 1949 and coverted into a snowmobile. Canx.
G-CAOV	DH.60X Moth (Certificate of Registration No. 309)	401		12. 9.27	DBR in fatal crash at Pine Ridge, Ont. on 27.7.28. Canx 30.4.32
G-CAOW	DH.60X Moth (Re-engined with DH Gipsy I 22.4.32) (Re-engined with DH Gipsy II 12.5.34) (Certificate of Registration No. 310, then Certificate of Registration No. 2987 issued 6.1.43)	402		12. 9.27	DBR at Sioux Lookout, Ont. on 25.2.29. Canx post 4/49.
G-CAOX	DH.60X Moth (Re-engined with DH Gipsy I 22.4.32) (Re-engined with DH Gipsy II 28.4.34)(Was rebuilt with a metal fuselage, possibly during conversion to the DH Gipsy engine)(Certificate of Registration No. 311)	403		20. 7.27	Forced landing in treed area due to engine failure 8 miles south of Nakina, Ont. on 12.8.36. Canx.
G-CAOY	DH.60X Moth (Re-engined with DH Gipsy I 22.4.32) (Re-engined with DH Gipsy II 29.5.34)(Certificate of Registration No. 359)	504		11. 5.28	Stalled during take-off from small lake, 15 miles from Gogama, Ont. on 7.8.41 & DBR. Canx.
G-CAOZ	DH.60X Moth (Re-engined with DH Gipsy I 22.4.32) (Re-engined with DH Gipsy II in 3/35)(Certificate of Registration No. 360)	505		11. 5.28	Stalled during take-off due to downdraft at Kwagama Lake, Ont. on 23.6.47 & DBR. Canx.
G-CAPA	DH.60X Moth (Re-engined with DH Gipsy I 22.4.32) (Re-engined with DH Gipsy II 12.5.34) (Certificate of Registration No. 361, then Certificate of Registration No. 7212 issued 9.6.48)	506		11. 5.28	To USA as N1510V. Canx 21.10.55.
G-CAPB	DH.60X Moth (Re-engined with DH Gipsy I 22.4.32) (Re-engined with DH Gipsy II 12.5.34) (Certificate of Registration No. 362, then Certificate of Registration No. 7213 issued 9.6.48)	507		11. 5.28	Stalled during take-off at local airport, Val d'Or, Que. on 19.9.48 & DBR. Canx.
G-CAPC	DH.60X Moth (Re-engined with DH Gipsy I 22.4.32) (Re-engined with DH Gipsy II 12.5.34)(Certificate of Registration No. 363)	508		11. 5.28	WFU on 14.4.37. Rebuilt with new fuselage as CF-OAU. Canx.
G-CAPD	Was reserved for Ontario Provincial Air Service in 1928 - NTU.				
G-CAPE	Curtiss HS-2L (Certificate of Registration No. 364)	-	A-1300 (US Navy)	15. 5.28	Hit telephone wires during landing approach and overturned near edge of lake at Pays Flat, Ont. on 4.5.31 & DBR. Canx.
G-CAPF	Curtiss HS-2L (Certificate of Registration No. 365)	-	A-1342 (US Navy)	21. 5.29	Severely damaged (hull) at Twin Lake, Ont. in 8/32. Canx 15.5.33.
G-CAPG	DH.61 Giant Moth (Re-engined with P&W Hornet A1G on 12.5.34) (Certificate of Registration No. 484)	329		18. 8.28	WFU on 14.2.41 due to engine unserviceability. Reduced to produce. Canx.
G-CAPH	DH.60G Gipsy Moth (Certificate of Registration No. 522)	909		18.10.28	DBR during landing at Abitibi Lake, Ont. in 6/29. Canx.

Regn	Type	c/n	Previous identity	Regn date	Fate or immediate subsequent identity (if known)
G-CAPI to G-CAPZ	Was reserved for Ontario Provincial Air Service - NTU.				
G-CAQA(1)	Avro 594 Avian III	R3/CN/115		. .28R	Severely damaged at Scarborough(?), Ont. on 28.5.28. Rebuilt & re-regd as G-CAUH on 3.10.28 - original markings not applied to aircraft. Canx.
G-CAQA(2)	Avro 594 Avian IIIA (Certificate of Registration No. 447)	R3/CN/149		16. 7.28	DBF in hangar fire at Sarnia, Ont. in 9/30. Canx.
G-CAQB to G-CAQZ	Not allotted.				
G-CARA	Fairchild FC-2 (Certificate of Registration No. 366, then Certificate of Registration No. 1381 issued 23.3.34, then Certificate of Registration No. 1451 issued 27.8.34, then Certificate of Registration No. 1477 issued 29.10.34)	93		16. 5.28	DBR in forced landing during take-off due to engine failure at Lac la Rouge, Sask. on 19.6.37. Canx.
G-CARB	Alexander Long Wing Eaglerock (Certificate of Registration No. 390)	266	NC1458	11. 6.28	Severely damaged at Smiths Falls, Ont. on 23.7.28. Rebuilt in 1928 and re-regd as CF-AAR. Canx.
G-CARC	Ford 4-AT-A Trimotor (Certificate of Registration No. 653, then Certificate of Registration No. 1512 issued 19.1.35, then Certificate of Registration No. 1729 issued 17.4.36)	4-AT-10	NC1007 G-CARC/NC1007	24. 5.28	(Severly damaged on 21.11.36). To USA in 1956. Canx.
G-CARD	DH.61 Giant Moth (May have been DH.61 c/n 336 which was exported to Canada; presumably became airframe for CF-OAK c/n DHC-141)	-		. .28R	NTU. Canx.
G-CARE	Fairchild FC-2 (Certificate of Registration No. 407, then Certificate of Registration No. 1318 issued 19.7.33)	97	NC5576	14. 6.28	Re-regd as CF-MAH on 2.4.35. Canx.
G-CARF	Curtiss MF Seagull	-		23. 5.28R	NTU. Canx.
G-CARG	Reilly Monoplane	-		25. 5.28	W/o while being test flown in 1928. Canx.
G-CARH	Fairchild FC-2 (Certificate of Registration No. 419)	110	NC5740	20. 6.28	DBR after hitting shore during overshot landing in squally weather 60 miles east of Great Bear Lake, NWT. on 31.7.32. (On display Western Canada Aviation Museum, Winnipeg)
G-CARI	Fairchild FC-2 (Certificate of Registration No. 420)	120		20. 6.28	Severely damaged at Hudson Bay, NWT. in 5/29. Further damage in storage while awaiting repair. Canx.
G-CARJ	Fairchild FC-2W2 (Certificate of Registration No. 466)	130		29. 7.28	DBR in accident on 9.8.29 (details?). Canx.
G-CARK	Atlantic Aircraft/Fokker Super Universal (Certificate of Registration No. 451)	802		19. 7.28	Declared unserviceable after CCA inspection. Canx 16.3.31.
G-CARL	Curtiss HS-2L (Certificate of Registration No. 414)	-	G-CYGU US Navy A-1288	31. 5.28	Canx 29.10.29. Reduced to spares at Roberval, Que.
G-CARM	Fairchild FC-2W2 (Certificate of Registration No. 517, then Certificate of Registration No. 1643 issued 7.12.35, then Certificate of Registration No. 1804 issued 24.6.36)	132	NC7033	11.10.28	DBF when gasoline cargo ignited when aircraft hit buoy at Gastineau Channel, Juneau, Alaska on 15.6.39. Canx.
G-CARN	Loening Amphibian (Certificate of Registration No. 424)	206		29. 6.28	Fatal crash on island after stalling during local flight from Beaumaris, Ont. on 9.8.28 & DBR. Canx.
G-CARO	Canadian Vickers HS-3L (Certificate of Registration No. 453)	CV-110	A-1143 (US Navy)	20. 7.28	DBR when it broke from moorings in severe storm and hull holed at Roberval, Que. on 1.6.29. Canx.
G-CARP	American Eagle (Certificate of Registration No. 405, then Certificate of Registration No. 642 issued 6.6.29)	185	NC5526	12. 6.28	CofA expired 2.9.36 & WFU. Canx 13.1.40.
G-CARQ	Loening Amphibian (Certificate of Registration No. 440)	202		5. 7.28	DBF in suspected arson while staked down at Rimouski airport, Que. on 5.6.30. Canx.
G-CARR	Stearman C3B (Re-engined with Wright J-4B in 7/30; reverted to Wright J-5 in 11/30) (Certificate of Registration No. 467, then Certificate of Registration No. 2706 issued 12.9.40, then Certificate of Registration No. 3110 issued 4.12.44, then Certificate of Registration No. 5285 issued 7.12.46)	134		18. 8.28	DBR when ski broke on hitting runway marker at take-off and groundlooped during landing at Riviere-du-Loup, Que. on 2.1.47. Scrapped. Canx.
G-CARS	Loening Amphibian (Certificate of Registration No. 432)	204		29. 6.28	DBF after hitting obstruction on ski take-off and fire broke out when engine restarted at Quesnel, BC. on 16.3.33. Canx.
G-CART	Fairchild FC-2W2 (Certificate of Registration No. 441)	126		6. 7.28	Canx 16.3.33. Wings used in building of Fairchild 71CM CF-AUA. On display in 1997 at Rockcliffe, Canada. (Also marked as NC6621)
G-CARU	DH.60X Moth (Re-engined with DH Gipsy I on 8.12.35)(Certificate of Registration No. 456, then Certificate of Registration No. 1224 issued 28.9.32, then Certificate of Registration No. 1355 issued 13.3.34)	640		23. 7.28	CofA expired 14.4.37 & WFU. Canx.
G-CARV	DH.60X Moth (Certificate of Registration No. 421)	610		23. 6.28	Canx 20.7.29. Used in 1929 in rebuild of G-CAUR.
G-CARW	DH.60X Moth (Certificate of Registration No. 422, then Certificate of Registration No. 547 issued 19.1.29, then Certificate of Registration No. 1241 issued 27.1.33)	611		23. 6.28	DBR when it stalled during landing after engine failure at emergency field at Strathburn, Ont. on 1.5.33. Canx.
G-CARX	DH.60X Moth (Certificate of Registration No. 460)	635		25. 7.28	DBR when it stalled and crashed into Elbow River whilst low flying at Calgary, Alta. on 25.5.30. Canx.
G-CARY	DH.60X Moth (Certificate of Registration No. 461, then Certificate of Registration No. 1113 issued 25.2.32, then Certificate of Registration No. 1531 issued 5.12.34)	636		25. 7.28	Severely damaged in forced landing due to engine failure at Pigeon Lake, Alta. (30 miles west of Millet) on 16.10.36. To Calgary Institute of Technology and Art for rebuild on 19.2.38 - never completed. Canx.
G-CARZ	DH.60X Moth (Certificate of Registration No. 433, then Certificate of Registration No. 571 issued 28.3.29, then Certificate of Registration No. 1112 issued 25.2.32, then Certificate of Registration No. 1219 issued 9.11.32, then Certificate of Registration No. 1603 issued 25.7.35)	633		29. 6.28	Dismantled. Canx as WFU 15.4.39.
G-CASA	Curtiss JN-4D (Certificate of Registration No. 437)	-		4. 7.28	Canx 2.1.30.
G-CASB	Swallow Biplane (Certificate of Registration No. 445, then Certificate of Registration No. 874 issued 30.5.30, then Certificate of Registration No. 1174 issued 29.7.32)	944	NC5567	10. 7.28	Canx as WFU 28.7.33. Dismantled.

Regn	Type	c/n	Previous identity	Regn date	Fate or immediate subsequent identity (if known)
G-CASC	Fokker F.VIIb-3m (Certificate of Registration No. 708)	5104		13.12.28	DBF in hangar fire at Winnipeg, Man. on 4.3.31. Canx.
G-CASD	Atlantic Aircraft/Fokker Universal (CofR No. 452)	431		19. 7.28	DBF when aircraft caught fire while engine being heated under hood with blow pot at Winnipeg, Man. 23.12.29. Canx.
G-CASE	Atlantic Aircraft/Fokker Universal (CofR No. 472, then (Certificate of Registration No. 1101 issued 1.3.32, then Certificate of Registration No. 1201 issued 22.9.32)	432		3. 8.28	DBR after sinking ehen float gear collapsed during landing at Gull Lake, Alta. on 10.6.33. Canx.
G-CASF	Atlantic Aircraft/Fokker Universal (CofR No. 483)	433		20. 8.28	DBR when aircraft capsized by strong gust after landing and drifted onto rocks at Allanwater Lake, Ont. on 2.6.30. Canx
G-CASG	Was allotted to Western Canada Airways Ltd. (for Atlantic Aircraft/Fokker Universal) - NTU.				
G-CASH	Was allotted to Western Canada Airways Ltd. (for Atlantic Aircraft/Fokker Universal) - NTU.				
G-CASI	Was allotted to Western Canada Airways Ltd. (for Atlantic Aircraft/Fokker Universal) - NTU.				
G-CASJ	Atlantic Aircraft/Fokker Super Universal (Certificate of Registration No. 465)	805		29. 7.28	Sank in forced landing after take-off from lake near Cat Lake, 100 miles north of Sioux Lookout, Ont. on 13.7.29 & DBR. (Parts stored Western Canada Aviation Museum, Winnipeg) Canx.
G-CASK	Atlantic Aircraft/Fokker Super Universal (Certificate of Registration No. 481)	803		17. 8.28	DBF when aircraft caught fire during refuelling at Fort McMurray, Alta. on 31.3.33. Canx.
G-CASL	Atlantic Aircraft/Fokker Super Universal (Certificate of Registration No. 482)	806		20. 8.28	Fatal crash when aircraft spun into ground due to unknown cause near Mazenod Lake, NWT. on 29.6.32. Canx.
G-CASM	Atlantic Aircraft/Fokker Super Universal (Certificate of Registration No. 511)	810		28. 9.28	DBF in hangar fire at Winnipeg, Man. on 4.3.31. Canx.
G-CASN	Atlantic Aircraft/Fokker Super Universal (Certificate of Registration No. 538)	821		17.12.28	DBF in hangar fire at Winnipeg, Man. on 4.3.31. Canx.
G-CASO	Atlantic Aircraft/Fokker Super Universal (Certificate of Registration No. 541)	822		5. 1.29	DBR when undercarriage collapsed during take-off from ice at Aylmer Lake, NWT. on 16.11.29. Canx.
G-CASP	Atlantic Aircraft/Fokker Super Universal (Certificate of Registration No. 542)	823		31.12.28	Blown out into Hudson Bay after dragging anchor during gale and sank during salvage attempt at Churchill, Man. on 26.8.29 & DBR. Canx.
G-CASQ	Atlantic Aircraft/Fokker Super Universal (Certificate of Registration No. 546, then Certificate of Registration No. 2021 issued 30.6.37)	824		16. 1.29	Undercarriage collapsed during forced landing due to weather at Disappointment Inlet, Vancouver Island, BC. on 17.11.38 & DBR. Canx.
G-CASR	Pheasant H-10 (Certificate of Registration No. 463, then Certificate of Registration No. 521 issued 12.12.30, then Certificate of Registration No. 1047 issued 14.9.31)	121	NC5411	27. 7.28	Damaged (details unknown) at North Battleford, Sask. on 31.7.32. Canx. Stored until rebuilt in 1964. (On display at Western Development Museum, Saskatoon, Sask.)
G-CASS	Standard J-1 (C/n is probably USAS serial)(Certificate of Registration No. 436)	41324		27. 6.28	Grounded at de Lesseps Field. Canx 10.10.28.
G-CAST	Swallow Land Plane (Certificate of Registration No. 431, then Certificate of Registration No. 1717 issued 15.6.36)	950	NC6049	21. 6.29	Hit telephone wires on take-off after forced landing at Foxwarren, Man. on 19.6.36 & DBR. Canx.
G-CASU	Waco 10 (Certificate of Registration No. 474)	1617		3. 8.28	DBF in London Air Transport hangar fire at London, Ont. on 26.1.29. Canx.
G-CASV	Waco 10 (Certificate of Registration No. 475)	1599		3. 8.28	DBF in London Air Transport hangar fire at London, Ont. on 26.1.29. Canx.
G-CASW	Canadian Vickers Vedette V (Certificate of Registration No. 448)	CV-91		16. 7.28	Crashed in fog north of Porcher Island, BC. on 15.8.28 & DBR. Canx.
G-CASX	Boeing B-1D (Certificate of Registration No. 429)	1029		27. 6.28	Ran into rain on flight from Butedale to Swanson Bay, BC. and hit water when pilot reached for cloth to clean windscreen at Graham Reach, BC. on 13.7.28 & DBR. Canx.
G-CASY	Hawk-Clark Y-Avro Mallard S-2 (Built using fuselage of G-CAAQ, fitted with a Hawk engine and new wings with a Clark Y section in 1928/29) (Certificate of Registration No. 865)	-		21. 5.30	CofA expired 20.5.31. Canx.
G-CASZ	Curtiss JN-4	-		25. 6.28	No CofR issued. Sold 13.8.28. Canx.
G-CATA	Fairchild FC-2 (Certificate of Registration No. 442)	43	NC4012	30. 6.28	WFU & stored 5.2.31 at Lac a la Tortue. Canx 18.5.34. Reduced to spares.
G-CATB	Swallow Land Biplane (Certificate of Registration No. 501)	908	NC4365	21. 9.28	Damaged by cause unknown at Guelph, Ont on 12.6.29. DBF while under repair and before new certificate issued at Toronto, Ont. on 25.7.29. Canx.
G-CATC	Travel Air 2000 (Certificate of Registration No. 506, then Certificate of Registration No. 919 issued 28.8.30, then Certificate of Registration No. 1263 issued 11.4.33, then Certificate of Registration No. 1658 issued 16.2.36)	641		25. 9.28	Severely damaged during take-off at St.Luc de Matane, Que. in 12/36. Sold on 16.2.37. Canx 31.7.38.
G-CATD	Travel Air 2000 (Certificate of Registration No. 470, then Certificate of Registration No. 1200 issued 19.9.32, then Certificate of Registration No. 1763 issued 24.7.36)	584	NC6080	7. 8.28	WFU 29.9.42 due to wartime restrictions. Sold in 2/43. Severely damaged when aircraft nosed up in slush on Saguenay River during forced landing due to engine failure while being flown illegally after reassembly at Chicoutimi, Que. on 23.2.42. Canx.
G-CATE	Curtiss JN-4C (Certificate of Registration No. 464, then Certificate of Registration No. 570 issued 5.4.29)	AB.24	G-CABX (Royal Air Force Canada)	13. 7.28	Grounded after inspection on 12.7.29. Stored. To Pioneer Museum at Wetaskiwin. (On display 5/99 Renolds Alberta Museum as C1347) Canx.
G-CATF	DH.60X Moth (Certificate of Registration No. 449)	623		17. 7.28	DBF in National Air Transport hangar fire at Toronto, Ont. on 12.11.35. Canx.
G-CATG	DH.60X Moth (Certificate of Registration No. 458)	617		25. 7.28	DBR when nosed up during forced landing when ski hit rock at Val Morin, Que. on 8.3.31. Canx.

Regn	Type	c/n	Previous identity	Regn date	Fate or immediate subsequent identity (if known)
G-CATH	DH.60X Moth (Re-engined with DH Gipsy I in 6/30) (Certificate of Registration No. 388, then Certificate of Registration No. 1634 issued 30.10.35, then Certificate of Registration No. 2442 issued 26.5.39, then Certificate of Registration No. 2451 issued 31.5.39)	484		31. 5.28	WFU in late 1939 with damaged float. DBF due to unknown cause at Trout Lake, Ont. 10.5.40. Engine to CF-CEG. Canx.
G-CATI	DH.60X Moth (Certificate of Registration No. 490)	618		25. 8.28	DBR when aicraft stalled in turn at low altitude on training flight at Ramsey Lake, Ont. on 5.4.31. Canx.
G-CATJ	DH.60X Moth (Certificate of Registration No. 459, then Certificate of Registration No. 1329 issued 17.8.33, then Certificate of Registration No. 1347 issued 19.10.33, then Certificate of Registration No. 1516 issued 22.1.35, then Certificate of Registration No. 1627 issued 28.9.35, then Certificate of Registration No. 1713 issued 30.5.36, then Certificate of Registration No. 2639 issued 20.5.40)	622		25. 7.28	Canx as WFU 10.7.40 due to wartime restrictions.
G-CATK	DH.60X Moth (Re-engined with ADC Cirrus III in 12/30)(Certificate of Registration No. 462, then Certificate of Registration No. 1141 issued 23.5.32, then Certificate of Registration No. 2029 issued 6.5.37, then Certificate of Registration No. 2479 issued 10.7.39, then Certificate of Registration No. 2598 issued 13.2.40, then Certificate of Registration No. 2702 issued 21.8.40)	612		27. 7.28	Canx as WFU 6.10.43 due to wartime restrictions.
G-CATL	Fairchild FC-2W2 (Certificate of Registration No. 495, then Certificate of Registration No. 1127 issued 20.4.32)	511		25. 8.28	DBF in fatal crash 4 miles south of Gronard Lake, NWT. near Cameron Bay when the port wing failed on 31.1.33. Canx.
G-CATM	Loening Amphibian (Certificate of Registration No. 488)	209		20. 8.28	Stalled in turn during landing approach at Thicket Portage, NWT. on 25.8.29 & DBR. Canx.
G-CATN	Alexander Combination Wing Eaglerock (CofR No. 446, then Certificate of Registration No. 1076 issued 15.12.31, then Certificate of Registration No. 1611 issued 30.8.35)	529	NC5899	12. 7.28	Canx 19.10.37. To Hemphill Schools Ltd., Vancouver, BC (for use as an instructional airframe).
G-CATO	Buhl CA-5 Airsedan (Certificate of Registration No. 485)	23	NC4356	18. 8.28	DBF in National Air Transport hangar fire at Toronto, Ont. on 12.11.35. Canx.
G-CATP	Buhl CA-3C Sport Airsedan (Certificate of Registration No. 519)	32	NC6872	18.10.28	DBF in National Air Transport hangar fire at Toronto, Ont. on 12.11.35. Canx.
G-CATQ	DH.60X Moth	-		. .28R	NTU - Canx.
G-CATR	Fairchild FC-2 (Rebuilt with fuselage from G-CATW c/n CV-111 in 1929) (Certificate of Registration No. 832)	CV-88		22.11.28	Severely damaged in severe windstorm at Charlottetown, PEI. on 9.2.33. Reduced to spares. Canx.
G-CATS	Fairchild FC-2 (Rebuilt as Model 51 in 5/29; rebuilt as Model 51(Convertible) in 5/33)(Re-engined with Wright J-6 in 9/33; then Wright J-5 in 2/36)(Certificate of Registration No. 563, then Certificate of Registration No. 749 issued 4.9.29, then Certificate of Registration No. 1270 issued 9.5.33)	CV-102		3. 8.28	WFU on 15.11.36. Reduced to spares. Canx.
G-CATT	Fairchild FC-2 (Certificate of Registration No. 529)	CV-103		13.11.28	DBF when engine backfired in air and flames broke out on landing at Millidge, Ont. on 2.7.30. Canx.
G-CATU	Fairchild FC-2 (Certificate of Registration No. 518, then Certificate of Registration No. 1003 issued 11.6.31, then Certificate of Registration No. 1117 issued 4.5.32)	CV-104		13.11.28	Port wing sheared off on hitting tree after take-off from Kenogamissi Lake (Timmins), Ont. on 19.2.33 & DBR. Canx.
G-CATV	Fairchild FC-2 (Certificate of Registration No. 530)	CV-105		13.11.28	Stalled in turn avoiding shore of lake & DBR at Lake Otatakin, Ont. on 15.8.29. Canx.
G-CATW	Fairchild FC-2 (Certificate of Registration No. 535)	CV-111		23.11.28	Canx 15.1.29. Fuselage used to rebuild G-CATR in 1929.
G-CATX	Ford 4-AT-B Trimotor	4-AT-26	NC5810	7. 8.28	Hit water while low flying in poor weather causing a fatal crash in Puget Sound, near Port Townsend, BC. on 25.8.28.
G-CATY	Boeing B-1E (Certificate of Registration No. 539)	1027		19. 7.28	WFU 24.3.31. Reduced to scrap. Canx.
G-CATZ	DH.60X Moth (Certificate of Registration No. 463, then Certificate of Registration No. 573 issued 6.4.29)	621		28. 7.28	DBF in fire at auto garage while undergoing repair at North Bay, Ont. on 27.10.31. Canx.
G-CAUA	DH.60X Moth (Certificate of Registration No. 468, then Certificate of Registration No. 1291 issued 6.6.33, then Certificate of Registration No. 1669 issued 19.3.36, then Certificate of Registration No. 1845 issued 3.11.36, then Certificate of Registration No. 2733 issued 14.11.40)	630		7. 8.28	Canx as WFU 14.11.41 due to wartime restrictions. Stored until 1962. (On display at Rockcliffe, Canada)
G-CAUB	DH.60X Moth (Certificate of Registration No. 469, then Certificate of Registration No. 1128 issued 22.5.32, then Certificate of Registration No. 1307 issued 28.6.33, then Certificate of Registration No. 1430 issued 20.6.34, then Certificate of Registration No. 2735 issued 9.11.40, then Certificate of Registration No. 2811 issued 27.5.41)	631		7. 8.28	Canx as WFU 8.11.41 due to wartime restrictions. Canx.
G-CAUC	DH.60X Moth (Certificate of Registration No. 473)	628		15. 8.28	DBR in fatal crash at Weston, Ont. on 15.12.29. Canx.
G-CAUD	DH.60X Moth (Certificate of Registration No. 478, then Certificate of Registration No. 1559 issued 13.5.35, then Certificate of Registration No. 1770 issued 6.8.36, then Certificate of Registration No. 1903 issued 9.3.37)	639		16. 8.28	DBR when a gust of wind caught aircraft during take-off near Bancroft, Ont. on 27.3.37. Canx.
G-CAUE	DH.60X Moth (Certificate of Registration No. 494) then Certificate of Registration No. 2060 issued 19.8.37, then Certificate of Registration No. 2359 issued 3.1.39)	637		30. 8.28	Stalled in turn avoiding trees 1½ miles from take-off when flown by unlicensed owners & DBR at Grimshaw, Alta. on 11.11.39. Canx.
G-CAUF	Boeing B-1E (Certificate of Registration No. 502)	1071		21. 9.28	Canx as WFU 7.5.32. Reduced to spares.
G-CAUG	Boeing B-1E	-		. .28R	NTU. Canx.
G-CAUH	Avro 594 Avian III (Certificate of Registration No. 516, then Certificate of Registration No. 745 issued 5.9.29, then Certificate of Registration No. 1228 issued 3.1.33, then Certificate of Registration No. 1607 issued 2.8.35, then Certificate of Registration No. 1706 issued 3.6.36, then Certificate of Registration No. 1768 issued 28.7.36)	R3/CN/115	G-CAQA	3.10.28	Grounded for major overhaul on 12.10.37. Canx.
G-CAUI	American Eagle Biplane (Certificate of Registration No. 486)	213	NC5777	9. 8.28	DBF at Regina, Sask. on 20.9.29. Canx.
G-CAUJ	Swallow Land Biplane (Certificate of Registration No. 492, then Certificate of Registration No. 1039 issued 13.6.31, then Certificate of Registration No. 1044 issued 17.9.31)	946		22. 8.28	Overturned on landing with broken undercarriage strut & DBR at St.Catherines, Ont. on 17.10.31. Canx.

Regn	Type	c/n	Previous identity	Regn date	Fate or immediate subsequent identity (if known)
G-CAUK	Swallow Land Biplane (Certificate of Registration No. 476)	958		15. 8.28	Stalled in turn in forced landing due to engine failure & DBR at Farnham, Que. on 21.12.28. Canx.
G-CAUL	American Eagle Biplane (Certificate of Registration No. 479)	147	NC5164	1. 8.28	Noticed smoke in air, landed and aircraft burned up at Shoal Lake, Man. on 19.7.29. Canx.
G-CAUM	DH.60X Moth (Re-engined with ADC Cirrus III in 12/37)(Certificate of Registration No. 503, then Certificate of Registration No. 1450 issued 2.8.34, then Certificate of Registration No. 2153 issued 13.12.37, then Certificate of Registration No. 5451 issued 3.8.46, then Certificate of Registration No. 6529 issued 20.11.47)	696		21. 9.28	Canx as WFU 20.10.48.
G-CAUN	DH.60X Moth	629		. .28R	DBR (details?) at Weston, Ont. on 21.9.28 before CofR issued. Canx.
G-CAUO	DH.60X Moth (Re-engined with DH Gipsy I (DH.60G) on 23.4.35)(Certificate of Registration No. 491, then Certificate of Registration No. 497 issued 6.9.28, then Certificate of Registration No. 512 issued 28.9.28, then Certificate of Registration No. 1159 issued 4.7.32, then Certificate of Registration No. 1319 issued 27.7.33, then Certificate of Registration No. 2455 issued 9.6.39)	634		25. 8.28	Canx as WFU in 6/42 due to wartime restrictions.
G-CAUP	DH.60X Moth (Re-engined with ADC Cirrus III in 7/37)(Certificate of Registration No. 489, then Certificate of Registration No. 1726 issued 26.6.36, then Certificate of Registration No. 2179 issued 10.2.38)	642		25. 8.28	Canx as WFU 10.2.39.
G-CAUQ	DH.60X Moth (Certificate of Registration No. 508)	638		8. 9.28	Fatal crash (details?) & DBR at Walkerville, Ont. on 20.5.31. Canx.
G-CAUR	DH.60G Gipsy Moth (Rebuilt with ADC Cirrus II and parts from G-CARV in 2/39, c/n canx.) (Certificate of Registration No. 527, then Certificate of Registration No. 757 issued 25.9.29)	860		26.10.28	Severely damaged at Cornwall, Ont. on 9.2.30 & WFU. Involved in attempted escape by army deserter after bank robbery at Chicoutimi, Que. with markings CF-AUR 12.11.43.
G-CAUS	Canadian Vickers Vedette V	CV-92		. 9.28R	NTU - To Chile. Canx.
G-CAUT	Canadian Vickers Vedette V (Re-engined with A-5 Lynx IV (Mk.II) in 1935) (Certificate of Registration No. 513)	CV-93		14. 9.28	CofA expired 14.9.29. Stored at Montreal. Re-regd as CF-MAF on 14.5.35. Canx.
G-CAUU	Canadian Vickers Vedette V (Certificate of Registration No. 520)	CV-98		12.10.28	To Chile in 1928. Canx.
G-CAUV	Canadian Vickers Vedette V	CV-99		.10.28R	NTU - To Chile. Canx.
G-CAUW	Canadian Vickers Vedette II	CV-100		. .28R	NTU - To RCAF as 108 on 17.1.29. Canx.
G-CAUX	Canadian Vickers Vedette II	CV-101		. .28R	NTU - To RCAF as 109 on 5.1.29. Canx.
G-CAUY	Canadian Vickers Vedette II	CV-118		. .28R	NTU - To RCAF as 110 on 10.1.29. Canx.
G-CAUZ	Alexander Eaglerock A-2 (Certificate of Registration No. 526)	647		23.10.28	Forced landing in clearing due to engine failure & DBR 4 miles east of Carmacks, YT. on 29.11.29. Canx.
G-CAVA	Monocoupe (Certificate of Registration No. 487)	81	NC6554	20. 8.28	Severely damaged at St.Hubert, Que. on 6.10.29. Scrapped post-7/30. Canx.
G-CAVB	Avro 594 Avian IIIA (Certificate of Registration No. 505, then Certificate of Registration No. 1121 issued 1.7.32, then Certificate of Registration No. 1575 issued 19.6.35, then Certificate of Registration No. 2020 issued 24.6.37, then Certificate of Registration No. 2344 issued 19.11.38, then Certificate of Registration No. 2736 issued 7.11.40)	R3/CN/163		25. 9.28	Sold in 2/41 & used as ground instructional airframe. Canx 25.2.41.
G-CAVC	DH.60X Moth	-		. .28R	NTU - Canx.
G-CAVD	Lincoln Page LP-3 (Re-engined with Curtiss OXX-6 in 7/34)(Certificate of Registration No. 493)	228	NC6694	19. 8.28	Canx as WFU 20.5.38.
G-CAVE	Martin Model 70 (Certificate of Registration No. 798)	96	NC2545	20. 8.28	CofA expired 18.4.31. Canx 25.6.31.
G-CAVF	DH.60X Moth (Certificate of Registration No. 498)	688		10. 9.28	Fatal crashed when aircraft stalled in turn afer take-off and crashed in spin at Leaside, Ont. 23.4.29 & DBF. Canx.
G-CAVG	DH.60X Moth (Certificate of Registration No. 499)	689		10. 9.28	Stalled in turn when engine failed after take-off at Charlottetown, PEI. on 2.11.30 & DBR. Canx.
G-CAVH	DH.60X Moth (Re-engined with DH Gipsy I (DH.60G) in 7/30) (Certificate of Registration No. 500, then Certificate of Registration No. 942 issued 27.7.30, then Certificate of Registration No. 1279 issued 26.5.33, then Certificate of Registration No. 2780 issued 20.3.41, then Certificate of Registration No. 2903 issued 23.12.41, then Certificate of Registration No. 3020 issued 13.7.43)	690		10. 9.28	Flew into snowstorm and hit tree at Hidden Lake, 26 miles ENE of Yellowknife, NWT. on 4.12.45 & DBR. Canx.
G-CAVI	DH.60X Moth (Re-engined with ADC Cirrus III in 11/35)(Certificate of Registration No. 534, then Certificate of Registration No. 1440 issued 1.8.34, then Certificate of Registration No. 2682 issued 25.6.40)	632		29.11.28	Canx as WFU 12.2.46. DBF in 2/47.
G-CAVJ	DH.60G Gipsy Moth (Certificate of Registration No. 515)	858		2.10.28	Capsized while being towed at seaplane base in windstorm at Montreal, Que. on 27.7.29 & DBR. Canx.
G-CAVK	DH.60G Gipsy Moth (Certificate of Registration No. 524, then Certificate of Registration No. 2248 issued 4.6.38, then Certificate of Registration No. 2262 issued 2.7.38)	813		23.10.28	Canx as WFU 15.4.40 due to wartime restrictions.
G-CAVL	Fairchild FC-2W2 (Certificate of Registration No. 509)	515		29. 9.28	Caught fire in hangar due to unknown cause at Newark Airport, NJ, USA. on 4.8.30 & DBF. Canx.
G-CAVM	Curtiss JN-4 (Certificate of Registration No. 507, then Certificate of Registration No. 719 issued 31.7.29)	11		21. 9.28	DBR at La Salle Airport, Montreal, Que. in 8/30. Canx.
G-CAVN	Fairchild FC-2W2 (Certificate of Registration No. 510)	522		29. 9.28	Damaged in precautionary landing due to weather & DBF when caught fire later due to battery short at Riverside, NB. on 19.2.30. Canx.
G-CAVO	Reid Rambler (Certificate of Registration No. 514)	1000		29. 9.28	Prototype dismantled 12.12.29 since cost of modification to standard type was prohibitive. Fuselage used for CF-BPB. Canx.
G-CAVP	Atlantic Aircraft/Fokker Super Universal	-		. 9.28R	NTU. Canx.
G-CAVQ	Monocoupe (Certificate of Registration No. 523)	233	NC7357	27. 9.28	Fatal crash when aircraft hit telephone wires on local flight whilst barnstorming & DBF at Khedive, Sask. on 3.4.29. Canx.
G-CAVR	Fairchild FC-2W2 (Certificate of Registration No. 525)	525		22.10.28	Dismantled in 3/35. Wings used to build G-CAVV. Canx.

Regn	Type	c/n	Previous identity	Regn date	Fate or immediate subsequent identity (if known)
G-CAVS	Fairchild FC-2	CV-112		16.10.28	No CofR issued. Airframe stored until 1934 then used to rebuild Fairchild FC-2 G-CANB. Canx.
G-CAVT	Canadian Vickers Vedette	-		. .28R	NTU. Canx.
G-CAVU	DH.60G Gipsy Moth (Certificate of Registration No. 572)	862		12. 4.29	Hit hydro lines on take-off from field becoming hung up on wires and caught fire at London, Ont. on 6.10.32. Canx.
G-CAVV	Fairchild FC-2W2 (Fuselage was made as a Model 71C, but aircraft was typed FC-2W2 due to wings from G-CAVR) (Certificate of Registration No. 1551)	1203		30. 3.35	Canx 26.2.38. Fuselage used to build Fairchild 71C CF-BJF.
G-CAVW	DH.60G Gipsy Moth (Certificate of Registration No. 532, then Certificate of Registration No. 666 issued 6.2.30, then Certificate of Registration No. 1029 issued 5.8.31)	859		26.11.28	To Trinidad as VP-TAA 8/31. Canx.
G-CAVX	DH.60M Moth (Certificate of Registration No. 536)	339	G-AAAR	30.11.28	Stalled during landing due to gust of wind at Wolfe Island, Ont. on 4.4.37. Canx.
G-CAVY	DH.60 Moth	-		. .28R	NTU. Canx.
G-CAVZ	DH.60 Moth	-		. .28R	NTU. Canx.
G-CAWA	Curtiss JN-4 (Possibly built from G-CAEX c/n 5061, but with "clipped" wings and no V-struts on ailerons) (Certificate of Registration No. 732)	61		20. 5.29	WFU on 8.4.31. Dismantled. Canx.
G-CAWB	Atlantic Aircraft/Fokker Super Universal (Certificate of Registration No. 548)	815	NC8045	28. 1.29	DBR when wing struck ice due to down draught after take-off at Takla Landing, BC. on 21.3.37. Canx.
G-CAWC	Alexander Combination Wing Eaglerock (Certificate of Registration No. 748, then Certificate of Registration No. 983 issued 19.3.31)	409	NC4209	20. 6.29	DBR when aircraft crashed in spin at Conestogo, Ont. on 3.11.31. Canx.
G-CAWD	Monocoupe (Certificate of Registration No. 533, then (Certificate of Registration No. 1410 issued 15.5.34, then Certificate of Registration No. 1744 issued 7.7.36, then Certificate of Registration No. 2136 issued 29.11.37)	155	NC6752	22.11.28	Stalled in turn when engine cut after take-off & DBR at Schist Lake, near Flin Flon, Man. on 2.12.37. Canx.
G-CAWE	Waco 10 (Certificate of Registration No. 537)	995	NC3336	6.12.28	Exhaust modified to discharge under wing, seam split and flames ignited fabric after take-off from Grandview, Man. on 13.8.29 & DBF. Canx.
G-CAWF	Pitcairn PA-6 Super Mailwing (Certificate of Registration No. 544)	16		5. 1.29	DBR at Union Valley, Alta. on 13.5.31. Canx.
G-CAWG	Pitcairn PA-6 Super Mailwing (Certificate of Registration No. 545)	17		5. 1.29	Forced landing due to engine failure in storm 3 miles south of Richelieu, Que. on 8.4.29 & DBR. Canx.
G-CAWH	Fairchild FC-2 (Certificate of Registration No. 540)	12	NC1523	18.12.28	Restored to USA as NC1523 on 12.4.29. Canx.
G-CAWI	Avro 594 Avian III (Certificate of Registration No. 543)	R3/CN/105		31.12.28	Forced landing due to fog near St.Anthony, Newfoundland & DBR (date?). CofA expired 31.12.29. Canx.
G-CAWJ to G-CAXO	Not allotted. Not allotted.				
G-CAXP	DH.60X Moth (Certificate of Registration No. 450)	626	G-EBXP	12. 5.28	To USA as NC9305 in 1930. Canx.

G-CY

G-CY

G-CYAA to G-CYZZ - Allocated to Canadian military aircraft from 6/20 until 1931.

Regn	Type	c/n	Previous identity	Regn date	Fate or immediate subsequent identity (if known)
G-CYAA	Avro 504K	-	H9622	18. 6.20	Canx 21.1.25.
G-CYAB	SE.5A	-	E3172	18. 6.20	Canx 30.4.26.
G-CYAC	Avro 504K	-	E362	18. 6.20	Damaged at Camp Borden on 8.8.21. Canx after 1/25.
G-CYAD	Airco DH.9A	-	E1000	18. 6.20	Crashed at Mordy on 23.8.20. Canx 18.2.29.
G-CYAE	Curtiss HS-2L	-	A-1248 (US Navy)	22. 7.20	Canx 31.7.27.
G-CYAF	Curtiss HS-2L	2901	A-1875 (US Navy)	22. 7.20	Canx 2.8.24.
G-CYAG	Curtiss HS-2L	-	A-1941 (US Navy)	25.10.20	Canx 26.9.23.
G-CYAH	Curtiss HS-2L	4122		25.10.20	Canx 26.11.24.
G-CYAI	Avro 504K	-	E363	19. 7.20	Canx 24.7.21.
G-CYAJ	Airco DH.9A	-	E998	19. 7.20	Canx 23.9.27.
G-CYAK	Airco DH.9A	-	E994	19. 7.20	Damaged in 1920 (details?). Canx 18.2.29.
G-CYAL	Avro 504K	-	H1917	19. 7.20	Damaged at Camp Borden on 12.8.20. Canx.
G-CYAM	Avro 504K	-	H9738	19. 7.20	Damaged at Camp Borden on 24.2.25. Canx 24.2.25.
G-CYAN	Airco DH.9A	-	E996	19. 7.20	Canx 23.9.27.
G-CYAO	Airco DH.9A	-	E1002	19. 6.20	Canx 1.2.22.
G-CYAP	Avro 504K	-	H2043	19. 7.20	To RCAF as 44. Canx.
G-CYAQ	Avro 504K	-	H2048	19. 7.20	To RCAF as 2. Canx.
G-CYAR	Avro 504K	-	H7461	19. 8.20	To RCAF as 1. Canx.
G-CYAS	Avro 504K	-	H2044	4. 8.20	Canx 25.1.25.
G-CYAT	Avro 504K	-	H9627	13. 8.20	To RCAF as 45. Canx.
G-CYAU	Avro 504K	-	H9629	13. 8.20	To RCAF as 46. Canx.
G-CYAV	Avro 504K	-	H9626	13. 8.20	To RCAF as 50. Canx.
G-CYAW	Avro 504K	-	H9628	13. 8.20	Damaged at Camp Borden on 26.8.21. Canx 8.3.22.
G-CYAX	Avro 504K	-	H2041	20. 4.21	To RCAF as 14. Canx.
G-CYAY	SE.5A	-	F9114	10. 9.20	Canx 25.2.29.
G-CYAZ	Airco DH.9A	-	E997	10. 9.20	Damaged at Winnipeg on 30.9.20. Canx 1.2.22.
G-CYBA	Curtiss HS-2L	-		24. 9.20	Canx 29.7.22.
G-CYBB	Curtiss HS-2L	-		30. 5.21	Canx 27.3.25.
G-CYBC	Bristol F.2b Fighter	4322	F4336	6. 8.20	Canx 7.2.22.

Regn	Type	c/n	Previous identity	Regn date	Fate or immediate subsequent identity (if known)
G-CYBD	Avro 504K	-	H9744	18. 9.20	Damaged at Camp Borden on 1.4.21. Canx 27.4.21.
G-CYBE	SE.5A	-	D8479	10. 9.20	Damaged at Camp Borden on 16.11.20. Canx 25.2.29.
G-CYBF	Airco DH.9A	-	E995	18. 9.20	Canx 18.2.29.
G-CYBG	Avro 504K	-	H9672	23.11.20	Damaged at Camp Borden on 18.10.21. Canx after 1/25.
G-CYBH	Avro 504K	-	H9624	18. 9.20	Damaged at Camp Borden on 22.10.25. Canx 15.1.26.
G-CYBI	Airco DH.9A	-	E992	17. 9.20	Canx 18.5.26.
G-CYBJ	SE.5A	-	D8472	29. 9.20	Damaged at Camp Borden on 21.10.21. Canx 30.4.26.
G-CYBK	Avro 504K	-	H9715	18. 9.20	Damaged at Camp Borden on 18.2.21. Canx after 1/25.
G-CYBL	Avro 504N (Originally regd as 504K)	-	H9625	18. 9.20	Canx 25.11.30. To RCAF as 53.
G-CYBM	Avro 504N (Originally regd as 504K, converted 17.1.27)	-	H9670	11.10.20	Canx 17.7.29. To RCAF as 52.
G-CYBN	Airco DH.9A	-	E993	11.10.20	Damaged at Camp Borden on 22.11.20. Canx 18.2.29.
G-CYBO	Airco DH.4B (Originally regd as DH.4)	-	F2705	30.11.20	Canx 30.11.28.
G-CYBP	SE.5A	-	F9016	7.10.20	Damaged at Beaton on 7.2.21. Canx 25.2.29.
G-CYBQ	SE.5A	-	D8487	12.10.20	Damaged at Camp Borden on 9.2.21. Canx 8.3.22.
G-CYBR	Avro 504K	-	H9745	12.10.20	Canx after 1/25.
G-CYBS	Avro 504K	-	H9740	12.10.20	Damaged at Camp Borden on 5.4.21. Canx after 1/25.
G-CYBT	Short Felixstowe F.3	-	N4016	3.10.21	Canx 29.9.22.
G-CYBU	Airco DH.4	-	F2709	26.10.20	Canx 30.11.28.
G-CYBV	Airco DH.4	-	F2710	29.11.20	Crashed at High River on 1.8.21. Canx.
G-CYBW	Airco DH.4	-	F2672	1. 2.21	Damaged at High River on 31.5.21. Canx.
G-CYBX	SE.5A	-	E3173	2.11.20	Damaged at Moorfield on 18.3.21. Canx 30.4.26.
G-CYBY	SE.5A	-	D8489	16.12.20	Damaged at Camp Borden on 28.1.21. Canx.
G-CYBZ	Avro 504K	-	H9742	15.11.20	Damaged at Camp Borden in 5/21. Canx 13.4.23.
G-CYCA	Avro 504K	-	H9690	12.10.20	Damaged at Rugby on 13.4.21. Canx 27.4.21.
G-CYCB	Avro 504K	-	H9737	12.10.20	Damaged at Camp Borden on 9.12.21. Canx 8.3.22.
G-CYCC	SE.5A	-	F9128	7.10.20	Canx 30.4.26.
G-CYCD	Avro 504N (Originally regd as 504K)	-	H9669	12.10.20	To RCAF as 51. Canx.
G-CYCE	SE.5A	-	F9117	3.11.20	Canx 30.4.26.
G-CYCF	Fairey IIIc Transatlantic	F.333	G-EARS N9256	4.10.20	Damaged at St.John on 7.10.20. Canx 7.10.20.
G-CYCG	Airco DH.9A	-	E1001	16.12.20	Damaged at Camp Borden on 20.12.20. Canx 23.9.27.
G-CYCH	Avro 504K	-	H9714	15.11.20	Damaged at Camp Borden on 22.3.21. Canx 27.4.21.
G-CYCI	Avro 504K	-	H9736	23.11.20	Damaged at Camp Borden in early-1921. Canx 17.4.21.
G-CYCJ	Avro 504K	-	H9732	23.11.20	Damaged at Barrie on 10.4.21. Canx 27.4.21.
G-CYCK	Avro 504K	-	H9717	23.11.20	Damaged at Camp Borden on 14.11.21. Canx 8.3.22. Rebuilt & re-regd as CF-CYC.
G-CYCL	Avro 504K	-	H9739	18. 1.21	Damaged at Camp Borden on 3.1.21. Canx 1.2.22.
G-CYCM	Avro 504K	-	H9741	19. 4.21	To ground instructional airframe in 1927. Canx 21.3.30.
G-CYCN	Curtiss JN-4	-	NC1048	13. 1.21	Canx 5.1.23.
G-CYCO	Curtiss JN-4	-	NC502	13. 1.21	Damaged at Camp Borden on 26.1.21. Canx.
G-CYCP	Curtiss JN-4	-	NC1343	13. 1.21	Canx 3.11.20.
G-CYCQ	SE.5A	-	F9136	3.11.20	Canx 25.2.29.
G-CYCR	Avro 504K	-	H9671	19. 4.21	Damaged at Camp Borden on 20.12.21. Canx 30.12.21.
G-CYCS	Avro 504K	-	H9621	14. 1.21	Damaged at Shelbourne on 15.2.21. Canx 3.2.28.
G-CYCT	Avro 504K	-	H9668	1. 2.21	Damaged at Camp Borden on 18.2.21. Canx after 1/25.
G-CYCU	Avro 504K	-	H9665	14. 1.21	Damaged at Barrie on 4.8.21. Canx 8.3.22.
G-CYCV	SE.5A	-	F9139	5. 1.21	Damaged at Camp Borden on 16.3.21. Canx 25.2.29.
G-CYCW	Airco DH.4	-	F2713	1. 2.21	Canx 30.11.28.
G-CYCX	Avro 504K	-	H2049	18. 1.21	To RCAF as 3. Canx.
G-CYCY	Avro 504K	-	H2046	19. 4.21	Damaged at Camp Borden on 11.4.21. Canx 27.4.21.
G-CYCZ	Avro 504K	-	H9630	22. 4.21	Canx 25.3.26.
G-CYDA	Avro 504K	-	H2045	1. 2.21	To RCAF as 13 (but marked as 13A). Canx.
G-CYDB	Airco DH.4	-	F2673	1. 2.21	Canx 4.12.24.
G-CYDC	Curtiss JN-4	-	NC240	5. 5.21	Canx 5.1.23.
G-CYDD	Curtiss JN-4	-	NC292	5. 5.21	Damaged at Camp Borden in 1921 (details?). Canx.
G-CYDE	Curtiss JN-4	-	NC610	7. 9.20	Damaged at Camp Borden on 15.12.20. Canx.
G-CYDF	Curtiss JN-4	-	NC826	5. 5.21	Damaged at Kingston on 8.9.21. Canx.
G-CYDG	Curtiss JN-4	-	NC438	5. 5.21	Canx 15.1.23.
G-CYDH	Short Felixstowe F.3	-	N4009	11. 7.21	Canx 11.1.23.
G-CYDI	Short Felixstowe F.3	-	N4010	30. 5.21	Canx 12.9.23.
G-CYDJ	Short Felixstowe F.3	-	N4011	28. 6.21	Canx 26.1.23.
G-CYDK	Airco DH.4	-	F2711	19. 4.21	Damaged at Waldenar on 23.4.22. Canx.
G-CYDL	Airco DH.4B (Originally regd as DH.4)	-	F2712	19. 4.21	Canx 30.11.28.
G-CYDM	Airco DH.4B (Originally regd as DH.4)	-	F2706	19. 4.21	Canx 30.11.28.
G-CYDN	Airco DH.4B (Originally regd as DH.4)	-	F2708	16. 3.21	Canx 2.2.25.
G-CYDO	Airco DH.9a	-	E999	16. 3.21	Damaged at Arthur on 17.5.21. Canx 23.9.27.
G-CYDP	Bristol F.2b Fighter	3520	D7869	19. 4.21	Canx after 1/25.
G-CYDQ	Short Felixstowe F.3	-	N4014	13. 4.21	Canx 12.9.23.
G-CYDR	Curtiss HS-2L	9332	A-1991 (US Navy)	28. 5.21	Canx 4.11.21.
G-CYDS	Curtiss HS-2L	9327	A-1986 (US Navy)	8. 7.21	Canx 8.8.21.
G-CYDT	Curtiss HS-2L	9331	A-1990 (US Navy)	23. 7.21	Canx 26.2.24.
G-CYDU	Curtiss HS-2L	-	A-1984 (US Navy)	7. 7.21	Damaged at Brit Col on 23.7.25. Canx.

Regn	Type	c/n	Previous identity	Regn date	Fate or immediate subsequent identity (if known)
G-CYDV	Curtiss JN-4	-	NC228	5. 5.21	Canx 15.1.23.
G-CYDW	Curtiss JN-4	-	NC264	5. 5.21	Canx 15.1.23.
G-CYDX	Curtiss HS-2L	459	A-1993 (US Navy)	27. 6.21	Canx 26.1.24.
G-CYDY	Curtiss HS-2L	4131	A-1992 (US Navy)	19. 7.21	DBR at Roberval, Que. on 10.8.22. Canx.
G-CYDZ	Sopwith 7F.1 Snipe	-	E7649	11. 2.21	Crashed on 22.10.23. Canx.
G-CYEA	Curtiss HS-2L	9360	A-2019 (US Navy)	12. 7.21	Damaged at Vancouver on 11.9.22. Canx.
G-CYEB	Curtiss HS-2L	950	A-1994 (US Navy)	6. 8.21	Canx 10.9.25.
G-CYEC	Airco DH.4B (Originally regd as DH.4)	-	F2714	26.10.20	Canx 30.11.28.
G-CYED	Curtiss HS-2L	-	A-1985 (US Navy)	27. 9.21	Canx 1.7.28.
G-CYEE	Avro 504K (Later converted to Seaplane)	-	E361	27. 8.21	Canx 11.7.28.
G-CYEF	Curtiss HS-2L	-	A-1988 (US Navy)	17.11.21	Damaged at Victoria Beach on 26.6.23. Canx.
G-CYEG	Avro 504K	-	H9729	26. 9.21	To ground instructional airframe in 1925. Canx 8.5.29.
G-CYEH	Avro 504N (Originally regd as 504K, converted 17.1.27)	-	H9727	27.10.21	To RCAF as 54. Canx.
G-CYEI	Avro 504N (Originally regd as 504K, converted 29.6.27)	-	H9666	27.10.21	To RCAF as 4. Canx.
G-CYEJ	Curtiss HS-2L	-	A-2223 (US Navy)	23. 5.22	Damaged at Parry Sound in 1922 (details?). Canx.
G-CYEK	Curtiss HS-2L	9363	A-2022 (US Navy)	19. 8.22	Damaged at Roberval on 21.9.22. Canx.
G-CYEL	Curtiss HS-2L	9328	A-9187 (US Navy)	2. 9.22	Canx 12.8.25.
G-CYEM	Airco DH.4	-	F2707	7. 6.22	Crashed at High River on 28.7.24. Canx 30.11.28.
G-CYEN	Short Felixstowe F.3	-	N4015	21. 8.22	Damaged at Victoria Beach on 8.9.22. Canx 12.9.23.
G-CYEO	Short Felixstowe F.3 (Certificate of Registration No. 215)	-	N4181	29. 9.22	Canx 11.1.23.
G-CYEP	Curtiss H-26	-	N4905	2. 2.22	Canx 2.1.24.
G-CYEQ	Martinsyde F.6	EA/500	G-EAPI	9.10.22	Canx 4.11.25.
G-CYER	Fairchild FC-2W2	-		. .	NTU - Canx.
G-CYES	Vickers 85 Viking IV	28/CV-7		15. 6.23	Canx 2.7.25.
G-CYET	Vickers 85 Viking IV	27/CV-8		12. 7.23	Damaged at Hilbre, Man. on 11.7.27. Canx.
G-CYEU	Canadian Vickers 85 Viking IV	CV-1		24. 7.23	WFU at Winnipeg, Man. Canx 4.5.34.
G-CYEV	Canadian Vickers 85 Viking IV	CV-2		15. 8.23	WFU at Cormorant Lake. Canx 20.2.31.
G-CYEW	Canadian Vickers 85 Viking IV	CV-3		31. 8.23	Damaged on 31.7.26 (details?). Canx.
G-CYEX	Canadian Vickers 85 Viking IV	CV-4		3.10.23	Damaged at Mannitoba on 25.8.29. Canx.
G-CYEY	Canadian Vickers 85 Viking IV	CV-5		17.10.23	WFU at Victoria Beach on 24.8.26. Canx.
G-CYEZ	Canadian Vickers 85 Viking IV	CV-6		9.11.23	WFU at Luc du Bonnet on 28.8.30. Canx.
G-CYFA to G-CYFD	Not allotted. Not allotted.				
G-CYFE	Avro 504K	-	H7462	16. 5.24	Canx at Camp Borden (details?).
G-CYFF	Avro 504K	-	H9558	20. 4.21	To RCAF as 15. Canx.
G-CYFG	Avro 504N (Originally regd as 504K)	2353	H9555	16. 5.24	To RCAF as 5. Canx.
G-CYFH	Avro 504N (Originally regd as 504K, converted 3.8.27)	-	H9722	16. 5.24	To RCAF as 6. Canx.
G-CYFI	Avro 504K	-	H2047	16. 5.24	Canx.
G-CYFJ	Avro 504K	-	H9553	6. 6.24	To RCAF as 7. Canx.
G-CYFK	Avro 504K	-	H9743	17. 4.23	Damaged at Richmond Hill on 27.7.26. Canx 7.10.26.
G-CYFL	Avro 504K	-	H9735	17. 4.23	To RCAF as 47. Canx.
G-CYFM	Avro 504K	-	H9631	18. 4.23	Crashed at Camp Borden on 2.7.24. Canx 31.3.26.
G-CYFN	Avro 504K	-	H9632	23. 6.24	To RCAF as 48. Canx.
G-CYFO	Avro 504K	-	H9556	18. 4.23	Damaged at Camp Borden on 2.10.24. Canx 31.3.26.
G-CYFP	Sopwith 1F.1 Camel	-	F6481	7.10.24	Lost in hangar fire at Camp Borden. Canx 18.10.28.
G-CYFQ	Sopwith 1F.1 Camel	-	F6473	17.11.24	Lost in hangar fire at Camp Borden. Canx 18.10.28.
G-CYFR	Sopwith 1F.1 Camel	-	F6310	17.11.24	Lost in hangar fire at Camp Borden. Canx 23.6.27.
G-CYFS	Canadian Vickers Vedette I	CV-9		17. 7.25	Canx 25.11.27.
G-CYFT	Avro 552A	CV-10		19.12.24	Canx 29.11.27.
G-CYFU	Avro 552A	CV-11		11. 3.25	Canx 29.9.28.
G-CYFV	Avro 552A	CV-12		11. 3.25	Canx 15.8.28.
G-CYFW	Avro 552A	CV-13		30. 3.25	Canx 22.2.28.
G-CYFX	Avro 552A	CV-14		30. 3.25	Canx 28.5.28.
G-CYFY	Avro 504N	R3/LY/10598		11. 9.24	To RCAF as 8. Canx.
G-CYFZ	Avro 504N	R3/LY/10617		14.10.24	To RCAF as 9. Canx.
G-CYGA(1)	Curtiss HS-2L	-	A-1307 (US Navy)	13.10.24	Canx 1.7.28.
G-CYGA(2)	Canadian Vickers Vedette II	CV-53	G-CAGA	2. 8.27	Canx 27.9.34. Re-regd as CF-SAE.
G-CYGB	Avro 552A	CV-20		12. 2.25	Damaged at Lac du Bonnett. Canx 30.12.27.
G-CYGC	Avro 552A	CV-21		26. 5.25	Damaged at Bowden Lake (details?). Canx 18.10.27.
G-CYGD	Avro 552A	CV-22		29. 5.25	Damaged at Moore Lake (details?). Canx 19.8.27.
G-CYGE	Avro 552A	CV-23		12. 6.25	Damaged at Long Lake (details?). Canx 16.1.28.
G-CYGF	Avro 552A	CV-24		16. 6.25	Canx 8.4.27.
G-CYGG	Avro 552A	CV-25		26. 6.25	Damaged at Lac du Bonnett (details?). Canx 17.2.28.
G-CYGH	Avro 552A	CV-26		26. 6.25	Damaged at Cormorant Lake on 15.8.25. Canx.
G-CYGI	Avro 552A	CV-27		30. 6.25	Canx 2.6.28.

Regn	Type	c/n	Previous identity	Regn date	Fate or immediate subsequent identity (if known)
G-CYGJ	Avro 552A	CV-28		9. 7.25	Canx 18.1.28.
G-CYGK	Avro Wright	CV-29		14. 7.25	Damaged at Orillia on 26.9.29. Canx.
G-CYGL	Curtiss HS-2L	117	A-1298 (US Navy)	8. 6.25	Canx 9.12.26.
G-CYGM	Curtiss HS-2L	-	A-1290 (US Navy)	19. 6.25	Canx 1.7.28.
G-CYGN	Curtiss HS-2L	-	A-1312 (US Navy)	31. 5.25	Canx 25.10.26.
G-CYGO	Curtiss HS-2L	-	A-1152 (US Navy)	25. 5.25	Canx 1.7.28.
G-CYGP	Curtiss HS-2L	107	A-1159 (US Navy)	8. 6.25	Canx 1.4.26.
G-CYGQ	Curtiss HS-2L	119	A-1303 (US Navy)	12. 8.25	Canx 25.9.28.
G-CYGR	Curtiss HS-2L	142	A-1315 (US Navy)	12. 8.25	Canx 25.9.28.
G-CYGS	Curtiss HS-2L	210	A-1392 (US Navy)	12. 8.25	Canx 8.5.28.
G-CYGT	Curtiss HS-2L	97	A-1279 (US Navy)	12. 8.25	Canx 1.7.28.
G-CYGU	Curtiss HS-2L	109	A-1288 (US Navy)	12. 8.25	Canx 13.4.28. Re-regd as G-CARL on 31.5.28.
G-CYGV	Canadian Vickers Varuna I	CV-30		2. 6.26	Canx 16.11.32.
G-CYGW	Canadian Vickers Vedette II	CV-32		20. 8.26	Canx.
G-CYGX	Canadian Vickers Vedette II	CV-33		10. 9.26	Canx 20.7.27.
G-CYGY	Canadian Vickers Vedette II	CV-34		10. 9.26	Canx 6.5.36. Re-regd as CF-SAD.
G-CYGZ	Canadian Vickers Vedette II	CV-35		3. 8.26	Canx at Lac du Bonnett (details?).
G-CYHA	Avro 504K	-	H2042	28. 8.25	Crashed at Camp Borden on 28.1.28. Canx 18.2.28.
G-CYHB	Not allotted.				
G-CYHC	Avro 504K	-	H9623	11. 6.26	To RCAF as 49. Canx.
G-CYHD	Avro 504K	-	H9633	11. 6.26	Crashed at Camp Borden on 19.12.27. Canx 20.1.28.
G-CYHE to G-CYUQ	Not allotted.				
G-CYUR	DH.80A Puss Moth	DHC.214		12. 3.31	Canx 12.8.36.
G-CYUS	DH.80A Puss Moth	DHC.215		14. 5.31	To ground instructional airframe as A-6. Canx.
G-CYUT	DH.80A Puss Moth	DHC.216		3. 5.31	Crashed when port wing failed at Ottawa on 21.3.32. Canx.
G-CYUU	DH.80A Puss Moth	DHC.217		1. 5.31	Canx 12.8.36.
G-CYUV	Fairchild 71B	FA.6		6. 6.31	Damaged at Great Bear Lake on 31.7.32. Canx.
G-CYUW	Fairchild 71B	FA.5		17. 5.31	To RCAF as 629. Canx.
G-CYUX	Bellanca CH-300	CV-171		29. 6.31	To RCAF as 601. Canx.
G-CYUY	Bellanca CH-300	CV-172		29. 6.31	To RCAF as 602. Canx.
G-CYUZ	Bellanca CH-300	CV-173		18. 7.31	To RCAF as 603. Canx.
G-CYVA	Bellanca CH-300	CV-174		18. 5.31	To RCAF as 604. Canx.
G-CYVB	Bellanca CH-300	CV-175		22. 5.31	To RCAF as 605. Canx.
G-CYVC	Bellanca CH-300	CV-176		1. 6.31	To RCAF as 606. Canx.
G-CYVD	DH.75A Hawk Moth	343	G-AAFW	4.12.29	Canx 8.10.35. To CF-CCA.
G-CYVE	Fairchild 71C (Originally regd as a 71B)	767/4		2.10.30	To RCAF as 630. Canx.
G-CYVF	Bellanca CH-300	188		20. 5.30	To RCAF as 607. Canx.
G-CYVG	Bellanca CH-300	189		5. 6.30	To RCAF as 608. Canx.
G-CYVH	Bellanca CH-300	190		8. 7.30	To RCAF as 609. Canx.
G-CYVI	Bellanca CH-300	191		6. 8.30	To RCAF as 610. Canx.
G-CYVJ	Bellanca CH-300	192		1. 8.30	To RCAF as 611. Canx.
G-CYVK	Bellanca CH-300	193		26. 7.30	To RCAF as 612. Canx.
G-CYVL	DH.75 Hawk Moth	707		19.12.30	Crashed at Longueil, Que. on 27.6.31. Canx.
G-CYVM	DH.75 Hawk Moth	708		9.11.30	Canx 5.10.34.
G-CYVN	Fairchild 71B	766/3		12. 7.30	To RCAF as 631. Canx.
G-CYVO	Fairchild 71B	765/2		8. 7.30	To RCAF as 632. Canx.
G-CYVP	Canadian Vickers Vedette V	CV-146		4. 2.30	Canx 29.12.30. Re-regd as CF-LIR.
G-CYVQ	Canadian Vickers Vancouver II	CV-164		16. 7.30	To RCAF as 902. Canx.
G-CYVR	Canadian Vickers Vancouver II	CV-165		24. 7.30	To RCAF as 903. Canx.
G-CYVS	Canadian Vickers Vancouver II	CV-166		28. 8.30	To RCAF as 904. Canx.
G-CYVT	Canadian Vickers Vancouver II	CV-167		15. 8.30	To RCAF as 905. Canx.
G-CYVU	Canadian Vickers Vancouver II	CV-168		2. 9.30	To RCAF as 906. Canx.
G-CYVV	Not allotted.				
G-CYVW	Not allotted.				
G-CYVX	Fairchild 71B	764/1		9. 7.30	To RCAF as 633. Canx.
G-CYVY	Fairchild 71B	763		30. 5.30	To RCAF as 634. Canx.
G-CYVZ	Fairchild 71B	762		30. 5.30	To RCAF as 635. Canx.
G-CYWA	Fairchild 71B	761		20. 5.30	To RCAF as 636. Canx.
G-CYWB	Fairchild 71	645		5. 4.30	To RCAF as 637. Canx.
G-CYWC	Fairchild 71	688		31. 3.30	To RCAF as 638. Canx.
G-CYWD	Fairchild 71	670		28. 3.30	To RCAF as 639. Canx.
G-CYWE	Fairchild 71	674		14. 3.30	To RCAF as 640. Canx.
G-CYWF	Fairchild 71	687		25. 3.30	Damaged at English Bay on 14.7.39. Canx.
G-CYWG	Fairchild 71	689		5. 4.30	To RCAF as 642. Canx.
G-CYWH	Fairchild 71	690		12. 4.30	To RCAF as 643. Canx.

Regn	Type	c/n	Previous identity	Regn date	Fate or immediate subsequent identity (if known)
G-CYWI	Canadian Vickers Vedette VI	CV-163		13. 5.30	To RCAF as 817. Canx.
G-CYWJ	Canadian Vickers Vedette VI	CV-162		5. 5.30	To RCAF as 808. Canx.
G-CYWK	Canadian Vickers Vedette VA	CV-161		1. 5.30	Damaged at Lac du Bonnet on 18.5.33. Canx.
G-CYWL	Canadian Vickers Vedette VA	CV-160		8. 5.30	To RCAF as 809. Canx.
G-CYWM	Canadian Vickers Vedette VA	CV-159		8. 5.30	To RCAF as 810. Canx.
G-CYWN	Canadian Vickers Vedette VA	CV-158		8. 5.30	To RCAF as 811. Canx.
G-CYWO	Canadian Vickers Vedette VA	CV-157		8. 5.30	To RCAF as 812. Canx.
G-CYWP	Canadian Vickers Vedette VA	CV-156		8. 5.30	To RCAF as 813. Canx.
G-CYWQ	Canadian Vickers Vedette VA	CV-155		8. 5.30	Damaged at Brighton on 23.9.37. Canx.
G-CYWR	Canadian Vickers Vedette V	CV-151	CF-AIV	25.10.29	Damaged on test flight on 4.11.29. Canx.
G-CYWS	Canadian Vickers Vedette V	CV-150	CF-AIU	6.11.29	Canx 18.10.35.
G-CYWT	Bellanca CH-300	139		16.10.29	Damaged on 1.3.30. Canx.
G-CYWU	Fairchild FC-2L	19		1.10.29	Canx 6.1.31.
G-CYWV	DH.60M Moth	1322		10. 9.29	Canx 20.6.31. Re-regd as CF-APB.
G-CYWW	DH.60G Gipsy Moth	1321		15.10.29	Canx 13.6.31. Re-regd as CF-APB.
G-CYWX	Fairchild 71	664		24. 6.29	Damaged on 5.7.29. Canx.
G-CYWY	DH.60G Gipsy Moth	1309		30. 7.29	To RCAF as 212. Canx.
G-CYWZ	Ford Trimotor	6-AT-1		28. 5.29	Canx 25.2.37. Re-regd as CF-BEP.
G-CYXA	Atlantic Aircraft/Fokker Super Universal	CV-131		12. 4.29	Canx 9.8.29. Re-regd as CF-AFL.
G-CYXB	Fairchild 71	625		30. 4.29	To RCAF as 644. Canx.
G-CYXC	Curtiss-Wright Rambler	1003		17.10.29	Canx 18.9.36. Re-regd as CF-CDY.
G-CYXD	Curtiss-Reid Rambler	1006		17.10.29	Damaged on 25.5.30. Canx.
G-CYXE	DH.60G Gipsy Moth	757		23. 4.29	Damaged at Demaine on 21.1.30. Canx.
G-CYXF	DH.60G Gipsy Moth	759		19. 4.29	Canx 5.5.31.
G-CYXG	DH.60G Gipsy Moth	758		5. 3.29	Canx 21.7.32. Re-regd as CF-APC.
G-CYXH	DH.60G Gipsy Moth	756		24. 4.29	Canx 9.12.29.
G-CYXI(1)	DH.60X Moth	530		13. 7.28	Re-regd as G-CAKH(2) in 7/28. Canx.
G-CYXI(2)	DH.60X Moth	463	G-CAKH	15. 8.28	Crashed just prior to delivery. Canx.
G-CYXJ	Pitcairn Mailwing	18		3. 4.28	Damaged on 24.7.31. Canx.
G-CYXK	Fairchild FC-2	CV-86		29. 8.28	To RCAF as 620. Canx.
G-CYXL	Fairchild FC-2	66		6. 5.28	Damaged on 4.7.31. Canx.
G-CYXM	Fairchild FC-2	64		6. 5.28	To RCAF as 613. Canx.
G-CYXN	Fairchild FC-2W	90		4. 6.28	To RCAF as 615. Canx.
G-CYXO	Fairchild FC-2W	88		13. 6.28	To RCAF as 616. Canx.
G-CYXP	Fairchild FC-2W	94		13. 6.28	To RCAF as 617. Canx.
G-CYXQ	Fairchild FC-2W	84		4. 6.28	To RCAF as 618. Canx.
G-CYXR	Fairchild FC-2W	82		13. 6.28	Crashed on 28.10.29. Canx.
G-CYXS	Canadian Vickers Vancouver I	CV-107		23. 8.29	Canx 3.10.34.
G-CYXT	Fairchild FC-2	CV-85		20. 7.28	Canx 24.4.30.
G-CYXU	Fairchild FC-2 (Later modified to FC-2L)	CV-84		13. 9.29	To RCAF as 614. Canx.
G-CYXV	Fairchild FC-2	CV-83		2. 8.28	To RCAF as 626. Canx.
G-CYXW	Fairchild FC-2	68		9. 5.28	To RCAF as 624. Canx.
G-CYXX	Fairchild FC-2	63		9. 5.28	Damaged at Regina on 22.4.30. Canx.
G-CYXY	Fairchild FC-2	65	RCAF 211	12. 4.28	To RCAF as 623. Canx.
G-CYXZ	Canadian Vickers Vedette II	CV-90		26. 7.28	Canx 13.5.32. Re-regd as CF-MAE.
G-CYYA	Canadian Vickers Vedette II	CV-76		16. 6.28	Canx 13.5.32. Re-regd as CF-MAC.
G-CYYB	Canadian Vickers Vedette II	CV-73		14. 6.28	Canx 25.11.31.
G-CYYC	Canadian Vickers Vedette II	CV-72		14. 6.28	Canx 13.5.32. Re-regd as CF-MAD.
G-CYYD	Canadian Vickers Vedette II	CV-71		18. 3.28	Canx 13.5.32. Re-regd as CF-MAB.
G-CYYE	Canadian Vickers Vedette II	CV-58		3. 3.28	Canx 23.5.29.
G-CYYF	Canadian Vickers Vedette II	CV-57		29. 3.28	Crashed on 17.7.30. Canx.
G-CYYG	DH.60X Moth (Only aircraft to retain its RCAF markings after transfer to the civil register)(Certificate of Registration No. 651, then Certificate of Registration No. 2271 issued 12.7.38, then Certificate of Registration No. 2851 issued 22.8.41)	503		4. 5.28	WFU due to wartime restrictions post 4/44. (On display 5/99 Reynolds Alberta Museum) Canx.
G-CYYH	DH.60X Moth	496		7. 7.28	Canx 20.11.29.
G-CYYI	DH.60X Moth	495		7. 7.28	WFU. To ground instructional airframe as A-2. Canx.
G-CYYJ	DH.60X Moth	490		27. 4.28	Canx 15.4.37. To RCAF as CF-CEF.
G-CYYK	DH.60X Moth	489		27. 4.28	WFU. To ground instructional airframe. Canx.
G-CYYL	DH.60X Moth	488		27. 4.28	Canx 15.4.37. Re-regd as CF-CED.
G-CYYM	DH.60X Moth	494		7. 7.28	Canx 9.5.31. Re-regd as CF-APM.
G-CYYN	DH.60X Moth	493		7. 7.28	Crashed on 10.6.29. Canx.
G-CYYO	DH.60X Moth	492		7. 7.28	Crashed on 16.6.29. Canx.
G-CYYP	DH.60X Moth	491		29. 5.28	Canx 16.1.29.
G-CYYQ	DH.60X Moth	487		5. 5.28	Crashed on 26.7.29. Canx.
G-CYYR	DH.60X Moth	486		5. 6.28	Canx 25.7.35. Re-regd as CF-CEB.
G-CYYS	DH.60X Moth	485		5. 6.28	Canx 3.9.36. Re-regd as CF-CDD.
G-CYYT	Fairchild FC-2	23		4.11.27	To RCAF as 627. Canx.
G-CYYU	Fairchild FC-2W	92		21. 5.28	To RCAF as 619. Canx.
G-CYYV	Fairchild FC-2	19		20.10.27	To RCAF as 625. Canx.
G-CYYW	DH.60X Moth	457		13. 1.28	Canx 3.12.29.
G-CYYX	DH.60X Moth	456		16. 1.28	Canx 3.12.29.
G-CYYY	DH.60M Moth	760		9. 4.29	Canx 18.11.36. Re-regd as CF-CEC.
G-CYYZ	Canadian Vickers Vedette V	CV-125		9. 7.29	Canx 23.8.33. Re-regd as CF-SAC.
G-CYZA(1)	Armstrong-Whitworth Atlas	AW.297		30.12.27	To RCAF as 17. Canx.
G-CYZA(2)	Canadian Vickers Vedette V	CV-128		27. 8.29	To RCAF as 805. Canx.
G-CYZB(1)	Armstrong-Whitworth Atlas	AW.260		30.12.27	To RCAF as 16. Canx.
G-CYZB(2)	Canadian Vickers Vedette V	CV-124		12. 7.29	To RCAF as 806. Canx.
G-CYZC	Canadian Vickers Vedette V	CV-127		15. 6.29	Canx 21.10.29.
G-CYZD	Canadian Vickers Vedette V	CV-123		12. 6.29	To RCAF as 816. Canx.

Regn	Type	c/n	Previous identity	Regn date	Fate or immediate subsequent identity (if known)
G-CYZE(1)	Armstrong-Whitworth Siskin IIIA	AW.281	RCAF 303 RCAF 21/G-CYZE	20.12.27	Restored to RCAF as 303. Canx.
G-CYZE(2)	Canadian Vickers Vedette V	CV-126		19. 6.29	To RCAF as 807. Canx.
G-CYZF(1)	Armstrong-Whitworth Siskin IIIA	-		20.12.27	To RCAF as 20. Canx.
G-CYZF(2)	Canadian Vickers Vedette V	CV-149		8. 8.29	Canx 13.5.32. Re-regd as CF-MAA.
G-CYZG	Douglas MO.2B	265	NC236	22. 8.27	Canx 8.1.30.
G-CYZH	Keystone Puffer	105		27. 6.27	Crashed on 16.7.29. Canx.
G-CYZI	Keystone Puffer	-		13. 6.27	Canx 22.10.34.
G-CYZJ	Canadian Vickers Vanessa II	CV-36	G-CAFG	26. 4.27	DBR when swamped in gale at Rimouski, Que. on 9.9.27. Canx.
G-CYZK	Canadian Vickers Vedette II	CV-52		17. 9.27	To RCAF as 11. Canx.
G-CYZL	Canadian Vickers Vedette II	CV-51		26. 8.27	Crashed on 18.6.29. Canx.
G-CYZM	Canadian Vickers Vedette II	CV-50		17. 5.27	Canx 21.6.33. Re-regd as CF-SAB.
G-CYZN	Canadian Vickers Vedette II	CV-41		15. 3.27	Canx 8.1.31.
G-CYZO	Canadian Vickers Vedette II	CV-40		24. 3.27	Crashed on 10.9.29. Canx.
G-CYZP	Canadian Vickers Varuna II	CV-49		8. 8.27	Damaged at Shileys Bay on 19.8.27. Canx.
G-CYZQ	Canadian Vickers Varuna II	CV-48		4. 8.27	Canx 12.12.30.
G-CYZR	Canadian Vickers Varuna II	CV-47		13. 6.27	Canx.
G-CYZS	Canadian Vickers Varuna II	CV-46		27. 5.27	Canx 19.12.30.
G-CYZT	Canadian Vickers Varuna II	CV-38		11. 5.27	Crashed on 21.7.30. Canx.
G-CYZU	Canadian Vickers Varuna II	CV-37		11. 5.27	Crashed on 9.6.27. Canx.
G-CYZV	Canadian Vickers Vrauna II	CV-39		12. 3.27	Canx 14.3.28.
G-CYZW	Canadian Vickers Vigil	CV-44		11. 4.28	Canx 3.11.30.
G-CYZX	Canadian Vickers Velos	CV-45		18.11.27	Sank on 30.11.28. Canx.
G-CYZY	Canadian Vickers Vista	-		. .27R	Not built. Canx.
G-CYZZ	Canadian Vickers Vista	CV-42		9.11.27	Canx 4.5.31.

INDIA

Regn	Type	c/n	Previous identity	Regn date	Fate or immediate subsequent identity (if known)
G-IA					G-IA

G-IAAA to G-IAAZ - Allocated to India from 1919 until 1928.

Regn	Type	c/n	Previous identity	Regn date	Fate or immediate subsequent identity (if known)
G-IAAA(1)	Handley Page O/7	HP.8		.10.19	WFU in 7/21. Canx.
G-IAAA(2)	Airco DH.9 Seaplane	-	H9129	. 3.26	Re-regd as G-IAAP. Canx.
G-IAAB(1)	Handley Page O/7	HP.9		.11.19	WFU in 7/21. Canx.
G-IAAB(2)	Airco DH.9	-	D3180	. 4.27	W/o in Turkey on 26.5.27. Canx.
G-IAAC(1)	Handley Page O/7	HP.11	G-EAPA	. 5.20	W/o in gale in 10/20. Canx.
G-IAAC(2)	Handley Page O/10	HP.34	G-EASX F308	. 2.21	Fate unknown. Canx.
G-IAAD	No details known.				
G-IAAE	No details known.				
G-IAAF	No details known.				
G-IAAG	Airco DH.9	-		. .	Identity unknown. Canx.
G-IAAH	No details known.				
G-IAAI	No details known.				
G-IAAJ	No details known.				
G-IAAK	No details known.				
G-IAAL	No details known.				
G-IAAM	No details known.				
G-IAAN	No details known.				
G-IAAO	No details known.				
G-IAAP	Airco DH.9	-	G-IAAA(2) H9129	. .	Re-regd as VT-AAP in 12/28. Canx.
G-IAAQ	Airco DH.9	-	E611	. .	Re-regd as VT-AAQ in 12/28. Canx.
G-IAAR	No details known.				
G-IAAS	Airco DH.9 Seaplane	-	D5686	. 6.25	Re-regd as VT-AAS in 4/29. Canx.
G-IAAT	Junkers	530		. 4.25	Re-regd as VT-AAV in 1929. Canx.
G-IAAU	DH.9	-		. .	Identity unknown. Canx.
G-IAAV	No details known.				
G-IAAW	Westland Widgeon III	WA.1694	G-EBRP	. 3.28	Re-regd as VT-AAM in 3/28. Canx.
G-IAAX	Avro 594 Avian III	R3/CN/110		. 3.28	Re-regd as VT-AAN in 3/28. Canx.
G-IAAY	Airco DH.9	-		. 1.28	Re-regd as VT-AAO in 1/28. Canx.
G-IAAZ	No details known.				

NEW ZEALAND

The New Zealand Civil Aviation Authority issued the registration marks G-NZAA to G-NZAS during 1921 and 1922, with marks G-NZAT to G-NZAZ plus G-NZEA to G-NZEF issued during 1928 and early 1929. A gap in the registration dates covering the years 1923 to 1927 was the result of civil aviation flying in New Zealand almost ceasing to exist for that period. As from 1.1.29 the designated country marks had changed to ZK-, ZL- and ZM- followed by three letter combination (eg; ZK-AAA).

Regn	Type	c/n	Previous identity	Regn date	Fate or immediate subsequent identity (if known)

G-NZ G-NZ

G-NZAA to G-NZAZ and G-NZEA to G-NZEF - Allocated to New Zealand from 1921 until 1929.

Regn	Type	c/n	Previous identity	Regn date	Fate or immediate subsequent identity (if known)
G-NZAA	Avro 504L	-	H2989	21.12.21	Canx.
G-NZAB	Avro 504K	-	H5240	28. 2.22	WFU at Longlands in 1923/24. Canx.
G-NZAC	Avro 504L	-	H2990	28. 2.22	Canx.
G-NZAD	DH.9	-	H5636	28. 2.22	To New Zealand Permanent AF as 5636 in 6/23. Canx.
G-NZAE	DH.9	-	H5627	28. 2.22	To New Zealand Permanent AF on 21.6.23. Canx.
G-NZAF	Avro 504K	GW.5476	E9432	28. 2.22	To New Zealand Permanent AF as E9432 on 21.6.23. Canx.
G-NZAG	Avro 504K	-	H1964	28. 2.22	To New Zealand Permanent AF as H1964 on 21.6.23. Canx.
G-NZAH	Airco DH.9	-	D3136	28. 2.22	To New Zealand Permanent AF as 3136 on 21.6.23. Canx.
G-NZAI	Supermarine Channel II	1142		28. 2.22	Broken up in 1927. Hull used as a boat until 1943. Canx.
G-NZAJ	Avro 504K	-	H2987	8. 3.22	To New Zealand Permanent AF as H2987 on 21.6.23. Canx.
G-NZAK	Avro 504K	-	E4242	8. 3.22	To New Zealand Permanent AF as E4242 on 21.6.23. Canx.
G-NZAL	Avro 504K	-	H1966	28. 3.22	To New Zealand Permanent AF as H1966. Canx.
G-NZAM	Airco DH.9	-	D3139	28. 3.22	To New Zealand Permanent AF as 3139 on 14.6.23. Canx.
G-NZAN	Avro 504K	-	E3142	28. 3.22	Canx.
G-NZAO	Avro 504K	-	H5241	28. 3.22	Canx.
G-NZAP	Avro 504K	GW.4568	E9424	28. 3.22	Canx.
G-NZAQ	DH.9	-	H5672	5. 4.22	Canx.
G-NZAR	Avro 504K	GW.4571	E9427	5. 4.22	Canx.
G-NZAS	Walsh Flying Boat	5D		24. 8.22	DBF at Kohimarama in 9/24. Canx.
G-NZAT	DH.60X Moth	500		1. 5.28	Re-regd as ZK-AAB. Canx.
G-NZAU	DH.60X Moth	591		4. 7.28	Crashed at Waikari on 9.7.28. Canx.
G-NZAV	Avro 594 Avian IIIA	R3/CN/174		17.12.28	Re-regd as ZK-AAC 4.1.29. Canx.
G-NZAW	DH.60G Gipsy Moth	866		. .29	Re-regd as ZK-AAL in 1929. Canx.
G-NZAX	DH.60G Gipsy Moth	867		19. 2.29	Re-regd as ZK-AAM. Canx.
G-NZAY	DH.60G Gipsy Moth	868		1. 5.29	Re-regd as ZK-AAH. Canx.
G-NZAZ	DH.60G Gipsy Moth	869		1. 5.29	Re-regd as ZK-AAI. Canx.
G-NZEA	DH.60G Gipsy Moth	914		3. 5.29	NTU. To ZK-AAJ. Canx.
G-NZEB	DH.60G Gipsy Moth	915		. 4.29	NTU. To ZK-AAK. Canx.
G-NZEC	DH.60G Gipsy Moth	927		15. 3.29	NTU. To ZK-AAD. Canx.
G-NZED	DH.60G Gipsy Moth	928		9.10.28	NTU. To ZK-AAE. Canx.
G-NZEE	Avro 594 Avian IIIA	R3/CN/162		12.10.28	NTU. To ZK-AAF 1.1.29. Canx.
G-NZEF	DH.60G Gipsy Moth	929		29.12.28	NTU. To ZK-AAG. Canx.

UNION of SOUTH AFRICA

Regn	Type	c/n	Previous identity	Regn date	Fate or immediate subsequent identity (if known)
G-UA					G-UA
G-UAAA to G-UABD - Allocated to the Union of South Africa from 1927 until 1/29.					
G-UAAA	DH.60 Moth	362		14. 4.27	Re-regd as ZS-AAA in 1/29. Canx.
G-UAAB	DH.60X Moth	435		22.11.27	Re-regd as ZS-AAB in 1/29. Canx.
G-UAAC	Avro 594 Avian II	R3/AV/122		. 8.27	Re-regd as ZS-AAC in 1929. Canx.
G-UAAD	DH.60X Moth	432	G-EBTJ	21.10.27	Re-regd as ZS-AAD in 1/29. Canx.
G-UAAE	DH.60X Moth	439		2.11.27	W/o at Pomeroy on 26.12.27. Canx.
G-UAAF	DH.60X Moth	440		2.11.27	Re-regd as ZS-AAF in 1/29. Canx.
G-UAAG	DH.60X Moth	442		15.11.27	W/o at Bloemfontein on 7.2.28. Canx.
G-UAAH	Westland Widgeon III	WA.1693		. .27	Re-regd as ZS-AAH in 1929. Canx.
G-UAAI	DH.60X Moth	479		2. 2.28	Re-regd as ZS-AAI in 1/29. Canx.
G-UAAJ	Klemm L.27-III	-		. .28	Re-regd as ZS-AAJ in 1929. Canx.
G-UAAK	Avro 594 Avian IIIA	R3/CN/200		. .28	Re-regd as ZS-AAK in 1929. Canx.
G-UAAL	DH.60X Moth	502		8. 3.28	Re-regd as ZS-AAL in 1/29. Canx.
G-UAAM	Boulton & Paul P.9	P.9/2	G-EASJ	. .28	Re-regd as ZS-AAM in 1929. Canx.
G-UAAN	DH.60X Moth	588		. 7.28	W/o on 30.8.28. Canx.
G-UAAO	DH.60X Moth	422	G-EBSR	3. 8.28	W/o at Baragwanath on 1.2.29. Canx.
G-UAAP(1)	DH.60X Moth	608		18. 7.28	Crashed at Zoutspan on 10.8.28. Rebuilt as VP-YAA. Canx.
G-UAAP(2)	DH.60X Moth	625		. .	Re-regd as ZS-AAP. Canx.
G-UAAQ	DH.60X Moth	534		1. 6.28	W/o at Roodepoort on 5.6.28. Canx.
G-UAAR	Avro 594 Avian II	R3/AV/113	G-EBWP	. 7.28	Re-regd as ZS-AAR. Canx.
G-UAAS	Avro 594 Avian III	R3/CN/109		. 7.28	Re-regd as ZS-AAS. Canx.
G-UAAT	Avro 594 Avian IIIA	R3/CN/167		.10.28	Re-regd as ZS-AAT. Canx.
G-UAAU	Avro 594 Avian IIIA	R3/CN/168		.10.28	Re-regd as ZS-AAU. Canx.
G-UAAV	Avro 594 Avian IV	R3/CN/225		. .28	Re-regd as ZS-AAV. Canx.
G-UAAW	DH.60X Moth	607		. 6.28	Re-regd as ZS-AAW in 1/29. Canx.
G-UAAX	DH.60X Moth	587		. 8.28	Re-regd as ZS-AAX. Canx.
G-UAAY	DH.60X Moth	-		. .28	Re-regd as ZS-AAY in 2/30. Canx.
G-UAAZ	Avro 594 Avian IIIA	R3/CN/159		. 9.28	Re-regd as ZS-AAZ. Canx.
G-UABA(1)	Vickers FB.27 Vimy	-		. . R	NTU. Crashed at Korosko, Egypt in 2/20 whilst on flight to South Africa. Canx.
G-UABA(2)	Vickers FB.27 Vimy (Fitted with engines and instruments from G-UABA(1))	-	(RAF)	. . R	NTU. Crashed on take-off from Bulawayo, Rhodesia in 2/20 whilst on delivery to South Africa. Canx.
G-UABB	Avro 594 Avian IIIA	R3/CN/175		.11.28	Re-regd as ZS-ABB. Canx.
G-UABC	DH.60X Moth	701		29.10.28	Re-regd as ZS-ABC in 1/29. Canx.
G-UABD	DH.60X Moth	698		9.11.28	Re-regd as ZS-ABD in 1/29. Canx.

SECTION 8 - REPUBLIC OF IRELAND REGISTER

The Irish equivalent of the PFA is the Society of Amateur Aircraft Constructors (SAAC), and various aircraft use a SAAC allocation as their construction number.

Regn	Type	c/n	Previous identity	Regn date	Fate or immediate subsequent identity (if known)
EI-AAA	Avro 594B Avian IIIA	R3/CN/170		5.10.28	To G-ABPU 9/31. Canx.
EI-AAB	Avro 594B Avian IIIA	R3/CN/171		1. 1.29	To G-ACGT 5/33. Canx.
EI-AAC	DH.60G Gipsy Moth	1000		11. 4.29	Canx 5.4.37. To G-AFKA 9/38.
EI-AAD	Desoutter II	D.30		20.10.30	To G-ABOM 5/31. Canx.
EI-AAE	DH.60M Moth	1556		27. 1.31	To G-ABPJ 8/31. Canx.
EI-AAF	DH.60G Gipsy Moth	1262	G-ABAH	3. 6.31	Crashed near Bundoran, Co.Donegal on 31.8.31. Canx 21.7.32.
EI-AAG	DH.60G Gipsy Moth	648	G-EBYV	2. 6.31	Restored as G-EBYV in 9/32. Canx 17.8.32.
EI-AAH	DH.60G Gipsy Moth	1808	G-ABGL	24. 8.31	Crashed off Dalkey, Co.Dublin on 24.5.33. Canx.
EI-AAI	DH.60G Gipsy Moth	1860	G-ABOW	24. 8.31	Collided with DH.83 G-ABWF over Limerick on 7.7.33. Canx.
EI-AAJ	DH.60G Gipsy Moth	1866	G-ABOZ	24. 8.31	Crashed at Little Sugarloaf Mountains, Co.Wicklow on 29.5.37. Canx.
EI-AAK	DH.60G Gipsy Moth	1276	G-ABBV	22. 8.31	Restored as G-ABBV 4/36. Canx.
EI-AAL	Comper C.L.A.7 Swift	S.31/7		17. 2.32	Crashed near Marseilles, France on 12.2.32. Canx.
EI-AAM	Avro 504K	-	G-AAYH H9833	15. 3.32	Scrapped in 1932. Canx.
EI-AAN	Avro 504K	-	G-ABHP J8371	23. 7.32	WFU in 1932. Scrapped. Canx.
	Note: One of EI-AAM/AAN crashed Tramore Strand, Waterford on 19.8.32.				
EI-AAO	Blackburn Bluebird IV	SB.249	G-ABJA	20. 5.32	Crashed at Tramore Strand, Waterford on 31.7.32. Canx.
EI-AAP	DH.83 Fox Moth	4003	(ZS-ADE)	20. 7.32	To G-AFKI in 9/38. Canx.
EI-AAQ	General Aircraft Monospar ST.4 Mk.I	ST.4/6	G-ABVS	20. 2.33	Restored as G-ABVS in 11/33. Canx.
EI-AAR	DH.60G Gipsy Moth	1030	G-AAEA	1. 5.33	Crashed at Ballygowan, Roffery, Saintfield, Co.Down on 21.12.34. Canx.
EI-AAS	Not allocated.				
EI-AAT	Spartan 3-Seater	61	G-ABRA	15. 6.33	w/o. Canx 5.2.35.
EI-AAU	DH.60G-III Gipsy Moth	5032		9. 9.33	Crashed at Kilcool, Co.Wicklow on 2.7.38; rebuilt as G-AFWX 8/39. Canx.
EI-AAV(1)	Miles M.2 Hawk	23	G-ACMX	. .34R	NTU - Remained as G-ACMX. Canx.
EI-AAV(2)	Civilian C.A.C.1 Coupe	0.1	G-AAIL	11. 5.35	Reduced to spares. Canx 24.1.49.
EI-AAW	DH.60G Gipsy Moth	1849	G-ACBU ZS-ADB	29. 5.34	Crashed Stone, Staffs on 26.11.35. Canx.
EI-AAX	Miles M.2 Hawk	24	G-ACNX	26. 3.34	Restored as G-ACNX 12/34. Canx.
EI-AAY	Not allocated.				
EI-AAZ	Bellanca 28-70	902		16.10.34	To USA as NR190M in 11/36. Canx.
EI-ABA	DH.60G Gipsy Moth	1105	G-AAJJ	29. 8.34	Crashed on 17.9.34 and restored as G-AAJJ 6/35. Canx.
EI-ABB	DH.60G Gipsy Moth	1142	G-AAKM	1. 3.35	Restored as G-AAKM 4/37. Canx.
EI-ABC	Robinson Redwing II	RA.4	G-ABMJ	17. 4.35	w/o 12.5.35. Canx.
EI-ABD	British Klemm L.25c-Ia Swallow	28	G-ACZK	22. 3.35	Sold to UK in 1939 and to RAF in 1940. Canx.
EI-ABE	DH.60G Gipsy Moth	1048	G-AASY	1. 3.35	Restored as G-AASY 2/38. Canx.
EI-ABF	Klemm L.32-X	668	G-ACLH CH-360	15.12.36	Scrapped at Dublin Airport in 1950. Canx 18.12.50.
EI-ABG	Southern Martlet	2/SH200	G-AAII	19. 6.36	w/o. Canx 9.11.48.
EI-ABH	Mignet HM.14 Pou du Ciel	-		9. 6.36	Scrapped. Canx.
EI-ABI(1)	DH.84 Dragon II	6076	G-ACPY	26. 5.36	Restored as G-ACPY 2/38. Canx.
EI-ABI(2)	DH.84 Dragon II	6105	EI-AFK G-AECZ/AV982/G-AECZ	12. 8.85	
EI-ABJ	Klemm L.25c-XI	413	G-ABZO D-7	22. 1.37	Crashed at Greystones, Co.Wicklow on 13.8.38. Canx.
EI-ABK	DH.86A Srs.I (Converted to DH.86B in 1937)	2338	G-ADVJ	16. 9.36	Restored as G-ADVJ 10/46. Canx.
EI-ABL	DH.87B Hornet Moth	8107		2. 3.37	To G-AFRE 12/38. Canx.
EI-ABM	DH.80A Puss Moth	2200	G-ABNZ	16.10.37	Restored as G-ABNZ 12/38. Canx.
EI-ABN	Aeronca C.3	A.609	G-AEFU	16. 6.37	Scrapped 1955. Canx 22.11.55.
EI-ABO	DH.87B Hornet Moth	8120		4. 5.37	To G-AFMP 12/38. Canx.
EI-ABP	DH.89A Dragon Rapide	6341	G-AENO EI-ABP/G-AENO	. 5.37	To VH-ADE 2/40. Canx.
EI-ABQ	Miles M.2 Hawk	23	G-ACMX (EI-AAV)/G-ACMX	17.12.38	Sold to UK in 8/39. Canx.
EI-ABR	Not allocated.				
EI-ABS	Not allocated.				
EI-ABT	DH.86B Srs.I	2336	G-ADUH	14.10.38	Restored as G-ADUH 11/46. Canx.
EI-ABU	Spartan 3-Seater II	102	G-ABYN	28. 4.39	Restored as G-ABYN 4/92. Canx 10.4.92.
EI-ABV	Lockheed 14-WF62	1497		23. 6.39	To VH-ADW 5/40. Canx.
EI-ABW	Lockheed 14-WF62	1498		23. 6.39	To VH-ADY 5/40. Canx.
EI-ABX	BA Swallow II	464	G-AFES	17. 7.39	Scrapped. Canx 13.12.55.
EI-ABY	BA Swallow II	431	G-AEIW	18. 8.39	Scrapped. Canx 13.12.55.
EI-ABZ	Piper J/4A Cub Coupe (Possibly c/n 4-689 ex.G-AFXY/NC24771)	1292		. .39R	NTU - Not delivered from UK and to RAF as HL530 in 10/41.
EI-ACA	Douglas DC-3-268B	2178		1. 4.40	Crashed and DBF at Shannon, Ireland on 18.6.46. Canx.
EI-ACB(1)	Douglas DC-3-268C	2261		. .40R	NTU - To NC19971 9/40. Canx.
EI-ACB(2)	Lockheed 414 Hudson I	1812	IAC AC-91 P5123	2. 8.45	To OO-API 5/47. Canx.
EI-ACC	Vickers-Supermarine 236 Walrus 1	6S/21840	IAC N-18 (L2301)	28. 8.45	To G-AIZG 12/46. Canx.
EI-ACD	Douglas C-47-DL Dakota	9140	42-32914	17.12.45	To CS-TAD 6/63. Canx.

Regn	Type	c/n	Previous identity	Regn date	Fate or immediate subsequent identity (if known)
EI-ACE	Douglas DC-3D	42956	NC37466	27. 2.46	To 9N-AAP 7/64. Canx.
EI-ACF	Douglas DC-3D	42957	NC37467	1. 3.46	Crashed on 1.1.53 Spernall, nr.Elmdon Airport. Canx.
EI-ACG	Douglas C-47-DL Dakota	4579	41-18487	15. 4.46	To EI-ALR 10/60. Canx.
EI-ACH	Douglas C-47A-20-DK Dakota	12893	42-93027	30. 1.46	To G-APUC 6/59. Canx.
EI-ACI	Douglas C-47-DL Dakota	9036	42-32810	8. 4.46	To EI-ALS 12/60. Canx.
EI-ACJ	Taylorcraft Plus D	203	LB344	20. 4.46	Crashed at Shannon on 18.1.47. Canx.
EI-ACK	Douglas C-47A-80-DL Dakota	19503	43-15037	29. 6.46	To 4X-AOC 2/60. Canx.
EI-ACL	Douglas C-47A-1-DK Dakota	11861	42-92098	13. 8.46	To HZ-AAL 6/58. Canx.
EI-ACM	Douglas C-47A-20-DK Dakota	12899	42-93032	21. 7.46	To HZ-AAN 6/58. Canx.
EI-ACN	Taylorcraft Plus D	226	LB379	23. 8.46	WFU. Canx 11.3.66.
EI-ACO	Auster J/1 Autocrat	2104		14. 9.46	To G-ALUE 7/49. Canx.
EI-ACP	Taylorcraft Plus D	192	G-AHSC LB333	3.10.46	DBR at Cooagh on 4.9.54. Canx.
EI-ACQ	Not allocated.				
EI-ACR	Lockheed L.749A-79-32 Constellation	2548	(VP-C..) (NC86534)	17. 9.47	To G-ALAK 22.6.48. Canx.
EI-ACS	Lockheed L.749A-79-32 Constellation	2549	(NC86535)	17. 9.47	To G-ALAL 22.6.48. Canx.
EI-ACT	Douglas C-47A-10-DK Dakota	12471	KG436 42-92647	4.10.46	To EI-ALT 1.61. Canx.
EI-ACU	Auster J/2 Arrow	2364		22. 2.47	DBR in gales at Shannon on 23.4.47. Canx.
EI-ACV	Percival P.28 Proctor I	K.426	G-AIRF Z7251	14.12.46	Scrapped. Canx 11.3.66.
EI-ACW	Miles M.65 Gemini 1A	6320		16. 6.47	To G-ALUG 7/49. Canx.
EI-ACX	Percival P.28 Proctor I	K.328	G-AIIJ P6319	18. 1.47	Scrapped. Canx 20.7.60.
EI-ACY	Auster J/1 Autocrat	2146	G-AIBK	20. 5.47	Crashed at Oughterard on 5.4.67. Canx.
EI-ACZ	Not allocated.				
EI-ADA	Lockheed L.749-79-32 Constellation	2554	(NC.....)	17. 9.47	To G-ALAM 22.6.48. Canx.
EI-ADB	Airspeed AS.65 Consul	5134	HN844	7. 7.47	To G-ALTZ 6/49. Canx.
EI-ADC	Airspeed AS.65 Consul	5151	HM980	24. 9.47	To AP-AGK 4/53. Canx.
EI-ADD	Lockheed L.749A-79-32 Constellation	2555	(NC.....)	8.10.47	To G-ALAN 22.6.48. Canx.
EI-ADE	Lockheed L.749A-79-32 Constellation	2566	(F-....)	24.10.47	To G-ALAO 22.6.48. Canx.
EI-ADF	Vickers 634 Viking 1B	208		4. 6.47	To G-AKTV 5.2.48. Canx 10.3.48.
EI-ADG	Vickers 634 Viking 1B	209		17. 6.47	To SU-AFN 11/48. Canx.
EI-ADH	Vickers 634 Viking 1B	210		23. 7.47	To SU-AFM 11/48. Canx.
EI-ADI	Vickers 634 Viking 1B	211		28. 7.47	To G-AKTU 5.2.48. Canx 10.3.48.
EI-ADJ	Vickers 634 Viking 1B	212		2. 8.47	To SU-AFO 12/48. Canx.
EI-ADK	Vickers 634 Viking 1B	213		9. 9.47	To SU-AFK 8/48. Canx.
EI-ADL	Vickers 634 Viking 1B	214		5. 9.47	To SU-AFL 8/48. Canx.
EI-ADM	Miles M.65 Gemini 1A	6520		17.12.47	To G-AFLT(2) 6/49. Canx.
EI-ADN	Auster J/2 Arrow	2391		31. 7.47	Crashed at Clogher Head, Co.Louth, Ireland on 1.12.47. Canx.
EI-ADO	PA-12 Super Cruiser	12-3278		4.11.47	To G-ARTH 9/61. Canx.
EI-ADP	DH.89A Dragon Rapide	6945	G-AHEB RL963	27. 8.47	Restored as G-AHEB 4/55. Canx.
EI-ADQ	Not allocated.				
EI-ADR	Piper J3C-50 Cub	2424	G-AFIZ	29. 1.48	WFU. Canx 1.11.55.
EI-ADS	British Klemm BK.1 Swallow	1	G-ACMK	25. 3.48	WFU. Canx 23.6.60.
EI-ADT	Miles M.38 Messenger 2A	6364	G-AJFG	6. 5.48	Restored as G-AJFG 12/66. Canx.
EI-ADU	Miles M.14A Hawk Trainer III	623	G-AKRI L8145	14. 5.48	Crashed at Weston on 23.5.48. Canx.
EI-ADV	PA-12 Super Cruiser	12-3459	NC4031H	11. 5.48	Badly damaged in forced landing at Maynooth west of Weston on 8.7.99.
EI-ADW	Douglas C-47B-5-DK Dakota	14662/26107	G-AGKL KJ935/43-48846	4. 6.48	Restored as G-AGKL 9/48. Canx.
EI-ADX	Douglas C-47B-15-DK Dakota	15283/26728	G-AGNC KK145/43-49467	4. 6.48	Restored as G-AGNC 9/48. Canx.
EI-ADY	Douglas C-47B-15-DK Dakota	15552/26997	G-AGNG KK216/43-49736	4. 6.48	Restored as G-AGNG 10/48. Canx.
EI-ADZ	Not allocated.				
EI-AEA	DH.89A Dragon Rapide	6433	G-AFMG Z7259/G-AFMG	26. 7.48	Crashed at Highfield Farm, Hutton Cranswick, near Driffield, Yorks on 4.10.49. Canx.
EI-AEB	Piper J3C-65 Cub	21967	G-AKBS	13. 8.48	To N9987F 9/51. Canx.
EI-AEC	BA Swallow II	493	G-AFHM	7. 9.48	WFU. Canx 9.2.55.
EI-AED	Not allocated.				
EI-AEE	Not allocated.				
EI-AEF	Not allocated.				
EI-AEG	Not allocated.				
EI-AEH	Not allocated.				
EI-AEI	Not allocated.				
EI-AEJ	Not allocated.				
EI-AEK	Not allocated.				
EI-AEL	Not allocated.				
EI-AEM	Not allocated.				
EI-AEN	Not allocated.				
EI-AEO	Not allocated.				
EI-AEP	Not allocated.				
EI-AEQ	Not allocated.				
EI-AER	Not allocated.				

Regn	Type	c/n	Previous identity	Regn date	Fate or immediate subsequent identity (if known)
EI-AES	Not allocated.				
EI-AET	Not allocated.				
EI-AEU	Not allocated.				
EI-AEV	Not allocated.				
EI-AEW	Not allocated.				
EI-AEX	Not allocated.				
EI-AEY	Not allocated.				
EI-AEZ	Not allocated.				
EI-AFA	Douglas C-47A-80-DL Dakota	19632	OY-AUB 43-15166	26.11.48	To 9N-AAL 10/63. Canx.
EI-AFB	Douglas C-47A-90-DL Dakota	20453	OY-DDO 43-15987	26.11.48	To VR-TBT 1/58. Canx.
EI-AFC	Douglas C-47A-90-DL Dakota	20135	SE-BAZ 43-15669	26.11.48	To 9N-AAO 6/64. Canx.
EI-AFD	BA Swallow II	468	G-AERR	21.12.48	Scrapped at Weston in 1962. Canx 6.3.53.
EI-AFE	Piper J3C-90 Cub	16687	OO-COR D-ELAB/N9945F/EI-AFE/N79076/NC79076	11. 3.49	
EI-AFF	BA L.25C Swallow II	406	G-ADMF	18. 5.49	Damaged in floods at Coonagh on 16.5.66. (On rebuild in private house 4/96)
EI-AFG	Auster J/1 Autocrat	2631	G-AJUT	24. 9.49	Restored as G-AJUT 1/54. Canx.
EI-AFH	Miles M.38 Messenger 2A	6701	G-AKBL	21. 2.50	Restored as G-AKBL 2/53. Canx.
EI-AFI	DH.82A Tiger Moth	82439	G-ALIZ N9369	3.10.49	Crashed and DBF at Weston on 9.1.50. Canx.
EI-AFJ	DH.82A Tiger Moth	83794	G-AHPZ T7280	14. 3.50	WFU in 10/65. Canx 11.3.66. Restored as G-AHPZ on 2.6.99.
EI-AFK	DH.84 Dragon II	6105	G-AECZ AV982/G-AECZ	16. 3.50	Canx 11.3.66. To EI-ABI(2) 8/85.
EI-AFL	Douglas C-47B-35-DK Dakota	16699/33447	G-ALXO KP228/44-77115	13. 5.50	Crashed into Mt.Snowdon on 10.1.52. Canx.
EI-AFM	Miles M.38 Messenger 2A	6377	G-AKBN	1. 9.50	Restored as G-AKBN 9/54. Canx.
EI-AFN	BA Swallow II	485	G-AFGV	23. 8.50	WFU. Canx 30.5.67. (Stored 1992)
EI-AFO	Avro 631 Cadet	730	IAC C-7	10.11.50	NTU - To EI-AGO 3/54. Canx.
EI-AFP	Bristol 170 Freighter 31E	12827	G-AINL WJ320/G-18-93/G-AINL	14. 3.52	Restored as G-AINL 10/52. Canx.
EI-AFQ	Bristol 170 Freighter 31E	12937	G-18-111 G-ALSJ	10. 6.52	Restored as G-ALSJ 10/55. Canx.
EI-AFR	Bristol 170 Freighter 31E	13072	G-18-116 G-AMLJ	17. 7.52	Restored as G-AMLJ 6/55. Canx.
EI-AFS	Bristol 170 Freighter 31E	13074	G-AMLL	5.12.52	Restored as G-AMLL 1/57. Canx.
EI-AFT	Bristol 170 Freighter 31E	13076	G-AMLN	23. 1.53	To F-BFUO 10/56. Canx.
EI-AFU	Not allocated.				
EI-AFV	Vickers 707 Viscount	30		5. 3.54	To G-APZB 2/60. Canx.
EI-AFW	Vickers 707 Viscount	31		5. 3.54	To VR-BBJ 2/60. Canx.
EI-AFX	Not allocated.				
EI-AFY	Vickers 707 Viscount	32		25. 3.54	To VR-BBH 1/60. Canx.
EI-AFZ	Not allocated.				
EI-AGA	BA Swallow II	500	G-AFIH	14. 6.52	Crashed near Weston on 1.3.59. Canx.
EI-AGB	Miles M.38 Messenger 2A	6332	G-AHFP	12. 1.53	Crashed Rosses Point, Co.Sligo on 1.5.53. Became spares use for G-AGOY. Canx.
EI-AGC	DH.82A Tiger Moth	84643	G-AMKI OH-ELB/G-AMKI/T6195	9. 5.53	Crashed at Killiney Strand on 15.7.55. Canx.
EI-AGD	Taylorcraft Plus D	108	G-AFUB HL534/G-AFUB	26. 5.53	Damaged in gales at Cork in 2/74. (On rebuild 4/96)
EI-AGE	Miles M.48 Messenger 3	4690	G-AGOY HB-EIP/G-AGOY/U-0247	17. 6.53	WFU and restored as G-AGOY. Canx 11.3.66.
EI-AGF	Miles M.65 Gemini 1A	6291	G-AJWF	18. 7.53	Restored as G-AJWF 11/53. Canx.
EI-AGG	DH.82A Tiger Moth	86173	G-AGRA NL690	14. 9.53	Crashed at Coonagh, Ireland prior to 12.2.54. Canx 2.6.54.
EI-AGH	BA Swallow II	488	G-AFHH	3.12.53	Crashed at Abbeyshrule on 18.4.59. Canx.
EI-AGI	Vickers 707 Viscount	34		2. 4.54	To G-APZC 1/60. Canx.
EI-AGJ	Auster J/1 Autocrat	2208	G-AIPZ	3.11.53	(On rebuild 6/96)
EI-AGK	DH.89A Dragon Rapide	6458	G-AKNV R5922	16.12.53	Restored as G-AKNV 6/55. Canx.
EI-AGL	DH.82A Tiger Moth	85549	G-ANEO DE582	11. 1.54	Restored as G-ANEO 4/58. Canx.
EI-AGM	Piper J3C-65 Cub	21967	N9987F EI-AEB/G-AKBS	9. 2.54	WFU in 1963. Canx 19.6.66.
EI-AGN	DH.82A Tiger Moth	82943	G-ANEM R5042	13. 3.54	To UK on 24.9.78 and restored as G-ANEM 4/82. Canx.
EI-AGO	Avro 631 Cadet	730	(EI-AFO) IAC C-7	10. 3.54	Not converted. Canx 11.3.66. To ZK-AVR.
EI-AGP	DH.82A Tiger Moth	3946	G-ANDM EI-AGP/G-ANDM/(G-ANDI)/N6642	5. 5.54	Restored as G-ANDM 5/81. Canx 27.5.81.
EI-AGQ	Avro 652A Anson I	-	G-ALXC MH182	24. 6.54	Restored as G-ALXC 9/56. Canx.
EI-AGR	DH.82A Tiger Moth	84296	T7932	17. 6.54	Crashed at Maynooth on 7.8.61. Canx.
EI-AGS	DH.82A Tiger Moth	85115	T6868	17. 6.54	Crashed at Lucan, near Weston on 30.9.56. Canx.
EI-AGT	DH.82A Tiger Moth	82190	N6940	7. 6.54	w/o on 16.6.57. Canx.
EI-AGU	Miles M.38 Messenger 2A	HPR.146	G-AJYZ	23. 6.54	Restored as G-AJYZ 6/57. Canx.
EI-AGV	DH.82A Tiger Moth	84590	T6123	16. 9.54	Crashed at Cahirciveen on 6.8.55. Canx.
EI-AGW	Avro 652A Anson C.19 Srs.2	1375	G-AIYK	9. 6.55	Restored as G-AIYK 12/56. Canx 8.12.56.
EI-AGX	Not allocated.				
EI-AGY	SAAB 91C Safir	91-318	SE-XBE	20. 8.55	To OE-DSA 2/58. Canx.

Regn	Type	c/n	Previous identity	Regn date	Fate or immediate subsequent identity (if known)
EI-AGZ	Not allocated.				
EI-AHA	DH.82A Tiger Moth	82494	N9440	30. 3.55	WFU in 10/65. Canx 18.3.66.
EI-AHB	DH.82A Tiger Moth	82699	R4758	30. 3.55	WFU. Canx 18.3.66.
EI-AHC	DH.82A Tiger Moth	82852	R4944	30. 3.55	Crashed at Weston in 1958. Canx 19.2.62.
EI-AHD	DH.82A Tiger Moth	83037	R5175	30. 3.55	WFU in 10/65. Canx 18.3.66.
EI-AHE	Not allocated.				
EI-AHF	DH.82A Tiger Moth	84531	T8258	30. 3.55	WFU. Canx 18.3.66.
EI-AHG	Douglas C-47B-25-DK Dakota		F-OAPD	9. 5.55	To CS-IAE 2/64. Canx.
		16013/32761	G-ANLI/Pakistan AF		H712/KN387/44-76429
EI-AHH	DH.82A Tiger Moth	86550	PG641	. 7.55R	NTU - To EI-AHM 8/55. Canx.
EI-AHI	DH.82A Tiger Moth	85347	G-APRA	17. 9.93	
			DE313		
EI-AHJ	DH.82A Tiger Moth	86414	NL984	21. 9.55	To N8722 12/69. Canx 1.12.69.
EI-AHK	DH.82A Tiger Moth	3991	N6718	20. 9.55	WFU. Canx 18.3.66.
EI-AHL	Miles M.38 Messenger 2A	6338	G-AIAJ	19.10.55	Restored as G-AIAJ 2/56. Canx.
EI-AHM	DH.82A Tiger Moth	86550	(EI-AHH)	20. 8.55	To G-APGM 1/86. Canx 6.11.85.
			PG641		
EI-AHN	Miles M.65 Gemini 1A	6470	G-AKEI	16. 3.56	Restored as G-AKEI 2/57. Canx.
EI-AHO	Avro 652A Anson I	-	G-AHNT	22. 2.56	Not delivered. Scrapped 3/58 Portsmouth, UK. Canx 18.3.66.
			MG866		
EI-AHP	DHC.1 Chipmunk 22A	C1/0164	WB728	31. 5.56	To G-AOZU 2/57. Canx.
	(Fuselage no. DHB/f/63)				
EI-AHQ	Not allocated.				
EI-AHR	DHC.1 Chipmunk 22A	C1/0184	WB735	31. 5.56	DBR 16.5.66 at Coonagh when River Shannon burst its banks.
	(Fuselage no. DHB/f/71)				Static exhibit at Charleville in 1974. Canx 18.4.80.
EI-AHS	Not allocated.				
EI-AHT	DHC.1 Chipmunk 22A	C1/0230	WD290	31. 5.56	To G-AOZV 12/56. Canx.
	(Fuselage no. DHB/f/115)				
EI-AHU	DHC.1 Chipmunk 22A	C1/0144	WB696	31. 5.56	To G-APLO 5/58. Canx.
	(Fuselage no. DHB/f/48)				
EI-AHV	DHC.1 Chipmunk 22A	C1/0256	WD319	31. 5.56	To G-AOZJ 1/57. Canx.
	(Fuselage no. DHB/f/139)				
EI-AHW	DHC.1 Chipmunk 22A	C1/0396	WG324	31. 5.56	To VH-UWG 4/58. Canx.
	(Fuselage no. DHB/f/284)				
EI-AHX	Not allocated.				
EI-AHY	DHC.1 Chipmunk 22A	C1/0139	WB691	31. 5.56	To HB-TUF 7/58. Canx.
	(Fuselage no. DHB/f/44)				
EI-AHZ	Not allocated.				
EI-AIA	Not allocated.				
EI-AIB	Not allocated.				
EI-AIC	Not allocated.				
EI-AID	Not allocated.				
EI-AIE	Not allocated.				
EI-AIF	Not allocated.				
EI-AIG	Not allocated.				
EI-AIH	Not allocated.				
EI-AII	Not allocated.				
EI-AIJ	Not allocated.				
EI-AIK	Not allocated.				
EI-AIL	Not allocated.				
EI-AIM	Not allocated.				
EI-AIN	Not allocated.				
EI-AIO	Not allocated.				
EI-AIP	Not allocated.				
EI-AIQ	Not allocated.				
EI-AIR	Not allocated.				
EI-AIS	Not allocated.				
EI-AIT	Not allocated.				
EI-AIU	Not allocated.				
EI-AIV	Not allocated.				
EI-AIW	Not allocated.				
EI-AIX	Not allocated.				
EI-AIY	Not allocated.				
EI-AIZ	Not allocated.				
EI-AJA	DHC.1 Chipmunk 22A	C1/0078	WB632	31. 5.56	To G-APMW 5/58. Canx.
	(Fuselage no. DHB/f/11)				
EI-AJB	DHC.1 Chipmunk 22A	C1/0245	WB710	31. 5.56	To VH-RSM 2/61. Canx.
	(Fuselage no. DHB/f/130)				
EI-AJC	DHC.1 Chipmunk 22A	C1/0061	WB620	21. 7.56	To G-ARTP 10/61. Canx.
	(Fuselage no. DHB/f/4)				
EI-AJD	DHC.1 Chipmunk 22A	C1/0072	WB630	21. 7.56	To VH-BWD 1/59. Canx.
	(Fuselage no. DHH/f/80)				
EI-AJE	DHC.1 Chipmunk 22A	C1/0214	WB764	21. 7.56	To G-APPK 10/58. Canx.
	(Fuselage no. DHB/f/97)				
EI-AJF	DHC.1 Chipmunk 22A	C1/0277	WD336	16. 7.56	To G-ARCR 8/60. Canx.
	(Fuselage no. DHB/f/158)				
EI-AJG	Beechcraft G35 Bonanza	D-4789		22. 8.56	To G-APTY 6/59. Canx.
EI-AJH	Auster J/5P Autocar	3191	G-AOHF	20.11.56	Restored as G-AOHF 3/57. Canx.
			(D-EFOR)		
EI-AJI	Vickers 808 Viscount	289		21. 5.57	Broken up 5/72. Canx as WFU 31.10.69.
EI-AJJ	Vickers 808 Viscount	290		21. 5.57	Broken up 5/72. Canx as WFU 31.12.69.
EI-AJK	Vickers 808 Viscount	291		21. 5.57	To HB-ILR 11/69. Canx 4.11.69.
EI-AJL	PA-23-160 Apache	23-903		30. 1.57	Crashed in River Shannon on 15.1.58. Canx.

Regn	Type	c/n	Previous identity	Regn date	Fate or immediate subsequent identity (if known)
EI-AJM	PA-22-150 Tri-Pacer	22-4962	N7105D	20. 5.57	To F-OBHV 4/58. Canx.
EI-AJN	PA-22-150 Tri-Pacer	22-5009		5. 4.57	To G-APTP 3/59. Canx.
EI-AJO	DH.89A Dragon Rapide 6	6884	G-AGSH NR808	26. 4.57	Restored as G-AGSH 7/57. Canx.
EI-AJP	DH.82A Tiger Moth	85348	G-AOUZ DE314	20. 4.57	To G-AOUZ 7/57. Canx.
EI-AJQ	Not allocated.				
EI-AJR	Percival P.28 Proctor I	K.238	G-AIKI P6179	28. 4.57	Restored as G-AIKI 9/57. Canx.
EI-AJS	Taylorcraft Auster 5D	1060	G-AOCR NJ673	20. 4.57	Restored as G-AOCR 7/57. Canx.
EI-AJT	PA-23-160 Apache	23-1258		1. 4.58	To G-APMY 15.5.58. Canx.
EI-AJU	PA-22-125 Tri-Pacer	22-113	XB-NOU	24. 1.58	To SE-CLU 7/59. Canx.
EI-AJV	Vickers 745D Viscount	228	G-16-3 (N7466)	26. 3.58	To G-APNG 6/58. Canx.
EI-AJW	Vickers 745D Viscount	225	G-16-4 (N7463)	26. 3.58	To G-APNF 6/58. Canx.
EI-AJX	Not allocated.				
EI-AJY	Cessna 310A	35335	N3635D	28. 4.58	To G-APNJ 6/58. Canx.
EI-AJZ	Not allocated.				
EI-AKA	Fokker F-27 Friendship 100	10105	PH-FAA	10. 9.57	To PH-FSF 6/66. Canx.
EI-AKB	Fokker F-27 Friendship 100	10106	PH-FAB	10. 9.57	To PI-C530 1/66. Canx.
EI-AKC	Fokker F-27 Friendship 100	10107	PH-FAC	10. 9.57	To PH-SAP 3/66. Canx.
EI-AKD	Fokker F-27 Friendship 100	10109	PH-FAE	10. 9.57	To PH-YFF 1/66. Canx.
EI-AKE	Fokker F-27 Friendship 100	10110	PH-FAF	10. 9.57	To PH-FSE 6/66. Canx.
EI-AKF	Fokker F-27 Friendship 100	10118	PH-FAN	10. 9.57	To PH-FSA 1/66. Canx.
EI-AKG	Fokker F-27 Friendship 100	10119	PH-FAO	10. 9.57	To PH-FSB 1/66. Canx.
EI-AKH(1)	Cessna 150	150-17030	N5530E	. .58R	NTU - To SE-CLY 9/59. Canx.
EI-AKH(2)	DH.89A Dragon Rapide	6870	G-AKSE NR794	14. 5.59	Restored as G-AKSE 1/61. Canx.
EI-AKI	PA-23-160 Apache	23-1385	N3421P	31. 5.58	To G-ARBN 6/60. Canx.
EI-AKJ	Vickers 808 Viscount	421		14. 6.58	To EI-AKO 2/59. Canx.
EI-AKK	Vickers 808 Viscount (Converted to freighter in 7/67)	422		14. 6.58	Seriously damaged 21.9.67 Bristol-Lulsgate, UK. Canx.
EI-AKL	Vickers 808 Viscount (Converted to freighter in 6/67)	423		14. 6.58	Canx as WFU 31.3.70. To D-ADAM 7/70.
EI-AKM	Piper J3C-65 Cub	15810	N88194 NC88194	17.11.58	(Stored with J.Molloy)
EI-AKN	Taylorcraft Auster 5	1021	F-BIAU G-AJAK/NJ625	2. 1.59	Restored as G-AJAK 4/61. Canx.
EI-AKO	Vickers 808 Viscount	421	EI-AKJ	18. 2.59	Canx as WFU 31.3.70. To D-ADAN 7/70.
EI-AKP	PA-22-160 Tri-Pacer	22-6666		15. 4.59	To G-APWR 9/59. Canx.
EI-AKQ	Not allocated.				
EI-AKR	Downer Bellanca 14-19-3	4125		20. 5.59	To G-ASRD 3/64. Canx.
EI-AKS	PA-18A-150 Super Cub	18-6670		15. 4.59	To G-APUI 5/59. Canx.
EI-AKT	Hiller UH-12E	2001	N5327V	13. 6.59	To VP-YSZ 12/60. Canx.
EI-AKU	DH.94 Moth Minor	94034	G-AFPD W6459/G-AFPD	9. 7.59	WFU in 1962. Canx 11.3.66.
EI-AKV	PA-24-250 Comanche (Officially regd with c/n 24-1190)	24-1205		11. 7.59	To G-APZF 1/60. Canx.
EI-AKW	PA-24-250 Comanche (Officially regd with c/n 24-1197)	24-1190		11. 7.59	To G-APZG 1/60. Canx.
EI-AKX	Not allocated.				
EI-AKY	PA-22-160 Tri-Pacer	22-6689		7. 7.59	To G-ARXK 2/62. Canx.
EI-AKZ	Not allocated.				
EI-ALA	Boeing 720-048B (Line No. 172)	18041	LN-TUU EI-ALA/N7083/EI-ALA	28. 9.60	To N734T 10/72. Canx.
EI-ALB	Boeing 720-048B (Line No. 182)	18042		28. 9.60	To N7081 9/64. Canx.
EI-ALC	Boeing 720-048B (Line No. 188)	18043	LN-TUV EI-ALC/N8790R/EI-ALC/9Y-TCS/EI-ALC/N7082/EI-ALC	28. 9.60	To OO-TEB 8/72. Canx.
EI-ALD	PA-23-160 Apache	23-1781		14. 9.59	To G-APBD 10/59. Canx.
EI-ALE	SCAN 30 Widgeon	19	VP-KNV F-BGTD	30. 9.59	To G-ARIX 2/60. Canx.
EI-ALF	PA-22-160 Tri-Pacer	22-7054		17.11.59	To G-APZL 1/60. Canx.
EI-ALG	Vickers 808 Viscount	312	VR-BAY G-APDX	26. 3.60	Broken up 5/72. Canx as WFU 31.10.69.
EI-ALH	Taylorcraft Plus D	106	G-AHLJ HH987/G-AFTZ	5. 5.60	
EI-ALI	Beechcraft 35-A33 Debonair	CD-214		11. 8.60	To G-ASHR 4/63. Canx.
EI-ALJ	Taylorcraft Plus D	154	G-AHAD LB283	5.10.59	Crashed after mid-air collision with D.31 Turbulent G-ARIZ near Limerick on 25.8.62. Canx.
EI-ALK	PA-23-160 Apache	23-1686		4.11.59	To G-APFV 12/59. Canx.
EI-ALL	Beechcraft M35 Bonanza	D-6236		30.10.59	To G-ATSR 3/66. Canx.
EI-ALM	Miles M.65 Gemini 3C	6488	G-AKGE	6.11.59	Restored as G-AKGE 11/61. Canx.
EI-ALN	Auster J/5L Aiglet Trainer	3143	G-AOFS	5. 4.60	Restored as G-AOFS 3/61. Canx.
EI-ALO	Cessna 180A	180-50012	G-APYJ N347TC/N9714B	21. 6.60	Restored as G-APYJ 6/61. Canx.
EI-ALP	Avro 643 Cadet II	848	G-ADIE	12. 9.60	Engine seizure 12.6.77 (Stored 12/98 Weston)
EI-ALQ	Not allocated.				
EI-ALR	Douglas C-47-DL Dakota	4579	EI-ACG 41-18487	2. 1.61	To French Navy as 18487 in 1/61. Canx.

Regn	Type	c/n	Previous identity	Regn date	Fate or immediate subsequent identity (if known)
EI-ALS	Douglas C-47-DL Dakota	9036	EI-ACI 42-32810	2. 1.61	To French Navy as 32810 in 1/61. Canx.
EI-ALT	Douglas C-47A-10-DK Dakota	12471	EI-ACT KG436/42-92647	2. 1.61	To French Navy as 12471 in 1/61. Canx.
EI-ALU	Avro 631 Cadet	657	G-ACIH	14. 3.61	(Stored 4/96 Dublin)
EI-ALV	Lockheed 12A	1226	G-AHLH NC18130	21. 3.61	To F-BUIE 11/73. Canx.
EI-ALW	PA-24-250 Comanche	24-2133	G-ARLK N7257P/N10F	29. 6.61	Restored as G-ARLK 3/64. Canx.
EI-ALX	Not allocated.				
EI-ALY	Percival P.44 Proctor 5	Ae.72	G-AHWO	28. 6.61	Not rebuilt following crash at Collinstown, Dublin on 5.5.59. Canx 15.2.66.
EI-ALZ	Not allocated.				
EI-AMA	Vickers 808 Viscount	258	CF-MCJ VR-BAX/G-APDW/(G-AOYI)	31.10.61	Broken up 8/96. Canx as WFU 6.1.70.
EI-AMB	Beagle A.61 Terrier 1	3720	G-ARLH VX109	28.10.61	Restored as G-ARLH 8/68. Canx.
EI-AMC(1)	Beagle A.61 Terrier 1	3730	VX926	.12.61R	NTU - To G-ASKJ 7/63. Canx.
EI-AMC(2)	Beechcraft B95A Travel Air	TD-504		18. 4.62	To G-ATRC 2/66. Canx.
EI-AMD	Socata MS.880B Rallye Club	5080		16. 4.62	WFU by 1979. Broken up 1980. Canx 8.6.81.
EI-AME	PA-28-160 Cherokee	28-206	G-ARUV	31. 1.62	To G-ATDA 4/65. Canx.
EI-AMF	Taylorcraft Plus D	157	G-ARRK G-AHUM/LB286	26. 4.62	Damaged in gales at Cork in 2/74. (For sale 6/97) Canx 3.4.70.
EI-AMG	Morane-Saulnier MS.885 Super Rallye	5097		30. 4.62	Crashed on 4.4.67. Canx 22.5.67. To G-AWXY 1/69.
EI-AMH	DHC.1 Chipmunk 22A (Fuselage no. DHB/f/4)	C1/0061	G-ARTP EI-AJC/WB620	19. 4.62	Restored as G-ARTP 11/64. Canx.
EI-AMI	PA-22-108 Colt	22-8835	G-ARSU	14. 6.62	Restored as G-ARSU 7/70. Canx 8.7.70.
EI-AMJ	PA-22-160 Tri-Pacer	22-6299	N9239D	7. 6.62	Crashed at Kilflynn on 28.5.68. Canx.
EI-AMK	Auster J/1 Autocrat	1838	G-AGTV	19. 9.62	WFU after engine failure 5.79 (Sold 4/95)(Stored 4/96)
EI-AML	DH.89A Dragon Rapide	6709	G-AKPA HG724	15. 6.62	To F-BLHZ 6/64. Canx.
EI-AMM	PA-24-180 Comanche	24-3239		10. 8.62	To G-ASFH 3/63. Canx.
EI-AMN	DH.89A Dragon Rapide	6907	G-ALGE YI-ABG/NR843	31. 7.62	To F-BLXX 8/64. Canx.
EI-AMO	Auster J/1B Aiglet	2792	G-ARBM VP-SZZ/VP-KKR	1. 9.62	Restored as G-ARBM. Canx 3/91.
EI-AMP	Aviation Traders ATL.98 Carvair	7480/6	G-ARZV N75298/YV-C-AVH/NC90431/41-10761	5. 2.63	To CF-EPX 7/68. Canx.
EI-AMQ	Not allocated.				
EI-AMR	Aviation Traders ATL.98 Carvair	10448/8	N88819 42-72343	5. 2.63	To CF-EPV 5/68. Canx.
EI-AMS	PA-22-150 Tri-Pacer	22-6089	N8931D	31. 8.62	Crashed at Dundalk, Ireland on 9.3.75. Canx 16.5.79.
EI-AMT	Cessna 185A	185-0288	N4088Y	25. 9.62	Crashed at Lugnaquilla Mountains, Co.Wicklow on 29.6.67. Canx.
EI-AMU	BA Swallow II	449	G-AELG	3. 9.62	Crashed at Abbeyshrule on 5.4.63. Canx 11.3.66.
EI-AMV	Percival P.44 Proctor 5	Ae.103	G-AIET	6.11.62	Crashed at Stowting, Kent on 16.10.63. Canx.
EI-AMW	Boeing 707-348C (Line No. 377)	18737	LX-LGV EI-AMW	21. 5.64	To 70-ACJ 5/79. Canx 18.5.79.
EI-AMX	Not allocated.				
EI-AMY	Auster J/1N Alpha	2634	G-AJUW	9. 4.63	Dismantled in 1974. (For rebuild 4/92, to Kildare area since)
EI-AMZ	Not allocated.				
EI-ANA	Taylorcraft Plus D	206	G-AHCG LB347	29. 8.63	(Stored 4/92)
EI-ANB	Miles M.75 Aries 1	75/1007	G-AOGA	27. 5.63	Restored as G-AOGA 9/63. Canx.
EI-ANC(1)	Nord 1002 Pingouin	-		. .63R	NTU. Canx.
EI-ANC(2)	Cessna 182A	34078	N6078B	9. 9.65	To G-ATNU 11/65. Canx.
EI-AND	Cessna 175A	56444	G-APYA N6944E	29. 8.63	Fatal crash in Irish Sea off Formby Point, Lancs 30.10.94. Wreck recovered from the sea 2m N of Angelsey on 3.1.95.
EI-ANE	BAC One-Eleven Srs.208AL	BAC.049		31. 3.65	To 5N-HTC 9/91. Canx 9/91.
EI-ANF	BAC One-Eleven Srs.208AL	BAC.050	AN-BBS EI-ANF	31. 3.65	To 5N-HTD 9/91. Canx 3/92.
EI-ANG	BAC One-Eleven Srs.208AL	BAC.051		31. 3.65	To 5N-HTA 9/91. Canx 11.6.91.
EI-ANH	BAC One-Eleven Srs.208AL	BAC.052		31. 3.65	To 5N-HTB 9/91. Canx 15.7.91.
EI-ANI	PA-23-150 Apache	23-1159	G-APCL	12.12.63	Restored as G-APCL 11/64. Canx.
EI-ANJ	Aviation Traders ATL.98 Carvair	10458/14	G-ASKD D-ANEK/(D-ABIB)/OO-SBO/F-BHVR/OO-SBO/N88721/42-72353	17. 6.64	To CF-EPW 6/68. Canx.
EI-ANK	Douglas DC-3C-S1C3G Dakota	9813	5N-AAO VR-NCO/VH-AFA(2)/"VHC-HM"/42-23951	9. 3.64	To G-ATBE 2/65. Canx.
EI-ANL	Douglas DC-4-1009 Skymaster	42911	LX-SAF ZS-CIH/NC6402	29. 5.64	To EI-APK 1/67. Canx.
EI-ANM	Douglas DC-7CF (Line No. 818)	45190	N302G HB-IBM	22. 7.64	Restored as N302G 2/66. Canx.
EI-ANN	DH.82A Tiger Moth	83161	G-ANEE T5418	6.10.64	Badly damaged Culmullen 18.10.64 (Stored in loft 5/96)
EI-ANO	Boeing 707-348C (Line No. 413)	18880	N318F EI-ANO/N318F/EI-ANO	24. 2.65	To 5A-DIX 5/81. Canx 19.5.81.
EI-ANP(1)	Beagle-Auster D5/180 Husky	3680	(5N-ADG)	. .65R	NTU - To 5H-MMV 11/66. Canx.
EI-ANP(2)	Omega 56 HAFB	05	G-AXJA	16. 1.70	DBR 3.10.75 when envelope destroyed at Abbeyshrule when gas cylinder exploded and basket transferred to EI-BBM. Canx 12.9.85. Canopy used by Bristol Project children.
EI-ANQ	Not allocated.				

Regn	Type	c/n	Previous identity	Regn date	Fate or immediate subsequent identity (if known)
EI-ANR	Lake LA-4-200 Skimmer	295	N1133L	17.11.64	To G-BOLL 5/88. Canx 4.5.88.
EI-ANS	Reims Cessna F.172F	0095		30.10.64	To G-ATWJ 6/66. Canx.
EI-ANT	Champion 7ECA Citabria	7ECA-38		13. 1.65	
EI-ANU(1)	Bolkow	-		. .64R	NTU. Canx.
EI-ANU(2)	PA-30-160 Twin Comanche C	30-1820	G-AXER N8676Y	15.12.69	Restored as G-AXER 1/70. Canx.
EI-ANV	Boeing 707-348C (Line No. 488)	19001	9G-ACR EI-ANV	22. 3.66	To 5A-DIY 6/81. Canx 16.6.81.
EI-ANW	SAN Jodel D.117	625	F-BIBG	23. 3.65	DBR at Enniskillen, Ireland on 21.5.76. Canx 12.9.85.
EI-ANX	Not allocated.				
EI-ANY	PA-18-95 Super Cub	18-7152	G-AREU N3096Z	18.11.64	Crashed off Spanish Point, Co.Clare on 15.4.78. Canx.
EI-ANZ	Not allocated.				
EI-AOA	PA-28-140 Cherokee	28-20238	N6206W	3. 6.66	To G-AXAB 2/69. Canx.
EI-AOB	PA-28-140 Cherokee	28-20667		28. 4.65	
EI-AOC	Douglas DC-7CF (Line No. 779)	45128	N2282 XA-LOC	23. 5.65	Restored as N2282 12/65. Canx.
EI-AOD(1)	Bensen B.8 Gyrocopter	-		. .65R	NTU. Canx.
EI-AOD(2)	Cessna 182J	182-57249	N3149F	13. 6.66	DBR at Castlebar on 21.8.87. Canx.
EI-AOE	Vickers 803 Viscount	177	PH-VIF	29.10.65	To HB-ILP 3/69. Canx 11/69.
EI-AOF	Vickers 803 Viscount	176	PH-VIE	3.12.65	Crashed 2 miles north of Ashbourne, Dublin on 22.6.67. Canx.
EI-AOG	Vickers 803 Viscount	172	PH-VIA	15. 3.66	WFU in 10/69. Canx 26.7.72.
EI-AOH	Vickers 803 Viscount	180	PH-VII	18. 5.66	WFU in 11/70. Canx 3.1.72.
EI-AOI	Vickers 803 Viscount	179	PH-VIH	16. 6.66	WFU in 10/71. Canx 3.1.72.
EI-AOJ	Vickers 803 Viscount	173	PH-VIB	27. 9.66	WFU in 11/70. Canx 22.1.73.
EI-AOK(1)	Vickers 803 Viscount	174	PH-VIC	. .66R	NTU - To EI-APD 10/66. Canx.
EI-AOK(2)	Reims Cessna F.172G	0208		14. 3.66	
EI-AOL	Vickers 803 Viscount	175	PH-VID	29.11.66	To G-AYTW 3/71. Canx 10.3.71.
EI-AOM	Vickers 803 Viscount	178	PH-VIG	29.11.66	Crashed 24.3.68 into Irish Sea, 80kms off the Wexford Coast, Ireland. Canx.
EI-AON	Beechcraft A23 Musketeer	M-227	N2327J	1. 5.65	Crashed at Ballybeggan Racecourse on 28.8.66. Canx.
EI-AOO	Cessna 150E	150-61225	G-BURH EI-AOO/N2125J	30. 4.65	Restored as G-BURH 6/93. Canx 5/93.
EI-AOP(1)	Cessna 150F	150-61586	N6286R	. 5.65R	NTU - To G-ATHZ 8/65. Canx.
EI-AOP(2)	DH.82A Tiger Moth	84320	G-AIBN T7967	24. 9.65	DBR at Culmullen, Ireland on 5.5.74. Canx 12.9.85. (Stored in loft 5/96)
EI-AOQ	Not allocated.				
EI-AOR	Douglas C-54B-1DC Skymaster	10441	F-BIUT OD-ACA/N226A/PP-CCI/42-72336	2. 6.65	To ZS-IGC 12/69. Canx 10.12.69.
EI-AOS	Cessna 310B	35578	G-ARIG EI-AOS/G-ARIG/N5378A	1.11.65	(In storage by 1978) Wfu and to scrapyard. Canx.
EI-AOT	PA-28-180 Cherokee C	28-2343		28. 6.65	To G-ATHR 8/65. Canx.
EI-AOU	Hughes H.269B (300)	45-0189		3. 9.65	To G-AVZC 12/67. Canx.
EI-AOV	Hughes H.269B (300)	45-0188		3. 9.65	To 5Y-ADV 7/66. Canx.
EI-AOW	Hughes H.269B (300)	65-0205		27.10.65	To 6Y-JFN 3/66. Canx.
EI-AOX	Not allocated.				
EI-AOY	CZL L-200D Morava	171329	(D-GLIN) EI-AOY/OK-SHB	24. 2.66	To D-GGDC 12/73. Canx.
EI-AOZ	Not allocated.				
EI-APA	PA-22-160 Tri-Pacer	22-7487	G-ARDV	14.12.65	Restored as G-ARDV 9/68. Canx.
EI-APB	Douglas C-47B-1-DK Dakota	14155/25600	G-AMWV KJ816/43-48339	21. 3.66	Restored as G-AMWV 8/67. Canx.
EI-APC	Bristol 170 Freighter 31E	13072	G-AMLJ OD-ACM/G-AMLJ/EI-AFR/G-18-116/G-AMLJ	2. 3.66	To F-BTYO 12/72. Canx.
EI-APD	Vickers 803 Viscount	174	(EI-AOK) PH-VIC	28.10.66	Stored 10/70. Broken up 5/71 Dublin, Ireland. Canx.
EI-APE	Hughes H.269B (300)	64-0108	N9382F	17. 2.66	Crashed Mount Kenya on 16.3.66. Canx.
EI-APF(1)	Reims Cessna F.150F (Wichita c/n 63470)	0056		. .66R	NTU - To OH-CEU 8/66. Canx.
EI-APF(2)	Reims Cessna F.150G	0112		6. 3.66	
EI-APG	Boeing 707-348C (Line No. 599)	19410	CF-TAI EI-APG/N8789R/EI-APG	24. 4.67	To ST-AIM 9/82. Canx 7.9.82.
EI-APH	Hughes H.269B (300)	16-0234		29. 4.66	To G-AWKC 5/68. Canx.
EI-API	Hughes H.269B (300)	36-0239		10. 5.66	To LN-OQF 8/69. Canx.
EI-APJ	Douglas C-47B-30-DK Dakota	16294/33042	G-AMYX XF619/G-AMYX/KN509/44-76710	13. 7.66	To N3102Q 9/67. Canx.
EI-APK	Douglas DC-4-1009	42911	EI-ANL LX-SAF/ZS-CIH/N6402	4. 1.67	To N6304D 6/69. Canx.
EI-APL	Hughes H.269B (300)	-		. .66R	NTU - Not delivered. Canx.
EI-APM	Bristol 170 Freighter 31E	13076	F-BFUO EI-AFT/G-AMLN	23.11.66	Crashed at Dublin on 12.6.67. Canx.
EI-APN	Hughes H.269B (300)	116-0284		24. 2.67	To G-AVVS 10/67. Canx.
EI-APO	Beagle B.206C Srs.1	B.044	G-ATZO	16. 3.67	Restored as G-ATZO 11/67. Canx.
EI-APP(1)	Boeing 737-248 (Line No. 147)	19424		9. 6.67R	NTU - To EI-ASA. Canx.
EI-APP(2)	Bell 206A JetRanger	79		22. 8.67	To CF-FKR 7/72. Canx 29.4.72.
EI-APQ	Not allocated.				
EI-APR	Not allocated. [Marks were reserved by Paddy Robinson]				
EI-APS(1)	Boeing 737-248 (Line No. 153)	19425		9. 5.67R	NTU - To EI-ASB. Canx.
EI-APS(2)	Schleicher ASK-14	14008	G-AWVV D-KOBB	24.11.69	(Also allocated glider marks EI-114)

Regn	Type	c/n	Previous identity	Regn date	Fate or immediate subsequent identity (if known)
EI-APT(1)	Fokker D.VII/65 Replica	01	F-BNDF	2. 6.67	To EI-APU .68.
EI-APT(2)	Fokker D.VII/65 Replica	02	EI-APU F-BNDG	. .68	To N903AC 5/85. Canx 28.5.85.
EI-APU(1)	Fokker D.VII/65 Replica	02	F-BNDG	2. 6.67	To EI-APT /68. Canx.
EI-APU(2)	Fokker D.VII/65 Replica	01	EI-APT F-BNDF	. .68	To N902AC 5/85. Canx 28.5.85.
EI-APV	Fokker D.VII/65 Replica	03	F-BNDH	2. 6.67	To N904AC 5/85. Canx 28.5.85.
EI-APW	Fokker DR.1 Triplane Replica	001	G-ATIY	29. 5.67	To N..... 5/85. Canx 28.5.85.
EI-APX	Not allocated.				
EI-APY	Fokker DR.1 Triplane Replica (Bitz b.)	002	G-ATJM	29. 5.67	To N78001 /70. Canx.
EI-APZ	Not allocated.				
EI-AQA	Not allocated.				
EI-AQB	Not allocated.				
EI-AQC	Not allocated.				
EI-AQD	Not allocated.				
EI-AQE	Not allocated.				
EI-AQF	Not allocated.				
EI-AQG	Not allocated.				
EI-AQH	Not allocated.				
EI-AQI	Not allocated.				
EI-AQJ	Not allocated.				
EI-AQK	Not allocated.				
EI-AQL	Not allocated.				
EI-AQM	Not allocated.				
EI-AQN	Not allocated.				
EI-AQO	Not allocated.				
EI-AQP	Not allocated.				
EI-AQQ	Not allocated.				
EI-AQR	Not allocated.				
EI-AQS	Not allocated.				
EI-AQT	Not allocated.				
EI-AQU	Not allocated.				
EI-AQV	Not allocated.				
EI-AQW	Not allocated.				
EI-AQX	Not allocated.				
EI-AQY	Not allocated.				
EI-AQZ	Not allocated.				
EI-ARA	Miles SE.5A Replica	SEM.7282	G-ATGV	29. 5.67	Crashed at Weston, Ireland on 15.9.70. Canx 12.9.85.
EI-ARB	Miles SE.5A Replica	SEM.7283	G-ATGW	29. 5.67	Fatal crash after collision in mid-air with Alouette II G-AWEE over sea 1½ miles North of Wicklow Bay while filming on 18.8.70. Canx 12.9.85.
EI-ARC	Pfalz D.III Replica	PPS/Pfalz/1	G-ATIF	29. 5.67	To N906AC 5/85. Canx 28.5.85.
EI-ARD	Pfalz D.III Replica	PT.16	G-ATIJ	29. 5.67	To N905AC 5.85. Canx 28.5.85.
EI-ARE	SNCAN Stampe SV-4C	386	F-BBIT	2. 6.67	Crashed into River Liffey on 16.9.70. Canx.
EI-ARF	Caudron C.277 Luciole	7546/135	F-BNMB G-ATIP/F-AQFB	23. 5.68	To N907AC 5/85. Canx 28.5.85.
EI-ARG	Morane Saulnier MS.230	1049	F-BGMR	6. 5.68	To G-BJCL 7/81. Canx 21.7.81.
EI-ARH	Slingsby T.56 SE.5A Replica (Currie Wot)	1590	"A5435" EI-ARH/G-AVOT	21. 6.67	(Reported at Flabob, California 5/86)
EI-ARI	Slingsby T.56 SE.5A Replica (Currie Wot)	1591	"A4850" EI-ARI/G-AVOU	21. 6.67	To N908AC 5.85. Canx 28.5.85.
EI-ARJ	Slingsby T.56 SE.5A Replica (Currie Wot)	1592	"A7001" EI-ARJ/G-AVOV	21. 6.67	To N909AC 5.85. Canx 28.5.85.
EI-ARK	Slingsby T.56 SE.5A Replica (Currie Wot)	1593	"A5202" EI-ARK/G-AVOW	21. 6.67	To N910AC 5.85. Canx 28.5.85.
EI-ARL	Slingsby T.56 SE.5A Replica (Currie Wot)	1595	"A6262" EI-ARL/G-AVOY	21. 6.67	To N912AC 5.85. Canx 28.5.85.
EI-ARM	Slingsby T.56 SE.5A Replica (Currie Wot)	1594	"A1313" "A5435"/EI-ARM/G-AVOX	21. 6.67	Regd with c/n 1595, ex G-AVOY (Probably sold in USA)
EI-ARN	Wren 460 (Converted Cessna 182H)	182-56196/26	N2096X	12. 6.67	Crashed at Edenderry, Ireland on 16.5.80. Wreck to Abbeyshrule. Canx 22.9.80.
EI-ARO	Beagle A.61 Terrier 2 (Conversion of Auster AOP.6 c/n 2487)	B.645	(G-ARLN) TW629	20. 6.67	Crashed at Castlebar in 9/68. Canx.
EI-ARP	Douglas C-47B-30-DK Dakota	16262/33010	G-AMWW KN492/44-76678	18. 5.67	Restored as G-AMWW 6/67. Canx.
EI-ARQ	Not allocated.				
EI-ARR	Douglas C-47A-20-DK Dakota	13164	G-AKJH KG572/42-93271	14. 6.67	Restored as G-AKJH 12/67. Canx.
EI-ARS(1)	Lockheed L.1049G-82 Super Constellation	4672	CS-TLF XA-NAX/HS-TCA	. 7.67R	NTU - Remained as CS-TLF. Canx.
EI-ARS(2)	Douglas C-54E-5-DO Skymaster	27289	(LN-TUR) EI-ARS/HB-ILU/N88887/44-9063	9.12.69	Restored as N88887 in 8/77. Canx 22.6.77.
EI-ART	Fairchild-Hiller FH.1100	45		20. 6.67	To G-AYTE 2/71. Canx.
EI-ARU	Brantly 305	1035	G-ATYB N12H	14. 8.67	Stored in UK. Canx 9.1.68.
EI-ARV	DH.104 Dove 8A	04525	G-ARSN	16. 8.67	To Irish Air Corps as 201 in 12/70. Canx 18.12.70.
EI-ARW	SAN Jodel DR.1050 Ambassadeur	118	F-BJJH	14. 8.67	Badly damaged in crash Nr.Carnmore 28.7.86 (Stored 4/96)
EI-ARX	Not allocated.				
EI-ARY	Reims Cessna F.150H	0239		23.10.67	Crashed at Farranfore on 14.6.70. Canx.
EI-ARZ	Not allocated.				
EI-ASA	Boeing 737-248 (Line No. 147)	19424	9J-ADZ EI-ASA/(EI-APP)	23. 6.67	To F-GHML 2/90. Canx.

Regn	Type	c/n	Previous identity	Regn date	Fate or immediate subsequent identity (if known)
EI-ASB	Boeing 737-248	19425	PP-SRX	23. 6.67	To OB-R-1314. Canx 10.12.87.
	(Line No. 153)		EI-ASB/SU-AYX/EI-ASB/(EI-APS)		
EI-ASC	Boeing 737-248QC	20218	EC-DZB	5. 8.69	To F-GGFJ 11/90. Canx.
	(Line No. 199)		EI-ASC/PP-SNY/EI-ASC		
EI-ASD	Boeing 737-248QC	20219		1. 9.69	To CC-CEI 10/95. Canx 24.11.95.
	(Line No. 208)				
EI-ASE	Boeing 737-248QC	20220		1. 9.69	To 9M-PMP. Canx 26.3.94.
	(Line No. 215)				
EI-ASF	Boeing 737-248C	20221	C6-BFB	9.10.69	To OO-PHC. Canx.
	(Line No. 227)		EI-ASF/CF-ASF/EI-ASF		
EI-ASG	Boeing 737-248C	20222	HR-SHD	5. 1.70	Stored 10/91 Dublin, Eire. Broken up 1/95. Canx 22.8.95.
	(Line No. 240)		EI-ASG/N7360F/		(Forward fuselage to Ryanair as cabin trainer)
			EI-ASG/SU-AYT/EI-ASG		
EI-ASH	Boeing 737-248C	20223	HR-TNS	5. 1.70	To CC-CSL 10/95. Canx 20.10.95.
	(Line No. 252)		EI-ASH/C-GTAR/EI-ASH/N80AF/EI-ASH/N7361F/EI-ASH/		
			C-GTAR/EI-ASH/C-GTAR/EI-ASH/CF-TAR/EI-ASH		
EI-ASI	Boeing 747-148	19744	(TF-...)	20. 7.70	To 5N-ZZZ 2/97. Canx 14.2.97.
	(Line No. 84)		EI-ASI/HS-VGB/EI-ASI		
EI-ASJ	Boeing 747-148	19745	TF-ABN	20. 7.70	To 5N-AAA. Canx 14.2.97.
	(Line No. 108)		EI-ASJ/"G-BZBO"/EI-ASJ/(TF-...)/EI-ASJ/G-BDPZ/EI-ASJ/HS-VGF/EI-ASJ		
EI-ASK	Boeing 737-222	19947	N9066U	30. 5.74	Restored as N9066U 10/75. Canx.
	(Line No. 187)		EI-ASK/N9066U		
EI-ASL	Boeing 737-248C	21011		14.10.74	To F-GKTK. Canx 11/93.
	(Line No. 411)				
EI-ASM	Boeing 707-351C	19263	9J-AEB	3. 7.75	To 9J-AEB 1/76. Canx.
	(Line No. 516)		N370US/(VR-HHK)/N370US		
EI-ASN	Boeing 707-349C	18976	N323F	27. 3.69	To 9J-ADY 3/75. Canx.
	(Line No. 449)				
EI-ASO	Boeing 707-349C	19354	S2-ACB	1. 4.69	To N324F 12/86. Canx 30.10.86.
	(Line No. 503)		EI-ASB/9J-AEC/EI-ASO/9J-AEC/EI-ASO/G-BAWP/EI-ASO/VH-EBZ/EI-ASO/N324F		
EI-ASP	Percival P.40 Prentice T.1		G-AOLU	17.10.67	Restored as G-AOLU 10/72. Canx.
	(Also c/n 5830/3)	B3/1A/PAC/283	VS356		
EI-ASQ	Not allocated.				
EI-ASR(1)	BN-2A Islander	-		. .68R	NTU. Canx.
EI-ASR(2)	McCandless M.4 Gyroplane (VW)	M.4/5	G-AXHZ	29. 9.69	(Stored 4/96)
	(Originally regd with c/n M.4/4)				
EI-ASS	Not allocated.				
EI-AST	Reims Cessna F.150H	0273		30. 1.68	
EI-ASU	Beagle A.61 Terrier 2	B.633	G-ASRG	10. 1.68	Canx 15.6.77. (On rebuild 4/96 at Trim)
			WE599		
EI-ASV	PA-28R-180 Cherokee Arrow	28R-30219	G-AVWP	12. 2.68	DBF at Farrenfore, Ireland on 13.5.82. Canx.
EI-ASW	Bell 206A JetRanger	180		17. 4.68	To G-BADS 9/72. Canx.
EI-ASX	Not allocated.				
EI-ASY	PA-32-300 Cherokee Six	32-40108	G-AVFT	21. 5.68	To F-OCSS 11/72. Canx.
EI-ASZ	Not allocated.				
EI-ATA	Beagle A.109 Airedale	B.535	G-AWGA	24. 6.68	Restored as G-AWGA 7/69. Canx.
			D-ENRU		
EI-ATB	Cessna 310N	310N-0054	N4154Q	2. 9.68	To G-AWTA 11/68. Canx.
EI-ATC	Cessna 310G	310G-0050	G-ARWF	8.10.69	Crashed at Carrickfin, Co.Donegal on 10.1.79. WFU & sold to
			N8950Z		USA for parting out as spares. Canx 8.93.
EI-ATD	Beagle A.109 Airedale	B.510	G-ARXC	24.10.68	Restored as G-ARXC 7/69. Canx.
EI-ATE(1)	Beagle A.109 Airedale	B.509	G-ARXB	. 2.69R	NTU - Not Imported & remained as G-ARXB. Canx.
EI-ATE(2)	Campbell-Bensen B.8MS Gyrocopter	CA/311	G-AWLM	17. 9.69	Restored as G-AWLM 3/73. Canx.
EI-ATF(1)	Beagle B.121 Pup 150	B121-022	G-AWRC	12.11.68	NTU - To OH-BGD 3/69. Canx.
			G-35-022		
EI-ATF(2)	Cessna 182G Skylane	182-55135	G-ASRR	29. 3.70	To (G-CBIL)/G-ASRR 6/78. Canx 28.5.78.
			N3735U		
EI-ATG	Helio H.395 Super Courier	523	G-ARMU	14. 3.69	Restored as G-ARMU 5/70. Canx 20.5.70.
			N4172D/N13B		
EI-ATH(1)	Cessna 337A Super Skymaster	337-0484	N5384S	. .68R	NTU - To G-AXHA 6/69. Canx.
EI-ATH(2)	Reims Cessna F.150J	0426		5. 3.69	Blown over in a storm at Cork 10.3.82 & progressively
					stripped at Abbeyshrule since. Canx 16.5.86.
EI-ATI	PA-23-250 Aztec D	27-4069	N6735Y	2. 1.69	Crashed at Ballyfree on 8.8.70, rebuilt at Kidlington
					during 11/70 & re-regd as G-AYWY 4/71. Canx 9.3.71.
EI-ATJ	Beagle B.121 Pup Srs.150	B121-029	G-35-029	10. 2.69	
EI-ATK	PA-28-140 Cherokee	28-24120	G-AVUP	18.10.68	Badly damaged in crash at Connaught on 14.2.87
					(Stored - spares use 4/96)
EI-ATL	Aeronca 7AC Champion	7AC-4674	N1119E	22. 9.69	Damaged in gales Weston 26.11.75 (In storage in 1978)
EI-ATM	Piccard Ax6 HAFB	105	N3255	22. 7.69	Canx as WFU 26.7.75.
			N5W		
EI-ATN	PA-28-140 Cherokee	28-24468	G-AWEW	8. 5.69	Ditched in sea off Cork on 22.9.73. Canx 1.7.81.
EI-ATO	Aérospatiale SE.316B Alouette III	1517	G-AWXG	8. 7.70	Crashed into Irish Sea on 26.5.71. Canx 4.7.72.
			F-WIEQ		Salvaged and rebuilt as F-ZBAG 9/73.
EI-ATP	Phoenix Luton LA-4A Minor	PAL/1124	G-ASCY	29. 8.69	To USA 7/73. (On display in Concourse E 10/94, Miami Intl
					Airport, FL)
EI-ATQ	Not allocated.				
EI-ATR	Sud Aviation SE.210 Caravelle VI-R	110	EC-ARL	6. 8.73	To B-2503 8/73. Canx 21.8.73.
EI-ATS	Socata MS.880B Rallye Club	1582		20. 4.70	(Stored 4/96 Abbeyshrule - gone by 11/98)
EI-ATT	Douglas DC-7CF	45184	PH-DSE	13. 2.69	To TR-LQC 8/71. Canx.
	(Line No. 816)				

Regn	Type	c/n	Previous identity	Regn date	Fate or immediate subsequent identity (if known)
EI-ATU	Douglas DC-7CF (Line No. 820)	45185	PH-DSF	24. 2.69	To TR-LNY 5/70. Canx 13.5.70.
EI-ATV(1)	Douglas DC-7CF (Line No. 829)	45186	PH-DSG	. 3.69R	NTU - To EI-ATW(2). Canx.
EI-ATV(2)	Douglas DC-7CF (Line No. 837)	45188	(EI-ATW) PH-DSI	19. 3.69	To TR-LNZ 8/69. Canx.
EI-ATW(1)	Douglas DC-7CF (Line No. 837)	45188	PH-DSI	. 3.69R	NTU - To EI-ATV(2). Canx.
EI-ATW(2)	Douglas DC-7CF (Line No. 829)	45186	(EI-ATV) PH-DSG	26. 3.69	To (VP-WBP)/TR-LOJ 5/69. Canx.
EI-ATX	Not allocated.				
EI-ATY	Hughes H.369HM (500M)	49-0036M		28. 5.69	To G-BDKL 10/75. Canx 16.10.75.
EI-ATZ	Not allocated.				
EI-AUA	Hughes H.369HE (500HE)	59-0102E	N9012F	9. 6.69	To G-AYNK 12/70. Canx 8.12.70.
EI-AUB	DH.82A Tiger Moth	86509	F-BGCP French AF/NM201	26. 8.69	To N82JS 10/75. Canx 7.10.75.
EI-AUC(1)	BN-2A Islander	-		.12.69R	NTU. Canx.
EI-AUC(2)	Reims Cessna FA.150K Aerobat	0040		10. 4.70	Badly damaged in forced landing north of Weston on 15.7.99.
EI-AUD	Socata MS.880B Rallye Club	1605		7. 7.70	Involved in an accident after 25.6.83 - at Abbeyshrule 8/83 in damaged state. To spares use. Canx 3.6.86.
EI-AUE	Socata MS.880B Rallye Club	1359	G-AXHU	1. 4.70	
EI-AUF	BN-2A Islander	151	G-AXXK G-51-151	28. 5.70	Restored as G-AXXK 12/73. Canx.
EI-AUG	Socata MS.894A Rallye Minerva	220 11080		17. 6.70	
EI-AUH	Reims Cessna F.172H	0727		28. 7.70	W/o at Kilkenny, Ireland in 5/72. Canx 28.8.86. Scrapped 1995.
EI-AUI	SNIAS SE.313B Alouette II	1648	G-BANR EI-AUI/Belgian Army OL-A/South Vietnam AF 1648	10. 7.70	To G-FILM 5/80. Canx 13.5.80.
EI-AUJ	Socata MS.880B Rallye Club	1370	G-AXHF F-BNGV	12. 6.70	Crashed at Inishman, Aran Islands on 27.8.81. (Stored 11/98 at Abbeyshrule)
EI-AUK	DH.104 Dove 6	04446	G-ANGU G-5-15	11. 8.70	Repossessed in the early 1970's & scrapped at Baginton. Canx 12.9.85.
EI-AUL	BN-2A-26 Islander	180	G-51-180	22. 6.70	To G-BAVT 4/73. Canx.
EI-AUM	Auster J/1 Autocrat	2612	G-AJRN (PH-...)/G-AJRN	11. 9.70	(On rebuild 6/96)
EI-AUN	Socata MS.880B Rally Club	1616	G-AXHH F-WNGU	10. 6.70	DBR near Dublin Airport on 15.7.80. Remains at Abbeyshrule. Canx 22.4.81.
EI-AUO	Reims Cessna FA.150K Aerobat	0074	"EI-ALL"	2. 3.71	(Was incorrectly painted as EI-ALL at Reims in 9/70 prior to delivery)
EI-AUP	Socata MS.880B Rallye Club	1143	G-AVVK	30. 9.70	DBR at Coonagh, Ireland on 1.9.83. Canx 19.5.88. (Stored - spares use 10/98 at Abbeyshrule)
EI-AUQ	Not allocated.				
EI-AUR	Bolkow Bo.208C Junior 3	600	G-ATOC D-ECGU	19.11.70	Canx 1.5.80.
EI-AUS	Auster J/5F Aiglet Trainer	2779	G-AMRL	10.11.70	Canx 4.6.76. (On rebuild 4/95)
EI-AUT	Forney F.1A Aircoupe	5731	G-ARXS D-EBSA/N3037G	21.12.70	(Stored 4/96)
EI-AUU	Morane-Saulnier MS.500	637	F-BJQG French Mil	30.10.70	To G-AZMH 1/72. Canx.
EI-AUV	PA-23-250 Aztec C	27-2554	(EI-BCJ) N80WT/EI-AUV/N80WT/OO-LAB/HB-LAB	30.11.70	Canx 13.1.84. Stored at Shannon 1984. Scrapped in 1985.
EI-AUW	Cessna 310K	310K-0190	N7090L	. .70R	NTU - To LX-ADP 6/74. Canx.
EI-AUX	Not allocated.				
EI-AUY	Morane-Saulnier MS.502 Cricquet	338	F-BCDG French Mil	30.11.70	(On display 7/99 at Duxford; painted in Luftwaffe c/s "CF+HF")
EI-AUZ	Not allocated.				
EI-AVA	Reims Cessna F.172K	0762		1. 7.71	w/o late 1979 Castlebridge, Ireland. Fuselage taken to UK 5/80 for disposal. Canx 11.7.79.
EI-AVB	Aeronca 7AC Champion	7AC-1790	7P-AXK ZS-AXK	14. 6.71	Canx 17.1.86. Reserved as N151JC 11/97.
EI-AVC	Reims Cessna F.337F Super Skymaster (Wichita c/n 01355)	0032	N4757	26. 8.71	
EI-AVD	PA-30-160 Twin Comanche B	30-1613	G-AVVI N8454Y	10. 6.71	Restored as G-AVVI 20.8.71. Canx 8/71.
EI-AVE(1)	BN-2A-26 Islander	623	G-AYJE	. .71R	NTU - Remained as G-AYJE & to CR-CAS 9/71. Canx.
EI-AVE(2)	PA-18-95 Super Cub	18-7375	G-ARCT	9. 1.73	Restored as G-ARCT. Canx 16.11.77.
EI-AVF	Cessna 337B Super Skymaster	337B-0555	5H-MNL N5455S	3. 3.71	To G-BBBL 6/73. Canx.
EI-AVG	Beechcraft 95-B55 Baron	TC-30	D-INOX HB-GCN/N8888Z	5.11.71	To D-IMGH 10/82. Canx 9.6.82.
EI-AVH	PA-28R-200 Cherokee Arrow B	28R-7135151		8. 9.71	To G-BAZU 6/73. Canx.
EI-AVI	Aérospatiale 316B Alouette III	1790		1. 9.71	Returned to SNIAS 1.3.73. To F-ZBAH(2) 9/81. Canx.
EI-AVJ	AW.650 Argosy 222	6801	CF-TAG G-ASXM	5.11.71	Restored as CF-TAG 11/71. Canx.
EI-AVK	Brantly B.2B	330	G-ASLO N2168U	19.10.71	Restored as G-ASLO 3/73. Canx.
EI-AVL	Auster J/5F Aiglet Trainer	2783	G-AMTD	24. 1.72	Restored as G-AMTD 10/84. Canx 16.10.84.
EI-AVM	Reims Cessna F.150L	0745		3. 3.72	
EI-AVN	Hughes 369HM (500M)	52-0214M	N9037F	15. 8.72	To G-RAMM 7/93. Canx 7/93.
EI-AVO	BN-2A-2 Islander	285	G-AZBV G-51-285	24. 3.72	To 4X-AYK 7/73. Canx 2.7.73.

Regn	Type	c/n	Previous identity	Regn date	Fate or immediate subsequent identity (if known)
EI-AVP(1)	Beagle A.109 Airedale	B.507	G-ARRO	. 6.72R	NTU - Remained as G-ARRO. Canx.
EI-AVP(2)	Aero Commander 680FP	1385-145	F-BNFG N6304U	28.12.72	To F-BNPE 5/75. Canx 2.5.75.
EI-AVQ	Not allocated.				
EI-AVR	Aero Commander 112	0073	(N1073J)	21. 5.73	To G-BDEJ 6/75. Canx 20.5.75.
EI-AVS	PA-30-160 Twin Comanche	30-123	G-AVGT N7105Y	7. 7.72	Restored as G-AVGT on 28.8.73. Canx.
EI-AVT	SNCAN Stampe SV-4C	399	F-BHQN F-BCQN	11. 9.72	Crashed near Castlebridge, Ireland on 6.6.76. Canx.
EI-AVU	AIA Stampe SV-4C	1060	F-BAUR	14. 7.72	To N901AC 5/85. Canx 28.5.85.
EI-AVV	American Aviation AA-1 Yankee	AA1-0445	G-AYLP	28. 8.72	Restored as G-AYLP 7/73. Canx.
EI-AVW	Auster J/1N Alpha	3384	G-APKD	15. 8.72	Canx 8.10.74. To VH-KSP 12/92.
EI-AVX	Not allocated.				
EI-AVY	Sud Aviation SE.210 Caravelle VI-R	109	EC-ARJ F-WJAM	6. 8.73	NTU - To B-2501 8/73. Canx 21.8.73.
EI-AVZ	Not allocated.				
EI-AWA	Bell 206B JetRanger II	897		7.12.72	To G-COIN 3/85. Canx 8.3.85.
EI-AWB	MBB Bo.105D	S.21	G-AZOM D-HDAD	31.10.72	Restored as G-AZOM 1/78. Canx 10.1.78.
EI-AWC	Sud SA.318C Alouette II	1997	G-AWFL	30. 1.73	Crashed at Vincent O'Brien Stables, Cashel, Co.Tipperary on 15.5.74. Canx 23.10.74.
EI-AWD	PA-22-160 Tri-Pacer	22-6411	G-APXV N9437D	17. 1.73	Blown over in gales Cork 12.81. (Stored .89)
EI-AWE	Reims Cessna F.150L	0877		22. 2.73	
EI-AWF	Reims Cessna F.337E Super Skymaster (Wichita c/n 01242)	0009	G-AYFB	26. 5.72	Restored as G-AYFB 9/75. Canx 12.9.75.
EI-AWG	Douglas DC-7CF (Line No. 965)	45471	N4041 SE-CCI/JA6305	10.11.72	DBR 3.3.74 Luton, UK. Canx.
EI-AWH	Cessna 210J Centurion	210-59067	G-AZCC (EI-AWH)/G-AZCC/5N-AIE/N1734C/(N6167F)	19. 1.73	
EI-AWI	Piccard AX-6 HAFB	642		16. 1.73	To USA. Canx 16.9.75.
EI-AWJ	Socata MS.893A Rallye Commodore 180	10664	G-AVAK	15.12.72	Restored as G-AVAK 9/82. Canx 13.9.82.
EI-AWK	Bell 212	30542	G-BALZ VR-BEK/N2961W	19. 3.73	Restored as G-BALZ 16.7.74.
EI-AWL	PA-28R-200 Cherokee Arrow II	28R-7235289	G-BAHZ	30. 1.73	Restored as G-BAHZ. Canx 17.9.79.
EI-AWM	IRMA BN-2A-8 Islander	653	G-AYXE	29. 5.73	To G-OWIN 3/83. Canx 21.3.83.
EI-AWN	Bell 212	30563	G-BARJ EI-AWN/G-BARJ	28. 5.73	Restored as G-BARJ 18.11.74.
EI-AWO	Douglas DC-7BF (Line No. 923)	45238	F-BTAY F-OCOQ/SE-ERS/N752Z/N341AA	3. 5.73	To N90712 6/74.
EI-AWP	DH.82A Tiger Moth	85931	F-BGCL French AF/DF195	4. 7.72	
EI-AWQ	Not allocated.				
EI-AWR	Malmo MFI-9 Junior (C/n originally quoted as 01-1963)	010	LN-HAG (SE-EBW)	12. 6.73	
EI-AWS	PA-34-200 Seneca II	34-7350007	G-BAGZ N15067	12. 6.73	Restored as G-BAGZ 5/77. Canx 6.5.77.
EI-AWT	PA-34-200 Seneca II	34-7350164	N55034	26. 6.73	To D-GNUT 10/76. Canx 6.8.76.
EI-AWU	Socata MS.880B Rallye Club	880	G-AVIM	12. 1.74	(Status uncertain)
EI-AWV	American Aviation AA-5 Traveler	AA5-0319	G-BASH N5419L	20. 7.73	Restored as G-BASH. Canx 26.8.80.
EI-AWW	Cessna 414 Chancellor II	414-0163	OY-AKI (N8233Q)	11. 5.73	To N414SD. Canx 14.2.94.
EI-AWX	Not allocated.				
EI-AWY	Mitsubishi MU-2B-35J	617	N467MA	11. 3.74	To (N467MA)/N8484T. Canx 13.10.80.
EI-AWZ	Not allocated.				
EI-AXA	Not allocated.				
EI-AXB	Not allocated.				
EI-AXC	Not allocated.				
EI-AXD	Not allocated.				
EI-AXE	Not allocated.				
EI-AXF	Not allocated.				
EI-AXG	Not allocated.				
EI-AXH	Not allocated.				
EI-AXI	Not allocated.				
EI-AXJ	Not allocated.				
EI-AXK	Not allocated.				
EI-AXL	Not allocated.				
EI-AXM	Not allocated.				
EI-AXN	Not allocated.				
EI-AXO	Not allocated.				
EI-AXP	Not allocated.				
EI-AXQ	Not allocated.				
EI-AXR	Not allocated.				
EI-AXS	Not allocated.				
EI-AXT	Not allocated.				
EI-AXU	Not allocated.				
EI-AXV	Not allocated.				
EI-AXW	Not allocated.				
EI-AXX	Not allocated.				

Regn	Type	c/n	Previous identity	Regn date	Fate or immediate subsequent identity (if known)
EI-AXY	Not allocated.				
EI-AXZ	Not allocated.				
EI-AYA	Socata MS.880B Rallye Club	2256	G-BAON	27. 7.73	
EI-AYB	Gardan GY-80-180 Horizon	156	F-BNQP	5.10.73	
EI-AYC	American Aviation AA-5 Traveler	AA5-0381	G-BAZF N5481L	5. 9.73	Restored as G-BAZF 7/76. Canx 9.7.76.
EI-AYD	American Aviation AA-5 Traveler	AA5-0300	G-BAZE N5400L	5. 9.73	
EI-AYE	PA-28R-200 Cherokee Arrow II	28R-7335297	(G-BBEH) N55837	7. 9.73	To G-BDKV 10/75. Canx 27.10.75.
EI-AYF	Reims Cessna FRA.150L Aerobat	0218		26. 3.74	
EI-AYG	PA-39-160 Twin Comanche C/R	39-91	G-AYZP N8933Y	21. 2.74	To G-BEFW 10/76. Canx.
EI-AYH	Cessna 172B	172-48211	G-ARFK N7711X	11.11.73	DBR at Elstree, UK on 3.1.81. Canx 21.1.81.
EI-AYI	Socata MS.880B Rallye Club	189	F-OBXE	21.11.73	Damaged at Dungany/Trim 25.3.83. Canx.
EI-AYJ	Cessna 182P Skylane II	182-62470	N52229	21. 3.74	w/o 19.9.76. Canx 16.6.81. Fuselage remains at Dublin, Ireland 1981.
EI-AYK	Reims Cessna F.172M Skyhawk II	1092		25. 3.74	
EI-AYL(1)	American American AA-5 Traveler	AA5-0383	G-BBDA	. .74R	NTU - Remained as G-BBDA. Canx.
EI-AYL(2)	Beagle A.109 Airedale	B.507	G-ARRO (EI-AVP)/G-ARRO	12. 3.74	Stored - for rebuild 4/96.
EI-AYM	American Aviation AA-5 Traveler	AA5-0440	G-BBLS	1. 3.74	Restored as G-BBLS 8/74. Canx 16.8.74.
EI-AYN	IRMA BN-2A-8 Islander	704	G-BBFJ	26. 3.74	(On overhaul 6/98)
EI-AYO(1)	Reims Cessna F.172M Skyhawk II	1137		. 5.74R	NTU - To PH-DMF 6/74. Canx.
EI-AYO(2)	Douglas DC-3A-197	1911	N655GP N65556/N255JB/N8695E/N333H/NC16071	5. 3.76	The Science Museum (On display 9/93) Wroughton. Canx 27.10.78.
EI-AYP	Bell 206B JetRanger II	1294		2. 7.74	To C-GOEV 7/75. Canx 9.7.75.
EI-AYQ	Not allocated.				
EI-AYR	Schleicher ASK-16	16022		5. 4.74	(Probably also EI-119)
EI-AYS	PA-22-108 Colt	22-8448	G-ARKT	28. 6.74	
EI-AYT(1)	PA-23 Aztec	-		. .74R	NTU - Canx.
EI-AYT(2)	American Aviation AA-5 Traveler	-		. .74R	NTU - Canx.
EI-AYT(3)	Socata MS.894A Rallye Minerva 220	11065	G-AXIU	6. 8.74	Badly damaged in forced landing en route Weston/Coonagh 12.11.89 (Stored - for spares 4/96)
EI-AYU	Brunswick LF-1 Zaunkoenig	V-2	G-ALUA VX190/D-YBAR	1. 5.74	Whilst returning to Germany for preservation it was impounded at Calais. Canx 21.5.76. To D-EBCQ 5/87.
EI-AYV(1)	American Aviation AA-5 Traveler	AA5-0471	G-BBRZ	. .74R	NTU - Remained as G-BBRZ. Canx.
EI-AYV(2)	Socata MS.892A Rallye Commodore 150	10482	F-BLSP	27. 8.74	
EI-AYW	PA-23-250 Aztec C	27-2933	N5801Y	6. 5.75	w/o at Shannon, Ireland in 9/80 & used for spares. Canx.
EI-AYX	Not allocated.				
EI-AYY	Evans VP-1	MD-01 & SAAC-03		18. 8.75	
EI-AYZ	Not allocated.				
EI-AZA	Not allocated.				
EI-AZB	Not allocated.				
EI-AZC	Not allocated.				
EI-AZD	Not allocated.				
EI-AZE	Not allocated.				
EI-AZF	Not allocated.				
EI-AZG	Not allocated.				
EI-AZH	Not allocated.				
EI-AZI	Not allocated.				
EI-AZJ	Not allocated.				
EI-AZK	Not allocated.				
EI-AZL	Not allocated.				
EI-AZM	Not allocated.				
EI-AZN	Not allocated.				
EI-AZO	Not allocated.				
EI-AZP	Not allocated.				
EI-AZQ	Not allocated.				
EI-AZR	Not allocated.				
EI-AZS	Not allocated.				
EI-AZT	Not allocated.				
EI-AZU	Not allocated.				
EI-AZV	Not allocated.				
EI-AZW	Not allocated.				
EI-AZX	Not allocated.				
EI-AZY	Not allocated.				
EI-AZZ	Not allocated.				
EI-BAA	Bristol 175 Britannia 307F	12921	G-ANCE G-18-3/(N6596C)/G-ANCE	20. 5.74	WFU 4/79. Broken up 5/81 Dublin for spares. Canx 27.5.81.
EI-BAB	Socata MS.894E Rallye Minerva 220GT	12195	(S9-NAF) EI-BAB/(G-BLPN)/EI-BAB	20. 6.74	To G-VAJT 7/89. Canx.
EI-BAC	PA-34-200 Seneca II	34-7450185	N43320	12. 7.74	To D-GDEB 9/76. Canx 18.3.76.
EI-BAD	Cessna 185A	185-0285	9XR-DA N4085Y	15. 7.74	NTU - To 5Y-BAD 9/74. Canx 17.9.74.
EI-BAE	PA-31-310 Turbo Navajo	31-700	G-AYUF N6790L	14. 6.74	Restored as G-AYUF 10/77. Canx 7.10.77.

Regn	Type	c/n	Previous identity	Regn date	Fate or immediate subsequent identity (if known)
EI-BAF	Thunder Ax6-56 HAFB	027	G-BCFU	31. 7.74	CofA expired 31.7.86. WFU in 1990 at Kinnitty, Ireland. To British Balloon Museum in 3/95. Canx 3.9.98 as removed from service.
EI-BAG	Cessna 172A	172-47571	G-ARAV N9771T	7. 8.74	Damaged late 5.78. Canx 3.4.80. (On rebuild 4/96)
EI-BAH	Rockwell Commander 681B Hawk	6060	F-BTFG N9142N	28. 1.75	To F-BXPV. Canx 3.11.75.
EI-BAI	CEA Jodel DR.1050/M1 Sicile Record	622	G-AYYO F-BMPZ	15. 9.74	Restored as G-AYYO 6/76. Canx 21.6.76.
EI-BAJ	SNCAN Stampe SV-4C	171	F-BBPN	17.10.74	Reportedly badly damaged in forced landing in 8/99.
EI-BAK	Naval Aircraft Factory N3N-3	2633	N45037 (EI-BAK)/N45037/2633	.10.74	To EI-BEY 5/78. Canx.
EI-BAL	Beagle A.109 Airedale	B.515	G-ARZS	17.10.74	(Stored 4/96)
EI-BAM	Bell 212	30655	G-BCPY	15.11.74	To ZK-HNK 8/83. Canx 18.8.83.
EI-BAN	Cameron O-65 HAFB (Irish Register originally quoted type as a Piccard Ax6 HAFB with same c/n)	148		31.12.74	To G-BKJT 10/82. Canx 11.10.82.
EI-BAO	Reims Cessna F.172G	0278	G-ATNH	11. 2.75	
EI-BAP	Piper J3C-90 Cub (L-4H-PI) (Frame No 10932; Official identity c/n 12499 & 44-80203, probably rebuilt 1945)	11098	F-BFBZ 44-80203/43-29807	30. 1.75	To G-SEED 1/80. Canx 2.1.80.
EI-BAQ	Not allocated.				
EI-BAR	Thunder Ax8-105 HAFB	014	G-BCAM	26. 2.75	
EI-BAS	Reims Cessna F.172M Skyhawk II	1262		2. 5.75	
EI-BAT	Reims Cessna F.150M	1196		2. 5.75	
EI-BAU	AIA Stampe SV-4C	1096	G-BALA F-BKOF/French Mil	29. 4.75	Restored as G-BALA. Canx 10.10.87.
EI-BAV	PA-22-108 Colt	22-8347	G-ARKO	30. 4.75	(Stored 4/96)
EI-BAW	PA-23-160 Apache	23-1686	G-APFV EI-ALK	12. 5.75	To G-MOLY 6/79. Canx 5.6.79.
EI-BAX	Not allocated.				
EI-BAY(1)	Cameron O-84 HAFB (Originally regd as Cameron Ax8-84 HAFB)	016	G-AYJZ	28. 5.75	Rebuilt as EI-BAY(2). Canx 1.80. To British Balloon Museum & Library.
EI-BAY(2)	Cameron V-77 HAFB	433	G-BFYK	. 1.80	Restored as G-BFYK 4/92. Canx 16.4.92.
EI-BAZ	Not allocated.				
EI-BBA	BN-2A-26 Islander	444	G-BCZV	12. 6.75	W/o at Inishmore, Ireland on 16.10.75. Used as spares. Canx 21.12.76.
EI-BBB	Rockwell Commander 112A	221	N1221J	25. 8.75	DBR at Weston, Ireland on 26.10.81. Canx.
EI-BBC	PA-28-180 Cherokee B	28-1049	G-ASEJ	18. 6.75	
EI-BBD	Evans VP-1	VP-1-No.2 & SAAC-02		13. 8.76	(On rebuild following an accident at Gowran Grange in 8/81)
EI-BBE	Champion 7FC Tri-Traveler	7FC-393	G-APZW	7. 9.75	(Tail wheel conversion equivalent to 7EC Traveler)
EI-BBF(1)	Evans VP-1	-		. .75R	NTU. Canx.
EI-BBF(2)	EAA P-2 Sport Biplane	1 & SAAC-01		5.11.86	To G-BPUA 3/89. Canx 20.1.89.
EI-BBG	Socata MS.880B Rallye 100ST	2592		27.10.75	(Stored 5/96)
EI-BBH	Bristol 175 Britannia 253F	13436	XM491	5. 9.75	To 9Q-CMO(2) 11/81. Canx 30.11.81.
EI-BBI	Socata MS.892E Rallye Commodore 150ST	2663		13.10.75	In damaged state at Abbeyshrule 4/86.
EI-BBJ	Socata MS.880B Rallye 100S	2361	F-BUVX	7.11.75	
EI-BBK	Beagle A.109 Airedale	B.509	G-ARXB (EI-ATE)/G-ARXB	18.11.75	In damaged state at Abbeyshrule 4/86. (Stored - for rebuild 4/96)
EI-BBL	Rockwell Commander 690A	11119	F-BPQQ N471SC/N57119	11.12.75	To N65169. Canx 9/90.
EI-BBM	Cameron O-65 HAFB (Originally regd as Cameron Ax7-56 HAFB)	195		14. 1.76	(Now uses original canopy from EI-BGT & basket from EI-ANP)
EI-BBN	Reims Cessna F.150M	1281		27. 4.76	Canx 23.6.98 as destroyed.
EI-BBO	Socata MS.893E Rallye 180GT	12522	F-BVNM	8. 3.76	
EI-BBP	Socata MS.893E Rallye 180GT	12483	F-BVNB	8. 3.76	Crashed nr Cahir, Co.Tipperary, Ireland on 20.9.76. Canx.
EI-BBQ	Not allocated.				
EI-BBR	BN-2A-26 Islander	472	F-BVOE G-BDJS	13. 3.76	DBR near Galway, Ireland on 7.7.80. Canx 12.9.85.
EI-BBS(1)	PA-30-160 Twin Comanche B	30-1002	G-ATSZ (AN-...)/G-ATSZ/N7912Y	. .76R	NTU - To EI-BPS 3/85. Canx.
EI-BBS(2)	PA-28-180 Cherokee Challenger G	28-7305474	G-BBHY N9508N	5. 4.76	Restored as G-BBHY 2/81. Canx 4.2.81.
EI-BBT	Aviamilano F.8L Falco 3	216	G-APXD	10. 6.76	To N304SF 7/81. Canx 7.7.81.
EI-BBU	Morane MS.880B Rallye Club	1951	G-AZKF	27. 7.76	DBR in 1980. Canx 19.6.81.
EI-BBV	Piper J3C-65 Cub (L-4J-PI) (Frame No. 12888)	13058	D-ELWY F-BEGB/44-80762	14. 6.76	Noted dismantled at Weston in 5.97 with marks taped over following an incident several weeks previously at Kilrush or Hackettstown.
EI-BBW	Socata MS.894A Rallye Minerva 220	12003	G-BCLT F-BTRL	10. 5.76	Restored as G-BCLT 4/89. Canx 31.3.89.
EI-BBX	Not allocated.				
EI-BBY	Bristol 175 Britannia 253F	13455	XL658	18. 6.76	DBR on landing at Shannon, Ireland 30.9.77. Broken up at Shannon, Ireland. Canx 12.9.85.
EI-BBZ	Not allocated.				
EI-BCA	Hiller 360 UH-12E	2292	G-BDYY XS705	19. 7.76	Crashed at Tallagh on 31.7.77. Canx 2.3.78. Restored as G-BDYY 30.11.78.
EI-BCB	Morane MS.880B Rallye Club 100T	2513	F-BVHU	25. 5.76	w/o on 19.12.76. Canx 25.6.81.
EI-BCC	Boeing 737-219 (Line No. 428)	21131	(PH-TVM) EI-BCC/ZK-NAQ/N8293V	9. 7.76	To N7362F 10/77. Canx 17.10.77.
EI-BCD	PA-34-200 Seneca	34-7250011	PH-AVM N1978T	19. 8.76	To G-BETT 6/77. Canx 26.5.77.
EI-BCE	BN-2A-26 Islander	519	G-BDUV	14. 9.76	

Regn	Type	c/n	Previous identity	Regn date	Fate or immediate subsequent identity (if known)
EI-BCF	Bensen B.8M Gyrocopter	47491	N.....	24. 8.76	(C/n also quoted as 47941 - which is correct?)
EI-BCG	Cessna T.310Q II	T310Q-0641	G-BAKE N8404F	15. 9.76	To D-IEBE 5/79. Canx 16.5.79.
EI-BCH	GEMS MS.892A Rallye Commodore 150	10561	G-ATIW	17. 9.76	Canx 20.3.80. WFU believed due to corrosion.
EI-BCI	Bristol 175 Britannia 253F	13449	(CS-...) EI-BCI/XL640	7.10.76	To G-BHAU 8/79. Canx 10.8.79.
EI-BCJ(1)	PA-23-250 Aztec C	27-2554	N80WT EI-AUV/N80WT/OO-LAB/HB-LAB	. .76R	NTU - Restored as EI-AUV 1/77. Canx.
EI-BCJ(2)	Aeromere F.8L Falco 3	204	G-ATAK D-ENYB	19. 1.77	(On rebuild 6/97)
EI-BCK	Reims Cessna F.172N Skyhawk II	1543		22.11.76	
EI-BCL	Cessna 182P Skylane II (Reims assembled with c/n 0045)	182-64300	N1366M	22.11.76	
EI-BCM	Piper J3C-65 Cub (L-4H-PI)	11983	F-BNAV N9857F/44-79687	26.11.76	
EI-BCN	Piper J3C-65 Cub (L-4H-PI)	12335	F-BFQE OO-PIE/44-80039	26.11.76	
EI-BCO	Piper J3C-65 Cub	"1"	F-BBIV	26.11.76	(Not yet converted and stored)
EI-BCP	Rollason-Druine D.62B Condor	RAE/618	G-AVCZ	27. 1.77	DBR whilst en-route Abbeyshrule-Gowran Grange on 16/17.8.80. Remains dumped at Abbeyshrule. Canx 16.1.81.
EI-BCQ	Not allocated.				
EI-BCR	Boeing 737-281 (Line No. 231)	20276	9Q-CNL JA8403	19. 1.77	To N20727/4X-BAG 10/96. Canx 26.7.96.
EI-BCS	Socata MS.880B Rallye Club 100T	2550	F-BVZV	4. 2.77	
EI-BCT	Cessna 411A	411A-0274	G-AVEK N3274R	10. 8.77	To G-BVGC 11/93. Canx 11/93.
EI-BCU	Socata MS.880B Rallye Club 100T	2595	F-BXTH	10. 2.77	(Stored dismantled 12/98 Weston)
EI-BCV	Reims Cessna F.150M Commuter	1415		16. 3.77	To G-BOBV 12/87. Canx 11.12.87.
EI-BCW	Socata MS.880B Rallye Club	1783	G-AYKE	18. 4.77	(Stored 6/97 Abbeyshrule - gone by 11/98)
EI-BCX	Not allocated.				
EI-BCY	Beechcraft A200 Super King Air	BB-208	SE-GRR	7. 4.77	To Irish Air Corps as 232. Canx.
EI-BCZ	Not allocated.				
EI-BDA	PA-22-108 Colt	22-8466	G-ARNC	13. 6.77	DBR at Cork, Ireland on 5.12.78. Canx 8.8.79.
EI-BDB	Socata MS.880B Rallye Club 100ST	2924		26. 4.77	DBR at Mt.Kippure, Dublin, Ireland on 28.7.78. Canx 25.6.81.
EI-BDC	Bristol 175 Britannia 253F	13448	XL639	24. 5.77	To G-BRAC 6/78. Canx 2.6.78.
EI-BDD	PA-34-200 Seneca	34-7250221	G-AZZS N5212T	29. 6.77	Restored as G-AZZS 6/83. Canx 20.6.83.
EI-BDE	Colt Ax7-77A HAFB (Original canopy c/n 003 replaced)	384		24. 5.77	To G-BJUY 12/81. Canx 12.9.85.
EI-BDF	Enstrom F-28A-UK	103	G-BAHU	6. 9.77	Restored as G-BAHU 2/81. Canx 2.2.81.
EI-BDG	Robin HR.100/210 Royal	145	G-BAEC	13. 7.77	Restored as G-BAEC 12/80. Canx 19.12.80.
EI-BDH	Socata MS.880B Rallye Club	1270	G-AWOB	18. 7.77	(Status uncertain - probably scrapped)
EI-BDI	MBB Bo.105C	S.211	D-HDGB	26. 7.77	Ditched off Donegal coast, nr Blasket Islands, Ireland on 3.6.81. Remains recovered and sold for scrap in UK. Canx 12.9.85.
EI-BDJ	Colt Ax7-77A HAFB	006		22. 7.77	Canx 25.4.78. To G-BFRG.
EI-BDK	Socata MS.880B Rallye Club 100T	2561	F-BXMZ	10. 8.77	(Stored 11/98 at Abbeyshrule)
EI-BDL	Evans VP-2	V2-2101 & PFA/7213 & SAAC-04		7. 9.77	
EI-BDM	PA-23-250 Aztec D	27-4166	G-AXIV N6826Y	7.10.77	Dismantled at Dublin in 4/85. (To SE Aviation Enthusiasts Museum) (Stored 4/96)
EI-BDN	PA-23-250 Aztec D	27-4306	G-AXOW N6946Y	14. 3.78	Restored as G-AXOW 5/79. Canx 15.3.79.
EI-BDO	Reims Cessna F.152 II	1457		11.11.77	Ditched at Youghal Harbour, Co.Cork, Ireland on 8.6.85. Wreck recovered & scrapped. Canx 22.8.86.
EI-BDP	Cessna 182P Skylane II	182-60867	G-AZLC N9327G	14.11.77	Damaged .88 (Derelict airframe stored 11/98 at Abbeyshrule) Canx as WFU 27.11.98.
EI-BDQ	Not allocated.				
EI-BDR	PA-28-180 Cherokee C	28-3980	G-BAAO LN-AEL/(SE-FAG)	8.12.77	
EI-BDS	Socata MS.894A Rallye Minerva 220	11678	F-BSFT	2.12.77	Canx 12.11.82.
EI-BDT(1)	Douglas C-47A-50-DL Dakota	10144	F-BCYX 42-24282	6.12.77R	NTU - remained as F-BCYX. Canx.
EI-BDT(2)	Douglas C-47B-30-DK Dakota	16124/32872	G-AMPZ TF-AIV/G-41-3-66/(PH-RIC)/G-AMPZ/OD-AEQ/G-AMPZ/KN442/44-76540	15. 9.78	Restored as G-AMPZ 1/82. Canx 28.1.82.
EI-BDU(1)	Douglas C-47-DL Dakota	4398	F-BCYT 41-18360	. 3.78R	NTU - remained as F-BCYT. Canx.
EI-BDU(2)	Douglas C-47-DL Dakota	9043	G-AKNB XY-ACN/G-AKNB/FD789/42-32817	20.10.78	Restored as G-AKNB 1/82. Canx 28.1.82.
EI-BDV	PA-32-260 Cherokee Six	32-99	G-ATVC N3269W	31. 1.78	DBR at Birr, Ireland on 14.1.79. Canx 12.9.85.
EI-BDW	PA-31-350 Navajo Chieftain	31-7852082	PH-EWD EI-BDW/N27606	19. 5.78	To OY-ATP 10/79. Canx 12.10.79.
EI-BDX	Not allocated.				
EI-BDY	Boeing 737-2E1 (Line No. 424)	21112	G-BNYT EI-BDY/C-GNDD/EI-BDY/CN-RML/EI-BDY/(EI-BEA)/C-GEPB/N70720/C-GEPB/N4039W/C-GEPB	31. 3.78	To CC-CYT 3/95. Canx 13.2.95.

Regn	Type	c/n	Previous identity	Regn date	Fate or immediate subsequent identity (if known)
EI-BDZ	Not allocated.				
EI-BEA(1)	Boeing 737-2E1	21112	C-GEPB	. .77R	NTU - To EI-BDY 3/78. Canx.
	(Line No. 424)		N70720/C-GEPB/N4039W/C-GEPB		
EI-BEA(2)	Socata MS.880B Rallye 100ST	3007		28. 2.78	(Fuselage only stored 12/98 Weston)
EI-BEB	Boeing 737-248	21714	VT-EWH	15. 3.79	To N1714T 10/97. Canx 20.10.97.
	(Line No. 565)		EI-BEB/VT-EWH/EI-BEB		
EI-BEC	Boeing 737-248	21715	VT-EWI	15. 3.79	To N1715Z 10/97. Canx 17.10.97.
	(Line No. 579)		EI-BEC/VT-EWI/EI-BEC/TF-VLM/EI-BEC		
EI-BED	Boeing 747-130	19748	D-ABYC	5. 1.79	Stored 10/94 Dublin, Eire. For spares use 1995. Stored 2/95
	(Line No. 44)				Marana, AZ. Broken up. Canx 25.7.96.
EI-BEE	Boeing 737-281	20413	C6-BEC	2. 5.80	To 4X-BAF. Canx 5/93.
	(Line No. 241)		(EI-BEE)/JA8406		
EI-BEF	Boeing 737-281	20449	OB-R-1263	8. 8.79	To N142AW 9/84. Canx 10.9.84.
	(Line No. 259)		EI-BEF/JA8408		
EI-BEG	Short SD.3-30 Var.100	SH3092	G-BKMU	30. 3.83	To EI-BEH 5/83. Canx.
			G-14-3092		
EI-BEH	Short SD.3-30 Var.100	SH3092	EI-BEG	6. 5.83	Restored as G-14-3092/G-BKMU 11/84. Canx 9.11.84.
			G-BKMU/G-14-3092		
EI-BEI	Not allocated (Was reserved for Aer Lingus Teoranta 23.11.77)				
EI-BEJ	Not allocated (Was reserved for Aer Lingus Teoranta 23.11.77)				
EI-BEK	Short SD.3-60 Var.200	SH3635	G-BLED	22. 2.84	To G-CLAS 7/93. Canx 7/93.
			G-14-3635		
EI-BEL	Short SD.3-60 Var.200	SH3636	G-BLEE	22. 2.84	To G-SBAC 2/92. Canx 7/91.
			G-14-3636		
EI-BEM	Short SD.3-60 Var.100	SH3642	G-BLGC	15. 6.84	Crashed near East Midlands, UK on 31.1.86. Canx 28.8.86.
			G-14-3642		
EI-BEN	Piper J3C-65 Cub (L-4J-PI)	12546	G-BCUC	28. 4.78	
	(Frame No. 12376)		F-BFMN/44-80250		
EI-BEO	Cessna 310Q II	310Q-0233	D-ICEG	13. 4.78	(Stored .95 - status uncertain .97)
			N7733Q		
EI-BEP	Socata MS.892A Rallye Commodore 150	11947	F-BTJT	14. 4.78	(Stored 4/96)
EI-BEQ	Not allocated.				
EI-BER	Boeing 707-331C	19212	N5771T	5. 5.78	To LX-FCV 10/78. Canx 6.10.78.
	(Line No. 588)				
EI-BES	Agusta-Bell 206B JetRanger II	8304	G-AZRU	13. 6.78	Restored as G-AZRU 8/80. Canx 26.8.80.
EI-BET	Reims Cessna F.337G Super Skymaster	0084	D-INAI	19. 5.78	To (G-BLOY)/G-BLSB 11/84. Canx 14.11.84.
	(Wichita c/n 01791)		(N53697)		
EI-BEU	Auster J/4 Archer	2069	G-AIJM	11. 5.78	Restored as G-AIJM 11.80. Canx 16.10.80.
EI-BEV	Agusta-Bell 206B JetRanger	8026	G-AVVH	12. 5.78	w/o at Kilruddery, Co.Wicklow, Ireland on 24.5.79.
			HP-644/G-AVVH		Canx 15.6.81.
EI-BEW	Beechcraft 95-D55 Baron	TE-610	D-IHAT	15. 6.78	To C-GIFY 8/81. Canx 6.8.81.
			(D-IKYK)/LN-TVC		
EI-BEX	Not allocated.				
EI-BEY	Naval Aircraft Factory N3N-3	2633	N45037	11. 5.78	To N..... 2/85. Canx 20.2.85.
			EI-BAK/N45037/(EI-BAK)/N45037/2633		
EI-BEZ	Not allocated.				
EI-BFA	Colt Ax7-77A HAFB	007		31. 5.78	To LN-CBB 8/78. Canx.
EI-BFB	Socata MS.880B Rallye 100ST	3044		12. 6.78	Fatal crash nr Weston on 18.10.87. (Wreck stored 2/95)
EI-BFC	Boeing 737-2H4	20336	EC-DZH	21. 7.78	To N709ML. Canx.
	(Line No. 239)		EI-BFC/(N332XV)/EI-BFC/N22SW/(N470AC)		
EI-BFD	Scheibe SF-28A Tandem Falke	5739	G-BBGA	1. 2.80	(Also flew as EI-122) Restored as G-BBGA 4/82.
			D-KOEI		Canx 27.4.82.
EI-BFE	Reims Cessna F.150G	0158	G-AVGM	3. 8.78	(On rebuild by D.McCarthy 4/90)
EI-BFF	Beechcraft A23-24 Musketeer Super III	MA-352	G-AXCJ	20. 8.78	
EI-BFG	Colt 77A HAFB	012		18. 6.78	To G-BHBB 9/79. Canx 14.9.79.
EI-BFH	Bell 212	30878	G-BFJG	19. 9.78	To 5N-AJL(2) 4/97. Canx 9.4.97.
EI-BFI	Socata MS.880B Rallye 100ST	2618	F-BXDK	10. 8.78	Crashed on 14.12.85. (Stored 4/96)
EI-BFJ	Beechcraft 200 Super King Air	BB-376	N4914M	29. 9.78	To Irish Air Corps as 234. Canx.
EI-BFK	Bell 206B JetRanger III	2401	N50005	20. 9.78	To G-BKPF 3/83. Canx 9.3.83.
EI-BFL	Rockwell Commander 690B	11465	N81767	17. 7.78	Restored as N81767 /79. Canx 20.4.79.
EI-BFM	Socata MS.893E Rallye 180GT	12958	F-GARN	12.10.78	
EI-BFN	Boeing 707-430C	17719	N64739	24. 8.78	To (N90498)/5A-CVA 4/79. Canx 17.1.79.
	(Line No. 106)		D-ABOC		
EI-BFO	Piper J3C-90 Cub (L-4J-PI)	12701	F-BFQJ	11. 9.78	
	(Frame No. 12531 - regd as c/n 8911)		N79856/NC79856/44-80405		
EI-BFP	Socata MS.880B Rallye 100ST	2942	F-GARR	6.10.78	(Stored 6/97)
EI-BFQ	Not allocated.				
EI-BFR	Socata MS.880B Rallye 100ST	2429	F-OCVK	9.11.78	
EI-BFS	Clutton FRED Srs.II	LAS.1803 & PFA/29-10141	G-BDSA	24.10.78	Restored as G-BDSA. Canx 6/93.
EI-BFT	Beechcraft 200 Super King Air	BB-438		7.12.78	To (G-BLLC)/G-LKOW 7/84. Canx 7.11.84.
EI-BFU	Boeing 707-344	17929	ZS-SAB	24.10.78	To VN-A304 11/78. Canx 28.10.78.
	(Line No. 154)		ZS-CKD		
EI-BFV	Socata MS.880B Rallye 100T	2415	F-BVAH	2. 2.79	Noted in damaged state at Birr 17.3.85. (Stored 8/93)
EI-BFW	Beechcraft 200 Super King Air	BB-461		8. 2.79	To N116PA 2/81. Canx 26.2.81.
EI-BFX	Not allocated.				
EI-BFY	Cessna 337D Super Skymaster	337-1077	G-AXRX	27.11.78	DBF at Clonmellon, Co.Wicklow, Ireland on 25.3.80.
			(G-AXBV)/N86098		Canx 17.6.81.

Regn	Type	c/n	Previous identity	Regn date	Fate or immediate subsequent identity (if known)
EI-BFZ	Not allocated.				
EI-BGA	Socata MS.880B Rallye 100ST	2549	G-BCXC	23.11.78	
			F-OCZQ		
EI-BGB	Socata MS.880B Rallye Club	1913	G-AZKB	22. 1.79	(Stored 6/97 Abbeyshrule - gone by 11/98)
EI-BGC	Socata MS.880B Rallye Club	1265	F-BRDC	22.12.78	
EI-BGD	Socata MS.880B Rallye Club	2287	F-BUJI	18.12.78	(Stored 11/98 Abbeyshrule)
			(D-EKHD)		
EI-BGE	Reims Cessna F.172M	1491	G-BEUR	21.12.78	Restored as G-BEUR 3/81. Canx 26.2.81.
EI-BGF	PA-28R-180 Cherokee Arrow	28R-30121	SE-FAS	30. 1.79	Fatal crash into mountain at Mynydd Prescelly,
					near Haverfordwest, Dyfed on 6.10.83. Canx.
EI-BGG	Socata MS.892E Rallye 150GT	12824	F-GAFS	30. 1.79	
EI-BGH(1)	Reims Cessna F.152 II	1607		. .79R	NTU - To EI-BGI(2) 5/79. Canx.
EI-BGH(2)	Reims Cessna F.172N Skyhawk II	1789	(EI-BGI)	30. 3.79	Severely damaged 5.5.80 Lambay Island, N of Dublin Airport.
					To G-BZGH 12/98. Canx 19.11.98.
EI-BGI(1)	Reims Cessna F.172N Skyhawk II	1789		. .79R	NTU - To EI-BGH(2) 3/79. Canx.
EI-BGI(2)	Reims Cessna F.152 II	1607	(EI-BGH)	14. 5.79	To G-BMHI 11/85. Canx 6.11.85.
EI-BGJ(1)	Cessna 414A Chancellor III		N6547C	. .79R	NTU - To EI-BGP 3/79. Canx.
		414A-0016			
EI-BGJ(2)	Reims Cessna F.152 II	1664		14. 5.79	
EI-BGK	Cessna P.206D Super Skylane	0548	N90WT	3. 5.79	w/o at Ardnamurchan on 16.6.89.
			G-BAMO/4X-ALP/4X-ALF/N8748Z		
EI-BGL	Rockwell Commander 690B	11507	N81850	20. 4.79	w/o at Jevington, near Eastbourne, UK on 13.11.84. Canx.
EI-BGM	Cessna 340A	340A-0056	OY-BUP	7. 3.79	To D-.... 2/80. Canx 27.2.80.
			N98610		
EI-BGN	Morane MS.880B Rallye Club	1853	TU-TJC	28. 3.79	Broken up 1983. Canx 10.8.83.
			F-OCRU		
EI-BGO	Canadair CL-44J	9	TF-LLH	24. 4.79	WFU on 3.1.86. Used for Rescue Training. Broken up 12/86
			CF-MKP-X		Dublin, Ireland. Canx 18.9.86.
EI-BGP	Cessna 414A Chancellor III		(EI-BGJ)	28. 3.79	To N414AS 11/92. Canx 25.11.92.
		414A-0016	N6574C		
EI-BGQ	Not allocated.				
EI-BGR(1)	Beechcraft 200 Super King Air		N2160L	.11.78R	NTU - To OY-CBK. Canx.
		BB-160			
EI-BGR(2)	Beechcraft 200 Super King Air		OY-CBV	9. 4.79R	NTU - Remained as OY-CBV. Canx.
		BB-192	SE-GRP		
EI-BGR(3)	PA-31P-425 Pressurized Navajo		OY-CBH	27.11.79	Restored as N66814 12/81. Canx 1.12.81.
		31P-7400174	SE-GUG/N66814		
EI-BGS	Socata MS.893E Rallye 180GT	12675	F-BXTY	25. 4.79	Badly damaged in gales at Claive, Co.Kildare in 3.91.
					(Wreck stored 4/96 Abbeyshrule - gone by 11/98)
EI-BGT	Colt 77A HAFB	041		14. 5.79	
	(Fitted with new envelope c/n 1092 - original to EI-BBM)				
EI-BGU	Socata MS.880B Rallye Club	875	F-BONM	9. 5.79	Wreck stored 6/95
EI-BGV	American Aviation AA-5 Traveler		G-BDCL	18. 7.79	Restored as G-BDCL 6/90. Canx.
		AA5-0773	N1373R		
EI-BGW	HS.125 Srs.1B/522	25080	G-BDYE	12. 6.79	To (C-GSOL)/C-GLEO 3/81. Canx 26.3.81.
			3D-AAB/VQ-ZIL		
EI-BGX	Not allocated.				
EI-BGY	Beechcraft A200 Super King Air			10. 7.79	To PH-BGY 9/79. Canx 11.9.79.
		BB-558			
EI-BGZ	Not allocated.				
EI-BHA	Beechcraft A200 Super King Air		OY-AUM	6. 2.80	Restored as OY-AUM 7/85. Canx 19.2.85.
		BB-626	EI-BHA		
EI-BHB	Socata MS.887 Rallye 125	2162	F-BUCH	7. 6.79	Dismantled fuselage noted at Abbeyshrule 9/91.
					(Stored 11/98)
EI-BHC	Reims Cessna F.177RG Cardinal	0010	G-AYTG	11. 7.79	
	(Wichita c/n 00117)				
EI-BHD	Socata MS.893E Rallye 180GT	13086	F-GBCF	6. 7.79	To G-DOOR 11/88. Canx 24.11.88.
EI-BHE	Agusta-Bell 206B JetRanger II	8405	OO-MHS	6. 7.79	To G-BHSM 7/80. Canx 24.7.80.
			F-BVEM		
EI-BHF	Socata MS.892A Rallye Commodore 150		F-BPBP	10. 7.79	
		10742			
EI-BHG(1)	Cessna 337 Super Skymaster	-		. .79R	NTU. Canx.
EI-BHG(2)	Beechcraft A200 Super King Air		9Q-CTK	14. 1.80	To (G-BLKN)/(G-ONPA)/G-HIGG 12/84. Canx 26.9.84.
		BB-160	N8493D/EI-BHG/OY-CBK/(EI-BGR)/N2160L		
EI-BHH	Reims Cessna FRA.150L Aerobat	0239	PH-ASH	7. 8.81	To G-BLPH 9/84. Canx 12.10.84.
EI-BHI	Bell 206B JetRanger II	906	G-BAKX	14. 8.79	
EI-BHJ	Miles M.65 Gemini 3C	HPR.141	G-ALZG	20. 8.79	Crashed at Corrigaline, Co.Cork, Ireland on 31.12.82. Canx.
EI-BHK	Socata MS.880B Rallye Club	1307	F-BRJE	20. 8.79	
EI-BHL	Beechcraft E90 King Air	LW-321	N60253	7. 9.79	
EI-BHM	Reims Cessna F.337E Super Skymaster		OO-PDC	1.11.79	To Dublin College of Technology, Instructional Airframe
	(Wichita c/n 01217)	0004	OO-PDG		5/92. Canx.
EI-BHN	Socata MS.893A Rallye Commodore 180		F-BRRO	11.10.79	(On overhaul 6/96)
		11422			
EI-BHO	Sikorsky S-61N Mk.II	61822	G-BPWB	2.11.79	Restored as G-BPWB 5/97. Canx.
			EI-BHO		
EI-BHP	Socata MS.893A Rallye Commodore 180		F-BSAA	12.10.79	
		11459			
EI-BHQ	Not allocated.				
EI-BHR	Enstrom 280C-UK Shark	1173	G-BGMX	8.10.79	Restored as G-BGMX 10/80. Canx 13.10.80.
			(F-GBOS)		
EI-BHS(1)	Beechcraft 76 Duchess	ME-327		5.10.79R	NTU. Canx 21.12.79.
EI-BHS(2)	Beechcraft 76 Duchess	ME-352		18. 1.80	To OY-BED 8/80. Canx 22.7.80.
EI-BHT	Beechcraft 77 Skipper	WA-77		17.10.79	

Regn	Type	c/n	Previous identity	Regn date	Fate or immediate subsequent identity (if known)
EI-BHU	Beechcraft 77 Skipper	WA-78	(LN-...) EI-BHU	17.10.79	DBR at Waterford, Ireland on 19.7.83. Canx 25.8.83.
EI-BHV	Champion 7EC Traveler	7EC-739	G-AVDU N9837Y	30.10.79	(On rebuild 5/92)
EI-BHW	Reims Cessna F.150F (Wichita c/n 62671)	0013	G-ATMK	22.11.79	
EI-BHX	Not allocated.				
EI-BHY	Socata MS.892E Rallye 150ST	2929	F-GARL	19.11.79	
EI-BHZ	Not allocated.				
EI-BIA	Reims Cessna FA.152 II	0366		30.11.79	Crashed at Thurles, Holycross on 28.9.80. Canx 16.6.81. Scrapped.
EI-BIB	Reims Cessna F.152 II	1724		30.11.79	Overran on landing at Carnmore in 11.81. Remains dumped at Abbeyshrule in 1982. To be rebuilt!
EI-BIC(1)	Reims Cessna F.172N Skyhawk II	2050		5.11.79R	NTU - To (EI-BIN)/LN-LGF 3/81. Canx.
EI-BIC(2)	Reims Cessna F.172N Skyhawk II	1965	(OO-HNZ)	15. 2.80	Badly damaged on landing at Castlebar on 13.4.95. (Stored 11/98 at Abbeyshrule)
EI-BID	PA-18-95 Super Cub (L-18C-PI)	18-1524	D-EAES ALAT/51-15524	30.11.79	(Possibly c/n 18-1571 ex 51-15571)
EI-BIE	Reims Cessna FA.152 Aerobat	0362		28. 2.80	To G-STAP. Canx 25.5.87.
EI-BIF	Socata MS.894A Rallye 235E Gabier	13121	HB-EYT N344RA	4. 1.80	To G-BWWG 10/96. Canx 19.8.96.
EI-BIG	Moravan Zlin 526 Trener Master	1086	D-EBUP OO-BUT	7.12.79	Damaged on landing in 9/91 (Stored 10/97)
EI-BIH	Socata TB-10 Tobago	109		28. 2.80	To G-LANA 7/81. Canx 13.7.81.
EI-BII	Boeing 737-2L9 (Line No. 480)	21279	OY-APH N1787B	1. 2.80	To F-GCGS 4/80. Canx 2.4.80.
EI-BIJ	Agusta-Bell 206B JetRanger II	8432	G-BCVZ	29. 1.80	
EI-BIK	PA-18-180 Super Cub	18-7909088	N82276	1. 2.80	Damaged when taxied into fuel drum at Gowran Grange in 8/81. Currently stored.
EI-BIL	Beechcraft G35 Bonanza	D-1168	G-APVW N9866F/4C-ACL/4X-ACI Israeli DF/AF 0604/ZS-BTE	30.11.79	Restored as G-APVW .85. Canx 15.11.85.
EI-BIM	Morane-Saulnier MS.880B Rallye Club	305	F-BKYJ(2)	28. 3.80	(Stored 6/97)
EI-BIN(1)	Reims Cessna F.172N Skyhawk II	2050	(EI-BIC)	18. 2.80R	NTU - To LN-LGF 3/81. Canx.
EI-BIN(2)	Reims Cessna F.152 II	1843		10. 2.81	To G-BLWV 2/85. Canx 21.2.85.
EI-BIO	Piper J3C-65 Cub (L-4J-PI)	12657	F-BGXP OO-GAE/44-80361	27. 5.80	
EI-BIP	Beechcraft 200 Super King Air	BB-687		10. 4.80	To SE-INI 10/83. Canx 2.10.83.
EI-BIQ	Not allocated.				
EI-BIR	Reims Cessna F.172M Skyhawk II	1225	F-BVXI	24. 3.80	
EI-BIS	Robin R.1180TD Aiglon	268		14. 5.80	
EI-BIT	Socata MS.887 Rallye 125	2169	F-BULQ	18. 3.80	
EI-BIU	Robin R.2112A Alpha	175		14. 5.80	
EI-BIV	Bellanca 8KCAB Super Decathlon	464-79	N5032Q	3. 6.80	
EI-BIW	Socata MS.880B Rallye Club	1144	F-BPGB	19. 5.80	
EI-BIX	Not allocated.				
EI-BIY	Agusta-Bell 47G-3B1	1575	G-BEHK XT110	3. 6.80	Restored as G-BEHK 1/81. Canx 7.1.81.
EI-BIZ	Not allocated.				
EI-BJA	Reims Cessna FRA.150L Aerobat	0143	G-AZTE	13. 3.80	Crashed near Rathcoole, Ireland on 4.4.86. Canx 29.8.86.
EI-BJB	Aeronca 7DC Champion	7AC-925	G-BKKM EI-BJB/N82296/NC82296	16. 4.80	
EI-BJC	Aeronca 7AC Champion	7AC-4927	N1366E NC1366E	2. 4.80	
EI-BJD	Mooney M.20K Srs.231	25-0389	C-GNWH (N4024H)	9. 7.80	To HB-DGE. Canx 13.8.81.
EI-BJE	Boeing 727-275 (Line No. 96)	19742	C-FPWD CF-PWD	26. 5.80	To 4R-ULH 6/85. Canx 14.6.85.
EI-BJF	American Aviation AA-5 Traveler	AA5-0568	F-BVRM N9568L	18. 6.80	To G-BMYI 9/86. Canx 19.8.86.
EI-BJG	Robin R.1180TD Aiglon	-		30. 4.80R	NTU. Canx.
EI-BJH	Slingsby Nipper T.66 RA.45 Srs.3 (Tipsy c/n 74)	S.104/1588	G-AVKK	3. 6.80	Restored as G-AVKK 6/85. Canx 7.5.85.
EI-BJI	Reims Cessna FR.172E Rocket	0040	G-BAAS SE-FBW/OY-DKN	23. 5.80	DBR at Edenderry, Ireland on 29.8.82. (Remains probably scrapped pre.90)
EI-BJJ	Aeronca 15AC Sedan	15AC-226	(G-BHXP) EI-BJJ/N1214H	6. 6.80	(Stored 3/98 Abbeyshrule)
EI-BJK	Socata MS.880B Rallye 110ST Galopin	3226	F-GBKY	8. 7.80	
EI-BJL	Cessna 551 Citation II (Unit No. 039) (Built as 550 Citation II c/n 550-0039)	551-0084	G-BJHH (N3273M)	25. 7.80	To N78FA. Canx 3/93.
EI-BJM	Cessna A.152 Aerobat	0936	(EAF) N761CC	18. 9.80	
EI-BJN	Cessna 501 Citation I/SP (Unit No. 555)	501-0175	N2072A	10. 7.80	To VR-BKP 12/88. Canx 9.12.88.
EI-BJO	Cessna R.172K Hawk XP II	3340	N758TD	6. 8.80	
EI-BJP	Boeing 737-275C (Line No. 139)	19743	C-FPWE CF-PWE	9. 9.80	To N331XV 9/86. Canx 30.9.86.
EI-BJQ	PA-31-350 Navajo Chieftain	-		. .80R	NTU. Canx.
EI-BJR	Bell 206B JetRanger	587	G-AYMW	28. 8.80	Restored as G-AYMW 1/81. Canx 14.1.81.

Regn	Type	c/n	Previous identity	Regn date	Fate or immediate subsequent identity (if known)
EI-BJS	American Aviation AA-5B Tiger	AA5B-0979	G-BFZR	3. 9.80	
EI-BJT	PA-38-112 Tomahawk	38-78A0818	G-BGEU	16.10.80	
			N9650N		
EI-BJU	Rockwell 690B Turbo Commander	11546	G-BHLI	. .80R	NTU - Remained as G-BHLI. Canx 9.4.81.
			N81632		
EI-BJV	Agusta-Bell 206B JetRanger III	8567	G-BTWW	17.10.80	Restored as G-BTWW. Canx 2.4.85.
EI-BJW	DH.104 Dove 5	04485	G-ASNG	7.11.80	Waterford Airport Fire Service (Still painted as G-ASNG).
			HB-LFF/G-ASNG/HB-LFF/G-ASNG/PH-IOM		Canx 29.1.94.
EI-BJX	PA-31-350 Navajo Chieftain	-		. .80R	NTU. Canx.
EI-BJY	Beechcraft 200 Super King Air	BB-800		16. 1.81	To N200GA 11/83. Canx 4.11.83.
EI-BJZ	Not allocated.				
EI-BKA	Aerotek Pitts S-2A Special	2165	N105JM	29. 9.80	w/o at Strandhill on 1.4.84. Canx.
EI-BKB	Aeronca 11AC Chief	11AC-1035	G-IVOR	5.11.80	Restored as G-IVOR. Canx 9.3.84.
			EI-BKB/N9397E		
EI-BKC	Aeronca 15AC Sedan	15AC-467	N1394H	5.11.80	
EI-BKD	Mooney M.20J Srs.201	24-0950	G-BHOK	4.12.80	To N311SM. Canx 10.11.94.
			N3818H		
EI-BKE	Morane MS.885 Super Rallye	278	F-BKUN	9. 2.81	DBR at Ballyclumack, Co.Wexford on 5.4.81. Canx 16.9.86.
			F-WKUN		(Wreck stored 4/96)
EI-BKF	Reims Cessna F.172H	0476	G-AVUX	4.12.80	
EI-BKG	Westland-Bell 47G-3B1	WA/354	G-BEHN	2. 1.81	Restored as G-BEHN 12/81. Canx 24.12.81.
	(Line No. WAN/45)		XT195		
EI-BKH	Partenavia P.68B Victor	147	G-PAUL	19. 1.81	To G-BJOF 11/81. Canx 4.11.81.
EI-BKI	PA-31-350 Navajo Chieftain	31-7405148	G-BDFN	9. 2.81	Restored as G-BDFN 11/81. Canx 4.11.81.
			5Y-ASI		
EI-BKJ	Douglas C-47B-15-DK Dakota	15124/26569	G-AMPY	. .81R	NTU - Remained as G-AMPY. Canx.
			N15751/G-AMPY/TF-FIO/G-AMPY/JY-ABE/"JY-AAE"/G-AMPY/KK116/43-49308		
EI-BKK	Taylor JT.1 Monoplane	PFA/1421	G-AYYC	2. 2.81	
EI-BKL	Reims Cessna FR.172F Rocket	0140	D-EBTQ	5. 3.81	Badly damaged in gales at Farrenfore, Ireland in 1/84.
			F-WLIT		Since broken up for spares & to UK 3/85. Canx 27.2.89.
EI-BKM	Zenair CH.200-RW-AA	2-471		2. 2.81	Canx at owner's request 28.2.94, and sold to UK.
EI-BKN	Socata MS.880B Rallye 100ST	3035	F-GBCK	18. 2.81	
EI-BKO	Boeing 707-321B	18832	N401	10. 4.81	NTU - To VN-81416 12.4.81. Canx 14.4.81.
	(Line No. 403)		N401PA/(OO-TYB)/N401PA		
EI-BKP	Zenair CH.200-AA	2-563		4. 3.81	To G-BPTO 3/89. Canx 13.3.89.
EI-BKQ	Not allocated.				
EI-BKR	Cessna 172N Skyhawk II	172-72969	G-BHKZ	2. 4.81	To G-BKRB 3/83. Canx 22.3.83.
	(Wren conversion)		N1207F		
EI-BKS	Eipper Quicksilver	IMA-001		15. 4.81	
EI-BKT	Agusta-Bell 206B JetRanger III	8562	D-HAFD	6. 4.81	
			HB-XIC		
EI-BKU	Socata MS.892A Rallye Commodore 150	10990	F-BRLG	21. 5.81	(Stored 11/98 Abbeyshrule)
EI-BKV	Beechcraft B200C Super King Air	BL-43		27. 4.81	To OY-BEP 11/81. Canx 2.11.81.
EI-BKW	Beechcraft 76 Duchess	ME-404	ST-AKB	29. 5.81	To N771AW. Canx 11.11.85.
			EI-BKW/N3834Z		
EI-BKX	Not allocated.				
EI-BKY	Beechcraft 99	U-124	N788C	8. 7.81	To SE-IOG 10/84. Canx 19.9.84.
EI-BKZ	Not allocated.				
EI-BLA	PA-23-250 Aztec C	27-3321	G-AYZO	24. 4.81	To N811SC /85. Canx 27.9.85.
			N6112Y/CF-THZ/N6112Y		
EI-BLB	SNCAN Stampe SV-4C	323	F-BCTE	27. 7.81	Fatal crash after striking power lines at the Albert Lock of the Jamestown Canal, near Drumsna, Co.Leitrim on 1.6.97.
EI-BLC	Boeing 707-347C	19964	N1502W	26. 7.81	To N707PD 11/81. Canx 2.11.81.
	(Line No. 733)		TF-VLG/N1502W		
EI-BLD	MBB Bo.105DB	S.381	D-HDLQ	21. 7.81	(Was noted at Dublin on 1.4.97 painted in British Army camouflage as "XZ170" - presumably for a film)
EI-BLE	Eipper Quicksilver	IMA-003		20. 8.81	Crashed in 8/81. Canx.
EI-BLF(1)	Eipper Quicksilver	-		. .81R	Not imported. Canx.
EI-BLF(2)	Hiway Demon	EC25PS/80-00205		30.11.81	Canx as TWFU 15.5.85.
EI-BLG	Agusta-Bell 206B JetRanger III	8614	G-BIGS	6. 7.81	To EI-PMI 9/96. Canx.
EI-BLH	Cessna 421C Golden Eagle III	421C-0647	G-NORX	13. 7.81	Restored to G-NORX 8/84. Canx 2.8.84.
			N88600		
EI-BLI	Beechcraft C90 King Air	LJ-985		20. 8.81	To N409ND 9/84. Canx 5.9.84.
EI-BLJ	Cessna T210H Turbo Centurion	T210-0337	G-AWGP	1. 2.82	Restored as G-AWGP. Canx 23.6.87.
			N6937R		
EI-BLK	PA-28-181 Cherokee Archer II	28-7790542	G-BIEP	7. 8.81	Restored as G-BIEP. Canx 20.11.85.
			N38342		
EI-BLL	Reims Cessna F.172P Skyhawk II	2122		21. 9.81	DBR at Tullamore, Ireland on 14.2.87. Canx.
EI-BLM	Hiway Skytrike II/MSD	AS.06		17. 8.81	Canx 23.7.87.
EI-BLN	Eipper Quicksilver MX	MX.01		26. 8.81	
EI-BLO	Eurowing Catto CP.16	260		21. 9.81	Stored at Longford in 1990. Canx.
EI-BLP	Short SD.3-30 Var.100	SH3078	G-BJLK	21. 9.81	Restored as G-BJLK. Canx 15.6.84.
			G-14-3078		
EI-BLQ	Not allocated.				
EI-BLR	PA-34-200T Seneca II	34-7570163	G-BDUN	.10.81R	NTU - Remained as G-BDUN. Canx.
			SE-GIA		
EI-BLS	Cessna 150M Commuter	150-76869	N45356	23.10.81	To G-BLVS 2/85. Canx 19.2.85.
EI-BLT	PA-38-112 Tomahawk	38-79A0998	G-BGZI	15.10.81	To G-OPSF 10/82. Canx 11.10.82.
EI-BLU	Evans VP-1	SAAC-05		13.10.81	

Regn	Type	c/n	Previous identity	Regn date	Fate or immediate subsequent identity (if known)
EI-BLV	Beechcraft 99	U-26	N746A N538MA/N538M	17.11.81	To OY-BEN 12/81. Canx 3.12.81.
EI-BLW	PA-23-250 Aztec C	27-3173	G-BBAV PH-KNV/LN-NPD/SE-EPW	16.11.81	In open storage at Shannon in 11/90. Still stored 8/97.
EI-BLX	Not allocated.				
EI-BLY	Sikorsky S-61N Mk.II	61-761	C-GPOH VH-IMQ/VH-PTF/N611EH	10.12.81	To G-BXSN 2/98. Canx.
EI-BLZ	Not allocated.				
EI-BMA	Socata MS.880B Rallye Club	1965	F-BTJR D-EOOM	26. 1.82	
EI-BMB(1)	Boeing 737-2L9 (Line No. 620)	22071	SU-BCJ OY-APN	. .81R	NTU - To G-BJSO 12/81. Canx.
EI-BMB(2)	Socata MS.880B Rallye 100T	2505	G-BJCO F-BVLB	5. 1.82	
EI-BMC	Hiway Demon/Skytrike 175	R217D		13. 1.82	Canx 6.7.94 as "aircraft sold".
EI-BMD	American Aerolights Eagle	715 E 2624		13. 1.82	Canx 9.9.87.
EI-BME	Beechcraft B200C Super King Air	BL-49	N3836E (XA-...)	11. 1.82	NTU - To N17KK. Canx 30.5.83.
EI-BMF	Aeromere-Laverda F.8L Super Falco Srs.IV	416	G-AWSU	28. 1.82	
EI-BMG	PA-28-140 Cherokee F	28-7325240	G-BFBF PH-SRF	28. 1.82	Restored as G-BFBF 1/83. Canx 13.1.83.
EI-BMH	Socata MS.880B Rallye Club	1277	(G-BIDS) F-BSTJ	19. 2.82	(UK marks were used unofficially)
EI-BMI	Socata TB-9 Tampico	203	F-GCOV	12. 5.82	
EI-BMJ	Socata MS.880B Rallye 100T	2594	F-BXTG	10. 3.82	
EI-BMK	Cessna 310Q II	310Q-0919	G-BBNS N69685	1. 3.82	WFU & sold to USA for parting out as spares. Canx 8.93.
EI-BML	PA-23-250 Aztec C	27-3405	G-ATSB G-ATZJ/N6179Y	26. 3.82	WFU at Abbeyshrule, Ireland. Canx 16.5.86.
EI-BMM	Reims Cessna F.152 II	1899		10. 3.82	
EI-BMN	Reims Cessna F.152 II	1912		10. 3.82	
EI-BMO	Robin R.2160i Acrobin	116	SE-GSZ	23. 4.82	To G-SBMO 2/99. Canx.
EI-BMP	Agusta-Bell 206B JetRanger III	8564	G-JUMP	28. 4.82	Crashed at Oughterard, Co.Galway on 29.7.82.
EI-BMQ	Not allocated.				
EI-BMR	Southdown Puma Lightning 159DS	007		31. 3.82	Canx 23.7.87.
EI-BMS	Reims Cessna F.177RG Cardinal	-		. .82R	Possibly NTU.
EI-BMT	American Aviation AA-5B Tiger	AA5B-0625	G-BFHS	28. 6.82	To G-PORK 2/84. Canx 25.1.84.
EI-BMU	Monnett Sonerai IIL	01224		19. 5.82	(Stored 8/96)
EI-BMV	American Aviation AA-5 Traveler	AA5-0200	G-BAEJ	28. 7.82	Badly damaged at Brittas Bay in 3/93. (Stored 6/97)
EI-BMW	Maddock Skytrike/Hiway Vulcan	LM-100		1. 6.82	
EI-BMX	Not allocated.				
EI-BMY	Boeing 737-2L9 (Line No. 479)	21278	D2-TBT F-GCGR/D2-TBT/F-GCGR/4R-ALC/OY-APG/N1787B	1. 7.82	To G-BKRO 4/83. Canx 20.4.83.
EI-BMZ	Not allocated.				
EI-BNA	Douglas DC-8-63CF (Line No. 371)	45989	LX-ACV (CX-BOU)/TF-ACV/LX-ACV/N779FT	15. 4.83	
EI-BNB	Lake LA-4-200 Buccaneer	650	N1057L	26. 8.82	To G-OSMR 3/96. Canx 7.3.96.
EI-BNC(1)	Reims Cessna F.172P Skyhawk II	-		. .82R	NTU. Canx.
EI-BNC(2)	Reims Cessna F.152 II	1894	N9097Y	5. 8.82	To G-BWEU 6/95. Canx 15.6.85.
EI-BND	Canadair Conroy CL-44-O	16	N447T	4.11.82	(Temp unregd 22.11.96) To 4K-GUP 8/97. Canx.
EI-BNE	Helio H.295 Super Courier	1706	N108R ZS-JEE/N68873	7.12.82	Restored as N108R 4/84, but DBR en-route to USA. Canx 11.4.84.
EI-BNF	Eurowing Goldwing	-		22. 9.82	
EI-BNG	Morane MS.892A Rallye Commodore 150	10455	F-BRGY D-EDZO	4.10.82	Canx.
EI-BNH	Hiway Skytrike	AS.09		18.10.82	
EI-BNI	Bell 412	33074	N10834	16.11.82	Crashed at Phndar, near Gilgit, Pakistan on 12.3.86 still marked as N10834. Canx 2.11.87. To VH-NSB 6/88.
EI-BNJ	Evans VP-2	-		24. 1.83	
EI-BNK	Cessna U.206F Stationair 6 II	U206-01706	G-HILL PH-ADN/D-EEXY/N9506G	23.12.82	
EI-BNL	Rand Robinson KR-2	-		13. 1.83	
EI-BNM(1)	Short SD.3-30 Var.200	SH3093	G-BKMV G-14-3093	. .83R	NTU - To N155DD 4/83. Canx.
EI-BNM(2)	Short SD.3-30 Var.100	SH3064	G-BIOF N280VY/N4270A/G-BIOF	17. 6.83	Restored as G-14-3064/G-BIOF. Canx 13.3.84.
EI-BNN	Short SC.7 Skyvan 3-200	SH1854	G-AWWS N7978/CF-VAN/G-AWWS/G-14-2	24. 5.83	To OY-JRL. Canx 7/90.
EI-BNO(1)	Cessna 210F Centurion	210-58735	G-ATMP N1835F/F-BIFU/N1835F	. .83R	NTU - To EI-BOD 6/83. Canx.
EI-BNO(2)	Aerospatiale AS.350B Ecureuil	1647	G-BKJY	4. 3.83	To G-JRBI 3/84. Canx 20.3.84.
EI-BNP	Rotorway 133 Executive	-		1. 3.83	NTU - Not imported (Not completed .89)
EI-BNQ	Not allocated.				
EI-BNR	American Aviation AA-5 Traveler (Regd with c/n 202 in error)	AA5-0203	N9992Q CS-AHJ	1. 3.83	DBR at Abbeyshrule, Ireland on 21.2.88. Canx 22.7.88. (Stored 4/96 - spares use)
EI-BNS	Boeing 737-212 (Line No. 288)	20521	C-FNAW CF-NAW/(CF-NAD)/9M-AQC	8. 4.83	To N130AW. Canx.
EI-BNT	Cvjetkovic CA-65	-		23. 3.83	

Regn	Type	c/n	Previous identity	Regn date	Fate or immediate subsequent identity (if known)
EI-BNU	Socata MS.880B Rallye Club	1204	F-BPQV	7. 4.83	
EI-BNV	PA-23-250 Aztec E	27-7305200	G-BBOK	26. 5.83	Restored as G-BBOK 2/87. Canx 2.2.87.
			N40482		
EI-BNW	Not to be allocated (for unknown reasons)				
EI-BNX	Not allocated.				
EI-BNY	Sud Aviation SN.601 Corvette	11	F-BTTV	26. 5.83	To F-WFPD. Canx 16.10.87.
			F-ODKS/TR-LWY/F-BTTS/N613AC/(F-WIFU)		
EI-BNZ	Not allocated.				
EI-BOA	Pterodactyl Microlight	-		3. 5.83	
EI-BOB	Mainair Tri-Flyer/Airwave Nimrod	165		3. 5.83	To G-MNIW 11/85. Canx 1.7.85.
		050/19181			
EI-BOC	Boeing 737-242C	20455	C-FNAQ	24. 5.83	Restored as C-FNAQ. Canx 14.11.83.
	(Line No. 254)		CF-NAQ		
EI-BOD	Cessna 210F Centurion	210-58735	(EI-BNO)	2. 6.83	DBR at Dunboyne, Co.Meath, Ireland 17.3.85. Canx 25.5.85.
			G-ATMP/N1835F/F-BIFU/N1835F		To Dodson Aviation Scrapyard, Ottawa, KS, USA.
EI-BOE	Socata TB-10 Tobago	301	F-GDBL	12. 9.83	
EI-BOF	Socata TB-10 Tobago	298	G-HILT	8. 8.83	To (G-BMYB)/G-HILT. Canx 18.8.86.
EI-BOG	Boeing 737-2L9	22071	G-BJSO	. .83R	NTU - To EI-BOJ 10/83. Canx.
	(Line No. 620)		(EI-BMB)/SU-BCJ/OY-APN		
EI-BOH	Eipper Quicksilver	-		8. 9.83	
EI-BOI	Reims Cessna F.150G	0204	G-AVEO	13. 9.83	Restored as G-AVEO 9/85. Canx 26.9.85.
EI-BOJ	Boeing 737-2L9	22071	G-GPAB	7.10.83	To VR-HKP. Canx 20.6.85.
	(Line No. 620)		G-BJSO/EI-BOJ/(EI-BOG)/G-BJSO/(EI-BMB)/SU-BCJ/OY-APN		
EI-BOK	PA-E23-250 Turbo Aztec E	27-7305223	G-BBRJ	10.11.83	Restored as G-BBRJ. Canx 9.10.92.
			N40493		
EI-BOL	PA-31-310 Turbo Navajo	31-776	G-AZIM	21. 9.83	To SE-INR 12.83. Canx 6.12.83.
			N7250L		
EI-BOM	Boeing 737-2T4ADV	22368	G-GPAA	9.11.84	To LV-WNA 9/95. Canx 18.8.95.
	(Line No. 707)		N52AF/EI-BOM/N52AF/(EI-BOM)/N52AF		
EI-BON	Boeing 737-2T4ADV	22369	EC-DUL	14. 3.85	To LV-WNB 9/95. Canx 18.8.95.
	(Line No. 708)		N56AF/(EI-BON)/N56AF		
EI-BOO	PA-E23-250 Aztec C	27-2754	G-ATCY	13. 4.84	To G-JANK 4/95. Canx 19.4.95.
			N5640Y		
EI-BOP	Socata MS.892A Rallye Commodore 150		G-BKGS	13. 3.84	Crashed on landing at Coonagh, Ireland on 29.3.86. Canx
		11748	F-BSXS		19.5.88. (Stored - spares use 10/98 at Abbeyshrule)
EI-BOQ	Not allocated.				
EI-BOR	Bell 222A	47021	LN-OSB	24. 2.84	
EI-BOS	Boeing 747-132SCD	19898	B-1860	7. 4.84	To N725PA. Canx 9.5.84.
	(Line No. 94)		N9898		
EI-BOT	Aerospatiale AS.350B Ecureuil	1613	G-BKFB	9. 4.84	DBR at Knocksedan, Co.Dublin on 15.4.91. Canx.
EI-BOU	Boeing 747-133	20013	C-FTOA	9. 5.84	To N749R .84. Canx.
	(Line No. 104)		CF-TOA		
EI-BOV	Rand Robinson KR-2	SAAC-11		7. 5.84	Damaged on landing at Carnmore in 3.91 (Stored 9/91)
EI-BOW	Cessna 182M Skylane	182-59403	G-AWXA	25. 9.84	Restored as G-AWXA. Canx 26.2.87.
			N70877		
EI-BOX	Duet	-		12.10.84	
EI-BOY	Practavia Pilot Sprite			12. 2.84	W/o near Enniskerry, Co.Wicklow on 12.12.87.
	(Regd as Murphy Sprite)	153 & SAAC-08			
EI-BOZ	Not allocated.				
EI-BPA	PA-E23-250 Aztec D	27-4577	G-AZFE	30. 5.84	Restored as G-AZFE. Canx 23.4.87.
			N13962		
EI-BPB	PA-28R-200 Cherokee Arrow D II		G-BAAR	28.11.84	To G-ODOG 8/96. Canx 23.7.96.
		28R-7235197	N11C		
EI-BPC	Rockwell 690B Turbo Commander	11546	(YV-280CP)	6.12.84	To N690SC. Canx 28.3.85.
			G-BHLI/(EI-BJU)/G-BHLI/N81632		
EI-BPD	Short SD.3-60 Var.100	SH3656	G-BLPU	25.10.84	To G-RMCT 11/92. Canx 27.11.92.
			G-14-3656		
EI-BPE	Viking Dragonfly	SAAC-16		15.10.84	
EI-BPF	Douglas DC-8-71CF	45897	EC-CCF	22.10.84	Restored as N8786R. Canx 20.3.85.
	(Line No. 313)		N8786R		
EI-BPG	Douglas DC-8-71CF	45898	EC-CCG	22.10.84	Restored as N8787R. Canx 22.2.85.
	(Line No. 320)		N8787R		
EI-BPH	Boeing 747-133	20013	N749R	8. 2.85	To N890FT. Canx 29.4.88.
	(Line No. 104)		EI-BOU/C FTOA/CF-TOA		
EI-BPI	Embraer EMB.110P1 Bandeirante		OY-ASY	4. 1.85	Restored as OY-ASY. Canx 5/93.
		110-308	PT-SCO		
EI-BPJ	Cessna 182A Skylane	182-34949	G-BAGA	4.12.84	Damaged pre.7.95 (Stored 11/98 at Abbeyshrule)
			N4849D		
EI-BPK	Sikorsky S-61N Mk.II	61-224	G-BEJL	28. 3.85	Restored as G-BEJL 6/85. Canx 18.6.85.
			N4606G		
EI-BPL	Reims Cessna F.172K	0758	G-AYSG	28. 3.85	
EI-BPM	Aerospatiale AS.350B Ecureuil	1805	G-BLSP	3. 4.85	To G-OFHL 6/93. Canx 6/93.
EI-BPN	Flexiform Striker	-		12. 3.85	
EI-BPO	Southdown Puma	1923		12. 3.85	
	(Also quotes ENo.82-00108 as c/n)				
EI-BPP	Eipper Quicksilver MX	3207		12. 3.85	(Stored 8/93)
EI-BPQ	Not allocated.				
EI-BPR	Boeing 737-2S3	21775	(EI-BRR)	2. 5.85	Restored as (G-BNZU)/G-BMOR. Canx 31.3.88.
	(Line No. 570)		G-BMOR		
EI-BPS	PA-30-160 Twin Comanche B	30-1002	(EI-BBS)	25. 3.85	Restored as G-ATSZ 10/95. Canx 25.10.95.
			G-ATSZ/(AN-...)/G-ATSZ/N7912Y		
EI-BPT	Skyhook Sabre	-		26. 3.85	
EI-BPU	Hiway Demon	-		26. 3.85	

Regn	Type	c/n	Previous identity	Regn date	Fate or immediate subsequent identity (if known)
EI-BPV	Boeing 737-2T5ADV (Line No. 641)	22024	G-BGTV	8. 4.85	To C-FHCP. Canx 2.4.86.
EI-BPW	Boeing 737-2S3 (Line No. 577)	21776	G-BMEC	14. 5.85	To N368DL. Canx 29.9.87.
EI-BPX	Not allocated.				
EI-BPY	Boeing 737-2S3 (Line No. 563)	21774	OO-TYD (EI-BPY)/G-BMHG/N1787B	16.11.85	To N367DL. Canx 20.10.87.
EI-BPZ	Not allocated.				
EI-BQA	Not allocated.				
EI-BQB	Not allocated.				
EI-BQC	Not allocated.				
EI-BQD	Not allocated.				
EI-BQE	Not allocated.				
EI-BQF	Not allocated.				
EI-BQG	Not allocated.				
EI-BQH	Not allocated.				
EI-BQI	Not allocated.				
EI-BQJ	Not allocated.				
EI-BQK	Not allocated.				
EI-BQL	Not allocated.				
EI-BQM	Not allocated.				
EI-BQN	Not allocated.				
EI-BQO	Not allocated.				
EI-BQP	Not allocated.				
EI-BQQ	Not allocated.				
EI-BQR	Not allocated.				
EI-BQS	Not allocated.				
EI-BQT	Not allocated.				
EI-BQU	Not allocated.				
EI-BQV	Not allocated.				
EI-BQW	Not allocated.				
EI-BQX	Not allocated.				
EI-BQY	Not allocated.				
EI-BQZ	Not allocated.				
EI-BRA(1)	Boeing 727-247A (Line No. 889)	20580	N2808W	. .85R	NTU - To EI-BRD 5/85. Canx.
EI-BRA(2)	Reims Cessna F.150J	0408	G-AWUU	16. 5.85	Restored as G-AWUU. Canx 7/89.
EI-BRB	Boeing 737-2S3 (Line No. 650)	22279	G-BMSM	6. 6.85	To N368DE. Canx 3.88.
EI-BRC	PA-31-350 Navajo Chieftain	31-7952247	G-WSSC N3543W	17. 5.85	Restored as G-WSSC. Canx 12.5.86.
EI-BRD	Boeing 727-247A (Line No. 889)	20580	(EI-BRA) N2808W	6. 5.85	To N502AV. Canx 25.3.87.
EI-BRE	Bell 212	30853	G-BIGB ZS-HHU/A2-ACJ/ZS-HHU/N16831	24. 4.85	To storage at Redhill 25.10.85. Canx 29.10.85. Restored as G-BIGB 6/86.
EI-BRF	Boeing 727-264 (Line No. 975)	20710	N788BR (N788QS)/N788BR/XA-CUE	20. 5.85	To N728ZV. Canx 30.9.85.
EI-BRG	HS.125 Srs.731	25281	N125DB N18GX/N1BG/N71BH	20. 6.85	To N70338 11/88. Canx.
EI-BRH	Mainair Gemini/Flash	316-585-3		15. 5.85	
EI-BRI	Swearingen SA.226TC Metro II	TC-386	N10117 HK-2561X/N10117	18.10.85	To N32AG. Canx 13.7.87.
EI-BRJ	Beechcraft 58 Baron	TH-1258	ST-AIK G-IASI/N38332/N2585J	6. 6.85	To N770AW. Canx 11.11.85.
EI-BRK	Flexiform Trike	LM.102		17. 6.85	
EI-BRL	Agusta-Bell 206B JetRanger II	8340	G-BFJW F-BXOX/D-HMOG/(D-HNWS)	9. 8.85	Restored as G-BFJW. Canx 29.10.85.
EI-BRM	Cessna 172Q	172-76147	N97033	17. 6.85	Collided in mid-air with F.152 EI-BRO over Bandon, Co.Cork 26.2.92 and w/o (The 152 landed safely at Cork). Canx.
EI-BRN	Boeing 737-2T4 (Line No. 750)	22529	N51AF	12. 8.85	To N703ML. Canx 24.12.86.
EI-BRO	Reims Cessna F.152 II	1957		12.11.85	To G-IBRO 10/95. Canx 25.8.95.
EI-BRP	Canadair CL-44J	35	9Q-CQS 5A-DGJ/5A-CVB/TL-AAL/5A-CVB/N4993U/TF-LLF/CF-PBG-X	4. 9.85	Stored 11/90 Southend, UK. Broken up 2/93 Stock, Essex, UK.
EI-BRQ	Not allocated.				
EI-BRR(1)	Boeing 737-2S3 (Line No. 570)	21775	G-BMOR	. .85R	NTU - To EI-BPR 5/85. Canx.
EI-BRR(2)	Boeing 747-133 (Line No. 121)	20014	EC-DXE C-FTOB/CF-TOB	6.11.85	To N621FE. Canx 10.10.86.
EI-BRS	Cessna P.172D	P172-57173	G-WPUI G-AXPI/9M-AMR/N11B/(N8573X)	2. 9.85	
EI-BRT	Flexwing M.17727	990059		5.11.85	Canx 20.5.96 at owner's request and scrapped, but stored 8/97 at Clane/Millicent Field, Ireland.
EI-BRU	Evans VP-1	V-12-84-CQ & SAAC-18		5.11.85	
EI-BRV	Hiway Skytrike/Demon	-		5.11.85	
EI-BRW	Hovey Delta Bird	-		5.11.85	
EI-BRX	Reims Cessna FRA.150L Aerobat	0160	G-BACM	9. 1.86	
EI-BRY	Cessna 210M Centurion	210-62725	G-BMGU ZS-KRZ/N6262B	6. 1.86	DBR at Clonsilla, Co.Dublin on 16.10.86. Canx 18.4.88.
EI-BRZ	Boeing 737-2E3 (Line No. 811)	22703	G-BNZT EC-DYZ/EI-BRZ/CC-BIN	31. 3.86	To G-IBTY. Canx 14.12.88.
EI-BSA	Gates LearJet 55	55-021	N700TG N3794B	15.11.85	To I-LOOK 3/86. Canx 2.4.86.

Regn	Type	c/n	Previous identity	Regn date	Fate or immediate subsequent identity (if known)
EI-BSB	Wassmer Jodel D.112	1067	G-AWIG F-BKAA	23. 6.87	
EI-BSC	Reims Cessna F.172N Skyhawk II	1651	G-NIUS	10.12.85	
EI-BSD	Enstrom F-28A	153	G-BBHE	10. 2.86	
EI-BSE	Avro 748 Srs.1/106	1549	G-ARRW	26. 3.86	Restored as G-ARRW. Canx.
EI-BSF	Avro 748 Srs.1/105	1544	EC-DTP G-BEKD/LV-HHF/LV-PUM	28. 5.86	WFU 7.1.87 at Dublin. Canx 26.7.94 at owner's request as dismantled. (Cabin crew trainer 11/95)
EI-BSG	Bensen B.80 Gyrocopter	HB		30. 1.86	(Stored 3/90)
EI-BSH	Colt 77A HAFB	792		10. 3.86	To G-BPLI 3/89. Canx 16.3.89.
EI-BSI	Douglas C-47B-35-DK Dakota	16631/33379	SU-BFY G-AMSN/KN673/44-77047	30. 3.86	Restored as G-AMSN 11/89. Canx 3.5.89.
EI-BSJ	Douglas C-47A-80-DL Dakota	19754	SU-BFY N920/60-SAA/60S-AAA/N161/43-15288	. 6.86R	NTU - To PH-DDZ 2.99. Canx.
EI-BSK	Socata TB-9 Tampico	618		9. 4.86	
EI-BSL	PA-34-220T Seneca III	34-8233041	N8468X	27. 6.86	
EI-BSM	Short SD.3-60 Var.100	SH3664	G-BLTO G-14-3664	. .86	Restored as G-BLTO. Canx 12.5.86.
EI-BSN(1)	Short SD.3-60 Var.100	SH3689	G-BMLD G-14-3689	. .86R	NTU - To EI-BSP 4/86. Canx.
EI-BSN(2)	Cameron O-65 HAFB	1278		14. 4.86	
EI-BSO	PA-28-140 Cherokee B	28-25449	C-GOBL N8241W	16. 4.86	
EI-BSP	Short SD.3-60 Var.100	SH3689	(EI-BSN) G-BMLD/G-14-3689	18. 4.86	To G-UBAC 4/93. Canx 4/93.
EI-BSQ	Colt Ax6-56Z HAFB	531	SE-ZBE	2. 7.86	Reported to have hit HT cables and envelope destroyed in early 1990. Canx 15.11.96 on owner's request as destroyed.
EI-BSR	Lake LA-4-200 Buccaneer	975	N3076P	11. 8.86	To D-ESAB 1/92. Canx 31.12.91.
EI-BSS	BAC One-Eleven 561RC	BAC.402	YR-BRB EI-BSS/YR-BRB/EI-BSS/YR-BRB/EI-BSS/YR-BSB	17.11.86	Restored as YR-BRB. Canx 6/93.
EI-BST	Bell 206B JetRanger II	1584	C-GTQH	1. 7.86	Ditched in the sea nr Dunquin, Co.Kerry on 24.9.91. Canx.
EI-BSU(1)	Reims Cessna F.172P Skyhawk II	-		. .86R	NTU. Canx.
EI-BSU(2)	Champion 7KCAB Citabria	124	N1621G	15. 6.87	
EI-BSV	Socata TB-20 Trinidad	579	G-BMIX	15. 8.86	
EI-BSW(1)	[Was reserved for "Follens"]			. .86R	NTU. Canx.
EI-BSW(2)	Solar Wings Pegasus XL-R	SW-TB-1124 & SW-WA-1122		22. 6.87	
EI-BSX	Piper J3C-65 Cub (Frame No 8999; official identity of c/n 13255 is incorrect - probably rebuilt 1945)	8912	G-ICUB F-BEGT/NC79805/45-4515/42-36788	25. 3.86	
EI-BSY	BAC One-Eleven 525FT	BAC.266	YR-BCN YU-ANM/YR-BCN/YU-AKN/YR-BCN	2. 3.87	Restored as YR-BCN. Canx 13.11.89.
EI-BSZ	BAC One-Eleven 525FT	BAC.272	YR-BCO YU-ANN/YR-BCO/G-TARO/YR-BCO	27. 4.87	Restored as YR-BCO. Canx 13.11.89.
EI-BTA	McDonnell Douglas DC-9-83 (MD-83) (Line No. 1270)	49391	(N9806F)	29. 4.86	To N16892. Canx 29.10.87.
EI-BTB	McDonnell Douglas DC-9-83 (MD-83) (Line No. 1272)	49392		1. 5.86	To N16893. Canx 26.1.88.
EI-BTC	McDonnell Douglas DC-9-83 (MD-83) (Line No. 1279)	49393	N6202D	2. 6.86	To N16894. Canx 5/92.
EI-BTD	McDonnell Douglas DC-9-83 (MD-83) (Line No. 1285)	49394		18. 6.86	To N16895. Canx 5/92.
EI-BTE	MBB Bo.105DBS-4	S.34	G-AZTI EC-DRY/G-AZTI/D-HDAN	6.10.86	Restored as G-AZTI. Canx 3.11.86.
EI-BTF	Boeing 737-3Y0 (Line No. 1353)	23684		19. 2.87	To F-GLTF 5/92. Canx 5/92.
EI-BTG	Douglas DC-8-71CF (Line No. 395)	46001	N872TV HB-IDM/N799FT/N863F	30. 1.87	To N706FT. Canx 19.5.87.
EI-BTH	Short SD.3-60 Var.300	SH3717	G-14-3717 G-BNFA/G-14-3717	26. 2.87	Restored as G-BNFA. Canx 21.3.94.
EI-BTI	Short SD.3-60 Var.300	SH3718	G-14-3718 G-BNFB/G-14-3718	26. 2.87	Restored as G-BNFB. Canx 19.4.94.
EI-BTJ	Short SD.3-60 Var.300	SH3719	G-14-3719 G-BNFC/G-14-3719	26. 2.87	W/o on Mt.Iligan, Philippines on 13.12.87. Canx.
EI-BTK	Short SD.3-60 Var.300	SH3720	G-14-3720 G-BNFD/G-14-3720	26. 2.87	Restored as G-BNFD. Canx 19.4.94.
EI-BTL	McDonnell Douglas DC-9-83 (MD-83) (Line No. 1343)	49399	(F-GGMA) EI-BTL/N6200N	26. 2.87	To F-GGMA 3/89. Canx.
EI-BTM	Boeing 737-317 (Line No. 1372)	23826		16. 4.87	To PP-SNV. Canx 21.5.87.
EI-BTN	Lockheed L.1011-385-50 Tristar	193C-1046	N702TT N702DA	27.10.87	Stored 12/93 Mojave, CA. Canx 31.5.96. Scrapped 1996.
EI-BTO	Short SD.3-60 Var.300	SH3727	G-BNMW G-14-3727	30.11.87	Restored as G-BNMW. Canx 27.5.94.
EI-BTP	Short SD.3-60 Var.300	SH3728	G-14-3728 EI-BTP/G-14-3728	8.12.87	To G-BNYF. Canx 25.5.94.
EI-BTQ	Boeing 747-2R7F (Line No. 354)	21650	LX-DCV	5.11.87	To N809FT. Canx 31.12.87.
EI-BTR	Boeing 737-2Q8 (Line No. 582)	21735	N133AW OO-TEM	19.11.87	To HA-LEA 12/88. Canx.
EI-BTS	Boeing 747-283M (Line No. 500)	22381	N4501Q EI-BTS/N4501Q/(OY-KHB)	20. 2.88	To N155FW 7/97. Canx 22.7.97.
EI-BTT	Boeing 737-375 (Line No. 1513)	23921		23. 2.88	To F-GLTT. Canx 8/92.

Regn	Type	c/n	Previous identity	Regn date	Fate or immediate subsequent identity (if known)
EI-BTU	McDonnell Douglas DC-9-83 (MD-83) (Line No. 1483)	49619	EC-FEB EC-642/N600DF/EI-BTU	1. 7.88	To N915PJ. Canx 2.2.94.
EI-BTV	McDonnell Douglas DC-9-83 (MD-83) (Line No. 1484)	49620	EC-EZU EC-531/EI-BTV	1. 7.88	To D-ALLV. Canx 12.4.95.
EI-BTW	Boeing 737-2Q8 (Line No. 642)	21960	G-BGTY	1. 6.88	To G-IBTW 4/89. Canx.
EI-BTX	McDonnell Douglas DC-9-82 (MD-82) (Line No. 1445)	49660	(N59842)	23. 3.88	
EI-BTY(1)	McDonnell Douglas DC-9-82 (MD-82) (Line No. 1452)	49661	(N11843)	. .86R	NTU - To EI-BWB 4/88. Canx.
EI-BTY(2)	McDonnell Douglas DC-9-82 (MD-82) (Line No. 1466)	49667	N12844	6. 5.88	
EI-BTZ	Boeing 737-2U4ADV (Line No. 761)	22576	N134AW G-OSLA	23. 3.88	To G-IBTZ 12/88. Canx.
EI-BUA	Cessna 172M Skyhawk II	172-65451	N5458H	8. 8.86	
EI-BUB	Short SC.7 Skyvan 3-100	SH1907	G-BKMD A40-SK/G-BAHK/G-14-79	1.12.86	Restored as G-BKMD 2/87. Canx 23.2.87.
EI-BUC	Jodel D.9 Bebe	RLS.1 & PFA/929	G-BASY	20. 1.87	
EI-BUD	Boeing 737-348QC (Line No. 1458)	23809	EC-FQP EC-279/EI-BUD/N1786B	21.10.87	To F-OGSY. Canx.
EI-BUE	Boeing 737-348QC (Line No. 1474)	23810	EC-FSC EC-375/EI-BUE	16.11.87	To F-OCHS. Canx.
EI-BUF	Cessna 210N Centurion II	210-63070	G-MCDS G-BHNB/N6496N	18.12.86	
EI-BUG	Socata ST-10 Diplomate	125	G-STIO OH-SAB	4. 2.87	
EI-BUH	Lake LA-4-200 Buccaneer	543	G-PARK G-BBGK/N39779	27. 5.87	
EI-BUI	Boeing 727-95 (Line No. 304)	19249	N7272V 4X-BAE/HK-2960/HK-2960X/G-BFGM/N1633	5. 5.87	Restored as N7272V. Canx 17.11.87.
EI-BUJ	Socata MS.892A Rallye Commodore 150	10737	G-FOAM G-AVPL	27. 2.87	Damaged pre .92 (Stored 6/97 Abbeyshrule - gone by 11/98)
EI-BUK	Cessna 402B	402B-1046	G-MOTE SE-GMG/(N98683)	24.10.86	To 5X-LCP. Canx 8/89.
EI-BUL	Whittaker MW.5 Sorcerer	1		4. 3.87	
EI-BUM	Cessna 404 Titan II	404-0650	N5313J	15. 5.87	To TL-ACB 12/94. Canx 29.11.94.
EI-BUN(1)	Cessna 551 Citation II (Unit No. 555)	551-0555	N1297Z	. .87R	NTU - To EI-BUY 7/87. Canx.
EI-BUN(2)	Beechcraft 76 Duchess	ME-371	(EI-BUO) N37001	26. 6.87	
EI-BUO(1)	Beechcraft 76 Duchess	ME-371	N37001	. 3.87R	NTU - To EI-BUN 6/87. Canx.
EI-BUO(2)	BAC One-Eleven 525FT	BAC.255	YR-BCL TC-AKA/YR-BCL/OE-ILC/YR-BCL	. 3.87R	NTU - To EI-BVG 3/88. Canx.
EI-BUO(3)	Aero Composites Sea Hawker (Now regd as Glass S.005E)	80		25. 8.87	Stored 6/97. (Damaged on landing at Strangford Lough in 9/91)
EI-BUP	Boeing 727-46 (Line No. 226)	18877	G-BAFZ HK-3270X/G-BAFZ/HK-3201X/G-BAFZ/JA8310	30.10.87	To N7046A 11.88. Canx 19.10.88.
EI-BUQ	BAC One-Eleven Srs.561RC	BAC.406	G-BNIH YR-BRF	. 3.87R	NTU - To EI-CAS 6/90. Canx.
EI-BUR	PA-38-112 Tomahawk	38-79A0363	G-BNDE N2541D	10. 7.87	
EI-BUS	PA-38-112 Tomahawk	38-79A0186	G-BNDF N2439C	10. 7.87	
EI-BUT	GEMS MS.893A Rallye Commodore 180 (Painted as a Galerien)	10559	SE-IMV F-BNBU	30. 7.87	
EI-BUU	Solar Wings Pegasus XL-R	SW-WA-1175	G-MTHK	. 8.87R	NTU - Remained as G-MTHK. Canx.
EI-BUV	Cessna 172RG Cutlass II	172RG-0710	N6449V	21. 5.87	Canx.
EI-BUW	Noble-Hardman Snowbird IIIA	SB-F001	77-DS (French)	8. 9.87	Badly damaged in crash Dromiskin, Co.Louth 1.6.92.
EI-BUX	Agusta A.109A	7147	N790SC (N466MP)/N790SC/N72521	10. 6.88	
EI-BUY	Cessna 551 Citation II (Unit No. 555)	551-0555	(EI-BUN) N1297Z	14. 7.87	To D-IRKE. Canx 15.6.92.
EI-BUZ	Robinson R-22 HP	0242	G-BMTM (N9081S)/ZS-HLL	2. 6.87	To N..... 3/96. Canx 14.3.96.
EI-BVA(1)	Boeing 737-2L9 (Line No. 620)	22071	VR-HKP EI-BOJ/G-GPAB/G-BJSO/EI-BOJ/(EI-BOG)/G-BJSO/(EI-BMB)/SU-BCJ/OY-APN	. .87R	NTU - To N281LF. Canx.
EI-BVA(2)	Cessna 404 Titan II	404-0237	SE-GYN LN-LML/SE-GYN/(N88723)	29. 7.87	To N404CP 9/93. Canx 16.9.93.
EI-BVB	Whittaker MW.6 Merlin	1		14. 9.87	
EI-BVC	Cameron N-65 HAFB	1566		21.10.87	Canx 20.5.98 as removed from service.
EI-BVD	Boeing 707-337B (Line No. 402)	18873	EL-AJS VT-DSI/N68655	. .87R	NTU - remained as EL-AJS. Canx.
EI-BVE	Jodel D.9 Bebe	547	G-AXYU	13.10.87	Restored as G-AXYU 7/95. Canx 28.5.95.
EI-BVF	Reims Cessna F.172N Skyhawk II	1777	G-BGHJ	30.10.87	
EI-BVG	BAC One-Eleven 525FT	BAC.255	YR-BCL EI-BVG/(EI-BUO)/YR-BCL/TC-AKA/YR-BCL/OE-ILC/YR-BCL	23. 3.88	Restored as YR-BCL 11/92. Canx 11/92.
EI-BVH	BAC One-Eleven 561RC	BAC.407	YR-BRG	31. 3.88	Restored as YR-BRG. Canx 10/93.
EI-BVI	BAC One-Eleven 525FT	BAC.256	YR-BCM OE-ILD/YR-BCM	30. 5.88	Restored as YR-BCM. Canx 10/93.
EI-BVJ(1)	Short SD.3-60 Var.100	SH3695	G-14-3695 (5N-AOX)/G-BMNK/G-14-3695	. 1.88R	NTU - To EI-BVM 3/88. Canx.
EI-BVJ(2)	AMF Chevvron 2-32	009		16. 2.88	

Regn	Type	c/n	Previous identity	Regn date	Fate or immediate subsequent identity (if known)
EI-BVK	PA-38-112 Tomahawk	38-79A0966	OO-FLG OO-HLG/N9705N	2. 3.88	
EI-BVL	Bell 412	33168	N320TQ	.12.88	To HB-XTA 2/89. Canx.
EI-BVM	Short SD.3-60 Var.100	SH3695	(EI-BVJ) G-14-3695/5N-AOX/G-BMNK/G-14-3695	7. 3.88	To G-TBAC 10/92. Canx 1.10.92.
EI-BVN	Bell 206B JetRanger II	2999	G-BKCM	29. 3.88	To N54AJ 1/93. Canx 23.12.92.
EI-BVO	Boeing 727-225F (Line No. 823)	20381	N8838E	11. 5.88	Restored as N8838E 10/88. Canx
EI-BVP	Cessna T303 Crusader	T303-00286	N5087V	12. 4.88	To N7079U 8/93. Canx 8.93.
EI-BVQ	Cameron Club 90SS HAFB (Club Orange Soft Drink Can shape)	1717		19. 7.88	To G-BWNP 3/96. Canx 16.2.96.
EI-BVR	Robinson R-22 Alpha	0452	G-WYRL N8556D	29. 4.88	W/o at Newhall, Naas, Co.Kildare, Ireland on 24.5.89.
EI-BVS	Cessna 172RG Cutlass II	172RG-0908	N9597B	12. 5.88	To N1937Z 9/97. Canx 4.9.97.
EI-BVT	Evans VP-2	V2-2129 & PFA/7221 & SAAC-20	G-BEIE	29. 4.88	
EI-BVU	Cessna 152 II	152-83182	N47184	7. 6.88	To G-BWEV 6/95. Canx 15.6.85.
EI-BVV	Cessna 152 II	152-85018	N6467P	7. 6.88	W/o at Mooretown, Ratoath, Co.Meath, Ireland on 27.9.88. Wreck at Dublin. Canx 8/91.
EI-BVW	Cessna 152 II	152-85123	N6093Q	7. 6.88	To G-IAFT 6/95. Canx 15.6.95.
EI-BVX	Embraer EMB.110P1 Bandeirante	110-419	N870AC PT-SGL	7. 6.88	To DQ-AFO 7/95. Canx 19.5.95.
EI-BVY	Heintz Zenith CH.200-AA-RW	2-582 & SAAC-26		7. 6.88	
EI-BVZ	Scheibe SF-25B Falke	46126	D-KADB	8. 7.88	Canx. at owner's request 3.3.94. To G-FEFE 4/94.
EI-BWA	Douglas DC-9-51 (Line No. 783)	47656	HB-ISM	2. 6.88	To SU-BKK. Canx 15.6.88.
EI-BWB	McDonnell Douglas DC-9-82 (MD-82) (Line No. 1452)	49661	(EI-BTY) (N11843)	6. 4.88	To SU-DAK. Canx.
EI-BWC(1)	McDonnell Douglas DC-9-83 (MD-83) (Line No. 1467)	49668	(N14845)	. 6.88R	To EC-163/EC-EIK. Canx.
EI-BWC(2)	Boeing 737-291 (Line No. 965)	23024	CS-TMC VT-EQJ/EI-BWC/N7399F	30. 9.88	To CS-TIS. Canx 6/92.
EI-BWD	McDonnell Douglas DC-9-83 (MD-83) (Line No. 1414)	49575	9Y-THT EI-BWD/EC-EFJ/EC-102	13. 4.88	
EI-BWE	McDonnell Douglas DC-9-83 (MD-83) (Line No. 1422)	49576	EC-EFK	29. 4.88	To F-GHED 1/89. Canx.
EI-BWF	Boeing 747-283M (Line No. 358)	21575	LX-OCV SE-DFZ/(EI-BWF)/N9727N/SE-DFZ/(SE-DEF)	12. 9.88	To N9727N. Canx 15.8.96.
EI-BWG	Douglas DC-8-71 (Line No. 507)	46099	F-GMFM (F-GFMF)/N917R/JA8041	. 8.88R	NTU - To 9J-AFL. Canx 13.10.89.
EI-BWH	Partenavia P.68C Victor	212	G-BHJP	11.12.87	
EI-BWI	BAC One-Eleven Srs.201AC	BAC.007	N101EX G-ASJC	20. 7.88	Restored as G-ASJC 10/90. Canx.
EI-BWJ	BAC One-Eleven Srs.201AC	BAC.009	N102EX (N29967)/G-ASJE	30. 8.88	Stored 3/91 Orlando International, FL. Broken up for spares. Canx 14.1.91.
EI-BWK	BAC One-Eleven Srs.201AC	BAC.011	N104EX G-ASJG	15. 7.88	To G-DBAF 7/90. Canx.
EI-BWL	BAC One-Eleven Srs.201AC	BAC.012	N105EX G-ASJH	20. 7.88	To G-OCNW 10/90. Canx.
EI-BWM	BAC One-Eleven Srs.201AC	BAC.013	N106EX G-ASJI	19. 7.88	To 9Q-CSJ. Canx 4/91.
EI-BWN	BAC One-Eleven Srs.203AE	BAC.020	N1546	13. 6.88	Stored 1/91 Orlando International, FL. Broken up. Canx 14.1.91.
EI-BWO	BAC One-Eleven Srs.203AE	BAC.041	N1547 (G-BLVO)/N1547	1. 9.88	DBF at Calabar, Nigeria on 29.7.97. Canx.
EI-BWP	BAC One-Eleven Srs.203AE	BAC.043	N1549 (G-BLVP)/N1549	29. 8.88	Stored 15.10.94 Southend, UK. Broken up 9/96. Canx 14.12.90.
EI-BWQ	BAC One-Eleven Srs.401AK	BAC.057	N170FE VR-CBI/N277NS/N5017	21. 7.88	To 9Q-CUG 9/90. Canx.
EI-BWR	BAC One-Eleven Srs.401AK	BAC.061	N171FE N40AS/N5021/N69HM/N5021	22. 7.88	To N682RW. Canx 6/90.
EI-BWS	BAC One-Eleven Srs.201AC	BAC.085	N107EX G-ASTJ	19. 7.88	To XA-RTN 1/91. Canx 14.1.91.
EI-BWT	BAC One-Eleven Srs.414EG	BAC.127	N174FE G-AZED/(N174FE)/G-AZED/(G-AZDG)/D-ANDY/G-16-3	22. 7.88	To 5N-BAB. Canx 4/91.
EI-BWU	Swearingen (Fairchild) SA.227AC Metro IV	AC-705	N2717K	29. 8.88	To ZK-NSU 4/90. Canx.
EI-BWV	Swearingen (Fairchild) SA.227AC Metro IV	AC-711	N2719B	1. 9.88	To ZK-NSY 4/90. Canx.
EI-BWW	Swearingen (Fairchild) SA.227AC Metro IV	AC-712	N2719C	12. 8.89	To ZK-NSZ 5/90. Canx.
EI-BWX	DHC.8-102 Dash Eight	113	C-FCTD C-GEOA	29. 9.88	To V2-LDQ. Canx 29.11.90.
EI-BWY	Boeing 737-291 (Line No. 923)	22744	N7358F (N34257)/N7358F	30. 9.88	To VT-EQH 11/88. Canx.
EI-BWZ	Boeing 737-291 (Line No. 957)	23023	CS-TMB VT-EQI/EI-BWZ/N7259F/(N67258)/N7359F	30. 9.88	To TF-ABI 5/92. Canx.
EI-BXA	Boeing 737-448 (Line No. 1742)	24474		28. 6.89	
EI-BXB	Boeing 737-448 (Line No. 1778)	24521		27.10.89	

Regn	Type	c/n	Previous identity	Regn date	Fate or immediate subsequent identity (if known)
EI-BXC	Boeing 737-448 (Line No. 1850)	24773		26. 4.90	
EI-BXD	Boeing 737-448 (Line No. 1867)	24866		1. 6.90	
EI-BXE	Boeing 737-548 (Line No. 1939)	24878		30.10.90	To EI-CDA 6/91. Canx.
EI-BXF	Boeing 737-548 (Line No. 1970)	24919		. .90R	To EI-CDB 5/91. Canx.
EI-BXG	Boeing 737-548 (Line No. 1975)	24968		. .90R	To EI-CDC 6/91. Canx.
EI-BXH	Boeing 737-548 (Line No. 1989)	24989		. .90R	To EI-CDD 7/91. Canx.
EI-BXI	Boeing 737-448 (Line No. 2036)	25052		29. 4.91	
EI-BXJ	Boeing 737-548 (Line No. 2050)	25115		. .90R	NTU - To EI-CDE 5/91. Canx.
EI-BXK	Boeing 737-448 (Line No. 2269)	25736		14. 4.92	
EI-BXL	Polaris F1B OK350 Microlight	M.561628		27. 6.91	
EI-BXM	Boeing 737-2T4C (Line No. 989)	23065	B-2504	. .91R	NTU - To N675MA. Canx.
EI-BXN(1)	Canadair CL.600-1A11 Challenger	1048	N601LS N600LS/N500LS/N600TT/N29687/C-GLXK	. 6.88R	NTU - To C-FSIP. Canx.
EI-BXN(2)	Microlight	?		. .89R	NTU. Canx. [Possibly Mainair Gemini/Flash 2A c/n 734-289-6 & W526 ex.G-MVOZ canx 25.9.89 to EI-... but restored as G-MVOZ on 1.4.93 !]
EI-BXN(3)	Boeing 737-2T4C (Line No. 992)	23066	B-2505	. .91R	NTU - To N676MA. Canx.
EI-BXO	Fouga (Valmet) CM-170 Magister	213	N18FM FM-28	21.11.88	(C/n unconfirmed) (Stored 4/96) (Sold to garage at Swords, nr.Dublin)
EI-BXP	PA-23-250 Turbo Aztec E	27-7305142	G-BSFL PH-NOA/9M-AUS/PH-NOA/N40378	1. 7.88	To N250MC 6/96. Canx 5.6.96.
EI-BXQ	Bell 206B JetRanger	348	G-BEWY 9Y-TDF	20. 7.88	To G-CULL 5/89. Canx 18.4.89.
EI-BXR	ATR-42-310	107	F-WWEE	13. 9.88	To F-GHPX 6/93. Canx 6/93.
EI-BXS	ATR-42-300	142	F-WWEN	24. 5.89	To HK-3943X 7/94. Canx 2.9.94.
EI-BXT	Rollason Druine D.62B Condor	RAE/626	G-AVZE	24. 8.88	
EI-BXU	PA-28-161 Cherokee Warrior II	28-7716097	G-BNUP N2282Q	3.10.88	To G-BYXU 1/99. Canx 7.1.99.
EI-BXV	Boeing 737-212 (Line No. 281)	20492	N7382F (N14250)/N7382F/9V-BCR	18.10.88	To VT-EQG 3/89. Canx 5.4.89.
EI-BXW	Boeing 737-291 (Line No. 909)	22743	N7357F (N34256)/N7357F	18.10.88	To CC-CEA 12/88. Canx.
EI-BXX	Agusta-Bell 206B JetRanger III	8560	G-JMVB G-OIML	15.11.88	
EI-BXY	Boeing 737-2S3 (Line No. 646)	22278	G-BJFH	16.12.88	To TF-ABN 3/93. Canx 1.4.93.
EI-BXZ	Flexiform Microlight	LPX.12		19.12.88	Canx 6.7.94 at owner's request. Aircraft dismantled.
EI-BYA	Thruster TST Mk.1	8504	G-MNDA	1. 2.89	
EI-BYB	Robinson R-22 Beta	0957	G-BPMK	1. 3.89	DBR near Enniskerry, Co.Wicklow, Ireland on 26.12.91. Canx 2/92.
EI-BYC	Bensen B.8MR Gyrocopter	-		24. 2.89	Canx 6.7.94 at owner's request. Aircraft dismantled.
EI-BYD(1)	Canadair CL.600-1A11 Challenger	1035	C-FEAQ N64FC/N122WF/N122TY/C-GLYA	. .89R	NTU - To VR-BLD .89. Canx.
EI-BYD(2)	Heintz Zenith CH-250 (Also quoted as c/n A2-866)	MS/FAS 2866		. 6.89R	NTU - To EI-BYL 6/89. Canx.
EI-BYD(3)	Cessna 150J Commuter	150-70878	N61193	20.11.89	
EI-BYE	PA-31-350 Navajo Chieftain	31-7305118	G-BFDA SE-GDR	29. 5.89	
EI-BYF	Cessna 150M Commuter	150-76654	N3924V	20.11.89	
EI-BYG	Socata TB-9 Tampico Club	928		22. 8.89	
EI-BYH	Cessna 340A/RAM II	340A-0316	N4146G	11. 5.89	To N56ME. Canx 14.5.96.
EI-BYI(1)	Short S.25 Sandringham (Short conversion c/n SH.55C from Sunderland GR.3)	SH974	G-BJHS N158J/VH-BRF/R.New Zealand AF NZ4108/ML814	. .89R	NTU - Remained as G-BJHS. Canx.
EI-BYI(2)	Colt 77A HAFB	1158	G-READ	9.10.93	Restored as G-READ 4/96. Canx 18.4.96.
EI-BYJ	Bell 206B JetRanger II	1897	N49725	23. 6.89	
EI-BYK	PA-23-250 Aztec E	27-7305075	G-BBEW N40262	6. 6.89	Restored as G-BBEW 8/98. Canx 10.8.98.
EI-BYL	Heintz Zenith CH-250 (Also quoted as c/n A2-866)	MS/FAS 2866	(EI-BYD)	14. 6.89	Stored at Strandhill, Sligo in 5/96.
EI-BYM	Cessna 500 Citation I (Unit No. 179)	500-0179	(N997S) N427DM/N111KR/N444J	8.11.89	To N179EA. Canx 4/91.
EI-BYN	Cessna 550 Citation II (Unit No. 188)	550-0171	N333CG (N984H)/N934H/N43D/(C-GDPE)/(N88797)	27. 7.89	To (N171VP)/N19AJ. Canx 4.2.94.
EI-BYO	ATR-42-310	161	F-WWEH	10.11.89	To OY-CIS. Canx 21.11.96.
EI-BYP(1)	ATR-42-300	236	F-WWES	. .91R	NTU - To 7Q-YKQ. Canx.
EI-BYP(2)	Cameron Concept-60 HAFB	3078		21. 5.93	To G-BWRT 10/96. Canx 21.10.96.
EI-BYQ	ATR-42-310	245	F-WWET	. .91R	NTU - To TS-LBA. Canx.
EI-BYR	Bell 206L-3 Long Ranger III	51284	(EI-LMG) EI-BYR/D-HBAD	15. 8.89	

Regn	Type	c/n	Previous identity	Regn date	Fate or immediate subsequent identity (if known)
EI-BYS	Robinson R-22 Beta	0832	G-OMJD	21. 9.89	w/o in 11/95. Canx 6.2.96 as scrapped.
EI-BYT	Aerospatiale AS.350B Ecureuil	1647	(F-GIIC)	13. 9.89	To F-GIJQ 4/93. Canx 1.4.93.
			EI-BYT/G-JRBI/EI-BNO(2)/G-BKJY		
EI-BYU	Short SD.3-60 Var.100	SH3632	OY-MMA	13.10.89	Restored as OY-MMA 10/90. Canx 30.10.90.
			G-BLCP		
EI-BYV	Hughes 369D (500D)	50-0696D	G-ITUP	16. 2.90	To TC-HMC 4/93. Canx 3/93.
			G-KSBF/G-BMJH		
EI-BYW	Thruster T.300	009-T300-370		25. 1.90	To G-MWWS 11/91. Canx 1.11.91.
EI-BYX	Champion 7GCAA Citbria	7GCAA-40	N546DS	4. 4.90	
EI-BYY	Piper J3C-85 Cub (L-4H-PI)	12494	EC-AQZ	12. 4.90	
	(Regd with c/n 22288 and officially		HB-OSG/44-80198		
	therefore ex.G-AKTJ/N3595K/NC3595K; actually frame no. 12322)				
EI-BYZ	PA-44-180 Seminole	44-7995202	N2193K	27. 6.90	To G-GSFT 10/98. Canx 12.10.98.
EI-BZA	Boeing 747-283B	22496	N4502R	18. 2.89	To N622FF 2/98. Canx 10.2.98.
	(Line No. 540)		(LN-RNB)		
EI-BZB	Airbus A.300C4-203F	083	RP-C3007	31. 1.89	To TC-MNG 11/97. Canx 11.11.97.
			EI-BZB/D-AHLB/F-WZES		
EI-BZC	DHC.8-102 Dash Eight	140	C-GFOD	30. 3.89	To V2-LDP 11/90. Canx.
EI-BZD	Douglas DC-10-30F	46976	C-GXRB	19. 4.89	To N602DC. Canx 6.5.92.
	(Line No. 254)		N8712Q		
EI-BZE	Boeing 737-3Y0	24464		2. 8.89	
	(Line No. 1753)				
EI-BZF	Boeing 737-3Y0	24465		7. 8.89	
	(Line No. 1755)				
EI-BZG	Boeing 737-3Y0	24466		2.10.89	DBR at Manila, Philippines on 11.5.90. Canx 5.12.90.
	(Line No. 1771)				
EI-BZH	Boeing 737-3Y0	24546		3. 1.90	To G-IGOC 5/98. Canx 1.5.98.
	(Line No. 1811)				
EI-BZI	Boeing 737-3Y0	24547		7. 2.90	To G-IGOE 5/98. Canx 19.5.98.
	(Line No. 1813)				
EI-BZJ	Boeing 737-3Y0	24677		29. 3.90	
	(Line No. 1837)				
EI-BZK	Boeing 737-3Y0	24678		4. 5.90	To G-IGOA 7/98. Canx 16.7.98.
	(Line No. 1853)				
EI-BZL	Boeing 737-3Y0	24680		4.10.90	
	(Line No. 1927)				
EI-BZM	Boeing 737-3Y0	24681		15.10.90	
	(Line No. 1929)				
EI-BZN	Boeing 737-3Y0	24770		30.10.90	
	(Line No. 1941)				
EI-BZO	Boeing 737-3Y0	23922	EC-EHZ	30. 8.89	To PP-VOM. Canx 18.10.89.
	(Line No. 1538)		EC-151		
EI-BZP	Boeing 737-3Y0	23923	EI-CEE	30. 8.89	To EC-898/EC-FJZ 11/91. Canx.
	(Line No. 1540)		G-TEAB/(N117AW)/EI-EZP/LN-AEQ/EI-BZP/EC-EIA/EC-152		
EI-BZQ	Boeing 737-3Y0	24462	(N116AW)	30. 8.89	To G-TEAA 4/90. Canx.
	(Line No. 1691)		EI-BZQ/EC-ENS/EC-244/N5573K		
EI-BZR	Boeing 737-3Y0	24463	YV-99C	7. 9.89	Restored as YV-99C. Canx 16.11.89.
	(Line No. 1701)		EI-BZR/EC-ENT/EC-245/N1779B		
EI-BZS	Boeing 737-3Y0	23747	EC-EBX	7. 9.89	To SE-DLN 9/89. Canx 26.9.89.
	(Line No. 1363)				
EI-BZT	Boeing 737-3Y0	23748	(OO-IIE)	11. 9.89	To EC-356/EC-FRP. Canx 3/93.
	(Line No. 1381)		PP-SOB/SE-DLO/PP-SOB/SE-DLO/EI-BZT/EC-EBY		
EI-BZU	Douglas DC-8-71F	45994	SE-DLH	24. 8.89	To N501SR. Canx 11.11.93.
	(Line No. 387)		EI-BZU/N8090U		
EI-BZV	McDonnell Douglas DC-9-83 (MD-83)			1. 9.89	To N509MD. Canx 14.9.89.
	(Line No. 1627)	49784			
EI-BZW	Douglas DC-9-15	47126	XA-SOH	17.11.89	To XA-LAC 9/90. Canx 18.10.90.
	(Line No. 405)				
EI-BZX	Douglas DC-9-15	47059	XA-SOA	17.11.89	To XA-RNQ 9/90. Canx 21.8.90.
	(Line No. 125)				
EI-BZY	Douglas DC-9-15	47084	XA-SOY	17.11.89	To XA-GDL 11/90. Canx 16.11.90.
	(Line No. 139)		XA-SOB		
EI-BZZ	Douglas DC-9-15	47122	XA-SOD	17.11.89	To XA-RKT 3/90. Canx 9.3.90.
	(Line No. 224)				
EI-CAA	Reims Cessna FR.172J Rocket	0486	G-BHTW	17. 8.89	Damaged 93/94. (Derelict airframe stored 10/98 at
			5Y-ATO		Abbeyshrule) Canx as WFU 27.11.98.
EI-CAB	Grob G-115A	8091	(D-EGVV)	23.10.89	To G-MERF 7/95. Canx 21.7.85.
EI-CAC	Grob G-115A	8092	(D-EGVV)	22.10.89	
EI-CAD	Grob G-115A	8104	(D-EGVV)	30. 1.90	To G-WIZB 9/98. Canx 2.9.98.
EI-CAE	Grob G-115A	8105	(D-EGVV)	5. 4.90	
EI-CAF	Bell 206B JetRanger II	2165	C-GTVH	23.10.89	To VH-JWK 9/94. Canx 7.1.94.
EI-CAG(1)	Boeing 767-2B1ER	25421		. .89R	NTU - To EI-CEM 1/92. Canx 6.1.92.
	(Line No. 407)				
EI-CAG(2)	Piper PA-31P Pressurised Navajo	-		. .89R	Possibly NTU.
EI-CAH	Gulfstream G.1159C Gulfstream IV		N17585	17.10.90	To ZS-NMO. Canx 6.5.94.
		1129			
EI-CAI	Boeing 747-123	20108	VH-EEI	22.10.89	To G-VMIA 3/90. Canx.
	(Line No. 87)		G-HIHO/(LX-NCV)/N14939/N9669		
EI-CAJ	O'Leary Biplane	-		4. 1.90	Canx 6.7.94 at owner's request. Aircraft dismantled.
EI-CAK	Douglas DC-8-63F	46121	(EI-CAV)	23. 8.90	To N786AL. Canx 13.7.94.
	(Line No. 500)		(EI-CAK)/TF-FLV/PH-DEK/(PI-C827)		
EI-CAL	Boeing 767-3Y0ER	24952	XA-RWW	19. 3.91	To N249WP/N24952. Canx 2.5.96.
	(Line No. 354)		EI-CAL		

Regn	Type	c/n	Previous identity	Regn date	Fate or immediate subsequent identity (if known)
EI-CAM	Boeing 767-3Y0ER	24953	XA-RWX	15. 2.93	To N632TW 1/97. Canx 3.1.97.
	(Line No. 405)		(EI-CAM)		
EI-CAN	Aerotech MW-5(K) Sorcerer		(G-MWGH)	15. 6.90	
		5K-0011-02			
EI-CAO	Cameron O-84 HAFB	2315		30. 7.90	To G-MOSY 4/96. Canx 17.4.96.
EI-CAP	Cessna R182 Skylane RG II		G-BMUF	27. 4.90	
		R182-00056	N7342W		
EI-CAQ	[This registration is being used by Aer Lingus as a "dummy" mark for ACARS testing]				
EI-CAR	Schweizer Hughes 269C (300C)	S.1454	N69A	30. 4.90	To G-PKPK 8/93. Canx 8/93.
EI-CAS(1)	Cessna P210N Pressurized Centurion		G-OPMB	. .90R	NTU - To EI-CAX 7/90. Canx.
	II	P210-00215	N4553K		
EI-CAS(2)	BAC One-Eleven 561RC	BAC.406	(EI-BUQ)	1. 6.90	Restored as YR-BRF 9/90. Canx.
			G-BNIH/YR-BRF		
EI-CAT	Cessna 421C Golden Eagle III		G-ICAT	17.12.90	Restored as N421PB 3/93. Canx 3/93.
		421C-0617	EI-CAT/G-OPEE/N421PB/N8507Z/G-OSSH/N88627		
EI-CAU	AMF Chevvron 2-32	022		14.11.90	
EI-CAV	Douglas DC-8-63F	46121	(EI-CAK)	. .90R	NTU - Reverted to EI-CAK. Canx.
	(Line No. 500)		TF-FLV/PH-DEK/(PI-C827)		
EI-CAW	Bell 206B JetRanger	780	N2947W	11. 7.90	
EI-CAX	Cessna P210N Pressurized Centurion		(EI-CAS)	9. 7.90	(On overhaul 6/98)
	II	P210-00215	G-OPMB/N4553K		
EI-CAY	Mooney M.20C Ranger	690074	N9272V	14.11.90	
EI-CAZ	Fairchild-Hiller FH-227D	519	SE-KBR	23. 9.91	WFU - To Norwich Airport Fire Service (Extant 2/99).
			C-FNAK/CF-NAK/N2735R/(N701U)		Canx 15.12.94.
EI-CBA	Douglas DC-9-15	47123	XA-SOE	17.11.89	Stored 1989 Waco, TX. Broken up. Canx 16.1.91.
	(Line No. 253)				
EI-CBB	Douglas DC-9-15	45785	XA-SOJ	17.11.89	To XA-RRY. Canx 18.12.89.
	(Line No. 64)		N1790U/HB-IFC		
EI-CBC	ATR-72-201	147	(N974NA)	5. 1.90	To EC-GQS 4/98. Canx 25.3.98.
			F-WWET		
EI-CBD	ATR-72-201	150	(N975NA)	7. 3.90	To EC-GUL 6/98. Canx 13.5.98.
			F-WWEI		
EI-CBE	McDonnell Douglas DC-9-83 (MD-83)		EC-EXX	21. 3.90	To SE-DPS. Canx 27.4.94.
	(Line No. 1332)	49398	EC-479/EI-CBE/G-PATA/N6202S/(G-LOGI)		
EI-CBF	ATR-42-310	176	(N426TE)	23. 2.90	To OY-MUK 5/99. Canx 19.4.99.
			F-WWEG		
EI-CBG	Douglas DC-9-51	47742	9Y-TFG	3. 4.90	To N662HA. Canx 29.4.97.
	(Line No. 857)				
EI-CBH	Douglas DC-9-51	47796	9Y-TGC	27. 4.90	To N661HA. Canx 2.5.97.
	(Line No. 903)				
EI-CBI	Douglas DC-9-51	48122	9Y-TGP	26. 7.90	To N660HA. Canx 29.4.97.
	(Line No. 972)				
EI-CBJ	DHC.8-102A Dash Eight	215	C-GFCF	25. 5.90	
EI-CBK	ATR-42-310	199	F-WWEM	25. 7.90	Stored 10/97 Calgary, Canada.
EI-CBL	Boeing 737-2K6	20957	HR-SHA	10.10.90	DBR at San Jose, Costa Rica on 17.11.91.
	(Line No. 377)				Canx 26.7.94 at owner's request as crashed.
EI-CBM	Lockheed L.1011-385-100 Tristar		A40-TS	27.10.90	To EL-AKG. Canx 5/91.
		193P-1068	JA8505		
EI-CBN	McDonnell Douglas DC-9-83 (MD-83)		EC-FEQ	6.11.90	To N902PJ. Canx 2.2.94.
	(Line No. 1357)	49401	EC-714/EI-CBN/EC-ECN/N6200N		
EI-CBO	McDonnell Douglas DC-9-83 (MD-83)		HB-IUL	6.11.90	
	(Line No. 1358)	49442	SE-DRU/TC-TRU/EI-CBO/EC-ECO/N6203D		
EI-CBP	Boeing 737-4Y0	24905		26. 2.91	To CS-TKE. Canx 16.3.94.
	(Line No. 2001)				
EI-CBQ	Boeing 737-3Y0	24907		19. 3.91	To UR-GAE. Canx 25.4.95.
	(Line No. 2013)				
EI-CBR	McDonnell Douglas DC-9-83 (MD-83)			3.12.90	
	(Line No. 1787)	49939			
EI-CBS	McDonnell Douglas DC-9-83 (MD-83)			10.12.90	
	(Line No. 1799)	49942			
EI-CBT	Boeing 737-4Y0	24692	N6069D	18.12.90	To PT-TEO 1/91. Canx 26.1.91.
	(Line No. 1885)		(HR-SHM)		
EI-CBU	McDonnell Douglas DC-9-87 (MD-87)		XA-RUO	. .91R	NTU - Remained as XA-RUO. Canx.
	(Line No. 1508)	49673	9V-TRY/(A3-RTA)		
EI-CBV	DHC.8-102A Dash Eight	270	C-GESR	30. 5.91	To V2-LDU 11/91. Canx.
EI-CBW	Airbus A.300B4-203	269	ZS-SDI	30. 5.91	To AP-BEL 4/93. Canx 4/93.
			LX-LGP/9V-STH/F-WZMB		
EI-CBX	McDonnell Douglas DC-9-83 (MD-83)		TC-INA	31. 7.91	To F-GPZA 4/98. Canx 31.3.98.
	(Line No. 1887)	49943	EI-CBX		
EI-CBY	McDonnell Douglas DC-9-83 (MD-83)			30. 7.91	
	(Line No. 1888)	49944			
EI-CBZ	McDonnell Douglas DC-9-83 (MD-83)		N6206F	13. 8.91	
	(Line No. 1889)	49945			
EI-CCA	Beechcraft A23-19A Musketeer Sport		G-AWTR	18. 7.90	
		MB-411	N2758B		
EI-CCB	PA-44-180 Seminole	44-7995179	N2093K	6. 9.90	(Stored 8/96)
EI-CCC	McDonnell Douglas DC-9-83 (MD-83)			27. 9.91	
	(Line No. 1898)	49946			
EI-CCD	Grob G-115A	8108	D-EIUD	15. 8.90	(Also reported as ex D-EIWD)
			(VH-...)/(D-EGVV)		
EI-CCE(1)	PA-12 Super Cruiser	12-3110	N4214M	. .90R	NTU - To EI-CFH 6/91. Canx.
			NC4214M		

Regn	Type	c/n	Previous identity	Regn date	Fate or immediate subsequent identity (if known)
EI-CCE(2)	McDonnell Douglas DC-9-83 (MD-83) (Line No. 1900)	49947		19. 9.91	
EI-CCF	Aeronca 11AC Chief	11AC-S-40	N3826E NC3826E	10. 1.91	
EI-CCG	Robinson R-22 Beta	1463		8. 8.90	Damaged in landing accident at Shannon on 30.12.92. Canx 5/93.
EI-CCH	Piper J3C-65 Cub	7278	N38801 NC30001	24. 1.91	
EI-CCI	American Aviation AA-5 Traveler	AA5-0773	G-BDCL EI-BGV/G-BDCL/N1373R	17. 9.90	Restored as G-BDCL 11/90. Canx.
EI-CCJ	Cessna 152 II	152-80174	N24251	9.10.90	(Stored - for sale 2/95)
EI-CCK	Cessna 152 II	152-79610	N757BM	9.10.90	(Damaged in heavy landing pre .95)
EI-CCL	Cessna 152 II	152-80382	N24791	9.10.90	Badly damaged in forced landing at Bray Head, Co.Wicklow on 4.5.93. (Status uncertain)
EI-CCM	Cessna 152 II	152-82320	N68679	9.10.90	
EI-CCN	Grob G-115A	8100	G-BSGE (VH-...)/(D-EGVV)	14.11.90	DBR in gales at Cork (date?). Canx 6.4.98 as destroyed. To G-BYFD 4/99.
EI-CCO	PA-44-180 Seminole (Regd with c/n 44-79951590)	44-7995190	N2135G	19. 2.91	To G-FSFT 10/98. Canx 12.10.98.
EI-CCP	Cessna 152 II	152-81625	G-BNOZ N65570	3.12.90	Restored as G-BNOZ 3/92. Canx 3/92.
EI-CCQ	Slingsby T.61F Venture T.2	1974	G-BSWL ZA655	15. 7.91	Restored as G-BSWL 11/97. Canx 19.11.97.
EI-CCR	Aero Commander 690D	15041	N68GA	13.12.90	To N82BA. Canx 27.1.94.
EI-CCS	Enstrom 280C-UK Shark	1173	G-SHXX G-BGMX/EI-BHR/G-BGMX/(F-GBOS)	28.11.90	Restored as G-BGMX. Canx 19.8.94.
EI-CCT	Robinson R-22 Mariner	0847M	(EI-KMA) G-STOI	3.12.90	To G-BXWW 6.98. Canx 27.5.98.
EI-CCU	BAC One-Eleven Srs.531FS	BAC.237	G-DJOS G-AYWB/VR-CAB/TI-LRL/TI-LRF/TI-1084C/(G-AYWB)	18.12.90	Restored as G-AYWB 11/94. Canx 1.11.94.
EI-CCV(1)	BAC One-Eleven Srs.518FG	BAC.201	G-FLRU G-AXMG/5B-DAF/G-AXMG	. .90R	NTU - To EI-CDO 5/91. Canx.
EI-CCV(2)	Cessna R172K Hawk XP II	R172-3039	N758EP	2. 3.91	
EI-CCW	BAC One-Eleven Srs.509EW	BAC.186	G-BSYN G-AWWZ	12. 4.91	Restored as G-AWWZ. Canx 27.4.94.
EI-CCX	BAC One-Eleven Srs.523FJ	BAC.211	G-EKPT G-AXLN/VR-CAL/TG-AYA/PP-SDU/G-AXLN	18.12.90	To 5N-EYI. Canx 26.10.94.
EI-CCY	American Aviation AA-1B Trainer	AA1B-0617	G-BDYC	19. 3.91	Fatal crash on take-off from Galway/Carnmore on 5.11.94. (Wreck stored 4/96)
EI-CCZ	Reims Cessna F.150L Commuter	0820	G-BABH	26. 3.91	Restored as G-BABH 3/95. Canx 16.3.95.
EI-CDA(1)	Hiller UH-12E	2292	G-BDYY XS705	. .91R	NTU - Remained as G-BDDY. Canx.
EI-CDA(2)	Boeing 737-548 (Line No. 1939)	24878	EI-BXE	26. 6.91	To YR-BGZ 6/99. Canx 22.6.99.
EI-CDB	Boeing 737-548 (Line No. 1970)	24919	EI-BXF	27. 5.91	
EI-CDC	Boeing 737-548 (Line No. 1975)	24968	EI-BXG	11. 6.91	
EI-CDD	Boeing 737-548 (Line No. 1989)	24989	EI-BXH	3. 7.91	
EI-CDE	Boeing 737-548 (Line No. 2050)	25115	PT-SLM EI-CDE/N1786B/(EI-BXJ)	21. 5.91	
EI-CDF	Boeing 737-548 (Line No. 2232)	25737		23. 3.92	
EI-CDG	Boeing 737-548 (Line No. 2261)	25738		7. 4.92	
EI-CDH	Boeing 737-548 (Line No. 2271)	25739		14. 4.92	
EI-CDI	McDonnell Douglas MD-11 (Line No.486)	48499		30.12.91	To PP-VPN 12/96. Canx 23.12.96.
EI-CDJ	McDonnell Douglas MD-11 (Line No.493)	48500	PK-GIH EI-CDJ	29. 3.92	To PP-VPO 4/97. Canx 10.4.97.
EI-CDK	McDonnell Douglas MD-11 (Line No.513)	48501		30. 9.92	To PP-VPP 9/97. Canx 23.9.97.
EI-CDL	McDonnell Douglas MD-11 (Line No.520)	48502		. .91R	NTU - To N9076Y/PK-GIG. Canx.
EI-CDM	McDonnell Douglas MD-11 (Line No.528)	48503		. .91R	NTU - To N9020U/PK-GII. Canx.
EI-CDN	McDonnell Douglas MD-11 (Line No.548)	48504	N9020Q	. .91R	NTU - To N9020Q/PK-GIJ. Canx.
EI-CDO	BAC One-Eleven Srs.518FG	BAC.201	(EI-CCV) G-FLRU/G-AXMG/5B-DAF/G-AXMG	3. 5.91	Restored as G-AXMG 5/94. Canx 6.5.94.
EI-CDP	Cessna 182L Skylane	182-58955	G-FALL OY-AHS/N4230S	20. 5.91	
EI-CDQ	Stolp SA.300 Starduster Too	HB.1980-1	C-GTLJ	26. 6.91	To G-UINN 3/98. Canx 16.3.98.
EI-CDR	Not allocated.				
EI-CDS	Boeing 737-548 (Line No. 2427)	26287		2. 2.93	To F-GJNV 4/99. Canx 9.3.99.
EI-CDT	Boeing 737-548 (Line No. 2463)	25165	PT-MNC EI-CDT	23. 3.93	To SE-DUT 4/98. Canx 23.4.98.
EI-CDU	Cessna 150F	150-62962	N8862G	17. 7.91	To G-BWGU 8/95. Canx 28.5.95.
EI-CDV	Cessna 150G	150-66677	N2777S	17. 7.91	

Regn	Type	c/n	Previous identity	Regn date	Fate or immediate subsequent identity (if known)
EI-CDW	Robinson R-22 Beta	1130	(EI-CFJ) G-BRTI/N8044U	30. 7.91	Restored as G-BRTI 2/97. Canx 6.12.96.
EI-CDX	Cessna 210K Centurion	210-59329	G-AYGN N9429M	14. 8.91	
EI-CDY	McDonnell Douglas DC-9-83 (MD-83) (Line No. 1905)	49948		27. 9.91	
EI-CDZ	Luscombe 8A Silvaire	3301	G-BSTX N71874/NC71874	23.10.91	Restored as G-BSTX 8/95. Canx 3.8.95.
EI-CEA	Boeing 767-3Y0ER (Line No. 408)	25411		. .91R	NTU - To PT-TAF 12/91. Canx.
EI-CEB	Airbus A.300B4-203A	240	SU-GAB F-WZMM	1.11.91	To VT-EVD. Canx 8.5.98.
EI-CEC	PA-31-350 Navajo Chieftain	31-7652017	G-BWSA G-BPJX/OY-BYP/LN-SAN/SE-GBD	23.10.91	To N961PA. Canx 3.4.96.
EI-CED	DHC.8-311A Dash Eight	283	C-GFUM	5.11.91	To PH-SDR. Canx 22.3.94.
EI-CEE	Boeing 737-3Y0 (Line No. 1540)	23923	G-TEAB (N117AW)/EI-EZP/LN-AEQ/EI-BZP/EC-EIA/EC-152	25.10.91	Restored as EI-BZP. Canx.
EI-CEF	Robinson R-22 HP	0266	G-BOBO N712BH/N100GV/N90763	4.11.91	To G-KRAY 5/95. Canx 22.5.95.
EI-CEG	Socata MS.893E Rallye 180GT	13083	SE-GTS	31.10.91	
EI-CEH	McDonnell Douglas DC-9-83 (MD-83) (Line No. 1913)	49950		19.11.91	To P4-MDE 3/95. Canx 2.3.95.
EI-CEI	Robinson R-22 Beta	1244	G-BRXZ	. .91R	NTU - To EI-CEJ 11/91. Canx.
EI-CEJ	Robinson R-22 Beta	1244	(EI-CEI) G-BRXZ	14.11.91	Restored as G-BRXZ 12/95. Canx 21.12.95.
EI-CEK	McDonnell Douglas DC-9-83 (MD-83) (Line No. 1596)	49631	EC-FMY EC-113/EI-CEK/EC-EPM/EC-261	13.12.91	
EI-CEL	Rans S-6 Coyote	D-190111		. .92R	NTU - To G-MWYF 1/92. Canx.
EI-CEM	Boeing 767-2B1ER (Line No. 407)	25421	(EI-CAG)	14. 1.92	To (ZS-SRB)/PT-TAK 10/95. Canx 21.10.95.
EI-CEN	Thruster T.300	9012-T300-500		2. 3.92	
EI-CEO	Boeing 747-259M (Line No. 372)	21730	HK-2980X HK-2300	28. 1.92	To N621FF 1/97. Canx 16.1.97.
EI-CEP	McDonnell Douglas DC-9-83 (MD-83) (Line No. 1984)	53122		14. 4.92	
EI-CEQ	McDonnell Douglas DC-9-83 (MD-83) (Line No. 1987)	53123		14. 4.92	
EI-CER	McDonnell Douglas DC-9-83 (MD-83) (Line No. 1993)	53125		20. 5.92	
EI-CES	Taylorcraft BC-65	2231	G-BTEG N27590/NC27590	25. 3.92	
EI-CET	Lockheed L.188CF Electra	1144	(G-FIJF) N668Q/N668F/N24AF/N138US	24. 7.92	To G-LOFE 1/99. Canx 4.1.99.
EI-CEU	Boeing 737-4Y0 (Line No. 1731)	24345	F-WQAE EI-CEU/SU-BLM/EI-CEU/EC-EPN/EC-308	14. 4.92	To VT-JAG 9/95. Canx 25.9.95.
EI-CEV	Boeing 737-4Y0 (Line No. 1661)	23979	EC-EMI EC-239	14. 4.92	To XA-SCA. Canx 6/92.
EI-CEW	Boeing 737-4Y0 (Line No. 1678)	23981	F-GNFS SU-BLL/EI-CEW/EC-EMY/EC-251	14. 4.92	To TC-AFZ. Canx 13.4.95.
EI-CEX	Lake LA-4-200 Buccaneer	1115	N8VG N3VC/N8544Z	18. 5.92	
EI-CEY	Boeing 757-2Y0 (Line No. 478)	26152		10. 8.92	
EI-CEZ	Boeing 757-2Y0 (Line No. 486)	26154		18. 9.92	
EI-CFA	SAAB 340B	340B-248	SE-G48	6. 6.91	To N248PX. Canx 10.7.85.
EI-CFB	SAAB 340B	340B-251	SE-G51	27. 6.91	To N251PX. Canx 21.6.95.
EI-CFC	SAAB 340B	340B-255	SE-G55	9. 8.91	To (N255PX)/OH-FAH. Canx 28.7.95.
EI-CFD	SAAB 340B	340B-257	SE-G57	23. 8.91	To N257PX. Canx 21.6.95.
EI-CFE	Robinson R-22 Beta	1709	G-BTHG	15. 5.91	
EI-CFF	PA-12 Super Cruiser	12-3928	N78544 NC78544	23. 5.91	
EI-CFG	Rousseau Piel CP.301B Emeraude	112	G-ARIW F-BIRQ	1. 6.91	
EI-CFH	PA-12 Super Cruiser	12-3110	(EI-CCE) N4214M/NC4214M	1. 6.91	
EI-CFI	PA-34-200T Seneca II	34-7870177	N9245C	15. 7.91	To G-BUNR 9/92. Canx 19.9.92.
EI-CFJ	Robinson R-22 Beta	1130	G-BRTI N8044U	26. 7.91	NTU (Registered in error) - To EI-CDW 7/91. Canx.
EI-CFK	Varga 2150A Kachina	VAC 155-80	G-BLWG OO-HTD/N8360J	23. 8.91	To G-DJCR 4/96. Canx 11.4.96.
EI-CFL	Airbus A.300B4	-		. .92R	NTU - Canx. [Was reserved for Air Tara Ltd]
EI-CFM	Cessna 172P Skyhawk II	172-74656	N53000	19. 5.92	Badly damaged in gales at Cork on 24.12.97.
EI-CFN	Cessna 172P Skyhawk II	172-74113	N5446K JA4172/N5446K	10. 5.92	
EI-CFO	Piper J3C-65 Cub	11947	OO-RAZ OO-RAF/44-79651	13. 5.92	
EI-CFP	Cessna 172P Skyhawk II Floatplane	172-74428	N52178	15. 7.91	
EI-CFQ	Boeing 737-3Y0 (Line No. 1625)	24255	OO-IID XA-RJP/G-MONL	6. 5.92	To HB-IID. Canx 5/93.
EI-CFR	Boeing 767-375ER (Line No. 430)	25865	N6063S (C-GCAW)	17. 7.92	To B-2561. Canx 11.92.

Regn	Type	c/n	Previous identity	Regn date	Fate or immediate subsequent identity (if known)
EI-CFS	Boeing 737-4Y0	26065		. .92R	NTU - To TC-JDY 6/92. Canx.
	(Line No. 2284)				
EI-CFT	Boeing 737-5Y0	25288		. .92R	NTU - To TC-JDU 6/92. Canx.
	(Line No. 2286)				
EI-CFU	Boeing 737-5Y0	25289		. .92R	NTU - To N6069D/TC-JDV 6/92. Canx.
	(Line No. 2288)				
EI-CFV	Socata MS.880B Rallye Club	1850	G-OLFS	13. 5.92	
			G-AYYZ		
EI-CFW	Cameron O-77 HAFB	2810	G-BUEV	12. 6.92	Restored as G-BUEV 3/93. Canx 3/93.
EI-CFX	Robinson R-22 Beta	0793	G-OSPI	16. 6.92	
EI-CFY	Cessna 172N Skyhawk II	172-68902	N734JZ	18. 6.92	
EI-CFZ	McDonnell Douglas DC-9-82 (MD-82)		N6206F	29. 7.92	
	(Line No. 1964)	53120			
EI-CGA	McDonnell Douglas DC-9-83 (MD-83)		F-GMPP	30. 6.92	To EC-898/EC-GBV. Canx 6.5.95.
	(Line No. 1467)	49668	EI-CGA/EC-EIK/EC-289/EC-EIK/EC-163/EI-BWC/(N14845)		
EI-CGB	Team Minimax	36		20. 8.92	(Previously thought to be a Medway Hybred (Rotax 227); possibly second use of marks?)
EI-CGC	Stinson 108-3 Station Wagon		OO-IAC	17. 7.92	
		108-5243	OO-JAC/N3B		
EI-CGD	Cessna 172M Skyhawk II	172-62309	OO-BMT	30. 7.92	
			N12846		
EI-CGE	Hiway Demon	EC-25PS-04		19. 8.92	Canx as TWFU 11.2.97.
	(C/n is engine type)				
EI-CGF	Phoenix Luton LA-5A Major		G-BENH	31. 7.92	
		PAL/1208 & PFA/1208	(G-ARWX)		
EI-CGG	Ercoupe 415C	3147	N2522H	10. 9.92	
			NC2522H		
EI-CGH	Cessna 210N Centurion II	210-63524	N6374A	16.11.92	
EI-CGI	McDonnell Douglas DC-9-83 (MD-83)		EC-EKM	19.10.92	
	(Line No. 1502)	49624	EC-279/EC-EKM/EC-178		
EI-CGJ	Solar Wings Pegasus XL-R	SW-WA-1506	G-MWTV	5. 4.93	
EI-CGK	Robinson R-22 Beta	0886	G-ROYY	21.11.92	
EI-CGL	Solar Wings Pegasus XL-R	SW-WA-1513	G-MWUE	14.11.92	Restored as G-MWUE 10/94. Canx 3.9.94.
EI-CGM	Solar Wings Pegasus XL-R	SW-WA-1502	G-MWVC	14.11.92	
EI-CGN	Solar Wings Pegasus XL-R	SW-WA-1529	G-MWXM	14.11.92	
EI-CGO	Douglas DC-8-63AF	45924	N353AS	25. 4.89	
	(Line No. 392)		(N791AL)/SE-DBH/OY-SBM/HS-TGZ/SE-DBH		
EI-CGP	PA-28-140 Cherokee C	28-26928	G-MLUA	25.11.92	
			G-AYJT/N11C		
EI-CGQ	Aerospatiale AS.350B Ecureuil	2076	G-BUPK	21. 1.93	
			JA9740		
EI-CGR	McDonnell Douglas DC-9-83 (MD-83)		F-GMCD	23.11.92	To EC-807/EC-GBY. Canx 27.3.95.
	(Line No. 1421)	49642	EC-EMT/EC-257/XA-TUR/EC-EKT/EC-190/SE-DHF/(EC-EFL)		
EI-CGS	McDonnell Douglas DC-9-83 (MD-83)		EC-EMG	1.12.92	To EC-805/EC-GBA. Canx 14.4.95.
	(Line No. 1538)	49626	EC-223/N2606Z		
EI-CGT	Cessna 152 II	152-82331	G-BPBL	10.12.92	
			N16SU/N68715		
EI-CGU	Robinson R-22 HP	0148	G-BSNH	10.12.92	Canx as WFU 16.4.97.
			N9065D		
EI-CGV	Piper J/5A Cub Cruiser	5-624	G-BPKT	11.12.92	
			N35372/NC35372		
EI-CGW	Powerchute Kestrel	00412	G-MWOB	20. 1.93	Canx 29.11.94.
EI-CGX(1)	Boeing 737-317	23177	PT-WBG	15. 1.93R	NTU - To EI-CHH 1/93. Canx.
	(Line No. 1216)		PP-SNU/C-FCPL		
EI-CGX(2)	Cessna 340	340-0106	(EI-CHH)	27. 3.93	Crashed nr.Knock on 19.8.94 - Stored Galway 1/95.
			N51388/G-BALM/N4553L		
EI-CGY	Douglas DC-8-71F	45976	PT-WBM	15. 1.93	Restored as PT-WBM. Canx 3/93.
	(Line No. 372)		PP-SOP/N8086U		
EI-CGZ	Boeing 737-2L9	21685	PT-WBA	15. 1.93	To UR-BFA. Canx 5.10.94.
	(Line No. 549)		PP-SNO/OY-APJ/G-BKAP/OY-APJ/9M-MBZ/OY-APJ		
EI-CHA	Boeing 737-3Y0	23747	PT-WBH	15. 1.93	To EC-377/EC-FRZ. Canx 3/93.
	(Line No. 1363)		PP-SOA/SE-DLN/EI-BZS/EC-EBX		
EI-CHB	Boeing 737-269	21206	PT-WBB	15. 1.93	To OB-1538. Canx 6/93.
	(Line No. 448)		PP-SNP/VR-BOX/9K-ACV		
EI-CHC	Boeing 737-2L9	21686	PT-WBC	15. 1.93	To TF-ABU 5/94. Canx 26.5.94.
	(Line No. 550)		PP-SNK/OY-APK/PP-SNK/OY-APK/9M-MBY/OY-APK		
EI-CHD	Boeing 737-317	23176	PT-WBF	15. 1.93	To N698SW. Canx 16.2.95.
	(Line No. 1213)		PP-SNT/C-FCPK		
EI-CHE	Boeing 737-317	23826	EC-FSA	15. 1.93	To N699SW. Canx 21.2.95.
	(Line No. 1372)		EC-376/EI-CHE/PT-WBI/PP-SNV/EI-BTM		
EI-CHF	PA-44-180 Seminole	44-7995112	G-BGJB	22. 2.93	
			N3046B		
EI-CHG	Enstrom 280C-UK Shark	1060	G-SHSS	3. 2.93	Restored as G-SHSS 6/96. Canx 6/96.
			(EI-...)/G-SHSS/G-BENO		
EI-CHH(1)	Cessna 340	340-0106	N51388	. .93R	NTU - To EI-CGX 3/93. Canx.
			G-BALM/N4553L		
EI-CHH(2)	Boeing 737-317	23177	(EI-CGX)	15. 1.93	To N302AL 2/97. Canx.
	(Line No. 1216)		PT-WBG/PP-SNU/C-FCPL		
EI-CHI	Mooney M.20C	20-1188	N6955V	27. 3.93	To G-BWTW 6/96. Canx 5.6.96.
EI-CHJ	Reims Cessna FR.172K Hawk XP II		G-BFIF	18. 2.93	To G-PJTM 10/98. Canx 20.7.98.
		0611			
EI-CHK	Piper J3C-65 Cub	23019	C-FHNS	10. 3.93	
			CF-HNS/N1492N/NC1492N		

Regn	Type	c/n	Previous identity	Regn date	Fate or immediate subsequent identity (if known)
EI-CHL	Bell 206L-3 Long Ranger III	51154	G-OIOM N32WT	15. 2.88	To N88EA 8/98. Canx 1.9.98.
EI-CHM	Cessna 150M Commuter	150-79288	G-BSZX (EI-...)/G-BSZX/N714MU	2. 3.93	
EI-CHN	Socata MS.880B Rallye Club	901	G-AVIO	22. 2.93	
EI-CHO	Lockheed L.188AF Electra	1068	(G-CHNX) N5535	25. 9.93	To G-CHNX 11/94. Canx 1.11.94.
EI-CHP	DHC.8-103 Dash Eight	258	VH-FNQ C-GFRP	7. 4.93	
EI-CHQ	Boeing 737-317 (Line No. 1098)	23173	PT-WBD PP-SNQ/C-FCPG	8. 4.93	To N946WP. Canx 2.6.95.
EI-CHR	CFM Shadow Srs.BD	063	G-MTKT	20. 5.93	
EI-CHS	Cessna 172M Skyhawk II	172-66742	G-BREZ N80775	26. 4.93	
EI-CHT	Solar Wings Pegasus XL-R	1449		16. 4.93	(Identity unconfirmed but possibly c/n SW-TB-1449)
EI-CHU	Boeing 737-317 (Line No. 1110)	23175	PT-WBE PP-SNS/C-FCPJ	7. 5.93	To N686SW 10/93. Canx 21.10.93.
EI-CHV	Agusta A.109A II	7149	VR-BMM HB-XTJ/D-HASV	10. 6.93	
EI-CHW	Lockheed L.188CF Electra	2003	SE-IVS C-GNWD/N852U/(N852ST)/N852/PH-LLB	28. 5.93	Stored 12/96 East Midlands, UK. Scrapped 8/98. Canx 20.3.98 as "removed from service".
EI-CHX	Lockheed L.188CF Electra	2006	SE-IVR N853U/PH-LLC	5. 8.93	To G-BYEF 12/98. Canx 11.12.98.
EI-CHY	Lockheed L.188CF Electra	2014	G-FIZU SE-IZU/(N857ST)/N857U/PH-LLG	20. 5.97	Restored as G-FIZU 12/98. Canx 22.12.98.
EI-CHZ	Lockheed L.188CF Electra	2015	SE-IVT C-GNWC/N858U/PH-LLH	10. 9.93	Stored at East Midlands Airport, UK in 6/98. Scrapped 18.8.98. Canx 15.12.98.
EI-CIA	Socata MS.880B Rallye Club	1218	G-MONA G-AWJK	26. 4.93	
EI-CIB	BAC One-Eleven Srs.501EX	BAC.191	G-AXJK	10. 6.93	Restored as G-AXJK 2/94. Canx 18.2.94.
EI-CIC	BAC One-Eleven Srs.501EX	BAC.177	G-AWYU	10. 6.93	Restored as G-AWYU 3/94. Canx 18.3.94.
EI-CID	BAC One-Eleven Srs.501EX	BAC.174	G-AWYR	4. 6.93	Restored as G-AWYR 6/94. Canx 28.3.94.
EI-CIE	BAC One-Eleven Srs.501EX	BAC.176	G-AWYT	4. 6.93	Restored as G-AWYT 1/94. Canx 18.1.94.
EI-CIF	PA-28-180 Cherokee C	28-2853	G-AVVV N8880J	12. 6.93	(Was rebuilt in 1967 using spare frame 28-3808S) (Stored dismantled 12/98 Weston)
EI-CIG	PA-18-150 Super Cub (Regd with frame no.18-7360)	18-7203	G-BGWF ST-AFJ/ST-ABN	12. 6.93	(Derelict fuselage 12/98 Weston)
EI-CIH	Ercoupe 415CD	4834	OO-AIA (PH-NDO)/N94723/NC94723	25. 6.93	
EI-CII	Not allocated.				
EI-CIJ	Cessna 340	340-0304	G-BBVE N69451	2. 7.93	
EI-CIK	Mooney M.20C Mk.21	2620	G-BFXC (EI-...)/G-BFXC/9H-ABD/G-BFXC/OH-MOA/N1349W	2. 7.93	
EI-CIL	Hughes 269C	40-0915	G-BOVY N1096K	7. 9.93	Restored as G-BOVY 8/95. Canx 22.8.95.
EI-CIM	Light Aero Avid Speedwing Mk.4	1125D		17. 8.93	
EI-CIN	Cessna 150K	150-71728	G-BSXG N6228G	6. 9.93	To G-OCIN 4/99. Canx 1.4.99.
EI-CIO	Bell 206L-3 Long Ranger III	51436	JA6075 N6546Q	24.10.93	
EI-CIP	Solar Wings Pegasus Quasar IITC	SW-WQT-0501	G-MWZS	11.11.93	Restored as G-MWZS. Canx 4.2.94.
EI-CIQ	ATR-42-312	113	DQ-FEQ F-WWEJ	16.11.93	To G-ZAPJ(2) 5/96. Canx 17.5.96.
EI-CIR	Cessna 551 Citation II (Unit No.144) (Originally built as Cessna 550 c/n 550-0128)	551-0174	N60AR EI-CIR/F-WLEF/9A-BPU/RC-BPU/YU-BPU/N220LA/N536M/N2631V	29.11.93	
EI-CIS	DHC.8-311A Dash Eight	342	D-BOBS C-GFHZ	7.12.93	To C-FTUY. Canx 19.12.94.
EI-CIT	DHC.8-311A Dash Eight	307	D-BOBE C-GEOA	16.11.93	To C-FTUX. Canx 19.12.94.
EI-CIU	DHC.8-311A Dash Eight	293	PT-OKD C-GDIU	30.12.93	To PH-SDS. Canx 3.6.94.
EI-CIV	PA-28-140 Cherokee Cruiser	28-7725232	G-BEXY N9639N	20.11.93	Badly damaged in gales at Cork on 24.12.97.
EI-CIW	McDonnell Douglas DC-9-82 (MD-82) (Line No. 1678)	49785	HL7271	30.12.93	
EI-CIX	Boeing 737-4Y0 (Line No. 2033)	24911	OY-MBK (PH-AHC)/(PH-OZB)/PT-WBJ/PP-SOJ/(TC-AGA)	7.12.93	To SE-DTB 3/95. Canx 20.3.95.
EI-CIY	Boeing 767-330ER (Line No. 381)	25208	D-ABUY	10.12.93	To I-AEIY 2/99. Canx 17.2.99.
EI-CIZ	Steen Skybolt	001	G-BSAO N303BC	12.12.93	
EI-CJA	Boeing 767-35HER (Line No. 445)	26387	S7-AAQ (I-AEJD)	22.12.93	
EI-CJB	Boeing 767-35HER (Line No. 456)	26388	S7-AAV (I-AEJE)	23.12.93	
EI-CJC	Boeing 737-204ADV (Line No. 867)	22640	G-BJCV CS-TMA/G-BJCV/C-GCAU/G-BJCV/C-GXCP/G-BJCV	25. 1.94	
EI-CJD	Boeing 737-204ADV (Line No. 946)	22966	G-BKHE (G-BKGU)	18. 2.94	

Regn	Type	c/n	Previous identity	Regn date	Fate or immediate subsequent identity (if known)
EI-CJE	Boeing 737-204ADV (Line No. 863)	22639	G-BJCU EC-DVE/G-BJCU	10. 3.94	
EI-CJF	Boeing 737-204ADV (Line No. 953)	22967	G-BTZF G-BKHF/(G-BKGV)	24. 3.94	
EI-CJG	Boeing 737-204ADV (Line No. 629)	22058	G-BGYK PP-SRW/G-BGYK/(G-BGRV)	25. 3.94	
EI-CJH	Boeing 737-204ADV (Line No. 621)	22057	G-BGYJ N8278V/(G-BGRU)	30. 3.94	
EI-CJI	Boeing 737-2E7 (Line No. 917)	22875	G-BMDF (PK-RI.)/G-BMDF/4X-BAB/N4570B	8. 7.94	
EI-CJJ	Not allocated - [Was reportedly reserved in 1993 for a Boeing 737-200 for Ryanair]				
EI-CJK	Airbus A.300B4-103	020	F-BUAR D-AMAY/(F-WLGB)	13. 1.94	
EI-CJL	Not allocated - [Was reportedly reserved in 1993 for a Boeing 737-200 for Ryanair]				
EI-CJM	Bell 206B JetRanger	1761	N281C N49582	3. 3.94	To EI-ONE 5/96. Canx.
EI-CJN	Not allocated.				
EI-CJO	Hoffmann H-36 Dimona	36113	G-BLCV	12. 2.94	Restored as G-BLCV 6/96. Canx 29.5.96.
EI-CJP	BAe 146 Srs.100	E1160	G-BVLJ A2-ABF/G-6-160	20. 5.94	Restored as G-BVLJ 4/95. Canx 3.4.95.
EI-CJQ	Not allocated.				
EI-CJR	SNCAN Stampe SV-4A	318	G-BKBK OO-CLR/F-BCLR	28. 2.94	
EI-CJS	Jodel Wassmer D.120A Paris-Nice	339	F-BOYF	28. 2.94	
EI-CJT	Slingsby Cadet III	830 & PCW-001	G-BPCW XA288	25. 2.94	
EI-CJU	Dornier Do.28D-2 Skyservant	4337	(N5TK) 5N-AOH/D-ILIF	10. 3.94	To G-BWCO 6/95. Canx 6/95.
EI-CJV	Moskito 2	004	D-MBGM	12. 3.94	
EI-CJW	Boeing 737-2P6ADV (Line No. 493)	21355	(N458TM) A40-BC	10. 3.94	Canx as destroyed 26.2.99 - believed following the accident at Atlanta on 2.11.98 while leased to Air Tran. (Was reserved were N463AT).
EI-CJX	Boeing 757-2Y0 (Line No. 555)	26160	N3519M N1786B/(B-2830)	31. 3.94	To N160GE 1/98. Canx 30.1.98.
EI-CJY	Boeing 757-2Y0 (Line No. 557)	26161	N3521N	13. 4.94	To N161GE 2/98. Canx 18.2.98.
EI-CJZ	Whittaker MW.6S Fatboy Flyer	PFA/164-11493	G-MWTW	24. 3.94	
EI-CKA	Robin DR.400/180R Remorqueur	1385	SE-GHM	30. 5.94	To G-ONGC 11/98. Canx 11.11.98.
EI-CKB	McDonnell Douglas DC-9-83 (MD-83) (Line No. 1332)	49400	9Y-THY G-PATB/N6202S/(G-DAIO)	7. 5.94	To N9407R. Canx 29.7.94.
EI-CKC	Auster J/1 Autocrat	1873	G-AGVN	8. 6.94	Restored as G-AGVN 5/95. Canx 18.5.95.
EI-CKD	Boeing 767-3Y0ER (Line No. 474)	26205	N6046P	13. 9.94	
EI-CKE	Boeing 767-3Y0ER (Line No. 505)	26208	N6009F	15. 9.94	
EI-CKF	Hunt Avon/Hunt Wing	JAH-8	G-MWPT	3. 6.94	Restored as G-MWPT 4/96. Canx 25.4.96.
EI-CKG	Hunt Avon Weightlifter	92009013		2. 7.94	
EI-CKH	PA-18-95 Super Cub	18-7248	G-APZK	3. 6.94	(Crashed near Glendalough, Co.Wicklow on 3.8.96)
EI-CKI	Thruster TST Mk.1	8078-TST-091	G-MVDI	3. 6.94	
EI-CKJ	Cameron N-77 HAFB	3305		6. 7.94	
EI-CKK	Boeing 737-2P6 (Line No. 528)	21612	A40-BH	12. 7.94	To HP-1340CMP 1/98. Canx 6.1.98.
EI-CKL	Boeing 737-2P6ADV (Line No. 496)	21356	A40-BD	5. 8.94	To LV-YIB 3/98. Canx 2.3.98.
EI-CKM	McDonnell Douglas DC-9-83 (MD-83) (Line No. 1655)	49792	TC-INC EI-CKM/D-ALLW/EI-CKM/XA-RPH/EC-FFF/EC-733/XA-RPH	10. 8.94	
EI-CKN	Whittaker MW.6S Fatboy Flyer	BCA.8942		29. 7.94	
EI-CKO	Hornet/Skyhook Cutlass Dual Trainer	83-00475	G-MMMV	24. 8.94	Canx 24.7.96 at owner's request as "removed from service".
EI-CKP	Boeing 737-2K2ADV (Line No. 668)	22296	PH-TVS PP-SRV/PH-TVS/LV-RBH/PH-TVS/LV-RAO/PH-TVS/EC-DVN/PH-TVS	7.10.94	
EI-CKQ	Boeing 737-2K2ADV (Line No. 888)	22906	PH-TVU G-BPLA/PH-TVU/C-FCAV/PH-TVU	20. 2.95	
EI-CKR	Boeing 737-2K2ADV (Line No. 647)	22025	PH-TVR C-FICP/PH-TVR/(D-AJAA)/PH-TVR	5. 5.95	
EI-CKS	Boeing 737-2T5ADV (Line No. 636)	22023	PH-TVX OE-ILE/PH-TVX/G-BGTW	1. 6.95	
EI-CKT	Mainair Gemini/Flash	307-585-3 & W47	G-MNCB	27. 9.94	
EI-CKU	Solar Wings Pegasus XL-R	SW-TB-1434 & SW-WA-1500	G-MWVB	14.10.94	
EI-CKV	Boeing 737-3Y0 (Line No. 1363)	23747	EC-FYE EC-667/XA-SIY/EC-FRZ/EC-377/EI-CHA/PT-WBH/PP-SOA/SE-DLN/EI-BZS/EC-EBX	23.12.94	To N331AW 11/97. Canx 19.11.97.
EI-CKW	Boeing 737-2P6 (Line No. 538)	21677	A40-BI	8.12.94	To HP-1339CMP 12/97. Canx 15.12.97.
EI-CKX	Wassmer Jodel D.112	1166	G-ASIS F-BKNR	7.12.94	
EI-CKY	Reims Cessna F.406 Caravan II	0018	PH-ALN OO-TIW/F-WZDZ	10. 2.95	To G-LEAF 3/96. Canx 7.3.96.
EI-CKZ	Jodel D.18	229		5. 4.95	
EI-CLA	HOAC DV-20 Katana	20106		24. 3.95	

Regn	Type	c/n	Previous identity	Regn date	Fate or immediate subsequent identity (if known)
EI-CLB	ATR-72-212	423	F-WWEB	23. 2.95	
EI-CLC	ATR-72-212	428	F-WWEF	24. 2.95	
EI-CLD	ATR-72-212	432	F-WWEL "F-WWLE"	3. 3.95	
EI-CLE	Quad City Challenger II	CH2-0894-UK-1193		13. 4.95	To G-MZNA 3/98. Canx 18.3.98.
EI-CLF	Fairchild-Hiller FH-227E	505	SE-KBP C-FNAI/CF-NAI/N7802M/PP-BUK/N7802M	12. 7.95	
EI-CLG(1)	BAe 146 Srs.300	E3155	G-BTNU (G-BSLS)/G-6-155	24. 2.95R	NTU - To EI-CLJ 3/96. Canx.
EI-CLG(2)	BAe 146 Srs.300	E3131	G-BRAB HS-TBL/G-BRAB/G-11-131	7. 6.95	
EI-CLH	BAe 146 Srs.300	E3146	G-BOJJ I-ATSC/G-BOJJ/G-6-146	2. 6.95	
EI-CLI	BAe 146 Srs.300	E3159	G-BVSA I-ATSD/G-6-159/G-5-159	19. 4.95	
EI-CLJ	BAe 146 Srs.300	E3155	(EI-CLG) G-BTNU/(G-BSLS)/G-6-155	1. 3.96	
EI-CLK	Boeing 737-2P6 (Line No. 564)	21733	A40-BJ	7. 3.95	To LV-YEB 1/98. Canx 27.1.98.
EI-CLL	Whittaker MW.6S Fatboy Flyer	1069		2. 4.95	
EI-CLM	Boeing 757-28A (Line No. 208)	24367	N381LF N240LA/C-GTSK/C-GNXI/C-GAWB	24. 3.95	To N701LF 12/97. Canx 11.12.97.
EI-CLN	Boeing 737-2C9ADV (Line No. 501)	21443	RA-73000 LX-LGH/N8277V	17. 5.95	To VP-BTA 7/99. Canx 16.7.99.
EI-CLO	Boeing 737-2C9ADV (Line No. 516)	21444	RA-73001 LX-LGI	16. 5.95	To VP-BTB 7/99. Canx 16.7.99.
EI-CLP	Boeing 757-2Y0 (Line No. 400)	25268	N400KL XA-TAE	14. 4.95	To C-GTSU. Canx 18.11.96.
EI-CLQ	Reims Cessna F.172N Skyhawk II	1653	G-BFLV	26. 5.95	
EI-CLR	Boeing 767-3Y0ER (Line No. 408)	25411	XA-EDE XA-TJD/SE-DKY/EI-CLR/XA-SKY/PT-TAF/(EI-CEA)	29. 5.95	
EI-CLS	Boeing 767-352ER (Line No. 583)	26262	N171LF (N808AM)	28. 7.95	
EI-CLT	Bell 206B JetRanger II	1727	N90158	17. 7.95	
EI-CLU	Boeing 757-28A (Line No. 676)	26274	N161LF	21. 6.95	To N751LF 1/98. Canx 14.1.98.
EI-CLV	Boeing 757-28A (Line No. 672)	26275	N151LF	19. 5.95	To N161LF 2/98. Canx 3.3.98.
EI-CLW	Boeing 737-3Y0 (Line No. 2248)	25187	XA-SAB	10. 6.95	
EI-CLX	Cessna 310Q II	310Q-1076	G-BBXL (N1223G)	5. 7.95	Restored as G-BBXL 12/97. Canx 11.12.97.
EI-CLY	BAe 146 Srs.300	E3149	G-BTZN N146PZ/ZP-CCY/N146PZ/G-BTZN/HS-TBN/G-11-149	16. 4.97	
EI-CLZ	Boeing 737-3Y0 (Line No. 2205)	25179	XA-RJR N3521N	27. 7.95	
EI-CMA	Boeing 757-236 (Line No. 362)	25054	XA-MMX N3502P/N5002K/(EC-668)/(G-BSNB)	11. 7.95	To N100FS. Canx 22.11.95.
EI-CMB	PA-28-140 Cherokee Cruiser	28-7725094	G-BELR N9541N	5. 9.95	
EI-CMC	Cessna 185A Skywagon	185-0491	G-BBEX 4X-ALD/N9992/N1691Z	26. 7.95	Restored as G-BBEX 8/95. Canx 9.8.95.
EI-CMD	Boeing 767-324ER (Line No. 568)	27392	N1785B (N48901)	28.12.95	To S7-RGV. Canx 25.1.96.
EI-CME	Boeing 767-324ER (Line No. 571)	27393	N1794B (N58902)	28.12.95	To S7-RGW. Canx 9.2.96.
EI-CMF	CFM Streak Shadow	050	G-MTFY	13. 9.95	(Probably simply a Shadow Srs.CD)
EI-CMG	Short SD.3-60 Var.300	SH3716	N360AR G-BNDM/G-14-3716	4.10.95	Restored as G-BNDM 4/97. Canx 3.1.97.
EI-CMH	Boeing 767-324ER (Line No. 593)	27568	N47904	20.11.95	To S7-RGU. Canx 9.2.96.
EI-CMI	Robinson R-22 Beta	1129	G-BRRZ N8050N	30.11.95	
EI-CMJ	ATR-72-212	467	F-WWLU	21.12.95	
EI-CMK	Eurowing Goldwing ST	76		22.12.95	
EI-CML	Cessna 150M	150-76786	G-BNSS N45207	5. 1.96	
EI-CMM	McDonnell Douglas DC-9-83 (MD-83) (Line No. 1784)	49937	G-COES N30010	1. 2.96	
EI-CMN	PA-12 Super Cruiser	12-1617	N2363M NC2363M	26. 1.96	
EI-CMO	Boeing 737-4Y0 (Line No. 1589)	23866	VT-EWL TC-ADA	26. 1.96	To B-2969. Canx 7.3.96.
EI-CMP	Douglas DC-9-32 (Line No. 189)	47089	N8270H EC-BIN	30. 1.96	To N939VV. Canx 5.2.96.
EI-CMQ	Boeing 767-3Q8ER (Line No. 619)	27993		27. 6.96	To I-AIMQ 2/99. Canx 26.2.99.
EI-CMR	Rutan LongEz	1716		2. 5.96	
EI-CMS	BAe 146 Srs.200A	E2044	N184US N361PS	24. 4.96	
EI-CMT	PA-34-200T Seneca II	34-7870088	G-BNER N2590M	23. 4.96	

Regn	Type	c/n	Previous identity	Regn date	Fate or immediate subsequent identity (if known)
EI-CMU	Mainair Mercury	1071-0296-7 & W873		3. 5.96	
EI-CMV	Cessna 150L	150-72747	G-MSES N1447Q	17. 5.96	
EI-CMW	Rotorway 152 Executive	3550		13. 5.96	
EI-CMX	Beechcraft 76 Duchess	ME-192	N60450	24. 6.96	To G-BXSK 2/98. Canx 9.2.98.
EI-CMY	BAe 146 Srs.200A	E2039	N177US N365PS	19. 6.96	
EI-CMZ(1)	BAe 146 Srs.200A	E2046	N187US N363PS	. .96R	NTU To EI-CNB 8/96. Canx.
EI-CMZ(2)	McDonnell Douglas DC-9-83 (MD-83) (Line No. 1269)	49390	9Y-THN	20. 7.96	
EI-CNA	Letov LK-2M Sluka (Full c/n is probably 8296s005)	829S005		28. 6.96	
EI-CNB	BAe 146 Srs.200A	E2046	(EI-CMZ) N187US/N363PS	3. 8.96	
EI-CNC	Team Minimax 1600	514		10. 9.96	
EI-CND	Reims Cessna F.406 Caravan II	0020	PH-FWF F-WZDS	. 8.96R	NTU - To PH-FWF/G-TURF 10/96. Canx.
EI-CNE	Boeing 737-4S3 (Line No. 2061)	25116	EC-GOA EI-CNE/EC-GFE/EC-997/OO-LTR/9M-MLF/N4249R/(G-BSRA)/N1789B	31.10.96	To EC-GUG 4/98. Canx 30.4.98.
EI-CNF	Boeing 737-4Y0 (Line No. 2201)	25180	EC-GHT EC-348/D-ABAJ/EC-FLD/EC-936	25.10.96	To EC-GOB 5/97. Canx 30.4.97.
EI-CNG	Air & Space 18-A Gyroplane	18-75	G-BALB N6170S	10. 9.96	
EI-CNH	Not allocated.				
EI-CNI	BAe 146 RJ85	E2299	G-6-299	26.11.96	
EI-CNJ	BAe 146 RJ85	E2300	G-6-300	2.12.96	
EI-CNK	BAe 146 RJ85	E2306	G-6-306	8. 5.97	
EI-CNL	Sikorsky S-61N Mk.II	61746	G-BDDA ZS-RBU/G-BDDA/ZS-RBU/G-BDDA/N91201/G-BDDA	19.12.96	
EI-CNM	PA-31-350 Navajo Chieftain	31-7305107	N1201H G-BBNT/N74958	16.12.96	
EI-CNN	Lockheed L.1011-385-1 Tristar 1	193K-1024	VR-HHV G-BAAA/N7852Q	30. 1.97	
EI-CNO	McDonnell Douglas DC-9-83 (MD-83) (Line No. 1494)	49672	EC-FTU EC-487/EC-EJQ/EC-150	19. 2.97	
EI-CNP	Boeing 737-266ADV (Line No. 451)	21192	TF-ABG N192GP/4R-ULO/SU-AYI	12. 3.97	To LV-... Canx 18.8.99.
EI-CNQ	BAe 146 Srs.200	E2031	G-OWLD N173US/N353PS	2. 7.97	
EI-CNR	McDonnell Douglas DC-9-83 (MD-83) (Line No. 1968)	53199	SE-DLU N13627	10. 4.97	
EI-CNS	Boeing 767-3Q8ER (Line No. 655)	27600	N6005C	16. 4.97	
EI-CNT	Boeing 737-230ADV (Line No. 694)	22115	D-ABFC	5.12.96	
EI-CNU	Cyclone Pegasus Quantum 15	7326		10. 4.97	
EI-CNV	Boeing 737-230ADV (Line No. 752)	22128	D-ABFX (D-ABFW)	26. 3.97	
EI-CNW	Boeing 737-230ADV (Line No. 772)	22133	D-ABHC (B-....)/D-ABHC/(D-ABHB)	31. 5.97	
EI-CNX	Boeing 737-230ADV (Line No. 745)	22127	D-ABFW N5573K/(D-ABFU)	4. 7.97	
EI-CNY	Boeing 737-230ADV (Line No. 649)	22113	D-ABFB N5573K	10.10.97	
EI-CNZ	Boeing 737-230ADV (Line No. 735)	22126	D-ABFU (D-ABFT)	5.11.97	
EI-COA	Boeing 737-230ADV (Line No. 848)	22637	CS-TES D-ABHX	16.12.97	
EI-COB	Boeing 737-230ADV (Line No. 727)	22124	D-ABFR	16. 1.98	
EI-COC	ATR-42-312	048	F-WQFT N4201G/F-WWED	24. 7.97	DBR on landing at Alghero, Italy on 20.1.98. Canx as destroyed 10.9.98.
EI-COD	ATR-42-312	052	F-WQBZ N4203G/F-WWEG	24. 7.97	
EI-COE	Europa Avn Europa	286		29. 5.97	
EI-COF	BAe 146 Srs.100	E1006	SE-DRH G-BKMN/(G-ODAN)	26. 5.97	Restored as G-BKMN 2/98. Canx 17.2.98.
EI-COG	Gyroscopic Rotorcraft Gyroplane	G.120		11. 3.98	(Imported from Australia in 1996, the design is a 2-seat side by side open cockpit gyro)
EI-COH	Boeing 737-430 (Line No. 2316)	27001	D-ABKB (VT-S..)/D-ABKB	6. 6.97	
EI-COI	Boeing 737-430 (Line No. 2323)	27002	D-ABKC	14.11.97	
EI-COJ	Boeing 737-430 (Line No. 2359)	27005	D-ABKK (D-ABKF)	21.11.97	
EI-COK	Boeing 737-430 (Line No. 2328)	27003	D-ABKD	23. 2.98	To 9H-ADO 4/99. Canx 9.4.99.
EI-COL	Lockheed L.1011-385-1 Tristar	193B-1036	(N660AT) N31014	1. 5.98	Stored Southend from 21.8.98. Broken up at Southend by 27.3.99. Canx 20.4.99.
EI-COM	Whittaker MW.6S Fatboy Flyer	1		10.10.97	
EI-CON	Boeing 737-2T5 (Line No. 730)	22396	PK-RIW EI-CON/PK-RIW/VT-EWF/A40-BM/C-GVRE/(EI-B..)/G-BHVH	21. 7.97	

Regn	Type	c/n	Previous identity	Regn date	Fate or immediate subsequent identity (if known)
EI-COO	Carlson Sparrow II	302		13. 8.97	
EI-COP	Reims Cessna F.150L Commuter	1058	G-BCBY PH-TGI/(G-BCBY)	26. 6.97	
EI-COQ	BAe 146 RJ70	E1254	9H-ACM (9H-ABW)/G-BVRJ	17.10.97	
EI-COR	Short SD.3-60 Var.300	SH3739	G-ZAPG G-CPTL/G-BOFI/G-14-3739	16. 9.97	To SX-BFW 1.99. Canx 23.12.98.
EI-COS	BAe ATP	2060	G-11-060	. .97R	NTU - To G-OBWO 6/98. Canx.
EI-COT	Reims Cessna F.172N Skyhawk II	1884	D-EIEF	24.11.97	
EI-COU	Boeing 737-4Y0 (Line No. 1885)	24690	SE-DRR PT-TDC/EC-GHK/EC-308/PT-TDA/EC-FBP/EC-603/TC-AFL	24.10.97	To EC-GUI 4/98. Canx 30.4.98.
EI-COV	HS.125 Srs.700B	257178	N621S N700CJ/G-5-747/VH-LMP/G-5-570/G-BMYX/G-5-530/4W-ACM/G-5-14	28. 5.98	
EI-COW	Lockheed L.1011-385-200F Tristar	193A-1158	N851MA D-AERN/N339EA	. .97R	NTU - To N260FA 9/98. Canx.
EI-COX	Boeing 737-230ADV (Line No. 726)	22123	D-ABFP	9. 1.98	
EI-COY	Piper J-3C-65 Cub	22519	N3319N NC3319N	5.11.97	
EI-COZ	PA-28-140 Cherokee C	28-26796	G-AYMZ N11C	5.11.97	
EI-CPA	McDonnell Douglas DC-9-83 (MD-83) (Line No. 1778)	49936	TC-INB G-HCRP/N3001D	3.12.97	To EC-GVI 6/98. Canx 10.6.98.
EI-CPB	McDonnell Douglas DC-9-83 (MD-83) (Line No. 1788)	49940	TC-IND G-TTPT/N30016	27.11.97	
EI-CPC	Airbus A.321-211	815	D-AVZT	8. 5.98	
EI-CPD	Airbus A.321-211	841	D-AVZA	16. 6.98	
EI-CPE	Airbus A.321-211	926	D-AVZQ	11.12.98	
EI-CPF	Airbus A.321-211	991	D-AVZE	9. 4.99	
EI-CPG	Airbus A.321-211	1023	D-AVZC	28. 5.99	
EI-CPH	Airbus A.321-211	1094	D-AVZ.	. .98R	(for delivery 10/99)
EI-CPI	Rutan LongEz	17	(ex)	18.12.97	
EI-CPJ	BAe 146 RJ70	E1258	9H-ACN (9H-ABX)/G-6-258	27. 3.98	
EI-CPK	BAe 146 RJ70	E1260	9H-ACO (9H-ABY)/G-6-260	27. 3.98	
EI-CPL	BAe 146 RJ70	E1267	9H-ACP (9H-ABZ)/G-6-267	31. 3.98	
EI-CPM	SAAB 2000	028	SE-KCF F-GMVR/(V7-9509)/SE-028	18. 3.98	
EI-CPN	Auster J/4	2073	G-AIJR	1. 4.98	
EI-CPO	Robinson R-22 B2 Beta	2775	G-BXUJ	23. 9.98	
EI-CPP	Piper J3C-65 Cub	12052	G-BIGH F-BFQV/OO-GAS/OO-GAZ/44-79756	23. 3.98	(Rebuilt 1994-98 at Glasthule, Dublin)
EI-CPQ	SAAB 2000	013	F-GTSA D-ADSA/SE-013	9. 4.98	To F-GTSL 4/99. Canx 1.4.99.
EI-CPR	Short SD.3-60 Var.200	SH3713	G-OBOH G-BNDJ/G-14-3713	1. 2.99	
EI-CPS	Beechcraft B58 Baron	TH-862	G-BEUL	21. 5.98	
EI-CPT	ATR-42-320	191	C-GIQS (ZS-NYP)/C-GIQS/F-WWEA	12. 6.98	
EI-CPU	Boeing 737-430 (Line No. 2344)	27004	D-ABKF (D-ABKK)/(D-ABKE)	15. 5.98	To SX-BFV 8/99. Canx 30.7.99.
EI-CPV	Boeing 767-38EER (Line No. 417)	25132	N132KR HL7268	4. 6.98	
EI-CPW	SAAB 2000	016	F-GTSC D-ADSC/SE-016	12. 6.98	
EI-CPX	Iniziative Industriali Italian Sky Arrow 650T	K.122 & SAAC-67		24. 6.98	
EI-CPY	BAe 146 Srs.100	E1003	N246SS (VH-NJA)/(N631AW)/N246SS/G-5-14/G-SCHH/G-5-14/G-SSCH/(G-BIAF)	13. 7.98	
EI-CPZ	Boeing 737-86N (Line No. 91)	28575	N1786B	. 8.98	NTU - To N575GE/VT-JNB 8/98. Canx.
EI-CQA	Not allocated.				
EI-CQB	Not allocated.				
EI-CQC	Not allocated.				
EI-CQD	Not allocated.				
EI-CQE	Not allocated.				
EI-CQF	Not allocated.				
EI-CQG	Not allocated.				
EI-CQH	Not allocated.				
EI-CQI	Not allocated.				
EI-CQJ	Not allocated.				
EI-CQK	Not allocated.				
EI-CQL	Not allocated.				
EI-CQM	Not allocated.				
EI-CQN	Not allocated.				
EI-CQO	Not allocated.				
EI-CQP	Not allocated.				
EI-CQQ	Not allocated.				
EI-CQR	Not allocated.				
EI-CQS	Not allocated.				
EI-CQT	Not allocated.				

Regn	Type	c/n	Previous identity	Regn date	Fate or immediate subsequent identity (if known)
EI-CQU	Not allocated.				
EI-CQV	Not allocated.				
EI-CQW	Not allocated.				
EI-CQX	Not allocated.				
EI-CQY	Not allocated.				
EI-CQZ	Not allocated.				
EI-CRA	Boeing 737-86N (Line No. 89)	28578	N578GE N170GD	. 8.98	NTU - To N578GE/VT-JNB 8/98. Canx.
EI-CRB	Lindstrand LBL-90A HAFB	550		23. 9.98	
EI-CRC	Boeing 737-46B (Line No. 1679)	24124	EC-GNC SU-SAB/EC-GHF/EC-309/SU-SAA/EC-FYG/EC-655/N689MA/G-BOPK	3.11.98	To EC-HCP 5/99. Canx 28.4.99.
EI-CRD	Boeing 767-31BER (Line No. 534)	26259	B-2565	29.10.98	
EI-CRE	McDonnell-Douglas DC-9-83 (MD-83) (Line No. 1601)	49854	D-ALLL	11.12.98	
EI-CRF	Boeing 767-31BER (Line No. 542)	25170	B-2566	4.12.98	
EI-CRG	Robin DR.400/180R Remorqueur	2021	D-EHEC	11.12.98	
EI-CRH	McDonnell-Douglas DC-9-83 (MD-83) (Line No. 1773)	49935	HB-IKM G-DCAC/N3004C	10. 2.99	
EI-CRI	Beechcraft 350 Super King Air	FL-66	VR-CRI N8266L	15. 9.95	To VP-CRI 11/98 / N199Y 1/99. Canx 30.11.98.
EI-CRJ	McDonnell-Douglas DC-9-83 (MD-83) (Line No. 1738)	53013	D-ALLP	27. 1.99	
EI-CRK	Airbus A.330-301	070	(EI-NYC) F-WWKV	18.11.94	
EI-CRL	Boeing 767-343ER (Line No. 743)	30008	(I-DEIB)	22. 3.99	
EI-CRM	Boeing 767-343ER (Line No. 736)	30009		8. 4.99	
EI-CRN	Boeing 737-228 (Line No. 952)	23008	(I-JETB) (N.....)/F-GBYI	18. 2.99	
EI-CRO	Boeing 767-3Q8ER (Line No. 747)	29383		16. 4.99	
EI-CRP	Boeing 737-73S (Line No. 187)	29078	N1014S N60436/N1787B	15. 4.99	
EI-CRQ	Boeing 737-73S (Line No. 211)	29080	N1782B "B2781N"/N1786B	14. 4.99	
EI-CRR	Aeronca 11AC Chief	11AC-1605	OO-ESM (OO-DEL)/OO-ESM	13. 4.99	
EI-CRS	Boeing 777-2Q8ER (Line No. 229)	29908		15. 7.99	
EI-CRT	Boeing 777-2Q8ER (Line No. ...)	28676	(HL....)	. .99R	(delivery due 10/99)
EI-CRU					
EI-CRV	Hoffmann H-36 Dimona	3674	OE-9319 HB-2081	2. 6.99	
EI-CRW	McDonnell-Douglas DC-9-83 (MD-83) (Line No. 1915)	49951	HB-IKN G-GMJM/N13627	8. 4.99	
EI-CRX	Socata TB-9 Tampico	1170	F-GKUL	21. 5.99	
EI-CRY	Medway Eclipser	160/138		2. 6.99	
EI-CRZ	Boeing 737-36E (Line No. 2769)	26322	EC-GGE EC-798	14. 4.99	
EI-CSA	Boeing 737-8AS (Line No. 210)	29916	N5573L N1786B	12. 3.99	
EI-CSB	Boeing 737-8AS (Line No. 298)	29917	N1786B	16. 6.99	
EI-CSC	Boeing 737-8AS (Line No. 307)	29918	N1786B	25. 6.99	
EI-CSD	Boeing 737-8AS (Line No. 341)	29919	N1786B	9. 8.99	
EI-CSE	Boeing 737-8AS (Line No. 362)	29920	N1786B	31. 8.99	
EI-CSF	Boeing 737-8AS (Line No. ...)	29921?		. 1.99R	(delivery due in 2000)
EI-CSG	Boeing 737-8AS (Line No. ...)	29922?		. 1.99R	(delivery due in 2000)
EI-CSH	Boeing 737-8AS (Line No. ...)	29923?		. 1.99R	(delivery due in 2000)
EI-CSI	Boeing 737-8AS (Line No. ...)	29924?		. 1.99R	(delivery due in 2000)
EI-CSJ	Boeing 737-8AS (Line No. ...)	29925?		. 1.99R	(delivery due in 2000)
EI-CSK	BAe 146 Srs.200A	E2062	N810AS N880DV/G-5-062/N406XV/(G-BNDR)/G-5-062	3. 4.98	
EI-CSL	BAe 146 Srs.200A	E2074	N812AS N881DV/G-5-074/G-BNND/HS-TBQ/G-BNND/N146SB/N192US/N368PS/(G-BNND)/G-5-074	8. 5.98	
EI-CSM	Boeing 737-8AS (Line No. ...)	29926?		. 1.99R	(delivery due in 2001)
EI-CSN	Boeing 737-8AS (Line No. ...)	29927?		. 1.99R	(delivery due in 2001)
EI-CSO	Boeing 737-8AS (Line No. ...)	29928?		. 1.99R	(delivery due in 2001)

Regn	Type	c/n	Previous identity	Regn date	Fate or immediate subsequent identity (if known)
EI-CSP	Boeing 737-8AS (Line No. ...)	29929?		. 1.99R	(delivery due in 2001)
EI-CSQ	Boeing 737-8AS (Line No. ...)	29930?		. 1.99R	(delivery due in 2001)
EI-CSR	Boeing 737-8AS (Line No. ...)	29931?		. 1.99R	(delivery due in 2002)
EI-CSS	Boeing 737-8AS (Line No. ...)	29932?		. 1.99R	(delivery due in 2002)
EI-CST	Boeing 737-8AS (Line No. ...)	29933?		. 1.99R	(delivery due in 2002)
EI-CSU	Boeing 737-36E (Line No. 2792)	27626	EC-GGZ EC-799	14. 4.99	
EI-CSV	Boeing 737-8AS (Line No. ...)	29934?		. 1.99R	(delivery due in 2002)
EI-CSW	Boeing 737-8AS (Line No. ...)	29935?		. 1.99R	(delivery due in 2002)
EI-CSX	Boeing 737-8AS (Line No. ...)	29936?		. 1.99R	(delivery due in 2003)
EI-CSY	Boeing 737-8AS (Line No. ...)	29937?		. 1.99R	(delivery due in 2003)
EI-CSZ	Boeing 737-8AS (Line No. ...)	29938?		. 1.99R	(delivery due in 2003)
EI-CTA	Boeing 737-8AS (Line No. ...)	29939?		. 1.99R	(delivery due in 2003)
EI-CTB	Boeing 737-8AS (Line No. ...)	29940?		. 1.99R	(delivery due in 2003)
EI-CTC	Medway Eclipser	158/137		2. 6.99	
EI-CTD	Airbus A.320-211	085	F-GJVZ F-WWDF	6. 5.99	
EI-CTE	McDonnell-Douglas DC-9-82 (MD-82) (Line No. 1633/18)	49517	B-540L B-2133	26. 4.99	To EC-HFS 7/99. Canx 30.7.99.
EI-CTF	McDonnell-Douglas DC-9-82 (MD-82) (Line No. 1690/22)	49521	B-2137	26. 4.99	To EC-HFT 8/99. Canx 7.8.99.
EI-CTG	Stoddard-Hamilton Glasair IIRG	721R	N721WR	3. 6.99	
EI-CTH					
EI-CTI	Reims Cessna FRA.150L Aerobat	0261	G-BCRN	29. 4.99	
EI-CTJ	McDonnell-Douglas DC-9-82 (MD-82) (Line No. 2069)	53147	HL7547 HL7203	11. 6.99	
EI-CTK	Sikorsky S-61N	61-489	PH-NZD	28. 4.99	
EI-CTL	Aerotech MW.5B Sorcerer	SR102-R440B-07	G-MTFH	21. 5.99	
EI-CTM	BAe 146 Srs.300	E3129	G-JEAL G-BXTN/HS-TBM/G-5-129	23. 3.99	
EI-CTN					
EI-CTO					
EI-CTP	McDonnell-Douglas DC-9-82 (MD-82) (Line No. 1482/10)	49509	B-2125	9. 6.99	To EC-H..
EI-CTQ	McDonnell-Douglas DC-9-82 (MD-82) (Line No. 1658/20)	49519	B-542L B-2135	9. 6.99	To EC-H..
EI-CTR					
EI-CTS					
EI-CTT	PA-28-161 Warrior II	28-7716305	N38974	14. 7.99	
EI-CTU					
EI-CTV	McDonnell-Douglas DC-9-82 (MD-82) (Line No. 1292/2)	49501	B-2107	23. 7.99	To EC-H..
EI-CTW					
EI-CTX	Boeing 737-228	23006	F-GBYG	26. 8.99	
EI-CTY	BAe 146 Srs.200	E2072	G-BNJI HB-IXC/N190US/N366PS/G-BNJI/G-5-072	7. 1.94	Restored as G-BNJI 7/96. Canx.
EI-CTZ					
EI-CUA					
EI-CUB	Piper J3C-65 Cub	16010	G-BPPV N88392/NC88392	17. 7.91	
EI-CUC					
EI-CUD					
EI-CUE					
EI-CUF					
EI-CUG					
EI-CUH					
EI-CUI					
EI-CUJ					
EI-CUK					
EI-CUL					
EI-CUM					
EI-CUN					
EI-CUO					
EI-CUP					
EI-CUQ					
EI-CUR					
EI-CUS					
EI-CUT					
EI-CUU					
EI-CUV					

Regn	Type	c/n	Previous identity	Regn date	Fate or immediate subsequent identity (if known)
EI-CUW					
EI-CUX					
EI-CUY					
EI-CUZ					
EI-CVA					
EI-CVB					
EI-CVC					
EI-CVD					
EI-CVE					
EI-CVF					
EI-CVG					
EI-CVH					
EI-CVI					
EI-CVJ					
EI-CVK					
EI-CVL					
EI-CVM					
EI-CVN					
EI-CVO					
EI-CVP					
EI-CVQ					
EI-CVR					
EI-CVS					
EI-CVT					
EI-CVU					
EI-CVV					
EI-CVW					
EI-CVX					
EI-CVY					
EI-CVZ					
EI-CWA					
EI-CWB					
EI-CWC					
EI-CWD					
EI-CWE					
EI-CWF					
EI-CWG					
EI-CWH					
EI-CWI					
EI-CWJ					
EI-CWK					
EI-CWL					
EI-CWM					
EI-CWN					
EI-CWO					
EI-CWP					
EI-CWQ					
EI-CWR					
EI-CWS					
EI-CWT					
EI-CWU					
EI-CWV					
EI-CWW					
EI-CWX					
EI-CWY					
EI-CWZ					
EI-CXA					
EI-CXB					
EI-CXC					
EI-CXD					
EI-CXE					
EI-CXF					
EI-CXG					
EI-CXH					
EI-CXI					
EI-CXJ					
EI-CXK					
EI-CXL					
EI-CXM					
EI-CXN					
EI-CXO					
EI-CXP					
EI-CXQ					
EI-CXR					
EI-CXS					
EI-CXT					
EI-CXU					
EI-CXV					
EI-CXW					
EI-CXX					
EI-CXY					
EI-CXZ					
EI-CYA					

Regn	Type	c/n	Previous identity	Regn date	Fate or immediate subsequent identity (if known)
EI-CYB					
EI-CYC					
EI-CYD					
EI-CYE					
EI-CYF					
EI-CYG					
EI-CYH					
EI-CYI					
EI-CYJ					
EI-CYK					
EI-CYL					
EI-CYM					
EI-CYN					
EI-CYO					
EI-CYP					
EI-CYQ					
EI-CYR					
EI-CYS					
EI-CYT					
EI-CYU					
EI-CYV					
EI-CYW					
EI-CYX					
EI-CYY					
EI-CYZ					
EI-CZA					
EI-CZB					
EI-CZC					
EI-CZD					
EI-CZE					
EI-CZF					
EI-CZG					
EI-CZH					
EI-CZI					
EI-CZJ					
EI-CZK					
EI-CZL					
EI-CZM					
EI-CZN					
EI-CZO					
EI-CZP					
EI-CZQ					
EI-CZR					
EI-CZS					
EI-CZT					
EI-CZU					
EI-CZV					
EI-CZW					
EI-CZX					
EI-CZY					
EI-CZZ					
EI-DAA					
EI-DAB					
EI-DAC					
EI-DAD					
EI-DAE					
EI-DAF					
EI-DAG					
EI-DAH					
EI-DAI					
EI-DAJ					
EI-DAK					
EI-DAL					
EI-DAM					
EI-DAN					
EI-DAO					
EI-DAP					
EI-DAQ					
EI-DAR					
EI-DAS					
EI-DAT					
EI-DAU					
EI-DAV					
EI-DAW					
EI-DAX					
EI-DAY					
EI-DAZ					
EI-DBA					
EI-DBB					
EI-DBC					
EI-DBD					
EI-DBE					
EI-DBF					

SECTION 9 - IRISH OUT-OF-SEQUENCE REGISTRATIONS

Regn	Type	c/n	Previous identity	Regn date	Fate or immediate subsequent identity (if known)
EI-DLA	Douglas DC-10-30	46958	N883LA	22. 6.94	
	(Line No.232)		EI-DLA/RP-C2003/(RP-C2000)/(PH-DTM)		
EI-DMT	PA-31-325 Turbo Navajo C	31-7512017	G-BFOM	1. 5.92	Reserved as F-GJHV .97, canx 22.9.97 on sale to France, but
			HB-LHH/N59933		restored as G-BFOM 21.1.98.
EI-DUB	Airbus A.330-301	055	F-WWKP	6. 5.94	
EI-DUN	Cessna 560 Citation V	560-0197	N197CV	. .93R	NTU - To XA-SJC 5/93. Canx.
			N12826		
EI-DWN	Cessna 421C Golden Eagle III	421C-0641	N422GC	5. 4.96	
			N307SP/ZS-KEP/N88582		
EI-EAA	Airbus A.300B4-203F	150	F-WQGT	2. 4.98	
			SU-BCC/F-WZMD		
EI-EAB	Airbus A.300B4-203F	199	F-WQFO	4. 6.98	
			SU-BDF/(SU-BCD)/F-WZMF		
EI-EAC	Airbus A.300B4-203F	250	N10970	20.11.98	
			N970C/F-WZMU		
EI-EAD	Airbus A.300B4-203F	289	"N-13972"	21. 5.99	
			N13972/(N972C)/N13972/N972C/F-WZMM		
EI-EA.	Airbus A.300B4-203F	152	OO-DLC	. .99R	
			N221EA/F-GBNP		
EI-EA.	Airbus A.300B4-203F	259	OO-DLD	. .99R	
			N865PA/TC-ALG/OB-1634/(AP-BFG)/SE-DSG/N72990/(N990C)/N232EA/F-GBNZ		
EI-EAT	Airbus A.300B4-203F	116	F-WQFR	16.12.97	
			D-ASAY/SU-BCB/F-WZES		
EI-ECA	Agusta A.109A II	7387	N109RP	28. 2.97	
			JA9662		
EI-EDR	PA-28R-200 Cherokee Arrow II	28R-7435265	G-BCGD	19.11.87	
			N9628N		
EI-EEC	PA-23-250 Aztec E	27-7554045	G-SATO	6. 2.92	
			G-BCXP/N54257		
EI-EIO	PA-34-200T Seneca II	34-7670274	N6257J	1.10.91	
EI-ELL	Medway Eclipser	157/136		2. 6.99	
EI-ETC	Aeronca 15AC Sedan	15AC-429	G-CETC	9.10.93	To N915TC. Canx 16.8.99.
			HB-ETC		
EI-EWW	Boeing 727-243F	21269	N17406	10.11.95	To OY-SEU 11/97. Canx 10.11.97.
	(Line No. 1230)		N576PE/I-DIRC/N40133		
EI-EXP	Short SD.3-30 Var.100	SH3092	G-BKMU	23. 7.92	WFU Exeter, UK. Scrapped 3/99 Exeter, UK, fuselage removed
			SE-IYO/G-BKMU		and transported to the grounds of Valley Nurseries, Beech,
			G-14-3092/EI-BEH/EI-BEG/G-BKMU/G-14-3092		near Alton, Hants in 4/99.
EI-FDX	Cessna 208A Caravan I	208A-00084	F-GEOH	7. 9.88	To N833FE. Canx 23.4.92.
			N833FE/(N9525F)		
EI-FEA	Fokker F-27 Friendship 600	10385	OO-FEA	14. 3.91	To N729FE 5/92. Canx 4.5.92.
			PH-FNH/OY-KAC/VH-TQN/PH-FNH		
EI-FEX	Cessna 208A Caravan I	208A-00016	SE-KRX	5.12.91	To N835FE. Canx 23.4.92.
			N804FE/(N9342F)		
EI-FKA	Fokker F.27-050	20118	PH-LMA	18. 1.89	To OY-EBB 9/99.
			(VH-FNM)/PH-EXB		
EI-FKB	Fokker F.27-050	20119	PH-LMB	17. 2.89	To OY-EDB 7/99. Canx 20.7.99.
			(VH-FNN)/PH-EXC		
EI-FKC	Fokker F.27-050	20177	PH-EXC	23. 2.90	
EI-FKD	Fokker F.27-050	20181	PH-EXG	12. 4.90	
EI-FKE	Fokker F.27-050	20208	PH-EXA	28. 1.91	
EI-FKF	Fokker F.27-050	20209	PH-EXE	8. 2.91	
EI-FKG	[Was reserved for Aer Lingus Commuter]			. .90R	NTU - Canx.
EI-FKH	[Was reserved for Aer Lingus Commuter]			. .90R	NTU - Canx.
EI-FKI	[Was reserved for Aer Lingus Commuter]			. .90R	NTU - Canx.
EI-FKJ	[Was reserved for Aer Lingus Commuter]			. .90R	NTU - Canx.
EI-FLY	Socata TB-9 Tampico	186	G-BIRA	13.10.93	Force landed on a golf course near Weston on 3.1.99.
EI-GER	Maule MX7-180A Star Rocket	20006C		7. 1.94	
EI-GFC	Socata TB-9 Tampico	141	G-BIAA	9.10.93	
EI-GHL	Bell 206B JetRanger III	3379	N16Q	4. 2.97	
			N2069A		
EI-GPA	Canadair CL.600-1A11 Challenger	1016	C-GWRT	6. 7.87	To VR-BKJ. Canx 1.2.89.
EI-GSM	Cessna 182S Skylane II	182-80188	N9541Q	17. 6.98	
EI-GWY	Cessna 172R Skyhawk II	172-80162	N9497F	31.12.97	
EI-HAM	Light-Aero Avid Flyer	1072-90		18.11.96	
EI-HCA	Boeing 727-225F	20382	N8839E	15. 4.94	
	(Line No. 825)				
EI-HCB	Boeing 727-223F	19492	N6817	2. 9.95	
	(Line No. 652)		EI-HCB/N6817		
EI-HCC	Boeing 727-223F	19480	N6805	26. 9.95	
	(Line No. 545)				
EI-HCD	Boeing 727-223F	20185	N6832	8.11.95	
	(Line No. 710)				
EI-HCE	Lockheed L.188CF Electra	1129	G-FIJV	17. 4.97	Restored as G-FIJV 9/98. Canx 25.9.98.
			C-FIJV/CF-IJV/N7143C		
EI-HCF	Lockheed L.188PF Electra	1138	G-FIJR	. .97R	NTU - Remained as G-FIJR. Canx.
			C-FIJR/CF-IJR/N134US		
EI-HCI	Boeing 727-223F	20183	N6830	23. 5.95	
	(Line No. 705)				

Regn	Type	c/n	Previous identity	Regn date	Fate or immediate subsequent identity (if known)
EI-HCS	Grob G-109B	6414	G-BMHR	18. 8.95	
EI-HER	Bell 206B JetRanger III	3408	G-HIER	1. 7.94	
			G-BRFD/N2069N		
EI-IRV	Aerospatiale AS.350B Ecureuil	1713	D-HENY	7.10.96	
EI-JAK	Pearce Jabiru UL	0144 & SAAC-68		9. 7.98	
EI-JBC	Agusta A.109A	7126	F-GATN	24. 7.97	
EI-JET	BAe 146 Srs.200	E2073	G-BVFV	23.12.93	Restored as G-BVFV 6/96. Canx.
			HB-IXD/N191US/N367PS/G-5-073		
EI-JFK	Airbus A.330-301	086	F-GMDE	11. 7.95	
EI-JTC	PA-31-350 Navajo Chieftain		G-POLO	27.11.93	To G-VIPY 10/97. Canx 9.10.97.
		31-7852143	N27750		
EI-JWM	Robinson R-22 Beta	1386	G-BSLB	21.11.92	
EI-KMA	Robinson R-22 Mariner	0847M	G-STOI	. .90R	NTU - To EI-CCT 12/90. Canx.
EI-KOC	Champion 7KCAB Citabria	253-70	N9070L	8.11.91	W/o at Weston, Ireland on 12.7.92. Canx 5/93.
EI-LAX	Airbus A.330-202	269	F-WWKV	29. 4.99	
EI-LCH	Boeing 727-281F	20466	N903PG	6. 2.95	
	(Line No. 865)		N527MD/HL7355/JA8332		
EI-LIT	MBB Bo.105S	S.434	A6-DBH	20. 2.96	
			Dubai 105/D-HDMH		
EI-LJG	Canadair CL.601-2B16 Challenger 3A		N608CC	10.11.88	To N601CJ. Canx 14.7.92.
		5023	C-GLYO		
EI-LJR	Dassault Falcon 2000	18	F-GMPR	21.11.97	To VP-CJA 12/97. Canx 12.12.97.
			F-WWMG		
EI-LMG	Bell 206L-3 Long Ranger III	51284	EI-BYR	.11.89R	NTU - remained as EI-BYR. Canx.
			D-HBAD		
EI-LRS	Schweizer Hughes 269C (300C)	S.1701	N41S	6. 3.95	
EI-MAC	Robinson R-22 Beta	1433	G-OHHL	18. 4.97	Broken-up in-flight en-route from Weston, Co.Wicklow to Sligo-Strandhill on 27.8.99.
EI-MAS	Canadair CL.601-2B16 Challenger 3R		C-FXIP	4. 2.97	To N601R 8/98. Canx 31.7.98.
		5194			
EI-MAT	Pearce Jabiru UL	0129 & SAAC-66		9. 7.98	To G-BYNR 7/99. Canx.
EI-MES	Sikorsky S-61N Mk.II	61-776	G-BXAE	27. 3.97	
			LN-OQO		
EI-MIP	Aerospatiale SA.365N Dauphin 2	6119	G-BLEY	20. 3.96	
			F-WTNM		
EI-MLA	Fokker F-27 Friendship 600QC	10304	HZ-KA8	. 2.97R	(Stored 3/99 Exeter, UK still marked as HZ-KA8)
			VH-FNO/PH-FIY		For sale 1999.
EI-NYC	Airbus A.330-301	070	F-WWKV	. .94R	NTU - To EI-CRK 11/94. Canx.
EI-ONE	Bell 206B JetRanger II	1761	EI-CJM	20. 5.96	
			N281C/N49582		
EI-ORD	Airbus A.330-301	059	(EI-USA)	6. 6.97	
			F-GMDD		
EI-PAK	Boeing 727-227F	21245	N16762	11. 3.96	To OY-SET 11/97. Canx 18.11.97.
	(Line No. 1202)		N569PE/(N443PS)/N444BN		
EI-PJM	Lake LA-250 Renegade	70	G-LAKE	. .92R	NTU - Remained as G-LAKE. Canx.
			N8415B		
EI-PMI	Agusta-Bell 206B JetRanger III	8614	EI-BLG	19. 9.96	
			G-BIGS		
EI-POD	Cessna 177B Cardinal	177B-02729	N1444C	3. 8.95	
EI-RRR	HS.125 Srs.700A	NA0318/257170	N80CL	. 9.99	
			N819M/G-5-14		
EI-RYR	Boeing-Stearman E75 (N2S-5) Kaydet		G-THEA	. 3.98R	NTU - Remained as G-THEA. Canx.
		75-5736A	N1733B/BuA.38122		
	(Original identity and c/n not confirmed correct - if USN serial is correct, c/n would be 75-7743)				
EI-SAI	Boeing 747SP-31	21962	UN-001	. 4.96R	NTU - To P4-AFE 4/96. Canx.
	(Line No. 439)		N601AA/N57202		
EI-SAR	Sikorsky S-61N	61-143	G-AYOM	26. 6.98	
	(Mitsubishi c/n M61-001)		N4585/JA9506/N94565		
EI-SHN	Airbus A.330-301	054	F-WWKJ	27. 4.94	
EI-SKY	Boeing 727-281F	20571	N905PG	5. 5.95	To OY-SEV 11/97. Canx 29.1.98.
	(Line No. 884)		N530MD/HL7367/JA8341		
EI-SNN	Cessna 650 Citation III	650-0183	N2614Y	10.10.90	To N820FJ. Canx 9.2.94.
EI-STR	Bell 407	53282	N44504	.10.98R	
EI-SXT	Canadair CL.601-2B16 Challenger 3R		C-FTNN	25. 4.95	
		5159	C-GLWR		
EI-TAM(1)	Canadair CL.601-2A12 Challenger		N372G	. .98R	NTU - To P4-TAM 3/98. Canx.
		3006	HB-IKX/(N3728)/N372G/C-GLXY		
EI-TAM(2)	Canadair CL.604-2B16 Challenger		C-GCCZ	28. 8.98	To VP-COJ 10/98. Canx 8.10.98.
		5367			
EI-TAR	Bell 222A	47029	N121NN	10. 9.98	
			N121NC/N120NC		
EI-TBG	Lockheed L.1011-385-1 Tristar		SE-DPV	26. 6.96	Canx 6.8.97 at owner's request. Flown to Bournemouth 4.8.97 for scrapping. Scrapping started 1/98, rear fuselage "chopped off" in 2/98.
		193B-1030	N31010		
EI-TCK	Cessna 421A Golden Eagle	421A-0038	G-AXAW	5.11.91	To N132CK 3.99. Canx 23.3.99.
			(EI-TCK)/G-AXAW/N2238Q		
EI-TKI	Robinson R-22 Beta	1195	G-OBIP	22. 8.91	
EI-TLA	Douglas DC-8-71F	45972	N8083U	26. 2.92	Restored as N8083U 4/94. Canx 8.3.94.
	(Line No. 358)				
EI-TLB(1)	Douglas DC-8-71F	45993	N8089U	. .92R	NTU - Remained as N8090U. Canx.
	(Line No. 382)				
EI-TLB(2)	Airbus A.300B4-103	012	F-GIJU	2. 4.96	
			G-BMNC/D-AMAX/F-WLGC		

Regn	Type	c/n	Previous identity	Regn date	Fate or immediate subsequent identity (if known)
EI-TLC	Douglas DC-8-71F (Line No. 388)	45995	N8091U	13. 4.92	Restored as N8091U 6/94. Canx 10.3.94.
EI-TLD	Douglas DC-8-71F (Line No. 277)	45812	N8072U	19. 6.92	To N500MH. Canx 11.11.93.
EI-TLE	Airbus A.320-231	429	D-AORX N429RX/F-WWIZ	25. 9.93	
EI-TLF	Airbus A.320-231	476	F-WWDR	10. 6.94	
EI-TLG	Airbus A.320-231	428	C-GMPG EI-TLG/C-GMPG/EI-TLG/(D-ANDY)/N391LF/F-WWIL	20. 5.94	
EI-TLH	Airbus A.320-231	247	G-OALA EI-TLH/N247RX/F-WWDK	22.12.94	
EI-TLI	Airbus A.320-231	405	N141LF HC-BTV/N441LF/F-WWDK	26. 5.95	
EI-TLJ	Airbus A.320-231	257	N257RX LZ-ABA/F-WWBI	29. 9.95	
EI-TLK	Airbus A.300B4-203	161	N226GE TC-JUV/N226EA/F-GBNU	12. 3.97	
EI-TLL	Airbus A.300B4-203	158	N225GE TC-JUY/N225EA/F-GBNT	20. 6.97	
EI-TLM	Airbus A.300B4-203	046	RP-C8882 SX-BEB/F-WZER/F-WZEK/F-WLGB	18. 9.97	
EI-TLN	Airbus A.300B4-203F	047	G-HLAA N740SC/F-BVGJ/F-WUAX	7.11.97	Restored as G-HLAA 7/98. Canx 8.7.98.
EI-TLO	Airbus A.320-232	758	F-WWDC	9. 1.98	
EI-TLP	Airbus A.320-232	760	F-WWDD	20. 1.98	
EI-TLQ	Airbus A.300B4-203A	131	6Y-JMK G-BIMB/(G-BILC)/F-WZEL	2. 4.98	
EI-TLR	Airbus A.320-231	414	B-HYR VR-HYR/F-WWIU	16. 6.98	
EI-TLS	Airbus A.320-231	430	(N430CR) B-HYS/VR-HYS/F-WWBH/F-WWHB	19. 8.98	
EI-TLT	Airbus A.320-231	415	B-HYV VR-HYV/F-WWBL	23. 4.99	
EI-TNT	Boeing 727-281F (Line No. 958)	20725	N902PG N526MD/HL7366/JA8346	10. 2.95	To OY-TNT 12/97. Canx 15.12.97.
EI-TVA	Boeing 737-43Q (Line No. 2827)	28489	B-18671	21.11.98	
EI-TVB	Boeing 737-43Q (Line No. 2838)	28493	B-18676	9.12.98	
EI-TVC	[Marks reserved for Virgin Express (Ireland) Ltd]			. .99R	
EI-TVD	[Marks reserved for Virgin Express (Ireland) Ltd]			. .99R	
EI-TVE	[Marks reserved for Virgin Express (Ireland) Ltd]			. .99R	
EI-TVF	[Marks reserved for Virgin Express (Ireland) Ltd]			. .99R	
EI-TVG	[Marks reserved for Virgin Express (Ireland) Ltd]			. .99R	
EI-TVH	[Marks reserved for Virgin Express (Ireland) Ltd]			. .99R	
EI-TVI	[Marks reserved for Virgin Express (Ireland) Ltd]			. .99R	
EI-TVJ	[Marks reserved for Virgin Express (Ireland) Ltd]			. .99R	
EI-TVK	[Marks reserved for Virgin Express (Ireland) Ltd]			. .99R	
EI-TVL	[Marks reserved for Virgin Express (Ireland) Ltd]			. .99R	
EI-TVM	[Marks reserved for Virgin Express (Ireland) Ltd]			. .99R	
EI-TVN	Boeing 737-36N (Line No. 3090)	28586	N1786B	19. 1.99	
EI-TVO	Boeing 737-36M (Line No. 2810)	28333	OO-VEB (OO-EBB)	6. 5.99	
EI-TVP	Boeing 737-3M8 (Line No. 2024)	25041	OO-LTL	30. 6.99	
EI-TVQ	[Marks reserved for Virgin Express (Ireland) Ltd]			. .99R	
EI-TVR	[Marks reserved for Virgin Express (Ireland) Ltd]			. .99R	
EI-TVS	[Marks reserved for Virgin Express (Ireland) Ltd]			. .99R	
EI-TVT	[Marks reserved for Virgin Express (Ireland) Ltd]			. .99R	
EI-TVU	[Marks reserved for Virgin Express (Ireland) Ltd]			. .99R	
EI-TVV	[Marks reserved for Virgin Express (Ireland) Ltd]			. .99R	
EI-TVW	[Marks reserved for Virgin Express (Ireland) Ltd]			. .99R	
EI-TVX	[Marks reserved for Virgin Express (Ireland) Ltd]			. .99R	
EI-TVY	[Marks reserved for Virgin Express (Ireland) Ltd]			. .99R	
EI-TVZ	[Marks reserved for Virgin Express (Ireland) Ltd]			. .99R	
EI-TWO	[Marks reserved for P.A.Wynne]	-		12.12.96R	
EI-UFO	PA-22-150 Tri-Pacer (Taildragger)	22-4942	G-BRZR N7045D	12. 2.94	
EI-UPS	Fairchild-Hiller FH-227B	-		. .90R	NTU - Canx.
EI-USA	Airbus A.330-301	059	F-GMDD	. 2.97R	NTU - To EI-ORD 6/97. Canx.
EI-VIP	Hughes 269C (300C)	21-1024	G-BOTS EI-VIP/G-BOTS/N13048/(N299SC)/N1105Z	27. 3.95	
EI-VIR	Airbus A.320-231	449	N449RX SX-BSV/(G-VSEE)/N449RX/F-WWIG	7. 4.95	To G-OUZO 11/95. Canx 8.11.95.
EI-WAC	PA-23-250 Aztec E	27-4683	G-AZBK N14077	26. 5.95	
EI-WAV	Bell 430	49028	N4213V	24.12.97	
EI-WCC	Robinson R-22 Beta	1044	G-OLUM	30.10.93	
EI-WDC	HS.125 Srs.3B	25132	G-OCBA EI-WDC/G-OCBA/G-MRFB/G-AZVS/OY-DKP	2. 7.94	
EI-WGV	Gulfstream G.1159 Gulfstream V	505	N505GV	21.11.97	

Regn	Type	c/n	Previous identity	Regn date	Fate or immediate subsequent identity (if known)
EI-WHE	Beechcraft B200 Super King Air	BB-1569	VP-CHE N20505	7. 5.98	
EI-XMA	Robinson R-22 Beta	0681	G-BNVC	20.10.87	
EI-XMC	Robinson R-22 Beta	1655		17. 5.91	Crashed in Dingle Harbour, Co.Kerry on 31.5.92. (Wreck stored)
EI-YAY	PA-38-112 Tomahawk	38-..A....		. 3.99R	

SECTION 10 - INTERNATIONAL CIVIL AIRCRAFT MARKINGS

Before the 1914-18 war, civil aeroplanes carried no official markings, and such markings as were used were of a purely individual nature, flying school fleet numbers, owner's or makers' names or trade marks, and the like. With the re-birth of civil flying in 1919, many countries initially started off with their own ideas on what type of registration markings should be used - Great Britain for example carried on what was in effect the military serial system, with the letter K followed by a group of three digits for any new aircraft.

It was not until the International Conference held in 1919 that the Air Convention came into being, laying down a definite system to which all civil aircraft throughout the world were supposed to adhere. Some of the larger countries were not parties to the agreement - Germany, Russia and the USA among them - but most of the world agreed to abide by the recommendations made.

Briefly, these recommendations were that all aircraft were to be allotted a five-letter group, the first to indicate the nationality, the remaining four to be the registration marking of the individual aircraft. These letters were to be prominently displayed on both sides of the fuselage, and across the full span of top and bottom of the mainplanes, the nationality letter being separated from the others by a hyphen. The nationality letter was, in addition, to be painted on each side of all tail surfaces. Furthermore the original order specified that the markings were to appear as black letters on a white panel, with the individual registration letters underlined in the case of private aircraft. It was not long, though, before many of these regulations fell into disuse, and while the system of lettering continued in most cases, the "black-on-white" rule was soon ignored, and most countries ceased to paint the nationality letter on the tail surfaces.

By 1929 the position was becoming a little involved; there were only 26 letters available for use as nationality markings, while some scores of countries were operating civil aircraft. Considerable duplication was therefore unavoidable. The International Commission for Air Navigation (I.C.A.N.) then drew up a fresh set of regulations, allotting one or two letters as nationality marks (in general, the bigger countries kept their old single-letter marks), followed by four or three letters respectively as individual markings, the nationality letters normally being in the group allotted to the country concerned in the International Telecommunications Convention for radio call-signs. At the same time, the tail markings were abolished, and the white panel officially dispensed with. Since then, the only major change has been the official adoption by I.C.A.O. (successor to I.C.A.N.) of the system in use for many years by the USA - much smaller lettering, fuselage markings moved up to the vertical tail surfaces, and wing markings painted on one wing only. This gives a much neater appearance to the aeroplane as a whole, and more scope for decorative work on the fuselage.

Below is a table of all known nationality markings in alphabetical order.

Nationality Mark	Country
A-	Austria
A-H	Hedjaz (Saudi Arabia)
A-N	Nicaragua
AN-	Nicaragua
AP-	Pakistan
A2-	Botswana
A3-	Tongo
A5-	Bhutan
A6-	United Arab Emirates
A7-	Qatar
A40-	Muscat and Oman
A9C-	Bahrein
B-	Formosa
B-	China (People's Republic)
B-	China (Republic of) [Taiwan]
B-A	Albania
B-B	Bulgaria
B-H	Hong Kong
B-L	Latvia
bHMAY-	Mongolia
BH-	Bosnia-Hercegovina (unofficially in 1993)
BR-	Burundi
C-	Colombia
C-B	Bolivia
C-C	Cuba
C-F	Canada
C-G	Canada
C-H	Canada (Hovercraft)
C-I	Canada (Microlight)
C-J	Canada
C-K	Canada
C-P	Portugal
C-R	Romania
C-U	Uruguay
C-V	Bolivia
CB-	Bolivia
CC-	Chile
CCCP-	USSR
CF-	Canada
CG-	Canada
CH-	Canada
CH-	Switzerland
CI-	Canada
CIS-	Commonwealth of Independent States (former USSR)
CJ-	Canada
CK-	Canada
CL-	Cuba
CN-	Morocco
CP-	Bolivia
CR-A	Mozambique
CR-B	Mozambique
CR-C	Cape Verde
CR-G	Portuguese Guinea (Guinea-Bissau)
CR-H	Mozambique
CR-I	Portuguese India
CR-L	Angola
CR-M	Mozambique
CR-S	Sao Tome Island
CR-T	Timor
CS-	Portugal
CU-	Cuba
CV-	Rumania
CX-	Uruguay
CY-	Ceylon
CZ-	Monaco
C2-	Nauru
C5-	Gambia
C6-	Bahamas
C9-	Mozambique
D-	Germany
D-	West Germany
D-	Mongolia
DDR-	East Germany
DM-	East Germany
DQ-	Fiji
DZ-	Danzig Free State
D2-	Angola
D4-	Cado Verde Islands
D6-	Comores Islands
E-A	Estonia
E-S	Ecuador
EA-	Spain
EB-	Spain
EC-	Spain
ED-	Spain
EE-	Spain
EF-	Spain
EG-	Spain
EH-	Spain
EI-	Irish Free State
EJ-	Irish Free State
EK-	Turkmenistan (unofficial)
EK-	Armenia
EL-	Liberia

Nationality Mark	Country
EP-	Iran
ER-	Moldova
ES-	Estonia
ET-	Ethiopia
EW-	Belarus
EX-	Kyrghyzstan
EY-	Tajikistan
EZ-	Saar Territory
EZ-	Turkmenistan
E3-	Eritrea (Government)
F-	France
F-D	French Morocco
F-KH	Cambodia
F-L	Laos
F-O	French Overseas Territories
F-OG	French Guinea/Antilles
F-VN	French Indochina (Vietnam)
FC-	"Free French"
G-	United Kingdom
G-AU	Australia
G-CA	Canada
G-CY	Canada (Military)
G-E	Great Britain
G-IA	India
G-NZ	New Zealand
G-UA	Union of South Africa
H-H	Haiti
H-M	Hungary
H-N	Netherlands
H-S	Siam (later Thailand)
HA-	Hungary
HB-	Switzerland
HB-	Liechtenstein
HC-	Ecuador
HH-	Haiti
HI-	Dominican Republic
HK-	Colombia
HL-	Republic of Korea (South)
HP-	Panama
HR-	Honduras
HS-	Thailand (Siam)
HZ-	Saudi Arabia
H4-	Solomon Islands
I-	Italy
J-	Japan
JA	Japan
JU-	Mongolia
JY-	Jordan
JZ-	Dutch East Indies
J2-	Djibouti
J3-	Grenada
J5-	Guinea-Bissau
J6-	St.Lucia
J7-	Dominica
J8-	St.Vincent/Grenadines
K-	USA
K-	Kuwait (unofficial)
K-S	Finland
KA-	Katanga (unofficial)
KW-	Cambodia
KKH-	Northern Cyprus (unofficial)
L-B	Czechoslovakia
L-G	Guatemala
L-L	Liberia
L-U	Luxembourg
LA-	Norway
LB-	Norway
LC-	Norway
LD-	Norway
LE-	Norway
LF-	Norway
LG-	Norway
LG-	Guatemala
LH-	Norway
LI-	Norway
LI-	Liberia
LJ-	Norway
LK-	Norway
LL-	Norway
LM-	Norway
LN-	Norway
LOD-	Lithuania (Balloons)
LQ-	Argentina (Government)
LR-	Lebanon
LV-	Argentina

Nationality Mark	Country
LX-	Luxembourg
LY-	Lithuania
LZ-	Bulgaria
M-	Spain
M-M	Spain (Military)
M-S	Mexico
MC-	Monaco
MI-	Marshall Islands
MONGOL-	Mongolia
MPR-	Mongolia
MT-	Mongolia
N	Norway
N	USA
NC	USA - Commercial
NM-	Cuba
NPC-	Philippines
NR	USA - Restricted
NS	USA - State-owned
NX	USA - Experimental
O-A	Peru
O-B	Belgium
O-P	Peru
OA-	Peru
OB-	Peru
OD-	Lebanon
OE-	Austria
OH-	Finland
OK-	Czech Republic/Czechia (Czechoslavakia)
OM-	Slovakia
OO-	Belgium
OO-C	Belgian Congo
OY-	Denmark
P-	Korea (North)
P-B	Brazil
P-P	Poland
PH-	The Netherlands
PI-	The Netherlands
PI-	Philippines
PJ-	Netherlands Antilles (Netherlands West Indies)
PK-	Indonesia (Netherlands East Indies)
PL-	Poland (Microlights)
PP-	Brazil
PT-	Brazil
PZ-	Surinam
P2-	Papua New Guinea
P4-	Aruba
P5-	North Korea
R-	Argentina
R-	Panama
R-R	Russia
R-Z	Lithuania
RA-	Russia
RB-	Belarus (allocated)
RC-	Croatia
RD-	Armenia (allocated)
RF-	Russia
RG-	Georgia (allocated)
RH-	Kyrgystan (allocated)
RI-	Indonesia
RK-	Kazakhstan (allocated)
RM-	Moldova (allocated)
RO-	Uzbekhistan (allocated)
RP-	Philippines
RP-	Tajikistan (allocated)
RR-	USSR
RR-	Russia (allocated)
RT-	Turkmenistan (allocated)
RV-	Iran (Persia)
RW-	Ukraine (allocated)
RX-	Panama
RY-	Lithuania
RDPL-	Laos
S-A	Sweden
S-G	Greece
S-P	Panama
SA-	Sweden
SA-	Saudi Arabia
SB-	Sweden
SC-	Sweden
SD-	Sweden
SE-	Sweden
SL-	Saar Territory
SN-	Sudan
SP-	Poland
SR-	Syria

Nationality Mark	Country
ST-	Sudan
SU-	Egypt
SX-	Greece
SSSR-	USSR
S2-	Bangladesh
S3-	Bangladesh (Military)
S5	Slovenia
S7-	Seychelles
S9-	Sao Tome Island
T-D	Denmark
TC-	Turkey
TF-	Iceland
TG-	Guatemala
TI-	Costa Rica
TJ-	TransJordan
TJ-	Cameroon
TL-	Central African Republic
TN-	Congo (Brazzaville)
TR-	Gabon
TS-	Saar Territory (unofficially)
TS-	Tunisia
TT-	Tchad
TU-	Cote d'Ivoire (Ivory Coast)
TY-	Benin (Dahomey)
TZ-	Mali
T1-	Australia (Microlights)
T2-	Australia (Microlights)
T3-	Kiribati
T7-	San Marino
T9-	Bosnia-Hercegovina
U-	Thailand (Microlights)
UH-	Hedjaz
UK-	Uzbekistan
UL-	Luxembourg
UN-	Jugoslavia
UN-	Kazakhstan
UN-	United Nations
UR-	Ukraine
URSS-	USSR
USSR-	USSR
VA-	Canada
VB-	Canada
VC-	Canada
VD-	Canada
VE-	Canada
VF-	Canada
VG-	Canada
VH-	Australia
VI-	Australia
VJ-	Australia
VK-	Australia
VL-	Australia
VM-	Australia
VN-	Vietnam
VO-	Newfoundland
VP-A	Gold Coast (including: Ashanti, Northern Territories of the Gold Coast and British Togoland) (Ghana)
VP-A	Anguilla
VP-B	Bahamas
VP-B	Bermuda
VP-C	Ceylon
VP-C	Cayman Islands
VP-F	Falkland Islands & dependencies
VP-G	British Guiana
VP-H	British Honduras (Belize)
VP-J	Jamaica and its dependencies
VP-K	Kenya
VP-L	Leeward/Windward Islands
VP-LA	Antigua
VP-LI	Antigua
VP-LK	St.Kitts
VP-LL	Anguilla
VP-LM	Monserrat
VP-LV	British Virgin Islands
VP-M	Malta
VP-N	Nyasaland
VP-P	The Islands of the Western Pacific High Commission
VP-R	Northern Rhodesia
VP-S	British Somaliland
VP-T	Trinidad and Tobago
VP-U	Uganda
VP-V	St.Vincent/Grenadines
VP-W	Rhodesia

Nationality Mark	Country
VP-W	Wei-hai-wei (China)
VP-X	The Colony and Protectorate of the Gambia
VP-Y	Southern Rhodesia
VP-Y	Rhodesia/Nyasaland
VP-Z	Zanzibar
VQ-B	Barbados
VQ-C	Cyprus
VQ-F	Fiji/Tonga/Friendly Islands
VQ-G	Grenada
VQ-H	St.Helena
VQ-L	St.Lucia
VQ-M	Mauritius
VQ-P	Palestine
VQ-S	Seychelles
VQ-T	Turks & Caicos Islands
VQ-ZA	Basutoland
VQ-ZB	Basutoland
VQ-ZC	Basutoland
VQ-ZD	Basutoland
VQ-ZE	Bechuanaland
VQ-ZF	Bechuanaland
VQ-ZG	Bechuanaland
VQ-ZH	Bechuanaland
VQ-ZI	Swaziland
VR-A	Aden (South Yemen)
VR-B	Bermuda
VR-C	Cayman Islands
VR-G	Gibraltar
VR-H	Hong Kong
VR-J	Johore
VR-L	Sierra Leone
VR-N	British Cameroons
VR-O	Sabah (North Borneo)
VR-R	Malaya
VR-S	Straits Settlements
VR-S	Singapore
VR-T	Tanganyika
VR-U	Brunei
VR-W	Sarawak
VS-	Brunei
VT-	India
V2-	Antigua/Barbuda
V3-	Belize
V4-	St.Kitts Nevis
V5-	Namibia
V6-	Micronesia
V7-	Marshall Islands
V8-	Brunei
X-A	Mexico
X-B	Mexico
X-C	China
X-H	Honduras
X-S	Serbia-Croatia-Slavonia (Jugoslavia)
XA-	Mexico - Commercial
XB-	Mexico - Private
XC-	Mexico - Government
XH-	Honduras
XT-	China
XT-	Burkina Faso (Upper Volta)
XU-	Kampuchea (Cambodia)
XV-	Vietnam (South)
XW-	Laos (Cambodia)
XY-	Myanmar (Burma)
XZ-	Myanmar (Burma)
Y-M	Danzig Free State
YA-	Afghanistan
YE-	Yemen
YI-	Iraq
YJ-	Vanuatu (New Hebrides)
YK-	Syria
YL-	Latvia
YM-	Danzig Free State
YN-	Nicaragua
YR-	Romania
YS-	El Salvador
YU-	Jugoslavia (Serbia)
YV-	Venezuela
Z-	Lithuania
Z-	Zimbabwe
ZA-	Albania
ZK-	New Zealand
ZK-	Cook Islands
ZL-	New Zealand
ZM-	New Zealand
ZP-	Paraguay

Nationality Mark	Country	Nationality Mark	Country
ZS-	Union of South Africa	60-	Somalia
ZS-	Republic of South Africa	60S-	Somalia
ZT-	Republic of South Africa	6V-	Senegal
ZU-	Republic of South Africa	6W-	Senegal (Military)
ZZ-	Zimbabwe (Gliders)	6Y-	Jamaica
Z3-	Macedonia	70-	South Yemen
3A-	Monaco	7P-	Lesotho
3B-	Mauritius	7Q-	Malawi
3C-	Equatorial Guinea	7T-	Algeria
3D-	Swaziland (Ngwane)	8P-	Barbados
3X-	Guinea	8Q-	Maldive Republic
4K-	Azerbaijan	8R-	Guyana
4L-	Georgia	9A-	Croatia
4P-	Palestine (unofficial allocation)	9G-	Ghana
4R-	Sri Lanka (Ceylon)	9H-	Malta
4W-	Yemen	9J-	Zambia
4X-	Israel	9K-	Kuwait
4YB-	Jordan	9L-	Sierra Leone
5A-	Libya	9M-	Malaysia
5B-	Cyprus	9N-	Nepal
5H-	Tanzania	90-	Democratic Republic of Congo (Kinshasa)
5N-	Nigeria	9Q-	Democratic Republic of Congo (Kinshasa)
5R-	Malagasy Republic (Madagascar)	9Q-	Zaire
5T-	Mauritania	9T-	Kinshasa/Zaire (Military)
5U-	Niger	9U-	Burundi
5V-	Togo	9V-	Singapore
5W-	Western Samoa	9XR-	Rwanda
5X-	Uganda	9Y-	Trinidad & Tobago
5Y-	Kenya		

B-CLASS MARKINGS

Manufacturer	Prefix	Manufacturer	Prefix	Manufacturer	Prefix
Armstrong-Whitworth	A	Armstrong-Whitworth	G-1	Flight Refuelling	G-33
Blackburn	B	Rolls-Royce (Bristol Engines)	G-1	Chrislea Aircraft Ltd	G-34
Boulton Paul	C	Blackburn	G-2	F G Miles Ltd/Beagle Aircraft	G-35
Bristol Aeroplane Company	D	Boulton Paul	G-3	College of Aeronautics	G-36
Cuncliffe Owen Aircraft	D	Portsmouth Aviation	G-4	Rolls-Royce	G-37
Portsmouth Aviation	D	Miles Aviation & Transport	G-4	DH Propellors Ltd	G-38
de Havilland	F	de Havilland	G-5	Folland Aircraft Ltd	G-39
Fairey	F	Fairey	G-6	Wiltshire School of Flying	G-40
Gloster	G	Gloster	G-7	Aviation Traders	G-41
Handley-Page	H	Slingsby Sailplanes	G-7	Armstrong Whitworth Motors Ltd	G-42
Hawker Aircraft	I	Handley-Page	G-8	Edgar Percival Ltd	G-43
George Parnell & Company	J	Hawker Aircraft	G-9	Agricultural Aviation Ltd	G-44
Reid & Sigrist Ltd	J	Reid & Sigrist Ltd	G-10	Bristol Siddeley Engines Ltd	G-45
A V Roe & Company	K	A V Roe & Company	G-11	Saunders Roe (Helicopter Div.)	G-46
Saunders Roe Ltd	L	Saunders Roe Ltd	G-12	Lancashire Aircraft Co.	G-47
Short Brothers	M	Short Brothers	G-14	Westland Aircraft Ltd	G-48
Supermarine	N	Supermarine	G-15	F G Miles Engineering	G-49
Vickers (Aviation)	O	Vickers (Aviation)	G-16	Alvis Ltd	G-50
Westland Aircraft	P	Westland Aircraft	G-17	Britten-Norman Ltd	G-51
Bristol Aircraft Company	R	Bristol Aeroplane Company	G-18	Marshalls of Cambridge	G-52
Spartan Aircraft	S	Heston Aircraft Ltd	G-19	NDN Aircraft	G-53
Heston Aircraft Ltd	S	General Aircraft Ltd	G-20	Cameron Balloons	G-54
General Aircraft Ltd	T	Phillips & Powis (Miles)	G-21	W Vinten	G-55
Phillips & Powis (Miles)	U	Airspeed Ltd	G-22	Edgley Aircraft Ltd	G-56
Airspeed Ltd	V	Percival Aircraft	G-23	Airship Industries Ltd	G-57
G & J Weir Ltd	W	Cuncliffe Owen Aircraft	G-24		G-58
Percival Aircraft	X	Auster Aircraft	G-25		G-59
British Aircraft Mfg. Ltd	Y	Slingsby Sailplanes	G-26		G-60
Cuncliffe OwenAircraft	Y	English Electric	G-27	Solar Wings	G-65
Auster Aircraft	Z	BEA Helicopter Unit	G-28	Cyclone	G-69
Slingsby Sailplanes	AB	D Napier & Son Ltd	G-29	FLS	G-70
		Pest Control Ltd	G-30		G-76
		Scottish Aviation	G-31	Eurocopter (Oxford)	G-79
		Cierva Autogiro Company	G-32		

AIR-BRITAIN SALES

Companion publications to the Business Jets International are also available by post-free mail order from

Air-Britain Sales Department (Dept BCR99)
19 Kent Road
GRAYS
Essex RM17 6DE

Visa / Mastercard accepted - please give full details of card number and expiry date.

* UNITED KINGDOM AND IRELAND REGISTERS HANDBOOK 1999 - £ 18.50
Current registers of all the UK and Irish register Aircraft, including non-British aircraft based in the UK. Alphabetical index by type. 600 pages. 35th annual edition.
Available in hardback format only.

* EUROPEAN REGISTERS HANDBOOK 1999 - £ 21.00
Current registers of over 45 Western and Eastern European countries.
Available in hardback format only.

* AIRLINE FLEETS 1999 - £ 18.50
Almost 3000 fleets listed plus leasing companies and "airliners in limbo". Available in hardback format only.

* BOEING 707/720/C-135 - £ 37.00
Chapters cover the evolution of the 707 family, C-135A modifications and current USAF structure. Includes Airline operators (128 pages) and individual aircraft histories (220 pages). Over 486 pages including 200 colour and almost 100 black and white photographs. A4 hardbound.

* BUSINESS JETS INTERNATIONAL 1999 - £ 16.00
Complete production lists of all purpose-built business jets with full 43,000+ cross-reference. Hardback format only available. 352 pages.

* BUSINESS TURBOPROP INTERNATIONAL 1996 - £ 12.50
Second edition detailing production lists of 58 turboprop types including Cessna 208/425/441, Aero Commander, Super King Air, PLUS (thanks to BN Historians) all Islanders and Trilanders with full 31,250+ cross-reference index.

* REGISTERS OF CANADA 1996/97 - £ 15.00
Current civil registers of Canada, over 300 pages, registration, type, p.i.'s, registration date (of last registration change) of all CF-, C-F, C-G and C-I microlight registers.

* CHIPMUNK - THE FIRST 50 YEARS - £ 19.00
The most comprehensive survey and production list ever produced with 250 photographs.

* BAC ONE-ELEVEN - £ 20.00
The complete development history and comprehensive production details, 240 A4 pages, hard cover.

* PIPER AIRCRAFT - £ 31.00
The most detailed book ever published covering the development and history of one of the world's best-known aircraft manufacturers. Liberally illustrated in colour and black and white, describes each of the Piper aircraft designed and built. With 464 A4 pages, hard cover.

* MILITARY TITLES -
Air-Britain also publishes a comprehensive range of military titles -

- RAF Serial Registers
- Detailed RAF Type "Files"
- Squadron Histories
- Royal Navy Aircraft Histories

Please write for details.

IMPORTANT NOTE - members receive substantial discounts on all of the above Air-Britain publications. For details of membership - see overleaf.